CODE OF ALABAMA
1975

———

1989 Replacement Index

———

Ready Reference Index
General Index

———

Prepared by

The Editorial Staff of the Publishers

Under the Direction of

Adrian D. Kowalsky, Richard W. Walter, Jr., Mark F. Dempsey,
and Suzan E. Gallihugh

———

VOLUME 24

———

Including legislation through the 1989 Regular Session

The Michie Company
Law Publishers
Charlottesville, Virginia
1989

Foreword to the Index

This volume contains the general index to the Code of Alabama. The index contains treatment of the laws compiled in the Code of Alabama, the constitutions of Alabama and the United States and the Rules of the Alabama Supreme Court. Statutory provisions are referred to in the index by section number (e.g., § 27-1-15). The constitutions, set out in Volumes 1 and 2, and the court rules, set out in Volume 23, are identified by abbreviations, a table of which follows this foreword. Index treatment for all legislation through the 1989 Regular Session has been included in this volume.

This index has been thoroughly examined and reworked since the publication of the 1988 replacement index, with the goal being to provide better access to the Code. This goal was accomplished by adding many group section references to the index. These new section references have replaced or supplemented thousands of index cross references.

A new feature is the ready reference index, which appears after the table of abbreviations. This brief index, which uses general terms with citations to large blocks of material, is designed for use by those who are familiar with the contents and language of the Code, but who need a reminder as to where in the Code material appears.

Also new to the index are two main headings, "short titles" and "popular names", the inclusion of which should also improve the usefulness of the index.

The general index is a topical index, not a random word index. Random entries in an index to statutes are misleading since they result in split or partial treatment. Thus, we have chosen to use a systematic arrangement of main topics or headings. Main headings treat the subject matter exhaustively unless references are made to other headings. Although the same subject matter is frequently repeated under different headings in the index, cross references are used to prevent the index from becoming too large and unwieldy. These cross references carry statute section numbers indicating the main treatment of the subject wherever possible.

Main headings were derived from the language of the Code of Alabama, from the phraseology used in the courts of Alabama or from terminology commonly used in the legal profession. In addition, an effort was made to employ phrases and terms commonly applied to Code of Alabama sections, such as frequently used nonlegal terms.

We solicit your help in keeping this index as usable as possible and ask that you inform us of any popular names that may have eluded us by returning the business reply cards found in the middle of this volume. You may also use the cards to tell us of any errors we may have made or improvements you think we should make. The Michie Company also maintains a **toll-free telephone number (1-800-446-3410)** for use by those needing immediate help in locating a particular section or by those desiring to make comments or suggestions. All suggestions, questions and comments receive serious consideration, and all communications receive a reply.

The general index does not attempt cover each topic in the vast field of law but refers only to the material contained in the Code of Alabama. A thorough knowledge of the format and terminology of the Code of Alabama is essential to the use of this index as a guide to subject matter.

A few basic rules for using this index are:

(1) *Gain familiarity with the contents of the Code of Alabama and the index.* Knowledge of the arrangement, terminology, topical treatment, analyses and reference system of both the Code of Alabama and the index is essential and must be acquired through examination and study.

(2) *Consult the principal subject and not the secondary subject.* Thus, for motor vehicle registration, look under motor vehicles and not under registration; for attorney fees, look under attorneys' fees and not under fees; for sales of alcoholic beverages, look under alcoholic beverages and not under sales.

(3) *Look for the noun and not the adjective.* Thus, for life insurance, look under insurance and not under life; for foreign corporations, look under corporations and not under foreign; for primary elections, look under elections and not under primaries. An exception to this rule is made for commonly used phrases or terms of art that are expressed in unitary phrases. Thus, for wrongful death, look under wrongful death and not under death; for declaratory judgments, look under declaratory judgments and not under judgments.

(4) *Consult the most pertinent subject.* Thus, for depositions, look under depositions and not under evidence or testimony or witnesses.

(5) *Consult allied headings.* If your search under one heading is to no avail, try another allied heading. Thus, if a search under the heading sheriffs is fruitless, try peace officers or police or other related headings. Each section has itemized entries, but perhaps the entries appear under headings that may not have initially occurred to you.

(6) *Use cross references.* Pay close attention to and make full use of the index cross references.

THE MICHIE COMPANY

Table of Abbreviations

ACJE .... Alabama Canons of Judicial Ethics
ACSF .... Alabama State Bar Client Security Fund Rules
AJICR .... Alabama Judicial Inquiry Commission Rules
ARAJC .... Rules Governing Appeals From Alabama Court of the Judiciary
ARAP .... Alabama Rules of Appellate Procedure
ARCP .... Alabama Rules of Civil Procedure
ARCrP .... Alabama Rules of Criminal Procedure
ARDE .... Alabama Rules of Disciplinary Enforcement
ARJA .... Alabama Rules of Judicial Administration
ARJC .... Rules of Procedure of the Alabama Court of the Judiciary
ARJP .... Alabama Rules of Juvenile Procedure
ARMCLE .... Alabama Rules for Mandatory Continuing Legal Education
ASCR .... Alabama Small Claims Rules
Const. Ala. .... Constitution of Alabama
Const. U. S. ...... Constitution of the United States

READY REFERENCE INDEX

A

AGRICULTURE.
Agricultural center, §§2-6-1 to
2-6-86.
Agricultural development
authority, §§2-3A-1 to
2-3A-16.
Agricultural liming materials,
§§2-23-1 to 2-23-11.
Agricultural research,
experimental and
extension work, §§2-30-1 to
2-30-62.
Board of agriculture and
industries, §§2-3-1 to
2-3-25.
Commercial alligator operators,
§§2-16A-1 to 2-16A-15.
Commercial feeds, §§2-21-1 to
2-21-34.
Commissioner of agriculture
and industries, §§2-2-1 to
2-2-73.
Commission merchants' sale of
farm produce, §§2-29-1 to
2-29-11.
Cooperatives and associations,
§§2-10-1 to 2-10-108.
Cotton, §§2-19-1 to 2-19-135.
Eggs, §§2-12-1 to 2-12-12.
Entomology, §§2-28-1 to
2-28-12.
Fairs and exhibits, §§2-7-1 to
2-7-53.
Farm crisis and transition
program, §§2-6A-1 to
2-6A-6.
Farmers' market authority,
§§2-5-1 to 2-5-17.
Fertilizer, §§2-22-1 to 2-22-23.
General provisions, §§2-1-1 to
2-1-10.
Grain dealers, §§2-31-1 to
2-31-19.
Honeybees and apiaries,
§§2-14-1 to 2-14-15.
Horticulture, §§2-28-1 to
2-28-12.
Hulls, §§2-20-1 to 2-20-6.
Livestock, §§2-15-1 to 2-15-317.
Livestock inspectors, §§2-4-1 to
2-4-4.
Marketing, grading and
standards, §§2-11-1 to
2-11-123.
Meat and poultry inspections,
§§2-17-1 to 2-17-38.
Milk and dairy products,
§§2-13-1 to 2-13-94.
Pesticides, §§2-27-1 to 2-27-63.
Plant pathology and tree
surgery, §§2-28-1 to
2-28-12.
Plants and trees, §§2-25-1 to
2-25-42.

AGRICULTURE—Cont'd
Poultry generally, §§2-16-1 to
2-16-42.
Poultry meat grading, §§2-18-1
to 2-18-3.
Promotion of agricultural
industries and products,
§§2-8-1 to 2-8-291.
Rabbit meat and food products,
§§2-17A-1 to 2-17A-5.
Seeds, §§2-26-1 to 2-26-76.
Soil-testing laboratories,
§§2-24-1 to 2-24-5.
Special funds, §§2-9-1 to 2-9-40.
Veterinarians, §§2-4-1 to 2-4-4.

ALCOHOLIC BEVERAGES.
Audit and collection of taxes on
beer or table wine by board
for benefit of local
governing bodies,
§§28-7A-1 to 28-7A-6.
Dry counties and
municipalities.
Regulation and control,
§§28-4-1 to 28-4-326.
Elections as to sale and
distribution.
Counties, §§28-2-1 to 28-2-25.
Municipalities, §§28-2A-1 to
28-2A-4.
Exclusive sales territories and
wholesalers, §§28-8-1 to
28-8-8.
General provisions, §§28-1-1 to
28-1-5.
Industrial alcohol.
Regulation of manufacture,
sale, etc., §§28-5-1 to
28-5-14.
Licensing code, §§28-3A-1 to
28-3A-26.
Native farm wine.
Regulation of production,
sale, etc., §§28-6-1 to
28-6-6.
Table wine.
Importation, distribution and
sale, §§28-7-1 to 28-7-24.
Wet counties.
Regulation and control,
§§28-3-1 to 28-3-286.
Wholesalers and suppliers of
beer.
Business relations between,
§§28-9-1 to 28-9-11.

ANIMALS.
Dogs biting or injuring persons.
Liability of owners, §§3-6-1
to 3-6-4.
Estrays, §§3-2-1 to 3-2-23.
Fences and livestock, §§3-4-1 to
3-4-7.
General provisions, §§3-1-1 to
3-1-29.
Rabies, §§3-7-1 to 3-7-13.

ANIMALS—Cont'd
Staking, pasturing upon
highways, §§3-3-1 to 3-3-3.
Stock laws, §§3-5-1 to 3-5-14.

ASSOCIATIONS.
Unincorporated professional
associations, §§10-10-1 to
10-10-16.

AVIATION.
Aeronautics, aircraft and
airports.
Regulation, §§4-2-1 to 4-2-95.
Aircraft control and warning
stations, §§4-7-1 to 4-7-3.
Airport authorities, §§4-3-1 to
4-3-80.
Airport county warrants and
certificates of indebtedness,
§§4-5-1 to 4-5-5.
Airport zoning, §§4-6-1 to
4-6-15.
General provisions, §4-1-1.
Helicopter pilots association,
§§4-9-1 to 4-9-7.
Municipal airports and
regulations, §§4-4-1 to
4-4-16.

B

BANKS AND FINANCIAL
INSTITUTIONS.
Banking emergencies,
§§5-10A-1 to 5-10A-17.
Bank merger, consolidation or
conversion, §§5-7A-1 to
5-7A-46.
Common trust funds, §§5-12A-1
to 5-12A-15.
Compliance with federal laws,
§§5-10A-1 to 5-10A-17.
Consumer finance, §§5-19-1 to
5-19-31.
Credit card act, §§5-20-1 to
5-20-10.
Credit unions, §§5-17-1 to
5-17-59.
Directors, officers and
employees, §§5-6A-1 to
5-6A-26.
Examinations of banks,
§§5-3A-1 to 5-3A-17.
General provisions, §§5-1A-1 to
5-1A-9.
George Wallace, Jr. plan for
Linked Deposits of 1988,
§§5-21-1 to 5-21-11.
Liquidation of banks, §§5-8A-1
to 5-8A-46.
Organization and operation of
banks, §§5-5A-1 to
5-5A-47.
Regional reciprocal banking,
§§5-13A-1 to 5-13A-10.

1

BANKS AND FINANCIAL INSTITUTIONS—Cont'd

Regional reciprocal savings institutions, §§5-14A-1 to 5-14A-8.

Reorganization of banks, §§5-9A-1 to 5-9A-6.

Reports of banks, §§5-3A-1 to 5-3A-17.

Retention of bank records, §§5-4A-1, 5-4A-2.

Savings and loan associations, §§5-16-1 to 5-16-53.

Small loans, §§5-18-1 to 5-18-24.

State banking department, §§5-2A-1 to 5-2A-125.

Trust business of banks and trust companies.

Regulation, §§5-11A-1 to 5-11A-37.

BUSINESS ASSOCIATIONS.

Corporations, §§10-1-1 to 10-7-4.

Nonprofit organizations' liability of officers, §§10-11-1 to 10-11-5.

Partnerships, §§10-8-1 to 10-9A-203.

Unincorporated professional associations, §§10-10-1 to 10-10-16.

C

CHILDREN AND MINORS.

Adoption of children, §§26-10-1 to 26-10-30.

Alabama uniform guardianship and protective act, §§26-2A-1 to 26-2A-160.

Bureau for information on missing persons, §§26-19-1 to 26-19-10.

Child abuse and neglect, §§26-16-1 to 26-16-53.

Child abuse generally, §§26-15-1 to 26-15-4.

Child protection, §§26-18-1 to 26-18-10.

General provisions, §§26-1-1 to 26-1-5.

Legitimation of children, §§26-11-1 to 26-11-3.

Parental consent to performing abortion upon minor, §§26-21-1 to 26-21-8.

Relief of minor children from disabilities of nonage, §§26-13-1 to 26-13-8.

Reporting of child abuse or neglect, §§26-14-1 to 26-14-13.

Sex crime records of employees supervising children, §§26-20-1 to 26-20-6.

Uniform parentage act, §§26-17-1 to 26-17-21.

CIVIL PRACTICE AND PROCEDURE.

Actions, §§6-5-1 to 6-5-605.

Damages, §§6-11-1 to 6-11-30.

Exemptions, §§6-10-1 to 6-10-126.

General provisions, §§6-1-1, 6-1-2.

Judgments, §§6-9-1 to 6-9-238.

Limitation of actions, §§6-2-1 to 6-2-40.

CIVIL PRACTICE AND PROCEDURE—Cont'd

Miscellaneous procedure, §§6-8-1 to 6-8-104.

Parties, §§6-7-1 to 6-7-103.

Process, §§6-4-1 to 6-4-22.

Remedies, §§6-6-1 to 6-6-757.

Venue, §§6-3-1 to 6-3-22.

COMMERCIAL CODE.

Bank deposits and collections, §§7-4-101 to 7-4-504.

Bulk transfers, §§7-6-101 to 7-6-111.

Commercial paper, §§7-3-101 to 7-3-805.

Comparative table of uniform acts-appendix, pp. 627 to 632.

General provisions, §§7-1-101 to 7-1-208.

Investment securities, §§7-8-101 to 7-8-406.

Letters of credit, §§7-5-101 to 7-5-117.

Repealer and effective date, §§7-10-101 to 7-10-104.

Sales, §§7-2-101 to 7-2-725.

Secured transactions, sales of accounts and chattel paper, §§7-9-101 to 7-9-507.

Transition provisions and effective date, §§7-11-101 to 7-11-108.

Warehouse receipts, bills of lading and other documents of title, §§7-7-101 to 7-7-603.

COMMERCIAL LAW AND CONSUMER PROTECTION.

Agency, §§8-2-1 to 8-2-9.

Alabama fraudulent transfer act, §§8-9A-1 to 8-9A-12.

Athlete agents regulatory act, §§8-26-1 to 8-26-41.

Bills of exchange, §§8-4-1 to 8-4-4.

Consumer finance, §§5-19-1 to 5-19-31.

Contracts, §§8-1-1 to 8-1-172.

Deceptive trade practices, §§8-19-1 to 8-19-15.

Disposal of molds, dies or patterns, §§8-28-1 to 8-28-4.

Distress merchandise sales, §§8-13-1 to 8-13-23.

Frauds, §§8-9-1 to 8-9-12.

Going out of business sales, §§8-13-1 to 8-13-23.

Goods and products.

Regulation, §§8-17-1 to 8-17-226.

Health studio services, §§8-23-1 to 8-23-13.

Interest and usury, §§8-8-1 to 8-8-15.

Motion picture fair competition, §§8-18-1 to 8-18-6.

Motor fuel marketing, §§8-22-1 to 8-22-18.

Motor vehicle manufacturers, wholesalers, etc., with motor vehicle dealers, §§8-20-1 to 8-20-12.

Nonnegotiable instruments, §§8-5-1 to 8-5-30.

Public auctions, §§8-14-1 to 8-14-24.

Public warehouses, §§8-15-1 to 8-15-38.

COMMERCIAL LAW AND CONSUMER PROTECTION—Cont'd

Rebates, discounts, drawbacks, return commissions, gifts or gratuities, §§8-11-1 to 8-11-5.

Rental-purchase agreements, §§8-25-1 to 8-25-6.

Repurchase of inventory from farm equipment retailers, §§8-21-1 to 8-21-14.

Restraint of trade or production, §§8-10-1 to 8-10-3.

Sale of checks, §§8-7-1 to 8-7-15.

Sales representative's commission contracts, §§8-24-1 to 8-24-5.

Securities, §§8-6-1 to 8-6-122.

Suretyship, §§8-3-1 to 8-3-42.

Trademarks, names, marks, devices and labels, §§8-12-1 to 8-12-44.

Trade secrets act, §§8-27-1 to 8-27-6.

Weights and measures, §§8-16-1 to 8-16-123.

CONSERVATION AND NATURAL RESOURCES.

Coastal areas.

Preservation, development, etc., §§9-7-1 to 9-7-22.

Caves, §§9-19-1 to 9-19-5.

Department of conservation and natural resources, §§9-2-1 to 9-2-130.

Environmental improvement authorities, §§9-6-1 to 9-6-17.

Fish.

Marketing, grading and standards, §§2-11-1 to 2-11-123.

Fish, game and wildlife, §§9-11-1 to 9-11-457.

Forests and forest products, §§9-13-1 to 9-13-250.

General provisions, §§9-1-1 to 9-1-6.

Geological survey, §§9-4-1 to 9-4-19.

Marine resources, §§9-12-1 to 9-12-184.

Mineral resources, §§9-16-1 to 9-16-135.

Minerals resource management committee, §§9-5-1 to 9-5-3.

Oil and gas, §§9-17-1 to 9-17-110.

Public lands, §§9-15-1 to 9-15-53.

Recreation capital development assistance fund, §§9-7A-1 to 9-7A-17.

Soil and water conservation cost-share grants, §§9-8A-1 to 9-8A-16.

Soil and water conservation generally, §§9-8-1 to 9-8-67.

Southern interstate nuclear compact, §§9-18-1 to 9-18-6.

Southern states energy compact, §§9-18A-1 to 9-18A-4.

State forestry commission, §§9-3-1 to 9-3-18.

CONSERVATION AND NATURAL RESOURCES —Cont'd

State parks, §§9-14-1 to 9-14-29.

Synfuels development authority, §§9-6A-1 to 9-6A-10.

Water conservation and irrigation, §§9-10-1 to 9-10-47.

Water management and drainage, §§9-9-1 to 9-9-80.

CONSTRUCTION AND INTERPRETATION, §§1-1-1 to 1-1-16.

CORPORATIONS.

Business corporations, §§10-2A-1 to 10-2A-339.

Corporations, particular, §§10-4-1 to 10-4-406.

General provisions, §§10-1-1 to 10-1-3.

Infant shareholders, §§10-6-1 to 10-6-4.

Nonprofit organizations' liability of officers, §§10-11-1 to 10-11-5.

Powers, rights and duties of certain corporations, §§10-5-1 to 10-5-14.

Prosecution of corporations, §§10-7-1 to 10-7-4.

CORRECTIONAL AND DETENTION FACILITIES.

Board of corrections, §§14-1-1 to 14-1-18.

Convict labor, §§14-5-1 to 14-5-11.

Corrections institution finance authority, §§14-2-1 to 14-2-36.

County convicts, §§14-4-1 to 14-4-14.

Deducations from sentences, §§14-9-1 to 14-9-44.

Discharging convicts, §§14-10-1 to 14-10-3.

Interstate corrections compact, §§14-13-1 to 14-13-3.

Jails, §§14-6-1 to 14-6-109.

Prisoners and prisons offenses, §§14-11-1 to 14-11-11.

Prison-made goods, §§14-7-1 to 14-7-23.

Prison system, §§14-3-1 to 14-3-60.

Schools at correctional units, §§14-12-1 to 14-12-4.

Temporary release programs, §§14-8-1 to 14-8-67.

COUNTIES AND MUNICIPAL CORPORATIONS.

Provisions applicable to counties and municipal corporations.

Alabama convention facilities act, §§11-100-1 to 11-100-8.

Ambulance service, §§11-87-1 to 11-87-5.

Apportionment of road and bridge taxes, §§11-83-1 to 11-83-3.

Community action agencies, §§11-96-1 to 11-96-6.

County industrial development authorities, §§11-92A-1 to 11-92A-22.

COUNTIES AND MUNICIPAL CORPORATIONS—Cont'd

Provisions applicable to counties and municipal corporations—Cont'd

Emergency telephone service, §§11-98-1 to 11-98-7.

Forest lands.

Acquisition and administration, §§11-84-1, 11-84-2.

Free public libraries, §§11-90-1 to 11-90-4.

General provisions, §§11-80-1 to 11-80-6.

Industrial parks, §§11-92-1 to 11-92-11.

Municipal and county bonds, §§11-81-1 to 11-81-227.

Officers and employees.

Group life, health, accident, etc., insurance, §§11-91-1 to 11-91-8.

Port authorities, §§11-94-1 to 11-94-25.

Public hospitals, §§11-95-1 to 11-95-21.

Recreation boards, §§11-86-1 to 11-86-6.

Regional planning and development, §§11-85-1 to 11-85-73.

Securities issued in anticipation of receipt of grants, §§11-81A-1 to 11-81A-7.

Securities redemption, §§11-82-1 to 11-82-7.

Solid waste disposal authorities, §§11-89A-1 to 11-89A-25.

Tax increment districts, §§11-99-1 to 11-99-10.

Tort claims and judgments, §§11-93-1 to 11-93-3.

Utility services facilities.

Construction and improvement, §§11-97-1 to 11-97-27.

Water, sewer and fire protection authorities, §§11-88-1 to 11-88-135.

Water, sewer, solid waste disposal and fire protection districts, §§11-89-1 to 11-89-19.

Provisions applicable to counties only.

Acquisition, erection, maintenance, etc., of buildings, property, roads, etc., generally, §§11-14-1 to 11-14-24.

Acquisition, etc., of lands for public purposes, etc., §§11-18-1 to 11-18-24.

Acquisition of waterworks plants or distribution systems, §§11-21-1 to 11-21-4.

Bonds of county officers, employees, etc., generally, §§11-2-1 to 11-2-34.

Burial places, graveyards and cemeteries, §§11-17-1 to 11-17-16.

Claims and demands, §§11-12-1 to 11-12-16.

COUNTIES AND MUNICIPAL CORPORATIONS—Cont'd

Provisions applicable to counties only—Cont'd

Codification and publication of laws, §§11-13-1 to 11-13-6.

Community antenna television facilities, §§11-27-1 to 11-27-3.

Comprehensive land-use management in flood-prone areas, §§11-19-1 to 11-19-24.

Coroner, §§11-5-1 to 11-5-13.

County commission, §§11-3-1 to 11-3-26.

County seats.

Relocation and erection of new courthouses, §§11-16-1 to 11-16-40.

Engineer, §§11-6-1 to 11-6-25.

Financial affairs generally, §§11-8-1 to 11-8-17.

General provisions, §§11-1-1 to 11-1-17.

Government capital improvement, §§11-29-1 to 11-29-7.

Industrial parks, §§11-23-1 to 11-23-8.

Law libraries, §§11-25-1 to 11-25-12.

Liability self-insurance funds, §§11-30-1 to 11-30-7.

Loans.

Making in anticipation of taxes, §§11-10-1 to 11-10-6.

Promotion of industry and trade, §§11-20-1 to 11-20-50.

Public building authorities, §§11-15-1 to 11-15-19.

Public construction warrants, §§11-28-1 to 11-28-7.

Public park and recreation boards, §§11-22-1 to 11-22-19.

Securities issued in anticipation of grants, §§11-11B-1 to 11-11B-8.

Self-insurance for compensation, hospitalization, etc., benefits, §§11-26-1 to 11-26-6.

Subdivisions.

Regulation, §§11-24-1 to 11-24-7.

Surveyors, §§11-7-1 to 11-7-12.

Treasurer or depository, §§11-4-1 to 11-4-50.

Warrants.

Issuance in anticipation of ad valorem taxes, §§11-11A-1 to 11-11A-5.

Issuance in anticipation of gasoline taxes, §§11-11-1 to 11-11-8.

Warrants for utility purposes, §§11-9-1 to 11-9-28.

COUNTIES AND MUNICIPAL
 CORPORATIONS—Cont'd
Provisions applicable to
 municipal corporations
 only.
 Abatement of weeds,
  §§11-67-1 to 11-67-28.
 Adoption of mayor-council
  form of government,
  §§11-43D-1 to 11-43D-22.
 Class C municipalities.
  Abandonment of
   commission form of
   government,
   §§11-44D-1 to
   11-44D-21.
 Class 1 municipalities.
  Horse racing, §§11-65-1 to
   11-65-47.
 Class 2 municipalities.
  Government, §§11-44C-1 to
   11-44C-93.
 Class 3 municipalities.
  Public transportation
   service, §§11-49A-1 to
   11-49A-20.
 Class 4 municipalities.
  Abandonment of
   commission form of
   government,
   §§11-44B-1 to
   11-44B-22.
  Mayor-council form of
   government,
   §§11-43B-1 to
   11-43B-32.
 Class 5 municipalities.
  Mayor/commission/city
   manager form of
   government,
   §§11-44E-1 to
   11-44E-221.
  Mayor-council form of
   government,
   §§11-43C-1 to
   11-43C-92.
 Class 7 municipalities.
  Abandonment of
   commission form of
   government,
   §§11-44A-1 to
   11-44A-32.
 Class 8 municipalities.
  Abandonment of
   commission form of
   government,
   §§11-44F-1 to
   11-44F-3.
 Commission form of
  government, §§11-44-1 to
  11-44-162.
  Abandonment in class 4
   municipalities,
   §§11-44B-1 to
   11-44B-22.
  Abandonment in class 6
   municipalities,
   §§11-44D-1 to
   11-44D-21.
  Abandonment in class 7
   municipalities,
   §§11-44A-1 to
   11-44A-32.
  Abandonment in class 8
   municipalities,
   §§11-44F-1 to
   11-44F-3.
 Corporate limits.
  Alteration, §§11-42-1 to
   11-42-213.

COUNTIES AND MUNICIPAL
 CORPORATIONS—Cont'd
Provisions applicable to
 municipal corporations
 only—Cont'd
 Council-manager form of
  government, §§11-43A-1
  to 11-43A-52.
 Downtown redevelopment
  authorities, §§11-54A-1
  to 11-54A-24.
 Elections, §§11-46-1 to
  11-46-145.
 General provisions, §§11-40-1
  to 11-40-36.
 Government of class 2
  municipalities,
  §§11-44C-1 to 11-44C-93.
 Historic preservation
  commissions and
  architectural review
  boards, §§11-68-1 to
  11-68-15.
 Horse racing in class 1
  municipalities, §§11-65-1
  to 11-65-47.
 Housing standards and
  unsafe buildings.
  Regulation, §§11-53-1 to
   11-53-4.
 Incorporation and
  dissolution, §§11-41-1 to
  11-41-28.
 Mayor and council, other
  officers, employees,
  departments, etc.,
  §§11-43-1 to 11-43-190.
 Mayor-council form of
  government.
  Class 4 municipalities,
   §§11-43B-1 to
   11-43B-32.
  Class 5 municipalities,
   §§11-43C-1 to
   11-43C-92.
 Medical clinic boards,
  §§11-58-1 to 11-58-15.
 Municipal electric authority,
  §§11-50A-1 to 11-50A-33.
 Municipal government
  capital improvement,
  §§11-66-1 to 11-66-7.
 Municipal special health care
  facility authorities,
  §§11-62-1 to 11-62-21.
 Ordinances and resolutions,
  §§11-45-1 to 11-45-11.
 Parking facilities, §§11-61-1
  to 11-61-3.
 Planning, zoning and
  subdivisions, §§11-52-1
  to 11-52-84.
 Post office projects, §§11-55-1
  to 11-55-12.
 Powers, duties and liabilities
  generally, §§11-47-1 to
  11-47-243.
 Promotion of industry, trade,
  commerce and pollution
  control, §§11-54-1 to
  11-54-211.
 Public athletic boards,
  §§11-59-1 to 11-59-17.
 Public building authorities,
  §§11-56-1 to 11-56-22.
 Public corporations' financial
  assistance, §§11-63-1 to
  11-63-4.
 Public improvements and
  assessments generally,
  §§11-48-1 to 11-48-106.

COUNTIES AND MUNICIPAL
 CORPORATIONS—Cont'd
Provisions applicable to
 municipal corporations
 only—Cont'd
 Public library authorities,
  §§11-57-1 to 11-57-26.
 Public park and recreation
  boards, §§11-60-1 to
  11-60-20.
 Public transportation service
  in class 3 municipalities,
  §§11-49A-1 to 11-49A-20.
 Public utilities, §§11-50-1 to
  11-50-533.
 Securities issued in
  anticipation of grants,
  §§11-64-1 to 11-64-7.
 Streets, highways, railroad
  bridges, ferries, etc.
  Regulation, construction,
   maintenance, etc.,
   §§11-49-1 to 11-49-106.
 Taxation, §§11-51-1 to
  11-51-207.

COURTS.
 Administrative office courts
  and department of court
  management, §§12-5-1 to
  12-5-21.
 Appellate proceedings,
  §§12-22-1 to 12-22-246.
 Circuit and district court
  personnel, §§12-17-1 to
  12-17-292.
 Circuit courts, §§12-11-1 to
  12-11-61.
 Court finances, §§12-19-1 to
  12-19-276.
 Court of criminal appeals,
  §§12-3-1 to 12-3-36.
 Court of the judiciary, §§12-7-1,
  12-7-2.
 Department of court
  management and
  administrative office of
  courts, §§12-5-1 to 12-5-21.
 District courts, §§12-12-1 to
  12-12-73.
 Evidence and witnesses,
  §§12-21-1 to 12-21-285.
 General provisions, §§12-1-1 to
  12-1-22.
 Judicial and other public
  records, §§12-20-1 to
  12-20-50.
 Judicial compensation
  commission, §§12-10-1 to
  12-10-5.
 Judicial conference, §§12-8-1 to
  12-8-8.
 Judicial inquiry commission,
  §12-6-1.
 Judicial retirement, §§12-18-1
  to 12-18-114.
 Judicial system study
  commission, §§12-9-1 to
  12-9-9.
 Juries, §§12-16-1 to 12-16-233.
 Juvenile proceedings, §§12-15-1
  to 12-15-120.
 Municipal courts, §§12-14-1 to
  12-14-71.
 Probate courts, §§12-13-1 to
  12-13-70.
 Reporter of decisions.
  Supreme court and courts of
   appeals, §§12-4-1 to
   12-4-4.

COURTS—Cont'd
Supreme court, §§12-2-1 to
12-2-160.

CRIMINAL LAW.
Abuse of public office,
§§13A-10-80 to 13A-10-82.
Alabama Anti-obscenity
enforcement act,
§§13A-12-200.1 to
13A-12-200.10.
Arson and explosives,
§§13A-7-40 to 13A-7-44.
Assaults, §§13A-6-20 to
13A-6-25.
Bribery and corrupt influence,
§§13A-10-60 to 13A-10-63.
Burglary and criminal trespass,
§§13A-7-1 to 13A-7-8.
Child pornography,
§§13A-12-170 to
13A-12-197.
Crimes and offenses.
Miscellaneous offenses,
§§13A-14-1 to 13A-14-5.
Criminal damage to property,
§§13A-7-20 to 13A-7-29.
Criminal liability, §§13A-2-1 to
13A-2-26.
Defenses, §§13A-3-1 to
13A-3-31.
Drug Crimes amendments act
of 1987, §§13A-12-210 to
13A-12-216.
Drug predator control act of
1987, §§13A-12-201 to
13A-12-205.
Escape and custody related
offenses, §§13A-10-30 to
13A-10-45.
Felons.
Registration, §§13A-11-180 to
13A-11-186.
Firearms and weapons,
§§13A-11-50 to 13A-11-84.
Forgery and related offenses,
§§13A-9-1 to 13A-9-20.
Frauds.
Business, §§13A-9-40 to
13A-9-52.
Fraudulent practices,
§§13A-9-40 to 13A-9-52.
Gambling offenses,
§§13A-12-20 to 13A-12-92.
General provisions, §§13A-1-1
to 13A-1-11.
Homicide, §§13A-6-1 to
13A-6-4.
Inchoate crimes, §§13A-4-1 to
13A-4-5.
Kidnapping, unlawful
punishment and related
offenses, §§13A-6-40 to
13A-6-45.
Libel and defamation,
§§13A-11-160 to
13A-11-164.
Obscenity and related offenses,
§§13A-12-130 to
13A-12-159.
Obstruction of justice and
judicial proceedings,
§§13A-10-120 to
13A-10-131.
Obstruction of public
administration, §§13A-10-1
to 13A-10-12.
Offenses against public health
and morals.
General provisions,
§§13A-12-1 to 13A-12-4.

CRIMINAL LAW—Cont'd
Offenses against public order
and safety.
Miscellaneous offenses,
§§13A-11-220 to
13A-11-224.
Offenses against the family,
§§13A-13-1 to 13A-13-7.
Offenses involving damage to
and intrusion upon
property.
Miscellaneous offenses,
§§13A-7-60, 13A-7-61.
Offenses involving theft.
Copying and sale of recorded
devices, §§13A-8-80 to
13A-8-86.
Shopping carts, §§13A-8-60
to 13A-8-64.
Perjury and related offenses,
§§13A-10-100 to
13A-10-109.
Privacy offenses, §§13A-11-30
to 13A-11-37.
Prostitution offenses,
§§13A-12-110 to
13A-12-113.
Public order and indecency
offenses, §§13A-11-1 to
13A-11-14.
Punishments and sentences,
§§13A-5-1 to 13A-5-59.
Restraints of trade,
§§13A-11-120 to
13A-11-123.
Robbery, §§13A-8-40 to
13A-8-44.
Pharmacies, §§13A-8-50 to
13A-8-52.
Sex offenders registration,
§§13A-11-200 to
13A-11-203.
Sexual offenses, §§13A-6-60 to
13A-6-70.
Sports offenses, §§13A-11-140
to 13A-11-143.
Theft and related offenses,
§§13A-8-1 to 13A-8-22.

CRIMINAL PROCEDURE.
Arrests, §§15-10-1 to 15-10-93.
Bail, §§15-13-1 to 15-13-82.
Child sexual abuse victim
protection act of 1989,
§§15-26-1 to 15-26-9.
Complaint.
Initiation of proceedings,
§§15-7-1 to 15-7-22.
Coroners' inquest, §§15-4-1 to
15-4-11.
Crime victims, §§15-23-1 to
15-23-46.
Defense of indigents, §§15-12-1
to 15-12-46.
Extradition and detainers,
§§15-9-1 to 15-9-88.
General provisions, §§15-1-1,
15-1-2.
Habeas corpus, §§15-21-1 to
15-21-34.
Indictments, §§15-8-1 to
15-8-150.
Insanity, §§15-16-1 to 15-16-71.
Jurisdiction and venue,
§§15-2-1 to 15-2-27.
Limitations on prosecution,
§§15-3-1 to 15-3-8.
Mentally retarded defendants,
§§15-24-1 to 15-24-7.
Pardons, paroles and probation,
§§15-22-1 to 15-22-77.

**CRIMINAL PROCEDURE
—Cont'd**
Peace and preserve order
proceedings, §§15-6-1 to
15-6-61.
Pleadings, §§15-15-1 to
15-15-44.
Preliminary hearings,
§§15-11-1 to 15-11-15.
Searches and seizures, §§15-5-1
to 15-5-31.
Sentence and punishment,
§§15-18-1 to 15-18-151.
Sex offenders, §15-20-1 to
15-20-5.
Sexual offenses and
exploitation.
Child victims and witnesses
in prosecutions,
§§15-25-1 to 15-25-6.
Trial arrangements, §§15-14-1
to 15-14-57.
Verdict, §§15-17-1 to 15-17-5.
Youthful offenders, §§15-19-1
to 15-19-7.

D

DECEDENTS' ESTATES.
Administration of estates,
§§43-2-1 to 43-2-813.
Adoption of adults.
Inheritance purposes,
§§43-4-1 to 43-4-4.
Escheats, §§43-6-1 to 43-6-9.
Probate code, §§43-8-1 to
43-8-298.
Uniform simultaneous death
act, §§43-7-1 to 43-7-8.

DOMESTIC RELATIONS.
Child custody and support,
§§30-3-1 to 30-3-99.
Divorce and alimony, §§30-2-1
to 30-2-55.
Domestic violence facilities,
§§30-6-1 to 30-6-13.
Husband and wife, §§30-4-1 to
30-4-98.
Marriage, §§30-1-1 to 30-1-18.
Protection from abuse, §§30-5-1
to 30-5-11.

E

EDUCATION.
Alabama High School of
Mathematics and Science,
§§16-26A-1 to 16-26A-7.
American Legion scholarships,
§§16-31-1 to 16-31-4.
Black Heritage Museum of
West Alabama act,
§§16-62-1 to 16-62-6.
Boards of school trustees,
§§16-10-1 to 16-10-11.
City boards of education,
§§16-11-1 to 16-11-27.
City superintendents of schools,
§§16-12-1 to 16-12-21.
Commission of higher
education, §§16-5-1 to
16-5-14.
Compact for education,
§§16-44-1 to 16-44-3.
County boards of education,
§§16-8-1 to 16-8-43.
County superintendents of
education, §§16-9-1 to
16-9-34.

EDUCATION—Cont'd
Department of education, §§16-2-1 to 16-2-8.
Dependents of blind parents. Educational benefits, §§16-33-1 to 16-33-12.
Drug abuse education, §§16-41-1 to 16-41-10.
Educational building authorities, §§16-17-1 to 16-17-19.
Educational television commission, §§16-7-1 to 16-7-6.
Educational television foundation authority, §§16-7A-1 to 16-7A-8.
Education authority, §§16-15-1 to 16-15-13.
Education of exceptional children, §§16-39-1 to 16-39-12.
Education study commission, §§16-6-1 to 16-6-6.
General provisions, §§16-1-1 to 16-1-27.
Guaranteed student loan program, §§16-33B-1 to 16-33B-8.
High schools generally, §§16-26-1 to 16-26-4.
Historical research, §§16-42-1 to 16-42-3.
Illiteracy, §§16-34-1 to 16-34-4.
Improving education programs, §§16-6A-1 to 16-6A-17.
Instruction as to certain subjects, §§16-40-1 to 16-40-8.
Interstate agreement on qualifications of educational personnel, §§16-23A-1 to 16-23A-3.
Lease and sale of school lands, §§16-20-1 to 16-20-9.
Libraries, §§16-21-1 to 16-21-3.
Local aid to state educational institutions, §§16-19-1 to 16-19-8.
Marine environmental sciences consortium, §§16-45-1 to 16-45-5.
Officers and employees generally, §§16-22-1 to 16-22-9.
Private colleges and universities facilities authority, §§16-18A-1 to 16-18A-13.
Public educational building authorities, §§16-18-1 to 16-18-21.
Public education employees' health insurance, §§16-25A-1 to 16-25A-17.
Public school and college authority, §§16-16-1 to 16-16-13.
Public school corporation, §§16-14-1 to 16-14-19.
Regulation of certain schools and courses of instruction, §§16-46-1 to 16-46-10.
Rehabilitation and crippled children service, §§16-38-1 to 16-38-9.
School attendance, §§16-28-1 to 16-28-24.
School children.
Immunization, §§16-30-1 to 16-30-5.

EDUCATION—Cont'd
School children—Cont'd
Mental and physical examinations, §§16-29-1 to 16-29-6.
School finances generally, §§16-13-1 to 16-13-217.
State board of education, §§16-3-1 to 16-3-37.
State courses of study committee, §§16-35-1 to 16-35-5.
State superintendent of education, §§16-4-1 to 16-4-21.
Stonewall Jackson memorial fund, §§16-32-1 to 16-32-3.
Student grant program, §§16-33A-1 to 16-33A-11.
Teachers' retirement system, §§16-25-1 to 16-25-47.
Teachers' tenure of employment, §§16-24-1 to 16-24-38.
Teacher training and certification, §§16-23-1 to 16-23-23.
Textbooks, §§16-36-1 to 16-36-39.
Trade schools and junior colleges, §§16-60-1 to 16-60-270.
Transportation of pupils, §§16-27-1 to 16-27-7.
Trust fund for eminent scholars, §§16-61-1 to 16-61-10.
United States flag and state flag, §§16-43-1 to 16-43-5.
Vocational education, §§16-37-1 to 16-37-8.

ELECTIONS.
Absentee voting, §§17-10-1 to 17-10-20.
Amendments to the constitution, §§17-17-1 to 17-17-6.
Ballots, §§17-8-1 to 17-8-46.
Canvassing returns; declaration of results, §§17-14-1 to 17-14-27.
Challenge of voters, §§17-12-1 to 17-12-8.
Conduct and management generally, §§17-7-1 to 17-7-21.
Congressional districts, §§17-20-1 to 17-20-4.
Contesting elections, §§17-15-1 to 17-15-63.
Counting of votes, §§17-13-1 to 17-13-11.
Election officers, §§17-6-1 to 17-6-16.
Elective officers, §§17-2-1 to 17-2-11.
Electronic vote counting systems, §§17-24-1 to 17-24-11.
Fair Campaign Practices Act, §§17-22A-1 to 17-22A-23.
General provisions, §§17-1-1 to 17-1-7.
Miscellaneous offenses, §§17-23-1 to 17-23-11.
Municipal corporations, §§11-46-1 to 11-46-145.
Precincts, §§17-5A-1 to 17-5A-10.

ELECTIONS—Cont'd
Presidential and vice-presidential electors, §§17-19-1 to 17-19-8.
Presidential preference primary elections, §§17-16A-1 to 17-16A-6.
Primary elections, §§17-16-1 to 17-16-89.
Qualifications of electors, §§17-3-1 to 17-3-13.
Registration, §§17-4-1 to 17-4-215.
Reimbursing counties for expenses of certain elections, §§17-21-1 to 17-21-6.
Special elections, §§17-18-1 to 17-18-7.
Voting machines, §§17-9-1 to 17-9-41.

EMINENT DOMAIN.
Acquisition of rights-of-way by private parties, §§18-3-1 to 18-3-22.
Erection of dams for mills, gins, factories or electric generators, §§18-2-1 to 18-2-21.
Generally, §§18-1A-1 to 18-1A-311.

F

FIDUCIARIES AND TRUSTS.
Fiduciaries in war service, §§19-2-1 to 19-2-5.
Generation-skipping tax. Preclusion or minimization, §§19-5-1 to 19-5-12.
Securities held by fiduciaries, §§19-4-1 to 19-4-42.
Trusts, §§19-3-1 to 19-3-303.
Uniform fiduciaries act, §§19-1-1 to 19-1-13.

FOOD, DRUGS AND COSMETICS.
Controlled substances, §§20-2-1 to 20-2-164.
Standards, labeling and adulteration, §§20-1-1 to 20-1-154.

G

GENERAL PROVISIONS.
Miscellaneous, §§1-3-1 to 1-3-8.

GUARDIANSHIP.
Appointment of curators, §§26-7A-1 to 26-7A-17.
Appointment of guardians, §§26-2-1 to 26-2-55.
Bonds of guardians, §§26-3-1 to 26-3-14.
General provisions, §§26-1-1 to 26-1-5.
Guardianship and commitment of incompetent veterans and dependents, §§26-9-1 to 26-9-19.
Removal of person or property of minors and wards, §§26-8-1 to 26-8-52.
Settlements of guardians, §§26-5-1 to 26-5-54.
Uniform guardianship and protective proceedings act, §§26-2A-1 to 26-2A-160.

H

HANDICAPPED PERSONS.
Crippled and disabled children, §§21-3-1 to 21-3-8.
Deaf and blind persons generally, §§21-1-1 to 21-1-62.
Governor's committee on employment the handicapped, §§21-5-1 to 21-5-10.
Hemophilia treatment, §§21-8-1 to 21-8-5.
Physically handicapped persons.
Accessibility to and use of public buildings and facilities, §§21-4-1 to 21-4-24.
Rehabilitation program for the homebound, §§21-6-1 to 21-6-5.
Rights of blind and otherwise physically disabled persons, §§21-7-1 to 21-7-10.
Workshops, home industries, etc., §§21-2-1 to 21-2-4.

HEALTH AND ENVIRONMENTAL CONTROL.
Agricultural nonpoint source financial assistance act, §§22-38-1 to 22-38-8.
Air pollution control act, §§22-28-1 to 22-28-23.
Ambulances, §§22-18-1 to 22-18-7.
Barber, manicure or beauty shops, §§22-17-1 to 22-17-11.
Cancer, §§22-13-1 to 22-13-13.
Consent for health services, §§22-8-1 to 22-8-9.
Dead bodies, §§22-19-1 to 22-19-144.
Determination of death, §§22-31-1 to 22-31-4.
Environmental management, §§22-22A-1 to 22-22A-16.
Fees for home health services, §§22-7-1 to 22-7-6.
General provisions, §§22-1-1 to 22-1-11.
Genetics service, §§22-10A-1 to 22-10A-3.
Hazardous waste.
Management, §§22-30-1 to 22-30-24.
Hospitals and other health care facilities generally, §§22-21-1 to 22-21-391.
Lead ban act, §§22-37-1 to 22-37-6.
Local health authorities, §§22-3-1 to 22-3-12.
Long-term residential health care recipient ombudsmen act, §§22-5A-1 to 22-5A-7.
Medicaid program, §§22-6-1 to 22-6-9.
Miscellaneous health laws, §§22-20-1 to 22-20-12.
Mothers and babies indigent care trust fund, §§22-12B-1 to 22-12B-4.
Nuisances menacing public health, §§22-10-1 to 22-10-3.

HEALTH AND ENVIRONMENTAL CONTROL—Cont'd
Perinatal health care, §§22-12A-1 to 22-12A-6.
Pollution control finance authority, §§22-29-1 to 22-29-23.
Quarantine laws and regulations, §§22-12-1 to 22-12-29.
Radiation, §§22-14-1 to 22-14-35.
Reporting notifiable diseases, §§22-11A-1 to 22-11A-37.
Sewage collection, treatment and disposal facilities, §§22-26-1 to 22-26-7.
Solid waste, §§22-27-1 to 22-27-27.
Southeast interstate low-level radioactive waste management compact, §§22-32-1 to 22-32-9.
State commission on physical fitness, §§22-5-1 to 22-5-9.
State health authorities, §§22-2-1 to 22-2-14.
State health planning and development, §§22-4-1 to 22-4-17.
Termination of life-support procedures, §§22-8A-1 to 22-8A-10.
Toxic substances in the workplace, §§22-33-1 to 22-33-15.
Underground storage tank and wellhead protection act, §§22-36-1 to 22-36-10.
Underground storage tank trust fund, §§22-35-1 to 22-35-13.
Vital statistics, §§22-9-1 to 22-9-79.
Water and wastewater systems and treatment plants, §§22-25-1 to 22-25-15.
Water pollution control, §§22-22-1 to 22-22-14.
Water pollution control authority, §§22-34-1 to 22-34-17.
Water well standards, §§22-24-1 to 22-24-12.
Waterworks and water supplies generally, §§22-23-1 to 22-23-54.

HIGHWAYS, ROADS, BRIDGES AND FERRIES.
Closing and vacating streets, alleys and highways, §§23-4-1 to 23-4-20.
Controlled access facilities, §§23-3-1 to 23-3-8.
Highways, §§23-1-1 to 23-1-317.
Industrial access roads and bridges, §§23-6-1 to 23-6-12.
Offenses, §§23-5-1 to 23-5-14.
Toll roads, bridges and ferries, §§23-2-1 to 23-2-161.

HOUSING.
Housing authorities, §§24-1-1 to 24-1-134.
Housing finance authority, §§24-1A-1 to 24-1A-9.
Manufactured buildings, §§24-4A-1 to 24-4A-7.

HOUSING—Cont'd
Manufactured housing commission, §§24-6-1 to 24-6-4.
Mobile homes, §§24-5-1 to 24-5-34.
Mowa Choctaw housing authority, §§24-7-1 to 24-7-6.
Redevelopment projects, §§24-2-1 to 24-2-10.
Urban renewal projects, §§24-3-1 to 24-3-9.

I

INSURANCE.
Adjusters, §§27-9-1 to 27-9-8.
Alcoholism treatment in group plans, §§27-20A-1 to 27-20A-4.
Assets, §§27-37-1 to 27-37-9.
Authorization of insurers, §§27-3-1 to 27-3-29.
Automobile clubs and associations, §§27-39-1 to 27-39-8.
Burial insurance policies, §§27-17-1 to 27-17-16.
Casualty insurance contracts, §§27-23-1 to 27-23-28.
Certified registered nurse anesthetist coverage, §§27-46-1 to 27-46-3.
Dental care services, §§27-19A-1 to 27-19A-11.
Department and commissioner of insurance, §§27-2-1 to 27-2-55.
Deposits.
Administration, §§27-6-1 to 27-6-16.
Disability insurance policies, §§27-19-1 to 27-19-58.
Fees and taxes, §§27-4-1 to 27-4-11.
Fraternal benefit societies, §§27-34-1 to 27-34-54.
Conversion, §§27-35-1 to 27-35-11.
General provisions, §§27-1-1 to 27-1-18.
Group and blanket disability insurance, §§27-20-1 to 27-20-7.
Group life insurance, §§27-18-1 to 27-18-16.
Health care plan, §§27-21-1 to 27-21-6.
Health maintenance organizations, §§27-21A-1 to 27-21A-32.
Holding companies, §§27-28-1 to 27-28-5.
Industrial life insurance, §§27-16-1 to 27-16-17.
Insurance guaranty association, §27-42-1 to 27-42-20.
Insurance holding company systems, §§27-29-1 to 27-29-14.
Insurance premium finance companies, §§27-40-1 to 27-40-18.
Investments of life, disability and burial insurance companies, §§27-41-1 to 27-41-41.

INSURANCE—Cont'd

Kinds of insurance; limits of risk; reinsurance, §§27-5-1 to 27-5-13.

Legal expense insurance, §§27-43-1 to 27-43-23.

Liabilities, §§27-36-1 to 27-36-7.

Life and disability insurance guaranty association, §§27-44-1 to 27-44-21.

Life and disability insurance representatives, §§27-8-1 to 27-8-28.

Life insurance and annuity contracts, §§27-15-1 to 27-15-29.

Mail order insurance, §§27-11-1 to 27-11-7.

Medical liability insurance, §§27-26-1 to 27-26-43.

Mutual aid associations, §§27-30-1 to 27-30-34.

Pharmaceutical insurance coverage, §§27-45-1 to 27-45-9.

Property, casualty and surety insurance representatives, §§27-7-1 to 27-7-38.

Property insurance contracts, §§27-22-1, 27-22-2.

Rates and rating organizations, §§27-13-1 to 27-13-105.

Reciprocal insurers, §§27-31-1 to 27-31-29.

Rehabilitation, reorganization, conservation and liquidation of insurers, §§27-32-1 to 27-32-41.

Separate accounts and variable annuities, §§27-38-1 to 27-38-6.

Stock and mutual insurers.
Organization and corporate procedures, §§27-27-1 to 27-27-61.

Surety insurance contracts, §§27-24-1 to 27-24-8.

The insurance contract, §§27-14-1 to 27-14-32.

Title insurance, §27-25-1.

Trade practices law, §§27-12-1 to 27-12-24.

Trusteed assets of alien insurers, §§27-33-1 to 27-33-16.

Unauthorized insurers and surplus lines, §§27-10-1 to 27-10-56.

L

LABOR AND INDUSTRIAL RELATIONS.

Child labor, §§25-8-1 to 25-8-31.

Coal mine safety, §§25-9-1 to 25-9-370.

Department of industrial relations, §§25-2-1 to 25-2-26.

Department of labor, §§25-3-1 to 25-3-5.

Employer's liability for certain injuries, §§25-6-1 to 25-6-4.

General provisions, §§25-1-1 to 25-1-2.

Labor unions and labor relations, §§25-7-1 to 25-7-54.

LABOR AND INDUSTRIAL RELATIONS—Cont'd

Small business assistance, §§25-10-1 to 25-10-10.

Unemployment compensation, §§25-4-1 to 25-4-152.

Workmen's compensation, §§25-5-1 to 25-5-257.

LEGISLATURE.

Alabama law institute, §§29-8-1 to 29-8-5.

Emergency interim succession, §§29-3-1 to 29-3-16.

General provisions, §§29-1-1 to 29-1-23.

Legislative council, §§29-6-1 to 29-6-7.

Legislative fiscal office, §§29-5-1 to 29-5-12.

Legislative reference service, §§29-7-1 to 29-7-7.

Permanent legislative committees, §§29-2-1 to 29-2-41.3.

Subordinate officers and employees, §§29-4-1 to 29-4-51.

M

MENTAL HEALTH.

Commitment, discharge and transfer of persons in state institutions, §§22-52-1 to 22-52-72.

Department of mental health and mental retardation; board of trustees, §§22-50-1 to 22-50-62.

Interstate compact on mental health, §§22-55-1 to 22-55-4.

Regional mental health programs and facilities, §§22-51-1 to 22-51-14.

Security medical facility, §§22-54-1 to 22-54-5.

Support of persons in state mental institutions, §§22-53-1 to 22-53-26.

MILITARY AFFAIRS AND CIVIL DEFENSE.

Armory commission, §§31-4-1 to 31-4-19.

Bonus for Southeast Asian war prisoners, §§31-7-1 to 31-7-5.

Department of veterans' affairs, §§31-5-1 to 31-5-14.

Emergency management, §§31-9-1 to 31-9-24.

General provisions, §§31-1-1 to 31-1-3.

Military code, §§31-2-1 to 31-2-133.

National guard.
Compensation for death, §§31-3-1 to 31-3-7.
Educational assistance, §§31-10-1 to 31-10-4.

Pensions for widows of Confederate veterans, §§31-8-1 to 31-8-33.

State Veterans' Homes, §§31-5A-1 to 31-5A-11.

Veterans' and dependents' educational benefits, §§31-6-1 to 31-6-17.

MOTOR VEHICLES.

Abandoned motor vehicles, §§32-13-1 to 32-13-8.

Department of public safety, §§32-2-1 to 32-2-44.

Driver training schools, §§32-14-1 to 32-14-24.

General provisions, §§32-1-1 to 32-1-7.

Highway and traffic safety coordination act, §§32-4-1 to 32-4-7.

Licenses and registration, §§32-6-1 to 32-6-331.

Motorcycles and motor-driven cycles, §§32-12-1 to 32-12-44.

Motor vehicle accidents, §§32-10-1 to 32-10-12.

Motor vehicle manufacturers, wholesalers, etc.
Dealings with motor vehicle dealers, §§8-20-1 to 8-20-12.

Motor vehicle safety-responsibility act, §§32-7-1 to 32-7-42.

Municipal testing stations, §§32-18-1 to 32-18-8.

Nonoriginal equipment manufacturer after market crash parts disclosure, §§32-17A-1 to 32-17A-3.

Regulation of operation of motor vehicles, etc., generally, §§32-5-1 to 32-5-316.

Renting, hiring and using motor vehicles, §§32-15-1 to 32-15-8.

Rescue squads, §§32-11-1 to 32-11-4.

Rules of the road, §§32-5A-1 to 32-5A-266.

Selling used motor vehicles, §§32-16-1 to 32-16-4.

State-owned motor vehicles, §§41-17-1 to 41-17-9.

State safety coordinating committee, §§32-3-1 to 32-3-7.

Trucks, trailers and semitrailers, §§32-9-1 to 32-9-32.

Uniform certificate of title and antitheft act, §§32-8-1 to 32-8-88.

Warranty work on motor vehicles, §§32-17-1, 32-17-2.

N

NAVIGATION AND WATERWAYS.

Ameraport deep draft harbor and terminal compact, §§33-9-1 to 33-9-2.

Ameraport offshore harbor and terminal commission, §§33-10-1 to 33-10-26.

Bear creek development authority, §§33-15-1 to 33-15-19.

Coosa valley development authority, §§33-16-1 to 33-16-15.

NAVIGATION AND WATERWAYS—Cont'd

Department of harbors and ports and state docks.

General provisions, §§33-1-1 to 33-1-36.

Development of docks along inland waterways, §§33-2-1 to 33-2-213.

Discharge of litter and sewage from watercraft, §§33-6-1 to 33-6-12.

Elk river development agency, §§33-12-1 to 33-12-10.

Harbor masters, §§33-3-1 to 33-3-6.

Obstructing navigation and dams, §§33-7-1 to 33-7-54.

Pilots and pilotage, §§33-4-1 to 33-4-57.

Port authority, §§33-13-1 to 33-13-13.

Registration and operation of vessels, §§33-5-1 to 33-5-36.

Tombigbee-Tennessee waterway development compact, §§33-8-1 to 33-8-4.

Tombigbee valley development authority, §§33-17-1 to 33-17-15.

P

PARTNERSHIPS.

Limited partnerships, §§10-9A-1 to 10-9A-203.

Partnerships generally, §§10-8-1 to 10-8-103.

PROFESSIONS AND OCCUPATIONS.

Accountants, §§34-1-1 to 34-1-22.

Architects, §§34-2-1 to 34-2-42.

Attorneys-at-law, §§34-3-1 to 34-3-108.

Auctioneers, §§34-4-1 to 34-4-54.

Barbers, §§34-5-1 to 34-5-16.

Billiard rooms, §§34-6-1 to 34-6-35.

Contractors, §§34-8-1 to 34-8-27.

Cosmetologists, §§34-7-1 to 34-7-47.

Counselors, §§34-8A-1 to 34-8A-23.

Dentists and dental hygienists, §§34-9-1 to 34-9-65.

Dietitians and nutritionists, §§34-34-1 to 34-34-4.

Electrical contractors, §§34-36-1 to 34-36-17.

Employment agencies, §§34-10-1 to 34-10-5.

Engineers and land surveyors, §§34-11-1 to 34-11-37.

Fire protection sprinkler systems, §§34-33-1 to 34-33-12.

Foresters, §§34-12-1 to 34-12-37.

Funeral services, §§34-13-1 to 34-13-152.

Hearing aid dealers and fitters, §§34-14-1 to 34-14-33.

Heating and air conditioning contractors, §§34-31-1 to 34-31-34.

PROFESSIONS AND OCCUPATIONS—Cont'd

Hotels, inns and other transient lodging places, §§34-15-1 to 34-15-20.

Impaired professionals' committee, §§34-38-1 to 34-38-8.

Interior designers, §§34-15A-1 to 34-15A-7.

Landscape architecture, §§34-17-1 to 34-17-27.

Medical technicians, §§34-18-1 to 34-18-47.

Midwives, §§34-19-1 to 34-19-10.

Nurses, §§34-21-1 to 34-21-63.

Nursing home administrators, §§34-20-1 to 34-20-16.

Optometrists, §§34-22-1 to 34-22-65.

Pharmacists and pharmacies, §§34-23-1 to 34-23-118.

Physicians and other practitioners of healing arts, §§34-24-1 to 34-24-384.

Plumbers and gas fitters, §§34-37-1 to 34-37-18.

Polygraph examiners, §§34-25-1 to 34-25-36.

Psychologists, §§34-26-1 to 34-26-48.

Real estate brokers, §§34-27-1 to 34-27-69.

Social workers, §§34-30-1 to 34-30-58.

Soil classifiers, §§34-32-1 to 34-32-19.

Speech pathologists and audiologists, §§34-28A-1 to 34-28A-44.

Transient merchants, §§34-35-1 to 34-35-9.

Veterinarians, §§34-29-1 to 34-29-94.

PROPERTY.

Annuity and mortality tables, §§35-16-1 to 35-16-4.

Boundaries, §§35-3-1 to 35-3-25.

Condominium ownership, §§35-8-1 to 35-8-22.

Conveyances and creation of estates, §§35-4-1 to 35-4-412.

Damages for destruction, injury or removal of trees, §§35-14-1 to 35-14-3.

Duty of care owed persons on premises for sporting or recreational purposes, §§35-15-1 to 35-15-28.

General provisions, §§35-1-1 to 35-1-3.

Landlord and tenant, §§35-9-1 to 35-9-100.

Liens, §§35-11-1 to 35-11-456.

Lost or unclaimed property, §§35-12-1 to 35-12-48.

Mortgages, §§35-10-1 to 35-10-51.

Partition, §§35-6-1 to 35-6-126.

Partition fences, §§35-7-1 to 35-7-7.

Salvage, §§35-13-1 to 35-13-10.

Surveys, §§35-2-1 to 35-2-82.

Uniform transfers to minors act, §§35-5A-1 to 35-5A-24.

PUBLIC OFFICERS AND EMPLOYEES.

Administration of funds of pension and retirement plans, §§36-31-1 to 36-31-3.

Attorney general, §§36-15-1 to 36-15-21.

Code of ethics, §§36-25-1 to 36-25-30.

Compensation for death or disability of peace officers, firemen, etc., §§36-30-1 to 36-30-23.

Constables, §§36-23-1 to 36-23-9.

Director of forensic sciences, §§36-18-1 to 36-18-5.

Eligibility for office; residence; commissions, §§36-2-1 to 36-2-10.

Fire fighters' personnel standards and education commission, §§36-32-1 to 36-32-12.

Fire marshal, §§36-19-1 to 36-19-44.

General provisions, §§36-1-1 to 36-1-7.

Governor, §§36-13-1 to 36-13-33.

Impeachment, §§36-11-1 to 36-11-25.

Law enforcement officers generally, §§36-21-1 to 36-21-105.

Maintenance, use, etc., of public property, records, etc., §§36-12-1 to 36-12-64.

Military service during war and national emergencies, §§36-8-1 to 36-8-6.

Miscellaneous offenses generally, §§36-10-1 to 36-10-16.

Notaries public, §§36-20-1 to 36-20-32.

Oaths of office, §§36-4-1 to 36-4-9.

Official bonds, §§36-5-1 to 36-5-68.

Preretirement death benefit program, §§36-27B-1 to 36-27B-6.

Protection of certain state officers and visitors, §§36-33-1 to 36-33-4.

Public employees individual retirement account fund, §§36-27A-1 to 36-27A-7.

Reimbursement of traveling and other expenses, §§36-7-1 to 36-7-42.

Rental of offices for state officers, §§36-24-1 to 36-24-4.

Salaries, §§36-6-1 to 36-6-11.

Secretary of state, §§36-14-1 to 36-14-15.

Sheriffs, §§36-22-1 to 36-22-65.

Social security, §§36-28-1 to 36-28-10.

State auditor, §§36-16-1 to 36-16-11.

State employees' health insurance plan, §§36-29-1 to 36-29-13.

State employees' retirement system, §§36-27-1 to 36-27-103.

PUBLIC OFFICERS AND
    EMPLOYEES—Cont'd
State personnel department
    and merit system,
    §§36-26-1 to 36-26-108.
State treasurer, §§36-17-1 to
    36-17-19.
Terms of office, §§36-3-1 to
    36-3-6.
Vacation of office; filling of
    vacancies, §§36-9-1 to
    36-9-17.

PUBLIC UTILITIES AND
    TRANSPORTATION.
Development of cogeneration
    facilities, §§37-12-1 to
    37-12-5.
Electric cooperatives, §§37-6-1
    to 37-6-49.
Electric membership
    corporations, §§37-7-1 to
    37-7-21.
Incorporation of railroad
    authorities as public
    corporations, §§37-13-1 to
    37-13-21.
Motor vehicle carriers, §§37-3-1
    to 37-3-34.
Municipal corporations,
    §§11-50-1 to 11-50-533.
Penal provisions, §§37-8-1 to
    37-8-280.
Power districts, §§37-5-1 to
    37-5-9.
Public service commission,
    §§37-1-1 to 37-1-157.
Public utilities other than
    transportation companies
    or motor vehicle carriers,
    §§37-4-1 to 37-4-131.
Railroad preservation,
    §§37-10-1 to 37-10-7.
Rapid rail transit compact,
    §37-11-1.
Regulation of air commerce,
    §§37-9-1 to 37-9-32.
Service territories for electric
    suppliers, §§37-14-1 to
    37-14-40.
Transportation companies,
    §§37-2-1 to 37-2-184.

PUBLIC WELFARE.
Assistance to needy blind
    persons, §§38-5-1 to 38-5-7.
Child care, §§38-7-1 to 38-7-18.
Child support programs,
    §§38-10-1 to 38-10-33.
Commission on the aging,
    §§38-3-1 to 38-3-6.
General provisions, §§38-1-1 to
    38-1-6.
Medical assistance to elderly
    persons, §§38-6-1 to 38-6-9.
Protection of aged or disabled
    adults, §§38-9-1 to 38-9-11.
Public assistance generally,
    §§38-4-1 to 38-4-13.
Relief and support of poor
    persons by counties,
    §§38-8-1 to 38-8-3.
State and county departments
    and boards of pensions and
    security, §§38-2-1 to
    38-2-12.
Welfare employment program,
    §§38-11A-1 to 38-11A-4.

PUBLIC WORKS.
Construction of public
    buildings with radioactive
    fallout protection, §§39-6-1,
    39-6-2.
Domestic products and resident
    workmen for public works,
    improvements, etc.,
    §§39-3-1 to 39-3-14.
General provisions, §§39-1-1,
    39-1-2.
Improvement authorities,
    §§39-7-1 to 39-7-34.
Public improvement contracts.
Actions or proceedings upon
    and properly let or
    executed, §§39-5-1 to
    39-5-6.
Letting, execution and
    administration.
State agencies generally,
    §§39-2-1 to 39-2-14.

S

SECURITIES.
Counties and municipal
    corporations.
Redemption of securities,
    §§11-82-1 to 11-82-7.
Securities issued in
    anticipation of grants,
    §§11-64-1 to 11-64-7.
Securities issued in
    anticipation of receipt of
    grants, §§11-81A-1 to
    11-81A-7.
Investment securities,
    §§7-8-101 to 7-8-406.
Securities generally, §§8-6-1 to
    8-6-122.
Securities held by fiduciaries,
    §§19-4-1 to 19-4-42.
Securities tax, §§40-24-1 to
    40-24-8.

STATE GOVERNMENT.
Aboriginal mounds, earthworks
    and other antiquities,
    §§41-3-1 to 41-3-6.
Academy of Honor, §§41-11-1
    to 41-11-6.
Administrative procedure,
    §§41-22-1 to 41-22-27.
Alabama community service
    grant program, §§41-24-1
    to 41-24-5.
Authorities, §§41-10-1 to
    41-10-406.
Boards and commissions,
    §§41-9-1 to 41-9-883.
Boundaries of state, §§41-2-1 to
    41-2-4.
Budget management, §§41-19-1
    to 41-19-12.
Bureau of tourism and travel,
    §§41-7-1 to 41-7-5.
Continuation or termination of
    state agencies, §§41-20-1 to
    41-20-16.
Department of archives and
    history, §§41-6-1 to
    41-6-53.
Department of economic and
    community affairs,
    §§41-23-1 to 41-23-32.
Department of energy,
    §§41-6A-1 to 41-6A-11.
Department of examiners of
    public accounts, §§41-5-1 to
    41-5-24.

STATE GOVERNMENT—Cont'd
Department of finance,
    §§41-4-1 to 41-4-263.
General provisions, §§41-1-1 to
    41-1-10.
Law enforcement planning
    agency, §§41-8A-1 to
    41-8A-13.
Penny trust fund, §§41-15A-1
    to 41-15A-5.
Public contracts, §§41-16-1 to
    41-16-125.
Public library service, §§41-8-1
    to 41-8-25.
Public records, §§41-13-1 to
    41-13-44.
Southern growth policies
    agreement, §§41-18-1 to
    41-18-3.
State code distribution,
    §§41-21-1 to 41-21-8.
State funds.
    Generally, §§41-14-1 to
    41-14-38.
State insurance fund, §§41-15-1
    to 41-15-13.
State-owned motor vehicles,
    §§41-17-1 to 41-17-9.
White House of the
    Confederacy, §§41-12-1 to
    41-12-3.

STATE SYMBOLS AND
    HONORS, §§1-2-1 to 1-2-22.

T

TAXATION.
Assessment of taxes.
    Generally, §§40-7-1 to
    40-7-100.
Compensation of tax assessors,
    tax collectors, revenue
    commissioners, license
    commissioners, etc.,
    §§40-6A-1 to 40-6A-8.
Controlled substances excise
    tax, §§40-17A-1 to
    40-17A-16.
Corporations, §§40-14-1 to
    40-14-103.
County boards of equalization,
    §§40-3-1 to 40-3-26.
Department of revenue,
    §§40-2-1 to 40-2-66.
Distribution of payments made
    in lieu of taxes, §§40-28-1
    to 40-28-4.
Dog race track pari-mutuel
    pool tax, §§40-26A-1 to
    40-26A-17.
Enforcement of tax laws,
    §§40-29-1 to 40-29-120.
Estate and inheritance taxes,
    §§40-15-1 to 40-15-21.
Exemptions from taxation and
    licenses, §§40-9-1 to
    40-9-61.
Financial institution excise tax,
    §§40-16-1 to 40-16-8.
Gasoline and other motor fuels;
    lubricating oils, §§40-17-1
    to 40-17-240.
General provisions, §§40-1-1 to
    40-1-48.
Generation-skipping transfer
    tax, §§40-15A-1 to
    40-15A-14.
Gummed cigarette papers,
    §§40-25A-1 to 40-25A-20.

TAXATION—Cont'd
Income taxes, §§40-18-1 to
40-18-176.
Licenses, §§40-12-1 to
40-12-425.
Minerals.
Severance taxes, §§40-13-1 to
40-13-36.
Motor carrier mileage tax,
§§40-19-1 to 40-19-17.
Multistate tax compact,
§§40-27-1 to 40-27-6.
Municipal corporations,
§§11-51-1 to 11-51-207.
Oil and gas, §§40-20-1 to
40-20-37.
Public utilities, §§40-21-1 to
40-21-107.
Rate of taxation, §§40-8-1 to
40-8-5.
Recordation tax, §§40-22-1 to
40-22-12.
Sale of land, §§40-10-1 to
40-10-166.
Sales and use taxes, §§40-23-1
to 40-23-110.
Securities tax, §§40-24-1 to
40-24-8.
Subjects of taxation and date
taxes due, §§40-11-1 to
40-11-5.
Supernumerary tax collectors,
tax assessors, license
commissioners, etc.,
§§40-6-1 to 40-6-8.

TAXATION—Cont'd
Tax assessors, §§40-4-1 to
40-4-8.
Tax collectors, §§40-5-1 to
40-5-46.
Tobacco tax, §§40-25-1 to
40-25-62.
Transient occupancy tax,
§§40-26-1 to 40-26-21.

U

UNITED STATES.
Cession of land by state,
§§42-3-1 to 42-3-3.
Condemnation of land or
rights-of-way, §§42-2-1 to
42-2-12.
General provisions, §§42-1-1,
42-1-2.

UNIVERSITIES AND
COLLEGES.
Alabama Agricultural and
Mechanical University,
§§16-49-1 to 16-49-55.
Alabama State University,
§§16-50-1 to 16-50-30.
Auburn University, §§16-48-1
to 16-48-12.
Black Heritage Museum of
West Alabama Act,
§§16-62-1 to 16-62-6.
Jacksonville State University,
§§16-52-1 to 16-52-16.

UNIVERSITIES AND
COLLEGES—Cont'd
Livingston University,
§§16-53-1 to 16-53-12.
Sylacauga Nurses Training
School, §§16-58-1 to
16-58-3.
Wallace-Folsom Prepaid
College Tuition Trust
Fund, §§16-63-1 to 16-63-8.
Troy State University,
§§16-56-1 to 16-56-15.
Tuskegee Institute, §§16-57-1
to 16-57-4.
University of Alabama,
§§16-47-1 to 16-47-204.
University of Montevallo,
§§16-54-1 to 16-54-18.
University of North Alabama,
§§16-51-1 to 16-51-15.
University of South Alabama,
§§16-55-1 to 16-55-9.

Y

YOUTH SERVICES.
Department of youth services
and youth services board,
§§44-1-1 to 44-1-77.
Interstate compact on juveniles,
§§44-2-1 to 44-2-26.
Regional custody and care of
youths under jurisdiction of
juvenile court, §§43-3-1 to
43-3-12.

GENERAL INDEX

A

ABANDONED MOTOR VEHICLES ACT.
General provisions, §§32-13-1 to 32-13-8.
See MOTOR VEHICLES.

ABANDONMENT.
Alleys.
Closing and vacating streets, alleys and highways.
General provisions, §§23-4-1 to 23-4-20.
See HIGHWAYS.
Animals.
Destruction, §3-1-8.
Bank accounts.
Uniform disposition of unclaimed property act.
General provisions, §§35-12-20 to 35-12-48.
See LOST OR UNCLAIMED PROPERTY.
Boats.
Notice to department, §33-5-16.
Cemeteries.
Municipal corporations, §§11-47-60 to 11-47-74.
See MUNICIPAL CORPORATIONS.
Children, §13A-13-5.
Coal mines.
Abandoned mine reclamation, §§9-16-120 to 9-16-134.
See COAL.
Contracts.
When recorded contract presumed abandoned, §35-4-75.
Dead bodies.
Distribution of unclaimed bodies for scientific study, §§22-19-20 to 22-19-30.
See DEAD BODIES.
Highways.
Closing and vacating streets, alleys and highways.
General provisions, §§23-4-1 to 23-4-20.
See HIGHWAYS.
Landlord and tenant.
Crops.
Seizure of crops, §35-9-12.
Lost or unclaimed property.
General provisions.
See LOST OR UNCLAIMED PROPERTY.

ABANDONMENT—Cont'd
Lost or unclaimed property —Cont'd
Uniform disposition of unclaimed property act.
General provisions, §§35-12-20 to 35-12-48.
See LOST OR UNCLAIMED PROPERTY.
Minors.
Relief from disabilities of nonage.
See MINORS.
Motor vehicles.
Abandoned motor vehicles.
General provisions, §§32-13-1 to 32-13-8.
See MOTOR VEHICLES.
Municipal corporations.
Cemeteries, §§11-47-60 to 11-47-74.
See MUNICIPAL CORPORATIONS.
Class 5 municipalities.
Mayor/commission/city manager form of government, §§11-44E-200 to 11-44E-202.
See MUNICIPAL CORPORATIONS.
Class 7 municipalities.
Commission form of government, §§11-44A-1 to 11-44A-160.
See MUNICIPAL CORPORATIONS.
Commission form of government.
General provisions, §§11-44-150 to 11-44-162.
See MUNICIPAL CORPORATIONS.
Parent and child.
Termination of parental rights.
Presumption, §26-18-7.
Presumptions.
Contracts.
When recorded contract presumed abandoned, §35-4-75.
Parent and child.
Termination of parental rights.
Arising from abandonment, §26-18-7.
Uniform disposition of unclaimed property act, §§35-12-22 to 35-12-29.
See LOST OR UNCLAIMED PROPERTY.

ABANDONMENT—Cont'd
Property.
Lost or unclaimed property.
General provisions.
See LOST OR UNCLAIMED PROPERTY.
Uniform disposition of unclaimed property act.
General provisions, §§35-12-20 to 35-12-48.
See LOST OR UNCLAIMED PROPERTY.
Salvage.
General provisions, §§35-13-1 to 35-13-10.
See SALVAGE.
Ships and shipping.
Notice to department, §33-5-16.
Shopping carts.
Abandonment on public streets, etc., §13A-8-62.
Streets.
Closing and vacating streets, alleys and highways.
General provisions, §§23-4-1 to 23-4-20.
See HIGHWAYS.

ABATEMENT, REVIVAL AND SURVIVAL OF ACTIONS, §§6-5-460 to 6-5-466.
Barred rights or remedies, Const. Ala., art. IV, §95.
Death of one or more defendants jointly sued, §6-5-466.
Equitable claims, §6-5-464.
Garnishment.
Revival on death of garnishee or contestant, §6-6-395.
Informers.
Actions by, §6-5-461.
Joint defendants.
Revival in case of death of one or more, §6-5-466.
Judgments.
Revival of judgments, §§6-9-190 to 6-9-196.
See JUDGMENTS.
Marriage.
Actions by or against unmarried women.
Abatement upon marriage, §6-5-460.
Personal representative.
Claims by and against in proceedings not of an equitable nature, §6-5-462.

**ABATEMENT, REVIVAL
AND SURVIVAL OF
ACTIONS**—Cont'd
**Personal representative
—Cont'd**
Substitution of personal
representative where no
action filed, §6-5-465.
Real property.
Survival of claims as to
which actions filed,
§6-5-463.
Wrongful death, §6-5-410.

ABATTOIRS.
General provisions.
See SLAUGHTERHOUSES.

**ABDUCTION AND
KIDNAPPING.**
General provisions,
§§13A-6-40 to 13A-6-45.
See KIDNAPPING.

ABETTING.
See AIDING AND ABETTING.

ABORIGINAL MOUNDS.
**Aboriginal mounds,
earthworks and other
antiquities,** §§41-3-1 to
41-3-6.
See HISTORY AND
ARCHIVES.

ABORTION.
Appeals.
Parental consent to
performing abortion
upon minors.
Waiver of written consent
requirements,
§26-21-4.
**Confidentiality of
information.**
Parental consent to
performing abortion
upon minors.
Disclosure of information.
Liability of physician,
§26-21-7.
Waiver of written consent
requirement.
Confidentiality of
proceedings,
§26-21-4.
Confidentiality of
records, §26-21-8.
Persons disclosing
guilty of
misdemeanor,
§26-21-8.
Liability of physician for
disclosure, §26-21-7.
Consent.
Parental consent to
performing abortions
upon minors, §§26-21-1
to 26-21-8. See within
this heading, "Parental
consent to performing
abortions upon minors."
Costs.
Parental consent to
performing abortion
upon minors, §26-21-4.
Definitions.
Parental consent to
performing abortions
upon minors, §26-21-2.

ABORTION—Cont'd
Emergencies.
Parental consent to
performing abortion
upon minors.
Medical emergencies.
Chapter inapplicable to,
§26-21-5.
Guardian and ward.
Parental consent to
performing abortions
upon minors.
Consent of legal guardian,
§26-21-3.
Hearings.
Parental consent to
performing abortion
upon minors.
Waiver of consent,
§26-21-4.
Inducing abortion, §13A-13-7.
Licenses.
Parental consent to
performing abortion
upon minors.
Forfeiture.
Violating chapter,
§26-21-6.
Medical emergencies.
Parental consent to
performing abortion
upon minors.
Chapter inapplicable to,
§26-21-5.
Minors.
Parental consent to
performing abortions
upon minors, §§26-21-1
to 26-21-8. See within
this heading, "Parental
consent to performing
abortions upon minors."
Misdemeanors.
Parental consent to
performing abortion
upon minors.
Confidentiality of records.
Disclosure, §26-21-8.
Violating chapter,
§26-21-6.
Notice.
Parental consent to
performing abortions
upon minors.
Pregnancy caused by
sexual intercourse
with minor's natural
father, etc.
Notice to minor's mother,
§26-21-3.
Waiver of written consent
requirement.
Notice by court to
minor's parents or
legal guardian,
§26-21-4.
**Parental consent to
performing abortions
upon minors,** §§26-21-1 to
26-21-8.
Appeals.
Waiver of written consent
requirement, §26-21-4.
Attorneys at law.
Waiver of written consent
requirement.
Representation of
minors, §26-21-4.

ABORTION—Cont'd
**Parental consent to
performing abortions
upon minors**—Cont'd
Confidentiality of
information.
Disclosure.
Liability of physician,
§26-21-7.
Misdemeanor, §26-21-8.
Waiver of written consent
requirement.
Confidentiality of
proceedings,
§26-21-4.
Confidentiality of records
and information,
§26-21-8.
Persons disclosing
guilty of
misdemeanor,
§26-21-8.
Liability of physician for
disclosure, §26-21-7.
Costs.
Waiver of written consent
requirement, §26-21-4.
Definitions, §26-21-2.
Emancipated minor.
Written consent.
Contents, §26-21-3.
Emergencies.
Medical emergencies.
Chapter inapplicable to,
§26-21-5.
Findings.
Legislative findings,
§26-21-1.
Guardian.
Legal guardian of minor.
Written consent
required, §26-21-3.
Hearings.
Waiver of consent,
§26-21-4.
Liability of physicians.
Disclosure of information,
§26-21-7.
Licenses.
Forfeiture.
Violating chapter,
§26-21-6.
Medical emergencies.
Chapter inapplicable to,
§26-21-5.
Misdemeanors.
Confidentiality of records.
Disclosure, §26-21-8.
Violations of chapter,
§26-21-6.
Mother of minor.
Pregnancy caused by
sexual intercourse
with minor's natural
father, etc.
Written notice to minor's
mother, §26-21-3.
Notice.
Minor's mother.
Pregnancy caused by
sexual intercourse
with minor's natural
father, etc.
Written notice to
minor's mother,
§26-21-3.
Waiver of written consent
requirement.
Notice by court to
parents or legal
guardian, §26-21-4.

ABORTION—Cont'd
Parental consent to performing abortions upon minors—Cont'd
Penalties.
Violations of chapter, §26-21-6.
Petitions.
Waiver of consent, §§26-21-3, 26-21-4.
Pleadings.
Waiver of consent.
Minors identified by initials only, §26-21-4.
Pregnancy caused by sexual intercourse with minor's natural father, adoptive father or stepfather or legal guardian.
Written notice to minor's mother, §26-21-3.
Purposes.
Legislative purposes, §26-21-1.
Records.
Waiver of consent, §26-21-4.
Confidentiality of records and information, §26-21-8.
Persons disclosing guilty of misdemeanor, §26-21-8.
Transcript recorded, §26-21-4.
Reports.
Persons performing abortions or agents, §26-21-8.
Unemancipated minor.
Written consent of parent or guardian.
Required, §26-21-3.
Venue.
Waiver of consent, §26-21-4.
Vital statistics.
Reports of persons performing abortions or agents, §26-21-8.
Waiver.
Written consent, §26-21-3.
Appeals, §26-21-4.
Confidentiality of identity of minor, §26-21-4.
Confidentiality of records and information, §26-21-8.
Liability of physician for disclosure, §26-21-7.
Contents, §26-21-3.
Costs, §26-21-4.
Disclosure of information.
Liability of physician, §26-21-7.
Emancipated minor.
Contents, §26-21-3.
Hearing, §26-21-4.
Identity of minor.
Confidential, §26-21-4.
Notice to parents or guardian by court.
Prohibited, §26-21-4.

ABORTION—Cont'd
Parental consent to performing abortions upon minors—Cont'd
Waiver—Cont'd
Written consent—Cont'd
Petition, §26-21-4.
Assistance to minor in preparing and filing, §26-21-4.
Contents, §26-21-4.
Oath required, §26-21-4.
Pleadings.
Minor identified by initials only, §26-21-4.
Priority of proceedings over other pending matters, §26-21-4.
Procedure, §26-21-4.
Required, §26-21-3.
Rights of minors, §26-21-4.
Venue, §26-21-4.
Written and specific factual findings.
Court to issue, §26-21-4.
Penalties.
Parental consent to performing abortion upon minors.
Violation of chapter, §26-21-6.
Petitions.
Parental consent to performing abortion upon minors.
Waiver of consent, §§26-21-3, 26-21-4.
Physicians.
Inducing or attempting to induce, §13A-13-7.
Parental consent to performing abortions upon minors.
Disclosure of information.
Liability of physicians, §26-21-7.
Generally, §§26-21-1 to 26-21-8. See within this heading, "Parental consent to performing abortions upon minors."
Pleadings.
Parental consent to performing abortion upon minors.
Waiver of consent.
Pleadings to identify minors by initials only, §26-21-4.
Records.
Parental consent to performing abortion upon minors.
Waiver of written consent requirement, §26-21-4.
Confidentiality, §26-21-8.
Persons disclosing guilty of misdemeanor, §26-21-8.
Transcript recorded, §26-21-4.

ABORTION—Cont'd
Reports.
Parental consent to performing abortion upon minors.
Reports to bureau of vital statistics, §26-21-8.
Venue.
Parental consent to performing abortion upon minors.
Waiver of consent, §26-21-4.
Vital statistics.
Reports by persons performing abortions or agents, §26-21-8.

ABSENTEE VOTING,
§§17-10-1 to 17-10-20.
See ELECTIONS.

ABSTRACTS OF TITLE.
Abstract companies.
Licenses, §40-12-41.
Ejectment, §6-6-283.
Forests and forestry.
State forests.
When abstract required, §9-13-42.
Judicial sales, §6-8-30.
Licenses.
Abstract companies, §40-12-41.
Mortgages and deeds of trust.
Failure to keep, §12-13-54.

ABUSE OF CHILDREN.
Child abuse and neglect, §§26-14-1 to 26-14-53.
See MINORS.

ABUTTING LANDOWNERS.
Assessments for public improvements, §11-48-14.
Fences.
Partition fences, §§35-7-1 to 35-7-7.
See PARTITION.
Highways.
Closing and vacating streets, alleys and highways.
Notice, §23-4-2.
Vacation of street or alley, §23-4-20.
Liens.
Improvements on public streets, etc.
General provisions, §§35-11-410 to 35-11-417.
See HIGHWAYS.
Liens.
Highways.
Improvements on public streets, etc.
General provisions, §§35-11-410 to 35-11-417.
See HIGHWAYS.
Municipal corporations.
Assessments for public improvements, §11-48-14.
Maps or plats.
Vacation of streets or alleys by abutting landowners, §35-2-54.
Validation, ratification, etc., §35-2-55.

ABUTTING LANDOWNERS
—Cont'd
Partition fences, §§35-7-1 to 35-7-7.
See PARTITION.
Public utilities.
Damages to abutting owners.
Liability of public utilities in municipal corporations, Const. Ala., art. XII, §227.
Streets or alleys.
Liens.
Improvements on public streets, etc.
General provisions, §§35-11-410 to 35-11-417.
See HIGHWAYS.
Vacation, §23-4-20.
Town surveys, plats or maps.
Vacation of streets or alleys by abutting landowners, §35-2-54.

ACADEMY OF HONOR,
§§41-11-1 to 41-11-6.
Appropriations, §41-11-6.
Chairman, §41-11-4.
Clerical assistance, §41-11-4.
Composition, §41-11-2.
Creation, §41-11-1.
Election of members, §§41-11-2, 41-11-3.
Meetings, §41-11-5.
Members, §§41-11-2, 41-11-3.
Nominations for new members, §41-11-3.
Purpose, §41-11-1.
Quorum, §41-11-5.
Rules and regulations, §41-11-5.
Secretary, §41-11-4.

ACCESSORIES.
See ACCOMPLICES AND ACCESSORIES.

ACCIDENTS.
Accident insurance.
See INSURANCE.
Automobile accidents.
General provisions, §§32-10-1 to 32-10-12.
See MOTOR VEHICLES.
Boats.
Generally, §33-5-25.
Coal.
Mine safety.
See COAL.
Fish and game.
Hunting deaths.
Reporting of accidents, §9-11-21.
Good Samaritan act.
Exemptions from liability, §6-5-332.
Insurance.
See INSURANCE.
Motor vehicles.
General provisions, §§32-10-1 to 32-10-12.
See MOTOR VEHICLES.
Railroads.
Precautions.
Failure to use to prevent accidents, §37-8-114.
Reports, §37-2-91.
Rescue squads.
See RESCUE SQUADS.

ACCIDENTS—Cont'd
Workmen's compensation.
General provisions, §§25-5-1 to 25-5-231.
See WORKMEN'S COMPENSATION.

ACCOMPLICES AND ACCESSORIES.
Aiding and abetting.
See AIDING AND ABETTING.
Criminal liability based upon behavior of another, §§13A-2-21 to 13A-2-25.
Accountability imposed by statute, §13A-2-21.
Complicity.
Promoting or assisting commission of offense, §13A-2-23.
Defenses.
Certain defenses not available, §13A-2-25.
Exceptions, §13A-2-23.
Innocent persons.
Causing innocent persons to engage in criminal behavior.
Accountability of persons causing, §13A-2-22.
Evidence.
Testimony for felony conviction, §12-21-222.
Hindering prosecution or apprehension, §§13A-10-42 to 13A-10-45.
Witnesses.
Testimony for felony conviction, §12-21-222.

ACCORD AND SATISFACTION.
Affirmative defense, ARCP, Rule 8 (c).
Contracts, §§8-1-20 to 8-1-23.

ACCOUNTANTS, §§34-1-1 to 34-1-22.
Advertising.
Evidence of unlawful practice, §34-1-20.
Unlawful use of title "certified public accountant," §34-1-16.
Agriculture.
Department of agriculture and industries.
Clerical work and records.
Accountant in charge of clerical work and records, §2-2-15.
Appeals.
Appeals from decision of board of public accountancy, §34-1-14.
Associations.
Professional corporations.
Generally. See within this heading, "Professional corporations."
Unincorporated professional associations.
Generally. See within this heading, "Unincorporated professional associations."
Board of public accountancy.
Appointment of members, §34-1-3.

ACCOUNTANTS—Cont'd
Board of public accountancy
—Cont'd
Certificates.
Power of board to issue, §34-1-4.
Chairman, §34-1-3.
Compensation of members, §34-1-3.
Created, §34-1-3.
Defined, §34-1-2.
Disciplinary investigations.
Confidentiality, §34-1-3.
Election of officers, §34-1-3.
Enlargement of board, §34-1-3.
Evidence.
Official records of board admissible in evidence, §34-1-3.
Examination, §34-1-4.
Expenses of members, §34-1-3.
Fees.
Disposition, §34-1-22.
Examinations, §34-1-4.
Hearings, §34-1-14.
Nonresident accountants.
Rules governing permits, §34-1-7.
Permits.
Nonresident accountants, §34-1-7.
Professional conduct.
Promulgation of rules, §34-1-3.
Qualification of members, §34-1-3.
Quorum, §34-1-3.
Reappointment of members, §34-1-3.
Records, §34-1-3.
Register.
Publication, §34-1-3.
Reinstatement of certificates, registration or permits, §34-1-15.
Rules and regulations.
Nonresident accountants, §34-1-7.
Professional conduct, §34-1-3.
Promulgation by board, §34-1-3.
Seal, §34-1-3.
Secretary-treasurer, §34-1-3.
Staff.
Employment, §34-1-3.
Terms, §34-1-3.
Vacancies, §34-1-3.
Vice-chairman, §34-1-3.
Censure.
Grounds for censure, §34-1-12.
Partnerships, professional associations or corporations, §34-1-13.
Certificates.
Censure of holder, §34-1-12.
Partnerships, professional associations or corporations, §34-1-13.
Fees, §34-1-4.
Granting, §34-1-4.
Holders of existing certificates, §34-1-4.
Illegal use of title "certified public accountant," §34-1-16.
Revocation, §34-1-12.
Reinstatement, §34-1-15.

ACCOUNTANTS—Cont'd
Certificates—Cont'd
Suspension, §34-1-12.
**Confidentiality of
information.**
Consent of client required for
transfer of working
papers, §34-1-21.
Disciplinary investigations,
§34-1-3.
Corporations.
Professional corporations.
Generally. See within this
heading, "Professional
corporations."
Definitions, §34-1-2.
Depositions.
Hearings, §34-1-14.
Education.
Continuing education
requirements, §34-1-11.
Qualifications of certified
public accountants,
§34-1-4.
Evidence.
Hearings, §34-1-14.
Records.
Admissibility of official
records of board,
§34-1-3.
Unlawful practice, §34-1-20.
Examination.
Certified public accountants,
§34-1-4.
Fees, §34-1-4.
Registration examination,
§34-1-8.
Waiver by board, §34-1-4.
Experience.
Qualifications of certified
public accountants,
§34-1-4.
Fees.
Disposition of fees and
charges, §34-1-22.
Examination fee, §34-1-4.
Foreign accountant
registration fee, §34-1-5.
Nonresident accountants.
Annual permit fees,
§34-1-7.
Permits.
Annual permit fee,
§34-1-11.
Nonresident accountants,
§34-1-7.
Registration.
Fees to be set by board,
§34-1-8.
Initial registration fee,
§34-1-8.
Foreign accountants.
Registration of foreign
accountants, §34-1-5.
Funds.
Deposit of fees and charges,
§34-1-22.
Disbursements from fund,
§34-1-22.
Hearings, §34-1-14.
Appeals, §34-1-14.
Appearance.
Failure to appear,
§34-1-14.
Attorney at law.
Accused entitled to
counsel, §34-1-14.
Counsel for board,
§34-1-14.

ACCOUNTANTS—Cont'd
Hearings—Cont'd
Charges.
Service and contents,
§34-1-14.
Commencement of
proceedings, §34-1-14.
Depositions, §34-1-14.
Evidence, §34-1-14.
Notice, §34-1-14.
Record, §34-1-14.
Subpoenas.
Attendance of witnesses,
§34-1-14.
Transcript, §34-1-14.
Witnesses.
Compelling attendance,
§34-1-14.
Confrontation and cross-
examination, §34-1-14.
Injunctions, §34-1-18.
Licenses.
Public accountants,
§40-12-43.
Certified public
accountants, §40-12-71.
**National society of public
accountants.**
Registration examinations.
Questions to adhere to
established standards,
§34-1-8.
Nonresident accountants.
Registration, §34-1-5.
Rules governing permits,
§34-1-7.
Temporary annual permits,
§34-1-7.
Notice.
Hearings, §34-1-14.
Offices.
Registration and supervision,
§34-1-10.
Resident manager, §34-1-10.
Partnerships.
Illegal use of title "certified
public accountants,"
§34-1-16.
Offices.
Registration and
supervision, §34-1-10.
Registration.
Composed of certified
public accountants,
§§34-1-6, 34-1-9.
Revocation, §34-1-13.
Suspension, §34-1-13.
Withdrawal of members.
Notification to board,
§34-1-9.
Penalties, §34-1-19.
Permits.
Annual permits, §34-1-11.
Censure of holder, §34-1-12.
Continuing education,
§34-1-11.
Expiration, §34-1-11.
Fees, §34-1-7.
Nonresident accountants.
Temporary annual permits,
§34-1-7.
Revocation, §34-1-12.
Partnerships, professional
associations or
corporations, §34-1-13.
Reinstatement, §34-1-15.
Suspension, §34-1-12.
Partnerships, professional
associations or
corporations, §34-1-13.

ACCOUNTANTS—Cont'd
Practice of accountancy.
Unlawful practice, §§34-1-16
to 34-1-20.
Professional corporations.
Admission or withdrawal of
shareholders.
Notification to board,
§34-1-9.
General provisions,
§§10-4-380 to 10-4-406.
See PROFESSIONAL
CORPORATIONS.
Illegal use of title "certified
public accountant,"
§34-1-16.
Offices.
Registration and
supervision, §34-1-10.
Registration, §§34-1-6,
34-1-9.
Revocation or suspension,
§34-1-13.
**Public accountancy act of
1973.**
Citation of act, §34-1-1.
**Qualifications of certified
public accountants,**
§34-1-4.
Registration qualifications,
§34-1-8.
Records.
Board to keep records of
proceedings, §34-1-3.
Disciplinary investigations.
Confidentiality, §34-1-3.
Hearings, §34-1-14.
Registration.
Censure of holder, §34-1-12.
Foreign accountants, §34-1-5.
Offices in state, §34-1-10.
Partnerships, professional
associations or
corporations composed of
certified public
accountants, §§34-1-6,
34-1-9.
Qualifications of public
accountants, §34-1-8.
Revocation, §34-1-13.
Reinstatement, §34-1-15.
Suspension, §34-1-12.
Partnerships, professional
associations or
corporations, §34-1-13.
Reports.
Confidentiality of working
papers, §34-1-21.
Rules and regulations.
Board of public accountancy.
Nonresident accountants,
§34-1-7.
Promulgation, §34-1-3.
**Seals and sealed
instruments.**
Board of public accountancy.
Seal of board, §34-1-3.
Short title of act, §34-1-1.
State treasurer.
Maintenance of fund for fees
and charges collected,
§34-1-22.
Subpoenas.
Hearings, §34-1-14.
Title.
Short title of act, §34-1-1.

ACCOUNTANTS—Cont'd
  Unincorporated professional associations.
    Admission or withdrawal of shareholders.
      Notification to board, §34-1-9.
    General provisions, §§10-10-1 to 10-10-16.
    See UNINCORPORATED PROFESSIONAL ASSOCIATIONS.
  Illegal use of title "certified public accountant," §34-1-16.
  Offices.
    Registration and supervision, §34-1-10.
  Registration, §§34-1-6, 34-1-9.
  Revocation, §34-1-13.
  Suspension, §34-1-13.
  Unlawful practice, §§34-1-16 to 34-1-20.
    Certain acts not prohibited, §34-1-17.
    Enumeration of unlawful acts, §34-1-16.
    Evidence, §34-1-20.
    Injunctions, §34-1-18.
    Penalties, §34-1-19.
  Witnesses.
    Hearings.
      Compelling attendance, §34-1-14.
      Confrontation and cross-examination, §34-1-14.
  Working papers.
    Ownership, §34-1-21.

ACCOUNTS AND ACCOUNTING.
  Accountants.
    General provisions, §§34-1-1 to 34-1-22.
    See ACCOUNTANTS.
  Alcoholic beverage control board.
    Maintenance, examination and audit, §28-3-52.
  Audits.
    See AUDITS.
  Banks and financial institutions.
    Common trust funds, §5-12A-14.
    Record of fiduciary accounts owning interest in fund, §5-12A-8.
  Catfish.
    Promotion of industry.
      Inspection of books and records of sellers, §2-8-291.
  Comptroller.
    General provisions.
      See COMPTROLLER.
  Condominiums.
    Records, §35-8-10.
  Conservators.
    Settlements of accounts of conservators, §§26-5-1 to 26-5-54.
    See CONSERVATORS.

ACCOUNTS AND ACCOUNTING—Cont'd
  Constitution of the United States.
    Receipts and expenditures of public money.
      Publication of statement and account, Const. U. S., Art. I, §9.
  Contractors.
    State licensing board, §34-8-25.
  Correctness of accounts.
    Evidence.
      Verified itemized statement, §12-21-111.
  Counties.
    County commissions.
      Powers and duties, §11-3-11.
    Depositories.
      Opening of accounts, §11-4-46.
    Treasurers.
      Annual account.
        Recordation and posting of copy, §11-4-28.
  Curators, §§26-7A-11 to 26-7A-13.
  Dental service corporations.
    Sales representatives.
      Funds received, §22-21-378.
  Department of examiners of public accounts, §§41-5-1 to 41-5-24.
    Assistants, §41-5-10.
    Attorney general.
      Legal assistance, §41-5-11.
    Audits.
      Periodic audits, §41-5-14.
      Reports.
        Examiners, §41-5-21.
    Bonds, surety.
      Assistants and employees, §41-5-10.
      Chief examiner, §41-5-5.
    Certification of official acts, §41-5-15.
    Charges.
      Settlement of charges, §41-5-22.
    Chief examiner.
      Appointment, §41-5-3.
        Not eligible for appointment to other offices during term, §41-5-4.
      Assistant chief examiner, §41-5-8.
        Authority, §41-5-15.
        Salary, §41-5-9.
      Bond, surety, §41-5-5.
      Delegation of power, §41-5-7.
      Depositions.
        Authority to take, §41-5-15.
      Duties, §41-5-6.
      Elections.
        Not eligible for election to other offices during term, §41-5-4.
      Head of department, §41-5-3.
      Local government records commission.
        Member of commission, §41-13-22.
      Oaths.
        Administering, §41-5-15.

ACCOUNTS AND ACCOUNTING—Cont'd
  Department of examiners of public accounts—Cont'd
    Chief examiner—Cont'd
      Oaths—Cont'd
        Oath of office, §41-5-5.
      Other office.
        Not eligible for appointment or election to, §41-5-4.
      Political affiliation, §41-5-4.
      Powers, §41-5-6.
        Delegation, §41-5-7.
      Qualifications, §41-5-4.
      Removal, §41-5-3.
      Salary, §41-5-9.
      State records commission.
        Member, §41-13-20.
      Subpoenas, §41-5-16.
      Succession, §41-5-3.
      Term, §41-5-3.
      Vacancies, §41-5-3.
      Witnesses, §41-5-16.
    Created, §41-5-1.
    Depositions.
      Authority, §41-5-15.
    Deputy examiner.
      Authority, §41-5-15.
    Disposition of money received, §41-5-24.
    District attorneys.
      Legal assistance, §41-5-11.
    Divisions of department, §41-5-1.
    Employees, §41-5-10.
    Examinations.
      Periodic examinations, §41-5-14.
    Head of department, §41-5-3.
    Legal assistance.
      Attorney general and district attorneys, §41-5-11.
    Legal counsel for department, §41-5-12.
      Assistant legal counsels, §41-5-13.
    Legislative committee on public accounts, §§41-5-18 to 41-5-20.
      Chairman, §41-5-18.
      Compensation, §41-5-19.
      Election, §41-5-18.
      Established, §41-5-18.
      Expenses, §41-5-19.
      Meetings, §41-5-19.
      Membership, §41-5-18.
      Reports, §41-5-20.
      Supervisory agency, §41-5-18.
      Terms, §41-5-18.
      Vacancies, §41-5-18.
      Vice-chairman, §41-5-18.
    Money received by department.
      Disposition, §41-5-24.
    Oaths.
      Administering, §41-5-15.
    Officers to keep uniform accounts, §41-5-23.
    Offices, §41-5-2.
    Receipts by department.
      Disposition of money received, §41-5-24.
    Reports.
      Audits.
        Examiners to make sworn reports, §41-5-21.

ACCOUNTS AND ACCOUNTING—Cont'd
Department of examiners of public accounts—Cont'd
Reports—Cont'd
Legislative committee on public accounts, §41-5-20.
Rules and regulations. Publication, §41-5-17.
Salaries.
Chief examiner and assistant chief examiner, §41-5-9.
Settlement of charges, §41-5-22.
Subpoenas, §41-5-16.
Witnesses, §41-5-16.
Division of control and accounts.
Generally, §41-4-50.
Itemization of accounts against state.
Required, §41-4-54.
Evidence.
Books of account as proof of accounts, §12-21-42.
Verified itemized statement as evidence of account's correctness, §12-21-111.
Examiners of public accounts.
Department of examiners of public accounts, §§41-5-1 to 41-5-24. See within this heading, "Department of examiners of public accounts."
Executors and administrators.
See EXECUTORS AND ADMINISTRATORS.
Governor's mansion advisory board.
Maintenance of account, §41-9-532.
Guardian and ward.
Curators, §§26-7A-11 to 26-7A-13.
Audit and examination of accounts, §26-7A-12.
Confirmation of curator's account, §26-7A-11.
Final records, §26-7A-13.
Deceased guardian.
Books of account kept by. Evidence, §12-21-32.
Evidence.
Books of account kept by, §12-21-32.
Settlement of conservators' accounts, §§26-5-1 to 26-5-54.
See CONSERVATORS.
Uniform guardianship and protective proceedings act.
Conservators.
Accounting to court, §26-2A-147.
Harbors and ports.
Certain expenditures, §33-1-1.
Income tax.
Inventory.
Use to determine income of taxpayer, §40-18-11.

ACCOUNTS AND ACCOUNTING—Cont'd
Income tax—Cont'd
Net income of individuals.
Computation on basis of taxpayer's annual accounting period, §40-18-13.
Returns.
Changes of accounting period, §40-18-30.
Rules and regulations.
Promulgation by department of revenue, §40-18-57.
Unnecessary examination or investigation, §40-18-56.
Insurance.
Mutual aid associations, §27-30-21.
Duty of officers and agents, §27-30-23.
Labor.
Accounts of employers.
Access by department of industrial relations, §25-2-22.
Legislative committee on public accounts, §§41-5-18 to 41-5-20.
Meat and meat products.
False statements or entries, §2-17-34.
Military affairs.
Adjutant general, §31-2-68.
Officers, §31-2-68.
Motor sports hall of fame commission.
Books of account, §41-9-477.
Motor vehicle carriers.
Public service commission.
Authority, §§37-3-7, 37-3-22.
Municipal corporations.
Class 5 municipalities.
Mayor/commission/city manager form of government.
Examination of accounts, §11-44E-54.
Clerks.
Maintenance, etc., of accounts, §11-43-102.
Commission form of government.
Examinations of accounts, §11-44-50.
Council-manager form of government.
See MUNICIPAL CORPORATIONS.
Examinations and reports as to municipal books and accounts, §11-43-85.
Mayor/commission/city manager form of government.
Examinations, §11-44E-54.
Weeds.
Abatement.
Class 2 municipalities. Cost, §11-67-7.
Class 5 municipalities. Cost, §11-67-26.

ACCOUNTS AND ACCOUNTING—Cont'd
Partnerships.
Dissolution.
Partner's right to account, §10-8-98.
Limited partnerships formed since January 1, 1972.
Dissolution.
Settling of accounts, §10-9A-144.
Partner accountable as fiduciary, §10-8-48.
Right of partner to formal accounting, §10-8-46.
Poultry.
False statements or entries, §2-17-34.
Public accounts.
Department of examiners of public accounts, §§41-5-1 to 41-5-24. See within this heading, "Department of examiners of public accounts."
Public officers and employees.
Uniform accounts.
Officers to keep uniform accounts, §41-5-23.
Public service commission.
See PUBLIC SERVICE COMMISSION.
Public utilities.
Uniform systems of accounts.
Public service commission to establish, §37-1-54.
Public works.
Improvement authorities.
Accounts and books. Generally, §39-7-28.
Railroads.
Intrastate operations separated, §37-1-55.
Reports.
Department of examiners of public accounts.
Audits, §41-5-21.
Savings and loan associations.
Accounts generally.
See SAVINGS AND LOAN ASSOCIATIONS.
Small loans.
Generally, §5-18-11.
Southern products mart authority.
Annual audit, §41-10-66.
Space science exhibit commission.
Maintenance and audit of account, §41-9-437.
State departments and agencies.
Department of examiners of public accounts.
Generally, §§41-5-1 to 41-5-24. See within this heading, "Department of examiners of public accounts."
Statement of account.
Verified itemized statement as evidence of accounts correctness, §12-21-111.
Transfers to minors.
Accounting by custodian, §35-5A-20.

**ACCOUNTS AND
    ACCOUNTING**—Cont'd
Transfers to minors—Cont'd
Custodians.
    Permission of court to
        account, §35-5A-20.
    Petition for accounting,
        §35-5A-20.
**USS Alabama battleship
    commission.**
Maintenance and audits of
    books of account,
    §41-9-350.
Vacation time-sharing plans.
Escrow accounts.
    Deficiency, §34-27-61.
    Defined, §34-27-50.
    Failure to place all funds
        in escrow accounts,
        §34-27-55.
    Failure to place 50 percent
        of cash, etc., received
        in escrow, §34-27-58.
Verified itemized statements.
Evidence of accounts
    correctness, §12-21-111.
**Water management and
    drainage.**
Board of water management
    commissioners.
    Annual audit of accounts,
        §9-9-18.
**Water pollution control
    authority, §22-34-11.**
Wills.
Executor's inventory or
    report on final
    settlement.
    Testator may exempt
        executor, §43-2-311.

ACIDS.
**Caustic or corrosive
    substances, §§8-17-20 to
    8-17-24.**

ACKNOWLEDGMENTS.
Attorneys at law.
Powers of attorney, §35-4-28.
Collateral.
Receipt or acknowledgment
    required, §8-1-3.
Conveyances.
See CONVEYANCES.
Corporations.
Forms, §35-4-29.
Deeds.
Conveyances generally.
    See CONVEYANCES.
Electric cooperatives.
Persons authorized to take.
    Officers, directors or
        members not
        disqualified, §37-6-25.
Environmental control.
Improvement authorities.
    Certificate of incorporation,
        §9-6-5.
Evidence.
Improper acknowledgments,
    §35-4-72.
Foreign countries.
Officers authorized to take in
    foreign countries,
    §35-4-26.
Forms, §35-4-29.
Improper acknowledgments.
Evidence, §35-4-72.
Leases.
Leases for more than 20
    years, §35-4-6.

ACKNOWLEDGMENTS
    —Cont'd
**Liens for improvements on
    public streets, etc.**
Satisfaction, §35-11-416.
**Mechanics' and
    materialmen's liens.**
Satisfaction, §35-11-231.
**Mortgages and deeds of
    trust.**
Conveyances generally.
    See CONVEYANCES.
Other states.
Officers authorized to take in
    other states, §35-4-26.
Powers of attorney, §35-4-28.
Real property.
Conveyances generally.
    See CONVEYANCES.
Recordation.
Form of acknowledgment of
    conveyances, §35-4-68.
Improperly acknowledged
    instruments as evidence,
    §35-4-72.
**Savings and loan
    associations.**
Public officers employed by
    or members of
    associations.
    Validation, §5-16-41.
**Seals and sealed
    instruments.**
Proof, §35-4-27.
Sewers.
Liens for improvements on
    public sewers.
    Satisfaction, §35-11-416.
Streets.
Liens for improvements.
    Satisfaction, §35-11-416.
Supreme court.
Justices.
    Taking, §12-2-3.
**Town surveys, plats or
    maps.**
Plats or maps, §35-2-51.
Wills.
Conveyances generally.
    See CONVEYANCES.

**ACQUIRED IMMUNE
    DEFICIENCY
    SYNDROME.**
**Sexually transmitted
    diseases.**
Notifiable diseases generally,
    §§22-11A-1 to 22-11A-38.
    See DISEASES.

ACTINOMYCOSIS.
**Notifiable diseases,
    §§22-11A-1 to 22-11A-38.**
See DISEASES.

ACTIONS.
**Abatement, revival and
    survival, §§6-5-460 to
    6-5-466.**
See ABATEMENT,
    REVIVAL AND
    SURVIVAL OF
    ACTIONS.
Adverse possession.
See ADVERSE
    POSSESSION.
Advertising.
Outdoor advertising.
    Nonconforming signs.
        Removal.
            Determination of just
                compensation,
                §23-1-282.

ACTIONS—Cont'd
Agents.
Acts committed by.
    Sufficient proof, §6-5-300.
Agriculture.
Mutual farming or trucking
    associations, §2-10-104.
Airport authorities, §4-3-50.
Alcoholic beverages.
Beer.
    Business relations between
        wholesalers and
        suppliers.
        Declaratory judgments,
            §28-9-11.
        Violations of provisions,
            §28-9-11.
Minors.
    Illegal liquor sales.
        Parents' or guardians'
            right, §6-5-70.
        Person injured as
            consequence,
            §6-5-71.
Alienation of affections.
Females 19 years of age or
    older.
    No civil claims for, §6-5-331.
Aliens.
Suits against state, Const. U.
    S., Amendment XI.
Arbitration and award.
Reference of controversy to
    arbitrators when no
    action pending, §6-6-2.
Assignments.
Contracts assigned by
    writing and not covered
    by uniform commercial
    code, §§8-5-26 to 8-5-30.
Associations.
Officers.
    Liability of officers of
        nonprofit associations,
        §§10-11-1 to 10-11-5.
Parties.
    Right to commence actions,
        §6-7-80.
Unincorporated associations.
    Actions relating to, ARCP,
        Rule 23.2.
Unincorporated professional
    associations, §10-10-3.
Attachment.
See ATTACHMENTS.
Attorney general.
Defense of suits against
    states, Const. Ala., amd.
    111.
Legal proceedings in name of
    state.
    Institution and
        prosecution, §36-15-12.
Litigation affecting state.
    Defending suits against
        state, Const. Ala.,
        amd. 111.
    Direction and control,
        §36-15-21.
Attorneys at law.
Legal services liability,
    §§6-5-570 to 6-5-581.
    See ATTORNEYS AT
        LAW.
Auctions and auctioneers.
Collection of compensation,
    §34-4-5.
Authorities.
Officers.
    Nonprofit organizations,
        §§10-11-1 to 10-11-5.

ACTIONS—Cont'd
Bad checks.
Rights of action of holders, §6-5-285.
Bailments.
Trespass to personal property, §6-5-263.
Banks and financial institutions.
Credit unions.
Rules and regulations.
Action to determine validity or applicability, §5-17-47.
Liquidation of insolvent banks.
Actions upon rejected claims, §5-8A-44.
Institution of civil action, §5-8A-22.
Savings and loan associations.
Powers, §5-16-24.
Superintendent of banks.
Representation in civil actions, §5-2A-23.
Bear Creek development authority.
Authority may sue and be sued, §33-15-6.
Bishop of diocese.
Powers of corporation, §10-4-4.
Boards and commissions.
Officers.
Liability of officers of nonprofit organizations, §§10-11-1 to 10-11-5.
Boats.
Discharge of litter and sewage, §33-6-10.
Bond issues.
Municipal special health care facility authorities.
Validity, §11-62-9.
Bonds, surety.
Official bonds, §§6-5-30, 6-5-31.
Boundaries.
Actions to determine boundaries, §§35-3-1 to 35-3-25.
See BOUNDARIES.
Breach of contracts.
Commercial code.
Claim or right arising out of breach.
Waiver or renunciation, §7-1-107.
Sales.
Breach, repudiation and excuse, §§7-2-601 to 7-2-616.
See COMMERCIAL CODE.
General provisions.
See CONTRACTS.
Business trusts, §19-3-66.
Change of venue.
See VENUE.
Checks.
Worthless checks.
Right of action of holders, §6-5-285.
Child support programs.
Disposition of payments collected, §38-10-8.

ACTIONS—Cont'd
Child support programs —Cont'd
Enforcement of child support.
Institution of actions, §38-10-7.
Persons owed duty of support.
Right to enforce support, §38-10-10.
Support owed by parents to child.
Child in department's custody or receiving maintenance payments.
Action to assure parent's support, §38-10-32.
Cigarettes.
Tax on gummed cigarette papers.
Collection, §40-25A-14.
Limitation of actions, §40-25A-11.
Claim and delivery.
Trial of right of property, §§6-6-160 to 6-6-168.
See PERSONAL PROPERTY.
Class actions, ARCP, Rule 23.
Coal.
Abandoned mine reclamation.
Landowner's actions, §9-16-128.
Surface mining control and reclamation.
Citizen's actions, §9-16-95.
Commencement of actions, ARCP, Rule 3.
Liens for improvements on public streets, etc., §35-11-413.
Limitation of actions.
See LIMITATION OF ACTIONS.
Mechanics' and materialmen's liens.
Enforcement of liens, §35-11-222.
Statute of limitations.
See LIMITATION OF ACTIONS.
Commercial code.
See COMMERCIAL CODE.
Commission merchants.
Sale of farm produce.
Institution of civil actions upon bonds, §2-29-4.
Condemnation.
Eminent domain.
See EMINENT DOMAIN.
Condominiums.
Generally, §35-8-12.
Constitution of Alabama.
Attorney general may be required to defend actions against state, etc., Const. Ala., amd. 111.
Corporations.
Right to sue and be sued, Const. Ala., art. XII, §240.
Removal after commencement of suit, Const. Ala., art. IV, §95.
Revival of barred rights or remedies, Const. Ala., art. IV, §95.

ACTIONS—Cont'd
Constitution of Alabama —Cont'd
Right to prosecute civil cause, Const. Ala., art. I, §10.
Constitution of the United States.
Actions to which United States a party, Const. U. S., Art. III, §2.
Consumer finance.
Creditors.
Affidavit, §5-19-11.
Contracts.
See CONTRACTS.
Conveyances.
Reformation, §§35-4-150 to 35-4-153.
Coosa Valley development authority.
Power to sue and be sued, §33-16-8.
Corporations.
Derivative actions, ARCP, Rule 23.1.
Form of complaint, ARCP, Form 25.
Dissolution.
Creditor's action, §10-2A-195.
Stockholder's suit, §10-2A-195.
Indemnification of directors, officers, etc., §10-2A-21.
Nonprofit corporations.
Officers liability, §§10-11-1 to 10-11-5.
Powers of corporations, §10-2A-20.
Right to sue and be sued, Const. Ala., art. XII, §240.
Corrections.
Institution finance authority.
Bond issues.
Contest of authorizing resolution, §14-2-15.
Power to maintain, §14-2-8.
Venue, §14-2-33.
Counterclaims.
General provisions, §§6-8-80 to 6-8-86.
See COUNTERCLAIMS.
Rules of civil procedure, ARCP, Rule 13.
Counties.
See COUNTIES.
Courts.
Litigation accountability, §§12-19-270 to 12-19-276.
See COURTS.
Creditor's actions.
General provisions, §§6-6-180 to 6-6-204.
See DEBTORS AND CREDITORS.
Credit unions.
Rules and regulations.
Determining validity or applicability, §5-17-47.
Criminal conversation.
Females 19 years of age or over.
No civil claims, §6-5-331.
Criminal law and procedure.
Effect of title on civil actions, §13A-1-8.

ACTIONS—Cont'd
Criminal law and procedure
  —Cont'd
  Justification and excuse.
    Civil remedy unimpaired,
      §13A-3-21.
Damages.
  See DAMAGES.
Death by wrongful act.
  See WRONGFUL DEATH.
Debtors and creditors.
  Creditor's actions.
    General provisions,
      §§6-6-180 to 6-6-204.
    See DEBTORS AND
      CREDITORS.
Decedents' estates.
  Waste, trespass, etc.
    Actions against executor or
      administrator, §6-5-90.
Deceit.
  Fraudulent deceit, §6-5-104.
  Generally, §6-5-103.
Declaratory judgments.
  General provisions, §§6-6-220
    to 6-6-232.
  See DECLARATORY
    JUDGMENTS.
  Rules of civil procedure,
    ARCP, Rule 57.
Deeds.
  Reformation, §§35-4-150 to
    35-4-152.
Defamation.
  General provisions, §§6-5-180
    to 6-5-189.
  See LIBEL AND
    SLANDER.
Desertion and nonsupport.
  Action initiated for
    enforcement of support.
  Payment of overdue
    support.
    Bond, security or other
      guarantee to secure,
      §30-3-6.
Detinue.
  General provisions, §§6-6-250
    to 6-6-264.
  See DETINUE.
  Rules of civil procedure.
    Seizure of personal
      property, ARCP, Rule
      64 (b).
Dismissal of actions.
  See DISMISSAL OF
    ACTIONS.
Education.
  County boards of education.
    Right to sue, §16-8-40.
  Private colleges and
    universities facilities
    authority, §16-18A-10.
Ejectment, §§6-6-280 to
  6-6-298.
  See EJECTMENT.
Election between actions,
  §6-5-440.
Electric cooperatives,
  §37-6-3.
Electricity.
  Service territories for electric
    suppliers.
    1984 act.
      Action for injunction or
        damages, §37-14-9.
    1985 act.
      Action for injunction or
        damages, §37-14-37.
Electric membership
  corporations, §37-7-10.

ACTIONS—Cont'd
Eminent domain.
  See EMINENT DOMAIN.
Endorsements.
  Contracts assigned by
    writing and not covered
    by uniform commercial
    code.
    Action to charge endorsers,
      §§8-5-26 to 8-5-30.
Environmental control.
  Environmental improvement
    authorities, §9-6-8.
Executors and
  administrators.
  Actions by and against.
    See EXECUTORS AND
      ADMINISTRATORS.
Exemptions from
  administration and
  payment of debts.
  Actions on property before
    set apart.
    Right to commence or
      defend, §6-10-67.
False imprisonment.
  See FALSE
    IMPRISONMENT.
Felonious injury.
  Civil action without criminal
    prosecution, §6-5-370.
Fences.
  Partition fences.
    Action to recover costs and
      expenses, §35-7-7.
Forcible entry and unlawful
  detainer, §§6-6-310 to
  6-6-353.
  See FORCIBLE ENTRY
    AND UNLAWFUL
    DETAINER.
Foreign causes of action.
  Enforcement.
    Jurisdiction of defendant
      obtained in state,
      §6-5-430.
Forests and forestry.
  Forest products.
    Privilege and severance
      taxes.
      Collection of delinquent
        taxes, §9-13-101.
Fraternal benefit societies.
  Conversion into stock or
    mutual life insurance
    company.
    Pending actions, §27-35-10.
Fraternal orders.
  Declaratory actions,
    §§10-4-174 to 10-4-178.
Fraud, §§6-5-100 to 6-5-104.
Frivolous actions.
  Litigation accountability,
    §§12-19-270 to 12-19-276.
  See COURTS.
Governor.
  Actions against state to
    recover lands, §36-13-3.
Guardian ad litem.
  Improper appointment,
    §6-7-103.
Harbors and ports.
  Docks department.
    Department may prosecute
      necessary actions,
      §33-1-21.
Hazardous substances.
  Cleanup fund.
    Actions for costs of
      cleanup, §22-30A-8.

ACTIONS—Cont'd
Hazardous substances
  —Cont'd
  Fees for disposal of
    hazardous waste or
    substances.
    Time limitations under
      chapter, §22-30B-14.
Hazardous waste.
  Fees for disposal of
    hazardous waste or
    substances.
    Time limit for actions
      under chapter,
      §22-30B-14.
Health care authorities.
  Powers of authority,
    §22-21-318.
Highways.
  Authority.
    Maintaining and
      defending, §23-1-175.
  Damages to highways,
    §32-5-9.
  Finance corporation.
    Maintaining and
      defending, §23-1-175.
Husband and wife.
  Alienation of affections.
    Abolished for female
      person 19 years of age
      or over, §6-5-331.
  Prosecution or defense of
    actions in name of
    husband by wife, §6-7-1.
  Torts.
    Wife's torts.
      To sue and be sued alone
        upon torts, §30-4-11.
Income tax.
  See INCOME TAX.
Insurance.
  Disability insurance.
    Provision in policy as to
      legal actions,
      §27-19-14.
  Enforcement of insurance
    code, §27-2-19.
  Insurers.
    Time to answer or plead,
      §27-3-25.
  Mail order insurance,
    §§27-11-4, 27-11-6.
  Reciprocal insurers, §27-31-4.
  Unauthorized insurers,
    §27-10-3.
Investment securities.
  Actions for price, §7-8-107.
  Purchaser.
    Action against purchaser
      for wrongful transfer,
      §7-8-315.
Joint tenants and tenants in
  common.
  Parties.
    Action against cotenant or
      coparcener, §6-7-40.
Judgments.
  Declaratory judgments.
    General provisions,
      §§6-6-220 to 6-6-232.
    See DECLARATORY
      JUDGMENTS.
    Rules of civil procedure,
      ARCP, Rule 57.
  General provisions.
    See JUDGMENTS.

ACTIONS—Cont'd

Labor unions.
Right to work law.
Denial of employment in
violation of article,
§25-7-35.
Landlord and tenant.
Use and occupation of land.
When reasonable
satisfaction may be
recovered, §35-9-100.
Legal services liability,
§§6-5-570 to 6-5-581.
See ATTORNEYS AT LAW.
Libel and slander, §§6-5-180
to 6-5-189.
See LIBEL AND SLANDER.
Licenses.
Recovery of tax, §40-12-2.
Limitation of actions.
See LIMITATION OF
ACTIONS.
Lis pendens, §§35-4-130 to
35-4-139.
See LIS PENDENS.
Litigation accountability,
§§12-19-270 to 12-19-276.
See COURTS.
Malpractice.
General provisions.
See MALPRACTICE.
Masters.
Rules of civil procedure,
ARCP, Rule 53.
Meat and meat products.
Violations.
Admissibility of evidence of
violations, §2-17-31.
**Mechanics' and
materialmen's liens.**
Enforcement of liens,
§§35-11-220 to 35-11-230.
See MECHANICS' AND
MATERIALMEN'S
LIENS.
**Mental health finance
authority.**
Power to sue and be sued,
§41-10-356.
Mentally ill.
Regional mental health
programs and facilities.
Liability of officers of
nonprofit
organizations,
§§10-11-1 to 10-11-5.
Military affairs.
See MILITARY AFFAIRS.
Mines and minerals.
Surface mining reclamation.
Enforcement of final order
of director, §9-16-11.
Minors.
See MINORS.
Monopolies.
By whom and against whom
action may be
commenced, §6-5-60.
Venue, §6-5-60.
**Mortgages and deeds of
trust.**
Reformation of deeds,
mortgages and
conveyances, §§35-4-150
to 35-4-153.
Motor vehicle carriers.
Mileage tax.
Collectible by civil action,
§40-19-3.
Other rights of action not
extinguished, §37-3-19.

ACTIONS—Cont'd

Motor vehicles.
Financial responsibility act.
Matters not to be evidence
in civil actions,
§32-7-12.
Safety-responsibility act.
Chapter not to prevent
other process, §32-7-41.
Used car sales.
Right of action dependent
upon compliance with
provisions of chapter,
§32-16-3.
Multiple actions.
Election between actions,
§6-5-440.
Municipal corporations.
Attorney general may be
required to defend suits,
Const. Ala., amd. 111.
Class 5 municipalities.
Mayor/commission/city
manager form of
government.
Succession of
government.
Continuance of
pending legal
actions,
§11-44E-146.
Historic preservation
commissions, §11-68-12.
Mayor/commission/city
manager form of
government.
Succession of government.
Continuance of pending
legal actions and
proceedings,
§11-44E-146.
Nuisances.
Enjoining and abating,
§§6-5-122, 11-47-118.
Rights of action.
Preserved and enforced.
Notwithstanding change
of name of
organization,
§11-40-4.
Negotiable instruments,
§§6-5-284 to 6-5-286.
Notice.
Filing notice of actions in lis
pendens record,
§35-4-131.
Nuisances.
Lewdness, assignation or
prostitution.
Action to abate and
perpetually enjoin,
§§6-5-142, 6-5-143,
6-5-148, 6-5-149.
See NUISANCES.
Municipal corporations.
Maintenance of civil
actions to enjoin and
abate, §§6-5-122,
11-47-118.
Public nuisances.
Abatement by
municipalities,
§6-5-122.
Right of action, §6-5-121.
Obscenity.
Violations of anti-obscenity
enforcement act.
Injunctive relief,
§13A-12-200.7.

ACTIONS—Cont'd

Oil and gas.
Conservation and regulation
of production.
See OIL AND GAS.
Parent and child.
See PARENT AND CHILD.
Parties.
General provisions.
See PARTIES.
Partition.
Fences.
Action to recover costs and
expenses, §35-7-7.
Trial of title or adverse claim
issues, §6-8-1.
Partnerships.
Limited partnerships.
Derivative actions,
§§10-9A-180 to
10-9A-183.
See PARTNERSHIPS.
Parties.
Maintaining action against
partnership in common
name or against any
associates, §6-7-70.
Peace officers.
Defense.
Payment of fees and costs
in certain cases,
§36-21-1.
Penalties.
Actions for statutory
penalties.
Commencement.
Who may commence,
§6-5-50.
Pending actions.
Lis pendens.
General provisions,
§§35-4-130 to 35-4-139.
See LIS PENDENS.
Personal property.
Detinue.
General provisions,
§§6-6-250 to 6-6-264.
See DETINUE.
Rules of civil procedure.
Seizure of personal
property, ARCP,
Rule 64 (b).
General provisions.
See PERSONAL
PROPERTY.
Replevin.
General provisions.
See REPLEVIN.
Trial of right of property,
§§6-6-160 to 6-6-168.
See PERSONAL
PROPERTY.
Pilots and pilotage.
Bond of pilot.
Actions on bonds, §33-4-40.
State pilotage commission.
Civil actions to recover
forfeitures, §33-4-12.
Polygraph examiners.
License required to maintain
actions, §34-25-30.
Poultry.
Violations.
Admissibility in evidence,
§2-17-31.
Power districts.
Bond issues.
Rights and remedies of
bondholders, §37-5-8.
Power to sue and be sued,
§37-5-3.

ACTIONS—Cont'd
Principal and agent.
Acts committed by agent.
Sufficient proof to sustain
allegation, §6-5-300.
Printing.
Public printing and binding.
Venue of actions on
contracts, §41-4-138.
Products liability, §§6-5-500
to 6-5-525.
See PRODUCTS LIABILITY.
Public lands.
School lands.
Clearing of title, §9-15-37.
**Public officers and
employees.**
Actions on official bonds,
§§6-5-30, 6-5-31.
Attorney general may be
required to defend suits
against officers, Const.
Ala., amd. 111.
Public service commission.
See PUBLIC SERVICE
COMMISSION.
Public utilities.
Utility services actions,
§§6-5-600 to 6-5-605.
See UTILITY SERVICES
ACTIONS.
Public welfare.
Persons owning property and
supported at public
charge.
Civil actions against
certain persons,
§38-1-5.
Public works.
Contracts.
Contract to let in violation
of law.
See PUBLIC WORKS.
Improvement districts,
§39-7-22.
Bond issues, §39-7-25.
Quo warranto, §§6-6-590 to
6-6-604.
See QUO WARRANTO.
Railroad authorities,
§37-13-7.
Suits against manager or
director of authority,
§37-13-10.
Railroads.
Accommodations for
passengers.
Orders of public service
commission.
Failure to comply with
orders, §37-2-113.
Action for damages not
barred, §37-2-116.
Real estate brokers.
Notice to commission of
actions against licensees,
§34-27-31.
Real property.
Adverse possession.
See ADVERSE
POSSESSION.
Ejectment, §§6-6-280 to
6-6-298.
See EJECTMENT.
Forcible entry and unlawful
detainer, §§6-6-310 to
6-6-353.
See FORCIBLE ENTRY
AND UNLAWFUL
DETAINER.

ACTIONS—Cont'd
Real property—Cont'd
General provisions.
See REAL PROPERTY.
Lis pendens, §§35-4-130 to
35-4-139.
See LIS PENDENS.
Redemption, §§6-5-247 to
6-5-257.
See REAL PROPERTY.
Receivers.
Commencement of actions
against receivers,
§6-6-626.
Recordation.
Lis pendens.
General provisions,
§§35-4-130 to 35-4-139.
See LIS PENDENS.
Records.
Orders, judgments and
decrees.
Copying into final record
not required,
§12-20-21.
Pleadings, motions or other
papers.
Original or copies final
record in civil actions,
§12-20-22.
**Reformation of deeds,
mortgages and
conveyances,** §§35-4-150
to 35-4-152.
Removal of actions.
After commencement of suit,
Const. Ala., art. IV, §95.
Change of venue.
See VENUE.
Probate courts.
Removal of estate
administration,
§12-11-41.
Replevin.
General provisions.
See REPLEVIN.
**Restitution to victims of
crimes.**
Civil action by victim of
crime.
Credit for restitution paid,
§15-18-75.
Revival of actions.
General provisions, §§6-5-460
to 6-5-466.
See ABATEMENT,
REVIVAL AND
SURVIVAL OF
ACTIONS.
**Right to prosecute civil
cause,** Const. Ala., art. I,
§10.
Right to work law.
Denial of employment in
violation of article,
§25-7-35.
Rules of civil procedure,
ARCP, Rules 1 to 86.
See RULES OF CIVIL
PROCEDURE.
Sales tax.
Street and highway
contractors.
Collection of tax by civil
action, §40-23-50.
Tax collectible by civil
action, §§40-23-21,
40-23-32.
Street and highway
contractors, §40-23-50.

ACTIONS—Cont'd
**Savings and loan
associations.**
Powers of associations,
§5-16-24.
Savings statute.
New action after adverse
decision, §6-2-39.
Sealed instruments.
Consideration of sealed
instruments.
Impeachment of and
inquiry into, §6-5-287.
Seduction.
See SEDUCTION.
Simultaneous actions.
Election between actions,
§6-5-440.
Slander.
General provisions, §§6-5-180
to 6-5-189.
See LIBEL AND
SLANDER.
Small loans.
Debts or evidences of
indebtedness.
Applicability of chapter to
actions, §5-18-21.
Sports.
Agents.
Jurisdiction determined by
damages claimed,
§8-26-36.
Parties to action against
agent, §8-26-36.
Transfer and assignment of
action, §8-26-36.
State.
Actions by the state, §§6-5-1
to 6-5-4.
Claims against state.
General provisions.
See CLAIMS AGAINST
STATE.
Suits against state, Const. U.
S., Amendment XI.
Attorney general may be
required to defend,
Const. Ala., amd. 111.
**State departments and
agencies.**
Sunset law.
Termination of agency.
Effect upon claims or
rights against
agency, §41-20-14.
Statute of limitations.
See LIMITATION OF
ACTIONS.
Superintendent of banks.
Representation in civil
actions, §5-2A-23.
Support and maintenance.
Action initiated for
enforcement of support.
Payment of overdue
support.
Bond, security, or other
guarantee to secure
payment, §30-3-6.
Suretyship.
Payments by surety pending
action, §8-3-8.
Surety may require creditor
to bring action against
principal, §8-3-13.

ACTIONS—Cont'd
Survival of actions.
General provisions, §§6-5-460 to 6-5-466.
See ABATEMENT, REVIVAL AND SURVIVAL OF ACTIONS.
Taxation.
See TAXATION.
Telephones.
Securities of telephone companies.
Penalties.
Actions to recover, §37-2-182.
Tombigbee Valley development authority.
Power to sue and be sued, §33-17-8.
Transportation companies.
Connecting carriers.
Joint actions against, §37-2-34.
Damages for loss, injury or delay in delivery, §37-2-62.
Joint actions against, §37-2-34.
Overcharges.
Recovery, §37-2-33.
Penalties.
Recovery, §§37-2-17, 37-2-45.
Rights of action not waived, §37-2-44.
Trespass.
See TRESPASS.
Trial.
General provisions.
See TRIAL.
Trial of right of property, §§6-6-160 to 6-6-168.
See PERSONAL PROPERTY.
Unemployment compensation.
Delinquent payments.
Collection, §25-4-134.
Limitation of actions, §25-4-145.
Uniform commercial code.
See COMMERCIAL CODE.
Unincorporated professional associations.
Laws governing actions, §10-10-3.
University of Montevallo.
Corporate powers, §16-54-1.
Use tax.
Actions to prevent or enjoin collection of tax, §40-23-87.
Delinquent taxes.
Actions to collect, §40-23-86.
Returns.
Failing or refusing to furnish returns, §40-23-88.
Utility services actions, §§6-5-600 to 6-5-605.
See UTILITY SERVICES ACTIONS.
Vacation time-sharing plans.
Commission notified of legal action against licensee, §34-27-69.
Venue.
General provisions.
See VENUE.

ACTIONS—Cont'd
Verdict.
General provisions.
See VERDICT.
Waste.
Right of action against executor or administrator, §6-5-90.
Water conservation and irrigation.
Agency.
Power to sue and be sued, §9-10-5.
Corporations.
Power to sue and be sued, §9-10-34.
Water management and drainage.
Districts.
Bond issues.
Proceedings upon default, §9-9-40.
Water system assistance authority.
Power to sue and be sued, §22-23A-6.
Welfare.
Persons owning property and supported at public charge.
Civil actions against certain persons, §38-1-5.
Wills.
Legatees.
Action against personal representative to recover legacy, §43-2-138.
Workmen's compensation.
Co-employee law suits.
See WORKMEN'S COMPENSATION.
Compensation by civil action, §§25-5-30 to 25-5-36.
General provisions.
See WORKMEN'S COMPENSATION.
Wrongful death.
See WRONGFUL DEATH.

ACTUARIAL TABLES.
Annuity and mortality tables, §§35-16-1 to 35-16-4.

ACTUARIES.
Licenses, §40-12-43.

ADDISON, MUNICIPALITY OF.
Economic development, Const. Ala., amd. 256.

ADJOINING OWNERS.
Abutting landowners.
General provisions.
See ABUTTING LANDOWNERS.

ADJUSTERS.
Insurance.
General provisions, §§27-9-1 to 27-9-8.
See INSURANCE.

ADMINISTRATIVE PROCEDURE ACT, §§41-22-1 to 41-22-27.
Agencies.
Adjudicative proceedings.
Commenced prior to October 1, 1983.
Disposition, §41-22-27.

ADMINISTRATIVE PROCEDURE ACT—Cont'd
Agencies—Cont'd
Administrative codes.
Availability, §41-22-7.
Contents, §41-22-7.
Publication, §41-22-7.
Alabama administrative monthly.
Cost to agencies for use, §41-22-7.
Codes, standards and regulations of other agencies.
Adoption by reference, §41-22-9.
Availability from adopting agency, §41-22-9.
Form of reference, §41-22-9.
Contested cases.
Application for rehearing, §41-22-17.
Contents, §41-22-17.
Decision on application, §41-22-17.
Effect on final order, §41-22-17.
Filing, §41-22-17.
Form, §41-22-17.
Service of application on parties of record, §41-22-17.
Argument.
Presentation of arguments, §41-22-12.
Disposition.
Stipulation, settlement, etc., §41-22-12.
Evidence.
Presentation of evidence, §41-22-12.
Rules of evidence in contested cases, §41-22-13.
Final decision.
Adoption of final decision.
Requirement of majority, §41-22-15.
Disqualification from participation.
Grounds, §41-22-18.
Final order, §41-22-16.
Contents, §41-22-16.
Copies.
Service of copies of final order, §41-22-16.
Form, §41-22-16.
Service of notice of final order, §41-22-16.
When rendered, §41-22-16.
Hearings.
Notice, §41-22-12.
Contents of notice, §41-22-12.
Failure to appear, procedure, §41-22-12.
Rehearings, §41-22-17.
Intervention, §41-22-14.
Oral proceedings.
Public attendance, §41-22-12.
Recordings and transcripts, §41-22-12.

ADMINISTRATIVE
PROCEDURE ACT—Cont'd
Agencies—Cont'd
Contested cases—Cont'd
Preliminary and
procedural actions or
rulings.
Judicial review,
§41-22-20.
Appeal from judgment
of circuit court,
§41-22-21.
Proposed order.
Disqualification for
participation.
Grounds, §41-22-18.
Finality, §41-22-15.
Use where official is
unfamiliar with
case, §41-22-15.
Records.
Contents, §41-22-12.
Rehearings.
Application, §41-22-17.
Grounds, §41-22-17.
Right to counsel,
§41-22-12.
Declaratory ruling,
§41-22-11.
Effect, §41-22-11.
Failure to issue ruling.
Effect, §41-22-11.
Judical review, §41-22-11.
Petition, §41-22-11.
Contents, §41-22-11.
Form, §41-22-11.
Defined, §41-22-3.
Existing rules.
Validity, review, etc.,
§41-22-27.
Joint committee on
administrative
regulation review.
Submission of proposed
rules, §41-22-23.
Licenses, §41-22-19.
Denial, §41-22-19.
Grant, §41-22-19.
Renewal, §41-22-19.
Revocation or suspension,
§41-22-19.
Rules.
Adoption, amendment or
repeal, §41-22-5.
Compliance with
provisions.
Validity of rules in
substantial
compliance,
§41-22-5.
Effect of provisions and
other procedural
requirements,
§41-22-5.
Notice of intent,
§41-22-5.
Submission of data by
interested persons,
§41-22-5.
Authority to prescribe,
§41-22-2.
Effective dates of rules,
§41-22-6.
Effect of rule.
Not made available to
public, §41-22-4.
Emergency rule.
Procedure for adoption,
§41-22-5.

ADMINISTRATIVE
PROCEDURE ACT—Cont'd
Agencies—Cont'd
Rules—Cont'd
Filing of copies with
legislative reference
service, §41-22-6.
Information as to
authorship of rules,
§41-22-6.
Petition for adoption,
amendment or repeal,
§41-22-8.
Form, §41-22-8.
Submission upon
procedure of petition,
§41-22-8.
Proceedings to contest
rules.
Limitation of actions,
§41-22-5.
Public access.
Permanent registers and
rules, §§41-22-4,
41-22-6.
Rules applicable to only
one county.
Omission from
publications,
§41-22-7.
Rules governing
organization, practice,
etc.
Adoption by agencies,
§41-22-4.
Uniform system for
numbering, §41-22-7.
Validity or applicability of
rules.
Actions for declaratory
judgment, §41-22-10.
Secretary.
Designation of secretary,
§41-22-6.
Legislative reference
service.
Filing with, §41-22-7.
Rules.
Filing of copies of rules
with secretary,
§41-22-6.
Alabama administrative
code, §41-22-7.
Alabama administrative
monthly, §41-22-7.
Applicability of chapter,
§§41-22-2, 41-22-25.
Committee.
Defined, §41-22-3.
Construction of chapter,
§41-22-25.
Contested case.
Agencies. See within this
heading, "Agencies."
Defined, §41-22-3.
Corrections.
Inmate community
reintegration under SIR
act.
Exemption of program,
§15-18-122.
Declaratory judgments.
Validity of agency rules,
§41-22-10.
Declaratory rulings.
Agencies, §41-22-11.
Definitions, §41-22-3.
Effective date of chapter,
§41-22-27.
Effect on substantive rights,
§41-22-2.

ADMINISTRATIVE
PROCEDURE ACT—Cont'd
Heating and air conditioning
contractors.
Board to comply with act,
§34-31-33.
Joint committee on
administrative
regulation review,
§§41-22-22 to 41-22-24.
Agencies.
Submission of proposed
rules, §41-22-23.
Chairman, §41-22-22.
Compensation, §41-22-22.
Composition, §41-22-22.
Creation, §41-22-22.
Expenses, §41-22-22.
Functions.
Generally, §41-22-22.
Legislature.
Disapproved rules.
Reconsideration,
§41-22-24.
Meetings, §41-22-22.
Proposed rules, §41-22-23.
Amendments by
committee, §41-22-23.
Approval or disapproval,
§41-22-23.
Criteria for review,
§41-22-23.
Submission by agency,
§41-22-23.
Legislature.
Intent of legislature,
§41-22-2.
Joint committee on
administrative
regulation review.
Disapproved rules.
Reconsideration,
§41-22-24.
License.
Defined, §41-22-3.
Licensing.
Defined, §41-22-3.
Probation.
Applicability, §15-18-8.1.
Purpose, §41-22-2.
Quorum.
Defined, §41-22-3.
Repeal of inconsistent laws,
§41-22-26.
Rule.
Defined, §41-22-3.
Short title, §41-22-1.
State departments and
agencies.
Generally. See within this
heading, "Agencies."

ADMIRALTY.
Constitution of the United
States, Const. U. S., Art. I,
§8.
Jurisdiction of courts, Const.
U. S., Art. III, §2.
Ships and shipping.
General provisions.
See SHIPS AND
SHIPPING.
Waters and watercourses.
General provisions.
See WATERS AND
WATERCOURSES.

ADOPTION, §§26-10-1 to 26-10-30.
  Adults for purposes of inheritance, §§43-4-1 to 43-4-4.
    Natural parents.
      Right of inheritance from, §43-4-3.
    Order of adoption.
      Notice to registrar of vital statistics, §43-4-2.
      Petition, §43-4-1.
      Recordation, §43-4-1.
    Petition for order of adoption, §43-4-1.
    Prior vested rights not affected, §43-4-4.
    Relationship of adopted person to adopter and children of adopter, §43-4-3.
    Rights of inheritance, §43-4-3.
  Advertising.
    Adoption agencies.
      Unlicensed agencies, §26-10-8.
  Annulment, §26-10-5.
  Appeals.
    Subsidized adoptions.
      Review of subsidy decisions, §26-10-29.
  Applicability of chapter, §26-10-10.
  Birth certificate, §26-10-4.
  Child care facilities.
    General provisions, §§38-7-1 to 38-7-18.
    See WELFARE.
  Child placement.
    Child-placing agencies.
      Defined, §38-7-2.
    Interstate compact on child placement, §§44-2-20 to 44-2-26.
    See MINORS.
  Consent.
    Parental consent, §26-10-3.
  Constitution of Alabama.
    Probate courts.
      Jurisdiction, Const. Ala., amd. 364.
    Special, private or local laws prohibited, Const. Ala., art. IV, §104.
  Decedents' estates.
    Adoption of adults for purposes of inheritance, §§43-4-1 to 43-4-4.
  Department of human resources.
    Adoption agencies.
      Licensing, §26-10-8.
    Investigation as to petition for adoption, §26-10-2.
    Order of adoption.
      Copy of order to be sent to department, §26-10-4.
    Probate judges.
      Reports to department. Required, §12-13-44.
    Records.
      Order of adoption, §26-10-4.
  District courts.
    Records of proceedings, §12-12-35.
    Transfer to district court from probate court, §12-12-35.

ADOPTION—Cont'd
  Ensuring child's adjustment.
    Requiring adopting person to remain home, §26-10-2.1.
  Fees.
    Investigation services, §26-10-4.1.
    Probate judges' fees, §12-19-90.
  Grandparents.
    Procedure for adoption, §26-10-7.
    Visitation rights, §26-10-5.
  Guardian and ward.
    Uniform guardianship and protective proceedings act.
      Minors.
        Termination of appointment, §26-2A-79.
  Hearings.
    Petition, §26-10-2.
    Subsidized adoption, §26-10-29.
  Hospitals.
    Child placing, §22-21-31.
  Inheritance.
    Adults for purposes of inheritance, §§43-4-1 to 43-4-4.
    Child adopted under law of foreign state, §26-10-6.
    Generally, §26-10-5.
  Inspections.
    Birth certificates, §26-10-4.
  Interstate compact on child placement, §§44-2-20 to 44-2-26.
    See MINORS.
  Investigations.
    Fees, §26-10-4.1.
    Petition for adoption, §26-10-2.
  Licenses.
    Adoption agencies, §26-10-8.
  Names.
    Change of name of child, §26-10-1.
  Nonresidents.
    Conditions precedent to bringing child into state, §38-7-15.
    Subsidized adoption.
      Effect of nonresidence of adopting parents, §26-10-27.
  Orders of adoption.
    Adults for purposes of inheritance.
      Notice to registrar of vital statistics, §43-4-2.
      Petition for order, §43-4-1.
      Recordation, §43-4-1.
    Final order.
      Entry of order, §26-10-4.
    Interlocutory order of adoption, §26-10-4.
  Parent and child.
    Consent of parents, §26-10-3.
    Termination of parental rights.
      Authority of one in custody to place for adoption, §26-18-10.
      Review of efforts to achieve adoption, §26-18-9.
  Penalties.
    Violations of chapter, §26-10-9.

ADOPTION—Cont'd
  Persons employed outside home.
    No rule or regulation to prevent adoption, §26-10-2.1.
  Petition.
    Adults for purposes of inheritance.
      Petition for order of adoption, §43-4-1.
    Contents, §26-10-1.
    Dismissal, §26-10-2.
    Filing, §26-10-1.
    Hearings, §26-10-2.
    Investigations, §26-10-2.
  Probate judges.
    Fees, §12-19-90.
    Reports, §12-13-44.
  Recordation.
    Adults for purposes of inheritance.
      Orders of adoption, §43-4-1.
  Records.
    Birth certificate, §26-10-4.
    District courts.
      Adoption proceedings, §12-12-35.
    Inspections, §26-10-5.
    Order of adoption, §26-10-4.
    Petition, §26-10-5.
    Subsidized adoption.
      Confidentiality, §26-10-28.
  Relatives.
    Procedure for adoption, §26-10-7.
  Reports.
    Probate judges, §12-13-44.
    Subsidized adoption, §26-10-26.
    Violations of chapter, §26-10-9.
  Rules and regulations.
    Subsidized adoptions, §26-10-30.
  Siblings.
    Procedure for adoption by siblings, §26-10-7.
  State board of health.
    Copy of final order of adoption, §26-10-4.
  Stepparents.
    Procedure for adoption by stepparents, §26-10-7.
  Subsidized adoption, §§26-10-20 to 26-10-30.
    Administration of program, §26-10-23.
    Appeals, §26-10-29.
    Certification for subsidy, §§26-10-24 to 26-10-26.
    Agreement between department and adopting family.
      Amount of subsidy, §26-10-25.
      Duration, §26-10-25.
      Form, §26-10-25.
      Limitations of subsidy, §26-10-25.
      Modification, §26-10-26.
      Termination of subsidy, §26-10-26.
    Procedure, §26-10-24.
    Child.
      Defined, §26-10-22.
    Citation, §26-10-20.
    Definitions, §26-10-22.
    Funds.
      Provision for funds, §26-10-23.

ADOPTION—Cont'd
Subsidized adoption—Cont'd
Hearing, §26-10-29.
Appeals, §26-10-29.
Nonresidents.
Effect of nonresidence,
§26-10-27.
Purpose of article, §26-10-21.
Records.
Confidentiality, §26-10-28.
Reports.
Annual report of parents,
§26-10-26.
Review of subsidy decisions,
§26-10-29.
Rules and regulations,
§26-10-30.
Short title, §26-10-20.
**Transfer of proceedings to
district court from
probate court,** §12-12-35.
Violations of chapter,
§26-10-9.
Visitation rights.
Natural grandparents,
§26-10-5.
Vital statistics, §26-10-4.
Birth certificate, §26-10-4.
Registrars.
Order of adoption,
§26-10-4.

ADULT EDUCATION.
Legislative appropriations,
§16-34-4.

ADULTERATION.
Alcoholic beverages,
§28-3A-25.
Beverages, §11-47-136.
Brake fluid, §§8-17-3, 8-17-5.
Candy, §20-1-23.
**Coal mixed with other
substances or with
different quality,**
§13A-9-52.
Cosmetics.
Adulteration and
misbranding, §§20-1-50
to 20-1-57.
See COSMETICS.
Drugs.
Adulteration and
misbranding.
See DRUGS.
Fertilizer, §2-22-17.
Food.
Adulteration and
misbranding.
See FOOD.
Fraud.
Deceptive business practices.
Selling adulterated
commodities,
§13A-9-41.
Grain, §2-20-4.
Ice cream, §2-13-12.
Meat and meat products.
See MEAT AND MEAT
PRODUCTS.
Mellorine, §20-1-137.
Milk and milk products.
Ice cream, §2-13-12.
Petroleum products.
Fraud and deceit in sale,
§8-17-134.
Prohibited, §8-17-83.
**Pharmacists and
pharmacies.**
Sale of adulterated drugs,
§34-23-9.
Poultry, §§2-17-18 to 2-17-20.

ADULTERATION—Cont'd
**Selling adulterated
commodities,** §13A-9-41.
Soft drinks, §20-1-28.

ADULTERY.
Elements of crime, §13A-13-2.

**ADULT PROTECTIVE
SERVICES,** §§38-9-1 to
38-9-11.
**Abuse, neglect and
exploitation,** §§38-9-7 to
38-9-10.
Initiation of charges, §38-9-7.
Method of reporting,
§38-9-8.
Penalties, §38-9-7.
Failure to make report,
§38-9-10.
Prohibited, §38-9-7.
Reports, §§38-9-8 to 38-9-10.
Content, §38-9-8.
Immunity for reporter,
§38-9-9.
Penalty for failure to make
report, §38-9-10.
Required, §38-9-8.
**Arrangements for protective
services.**
When persons eligible,
§38-9-4.
Citation of chapter, §38-9-1.
Definitions, §38-9-2.
**Department of pensions and
security.**
Duty to ascertain persons in
need of care and
protection, §38-9-4.
Exemption of officers and
agents from civil
liability, §38-9-11.
Liability of department for
protective services,
§38-9-4.
**Emergency protective
services,** §38-9-5.
Hearings.
Emergency protective
services, §38-9-5.
Protective placement,
§38-9-6.
Intent of legislature, §38-9-3.
**Legislative findings and
intent,** §38-9-3.
Penalties.
Abuse, neglect and
exploitation, §38-9-7.
Failure to report, §38-9-10.
Protective placement,
§38-9-6.
Reports.
Abuse, neglect and
exploitation, §§38-9-8 to
38-9-10.
**Services to conform to
wishes of person to be
served,** §38-9-4.

ADULTS.
Adoption.
Adults for purposes of
inheritance, §§43-4-1 to
43-4-4.
Education.
Legislative appropriations,
§16-34-4.
Protective services.
General provisions, §§38-9-1
to 38-9-11.
See ADULT PROTECTIVE
SERVICES.

AD VALOREM TAXES.
See TAXATION.

ADVANCEMENTS.
Decedents' estates, §§43-8-49
to 43-8-54.
See DECEDENTS'
ESTATES.

ADVERSE POSSESSION.
**Conveyances by governor or
state agency or
institution.**
Conveyances in cases of
adverse possession,
§35-4-391.
Ejectment.
Proceedings upon defendant's
suggestion, §6-6-286.
Public lands.
Conveyances by governor or
state agency or
institution.
Conveyances in cases of
adverse possession,
§35-4-391.
School lands.
When title acquired by
adverse possession,
§16-20-6.
Time.
Construction of section,
§6-5-200.
When claim may be defended
or prosecuted, §6-5-200.
When title to land conferred
or defeated, §6-5-200.

ADVERTISING.
Accountants.
Evidence of unlawful
practice, §34-1-20.
Unlawful use of title
"certified public
accountant," §34-1-16.
Actions.
Outdoor advertising.
Nonconforming signs.
Removal.
Determination of just
compensation,
§23-1-282.
Adoption agencies.
Advertising by unlicensed
agencies prohibited,
§26-10-8.
Alcoholic beverages.
Antiadvertising liquor law,
§28-3-16.
Display of advertising of
table wine, §28-7-23.
Wet counties, §28-3-16.
Bait advertising.
Class A misdemeanor,
§13A-9-43.
Elements of crime,
§13A-9-43.
Television or radio
broadcasting stations.
Limitation on criminal
liability, §13A-9-44.
Bids for construction.
Awards of contracts,
§23-2-145.
Billboards.
Outdoor advertising.
Generally, §§23-1-270 to
23-1-288. See within
this heading, "Outdoor
advertising."
Butter.
Substitutes for butter,
§2-13-19.

ADVERTISING—Cont'd

Catfish.
Sale of catfish products,
§2-11-33.

Cheese.
Substitutes for cheese,
§2-13-19.

Chiropractors, §34-24-121.
Unlawful advertising,
§34-24-166.

Counties.
Public roads, bridges and
ferries.
Advertising for bids,
§§23-1-92, 23-1-93.

Definitions.
Outdoor advertising,
§23-1-271.

**Dentists and dental
hygienists,** §§34-9-19,
34-9-20.

Drugs.
Imitation controlled
substances.
Advertising prohibited,
§20-2-143.

Elections.
Fair campaign practices.
Cards, pamphlets, etc., to
contain identification,
§17-22A-13.
Identification as paid
political
advertisement,
§17-22A-12.

**Executors and
administrators.**
Distribution or division on
final settlement.
Sale of property,
§§43-2-455, 43-2-624.
Payment of debts.
Sale of property, §43-2-455.

False advertising, §13A-9-42.
Television or radio
broadcasting stations.
Limitation on criminal
liability, §13A-9-44.

**Health maintenance
organizations.**
Untrue or misleading
advertising, §27-21A-13.

**Hearing aid dealers and
fitters.**
False advertising, §34-14-9.

**Heating and air conditioning
contractors.**
Only certified contractors to
advertise, §34-31-24.

Highways.
Rights of way.
Prohibited on highway
rights of way, §23-1-6.

Impotency.
Advertisements concerning
impotency, §22-20-12.

Indictments.
Unregistered securities.
Form of indictment,
§15-8-150.

Licenses, §40-12-45.

Mellorine.
False and misleading
advertising, §20-1-136.

Milk and milk products.
Substitutes for butter and
cheese, §2-13-19.

ADVERTISING—Cont'd

Motor vehicles.
Signs, signals or markers
bearing commercial
advertising prohibited,
§32-5A-36.

Municipal corporations.
Authorized, §11-47-9.
Costs, §11-47-10.
Municipal resources,
§11-47-11.
Streets.
Municipal connecting link
roads.
Use of advertising signs,
§23-1-113.

Oil and gas.
Leases by state.
Costs for necessary legal
advertisements,
§9-17-66.

Optometrists.
Unauthorized advertising,
§34-22-23.

Outdoor advertising,
§§23-1-270 to 23-1-288.
Actions.
Nonconforming signs.
Removal.
Determination of just
compensation,
§23-1-282.
Adjacent area.
Defined, §23-1-271.
Erection and maintenance
of signs.
Prohibited, §23-1-273.
Citation of division,
§23-1-270.
Controversies, §23-1-278.
Declaration of policy,
§23-1-272.
Definitions, §23-1-271.
Enforcement of division,
§23-1-278.
Equitable proceedings to
enforce, §23-1-278.
Erection and maintenance of
signs, §§23-1-273 to
23-1-277.
Adjacent areas.
Prohibited, §23-1-273.
Areas outside urban
centers.
Prohibited beyond limit
of adjacent areas,
§23-1-273.
Controls, §23-1-274.
Criteria, §23-1-274.
Date of erection.
Appearing on signs,
§23-1-276.
Exceptions, §23-1-277.
Identification tags or
decals.
Exceptions, §§23-1-275,
23-1-277.
Lighting, §23-1-274.
Name and address of
owner.
Appearing on signs,
§23-1-277.
Permits.
Applications, §23-1-275.
Exceptions, §23-1-277.
Fees, §23-1-275.
Disposition, §23-1-287.
Issuance, §23-1-275.
Required, §23-1-275.
Exceptions, §23-1-277.
Size of signs, §23-1-274.

ADVERTISING—Cont'd

Outdoor advertising—Cont'd
Erection and maintenance of
signs—Cont'd
Spacing of signs, §23-1-274.
Tags.
Identification tags or
decals.
Exceptions, §§23-1-275,
23-1-277.
Highways.
Rights of way.
Prohibited on, §23-1-6.
Maintenance of signs,
§§23-1-273 to 23-1-277.
Municipal connecting link
roads, §23-1-113.
Nonconforming signs,
§§23-1-279 to 23-1-285.
Removal, §23-1-279.
Just compensation,
§23-1-279.
Acceptance of federal
funds, §23-1-285.
Action to determine,
§23-1-282.
Availability of funds,
§23-1-283.
Determination,
§23-1-282.
For what compensation
paid, §23-1-281.
Sufficient federal funds
required,
§23-1-283.
To whom paid,
§23-1-282.
When paid, §23-1-280.
Penalties.
Vioaltions, §23-1-288.
Policy.
Declaration of policy,
§23-1-272.
Removal of signs.
Nonconforming signs,
§§23-1-279 to 23-1-285.
Violations, §23-1-278.
Rules and regulations.
Penalties.
Violations, §23-1-288.
Promulgation, §23-1-286.
Removal of signs.
Violations, §23-1-278.
Short title of division,
§23-1-270.
Traffic signs or signals
bearing commercial
advertising prohibited,
§32-5A-36.
United States.
Federal funds.
Director authorized to
accept, §23-1-285.
Secretary of transportation.
Agreements with,
§23-1-284.
Violations.
Penalties, §23-1-288.

Peace officers.
State or federal peace officer
magazines.
Solicitation of
advertisements,
§13A-14-5.

Penalties.
Outdoor advertising,
§23-1-288.

ADVERTISING—Cont'd
  Permits.
    Outdoor advertising.
      Erection and maintenance
        of signs. See within
        this heading, "Outdoor
        advertising."
  Petroleum products.
    Reclaimed or re-refined oil,
      §8-17-112.
  Physical therapists.
    Unethical advertising,
      §34-24-217.
  Podiatrists.
    False or misleading
      advertising, §34-24-276.
    False or misleading
      statements in
      advertising, §34-24-231.
  Political signs.
    Outdoor advertising
      generally, §§23-1-270 to
      23-1-288. See within this
      heading, "Outdoor
      advertising."
  Prostatic troubles.
    Advertisements concerning,
      §22-20-12.
  Railroads, §§37-2-114,
    37-8-200.
  Real estate brokers.
    Unlawful advertising,
      §34-27-36.
  Rental-purchase agreements.
    Required provisions, §8-25-5.
  Rules and regulations.
    Outdoor advertising.
      Penalties.
        Violations, 23-1-288.
      Promulgation, §23-1-286.
      Removal of signs.
        Violations of rules and
        regulations,
        §23-1-278.
  Sales.
    Going out of business or
      distress merchandise
      sales, §8-13-16.
    License.
      Display, §8-13-2.
  Seeds.
    Prohibited acts, §2-26-11.
  Sexual weakness, §22-20-12.
  Ships and shipping.
    Name of country of registry
      to be stated, §33-1-34.
  Signs.
    Outdoor advertising.
      Generally, §§23-1-270 to
      23-1-288. See within
      this heading, "Outdoor
      advertising."
  Small loans, §5-18-13.
  **Space science exhibit
    commission.**
    Exhibits and facilities,
      §41-9-436.
  Sports.
    Agents, §8-26-33.
      False information or
      promises concerning
      employment
      prohibited, §8-26-33.
  Tags.
    Outdoor advertising.
      Erection or maintenance of
      signs.
        Identification tags or
        decals, §23-1-275.

ADVERTISING—Cont'd
  **Toll road, bridge and tunnel
    authority.**
    Bids for construction,
      §23-2-145.
  United States.
    Outdoor advertising.
      Federal funds.
        Director authorized to
        accept, §23-1-285.
      Secretary of transportation.
        Agreements with,
        §23-1-284.
  Use tax.
    Advertising assumption or
      absorption by sellers
      prohibited, §40-23-67.
  Vacation time-sharing plans.
    Failure to follow rules of
      advertising, §34-27-51.
  Welfare.
    Child care facilities,
      §38-7-12.
    Penalties, §38-7-16.

AERONAUTICS.
  General provisions, §§4-1-1 to
    4-7-3.
  See AVIATION.

AFFIDAVITS.
  Alcoholic beverages.
    Dry counties.
      See ALCOHOLIC
        BEVERAGES.
  Anatomical gifts.
    Filing of gift made by
      execution of affidavit,
      §22-19-60.
  Attachments.
    See ATTACHMENTS.
  **Banks and financial
    institutions.**
    Fiduciary accounts.
      Transfers.
        Filing of affidavit in
        office of judge of
        probate, §5-11A-34.
  Consumer finance.
    Actions by creditors.
      Affidavit to be filed before
      bringing, §5-19-11.
  Conveyances, §§35-4-69 to
    35-4-71.
  Court costs, §12-19-70.
  Dams.
    Application to erect, §18-2-2.
  Deeds.
    Conveyances generally,
      §§35-4-69 to 35-4-71.
  District attorneys.
    Commencing prosecution on
      own affidavit,
      §12-17-194.
  Docket fees, §12-19-70.
  Elections.
    Absentee voting, §§17-10-7,
      17-10-8.
  Eminent domain.
    Counties.
      Proceeding without
      affidavit, §18-1A-270.
    State.
      Proceeding without
      affidavit, §18-1A-270.
  Evidence.
    Admissibility as evidence,
      §35-4-70.
  Fees.
    Probate judges' fees,
      §12-19-90.

AFFIDAVITS—Cont'd
  Gambling.
    Gambling places.
      Court to examine affiant
      under oath,
      §13A-12-54.
  Garnishment.
    Amount due plaintiff,
      §6-6-391.
  Hardship affidavits.
    Court costs, §12-19-70.
  Highways.
    Department.
      Power to take affidavits,
      §23-1-39.
  Income tax.
    Making false affidavits,
      §40-18-52.
  Judicial sales.
    Notices.
      Publication.
        Existence of agreement
        between officer and
        publisher and that
        sum charged is
        lowest, §6-8-65.
  Landlord and tenant.
    Liens for advances and rent
      of lands, §35-9-35.
    Possession wrongfully
      withheld.
      See LANDLORD AND
        TENANT.
  Licenses.
    False affidavits, §40-12-8.
  Liens.
    Attachment.
      Required before issue,
      §35-11-5.
  Marine resources.
    Boats.
      Licenses.
        Tonnage of vessel,
        §9-12-85.
  **Mortgages and deeds of
    trust.**
    Conveyances generally,
      §§35-4-69 to 35-4-71.
  New trial.
    Time for serving affidavits,
      ARCP, Rule 59 (c).
  Nonresidents.
    Taking of affidavits outside
      state, §12-21-4.
  Outside state.
    Taking of affidavits outside
      state, §12-21-4.
  Personal property.
    Trial of right of property,
      §§6-6-160, 6-6-161.
  Pilots.
    Affidavit to accompany
      application for license,
      §33-4-34.
  Probate judges.
    Fees, §12-19-90.
    Recordation, §35-4-71.
  Property.
    Seizure of person or property.
      Procedure for seizure of
      property, ARCP, Rule
      64 (b).
  **Public officers and
    employees.**
    Public property, papers, etc.
      Recovery of papers,
      property, etc., by
      successors to office,
      §§36-12-22 to 36-12-24.
  Purchases and stores.
    Vendor's affidavit, §41-4-112.

AFFIDAVITS—Cont'd
Quarantine.
Persons desiring to enter or remain in certain places, §22-12-29.
Recordation.
Record as notice of facts recited, §35-4-69.
Recordation by probate judge, §35-4-71.
Records.
Final record, §12-20-22.
Rules of civil procedure.
Seizure of person or property.
Procedure for seizure of property, ARCP, Rule 64 (b).
Searches and seizures.
Seizure of person or property.
Procedure for seizure of property, ARCP, Rule 64 (b).
Summary judgment, ARCP, Rule 56 (e) to (g).
Supreme court.
Justices.
Taking of affidavits, §12-2-3.
Time for motions supported by affidavits, ARCP, Rule 6 (d).

AFFRAYS.
Indictments.
Form of indictment, §15-8-150.

AFRICAN DEVELOPMENT BANK.
Insurance.
Investments of certain insurance companies.
Obligations of African development bank, §27-41-14.

AFRICATOWN, U.S.A. STATE PARK, §§41-10-230 to 41-10-240.
Administration.
Agreements with city of Prichard, §41-10-234.
Advisory committee.
Establishment, organization and duties, §41-10-236.
Africatown, U.S.A. historic preservation authority.
Defined, §41-10-231.
Duties, §41-10-238.
Establishment, §41-10-238.
Boundaries.
Description, §41-10-233.
Citation of article, §41-10-230.
City of Prichard.
Development and administration, §41-10-234.
Commemorative markers and plaques, §41-10-235.
Development.
City of Prichard, §41-10-234.
Established, §41-10-233.
Inclusion in listing of state parks, §41-10-232.
Institute of ethnic science and technology.
Functions, §41-10-237.
Property rights.
Injunction to protect, §41-10-240.
Not to be affected by article, §41-10-239.

AFRICATOWN, U.S.A. STATE PARK—Cont'd
Short title of article, §41-10-230.
Use, §41-10-232.

AGE.
Aged persons.
General provisions.
See AGED PERSONS.
Alcoholic beverages.
Employment of underage person, §28-1-5.
Minimum age for purchasing, consuming, possessing, etc., §28-1-5.
Congress.
Representative in congress, Const. U. S., Art. I, §2.
Senator, Const. U. S., Art. I, §3.
Constitution of the United States.
Congress.
Representative in congress, Const. U. S., Art. I, §2.
Senator, Const. U. S., Art. I, §3.
Elections.
Right to vote not to be abridged on account of age, Const. U. S., Amendment XXVI.
Voting by persons eighteen years of age, Const. U. S., Amendment XXVI.
President of the United States, Const. U. S., Art. II, §1.
Vice-president, Const. U. S., Amendment XII.
Criminal law and procedure.
Immaturity as defense, §13A-3-3.
Education.
Attendance.
See EDUCATION.
Majority.
Age of majority.
Contracting for educational loans, §26-1-5.
Elderly persons.
General provisions.
See AGED PERSONS.
Elections.
Qualifications of voters, Const. Ala., art. VIII, §177.
Right to vote.
Not to be abridged on account of age, Const. U. S., Amendment XXVI.
Persons eighteen years of age, Const. U. S., Amendment XXVI.
Emancipation of minors.
Relief from disabilities of nonage, §§26-13-1 to 26-13-8; Const. Ala., art. IV, §104.
See MINORS.
Fraternal benefit societies.
Members, §27-34-21.
Funerals.
Embalmers.
Licenses.
Qualifications of applicants, §34-13-92.

AGE—Cont'd
Insurance.
Adjusters, §27-9-3.
Annuity contracts.
Misstatement of age, §27-15-20.
Disability insurance.
Age limit, §27-19-36.
Misstatement of age, §27-19-18.
Industrial life insurance policies.
Misstatement, §27-16-7.
Life insurance policies.
Misstatement, §27-15-6.
Pure endowment contracts.
Misstatement of age, §27-15-20.
Jury.
Challenges, §12-16-150.
Qualifications, §12-16-60.
Majority.
Age of majority, §26-1-1.
Contracting for educational loans, §26-1-5.
Uniform guardianship and protective proceedings act.
Termination of appointment, §26-2A-79.
Relief of from disabilities of nonage, §§26-13-1 to 26-13-8; Const. Ala., art. IV, §104.
See MINORS.
Marriage.
Minimum age, §30-1-4.
Military affairs.
Naval militia, §31-2-4.
State militia, §31-2-2.
Unorganized militia, §31-2-5.
Minors.
General provisions.
See MINORS.
Majority.
Age of majority, §26-1-1.
Relief from disabilities of nonage, §§26-13-1 to 26-13-8; Const. Ala., art. IV, §104.
See MINORS.
Motor vehicles.
Driver training schools.
Persons under 16 years of age operating motor vehicles, §32-5-64.
Persons under 16 years of age operating motor vehicles.
Permitting, §32-5-65.
Prohibited, §32-5-64.
Nonage.
Relief from disabilities of nonage, §§26-13-1 to 26-13-8; Const. Ala., art. IV, §104.
See MINORS.
Old age.
General provisions.
See AGED PERSONS.
Peace officers, §36-21-46.
Pilots and pilotage.
Apprentices.
Age limitations, §33-4-31.
Compulsory retirement of bar pilots, §33-4-53.
Requirements, §33-4-31.
President of the United States, Const. U. S., Art. II, §1.

AGE—Cont'd
Vice-president, Const. U. S.,
    Amendment XII.
Wills.
    Who may make will,
    §43-8-130.

AGED PERSONS.
Adult protective services,
    §§38-9-1 to 38-9-11.
    See ADULT PROTECTIVE
        SERVICES.
Appeals.
    Medical assistance to elderly
        persons, §38-6-7.
Assistance.
    Medical assistance to elderly
        persons, §§38-6-1 to
        38-6-9. See within this
        heading, "Medical
        assistance to elderly
        persons."
    Old age pensions.
        Eligibility, §38-4-1.
    State.
        Authorization to
            participate in
            programs to provide
            assistance to the aged,
            §38-1-6.
Buildings.
    Accessibility to and use of
        public buildings,
        §§21-4-1 to 21-4-7.
        See PUBLIC BUILDINGS.
Commission on the aging,
    §§38-3-1 to 38-3-6.
    Appointment, §38-3-1.
    Chairman, §38-3-2.
    Compensation, §38-3-4.
    Composition, §38-3-1.
    Confidential secretary,
        §38-3-5.
    Coordination of activities,
        §38-3-2.
    Creation, §38-3-1.
    Duties, §38-3-2.
    Executive director, §38-3-5.
    Expenses, §38-3-4.
    Gifts, §38-3-6.
    Membership, §38-3-1.
    Officers, §38-3-2.
    Personnel.
        Appointment, §38-3-5.
    Qualification of members,
        §38-3-1.
    Reports.
        Duty to give to legislature,
            §38-3-2.
    Request of money.
        Authority to receive,
            §38-3-6.
    Salary, §38-3-4.
    Statistics.
        Duty to gather, §38-3-2.
    Subcommittees.
        Authority to create,
            §38-3-3.
Counties.
    Programs to provide
        assistance to the aged.
        Authority to participate in
            programs, §38-1-6.
    Recreational, social and
        cultural facilities.
        Planning, establishment,
            etc., §11-80-5.

AGED PERSONS—Cont'd
Curators.
    General provisions,
        §§26-7A-1 to 26-7A-17.
        See GUARDIAN AND
            WARD.
Definitions.
    Medical assistance, §38-6-2.
Drugs.
    Sales tax.
        Exemptions.
            Gross proceeds of sale to
                persons 65 years or
                older, §40-23-4.
Elections.
    Accessibility to registration
        and polling places,
        §§21-4-20 to 21-4-24.
Fraud.
    Medical assistance to elderly
        persons.
        Penalty, §38-6-8.
Gifts.
    Commission on the aging.
        Authority to receive,
            §38-3-6.
Guardian and ward.
    Curators.
        General provisions,
            §§26-7A-1 to 26-7A-17.
            See GUARDIAN AND
                WARD.
    Uniform guardianship and
        protective proceedings
        act, §§26-2A-1 to
        26-2A-160.
        See GUARDIAN AND
            WARD.
Health.
    Long term quality health
        care, §§22-6-20 to
        22-6-27.
        See LONG TERM
            QUALITY HEALTH
            CARE.
    Medicaid program, §§22-6-1
        to 22-6-6.
        See HEALTH.
Hearings.
    Medical assistance to elderly
        persons, §38-6-7.
Income tax.
    Voluntary check-off
        designations, §40-18-147.
**Long term quality health
    care.**
    General provisions, §§22-6-20
        to 22-6-27.
        See LONG TERM
            QUALITY HEALTH
            CARE.
Medicaid program, §§22-6-1
    to 22-6-6.
    See HEALTH.
**Medical assistance to elderly
    persons,** §§38-6-1 to
    38-6-9.
    Administration of program,
        §38-6-1.
    Appeals, §38-6-7.
    Definitions, §38-6-2.
    Department of human
        resources, §38-6-1.
    Determination of scope and
        kind of medical
        assistance, §38-6-3.
    Eligibility for assistance,
        §§38-6-4 to 38-6-6.
        Determination.
            Procedures, §38-6-6.
            Rules, §38-6-4.

AGED PERSONS—Cont'd
**Medical assistance to elderly
    persons**—Cont'd
    Eligibility for assistance
        —Cont'd
        Persons eligible for
            assistance, §38-6-5.
    Fraud.
        False representations.
            Penalties, §38-6-8.
    Hearings.
        Applicants or recipients,
            §38-6-7.
    Long term quality health
        care, §§22-6-20 to
        22-6-27.
        See LONG TERM
            QUALITY HEALTH
            CARE.
    Payments of assistance.
        Eligibility for assistance,
            §38-6-5.
    Penalties.
        False representations,
            §38-6-8.
    Physicians, §38-6-2.
        Participation in program,
            §38-6-2.
        Right to choose
            practitioner, §38-6-2.
    Program authorized, §38-6-1.
    Rules and regulations.
        Determination of eligibility
            for assistance, §38-6-4.
    Scope of medical assistance.
        Determination, §38-6-3.
    Social security.
        Conflicts with social
            security act.
            Suspension of provisions
                of chapter, §38-6-9.
        Eligibility for medical
            assistance, §§38-6-4,
            38-6-5.
Municipal corporations.
    Programs to provide
        assistance to the aged.
        Authority to participate,
            §38-1-6.
    Recreational, social and
        cultural facilities.
        Planning, establishment,
            etc., §11-80-5.
Penalties.
    Medical assistance to elderly
        persons, §38-6-8.
Pensions.
    Eligibility, §38-4-1.
Public assistance generally.
    See WELFARE.
Public buildings.
    Accessibility to and use of
        public buildings,
        §§21-4-1 to 21-4-7.
        See PUBLIC BUILDINGS.
Recreation.
    Counties and municipalities.
        Planning, establishment,
            etc., of facilities,
            §11-80-5.
Reports.
    Commission on the aging,
        §38-3-2.
Rules and regulations.
    Medical assistance to elderly
        persons.
        Determination of eligibility
            for assistance, §38-6-4.
Salaries.
    Commission on the aging,
        §38-3-4.

AGED PERSONS—Cont'd
Sales tax.
Exemptions.
Gross proceeds from sales
to persons 65 years or
older, §40-23-4.
Senior citizens hall of fame,
§§41-9-740 to 41-9-745.
Chairman, §41-9-743.
Composition, §41-9-741.
Election of members,
§41-9-742.
Chairman, §41-9-743.
Establishment, §41-9-740.
Expenses, §41-9-745.
Meetings, §41-9-744.
Purpose, §41-9-740.
Rules and regulations,
§41-9-744.
Secretary, §41-9-743.
Social security.
Medical assistance to elderly
persons, §§38-6-1 to
38-6-9. See within this
heading, "Medical
assistance to elderly
persons."
State.
Programs to provide
assistance to the aged.
Authority to participate in
programs, §38-1-6.
Statistics.
Commission on the aging.
Duty to gather, §38-3-2.
Taxation.
Exemptions from taxation.
Homestead exemptions,
§40-9-19.
Verification of eligibility
by mail, §40-9-21.1.
Principal residence of
persons 65 years or
older, §40-9-21.
Verification of eligibility
by mail, §40-9-21.1.
Sales tax.
Medicines prescribed for
persons 65 years or
older.
Exemption from tax,
§40-23-62.
Use tax.
Medicines prescribed for
persons 65 years or
older.
Exemption from tax,
§40-23-62.
**Uniform guardianship and
protective proceedings
act,** §§26-2A-1 to
26-2A-160.
See GUARDIAN AND
WARD.
Use tax.
Medicines prescribed for
persons 65 years or
older.
Exemptions, §40-23-62.
Welfare.
Medical assistance to elderly
persons, §§38-6-1 to
38-6-9. See within this
heading, "Medical
assistance to elderly
persons."
Public assistance generally.
See WELFARE.

AGENCIES.
Community action agencies,
§§11-96-1 to 11-96-6.
See COMMUNITY ACTION
AGENCIES.
State agencies.
General provisions.
See STATE
DEPARTMENTS AND
AGENCIES.

AGENTS.
Actions.
Acts committed by.
Sufficient proof, §6-5-300.
Agriculture.
Acts or omissions of officers
or agents, §2-1-2.
Commissioner of agriculture
and industries, §2-2-13.
Power to employ, §2-2-8.
**Alabama Agricultural and
Mechanical University.**
Default, §16-49-3.
Alabama State University.
Default, etc., of agents,
§16-50-3.
Alcoholic beverages.
Dry counties.
Enforcement of chapter.
Self-incrimination,
§28-4-320.
Punishment, §28-4-30.
Athletic agents, §§8-26-1 to
8-26-41.
See SPORTS.
Authority, §§8-2-1 to 8-2-6.
Apparent authority.
Principal bound by agent's
acts, §8-2-6.
General agents.
Authority to receive price,
§8-2-2.
Generally, §8-2-1.
Person acting as agent.
Warranty of authority
assumed, §8-2-5.
Purpose of agency.
Authority to effect, §8-2-4.
Representation of authority,
§8-2-4.
Special agents.
Authority to receive price,
§8-2-3.
**Banks and financial
institutions.**
Fiduciary accounts.
Transfers.
Appointment of related
institution as agent,
§§5-11A-33,
5-11A-37.
Bishop of diocese.
Employment, §10-4-4.
Boats.
Special agents to sell boat
licenses, §33-5-20.
Bribery.
Commercial bribery,
§13A-11-120.
Checks.
Sale of checks.
Agents of licensees,
§8-7-10.
Claims against agent.
Setoff against principal's
claim, §8-2-9.
Claims by and against state.
Prosecuted in person or by
counsel or agent,
§41-9-63.

AGENTS—Cont'd
Commercial code.
Bank deposits and
collections.
Agency status of collecting
banks, §7-4-201.
Commercial paper.
Conversion.
Innocent representative,
§7-3-419.
Signature by authorized
representative,
§7-3-403.
Signature in ambiguous
capacity deemed
endorsement, §7-3-402.
Warranties on presentment
and transfer, §7-3-417.
Words describing payee,
§7-3-117.
Investment securities.
Conversion.
No conversion by good
faith delivery,
§7-8-318.
Effect of signature of
transfer agent,
§§7-8-208, 7-8-312.
Corporations.
Foreign corporations.
Registered agents.
See CORPORATIONS.
General provisions.
See CORPORATIONS.
Nonprofit corporations.
See CORPORATIONS.
Cotton.
Appropriation of cotton from
bale by agent having
custody, §2-19-4.
**County industrial
development authorities.**
Liability, §11-92A-12.
Criminal law and procedure.
Commercial bribery,
§13A-11-120.
Employment agencies,
§§34-10-1 to 34-10-5.
Evidence.
Missing persons.
Presumption of signer's
authority, §12-21-91.
Fiduciaries generally.
See FIDUCIARIES.
Fraternal benefit societies,
§§27-34-43, 27-34-44.
General agents.
Authority to receive price,
§8-2-2.
Health care service plans.
Certificates for agents,
§10-4-111.
**Industrial development
corporations.**
Appointment, §10-4-136.
Powers of corporation,
§10-4-133.
Insurance.
General provisions.
See INSURANCE.
Life and disability insurance
representatives, §§27-8-1
to 27-8-28.
See INSURANCE.
Property, casualty and surety
insurance
representatives, §§27-7-1
to 27-7-34.
See INSURANCE.

AGENTS—Cont'd

Investment securities.
Conversion.
No conversion by good faith delivery, §7-8-318.
Effect of signature of transfer agent, §§7-8-208, 7-8-312.

Jacksonville State University.
Default, etc., not to work forfeiture, §16-52-11.

Land agents.
Public lands, §9-2-130.

Liability of principal.
Apparent authority, §8-2-6.
Negligence and omission of agent, §8-2-7.

Limitation of actions.
Commencement of limitation.
Principal against agent, §6-2-6.

Livingston University.
Default, etc., not to work forfeiture, §16-53-11.

Missing persons.
Presumption of signer's authority, §12-21-91.

Motor vehicles.
Uniform certificate of title and antitheft act.
Designated agents.
See MOTOR VEHICLES.

Municipal corporations.
Bonds, surety.
Recordation, §36-5-3.
Principal responsible for negligence, §8-2-7.
Torts.
Liability for negligence of agents, etc., §§11-47-190 to 11-47-192.
Waterworks and sewer boards.
Management and operation as agents of municipality, §§11-50-290, 11-50-291.

Notice.
Claim against agent before notice of agency.
Setoff against principal's claim by person having, §8-2-9.
Notice of whatever either has notice of, §8-2-8.

Nurseries.
Registration, §2-25-7.

Partnerships.
Dissolution.
Binding of partnership by partner after dissolution, §10-8-95.
Effect on authority of partners, §10-8-94.
Liability of partner by estoppel, §10-8-55.
Limited partnerships.
Maintenance, §10-9A-3.
Partners as agents of partnership, §10-8-49.

Principal.
Liability of principal.
Apparent authority.
Principal bound by agent's acts, §8-2-6.

AGENTS—Cont'd

Principal—Cont'd
Liability of principal—Cont'd
Negligence and omission of agent in transacting agency, §8-2-7.

Prisons and prisoners.
Work release program.
Inmate not deemed agent of board of corrections, §14-8-5.

Public lands.
Land agent, §9-2-130.

Purpose of agency.
Authority to effect, §8-2-4.

Real estate brokers,
§§34-27-1 to 34-27-69.
See REAL ESTATE BROKERS.

Rebates.
Taking by agents.
Commission merchants, §8-11-5.
Railroad, manufacturing or mining corporation agents, §8-11-4.

Securities.
Civil liabilities, §8-6-19.

Special agents.
Authority to receive price, §8-2-3.

Sports, §§8-26-1 to 8-26-41.
See SPORTS.

Taxation.
Liability of agents, §40-1-7.
Returns.
Separate returns in individual and fiduciary capacity, §40-7-20.

Troy State University.
Default, etc., not to work forfeiture, §16-56-11.

Unincorporated professional associations.
Disqualification to practice.
Withdrawal of agents, §10-10-13.
Professional services rendered through officers or employees, §10-10-12.

University of Montevallo.
Records of transactions.
Required, §16-54-10.

University of North Alabama.
Default, etc., not to work forfeiture, §16-51-11.

Warranty.
Person acting as agent.
Warranty of authority assumed, §8-2-5.

AGISTERS.

Animals.
Lien on animals for feeding, boarding or training, §35-11-71.

Birds.
Lien on birds for feeding, boarding or training, §35-11-71.

Liens.
Birds or animals.
Lien for feeding, boarding or training, §35-11-71.
Livestock.
Lien on stock for pasturage or training, §35-11-70.

AGISTERS—Cont'd

Livestock.
Lien on stock for pasturage or training, §35-11-70.

AGRICULTURAL AND CONSERVATION DEVELOPMENT COMMISSION.

Soil and water conservation.
Cost-share grants.
See SOIL AND WATER CONSERVATION.

AGRICULTURAL LIMING MATERIAL.

General provisions, §§2-23-1 to 2-23-11.
See LIME.

AGRICULTURE.

Accountants.
Department of agriculture and industries.
Accountant in charge of clerical work and records, §2-2-15.

Actions.
Mutual farming or trucking associations, §2-10-104.

Acts or omissions of officers or agents, §2-1-2.

Agencies.
Cooperation required, §2-1-5.
Meetings, §2-1-5.

Agents.
Acts or omissions of officers or agents, §2-1-2.
Commissioner of agriculture and industries.
Appointment, §2-2-13.
Bonds, surety, §2-2-13.
Power to employ, §2-2-8.

Agricultural and industrial exhibit commission,
§§2-7-1 to 2-7-7. See within this heading, "Fairs and exhibits."

Agricultural center.
Agricultural markets and coliseum corporation, §§2-6-70 to 2-6-86. See within this heading, "Agricultural markets and coliseum corporation."
Board.
Employees, §2-6-3.
Establishment, organization and duties, §2-6-1.
Fairs and exhibits.
State aid to agricultural fairs. See within this heading, "Fairs and exhibits."
Lease of corporation's properties to board, §2-6-27.
Rental payments.
State treasurer to disburse, §2-6-34.
Rules and regulations, §2-6-1.
State aid to agricultural fairs, §2-7-32.

AGRICULTURE—Cont'd
  Agricultural center—Cont'd
    Coliseum.
      Agricultural markets and
        coliseum corporation,
        §§2-6-70 to 2-6-86. See
        within this heading,
        "Agricultural markets
        and coliseum
        corporation."
      Construction by
        corporation, §2-6-32.
      Conveyance to corporation
        by state, §2-6-26.
      Lease of coliseum,
        §§2-6-27, 2-6-50 to
        2-6-54.
        Agricultural center fund,
          §2-6-53.
        Appropriations, §2-6-53.
        Authorized, §2-6-51.
        Definitions, §2-6-50.
        Operation of leased
          properties, §2-6-52.
        Rentals, §2-6-54.
        State.
          Lease not to constitute
            debt of state,
            §2-6-54.
    Corporation.
      Authority for
        incorporation, §2-6-22.
      Bond issues.
        Execution of bonds,
          §2-6-29.
        Exemption from
          taxation, §2-6-37.
        Investments, §2-6-36.
        Issuance, §2-6-28.
        Limitation of action to
          contest validity, etc.,
          §2-6-35.
        Notice of bond
          resolution, §2-6-35.
        Pledge for bonds,
          §2-6-30.
        Proceeds from sale.
          Use of proceeds,
            §2-6-31.
        Refunding bonds,
          §2-6-33.
        Resolution.
          Notice, §2-6-35.
        Sale of bonds, §2-6-28.
        Use of proceeds from
          sale, §2-6-31.
        Taxation.
          Exemption from
            taxation, §2-6-37.
        Validity.
          Limitation of action to
            contest validity,
            §2-6-35.
      Certificate of incorporation,
        §2-6-23.
      Coliseum.
        Construction, §2-6-32.
        Conveyance, §2-6-26.
        Lease of coliseum,
          §§2-6-27, 2-6-50 to
          2-6-54.
      Composition, §2-6-24.
      Conveyance of lands to,
        §2-6-26.
      Definitions, §2-6-20.
      Directors, §2-6-24.
      Dissolution, §2-6-38.
      Exemption from taxation,
        §2-6-37.

AGRICULTURE—Cont'd
  Agricultural center—Cont'd
    Corporation—Cont'd
      Lease of properties to
        board, §2-6-27.
      Rental payments,
        §2-6-34.
      Legislative findings and
        intent, §2-6-21.
      Officers, §2-6-24.
      Powers, §2-6-25.
      Procedure for
        incorporation, §2-6-22.
      Property.
        Conveyance to state,
          §2-6-38.
        Exemption from
          taxation, §2-6-37.
        Lease of properties to
          board, §2-6-27.
        Rental payments,
          §2-6-34.
      Record of proceedings,
        §2-6-24.
      State.
        Conveyance of properties
          to state, §2-6-38.
      Taxation.
        Exemption from
          taxation, §2-6-37.
      Venue of actions under
        article, §2-6-35.
    Definitions.
      Corporation, §2-6-20.
      Lease of coliseum, §2-6-50.
    Employees, §2-6-3.
    Fund, §2-6-53.
    Records.
      Corporation.
        Record of proceedings,
          §2-6-24.
    Rules and regulations.
      Agricultural center board,
        §2-6-1.
  **Agricultural development
    authority,** §§2-3A-1 to
    2-3A-16. See within this
    heading, "Development
    authority."
  **Agricultural experiment
    station system,** §§2-30-40
    to 2-30-44.
  Agricultural fund, §§2-9-1 to
    2-9-7.
    Board of agriculture and
      industries.
      Payment of salaries and
        expenses of board,
        §2-9-5.
    Commissioner of agriculture
      and industries.
      Authority, §2-9-4.
      Payment of salaries and
        expenses of
        commissioner, §2-9-5.
    Delinquent fee payments,
      §2-9-2.
    Department of agriculture
      and industries.
      Payment of salary and
        expenses of
        department employees,
        §2-9-5.
    Expenditures.
      Purpose, §2-9-3.
      Pursuant to budget and
        allotment, §2-9-7.
    Payments from fund, §2-9-6.
    Purpose for which fund may
      be expended, §2-9-3.

AGRICULTURE—Cont'd
  Agricultural fund—Cont'd
    Requisitions for payments
      from fund, §2-9-6.
    Source of fund, §2-9-1.
    Unappropriated or
      unexpended funds,
      §2-9-7.
    Warrants for payments from
      fund, §2-9-6.
    Withdrawals, §2-9-7.
  **Agricultural markets and
    coliseum corporation,**
    §§2-6-70 to 2-6-86.
    Authority for incorporation,
      §2-6-72.
    Board of directors, §2-6-74.
    Certificate of incorporation,
      §2-6-73.
    Definitions, §2-6-70.
    Dissolution, §2-6-86.
    Incorporation.
      Authority and procedure,
        §2-6-72.
      Certificate, §2-6-73.
    Investments, §2-6-84.
    Legislative findings, §2-6-71.
    Market facilities.
      Construction, §2-6-79.
    Powers, §2-6-75.
    Procedure for incorporation,
      §2-6-72.
    Purpose, §2-6-71.
    Refunding securities, §2-6-81.
    Renovation of coliseum,
      §2-6-80.
    Securities.
      Amount, §2-6-76.
      Execution, §2-6-77.
      Exemption from taxation,
        §2-6-85.
      Interest, §2-6-76.
        Payment by state
          treasurer, §2-6-82.
      Investment, §2-6-84.
      Issuance, §2-6-76.
        Notice, §2-6-83.
      Principal and interest,
        §2-6-82.
      Proceeds.
        Disposition, §2-6-78.
      Refunding securities,
        §2-6-81.
      Sale, §2-6-76.
        Disposition of proceeds,
        §2-6-78.
      Taxation.
        Exemption, §2-6-85.
      Validity.
        Limitation of actions,
        §2-6-83.
    Taxation.
      Exemption of securities,
        §2-6-85.
    Venue.
      Actions under article,
        §2-6-83.
  **Alabama agricultural and
    mechanical university.**
    General provisions, §§16-49-1
      to 16-49-55.
    See ALABAMA
      AGRICULTURAL
      AND MECHANICAL
      UNIVERSITY.
  Alabama extension service,
    §§2-30-1 to 2-30-4.
    Appropriations, §2-30-4.

AGRICULTURE—Cont'd
Alabama extension service
—Cont'd
Auburn university.
Operated in connection
with Auburn
university, §2-30-1.
Board of agriculture and
industries.
Assistance from specialists
and scientists, §2-3-5.
Commissioner member of
board, §2-3-1.
Creation, §2-30-1.
Director, §2-30-1.
Duties, §2-30-2.
Employees, §2-30-3.
Forests and forestry.
Research and educational
programs, §§2-30-20 to
2-30-24.
Purposes of extension service,
§2-30-2.
Seeds.
Registration of symbol of
seeds or plant parts.
Cooperation, §2-26-52.
Alligator farms, §§9-12-200 to
9-12-214.
See ALLIGATOR FARMS.
Analyses.
Adulterated, misbranded or
substandard articles,
§§2-2-32 to 2-2-37.
Appeals.
Marketing associations.
Orders, §2-10-32.
Refusal of permit, §2-10-25.
Temporary permit
pending appeal,
§2-10-26.
Appropriations.
Markets.
Local appropriations
authorized, §2-5-17.
Associations.
Incorporated marketing
associations, §§2-10-50 to
2-10-74. See within this
heading, "Marketing
associations."
Marketing associations,
§§2-10-20 to 2-10-74. See
within this heading,
"Marketing
associations."
Mutual farming or trucking
associations, §§2-10-90 to
2-10-108. See within this
heading, "Mutual
farming or trucking
associations."
Attachment.
Liens.
Superintendents and
laborers, §§35-11-92 to
35-11-94.
Attorney general.
Board of agriculture and
industries.
Legal advisor to board,
§2-3-6.
Auburn university.
Alabama extension service.
Generally, §§2-30-1 to
2-30-4.
Operated in connection
with, §2-30-1.

AGRICULTURE—Cont'd
Auburn university—Cont'd
Board of agriculture and
industries.
Assistance from specialists
and scientists of
Auburn university,
§2-3-5.
Authorities.
Agricultural development
authority, §§2-3A-1 to
2-3A-16. See within this
heading, "Development
authority."
Farmers' market authority,
§§2-5-1 to 2-5-17. See
within this heading,
"Farmers' market
authority."
**Board of agriculture and
industries.**
Alabama extension service.
Assistance from specialists
and scientists, §2-3-5.
Attorney general.
Legal advisor, §2-3-6.
Auburn university.
Assistance from specialists
and scientists, §2-3-5.
Bread, flour, cornmeal and
grits.
Administration and
enforcement, §20-1-78.
Bulbs.
Promotion of industry.
Certification of growers
association,
§§2-8-123, 2-8-124.
Catfish.
Promotion of industry.
Certification of
producers'
association, §2-8-274.
Rules and regulations,
§2-8-289.
Cattle.
Promotion of cattle
industry, §§2-8-1 to
2-8-22.
See LIVESTOCK.
Commissioner of agriculture
and industries.
Member of board, §2-3-1.
Compensation, §2-3-3.
Composition, §2-3-1.
Cooperative extension
service.
Director member of board,
§2-3-1.
Cosmetics.
Rules and regulations,
§20-1-2.
District attorneys.
Duties, §2-3-6.
Drugs.
Rules and regulations,
§20-1-2.
Standards of purity,
§20-1-21.
Duties, §2-3-4.
Eggs and egg products.
Promotion of industry.
Certification of
producers'
association, §2-8-154.
Rules and regulations,
§2-8-167.
Expenses, §2-3-3.
Payment, §2-9-5.
Farmer members, §2-3-2.

AGRICULTURE—Cont'd
**Board of agriculture and
industries**—Cont'd
Food.
Rules and regulations,
§20-1-2.
Standards of purity,
§20-1-1.
Fruits.
Promotion of industry.
Certification of growers
association,
§§2-8-123, 2-8-124.
Governor.
Appointment of members,
§2-3-2.
Ex officio chairman, §2-3-1.
Grain.
Grading and standards of
grain.
Powers of board,
§2-11-91.
Industry members, §2-3-2.
Legal advisor.
Attorney general, §2-3-6.
Marketing associations.
Violations of purposes of
organization, etc.,
§§2-10-31, 2-10-32.
Marketing of agricultural
products.
Powers, §2-11-3.
Rules and regulations,
§2-11-8.
Meetings.
Staff members
representing superior
at meetings, §2-3-3.
Milk and milk products.
Power of board, §2-13-2.
Notice, §2-2-17.
Nurseries.
Insect and disease control.
See NURSERIES.
Nuts, bulbs, fruits and
vegetables.
Promotion of industry.
Certification of growers'
association,
§§2-8-123, 2-8-124.
Oleomargarine.
Changes of specifications
as to addition of
vitamins, §20-1-112.
Per diem, §2-3-3.
Plants.
Insect and disease control.
See NURSERIES.
Rules and regulations.
Catfish, §2-8-289.
Copies furnished to probate
judges, §2-2-17.
Duties of district attorneys,
§2-3-6.
Eggs and egg products,
§2-8-167.
Evidence, §2-2-17.
Marketing of agricultural
products, §2-11-8.
Salary, §2-9-5.
Seeds.
Rules and regulations,
§2-26-3.
Soybeans.
Promotion of soybean
industry.
Certificate of producers'
association, §2-8-84.

AGRICULTURE—Cont'd
Board of agriculture and industries—Cont'd
Swine.
Promotion of swine industry, §§2-8-40 to 2-8-62.
See LIVESTOCK.
Terms, §2-3-2.
Vegetables.
Promotion of industry.
Certification of growers association, §§2-8-123, 2-8-124.
Warehouses.
Standards, records, rules and regulations, §8-15-2.
Weights and measures, §8-16-15.
Bond issues.
Agricultural center.
Corporations. See within this heading, "Agricultural center."
Agricultural markets and coliseum corporation.
Securities. See within this heading, "Agricultural markets and coliseum corporation."
Development authority, §§2-3A-8 to 2-3A-10.
Bonds, surety.
Commissioner of agriculture and industries, §2-2-3.
Employees' bonds, §2-2-13.
Equivalence to bonds, §§2-2-70 to 2-2-73.
Applicability of trust fund agreements.
Issued in lieu of bond, §2-2-72.
Declaration of legislature, §2-2-70.
Forms, §2-2-71.
Rules and regulations, §2-2-73.
Substitution of bond equivalent, §2-2-71.
Trust fund agreement.
Applicability where agreement issued in lieu of bond, §2-2-72.
When substitution permitted, §2-2-71.
Marketing associations, §2-10-33.
Marketing of agricultural products.
Employees and inspectors, §2-11-9.
Brands and marks.
Grading and standards of farm products and fish, §§2-11-50 to 2-11-59. See within this heading, "Grading and standards of farm products and fish."
Misbranded articles, §§2-2-31 to 2-2-37. See within this heading, "Misbranding."
Bulbs.
Board of agriculture and industries.
Promotion of industry.
Certification of growers associations, §§2-8-123, 2-8-124.

AGRICULTURE—Cont'd
Bulbs—Cont'd
Fruits and vegetables generally.
See FRUITS AND VEGETABLES.
Catfish.
Board of agriculture and industries.
Promotion of industry.
Certification of producers' association, §2-8-274.
Coliseum.
Agricultural center.
Generally. See within this heading, "Agricultural center."
Agricultural markets and coliseum corporation, §§2-6-70 to 2-6-86. See within this heading, "Agricultural markets and coliseum corporation."
Commercial feed law of 1978, §§2-21-16 to 2-21-34.
See FEEDS.
Commissioner of agriculture and industries.
Agents, §2-2-13.
Power to employ, §2-2-8.
Agricultural and industrial exhibit commission.
Member of commission, §2-7-1.
Agricultural center corporation.
Composition, §2-6-24.
Agricultural fund.
Authority, §2-9-4.
Analyses.
Duties, §2-2-33.
Assistance from other state agencies, §2-2-8.
Assistants, §2-2-13.
Designation, §2-2-10.
Power to employ, §2-2-8.
Board of agriculture and industries.
Member of board, §2-3-1.
Bonds, surety, §2-2-3.
Employees' bonds, §2-2-13.
Bread, flour, cornmeal and grits.
Powers and duties, §20-1-78.
Catfish.
Marketing of catfish, §§2-11-30 to 2-11-40.
See CATFISH.
Promotion of industry.
Enforcement duties, §2-8-290.
Cattle.
Promotion of cattle industry.
Enforcement duties, §2-8-21.
Chief executive officer of department, §2-2-1.
Commercial feed law of 1978.
Enforcement, §2-21-18.
Commission merchants.
Sale of farm produce by commission merchants.
See COMMISSION MERCHANTS.
Compensation, Const. Ala., art. V, §118.

AGRICULTURE—Cont'd
Commissioner of agriculture and industries—Cont'd
Confidential information, §2-2-6.
Constitution of Alabama.
Compensation, Const. Ala., art. V, §118.
Duties, Const. Ala., art. V, §137; amd. 111.
Executive department.
Member of department, Const. Ala., art. V, §112.
Fees.
Restrictions on receipt, Const. Ala., art. V, §137; amd. 111.
Mental unsoundness, Const. Ala., art. V, §136.
Qualifications, Const. Ala., art. V, §132.
Residency requirements, Const. Ala., art. V, §118.
Succession.
Ineligible to succeed self, Const. Ala., art. V, §116.
One additional term, Const. Ala., amd. 282.
Term of office, Const. Ala., art. V, §116; amd. 282.
Vacancy in office, Const. Ala., art. V, §136.
Cosmetics.
Enforcement, §20-1-1.
Right of entry, §20-1-3.
Cotton.
Boll weevil eradication.
Duties, §2-19-122.
Right of entry, §2-19-123.
Gins.
Rules and regulations, §2-19-62.
Registration of cotton buyers, §2-19-103.
List.
Publication by commissioner, §2-19-105.
Department of agriculture and industries.
Appointment of legal council, §2-2-12.
Chief executive officer, §2-2-1.
Organization into divisions, §2-2-11.
Drugs.
Enforcement, §20-1-1.
Right of entry, §20-1-3.
Duties, §§2-2-8, 2-2-9, 2-2-11; Const. Ala., art. V, §137; amd. 111.
Eggs and egg products.
Enforcement, §2-12-8.
Promotion of industry.
Enforcement, §2-8-168.
Election.
Constitutional provisions, Const. Ala., art. V, §115.

AGRICULTURE—Cont'd
Commissioner of agriculture and industries—Cont'd
Election—Cont'd
Contest of elections, Const. Ala., art. V, §115.
State officers generally, §§17-15-50 to 17-15-63.
See ELECTIONS.
General elections.
Offices for which general election held, §17-2-2.
Time, §17-2-3.
Returns, Const. Ala., art. V, §114.
Opening, Const. Ala., art. V, §115.
Publication, Const. Ala., art. V, §115.
State officers elected by the people, §17-2-1.
Tie votes, Const. Ala., art. V, §115.
Time, Const. Ala., art. V, §114.
Employees, §2-2-13.
Power to employ, §2-2-8.
Enforcement of laws, §2-2-16.
Executive department.
Member of department, Const. Ala., art. V, §112.
Expenses, §2-9-5.
Feeds.
Commercial feed law of 1978.
Enforcement, §2-21-18.
Fees.
Restrictions on receipt, Const. Ala., art. V, §137; amd. 111.
Fertilizer.
See FERTILIZER.
Food.
Enforcement, §20-1-1.
Right of entry, §20-1-3.
Fruits and vegetables.
Grading and standards.
Powers, §2-11-76.
Rules and regulations, §2-11-77.
Funds.
Agricultural fund.
Authority, §2-9-4.
Grading and standards of farm products and fish.
See within this heading, "Grading and standards of farm products and fish."
Grain.
Grading and standards.
Duties, §2-11-90.
Grain dealers.
See GRAIN DEALERS.
Handbooks.
Publication, §2-2-7.
Honeybees and apiaries.
See HONEYBEES AND APIARIES.
Impeachment, Const. Ala., art. VII, §173.
Inspections.
Books and records, §2-2-6.
Samples, §2-2-37.
Investigations.
Marketing associations, §2-10-29.
Powers, §2-2-8.

AGRICULTURE—Cont'd
Commissioner of agriculture and industries—Cont'd
Landscaping.
Horticulture and floriculture work.
Permits, §§2-28-5, 2-28-7.
Lime.
Right of entry, §2-23-6.
Livestock.
See LIVESTOCK.
Livestock theft investigator.
Appointment, §2-2-14.
Marketing associations, §§2-10-2, 2-10-29 to 2-10-32.
Marketing of agricultural products.
Agreements with other agricultural agencies, §2-11-8.
Powers, §2-11-3.
Markets.
Supervision of operation, §2-3-22.
Meat and meat products.
See MEAT AND MEAT PRODUCTS.
Mental unsoundness, Const. Ala., art. V, §136.
Milk and milk products.
Health regulations.
See MILK AND MILK PRODUCTS.
Permits, §2-13-86.
Notice.
Rules and regulations, §2-2-16.
Nurseries.
Insect and disease control.
See NURSERIES.
Pamphlets, §2-2-7.
Penalties.
Entomology, plant pathology, tree surgery, etc., violations, §2-2-18.
Pesticide violations, §2-2-18.
Pest control.
Permits, §§2-28-5, 2-28-7.
Pesticides.
Application of pesticides, §§2-27-54, 2-27-57.
Plants.
Insect and disease control.
See NURSERIES.
Pathologists.
Permits, §§2-28-5, 2-28-7.
Poultry.
See POULTRY.
Powers, §§2-2-8, 2-2-9.
Publication of handbooks, pamphlets, etc., §2-2-7.
Qualifications, §2-2-2; Const. Ala., art. V, §132.
Records.
Inspection, §2-2-6.
Reports, §2-2-7.
Residency requirements, Const. Ala., art. V, §118.
Rules and regulations, §2-2-16.
Grading and standards of farm products and fish, §2-11-51.
Grading and standards of fruits and vegetables, §2-11-77.
Salary, §2-2-5.

AGRICULTURE—Cont'd
Commissioner of agriculture and industries—Cont'd
Samples.
Inspection, §2-2-37.
Seeds.
Powers and duties, §2-26-2.
Soil testing laboratories, §§2-24-2, 2-24-4, 2-24-5.
Soybeans.
Promotion of soybean industry.
Enforcement, §2-8-101.
Statistics.
Generally, §§2-2-50 to 2-2-53.
Substandard articles.
Tests or analyses.
Duties, §2-2-33.
Succession.
Ineligible to succeed self, Const. Ala., art. V, §116.
One additional term, Const. Ala., amd. 282.
Swine.
Promotion of swine industry.
Enforcement, §2-8-61.
Term of office, §2-2-4; Const. Ala., art. V, §116; amd. 282.
Tests.
Duties, §2-2-33.
Vacancy in office, §2-2-4; Const. Ala., art. V, §136.
Warehouses.
Inspection, §8-15-11.
Supervision, §8-15-1.
Weights and measures, §§8-16-5 to 8-16-7, 8-16-11.
Witnesses.
Examination, §2-2-6.
Commission merchants.
General provisions, §§2-29-1 to 2-29-11.
See COMMISSION MERCHANTS.
Sales representatives commission contracts, §§8-24-1 to 8-24-5.
Conflict of laws.
Incorporated marketing associations, §2-10-68.
Containers of farm products.
Standards, §§8-16-16, 8-16-17.
Contracts, §2-10-65.
Incorporated marketing associations.
Marketing contracts, §2-10-65.
Cooperation.
Cooperation of agricultural agencies, §2-1-5.
Cooperatives.
Defined, §2-1-1.
Marketing associations, §§2-10-20 to 2-10-74. See within this heading, "Marketing associations."
Mutual farming or trucking associations, §§2-10-90 to 2-10-108. See within this heading, "Mutual farming or trucking associations."

AGRICULTURE—Cont'd
Cooperatives—Cont'd
Names.
Use of word "cooperative" in name, §2-10-1.
Corporations.
Acts or omissions of officers or agents, §2-1-2.
Agricultural center. See within this heading, "Agricultural center."
Agricultural markets and coliseum corporation, §§2-6-70 to 2-6-86. See within this heading, "Agricultural markets and coliseum corporation."
Marketing associations.
Incorporated marketing associations, §§2-10-50 to 2-10-74. See within this heading, "Marketing associations."
Cotton.
General provisions, §§2-19-1 to 2-19-135.
See COTTON.
Counties.
Acquisition of lands for public purposes.
Use for agricultural purposes, §11-18-2.
County appropriations for extension work, §2-30-4.
Exhibit of agricultural resources, §11-3-11.
Farmers' market authority.
Appropriations, §2-5-17.
Promotion, §11-3-11.
Crops.
General provisions.
See CROPS.
Partition, §§35-6-110 to 35-6-126.
See PARTITION.
Definitions, §2-1-1.
Agricultural center corporation, §2-6-20.
Lease of coliseum buildings and facilities, §2-6-50.
Agricultural development authority, §2-3A-2.
Agricultural markets and coliseum corporation, §2-6-70.
Development authority, §2-3A-2.
Marketing associations, §2-10-20.
Incorporated marketing associations, §2-10-50.
Mutual farming or trucking associations, §2-10-90.
State aid to agricultural fairs, §2-7-20.
Department of agriculture and industries.
Accountant in charge of clerical work, §2-2-15.
Commissioner.
Chief executive officer, §2-2-1.
Legal counsel.
Appointment by, §2-2-12.
Organization into divisions, §2-2-11.
Cosmetics.
Enforcement of chapter, §20-1-1.

AGRICULTURE—Cont'd
Department of agriculture and industries—Cont'd
Division, §2-26-4.
Organization of department into divisions, §2-2-11.
Qualifications of division heads, §2-2-15.
Drugs.
Enforcement of chapter, §20-1-1.
Eggs and egg products.
Invoices.
Furnishing duplicate copies, §2-12-7.
Employees.
Assignment of duties, §2-2-11.
Insurance, §2-9-22.
Salaries and expenses, §2-9-5.
Estrays.
Investigation of seizure, §3-2-3.
Notice as to seizure, §3-2-2.
Expenses of employees.
Payment, §2-9-5.
Food.
Enforcement of chapter, §20-1-1.
Investigations.
Seed investigation and arbitration committee, §§2-26-70 to 2-26-76.
See SEEDS.
Legal counsel.
Appointment, §2-2-12.
Livestock.
See LIVESTOCK.
Organization into divisions, §2-2-11.
Records, §2-2-15.
Salaries.
Payment, §2-9-5.
Seeds.
Rules and regulations.
Tree or shrub seeds, §2-26-4.
Statistics, §§2-2-50 to 2-2-53.
Development authority, §§2-3A-1 to 2-3A-16.
Board, §2-3A-4.
Bond issues, §§2-3A-8 to 2-3A-10.
Proceeds from sale, §2-3A-9.
Refunding bonds, §2-3A-10.
Sale, §2-3A-9.
Code of ethics.
Applicability of, §2-3A-13.
Cumulative nature of provisions, §2-3A-15.
Declaration of purpose, §2-3A-1.
Definitions, §2-3A-2.
Dissolution of authority, §2-3A-14.
Freedom of authority from state supervision and control, §2-3A-13.
Incorporation of authority, §2-3A-3.
Legislative findings, §2-3A-1.
Legislative oversight committee, §2-3A-6.
Liberal construction of chapter, §2-3A-16.
Meetings.
Open meetings, §2-3A-7.
Officers, §2-3A-5.

AGRICULTURE—Cont'd
Development authority —Cont'd
Powers, §2-3A-7.
Supervision and control of state.
Freedom of authority from, §2-3A-13.
Taxation.
Exemption from, §2-3A-11.
Usury and interest laws.
Exemption from, §2-3A-12.
Director of finance.
Agricultural center corporation.
Composition, §2-6-24.
District attorneys.
Duties, §2-3-6.
Eggs and egg products, §§2-12-1 to 2-12-12.
See EGGS AND EGG PRODUCTS.
Elections.
Commissioner of agriculture and industries. See within this heading, "Commissioner of agriculture and industries."
Eminent domain.
Farmers' market authority.
No right of eminent domain, §2-5-6.
Equivalence to bonds, §§2-2-70 to 2-2-73.
Estrays.
Determination of ownership, §2-15-25.
Investigation of seizure by department, §3-2-3.
Notice as to seizure, §3-2-2.
Evidence.
Analysis of products.
Admissibility of certificate, §2-2-35.
Marketing of agricultural products.
Certificate of inspection or classification as evidence, §2-11-7.
Notices, §2-2-17.
Prima facie evidence of possession with intent to sell, §2-1-3.
Rules and regulations, §2-2-17.
Exhibits.
Agricultural and industrial exhibit commission, §§2-7-1 to 2-7-7. See within this heading, "Fairs and exhibits."
State aid to agriculture fairs, §§2-7-20 to 2-7-32. See within this heading, "Fairs and exhibits."
State aid to livestock shows, §§2-7-50 to 2-7-53.
Experiment station system, §§2-30-40 to 2-30-44.
Auburn university.
Operated in connection with, §2-30-40.
Creation, §2-30-40.
Director, §2-30-40.
Annual report, §2-30-43.
Researches and experiments, §2-30-43.
Duties of system, §2-30-41.
Employees, §2-30-44.

AGRICULTURE—Cont'd
Experiment station system
—Cont'd
Experimental fields,
§2-30-42.
Objects of system, §2-30-41.
Purposes of system, §2-30-41.
Reports, §2-30-43.
Roads.
Construction and
maintenance, §23-1-43.
Supervision of researches and
experiments, §2-30-43.
Extension service, §§2-30-1 to
2-30-4.
Fairs and exhibits, §§2-7-1 to
2-7-53.
Agricultural and industrial
exhibit commission,
§§2-7-1 to 2-7-7.
Establishment and
organization, §2-7-1.
Grants to state fair
authority, §§2-7-2 to
2-7-6.
Appropriations used for
prizes, §2-7-2.
Payment to authority,
§2-7-5.
Premiums or prizes in
excess of annual
appropriation,
§2-7-3.
Expenditures.
Limited to prizes,
§2-7-5.
Free space for exhibits,
§2-7-5.
Meetings.
Meetings to consider
distribution of
prizes at state fair,
§2-7-4.
Payment of
appropriation,
§2-7-5.
Per diem expenses,
§2-7-4.
Prizes, §§2-7-3 to 2-7-5.
Appropriations used
for, §2-7-2.
Distribution, §§2-7-3,
2-7-4.
Expenditures limited
to prizes, §2-7-5.
Premiums or prizes in
excess of annual
appropriation,
§2-7-3.
Reports, §2-7-6.
Space for exhibits.
Free space, §2-7-5.
Travel allowances,
§2-7-4.
Unexpended funds.
Return, §2-7-6.
South Alabama state fair
association.
Annual payment to
association, §2-7-7.
Definitions.
State aid to agricultural
fairs, §2-7-20.
Livestock shows.
State aid to livestock
shows, §§2-7-50 to
2-7-53.
Reports.
State fair authority, §2-7-6.

AGRICULTURE—Cont'd
Fairs and exhibits—Cont'd
Rules and regulations.
State aid to agricultural
fairs, §2-7-32.
South Alabama state fair
association.
Annual payment to
association, §2-7-7.
State aid to agricultural
fairs, §§2-7-20 to 2-7-32.
Administrative purposes.
Expenditures, §2-7-23.
Amount payable to fairs,
§§2-7-27 to 2-7-29.
Generally, §2-7-27.
Limitations, §2-7-29.
Special merit awards,
§2-7-28.
Definitions, §2-7-20.
Disbursement of funds,
§2-7-21.
Eligibility.
Fairs receiving direct
legislative
appropriations
ineligible, §2-7-30.
Payments to fairs, §2-7-26.
Prizes.
Approval, §2-7-26.
Filing of statement of
prizes to be awarded,
§2-7-25.
Special awards
committee, §2-7-31.
Special merit awards,
§2-7-28.
Statement of awards.
Filing, §2-7-25.
Verified statement,
§2-7-26.
Types of awards, §2-7-24.
Qualifications for receipt of
aid, §2-7-22.
Rules and regulations by
board, §2-7-32.
State aid to livestock shows,
§§2-7-50 to 2-7-53.
**Farm crisis and transition
program,** §§2-6A-1 to
2-6A-6.
Commission, §§2-6A-2,
2-6A-4.
Advisory committee,
§2-6A-2.
Chairman, §2-6A-2.
Composition, §2-6A-2.
Offices.
Regional districts and
offices, §2-6A-4.
Powers and duties.
Generally, §2-6A-2.
Regional districts, §2-6A-4.
Rules and regulations,
§2-6A-2.
Use of physical facilities of
other agencies,
§2-6A-2.
Contributions, §2-6A-6.
Coordinator, §§2-6A-3 to
2-6A-5.
Duties, §2-6A-3.
Employment, §2-6A-3.
Regional coordinator.
Duties, §2-6A-5.
Selection, §2-6A-4.
Established, §2-6A-2.
Policy, §2-6A-1.
Private contributions,
§2-6A-6.

AGRICULTURE—Cont'd
Farm equipment.
Liens.
Owners of hay baling
machines or presses,
§§35-11-290,
35-11-291.
Repurchase of inventory from
retailers, §§8-21-1 to
8-21-14.
See FARM EQUIPMENT.
Farmers' market authority,
§§2-5-1 to 2-5-17.
Administrator, §2-5-4.
Adulteration.
Sale of articles unfit for
food to be prohibited,
§2-5-9.
Chairman, §2-5-2.
Charges.
Market charges, §2-5-8.
Classes for produce, §2-5-7.
Compensation of members,
§2-5-3.
Composition, §2-5-2.
Counties.
Local appropriations
authorized, §2-5-17.
Cull produce.
Sale of cull produce, §2-5-7.
Duties, §2-5-1.
Ejection of persons from
markets, §2-5-11.
Eminent domain.
No right of eminent
domain, §2-5-6.
Enforcement of chapter.
Rules and regulations to
enforce, §2-5-10.
Establishment, §2-5-1.
Establishment of farmers'
markets, §2-5-5.
Expenses of members, §2-5-3.
Facilitating sale and
exchange of products,
§2-5-13.
Fixing minimum prices,
§2-5-12.
Funds.
Disposition, §2-5-14.
Grades for produce, §2-5-7.
Lease of space or facilities,
§2-5-16.
Location of markets.
Regulation of location,
§2-5-6.
Meetings, §2-5-3.
Minumum prices.
Fixing, §2-5-12.
Municipal corporations.
Local appropriations
authorized, §2-5-17.
Per diem, §2-5-3.
Powers, §2-5-1.
Prices.
Fixing minimum prices,
§2-5-12.
Qualifications of members,
§2-5-2.
Rules and regulations.
Conduct of market, §2-5-7.
Ejection of persons from
markets for violations,
§2-5-11.
Enforcement of chapter,
§2-5-10.
Sales by producer to
consumer outside
markets, §2-5-15.

AGRICULTURE—Cont'd
Farmers' market authority
—Cont'd
Substandard articles.
Sale of articles unfit for
food to be prohibited,
§2-5-9.
Terms of members, §2-5-2.
Unfit articles.
Sale for food to be
prohibited, §2-5-9.
Vice-chairman, §2-5-2.
Violations of chapter.
Ejection of persons from
markets for violations,
§2-5-11.
Farmers' markets.
Authority, §§2-5-1 to 2-5-17.
See within this heading,
"Farmers' market
authority."
Generally. See within this
heading, "Markets."
Farm products.
Advances.
Lien for advances.
Failure to apply farm
produce to payment
of lien, §2-1-4.
Analysis, §§2-2-32 to 2-2-37.
Commission merchants.
General provisions,
§§2-29-1 to 2-29-11.
See COMMISSION
MERCHANTS.
Decedents' estates.
Sale of farm products,
§43-2-419.
Defined, §2-29-1.
Executors and
administrators.
Sale of farm products,
§43-2-419.
Grading and standards of
farm products and fish,
§§2-11-50 to 2-11-59. See
within this heading,
"Grading and standards
of farm products and
fish."
Hindering transportation,
§13A-11-221.
Liens.
Rent or advances.
Failure to apply farm
produce to payment,
§2-1-4.
Marketing of agricultural
products, §§2-11-1 to
2-11-11. See within this
heading, "Marketing of
agricultural products."
Markets. See within this
heading, "Markets."
Misbranding, §§2-2-31 to
2-2-37. See within this
heading, "Misbranding."
Rent.
Lien for rent.
Failure to apply farm
produce to payment
of lien, §2-1-4.
Sale by commission
merchants.
General provisions,
§§2-29-1 to 2-29-11.
See COMMISSION
MERCHANTS.
Samples.
Inspection, §2-2-37.

AGRICULTURE—Cont'd
Farm products—Cont'd
Standards.
Grading and standards of
farm products and fish,
§§2-11-50 to 2-11-59.
See within this
heading, "Grading and
standards of farm
products and fish."
Statistics, §§2-2-50 to 2-2-53.
Substandard articles,
§§2-2-30 to 2-2-37. See
within this heading,
"Substandard articles."
Feeds.
Commercial feed law of 1978,
§§2-21-16 to 2-21-34.
See FEEDS.
Fees.
Commissioner of agriculture
and industries.
Restrictions on receipt,
Const. Ala., art. V,
§137; amd. 111.
Delinquent payment of
license or permit fee,
§2-9-2.
Grading and standards of
farm products and fish.
Disposition of fees,
§2-11-58.
Marketing associations.
Incorporated marketing
associations, §§2-10-73,
2-10-74.
Permit fee, §2-10-21.
Marketing of agricultural
products.
Disposition of fees,
§2-11-11.
Inspectors, §2-11-6.
Mutual farming or trucking
associations.
Articles of incorporation.
Fees for filing, §2-10-107.
Membership fees, §2-10-96.
Permit fee, §2-10-105.
Fertilizer.
General provisions, §§2-22-1
to 2-22-23.
See FERTILIZER.
Fruits.
Grading and standards,
§§2-11-50 to 2-11-59.
See FRUITS AND
VEGETABLES.
Promotion of industry,
§§2-8-120 to 2-8-137.
See FRUITS AND
VEGETABLES.
Funds.
Agricultural center fund,
§2-6-53.
Agricultural fund, §§2-9-1 to
2-9-7. See within this
heading, "Agricultural
fund."
Egg inspection fund, §2-9-40.
Farmers' market authority.
Disposition of funds,
§2-5-14.
Refunds.
Funds improperly or
illegally collected,
§2-1-6.
Shipping point inspection
fund, §§2-9-20 to 2-9-22.

AGRICULTURE—Cont'd
Garnishment.
Liens of agricultural
superintendents and
laborers, §35-11-95.
Gasoline tax.
Refunds.
Gasoline used for
agricultural
purposes,
§§40-17-100 to
40-17-108.
See GASOLINE.
Geological survey, §§9-4-1 to
9-4-19.
See GEOLOGICAL
SURVEY.
Governor.
Agricultural center
corporation.
Composition, §2-6-24.
Board of agriculture and
industries.
Appointment of members,
§2-3-2.
Ex officio chairman of
board, §2-3-1.
**Grading and standards of
farm products and fish,**
§§2-11-50 to 2-11-59.
Alteration, §2-11-52.
Applicability of article,
§2-11-50.
Article cumulative, §2-11-59.
Brands, labels or trademarks,
§§2-11-53 to 2-11-55.
Certificate of inspection,
§2-11-56.
Charges, §2-11-58.
Commissioner of agriculture
and industries.
Inspections, §§2-11-56,
2-11-57.
Obstructing performance of
duty, §2-11-57.
Rules and regulations,
§2-11-51.
Establishment, §2-11-52.
Publicity, §2-11-54.
Fees, §2-11-58.
Fruits and vegetables,
§§2-11-70 to 2-11-79.
See FRUITS AND
VEGETABLES.
Grain, §§2-11-90 to 2-11-103.
See GRAIN.
Inspections, §2-11-56.
Certificate of inspection,
§2-11-56.
Right of entry, §2-11-57.
Samples, §2-11-57.
Publicity as to establishment,
§2-11-54.
Rules and regulations,
§2-11-51.
Saltwater fish and seafood.
Article not applicable to,
§2-11-50.
Samples, §2-11-57.
Grain.
Grading and standards,
§§2-11-90 to 2-11-103.
See GRAIN.
Promotion of industry,
§§2-8-230 to 2-8-252.
See GRAIN.

AGRICULTURE—Cont'd
Hay.
　Liens.
　　Owners of hay baling
　　　machines or presses,
　　　§§35-11-290,
　　　35-11-291.
　Motor vehicles.
　　Loads fastened by cables or
　　　chains, §32-5-75.
Highways.
　Experiment station system.
　　Construction and
　　　maintenance.
　　　State highway
　　　　department,
　　　　§23-1-43.
Honey.
　General provisions,
　　§§2-11-120 to 2-11-123.
Honeybees and apiaries.
　General provisions, §§2-14-1
　　to 2-14-15.
　See HONEYBEES AND
　　APIARIES.
Income tax.
　Estimated tax.
　　Farmers declaration,
　　　§40-18-83.
　Exempt organizations,
　　§§40-18-32.
Incorporated marketing
　associations, §§2-10-50 to
　2-10-74. See within this
　heading, "Marketing
　associations."
Information.
　Duty to furnish, §2-1-5.
　Statistics.
　　Use of information
　　　gathered under article,
　　　§2-2-53.
Insecticides.
　General provisions, §§2-27-1
　　to 2-27-63.
　See PESTICIDES.
Inspections.
　Commissioner of agriculture
　　and industries, §2-2-37.
　Marketing of agricultural
　　products, §§2-11-1 to
　　2-11-11. See within this
　　heading, "Marketing of
　　agricultural products."
　Samples, §2-2-37.
　Shipping point inspection
　　fund, §§2-9-20 to 2-9-22.
Insurance.
　Department of agriculture
　　and industries.
　　Insurance for employees,
　　　§2-9-22.
Inventories.
　Farm equipment.
　　Repurchase of inventory
　　　from retailers, §§8-21-1
　　　to 8-21-14.
　　See FARM
　　　EQUIPMENT.
Labels.
　Grading and standards of
　　farm products and fish,
　　§§2-11-50 to 2-11-59. See
　　within this heading,
　　"Grading and standards
　　of farm products and
　　fish."
Labor.
　Statistics, §§2-2-50 to 2-2-53.
Laboratories.
　Establishment, §2-2-36.

AGRICULTURE—Cont'd
Laboratories—Cont'd
　Operation, §2-2-36.
　Soil-testing laboratories,
　　§§2-24-1 to 2-24-5.
　Where analyses to be made,
　　§2-2-34.
Laborers.
　Liens.
　　Superintendents and
　　　laborers, §§35-11-91 to
　　　35-11-97. See within
　　　this heading, "Liens."
Leases.
　Agricultural center.
　　Lease of coliseum building
　　　and facilities, §§2-6-27,
　　　2-6-50 to 2-6-54.
Licenses.
　Farm products.
　　Municipalities not to
　　　charge farmers for
　　　sale, §11-51-105.
　Fees.
　　Delinquent payments,
　　　§2-9-2.
　Marketing of agricultural
　　products.
　　Inspectors, §2-11-6.
Liens.
　Attachment.
　　Superintendents' and
　　　laborers' liens,
　　　§§35-11-91 to 35-11-97.
　Cotton.
　　Gins, §§35-11-290,
　　　35-11-291.
　Farm products.
　　Lien for rent or advances.
　　　Failure to apply farm
　　　　produce to payment,
　　　　§2-1-4.
　Hay baling machines or
　　presses, §§35-11-290,
　　35-11-291.
　Laborers, §§35-11-91 to
　　35-11-97.
　Peanut machines or pickers,
　　§§35-11-290, 35-11-291.
　Plantation superintendents,
　　§§35-11-91 to 35-11-97.
　Plants for drying or
　　processing seeds,
　　§§35-11-290, 35-11-291.
　Sharecroppers.
　　Liens of tenants in
　　　common, §§35-11-350,
　　　35-11-351.
　Superintendents and
　　laborers, §§35-11-91 to
　　35-11-97.
　　Advances.
　　　Satisfaction of claims for
　　　　advances, §35-11-96.
　　Attachment, §§35-11-92 to
　　　35-11-94.
　　Claims for rent and
　　　advances, §35-11-96.
　　Crops leviable,
　　　§35-11-94.
　　Declaration, §35-11-91.
　　Enforcement, §35-11-92.
　　Garnishment, §35-11-95.
　　Prior liens.
　　　Satisfaction, §§35-11-96,
　　　　35-11-97.
　　Rent.
　　　Satisfaction, §35-11-96.
　　Tenants in common,
　　　§§35-11-350, 35-11-351.

AGRICULTURE—Cont'd
Lime.
　Agricultural liming
　　materials, §§2-23-1 to
　　2-23-11.
　See LIME.
Livestock.
　General provisions, §§2-15-1
　　to 2-15-317.
　See LIVESTOCK.
Machinery and equipment.
　Farm equipment.
　　Repurchase of inventory
　　　from retailers, §§8-21-1
　　　to 8-21-14.
　　See FARM
　　　EQUIPMENT.
　Farm tractors.
　　See MOTOR VEHICLES.
　Sales tax, §§40-23-37,
　　40-23-38.
　Use tax.
　　Administrative provisions,
　　　§40-23-64.
　　Enforcement, §40-23-64.
　　Imposed, §40-23-63.
　　Persons liable, §40-23-63.
　　Weight, §40-23-63.
Marketing associations,
　§§2-10-20 to 2-10-74.
　Appeals.
　　Orders of board, §2-10-32.
　　Refusal of permit, §2-10-25.
　　Temporary permit
　　　pending appeal,
　　　§2-10-26.
　Board of agriculture and
　　industries.
　　Violation of purposes of
　　　organization, etc.
　　Hearings, §2-10-31.
　　Orders, §2-10-32.
　Commissioner of agriculture
　　and industries.
　　Investigations, §2-10-29.
　　Permits.
　　　Duties, §2-10-22.
　　Violations of purposes of
　　　organizations, etc.,
　　　§2-10-30.
　　Hearings, §2-10-31.
　　Orders, §2-10-32.
　Definitions.
　　"Association," §2-10-20.
　　Incorporated marketing
　　　associations, §2-10-50.
　Dissolution, §2-10-35.
　Fees.
　　Incorporated marketing
　　　associations, §§2-10-73,
　　　2-10-74.
　Incorporated marketing
　　associations, §§2-10-50 to
　　2-10-74.
　　Agreements between
　　　associations, §2-10-70.
　　Articles of incorporation.
　　　Acknowledgment,
　　　　§2-10-56.
　　　Amendments, §2-10-57.
　　　Contents, §2-10-56.
　　　Fees for filing, §2-10-74.
　　　Filing, §2-10-56.
　　　　Fees for filing,
　　　　　§2-10-74.
　　　Signing, §2-10-56.
　　Bylaws, §2-10-58.
　　Conflicting laws not
　　　applicable, §2-10-68.

AGRICULTURE—Cont'd
Marketing associations
—Cont'd
Incorporated marketing
associations—Cont'd
Contracts.
Marketing contracts,
§2-10-65.
Debts.
Member's liability for
association's debts,
§2-10-62.
Definitions, §2-10-50.
Directors.
Contracts with
association, §2-10-60.
Referring questions to
entire membership,
§2-10-64.
Removal, §2-10-63.
Selection, §2-10-60.
Vacancies, §2-10-60.
Fees.
Filing articles of
incorporation,
§2-10-74.
Probate judges and
secretary of state,
§2-10-73.
General corporation laws.
Applicability, §2-10-72.
Members.
Certificate of
membership,
§2-10-62.
Liability for association's
debts, §2-10-62.
Meetings, §2-10-59.
Referring questions to
entire membership,
§2-10-64.
Who may become
members, §2-10-55.
Monopolies.
Association not a
monopoly, §2-10-71.
Mutual farming or
trucking associations.
Incorporated marketing
associations not
affected by article,
§2-10-108.
Nonprofit associations,
§2-10-51.
Objects, §2-10-53.
Officers, §2-10-61.
Removal, §2-10-63.
Other corporations.
Association may form,
own or control,
§2-10-69.
Powers, §2-10-54.
Reports, §2-10-67.
Stock, §2-10-62.
Exchange of stock,
§2-10-66.
Stockholders.
Who may become
stockholders,
§2-10-55.
Who may form, §2-10-52.
Investigations, §2-10-29.
Mortgages and deeds of trust,
§2-10-27.
Mutual farming or trucking
associations, §§2-10-90 to
2-10-108. See within this
heading, "Mutual
farming or trucking
associations."

AGRICULTURE—Cont'd
Marketing associations
—Cont'd
Permits, §§2-10-21 to
2-10-26.
Appeals.
Refusal of permit,
§2-10-25.
Temporary permit
pending appeal,
§2-10-26.
Application for permit.
Duty of commissioner,
§2-10-22.
Fee, §2-10-21.
Fee, §2-10-21.
Renewal fee, §2-10-23.
Issuance, §2-10-23.
Refusal, §2-10-24.
Appeal, §2-10-26.
Notice, §2-10-25.
Temporary permit
pending appeal,
§2-10-26.
Renewal fee, §2-10-23.
Required, §2-10-21.
Temporary permit.
Pending appeal of refusal
of permit, §2-10-26.
Reports.
Annual report, §2-10-28.
Incorporated marketing
associations, §2-10-67.
Violations of purposes,
§2-10-30.
Hearings, §2-10-31.
Orders, §2-10-32.
Stock.
Authority to acquire stock,
§2-10-27.
Violation of purposes of
organization, etc.,
§§2-10-30 to 2-10-34.
Appeals, §2-10-32.
Bonds, surety.
Person in charge,
§2-10-33.
Closing out association.
Payment of expense,
§2-10-34.
Commissioner to report
association violating,
§2-10-30.
Hearings, §2-10-31.
Orders, §2-10-32.
Appeal, §2-10-32.
Receivership, §2-10-32.
Bonds required of person
in charge, §2-10-33.
Payment of expense of
operating or closing
out association,
§2-10-34.
**Marketing of agricultural
products,** §§2-11-1 to
2-11-11.
Applicability of article,
§2-11-2.
Board of agriculture and
industries.
Powers, §2-11-3.
Rules and regulations,
§2-11-8.
Bonds, surety.
Employees and inspectors,
§2-11-9.
Bulk.
Marketing in bulk, §2-11-2.
Catfish, §§2-11-30 to 2-11-40.
See CATFISH.

AGRICULTURE—Cont'd
**Marketing of agricultural
products**—Cont'd
Certificate of inspection or
classification.
Evidence, §2-11-7.
Commissioner of agriculture
and industries.
Agreements with other
agricultural agencies,
§2-11-8.
Powers, §2-11-3.
Effective date of standards,
§2-11-4.
Employees.
Bonds, surety, §2-11-9.
Offenses, §2-11-10.
Evidence.
Certificate of inspection or
classification, §2-11-7.
Federal government.
Cooperation with federal
government, §2-11-5.
Federal standards, §2-11-5.
Fees.
Disposition, §2-11-11.
Inspectors, §2-11-6.
Fines.
Disposition, §2-11-11.
Inspections.
Certificates as evidence,
§2-11-7.
Inspectors, §2-11-6.
Bonds, surety, §2-11-9.
Offenses, §2-11-10.
Licenses.
Inspectors, §2-11-6.
Purposes of article, §2-11-1.
Rules and regulations,
§2-11-8.
Standards.
Effective date, §2-11-4.
Federal standards, §2-11-5.
Information, §2-11-4.
Violations, §2-11-11.
Unlawful acts, §2-11-6.
Markets.
Acquisition of sites, §2-3-20.
Adulteration.
Sale of articles unfit for
food to be prohibited,
§2-5-9.
Agricultural markets and
coliseum corporation,
§§2-6-70 to 2-6-86. See
within this heading,
"Agricultural markets
and coliseum
corporation."
Approach roads.
Construction, §2-3-21.
Charges by farmers' market
authority, §2-5-8.
Charges for space, services
and facilities, §2-3-20.
Classes for produce, §2-5-7.
Commissioner of agriculture.
Supervision of operation,
§2-3-22.
Construction, §§2-3-20,
2-3-21.
Cull produce.
Sale, §2-5-7.
Ejection of persons from
markets, §2-5-11.
Establishment, §2-5-5.
Farmers' market authority,
§§2-5-1 to 2-5-17. See
within this heading,
"Farmers' market
authority."

AGRICULTURE—Cont'd
Markets—Cont'd
Grades for produce, §2-5-7.
Lease of space or facilities,
§2-5-16.
Livestock.
General provisions,
§§2-15-1 to 2-15-317.
See LIVESTOCK.
Location, §2-5-6.
Prices.
Fixing minimum prices,
§2-5-12.
Roads.
Construction, §2-3-21.
Rules and regulations,
§2-3-23.
Conduct of market, §2-5-7.
Sales by producer to
consumer outside
markets, §2-5-15.
State farmers' market
committee.
Establishment,
organization and
duties, §2-3-24.
Reports, §2-3-25.
Storage, §2-3-20.
Substandard articles.
Sales prohibited, §2-5-9.
Supervision of operation.
Commissioner of
agriculture, §2-3-22.
Unfit articles.
Sales prohibited, §2-5-9.
Meetings.
Agricultural agencies, §2-1-5.
Misbranding, §§2-2-31 to
2-2-37.
Analysis, §§2-2-32 to 2-2-36.
Duties of commissioner,
§2-2-33.
Establishment and
operation of
laboratory, §2-2-36.
Evidence.
Certificate of analysis,
§2-2-35.
Violations of title.
Procedure when analysis
shows, §2-2-32.
Where analyses to be
made, §2-2-34.
Commissioner of agriculture
and industries.
Tests or analyses.
Duties, §2-2-33.
Condemnation, §2-2-31.
Evidence.
Certificate of analysis,
§2-2-35.
Laboratories, §2-2-36.
Where analyses to be
made, §2-2-34.
Samples.
Inspection, §2-2-37.
Seizure, §2-2-31.
Tests.
Duty of commissioner,
§2-2-33.
Monopolies.
Incorporated marketing
associations.
Association not a
monopoly, §2-10-71.
**Mortgages and deeds of
trust.**
Marketing associations,
§2-10-27.

AGRICULTURE—Cont'd
Motor fuels.
Sales tax.
Exemption of diesel fuel
used for off-highway
purposes, §40-23-4.
Use tax.
Exemption of diesel fuel
used for off-highway
agricultural purposes,
§40-23-62.
Motor vehicle carriers.
Vehicles hauling agricultural
commodities.
Exemptions from chapter,
§37-3-4.
Motor vehicles.
Tractors.
See MOTOR VEHICLES.
Municipal corporations.
Farmers' market authority.
Local appropriations
authorized, §2-5-17.
Sale, etc., of farm products.
Municipalities not to
charge farmers for
sale, §11-51-105.
Regulation, §2-29-10.
**Mutual farming or trucking
associations,** §§2-10-90 to
2-10-108.
Actions, §2-10-104.
Applicability of article.
Existing associations,
§2-10-106.
Incorporated marketing
associations not
affected, §2-10-108.
Articles of incorporation,
§2-10-92.
Fees for filing, §2-10-107.
Filing.
Fees for filing, §2-10-107.
Board of directors, §2-10-94.
Bylaws.
Adoption, §2-10-93.
Definitions, §2-10-90.
Directors.
Board of directors,
§2-10-94.
Dividends.
Patronage dividends,
§2-10-103.
Existing associations.
Applicability of article,
§2-10-106.
Expenses.
Charges for expenses,
§2-10-103.
Federation of associations,
§§2-10-100 to 2-10-102.
Authorized, §2-10-100.
Management, §2-10-101.
Organization, §2-10-101.
Powers, §2-10-102.
Fees.
Filing articles of
incorporation,
§2-10-107.
Members, §2-10-96.
Permit fee, §2-10-105.
Formation, §2-10-92.
Incorporated marketing
associations.
Not affected by article,
§2-10-108.
Members, §§2-10-96, 2-10-97.
Officers, §2-10-95.
Organization, §2-10-93.
Stock, §2-10-98.

AGRICULTURE—Cont'd
**Mutual farming or trucking
associations**—Cont'd
Patronage dividends,
§2-10-103.
Permits.
Fee, §2-10-105.
Powers, §2-10-99.
Purposes of article, §2-10-91.
Reserve.
Charges for creating
reserve, §2-10-103.
Stock.
Organization with capital
stock, §2-10-98.
Taxation, §2-10-105.
Names.
Cooperatives.
Use of word "cooperative"
in name, §2-10-1.
Notice.
Evidence of notices, §2-2-17.
Rules and regulations,
§2-2-16.
Nuisances.
Farming not deemed
nuisance after operating
one year, §6-5-127.
Nuts.
General provisions.
See NUTS.
Promotion of industry,
§§2-8-120 to 2-8-137.
See NUTS.
Officers.
Acts or omissions, §2-1-2.
Partnerships.
Acts or omissions of officers
or agents, §2-1-2.
Peanuts.
See PEANUTS.
Penalties.
Pesticide, entomology, plant
pathology, tree surgery,
etc., violations, §2-2-18.
Violation of title, §2-1-9.
Permits.
Fees.
Delinquent payments,
§2-9-2.
Mutual farming or
trucking associations,
§2-10-105.
Marketing associations,
§§2-10-21 to 2-10-26. See
within this heading,
"Marketing
associations."
Personal property.
Sale of farm products,
§43-2-419.
Pesticides.
General provisions, §§2-27-1
to 2-27-63.
See PESTICIDES.
Plantation superintendents.
Liens.
Superintendents and
laborers, §§35-11-91 to
35-11-97. See within
this heading, "Liens."
Possession.
Prima facie evidence, §2-1-3.
Poultry.
General provisions, §§2-16-1
to 2-16-42.
See POULTRY.
Inspections, §§2-17-1 to
2-17-38.
See POULTRY.

AGRICULTURE—Cont'd
Recordation.
Taxation.
Farm loans.
Exemption from tax, §40-22-5.
Production credit corporations and associations.
Exemption, §40-22-4.
Records.
Agricultural center corporation.
Record of proceedings, §2-6-24.
Reports.
Commissioner of agriculture and industries, §2-2-7.
Marketing associations, §2-10-28.
Incorporated marketing associations, §2-10-67.
Violations of purposes of organization, §2-10-30.
Markets.
State farmers' market committee, §2-3-25.
State fair authority, §2-7-6.
Roads.
Experiment station system.
Construction and maintenance.
State highway department, §23-1-43.
Rules and regulations.
Agricultural center board, §2-6-1.
Bond equivalence.
Implementation of provisions, §2-2-73.
Copies furnished to probate judges, §2-2-17.
Evidence, §2-2-17.
Fairs and exhibits.
State aid to agricultural fairs, §2-7-32.
Farmers' market authority.
Conduct of market, §2-5-7.
Ejection of persons from markets for violations, §2-5-11.
Enforcement of chapters, §2-5-10.
Grading and standards of farm products and fish, §2-11-51.
Marketing of agricultural products, §2-11-8.
Markets, §2-3-23.
Conduct of market, §2-5-7.
Notice, §2-2-16.
Promulgation, §2-2-16.
Salaries.
Commissioner of agriculture and industries, §2-2-5.
Sales.
Evidence.
Prima facie evidence, §2-1-3.
Suspension of sale, §2-2-30.
Sales tax.
Exemptions, §40-23-4.
Machinery and equipment, §§40-23-37, 40-23-38.

AGRICULTURE—Cont'd
Securities.
Agricultural markets and coliseum corporation. See within this heading, "Agricultural markets and coliseum corporation."
Seeds.
General provisions, §§2-26-1 to 2-26-76.
See SEEDS.
Shipping point inspection fund, §§2-9-20 to 2-9-22.
Creation of fund, §2-9-20.
Department of agriculture and industries.
Insurance for employees, §2-9-22.
Expenditures, §2-9-21.
Insurance for employees, §2-9-22.
Moneys paid into fund, §2-9-20.
Soil-testing laboratories, §§2-24-1 to 2-24-5.
Approval by commissioner, §2-24-2.
False or fraudulent representations as to approval, §2-24-5.
Auburn university.
Agricultural soil-testing laboratory not affected by chapter, §2-24-4.
Board of agriculture and industries.
Rules and regulations, §2-24-3.
Certification by commissioner, §2-24-2.
False or fraudulent representations, §2-24-5.
Not mandatory, §2-24-4.
Commissioner of agriculture and industries.
Approval and certification, §2-24-2.
Certification not mandatory, §2-24-4.
False or fraudulent representations, §2-24-5.
Purpose of chapter, §2-24-1.
Rules and regulations, §2-24-3.
Soybeans.
Promotion of industry, §§2-8-80 to 2-8-103.
See SOYBEANS.
Standards.
Grading and standards of farm products and fish, §§2-11-50 to 2-11-59. See within this heading, "Grading and standards of farm products and fish."
Marketing of agricultural products, §§2-11-1 to 2-11-11. See within this heading, "Marketing of agricultural products."
State board of agriculture and industries. See within this heading, "Board of agriculture and industries."

AGRICULTURE—Cont'd
State treasurer.
Agricultural center corporation.
Lease of corporations properties to board.
Disbursement of rental payments, §2-6-34.
Statistics, §§2-2-50 to 2-2-53.
Expenses of compiling, §2-2-52.
Federal statistician.
Designation, §2-2-51.
Generally, §2-2-50.
Use of information, §2-2-53.
Stock and stockholders.
Marketing associations.
Authority to acquire stock, §2-10-27.
Incorporated marketing associations.
Exchange of stock, §2-10-66.
Stock of associations, §2-10-62.
Mutual farming or trucking associations.
Organization with capital stock, §2-10-98.
Substandard articles, §§2-2-30 to 2-2-37.
Analysis, §§2-2-32 to 2-2-36.
Duty of commissioner to have analyses made, §2-2-33.
Establishment and operation of laboratory, §2-2-36.
Evidence.
Certificate of analysis, §2-2-35.
Violations.
Procedure when analysis shows, §2-2-32.
Where analyses to be made, §2-2-34.
Commissioner of agriculture and industries.
Tests or analyses.
Duties, §2-2-33.
Condemnation, §2-2-31.
Evidence.
Certificate of analysis, §2-2-35.
Farmers' market authority.
Sale of articles unfit for food to be prohibited, §2-5-9.
Laboratories, §2-2-36.
Where analysis to be made, §2-2-34.
Samples.
Commissioner authorized to inspect and secure, §2-2-37.
Seizure, §2-2-31.
Suspension of sale, §2-2-30.
Tests.
Duties of commissioner, §2-2-33.
Superintendents.
Liens.
Superintendents and laborers, §§35-11-91 to 35-11-97. See within this heading, "Liens."

AGRICULTURE—Cont'd
  Suspension of sale of article,
    §§2-2-30 to 2-2-37.
  Commissioner of agriculture
    and industries.
    Tests or analyses.
      Duties, §2-2-33.
  Condemnation of adulterated
    article, §2-2-31.
    Duty of commissioner,
      §2-2-33.
  Establishment and
    operation of
    laboratory, §2-2-36.
  Evidence.
    Certificate of analysis,
      §2-2-35.
  Evidence.
    Certificate of analysis,
      §2-2-35.
  Farmers' market authority.
    Sale of articles unfit for
    food to be prohibited,
    §2-5-9.
  Laboratories, §2-2-36.
  Violations.
    Procedure when analysis
    shows, §2-2-32.
    Where analyses to be
    made, §2-2-34.
  Samples.
    Commissioner authorized
    to inspect and secure,
    §2-2-37.
  Seizure of adulterated article,
    §2-2-31.
  Tests.
    Duty of commissioner,
    §2-2-33.
    Where analyses to be
    made, §2-2-34.
  Taxation.
    Agricultural markets and
    coliseum corporation.
    Exemption of securities,
    §2-6-85.
    Exemptions, §40-9-1.
    Recordation tax, §§40-22-4,
    40-22-5.
    Sales tax, §40-23-4.
    Gasoline.
      Refunds.
      Gasoline used for
      agricultural
      purposes,
      §§40-17-100 to
      40-17-108.
      See GASOLINE.
    Mutual farming or trucking
    associations, §2-10-105.
    Sales tax. See within this
    heading, "Sales tax."
    Use tax. See within this
    heading, "Use tax."
  Tests.
    Adulterated, misbranded or
    substandard articles.
    Duty of commissioner,
    §2-2-33.
  Tractors.
    See MOTOR VEHICLES.
  Trademarks.
    Grading and standards of
    farm products and fish,
    §§2-11-53 to 2-11-55.
  Transportation companies.
    Special rates for agricultural
    enterprises, §37-2-15.

AGRICULTURE—Cont'd
  Trucking associations.
    Mutual farming or trucking
    associations, §§2-10-90 to
    2-10-108. See within this
    heading, "Mutual
    farming or trucking
    associations."
  United States.
    Offense under federal
    jurisdiction, §2-1-10.
  Universities and colleges.
    Alabama agricultural and
    mechanical university.
    General provisions,
      §§16-49-1 to 16-49-55.
    See ALABAMA
      AGRICULTURAL
      AND
      MECHANICAL
      UNIVERSITY.
  Use tax.
    Diesel fuel used for off-
    highway agricultural
    purposes.
      Exemption, §40-23-62.
    Machinery and equipment,
    §§40-23-63, 40-23-64.
      Administrative provisions,
      §40-23-64.
      Enforcement, §40-23-64.
      Persons liable, §40-23-63.
      Tax imposed, §40-23-63.
      Weight, §40-23-63.
  Vegetables.
    Grading and standards,
    §§2-11-50 to 2-11-59.
    See FRUITS AND
      VEGETABLES.
    Promotion of industry,
    §§2-8-120 to 2-8-137.
    See FRUITS AND
      VEGETABLES.
  Violations of title.
    Offense under federal
    jurisdiction, §2-1-10.
    Penalty, §2-1-9.
  Water pollution.
    Agricultural nonpoint source
    pollution, §§22-38-1 to
    22-38-8.
    See WATER POLLUTION.
  Weights and measures.
    General provisions, §§8-16-1
    to 8-16-123.
    See WEIGHTS AND
      MEASURES.
  Witnesses.
    Commissioner of agriculture
    and industries.
      Examination of witnesses,
      §2-2-6.
  Workers.
    Liens.
      Superintendents and
      laborers, §§35-11-91 to
      35-11-97. See within
      this heading, "Liens."

AIDING AND ABETTING.
  **Accomplices and
    accessories.**
    See ACCOMPLICES AND
    ACCESSORIES.
  Escape.
    Hindering apprehension of
    escapee, §13A-10-45.
    Permitting or facilitating,
    §§13A-10-34, 13A-10-35.

AIDING AND ABETTING
  —Cont'd
  **Liability based upon
    behavior of another,**
    §13A-2-23.

AIDS.
  **Sexually transmitted
    diseases.**
    Notifiable diseases generally,
    §§22-11A-1 to 22-11A-38.
    See DISEASES.

AIRBOATS.
  Prohibition on use, §9-2-15.1.

AIR COMMERCE, §§37-9-1 to
  37-9-32.
  Air carriers.
    Accounts, §37-9-29.
    Aircraft and other
    equipment.
      Exemption from taxation,
      §40-9-1.
    Alcoholic beverages.
      Exemption of sales from
      taxation.
      Hub operations,
      §28-3-207.
    Buildings.
      Access, §37-9-29.
    Classifications.
      Establishment, §37-9-10.
    Common carriers.
      Certificates.
      Generally, §§37-9-16 to
      37-9-25. See within
      this heading,
      "Certificates and
      permits."
      Defined, §37-9-2.
    Contract carriers.
      Defined, §37-9-2.
      Permits.
      Generally, §§37-9-16 to
      37-9-25. See within
      this heading,
      "Certificates and
      permits."
    Credit.
      Extension, §37-9-28.
    Defined, §37-9-2.
    Exemption from chapter,
    §37-9-10.
    Facilities.
      Duties, §37-9-28.
    Franchise tax.
      Foreign corporations,
      §40-14-41.
    Gasoline tax.
      Exemptions, §40-17-31.
    Inquiries into business,
    §37-9-9.
    Lands.
      Access, §37-9-29.
    Personal property.
      Leasing or renting.
      Licensing exemptions,
      §40-12-223.
    Preferences.
      Undue preferences,
      §37-9-28.
    Rates, fares and charges.
      Generally. See within this
      heading, "Rates, fares
      and charges."
    Records, §37-9-29.
    Reports, §37-9-29.
    Sales tax exemptions,
    §40-23-4.
    Service, §37-9-28.
    Use tax exemptions,
    §40-23-62.

AIR COMMERCE—Cont'd
Aviation generally, §§4-1-1 to 4-9-7.
See AVIATION.
Bonds, surety.
Brokers, §37-9-24.
Certificates and permits, §37-9-18.
Brokers.
Bonds, surety, §37-9-24.
Classifications, §37-9-10.
Defined, §37-9-2.
Exemption from chapter, §37-9-10.
Inquiries into business, §37-9-9.
Licenses, §37-9-24.
Public service commission.
Powers, §37-9-24.
Certificates and permits, §§37-9-16 to 37-9-25.
Additional air transportation.
Investigations to determine need, §37-9-17.
Proceedings to furnish, §37-9-17.
Alteration, §37-9-21.
Amendment, §37-9-21.
Application, §37-9-17.
Bonds, surety, §37-9-18.
Charter flights, §37-9-20.
Conditions, §37-9-20.
Contents, §37-9-20.
Denial, §37-9-19.
Duration, §37-9-20.
Effective date, §37-9-20.
Emergency landings, §37-9-20.
Extension of existing service, §37-9-22.
Fees, §37-9-25.
Hearing, §37-9-17.
Insurance, §37-9-18.
Issuance, §37-9-19.
Landing points, §37-9-20.
Lease, §37-9-23.
Limitations, §37-9-20.
Modification, §37-9-21.
Notice, §37-9-17.
Required, §37-9-16.
Revocation, §37-9-21.
Standards.
Issuance or denial, §37-9-19.
Suspension, §37-9-21.
Take-off points, §37-9-20.
Temporary authorization, §37-9-19.
Terms, §37-9-20.
Transfers, §37-9-23.
Charges.
Generally. See within this heading, "Rates, fares and charges."
Commission.
Defined, §37-9-2.
Generally. See within this heading, "Public service commission."
Common carriers.
Air carriers.
Certificates and permits, §§37-9-16 to 37-9-25.
See within this heading, "Certificates and permits."
Defined, §37-9-2.
Generally. See within this heading, "Air carriers."

AIR COMMERCE—Cont'd
Contract carriers.
Certificates and permits, §§37-9-16 to 37-9-25. See within this heading, "Certificates and permits."
Defined, §37-9-2.
Generally. See within this heading, "Air carriers."
Declaration of policy, §37-9-5.
Definitions, §§37-9-2, 37-9-3.
Interstate commerce, §37-9-4.
Fares.
Generally. See within this heading, "Rates, fares and charges."
Fees.
Certificates and permits, §37-9-25.
Gasoline tax.
Exemptions from tax, §40-17-31.
Insurance.
Common carriers and contract carriers, §37-9-18.
Interstate commerce.
Exemptions from regulation, §37-9-4.
Rates, services, etc.
Powers of commission, §37-9-13.
Interstate cooperation, §37-9-12.
Licenses.
Brokers, §37-9-24.
Personal property.
Air carriers leasing or renting.
Exemptions, §40-12-223.
Penalties, §37-9-31.
Permits, §§37-9-16 to 37-9-25.
See within this heading, "Certificates and permits."
Personal property.
Air carriers leasing or renting.
License exemptions, §40-12-223.
Policy.
Declaration, §37-9-5.
Property rights in use of airspace.
Chapter not to confer, §37-9-6.
Public service commission.
Administration of chapter, §37-9-8.
Brokers.
Powers, §37-9-24.
Compensation of members, §37-9-32.
Conflicts of interest, §37-9-15.
Cooperation with state and federal authorities, §37-9-12.
Inquiries into business of air carriers, brokers, etc., §37-9-9.
Inspections, §37-9-29.
Interstate rates, services, etc.
Powers, §37-9-13.
Proceedings before commission, §37-9-14.
Rates, fares and charges. See within this heading, "Rates, fares and charges."

AIR COMMERCE—Cont'd
Public service commission —Cont'd
Rules, regulations and orders, §37-9-8.
Noncompliance, §37-9-11.
Scope of control, §37-9-7.
Rates, fares and charges.
Changes, §37-9-27.
Excessive rates, §37-9-30.
Joint rates.
Filing, §37-9-27.
Public service commission.
Authority, §37-9-28.
Reasonable rates, fares and charges.
Establishment, enforcement, etc., §37-9-28.
Reasonable rates, §37-9-28.
Refunds or remittances, §37-9-27.
Excessive rates, §37-9-30.
Tariff, §37-9-27.
Records.
Air carriers, §37-9-29.
Reports.
Air carriers, §37-9-29.
Routes.
Abandonment or discontinuance, §37-9-26.
Rules and regulations.
Public service commission, §37-9-8.
Sales tax.
Air carriers.
Exemptions, §40-23-4.
Scope of chapter, §37-9-7.
Taxation.
Exemptions from taxation.
Air carriers.
Aircraft and other equipment, §40-9-1.
Alcoholic beverage sales.
Hub operations, §28-3-207.
Gasoline tax, §40-17-31.
Sales tax, §40-23-4.
Use tax, §40-23-62.
Time tables, §37-9-28.
Title of chapter, §37-9-1.
United States.
Cooperation with federal authorities, §37-9-12.
Mail service exempt from chapter, §37-9-3.
Use tax.
Air carriers.
Exemptions, §40-23-62.
Violations of chapter, §37-9-11.

AIR CONDITIONING.
Contractors.
General provisions, §§34-31-1 to 34-31-34.
See HEATING AND AIR CONDITIONING CONTRACTORS.
Licenses.
Plants and equipment, §40-12-46.

AIRCRAFT.
General provisions.
See AVIATION.

AIR NATIONAL GUARD.
See MILITARY AFFAIRS.

AIR POLLUTION, §§22-28-1 to
22-28-23.
Advisory committees,
§22-28-10.
**Air pollution control
commission.** See within
this heading, "Control
commission."
**Alabama air pollution
control act.**
Short title of chapter,
§22-28-1.
Authorities.
Environmental improvement
authorities, §§9-6-1 to
9-6-17.
See ENVIRONMENTAL
IMPROVEMENT
AUTHORITIES.
Control commission.
Providing information to
commission, §22-28-18.
Rules and regulations.
Adoption, §22-28-15.
Authority, §22-28-14.
Counties.
Local air pollution control
programs, §22-28-23.
Declaration of policy,
§22-28-3.
Definitions, §22-28-2.
Emergencies, §22-28-21.
Emissions.
Control requirements,
§22-28-11.
Variances, §22-28-13.
Motor vehicle emissions,
§22-28-12.
Sampling and providing
information on
emissions, §22-28-18.
**Environmental improvement
authorities,** §§9-6-1 to
9-6-17.
See ENVIRONMENTAL
IMPROVEMENT
AUTHORITIES.
Hearings.
Rules and regulations,
§22-28-15.
Income tax.
Corporations.
Deductions invested in air
pollution control,
§40-18-35.
Information, §22-28-20.
Injunctions, §22-28-22.
Inspections, §22-28-19.
**Local air pollution control
programs,** §22-28-23.
Motor vehicles emissions,
§22-28-12.
Municipal corporations.
Local air pollution control
programs, §22-28-23.
Penalties, §22-28-22.
Permits, §22-28-16.
Plans.
Review of plans, §22-28-17.
Programs.
Local air pollution control
programs, §22-28-23.
Purpose of chapter, §22-28-3.
Records, §22-28-9.
Availability of records,
§22-28-20.
Powers, §22-28-10.
Reports, §22-28-20.
Right of entry.
Inspections, §22-28-19.

AIR POLLUTION—Cont'd
Rules and regulations,
§§22-18-13 to 22-18-15.
Adoption, §22-28-15.
Control commission.
Authority of commission,
§22-28-14.
Hearings, §22-28-15.
Variances, §22-28-13.
Sales tax exemptions,
§40-23-4.
Samples, §§22-28-18, 22-28-19.
Short title of chapter,
§22-28-1.
Specifications.
Review of specifications,
§22-28-17.
Subpoenas, §22-28-22.
Taxation.
Income tax.
Corporations.
Deductions invested in
air pollution control,
§40-18-35.
Use tax exemptions,
§40-23-62.
Tests, §22-28-19.
Use tax exemptions,
§40-23-62.
Variances, §22-28-13.
Violations of chapter,
§22-28-22.

AIRPORTS.
Counties.
See COUNTIES.
General provisions.
See AVIATION.
Municipal airports.
General provisions, §§4-4-1 to
4-4-16.
See MUNICIPAL
CORPORATIONS.

**ALABAMA ACADEMY OF
HONOR,** §§41-11-1 to
41-11-6.
See ACADEMY OF HONOR.

**ALABAMA
ADMINISTRATIVE
CODE,** §41-22-7.

**ALABAMA
ADMINISTRATIVE
MONTHLY,** §41-22-7.

**ALABAMA AGRICULTURAL
AND MECHANICAL
UNIVERSITY,** §§16-49-1 to
16-49-55.
Agents.
Default, §16-49-3.
**American legion
scholarships,** §§16-31-1 to
16-31-4.
Autonomy.
Degree of autonomy,
§16-49-1.
**Black archives, research
center and museum,**
§§16-49-50 to 16-49-55.
See HISTORY AND
ARCHIVES.
Board of trustees, §§16-49-20
to 16-49-30.
Appointment of members,
§16-49-20.
Body corporate, §16-49-21.
Compensation of members,
§16-49-20.
Composition, §16-49-20.
Conflicts of interest,
§16-49-29.

**ALABAMA AGRICULTURAL
AND MECHANICAL
UNIVERSITY—Cont'd**
Board of trustees—Cont'd
Courses of instruction,
§16-49-23.
Creation, §16-49-20.
Default, §16-49-3.
Degrees, §16-49-23.
Duties, §16-49-22.
Endowment funds.
Investment, §16-13-2.
Expenses of members,
§16-49-28.
Faculty.
Appointment, removal,
etc., §16-49-23.
Jurisdiction, §16-49-24.
Meetings, §16-49-26.
Name, §16-49-21.
Powers, §§16-49-22 to
16-49-24.
President of university.
Appointment, §16-49-23.
Qualifications of members,
§16-49-20.
Quorum, §16-49-27.
Recommendation of programs
to qualify for federal
funds, §16-49-1.
Reports to legislature,
§16-49-30.
Terms of members,
§16-49-20.
Vacancies, §16-49-25.
Body corporate, §16-49-21.
**Commission of higher
education.**
General provisions, §§16-5-1
to 16-5-14.
See UNIVERSITIES AND
COLLEGES.
Conflicts of interest.
Board of trustees, §16-49-29.
Corporation.
Body corporate, §16-49-21.
Courses of instruction,
§16-49-23.
Degrees.
Powers of board of trustees,
§16-49-23.
Faculty, §16-49-23.
Eminent scholars trust fund,
§§16-61-1 to 16-61-10.
See UNIVERSITIES AND
COLLEGES.
Existing policies, procedures,
etc., §16-49-2.
Federal funds.
Recommendation to qualify
for federal funds,
§16-49-1.
Gifts, §16-49-3.
Grants, §16-49-3.
History and archives.
State Black archives,
research center and
museum, §§16-49-50 to
16-49-55.
See HISTORY AND
ARCHIVES.
Jurisdiction.
Board of trustees, §16-49-24.
Legislature.
Reports to legislature,
§16-49-30.

ALABAMA AGRICULTURAL AND MECHANICAL UNIVERSITY—Cont'd
Museums.
State Black archives, research center and museum, §§16-49-50 to 16-49-55.
See HISTORY AND ARCHIVES.
Names.
Board of trustees, §16-49-21.
Grants or gifts not to fail because of misnomer, etc., §16-49-3.
Officers and employees.
Existing policies, procedures, etc., relative to, §16-49-2.
Police.
General provisions.
See UNIVERSITIES AND COLLEGES.
University police officers, §16-49-4.
President of university, §16-49-23.
Programs.
Recommendation to qualify for federal, etc., funds, §16-49-1.
Reports.
Board of trustees, §16-49-30.
Research center.
Black archives, research center and museum, §§16-49-50 to 16-49-55.
See HISTORY AND ARCHIVES.
Salaries, §16-49-23.
Scholarships.
American legion scholarships, §§16-31-1 to 16-31-4.
Students.
Existing policies, procedures, etc., relative to students, §16-49-2.
Trustees.
Board of trustees, §§16-49-20 to 16-49-30. See within this heading, "Board of trustees."
Universities and colleges generally.
See UNIVERSITIES AND COLLEGES.

ALABAMA AGRICULTURAL DEVELOPMENT AUTHORITY.
Agriculture.
Development authority, §§2-3A-1 to 2-3A-16.
See AGRICULTURE.

ALABAMA AGRICULTURAL MARKETS AND COLISEUM CORPORATION, §§2-6-70 to 2-6-86.
See AGRICULTURE.

ALABAMA BOYS' INDUSTRIAL SCHOOLS.
See YOUTH SERVICES.

ALABAMA CITY.
Property tax, Const. Ala., amd. 17.

ALABAMA COLLEGE, §§16-54-1 to 16-54-18.
See UNIVERSITY OF MONTEVALLO.

ALABAMA CONVENTION FACILITIES ACT.
General provisions, §§11-100-1 to 11-100-8.
See CONVENTION FACILITIES.

ALABAMA COORDINATE SYSTEMS, §§35-2-1 to 35-2-9.
See SURVEYS AND SURVEYORS.

ALABAMA CORRECTIONS INSTITUTION FINANCE AUTHORITY.
Corrections.
Institution finance authority, §§14-2-1 to 14-2-36.
See CORRECTIONS.

ALABAMA CREDIT UNION LEAGUE, §§5-17-25 to 5-17-28.

ALABAMA EXTENSION SERVICE, §§2-30-1 to 2-30-4.

ALABAMA FRESH PURSUIT ACT, §15-10-74.

ALABAMA GIRLS' INDUSTRIAL SCHOOL, §§16-54-1 to 16-54-18.
See UNIVERSITY OF MONTEVALLO.

ALABAMA GIRLS' TECHNICAL INSTITUTE, §§16-54-1 to 16-54-18.
See UNIVERSITY OF MONTEVALLO.

ALABAMA HERITAGE TRUST FUND.
Constitution of Alabama, Const. Ala., amd. 394.

ALABAMA HIGH SCHOOL OF MATHEMATICS AND SCIENCE, §§16-26A-1 to 16-26A-7.

ALABAMA HIGHWAY AUTHORITY.
Highways.
Authority, §§23-1-150 to 23-1-160.
See HIGHWAYS.

ALABAMA HIGHWAY FINANCE CORPORATION.
Highways.
Finance corporation, §§23-1-170 to 23-1-181.
See HIGHWAYS.

ALABAMA HISTORICAL COMMISSION, §§41-9-240 to 41-9-262.
See HISTORY AND ARCHIVES.

ALABAMA INDUSTRIAL SCHOOLS.
See YOUTH SERVICES.

ALABAMA INSTITUTE FOR DEAF AND BLIND.
Handicapped persons.
Institute for deaf and blind, §§21-1-1 to 21-1-26.
See HANDICAPPED PERSONS.

ALABAMA INSTITUTE OF AVIATION TECHNOLOGY AT OZARK.
Vocational trade school.
To be operated as additional vocational trade school, §16-60-198.

ALABAMA LAW ENFORCEMENT PLANNING AGENCY, §§41-8A-1 to 41-8A-13.
See LAW ENFORCEMENT PLANNING AGENCY.

ALABAMA LAW INSTITUTE, §§29-8-1 to 29-8-5.
Advisory capacity, §29-8-5.
Compensation.
Generally, §29-8-2.
Director, §29-8-2.
Duties, §29-8-4.
Establishment, §29-8-1.
Governing council, §29-8-1.
Judicial system study commission.
Assistance of commission by institute, §12-9-7.
Membership, §29-8-1.
Plan of membership.
Adoption of plan, §29-8-3.
Purposes and duties, §29-8-4.
Reports, §29-8-5.

ALABAMA MENTAL HEALTH FINANCE AUTHORITY, §§41-10-350 to 41-10-371.
See MENTAL HEALTH FINANCE AUTHORITY.

ALABAMA POLYTECHNIC INSTITUTE.
General provisions, §§16-48-1 to 16-48-12.
See AUBURN UNIVERSITY.

ALABAMA PORT AUTHORITY.
Harbors and ports.
Port authorities, §§33-13-1 to 33-13-13.
See HARBORS AND PORTS.

ALABAMA PRIVATIZATION ACT.
Utility services facilities, §§11-97-1 to 11-97-27.
See UTILITY SERVICES FACILITIES.

ALABAMA RULES OF CIVIL PROCEDURE, ARCP, Rules 1 to 86.
See RULES OF CIVIL PROCEDURE.

ALABAMA SCHOOL OF TRADES, §§16-60-210 to 16-60-221.
See TRADE SCHOOLS.

ALABAMA STATE UNIVERSITY, §§16-50-1 to 16-50-30.
Agents.
Default, etc., of agents, §16-50-3.
American legion scholarships, §§16-31-1 to 16-31-4.
Autonomy, §16-50-1.

ALABAMA STATE UNIVERSITY—Cont'd

Board of trustees.
Appointment of members, §16-50-20.
Body corporate, §16-50-21.
Compensation of members, §16-50-20.
Composition, §16-50-20.
Conflicts of interest, §16-50-29.
Course of instruction.
　Powers of board, §16-50-23.
Creation, §16-50-20.
Default, etc., of trustees, §16-50-3.
Degrees.
　Powers of board, §16-50-23.
Duties, §16-50-22.
Endowment funds.
　Investment, §16-13-2.
Expenses of members.
　Certificate for payment, §16-50-28.
Faculty.
　Powers of board, §16-50-23.
Jurisdiction, §16-50-24.
Meetings, §16-50-26.
Name, §16-50-21.
Powers, §§16-50-22, 16-50-23.
　Transfer of powers from state board of education, §16-50-24.
President of university.
　Powers of board, §16-50-23.
Qualifications of members, §16-50-20.
Quorum, §16-50-27.
Reports to legislature, §16-50-30.
Terms of members, §16-50-20.
Tuition.
　Powers of board, §16-50-23.
Vacancies in office, §16-50-25.
Body corporate, §16-50-21.
Commission of higher education.
General provisions, §§16-5-1 to 16-5-14.
See UNIVERSITIES AND COLLEGES.
Conflicts of interest.
Board of trustees, §16-50-29.
Corporation.
Body corporate, §16-50-21.
Course of instruction.
Board of trustees.
　Powers of board, §16-50-23.
Degrees.
Board of trustees.
　Powers of board, §16-50-23.
Faculty, §16-50-23.
Eminent scholars trust fund, §§16-61-1 to 16-61-10.
See UNIVERSITIES AND COLLEGES.
Existing policies, procedures, etc., §16-50-2.
Federal funds.
Recommendation to qualify for federal funds, §16-50-1.
Funds.
Eminent scholars trust fund, §§16-61-1 to 16-61-10.
See UNIVERSITIES AND COLLEGES.

ALABAMA STATE UNIVERSITY—Cont'd

Gifts, §16-50-3.
Recommendation to qualify for federal, etc., funds, §16-50-1.
Grants, §16-50-3.
Recommendation of programs to qualify for federal, etc., funds, §16-50-1.
Jurisdiction.
Board of trustees, §16-50-24.
Legislature.
Reports to legislature, §16-50-30.
Marine environmental sciences consortium, §§16-45-1 to 16-45-5.
Names.
Board of trustees, §16-50-21.
Grants or gifts not to fail because of misnomer, etc., §16-50-3.
Officers and employees.
Default, etc., §16-50-3.
Existing policies, procedures, etc., relative to, §16-50-2.
Organization of university, §16-50-23.
Police.
Generally, §§16-22-1, 16-22-2.
University police officers, §16-50-4.
President of university, §16-50-23.
Reports.
Board of trustees, §16-50-30.
Salaries, §16-50-23.
Scholarships.
American legion scholarships, §§16-31-1 to 16-31-4.
Students.
Existing policies, procedures, etc., relative to students, §16-50-2.
Trustees.
Board of trustees. See within this heading, "Board of trustees."
Tuition.
Board of trustees.
　Powers of board, §16-50-23.
Universities and colleges generally.
See UNIVERSITIES AND COLLEGES.

ALABAMA TECHNICAL COLLEGE.
Merger of institutions, §16-60-270.
New college designated and named, §16-60-270.

ALABAMA TECHNICAL INSTITUTE AND COLLEGE FOR WOMEN, §§16-54-1 to 16-54-18.
See UNIVERSITY OF MONTEVALLO.

ALABAMA TRAINING SCHOOL FOR GIRLS.
See YOUTH SERVICES.

ALABAMA TRUST FUND, Const. Ala., amd. 450.

ALABAMA WATER SYSTEM ASSISTANCE AUTHORITY.
General provisions, §§22-23A-1 to 22-23A-17.
See WATER SYSTEM ASSISTANCE AUTHORITY.

ALABASTER, CITY OF.
Taxation.
Additional ad valorem tax in city, Const. Ala., amd. 409.

ALARMS.
False alarms.
Rendering false alarms, §13A-10-8.

ALBANY, MUNICIPALITY OF.
Property tax, Const. Ala., amd. 13.

ALCOHOL.
Alcoholic beverages.
General provisions, §§28-1-1 to 28-9-11.
See ALCOHOLIC BEVERAGES.
Alcoholism.
Treatment.
　Group plans, §§27-20A-1 to 27-20A-4.
Education.
Alcohol abuse education, §§16-41-4 to 16-41-10.
See EDUCATION.
Industrial alcohol, §§28-5-1 to 28-5-14.
See INDUSTRIAL ALCOHOL.
Motor vehicles.
Driving under the influence.
See MOTOR VEHICLES.

ALCOHOLIC BEVERAGES.
Abatement.
Dry counties.
　Abatement of liquor nuisances, §§28-4-220 to 28-4-232. See within this heading, "Dry counties."
Actions.
Beer.
　Business relations between wholesalers and suppliers.
　　Declaratory judgments, §28-9-11.
　　Violations of provisions, §28-9-11.
Minors.
　Illegal liquor sales.
　　Parent or guardian, §6-5-70.
　　Person injured in consequence, §6-5-71.
Adulteration, §28-3A-25.
Advertising.
Table wine, §28-7-23.
Wet counties, §28-3-16.
Age.
Employment of underage person, §28-1-5.
Lounges, §28-3A-11.
Minimum age for purchasing, consuming, possessing, etc., §28-1-5.

ALCOHOLIC BEVERAGES
—Cont'd
Agents.
Dry counties.
Enforcement of chapter.
Self-incrimination,
§28-4-320.
Sales.
Agents assisting friends
of sellers.
Punishment, §28-4-30.
Air carriers.
Exemption of sales from
taxation.
Hub operations, §28-3-207.
Licenses.
Retail common carrier
liquor license,
§28-3A-18.
Airport authority.
Special retail license,
§28-3A-19.
Alcohol abuse education,
§§16-41-4 to 16-41-10.
See EDUCATION.
**Alcoholic beverage control
board,** §§28-3-40 to
28-3-55.
Accounts, §28-3-52.
Administration of chapter,
§28-3-42.
Administrator, §28-3-42.
Cost of evidence fund,
§28-3-55.
Appointment of members,
§28-3-40.
Beer.
Supervision of sale and
distribution, §28-3-45.
Bond of members, §28-3-40.
Books.
Maintenance, §28-3-52.
Compensation of members,
§28-3-41.
Composition, §28-3-40.
Conflicts of interest,
§28-3-40.
Disposition of moneys
received, §28-3-53.
Dry counties.
Contraband.
Delivery of liquors and
beverages to board,
§28-4-273.
Duties, §28-3-43.
Earnings.
Additional "mark up"
credited to general
fund, §28-3-53.2.
Disposition of moneys
received, §28-3-53.
Distribution of funds
accumulated as
working capital,
§28-3-53.1.
Use of moneys realized,
§28-3-53.1.
Examination of board,
§28-3-43.
Functions, §28-3-43.
Governor.
Annual report to, §28-3-42.
Inspections, §28-3-50.
Law enforcement officers and
investigators.
Badge and pistol as part of
retirement benefits,
§36-21-8.
Malt beverages.
Supervision of sale and
distribution, §28-3-45.

ALCOHOLIC BEVERAGES
—Cont'd
**Alcoholic beverage control
board**—Cont'd
Meetings, §28-3-40.
Office, §28-3-40.
Permits.
Transportation of wine for
sacramental purposes,
§§28-4-182, 28-4-183.
Possession by officers, etc.,
for personal use,
§28-3-42.
Powers, §28-3-43.
Qualifications of members,
§28-3-40.
Quorum, §28-3-40.
Records, §28-3-52.
Removal of members,
§28-3-40.
Reports, §28-3-42.
Rules and regulations,
§§28-3-49 to 28-3-51.
Inspections, §28-3-50.
Introduction in evidence,
§28-3-49.
Promulgation, amendment,
etc., by board,
§28-3-49.
Stamps, crowns or lids,
§28-3-51.
Safety coordinating
committee.
Member of committee,
§32-3-1.
Sales tax exemption,
§11-51-200.
Suspension of members,
§28-3-40.
Table wine.
Issuance of licenses,
§28-7-5.
Regulations, §28-7-17.
Taxation.
Additional "mark up"
credited to general
fund, §28-3-53.2.
Audit and collection of
taxes on beer or table
wine for benefit of
local governing bodies
generally, §§28-7A-1 to
28-7A-6. See within
this heading,
"Taxation."
Collection of licenses and
taxes, §28-3-45.
Disposition, §28-3-53.
Delay in distribution of
certain funds,
§28-3-53.1.
Powers, §28-3-46.
Refunds, §28-3-54.
Sales tax exemption,
§11-51-200.
Term of members, §28-3-40.
Transportation of beverages.
Lease of trucks, §28-3-44.
Allowable quantities.
Dry counties.
Private use, §§28-4-200,
28-4-201.
Arbitration.
Beer.
Business relations between
wholesalers and
suppliers, §28-9-8.
Assignments.
Licenses, §28-3A-23.
Table wine licenses, §28-7-14.

ALCOHOLIC BEVERAGES
—Cont'd
Audits.
Alcoholic beverage control
board, §28-3-52.
Invoices, books, papers, etc.,
§28-3-7.
Aviation.
Licenses.
Airport authority,
§28-3A-19.
Common carriers,
§28-3A-18.
Bankruptcy and insolvency.
Licenses.
Cancellation upon
bankruptcy, §28-3A-23.
Table wine licenses.
Bankruptcy, §28-7-14.
Beer.
Alcoholic beverage control
board.
Collection of licenses and
taxes, §28-3-45.
Business relations between
wholesalers and
suppliers, §§28-9-1 to
28-9-11.
Actions.
Declaratory judgments,
§28-9-11.
Violations of provisions,
§28-9-11.
Agreements.
Amendment, §28-9-6.
Cancellation, §28-9-6.
Defined, §28-9-2.
Existing agreements,
§28-9-10.
Failure to provide
written agreement.
Prohibited, §28-9-4.
Successor to business,
§28-9-10.
Termination, §28-9-6.
Transferee of business,
§28-9-10.
Waiver of rights by
wholesalers.
Null and void, §28-9-9.
Ancillary business.
Defined, §28-9-2.
Applicability of provisions.
Existing agreements,
§28-9-10.
Arbitration procedures,
§28-9-8.
Coercion, §28-9-4.
Damages.
Violations of provisions,
§28-9-11.
Declaratory judgments,
§28-9-11.
Definitions, §28-9-2.
Good faith.
Amendment or
cancellation of
agreement.
Proof of good faith,
§28-9-6.
Defined, §28-9-2.
Dispute settlements,
§28-9-9.
Injunctions, §28-9-11.
Legislative declaration,
§28-9-1.
Notice.
Amendment or
cancellation of
agreement, §28-9-6.

ALCOHOLIC BEVERAGES
—Cont'd
Beer—Cont'd
Business relations between
wholesalers and
suppliers—Cont'd
Notice—Cont'd
Arbitration procedures,
§28-9-8.
Transfer of wholesaler's
business, §28-9-5.
Prohibited acts.
Suppliers, §28-9-4.
Wholesalers, §28-9-5.
Purpose of provisions,
§28-9-1.
Retaliatory action.
Defined, §28-9-2.
Prohibited acts, §28-9-4.
Sales territory.
Defined, §28-9-2.
Suppliers.
Coercion of wholesalers,
§28-9-4.
Defined, §28-9-2.
Liability.
Acts diminishing value
of wholesaler's
business, §28-9-8.
Violations of
provisions,
§28-9-11.
Prohibited acts, §28-9-4.
Sales of beer through
wholesalers, §28-9-3.
Successor to supplier's
business.
Agreements to apply
to, §28-9-10.
Violations of provisions,
§28-9-11.
Waiver of rights by
wholesalers.
Null and void, §28-9-9.
Wholesalers.
Coercion of wholesalers
by suppliers, §28-9-4.
Defined, §28-9-2.
Prohibited acts, §28-9-5.
Sales by beer suppliers
through wholesalers,
§28-9-3.
Transfer of wholesaler's
business, §28-9-7.
Agreements to apply to
transferee,
§28-9-10.
Consent of supplier,
§28-9-7.
Defined, §28-9-2.
Notice to supplier,
§28-9-5.
Prohibited acts by
supplier as to,
§28-9-4.
Prohibited acts by
wholesaler as to,
§28-9-5.
Waiver of rights.
Null and void, §28-9-9.
Clubs.
Authority to purchase beer,
§28-3A-12.
Containers, §28-3A-23.
Definitions, §28-3-1.
Business relations between
wholesalers and
suppliers, §28-9-2.
Draft or keg beer.
Manner of sale, §28-3A-23.

ALCOHOLIC BEVERAGES
—Cont'd
Beer—Cont'd
Excise tax, §§28-3-190 to
28-3-199.
Administration, §28-3-190.
Collection, §28-3-190.
Disposition of proceeds,
§28-3-190.
Distributors.
Exemptions, §28-3-191.
Enforcement, §28-3-190.
Escrow fund, §28-3-196.
Exclusive nature of tax,
§28-3-190.
Fees.
County and municipal
license fees,
§28-3-194.
Legislative intent,
§28-3-195.
Levy of tax, §28-3-190.
License fees, §28-3-194.
Local taxes and licenses.
Repealer provision,
§28-3-199.
Meaning of words and
phrases, §28-3-198.
Penalties, §28-3-190.
Violations, §28-3-192.
Wholesalers.
Failure to timely pay
tax, §28-3-193.
Repeal of certain local
taxes and licenses,
§28-3-199.
Revenue loss phase-out
system, §28-3-196.
Supplemental revenue loss
phase-out revenue
system, §28-3-197.
Unlawful acts and offenses,
§28-3-192.
Wholesalers.
Delinquent payments.
Penalty, §28-3-193.
Exemptions, §28-3-191.
Words and phrases.
Meaning, §28-3-198.
Importers.
Reports of beer shipments,
§28-3A-7.
Keg beer.
Manner of sale, §28-3A-23.
Levelized beer tax,
§§28-3-190 to 28-3-199.
Licenses.
Generally, §§28-3A-1 to
28-3A-26. See within
this heading,
"Licenses."
On and off premises
consumption.
Retail license,
§§28-3A-16,
28-3A-17.
Malt beverages.
Collection of licenses and
taxes, §28-3-45.
Defined, §28-3-1.
On and off premises
consumption.
Off-premises consumption,
§§28-3A-16, 28-3A-17.
Reports.
Manufacturer's reports,
§28-3A-6.
Suppliers.
Business relations with
wholesalers, §§28-9-1
to 28-9-11.

ALCOHOLIC BEVERAGES
—Cont'd
Beer—Cont'd
Taxation.
Excise tax, §§28-3-190 to
28-3-199.
Malt or brewed beverages.
See within this
heading, "Taxation."
Wholesalers.
Business relations with
suppliers, §§28-9-1 to
28-9-11.
Excise tax.
Generally, §§28-3-190 to
28-3-199.
Importing beer, §28-3A-9.
Billiard rooms.
Sale prohibited, §34-6-12.
Blood tests.
Motor vehicles.
Driving under the
influence.
Chemical tests for
intoxication.
See MOTOR
VEHICLES.
Bonds, surety.
Abatement of liquor
nuisances.
Preliminary injunctions,
§28-4-224.
Alcoholic beverage control
board, §28-3-40.
Dry counties.
Recovery of vehicles seized,
§§28-4-287, 28-4-288.
Table wine.
Bond to acquire license
application, §28-7-6.
Wholesaler's license,
§28-7-9.
Bone dry law, §§28-4-1 to
28-4-326. See within this
heading, "Dry counties."
Brewers.
Defined, §28-4-22.
Buses.
Licenses.
Retail common carrier
liquor license,
§28-3A-18.
Carriers.
Dry counties.
Transportation of
prohibited beverages.
Common carriers. See
within this heading,
"Dry counties."
Licenses.
Retail common carrier
liquor license,
§28-3A-18.
Records.
Examination, §28-3-6.
Wine for sacramental or
religious purposes.
Maintenance and
inspection,
§28-4-118.
Shipments from outside
state, §28-4-184.
Stamps, crowns or lids.
Affixing to articles on
interstate common
carriers, §28-3-51.
Statements of consignments
and deliveries, §28-3-6.

ALCOHOLIC BEVERAGES
—Cont'd
Chemical tests for
    intoxication.
    Motor vehicles.
    Driving under the
        influence.
        See MOTOR VEHICLES.
Child labor.
    Employment of persons
        under 19 years of age
        prohibited, §25-8-12.
Churches.
    Dry counties.
        Wine for sacramental or
            religious purposes. See
            within this heading,
            "Dry counties."
Closing of licensed places.
    Emergencies.
        Temporary closings,
            §28-3-47.
Clubs.
    Beer.
        Authority to purchase,
            §28-3A-12.
        Defined, §28-3-1.
        Dry counties.
            Keeping of prohibited
                liquors and beverages
                in lockers, rooms, etc.,
                §28-4-23.
            Unlawful drinking places.
                Forfeiture of charters of
                    clubs, §28-4-72.
        Licenses, §28-3A-12.
            Fees, §28-3A-21.
        Sunday sales, §28-3A-12.
    Wine.
        Authority to purchase,
            §28-3A-12.
Coal.
    Mine safety.
        Entry into mines while
            intoxicated, §25-9-27.
C.O.D.
    Dry counties.
        Transportation of
            prohibited beverages,
            §28-4-114.
Commercial code.
    Sales.
        Implied warranty of
            merchantability,
            §7-2-314.
        Warehouse receipts.
            Storage under government
                bond, §7-7-201.
Common carriers.
    Dry counties.
        Transportation of
            prohibited beverages.
            See within this
            heading, "Dry
            counties."
    Licenses.
        Fees, §28-3A-21.
        Retail common carriers,
            §28-3A-18.
    Stamps, crowns or lids.
        Rules and regulations for
            affixing, §28-3-51.
Condemnation.
    Dry counties.
        Contraband, §§28-4-250 to
            28-4-299. See within
            this heading, "Dry
            counties."
Conflicts of interest.
    Alcoholic beverage control
        board, §28-3-40.

ALCOHOLIC BEVERAGES
—Cont'd
Conflicts of interest—Cont'd
    Interlocking businesses and
        interests prohibited,
        §28-7-22.
Constitution of the United
    States, Const. U. S.,
    Amendments XVIII, XXI.
Containers.
    Beer, §28-3A-23.
    Dry counties.
        Wine for sacramental or
            religious purposes.
            Labeling of containers,
                §28-4-119.
    Original containers,
        §28-3A-6.
    Transportation in other than
        original containers,
        §28-3A-25.
    Wholesalers.
        Sales in original
            containers, §28-3A-9.
    Wine, §28-3A-23.
Contraband.
    Confiscation.
        Interfering with
            confiscation, §28-3-19.
    Dry counties, §§28-4-250 to
        28-4-299. See within this
        heading, "Dry counties."
    Possession of illegally
        manufactured,
        transported or imported
        beverages, §28-1-1.
    Unregistered labels,
        §28-3A-6.
    Wet counties, §§28-3-240 to
        28-3-244.
Control board, §§28-3-40 to
    28-3-55. See within this
    heading, "Alcoholic
    beverage control board."
Cost of evidence fund.
    Use, §28-3-55.
Counterfeiting and forgery.
    Stamps, crowns or lids,
        §28-3-228.
Counties.
    Dry counties, §§28-4-1 to
        28-4-326. See within this
        heading, "Dry counties."
    Elections.
        Sale and distribution. See
            within this heading,
            "Elections."
    Privilege or license taxes.
        Authorized, §28-3A-21.
    Taxation.
        Audit and collection of
            taxes for benefit of
            local governing body,
            §§28-7A-1 to 28-7A-6.
            See within this
            heading, "Taxation."
    Wet counties, §§28-3-1 to
        28-3-286. See within this
        heading, "Wet counties."
Crowns.
    Tax or identification stamps,
        crowns or lids.
        Generally, §§28-3-220 to
            28-3-229. See within
            this heading, "Stamps,
            crowns and lids."

ALCOHOLIC BEVERAGES
—Cont'd
Damages.
    Beer.
        Business relations between
            wholesalers and
            suppliers.
            Violations of provisions,
                §28-9-11.
Declaratory judgments.
    Beer.
        Business relations between
            wholesalers and
            suppliers, §28-9-11.
Definitions, §28-3-1.
    Beer, §28-3-1.
        Business relations between
            wholesalers and
            suppliers, §28-9-2.
    Brewers, §28-4-22.
    Distillers, §28-4-1.
    Native farm wine, §28-6-1.
    Sales.
        Exclusive sales territories,
            §28-8-7.
Delivery of alcoholic
    beverages.
    From out-of-state, §28-1-4.
Denatured alcohol, §§28-5-1
    to 28-5-14.
    See INDUSTRIAL
        ALCOHOL.
Dentists.
    Acquisition, dispensing, etc.,
        §28-3-15.
Detinue.
    Dry counties.
        Contraband.
            Recovery by detinue
                during pendency of
                proceedings,
                §28-4-265.
Discrimination.
    State retaliating against
        Alabama products,
        §28-3-13.
Distillers.
    Defined, §28-4-1.
Distribution.
    Elections.
        Sale and distribution. See
            within this heading,
            "Elections."
Distributors.
    Not to be manufacturers or
        retailers, §28-3-4.
    Reports, §§28-3-9, 28-3-10.
    Separation of financial and
        business interests,
        §28-3-4.
    Shipment or delivery within
        state, §28-3-8.
    Stamps, crowns or lids,
        §§28-3-220 to 28-3-229.
        See within this heading,
        "Stamps, crowns or lids."
District attorneys.
    Dry counties.
        Enforcement of chapter,
            §§28-4-314, 28-4-315.
Dram shop act.
    Persons injured in
        consequence of illegal
        liquor sales, §6-5-71.
Driving under the influence.
    See MOTOR VEHICLES.
Drug abuse education,
    §§16-41-1 to 16-41-10.
    See EDUCATION.

ALCOHOLIC BEVERAGES
—Cont'd
Druggists.
Dry counties.
Druggists and physicians,
§§28-4-150 to 28-4-166.
See within this
heading, "Dry
counties."
Drunken driving.
Motor vehicles.
Driving under the
influence.
See MOTOR VEHICLES.
Drunkenness.
See DRUNKENNESS.
Dry counties, §§28-4-1 to
28-4-326.
Abatement of liquor
nuisances, §§28-4-220 to
28-4-232.
Authorization, §28-4-220.
Costs.
Payment of costs in
proceedings,
§28-4-229.
Evidence, §28-4-323.
Rules of evidence,
§28-4-231.
Injunctions.
Persons who may be
enjoined, §28-4-230.
Preliminary injunctions,
§§28-4-223, 28-4-224.
Joinder of parties,
§28-4-230.
Judgments.
Enforcement of
judgments,
§28-4-231.
Entry of judgments,
§28-4-232.
Jurisdiction, §28-4-231.
Petition, §§28-4-220 to
28-4-222.
Contents, §28-4-222.
Filing, §28-4-220.
Persons against whom
petition may be
filed, §28-4-221.
Verification, §28-4-222.
Preliminary injunctions.
Bonds, surety, §28-4-224.
Issuance, §28-4-223.
Procedure generally,
§28-4-220.
Seizure, §§28-4-225 to
28-4-229, 28-4-232.
Costs, §28-4-229.
Destruction of liquor and
beverages,
§28-4-227.
Entry of judgment for
destruction,
§28-4-232.
Disposition of liquor and
beverages,
§§28-4-227, 28-4-228.
Restoration to owner,
§28-4-228.
Writ.
Application, §28-4-225.
Contents, §28-4-226.
Fees and allowances,
§28-4-229.
Issuance, §28-4-225.
Unlawful drinking places,
§28-4-71.

ALCOHOLIC BEVERAGES
—Cont'd
Dry counties—Cont'd
Affidavits.
Transportation of
prohibited beverages.
Nonbeverage use,
§28-4-117.
Agents.
Enforcement of chapter.
Self-incrimination,
§28-4-320.
Punishment, §28-4-30.
Applicability of chapter,
§28-4-4.
Dry municipalities,
§28-4-5.
Arts.
Sales for use in arts,
§28-4-152.
Barter, §§28-4-20,
28-4-21.
Bonds, surety.
Recovery of vehicles seized,
§§28-4-287, 28-4-288.
Brewers, §28-4-22.
Classification as dry
counties.
Elections, §28-2-1.
Clubs.
Keeping of prohibited
liquors and beverages,
§28-4-23.
Unlawful drinking places.
Forfeiture of charters,
§28-4-72.
Concealment.
Person concealing self.
Sale, barter, etc., of
prohibited liquor,
§§28-4-26, 28-4-27.
Containers.
Contraband, §§28-4-292,
28-4-293.
Contraband, §§28-4-250 to
28-4-299.
Abatement of liquor
nuisances, §§28-4-220
to 28-4-232.
Answer by persons
claiming right in
liquors and beverages
seized, §28-4-268.
Authorization of forfeiture
and condemnation,
§28-4-250.
Containers, §§28-4-292,
28-4-293.
Delivery of liquors and
beverages to alcoholic
beverage control board,
§28-4-273.
Depots.
Search warrants.
Issuance, §28-4-263.
Destruction, §28-4-273.
Report by officers seizing
beverages,
§28-4-294.
Detinue during pendency
of proceedings under
article, §28-4-265.
Disposition of property
seized, §28-4-264.
Druggists.
Search of premises of
bona fide druggists,
§28-4-297.

ALCOHOLIC BEVERAGES
—Cont'd
Dry counties—Cont'd
Contraband—Cont'd
Evidence.
Disposition of prohibited
beverages held as
evidence, §28-4-295.
Fees of officers making
seizures, §28-4-325.
Forfeiture and
condemnation,
§§28-4-250, 28-4-269 to
28-4-279, 28-4-293,
28-4-299.
Appeals, §§28-4-276 to
28-4-278.
Authorization,
§28-4-276.
Bond, surety,
§28-4-277.
Circuit court
proceedings,
§28-4-277.
Costs, §28-4-277.
Eligibility, §28-4-277.
Final judgment,
§28-4-278.
Jury trial, §28-4-277.
Persons entitled to
appeal, §28-4-277.
Procedure, §28-4-276.
Circuit courts,
§§28-4-277, 28-4-279.
Costs, §28-4-275.
Destruction of beverages,
§28-4-273.
Dismissal, §28-4-274.
Entry of judgment of
dismissal, §28-4-274.
Entry of judgment of
forfeiture, §28-4-273.
Fees and allowances,
§28-4-280.
Hearings, §28-4-273.
Immunity from
prosecution,
§28-4-272.
Issues.
Generally, §28-4-269.
Multiple claimants,
§28-4-270.
Judgments.
Appeals, §§28-4-276 to
28-4-278.
Dismissal, §28-4-274.
Final judgment,
§28-4-278.
Forfeiture, §28-4-273.
Notice.
Defects or
irregularities in
notice, §28-4-281.
Officers attending and
prosecuting.
Allowances and fees,
§28-4-280.
Parties.
Generally, §28-4-269.
Multiple claimants,
§28-4-270.
Procedure generally,
§28-4-250.
Prosecution of action,
§28-4-271.
Recovery of beverages
seized.
Barring actions to
recover, §28-4-265.

ALCOHOLIC BEVERAGES
—Cont'd
Dry counties—Cont'd
Contraband—Cont'd
Forfeiture and
condemnation—Cont'd
Return to place or person
from which taken,
§28-4-274.
Style of action,
§28-4-269.
Trial, §28-4-269.
Conduct, §28-4-273.
Witnesses, §28-4-272.
Notice.
Defects or irregularities.
Correction, §28-4-281.
General notice.
Delivery, §28-4-267.
Issuance, §28-4-266.
Posting, §28-4-267.
Officers seizing prohibited
beverages.
Preparation of return,
§28-4-294.
Reports, §28-4-294.
Physicians.
Search of premises of
bona fide physicians,
§28-4-298.
Property rights, §28-4-293.
Railroads.
Search warrants.
Issuance, §28-4-263.
Receptacles, etc., §28-4-292.
Forfeiture, disposition,
etc., §28-4-293.
Property rights,
§28-4-293.
Sale, §28-4-292.
Seizure, §28-4-293.
Recovery.
Final judgment of
condemnation,
§28-4-265.
Notice of show cause
hearing, §§28-4-266,
28-4-267.
Replevin or detinue,
§28-4-265.
Replevin, §28-4-265.
Reports.
Officers seizing
prohibited
beverages,
§28-4-294.
Resale, §28-4-296.
Sale of confiscated
beverages, §28-4-299.
Deposit with control
board, §28-4-296.
Proceeds, §28-4-299.
Search warrants.
Depositions, §28-4-255.
Depots.
Issuance, §28-4-263.
Disposition of property
seized, §28-4-264.
Execution.
Allowances and fees,
§28-4-280.
Giving of receipt,
§28-4-260.
Limitation period,
§28-4-261.
Persons authorized to
execute, §28-4-258.
Time, §28-4-259.
Fees and allowances of
officers executing,
§28-4-280.

ALCOHOLIC BEVERAGES
—Cont'd
Dry counties—Cont'd
Contraband—Cont'd
Search warrants—Cont'd
Form, §28-4-257.
Issuance, §§28-4-251 to
28-4-256.
Affidavit of probable
cause, §28-4-254.
Authorization,
§28-4-251.
Depositions, §28-4-255.
Grounds, §28-4-253.
Judges, §28-4-256.
Persons authorized to
issue, §28-4-252.
Procedure, §28-4-251.
Standard, §28-4-254.
Officers executing,
§28-4-258.
Fees and allowances,
§28-4-280.
Persons authorized to
execute, §28-4-258.
Persons authorized to
issue, §28-4-252.
Probable cause.
Contents of affidavit
supporting,
§28-4-254.
Railroads.
Issuance, §28-4-263.
Receipts.
Giving, §28-4-260.
Return of warrant,
§28-4-262.
Copies, §28-4-262.
Limitation period for
return, §28-4-261.
Steamboats, §28-4-263.
Watercraft, §28-4-263.
Seizure, §28-4-293.
Abatement of liquor
nuisances,
§§28-4-225 to
28-4-229.
Disposition of property,
§28-4-264.
Search warrants,
§§28-4-251 to
28-4-263.
Steamboats.
Search warrants,
§28-4-263.
Stills, etc., §§28-4-282 to
28-4-284.
Contraband, §28-4-282.
Destruction, §28-4-282.
Forfeiture, §28-4-282.
Enforcement,
§28-4-283.
Sale of property,
§28-4-284.
Unlawful disposition,
§28-4-297.
Vehicles, etc., used to
transport prohibited
beverages, §§28-4-285
to 28-4-290.
Advertisement and sale,
§28-4-290.
Bonds, surety.
Failure of bondsmen to
deliver upon
affirmance of
judgment,
§28-4-288.

ALCOHOLIC BEVERAGES
—Cont'd
Dry counties—Cont'd
Contraband—Cont'd
Vehicles, etc., used to
transport prohibited
beverages—Cont'd
Bonds, surety—Cont'd
Recovery of vehicle
pending appeal,
§§28-4-287,
28-4-288.
Condemnation generally,
§28-4-285.
Confiscation, §28-4-285.
Costs, §28-4-289.
Declared contraband,
§28-4-285.
Failure to deliver vehicle
upon entry of
judgment, §28-4-287.
Forfeiture, §28-4-285.
Institution of
proceedings,
§28-4-286.
Intervention, §28-4-286.
Parties, §28-4-286.
Recovery of vehicles,
§§28-4-286 to
28-4-288.
Bond for recovery
pending
condemnation
action, §§28-4-287,
28-4-288.
Replevin or detinue,
§28-4-286.
Sale of vehicles, etc., by
sheriff or court,
§28-4-290.
Proceeds, §28-4-291.
Seizure, §28-4-285.
Watercraft.
Search warrants,
§28-4-263.
Control board.
Contraband.
Delivery to alcoholic
beverage control
board, §28-4-273.
Definitions, §28-4-1.
Delivery of prohibited
beverages generally,
§§28-4-110 to 28-4-137.
Distillation, §28-4-24.
District attorneys.
Enforcement of chapter,
§§28-4-314, 28-4-315.
Domestic use.
Applicability of laws as to
domestic use, §28-4-3.
Druggists and physicians,
§§28-4-150 to 28-4-166.
Affidavits.
Physicians authorized to
prescribe alcohol for
medicinal purposes,
§28-4-156.
Authorization to prescribe.
Physician's affidavit,
§28-4-156.
Brandy.
Prescription, §28-4-162.
Contraband.
Search of premises of
bona fide druggists
or physicians,
§28-4-298.

ALCOHOLIC BEVERAGES
—Cont'd
Dry counties—Cont'd
Druggists and physicians
—Cont'd
Drugstores in which
prescribing physician
has financial interest,
§28-4-160.
Examinations prior to
issuing prescription for
pure alcohol,
§28-4-154.
Gin.
Prescription, §28-4-162.
Jails.
Sale to prisoners by
persons in charge of
jails, §28-4-165.
Jamaica ginger.
Prescription, sale,
dispensing, etc.,
§28-4-163.
Penalties, §28-4-166.
Prescriptions, §§28-4-155 to
28-4-164.
Authorization to
prescribe.
Physician's affidavit,
§28-4-156.
Brandy, §28-4-162.
Compounding, §28-4-151.
Contents, §28-4-157.
Copies.
Evidence, §28-4-161.
Filing, §28-4-159.
Disposition of
prescription when
filled by druggist,
§28-4-160.
Evidentiary, §28-4-161.
Failure to comply with
requirements,
§28-4-164.
Filling, §28-4-160.
Form, §28-4-158.
Gin, §28-4-162.
Grand jury.
Examination,
§28-4-159.
Jamaica ginger,
§28-4-163.
Limitation as to amount
of alcohol, §28-4-160.
Professional opinion of
physician that
alcohol used for
medicinal purposes,
§28-4-155.
Pure alcohol.
Sales for medicinal
purposes,
§28-4-154.
Recordation, §28-4-161.
Rum, §28-4-162.
Whiskey, §28-4-162.
Prisoners.
Sale, delivery, etc.,
§28-4-165.
Professional opinion of
physician.
Use by patient for
medicinal purposes,
§28-4-155.
Purchase by physicians,
§28-4-153.
Pure alcohol.
Sales for medicinal
purposes, §28-4-154.
Retail druggists.
Sales, §28-4-152.

ALCOHOLIC BEVERAGES
—Cont'd
Dry counties—Cont'd
Druggists and physicians
—Cont'd
Retail druggists—Cont'd
Use for compounding of
prescriptions,
§28-4-151.
Rum.
Prescription, §28-4-162.
Sales.
Jamaica ginger,
§28-4-163.
Limitation as to amount,
§28-4-160.
Pure alcohol.
Sales for medicinal
purposes,
§28-4-154.
Retail druggists,
§§28-4-151, 28-4-152.
Wholesale druggists,
§28-4-150.
Searches and seizures.
Premises of bona fide
druggists or
physicians,
§28-4-298.
Statements.
Evidentiary effect of
certified copy,
§28-4-161.
Execution of statement,
§28-4-152.
Recordation, §28-4-161.
Wholesale druggist.
Monthly statements,
§28-4-150.
Transportation of
beverages for
nonbeverage use,
§§28-4-117 to 28-4-119.
Use.
Druggists, §28-4-151.
Physicians, §28-4-153.
Unauthorized use,
§28-4-164.
Purposes, §28-4-152.
Violations of article.
Penalties, §28-4-166.
Whiskey.
Prescription, §28-4-162.
Wholesale druggists.
Sales.
Monthly statements,
§28-4-150.
Dry municipalities.
Applicability of chapter,
§28-4-5.
Elections as to sale and
distribution. See within
this heading, "Elections."
Enforcement of chapter,
§§28-4-310 to 28-4-326.
Affidavits.
Amendment, §28-4-313.
Contents, §28-4-321.
Continuation of
prosecution,
§28-4-313.
Proof, §28-4-321.
Prosecutions for
violations begun by
affidavit, §28-4-313.
Several charges,
§28-4-322.
Sufficiency, §28-4-321.
Agents.
Self-incrimination,
§28-4-320.

ALCOHOLIC BEVERAGES
—Cont'd
Dry counties—Cont'd
Enforcement of chapter
—Cont'd
Attorney general.
Instructions for
enforcement,
§28-4-312.
Charges.
Contents and sufficiency,
§28-4-321.
Proof of charges,
§28-4-321.
Several charges,
§28-4-322.
Complaints.
Amendment, §28-4-313.
Contents, §28-4-321.
Proof, §28-4-321.
Several charges,
§28-4-322.
Sufficiency, §28-4-321.
District attorneys.
Institution of
prosecutions,
§28-4-314.
Reports to grand juries,
§28-4-314.
Sheriffs to cooperate
with, §28-4-315.
Fees of officers making
seizures, §28-4-325.
Governor.
Supervision of
enforcement,
§28-4-310.
Grand jury proceedings.
District attorneys to
institute
prosecutions for or
make reports to
grand juries as to
violations, §28-4-314.
Duty to present
indictments,
§28-4-319.
Right to demand,
§28-4-313.
Witnesses, §§28-4-316 to
28-4-318.
Indictments.
Contents, §28-4-321.
Duty of grand jury,
§28-4-319.
Proof, §28-4-321.
Prosecutions begun by
indictment,
§28-4-313.
Right to demand grand
jury indictment,
§28-4-313.
Several charges,
§28-4-322.
Sufficiency, §28-4-321.
Injunctions, §28-4-324.
Inspectors.
Appointment, §28-4-311.
Offer and payment of
rewards, §28-4-311.
Instructions for officers for
enforcement,
§28-4-312.
Judgments.
Separate counts,
§28-4-322.
Penalties, §28-4-326.
Proof of charges, §28-4-321.

ALCOHOLIC BEVERAGES
—Cont'd
Dry counties—Cont'd
Enforcement of chapter
—Cont'd
Reports.
Failure of officer to
make report,
§28-4-311.
Officers with duty of
enforcing laws,
§28-4-310.
Rewards.
Inspectors.
Offer and payment,
§28-4-311.
Manufacture.
Convictions for
violations,
§28-4-25.
Stills.
Convictions for
possession,
§28-4-54.
Sheriffs.
Cooperation with district
attorneys, §28-4-315.
Witnesses.
Agents and principals.
Self-incrimination,
§28-4-320.
Grand jury proceedings,
§§28-4-316 to
28-4-318.
Immunity from
prosecution,
§28-4-321.
Initial interrogation,
§28-4-317.
Evidence.
Abatement of liquor
nuisances, §28-4-231.
Contraband.
Disposition, §28-4-295.
Renting or permitting use
of premises for sale,
manufacture, etc.,
§§28-4-92, 28-4-93.
Unlawful drinking places,
§28-4-73.
Exchange.
Penalties, §28-4-21.
Prohibited, §28-4-20.
Fees.
Officers making seizures,
§28-4-325.
Forfeiture generally,
§§28-4-250 to 28-4-299.
Injunctions.
Abatement of liquor
nuisances.
Persons who may be
enjoined, §28-4-230.
Preliminary injunctions,
§§28-4-223, 28-4-224.
Violations of chapter,
§28-4-324.
Inspectors.
Enforcement of chapter.
Appointment, §28-4-311.
Offer and payment of
rewards, §28-4-311.
Jails.
Sale, delivery, etc., of
liquors to prisoners,
§28-4-165.
Jurisdiction.
Abatement of liquor
nuisances, §28-4-231.

ALCOHOLIC BEVERAGES
—Cont'd
Dry counties—Cont'd
Labels.
Wine for sacramental or
religious purposes,
§28-4-119.
Manufacture.
Prohibited, §28-4-24.
Renting or permitting use
of premises, §§28-4-90
to 28-4-93.
Rewards.
Conviction for violation
of section prohibiting
manufacture,
§28-4-25.
Mechanical purposes.
Sales for use for,
§28-4-152.
Medicinal purposes.
Generally, §§28-4-150 to
28-4-166.
Minors.
Common carriers
delivering to minor
from another state,
§28-4-125.
Moonshiners.
Stills generally, §§28-4-50
to 28-4-55.
Motor vehicles.
Contraband.
Vehicles, etc., used to
transport prohibited
beverages,
§§28-4-285 to
28-4-290.
Storage, possession, etc., in
passenger area or in
view of passengers,
§28-4-200.
Municipalities.
Dry municipalities.
Applicability of chapter,
§28-4-5.
Nuisances.
Abatement of liquor
nuisances, §§28-4-220
to 28-4-232.
Unlawful drinking places,
§28-4-71.
Offer for sale, §§28-4-20,
28-4-21.
Penalties.
Druggists and physicians,
§28-4-166.
General penalty, §28-4-326.
Private use, §28-4-201.
Sale.
Agents assisting friends
of sellers, §28-4-30.
Offer for sale, §28-4-21.
Stills, §28-4-52.
Pharmacists.
Sale, purchase and
prescription generally,
§§28-4-150 to 28-4-166.
Physicians.
Sale, purchase and
prescription generally,
§§28-4-150 to 28-4-166.
Possession.
Penalties, §28-4-21.
Prohibited, §§28-4-2,
28-4-20.

ALCOHOLIC BEVERAGES
—Cont'd
Dry counties—Cont'd
Prescriptions.
Sale, purchase and
prescription by
druggists and
physicians, §§28-4-155
to 28-4-164.
Prisoners.
Sale, delivery, etc., of
liquors to prisoners,
§28-4-165.
Private use, §§28-4-200,
28-4-201.
Vehicles.
Storage, possession, etc.,
in passenger area or
in view of
passengers,
§28-4-200.
Violations of article.
Penalties, §28-4-201.
Purchase.
Druggists and physicians,
§§28-4-150 to 28-4-166.
Receipt.
Receipt of order for
prohibited liquors or
beverages, §28-4-29.
Receipt of prohibited
beverages, §§28-4-111,
28-4-112.
Records.
Common carriers.
Transportation of
prohibited
beverages,
§§28-4-131 to
28-4-133.
Wine for sacramental or
religious purposes.
Shipment from outside
state, §28-4-184.
Rectifier of spirits.
Conduct of business,
§28-4-22.
Renting or permitting use of
premises for sale,
manufacture, etc.,
§§28-4-90 to 28-4-93.
Evidence, §§28-4-92,
28-4-93.
Storage, §28-4-92.
Forfeiture of rights of
lessee, §28-4-91.
Prohibited, §28-4-90.
Rights of lessee.
Forfeiture, §28-4-91.
Reports.
Contraband.
Destruction, delivery,
etc., §28-4-264.
Enforcement of chapter,
§§28-4-310, 28-4-311.
Retailers.
Conduct of business,
§28-4-22.
Rewards.
Inspectors.
Offer and payment,
§28-4-311.
Manufacture.
Allowance for furnishing
evidence of violation,
§28-4-25.
Stills.
Allowance for furnishing
evidence of violation
of section 28-4-50,
§28-4-54.

ALCOHOLIC BEVERAGES
—Cont'd
Dry counties—Cont'd
Sale, §28-3A-25.
Agents or assisting friends
of sellers.
Punishment, §28-4-30.
Concealment.
Enforcement of section
28-4-26, §28-4-27.
Persons, concealing self
in house, room, etc.,
§28-4-26.
Penalties, §28-4-21.
Agents or assisting
friends of sellers,
§28-4-30.
Storage, §28-4-28.
Unauthorized sale, §28-4-2.
Scientific purposes.
Sales for scientific
purposes, §28-4-152.
Searches and seizures.
Abatement of liquor
nuisances.
Seizure, §§28-4-225 to
28-4-229, 28-4-332.
Warrants, §§28-4-251 to
28-4-263.
Sheriffs.
Enforcement of chapter.
Cooperation with district
attorneys, §28-4-315.
Stills.
Possession by sheriff,
etc., enforcing law,
§28-4-53.
Rewards.
Furnishing evidence to
support
convictions for
violations of
section 28-4-50,
§28-4-54.
Ships and shipping.
Search warrants,
§28-4-263.
Signs containing names of
prohibited beverages,
§28-4-31.
Solicitation, §28-4-29.
Steamboats.
Search warrants,
§28-4-263.
Stills, §§28-4-50 to 28-4-55.
Contraband, §§28-4-282 to
28-4-284.
Manufacture, sale,
possession, etc.,
§28-4-50.
Penalty for violation,
§28-4-52.
Operation, etc., upon
premises by another,
§28-4-55.
Parts.
Unexplained possession,
§28-4-51.
Penalties.
Violations of section
28-4-50, §28-4-52.
Rewards.
Sheriffs.
Furnishing evidence to
support
convictions for
violations of
section 28-4-50,
§28-4-54.

ALCOHOLIC BEVERAGES
—Cont'd
Dry counties—Cont'd
Stills—Cont'd
Sheriffs.
Possession, etc., by
sheriff, etc.,
enforcing law,
§28-4-53.
Rewards.
Furnishing evidence to
support
convictions for
violations of
sections 28-4-50,
§28-4-54.
Storage, §28-4-28.
Transportation of prohibited
beverages, §§28-4-110 to
28-4-137.
Bills of exchange.
Presentation, collection,
etc., §28-4-126.
C.O.D., §28-4-114.
Common carriers.
Acceptance from common
carrier, §28-4-111.
Delivery from another
state with intent
to use in violation
of law, §28-4-123.
Books.
Examinations,
§28-4-133.
Carriage.
Delivery into state,
§28-4-110.
Consignments.
Delivery from another
state to person
other than
consignee,
§28-4-124.
Fictitious persons or
names.
Delivery from another
state to person
under fictitious
name, §28-4-121.
Minors.
Delivery to minor of
liquors from
another state,
§28-4-125.
Penalties, §28-4-136.
Receipt from common
carrier, §28-4-111.
Records, §§28-4-131 to
28-4-133.
Acquisition, §28-4-132.
Duty to maintain,
§28-4-131.
Evidence, §28-4-132.
Examination,
§28-4-133.
Inspection, §28-4-132.
Statement, §§28-4-127 to
28-4-130.
Contents, §28-4-127.
Copies, §28-4-130.
Demand upon failure
to file, §28-4-128.
Evidence, §28-4-130.
Filing, §§28-4-127 to
28-4-129.
Injunctions, §28-4-128.
Inspection, §28-4-129.
Mandamus, §28-4-128.
Notice of further
refusal or neglect
to file, §28-4-128.

ALCOHOLIC BEVERAGES
—Cont'd
Dry counties—Cont'd
Transportation of prohibited
beverages—Cont'd
Common carriers—Cont'd
Statement—Cont'd
Required statement,
§28-4-127.
Transportation with
intent to violate
laws of state,
§28-4-120.
Violations of article.
Penalties, §28-4-136.
Companies.
Conduct of business,
§28-4-116.
Forfeiture of charter,
§28-4-116.
Consignments.
Delivery from another
state to person other
than consignee,
§28-4-124.
Order of receipt,
§28-4-122.
Distribution.
Receipt, §28-4-112.
Drafts.
Presentation, collection,
etc., §28-4-126.
Evidence.
Common carriers.
Statements, §28-4-130.
Delivery to stores, shops,
dwellings, etc., from
which sale
prohibited, §28-4-93.
Fictitious persons or
names.
Delivery to person under
fictitious name,
§28-4-121.
Five gallon act, §28-4-115.
Interstate transportation.
Applicability of article,
§28-4-137.
Minors.
Delivery by common
carrier from another
state, §28-4-125.
Nonbeverage use.
Affidavits, §28-4-117.
Labeling of packages,
§28-4-119.
Records, §28-4-118.
Orders.
Presentation, collection,
etc., of draft, bill of
exchange, etc.,
§28-4-126.
Receipt, §28-4-122.
Penalties, §28-4-136.
Receipt.
Common carriers,
§28-4-111.
Storage, distribution,
etc., for another,
§28-4-112.
Records.
Common carriers,
§§28-4-131 to
28-4-133.
Nonbeverage use,
§28-4-118.
Storage.
Receipt for storage for
another, §28-4-112.

ALCOHOLIC BEVERAGES
—Cont'd
Dry counties—Cont'd
Transportation of prohibited
beverages—Cont'd
Venue.
Where certain offenses
deemed committed,
§28-4-135.
Violations of article.
Common carriers.
Examination of books,
etc., in connection
with prosecutions,
§28-4-133.
District attorneys.
Duties in cases of
grand jury
indictments,
§28-4-136.
Jurisdiction, §28-4-135.
Penalties, §28-4-136.
Venue, §28-4-135.
Witnesses, §28-4-134.
Wine for sacramental or
religious purposes.
Affidavits, §28-4-117.
Labeling, §28-4-119.
Records, §28-4-118.
Shipment from outside
state, §28-4-184.
Within state.
From point to point or
along public streets
or highways,
§28-4-113.
Witnesses, §28-4-134.
Unauthorized possession,
sale, delivery, use, etc.,
§28-4-2.
Unlawful drinking places,
§§28-4-70 to 28-4-73.
Abatement, §28-4-71.
Clubs.
Forfeiture of charters,
§28-4-72.
Evidence, §28-4-73.
Incorporated associations.
Forfeiture of charters,
§28-4-72.
Informations, indictments,
etc., §28-4-73.
Maintenance prohibited,
§28-4-70.
Nuisances, §28-4-71.
Watercraft.
Search warrants,
§28-4-263.
Wholesalers.
Conduct of business,
§28-4-22.
Wine for sacramental or
religious purposes,
§§28-4-180 to 28-4-184.
Applicability of laws,
§28-4-3.
Labeling of packages or
containers, §28-4-119.
Permit for shipping wine
from outside state,
§§28-4-182, 28-4-183.
Purchase, §28-4-181.
Persons authorized to
purchase, §28-4-180.
Records.
Transportation,
§28-4-118.
Shipment from outside
state, §28-4-184.
Sale, §28-4-181.

ALCOHOLIC BEVERAGES
—Cont'd
Dry counties—Cont'd
Wine for sacramental or
religious purposes
—Cont'd
Shipment from outside
state.
Permit for shipping
wine, §§28-4-182,
28-4-183.
Records, §28-4-184.
Transportation.
Affidavits, §28-4-117.
Alcoholic beverage
control board.
Permit for wine to be
shipped from
outside state,
§§28-4-182,
28-4-183.
Labeling of packages,
§28-4-119.
Records, §28-4-118.
Shipment from outside
state, §28-4-184.
Words.
Designating business by
dealers in beverages,
§28-4-31.
Education.
Drug abuse education.
General provisions,
§§16-41-1 to 16-41-10.
See EDUCATION.
Keeping on school premises,
§16-1-10.
Selling, etc., to school
children, §16-1-10.
Elections.
Election officers.
Consuming during election,
§17-6-16.
Municipal elections,
§11-46-132.
Municipal corporations.
Drunkenness at or about
polling place,
§§11-46-68, 11-46-139.
Officers of election.
Consuming during
election,
§§11-46-132, 17-6-16.
Polling places.
Intoxication at polling
place.
Municipal elections,
§11-46-139.
Primary elections,
§17-16-47.
Poll watchers.
Consuming during election,
§17-6-16.
Municipal elections,
§§11-46-65,
11-46-132.
Protection against
intoxicating liquors at
elections, Const. Ala.,
art. VIII, §191.
Sale and distribution.
Certain municipalities.
Distribution of funds,
§28-2A-2.
Elections in
municipalities in
same county.
Population of 4,000 or
more, §28-2A-4.
Intent of legislature,
§28-2A-3.

ALCOHOLIC BEVERAGES
—Cont'd
Elections—Cont'd
Sale and distribution—Cont'd
Certain municipalities
—Cont'd
Procedure, §28-2A-1.
Classification of counties
as wet or dry counties.
Procedure, §28-2-1.
Dry counties.
Laws applicable in dry
counties, §28-2-1.
Procedure, §28-2-1.
Special method
referendum.
Adoption of article,
§28-2-21.
Applicability of other
provisions, §28-2-25.
Approval of sale and
distribution.
Conditions governing
sale, §28-2-22.
Conflicts of law.
Applicability of other
provisions of title,
§28-2-25.
Counties not authorized
to conduct referenda,
§28-2-24.
Question to be asked
voters, §28-2-21.
Request for election,
§28-2-21.
Short title of article,
§28-2-20.
Wet counties not
authorized to
conduct referenda,
§28-2-24.
Watchers.
Drinking of intoxicating
liquors by watcher,
§§11-46-65, 11-46-136.
Emergencies.
Temporary closings of
licensed places, §28-3-47.
Ethyl alcohol.
Industrial alcohol.
General provisions,
§§28-5-1 to 28-5-14.
See INDUSTRIAL
ALCOHOL.
Wet counties.
Applicability of provisions
of chapter to, §28-3-3.
Evidence.
Alcoholic beverage control
board.
Regulations as to table
wine, §28-7-17.
Cost of evidence fund.
Use, §28-3-55.
Dry counties.
Abatement of liquor
nuisances, §28-4-231.
Admissibility.
Similarity in color, odor
and general
appearance,
§28-4-323.
Contraband.
Disposition upon
convictions,
§28-4-295.
Renting or permitting use
of premises for sale,
manufacture, etc.,
§§28-4-92, 28-4-93.
Separate counts, §28-4-322.

ALCOHOLIC BEVERAGES
—Cont'd
Evidence—Cont'd
Dry counties—Cont'd
Testimony of persons
purchasing prohibited
beverages, §28-4-321.
Unlawful drinking places,
§28-4-73.
Exclusionary rule, §28-1-2.
Illegal searches.
Admissibility of evidence
obtained by, §28-1-2.
Excise taxes.
Beer, §§28-3-190 to 28-3-199.
See within this heading,
"Beer."
Malt or brewed beverages,
§28-3-184.
Containers.
Identification on
containers,
§28-3-187.
Definitions, §28-3-183.
Failure to pay, §28-3-186.
Illegal possession of
unidentified malt or
brewed beverages,
§28-3-186.
Reports, §28-3-185.
Exclusionary rule, §28-1-2.
Exclusive sales territories,
§§28-8-1 to 28-8-8. See
within this heading,
"Sales."
Fairs.
Special retail license for fair
authority, §28-3A-19.
Federal reservations.
Shipment to federal
reservations, §28-3-8.
Fees.
Disposition, §28-3A-22.
Dry counties.
Officers making seizures,
§28-4-325.
Licenses. See within this
heading, "Licenses."
Food stamps.
Illegal possession of food
stamps, §13A-9-92.
Forfeitures.
Dry counties.
Contraband, §§28-4-250 to
28-4-299. See within
this heading, "Dry
counties."
Wet counties.
Contraband.
Confiscation generally.
See within this
heading, "Wet
counties."
Franchises.
Special retail license,
§28-3A-19.
Governor.
Alcoholic beverage control
board.
Annual report to governor,
§28-3-42.
Dry counties.
Supervision of
enforcement,
§28-4-310.
Grand jury.
Dry counties.
Enforcement of chapter.
See within this
heading, "Dry
counties."

ALCOHOLIC BEVERAGES
—Cont'd
Hearings.
Licenses, §28-3A-24.
Hotels.
Defined, §28-3-1.
Licenses generally. See
within this heading,
"Licenses."
Hours of sale, §28-3A-25.
Identification.
Stamps, crowns or lids. See
within this heading,
"Stamps, crowns or lids."
Impeachment.
Intemperance as grounds for,
§36-11-1.
Importers.
Filing lists of labels,
§28-3A-7.
Licenses. See within this
heading, "Licenses."
Records, §28-3A-7.
Reports.
Beer and wine shipments,
§28-3A-7.
Table wine.
License, §28-7-10.
Wholesalers.
Beer and table wine,
§28-3A-9.
Indictments.
Buying, selling, possessing,
etc., prohibited liquors,
§15-8-150.
Dry counties.
Enforcement of chapter.
See within this
heading, "Dry
counties."
Industrial alcohol.
General provisions, §§28-5-1
to 28-5-14.
See INDUSTRIAL
ALCOHOL.
Injunctions.
Beer.
Business relations between
wholesalers and
suppliers, §28-9-11.
Dry counties.
Abatement of liquor
nuisances.
Persons who may be
enjoined, §28-4-230.
Preliminary injunctions,
§§28-4-223, 28-4-224.
Enforcement of chapter,
§28-4-324.
Inspections.
Alcoholic beverage control
board, §28-3-50.
Dry counties.
Appointment of inspectors,
§28-4-311.
Invoices, books, papers, etc.,
§28-3-7.
Manufacturers, §28-3A-6.
Refusing to allow inspection,
§28-3A-25.
Rules and regulations,
§28-3-50.
Wet counties.
Refusing to permit,
§28-3-19.
Insurance.
Disability insurance.
Optional policy provision,
§27-19-26.

ALCOHOLIC BEVERAGES
—Cont'd
Interstate commerce.
Dry counties.
Transportation of
prohibited beverages,
§28-4-127.
Invoices.
Audit by board, §28-3-7.
Inspection by board, §28-3-7.
Preservation, §28-3-7.
Selling or shipping to
persons, firms, etc., in
another state or to
federal government,
§28-3-11.
Jails.
Dry counties.
Sale, delivery, etc., of
liquors to prisoners,
§28-4-165.
Furnishing to prisoners,
§14-6-18.
Jurisdiction.
Dry counties.
Abatement of liquor
nuisances, §28-4-231.
Labels.
Dry counties.
Wine for sacramental or
religious purposes,
§28-4-119.
Importers.
Filing with board,
§28-3A-7.
Manufacturers.
Filing labels with board,
§28-3A-6.
Table wine.
Registration of labels,
§28-7-11.
Wine.
Unregistered labels,
§28-3A-6.
Leases.
Dry counties.
Renting or permitting use
of premises for sale,
manufacture, etc.,
§§28-4-90 to 28-4-93.
Legal hours of sale,
§28-3A-25.
Levelized beer tax.
Excise tax on beer,
§§28-3-190 to 28-3-199.
See within this heading,
"Beer."
Levelized wine tax, §28-7-16.
Licenses, §§28-3A-1 to
28-3A-26.
Airport authority, §28-3A-19.
Applications, §28-3A-4.
Renewal, §28-3A-5.
Retail liquor license,
§28-3A-23.
Assignment, §28-3A-23.
Table wine licenses,
§28-7-14.
Bankruptcy.
Cancellation upon,
§28-3A-23.
Beer.
On and off premises
consumption.
Retail license, §28-3A-16.
Board.
Disposition of moneys
received by, §28-3-53.
Issuance, §28-3A-3.
Citation, §28-3A-1.

ALCOHOLIC BEVERAGES
—Cont'd
Licenses—Cont'd
Civic center authority,
§28-3A-19.
Clubs, §28-3A-12.
Beer.
Authority to purchase,
§28-3A-12.
Wine.
Authority to purchase
table wine,
§28-3A-12.
Common carriers.
Fees, §28-3A-21.
Retail common carrier
license, §28-3A-18.
Containers.
Original containers,
§28-3A-6.
Display of licenses.
Table wine, §28-7-14.
Fair authorities, §28-3A-19.
Fees.
Application fee, §28-3A-4.
Disposition, §§28-3-53,
28-3A-22.
Licenses issued by board,
§28-3A-21.
Schedule, §28-3A-21.
Table wine, §28-7-13.
Application fees, §28-7-6.
Payment and collection
of fees, §28-7-13.
Transfer fee, §28-3A-23.
Fines.
Suspension or revocation of
license, §28-3A-24.
Food stamps.
Illegal possession of food
stamps.
Revocation of liquor
license, §13A-9-92.
Franchises, §28-3A-19.
Hearings.
Hearing commission,
§28-3A-24.
Suspension or revocation,
§28-3A-24.
Importers, §28-3A-7.
Fees, §28-3A-21.
Table wine license,
§28-7-10.
Inspections.
Refusing to allow
inspection, §28-3A-25.
Issuance, §28-3A-23.
Authority of board,
§28-3A-3.
Table wine license, §28-7-7.
Lounges.
Fees, §28-3A-21.
Retail liquor license,
§28-3A-11.
Manufacturers, §28-3A-6.
Fee, §28-3A-21.
Minors.
Selling, etc., to minors,
§28-3A-25.
Native farm wine.
Privilege license tax,
§28-6-4.
Sales, §28-6-2.
Off-premises consumption,
§28-3A-17.
Optometrists.
Habitual drunkenness,
§34-22-23.
Penalties, §28-3A-25.
Delinquent renewal,
§28-3A-5.

ALCOHOLIC BEVERAGES
—Cont'd
Licenses—Cont'd
Purposes for issuance of
license, §28-3A-3.
Racing commission,
§28-3A-19.
Railroads, §28-3A-18.
Records.
Failure to keep records,
§28-3A-25.
Manufacturer's daily
records, §28-3A-6.
Renewal, §28-3A-5.
Eligibility after revocation,
§28-3A-24.
Table wine, §28-7-12.
Reports.
Manufacturer's, §28-3A-6.
Restaurants, §28-3A-13.
Fees, §28-3A-21.
Retailers.
Beer.
On and off premises
consumption,
§28-3A-16.
Club liquor retail license,
§28-3A-12.
Common carrier liquor
license, §28-3A-18.
Fees, §28-3A-21.
Lounge retail liquor
license, §28-3A-11.
Off-premises consumption,
§28-3A-15.
On-premises wine sales,
§28-3A-14.
Restaurants, §28-3A-13.
Separate license,
§28-3A-23.
Special events, §28-3A-20.
Special retail license,
§28-3A-19.
Table wine, §28-7-8.
Revocation, §28-3A-24.
Food stamps.
Illegal possession,
§13A-9-92.
Second or subsequent
conviction, §28-3A-26.
Table wine license,
§28-7-15.
Seizure of unregistered
goods, §28-3A-6.
Shipping lines, §28-3A-18.
Short title, §28-3A-1.
Special events retail license,
§28-3A-20.
Fees, §28-3A-21.
Special retail license,
§28-3A-19.
Fee, §28-3A-21.
State parks, §28-3A-19.
Suspension, §28-3A-24.
Table wine licenses,
§28-7-15.
Table wine.
Administration of chapter,
§28-7-13.
Application, §28-7-6.
Assignment, §28-7-14.
Bankruptcy of licensee,
§28-7-14.
Board.
Authority to issue,
§28-7-5.
Bond, §28-7-6.
County approval, §28-7-5.
Display, §28-7-14.
Fees.
Filing fee, §28-7-6.

ALCOHOLIC BEVERAGES
—Cont'd
Licenses—Cont'd
Table wine—Cont'd
Fees—Cont'd
Payment and collection
of fees, §28-7-13.
Grant, §28-7-14.
Importer's license,
§28-7-10.
Issuance, §28-7-7.
License tax, §28-7-13.
Municipal approval,
§28-7-5.
Off-premises consumption,
§28-3A-15.
On-premises consumption,
§28-3A-14.
Payment and collection of
fees, §28-7-13.
Renewal, §28-7-12.
Retailer's license, §28-7-8.
Separate licenses, §28-7-14.
Suspension or revocation,
§28-7-15.
To whom licenses granted,
§28-7-14.
Wholesaler's license,
§28-7-9.
To whom issued, §28-3A-23.
Unlawful acts, §28-3A-25.
Violations, §28-3A-25.
Second or subsequent
conviction, §28-3A-26.
Warehouses, §28-3A-10.
Fees, §28-3A-21.
Wet counties, §28-3A-19.
When due and payable,
§28-3A-5.
Wholesalers, §28-3A-8.
Fees, §28-3A-21.
Selling without license,
§28-3A-9.
Table wine, §28-7-9.
Unlawful acts and offenses,
§28-3A-25.
Lids.
Tax and identification
stamps, crowns or lids.
See within this heading,
"Stamps, crowns or lids."
Local option.
Elections.
Sale and distribution. See
within this heading,
"Elections."
Lounges.
Age, §28-3A-11.
Dancing, §28-3A-11.
Licenses, §§28-3A-11,
28-3A-21.
Malt beverages.
Alcoholic beverage control
board.
Collection of licenses and
taxes, §28-3-45.
Defined, §28-3-1.
Excise taxes, §§28-3-183 to
28-3-187.
Manufacture.
Dry counties. See within this
heading, "Dry counties."
Illegal manufacture.
Possession of illegally
manufactured
beverages, §28-1-1.
Wet counties.
Laws as to illicit liquor
not repealed by
chapter, §28-3-18.

ALCOHOLIC BEVERAGES
—Cont'd
Manufacturers.
Defined, §28-3-1.
Inspection, §28-3A-6.
Licenses, §§28-3A-6,
28-3A-11.
Generally. See within this
heading, "Licenses."
Not to be distributors,
wholesalers or retailers,
§28-3-4.
Original containers,
§28-3-6.
Out-of-state manufacturers.
Delivery within state,
§28-1-4.
Principal place of business,
§28-3A-6.
Records, §28-3A-6.
Reports.
Beer and wine shipments,
§28-3A-6.
Separation of financial and
business interests,
§28-3-4.
Stamps, crowns or lids. See
within this heading,
"Stamps, crowns or lids."
Stills.
Dry counties. See within
this heading, "Dry
counties."
Table wine. See within this
heading, "Wine."
Violations of licensing act,
§28-3A-25.
Military affairs.
Interference with
performance of troops,
§31-2-126.
Invoices and receipts of goods
shipped to federal
government for military
purposes, §28-3-11.
National guard.
Commanders closing
certain places and
forbidding sale,
§31-2-124.
Compensation for death of
national guardsmen.
When dependents not
entitled to
compensation,
§31-3-2.
Penalties.
Unauthorized sale or
possession, §28-1-3.1.
Possession by eligible persons
of beverages purchased
from military stores,
§28-1-3.1.
Shipment to military
reservations within
state, §28-3-8.
Unauthorized sale or
possession, §28-1-3.1.
Mines and minerals.
Coal mine safety, §25-9-27.
Minors.
Consent as to alcohol
toxicity, §22-8-6.
Delivery by common carrier
to minor from another
state, §28-4-125.
Employment of underage
person, §28-1-5.
Illegal liquor sales.
Right of action by parent
or guardian, §6-5-70.

ALCOHOLIC BEVERAGES
—Cont'd
Minors—Cont'd
Illegal liquor sales—Cont'd
Right of action of person
injured in consequence,
§6-5-71.
Minimum age for purchasing,
etc., §28-1-5.
Schools.
Keeping on school
premises, §16-1-10.
Selling, etc., to school
children, §16-1-10.
Selling, etc., to minors,
§28-3A-25.
Wine.
Selling to minor, §28-7-15.
Moonshiners.
Stills.
Dry counties. See within
this heading, "Dry
counties."
Motor vehicles.
Chemical tests for
intoxication.
Driving under the
influence.
See MOTOR VEHICLES.
Contraband.
Dry counties. See within
this heading, "Dry
counties."
Drivers' licenses.
Grounds for revocation,
§32-5A-195.
Persons to whom license
not to be issued,
§32-6-7.
Driving under the influence.
See MOTOR VEHICLES.
Dry counties.
Contraband.
Vehicles, etc., used to
transport prohibited
beverages,
§§28-4-285 to
28-4-290. See within
this heading, "Dry
counties."
Storage, etc., in passenger
area of vehicles or in
view of passengers,
§28-4-200.
Renting to intoxicated
person, §32-15-2.
Municipal corporations.
Elections.
Commission form.
Officers of election.
Drinking during
election,
§11-46-132.
Drunkenness at polling
place, §§11-46-68,
11-46-139.
Officers of election.
Drinking during election,
§§11-46-65,
11-46-132,
11-46-136, 17-6-16.
Watchers.
Consumption during
election, §§11-46-65,
11-46-136.
Emergencies.
Temporary closing of
licensed places,
§28-3-47.

ALCOHOLIC BEVERAGES
—Cont'd
Municipal corporations
—Cont'd
Licenses.
Retail liquor license
applications.
Approval by governing
authority,
§28-3A-23.
Privilege or license tax,
§28-3A-21.
Sales tax.
Exemption, §11-51-200.
Suppression of intemperance,
§11-47-112.
Taxation.
Audit and collection of
taxes for benefit of
local governing body,
§§28-7A-1 to 28-7A-6.
See within this
heading, "Taxation."
Temperance.
Promotion, §11-47-112.
Traffic in certain beverages.
Suppression, §11-47-112.
Native farm wine, §§28-6-1 to
28-6-6.
Notice.
Beer.
Business relations between
wholesalers and
suppliers.
Amendment or
cancellation of
agreement, §28-9-6.
Arbitration procedures,
§28-9-8.
Transfer of wholesaler's
business, §28-9-5.
Nuisances.
Dry counties.
Abatement of liquor
nuisances, §§28-4-220
to 28-4-232. See within
this heading, "Dry
counties."
Optometrists.
Licenses.
Habitual drunkenness,
§34-22-23.
Out-of-state manufacturers.
Delivery within state,
§28-1-4.
Packages.
Breaking of packages,
§28-3-50.
Containers. See within this
heading, "Containers."
Parent and child.
Illegal sales to minors.
Right of action, §6-5-70.
Penalties.
Dry counties. See within this
heading, "Dry counties."
Licenses.
Violations, §28-3A-25.
Manufacturers.
Unlawful acts, §28-3A-25.
Military affairs.
Unauthorized sale or
possession, §28-1-3.1.
Table wine, §28-7-15.
Wet counties, §28-3-20.
Penitentiary.
Introducing into
penitentiary, §14-3-60.

ALCOHOLIC BEVERAGES
—Cont'd

Pharmacists.
Dry counties.
Druggists and physicians
generally, §§28-4-150
to 28-4-166. See within
this heading, "Dry
counties."

Physicians.
Acquisition, dispensing, etc.
Purposes, §28-3-15.
Dry counties.
Druggists and physicians
generally, §§28-4-150
to 28-4-166. See within
this heading, "Dry
counties."

Pilots and pilotage.
Branches.
Grounds for depriving pilot
of branch, §33-4-46.

Possession.
Certain quantities purchased
from military stores,
§28-1-3.1.
Dry counties. See within this
heading, "Dry counties."

Prescriptions.
Dry counties.
Druggists and physicians,
§§28-4-155 to 28-4-164.
See within this
heading, "Dry
counties."

Presumptions.
Stamps, crowns or lids.
Sale without proper
stamps, §28-3-224.

Prisons and prisoners.
Dry counties.
Sale to prisoners,
§28-4-165.

Public intoxication,
§13A-11-10.

**Public officers and
employees.**
Impeachment.
Intemperance as grounds,
§36-11-1.

Railroads.
Conductors, §37-8-161.
Dry counties.
Search warrants.
Issuance, §28-4-263.
Engineers, §37-8-161.
Intoxication of employees,
§37-8-161.
Licenses, §28-3A-18.
Public drinking in passenger
cars or in waiting rooms,
§37-8-160.

Records.
Alcoholic beverage control
board, §28-3-52.
Carriers.
Examination, §28-3-6.
Wine for sacramental or
religious purposes,
§28-4-118.
Shipments from outside
state, §28-4-184.
Failure to keep, §28-3A-25.
Importers, §28-3A-7.
Manufacturer's daily records,
§28-3A-6.
Stamps, crowns or lids,
§28-3-225.

ALCOHOLIC BEVERAGES
—Cont'd

Records—Cont'd
Wine for sacramental or
religious purposes,
§28-4-118.
Shipment from outside
state, §28-4-184.

Referendum.
Elections.
Sale and distribution. See
within this heading,
"Elections."

Registration.
Labels.
Table wine, §28-7-11.
Licenses.
Seizure of unregistered
goods, §28-3A-6.

Religion.
Dry counties.
Wine for sacramental or
religious purposes,
§§28-4-180 to 28-4-184.
Wet counties.
Wine for sacramental or
religious purposes,
§28-3-15.

Rent.
Dry counties.
Renting premises for sale,
manufacture, etc.,
§§28-4-90 to 28-4-93.

Replevin.
Dry counties.
Contraband, §28-4-265.

Reports.
Alcoholic beverage control
board, §28-3-42.
Distributors, §28-3-9.
Orders by persons without
state, §28-3-10.
Dry counties.
Enforcement of chapter,
§§28-4-310, 28-4-311.
Officer's reports, §28-4-294.
Importers.
Beer and wine shipments,
§28-3A-7.
Manufacturers.
Beer and wine shipments,
§28-3A-6.
Native farm wine, §28-6-4.
Stamps, crowns or lids.
Purchase, etc., of articles
without, §28-3-12.
Taxation.
Malt or brewed beverages.
Excise tax, §28-3-185.
Wholesalers, §28-3-9.

Restaurants.
Defined, §28-3-1.
Licenses, §§28-3A-13,
28-3A-21.
Sales.
Authority to sell,
§28-3A-13.

Retailers.
Club liquor retailers.
Licenses, §28-3A-12.
Defined, §§28-3-1, 28-4-1.
Dry counties.
Conduct of business,
§28-4-22.
Invoices.
Shipments of alcoholic
beverages received
from without state.
Retail dealers to furnish
duplicate invoices to
board, §28-3-5.

ALCOHOLIC BEVERAGES
—Cont'd

Retailers—Cont'd
Licenses. See within this
heading, "Licenses."
Restaurants.
Licenses, §28-3A-13.
Separation of financial and
business interests,
§28-3-4.
Stamps, crowns or lids. See
within this heading,
"Stamps, crowns or lids."
Where beverages sold,
§28-3A-23.
Wine.
Off-premises consumption.
License, §28-3A-15.
On-premises consumption.
License, §28-3A-14.
Table wine, §§28-7-5,
28-7-20.

Rewards.
Dry counties.
Furnishing evidence of
violation of section
prohibiting
manufacture, §28-4-25.
Inspectors.
Offer and payment for
convictions,
§28-4-311.
Stills.
Furnishing evidence to
support convictions
for violations of
section 28-4-50,

Riots.
Temporary closing of licensed
places, §28-3-47.

Rules and regulations.
Generally, §28-3-49.
Inspections.
Breaking of packages,
§28-3-50.
Native farm wine, §28-6-5.
Stamps, crowns or lids.
Interstate common carrier,
§28-3-51.
Table wine, §28-7-17.
Wet counties.
Penalties, §28-3-20.

Sacramental purposes.
Wine for sacramental or
religious purposes.
Dry counties, §§28-4-180 to
28-4-184.
Wet counties, §28-3-15.

Sales.
Clubs, §28-3A-12.
Commercial code.
Implied warranty of
merchantability,
§7-2-314.
Contraband.
Dry counties, §§28-4-296,
28-4-299.
Wet counties.
Confiscation and sale,
§§28-3-240 to
28-3-244.
Defined, §28-3-1.
Dry counties. See within this
heading, "Dry counties."
Elections.
Sale and distribution. See
within this heading,
"Elections."

ALCOHOLIC BEVERAGES
—Cont'd
Sales—Cont'd
Exclusive sales territories, §§28-8-1 to 28-8-8.
Agreements, §§28-8-2 to 28-8-4.
Definitions, §28-8-7.
Designation, §28-8-2.
Modification, §28-8-4.
Exclusive wholesalers.
Designation, §28-8-2.
Service and quality control, §28-8-5.
Verification of reporting and payment of taxes, §28-8-6.
Intent of legislature, §28-8-1.
Penalties, §28-8-8.
Policy of legislature, §28-8-1.
Resale prices.
Territorial agreement may not establish or maintain, §28-8-3.
Unlawful acts and offenses, §28-8-8.
Hours of sale, §28-3A-25.
Legal hours of sale, §28-3A-25.
Licenses generally. See within this heading, "Licenses."
Minors.
Generally. See within this heading, "Minors."
National guard.
Commanders closing certain places and forbidding sale, §31-2-124.
Native farm wine.
Authorized buyers, §28-6-3.
Licenses required, §28-6-2.
Original containers, §28-3A-6.
Restaurants, §28-3A-13.
Stamps, crowns or lids, §28-3-225.
Unauthorized sales, §§28-3-222, 28-3-224.
State liquor stores. See within this heading, "State liquor stores."
Taxation. See within this heading, "Taxation."
Wet counties.
Contraband.
Confiscation and sale, §§28-3-240 to 28-3-244.
Legal hours of sale, §28-3A-25.
Wine.
Generally. See within this heading, "Wine."
Within certain distances of colleges, etc., §28-3-17.
Sales tax.
Additional state sales tax, §§28-3-280 to 28-3-286.
See within this heading, "Taxation."
Schools.
Keeping on school premises, §16-1-10.
Selling to school children, §16-1-10.

ALCOHOLIC BEVERAGES
—Cont'd
Scientific purposes.
Wet counties.
Acquisition by physicians, dentists, etc., §28-3-15.
Searches and seizures.
Contraband liquors and beverages.
Dry counties.
Contraband generally, §§28-4-250 to 28-4-299. See within this heading, "Dry counties."
Wet counties.
Contraband.
Confiscation and sale, §§28-3-240 to 28-3-244.
Exclusionary rule, §28-1-2.
Sheriffs.
Dry counties. See within this heading, "Dry counties."
Ships and shipping.
Dry counties.
Search warrants.
Issuance for search of watercraft, §28-4-263.
Intoxication of persons employed upon vessels, §37-8-161.
Licenses.
Retail common carrier license, §28-3A-18.
Signs.
Dry counties.
Exhibition of signs, §28-4-31.
Wet counties, §28-3-16.
Stamps, crowns or lids.
Affixing.
Failure, §28-3-226.
Manner and time, §28-3-223.
Required, §§28-3-220, 28-3-221.
Rules and regulations, §§28-3-50, 28-3-51.
Alcoholic beverage control board.
Rules and regulations, §§28-3-50, 28-3-51.
Amount.
Affixing in amount of tax, §28-3-222.
Articles offered for sale without.
Confiscation, §28-3-222.
Reports, §28-3-12.
Common carriers.
Rules and regulations for interstate common carrier, §28-3-51.
Confiscation.
Articles offered for sale without, §28-3-222.
Counterfeiting, §28-3-228.
Design, §28-3-48.
Board to design, §28-3-221.
Designation, §28-3-48.
Distribution, §28-3-225.
Failure to properly affix, §28-3-226.
Form, §28-3-48.
Interstate common carriers.
Rules and regulations, §28-3-51.
Lien for judgment in favor of state, §28-3-226.

ALCOHOLIC BEVERAGES
—Cont'd
Stamps, crowns or lids
—Cont'd
Manner for affixing, §28-3-223.
Interstate common carriers, §28-3-51.
Manufacture, §28-3-225.
Native farm wine, §28-6-5.
Presumption as to sale without, §28-3-224.
Purchase by manufacturers, §28-3-225.
Records.
Persons using to pay costs of quarterly examinations by board examiners, §28-3-225.
Removal for use or reuse, §28-3-227.
Reports.
Purchase, receipt, etc., of beverages not having, §28-3-12.
Reproduction, §28-3-228.
Restoration for use or reuse, §28-3-227.
Rules and regulations.
Affixing, §28-3-50.
Interstate common carriers, §28-3-51.
Sales, §28-3-225.
Without proper stamps.
Confiscation, §28-3-222.
Presumptions, §28-3-224.
Time for affixing, §28-3-223.
Unattached stamps, crowns or lids.
Unauthorized possession, §28-3-229.
Unauthorized sale, §28-3-227.
Wholesalers, distributors, etc.
Stamping, §28-3-224.
State liquor stores.
Location.
Distance from certain institutions, §28-3-17.
Profits.
Disposition, §28-3-74.
Taxation.
Additional tax.
Alcoholic beverage control board store fund, §28-3-200.
Steamship companies.
Dry counties.
Search warrants.
Issuance, §28-4-263.
Intoxication of employees, §37-8-161.
Stills.
Dry counties. See within this heading, "Dry counties."
Possession, §28-1-1.
Rewards, §28-5-54.
Wet counties.
Possession of illicit apparatus not repealed by chapter, §28-3-18.
Storage.
Dry counties, §28-4-28.
Wholesalers, §28-3A-23.
Stores.
State liquor stores. See within this heading, "State liquor stores."
Sundays.
Clubs, §28-3A-12.
Legal hours of sale, §28-3A-25.

ALCOHOLIC BEVERAGES
—Cont'd

Table wine, §§28-7-1 to 28-7-24. See within this heading, "Wine."

Taxation.

Additional state sales tax, §§28-3-280 to 28-3-286.
Amount of tax, §28-3-280.
Article cumulative, §28-3-285.
Collection, §28-3-281.
Distribution, §28-3-281.
Effective date, §28-3-286.
Levy of tax, §28-3-280.
Local taxes or fees.
Prohibited, §28-3-284.
Rules and regulations, §28-3-283.
Use of proceeds, §28-3-282.
Additional ten percent tax, §28-3-205.
Administration of taxes.
Powers of board, §28-3-46.
Air carriers.
Exemptions.
Hub operations in state, §28-3-207.
Alcoholic beverage control board.
Additional "mark up" credited to general fund, §28-3-53.2.
Collection, §28-3-45.
Disposition, §28-3-53.
Distribution of funds, §28-3-53.1.
Municipal sales tax.
Exemption, §11-51-200.
Powers, §28-3-46.
Refunds, §28-3-54.
Audit and collection of taxes for benefit of local governing bodies, §§28-7A-1 to 28-7A-6.
Authorized, §§28-7A-2, 28-7A-6.
Books and records, §28-7A-6.
Definitions, §28-7A-1.
Disposition, §28-7A-3.
Due date, §28-7A-3.
Fee, §§28-7A-3, 28-7A-4.
Forms, §28-7A-5.
Reports, §28-7A-5.
Retention or reclamation of authority by local governing body, §28-7A-2.
Rulemaking power of board, §28-7A-5.
Beer.
Excise tax, §§28-3-190 to 28-3-199. See within this heading, "Beer."
Contraband.
Tax due and assessed.
Collection, §28-3-242.
Crowns. See within this heading, "Stamps, crowns or lids."
Delinquent taxes, §28-3-14.
Enforcement.
Powers of board, §28-3-46.
Excise tax.
Beer, §§28-3-190 to 28-3-199. See within this heading, "Beer."
Malt or brewed beverages, §§28-3-183 to 28-3-187.

ALCOHOLIC BEVERAGES
—Cont'd

Taxation—Cont'd

License taxes.
Wine wholesalers, importers, etc., §28-7-13.
Lids. See within this heading, "Stamps, crowns or lids."
Lien for taxes, §28-3-14.
Liquor, §§28-3-200 to 28-3-206.
Malt or brewed beverages.
Alcoholic beverage control board.
Collection, §28-3-45.
Audit and collection of taxes for benefit of local governing bodies, §§28-7A-1 to 28-7A-6.
Elections as to sale and distribution.
Special method referendum.
Levy and collection, §28-2-23.
Excise tax, §§28-3-183 to 28-3-187.
Collection, §28-3-184.
Containers.
Identification, §28-3-187.
Definitions, §28-3-183.
Disposition of funds, §28-3-184.
Exemptions, §28-3-185.
Identification on containers, §28-3-187.
Illegal possession of unidentified malt or brewed beverages, §28-3-186.
Levy, §28-3-184.
Penalties.
Failure to pay, §28-3-186.
Violations, §28-3-187.
Reports, §28-3-185.
Native farm wine.
Excise tax, §28-6-4.
Refunds.
Overpayment or erroneous payment of taxes, §28-3-54.
Spirituous or vinous liquors, §§28-3-200 to 28-3-206.
Additional five percent tax, §28-3-203.
Limitation on collectors, §28-3-206.
Additional ten percent tax.
Alcoholic beverage control board store fund, §28-3-200.
Generally, §28-3-201.
Limitation on collectors, §28-3-206.
Purposes, §28-3-202.
Additional three percent tax, §28-3-204.
Limitation on collectors, §28-3-206.
Alcoholic beverage control board.
Collection, §28-3-45.
Audit and collection of taxes for benefit of local governing bodies, §§28-7A-1 to 28-7A-6.

ALCOHOLIC BEVERAGES
—Cont'd

Taxation—Cont'd

Spirituous or vinous liquors
—Cont'd
Collector's bottles of liquor.
Limitation on additional tax, §28-3-206.
Gift packs of wine.
Limitation on additional tax, §28-3-206.
Stamps, crowns or lids. See within this heading, "Stamps, crowns or lids."
Table wine.
Applications of certain taxes, §28-7-24.
Audit and collection of taxes for benefit of local governing bodies, §§28-7A-1 to 28-7A-6.
Tax on sale of table wine, §28-7-16.
Tax levied on gross receipts, §40-23-2.
Unpaid taxes and penalties, §28-3-14.
Wine, §§28-3-200 to 28-3-206.

Transportation.

Alcoholic beverage control board.
Lease of trucks for transportation, §28-3-44.
Dry counties.
Transportation of prohibited beverages, §§28-4-110 to 28-4-137.
See within this heading, "Dry counties."
Possession of illegally transported beverages, §28-1-1.
Unlawful acts, §28-3A-25.

Unlawful drinking places.

Dry counties, §§28-4-70 to 28-4-73.

Warehouses.

Licenses, §§28-3A-10, 28-3A-21.
Receipts.
Storage under government bond, §7-7-201.

Warrants.

Dry counties.
Contraband, §§28-4-251 to 28-4-263.

Weapons.

Delivery of pistols to drunkards, §13A-11-76.
Possession of pistols by drunkards, §13A-11-72.

Wet counties.

Advertising, §28-3-16.
Alcoholic beverage control board. See within this heading, "Alcoholic beverage control board."
Beer.
General provisions. See within this heading, "Beer."
Classes of businesses regulated.
Separation of financial and business interests between classes, §28-3-4.

ALCOHOLIC BEVERAGES
—Cont'd
Wet counties—Cont'd
Classification as wet
counties.
Elections, §28-2-1.
Construction of chapter,
§28-3-2.
Contraband.
Confiscation and sale,
§§28-3-240 to 28-3-244.
Definitions, §28-3-1.
Elections.
Sale and distribution. See
within this heading,
"Elections."
Ethyl alcohol.
Applicability of provisions,
§28-3-3.
Inspections.
Refusing to permit,
§28-3-19.
Licenses generally. See
within this heading,
"Licenses."
Penalties, §§28-3-20 to
28-3-22.
Hard labor in lieu of jail
sentence, §28-3-21.
Minimum penalties,
§28-3-22.
Remittance, §28-3-22.
Violations of chapter,
§28-3-20.
Prohibited acts, §28-3-19.
Purpose of chapter, §28-3-2.
Religious purposes.
Acquisition of wine by
ministers, pastors, etc.,
§28-3-15.
Rules and regulations.
Penalties for violations,
§28-3-20.
Sacramental or religious
purposes.
Acquisition of wine by
ministers, pastors, etc.,
§28-3-15.
Sales.
Generally. See within this
heading, "Sales."
Legal hours of sale,
§28-3A-25.
Signs.
Advertising, §28-3-16.
State liquor stores. See
within this heading,
"State liquor stores."
Taxation. See within this
heading, "Taxation."
Violations of chapter.
Hard labor in lieu of jail
sentence, §28-3-21.
Penalties, §28-3-20.
Wholesalers.
Beer, §§28-3-191, 28-3-193.
Containers.
Sales in original
containers, §28-3A-8.
Defined, §§28-3-1, 28-4-1.
Exclusive sales territories.
See within this heading,
"Sales."
Licenses. See within this
heading, "Licenses."
Not to be manufacturers or
retailers, §28-3-4.
Place of sale, §28-3A-23.
Reports, §28-3-9.
Filing, §28-3-9.

ALCOHOLIC BEVERAGES
—Cont'd
Wholesalers—Cont'd
Reports—Cont'd
Orders by persons without
state, §28-3-10.
Separation of financial and
business interests,
§28-3-4.
Shipment or delivery within
state, §28-3-8.
Stamps, crowns or lids. See
within this heading,
"Stamps, crowns or lids."
Storage, §28-3A-23.
Table wine. See within this
heading, "Wine."
Wine.
Table wine. See within this
heading, "Wine."
Wine.
Advertising.
Table wine, §28-7-23.
Alcoholic beverage control
board.
Collection of licenses and
taxes, §28-3-45.
Supervision of sale and
distribution, §28-3-45.
Clubs.
Authority to purchase
wine, §28-3A-12.
Containers, §28-3A-23.
Defined, §28-3-1.
Delivery.
Wine made from fruit
grown on own
premises.
Inapplicability of
provisions, §28-4-3.
Domestic use.
Wines made from fruit
grown on own
premises.
Inapplicability of
provisions, §28-4-3.
Importers.
Reports, §28-3A-7.
Interlocking businesses and
interests prohibited,
§28-7-22.
Labels.
Unregistered labels,
§28-3A-6.
Levelized wine tax, §28-7-16.
Licenses. See within this
heading, "Licenses."
Minors.
Selling to minor, §28-7-15.
Native farm wine.
Board.
Defined, §28-6-1.
Definitions, §28-6-1.
Importation of materials.
Applications, §28-6-4.
Interpretation and
construction, §28-6-6.
Licenses.
Privilege license tax,
§28-6-4.
Sales, §28-6-2.
Native farm winery.
Defined, §28-6-1.
Person.
Defined, §28-6-1.
Reports, §28-6-4.
Rules and regulations,
§28-6-5.
Sales.
Authorized buyers,
§28-6-3.

ALCOHOLIC BEVERAGES
—Cont'd
Wine—Cont'd
Native farm wine—Cont'd
Sales—Cont'd
Licenses required,
§28-6-2.
Stamps, crowns or lids,
§28-6-5.
Taxation.
Excise tax, §28-6-4.
Off-premises consumption.
Retail license, §28-3A-15.
On-premises consumption.
Retail license, §28-3A-14.
Possession.
Wine made from fruit
grown on own
premises.
Inapplicability of
provisions, §28-4-3.
Reports.
Shipments of wine,
§28-3A-6.
Retailers.
Table wine.
Sale by wine retailers in
certain counties,
§28-3-168.
Sacramental or religious
purposes.
Dry counties, §§28-4-180 to
28-4-184.
Wet counties, §28-3-15.
Wines made from fruit
grown on own
premises.
Inapplicability of
provisions, §28-4-3.
Sales.
Table wine.
Sale by retailers in
certain counties,
§28-3-168.
Table wine, §§28-7-1 to
28-7-24.
Advertising, §28-7-23.
Bankruptcy or insolvency
of licensee, §28-7-14.
Board.
Issuance of licenses,
§28-7-5.
Regulations of board,
§28-7-17.
Bonds, surety, §28-7-6.
Wholesaler's license,
§28-7-9.
Citation, §28-7-1.
Importers.
Licenses, §28-7-5.
Interlocking businesses
and interests
prohibited, §28-7-22.
Labels.
Registration, §28-7-11.
Legislative intent, §28-7-2.
Licenses. See within this
heading, "Licenses."
Manufacturers.
Interlocking businesses
and interests,
§28-7-22.
Licenses, §28-7-5.
Sales, §28-7-18.
Penalties, §28-7-15.
Purpose of chapter,
§28-7-2.
Registration of labels,
§28-7-11.
Repealer, §28-7-24.

ALCOHOLIC BEVERAGES
—Cont'd
Wine—Cont'd
Table wine—Cont'd
Retailers.
Licenses, §28-7-5.
Sales, §28-7-20.
Sales.
Manufacturers, §28-7-18.
Minors, §28-7-15.
Retailers, §28-3-168.
To whom sold, §28-7-4.
Wholesalers, §28-7-19.
Short title, §28-7-1.
Storage, §28-7-14.
Taxation.
Applications of certain
taxes, §28-7-24.
License tax, §28-7-13.
Sales, §28-7-16.
Violations of chapter,
§28-7-15.
Wholesalers.
Importing, §28-3A-9.
Licenses, §28-7-5.
Sales, §28-7-19.
Storage, §28-7-14.
Who may sell, §28-7-4.
Taxation generally. See
within this heading,
"Taxation."
Transportation.
Wine made from fruit
grown on own
premises.
Inapplicability of
provisions, §28-4-3.
Wines made from fruit grown
on own premises.
Generally, §28-4-3.
Witnesses.
Dry counties.
Enforcement of chapter.
See within this
heading, "Dry
counties."

ALCOHOLISM.
Consent for health services.
Minors, §22-8-6.
Guardian and ward.
Curators.
Appointment generally,
§§26-7A-1 to 26-7A-17.
See GUARDIAN AND
WARD.
Uniform guardianship and
protective proceedings
act, §§26-2A-1 to
26-2A-160.
See GUARDIAN AND
WARD.
Minors.
Consent for health services,
§22-8-6.
Treatment.
Group plans, §§27-20A-1 to
27-20A-4.
"Alcoholism" defined,
§27-20A-1.
Applicability of chapter,
§27-20A-2.
Benefits required,
§27-20A-3.
Coverage, §27-20A-4.
Definitions, §27-20A-1.
Detoxification.
Defined, §27-20A-1.
Outpatient treatment.
Defined, §27-20A-1.

ALICEVILLE,
MUNICIPALITY OF.
Property tax, Const. Ala.,
amd. 8.

ALIENATION OF
AFFECTIONS.
**Action abolished for female
persons 19 years of age
or over,** §6-5-331.

ALIENS.
Actions.
Suits against state, Const. U.
S., Amendment XI.
Congress.
Eligibility to be
representative, Const. U.
S., Art. I, §2.
Constitution of Alabama.
Property rights of aliens,
Const. Ala., art. I, §34.
**Constitution of the United
States.**
Eligibility to be
representative, Const. U.
S., Art. I, §2.
Naturalization, Const. U. S.,
Art. I, §8.
Presidency.
Ineligibility for presidency,
Const. U. S., Art. II,
§1.
Suits against state, Const. U.
S., Amendment XI.
**Executors and
administrators.**
Foreign executors and
administrators,
§§43-2-210 to 43-2-214.
Funds due foreign residents.
Payment to consular officer,
§6-8-20.
Naturalization, Const. U. S.,
Art. I, §§8, 9.
Personal property.
Right of aliens, §35-1-1.
**President of the United
States.**
Ineligible for presidency,
Const. U. S., Art. II, §1.
Property rights, §35-1-1;
Const. Ala., art. I, §34.
Real property.
Rights of aliens, §35-1-1.
Suits against state, Const. U.
S., Amendment XI.
**Unemployment
compensation.**
Disqualifications, §25-4-78.
Wills.
Intestate succession.
Status not a
disqualification to
inheriting, §43-8-56.
Probate of foreign will,
§43-8-175.

ALIMONY.
General provisions, §§30-2-1
to 30-2-55.
See DIVORCE AND
ALIMONY.

ALKALIES.
Regulation generally,
§§8-17-20 to 8-17-24.

ALLEYS.
Abandonment.
Closing and vacating streets,
alleys and highways,
§§23-4-1 to 23-4-20.
See HIGHWAYS.

ALLEYS—Cont'd
Abutting landowners.
Closing and vacating streets,
alleys and highways.
Notice, §23-4-2.
Procedure, §23-4-20.
**Closing and vacating streets,
alleys and highways,**
§§23-4-1 to 23-4-20.
See HIGHWAYS.
**Improvements on public
streets, etc.**
Liens, §§35-11-410 to
35-11-417.
See HIGHWAYS.
Liens.
Improvements on public
streets, etc., §§35-11-410
to 35-11-417.
See HIGHWAYS.
Vacating, §§23-4-1 to 23-4-20.
See HIGHWAYS.

ALLIGATOR FARMS,
§§9-12-200 to 9-12-214.
Bills of sale.
Retention, §9-12-207.
Commissioner.
Defined, §9-12-200.
Dealers.
Licenses, §9-12-206.
Parts dealers.
Defined, §9-12-200.
Parts transaction form,
§9-12-207.
Definitions, §9-12-200.
Department.
Defined, §9-12-200.
Endangerment of species.
Effect of federal declaration
of endangerment,
§9-12-213.
Fees.
Disposition of revenue,
§9-12-213.
Licenses, §9-12-202.
Expiration and renewal,
§9-12-203.
Parts dealers, §9-12-206.
Restaurant licenses,
§9-12-206.
Retailers' licenses,
§9-12-206.
Forfeitures.
Violations of chapter,
§9-12-214.
Forms.
Parts transaction form,
§9-12-207.
Licenses.
Cancellation, §9-12-214.
Dealers, §9-12-206.
Endangerment of species.
Effect on license,
§9-12-213.
Expiration and renewal,
§9-12-203.
Fees, §§9-12-202, 9-12-206.
Expiration and renewal,
§9-12-203.
Issuance, §9-12-202.
Restaurant licenses,
§9-12-206.
Retailer's license, §9-12-206.
Ownership, §9-12-205.
Parts.
Defined, §9-12-200.
License for dealers,
§9-12-206.
Property rights in parts,
§9-12-205.

ALLIGATOR FARMS—Cont'd
Parts—Cont'd
Tags.
Attachment to part,
carcass, etc., §9-12-208.
Transportation, sale, etc.,
§9-12-204.
Transaction forms, §9-12-207.
Penalties, §9-12-211.
Propagation of alligators,
§9-12-201.
Property rights in alligators
and parts, §9-12-205.
Records.
Bill of sale, §9-12-207.
Restaurants.
Licenses, §9-12-206.
Retailers.
Licenses, §9-12-206.
Sales.
Restrictions on buyers,
§9-12-204.
Severance tax.
Skins, §9-12-210.
Disposition of revenue,
§9-12-212.
Skins.
Severance tax, §9-12-210.
Disposition of revenue,
§9-12-212.
Tags.
Attachment of tags,
§9-12-209.
Requirement of tags,
§9-12-204.
Shipment requires tag,
§9-12-209.
Tags.
Parts and skins.
Attachment to part,
carcass, etc., §9-12-208.
Transportation, sale, etc.,
requires tag,
§9-12-204.
Taxation.
Disposition of revenue,
§9-12-212.
Severance tax on skins,
§9-12-210.
Payment prerequisite to
sale or shipment,
§9-12-204.
Transportation.
Carcasses, parts, etc.
Tags required, §9-12-204.
Definition of "transport,"
§9-12-200.
Violations of chapter.
Cancellation of license,
§9-12-214.
Penalty, §9-12-211.

ALMONDS.
General provisions.
See NUTS.
Promotion of industry,
§§2-8-120 to 2-8-137.
See NUTS.

ALTERATION OF
INSTRUMENTS.
Commercial code.
See COMMERCIAL CODE.

ALUM.
Barbers.
Use of alum, §22-17-7.
Cosmetologists.
Use of alum, §22-17-7.

AMATEUR RADIO
OPERATORS.
Motor vehicle tags and
plates.
See MOTOR VEHICLES.

AMBASSADORS AND
CONSULS.
Constitution of the United
States, Const. U. S., Art.
II, §§2, 3; Art. III, §2.

AMBULANCES, §§22-18-1 to
22-18-7.
Advisory board, §22-18-5.
Applicability of chapter.
Exceptions, §22-18-2.
Attendants.
Ambulances to be under
direction of, §22-18-4.
Licenses. See within this
heading, "Licenses."
Training, §22-18-3.
Chapter cumulative,
§22-18-7.
Counties.
Ambulance service, §§11-87-1
to 11-87-5.
Definitions, §22-18-1.
Drivers.
Licenses. See within this
heading, "Licenses."
Training, §22-18-3.
Exceptions to chapter,
§22-18-2.
Fees.
Licenses, §22-18-4.
Licenses.
Fees, §22-18-4.
Taxes and registration
fees, §40-12-247.
Operators' licenses,
§§22-18-3, 22-18-4.
Rules and regulations,
§22-18-3.
Taxes and registration fees,
§40-12-247.
Motor vehicle carriers.
Exemptions from chapter,
§37-3-4.
Municipal corporations,
§§11-87-1 to 11-87-5,
22-18-7.
Operation.
Rules and regulations,
§22-18-3.
Operators.
Licenses, §§22-18-3, 22-18-4.
Penalties.
Violations, §22-18-6.
Rescue squads.
See RESCUE SQUADS.
Rules and regulations.
Advisory board, §22-18-5.
Licenses, §22-18-3.
Operation, §22-18-3.
Training, §22-18-3.
Violations, §22-18-6.
Speed limits.
When speed limit not
applicable, §32-5A-7.
Stopping, standing and
parking.
Certain privileges available,
§32-5A-7.
Stop signals and stop signs.
Authorized to proceed past,
§32-5A-7.
Surplus property.
Volunteer nonprofit
ambulance services.
Transfers to, §41-4-33.2.

AMBULANCES—Cont'd
Training drivers and
attendants, §22-18-3.
Violations of chapter or
rules and regulations,
§22-18-6.

AMENDMENTS.
Code of Alabama.
References to sections, titles,
etc., §1-1-15.
Constitution of Alabama.
See CONSTITUTION OF
ALABAMA.
Constitution of the United
States.
See CONSTITUTION OF
THE UNITED STATES.
Corporations.
See CORPORATIONS.
Electric cooperatives.
Articles of incorporation,
§37-6-7.
Bylaws, §37-6-8.
Garnishment.
Applicability of section
6-6-143, §6-6-371.
Indictments, §§15-8-90,
15-8-91.
Judgments.
Clerical mistakes. ARCP,
Rule 60 (a).
Lame Duck amendment.
Congress.
Changing meeting of
congress, Const. U. S.,
Amendment XX.

A MENSA ET THORO
DIVORCE, §§30-2-30,
30-2-31.

AMERAPORT.
Deep draft harbor and
terminal compact.
Authorization, §33-9-2.
Definitions, §33-9-1.
Governor.
Authority to execute,
§33-9-2.
Provisions.
Generally, §33-9-2.
Offshore harbor and
terminal commission,
§§33-10-1 to 33-10-26.
Appointment of
commissioners, §33-10-3.
Bond issues.
Exemption from taxation,
§33-10-25.
Issuance, §33-10-24.
Servicing of bonds,
§33-10-25.
Chairman.
Designation by governor,
§33-10-3.
President at meetings,
§33-10-5.
Coastal environment.
Protection, §33-10-20.
Commodities.
Terminals, §33-10-19.
Compensation of members,
§33-10-4.
Composition, §33-10-3.
Contracts.
Intergovernmental
contracts, §33-10-23.
Other agencies, §33-10-16.
Public utilities, §33-10-21.
Creation, §33-10-2.
Definitions, §33-10-1.

AMERAPORT—Cont'd
Offshore harbor and terminal commission—Cont'd
Duties.
Generally, §33-10-14.
Employees.
Compensation, §33-10-10.
Executive director to employ, §33-10-9.
Equipment.
Purchase of equipment, §33-10-22.
Executive director.
Commission to employ, §33-10-6.
Compensation, §33-10-9.
Duties, §33-10-7.
Minutes, files and records, §33-10-8.
Personnel.
Employment, §33-10-9.
Records.
Duties, §33-10-8.
Secretary to board of commissioners, §33-10-9.
Term, §33-10-6.
Existence.
When commission to cease to exist, §33-10-26.
Expenses of members, §33-10-4.
Governor.
Appointment of commissioners, §33-10-3.
Ex officio member, §33-10-3.
Information collected by commission.
Property of state, §33-10-13.
Jurisdiction, §33-10-17.
Waterbottoms.
Right to acquire, §33-10-17.
Leases.
Oysters.
Compensation of oyster lessees, §33-10-19.
State lands, §33-10-19.
Waterbottoms, §33-10-18.
Meetings, §33-10-5.
Officers.
Designation by governor, §33-10-3.
Other agencies.
Contracts with, §33-10-16.
Oysters.
Compensation of oyster lessees, §33-10-19.
Petroleum.
Terminals, §33-10-19.
Policy.
Commission to formulate, §33-10-14.
Powers.
Enumerated, §33-10-15.
Generally, §33-10-14.
Promotion, operation, etc., of development program, §33-10-16.
Protection of coastal environment, §33-10-20.
Public utilities.
Contracts, §33-10-21.
Purpose of chapter, §33-10-2.
Qualifications, §33-10-3.
Quorum, §33-10-5.

AMERAPORT—Cont'd
Offshore harbor and terminal commission—Cont'd
Records.
Executive director.
Duties, §33-10-8.
Open to inspection, §33-10-13.
Removal of members, §33-10-3.
Rules and regulations, §33-10-11.
Solicitation of money and other assistance, §33-10-12.
State lands.
Leases, §33-10-19.
Taxation.
Exemption from taxation, §33-10-25.
Terminals.
Petroleum and commodity terminal, §33-10-19.
Termination, §33-10-26.
Terms of members, §33-10-3.
United States congress.
When commission to cease to exist.
Authorization of bistate compact, §33-10-26.
Vacancies, §33-10-3.
Vehicles.
Purchase of vehicles, §33-10-22.
Waterbottoms.
Lease of state-owned waterbottoms, §33-10-18.
Right to acquire, §33-10-17.

AMERICAN CANCER SOCIETY.
Taxation.
Exemptions, §40-9-12.

AMERICAN LEGION.
Scholarships.
See UNIVERSITIES AND COLLEGES.
Taxation.
Exemption from sales and use taxes, §40-23-5.
Property exempt, §40-9-1.

AMERICAN-MADE PRODUCTS AND LABOR.
Public works, §39-3-1.

AMICUS CURIAE.
Briefs, ARAP, Rules 28 (e), 29.

AMMONIA.
Regulation of caustic or corrosive substances, §§8-17-20 to 8-17-24.

AMMUNITION.
See WEAPONS.

AMPHETAMINES.
Controlled substances.
General provisions, §§20-2-1 to 20-2-144.
See DRUGS.

AMUSEMENT PARKS.
Licenses, §40-12-47.

AMUSEMENTS.
Billiard rooms.
See BILLIARD ROOMS.
Blind persons.
Right to use, §21-7-3.

AMUSEMENTS—Cont'd
Boxing and wrestling.
See BOXING AND WRESTLING.
Handicapped persons.
Right to use of places of public amusement, §21-7-3.
Horse racing, §§11-65-1 to 11-65-46, 13A-12-31.
See HORSE RACING.
Licenses.
Amusement parks, §40-12-47.
Municipal corporations, §§11-51-102, 11-51-104.
Revocation of licenses, §11-51-103.
Municipal corporations.
Houses of amusement.
Closing, §11-51-102.
Licenses, §§11-51-102, 11-51-104.
Revocation of licenses of houses of public entertainment, §11-51-103.
Provision of music and other exhibitions, §11-47-19.
Pool halls.
General provisions.
See BILLIARD ROOMS.
Sales tax.
Tax levied on gross receipts, §40-23-2.
Sports generally.
See SPORTS.
Wildlife.
Exhibitions, §§9-11-320 to 9-11-328.
See FISH AND GAME.

ANARCHY AND SUBVERSIVE ACTIVITIES.
Civil defense.
Employment of subversives, §31-9-20.
Treason.
See TREASON.

ANATOMICAL GIFTS.
Acquisition and transportation of donor organs, bones and tissues.
Adherence to quality assurance standards, §22-19-123.
Certification, §22-19-122.
Compliance with provisions.
Immunity of persons complying, §22-19-125.
Construction with other laws, §22-19-126.
Definitions, §22-19-121.
Federal standards.
State standards to be consistent with, §22-19-126.
Immunity.
Persons complying with provisions, §22-19-125.
Intent of provisions, §22-19-120.
Legislative declaration, §22-19-120.
Proficiency standards, §22-19-122.
Quality assurance.
Adherence to standards, §22-19-123.
Defined, §22-19-121.

ANATOMICAL GIFTS—Cont'd
Acquisition and transportation of donor organs, bones and tissues—Cont'd
Quality assurance—Cont'd
Promulgation of measures, §22-19-122.
Updating of standards, §22-19-122.
Violations of provisions. Sanctions, §22-19-124.
Affidavits.
Filing of gift made by, §22-19-60.
Amendment of gift, §22-19-46.
Consent.
Lifesaving organ procurement act.
Request for consent, §22-19-142.
Death.
Powers, duties and liabilities upon death, §22-19-47.
Definitions, §22-19-41.
Acquisition and transportation of donor organs, bones and tissues, §22-19-121.
Lifesaving organ procurement act, §22-19-141.
Delivery or deposit of gift document, §22-19-45.
Department of public safety.
Gift made by execution of affidavit.
Filing with department, §22-19-60.
Immunity from civil liability, §22-19-61.
Documents.
Amendment of gift document, §22-19-46.
Delivery or deposit of gift document, §22-19-45.
Revocation of gift document, §22-19-46.
Donees.
Duties upon death, §22-19-47.
Institutions or persons who may become donees, §22-19-43.
Liabilities upon death, §22-19-47.
Powers upon death, §22-19-47.
Rights of donees, §22-19-42.
Donors.
Eye enucleation licenses.
Compliance with uniform anatomical gift act, §34-13-152.
General provisions, §§34-13-150 to 34-13-152.
Who may donate, §22-19-42.
Driver's license or nondriver identification card.
Department of public safety.
Filing of affidavit, §22-19-60.
Immunity from civil liabiity, §22-19-61.
Effect of expiration, revocation, renewal, etc., §22-19-60.

ANATOMICAL GIFTS—Cont'd
Driver's license or nondriver identification card —Cont'd
Gift made by execution of affidavit.
Filing with department of public safety, §22-19-60.
Notice of intent to make gift, §22-19-60.
Specific gift to be noted, §22-19-60.
Duties upon death, §22-19-47.
Eligibility.
Donees, §22-19-43.
Donors, §22-19-42.
Execution of gift.
Affidavit to be filed with department of public safety, §22-19-60.
Modes of executing, §22-19-44.
Eyes.
Donor eye enucleation licenses.
Compliance with uniform anatomical gift act, §34-13-152.
General provisions, §§34-13-150 to 35-13-152.
Eye enucleation, §§22-19-100 to 22-19-104.
How gift executed, §22-19-44.
Affidavit, §22-19-60.
Intent to make gift.
Notice on driver's license or nondriver identification card, §22-19-60.
Liabilities upon death, §22-19-47.
Lifesaving organ procurement act, §§22-19-140 to 22-19-144.
Compliance with provisions. Immunity of persons complying, §22-19-143.
Consent to anatomical gift. Request for, §22-19-142.
Construction with other laws, §22-19-144.
Definitions, §22-19-141.
Immunity of persons complying with provisions, §22-19-143.
Intent of provisions, §22-19-140.
Request for consent to anatomical gift, §22-19-142.
Motor vehicles.
Anatomical gifts by holders of drivers' licenses. See within this heading, "Driver's license or nondriver identification card."
Part of body.
Who may donate, §22-19-42.
Powers upon death, §22-19-47.
Purposes for which gifts may be made, §22-19-43.
Revocation of gift, §22-19-46.
Rights of donees, §22-19-42.
Short title of article, §22-19-40.

ANATOMICAL GIFTS—Cont'd
Transportation of donor organs, bones and tissues.
Generally, §§22-19-120 to 22-19-126. See within this heading, "Acquisition and transportation of donor organs, bones and tissues."
Who may donate, §22-19-42.
ANESTHESIA.
Dentists.
Use of anesthesia, §§34-9-60 to 34-9-65.
See DENTISTS.
ANIMALS.
Abandonment.
Destruction of certain abandoned animals, §3-1-8.
Abused animals.
Care and keeping, §3-1-13.
Agisters.
Lien for feeding, §35-11-71.
Aviation.
Domestic animals or fowl on airports, landing fields, etc., §4-2-6.
Boarding.
Lien on animals for boarding, §35-11-71.
Burial, §3-1-28.
Burning of bodies, §3-1-28.
Chicks.
Sale as pets or novelties, §3-1-15.
Coal.
Mine safety.
Hoisting of animals, §25-9-210.
Underground stables, §25-9-153.
Cockfighting, §13A-12-4.
Commercial code.
Sale of unborn animals, §7-2-105.
Identification of goods, §7-2-501.
Council on animal and environmental health, §§22-2-9, 22-2-10.
Counties.
Acquisition of lands for public purposes.
Use for betterment of animal life, §11-18-2.
Prevention of cruelty to animals.
Employment of persons to enforce laws, §3-1-16.
Cruelty to animals.
See CRUELTY TO ANIMALS.
Dangerous animals.
Liability of owner, §3-1-3.
Dead animals.
Burial or burning of bodies, §3-1-28.
Depositing in running streams, §22-20-9.
Depositing in water supplies, §22-20-8.
Solid waste disposal act.
See GARBAGE AND TRASH.
Defined, §3-5-1.

ANIMALS—Cont'd
Destruction.
Societies for prevention of
cruelty to animals.
Abandoned animals,
§3-1-8.
Wanton, malicious, etc.,
destruction, §3-1-10.
Tender of compensation,
§3-1-11.
Trespassing by animal as
mitigation or
justification of offense,
§3-1-11.
Diseases.
Nuisances menacing public
health.
See HEALTH.
Rabies, §§3-7-1 to 3-7-13.
See RABIES.
Dogs.
See DOGS.
Ducklings.
Sale, §3-1-15.
Education.
Humane treatment of
animals taught,
§16-40-4.
Estrays.
See ESTRAYS.
Exhibitions.
Possession of wildlife for
public exhibition
purposes.
See FISH AND GAME.
Feeding.
Lien on animals for feeding,
§35-11-71.
Fences, §§3-4-1 to 3-4-7.
See LIVESTOCK.
Game laws.
See FISH AND GAME.
Health.
Council on animal and
environmental health,
§§22-2-9, 22-2-10.
Nuisances menacing public
health, §§22-10-1 to
22-10-3.
Highways.
Pasturing on highway rights
of way, §§3-3-1 to 3-3-3.
Hunting.
General provisions.
See FISH AND GAME.
Income tax.
Deductions of contributions
for prevention of cruelty,
§§40-18-15, 40-18-35.
Indictments.
Cruelty to animals,
§15-8-150.
Offenses concerning animals.
Description of animal in
indictment, §15-8-34.
Wanton, malicious, etc.,
destruction, §15-8-150.
Injury to animals.
Cruelty to animals,
§13A-11-14.
Wanton, malicious, etc.,
injury.
Prohibited, §3-1-10.
Proof of trespassing by
animal in mitigation
or justification,
§3-1-11.
Tender of compensation,
§3-1-11.

ANIMALS—Cont'd
Liens.
Feeding, boarding or
training, §35-11-71.
Livestock.
See LIVESTOCK.
Owners of stallions, jacks,
bulls, etc.
See LIVESTOCK.
Veterinarians, §§35-11-390,
35-11-391.
Livestock.
See LIVESTOCK.
Marine mammals.
Protection, §§9-11-390 to
9-11-398.
See MARINE MAMMAL
PROTECTION.
Motor vehicles.
Certificate of title.
Animal-drawn vehicles.
Exemption, §32-8-31.
Horse-drawn wagons.
Reflectors or similar
warning devices,
§32-5-245.
Lamps.
Animal-drawn vehicles,
§32-5-240.
Persons riding animals or
driving animal-drawn
vehicles, §32-5A-5.
Reflective devices on ridden
animals, §32-5-249.
Municipal corporations.
Running at large.
Destruction, §11-47-110.
Impoundment, etc.,
§11-47-110.
Violations of ordinances
prohibiting.
Summons and complaint
in lieu of arrest,
§11-40-10.1.
Neglected animals.
Care and keeping, §3-1-13.
Purchase.
Domestic animals or fowl.
Between sunset and
sunrise prohibited,
§3-1-20.
Rabbits.
Sale of baby rabbits, §3-1-15.
Slaughter, etc., for human
consumption.
See MEAT AND MEAT
PRODUCTS.
Rabies.
General provisions, §§3-7-1 to
3-7-13.
See RABIES.
Running at large.
Estrays.
See ESTRAYS.
Livestock.
See LIVESTOCK.
Municipal corporations.
Impoundment and
destruction of animals
running at large,
§11-47-110.
Violations of ordinances
prohibiting.
Summons and complaint
in lieu of arrest,
§11-40-10.1.
Rabies.
See RABIES.

ANIMALS—Cont'd
Sales.
Chicks as pets or novelties,
§3-1-15.
Between sunset and
sunrise, §3-1-20.
Rabbits.
Sale of baby rabbits as
pets, §3-1-15.
Veterinarians' liens.
Sale of animal to enforce
lien, §35-11-391.
**Societies for prevention of
cruelty to animals.**
Care and keeping of
neglected or abused
animals, §3-1-13.
Destruction of certain
abandoned animals,
§3-1-8.
Spotlighting, §32-5-17.
**Staking on highway rights
of way.**
Estrays, §3-3-3.
Trainers.
Lien on animals for feeding,
etc., §35-11-71.
Trespass.
Wanton, malicious, etc.,
destruction, injury, etc.,
Mitigation or justification
of offense, §3-1-11.
Trusts and trustees.
Principal and income.
Principal comprising
animals, §19-3-277.
Veterinarians.
See VETERINARIANS.
Vicious animals.
Liability of owner, §3-1-3.
**Wanton, malicious, etc.,
destruction or injury,**
§§3-1-10, 3-1-11.
Waters and watercourses.
Depositing dead animals or
fowl in running streams,
§22-20-9.
**Water supply and
waterworks.**
Dead animals.
Depositing in water
supplies, §22-20-8.
Wild animals.
Butchering, etc., of legally
taken wild animals,
§22-20-6.

ANNEXATION.
Constitution of Alabama.
Acquisition of foreign
territory, Const. Ala.,
art. IV, §90.
Education.
Territory embracing schools.
Agreements and
arbitration.
Appointment of board of
arbitration, §16-8-21.
Hearing by board of
arbitration, §16-8-22.
Retention of control by
county boards,
§16-8-20.
When arbitration
required, §16-8-21.
Municipal corporations,
§§11-42-1 to 11-42-88.
See MUNICIPAL
CORPORATIONS.

ANNEXATION—Cont'd
State.
Acquisition of foreign
territory, Const. Ala.,
art. IV, §90.
**Water management and
drainage.**
Districts.
Annexation of land to
district, §9-9-50.

ANNISTON, CITY OF.
Cerebral palsy center.
Appropriation for.
Authorized, Const. Ala.,
amd. 494.
Industrial parks.
Acquisition and development,
Const. Ala., amd. 376.
Property tax, Const. Ala.,
amds. 8, 350.
School tax.
Application of special school
taxes, Const. Ala., amd.
281.
Special property tax for
educational purposes,
Const. Ala., amd. 350.
Special school tax, Const.
Ala., amd. 232.

ANNUITIES.
**Annuity and mortality
tables.**
See ANNUITY AND
MORTALITY TABLES.
Commercial code.
Secured transactions.
Transfer of interest or
claim in annuities
excluded, §7-9-104.
Education.
Tax sheltered annuities.
Salary deductions,
§16-22-6.
General provisions.
See INSURANCE.
Peace officers.
Annuity and benefit fund.
See PEACE OFFICERS.
Secured transactions.
Transfer of interest or claim
in annuities excluded,
§7-9-104.

**ANNUITY AND MORTALITY
TABLES.**
Contents of annuity tables.
§35-16-1.
Evidence, §35-16-2.
Annuity tables, §35-16-2.
Mortality tables, §35-16-4.
Publication, §35-16-1.
Annuity tables, §35-16-1.
Mortality tables, §35-16-3.

ANNULMENT.
Adoption, §26-10-5.
Marriage.
See MARRIAGE.
Partition.
Circuit courts, §35-6-50.

ANTE LITEM NOTICE.
Municipal corporations.
Liability for negligence of
agents, etc., §11-47-192.

ANTENNAS.
**Community antenna
television facilities,**
§§11-27-1 to 11-27-3,
23-1-59.

ANTHRAX.
Notifiable diseases,
§§22-11A-1 to 22-11A-38.
See DISEASES.

ANTIQUES.
Criminal simulation,
§13A-9-10.
Motor vehicles, §§40-12-290 to
40-12-296.
See MOTOR VEHICLES.
Weapons.
Antique pistols, §13A-11-83.

ANTITHEFT ACT.
**Uniform certificate of title
and antitheft act,**
§§32-8-1 to 32-8-88.
See MOTOR VEHICLES.

APARTMENTS.
Condominiums, §§35-8-1 to
35-8-22.
See CONDOMINIUMS.
Landlord and tenant.
See LANDLORD AND
TENANT.
Vacation time-sharing plans,
§§34-27-50 to 34-27-69.
See VACATION TIME-
SHARING PLANS.

APIARIES, §§2-14-1 to 2-14-15.
See HONEYBEES AND
APIARIES.

APOTHECARIES.
General provisions, §§34-23-1
to 34-23-118.
See PHARMACISTS AND
PHARMACIES.

APPEALS.
Abolished courts of record.
Appeal from judgments or
decrees, §12-22-3.
Abortion.
Parental consent to
performing abortion
upon minors.
Waiver of written consent
requirements,
§26-21-4.
Accountants.
Board of public accountancy,
§34-1-14.
Adoption.
Subsidized adoptions,
§26-10-29.
Affirmation of judgment.
Execution upon affirmation,
§12-22-75.
Stayed judgment, §§12-22-72
to 12-22-74.
Aged persons.
Medical assistance to elderly
persons, §38-6-7.
Agreements in writing,
ARAP, Rule 47.
Agriculture.
Marketing associations.
Refusal of permit, §2-10-25.
Temporary permit
pending appeal,
§2-10-26.
Violation of purpose of
organization, etc.,
§2-10-32.
Airports.
Zoning, §4-6-11.
Amicus curiae.
Briefs, ARAP, Rules 28 (e),
29.

APPEALS—Cont'd
Appealable judgments,
§12-22-2.
Appeal as of right.
Final judgments, §12-22-2.
Rules of appellate procedure.
See within this heading,
"Rules of appellate
procedure."
Appeal by permission.
Rules of appellate procedure.
See within this heading,
"Rules of appellate
procedure.
Appendix to briefs. See
within this heading,
"Briefs."
Arbitration and award,
§6-6-15.
Argument.
Certified questions from
federal courts, ARAP,
Rule 18 (g).
Oral argument. See within
this heading, "Oral
argument."
Assessments.
Municipal corporations.
See MUNICIPAL
CORPORATIONS.
Taxation.
See TAXATION.
Assignment of error.
Not required, ARAP, Rule
20.
Attorneys at law.
Disciplinary proceedings.
Rules of disciplinary
enforcement.
Appeals to supreme
court, ARDE, Rule 8.
Roll of attorneys, ARAP,
Rule 46.
Auctioneers.
Revocation or suspension of
license, §34-4-30.
Aviation.
Aeronautics commission.
Failure to file appeal of
orders of commission,
§4-2-51.
Procedure for appeal of
orders, §4-2-50.
Airports.
Zoning, §4-6-11.
Bail and recognizance.
Affirmation or dismissal of
appeal.
Duty of defendant to
surrender, §12-22-244.
Denial of bail, §15-13-8.
Forfeiture of undertaking.
Proceedings when
undertaking forfeited,
§12-22-246.
Reversal of conviction and
case remanded.
Effect of undertaking,
§12-22-245.
Stay of sentence when
question of law reserved
and admission to bail,
§§12-22-170, 12-22-171.
Writs of error.
Admission of defendant to
bail, §12-22-222.
**Banks and financial
institutions.**
Refusal to permit
incorporation, §5-5A-8.
Reorganization, §5-9A-5.

APPEALS—Cont'd
Barbers.
Board of barber examiners,
§34-5-8.
Bonds, surety.
Costs on appeal. See within
this heading, "Costs on
appeal."
Stay by supersedeas bond,
ARAP, Rule 8 (a).
Stay pending appeal, ARAP,
Rule 8 (c).
Briefs.
Amicus curiae, ARAP, Rules
28 (e), 29.
Appellants' briefs, ARAP,
Rule 28 (a).
Appellees' briefs, ARAP,
Rule 28 (b).
Appendix, ARAP, Rule 28 (f).
Arrangement, ARAP, Rule
30 (e).
Contents, ARAP, Rule 30.
Copies, ARAP, Rule 30 (b).
Costs, ARAP, Rule 35 (c).
Costs of producing, ARAP,
Rule 30 (c).
Exhibits.
Reproduction of exhibits,
ARAP, Rule 30 (f).
Filing.
Duty of appellant,
ARAP, Rule 30 (b).
Time, ARAP, Rule 30
(b).
Form, ARAP, Rule 32 (a).
Option to use either
appendix or record,
ARAP, Rule 30 (a).
Preparation.
Duty of appellant,
ARAP, Rule 30 (b).
Record in lieu of appendix,
ARAP, Rule 30 (g).
Time, ARAP, Rule 30 (b).
Transmittal to appellate
clerk.
Form, ARAP, Form 9.
Certified questions from
federal courts, ARAP,
Rule 18 (g).
Copies.
Number, ARAP, Rule 31
(b).
Cross appeals, ARAP, Rule
28 (h).
Filing.
Copies, ARAP, Rule 31 (b).
Failure, ARAP, Rule 31
(c).
Time, ARAP, Rule 31 (a).
Extension, ARAP, Rule
31 (d).
Form, ARAP, Rule 32 (a).
Length, ARAP, Rule 28 (g).
Multiple appellants or
appellees, ARAP, Rule
28 (i).
Record on appeal.
Costs of producing, ARAP,
Rule 30 (c).
References in briefs to,
ARAP, Rules 28 (e), 30
(d).
References in briefs to
parties, ARAP, Rule 28
(d).
Reply brief, ARAP, Rule 28
(c).

APPEALS—Cont'd
Briefs—Cont'd
Review of decisions of courts
of appeal, ARAP, Rule
39.
Rules and regulations.
Reproduction, ARAP, Rule
28 (f).
Service of briefs.
Forms for certificates of
service, ARAP, Forms
7, 8.
Number of copies to be
served, ARAP, Rule 31
(b).
Time, ARAP, Rule 31 (a).
Statutes.
Reproduction, ARAP, Rule
28 (f).
Time for serving and filing,
ARAP, Rule 31 (a).
Extension, ARAP, Rule 31
(d).
Capital punishment.
Automatic review, §13A-5-55.
Stay pending appeal, ARAP,
Rule 8 (d).
Cemeteries.
County cemeteries.
Appeals from assessment of
damages, §§11-17-7 to
11-17-11.
Certificate of judgment.
Issuance, ARAP, Rule 41 (a).
Stay pending petitions for
certiorari to courts of
appeals, ARAP, Rule 41
(b).
Certiorari.
Certificate of judgment.
Stay pending petitions for
certiorari to courts of
appeals, ARAP, Rule
41 (b).
Dismissal of petition, ARAP,
Rule 2 (c).
Judgments on applications
for remedial writs,
§12-22-6.
Petition for certiorari.
Dismissal, ARAP, Rule 2
(c).
Form of writ to courts of
appeals, ARAP, Form
22.
Review of decisions of
courts of appeal,
ARAP, Rule 39.
Charge to jury, §12-16-13.
Chiropractors.
Licenses.
Refusal, revocation or
suspension,
§34-24-175.
Cigarettes.
Taxation.
Gummed cigarette papers.
Assessment of tax,
§§40-25A-10,
40-25A-11.
Circuit courts.
Appeals from district court.
See DISTRICT COURTS.
General provisions.
See CIRCUIT COURTS.
Coal.
Surface mining control and
reclamation.
Division of hearings and
appeals, §9-16-77.

APPEALS—Cont'd
Coal—Cont'd
Surface mining control and
reclamation—Cont'd
Procedure for appeals,
§9-16-79.
Condemnation.
See EMINENT DOMAIN.
Confession of judgment.
Release of errors, §12-22-1.
Consolidated appeals, ARAP,
Rule 3 (b).
Constitution of Alabama.
Constitutional questions,
ARAP, Rule 44.
Criminal cases.
Statute held
unconstitutional,
§12-22-91.
Justices of the peace, Const.
Ala., art. VI, §168.
**Constitution of the United
States.**
Constitutional questions,
ARAP, Rule 44.
Criminal cases.
Statute held
unconstitutional,
§12-22-91.
Review of facts tried by jury,
Const. U. S., Amendment
VII.
Consumer finance.
Orders of administrator,
§5-19-26.
Contempt.
By attorney or officer,
§12-1-11.
Rules of appellate procedure.
Penalty for willful
noncompliance, ARAP,
Rule 48.
Contractors.
Decisions of state licensing
board, §34-8-27.
Corporations.
Probate judge, §10-2A-331.
Secretary of state,
§10-2A-331.
Taxation of corporate shares
of stock.
Assessment, §40-14-71.
Cosmetologists.
Board of cosmetology,
§34-7-47.
Costs on appeal.
Against whom taxed, ARAP,
Rule 35 (a).
Appendix to briefs, ARAP,
Rule 35 (c).
Bonds and security for costs.
Liability to appellee for
taking insufficient
surety, §12-22-41.
Probate courts, §§12-22-24,
12-22-25.
Recording of order fixing
supersedeas bond,
§12-22-40.
Briefs.
Appendix.
Costs of producing,
ARAP, Rule 30 (c).
Filing, ARAP, Rule 30
(b).
Certified questions from
federal courts, ARAP,
Rule 18 (f).
Clerk to insert in certificate
of judgment, ARAP, Rule
35 (d).

APPEALS—Cont'd
Costs on appeal—Cont'd
Execution by lower courts for
unpaid costs, §12-22-76.
Highways.
Closing and vacating
streets, alleys and
highways.
Bond, §23-4-5.
Impeachment.
Appeals to supreme court.
Security for costs
required, §36-11-16.
Penalties.
Affirmation of stayed
judgment generally,
§12-22-72.
Frivolous appeal, ARAP,
Rule 38.
Probate courts, §§12-22-24,
12-22-25, 12-22-27.
Record on appeal.
Costs of copies, ARAP,
Rule 35 (c).
Security for costs.
Appeal by permission,
ARAP, Rule 5 (c).
Civil cases, ARAP, Rule 7.
State.
Costs for and against state
of Alabama, ARAP,
Rule 35 (b).
Unpaid costs.
Execution by lower courts
for unpaid costs,
§12-22-76.
Counterclaims and cross-
claims, ARCP, Rule 13 (j).
Counties.
Bond issues.
Validation.
Judgment of circuit
court, §6-6-754.
Cemeteries.
Appeals from assessment of
damages, §§11-17-7 to
11-17-11.
Public roads, bridges and
ferries.
Eminent domain, §23-1-82.
Court of civil appeals.
See COURT OF CIVIL
APPEALS.
Court of criminal appeals.
See COURT OF CRIMINAL
APPEALS.
Credit unions.
Appeals to board from
actions of administrator,
§5-17-55.
Suspension of director,
officer, etc., §5-17-8.
Criminal cases.
Affirmation of judgment.
Capital cases, §12-22-243.
Duty of defendant on bail
to surrender,
§12-22-244.
Appeals to circuit courts.
See CIRCUIT COURTS.
Automatic appeals.
Consideration, §12-22-241.
From death sentence,
§12-22-150.
Bail, §§12-22-244 to
12-22-246.
Bond.
Felonies, §12-22-170.
Misdemeanors, §12-22-171.

APPEALS—Cont'd
Criminal cases—Cont'd
Capital cases.
Affirmation of judgment,
§12-22-243.
Automatic appeal,
§12-22-150.
Circuit courts.
Appeals to circuit courts.
See CIRCUIT COURTS.
Clerks of court, §12-22-220.
Completion of record.
Mechanics of completion,
ARAP, Rule 11 (b).
Composition of record,
ARAP, Rule 10 (c).
Court of criminal appeals.
Appeals to court of
criminal appeals.
See COURT OF
CRIMINAL
APPEALS.
Death sentence.
Affirmation of judgment,
§12-22-243.
Automatic appeal,
§12-22-150.
Scope of review, ARAP,
Rule 45A.
Dismissal of appeal.
Dismissal if not prosecuted
to term returnable,
§12-22-221.
Duty of defendant on bail
to surrender upon
dismissal, §12-22-244.
Entry of order granting on
court's minutes,
§12-22-221.
Habeas corpus, §12-22-90.
Indigent persons.
In forma pauperis
proceedings, ARAP,
Rule 24.
Forms, ARAP, Form 15.
Providing record on appeal,
§§12-22-190 to
12-22-201.
New trial.
Automatic appeals.
Granting of new trial,
§12-22-241.
Granting of new trial,
§12-22-242.
Record on appeal.
Completion and
transmission, ARAP,
Rule 11 (b).
Composition of record,
ARAP, Rule 10 (c).
Providing record on appeal
for indigents.
Applicability of division,
§12-22-191.
Appropriations,
§12-22-201.
Burden of proof as to
sufficient funds,
§12-22-195.
Costs.
Estimate, §12-22-193.
When appeal
unfavorable,
§12-22-199.
Denial of petition for
appeal under
division, §12-22-198.
Disbursements.
Approval of governor,
§12-22-201.

APPEALS—Cont'd
Criminal cases—Cont'd
Record on appeal—Cont'd
Providing record on appeal
for indigents—Cont'd
Estimate of costs and
fees, §12-22-193.
Examination of
petitioner,
§12-22-193.
Fees.
Estimate of fees,
§12-22-193.
Payment, §12-22-197.
Financial information.
Ascertainment,
§12-22-193.
Entry on minutes of
court, §12-22-196.
Report on financial
condition of
petitioner,
§12-22-194.
Governor.
Approval of
disbursement of
funds, §12-22-201.
Inadequate record,
§12-22-198.
Order to prepare record,
§12-22-197.
Payment and
transmission of fees,
§12-22-197.
Petition for appeal under
division, §12-22-192.
Appeals from denial of
petition,
§12-22-198.
Purpose of division,
§12-22-190.
Reports.
Financial condition of
petitioner,
§12-22-194.
Rules and regulations,
§12-22-200.
Subpoena of witnesses,
§12-22-193.
Unfavorable appeal.
Judgment for costs,
§12-22-199.
Witnesses.
Subpoena, §12-22-193.
Release in criminal cases,
ARAP, Rule 9.
Reversal of judgment,
§12-22-242.
Automatic appeals,
§12-22-241.
Effect of undertaking when
conviction reversed
and case remanded,
§12-22-245.
Scope of review.
Cases other than death
cases, ARAP, Rule
45B.
State appeals.
Statute held
unconstitutional,
§12-22-91.
Stays pending appeal.
Death sentence.
Automatic stay,
§12-22-150; ARAP,
Rule 8 (d).
Felonies.
Question of law reserved
and admission on
bail, §12-22-170.

APPEALS—Cont'd
Criminal cases—Cont'd
Stays pending appeal
—Cont'd
Misdemeanors.
Confessed judgments,
§12-22-172.
Question of law reserved
and admission to
bail, §12-22-171.
Question of law reserved
and admission to bail.
Felonies, §12-22-170.
Misdemeanors,
§12-22-171.
Waiver of stayed sentence,
§12-22-173.
Writs of error, §12-22-222.
Subpoenas.
Appeals to circuit courts.
Issuance, execution and
return, §12-22-111.
Supreme court.
Appeals to supreme court,
§§12-22-130 to
12-22-133.
Time for taking appeal as of
right, ARAP, Rule 4 (b).
Transmission of record.
Mechanics of transmission,
ARAP, Rule 11 (b).
Unconstitutionality.
Statute held
unconstitutional,
§12-22-91.
Waiver of stayed sentence,
§12-22-173.
When granted, §12-22-220.
Writs of error.
Bail.
Admission of defendant
to bail, §12-22-222.
By whom granted,
§12-22-220.
Failure to appear,
§12-22-222.
Stay of proceedings on
judgment, §12-22-222.
Damages.
Frivolous appeal, ARAP,
Rule 38.
Dams.
Erection.
Assessment of damages,
§18-2-19.
Death.
Substitution of parties,
ARAP, Rule 43 (a).
Death sentence.
Automatic appeal,
§12-22-150.
Scope of review, ARAP, Rule
45A.
Stay pending appeal,
§12-22-150; ARAP, Rule
8 (d).
Decedents' estates.
Appeals from probate court,
§§12-22-20 to 12-22-27.
See PROBATE COURTS.
Judgment on partial or
annual settlement of
estate, §12-22-4.
Defenses.
Litigation on merits after
loss on certain defenses
not to bar raising of
same defenses on appeal,
§6-8-101.

APPEALS—Cont'd
Definitions.
Rules of appellate procedure,
ARAP, Rule 51.
Dentists.
Board of dental examiners.
Judicial review of orders,
§34-9-25.
**Department of industrial
relations.**
Board of appeals.
See LABOR.
Discovery pending appeal,
ARCP, Rule 27 (b).
Diseases.
Notifiable diseases.
Commitment, §22-11A-36.
Dismissal.
Execution upon dismissal of
appeal, §12-22-75.
Penalties for noncompliance
with rules, ARAP, Rule
2 (a).
Record on appeal.
Failure to cause timely
completion, ARAP,
Rule 12 (c).
Voluntary dismissal, ARAP,
Rule 42.
District courts.
Appeals from district courts,
§§12-12-70 to 12-12-73.
Dockets.
Docketing appeals, ARAP,
Rule 12 (a).
Fees, ARAP, Rules 12 (a),
35A.
Dower.
Ascertainment and payment,
§35-4-192.
Drugs.
Controlled substances.
Manufacturers and
distributors.
Denial, refusal,
revocation or
suspension, §20-2-53.
Education.
See EDUCATION.
Eggs and egg products.
Revocation of permits for
sale, §2-12-4.
Elections.
See ELECTIONS.
Electricity.
Service territories for electric
suppliers.
1984 act.
Validity of provisions,
§37-14-13.
1985 act.
Validity of provisions,
§37-14-38.
Eminent domain.
See EMINENT DOMAIN.
Engineers.
Board of registration.
Appeals from decisions of
board, §34-11-13.
Entry of judgment, ARAP,
Rule 36 (b).
Environmental management.
Commission.
Hearings and procedures
before commission,
§22-22A-7.
Error.
Assignment not required,
ARAP, Rule 20.
Error without injury, ARAP,
Rule 45.

APPEALS—Cont'd
Error—Cont'd
Writs of error.
Criminal cases,
§§12-22-220,
12-22-222.
Estate and inheritance tax,
§40-15-20.
Evidence.
Criminal cases.
Appeals to circuit courts.
Rules, §12-22-114.
Excessive judgments,
§12-22-71.
Executions.
Execution upon dismissal or
affirmation, §12-22-75.
Unpaid costs.
Execution, §12-22-76.
**Executors and
administrators.**
Appeals from probate court,
§§12-22-20 to 12-22-27.
See PROBATE COURTS.
Compelling conveyances,
§35-4-321.
Judgment on partial or
annual settlement of
estate, §12-22-4.
**Exemptions from
administration and
payment of debts.**
Report of appraisers or
commissioners.
Exceptions, §6-10-91.
Exhibits.
Appendix to briefs.
Reproduction of exhibits,
ARAP, Rule 30 (f).
Form of request for original
to be filed, ARAP, Form
20.
Record on appeal.
Custody of exhibits, ARAP,
Rule 11 (e).
Use of physical exhibits at
oral argument, ARAP,
Rule 34 (e).
Experts.
Appointment.
Appointment and use of
appellate experts, ARAP,
Rule 33A.
Extraordinary writs.
Review in supreme court of
decisions of courts of
appeals, ARAP, Rule 21.
Fees.
Docket fee, ARAP, Rules 12
(a), 35A.
Final judgments.
Appeal as of right, §12-22-2.
Fires and fire prevention.
Orders of fire marshal.
Appeal from circuit court
to court of civil
appeals, §36-19-13.
Appeal to circuit court,
§36-19-12.
Fish and game.
Violations of laws, §§9-11-8,
9-11-12.
**Forcible entry and unlawful
detainer,** §§6-6-350 to
6-6-353.
Forests and forestry.
Forest products.
Privilege and severance
taxes.
Assessment of taxes by
department,
§§9-13-96, 9-13-98.

APPEALS—Cont'd

Forms.

Rules of appellate procedure.
See within this heading,
"Rules of appellate
procedure."

Fraternal benefit societies.

Review of decisions and
findings of commissioner
of insurance, §27-34-52.

Frivolous appeal.

Damages, ARAP, Rule 38.
Litigation accountability,
§§12-19-270 to 12-19-276.
See COURTS.

Funerals.

Decisions of board of funeral
service, §§34-13-6,
34-13-31.

Garnishment, §6-6-464.

Ginseng.

Refusal or recall of permits
or certificates, §9-13-249.

Grain.

Grading and standards,
§2-11-97.

Grain dealers.

Judicial review of rulings of
commissioner, §2-31-15.

Guardian ad litem.

Probate courts.
Appeals from probate
courts, §12-22-26.

Guardian and ward.

Curators.
Appointment, §26-7A-16.
Probate courts.
Appeals from probate
courts, §12-22-26.
Uniform guardianship and
protective proceedings
act, §26-2A-36.

Guilty pleas.

No right of appeal,
§15-15-26.

Habeas corpus, ARAP, Rule
22.

Harmless error.

Error without injury, ARAP,
Rule 45.

Health.

State health planning and
development, §22-4-5.

**Hearing aid dealers and
fitters.**

Suspension or revocation of
license, §34-14-9.

**Heating and air conditioning
contractors,** §34-31-34.

Highways.

Closing and vacating streets,
alleys and highways,
§23-4-5.

Holidays.

Rules of appellate procedure,
ARAP, Rule 26 (a).

Horse racing.

Review of commission action,
§11-65-12.

Hospitals.

Licenses.
Judicial review of
suspension or
revocation, §22-21-26.
Liens of hospitals,
§35-11-373.

**Hotels, inns and other
transient lodging places.**

Transient occupancy tax.
Assessment, §40-26-13.

APPEALS—Cont'd

Illegitimacy.

Determination of paternity,
§26-17-20.

Impeachment.

Appeals to supreme court,
§§36-11-15, 36-11-16.

Income tax.

Assessments, §40-18-40.
Setoff debt collection,
§40-18-104.
Withholding tax.
Appeals of employer,
§40-18-74.

Indigent persons.

Appointment and
compensation of counsel,
§15-12-22.
Calculation of rates,
§15-12-24.
Criminal cases.
Providing record on appeal
for indigents,
§§12-22-190 to
12-22-201. See within
this heading,
"Criminal cases."
In forma pauperis
proceedings, ARAP, Rule
24.
Forms, ARAP, Form 15.
Proceedings.
In forma pauperis, ARAP,
Rule 24.
Forms, ARAP, Form 15.

Industrial relations.

Department of industrial
relations, §25-2-13.

Industrial revenue bonds.

Appeals to securities
commission, §8-6-117.

**In forma pauperis
proceedings,** ARAP, Rule
24.
Criminal cases.
Providing record on appeal
for indigents,
§§12-22-190 to
12-22-201. See within
this heading,
"Criminal cases."
Forms, ARAP, Form 15.

Injunctions.

Pending appeal, ARCP, Rule
62 (c).
Remedial writs, §12-22-6.
Temporary restraining
orders.
Applications for, §12-22-7.

Insurance.

See INSURANCE.

Interest.

Judgments, ARAP, Rule 37.

Jails.

Inspection of jails.
When new construction
required, §14-6-82.
Tubercular prisoners.
Persons confined pending
appeal, §14-6-61.

Judgments.

Appealable judgments,
§12-22-2.
Certificate of judgment.
Date of issuance, ARAP,
Rule 41 (a).
Stay pending petitions for
certiorari, ARAP, Rule
41 (b).
Entry of judgment, ARAP,
Rule 36 (b).

APPEALS—Cont'd

Judgments—Cont'd

Final judgments.
Appeal as of right,
§12-22-2.
Interest on judgments,
ARAP, Rule 37.
Juvenile courts, §12-15-120.

Jury.

Charge to jury, §12-16-13.
Disqualification of jurors,
§12-16-60.

Justices of the peace, Const.
Ala., art. VI, §168.

Juvenile proceedings,
§12-15-120; ARJP, Rule 28.
Counsel for indigent
juveniles, §15-12-22.
Calculation of rates,
§15-12-24.
District attorneys.
Representation of state,
§12-15-5.
Indigent persons.
Appointment and
compensation of
counsel, §15-12-22.
Calculation of rates,
§15-12-24.

Landlord and tenant.

Possession wrongfully
withheld, §35-9-87.

Landscaping.

Horticulture and floriculture
work.
Denial or revocation of
permits, §2-28-7.

Life estates.

Ascertainment and payment,
§35-4-192.

Limitation of actions.

Actions against surety in
courts of the United
States or other state.
Four year limitation,
§6-2-36.
Arrest or reversal of
judgment on appeal.
Recommencement of
action, §6-2-38.

Liquefied petroleum gas.

Directive order of
discontinuance,
§9-17-108.

Litigation accountability,
§§12-19-270 to 12-19-276.
See COURTS.

Livestock.

Running at large, §3-5-12.

Mandamus, §12-22-6.
Review in supreme court of
decisions of courts of
appeals, ARAP, Rule 21.

Marine resources.

Violation of chapter,
§§9-12-6, 9-12-7.

Mentally ill.

See MENTALLY ILL.

Military affairs.

Compensation for death of
national guardsmen.
Decision of awarding
authority to be final,
§31-3-7.

Milk and milk products.

Health regulations.
Appeal from order or
action of commissioner,
§2-13-90.

APPEALS—Cont'd

Minors.
Juvenile proceedings. See within this heading, "Juvenile proceedings."

Motions.
Caption, ARAP, Rule 32 (c).
Form, ARAP, Rule 32 (b).
Rules of appellate procedure. See within this heading, "Rules of appellate procedure."

Motor fuels.
Distributors of motor fuels. Decisions of department of revenue, §40-12-203.

Motor vehicle carriers.
Final action or order of commission, §37-3-29.
Mileage tax.
Appeals by taxpayers of assessments, §40-19-9.

Motor vehicles.
See MOTOR VEHICLES.

Municipal corporations.
See MUNICIPAL CORPORATIONS.

Municipal courts.
See MUNICIPAL COURTS.

New trial.
Automatic appeals on granting, §12-22-241.
Grant or refusal of motion for new trial, §12-22-10.

Next friend.
Probate courts.
Appeals from probate courts, §12-22-26.

Notice of appeal.
Content, ARAP, Rule 3 (c).
Filing, ARAP, Rule 3 (a).
Forms, ARAP, Rule 3 (c); ARAP, Forms 1, 2, 11, 12.
Service, ARAP, Rule 3 (d).

Nurseries.
Insect and disease control.
Appeals to state board from actions of commissioner, §2-25-18.

Nurses.
Denial, suspension or revocation of license, §34-21-25.

Nursing homes.
Board of examiners of nursing home administrators, §34-20-6.

Oil and gas.
Conservation and regulation of production.
Injunctions, §9-17-18.

Opinions.
Sending copies of opinions, ARAP, Rule 36 (a).

Optometrists.
Disciplinary actions against licensees, §34-22-8.

Oral argument.
Certified questions from federal courts, ARAP, Rule 18 (h).
Content, ARAP, Rule 34 (c).
Exhibits.
Use of physical exhibits, ARAP, Rule 34 (e).
Motions, ARAP, Rule 27 (c).
Nonappearance of parties, ARAP, Rule 34 (d).
Notice, ARAP, Rule 34 (a).

APPEALS—Cont'd

Oral argument—Cont'd
Order, ARAP, Rule 34 (c).
Postponement, ARAP, Rule 34 (a).
Review of decisions of courts of appeal, ARAP, Rule 39.
Time allowed, ARAP, Rule 34 (b).

Orders of court.
Notice, ARAP, Rule 17 (a).

Parent and child.
Determination of paternity, §26-17-20.
Termination of parental rights.
Precedence of appeals, §26-18-2.

Parties.
Substitution of parties, ARAP, Rule 43.

Partition.
Crops, §35-6-124.

Peace bonds, §§15-6-40 to 15-6-43.

Penalties.
Disposition of appeals.
Affirmation of stayed judgment generally, §12-22-72.
Frivolous appeal, ARAP, Rule 38.

Pest control.
Denial or revocation, §2-28-7.

Pesticides.
Application.
Licenses.
Suspension, revocation or modification, §2-27-54.

Pharmacists and pharmacies.
Board of pharmacy, §34-23-94.

Physical therapists.
Refusal, revocation or suspension of licenses, §34-24-194.

Physicians.
Foreign medical school graduates.
Off-shore medical schools, §34-24-82.
Revocation or suspension of licenses, §34-24-367.

Pilots and pilotage.
Apprentices.
Discharge, §33-4-33.

Plant pathologists.
Denial or revocation of permits, §2-28-7.

Polygraph examiners.
Refusal, suspension or revocation of licenses, §34-25-35.

Poor persons. See within this heading, "Indigent persons."

Post-conviction remedies.
Court to which appeal taken, ARCrP, Rule 20.10 (a).
Release of petitioners, ARCrP, Rule 20.10 (b).
Who may appeal, ARCrP, Rule 20.10 (a).

Prehearing conference, ARAP, Rule 33.
Form of request, ARAP, Form 21.

APPEALS—Cont'd

Probate court.
Appeals from probate court. See PROBATE COURTS.

Prohibition, writ of, §12-22-6.
Review in supreme court of decisions of courts of appeals, ARAP, Rule 21.

Psychologists.
Refusal, suspension or revocation of licenses, §34-26-48.

Public officers and employees.
Substitution of parties, ARAP, Rule 43 (b).

Public service commission.
See PUBLIC SERVICE COMMISSION.

Public utilities.
Purchase of property by governmental agency.
Forced sales, §37-4-63.
Taxation.
Protest of incorrect valuation, §40-21-24.
Valuation of utility property, §37-4-21.
Appeals of commission order, §37-4-19.
Appeals to supreme court, §37-4-21.

Quo warranto.
See QUO WARRANTO.

Radio utilities.
Final actions or orders of public service commission, §37-4-114.

Real estate brokers.
Disciplinary actions, §34-27-38.

Receivers.
Appointing or refusing to appoint, §12-22-9.
By clerk or register of circuit court, §6-6-621.

Record on appeal.
Agreed statement, ARAP, Rule 10 (e).
Briefs.
References to record, ARAP, Rules 28 (e), 30 (d).
Certification.
Fees.
Probate judges' fees, §12-19-90.
Completion.
Certificate, ARAP, Form 5.
Dismissal for failure to timely complete, ARAP, Rule 12 (c).
Extension of time, ARAP, Rule 11 (c).
Forms of certificates, ARAP, Forms 4 to 6, 13, 14.
Mechanics, ARAP, Rule 11 (a), (b).
Reduction in time, ARAP, Rule 11 (c).
Composition, ARAP, Rule 10 (b), (c).
Correction, ARAP, Rule 10 (f).
Costs of copies, ARAP, Rule 35 (c).
Criminal cases. See within this heading, "Criminal cases."
Custody, ARAP, Rule 17 (b).

APPEALS—Cont'd

Record on appeal—Cont'd

Delayed or defective record.
Liability of clerk, etc., for delayed or defective record, §12-22-60.
Dismissal for failure to cause timely completion, ARAP, Rule 12 (c).
Electronic recording devices, ARAP, Rule 14.
Exhibits.
Custody of exhibits, ARAP, Rule 11 (e).
Filing.
Appeal by permission, ARAP, Rule 5 (c).
Notice, ARAP, Rule 12 (b).
Forms, ARAP, Forms 3 to 6, 10, 13, 14.
Indigent persons.
Criminal cases. See within this heading, "Criminal cases."
In lieu of appendix, ARAP, Rule 30 (g).
Modification, ARAP, Rule 10 (f).
Notice of filing, ARAP, Rule 12 (b).
Omitted parts, ARAP, Rule 10 (a).
Option to use either appendix or record, ARAP, Rule 30 (a).
Preliminary hearing in appellate court, ARAP, Rule 11 (d).
Recording devices.
Use, ARAP, Rule 14.
Statement of evidence or proceedings, ARAP, Rule 10 (d).
Transmission.
Forms, ARAP, Forms 10, 14.
Mechanics, ARAP, Rule 11 (a), (b).
Original item from trial court, ARAP, Rule 13.
Videotape recording, ARAP, Rule 14.

Rehearing.

Applications, ARAP, Rule 40.
Denial of petition for certiorari, ARAP, Rule 39 (j).
Form, ARAP, Rule 32 (b).

Reversal.

Procedure upon reversal, §12-22-70.

Right of appeal.

Rules of appellate procedure. See within this heading, "Rules of appellate procedure."

Rules and regulations.

Briefs.
Reproduction, ARAP, Rule 28 (f).

Rules of appellate procedure.

Agreements in writing, ARAP, Rule 47.
Amicus curiae.
Briefs, ARAP, Rule 29.
Appealability of order not otherwise appealable.
Form of certificate of trial judge, ARAP, Form 17.

APPEALS—Cont'd

Rules of appellate procedure —Cont'd

Appeal as of right.
Consolidated appeals, ARAP, Rule 3 (b).
How taken, ARAP, Rule 3.
Joint appeals, ARAP, Rule 3 (b).
Notice.
Content, ARAP, Rule 3 (c).
Filing, ARAP, Rule 3 (a).
Form, ARAP, Rule 3 (c).
Service, ARAP, Rule 3 (d).
Service of notice, ARAP, Rule 3 (d).
When taken, ARAP, Rule 4.
Appeal by permission.
Costs, ARAP, Rule 5 (c).
Effect on trial court proceedings, ARAP, Rule 5 (d).
Form of papers, ARAP, Rule 5 (e).
Grant of permission, ARAP, Rule 5 (c).
Number of copies, ARAP, Rule 5 (e).
Petition, ARAP, Rule 5.
Form, ARAP, Form 16.
Record on appeal.
Filing, ARAP, Rule 5 (c).
Security for costs, ARAP, Rule 5 (c).
Argument.
Certified questions from federal courts, ARAP, Rule 18 (g).
Assignment of error.
Not required, ARAP, Rule 20.
Attorneys at law.
Roll of attorneys, ARAP, Rule 46.
Briefs.
Amicus curiae, ARAP, Rules 28 (e), 29.
Appellants' briefs, ARAP, Rule 28 (a).
Appellees' briefs, ARAP, Rule 28 (b).
Appendix, ARAP, Rule 29.
Arrangement, ARAP, Rule 30 (e).
Contents, ARAP, Rule 30 (b).
Determination, ARAP, Rule 30 (c).
Copies, ARAP, Rule 30 (b).
Costs, ARAP, Rule 35 (c).
Exhibits.
Reproduction, ARAP, Rule 30 (f).
Filing.
Duty to file, ARAP, Rule 30 (b).
Form, ARAP, Rule 32 (a).
Option to use either appendix or record, ARAP, Rule 30 (a).
Preparation.
Duty to prepare, ARAP, Rule 30 (b).

APPEALS—Cont'd

Rules of appellate procedure —Cont'd

Briefs—Cont'd
Appendix—Cont'd
Record in lieu of appendix, ARAP, Rule 30 (g).
Time for filing, ARAP, Rule 30 (b).
Transmittal.
Form of letter of transmittal, ARAP, Form 9.
Certified questions from federal courts, ARAP, Rule 18 (g).
Copies.
Number to be filed and served, ARAP, Rule 31 (b).
Cross appeals, ARAP, Rule 28 (h).
Filing.
Extension of time, ARAP, Rule 31 (d).
Failure to file, ARAP, Rule 31 (c).
Number of copies, ARAP, Rule 31 (b).
Time, ARAP, Rule 31 (a).
Extension, ARAP, Rule 31 (d).
Form, ARAP, Rule 32 (a).
Length, ARAP, Rule 28 (g).
Multiple appellants or appellees, ARAP, Rule 28 (i).
Record on appeal.
References to record, ARAP, Rules 28 (e), 30 (d).
References in briefs to parties, ARAP, Rule 28 (d).
Reply brief, ARAP, Rule 28 (c).
Review of decisions of courts of appeal, ARAP, Rule 39.
Rules and regulations.
Reproduction, ARAP, Rule 28 (f).
Service of briefs.
Form, ARAP, Forms 7, 8.
Number of copies, ARAP, Rule 31 (b).
Time, ARAP, Rule 31 (a).
Statutes.
Reproduction of statutes, ARAP, Rule 28 (f).
Time for serving and filing, ARAP, Rule 31 (a).
Extension, ARAP, Rule 31 (d).
Captions, ARAP, Rule 32 (c).
Certificate of judgment.
Date of issuance, ARAP, Rule 41 (a).
Stay pending petitions for certiorari to courts of appeals, ARAP, Rule 41 (b).

APPEALS—Cont'd
Rules of appellate procedure
—Cont'd
Certified questions from
federal courts, ARAP,
Rule 18.
Form, ARAP, Form 18.
Certiorari.
Dismissal of petition,
ARAP, Rule 2 (c).
Petition for certiorari.
Form of petition to
courts of appeals,
ARAP, Form 22.
Review of decisions of
courts of appeal,
ARAP, Rule 39.
Stay pending petitions for
certiorari to courts of
appeals, ARAP, Rule
41 (b).
Clerks of court.
Duties, ARAP, Rule 17.
Consolidated appeals, ARAP,
Rule 3 (b).
Constitutional questions,
ARAP, Rule 44.
Contempt.
Willful noncompliance,
ARAP, Rule 48.
Costs.
Against whom taxed,
ARAP, Rule 35 (a).
Appendix to briefs, ARAP,
Rule 35 (c).
Producing, ARAP, Rule
30 (c).
Certified questions from
federal courts, ARAP,
Rule 18 (f).
Clerk to insert in
certificate of judgment,
ARAP, Rule 35 (d).
Record on appeal, ARAP,
Rule 35 (c).
Security for costs.
Appeals by permission,
ARAP, Rule 5 (c).
Civil cases, ARAP, Rule
7.
State.
Costs for and against
state, ARAP, Rule
35 (b).
Court sitting in divisions,
ARAP, Rule 16.
Criminal cases.
In forma pauperis
proceedings, ARAP,
Rule 24 (b).
Record on appeal.
Completion and
transmission of
record, ARAP, Rule
11 (b).
Composition, ARAP,
Rule 10 (c).
Release in criminal cases,
ARAP, Rule 9.
Statement of evidence or
proceedings, ARAP,
Rule 10 (d).
When appeal taken, ARAP,
Rule 4 (b).
Cross appeals.
Briefs, ARAP, Rule 28 (h).
Death of a party.
Substitution, ARAP, Rule
43 (a).

APPEALS—Cont'd
Rules of appellate procedure
—Cont'd
Death sentence.
Scope of review, ARAP,
Rule 45A.
Stay pending appeal,
ARAP, Rule 8 (d).
Definitions, ARAP, Rule 51.
Dismissal.
Failure to complete record,
ARAP, Rule 12 (c).
Petition for certiorari,
ARAP, Rule 2 (c).
Voluntary dismissal,
ARAP, Rule 42.
Divisions.
Court sitting in divisions,
ARAP, Rule 16.
Docketing appeal, ARAP,
Rule 12 (a).
Fees, ARAP, Rule 35A.
Effective date of rules,
ARAP, Rule 49.
Entry of judgment, ARAP,
Rule 36 (b).
Error.
Assignment not required,
ARAP, Rule 20.
Error without injury,
ARAP, Rule 45.
Exhibits.
Appendix to briefs.
Reproduction, ARAP,
Rule 30 (f).
Form of request for
original to be filed,
ARAP, Form 20.
Record on appeal.
Custody, ARAP, Rule 11
(e).
Use at oral argument,
ARAP, Rule 34 (e).
Experts.
Appointment and use of
appellate experts,
ARAP, Rule 33A.
Extraordinary writs, ARAP,
Rule 21.
Federal courts.
Certified questions from
federal courts, ARAP,
Rule 18.
Forms, ARAP, Form 18.
Fees.
Docket fee, ARAP, Rules
12 (a), 35A.
Filing of papers, ARAP, Rule
25 (a).
Appendix to briefs.
Duty to file, ARAP, Rule
30 (b).
Briefs, ARAP, Rule 31.
Form of request for
original to be filed,
ARAP, Form 20.
Forms, ARAP, Rule 50.
Appendix to briefs.
Transmittal to appellate
clerk, ARAP, Form
9.
Briefs.
Certificate of service,
ARAP, Forms 7, 8.
Captions, ARAP, Rule 32
(c).
Certified questions from
federal courts, ARAP,
Form 18.

APPEALS—Cont'd
Rules of appellate procedure
—Cont'd
Forms—Cont'd
Certiorari.
Form of petition to
courts of appeals,
ARAP, Form 22.
Filing of papers.
Request for original to
be filed, ARAP,
Form 20.
In forma pauperis
proceedings, ARAP,
Form 15.
Mandamus, ARAP, Form
19.
Notice of appeal, ARAP,
Forms 1, 2, 11, 12.
Papers, ARAP, Rule 32 (b).
Permission to appeal,
ARAP, Form 16.
Prehearing conference.
Request, ARAP, Form
21.
Record on appeal, ARAP,
Forms 3 to 6, 10, 13,
14.
Summary of rulings and
actions adverse to
appellant, ARAP,
Form 23.
Frivolous appeal, ARAP,
Rule 38.
Habeas corpus, ARAP, Rule
22.
Harmless error.
Error without injury,
ARAP, Rule 45.
Holidays, ARAP, Rule 26 (a).
In forma pauperis
proceedings, ARAP, Rule
24.
Forms, ARAP, Form 15.
Injunction pending appeal,
ARAP, Rule 8.
Interest on judgments,
ARAP, Rule 37.
Joint appeals, ARAP, Rule 3
(b).
Judgments.
Certificate of judgment.
Date of issuance, ARAP,
Rule 41.
Stay pending petitions
for certiorari to
courts of appeals,
ARAP, Rule 41 (b).
Entry of judgment, ARAP,
Rule 36 (b).
Interest on judgments,
ARAP, Rule 37.
Jurisdiction.
Certified questions from
federal courts, ARAP,
Rule 18 (b).
Mandamus.
Directed to judge or judges,
ARAP, Rule 21.
Form of petition for writ of
mandamus, ARAP,
Form 19.
Motions.
Caption, ARAP, Rule 32
(c).
Content, ARAP, Rule 27
(a).
Copies, ARAP, Rule 27 (d).
Determination for
procedural orders,
ARAP, Rule 27 (b).

APPEALS—Cont'd
  Rules of appellate procedure
  —Cont'd
    Motions—Cont'd
      Form of papers, ARAP,
        Rules 27 (d), 32 (b).
      Oral argument not
        permitted, ARAP, Rule
        27 (c).
      Procedural orders, ARAP,
        Rule 27 (b).
      Reply, ARAP, Rule 27 (a).
      Response, ARAP, Rule 27
        (a).
      Stay pending appeal,
        ARAP, Rule 8 (b).
    Noncompliance.
      Contempt for willful
        noncompliance, ARAP,
        Rule 48.
    Notice of appeal.
      Content, ARAP, Rule 3 (c).
      Filing, ARAP, Rule 3 (a).
      Forms, ARAP, Forms 1, 2,
        11, 12.
      Service, ARAP, Rule 3 (d).
    Opinions.
      Sending copies of opinions,
        ARAP, Rule 36 (a).
    Oral argument.
      Certified questions from
        federal courts, ARAP,
        Rule 18 (h).
      Content, ARAP, Rule 34
        (c).
      Exhibits.
        Use, ARAP, Rule 34 (e).
      Motions.
        Oral argument not
          permitted, ARAP,
          Rule 27 (c).
      Nonappearance of parties,
        ARAP, Rule 34 (d).
      Notice, ARAP, Rule 34 (a).
      Order, ARAP, Rule 34 (c).
      Postponement, ARAP, Rule
        34 (a).
      Review of decisions of
        courts of appeal,
        ARAP, Rule 39.
      Time allowed, ARAP, Rule
        34 (b).
    Orders of court.
      Notice, ARAP, Rule 17 (a).
    Overruling cases, ARAP,
      Rule 15.
    Papers.
      Custody, ARAP, Rule 17
        (b).
    Parties.
      Death.
        Substitution, ARAP,
          Rule 43 (a).
      Public officers.
        Substitution of parties,
          ARAP, Rule 43 (b).
      Substitution of parties,
        ARAP, Rule 43.
    Penalties for noncompliance,
      ARAP, Rule 2 (a).
    Petitions.
      Extraordinary writs,
        ARAP, Rule 21.
      Mandamus, ARAP, Rule
        21.
      Prohibition, writ of, ARAP,
        Rule 21.
    Prehearing conference,
      ARAP, Rule 33.
      Form of request, ARAP,
        Form 21.

APPEALS—Cont'd
  Rules of appellate procedure
  —Cont'd
    Prohibition, writ of.
      Directed to judge or judges,
        ARAP, Rule 21.
    Public officers.
      Substitution of parties,
        ARAP, Rule 43 (b).
    Record on appeal.
      Agreed statement, ARAP,
        Rule 10 (e).
      Briefs.
        References, ARAP, Rules
          28 (e), 30 (d).
      Completion of record.
        Extension of time,
          ARAP, Rule 11 (c).
        Failure to timely
          complete, ARAP,
          Rule 12 (c).
        Forms of certificates,
          ARAP, Forms 4 to 6,
          13, 14.
        Reporter's transcript,
          ARAP, Form 5.
        Mechanics, ARAP, Rule
          11 (a), (b).
        Reduction in time,
          ARAP, Rule 11 (c).
      Composition, ARAP, Rule
        10 (b), (c).
      Correction, ARAP, Rule 10
        (f).
      Costs of copies, ARAP,
        Rule 35 (c).
      Custody, ARAP, Rule 17
        (b).
      Electronic recording
        devices, ARAP, Rule
        14.
      Exhibits.
        Custody, ARAP, Rule 11
          (e).
      Failure to timely complete,
        ARAP, Rule 12 (c).
      Filing of record.
        Appeal by permission,
          ARAP, Rule 5 (c).
        Notice, ARAP, Rule 12
          (b).
      Forms, ARAP, Forms 3 to
        6, 10, 13, 14.
      In lieu of appendix, ARAP,
        Rule 30 (g).
      Modification, ARAP, Rule
        10 (f).
      Notice of filing, ARAP,
        Rule 12 (b).
      Omitted parts, ARAP, Rule
        10 (a).
      Option to use either
        appendix or record,
        ARAP, Rule 30 (a).
      Preliminary hearing in
        appellate court, ARAP,
        Rule 11 (d).
      Recording devices.
        Use, ARAP, Rule 14.
      Statement of evidence or
        proceedings, ARAP,
        Rule 10 (d).
      Transmission,
        Forms, ARAP, Forms 10,
          14.
        Mechanics, ARAP, Rule
          11 (a), (b).
        Original item from trial
          court, ARAP, Rule
          13.

APPEALS—Cont'd
  Rules of appellate procedure
  —Cont'd
    Record on appeal—Cont'd
      Videotape recording,
        ARAP, Rule 14.
    Rehearing.
      Applications, ARAP, Rule
        40.
      Denial of petition for
        certiorari, ARAP,
        Rule 39 (j).
      Form, ARAP, Rule 32
        (b).
      Review of decisions of courts
        of appeal, ARAP, Rule
        39.
      Extraordinary writs,
        ARAP, Rule 21.
      Mandamus, ARAP, Rule
        21.
      Prohibition, writ of, ARAP,
        Rule 21.
    Scope of review, ARAP, Rule
      45B.
    Scope of rules, ARAP, Rule
      1.
    Service of process.
      Briefs, ARAP, Rule 31.
      Constitutional questions,
        ARAP, Rule 44.
      Extraordinary writs.
        Petitions, ARAP, Rule
          21.
      Mandamus.
        Petitions, ARAP, Rule
          21.
      Manner of service, ARAP,
        Rule 25 (c).
      Notice of appeal, ARAP,
        Rule 3 (d).
      Prohibition, writ of.
        Petitions, ARAP, Rule
          21.
      Proof of service, ARAP,
        Rule 25 (d).
      Required, ARAP, Rule 25
        (b).
      Review of decisions of
        courts of appeal,
        ARAP, Rule 39.
    Stay pending appeal.
      Bonds, surety.
        Conditioning stay upon,
          ARAP, Rule 8 (c).
        Principals and sureties,
          ARAP, Rule 8 (c).
        Supersedeas bond,
          ARAP, Rule 8 (a).
      Criminal cases, ARAP,
        Rule 8 (d).
      Death sentence, ARAP,
        Rule 8 (d).
      Motion for stay, ARAP,
        Rule 8 (b).
      Supersedeas bond, ARAP,
        Rule 8 (a).
    Suspension of rules, ARAP,
      Rule 2 (b).
    Time.
      Computation, ARAP, Rule
        26 (a).
      Enlargement, ARAP, Rule
        26 (b).
    Title of rules, ARAP, Rule
      49.
    Voluntary dismissal, ARAP,
      Rule 42.
    Written agreements, ARAP,
      Rule 47.

APPEALS—Cont'd

Rules of civil procedure.

Counterclaims and cross-claims, ARCP, Rule 13 (j).

Discovery pending appeal, ARCP, Rule 27 (b).

Stay upon appeal, ARCP, Rule 62 (d).

Rules of criminal procedure.

Post-conviction remedies, ARCrP, Rule 20.10.

State from pre-trial ruling, ARCrP, Rule 17.

Sales tax.

Assessments, §40-23-18.

Savings and loan associations.

From orders of commissioner or board, §5-2A-63.

Securities.

Action of commission, §8-6-32.

Security for costs on appeal.

See within this heading, "Costs on appeal."

Security to keep the peace, §§15-6-40 to 15-6-42.

See PEACE BONDS.

Service of process.

Rules of appellate procedure. See within this heading, "Rules of appellate procedure."

Small claims, ASCR, Rule M.

Small loans.

From act of bureau or supervisor, §5-2A-82.

Review of orders of supervisor, §5-18-20.

Social workers.

Disciplinary proceedings, §34-30-5.

Speech pathologists and audiologists.

Revocation or suspension of licenses, §34-28A-26.

Sports.

Agents.

Disputes, §8-26-38.

Registration.

Refusal, §8-26-7.

State.

Costs for and against state, ARAP, Rule 35 (b).

Criminal cases.

Statute held unconstitutional, §12-22-91.

Statutes.

Briefs.

Reproduction in briefs, ARAP, Rule 28 (f).

Stays, ARCP, Rule 62 (d); ARAP, Rule 8.

Certificate of judgment, ARAP, Rule 41 (b).

Criminal cases. See within this heading, "Criminal cases."

Writs of error.

Stay of proceedings on judgment, §12-22-222.

Subpoenas.

Appeals to circuit courts. Criminal cases, §12-22-111.

Supersedeas.

Recording of order fixing, §12-22-40.

Remedial writs, §12-22-6.

APPEALS—Cont'd

Supreme court.

Criminal cases, §§12-22-130 to 12-22-133.

Surveys and surveyors.

Board of registration.

Appeals from decisions of board, §34-11-13.

Taxation.

General provisions.

See TAXATION.

Income tax.

See INCOME TAX.

Teachers.

See EDUCATION.

Time for taking appeal.

Civil cases.

Appeal as of right, ARAP, Rule 4 (a).

Criminal cases.

Appeal as of right, ARAP, Rule 4 (b).

Transcripts.

Record on appeal. See within this heading, "Record on appeal."

Tree surgeons.

Denial or revocation of permits, §2-28-7.

Unemployment compensation, §§25-4-92 to 25-4-97.

See UNEMPLOYMENT COMPENSATION.

United States.

Condemnation of land or rights-of-way.

Assessment of damages, §42-2-9.

Granting or refusal of application, §42-2-6.

Use tax.

Redeterminations, §40-23-73.

Veterinarians.

Disciplinary action, §34-29-83.

Videotape recording.

Record on appeal, ARAP, Rule 14.

Voluntary dismissal, ARAP, Rule 42.

Warehouses.

Denial of permits, §8-15-6.

Water management and drainage.

Districts.

Board of viewers, §9-9-30.

Inclusion or exclusion of property, §9-9-12.

Drainage subdistricts.

Failure to appeal, §9-9-80.

Orders of commission, §9-9-77.

Welfare, §§38-4-4 to 38-4-6, 38-7-9.

Workmen's compensation.

Determination of disputed compensation claims generally, §25-5-81.

Writs.

Remedial writs, §6-6-641.

Writs of error.

Criminal cases, §§12-22-220, 12-22-222.

Zoning.

Airports, §4-6-11.

Municipal corporations, §§11-52-80, 11-52-81.

APPLIANCES.

Land clearing or improvements.

Liens, §§35-11-430, 35-11-431.

Nuisances menacing public health.

Summary destruction without compensation, §22-10-3.

Unclaimed property.

Disposition of unclaimed articles left for service, §35-12-6.

APPORTIONMENT.

Congress, Const. U. S., Art. I, §§2, 3; Amendments XIV, XVII.

Constitution of Alabama.

See CONSTITUTION OF ALABAMA.

Constitution of the United States.

Congress, Const. U. S., Amendments XIV, XVII.

Legislature of Alabama.

See LEGISLATURE.

APPRAISALS AND APPRAISERS.

Eminent domain, §§18-1A-21, 18-1A-22.

Required, §18-1A-21.

Executors and administrators.

Collection, inventory and appraisement of personal property.

See EXECUTORS AND ADMINISTRATORS.

Exemptions from administration and payment of debts.

See EXEMPTIONS FROM ADMINISTRATION AND PAYMENT OF DEBTS.

Salvage, §§35-13-2, 35-13-16.

Savings and loan associations, §5-16-5.

Taxation, §40-1-6.

APPRENTICES.

Auctioneers, §§34-4-2, 34-4-5, 34-4-32.

Barbers, §34-5-5.

Cosmetologists.

See COSMETOLOGISTS.

Funeral professionals, §§34-13-130 to 34-13-134.

Pilots and pilotage, §§33-4-31 to 33-4-36.

See PILOTS AND PILOTAGE.

APPROPRIATIONS.

Academy of honor.

Amount and use, §41-11-6.

Agriculture.

Markets.

Local appropriations, §2-5-17.

Armories.

Maintenance of armories, §31-4-19.

Unexpended regular military appropriations.

Disposition, §31-2-15.

Budgets.

See BUDGETS.

APPROPRIATIONS—Cont'd

Charities.
Institutions not under
absolute control of state.
Const. Ala., art. IV,
§73.
Civil defense, §31-9-24.
Code of Alabama, §41-21-8.
Community action agencies,
§11-96-1.
Congress, Const. U. S., Art. I,
§§7, 9.
Constitution of Alabama.
See CONSTITUTION OF
ALABAMA.
**Constitution of the United
States,** Const. U. S., Art. I,
§9.
Army, Const. U. S., Art. I,
§8.
Revenue bills, Const. U. S.,
Art. I, §7.
Convention facilities,
§§11-100-4, 11-100-7.
Counties.
See COUNTIES.
**Economic and community
affairs.**
Transfer of appropriations to
department, §41-23-3.
Education.
Educational reform.
Commission, §16-6A-5.
Institutions not under
absolute control of state,
Const. Ala., art. IV,
§73.
Teachers.
Employment of teacher
aides, §16-1-1.1.
Transfer of appropriated
funds among line items,
§16-13-40.
Emergencies, §41-4-94.
**Energy management and
conservation.**
Operation of department of
energy, §41-6A-10.
Fires and fire prevention.
Survivor's education
assistance act.
Annual appropriations
from state general
fund, §36-21-105.
Forests and forestry.
Forest products.
Privilege and severance
taxes.
Appropriation of tax
receipts for use of
state forestry
commission,
§9-13-84.
Geological survey, §§9-4-8,
9-4-9.
Governor.
Restrictions of allotments by
governor, §41-4-90.
Hazardous substances.
Cleanup fund, §22-30A-3.
Health.
Municipal corporations.
Appropriations by
municipalities for
public health work,
§22-2-2.

APPROPRIATIONS—Cont'd

Hospitals.
See HOSPITALS.
Income tax.
Homestead exemptions.
Replacement of revenues
lost by reason of
exemption of
homesteads, §40-18-58.
Indians.
Indian affairs commission.
Perpetual appropriation,
§41-9-715.
Insurance.
Appropriations to certain
universities.
Determining
reimbursement for
patient care activities,
§27-1-11.1.
Judicial conference.
Chief justice may direct use,
§12-8-8.
Legislature.
See LEGISLATURE.
**Long term quality health
care,** §22-6-24.
Marine resources.
Gulf states marine fisheries
compact.
Commission.
Operating expenses,
§9-12-184.
Military affairs.
Armories.
Disbursement for
maintenance of
armories, §31-4-19.
Payment of commission
expenses or
obligations, §31-4-6.
Counties or municipalities.
Local units, §31-2-129.
National guard, §31-2-108.
Active military service,
§31-2-133.
Regular military
appropriations,
§31-2-132.
Revolving fund, §31-2-131.
State defense force, §31-2-10.
Unexpended appropriations,
§31-2-15.
Motor vehicle carriers,
§37-3-31.
Municipal corporations.
See MUNICIPAL
CORPORATIONS.
Music.
Hall of fame board,
§41-9-684.
**Office of state planning and
federal programs.**
Transfer to office, §41-9-212.
Peace officers.
Hall of fame, §41-9-873.
Survivor's education
assistance act,
§36-21-105.
Prisons and prisoners.
Convict labor.
Purchase of state lands,
§14-3-2.
**Public officers and
employees.**
State employees' health
insurance plan,
§36-29-13.

APPROPRIATIONS—Cont'd

Railroads.
Preservation, §37-10-7.
**St. Stephens historical
commission.**
Counties and municipalities.
Authorization to
appropriate,
§41-9-336.
**Southeast interstate low-
level radioactive waste
management compact,**
§22-32-5.
State parks.
Counties and municipalities.
Improvement, operation,
etc., §9-14-6.
Supreme court.
Purposes, §12-2-20.
Tennessee Valley Authority.
Exhibit commission.
Bond issues.
Payment of principal and
interest, §41-9-783.
United States, Const. U. S.,
Art. I, §9.
**University of South
Alabama.**
Insurance.
Patient care
reimbursement,
§27-1-11.1.
Veterans.
Pensions for widows of
confederate veterans,
§31-8-19.
Welfare.
See WELFARE.

ARBITRATION AND AWARD,
§§6-6-1 to 6-6-16.
Actions.
Referral to arbitrators when
no action pending,
§6-6-2.
Alcoholic beverages.
Beer.
Business relations between
wholesalers and
suppliers, §28-9-8.
Appeals, §6-6-15.
Arbitrators.
Depositions,
§6-6-7.
Duties, §6-6-4.
Majority vote, §6-6-5.
Naming, §6-6-3.
Oath, §6-6-6.
Administering, §6-6-7.
Reference of controversy to
when no action pending,
§6-6-2.
Subpoena, §§6-6-7 to
6-6-9.
Substitutions, §6-6-5.
Witnesses.
Subpoena, §§6-6-7 to
6-6-9.
Attorneys at law.
Legal services liability.
Voluntary arbitration,
§6-5-575.
Award, §§6-6-12 to
6-6-15.
Appeals, §6-6-15.
Enforcement, §6-6-13.
Finality, §6-6-14.
Force and effect, §6-6-12.
Proceedings when not
performed, §6-6-12.

ARBITRATION AND AWARD —Cont'd

Canons of judicial ethics.
Judge not to act as arbitrator, ACJE, Canon 5E.
Common-law arbitration not precluded, §6-6-16.
Constables.
Fees and charges, §6-6-10.
Constitution of Alabama.
Adoption of laws to provide for, Const. Ala., art. IV, §84.
Contracts.
Specific performance.
Agreement to arbitrate, §8-1-41.
Courts.
Duty to encourage, §6-6-1.
Decedents' estates.
Settlements and distributions.
Arbitration on settlement of estates, §§43-2-600 to 43-2-607.
See EXECUTORS AND ADMINISTRATORS.
Defenses.
Affirmative defense, ARCP, Rule 8 (c).
Education.
Annexing to city territory embracing schools.
Appointment of board, §16-8-21.
Hearing by board, §16-8-22.
When arbitration required, §16-8-21.
Eminent domain.
Arbitration of compensation, §§18-1A-250 to 18-1A-257.
See EMINENT DOMAIN.
Executors and administrators.
Settlements and distributions.
Arbitration on settlement of estates, §§43-2-600 to 43-2-607.
See EXECUTORS AND ADMINISTRATORS.
Fees and charges.
Arbitrators, §6-6-10.
Refusal to deliver award until paid, §6-6-11.
Constables, §6-6-10.
Payment, §6-6-10.
Refusal to testify or deliver award until paid, §6-6-11.
Recovery by party not liable, §6-6-11.
Sheriffs, §6-6-10.
Witnesses, §6-6-10.
Refusal to testify until paid, §6-6-11.
Judge not to act as arbitrator, ACJE, Canon 5E.
Labor unions.
Local boards of arbitration, §§25-7-50 to 25-7-54.
Malpractice.
Settlement, §6-5-485.
Oaths.
Arbitrators, §§6-6-6, 6-6-7.

ARBITRATION AND AWARD —Cont'd

Single-tax and other mutual economic associations.
Disputes arising under real estate leases, §10-4-194.
Statement of dispute, §6-6-3.
Submission to arbitrators, §6-6-3.
Subpoena of witnesses, §§6-6-7 to 6-6-9.
Taxation.
Multistate tax compact, §40-27-1.
Unions.
Local boards of arbitration, §§25-7-50 to 25-7-54.
Witnesses.
List.
Delivery with submissions, §6-6-3.
Subpoena power, §§6-6-7 to 6-6-9.

ARCHAEOLOGY.
Aboriginal mounds, earthworks and other antiquities, §§41-3-1 to 41-3-6.
See HISTORY AND ARCHIVES.

ARCHITECTS, §§34-2-1 to 34-2-42.
Associations.
Professional corporations.
See PROFESSIONAL CORPORATIONS.
Unincorporated professional associations.
See UNINCORPORATED PROFESSIONAL ASSOCIATIONS.
Board of registration, §§34-2-38 to 34-2-42.
Appointment of members, §34-2-38.
Bylaws, §34-2-39.
Certificate of appointment, §34-2-39.
Chairman, §34-2-40.
Composition, §34-2-38.
Creation, §34-2-38.
Expenses of members, §34-2-41.
Fund of board, §34-2-41.
Meetings, §34-2-40.
Powers and duties, §34-2-39.
Qualifications of members, §34-2-38.
Reports, §34-2-42.
Rules and regulations.
Promulgation by board, §34-2-39.
Seal of board, §34-2-39.
Secretary, §34-2-40.
Terms of office, §34-2-38.
Vacancies, §34-2-38.
Certificate of registration, §§34-2-33, 34-2-34.
Compliance with chapter, §34-2-31.
Conservation and natural resources.
Buildings and facilities.
Contracts for architectural services, §9-2-42.
Construction of chapter, §34-2-31.

ARCHITECTS—Cont'd
Corporations.
Certificate of authorization, §34-2-35.
Renewal.
Fee, §34-2-35.
Practice of architecture, §34-2-37.
Professional corporations.
See PROFESSIONAL CORPORATIONS.
Declaration of legislative policy, §34-2-31.
Definitions.
Practice of architecture, §34-2-30.
Emeritus status architect, §34-2-33.
Certificate of registration.
Renewal, §34-2-33.
Employees.
Exemptions from chapter, §34-2-32.
Engineers.
Interprofessional privileges, §34-2-32.
Examinations.
Registration examination, §34-2-33.
Exemptions from chapter, §34-2-32.
Fees.
Registration fees, §34-2-33.
Funds.
Board of registration fund, §34-2-41.
Governor.
Board of registration.
Annual report to governor, §34-2-42.
Harbors and ports.
Acquisition and operation of wharves, docks, warehouses by state.
Consultation with architects, §33-1-12.
Director of state docks.
Appointment of architects, §33-1-5.
Injunction, §34-2-36.
Landscape architects, §§34-17-1 to 34-17-27.
See LANDSCAPE ARCHITECTS.
Licenses, §40-12-48.
Partnerships.
Certificates of authorization, §34-2-35.
Practice of architecture, §34-2-37.
Penalties.
Registration.
Registered architect's seal, §34-2-35.
Unlawful acts, §34-2-36.
Practice of architecture.
Defined, §34-2-30.
Partnerships, §34-2-37.
Registration, §§34-2-32 to 34-2-35.
Certificate of registration, §§34-2-33, 34-2-34.
Exemptions from requirements of chapter, §34-2-32.
Interprofessional privileges, §34-2-32.
Fees, §34-2-33.
Hearing.
Refusal to issue certificate, §34-2-34.

ARCHITECTS—Cont'd
 Registration—Cont'd
  Hearing—Cont'd
   Revocation or suspension of
    certificate, §34-2-34.
  Penalties.
   Registered architect's seal,
    §34-2-35.
  Qualifications of applicants,
   §34-2-33.
  Refusal to issue certificate,
   §34-2-34.
  Revocation or suspension of
   certificate, §34-2-34.
  Seals.
   Registered architect's seal,
    §34-2-35.
  Violations.
   Registered architect's seal,
    §34-2-35.
 Reports.
  Board of registration,
   §34-2-42.
 Seals.
  Board of registration.
   Seal of board, §34-2-39.
  Registered architect's seal,
   §34-2-35.
 **Unincorporated professional
  associations.**
  General provisions.
   See UNINCORPORATED
    PROFESSIONAL
    ASSOCIATIONS.
  Practice of architecture by
   associations, §34-2-37.
 Violations.
  Registration.
   Registered architect's seal,
    §34-2-35.

ARCHIVES.
 See HISTORY AND
  ARCHIVES.

ARMED FORCES.
 **General provisions, §§31-2-1
  to 31-2-133.**
  See MILITARY AFFAIRS.

**ARMORIES, §§31-4-1 to
 31-4-19.**
 Appropriations.
  Maintenance of armories,
   §31-4-19.
  Unexpended regular military
   appropriations.
   Disposition, §31-2-15.
 Armory boards, §31-4-15.
 **Armory commission, §§31-4-1
  to 31-4-19.**
  See MILITARY AFFAIRS.
 Athletic matches, §31-2-56.
 Bond issues.
  Counties.
   Public improvement bonds.
    See COUNTIES.
  Municipal corporations.
   Public improvement bonds.
    See MUNICIPAL
     CORPORATIONS.
 **Commission, §§31-4-1 to
  31-4-19.**
  See MILITARY AFFAIRS.
 Construction.
  Approval, inspection and
   supervision, §31-4-13.
 **Contests held in armories,
  §31-2-56.**
 Counties.
  Acquisition of lands,
   §11-18-2.

ARMORIES—Cont'd
 Counties—Cont'd
  Bond issues.
   Public improvement bonds.
    See COUNTIES.
  Cooperation of counties for
   acquisition of buildings,
   §31-4-9.
  Sale of real estate and
   buildings to local
   national guard,
   §31-2-130.
  Sites.
   Conveyance of public
    lands, §31-4-11.
 **Deposit of arms and
  equipment, §31-2-23.**
 **Designation by governor,
  §31-2-15.**
 **Disposition generally,
  §31-4-14.**
 **Exhibitions held in armories,
  §31-2-56.**
 Governor.
  Designation by governor,
   §31-2-15.
 Inspection, §31-4-13.
 Leases, §31-4-16.
 Maintenance.
  Appropriations, §31-4-19.
 **Management and care,
  §31-4-15.**
 Municipal corporations.
  Conveyance of public lands,
   §31-4-11.
  Cooperation for acquisition of
   buildings, §31-4-9.
  Public improvement bonds.
   See MUNICIPAL
    CORPORATIONS.
  Seal of real estate and
   buildings to local
   national guard,
   §31-2-130.
 Officers of control, §31-4-15.
 Public lands.
  Counties or municipalities.
   Conveyance of public
    lands, §31-4-11.
 Real property.
  Exemptions from taxation,
   §31-4-12.
 Renting armories, §31-4-15.
 Sale.
  Duties of armory commission,
   §31-4-16.
 Sites.
  Counties or municipalities.
   Conveyance of public
    lands, §31-4-11.
 Taxation.
  Exemption of property,
   §31-4-12.
 Use generally, §31-4-14.

ARMS.
 General provisions.
  See WEAPONS.

ARMY NATIONAL GUARD.
 See MILITARY AFFAIRS.

ARRAIGNMENT.
 Desertion and nonsupport.
  Representation prior to
   arraignment.
   Matters to be ascertained,
    §15-12-20.
 Indigent persons.
  Matters affecting
   representation to be
   ascertained before
   arraignment, §15-12-20.

ARRAIGNMENT—Cont'd
 Paternity.
  Representation prior to
   arraignment.
   Matters to be ascertained,
    §15-12-20.
 Preliminary hearings.
  General provisions, §§15-11-1
   to 15-11-15.
  See PRELIMINARY
   HEARINGS.
 Rules of criminal procedure.
  Necessity, ARCrP, Rule 19.
 Youthful offenders, §15-19-1.

ARREST, §§15-10-1 to 15-10-93.
 **Arrest before indictment,
  §§15-10-1 to 15-10-14.**
  Another county.
   Authority to pursue in
    another county,
    §15-10-11.
   Endorsement when
    executed in different
    county, §15-10-10.
  Appearance.
   When defendant taken
    before judge or
    magistrate, §15-10-12.
  Breaking and entering of
   dwelling house.
   Authority of officer,
    §15-10-1.
   Without warrant,
    §15-10-4.
   With warrant, §15-10-2.
  Capital felony.
   Notice to governor or chief
    justice, §15-10-8.
  Duty of arresting officer.
   Arrest without warrant,
    §15-10-4.
  Endorsement.
   Execution in different
    county, §15-10-10.
   Liability of judge or
    magistrate, §15-10-13.
   When warrant endorsed,
    §15-10-13.
  Escape.
   Rearrest, §15-10-9.
  Execution where warrant to
   be executed, §15-10-10.
  Goods held for sale.
   Person suspected of
    larceny, §15-10-14.
  Merchants.
   Detention and arrest of
    person suspected of
    larceny, §15-10-14.
  Notice.
   Capital felonies.
    Notice to governor or
     chief justice,
     §15-10-8.
  Officers authorized to make
   arrests, §15-10-1.
   Breaking and entering of
    dwelling house.
    Without warrant,
     §15-10-4.
    With warrant, §15-10-2.
  Presence of judge or
   magistrate.
   Offense committed in
    presence, §15-10-6.
  Private persons.
   Arrests by, §15-10-7.
  Pursuit in another county on
   warrant from municipal
   court, §15-10-11.

ARREST—Cont'd
Arrest before indictment
—Cont'd
Rearrest, §15-10-9.
Warrants.
Arrest without warrant.
Driving under the
influence, §32-5-171.
When authorized,
§15-10-3.
Breaking and entering of
dwelling house.
Without warrant,
§15-10-4.
With warrant, §15-10-2.
Execution.
When officer may
execute, §15-10-2.
Where warrant executed,
§15-10-10.
When defendant taken
before judge or
magistrate issuing,
§15-10-12.
Arrest in other counties,
§§15-10-70 to 15-10-74.
Application for removal
order, §15-10-71.
Duty of arresting officer,
§15-10-70.
Endorsement of removal
order, §15-10-72.
Fresh pursuit, §15-10-74.
Guard.
Prisoners charged with
misdemeanors,
§15-10-73.
Removal of prisoner,
§15-10-73.
Misdemeanors.
Guards for prisoners,
§15-10-73.
Removal order.
Application, §15-10-71.
Endorsement, §15-10-72.
Granting, §15-10-71.
Guards, §15-10-73.
Bail and recognizance.
After conditional judgment,
§15-13-63.
Discharge of bail by arrest
and surrender of
defendant, §15-13-62.
General provisions.
See BAIL AND
RECOGNIZANCE.
Bench warrants, §15-10-60.
Boats.
Fees of arresting officer,
§33-5-34.
Citizens' arrest, §15-10-7.
Civil defense.
Orders, rules and regulations
of governor.
Arrest for violating,
§31-9-15.
Complaints, §§15-7-1 to
15-7-4.
Arrest warrant.
Contents, §15-7-4.
Form, §15-7-4.
Issuance, §15-7-3.
Complainant.
Examination, §15-7-2.
Definitions, §15-7-1.
Warrant of arrest, §15-7-4.
Depositions, §15-7-2.
Examinations, §15-7-2.
Witnesses.
Examination of witnesses,
§15-7-2.

ARREST—Cont'd
Congress.
Arrest of members, Const. U.
S., Art. I, §6.
Privilege from, Const. U. S.,
Art. I, §6.
Constitution of Alabama,
Const. Ala., art. I, §7.
Militia.
Immunity of members,
Const. Ala., art. XV,
§275.
**Constitution of the United
States.**
Privilege from arrest, Const.
U. S., Art. I, §6.
Counties.
Arrest in other counties,
§§15-10-70 to 15-10-74.
Domestic violence.
Reports.
Whether or not arrest
made, §15-22-31.
Education.
Truancy, §16-28-17.
Elections.
Electors attending, going to
or returning from
elections, §17-1-6; Const.
Ala., art. VIII, §192.
Escape.
Rearrest, §15-10-9.
Extradition.
General provisions, §§15-9-1
to 15-9-88.
See EXTRADITION.
Fees.
Forests and forestry.
Arresting officers,
§9-13-24.
Fingerprinting, §§15-10-90,
15-10-91.
Fire marshal.
Power, §36-19-18.
Fish and game.
Violations, §§9-11-8, 9-11-12.
Force.
Resisting arrest prohibited,
§13A-3-28.
Use of force, §13A-3-27.
Forests and forestry.
Fees.
Arresting officers,
§9-13-24.
Fresh pursuit, §15-10-74.
Fugitives from justice.
Rewards.
Information leading to
arrest and conviction,
§15-9-1.
Gambling.
Gambling places.
Arrest of occupants,
§13A-12-56.
Municipal corporations,
§11-47-111.
Ginseng.
Enforcement of provisions,
§9-13-250.
Governor.
Notice of arrest.
Capital felony, §15-10-8.
History and archives.
Tannehill furnace and
foundry commission.
Police, §41-9-325.

ARREST—Cont'd
Indictments.
Arrest before indictment,
§§15-10-1 to 15-10-14.
See within this heading,
"Arrest before
indictment."
Defendant present after
indictment, §15-10-30.
Warrant of arrest twice
returned not found,
ARJA, Rule 16.
Jails.
Copy of arrest writ to be
delivered to jailer,
§15-10-46.
Larceny.
Goods held for sale.
Persons suspected of
larceny, §15-10-14.
Legislature.
Privilege from arrest,
§29-1-7.
Constitutional provisions,
Const. Ala., art. IV,
§56.
Libel and slander.
Reports of arrests.
Privileged information,
§13A-11-161.
Livestock.
Sanitary and disease control
laws.
Appearance upon arrest,
§2-2-14.1.
Theft.
Appearance upon arrest,
§2-2-14.1.
Magistrates.
District court magistrates
agency division.
Authority, ARJA, Rule 18.
Municipal court magistrates
agency division.
Authority, ARJA, Rule 18.
Marine resources, §§9-2-86,
9-12-3.
Merchants.
Persons suspected of larceny
of goods held for sale,
§15-10-14.
Military affairs.
Exemption of members of
militia, §31-2-79; Const.
Ala., art. XV, §275.
Militia.
Immunity of members,
§31-2-79; Const. Ala.,
art. XV, §275.
Motor vehicles.
See MOTOR VEHICLES.
Municipal corporations.
Gambling, §11-47-111.
Motor vehicle arrest.
Disposition of fines and
forfeitures,
§32-5A-10.
Police.
Summons and complaint in
lieu of arrest,
§11-40-10.1.
Municipal courts.
Warrants, §§12-14-4 to
12-14-32.
See MUNICIPAL
COURTS.
Parole.
Power of officers, §15-22-74.
Retaking of parolee without
warrant, §15-22-31.

ARREST—Cont'd
Peace bonds, §§15-6-21,
  15-6-22, 15-6-25.
Preliminary hearings,
  §§15-11-1 to 15-11-15.
  See PRELIMINARY
  HEARINGS.
Prisons and prisoners.
  Officers and guards.
  Escaped convicts, §14-3-15.
  Powers of arrest, §14-3-14.
Private persons.
  Arrests by, §15-10-7.
Privilege from arrest.
  Constitutional provision.
  Congress, Const. U. S.,
    Art. I, §6.
  Militia, §31-2-79; Const.
    Ala., art. XV, §275.
Probation.
  Violations of probation
    terms, §15-22-54.
Quarantine.
  Without warrants, §22-12-26.
Railway policemen.
  Powers of arrest, §37-2-153.
Records.
  Criminal justice information
    center, §§41-9-590 to
    41-9-648.
  See CRIMINAL LAW AND
    PROCEDURE.
Resisting arrest, §13A-10-41.
  Use of force, §13A-3-28.
Securities.
  Director.
  Warrants of arrest,
    §8-6-22.
  Securities commission.
  Warrants of arrest,
    §8-6-21.
Sex offenses.
  Reports.
  Failure to report arrest,
    §15-20-4.
  Law enforcement officers,
    §15-20-2.
Ships and shipping.
  Fees of arresting officer,
    §33-5-34.
Shoplifting, §15-10-14.
State parks.
  Deputy police officers, §9-2-9.
  Powers of director of division,
    §9-2-9.
Stores.
  Persons suspected of larceny
    of goods held for sale,
    §15-10-14.
**Tannehill furnace and
  foundry commission.**
  Police powers of commission,
    §41-9-325.
Taxation.
  Department of revenue.
  Agents and employees.
  Arrest fee, §40-2-10.
Trees and timber.
  Fees.
  Arresting officers,
    §9-13-24.
Truancy, §16-28-17.
**Unemployment
  compensation.**
  Fee, §25-4-147.
Warrants.
  Arrest before indictment,
    §§15-10-1 to 15-10-14.
  See within this heading,
    "Arrest before
    indictment."

ARREST—Cont'd
Warrants—Cont'd
  Bench warrants, §15-10-60.
  Coroner's inquests.
  Issuance and execution of
    warrant for accused,
    §15-4-9.
  Fish and game.
  Violations of laws,
    §§9-11-8, 9-11-12.
  Issuance upon complaint,
    §15-7-4.
  When issued, §15-7-3.
  Municipal courts, §§12-14-4,
    12-14-32.
  Return not found.
  Withdrawal and filing of
    indictments, ARJA,
    Rule 16.
Weights and measures.
  Power of commissioner and
    sealers, §8-16-11.
Writ of arrest, §§15-10-40 to
  15-10-46.
  Bail and recognizance.
  Amount to be endorsed on
    writ of arrest,
    §15-13-7.
  Execution, §15-10-44.
  Adjoining county,
    §15-10-45.
  Felony.
  Form of writ, §15-10-41.
  Form.
  Felony, §15-10-41.
  Misdemeanor, §15-10-42.
  Issuance, §15-10-40.
  Jailer.
  Delivery of copy of writ,
    §15-10-46.
  Misdemeanor.
  Form of writ, §15-10-42.
  Number of writs, §15-10-43.
  Return, §15-10-47.
  Sheriff.
  Execution of writ by
    sheriffs or deputy,
    §15-10-44.

ARSON, §§13A-7-40 to 13A-7-43.
Definitions, §13A-7-40.
Explosives and explosions.
  General provisions.
  See EXPLOSIVES AND
    EXPLOSIONS.
First degree arson.
  Class A felony, §13A-7-41.
  Elements of crime,
    §13A-7-41.
Force.
  Use of deadly physical force,
    §13A-3-25.
Indictments.
  Form, §15-8-150.
Insurance.
  Insurers suspecting.
  Notice to fire marshal or
    law-enforcement
    agency, §36-19-42.
Justification.
  Second degree arson,
    §13A-7-42.
  Third degree arson,
    §13A-7-43.
Limitations on prosecution,
  §15-3-5.
Second degree arson.
  Class B felony, §13A-7-42.
  Elements of crime,
    §13A-7-42.
  Justification, §13A-7-42.

ARSON—Cont'd
Third degree arson.
  Class A misdemeanor,
    §13A-7-43.
  Elements of crime,
    §13A-7-43.
  Justification, §13A-7-43.

ART.
Art commission, §§41-9-20 to
  41-9-22.
  Appointment of members,
    §41-9-21.
  Books, §41-9-22.
  Compensation, §41-9-21.
  Composition, §41-9-21.
  Creation, §41-9-20.
  Duties, §41-9-22.
  Employees, §41-9-22.
  Meetings, §41-9-22.
  Officers, §41-9-22.
  Powers, §41-9-22.
  Publications, §41-9-23.
  Qualifications of members,
    §41-9-21.
  Reports.
  Annual report to governor,
    §41-9-23.
  Rules and regulations,
    §41-9-22.
  Terms of members, §41-9-21.
Canons of judicial ethics.
  Permitted activities, ACJE,
    Canons 5A, 5G.
Commission, §§41-9-20 to
  41-9-22.
Council on the arts, §§41-9-40
  to 41-9-47.
  Advisors, §41-9-43.
  Appointment of members,
    §41-9-41.
  Assistance, §41-9-46.
  Compensation, §41-9-42.
  Composition, §41-9-41.
  Consultants, §41-9-43.
  Data, §41-9-46.
  Debts.
  Liability, §41-9-44.
  Duties, §41-9-45.
  Establishment, §41-9-41.
  Executive director, §41-9-43.
  Legislative findings,
    §41-9-40.
  Liability upon debts or
    obligations, §41-9-44.
  National foundation on the
    arts and humanities.
  Agency to receive funds
    from, §41-9-46.
  Obligations.
  Liability, §41-9-44.
  Officers, §41-9-42.
  Powers, §41-9-44.
  Public policy, §41-9-40.
  Qualifications of members,
    §41-9-41.
  Reappointment of members,
    §41-9-42.
  Reports, §41-9-47.
  Terms of members, §41-9-42.
  Vacancies, §41-9-42.
Counties.
  Art galleries.
  Acquisition of lands,
    §11-18-2.
  Establishment, §11-47-16.
Criminal simulation,
  §13A-9-10.

ART—Cont'd
Evidence.
Facts of general notoriety
and interest, §12-21-108;
ARCP, Rule 44 (g).
Income tax.
Art development fund.
Voluntary check-off
designations,
§§40-18-140,
40-18-141.
Judges.
Permitted activities, ACJE,
Canons 5A, 5G.
Municipal corporations.
Art galleries.
Establishment, §11-47-16.
**National foundation on the
arts and humanities.**
Council on the arts.
Agency to receive funds
from, §41-9-46.
Reports.
Art commission, §41-9-23.
Council on the arts, §41-9-47.
Rules and regulations,
§41-9-22.
Societies for promoting arts.
Corporations.
Public societies, §§10-4-20
to 10-4-26.
See CORPORATIONS.
**University of Alabama
museums,** §§16-47-190 to
16-47-204.
See UNIVERSITY OF
ALABAMA.

**ARTICLES OF
INCORPORATION.**
See CORPORATIONS.

**ARTIFICIAL
INSEMINATION.**
Livestock, §§2-30-60 to
2-30-62.
Parent and child.
Effect, §26-17-21.

ARTIFICIAL SWEETENERS.
Soft drinks, §20-1-28.

ASBESTOS.
Commencement of actions.
Injuries resulting from
exposure to asbestos,
§6-2-30.
Contractors accreditation,
§§22-39-1 to 22-39-5.
Accreditation agencies.
Safe-state program,
§22-39-4.
Certification of removal
projects, §22-39-5.
Penalties.
Violations, §22-39-5.
Citation of chapter.
Short title, §22-39-2.
Designing and publishing
accreditation plans.
Safe-state program,
§22-39-4.
Fees.
Safe-state program.
Authorized to charge,
§22-39-4.
Penalties.
Removal projects.
Violations of certification
requirements,
§22-39-5.
Purposes of chapter,
§22-39-1.

ASBESTOS—Cont'd
Contractors accreditation
—Cont'd
Removal projects.
Certification, §22-39-5.
Penalties.
Violations, §22-39-5.
Required.
Services requiring
accreditation, §22-39-3.
Safe-state program.
Certification of asbestos
removal projects,
§22-39-5.
Designated as accreditation
agency, §22-39-4.
Designing and publishing
accreditation plans.
§22-39-4.
Fees.
Authorized to charge,
§22-39-4.
Training periods.
Establishing and
publishing, §22-39-4.
Services requiring
accreditation, §22-39-3.
Short title, §22-39-2.
Title of chapter.
Short title, §22-39-2.
Training periods.
Safe-state program.
Establishing and
publishing, §22-39-4.
University of Alabama.
Safe-state program.
Designated as
accreditation agency,
§22-39-4.
Fees.
Contractors accreditation.
Safe-state program.
Authorized to charge,
§22-39-4.
Limitation of actions.
Injuries resulting from
exposure to asbestos,
§6-2-30.
Penalties.
Contractors accreditation.
Certification of removal
projects.
Violations, §22-39-5.
University of Alabama.
Contractors accreditation.
Safe-state program.
Division of university.
Designated
accreditation
agency, §22-39-4.

**ASHLAND, MUNICIPALITY
OF.**
Property tax, Const. Ala.,
amd. 8.

ASPHALT.
Plants.
Inspection prerequisite to
eligibility to bid on sale
of mix, §39-1-2.

ASSAULT AND BATTERY.
**Assault with intent to
ravish.**
Exclusion of persons from
courtroom, Const. Ala.,
art. VI, §169.
Complaint.
Form, ARCP, Form 17.
Criminal coercion, §13A-6-25.

ASSAULT AND BATTERY
—Cont'd
Education.
Reports of physical assaults
on students and school
personnel, §16-1-24.
Evidence.
Vulgar evidence.
Exclusion, §§12-21-9,
12-21-202.
First degree assault,
§13A-6-20.
Indictments.
Form, §15-8-150.
Limitation of actions, §6-2-34.
Menacing, §13A-6-23.
Military affairs.
Duty to disperse when shot
fired, etc., at national
guard, §31-2-121.
Assault on national guard
members, §31-2-119.
Protection of national guard
troops from assault,
§31-2-120.
Pleadings.
Form of complaint, ARCP,
Form 17.
Reckless endangerment,
§13A-6-24.
Second degree assault,
§13A-6-21.
Teachers.
Reports of assaults on
teachers, §16-1-24.
Third degree assault,
§13A-6-22.

ASSEMBLY.
Legislature.
See LEGISLATURE.
Peace officers.
Killing dogs used by peace
officers.
Violating section during
orderly demonstration.
Inapplicability of section,
§13A-11-15.
Right of assembly, Const.
Ala., art. I, §25.
Unlawful assembly,
§13A-11-5.
Failure of disorderly persons
to disperse, §13A-11-6.

ASSESSMENTS.
Appeals.
Taxation generally.
See TAXATION.
Attorneys at law.
Client security fund.
Fees, ACSF, Rule 8.
**Banks and financial
institutions,** §§5-2A-20,
5-2A-21.
Catfish.
Promotion of industry,
§§2-8-272 to 2-8-283.
See CATFISH.
Cemeteries.
County cemeteries, §§11-17-1
to 11-17-16.
See COUNTIES.
Condominiums.
Association, §35-8-9.
Liens, §35-8-17.
Special assessments,
§35-8-15.
Cotton.
Promotion of cotton products.
See COTTON.

ASSESSMENTS—Cont'd
  Counties.
    See COUNTIES.
  Dams.
    Erection of dams for mills,
      gins, factories or electric
      generators.
      See DAMS.
  Elections.
    Primary elections.
      Assessments and other
        qualifications for
        candidates, §17-16-15.
  Eminent domain, §18-1A-293.
  Estate and inheritance tax,
    §§40-15-6, 40-15-15.
  Forest fire protection,
    §§9-13-180 to 9-13-187.
    See FORESTS AND
      FORESTRY.
  Fruits and vegetables.
    Promotion of industry,
      §§2-8-124 to
      2-8-136.
    See FRUITS AND
      VEGETABLES.
  Income tax.
    See INCOME TAX.
  Insurers.
    Generally.
      See INSURANCE.
    Life and disability insurance
      guaranty association.
      See INSURANCE.
    Reciprocal insurers.
      Assessments on
        subscribers.
      See INSURANCE.
  Municipal corporations.
    Assessments for public
      improvements, §§11-48-1
      to 11-48-106.
    See MUNICIPAL
      CORPORATIONS.
    Sales and use taxes.
      See MUNICIPAL
      CORPORATIONS.
    Taxation.
      Assessment of property
        taxes.
      See MUNICIPAL
        CORPORATIONS.
  Public improvements.
    Municipal corporations.
      Assessments for public
        improvements,
        §§11-48-1 to 11-48-106.
      See MUNICIPAL
        CORPORATIONS.
  Sales tax.
    See SALES TAX.
  Savings and loan
    associations.
    Fees, §5-16-38.1.
  Taxation.
    Estate and inheritance tax,
      §§40-15-6, 40-15-15.
    General provisions.
      See TAXATION.
    Sales tax.
      See SALES TAX.

ASSETS.
  Banks.
    See BANKS AND
      FINANCIAL
      INSTITUTIONS.
  Corporations.
    See CORPORATIONS.

ASSETS—Cont'd
  Creditor's actions.
    Discovery of assets.
      See DEBTORS AND
        CREDITORS.
  Discovery of assets.
    Creditor's actions.
      See DEBTORS AND
        CREDITORS.
    Insurance guaranty
      association, §27-42-20.
  Insurers.
    See INSURANCE.
  Savings and loan
    associations.
    See SAVINGS AND LOAN
      ASSOCIATIONS.

ASSIGNATION.
  Nuisances.
    Lewdness, assignation or
      prostitution, §§6-5-140 to
      6-5-146.
    See NUISANCES.

ASSIGNED RISKS.
  Safety-responsibility act,
    §§32-7-1 to 32-7-42.
    See MOTOR VEHICLES.

ASSIGNMENTS.
  Actions.
    Endorsers or assignors on
      contracts assigned by
      writing and not covered
      by uniform commercial
      code, §§8-5-26 to 8-5-30.
    Applicability of provisions,
      §8-5-29.
    Costs, §8-5-30.
    Excused from bringing
      action, obtaining
      judgment, etc., §8-5-28.
    Execution.
      Issuance, §8-5-26.
    Judgment.
      Excuse from obtaining,
        §8-5-28.
      Inability of maker to
        pay.
        Proof, §8-5-26.
      Issuance of execution,
        §8-5-26.
    Time for bringing, §8-5-26.
      Extension or waiver,
        §8-5-27.
  Alcoholic beverages.
    Licenses, §28-3A-23.
    Table wine licenses, §28-7-14.
  Bills.
    Transfer of bill given for
      purchase money of lands.
      Effect, §8-5-24.
  Bonds.
    Assignable by endorsement,
      §8-5-20.
    Transfer of bond given for
      purchase money of lands.
      Effect, §8-5-24.
  Buildings.
    Liens for rent of buildings.
    Lien, rights and remedies
      vested in assignee,
      §35-9-65.
  Child support programs.
    Recipients of aid.
      Acceptance deemed
        assignment of right,
        §§38-10-4, 38-10-5.

ASSIGNMENTS—Cont'd
  Child support programs
    —Cont'd
    Support owed by parents to
      child.
    Child in custody of
      department or
      receiving maintenance
      payments.
      Assignment to
        department,
        §38-10-31.
  Commercial code.
    General provisions.
      See COMMERCIAL CODE.
    Secured transactions.
      See COMMERCIAL CODE.
  Consumer finance, §5-19-8.
  Contracts.
    Assignable by endorsement,
      §8-5-20.
    Endorsers or assignors on
      contracts assigned by
      writing and not covered
      by uniform commercial
      code. See within this
      heading, "Actions."
    Notice of assignment.
      Subject to payments,
        setoffs and discounts
        prior to, §8-5-25.
  Creditors.
    Assignments for benefit of.
      See ASSIGNMENTS FOR
        BENEFIT OF
        CREDITORS.
  Crops.
    Partition of crops, §35-6-126.
    Right to assign interest,
      §8-5-22.
  Endorsements.
    Bonds.
      Assignable by
        endorsement, §8-5-20.
    Contracts.
      Assignable by
        endorsement, §8-5-20.
    Endorsers or assignors on
      contracts assigned by
      writing and not covered
      by uniform commercial
      code. See within this
      heading, "Actions."
  Insurance.
    Policies, §27-14-21.
  Investment securities.
    Partial assignment, §7-8-308.
  Judgments.
    Endorsers or assignors on
      contracts assigned by
      writing and not covered
      by uniform commercial
      code. See within this
      heading, "Actions."
    Right of assignee to have
      execution, §6-9-196.
  Landlord and tenant.
    Liens for advances and rent
      of lands.
      Assignment of claim,
        §35-9-33.
    Liens for rent of buildings.
      Vesting in assignee of
        claim for rent,
        §35-9-65.
  Mechanics' and
    materialmen's liens,
    §35-11-233.

ASSIGNMENTS—Cont'd
  Motor vehicles.
    Uniform certificate of title
      and antitheft act.
      Security interests,
        §32-8-63.
  Notes.
    Transfer of note given for
      purchase money of lands,
      §8-5-24.
  Notice.
    Payments, setoffs and
      discounts prior to notice,
      §8-5-25.
  Paper circulated as money.
    Notice of assignment.
      Subject to payments,
        setoffs and discounts
        prior to, §8-5-25.
  Partition.
    Crops.
      Article applicable to
        assignees, §35-6-126.
  Partnerships, §§10-8-72,
    10-8-102.
    Limited partnerships.
      Assignment of partnership
        interest, §10-9A-121.
      Right to become limited
        partner, §10-9A-123.
    Partner's interest, §§10-8-41,
      10-8-72.
    Rights of assignees, §10-8-41.
  **Peace officers' annuity and
    benefit fund.**
    Benefits, annuities, etc., not
      subject, §36-21-77.
  Public utilities.
    Taxation.
      Duties of assignees,
        §40-21-33.
  Purchase money of lands.
    Transfer of bill, note, etc.,
      given for.
      Effect, §8-5-24.
  Radio utilities.
    Certificate of public
      convenience and
      necessity, §37-4-105.
  Railroads.
    Property injury claims,
      §8-5-23.
  Sales.
    Accounts.
      See COMMERCIAL CODE.
  Secured transactions.
    See COMMERCIAL CODE.
  Sewers.
    Liens for improvements on
      public sewers,
      §35-11-417.
  Streets.
    Liens for improvements on
      public streets,
      §35-11-417.
  **Trademarks and service
    marks.**
    Mark and registration,
      §8-12-11.
  **Unemployment
    compensation.**
    Assignment of right to
      benefits void, §25-4-140.
  Uniform commercial code.
    General provisions.
      See COMMERCIAL CODE.
    Secured transactions.
      See COMMERCIAL CODE.
  Veterans.
    Bonus for Southeast Asian
      war prisoners, §31-7-2.

ASSIGNMENTS—Cont'd
  Wages.
    Future wages, §8-5-21.
  Workmen's compensation.
    Acceptance of assignment of
      compensation claim,
      §25-5-231.
    Claims not to be assignable,
      §25-5-86.
    Pneumoconiosis.
      Assignment of benefits
        void, §25-5-179.

**ASSIGNMENTS FOR
BENEFIT OF
CREDITORS.**
  Bulk transfers.
    Transfers excepted from
      article, §7-6-103.
  Commercial code.
    Bulk transfers.
      Transfers excepted from
        article, §7-6-103.
    Secured transactions.
      Priority over unperfected
        security interests,
        §7-9-301.
  Deeds of assignment.
    Recordation, §35-4-57.
  Recordation.
    Deeds of assignment,
      §35-4-57.
  Secured transactions.
    Priority over unperfected
      security interests,
      §7-9-301.

ASSISTANCE.
  Aged persons.
    Medical assistance to elderly
      persons, §§38-6-1 to
      38-6-9.
    See AGED PERSONS.
  Blind persons.
    Assistance to needy blind
      persons, §§38-5-1 to
      38-5-7.
    See BLIND PERSONS.
  Counties.
    Relief and support of poor
      persons.
    See INDIGENT PERSONS.
  Social security.
    General provisions.
      See SOCIAL SECURITY.
    Public employees, §§36-28-1
      to 36-28-10.
  Welfare generally.
    See WELFARE.

ASSOCIATIONS.
  Accountants.
    Unincorporated professional
      associations.
    See ACCOUNTANTS.
  Actions.
    Commencement against,
      §6-7-81.
    Right to commence actions,
      §6-7-80.
    Officers.
      Liability of officers of
        nonprofit associations,
        §§10-11-1 to 10-11-5.
    Unincorporated associations.
      Actions relating to, ARCP,
        Rule 23.2.
  Agriculture.
    Marketing associations,
      §§2-10-20 to 2-10-74.
    See AGRICULTURE.

ASSOCIATIONS—Cont'd
  Agriculture—Cont'd
    Mutual farming or trucking
      associations, §§2-10-90 to
      2-10-108.
    See AGRICULTURE.
  Attorneys at law.
    State bar.
      See ATTORNEYS AT
        LAW.
  **Automobile clubs and
    associations,** §§27-39-1 to
    27-39-8.
    See INSURANCE.
  Aviation.
    Helicopter pilots association,
      §§4-9-1 to 4-9-7.
    See AVIATION.
  Bar association.
    State bar.
      See ATTORNEYS AT
        LAW.
  Charter.
    Granting.
      Special, private or local
        laws prohibited, Const.
        Ala., art. IV, §104.
  Churches.
    State conventions or
      associations of churches,
      §§10-4-60 to 10-4-63.
  Condominiums.
    See CONDOMINIUMS.
  Constitution of Alabama.
    Regulation of associations,
      Const. Ala., art. IV,
      §103.
  Corporations.
    General provisions, §§10-1-1
      to 10-7-4.
    See CORPORATIONS.
  Definitions.
    Liability of officers of
      nonprofit organizations,
      §10-11-2.
  Education.
    Association of school board
      members.
      Generally, §16-1-6.
    Teachers' retirement
      system.
      Eligibility, §16-25-10.1.
  Electric cooperatives,
    §§37-6-1 to 37-6-49.
    See ELECTRIC
      COOPERATIVES.
  Fraternal orders, §§10-4-170
    to 10-4-178.
    See FRATERNAL ORDERS.
  Helicopter pilots association,
    §§4-9-1 to 4-9-7.
    See AVIATION.
  Hospitals.
    Public hospital associations,
      §§22-21-50 to 22-21-57.
    See HOSPITALS.
  Immunity.
    Officers.
      Liability of officers of
        nonprofit associations,
        §§10-11-1 to 10-11-5.
  Insurance.
    Automobile clubs and
      associations, §§27-39-1 to
      27-39-8.
    See INSURANCE.
    Insurance guaranty
      association, §§27-42-1 to
      27-42-20.
    See INSURANCE.

ASSOCIATIONS—Cont'd
Insurance—Cont'd
Life and disability insurance guaranty association, §§27-44-1 to 27-44-21. See INSURANCE.
Mutual aid associations, §§27-30-1 to 27-30-33. See INSURANCE.
Interest.
Maximum rates of interest. Credit sales of $2,000 or more to associations, §8-8-5.
Loans of $2,000 or more to associations, §8-8-5.
Judgments.
Actions against unincorporated associations, §6-7-81.
Labor.
Unions and labor relations, §§25-7-1 to 25-7-25. See LABOR.
Liability of officers of nonprofit organizations, §§10-11-1 to 10-11-5.
Licenses.
Exemptions from licenses. Disabled veterans. Inapplicability to associations, §40-12-348.
Veterans of World War II. Inapplicability to associations, §40-12-375.
Literary or social societies.
Conveyances, §§35-4-340 to 35-4-344.
Merchants.
Retail merchants associations, §10-4-260.
Wholesale merchants associations, §10-4-280.
Motor vehicles.
Automobile clubs and associations, §§27-39-1 to 27-39-8. See INSURANCE.
Mutual aid associations.
General provisions, §§27-30-1 to 27-30-33. See INSURANCE.
Single-tax and other mutual economic associations, §§10-4-190 to 10-4-194.
Negligence.
Liability of officers of nonprofit associations, §§10-11-1 to 10-11-5.
Nonprofit corporations.
General provisions, §§10-3A-1 to 10-3A-225. See CORPORATIONS.
Nonprofit organizations.
Liability of officers, §§10-11-1 to 10-11-5.
Officers.
Liability of officers of nonprofit organizations, §§10-11-1 to 10-11-5.
Applicability of provisions, §§10-11-4, 10-11-5.
Definitions, §10-11-2.
Immunity from suit, §10-11-3.
Legislative intent, §10-11-1.
Scope of provisions, §§10-11-4, 10-11-5.

ASSOCIATIONS—Cont'd
Officers—Cont'd
Liability of officers of nonprofit organizations —Cont'd
Subsidiaries. For-profit subsidiary not immune, §10-11-3.
Willful misconduct. Exception to immunity from suit, §10-11-3.
Parties.
Actions against associations. Commencement, §§6-7-80, 6-7-81.
Satisfaction of judgment, §6-7-81.
Partnerships, §§10-8-1 to 10-8-103. See PARTNERSHIPS.
Professional corporations, §§10-4-380 to 10-4-406. See PROFESSIONAL CORPORATIONS.
Retail merchants associations, §10-4-260.
Savings and loan associations, §§5-16-1 to 5-16-53. See SAVINGS AND LOAN ASSOCIATIONS.
Service of process.
How served, ARCP, Rule 4 (c).
Single-tax and other mutual economic associations, §§10-4-190 to 10-4-194.
Social workers.
Professional associations, §34-30-31.
Taxation.
Exemptions from taxation. Association formed for social or literary advancement, §40-9-16.
Torts.
Liability of officers of nonprofit associations, §§10-11-1 to 10-11-5.
Unincorporated associations.
Actions relating to unincorporated associations, ARCP, Rule 23.2.
Unincorporated professional associations, §§10-10-1 to 10-10-16. See UNINCORPORATED PROFESSIONAL ASSOCIATIONS.
Unincorporated professional associations, §§10-10-1 to 10-10-16. See UNINCORPORATED PROFESSIONAL ASSOCIATIONS.
Wholesale merchants associations, §10-4-280.

ASSUMPTION OF RISK.
Affirmative defense, ARCP, Rule 8 (c).

ATHENS, MUNICIPALITY OF.
Property tax, Const. Ala., amd. 8.

ATHENS STATE COLLEGE.
Teachers retirement system.
Purchase of credit for total years of service rendered by employees participating in system, §16-25-13.1.

ATHLETICS.
Agents.
Sports. Generally, §§8-26-1 to 8-26-41. See SPORTS.
Athletic commission, §41-9-90.1.
General provisions.
See SPORTS.

ATMORE, MUNICIPALITY OF.
Property tax, Const. Ala., amd. 8.

ATOMIC ENERGY.
Compacts.
Southeast interstate low-level radioactive waste management compact, §§22-32-1 to 22-32-9.
Control.
State radiation control agency. See within this heading, "Radiation."
Counties.
Radiation. Effect of chapter on local ordinances, §22-14-15.
Definitions.
Radiation, §22-14-1.
Disposal of nuclear waste.
Nonconsent of state to acquisition of land by federal government, §22-14-16.
Electric generating facilities.
Employees, §§22-14-30 to 22-14-34.
Cost of implementing article, §22-14-35.
Equivalent background investigation sufficient, §22-14-34.
Fingerprints. Required, §22-14-31.
Submission of cards to FBI, §22-14-32.
Inquiry into employee's criminal history, §22-14-30.
Search of criminal records by department, §22-14-31.
Fees, §22-14-31.
Liability of department, §22-14-33.
Eminent domain.
Disposal of nuclear waste. Nonconsent of state to acquisition of land by federal government, §22-14-16.
Exposure to radiation.
Workmen's compensation. Occupational exposure to radiation, §§25-5-190 to 25-5-201. See WORKMEN'S COMPENSATION.

ATOMIC ENERGY—Cont'd
Fallout protection.
Public buildings.
Construction with
radioactive fallout
protection.
See PUBLIC WORKS.
Fees.
Employees.
Search of criminal records
by department,
§22-14-31.
Fingerprints.
Employees.
Electric generating
facilities, §§22-14-31,
22-14-32.
Governor.
Radiation.
Agreements with federal
government, §22-14-9.
Health.
Radiation, §§22-14-1 to
22-14-35. See within this
heading, "Radiation."
Inspections.
State radiation control
agency, §22-14-7.
Cooperative agreements,
§22-14-10.
Licenses.
Exemptions.
Nuclear fuel assemblies,
§40-9-22.
Radioactive materials. See
within this heading,
"Radiation."
**Low-level radioactive waste
generators,** §§22-14-20 to
22-14-22.
Municipal corporations.
Radiation.
Effect of chapter on local
ordinances, §22-14-15.
Ordinances.
Radiation.
Effect of chapter on local
ordinances, §22-14-15.
Penalties.
Radiation.
Violations, §22-14-14.
Public buildings.
Construction with radioactive
fallout protection,
§§39-6-1, 39-6-2.
Radiation, §§22-14-1 to
22-14-35.
Administrative action,
§22-14-11.
Advisory board of health,
§22-14-5.
Agreements with federal
government, §22-14-9.
By-product materials.
Defined, §22-14-1.
Compensation for
occupational exposure to
radiation.
See WORKMEN'S
COMPENSATION.
Declaration of policy,
§22-14-2.
Definitions,
§22-14-1.
Exposure to radiation.
Workmen's compensation.
Occupational exposure to
radiation, §§25-5-190
to 25-5-201.
See WORKMEN'S
COMPENSATION.

ATOMIC ENERGY—Cont'd
Radiation—Cont'd
Federal government.
Agreements with federal
government, §22-14-9.
Governor.
Agreements with federal
government, §22-14-9.
Impoundment.
Ionizing radiation sources,
§22-14-13.
Inspections, §22-14-7.
Cooperative agreements,
§22-14-10.
Ionizing radiation.
Defined, §22-14-1.
Impounding of sources,
§22-14-13.
Licenses.
Defined, §22-14-1.
Federal license.
Effect of agreements
with federal
government,
§22-14-9.
Persons dealing with
radioactive materials,
§22-14-6.
Orders directing compliance,
§22-14-12.
Ordinances.
Effect of chapter on local
ordinances, §22-14-15.
Penalty for violations,
§22-14-14.
Person.
Defined, §22-14-1.
Persons dealing with
radioactive materials.
Licensing or registration,
§22-14-6.
Public buildings.
Construction with
radioactive fallout
protection.
See PUBLIC WORKS.
Purpose of chapter, §22-14-3.
Records, §22-14-8.
Registration.
Persons dealing with
radioactive materials,
§22-14-6.
Reports, §22-14-8.
Right of entry, §22-14-7.
Rules and regulations,
§22-14-8.
Source materials.
Defined, §22-14-1.
Ionizing radiation sources.
Impounding, §22-14-13.
Southeast interstate low-
level radioactive waste
management compact,
§§22-32-1 to 22-32-9.
Special nuclear material.
Defined, §22-14-1.
State radiation control
agency.
Administrative action,
§22-14-11.
Director, §22-14-4.
Duties, §22-14-4.
Inspections, §22-14-10.
Judicial review of actions,
§22-14-11.
Powers, §22-14-4.
Rules and regulations,
§22-14-8.

ATOMIC ENERGY—Cont'd
Radiation—Cont'd
State radiation control
agency—Cont'd
State board of health
designated state
radiation control
agency, §22-14-4.
Training programs,
§22-14-10.
Training programs,
§22-14-10.
Violations of chapter,
§22-14-14.
Orders enjoining or
directing compliance,
§22-14-12.
Records.
Radiation, §22-14-8.
Reports.
Radiation, §22-14-8.
Rules and regulations.
Radiation, §22-14-8.
**Southeast interstate low-
level radioactive waste
management compact,**
§§22-32-1 to 22-32-9.
**Southern interstate nuclear
compact,** §§9-18-1 to
9-18-6.
Advisory committee, §9-18-1.
Board, §9-18-1.
Budget, §9-18-4.
Contracts with board of
control of employees
retirement system,
§9-18-3.
Member, §9-18-2.
Powers, §9-18-1.
Budget, §9-18-4.
Employees retirement
system.
Contracts of board of
control with board,
§9-18-3.
Enactment, §9-18-1.
Finances, §9-18-1.
Policy and purpose, §9-18-1.
State departments and
agencies.
Cooperation with board,
§9-18-6.
Supplementary agreements,
§9-18-1.
When effective, §9-18-5.
**Southern states energy
compact,** §§9-18A-1 to
9-18A-4.
**State radiation control
agency.** See within this
heading, "Radiation."
Taxation.
Exemptions.
Nuclear fuel assemblies,
§40-9-22.
United States.
Disposal of nuclear waste.
Nonconsent of state to
acquisition of land by
federal government,
§22-14-16.
Radiation.
Agreements with federal
government, §22-14-9.
Workmen's compensation.
Radiation.
Occupational exposure to
radiation, §§25-5-190
to 25-5-201.
See WORKMEN'S
COMPENSATION.

ATTACHMENTS.
 Actions.
  Actions by defendant,
   §§6-6-148, 6-6-149.
  Trial proceedings. See within
   this heading, "Trial
   proceedings."
 Adjoining counties.
  Execution of attachments,
   §15-10-45.
 Affidavits.
  Amendment, §6-6-143.
  Return, §6-6-53.
  Special facts and
   circumstances.
   Determination of amount
    of levy required,
    §6-6-46.
 Agriculture.
  Liens.
   Superintendents and
    laborers, §§35-11-92 to
    35-11-94.
 Amendments, §6-6-143.
 Ancillary attachments.
  Aid of pending action,
   §6-6-120.
  Dismissal of attachment,
   §6-6-121.
  Evasion of service of process
   by defendants, §6-6-121.
 Applicability of article.
  Private corporations, §6-6-30.
 Bills of lading.
  Attachment of goods covered
   by negotiable document,
   §7-7-602.
 Blacksmiths' liens,
  §35-11-111.
  Joinder, §35-11-112.
 Boats.
  Liens of owners of booms and
   bulkheads, §35-11-311.
 Bonds, surety.
  Action on attachment bond,
   §6-6-148.
  Amendments, §6-6-143.
  Execution by plaintiff,
   §6-6-45.
  Return of bond, §6-6-53.
 Booms and bulkheads.
  Liens of owners, §35-11-311.
 Buildings.
  Liens for rent of buildings,
   §§35-9-60 to 35-9-65.
 Bulk transfers.
  Limitation of levies,
   §7-6-111.
 Bulls.
  Liens of owners, §35-11-331.
 Business trusts.
  Property subject to
   attachment, §19-3-66.
 Circuit courts.
  Fees, §12-19-75.
  Issuance by judge or clerk,
   §6-6-43.
 Commercial code.
  Bank deposits and
   collections.
   When items subject to
    legal process, §7-4-303.
  Bulk transfers.
   Limitation of levies,
    §7-6-111.
  Documents of title.
   Attachment of goods
    covered by negotiable
    document, §7-7-602.

ATTACHMENTS—Cont'd
 Commercial code—Cont'd
  Investment securities.
   Levy upon security,
    §7-8-317.
  Secured transactions.
   Debtor's rights in
    collateral, §7-9-311.
 Complaint.
  Filing in actions begun by
   attachment.
   Default judgment,
    §6-6-141.
   Summons, §6-6-141.
   Time, §6-6-140.
 Constables.
  Service of attachments when
   office vacant, §36-23-8.
 Construction and
  interpretation, §6-6-143.
 Contempt.
  Attachments for contempt,
   §12-1-8.
 Contracts.
  Breach, §6-6-41.
 Corporations.
  Applicability to private
   corporations, §6-6-30.
  Domestic corporations.
   Right to process of
    attachment, §6-6-49.
  Foreign corporations,
   §§6-6-49 to 6-6-51.
 Cotton gins.
  Liens of owners, §35-11-291.
 Crops.
  Landlord and tenant.
   Advances and rent,
    §35-9-32.
  Liens of agricultural
   superintendents and
   laborers, §§35-11-91 to
   35-11-97.
  See AGRICULTURE.
  Liens of tenants in common,
   §35-11-351.
 Damages.
  Actions sounding in damages
   merely, §6-6-41.
 Debts.
  Collections, §6-6-41.
 Defendant.
  Action by defendant.
   Attachment bond for
    damages, §6-6-148.
   Venue, §6-6-149.
  Judgments.
   Suspending entry of
    judgment, §6-6-145.
 Discharge of levy, §6-6-45.
 District courts.
  Fees, §12-19-75.
  Issuance, §6-6-43.
 Execution.
  Endorsement of levy or
   service on writ, §6-6-70.
  Execution in any county,
   §6-6-73.
  Execution upon judgment by
   plaintiff, §6-6-147.
  Levy. See within this
   heading, "Levy."
  Sundays, §6-6-52.
 Executors and
  administrators.
  Judgments.
   Suspending entry of
    judgment against,
    §6-6-144.
  Right to commence, §6-6-47.

ATTACHMENTS—Cont'd
 Executors and
  administrators—Cont'd
  Settlements and
   distributions.
   Compelling settlement
    where authority
    ceased, §43-2-555.
 Exemptions from levy and
  sale under process.
  General provisions.
   See EXEMPTIONS FROM
    LEVY AND SALE
    UNDER PROCESS.
 Fees, §12-19-75.
 Form, §6-6-40.
 Fraternal benefit societies.
  Exemption of benefits, etc.,
   from attachment,
   §27-34-27.
 Fraudulent conveyances,
  §6-6-42.
 Garnishees.
  Proceedings with, §§6-6-70,
   6-6-71.
 Garnishment.
  General provisions.
   See GARNISHMENT.
 Habeas corpus.
  Compelling obedience of writ,
   §15-21-30.
 Hay.
  Liens of owners of bailing
   machines or presses,
   §35-11-291.
 Hearings.
  Sale of property levied on.
   Order for receipt of sale
    proceeds by plaintiff
    pending action,
    §6-6-78.
  Seizure of person or property.
   Procedure for seizure of
    property, ARCP, Rule
    64 (b).
 Insurers.
  Delinquency proceedings,
   §27-32-21.
 Investment securities.
  Levy upon security, §7-8-317.
 Issuance.
  Cases in which issued,
   §6-6-42.
  Matters for which issued,
   §6-6-41.
  Oath of plaintiff, §6-6-44.
  Sundays, §6-6-52.
  Who may issue, §6-6-43.
 Jacks.
  Liens of owners, §35-11-331.
 Joint tenants and tenants in
  common.
  Liens of tenants in common,
   §35-11-351.
 Judgments.
  Default judgments, §6-6-141.
  Execution upon judgment by
   plaintiff, §6-6-147.
  Suspending entry of
   judgment.
   Against defendant while
    claims settled,
    §6-6-145.
   Against executor or
    administrator,
    §6-6-144.

ATTACHMENTS—Cont'd

Landlord and tenant.
Liens for advances and rent of lands, §§35-9-30 to 35-9-42.
See LANDLORD AND TENANT.

Levy.
Discharge, §6-6-45.
Endorsement of levy or service on writ, §6-6-70.
Indemnification of sheriff, §6-6-80.
Joint or separate property, §6-6-72.
Notice.
Nonresident defendant, §6-6-81.
Resident defendant, §6-6-82.
Property on which attachments may be levied, §6-6-70.
Reduction of sum, §6-6-46.
Special facts and circumstances.
Additional affidavit, §6-6-46.

Liens.
See LIENS.

Livestock.
Liens of owners of stallions, jacks, bulls, etc., §35-11-331.

Lumber.
Employees' or laborers' liens, §35-11-273.
Sawmill owners' or operators' liens, §35-11-251.

Machinery liens.
Liens for production, manufacture or repair, §35-11-111.

Motor vehicle liens.
Production, manufacture or repair, §35-11-111.

Municipal corporations.
Licenses.
Collection of license taxes, §11-51-160.
Taxation.
Collection in anticipation of nonpayment, §11-51-26.

Nonresidents.
Issuance when defendant resides out of state, §6-6-42.
One nonresident against another, §6-6-48.
Security for costs, §6-6-50.

Notice.
Levy.
Nonresident defendant, §6-6-81.
Resident defendant, §6-6-82.
Sale of property levied on.
Order for receipt of sale proceeds by plaintiff pending action, §6-6-78.

Oaths.
Oath of plaintiff, §6-6-44.

Partnerships.
Exemption of partner's interest, §10-8-72.

Peace officers' annuity and benefit fund.
Benefits, annuities, etc., not subject, §36-21-77.

ATTACHMENTS—Cont'd

Peanuts.
Liens of owners of peanut machines or pickers, §35-11-291.

Plaintiff.
Bond.
Execution, §6-6-45.
Execution upon judgment, §6-6-147.
Indemnification of sheriff, §6-6-80.
Oath, §6-6-44.
Restoration of property to claimant at plaintiff's cost, §6-6-146.

Probate courts.
Issuance by judge, §6-6-43.

Public officers and employees.
State employees' retirement system.
Exemption of pension, annuity, etc., §36-27-28.

Railroad laborers' and employees' liens.
See RAILROADS.

Replevin of property.
General provisions.
See REPLEVIN.

Restitution to victims of crimes.
Employment income withholding order.
Authority to attach assets of defendant, §15-18-144.
Priority of orders, §15-18-150.

Rules of civil procedure.
Seizure of person or property.
Procedure for seizure of property, ARCP, Rule 64 (b).

Sale.
Perishables.
Proceedings against sheriff and sureties, §6-6-79.
Sale of property levied on where perishable, §6-6-77.
Proceeds.
Order for receipt by plaintiff pending action upon executing refunding bond, §6-6-78.

Sawmills.
Employees' or laborers' liens, §35-11-273.
Owners' or operators' liens, §35-11-251.

Searches and seizures.
Seizure of person or property, ARCP, Rule 64 (b).

Secured transactions.
Debtor's rights in collateral, §7-9-311.

Seeds.
Liens of owners of plants for drying or processing planting seeds, §35-11-291.

Sheriffs.
Holding of attached property, §6-6-73.
Levy.
Indemnification by plaintiff, §6-6-80.

ATTACHMENTS—Cont'd

Sheriffs—Cont'd
Sale of perishables.
Proceedings against sheriff for money received, §6-6-79.

Stallions.
Liens of owners, §35-11-331.

Stumpage.
Liens for stumpage, §35-11-21.

Sundays.
Issuance and execution, §6-6-52.

Trees and timber.
Liens for stumpage, §35-11-21.
Timber employees' or laborers' liens, §35-11-273.

Trial proceedings.
Complaint, §§6-6-140, 6-6-141.
Default judgments, §6-6-141.
Dismissal of attachment, §§6-6-142, 6-6-143.
Judgments. See within this heading, "Judgments."

Unemployment compensation.
Benefits.
Exemption, §25-4-140.
Delinquent contributions.
Procedures for collection, §25-4-134.

Venue.
Actions by defendant, §6-6-149.

Veterans.
Bonus for Southeast Asian war prisoners.
Attachments prohibited, §31-7-2.

Warehouse receipts.
Attachment of goods covered by negotiable document, §7-7-602.

Witnesses in adjoining counties, §12-21-183.

Woodworkmen's liens, §35-11-111.
Joinder, §35-11-112.

Workmen's compensation.
Exemption of claims, §25-5-86.
Pneumoconiosis.
Benefits exempt, §25-5-179.

Writs.
Alias writs, §6-6-75.
Branch writs, §6-6-74.
Endorsement, §6-6-70.
New writs of garnishment, §6-6-75.
Seizure of person or property.
Procedure for seizure of property.
Writs of seizure or attachment, ARCP, Rule 64 (b).

ATTAINDER.
Bill of attainder.
Constitutional provisions, Const. U. S., Art. I, §§9, 10; Art. III, §3.

ATTALLA, MUNICIPALITY OF.
Property tax, Const. Ala., amd. 31.

ATTEMPTS.
  Drugs.
    Controlled substances.
      Attempt to commit crime,
        §13A-12-203.
      Included offenses,
        §13A-12-205.
  Elements of crime, §13A-4-2.
  Impossibility of commission,
    §13A-4-2.
  Renunciation of criminal
    intent, §13A-4-2.
  Specific offenses
    enumerated, §13A-4-2.

ATTORNEY GENERAL.
  Actions.
    Legal proceedings in name of
      state.
      Institution and
        prosecution, §36-15-12.
    Litigation affecting state.
      Defense of suits against,
        Const. Ala., amd. 111.
      Direction and control,
        §36-15-21.
      Employment of attorneys,
        §36-15-21.
    Suits against states.
      Defense, Const. Ala., amd.
        111.
  Agriculture.
    Board of agriculture and
      industries.
      Legal advisor, §2-3-6.
  Alcoholic beverages.
    Dry counties.
      Instructions for
        enforcement of laws,
        §28-4-312.
  Armory commission.
    Member, §31-4-1.
  Assistant attorney general.
    Absence of attorney general.
      Assistants to act,
        §36-15-17.
    Appointment, §36-15-6.
    Bonds, §36-15-8.
    Highway department.
      Chief and assistant
        counsels.
        Commissioned as
          assistant attorneys
          general, §23-1-26.
    Insurance.
      Assignment to department
        of insurance, §27-2-11.
    Private practice.
      Prohibited, §36-15-9.
    Public service commission.
      Appointment as legal
        advisor to, §36-15-7.
  Attending criminal and civil
    proceedings in which
    state party, §12-3-32.
  Banks and financial
    institutions.
    Legal counsel for
      department, §5-2A-23.
  Bond, §36-15-2.
    Assistant attorneys general,
      §36-15-8.
  Charitable fraud.
    Enforcement of provisions,
      §13A-9-76.
  Claims against state.
    Defense of suits, Const. Ala.,
      amd. 111.
  Clerical assistants.
    Employment, §36-15-11.

ATTORNEY GENERAL
  —Cont'd
  Coal.
    Surface mining control and
      reclamation.
      Actions to suspend or
        revoke permit,
        §9-16-93.
  Commissions.
    Payment into state treasury,
      §36-15-4.
  Compensation, Const. Ala.,
    art. V, §118.
  Constitutional validity of
    statutes, ordinances, etc.,
    questioned.
    Notice to attorney general,
      §6-6-227; ARAP, Rule
      44.
  Constitution of Alabama.
    Compensation, Const. Ala.,
      art. V, §118.
    Defending suits against
      state, etc., Const. Ala.,
      amd. 111.
    Duties, Const. Ala., art. V,
      §137; amd. 111.
    Executive department.
      Member, Const. Ala., art.
        V, §112.
    Fees.
      Restrictions on receipt,
        Const. Ala., art. V,
        §137; amd. 111.
    Mental unsoundness, Const.
      Ala., art. V, §136.
    Qualifications, Const. Ala.,
      art. V, §132.
    Residency requirements,
      Const. Ala., art. V, §118.
    Succession.
      Ineligible to succeed self,
        Const. Ala., art. V,
        §116.
      One additional term,
        Const. Ala., amd. 282.
    Term of office, Const. Ala.,
      art. V, §116; amd. 282.
    Vacancy in office, Const.
      Ala., art. V, §136.
    Validity of statutes,
      ordinances, etc.,
      questioned.
      Notice to attorney general,
        §6-6-227; ARAP, Rule
        44.
  Counties.
    Defense of actions against,
      Const. Ala., amd. 111.
    Duty to give opinions,
      §36-15-18.
      Certificate of officer,
        §36-15-20.
      Moot or private questions
        not submitted,
        §36-15-20.
      Written opinion protects
        officer, etc., §36-15-19.
  Court of civil appeals.
    Attending civil suits where
      state party, §12-3-32.
  Court of criminal appeals.
    Attending criminal cases
      where state party,
      §12-3-32.
  Criminal cases.
    Direction of prosecution,
      §36-15-14.
  Deceptive trade practices.
    Powers and duties, §8-19-4.

ATTORNEY GENERAL
  —Cont'd
  Department of examiners of
    public accounts.
    Legal assistance, §41-5-11.
  Deputy attorney general,
    §36-15-5.
  Director of forensic sciences.
    Appointment, §36-18-1.
  District attorneys.
    Advising, §36-15-15.
  Duties, §36-15-1; Const. Ala.,
    art. V, §137; amd. 111.
  Elections.
    Fair campaign practices.
      Prosecution of violations,
        §17-22A-22.
  Environmental management
    department.
    Powers not affected by
      chapter, §22-22-13.
    Representation of
      department, §22-22A-5.
  Executive assistant,
    §36-15-10.
  Executive department.
    Member of department,
      Const. Ala., art. V, §112.
  Expenses, §36-15-16.
  Fees.
    Criminal cases, §12-19-190.
    Payment into state treasury,
      §36-15-4.
    Restrictions on receipt,
      Const. Ala., art. V, §137;
      amd. 111.
  Forests and forestry.
    State forests.
      Gifts of land.
        Duties, §9-13-1.
  Foundations.
    Powers not impaired,
      §10-4-210.
  Fraud.
    Charitable fraud.
      Enforcement of provisions,
        §13A-9-76.
  Grand juries.
    Appearance before,
      §36-15-13.
  Highways.
    Department.
      Chief and assistant
        counsels.
        Commissioned as
          assistant attorneys
          general, §23-1-26.
    Finance corporation.
      Vice-president, §23-1-174.
  Impeachment, Const. Ala.,
    art. VII, §173.
    Duty to institute and
      prosecute proceedings,
      §36-11-4.
    General provisions.
      See IMPEACHMENT.
  Insurance.
    Assistant attorney general.
      Assignment to department,
        §27-2-11.
    Enforcement of code,
      §27-2-19.
  Local government records
    commission.
    Member, §41-13-22.
  Mental unsoundness, Const.
    Ala., art. V, §136.
  Military affairs.
    Armory commission.
      Member, §31-4-1.

ATTORNEY GENERAL
—Cont'd

Military affairs—Cont'd

Arms and equipment.

Proceedings when soldiers unable to account for property or money, §31-2-34.

Motor vehicles.

Safety coordinating committee. Member, §32-3-1.

Municipal corporations.

Defense of actions against, Const. Ala., amd. 111.

Duty to give opinions to officers, §36-15-18.

Certificate requesting, §36-15-20.

Moot or private questions, §36-15-20.

Resolution required, §36-15-20.

Written opinion protects officer, §36-15-19.

Ordinance or franchise unconstitutional.

Entitled to be heard, §6-6-227.

Service upon attorney general, §6-6-227; ARAP, Rule 44.

Notice.

Constitutional validity of ordinances, etc., questioned.

Attorney general to be notified, §6-6-227; ARAP, Rule 44.

Oath of office.

General provisions, §§36-4-1 to 36-4-7.

See PUBLIC OFFICERS AND EMPLOYEES.

Obscenity.

Anti-obscenity enforcement act.

Injunctive relief, §13A-12-200.7.

Forfeiture actions, §13A-12-200.8.

Opinions.

Certificate of officer requesting, §36-15-20.

Duty to give, §36-15-18.

Moot or private questions, §36-15-20.

Written opinion protects officer, governing body, etc., §36-15-19.

Ordinances.

Constitutionality questioned.

Notice to attorney general, §6-6-227; ARAP, Rule 44.

Pharmacists and pharmacies.

Board of pharmacy.

Counsel to board, §34-23-93.

Protection of certain state officers and visitors.

General provisions, §§36-33-1 to 36-33-4.

Public officers generally, §§36-1-1 to 36-33-4.

See PUBLIC OFFICERS AND EMPLOYEES.

Public service commission.

Appointment of assistant as legal advisor, §36-15-7.

ATTORNEY GENERAL
—Cont'd

Public service commission
—Cont'd

Consumers.

Assistant representing consumers before commission, §37-1-16.

Representing commission, §37-1-64.

Special counsel.

Employment, §37-1-64.

Qualifications, Const. Ala., art. V, §132.

Railroads.

Noncompliance with commission order.

Civil action, §37-2-113.

Failure of commission to notify, §37-8-111.

Records.

Local government records commission.

Member, §41-13-22.

Residency requirements, Const. Ala., art. V, §118.

Safety coordinating committee.

Member, §32-3-1.

Salary, §36-15-3.

Sales tax.

Violations.

Injunctions, §40-23-27.

Speech pathologists and audiologists.

Assistance in enforcement, §34-28A-4.

State parks.

Concessions within park areas.

Approval of contracts for maintenance and operation, §9-14-28.

State records commission.

Member, §41-13-20.

Statutes unconstitutional.

Allegations entitled to be heard, §6-6-227.

Notice to attorney general, §6-6-227; ARAP, Rule 44.

Served with copy of proceedings, §6-6-227.

Stenographers.

Appointment, §36-15-6.

Subpoenas, §36-15-13.

Succession.

Ineligible to succeed self, Const. Ala., art. V, §116.

Supreme court library fund.

Use for purchase of law books, §12-2-158.

Use tax.

Delinquent taxes.

Actions to collect, §40-23-86.

Vacancy in office, Const. Ala., art. V, §136.

Welfare.

Child care facilities.

Operating without license.

Report for prosecution, §38-7-10.

ATTORNEYS AT LAW.

Accountants.

Hearings before board.

Accused entitled to counsel, §34-1-14.

Attorney for the board, §34-1-14.

ATTORNEYS AT LAW—Cont'd

Acknowledgments.

Powers of attorney, §35-4-28.

Actions.

Legal services liability, §§6-5-570 to 6-5-581. See within this heading, "Legal services liability."

Alabama law institute, §§29-8-1 to 29-8-5.

Appeals.

Disciplinary proceedings.

Rules of disciplinary enforcement.

Appeals to supreme court, ARDE, Rule 8.

Roll of attorneys, ARAP, Rule 46.

Appearance.

Without authority, §§34-3-22, 34-3-23.

Appointed counsel.

Defense of indigents, §§15-12-1 to 15-12-25.

See INDIGENT PERSONS.

Post-conviction remedies, ARCrP, Rule 20.7 (c).

Public defenders, §§15-12-40 to 15-12-46.

See PUBLIC DEFENDERS.

Arbitration and award.

Legal services liability.

Settlement of disputes by voluntary arbitration, §6-5-575.

Assessments.

Client security fund.

Fees, ACSF, Rule 8.

Associations.

Bar associations. See within this heading, "State bar."

Professional corporations.

See PROFESSIONAL CORPORATIONS.

Unincorporated professional associations.

See UNINCORPORATED PROFESSIONAL ASSOCIATIONS.

Attorney general.

See ATTORNEY GENERAL.

Auctions and auctioneers.

Board of auctioneers.

Legal assistance, §34-4-51.

Authority.

Generally, §34-3-21.

Bar association. See within this heading, "State bar."

Board of commissioners, §§34-3-40 to 34-3-44.

Annual meeting, §34-3-16.

Board of examiners.

Authority to establish, §34-3-2.

Building foundation, §§34-3-101 to 34-3-108.

See within this heading, "State bar."

Compensation, §34-3-44.

Composition, §34-3-40.

Disciplinary proceedings against attorneys. See within this heading, "Disciplinary proceedings."

Election, §34-3-41.

Established, §34-3-40.

Fund, §34-3-44.

Nominations, §34-3-42.

Powers, §34-3-43.

ATTORNEYS AT LAW—Cont'd
Board of commissioners
—Cont'd
Rules and regulations,
§34-3-43.
State bar building
foundation, §§34-3-100 to
34-3-108. See within this
heading, "State bar."
Terms, §34-3-40.
Vice president, §34-3-16.
Board of examiners.
Authority of commissioners
to establish, §34-3-2.
Bribery.
Commercial bribery,
§13A-11-120.
Buildings.
State bar building
foundation. See within
this heading, "State bar."
Canons of judicial ethics.
Disciplinary measures.
Judge to take or initiate,
ACJE, Canon 3B.
Practice of law.
Judge not to practice law,
ACJE, Canon 5F.
Capital punishment.
Appointment of counsel for
indigents, §13A-5-54.
Champerty, §34-3-24.
Child abuse or neglect.
Appointment of attorney,
§26-14-11.
Clerks of court.
Attorneys not deemed
sufficient sureties on
official bond, §36-5-13.
Practice of law before court
prohibited, §34-3-8.
Register or clerk of circuit
court, §§34-3-10,
34-3-14.
Client security fund.
Actions.
Subrogation and amount of
reimbursement, ACSF,
Rule 10.
Assessments.
Fees, ACSF, Rule 8.
Effect of failure to pay,
ACSF, Rule 17.
Assumption of risk or loss.
Person, firm or association
compensated for.
Reimbursement
prohibited, ACSF,
Rule 15.
Attorneys' fees.
Prohibited, ACSF, Rule 12.
Claimants.
Defined, ACSF, Rule 2.
Committee.
Appointment, ACSF, Rule
4.
Chairman, ACSF, Rule 4.
Compensation, ACSF, Rule
4.
Composition, ACSF, Rule
4.
Conflict of interest, ACSF,
Rule 13.
Defined, ACSF, Rule 2.
Duties, ACSF, Rule 6.
Expenses, ACSF, Rule 4.
Immunity, ACSF, Rule 14.
Meetings, ACSF, Rule 5.
Members, ACSF, Rule 4.
Processing applications,
ACSF, Rule 7.

ATTORNEYS AT LAW—Cont'd
Client security fund—Cont'd
Committee—Cont'd
Quorum, ACSF, Rule 5.
Reports, ACSF, Rule 6.
Responsibilities, ACSF,
Rule 6.
Rules of procedure, ACSF,
Rule 6.
Secretary, ACSF, Rule 4.
Terms of office, ACSF,
Rule 4.
Treasurer, ACSF, Rule 15.
Vacancies, ACSF, Rule 4.
Confidentiality of
applications, proceedings
and reports, ACSF, Rule
11.
Conflict of interest, ACSF,
Rule 13.
Construction and
interpretation.
Severability of rules,
ACSF, Rule 16.
Definitions, ACSF, Rule 2.
Disciplinary proceedings.
Rules of disciplinary
enforcement.
Suspension for
noncompliance with
rules, ARDE, Rule 3.
Dishonest conduct.
Defined, ACSF, Rule 2.
Reimbursement for loss or
damage resulting from,
ACSF, Rule 15.
Fees.
Assessments, ACSF, Rule
8.
Effect of failure to pay,
ACSF, Rule 17.
Attorneys' fees.
Prohibited, ACSF, Rule
12.
Immunity.
Committee, ACSF, Rule
14.
Incompetence.
Reimbursement for loss or
damage resulting from,
ACSF, Rule 15.
Limitation on payment of
claims, ACSF, Rule 9.
Malpractice.
Reimbursement for loss or
damage resulting from,
ACSF, Rule 15.
Non-reimbursable losses.
Defined, ACSF, Rule 2.
Payment of claims.
Duty of committee, ACSF,
Rule 6.
Limitation on payment,
ACSF, Rule 9.
Maximum amount, ACSF,
Rule 9.
Reimbursable losses.
Defined, ACSF, Rule 2.
Reimbursement, ACSF, Rule
3.
Confidentiality, ACSF,
Rule 11.
Contents, ACSF, Rule 3.
Filing, ACSF, Rule 3.
Form, ACSF, Rule 3.
Processing, ACSF, Rule 7.
Service upon lawyer,
ACSF, Rule 3.
Reports.
Committee, ACSF, Rule 6.

ATTORNEYS AT LAW—Cont'd
Client security fund—Cont'd
Restitution.
Prosecution of claims for.
Duty of committee,
ACSF, Rule 6.
Rules of procedure.
Committee, ACSF, Rule 6.
Scope of rules, ACSF, Rule 1.
Severability of rules, ACSF,
Rule 16.
Subrogation, ACSF, Rule 10.
Suspension.
Effect of failure to pay
assessed fees, ACSF,
Rule 17.
Compensation.
Receiving compensation from
attorney, §34-3-25.
**Confidentiality of
information.**
Client security fund.
Applications for
reimbursement, ACSF,
Rule 11.
Conflicts of interest.
Client security fund.
Committee, ACSF, Rule
13.
Conservators.
Settlements of accounts of
guardians.
Fees, §26-5-13.
Conspiracy.
Practicing law without
license.
Conspiring in violation,
§34-3-7.
Constables.
Attorneys not deemed
sufficient sureties on
official bonds, §36-5-13.
**Constitution of the United
States.**
Right to have counsel, Const.
U. S., Amendment VI.
Consumer finance.
Contractual provisions for
fees, §5-19-10.
Contempt.
Appeal to appellate court,
§12-1-11.
Continuing legal education.
Rules. See within this
heading, "Rules for
mandatory continuing
legal education."
Conviction of crime.
Disciplinary proceedings,
ARDE, Rule 14.
Coroners.
Attorneys not deemed
sufficient sureties,
§36-5-13.
Corporations.
Professional corporations.
See PROFESSIONAL
CORPORATIONS.
Court appointed counsel.
Defense of indigents,
§§15-12-1 to 15-12-25.
See INDIGENT PERSONS.
Court of criminal appeals.
Staff attorneys, §12-3-35.
Credit union administration.
Employment of attorneys and
special counsel, §5-17-50.
Criminal procedure.
Counsel for accused, Const.
U. S., Amendment VI.

ATTORNEYS AT LAW—Cont'd
Death.
Appointment of counsel to protect client's interests, ARDE, Rule 21.
Definitions.
Client security fund, ACSF, Rule 2.
Legal services liability, §6-5-572.
Practice of law, §34-3-6.
Depositions.
Disciplinary proceedings, ARDE, Rule 13.
Disability.
Disciplinary proceedings. See within this heading, "Disciplinary proceedings."
Disappearance.
Appointment of counsel to protect client's interests, ARDE, Rule 21.
Disbarment. See within this heading, "Disciplinary proceedings."
Disciplinary proceedings.
Admonition.
Private informal admonition, ARDE, Rule 3.
Appeals.
Perfection of appeal, ARDE, Rule 18.
Reinstatement, ARDE, Rule 19.
Rejection of tendered conditional guilty plea, ARDE, Rule 16.
Supreme court, ARDE, Rule 8.
Approval of rules and regulations by court, §34-3-81.
Assignment of cases, ARDE, Rule 5.
Censure.
Public censure, ARDE, Rule 3.
Client security fund.
Suspension for noncompliance with, ARDE, Rule 3.
Complainants.
Refusal to proceed, compromise, etc., ARDE, Rule 10.
Conditional guilty plea, ARDE, Rule 16.
Confidentiality, ARDE, Rule 22.
Continuing legal education.
Mandatory rules.
Suspension for noncompliance with, ARDE, Rule 3.
Conviction of crime, ARDE, Rule 14.
Death.
Appointment of counsel to protect client's interests, ARDE, Rule 21.
Depositions, ARDE, Rule 13.
Disappearance.
Appointment of counsel to protect client's interests, ARDE, Rule 21.
Disciplinary board of state bar, ARDE, Rule 4.

ATTORNEYS AT LAW—Cont'd
Disciplinary proceedings —Cont'd
Disciplinary commission, ARDE, Rule 6.
Discovery, ARDE, Rule 13.
Evidence.
Power of subpoena, §34-3-82.
Right of accused member to introduce evidence, §34-3-83.
Fees.
Payment of witnesses, §34-3-84.
Formal charges.
Conditional guilty plea, ARDE, Rule 16.
Filing and service, ARDE, Rule 12.
Time limit, ARDE, Rule 23.
General counsel for state bar.
Investigation by, ARDE, Rule 8.
Powers and duties, ARDE, Rule 7.
Grievance committee.
Failure to submit report within one year, ARDE, Rule 8.
Formal charges by, ARDE, Rule 8.
Investigation by, ARDE, Rule 8.
Records, ARDE, Rule 8.
Grounds for discipline, ARDE, Rule 2.
Hearings, ARDE, Rule 8.
Immunity, ARDE, Rule 9.
Incompetence or incapacity, ARDE, Rule 20.
Appointment of counsel to protect client's interests, ARDE, Rule 21.
Initiation of proceedings, §34-3-89.
Investigations.
General counsel, ARDE, Rule 8.
Grievance committee, ARDE, Rule 8.
Jurisdiction.
Rules of disciplinary enforcement, ARDE, Rule 1.
Limitation of actions, ARDE, Rule 23.
Nonresidents.
Reciprocal discipline, ARDE, Rule 17.
Notice.
Charges, §34-3-83.
Reinstatement, ARDE, Rule 19.
Suspension or disbarment, ARDE, Rule 18.
Oaths and affirmations, ARDE, Rule 13.
Pending civil or criminal litigation, ARDE, Rule 11.
Plea bargaining, ARDE, Rule 16.
Pre-trial proceedings, ARDE, Rule 13.
Procedure generally, §34-3-80.

ATTORNEYS AT LAW—Cont'd
Disciplinary proceedings —Cont'd
Prosecution counsel.
Appointment by board of commissioners, §34-3-80.
Reciprocal discipline, ARDE, Rule 17.
Records.
Confidentiality, ARDE, Rule 22.
Disbarment on consent, ARDE, Rule 15.
Expungement of records, ARDE, Rule 8.
Grievance committee, ARDE, Rule 8.
Maintenance by attorney, ARDE, Rule 18.
Proceedings to be recorded, §34-3-85.
Reinstatement, ARDE, Rule 19.
Disabled attorneys, ARDE, Rule 20.
Removal or suspension of attorney, ARDE, Rule 3.
Appointment of counsel to protect client's interests, ARDE, Rule 21.
Causes, §§34-3-86, 34-3-87.
Cumulative, §34-3-88.
Clien security fund rules.
Noncompliance with, ARDE, Rule 3.
Conditional guilty plea, ARDE, Rule 16.
Conduct during suspension, ARDE, Rule 16.
Consent by attorney to disbarment, ARDE, Rule 15.
Consent by attorney to discipline, ARDE, Rule 16.
Fixed period of time, ARDE, Rule 3.
Notice to clients, ARDE, Rule 18.
Publication of notice, ARDE, Rule 18.
Order of disbarment on consent, ARDE, Rule 15.
Orders of suspension or disbarment, ARDE, Rule 18.
Reinstatement, ARDE, Rule 19.
Rules for mandatory continuing legal education.
Noncompliance, ARDE, Rule 3.
Temporary suspension, ARDE, Rule 3.
Reprimand.
Private reprimand, ARDE, Rule 3.
Rights of accused member, §34-3-83.
Rules and regulations.
Approval by court, §34-3-81.
Establishment, §34-3-80.

ATTORNEYS AT LAW—Cont'd
Disciplinary proceedings
—Cont'd
Rules of disciplinary
  enforcement.
Admonition.
  Private informal
    admonition, ARDE,
    Rule 3.
Appeals.
  Perfection of appeal,
    ARDE, Rule 18.
  Reinstatement, ARDE,
    Rule 19.
  Rejection of tendered
    conditional guilty
    plea, ARDE, Rule
    16.
  Supreme court, ARDE,
    Rule 8.
Assignment of cases,
  ARDE, Rule 5.
Censure.
  Public censure.
    Type of discipline,
      ARDE, Rule 3.
Client security fund rules.
  Suspension for
    noncompliance with,
    ARDE, Rule 3.
Complainants.
  Refusal to proceed,
    compromise, etc.,
    ARDE, Rule 10.
Confidentiality, ARDE,
  Rule 22.
Consent of attorney.
  Disbarment, ARDE, Rule
    15.
  Discipline, ARDE, Rule
    16.
Continuing legal
  education.
  Noncompliance with
    mandatory rule.
    Suspension for, ARDE,
      Rule 3.
Conviction of crime,
  ARDE, Rule 14.
Death.
  Appointment of counsel
    to protect client's
    interests, ARDE,
    Rule 21.
Depositions, ARDE, Rule
  13.
Disappearance.
  Appointment of counsel
    to protect client's
    interests, ARDE,
    Rule 21.
Disbarment.
  Appointment of counsel
    to protect client's
    interests, ARDE,
    Rule 21.
  Consent, ARDE, Rule 15.
  Notice of disbarment.
    Publication, ARDE,
      Rule 18.
  Order of disbarment,
    ARDE, Rule 18.
  Reinstatement, ARDE,
    Rule 19.
  Type of discipline,
    ARDE, Rule 3.
Disciplinary board of state
  bar, ARDE, Rule 4.
Formal hearing, ARDE,
  Rule 8.

ATTORNEYS AT LAW—Cont'd
Disciplinary proceedings
—Cont'd
Rules of disciplinary
  enforcement—Cont'd
Disciplinary commission,
  ARDE, Rule 6.
Discovery, ARDE, Rule 13.
Effective date of rules,
  ARDE, Rule 24.
Evidence.
  Subpoena of evidence,
    §34-3-82.
Expungement of records,
  ARDE, Rule 8.
Formal charges.
  Conditional guilty plea,
    ARDE, Rule 16.
  Filing and service,
    ARDE, Rule 12.
  Time limit, ARDE, Rule
    23.
General counsel for state
  bar.
  Investigation by, ARDE,
    Rule 8.
  Powers and duties,
    ARDE, Rule 7.
Grievance committee.
  Failure to submit report
    within one year,
    ARDE, Rule 8.
  Formal charges by,
    ARDE, Rule 8.
  Investigation by, ARDE,
    Rule 8.
  Records, ARDE, Rule 8.
Grounds for discipline,
  ARDE, Rule 2.
Guilty plea.
  Conditional guilty plea,
    ARDE, Rule 16.
Hearings.
  Formal hearing, ARDE,
    Rule 8.
Immunity, ARDE, Rule 9.
Incapacity.
  Appointment of counsel
    to protect client's
    interests, ARDE,
    Rule 21.
  Proceedings where
    attorney alleged to
    be incapacitated,
    ARDE, Rule 20.
Incompetence.
  Appointment of counsel
    to protect client's
    interests, ARDE,
    Rule 21.
  Proceedings where
    attorney declared
    incompetent, ARDE,
    Rule 20.
Investigations.
  General counsel, ARDE,
    Rule 8.
  Grievance committee,
    ARDE, Rule 8.
Jurisdiction, ARDE, Rule
  1.
Limitation of actions,
  ARDE, Rule 23.
Nonresidents.
  Reciprocal discipline,
    ARDE, Rule 17.
Notice.
  Reinstatement, ARDE,
    Rule 19.

ATTORNEYS AT LAW—Cont'd
Disciplinary proceedings
—Cont'd
Rules of disciplinary
  enforcement—Cont'd
Notice—Cont'd
  Suspension or
    disbarment, ARDE,
    Rule 18.
Oaths and affirmations,
  ARDE, Rule 13.
Pending civil or criminal
  litigation.
  Matters involving
    related litigation,
    ARDE, Rule 11.
Powers of court, ARDE,
  Rule 1.
Pre-trial proceedings,
  ARDE, Rule 13.
Reciprocal discipline,
  ARDE, Rule 17.
Records.
  Confidentiality, ARDE,
    Rule 22.
  Disbarment on consent,
    ARDE, Rule 15.
  Expungement of records,
    ARDE, Rule 8.
  Grievance committee,
    ARDE, Rule 8.
  Maintenance by
    attorney, ARDE,
    Rule 18.
  Reinstatement, ARDE,
    Rule 19.
  Disabled attorneys,
    ARDE, Rule 20.
Reprimand.
  Private reprimand,
    ARDE, Rule 3.
Service of process, ARDE,
  Rule 12.
Subpoenas, ARDE, Rule
  13.
Supreme court, ARDE,
  Rule 8.
  Appeals to, ARDE, Rule
    8.
Types of discipline, ARDE,
  Rule 3.
Witnesses, ARDE, Rule 13.
Service of papers and notices,
  ARDE, Rule 12.
Service of process, ARDE,
  Rule 12.
Subpoenas, §34-3-82; ARDE,
  Rule 13.
Supreme court.
  Appeals to, ARDE, Rule 8.
Who may initiate
  proceedings, §34-3-89.
Witnesses, ARDE, Rule 13.
  Confrontation, §34-3-83.
  Payment of witnesses,
    §34-3-84.
  Power of subpoena,
    §34-3-82.
Discovery.
Disciplinary proceedings,
  ARDE, Rule 13.
Diseases.
Notifiable diseases.
  Commitment of afflicted
    persons.
    Appointment of attorney,
      §22-11A-29.
    Attorneys' fees,
      §22-11A-35.

ATTORNEYS AT LAW—Cont'd
District attorneys.
See DISTRICT
ATTORNEYS.
Domestic relations.
Protection from abuse.
Hearing on petition for
relief.
Right to counsel, §30-5-6.
Durable power of attorney,
§26-1-2.
Duties of attorneys.
Generally, §34-3-20.
Education.
Rules for mandatory
continuing legal
education, ARMCLE,
Rules 1 to 8. See within
this heading, "Rules for
mandatory continuing
legal education."
Elections.
Board of commissioners,
§34-3-41.
Evidence.
Appearance without
authority.
Proof, §34-3-23.
Disciplinary proceedings.
Right to introduce
evidence, §34-3-83.
Subpoenas, §34-3-82;
ARDE, Rule 13.
Privileges, §12-21-161.
Examinations.
Board of examiners.
Authority of commissioners
to establish, §34-3-2.
Certified graduates of certain
law schools.
Authorized to take bar
exam, §34-3-2.1.
**Executors and
administrators.**
Attorney's fees, §43-2-682.
Expungement of records.
Disciplinary proceedings,
ARDE, Rule 8.
Fees.
Admission fees, §34-3-3.
Disposition, §34-3-4.
Attorneys' fees.
See ATTORNEYS' FEES.
Client security fund, ACSF,
Rules 1 to 16. See within
this heading, "Client
security fund."
Disciplinary proceedings.
Witness fees, §34-3-84.
License fees.
Disposition of fees, §34-3-4.
Effect of default, §34-3-5.
Felonies.
Removal, §34-3-86.
Foundations.
State bar building
foundation. See within
this heading, "State bar."
Funds.
Board of commissioners of
state bar, §34-3-44.
Client security fund, ACSF,
Rules 1 to 16. See within
this heading, "Client
security fund."
State bar building
foundation.
Disbursement of
appropriations,
§34-3-107.

ATTORNEYS AT LAW—Cont'd
Garnishment.
Money in hands of attorney,
§6-6-412.
Guardian ad litem.
Appointment by court,
§15-12-21.
Hearings.
Disciplinary proceedings,
ARDE, Rule 8.
Highway department.
Legal division, §§23-1-25 to
23-1-31.
See HIGHWAYS.
Immunity.
Client security fund.
Immunity of committee,
ACSF, Rule 14.
Disciplinary proceedings,
ARDE, Rule 9.
Incompetence or incapacity,
ARDE, Rule 20.
Appointment of counsel to
protect client's interest,
ARDE, Rule 21.
Indigent persons.
Defense of indigents.
General provisions,
§§15-12-1 to 15-12-25.
See INDIGENT
PERSONS.
Public defenders,
§§15-12-40 to 15-12-46.
See PUBLIC
DEFENDERS.
Insurance.
Legal expense insurance,
§§27-43-1 to 27-43-22.
See INSURANCE.
**Interference with judicial
proceedings,** §13A-10-130.
Interpleader.
Attorneys' fees, ARCP, Rule
22 (c).
Interrogatories to jury.
Court to provide attorneys
with questions or
interrogatories, ARCP,
Rule 49 (d).
Investigations.
Disciplinary proceedings,
ARDE, Rule 8.
Judges.
Canons of judicial ethics. See
within this heading,
"Canons of judicial
ethics."
Practice of law prohibited,
§§34-3-11, 34-3-14.
Canons of judicial ethics,
ACJE, Canon 5F.
Constitutional provisions,
Const. Ala., art. VI,
§162.
Jurisdiction.
Disciplinary proceedings,
ARDE, Rule 1.
Jury.
Disqualification.
Relation of juror to
attorney, §12-16-150.
Juvenile proceedings.
Appearance of counsel,
ARJP, Rule 14.
Appointment of counsel,
§12-15-63.
Fees.
Issuance of order for
payment, §12-15-11.

ATTORNEYS AT LAW—Cont'd
Juvenile proceedings—Cont'd
Fees—Cont'd
Liability of counties,
§12-15-10.
Repeal of provisions,
§12-15-10.1.
Involuntary commitment,
§12-15-90.
Right to counsel, ARJP, Rule
22.
Notice, §12-15-63.
Legal education.
Rules for mandatory
continuing legal
education, ARMCLE,
Rules 1 to 8. See within
this heading, "Rules for
mandatory continuing
legal education."
Legal services liability,
§§6-5-570 to 6-5-581.
Advance payments.
Not admission of liability,
§6-5-576.
Payments in excess of
award, §6-5-576.
Applicability of article,
§6-5-581.
Arbitration.
Voluntary arbitration,
§6-5-575.
Breach of the standard of
care.
Defined, §6-5-572.
Citation of article, §6-5-571.
Defenses, §6-5-579.
Definitions, §6-5-572.
Effect of article on
inconsistent provisions of
law, §6-5-581.
Effect of compliance,
§6-5-578.
Evidence, §6-5-577.
Intent of legislature,
§6-5-570.
Limitation of action,
§6-5-574.
One form of action.
Creation, §6-5-573.
Rules of evidence and
procedures, §6-5-577.
Rules of professional conduct.
Effect of violations,
§6-5-578.
Settlement of disputes.
Voluntary arbitration,
§6-5-575.
Short title of article,
§6-5-571.
Standards of care, §6-5-580.
Defined, §6-5-572.
Underlying action.
Severability, §6-5-579.
Licenses, §40-12-49.
Fees.
Disposition, §34-3-4.
Effect of default, §34-3-5.
Practicing law without
license.
Conspiring in violation,
§34-3-7.
Liens.
Attorneys' fees, §34-3-61.
Limitation of actions.
Disciplinary proceedings,
ARDE, Rule 23.
Legal services liability
actions, §6-5-574.

ATTORNEYS AT LAW—Cont'd
Litigation accountability.
Fees.
Approval of stipulations,
§12-19-274.
Assessment against party
bringing action
without substantial
justification,
§12-19-272.
Negotiated in private,
§12-19-274.
Malpractice, §§6-5-570 to
6-5-581. See within this
heading, "Legal services
liability."
Meetings.
Annual meeting of state bar,
§34-3-16.
**Mental health finance
authority.**
Power to employ attorneys,
§41-10-356.
Mentally ill.
Commitment.
Involuntary commitment.
Appointment of attorney,
§§22-52-4, 22-52-5.
Payment of fees,
§22-52-14.
Criminal law and procedure.
Release of criminal
psychopaths.
Appointed counsel,
§15-16-65.
Military affairs.
Actions against national
guard members for acts
or omissions performed
in official capacity,
§§31-2-89, 31-2-90.
Misconduct.
Disciplinary proceedings. See
within this heading,
"Disciplinary
proceedings."
**Motion picture fair
competition.**
Attorneys' fees in civil
actions, §8-18-6.
Motions.
Signing, ARCP, Rule 11.
Nonresidents.
Disciplinary proceedings.
Reciprocal discipline,
ARDE, Rule 17.
Oaths.
Admission oath, §34-3-15.
Partition.
Fees, §34-3-60.
Penalties.
Certain ministerial officers
practicing law, §34-3-9.
Circuit court.
Practicing law by register
or clerk of circuit
court, §34-3-10.
Clerk or employee practicing
before court, §34-3-8.
Register or clerk of circuit
court, §34-3-10.
Disciplinary proceedings
against attorneys. See
within this heading,
"Disciplinary
proceedings."
Encouraging litigation,
§34-3-24.
Judges.
Practice of law, §34-3-11.

ATTORNEYS AT LAW—Cont'd
Penalties—Cont'd
Officers with authority to
take complaints and
issue warrants practicing
before own court,
§34-3-13.
Partner of district attorney
prohibited from
defending certain cases,
§34-3-12.
Practicing law without
license, §34-3-7.
Receiving compensation from
attorney, §34-3-25.
Removal or suspension of
attorneys. See within
this heading,
"Disciplinary
proceedings."
Soliciting business, §34-3-24.
Pilots and pilotage.
Revocation or suspension of
licenses.
Representation of pilot,
§33-4-45.
Pleadings.
Signing, ARCP, Rule 11.
Post-conviction remedies.
Appointment of counsel,
ARCrP, Rule 20.7 (c).
Powers of attorney.
Acknowledgments, §35-4-28.
Conveyances generally.
See CONVEYANCES.
Durable power of attorney,
§26-1-2.
Veterans.
Department of veterans'
affairs.
Execution, §31-5-4.
Practice of law.
Any person may manage his
own case, §34-3-19.
Appearance without
authority, §34-3-22.
Proof, §34-3-23.
Assistant attorneys general.
Private practice prohibited,
§36-15-9.
Exception, §36-15-9.
Authority of attorneys in
case.
Generally, §34-3-21.
Certain ministerial officers
prohibited, §34-3-9.
Clerk or employee prohibited
from practicing before
court, §34-3-8.
Defined, §34-3-6.
Disciplinary proceedings. See
within this heading,
"Disciplinary
proceedings."
District attorney.
Partner of district attorney
prohibited, §34-3-12.
Duties of attorneys.
Generally, §34-3-20.
Judges not to practice law,
§§34-3-11, 34-3-14.
Canons of judicial ethics,
ACJE, Canon 5F.
Constitutional provisions,
Const. Ala., art. VI,
§162.
Lawyers not engaged in
active practice, §34-3-18.
Lay practice, §34-3-19.
Oath of admission, §34-3-15.

ATTORNEYS AT LAW—Cont'd
Practice of law—Cont'd
Officers and deputies
disqualified from
practicing, §34-3-14.
Officers with authority to
take complaints and
issue warrants not to
practice before own
court, §34-3-13.
Practice of law by register or
clerk of circuit court,
§§34-3-10, 34-3-14.
Practice without license,
§34-3-7.
Probate court clerk, §34-3-14.
Removal or suspension of
attorneys. See within
this heading,
"Disciplinary
proceedings."
Sheriffs and deputies.
Not to practice law,
§34-3-14.
Unlawful practice of law,
§34-3-1.
Practicing without license,
§34-3-7.
Who may practice as
attorneys, §34-3-6.
Preliminary hearings.
Appearance by counsel for
defendant, §15-11-7.
Privileges.
Attorney-client privilege,
§12-21-161.
Probate courts.
Bonds, surety of judges.
Attorneys not deemed
sufficient sureties,
§36-5-13.
Professional corporations.
See PROFESSIONAL
CORPORATIONS.
Public defenders, §§15-12-40
to 15-12-46.
See PUBLIC DEFENDERS.
**Public officers and
employees.**
Bar association.
Qualified lawyers holding
public office as
members, §34-3-17.
Certain ministerial officers
prohibited from
practicing law, §34-3-9.
Clerk or employee prohibited
from practicing before
court, §34-3-8.
Register or clerk of circuit
court, §34-3-10.
Court officers disqualified
from practicing law,
§34-3-14.
Officers with authority to
take complaints and
issue warrants not to
practice before own
court, §34-3-13.
Sheriffs disqualified from
practicing law, §34-3-14.
Public service commission.
Party heard by attorney,
§37-1-88.
Special counsel, §§37-1-12,
37-1-64.
Rebates, §8-11-5.
Reciprocity.
Disciplinary proceedings,
ARDE, Rule 17.

ATTORNEYS AT LAW—Cont'd
Records.
Disciplinary proceedings,
§34-3-85.
**Removal or suspension of
attorneys.** See within this
heading, "Disciplinary
proceedings."
**Roll of attorneys, ARAP,
Rule 46.**
Rules and regulations.
Board of commissioners,
§34-3-43.
Client security fund, ACSF,
Rules 1 to 16. See within
this heading, "Client
security fund."
Disciplinary proceedings. See
within this heading,
"Disciplinary
proceedings."
**Rules for mandatory
continuing legal
education, ARMCLE,
Rules 1 to 8.**
Commission.
Established, ARMCLE,
Rule 1.
Reports, ARMCLE, Rule 5.
Contents of programs,
ARMCLE, Rule 7.
Credits, ARMCLE, Rule 4.
Disciplinary proceedings.
Rules of disciplinary
enforcement.
Suspension for
noncompliance with
rules for mandatory
continuing legal
education, ARDE,
Rule 3.
Exemptions, ARMCLE, Rule
2.
Members, ARMCLE, Rule 1.
Noncompliance with rules.
Sanctions, ARMCLE, Rule
6.
Powers and duties.
Generally, ARMCLE, Rule
1.
Presentation of programs,
ARMCLE, Rule 7.
Reports.
Commission to file annual
report, ARMCLE, Rule
5.
Requirements.
Additional policies,
ARMCLE, Rule 8.
Generally, ARMCLE, Rule
3.
Sanctions for noncompliance,
ARMCLE, Rule 6.
Scope of rules, ARMCLE,
Rule 2.
Standards for continuing
education, ARMCLE,
Rule 3.
Additional policies,
ARMCLE, Rule 8.
Rules of criminal procedure.
Post-conviction remedies.
Appointment of counsel,
ARCrP, Rule 20.7 (c).
Securities.
Director.
Appointment of legal
counsel, §8-6-58.
Service of process.
Disciplinary proceedings,
ARDE, Rule 12.

ATTORNEYS AT LAW—Cont'd
Sheriffs.
Attorneys deemed sufficient
sureties on official bonds,
§36-5-13.
Practice of law prohibited,
§34-3-14.
**Signing of pleadings,
motions or other papers,
ARCP, Rule 11.**
State bar.
Admission fees.
Disposition of fees, §34-3-4.
Alabama law institute.
See ALABAMA LAW
INSTITUTE.
Annual meeting, §34-3-16.
Board of commissioners,
§§34-3-40 to 34-3-44.
Building foundation,
§§34-3-100 to 34-3-108.
Appropriations, §34-3-107.
Board of trustees,
§34-3-103.
Certificate of incorporation,
§34-3-102.
Conveyance of real
property, §34-3-106.
Exemptions from taxation,
§34-3-105.
Incorporation.
Application, §34-3-101.
Certificate, §34-3-102.
Legislative findings and
intent, §34-3-100.
Nonprofit nature,
§34-3-108.
Officers, §34-3-103.
Powers, §34-3-104.
Public nature, §34-3-108.
State to convey certain
land to foundation,
§34-3-106.
Client security fund, ACSF,
Rules 1 to 16. See within
this heading, "Client
security fund."
Disciplinary board. See
within this heading,
"Disciplinary
proceedings."
Election of officers, §34-3-16.
Expenses of board members,
§34-3-16.
Fees.
Admission fees, §34-3-3.
Funds.
Client security fund,
ACSF, Rules 1 to 16.
See within this
heading, "Client
security fund."
Lawyers holding public office
authorized to become
members, §34-3-17.
Lawyers not engaged in
active practice
authorized to become
members, §34-3-18.
Meeting.
Annual meeting of bar,
§34-3-16.
Secretary.
Compensation, §34-3-16.
Election, §34-3-16.
Student loan program.
Legal counsel for program,
§16-33B-8.

ATTORNEYS AT LAW—Cont'd
Subpoenas.
Disciplinary proceedings,
ARDE, Rule 13.
Subpoena of witnesses and
evidence, §34-3-82.
Subrogation.
Client security fund, ACSF,
Rule 10.
**Summary proceedings
involving officials.**
Failure to pay money or
deliver personal property
recovered in capacity as
attorney, §6-6-740.
Supreme court.
Disciplinary proceedings.
Appeals to supreme court,
ARDE, Rule 8.
Roll of attorneys, ARAP,
Rule 46.
Special judges.
Appointment of members
of bar, §12-2-14.
Staff attorneys, §12-2-21.
Taxation.
Taxing authorities acting as
attorney for taxpayer,
§40-1-20.
Trusts and trustees.
Fees, §34-3-60.
**Unemployment
compensation.**
Fees for attorneys or agents,
§25-4-139.
**Unincorporated professional
associations.**
See UNINCORPORATED
PROFESSIONAL
ASSOCIATIONS.
United States.
Condemnation of land or
rights-of-way.
Appointment of counsel for
infants and persons of
unsound mind, §42-2-4.
**Unlawful practice of law,
§34-3-1.**
Practicing without license,
§34-3-7.
Verdict.
Attorneys provided with
questions or
interrogatories for jury,
ARCP, Rule 49 (d).
Veterans.
Powers of attorney.
Department of veterans'
affairs.
Execution, §31-5-4.
**Water system assistance
authority.**
Power to appoint and
employ, §22-23A-6.
Welfare.
Department of human
resources.
Legal counsel, §38-2-4.
Witnesses.
Disciplinary proceedings. See
within this heading,
"Disciplinary
proceedings."
Testimony of attorney for or
against client,
§12-21-161.
Workmen's compensation.
Disputed claims for
compensation.
Attorneys' fees, §25-5-90.

ATTORNEYS AT LAW—Cont'd
Workmen's compensation
  —Cont'd
  Fees.
    Settlements with third
      parties, §25-5-11.
    Persons not authorized to
      practice law, §25-5-227.
    Solicitation of employment,
      §25-5-226.
Youth services.
  Department of youth
    services.
    Legal counsel, §44-1-23.

ATTORNEYS' FEES.
Conservators.
  Settlements of accounts of
    conservators, §26-5-13.
Court appointed counsel.
  Defense of indigents,
    §§15-12-1 to 15-12-25.
    See INDIGENT PERSONS.
Diseases.
  Notifiable diseases.
    Commitment proceedings,
      §22-11A-35.
Disputed amount, §34-3-62.
Interpleader, ARCP, Rule 22
  (c).
Involuntary commitment of
  mentally ill, §22-52-14.
Juvenile proceedings,
  §§12-15-10, 12-15-11.
  Repeal of provisions,
    §12-15-10.1.
Liens for attorneys' fees,
  §34-3-61.
Litigation accountability.
  Approval of stipulations,
    §12-19-274.
  Assessment against party
    bringing action without
    substantial justification,
    §12-19-272.
  Negotiated in private,
    §12-19-274.
Motion picture fair
  competition.
  Award of attorneys' fees,
    §8-18-6.
Partition and trust
  proceedings, §34-3-60.
Receiving compensation
  from attorney, §34-3-25.
Unemployment
  compensation.
  Limitation of fees, §25-4-139.

ATTORNMENT.
Conveyances.
  Attornment of tenant
    unnecessary, §35-4-32.
Landlord and tenant.
  Prohibited generally, §35-9-1.

AUBURN, MUNICIPALITY
  OF.
Property tax, Const. Ala.,
  amd. 8.
Recreation.
  Special property tax for
    recreational purposes,
    Const. Ala., amd. 242.
School tax.
  Special property tax for
    educational purposes,
    Const. Ala., amd. 148.

AUBURN UNIVERSITY,
  §§16-48-1 to 16-48-12.
Agriculture.
  Agricultural experiment
    station system.
    Employees.
      Membership in teachers'
        retirement system,
        §16-25-6.
    Operated in connection
      with Auburn
      university, §2-30-40.
  Alabama extension service,
    §§2-30-1 to 2-30-4.
  See AGRICULTURE.
  Board of agriculture and
    industries.
    Assistance from specialists
      and scientists of
      Auburn university,
      §2-3-5.
Alabama extension service.
  General provisions, §§2-30-1
    to 2-30-4.
American Legion
  scholarships.
  See UNIVERSITIES AND
    COLLEGES.
Board of trustees, Const.
  Ala., art. XIV, §266; amd.
  161.
  Divided into classes,
    §16-48-5.
  Endowment funds.
    Investment, §16-13-2.
  Expenses, §16-48-9.
  Meetings, §16-48-7.
  Powers, §16-48-4.
  Quorum, §16-48-8.
  Report made to legislature,
    §16-48-11.
  Vacancies, §16-48-6.
Body corporate, §16-48-1.
Bond issues.
  Construction and
    improvement purposes,
    Const. Ala., amd. 120.
Commission of higher
  education.
  General provisions.
    See UNIVERSITIES AND
      COLLEGES.
Conduct, §16-48-4.
Constitution of Alabama.
  Board of trustees, Const.
    Ala., art. XIV, §266;
    amd. 161.
  Bonds, Const. Ala., amd. 120.
  Location.
    Change, Const. Ala., art.
      XIV, §267.
Corporation.
  Body corporate, §16-48-1.
  Powers.
    Corporate powers,
      §16-48-2.
Degrees.
  Powers of board of trustees,
    §16-48-4.
Ejectment.
  Recovery of lands by or in
    name of state for
    university, §6-6-281.
Eminent domain.
  General provisions.
    See EMINENT DOMAIN.

AUBURN UNIVERSITY
  —Cont'd
Employees.
  State employees' retirement
    system.
  Employees of cooperative
    extension service.
    Participation in systems,
      §36-27-7.
Extension service.
  Alabama extension service,
    §§2-30-1 to 2-30-4.
Faculty.
  Appointment by trustees,
    §16-48-4.
  Eminent scholars trust fund,
    §§16-61-1 to 16-61-10.
  See UNIVERSITIES AND
    COLLEGES.
Federal grant.
  Interest on federal fund paid
    by state, §16-48-3.
Funds.
  Eminent scholars trust fund,
    §§16-61-1 to 16-61-10.
  See UNIVERSITIES AND
    COLLEGES.
  Federal fund.
    Interest on federal fund
      paid by state, §16-48-3.
Gifts.
  Preserved, §16-48-10.
Legislature.
  Report made to legislature,
    §16-48-11.
Location.
  Change, Const. Ala., art.
    XIV, §267.
Marine environmental
  sciences consortium,
  §§16-45-1 to 16-45-5.
Organization, §16-48-4.
Police, §16-48-12.
  Generally, §§16-22-1,
    16-22-2.
Powers.
  Corporate powers, §16-48-2.
President.
  Agricultural and industrial
    exhibit commission.
    Member of commission,
      §2-7-1.
Reports, §16-48-11.
Salaries.
  Powers of board of trustees,
    §16-48-4.
Sales tax.
  Tax levied on gross receipts,
    §40-23-2.
Scholarships.
  American Legion
    scholarships.
    See UNIVERSITIES AND
      COLLEGES.
Seeds.
  Registration of symbol of
    seeds or plant parts.
    Cooperation of experiment
      station, §2-26-52.
Soil and water conservation.
  Water resources research
    institute.
    General provisions, §§9-8-1
      to 9-8-4.
Soil-testing laboratory.
  Not affected by chapter,
    §2-24-4.

AUBURN UNIVERSITY —Cont'd

State employees' retirement system.
Employees of cooperative extension service.
Participation in systems, §§36-27-7, 36-27-7.1.

Trustees.
Board of trustees. See within this heading, "Board of trustees."

Tuition.
Powers of board of trustees, §16-48-4.

Universities and colleges generally.
See UNIVERSITIES AND COLLEGES.

Water resources research institute.
General provisions, §§9-8-1 to 9-8-4.

AUCTIONS AND AUCTIONEERS, §§34-4-1 to 34-4-54.

Abandoned motor vehicles.
Authority to sell, §32-13-3.

Actions.
Collection of compensation, §34-4-5.

Applicability of chapter.
Exemptions from chapter, §34-4-3.
Limitations on authority of political subdivisions, §34-4-6.

Apprentice auctioneer.
Action for compensation.
Apprentice not authorized to initiate, §34-4-5.
Defined, §34-4-2.
Licenses.
Generally. See within this heading, "Licenses."
Revocation or suspension of auctioneer's license.
Effect on license of apprentice, §34-4-32.

Attorneys at law.
Board of auctioneers.
Legal assistance, §34-4-51.

Auctioneer.
Defined, §34-4-2.

Audits.
Board of auctioneers, §34-4-54.

Board of auctioneers.
Appointment, §34-4-50.
Audit of accounts, §34-4-54.
Certificates of appointment, §34-4-51.
Compensation, §34-4-53.
Complaints.
Prosecution, §34-4-51.
Composition, §34-4-50.
Defined, §34-4-2.
Enforcement of chapter, §34-4-4.
Evidence.
Copies of records and papers, §34-4-50.
Funds.
Collection and disbursement, §34-4-54.
Immunity of members, §34-4-30.
Legal assistance, §34-4-51.

AUCTIONS AND AUCTIONEERS—Cont'd

Board of auctioneers—Cont'd
Licenses. See within this heading, "Licenses."
Meetings, §34-4-52.
Officers, §34-4-50.
Quasi judicial body, §34-4-30.
Quorum, §34-4-52.
Records.
Copies as evidence, §34-4-50.
Proceedings, §34-4-54.
Revocation or suspension of licenses. See within this heading, "Licenses."
Rules and regulations, §34-4-50.
Seal, §34-4-50.
Terms of office, §34-4-50.

Bonds, surety.
License accompanied by, §34-4-24.

Business of auctioneering.
Defined, §34-4-2.

Citation of chapter, §34-4-1.

Commercial code.
Bulk transfers, §7-6-108.
Sale by auction, §7-2-328.

Compensation.
Actions for collection, §34-4-5.

Counties.
Limitations on authority, §34-4-6.

Definitions, §34-4-2.

Drugs.
Notice of sale of drugs, §34-23-6.

Enforcement of chapter.
Generally, §34-4-4.
Penalties for violation, §34-4-7.

Evidence.
Board of auctioneers.
Copies of records and papers, §34-4-50.

Examinations.
License examination, §34-4-21.

Exemptions from provisions of chapter, §34-4-3.

Fees.
Actions for collection of fees, §34-4-5.
Examination fees, §34-4-21.

Fraud.
Memorandum of auctioneer.
Sufficiency as note of contract, §8-9-3.

Gold, silver, watches, jewelry, china, etc., §§8-14-20 to 8-14-24.
Boosters.
Unlawful, §8-14-22.
By-bidders.
Unlawful, §8-14-22.
Cappers.
Unlawful, §8-14-22.
Hours of sale, §8-14-21.
Penalties, §8-14-24.
Sale at auction restricted, §8-14-20.
Violation of article, §8-14-24.
Warranties.
Descriptions of goods considered, §8-14-23.

Goods.
Defined, §34-4-2.

AUCTIONS AND AUCTIONEERS—Cont'd

Licenses, §40-12-50.
Address.
Change of address, §34-4-21.
Mailing address, §34-4-26.
Appeals.
Revocation or suspension, §34-4-30.
Applications, §34-4-21.
Apprentice auctioneer.
Revocation or suspension.
Effect on license of apprentice, §34-4-32.
Associations.
Effect of license issued to association, §34-4-28.
Board of auctioneers. See within this heading, "Board of auctioneers."
Bond, §34-4-24.
Certificates, §34-4-21.
Corporations.
Effect of license issued to corporation, §34-4-28.
Evidence of rights and privileges, §34-4-23.
Examinations, §34-4-21.
Expiration, §34-4-21.
Fees, §34-4-21.
Issuance, §34-4-21.
Nonresidents, §34-4-25.
Partnerships.
Effect of license issued to partnership, §34-4-28.
Privilege licenses, §34-4-27.
Qualifications of applicants, §34-4-21.
Register of applicants, §34-4-22.
Renewal, §34-4-21.
Required, §34-4-20.
Revocation or suspension, §§34-4-29 to 34-4-32.
Effect on license of apprentice auctioneer, §34-4-32.
Grounds, §34-4-29.
Judgment in damage action against licensee, §34-4-31.
Hearing, §34-4-29.
Procedure for hearing, §34-4-30.
Immunity of board, §34-4-30.
Judicial review of decision, §34-4-30.
Notice of charges, §34-4-29.
Procedure generally, §34-4-29.
Rights and privileges.
License as evidence of, §34-4-23.
Transferability, §34-4-28.

Medicines.
Notice of sale of drugs and medicines, §34-23-6.

Mental health finance authority.
Bond issues.
Sale of bonds at public auction, §41-10-360.

Motor vehicles.
Abandoned motor vehicles.
Authority to sell, §32-13-3.

Municipal corporations.
Licensing of auction sales, §11-51-97.

AUCTIONS AND AUCTIONEERS—Cont'd

Municipal corporations —Cont'd
Limitation on authority to tax, §34-4-6.

Nonresidents.
Licensing of nonresidents, §34-4-25.

Pawnbrokers.
Sale of pledges.
Public auction, §8-1-81.

Penalties.
Violation of article, §§8-14-24, 34-4-7.

Persons.
Defined, §34-4-2.

Pharmacists and pharmacies.
Notice of auction sales of drugs and medicines, §34-23-6.

Political subdivisions.
Limitations on authority, §34-4-6.

Privilege licenses, §34-4-27.

Public lands.
Sale generally.
See PUBLIC LANDS.

Public sales.
Consideration for bidding or not bidding, §8-1-100.
Contracts in violation void, §8-1-102.

Rebates.
Taking by auctioneer, §8-11-5.

Records.
Board of auctioneers.
Copies as evidence, §34-4-50.
Proceedings, §34-4-54.
Sale of personal property at auction, §8-14-1.

Revocation or suspension of licenses. See within this heading, "Licenses."

Rights and privileges.
License as evidence of, §34-4-23.

Rules and regulations, §34-4-4.

Seals.
Board of auctioneers, §34-4-50.

Short title of chapter, §34-4-1.

Southeast interstate low-level radioactive waste management compact.
Seizure of source of ionizing radiation.
Unredeemed equipment auctioned, §22-32-8.

Taxation.
Assessment against auctioneers, §40-7-44.
Limitations on authority of political subdivisions, §34-4-6.
Subjects of taxation, §40-11-1.

Title.
Short title of chapter, §34-4-1.

Warranty.
Gold, silver, watches, jewelry, china, etc.
Descriptions of goods considered warranties, §8-14-23.

AUDIOLOGISTS.

General provisions, §§34-28-1 to 34-28A-44.
See SPEECH PATHOLOGISTS AND AUDIOLOGISTS.

AUDITA QUERELA.

Rules of civil procedure.
Writ abolished, ARCP, Rule 60 (b).

AUDITORS.

Accountants, §§34-1-1 to 34-1-22.
See ACCOUNTANTS.

Accounts and accounting.
See ACCOUNTS AND ACCOUNTING.

Audits generally.
See AUDITS.

Masters, ARCP, Rule 53.

Municipal corporations.
Duties, §§11-43-3, 11-43-103.

State auditor.
See STATE AUDITOR.

AUDITS.

Accountants, §§34-1-1 to 34-1-22.
See ACCOUNTANTS.

Accounts and accounting.
See ACCOUNTS AND ACCOUNTING.

Alcoholic beverages.
Alcoholic beverage control board.
Books, records and accounts of board, §28-3-52.
Invoices, books, papers, etc., §28-3-7.

Auctions and auctioneers.
Board of auctioneers, §34-4-54.

Banks and financial institutions.
See BANKS AND FINANCIAL INSTITUTIONS.

Barbers.
Board of barber examiners, §34-5-12.

Cahaba trace commission, §41-9-809.

Catfish.
Promotion of industry.
Certified association, §2-8-288.

Chiropractors.
Board of chiropractic examiners, §34-24-143.

Community action agencies, §11-96-3.

Conservators.
Settlements of accounts of guardians.
Partial settlement, §26-5-4.

Counties.
Claims and demands against counties, §11-12-4.
County commissions.
Powers and duties, §11-3-11.
Department of examiners of public accounts.
Periodic audits, §41-5-14.

AUDITS—Cont'd

Counties—Cont'd
Warrants for construction of public buildings, bridges and roads.
Issuance of warrants deemed audit and allowance of claim, §11-28-6.
Waterworks systems warrants.
Issuance of warrants deemed audit and allowance of claim, §11-9-26.

Credit unions.
Supervisory committee.
Powers and duties, §5-17-13.

Crime victims compensation.
Financial affairs of commission, §15-23-7.

Dentists.
Board of dental examiners, §34-9-42.

Department of examinations of public accounts, §§41-5-1 to 41-5-24.
See ACCOUNTS AND ACCOUNTING.

Education.
City boards of education, §16-11-22.
Department of examiners of public accounts.
Audits of certain institutions, §16-1-22.
Educational institutions.
Student grant program, §16-33A-8.
Insurance.
Risk management cooperatives, §16-8-42.1.
Textbooks.
Accounting books and records, §16-36-31.

Educational television foundation authority, §16-7A-4.

Eggs and egg products.
Promotion of industry.
Growers' association, §2-8-166.

Executors and administrators.
Settlements and distributions, §43-2-507.
Compelling settlement, §43-2-531.
Authority ceased, §43-2-556.

Funerals.
Board of funeral service, §34-13-29.

Guardian and ward.
Curators, §26-7A-12.

Harbors and ports.
Certain expenditures, §33-1-1.

Hospitals.
Publicly-owned medical institutions, §22-21-4.

Indians.
Indian affairs commission, §41-9-717.

Licenses.
Actuaries or auditors, §40-12-43.

AUDITS—Cont'd

Livestock.

Promotion of cattle industry.
Owners' associations,
§2-8-19.
Promotion of swine industry.
Producers' associations,
§2-8-59.

Military affairs.

Adjutant general, §31-2-68.
Officers, §31-2-68.

Motor sports hall of fame commission, §41-9-477.

Municipal corporations.

Boards of water and sewer
commissioners,
§11-50-355.
Bond issues, §11-81-68.
Claims against municipality,
§11-43-101.
Commission form of
government.
Optional form A,
§11-44-95.
Optional form B,
§11-44-139.
Transportation service in
Class 3 municipalities,
§11-49A-18.

Office of prosecution services, §12-17-233.

Peace officers' annuity and benefit fund, §36-21-75.

Public accounts.

Department of examiners of
public accounts, §§41-5-1
to 41-5-24.
See ACCOUNTS AND
ACCOUNTING.

Public works.

Improvement authorities,
Special audit, §39-7-28.

Sales.

Going out of business or
distress merchandise
sales.
License applications.
Cost, §8-13-6.

Savings and loan associations, §5-16-36.

Seeds.

Records of receipts, sales and
deliveries, §2-26-10.

Southern products mart authority, §41-10-66.

Soybeans.

Promotion of soybean
industry.
Producers' associations,
§2-8-99.

Space science exhibit commission, §41-9-437.

State auditor.

See STATE AUDITOR.

State parks.

Revolving fund, §9-2-107.

Student grant program.

Educational institutions,
§16-33A-8.
False statements and
representations,
§16-33A-10.

Student loan program.

Institutions.
Approved and eligible
institutions, §16-33B-5.

Taxation.

Multistate tax compact.
Interstate audits, §40-27-1.
Force and effect,
§40-27-6.

AUDITS—Cont'd

Tennessee Valley authority.

Exhibit commission,
§41-9-785.

USS Alabama battleship commission, §41-9-350.

Water management and drainage.

Board of water management
commissioners, §9-9-18.

AUGUSTA COUNTY.

Probate judge.

Compensation, Const. Ala.,
amd. 493.

AUTAUGA COUNTY.

Economic development,
Const. Ala., amd. 183.

AUTHENTICATION OF DOCUMENTS.

See EVIDENCE.

AUTHORITIES.

Actions.

Liability of officers of
nonprofit organizations,
§§10-11-1 to 10-11-5.

Africatown, U.S.A. historic preservation authority,
§§41-10-230 to 41-10-240.
See AFRICATOWN, U.S.A.
STATE PARK.

Agricultural development authority.

Agriculture.
Development authority,
§§2-3A-1 to 2-3A-16.
See AGRICULTURE.

Airport authorities, §§4-3-1 to 4-3-80.

See AVIATION.

Alabama building authority,
§41-10-1.

Alabama educational television foundation authority, §§16-7A-1 to 16-7A-8.

See EDUCATIONAL
TELEVISION
FOUNDATION
AUTHORITY.

Alabama education authority, §§16-15-1 to 16-15-13.

See EDUCATION.

Alabama highway authorities.

See HIGHWAYS.

Alabama port authority,
§§33-13-1 to 33-13-13.
See HARBORS AND PORTS.

Alabama public school and college authority,
§§16-16-1 to 16-16-13.
See EDUCATION.

Alabama trade school and junior college authority,
§§16-60-80 to 16-60-96.
See JUNIOR COLLEGES.

Bear creek development authority, §§33-15-1 to 33-15-19.

See BEAR CREEK
DEVELOPMENT
AUTHORITY.

Bond issues.

Consent of department of
finance, §41-4-16.

AUTHORITIES—Cont'd

Bridges.

Toll road, bridge and tunnel
authority, §§23-2-140 to
23-2-161.
See TOLL ROAD, BRIDGE
AND TUNNEL
AUTHORITY.

Buildings.

Alabama building authority,
§41-10-1.
Alabama building finance
authority, §41-10-2.
Counties.
Public building authorities,
§§11-15-1 to 11-15-19.
See COUNTIES.

Cemetery authority.

Defined, §34-13-1.

Commercial development authorities.

Class 1 municipalities,
§§11-54-170 to 11-54-192.
See MUNICIPAL
CORPORATIONS.

Coosa valley development authority, §§33-16-1 to 33-16-15.

See COOSA VALLEY
DEVELOPMENT
AUTHORITY.

Corrections.

Alabama corrections
institution finance
authority, §§14-2-1 to
14-2-36.
See CORRECTIONS.

Disposal authorities,
§§11-89A-1 to 11-89A-25.
See SOLID WASTE.

Downtown redevelopment authorities, §§11-54A-1 to 11-54A-24.

See DOWNTOWN
REDEVELOPMENT
AUTHORITIES.

Educational building authorities, §§16-17-1 to 16-17-19.

See EDUCATION.

Educational television foundation authority,
§§16-7A-1 to 16-7A-8.
See EDUCATIONAL
TELEVISION
FOUNDATION
AUTHORITY.

Electricity.

Municipal electric authority,
§§11-50A-1 to 11-50A-33.
See MUNICIPAL
CORPORATIONS.

Environmental improvement authorities, §§9-6-1 to 9-6-17.

See ENVIRONMENTAL
IMPROVEMENT
AUTHORITIES.

Farmers' market authority,
§§2-5-1 to 2-5-17.
See AGRICULTURE.

Garbage and trash.

Solid waste.
Disposal authorities,
§§11-89A-1 to
11-89A-25.
See SOLID WASTE.

AUTHORITIES—Cont'd
Harbors and ports.
Port authorities, §§33-13-1 to
33-13-13.
See HARBORS AND
PORTS.
Health care authorities,
§§22-21-310 to 22-21-356.
See HEALTH CARE
AUTHORITIES.
Highways.
Federal aid highway finance
authority, §§23-1-301 to
23-1-317.
See HIGHWAYS.
**Historical preservation
authorities.**
See HISTORICAL
PRESERVATION
AUTHORITIES.
Historic Blakeley authority,
§§41-10-170 to 41-10-182.
See HISTORIC BLAKELEY
AUTHORITY.
Hospitals.
County and municipal
hospital authority,
§§22-21-170 to 22-21-191.
See HOSPITALS.
Municipal hospital building
authorities, §§22-21-130
to 22-21-156.
See HOSPITALS.
Housing authorities, §§24-1-4
to 24-1-134
See HOUSING
AUTHORITIES.
Housing finance authority,
§§24-1A-1 to 24-1A-21.
See HOUSING FINANCE
AUTHORITY.
Immunity.
Liability of officers of
nonprofit organizations,
§§10-11-1 to 10-11-5.
Improvement authorities,
§§39-7-1 to 39-7-34.
See PUBLIC WORKS.
**Industrial development
authority,** §§41-10-20 to
41-10-32.
See INDUSTRIAL
DEVELOPMENT
AUTHORITY.
Judicial building authority,
§§41-10-260 to 41-10-284.
See JUDICIAL BUILDING
AUTHORITY.
Junior colleges.
Trade school and junior
college authority,
§§16-60-80 to 16-60-96.
See JUNIOR COLLEGES.
**Liability of officers of
nonprofit organizations,**
§§10-11-1 to 10-11-5.
Libraries.
Public library authorities,
§§11-57-1 to 11-57-26.
See MUNICIPAL
CORPORATIONS.
**Mental health finance
authority,** §§41-10-350 to
41-10-371.
See MENTAL HEALTH
FINANCE
AUTHORITY.

AUTHORITIES—Cont'd
Municipal corporations.
Commercial development
authorities in Class 1
municipalities,
§§11-54-170 to 11-54-192.
See MUNICIPAL
CORPORATIONS.
Negligence.
Liability of officers of
nonprofit organizations,
§§10-11-1 to 10-11-5.
Nonprofit organizations.
Liability of officers of
nonprofit organizations,
§§10-11-1 to 10-11-5.
**Pollution control finance
authority,** §§22-29-1 to
22-29-23.
See WATER POLLUTION.
Port authority, §§33-13-1 to
33-13-13.
See HARBORS AND PORTS.
Products marts.
See PRODUCTS MARTS.
Public building authorities.
Counties, §§11-15-1 to
11-15-19.
See COUNTIES.
Municipal corporations,
§§11-56-1 to 11-56-22.
See MUNICIPAL
CORPORATIONS.
**Public school and college
authority,** §§16-16-1 to
16-16-13.
See EDUCATION.
Public works.
Improvement authorities,
§§39-7-1 to 39-7-34.
See PUBLIC WORKS.
Railroad authorities,
§§37-13-1 to 37-13-21.
See RAILROAD
AUTHORITIES.
**Shakespeare festival theatre
finance authority,**
§§41-10-200 to 41-10-215.
See SHAKESPEARE
FESTIVAL THEATRE
FINANCE
AUTHORITY.
Solid waste.
Disposal authorities,
§§11-89A-1 to 11-89A-25.
See SOLID WASTE.
**Southern products mart
authority.**
See PRODUCTS MARTS.
**Space science exhibit
finance authority,**
§§41-10-300 to 41-10-332.
See SPACE SCIENCE
EXHIBIT FINANCE
AUTHORITY.
**State products mart and
coliseum authority.**
See PRODUCTS MARTS.
Supercomputer authority,
§§41-10-390 to 41-10-406.
See SUPERCOMPUTER
AUTHORITY.
**Synfuels development
authority,** §§9-6A-1 to
9-6A-10.
See SYNFUELS
DEVELOPMENT
AUTHORITY.

AUTHORITIES—Cont'd
**Tombigbee valley
development authority,**
§§33-17-1 to 33-17-15.
See TOMBIGBEE VALLEY
DEVELOPMENT
AUTHORITY.
Torts.
Liability of officers of
nonprofit organizations,
§§10-11-1 to 10-11-5.
**Trade school and junior
college authority,**
§§16-60-80 to 16-60-96.
See JUNIOR COLLEGES.
**Transportation service in
Class 3 municipalities.**
See MUNICIPAL
CORPORATIONS.
Water pollution.
Pollution control finance
authority, §§22-29-1 to
22-29-23.
See WATER POLLUTION.
Water pollution control
authority, §§22-34-1 to
22-34-17.
See WATER POLLUTION
CONTROL
AUTHORITY.
**Water, sewer and fire
protection authorities,**
§§11-88-1 to 11-88-111.
See WATER, SEWER AND
FIRE PROTECTION
AUTHORITIES.
**Water system assistance
authority,** §§22-23A-1 to
22-23A-17.
See WATER SYSTEM
ASSISTANCE
AUTHORITY.
AUTOMOBILES.
Clubs and associations,
§§27-19-1 to 27-19-8.
See INSURANCE.
General provisions, §§32-1-1
to 32-18-8.
See MOTOR VEHICLES.
**Motor sports hall of fame
commission,** §§41-9-470 to
41-9-478.
See MOTOR SPORTS HALL
OF FAME
COMMISSION.
AUTOPSIES.
Coroners.
See CORONERS.
Insurance.
Disability insurance.
Provision in policy,
§27-19-13.
State toxicologist.
General provisions.
See STATE
TOXICOLOGIST.
AVIATION, §§4-2-1 to 4-2-95.
Abatement.
Municipal corporations.
Navigational hazards.
Removal, §4-4-10.
Aeronautics commission,
§§4-2-30 to 4-2-50.
Appeal of orders.
Failure to file appeal,
§4-2-51.
Procedure for appeal,
§4-2-50.
Appointment of members,
§4-2-30.

AVIATION—Cont'd
Aeronautics commission
—Cont'd
Compensation of members,
§4-2-30.
Composition, §4-2-30.
Created, §4-2-30.
Donations, §4-2-41.
Duties, §4-2-33.
Delegation to director of
aeronautics, §4-2-35.
Employees, §4-2-32.
Enforcement of aeronautics
laws, §4-2-47.
Expenditures, §4-2-32.
Federal government.
Intervention in certain
controversies, §4-2-46.
Fiscal year, §4-2-31.
Foreign states.
Intervention in certain
controversies, §4-2-46.
Functions, §4-2-34.
Grants, §4-2-41.
Hearings, §4-2-48.
Reports, §4-2-49.
Inspections, §4-2-50.
Intervention in certain
controversies, §4-2-46.
Investigations, §4-2-48.
Reports, §4-2-49.
Loans, §4-2-41.
Meetings, §4-2-31.
Offices, §4-2-32.
Orders.
Appeals.
Failure to file appeal,
§4-2-51.
Procedure for appeal,
§4-2-50.
Enforcement, §4-2-48.
Reasons to accompany
orders, §4-2-50.
Rehearing, §4-2-50.
Service upon interested
persons, §4-2-50.
Organization, §4-2-31.
Powers, §4-2-33.
Delegation to director of
aeronautics, §4-2-35.
Enforcement powers,
§4-2-47.
Qualifications of members,
§4-2-30.
Removal of members,
§4-2-30.
Reports.
Annual report to governor,
§4-2-31.
Investigations, hearings,
etc., §4-2-49.
Rules and regulations,
§4-2-37.
State airports.
General provisions.
§§4-2-90 to 4-2-95. See
within this heading,
"Airports."
Joint activities with other
governmental
agencies, §4-2-92.
Subpoenas.
Enforcement, §4-2-48.
Terms of members, §4-2-30.
Air commerce.
General provisions.
See AIR COMMERCE.
Aircraft.
Certificates.
Display, §4-2-78.
Operation without, §4-2-76.

AVIATION—Cont'd
Aircraft—Cont'd
Certificates—Cont'd
Possession, §4-2-78.
Exceptions to regulations,
§4-2-80.
Licenses.
Display, §4-2-78.
Operation without, §4-2-76.
Possession, §4-2-78.
Permits.
Display, §4-2-78.
Operation without, §4-2-76.
Possession, §4-2-78.
Registration.
State registration.
Possession, display, etc.,
§4-2-78.
Regulation, §4-2-72.
Stations.
Control and warning
stations, §§4-7-1 to
4-7-3.
Suspension of operations,
§4-2-79.
Airmen.
Certificates.
Display, §4-2-78.
Operation without, §4-2-76.
Possession, §4-2-78.
Exceptions to regulations,
§4-2-80.
Helicoper pilots association,
§§4-9-1 to 4-9-7. See
within this heading,
"Helicopter pilots
association."
Licenses.
Display, §4-2-78.
Operation without, §4-2-76.
Possession, §4-2-78.
Permits.
Display, §4-2-78.
Operation without, §4-2-76.
Possession, §4-2-78.
Regulation, §4-2-72.
Airports.
Acquisition, construction, etc.
Bond issues.
Authority of counties
and municipalities,
§4-1-1.
Certificate of approval.
Application prior to
acquisition of
property, §4-2-73.
Compliance with federal
laws, §4-2-39.
Contracts.
Law governing, §4-2-43.
Cooperation with federal
government, §4-2-39.
Federal funding.
Authority to accept,
§4-2-40.
Compliance with federal
laws, §4-2-39.
Disposition, §4-2-44.
Conditions, §4-2-40.
Financial and technical
assistance to
municipalities, §4-2-38.
Municipal airports.
Acquisition of lands by
condemnation,
§4-4-6.
Authority to acquire,
establish, etc.,
§4-4-2.
Methods of acquisition,
§4-4-5.

AVIATION—Cont'd
Airports—Cont'd
Acquisition, construction, etc
—Cont'd
State airports, §4-2-90.
Air rights.
Acquisition, §4-6-13.
Animals.
Prohibited upon premises
of airports, §4-2-6.
Appeals.
Zoning, §4-6-11.
Approach plans.
Formulation, adoption, etc.,
§4-2-78.
Authorities, §§4-3-1 to
4-3-80.
Actions, §4-3-23.
Alternate procedure for
incorporation, §§4-3-40
to 4-3-61.
Actions, §4-3-50.
Approval of application
by governing body,
§4-3-41.
Article cumulative,
§4-3-62.
Board of directors,
§4-3-45.
Bond issues, §§4-3-51 to
4-3-58.
Delivery, §4-3-53.
Denominations,
§4-3-51.
Disposition of proceeds,
§4-3-55.
Execution, §4-3-53.
Exemptions from
taxation, §4-3-59.
Form, §4-3-51.
Interest, §§4-3-51,
4-3-54.
Investments, §§4-3-57,
4-3-58.
Issuance, §4-3-51.
Limitation of actions,
§4-3-52.
Notice of bond,
§4-3-52.
Principal and interest,
§§4-3-51, 4-3-54.
Publication of notice,
§4-3-52.
Refunding bonds,
§4-3-56.
Sale, §§4-3-51, 4-3-55.
Security for payment,
§4-3-54.
Terms, §4-3-51.
Certificate of
incorporation,
§§4-3-42 to 4-3-44.
Amendments, §4-3-44.
Contents, §4-3-42.
Execution, §4-3-43.
Modification, §4-3-44.
Recordation, §4-3-43.
Civil actions against
authority, director,
etc., §4-3-50.
Contracts.
Exemption from state
restrictions,
§4-3-60.
Counties.
Assistance, §4-3-49.
Cooperation, §4-3-49.
Investment of funds in
bonds, §4-3-57.
Definitions, §4-3-40.
Directors, §4-3-45.

AVIATION—Cont'd
　Airports—Cont'd
　　Authorities—Cont'd
　　　Alternate procedure for
　　　　incorporation—Cont'd
　　　　Dissolution.
　　　　　Procedure, §4-3-61.
　　　　Eminent domain.
　　　　　Powers, §4-3-47.
　　　　Federal aid.
　　　　　Receipt and
　　　　　　expenditure,
　　　　　　§4-3-48.
　　　　Filing of application for
　　　　　incorporation,
　　　　　§4-3-41.
　　　　Grants, §4-3-48.
　　　　Insurance.
　　　　　Eligibility of bond
　　　　　　issues as
　　　　　　investments,
　　　　　　§4-3-58.
　　　　Limitation of actions.
　　　　　Challenge of
　　　　　　proceedings for
　　　　　　issuance of bonds,
　　　　　　§4-3-52.
　　　　Loans.
　　　　　Federal, state and
　　　　　　local loans,
　　　　　　§4-3-48.
　　　　Local aid.
　　　　　Receipt and
　　　　　　expenditure,
　　　　　　§4-3-48.
　　　　Municipalities.
　　　　　Assistance, §4-3-49.
　　　　　Cooperation, §4-3-49.
　　　　　Investment of funds in
　　　　　　bond issues,
　　　　　　§4-3-57.
　　　　Notice.
　　　　　Bond issues, §4-3-52.
　　　　Officers, §4-3-46.
　　　　Personnel, §4-3-46.
　　　　Powers generally,
　　　　　§4-3-47.
　　　　Provisions of article
　　　　　cumulative, §4-3-62.
　　　　Purchases.
　　　　　Exemption from state
　　　　　　restrictions,
　　　　　　§4-3-60.
　　　　State aid.
　　　　　Receipt and
　　　　　　expenditure,
　　　　　　§4-3-48.
　　　　Taxation.
　　　　　Concessionaires,
　　　　　　§4-3-59.
　　　　　Exemption, §4-3-59.
　　　　Trusts and trustees.
　　　　　Eligibility of bond
　　　　　　issues as
　　　　　　investments,
　　　　　　§4-3-58.
　　　　Zoning.
　　　　　Powers of zoning,
　　　　　　§4-3-60.
　　　Board of directors, §4-3-5.
　　　　Alternate procedure for
　　　　　incorporation,
　　　　　§4-3-45.
　　　Bond issues.
　　　　Alternate procedure for
　　　　　incorporation,
　　　　　§§4-3-51 to 4-3-59.
　　　　Counties.
　　　　　Investment, §4-3-20.
　　　　Delivery, §4-3-16.
　　　　Denominations, §4-3-14.

AVIATION—Cont'd
　Airports—Cont'd
　　Authorities—Cont'd
　　　Bond issues—Cont'd
　　　　Execution of bonds,
　　　　　§4-3-16.
　　　　Exemption from
　　　　　taxation, §4-3-8.
　　　　Form, §4-3-14.
　　　　Insurance companies.
　　　　　Eligibility as
　　　　　　investments,
　　　　　　§4-3-21.
　　　　Investment of county,
　　　　　municipal, etc.,
　　　　　funds in bonds,
　　　　　§4-3-20.
　　　　Issuance, §4-3-14.
　　　　　Limitation period,
　　　　　　§4-3-15.
　　　　Limitation period for
　　　　　proceedings to
　　　　　challenge validity,
　　　　　etc., §4-3-15.
　　　　Maturity, §4-3-14.
　　　　Municipal corporations.
　　　　　Investment, §4-3-20.
　　　　Notice of bond
　　　　　resolutions, §4-3-15.
　　　　Refunding bonds,
　　　　　§4-3-19.
　　　　Resolutions.
　　　　　Publication of notice of
　　　　　　bond resolutions,
　　　　　　§4-3-15.
　　　　Sale, §4-3-14.
　　　　　Use of proceeds,
　　　　　　§4-3-18.
　　　　Savings banks.
　　　　　Eligibility as
　　　　　　investments,
　　　　　　§4-3-21.
　　　　Security of bonds,
　　　　　§4-3-17.
　　　　Terms, §4-3-14.
　　　　Validity.
　　　　　Limitation period for
　　　　　　proceedings to
　　　　　　challenge, §4-3-15.
　　　Certificate of incorporation,
　　　　§§4-3-2 to 4-3-4.
　　　　Alternate procedure for
　　　　　incorporation,
　　　　　§§4-3-41 to 4-3-44.
　　　　Approval, §4-3-2.
　　　　Contents, §4-3-3.
　　　　Execution, §4-3-4.
　　　　Form, §4-3-2.
　　　　Recordation, §4-3-4.
　　　Contracts.
　　　　Certain contracts
　　　　　validated, §4-3-23.
　　　　Exemption from state
　　　　　restrictions, §4-3-10.
　　　　Alternate procedure
　　　　　for incorporation,
　　　　　§4-3-60.
　　　Counties.
　　　　Assistance and
　　　　　cooperation, §4-3-13.
　　　　Alternate procedure
　　　　　for incorporation,
　　　　　§4-3-49.
　　　　Investment of county
　　　　　funds, §4-3-20.
　　　　Alternate procedure
　　　　　for incorporation,
　　　　　§4-3-57.

AVIATION—Cont'd
　Airports—Cont'd
　　Authorities—Cont'd
　　　Definitions, §4-3-1.
　　　　Alternate procedure for
　　　　　incorporation,
　　　　　§4-3-40.
　　　Directors, §4-3-5.
　　　　Alternate procedure for
　　　　　incorporation,
　　　　　§4-3-45.
　　　　Immunity, §4-3-7.
　　　　Alternate procedure
　　　　　for incorporation,
　　　　　§§4-3-45, 4-3-50.
　　　Dissolution.
　　　　Procedure, §4-3-22.
　　　　Alternate procedure
　　　　　for incorporation,
　　　　　§4-3-61.
　　　Eminent domain.
　　　　Alternate procedure for
　　　　　incorporation,
　　　　　§4-3-47.
　　　Exemption from taxation,
　　　　§4-3-8.
　　　　Alternate procedure for
　　　　　incorporation,
　　　　　§4-3-59.
　　　Federal aid, §4-3-12.
　　　　Alternate procedure for
　　　　　incorporation,
　　　　　§4-3-48.
　　　Immunity, §4-3-7.
　　　　Alternate procedure for
　　　　　incorporation,
　　　　　§4-3-50.
　　　Income.
　　　　Exemption from
　　　　　taxation, §4-3-8.
　　　　Alternate procedure
　　　　　for incorporation,
　　　　　§4-3-59.
　　　Incorporation.
　　　　Procedure, §4-3-2.
　　　　Alternate procedure,
　　　　　§§4-3-41 to 4-3-62.
　　　Liability.
　　　　Immunity, §4-3-7.
　　　　Alternate procedure
　　　　　for incorporation,
　　　　　§4-3-50.
　　　Municipal corporations.
　　　　Assistance and
　　　　　cooperation, §4-3-13.
　　　　Alternate procedure
　　　　　for incorporation,
　　　　　§4-3-49.
　　　　Bond issues.
　　　　　Investment in funds,
　　　　　　§4-3-57.
　　　　　Borrowing of money to
　　　　　　assist authority,
　　　　　　§4-3-80.
　　　Negligence.
　　　　Immunity of authority
　　　　　and directors, §4-3-7.
　　　　Alternate procedure
　　　　　for incorporation,
　　　　　§4-3-50.
　　　Officers, §4-3-6.
　　　　Alternate procedure for
　　　　　incorporation,
　　　　　§4-3-46.
　　　Personnel.
　　　　Alternate procedure for
　　　　　incorporation,
　　　　　§4-3-46.

AVIATION—Cont'd
Airports—Cont'd
  Authorities—Cont'd
    Powers, §4-3-11.
      Zoning powers, §4-3-10.
        Alternate procedure
          for incorporation,
          §4-3-60.
    Property.
      Exemptions from
        taxation.
        Alternate procedure
          for incorporation,
          §4-3-59.
    Publication of notice of
      bond resolutions.
      Alternate procedure for
        incorporation,
        §4-3-52.
    Purchasing restrictions.
      Exemptions from state
        restrictions.
      Alternate procedure
        for incorporation,
        §4-3-60.
    Refunding bonds.
      Alternate procedure for
        incorporation,
        §4-3-56.
    State aid.
      Alternate procedure for
        incorporation,
        §4-3-48.
    Zoning.
      Powers.
        Alternate procedure
          for incorporation,
          §4-3-60.
  Bond issues.
    Airport authorities,
      §§4-3-14 to 4-3-21.
    Authority to issue bonds
      for acquisition,
      improvement, etc.,
      §§4-1-1, 4-4-11.
    Municipal corporations.
      General provisions.
      See MUNICIPAL
        CORPORATIONS.
  Certificates of approval.
    Applications.
      Required prior to
        acquisition, §4-2-73.
    Hearings, §4-2-74.
    Notice, §4-2-74.
    Order, §4-2-74.
    Revocation, §4-2-79.
  Concessions, §4-2-94.
    Liens of concessionaires,
      §4-4-9.
    Municipal airports.
      Grant of concessions,
        §4-4-8.
    Taxation, §4-3-8.
  Condemnation.
    Municipal airports.
      Acquisition of lands,
        §4-4-6.
    State airports.
      Abandonment of
        proceedings, §4-2-93.
      Power of condemnation,
        §4-2-90.
        Exercise in name of
          state, §4-2-90.
  Constitution of Alabama.
    Construction, maintenance,
      etc., Const. Ala., amd.
      58.

AVIATION—Cont'd
Airports—Cont'd
  Contracts.
    Law governing contracts,
      §4-2-43.
  Control and warning
    stations, §§4-7-1 to 4-7-3.
  Acquisition of property,
    §4-7-1.
  Condemnation proceedings.
    City may pay awards
      and costs, §4-7-2.
  Conveyance of property,
    §4-7-1.
  Cooperation with federal
    government, §4-7-3.
  Eminent domain.
    City may pay awards
      and costs, §4-7-2.
  Establishment.
    Cooperation with federal
      government, §4-7-3.
  Operation.
    Cooperation with federal
      government, §4-7-3.
  Sites.
    Cities may furnish,
      §4-7-1.
    Condemnation
      proceedings.
      City may pay awards
        and costs, §4-7-2.
    Procedure for acquisition
      and conveyance,
      §4-7-1.
  Counties.
    Authorities, §§4-3-1 to
      4-3-80.
    Bond issues.
      Authority to issue bonds,
      §§4-1-1, 4-4-11.
    Warrants and certificates
      of indebtedness,
      §§4-5-1 to 4-5-5.
    Zoning, §§4-6-1 to 4-6-15.
  County boards of health.
    Duties, §22-3-2.
  Definitions, §4-6-2.
    Airport authorities, §4-3-1.
    Alternate procedure for
      incorporation,
      §4-3-40.
    Municipal airports, §4-4-1.
  Development fund.
    State airports development
      fund, §4-2-42.
  Easements.
    Acquisition, §4-6-13.
      State airports, §4-2-91.
  Eminent domain. See within
    this heading, "Eminent
    domain."
  Exceptions to regulations,
    §4-2-80.
  Fowl.
    Prohibited upon premises
      of airports, §4-2-6.
  Funds.
    State airports development
      fund, §4-2-42.
  Hazards.
    Navigational hazards. See
      within this heading,
      "Navigational
      hazards."
  Health.
    Duties of county boards,
      §22-3-2.
  Highways.
    Use of highway leading to
      or from airport, §4-3-9.

AVIATION—Cont'd
Airports—Cont'd
  Improvement.
    Authority of counties and
      municipalities to issue
      bonds, §4-1-1.
  Industrial development
    authority.
    Exercise of powers granted
      to airport authorities,
      §41-10-26.1.
  Inspections, §4-2-50.
  Licenses, §4-2-72.
    Display, §4-2-78.
    Hearings, §4-2-74.
    Issuance, §4-2-75.
    Limitation of operations,
      §4-2-73.
    Notice, §4-2-74.
    Operation of airport
      without license,
      §4-2-73.
    Order, §4-2-74.
    Revocation, §4-2-79.
  Motor vehicles.
    Trespass and operation on
      airports, §4-2-7.
  Municipal airports.
    General provisions, §§4-4-1
      to 4-4-16.
    See MUNICIPAL
      CORPORATIONS.
    Zoning, §§4-6-1 to 4-6-15.
  Municipal regulations,
    §4-4-14.
  Navigational hazards.
    Zoning. See within this
      heading, "Navigational
      hazards."
  Operation.
    Limitation of operations,
      §4-2-73.
    Prohibited without license,
      §4-2-73.
    State airports, §4-2-90.
  Parks.
    Municipal airports.
      Use of parks for airports,
        §4-4-3.
  Permits.
    Zoning permits, §4-6-8.
  Proposed airports.
    Application for certificate
      of approval required,
      §4-2-73.
  Records.
    Zoning, §4-6-10.
  Roads.
    Use of public roads leading
      to or from airport,
      §4-3-9.
  Sale.
    Municipal airports,
      §4-4-13.
  Sites.
    Approval, §4-2-72.
  Solicitation of votes.
    Property.
      Exemption from
        taxation, §4-3-8.
    Provisions of chapter
      cumulative, §4-3-24.
    Publication of notice of
      bond resolutions,
      §4-3-15.
    Purchasing restrictions.
      Exemption from state
        restrictions, §4-3-10.
    Refunding bonds, §4-3-19.
    State aid, §4-3-12.

AVIATION—Cont'd
  Airports—Cont'd
    Solicitation of votes—Cont'd
      Streets, highways, etc.
        Tax or license for use
          leading to or from
          airport prohibited,
          §4-3-9.
    Taxation.
      Tax for use of public
        streets, etc., leading
        to or from airport
        prohibited, §4-3-9.
    Zoning.
      Exemption from state
        zoning restrictions,
        §4-3-10.
      Powers, §4-3-10.
  State airports, §§4-2-90 to
    4-2-95.
    Acquisition, §4-2-90.
    Aeronautics commission.
      Joint activities with
        other governmental
        agencies, §4-2-92.
    Concessions.
      Airport concessions,
        §4-2-94.
    Condemnation.
      Abandonment
        proceedings, §4-2-93.
      Power of condemnation,
        §§4-2-90, 4-2-93.
    Construction, §4-2-90.
    Development fund, §4-2-42.
    Disposition, §4-2-90.
    Easements, §4-2-91.
    Eminent domain.
      Abandonment
        proceedings, §4-2-93.
      Power of condemnation,
        §§4-2-90, 4-2-93.
    Examinations.
      Right of entry, §4-2-93.
    Exclusive use.
      Grant of right
        prohibited, §4-2-90.
    Joint activities with other
      governmental
      agencies, §4-2-92.
    Lease of property, airports
      or space.
      Improvements, etc.,
        §4-2-94.
      Charges or rental,
        §4-2-95.
    Liens for services, §4-2-95.
    Operation, §4-2-90.
    Protection privileges,
      §4-2-91.
    Right of entry, §4-2-93.
    Sale of property, etc., to
      other governmental
      bodies, §4-2-94.
    Services.
      Charges or rental,
        §4-2-95.
      Liens for services,
        §4-2-95.
    Surveys.
      Right of entry for
        surveys, §4-2-93.
    Streets.
      Use of public streets
        leading to or from
        airport, §4-3-9.
    Suspension of operations of
      aircraft, §4-2-79.
    Trespass.
      Vehicles, §4-2-7.

AVIATION—Cont'd
  Airports—Cont'd
    Warning stations, §§4-7-1 to
      4-7-3.
    Warrants for payment of
      money.
      County warrants and
        certificates of
        indebtedness, §§4-5-1
        to 4-5-5.
    Zoning, §§4-6-1 to 4-6-15.
      Abatement of violations,
        §4-6-12.
      Administration of
        regulations, §4-6-9.
      Administrative agency,
        §4-6-10.
      Appeals, §4-6-11.
      Airport authorities,
        §4-3-10.
      Alternate procedure for
        incorporation,
        §4-3-60.
      Air rights.
        Acquisition, §4-6-13.
      Appeals, §4-6-11.
      Applicability of chapter.
        Existing municipal
          zoning ordinances,
          boundaries, etc.,
          §4-6-14.
      Boundaries.
        Existing municipal
          zoning boundaries,
          §4-6-14.
      Commission, §4-6-5.
      Comprehensive zoning
        regulations.
        Relation of airport
          zoning regulations,
          §4-6-15.
      Definitions, §4-6-2.
      Easements.
        Acquisition, §4-6-13.
      Enforcement of
        regulations, §4-6-9.
      Existing municipal zoning
        ordinances,
        boundaries, etc.
        Chapter not to affect,
          §4-6-14.
      Hazards. See within this
        heading, "Navigational
        hazards."
      Nonconforming uses,
        §4-6-7.
      Permits, §4-6-8.
      Records.
        Official actions of
          administrative
          agency, §4-6-10.
      Regulations.
        Abatement of violations,
          §4-6-12.
        Administration, §4-6-9.
        Adoption, §4-6-6.
        Authority of counties
          and municipalities to
          adopt, §4-6-4.
        Comprehensive zoning
          regulations.
          Relation of airport
            zoning regulations,
            §4-6-15.
        Correction of violations,
          §4-6-12.
        Enforcement, §4-6-9.
        Standards for adoption,
          §4-6-7.

AVIATION—Cont'd
  Airports—Cont'd
    Zoning—Cont'd
      Regulations—Cont'd
        Violations of regulations.
          Remedies for
          correction,
          abatement, etc.,
          §4-6-12.
      Remedies.
        Violations of regulations,
          §4-6-12.
      Short title of chapter,
        §4-6-1.
      Variances, §4-6-8.
      Violations of regulations.
        Remedies, §4-6-12.
  Air schools.
    Certificate.
      Operation without, §4-2-77.
      Regulation, §4-2-72.
    Licenses.
      Operation without, §4-2-77.
    Permits.
      Operation without, §4-2-77.
    Regulation, §4-2-72.
    Suspension of operations,
      §4-2-79.
  Airspace.
    Reservations, §4-2-71.
    State sovereignty over
      airspace, §4-2-70.
  **Alabama institute of
    aviation technology at
    Ozark.**
    Vocational trade school.
      Operated as additional
        vocational trade
        school, §16-60-198.
  Alcoholic beverages.
    Licenses.
      Retail common carrier
        liquor license,
        §28-3A-18.
      Special retail license for
        airport authority,
        §28-3A-19.
  Animals.
    Domestic animals or fowl on
      airports, §4-2-6.
  Appeals.
    Aeronautics commission.
      Failure to file appeal,
        §4-2-51.
      Procedure, §4-2-50.
    Airports.
      Zoning, §4-6-11.
  Authorities.
    Airport authorities. See
      within this heading,
      "Airports."
  Blind persons.
    Right to use of public
      conveyances and
      transportation facilities,
      §21-7-3.
  Bond issues.
    Airport authorities. See
      within this heading,
      "Airports."
    Space science exhibit
      commission.
      See SPACE SCIENCE
        EXHIBIT
        COMMISSION.
  Carriers.
    Air commerce.
      See AIR COMMERCE.
  Commerce.
    General provisions.
      See AIR COMMERCE.

AVIATION—Cont'd
Commercial code.
Secured transactions.
Security interest in
airplanes, §7-9-103.
Commissions.
Aeronautics commission,
§§4-2-30 to 4-2-50. See
within this heading,
"Aeronautics
commission."
Space science exhibit
commission, §§41-9-430
to 41-9-439.
See SPACE SCIENCE
EXHIBIT
COMMISSION.
Conflicting laws.
Repeal, §4-2-13.
Constitution of Alabama.
Construction, maintenance,
etc., of airports and air
navigation facilities by
state, Const. Ala., amd.
58.
Contracts.
Airports.
Acquisition, construction,
etc., §4-2-43.
Contracts made during flight,
§4-2-5.
**Control and warning
stations,** §§4-7-1 to 4-7-3.
Counties.
Airports.
General provisions.
See COUNTIES.
Zoning, §§4-6-1 to 4-6-15.
See within this
heading, "Airports."
Criminal law and procedure.
Jurisdiction of crimes, §4-2-4.
Definitions, §4-2-3.
Airport authorities, §4-3-1.
Alternate procedure for
incorporation, §4-3-40.
Airports, §4-6-2.
Airport authorities, §4-3-1.
Municipal airports, §4-4-1.
Department.
State aeronautics
department. See within
this heading, "State
aeronautics department."
Director of aeronautics.
Appointment, §4-2-35.
Assistant director, §4-2-35.1.
Compensation, §4-2-35.
Duties, §4-2-36.
Delegation of duties by
commission, §4-2-35.
Hearings, §4-2-48.
Reports, §4-2-49.
Investigations, §4-2-48.
Reports, §4-2-49.
Orders.
Enforcement, §4-2-48.
Powers, §4-2-36.
Delegation of powers by
commission, §4-2-35.
Qualifications, §4-2-35.
Reports.
Investigation, hearings,
etc., §4-2-49.
Subpoenas.
Enforcement, §4-2-48.
Term of office, §4-2-35.
Easements.
Airports.
Acquisition of easements,
§4-6-13.

AVIATION—Cont'd
Education.
Air schools. See within this
heading, "Air schools."
Ground schools, §4-2-77.
Helicopter pilots association,
§§4-9-1 to 4-9-7. See
within this heading,
"Helicopter pilots
association."
Eminent domain.
Aircraft, control and warning
stations.
City may pay awards and
costs, §4-7-2.
Airport authorities.
Alternate procedure for
incorporation, §4-3-47.
Municipal airports.
Acquisition of lands by
condemnation, §4-4-6.
State airports.
Abandonment of
proceedings, §4-2-93.
Power of condemnation,
§§4-2-90, 4-2-93.
**Enforcement of aeronautics
laws,** §4-2-47.
Exhibitions.
Space science exhibit
commission, §§41-9-430
to 4-9-439.
See SPACE SCIENCE
EXHIBIT
COMMISSION.
Fish and game.
Use of aircraft for hunting,
etc., prohibited, §4-2-9.
Fowl.
Domestic fowl on airports,
§4-2-6.
Funds.
Airports.
Federal funding, §§4-2-39,
4-2-40, 4-2-44, 4-3-12,
4-3-48.
Helicopter pilots association,
§§4-9-4, 4-9-5.
Special funds, §4-2-42.
State aeronautics department
fund, §§4-2-41, 4-2-45.
State airports development
fund, §4-2-42.
Governor.
Aeronautics commission.
Annual report, §4-2-31.
Ground schools.
Certificates.
Operation without, §4-2-77.
Licenses.
Operation without, §4-2-77.
Permits.
Operation without, §4-2-77.
Hall of fame.
Board, §§41-9-720 to
41-9-722.
Appointment of members,
§41-9-721.
Appropriations.
Legislative
appropriations,
§41-9-722.
Composition, §41-9-721.
Created, §41-9-720.
Expenses, §41-9-721.
Function, §41-9-720.
Organization, §41-9-721.
Purpose, §41-9-720.
Taxation.
Exemptions, §41-9-722.
Terms of office, §41-9-721.

AVIATION—Cont'd
Handicapped persons.
Right to use of public
conveyances and
transportation facilities,
§21-7-3.
Hazards.
Navigational hazards. See
within this heading,
"Navigational hazards."
Hearings.
Aeronautics commission,
§4-2-48.
Reports, §4-2-49.
Helicopter pilots association,
§§4-9-1 to 4-9-7.
Board of directors.
Duties, §4-9-2.
Powers and duties, §4-9-2.
Rules and regulations,
§4-9-3.
Board of special directors,
§4-9-7.
Duties, §4-9-3.
Education and instruction
fund, §4-9-4.
Establishment, §4-9-1.
Federal aid.
Designation as state
agency for purpose of
receiving, §4-9-5.
Funds.
Education and instruction
fund, §4-9-4.
Powers and duties, §4-9-3.
Rules and regulations,
§4-9-3.
Superintendent of education.
Supervision of association,
§4-9-6.
Hunting.
Use of aircraft for hunting,
etc., prohibited, §4-2-9.
**Institute of aviation
technology at Ozark.**
Vocational trade school.
Operated as additional
vocational trade
school, §16-60-198.
Instructors.
Air schools, §4-2-77.
Interstate commerce.
Aircraft.
Exceptions to regulations,
§4-2-80.
Jurisdiction.
Crimes and torts, §4-2-4.
Landing fields. See within
this heading, "Airports."
Maps.
Recording of aerial
photographs or maps,
§§35-2-80 to 35-2-82.
Motor fuels.
Additional excise tax.
Aircraft.
Exemptions, §40-17-220.
Motor vehicles.
Trespass and operation of
vehicles on airports,
§4-2-7.
Municipal corporations.
Airports.
General provisions.
See MUNICIPAL
CORPORATIONS.
Zoning. See within this
heading, "Airports."

AVIATION—Cont'd
  Navigational facilities.
    Inspections.
      Authority of aeronautics
        commission to inspect,
        §4-2-50.
  Navigational hazards.
    Abatement, §4-6-12.
    Alteration.
      Declared public purpose,
        §4-6-3.
    Contrary to public interest,
      §§4-2-71, 4-6-3.
    Correction, §4-6-12.
    Definitions, §4-6-2.
    Elimination.
      Declared public purpose,
        §4-6-3.
    Lights.
      Installation upon hazards,
        §4-6-8.
      Municipal corporations,
        §4-4-10.
    Markers.
      Installation upon hazards,
        §4-6-8.
      Municipal corporations,
        §4-4-10.
    Municipal corporations.
      Markers or lights on
        hazards, §4-4-10.
  Penalties.
    Violations of chapter,
      §4-2-12.
  Photography.
    Recording of aerial
      photographs or maps,
      §§35-2-80 to 35-2-82.
  Pilots.
    General provisions. See
      within this heading,
      "Airmen."
    Helicopter pilots association,
      §§4-9-1 to 4-9-7. See
      within this heading,
      "Helicopter pilots
      association."
  Purpose of chapter, §4-2-2.
  Quarantine.
    Refusal of freight, §22-12-21.
    Supervision of public
      conveyances, §22-12-21.
    Transportation of person or
      thing in violation,
      §22-12-22.
  Railroads.
    Operation of transportation
      methods, §10-5-9.
  **Reckless operation of
    aircraft,** §4-2-10.
  Recordation.
    Aerial photographs or maps,
      §§35-2-80 to 35-2-82.
  Records.
    Airports.
      Zoning, §4-6-10.
  Repeal of conflicting laws,
    §4-2-13.
  Reports.
    Aeronautics commission.
      Annual report to governor,
        §4-2-31.
      Hearings, §4-2-49.
  Reservations.
    Airspace reservations,
      §4-2-71.
  Right of entry.
    Airport surveys and
      examinations, §4-2-93.

AVIATION—Cont'd
  Rules and regulations.
    Aeronautics commission,
      §4-2-37.
    Airports.
      Zoning. See within this
        heading, "Airports."
  Schools.
    Air schools. See within this
      heading, "Air schools."
    Ground schools, §4-2-77.
  Secured transactions.
    Determination of validity
      and perfection of security
      interest in airplane,
      §7-9-103.
  Service of process.
    Aeronautics commission.
      Orders.
        Service upon interested
          persons, §4-2-50.
  **Space science exhibit
    commission.**
    General provisions.
      See SPACE SCIENCE
        EXHIBIT
        COMMISSION.
  State.
    Sovereignty over airspace,
      §4-2-70.
  **State aeronautics
    department.**
    Composition, §4-2-30.
    Created, §4-2-30.
    Disbursement of funds,
      §4-2-45.
    Expenses, §4-2-45.
    Funds.
      Disbursement, §4-2-45.
      Expenditures from fund,
        §4-2-41.
    Short title of chapter, §4-2-1.
  State airports, §§4-2-90 to
    4-2-95.
  Subpoenas.
    Enforcement, §4-2-48.
  Taxation.
    Air commerce.
      Exemptions from taxation.
      Air carriers.
        See AIR COMMERCE.
    Airport authorities.
      Exemption from taxation,
        §4-3-8.
      Alternate procedure for
        incorporation,
        §4-3-59.
    Motor fuels.
      Additional excise tax.
      Aircraft.
        Exemptions, §40-17-220.
  Torts.
    Jurisdiction, §4-2-4.
    State, municipal, etc.,
      immunity from tort
      liability, §4-2-4.
  Trade schools.
    Alabama institute of aviation
      technology at Ozark.
      To be operated as
        additional vocational
        trade school,
        §16-60-198.
  Transportation companies.
    Air commerce, §§37-9-1 to
      37-9-32.
      See AIR COMMERCE.
    General provisions, §§37-2-1
      to 37-2-184.
      See TRANSPORTATION
        COMPANIES.

AVIATION—Cont'd
  Trespass.
    Vehicles.
      Trespass and operation on
        airports, landing fields,
        etc., §4-2-7.
  **Unauthorized use,
    possession, etc., of
    aircraft,** §4-2-11.
  United States.
    Airports.
      Federal funding.
        Acquisition, construction,
          etc. See within this
          heading, "Airports."
      Airport authorities,
        §4-3-12.
        Alternate procedure
          for incorporation,
          §4-3-48.
  Violations of chapter,
    §4-2-12.
  Warning stations.
    Control and warning
      stations, §§4-7-1 to 4-7-3.
  **Warrants for payment of
    money.**
    Airports.
      Warrants and certificates
        of indebtedness for
        airport purposes,
        §§4-5-1 to 4-5-5.
  Weapons.
    Discharging firearm into
      aircraft, §13A-11-61.
  Zoning.
    Airports. See within this
      heading, "Airports."

A VINCULO DIVORCE,
  §§30-2-1 to 30-2-11.
  See DIVORCE AND
    ALIMONY.

AWARDS.
  Arbitration and award.
    General provisions, §§6-6-1 to
      6-6-11.
      See ARBITRATION AND
        AWARD.
  Damages.
    See DAMAGES.

B

BACTERIOLOGISTS.
  Licenses, §40-12-126.

BAD CHECKS.
  Actions.
    Holder of worthless
      instruments.
      Right of action, §6-5-285.
  Charge for bad checks.
    Imposition authorized,
      §8-8-15.
    Not deemed interest, finance
      or other charge, §8-8-15.
  District attorneys.
    Special services division.
      Worthless check unit,
        §12-17-224.
  **Negotiating worthless
    instruments,** §§13A-9-13.1
    to 13A-9-13.3.
  Penalty and service charge,
    §8-8-15.
  Service charge, §8-8-15.
  Taxation.
    Payment of tax with bad
      check, §40-29-70.

BAGGAGE.

Hotels.

See HOTELS, INNS AND OTHER TRANSIENT LODGING PLACES.

Liens.

Hotel keepers.
Liens generally, §§35-11-130, 35-11-131.
Restaurant keepers.
Liens generally, §§35-11-130, 35-11-131.

Motor vehicle carriers, §§37-3-7, 37-3-12.

Penitentiary.

Search of convict's baggage, §14-3-35.

Seizures.

Liens of hotel and restaurant keepers.
Seizure and sale of goods and baggage of guests, §35-11-131.

Transportation companies.

Passengers.
Personal baggage, §§37-2-35 to 37-2-39.

BAIL AND RECOGNIZANCE, §§15-13-1 to 15-13-82.

Admission to bail.

Defined, §15-13-1.

Amount.

Endorsement on writ of arrest, §15-13-7.
Presumption of aggravated offense when fixing amount, §15-7-22.

Appeals.

Affirmation of conviction or dismissal of appeal.
Duty of defendant on bail to surrender, §12-22-244.
Denial of bail, §15-13-8.
Forfeiture of undertaking.
Proceedings when undertaking forfeited, §12-22-246.
Reversal of conviction and case remanded.
Effect of undertaking, §12-22-245.
Stay of sentence, §§12-22-170, 12-22-171.
Writs of error.
Admission of defendant to bail, §12-22-222.

Appearance.

Forfeiture for failure of defendant to appear, §15-13-80.

Applications.

Limitation on number, §15-13-8.

Arrest.

After conditional judgment, §15-13-63.
Discharge of bail by arrest and surrender of defendant, §15-13-62.

Bail bondsmen.

Judicial and ministerial officers prohibited, §15-13-24.

Bail jumping.

Discretionary bail schedule, ARJA, Rule 2.

BAIL AND RECOGNIZANCE —Cont'd

Bail jumping—Cont'd

First degree bail jumping.
Class C felony, §13A-10-39.
Defenses to prosecution, §13A-10-39.
Elements, §13A-10-39.
Second degree bail jumping.
Class A misdemeanor, §13A-10-40.
Defenses to prosecution, §13A-10-40.
Elements, §13A-10-40.

Bail taken in open court.

Bail not taken in open court.
Form and requisites, §15-13-21.
Entry in minutes, §15-13-20.
Form of entry, §15-13-20.

Bond issues.

Deposit of federal or state bonds in lieu of cash, §15-13-43.

Bondsmen.

Bond required for bondsmen, §15-13-22.
Undertaking of bail. See within this heading, "Undertaking of bail."

Capital offenses, §15-13-3.

Capital punishment.

Discretionary bail schedule.
Capital felonies, ARJA, Rule 2.

Cash deposit.

Application in satisfaction of fine, §15-13-42.
Exoneration of bail, §15-13-41.
Forfeiture of deposit, §15-13-80.
Government bonds in lieu of cash, §15-13-43.
Permitted after bail given and prior to forfeiture, §15-13-41.
Refund of surplus, §15-13-42.
Return of deposit upon surrender by defendant, §15-13-65.
When authorized in lieu of bail, §15-13-40.

Clerks of court.

Return of undertakings to clerk, §15-13-25.

Conditional judgment.

Arrest of defendant after conditional judgment, §15-13-63.
Entry, §15-13-81.
Execution and return of notice, §15-13-81.
Exoneration of bail, §15-13-62.
Notice to defendant, §15-13-81.
When excuses for default heard, §15-13-82.
When set aside or made absolute, §15-13-82.

Constitution of Alabama.

Excessive bail, Const. Ala., art. I, §16.
Right to bail, Const. Ala., art. I, §16.

Constitution of the United States.

Excessive bail, Const. U. S., Amendment VIII.

BAIL AND RECOGNIZANCE —Cont'd

Courts.

Officers.
Signing of bond for appearance or release of prisoner, §36-10-11.
Taking bail in open court.
Bail not taken in open court.
Form and requisites, §15-13-21.
Entry in minutes, §15-13-20.

Definitions, §15-13-1.

Discharge of bail.

Surrender of defendant prior to conditional judgment, §15-13-62.
When bail not deemed discharged, §15-13-61.

Discharge of defendant.

By arresting officer, §15-7-20.
By judge or magistrate, §15-7-21.
Certification and delivery of warrant with undertaking, §15-7-21.
Presumption of aggravated offense when fixing amount, §15-7-22.

Discretionary bail schedule, ARJA, Rule 2.

Drugs.

Municipal ordinance violations.
Discretionary bail schedule, ARJA, Rule 2.

Entry.

Form, §15-13-20.
Open court.
Entry in minutes when taken in open court, §15-13-20.

Escape.

Discretionary bail schedule, ARJA, Rule 2.

Extradition.

See EXTRADITION.

Factors considered in setting bail, ARJA, Rule 2.

Felonies.

Discharge of defendant upon posting of bail, §15-13-6.
Discretionary bail schedule, ARJA, Rule 2.
Fixing of bail for felony, §15-13-6.

Forfeiture.

Appeals.
Proceedings when undertaking forfeited, §12-22-246.
Cash deposited in lieu of bail, §15-13-80.
Failure of defendant to appear, §15-13-80.
Government bonds deposited in lieu of cash.
Sale of bonds, §15-13-43.
When excuses for default heard, §15-13-82.

Forms.

Bail not taken in open court, §15-13-21.
Bail taken in open court, §15-13-20.
Conditional judgment, §15-13-81.

BAIL AND RECOGNIZANCE
—Cont'd
Habeas corpus.
Admission to bail if charged
with bailable offense,
§15-21-22.
Failure to appear, §15-21-20.
Forfeiture of bail, §15-21-22.
Persons entitled to prosecute
writ.
Persons confined for failure
to enter into
undertaking to keep
the peace, §15-21-2.
Procedure when sufficient
bail not offered,
§15-21-22.
Transmission of bail to clerk
of court, §15-21-22.
Without notice, §15-21-13.
Homicide.
Discretionary bail schedule.
Murder, ARJA, Rule 2.
Judges.
Signing of bond for
appearance or release of
prisoner.
Prohibited, §36-10-11.
Magistrates.
District court magistrates
agency division.
Authority of magistrates
in, ARJA, Rule 18.
Municipal court magistrates
agency division.
Authority of magistrates
in, ARJA, Rule 18.
Mentally ill.
Execution for
acknowledgment of
undertaking, §15-13-23.
Minors.
Execution for
acknowledgment of
undertaking, §15-13-23.
Misdemeanors.
Discharge of defendant by
sheriff after indictment,
§15-13-5.
Discretionary bail schedule,
ARJA, Rule 2.
When new bail allowed,
§15-13-64.
Motor vehicles.
General provisions.
See MOTOR VEHICLES.
Traffic related offenses.
Discretionary bail
schedule, ARJA, Rule
2.
Municipal courts.
Admission to bail of persons
charged with violations
of municipal ordinances,
§12-14-5.
Waiver of appearance
bond, §12-14-5.
New undertaking.
When required, §15-13-26.
Officers.
Judicial and ministerial
officers prohibited from
signing bonds, etc.,
§15-13-24.
Opportunity to give bail.
Prisoners entitled to
opportunity, §15-13-4.

BAIL AND RECOGNIZANCE
—Cont'd
Penitentiary.
Commission of offense during
incarceration.
When eligible for bail,
§14-3-56.
Personal recognizance,
§15-13-4; ARJA, Rule 2.
Preliminary hearings.
Amount to be endorsed on
commitment, §15-11-11.
Commitment of defendant to
bail, §15-11-3.
Default.
Certification to circuit
court, §15-11-4.
District court certificate as
presumptive evidence,
§15-11-4.
Issuance of alias warrant
upon default, §15-11-5.
Discharge of defendant,
§15-11-11.
When defendant committed
to bail, §15-11-10.
Qualifications for bail,
§15-13-22.
Infants, §15-13-23.
Insane persons, §15-13-23.
**Release on personal
recognizance,** §15-13-4.
Returns.
Undertakings returned to
clerk of court, §15-13-25.
Right to bail, §15-13-2; Const.
Ala., art. I, §16.
Exceptions, §15-13-3.
Persons charged with capital
offense, §15-13-3.
Prisoners entitled to
opportunity to give bail,
§15-13-4.
Schedule.
Discretionary bail schedule,
ARJA, Rule 2.
Setting bail.
Factors considered, ARJA,
Rule 2.
Surrender of defendant.
Agent may be authorized to
arrest defendant,
§15-13-62.
Exoneration of bail,
§15-13-62.
Required to exonerate bail,
§15-13-64.
Return of cash deposit upon
surrender, §15-13-65.
Taking of bail.
Defined, §15-13-1.
Open court.
Bail not taken in open
court.
Form and requisites,
§15-13-21.
Entry into minutes,
§15-13-20.
Undertaking of bail.
Extent undertaking binds
parties thereto,
§15-13-60.
Judicial and ministerial
officers prohibited,
§15-13-24.
Qualifications, §15-13-22.
When new undertaking may
be required, §15-13-26.
Writs of error.
Admission of defendant to
bail, §12-22-222.

BAILIFFS.
Additional positions.
Authorization by
administrative director
of courts, §12-17-310.
Circuit courts, ARJA, Rule
11.
Compensation, §12-17-311.
District courts, ARJA, Rule
11.
Existing positions continued,
§12-17-310.
Number of bailiffs,
§12-17-311.

BAILMENTS.
Actions.
Trespass to personal
property, §6-5-263.
Commercial code.
Investment securities.
No conversion by good
faith delivery,
§7-8-318.
Sales.
Seller's remedy of stoppage
of delivery in transit,
§7-2-705.
Investment securities.
No conversion by good faith
delivery, §7-8-318.

BAIT.
General provisions.
See FISH AND GAME.
Marine resources.
Licenses.
Shrimp bait dealers,
§§9-12-54.1 to
9-12-54.7.
See MARINE
RESOURCES.

BALDWIN COUNTY.
Barbers.
Chapter not applicable to
Baldwin county,
§34-5-15.
Court costs and charges,
Const. Ala., amd. 229.
Hospitals.
Special district tax for public
hospital purposes, Const.
Ala., amds. 230, 471.
Libraries.
Special property tax for
public library purposes,
Const. Ala., amd. 319.
Officers.
Compensation of certain
officers, Const. Ala.,
amd. 229.
Roads.
Districts to build and
maintain public roads,
Const. Ala., amd. 15.
School tax.
Additional tax for school
purposes, Const. Ala.,
amd. 162.
Seawalls.
Districts to build and
maintain seawalls,
Const. Ala., amd. 15.
**Water supply and
waterworks.**
Wells.
Inapplicability of chapter,
§22-24-12.

BALLET.
Sales tax.
Exemption.
Gross proceeds from sales
of admissions exempt,
§40-23-4.

BALLOTS.
Elections generally.
See ELECTIONS.
Municipal elections.
See MUNICIPAL
CORPORATIONS.

BANDS.
Counties.
Appropriations for bands,
§11-80-4.
Municipal corporations.
Appropriations for municipal
bands, §11-80-4.

BANG'S DISEASE.
Cattle.
General provisions,
§§2-15-190 to 2-15-197.
See LIVESTOCK.

**BANKRUPTCY AND
INSOLVENCY.**
Alcoholic beverages.
Cancellation of license upon
bankruptcy of licensee,
§28-3A-23.
Licenses.
Table wine licenses.
Bankruptcy of licensee,
§28-7-14.
**Banks and financial
institutions.**
See BANKS AND
FINANCIAL
INSTITUTIONS.
Blind persons.
Assistance to needy blind
persons.
Assistance not to pass
through trustee,
§38-5-5.
Bulk transfers.
Trustees in bankruptcy.
Transfers excepted from
article, §7-6-103.
Commercial code.
See COMMERCIAL CODE.
Congress.
Powers of congress, Const. U.
S., Art. I, §8.
**Constitution of the United
States.**
Powers of congress, Const. U.
S., Art. I, §8.
Corporations, §§10-2A-2,
10-2A-309.
Criminal law and procedure.
Financial statements.
Issuing false statements,
§13A-9-49.
Decedents' estates.
Insolvent estates, §§43-2-700
to 43-2-813.
See EXECUTORS AND
ADMINISTRATORS.
Decrees.
Recordation, §35-4-52.
Discharge in bankruptcy.
Affirmative defense, ARCP,
Rule 8 (c).
Drugs.
Notice of bankruptcy sale of
drugs and medicines,
§34-23-6.

**BANKRUPTCY AND
INSOLVENCY**—Cont'd
**Executors and
administrators.**
Insolvent estates, §§43-2-700
to 43-2-813.
See EXECUTORS AND
ADMINISTRATORS.
Financial statements.
Issuing false statements,
§13A-9-49.
Fraud.
Fraud in insolvency,
§13A-9-48.
Fraudulent transfers.
When debtor deemed to be
insolvent, §8-9A-2.
Insurance.
Life and disability insurance
guaranty association.
Insolvent insurers.
See INSURANCE.
Insurance companies.
Holding companies.
Delinquency proceedings,
§27-29-11.
**Levy and sale under
process.**
Exemptions from, §6-10-11.
Medicines.
Notice of sales of medicines,
§34-23-6.
Orders.
Recordation, §35-4-52.
Parties.
Proceedings when defendant
involved in bankruptcy,
§6-7-30.
Partnerships.
Dissolution, §10-8-91.
Petitions.
Recordation, §35-4-52.
**Pharmacists and
pharmacies.**
Notice of sale of drugs and
medicines, §34-23-6.
Receivers.
General provisions.
See RECEIVERS.
Recordation.
Petitions, decrees or orders of
bankruptcy, §35-4-52.
Rules of civil procedure.
Discharge in bankruptcy.
Affirmative defense,
ARCP, Rule 8 (c).
Sales.
Going out of business or
distressed merchandise
sales, §§8-13-1 to
8-13-23.
See SALES.
Secured transactions.
Trustees in bankruptcy.
Priority over unperfected
security interests,
§7-9-301.
Trustees in bankruptcy.
Secured transactions.
Priority over unperfected
security interests,
§7-9-301.
**Unemployment
compensation.**
Employers.
Effect of bankruptcy of
employer, §25-4-135.
Uniform commercial code.
See COMMERCIAL CODE.

**BANKS AND FINANCIAL
INSTITUTIONS,** §§5-1A-1
to 5-21-9.
Acceptances.
Drafts or bills of exchange.
Authority, §5-5A-25.
Limitations, §5-5A-26.
Accounts.
Common trust funds.
Generally, §5-12A-14.
Record of fiduciary
accounts owning
interest in fund,
§5-12A-8.
Fiduciary accounts.
Transfers, §§5-11A-30 to
5-11A-37. See within
this heading,
"Fiduciary accounts."
Savings and loan
associations.
See SAVINGS AND LOAN
ASSOCIATIONS.
Actions.
Credit unions.
Rules and regulations.
Adopting, amending or
repealing.
Action to determine
validity or
applicability,
§5-17-47.
Liquidation of insolvent
banks.
Actions upon rejected
claims, §5-8A-44.
Institution of civil action,
§5-8A-22.
Savings and loan
associations.
Powers, §5-16-24.
Superintendent of banks.
Representation in civil
actions, §5-2A-23.
**Administration of common
trust funds,** §§5-12A-1 to
5-12A-15.
Accounts and accounting.
Generally, §5-12A-14.
Record of fiduciary
accounts owning
interest in fund,
§5-12A-8.
Assets.
Ownership of assets,
§5-12A-11.
Audits.
Annual audit, §5-12A-9.
Common trust fund plan.
Amendment of plan,
§5-12A-5.
Approval, §5-12A-4.
Provisions of plan,
§5-12A-4.
Required provisions,
§5-12A-4.
Control of fund, §5-12A-11.
Definitions, §5-12A-1.
Establishment of funds.
Trust institutions may
establish, §5-12A-2.
Extent of fund, §5-12A-8.
Funds differing from funds
permitted by chapter,
§5-12A-13.
Instrument under which
trust fund acts.
Control of investments by
instrument, §5-12A-6.

BANKS AND FINANCIAL INSTITUTIONS—Cont'd
Administration of common trust funds—Cont'd
Investments by trust institutions, §5-12A-3.
Control of investments by instrument under which trust acts, §5-12A-6.
Investment of estate moneys in fund, §5-12A-7.
Management of fund, §5-12A-11.
Mistakes in administration of fund, §5-12A-12.
Ownership of assets, §5-12A-11.
Records, §5-12A-11.
Fiduciary accounts owning interest in fund, §5-12A-8.
Taxation, §5-12A-15.
Trust institutions may establish, maintain and administer common trust funds, §5-12A-2.
Valuation of securities in fund.
Quarterly valuation, §5-12A-10.
Withdrawals from common trust funds, §5-12A-7.
Affidavits.
Fiduciary accounts.
Transfers.
Filing of affidavit in office of judge of probate, §5-11A-34.
Agents.
Fiduciary accounts.
Transfers.
Appointment of related institution as agent, §§5-11A-33, 5-11A-37.
Amendments.
Incorporation.
Certificates of incorporation, §5-5A-17.
Annuity tables, §§35-16-1 to 35-16-4.
Appeals.
Credit unions.
Board.
Appeals to board from action of administrator, §5-17-55.
Refusal to permit incorporation, §5-5A-8.
Reorganization, §5-9A-5.
Savings and loan associations.
Appeals from order of commissioner or board, §5-2A-63.
Applicability of title.
Effect of repeal of prior acts, §5-1A-8.
Inconsistent provisions in other laws superseded, §5-1A-6.
Supervisory provisions not applicable to national banks, §5-1A-5.
Assessments.
Annual assessments.
Amount, §5-2A-20.

BANKS AND FINANCIAL INSTITUTIONS—Cont'd
Assessments—Cont'd
Annual assessments—Cont'd
Collection.
Assessment and forfeiture, §5-2A-21.
Disposition of revenue, §5-2A-20.
Failure to pay.
Forfeiture, §5-2A-21.
Payment.
Forfeiture for failure to pay, §5-2A-21.
When payable, §5-2A-20.
When payable, §5-2A-20.
Savings and loan associations.
Fees, §5-16-38.1.
Assets.
Common trust funds.
Ownership of assets, §5-12A-11.
Federal deposit insurance corporation.
Loans from and sale of assets to corporation, §5-8A-34.
Liquidation. See within this heading, "Liquidation."
Pledge of assets as security for certain deposits, §5-5A-28.
Receivers.
Passage of title to assets, etc., of banking institution to receiver, §5-8A-25.
Savings and loan associations.
See SAVINGS AND LOAN ASSOCIATIONS.
Attorney general.
Legal counsel for state banking department, §5-2A-23.
Audits.
Administration of common trust funds annual audit, §5-12A-9.
Common trust funds.
Annual audit, §5-12A-9.
Credit unions.
Supervisory committee, §5-17-13.
Examination of banks, §§5-3A-1 to 5-3A-17. See within this heading, "Examination of banks."
Independent audits, §5-2A-22.
Reports.
Independent audits.
Report in lieu of audit, §5-2A-22.
Required annually, §5-3A-1.
Savings and loan associations, §5-16-36.
Automatic unmanned cash dispensing machine, §5-5A-30.
Bank.
Defined, §5-1A-2.
Use of words restricted, §5-1A-3.
Banker.
Use of words restricted, §5-1A-3.
Bank examiners. See within this heading, "Examination of banks."

BANKS AND FINANCIAL INSTITUTIONS—Cont'd
Bank holding companies.
Defined, §5-1A-2.
Regional reciprocal banking.
General provisions, §§5-13A-1 to 5-13A-10. See within this heading, "Regional reciprocal banking."
Banking.
Emergencies.
Authorization of banks to postpone certain banking activities, §5-10A-1.
Use of words restricted, §5-1A-3.
Banking board.
Appeals.
Refusal to permit incorporation, §5-5A-8.
Appointment of members, §5-2A-40.
Chairman, §5-2A-40.
Compensation of members, §5-2A-45.
Composition, §5-2A-40.
Defaults.
Proceedings as to defaults, §5-8A-20.
Examination of banks.
Disclosure.
Condition or affairs of banks by board, §5-3A-3.
Governor.
Appointment of members, §5-2A-40.
Limitation of liability.
Board members and employees, §5-2A-16.
Liquidation of bank without assent of board, §5-8A-21.
Meetings.
Confidential, §5-3A-11.
Notice, §5-2A-41.
Place, §5-2A-42.
Misconduct of bank.
Proceedings, §5-8A-20.
Notice.
Meetings, §5-2A-41.
Qualifications of members, §5-2A-44.
Quorum, §5-2A-43.
Removal of members, §5-2A-6.
Superintendent of banks.
Generally, §§5-2A-3 to 5-2A-16. See within this heading, "Superintendent of banks."
Terms of members, §5-2A-40.
Vacancies.
Filling, §5-2A-44.
Bankruptcy and insolvency.
Liquidation, §§5-8A-1 to 5-8A-46. See within this heading, "Liquidation." .
Preference of certain creditors in case of insolvency, Const. Ala., art. XIII, §250.
Repeal of section 250, Const. Ala., amd. 5.
Receipt of deposits in failing financial institutions, §13A-9-50.

**BANKS AND FINANCIAL
INSTITUTIONS**—Cont'd
**Bills or notes issued as
money.**
Authority to issue, Const.
Ala., art. XIII, §248.
Redeemable in gold or silver,
Const. Ala., art. XIII,
§249.
Bonds, surety.
Agreements between
principal and sureties on
bond for bank deposits,
§5-5A-35.
Bank examiners, §5-2A-19.
Credit unions.
See CREDIT UNIONS.
Liquidation.
Solvent banks.
Directors, §5-8A-1.
Officers and employees,
§6-6A-3.
Regulation of trust business.
Exemptions.
Trust companies acting
as administrators,
§5-11A-9.
Superintendent of banks.
Deputy superintendent of
banks, §5-2A-15.
Trust business.
Deposit of security for
operation of trust
business. See within
this heading,
"Regulation of trust
business."
Branch banks.
Consolidation, merger or
transfer.
Applicability of article to
branch banks, §5-7A-6.
Establishment, §5-5A-20.
Repeal of conflicting laws,
§5-5A-20.
Validation of existing branch
banks, §5-5A-20.
Bureau of credit unions.
Generally, §§5-2A-100 to
5-2A-103.
Transfer of jurisdiction,
§5-17-7.
Bureau of loans.
See SMALL LOANS.
Bureau of savings and loan,
§§5-2A-60, 5-2A-61.
Savings and loan board,
§§5-2A-63, 5-16-2.
Capital.
Credit unions, §5-17-4.
Defined, §5-1A-2.
Savings and loan
associations.
See SAVINGS AND LOAN
ASSOCIATIONS.
Capital stock. See within this
heading, "Stock and
stockholders."
Certificate of incorporation.
See within this heading,
"Incorporation."
Certificates of deposit,
§5-5A-36.
Charter.
Renewal of existing charter
not required, Const. Ala.,
amd. 51.
Vacation of bank charter.
Institution of proceedings,
§5-8A-22.

**BANKS AND FINANCIAL
INSTITUTIONS**—Cont'd
Checks.
Bad checks.
Generally.
See BAD CHECKS.
Negotiating worthless
instruments,
§§13A-9-13.1 to
13A-9-13.3.
Commercial code.
Commercial paper,
§§7-3-101 to 7-3-805.
See COMMERCIAL
CODE.
General provisions.
See CHECKS.
Citation of act, §5-1A-1.
Clearinghouse certificates.
Emergencies.
Discharge of deposits,
§5-10A-12.
Issuance and reissuance,
§5-10A-13.
Closing.
Holidays, §1-3-8.
Permitted on one business
day of each week,
§5-5A-32.
Collections.
Commercial code.
Bank deposits and
collections, §§7-4-101
to 7-4-504.
See COMMERCIAL
CODE.
Commencement of business.
Examination prior to
commencement,
§5-5A-11.
Incorporation. See within
this heading,
"Incorporation."
Permits to transact business.
See within this heading,
"Permits."
Savings and loan
associations, §5-16-12.
Commercial code.
Bank deposits and
collections, §§7-4-101 to
7-4-504.
See COMMERCIAL CODE.
General provisions, §§7-1-101
to 7-11-108.
See COMMERCIAL CODE.
Negotiable instruments
generally.
See NEGOTIABLE
INSTRUMENTS.
Sale of checks, §§8-7-1 to
8-7-15.
See CHECKS.
Travelers' checks.
Sale of checks generally,
§§8-7-1 to 8-7-15.
See CHECKS.
Common trust funds.
Administration, §§5-12A-1 to
5-12A-15. See within this
heading, "Administration
of common trust funds."
Conflict of laws.
Regional reciprocal banking.
Applicable law, §5-13A-6.
Construction with other
laws, §5-13A-10.
Resolution, §5-1A-6.

**BANKS AND FINANCIAL
INSTITUTIONS**—Cont'd
Conflicts of interest.
Directors, officers and
employees.
Receiving commission to
procure loans,
purchases, discounts,
etc., §5-6A-22.
State banking department.
Loans, gifts, favors, etc.,
from banks, employees,
etc.
Prohibited, §5-3A-9.
**Consolidation, merger or
transfer,** §§5-7A-1 to
5-7A-6.
Branch banks.
Applicability of article,
§5-7A-6.
Certificate of approval.
Issuance by
superintendent,
§5-7A-4.
Dissenting shareholders.
Rights, §5-7A-44.
Examinations, §5-7A-5.
General or local laws not
affected, §5-7A-46.
Permitted, §5-7A-1.
Place of business.
Transfer of place of
business, §5-7A-1.
Proceedings to effect,
§5-7A-2.
Certificate of proceedings
to be forwarded to
superintendent of
banks, §5-7A-3.
Refusal of consent, §5-7A-6.
Resulting banks, §5-7A-45.
Superintendent of banks,
§§5-7A-3 to 5-7A-6.
Appeal of refusal of
consent, §5-7A-6.
Certificate of proceedings
to be forwarded to
superintendent,
§5-7A-3.
Issuance of certificate of
approval by
superintendent,
§5-7A-4.
Written consent required,
§5-7A-5.
Constitution of Alabama.
See CONSTITUTION OF
ALABAMA.
**Construction and
interpretation.**
Credit unions.
See CREDIT UNIONS.
Regional reciprocal banking,
§§5-13A-9, 5-13A-10.
Contracts.
Industrial development
corporations, §10-4-133.
Receiver.
Assumption or rejection of
executory contracts,
§5-8A-35.
Savings and loan
associations.
See SAVINGS AND LOAN
ASSOCIATIONS.
Conversion.
Credit unions, §5-17-22.
Dissenting shareholders.
Rights, §5-7A-44.
General or local laws not
affected, §5-7A-46.

BANKS AND FINANCIAL INSTITUTIONS—Cont'd

Conversion—Cont'd

National banks into state banks, §§5-7A-20 to 5-7A-24.

Articles of incorporation. Execution, §5-7A-21.

Declaration of incorporation, §5-7A-23.

Duties of bank upon issuance of certificate, §5-7A-22.

Fee, §5-7A-20.

Incorporation. Declaration of incorporation, §5-7A-23.

Officers and employees. Powers and duties upon issuance of certificate, §5-7A-22.

Organization certificate. Execution, §5-7A-21.

Powers of bank upon issuance of certificate, §5-7A-22.

Stock and stockholders. Continuation of previous shares, §5-7A-21.

Issuance of stock by state bank, §5-7A-24.

Powers and duties of stockholders upon issuance of certificate, §5-7A-22.

Procedure for conversion, §5-7A-20.

Resulting banks, §5-7A-45.

Savings and loan associations. See SAVINGS AND LOAN ASSOCIATIONS.

State banks into or consolidation with national banks, §§5-7A-40 to 5-7A-43.

Authorized, §5-7A-40.

Exchange of stock, §5-7A-40.

Identity, obligations, etc., of state bank or trust company. Continuation, §5-7A-43.

Property of state bank. Transfer to national bank, §5-7A-42.

Stock and stockholders. Exchange of stock, §5-7A-40.

Meeting of stockholders for purpose of conversion or consolidation, §5-7A-41.

Corporations.

Applicability to corporations provisions, §10-2A-336.

Credit unions. See CREDIT UNIONS.

Engaging in banking business. Restrictions, §5-1A-4.

Incorporation. See within this heading, "Incorporation."

BANKS AND FINANCIAL INSTITUTIONS—Cont'd

Corporations—Cont'd

Names. Use of words "banks," "banker," "banking," etc., restricted, §5-1A-3.

Restrictions on engaging in banking business, §5-1A-4.

Savings and loan associations. Applicability of corporation provisions, §10-2A-336.

Counties.

County boards of health. Duties, §22-3-2.

Deposit of county funds. Pledge of assets as security, §5-5A-28.

Depositories. See COUNTIES.

Industrial development corporations. Occupational license tax, §10-4-144.

Industry and trade. Projects for promotion. Investment in bonds by savings banks, §11-20-10.

Credit.

Letters of credit. Commercial code, §§7-5-101 to 7-5-117. See COMMERCIAL CODE.

Credit card banks, §§5-20-3, 5-20-4, 5-20-6 to 5-20-9.

Creditors.

Liquidation. Insolvent banks, §§5-8A-1 to 5-8A-46. See within this heading, "Liquidation."

Credit unions.

General provisions. See CREDIT UNIONS.

Criminal law and procedure.

Failing financial institutions. Receiving deposits in, §13A-9-50.

Death.

Credit unions. See CREDIT UNIONS.

Savings and loan associations. See SAVINGS AND LOAN ASSOCIATIONS.

Decedents' estates.

Credit unions. Disposition of shares or deposit account of decedent, §5-17-16.

Disposition of deposits of deceased persons, §5-5A-38.

Time for payment, §5-5A-39.

Payment of deposit of deceased person, §5-5A-41.

Savings and loan associations. Disposition of deceased persons' accounts, §5-16-46.

BANKS AND FINANCIAL INSTITUTIONS—Cont'd

Defaults.

Proceedings by superintendent before banking board, §5-8A-20.

Definitions, §5-1A-2.

Administration of common trust funds, §5-12A-1.

Credit unions, §5-17-1.

Deposits, §5-5A-28.

Examinations of banks. Affiliate, §5-3A-1.

Excise tax, §40-16-1.

Fidicuary accounts. Transfers. Related, §5-11A-36.

Industrial development corporations, §10-4-130.

Regional reciprocal banking, §5-13A-2.

Savings and loan associations, §§5-14A-2, 5-16-2.

Department.

State banking department generally. See within this heading, "State banking department."

Deposits.

Adverse claims to deposits, §5-5A-42.

Agreement as to person or purpose for which deposit made and payable, §5-1A-9.

Bonds, surety. Agreements between principal and sureties on bond for bank deposits, §5-5A-35.

Certificates of deposit. Maturity of certificates issued for more than ninety days. Notice, §5-5A-36.

Notice. Maturity of certificates issued for more than ninety days, §5-5A-36.

Commercial code. Bank deposits and collections, §§7-4-101 to 7-4-504. See COMMERCIAL CODE.

Credit unions. See CREDIT UNIONS.

Death of depositor or trustee, §§5-5A-38 to 5-5A-41.

Disposition of deposits of deceased persons, §5-5A-38.

Time for payment, §5-5A-39.

Joint deposits. Payment of deposits made in names of two persons upon death of one, §5-5A-41.

Trusts and trustees. Disposition of deposits in trust for another upon death of trustee, §5-5A-40.

Debtor-creditor relationship, §5-1A-9.

Defined, §5-5A-28.

BANKS AND FINANCIAL INSTITUTIONS—Cont'd
Deposits—Cont'd
Directors, officers and
employees.
Overdrawing own account,
§5-6A-22.
Failing financial institutions.
Receiving deposits in,
§13A-9-50.
Insurance. See within this
heading, "Insurance of
deposits."
Joint deposits.
Death.
Payment of deposits
made in names of
two persons upon
death of one,
§5-5A-41.
Minors. See within this
heading, "Minors."
Powers of banks, §5-5A-18.
Public funds.
Pledge of assets of banks
as security for deposit
of public funds,
§5-5A-28.
Records.
Disclosure of customer's
financial records,
§5-5A-43.
Savings and loan
associations.
See SAVINGS AND LOAN
ASSOCIATIONS.
Scrip, clearinghouse
certificates or emergency
currency, §5-10A-12.
Special deposits.
Powers of banks, §5-5A-18.
Taxation.
Money on deposit.
Exemption, §40-9-1.
Trusts and trustees.
Death of trustee.
Disposition of deposit in
trust for another
upon death of
trustee, §5-5A-40.
**Directors, officers and
employees, §§5-6A-1 to
5-6A-26.**
Bonds, surety.
Officers and employees,
§5-6A-3.
Capital stock.
Fraudulent representations
as to capital stock,
§5-6A-25.
Purchase, reduction or
payment not in
accordance with law,
§5-6A-20.
Commissions.
Receipt of commission to
procure loans,
purchase, discounts,
etc., §5-6A-22.
Conflicts of interest.
Receipts of commission,
etc., to procure loans,
purchases, discounts,
etc., §5-6A-22.
Conversion of national banks
into state banks.
Powers and duties of
officers and employees
upon issuance of
certificate, §5-7A-22.

BANKS AND FINANCIAL INSTITUTIONS—Cont'd
**Directors, officers and
employees**—Cont'd
Conversion of national banks
into state banks—Cont'd
Powers of directors,
§5-7A-21.
Credit unions.
Directors.
See CREDIT UNIONS.
Officers.
See CREDIT UNIONS.
Deposits.
Overdrawing on account,
§5-6A-22.
Discounts.
Illegal discounts of notes,
§5-6A-20.
Notes.
Illegal discounts,
§5-6A-20.
Receipt of commissions,
etc., to procure
discounts, §5-6A-22.
Dividends.
Declaration of unearned
dividend, §5-6A-20.
Fraud, §§5-6A-23 to 5-6A-25.
Bank property.
Receipt or possession
with intent to
defraud, §5-6A-23.
Books and accounts of
bank.
Making false entries,
§5-6A-24.
Capital stock.
Fraudulent
representation as to
capital stock,
§5-6A-25.
Gifts.
Receipt of gifts to procure
loans, purchases,
discounts, etc.,
§5-6A-22.
Industrial development
corporations.
Directors.
See INDUSTRIAL
DEVELOPMENT
CORPORATIONS.
Employees, §10-4-133.
Officers.
See INDUSTRIAL
DEVELOPMENT
CORPORATIONS.
Liquidation.
Solvent banks, §5-8A-1.
Bond, surety, §5-8A-1.
Loans.
Concealment of loans.
Penalties, §5-6A-21.
Loans to bank officers and
employees, §5-6A-26.
Making loans with stock of
lending bank as
security, §5-6A-20.
Receipt of commissions to
procure loans,
§5-6A-22.
Meetings of board of
directors, §5-6A-3.
Oath of directors, §5-6A-2.
Overdrawing own account,
§5-6A-22.
Penalties.
Concealment of loans.
Purchase of securities,
etc., §5-6A-21.

BANKS AND FINANCIAL INSTITUTIONS—Cont'd
**Directors, officers and
employees**—Cont'd
Penalties—Cont'd
Conflicts of interest.
Receiving commissions
for procuring loans,
discounts, etc.,
§5-6A-22.
Declaration of unearned
dividends, discounts of
notes, etc., §5-6A-20.
False reports, §5-6A-25.
Fraudulent representations
as to capital stock,
§5-6A-25.
Liability for knowing and
willful violation of title
5, §5-5A-47.
Overdrawing own account,
§5-6A-22.
Receipt of commissions,
etc., to procure loans,
purchases, discounts,
etc., §5-6A-22.
Purchases.
Receipt of commissions to
procure purchases,
§5-6A-22.
Removal procedure,
§5-2A-12.
Residence of directors,
§5-6A-1.
Rewards.
Receipt of rewards to
procure loans,
purchases, discounts,
etc., §5-6A-22.
Savings and loan
associations.
Directors.
See SAVINGS AND
LOAN
ASSOCIATIONS.
Officers and employees.
See SAVINGS AND
LOAN
ASSOCIATIONS.
Securities.
Concealment of purchases,
§5-6A-21.
Stock.
Directors to own stock,
§5-6A-1.
Discounts.
Directors, officers and
employees.
Receiving commission to
procure discounts, etc.,
§5-6A-22.
Illegal discounts of notes,
§5-6A-20.
Discovery.
Production of documents and
things.
Powers of superintendent
and bank examiners,
§5-3A-6.
District attorneys.
Superintendent of banks.
Representation in civil
actions, §5-2A-23.
Dividends.
Credit unions, §5-17-20.
Liquidation of insolvent
banks.
Payment of dividends to
creditors, §5-8A-45.

**BANKS AND FINANCIAL
   INSTITUTIONS**—Cont'd
Dividends—Cont'd
Penalties.
   Declaration of unearned
      dividends, §5-6A-20.
   Required surplus fund,
      §5-5A-21.
Savings and loan
   associations.
   See SAVINGS AND LOAN
      ASSOCIATIONS.
Unearned dividends.
   Declaration of unearned
      dividends, §5-6A-20.
Drafts.
Letters of credit, §§7-5-101 to
   7-5-117.
   See COMMERCIAL CODE.
Duration.
Duration of corporations not
   limited, Const. Ala.,
   amd. 51.
Education.
Public school funds.
   Pledge of assets of banks
      as security for public
      school funds, §5-5A-28.
Effect of repeal of prior acts,
   §5-1A-8.
Embezzlement.
See EMBEZZLEMENT.
Emergencies, §§5-10A-1 to
   5-10A-17.
Applicability of sections in
   emergencies, §5-10A-5.
Banking board.
   Authorization of banks to
      postpone certain
      banking activities,
      §5-10A-1.
Certificates of indebtedness.
   Issuance, §5-10A-14.
Compliance with chapter not
   to entail liability,
   §5-10A-16.
Deposits.
   Authorization of banks to
      postpone certain
      banking activities,
      §5-10A-1.
   Discharging deposits,
      §5-10A-12.
   Scrip, clearinghouse
      certificates or
      emergency currency.
      Discharge, §5-10A-12.
Duration of emergency
   action, §5-10A-5.
Expenses.
   Payment of expenses of
      bank operating
      without receivership
      liquidation, §5-10A-7.
Holidays.
   Declaration of banking
      holidays, §5-10A-3.
   Extension of banking
      holiday, §5-10A-4.
Liabilities.
   Authorization of banks to
      postpone certain
      banking activities,
      §5-10A-1.
Liquidation.
   Payment of expenses of
      bank operating
      without receivership
      liquidation, §5-10A-7.

**BANKS AND FINANCIAL
   INSTITUTIONS**—Cont'd
Emergencies—Cont'd
Loans.
   Authorization of banks to
      postpone certain
      banking activities,
      §5-10A-1.
Notes.
   Issuance, §5-10A-14.
Operating expenses.
   Payment of expenses of
      bank operating
      without receivership
      liquidation, §5-10A-7.
Reorganization without
   receivership liquidation.
   Authorization and
      approval, §5-10A-15.
Rules and regulations.
   Extension of emergency
      rules or regulations,
      §5-10A-4.
Scrip, clearinghouse
   certificates or emergency
   currency.
   Discharge of deposits,
      §5-10A-12.
   Issuance and reissuance,
      §5-10A-13.
Segregation of assets.
   Adjustments, §5-10A-11.
   Authorization of banks to
      postpone certain
      banking activities,
      §5-10A-1.
   Commingling of items in
      classes of deposits,
      §5-10A-10.
   Distribution upon
      receivership
      liquidation of bank,
      §5-10A-8.
   Identification of segregated
      items, §5-10A-11.
   Liquidation.
      Distribution of
         segregated assets
         upon receivership
         liquidation,
         §5-10A-8.
   Manner of segregation,
      §§5-10A-8, 5-10A-9.
Services or labor during
   emergency.
   Issuance of notes or
      certificates of
      indebtedness,
      §5-10A-14.
Superintendent of banks.
   Authorization of banks to
      postpone certain
      banking facilities,
      §5-10A-1.
Emergency currency.
Discharge of deposits,
   §5-10A-12.
Issuance and reissuance,
   §5-10A-13.
**Engaging in banking
   business.**
Restrictions, §5-1A-4.
Examination of banks,
   §§5-3A-1 to 5-3A-17; Const.
   Ala., art. XIII, §254.
Bank examiners.
   Bonds, surety, §5-2A-19.
   Commission of office,
      §5-2A-18.
   Duties.
      Generally, §5-2A-17.

**BANKS AND FINANCIAL
   INSTITUTIONS**—Cont'd
Examination of banks
   —Cont'd
Bank examiners—Cont'd
   False reports by bank
      examiners, §5-3A-10.
   Oath, §5-2A-17.
   Production of documents.
      Power to compel,
         §5-3A-6.
   Reports, §5-3A-8.
      Use of reports in
         liquidation
         proceedings,
         §5-8A-26.
   Witnesses.
      Powers as to witnesses,
         §5-3A-6.
Banking board.
   Disclosure of condition or
      affairs of bank by
      board, §5-3A-3.
Commencement of business.
   Examination prior to
      commencement,
      §5-5A-11.
Consolidation, merger or
   transfer, §5-7A-5.
Definitions.
   Affiliate, §5-3A-1.
Discovery.
   Powers of superintendent
      and bank examiners,
      §5-3A-6.
Expenses.
   Special examinations,
      §5-3A-4.
Federal deposit insurance
   corporation.
   Acceptance of
      examinations as
      reports of FDIC,
      §5-3A-2.
Foreign banks.
   Examination of agencies of
      foreign banks, §5-3A-5.
   Powers of superintendent
      and bank examiners,
      §5-3A-6.
Items to be examined,
   §5-3A-1.
Production of documents.
   Powers of superintendent
      and bank examiners,
      §5-3A-6.
Reports.
   Confidential, §5-3A-11.
   False reports by bank
      examiners, §5-3A-10.
   Publication of reports of
      examination for
      limited purposes,
      §5-3A-8.
   Superintendent and bank
      examiners, §5-3A-8.
   Use of reports in
      liquidation
      proceedings,
      §5-8A-26.
   Verification of false report
      of condition of bank,
      §5-3A-17.
Required, §5-3A-1.
Special examinations.
   Expenses, §5-3A-4.
Times of examination,
   §5-3A-1.

BANKS AND FINANCIAL INSTITUTIONS—Cont'd
Examination of banks
—Cont'd
Witnesses.
Powers of superintendent
and bank examiners,
§5-3A-6.
Excise tax, §§40-16-1 to
40-16-8.
Appeal from final
assessments, §40-16-4.
Assessment, §40-16-4.
Credits for other taxes,
§40-16-8.
Definitions, §40-16-1.
Delinquency.
Penalty, §40-16-5.
Distributions, §40-16-6.
Due date, §40-16-5.
Extension, §40-16-5.
Exemptions, §40-16-8.
Levy, §40-16-4.
Payment, §40-16-6.
Time, §40-16-5.
Extension, §40-16-5.
Penalties.
Delinquency, §40-16-5.
Production credit
associations.
Taxable under chapter,
§40-16-2.
Refunds, §40-16-7.
Returns, §40-16-3.
**Executors and
administrators.**
Accounts, §5-16-43.
Conversion of state banks
with national banks.
Continuation of obligations
of state bank,
§5-7A-43.
Disposition of deposits of
deceased persons,
§5-5A-38.
Time for payment,
§5-5A-39.
Fiduciary accounts.
Transfers, §§5-11A-30 to
5-11A-37. See within
this heading,
"Fiduciary accounts."
Powers of banks, §5-5A-18.
Failing financial institutions.
Receiving deposits in,
§13A-9-50.
**Federal deposit insurance
corporation.**
Incorporation.
Membership in required,
§5-5A-12.
Insurance of deposits. See
within this heading,
"Insurance of deposits."
Loans from and sale of assets
to corporation, §5-8A-34.
Membership in required,
§5-5A-12.
Subrogation, §5-8A-31.
Federal laws.
Authorization of compliance
by banks, §5-10A-6.
Compliance with not to
entail liability,
§5-10A-16.
Operation of banks under
federal laws, §5-10A-6.
Public officers not to incur
liability or penalties for
compliance, §5-10A-17.

BANKS AND FINANCIAL INSTITUTIONS—Cont'd
Federal reserve system.
Maintenance of reserve by
member banks, §5-5A-19.
Fees.
Credit unions.
See CREDIT UNIONS.
Expenses.
Paid from annual expenses
of banks, §5-2A-20.
Incorporation, §5-5A-13.
Filing fees, §5-5A-13.
Industrial development
corporations.
Incorporation, §10-4-131.
Officers and employees.
Salaries to be paid from
annual assessment of
banks, §5-2A-20.
Permits, §5-5A-1.
Filing fees for
incorporation,
§5-5A-13.
Savings and loan
associations.
Assessment for, §5-16-38.1.
Fiduciaries.
Conversion of state banks
with national banks.
Continuation of obligations
of state bank,
§5-7A-43.
Credit unions.
Power to accept deposit of
fiduciary funds,
§5-17-4.
Regulation of trust business.
Securities.
Authority of trust
company to purchase
its own securities in
fiduciary capacity,
§5-11A-12.
Savings and loan
associations, §5-16-43.
Fiduciary accounts.
Transfers, §§5-11A-30 to
5-11A-37.
Abandonment.
Filing of notice,
§5-11A-34.
Affidavits.
Filing in office of judge
of probate,
§5-11A-34.
Agents.
Appointment of related
institution as agent,
§§5-11A-33,
5-11A-37.
Approval of superintendent
of banking, §5-11A-31.
Authorized where transfer
between related
institutions,
§5-11A-30.
Definitions.
Related, §5-11A-36.
Hearing on objection,
§5-11A-33.
Notice, §5-11A-32.
Abandonment of
transfer.
Filing, §5-11A-34.
Objections, §5-11A-33.
Related.
Defined, §5-11A-36.

BANKS AND FINANCIAL INSTITUTIONS—Cont'd
Fiduciary accounts—Cont'd
Transfers—Cont'd
Transferee bank, trust
company or trust
department as
fiduciary, §5-11A-35.
Effect, §5-11A-35.
Foreign banks.
Examination of agencies of
foreign banks, §5-3A-5.
Powers of superintendent and
bank examiners,
§5-3A-6.
Fraud.
Capital stock.
Fraudulent
representations,
§5-6A-25.
Directors, officers and
employees.
Bank property.
Receipt or possession
within intent to
defraud, §5-6A-23.
Books and accounts of
bank.
Making false entries,
§5-6A-24.
Capital stock.
Fraudulent
representations,
§5-6A-25.
Records.
Directors, officers and
employees.
Making false entries,
§5-6A-24.
Gifts.
Directors, officers and
employees.
Receipt of gifts to procure
loans, purchases,
discounts, etc.,
§5-6A-22.
Governor.
Banking board.
Appointment of members,
§5-2A-40.
Superintendent of banks.
Annual report to governor,
§5-2A-13.
Grand jury.
Credit unions.
Violations of credit union
laws.
Administrator to submit
to grand jury,
§5-17-49.
Superintendent of banks.
Reports of criminal
violations to grand
juries, §5-2A-14.
Guardian and ward.
Administration of common
trust funds generally,
§§5-12A-1 to 5-12A-15.
See within this heading,
"Administration of
common trust funds."
Fiduciary accounts.
Transfers, §§5-11A-30 to
5-11A-37. See within
this heading,
"Fiduciary accounts."
Powers of banks, §5-5A-18.
Health.
Authority and jurisdiction of
state board of health,
§22-2-2.

BANKS AND FINANCIAL INSTITUTIONS—Cont'd

Health—Cont'd
Duties of county boards of
   health, §22-3-2.
Hearings.
Fiduciary accounts.
   Transfers.
      Objections, §5-11A-33.
Holidays.
Closing of banks.
   Certain holidays, §1-3-8.
   Closing one business day of
      each week, §5-5A-32.
Transaction of business on
   legal holidays, §5-5A-30.
Liability for transaction,
   §5-5A-31.
Housing.
Investments and loans,
   §5-5A-23.
Income tax.
Corporations.
   Deductions.
      Amounts received as
         dividends from
         national banks,
         §40-18-38.
   Exemptions.
      Federal land banks,
         §40-18-32.
      Savings and loan
         associations, §40-18-32.
Incorporation.
Affidavit of proposed
   incorporators, §5-5A-3.
Amendments.
   Certificates of
      incorporation,
      §5-5A-17.
Appeal from refusal to
   permit incorporation to
   banking board, §5-5A-8.
Articles of incorporation.
   Conversion of national
      banks into state banks.
      Execution of articles of
         incorporation,
         §5-7A-1.
Banking board.
   Appeals from refusal to
      permit incorporation to
      banking board,
      §5-5A-8.
Capital stock.
   Minimum amount required
      for incorporation,
      §5-5A-14.
Certificate of incorporation.
   Amendment, §5-5A-17.
      Approval of amended
         certificate, §5-5A-17.
   Authorization of issuance
      by superintendent of
      banks, §5-5A-6.
   Filing, §5-5A-7.
   Issuance.
      Certificate of
         incorporation,
         §5-5A-6.
   Recordation, §5-5A-7.
   Savings and loan
      associations.
      See SAVINGS AND
         LOAN
         ASSOCIATIONS.
   Submission of proposed
      certificate, §5-5A-3.

BANKS AND FINANCIAL INSTITUTIONS—Cont'd

Incorporation—Cont'd
Certificate of incorporation
   —Cont'd
   Superintendent of banks.
      Issuance of certificates of
         incorporation,
         §5-5A-6.
Conversion of national banks
   into state banks.
   Declaration of
      incorporation,
      §5-7A-23.
   Execution of articles of
      incorporation and
      organization
      certificate, §5-7A-21.
Federal deposit insurance
   corporation.
   Membership in required,
      §5-5A-12.
Fees, §5-5A-13.
   Filing fees, §5-5A-13.
Fitness of stockholders.
   Investigation as to fitness,
      §5-5A-4.
Industrial development
   corporations.
   See INDUSTRIAL
      DEVELOPMENT
      CORPORATIONS.
Intention to incorporate.
   Deferment of notice,
      §5-5A-2.
   Notice of intention,
      §5-5A-2.
Necessity for bank.
   Investigation as to
      necessity, §5-5A-4.
Notice.
   Intention to incorporate,
      §5-5A-2.
Objections to incorporation,
   §5-5A-5.
Procedure, §5-5A-1.
Recordation of certificate of
   incorporation, §5-5A-7.
Refusal to permit
   incorporation, §5-5A-8.
   Judicial review of refusal,
      §5-5A-9.
Savings and loan
   associations.
   See SAVINGS AND LOAN
      ASSOCIATIONS.
Indebtedness.
Limits, §5-5A-22.
**Industrial development
   corporations,** §§10-4-130
   to 10-4-152.
See INDUSTRIAL
   DEVELOPMENT
   CORPORATIONS.
Injunctions.
Receivers.
   Liquidation of insolvent
      banks.
      Application against
         acquisition of
         possession of
         business and
         property by receiver,
         §5-8A-27.
Insolvent banks.
Liquidation, §§5-8A-1 to
   5-8A-46. See within this
   heading, "Liquidation."

BANKS AND FINANCIAL INSTITUTIONS—Cont'd

Insurance of deposits.
Federal deposit insurance
   corporation.
   Loans from and sale of
      assets to corporation,
      §5-8A-34.
   Membership in required,
      §5-5A-12.
   Subrogation, §5-8A-31.
Savings and loan
   associations, §§5-16-24,
   5-16-51.
Security not required when
   deposit insured,
   §5-5A-29.
Interest.
General provisions.
   See INTEREST.
Maximum rates of interest,
   §§8-8-1 to 8-8-15; Const.
   Ala., art. XIII, §252.
See INTEREST.
Inventories.
Liquidation of insolvent
   banks.
   Inventory of assets of
      bank, §5-8A-41.
Investments.
Credit unions, §5-17-4.
Housing.
   Investments regarding
      housing, §5-5A-23.
Savings and loan
   associations.
   See SAVINGS AND LOAN
      ASSOCIATIONS.
Investment securities,
   §§7-8-101 to 7-8-406.
See COMMERCIAL CODE.
Joint deposits.
Credit unions, §5-17-15.
Death.
   Payment of deposits made
      in names of two
      persons upon death of
      one, §5-5A-41.
Savings and loan
   associations, §§5-16-44,
   5-16-45.
Judgments.
Reorganization.
   Entry of judgment,
      §5-9A-4.
Sale of bonds or securities
   deposited with treasurer
   for satisfaction of
   judgment against trust
   company, §5-11A-8.
Legislature.
Authority restricted, Const.
   Ala., art. XIII, §247.
Letters of credit.
Commercial code, §§7-5-101
   to 7-5-117.
See COMMERCIAL CODE.
Libel and slander.
False, etc., statements
   affecting financial
   standing of bank,
   §5-5A-46.
Licenses.
Industrial development
   corporations.
   Occupational license taxes,
      §10-4-144.
Municipal licenses.
   Schedule of tax,
      §11-51-130.

**BANKS AND FINANCIAL
INSTITUTIONS**—Cont'd
Licenses—Cont'd
Savings and loan
associations.
Municipal license
schedules, §11-51-131.
Liens.
Credit unions.
Lien on shares and
deposits of members,
§5-17-14.
Liquidation of insolvent
banks.
Creation of liens against
bank in possession of
superintendent,
§5-8A-28.
Savings and loan
associations.
Accounts, §5-16-26.
**Liquidation, §§5-8A-1 to
5-8A-46.**
Credit unions, §§5-17-21,
5-17-28.
Insolvent banks.
Actions.
Institution of civil action,
§5-8A-22.
Rejected claims,
§5-8A-44.
Agent to assist.
Compensation.
Payment, §5-8A-37.
Assets.
Acquisition of possession
of property and
business of bank by
superintendent.
Notice to holders of
bank assets,
§5-8A-23.
Inventory of assets of
bank, §5-8A-41.
Segregated assets.
Distribution, §5-10A-8.
Assistance in liquidation.
Compensation, §5-8A-36.
Payment, §5-8A-37.
Employment by
superintendent,
§5-8A-36.
Banking board.
Liquidation of bank by
superintendent
without assent of
banking board,
§5-8A-21.
Business of bank.
Acquisition by receiver.
Injunction against
acquisition of
business by
receiver or
superintendent,
§5-8A-27.
Acquisition by
superintendent,
§5-8A-23.
Resumption of business
of bank in possession
of superintendent,
§5-8A-29.
Capital stock.
Correction of
impairments.
Proceedings of bank as
to correction,
§5-2A-11.

**BANKS AND FINANCIAL
INSTITUTIONS**—Cont'd
Liquidation—Cont'd
Insolvent banks—Cont'd
Capital stock—Cont'd
Correction of
impairments—Cont'd
Proceedings of
superintendent of
banks, §5-2A-10.
Claims against bank.
Filing, §5-8A-39.
Late claims, §5-8A-44.
List of claims.
Filing, §5-8A-41.
Notice for, §5-8A-39.
Objections to claims,
§5-8A-42.
Payment of dividends to
creditors, §5-8A-45.
Preferred claims,
§5-8A-40.
Rejection of claims,
§5-8A-43.
Actions upon rejected
claims, §5-8A-44.
Claims of bank.
Collection, §5-8A-30.
Sale, §5-8A-32.
Counsel in liquidation.
Compensation, §5-8A-36.
Payment, §5-8A-37.
Employment, §5-8A-36.
Creditors.
Payment of dividends to
creditors, §5-8A-45.
Debts due bank.
Collection, §5-8A-30.
Sale, §5-8A-32.
Defaults or misconduct of
bank.
Proceedings by
superintendent
before banking
board, §5-8A-20.
Deposit of funds collected
by receiver, §5-8A-38.
Dissolution of bank,
§5-8A-46.
Distribution.
Final distribution,
§5-8A-46.
Dividends.
Payment to creditors,
§5-8A-45.
Final distribution,
§5-8A-46.
Transfer of funds,
§5-8A-46.
Funds collected by
receiver.
Deposit, §5-8A-38.
Impairment of capital
stock.
Proceedings of bank as
to correction,
§5-2A-11.
Proceedings of
superintendent of
banks as to
correction, §5-2A-10.
Injunctions.
Acquisition of possession
of business and
property by receiver
or superintendent,
§5-8A-27.
Inventory of assets of
bank, §5-8A-41.

**BANKS AND FINANCIAL
INSTITUTIONS**—Cont'd
Liquidation—Cont'd
Insolvent banks—Cont'd
Liens.
Creation of liens against
bank in possession of
superintendent,
§5-8A-28.
Litigation expenses,
§5-8A-36.
Approval, §5-8A-36.
Loans.
Negotiation of loans, etc.,
on behalf of closed
bank, §5-8A-33.
Losses.
How charged, §5-2A-11.
Property.
Acquisition of possession
by receiver.
Injunction against
acquisition,
§5-8A-27.
Acquisition of possession
by superintendent,
§5-8A-23.
Sale, §5-8A-32.
Receivers.
Appointment, §5-8A-24.
Assumption or rejection
of executory
contracts, §5-8A-35.
Final distribution,
§5-8A-46.
Funds collected by
receiver.
Deposit, §5-8A-38.
Property and business of
bank.
Injunction against
acquisition of
possession of
business and
property by
receiver, §5-8A-27.
Termination of
receivership,
§5-8A-46.
Reports.
Use of bank examiner's
reports in
liquidation
proceedings,
§5-8A-26.
Resumption of bank in
possession of
superintendent,
§5-8A-29.
Segregation of assets.
Distribution of
segregated assets,
§5-10A-8.
Superintendent of banks.
Defaults or misconduct of
bank.
Proceedings before
banking board,
§5-8A-20.
Liens.
Creation of liens
against bank in
possession of
superintendent,
§5-8A-28.
Liquidation without
assent of banking
board, §5-8A-21.

BANKS AND FINANCIAL INSTITUTIONS—Cont'd

Liquidation—Cont'd

Insolvent banks—Cont'd

Superintendent of banks —Cont'd

Proceedings as to correction of impairment of capital stock, §5-2A-10.

Property and business of bank.

Acquisition by superintendent, §5-8A-23.

Injunction against acquisition of possession of business and property by superintendent, §5-8A-27.

Report and order correction of unsafe and unsound matters, §5-2A-12.

Termination of receivership, §5-8A-46.

Unsafe and unsound matters.

Superintendent to report and order correction, §5-2A-12.

Savings and loan associations.

Involuntary liquidation, §5-16-37.

Voluntary dissolution.

See SAVINGS AND LOAN ASSOCIATIONS.

Segregation of assets.

Distribution of segregated assets, §5-10A-8.

Solvent banks, §5-8A-1.

Directors.

Bonds, surety, §5-8A-1.

Loans.

Bureau of loans.

See SMALL LOANS.

Closed banks.

Negotiation of loans, etc., §5-8A-33.

Concealment of loans, §5-6A-21.

Credit unions.

See CREDIT UNIONS.

Directors, officers and employees. See within this heading, "Directors, officers and employees."

Federal deposit insurance corporation.

Loans from and sale of assets to corporation, §5-8A-34.

Housing.

Loans regarding housing, §5-5A-23.

Industrial development corporations.

See INDUSTRIAL DEVELOPMENT CORPORATIONS.

Limitations on loans, §5-5A-22.

BANKS AND FINANCIAL INSTITUTIONS—Cont'd

Loans—Cont'd

Liquidation of insolvent banks.

Negotiation of loans, etc., on behalf of closed banks, §5-8A-33.

Maximum loans, §5-5A-22.

Powers of banks, §5-5A-18.

Savings and loan associations.

See SAVINGS AND LOAN ASSOCIATIONS.

Small loans.

See SMALL LOANS.

State banking department.

Conflicts of interest, §5-3A-9.

Stock and stockholders.

Making loans with stock of lending bank as security, §5-6A-20.

Losses.

How charged, §5-2A-11.

Industrial development corporations, §10-4-136.

Savings and loan associations, §5-16-16.

Machines.

Use of automatic unmanned cash dispensing machine, §5-5A-30.

Merger.

Generally, §§5-7A-1 to 5-7A-6. See within this heading, "Consolidation, merger or transfer."

Minors.

Deposits, §§5-5A-37 to 5-5A-39.

Disposition of deposits of deceased persons, §5-5A-38.

Time for payment, §5-5A-39.

Rights of minors, §5-5A-37.

Savings and loan associations.

Accounts, §5-16-43.

Misconduct of bank.

Proceedings by superintendent before banking board, §5-8A-20.

Mortality tables.

Annuity and mortality tables, §§35-16-1 to 35-16-4.

Mortgages and deeds of trust.

Industrial development corporations, §§10-4-133, 10-4-142.

Investments and loans with respect to housing, §5-5A-23.

Powers of banks, §5-5A-18.

Municipal corporations.

Deposits.

Pledge of assets of banks as security for deposits, §5-5A-28.

Industrial development corporations.

Occupational license taxes, §10-4-144.

Licenses.

Schedule of license tax, §11-51-130.

BANKS AND FINANCIAL INSTITUTIONS—Cont'd

Municipal corporations —Cont'd

Savings and loan associations.

Schedule of license tax, §11-51-131.

Names.

Corporations.

Use of words "banks," "banker," "banking," etc., restricted, §5-1A-3.

Savings and loan associations, §5-16-9.

Use of word "trust" in corporate or partnership name, §§5-11A-1, 5-11A-4.

National banks.

Applicability of title.

Supervisory provisions not applicable to national banks, §5-1A-5.

Conversion.

National banks into state banks, §§5-7A-20 to 5-7A-24.

State banks with national banks, §§5-7A-40 to 5-7A-43.

Defined, §5-1A-2.

State banks.

Powers of federally chartered or regulated banks.

State banks to have, §5-5A-18.1.

Supervisory provisions of title.

Not applicable to national banks, §5-1A-5.

Negotiable instruments.

Bad checks.

Generally.

See BAD CHECKS.

Negotiating worthless instruments, §§13A-9-13.1 to 13A-9-13.3.

Checks generally.

See CHECKS.

Commercial code.

Bank deposits and collections, §§7-4-101 to 7-4-504.

See COMMERCIAL CODE.

Commercial paper, §§7-3-101 to 7-3-805.

See COMMERCIAL CODE.

General provisions.

See NEGOTIABLE INSTRUMENTS.

Newspapers.

Publication of semi-annual reports, §5-3A-14.

Notice.

Banking board.

Meetings, §5-2A-41.

Certificates of deposit.

Maturity of certificates issued for more than ninety days, §5-5A-36.

Fiduciary accounts.

Transfers, §5-11A-32.

Abandonment.

Filing of notice, §5-11A-34.

BANKS AND FINANCIAL INSTITUTIONS—Cont'd

Notice—Cont'd
Intention to incorporate, §5-5A-2.
Liquidation.
Insolvent banks, §§5-8A-23, 5-8A-39.
Oaths.
Bank examiners, §5-2A-17.
Directors, §5-6A-2.
Organization.
Credit unions, §§5-17-2, 5-17-7.
Incorporation. See within this heading, "Incorporation."
Industrial development corporations, §10-4-132.
Reorganization, §§5-9A-1 to 5-9A-6. See within this heading, "Reorganization."
Penalties.
Annual assessment of banks.
Forfeiture for failure to pay, §5-2A-21.
Capital stock.
Fraudulent representations, §5-6A-25.
Conflicts of interest.
Directors, officers and employees.
Receiving commissions for procuring loans, discounts, etc., §5-6A-22.
Directors, officers and employees. See within this heading, "Directors, officers and employees."
Discounts.
Illegal discounts of notes, etc., §5-6A-20.
Dividends.
Declarations of unearned dividends, discounts of notes, etc., §5-6A-20.
False statements affecting financial standing of bank, §5-5A-46.
Liability of directors for knowing and willful violation of title 5, §5-5A-47.
Loans.
Concealment of loans, §5-6A-21.
Overdrawing account.
Directors, officers and employees, §5-6A-22.
Permits.
Penalty for failure to obtain, §5-5A-10.
Reports.
Failure to pay for publication of bank report by bank superintendent, §5-3A-16.
False reports, etc., as to condition of bank, §5-6A-25.
Runs on banks.
Initiation of runs on banks, §5-5A-45.
Perjury.
False reports by bank examiners, §5-3A-10.

BANKS AND FINANCIAL INSTITUTIONS—Cont'd

Perjury—Cont'd
False swearing, etc., before bank examiner or superintendent, §5-3A-7.
Permits.
Application, §5-5A-1.
Cost, §5-5A-1.
Fees, §5-5A-1.
Filing fees for incorporation, §5-5A-13.
Issuance, §5-5A-11.
Penalty for failure to obtain, §5-5A-10.
Recordation, §5-5A-11.
Required, §5-5A-10.
Savings and loan associations, §5-2A-62.
Photography.
Reproduction of records and books, §5-4A-1.
Place of business.
Transfer, §5-7A-1.
Credit unions, §5-17-23.
Pledge and collateral security.
Assets of banks.
Pledge of assets as security for certain deposits, §5-5A-28.
Housing.
Investments and loans regarding housing, §5-5A-23.
Insurance of deposits.
Security not required when deposits insured, §5-5A-29.
Powers of banks, §5-5A-18.
Savings and loan associations, §§5-16-24, 5-16-26.
Powers.
Conversion of national banks into state banks.
Powers and duties of banks upon issuance of certificate, §5-7A-22.
Credit unions.
Expanding powers.
See CREDIT UNIONS.
Generally, §5-17-4.
Generally, §5-5A-18.
Industrial development corporations, §10-4-133.
Savings and loan associations, §5-16-24.
Property.
Conversion of state bank with national bank.
Transfer of property of state bank to national bank, §5-7A-42.
Credit unions.
Powers, §5-17-4.
Industrial development corporations, §§10-4-133, 10-4-142.
Insolvent banks.
Liquidation generally, §§5-8A-1 to 5-8A-46. See within this heading, "Liquidation."
Savings and loan associations.
See SAVINGS AND LOAN ASSOCIATIONS.

BANKS AND FINANCIAL INSTITUTIONS—Cont'd

Proposed banks.
Incorporation. See within this heading, "Incorporation."
Public funds.
Security.
State departments and agencies.
Pledge of assets of banks as security for public funds, §5-5A-28.
Public officers and employees.
Federal laws.
Officers not to incur liability or penalties for compliance, §5-10A-17.
Savings and loan associations.
Acknowledgment, etc., of instruments, §5-16-41.
Superintendent of banks.
Officers not to incur liability or penalties for compliance with orders, §5-10A-17.
Receivers.
Contracts.
Assumption or rejection of executory contracts, §5-8A-35.
Deposit of funds collected, §5-8A-38.
Injunctions.
Liquidation of insolvent banks.
Application by bank for injunction against acquisition of business and property, §5-8A-27.
Insolvent banks.
Liquidation generally, §§5-8A-1 to 5-8A-46. See within this heading, "Liquidation."
Passage of title to assets, etc., of banking institution to receiver, §5-8A-25.
Powers of banks, §5-5A-18.
Receivership court.
Defined, §5-1A-2.
Termination of receivership, §5-8A-46.
Recordation.
Certificate of incorporation, §5-5A-7.
Credit unions.
Seal, §5-17-43.
Permit to transact business, §5-5A-11.
Records.
Assets.
Ownership of assets, §5-12A-11.
Common trust funds.
Record of fiduciary accounts owning interest in fund, §5-12A-8.
Control of fund, §5-12A-11.
Copying, §5-4A-1.
Deposits.
Adverse claims to deposits, §5-5A-42.

BANKS AND FINANCIAL INSTITUTIONS—Cont'd
Records—Cont'd
Disclosure of customer's
    financial records,
    §5-5A-43.
Fraud.
    Directors, officers and
        employees.
    Making false entries,
        §5-6A-24.
Management of fund,
    §5-12A-11.
Ownership of assets,
    §5-12A-11.
Reproductions, §5-4A-1.
Retention of bank records.
    Applicability of chapter to
        state and national
        banks, §5-4A-2.
    Disposition of records after
        retention for
        prescribed period,
        §5-4A-1.
    Period of retention.
        Required period, §5-4A-1.
    Reproduction of records
        and books, §5-4A-1.
    Required, §5-4A-1.
Savings and loan
    associations.
    See SAVINGS AND LOAN
        ASSOCIATIONS.
Regional reciprocal banking,
    §§5-13A-1 to 5-13A-10.
Acquisition.
    Alabama bank holding
        company or Alabama
        bank, §§5-13A-3,
        5-13A-8.
    Definition of "acquires,"
        §5-13A-2.
    Prohibited transactions,
        §5-13A-4.
Bank holding companies.
    Alabama bank holding
        companies.
    Defined, §5-13A-2.
    Divestiture.
        Prohibited transactions,
            §5-13A-4.
    Regional bank holding
        companies.
    Acquisition of Alabama
        bank holding
        company or Alabama
        bank, §5-13A-3.
    Applications,
        §§5-13A-3,
        5-13A-8.
Citation of act.
    Short title, §5-13A-1.
Conflict of laws. §5-13A-6.
    Construction with other
        laws, §5-13A-10.
Construction and
    interpretation.
    Construction with other
        laws, §5-13A-10.
Severability of provisions,
    §5-13A-9.
Definitions, §5-13A-2.
Divestiture.
    Prohibited transactions,
        §5-13A-4.
Enforcement of provisions,
    §5-13A-5.
Severability of provisions,
    §5-13A-9.
Short title of act, §5-13A-1.

BANKS AND FINANCIAL INSTITUTIONS—Cont'd
Regional reciprocal banking
    —Cont'd
Superintendent of banks.
    Cease and desist orders,
        §5-13A-5.
    Cooperation with other
        bank regulatory
        agencies, §5-13A-7.
    Definition of
        "superintendent,"
        §5-13A-2.
    Enforcement of provisions,
        §5-13A-5.
Title of act.
    Short title, §5-13A-1.
Regulation of trust business,
    §§5-11A-1 to 5-11A-12.
Amenability of trust
    companies to banking
    laws, §5-11A-1.
Authority of trust company
    to purchase its own
    securities in fiduciary
    capacity, §5-11A-12.
Banking laws.
    Amenability of trust
        companies to banking
        laws, §5-11A-1.
Capital stock.
    Requirements for trust
        companies, §5-11A-3.
Deposit of security for
    operation of trust
    business.
    Amount required,
        §5-11A-5.
    Certificate of deposit,
        §5-11A-7.
    Charges against deposit,
        §5-11A-5.
    Disposition of deposit in
        trust for another upon
        death of trustee,
        §5-5A-40.
    Executors and
        administrators.
    Exemption of trust
        companies from bond
        requirement,
        §5-11A-9.
    Form, §5-11A-5.
    Interest on deposits with
        treasurer payable to
        trust company,
        §5-11A-11.
    Purpose of deposit,
        §5-11A-7.
    Required amount,
        §5-11A-5.
    Sale of bonds or securities
        for satisfaction of
        judgment against trust
        company, §5-11A-8.
    Treasurer to decline
        certain bonds or
        securities, §5-11A-6.
    Veterans.
        Exemption of trust
            companies from bond
            requirement,
            §5-11A-9.
    Withdrawal of bonds or
        securities from deposit
        with trustees,
        §5-11A-10.
    Withdrawal of deposit,
        §5-11A-5.

BANKS AND FINANCIAL INSTITUTIONS—Cont'd
Regulation of trust business
    —Cont'd
Fiduciaries.
    Securities.
        Authority of trust
            company to purchase
            its own securities in
            fiduciary capacity,
            §5-11A-12.
Judgment against trust
    company.
    Sale of bonds or securities
        deposited with
        treasurer for
        satisfaction of
        judgment, §5-11A-8.
Names.
    Use of word "trust " in
        corporate or
        partnership name,
        §§5-11A-1, 5-11A-4.
Operation of trust
    departments by banks,
    §5-11A-1.
Securities.
    Authority of trust company
        to purchase its own
        securities in fiduciary
        capacity, §5-11A-12.
Superintendent of banks.
    Written approval of
        superintendent to
        conduct trust business,
        §5-11A-2.
Trust departments.
    Operation by banks,
        §5-11A-1.
Written approval of
    superintendent to
    conduct trust business,
    §5-11A-2.
Reorganization, §§5-9A-1 to
    5-9A-6.
Appeals, §5-9A-5.
Authorization and approval
    of reorganization without
    receivership liquidation,
    §5-10A-15.
Cooperation of
    superintendent, §5-9A-1.
Entry of judgment, §5-9A-4.
Hearing upon plan, §5-9A-4.
Judgment.
    Appeals, §5-9A-5.
    Entry of judgment,
        §5-9A-4.
Manner of reorganization not
    exclusive, §5-9A-6.
Plan of reorganization,
    §§5-9A-1 to 5-9A-4.
    Entry of judgment on plan,
        §5-9A-4.
    Hearing upon plan,
        §5-9A-4.
    Preparation by
        superintendent,
        §5-9A-1.
    Publication of plan,
        §5-9A-3.
    Submission to board of
        directors, §5-9A-1.
    Submission to court for
        confirmation and
        approval, §5-9A-2.
Publication of plan, §5-9A-3.
Savings and loan
    associations.
    See SAVINGS AND LOAN
        ASSOCIATIONS.

BANKS AND FINANCIAL INSTITUTIONS—Cont'd
Reorganization—Cont'd
Superintendent of banks.
Cooperation in
reorganization,
§5-9A-1.
Repeal of prior acts.
Effect, §5-1A-8.
Reports.
Condition of bank.
False reports as to
condition of bank,
§5-6A-25.
Credit unions.
See CREDIT UNIONS.
Examination of banks.
Confidential, §5-3A-11.
False reports by bank
examiners, §5-3A-10.
Publication of reports for
limited purposes,
§5-3A-8.
Reports by examiners or
superintendent.
Use of reports in
liquidation
proceedings,
§5-8A-26.
Superintendent and bank
examiners.
Duties, §5-3A-8.
False report of condition of
bank.
Verification, §5-3A-17.
Federal deposit insurance
corporation.
Acceptance of reports of
FDIC, §5-3A-2.
Governor.
Annual report from
superintendent of
banks, §5-2A-13.
Grand jury.
Reports by superintendent
of banks of criminal
violations, §5-2A-14.
Independent audits.
Report in lieu of audit,
§5-2A-22.
Industrial development
corporations.
Annual report, §10-4-147.
Liquidation of insolvent
banks.
Use of bank examiner's
reports in court in
liquidation
proceedings, §5-8A-26.
Penalties.
Failure to pay for
publication by
superintendent,
§5-3A-16.
Savings and loan
associations, §5-16-36.
Semi-annual reports, Const.
Ala., art. XIII, §254.
Form, §5-3A-14.
Newspapers.
Publication, §5-3A-14.
Penalty for late report,
§5-3A-14.
Publication, §5-3A-14.
Failure to pay for
publication by
superintendent,
§5-3A-16.
Republication, §5-3A-15.
Required, §5-3A-12.

BANKS AND FINANCIAL INSTITUTIONS—Cont'd
Reports—Cont'd
Semi-annual reports—Cont'd
Special reports of banks,
§5-3A-13.
Verification, §5-3A-12.
Special reports.
Semi-annual reports,
§5-3A-13.
Superintendent of banks. See
within this heading,
"Superintendent of
banks."
Verification.
False report of condition of
bank, §5-3A-17.
Reprographics.
Reproduction of records and
books, §5-4A-1.
Reserves.
Credit unions, §5-17-19.
Deficiencies, §5-5A-18.
Generally, §5-5A-18.
Maintenance, §5-5A-19.
Required reserve fund,
§5-5A-18.
Savings and loan
associations.
See SAVINGS AND LOAN
ASSOCIATIONS.
Residence.
Directors, §5-6A-1.
Rewards.
Directors, officers and
employees.
Receipt of rewards to
procure loans,
purchases, discounts,
etc., §5-6A-22.
Rules and regulations.
Credit unions.
See CREDIT UNIONS.
Emergencies.
Promulgation by
superintendent or
banking board,
§§5-2A-9, 5-10A-2,
5-10A-3.
Superintendent of banks.
Emergency regulations,
§§5-2A-9, 5-10A-2,
5-10A-3.
Interpretation, §5-2A-8.
Issuance by
superintendent,
§5-2A-7.
Judicial review, §5-2A-9.
Promulgation, §5-2A-8.
Procedure, §5-2A-9.
Runs on banks.
Penalties.
Initiation of runs on banks,
§5-5A-45.
Sale of checks, §§8-7-1 to
8-7-15.
See CHECKS.
**Savings and loan
associations.**
General provisions, §§5-16-1
to 5-16-53.
See SAVINGS AND LOAN
ASSOCIATIONS.
Schools.
Deposit of public school
funds.
Pledge of assets of banks
as security, §5-5A-28.

BANKS AND FINANCIAL INSTITUTIONS—Cont'd
Scrip.
Emergencies.
Discharge of deposits,
§5-10A-12.
Issuance and reissuance of
scrip, §5-10A-13.
Secured transactions.
Savings and loan
associations.
Transfers of accounts
excluded from article,
§7-9-104.
Transfer of accounts excluded
from provisions of
article, §7-9-104.
Securities.
Directors, officers and
employees.
Concealment of loans,
§5-6A-21.
Industrial development
corporations.
Applicability of securities
laws, §10-4-152.
Investment securities,
§§7-8-101 to 7-8-406.
See COMMERCIAL CODE.
Regulation of trust business.
Authority of trust company
to purchase its own
securities in fiduciary
capacity, §5-11A-12.
Savings and loan
associations.
See SAVINGS AND LOAN
ASSOCIATIONS.
Semiannual reports. See
within this heading,
"Reports."
Ships and shipping.
Drafts or bills of exchange
arising from transactions
involving shipment of
goods.
Acceptance.
Authority, §5-5A-25.
Limitations, §5-5A-26.
Short title, §5-1A-1.
Small loans.
See SMALL LOANS.
Specie.
Basis, Const. Ala., art. XIII,
§248.
Bills or notes issued as
money.
Redeemable in specie,
Const. Ala., art. XIII,
§249.
Payments.
Laws not to sanction
suspension, Const.
Ala., art. XIII, §249.
State banking department.
Attorney general.
Legal counsel, §5-2A-23.
Bureaus.
Bureau of credit unions.
See CREDIT UNIONS.
Bureau of loans.
See SMALL LOANS.
Bureau of savings and
loans.
See SAVINGS AND
LOAN
ASSOCIATIONS.

BANKS AND FINANCIAL INSTITUTIONS—Cont'd

State banking department —Cont'd

Conflicts of interest.
Loans, gifts, favors, etc., to banking department employees from banks, employees, etc.
Prohibited, §5-3A-9.
Creation of department, §5-2A-1.
Legal counsel, §5-2A-23.
Loans.
Conflicts of interest, §5-3A-9.
Offices, §5-2A-2.
Superintendent of banks. See within this heading, "Superintendent of banks."
Venue, §5-2A-2.

State board of health.
Authority and jurisdiction, §22-2-2.

State departments and agencies.
Deposit of public funds.
Pledge of assets of banks as security for deposits, §5-5A-28.

Stock and stockholders.
Acquisition of majority of voting shares of bank, §5-5A-44.
Procedure, §5-5A-44.
Affidavit of proposed stockholders, §5-5A-3.
Capital stock.
Decrease, §5-5A-15.
Illegal decrease, §5-6A-20.
Dividing, withdrawing, paying, etc.
Except in accordance with law, §5-6A-20.
Fraudulent representations, §5-6A-25.
Impairment.
Proceedings of bank as to correction, §5-2A-11.
Proceedings of superintendent of banks as to correction, §5-2A-10.
Increase, §5-5A-15.
Issuance.
Prior written approval of superintendent required, §5-5A-16.
Minimum amount required for incorporation, §5-5A-14.
Ownership of capital stock of other banks, §5-5A-27.
Purchase of own stock, §5-5A-27.
Trust companies.
Requirements for trust companies, §5-11A-3.
Conversion of national banks into state banks.
Continuation of shares, §5-7A-21.
Issuance of stock by state banks, §5-7A-24.

BANKS AND FINANCIAL INSTITUTIONS—Cont'd

Stock and stockholders —Cont'd

Conversion of national banks into state banks—Cont'd
Powers and duties of stockholders upon issuance of certificate, §5-7A-22.
Conversion of state banks with national banks.
Exchange of stock, §5-7A-40.
Meeting of stockholders for purpose of conversion or consolidation, §5-7A-41.
Directors.
Required to own stock, §5-6A-1.
Fitness of stockholders.
Investigation as to fitness, §5-5A-4.
Industrial development corporations.
See INDUSTRIAL DEVELOPMENT CORPORATIONS.
Liquidation generally. See within this heading, "Liquidation."
Loans.
Secured by own stock, §5-5A-27.
Own stock.
Illegal purchase of own stock, §5-6A-20.
Loans secured by own stock, §5-5A-27.
Purchase of own stock, §5-5A-27.
Illegal purchase of own stock, §5-6A-20.
Pledge and collateral security.
Loans secured by owned stock, §5-5A-27.
Proposed stockholders.
Affidavit, §5-5A-3.
Disclosure to stockholders, §5-5A-3.
State and political subdivisions thereof not to be stockholders, Const. Ala., art. XIII, §253.
Superintendent of banks.
Issuance of capital stock.
Approval of superintendent required, §5-5A-16.
Trust companies.
Capital stock requirements, §5-11A-3.
Voting shares.
Acquisition of majority of voting shares of bank, §5-5A-44.
Procedure, §5-5A-44.

Sundays.
Transaction of business on Sundays, §5-5A-30.

Superintendent of banks,
§§5-2A-3 to 5-2A-16.
Actions.
Representation in civil actions, §5-2A-23.
Appointment, §5-2A-3.
Assistants.
Appointment, §5-2A-15.

BANKS AND FINANCIAL INSTITUTIONS—Cont'd

Superintendent of banks —Cont'd

Banking board.
Defaults or misconduct of bank.
Proceedings before banking board, §5-8A-20.
Ex officio member and chairman of board, §5-2A-40.
Liquidation of bank by superintendent without assent of banking board, §5-8A-21.
Bonds, surety, §5-2A-4.
Deputy superintendent of banks, §5-2A-15.
Capital stock.
Correction of impairments.
Proceedings of superintendent of banks, §5-2A-10.
Consolidation, §§5-7A-3 to 5-7A-6.
Credit cards, §§5-20-3, 5-20-7.
Criminal violations.
Report of criminal violations to grand juries, §5-2A-14.
Defaults.
Proceedings by superintendent before banking board, §5-8A-20.
Defined, §5-1A-2.
Deputy.
Bond, §5-2A-15.
District attorneys.
Representation in civil actions, §5-2A-23.
Emergencies, §5-10A-1.
Employees.
Appointment, §5-2A-15.
Executed papers.
Recordation, §5-2A-5.
Expansion of banking powers, §5-2A-7.
Fiduciary accounts.
Transfers.
Approval, §5-11A-31.
Filling of vacancies, §5-2A-3.
Governor.
Annual report to governor, §5-2A-13.
Limitation of liability of superintendent or employees, §5-2A-16.
Liquidation.
Insolvent banks. See within this heading, "Liquidation."
Misconduct of bank.
Proceedings before banking board, §5-8A-20.
Oath, §5-2A-4.
Orders of superintendent.
Public officers not to incur liability or penalties for compliance, §5-10A-17.
Production of documents.
Power to compel, §5-3A-6.
Qualifications, §5-2A-3.
Recordation of executed papers, §5-2A-5.

BANKS AND FINANCIAL INSTITUTIONS—Cont'd

Superintendent of banks —Cont'd

Regional reciprocal banking. Cease and desist orders, §5-13A-5.

Cooperation with other bank regulatory agencies, §5-13A-7.

Definition of "superintendent," §5-13A-2.

Enforcement of provisions, §5-13A-5.

Regulation of trust business. Written approval of superintendent to conduct trust business, §5-11A-2.

Removal, §5-2A-6.

Reorganization, §5-9A-1.

Reports, §§5-2A-12 to 5-2A-14.

Annual report to governor, §5-2A-13.

Criminal violations. Reports to grand juries, §5-2A-14.

Publication and distribution of annual report, §5-2A-13.

Publication of bank reports, §5-3A-14.

Unsafe and unsound matters, §5-2A-12.

Representation in civil actions, §5-2A-23.

Rules and regulations, §§5-2A-7 to 5-2A-9.

Emergency regulations, §5-2A-9.

Interpretation, §5-2A-8.

Issuance by superintendent, §5-2A-7.

Judicial review, §5-2A-9.

Promulgation, §5-2A-8.

Procedure, §5-2A-9.

Seal of office, §5-2A-5.

Small loan companies. Examination, §5-2A-24.

Stock and stockholders. Issuance of capital stock. Approval of superintendent required, §5-5A-16.

Supervision of state banking department, §5-2A-3.

Surety bond, §5-2A-4.

Term of office, §5-2A-3.

Unsafe and unsound matters. Report and order for correction, §5-2A-12.

Vacancies, §5-2A-3.

Witnesses. Powers as to witnesses, §5-3A-6.

Suretyship.

Agreements between principal and sureties on bond for deposit of money and assets in bank, §5-5A-35.

Surplus.

Defined, §5-1A-2.

Industrial development corporations. Earned surplus, §10-4-145.

Surplus fund, §5-5A-21.

BANKS AND FINANCIAL INSTITUTIONS—Cont'd

Tables.

Annuity and mortality tables, §§35-16-1 to 35-16-4.

Taxation.

Common trust funds. Generally, §5-12A-15.

Credit unions, §5-17-24.

Equalization of taxation of state and national bank, §40-1-9.

Excise tax, §§40-16-1 to 40-16-8. See within this heading, "Excise tax."

Industrial development corporations, §10-4-143.

Money on deposit. Exemption from taxation, §40-9-1.

Officers. Failure to make, swear to and deliver required statements, §40-1-19.

Savings and loan associations. Exemptions of certain organizations from income tax, §10-18-32.

Termination of business.

Const. Ala., art. XIII, §251.

Duration of corporations not limited, Const. Ala., amd. 51.

Liquidation, §§5-8A-1 to 5-8A-46. See within this heading, "Liquidation." §5-5A-16.

Travelers' checks.

Sale of checks generally, §§8-7-1 to 8-7-15.

See CHECKS.

Trusts and trustees.

Administration of common trust funds, §§5-12A-1 to 5-12A-15. See within this heading, "Administration of common trust funds."

Credit unions. Reports for trust beneficiaries, §5-17-15.

Fiduciary accounts. Transfers, §§5-11A-30 to 5-11A-37. See within this heading, "Fiduciary accounts."

Regulation of trust business, §§5-11A-1 to 5-11A-12. See within this heading, "Regulation of trust business."

Savings and loan associations, §§5-16-43, 5-16-47.

Unclaimed property.

Uniform disposition of unclaimed property act, §§35-12-20 to 35-12-48.

See LOST OR UNCLAIMED PROPERTY.

Undivided profits.

Defined, §5-1A-2.

Uniform commercial code.

General provisions, §§7-1-101 to 7-11-108.

See COMMERCIAL CODE.

BANKS AND FINANCIAL INSTITUTIONS—Cont'd

USS Alabama battleship commission.

Bond issues. Legal investments for banks, §41-9-353.

Borrowing from bank. Commission may borrow from bank pending loan from state docks department, §41-9-355.

Vending machines.

Use of automatic unmanned cash dispensing machines, §5-5A-30.

Veterans.

Regulation of trust business. Exemption of trust companies acting as administrator from bond requirement, §5-11A-9.

Veterans' day. Observance by closing of schools, banks and government offices, §1-3-8.

Water conservation and irrigation.

Corporations. Bond issues. Investments, §9-10-39.

Witnesses.

Powers of superintendents and bank examiners, §5-3A-6.

BAR ASSOCIATION.

Alabama state bar.

See ATTORNEYS AT LAW.

BARBED WIRE FENCES.

Livestock.

See LIVESTOCK.

BARBERS.

Alum.

Use of alum, §22-17-7.

Appeals.

Board of barber examiners. Decision of board, §34-5-8.

Applicability of chapter.

Counties. Chapter not applicable to certain counties, §34-5-15.

Exemptions from chapter, §34-5-3.

Other provisions not repealed, §34-5-14.

Apprentices.

Qualifications for certification, §34-5-5.

Audits.

Board of barber examiners. Annual audit of board's accounts, §34-5-12.

Barber colleges.

Certification. Establishment of new colleges, §34-5-7.

Generally, §34-5-6.

Separate locations. Certification for each location, §34-5-7.

Courses of instruction, §34-5-7.

Curriculum, §34-5-7.

Fees, §34-5-10.

Instructors. Certification, §34-5-4.

BARBERS—Cont'd
Barber colleges—Cont'd
New colleges.
Establishment of new
colleges, §34-5-7.
Board of barber examiners.
Appointment of members,
§34-5-13.
Authority of board, §34-5-8.
Creation, §34-5-13.
Deposit of funds and receipts,
§34-5-12.
Establishment, §34-5-13.
Expenses of board, §34-5-12.
Expenses of members,
§34-5-13.
Funds.
Audit of accounts,
§34-5-12.
Deposit and use of funds,
§34-5-12.
Health department.
Advice and cooperation of
department, §34-5-13.
Officers.
Bond of officers, §34-5-13.
Election of officers,
§34-5-13.
Salaries, §34-5-13.
Qualifications of members,
§34-5-13.
Records, §34-5-13.
Refusal to license or certify,
§34-5-8.
Rules and regulations,
§34-5-13.
Terms of office, §34-5-13.
Vacancies.
Filling vacancies, §34-5-13.
Bonds, surety.
Board of barber examiners.
Bond of officers, §34-5-13.
Certificates.
Apprentices.
Qualifications for
certification, §34-5-5.
Barber colleges, §§34-5-6,
34-5-7.
Display of certificate,
§34-5-11.
Exemptions from provisions
of chapter, §34-5-3.
Fees, §34-5-10.
Instructors at barber
colleges, §34-5-4.
Qualifications for
certification as barber or
apprentice, §34-5-5.
Refusal to certify, §34-5-8.
Renewal of certificate,
§34-5-9.
Required, §34-5-2.
Exemptions from chapter,
§34-5-3.
Restoration of certificate,
§34-5-9.
Revocation and suspension,
§34-5-8.
Cleansing of hands, §22-17-5.
Counties.
Chapter not applicable to
certain counties,
§34-5-15.
Definitions, §22-17-1.
Practice of barbering,
§34-5-1.
Diseases.
Service by persons having
skin or venereal disease,
§22-17-8.

BARBERS—Cont'd
Diseases—Cont'd
Service of persons having
inflamed, etc., skin,
§22-17-9.
Treatment of skin diseases
prohibited, §22-17-10.
Dormitories.
Use of shop as dormitory,
§22-17-11.
Education.
Barber colleges. See within
this heading, "Barber
colleges."
Enforcement of chapter.
Penalties for violations,
§34-5-16.
Equipment.
Maintenance.
Duty of manager, §22-17-3.
Examinations.
Board of barber examiners.
See within this heading,
"Board of barber
examiners."
Fees, §34-5-10.
Instructors in barber
colleges.
Certification of instructors,
§34-5-4.
Licenses, §34-5-2.
**Exemptions from provisions
of chapter, §34-5-3.**
Fees, §§34-5-8 to 34-5-10.
Generally, §34-5-10.
Renewal of certificate or
license, §34-5-9.
Restoration of certificate or
license, §34-5-9.
Witnesses.
Proceedings before board of
barber examiners,
§34-5-8.
Headrests, §22-17-6.
Health, §§22-17-1 to 22-17-11.
Alum.
Use of alum, §22-17-7.
Applicability of chapter,
§22-17-2.
Board of barber examiners.
Advice and cooperation of
health department,
§34-5-13.
Cleansing of hands, §22-17-5.
Definitions, §22-17-1.
Dormitories.
Use of shop as dormitory
prohibited, §22-17-11.
Equipment.
Duty of manager as to
maintenance, §22-17-3.
Hands.
Cleansing of hands,
§22-17-5.
Headrests, §22-17-6.
Infections.
Treatment of infections
prohibited, §22-17-10.
Maintenance of shop and
equipment.
Duty of manager, §22-17-3.
Reusing certain materials
prohibited, §22-17-7.
Shop.
Duty of manager as to
maintenance, §22-17-3.
Skin diseases.
Service by persons having
skin disease, §22-17-8.

BARBERS—Cont'd
Health—Cont'd
Skin diseases—Cont'd
Service of persons having
inflamed, etc., skin,
§22-17-9.
Treatment prohibited,
§22-17-10.
Treatment of skin diseases or
infections prohibited,
§22-17-10.
Venereal diseases.
Service by persons having
venereal disease,
§22-17-8.
Waste disposal, §22-17-4.
Water connections, §22-17-4.
Infections.
Treatment of infections
prohibited, §22-17-10.
Licenses, §40-12-58.
Examinations for licenses,
§34-5-2.
Fees, §34-5-10.
Refusal to license, §34-5-8.
Renewal of license, §34-5-9.
Restoration of license,
§34-5-9.
Revocation and suspension,
§34-5-8.
Penalties.
Violations of chapter,
§34-5-16.
Practice of barbering.
Certificate required, §34-5-2.
Defined, §34-5-1.
Students in certified barber
colleges, §34-5-2.
Records.
Board of barber examiners,
§34-5-13.
**Refusal, revocation and
suspension of licenses
and certificates.**
Appeals from decision of
board, §34-5-8.
Conduct of hearings, §34-5-8.
Grounds for refusal to issue
or renew, §34-5-8.
Notice of decision, §34-5-8.
Subpoena power of board,
§34-5-8.
Witnesses.
Compelling attendance,
§34-5-8.
**Renewal or restoration of
certificate or license,**
§34-5-9.
Fees, §34-5-10.
Repeals.
Chapter not to repeal other
provisions, §34-5-14.
Rules and regulations.
Board of barber examiners,
§34-5-13.
Sewers.
Waste disposal, §22-17-4.
Shops.
Duty of manager as to
maintenance, §22-17-3.
Use as dormitory prohibited,
§22-17-11.
Skin diseases.
Service by persons having
skin disease, inflamed,
etc., skin, §§22-17-8,
22-17-9.
Treatment of skin diseases
prohibited, §22-17-10.

BARBERS—Cont'd
Venereal diseases.
Service by persons having
venereal disease,
§22-17-8.
Waste disposal, §22-17-4.
Water connections, §22-17-4.

BARBITURATES.
Controlled substances.
See DRUGS.

BARBOUR COUNTY.
Court costs and charges,
Const. Ala., amd. 290.
Probate judge.
Compensation, Const. Ala.,
amd. 290.
Property tax.
Special property tax, Const.
Ala., amd. 143.
Sheriff.
Compensation, Const. Ala.,
amd. 290.

BARLEY.
General provisions.
See GRAIN.

BARREL.
**Weight per barrel of certain
commodities.**
Commissioner of agriculture
and industry.
Authority to promulgate
rules, §8-16-94.

BASEBALL.
Agents.
Generally, §§8-26-1 to
8-26-41.
See SPORTS.
Licenses.
Baseball parks, §40-12-59.

BASKETBALL.
Agents.
Generally, §§8-26-1 to
8-26-41.
See SPORTS.

BASKETS.
Fish and game.
Catching of nongame fish
with wire baskets,
§§9-11-190 to 9-11-198.
See FISH AND GAME.

BASS.
Fish and game generally.
See FISH AND GAME.
Largemouth bass.
State fresh water fish, §1-2-9.

BASTARDS.
General provisions.
See ILLEGITIMACY.
Paternity.
Determination of paternity,
§§26-17-1 to 26-17-21.
See PARENT AND
CHILD.

BATTERY.
See ASSAULT AND
BATTERY.

BATTLESHIP COMMISSION.
**USS Alabama battleship
commission.**
General provisions,
§§41-9-340 to 41-9-358.
See USS ALABAMA
BATTLESHIP
COMMISSION.

**BATTLESHIP COMMISSION
—Cont'd**
**USS Alabama battleship
commission—Cont'd**
Motor vehicles.
Tags and plates.
Special tag number for
chairman, §32-6-55.

**BAYOU LA BATRE,
MUNICIPALITY OF.**
Economic development.
Promotion of industrial,
commercial and
agricultural
development, Const.
Ala., amds. 220, 261.

BEACHES.
Coastal areas.
Environmental management
board.
Transfer of functions, etc.,
§22-22A-10.
General provisions, §§9-7-1 to
9-7-22.
See COASTAL AREAS.
Motor vehicles.
Operation of vehicles on
beaches of Gulf of
Mexico.
Prohibited, §32-1-7.

BEANS.
Soybeans.
Constitution of Alabama,
Const. Ala., amds. 315,
401.
Crops generally.
See CROPS.
General provisions, §§2-8-80
to 2-8-103.
See SOYBEANS.

**BEAR CREEK
DEVELOPMENT
AUTHORITY,** §§33-15-1 to
33-15-19.
Actions.
Authority may sue and be
sued, §33-15-6.
Advisory board.
Establishment by directors,
§33-15-18.
Authorization, §33-15-2.
Bonds and other obligations.
Contracts to secure bonds,
§33-15-9.
Directors.
Chairman to sign,
§33-15-8.
Statutory mortgage lien.
Resolution of board of
directors, §33-15-10.
Execution, §33-15-8.
Interest.
Security for payment,
§33-15-9.
Issuance by authority,
§33-15-8.
Consent of department of
finance not required
for issuance, §33-15-14.
Public hearing not
prerequisite to
issuance, §33-15-14.
Liens.
Statutory mortgage lien,
§33-15-10.
Negotiable instruments,
§33-15-8.

**BEAR CREEK
DEVELOPMENT
AUTHORITY—Cont'd**
**Bonds and other obligations
—Cont'd**
Principal.
Security for payment,
§33-15-9.
Proceeds.
Use of proceeds from sale,
§33-15-11.
Refunding bonds, §33-15-8.
Sale.
Public or private sale,
§33-15-8.
Use of proceeds from sale,
§33-15-11.
Security for payment of
principal and interest,
§33-15-9.
Taxation.
Exemption from taxation,
§33-15-12.
Bylaws, §33-15-6.
Constitution of Alabama.
Development of Bear Creek
watershed area, Const.
Ala., amd. 247.
Construction of chapter,
§33-15-19.
Contracts.
Authority may enter into
contracts, §33-15-6.
Contracts to secure bonds
and other obligations,
§33-15-9.
**Cooperation of state
agencies,** §33-15-17.
Counties.
Monetary contributions by
certain counties,
§33-15-13.
Definitions, §33-15-1.
Development plans.
Formulation and execution,
§33-15-6.
Directors.
Advisory board.
Establishment by directors,
§33-15-18.
Appointment, §33-15-4.
Bonds and other obligations.
Signature by chairman,
§33-15-8.
Statutory mortgage lien.
Resolution of board of
directors, §33-15-10.
Chairman.
Bond issues.
Signature by chairman,
§33-15-8.
Compensation, §33-15-5.
Composition of board,
§33-15-4.
Expenses, §33-15-5.
Meetings.
Initial meeting, §33-15-5.
Qualifications, §33-15-4.
Quorum, §33-15-5.
Reports.
Annual report to governor,
§33-15-15.
Terms, §33-15-4.
Vacancies, §33-15-4.
Duties.
Generally, §33-15-6.
Eminent domain.
Acquisition of certain
property or rights not
authorized, §33-15-5.
Establishment, §33-15-2.

BEAR CREEK DEVELOPMENT AUTHORITY—Cont'd
Financing, §33-15-6.
Annual reports of directors, §33-15-15.
Freedom of authority from supervision and control, §33-15-14.
Functions.
Generally, §33-15-6.
Highways.
Use of public roads, §33-15-16.
Incorporation.
Certificate of incorporation.
Presentation to probate judge, §33-15-3.
Signing, §33-15-3.
Perpetual succession in corporate name, §33-15-6.
Procedure, §33-15-3.
Public corporation, §33-15-2.
Liens.
Statutory mortgage lien, §33-15-10.
Management and operation, §33-15-6.
Mortgages and deeds of trust.
Exemption from taxation, §33-15-12.
Statutory mortgage lien, §33-15-10.
Municipal corporations.
Monetary contributions by certain municipalities, §33-15-13.
Park rangers.
Appointment, §33-15-6.
Permits.
User permits required, §33-15-7.
Political subdivision of state, §33-15-2.
Powers.
Generally, §33-15-6.
Probate judge.
Certificate of incorporation.
Presentation to judge, §33-15-3.
Public corporation, §33-15-2.
Public utilities.
Eminent domain.
Acquisition of certain property controlled by utilities, §33-15-5.
Purpose, §33-15-2.
Railroads.
Eminent domain.
Acquisition of property controlled by railroads, §33-15-5.
Rates, fees and charges.
Fixing, §33-15-7.
Schedule of rates and charges, §33-15-7.
Services rendered by authority, §33-15-7.
Real property.
Eminent domain.
Acquisition of certain property or rights not authorized, §33-15-5.
Land acquisition, §33-15-6.
Taxation.
Exemption from taxation, §33-15-12.

BEAR CREEK DEVELOPMENT AUTHORITY—Cont'd
Reports.
Annual reports of directors, §33-15-15.
Rights of way.
Authority to use rights of way on all public roads in the state, §33-15-16.
Seal.
Corporate seal, §33-15-6.
Services.
Rates, fees and charges for services rendered, §33-15-7.
State agencies.
Cooperation, §33-15-17.
Supervision and control.
Freedom of authority, §33-15-14.
Taxation.
Bonds and other obligations.
Exemption from taxation, §33-15-12.
User permits.
Required, §33-15-7.
Watershed.
Defined, §33-15-1.

BEAUTICIANS.
General provisions.
See COSMETOLOGISTS.

BEAUTIFICATION.
Beautification board, §§41-9-490 to 41-9-498.
Appointment of members, §41-9-491.
Appropriations, §41-9-498.
Boards and commissions.
Cooperation with beautification board, §41-9-497.
Compensation of members, §41-9-495.
Composition, §41-9-490.
Creation, §41-9-490.
Criticisms, §41-9-497.
Duties, §41-9-496.
Expenses of members, §41-9-495.
Meetings, §41-9-494.
Open to public, §41-9-494.
Officers, §41-9-494.
Powers, §41-9-496.
Qualifications of members, §41-9-491.
Residency, §41-9-492.
Quorum, §41-9-494.
Recommendations, §41-9-497.
Records.
Proceedings of board.
Maintenance and examination of record, §41-9-494.
Reports, §41-9-497.
Residency, §41-9-492.
Terms of members, §41-9-491.
Vacancies, §41-9-493.
Ferries.
Contracts and regulations relative to federal assistance, §23-1-1.
Highway beautification.
Bridges, §23-1-1.
Federal assistance, §23-1-1.
Junkyard control, §§23-1-240 to 23-1-251.
See JUNKYARD CONTROL.

BEAUTIFICATION—Cont'd
Highway beautification —Cont'd
Outdoor advertising, §§23-1-270 to 23-1-288.
See ADVERTISING.
Scenic enhancement, §§23-1-220 to 23-1-223.

BEAVER.
General provisions.
See FISH AND GAME.
Hunting, §9-11-262.

BEDDING.
Jails.
Furnishing of bedding, §§14-6-19, 14-6-93.
Nuisances menacing public health, §§22-10-1 to 22-10-3.

BEEF.
General provisions.
See MEAT AND MEAT PRODUCTS.

BEER.
See ALCOHOLIC BEVERAGES.

BEES.
Honeybees and apiaries, §§2-14-1 to 2-14-15.
See HONEYBEES AND APIARIES.

BEGGARS.
Loitering for purpose of begging, §13A-11-9.
Maiming one's self to obtain alms, §13A-14-1.

BENCH MARKS.
Establishment along highways, §9-4-11.

BENCH WARRANTS.
Defined, §15-10-60.
Procedure, §15-10-60.

BENEVOLENT SOCIETIES.
Corporations.
Public societies, §§10-4-20 to 10-4-28.
See CORPORATIONS.
Fraternal benefit societies.
See FRATERNAL BENEFIT SOCIETIES.

BEQUESTS.
Death of devisee.
Before testator, §43-8-224.
Existing trust.
Bequest to trustee of, §43-8-140.
General provisions.
See WILLS.

BESSEMER, MUNICIPALITY OF.
Property tax, Const. Ala., amd. 8.

BETTING.
Bingo.
See BINGO.
Dog racing.
Pari-mutuel betting.
Legalized betting not affected by gambling article, §13A-12-31.
Taxation, §40-11-5.
General provisions.
See GAMBLING.
Horse racing, §§11-65-1 to 11-65-47.
See HORSE RACING.

BETTING—Cont'd
Lotteries.
General provisions, §§13A-12-20, 13A-12-22, 13A-12-29, 13A-12-70 to 13A-12-75.
See LOTTERIES.
Misdemeanors.
Class A misdemeanor.
Gambling.
See MISDEMEANORS.
Pari-mutuel betting.
Legalized pari-mutuel betting not affected by gambling article, §13A-12-31.

BEVERAGE CONTAINERS.
Alcoholic beverages.
Containers.
See ALCOHOLIC BEVERAGES.
Evidence.
Presumptive evidence of unlawful use or purchase, §8-12-22.
Milk and milk products.
Marked containers, §§8-12-40 to 8-12-44, 8-16-95 to 8-16-97.
See MILK AND MILK PRODUCTS.
Names, marks, etc.
Defacing, §8-12-21.
Registration, §8-12-20.
Refilling, §8-12-21.
Searches and seizures.
Issuance of warrant for containers unlawfully used or held, §8-12-23.
Trafficking, §8-12-21.

BEVERAGES.
Adulterated beverages.
Inspection.
Municipal corporations, §11-47-136.
Prohibition of sale, etc.
Municipal corporations, §11-47-136.
Alcoholic beverages.
General provisions, §§28-1-1 to 28-9-11.
See ALCOHOLIC BEVERAGES.
Commercial code.
Sales.
Implied warranty of merchantability, §7-2-314.
Destruction.
Nuisances menacing public health.
Summary destruction of property without compensation, §22-10-3.
Health.
Nuisances menacing public health, §§22-10-1 to 22-10-3.
Industrial alcohol.
Beverage use, §§28-5-7, 28-5-8.
Inspections.
Municipal corporations, §11-47-136.
Intoxicating beverages.
General provisions, §§28-1-1 to 28-9-11.
See ALCOHOLIC BEVERAGES.

BEVERAGES—Cont'd
Licenses.
Cereal beverages, carbonated or other soft drinks.
Retailers, §40-12-69.
Wholesalers, §40-12-70.
Milk.
See MILK AND MILK PRODUCTS.
Municipal corporations.
Impure, adulterated, etc., drink.
Prohibition of sale, etc., §11-47-136.
Provision for inspections, §11-47-136.
Nuisances menacing public health, §§22-10-1 to 22-10-3.

BIBB COUNTY.
Court costs and charges,
Const. Ala., amds. 306, 332.
Economic development,
Const. Ala., amd. 312.
Officers.
Compensation of certain officers, Const. Ala., amd. 332.
Sheriff.
Compensation of sheriff, Const. Ala., amd. 306.

BIBLES.
Penitentiary.
Board of corrections to supply, §14-3-46.

BICYCLES, §§32-5A-260 to 32-5A-266.
Application of regulations, §32-5A-266.
Brakes, §32-5A-265.
Carrying articles, §32-5A-264.
Clinging to vehicles, §32-5A-262.
Defined, §32-1-1.1.
Guardians.
Violations of regulations.
Guardians not to authorize or permit, §32-5A-266.
Lamps, §32-5A-265.
Licenses.
Dealers, §40-12-62.
Tags, §40-12-62.
Limited-access highways.
Restrictions on use, §32-5A-92.
Minors.
Violations.
Parents or guardians of child not to authorize violations, §32-5A-266.
Motorcycles.
See MOTORCYCLES.
Motor-driven cycles, §§32-12-20 to 32-12-27.
See MOTORCYCLES.
Number of persons riding bicycle at one time, §32-5A-261.
Parent and child.
Violations of regulations.
Parent not to permit or authorize violations, §32-5A-266.
Parks, §32-5A-263.
Reflective devices, §32-5A-265.

BICYCLES—Cont'd
Riding on bicycles, §32-5A-261.
Where bicycle to be ridden, §32-5A-263.
Rights of persons riding bicycles, §32-5A-260.
Traffic laws applicable, §32-5A-260.
Violations of regulations, §32-5A-266.

BIDS AND BIDDING.
County industrial development authorities.
Exemption from competitive bid laws, §11-92A-19.
Fires and fire prevention.
Sprinkler systems.
Awarding of contracts, §34-33-10.
Copies of chapter furnished to invited bidders, §34-33-10.
Health.
Medicaid program.
Eyewear.
Prescription eyewear for recipients, §22-6-7.1.
Health care authorities.
Competitive bidding laws.
Applicability, §22-21-335.
Mental health finance authority.
Bond issues.
Sale of bonds, §41-10-360.
Public contracts.
Competitive bidding, §§41-16-20 to 41-16-63.
See CONTRACTS.
Utility services facilities.
Exemption from competitive bid laws, §11-97-20.

BIGAMY.
Defenses to prosecution, §13A-13-1.
Elements of crime, §13A-13-1.
Indictments.
Form of indictment, §15-8-150.
Persons married outside state, §13A-13-1.

BILLBOARDS.
Outdoor advertising, §§23-1-270 to 23-1-288.
See ADVERTISING.

BILLIARD ROOMS, §§34-6-1 to 34-6-35.
Alcoholic beverages.
Sale prohibited, §34-6-12.
Applicability of chapter.
Exemptions from chapter, §34-6-15.
Authority of municipalities, §34-6-3.
Bonds, surety.
Licensee's bond, §34-6-32.
Cleanliness.
Billiard rooms to be kept clean and sanitary, §34-6-5.
Counties.
Commercial operation of tables.
Authorized, §34-6-8.1.
License.
Required, §34-6-8.1.

BILLIARD ROOMS—Cont'd
Counties—Cont'd
Keeping or operating billiard
tables outside
incorporated cities or
towns, §34-6-8.
Minors.
Playing billiards permitted
in certain counties,
§34-6-9.
Definitions, §34-6-1.
Doors.
Secret doors, trapdoors, etc.,
prohibited, §34-6-7.
Exemptions from chapter,
§34-6-15.
Gambling.
Betting, §34-6-14.
Permitting gambling devices
in billiard room,
§34-6-13.
Prohibited, §34-6-12.
Health.
Compliance with health and
sanitation ordinances
and regulations, §34-6-5.
Hours of operation, §34-6-4.
Inspection of billiard rooms,
§34-6-2.
Interior view.
Clear view of interior
required, §34-6-6.
Licenses.
Application to city clerk,
§34-6-34.
Application to probate judge,
§34-6-32.
Bond, §34-6-32.
Clerk.
Application to city clerk,
§34-6-34.
Credit for unused portion of
surrendered license,
§34-6-33.
Forfeiture of license,
§34-6-33.
Issuance, §34-6-32.
No license issued where
prohibited by city
ordinance, §34-6-35.
Municipal corporations,
§11-51-102.
Annexation.
Territory exempt from
taxation, §11-42-81.
Application to city clerk,
§34-6-34.
No license issued where
billiard room
prohibited by
ordinance, §34-6-35.
Revocation, §11-51-103.
Operating without license,
§34-6-30.
Penalties.
Operating without license,
§34-6-30.
Pool tables, §40-12-146.
Municipal corporations,
§§11-51-102,
11-51-103.
Probate judge.
Application to judge,
§34-6-32.
Authority to grant license,
§34-6-31.
Qualifications of applicants,
§34-6-32.

BILLIARD ROOMS—Cont'd
Licenses—Cont'd
Surrender of license,
§34-6-33.
Credit for unused portion,
§34-6-33.
Minors.
Certification as to age,
§34-6-9.
Misrepresentation of age,
§34-6-9.
Penalties.
False certification by
minor of age, §34-6-9.
Permitting minors to play
pool or billiards,
§34-6-10.
Permitting minors to play
billiards or pool,
§34-6-10.
Playing billiards prohibited,
§34-6-9.
Exceptions in certain
counties, §34-6-9.
Posting of law as to minors,
§34-6-11.
Municipal corporations.
Authority of municipalities,
§34-6-3.
Closing, §11-51-102.
Keeping or operating billiard
tables outside
incorporated cities or
towns, §§34-6-8, 34-6-8.1.
Licenses. See within this
heading, "Licenses."
Notice.
Posting of law as to minors,
§34-6-11.
Penalties.
Licenses.
Operating without license,
§34-6-30.
Minors.
Permitting minors to play
billiards or pool,
§34-6-10.
Violations of chapter,
§34-6-16.
Probate judge.
Licenses, §§34-6-31, 34-6-32.
Rules and regulations.
Compliance with health
department regulations,
§34-6-5.
Sales tax.
Tax levied on gross receipts,
§40-23-2.
**Screens, blinds, partitions,
etc.**
Obstructing interior view of
billiard room prohibited,
§34-6-6.
**Secret doors, connections,
etc.**
Prohibited, §34-6-7.
Signs.
Posting of law as to minors,
§34-6-11.
Time.
Hours when billiard room
may be operated,
§34-6-4.
Windows.
Secret windows, etc., for
gambling purposes
prohibited, §34-6-7.
View into interior not to be
obstructed, §34-6-6.

BILL OF RIGHTS.
Constitution of Alabama.
Declaration of rights, Const.
Ala., art. I, §§1 to 36.
See CONSTITUTION OF
ALABAMA.
**Constitution of the United
States,** Const. U. S.,
Amendments I to X.

BILLS OF ATTAINDER.
Constitutional provisions,
Const. U. S., Art. I, §§9,
10; Art. III, §3.
Treason.
Bills of attainder of treason
by legislature prohibited,
Const. Ala., art. I, §19.

BILLS OF EXCHANGE.
Commercial code.
Commercial paper generally,
§§7-3-101 to 7-3-805.
See COMMERCIAL CODE.
Damages on protest.
Nonacceptance, §§8-4-1,
8-4-4.
Nonpayment, §8-4-1.
Applicability of rate of
exchange.
Determination of
damages, §8-4-3.
Damages in place of all
charges except costs,
§8-4-2.
**Negotiable instruments
generally.**
See NEGOTIABLE
INSTRUMENTS.
Rate of exchange.
Applicability in determining
amount due and
damages for
nonpayment, §8-4-3.

BILLS OF LADING.
Commercial code.
See COMMERCIAL CODE.
Documents of title, §§7-7-101
to 7-7-603.
See COMMERCIAL CODE.
Motor vehicle carriers,
§37-3-23.
Seeds.
Maintenance by trucks, etc.,
transporting seed for
sale, §2-26-10.
Transportation companies,
§§37-2-21 to 37-2-26.
See TRANSPORTATION
COMPANIES.

BILLS OF REVIEW.
Rules of civil procedure.
Abolished, ARCP, Rule 60
(b).

BINGO.
Jefferson county.
Operation of bingo games in
Jefferson county, Const.
Ala., amd. 386.
Madison county.
Operation of bingo games,
Const. Ala., amd. 387.
Mobile county.
Operation of bingo games in,
Const. Ala., amd. 440.
Montgomery county.
Operation of bingo games,
Const. Ala., amd. 413.

BIRDS.
Agisters.
Lien for feeding, boarding or training, §35-11-71.
Boarding.
Lien for boarding, §35-11-71.
Feeding.
Lien for feeding, §35-11-71.
Game laws.
See FISH AND GAME.
Hunting.
See FISH AND GAME.
Liens.
Feeding, boarding or training, §35-11-71.
Quail.
Commercial quail breeding. See FISH AND GAME.
State bird, §1-2-7.
State game bird, §1-2-17.
Training.
Lien for training, §35-11-71.
Turkey.
State game bird, §1-2-17.
Yellow-hammer.
State bird, §1-2-7.

BIRMINGHAM BUILDING TRADES TOWERS.
Licenses.
Exemptions, §40-9-12.
Taxation.
Exemptions, §40-9-12.

BIRMINGHAM FOOTBALL FOUNDATION, INC.
Licenses.
Exemptions, §40-9-12.
Taxation.
Exemptions, §40-9-12.

BIRMINGHAM, MUNICIPALITY OF.
Circuit courts at Birmingham.
Vacancies in office of judge, Const. Ala., amd. 83.
Property tax, Const. Ala., amd. 8.
Special ad valorem tax for paying principal and interest on bonds, Const. Ala., amd. 240.

BIRMINGHAM SOUTHERN COLLEGE.
Marine environmental sciences consortium, §§16-45-1 to 16-45-5.

BIRTH DEFECTS.
Genetic service, §§22-10A-1 to 22-10A-3.

BIRTHS.
Certificates.
See VITAL STATISTICS.
Midwives.
Practice of midwifery, §§34-19-2 to 34-19-10.
Prevention of infantile blindness, §22-20-2.
Reports of death, §22-9-78.
See MIDWIVES.
Vital statistics.
See VITAL STATISTICS.

BISHOP OF DIOCESE, §§10-4-1 to 10-4-9.
Actions.
Powers of corporation, §10-4-4.
Administrator.
Appointment to act while bishopric vacant, §10-4-6.

BISHOP OF DIOCESE—Cont'd
Agents.
Employment, §10-4-4.
Bond issues.
Powers of corporation, §10-4-4.
Certificate of incorporation, §10-4-3.
Fees, §10-4-8.
Prima facie evidence, §10-4-9.
Dissolution.
Generally, §10-4-7.
Powers of corporation, §10-4-4.
Evidence.
Records and certificates prima facie evidence, §10-4-9.
Fees, §10-4-8.
Incorporation, §§10-4-1 to 10-4-3.
Application, §10-4-2.
Authority to incorporate, §10-4-1.
Certificate of incorporation, §10-4-3.
Proceedings to incorporate, §10-4-2.
Name.
Corporate name, §10-4-4.
Officers.
Appointment, §10-4-4.
Powers of corporation, §10-4-4.
Property.
Power of corporation, §10-4-4.
Records.
Prima facie evidence, §10-4-9.
Seals and sealed instruments.
Corporate seal, §10-4-4.
Secretary of state.
Application for corporation, §10-4-2.
Fees to be paid secretary of state, §10-4-8.
Succession.
Certificate of succession by successor of bishop, §10-4-5.
Fees, §10-4-8.
Prima facie evidence, §10-4-9.
Vacancy of bishopric.
Appointment of administrator, §10-4-6.

BLACK ARCHIVES, RESEARCH CENTER AND MUSEUM, §§16-49-50 to 16-49-55.
See HISTORY AND ARCHIVES.

BLACK HERITAGE MUSEUM OF WEST ALABAMA, §§16-62-1 to 16-62-6.
Citation of chapter, §16-62-1.
Curator, §16-62-4.
Definitions, §16-62-2.
Duties, §16-62-5.
Functions, §16-62-5.
Grants.
Authority to accept, §16-62-6.
Purpose of chapter, §16-62-3.
Short title of chapter, §16-62-1.

BLACK HERITAGE MUSEUM OF WEST ALABAMA —Cont'd
Stillman College.
Authority to accept funds, grants and services, §16-62-6.

BLACKLISTS.
Maintaining, §13A-11-123.

BLACKSMITHS.
Liens.
Attachment.
Joinder of persons having liens on same property, §35-11-112.
Right to enforce lien by attachment, §35-11-111.
Declaration of lien, §35-11-110.
Enforcement.
Joinder of persons having liens on same property, §35-11-112.
Right to enforce by attachment, §35-11-111.

BLANKET MORTGAGES.
Condominium property, §35-8-18.
Mortgages and deeds of trust generally.
See MORTGAGES AND DEEDS OF TRUST.

BLASTING.
Coal.
Mine safety.
Explosives and blasting, §§25-9-130 to 25-9-137.
See COAL.
General provisions.
See EXPLOSIVES AND EXPLOSIONS.

BLEACH.
Caustic or corrosive substances.
General provisions, §§8-17-20 to 8-17-24.
Eye protective devices.
Pupils and teachers, §16-1-7.

BLIND PERSONS.
Alabama institute for deaf and blind, §§21-1-1 to 21-1-26.
See HANDICAPPED PERSONS.
Amusements.
Right to use of places of public amusement, §21-7-3.
Assistance to needy blind persons, §§38-5-1 to 38-5-7.
Amount of assistance, §38-5-1.
Retention of certain property by applicant, §38-5-4.
Bankruptcy.
Assistance not to pass through trustee, §38-5-5.
Definitions, §38-1-1.
Eligibility, §38-4-1.
To whom assistance payable, §38-5-2.

BLIND PERSONS—Cont'd

Assistance to needy blind persons—Cont'd
Examinations.
Freedom of choice in selection of specialists, §38-1-2.
Hospitalization.
Cost not to constitute lien on property, §38-5-5.
Relatives.
Not legally liable for cost, §38-5-6.
Inalienability of aid, §38-5-5.
Injunctions.
Freedom of choice in selection of specialists to make examinations, §38-1-2.
Intent of chapter, §38-5-3.
Liens.
Hospitalization.
Cost not to constitute lien on property, §38-5-5.
Payment of assistance.
Amount, §38-5-1.
Eligibility for assistance, §§38-4-1, 38-5-2.
Certain property retained by applicant, §38-5-4.
To whom assistance payable, §38-5-2.
Property.
Retention of certain property by applicant, §38-5-4.
Public assistance generally.
See WELFARE.
Purpose of chapter, §38-5-3.
Relatives.
Liability to support, hospital and medical care, etc.
Relatives not legally liable, §38-5-6.
Social security.
Conflicts with social security act, §38-5-7.
Aviation.
Right to use of public conveyances and transportation facilities, §21-7-3.
Bankruptcy and insolvency.
Assistance to needy blind persons.
Assistance not to pass through trustee, §38-5-5.
Boats.
Right to use of public conveyances and transportation facilities, §21-7-3.
Buildings.
Accessibility to and use of public buildings and facilities by physically handicapped persons, §§21-4-1 to 21-4-7.
See PUBLIC BUILDINGS.
Operation of vending stands by blind persons in public buildings, §21-1-41.
Right to full use of public buildings, §21-7-2.

BLIND PERSONS—Cont'd

Buses.
Right to use of public conveyances and transportation facilities, §21-7-3.
Canes.
White canes. See within this heading, "White canes."
Common carriers.
Right to use of public conveyances and transportation facilities, §21-7-3.
Constitution of Alabama.
Exemptions from poll tax, Const. Ala., amd. 109.
Institute for deaf and blind.
Bonds for construction and improvement purposes, Const. Ala., amd. 117.
Counties.
Employment by counties, §21-7-8.
Damages.
Liability for damages caused by guide dogs, §21-7-4.
Definitions.
Blind-made products or services, §21-1-60.
Generally, §21-1-3.
Operation of vending stands by blind persons, §21-1-40.
Dogs.
Guide dogs. See within this heading, "Guide dogs."
Education.
Educational benefits for dependents of blind parents, §§16-33-1 to 16-33-12.
See UNIVERSITIES AND COLLEGES.
Employment by public schools, §21-7-8.
Exceptional children, §§16-39-1 to 16-39-12.
See EDUCATION.
Institute for deaf and blind, §§21-1-1 to 21-1-26.
See HANDICAPPED PERSONS.
Elections.
Accessibility to registration and polling places, §§21-4-20 to 21-4-24.
Ballots.
Assistance in casting, §17-8-29.
Municipal elections.
Assistance to disabled voters, §§11-46-40, 11-46-111, 11-46-122, 11-46-138.
Deception of disabled voters by marker, etc., §§11-46-64, 11-46-135.
False declaration requesting assistance, §11-46-138.
Mayor-council form.
Assistance of disabled voters, §11-46-40.
Voting machines, §11-46-51.
Voting machines.
Assistance at polls, §17-9-25.

BLIND PERSONS—Cont'd

Employment.
By state, political subdivisions, public schools, etc., §21-7-8.
Evidence.
How blindness proved, §1-1-3.
Examinations.
Assistance to needy blind persons.
Freedom of choice in selection of specialists to make examinations, §38-1-2.
Guide dogs.
Crossing public streets with guide dogs, §32-5A-220.
Duty of drivers to blind or partially blind pedestrians using guide dog, §21-7-6.
Failure to use guide dog.
Rights of blind persons not using guide dog, §21-7-7.
Housing accommodations.
Right to housing accommodations, §21-7-9.
Liability for damages caused by guide dogs, §21-7-4.
Refusal to permit guide dog accompanying blind person to enter place of public accommodation, public conveyance, etc., §3-1-7.
Right of blind or partially blind persons to be accompanied by guide dog, §21-7-4.
Rights of blind persons not using guide dog, §21-7-7.
Home industries.
Workshops, home industries, etc., §§21-2-1 to 21-2-4.
Hospitals.
Assistance to needy blind persons.
Cost of hospitalization.
Not to constitute lien on property, §38-5-5.
Relatives not legally liable, §38-5-6.
Hotels, inns and other transient lodging places.
Right to use of public lodging places, §21-7-3.
Housing.
Right to housing accommodations, §21-7-9.
Infantile blindness.
Notifiable diseases generally, §§22-11A-1 to 22-11A-38.
See DISEASES.
Prevention, §22-20-2.
Injunctions.
Freedom of choice in selection of specialists to make examinations, §38-1-2.
Institute for deaf and blind, §§21-1-1 to 21-1-26.
See HANDICAPPED PERSONS.
Liability.
Damages caused by guide dogs, §21-7-4.

BLIND PERSONS—Cont'd
Liability—Cont'd
Hospitalization costs.
Relatives not legally liable,
§38-5-6.
Libraries.
Operation of library service
by department of adult
blind and deaf, §21-1-15.
Licenses.
Exemptions from licenses,
§40-12-330.
Vending stands.
Preference in issuance of
licenses, §21-1-41.
Liens.
Assistance to needy blind
persons.
Hospitalization.
Cost not to constitute
lien on property,
§38-5-5.
Lodging places.
Right to use of public lodging
places, §21-7-3.
Midwives.
Infantile blindness.
Prevention, §22-20-2.
Minors.
Infantile blindness.
Notifiable diseases,
§§22-11A-1 to
22-11A-38.
See DISEASES.
Prevention, §22-20-2.
Motor vehicles.
Guide dogs, §§21-7-6, 21-7-7.
Right to use of public
conveyances and
transportation facilities,
§21-7-3.
Municipal corporations.
Elections.
Assistance to disabled
voters, §§11-46-40,
11-46-111, 11-46-122,
11-46-138.
Deception of disabled
voters by marker, etc.,
§§11-46-64, 11-46-135.
False declaration
requesting assistance,
§11-46-138.
Mayor-council form.
Assistance of disabled
electors, §11-46-40.
Voting machines,
§11-46-51.
Employment by
municipalities, §21-7-8.
Needy blind persons.
Assistance, §§38-5-1 to
38-5-7. See within this
heading, "Assistance to
needy blind persons."
Nurses.
Infantile blindness.
Prevention, §22-20-2.
Parent and child.
Educational benefits for
dependents of blind
parents, §§16-33-1 to
16-33-12.
See UNIVERSITIES AND
COLLEGES.
Pedestrians.
Duty of drivers to blind or
partially blind
pedestrians carrying
cane or using guide dog,
§21-7-6.

BLIND PERSONS—Cont'd
Pedestrians—Cont'd
Rights of blind persons not
using cane or guide dog,
§21-7-7.
Penalties.
Sale, etc., of blind-made
products or services.
Penalties for violation of
article, §21-1-62.
Physicians.
Assistance to needy blind
persons.
Freedom of choice in
selection of specialists,
§38-1-2.
Infantile blindness.
Prevention, §22-20-2.
Poll tax.
Exemptions from poll tax,
Const. Ala., amd. 109.
Products.
Sale, etc., of blind-made
products or services,
§§21-1-60 to 21-1-62.
Proof of blindness.
How blindness proved,
§1-1-3.
Property.
Assistance to needy blind
persons.
Hospitalization.
Cost not to constitute
lien, §38-5-5.
Retention of certain
property by applicant,
§38-5-4.
Public accommodations.
Right to use, §21-7-3.
Public buildings.
Accessibility to and use of
buildings and facilities,
§§21-4-1 to 21-4-7.
See PUBLIC BUILDINGS.
Operation of vending stands
in public buildings,
§21-1-41.
Right to full use of public
buildings and facilities,
§21-7-2.
Public lands.
Operation of vending stands
on properties of state,
§21-1-41.
Railroads.
Right to use of public
conveyances and
transportation facilities,
§21-7-3.
Register of blind persons.
Preparation and
maintenance, §21-1-16.
Resorts.
Right to use of public resorts,
§21-7-3.
**Rights of blind and other
physically disabled
persons,** §§21-7-1 to
21-7-10.
See HANDICAPPED
PERSONS.
**Sale, etc., of blind-made
products or services,**
§§21-1-60 to 21-1-62.
Certification of products or
services as blind-made,
§21-1-61.
Definition of blind-made
products or services,
§21-1-60.

BLIND PERSONS—Cont'd
**Sale, etc., of blind-made
products or services**
—Cont'd
Penalties for violations of
article, §21-1-62.
Violations of article.
Penalties for violations,
§21-1-62.
Sales taxes.
Division of rehabilitation and
crippled children service.
Business enterprise
program.
Blind vendors.
Exemption from sales
or use taxes,
§40-23-5.
Scholarships.
Educational benefits for
dependents of blind
parents, §§16-33-1 to
16-33-12.
See UNIVERSITIES AND
COLLEGES.
Seeing eye dogs. See within
this heading, "Guide dogs."
Ships and shipping.
Right to use of public
conveyances and
transportation facilities,
§21-7-3.
Sidewalks.
Right to full use of
sidewalks, §21-7-2.
Silver nitrate.
Prevention of infantile
blindness, §22-20-2.
Social security.
Assistance to needy blind
persons, §38-5-7.
State.
Employment by state,
§21-7-8.
Streets.
Right of way, §32-5A-220.
Right to full use of streets,
§21-7-2.
Transportation.
Right to use of public
conveyances and
transportation facilities,
§21-7-3.
Universities and colleges.
Educational benefits for
dependents of blind
parents, §§16-33-1 to
16-33-12.
See UNIVERSITIES AND
COLLEGES.
Vending stands.
Licenses.
Preference in issuance of
licenses, §21-1-41.
Operation by blind persons.
Definitions, §21-1-40.
Public buildings and
property, §21-1-41.
White canes.
Duty of drivers to blind or
partially blind
pedestrians carrying
cane, §21-7-6.
Failure to use cane.
Rights of blind persons not
using cane, §21-7-7.
Rights of blind persons not
using cane, §21-7-7.
White cane safety day.
Annual proclamation,
§21-7-10.

BLIND PERSONS—Cont'd
Workmen's compensation,
§25-5-57.
Workshops, home industries,
etc., for blind persons,
§§21-2-1 to 21-2-4.
BLOOD.
Blood tests.
Alcohol.
Chemical tests for
intoxication,
§§32-5-190 to 32-5-194,
32-5A-194.
Dead bodies.
Blood and urine samples,
§§22-19-80 to 22-19-82.
Drunkenness.
Chemical tests for
intoxication,
§§32-5-190 to 32-5-194,
32-5A-194.
Motor vehicles.
Chemical tests for
intoxication,
§§32-5-190 to 32-5-194,
32-5A-194.
Paternity proceedings,
§26-17-12.
Syphilis.
Marriage license.
Examination for syphilis,
§22-11A-15.
Commercial code.
Implied warranty, §7-2-314.
Donations.
Minors.
Persons 17 or older,
§26-1-3.
Prisoners.
Deductions from sentences,
§14-9-3.
BLOUNT COUNTY.
Court costs and charges,
Const. Ala., amd. 344.
Economic development.
Municipalities in Blount
county, Const. Ala., amd.
95.
Officers.
Compensation of certain
officers, Const. Ala.,
amd. 344.
Taxation.
Offices of tax assessor and
tax collector.
Consolidation, Const. Ala.,
amd. 430.
BLUE LAWS.
Certain acts prohibited on
Sunday, §§13A-12-1,
13A-12-2.
Sunday sales.
See SUNDAYS.
BLUEPRINTS.
Licenses.
Blueprint makers, §40-12-63.
BLUE SKY LAW, §§8-6-1 to
8-6-60.
See SECURITIES.
BOARDINGHOUSES.
See HOTELS, INNS AND
OTHER TRANSIENT
LODGING PLACES.
**BOARDS AND
COMMISSIONS.**
Accountants.
Board of public accountancy.
See ACCOUNTANTS.

**BOARDS AND
COMMISSIONS**—Cont'd
Actions.
Officers.
Liability of officers of
nonprofit
organizations,
§§10-11-1 to 10-11-5.
Adjustment of claims.
Board of adjustment,
§§41-9-60 to 41-9-74.
See CLAIMS AGAINST
STATE.
Aged persons.
Commission on the aging,
§§38-3-1 to 38-3-6.
See AGED PERSONS.
Agriculture.
Agricultural center.
Board.
See AGRICULTURE.
Board of agriculture and
industries.
See AGRICULTURE.
Fairs and exhibits.
Agricultural and industrial
exhibit commission,
§§2-7-1 to 2-7-7.
See AGRICULTURE.
Farm crisis and transition
commission, §§2-6A-2,
2-6A-4.
Air pollution control
commission.
See AIR POLLUTION.
Alabama commission of
higher education,
§§16-5-1 to 16-5-14.
See UNIVERSITIES AND
COLLEGES.
Alabama educational
television commission,
§§16-7-1 to 16-7-6, 16-7A-7.
See EDUCATION.
Alabama education study
commission, §§16-6-1 to
16-6-6.
See EDUCATION.
Alabama historical
commission, §§41-9-240 to
41-9-262.
See HISTORY AND
ARCHIVES.
Alabama Indian affairs
commission, §§41-9-708 to
41-9-717.
See INDIANS.
Alcoholic beverage control
board.
See ALCOHOLIC
BEVERAGES.
Ameraport offshore harbor
and terminal
commission, §§33-10-1 to
33-10-26.
See AMERAPORT.
Arbitration and award.
Unions and labor relations.
Local boards of arbitration,
§§25-7-50 to 25-7-54.
Architects.
Board of registration,
§§34-2-38 to 34-2-42.
Armory commission, §§31-4-1
to 31-4-19.
See MILITARY AFFAIRS.
Art commission, §§41-9-20 to
41-9-22.

**BOARDS AND
COMMISSIONS**—Cont'd
Athletics.
Athlete agent regulatory
commission.
See SPORTS.
Athletic commission,
§41-9-90.1.
Motor sports hall of fame
commission, §§41-9-470
to 41-9-478.
See MOTOR SPORTS
HALL OF FAME
COMMISSION.
Sports hall of fame board,
§§41-9-450 to 41-9-454.
Attorneys at law.
Board of commissioners.
See ATTORNEYS AT
LAW.
Board of examiners, §34-3-2.
State bar.
Building foundation.
Board of trustees,
§34-3-103.
Auctioneers.
Board of auctioneers.
See AUCTIONS AND
AUCTIONEERS.
Audiologists.
Board of examiners,
§§34-28A-40 to
34-28A-44.
Aviation.
Aeronautics commission.
See AVIATION.
Hall of fame board,
§§41-9-720 to 41-9-722.
Space science exhibit
commission, §§41-9-430
to 41-9-439.
See SPACE SCIENCE
EXHIBIT
COMMISSION.
Banking board.
See BANKS AND
FINANCIAL
INSTITUTIONS.
Barbers.
Board of barber examiners.
See BARBERS.
Bar examiners, §34-3-2.
Beautification board,
§§41-9-490 to 41-9-498.
See BEAUTIFICATION.
Bond issues.
Consent of department of
finance prerequisite to
issuance, §41-4-16.
Boxing and wrestling.
Athletic commission,
§41-9-90.1.
Building commission.
See BUILDINGS.
Cahaba trace commission,
§§41-9-800 to 41-9-810.
See CAHABA TRACE
COMMISSION.
Capitol.
State capitol preservation
commission, §41-9-261.
Cemeteries.
County cemeteries.
Commission, §§11-17-1 to
11-17-4.
Chiropractors.
Board of chiropractic
examiners, §§34-24-140
to 34-24-145.
See CHIROPRACTORS.

BOARDS AND COMMISSIONS—Cont'd

City boards of education.
See EDUCATION.

Claims against the state.
Board of adjustment.
Executive or secret sessions prohibited, §13A-14-2.
General provisions, §§41-9-61 to 41-9-71.
See CLAIMS AGAINST STATE.
Legal representation, §41-4-204.

Coal.
Abandoned mine reclamation.
Interagency cooperation, §9-16-131.
Surface mining control and reclamation.
Commission, §§9-16-73, 9-16-74, 9-16-77.

Coastal areas board.
See COASTAL AREAS.

Conservation and natural resources.
Advisory board, §§9-2-14 to 9-2-15.1.

Continuation.
Sunset law generally.
See STATE DEPARTMENTS AND AGENCIES.

Continuing women's commission, §§41-9-410 to 41-9-414.

Contractors.
State licensing board, §§34-8-20 to 34-8-27.
See CONTRACTORS.

Corrections.
Board of corrections.
See CORRECTIONS.

Cosmetology.
Board of cosmetology.
See COSMETOLOGISTS.

Counseling.
Board of examiners in counseling.
See COUNSELORS.

County commissions.
See COUNTIES.

County jury commissions.
See JURY.

Credit unions.
Board.
General provisions, §§5-17-51, 5-17-55 to 5-17-58.
Removal of members, §5-17-44.

Crime victims compensation.
Commission.
See CRIME VICTIMS COMPENSATION.

Criminal justice advisory commission, §§41-9-570 to 41-9-574.

Criminal justice information center.
Commission.
See CRIMINAL LAW AND PROCEDURE.

Criminal law and procedure.
Executive or secret sessions of certain boards, §13A-14-2.

BOARDS AND COMMISSIONS—Cont'd

Dentists.
Board of dental examiners.
See DENTISTS.

Dietitians and nutritionists.
Board of examiners for dietetics/nutrition practice, §34-34A-6.

Education.
Boards of education.
City boards of education, §§16-11-1 to 16-11-27.
See EDUCATION.
County boards of education, §§16-8-1 to 16-8-43.
See EDUCATION.
General provisions.
See EDUCATION.
State board of education, §§16-3-1 to 16-3-37.
See EDUCATION.
Educational reform.
Commission, §§16-6A-5 to 16-6A-8.
School trustees.
Boards of school trustees.
See EDUCATION.
Teachers.
State tenure commission, §§16-24-30 to 16-24-38.
See EDUCATION.

Educational television commission, §§16-7-1 to 16-7-7.
See EDUCATION.

Elections.
Registrars.
See ELECTIONS.

Electrical contractors.
Board of electrical contractors.
See ELECTRICAL CONTRACTORS.

Electric membership corporations.
Board of directors.
Fund, §34-36-17.
General provisions, §§34-36-4 to 34-36-6.

Engineers.
Board of registration.
See ENGINEERS.

Environmental management commission.
Defined, §22-22A-3.
General provisions, §§22-22A-6 to 22-22A-8.

Ethics.
State ethics commission, §§26-5-3, 26-5-4.

Executive mansion.
Governor's mansion advisory board, §§41-9-530 to 41-9-532.

Executive or secret sessions of certain boards, §13A-14-2.

Fees.
Disposition of departmental and institutional fees, receipts, etc., §41-4-92.

Fires and fire prevention.
Personnel standards and education.
Commission, §§36-32-1 to 36-32-12.
See FIRES AND FIRE PREVENTION.

BOARDS AND COMMISSIONS—Cont'd

Foreign trade and relations commission, §§41-9-660 to 41-9-664.

Forests and forestry.
Foresters.
Board of registration.
Defined, §34-12-1.
General provisions, §§34-12-30 to 34-12-37.
See FORESTS AND FORESTRY.
Revocation or suspension of licenses, §34-12-9.
State forestry commission.
See FORESTS AND FORESTRY.

Fort Morgan historical commission, §41-9-260.

Funeral service.
Board of funeral service.
See FUNERALS.

Gorgas memorial board.
Generally, §41-9-220.

Governor.
Governor's mansion advisory board, §§41-9-530 to 41-9-532.

Health.
County boards of health, §§22-3-1 to 22-3-3.
Physical fitness commission, §§22-5-1 to 22-5-9.
See HEALTH.
State board of health, §§22-2-1 to 22-2-3.

Hearing aid dealers.
Board of hearing aid dealers.
See HEARING AID DEALERS AND FITTERS.

Hobson memorial board, §41-9-222.

Hospitals.
County hospital boards, §§22-21-70 to 22-21-83.
See HOSPITALS.
State board of health.
See HOSPITALS.

Human resources.
Board of human resources, §38-2-2.
County boards of human resources.
See WELFARE.

Immunity.
Officers.
Liability of officers of nonprofit organizations, §§10-11-1 to 10-11-5.

Improvement authorities.
Board of trustees, §§39-7-14 to 39-7-17, 39-7-28.

Industrial development board.
Advisory board, §§41-9-185 to 41-9-188.
Counties, §§11-20-30 to 11-20-50.
See COUNTIES.
Generally, §41-9-187.
Municipal corporations, §§11-54-80 to 11-54-101.
See MUNICIPAL CORPORATIONS.

BOARDS AND
COMMISSIONS—Cont'd
Insurance.
State employees' insurance
board.
See PUBLIC OFFICERS
AND EMPLOYEES.
Jacksonville state
university.
Board of trustees, §§16-52-1
to 16-52-10.
See JACKSONVILLE
STATE UNIVERSITY.
Judicial compensation
commission, §§12-10-1 to
12-10-5.
Judicial inquiry commission.
See JUDGES.
Judicial system study
commission, §§12-9-1 to
12-9-9.
See JUDICIAL SYSTEM
STUDY COMMISSION.
Jury commissions.
County jury commissions.
See JURY.
Labor.
Department of labor
relations.
Board of appeals.
See LABOR.
LaGrange historical
commission.
Generally, §41-9-270.
Landscape architects.
Board of examiners.
General provisions,
§§34-17-1 to 34-17-3.
Rules and regulations.
Examination, §34-17-22.
Secretary.
Landscape architects'
fund.
Duties, §34-17-6.
Liability.
Officers.
Liability of officers of
nonprofit
organizations,
§§10-11-1 to 10-11-5.
Library board.
Alabama public library
service.
Executive board, §§41-8-2,
41-8-3.
Library boards.
General provisions,
§§11-90-2, 11-90-3.
Liquefied petroleum gas
board, §§9-17-101 to
9-17-104, 9-17-106.
Litter.
Beautification board,
§§41-9-490 to 41-9-498.
See BEAUTIFICATION.
Livingston university.
Board of trustees, §§16-53-1
to 16-53-11.
See LIVINGSTON
UNIVERSITY.
Marine resources.
Fishing reef ship commission,
§9-12-142.
Medical association board of
censors.
Constituted as board of
medical examiners,
§34-24-53.

BOARDS AND
COMMISSIONS—Cont'd
Medical clinic boards,
§§11-58-1 to 11-58-15.
See MUNICIPAL
CORPORATIONS.
Medical examiners.
State board of medical
examiners.
See PHYSICIANS.
Medical technicians.
Board of examiners.
Annulment or revocation of
certificate, §34-18-24.
General provisions,
§§34-18-40 to 34-18-47.
See MEDICAL
TECHNICIANS.
Meetings.
Executive or secret sessions.
Prohibited as to certain
boards, §13A-14-2.
Men's hall of fame.
Board, §41-9-850.
Mental health board.
See MENTALLY ILL.
Mental health capital outlay
oversight commission,
§22-50-25.
Military affairs.
Armory commission, §§34-4-1
to 34-4-19.
See MILITARY AFFAIRS.
Motor sports hall of fame
commission, §§41-9-470 to
41-9-478.
See MOTOR SPORTS HALL
OF FAME
COMMISSION.
Motor vehicles.
Drivers' licenses.
Medical advisory board,
§§32-6-40 to 32-6-48.
See MOTOR VEHICLES.
Municipal corporations.
General provisions.
See MUNICIPAL
CORPORATIONS.
Music.
Hall of fame board,
§§41-9-680 to 41-9-684.
Negligence.
Officers.
Liability of officers of
nonprofit
organizations,
§§10-11-1 to 10-11-5.
Nurses.
Board of nursing.
Disciplinary proceedings,
§34-21-25.
General provisions,
§§34-21-1 to 34-21-5.
Nursing home
administrators.
Board of examiners of
nursing home
administrators.
Disciplinary proceedings,
§§34-20-14, 34-20-15.
General provisions,
§§34-20-1 to 34-20-8.
See NURSING HOMES.
Officers.
Liability of officers of
nonprofit organizations,
§§10-11-1 to 10-11-5.

BOARDS AND
COMMISSIONS—Cont'd
Oil and gas.
Conservation and regulation
of production.
Oil and gas board.
See OIL AND GAS.
Pardons and paroles.
Board of pardons and
paroles.
See PAROLE.
Peace officers.
Hall of fame.
Board, §§41-9-870,
41-9-871.
Standards and training
commission, §§36-21-40
to 36-21-51.
See PEACE OFFICERS.
Personnel.
State personnel board.
See PUBLIC OFFICERS
AND EMPLOYEES.
Pharmacy.
Board of pharmacy.
See PHARMACISTS AND
PHARMACIES.
Physical fitness, §§22-5-1 to
22-5-9.
See HEALTH.
Physical therapy.
Board of physical therapy,
§§34-24-191 to 34-24-195.
Physicians.
Licenses.
Medical licensure
commission.
See PHYSICIANS.
State board of medical
examiners.
See PHYSICIANS.
State licensing board for
healing arts.
Board of chiropractic
examiners.
Generally, §§34-24-140
to 34-24-145.
See
CHIROPRACTORS.
Licenses.
Suspension or revocation
generally.
See PHYSICIANS.
State board of medical
examiners generally.
See PHYSICIANS.
Pilots.
State pilotage commission.
See PILOTS AND
PILOTAGE.
Planning.
Municipal planning
commissions.
See MUNICIPAL
CORPORATIONS.
Regional planning and
development.
See PLANNING.
Plumbers and gas fitters
examining board.
See PLUMBING.
Podiatry.
Board of podiatry,
§§34-24-250 to 34-24-257.
See PODIATRISTS.
Polygraph examiners.
See POLYGRAPH
EXAMINERS.
Power districts.
Board of directors.
See POWER DISTRICTS.

BOARDS AND COMMISSIONS—Cont'd

Psychologists.
Board of examiners.
See PSYCHOLOGISTS.

Public service commission.
Air commerce.
See AIR COMMERCE.
Elections.
See ELECTIONS.
Explosives.
Transportation, §§37-8-183, 37-8-184.
General provisions.
See PUBLIC SERVICE COMMISSION.
Motor vehicle carriers.
See MOTOR VEHICLE CARRIERS.
Municipal corporations.
See MUNICIPAL CORPORATIONS.
Pipelines.
Gas pipeline systems.
See PIPELINES.
Power districts, §37-5-2.
Public utilities.
See PUBLIC UTILITIES.
Radio.
Utilities.
See RADIO.
Railroads.
See RAILROADS.
Telephones.
See TELEPHONES.

Real estate commission.
See REAL ESTATE BROKERS.

Records.
Local government records commission, §§41-13-22 to 41-13-25.
State records commission, §§41-13-20, 41-13-21, 41-13-24, 41-13-25.
See RECORDS.

Recreation boards.
General provisions, §§11-86-1 to 11-86-6.
See PARKS AND RECREATION.
Municipalities.
Joint actions with counties, §11-86-5.
Public park and recreation boards, §§11-60-1 to 11-60-20.
See MUNICIPAL CORPORATIONS.

Regional planning and development.
See PLANNING.

Registrars.
See ELECTIONS.

Reports.
Printing, §41-4-141.
Time for making, §41-4-141.

St. Stephens historical commission, §§41-9-335 to 41-9-337.

Sanitation.
Beautification board, §§41-9-490 to 41-9-498.
See BEAUTIFICATION.

Savings and loan board, §§5-2A-63, 5-16-2.

School trustees.
Boards of school trustees.
See EDUCATION.

BOARDS AND COMMISSIONS—Cont'd

Science.
Space science exhibit commission, §§41-9-430 to 41-9-439.
See SPACE SCIENCE EXHIBIT COMMISSION.

Secret sessions of certain boards, §13A-14-2.

Securities commission.
See SECURITIES.

Soil and water conservation.
Cost-share grants.
Agricultural and conservation development commission.
See SOIL AND WATER CONSERVATION.

Southeast interstate low-level radioactive waste management compact, §§22-32-1 to 22-32-9.

Space science exhibit commission, §§41-9-430 to 41-9-439.
See SPACE SCIENCE EXHIBIT COMMISSION.

Speech pathologists and audiologists.
Board of examiners.
See SPEECH PATHOLOGISTS AND AUDIOLOGISTS.

Sports.
Agents.
Athlete agent regulatory commission.
See SPORTS.
Athletic commission, §41-9-90.1.
Motor sports hall of fame commission, §§41-9-470 to 41-9-478.
See MOTOR SPORTS HALL OF FAME COMMISSION.
Sports hall of fame board, §§41-9-450 to 41-9-454.

Sunset law, §§41-20-1 to 41-20-16.
See STATE DEPARTMENTS AND AGENCIES.

Sunshine law.
Executive or secret sessions.
Prohibited as to certain boards, §13A-14-2.

Surveys and surveyors.
Board of registration.
See SURVEYS AND SURVEYORS.
Division of land surveys.
Advisory board, §§35-2-25 to 35-2-29, 35-2-32.

Tannehill furnace and foundry commission, §§41-9-320 to 41-9-330.
See HISTORY AND ARCHIVES.

Taxation.
County boards of equalization, §§40-3-1 to 40-3-26.
See TAXATION.

Teachers.
State tenure commission, §§16-24-30 to 16-24-38.
See EDUCATION.

BOARDS AND COMMISSIONS—Cont'd

Tennessee Valley authority.
Exhibit commission, §§41-9-780 to 41-9-787.
See TENNESSEE VALLEY AUTHORITY.

Termination, §§41-20-1 to 41-20-16.
See STATE DEPARTMENTS AND AGENCIES.

Torts.
Officers.
Liability of officers of nonprofit organizations, §§10-11-1 to 10-11-5.

Troy state university.
Board of trustees.
See TROY STATE UNIVERSITY.

Uniform state laws.
Commission on uniform state laws.
See UNIFORM LAWS.

Unions and labor relations.
Local boards of arbitration.
See LABOR.

Universities and colleges.
Commission of higher education, §§16-5-1 to 16-5-14.
See UNIVERSITIES AND COLLEGES.

University of Alabama.
Board of trustees.
See UNIVERSITY OF ALABAMA.

University of North Alabama.
Board of trustees.
See UNIVERSITY OF NORTH ALABAMA.

University of South Alabama.
Board of trustees.
Endowment funds.
Investment, §16-13-2.
General provisions, §§16-55-1 to 16-55-6.
See UNIVERSITY OF SOUTH ALABAMA.

USS Alabama battleship commission, §§41-9-340 to 41-9-358.
See USS ALABAMA BATTLESHIP COMMISSION.

Veterans' affairs.
Board of veterans' affairs, §§31-5-2, 31-5-3.

Veterinarians.
Board of veterinary medicine, §§34-29-63 to 34-29-70.
See VETERINARIANS.

Water management commissioners.
Board of water management commissioners.
See WATER MANAGEMENT AND DRAINAGE.

Welfare.
Board of human resources.
See WELFARE.

Women.
Continuing women's commission, §§41-9-410 to 41-9-414.

BOARDS AND
    COMMISSIONS—Cont'd
Women—Cont'd
  Hall of fame board,
    §§41-9-550 to 41-9-554.
  Youth services board,
    §§44-1-29, 44-1-50 to
    44-1-56.
  See YOUTH SERVICES.

BOATS, §§33-5-1 to 33-5-6.
  Abandonment.
  Notice to department of
    conservation and natural
    resources, §33-5-16.
  Accidents, §33-5-25.
  Actions.
  Discharge of litter and
    sewage from watercraft.
  Prosecutions under
    chapter, §33-6-10.
  Agents.
  Special agents to sell boat
    licenses, §33-5-20.
  Airboats.
  Advisory board of
    conservation and natural
    resources.
  Prohibition on use of
    airboats, §9-2-15.1.
  Applicability of chapter,
    §33-5-2.
  Aquaplanes.
  Safety regulations, §33-5-26.
  Arrests.
  Fees of arresting officer,
    §33-5-34.
  Attachment.
  Liens of owners of booms and
    bulkheads, §35-11-311.
  Blind persons.
  Right to use of public
    conveyances and
    transportation facilities,
    §21-7-3.
  Booms and bulkheads.
  See BOOMS AND
    BULKHEADS.
  Certificates of registration.
  See within this heading,
    "Registration of vessels."
  Change of ownership.
  Registration.
    Filing new application for
      registration, §33-5-15.
  Classification of vessels.
  Fees.
    Schedule of fees, §33-5-17.
  Counties.
  Local regulation, §33-5-31.
  Numbering.
    Exemption from
      numbering provisions.
    Boats owned by counties,
      §33-5-19.
  Death.
  Accidents involving death.
    Report required, §33-5-25.
  Declaration of policy,
    §33-5-1.
  Definitions, §33-5-3.
  Discharge of litter and
    sewage from watercraft,
    §33-6-1.
  Sailboard, §33-5-22.1.
  Department of conservation
    and natural resources.
  Certificates of registration
    and numbers.
  Issuance by department,
    §33-5-10.

BOATS—Cont'd
Department of conservation
    and natural resources
    —Cont'd
  Change of address.
    Notice to department,
      §33-5-16.
  Commissioner.
    Discharge of litter and
      sewage from
      watercraft.
    Rules, regulations and
      orders.
    Approval by
      commissioner,
      §33-6-4.
  Rules and regulations.
    Admissibility as
      evidence, §33-5-30.
  Safety lights.
    Standards, §33-5-22.
  Supplying information to
    federal agencies,
    §33-5-8.
  Warning citations,
    §33-5-36.
  Destruction or abandonment.
    Notice to department,
      §33-5-16.
  Enforcement of chapter,
    §33-5-6.
  Liveries.
    Inspection of liveries by
      department, §33-5-21.
  Records.
    Keeping of records
      pursuant to chapter,
      §33-5-7.
  Rules and regulations
    generally. See within
    this heading, "Rules and
    regulations."
  Transfer of interest.
    Notice to department,
      §33-5-16.
Destruction.
  Notice to department of
    conservation and natural
    resources, §33-5-16.
Discharge of litter and
    sewage from watercraft,
    §§33-6-1 to 33-6-12.
  Actions.
    Prosecutions under
      chapter, §33-6-10.
  Applicability of chapter,
    §33-6-12.
  Board of health.
    Enforcement of chapter,
      rules and regulations,
      §33-6-10.
    Expenditures by board,
      §33-6-9.
    Marine toilets.
      Certification and
        approval by board of
        health, §33-6-6.
    Orders, §33-6-5.
    Public education program,
      §33-6-8.
  Commissioner of
    conservation and natural
    resources.
    Rules and regulations.
    Approval by
      commissioner,
      §33-6-4.
  Complaints.
    Violations of chapter,
      §33-6-10.

BOATS—Cont'd
Discharge of litter and
    sewage from watercraft
    —Cont'd
  Control and regulations.
    Methods of control, §33-6-5.
  Enforcement of chapter.
    Rules, regulations, etc.,
      §33-6-10.
  Expenditures.
    Board of health
      expenditures, §33-6-9.
  Fines.
    Disposition, §33-6-11.
  Governor.
    Rules and regulations.
    Approval by governor,
      §33-6-4.
  Litter.
    Defined, §33-6-1.
  Marinas.
    Receptacles.
    On-shore trash
      receptacles at
      marinas, §33-6-7.
  Marine toilets.
    Approval by board of
      health, §33-6-6.
    Certification, §33-6-6.
    Defined, §33-6-1.
    Discharge of untreated
      sewage, §33-6-3.
    Federal standards.
      Compatibility, §33-6-5.
    Manufacturers.
      Certification by
        manufacturer,
        §33-6-6.
    Restrictions on use,
      §33-6-3.
    Standards.
      Compatibility of federal
        standards, §33-6-5.
  Ordinances.
    Conflicts with other
      ordinances, §33-6-12.
  Penalties.
    Fines.
      Disposition under
        chapter, §33-6-11.
    Violations, §33-6-10.
  Permits.
    Rules and regulations of
      board of health,
      §33-6-5.
  Public education program,
    §33-6-8.
  Receptacles.
    On-shore trash receptacles
      at marinas, etc.,
      §33-6-7.
  Rules and regulations.
    Adoption by board of
      health, §33-6-4.
    Applicability, §33-6-12.
    Commissioner of
      conservation and
      natural resources.
    Approval by
      commissioner,
      §33-6-4.
    Compatibility with federal
      standards, §33-6-5.
    Conflicts with other
      regulations, ordinances
      or laws, §33-6-12.
    Contents, §33-6-5.
    Enforcement, §33-6-10.
    Governor.
      Approval by governor,
        §33-6-4.

BOATS—Cont'd
Discharge of litter and sewage from watercraft —Cont'd
Sewage.
Defined, §33-6-1.
Violations, §33-6-10.
Warrants.
Violations, §33-6-10.
Watercraft.
Defined, §33-6-1.
District courts.
Jurisdiction of offenses, §33-5-32.
Drugs.
Prohibited operations, §33-5-24.
Duty of care owed persons on premises for sporting or recreational purposes, §§35-15-1 to 35-15-5.
Equipment.
Flame arrestors.
Motorboats required to have flame arrestors on carburetors, §33-5-22.
Lights, §33-5-22.
Local regulation, §33-5-31.
Muffling devices, §33-5-23.
Safety devices generally, §33-5-22.
Sailboards.
Hull deemed flotation device, §33-5-22.1.
Sirens prohibited, §33-5-23.
Toilets.
Marine toilets. See within this heading, "Discharge of litter and sewage from watercraft."
Evidence.
Accident reports.
Use as evidence in trials, §33-5-25.
Rules and regulations of commissioner.
Admissibility as evidence, §33-5-30.
Exhibitions,
Fees.
Arrests.
Fees of arresting officer, §33-5-34.
Certificates of registration and numbers, §33-5-10.
Classification of vessels.
Schedule of fees, §33-5-17.
Violations.
Fees in certain prosecutions, §33-5-33.
Fees of arresting officer, §33-5-34.
Fines.
Disposition, §33-5-32.
Fishing boats.
Marine resources.
See MARINE RESOURCES.
Flags, §33-5-22.
Foreign vessels.
Numbering, §33-5-15.
Funds.
Certificates of registration and numbers.
Use of funds received, §33-5-10.

BOATS—Cont'd
Garbage and trash.
Discharge of litter and sewage from watercraft, §§33-6-1 to 33-6-12. See within this heading, "Discharge of litter and sewage from watercraft."
Marinas.
On-shore trash receptacles at marinas, §33-6-7.
Handicapped persons.
Right to use of public conveyances and transportation facilities, §21-7-3.
Injuries.
Accidents involving injuries.
Report required, §33-5-25.
Inspections.
Certificates of registration and number.
Availability of certificate for inspection, §33-5-11.
Liveries.
Inspection by department of conservation and natural resources, §33-5-21.
Jurisdiction.
District courts.
Jurisdiction of offenses, §33-5-32.
Length.
Capacity plate.
Required, §33-5-22.
Defined, §33-5-3.
Licenses.
Foreign vessels.
Operation without license, §33-5-15.
Marine resources.
General provisions.
See MARINE RESOURCES.
Sale.
Special agents to sell boat licenses, §33-5-20.
Sheriffs.
Sale of licenses, §33-5-20.
Special agents to sell, §33-5-20.
Term of license, §33-5-13.
Liens.
Declaration of lien on watercraft, §35-11-60.
Lights, §33-5-22.
Litter.
Discharge of litter and sewage from watercraft, §§33-6-1 to 33-6-12. See within this heading, "Discharge of litter and sewage from watercraft."
Liveries, §33-5-21.
Local regulation, §33-5-31.
Marinas.
On-shore trash receptacles at marinas, §33-6-7.
Marine police.
See MARINE POLICE.
Marine resources.
See MARINE RESOURCES.
Motorboats.
Carburetors.
Flame arrestors.
Required, §33-5-22.
Muffling devices, §33-5-23.
Municipal corporations.
Local regulation, §33-5-31.

BOATS—Cont'd
Municipal corporations —Cont'd
Numbering.
Exemption.
Boats owned by municipalities, §33-5-19.
Negligence.
Operation in reckless or negligent manner, §33-5-24.
Notice.
Change of address, §33-5-16.
Transfer of interest, §33-5-16.
Numbering.
Certificates of number.
Term of certificate, §33-5-13.
Display of numbers, §§33-5-9, 33-5-11.
Exemption. §33-5-19.
Foreign vessels, §33-5-15.
Local regulation, §33-5-31.
Numbering system, §33-5-12.
Only authorized number to be used, §33-5-18.
Owners.
Change of address.
Notice to department of conservation and natural resources, §33-5-16.
Change of ownership.
Registration.
Filing new application form, §33-5-15.
Defined, §33-5-3.
Parades and tournaments.
Protection from marine traffic interference and hazards, §33-5-27.
Regulations, §33-5-27.
Penalties.
Discharge of litter and sewage from watercraft, §§33-6-10, 33-6-11.
Disposition of fines, §33-5-32.
Prohibited operations, §33-5-24.
Second offenses, §33-5-24.
Violations of chapter generally, §33-5-35.
Police.
Marine police.
See MARINE POLICE.
Policy.
Declaration of policy, §33-5-1.
Races and regattas, §33-5-27.
Records.
Keeping of records, §33-5-7.
Registration of vessels.
Certificates of registration.
Application, §33-5-11.
Change of ownership.
Filing new application form, §33-5-15.
Contents, §33-5-11.
Duplicate certificates, §33-5-16.
Fees, §33-5-10.
Funds.
Use of funds received under chapter, §33-5-10.
Inspection.
Availability for inspection, §33-5-11.

BOATS—Cont'd
Registration of vessels
—Cont'd
Certificates of registration
—Cont'd
Issuance, §§33-5-10,
33-5-11.
By whom issued,
§33-5-10.
Revocation or suspension.
Second and third
offenses, §33-5-24.
Size, §33-5-11.
Termination of certificate.
Grounds, §33-5-16.
Term of certificate,
§33-5-13.
Fees.
Schedule of fees, §33-5-17.
Numbering. See within this
heading, "Numbering."
Rentals.
Liveries, §33-5-21.
Reports.
Accident reports.
Death, injury or property
damage, §33-5-25.
Rules and regulations.
Discharge of litter and
sewage from watercraft.
See within this heading,
"Discharge of litter and
sewage from watercraft."
Evidence.
Admissibility as evidence,
§33-5-30.
Filing, §33-5-29.
Power of commissioner to
promulgate, §33-5-28.
Publication, §33-5-29.
Safety.
Declaration of policy, §33-5-1.
Equipment generally. See
within this heading,
"Equipment."
Lights, §33-5-22.
Liveries.
Safety provisions relative
to boat liveries,
§33-5-21.
Water skis.
Safety regulations,
§33-5-26.
Sailboards.
Defined, §33-5-22.1.
Hull deemed flotation device,
§33-5-22.1.
Sales tax, §40-23-2.
Salt water fishing.
Marine resources generally.
See MARINE
RESOURCES.
Salvage.
See SALVAGE.
Sewage.
Discharge of litter and
sewage from watercraft,
§§33-6-1 to 33-6-12. See
within this heading,
"Discharge of litter and
sewage from watercraft."
Sheriffs.
Licenses.
Special agents to sell boat
licenses.
Sheriffs designated as
special agents,
§33-5-20.
Ships and shipping.
See SHIPS AND SHIPPING.

BOATS—Cont'd
Sirens.
Prohibited, §33-5-23.
Skindivers.
Flags.
Required, §33-5-22.
Skis.
Water skis.
Operation of boat near
water skis, §33-5-24.
Safety regulations,
§33-5-26.
Toilets.
Marine toilets. See within
this heading, "Discharge
of litter and sewage from
watercraft."
Torts.
Duty of care owed persons on
premises for sporting or
recreational purposes,
§§33-15-1 to 33-15-5.
See PARKS AND
RECREATION.
Negligence.
Operation in a reckless or
negligent manner,
§33-5-24.
Transfer of interest.
Notice to department of
conservation and natural
resources, §33-5-16.
Trash receptacles.
On-shore trash receptacles at
marinas, §33-6-7.
Trespass.
Fastening boats on booms,
bulkheads or piles
without consent of
owner, §33-7-9.
Warnings.
Trespass after warning on
booms, bulkheads or
piles erected by
riparian proprietors,
§33-7-9.
United States.
Commissioner of
conservation and natural
resources.
Supplying information to
federal agencies,
§33-5-8.
Discharge of litter and
sewage from watercraft.
Standards for marine
toilets, §33-6-5.
Numbering.
Exemption.
Boats owned by United
States, §33-5-19.
Violations.
District courts.
Jurisdiction of offenses,
§33-5-32.
Fees.
Arresting officer, §33-5-34.
Fees in certain
prosecutions, §33-5-33.
Fines.
Disposition, §33-5-32.
Penalty for violations of
chapter generally,
§33-5-35.
Warning citations, §33-5-36.
Warning citations, §33-5-36.
Warrants.
Discharge of litter and
sewage from watercraft.
Violations of chapter,
§33-6-10.

BOATS—Cont'd
Water skis.
Operation of boats near
water skis, §33-5-24.
Safety regulations, §33-5-26.

BOLL WEEVILS.
Eradication in cotton,
§§2-19-120 to 2-19-135.
See COTTON.

BOMBS.
Explosives generally.
See EXPLOSIVES AND
EXPLOSIONS.
False reporting, §13A-11-11.
Fire bombs.
Motor vehicles.
Throwing into occupied
vehicles, §32-5-11.
Indictments.
Setting off explosives near
dwellings.
Form of indictment,
§15-8-150.

BONA FIDE PURCHASERS.
Commercial code.
See COMMERCIAL CODE.

BOND ISSUES.
Aged persons.
Special health care facility
authorities.
See MUNICIPAL
CORPORATIONS.
Agriculture.
Agricultural center.
Corporation.
See AGRICULTURE.
Agricultural markets and
coliseum corporation.
Securities.
See AGRICULTURE.
Development authority,
§§2-3A-8 to 2-3A-10.
Airport authorities.
See AVIATION.
Airports.
Authority of counties and
municipalities to issue
bonds for acquisition,
improvement, etc.,
§4-1-1.
Alabama building authority,
§41-10-1.
Alabama highway authority.
See HIGHWAYS.
**Alabama highway finance
corporation.**
See HIGHWAYS.
Alabama port authority.
See HARBORS AND PORTS.
Ameraport.
Offshore harbor and terminal
commission, §§33-10-24,
33-10-25.
Armory commission.
Financing or refinancing of
armories, etc., §31-4-5.
Auburn university.
Construction and
improvement purposes,
Const. Ala., amd. 120.
Authorities.
Consent of department of
finance prerequisite to
issuance, §41-4-16.
Bail and recognizance.
Deposit of federal or state
bonds in lieu of cash,
§15-13-43.

BOND ISSUES—Cont'd
**Bear creek development
authority.**
See BEAR CREEK
DEVELOPMENT
AUTHORITY.
Bishop of diocese.
Powers of corporation,
§10-4-4.
Boards and commissions.
Consent of department of
finance prerequisite to
issuance, §41-4-16.
Bridges.
General provisions.
See BRIDGES.
Interstate highway system.
See BRIDGES.
Public improvement bonds.
Certain revenue producing
undertakings,
§§11-81-140 to
11-81-150.
See COUNTIES.
Buildings.
Alabama building authority,
§41-10-1.
Commercial code.
Investment securities,
§§7-8-101 to 7-8-406.
See COMMERCIAL CODE.
**Commercial development
authorities.**
Municipal corporations.
See MUNICIPAL
CORPORATIONS.
**Conservation and natural
resources.**
Department.
Issuance.
No authority to issue,
§9-2-24.
Constitution of Alabama.
Acts relating to bonded debt
of state.
Governor authorized to act
thereunder, Const.
Ala., art. XVII, §283.
Validation, Const. Ala.,
art. XVII, §283.
Amendments.
Certain county revenue
securities not to
constitute bonds or
indebtedness, Const.
Ala., amd. 398.
Municipal corporations.
Issuance, Const. Ala., art.
XII, §222.
Revenue bonds, Const.
Ala., amd. 107.
Obligations and liabilities of
corporations, etc., held or
owned by state, counties
or municipalities, Const.
Ala., art. IV, §100.
Public corporations.
Bonds and other securities
issued by certain
public corporations,
Const. Ala., amd. 108.
Refunding bonds for existing
indebtedness, Const.
Ala., art. XI, §213; amd.
26.

BOND ISSUES—Cont'd
Constitution of Alabama
—Cont'd
Research institute.
Bonds for construction and
improvement purposes
at University of
Alabama research
institute, Const. Ala.,
amd. 157.
Special, private or local laws
prohibited, Const. Ala.,
art. IV, §104.
Convention facilities.
Faith and credit of state not
pledged, §11-100-7.
Refunding or refinancing of
bonds.
Application of payments
and credits, §11-100-8.
**Coosa Valley development
authority,** §§36-16-2,
36-16-12 to 36-16-14.
Corporations, §10-2A-71.
Corrections.
Alabama corrections
institution finance
authority.
See CORRECTIONS.
Counties.
See COUNTIES.
**County industrial
development authorities,**
§11-92A-14.
Investments.
Authorized investments,
§11-92A-16.
Refunding bonds,
§11-92A-14.
Sale of bonds, §11-92A-14.
Application of proceeds,
§11-92A-16.
Security for bonds,
§§11-92A-15, 11-92A-16.
Taxation.
Exemption, §§11-92A-16,
11-92A-19.
Validation of bonds,
§11-92A-14.
Coupons.
Registered bonds.
Issuance without, §41-1-7.
Definitions.
Private activity bonds.
State ceiling, §41-10-36.
Docks.
Bonds for state docks
facilities.
General provisions,
§§33-2-180 to 33-2-196;
Const. Ala., amd. 213.
See HARBORS AND
PORTS.
Development of docks and
other facilities along
inland waterways.
See WATERS AND
WATERCOURSES.
**Downtown redevelopment
authorities,** §§11-54A-10
to 11-54A-15.
See DOWNTOWN
REDEVELOPMENT
AUTHORITIES.
Education.
General provisions.
See EDUCATION.
Elections.
Counties.
See COUNTIES.

BOND ISSUES—Cont'd
Elections—Cont'd
Municipal corporations.
See MUNICIPAL
CORPORATIONS.
Electric cooperatives,
§§37-6-28, 37-6-29.
**Electric membership
corporations,** §§37-7-12 to
37-7-15.
**Elk river development
agency.**
Exemption from taxation,
§33-12-5.
**Environmental improvement
authorities,** §§9-6-9 to
9-6-12.
Facsimile signatures.
Execution of bonds with
facsimile signatures,
§1-3-3.
Health.
Special health care facility
authorities.
See MUNICIPAL
CORPORATIONS.
Highways.
See HIGHWAYS.
**Historical preservation
authorities.**
See HISTORICAL
PRESERVATION
AUTHORITIES.
Historic Blakeley authority.
Authorized, §41-10-176.
Hospitals.
General provisions.
See HOSPITALS.
Public improvement bonds.
Counties.
See COUNTIES.
Municipal corporations.
See MUNICIPAL
CORPORATIONS.
**Hotels, inns and other
transient lodging places.**
Municipal corporations.
Acquisition of projects for
promotion of hotel
services.
See MUNICIPAL
CORPORATIONS.
Housing authorities.
General provisions.
See HOUSING
AUTHORITIES.
Housing finance authority.
See HOUSING FINANCE
AUTHORITY.
Improvement authorities,
§§39-7-22 to 39-7-26.
Income tax.
Exemptions.
Interest on obligations of
the state of Alabama,
§40-18-14.
United States.
Interest or other income
received from
obligations of United
States, §40-18-4.
**Industrial access roads and
bridges,** §23-6-8.
Disposition of proceeds,
§23-6-9.
Refunding bonds, §23-6-9.

BOND ISSUES—Cont'd

Industrial development authority, §§41-10-27 to 41-10-31.

General provisions.
See INDUSTRIAL DEVELOPMENT AUTHORITY.

Private activity bonds.
State ceiling, §§41-10-35 to 41-10-43. See within this heading, "Private activity bonds."

Industrial development boards.
Municipal boards, §§11-54-89 to 11-54-92, 11-54-96.

Industrial development corporations, §§10-4-139, 10-4-140.

Industrial revenue bonds, §§8-6-110 to 8-6-122.
See INDUSTRIAL REVENUE BONDS.

Inland waterways.
Development of docks and other facilities along inland waterways.
See WATERS AND WATERCOURSES.

Interest.
Payment.
State treasurer, §§36-17-8, 36-17-10 to 36-17-15.
See STATE TREASURER.

Invalid or unissued bonds.
Refund of money paid for invalid or unissued bonds, §§41-4-62, 41-4-63.

Investment securities, §§7-8-101 to 7-8-406.
See COMMERCIAL CODE.

Judicial building authority.
See JUDICIAL BUILDING AUTHORITY.

Junior colleges.
Trade school and junior college authority, §§16-60-90 to 16-60-93.

Letters of credit.
Municipalities, counties, public corporations, boards of education, etc.
Authority as security for bonds, notes, etc., §11-80-7.

Libraries.
Public library authorities, §§11-57-1 to 11-57-26.
See MUNICIPAL CORPORATIONS.

Limitation of actions.
Action to test validity of municipal bond election, §§6-2-40, 11-81-61.
Contesting validity of issuance, sale, etc., §11-81-14.

Medical clinic boards, §§11-58-1 to 11-58-15.
See MUNICIPAL CORPORATIONS.

Mental health finance authority.
See MENTAL HEALTH FINANCE AUTHORITY.

BOND ISSUES—Cont'd

Military affairs.
Armory commission.
Financing or refinancing of armories, §31-4-5.

Minors.
Ownership of securities by minors generally, §§8-6-90 to 8-6-95.
See SECURITIES.

Motor sports hall of fame commission, §§41-9-473 to 41-9-476.

Municipal corporations.
Debt limit.
See CONSTITUTION OF ALABAMA.
General provisions.
See MUNICIPAL CORPORATIONS.

Payment.
Refund of money paid for invalid or unissued bonds, §§41-4-62, 41-4-63.
When bonds of state payable, §41-1-4.

Penal and correctional facilities.
Improvement of prisons and other facilities, Const. Ala., amd. 374.

Pollution control finance authority, §§22-29-8 to 22-29-15, 22-29-22.
See WATER POLLUTION.

Port authorities.
See HARBORS AND PORTS.

Post-office projects.
Municipal corporations, §§11-55-1 to 11-55-13.
See MUNICIPAL CORPORATIONS.

Power districts, §§37-5-3, 37-5-5 to 37-5-8.

Private activity bonds.
State ceiling.
Allocation.
Application, §41-10-37.
Carryforward allocation procedure, §41-10-39.
Confirmation of prior allocations, §41-10-43.
Duty of fairness and impartiality in granting, §41-10-40.
Formula, §41-10-38.
Procedure, §41-10-37.
Certifications.
Resignation of official, §41-10-42.
Definition, §41-10-36.
Forms, §41-10-41.
Intent of legislature, §41-10-35.
Legislative findings, §41-10-35.
Rules and regulations, §41-10-41.

Public corporations, Const. Ala., amd. 108.

Public utilities.
Counties.
See COUNTIES.
Municipal corporations.
See MUNICIPAL CORPORATIONS.
Provisions of article inapplicable to certain notes, §37-4-13.

BOND ISSUES—Cont'd

Public works.
Improvement authorities, §§39-7-22 to 39-7-26.

Railroad authorities, §§37-13-1, 37-13-11 to 37-13-19.
See RAILROAD AUTHORITIES.

Randolph county.
Funding county facilities.
County facilities building fund, Const. Ala., amd. 444.
Securities, Const. Ala., amd. 442.

Redevelopment projects.
Investment by public bodies, etc., in bonds, etc., issued by housing authorities, etc., §24-2-9.
Issuance, §24-2-3.

Refunds.
Money paid for invalid or unissued bonds, §§41-4-62, 41-4-63.

Registration.
Issuance without coupons, §41-1-7.

Remedies.
County bonds and obligations.
Validation.
See COUNTIES.
Municipal corporations.
Validation of city obligations.
See MUNICIPAL CORPORATIONS.

Roads.
Highways.
See HIGHWAYS.

Seals.
Execution of bonds with seals, §1-3-3.

Securities.
Generally.
See SECURITIES.
Investment securities, §§7-8-101 to 7-8-406.
See COMMERCIAL CODE.

Sewers.
Municipal corporations.
See MUNICIPAL CORPORATIONS.

Shakespeare festival theatre finance authority, §§41-10-206 to 41-10-208.

Signatures.
Execution of bonds with facsimile signatures, §1-3-3.

Sinking fund.
Use of funds in sinking fund, §§41-4-10 to 41-4-15.
See FINANCE.

Soil and water conservation.
Watershed conservancy districts, §§9-8-61, 9-8-62.

Southern products mart authority.
See PRODUCTS MARTS.

Space science exhibit commission.
See SPACE SCIENCE EXHIBIT COMMISSION.

State.
When bonds of state payable, §41-1-4.

BOND ISSUES—Cont'd
State parks.
Acquisition, development, etc., of parks and park facilities, Const. Ala., amd. 267.
State products mart and coliseum authority, §§41-10-55 to 41-10-65, 41-10-69.
See PRODUCTS MARTS.
State treasurer, §§36-17-8, 36-17-10 to 36-17-15.
See STATE TREASURER.
Tannehill furnace and foundry commission.
Issuance of revenue bonds, §41-9-326.
Taxation.
Exemption from taxation.
County and municipal bonds, §40-9-1.
Taxation.
Exemptions from taxation, §§11-89-16, 33-16-12, 40-9-1.
Alabama state bonds, §40-9-1.
County and municipal bonds, §§11-81-29, 40-9-1.
Highways, §23-1-157.
Housing and finance authority, §24-1A-12.
Tennessee Valley authority, §41-9-786.
United States bonds, §40-9-1.
Income tax, §§40-18-4, 40-18-14.
Subjects of taxation, §40-11-1.
Telephone companies.
Securities of telephone companies, §§37-2-170 to 37-2-184.
See TELEPHONES.
Tennessee Valley authority.
Exhibit commission.
Exclusive obligation of commission, §41-9-783.
Exemption from taxation, §41-9-786.
Payment of principal and interest.
Appropriation and pledge of amounts retained by state, §41-9-783.
Toll road, bridge and tunnel authority.
See TOLL ROAD, BRIDGE AND TUNNEL AUTHORITY.
Tombigbee Valley development authority, §§33-17-2, 33-17-12 to 33-17-14.
Trade school and junior college authority, §§16-60-90 to 16-60-93.
Transfer.
Investment securities.
See COMMERCIAL CODE.
Uniform commercial code.
Investment securities, §§7-8-101 to 7-8-406.
See COMMERCIAL CODE.
Unissued bonds.
Refund of money paid for unissued bonds, §§41-4-62, 41-4-63.

BOND ISSUES—Cont'd
United States.
Taxation.
Exemption, §40-9-1.
Universities and colleges.
Issuance of revenue securities by institutions of learning, Const. Ala., amd. 160.
University of Alabama.
Medical center.
Bonds for construction and improvement purposes, Const. Ala., amd. 119.
School of medicine.
Issuance of bonds, §16-47-95.
USS Alabama battleship commission, §§41-9-352, 41-9-353.
Utility services facilities, §§11-97-9 to 11-97-12, 11-97-25.
Validation.
County bonds and obligations.
See COUNTIES.
Municipal corporations.
See MUNICIPAL CORPORATIONS.
Warehouses.
Counties.
Public improvement bonds.
See COUNTIES.
Municipal corporations.
Public improvement bonds.
See MUNICIPAL CORPORATIONS.
Water conservation and irrigation.
Agency, §§9-10-5, 9-10-8.
Corporations, §§9-10-34, 9-10-36 to 9-10-41.
See WATER CONSERVATION AND IRRIGATION.
Water management and drainage.
Districts, §§9-9-15, 9-9-36 to 9-9-40.
Water pollution control authority.
Anticipation of bonds.
Certificates or notes in anticipation of bonds, §22-34-9.
Authorization to issue, §22-34-7.
Certificates of notes in anticipation of bonds, §22-34-9.
Dedicated source of revenue to repay money, §22-34-11.
Definitions, §22-34-1.
Interest.
Exemption from usury laws, §22-34-14.
Investment in authority bonds.
Legal investments, §22-34-12.
Negotiability, §22-34-16.
Obligations only of authority, §22-34-17.
Refunding bonds, §22-34-10.
Sale, §22-34-8.
Special obligation bonds, §22-34-17.
State not indebted, §22-34-17.

BOND ISSUES—Cont'd
Water pollution control authority—Cont'd
Tax exemption, §22-34-13.
Usury.
Exemption from usury laws, §22-34-14.
Water pollution control finance authority, §§22-29-8 to 22-29-15, 22-29-22.
See WATER POLLUTION.
Waters and watercourses.
Development of docks and other facilities along inland waterways.
See WATERS AND WATERCOURSES.
Navigable waterway between Demopolis and Tennessee river and Tombigbee Valley projects, Const. Ala., amd. 355.
Water, sewer and fire protection authorities, §§11-88-1 to 11-88-111.
See WATER, SEWER AND FIRE PROTECTION AUTHORITIES.
Water, sewer and fire protection districts, §§11-89-1 to 11-89-19.
See WATER, SEWER AND FIRE PROTECTION DISTRICTS.
Water system assistance authority.
Approval not required, §22-23A-15.
Authority to issue and sell, §22-23A-7.
Refunding bonds, §22-23A-10.
Defined, §22-23A-1.
Exclusively obligations of authority, §22-23A-17.
Interest, §22-23A-7.
Exemption, §22-23A-14.
Investments in, §22-23A-12.
Loans in anticipation of issuance, §22-23A-9.
Negotiable instruments.
Bonds and coupons deemed, §22-23A-16.
Notice of public sale, §22-23A-8.
Power to issue, §22-23A-6.
Proceeds.
Defined, §22-23A-1.
Publication.
Notice of public sale, §22-23A-8.
Refunding bonds.
Authority to issue, §22-23A-10.
Sales.
Procedure, §22-23A-8.
Security for payment of principal and interest, §22-23A-7.
Taxation.
Exemption from taxation, §22-23A-13.
Terms, §22-23A-7.

BONDS, SURETY.
Accounts and accounting.
Department of examiners of public accounts, §§41-5-5, 41-5-10.

BONDS, SURETY—Cont'd
Actions on official bonds,
§§6-5-30, 6-5-31.
See PUBLIC OFFICERS
AND EMPLOYEES.
Administrators and
executors, §§43-2-80 to
43-2-93.
See EXECUTORS AND
ADMINISTRATORS.
Agriculture.
Commissioner of agriculture
and industries, §2-2-3.
Employees' bonds, §2-2-13.
Equivalence to bond,
§§2-2-70 to 2-2-73.
Marketing of agricultural
products.
Employees and inspectors,
§2-11-9.
Air commerce, §§37-9-18,
37-9-24.
Alcoholic beverages.
See ALCOHOLIC
BEVERAGES.
Appeals.
Costs on appeal.
See APPEALS.
Stay by supersedeas bond,
ARAP, Rule 8 (a).
Stay pending appeal, ARAP,
Rule 8 (c).
Attachment.
Action by defendant on
attachment bond for
damages, §6-6-148.
Amendments, §6-6-143.
Execution by plaintiff,
§6-6-45.
Return of bond, §6-6-53.
Sale of property levied on.
Order for receipt of sale
proceeds upon
executing refunding
bond.
See ATTACHMENTS.
Attorney general, §36-15-2.
Assistant attorneys general,
§36-15-8.
Attorneys at law.
Not deemed sufficient
sureties on certain
official bonds, §36-5-13.
Auctions and auctioneers.
License to be accompanied by
bond, §34-4-24.
Bail and recognizance.
See BAIL AND
RECOGNIZANCE.
Banks and financial
institutions.
Agreements between
principal and sureties on
bond for bank deposits,
§5-5A-35.
Bank examiners, §5-2A-19.
Credit unions.
See CREDIT UNIONS.
Liquidation.
Solvent banks.
Directors, §5-8A-1.
Officers and employees,
§5-6A-3.
Regulation of trust business.
Exemptions.
Trust companies
exempted from bond
requirements,
§5-11A-9.

BONDS, SURETY—Cont'd
Banks and financial
institutions—Cont'd
Superintendent of banks,
§5-2A-4.
Deputy superintendent,
§5-2A-15.
Barbers.
Board of barber examiners.
Bond of officers, §34-5-13.
Billiard rooms.
Licensee's bond, §34-6-32.
Catfish.
Promotion of industry.
Treasurer of certified
association, §2-8-285.
Cemeteries.
County cemeteries.
Appeals from assessment of
damages, §11-17-8.
Checks.
Sale of checks.
See CHECKS.
Chiropractors.
Board of chiropractic
examiners.
Bond of executive
secretary, §34-24-144.
Bond of secretary-
treasurer, §34-24-144.
Circuit courts.
Clerks of court, §12-17-91.
Registers, §12-17-111.
Clerks of court, §12-17-91.
Attorneys not deemed
sufficient sureties on
official bonds of certain
clerks, §36-5-13.
Coal.
Surface mining control and
reclamation.
Performance bonds and
bond releases,
§9-16-89.
Commissioner of labor,
§25-3-2.
Commission merchants.
Sale of farm produce,
§2-29-4.
Comptroller, §41-4-7.
Conservation and natural
resources.
Commissioner, §9-2-5.
Department.
Certain officers and
employees, §9-2-18.
Conservators, §26-3-1.
Additional bond.
Requirement, §26-3-7.
Failure to give, §26-3-7.
Conditionally executed
bonds.
Liability of sureties,
§26-3-11.
General conservators of
county, §26-3-5.
Liability of sureties.
Conditionally executed
bonds, §26-3-11.
Discharge from liability.
Application, §26-3-8.
New bond required,
§26-3-9.
Neglect in taking.
Liability of probate judge,
§26-3-13.
New bond.
Application for discharge
from liability of surety.
Effect of giving new
bond, §26-3-9.

BONDS, SURETY—Cont'd
Conservators—Cont'd
New bond—Cont'd
Application for discharge
from liability of surety
—Cont'd
Required, §26-3-8.
Failure to give,
§26-3-8.
Requirement, §26-3-7.
Failure to give, §26-3-7.
Omission in taking.
Liability of probate judge,
§26-3-13.
Recordation, §26-3-12.
Reductions.
Partial settlement of
estate, §26-3-14.
Settlement of estate.
Reduction upon partial
settlement, §26-3-14.
Settlements of accounts of
conservators.
Death of conservator.
Enforcement of
judgments against
sureties, §26-5-54.
Filing of account and
vouchers for final
settlement by
sureties, §26-5-50.
Succeeding conservator.
Requiring sureties to
make settlement,
§26-5-52.
Statutory bonds.
Force and effect of
statutory bonds given
bonds of certain
conservators, §26-3-10.
Testamentary conservators.
Relief from requirement of
giving bond, §26-3-3.
Requirement by probate
court of bond,
§26-3-4.
Uniform guardianship and
protective proceedings
act, §26-2A-139.
Terms and requirements,
§26-2A-140.
Constables.
Generally, §36-23-4.
Liability of constable and
sureties, §36-23-9.
Contractors.
State licensing board.
Bond of secretary-
treasurer, §34-8-22.
Coroners, §11-5-3.
Additional bond.
Effect of failure to give,
§11-5-9.
When required, §11-5-9.
Attorneys not deemed
sufficient sureties on
coroner bonds, §36-5-13.
Corporations.
Receivers, §10-2A-197.
Corrections.
Board of corrections.
Officers and employees,
§14-1-5.
Commissioner of corrections,
§14-1-1.4.
Cosmetology.
Board of cosmetology.
Bonds of members and
treasurer, §34-7-41.

BONDS, SURETY—Cont'd

Cotton.
Promotion of cotton products.
Treasurer of commission,
§2-8-204.
Counties.
See COUNTIES.
Court of civil appeals.
Clerk of court, §12-3-24.
Court of criminal appeals.
Clerk of court, §12-3-21.
Courts.
Officials and employees of
unified judicial system.
Bonding of court officials
and employees, ARJA,
Rule 1.
Credit unions.
Bureau of credit unions.
Supervisor, §5-2A-100.
Credit union administration.
Administrator, §5-17-42.
Examiners and office
assistants, §5-17-54.
**Crime victims compensation
commission,** §15-23-4.
Dental service corporations,
§22-21-370.
Dentists.
Board of dental examiners.
Bond of secretary-treasurer
of board, §34-9-42.
**Department of examiners of
public accounts,** §§41-5-5,
41-5-10.
Desertion and nonsupport.
Payment of overdue support.
Bond, security or other
guarantee to secure,
§30-3-6.
Detinue.
See DETINUE.
**Director of industrial
relations,** §25-2-6.
District courts.
Appeals bond, §12-12-73.
**Downtown redevelopment
authorities.**
Treasurer, §11-54A-8.
Education.
City superintendents of
schools, §16-11-7.
County superintendent of
education, §16-9-3.
Secretary of county boards
of education, §16-8-7.
Public school funds.
Bonding of persons
handling public school
funds, §§16-13-8,
16-13-9.
State superintendent of
education, §16-4-3.
Treasurer of city school
boards, §16-11-7.
Eggs and egg products.
Promotion of industry.
Treasurer of growers'
association, §2-8-163.
Ejectment.
Retention of possession if
crop planted or growing
within time period.
Force and effect of bond,
§6-6-294.
Elections.
Contests.
Examination of ballots,
voting machines, etc.,
§17-8-46.

BONDS, SURETY—Cont'd

Eminent domain.
Entry upon property,
§18-1A-52.
Proceedings by state or
county without bond,
§18-1A-270.
Equivalence to bonds.
Agriculture, §§2-2-70 to
2-2-73.
Evidence.
Official bonds.
Copies of required official
bonds, §12-21-104.
Proof of bonds or
recognizances,
§36-5-21.
Executions.
Forthcoming bonds,
§§6-9-160, 6-9-161.
Indemnity bond, §6-9-81.
Lien of execution.
Destruction upon execution
of bond for appeal, etc.,
§6-9-61.
**Executors and
administrators,** §§43-2-80
to 43-2-93.
See EXECUTORS AND
ADMINISTRATORS.
**Exemptions from levy and
sale under process.**
Contest of exemption claim,
§§6-10-27, 6-10-36.
Fiduciaries.
Fiduciaries in war service,
§19-2-5.
Finance.
Department of finance.
Officers and chiefs of
divisions, §41-4-7.
Director of finance, §41-4-31.
Fire marshal, §27-2-10.
Fish and game.
Fur dealers.
Nonresidents, §9-11-253.
Game and fish division.
Director, §9-2-63.
Licenses.
Special agents, §9-11-39.
Payable to probate judge
or license
commissioner,
§9-11-40.
Wardens, §9-2-64.
**Forcible entry and unlawful
detainer.**
Appeals.
Suspension of writ of
restitution or
possession.
Defendant posting of
bond, §6-6-351.
Forests and forestry.
Board of registration for
foresters.
Bond of secretary,
§34-12-36.
State forester, §9-3-5.
**Forthcoming and delivery
bonds.**
Executions, §§6-9-160,
6-9-161.
Fraternal benefit societies.
Articles of incorporation,
§27-34-10.

BONDS, SURETY—Cont'd

Fruits and vegetables.
Promotion of industry.
Treasurer of growers'
organization.
Bond of treasurer,
§2-8-137.
Funerals.
Board of funeral service.
Bond of treasurer,
§34-13-23.
Game and fish.
Wardens.
Deputy game and fish
wardens, §9-11-17.
Garnishment.
See GARNISHMENT.
Gas fitters.
Plumbers and gas fitters
examining board.
Secretary-treasurer,
§34-37-5.
Grain.
Promotion of grain industry.
Treasurer of association,
§2-8-245.
Grain dealers, §§2-31-4,
2-31-5.
Default.
Action by commission upon
default, §2-31-8.
Suspension or revocation of
license for failure to
keep bond, §2-31-7.
Trust fund agreement in lieu
of bond requirements,
§2-31-5.
Grand jury.
County officers.
Examination of bonds of
county officers,
§12-16-192.
Guardian and ward.
Curators.
Appointment, §26-7A-8.
Uniform guardianship and
protective proceedings
act.
Conservators, §26-2A-139.
Foreign conservators,
§26-2A-160.
Terms and requirements,
§26-2A-140.
Harbors and ports.
Director of state docks.
Bond required, §33-1-3.
Docks department.
Bonds required of certain
employees, §33-1-6.
Harbor masters and deputies,
§33-3-5.
Secretary-treasurer of docks
department, §33-1-7.
Hazardous wastes.
Storage and disposal sites.
Permits.
Required, §22-30-12.
Transportation.
Permits.
Required, §22-30-12.
Treatment facilities.
Permits.
Required, §22-30-12.
Health.
County health officers,
§22-3-7.
State health officer, §22-2-8.
Health studio services,
§8-23-3.

BONDS, SURETY—Cont'd
Hearing aid dealers and fitters.
Temporary licenses, §34-14-7.
Heating and air conditioning contractors.
Performance bonds, §34-31-28.
Requirement of bond authorized, §34-31-30.
Highway patrol, §§32-2-23, 32-2-24.
Highways.
Contracts.
Bid guaranty, §23-1-2.
Department.
Chief engineer, §23-1-22.
Director, §23-1-21.
Director, §23-1-21.
Utilities.
Digging up of roads.
Restoration of road, §23-1-4.
Historic Blakeley authority.
Treasurer, §41-10-174.
Horse racing.
Racetracks.
Operators, §11-65-20.
Owners, §11-65-17.
Indians.
Indian affairs commission, §41-9-717.
Industrial alcohol.
Collection of penalties on bonds, §28-5-9.
Permittees, §28-5-4.
Industrial relations.
Director, §25-2-6.
Injunctions, ARCP, Rule 65 (c).
Insurance.
Chief receivership division, §27-2-51.
Commissioner of insurance, §27-2-3.
Legal expense insurance, §27-43-9.
Junior colleges.
Franklin, Marion and Winston counties.
Treasurer's bond, §16-60-31.
Jackson and DeKalb counties.
Treasurer's bond, §16-60-61.
Labor.
Commissioner of labor, §25-3-2.
Director of industrial relations, §25-2-6.
Landlord and tenant.
Liens for advances and rent of lands, §35-9-35.
Licenses.
Bond makers, §40-12-64.
Brokers, §40-12-162.
Fish and game, §§9-11-39, 9-11-40.
License inspectors, §40-12-11.
Liens.
Attachment.
Bond required before issue of attachment, §35-11-5.
Limitation of actions.
Chapter inapplicable, §6-2-2.

BONDS, SURETY—Cont'd
Limitation of actions.
Action against surety to any replevy or forthcoming bond executed in courts of the United States or other state.
Four-year limitation, §6-2-36.
Liquefied petroleum gas, §§9-17-104, 9-17-105.
Lis pendens.
Release of land from lien upon execution of bond, §35-4-137.
Livestock.
Dealers, §§2-15-133, 2-15-134.
Market operators, §2-15-63.
Promotion of cattle industry.
Treasurers of cattle owners' associations, §2-8-16.
Promotion of swine industry.
Treasurers of swine producers' associations, §2-8-56.
Weighing livestock at markets.
Bond of permittee, §2-15-93.
Marine resources.
See MARINE RESOURCES.
Mechanics' and materialmen's liens.
Transfer of lien on real property to other security.
Requirements as to bond, §35-11-233.
Medical technicians.
Secretary-treasurer of board, §34-18-45.
Mentally ill.
Support of persons in state mental institutions, §§22-53-5, 22-53-26.
Military affairs.
See MILITARY AFFAIRS.
Mines and minerals.
See MINES AND MINERALS.
Motor fuels.
Diesel fuel tax.
Application for license for sale, withdrawal or use, §40-17-14.
Distributors of motor fuels.
Licenses, §40-12-194.
Motor vehicle carriers.
Brokers.
Bond required for issuance of license, §37-3-15.
Certificates of public convenience and necessity.
Bond required, §37-3-18.
Contract carrier permit.
Bond required, §37-3-18.
Fuel tax.
Motor carriers to give bond, §40-17-143.
Mileage tax.
Bond or other security for collection of tax, §40-19-16.
Motor vehicles.
See MOTOR VEHICLES.
Municipal corporations.
See MUNICIPAL CORPORATIONS.

BONDS, SURETY—Cont'd
Municipal courts.
Appeal bonds.
Designation of other municipal officers to approve, §12-14-31.
Appearance bonds.
Designation of other municipal officers to approve, §12-14-31.
Inability to pay fines and costs.
Defendant's bond, §12-14-11.
Notaries public, §36-20-3.
Notaries public for state at large, §36-20-31.
Nuisances.
Lewdness, assignation or prostitution.
Bond for preliminary injunction or temporary restraining order prior to hearing, §6-5-144.
Closing place pending final decision.
Release of property on bond, §6-5-148.
Nurses.
Board of nursing.
Bond of executive officer, §34-21-2.
Official bonds.
County officers, employees, etc.
See COUNTIES.
General provisions.
See PUBLIC OFFICERS AND EMPLOYEES.
Optometrists.
Board of optometry.
Bond of members, §34-22-41.
Partition.
Crops.
Forthcoming bond, §35-6-114.
Peace bonds.
See PEACE BONDS.
Peace officers.
Annuity and benefit fund.
Board of commissioners.
Members and employees handling funds, §36-21-63.
Peddlers.
Sales tax.
Itinerant vendors to file bond, §40-23-24.
Personal property.
Trial of right of property.
See PERSONAL PROPERTY.
Pest control.
Subterranean termite eradication and control work, §2-28-10.
Pesticides.
Application, §2-27-56.
Pharmacists and pharmacies.
Board of pharmacy.
Secretary and treasurer to furnish bond, §34-23-91.
State drug inspectors, §34-23-3.
Pilots and pilotage.
See PILOTS AND PILOTAGE.

BONDS, SURETY—Cont'd
Pipelines.
Highways.
Digging up of roads, §23-1-4.
Plumbing.
Certification of plumbers and gas fitters.
Revocation of certificates.
Issuance of license to licensee with prior revoked license, §34-37-12.
Master plumbers and gas fitters, §34-37-13.
Plumbers and gas fitters examining board.
Executive director, §34-37-5.
Podiatrists.
Board of podiatry.
Bond of secretary-treasurer, §34-24-254.
Polygraph examiners.
Licensees required to furnish, §34-25-21.
Printing.
Public printing and binding, §§41-4-133, 41-4-136.
Printer of acts and journals, §41-4-160.
Prisons and prisoners.
Superintendent of public works, §14-4-12.
Probate courts.
Attorneys at law.
Not deemed sufficient sureties on certain official bonds, §36-5-13.
Chief clerk, §12-13-13.
Judges, §12-13-33.
Persons who may institute civil actions on bonds of judges, §12-13-34.
Proceedings against sureties, ARCP, Rule 65.1.
Public building or construction contracts.
See CONTRACTS.
Public officers and employees.
County officers, employees, etc.
See COUNTIES.
General provisions.
See PUBLIC OFFICERS AND EMPLOYEES.
Public service commission.
See PUBLIC SERVICE COMMISSION.
Public works.
See PUBLIC WORKS.
Purchasing agent, §41-4-7.
Railroads.
Highways.
Digging up of roads, §23-1-4.
Railway policemen, §37-2-151.
Real estate brokers.
Disciplinary actions.
Appeal bond, §34-27-38.
Receivers.
Appointment, §6-6-622.
Replevin bond.
See REPLEVIN.
Rules of civil procedure.
Proceedings against sureties, ARCP, Rule 65.1.

BONDS, SURETY—Cont'd
St. Stephens historical commission.
Treasurer, §41-9-335.
Sale of checks.
See CHECKS.
Sales.
Going out of business or distress merchandise sales.
License.
Bond required of applicant, §8-13-4.
Sales tax.
Agents of department.
Bond required, §40-23-30.
Itinerant vendors, §40-23-24.
Savings and loan associations.
Commissioner.
Guarantee of amount subscribed by incorporators, §5-16-4.
Secretary of state.
See SECRETARY OF STATE.
Securities.
Dealers, §8-6-3.
Director, §8-6-59.
Salesmen, §8-6-3.
Securities commission.
Employees, §8-6-59.
Security to keep the peace.
See PEACE BONDS.
Sheriffs, §36-22-1.
Attorneys not deemed sufficient sureties on official bonds of sheriffs, §36-5-13.
Deputy sheriffs.
Attorneys not deemed sufficient sureties on official bonds of deputies, §36-5-13.
Small loans.
Bureau of loans.
Supervisor, §5-2A-80.
Solid waste.
Disposal authorities.
See SOLID WASTE.
Southeast interstate low-level radioactive waste management compact.
Contractors or leasors, §22-32-5.
Soybeans.
Promotion of soybean industry.
Bond of treasurer of soybean producers' association, §2-8-96.
Sports.
Agents.
Registration.
Assignment of deposits or accounts to commission in lieu of bond, §8-26-14.
Conditions of surety bond, §8-26-15.
Damages.
Not limited to amount of bond, §8-26-15.
Insurance.
Malpractice coverage in lieu of bond, §8-26-14.
Renewal, §8-26-9.
Surety bond required prior to issuance, §8-26-14.

BONDS, SURETY—Cont'd
Sports—Cont'd
Agents—Cont'd
Registration—Cont'd
Suspension.
Failure to maintain coverage, §8-26-16.
To whom bond payable, §8-26-15.
State auditor, §36-16-4.
State fire marshal, §27-2-10.
State officers and employees generally.
See PUBLIC OFFICERS AND EMPLOYEES.
State parks.
Concessions within state park areas.
Contracts for maintenance and operation, §9-14-23.
Division of parks.
Director, §9-2-102.
State treasurer.
Amount, §36-17-1.
Jurisdiction of action upon, §36-17-2.
Payments made to treasurer, §36-17-19.
Subdivisions.
County regulation of subdivisions.
Bonds posted by developers, §11-24-2.
Supersedeas.
Recording of order fixing supersedeas bond, §12-22-40.
Support and maintenance.
Payment of overdue support.
Bond, security or other guarantee to secure, §30-3-6.
Supreme court.
Clerk of court, §12-2-91.
Additional bond, §12-2-92.
Marshal, §12-2-153.
Tannehill furnace and foundry commission.
Requirement of bond from treasurer, §41-9-323.
Taxation.
Commissioner of revenue, §40-2-43.
Department of revenue.
Employees, §40-2-4.
Legal counsel, §40-2-62.
Lien for taxes.
Release of lien, §40-29-20.
Tax assessors, §40-4-1.
Tax collectors, §40-5-3.
Transfers to minors.
Custodians, §35-5A-16.
Transient merchants, §34-35-7.
Trusts and trustees.
See TRUSTS AND TRUSTEES.
Tuskegee Institute.
Treasurer, §16-57-1.
University of Montevallo.
Treasurer of university, §16-54-8.
Use tax.
Deposit of security.
Department may require, §40-23-75.
USS Alabama battleship commission.
Requirement of bond from treasurer, §41-9-342.

BONDS, SURETY—Cont'd

Utilities.
Highways.
Digging up of roads,
§23-1-4.
Vacation time-sharing plans,
§34-27-51.
Applicants for licenses,
§34-27-69.
Venue.
Breach of official bond,
§6-3-8.
Veterans, §31-5-11.
Visitation.
Compliance with visitation
order.
Bond, security, or other
guarantee to secure
compliance, §30-3-6.
Warehouses.
See WAREHOUSES.
Water management and
drainage.
Board of water management
commissioners, §9-9-41.
Districts.
Construction of
improvements.
Contractors.
See WATER
MANAGEMENT
AND DRAINAGE.
Employees, §9-9-41.
Treasurer, §9-9-16.
Weights and measures.
See WEIGHTS AND
MEASURES.
Welfare.
Commodity distributor,
§38-2-13.
Department of human
resources.
Officers, §38-2-13.
Wells.
Well driller's license,
§22-24-8.

BONE DRY LAW.

Dry counties, §§28-4-1 to
28-4-326.
See ALCOHOLIC
BEVERAGES.

BONE MARROW DONATION.

Minors.
Consent of minors and
parents, §22-8-9.

BOOKMAKING.

Defined, §13A-12-20.
Gambling generally.
See GAMBLING.
Horse racing.
Pari-mutuel betting.
See HORSE RACING.

BOOKS.

Evidence.
Production of books, etc.,
§§12-21-1 to 12-21-3.
Penitentiary.
Board of corrections to
supply reading material,
§14-3-46.
Records.
See RECORDS.
Textbooks.
See EDUCATION.

BOOMS AND BULKHEADS.

Anchorage.
State docks department.
Powers of department to
regulate, §33-3-2.

BOOMS AND BULKHEADS

—Cont'd

Attachment.
Liens of owners of booms and
bulkheads, §35-11-311.
Boats.
Charges for tying up,
§35-11-310.
Charges for tying up,
§35-11-310.
Constitution of Alabama.
Districts to build and
maintain seawalls,
Const. Ala., amd. 15.
Construction.
Licenses, §33-1-28.
Licenses.
Construction, §33-1-28.
Liens of owners.
Attachment, §35-11-311.
Declaration of lien,
§35-11-310.
Enforcement of lien,
§35-11-311.
Liens generally.
See LIENS.
State docks department.
Anchorage, berthage and
moorage.
Powers of department to
regulate, §33-3-2.
General provisions.
See HARBORS AND
PORTS.
Licenses.
Construction, §33-1-28.
Trees and timber.
Opening or cutting loose of
boom without authority,
§33-7-8.
Turning logs, timber or
lumber out of boom
without notice to owner,
§33-7-7.
Trespass.
Warnings.
Trespass after warning on
booms, bulkheads or
piles erected by
riparian proprietors,
§33-7-9.

BOOTLEGGING.

Alcoholic beverages.
Stills.
See ALCOHOLIC
BEVERAGES.
Copying and sale of
recorded devices
generally.
See RECORDED DEVICES.

BOTTLES.

Beverage containers
generally.
See BEVERAGE
CONTAINERS.
Licenses.
Bottlers, §40-12-65.
Names, marks, etc., on
beverage containers.
See BEVERAGE
CONTAINERS.

BOUNDARIES.

Actions to determine,
§§35-3-1 to 35-3-25.
Authorization of proceedings,
§35-3-1.
Circuit court.
Duty to determine claims
and make order,
§35-3-2.

BOUNDARIES—Cont'd

Actions to determine—Cont'd
Determination of boundaries
in pending actions.
Article not exclusive,
§35-3-25.
Map or plat.
Surveyor, §35-3-24.
Order for survey on motion
of court, §35-3-20.
Order for survey on motion
of party.
Appointment of surveyor,
§35-3-22.
Continuance, §35-3-21.
Costs, §35-3-22.
Deposit of costs,
§35-3-23.
Filing, §35-3-21.
Notice to show cause,
§35-3-21.
Provisions of article not
exclusive, §35-3-25.
Reports.
Surveyor, §35-3-24.
Surveyor.
Compensation, §35-3-25.
Duty to make survey,
§35-3-24.
Map or plat, §35-3-24.
Order for survey on
motion.
By court, §35-3-20.
By party, §35-3-22.
Report, §35-3-24.
Determination of claims.
Duty of court, §35-3-2.
Established lines.
Conclusiveness of
established lines,
§35-3-1.
Judgment, §35-3-3.
Landmarks, §35-3-3.
Proceedings authorized,
§35-3-1.
Right to maintain action,
§35-3-2.
Alabama coordinate system.
See SURVEYS AND
SURVEYORS.
Bridges.
Rivers forming boundaries
between states.
Agreements and contracts
with adjoining states
and federal
government, §23-1-57.
Cemeteries.
County cemeteries.
Establishment of
boundaries, §11-17-3.
Marking of boundaries,
§11-17-3.
Petition for appointment of
commission to mark
boundaries, §11-17-1.
Coal.
Boundaries and adjacent land
owners, §§25-9-320 to
25-9-322.
Constitution of Alabama,
Const. Ala., art. II, §§37 to
41.

BOUNDARIES—Cont'd
Contracts.
Bridges.
Rivers forming boundaries
between states.
Agreements and
contracts with
adjoining states and
federal government,
§23-1-57.
Coordinate system.
Alabama coordinate system,
§§35-2-1 to 35-2-9.
See SURVEYS AND
SURVEYORS.
Costs.
Determination of boundaries
in pending actions,
§35-3-22.
Deposit of costs, §35-3-23.
Counties.
General provisions.
See COUNTIES.
Offense committed on or near
county boundary.
Venue, §15-2-7.
Criminal law and procedure.
Offense committed on or near
county boundary.
Venue, §15-2-7.
Determination.
Actions to determine
boundaries. See within
this heading, "Actions to
determine."
Disputed boundary lines.
Ejectment.
Proceedings upon
defendant's suggestion,
§6-6-285.
District courts.
Boundaries of districts for
election of judges,
§12-17-60.
Change in boundaries,
§12-1-5.
Education.
Compulsory school
attendance districts,
§16-9-17.
Public school funds.
Apportionment of county
funds when boundaries
have been changed,
§16-13-35.
School tax district.
Boundaries fixed by county
board, §16-13-191.
Duration of boundaries,
§16-13-192.
Ejectment.
Disputed boundary lines.
Proceedings upon
defendant's suggestion,
§6-6-285.
Elections.
See ELECTIONS.
Fish and game.
Wildlife management areas,
§9-11-301.
Florida.
Boundary between Alabama
and Florida.
Generally, §41-2-3.
Precise location at mouth
of Perdido river and
surrounding area,
§41-2-4.
Georgia.
Boundary between Alabama
and Georgia, §41-2-2.

BOUNDARIES—Cont'd
Housing authorities.
County housing authorities,
§24-1-62.
Municipal housing
authorities, §24-1-23.
Regional and consolidated
housing authorities,
§24-1-103.
Application to secretary of
state.
Required for change in
area of operation,
§24-1-106.
Decrease of area of
operation.
Procedure for decrease,
§24-1-105.
Hearings.
Public hearings required
for change in area of
operation, §24-1-106.
Increase of area of
operation.
Procedure for increase,
§24-1-104.
Operation of authorities in
municipality outside
area of operation,
§24-1-111.
Judgments.
Actions to determine
boundaries, §35-3-3.
Military affairs.
Commanders of national
guard troops may
prescribe boundaries
around jails, public
buildings, etc., from
which public excluded,
§31-2-123.
Municipal corporations.
See MUNICIPAL
CORPORATIONS.
School tax district.
Boundaries fixed by county
board, §16-13-191.
Duration of boundaries,
§16-13-192.
Soil and water conservation.
Districts.
Changes, §9-8-23.
Watershed conservancy
districts, §9-8-52.
Addition of lands to
districts, §9-8-63.
Detachment of lands from
districts, §9-8-64.
State boundaries.
Boundary between Alabama
and Florida.
Generally, §41-2-3.
Defined, Const. Ala., art. II,
§37.
Description.
General description,
§41-2-1.
Florida.
Boundary between
Alabama and Florida.
Generally, §41-2-3.
Precise location at mouth
of Perdido river and
surrounding area,
§41-2-4.
General description, §41-2-1.
Georgia.
Boundary between
Alabama and Georgia,
§41-2-2.

BOUNDARIES—Cont'd
Wildlife management areas,
§9-11-301.
BOUNTIES.
Fish and game.
See FISH AND GAME.
BOWIE KNIVES.
Minors.
Sale to minor prohibited,
§13A-11-57.
Weapons generally.
See WEAPONS.
BOWLING ALLEYS.
Licenses, §40-12-66.
Municipal corporations,
§11-51-102.
Revocation of licenses,
§11-51-103.
Municipal corporations.
Closing, §11-51-102.
Licenses, §11-51-102.
Revocation, §11-51-103.
BOXING AND WRESTLING.
Athletic commission,
§41-9-90.1.
Conflicts of interest.
Athletic commission,
§41-9-90.1.
Fees.
Collection of license and
permit fees, §41-9-96.
Penalties.
Athletic commission,
§41-9-90.1.
Permits and licenses.
Fees and taxes.
Collection by commissioner
of revenue, §41-9-96.
Revenue department.
Collection of fees and taxes.
Distribution of proceeds,
§41-9-96.
Rules and regulations.
Athletic commission,
§41-9-90.1.
Sales tax.
Tax levied on gross receipts,
§40-23-2.
Sports generally.
See SPORTS.
Taxation.
Commissioner of revenue to
collect, §41-9-96.
Distribution of proceeds,
§41-9-96.
Sales tax.
Tax levied on gross
receipts, §40-23-2.
**BOYCOTTING AND
BLACKLISTING.**
Insurance, §27-12-8.
Maintaining, §13A-11-123.
BOY SCOUTS OF AMERICA.
Licenses.
Exemptions, §40-9-12.
Taxation.
Exemptions, §40-9-12.
BRAIN DEATH ACT.
Determination of death,
§§22-31-1 to 22-31-4.
BRAKE FLUID, §§8-17-1 to
8-17-9.
Adulteration.
Sale prohibited, §8-17-5.
When deemed adulterated,
§8-17-3.

BRAKE FLUID—Cont'd
  Condemnation for violations,
    §8-17-7.
  Definitions, §8-17-1.
  Distribution.
    Registration and permit,
    §8-17-2.
  Inspections, §8-17-8.
  Misbranding.
    Sale prohibited, §8-17-5.
    When deemed misbranded,
    §8-17-4.
  Penalties.
    Violations of article, §8-17-9.
  Permits.
    Sale or distribution, §8-17-2.
  Registration.
    Sale or distribution, §8-17-2.
    Unregistered sale
    prohibited, §8-17-5.
  Rules and regulations.
    Promulgation, §8-17-6.
  Sale.
    Prohibited if misbranded,
    adulterated or
    unregistered, §8-17-5.
    Registration and permit,
    §8-17-2.
    Suspension from sale for
    violations, §8-17-7.
  Seizure for violations,
    §8-17-7.
  Testing, §8-17-8.
  Violations of article.
    Penalty, §8-17-9.
    Suspension from sale, seizure
    and condemnation for
    violations, §8-17-7.

BRAKES.
  Motorcycles, §§32-5-212,
    32-12-24.
  Motor vehicles, §32-5-212.

BRANCH BANKS, §§5-5A-20,
  5-7A-6.
  Banks generally.
    See BANKS AND
      FINANCIAL
      INSTITUTIONS.

BRANDS AND MARKS.
  Agriculture.
    Grading and standards of
    farm products and fish,
    §§2-11-50 to 2-11-59.
    See AGRICULTURE.
    Misbranding, §§2-2-31 to
    2-2-37.
    See AGRICULTURE.
  Caustic or corrosive
    substances.
    Approval and registration of
    brands and labels,
    §8-17-23.
  Commercial feeds.
    Brand name.
      Defined, §2-21-17.
      Misbranding, §2-21-21.
  Cosmetics.
    Adulteration and
      misbranding of
      cosmetics.
    See COSMETICS.
  Cotton, §§2-19-3, 2-19-16.
  Drugs.
    Adulteration and
      misbranding of drugs.
    See DRUGS.
    Pharmacists and pharmacies.
    Sale of adulterated drugs,
    §34-23-9.

BRANDS AND MARKS
  —Cont'd
  Drugs—Cont'd
    Pharmacists and pharmacies
    —Cont'd
      Substitution of brands,
      §34-23-8.
  Explosives.
    Transportation of explosives.
      Marking of packages
      containing explosives,
      §37-8-182.
  Feeds.
    Commercial feeds.
      Brand name.
        Defined, §2-21-17.
        Misbranding, §2-21-21.
  Fertilizer.
    Misbranding, §2-22-16.
  Food.
    Adulteration and
      misbranding of foods,
      §§20-1-20 to 20-1-32.
    See FOOD.
  Grain.
    Sacks, bags, etc.
      Marking, §2-20-1.
  Honeybees and apiaries.
    Hive-bodies and supers.
      Owners, etc., to mark,
      §2-14-7.
  Ice cream.
    Misbranded ice cream,
    §2-13-13.
  Indictments.
    Alteration, etc., of brands
    and marks.
      Form of indictments,
      §15-8-150.
  Labels generally.
    See LABELS.
  Linseed oil.
    Mixture or substitute to be
    marked as such,
    §8-17-43.
  Livestock.
    See LIVESTOCK.
  Meat and meat products.
    See MEAT AND MEAT
      PRODUCTS.
  Mellorine.
    Misbranding, §§20-1-135,
    20-1-137.
  Milk and milk products.
    Marked containers.
      See MILK AND MILK
      PRODUCTS.
  Misbranding.
    Agriculture, §§2-2-31 to
    2-2-37.
    See AGRICULTURE.
    Brake fluid, §§8-17-4, 8-17-5.
    Caustic or corrosive
    substances.
      Confiscation, §8-17-22.
      Defined, §8-17-20.
      Selling in, §8-17-21.
    Cosmetics.
      Adulteration and
      misbranding of
      cosmetics.
      See COSMETICS.
    Drugs.
      Adulteration and
      misbranding of drugs.
      See DRUGS.
      Pharmacists and
      pharmacies.
        Sale of adulterated
        drugs, §34-23-9.

BRANDS AND MARKS
  —Cont'd
  Misbranding—Cont'd
    Feed.
      Commercial feed, §2-21-21.
    Fertilizer, §2-22-16.
    Food.
      Adulteration and
      misbranding of foods.
      See FOOD.
    Indictment.
      Form of indictment,
      §15-8-150.
    Meat and meat products,
      §§2-17-18 to 2-17-20.
    Mellorine, §§20-1-135,
      20-1-137.
    Poultry, §§2-17-10, 2-17-18 to
      2-17-20.
  Personal property.
    Defacing identifying mark on
    encumbered personal
    property, §8-12-3.
    Presumption of guilt by
    possession, §8-12-3.
  Plant parts.
    Registration of symbol of
    seeds or plant parts,
    §§2-26-50 to 2-26-52.
  Poultry.
    See POULTRY.
  Seeds.
    Registration of symbol of
    seeds or plant parts,
    §§2-26-50 to 2-26-52.
  Service marks.
    Registration of trademarks
    and service marks,
    §§8-12-6, 8-12-8 to
    8-12-18.
    See TRADEMARKS.
  Trademarks.
    See TRADEMARKS.

BRASS KNUCKLES.
  Possession or use
    prohibited, §13A-11-53.
  Weapons generally.
    See WEAPONS.

BRAZIL NUTS.
  See NUTS.

BREACH OF CONTRACT.
  Commercial code.
    See COMMERCIAL CODE.
  General provisions.
    See CONTRACTS.

BREAD, FLOUR, CORNMEAL
  AND GRITS, §§20-1-70 to
  20-1-78.
  Applicability of article,
    §20-1-72.
  Board of agriculture and
    industries.
    Powers and duties, §20-1-78.
  Commissioner of agriculture
    and industries.
    Powers and duties, §20-1-78.
  Dams.
    Erection of dams for mills,
    gins, factories or electric
    generators.
    See DAMS.
  Definitions, §20-1-71.
  Enforcement.
    Rules and regulations,
    §20-1-78.
  Enrichment.
    Bread, §20-1-76.
    Defined, §20-1-71.

**BREAD, FLOUR, CORNMEAL
AND GRITS**—Cont'd
Label requirements.
Requirements as to labeling,
§20-1-77.
**Minimum requirements as to
amounts of vitamins and
other ingredients.**
Bread, §20-1-75.
Cornmeal, §20-1-73.
Flour, §20-1-74.
Grits, §20-1-73.
Orders.
Publication and effective
date, §20-1-78.
Requirements.
Labeling, §20-1-77.
Rules and regulations.
Publication and effective
date, §20-1-78.
Short title of article,
§20-1-70.
Weights and measures.
Cornmeal and grits to be sold
in 5 to 200 pound
packages, §8-16-102.
Exceptions, §8-16-102.
Flour to be sold in packages
of 5 to 200 pounds,
§8-16-103.

BREAKING AND ENTERING.
Burglary.
See BURGLARY.

BREEDING.
Fish and game propagation.
See FISH AND GAME.

**BREWTON, MUNICIPALITY
OF.**
Property tax, Const. Ala.,
amd. 8.

BRIBERY.
Agents.
Commercial bribery,
§13A-11-120.
Attorneys at law.
Commercial bribery,
§13A-11-120.
Benefits.
Defined, §13A-10-60.
Commercial bribery.
Class A misdemeanor,
§13A-11-120.
Elements of crime,
§13A-11-120.
Receiving a commercial
bribe, §13A-11-121.
Compounding, §13A-10-7.
**Conflicts of interest
generally.**
See CONFLICTS OF
INTEREST.
Constitution of Alabama.
Corrupt solicitation.
Offense of corrupt
solicitation to be
defined by law, Const.
Ala., art. IV, §81.
Offer, gift, etc., of money,
etc., to executive or
judicial officers or
members of legislature to
influence official acts,
Const. Ala., art. IV, §80.
Solicitation, acceptance, etc.,
of bribes by legislators,
Const. Ala., art. IV, §81.
**Constitution of the United
States,** Const. U. S., Art.
II, §4.

BRIBERY—Cont'd
Crime victims compensation.
Penalties for influence
peddling, §15-23-18.
Definitions, §§13A-10-60,
13A-10-100.
Elections.
Bribing or attempting to
influence voter, §17-23-3.
Candidates.
Barred by bribery,
§17-23-6.
Contests.
Grounds of contest,
§17-15-1.
Municipal elections,
§§11-46-67, 11-46-68.
Employers and employees.
Commercial bribery,
§13A-11-120.
**Executors and
administrators.**
Commercial bribery,
§13A-11-120.
Fiduciaries.
Commercial bribery,
§13A-11-120.
Funerals.
Obtaining licenses by
bribery, §34-13-7.
Indictments.
Form of indictment,
§15-8-150.
Jurat.
Defined, §13A-10-100.
Jury.
Bribing a juror, §13A-10-125.
Receiving a bribe by a juror,
§13A-10-126.
Legislature, Const. Ala., art.
IV, §§79 to 81.
Protection of members from
bribes, Const. Ala., art.
IV, §53.
Municipal corporations.
Class 5 municipalities.
Mayor/commission/city
manager form of
government.
Elections, §11-44E-161.
Misdemeanor,
§11-44E-164.
Persons appointed by
city manager or
seeking
appointment.
Rendering or paying
money, service or
other valuable
things,
§11-44E-94.
Elections.
Commission form,
§§11-46-138,
11-46-139.
Mayor/commission/city
manager form of
government,
§11-44E-161.
Misdemeanor,
§11-44E-164.
Mayor-council form,
§§11-46-67, 11-46-68.
Offering or accepting
bribes for votes,
§11-44-53.
Oath.
Defined, §13A-10-100.
Official proceeding.
Defined, §13A-10-100.

BRIBERY—Cont'd
Party officers.
Defined, §13A-10-60.
Pecuniary benefit.
Defined, §13A-10-60.
Trading in public office.
Conferring pecuniary
benefits upon public
servants, §13A-10-63.
**Public officers and
employees.**
Conflicts of interest
generally.
See CONFLICTS OF
INTEREST.
Public servants.
Class C felony, §13A-10-61.
Conflicts of interest.
Failure to disclose,
§13A-10-62.
Defenses to prosecution,
§13A-10-61.
Defined, §13A-10-60.
Elements of crime,
§13A-10-61.
Sports bribery.
See SPORTS.
Trading in public office,
§13A-10-63.
**Vice-president of the United
States,** Const. U. S., Art.
II, §4.
Witnesses, §13A-10-121.
Receiving a bribe by a
witness, §13A-10-122.

BRIDGES.
Alabama bridge commission.
Bond issues.
Bonds to pay or retire
Alabama bridge
commission bonds,
Const. Ala., amd. 42.
Beautification.
Contracts.
Federal assistance, §23-1-1.
Rules and regulations.
Federal assistance.
Promulgation and
enforcement,
§23-1-1.
Bond issues, Const. Ala., amd.
21.
Alabama bridge commission
bonds.
Bonds to pay or retire
Alabama bridge
commission bonds,
Const. Ala., amd. 42.
Interstate highway system.
See within this heading,
"Interstate highway
system."
Public improvement bonds.
Certain revenue producing
undertakings.
Counties.
See COUNTIES.
Municipal corporations,
§§11-81-140 to
11-81-150.
See COUNTIES.
United States.
Bond issue for acquiring
bridges in conjunction
with United States,
Const. Ala., amd. 87.

BRIDGES—Cont'd
Boundaries.
Rivers forming boundaries
between states.
Contracts with adjoining
states and federal
government, §23-1-57.
Chartering.
Special, private or local laws
prohibited, Const. Ala.,
art. IV, §104.
Condemnation.
Power of eminent domain in
internal improvement
corporations, §10-5-1.
Conflicts of interest.
Construction and
maintenance of roads
and bridges.
Department.
Employees and director,
§23-1-58.
Constitution of Alabama.
Bond issues, Const. Ala.,
amd. 21.
Alabama bridge
commission.
Bonds to pay or retire
Alabama bridge
commission bonds,
Const. Ala., amd. 42.
United States.
Bond issue for acquiring
bridges in
conjunction with
United States,
Const. Ala., amd. 87.
Construction, maintenance,
etc., of bridges, Const.
Ala., amds. 12, 58.
State not to engage in
internal improvements
or lend money or credit
for improvements.
Exception as to bridges,
Const. Ala., amd. 1.
Construction, Const. Ala.,
amds. 12, 58.
Conflicts of interest.
Department.
Employees and director
of department,
§23-1-58.
Contracts.
Federal assistance, §23-1-1.
Coosa Valley development
authority, §33-16-9.
Counties.
Application by counties for
construction of state
bridges, §23-1-48.
Consultation with highway
department, §23-1-40.
Engineers.
Competent engineers.
Department to furnish,
§23-1-49.
Interstate highway system.
Newly constructed bridge
deemed part of
existing facility,
§23-2-121.
Quarries.
Acquisition of land,
§23-1-3.
Rules and regulations.
Federal assistance.
Promulgation and
enforcement,
§23-1-1.

BRIDGES—Cont'd
Construction—Cont'd
Rules and regulations
—Cont'd
Promulgation, §§23-1-1,
23-1-59.
Supervision.
Engineers.
Competent engineers,
§23-1-49.
Highway department,
§23-1-40.
Contracts.
Adjoining states.
Rivers forming boundaries
between states,
§23-1-57.
Beautification of bridges,
§23-1-1.
Bid guaranty, §23-1-2.
Coosa Valley development
authority, §33-16-9.
Federal government.
Agreements and contracts
with federal
government.
Rivers forming
boundaries between
states, §23-1-57.
Maintenance of bridges.
Federal assistance, §23-1-1.
Prisons and prisoners.
Convict labor.
Use on public roads and
bridges, §23-1-37.
Public utilities.
Rights of way.
Entering into with
highway
department,
§23-1-59.
**Coosa Valley development
authority.**
Contracts for construction,
reconstruction, etc.,
§33-16-9.
Duties and obligations in
regard to, §33-16-7.
Counties.
Bond issues generally.
See COUNTIES.
Construction or maintenance
of state bridges.
Application by counties for
construction or
maintenance, §23-1-48.
Consultation with highway
department, §23-1-40.
Navigable streams.
Expenditure of county
funds, §11-3-15.
Joint operation by several
counties, §11-3-16.
Public roads, bridges and
ferries.
See COUNTIES.
Warrant for construction of
public buildings, bridges
and roads, §§11-28-1 to
11-28-7.
See COUNTIES.
Drawbridges.
Railroad drawbridges.
Steamboats passing
through, §37-2-88.
Eminent domain.
Power of eminent domain in
internal improvement
corporations, §10-5-1.
Fishing from bridges,
§32-5A-216.

BRIDGES—Cont'd
Highways.
Department.
Rules and regulations.
Promulgation, §23-1-59.
General provisions.
See HIGHWAYS.
**Industrial access roads and
bridges,** §§23-6-1 to
23-6-12.
See INDUSTRIAL ACCESS
ROADS AND BRIDGES.
Injuries.
Rules and regulations.
Prevention of unnecessary
injuries.
Promulgation by
highway
department,
§23-1-59.
Interstate highway system.
Toll bridges designated as
parts of interstate
highway system.
Bond issues.
Payment of outstanding
indebtedness,
§23-2-122.
Construction.
When newly constructed
bridge deemed part
of existing facility,
§23-2-121.
Tolls.
Free facilities after
payment of
outstanding
indebtedness,
§23-2-122.
Licenses.
Special, private or local laws
prohibited, Const. Ala.,
art. IV, §104.
Maintenance.
Conflicts of interest.
Department.
Employees and director
of department,
§23-1-58.
Contracts.
Federal assistance, §23-1-1.
Counties.
Application by counties for
maintenance of state
bridges, §23-1-48.
Engineers.
Competent engineers.
Department to furnish,
§23-1-49.
Municipal corporations.
Authority of state highway
department, §23-1-47.
Quarries.
Acquisition of land,
§23-1-3.
Rules and regulations.
Federal assistance.
Promulgation and
enforcement,
§23-1-1.
Promulgation, §§23-1-1,
23-1-59.
Standards.
Establishment, §23-1-40.
Supervision.
Engineers.
Competent engineers,
§23-1-49.
Highway department,
§23-1-40.

BRIDGES—Cont'd
Motor vehicles.
Pedestrians.
Entry restricted by signals, gates or barriers, §32-5A-222.
Speed limitations on bridges, §§32-5-92, 32-5A-176.
Trucks, trailers and semitrailers.
Weight on bridges, §32-9-20.
Weight restrictions.
Rules and regulations.
Promulgation by highway department, §23-1-59.
Municipal corporations.
Access roads or bridges to certain facilities.
Aid for development by municipalities, §23-1-91.
Aid by benefited municipalities, §23-1-90.
Architectural review boards.
Applicability of provisions to bridges, §11-68-15.
Counties.
Operation, etc., of bridges over navigable streams.
Authority of counties where bridges in municipal corporations, §11-3-17.
Establishment within municipalities, §23-1-86.
Historic preservation commissions.
Applicability of provisions to bridges, §11-68-15.
Maintenance.
Authority of state highway department, §23-1-47.
Railroads.
Bridges, tunnels, etc.
Requirement of construction and maintenance within limits of certain cities, §§11-49-40 to 11-49-45.
See MUNICIPAL CORPORATIONS.
Speed limits on bridges.
Signs stating maximum speed, §32-5-92.
Streets.
Taxation.
Apportionment of road and bridge taxes between counties and municipalities, §§11-83-1 to 11-83-3.
Prisons and prisoners.
Convict labor.
Use on public roads and bridges, §23-1-37.
Property.
Eminent domain.
Power of eminent domain in internal improvement corporation, §10-5-1.

BRIDGES—Cont'd
Public utilities.
Rights of way.
Rules and regulations.
Promulgation by highway department, §23-1-59.
Railroads.
Drawbridges.
Steamboats passing through railroad drawbridges, §37-2-88.
Grade crossings.
See RAILROADS.
Municipal corporations.
Bridges, tunnels, etc.
Requirement of construction and maintenance within limits of certain cities, §§11-49-40 to 11-49-45.
See MUNICIPAL CORPORATIONS.
Repairs. See within this heading, "Maintenance."
Rights of way.
Public utilities.
Contracts.
Highway department entering into contracts, §23-1-59.
Rules and regulations.
Promulgation by highway department, §23-1-59.
Rules and regulations.
Beautification of bridges, §23-1-1.
Construction of bridges, §§23-1-1, 23-1-59.
Highway department.
Promulgation, §23-1-59.
Injuries.
Prevention of unnecessary injuries, §23-1-59.
Maintenance of bridges.
Federal assistance.
Promulgation and enforcement, §23-1-1.
Promulgation, §§23-1-1, 23-1-59.
Motor vehicles.
Weight restrictions, §23-1-59.
Public utilities.
Rights of way, §23-1-59.
Trespass, §23-1-59.
Weight restrictions, §23-1-59.
Signs.
Expenditure of state funds.
Erection and maintenance of signs.
Signs designating bridge in honor or memory of individual, §23-1-8.1.
Speed limitations, §§32-5-92, 32-5A-176.
Erection of signs stating maximum speeds on bridges, §§32-5-92, 32-5A-176.

BRIDGES—Cont'd
State parks.
Repair and maintenance.
Bridges within state parks system and state owned public fishing lake areas, §9-14-5.
Synfuels development authority.
Contracts for construction, reconstruction, etc.
Supervision or performance by highway department, §9-6A-8.
Tolls.
Toll bridges designated as parts of interstate highway system, §§23-2-121, 23-2-122.
Toll road, bridge and tunnel authority, §§23-2-140 to 23-2-161.
See TOLL ROAD, BRIDGE AND TUNNEL AUTHORITY.
Tombigbee Valley development authority.
Duties and obligations as to highway bridges, §33-17-7.
Trespass.
Rules and regulations, §23-1-59.
United States.
Bond issue for acquiring, etc., bridges in conjunction with United States, Const. Ala., amd. 87.
Contracts.
Rivers forming boundaries between states, §23-1-57.
Water management and drainage.
Districts.
Construction of improvements.
Cost of construction when ditch, drain or watercourse crosses public highway, §9-9-46.
Weights and measures.
Weight on bridges, §32-9-20.
Rules and regulations, §23-1-59.

BRIEFS.
Appeals.
See APPEALS.
Rules of appellate procedure.
See APPEALS.

BROKERS.
Air commerce.
See AIR COMMERCE.
Insurance.
See INSURANCE.
Licenses.
See LICENSES.
Real estate brokers.
See REAL ESTATE BROKERS.
Rebates, §8-11-5.

BROTHELS.
See PROSTITUTION.

BRUCELLOSIS.
  Cattle.
    Brucellosis or Bang's disease,
      §§2-15-2, 2-15-190 to
      2-15-197.
    See LIVESTOCK.

BRYCE HOSPITAL.
  Hospitals generally.
    See HOSPITALS.

BUBONIC PLAGUE.
  Notifiable diseases
    generally, §§22-11A-1 to
    22-11A-38.
    See DISEASES.

BUDGETS.
  Appropriations.
    Allotments of appropriations,
      §41-4-91.
    Availability, §41-4-90.
    Effect, §41-4-90.
    Emergency appropriations,
      §41-4-94.
    Estimates of appropriations.
      See within this heading,
      "Estimates of
      appropriations."
    Lapsing of appropriations,
      §41-4-93.
    Restriction of allotments by
      governor, §41-4-90.
    Wrongfully expended
      appropriations, §41-4-95.
  Budget management act,
    §§41-19-1 to 41-19-12.
    Administration of budget.
      Formulation and
        presentation to
        agencies and
        departments, §41-19-7.
      Responsibility of governor,
        §41-19-4.
    Appropriations.
      Authority of agencies and
        departments to
        administer, §41-19-10.
      Approval of annual plans for
        operation of programs,
        §41-19-10.
      Balancing of authorized
        expenditures and
        estimated revenues.
        Responsibility of
          legislature, §41-19-9.
      Citation of chapter, §41-19-1.
      Definitions, §41-19-2.
      Department of finance.
        Preparation of information.
          Failure of agency to
          prepare, §41-19-6.
        Program and financial
          information.
          Submission to
            department,
            §41-19-6.
      Reports.
        Operation of agencies
          and departments.
          Quarterly reports,
            §41-19-10.
        Performance reports.
          Submission to
            department,
            §41-19-11.
      Financial information.
        Submission to department
          of finance, §41-19-6.

BUDGETS—Cont'd
  Budget management act
    —Cont'd
    Governor.
      Information.
        Summary of information.
          Compilation and
          submission to
          governor, §41-19-6.
      Proposed program and
        financial plan.
        Formulation and
          presentation,
          §41-19-7.
      Responsibility as to
        preparation and
        administration,
        §41-19-4.
    Information.
      Preparation by department
        of finance upon failure
        of agency, §41-19-6.
      Summary.
        Compilation and
          submission to
          governor, §41-19-6.
    Legislature.
      Consideration of program
        and financial plan.
        Responsibilities,
          §41-19-8.
      False budget or fiscal
        information.
      Preparation for
        presentation,
        §41-19-12.
      Formulation and
        presentation to
        legislature, §41-19-7.
    Program and financial
      plan.
      Adoption.
        Responsibilities,
          §41-19-8.
      Balancing of authorized
        expenditures and
        estimated revenues,
        §41-19-9.
    Preparation of budget.
      Responsibility of
        department of finance,
        §41-19-5.
      Responsibility of governor,
        §41-19-4.
    Purpose of chapter, §41-19-3.
    Reports.
      Department of finance.
        Operations of agencies
          and departments.
          Quarterly reports,
            §41-19-10.
        Performance reports,
          §41-19-11.
      Review of annual plans for
        operation of programs,
        §41-19-10.
      Salaries.
        Granting of increases.
          Agencies and
          departments,
          §41-19-10.
    Title of chapter, §41-19-1.
  Budget officers. See within
    this heading, "Division of
    the budget."
  Contents of budget, §41-4-83.
  Counties.
    See COUNTIES.
  Court of Alabama.
    Legislative budgets, Const.
    Ala., amd. 448.

BUDGETS—Cont'd
  District attorneys.
    Procedure, §12-17-221.
  Division of the budget.
    Budget officers.
      Appointment, §41-4-81.
      Full time service, §41-4-6.
      Head of division, §41-4-81.
      Oath of office, §41-4-6.
    Duties, §41-4-80.
    Established, §41-4-80.
    Functions, §41-4-80.
    Head of division, §41-4-81.
  Domestic violence facilities.
    Submission to office, §30-6-6.
  Education.
    Budget systems.
      See EDUCATION.
  Emergency appropriations,
    §41-4-94.
  Estimates of appropriations.
    Preparation by department of
      finance, §41-4-85.
    Submission to department of
      finance, §41-4-84.
    Supplemental estimates for
      additional
      appropriations, §41-4-89.
  Final budget.
    Formulation, §41-4-88.
  Form of budget, §41-4-83.
  Hearings.
    Tentative budget, §41-4-87.
  Law-enforcement planning
    agency.
    Submission to governor of
      annual budget,
      §41-8A-12.
  Legislature.
    Contents of annual budget of
      legislature, §29-1-22.
    Legislative budgets.
      Generally, Const. Ala.,
      amd. 448.
    Legislative fiscal office.
      Evaluation of budgetary
      matters, §29-5-10.
    Presentation by legislature of
      annual budget, §29-1-22.
    Transmission of budget to
      legislature, §41-4-82.
  Municipal corporations.
    Class 5 municipalities.
      Mayor/commission/city
        manager form of
        government.
      Commission.
        Power to adopt
          budgets,
          §11-44E-44.
      Fiscal year, §11-44E-110.
      Five year plan,
        §11-44E-112.
      Preparation of budgets
        by city manager,
        §11-44E-92.
      Submission of budgets by
        city manager,
        §11-44E-111.
    Transportation service in
      class 3 municipalities.
      Annual budget,
        §11-49A-18.
  Office of prosecution
    services.
    Transfer of budget excesses,
      §12-17-233.1.
  Penalties.
    Violations of article,
      §41-4-96.

BUDGETS—Cont'd
Schools.
Budget system.
See EDUCATION.
Tentative budget.
Hearings, §41-4-87.
Preparation, §41-4-86.
Transmission of budget to legislature, §41-4-82.
Universities and colleges.
Proposal and recommendations, §16-5-9.
Veterans.
State veterans' homes.
Budget request, §31-5A-9.
Violations of article.
Penalties for violations, §41-4-96.
Welfare.
Department of human resources, §38-2-3.
Youth services.
Youth services board, §44-1-56.

BUILDING AND LOAN ASSOCIATIONS.
Savings and loan associations.
See SAVINGS AND LOAN ASSOCIATIONS.

BUILDINGS.
Aged persons.
Accessibility to and use of public buildings by physically handicapped persons, §§21-4-1 to 21-4-7.
See PUBLIC BUILDINGS.
Alabama building authority.
Continuation, §41-10-1.
Dissolution, §41-10-1.
Alabama building corporation, §41-10-3.
Alabama building finance authority, §41-10-2.
Appliances, machinery and equipment used for land clearing or improvements.
Liens, §§35-11-430, 35-11-431.
Armories generally.
See ARMORIES.
Armory commission. See within this heading, "Military affairs."
Assignments.
Liens for rent of buildings.
Lien, rights and remedies vested in assignee of claim for rent, §35-9-65.
Attachments.
Landlord and tenant.
Liens of landlord.
Rent of buildings, §§35-9-60 to 35-9-65.
See LANDLORD AND TENANT.
Blind persons.
Accessibility to and use of public buildings and facilities, §§21-4-1 to 21-4-7.
See PUBLIC BUILDINGS.
Right to full use of public buildings, §21-7-2.

BUILDINGS—Cont'd
Bond issues.
Alabama building authority, §41-10-1.
Building commission.
Agents.
Appointment, §41-9-141.
Compensation of members, §41-9-140.
Composition, §41-9-140.
Conservation and natural resources.
Construction or modification of buildings and facilities.
Approval of commission not required as to certain contracts, §9-2-44.
Creation, §41-9-140.
Duties, §41-9-141.
Election.
Legislative members, §41-9-140.
Employees.
Appointment, §41-9-141.
Energy conservation building code.
Director of technical staff of commission.
Powers and duties as to promulgation, adoption and modification of code, §41-9-172.
Expenses of members, §41-9-140.
Funds.
Approval and allocation of funds, §41-9-141.
Meetings, §41-9-140.
Notice of meetings required, §41-9-141.
Minimum building standards code. See within this heading, "Minimum building standards code."
Notice of meetings.
Required, §41-4-141.
Officers, §41-9-140.
Appointment, §41-9-141.
Powers, §41-9-141.
Public works.
Radioactive fallout protection.
State funded public buildings or structures.
Powers and duties of commission, §39-6-1.
Rules and regulations.
Adoption, §41-9-141.
Vacancies.
Filling vacancies of legislative members, §41-9-140.
Burglary.
Defined, §13A-7-1.
Code.
Energy conservation building code, §§41-9-170 to 41-9-174.
Minimum building standards code, §§41-9-160 to 41-9-166. See within this heading, "Minimum building standards code."

BUILDINGS—Cont'd
Commercial code.
Sales.
Goods to be severed from realty, §7-2-107.
Commissions.
Building commission. See within this heading, "Building commission."
Conservation and natural resources.
Buildings and facilities, §§9-2-40 to 9-2-44.
Contractors.
General provisions.
See CONTRACTORS.
Corporation.
Alabama building corporation, §41-10-3.
Counties.
See COUNTIES.
Definitions.
Energy conservation building code, §41-9-170.
Minimum building standards code, §41-9-160.
Education.
See EDUCATION.
Eggs and egg products.
Inspection of buildings, §2-12-10.
Energy conservation building code, §§41-9-170 to 41-9-174.
Adoption.
Director of technical staff of building commission.
Powers and duties, §41-9-172.
Definitions, §41-9-170.
Director of technical staff of building commission.
Promulgation, adoption and modification of code.
Powers and duties, §41-9-172.
Distribution, §41-9-171.
Enforcement, §41-9-171.
Modification.
Director of technical staff of building commission.
Powers and duties, §41-9-172.
Promulgation, §41-9-171.
Director of technical staff of building commission.
Powers and duties, §41-9-172.
Standards to be included in code, §41-9-172.
Thermal and lighting efficiency guidelines.
Formulation by director, §41-9-174.
Training and assistance in implementing provisions.
Preparation and offering by director, §41-9-173.
Factory-built housing.
Manufactured buildings generally, §§24-4A-1 to 24-4A-7.
See MANUFACTURED BUILDINGS.
Finance.
Alabama building finance authority, §41-10-2.

BUILDINGS—Cont'd
Fire marshal.
  See FIRES AND FIRE
    PREVENTION.
Fish and game.
  Propagation of fish and
    game.
  Erection or purchase of
    buildings, §9-11-2.
Frank Lee youth center.
  Trade schools, §16-60-172.
Handicapped persons.
  Accessibility to and use of
    public buildings and
    facilities by physically
    handicapped persons,
    §§21-4-1 to 21-4-7.
  See PUBLIC BUILDINGS.
Harbors and ports.
  Displaced persons.
    Payment of relocation
      expenses of persons
      displaced by projects,
      §33-1-36.
  Exchange of property and
    relocation of buildings by
    department, §33-1-20.
  Insurance.
    State docks department.
      Authority to carry
        insurance, §33-1-25.
Health.
  Nuisances menacing public
    health, §§22-10-1 to
    22-10-3.
Hotels, inns and other
    transient lodging places.
  See HOTELS, INNS AND
    OTHER TRANSIENT
    LODGING PLACES.
Housing generally.
  See HOUSING.
Insanitary buildings.
  Nuisances menacing public
    health, §§22-10-1 to
    22-10-3.
Insurance.
  See INSURANCE.
Junior colleges.
  Approval of plans, §16-60-89.
  Expenditures for building,
    §16-60-89.
Landlord and tenant.
  Liens.
    Rent of buildings,
      §§35-9-60 to 35-9-65.
    See LANDLORD AND
      TENANT.
Libraries.
  Erection.
    Powers and duties of
      library boards,
      §11-90-3.
Liens.
  Landlord and tenant.
    Liens.
      Rent of buildings,
        §§35-9-60 to 35-9-65.
      See LANDLORD AND
        TENANT.
  Mechanics' and
    materialmen's liens.
    General provisions,
      §§35-11-210 to
      35-11-234.
    See MECHANICS' AND
      MATERIALMEN'S
      LIENS.
  Homestead exemptions,
    Const. Ala., art. X,
    §207.

BUILDINGS—Cont'd
Liens—Cont'd
  Mechanics' and
    materialmen's liens
    —Cont'd
    Improvements on public
      streets, etc.
    Liens, §§35-11-410 to
      35-11-417.
    See HIGHWAYS.
Lighting efficiency
    guidelines.
  Formulation by director,
    §41-9-174.
Livingston University.
  Board of trustees.
    Authority of board,
      §16-53-2.
Manufactured buildings.
  General provisions,
    §§24-4A-1 to 24-4A-7.
  See MANUFACTURED
    BUILDINGS.
Mechanics' and
    materialmen's liens.
  General provisions,
    §§35-11-210 to 35-11-234.
  See MECHANICS' AND
    MATERIALMEN'S
    LIENS.
  Homestead exemptions,
    Const. Ala., art. X, §207.
  Improvements on public
    streets, etc.
    Liens, §§35-11-410 to
      35-11-417.
    See HIGHWAYS.
Military affairs.
  Armory commission.
    Acquisition and
      construction of
      buildings, §31-4-8.
  Counties or municipalities.
    Cooperation with armory
      commission for
      acquisition of
      buildings, §31-4-9.
    Sale of real estate and
      buildings to local
      national guard units,
      §31-2-130.
  Donations.
    Reversion of donations,
      §31-4-19.
Minimum buildings
    standards code,
    §§41-9-160 to 41-9-166.
  Applicability, §41-9-162.
  Changes in code, §41-9-164.
  Conservation and natural
    resources.
    Construction or
      modification of
      buildings and
      facilities.
      Compliance with state
        building code,
        §9-2-44.
  Counties.
    Adoption of code by
      counties, §41-9-166.
  Definitions, §41-9-160.
  Distribution, §41-9-161.
  Enforcement, §§41-9-161,
    41-9-165.
  Hotels.
    Defined, §41-9-160.
    Operation of hotel not
      conforming to code,
      §41-9-163.

BUILDINGS—Cont'd
Minimum buildings
    standards code—Cont'd
  Moving picture theaters.
    Defined, §41-9-160.
    Operation of theater not
      conforming to code,
      §41-9-163.
  Municipal corporations.
    Adoption by municipalities,
      §41-9-166.
  Nonconforming statutes,
    §41-9-163.
  Promulgation, §41-9-161.
  Requirements of code,
    §41-9-163.
  Schoolhouses.
    Construction of public
      schoolhouse not
      conforming to code,
      §41-9-163.
    Defined, §41-9-160.
  State building and
    construction.
    Defined, §41-9-160.
    Erection and acquisition
      not conforming to code,
      §41-9-163.
Municipal corporations.
  See MUNICIPAL
    CORPORATIONS.
Nuisances.
  Health nuisances, §§22-10-1
    to 22-10-3.
  Municipal corporations.
    Minimum housing
      standards and
      regulation of unsafe
      buildings.
      Power to enjoin or abate
        public nuisances not
        impaired by chapter,
        §11-53-3.
Prefabricated housing.
  Manufactured buildings
    generally, §§24-4A-1 to
    24-4A-7.
  See MANUFACTURED
    BUILDINGS.
Public buildings generally.
  See PUBLIC BUILDINGS.
Public works.
  See PUBLIC WORKS.
Redevelopment projects.
  General provisions, §§24-2-1
    to 24-2-10.
  See REDEVELOPMENT
    PROJECTS.
Rent of buildings.
  Liens, §§35-9-60 to 35-9-65.
  See LANDLORD AND
    TENANT.
Rules and regulations.
  Building commission.
    Adoption, §41-9-141.
Schools.
  See EDUCATION.
Snead Junior College.
  Governor authorized to
    accept, §16-60-150.
Southern Union College.
  Acceptance of facilities by
    governor, §16-60-130.
Standards.
  Minimum building standards
    code, §§41-9-160 to
    41-9-166. See within this
    heading, "Minimum
    building standards code."

BUILDINGS—Cont'd
State building commission.
Armory.
Approval, inspection and supervision of armory construction, §31-4-13.
Subdivisions.
Counties.
Regulation of subdivisions by counties.
See COUNTIES.
Surveys and surveyors.
County surveyors.
Rights as to buildings not lost by straightening or location of section, etc., lines, §11-7-10.
Thermal efficiency guidelines.
Formulation by director of building commission, §41-9-174.
Trade schools.
Approval of plans, §16-60-89.
Expenditures for building, §16-60-89.
Frank Lee youth center, §16-60-172.
Urban renewal projects.
General provisions, §§24-3-1 to 24-3-10.
See URBAN RENEWAL PROJECTS.
Weapons.
Discharging firearm into building, §13A-11-61.

BULKHEADS.
See BOOMS AND BULKHEADS.

BULK TRANSFERS.
Commercial code, §§7-6-101 to 7-6-111.
See COMMERCIAL CODE.
Grain, §2-20-3.

BULLDOZERS.
Liens.
Appliances, machinery and equipment used for land clearing or improvements, §§35-11-430, 35-11-431.

BULLETS.
Brass or steel teflon-coated handgun ammunition.
Possession or sale, §13A-11-60.
Motor vehicle accidents.
Garages to report bullet damage, §32-10-10.
Weapons generally.
See WEAPONS.

BULLOCK COUNTY.
Development authority.
Membership and powers, Const. Ala., amd. 431.
Economic and industrial development promotion, Const. Ala., amd. 429.
Economic development, Const. Ala., amd. 128.
Officers.
Compensation of certain officers, Const. Ala., amd. 231.
Probate court.
Compensation of judge, Const. Ala., amd. 414.

BULLOCK COUNTY—Cont'd
Probate court—Cont'd
Judge not to serve on county governing body, Const. Ala., amd. 414.
School tax.
License taxes for school purposes, Const. Ala., amd. 163.

BULLS.
Liens.
Owners of stallions, jacks, bulls, etc., §§35-11-330, 35-11-331.

BUOYS.
Oyster reefs.
Damaging or removing buoys or markers, §9-12-62.

BURDEN OF PROOF.
Commercial code.
General provisions.
See COMMERCIAL CODE.
Criminal law and procedure.
Where offense was committed.
Proving at trial, §15-8-31.
Education.
Attendance.
Burden of proof on person in loco parentis, §16-28-13.
Eminent domain.
Amount of compensation, §18-1A-153.
Hearing on preliminary objections, §18-1A-94.
Evidence generally.
See EVIDENCE.
Investment securities.
Action on securities, §7-8-105.
Marine resources.
Residency, §9-12-1.
Physicians.
Foreign medical school graduates.
Off-shore medical schools.
Certificate of qualification.
Proof required, §34-24-83.
Substantial equivalence of program to accredited schools.
Burden of demonstrating, §34-24-80.
Post-conviction remedies, ARCrP, Rule 20.3.
Railroads.
Compliance with requirements of sections 37-2-80 through 37-2-82.
Burden of proof on company, §37-2-83.
Rules of criminal procedure.
Post-conviction remedies, ARCrP, Rule 20.3.
Substantial evidence.
Proof by substantial evidence, §12-21-12.
Uniform commercial code.
See COMMERCIAL CODE.
Welfare.
Child care facilities.
Relationship to child, §38-7-16.
Workmen's compensation.
Misconduct of employees, §25-5-36.

BURDEN OF PROOF—Cont'd
Workmen's compensation —Cont'd
Occupational diseases, §25-5-120.
Radiation.
Occupational exposure to radiation, §25-5-200.

BUREAUS.
Credit unions.
Bureau of credit unions, §§5-2A-100 to 5-2A-103, 5-17-7.
Evidence.
Authentication of paper or document, §12-21-72.
Loans.
Bureau of loans.
See SMALL LOANS.
Publicity.
Bureau of tourism and travel, §§41-7-1 to 41-7-5.
Reports.
Printing, §41-4-141.
Time for making, §41-4-141.
Savings and loan associations.
Bureau of savings and loans, §§5-2A-60, 5-2A-61.
Tourists.
Bureau of tourism and travel, §§41-7-1 to 41-7-5.

BURGLARY.
Buildings.
Defined, §13A-7-1.
Definitions, §13A-7-1.
Dwellings.
Defined, §13A-7-1.
Enter or remain unlawfully.
Defined, §13A-7-1.
First degree burglary.
Class A felony, §13A-7-5.
Elements of crime, §13A-7-5.
Indictments.
Form of indictment, §15-8-150.
Premises.
Defined, §13A-7-1.
Second degree burglary.
Class B felony, §13A-7-6.
Elements of crime, §13A-7-6.
Third degree burglary.
Class C felony, §13A-7-7.
Elements of crime, §13A-7-7.
Tools.
Possession of burglar's tools.
Class C felony, §13A-7-8.
Generally, §13A-7-8.
Use of force in defense of persons or property.
When deadly physical force justified, §13A-3-23.

BURIAL.
Animals, §3-1-28.
Cemeteries.
County cemeteries, §§11-17-1 to 11-17-16.
See COUNTIES.
General provisions.
See CEMETERIES.
Municipal cemeteries, §§11-47-40 to 11-47-74.
See MUNICIPAL CORPORATIONS.
Charities.
Preservation, repair, etc., of public or private burial places, etc., §11-17-13.

BURIAL—Cont'd
County cemeteries, §§11-17-1
to 11-17-16.
See COUNTIES.
Indian burial grounds.
Aboriginal mounds,
earthworks and other
antiquities, §§41-3-1 to
41-3-6.
See HISTORY AND
ARCHIVES.
Indigent persons.
Counties.
Burial of persons dying
with no estate, §38-8-2.
Insurance, §§27-17-1 to
27-17-15.
See INSURANCE.
Licenses.
Coffins and caskets.
Agents, §40-12-79.
Dealers, §40-12-79.
Manufacturers, §40-12-78.
Municipal cemeteries.
General provisions,
§§11-47-40 to 11-47-74.
See MUNICIPAL
CORPORATIONS.
Permits.
Filing, §22-9-7.
Out-of-state burials,
§22-9-75.
Processing of permits,
§22-9-7.
Required, §22-19-3.
Ministers at funerals to
ascertain if permit
secured, §22-19-4.
**Receipts for burial, removal
or other disposition of
dead human bodies,**
§22-9-73.
Wording of receipt for in-
state interment,
§22-9-74.
Sextons.
Duties of sextons, §22-9-76.
Societies, §§10-4-20 to 10-4-28.
See CEMETERIES.
Workmen's compensation.
Expenses, §25-5-67.

BURNING.
Arson.
See ARSON.
Fires and fire prevention.
See FIRES AND FIRE
PREVENTION.

BUSES.
Alcoholic beverages.
Licenses.
Retail common carrier
liquor license,
§28-3A-18.
Blind persons.
Right to use of public
conveyances and
transportation facilities,
§21-7-3.
Employees.
Biweekly payment of wages,
§37-8-270.
Handicapped persons.
Right to use of public
conveyances and
transportation facilities,
§21-7-3.
Motor vehicle carriers.
See MOTOR VEHICLE
CARRIERS.

BUSES—Cont'd
Motor vehicles generally.
See MOTOR VEHICLES.
Quarantine.
Free rides on public
transports for quarantine
officers, §22-12-23.
Supervision of public
conveyances affected by
quarantine, §22-12-21.
Transportation of person or
thing in violation of
quarantine, §22-12-22.
School buses, §§16-27-1 to
16-27-7.
See EDUCATION.
Transportation companies.
General provisions.
See TRANSPORTATION
COMPANIES.
Venue.
Violations committed on
buses, §37-8-94.
Violations.
Venue for violations
committed on buses,
§37-8-94.
Wages of employees.
Biweekly payment of wages,
§37-8-270.

BUSHEL.
**Weight per bushel of certain
commodities,** §8-16-94.
Commissioner of agriculture
and industries.
Authority to promulgate
rules, §8-16-94.

BUSHES.
Plants generally.
See PLANTS.

BUSINESS ASSISTANCE.
Small business assistance,
§§25-10-1 to 25-10-10.
See SMALL BUSINESS
ASSISTANCE.

BUSINESS CORPORATIONS.
**Alabama business
corporation act,**
§§10-2A-1 to 10-2A-339.
See CORPORATIONS.

BUSINESS RECORDS,
§§12-21-42 to 12-21-44;
ARCP, Rule 44 (h).

BUTCHERS.
Records, §§2-15-3, 2-15-27.
Cattle.
Butchers to maintain
records as to cows
butchered, §2-15-3.
Inspections, §2-15-3.

BUTLER COUNTY.
Barbers.
Chapter not applicable to
Butler county, §34-5-15.
Court costs and charges,
Const. Ala., amd. 353.
Officers.
Compensation, Const. Ala.,
amd. 353.
School tax.
Special property tax for
educational purposes,
Const. Ala., amd. 131.

BUTTER.
See MILK AND MILK
PRODUCTS.

BUTTERFLIES.
**Monarch butterfly
designated state insect,**
§1-2-25.

BYLAWS.
**Bear creek development
authority,** §33-15-6.
Condominiums, §§35-8-8,
35-8-10, 35-8-11.
Corporations.
See CORPORATIONS.
Credit unions.
Amendments, §5-17-9.
Education.
Insurance.
Risk management
cooperatives.
Filing.
Bylaws, §16-8-42.1.
Electric cooperatives.
See ELECTRIC
COOPERATIVES.
**Environmental improvement
authorities.**
Adoption and alteration,
§9-6-8.
Evidence.
Municipal bylaws, §12-21-95.
**Industrial development
corporations.**
Adoption, §10-4-132.
Municipal corporations.
See MUNICIPAL
CORPORATIONS.
**Savings and loan
associations.**
See SAVINGS AND LOAN
ASSOCIATIONS.
**Water conservation and
irrigation.**
Agency.
Adoption, §9-10-5.

C

CABINS.
Vacation time-sharing plans,
§§34-27-50 to 34-27-69.
See VACATION TIME-
SHARING PLANS.

CABLE TV.
**Community antenna
television facilities,**
§§11-27-1 to 11-27-3,
23-1-59.

CADAVERS.
Dead bodies generally.
See DEAD BODIES.

CAFES.
General provisions.
See RESTAURANTS.

CAFETERIAS.
General provisions.
See RESTAURANTS.

**CAHABA TRACE
COMMISSION,** §§41-9-800
to 41-9-810.
Appointment, §41-9-800.
New members, §41-9-802.
Audits, §41-9-809.
Chairman, §41-9-801.
Compensation, §41-9-804.
Composition, §41-9-800.
Conflicts of interest,
§41-9-804.
Creation, §41-9-800.

CAHABA TRACE
COMMISSION—Cont'd
Executive committee,
§41-9-803.
Expenses, §41-9-804.
Fund.
Composition, §41-9-805.
Establishment, §41-9-805.
Use, §41-9-805.
Headquarters, §41-9-802.
Meetings, §41-9-802.
Obligations.
Obligation of state not
created by commission
obligations, §41-9-808.
Officers, §41-9-802.
Powers.
Generally, §41-9-806.
Quorum, §41-9-802.
Records.
Revenues and expenditures,
§41-9-809.
Rules and regulations.
Adoption, §41-9-803.
State park or museum.
Not authorized by article,
§41-9-810.
Taxation.
Exemption from taxation,
§41-9-807.
Terms of office, §41-9-801.

CALERA, MUNICIPALITY
OF.
Property tax, Const. Ala.,
amd. 17.

CALHOUN COUNTY.
Cerebral palsy center.
Appropriation by city of
Anniston.
Authorized, Const. Ala.,
amd. 494.
Court costs and charges,
Const. Ala., amd. 412.
Industrial sites and
industrial park projects,
Const. Ala., amd. 415.
Officers.
Regulation of salaries, etc., of
certain public officers,
Const. Ala., amd. 33.
School taxes.
Special school tax, Const.
Ala., amd. 68.
Special tax in school
districts, Const. Ala.,
amds. 291, 335.
Use of special school tax
funds.
Refunding of bonds, etc.,
Const. Ala., amd. 165.

CAMDEN, MUNICIPALITY
OF.
Property tax, Const. Ala.,
amd. 8.

CAMELLIA.
State flower, §1-2-11.

CAMPAIGN
EXPENDITURES.
General provisions.
See ELECTIONS.

CAMPS AND CAMPING.
Duty of care owed persons
on premises for sporting
or recreational purposes,
§§35-15-1 to 35-15-5.

CAMPS AND CAMPING
—Cont'd
Forests and forestry.
Fires and fire prevention.
Campfires.
Emergency drought
conditions,
§9-13-141.
Military camps.
Annual encampments,
§31-2-37.
Enforcement of sanitation
laws, §31-2-40.
Torts.
Duty of care owed persons on
premises for sporting or
recreational purposes,
§§35-15-1 to 35-15-5.

CANADIAN INSURERS.
Trusteed assets, §27-33-16.
Investments of life, disability
and burial insurance
companies, §§27-41-13,
27-41-15, 27-41-17.

CANALS.
Common carriers, Const.
Ala., art. XII, §242.
Companies, Const. Ala., art.
XII, §242.
Transportation companies
generally.
See TRANSPORTATION
COMPANIES.
Constitution of Alabama.
Canal companies, Const.
Ala., art. XII, §242.
Navigable waterway between
Demopolis and
Tennessee river, Const.
Ala., amd. 270.
Navigable waterway between
Montgomery and
Gadsden and to the
Alabama-Georgia
boundary, Const. Ala.,
amd. 287.
Public highways.
When deemed, Const. Ala.,
art. XII, §242.
Construction.
Condemnation, §10-5-4.
Dwellings.
Construction through
curtilage, §10-5-5.
Dams.
Erection.
Construction of canal
through adjoining
lands.
Proceedings, §18-2-16.
Dwellings.
Construction through
curtilage, §10-5-5.
Eminent domain.
Condemnation of ways and
rights of way, §10-5-4.
Power of eminent domain in
internal improvement
corporations, §10-5-1.
Housing.
Construction through
curtilage, §10-5-5.
Manufacturers.
Connections to public ways.
Construction and
operation, §10-5-13.
Operation outside state and
making extensions
within state, §10-5-12.

CANALS—Cont'd
Mines and minerals.
Connections to public ways.
Construction and
operation, §10-5-13.
Operation outside state and
making extensions
within state, §10-5-12.
Municipal corporations.
Construction and
maintenance.
Authorized, §11-50-50.
Operation.
Condemnation of ways and
rights of way, §10-5-4.
Outside state.
Operation outside state,
§10-5-12.
Quarries.
Connections to public ways.
Construction and
operation, §10-5-13.
Operation outside state and
making extensions
within state, §10-5-12.
Railroads.
Operation of canals outside
state and making
extensions within state,
§10-5-12.
Taxation, §40-11-1.
Transportation companies.
General provisions.
See TRANSPORTATION
COMPANIES.

CANCER, §§22-13-1 to 22-13-13.
Cancer detection month.
Designation, §22-13-5.
Educational campaigns,
§22-13-4.
Examinations.
Disabled persons, §22-13-9.
Females, §22-13-6.
Free examinations for
indigent persons,
§22-13-8.
Indigent persons.
Free examinations,
§22-13-8.
Laboratory examination,
§22-13-11.
Males, §22-13-7.
Physicians' reports,
§22-13-10.
Reporting blanks,
§22-13-10.
Uniform examination,
§22-13-10.
Statewide seminars,
§22-13-4.
Counties.
Lurleen B. Wallace memorial
cancer hospital fund.
Appropriations by counties,
§11-8-12.
Detection month. See within
this heading, "Cancer
detection month."
Disabled persons.
Examinations, §22-13-9.
Education.
Campaigns, §22-13-4.
Plan, §22-13-3.
Statewide seminars,
§22-13-4.
Examinations.
Disabled persons, §22-13-9.
Females, §22-13-6.
Free examinations.
Indigent persons, §22-13-8.

CANCER—Cont'd
Examinations—Cont'd
Indigent persons.
Free examinations,
§22-13-8.
Laboratory examination,
§22-13-11.
Males, §22-13-7.
Physicians' reports,
§22-13-10.
Reporting blanks, §22-13-10.
Uniform examination,
§22-13-10.
Expenses of chapter.
Payment, §22-13-13.
Females.
Examinations, §22-13-6.
Financial aid for indigents,
§22-13-2.
Hospitals.
Lurleen B. Wallace memorial
cancer hospital fund.
Appropriations by counties,
§11-8-12.
Standards.
Requirements for cancer
units, §22-13-1.
Indigent persons.
Examinations.
Free examinations,
§22-13-8.
Financial aid for indigents,
§22-13-2.
Plan for care of indigents,
§22-13-1.
Laboratories.
Examination.
Specimens, §22-13-11.
**Lurleen B. Wallace memorial
cancer hospital fund.**
Appropriations by counties,
§11-8-12.
Free examinations, §22-13-8.
Males.
Examinations, §22-13-7.
Physicians.
Reports, §22-13-10.
Reports.
Physicians, §22-13-10.
Seminars.
Statewide seminars,
§22-13-4.
Standards.
Minimum standards for
cancer units, §22-13-1.
Test of specimens, §22-13-11.
Units.
Standard requirements.
Establishment and
designation, §22-13-1.
Women.
Examinations, §22-13-6.

CANCER SOCIETY.
Licenses.
Exemptions from licenses,
§40-9-12.
Taxation.
Exemptions, §40-9-12.

CANDIDATES.
See ELECTIONS.

CANDY.
Adulteration.
When deemed adulterated,
§20-1-23.

CANES.
Blind persons.
White canes.
See BLIND PERSONS.

**CANONS OF JUDICIAL
ETHICS.**
Adjudicative responsibilities.
Standards of performance,
ACJE, Canon 3A.
Administration of justice.
Avoiding conduct prejudicial
to the administration of
justice, ACJE, Canon 2B.
Improvement.
Judge may engage in
activities to improve
the administration of
justice, ACJE, Canon
4.
**Administrative
responsibilities,** ACJE,
Canon 3B.
Appointments.
Compensation of appointees,
ACJE, Canon 3B.
Extra-judicial appointments.
Judge not to accept, ACJE,
Canon 5G.
Merit.
Power of appointment to be
exercised only on basis
of merit, ACJE, Canon
3B.
Unnecessary appointments
prohibited, ACJE, Canon
3B.
Arbitration and award.
Judge not to act as
arbitrator, ACJE, Canon
5E.
Art.
Permitted activities, ACJE,
Canons 5A, 5G.
Attorneys at law.
Disciplinary measures.
Against lawyer for
unprofessional conduct,
ACJE, Canon 3B.
Practice of law.
Judge not to practice law,
ACJE, Canon 5F.
Unprofessional conduct.
Disciplinary measures
against lawyer for
unprofessional conduct,
ACJE, Canon 3B.
Avocational activities.
Permitted activities, ACJE,
Canon 5A.
Bequests.
Acceptance prohibited if
bequest reflects
expectation of judicial
favor, ACJE, Canon 5C.
Bias.
Disqualification for personal
bias, ACJE, Canon 3C.
Broadcasting.
When permitted in
courtroom, ACJE, Canon
3A.
Campaign conduct.
Generally, ACJE, Canon 7B.
**Candidates for judicial
office.**
Breach of canons.
Jurisdiction of supreme
court, ACJE, Canon
7C.
Campaign conduct, ACJE,
Canon 7B.
Political activity, ACJE,
Canon 7A.

**CANONS OF JUDICIAL
ETHICS**—Cont'd
Ceremonial occasions.
Judge may represent his
county, state or locality,
ACJE, Canon 5G.
Character witnesses.
Judge not to testify
voluntarily as character
witness, ACJE, Canon
2C.
Charitable activities.
Permitted activities, ACJE,
Canon 5B.
Civic activities.
Permitted activities, ACJE,
Canon 5B.
Compensation.
Appointees, ACJE, Canon
3B.
Extra-judicial activities.
Restrictions, ACJE, Canon
6.
Quasi-judicial activities.
Restrictions, ACJE, Canon
6.
Compliance with law.
Judge to comply with law,
ACJE, Canon 2A.
Confidentiality.
Information not to be used
for other purposes,
ACJE, Canon 5C.
Conflicts of interest.
Procedure for determining,
ACJE, Canon 6C.
Construction of code, ACJE,
Canon 1.
Court officials.
Standards of fidelity and
diligence.
Judge to require, ACJE,
Canon 3B.
Cultural activities.
Extra-judicial appointment,
ACJE, Canon 5G.
Permitted activities, ACJE,
Canon 5A.
Decorum.
Maintenance at all times,
ACJE, Canon 2B.
Proceedings before judge.
Judge to maintain decorum
in proceedings, ACJE,
Canon 3A.
Diligence.
Judge to perform duties
diligently, ACJE, Canon
3.
Disciplinary measures.
Unprofessional conduct.
Against a judge or lawyer
for unprofessional
conduct, ACJE, Canon
3B.
Disqualification.
Remittal of disqualification,
ACJE, Canon 3D.
Standards of conduct, ACJE,
Canon 3C.
Duties of office.
Adjudicative responsibilities.
Standards of performance,
ACJE, Canon 3A.
Administrative
responsibilities.
Standards of performance,
ACJE, Canon 3B.

**CANONS OF JUDICIAL
ETHICS**—Cont'd
Duties of office—Cont'd
Conflict with judicial duties.
Regulation of extra-judicial
activities to minimize,
ACJE, Canon 5.
Diligence.
Judge to perform duties
diligently, ACJE,
Canon 3.
Disqualification.
Remittal of
disqualification, ACJE,
Canon 3D.
Standards of conduct,
ACJE, Canon 3C.
Extra-judicial activities.
Minimize risk of conflict
with judicial duties,
ACJE, Canon 5.
Impartiality.
Judge to perform duties
impartially, ACJE,
Canon 3.
Educational activities.
Judge may accept extra-
judicial appointment,
ACJE, Canon 5G.
Elections.
Political activity. See within
this heading, "Political
activity."
Estates.
Conservator of estates.
Conservator of all estates
under his jurisdiction,
ACJE, Canon 3B.
Evidence.
Electronic presentation.
Discretion of trial judge,
ACJE, Canon 3A.
Personal knowledge of
disputed evidentiary
facts.
Qualification, ACJE,
Canon 3C.
Photographic presentation.
Discretion of trial judge or
appellate court, ACJE,
Canon 3A.
**Executors and
administrators.** See
within this heading,
"Fiduciaries."
Expenses.
Extra-judicial activities.
Restrictions on
reimbursement, ACJE,
Canon 6B.
Quasi-judicial activities.
Restrictions on
reimbursement, ACJE,
Canon 6B.
Extra-judicial activities.
Compensation.
Restrictions, ACJE, Canon
6A.
Expenses.
Restrictions on
reimbursement, ACJE,
Canon 6B.
Minimize risk of conflict with
judicial duties, ACJE,
Canon 5.
Quasi-judicial activities.
Permitted activities, ACJE,
Canon 4.

**CANONS OF JUDICIAL
ETHICS**—Cont'd
Family relationships.
Disqualification where
relative has a financial
interest, ACJE, Canon
3C.
Nepotism.
Prohibited in
appointments, ACJE,
Canon 3B.
Not to influence conduct or
judgment, ACJE, Canon
2C.
Favoritism.
Prohibited in appointments,
ACJE, Canon 3B.
Fiduciaries.
Disqualification where judge
has fiduciary interest,
ACJE, Canon 3C.
Permitted fiduciary
activities, ACJE, Canon
5D.
Restrictions on fiduciary
activities, ACJE, Canon
5D.
Financial interests.
Conflicts of interest.
Procedure for determining,
ACJE, Canon 6C.
Disclosure statement of
financial interests.
Filing, ACJE, Canon 6C.
Disqualification, ACJE,
Canon 3C.
Permitted financial
activities, ACJE, Canon
5C.
Reports.
Judge to regularly file
reports of financial
interests, ACJE,
Canon 6C.
Statement of economic
interests.
Disclosure statement of
financial interests.
Filing, ACJE, Canon 6C.
Filing, ACJE, Canon 6C.
Gifts.
Prohibited if gift reflects
expectation of judicial
favor, ACJE, Canon 5C.
Guardian and ward. See
within this heading,
"Fiduciaries."
Hearings.
Adjudicative responsibilities.
Standards of performance,
ACJE, Canon 3A.
Historical activities.
Judge may accept
appointment, ACJE,
Canon 5G.
Honorable judiciary.
Indispensable to justice,
ACJE, Canon 1.
Impartiality.
Disqualification where
impartiality may be
questioned, ACJE,
Canon 3C.
Judge to perform duties
impartially, ACJE,
Canon 3.
Promoting public confidence
in impartiality of
judiciary, ACJE, Canon
2A.

**CANONS OF JUDICIAL
ETHICS**—Cont'd
Impropriety.
Appearance of impropriety.
Judge to avoid in all his
activities, ACJE,
Canon 2.
Avoidance of impropriety,
ACJE, Canon 2.
Independence of judiciary.
Judge to uphold, ACJE,
Canon 1.
Influence.
Prestige of office.
Judge not to lend prestige
to advance interests of
others, ACJE, Canon
2C.
Special position of influence.
Judge not to convey or
permit others to
convey impression that
they are in special
position to influence
him, ACJE, Canon 2C.
Information.
Acquired in judicial capacity.
Not to be used for other
purposes, ACJE,
Canon 5C.
Integrity of judiciary.
Judge to uphold, ACJE,
Canon 1.
Promoting public confidence
in integrity, ACJE,
Canon 2A.
Law.
Improvement of the law.
Judge may engage in
activities to improve
the law, ACJE, Canon
4.
Lecturing.
Permitted activities, ACJE,
Canons 4A, 5A.
Legal system.
Improvement.
Judge may engage in
activities to improve
the legal system,
ACJE, Canon 4.
Loans.
Acceptance prohibited if loan
reflects expectation of
judicial favor, ACJE,
Canon 5C.
**Matters under submission or
advisement.**
Prompt disposition, ACJE,
Canon 3A.
Mediators.
Judge not to act as mediator,
ACJE, Canon 5E.
Nepotism.
Prohibited in appointments,
ACJE, Canon 3B.
Officers.
Court officials.
Standards of fidelity and
diligence.
Judge to require, ACJE,
Canon 3B.
Photography.
When taking of photographs
in courtroom permitted,
ACJE, Canon 3A.
Political activity.
Campaign conduct, ACJE,
Canon 7B.
Conduct generally, ACJE,
Canon 7A.

CANONS OF JUDICIAL ETHICS—Cont'd
Political activity—Cont'd
Refraining from political activity inappropriate to judicial office, ACJE, Canon 7.
Practice of law.
Judge not to practice law, ACJE, Canon 5F.
Prejudice.
Avoidance of prejudicial conduct, ACJE, Canon 2B.
Disqualification, ACJE, Canon 3C.
Prestige of office.
Judge not to lend prestige to advance private interests, ACJE, Canon 2C.
Public comment.
Abstinence from public comment concerning proceedings before court, ACJE, Canon 3A.
Public confidence.
Promoting public confidence in integrity and impartiality of judiciary, ACJE, Canon 2A.
Quasi-judicial activities.
Compensation.
Restrictions, ACJE, Canon 6A.
Expenses.
Restrictions on reimbursement, ACJE, Canon 6B.
Permitted activities, ACJE, Canon 4.
Radio.
When broadcasting in courtroom permitted, ACJE, Canon 3A.
Recording.
Electronic recording.
When permitted, ACJE, Canon 3A.
Recreational activities.
Permitted activities, ACJE, Canon 5A.
Relatives.
Disqualification where relative has a financial interest, ACJE, Canon 3C.
Influence.
Family relationships not to influence conduct or judgment, ACJE, Canon 2C.
Nepotism.
Prohibited in appointments, ACJE, Canon 3B.
Reports.
Financial interests.
Judge to regularly file reports of financial interests, ACJE, Canon 6C.
Respect for law.
Judge to respect the law, ACJE, Canon 2A.
Responsibilities.
Adjudicative responsibilities.
Standards of performance, ACJE, Canon 3A.

CANONS OF JUDICIAL ETHICS—Cont'd
Responsibilities—Cont'd
Administrative responsibilities.
Standards of performance, ACJE, Canon 3B.
Restrictions on conduct.
Extra-judicial activities, ACJE, Canon 5.
Financial activity, ACJE, Canon 6.
Judge to avoid impropriety and appearance of impropriety, ACJE, Canon 2.
Political activity, ACJE, Canon 7.
Quasi-judicial activities, ACJE, Canon 4.
Social activities.
Permitted activities, ACJE, Canon 5A.
Social relationships.
Not to influence conduct or judgment, ACJE, Canon 2C.
Solicitation of funds.
Judge not to solicit funds, ACJE, Canon 5B.
Speaking.
Permitted activities, ACJE, Canons 4A, 5A.
Sports.
Permitted activities, ACJE, Canon 5A.
Standards of conduct.
Adjudicative responsibilities, ACJE, Canon 3A.
Administrative responsibilities, ACJE, Canon 3B.
Disqualification, ACJE, Canon 3C.
Remittal of disqualification, ACJE, Canon 3D.
Judge to participate in establishing, etc., ACJE, Canon 1.
Standards of performance, ACJE, Canon 3B.
Television.
When broadcasting in courtroom permitted, ACJE, Canon 3A.
Temperance.
Maintenance at all times, ACJE, Canon 2B.
Testimony.
Character witnesses.
Judge not to testify voluntarily as a character witness, ACJE, Canon 2C.
Time.
Prompt disposition of business, ACJE, Canon 3A.
Trustees. See within this heading, "Fiduciaries."
Witnesses.
Character witness.
Judge not to testify voluntarily, ACJE, Canon 2C.
Disqualification of judge where judge has been a material witness, ACJE, Canon 3C.

CANONS OF JUDICIAL ETHICS—Cont'd
Writing.
Permitted activities, ACJE, Canons 4A, 5A.

CANTEENS.
Military canteens.
Exemptions from taxation, §31-2-81.

CAPACITY.
Corporations.
Nonprofit corporations.
When lack of capacity may be asserted, §10-3A-21.
Powers of corporations, §10-2A-20.
Deeds.
Capacity to convey deeds, §35-4-1.
Determination, ARCP, Rule 17 (b).
Pleadings, ARCP, Rule 9 (a).

CAPITAL IMPROVEMENTS.
Counties, §§11-29-1 to 11-29-7.
See COUNTIES.

CAPITAL OFFENSES, §§13A-5-39 to 13A-5-59.
Application of article.
Conduct after effective date, §13A-5-57.
Finding of unconstitutionality, §13A-5-59.
Conduct after effective date.
Application of article, §13A-5-57.
Definitions, §13A-5-39.
Enumeration, §13A-5-40.
Evidence.
Sentence hearing.
Admissibility of evidence, §13A-5-45.
Finding of unconstitutionality.
Application of article, §13A-5-59.
Forms.
Indictment and verdict forms.
Supreme court to promulgate, §13A-5-56.
Guilty plea, §13A-5-42.
Burden of proof upon state, §13A-5-42.
Sentencing, §13A-5-42.
Waiver.
Effective waiver, §13A-5-42.
Interpretation of article, §13A-5-58.
Jury.
Sentence hearing.
Advisory verdict, §13A-5-46.
Vote required, §13A-5-46.
Waiver of right to advisory verdict, §13A-5-46.
Instructions to jury, §13A-5-46.
Sentence hearing conducted before jury, §13A-5-46.
Waiver, §13A-5-46.
Separation of jury, §13A-5-46.

CAPITAL OFFENSES—Cont'd
Jury—Cont'd
Sentence hearing—Cont'd
Trial jury to sit for
sentence hearing,
§13A-5-46.
Exception, §13A-5-46.
Jury instructions, §13A-5-46.
Supreme court to
promulgate, §13A-5-56.
Lesser included offenses,
§13A-5-41.
Sentence hearing.
Burden of proof, §13A-5-45.
Delay, §13A-5-45.
Evidence.
Admissibility of evidence,
§13A-5-45.
Jury.
Advisory verdict,
§13A-5-46.
Vote required,
§13A-5-46.
Waiver of right to
advisory verdict,
§13A-5-46.
Instructions to jury,
§13A-5-46.
Sentence hearing
conducted before jury,
§13A-5-46.
Waiver, §13A-5-46.
Separation of jury,
§13A-5-46.
Trial jury to sit for
sentence hearing,
§13A-5-46.
Exception, §13A-5-46.
Mistrial, §13A-5-46.
Mitigating and aggravating
circumstances,
§13A-5-45.
Statements and arguments,
§13A-5-45.
Sentencing.
Aggravating circumstances.
Consideration of in,
§13A-5-50.
Enumerated, §13A-5-49.
Presentation of arguments,
§13A-5-47.
Process of weighing.
Defined, §13A-5-48.
Consideration of aggravating
circumstances in
sentence determination,
§13A-5-50.
Determination of sentence by
court, §13A-5-47.
Findings.
Court to enter written
findings, §13A-5-47.
Guilty plea.
Sentencing after guilty
plea, §13A-5-42.
Hearing. See within this
heading, "Sentence
hearing."
Mitigating circumstances.
Enumeration, §13A-5-51.
Generally, §13A-5-51.
Inclusion of defendant's
character, record, etc.,
§13A-5-52.
Presentation of arguments,
§13A-5-47.
Process of weighing.
Defined, §13A-5-48.
Pre-sentence investigation
report, §13A-5-47.

CAPITAL OFFENSES—Cont'd
Sentencing—Cont'd
Process of weighing
aggravating and
mitigating
circumstances.
Defined, §13A-5-48.
Recommendation of jury.
Court not bound by
sentence recommended
by jury, §13A-5-47.
Trial, §13A-5-43.
Waiver by defendant of
jury participation in
sentence hearing,
§13A-5-44.
Supreme court.
Forms.
Supreme court to
promulgate, §13A-5-56.
Jury instructions.
Supreme court to
promulgate, §13A-5-56.
Trial.
Discharge of defendant,
§13A-5-43.
Jury.
Selection and separation,
§13A-5-44.
Lesser included offenses,
§13A-5-43.
Procedure, §13A-5-43.
Sentencing, §13A-5-43.
Waiver by defendant of
jury participation in
sentence hearing,
§13A-5-44.

CAPITAL PUNISHMENT.
Appeals.
Automatic appeal,
§12-22-150.
Automatic review of
conviction and sentence
of death, §13A-5-55.
Scope of review in death
cases, ARAP, Rule 45A.
Stay pending appeal,
§12-22-150; ARAP, Rule
8 (d).
Attorneys at law.
Appointment of experienced
counsel for indigent
defendants, §13A-5-54.
Bail and recognizance.
Discretionary bail schedule.
Capital felonies, ARJA,
Rule 2.
Persons charged with capital
offense, §15-13-3.
Capital offenses, §§13A-5-39
to 13A-5-59.
See CAPITAL OFFENSES.
Commutation of sentence.
Authority of governor, Const.
Ala., amd. 38.
Postponing execution of
sentence pending
commutation,
§15-18-100.
Compensation of sheriff,
§15-18-80.
Confinement until execution,
§15-18-81.
Costs.
Payment for transportation
of body, §15-18-85.
Courts.
Authority of court following
review, §13A-5-53.

CAPITAL PUNISHMENT
—Cont'd
Courts—Cont'd
Specific determinations to be
made by court,
§13A-5-53.
Courts-martial, §31-2-83.
Definitions.
Automatic appeal from death
sentence, §12-22-150.
Delivery of condemned
person, §15-18-80.
Electrocution.
Execution by electrocution,
§15-18-82.
Permissible legal
punishments, §15-18-1.
Escape.
Rearrest and execution of
person escaping before
execution, §15-18-84.
Indigent persons.
Appointment of experienced
counsel, §13A-5-54.
Mentally ill.
Examination of defendant,
§15-16-22.
Limitations on jurisdiction to
suspend execution,
§15-16-23.
Order upon restoration of
sanity, §15-16-23.
Suspending execution of
death sentence,
§15-16-23.
Militia.
Imposition by courts-martial,
§31-2-83.
Minute entries.
Old-style minute entries for
appeals,
Rules of criminal
procedure, ARCrP,
Rule 22.
Pardons.
Person having death
sentence commuted to
life imprisonment,
§15-22-27.
Postponing execution of
sentence pending
pardons, §15-18-100.
Persons who may be present
at execution, §15-18-83.
Postponing execution of
sentence pending
commutation or pardon,
§15-18-100.
Pregnancy.
Procedure when condemned
female believed
pregnant, §15-18-86.
Reprieves.
Authority of governor to
grant, Const. Ala., amd.
38.
Return of execution
warrant, certificate and
statements, §15-18-85.
Review.
Authority of court following
review, §13A-5-53.
Conviction and death
sentence subject to
automatic review,
§13A-5-55.
Remanding, §13A-5-53.
Scope of review, §13A-5-53.

CAPITAL PUNISHMENT
—Cont'd
Rewards.
Information leading to arrest
and conviction for capital
crimes, §15-9-1.
**Rules of appellate
procedure.**
Scope of review, ARAP, Rule
45A.
Rules of criminal procedure.
Minute entries.
Old-style minute entries,
ARCrP, Rule 22.
Stays.
Stay pending appeal,
§12-22-150; ARAP, Rule
8 (d).
Visitation.
Certain persons may visit
condemned person,
§15-18-81.
Warrant.
Issuance and delivery for
execution, §15-18-80.
Return of execution warrant,
§15-18-85.
Where execution conducted,
§15-18-82.
Who conducts execution,
§15-18-82.

CAPITATION TAX.
**Constitution of the United
States,** Const. U. S., Art. I,
§9.
Election.
Denial or abridgement of
right to vote for failure
to pay tax prohibited,
Const. U. S.,
Amendment XXIV.

CAPITOL.
Advisory committee.
Appointment of members,
§41-9-510.
Compensation of members,
§41-9-510.
Composition, §41-9-510.
Creation, §41-9-510.
Duties, §41-9-513.
Meetings, §41-9-511.
Officers, §41-9-511.
Qualifications of members,
§41-9-510.
Terms of members,
§41-9-510.
Director of finance.
Duty as to offices and rooms
in Capitol, §41-4-34.
Gardener.
Employment, §41-4-183.
Grounds.
Gardener.
Employment, §41-4-183.
Protection.
Montgomery city council
authorized to adopt
ordinances, §41-4-186.
Guides.
Merit system.
State capitol guides
classified as "capitol
hostesses," §36-26-46.

CAPITOL—Cont'd
History and archives.
Alabama historical
commission.
Restoration and
preservation of
Capitol.
Designation of
commission as
agency, §41-9-261.
Landscaping.
Gardener.
Employment, §41-4-183.
**Legislation to change seat of
government of state,**
Const. Ala., art. IV, §78.
Legislature.
Control of space when
legislature convenes
outside capitol, §29-1-19.
Use of space, §29-1-19.
Montgomery.
See MONTGOMERY, CITY
OF.
Offices.
Duty of director of finance,
§41-4-34.
Police.
Color of uniform, §41-4-184.
Employment, §41-4-182.
Equipment.
Necessary equipment to be
furnished, §41-4-185.
Insurance.
Authority to insure,
§41-4-185.
Limits as to amount,
§41-4-185.
Payment for insurance,
§41-4-185.
Merit system.
Classified service,
§36-26-66.
Powers, §41-4-184.
Preservation.
Alabama historical
commission.
Designation as agency
responsible, §41-9-261.
Public service commission.
Domicile of commission,
§37-1-10.
Residence of commissioners,
§37-1-9.
Restoration.
Alabama historical
commission.
Designation as agency
responsible, §41-9-261.
Rooms.
Duty of director of finance,
§41-4-34.
**State capitol preservation
commission.**
Designation as agency
responsible, §41-9-261.
Streets.
Legislature authorized to
control streets adjacent
to Capitol, §29-1-19.1.

**CARBON HILL,
MUNICIPALITY OF.**
Economic development,
Const. Ala., amd. 277.
Property tax, Const. Ala.,
amd. 8.

CAR COMPANIES.
**Transportation companies
generally.**
See TRANSPORTATION
COMPANIES.

**CARDIOPULMONARY
RESUSCITATION.**
Education.
Instruction and techniques,
§16-40-8.

CARNIVALS.
Licenses, §40-12-163.

CARRIAGES.
Municipal corporations.
Licensing, §11-51-101.

CARRIERS.
Air carriers.
See AIR COMMERCE.
Alcoholic beverages.
Dry counties.
Transportation of
prohibited beverages,
§§28-4-110 to 28-4-137.
See ALCOHOLIC
BEVERAGES.
Licenses.
Retail common carrier,
§28-3A-18.
Records.
Carriers to permit
examination, §28-3-6.
Statements of consignments
and deliveries.
Furnishing to board,
§28-3-6.
Bills of lading, §§7-7-101 to
7-7-603.
See COMMERCIAL CODE.
Blind persons.
Right to use of public
conveyances and
transportation facilities,
§21-7-3.
Canal companies, Const. Ala.,
art. XII, §242.
**Certificates of public
convenience and
necessity.**
General provisions.
See MOTOR VEHICLE
CARRIERS.
Claims.
Soliciting claims from
shippers or consignees
against carriers,
§37-8-280.
Commercial code.
Bills of lading, §§7-7-101 to
7-7-603.
See COMMERCIAL CODE.
Constitution of Alabama.
Railroads, Const. Ala., art.
XII, §242.
Regulation of common
carriers, Const. Ala., art.
IV, §103.
Contract carriers.
See MOTOR VEHICLE
CARRIERS.
Criminal law and procedure.
Force.
Use by persons responsible
for maintenance of
order, §13A-3-24.
Hindering transportation of
commodities,
§13A-11-221.

CARRIERS—Cont'd
  Damages.
    Limitation of liability.
      Carrier issuing bill of
        lading, §7-7-309.
  Duty of care.
    Carrier issuing bill of lading,
      §7-7-309.
  Explosives.
    Transportation of explosives.
      See EXPLOSIVES AND
        EXPLOSIONS.
  Fish and game.
    Transporting protected birds
      or game.
      Liabilities, §9-11-256.
  Free tickets.
    Free passage on common
      carriers, §37-1-15.
  Handicapped persons.
    Right to use of public
      conveyances and
      transportation facilities,
      §21-7-3.
  **Hindering transportation of
    commodities,**
    §13A-11-221.
  Indigent persons.
    Free tickets, §37-1-15.
  Liability.
    Common-law liability of
      common carrier.
      Bills of lading or receipts,
        §37-2-21.
    Contractual limitation of
      liability.
      Carrier issuing bill of
        lading, §7-7-309.
  Liens.
    Lien of carrier, §7-7-307.
      Enforcement, §7-7-308.
  Limitation of actions.
    Actions by or against
      carriers for recovery of
      charges, §6-2-38.
  Mileage tax.
    Motor carrier mileage tax.
      See MOTOR VEHICLE
        CARRIERS.
  Motor vehicle carriers.
    See MOTOR VEHICLE
      CARRIERS.
  Municipal corporations.
    Annexation.
      Territory exempt from
        taxation.
        Assessment and
          collection of
          privilege or license
          tax from operators,
          §11-42-84.
  Negligence.
    Contractual limitation of
      liability.
      Bill of lading, §7-7-309.
    Duty of carrier.
      Carrier issuing bill of
        lading, §7-7-309.
  Pipelines.
    See PIPELINES.
  Public service commission.
    Free tickets.
      Persons passing free of
        charge, §37-1-15.
  Railroads.
    General provisions.
      See RAILROADS.
  Rates.
    Motor vehicle carriers.
      See MOTOR VEHICLE
        CARRIERS.

CARRIERS—Cont'd
  Rates—Cont'd
    Reduced rates for certain
      purposes, §37-2-40.
  Solicitation.
    Claims from shippers or
      consignees against
      carriers, §37-8-280.
  Tariffs of common carriers.
    See MOTOR VEHICLE
      CARRIERS.
  Taxation.
    Motor vehicle carriers.
      See MOTOR VEHICLE
        CARRIERS.
  Tickets.
    Free tickets.
      Persons passing free of
        charge, §37-1-15.
    Transportation companies.
      List of tickets, passes, etc.,
        to be filed with public
        service commission,
        §37-2-8.
  Tobacco.
    Sales tax.
      Common carriers,
        §§40-25-10, 40-25-11.
  Transportation companies.
    See TRANSPORTATION
      COMPANIES.
  **Unsolicited goods delivered
    by common carrier.**
    Disposition, §35-1-3.

**CARROLLTON,
  MUNICIPALITY OF.**
  Property tax, Const. Ala.,
    amd. 8.

**CARRYING CONCEALED
  WEAPONS.**
  See WEAPONS.

CARS.
  Motor vehicles.
    See MOTOR VEHICLES.
  Railroad cars.
    Procuring without bona fide
      intention for use,
      §37-8-148.

CARTS.
  Municipal corporations.
    Licensing, §11-51-101.

CASKETS.
  Licenses.
    Dealers and agents,
      §40-12-79.
    Manufacturers, §40-12-78.
  Sales.
    Notice and certificates to be
      enclosed in sold casket,
      §22-9-77.
    Record and report of casket
      sales, §22-9-77.

CASUALTY INSURANCE.
  See INSURANCE.

CATFISH, §§2-8-270 to 2-8-291.
  Accounts and accounting.
    Promotion of industry.
      Inspection of books and
        records of sellers,
        §2-8-291.
  Advertising.
    Requirements for sale of
      catfish products,
      §2-11-33.

CATFISH—Cont'd
  Assessments.
    Promotion of industry.
      Collection of assessments,
        §2-8-281.
        Remission of collections,
          §2-8-282.
      Deductions for expenses,
        §2-8-281.
      Expenditure, §2-8-286.
      Limitations on amount,
        §2-8-279.
      Penalty for failure to
        deduct and pay over,
        §2-8-291.
      Referendum, §2-8-272.
        Application of producers'
          association for
          certification and
          approval pr
        Canvass of results,
          §2-8-279.
        Certified associations.
          Authority to conduct,
            §2-8-275.
        Conduct, §2-8-273.
          Action by state board
            of agriculture and
            industries,
            §2-8-274.
        Conducting referendum,
          §2-8-277.
        Declaration of public
          interest, §2-8-272.
        Eligibility to vote in,
          §2-8-278.
        Expenses, §2-8-277.
        Majority vote required
          for approval of
          assessment,
          §2-8-279.
        Notice, §2-8-276.
        Question to be voted on,
          §2-8-278.
        Subsequent referendums,
          §2-8-280.
      Refund of assessment to
        purchaser of catfish
        feed, §2-8-283.
  Audits.
    Promotion of industry.
      Annual audit of certified
        association, §2-8-288.
  Bonds, surety.
    Promotion of industry.
      Treasurer of certified
        association, §2-8-285.
  Definitions.
    Marketing of catfish,
      §2-11-31.
  Elections.
    Promotion of industry.
      Assessments.
        Referendum on
          assessment,
          §§2-8-272 to 2-8-280.
  Game laws.
    See FISH AND GAME.
  Inspections.
    Promotion of industry.
      Seller's inspection of books
        and records of seller,
        §2-8-291.
  Labels.
    Requirements as to labeling
      for sale of catfish
      products, §2-11-33.
  Marketing of catfish,
    §§2-11-30 to 2-11-40.
    Administration of article,
      §2-11-32.

CATFISH—Cont'd
Marketing of catfish—Cont'd
Advertisements, §2-11-33.
Commissioner of agriculture
and industries.
Administration of article,
§2-11-32.
Cooperation with state and
federal agencies,
§2-11-37.
Publication of information
as to sale, etc.,
§2-11-36.
Rules and regulations.
Promulgation,
amendment, etc.,
§2-11-35.
Condemnation of catfish.
Catfish sold in violation of
article, §2-11-39.
Definitions, §2-11-31.
Enforcement of chapter.
Proceedings for
enforcement, §2-11-38.
Federal agencies.
Cooperation of
commissioner,
§2-11-37.
Labeling.
Requirements, §2-11-33.
Penalties.
Violations of article,
§§2-11-39, 2-11-40.
Publication by commissioner
of information as to sale,
etc., §2-11-36.
Resale.
Information to be provided
to persons, etc., to
whom catfish
distributed or sold for
resale, §2-11-34.
Rules and regulations.
Proceedings for
enforcement, §2-11-38.
Promulgation, amendment,
etc., by commissioner,
§2-11-35.
Seizure of catfish.
Catfish sold in violation of
article, §2-11-39.
Short title of article,
§2-11-30.
State agencies.
Cooperation of
commissioner,
§2-11-37.
Suspension from sale of
catfish.
Catfish sold in violation of
article, §2-11-39.
Violations of article.
Penalty for violations for
which no civil penalty
provided, §2-11-40.
Suspension from sale,
seizure and
condemnation of
catfish sold in
violation of article,
§2-11-39.
Monopolies.
Promotion of industry.
Activities to promote
industry not illegal or
in restraint of trade,
§2-8-271.
Notice.
Promotion of industry.
Referendum of
assessments, §2-8-276.

CATFISH—Cont'd
Penalties.
Marketing of catfish.
Violations of article,
§§2-11-39, 2-11-40.
Promotion of industry.
Failure to deduct and pay
over assessments,
§2-8-291.
Promotion of industry.
Agreements with certified
associations of other
states, §2-8-287.
Assessments.
Collection, §2-8-281.
Deductions for expenses,
§2-8-281.
Expenditures, §2-8-286.
Expenses.
Deductions for, §2-8-281.
Limitations on
assessments, §2-8-279.
Subsequent referendums,
§2-8-280.
Penalty for failure to
deduct and pay over,
§2-8-291.
Referendum, §2-8-272.
Application for approval
to conduct.
Action by board,
§2-8-274.
Generally, §2-8-273.
Authority of certified
association to
conduct, §2-8-275.
Canvass of results,
§2-8-279.
Conduct, §2-8-277.
Declared to be in public
interest, §2-8-272.
Eligibility to vote,
§2-8-278.
Expense.
Payment, §2-8-277.
Majority vote required
for approval,
§2-8-279.
Notice, §2-8-276.
Question to be voted on,
§2-8-278.
Refund to purchaser of
catfish feed, §2-8-283.
Conditions, §2-8-283.
Remittances to treasurer of
certified association,
§2-8-282.
Audit of certified association.
Annual audit, §2-8-288.
Authorized activities not
illegal or in restraint of
trade, §2-8-271.
Board of agriculture and
industries.
Rules and regulations,
§2-8-289.
Bonds, surety.
Treasurer of certified
association, §2-8-285.
Certification of association.
Application for
certification, §2-8-273.
Revocation of certification,
§2-8-290.
Commissioner of agriculture
and industries.
Enforcement duties,
§2-8-290.
Enforcement duties of
commissioner, §2-8-290.

CATFISH—Cont'd
Promotion of industry
—Cont'd
Examination of certified
association by
department of examiners
of public accounts,
§2-8-288.
Intent of legislature,
§2-8-270.
Joint programs with other
states, §2-8-287.
Legislative purpose and
intent, §2-8-270.
Penalty for failure to deduct
and pay over
assessments, §2-8-291.
Purpose of legislature,
§2-8-270.
Rules and regulations,
§2-8-289.
Sales.
Occasional sales between
producers.
Exempt from provisions,
§2-8-284.
Sellers.
Inspection of books and
records, §2-8-291.
Statement of certified
association.
Publication, §2-8-288.
Treasurer of certified
association.
Bond of treasurer,
§2-8-285.
Remittances to treasurer,
§2-8-282.
Referendum.
Promotion of industry.
Assessments.
Referendum on
imposition of
assessment,
§§2-8-272 to 2-8-280.
Rules and regulations.
Marketing of catfish,
§2-11-35.
Proceedings for
enforcement, §2-11-38.
Promotion of industry,
§2-8-289.
Sales.
Generally, §§2-11-30 to
2-11-40. See within this
heading, "Marketing of
catfish."
Promotion of industry.
Occasional sales between
producers.
Exemption from
provisions of
chapter, §2-8-284.
Searches and seizures.
Marketing of catfish.
Seizure of catfish sold in
violation of provisions
of article, §2-11-39.

**CATHOLIC MARITIME CLUB
OF MOBILE, INC.**
Licenses.
Exemptions, §40-9-12.
Taxation.
Exemptions, §40-9-12.

CATS.
Rabies.
General provisions, §§3-7-1 to
3-7-13.
See RABIES.

CATTLE.
  Bulls.
    Liens of owners, §§35-11-330,
      35-11-331.
  Dipping of cattle.
    General provisions.
      See LIVESTOCK.
    Indemnification by counties
      of owners for injuries,
      etc., caused by dipping of
      cattle, §§11-12-1 to
      11-12-3.
  Estrays.
    General provisions.
      See ESTRAYS.
  General provisions.
    See LIVESTOCK.
  Liens.
    Owners of stallions, jacks,
      bulls, etc., §§35-11-330,
      35-11-331.
  Livestock.
    See LIVESTOCK.
  Running at large.
    General provisions.
      See ESTRAYS.

CATTLE RUSTLING, §§2-15-40
  to 2-15-48.
  See LIVESTOCK.

C.A.T.V.
  **Community antenna
    television facilities
    generally, §§11-27-1 to
    11-27-3, 23-1-59.**

CAUSES OF ACTION.
  See ACTIONS.

**CAUSTIC OR CORROSIVE
  SUBSTANCES, §§8-17-20 to
  8-17-24.**
  Brands.
    Approval and registration,
      §8-17-23.
  Definitions, §8-17-20.
  Education.
    Eye protective devices for
      pupils and teachers,
      §16-1-7.
  Enforcement of article,
    §8-17-23.
  Eye protective devices.
    Pupils and teachers, §16-1-7.
  Labels.
    Approval and registration,
      §8-17-23.
  Misbranded containers.
    Confiscation, §8-17-22.
    Defined, §8-17-20.
    Selling in, §8-17-21.
  Penalties.
    Violations of article,
      §8-17-24.
  Sales.
    Misbranded containers,
      §8-17-21.

CAVES, §§2-19-1 to 2-19-5.
  Cave related activities.
    Equipment failure.
      Liability, §9-19-2.
    Injuries while engaged in.
      Liability, §9-19-2.
  Definitions, §9-19-1.
  Injuries.
    Cave related activities.
      Liability for injury while
        engaged in, §9-19-2.
  Litter.
    Prohibited acts, §9-19-3.
  Misdemeanors.
    Damage, litter, etc., §9-19-3.

CAVES—Cont'd
  Misdemeanors—Cont'd
    Penalties for misdemeanors,
      §9-19-5.
    Pollution of underground
      water resources, §9-19-4.
  Pollution.
    Underground water
      resources.
      Risk of pollution.
        Misdemeanor, §9-19-4.
  Vandalism.
    Prohibited acts, §9-19-3.
  Water resources.
    Pollution of underground
      water resources.
      Risk of pollution.
        Misdemeanor, §9-19-4.

CEMENT.
  Laboratories.
    Testing laboratory,
      §16-47-14.
  University of Alabama.
    Testing laboratories,
      §16-47-14.

CEMETERIES.
  Abandonment.
    Municipal corporations,
      §§11-47-60 to 11-47-74.
    See MUNICIPAL
      CORPORATIONS.
  **Aboriginal mounds,
    earthworks and other
    antiquities, §§41-3-1 to
    41-3-6.**
    See HISTORY AND
      ARCHIVES.
  Appeals.
    County cemeteries.
      Appeals from assessment of
        damages, §§11-17-7 to
        11-17-11.
  Assessments.
    County cemeteries, §§11-17-1
      to 11-17-16.
    See COUNTIES.
  Authority.
    Cemetery authority.
      Defined, §34-13-1.
  Bonds, surety.
    County cemeteries.
      Appeals from assessment of
        damages, §11-17-8.
  Boundaries.
    County cemeteries.
      Establishment of
        boundaries, §11-17-3.
      Marking of boundaries,
        §11-17-3.
      Petition for appointment of
        commission to mark
        boundaries, §11-17-1.
  Burial insurance.
    General provisions, §§27-17-1
      to 27-27-15.
    See INSURANCE.
    Investments of life, disability
      and burial insurance
      companies, §§27-41-1 to
      27-41-41.
    See INSURANCE.
  **Burial societies, §§10-4-20 to
    10-4-28.**
    Borrowing money, §10-4-24.
    Effect of recital in minutes
      on proceedings,
      §10-4-26.
    Certificate of incorporation,
      §10-4-20.
    Incorporation, §10-4-20.

CEMETERIES—Cont'd
  Burial societies—Cont'd
    Loans, §10-4-26.
    Mortgages and deeds of trust.
      Securing loans, §10-4-24.
      Effect of recital in
        minutes on
        proceedings,
        §10-4-26.
    Powers of corporations,
      §10-4-21.
    Special powers, §10-4-27.
    Property.
      Sale and conveyance,
        §10-4-26.
    Service of process.
      Validity of service on
        trustee, §10-4-23.
    Special powers, §10-4-27.
    Trustees, §10-4-20.
      Chairman and members of
        board, §10-4-28.
      Validity of service of
        process on trustee,
        §10-4-23.
  Charities.
    Conveyances, devises, etc.,
      for preservation, repair,
      etc., deemed to create
      charitable trusts,
      §11-17-13.
    Trusts and trustees.
      Burial societies,
        cemeteries, etc.,
        empowered to act as
        trustees, §11-17-14.
      Perpetual trusts,
        §11-17-15.
      Validation of prior
        conveyances, bequests,
        etc., §11-17-16.
  Coffins and caskets.
    Licenses, §§40-12-78,
      40-12-79.
    Sales, §22-9-77.
  Commission.
    County cemeteries, §§11-17-1
      to 11-17-16.
    See COUNTIES.
  Conveyances.
    Charitable trusts.
      Burial socieites,
        cemeteries, etc.,
        empowered to accept
        and to act as trustees,
        §11-17-14.
    Conveyances, devises, etc.,
      for preservation,
      repair, etc., of public
      or private burial
      places, etc., §11-17-13.
    Perpetual trusts,
      §11-17-15.
    Validation, etc., of prior
      conveyances,
      §11-17-16.
  Corporations.
    Burial societies, §§10-4-20 to
      10-4-28. See within this
      heading, "Burial
      societies."
  **Counties, §§11-17-1 to
    11-17-16.**
    See COUNTIES.
  Criminal law and procedure.
    Desecration of venerated
      objects, §13A-11-12.
  Damages.
    County cemeteries, §§11-17-1
      to 11-17-16.
    See COUNTIES.

CEMETERIES—Cont'd
Dead bodies generally.
   See DEAD BODIES.
Definitions, §34-13-1.
Desecration of venerated
   objects, §13A-11-12.
Eminent domain.
   Rights of way.
   Private parties.
      Acquisition, §18-3-20.
      Application to probate
         court, §18-3-22.
      Compensation.
         Payment, §18-3-21.
      Damages.
         Payment, §18-3-21.
      Width, §18-3-20.
      Yards, gardens, orchards,
         etc., §18-3-21.
Establishing, §22-20-4.
Exemptions from levy and
   sale under process.
   Burial place, §6-10-5.
Extension, §22-20-4.
Flower decorations, shrubs
   or plants.
   Injury to prohibited,
      §13A-7-23.1.
Funerals.
   General provisions.
   See FUNERALS.
Graves.
   Removing dead body from
      grave.
   See DEAD BODIES.
   Tombstones.
      Defacing, §13A-7-23.1.
Graveyard owners, §§10-4-20
   to 10-4-28. See within this
   heading, "Burial societies."
Hearings.
   County cemeteries.
      Appeals from assessment of
         damages, §§11-17-9,
         11-17-10.
Indians.
   Aboriginal mounds,
      earthworks and other
      antiquities, §§41-3-1 to
      41-3-6.
   See HISTORY AND
      ARCHIVES.
Insurance.
   Burial insurance.
      General provisions,
         §§27-17-1 to 27-17-15.
      See INSURANCE.
      Investments of life,
         disability and burial
         insurance companies,
         §§27-41-1 to 27-41-41.
      See INSURANCE.
Jury.
   County cemeteries.
      Appeals from assessment of
         damages.
      Establishment of
         damages by jury,
         §11-17-10.
      Summoning and
         impaneling of jurors,
         §11-17-9.
Licenses.
   Coffins and caskets.
      Dealers and agents,
         §40-12-79.
      Manufacturers, §40-12-78.
   Tombstones.
      Selling or erecting,
         §40-12-131.
Location, §22-20-4.

CEMETERIES—Cont'd
Misdemeanors.
   Defacing or injuring tomb,
      gravestone, flowers, etc.,
      §13A-7-23.1.
Monuments.
   Tombstones, §§13A-7-23.1,
      40-12-131.
Municipal corporations,
   §§11-47-40 to 11-47-74.
   See MUNICIPAL
      CORPORATIONS.
Owners.
   Graveyard owners, §§10-4-20
      to 10-4-28. See within
      this heading, "Burial
      societies."
Preservation.
   Declared charitable purposes,
      §11-17-13.
Repairs.
   Declared charitable purposes,
      §11-17-13.
Rights of way.
   Eminent domain.
      Private parties, §§18-3-20
         to 18-3-22.
Service of process.
   Burial societies.
      Validity of service of
         process on trustee,
         §10-4-23.
Taxation.
   Exemption, §40-9-1.
Tombstones.
   Defacing, §13A-7-23.1.
   Licenses.
      Selling or erecting,
         §40-12-131.
Trusts and trustees.
   Charitable trusts.
      Burial societies,
         cemeteries, etc.,
         empowered to accept
         conveyances, devises,
         etc., and to act as
         trustees, §11-17-14.
      Conveyances, devises, etc.,
         for preservation of
         burial places,
         §11-17-13.
      Perpetual trust, §11-17-15.
      Validation of prior
         conveyances,
         §11-17-16.
Wills.
   Charitable trusts.
      Burial societies,
         cemeteries, etc.,
         empowered to accept
         conveyances and to act
         as trustees, §11-17-14.
      Devises for preservation,
         repair, etc., of public
         or private burial
         places, etc., deemed to
         create, §11-17-13.
      Perpetual trusts,
         §11-17-15.
      Validation, etc., of prior
         conveyances, bequests,
         etc., §11-17-16.

CENSORSHIP.
Education.
   Communism, §§16-36-10,
      16-40-3.

CENSUS.
Constitution of the United
   States, Const. U. S., Art. I,
   §§2, 9.

CENSUS—Cont'd
Education.
   Decennial school census,
      §§16-4-15, 16-8-31;
      Const. Ala., art. XIV,
      §268.
   Cities, §16-11-10.
   City superintendents of
      schools, §16-12-13.
   County superintendents of
      education, §16-9-29.
   Enumerators, §16-8-32.
   Municipal census.
      Effect as to conduct of
         school census,
         §11-47-91.
Legislature.
   Apportionment of house
      based on decennial
      census of United States,
      Const. Ala., art. IX,
      §198.
Municipal corporations.
   False enumeration,
      §11-43-15.
   General provisions,
      §§11-47-90 to 11-47-95.
   Incorporation.
      Census enumeration of
         inhabitants, §11-41-4.
Reclassification date, §1-3-5.
Schools. See within this
   heading, "Education."

CEREALS.
Grain generally.
   See GRAIN.

CERTIFICATES OF
   CONVENIENCE AND
   NECESSITY.
Motor vehicle carriers.
   See MOTOR VEHICLE
      CARRIERS.
Transportation companies,
   §§37-2-4, 37-2-4.1.

CERTIFICATES OF
   DEPOSIT.
Commercial paper generally.
   See COMMERCIAL CODE.

CERTIFICATES OF
   INDEBTEDNESS.
General provisions.
   See BOND ISSUES.

CERTIFICATES OF NEED.
Health facilities, §§22-21-260
   to 22-21-276.
   See HOSPITALS.

CERTIFIED MAIL.
   See MAIL.

CERTIFIED PUBLIC
   ACCOUNTANTS.
Accountants generally.
   See ACCOUNTANTS.

CERTIORARI.
Appeals.
   Judgments on applications
      for remedial writs,
      §12-22-6.
Certificate of judgment.
   Stay of certificate pending
      petitions for certiorari to
      courts of appeals, ARAP,
      Rule 41 (b).
Circuit courts.
   Judges.
      Writs of certiorari to
         district and municipal
         courts, §12-17-28.

CERTIORARI—Cont'd
Court of civil appeals.
Powers of judges as to
issuance of writs,
§12-3-8.
Court of criminal appeals.
Powers of judges as to
issuance of writs,
§12-3-8.
Forms.
Petition for writ of certiorari
to a court of appeals,
ARAP, Form 22.
Issuance of writs.
Powers of justices, §12-2-2.
**Judgments on applications
for remedial writs,**
§12-22-6.
Petition for certiorari.
Form of petition for writ of
certiorari to a court of
appeals, ARAP, Form 22.
Review of decisions of courts
of appeals, ARAP, Rule
39.
Supreme court.
Issuance of writs.
Powers of justices, §12-2-2.
Petition for certiorari.
Review of decisions of
courts of appeal,
ARAP, Rule 39.

**CESSION OF LAND BY
STATE,** §§42-3-1 to 42-3-3.

CESSPOOLS.
Creating hazards,
§13A-11-220.

CHAMBERS COUNTY.
Court costs and charges,
Const. Ala., amd. 103.
Fire and rescue fund, Const.
Ala., amd. 476.
Hospitals.
Special tax for hospital and
public health purposes.
Use of proceeds, Const.
Ala., amd. 307.
Officers.
Offices, terms and
compensation, Const.
Ala., amd. 103.
School tax.
Special ad valorem tax for
school purposes, Const.
Ala., amd. 102.

**CHAMPERTY AND
MAINTENANCE.**
Generally, §34-3-24.

CHANCERY COURTS.
Constitution of Alabama.
See CONSTITUTION OF
ALABAMA.
Registers in chancery.
See CIRCUIT COURTS.

CHANCROID.
Notifiable diseases,
§§22-11A-1 to 22-11A-38.
See DISEASES.
Venereal diseases generally.
See VENEREAL DISEASES.

CHANGE BILLS.
Interest.
Unauthorized change bills
not exceeding $1.00,
§8-8-9.

CHANGE OF NAME.
See NAMES.

CHANGE OF VENUE.
See VENUE.

CHARITABLE FRAUD,
§§13A-9-70 to 13A-9-76.
See FRAUD.

CHARITIES.
Appropriations.
Appropriations to charitable
institutions not under
absolute control of state,
Const. Ala., art. IV, §73.
Burial.
Preservation, repair, etc., of
public or private burial
places, etc., declared
charitable purposes,
§11-17-13.
Cemeteries.
Preservation, repair, etc., of
public or private burial
places, etc., declared
charitable purposes,
§11-17-13.
Trusts and trustees.
Burial societies,
cemeteries, etc.,
empowered to accept
conveyances, devises,
etc., and to act as
trustees, §11-17-14.
Perpetual trusts,
§11-17-15.
Validation of prior
conveyances, bequests,
etc., §11-17-16.
Constitution of Alabama.
Appropriations to charitable
institutions not under
absolute control of state,
Const. Ala., art. IV, §73.
Corporations.
Nonprofit corporations.
See CORPORATIONS.
Counties.
Cemeteries.
Preservation, repair, etc.,
declared charitable
purposes, §11-17-13.
Trusts and trustees.
Conveyances, devises, etc.,
for preservation,
repair, etc., of public
or private burial places
deemed to create
charitable trusts,
§11-17-13.
Education.
State board of education.
Supervision of educational
work of special
institutions, §16-3-20.
Finance.
Department of finance.
Powers and duties of
department as to
eleemosynary
institutions, §41-4-8.
Food.
Nonliability of good faith
donors and distributors
of canned or perishable
food, §20-1-6.
Foundations.
Generally, §10-4-210.
Private foundations,
charitable trusts and
split interest trusts,
§§19-3-300 to 19-3-303.

CHARITIES—Cont'd
Foundations—Cont'd
State bar building
foundation, §§34-3-100 to
34-3-108.
See ATTORNEYS AT
LAW.
Fraternal benefit societies.
Generally.
See FRATERNAL
BENEFIT SOCIETIES.
Fraternal orders.
General provisions,
§§10-4-170 to 10-4-179.
See FRATERNAL
ORDERS.
Fraud.
Charitable fraud, §§13A-9-70
to 13A-9-76.
See FRAUD.
Income tax.
Corporations.
Deductions.
Contributions or gifts to
charitable
institutions,
§40-18-35.
Deductions.
Contributions or gifts made
to charitable
institutions, §40-18-15.
Jefferson county.
Bingo games.
Operation by nonprofit
organizations, Const.
Ala., amd. 386.
Judges.
Permitted activities, ACJE,
Canon 5B.
Licenses.
Exemptions, §§40-9-12,
40-9-13.
Madison county.
Bingo.
Operation of bingo games
by nonprofit
organizations in
Madison county, Const.
Ala., amd. 387.
Motor vehicle carriers.
Discounts.
Exemptions, §37-8-28.
Free passage.
Exemptions, §37-8-28.
Rebates.
Exemptions, §37-8-28.
Municipal corporations.
Assessments for public
improvements.
Property owned by
charitable
organizations.
Reduction or abatement,
§11-48-30.
Nonprofit corporations.
See CORPORATIONS.
**Public officers and
employees.**
Payroll deductions, §§36-1-4,
36-1-4.1.
Railroads.
Discounts.
Exemptions, §37-8-28.
Free passes, rebates or
discounts.
Exemptions, §37-8-28.
Rebates.
Exemptions, §37-8-28.
Taxation.
Exemptions from taxation,
§40-9-12.

CHARITIES—Cont'd
 Taxation—Cont'd
  Property exempt, §40-9-1.
 Transportation companies.
  Discounts.
   Exemptions, §37-8-28.
  Free passes.
   Exemptions, §37-8-28.
  Free transportation or
    reduced rates for
    charitable purposes,
    §37-2-40.
  Rebates.
   Exemptions, §37-8-28.
 Trusts and trustees.
  Cemeteries, §§11-17-13 to
    11-17-16.
  Charitable trusts.
   Private foundations,
     charitable trusts and
     split interest trusts,
     §§19-3-300 to 19-3-303.

CHASTITY.
 Libel and slander.
  Words falsely imputing
    woman's chastity
    actionable, §6-5-181.

CHATTAHOOCHEE RIVER.
 Historic Chattahoochee
   compact, §41-9-311.

CHATTEL MORTGAGES.
 Fraud, §8-9-1.
 Secured transactions,
   §§7-9-101 to 7-9-507.
  See COMMERCIAL CODE.
 Trial of right of property.
  Claims based on mortgage,
    §6-6-164.

CHATTELS.
 Attachment generally.
  See ATTACHMENTS.
 Detinue.
  General provisions, §§6-6-250
    to 6-6-264.
  See DETINUE.
 Personal property.
  See PERSONAL
    PROPERTY.
 Replevin.
  See REPLEVIN.
 Trees and timber.
  Conveyances of standing
    timber.
   When standing timber and
     trees, etc., deemed
     chattels, §35-4-363.

CHECKS.
 Actions.
  Holder of worthless check,
    draft or order.
   Right of action, §6-5-285.
 Agents.
  Sale of checks.
   Agents of licensees,
     §8-7-10.
 Bad checks.
  Charge for bad checks.
   Imposition authorized,
     §8-8-15.
   Not deemed finance
     charge, §8-8-15.
  Negotiating worthless
    instruments,
    §§13A-9-13.1 to
    13A-9-13.3.
  Penalty and service charge,
    §8-8-15.

CHECKS—Cont'd
 Bad checks—Cont'd
  Sales.
   Power to transfer title,
     §7-2-403.
  Service charge, §8-8-15.
  Taxation.
   Payment of tax with bad
     check, §40-29-70.
 Bonds, surety.
  Sale of checks. See within
    this heading, "Sale of
    checks."
 Commercial paper.
  General provisions, §§7-3-101
    to 7-3-805.
  See COMMERCIAL CODE.
 Counties.
  Issuance of orders not first
    approved by county
    commission, §11-8-9.
  Persons authorized to draw
    checks on county
    treasury or depository,
    §11-8-9.
 Criminal law and procedure.
  Negotiating worthless
    instruments,
    §§13A-9-13.1 to
    13A-9-13.3.
 District attorneys.
  Special services division.
   Worthless check unit,
     §12-17-224.
 Fees.
  Sale of checks, §§8-7-6, 8-7-9.
 Fiduciaries.
  Drawn by and payable to
    fiduciary, §19-1-6.
  Third persons.
   Check drawn by fiduciary
     payable to third
     person, §19-1-5.
 Licenses.
  Sale of checks. See within
    this heading, "Sale of
    checks."
 Negotiable instruments.
  Commercial paper, §§7-3-101
    to 7-3-805.
   See COMMERCIAL CODE.
  Generally.
   See NEGOTIABLE
     INSTRUMENTS.
 Negotiating worthless
   instruments, §§13A-9-13.1
   to 13A-9-13.3.
 Payment.
  Par payment, §5-5A-33.
  Postdated checks, §5-5A-34.
 Returned checks.
  Service charge, §8-8-15.
 Sale of checks, §§8-7-1 to
   8-7-15.
  Agents of licensees, §8-7-10.
  Bonds, surety.
   Adjustment, §8-7-11.
   Increase, §8-7-14.
   Licenses, §§8-7-7, 8-7-14.
  Definitions, §8-7-2.
  Employees of licensees,
    §8-7-10.
  Fees.
   Investigation fee, §8-7-6.
   License fee, §§8-7-6, 8-7-9.
  License.
   Application, §8-7-5.
   Bond, surety, §8-7-7.
    Increase of bond, §8-7-14.
   Denial.
    Judicial review, §8-7-12.

CHECKS—Cont'd
 Sale of checks—Cont'd
  License—Cont'd
   Denial—Cont'd
    Procedure, §8-7-12.
   Fees.
    Investigation fee, §8-7-6.
    License fee, §§8-7-6,
      8-7-9.
   Financial statement,
     §8-7-7.
   Issuance, §8-7-8.
   Required, §8-7-3.
    Exemptions, §8-7-4.
   Revocation.
    Grounds, §8-7-13.
    Judicial review, §8-7-12.
    Procedure, §8-7-12.
   Offices.
    List of offices.
     Annual and
       supplemental
       listings, §8-7-11.
    Application for license,
      §8-7-7.
   Penalties.
    Violations of chapter,
      §8-7-15.
   Representatives of licensees,
     §8-7-10.
   Title of chapter.
    Short title, §8-7-1.
   Violations of chapter.
    Penalties, §8-7-15.
 Travelers' checks.
  Sale of checks generally,
    §§8-7-1 to 8-7-15. See
    within this heading,
    "Sale of checks."
 Uniform commercial code.
  Commercial paper, §§3-7-101
    to 3-7-805.
   See COMMERCIAL CODE.
 Worthless checks.
  Generally. See within this
    heading, "Bad checks."
  Negotiating worthless
    instruments,
    §§13A-9-13.1 to
    13A-9-13.3.

CHEESE.
 Imitation cheese, §§2-13-16 to
   2-13-19.
 Milk products generally.
  See MILK AND MILK
    PRODUCTS.

CHEMICALS.
 Caustic or corrosive
   substances, §§8-17-20 to
   8-17-24.
 Controlled substances.
  Crimes amendment act,
    §§13A-12-210 to
    13A-12-216.
   See DRUGS.
  General provisions, §§20-2-1
    to 20-2-144.
   See DRUGS.
 Driving under the influence.
  Chemical tests for
    intoxication, §§32-5-190
    to 32-5-194.
 Drugs.
  See DRUGS.
 Industrial alcohol, §§28-5-1 to
   28-5-14.
  See INDUSTRIAL
    ALCOHOL.

CHEMICALS—Cont'd
Pharmacists and pharmacies generally.
See PHARMACISTS AND PHARMACIES.

CHEMISTRY.
Licenses, §40-12-126.

CHEROKEE COUNTY.
Officers.
Regulation of salaries, etc., of certain public officers, Const. Ala., amd. 43.
School tax.
Special school district tax, Const. Ala., amd. 78.

CHESTNUTS.
See NUTS.

CHEWING TOBACCO.
Tobacco generally.
See TOBACCO.

CHICKENPOX.
Notifiable diseases, §§22-11A-1 to 22-11A-38.
See DISEASES.

CHICKENS.
Eggs and egg products.
General provisions.
See EGGS AND EGG PRODUCTS.
Hatcheries and chick dealers, §§2-16-1 to 2-16-9.
See POULTRY.
Poultry, waste, dead poultry and unhatched or unused eggs, §§2-16-40 to 2-16-42.
Poultry generally.
See POULTRY.

CHIEF JUSTICE OF THE SUPREME COURT.
See SUPREME COURT.

CHILD ABUSE.
Domestic violence facilities, §§30-6-1 to 30-6-13.
See DOMESTIC VIOLENCE FACILITIES.
General provisions.
See MINORS.
Protection from abuse generally, §§30-5-1 to 30-5-11.
See DOMESTIC RELATIONS.

CHILD CARE FACILITIES, §§38-7-1 to 38-7-17.
See WELFARE.

CHILD CUSTODY AND SUPPORT.
Child support programs, §§38-10-1 to 38-10-33.
See CHILD SUPPORT PROGRAMS.
Generally.
See MINORS.
Uniform child custody jurisdiction act, §§30-3-20 to 30-3-44.
See MINORS.

CHILDHAVEN, INC.
Licenses.
Exemptions, §40-9-12.
Taxation.
Exemptions, §40-9-12.

CHILD LABOR.
See LABOR.

CHILD PASSENGER RESTRAINTS.
Contributory negligence.
Failure to wear system not contributory negligence, §32-5-222.
Penalty for violation, §32-5-222.
Required, §32-5-222.

CHILD PORNOGRAPHY.
Obscene materials containing visual reproduction of children, §§13A-12-190 to 13A-12-198.
See OBSCENITY.

CHILD PROTECTION.
Termination of parental rights, §§26-18-1 to 26-18-10.
See PARENT AND CHILD.

CHILDREN.
Minors generally.
See MINORS.
Missing persons.
See MISSING PERSONS.

CHILDREN'S TRUST FUND, §§26-16-30 to 26-16-33.

CHILD SUPPORT.
Custody and support.
See MINORS.
Department.
Right of department to support owed by parents to child, §§38-10-30 to 38-10-32.
Desertion and nonsupport.
General provisions.
See DESERTION AND NONSUPPORT.
Interstate income withholding.
Additional remedies, §30-3-92.
Adoption of another state's support order, §30-3-95.
Amendment of withholding order.
Amendment of support order, §30-3-96.
Choice of law, §30-3-94.
Costs.
Court costs, §30-3-97.
Defenses, §30-3-94.
Definitions, §30-3-91.
Docket fees, §30-3-97.
Documents filed with clerk, §30-3-93.
Entry of income withholding order, §30-3-95.
Evidence, §30-3-94.
Request by another state for evidence from person in this state, §30-3-99.
Hearings.
Prima facie cases, §30-3-94.
Obligor obtaining employment or income in another state.
Notification of agency requesting withholding, §30-3-96.
Petition for adoption of support order in another jurisdiction, §30-3-93.
Purpose of article, §30-3-90.
Service on obligor, §30-3-93.

CHILD SUPPORT—Cont'd
Interstate income withholding—Cont'd
Short title of article, §30-3-90.
Voluntary income withholding, §30-3-98.
Withholding by court of this state, §30-3-93.
Programs, §§38-10-1 to 38-10-33.
See CHILD SUPPORT PROGRAMS.
Withholding orders.
Answer by employer, §30-3-64.
Liability for failure to answer, §30-3-69.
Change of address.
Obligee to give notice of change, §30-3-65.
Termination of order when unable to deliver payments, §30-3-65.
Compliance with orders.
Employers who comply not liable for wrongful withholding, §30-3-68.
Content, §30-3-61.
Costs, §30-3-63.
Definitions, §30-3-60.
Discharging of employee due to order.
Employers not to discharge, §30-3-70.
Duration, §30-3-61.
Effective date, §30-3-62.
Entry of support and withholding orders by different courts, §30-3-62.
Existing support orders, §30-3-62.
Expenses of employer.
Authority to deduct fee for expenses, §30-3-51.
Failure or refusal to withhold.
Liability of employer, §30-3-69.
Fees.
Employer authorized to deduct fee, §30-3-71.
Filing of fees and costs, §30-3-63.
Garnishment.
Withholding orders to have priority, §30-3-67.
Hearings, §30-3-62.
Hiring person due to order.
Employer not to refuse to hire, §30-3-70.
Issuance, §30-3-62.
Maximum amount prescribed, §30-3-67.
Modification by court, §30-3-64.
New employer.
Obligor and employer to give notice of change of employer, §30-3-66.
Service of order on new employer, §30-3-66.
Notice of change of address.
Obligee to give notice, §30-3-65.
Termination of order when unable to deliver payments, §30-3-65.

CHILD SUPPORT—Cont'd
Withholding orders—Cont'd
Notice of change of employer.
Obligor and employer to
give notice, §30-3-66.
Order binding on employer,
§30-3-64.
Petitions, §30-3-62.
Filing, §30-3-62.
Fees, §30-3-63.
Required, §30-3-61.
Service on employer,
§30-3-61.
Termination of withholding,
§30-3-62.
Wrongful withholding.
Employers who comply not
liable, §30-3-68.

CHILD SUPPORT
PROGRAMS, §§38-10-1 to
38-10-33.
Actions.
Enforcement of child support.
Institution of actions,
§38-10-7.
Payments collected pursuant
to judicial actions.
Disposition, §38-10-8.
Persons owed duty of
support.
Right to enforce support,
§38-10-10.
Right of department to
support owed.
Child in department's
custody or receiving
payments.
Action to assure support,
§38-10-32.
ADC.
Defined, §38-10-2.
ADC foster care.
Defined, §38-10-2.
AFDC.
Defined, §38-10-2.
Aid.
Conditions of eligibility,
§§38-10-4, 38-10-5.
Defined, §38-10-2.
Payment.
Creation of debt to
department, §38-10-6.
Disposition of payments,
§38-10-8.
Liability to department,
§38-10-6.
Recipients of aid.
Acceptance deemed
assignment to
department of right to
child support,
§§38-10-4, 38-10-5.
Aid to dependent children.
Defined, §38-10-2.
**Aid to families with
dependent children.**
Defined, §38-10-2.
Assignments.
Acceptance deemed
assignment of right to
support to department,
§§38-10-4, 38-10-5.
Right of department to
support owed.
Child in custody or
receiving payments.
Assignment to
department of right,
§38-10-31.

**CHILD SUPPORT
PROGRAMS**—Cont'd
**Authorization by
department,** §38-10-3.
Citation, §38-10-1.
**Construction and
interpretation.**
Provisions of chapter,
§38-10-11.
Debts owed to department.
Liability for debts created
upon payment of aid,
§38-10-6.
Definitions, §38-10-2.
Right of department to
support owed, §38-10-30.
Department.
Defined, §38-10-2.
**Disposition of payments
collected pursuant to
judicial actions,** §38-10-8.
Enforcement.
Child support obligations.
Institution of actions,
§38-10-7.
Reciprocal state enforcement
of duty to support,
§§30-4-80 to 30-4-98.
See DESERTION AND
NONSUPPORT.
Income withholding.
Department as agency to
administer, §38-10-3.
Investigations.
Ability of parents to furnish
support.
Conducting by department,
§38-10-9.
Minors.
Recipients of aid.
Assignments to department
deemed binding,
§38-10-5.
Penalties.
Violations.
Falsification of financial
reports, §38-10-9.
Perjury.
Falsification of financial
reports, §38-10-9.
Purpose of chapter,
§38-10-11.
Recipients of aid.
Acceptance deemed
assignment of
department of right to
child support, §§38-10-4,
38-10-5.
Minors.
Assignments to department
deemed binding,
§38-10-5.
Reports.
Parents to report financial
status.
Violations, §38-10-9.
**Right of department to
support owed.**
Child in custody or receiving
payments.
Action to assure parents
provide support,
§38-10-32.
Assignment to department
of right to support,
§38-10-31.
Collections.
Paid to department,
§38-10-33.
Definitions, §38-10-30.

**CHILD SUPPORT
PROGRAMS**—Cont'd
**Right of department to
support owed**—Cont'd
Child in custody or receiving
payments—Cont'd
Payment of support.
Collection paid to
department,
§38-10-33.
Support.
Collection paid to
department,
§38-10-33.
Short title, §38-10-1.
Subrogation.
Recipients of aid.
Department subrogated to
right of child or
recipients to, §38-10-4.
**Uniform reciprocal
enforcement of support
act.**
Reciprocal state enforcement
of duty to support,
§§30-4-80 to 30-4-98.
See DESERTION AND
NONSUPPORT.
Violations.
Penalties.
Falsification of financial
reports, §38-10-9.

CHILTON COUNTY.
Constitution of Alabama.
Amendments.
Special property tax,
Const. Ala., amd. 402.
Court costs and charges,
Const. Ala., amd. 346.
Economic development.
Special property tax for rural
and industrial
development, Const.
Ala., amd. 166.
Industrial development.
Special property tax, Const.
Ala., amd. 166.
Officers.
Compensation of certain
officers, Const. Ala.,
amd. 346.
Rural development.
Special property tax, Const.
Ala., amd. 166.
Vocational trade school.
Special property tax for
acquiring, etc., Const.
Ala., amd. 166.

CHINA.
Auction sales.
Gold, silver, watches,
jewelry, china, etc.,
§§8-14-20 to 8-14-24.

CHIROPODISTS.
General provisions,
§§34-24-230 to 34-24-276.
See PODIATRISTS.
Insurance.
Health insurance.
Payment for services,
§27-1-15.
Licenses.
See PODIATRISTS.

CHIROPRACTORS,
§§34-24-120 to 34-24-176.
Advertising, §34-24-121.
Refusal, revocation or
suspension of license.
Unlawful advertising as
grounds, §34-24-166.
Appeals.
Licenses.
Refusal, revocation or
suspension,
§34-24-175.
Audits.
Board of chiropractic
examiners.
Audit of accounts,
§34-24-143.
**Authority of licensed
chiropractors,** §34-24-120.
**Board of chiropractic
examiners,** §§34-24-140 to
34-24-145.
Annual caucus, §34-24-140.
Appointment of members,
§34-24-140.
Audit of board, §34-24-143.
Compensation of members,
§34-24-142.
Composition, §34-24-140.
Created, §34-24-140.
Directory.
Publication, §34-24-140.
Executive secretary.
Accounts, §34-24-143.
Bond, §34-24-144.
Expenditures, §34-24-142.
Expenses of members,
§34-24-142.
Funds.
Audit, §34-24-143.
Disposition of funds,
§34-24-143.
Secretary-treasurer to
record, §34-24-143.
Governor.
Appointment of members,
§34-24-140.
Removal of members,
§34-24-141.
Investigators, inspectors,
attorneys and other
agents and employees.
Employment, §34-24-140.
Meetings, §34-24-144.
Oaths of office, §34-24-141.
Organization, §34-24-144.
President.
Election, §34-24-144.
Qualifications of members,
§34-24-140.
Quorum, §34-24-144.
Records.
Secretary-treasurer or
executive secretary to
keep records,
§34-24-143.
Removal from office,
§34-24-141.
Rules and regulations,
§34-24-144.
Licenses, §34-24-165.
Seal, §34-24-144.
Secretary-treasurer.
Accounts of secretary-
treasurer, §34-24-143.
Bond, §34-24-144.
Election, §34-24-144.
Terms of office, §34-24-141.

CHIROPRACTORS—Cont'd
**Board of chiropractic
examiners**—Cont'd
Vacancies.
Filling vacancies on board,
§§34-24-140,
34-24-141.
Bonds, surety.
Board of chiropractic
examiners.
Bond of executive
secretary, §34-24-144.
Bond of secretary-
treasurer, §34-24-144.
Compromise and settlement.
Licenses.
Refusal, revocation or
suspension.
Contested cases,
§34-24-168.
Costs.
Licenses.
Refusal, revocation or
suspension,
§34-24-170.
Definitions.
Chiropractic, §34-24-120.
Diagnosis.
Authority of licensed
chiropractors,
§34-24-120.
Duties of chiropractors,
§34-24-122.
Enforcement of provisions.
Authority of board to
promulgate rules and
regulations, §34-24-165.
Evidence.
Licenses.
Refusal, revocation or
suspension.
Rules of evidence.
Applicability,
§34-24-173.
Examinations.
Licensure, §34-24-161.
Extern programs, §34-24-145.
Fees.
Disposition of funds received,
§34-24-165.
Licenses, §34-24-160.
Issuance of license within
two years after
revocation or refusal,
§34-24-172.
Persons practicing on
January 1, 1960,
§34-24-163.
Reinstatement of license,
§34-24-176.
Renewal fee, §34-24-165.
Unlawful fee arrangements
as grounds for revocation
or suspension of license,
§34-24-166.
Fraud.
Refusal, revocation or
suspension of licenses.
Fraud as grounds,
§34-24-166.
Governor.
Board of chiropractic
examiners.
Appointment, §34-24-140.
Removal, §34-24-141.
Hall of fame.
Board.
Appropriations, §41-9-883.
Creation, §41-9-880.

CHIROPRACTORS—Cont'd
Hall of fame—Cont'd
Board—Cont'd
Donations, contributions,
etc.
Solicitation and
acceptance,
§41-9-882.
Expenditures, §41-9-883.
Meetings, §41-9-880.
Purpose, §41-9-881.
Quorum, §41-9-880.
Rules and regulations.
Adoption, §41-9-881.
Taxation.
Exemption, §41-9-882.
Insurance.
Payment for health services
of chiropractor, §27-1-10.
Selection of practitioner.
Insured to have exclusive
right to select,
§27-1-10.
Licenses, §40-12-136.
Annual renewal, §34-24-165.
Application, §34-24-160.
Examination, §34-24-161.
Fees, §34-24-160.
Issuance of license within
two years after
revocation or refusal,
§34-24-172.
Persons practicing on
January 1, 1960,
§34-24-163.
Reinstatement of license,
§34-24-176.
Renewal fee, §34-24-165.
General provisions.
See PHYSICIANS.
Issuance.
Generally, §34-24-161.
Persons practicing on
January 1, 1960,
§34-24-163.
Within two years after
revocation or refusal of
license, §34-24-172.
Preceptorship and extern
program.
Limited licenses,
§34-24-145.
Expiration, §34-24-145.
Issuance, §34-24-145.
Qualifications of applicant,
§34-24-160.
Recording with judge of
probate, §34-24-164.
Refusal, revocation or
suspension.
Appeal from final decision,
§34-24-175.
Costs, §34-24-170.
Evidence.
Rules of evidence.
Applicability,
§34-24-173.
Fines, §34-24-170.
Grounds, §34-24-166.
Hearing.
Notice, §34-24-167.
Rules and regulations,
§34-24-168.
Issuance of license within
two years after
revocation or refusal,
§34-24-172.
Notice of hearing,
§34-24-167.

CHIROPRACTORS—Cont'd
　Licenses—Cont'd
　　Refusal, revocation or
　　　suspension—Cont'd
　　　Orders.
　　　　Final order.
　　　　　Form and content,
　　　　　　§34-24-174.
　　　　Procedure generally,
　　　　　§34-24-167.
　　　　Renewal of license.
　　　　　Failure to renew,
　　　　　　§34-24-165.
　　　　Rules of evidence.
　　　　　Applicability,
　　　　　　§34-24-173.
　　　　Settlement of contested
　　　　　cases, §34-24-168.
　　　　Subpoenas, §34-24-173.
　　　　Witnesses, §34-24-173.
　　　Reinstatement, §34-24-176.
　　　Renewal, §34-24-165.
　　　Revocation of license for
　　　　failure to renew,
　　　　§34-24-165.
　　　Replacement, §34-24-161.
　　　Required, §34-24-123.
　　　Rules and regulations.
　　　　Refusal, revocation or
　　　　　suspension of licenses,
　　　　　§34-24-168.
　Notice.
　　Refusal, revocation or
　　　suspension of licenses.
　　　Notice of hearing,
　　　　§34-24-167.
　Oaths.
　　Board of chiropractic
　　　examiners.
　　　Oath of members,
　　　　§34-24-141.
　Orders.
　　Licenses.
　　　Refusal, revocation or
　　　　suspension.
　　　　Form and content,
　　　　　§34-24-174.
　Peer review committees.
　　Exemption from liability,
　　　§6-5-333.
　Penalties.
　　Licenses.
　　　Refusal, revocation or
　　　　suspension.
　　　　Fines, §34-24-170.
　　Violations of article,
　　　§34-24-123.
　**Powers of licensed
　　chiropractors, §34-24-120.**
　**Preceptorship and extern
　　program.**
　　Authorized, §34-24-145.
　　Eligibility, §34-24-145.
　　Establishment, §34-24-145.
　　Limited licenses.
　　　Expiration, §34-24-145.
　　　Issuance, §34-24-145.
　　Rules and regulations.
　　　Implementation of
　　　　programs, §34-24-145.
　Probate courts.
　　Licenses to be recorded with
　　　judge of probate,
　　　§34-24-164.
　**Professional standards
　　review committees.**
　　Exemption from liability,
　　　§6-5-333.

CHIROPRACTORS—Cont'd
　Records.
　　Board of chiropractic
　　　examiners.
　　　Secretary-treasurer or
　　　　executive secretary to
　　　　keep, §34-24-143.
　Registration.
　　General provisions.
　　　See PHYSICIANS.
　Rights of chiropractors,
　　§34-24-122.
　Rules and regulations.
　　Authority of board,
　　　§34-24-165.
　　Board of chiropractic
　　　examiners.
　　　Authority of board,
　　　　§34-24-144.
　　　Licenses, §34-24-165.
　　Licenses.
　　　Refusal, revocation or
　　　　suspension,
　　　　§34-24-168.
　　Preceptorship and extern
　　　program.
　　　Establishment and
　　　　implementation of
　　　　program, §34-24-145.
　Signs.
　　Place of practice, §34-24-161.
　**State licensing board for
　　healing arts.**
　　See PHYSICIANS.
　Subpoenas.
　　Licenses.
　　　Refusal, revocation or
　　　　suspension.
　　　　Compelling attendance of
　　　　　witnesses and
　　　　　production of
　　　　　documents and
　　　　　things, §34-24-173.
　Universities and colleges.
　　Chiropractic students
　　　enrolled in board
　　　approved chiropractic
　　　colleges.
　　　Preceptorship and extern
　　　　programs, §34-24-145.
　**Utilization review and
　　quality control
　　committees.**
　　Exemption from liability,
　　　§6-5-333.
　Witnesses.
　　Licenses.
　　　Refusal, revocation or
　　　　suspension,
　　　　§34-24-173.

CHLORINE.
　**Regulation of caustic or
　　corrosive substances,**
　　§§8-17-20 to 8-17-24.

CHOCTAW COUNTY.
　Probate judge.
　　Compensation, Const. Ala.,
　　　amd. 495.
　School tax.
　　Additional tax for school
　　　purposes, Const. Ala.,
　　　amd. 167.

CHOLERA.
　Hog cholera, §§2-15-230 to
　　2-15-274.
　　See LIVESTOCK.
　**Notifiable diseases
　　generally,** §§22-11A-1 to
　　22-11A-38.
　　See DISEASES.

CHOSES IN ACTION.
　Debts generally.
　　See DEBTS.
　Personal property generally.
　　See PERSONAL
　　　PROPERTY.
　Recordation.
　　Choses in action not personal
　　　property within division,
　　　§35-4-55.

CHURCHES.
　Alcoholic beverages.
　　Dry counties.
　　　Wine for sacramental or
　　　　religious purposes.
　　　　See ALCOHOLIC
　　　　　BEVERAGES.
　Associations.
　　State conventions or
　　　associations of churches,
　　　§§10-4-60 to 10-4-63.
　Bishop of diocese, §§10-4-1 to
　　10-4-9.
　　See BISHOP OF DIOCESE.
　Buses, §32-5A-154.
　Conventions.
　　State conventions or
　　　associations of churches,
　　　§§10-4-60 to 10-4-63.
　Corporations.
　　Nonprofit corporations.
　　　See CORPORATIONS.
　　State conventions or
　　　associations of churches,
　　　§§10-4-60 to 10-4-63.
　County boards of health.
　　Duties, §22-3-2.
　**Exemptions from levy and
　　sale under process.**
　　Church pew or seat, §6-10-5.
　Freedom of religion, Const.
　　Ala., art. I, §3.
　Health.
　　Authority and jurisdiction of
　　　state board of health,
　　　§22-2-2.
　　Duties of county boards of
　　　health, §22-3-2.
　Hospitals.
　　Conventions or associations
　　　of churches.
　　　Establishment of hospitals,
　　　　§10-4-61.
　Municipal corporations.
　　Cemeteries.
　　　Removal of remains, etc.,
　　　　from cemeteries owned
　　　　by churches, etc.,
　　　　§11-47-74.
　Nonprofit corporations.
　　General provisions.
　　　See CORPORATIONS.
　　State conventions or
　　　associations of churches,
　　　§§10-4-60 to 10-4-63.
　Orphanages.
　　Conventions or associations
　　　of churches.
　　　Establishment of, §10-4-61.
　Parochial schools.
　　See EDUCATION.
　Real property.
　　Conveyance by church
　　　corporation, §10-4-25.
　　Independence in control of
　　　real property, §10-4-22.
　　Sale by church corporation,
　　　§10-4-25.

CHURCHES—Cont'd
Schools.
Absence must be explained, §16-28-15.
Ages of children required to attend school, §16-28-3.
Attendance reports, §16-28-8.
Defined, §16-28-1.
Enrollment reports, §16-28-7.
Evidence.
Attendance register and rules and regulations as evidence, §16-28-23.
Gasoline tax.
Exemptions, §40-17-31.
Lubricating oils and greases.
Tax exemption, §40-17-171.
Motor fuels.
Additional excise tax on gasoline, motor fuel and lubricating oil.
Exemptions, §40-17-220.
Parochial schools.
Drug abuse education.
Exclusion of teacher or administrator from participation prohibited, §16-41-5.
Establishment of schools, §10-4-61.
School funds not to be used for support, Const. Ala., art. XIV, §263.
Physical education.
Exemption of church schools, §16-40-1.
Waiver of exemptions specified in chapter, §16-28-24.
Sextons.
Duties, §22-9-76.
Reports, §22-9-76.
State board of health.
Authority and jurisdiction, §22-2-2.
State conventions or associations of churches, §§10-4-60 to 10-4-63.
Confirmation of corporate existence, §10-4-63.
Existence.
Confirmation of corporate existence, §10-4-63.
Perpetual existence, §10-4-62.
Hospitals.
Establishment by, §10-4-61.
National conventions or associations.
Establishment of schools, hospitals, orphanages, etc., §10-4-61.
Orphanages.
Establishment by state, sectional or national conventions or associations, §10-4-61.
Perpetual existence, §10-4-62.
Powers of conventions or associations, §10-4-60.
Ratification of corporate existence, §10-4-63.
Schools.
Establishment by state, sectional or national conventions or associations, §10-4-61.

CHURCHES—Cont'd
State conventions or associations of churches —Cont'd
Sectional conventions or associations.
Establishment of schools, hospitals, orphanages, etc., §10-4-61.
Universities and colleges.
Conventions or associations of churches.
Establishment by, §10-4-61.
Wine for sacramental or religious purposes.
Dry counties.
See ALCOHOLIC BEVERAGES.

CIDER.
Name, marks, etc., on beverage containers, §§8-12-20, 8-12-21.

CIGARETTES.
Actions.
Tax on gummed cigarette papers.
Collection of tax by civil suit, §40-25A-14.
Limitation of actions, §40-25A-11.
Appeals.
Taxation.
Gummed cigarette papers.
Assessment of tax, §§40-25A-10, 40-25A-11.
Criminal law and procedure.
Selling cigarettes to minors, §13A-12-3.
Definitions.
Tax on gummed cigarette papers, §40-25A-1.
Executions.
Tax on gummed cigarette papers.
Execution on final assessment, §40-25A-13.
Licenses.
Cigars, cigarettes, cheroots, etc., §§40-12-72, 40-12-73.
Municipal license tax on vending machines, §11-51-98.
Taxation.
Gummed cigarette papers, §§40-25A-3, 40-25A-12.
Limitation of actions.
Taxation.
Gummed cigarette papers.
Assessments and actions to collect tax, §40-25A-11.
Minors.
Selling cigarettes to minors, §13A-12-3.
Municipal corporations.
License tax on vending machines, §11-51-98.
Penalties.
Taxation.
Gummed cigarette papers.
See within this heading, "Taxation."
Sale.
Minors.
Selling to minors, §13A-12-3.

CIGARETTES—Cont'd
Taxation.
Gummed cigarette papers, §§40-25A-1 to 40-25A-12.
Amount, §40-25A-2.
Appeals.
Assessment of tax, §40-25A-11.
Prima facie correctness of assessment on appeal, §40-25A-10.
Assessment of tax.
Appeals, §40-25A-11.
Prima facie correctness of assessment on appeal, §40-25A-10.
Deficiencies, §40-25A-9.
Execution on final assessment, §40-25A-13.
Finalizing assessment, §40-25A-10.
Hearing, §40-25A-10.
Limitations on assessments and actions to collect tax, §40-25A-11.
Taxpayer failing to make returns, §40-25A-8.
Collection.
Actions, §40-25A-14.
Limitations on assessments and actions to collect tax, §40-25A-11.
Excise tax collected.
Procedure on, §40-25A-18.
Limitations on assessments and actions to collect tax, §40-25A-11.
Construction and interpretation.
Effect on other licenses and taxes, §40-25A-12.
Definitions, §40-25A-1.
Department of revenue.
Enforcement of provisions, §40-25A-16.
Rules and regulations, §40-25A-16.
Disposition of proceeds, §40-25A-19.
Executions.
Final assessment.
Execution on, §40-25A-13.
Levy, §40-25A-2.
Licenses.
Effect of tax on other licenses, §40-25A-12.
Required, §40-25A-3.
Limitation of actions.
Assessments and actions to collect tax, §40-25A-11.
Payment, §40-25A-4.
Delinquent payments.
Penalty and interest, §40-25A-7.
Refund of excess payments, §40-25A-9.
Penalties.
Deficiencies, §40-25A-9.

CIGARETTES—Cont'd
Taxation—Cont'd
Gummed cigarette papers
—Cont'd
Penalties—Cont'd
Delinquent payment,
§40-25A-7.
Excess payments.
Refund, §40-25A-9.
Failure to make reports
or keep records,
§40-25A-6.
Failure to make returns,
§40-25A-8.
Proceeds.
Deduction of operating
expenses,
§40-25A-20.
Disposition, §40-25A-19.
Records.
Examination, §40-25A-5.
Failure to keep.
Penalty, §40-25A-6.
Required, §40-25A-5.
Reports.
Failure to report.
Penalty, §40-25A-6.
Restraint of violators from
continuing in business,
§40-25A-15.
Returns.
Assessment of tax on
taxpayer failing to
make returns,
§40-25A-8.
Extensions for making
returns, §40-25A-17.
Failure to make returns.
Assessment of tax,
§40-25A-8.
Penalty and interest,
§40-25A-8.
Rules and regulations.
Department of revenue,
§40-25A-16.
Statements.
Monthly statement,
§40-25A-4.
Violations of provisions.
Restraint of violators
from continuing in
business,
§40-25A-15.
Tobacco taxes.
General provisions,
§§40-25-1 to 40-25-62.
See TOBACCO.
Vending machines.
Municipal license tax,
§11-51-98.

CIRCUIT COURTS, §§12-11-1
to 12-11-61.
Adjournment.
Absence of judge adjourns
court, §12-17-29.
Administration.
Rules of judicial
administration.
See COURTS.
**Administrative fee for
periodic payments,**
§12-19-26.
Administrative personnel.
Coordination of functions and
duties, §12-5-13.
Always open, ARCP, Rule 77
(a).

CIRCUIT COURTS—Cont'd
Appeals.
Criminal cases.
Appeals to circuit court,
§§12-22-111 to
12-22-114.
Fires and fire prevention.
Orders of fire marshal,
§36-19-12.
Appeal from circuit court
to court of civil
appeals, §36-19-13.
From circuit courts.
Final judgments, §12-22-2.
From district courts.
Costs of appeal to circuit
courts, §12-19-150.
Counterclaims.
Statement of compulsory
counterclaim as
amendment to
proceedings, ARCP,
Rule 13 (j).
General provisions,
§§12-12-70 to 12-12-73.
Jurisdiction, §12-11-30.
Municipal courts, §§12-14-70,
12-14-71, 12-19-150,
12-19-153.
Attachment.
Fees, §12-19-75.
Issuance by judge or clerk,
§6-6-43.
Bailiffs, ARJA, Rule 11.
See BAILIFFS.
Bonds, surety.
Clerks of court, §12-17-91.
Registers, §12-17-111.
Boundaries.
Actions to determine
boundaries generally,
§§35-3-1 to 35-3-25.
See BOUNDARIES.
Change in boundaries.
Procedure when bill to
change boundaries
introduced in
legislature, §12-1-5.
Calendars, ARCP, Rule 79 (c).
Management, ARJA, Rule
16.
Certiorari.
Judges.
Writs of certiorari to
district and municipal
courts, §12-17-28.
Chambers.
Orders in chambers, ARCP,
Rule 77 (b).
Civil jurisdiction, §12-11-30.
Clerks of court.
Attachments.
Issuance, §6-6-43.
Authority, §12-17-93.
Bessemer division of tenth
judicial circuit.
Deputy clerk, §12-17-98.
Bonds, surety, §12-17-91.
Books and records, ARCP,
Rule 79.
Calendars, ARCP, Rule 79
(c).
Clerks generally.
See CLERKS OF COURT.
Convicts.
Duty of clerk when convict
indicted, §12-17-96.
Costs on appeal.
Execution for unpaid costs,
§12-22-76.

CIRCUIT COURTS—Cont'd
Clerks of court—Cont'd
Deputies.
Bessemer division of tenth
judicial circuit,
§12-17-98.
Compensation.
Supplemental salary for
elected deputies,
§12-17-99.
Elections.
Deputy circuit clerks in
counties having
more than five
circuit judges,
§17-2-8.
Supplemental salary for
elected deputies circuit
clerks, §12-17-99.
District courts.
Clerk of circuit court ex
officio clerk of district
court, §12-17-160.
Dockets.
Civil docket, ARCP, Rule
79 (a).
Duties of clerks, §12-17-94.
Duties, §12-17-94; ARJA,
Rule 4.
Failure to perform,
§12-17-94.
Election, Const. Ala., art. VI,
§165; amd. 328.
Deputy circuit clerks in
counties having more
than five circuit
judges, §17-2-8.
Failure to elect successor
vacates office, §36-9-5.
State and county officers
elected by the people,
§17-2-1.
Employees.
Employees in offices of
clerks to be paid by
state, §12-17-80.
Ex officio clerk of district
court, §12-17-160.
Fees.
Indices.
Fees for keeping indexes
not allowed,
§12-19-98.
Monthly reports as to fees
collected, §12-1-19.
Files of cases, ARCP, Rule
79.
Fines.
Monthly reports as to fines
collected, §12-1-19.
Hours office open, ARCP,
Rule 77 (c).
Impeachment, Const. Ala.,
art. VII, §175.
General provisions.
See IMPEACHMENT.
Subject to impeachment,
§36-11-1.
Indices, ARCP, Rule 79 (c).
Fees for keeping indexes
not allowed, §12-19-98.
Microfilm, ARCP, Rule 79
(b).
Minute book, ARCP, Rule 79
(b).
Notice of orders or
judgments, ARCP, Rule
77 (d).

CIRCUIT COURTS—Cont'd
Clerks of court—Cont'd
Offices, §12-17-90; ARCP,
  Rule 77 (c).
Office hours.
  Effect of closing offices
    on computation of
    time periods, ARJA,
    Rule 5.
  Routine work days,
    ARJA, Rule 5.
  Saturdays, Sundays and
    other holidays,
    ARJA, Rule 5.
  Conflicting state and
    county holidays,
    ARJA, Rule 5.
  Severe weather,
    hazardous or other
    emergency
    conditions, ARJA,
    Rule 5.
Orders by clerk, ARCP, Rule
  77 (c).
Payment of judgment.
  When sheriff's commissions
    to be collected,
    §12-17-95.
Pending actions.
  Taking file in pending
    action from office of
    clerk, §12-20-25.
Prisoners.
  Commitment or discharge.
    Duty of sheriff to report
      to clerk, §14-6-15.
Receivers.
  Appointment, §6-6-620.
  Appeal, §6-6-621.
Record on appeal.
  Liability of clerk for
    delayed or defective
    record, §12-22-60.
Records, ARCP, Rule 79.
  Duties of clerks, §12-17-94.
  Taking file in pending
    action from office of
    clerk, §12-20-25.
Registers.
  Clerk may serve as
    register in chancery,
    Const. Ala., art. VI,
    §165.
Reports.
  Monthly reports as to
    fines, fees, etc.,
    collected, §12-1-19.
Rules of judicial
  administration.
  See COURTS.
Salary.
  Annual salary, §12-17-81.
  Deputies.
    Supplemental salary,
      §12-17-99.
    Payment by state,
      §§12-17-80, 12-17-92.
  Secretarial services,
    §12-17-341; ARJA, Rule
    15.
Sheriffs' commissions.
  When sheriffs' commissions
    to be collected,
    §12-17-95.
State.
  Circuit clerks employees in
    offices of clerks to be
    paid by state,
    §12-17-80.

CIRCUIT COURTS—Cont'd
Clerks of court—Cont'd
Successors.
  Duty to pay over money to
    successor, §12-17-97.
Summary proceedings
  involving officials.
  Clerks and registers in
    general, §§6-6-700,
    6-6-723.
Summons and process.
  Duties of clerks, §12-17-94.
Supernumerary clerks,
  §§12-17-140 to 12-17-147.
  See within this heading,
    "Supernumerary clerks
    and registers."
Supernumerary fund.
  Contributions by clerks to
    supernumerary fund,
    §12-17-143.
Teachers' retirement system.
  Purchase of service credit
    for full time
    employment in office of
    clerk, §16-25-11.4.
Term of office, Const. Ala.,
  art. VI, §165.
  Incumbents.
    Terms of incumbents not
      abridged, Const.
      Ala., art. VI, §172.
Vacancies in office,
  §12-17-90.
  Failure to elect successor,
    §36-9-5.
  Filling, Const. Ala., art.
    VI, §165.
  Vacancies in office of clerk
    in counties where
    supernumerary holds
    commission,
    §12-17-141.
Coal.
Abandoned mine
  reclamation.
  Review of landowner's
    actions, §9-16-128.
Conservators.
Removal of conservatorship
  from probate courts,
  §26-2-2.
**Consolidation of courts in
  counties having two or
  more courts of record,**
  Const. Ala., art. VI, §148.
Constables.
Fees due constables for
  services in connection
  with circuit court
  proceedings, §12-19-94.
Constitution of Alabama.
See CONSTITUTION OF
  ALABAMA.
Consumer finance.
Appeals from orders of
  administrator, §5-19-26.
Contempt.
Jurisdiction, §12-11-30.
Corporations.
Jurisdiction.
  Public utility corporations.
    Jurisdiction to sell
      property and
      franchises of
      corporations,
      §12-11-32.
**Correction of errors in
  probate court.**
Settlements of estates,
  §12-11-60.

CIRCUIT COURTS—Cont'd
Costs.
General provisions.
  See COSTS.
Municipal corporations.
  Docket fees, fines, etc.,
    collected in municipal
    ordinance cases.
    Inapplicability of
      provisions,
      §12-19-155.
  Prescribed costs for circuit
    courts to be exclusive,
    §12-19-156.
Counties.
Circuit court in every county,
  §12-11-1.
Telephones.
  Procuring and providing
    telephones for offices,
    §11-3-11.
Utilities for courthouse
  offices, §11-12-13.
County personnel.
County court personnel
  serving circuit courts to
  become employees of
  state, §12-17-1.
Courthouses.
Circuit court to be held in
  each county at
  courthouse, §12-11-3.
Court reporters. See within
  this heading, "Reporters."
Courts generally.
See COURTS.
Criminal cases.
Appeals to circuit courts,
  §§12-22-111 to 12-22-114.
  Arrest.
    Warrant of arrest for
      defendant failing to
      appear, §12-22-112.
  Complaint.
    Statement of cause of
      complaint,
      §12-22-113.
  De novo trial in circuit
    court, §12-22-113.
  Evidence.
    Rules as to evidence
      governing appeals,
      §12-22-114.
  Failure to appear.
    Defendant, §12-22-112.
    Witnesses, §12-22-111.
  Liability of defendant
    failing to appear,
    §12-22-112.
  Rules as to evidence, etc.,
    governing appeals,
    §12-22-114.
  Statement of cause of
    complaint, §12-22-113.
  Subpoenas for witnesses.
    Issuance, execution and
      return, §12-22-111.
  Trial.
    De novo trial in circuit
      court, §12-22-113.
  Witnesses.
    Liability of witnesses
      failing to appear,
      §12-22-111.
    Subpoenas, §12-22-111.
Jurisdiction, §12-11-30.
Vesting, §12-1-3.

CIRCUIT COURTS—Cont'd
Decedents' estates.
Administration of estates in
circuit court.
Proceedings on
administration,
§12-11-40.
Removal of administration
from probate court,
§12-11-41.
Settlements of estates.
Correction of errors in
probate court,
§12-11-60.
Deemed always open, ARCP,
Rule 77 (a).
Definition of circuit, §1-1-1.
District attorneys.
General provisions.
See DISTRICT
ATTORNEYS.
Special sessions, §§12-2-34,
12-2-35, 12-2-37.
District courts.
Appeals from district courts.
See within this heading,
"Appeals."
Superintendence of district
courts, §12-11-30.
Supervision by presiding
circuit judges, §12-12-10.
Transfer of cases between
circuit and district court,
§12-11-9.
**Division of state into
circuits,** §12-11-2; Const.
Ala., art. VI, §142; amd.
328.
Certain counties need not be
included in circuit
divisions, Const. Ala.,
art. VI, §147.
Minimum number of counties
in circuit divisions,
Const. Ala., art. VI,
§147.
Dockets.
Civil docket, ARCP, Rule 79
(a).
Clerks of court.
Duties, §12-17-94.
Fees.
See DOCKETS.
Registers.
Duties, §12-17-114.
Drugs.
Controlled substances.
Manufacturers and
distributors.
Registration.
Review for denial,
nonrenewal,
suspension or
revocation,
§20-2-53.
Elections.
Clerks of court.
Absentee voting.
See ELECTIONS.
Deputy circuit clerks in
counties having more
than five circuit
judges, §17-2-8.
Election officials.
See ELECTIONS.
General elections.
Offices for which general
election held,
§17-2-2.

CIRCUIT COURTS—Cont'd
Elections—Cont'd
Clerks of court—Cont'd
State and county officers
elected by the people,
§17-2-1.
Judges, Const. Ala., art. VI,
§152.
Canons of judicial ethics.
Political activity, ACJE,
Canons 7, 7A, 7B.
Constitution of Alabama,
Const. Ala., art. VI,
§§152, 159; amd. 328.
General elections.
Offices for which general
election held,
§17-2-2.
Probate judges.
Failure to perform.
Duties to devolve upon
circuit court,
§17-1-4.
Misdemeanor, §17-1-5.
Penalty, §17-1-5.
State and county officers
elected by the people,
§17-2-1.
Two or more judges
running at the same
time.
Designation by number,
§17-7-20.
When circuit court judges
to be elected, §17-2-7.
Registration.
Appeals from refusal of
registration, §17-4-124.
Eminent domain generally.
See EMINENT DOMAIN.
Enumeration of circuits,
§12-11-2.
Equitable jurisdiction,
§12-11-31.
Cases of which circuit courts
take cognizance in
equitable matters,
§12-11-33.
Executions.
Fees, §12-19-75.
**Executors and
administrators.**
Appointment of personal
representatives,
§12-11-40.
Proceedings on
administration of estates
in circuit court,
§12-11-40.
Removal of administration of
estates from probate
court, §12-11-41.
Fees.
Administrative fee for
periodic payments.
Notice of fee, §12-19-26.
Payment to general fund,
§12-19-26.
Applicability of provisions,
§12-19-25.
Attachment fees, §12-19-75.
Clerks of court.
Indices.
Fees for keeping indexes
not allowed,
§12-19-98.
Monthly reports as to fees
collected, §12-1-19.
Costs generally.
See COSTS.

CIRCUIT COURTS—Cont'd
Fees—Cont'd
Defendant service fees,
§12-19-73.
Docket fees.
See DOCKETS.
Execution fees, §12-19-75.
Garnishment fees, §12-19-75.
Issuance of witness
subpoenas, §12-19-74.
Jurors' fees, §12-19-110.
Motor vehicles.
Filing a report of sale of
abandoned motor
vehicle, §12-19-76.
Prescribed fees for circuit
courts to be exclusive,
§12-19-156.
Reporters.
Taxed as costs in case
utilizing reporter,
§12-17-277.
Transcript fees, §12-17-276.
Witnesses' fees generally.
See WITNESSES.
**Forcible entry and unlawful
detainer.**
Appeal from district court,
§6-6-350.
Issuance of writ of
restitution or
possession, §6-6-352.
Frivolous actions.
Litigation accountability,
§§12-19-270 to 12-19-276.
See COURTS.
Garnishment.
Fees, §12-19-75.
Hearings.
Conduct in open court,
ARCP, Rule 77 (b).
Holidays.
Clerks of court and registers.
Office hours.
Conflicting state and
county holidays,
ARJA, Rule 5.
Saturdays, Sundays and
other holidays,
ARJA, Rule 5.
Hours open, ARCP, Rule 77
(a).
Impeachment.
Proceedings in circuit court,
§§36-11-13, 36-11-14.
Indices, ARCP, Rule 79 (c).
Fees for keeping indexes not
allowed, §12-19-98.
Indigent persons.
Defense of indigents.
Circuit indigent defense
commission, §5-12-4.
Injunctions.
Judges may grant, §6-6-500.
Power of circuit judges to
issue writs of injunction
returnable to courts of
chancery, Const. Ala.,
art. VI, §144.
Jails.
Commitment of prisoners.
Duty of sheriff to report to
clerk, §14-6-15.
Discharge of prisoners.
Duty of sheriff to report to
clerk, §14-6-15.
Lists of confined prisoners.
Furnishing to circuit
courts, §14-6-14.

CIRCUIT COURTS—Cont'd
Judges.
Absence of judge adjourns court, §12-17-29.
Appointment.
Initial appointment of judges for newly created circuits, Const. Ala., art. VI, §159.
Assignment of judges.
Temporary assignments, ARJA, Rule 13.
Attachments.
Issuance, §6-6-43.
Attendance.
Failure of judges to attend regular terms of court, Const. Ala., art. VI, §161.
Authority, §12-17-26.
Outside own circuit, §12-17-27.
Candidates for judgeship.
Designation of judgeship for which they are candidate, §12-17-21.
Canons of judicial ethics.
See CANONS OF JUDICIAL ETHICS.
Certiorari.
Writs of certiorari to district and municipal courts, §12-17-28.
Compensation, Const. Ala., art. VI, §150.
Retired judges on active duty status, §12-18-10.
Special judges, ARJA, Rule 14.
Conferences, seminars, etc.
Effect of failure to attend when attendance ordered, §12-1-18.
Reimbursement of travel expenses of judges attending, §12-1-18.
Death.
Retirement benefits.
Payment to spouses upon death of judges, §12-18-10.
Supernumerary judges.
Contribution for payment of benefits to spouse upon death of judge, §12-18-32.
Election by surviving spouses to obtain retirement benefits under provisions of article 1 of chapter, §12-18-33.
Different circuits.
Ordering of judges to attend and hold court in other circuits, §12-2-36.
Disability benefits, §12-18-10.
District attorneys.
Credit for time of service, §12-18-8.1.
District courts.
Supervision by presiding circuit judges, §12-12-10.
Writs of certiorari to district courts, §12-17-28.
Dual office holding, Const. Ala., art. VI, §150.

CIRCUIT COURTS—Cont'd
Judges—Cont'd
Duties, §12-17-26.
Retired judges, §12-18-7.
Retired judges on active duty status, §12-18-10.
Elections.
Canons of judicial ethics.
Political activity of judges, ACJE, Canons 7, 7A, 7B.
Generally. See within this heading, "Elections."
Expenses.
Travel expenses.
Reimbursement of travel expenses for attending conferences, seminars, etc., §12-1-18.
Extra judges.
Appointment of relief judges to assist in clearing dockets, §12-17-25.
General provisions.
See JUDGES.
Holding court for each other, Const. Ala., art. VI, §144.
Impeachment, Const. Ala., art. VII, §174.
Impeachment generally. See IMPEACHMENT.
Subject to impeachment, §36-11-1.
Incompetence.
Procedure when judge incompetent, Const. Ala., art. VI, §160.
Injunctions.
Power of circuit judges to issue writs returnable to courts of chancery, Const. Ala., art. VI, §144.
Jury box.
Emptying and refilling by circuit court judge, §12-16-45.
Municipal courts.
Writs of certiorari to municipal courts, §12-17-28.
Newly created circuits.
Initial appointment or election of judges, Const. Ala., art. VI, §159.
Numbering of judgeships in circuits with more than one judge, §12-17-21.
Number of judges, Const. Ala., amd. 328.
Increase or decrease in number.
Procedure when bill introduced in legislature, §12-1-5.
Number of resident judges in circuits, §12-17-20.
Oath of office.
Retired judges, §12-18-7.
Other circuits.
Ordering of judges to attend and hold court, etc., in other circuits, §12-2-36.

CIRCUIT COURTS—Cont'd
Judges—Cont'd
Pensions, §§12-18-1 to 12-18-41.
Powers.
County law libraries.
Appointment of librarians and custodians, §11-25-5.
Retired judges, §12-18-7.
Retired judges on active duty status, §12-18-10.
Presiding judges.
Selection, §12-17-23; ARJA, Rule 6.
Supervision of judges and other court personnel, §12-17-24.
Temporary assignment of judges and other court personnel, ARJA, Rule 13.
Qualifications, Const. Ala., art. VI, §154.
Receivers.
Appointment, §6-6-620.
Relief judges.
Appointment to assist in clearing dockets, §12-17-25.
Residence requirements, §12-17-22; Const. Ala., art. VI, §142.
Retirement, §§12-18-1 to 12-18-41.
Active duty status, §12-18-10.
Applicability of article to future additional state judicial offices, §12-18-12.
Applicability of article to judges elected or appointed after September 18, 1973, §12-18-5.
Benefits, §12-18-10.
Age sixty, §12-18-40.
Death.
Payment of benefits to spouses, §12-18-10.
Forfeiture of right to receive upon failure to file declaration of intention to retire, §12-18-7.
Compensation of retired judges on active duty status, §12-18-10.
Construction of article, §12-18-13.
Contributions to retirement fund by judges, §12-18-5.
Refund of contributions upon termination of service prior to eligibility for benefits, §12-18-8.
Transfer into judicial retirement fund, §12-18-8.
Credit for service as district or county court judge, §12-18-41.
Death.
Payment of benefits to spouses upon death of judges, §12-18-10.

CIRCUIT COURTS—Cont'd
Judges—Cont'd
Retirement—Cont'd
Declaration as to intention
to retire, §12-18-7.
Duties of retired judges,
§12-18-7.
Retired judges on active
duty status,
§12-18-10.
Election by judges holding
office on September 18,
1973, to come under
provisions of article,
§12-18-5.
Eligibility for retirement,
§12-18-6.
Entitlement to retirement
and receipt of pension,
§12-18-4.
Forfeiture of benefits upon
failure to file
declaration of
intention to retire,
§12-18-7.
Former county court
judges, district
attorneys or assistant
district attorneys
serving as circuit
judges on January 16,
1977.
Election to come under
provisions of article
1 of chapter,
§12-18-55.
Intention to retire.
Declaration as to
intention, §12-18-7.
Judicial retirement fund.
See JUDGES.
Military service.
Granting of credit for
military service,
§12-18-5.
Oath of retired judges,
§12-18-7.
Powers of retired judges,
§12-18-7.
Retired judges on active
duty status,
§12-18-10.
Prior service.
Crediting to circuit court
judges credit toward
supernumerary
status in position
other than circuit
judge, §12-18-11.
Receipt of credit for prior
service under
employees'
retirement system,
§12-18-8.
Prior to eligibility for
benefits.
Refund of contributions
to judicial
retirement fund,
§12-18-8.
Retirement order, §12-18-4.
Spouses.
Payment of benefits to
spouses upon death
of judges, §12-18-10.
State and local governing
bodies authorized to
pick up member
contributions,
§12-18-5.

CIRCUIT COURTS—Cont'd
Judges—Cont'd
Retirement—Cont'd
Time of service as full-time
state prosecutor,
§12-18-8.1.
Vacancies in office,
§12-18-9.
Salaries, §12-17-30; Const.
Ala., art. VI, §150.
Retired judges on active
duty status, §12-18-10.
Supplements, §12-17-30.
Secretarial services,
§12-17-340; ARJA, Rule
10.
Special judges.
Appointment, §12-1-14.
Compensation, ARJA, Rule
14.
Oath of office, §12-1-14.
Powers, §12-1-14.
Qualifications, §12-1-14.
Special sessions of court.
Forfeiture by judge failing
to order or attend
special session,
§12-2-37.
Supernumerary judges,
§§12-18-30 to 12-18-34.
Continuation of laws
concerning duties,
benefits, etc.,
§12-17-40.
Death.
Contribution for
payment to spouse of
supernumerary
judge upon death of
judge, §12-18-32.
Election by surviving
spouses to obtain
retirement benefits,
§12-18-33.
Prior service credit,
§12-18-11.
Retirement, §§12-18-30 to
12-18-34.
Benefits.
Contribution for
payment to spouse
of supernumerary
judge upon death
of judge,
§12-18-32.
Death.
Election by surviving
spouses to obtain
benefits under
provisions of
article 1 of
chapter, §12-18-33.
Effective date of article,
§12-18-34.
Election of judges
becoming
supernumerary
judges prior to
September 18, 1973
to come under
provisions of article
1, §12-18-30.
Supervision by presiding
judge, §12-17-24.
Temporary assignments,
ARJA, Rule 13.

CIRCUIT COURTS—Cont'd
Judges—Cont'd
Terms of office, Const. Ala.,
art. VI, §155.
Incumbents.
Terms of incumbents not
abridged, Const.
Ala., art. VI, §172.
Travel expenses.
Reimbursement of
expenses of attending
conferences, seminars,
etc., §12-1-18.
Vacancies, §12-18-9; Const.
Ala., art. VI, §158.
Judgments.
Notice of judgments, ARCP,
Rule 77 (d).
Record of final judgments in
minute book or on
microfilm, ARCP, Rule
79 (b).
Judicial circuits.
Certain statutes relative to
judicial circuits
continued in effect,
§12-1-22.
Jurisdiction, Const. Ala., art.
VI, §143; amd. 328.
Appellate jurisdiction,
§12-11-30.
Civil jurisdiction, §12-11-30.
Contempt, §12-11-30.
Criminal jurisdiction,
§12-11-30.
Vesting, §12-1-3.
Equitable jurisdiction,
§12-11-31.
Cases of which circuit
courts take cognizance
in equitable matters,
§12-11-33.
Funeral services.
Prosecutions arising under
chapter, §34-13-5.
Generally, §12-11-30.
Juvenile proceedings,
§§12-12-34, 12-15-2.
Legislature may confer
jurisdiction of circuit and
chancery court on either
court, Const. Ala., art.
VI, §148.
Partition, §35-6-20.
Public utility corporations.
Sale of property, §12-11-32.
Superintendence of district,
municipal and probate
courts, §12-11-30.
Jurors.
Fees, §12-19-110.
Juries generally.
See JURY.
Juvenile proceedings.
Commitment proceedings.
Transfer of cases,
§12-11-10.
General provisions.
See JUVENILE
PROCEEDINGS.
Jurisdiction, §§12-12-34,
12-15-2.
Landlord and tenant.
Possession wrongfully
withheld.
Removal of action to
circuit court, §35-9-83.
Litigation accountability.
General provisions,
§§12-19-270 to 12-19-276.
See COURTS.

CIRCUIT COURTS—Cont'd

Location.

Circuit court in every county, §12-11-1.

Circuit court to be held in each county at courthouse, §12-11-3.

Maps and plats.

Town surveys, maps or plats. Vacation and annulment by circuit court, §§35-2-58 to 35-2-62.

Military affairs.

Ordering out of troops. Request of judge to governor, §31-2-111.

Mines and minerals.

Abandoned mine reclamation. Review of landowner's actions, §9-16-128.

Motion day, ARCP, Rule 78.

Motor vehicle carriers.

Appeals from final action or orders of commission to circuit court, §37-3-29.

Motor vehicles.

Abandoned motor vehicles. Fee for filing a report of sale, §12-19-76.

Municipal corporations.

Appeals from judgments of circuit courts, §12-14-71.

Assessments for public improvements. See MUNICIPAL CORPORATIONS.

Costs.

Docket fees, fines, etc., collected in municipal ordinance cases. Distribution, Inapplicability of provisions, §12-19-155.

Prosecution assistance by municipality, ARJA, Rule 17.

Town surveys, maps or plats. Vacation and annulment of map or plat, §§35-2-58 to 35-2-62.

Municipal courts.

Appeals, §§12-14-70, 12-14-71, 12-19-150, 12-19-153.

Superintendence of municipal courts, §12-11-30.

Notice.

Fees.

Administrative fee for periodic payments. Notice of fee, §12-19-26.

Orders or judgments, ARCP, Rule 77 (d).

Number of circuits, §12-11-2.

Officers and employees.

Benefits.

State assumption of retirement and other employee benefits, §12-17-4.

Compensation.

Clerks of court. See within this heading, "Clerks of court."

Establishment of rates of compensation, §12-17-2.

Conferences, seminars, etc., §12-1-18.

CIRCUIT COURTS—Cont'd

Officers and employees —Cont'd

Controversies as to composition of court personnel. Determination of controversies, §12-17-1.

County personnel serving circuit courts to become employees of state, §12-17-1.

Expenses.

Expenses incurred at locations other than principal court site. Reimbursement, §12-17-3.

Reimbursement of officers and employees attending conferences, seminars, etc., §12-1-18.

Job descriptions. Establishment, §12-17-2.

Merit system, §12-17-1.

Retirement system, §12-17-1.

State assumption of retirement and other employee benefits, §12-17-4.

State employee personnel system. Court personnel included in, §12-17-2.

Supervision by presiding judges, §12-17-24.

Orders of court.

Notice of orders, ARCP, Rule 77 (d).

Record of appealable orders in minute book or on microfilm, ARCP, Rule 79 (b).

Papers.

Substitution of lost or destroyed papers or records in civil cases, §§12-20-26 to 12-20-31. See COURTS.

Partition.

Annulment of partition, §35-6-50.

General provisions, §§35-6-20 to 35-6-25. See PARTITION.

Pensions.

Judges.

Retirement.

Generally, §§12-18-1 to 12-18-41. See within this heading, "Judges."

Judicial retirement fund. See JUDGES.

Pipelines.

Gas pipeline systems. Jurisdiction of circuit court, §37-4-86.

Probate courts.

Administration of estates. Removal of administration from probate court, §12-11-41.

Correction of errors in probate court. Irregular sales of lands under decrees of court of probate may be confirmed, §12-11-61.

CIRCUIT COURTS—Cont'd

Probate courts—Cont'd

Settlements of estates. Correction of errors in probate court, §12-11-60.

Superintendence of probate courts, §12-11-30.

Process.

Special sessions, §12-11-7.

Public defenders.

General provisions. See PUBLIC DEFENDERS.

Public service commission.

Appeals.

Right of appeal to circuit court of Montgomery county, §37-1-120.

Orders of commission. Power of circuit court to compel compliance, §37-1-104.

Public utilities.

Appeals.

Purchase of property by municipality or governmental agency. Forced sales. Appeals to circuit court, §37-4-63.

Jurisdiction to sell property and franchises, §12-11-32.

Railroads.

Judgment confirming commission award regulating railroad's business with connecting line. Violation of circuit court judgment, §37-8-118.

Receivers.

Appointment, §§6-6-620, 6-6-621.

Recordation generally. See RECORDATION.

Records.

Clerks of court. See within this heading, "Clerks of court."

Courts generally. See COURTS.

Registers. See within this heading, "Registers."

Redemption of real estate.

Settlement and adjustment of rights and equities when complaint filed, §6-5-256.

Registers.

Appointment, Const. Ala., art. VI, §163.

Bonds, surety, §12-17-111.

Clerks of court. Clerk may serve as register in chancery, Const. Ala., art. VI, §165.

Compensation, Const. Ala., art. VI, §163.

Annual salary, §12-17-81.

Registers to be paid by state, §12-17-80.

Contempt. Punishment for contempt by registers, §12-17-121.

Costs on appeal. Execution for unpaid costs, §12-22-76.

CIRCUIT COURTS—Cont'd
Registers—Cont'd
Dockets.
Duties of register,
§12-17-114.
Duties, §12-17-114; ARJA,
Rule 4.
Failure to perform,
§12-17-114.
Employees.
Compensation, §12-17-112.
Employees in offices of
registers to be paid by
state, §12-17-80.
Endorsement of papers with
date of filing, §12-17-115.
Fees.
Indices.
Fees for keeping indexes
not allowed,
§12-19-98.
Uniformity of fees, Const.
Ala., art. VI, §163.
Fiduciary funds in hands of
officials, §§19-3-80 to
19-3-87.
See FIDUCIARIES.
Indices.
Fees for keeping indexes
not allowed, §12-19-98.
General direct and reverse
indices, §12-17-117.
Injunctions, §12-17-116.
Office.
Place of office, §12-17-113.
Office hours.
Closing offices.
Effect on computation of
time periods, ARJA,
Rule 5.
Routine work days, ARJA,
Rule 5.
Saturdays, Sundays and
other holidays, ARJA,
Rule 5.
Conflicting state and
county holidays,
ARJA, Rule 5.
Severe weather, hazardous
or other emergency
conditions, ARJA, Rule
5.
Office not to be filled when
vacancy occurs,
§12-17-110.
Place of office, §12-17-113.
Preservation of office of
register, ARCP, Rule 81
(d).
Qualifications, Const. Ala.,
art. VI, §163.
Reappointment.
Registers holding office on
October 10, 1975,
§12-17-110.
Receivers.
Appointment, §6-6-620.
Appeal, §6-6-621.
Record on appeal.
Liability of register for
delayed or defective
record, §12-22-60.
Records.
Indices.
General direct and
reverse indices,
§12-17-117.
Open to examination,
§12-17-119.
Recopying, §12-17-118.

CIRCUIT COURTS—Cont'd
Registers—Cont'd
Records—Cont'd
Taking file in pending
action from office of
register, §12-20-25.
Removal, §12-17-110; Const.
Ala., art. VI, §166.
Rules of judicial
administration.
See COURTS.
Salaries, Const. Ala., art. VI,
§163.
Annual salary, §12-17-81.
Registers and employees in
offices of registers to
be paid by state,
§12-17-80.
Successors.
Payment of money to
successor, §12-17-120.
Summary proceedings
involving officials.
Clerks and registers in
general, §§6-6-700,
6-6-723.
Supernumerary clerks and
registers, §§12-17-140 to
12-17-147. See within
this heading,
"Supernumerary clerks
and registers."
Supernumerary fund.
Contributions by registers
to supernumerary
fund, §12-17-143.
Terms of office, Const. Ala.,
art. VI, §163.
Incumbents.
Terms of incumbents not
abridged, Const.
Ala., art. VI, §172.
Vacancies.
Office not to be filled when
vacancy occurs,
§12-17-110.
Vacancies in office of
register in counties
where supernumerary
holds commission,
§12-17-141.
Reporters, §§12-17-270 to
12-17-293.
Additional positions.
Authorization by
administrative director
of courts, §12-17-271.
Appointment, §12-17-270.
Compensation, §12-17-274.
Supernumerary reporters,
§12-17-292.
Appropriation for
salaries, §12-17-293.
Continuation of existing
positions, §12-17-271.
Costs.
Fee for court reporter.
Taxed as costs in cases
utilizing reporter,
§12-17-277.
Duties, §12-17-275.
Supernumerary reporters,
§12-17-291.
Existing positions continued,
§12-17-271.
Fees.
Taxed as costs in cases
utilizing reporter,
§12-17-277.
Transcript fees, §12-17-276.

CIRCUIT COURTS—Cont'd
Reporters—Cont'd
Oath, §12-17-273.
Supernumerary reporters,
§12-17-291.
Official court reporters,
ARJA, Rule 12.
Powers.
Supernumerary reporters,
§12-17-291.
Qualifications, §12-17-270.
Removal, §12-17-270.
Reporter of decisions of
supreme court and courts
of appeals.
State employees'
retirement system.
Election by official court
reporter to be
covered by
employees'
retirement system,
§36-27-52.
Roving reporters.
Special roving reporters,
§12-17-272; ARJA,
Rule 12.
Salaries, §12-17-274.
Supernumerary reporters,
§12-17-292.
Appropriation for
salaries, §12-17-293.
Special court reporters.
Requests for, ARJA, Rule
12.
Roving reporters,
§12-17-272; ARJA,
Rule 12.
State employees' retirement
system.
Election by to be covered
by system, §36-27-52.
Supernumerary circuit court
reporters, §§12-17-290 to
12-17-293.
Appropriation for salaries,
§12-17-293.
Compensation, §12-17-293.
Duties, §12-17-291.
Oath, §12-17-291.
Powers, §12-17-291.
Qualifications for
becoming, §12-17-290.
Salary, §12-17-293.
Term, §12-17-292.
Term of office, §12-17-270.
Supernumerary reporters,
§12-17-292.
Transcript fees, §12-17-276.
Reports.
Clerks of court.
Monthly reports as to
fines, fees, etc.,
collected, §12-1-19.
Retirement.
Judges.
Generally, §§12-18-1 to
12-18-41. See within
this heading, "Judges."
Judicial retirement fund.
See JUDGES.
Officers and employees,
§§12-17-1, 12-17-4.
Rules of civil procedure.
See RULES OF CIVIL
PROCEDURE.
**Rules of judicial
administration generally.**
See COURTS.

CIRCUIT COURTS—Cont'd
Salaries.
Clerks of court. See within this heading, "Clerks of court."
Judges. See within this heading, "Judges."
Officers and employees.
Establishment of notes of compensation, §12-17-2.
Registers. See within this heading, "Registers."
Reporters, §§12-17-274, 12-17-292, 12-17-293.
Savings and loan associations.
Appeals from orders of savings and loan board, §5-2A-63.
Seals and sealed instruments.
Seal of court, ARJA, Rule 24.
Secretaries.
Clerks of court.
Secretaries for clerks, §12-17-341; ARJA, Rule 15.
Judicial secretaries, §12-17-340.
Service of process.
Defendant service fees, §12-19-73.
Fee for issuance of witness subpoenas, §12-19-74.
Sessions of court.
Defined, §12-11-8.
Regular sessions.
Provision for regular sessions, §12-11-5.
Special sessions.
District attorneys, §§12-2-34, 12-2-35, 12-2-37.
Notice of special sessions, §12-11-6.
Ordering by chief justice, §12-2-33.
Process for special sessions, §12-11-7.
Provisions for special sessions, §12-11-5.
Witnesses, §12-11-7.
Small loans.
Appeals from acts of bureau or supervisor, §5-2A-82.
Solicitors, Const. Ala., art. VI, §167.
Abolition of office, §12-12-9.
Designation of circuit solicitor as district attorney, Const. Ala., amd. 226.
District attorneys.
General provisions.
See DISTRICT ATTORNEYS.
Performance of functions by assistant district attorneys, §12-12-9.
Impeachment, Const. Ala., art. VII, §174.
Sundays.
Clerks of court and registers.
Office hours.
Saturdays, Sundays and other holidays, ARJA, Rule 5.
Supernumerary circuit judges. See within this heading, "Judges."

CIRCUIT COURTS—Cont'd
Supernumerary clerks and registers, §§12-17-140 to 12-17-147.
Applicability of division, §§12-17-140, 12-17-145.
Compensation, §12-17-142.
Contributions.
Contributions to other plans.
Refund, §12-17-146.
Contributions to supernumerary fund, §12-17-143.
Inclusion of prior service credit, §12-17-147.
Return of contributions upon termination of service, §12-17-147.
Death prior to receiving benefits equal to total contributions, §12-17-147.
Fund, §12-17-143.
Oath of office, §12-17-141.
Officials covered by division, §12-17-145.
Prior service credit, §12-17-144.
Qualifications for supernumerary status, §12-17-140.
Service credit.
Prior service credit, §12-17-144.
Termination of service.
Return of contributions upon termination of service, §12-17-147.
Death prior to receiving supernumerary benefits equal to total contributions, §12-17-147.
Term of office, §12-17-142.
Vacancies in office of clerk or register in counties where supernumerary holds commission, §12-17-141.
Supernumerary reports, §§12-17-290 to 12-17-293.
Suretyship.
Court in which complaints filed, §8-3-15.
Teachers' retirement system.
Clerks of court.
Purchase of service credit for full time employment in office of clerk, §16-25-11.4.
Transfer of cases.
Between circuit and district court, §12-11-9.
Involuntary juvenile commitment proceedings, §12-11-10.
Transfer to another court in same county, §12-11-11.
Trial.
Conduct in open court, ARCP, Rule 77 (b).
Trusts and trustees.
Removal of trust estate to another state.
Power of circuit court to authorize removal of trust estate, §19-3-190.
Utilities.
Courthouse offices, §11-12-13.

CIRCUIT COURTS—Cont'd
When held, Const. Ala., art. VI, §144.
When open, §12-11-4.
Where held, Const. Ala., art. VI, §144.
Wills.
Contesting validity after admission to probate, §§43-8-199, 43-8-202.
Witnesses.
Criminal cases, §12-22-111.
Fees generally.
See WITNESSES.
Special sessions, §12-11-7.
Workmen's compensation.
Determination of disputed compensation claims, §25-5-81.
Rules.
Chief justice of supreme court to prepare uniform rules for circuit courts, §25-5-12.

CIRCUIT SOLICITORS.
See CIRCUIT COURTS.

CIRCUSES.
Licenses, §40-12-74.

CISTERNS.
Municipal corporations.
Construction, regulation, etc., of public cisterns, etc., §11-47-140.

CITIES AND TOWNS.
General provisions.
See MUNICIPAL CORPORATIONS.

CITIZENS' ARREST.
Arrest by private persons, §15-10-7.

CITIZENS' BAND RADIOS.
Motor vehicle tags and plates.
See MOTOR VEHICLES.

CITIZENSHIP.
Constitutional provisions, Const. U. S., Art. IV, §2.
Rights and immunities of citizens, Const. U. S., Amendment XIV.
Jury.
Qualifications of jurors, §12-16-60.
Pilots and pilotage.
Qualifications of pilots, §33-4-31.
Rights and immunities of citizens, Const. U. S., Amendment XIV.

CITRONELLE, MUNICIPALITY OF.
Property tax, Const. Ala., amd. 13.

CIVIC CENTERS.
Constitution of Alabama.
Bonds for civic centers in certain counties, Const. Ala., amds. 238, 280.

CIVIC ORGANIZATIONS.
Exemptions from taxation, §11-54-61.
Fraternal benefit societies.
See FRATERNAL BENEFIT SOCIETIES.

CIVIC ORGANIZATIONS
—Cont'd
Municipal corporations.
Projects for provision of
buildings for national
organizations, §§11-54-50
to 11-54-62.
See MUNICIPAL
CORPORATIONS.

CIVIL ACTIONS.
See ACTIONS.

CIVIL AIR PATROL.
Motor vehicles.
License taxes and
registration fees.
Exemption, §40-12-244.
Tags and plates.
Amateur radio operators
licensed by civil air
patrol, §§32-6-90 to
32-6-93.

CIVIL DEFENSE, §§31-9-1 to
31-9-24.
Advisory council.
Insurance for civil defense
workers and trainees.
Recommendation of
council, §31-9-21.
Agency.
Emergency management
agency, §31-9-4.
**Anarchy and subversive
activities.**
Employment of subversives
by civil defense
organizations, §31-9-20.
Appropriations.
Regular and emergency
appropriations, §31-9-24.
Arrest.
Arrest without warrant.
Orders, rules and
regulations of
governor.
Arrest for violating or
attempting to
violate, §31-9-15.
Citation, §31-9-1.
Civil defense workers.
Defined, §31-9-16.
Employment of subversives
by civil defense
organizations, §31-9-20.
Insurance.
Compensation insurance
for workers, §31-9-21.
Loyalty oath, §31-9-20.
Powers and duties, §31-9-16.
Privileges and immunities,
§31-9-16.
Compacts.
Mutual interstate aid
agreements and
compacts, §31-9-7.
**Construction and
interpretation.**
Chapter to be liberally
construed, §31-9-23.
Contracts.
Insurance.
Compensation insurance
for civil defense
workers and trainees,
§31-9-21.
Counties.
Employees.
Powers and duties of
employees rendering
outside aid, §31-9-11.

CIVIL DEFENSE—Cont'd
Counties—Cont'd
Immunity from liability for
torts resulting from civil
defense activities,
§31-9-16.
Officers.
Military service in time of
national emergency or
war.
See COUNTIES.
Powers with respect to civil
defense generally,
§31-9-10.
State grants to political
subdivisions, §31-9-24.
Declarations of necessity,
§31-9-2.
Definitions, §31-9-3.
**Director of emergency
management agency,**
§31-9-4.
Emergencies.
Appropriations, §31-9-24.
Powers of governor during
emergencies, §31-9-8.
Proclamation by governor,
§31-9-8.
Emergency management act.
Generally, §§31-9-1 to
31-9-24.
**Emergency management
agency.**
Creation, §31-9-4.
Director.
Appointment, §31-9-4.
Duties, §31-9-4.
Employment of personnel,
§31-9-4.
Head of agency, §31-9-4.
Head of agency.
Director of emergency
management, §31-9-4.
Personnel.
Appointment by director,
§31-9-4.
**Findings and declarations of
necessity,** §31-9-2.
Gifts.
Acceptance by governor of
gifts from private
persons, §31-9-18.
Governor.
Emergency powers of
governor, §31-9-8.
Federal government.
Governor may accept
services, §31-9-18.
Mutual interstate aid
agreements and
compacts, §31-9-7.
Orders, rules and regulations
of governor.
Arrest without warrant for
violating or attempting
to violate, §31-9-15.
Distribution, §31-9-13.
Effect, §31-9-13.
Enforcement, §31-9-14.
Plan and program for civil
defense of state.
Governor to prepare,
§31-9-6.
Powers and duties generally,
§31-9-6.
Private persons.
Acceptance of services from
private persons,
§31-9-18.
Proclamation of emergency,
§31-9-8.

CIVIL DEFENSE—Cont'd
Insurance.
Civil defense workers and
trainees.
Compensation insurance,
§31-9-21.
**Liberal construction of
chapter,** §31-9-23.
Licenses.
Exemptions of civil defense
workers from license
requirements, §31-9-16.
Shelters.
Liability of persons
granting use, §31-9-17.
Local organizations.
Defined, §31-9-3.
Directors.
Mutual aid agreements.
Powers and duties of
directors as to
mutual aid
agreements, §31-9-9.
Establishment, §31-9-10.
Mutual aid agreements.
Powers and duties of
directors as to, §31-9-9.
Powers, §31-9-10.
Mobile support units.
Operation in other states,
§31-9-12.
Reimbursement of expenses
of operation of units of
other states, §31-9-12.
Municipal corporations.
Employees.
Powers and duties of
employees rendering
outside aid, §31-9-11.
Officers.
Military service in time of
national emergency of
war.
See MUNICIPAL
CORPORATIONS.
Powers with respect to civil
defense generally,
§31-9-10.
State grants to political
subdivisions, §31-9-24.
Torts.
Immunity of municipalities
from liability for torts
resulting from civil
defense activities,
§31-9-16.
Oaths.
Loyalty oath, §31-9-20.
Other states.
Mobile support units.
Reimbursement of
expenses of operation,
§31-9-12.
Penalties.
Violations, §31-9-22.
**Political activities by civil
defense organizations,**
§31-9-19.
Political subdivisions.
Defined, §31-9-3.
Employees.
Powers, duties, etc., of
employees rendering
outside aid, §31-9-11.
Powers with respect to civil
defense, §31-9-10.

CIVIL DEFENSE—Cont'd
Political subdivisions
—Cont'd
Torts.
Immunity of political
subdivisions from
liability for torts
resulting from civil
defense activities,
§31-9-16.
**Public officers and
employees.**
Military service in time of
national emergency or
war.
County officers.
See COUNTIES.
General provisions,
§§36-8-1 to 36-8-6.
See PUBLIC OFFICERS
AND EMPLOYEES.
Municipal officers.
See MUNICIPAL
CORPORATIONS.
Public policy, §31-9-2.
Purpose of chapter, §31-9-2.
Real property.
Shelters.
Liability of persons
granting for use of real
estate for shelters,
§31-9-17.
Short title, §31-9-1.
State.
Torts.
Immunity form liability
resulting from civil
defense activities,
§31-9-16.
**State grants to political
subdivisions,** §31-9-24.
**State officers and
employees.**
Military service in times of
national emergency or
war, §§36-8-1 to 36-8-6.
See PUBLIC OFFICERS
AND EMPLOYEES.
Title, §31-9-1.
Torts.
Immunity of state from
liability for torts,
§31-9-16.
Shelters.
Exemption from tort
liability.
Persons granting use,
§31-9-17.
United States.
Acceptance of services from
federal government by
governor, §31-9-18.
Warrants.
Governor.
Orders, rules and
regulations of
governor.
Arrest without warrant
for violating or
attempting to
violate, §31-9-15.

**CIVIL PROCEDURAL
RULES.**
See RULES OF CIVIL
PROCEDURE.

CIVIL SERVICE.
Merit system.
General provisions.
See PUBLIC OFFICERS
AND EMPLOYEES.

CIVIL SERVICE—Cont'd
**Municipalities having less
than 5,000 inhabitants,**
§11-43-5.1.
**Municipal law enforcement
officers,** §§11-43-180 to
11-43-190.
See MUNICIPAL
CORPORATIONS.

CLAIM AND DELIVERY.
Personal property.
Trial of right of property,
§§6-6-160 to 6-6-168.
See PERSONAL
PROPERTY.

CLAIMS.
Fraudulent transfers.
Extinguishment for claim for
relief, §8-9A-9.
Frivolous claims.
Litigation accountability,
§§12-19-270 to 12-19-276.
See COURTS.
Insurance.
See INSURANCE.

CLAIMS AGAINST STATE.
Agents.
Claimant may prosecute
claim against state in
person or by counsel or
agent, §41-9-63.
**Appropriations for payment
of awards,** §41-9-73.
Attorney general.
Attorney general may be
required to defend suits
against state, Const.
Ala., amd. 111.
**Award for payment of
damages.**
Appropriations for payment
of awards, §41-9-73.
Board of corrections officials.
Payment by board of
adjustment, §41-9-74.
Entry of award, §§41-9-68,
41-9-69.
Limitation on amount of
award for personal injury
or death, §41-9-70.
Secretary of board to deliver
certified copy of awards,
§41-9-71.
Warrants.
Comptroller to draw
warrant in favor of
persons, etc., found
entitled to damages,
§41-9-71.
Payment by treasurer of
warrants drawn
pursuant to findings
and awards of board,
§41-9-72.
Barred claims.
Claims based on void
warrants, §41-4-60.
Board of adjustment,
§§41-9-60 to 41-9-74.
Award for payment of
damages.
Limitation on amount of
award for personal
injury or death,
§41-9-70.
Secretary to deliver
certified copy of
awards, §41-9-71.

CLAIMS AGAINST STATE
—Cont'd
Board of adjustment—Cont'd
Clerical help.
Employment for
investigation of claims,
etc., §41-9-67.
Composition, §41-9-61.
Counties.
Employees of counties not
within jurisdiction of
board, §41-9-62.
Creation, §41-9-61.
Evidence.
Board may adopt rules of
evidence, §41-9-66.
Executive or secret sessions.
Prohibited, §13A-14-2.
Findings.
Secretary to deliver
certified copy of
findings, §41-9-71.
Forms.
Board may prescribe forms,
§41-9-66.
History of cases.
Secretary of board to
prepare, §41-9-71.
Interviews.
Conduct, §41-9-61.
Investigation of claims.
Employment of clerical
help for investigation,
§41-9-67.
Jurisdiction.
Claims within jurisdiction
of board, §41-9-62.
Legal division of department
of finance.
Representation of board of
adjustment, §41-4-204.
Meetings.
Attorney general to attend
meetings of board,
§41-9-61.
Municipal corporations.
Employees of
municipalities not
within jurisdiction of
board, §41-9-62.
Officers, §41-9-61.
Production of documents, etc.
Powers of board as to
requirement of
production, §41-9-67.
Purpose of division, §41-9-60.
Quarters, §41-9-61.
Quorum, §41-9-61.
Records of cases.
Board to supervise.
Preparation of records,
§41-9-61.
Rules of evidence and
procedure.
Board may adopt, §41-9-66.
Views.
Board may take views,
§41-9-61.
Civil defense.
Immunity from liability
arising from civil defense
activities, §31-9-16.
**Compromise of claims in
favor of state,** §41-1-3.
Comptroller.
May require proof of
correctness of claim,
§41-4-61.
Constitutional provisions,
Const. U. S., Amendment
XI.

CLAIMS AGAINST STATE
—Cont'd
Correctness of claim.
Comptroller may require
proof, §41-4-61.
Damages.
Board of corrections.
Payment by board of
adjustment, §41-9-74.
Determination of agency,
commission, etc., of state
inflicting injury or
damage, §41-9-69.
Determination of amount of
damage, §41-9-68.
Entry of award for payment
of damages.
Payment out of funds
appropriated to
agency, commission,
etc., inflicting damage,
§41-9-69.
Limitation on amount of
award for personal injury
or death, §41-9-70.
Warrants.
Comptroller to draw
warrant in favor of
persons, etc., found
entitled to damages,
§41-9-71.
Death.
Claims against state for
death to be made by
personal representative,
§41-9-64.
Limitation on amount of
award for death,
§41-9-70.
Evidence.
Board of adjustment may
adopt rules of evidence,
§41-9-66.
**Executors and
administrators.**
Claims against state for
death to be made by
personal representative,
§41-9-64.
Forms.
Board of adjustment.
Board may prescribe forms,
§41-9-66.
Injury.
Determination of agency,
commission, etc., of state
inflicting injury,
§41-9-69.
Determination of amount of
injury, §41-9-68.
Investigation of claims.
Board of adjustment.
Employment of clerical
help for investigation,
§41-9-67.
Jurisdiction.
Board of adjustment,
§41-9-62.
Limitation of actions.
Award for personal injury or
death.
Limitation on amount of
award, §41-9-70.
Presentation of claims
against state, §41-9-65.
Personal injury.
Limitation on amount of
award for personal
injury, §41-9-70.

CLAIMS AGAINST STATE
—Cont'd
**Presentation of claims
against state.**
Limitation periods, §41-9-65.
**Proof of correctness of
claim.**
Comptroller may require,
§41-4-61.
**Prosecution of claim against
state.**
Claimant may prosecute in
person or by counsel or
agent, §41-9-63.
Rewards.
Arrest and conviction of
criminals.
Deciding entitlement to
reward, §15-9-4.
State auditor.
Proof of correctness of claim.
Authority to require,
§36-16-2.
Void warrants.
Claims based on void
warrants barred,
§41-4-60.
Warrants.
Comptroller to draw warrant
in favor of persons found
entitled to damages,
§41-9-71.
Payment by treasurer of
warrants drawn
pursuant to findings and
awards of board,
§41-9-72.
Wrongful death.
Claims for death to be made
by personal
representative, §41-9-64.
Limitation on amount of
award for death,
§41-9-70.

CLAIRVOYANTS.
Licenses.
Fee, §40-12-104.

CLARKE COUNTY.
Court costs and charges,
Const. Ala., amd. 416.
Economic development,
Const. Ala., amd. 217.
Fire districts, Const. Ala.,
amd. 464.
Fires and fire prevention.
Fire districts, Const. Ala.,
amd. 464.
Probate judge.
Compensation, Const. Ala.,
amd. 478.
School tax.
Additional tax for school
purposes, Const. Ala.,
amd. 168.

CLASS ACTIONS.
Rules of civil procedure,
ARCP, Rule 23.

CLAY.
Sale of right to quarry clay,
§35-4-381.

CLAY COUNTY.
Barbers.
Chapter not applicable to
Clay county, §34-5-15.
Courts.
Costs and charges, Const.
Ala., amd. 359.

CLAY COUNTY—Cont'd
Officers.
Compensation, Const. Ala.,
amd. 359.
School tax.
Special school tax in Clay
county, Const. Ala., amd.
169.

**CLAYTON, MUNICIPALITY
OF.**
Property tax, Const. Ala.,
amd. 17.

**CLEANERS, DYERS AND
PRESSERS.**
Licenses.
Cleaning and pressing
establishments,
§40-12-75.
Diaper services, §40-12-117.
Hat-cleaning establishments,
§40-12-109.
Laundered towel, apron, etc.,
rentals, §40-12-117.
Laundries, §40-12-118.
Liens.
Declaration of lien,
§35-11-170.
Enforcement of lien,
§35-11-171.
Sale of articles, §35-11-171.
Lost or unclaimed property.
Disposition of unclaimed
articles left for service,
§35-12-6.

**CLEARINGHOUSE
CERTIFICATES,**
§§5-10A-12, 5-10A-13.

CLEBURNE COUNTY.
Court costs and charges,
Const. Ala., amds. 331,
347.
Officers.
Compensation, Const. Ala.,
amds. 331, 347.
School tax.
Special school district taxes,
Const. Ala., amd. 123.

CLERGY.
Corporations.
Conference of ministers,
§§10-4-40 to 10-4-43.
Fraud.
Fraudulently pretending to
be clergyman, §13A-14-4.
Funerals.
Burial permits.
Ministers at funerals to
ascertain if permit has
been secured, §22-19-4.
Prisons and prisoners.
Chaplains, §14-3-12.
Privileged communications.
Legal or quasi-legal
proceedings, §12-21-166.

CLERKS OF COURT.
Attorneys at law.
Attorneys not deemed
sufficient sureties on
official bond of certain
clerks, §36-5-13.
Practice of law by clerks.
Prohbiited, §34-3-8.
Register or clerk of
circuit court,
§§34-3-10, 34-3-14.

CLERKS OF COURT—Cont'd
Bonds, surety, ARJA, Rule 1.
Attorneys not deemed
sufficient sureties on
official bonds of certain
clerks, §36-5-13.
Circuit court clerks.
See CIRCUIT COURTS.
Constitution of Alabama.
See CONSTITUTION OF
ALABAMA.
Court of civil appeals.
See COURT OF CIVIL
APPEALS.
Court of criminal appeals.
See COURT OF CRIMINAL
APPEALS.
District courts.
See DISTRICT COURTS.
**Fiduciary funds in hands of
officials,** §§19-3-80 to
19-3-87.
See FIDUCIARIES.
**Financial systems for
receipt, deposit and
disbursement of funds.**
Assistance in development,
ARJA, Rule 28.
Funds.
Fiduciary funds in hands of
officials, §§19-3-80 to
19-3-87.
See FIDUCIARIES.
Guardian and ward.
Uniform guardianship and
protective proceedings
act.
Records and certified
copies.
Duties, §26-2A-34.
Impeachment, Const. Ala.,
art. VII, §175.
General provisions.
See IMPEACHMENT.
Motor vehicles.
Uniform traffic infractions.
Fines and court costs paid
to, ARJA, Rule 19.
Municipal courts.
Monthly reports as to fines
collected, §12-1-19.
Pending actions.
Taking file in pending action
from office of clerk,
§12-20-25.
**Rules of judicial
administration.**
See COURTS.
**Selection of clerks of
inferior courts,** Const.
Ala., art. VI, §164; amd.
271.
**State employees' retirement
system.**
Election by official court
reporter to be covered
by, §36-27-52.
**Summary proceedings
involving officials.**
Clerks and registers in
general, §§6-6-700,
6-6-723.
**Supernumerary clerks and
registers,** §§12-17-140 to
12-17-147.
See CIRCUIT COURTS.
Supreme court.
See SUPREME COURT.

CLERKS OF COURT—Cont'd
Trusts and trustees.
Fiduciary funds in hands of
officials, §§19-3-80 to
19-3-87.
See FIDUCIARIES.
Workmen's compensation.
Report of disposition of cases.
Circuit court clerks to
report, §25-5-6.
Writs of error.
Duty of clerk, §12-22-220.

CLINICS.
Medical clinic boards,
§§11-58-1 to 11-58-15.
See MUNICIPAL
CORPORATIONS.

CLIO, MUNICIPALITY OF.
Property tax, Const. Ala.,
amd. 17.

CLOSE CORPORATIONS,
§§10-2A-300 to 10-2A-313.
See CORPORATIONS.

CLUBS.
Alcoholic beverages.
See ALCOHOLIC
BEVERAGES.
Shrine motorcycle clubs,
§§32-6-190, 32-6-191.
Societies generally.
See SOCIETIES.

COAL.
**Abandoned mine
reclamation,** §§9-16-120 to
9-16-134.
Acquisition and disposition of
lands, §9-16-127.
Actions.
Landowner's actions,
§9-16-128.
Prior right of purchase,
§9-16-128.
Review by director or
court, §9-16-128.
Boards and commissions.
Interagency cooperation,
§9-16-131.
Definitions, §9-16-121.
Director.
Functions, §9-16-133.
Landowner's actions.
Review by director,
§9-16-128.
Powers, §9-16-133.
Disposition of lands,
§9-16-127.
Eligibility for reclamation.
Lands and waters eligible,
§9-16-124.
Filling voids, §9-16-130.
Funds.
Creation of abandoned
mine reclamation fund,
§9-16-122.
Priorities of expenditures
of monies from fund,
§9-16-123.
Purposes of abandoned
mine reclamation fund,
§9-16-122.
Special abandoned mine
reclamation trust fund,
§9-16-135.
Injunctive relief, §9-16-132.
Insurance.
Workmen's compensation,
§9-16-134.
Interagency cooperation,
§9-16-131.

COAL—Cont'd
**Abandoned mine
reclamation**—Cont'd
Landowner's actions,
§9-16-128.
Prior right of purchase,
§9-16-128.
Review by director or
court, §9-16-128.
Lands and waters eligible for
reclamation, §9-16-124.
Legislative intent, §9-16-120.
Liens.
Property subject to lien,
§9-16-129.
Amount, §9-16-129.
Priority, §9-16-129.
Statement by director,
§9-16-129.
Priorities of reclamation,
§9-16-123.
Program of reclamation,
§9-16-125.
Property subject to lien,
§9-16-129.
Amount, §9-16-129.
Priority, §9-16-129.
Statement by director,
§9-16-129.
Right of entry, §9-16-126.
Sealing tunnels, §9-16-130.
Shafts.
Sealing shafts, §9-16-130.
Special abandoned mine
reclamation trust fund,
§9-16-135.
State departments and
agencies.
Interagency cooperation,
§9-16-131.
Tunnels.
Sealing tunnels, §9-16-130.
Voids.
Filling voids, §9-16-130.
Workmen's compensation,
§9-16-134.
Accidents.
Coal mine safety. See within
this heading, "Mine
safety."
Actions.
Abandoned mine
reclamation.
Landowner's actions,
§9-16-128.
Surface mining control and
reclamation.
Citizen's actions, §9-16-95.
Adjacent landowners,
§§25-9-320 to 25-9-322.
Adulteration.
Coal mixed with other
substances or with
different quality,
§13A-9-52.
Alcoholic beverages.
Mine safety.
Entry into mines while
intoxicated, §25-9-27.
Transporting intoxicating
liquor into mine,
§25-9-27.
Animals.
Mine safety.
Hoisting of animals,
§25-9-210.
Underground stables,
§25-9-153.

COAL—Cont'd

Appeals.
Surface mining control and reclamation.
Division of hearings and appeals, §9-16-77.
Procedure for appeals, §9-16-79.

Attorney general.
Surface mining control and reclamation.
Suspension or revocation of permit.
Actions by attorney general, §9-16-93.

Blasting.
Coal mine safety, §§25-9-130 to 25-9-137.
Explosives.
Reports.
Premature explosions, §25-9-137.
Surface mining control and reclamation.
Permit for blasting plan, §9-16-83.

Boards and commissions.
Abandoned mine reclamation.
Interagency cooperation, §9-16-131.

Bonds, surety.
Surface mining control and reclamation.
Performance bonds and bond releases, §9-16-89.

Boundaries and adjacent landowners, §§25-9-320 to 25-9-322.
Distance of mine workings from boundary line of mine owner's coal rights, §25-9-320.
Inspections.
Refusal to permit adjacent landowner or lessee to inspect mine, §25-9-322.
Petitions.
Survey of mine upon petition of adjacent landowner, §25-9-321.
Refusal to permit adjacent landowner or lessee to inspect mine, §25-9-322.
Survey of mine upon petition of adjacent landowner, §25-9-321.

Child labor.
Persons under 18 not to work in or about mines, §25-9-30.

Circuit courts.
Abandoned mine reclamation.
Review of landowner's actions, §9-16-128.

Coal mine safety law, §§25-9-1 to 25-9-370. See within this heading, "Mine safety."

Conflicts of interest.
Certain persons not to have interest in Alabama coal mines, §25-9-4.
Surface mining commission, §9-16-76.

COAL—Cont'd

Contempt.
Mine safety.
Contempt proceedings, §25-9-23.

Convict labor.
Working convicts in coal mines, §14-5-3.
Penalties, §14-5-4.

Counties.
Severance tax.
Political subdivisions of state prohibited from levying, §40-13-9.

Criminal law and procedure.
Sale and delivery of coal mixed with other substances or materials or with different quality of coal, §13A-9-52.

Damages.
Unauthorized removal, §9-1-6.

Definitions.
Abandoned mine reclamation, §9-16-121.
Mine safety, §25-9-2.
Severance tax of 1971, §40-13-1.
Severance tax of 1977, §40-13-30.
Surface mining control and reclamation, §9-16-72.

Disasters.
Coal mine safety, §25-9-63.

Diseases.
Pneumoconiosis.
Compensation for pneumoconiosis for coal miners, §§25-5-140 to 25-5-152.
See WORKMEN'S COMPENSATION.

Drunkenness.
Mine safety.
Entry into mine while intoxicated, §25-9-27.

Dust.
Coal mine safety.
Accumulation of coal dust, §25-9-110.
Methods for allaying dust at source, §25-9-110.
Rock dusting, §25-9-111.

Electrical equipment.
Mine safety, §§25-9-170 to 25-9-176. See within this heading, "Mine safety."

Employment in mines.
Persons under 18 not to work in or about mines, §25-9-30.
Prisons and prisoners.
Working convicts in coal mines, §14-5-3.
Penalties, §14-5-4.
Solicitation of funds from employees for purposes of retaining or procuring employment, §25-9-28.

Energy.
Cogeneration facilities.
Purchase of coal produced in Alabama required, §37-12-5.

COAL—Cont'd

Environmental protection performance standards.
Surface mining control and reclamation.
Permits to conduct surface mining operations, §9-16-90.

Explosives and blasting.
Coal mine safety.
Generally, §§25-9-130 to 25-9-137. See within this heading, "Mine safety."
Surface mining operations, §§25-9-276 to 25-9-280.
Reports.
Premature explosions, §25-9-137.

Farms.
Surface mining control and reclamation.
Permits.
Issuance to mine on prime farm land, §9-16-85.

Fees.
Certificate of competence for fire bosses and mine foreman, §25-9-10.

Fire bosses.
Certificate of competency, §§25-9-8 to 25-9-15. See within this heading, "Mine safety."
Generally. See within this heading, "Mine safety."

Fire prevention.
Mine safety. See within this heading, "Mine safety."

Foreman.
Mine foreman.
Certificate of competency, §§25-9-8 to 25-9-15. See within this heading, "Mine safety."
Mine safety, §§25-9-17 to 25-9-19, 25-9-361.

Forgery and counterfeiting.
Mine safety.
Certificates of competency for fire bosses and mine foreman, §25-9-14.

Funds.
Abandoned mine reclamation, §9-16-122.
Priority of expenditures of monies from fund, §9-16-123.
Special abandoned mine reclamation trust fund, §9-16-135.
Surface mining control and reclamation.
Alabama surface mining fund, §9-16-103.
Reimbursement and funding, §9-16-104.

Gases.
Coal mine safety, §§25-9-80 to 25-9-91. See within this heading, "Mine safety."

Geological survey.
General provisions, §§9-4-1 to 9-4-19.
See GEOLOGICAL SURVEY.

COAL—Cont'd
Hearings.
Surface mining control and reclamation.
Designation of areas unsuitable for surface coal mining.
Review and public hearing, §9-16-96.
Division of hearings and appeals, §9-16-77.
Hearing officers.
Offices and facilities, §9-16-78.
Powers, §9-16-78.
Permits.
Suspension or revocation of permit, §9-16-93.
Procedure for hearings, §9-16-79.
Hoisting and haulage, §§25-9-210 to 25-9-216. See within this heading, "Mine safety."
Injunctions.
Abandoned mine reclamation, §9-16-132.
Mine safety.
Enforcement of chapter, §25-9-368.
Surface mining control and reclamation.
Suspension or revocation of permits.
Actions by attorney general, §9-16-93.
Inspections.
Adjacent landowner or lessee refusing, §25-9-322.
Mine safety. See within this heading, "Mine safety."
Surface mining control and reclamation.
By authority, §9-16-93.
Records, equipment, premises, etc.
Authority to inspect, §9-16-92.
Violation of provisions, §9-16-92.
Inspectors.
Mine safety. See within this heading, "Mine safety."
Insurance.
Abandoned mine reclamation.
Workmen's compensation, §9-16-134.
Surface mining control and reclamation.
Permit insurance, §9-16-83.
Labor.
Child labor.
Persons under 18 not to work in or about mines, §25-9-30.
Solicitation of funds from employees for purposes of retaining or procuring employment, §25-9-28.
Leases.
Inspections.
Refusal to permit adjacent landowner or lessee to inspect mine, §25-9-322.
Surface mining control and reclamation.
Certain lands leased, §9-16-101.

COAL—Cont'd
Licenses.
Coal and coke dealers.
Maintaining yards, §40-12-76.
Not maintaining yards, §40-12-77.
Surface mining control and reclamation, §9-16-81.
Liens.
Abandoned mine reclamation.
Property subject to lien, §9-16-129.
Lignite.
Severance tax of 1977 generally. See within this heading, "Severance tax of 1977."
Machinery.
Mine safety. See within this heading, "Mine safety."
Maps.
Contents, §25-9-300.
Examination, §25-9-300.
Failure to furnish, §25-9-301.
Filing, §25-9-300.
Incomplete, inaccurate or imperfect maps, §25-9-302.
Refusal to furnish, §25-9-301.
Required, §25-9-300.
Surveys of mines. See within this heading, "Surveys of mines."
Miners.
Payment by weight, §§25-9-340 to 25-9-345.
Prisons and prisoners.
Convict labor.
Working convicts in coal mines, §14-5-3.
Penalties, §14-5-4.
Mine safety, §§25-9-1 to 25-9-370.
Abandoned areas.
Inspection by foreman, §25-9-19.
Reports, §25-9-88.
Sealing, testing, etc., of abandoned workings, §25-9-85.
Testing of abandoned workings, §25-9-85.
Abstract of chapter.
Defacing, etc., of abstract, §25-9-364.
Posting at mines, §25-9-364.
Accidents.
Disasters, §25-9-63.
Investigations.
Major accidents, §25-9-61.
Major accidents.
Reports and investigations, §25-9-61.
Notice of injuries, §25-9-60.
Reports.
Major accidents, §25-9-61.
Treatment of injuries, §25-9-60.
Adjacent landowners, §§25-9-320 to 25-9-322.
Air.
General provisions, §§25-9-80 to 25-9-91.

COAL—Cont'd
Mine safety—Cont'd
Air—Cont'd
Surface mining operations.
Safety devices and practices for compressed air receivers, etc., §25-9-281.
Alabama mining academy, §§16-60-260 to 16-60-264.
Alcoholic beverages.
Entry into mine while intoxicated, §25-9-27.
Transporting intoxicating liquor into mine, §25-9-27.
Animals.
Hoisting of animals, §25-9-210.
Underground stables, §25-9-153.
Barriers, §25-9-271.
Blasting, §§25-9-130 to 25-9-137.
Boundaries and adjacent landowners, §§25-9-320 to 25-9-322.
Buildings.
Surface structures, §§25-9-250 to 25-9-254.
Cables.
Blasting cables, §25-9-135.
Trailing cables, §25-9-175.
Cages.
Safety features, §25-9-210.
Certificate of competency for fire bosses and mine foreman, §§29-9-10 to 25-9-15.
Applications.
False statements or misrepresentations in applications, §25-9-14.
Board of examiners, §25-9-9.
Cancellation, §25-9-15.
Counterfeit certificates, §25-9-14.
Examinations, §25-9-10.
Board of examiners, §25-9-9.
Fees, §25-9-10.
False certificates.
Uttering false certificates, §25-9-14.
False statements in applications, §25-9-14.
Fees, §25-9-10.
Forged certificates, §25-9-14.
Lost certificates.
Replacement, §25-9-13.
Misrepresentations in applications, §25-9-14.
Qualifications of applicants, §§25-9-11, 25-9-12.
Replacement of lost certificates, §25-9-13.
Required, §25-9-8.
Revocation, §25-9-15.
Suspension, §25-9-15.
Uttering false certificates, §25-9-14.
Checking systems.
Identification of persons underground, §25-9-41.

COAL—Cont'd

Mine safety—Cont'd

Chief of division.

Review by chief of orders of inspectors, §25-9-366.

Suspension of mine operations for violations imminently hazardous to workmen. Review by chief of orders of inspectors, §25-9-366.

Child labor.

Persons under 18 not to work in or about mines, §25-9-30.

Cleaning plants.

Maintenance in cleaning plants, §25-9-250.

Clothing.

Use of protective clothing, etc., §25-9-40.

Coal dust.

Accumulation, §25-9-110.

Methods for allaying dust at source, §25-9-110.

Compliance with chapter.

Employees to comply with chapter and rules of operators, §25-9-362.

Generally, §25-9-360.

Superintendent, mine foreman, etc., §25-9-361.

Suspension of compliance, §25-9-360.

Conflicts of interest.

Certain persons not to have interest in Alabama coal mines, §25-9-4.

Contempt proceedings, §25-9-23.

Correction of unsafe conditions, §25-9-24.

Coursing of air, §25-9-84.

Damages.

Correction, §25-9-90.

Duty of employees to report, §25-9-90.

Definitions, §25-9-2.

Department of industrial relations.

Legal representation of department, §25-9-369.

Devices.

Safety devices and practices.

Hoisting and haulage, §25-9-215.

Disasters, §25-9-63.

Division of safety and inspections.

Chief of division.

Conflicts of interest, §25-9-4.

Qualifications, §25-9-5.

Residence, §25-9-5.

Conflicts of interest, §25-9-4.

Drills.

Electric drills, §25-9-175.

Drunkenness.

Entry into mine while intoxicated, §25-9-27.

Dust.

Accumulation of coal dust, §25-9-110.

Methods for allaying dust at source, §25-9-110.

COAL—Cont'd

Mine safety—Cont'd

Dust—Cont'd

Rock dusting, §25-9-111.

Electrical equipment, §§25-9-170 to 25-9-176.

Cables for portable equipment, §25-9-175.

Circuit breakers, etc., §25-9-173.

Conversion equipment, §25-9-170.

Drills.

Electric drills, etc., §25-9-175.

Electricity, §25-9-230.

Examinations, §25-9-230.

Face equipment, §25-9-230.

Feeder wires, §25-9-171.

Grounding of frames, casings and other electrical equipment, §§25-9-172, 25-9-274.

Inspections, §25-9-274.

Insulating platforms, §§25-9-173, 25-9-274.

Lights, §25-9-176.

Power wires and circuits, §25-9-171.

Circuit breakers, §25-9-173.

Signal wires, §25-9-171.

Surface mining operations, §25-9-274.

Surface structures and practices.

Use of electrical equipment, §25-9-250.

Telephones, §25-9-174.

Wires, §25-9-171.

Trailing cables, §25-9-175.

Transformers, §25-9-170.

Trolley wires, §25-9-171.

Wires.

Power wires and circuits, §25-9-171.

Employees.

Appointment, §25-9-3.

Employment.

Solicitation of funds from employees for purposes of retaining or procuring employment, §25-9-28.

Enforcement of chapter, §§25-9-360 to 25-9-370.

Abstract of chapter.

Defacing, etc., §25-9-364.

Posting at mines, §25-9-364.

Employees to comply with chapter and rules of operators, §25-9-362.

Generally, §25-9-360.

Injunctions, §25-9-368.

Legal representation of department, §25-9-369.

Penalties.

Unlawful acts for which no other penalty provided, §25-9-370.

Posting abstract of chapter at mines, §25-9-364.

Reports.

Quarterly reports of mine operators, §25-9-363.

Representation of department, §25-9-369.

COAL—Cont'd

Mine safety—Cont'd

Enforcement of chapter —Cont'd

Review by chief of orders of inspectors, §25-9-366.

Superintendent, mine foreman, etc., to ensure compliance with chapter, §25-9-361.

Suspension of compliance with chapter, §25-9-360.

Suspension of mine operations for violations imminently hazardous to workmen.

Inspectors may order suspension, §25-9-365.

Judicial review of orders suspending mine operations, §25-9-367.

Review by chief of orders of inspectors, §25-9-366.

Unlawful acts for which no other penalty provided, §25-9-370.

Engineers.

Hoist engineers, §25-9-210.

Entering mines.

Intoxication.

Entry into mines while intoxicated, §25-9-27.

Persons not employees not to enter mines without consent of operator, §25-9-26.

Escapeways.

Requirements, §25-9-42.

Examinations.

Gases and other dangerous conditions, §25-9-86.

Use of flame safety lamps, §25-9-87.

Explosives and blasting, §§25-9-130 to 25-9-137.

Airdox.

Use of airdox, §25-9-130.

Black blasting powder.

Use, §25-9-130.

Cables.

Blasting cables, §25-9-135.

Cardox.

Use of cardox, §25-9-130.

Detonators.

Surface storage, §25-9-131.

Underground storage, §25-9-133.

Underground transportation, §25-9-132.

Dynamite.

Use of dynamite, §25-9-130.

Methods.

Permissible blasting methods, §25-9-130.

Misfires, §25-9-136.

Permissible explosives and blasting methods, §25-9-130.

COAL—Cont'd
Mine safety—Cont'd
Explosives and blasting
—Cont'd
Practices and procedures.
Blasting practices and
procedures,
§25-9-134.
Premature explosions.
Report, §25-9-137.
Reports.
Premature explosions,
§25-9-137.
Storage.
Black blasting powder,
§25-9-130.
Surface storage of
explosives and
detonators,
§25-9-131.
Underground storage of
explosives and
detonators,
§25-9-133.
Surface mining operations,
§§25-9-276 to 25-9-280.
Transportation.
Underground
transportation of
explosives and
detonators,
§25-9-132.
Fans, §25-9-230.
Main fans, §25-9-80.
Fees.
Certificate of competency
for fire bosses and
mine foreman,
§25-9-10.
Fire bosses.
Authorization to act as fire
boss.
Persons authorized to
act, §25-9-17.
Certificate of competency,
§§25-9-8 to 25-9-15.
Compliance with and
ensuring compliance
with chapter,
§25-9-361.
Duties.
Failure to perform
required duties,
§25-9-16.
Failure to perform required
duties, §25-9-16.
Persons authorized to act
as fire boss, §25-9-17.
Temporary fire bosses,
§25-9-17.
Fire prevention and control.
Electrical equipment,
§§25-9-170 to 25-9-176.
Flammable liquids.
Storage in lamp houses,
§25-9-251.
Surface structures,
§25-9-254.
Storage of flammable
liquids in lamp
houses, §25-9-251.
Underground fire
prevention and control,
§§25-9-150 to 25-9-155.
First aid equipment.
Maintenance, etc.,
§25-9-60.
Surface mining operations,
§25-9-282.

COAL—Cont'd
Mine safety—Cont'd
Flammable liquids.
Storage in lamp houses,
§25-9-251.
Foreman.
Abandoned areas of mines.
Inspection by foreman,
§25-9-19.
Certificate of competency,
§§25-9-8 to 25-9-15.
Compliance with and
ensuring compliance
with chapter,
§25-9-361.
Inspection of working
places and abandoned
areas of mines by
foreman, §25-9-19.
Qualifications in
underground mines,
§25-9-18.
Temporary foreman,
§25-9-17.
Underground mines.
Qualifications in
underground mines,
§25-9-18.
Working places.
Inspection by foreman,
§25-9-19.
Forgery and counterfeiting.
Certificates of competency
for fire bosses and
mine foreman,
§25-9-14.
Gases and ventilation,
§§25-9-80 to 25-9-91.
Abandoned workings.
Sealing, testing, etc.,
§25-9-85.
Accumulations.
Workings approaching
inaccessible
accumulations,
§25-9-89.
Correction of damage or
unsafe conditions,
§25-9-90.
Coursing of air, §25-9-84.
Detectors.
Methane detectors,
§25-9-81.
Examinations for gases
and other dangerous
conditions, §25-9-86.
Fans, §25-9-230.
Main fans, §25-9-80.
Flame safety lamps,
§25-9-87.
Instruments for
measurement of air
and gases in mines,
§25-9-21.
Lamps.
Use of flame safety
lamps, §25-9-87.
Machinery.
Certain machinery
prohibited
underground,
§25-9-214.
Measurement of air and
gases in mines.
Instruments for
measurement,
§25-9-21.
Methane detectors,
§25-9-81.
Procedure as to gases and
air quality, §25-9-82.

COAL—Cont'd
Mine safety—Cont'd
Gases and ventilation
—Cont'd
Prohibited acts, §25-9-91.
Reports.
Duty of employees to
report damages or
unsafe conditions,
§25-9-90.
Reports as to ventilation,
gas content,
reopening of mines,
etc., §25-9-88.
Standards as to gases and
air quality, §25-9-82.
Volume of air.
Standards as to
volume, §25-9-83.
Surface mining operations.
Safety devices and
practices for
compressed air
receivers, etc.,
§25-9-281.
Volume of air.
Standards as to volume
of air, §25-9-83.
Gloves.
Use of protective gloves,
§25-9-40.
Goggles.
Use of protective goggles,
§25-9-40.
Grease.
Use, storage, etc.,
§25-9-152.
Hoisting and haulage,
§§25-9-210 to 25-9-216.
Animals.
Hoisting of animals,
§25-9-210.
Cages.
Safety features,
§25-9-210.
Devices.
Safety devices,
§25-9-215.
Engineers.
Hoist engineers,
§25-9-210.
Engines.
Safety features of hoist
engines, §25-9-210.
Equipment.
Maintenance, etc.,
§25-9-211.
Locomotives.
Maintenance, etc.,
§25-9-211.
Safety devices,
§25-9-215.
Machinery.
Certain machinery
prohibited
underground,
§25-9-214.
Maintenance, etc., of mine
locomotives and other
haulage equipment,
§25-9-211.
Practices.
Safety practices,
§25-9-215.
Roads.
Clearances on haulage
roads, §25-9-213.
Construction,
installation and
maintenance,
§25-9-212.

COAL—Cont'd
  Mine safety—Cont'd
    Hoisting and haulage
      —Cont'd
      Roads—Cont'd
        Crossovers on haulage
          roads, §25-9-213.
        Shelter holes on haulage
          roads, §25-9-213.
        Track of haulage roads.
          Construction,
            installation and
            maintenance,
            §25-9-212.
      Ropes.
        Safety features of hoist
          ropes, §25-9-210.
      Safety devices and
        practices, §25-9-215.
      Safety features of cages,
        hoist engines, hoist
        ropes and hoist
        shafts, §25-9-210.
      Shafts.
        Safety features of hoist
          shafts, §25-9-210.
      Signal codes, etc.,
        §25-9-210.
      Timber.
        Hoisting of timber,
          §25-9-210.
      Tools.
        Hoisting of tools,
          §25-9-210.
      Track of haulage roads.
        Construction,
          installation and
          maintenance,
          §25-9-212.
      Transportation of men,
        §25-9-216.
    Identification of persons
      underground.
      Checking systems,
        §25-9-41.
    Injunctions, §25-9-368.
    Injuries.
      Notice of injuries, §25-9-60.
      Treatment of injuries,
        §25-9-60.
    Inspections.
      Abandoned areas of mines.
        Inspection by foreman,
          §25-9-19.
      Accompanying of
        inspectors, §25-9-7.
      Division of safety and
        inspections, §§25-9-4,
        25-9-5.
      Electrical equipment,
        §25-9-274.
      Foreman.
        Inspection of working
          places and
          abandoned areas of
          mines, §25-9-19.
      Instruments for
        measurement of air
        and gases in mines,
        §25-9-21.
      Refusal to permit adjacent
        landowner or lessee to
        inspect mine,
        §25-9-322.
      Schedule of inspections,
        §25-9-20.
      Surface mining operations,
        §§25-9-273, 25-9-274.
      Working places.
        Inspection by foreman,
          §25-9-19.

COAL—Cont'd
  Mine safety—Cont'd
    Inspectors.
      Accompanying of
        inspectors on
        inspections by
        representatives of
        miners, §25-9-7.
      Appointment of mine
        inspectors, §25-9-3.
      Conflicts of interest,
        §25-9-4.
      Duties, §25-9-7.
      Ordering suspension of
        mine operations for
        violations imminently
        hazardous to workmen,
        §25-9-365.
      Qualifications, §25-9-6.
      Reports.
        Mine examination
          reports, §25-9-7.
      Residence, §25-9-6.
      Review by chief of orders
        of inspectors,
        §25-9-366.
      Suspension of mine
        operations for
        violations imminently
        hazardous to workmen.
        Judicial review of orders
          suspending mine
          operations,
          §25-9-367.
        Review by chief of orders
          of inspectors,
          §25-9-366.
    Intoxication.
      Entry into mine while
        intoxicated, §25-9-27.
    Investigations.
      Accidents.
        Major accidents,
          §25-9-61.
    Lamp houses.
      Storage of flammable
        liquids in lamp houses,
        §25-9-251.
    Lamps.
      Use of flame safety lamps,
        §25-9-87.
    Lights.
      Electric lights, §25-9-176.
    Locomotives.
      Maintenance, etc.,
        §25-9-211.
    Lubricants.
      Use, storage, etc.,
        §25-9-152.
    Machinery.
      Certain machinery
        prohibited
        underground,
        §25-9-214.
      Face equipment, §25-9-230.
      Operation and
        maintenance.
        Face equipment,
          §25-9-230.
        Repairmen.
          Operation by
            repairmen,
            §25-9-232.
        Shop equipment,
          §25-9-231.
      Repairmen.
        Operation by repairmen,
          §25-9-232.
      Shop equipment, §25-9-231.

COAL—Cont'd
  Mine safety—Cont'd
    Machinery—Cont'd
      Surface mining operations.
        Guarding of exposed
          engines, wheels, etc.,
          §25-9-275.
    Maps of mines, §§25-9-300 to
      25-9-302.
    Methane detectors, §25-9-81.
    Mining academy.
      Alabama mining academy,
        §§16-60-260 to
        16-60-264.
    Minors.
      Persons under 18 not to
        work in or about
        mines, §25-9-30.
    Oil.
      Use, storage, etc.,
        §25-9-152.
    Openings.
      Requirements for mine
        openings, §25-9-42.
    Operators.
      Quarterly reports,
        §25-9-363.
    Rules.
      Employees to comply
        with rules of
        operators, §25-9-362.
    Penalties.
      Unlawful acts for which no
        other penalty provided,
        §25-9-370.
    Power wires and circuits,
      §25-9-171.
    Protective clothing.
      Use of protective clothing,
        §25-9-40.
    Pumps, §25-9-230.
    Purpose of chapter, §25-9-1.
    Reopening of mines.
      Reports, §25-9-88.
    Reports.
      Abandoned areas, §25-9-88.
      Accidents.
        Major accidents,
          §25-9-61.
      Damage or unsafe
        conditions, §25-9-90.
      Enforcement of chapter.
        Quarterly reports of
          mine operators,
          §25-9-363.
      Explosives and blasting.
        Report of premature
          explosions,
          §25-9-137.
      Fires.
        Operators to report fires,
          §25-9-155.
      Gas content, §25-9-88.
        Duty of employees to
          report damage or
          unsafe conditions,
          §25-9-90.
      Mine examination reports,
        §25-9-7.
      Quarterly reports of mine
        operators, §25-9-363.
      Reopening of mines,
        §25-9-88.
      Surface mining operations.
        Increase in hazards of pit
          operations to be
          reported, §25-9-284.
      Unsafe conditions,
        §25-9-24.

COAL—Cont'd
  Mine safety—Cont'd
    Reports—Cont'd
      Ventilation, §25-9-88.
      Duty of employees to
        report damage or
        unsafe conditions,
        §25-9-90.
    Rescue crews.
      Chief.
        Assignments by,
          §25-9-70.
        Jurisdiction in rescue
          and recovery work,
          §25-9-68.
      Compensation, §§25-9-65,
        25-9-69.
      Employment, §25-9-65.
      Existing conditions.
        Crews to be informed of,
          §25-9-70.
      Federal regulations.
        Applicability to rescue
          and recovery work,
          §25-9-70.
      Physical examination of
        crew members,
        §25-9-67.
      Qualifications, §25-9-67.
      Removal of crew members,
        §25-9-66.
      Training, §§25-9-65,
        25-9-66.
      Wages, §§25-9-65, 25-9-69.
      Workmen's compensation
        benefits, §§25-9-65,
        25-9-69.
    Rescue stations.
      Establishment, §25-9-64.
    Respiratory equipment,
      §25-9-40.
    Roads.
      Haulage roads, §§25-9-212,
        25-9-213.
    Rock dusting, §25-9-111.
    Roof support, §§25-9-190 to
      25-9-192.
      Correction of unsafe
        conditions, §25-9-190.
      Examination of roof, faces,
        ribs, etc., §25-9-190.
      Installation, etc., of
        timbering or other roof
        support systems,
        §25-9-191.
      Maintenance of supply of
        timbers or other roof
        supports, §25-9-192.
      Precautions against unsafe
        conditions, §25-9-190.
      Supply of timbers or other
        roof supports.
        Maintenance of supply,
          §25-9-192.
      Systems.
        Installation, etc., of
          timbering or other
          roof support systems,
          §25-9-191.
      Testing of roof, faces, ribs,
        etc., §25-9-190.
      Unsafe conditions.
        Correction and
          precautions against
          unsafe conditions,
          §25-9-190.
    Scales and weighing,
      §§25-9-340 to 25-9-345.
    Shafts.
      Requirements, §25-9-42.

COAL—Cont'd
  Mine safety—Cont'd
    Shafts—Cont'd
      Safety features of hoist
        shafts, §25-9-210.
    Short title of chapter,
      §25-9-1.
    Stables.
      Underground stables,
        §25-9-153.
    Storage.
      Flammable liquids.
        Storage in lamp houses,
          §25-9-251.
    Subpoenas.
      Expenses of executing,
        §25-9-23.
    Superintendents.
      Compliance with and
        ensuring compliance
        with chapter,
        §25-9-361.
    Supervisors.
      Compliance with and
        ensuring compliance
        with chapter,
        §25-9-361.
      Giving of orders requiring
        violation of chapter,
        §25-9-29.
    Surface mining operations,
      §§25-9-270 to 25-9-284.
      Access to pits.
        Maintenance, etc., of
          means of access,
          §25-9-272.
      Applicability of provisions,
        §25-9-270.
      Barriers, §25-9-271.
      Blasting.
        Handling of explosives
          during blasting
          operations,
          §25-9-280.
        Practices and procedures,
          §§25-9-278, 25-9-279.
        Warnings, guards, etc.,
          §25-9-280.
      Compressed air receivers,
        cylinders, etc.
        Safety devices and
          practices, §25-9-281.
      Draglines.
        Operation, inspection
          and maintenance,
          §25-9-273.
      Electrical blasting
        practices and
        procedures, §25-9-279.
      Electrical equipment.
        Generally, §25-9-274.
      Explosives and blasting,
        §§25-9-276 to 25-9-280.
        Blasting agent defined,
          §25-9-276.
        Definitions, §25-9-276.
        Guards, §25-9-280.
        Handling of explosives
          and detonators,
          §25-9-277.
          Handling during
            blasting
            operations,
            §25-9-280.
        Practices and procedures,
          §25-9-278.
        Electrical blasting,
          §25-9-279.
        Storage of explosives and
          detonators,
          §25-9-276.

COAL—Cont'd
  Mine safety—Cont'd
    Surface mining operations
      —Cont'd
      Explosives and blasting
        —Cont'd
        Transportation of
          explosives and
          detonators,
          §25-9-276.
        Use of explosives and
          detonators,
          §25-9-277.
        Warnings, §25-9-280.
      Exposed engines, wheels,
        etc.
        Guarding, §25-9-275.
      First aid equipment,
        §25-9-282.
      Hazards.
        Increase in hazards of pit
          operations to be
          reported, §25-9-284.
      Increase in hazards of pit
        operations to be
        reported, §25-9-284.
      Inspections.
        Electrical equipment,
          §25-9-274.
        Shovels and draglines,
          §25-9-273.
      Ladders.
        Maintenance of means of
          access to pits,
          §25-9-272.
      Loose material, §25-9-271.
      Machinery.
        Guarding of exposed
          engines, wheels, etc.,
          §25-9-275.
      Open pits.
        Access.
          Maintenance of means
            of access to pits,
            §25-9-272.
        Increase in hazards of pit
          operations to be
          reported, §25-9-284.
        Maintenance, etc.,
          §25-9-271.
        Overburden, §25-9-271.
      Reports.
        Increase in hazards of pit
          operations to be
          reported, §25-9-284.
      Shovels.
        Operation, inspection
          and maintenance,
          §25-9-273.
      Slope of material,
        §25-9-271.
      Toilets.
        Provision of sanitary
          toilets, §25-9-283.
      Tools.
        Safety of tools,
          §25-9-275.
      Trailing cables, §25-9-274.
      Water.
        Provision of potable
          drinking water and
          drinking cups or
          fountains, §25-9-283.
    Surface structures and
      practices, §§25-9-250 to
      25-9-254.
      Cleaning plants.
        Maintenance in cleaning
          plants, §25-9-250.

COAL—Cont'd
  Mine safety—Cont'd
    Surface structures and
      practices—Cont'd
    Electrical equipment.
      Use of electrical
        equipment,
        §25-9-250.
    Elevated platforms,
      §25-9-252.
    Fire prevention in surface
      structures, §25-9-254.
    Flammable liquids.
      Storage in lamp houses,
        §25-9-251.
    Housekeeping practices,
      §25-9-253.
    Lamp houses.
      Storage of flammable
        liquids in lamp
        houses, §25-9-251.
    Runways, §25-9-252.
    Stairways.
      Maintenance, etc.,
        §25-9-252.
    Storage of flammable
      liquids in lamp houses,
      §25-9-251.
    Tipples.
      Maintenance in tipples
        and cleaning plants,
        §25-9-250.
    Surveys of mines. See within
      this heading, "Surveys of
      mines."
    Suspension of mine
      operations for violations
      imminently hazardous to
      workmen.
      Inspectors may order
        suspension, §25-9-365.
      Judicial review of orders
        suspending mine
        operations, §25-9-367.
      Review by chief of orders
        of inspectors,
        §25-9-366.
    Telephones, §25-9-174.
    Wires, §25-9-171.
    Timber.
      Hoisting of timber,
        §25-9-210.
    Tipples.
      Maintenance in tipples,
        §25-9-250.
    Toilets.
      Surface mining operations.
        Provision of sanitary
        toilets, §25-9-283.
    Tools.
      Hoisting of tools,
        §25-9-210.
      Surface mining operations.
        Safety of tools,
        §25-9-275.
    Torches.
      Use of torches, §25-9-150.
    Trailing cables, §25-9-230.
      Surface mining operations,
      §25-9-274.
    Transportation of men,
      §25-9-216.
    Trolley wires, §25-9-171.
    Underground fire prevention
      and control, §§25-9-150
      to 25-9-155.
    Animals.
      Underground stables,
        §25-9-153.

COAL—Cont'd
  Mine safety—Cont'd
    Underground fire prevention
      and control—Cont'd
    Assistance of chief in
      extinguishing fires,
      §25-9-155.
    Building fires in mines,
      §25-9-150.
    Burning, §25-9-150.
    Discovery of fire.
      Procedure upon
        discovery, §25-9-154.
    Examinations for fire,
      §25-9-151.
    Fire extinguishing
      equipment, §25-9-152.
    Oil, grease and lubricants.
      Use, storage, etc.,
        §25-9-152.
    Procedure upon discovery
      of fire, §25-9-154.
    Reports.
      Operators to report fires,
        §25-9-155.
    Stables.
      Underground stables,
        §25-9-153.
    Torches.
      Use of torches,
        §25-9-150.
    Welding, §25-9-150.
    Unsafe conditions.
      Correction, §25-9-24.
      Examinations for gases
        and other dangerous
        conditions, §25-9-86.
      Gases and ventilation
        generally, §§25-9-80 to
        25-9-91.
      Reports, §25-9-24.
        Duty of employees to
          report, §25-9-90.
      Roof support.
        Correction and
          precautions against
          unsafe conditions,
          §25-9-190.
      Suspension of mine
        operations.
        Inspectors may order
          suspension,
          §25-9-365.
        Review of orders,
          §§25-9-366,
          25-9-367.
    Ventilation, §§25-9-80 to
      25-9-91.
    Violations of chapter.
      Giving of orders requiring
        violation of chapter,
        §25-9-29.
      Injunctions, §25-9-368.
      Penalties for unlawful acts
        for which no other
        penalty provided,
        §25-9-370.
      Suspension of mine
        operations.
        Inspectors may order
          suspension,
          §25-9-365.
        Judicial review of orders,
          §25-9-367.
        Review by chief of orders
          of inspectors,
          §25-9-366.

COAL—Cont'd
  Mine safety—Cont'd
    Water.
      Inaccessible accumulations
        of water.
        Procedure when
          workings
          approaching,
          §25-9-89.
      Removal of large and
        dangerous
        accumulations of water
        in adjoining mines,
        §25-9-62.
      Surface mining operations.
        Provision of potable
          drinking water and
          drinking cups or
          fountains, §25-9-283.
    Weights and measures,
      §§25-9-340 to 25-9-345.
    Welding, §25-9-150.
    Witnesses.
      Attendance, §25-9-24.
      Contempt proceedings,
        §25-9-23.
      Proceedings under chapter,
        §25-9-22.
    Working places of mines.
      Inspection by foreman,
        §25-9-19.
  Minors.
    Persons under 18 not to work
      in or about mines,
      §25-9-30.
  Motor vehicle carriers.
    Vehicles hauling coal.
      Exemptions from chapter,
      §37-3-4.
  Municipal corporations.
    Severance tax.
      Political subdivisions of
        state prohibited from
        levying, §40-13-9.
  Notice.
    Surface mining control and
      reclamation.
      Suspension or revocation of
        permits.
        Public hearing, §9-16-93.
  Penalties.
    Mine safety.
      Unlawful acts for which no
        other penalty provided,
        §25-9-370.
    Prisons and prisoners.
      Convict labor.
        Working convicts in coal
          mines, §14-5-4.
    Severance tax of 1971,
      §§40-13-7, 40-13-10.
    Severance tax of 1977,
      §§40-13-34, 40-13-35.
    Surface mining control and
      reclamation.
      Conflicts of interest,
        §9-16-76.
      Permits.
        Violations of provisions,
        §9-16-93.
  Permits.
    Surface mining control and
      reclamation. See within
      this heading, "Surface
      mining control and
      reclamation."

COAL—Cont'd
Petitions.
Surface mining control and reclamation.
Designation of areas unsuitable for surface coal mining, §9-16-96.
Review and public hearing, §9-16-96.
Pneumoconiosis.
Compensation for pneumoconiosis of coal miners.
See WORKMEN'S COMPENSATION.
Prisons and prisoners.
Coal mines.
Working convicts in coal mines, §14-5-3.
Penalties, §14-5-4.
Records.
Severance tax of 1977.
Inspection of records, §40-13-34.
Surface mining control and reclamation.
Confidentiality of records, §9-16-100.
Division of surface mining control and reclamation.
Transfer of records, §9-16-80.
Permits.
Maintenance of records, etc., by permittee, §9-16-92.
Reports.
Blasting and explosives.
Premature explosions, §25-9-137.
Mine safety. See within this heading, "Mine safety."
Severance tax of 1971. See within this heading, "Severance tax of 1971." ittee,
Surface mining control and reclamation.
Sales of coal, §9-16-102.
Right of entry.
Abandoned mine reclamation, §9-16-126.
Roof support, §§25-9-190 to 25-9-192.
Rules and regulations.
Surface mining control and reclamation.
Commission.
Revision of rules.
Oversight committee to be consulted, §9-16-73.
Emergency rules, §9-16-75.
Procedure for rule making, §9-16-75.
Underground coal mining operations, §9-16-91.
Safety.
Mine safety, §§25-9-1 to 25-9-370. See within this heading, "Mine safety."
Salaries.
Surface mining commission, §9-16-73.
Sales.
Coal mixed with other substances or with different quality of coal, §13A-9-52.

COAL—Cont'd
Scales and weighing, §§25-9-340 to 25-9-345.
Access to scales, §25-9-344.
Accurate weighing.
Failure of mine operators to weigh coal accurately, §25-9-345.
Check weighman.
Miners may furnish check weighman to examine scales, §25-9-342.
Testing of scales, §25-9-343.
Coal to be weighed and credited to miner, §25-9-341.
Correct weighing.
Failure of mine operators to weigh coal correctly, §25-9-345.
Credit to miner.
Coal to be weighed and credited to miner, §25-9-341.
Examination of scales.
Miners may furnish check weighman to examine scales, §25-9-342.
Failure of mine operators to weigh coal accurately and correctly, §25-9-345.
Owners to provide scales at mines where miners paid by weight, §25-9-340.
Provision of scales.
Owners to provide scales at mines where miners paid by weight, §25-9-340.
Testing of scales, §25-9-343.
Weights and measures. See within this heading, "Weights and measures."
Severance tax of 1971, §§40-13-1 to 40-13-10.
Amount of tax, §40-13-2.
Commissioner may ascertain where producer fails to report, §40-13-7.
Counties.
Political subdivisions of state prohibited from levying tax, §40-13-9.
Definitions, §40-13-1.
General fund.
Credit of proceeds to state general fund, §40-13-6.
Levy of excise and privilege tax, §40-13-2.
Political subdivisions of state prohibited from levying, §40-13-9.
Municipal corporations.
Political subdivisions of state prohibited from levying tax, §40-13-9.
Penalties.
Civil penalties.
Failure of producer to report, §40-13-7.
Criminal penalties, §40-13-10.
Proceeds.
Appropriation, §40-13-5.
Credit of proceeds to state general fund, §40-13-6.
Deposit, §40-13-5.
Disbursement, §40-13-5.

COAL—Cont'd
Severance tax of 1971
—Cont'd
Proceeds—Cont'd
General fund.
Credit of proceeds to state general fund, §40-13-6.
Rate of tax, §40-13-2.
Reports.
Coal shipped through seaport facility, §40-13-6.
Failure of producer to report.
Civil penalty, §40-13-7.
Commissioner may ascertain and assess amount of tax due, §40-13-7.
Production of information and records, §40-13-7.
Monthly report of producer, §40-13-3.
Monthly report of purchasers and transporters, §40-13-4.
Termination of tax, §40-13-8.
Severance tax of 1977, §§40-13-30 to 40-13-36.
Amount of tax, §40-13-31.
Collection of excise and privilege tax, §40-13-31.
Deposit and distribution of proceeds, §40-13-32.
Construction of article, §40-13-36.
Definitions, §40-13-30.
Deposit of proceeds, §40-13-32.
Distribution of proceeds, §40-13-32.
Proration where police jurisdictions overlap, §40-13-33.
Forms.
Issuance, §40-13-34.
Inspection of books, §40-13-34.
Levy of excise and privilege tax, §40-13-31.
Penalties.
Criminal penalties, §40-13-35.
Delinquent penalty, §40-13-34.
Proceeds.
Deposit, §40-13-32.
Distribution, §40-13-32.
Proration where police jurisdictions overlap, §40-13-33.
Records.
Inspection, §40-13-34.
Rules and regulations.
Promulgation, §40-13-34.
Stables.
Mine safety.
Underground stables, §25-9-153.
State departments and agencies.
Abandoned mine reclamation.
Interagency cooperation, §9-16-131.
Subpoenas.
Mine safety.
Expenses of executing subpoenas, §25-9-23.

COAL—Cont'd
Surface mining control and reclamation.
Abandoned mine reclamation, §§9-16-120 to 9-16-134. See within this heading, "Abandoned mine reclamation."
Actions.
Citizen's actions, §9-16-95.
Appeals.
Division of hearings and appeals, §9-16-77.
Procedure, §9-16-79.
Applicability of provisions.
Operations not subject to article, §9-16-99.
Bonds.
Performance bonds and bond releases, §9-16-89.
Citation of act, §9-16-70.
Citizen's actions, §9-16-95.
Commission.
Appointment, §9-16-73.
Compensation, §9-16-73.
Composition, §9-16-73.
Conflicts of interest, §9-16-76.
Penalty for violation of provisions, §9-16-76.
Creation, §9-16-73.
Director, §9-16-73.
Division of hearings and appeals.
Appointment of hearing officers, §9-16-77.
Authority, §9-16-77.
Creation, §9-16-77.
Powers, §9-16-77.
Functions, §9-16-74.
Funds, §9-16-73.
Meetings, §9-16-73.
Office, §9-16-73.
Powers.
Generally, §9-16-74.
Principal office, §9-16-73.
Qualifications of members, §9-16-73.
Quorum, §9-16-73.
Removal of members, §9-16-73.
Rules and regulations.
Revisions.
Oversight committee to be consulted, §9-16-73.
Staff, §9-16-73.
Vacancies in office, §9-16-73.
Constitutionality of article, §9-16-105.
Cumulative nature of provisions, §9-16-106.
Declaration of public policy, §9-16-71.
Definitions, §9-16-72.
Division of surface mining control and reclamation.
Authority, §9-16-80.
Chief.
Appointment, §9-16-80.
Authority, §9-16-80.
Compensation, §9-16-80.
Power, §9-16-80.
Creation, §9-16-80.
Powers, §9-16-80.
Transfer of books, records, powers, rights and personnel, §9-16-80.

COAL—Cont'd
Surface mining control and reclamation—Cont'd
Effective date, §9-16-107.
Emergency rules, §9-16-75.
Exemptions.
Areas exempt from mining operations, §9-16-96.
Experimental practices, §9-16-98.
Funds.
Alabama surface mining fund, §9-16-103.
Reimbursement and funding, §9-16-104.
Hearing officers.
Offices and facilities.
Location, §9-16-78.
Powers, §9-16-78.
Hearings.
Designation of areas unsuitable for surface coal mining.
Review and public hearing, §9-16-96.
Division of hearings and appeals, §9-16-77.
Permits.
Suspension or revocation of permit, §9-16-93.
Procedure, §9-16-79.
Witness fees, §9-16-78.
Inspections.
By authority, §9-16-93.
Records, equipment, premises, etc.
Authority to inspect, §9-16-92.
Violation of provisions, §9-16-92.
Right of entry, §9-16-92.
Leases of certain lands, §9-16-101.
Legislative intent, §9-16-71.
Licenses, §9-16-81.
Application for license.
Contents, §9-16-81.
Filing, §9-16-81.
Qualifications of applicants, §9-16-81.
Fees, §9-16-81.
Issuance, §9-16-81.
Required, §9-16-81.
Term, §9-16-81.
Notice.
Suspension or revocation of permits.
Public hearing, §9-16-93.
Operations not subject to article, §9-16-99.
Oversight committee.
Chairman.
Selection, §9-16-73.
Compensation, §9-16-73.
Composition, §9-16-73.
Created, §9-16-73.
Duties.
Consulted on proposed revisions of commission's rules and regulations, §9-16-73.
Meetings, §9-16-73.
Permits, §9-16-82.
Appeal of applications, §9-16-88.
Application, §9-16-82.
Appeal of application, §9-16-88.
Contents of application, §9-16-83.

COAL—Cont'd
Surface mining control and reclamation—Cont'd
Permits—Cont'd
Application—Cont'd
Copy filed for public inspection, §9-16-83.
Review of applications, §9-16-88.
Revisions, §9-16-86.
Approval by authority, §9-16-85.
Attorney general.
Actions by attorney general, §9-16-93.
Blasting plan, §9-16-83.
Cessation of operation, §9-16-93.
Denial by authority, §9-16-85.
Environmental protection performance standards, §9-16-90.
Exploration of coal, §9-16-87.
Hearing.
Suspension or revocation of permit, §9-16-93.
Injunctive relief, §9-16-93.
Insurance, §9-16-83.
Issuance.
Prime farm land mining, §9-16-85.
Modification by authority, §9-16-86.
Notice.
Public hearing.
Suspension or revocation of permit, §9-16-93.
Penalties.
Violations of provisions, §9-16-93.
Prime farm land.
Issuance to mine, §9-16-85.
Reclamation plan, §9-16-83.
Contents, §9-16-84.
Requirements, §9-16-84.
Records.
Maintenance of records, etc., by permittee, §9-16-92.
Renewal, §9-16-82.
Required, §9-16-82.
Revisions, §9-16-86.
Application, §9-16-86.
By authority, §9-16-86.
Revocation of permit, §9-16-93.
Public hearing, §9-16-93.
Notices and orders, §9-16-93.
Successor in interest, §9-16-82.
Suspension of permit, §9-16-93.
Public hearing, §9-16-93.
Notices and orders, §9-16-93.
Term, §9-16-82.
Termination, §9-16-82.
Underground coal mining operations, §9-16-91.
Violation schedule.
Filing of, §9-16-85.

COAL—Cont'd
Surface mining control and reclamation—Cont'd
Petitions.
Designation of areas unsuitable for surface coal mining.
Right to petition, §9-16-96.
Plan of reclamation, §9-16-84.
Contents, §9-16-84.
Permits, §9-16-83.
Public policy.
Declaration of policy, §9-16-71.
Records.
Confidentiality of records, §9-16-100.
Division of surface mining control and reclamation.
Transfer of records, §9-16-80.
Permits.
Maintenance of records, etc., by permittee, §9-16-92.
Reimbursement and funding, §9-16-104.
Repeals.
Certain laws not repealed, §9-16-106.
Reports.
Sales of coal, §9-16-102.
Rule making procedure, §9-16-75.
Sales of coal.
Reports of certain coal sales, §9-16-102.
Short title, §9-16-70.
Title of article, §9-16-70.
Underground coal mining operations.
Applicability of article, §9-16-91.
Effect on surface operations, §9-16-91.
Permit requirements, §9-16-91.
Rules and regulations.
Promulgation of, §9-16-91.
Suspension of underground coal mining, §9-16-91.
Unsuitable areas for surface coal mining.
Designation of areas, §9-16-96.
Right to petition, §9-16-96.
Review and public hearing, §9-16-96.
Validity of article, §9-16-105.
Water rights and replacement, §9-16-97.
Witnesses.
Fees, §9-16-78.
Surveys of mines.
Adjacent landowners.
Survey upon petition of adjacent landowner, §25-9-321.
Final survey, §25-9-304.
Intermediate surveys, §25-9-303.
Maps of mines. See within this heading, "Maps."

COAL—Cont'd
Surveys of mines—Cont'd
Petition of adjacent landowner.
Survey of mine upon petition, §25-9-321.
Taxation.
Severance tax of 1977, §§40-13-30 to 40-13-36.
See within this heading, "Severance tax of 1977."
Severance tax of 1971, §§40-13-1 to 40-13-10.
See within this heading, "Severance tax of 1971."
Use tax.
Exemptions, §40-23-62.
Telephones.
Mine safety, §25-9-174.
Telephone wires, §25-9-171.
Unauthorized removal.
Damages.
Legislative intent, §9-1-6.
Measure of damages, §9-1-6.
Public policy, §9-1-6.
Retroactive application of section, §9-1-6.
Underground coal mining operations, §9-16-91.
Applicability of article, §9-16-91.
Effect on surface operations, §9-16-91.
Permit requirements, §9-16-91.
Rules and regulations.
Promulgation of, §9-16-91.
Suspension of underground coal mining, §9-16-91.
Use tax.
Exemptions, §40-23-62.
Ventilation.
Coal mine safety.
Gases and ventilation, §§25-9-80 to 25-9-91.
See within this heading, "Mine safety."
Water.
Accumulations of water.
Accumulations of water in adjoining mines, §25-9-62.
Water rights and replacement, §9-16-97.
Weights and measures.
Delivery tickets, §8-16-99.
Liquid substances in coal, coke or charcoal.
Restriction, §8-16-98.
Sale by weight, §8-16-98.
Scales and weighing. See within this heading, "Scales and weighing."
"Ton" defined, §8-16-98.
Weighing at time of purchase at request of purchaser, §8-16-100.
Witnesses.
Mine safety.
Attendance of witnesses, §25-9-23.
Contempt proceedings, §25-9-23.
Witnesses at proceedings under chapter, §25-9-22.

COAL—Cont'd
Witnesses—Cont'd
Surface mining control and reclamation.
Fees for witnesses and proceedings, §9-16-78.
Workmen's compensation.
Coal mines.
See WORKMEN'S COMPENSATION.

COASTAL AREAS, §§9-7-1 to 9-7-22.
Board.
Defined, §9-7-10.
Duties.
Coastal area management program.
Development, §9-7-15.
Generally, §9-7-14.
Environmental management.
Transfer of functions, personnel, etc., of board, §22-22A-10.
Powers.
Funds, facilities, etc.
Acceptance, use and disposition, §9-7-14.
Generally, §9-7-14.
Coastal area management program.
Approval by governor, §9-7-17.
Development, §9-7-15.
Conservation and natural resources.
Department.
Permissible uses, §9-7-13.
Declaration of state policy, §9-7-12.
Definitions, §9-7-10.
Department.
Permissible uses.
Determination of additional permissible uses, §9-7-13.
Permits.
Activities of persons within coastal area to be consistent with program, §9-7-20.
Rules and regulations.
Promulgation, §9-7-16.
Environmental management.
Board.
Transfer of functions, personnel, etc., of board to office of state planning and federal programs, §22-22A-10.
Federal permits.
Applications.
Filing copies with board, §9-7-20.
Governor.
Coastal area management program.
Approval, §9-7-17.
Legislative findings, §9-7-11.
Local governments.
Regulation of uses of land within coastal areas, §9-7-20.
Management program, §§9-7-15, 9-7-17.
Marine environmental sciences consortium.
Permissible uses, §9-7-13.
Marine resources division.
Permissible uses, §9-7-13.

COASTAL AREAS—Cont'd

Mississippi-Alabama sea grant consortium.
Permissible uses, §9-7-13.

Motor vehicles.
Operation of vehicles on beaches and sand dunes of Gulf of Mexico. Prohibited, §32-1-7.

Permissible uses, §9-7-13.
Determination of additional permissible uses, §9-7-13.

Permits.
Department.
Activities of persons within coastal area to be consistent with program, §9-7-20.
Federal permits.
Filing copies of application with board, §9-7-20.
Requirements, §9-7-20.

Policies.
Declaration of state policy, §9-7-12.

Purposes of chapter, §9-7-11.

Rules and regulations.
Promulgation by department, §9-7-16.

Uses.
Permissible uses, §9-7-13.

COAT OF ARMS.

State coat of arms, §§1-2-1 to 1-2-3.

COCAINE.

Controlled substances generally, §§20-2-1 to 20-2-144.
See DRUGS.

COCKFIGHTING.

Keeping cockpit, §13A-12-4.
Prohibited, §13A-12-4.

CODEINE.

Controlled substances generally, §§20-2-1 to 20-2-144.
See DRUGS.

CODE OF ALABAMA, §§1-1-1 to 1-1-16.

Amendments.
References to sections, titles, etc., apply to amendments thereto, §1-1-15.

Appropriations, §41-21-8.

Articles.
References to articles, §1-1-15.

Catchlines of sections.
Not part of law, §1-1-14.

Chapters.
References to chapters, §1-1-15.

Classification of code, §1-1-14.

Compilation of certain sections.
Preparation and publication, §41-21-7.

Computation of time, §1-1-4.

Construction and interpretation, §§1-1-1 to 1-1-16.
See CONSTRUCTION AND INTERPRETATION.

Defenses.
Existing defenses preserved, §1-1-9.

CODE OF ALABAMA—Cont'd

Definitions.
See DEFINITIONS.

Distribution.
County law libraries, §11-25-10.
Duplicate copies.
Replacement of lost or destroyed sets, §41-21-3.
Effect of failure to follow code, §41-21-5.
Receipts.
Taking of receipts from officers, §41-21-6.
Record book, §41-21-6.
Secretary of state.
State departments and agencies, §41-21-1.
State departments and agencies.
Secretary of state, §41-21-1.

Divisions.
References to divisions, §1-1-15.

Gender.
Masculine includes feminine and neuter, §1-1-2.

Law libraries.
Counties.
Distribution of code to libraries, §11-25-10.

Legislative reference service.
See LEGISLATURE.

Lost or destroyed sets.
Furnishing of duplicate copies, §41-21-3.

Municipal corporations.
Corporate limits not altered or affected by adoption of code, §11-40-5.

Notes.
Not part of law, §1-1-14.

Organization of code, §1-1-14.

Plural includes singular, §1-1-2.

Population acts.
Not repealed, §1-1-10.

Public offenses.
Certain acts or omissions not public offenses, §1-1-6.

Public officers and employees.
Severance of connection with office.
Duty as to disposition of sets of code, §41-21-5.

Publisher.
Sale of code, §41-21-4.

References to sections, titles, etc., §1-1-15.

Remedies.
Existing remedies preserved, §1-1-9.

Repeals.
Certain statutes saved from repeal, §1-1-10.
Previous validating acts not repealed, §1-1-13.
Repealed laws not revived, §1-1-11.
Uncodified statutes of public, general and permanent nature, §1-1-10.

Reprints.
Preparation and publication of compilations or abridgements, §41-21-7.

CODE OF ALABAMA—Cont'd

Rights.
Existing rights preserved, §1-1-9.

Rules of supreme court.
Adoption of code not to affect, §6-1-1.

Sale.
Publisher, §41-21-4.

Sections.
Catchlines of sections not part of law, §1-1-14.
References to sections, §1-1-15.

Severability of provisions of code, §1-1-16.

Singular includes plural, §1-1-2.

Statutes.
See STATUTES.

Storage.
Additional sets of code, §41-21-2.

Tenses, §1-1-2.

Time.
Computation of time, §1-1-4.

Title.
Sets of code.
Vesting of title, §41-21-5.

Uncodified statutes of public, general and permanent nature repealed, §1-1-10.

University of Alabama.
Furnished to law department, §16-47-8.

Validating acts.
Previous validating acts not repealed, §1-1-13.

CODE OF ETHICS, §§36-25-1 to 36-25-30.

See PUBLIC OFFICERS AND EMPLOYEES.

CODICILS.

Wills generally.
See WILLS.

COFFEE COUNTY.

Courts.
Costs and charges, Const. Ala., amd. 360.

Economic and industrial development promotion, Const. Ala., amd. 429.

Officers and employees.
Compensation, Const. Ala., amd. 360.
Reorganization of certain offices, Const. Ala., amd. 377.

School tax.
Additional taxes for school purposes, Const. Ala., amd. 206.
Warrants payable from proceeds of special school taxes, Const. Ala., amd. 216.

Taxation.
Establishment of consolidated and unified tax system, Const. Ala., amd. 377.

COFFINS, §§40-12-77 to 40-12-79.

COGENERATION FACILITIES, §§37-12-1 to 37-12-5.

COHABITATION.
Termination of alimony upon cohabitation with member of opposite sex, §30-2-55.

COIN-OPERATED MACHINES.
Sales tax.
Tax levied on gross receipts, §40-23-2.
Vending machines.
See VENDING MACHINES.

COLBERT COUNTY.
Drainage districts, Const. Ala., amd. 45.
Form of government.
Laws changing form of government, Const. Ala., amd. 144.
Malaria control.
Drainage districts, Const. Ala., amd. 45.
Officers.
Compensation, allowances, etc., Const. Ala., amd. 136.
Laws changing term of office, compensation, allowances, etc., of officers, Const. Ala., amd. 144.
School tax.
Special school tax in school districts Nos. 1 and 2, Const. Ala., amd. 293.
Special tax by school districts, Const. Ala., amd. 130.

COLD STORAGE PLANTS.
Licenses, §40-12-137.

COLISEUM.
Agricultural center.
See AGRICULTURE.
State products mark and coliseum authority, §§41-10-80 to 41-10-109.
See PRODUCTS MARTS.

COLLATERAL SECURITY.
General provisions.
See PLEDGE AND COLLATERAL SECURITY.
Secured transactions, §§7-9-101 to 7-9-507.
See COMMERCIAL CODE.

COLLECTION AGENCIES.
Licenses, §40-12-80.

COLLECTIVE BARGAINING.
Labor unions generally.
See LABOR.

COLLEGES.
General provisions.
See UNIVERSITIES AND COLLEGES.
Junior colleges.
See JUNIOR COLLEGES.

COLOR OF TITLE.
Ejectment.
Liability of person holding possession under color of title, §6-6-289.

COLUMBIANA, MUNICIPALITY OF.
Property tax, Const. Ala., amd. 8.

COMMENCEMENT OF ACTIONS.
General provisions.
See ACTIONS.
Statute of limitations.
See LIMITATION OF ACTIONS.

COMMERCE.
See TRADE AND COMMERCE.

COMMERCIAL ALLIGATOR OPERATIONS, §§9-12-200 to 9-12-214.
See ALLIGATOR FARMS.

COMMERCIAL CODE, §§7-1-101 to 7-11-108.
Acceleration.
Option to accelerate at will, §7-1-208.
Acceptance under reservation of rights, §7-1-207.
Actions.
Defined, §7-1-201.
Investment securities.
Actions for price, §7-8-107.
Purchaser.
Action against purchaser based upon wrongful transfer, §7-8-315.
Agents.
Bank deposits and collections.
Agency status of collecting banks, §7-4-201.
Commercial paper.
Conversion.
Innocent representative, §7-3-419.
Signature by authorized representative, §7-3-403.
Signature in ambiguous capacity deemed indorsement, §7-3-402.
Warranties on presentment and transfer, §7-3-417.
Words describing payee, §7-3-117.
Investment securities.
Conversion.
No conversion by good faith delivery, §7-8-318.
Effect of signature of transfer agent, §§7-8-208, 7-8-312.
Representative defined, §7-1-201.
Aggrieved party.
Defined, §7-1-201.
Agreements.
Defined, §§7-1-201, 7-2-106.
Airplanes.
Secured transactions.
Determination of validity and perfection of security interest in airplane, §7-9-103.
Alcoholic beverages.
Sales.
Implied warranty of merchantability, §7-2-314.
Warehouse receipts.
Storage under government bond, §7-7-201.

COMMERCIAL CODE—Cont'd
Alteration of instruments.
Bank deposits and collections.
Customer's duty to discover and report alteration, §7-4-406.
Commercial paper.
Unauthorized completion, §7-3-115.
Documents of title.
Bills of lading, §7-7-306.
Warehouse receipts, §7-7-208.
Investment securities.
Completion or alteration, §7-8-206.
Animals.
Sale of unborn animals, §7-2-105.
Identification of goods, §7-2-501.
Annuities.
Secured transactions.
Transfer of interest or claim in annuities excluded, §7-9-104.
Application of title.
Effective date, §7-10-101.
Territorial application, §7-1-105.
Assignments.
Investment securities.
Partial assignment, §7-8-308.
Letters of credit, §7-5-116.
Sales.
Rights of buyer or seller, §7-2-210.
Secured transactions. See within this heading, "Secured transactions."
Assignments for benefit of creditors.
Bulk transfers.
Transfers excepted from article, §7-6-103.
Secured transactions.
Priority over unperfected security interests, §7-9-301.
Attachment.
Bank deposits and collections.
When items subject to legal process, §7-4-303.
Bulk transfers.
Limitation of levies, §7-6-111.
Documents of title.
Attachment of goods covered by negotiable document, §7-7-602.
Investment securities.
Levy upon security, §7-8-317.
Secured transactions.
Debtor's rights in collateral, §7-9-311.
Auctions and auctioneers.
Bulk transfers, §7-6-108.
Duties and liabilities of auctioneers, §7-6-108.
Sale by auction, §7-2-328.
Bailments.
Investment securities.
No conversion by good faith delivery, §7-8-318.

COMMERCIAL CODE—Cont'd
Bailments—Cont'd
Sales.
Seller's remedy of stoppage
of delivery in transit,
§7-2-705.
Bank deposits and
collections, §§7-4-101 to
7-4-504.
Account.
Defined, §7-4-104.
Alteration of instruments.
Customer's duty to discover
and report, §7-4-406.
Applicability of article,
§7-4-102.
Attachment and
garnishment.
When items subject to
legal process, §7-4-303.
Banking day.
Defined, §7-4-104.
Branch or separate offices
deemed separate bank,
§7-4-106.
Burden of proof.
Stop-payment order.
Burden of proof of loss,
§7-4-403.
Care.
Certain actions
constituting ordinary
care, §7-4-103.
Citation of article, §7-4-101.
Claims.
Warranties of customer
and collecting bank on
transfer or
presentment of items.
Time for claims,
§7-4-207.
Clearinghouse.
Defined, §7-4-104.
Effect, §7-4-103.
Collection by depositary and
collecting banks,
§§7-4-201 to 7-4-214.
Action.
When action seasonable,
§7-4-202.
Agency status.
Item indorsed "pay any
bank," §7-4-201.
"Pay any bank."
Item indorsed "pay any
bank," §7-4-201.
Presumption and
duration of agency
status of collecting
banks, §7-4-201.
Provisional status of
credits, §7-4-201.
Bills of lading.
Warranties of collecting
bank as to bills,
§7-7-508.
Charge-back.
Right of charge-back,
§7-4-212.
Claims.
Time for claims,
§7-4-207.
Delayed, §7-4-108.
Direct return, §7-4-212.
Documents of title.
Warranties of collecting
bank as to
documents, §7-7-508.
Duration of agency status
of collecting banks,
§7-4-201.

COMMERCIAL CODE—Cont'd
Bank deposits and
collections—Cont'd
Collection by depositary and
collecting banks—Cont'd
Holder in due course.
When bank gives value
for purposes of
holder in due course,
§7-4-209.
Indorsements.
Missing indorsement.
Supplying missing
indorsement,
§7-4-205.
Prior indorsement.
No notice from prior
indorsement,
§7-4-205.
Supplying missing
indorsement,
§7-4-205.
Insolvency, §7-4-214.
Instructions.
Effect of instructions,
§7-4-203.
Media of remittance,
§7-4-211.
Methods of sending and
presenting, §7-4-204.
Payment.
Final payment of item
by payor bank,
§7-4-213.
Provisional debits and
credits.
When provisional
debits and credits
become final,
§7-4-213.
Suspends payments.
Defined, §7-4-104.
When provisional debits
and credits become
final, §7-4-213.
Payor banks.
Suspension of payment,
§7-4-214.
Preference, §7-4-214.
Presentment.
By notice of item not
payable by, through
or at a bank,
§7-4-210.
Liability of secondary
parties, §7-4-210.
Methods of sending and
presenting, §7-4-204.
Warranties.
Warranties of
customer and
collecting bank on
transfer or
presentment of
items, §7-4-207.
Process of posting,
§7-4-109.
Refund.
Right of refund,
§7-4-212.
Remittance.
Media of remittance,
§7-4-211.
Provisional and final
settlement in
remittance cases,
§7-4-211.
Responsibility for
collection, §7-4-202.

COMMERCIAL CODE—Cont'd
Bank deposits and
collections—Cont'd
Collection by depositary and
collecting banks—Cont'd
Security interests.
Applicability of filing
provisions, §7-9-302.
Sending and presenting.
By notice of item not
payable by, through
or at a bank,
§7-4-210.
Liability of secondary
parties, §7-4-210.
Direct to payor bank,
§7-4-204.
Methods of sending and
presenting, §7-4-204.
Warranties.
Warranties of
customer and
collecting bank on
transfer or
presentment of
items, §7-4-207.
Status.
Agency status.
Presumption and
duration of agency
status of collecting
banks, §7-4-201.
Provisional status of
credits, §7-4-201.
Supplying missing
indorsements,
§7-4-205.
No notice from prior
indorsement,
§7-4-205.
Time.
Finality of provisional
debits and credits,
§7-4-213.
Time for claims,
§7-4-207.
Transfer between banks,
§7-4-206.
Warranties of customer
and collecting banks
on transfer,
§7-4-207.
Value.
When bank gives value
for purposes of
holder in due course,
§7-4-209.
Warehouse receipts.
Warranties of collecting
bank as to receipts,
§7-7-508.
Warranties.
Claims.
Time for claims,
§7-4-207.
Warehouse receipts.
Warranties of
collecting bank as
to receipts,
§7-7-508.
Warranties of customer
and collecting bank
on transfer or
presentment of
items, §7-4-207.
When action seasonable,
§7-4-202.
When provisional debits
and credits become
final, §7-4-213.

COMMERCIAL CODE—Cont'd
**Bank deposits and
collections**—Cont'd
Collection by depositary and
collecting banks—Cont'd
Withdrawal.
When certain credits
become available for
withdrawal,
§7-4-213.
Collection of documentary
drafts, §§7-4-501 to
7-4-504.
Definition of documentary
draft, §7-4-104.
Dishonor.
Duty to notify customer
of dishonor,
§7-4-501.
Referee in case of need,
§7-4-503.
Report of reasons for
dishonor, §7-4-503.
Handling of documentary
drafts, §7-4-501.
"On arrival" drafts.
Presentment, §7-4-502.
Presentment.
Duty to send for
presentment,
§7-4-501.
"On arrival" drafts,
§7-4-502.
Responsibility of
presenting bank for
documents and
goods, §7-4-503.
Privilege of presenting
bank to deal with
goods, §7-4-504.
Security interest for
expenses, §7-4-504.
Referee, §7-4-503.
Responsibility of
presenting bank for
documents and goods,
§7-4-503.
Security interest for
expenses, §7-4-504.
Conflict of laws.
Liability of bank, §7-4-102.
Customer.
Defined, §7-4-104.
Damages.
Certain action constituting
ordinary care,
§7-4-103.
Limitation by agreements,
§7-4-103.
Measure of damages,
§7-4-103.
Definitions.
Banks generally, §7-4-105.
Collecting bank, §7-4-105.
Depositary bank, §7-4-105.
Generally, §7-4-104.
Index, §7-4-104.
Intermediary bank,
§7-4-105.
Payor bank, §7-4-105.
Posting.
Process of posting,
§7-4-109.
Presenting bank, §7-4-105.
Process of posting,
§7-4-109.
Remitting bank, §7-4-105.
Delays, §7-4-108.

COMMERCIAL CODE—Cont'd
**Bank deposits and
collections**—Cont'd
Depositary and collecting
banks.
Collection by, §§7-4-201 to
7-4-214.
Defined, §7-4-105.
Documentary drafts.
Collection, §§7-4-501 to
7-4-504.
Defined, §7-4-104.
Executions.
When items subject to
legal process, §7-4-303.
Federal reserve regulations.
Effect, §7-4-103.
Forgery.
Customer's duty to discover
and report, §7-4-406.
Intermediary banks.
Defined, §7-4-105.
Item.
Defined, §7-4-104.
Payment.
Properly payable.
Defined, §7-4-104.
Suspends payment.
Defined, §7-4-104.
Payor banks.
Alteration of instruments.
Customer's duty to
discover and report
unauthorized
alteration, §7-4-406.
Attachment and
garnishment.
When items subject to
legal process,
§7-4-303.
Certifying items.
Order in which items
may be certified,
§7-4-303.
Charging items.
Order in which items
may be charged,
§7-4-303.
Clearinghouse.
Defined, §7-4-104.
Collection by depositary
and collecting banks.
Final payment of item
by payor bank,
§7-4-213.
Sending direct to payor
bank, §7-4-204.
Suspension of payment,
§7-4-214.
Customer relationship.
Customer's duty to
discover and report
unauthorized
signature or
alteration, §7-4-406.
Customer's right to stop
payment, §7-4-403.
Burden of proof of loss,
§7-4-403.
Death of customer,
§7-4-405.
Definition of customer,
§7-4-104.
Dishonor.
Liability to customer
for wrongful
dishonor, §7-4-402.

COMMERCIAL CODE—Cont'd
**Bank deposits and
collections**—Cont'd
Payor banks—Cont'd
Customer relationship
—Cont'd
Improper payment.
Bank's right to
subrogation on
improper payment,
§7-4-407.
Incompetence of
customer, §7-4-405.
No obligation to pay
check more than six
months old,
§7-4-404.
Stop-payment order.
Bank's right to
subrogation on
improper payment,
§7-4-407.
Customer's right to
stop payment,
§7-4-403.
Subrogation.
Bank's right to
subrogation on
improper payment,
§7-4-407.
When bank may charge
customer's account,
§7-4-401.
Wrongful dishonor.
Bank's liability to
customer,
§7-4-402.
Death of customer,
§7-4-405.
Defined, §7-4-105.
Delays, §7-4-108.
Responsibility for late
return of item,
§7-4-302.
Dishonor.
Liability to customer for
wrongful dishonor,
§7-4-402.
Time of dishonor,
§7-4-301.
Executions.
When items subject to
legal process,
§7-4-303.
Forgery.
Customer's duty to
discover and report,
§7-4-406.
Incompetence of customer,
§7-4-405.
Late return of item.
Responsibility, §7-4-302.
Legal process.
When items subject to
legal process,
§7-4-303.
Notice.
When items subject to
notice, §7-4-303.
Order in which items may
be charged or certified,
§7-4-303.
Payment.
Definition of suspending
payment, §7-4-104.
Final payment, §7-4-213.
Improper payment.
Bank's right to
subrogation on
improper payment,
§7-4-407.

COMMERCIAL CODE—Cont'd
Bank deposits and collections—Cont'd
Payor banks—Cont'd
Payment—Cont'd
No obligation to pay check more than six months old, §7-4-404.
Recovery of payment by return of items, §7-4-301.
Posting.
Deferred posting, §7-4-301.
Process of posting, §7-4-109.
Recovery of payment by return of items, §7-4-301.
Responsibility for late return of item, §7-4-302.
Set-offs.
When items subject to set-off, §7-4-303.
Signature.
Unauthorized signature.
Customer's duty to discover and report, §7-4-406.
Stopping payment.
Bank's right to subrogation on improper payment, §7-4-407.
Burden of proof of loss, §7-4-403.
Customer's right, §7-4-403.
Duration of order, §7-4-403.
When items subject to stop order, §7-4-303.
Subrogation.
Right to subrogation on improper payments, §7-4-407.
Suspension of payments, §7-4-214.
Defined, §7-4-104.
Time of dishonor, §7-4-301.
Unauthorized signature or alteration.
Customer's duty to discover and report, §7-4-406.
When bank may charge customer's account, §7-4-401.
When items subject to notice, stop order, legal process or set-off, §7-4-303.
Wrongful dishonor.
Liability to customer, §7-4-402.
Posting.
Deferred posting, §7-4-301.
Process of posting, §7-4-109.
Presenting bank.
Defined, §7-4-105.
Presumptions.
Agency status of collecting banks, §7-4-201.
Provisional status of credits, §7-4-201.
Receipt of items.
Time of receipt, §7-4-107.

COMMERCIAL CODE—Cont'd
Bank deposits and collections—Cont'd
Remitting bank.
Defined, §7-4-105.
Secured transactions.
Collection by depositary and collecting banks.
Security interest of collecting bank in items, accompanying documents and proceeds, §7-4-208.
Collection of documentary drafts.
Privilege of presenting bank to deal with goods.
Security interest for expenses, §7-4-504.
Separate or branch offices deemed separate banks, §7-4-106.
Set-offs.
When items subject to set-offs, §7-4-303.
Settle.
Defined, §7-4-104.
Short title of article, §7-4-101.
Stopping payment.
Bank's right to subrogation on improper payment, §7-4-407.
Burden of proof of loss, §7-4-403.
Customers' right, §7-4-403.
Duration of order, §7-4-403.
When items subject to stop order, §7-4-303.
Time.
Afternoon.
Defined, §7-4-104.
Collection by depositary and collecting banks.
Claims for breach of warranty, §7-4-207.
Finality of provisional debits and credits, §7-4-213.
Time for claims, §7-4-207.
Delays, §7-4-108.
Midnight deadline.
Defined, §7-4-104.
Receipt of items, §7-4-107.
Time of dishonor, §7-4-301.
When action seasonable, §7-4-202.
Unauthorized signature or alteration.
Customer's duty to discover and report, §7-4-406.
Variation of article by agreement, §7-4-103.
When action seasonable, §7-4-202.
Withdrawal.
When certain credits become available to withdrawal, §7-4-213.
Bankruptcy and insolvency.
Bank deposits and collections.
Suspension of payments by payor or collecting banks, §7-4-214.

COMMERCIAL CODE—Cont'd
Bankruptcy and insolvency—Cont'd
Bulk transfers.
Trustees in bankruptcy.
Transfers excepted from article, §7-6-103.
Buyer's insolvency.
Seller's remedies, §7-2-702.
Commercial paper.
Defenses against holder in due course, §7-3-305.
Definitions, §7-1-201.
Letters of credit.
Insolvency of bank holding funds for documentary credit, §7-5-117.
Secured transactions.
Trustees of bankruptcy.
Priority over unperfected security interests, §7-9-301.
Seller's insolvency.
Buyer's right to goods on seller's insolvency, §7-2-502.
Banks and financial institutions.
Branches.
Defined, §7-1-201.
Commercial paper. See within this heading, "Commercial paper."
Defined, §7-1-201.
Deposits and collections, §§7-4-101 to 7-4-504. See within this heading, "Bank deposits and collections."
Instructions.
Effect of instructions, §7-4-203.
Sales.
Banker's credit term, §7-2-325.
Secured transactions.
Transfer of accounts excluded from article, §7-9-104.
Bearer.
Defined, §7-1-201.
Beverages.
Sales.
Implied warranty of merchantability, §7-2-314.
Bills of lading.
Defined, §7-1-201.
General provisions, §§7-7-101 to 7-7-603. See within this heading, "Documents of title."
Overseas shipment.
Form of bill, §7-2-323.
Third-party documents.
Prima facie evidence, §7-1-202.
Blood.
Implied warranty, §7-2-314.
Bona fide purchasers.
Bulk transfers.
Subsequent transfers, §7-6-110.
Investment securities.
Adverse claim, §7-8-301.
Defined, §7-8-302.
Enforcement of completed or altered instruments, §7-8-206.
Title acquired by bona fide purchaser, §7-8-301.

COMMERCIAL CODE—Cont'd
Bona fide purchasers
—Cont'd
Sales.
Title acquired, §7-2-403.
Secured transactions.
Rights of third parties,
§§7-9-307 to 7-9-309.
Bond issues.
Investment securities
generally, §§7-8-101 to
7-8-406. See within this
heading, "Investment
securities."
Breach of contract.
Claim or right arising out of
breach.
Waiver or renunciation,
§7-1-107.
Sales.
Breach, repudiation and
excuse. See within this
heading, "Sales."
Waiver or renunciation of
claim or right after
breach, §7-1-107.
Buildings.
Sales.
Goods to be severed from
realty, §7-2-107.
**Bulk transfers, §§7-6-101 to
7-6-111.**
Applicability of article,
§7-6-102.
Exceptions, §7-6-103.
Assignments for benefit of
creditors.
Transfers excepted from
article, §7-6-103.
Attachment and
garnishment.
Limitation of actions and
levies, §7-6-111.
Auctioneer.
Defined, §7-6-108.
Duties and liabilities of
auctioneer, §7-6-108.
Auction sales, §7-6-108.
Bankruptcy and insolvency.
Trustees in bankruptcy.
Transfers excepted from
article, §7-6-103.
Bona fide purchasers.
Subsequent transfers,
§7-6-110.
Bulk transfers subject to
article, §7-6-102.
Exceptions, §7-6-103.
Citation of article.
Short title, §7-6-101.
Corporations.
Exception of sales on
dissolution or
reorganization from
article, §7-6-103.
Creditors.
List of creditors, §7-6-104.
Notice to creditors,
§7-6-105.
Content, §7-6-107.
Delivery, §7-6-107.
What creditors protected,
§7-6-109.
Defined, §7-6-102.
Enterprises subject to article,
§7-6-102.
Exceptions, §7-6-103.
Equipment.
Transfer of equipment,
§7-6-102.

COMMERCIAL CODE—Cont'd
Bulk transfers—Cont'd
Exceptions from article,
§7-6-103.
Executions.
Limitation of actions and
levies, §7-6-111.
Sales excepted from article,
§7-6-103.
Executors and
administrators.
Transfers excepted from
article, §7-6-103.
Fiduciaries.
Transfers excepted from
article, §7-6-103.
Garnishment.
Limitation of actions and
levies, §7-6-111.
Judicial sales and renting.
Transfers excepted from
article, §7-6-103.
Levies.
Limitation of levies,
§7-6-111.
Limitation of actions and
levies, §7-6-111.
Notice.
Contents, §7-6-107.
Creditors.
Contents and delivery,
§7-6-107.
Notice to creditors,
§7-6-105.
Delivery, §7-6-107.
Notice to creditors,
§7-6-105.
Contents, §7-6-107.
Delivery, §7-6-107.
Scope, §7-6-105.
Property.
Schedule of property,
§7-6-104.
Protection of creditors,
§7-6-109.
Schedule of property,
§7-6-104.
Secured transactions.
Applicability of bulk
transfer laws,
§7-9-111.
Short title of article,
§7-6-101.
Subsequent transfers,
§7-6-110.
Transfers.
Excepted from article,
§7-6-103.
Limitation of actions and
levies, §7-6-111.
Subsequent transfers,
§7-6-110.
What creditors protected,
§7-6-109.
Burden of establishing.
Defined, §7-1-201.
Burden of proof.
Bank deposits and
collections.
Order to stop payment.
Burden of proof of loss,
§7-4-403.
Commercial paper.
Establishing that
completion is
unauthorized,
§7-3-115.
Order to stop payment.
Burden of proof of loss,
§7-4-403.

COMMERCIAL CODE—Cont'd
Burden of proof—Cont'd
Definition of burden of
establishing, §7-1-201.
Investment securities.
Action on securities,
§7-8-105.
Option to accelerate at will.
Burden of establishing lack
of good faith, §7-1-208.
Sales.
Burden of establishing
breach after
acceptance, §7-2-607.
**Buyer in ordinary course of
business.**
Defined, §7-1-201.
Cancellation.
Sales contracts, §7-2-209.
Effect of cancellation or
rescission on claims for
antecedent breach,
§7-2-720.
Captions.
Section captions, §7-1-109.
Certificates of deposit.
Commercial paper generally.
See within this heading,
"Commercial paper."
**Chattel mortgages and deeds
of trust.**
Secured transactions
generally, §§7-9-101 to
7-9-507. See within this
heading, "Secured
transactions."
Checks.
Generally, §§7-3-101 to
7-3-805. See within this
heading, "Commercial
paper."
Collections.
Bank deposits and
collections, §§7-4-101 to
7-4-504. See within this
heading, "Bank deposits
and collections."
**Commercial paper, §§7-3-101
to 7-3-805.**
Acceleration of instrument.
Notice to purchaser that
instrument is overdue,
§7-3-304.
Acceptance.
Acceptor.
Contract of acceptor,
§7-3-413.
Accrual of cause of action
against acceptor,
§7-3-122.
Assignment.
Drawee must accept
check or draft,
§7-3-409.
Certification of check,
§7-3-411.
Contract of acceptor,
§7-3-413.
Defined, §7-3-410.
Dishonor.
Acceptance varying
draft, §7-3-412.
Drafts.
Acceptance varying
draft, §7-3-412.
Drawee.
Not liable until
acceptance,
§7-3-409.

COMMERCIAL CODE—Cont'd
Commercial paper—Cont'd
Acceptance—Cont'd
Drawer.
Certification of check
discharges drawer,
§7-3-412.
Finality of acceptance,
§7-3-418.
Incomplete drafts,
§7-3-410.
Operation of acceptance,
§7-3-410.
Presentment.
Time allowed for
acceptance, §7-3-506.
Time allowed for
acceptance after
presentment, §7-3-506.
Varying draft, §7-3-412.
Writing required, §7-3-410.
Accommodation party.
Contract of accommodation
party, §7-3-415.
Defined, §7-3-415.
Not notice of claim or
defense, §7-3-304.
Actions.
Accrual of cause of action,
§7-3-122.
Agents.
Conversion.
Innocent representative,
§7-3-419.
Signature by authorized
representative,
§7-3-403.
Signature in ambiguous
capacity deemed
indorsement, §7-3-402.
Warranties on presentment
and transfer, §7-3-417.
Words describing payee,
§7-3-117.
Alteration of instruments.
Effect of alteration,
§7-3-407.
Negligence contributing to
alteration, §7-3-406.
Notice of claim or defense
to purchaser, §7-3-304.
Unauthorized completion,
§7-3-115.
Warranty that instrument
not altered, §7-3-417.
What constitutes, §7-3-407.
Ambiguity.
Signature in ambiguous
capacity, §7-3-402.
Terms, §7-3-118.
Antedating, §7-3-114.
Not notice of claim or
defense, §7-3-304.
Assignments.
Check not assignment,
§7-3-409.
Bank deposits and
collections, §§7-4-101 to
7-4-504. See within this
heading, "Bank deposits
and collections."
Bankruptcy and insolvency.
Defenses against holder in
due course, §7-3-305.
Banks.
Branch or separate offices
deemed separate
banks, §7-4-106.
Certification of check.
Acceptance, §7-3-411.

COMMERCIAL CODE—Cont'd
Commercial paper—Cont'd
Banks—Cont'd
Deposits and collections,
§§7-4-101 to 7-4-504.
See within this
heading, "Bank
deposits and
collections."
Instructions.
Effect of instructions,
§7-4-203.
Instruments payable at
bank, §7-3-121.
Instruments payable
through banks,
§7-3-120.
Bearer.
Defined, §7-1-201.
Instruments not payable to
bearer, §7-3-805.
Payable to bearer,
§7-3-111.
Burden of proof.
Burden of establishing.
Defined, §7-1-201.
Genuineness or
authorization of
signatures, §7-3-307.
Order to stop payment.
Burden of proof of loss,
§7-4-403.
Signatures, defenses and
due course.
Burden of establishing,
§7-3-307.
Cancellation.
Cancellation of
indorsement, §7-3-605.
Discharge by cancellation
or reacquisition,
§7-3-208.
Indorsements.
Cancellation of
indorsement,
§7-3-208.
Right to rescind
negotiation, §7-3-207.
Certificates of deposit.
Defined, §7-3-104.
Form, §7-3-104.
Checks.
Acceptance.
Certification of check,
§7-3-411.
Assignment.
Check not assignment,
§7-3-409.
Bad checks.
Power to transfer title
when check
dishonored, §7-2-403.
Bank's right to subrogation
on improper payment,
§7-4-407.
Certification, §7-3-411.
Defined, §7-3-104.
Effect on underlying
obligations, §7-3-802.
Form, §7-3-104.
Incompetence of maker.
Accept on payment,
§7-4-405.
Payment by check,
§7-2-511.
Sales.
Payment by check,
§7-2-511.
Power to transfer title
when check
dishonored, §7-2-403.

COMMERCIAL CODE—Cont'd
Commercial paper—Cont'd
Checks—Cont'd
Stale check.
No obligation to pay
check more than six
months old,
§7-4-404.
Notice of claim or
defense, §7-3-304.
Stop-payment order.
Relationship between
payor banks and
customer, §7-4-403.
Citation of article, §7-3-101.
Claim.
Notice of claim.
Notice to purchaser,
§7-3-304.
Conditions precedent.
Defense of nonperformance
of any condition
precedent, §7-3-306.
Confession of judgment.
Terms and omissions not
affecting negotiability,
§7-3-112.
Consideration.
Defense of want or failure
of consideration,
§§7-3-306, 7-3-408.
Failure of consideration,
§7-3-408.
Taking for value, §7-3-303.
Want of consideration,
§7-3-408.
Construction and
interpretation.
Ambiguous terms,
§7-3-118.
Rules of construction,
§§7-3-102, 7-3-118.
Conversion.
Innocent representative,
§7-3-419.
When instrument
converted, §7-3-419.
Corporations.
Exceeding powers.
Negotiation effective
although subject to
rescission, §7-3-207.
Payee described as agent
or officer, §7-3-117.
Signature by authorized
representative,
§7-3-403.
Date, §7-3-114.
Acceptor failing to date
acceptance, §7-3-410.
Antedating, §7-3-114.
Not notice of claim or
defense, §7-3-304.
Failure to date, §7-3-114.
Negotiability.
Not affected by
antedating,
postdating or
nondating, §7-3-114.
Postdating, §7-3-114.
Not notice of claim or
defense, §7-3-304.
Defenses.
Against one not holder in
due course, §7-3-306.
Available against holder in
due course, §7-3-305.
Burden of establishing,
§7-3-307.

COMMERCIAL CODE—Cont'd
Commercial paper—Cont'd
Defenses—Cont'd
Holder in due course.
Defenses available
against holder in
due course, §7-3-305.
Notice of defense.
Notice to purchaser,
§7-3-304.
Want or failure of
consideration,
§7-3-408.
Warranty against defenses,
§7-3-417.
Definitions, §7-3-102.
Acceptance, §7-3-410.
Accommodation party,
§7-3-415.
Alteration of instruments,
§7-3-407.
Certificate of deposits,
§7-3-104.
Checks, §7-3-104.
Dishonor, §7-3-507.
Drafts, §7-3-104.
Holder in due course,
§7-3-302.
Index of definitions,
§7-3-102.
Instruments, §7-3-102.
Issue, §7-3-102.
Money, §7-3-107.
Negotiable instruments,
§7-3-104.
Notes, §7-3-104.
Order, §7-3-102.
Unconditional order,
§7-3-105.
Presentment, §7-3-504.
Promises, §7-3-102.
Unconditional promise,
§7-3-105.
Protest, §7-3-509.
Restrictive indorsement,
§7-3-205.
Secondary party, §7-3-102.
Sum certain, §7-3-106.
Transfer without recourse,
§7-3-417.
Unconditional promise or
order, §7-3-105.
Delivery.
Defenses of nondelivery or
delivery for a special
purpose, §7-3-306.
Defined, §7-1-201.
Delivery for a special
purpose.
Defenses, §7-3-306.
Issue defined, §7-3-102.
Negotiation, §7-3-202.
Nondelivery.
Defense of nondelivery,
§7-3-306.
Demand.
Accrual of cause of action
against obligor of
demand or time
certificate of deposit,
§7-3-122.
Payable on demand,
§§7-3-104, 7-3-108.
Presentment and demand
for acceptance or
payment, §7-3-504.
Destroyed instruments,
§7-3-804.
Discharge.
Cancellation, §7-3-605.

COMMERCIAL CODE—Cont'd
Commercial paper—Cont'd
Discharge—Cont'd
Certification of check.
Discharge against
drawer and prior
indorsers, §7-3-411.
Collateral.
Impairment of collateral,
§7-3-606.
Discharge of one party
discharges another
party, §7-3-601.
Extent of discharge,
§7-3-601.
Generally, §7-3-601.
Holder in due course.
Effect of discharge
against holder in
due course, §7-3-602.
Impairment of recourse or
collateral, §7-3-606.
Instruments payable to two
or more persons,
§7-3-116.
Payment.
Discharge upon payment,
§7-3-603.
Tender of payment,
§7-3-604.
Recourse.
Impairment of recourse,
§7-3-606.
Renunciation, §7-3-605.
Satisfaction.
Discharge upon
satisfaction,
§7-3-603.
Underlying obligations.
Effect of taking
instrument,
§7-3-802.
Unexcused delay in
presentment, notice of
dishonor or protest,
§7-3-502.
Dishonor.
Acceptance varying draft,
§7-3-412.
Bank deposits and
collections.
Payor banks, §7-4-301.
Wrongful dishonor.
Liability of bank to
customer,
§7-4-402.
Certificate of dishonor.
Protest a certificate of
dishonor, §7-3-509.
Defined, §7-3-507.
Evidence of dishonor,
§7-3-510.
Holder's right of recourse,
§7-3-507.
Indorsement.
Return of instrument for
lack of indorsement
not dishonor,
§7-3-507.
Power to transfer title
when check
dishonored, §7-2-403.
Recourse.
Holder's right, §7-3-507.
Re-presentment.
Term allowing re-
presentment in
event of dishonor,
§7-3-507.
When instrument is
dishonored, §7-3-507.

COMMERCIAL CODE—Cont'd
Commercial paper—Cont'd
Dishonor—Cont'd
Wrongful dishonor.
Liability of bank to
customer, §7-4-402.
Drafts.
Acceptance.
Acceptance varying
draft, §7-3-412.
Assignment.
Draft not assignment,
§7-3-409.
Defined, §7-3-104.
Drafts in a set, §7-3-801.
Form, §7-3-104.
International sight draft.
Letter of advice of
international sight
draft, §7-3-701.
Parts.
Drafts in a set, §7-3-801.
Drawer.
Contract of drawer,
§7-3-413.
Notice of dishonor.
When unexcused delay
in notice of dishonor
discharges drawer,
§7-3-502.
Presentment.
When unexcused delay
in necessary
presentment
discharges drawer,
§7-3-502.
Protest.
Unexcused delay
discharges drawer,
§7-3-502.
Secondary parties defined,
§7-3-102.
Duress.
Defenses against holder in
due course, §7-3-305.
Negotiation effective
although subject to
rescission, §7-3-207.
Evidence.
Accommodation party.
Proof of accommodation,
§7-3-415.
Certificate of notary as to
presentment for
acceptance, etc., of
instrument governed
by commercial law,
§12-21-105.
Dishonor.
Evidence of dishonor,
§7-3-510.
Notice of dishonor,
§7-3-510.
Fiduciaries.
Notice of claim or defense
to purchaser, §7-3-304.
Signature by authorized
representative,
§7-3-403.
Signature in ambiguous
capacity deemed
indorsement, §7-3-402.
Words describing payee,
§7-3-117.
Forgery.
Conversion of instrument,
§7-3-419.
Notice of claim or defense
to purchaser, §7-3-304.

COMMERCIAL CODE—Cont'd
Commercial paper—Cont'd
Forgery—Cont'd
  Unauthorized signature,
    §7-3-404.
  Negligence contributing
    to unauthorized
    signature, §7-3-406.
Forms.
  Certificate of deposit,
    §7-3-104.
  Check, §7-3-104.
  Draft, §7-3-104.
  Negotiable instrument,
    §7-3-104.
  Note, §7-3-104.
  Required forms, §7-3-104.
Fraud.
  Negotiation effective
    although subject to
    rescission, §7-3-207.
Guarantor.
  Contract of guarantor,
    §7-3-416.
Holder.
  Claim.
    Notice to purchaser,
      §7-3-304.
  Defense.
    Notice to purchaser,
      §7-3-304.
  Defined, §7-1-201.
  Discharge.
    Effect of discharge
      against holder in
      due course, §7-3-602.
  Holder in due course.
    Burden of establishing,
      §7-3-307.
    Defenses against holder
      in due course,
      §7-3-305.
    Defined, §7-3-302.
    Discharge.
      Effect of discharge
        against holder in
        due course,
        §7-3-602.
    Instruments not payable
      to order or to bearer,
      §7-3-805.
    Negotiation not subject
      to rescission,
      §7-3-207.
    Payee, §7-3-302.
    Purchaser of limited
      interest, §7-3-302.
    Rights of holder in due
      course, §7-3-305.
    Taking for value,
      §7-3-303.
    Value.
      Taking for value,
        §7-3-303.
      When bank gives
        value for purposes
        of holder in due
        course, §7-4-209.
    Who does not become,
      §7-3-302.
      Instruments not
        payable to order or
        to bearer,
        §7-3-805.
  Notice to purchaser.
    Notice of claim or
      defense, §7-3-304.
  Rights of holder, §7-3-301.
    Holder in due course,
      §7-3-305.

COMMERCIAL CODE—Cont'd
Commercial paper—Cont'd
Holder—Cont'd
  Rights of holder—Cont'd
    Rights of one not holder
      in due course,
      §7-3-306.
    Taking for value, §7-3-303.
    Value.
      Taking for value,
        §7-3-303.
      When bank gives value
        for purposes of
        holder in due course,
        §7-4-209.
Honor.
  Defined, §7-1-201.
Incomplete instruments.
  Acceptance of incomplete
    drafts, §7-3-410.
  Notice of claim or defense
    to purchaser, §7-3-115.
Indorsement.
  Ambiguity of signature.
    Signature in ambiguous
      capacity deemed
      indorsement,
      §7-3-402.
  Blank indorsement,
    §7-3-204.
  Cancellation, §7-3-605.
    Cancellation upon
      reacquisition,
      §§7-3-208, 7-3-605.
  Collection by depositary
    and collecting banks.
    Supplying missing
      indorsement,
      §7-4-205.
  Contract of indorsers,
    §7-3-414.
  Dishonor.
    Return of instrument for
      lack of indorsement
      not dishonor,
      §7-3-507.
  Generally, §7-3-202.
  Impostors, §7-3-405.
  Indorsers.
    Accrual of cause of
      action against
      indorsers, §7-3-122.
    Certification of check
      discharges indorsers,
      §7-3-411.
    Contract of indorsers,
      §7-3-414.
    Order of liability,
      §7-3-414.
  Delay in necessary
    presentment, notice
    of dishonor or
    protest.
    Unexcused delay
      discharges
      indorser, §7-3-502.
  Presentment.
    Unexcused delay in
      presentment
      discharges
      indorser, §7-3-502.
  Protest.
    Unexcused delay in
      protest discharges
      indorser, §7-3-502.
  Secondary parties
    defined, §7-3-102.
  Unexcused delay
    discharges indorser,
    §7-3-502.

COMMERCIAL CODE—Cont'd
Commercial paper—Cont'd
Indorsement—Cont'd
  Missing indorsements.
    Collection by depositary
      and collecting banks.
      Supplying missing
        indorsement,
        §7-4-205.
  Negotiation, §7-3-202.
  Reacquisition, §7-3-208.
  Restrictive indorsement.
    Defined, §7-3-205.
    Effect of restrictive
      indorsement,
      §7-3-206.
    Innocent representative,
      §7-3-419.
  Signature.
    Signature in ambiguous
      capacity deemed
      indorsement,
      §7-3-402.
    Signature in name of
      payee, §7-3-405.
    Special indorsement,
      §7-3-204.
  Transfer.
    Right to have
      indorsement of
      transferor, §7-3-201.
    Wrong or misspelled name,
      §7-3-203.
Innocent representative,
  §7-3-419.
Interest.
  Ambiguous terms and
    rules of construction,
    §7-3-118.
  Rate, §7-3-122.
International sight draft.
  Letter of advice, §7-3-701.
Intervention.
  Notice to third party of
    suit, §7-3-803.
Irregular instrument.
  Notice of claim or defense
    to purchaser, §7-3-304.
Issues.
  Defined, §7-3-102.
Larceny.
  Defenses, §7-3-306.
  Stolen instruments,
    §7-3-804.
Letter of advice.
  International sight draft,
    §7-3-701.
Liability of parties, §§7-3-401
  to 7-3-419.
  Acceptance varying draft,
    §7-3-412.
  Acceptor.
    Contract of acceptor,
      §7-3-413.
  Accommodation party.
    Contract of
      accommodation
      party, §7-3-415.
  Alteration of instruments,
    §7-3-407.
    Negligence contributing
      to alteration of
      instrument,
      §7-3-406.
  Assignment.
    Acceptance necessary,
      §7-3-409.
    Check or draft not
      assignment,
      §7-3-409.

COMMERCIAL CODE—Cont'd
Commercial paper—Cont'd
Liability of parties—Cont'd
Certification of check,
§7-3-411.
Contracts of parties,
§§7-3-413 to 7-3-416.
Drawee.
Acceptance necessary,
§7-3-409.
Drawer.
Contract of drawer,
§7-3-413.
Forgery.
Unauthorized signatures,
§7-3-404.
Guarantor.
Contract of guarantor,
§7-3-416.
Impostors, §7-3-405.
Indorsers.
Contract of indorser,
§7-3-414.
Order of liability,
§7-3-414.
Maker.
Contract of maker,
§7-3-413.
Signature.
Authorized
representative,
§7-3-403.
Deemed indorsement
when in ambiguous
capacity, §7-3-402.
Impostors, §7-3-405.
Person not liable unless
signature appears,
§7-3-401.
Unauthorized signatures,
§7-3-404.
Negligence
contributing to
unauthorized
signature,
§7-3-406.
Want or failure of
consideration,
§7-3-408.
Warranties on presentment
and transfer, §7-3-417.
Limitations on scope of
article, §7-3-103.
Lost instruments, §7-3-804.
Maker.
Accrual of cause of action
against maker,
§7-3-122.
Contract of maker,
§7-3-413.
Mentally ill.
Defenses against holder in
due course, §7-3-305.
Negotiation effective
although subject to
rescission, §7-3-207.
Minors.
Defenses against holder in
due course, §7-3-305.
Negotiation effective
although subject to
rescission, §7-3-207.
Misrepresentation.
Defenses against holder in
due course, §7-3-305.
Mistake.
Negotiation effective
although subject to
rescission, §7-3-207.
Money.
Defined, §7-3-107.

COMMERCIAL CODE—Cont'd
Commercial paper—Cont'd
Money—Cont'd
Instrument payable in
money, §7-3-107.
Name.
Misspelled name, §7-3-203.
Wrong name, §7-3-203.
Negligence.
Contributing to alteration
or unauthorized
signature, §7-3-406.
Negotiability.
Date, antedating and
postdating not
affecting negotiability,
§7-3-114.
Incomplete instruments,
§7-3-115.
Seal not affecting
negotiability, §7-3-113.
Terms and omissions not
affecting negotiability,
§7-3-112.
Writings.
Other writings affecting
instrument,
§7-3-119.
Negotiation, §7-3-202.
Effective to transfer
although subject to
rescission, §7-3-207.
Holder in due course.
Negotiation as against
subsequent holder in
due course not
subject to rescission,
§7-3-207.
Notes.
Defined, §7-3-104.
Form, §7-3-104.
Notice of claim or defense.
Notice to purchaser,
§7-3-304.
Notice of dishonor.
Death of party, §7-3-508.
Delay.
Effect of unexcused
delay, §7-3-502.
Excused delay, §7-3-511.
Evidence of notice,
§7-3-510.
Excused notice, §7-3-511.
Generally, §7-3-508.
How given, §7-3-508.
Mail, §7-3-508.
Time.
When given, §7-3-508.
Waiver of notice, §7-3-511.
When given, §7-3-508.
When necessary, §7-3-501.
Not necessary to charge
guarantor, §7-3-416.
Notice to third party,
§7-3-803.
Obligation.
Effect of instrument on
obligation for which it
is given, §7-3-802.
Omissions.
Terms and omissions not
affecting negotiability,
§7-3-112.
Order.
Defined, §7-3-102.
Form of negotiable
instruments, §7-3-104.
Instruments not payable to
order, §7-3-805.
Payable to order,
§§7-3-104, 7-3-110.

COMMERCIAL CODE—Cont'd
Commercial paper—Cont'd
Order—Cont'd
Required unconditional
order to pay sum
certain, §7-3-104.
Unconditional order.
Required unconditional
order, §7-3-104.
When order
unconditional,
§7-3-105.
Overdue instruments.
Notice of claim or defense
to purchaser, §7-3-304.
Parties.
Notice to third party,
§7-3-803.
Payment.
Banks.
Payable at bank,
§7-3-121.
Payable through bank,
§7-3-120.
Bearer.
Instruments not payable
to bearer, §7-3-805.
Payable to bearer,
§7-3-104.
When instrument
payable to bearer,
§7-3-111.
Demand.
Payable on demand,
§7-3-104.
What instruments
payable on demand,
§7-3-108.
Discharge.
Discharge upon payment,
§7-3-603.
Tender of payment,
§7-3-604.
Finality of payment,
§7-3-418.
Guarantor.
Contract of guarantor,
§7-3-416.
Money.
When payable in money,
§7-3-107.
Order.
Instruments not payable
to order, §7-3-805.
Payable to order,
§§7-3-104, 7-3-110.
When instrument
payable to order,
§7-3-110.
Payable to bearer,
§§7-3-104, 7-3-111.
Instruments not payable
to bearer, §7-3-805.
Payable to order,
§§7-3-104, 7-3-110.
Instruments not payable
to order, §7-3-805.
Presentment.
Time allowed for
payment, §7-3-506.
Tender of payment.
Discharge, §7-3-604.
Time.
Allowed for payment
after presentment,
§7-3-506.
Payable at definite time,
§7-3-104.
When payable at definite
time, §7-3-109.

COMMERCIAL CODE—Cont'd
Commercial paper—Cont'd
Payment—Cont'd
Two or more persons.
Instruments payable to
two or more persons,
§7-3-116.
Words of description.
Instruments payable
with words of
description, §7-3-117.
Postdating, §7-3-114.
Not notice of claim or
defense, §7-3-304.
Presentment.
Acceptance.
Time allowed for
acceptance, §7-3-506.
Defined, §7-3-504.
Delay.
Effect of unexcused
delay, §7-3-502.
Excused delay, §7-3-511.
Dishonor.
When instrument is
dishonored, §7-3-507.
Excused presentment,
§7-3-511.
Protest or notice of
dishonor or delay
therein, §7-3-511.
How presentment made,
§7-3-504.
Mail.
Presentment by mail,
§7-3-504.
Party to whom
presentment made.
Rights, §7-3-505.
Payment.
Time allowed for
payment, §7-3-506.
Re-presentment.
Term allowing re-
presentment in
event of dishonor,
§7-3-507.
Rights of party to whom
presentment made,
§7-3-505.
Time allowed for
acceptance or payment,
§7-3-506.
Time of presentment,
§7-3-503.
Waiver of presentment,
§7-3-511.
Protest or notice of
dishonor or delay
therein, §7-3-511.
Warranties on
presentment, §7-3-417.
When necessary, §7-3-501.
Not necessary to charge
guarantor, §7-3-416.
Presumptions.
Date presumed correct,
§7-3-114.
Genuineness or
authorization of
signatures, §7-3-307.
Promises.
Defined, §7-3-102.
Form of negotiable
instruments, §7-3-104.
Required unconditional
promise to pay,
§7-3-104.
Unconditional promise.
Required unconditional
promise, §7-3-104.

COMMERCIAL CODE—Cont'd
Commercial paper—Cont'd
Promises—Cont'd
Unconditional promise
—Cont'd
When promise
unconditional,
§7-3-105.
Protest.
Defined, §7-3-509.
Delay.
Excused delay, §7-3-511.
Unexcused delay
discharges drawer or
indorser, §7-3-502.
Excused protest, §7-3-511.
Generally, §7-3-509.
Noting for protest,
§7-3-509.
Time due, §7-3-509.
Waiver of protest, §7-3-511.
When necessary, §7-3-501.
Not necessary to charge
guarantor, §7-3-416.
Purchaser.
Notice of claim or defense,
§7-3-304.
Renunciation.
Discharge, §7-3-605.
Required form, §7-3-104.
Rescission.
Cancellation of
indorsement, §7-3-605.
Right to rescind
negotiation, §7-3-207.
Res judicata.
Effect of notice to party
answerable over,
§7-3-803.
Scope of article.
Limitations on scope,
§7-3-103.
Seal.
Does not affect
negotiability, §7-3-113.
Secondary parties.
Defined, §7-3-102.
Short title, §7-3-101.
Sight draft.
International sight draft.
Letter of advice,
§7-3-701.
Signature.
Ambiguous capacity.
Deemed indorsement
when in ambiguous
capacity, §7-3-402.
Authorized representative.
Signature by authorized
representative,
§7-3-403.
Warranty that signature
authorized, §7-3-417.
Burden of establishing,
§7-3-307.
Forgery.
Unauthorized signatures,
§7-3-404.
How made, §7-3-401.
Impostors, §7-3-405.
Incomplete instruments at
time of signing,
§7-3-115.
Liability.
Person not liable unless
signature appears,
§7-3-401.
Misspelled name, §7-3-203.
Name.
Wrong or misspelled
name, §7-3-203.

COMMERCIAL CODE—Cont'd
Commercial paper—Cont'd
Signature—Cont'd
Payee.
Signature in name of
payee intending
payee to have no
interest, §7-3-405.
Presumptions.
Genuineness or
authorization,
§7-3-307.
Representative.
Signature by authorized
representative,
§7-3-403.
Required signature,
§7-3-104.
Striking out signature.
Discharge, §7-3-605.
Unauthorized signature,
§7-3-404.
Negligence contributing
to unauthorized
signature, §7-3-406.
Warranty that signature
genuine and
authorized, §7-3-417.
Wrong name, §7-3-203.
Stolen instruments, §7-3-804.
Sum certain, §7-3-106.
Defined, §7-3-106.
Required, §7-3-104.
Tender of payment.
Discharge, §7-3-604.
Terms.
Not affecting negotiability,
§7-3-112.
Theft.
Defenses, §7-3-306.
Stolen instruments,
§7-3-804.
Third parties.
Notice to third party,
§7-3-803.
Time.
Acceptance.
Time allowed for
acceptance after
presentment,
§7-3-506.
Date, §7-3-114.
Definite time, §7-3-109.
Notice of dishonor.
When given, §7-3-508.
Payment.
Payable at definite time,
§§7-3-104, 7-3-109.
Time allowed for
payment after
presentment,
§7-3-506.
Presentment, §7-3-503.
Time allowed for
acceptance or
payment, §7-3-506.
Protest.
Time protest due,
§7-3-509.
Title.
Warranty of title, §7-3-417.
Transfer.
Blank indorsement,
§§7-3-204, 7-3-304.
Generally, §§7-3-201 to
7-3-208.
Negotiation, §7-3-202.
Effective to transfer
although subject to
rescission, §7-3-207.
Reacquisition, §7-3-208.

COMMERCIAL CODE—Cont'd
Commercial paper—Cont'd
Transfer—Cont'd
Restrictive indorsement,
§7-3-205.
Effect, §7-3-206.
Right of indorsement of
transferor, §7-3-201.
Rights vested in transferee,
§7-3-201.
Special indorsement,
§7-3-204.
Warranties on transfer,
§7-3-417.
Without recourse, §7-3-417.
Wrong or misspelled name,
§7-3-203.
Unauthorized completion,
§7-3-115.
Value.
Defined, §7-1-201.
Taking for value, §7-3-303.
Waiver.
Presentment, protest or
notice of dishonor,
§7-3-511.
Warranty on presentment
and transfer, §7-3-417.
Words of description.
Payable with words of
description, §7-3-117.
Writing.
Acceptances, §7-3-410.
Other writings affecting
instrument and
negotiability, §7-3-119.
Required, §7-3-104.
Conditional sales.
Secured transactions
generally, §§7-9-101 to
7-9-507. See within this
heading, "Secured
transactions."
Confession of judgment.
Commercial paper, §7-3-112.
Conflict of laws.
Bank deposits and
collections, §7-4-102.
Investment securities.
Registration of transfer,
§7-8-106.
Validity of security,
§7-8-106.
Parties' power to choose
applicable law, §7-1-105.
Secured transactions.
Multiple state transactions.
Perfection of security
interest, §7-9-103.
Perfection of security
interest in multiple
state transactions,
§7-9-103.
Removal of collateral,
§7-9-401.
Consignment, §7-9-114.
Conspicuous.
Defined, §7-1-201.
**Construction and
interpretation.**
Commercial paper.
Ambiguous terms and
rules of construction,
§7-3-118.
Course of dealing, §7-1-205.
Definitions. See within this
heading, "Definitions."
Documents of title.
Construction against
negative implication,
§7-7-105.

COMMERCIAL CODE—Cont'd
**Construction and
interpretation**—Cont'd
Implicit repeal.
Construction against
implicit repeal,
§7-1-104.
Option to accelerate at will,
§7-1-208.
Overseas, §7-2-323.
Reasonable time, §7-1-204.
Rules of construction,
§7-1-102.
Sales contracts.
Course of performance or
practical construction,
§7-2-208.
Offer and acceptance,
§7-2-206.
Seasonably, §7-1-204.
Time, §7-1-204.
Usage of trade, §7-1-205.
Contracts.
Battle of forms.
Sales contracts, §7-2-202.
Breach of contract.
Sales contracts.
Breach, repudiation and
excuse. See within
this heading,
"Sales."
Waiver or renunciation of
claim or right after
breach, §7-1-107.
Defined, §§7-1-201, 7-2-106.
Documents of title.
Contractual limitation of
liability, §7-7-309.
When adequate compliance
with commercial
contract, §7-7-509.
Limitation of actions.
Contracts for sale,
§7-2-725.
Obligation of good faith,
§7-1-203.
Parol and extrinsic evidence,
§7-2-202.
Reservation of rights.
Performance or acceptance
under reservation of
rights, §7-1-207.
Sales of goods generally,
§§7-2-101 to 7-2-725. See
within this heading,
"Sales."
Secured transactions. See
within this heading,
"Secured transactions."
Statute of frauds.
Sales contracts, §7-2-201.
Modification, §7-2-209.
Time.
Fixing reasonable time,
§7-1-204.
Corporations.
Bulk transfers.
Exception of sales on
dissolution or
reorganization,
§7-6-103.
Commercial paper.
Corporation exceeding
powers.
Negotiation effective
although subject to
rescission, §7-3-207.
Payee described as agent
or officer, §7-3-117.

COMMERCIAL CODE—Cont'd
Corporations—Cont'd
Commercial paper—Cont'd
Signature by authorized
representative,
§7-3-403.
Investment securities
generally, §§7-8-101 to
7-8-406. See within this
heading, "Investment
securities."
Secured transactions.
Filing.
Applicability of filing
provisions, §7-9-302.
Course of dealing, §7-1-205.
Implied warranties, §7-2-314.
Sales.
Used to explain terms of
contracts, §7-2-202.
Creditors.
Defined, §7-1-201.
Sales.
Rights of creditors,
§§7-2-326, 7-2-402.
Secured transactions
generally, §§7-9-101 to
7-9-507. See within this
heading, "Secured
transactions."
Credit union.
Secured transactions.
Transfer of accounts
excluded from
provisions of article,
§7-9-104.
Crops.
Sales.
Definition of goods,
§7-2-105.
Goods to be severed from
realty, §7-2-107.
Identification of goods,
§7-2-501.
Secured transactions.
Classification of goods,
§7-9-109.
Description of land,
§7-9-203.
Financing statement,
§7-9-402.
Place of filing, §7-9-401.
When security interest
attaches, §7-9-204.
Warehouse receipts.
Storage under government
bond, §7-7-201.
Custom.
Course of dealing and usage
of trade, §7-1-205.
Damages.
Bank deposits and
collections.
Certain action constituting
ordinary care,
§7-4-103.
Limitation by agreements,
§7-4-103.
Measure of damages,
§7-4-103.
Documents of title.
Limitation of liability in
bill of lading, §7-7-309.
Limitation of
warehouseman's
liability, §7-7-204.
Sales.
Effect of cancellation or
rescission on claims for
antecedent breach,
§7-2-720.

COMMERCIAL CODE—Cont'd
  Damages—Cont'd
    Sales—Cont'd
      Liquidation or limitation of
        damages, §§7-2-718,
        7-2-719.
      Seller's damages for
        repudiation, §7-2-708.
      Seller's incidental
        damages, §7-2-710.
      Third parties.
        Who can sue third
          parties for injury to
          goods, §7-2-722.
  Death.
    Bank deposits and
      collections.
      Death of customer.
        Authority of payor or
          collecting bank,
          §7-4-405.
  Definitions.
    Action, §7-1-201.
    Aggrieved party, §7-1-201.
    Agreement, §§7-1-201,
      7-2-106.
    Bank, §7-1-201.
    Bank deposits and
      collections. See within
      this heading, "Bank
      deposits and collections."
    Bearer, §7-1-201.
    Bill of lading, §7-1-201.
    Branch, §7-1-201.
    Bulk transfer, §7-6-102.
    Burden of establishing,
      §7-1-201.
    Buyer in ordinary course of
      business, §7-1-201.
    Commercial paper. See
      within this heading,
      "Commercial paper."
    Conspicuous, §7-1-201.
    Contract, §§7-1-201, 7-2-106.
    Creditors, §7-1-201.
    Defendant, §7-1-201.
    Delivery, §7-1-201.
    Documents of title, §§7-1-201,
      7-7-102.
    Effective date and transition
      provisions, §7-11-101.
    Fault, §7-1-201.
    Fungible, §7-1-201.
    Genuine, §7-1-201.
    Good faith, §7-1-201.
    Holder, §7-1-201.
    Honor, §7-1-201.
    Insolvency proceedings,
      §7-1-201.
    Insolvent, §7-1-201.
    Investment securities. See
      within this heading,
      "Investment securities."
    Letters of credit, §7-5-103.
    Merchant, §7-2-104.
    Money, §7-1-201.
    Notice, §7-1-201.
    Organization, §7-1-201.
    Party, §7-1-201.
    Person, §7-1-201.
    Presumption, §7-1-201.
    Purchase, §7-1-201.
    Purchaser, §7-1-201.
    Remedy, §7-1-201.
    Representative, §7-1-201.
    Rights, §7-1-201.
    Sales, §§7-2-103 to 7-2-106.
    Secured transactions. See
      within this heading,
      "Secured transactions."
    Security interest, §7-1-201.

COMMERCIAL CODE—Cont'd
  Definitions—Cont'd
    Send, §7-1-201.
    Signed, §7-1-201.
    Surety, §7-1-201.
    Telegram, §7-1-201.
    Term, §7-1-201.
    Unauthorized, §7-1-201.
    Value, §7-1-201.
    Warehouse receipt, §7-1-201.
    Written, §7-1-201.
  Delivery.
    Defined, §7-1-201.
  Deposits.
    Bank deposits and
      collections, §§7-4-101 to
      7-4-504. See within this
      heading, "Bank deposits
      and collections."
  Detinue.
    Investment securities.
      Action against purchaser
        based upon wrongful
        transfer, §7-8-315.
  Documentary drafts.
    Collection of documentary
      drafts, §§7-4-501 to
      7-4-504.
    General provisions, §§7-3-101
      to 7-3-805. See within
      this heading,
      "Commercial paper."
    Letters of credit, §§7-5-101 to
      7-5-117. See within this
      heading, "Letters of
      credit."
  Documents.
    Prima facie evidence by
      third-party documents,
      §7-1-202.
  Documents of title, §§7-7-101
    to 7-7-603.
    Alteration of instruments.
      Bills of lading, §7-7-306.
      Warehouse receipts,
        §7-7-208.
    Applicability of article,
      §7-7-103.
    Attachment of goods covered
      by negotiable document,
      §7-7-602.
    Bailee.
      Defined, §7-7-102.
    Bills of lading.
      Altered bills, §7-7-306.
      Bills of lading in a set,
        §7-7-304.
      Care.
        Contractual limitation of
          carrier's liability,
          §7-7-309.
        Duty of carrier, §7-7-309.
      Change of instructions,
        §7-7-303.
      Destination bills, §7-7-305.
      Diversion, §7-7-303.
      Duty of care, §7-7-309.
      Handling.
        Improper handling,
          §7-7-301.
      Instructions.
        Change of instructions,
          §7-7-303.
      Liability for nonreceipt or
        misdescription,
        §7-7-301.
      "Said to contain,"
        §7-7-301.
      "Shipper's weight, load
        and count," §7-7-301.

COMMERCIAL CODE—Cont'd
  Documents of title—Cont'd
    Bills of lading—Cont'd
      Liability of carrier.
        Contractual limitation of
          liability of carrier,
          §7-7-309.
        Duty of care, §7-7-309.
      Lien of carrier, §7-7-307.
        Enforcement, §7-7-308.
      Limitation of actions.
        Limitations in bill of
          lading or tariff,
          §7-7-309.
      Misdescription.
        Liability for
          misdescription,
          §7-7-301.
      Negotiable bill of lading,
        §7-7-104.
      Nonnegotiable bill of
        lading, §7-7-104.
      Nonreceipt.
        Liability for nonreceipt,
          §7-7-301.
      Reconsignment, §7-7-303.
      "Said to contain," §7-7-301.
      Set.
        In a set, §7-7-304.
        "Shipper's weight, load and
          count," §7-7-301.
      Through bills of lading and
        similar documents,
        §7-7-302.
    Citation of article.
      Short title, §7-7-101.
    Claims.
      Conflicting claims,
        §7-7-603.
    Conflicting claims, §7-7-603.
    Consignee.
      Defined, §7-7-102.
    Consignor.
      Defined, §7-7-102.
    Construction against
      negative implication,
      §7-7-105.
    Defeated.
      Document of title to goods
        defeated in certain
        cases, §7-7-503.
    Definitions, §7-7-102.
      Bailees, §7-7-102.
      Consignee, §7-7-102.
      Consignor, §7-7-102.
      Delivery order, §7-7-102.
      Documents, §7-7-102.
      Goods, §7-7-102.
      Index of definitions,
        §7-7-102.
      Issuer, §7-7-102.
      Warehouseman, §7-7-102.
      Warehouse receipts,
        §7-1-201.
    Delivery.
      Excuse, §7-7-403.
      Good faith delivery.
        No liability for good
          faith delivery
          pursuant to receipt
          or bill, §7-7-404.
      No liability for good faith
        delivery pursuant to
        receipt or bill,
        §7-7-404.
      Obligation of
        warehouseman or
        carrier to deliver,
        §7-7-403.
      Seller's stoppage of
        delivery, §7-7-504.

COMMERCIAL CODE—Cont'd
Documents of title—Cont'd
Delivery—Cont'd
Without indorsement,
§7-7-506.
Delivery order.
Defined, §7-7-102.
Destroyed documents,
§7-7-601.
Duplicates, §7-7-402.
Evidence.
Prima facie evidence by
third-party documents,
§7-1-202.
Executions.
Lien on goods covered by
negotiable document,
§7-7-602.
Goods.
Defined, §7-7-102.
Guarantee.
Indorser not guarantor for
other parties, §7-7-505.
Indorsement.
Compelling indorsement.
Right to compel,
§7-7-506.
Delivery without
indorsement, §7-7-506.
Indorser not guarantor for
other parties, §7-7-505.
Power to compel
indorsement, §7-7-506.
Injunctions.
Enjoining negotiation of
document, §7-7-602.
Interpleader, §7-7-603.
Irregularities in issue or
conduct of issuer,
§7-7-401.
Issuance.
Irregularities in issue,
§7-7-401.
Overissue, §7-7-402.
Issuer.
Conduct.
Irregularities in issue or
conduct of issuer,
§7-7-401.
Defined, §7-7-102.
Irregularities in conduct of
issuer, §7-7-401.
Laws not repealed, §7-10-104.
Liability.
No liability for good faith
delivery pursuant to
receipt or bill,
§7-7-404.
Liens.
Warehouseman, §7-7-209.
Enforcement of lien,
§7-7-210.
Limitation of actions.
Limitations in bill of
lading or tariff,
§7-7-309.
Limitations on warehouse
receipt or tariff,
§7-7-204.
Warehouse receipts.
Contractual limitation of
warehouseman's
liability, §7-7-204.
Lost documents, §7-7-601.
Missing documents, §7-7-601.
Negative implication.
Construction against,
§7-7-105.
Negotiability, §7-7-104.
Nonnegotiable documents,
§7-7-104.

COMMERCIAL CODE—Cont'd
Documents of title—Cont'd
Negotiation.
Absence of due negotiation.
Rights acquired in the
absence of due
negotiation,
§7-7-504.
Attachment of goods
covered by negotiable
document, §7-7-602.
Contract.
When adequate
compliance with
commercial contract,
§7-7-509.
Defeated.
Document of title to
goods defeated in
certain cases,
§7-7-503.
Delivery.
Seller's stoppage of
delivery, §7-7-504.
Without indorsement,
§7-7-506.
Diversion.
Effect of diversion,
§7-7-504.
Document of title to goods
defeated in certain
cases, §7-7-503.
Due negotiation.
Absence of due
negotiation.
Rights acquired in
absence, §7-7-504.
Indorsement, §7-7-501.
Requirements of due
negotiation,
§7-7-501.
Rights acquired by due
negotiation,
§7-7-502.
Rights acquired in the
absence of due
negotiation,
§7-7-504.
Form of negotiation,
§7-7-501.
Indorsement.
Compelling indorsement,
§7-7-506.
Delivery without
indorsement,
§7-7-506.
Due negotiation,
§7-7-501.
Form of negotiation,
§7-7-501.
Indorser not a guarantor
for other parties,
§7-7-505.
Nonnegotiable
documents, §7-7-501.
Power to compel,
§7-7-506.
Right to compel,
§7-7-506.
Warranties, §7-7-507.
Collecting bank.
Warranties of
collecting bank as
to documents,
§7-7-508.
Nonnegotiable documents,
§7-7-104.
Indorsement, §7-7-501.
Rights acquired by due
negotiation, §7-7-502.

COMMERCIAL CODE—Cont'd
Documents of title—Cont'd
Nonnegotiable documents
—Cont'd
Warranties.
Collecting bank,
§7-7-508.
Negotiation or transfer
of receipt or bill,
§7-7-507.
When adequate compliance
with commercial
contract, §7-7-509.
Obligation of warehouseman
or carrier to deliver,
§7-7-403.
Overissue, §7-7-402.
Relation of article to titles,
statute, tariff, etc.,
§7-7-103.
Repealed.
Laws not repealed,
§7-10-104.
Sales.
When documents
deliverable on
acceptance and on
payment, §7-2-514.
Short title of article,
§7-7-101.
Stolen documents, §7-7-601.
Storage.
Termination of storage at
warehouseman's
option, §7-7-206.
Suretyship.
Indorser not guarantor for
other parties, §7-7-505.
Tariffs.
Relation of article to tariff,
§7-7-103.
Transfer.
Warranties, §7-7-507.
Treaty.
Relation of article to
treaty, §7-7-103.
United States statutes.
Relation of article to
statute, §7-7-103.
Warehousemen.
Defined, §7-7-102.
Warehouse receipts.
Agricultural commodities.
Stored under government
bond, §7-7-201.
Alcoholic beverages.
Distilled spirits stored
under government
bond, §7-7-201.
Altered warehouse
receipts, §7-7-208.
Contractual limitation of
warehouseman's
liability, §7-7-204.
Crops.
Stored under government
bond, §7-7-201.
Defined, §7-1-201.
Distilled spirits stored
under government
bond, §7-7-201.
Duty of care, §7-7-204.
Form of warehouse receipt,
§7-7-202.
Fungible goods, §7-7-207.
Title of buyer in
ordinary course of
business, §7-7-205.
Goods must be kept
separate, §§7-7-204,
7-7-207.

COMMERCIAL CODE—Cont'd
  Documents of title—Cont'd
    Warehouse receipts—Cont'd
      Issuance.
        Who may issue, §7-7-201.
      Liability.
        Contractual limitation of
          warehouseman's
          liability, §7-7-204.
        Nonreceipt or
          misdescription,
          §7-7-203.
      Lien of warehouseman,
        §7-7-209.
        Enforcement, §7-7-210.
      Limitation of actions.
        Contractual limitation of
          warehouseman's
          liability, §7-7-204.
      Misdescription.
        Liability for, §7-7-203.
      Negotiable warehouse
        receipts, §7-7-104.
      Nonnegotiable warehouse
        receipts, §7-7-104.
      Nonreceipts.
        Liability for, §7-7-203.
      Storage.
        Under government bond,
          §7-7-201.
      Termination of storage at
        warehouseman's
        option, §7-7-206.
      Terms.
        Essential terms,
          §7-7-202.
        Optional terms, §7-7-202.
      Title under warehouse
        receipt defeated in
        certain cases, §7-7-205.
      Who may issue, §7-7-201.
    Warranties.
      Collecting banks.
        Warranties of collecting
          bank as to
          documents, §7-7-508.
      Negotiation or transfer of
        receipt or bill,
        §7-7-507.
  Drafts.
    Collectin of documentary
      drafts, §§7-4-501 to
      7-4-504.
    General provisions, §§7-3-101
      to 7-3-805. See within
      this heading,
      "Commercial paper."
    Letters of credit, §§7-5-101 to
      7-5-117. See within this
      heading, "Letters of
      credit."
  Duress.
    Commercial paper.
      Defenses against holder in
        due course, §7-3-305.
      Negotiation effective
        although subject to
        rescission, §7-3-207.
  Duties.
    Obligation of good faith,
      §7-1-203.
  **Effective date and transition
    provisions.**
    Change of place of filing,
      §7-11-105.
    Change of requirement of
      filing, §7-11-104.
    Definitions, §7-11-101.
    Filing requirements.
      Change of place of filing,
        §7-11-105.

COMMERCIAL CODE—Cont'd
  **Effective date and transition
    provisions**—Cont'd
    Filing requirements—Cont'd
      Changes generally,
        §7-11-104.
      Required refilings,
        §7-11-106.
    General rule, §7-11-103.
    Preservation of old transition
      provisions, §7-11-102.
    Presumption that rule of law
      continues unchanged,
      §7-11-108.
    Priorities, §7-11-107.
  Effective date of title,
    §7-10-101.
  Electricity.
    Secured transactions.
      Applicability of filing
        provisions, §7-9-302.
  Evidence.
    Commercial paper.
      Certificate of notary as to
        presentment for
        acceptance, etc.,
        §12-21-105.
    Proof of accommodation
      party, §7-3-415.
    Parol or extrinsic evidence.
      Sales contracts, §7-2-202.
    Prima facie evidence by
      third-party documents,
      §7-1-202.
    Sales.
      Contracts.
        Parol or extrinsic
          evidence, §7-2-202.
      Preserving evidence of
        goods in dispute,
        §7-2-515.
      Remedies.
        Admissibility of market
          quotations, §7-2-724.
        Proof of market price,
          §7-2-723.
    Usage of trade, §7-1-205.
  Executions.
    Bank deposits and
      collections.
      When items subject to
        legal process, §7-4-303.
    Bulk transfers.
      Limitation of levies,
        §7-6-111.
      Sales excepted from article,
        §7-6-103.
    Documents of title.
      Lien on goods covered by
        negotiable document,
        §7-7-602.
    Investment securities.
      Levy upon security,
        §7-8-317.
    Secured transactions.
      Debtor's rights in
        collateral, §7-9-311.
      Priority over unperfected
        security interests,
        §7-9-301.
  **Executors and
    administrators.**
    Bulk transfers.
      Transfers excepted from
        article, §7-6-103.
    Representative defined,
      §7-1-201.
  **Factors and commission
    merchants.**
    Sales. See within this
      heading, "Sales."

COMMERCIAL CODE—Cont'd
  Fault.
    Defined, §7-1-201.
  Fees.
    Secured transactions.
      Filing.
        Central filing system.
          Implementation,
          §7-9-410.
  Fiduciaries.
    Bulk transfers.
      Transfers excepted from
        article, §7-6-103.
    Commercial paper.
      Notice of claim or defense
        to purchaser, §7-3-304.
      Signature by authorized
        representative,
        §7-3-403.
      Signature in ambiguous
        capacity deemed
        indorsement, §7-3-402.
      Words describing payee,
        §7-3-117.
    Representative defined,
      §7-1-201.
    Simplification of fiduciary
      security transfers.
      Uniform act not repealed,
        §7-10-104.
    Uniform act for the
      simplification of
      fiduciary security
      transfers.
      Uniform act not repealed,
        §7-10-104.
  Fish.
    Secured transactions.
      When security interest
        attaches, §7-9-204.
  Fixtures.
    Secured transactions.
      Financing statement,
        §7-9-402.
      Place of filing, §7-9-401.
      Priority of security
        interests in fixtures,
        §7-9-313.
  Food.
    Sales.
      Implied warranty of
        merchantability,
        §7-2-314.
  Forgery.
    Bank deposits and
      collections.
      Customer's duty to discover
        and report
        unauthorized signature
        or alteration, §7-4-406.
    Commercial paper.
      Conversion of instrument,
        §7-3-419.
      Notice of claim or defense
        to purchaser, §7-3-304.
      Unauthorized signatures,
        §7-3-404.
      Negligence contributing
        to unauthorized
        signature, §7-3-406.
    Investment securities.
      Effect of unauthorized
        indorsement,
        §§7-8-205, 7-8-315.
  Fraud.
    Creditors.
      Right of seller's creditors
        against sold goods,
        §7-2-402.

COMMERCIAL CODE—Cont'd
Fraud—Cont'd
  Misrepresentation of buyer's
    solvency.
      Seller's remedies, §7-2-702.
  Sales.
    Remedies for fraud,
      §7-2-721.
    Transfer of title obtained
      by fraud, §7-2-403.
Frauds, statute of. See within
  this heading, "Statute of
  frauds."
Fraudulent conveyances.
  Rights of seller's creditors
    against sold goods,
    §7-2-402.
Funds.
  Uniform commercial code
    and farm products
    central index system
    fund.
      Creation, §7-9-307.
      Deposits, §7-9-307.
      Use, §7-9-307.
Fungible.
  Defined, §7-1-201.
Garnishment.
  Bank deposits and
    collections.
    When items subject to
      legal process, §7-4-303.
  Bulk transfers.
    Limitation of levies,
      §7-6-111.
  Secured transactions.
    Debtor's rights in
      collateral, §7-9-311.
General repealer, §7-10-103.
Genuine.
  Defined, §7-1-201.
Good faith.
  Defined, §7-2-103.
  Exercising option to
    accelerate, §7-1-208.
  Obligation of good faith,
    §7-1-203.
Guaranty.
  Commercial paper.
    Contract of guarantor,
      §7-3-416.
  Investment securities.
    Effect of guaranteeing
      signature or
      indorsement, §7-8-312.
    Indorser not guarantor,
      §7-8-308.
Holder.
  Defined, §7-1-201.
Honor.
  Defined, §7-1-201.
Housing finance authority.
  Applicability of certain
    provisions, §24-1A-11.
Human blood or tissue.
  Implied warranty, §7-2-314.
Implied warranties.
  Sales.
    Warranties. See within
      this heading, "Sales."
Indorsements.
  Bank deposits and
    collections, §7-4-205.
  Commercial paper. See
    within this heading,
    "Commercial paper."
  Documents of title, §§7-7-505,
    7-7-506.
  Investment securities. See
    within this heading,
    "Investment securities."

COMMERCIAL CODE—Cont'd
Indorsements—Cont'd
  Unauthorized indorsement.
    Defined, §7-1-201.
Injunctions.
  Documents of title.
    Enjoining negotiation of
      document, §7-7-602.
  Investment securities.
    Enjoining transfer,
      §§7-8-315, 7-8-317.
Insolvency. See within this
  heading, "Bankruptcy and
  insolvency."
Inspections.
  Sales. See within this
    heading, "Sales."
Installment contracts.
  Sales, §7-2-612.
Insurance.
  Policy or certificate as prima
    facie evidence, §7-1-202.
  Sales.
    C.I.F. and C. & F. terms,
      §7-2-320.
    Net landed weights,
      §7-2-321.
    Insurable interest in goods,
      §7-2-501.
  Secured transactions.
    Transfer of interest or
      claim in policy or
      annuity excluded,
      §7-9-104.
Interest.
  Commercial paper.
    Ambiguous terms and
      rules of construction,
      §7-3-118.
    Interest rates, §7-3-122.
Interpleader.
  Documents of title.
    Determination of
      conflicting claims,
      §7-7-603.
Intervention.
  Commercial paper.
    Notice to third party of
      suit, §7-3-803.
  Sales.
    Notice of claim or
      litigation to person
      answerable over,
      §7-2-607.
Inventories.
  Secured transactions.
    Classification of goods,
      §7-9-109.
Investment securities,
  §§7-8-101 to 7-8-406.
  Actions.
    Action against purchaser
      based upon wrongful
      transfer, §7-8-315.
    Actions for price, §7-8-107.
    Wrongful transfer.
      Action against
      purchaser, §7-8-315.
  Adverse claims, §7-8-301.
    Notice to purchaser,
      §§7-8-304, 7-8-305.
  Agents.
    Conversion.
      No conversion by good
      faith delivery,
      §7-8-318.
    Effect of signature of
      transfer agent,
      §§7-8-208, 7-8-312.
  Alterations of instrument,
    §7-8-206.

COMMERCIAL CODE—Cont'd
Investment securities—Cont'd
  Assignment.
    Partial assignment,
      §7-8-308.
  Attachment.
    Levy upon security,
      §7-8-317.
  Bailment.
    No conversion by good
      faith delivery,
      §7-8-318.
  Bearer form.
    Defined, §7-8-102.
    Indorsement of security in
      bearer form, §7-8-310.
  Bona fide purchaser.
    Enforcement of completed
      or altered instrument,
      §7-8-206.
  Broker.
    Defined, §7-8-303.
    Purchaser's broker as
      holder, §7-8-313.
  Burden of proof.
    Action on securities,
      §7-8-105.
  Central depository system.
    Transfer or pledge within a
      central depository
      system, §7-8-320.
  Citation of article.
    Short title, §7-8-101.
  Clearing corporation.
    Defined, §7-8-102.
  Completion of instrument,
    §7-8-206.
  Conflict of laws.
    Registration of transfer.
      Rights and duties of
      issuer, §7-8-106.
    Validity of securities,
      §7-8-106.
  Conversion.
    Delivery.
      No conversion by good
      faith delivery,
      §7-8-318.
  Custodian bank.
    Defined, §7-8-102.
  Definitions, §7-8-102.
    Adverse claims, §7-8-301.
    Bearer form, §7-8-102.
    Bona fide purchaser,
      §7-8-302.
    Broker, §7-8-303.
    Clearing corporation,
      §7-8-102.
    Custodian bank, §7-8-102.
    Index of definitions,
      §7-8-102.
    Issuer, §7-8-201.
    Overissue, §7-8-104.
    Registered forms, §7-8-102.
    Securities, §7-8-102.
    Subsequent purchaser,
      §7-8-102.
  Delivery.
    Action for price, §7-8-107.
    Conversion.
      No conversion by good
      faith delivery,
      §7-8-318.
    Duty to deliver, §7-8-314.
    Effect of delivery without
      indorsement, §7-8-307.
    Effect of indorsement
      without delivery,
      §7-8-309.
    Purchaser's broker as
      holder, §7-8-313.

COMMERCIAL CODE—Cont'd
Investment securities—Cont'd
Delivery—Cont'd
Remedy to recover the
price upon delivery,
§7-8-107.
Securities deliverable,
§7-8-107.
When delivery to
purchaser occurs,
§7-8-313.
When duty to deliver
completed, §7-8-314.
Depository system.
Transfer or pledge within a
central depository
system, §7-8-320.
Destroyed securities,
§7-8-405.
Detinue.
Action against purchaser
based upon wrongful
transfer, §7-8-315.
Executions.
Levy upon security,
§7-8-317.
Fiduciaries.
Uniform act for
simplification of
fiduciary security
transfers.
Not repealed, §7-10-104.
Forgery.
Effect of unauthorized
signature on issue,
§7-8-205.
Indorsement, §7-8-311.
Effect of unauthorized
indorsement,
§7-8-315.
Frauds, statute of, §7-8-319.
Guarantee.
Effect of guaranteeing
signature or
indorsement, §7-8-312.
Indorsements.
Assurance that
indorsements are
effective, §7-8-402.
Bearer form.
Indorsement of security
in bearer form,
§7-8-310.
Effect of delivery without
indorsement, §7-8-307.
Effect of guaranteeing
signature or
indorsement, §7-8-312.
Effect of indorsement
without delivery,
§7-8-309.
Effect of unauthorized
indorsement,
§§7-8-311, 7-8-315.
Forgery, §7-8-311.
Generally, §7-8-308.
How made, §7-8-308.
Indorsement of security in
bearer form, §7-8-310.
Indorser not a guarantor,
§7-8-308.
Partial assignment,
§7-8-308.
Registration.
Assurance that
indorsements are
effective, §7-8-402.
Right to compel
indorsement, §7-8-307.
Special indorsement,
§7-8-308.

COMMERCIAL CODE—Cont'd
Investment securities—Cont'd
Injunctions.
Enjoining transfer,
§§7-8-315, 7-8-317.
Issue and issuer.
Alteration of instruments,
§7-8-206.
Completion of instrument,
§7-8-206.
Defects.
Notice of defects.
Staleness as notice of
defects, §7-8-203.
Staleness as notice of
defects or defenses,
§7-8-203.
Defenses.
Issuer's defenses,
§7-8-202.
Notice of defects or
defenses, §7-8-202.
Staleness as notice of
defects or defenses,
§7-8-203.
Definitions.
Issuer, §7-8-201.
Effect of unauthorized
signature on issue,
§7-8-205.
Issuer's lien, §7-8-103.
Lien of issuer, §7-8-103.
Notice.
Notice of defect or
defense, §7-8-202.
Staleness as notice of
defects or defenses,
§7-8-203.
Overissue, §7-8-104.
Effect of overissue,
§7-8-104.
Owner.
Registered owners.
Rights of issuer with
respect to
registered owners,
§7-8-207.
Registered owners.
Rights of issuer with
respect to registered
owners, §7-8-207.
Registration.
Duty of issuer to register
transfer, §7-8-401.
Limited duty of inquiry,
§7-8-403.
Responsibility.
Issuer's responsibility,
§7-8-202.
Rights and duties of issuer
governed by law of
jurisdiction of issuer,
§7-8-106.
Signature.
Effect of signature of
authenticating
trustee, registrar or
transfer agent,
§7-8-208.
Staleness as notice of
defects or defenses,
§7-8-203.
Transfer.
Duty of issuer to register
transfer, §7-8-401.
Effect of issuer's
restrictions on
transfer, §7-8-204.

COMMERCIAL CODE—Cont'd
Investment securities—Cont'd
Issue and issuer—Cont'd
Transfer—Cont'd
Effect of signature of
authenticating
trustee, registrar or
transfer agent,
§7-8-208.
Warranties.
Effect of signature of
authenticating
trustee, registrar or
transfer agent,
§7-8-208.
Who is "issuer," §7-8-201.
Larceny.
Stolen securities, §7-8-405.
Lien.
Issuer's lien, §7-8-103.
Lost securities, §7-8-405.
Negotiable instruments,
§7-8-105.
Presumptions, §7-8-105.
Notice.
Issue and issuer, §§7-8-202,
7-8-203.
Registration.
Notice to authenticating
trustee, transfer
agent or registrar,
§7-8-406.
Staleness as notice of
adverse claims,
§§7-8-304, 7-8-305.
Overissue.
Defined, §7-8-104.
Effect of overissue,
§7-8-104.
Pledge.
Within a central depository
system, §7-8-320.
Presentment.
Warranties on
presentment, §7-8-306.
Presumptions as to
negotiability, §7-8-105.
Purchase.
Action against purchaser
based upon wrongful
transfer, §7-8-315.
Action for price, §7-8-107.
Adverse claims.
Construed, §7-8-301.
Notice to purchaser of
adverse claims,
§7-8-304.
Staleness as notice of
adverse claims,
§7-8-305.
Assignment.
Special assignment,
§7-8-308.
Attachment or levy upon
security, §7-8-317.
Bearer form.
Indorsement of security
in bearer form,
§7-8-310.
Bona fide purchaser.
Defined, §7-8-302.
Title acquired by,
§7-8-301.
Broker.
Defined, §7-8-303.
Purchaser's broker as
holder, §7-8-313.

COMMERCIAL CODE—Cont'd
Investment securities—Cont'd
Purchase—Cont'd
Central depository system.
Transfer or pledge
within a central
depository system,
§7-8-320.
Conversion.
No conversion by good
faith delivery,
§7-8-318.
Defined, §7-1-201.
Delivery.
Actions to recover
purchase price,
§7-8-107.
Duty to deliver, §7-8-314.
Effect of delivery without
indorsement,
§7-8-307.
Effect of indorsement
without delivery,
§7-8-309.
No conversion by good
faith delivery,
§7-8-318.
Purchaser's broker as
holder, §7-8-313.
When delivery to
purchaser occurs,
§7-8-313.
When duty to deliver
completed, §7-8-314.
Frauds, statute of,
§7-8-319.
Indorsement.
Bearer form.
Indorsement of
security in bearer
form, §7-8-310.
Effect of delivery without
indorsement,
§7-8-307.
Effect of guaranteeing
signature or
indorsement,
§7-8-312.
Effect of unauthorized
indorsement,
§§7-8-311, 7-8-315.
Forgery, §7-8-311.
Generally, §7-8-308.
How made, §7-8-308.
Indorsement of security
in bearer form,
§7-8-310.
Indorser not a guarantor,
§7-8-308.
Partial assignment,
§7-8-308.
Right to compel
indorsement,
§7-8-307.
Special indorsement,
§7-8-308.
Levy or attachment upon
security, §7-8-317.
Notice.
Staleness as notice of
adverse claims,
§7-8-305.
Pledge within a central
depository system,
§7-8-320.
Presentment.
Warranties on
presentment,
§7-8-306.
Remedy to recover agreed
price, §7-8-107.

COMMERCIAL CODE—Cont'd
Investment securities—Cont'd
Purchase—Cont'd
Rights acquired by
purchaser, §7-8-301.
Signature.
Effect of guaranteeing
signature or
indorsement,
§7-8-312.
Specific performance.
Right to obtain
possession of
security wrongfully
transferred,
§7-8-315.
Staleness as notice of
adverse claims,
§7-8-305.
Statute of frauds, §7-8-319.
Title.
Acquired by bona fide
purchaser, §7-8-301.
Transfer.
Action against purchaser
based upon wrongful
transfer, §7-8-315.
Enjoining transfer,
§7-8-315.
Purchaser's right to
requisites for
registration of
transfer on books,
§7-8-316.
Registration.
Duty of authenticating
trustee, transfer
agent or registrar,
§7-8-406.
Warranties on transfer,
§7-8-306.
Within central
depository system,
§7-8-320.
Warranties on presentment
and transfer, §7-8-306.
Purchaser.
Bona fide purchaser.
Adverse claim, §7-8-301.
Subsequent purchaser.
Defined, §7-8-102.
Registered form.
Defined, §7-8-102.
Registration.
Assurance that
indorsements are
effective, §7-8-402.
Conflict of laws.
Rights and duties of
issuer, §7-8-106.
Destroyed securities,
§7-8-405.
Duty of authenticating
trustee, transfer agent
or registrar, §7-8-406.
Duty of inquiry.
Limited duty, §7-8-403.
Duty of issuer to register
transfer, §7-8-401.
Effect of signature of
authenticating trustee,
registrar or transfer
agent, §7-8-208.
Indorsements.
Assurance that
indorsements are
effective, §7-8-402.
Inquiry.
Limited duty of inquiry,
§7-8-403.

COMMERCIAL CODE—Cont'd
Investment securities—Cont'd
Registration—Cont'd
Issuer.
Duty of issuer to register
transfer, §7-8-401.
Limited duty of inquiry,
§7-8-403.
Liability for registration,
§7-8-404.
Limited duty of inquiry,
§7-8-403.
Lost securities, §7-8-405.
Nonliability for
registration, §7-8-404.
Notice to authenticating
trustee, transfer agent
or registrar, §7-8-406.
Purchaser's right to
requisites for
registration of
transfer, §7-8-316.
Rights of issuer with
respect to registered
owners, §7-8-207.
Stolen securities, §7-8-405.
Transfer.
Duty of authenticating
trustee, transfer
agent or registrar,
§7-8-406.
Security.
Defined, §7-8-102.
Short title of article,
§7-8-101.
Signatures.
Assurance that
indorsements are
effective, §7-8-402.
Burden of proof, §7-8-105.
Effect of guaranteeing
signature or
indorsement, §7-8-312.
Effect of signature of
authenticating trustee,
registrar or transfer
agent, §7-8-208.
Effect of unauthorized
signature on issue,
§7-8-205.
Specific performance.
Right to obtain possession
of security wrongfully
transferred, §7-8-315.
Staleness as notice of adverse
claims, §7-8-305.
Statute of frauds, §7-8-319.
Stolen securities, §7-8-405.
Suretyship.
Indorser not a guarantor,
§7-8-308.
Title.
Acquired by bona fide
purchaser, §7-8-301.
Transfer.
Action against purchaser
based on wrongful
transfer, §7-8-315.
Central depository system.
Transfer within central
depository system,
§7-8-320.
Effect of signature of
authenticating trustee,
registrar or transfer
agent, §7-8-208.
Enjoining transfer,
§§7-8-315, 7-8-317.
Issuer.
Duty of issuer to register
transfer, §7-8-401.

COMMERCIAL CODE—Cont'd
Investment securities—Cont'd
Transfer—Cont'd
Purchaser's right to
requisites for
registration of transfer
on books, §7-8-316.
Registration.
Duty of authenticating
trustee, transfer
agent or registrar,
§7-8-406.
Duty of issuer to register
transfer, §7-8-401.
Warranties on transfer,
§7-8-306.
Wrongful transfer.
Action against purchaser
based upon wrongful
transfer, §7-8-315.
Transfer agent.
Effect of signature,
§7-8-312.
Validity of security governed
by law of jurisdiction of
issuers, §7-8-106.
Warranties.
Effect of signature of
authenticating trustee,
registrar or transfer
agent, §7-8-208.
On presentment and
transfer, §7-8-306.
Judgments.
Commercial paper.
Confession of judgment,
§7-3-112.
Secured transactions.
Transactions excluded from
provisions of article,
§7-9-104.
Jurisdiction.
Secured transactions.
Multiple state transactions.
Perfection of security
interest, §7-9-103.
Landlord and tenant.
Landlord's lien.
Applicability of secured
transactions provision,
§7-9-104.
Larceny.
Commercial paper.
Defenses, §7-3-306.
Stolen instruments,
§7-3-804.
Investment securities,
§7-8-405.
Sales.
Power to transfer voidable
title, §7-2-403.
Letters of credit, §§7-5-101 to
7-5-117.
Advice of credit, §7-5-107.
Advising banks.
Defined, §7-5-103.
Anticipatory repudiation.
Remedy, §7-5-115.
Assignment, §7-5-116.
Beneficiaries.
Defined, §7-5-103.
Citation of article.
Short title, §7-5-101.
Claim or lien.
Presenter's reservation of,
§7-5-110.
Confirming banks.
Defined, §7-5-103.

COMMERCIAL CODE—Cont'd
Letters of credit—Cont'd
Consent.
Withholding honor or
rejection by consent,
§7-5-112.
Consideration, §7-5-105.
Credit.
Advice of credit, §7-5-107.
Availability in portions,
§7-5-110.
Beneficiaries.
Defined, §7-5-103.
Confirmation, §7-5-107.
Defined, §7-5-103.
Effect of establishment of
credit, §7-5-106.
Error in statement of
terms, §7-5-107.
Establishment.
Consideration, §7-5-105.
Effect of establishment of
credit, §7-5-106.
Time and effect of
establishment,
§7-5-106.
Exhaustion of credit,
§7-5-108.
Notation of credit.
Defined, §7-5-108.
Portions.
Availability in portions,
§7-5-110.
Time and effect of
establishment.
Credit, §7-5-106.
Customers.
Defined, §7-5-103.
Issuer's obligation to its
customer, §7-5-109.
Definitions, §7-5-103.
Dishonor.
Remedy for improper
dishonor, §7-5-115.
Documentary drafts.
Defined, §7-5-103.
Exhaustion of credit,
§7-5-108.
Formal requirements,
§7-5-104.
Signing, §7-5-104.
Honor.
Issuer's duty and privilege
to honor, §7-5-114.
Time allowed for honor,
§7-5-112.
Withholding honor by
consent, §7-5-112.
Indemnities, §7-5-113.
Insolvency of bank holding
funds for documentary
credit, §7-5-117.
Issuers.
Customers.
Defined, §7-5-103.
Defined, §7-5-103.
Duty and privilege to
honor, §7-5-114.
Honor.
Duty and privilege to
honor, §7-5-114.
Insolvency of bank holding
funds for documentary
credit, §7-5-117.
Obligation to its customers,
§7-5-109.
Reimbursement.
Right to reimbursement,
§7-5-114.

COMMERCIAL CODE—Cont'd
Letters of credit—Cont'd
Lien or claim.
Presenter's reservation of
lien or claim, §7-5-110.
"Notation credit," §7-5-108.
Presentments.
Presenter.
Defined, §7-5-112.
Warranties on
presentment, §7-5-111.
Reimbursement.
Right of issuers to
reimbursement,
§7-5-114.
Rejection.
By consent, §7-5-112.
Time allowed for rejection,
§7-5-112.
Withholding by consent,
§7-5-112.
Repudiation.
Remedy for anticipatory
repudiation, §7-5-115.
Requirements.
Formal requirements,
§7-5-104.
Sales.
Letters of credit term,
§7-2-325.
Scope of article, §7-5-102.
Short title, §7-5-101.
Signing, §7-5-104.
Statement.
Error in statement of
terms.
Credit, §7-5-107.
Time.
Allowed for honor or
rejection, §7-5-112.
Establishment of credit,
§7-5-106.
Transfer.
Generally, §7-5-116.
Warranties on transfer,
§7-5-111.
Warranty.
Transfer and presentment,
§7-5-111.
Liens.
Bills of lading.
Carrier's lien, §7-7-307.
Enforcement, §7-7-308.
Carrier's lien, §7-7-307.
Enforcement, §7-7-308.
Investment securities.
Issuer's lien, §7-8-103.
Letters of credit.
Presenter's reservation,
§7-5-110.
Secured transactions. See
within this heading,
"Secured transactions."
Transactions excluded from
provisions as to secured
transactions, §7-9-104.
Warehouseman, §7-7-209.
Enforcement of lien,
§7-7-210.
Limitation of actions.
Bills of lading.
Limitations in bill of
lading or tariff,
§7-7-309.
Bulk transfers, §7-6-111.
Documents of title.
Limitations in bill of
lading or tariff,
§7-7-309.
Duration of financing
statements, §7-9-403.

COMMERCIAL CODE—Cont'd
Limitation of actions—Cont'd
Sales.
Contracts for sale,
§7-2-725.
Livestock.
Sale of unborn young.
Definition of goods,
§7-2-105.
Identification of goods,
§7-2-501.
Secured transactions.
Classification of goods,
§7-9-109.
When security interest
attaches, §7-9-204.
Lost or unclaimed property.
Commercial paper.
Lost instruments, §7-3-804.
Documents of title.
Lost, stolen or destroyed
documents of title,
§7-7-601.
Investment securities,
§7-8-405.
Market price, §§7-2-723,
7-2-724.
Mentally ill.
Bank deposits and
collections.
Incompetence of customer.
Authority of payor or
collecting bank,
§7-4-405.
Commercial paper.
Defenses against holder in
due course, §7-3-305.
Negotiation effective
although subject to
rescission, §7-3-207.
Mines and minerals.
Sales.
Goods to be severed from
realty, §7-2-107.
Secured transactions.
Description of land,
§7-9-203.
Multiple state transactions.
Perfection of security
interest, §7-9-103.
When security interest
attaches, §7-9-204.
Minors.
Commercial paper.
Defenses against holder in
due course, §7-3-305.
Negotiation effective
although subject to
rescission, §7-3-207.
Misrepresentation.
Commercial paper.
Defenses against holder in
due course, §7-3-305.
Sales.
Remedies, §7-2-721.
Solvency of buyer.
Seller's remedies on
discovery of buyer's
insolvency, §7-2-702.
Mistake.
Letters of credit.
Error in statement of
terms, §7-5-107.
Negotiation effective
although subject to
rescission, §7-3-207.
Money.
Defined, §7-1-201.

COMMERCIAL CODE—Cont'd
**Mortgages and deeds of
trust.**
Secured transactions.
Financing statement,
§7-9-402.
Generally. See within this
heading, "Secured
transactions."
Motor vehicles.
Secured transactions.
Applicability of filing
provisions, §7-9-302.
Multiple state transactions.
Secured transactions.
Perfection of security
interest, §7-9-103.
Negligence.
Commercial paper.
Negligence contributing to
alteration or
unauthorized
signature, §7-3-406.
Negotiable instruments.
Commercial paper, §§7-3-101
to 7-3-805. See within
this heading,
"Commercial paper."
Documents of title. See
within this heading,
"Documents of title."
Evidence.
Certificate of notary as to
presentment for
acceptance, etc.,
§12-21-105.
Notes.
General provisions. See
within this heading,
"Commercial paper."
Notice.
Bulk transfers.
Notice to creditors,
§7-6-105.
Content and delivery,
§7-6-107.
Commercial paper.
Notice to purchasers of
claim or defense,
§7-3-304.
Third party.
Notice to third party of
suit, §7-3-803.
Defined, §7-1-201.
Investment securities.
Issue and issuer.
Notice of defect or
defense, §7-8-202.
Staleness as notice of
defects or defenses,
§7-8-203.
Purchase.
Notice to purchaser of
adverse claims,
§7-8-304.
Staleness as notice of
claims, §7-8-305.
Registration.
Notice to authenticating
trustee, transfer
agent or registrar,
§7-8-406.
Sales. See within this
heading, "Sales."
Oil and gas.
Sales.
Goods to be severed from
realty, §7-2-107.
Secured transactions.
Applicability of filing
provisions, §7-9-302.

COMMERCIAL CODE—Cont'd
Oil and gas—Cont'd
Secured transactions—Cont'd
Description of land,
§7-9-203.
When security interest
attaches, §7-9-204.
Options.
Acceleration at will,
§7-1-208.
Contracts for sale, §7-2-311.
Organization.
Defined, §7-1-201.
Parol evidence.
Sales contracts.
Parol or extrinsic evidence,
§7-2-202.
Parties.
Aggrieved party.
Defined, §7-1-201.
Commercial paper. See
within this heading,
"Commercial paper."
Defendants.
Defined, §7-1-201.
Defined, §7-1-201.
Third parties.
Notice to third parties of
suits, §7-2-607.
Who can sue third parties
for injuries to goods,
§7-2-722.
Patents.
Sales.
Buyer's obligation against
infringement, §7-2-312.
Notice of claim or
litigation to person
answerable over,
§7-2-607.
Warranty against
infringement, §7-2-312.
**Performance under
reservation of rights,**
§7-1-207.
Person.
Defined, §7-1-201.
Pipelines.
Secured transactions.
Applicability of filing
provisions, §7-9-302.
Pleading.
Interpleader and
intervention.
Commercial paper.
Notice to third party of
suit, §7-3-803.
Sales.
Notice of claim or
litigation to person
answerable over,
§7-2-607.
**Pledge and collateral
security.**
Investment securities.
Pledge within central
depository system,
§7-8-320.
Secured transactions. See
within this heading,
"Secured transactions."
Presumptions.
Bank deposits and
collections.
Agency status of collecting
banks, §7-4-201.
Provisional status of
credits, §7-4-201.
Commercial paper.
Date presumed correct,
§7-3-114.

COMMERCIAL CODE—Cont'd
Presumptions—Cont'd
Commercial paper—Cont'd
Genuiness or authorization
of signatures, §7-3-307.
Defined, §7-1-201.
Investment securities.
Action on securities,
§7-8-105.
Sales.
Burden of establishing
breach after
acceptance, §7-2-607.
Principles of law.
Supplementary general
principles of law
applicable, §7-1-103.
Promissory notes.
Commercial paper generally,
§§7-3-101 to 7-3-805. See
within this heading,
"Commercial paper."
Protests.
Performance or acceptance
under protest, §7-1-207.
Purchasers.
Bona fide purchasers. See
within this heading,
"Bona fide purchasers."
Defined, §7-1-201.
Purchases.
Defined, §7-1-201.
Purposes, §7-1-102.
Railroads.
Secured transactions.
Applicability of filing
provisions, §7-9-302.
Determination of validity
and perfection of
security interest in
rolling stock, §7-9-103.
Transactions excluded from
provisions of article,
§7-9-104.
Real property.
Sales.
Goods to be severed from
realty, §7-2-107.
Price payable in realty,
§7-2-304.
Secured transactions. See
within this heading,
"Secured transactions."
Receivers.
Secured transactions.
Priority over unperfected
security interests,
§7-9-301.
Recordation.
Sales.
Goods to be severed from
realty, §7-2-107.
Releases.
Secured transactions.
Termination statement,
§7-9-404.
Remedies.
Defined, §7-1-201.
Liberal administration of
remedies, §7-1-106.
Performance or acceptance
under reservation of
rights, §7-1-207.
Sales. See within this
heading, "Sales."
Repeal.
Construction against implicit
repeal of code, §7-1-104.
General repealer, §7-10-103.
Laws not repealed, §7-10-104.

COMMERCIAL CODE—Cont'd
Repeal—Cont'd
Provision for transition,
§7-10-102.
Specific repealer, §7-10-102.
Replevin.
Sales.
Buyer's right to replevin,
§7-2-716.
Representatives.
Defined, §7-1-201.
Rescission.
Sales contracts, §7-2-209.
Effect of cancellation or
rescission on claims for
antecedent breach,
§7-2-720.
Reservation of rights.
Performance or acceptance
under reservation of
rights, §7-1-207.
Res judicata.
Commercial paper.
Effect of notice to person
answerable over,
§7-3-803.
Retail installment sales.
Secured transactions.
Validity of security
agreement, §7-9-201.
Rights.
Defined, §7-1-201.
Rules and regulations.
Secured transactions.
Filing.
Central filing system.
Implementation,
§7-9-410.
Rules of construction,
§7-1-102.
Salaries.
Secured transactions.
Transactions excluded from
provisions of article,
§7-9-104.
Sales, §§7-2-101 to 7-2-725.
Acceptance of goods.
Breach, repudiation and
excuse.
Buyer's rights on
improper delivery,
§7-2-601.
Burden of establishing
breach after
acceptance, §7-2-607.
Buyer's damages for breach
in regard to accepted
goods, §7-2-714.
Buyer's rights on improper
delivery, §7-2-601.
Effect of acceptance,
§7-2-607.
Installment contracts,
§7-2-612.
Revocation of acceptance in
whole or in part,
§7-2-608.
Seller's damages for
nonacceptance,
§7-2-708.
What constitutes
acceptance, §7-2-606.
When documents
deliverable on
acceptance, §7-2-514.
Agreement.
Defined, §7-2-106.
Animals.
Identification of goods,
§7-2-501.

COMMERCIAL CODE—Cont'd
Sales—Cont'd
Animals—Cont'd
Sale of unborn young,
§7-2-105.
Anticipatory repudiation.
Generally, §7-2-610.
Retraction of anticipatory
repudiation, §7-2-611.
Approval.
Sale on approval, §7-2-326.
Risk of loss, §7-2-327.
Special incidents,
§7-2-327.
Assignments.
Rights of buyer or seller,
§7-2-210.
Auctions.
Sale by auction, §7-2-328.
Bailments.
Seller's remedy of stoppage
of delivery in transit,
§7-2-705.
Bankruptcy and insolvency.
Buyer's right to goods on
seller's insolvency,
§7-2-502.
"Battle of forms."
Additional terms in
acceptance or
confirmation, §7-2-207.
Sales contracts, §7-2-202.
Bills of lading.
Form of bill of lading
required in overseas
shipment, §7-2-323.
Blood.
Implied warranty,
§7-2-314.
Bona fide purchasers.
Title acquired, §7-2-403.
Breach, repudiation and
excuse, §§7-2-601 to
7-2-616.
Absence of breach.
Risk of loss in absence,
§7-2-509.
Acceptance of goods.
Burden of establishing
breach after
acceptance, §7-2-607.
Buyer's damages for
breach in regard to
accepted goods,
§7-2-714.
Buyer's rights on
improper delivery,
§7-2-601.
Effect of acceptance,
§7-2-607.
Installment contracts,
§7-2-612.
Revocation of acceptance
in whole or in part,
§7-2-608.
Seller's damages for
nonacceptance,
§7-2-708.
What constitutes
acceptance of goods,
§7-2-606.
Antecedent breach.
Effect of cancellation or
rescission on claims
for antecedent
breach, §7-2-720.
Anticipatory repudiation.
Generally, §7-2-610.

COMMERCIAL CODE—Cont'd

Sales—Cont'd

Breach, repudiation and
excuse—Cont'd

Anticipatory repudiation
—Cont'd

Retraction of
anticipatory
repudiation,
§7-2-611.

Assurance of performance.
Right to adequate
assurance of
performance,
§7-2-609.

Burden of establishing
breach after
acceptance, §7-2-607.

Casualty to identified
goods, §7-2-613.

Cover.
Merchant buyer's duties
as to rightfully
rejected goods,
§7-2-603.

Cure by seller of improper
tender or delivery,
§7-2-508.

Damages.
Buyer's damages for
repudiation,
§7-2-713.

Seller's damages for
repudiation,
§7-2-708.

Delivery.
Buyer's rights on
improper delivery,
§7-2-601.

Doubtfulness of
performance.
Right to adequate
assurance of
performance,
§7-2-609.

Failure of presupposed
conditions, §7-2-615.

Procedure on notice
claiming excuse,
§7-2-616.

Identification of goods.
Casualty to identified
goods, §7-2-613.

Improper tender or
delivery.
Cure by seller, §7-2-508.

Installment contract
breach, §7-2-612.

Notice of breach, §7-2-607.

Notice of claim or
litigation to person
answerable over,
§7-2-607.

Notice of failure of
presupposed
conditions, §7-2-615.

Procedure on notice
claiming excuse,
§7-2-616.

Perishable goods.
Buyer's options as to
salvage of rightfully
rejected goods,
§7-2-604.

Merchant buyer's duties
as to rightfully
rejected goods,
§7-2-603.

COMMERCIAL CODE—Cont'd

Sales—Cont'd

Breach, repudiation and
excuse—Cont'd

Presupposed conditions.
Excuse by failure of
presupposed
conditions, §7-2-615.

Procedure on notice
claiming excuse,
§7-2-616.

Rejection of goods.
Buyer's options as to
salvage of rightfully
rejected goods,
§7-2-604.

Buyer's rights on
improper delivery,
§7-2-601.

Cover.
Merchant buyer's
duties as to
rightfully rejected
goods, §7-2-603.

Installment contracts,
§7-2-612.

Manner and effect of
rightful rejection,
§7-2-602.

Merchant buyer's duties
as to rightfully
rejected goods,
§7-2-603.

Perishable goods,
§§7-2-603, 7-2-604.

Waiver of buyer's
objections by failure
to particularize,
§7-2-605.

Replacement, §7-2-508.

Revocation of acceptance,
§7-2-608.

Risk of loss.
Effect of breach on risk
of loss, §7-2-510.

In absence of breach,
§7-2-509.

Substituted performance,
§7-2-614.

Waiver or renunciation of
claim or right after
breach, §7-1-107.

Buildings.
Contract for sale of
building, §7-2-107.

Bulk transfers, §§7-6-101 to
7-6-111. See within this
heading, "Bulk
transfers."

Burden of proof.
Burden of establishing
breach after
acceptance, §7-2-607.

Buyer.
Defined, §7-2-103.

In ordinary course of
business.
Defined, §7-1-201.

Insolvency of seller.
Buyer's right to goods,
§7-2-502.

Checks.
Payment by check,
§7-2-511.

C.I.F. and C. & F. terms,
§7-2-320.

Form of bill of lading in
overseas shipment,
§7-2-323.

Net landed weights,
§7-2-321.

COMMERCIAL CODE—Cont'd

Sales—Cont'd

C.I.F. and C. & F. terms
—Cont'd

Payment on arrival,
§7-2-321.

Warranty of condition on
arrival, §7-2-321.

Citation of article, §7-2-101.

C.O.D. terms.
Buyer not entitled to
inspect goods before
payment, §7-2-513.

Commercial unit.
Defined, §7-2-105.

Conditional sales.
Secured transactions
generally, §§7-9-101 to
7-9-507. See within
this heading, "Secured
transactions."

Confirmed credit term,
§7-2-325.

Consequential damages.
Buyer's remedies, §7-2-715.

Consignment sales, §7-2-326.
Sale or return, §7-2-326.
Risk of loss, §7-2-327.
Special incidents,
§7-2-327.

Construction and
interpretation.
Course of performance or
practical construction
of contracts, §7-2-208.

Exclusion or modification
of warranties,
§7-2-316.

Offer and acceptance in
formation of contract,
§7-2-206.

Contracts.
Absence of specific time
provisions, §7-2-309.

Absence of specified place
for delivery, §7-2-308.

Assignment of rights,
§7-2-210.

"Battle of forms," §7-2-207.

Cancellation, §7-2-209.
Defined, §7-2-106.

Effect of cancellation on
claims for
antecedent breach,
§7-2-720.

Collateral contracts.
Remedies for breach not
impaired, §7-2-701.

Construction.
Course of performance or
practical
construction,
§7-2-208.

Cooperation respecting
performance, §7-2-311.

Course of dealing.
Used to explain terms of
contracts, §7-2-202.

Course of performance,
§7-2-202.

Definitions, §7-2-106.

Delivery in single lots or
several lots, §7-2-307.

Exclusive dealings,
§7-2-306.

Final written expression,
§7-2-202.

Firm offers, §7-2-205.

Formal requirements,
§7-2-201.

COMMERCIAL CODE—Cont'd
Sales—Cont'd
  Contracts—Cont'd
    Formation.
      Generally, §7-2-204.
      Offer and acceptance,
        §7-2-206.
    General obligations of
      parties, §7-2-301.
    Identification of goods,
      §7-2-501.
    Installment contracts,
      §7-2-612.
    Limitation of actions,
      §7-2-725.
    Liquidation or limitation of
      damages, §§7-2-718,
      7-2-719.
    Modification.
      By agreement of parties,
        §7-2-209.
      Liquidation or limitation
        of damages,
        §7-2-719.
      Procedure on notice
        claiming excuse by
        failure of
        presupposed
        conditions, §7-2-616.
    Notice of termination,
      §7-2-309.
    Obligations.
      General obligations of
        parties, §7-2-301.
    Offer and acceptance.
      Additional terms in
        acceptance or
        confirmation,
        §7-2-207.
      "Battle of forms."
        Additional terms in
        acceptance or
        confirmation,
        §7-2-207.
      Firm offers, §7-2-205.
      Generally, §7-2-206.
      Irrevocable offers,
        §7-2-205.
      Methods of acceptance,
        §7-2-206.
    Open price term, §7-2-305.
    Options, §7-2-311.
    Output of seller, §7-2-306.
    Parol or extrinsic evidence,
      §7-2-202.
    Performance.
      Cooperation respecting
        performance,
        §7-2-311.
      Course of performance,
        §7-2-208.
      Delegation of
        performance,
        §7-2-210.
      Right to adequate
        assurance of
        performance,
        §7-2-609.
    Presupposed conditions.
      Excuse by failure of
        presupposed
        conditions, §7-2-615.
    Price payable in money,
      goods, etc., §7-2-304.
    Recordation.
      Goods to be severed from
        realty, §7-2-107.
    Remedies for breach of
      collateral contracts not
      impaired, §7-2-701.

COMMERCIAL CODE—Cont'd
Sales—Cont'd
  Contracts—Cont'd
    Requirements of buyer,
      §7-2-306.
      Formal requirements,
        §7-2-201.
    Resale.
      Seller's resale including
        contract for resale,
        §7-2-706.
    Rescission, §7-2-209.
      Effect of rescission on
        claims for
        antecedent breach,
        §7-2-720.
    Risk of loss.
      Allocation or division of
        risks, §7-2-303.
    Seals inoperative, §7-2-203.
    Statute of frauds, §7-2-201.
      Kinds of personal
        property not
        otherwise covered,
        §7-1-206.
      Modification of contract,
        §7-2-209.
      When writing not
        required, §7-2-201.
    Statute of limitations in
      contracts for sale,
      §7-2-725.
    Termination.
      Defined, §7-2-106.
      Notice of termination,
        §7-2-309.
    Terms.
      Liquidation or limitation
        of damages,
        §§7-2-718, 7-2-719.
    Unconscionable contract or
      clause, §7-2-302.
    Usage of trade.
      Used to explain terms of
        contracts, §7-2-202.
    Void contracts.
      Casualty to identified
        goods, §7-2-613.
    Waiver of executory
      portion, §7-2-209.
    Written expression.
      Final written expression,
        §7-2-202.
  Course of dealing.
    Implied warranties,
      §7-2-314.
  Course of performance,
    §7-2-208.
    Used to explain terms of
      contracts, §7-2-202.
  Cover.
    Buyer's inability to effect
      cover.
      Right to specific
        performance,
        §7-2-716.
    Buyer's remedies,
      §§7-2-711, 7-2-712.
    Merchant buyer's duties as
      to rightfully rejected
      goods, §7-2-603.
  Credit.
    Running of credit.
      Open time for running of
        credit, §7-2-310.
  Creditors' rights.
    Approval.
      Sale on approval,
        §7-2-326.
    Consignment sales,
      §7-2-326.

COMMERCIAL CODE—Cont'd
Sales—Cont'd
  Creditors' rights—Cont'd
    Rights of seller's creditors
      against goods sold,
      §7-2-402.
    Sale on approval, §7-2-326.
    Sale or return, §7-2-326.
  Crops.
    Contract for sale, §7-2-107.
    Identification of goods,
      §7-2-501.
  Cure by seller.
    Improper tender or
      delivery, §7-2-508.
  Damages.
    Buyer's damages, §§7-2-713
      to 7-2-718.
    Market price.
      Admissibility of market
        quotations, §7-2-724.
      Proof of market price,
        §7-2-723.
      Time and place,
        §7-2-723.
    Proof of market price,
      §7-2-723.
  Definitions, §§7-2-103 to
    7-2-106.
    Index, §7-2-103.
  Delivery.
    Absence of specified place
      for delivery, §7-2-308.
    Authority to ship under
      reservation, §7-2-310.
    Buyer's rights on improper
      delivery, §7-2-601.
    Cure by seller of improper
      tender or delivery,
      §7-2-508.
    Damages.
      Buyer's damages for
        nondelivery,
        §7-2-713.
    Defined, §7-1-201.
    Delivery ex-ship, §7-2-322.
    Delivery on condition,
      §7-2-507.
    Documents of title.
      When documents
        deliverable on
        acceptance and on
        payment, §7-2-514.
    Effect of seller's tender,
      §7-2-507.
    Excuse by failure of
      presupposed
      conditions, §7-2-615.
    Ex-ship, §7-2-322.
    General obligation of
      seller, §7-2-301.
    Improper tender or
      delivery.
      Buyer's rights on
        improper delivery,
        §7-2-601.
      Cure by seller, §7-2-508.
    Manner of seller's tender of
      delivery, §7-2-503.
    No arrival, no sale term,
      §7-2-324.
    Nonconforming tender or
      delivery.
      Cure or replacement by
        seller, §7-2-508.
    Nondelivery.
      Buyer's damages for
        nondelivery,
        §7-2-713.
    Place of delivery, §7-2-308.
    Replacement, §7-2-508.

COMMERCIAL CODE—Cont'd
Sales—Cont'd
Delivery—Cont'd
Seller's remedy of stoppage
of delivery in transit,
§7-2-705.
Shipment by seller,
§7-2-504.
Shipment under
reservation.
Authority to ship under
reservation,
§7-2-310.
Single lots or several lots,
§7-2-307.
Stoppage in transit,
§7-2-705.
Substituted performance,
§7-2-614.
Deposits.
Liquidation or limitation of
damages, §7-2-718.
Disclaimer of warranties,
§7-2-316.
Disputed goods.
Preserving evidence of
goods in dispute,
§7-2-515.
Documents of title.
When deliverable on
acceptance and when
on payment, §7-2-514.
Entrusting, §7-2-403.
Evidence.
Parol or extrinsic evidence,
§7-2-202.
Preserving evidence of
goods in dispute,
§7-2-515.
Exclusions from article.
Certain security and other
transactions excluded,
§7-2-102.
Exclusive dealings, §7-2-306.
Express warranties, §7-2-313.
Cumulation and conflict,
§7-2-317.
Factors.
Consignment sales,
§7-2-326.
Entrusting, §7-2-403.
Rights of creditors,
§7-2-326.
Sale on approval, §7-2-326.
Sale or return, §7-2-326.
Title.
Power to transfer title,
§7-2-403.
F.A.S. terms, §7-2-319.
Financing agency.
Defined, §7-2-104.
Rights of financing agency,
§7-2-506.
Fitness for a particular
purpose.
Implied warranty,
§7-2-315.
F.O.B. terms, §7-2-319.
Form of bill of lading in
overseas shipment,
§7-2-323.
Fraud.
Transfer of title obtained
by fraud, §7-2-403.
Good faith.
Defined, §7-2-103.
Purchase of goods,
§7-2-403.
Goods.
Conforming to contract,
§7-2-106.

COMMERCIAL CODE—Cont'd
Sales—Cont'd
Goods—Cont'd
Definitions, §7-2-105.
Fungible goods, §7-1-201.
Fungible goods.
Defined, §7-1-201.
Severance from realty,
§7-2-107.
Recordation, §7-2-107.
Specially manufactured
goods.
Writing not required,
§7-2-201.
Transferability, §7-2-105.
Human blood and tissues.
Implied warranty,
§7-2-314.
Identification of goods.
Breach of contract.
Seller's right to identify
goods to the contract
notwithstanding
breach, §7-2-704.
Casualty to identified
goods, §7-2-613.
Manner of identification,
§7-2-501.
Seller's right to identify
goods to the contract
notwithstanding
breach, §7-2-704.
Impossibility of performance.
Excuse by failure of
presupposed
conditions, §7-2-615.
Procedure on notice
claiming excuse,
§7-2-616.
Substituted performance,
§7-2-614.
Incidental damages.
Buyer's remedies, §7-2-715.
Seller's incidental
damages, §7-2-710.
Infringement.
Buyer's obligation against
infringement, §7-2-312.
Warranty against
infringement, §7-2-312.
Insolvency.
Buyer's right to goods on
seller's insolvency,
§7-2-502.
Seller's remedies on
discovery of buyer's
insolvency, §7-2-702.
Inspection of goods.
Buyer's right to inspect
goods, §7-2-513.
Disputed goods.
Preserving evidence of
goods in dispute,
§7-2-515.
Payment by buyer before
inspection, §7-2-512.
Preserving evidence of
goods in dispute,
§7-2-515.
Installment contracts,
§7-2-612.
Breach, §7-2-612.
Insurance.
C.I.F. and C. & F. terms.
Form of bill of lading in
overseas shipment,
§7-2-323.
Payment on arrival,
§7-2-321.
Warranty of condition on
arrival, §7-2-321.

COMMERCIAL CODE—Cont'd
Sales—Cont'd
Larceny.
Power to transfer voidable
title, §7-2-403.
Limitation of actions,
§7-2-725.
Liquidation of damages,
§7-2-718.
Livestock.
Manner of identification,
§7-2-501.
Lot.
Defined, §7-2-105.
Market price.
Admissibility of market
quotations, §7-2-724.
Proof of market price,
§7-2-723.
Time and place, §7-2-723.
Merchant.
Between merchants.
Defined, §7-2-104.
Defined, §7-2-104.
Merchantability.
Implied warranty of
merchantability,
§7-2-314.
Minerals.
Contract for sale of
minerals, §7-2-107.
Models.
Express warranties by
model, §7-2-313.
No arrival, no sale term,
§7-2-324.
Notice.
Breach, §7-2-607.
Claim or litigation to
person answerable
over, §7-2-607.
Contracts.
Notice of breach,
§7-2-607.
Excuse by failure of
presupposed
conditions, §7-2-615.
Procedure on notice
claiming excuse,
§7-2-616.
Resale by seller.
Notice to buyer,
§7-2-706.
Termination, §7-2-309.
Offer and acceptance,
§§7-2-205 to 7-2-207.
Options, §7-2-311.
Output or requirements,
§7-2-306.
Overseas shipments.
Construction of "overseas,"
§7-2-323.
Form of bill of lading
required in overseas
shipment, §7-2-323.
Letter of credit or banker's
credit terms, §7-2-325.
Parol or extrinsic evidence.
Sales contracts, §7-2-202.
Payment.
Before inspection, §7-2-512.
Check payment, §7-2-511.
General obligation of
buyer, §7-2-301.
Inspection of goods.
Buyer's right to inspect
goods prior to
payment, §7-2-513.
Payment before
inspection, §7-2-512.
Open price term, §7-2-305.

COMMERCIAL CODE—Cont'd
  Sales—Cont'd
    Payment—Cont'd
      Open time for payment,
        §7-2-310.
      Price payable in money,
        goods, etc., §7-2-304.
      Seller's action for the price,
        §7-2-709.
      Substituted performance,
        §7-2-614.
      Tender of payment by
        buyer, §7-2-511.
      When documents
        deliverable on
        payment, §7-2-514.
    Performance, §§7-2-501 to
      7-2-515.
      Assurance of performance.
        Right to adequate
          assurance, §7-2-609.
      Cooperation respecting
        performance, §7-2-311.
      Course of performance,
        §7-2-208.
      Delivery on condition,
        §7-2-507.
      Doubtfulness of
        performance.
        Right to adequate
          assurance of
          performance,
          §7-2-609.
      General obligations of
        parties, §7-2-301.
      Impossibility of
        performance.
        Excuse by failure of
          presupposed
          conditions, §7-2-615.
        Procedure on notice
          claiming excuse,
          §7-2-616.
        Substituted performance,
          §7-2-614.
      Manner of tender of
        delivery, §7-2-503.
      Right to adequate
        assurance of
        performance, §7-2-609.
      Shipment by seller,
        §7-2-504.
      Seller's shipment under
        reservation,
        §7-2-505.
      Substituted performance,
        §7-2-614.
      Tender of delivery.
        Cure by seller of
          improper tender,
          §7-2-508.
        Effect of seller's tender,
          §7-2-507.
        Manner of tender,
          §7-2-503.
        Tender of payment by
          buyer, §7-2-511.
    Perishable goods.
      Buyer's options as to
        salvage of rightfully
        rejected goods,
        §7-2-604.
      Merchant buyer's duties as
        to rightfully rejected
        goods, §7-2-603.
    Present sale.
      Defined, §7-2-106.
    Preserving evidence of goods
      in dispute, §7-2-515.
    Prices.
      Action for price, §7-2-709.

COMMERCIAL CODE—Cont'd
  Sales—Cont'd
    Prices—Cont'd
      Admissibility of market
        quotations, §7-2-724.
      Deduction of damages from
        price, §7-2-717.
      Open price term, §7-2-305.
      Prices payable in money,
        goods, realty, etc.,
        §7-2-304.
      Proof of market price,
        §7-2-723.
      Time and place of market
        price, §7-2-723.
    Quantity.
      Output or requirements
        contracts, §7-2-306.
    Real property.
      Goods to be severed from
        realty, §7-2-107.
    Receipt.
      Defined, §7-2-103.
    Rejection of goods.
      Buyer's options as to
        salvage of rightfully
        rejected goods,
        §7-2-604.
      Buyer's rights on improper
        delivery, §7-2-601.
      Cover.
        Merchant buyer's duties
          as to rightfully
          rejected goods,
          §7-2-603.
      Effect of rightful rejection,
        §7-2-602.
      Installment contracts,
        §7-2-612.
      Manner of rightful
        rejection, §7-2-602.
      Merchant buyer's duties as
        to rightfully rejected
        goods, §7-2-603.
      Perishable goods.
        Buyer's options as to
          salvage of rightfully
          rejected goods,
          §7-2-604.
        Merchant buyer's duties
          as to rightfully
          rejected goods,
          §7-2-603.
      Waiver of buyer's
        objections by failure to
        particularize, §7-2-605.
    Remedies, §§7-2-701 to
      7-2-725.
      Anticipatory repudiation,
        §7-2-610.
      Assurance of performance.
        Right to adequate
          assurance of
          performance,
          §7-2-609.
      Breach of collateral
        contracts.
        Remedies for breach of
          collateral contracts
          not impaired,
          §7-2-701.
      Breach of warranty.
        Limitation of remedies,
          §7-2-316.
      Buyer's remedies.
        Breach of warranty.
          Limitation of remedies,
          §7-2-316.
        Consequential damages,
          §7-2-715.

COMMERCIAL CODE—Cont'd
  Sales—Cont'd
    Remedies—Cont'd
      Buyer's remedies—Cont'd
        Cover, §§7-2-711,
          7-2-712.
        Buyer's right to
          replevin if unable
          to effect cover,
          §7-2-716.
        Damages for breach in
          regard to accepted
          goods, §7-2-714.
        Damages for nondelivery
          or repudiation,
          §7-2-713.
        Deduction of damages
          from price, §7-2-717.
        Generally, §7-2-711.
        Incidental damages,
          §7-2-715.
        Price.
          Deduction of damages
            from price,
            §7-2-717.
        Procurement of
          substitute goods,
          §7-2-712.
        Replevin, §7-2-716.
        Security interest in
          rejected goods,
          §7-2-711.
        Specific performance,
          §7-2-716.
      Claims for antecedent
        breach.
      Effect of cancellation or
        rescission on,
        §7-2-720.
      Contractual modification or
        limitation of remedies,
        §7-2-719.
      Fraud.
        Remedies for fraud,
          §7-2-721.
      Injury to goods.
        Who can sue third
          parties for injury to
          goods, §7-2-722.
      Limitation of actions,
        §7-2-725.
      Limitation of remedies,
        §7-2-719.
        Breach of warranty,
          §7-2-316.
      Liquidation or limitation of
        damages, §7-2-718.
      Deposits, §7-2-718.
      Market price.
        Admissibility of market
          quotations, §7-2-724.
        Proof of market price,
          §7-2-723.
        Time and place,
          §7-2-723.
      Seller's remedies.
        Action for the price,
          §7-2-709.
        Damages for
          nonacceptance or
          repudiation,
          §7-2-708.
        Discovery of buyer's
          insolvency, §7-2-702.
        Generally, §§7-2-703,
          7-2-704.
        Incidental damages,
          §7-2-710.
        Person in the position of
          a seller, §7-2-707.

COMMERCIAL CODE—Cont'd
Sales—Cont'd
  Remedies—Cont'd
    Seller's remedies—Cont'd
      Resale including contract
        for resale, §7-2-706.
      Right to identify goods to
        the contract
        notwithstanding
        breach, §7-2-704.
      Right to salvage
        unfinished goods,
        §7-2-704.
      Stoppage of delivery in
        transit or otherwise,
        §7-2-705.
      Statute of limitations in
        contracts for sale,
        §7-2-725.
    Third parties.
      Who can sue third
        parties for injury to
        goods, §7-2-722.
  Replacement, §7-2-508.
  Replevin.
    Buyer's right to replevin,
      §7-2-716.
  Requirements contracts,
    §7-2-306.
  Resales.
    Merchant buyer's duties as
      to rightfully rejected
      goods, §7-2-603.
    Sale or return, §7-2-326.
      Risk of loss, §7-2-327.
      Special incidents,
        §7-2-327.
    Seller's resale including
      contract for resale,
      §7-2-706.
  Res judicata.
    Effect of notice to person
      answerable over,
      §7-2-607.
  Risk of loss.
    Allocation or division of
      risks, §7-2-303.
    Breach.
      Effect of breach on risk
        of loss, §7-2-510.
      Risk in absence of
        breach, §7-2-509.
    C.I.F. and C. & F. terms,
      §7-2-320.
    Form of bill of lading in
      overseas shipment,
      §7-2-323.
    Net landed weights,
      §7-2-321.
    Payment on arrival,
      §7-2-321.
    Warranty of condition on
      arrival, §7-2-321.
    Delivery ex-ship, §7-2-322.
    Effect of breach on risk of
      loss, §7-2-510.
    F.O.B. and F.A.S. terms,
      §7-2-319.
    Form of bill of lading
      required in overseas
      shipment, §7-2-323.
    Generally, §7-2-509.
    In absence of breach,
      §7-2-509.
    Sale on approval, §7-2-327.
    Sale or return, §7-2-327.
  Sale on approval, §7-2-326.
    Risk of loss, §7-2-327.
    Special incidents, §7-2-327.
  Sale or return, §7-2-326.
    Risk of loss, §7-2-327.

COMMERCIAL CODE—Cont'd
Sales—Cont'd
  Sale or return—Cont'd
    Special incidents, §7-2-327.
  Salvage.
    Buyer's options as to
      salvage of rightfully
      rejected goods,
      §7-2-604.
    Seller's remedies.
      Right to salvage
        unfinished goods,
        §7-2-704.
  Samples.
    Express warranties by
      sample, §7-2-313.
  Scope of article, §7-2-102.
  Seals inoperative, §7-2-203.
  Secured transactions.
    Alienability of debtor's
      rights, §7-9-311.
    Buyer's security interest in
      rejected goods,
      §7-2-711.
    Default.
      Disposition of collateral,
        §§7-9-504 to 7-9-507.
    Exclusions from article,
      §7-2-102.
    Reservation for security,
      §7-2-501.
    Reservation of title,
      §§7-2-310, 7-2-401.
    Security interests arising
      under article on sales,
      §7-9-113.
    Shipment under
      reservation, §7-2-505.
    Warranty against liens or
      encumbrances,
      §7-2-312.
  Seller.
    Defined, §7-2-103.
  Severance from realty.
    Goods to be severed,
      §7-2-107.
  Shipment by seller, §7-2-504.
  Shipment under reservation,
    §7-2-505.
    Authority to ship under
      reservation, §7-2-310.
  Short title, §7-2-101.
  Specially manufactured
    goods.
    When writing not required
      for contract, §7-2-201.
  Specific performance.
    Buyer's right to specific
      performance, §7-2-716.
  Statute of frauds, §7-2-201.
    Kinds of personal property
      not otherwise covered,
      §7-1-206.
    Modification of contract,
      §7-2-209.
    Sales contracts, §7-2-201.
    When writing not required,
      §7-2-201.
  Statute of limitations in
    contracts for sale,
    §7-2-725.
  Tender of delivery by seller.
    Cure by seller of improper
      tender or delivery,
      §7-2-508.
    Effect of seller's tender,
      §7-2-507.
    Manner of tender of
      delivery, §7-2-503.
  Tender of payment by buyer,
    §7-2-511.

COMMERCIAL CODE—Cont'd
Sales—Cont'd
  Terms.
    Absence of specific time
      provisions, §7-2-309.
    Absence of specified place
      for delivery, §7-2-308.
    Banker's credit, §7-2-325.
    C.I.F. and C. & F. terms,
      §7-2-320.
      Form of bill of lading in
        overseas shipment,
        §7-2-323.
      Net landed weights,
        §7-2-321.
      Payment on arrival,
        §7-2-321.
      Warranty of condition on
        arrival, §7-2-321.
    C.O.D. terms.
      Buyer not entitled to
        inspect goods before
        payment, §7-2-513.
    Confirmed credit, §7-2-325.
    Delivery ex-ship, §7-2-322.
    Exclusive dealings,
      §7-2-306.
    F.O.B. and F.A.S. terms,
      §7-2-319.
      Form of bill of lading in
        overseas shipment,
        §7-2-323.
    Letter of credit, §7-2-325.
    No arrival, no sale,
      §7-2-324.
    Open price term, §7-2-305.
    Quantity.
      Output or requirements
        contracts, §7-2-306.
  Third parties.
    Injury to goods.
      Who can sue third
        parties for injury to
        goods, §7-2-722.
  Timber.
    Contract for sale of timber,
      §7-2-107.
  Time.
    Absence of specific time
      provisions, §7-2-309.
    Notice of termination,
      §7-2-309.
    Open time for payment or
      running of credit,
      §7-2-310.
  Title.
    Creditors' rights, §7-2-402.
    Entrusting, §7-2-403.
    Fraud.
      Transfer of title obtained
        by fraud, §7-2-403.
    Good faith purchase of
      goods, §7-2-403.
    Larceny.
      Power to transfer
        voidable title,
        §7-2-403.
    Passing of title, §7-2-401.
      Limited applicability of
        section, §7-2-401.
      Reservation for security,
        §7-2-401.
    Power to transfer,
      §7-2-403.
    Reservation for security,
      §7-2-401.
    Retention of title, §7-2-505.
    Shipment under
      reservation, §7-2-505.
    Transfer, §7-2-403.

COMMERCIAL CODE—Cont'd
Sales—Cont'd
Title—Cont'd
Warranty of title and
against infringement,
§7-2-312.
Transplants.
Implied warranty,
§7-2-314.
Unconscionable contract or
clause, §7-2-302.
Usage of trade.
Implied warranties,
§7-2-314.
Used to explain terms of
contracts, §7-2-202.
Waiver.
Buyer's objections by
failure to particularize,
§7-2-605.
Warranties.
Breach of warranty.
Limitation of remedies
for breach, §7-2-316.
C.I.F. and C. & F. terms.
Warranty of condition on
arrival, §7-2-321.
Conflict of warranty,
§7-2-317.
Course of dealing,
§7-2-314.
Cumulation of warranties,
§7-2-317.
Disclaimer of warranties,
§7-2-316.
Exclusion, §7-2-316.
Persons to whom
warranties extend,
§7-2-318.
Express warranties,
§7-2-313.
Cumulation and conflict,
§7-2-317.
Third-party beneficiaries,
§7-2-318.
Fitness for a particular
purpose, §7-2-315.
Implied warranties.
Course of dealing,
§7-2-314.
Cumulation and conflict,
§7-2-317.
Fitness for a particular
purpose, §7-2-315.
Merchantability,
§7-2-314.
Third-party warranties,
§7-2-318.
Transplants, §7-2-314.
Usage of trade, §7-2-314.
Merchantability, §7-2-314.
Modification, §7-2-316.
Persons to whom
warranties extend,
§7-2-318.
Where security
agreement exists,
§7-9-206.
Notice of claim or
litigation to person
answerable over,
§7-2-607.
Third-party beneficiaries,
§7-2-318.
Usage of trade, §7-2-314.
Warranty of title and
against infringement,
§7-2-312.

COMMERCIAL CODE—Cont'd
Salvage.
Sales.
Seller's right to salvage
unfinished goods,
§7-2-704.
**Savings and loan
association.**
Secured transactions.
Transfer of accounts
excluded from
provisions of article,
§7-9-104.
**Seals and sealed
instruments.**
Commercial paper.
Negotiability not affected,
§7-3-113.
Contracts for sale.
Seal inoperative, §7-2-203.
Secretary of state.
Secured transactions.
Filing.
Central index system
program.
Secretary to
promulgate
regulations,
§7-9-410.
Place of filing, §7-9-401.
Section captions, §7-1-109.
Secured transactions,
§§7-9-101 to 7-9-507.
Accessions, §7-9-314.
Accounts.
Defined, §7-9-106.
Multiple state transactions.
Perfection of security
interest, §7-9-103.
When security interest
attaches, §7-9-204.
After-acquired collateral.
When after-acquired
collateral not security
for antecedent debt,
§7-9-108.
When security interest
attaches, §7-9-204.
Airplanes.
Determination of validity
and perfection of
security interest in
plane, §7-9-103.
Alienability of debtor's
rights, §7-9-311.
Judicial process, §7-9-311.
Annuities.
Transfer of interest or
claim in annuity
excluded, §7-9-104.
Antedecent debt.
When after-acquired
collateral not security
for antecedent debt,
§7-9-108.
Applicability of article,
§§7-9-102 to 7-9-104.
Security interests to which
filing provisions of
article do not apply,
§7-9-302.
Assignments.
Accounts or contract
rights.
Defenses against
assignee, §7-9-318.
Identification and proof
of assignment,
§7-9-318.

COMMERCIAL CODE—Cont'd
Secured transactions—Cont'd
Assignments—Cont'd
Accounts or contract rights
—Cont'd
Modification of contract
after notification of
assignment,
§7-9-318.
Proof of assignment,
§7-9-318.
Term prohibiting
assignment
ineffective, §7-9-318.
Agreement not to assert
defenses against
assignee, §7-9-206.
Security interest, §7-9-405.
Assignments for benefit of
creditors.
Priority over unperfected
security interests,
§7-9-301.
Attachment.
Attachment and
enforceability of
security interest,
§7-9-203.
Debtor's rights in
collateral, §7-9-311.
Bank deposits and
collections.
Collection by depositary
and collecting banks.
Security interest of
collecting bank in
items, accompanying
documents and
proceeds, §7-4-208.
Security interests to
which filing
provisions of article
do not apply,
§7-9-302.
Collection of documentary
drafts, §7-4-504.
Bankruptcy and insolvency.
Trustees in bankruptcy.
Priority over unperfected
security interests,
§7-9-301.
Banks.
Financial institutions.
Transfer of accounts
excluded from
article, §7-9-104.
Bulk transfer laws.
Applicability, §7-9-111.
Buyer of goods and
protection, §7-9-307.
Funds.
Uniform commercial code
and farm products
central index system
fund.
Fees and charges to be
deposited into
fund, §7-9-307.
Chattel paper.
Defined, §7-9-105.
Multiple state transactions.
Perfection of security
interest, §7-9-103.
Purchase of chattel paper,
§7-9-308.
Citation of article.
Short title, §7-9-101.
Classification of goods,
§7-9-109.

COMMERCIAL CODE—Cont'd
Secured transactions—Cont'd
Collateral.
After-acquired collateral.
When after-acquired
collateral not
security for
antecedent debt,
§7-9-108.
Alienability of debtor's
rights, §7-9-311.
Conflicting security
interests.
Priorities among
conflicting security
interests in the same
collateral, §7-9-312.
Default.
Acceptance of collateral
as discharge of
obligation, §7-9-505.
Compulsory disposition
after default,
§7-9-505.
Debtor's right to redeem,
§7-9-506.
Disposition after default,
§7-9-504.
Compulsory
disposition,
§7-9-505.
Redemption of collateral.
Debtor's right to
redeem, §7-9-506.
Secured party's right to
dispose of collateral
after default,
§7-9-504.
Effect of disposition,
§7-9-504.
Defined, §7-9-105.
Disposition after default,
§7-9-504.
Compulsory disposition,
§7-9-505.
List of collateral.
Request for list of
collateral, §7-9-208.
Priorities among
conflicting security
interests in the same
collateral, §7-9-312.
Redemption of collateral.
Debtor's right to redeem
after default,
§7-9-506.
Release of collateral,
§7-9-406.
Request for list of
collateral, §7-9-208.
Rights and duties when
collateral in secured
party's possession,
§7-9-207.
Secured party's rights on
disposition of
collateral, §7-9-306.
Statement of release of
collateral, §7-9-406.
Title to collateral.
Immaterial, §7-9-202.
Use or disposition of
without accounting
permissible, §7-9-205.
Contract or tort liability
not imposed on
secured party,
§7-9-317.

COMMERCIAL CODE—Cont'd
Secured transactions—Cont'd
Collateral—Cont'd
When after-acquired
collateral not security
for antecedent debt,
§7-9-108.
Where collateral is not
owned by debtor,
§7-9-112.
Conflicting security interests.
Priorities among
conflicting security
interests in the same
collateral, §7-9-312.
Conflict of laws.
Multiple state transactions.
Perfection of security
interest, §7-9-103.
Perfection of security
interest.
Multiple state
transactions,
§7-9-103.
Removal of collateral,
§7-9-401.
Consignment, §7-9-114.
Consumer goods.
Classification of goods,
§7-9-109.
Defined, §7-9-109.
Filing.
Security interests to
which filing
provisions of article
do not apply,
§7-9-302.
When security interest
attaches, §7-9-204.
Contract rights.
Filing.
Applicability of filing
provisions, §7-9-302.
Place of filing, §7-9-401.
Multiple state transactions.
Perfection of security
interest, §7-9-103.
Place of filing, §7-9-401.
When security interest
attaches, §7-9-204.
Corporations.
Filing.
Applicability of filing
provisions, §7-9-302.
Credit unions.
Transfer of accounts
excluded from article,
§7-9-104.
Crops.
Classification of goods,
§7-9-109.
Description of land,
§7-9-203.
Formal requisites of
financing statement,
§7-9-402.
Place of filing, §7-9-401.
When security interest
attaches, §7-9-204.
Debtor's contracts.
Account debtor.
Defined, §7-9-105.
Definition of debtor,
§7-9-105.
Secured party not obligated
on contract of debtor,
§7-9-317.
Debtor's rights.
Alienability, §7-9-311.
Judicial process,
§7-9-311.

COMMERCIAL CODE—Cont'd
Secured transactions—Cont'd
Debtor's rights—Cont'd
Definition of debtor,
§7-9-105.
Default, §§7-9-501 to 7-9-507.
Collateral.
Acceptance of collateral
as discharge of
obligation, §7-9-505.
Compulsory disposition,
§7-9-505.
Debtor's right to redeem,
§7-9-506.
Disposition after default,
§7-9-504.
Compulsory
disposition,
§7-9-505.
Redemption.
Debtor's right to
redeem, §7-9-506.
Secured party's right to
dispose of collateral
after default,
§7-9-504.
Effect of disposition,
§7-9-504.
Collection rights of secured
party, §7-9-502.
Debtor's right to redeem
collateral, §7-9-506.
Discharge of obligation.
Acceptance of collateral
as discharge of
obligation, §7-9-505.
Generally, §7-9-501.
Personal property.
Procedure when security
agreement covers
both real and
personal property,
§7-9-501.
Real property.
Procedure when security
agreement covers
both real and
personal property,
§7-9-501.
Redemption of collateral.
Debtor's right to redeem,
§7-9-506.
Right of secured party to
take possession after
default, §7-9-503.
Sales.
Disposition of collateral,
§§7-9-504 to 7-9-507.
Secured party.
Collection rights of
secured party,
§7-9-502.
Failure to comply.
Liability, §7-9-507.
Liability for failure to
comply with
provisions, §7-9-507.
Right to dispose of
collateral after
default, §7-9-504.
Effect of disposition,
§7-9-504.
Right to take possession
after default,
§7-9-503.
Defenses.
Against assignee of
account, §7-9-318.
Agreement not to assert
defenses against
assignee, §7-9-206.

COMMERCIAL CODE—Cont'd
Secured transactions—Cont'd
Definitions, §7-9-105.
  Account, §7-9-106.
  Account debtor, §7-9-105.
  Attached, §7-9-105.
  Certificate of deposit,
    §7-9-105.
  Chattel paper, §7-9-105.
  Collateral, §7-9-105.
  Construction mortgage,
    §7-9-105.
  Consumer goods, §7-9-109.
  Debtor, §7-9-105.
  Deposit account, §7-9-105.
  Document, §7-9-105.
  Encumbrance, §7-9-105.
  Equipment, §7-9-109.
  Farm products, §7-9-109.
  Fixture, §7-9-105.
  General intangibles,
    §7-9-106.
  Generally, §7-9-105.
  Goods, §7-9-105.
  Index, §7-9-105.
  Instrument, §7-9-105.
  Inventory, §7-9-109.
  Mortgage, §7-9-105.
  Proceeds, §7-9-306.
  Purchase money security
    interest, §7-9-107.
  Pursuant to commitment,
    §7-9-105.
  Secured party, §7-9-105.
  Security agreement,
    §7-9-105.
  Timber to be cut, §7-9-105.
  Utility, §7-9-105.
Delivery.
  Defined, §7-1-201.
Description.
  Sufficiency of description,
    §7-9-110.
Documents.
  Defined, §7-9-105.
  Multiple state transactions.
    Perfection of security
      interest, §7-9-103.
  Perfected security interest
    in documents or goods
    covered by documents,
    §7-9-304.
  Purchasers of documents.
    Protection, §7-9-309.
Effective date and transition
  provisions, §§7-11-101 to
  7-11-108.
Electricity.
  Applicability of filing
    provisions, §7-9-302.
Equipment.
  Defined, §7-9-109.
Exclusions from article,
  §7-9-104.
  Security interests to which
    filing provisions of
    article do not apply,
    §7-9-302.
Executions.
  Debtor's rights in
    collateral, §7-9-311.
  Priority over unperfected
    security interests,
    §7-9-301.
Farm products.
  Defined, §7-9-109.
Fees.
  Assignment of security
    interest, §7-9-405.
  Prescribed fees in lieu of
    all others, §7-9-409.

COMMERCIAL CODE—Cont'd
Secured transactions—Cont'd
Fees—Cont'd
  Release of collateral,
    §7-9-406.
  Termination statement,
    §7-9-404.
Filing.
  Assignment of security
    interest, §7-9-405.
  Fees of filing officer,
    §7-9-405.
  Central index system
    program.
    Public training, §7-9-410.
    Rules and regulations,
      §7-9-410.
    User training, §7-9-410.
  Collateral.
    Release of collateral,
      §7-9-406.
    Duties of filing officer,
      §7-9-406.
    Removal of collateral,
      §7-9-401.
  Conflict of laws, §§7-9-103,
    7-9-401.
  Duration of filing,
    §7-9-403.
  Duties of filing officer,
    §§7-9-403 to 7-9-406.
  Effect of lapsed filing,
    §7-9-403.
  Erroneous filing, §7-9-401.
  Fees.
    Assignment of security
      interest, §7-9-405.
    Financing statement,
      §7-9-403.
      Assignment, §7-9-405.
    Prescribed fees in lieu of
      all others, §7-9-409.
    Release of collateral,
      §7-9-406.
    Statement of release of
      collateral, §7-9-406.
    Termination statement,
      §7-9-404.
  Filing officer.
    Duties, §§7-9-403 to
      7-9-406.
    Information from filing
      officer, §7-9-407.
  Financing statement,
    §7-9-402.
    Amendments, §7-9-402.
    Formal requisites,
      §7-9-402.
  Formal requisites of
    financing statements,
    §7-9-402.
  Information from filing
    officer, §7-9-407.
  Lapsed filing.
    Effect of lapsed filing,
      §7-9-403.
  Perfected security
    interests.
    Perfection by permissive
      filing, §7-9-304.
    Temporary perfection
      without filing or
      transfer of
      possession, §7-9-304.
    When possession by
      secured party
      perfects without
      filing, §7-9-305.
  Permissive filing.
    Perfection by permissive
      filing, §7-9-304.

COMMERCIAL CODE—Cont'd
Secured transactions—Cont'd
Filing—Cont'd
  Place of filing, §7-9-401.
  Refiling.
    Required, §7-11-106.
  Removal of collateral,
    §7-9-401.
    Incoming goods already
      subject to security
      interest, §7-9-103.
    Required refilings,
      §7-11-106.
  Secretary of state.
    Place of filing, §7-9-401.
  Security interests to which
    filing provisions of
    article do not apply,
    §7-9-302.
  Termination statement,
    §7-9-404.
  Transition provision on
    change of place of
    filing, §7-11-105.
  Transition provision on
    change of requirement
    of filing, §7-11-104.
  What constitutes filing,
    §7-9-403.
  When required to perfect
    security interest,
    §7-9-302.
Financing statements,
  §7-9-402.
  Amendments, §7-9-402.
  Assignment, §7-9-405.
  Covering consigned or
    leased goods, §7-9-408.
  Duration, §7-9-403.
  Fees for filing, §7-9-403.
  Formal requisites,
    §7-9-402.
  Mortgage as financing
    statement, §7-9-402.
Fish.
  When security interest
    attaches, §7-9-204.
Fixtures.
  Formal requisites of
    financing statement,
    §7-9-402.
  Place of filing, §7-9-401.
  Priority of security
    interests in fixtures,
    §7-9-313.
Fungible.
  Defined, §7-1-201.
Garnishment.
  Debtor's rights in
    collateral, §7-9-311.
General intangibles.
  Defined, §7-9-106.
  Multiple state transactions.
    Perfection of security
      interest, §7-9-103.
Goods.
  Certificate of title goods.
    Multiple state
      transactions.
      Perfection of security
        interest, §7-9-103.
  Classification of goods,
    §7-9-109.
  Consumer goods.
    Defined, §7-9-109.
  Defined, §7-9-105.
  Incoming goods already
    subject to security
    interest, §7-9-103.
  Protection of buyers of
    goods, §7-9-307.

COMMERCIAL CODE—Cont'd
Secured transactions—Cont'd
Instruments.
  Defined, §7-9-105.
  Multiple state transactions.
    Perfection of security
      interest, §7-9-103.
  Perfected security interest
    in instruments,
    §7-9-304.
  Purchase, §7-9-308.
  Protection, §7-9-309.
Insurance.
  Transfer of interest or
    claim in policy or
    annuity excluded,
    §7-9-104.
Intangibles.
  General intangibles.
    Multiple state
      transactions.
      Perfection of security
        interest, §7-9-103.
Inventory.
  Classification of goods,
    §7-9-109.
  Defined, §7-9-109.
Judgments and decrees.
  Transactions excluded from
    article, §7-9-104.
Jurisdiction.
  Multiple state transactions.
    Perfection of security
      interest, §7-9-103.
Landlord and tenant.
  Landlord's lien, §7-9-310.
  Applicability of secured
    transactions article,
    §7-9-104.
Liens.
  Landlord's lien, §7-9-310.
  Priority of certain liens
    arising by operation of
    law, §7-9-310.
  Priority over unperfected
    security interests,
    §7-9-301.
  Transactions excluded from
    article, §7-9-104.
Limitation of actions.
  Duration of financing
    statements, §7-9-403.
Livestock.
  Classification of goods,
    §7-9-109.
  When security interest
    attaches, §7-9-204.
Mines and minerals.
  Description of land,
    §7-9-203.
  Multiple state transactions.
    Perfection of security
      interest, §7-9-103.
  When security interest
    attaches minerals,
    §7-9-204.
Mobile goods.
  Multiple state transactions.
    Perfection of security
      interest, §7-9-103.
Money.
  Perfection of security
    interest in money,
    §7-9-304.
Mortgages.
  Financing statement,
    §7-9-402.
Motor vehicles.
  Applicability of filing
    provisions, §7-9-302.

COMMERCIAL CODE—Cont'd
Secured transactions—Cont'd
Multiple state transactions.
  Perfection of security
    interest, §7-9-103.
Oil and gas.
  Applicability of filing
    provisions, §7-9-302.
  Description of land,
    §7-9-203.
  When security interest
    attaches, §7-9-204.
Perfected security interest,
  §7-9-301.
  Continuity of perfection,
    §7-9-303.
  Documents.
    Perfection in documents
      and goods covered by
      documents, §7-9-304.
  Effect of lapsed filing,
    §7-9-403.
  Goods covered by
    documents.
    Perfection in goods
      covered by
      documents, §7-9-304.
  Instruments.
    Perfection in
      instruments,
      §7-9-304.
  Lapsed filing.
    Effect, §7-9-403.
  Money.
    Perfection in money,
      §7-9-304.
  Multiple state transactions,
    §7-9-103.
  Permissive filing.
    Perfection by permissive
      filing, §7-9-304.
  Possession by secured
    party.
    When possession perfects
      without filing,
      §7-9-305.
  Temporary perfection.
    Without filing or
      transfer of
      possession, §7-9-304.
  When filing is required to
    perfect, §7-9-302.
  When possession by
    secured party perfects
    without filing,
    §7-9-305.
  When security interest is
    perfected, §7-9-303.
Pipelines.
  Applicability of filing
    provisions, §7-9-302.
Policy of article, §7-9-102.
Priorities.
  Accessions, §7-9-314.
  Among conflicting security
    interests in the same
    collateral, §7-9-312.
  Arising by operation of
    law, §7-9-310.
  Commingling of goods.
    When goods are
      commingled,
      §7-9-315.
  Fixtures.
    Security interests in
      fixtures, §7-9-313.
  Knowledge, §7-9-401.
  Liens arising by operation
    of law, §7-9-310.

COMMERCIAL CODE—Cont'd
Secured transactions—Cont'd
Priorities—Cont'd
  Persons who take priority
    over unperfected
    security interests,
    §7-9-301.
  Processing of goods.
    When goods are
      processed, §7-9-315.
  Subject to subordination,
    §7-9-316.
  Subordination by
    agreement, §7-9-316.
  Transition provisions,
    §7-11-107.
  Unperfected security
    interests, §7-9-301.
  When goods are
    commingled or
    processed, §7-9-315.
Proceeds.
  Defined, §7-9-306.
  Description in security
    agreements, §7-9-203.
Protection of buyers of goods,
  §7-9-307.
Protection of purchasers of
  instruments and
  documents, §7-9-309.
Railroads.
  Applicability of filing
    provisions, §7-9-302.
  Determination of validity
    and perfection of
    security interest in
    rolling stock, §7-9-103.
  Transactions excluded from
    article, §7-9-104.
Real property.
  Defaults.
    Procedure when security
      agreement covers
      both real and
      personal property,
      §7-9-501.
  Formal requisites of
    financing statement,
    §7-9-402.
  Priority of security
    interests in fixtures,
    §7-9-313.
  Sufficiency of description,
    §7-9-110.
Receivers.
  Priority over unperfected
    security interests,
    §7-9-301.
Releases.
  Termination statement,
    §7-9-404.
Retail installment sales.
  Validity of security
    agreement, §7-9-201.
Salaries.
  Transactions excluded from
    article, §7-9-104.
Sales.
  Alienability of debtor's
    rights, §7-9-311.
  Default.
    Disposition of collateral,
      §§7-9-504 to 7-9-507.
  Security interests arising
    under article on sales,
    §7-9-113.
Savings and loan association.
  Transfer of accounts
    excluded from article,
    §7-9-104.

COMMERCIAL CODE—Cont'd
  Secured transactions—Cont'd
  Secretary of state.
    Place of filing, §7-9-401.
  Secured party.
    Default, §§7-9-501 to
        7-9-507.
    Defined, §7-9-105.
    Not obligated on contract
        of debtor, §7-9-317.
    Rights on disposition of
        collateral, §7-9-306.
  Securities.
    Restriction on transfer,
        §§7-8-204, 10-2A-41.
  Security agreement.
    Advances.
      Future advances,
          §7-9-204.
    After-acquired property,
        §7-9-204.
    Agreement not to assert
        defenses against
        assignee, §7-9-206.
    Collateral.
      List of collateral.
        Request for list,
            §7-9-208.
      Rights and duties when
          collateral is in
          secured party's
          possession, §7-9-207.
      Title to collateral
          immaterial,
          §7-9-202.
      Use or disposition
          without accounting
          permissible,
          §7-9-205.
        Contract or tort
            liability not
            imposed on
            secured party,
            §7-9-317.
    Defenses.
      Agreement not to assert
          defenses against
          assignee, §7-9-206.
    Defined, §7-9-105.
    Description in a security
        agreement, §7-9-203.
    Formal requisites,
        §7-9-203.
    Modification of sales
        warranties where
        security agreement
        exists, §7-9-206.
    Proceeds, §7-9-203.
    Requisites.
      Formal requisites,
          §7-9-203.
    Rights and duties when
        collateral is in secured
        party's possession,
        §7-9-207.
    Sales.
      Reservation for security,
          §7-2-505.
    Sales warranties.
      Modification of sales
          warranties where
          security agreement
          exists, §7-9-206.
    Statement of account.
      Request for statement of
          account, §7-9-208.
    Title to collateral
        immaterial, §7-9-202.

COMMERCIAL CODE—Cont'd
  Secured transactions—Cont'd
  Security agreement—Cont'd
    Use or disposition of
        collateral without
        accounting
        permissible, §7-9-205.
      Contract or tort liability
          not imposed on
          secured party,
          §7-9-317.
    Validity.
      General validity of
          security agreement,
          §7-9-201.
    When security interest
        attaches, §7-9-204.
  Security interest.
    Assignment, §7-9-405.
    Attachment, §7-9-203.
    Bank deposits and
        collections.
      Collection of
          documentary drafts,
          §7-4-504.
      Security interest of
          collecting bank in
          items, accompanying
          documents and
          proceeds, §7-4-208.
    Conflicting security
        interests.
      Priorities among
          conflicting security
          interests in the same
          collateral, §7-9-312.
    Defined, §§7-1-201,
        7-9-107.
    Documents.
      Perfection in documents
          and goods covered by
          documents, §7-9-304.
    Enforceability, §7-9-203.
    Instruments.
      Perfection in
          instruments,
          §7-9-304.
    Money.
      Perfection in money,
          §7-9-304.
    Priority over unperfected
        security interests,
        §7-9-301.
    Purchase money security
        interest.
      Defined, §7-9-107.
    Sales.
      Buyer's security interest
          in rejected goods,
          §7-2-711.
      Reservation for security,
          §7-2-505.
      Reservation of title for
          security, §§7-2-310,
          7-2-401.
      Security interests arising
          under article on
          sales, §7-9-113.
    Unperfected security
        interests.
      Effect of lapsed filing,
          §7-9-403.
      Priority over, §7-9-301.
    When security interest
        attaches, §7-9-204.
  Set-off.
    Transactions excluded from
        article, §7-9-104.
  Ships and shipping.
    Transactions excluded from
        article, §7-9-104.

COMMERCIAL CODE—Cont'd
  Secured transactions—Cont'd
  Short title of article,
      §7-9-101.
  Small loans.
    Validity of security
        agreement, §7-9-201.
  Subject matter of article,
      §7-9-102.
    Security interests to which
        filing provisions of
        article do not apply,
        §7-9-302.
  Subordination.
    Priority subject to
        subordination,
        §7-9-316.
  Sufficiency of description,
      §7-9-110.
  Telephones and telegraphs.
    Applicability of filing
        provisions, §7-9-302.
  Termination statement.
    Fees for filing, §7-9-404.
    Filing, §7-9-404.
  Third parties.
    Rights of third parties
        generally, §§7-9-301 to
        7-9-318.
  Timber.
    Defined, §7-9-105.
    Description of land,
        §7-9-203.
    Formal requisites of
        financing statement,
        §7-9-402.
    Place of filing, §7-9-401.
  Time.
    Duration of financing
        statement, §7-9-403.
  Title to collateral.
    Immaterial, §7-9-202.
  Torts.
    Transfer of claims excluded
        from article, §7-9-104.
  Transactions excluded from
      article, §7-9-104.
  Transition provisions.
    Presumption that rule of
        law continues
        unchanged, §7-11-108.
  Unperfected security
      interests.
    Effect of lapsed filing,
        §7-9-403.
    Lapsed filing.
      Effect, §7-9-403.
    Lien creditor.
      Rights, §7-9-301.
    Persons who take priority
        over, §7-9-301.
  Usury.
    Validity of security
        agreement, §7-9-201.
  Validity.
    Security agreement.
      General validity of
          security agreement,
          §7-9-201.
  Wages.
    Transactions excluded from
        article, §7-9-104.
  Warranty.
    Sales warranties.
      Modification where
          security agreement
          exists, §7-9-206.
  Water supply and
      waterworks.
    Applicability of filing
        provisions, §7-9-302.

COMMERCIAL CODE—Cont'd

Securities.
Investment securities,
§§7-8-101 to 7-8-406. See
within this heading,
"Investment securities."

Send.
Defined, §7-1-201.

Setoff.
Bank deposits and
collections.
When items subject to
setoffs, §7-4-303.
Secured transactions.
Transactions excluded from
provisions of article,
§7-9-104.

Severability of provisions,
§7-1-108.

Ships and shipping.
Documents of title.
General provisions,
§§7-7-101 to 7-7-603.
See within this
heading, "Documents
of title."
Sales. See within this
heading, "Sales."
Secured transactions.
Transactions excluded from
provisions of article,
§7-9-104.

Short title, §7-1-101.

Signatures.
Bank deposits and
collections.
Customer's duty to discover
and report
unauthorized
signature, §7-4-406.
Commercial paper. See
within this heading,
"Commercial paper."
Investment securities.
Assurance that
indorsements are
effective, §7-8-402.
Burden of proof, §7-8-105.
Effect of guaranteeing
signature or
indorsement, §7-8-312.
Effect of signature of
authenticating trustee,
registrar or transfer
agent, §7-8-208.
Effect of unauthorized
signature on issue,
§7-8-205.
Letters of credit, §7-5-104.
Unauthorized signature.
Defined, §7-1-201.

Signed.
Defined, §7-1-201.

Small loans.
Secured transactions.
Validity of security
agreement, §7-9-201.

Specific performance.
Investment securities.
Right to obtain possession
of security wrongfully
transferred, §7-8-315.
Sales.
Buyer's right to specific
performance, §7-2-716.

Specific repealer, §7-10-102.

Statute of frauds.
Investment securities,
§7-8-319.

COMMERCIAL CODE—Cont'd

Statute of frauds—Cont'd
Kinds of personal property
not otherwise covered,
§7-1-206.
Sales contract, §7-2-201.
Investment securities,
§7-8-319.
Modification of sales
contracts, §7-2-209.

Stoppage in transit.
Documents of title.
Seller's stoppage of
delivery, §7-7-504.
Sales.
Seller's remedies, §7-2-705.

Stop-payment order.
Bank's right to subrogation
on improper payment,
§7-4-407.
Relationship between payor
bank and customer,
§7-4-403.

Subrogation.
Bank deposits and
collections.
Payor bank's right to
subrogation on
improper payment,
§7-4-407.

Surety.
Defined, §7-1-201.

Suretyship.
Documents of title.
Indorser not guarantor for
other parties, §7-7-505.
Investment securities.
Indorser not a guarantor,
§7-8-308.

Telegram.
Defined, §7-1-201.

Telephones.
Secured transactions.
Applicability of filing
provisions, §7-9-302.

Theft.
Commercial paper.
Defenses, §7-3-306.
Stolen instruments,
§7-3-804.

Third parties.
Sales.
Who can sue third parties
for injury to goods,
§7-2-722.
Secured transactions.
Rights of third parties
generally, §§7-9-301 to
7-9-318.

Time.
Bank deposits and
collections. See within
this heading, "Bank
deposits and collections."
Commercial paper. See
within this heading,
"Commercial paper."
Letters of credit.
Establishment of credit,
§7-5-106.
Time allowed for honor or
rejection, §7-5-112.
Reasonable time, §7-1-204.
Sales, §§7-2-309, 7-2-310.
"Seasonably" construed,
§7-1-204.
Secured transactions.
Duration of financing
statement, §7-9-403.

COMMERCIAL CODE—Cont'd

Tissue.
Human blood and tissues.
Implied warranty,
§7-2-314.

Title.
Documents of title, §§7-7-101
to 7-7-603. See within
this heading,
"Documents of title."
Investment securities.
Title acquired by bona fide
purchaser, §7-8-301.
Power to transfer, §7-2-403.
Retention of title, §7-2-505.
Rights of seller's creditors
against sold goods,
§7-2-402.
Sales. See within this
heading, "Sales."
Secured transactions.
Title to collateral
immaterial, §7-9-202.

Torts.
Secured transactions.
Transfer of claims excluded
from provisions of
article, §7-9-104.

Transition to title.
Provision for transition,
§7-10-102.

Transplants.
Implied warranty, §7-2-314.

Trees and timber.
Sales.
Goods to be severed from
realty, §7-2-107.
Secured transactions.
Description of land,
§7-9-203.
Financing statement,
§7-9-402.
Place of filing, §7-9-401.

Usage of trade, §7-1-205.
Implied warranties, §7-2-314.

Usury.
Secured transactions.
Validity of security
agreement, §7-9-201.

Value.
Defined, §7-1-201.

Variation by agreement,
§7-1-102.

Wages.
Secured transactions.
Transactions excluded from
provisions of article,
§7-9-104.

Waiver.
Commercial paper.
Waiver of presentment,
protest or notice of
dishonor, §7-3-511.
Sales contracts, §7-2-209.

Warehouse receipts.
General provisions. See
within this heading,
"Documents of title."

Warranty.
Bank deposits and
collections.
Collection by depositary
and collecting banks.
See within this
heading, "Bank
deposits and
collections."
Commercial paper.
Warranties on presentment
and transfer, §7-3-417.

COMMERCIAL CODE—Cont'd
Warranty—Cont'd
Documents of title.
Warranties of collecting
bank, §7-7-508.
Implied warranty.
Human blood and tissues,
§7-2-314.
Investment securities.
Effect of signature of
authenticating trustee,
registrar or transfer
agent, §7-8-208.
Warranties on presentment
and transfer, §7-8-306.
Letters of credit.
Warranties on transfer and
presentment, §7-5-111.
Sales. See within this
heading, "Sales."
Secured transactions.
Modification of sales
warranties where
security agreement
exists, §7-9-206.
**Water supply and
waterworks.**
Secured transactions.
Applicability of filing
provisions, §7-9-302.
Weights and measures.
Official certificate as prima
facie evidence, §7-1-202.
Written.
Defined, §7-1-201.

**COMMERCIAL
DEVELOPMENT
AUTHORITIES.**
Municipal corporations.
Authorities in class 1
municipalities,
§§11-54-170 to
11-54-192.
See MUNICIPAL
CORPORATIONS.

COMMERCIAL FEED LAW,
§§2-21-1 to 2-21-34.
See FEEDS.

COMMERCIAL PAPER.
Commercial code, §§7-3-101
to 7-3-805.
See COMMERCIAL CODE.
Negotiable instruments.
See NEGOTIABLE
INSTRUMENTS.

**COMMERCIAL WEIGHING
AND MEASURING
TECHNICIANS.**
Registration, §§8-16-120 to
8-16-123.

COMMISSION MERCHANTS.
Actions.
Sale of farm produce.
Institution of civil actions
upon bonds, §2-29-4.
Agriculture.
Sale of farm produce,
§§2-29-1 to 2-29-11. See
within this heading,
"Sale of farm
produce."
Bonds, surety.
Sale of farm produce,
§2-29-4.
Cotton.
Appropriation of cotton from
bale by commission
merchant having
custody, §2-19-4.

COMMISSION MERCHANTS
—Cont'd
Definitions.
Sale of farm produce,
§2-29-1.
Fees.
Sale of farm produce.
Permit fee, §2-29-2.
Licenses, §40-12-81.
Liens.
Secured transactions,
§§7-9-101 to 7-9-507.
See COMMERCIAL CODE.
Permits.
Sale of farm produce. See
within this heading,
"Sale of farm produce."
Rebates, §8-11-5.
Records.
Sale of farm produce.
Maintenance of records,
§2-29-7.
Sale of farm produce,
§§2-29-1 to 2-29-11.
Actions.
Institution of civil actions
upon bonds, §2-29-4.
Applicability of provisions of
chapter, §2-29-11.
Bonds, surety, §2-29-4.
Complaints against
commission merchants.
Investigation, §2-29-8.
Definitions, §2-29-1.
Fees.
Permit fee, §2-29-2.
Investigations, §2-29-8.
Municipal corporations.
Regulation of sale, etc., of
farm products by
farmers or other
producers, §2-29-10.
Permits.
Application for permit,
§2-29-2.
Denial or revocation.
Authorization, §2-29-5.
Conduct of proceedings
as to revocation,
§2-29-8.
Grounds, §2-29-5.
Proceedings for review,
§2-29-6.
Duration, §2-29-2.
Expiration date, §2-29-3.
Fee, §2-29-2.
Investigation of applicants,
§2-29-8.
Issuance, §2-29-2.
Required, §2-29-2.
Prohibited acts, §2-29-9.
Records.
Maintenance of records as
to handling, storage or
sale of farm products,
§2-29-7.
**Sales representative's
commission contracts,**
§§8-24-1 to 8-24-5.

COMMISSIONS.
Boards and commissions.
See BOARDS AND
COMMISSIONS.
Public officers' commissions.
See PUBLIC OFFICERS
AND EMPLOYEES.

COMMON CARRIERS.
See CARRIERS.

COMMON LAW.
Arbitration.
Common-law arbitration not
precluded, §6-6-16.
Carriers.
Common-law liability of
common carriers.
Bills of lading or receipts,
§37-2-21.
**Constitution of the United
States.**
Suits at common law, Const.
U. S., Amendment VII.
**English common law
adopted,** §1-3-1.
Evidence.
Proof of unwritten or
common law of other
states and territories,
§12-21-65.
Indictments.
Offenses charged or described
as at common law,
§15-8-20.

COMMON TRUST FUNDS.
**Banks and financial
institutions.**
Administration of common
trust funds, §§5-12A-1 to
5-12A-15.
See BANKS AND
FINANCIAL
INSTITUTIONS.

COMMUNICABLE DISEASES.
See DISEASES.

COMMUNICATIONS.
Harassing communications,
§13A-11-8.

COMMUNISM.
Censorship, §16-40-3.
Education.
Instruction in history,
doctrines, etc., of
communism, §16-40-3.
Propaganda.
Instruction in history,
doctrines, etc., of
communism, §16-40-3.
Textbooks.
Contract to exclude
communist authors,
§16-36-10.

**COMMUNITY ACTION
AGENCIES,** §§11-96-1 to
11-96-6.
**Allocation of appropriated
funds,** §11-96-2.
Appropriations.
Contributions.
County and municipal
governments,
§11-80-4.1.
County and municipal
governments, §11-80-4.1.
Funds, §11-96-1.
Audits.
Bi-annual audit, §11-96-3.
Community action program.
Administration, §11-96-5.
Components of program,
§11-96-5.
Defined, §11-96-5.
**Consultation with
neighborhood based
organizations,** §11-96-3.
**Continuation of certain
community action
agencies,** §11-96-6.
Defined, §11-96-3.

COMMUNITY ACTION AGENCIES—Cont'd

Delegation of responsibility,
§11-96-3.

Funds.
Allocation, §11-96-2.
Appropriation, §11-96-1.

Governing board, §11-96-3.

Limited purpose agencies,
§11-96-4.

Powers and duties, §11-96-3.

Selection of board members,
§11-96-3.

Service area, §11-96-3.

COMMUNITY ANTENNA TELEVISION FACILITIES, §§11-27-1 to 11-27-3, 23-1-59.

COMMUNITY COLLEGES.

Junior colleges.
See JUNIOR COLLEGES.

School buses.
Transportation of students on
public school buses,
§16-27-2.

Universities and colleges generally.
See UNIVERSITIES AND
COLLEGES.

COMMUNITY DEVELOPMENT.

Economic and community affairs, §§41-23-1 to
41-23-6.
See ECONOMIC AND
COMMUNITY
AFFAIRS.

Enterprise zones, §§41-23-20
to 41-23-32.
See ENTERPRISE ZONES.

COMMUNITY SERVICES GRANTS.

Definitions, §41-24-1.

Evaluation of proposal.
Criteria used, §41-24-5.

Heads of grant-making agencies.
Authority and
responsibilities, §41-24-4.

Intent of legislature,
§41-24-2.

Purpose of chapter, §41-24-2.

Purpose of grants, §41-24-3.

COMMUTATION OF SENTENCES.
See SENTENCING.

COMPACTS.

Ameraport deep draft harbor and terminal compact, §§33-9-1, 33-9-2.

Atomic energy.
Southern interstate nuclear
compact, §§9-18-1 to
9-18-6.
See ATOMIC ENERGY.

Civil defense.
Mutual interstate aid
agreements and
compacts, §31-9-7.

Constitution of the United States.
Between state and foreign
power, Const. U. S., Art.
I, §10.
Between the states, Const. U.
S., Art. I, §10.

COMPACTS—Cont'd

Corrections.
Interstate corrections
compact, §§14-13-1 to
14-13-3.

Detainers.
Mandatory disposition of
detainers, §§15-9-80 to
15-9-88.
See DETAINERS.

Drivers' licenses.
Alabama driver license
compact, §§32-6-30 to
32-6-36.
See MOTOR VEHICLES.

Education.
Compact for education,
§§16-44-1 to 16-44-3.
Interstate agreement on
qualifications of
educational personnel,
§§16-23A-1 to 16-23A-3.

Forest fires.
Southeastern interstate
forest fire protection
compact, §§9-13-200,
9-13-201.

Gulf states marine fisheries compact, §§9-12-180 to
9-12-184.

Historic Chattahoochee compact, §41-9-311.

Income tax.
Multistate tax compact.
Allocation and
apportionment of
deduction and
exemptions, §40-18-22.

Infants.
Interstate compact on child
placement, §§44-2-20 to
44-2-26.
See MINORS.

Interstate compact on juveniles, §§44-2-1 to
44-2-67.
See YOUTH SERVICES.

Interstate library compact,
§§41-8-20 to 41-8-25.

Juveniles.
Interstate compact on
juveniles, §§44-2-1 to
44-2-7.
See YOUTH SERVICES.

Libraries.
Interstate library compact,
§§41-8-20 to 41-8-25.

Marine resources.
Gulf states marine fisheries
compact, §§9-12-180 to
9-12-184.

Mental health.
Interstate compact on mental
health, §§22-55-1 to
22-55-4.

Minors.
Interstate compact on
juveniles, §§44-2-1 to
44-2-7.
See YOUTH SERVICES.

Motor vehicle carriers.
Mileage tax.
Reciprocal agreements
with other states,
§40-19-11.

Motor vehicles.
Alabama driver license
compact, §§32-6-30 to
32-6-36.
See MOTOR VEHICLES.

COMPACTS—Cont'd

Multistate tax compact,
§§40-27-1 to 40-27-6.
See TAXATION.

Nuclear compact.
Southern interstate nuclear
compact, §§9-18-1 to
9-18-6.
See ATOMIC ENERGY.

Parole.
Interstate compacts,
§15-22-1.

Probation.
Interstate compacts,
§15-22-1.

Railroads.
Rapid rail transit compact.
Execution and text of
compact, §37-11-1.

Rapid rail transit compact.
Execution and text, §37-11-1.

Southeastern interstate forest fire protection compact, §§9-13-200,
9-13-201.

Southeast interstate low-level radioactive waste management compact, §§22-32-1 to 22-32-9.

Southern growth policies agreements, §§41-18-1 to
41-18-3.

Southern interstate nuclear compact, §§9-18-1 to
9-18-6.
See ATOMIC ENERGY.

Southern states energy compact, §§9-18A-1 to
9-18A-4.

State.
Compacts between the states
or with foreign powers,
Const. U. S., Art. I, §10.

Taxation.
Multistate tax compact,
§§40-27-1 to 40-27-6.
See TAXATION.

Tombigbee-Tennessee waterway development compact, §§33-8-1 to
33-8-4.

Universities and colleges.
Authority to make interstate
educational agreements,
§16-3-34.

Youth services.
Interstate compact on
juveniles, §§44-2-1 to
44-2-7.
See YOUTH SERVICES.

COMPETITIVE BID LAW.

Public contracts, §§41-16-1 to
41-16-125.
See CONTRACTS.

COMPLAINTS.

Arrest.
Initiation of proceedings by
complaint, §§15-7-1 to
15-7-4.

Attachment.
Filing in actions begun by
attachment, §§6-6-140,
6-6-141.

Eminent domain.
See EMINENT DOMAIN.

Pleadings generally.
See PLEADINGS.

Rules of criminal procedure.
See RULES OF CRIMINAL
PROCEDURE.

COMPOUNDING.
Class A misdemeanor,
§13A-10-7.
Defenses to prosecution,
§13A-10-7.
Elements of crime, §13A-10-7.

COMPROMISE AND
SETTLEMENT.
Chiropractors.
Licenses.
Refusal, revocation or
suspension.
Contested cases,
§34-24-168.
Class actions, ARCP, Rule 23
(e).
Conservators.
Settlements of accounts of
conservators, §§26-5-1 to
26-5-54.
See CONSERVATORS.
Courts.
Duty to encourage, §6-6-1.
Debts.
Evidence.
Written settlements for
composition of debts,
§12-21-31.
Discharges.
Pro tanto settlements.
Effect of discharges entered
pursuant to,
§12-21-109.
Eminent domain, §18-1A-4.
Evidence.
Written settlements for
composition of debts,
§12-21-31.
Executors and
administrators.
See EXECUTORS AND
ADMINISTRATORS.
Guardian and ward.
Settlements of accounts of
conservators, §§26-5-1 to
26-5-54.
See CONSERVATORS.
Uniform guardianship and
protective proceedings
act.
Conservators.
Final consent
settlements,
§26-2A-158.
Judgments.
Pro tanto settlements.
Effect of judgments entered
pursuant to,
§12-21-109.
Malpractice.
Judgments and settlements.
See MALPRACTICE.
Pro tanto settlements.
Effect of receipts, releases,
discharges and
judgments entered
pursuant to, §12-21-109.
Receipts.
Pro tanto settlements.
Effect of receipts entered
pursuant to,
§12-21-109.
Releases.
Pro tanto settlements.
Effect of releases entered
pursuant to,
§12-21-109.

COMPROMISE AND
SETTLEMENT—Cont'd
Savings and loan
associations.
Power of directors to
compromise and settle
any debts and claims,
§5-16-24.
Workmen's compensation,
§25-5-56.
Occupational diseases.
Settlements between
parties, §25-5-121.
Pneumoconiosis.
Settlements between
parties, §25-5-150.
Radiation.
Occupational exposure to
radiation.
Settlements between
parties, §25-5-201.
Reports of settlements,
§25-5-5.
Third parties.
Attorney's fees in
settlements with third
parties, §25-5-11.

COMPTROLLER.
Appointment, §41-4-51.
Bond issues.
Refund of money paid for
invalid or unissued
bonds, §§41-4-62,
41-4-63.
Bonds, surety, §41-4-7.
Division of control and
accounts.
Head of division, §41-4-51.
Education.
Budget system.
Estimate of funds,
§16-13-141.
Elections.
Amendments to constitution
of Alabama.
Duty of comptroller to
ascertain expenses and
file same, §17-17-6.
Expenses of state officers
and employees, §41-4-57.
Full time service, §41-4-6.
Inactive funds.
Closing out inactive funds
and transferring balance
to general fund,
§41-4-64.
Oath of office, §41-4-6.
Proof of correctness of
claim.
Comptroller may require,
§41-4-61.
Receipt of revenue.
Restrictions on receipt,
§41-4-52.
Refund of money paid for
invalid or unissued
bonds, §§41-4-62, 41-4-63.
Taxation.
Refund of taxes paid by
mistake or error,
§40-10-162.
Land sold for taxes not due
at time of sale,
§40-10-103.
Warrants.
Drawing warrants in favor of
defaulters.
Restrictions on drawing
warrants in favor of
defaulters, §41-4-53.

COMPTROLLER—Cont'd
Warrants—Cont'd
Duplicate warrants.
Issuance when originals
lost, §41-4-58.
Execution of warrants.
When warrant deemed
duly executed,
§41-4-59.

COMPUTERS.
Computer crimes.
Citation of article,
§13A-8-100.
Computer equipment or
supplies.
Acts constituting offenses
against, §13A-8-103.
Punishment, §13A-8-103.
Definitions, §13A-8-101.
Intellectual property.
Acts constituting offenses
against, §13A-8-102.
Punishment, §13A-8-102.
Short title of article,
§13A-8-100.
Costs.
Dissemination of computer-
based court information,
ARJA, Rule 33.
Data and data systems.
See DATA.
Dissemination of computer-
based court information,
ARJA, Rule 33.
Applications, ARJA, Rule 33.
Costs, ARJA, Rule 33.
Criteria to determine release
of data, ARJA, Rule 33.
Forms, ARJA, Rule 33.
Information for release of
data, ARJA, Rule 33.
Policies and procedures,
ARJA, Rule 33.
Release of data.
Criteria to determine,
ARJA, Rule 33.
Information for, ARJA,
Rule 33.
Forms.
Dissemination of computer-
based court information,
ARJA, Rule 33.
Supercomputer authority,
§§41-10-390 to 41-10-406.
See SUPERCOMPUTER
AUTHORITY.

CONCEALED WEAPONS.
General provisions.
See WEAPONS.

CONCERT HALLS.
Establishment, acquisition,
administration, etc.,
§11-47-16.

CONCERTS.
Licenses, §40-12-82.

CONDEMNATION.
Alcoholic beverages.
Dry counties.
Contraband, §§28-4-250 to
28-4-299.
See ALCOHOLIC
BEVERAGES.
Brake fluid.
Condemnation for violations,
§8-17-7.

CONDEMNATION—Cont'd

Counties.
Eminent domain.
See EMINENT
DOMAIN.
General provisions.
See COUNTIES.
Electric utilities, §§37-4-130,
37-4-131.
Fertilizer.
Noncomplying fertilizer,
§2-22-21.
Forests and forestry.
Timber theft equipment,
§§9-13-220 to 9-13-227.
See TREES AND TIMBER.
General provisions.
See EMINENT DOMAIN.
Highways.
Eminent domain.
See HIGHWAYS.
Rights of ways.
Private parties, §§18-3-1 to
18-3-3.
Jails.
Inspection of jails.
Power to condemn jails,
§14-6-83.
Motor vehicles.
Nighttime hunting of deer,
§9-11-252.1.
Timber theft equipment,
§§9-13-220 to 9-13-227.
See TREES AND TIMBER.
United States.
Condemnation of land or
rights of way, §§42-2-1 to
42-2-12.
See UNITED STATES.
Weights and measures.
Nonstandard weights and
measures, §8-16-9.

CONDOMINIUMS, §§35-8-1 to
35-8-22.
Accounts and accounting.
Records, §35-8-10.
Actions.
Generally, §35-8-12.
Unit owners, §35-8-12.
Administration of property.
Duties and responsibilities of
association, §35-8-9.
Applicability of chapter,
§35-8-3.
Assessments.
Association, §35-8-9.
Liens in favor of
association, §35-8-17.
Special assessments,
§35-8-15.
Association.
Actions by and against
association, §35-8-12.
Administration and
management of property.
Duties and responsibilities
of association, §35-8-9.
Assessments, §35-8-9.
Liens in favor of
association,
§35-8-17.
Bylaws, §35-8-10.
Defined, §35-8-2.
Duties and responsibilities.
Administration and
management of
property, §35-8-9.
Liability, §35-8-12.
Liens in favor of association,
§35-8-17.

CONDOMINIUMS—Cont'd

Association—Cont'd
Powers, §35-8-9.
Service of process on
association, §35-8-12.
Units.
Purchase of units, §35-8-9.
Building laws.
Construction and application
of building laws,
ordinances and
regulations, §35-8-21.
Bylaws.
Amendments, §35-8-10.
Association, §35-8-10.
Contents, §35-8-10.
Recordation, §35-8-11.
Common elements.
Defined, §35-8-2.
Generally, §35-8-6.
Maintenance, repair, etc., by
association, §35-8-9.
Prohibited work, §35-8-14.
Common expenses.
Defined, §35-8-2.
Generally, §35-8-13.
Powers of association to
assess and collect funds
to pay for common
expenses, §35-8-9.
Common surplus.
Defined, §35-8-2.
Limited common surplus.
Defined, §35-8-2.
Condominium property.
Administration and
management.
Duties and responsibilities
of association, §35-8-9.
Blanket mortgage on
condominium property,
§35-8-18.
Defined, §35-8-2.
Establishment, §35-8-7.
Liens against condominium
property, §35-8-16.
Removal, §35-8-20.
**Construction and
interpretation.**
Building or zoning laws,
ordinances and
regulations, §35-8-21.
Chapter to be liberally
construed, §35-8-22.
Conveyances.
Common and limited
common elements.
Undivided interest in
common and limited
common elements,
§35-8-6.
Declaration.
Contents, §35-8-7.
Defined, §35-8-2.
Establishment of
condominium property,
§35-8-7.
Plans for unit.
Recorded as part of
declaration or as
amendment, §35-8-8.
Recordation, §35-8-7.
Deeds.
Recordation, §35-8-11.
Units, §35-8-8.
Definitions, §35-8-2.
Elements.
Common elements. See
within this heading,
"Common elements."

CONDOMINIUMS—Cont'd

Elements—Cont'd
Private elements.
Defined, §35-8-2.
Expenses.
Common expenses. See
within this heading,
"Common expenses."
Insurance.
Powers of association,
§35-8-9.
Investments.
Mortgage investments on
condominium property,
§35-8-19.
**Joint tenants and tenants in
common.**
Removal of condominium
property.
Property deemed to be
owned in common,
§35-8-20.
Leases.
Common and limited
common elements.
Lease includes undivided
interest in common
and limited common
elements, §35-8-6.
Units, §35-8-8.
**Liberal construction of
chapter,** §35-8-22.
Liens.
Against condominium
property.
Generally, §35-8-16.
In favor of association,
§35-8-17.
Mortgages and deeds of trust.
See within this heading,
"Mortgages and deeds of
trust."
Recordation, §35-8-11.
Termination of condominium,
§35-8-20.
Limited common elements.
See within this heading,
"Common elements."
Limited common expenses.
See within this heading,
"Common expenses."
Limited common surplus,
§35-8-2.
Management of property.
Duties and responsibilities of
association, §35-8-9.
**Mortgages and deeds of
trust.**
Blanket mortgage on
condominium property,
§35-8-18.
Common and limited
common elements.
Mortgage includes
undivided interest in
common and limited
common elements,
§35-8-6.
Investments.
Mortgage investments on
condominium property,
§35-8-19.
Recordation, §35-8-11.
Units, §35-8-8.
Ordinances.
Building or zoning
ordinances.
Construction and
application, §35-8-21.
Ownership of units, §35-8-5.

CONDOMINIUMS—Cont'd
Person.
Defined, §35-8-2.
Plans for units.
Recorded as part of
declaration, §35-8-8.
Possession of units, §35-8-5.
Private elements.
Defined, §35-8-2.
Prohibited work, §35-8-14.
Property.
Condominium property. See
within this heading,
"Condominium
property."
Real property.
Units to constitute real
property, §35-8-4.
Recordation.
Bylaws, §35-8-8.
Declaration, §35-8-7.
Documents and instruments,
§35-8-11.
Records.
Accounting records, §35-8-10.
Rules and regulations.
Building or zoning
regulations.
Construction and
application, §35-8-21.
Service of process.
Association, §35-8-12.
Short title of chapter,
§35-8-1.
Surplus.
Common surplus, §35-8-2.
Taxation, §35-8-15.
**Termination of
condominium,** §35-8-20.
Time-sharing.
Vacation time-sharing plans,
§§34-27-50 to 34-27-69.
See VACATION TIME-
SHARING PLANS.
Units.
Actions by and against unit
owners, §35-8-12.
Bylaws.
Recordation, §35-8-8.
Change of units.
Amendment to declaration,
§35-8-9.
Deeds, §35-8-8.
Defined, §35-8-2.
Enjoyment, §35-8-5.
Identification, §35-8-8.
Inclusions in unit, §35-8-5.
Leases, §35-8-8.
Liability of owners, §35-8-12.
Maintenance, repair, etc.
Prohibited work, §35-8-14.
Meetings of unit owners,
§35-8-10.
Mortgages and deeds of trust,
§35-8-8.
Ownership, §35-8-5.
Plans for units.
Recorded as part of
declaration, §35-8-8.
Possession, §35-8-5.
Real property.
Units to constitute real
property, §35-8-4.
Removal of unit from
condominium property,
§35-8-20.
Vacation time-sharing plans,
§§34-27-50 to 34-27-69.
See VACATION TIME-
SHARING PLANS.

CONDOMINIUMS—Cont'd
Wills.
Common and limited
common elements.
Devise includes undivided
interest in common
and limited common
elements, §35-8-6.
Zoning.
Construction and application
of zoning laws,
ordinances and
regulations, §35-8-21.

CONFECTIONERY.
Adulteration.
When deemed adulterated,
§20-1-23.

CONFEDERACY.
**Department of archives and
history.**
Collection of data as to
Alabama soldiers in war
between states, §41-6-13.
Memorials.
Division of parks.
Director.
Powers and duties.
Cooperation with
citizens'
committees,
§9-2-105.
General provisions,
§9-2-104.
**White House of the
Confederacy,** §§41-12-1 to
41-12-3.

CONFEDERATE VETERANS.
**Old age assistance to
widows.**
Appropriation from
confederate pension
funds, §38-4-12.
Eligibility, §38-4-11.
Pensions for widows,
§§31-8-1 to 31-8-33.
See VETERANS.

**CONFESSION OF
JUDGMENT.**
See JUDGMENTS.

**CONFIDENTIALITY OF
INFORMATION.**
Abortion.
Parental consent.
Waiver.
Confidentiality of records
and information,
§26-21-8.
Persons disclosing,
§26-21-8.
Liability of physician for
disclosure, §26-21-7.
Proceedings confidential
and anonymous,
§26-21-4.
Accountants.
Disciplinary investigations,
§34-1-3.
Transfer of working papers.
Consent of client required,
§34-1-21.
Attorneys at law.
Client security fund.
Applications for
reimbursement, ACSF,
Rule 11.

**CONFIDENTIALITY OF
INFORMATION**—Cont'd
Diseases.
Notifiable diseases.
Third parties.
Notification of diseases,
§22-11A-38.
**Hazardous waste or
substances.**
Fees for disposal of
hazardous waste or
substances.
Confidentiality of fee
reports, §22-30B-15.
**Health maintenance
organizations.**
Medical information,
§27-21A-25.
Privileges generally.
See PRIVILEGES.

CONFLICT OF LAWS.
Agriculture.
Incorporated marketing
associations.
Conflicting laws not
applicable, §2-10-68.
Appeals.
Probate judge, §10-2A-331.
Secretary of state,
§10-2A-331.
**Banks and financial
institutions.**
Regional reciprocal banking.
Applicable law, §5-13A-6.
Construction with other
laws, §5-13A-10.
Commercial code.
Bank deposits and
collections, §7-4-102.
Investment securities.
Registration of transfer,
§7-8-106.
Validity of security,
§7-8-106.
Parties' power to choose
applicable law, §7-1-105.
Secured transactions.
Multiple state transactions.
Perfection of security
interest, §7-9-103.
Removal of collateral,
§7-9-401.
Corporations.
Close corporations,
§10-2A-313.
Counties.
Land-use management in
flood-prone areas.
Conflict of regulations with
other local ordinances,
regulations, etc.,
§11-19-23.
Credit cards.
Repeal of conflicting laws,
§5-20-10.
Foreign causes of action.
Enforcement when
jurisdiction of defendant
can be obtained in this
state, §6-5-430.
Health.
Municipal and general health
laws.
Conflicts between
municipal and general
health laws, §22-1-2.
Housing authorites.
County housing authorities,
§24-1-84.

CONFLICT OF LAWS—Cont'd
Housing authorites—Cont'd
Municipal housing
authorities, §24-1-45.
Investment securities.
Registration of transfer,
§7-8-106.
Validity of security, §7-8-106.
**Law-enforcement planning
agency.**
Omnibus crime control and
safe streets act of 1968.
Effect of chapter in event
provisions conflict,
§41-8A-13.
Mentally ill.
Repeal of conflicting laws,
§22-50-24.
Mobile homes.
Anchoring.
Certain local laws,
municipal ordinances,
etc., not repealed,
§24-5-34.
Municipal corporations.
Boards of water and sewer
commissioners,
§11-50-358.
Health laws.
Conflicts between
municipal and general
health laws, §22-1-2.
Municipalities not to pass
laws in conflict with
general laws of state,
Const. Ala., art. IV, §89.
Zoning, §11-52-82.
Plumbing.
Other laws repealed,
§34-37-18.
Probate judge.
Administration of chapter,
§10-2A-330.
Appeals, §10-2A-331.
Powers, §10-2A-330.
Public service commission.
Appeal of rate cases.
Repeal of conflicting laws,
§37-1-144.
Redevelopment projects,
§24-2-10.
Secretary of state.
Administration of chapter,
§10-2A-330.
Appeals, §10-2A-331.
Powers, §10-2A-330.
Secured transactions.
Multiple state transactions.
Perfection of security
interest, §7-9-103.
Perfection of security interest
in multiple state
transactions, §7-9-103.
Removal of collateral,
§7-9-401.
Trusts and trustees.
Investment of trust estate.
Repeal of conflicting
statutes, §19-3-120.
Urban renewal projects,
§24-3-9.
Zoning, §11-52-82.

CONFLICTS OF INTEREST.
Abuse of public office.
General provisions.
See PUBLIC OFFICERS
AND EMPLOYEES.
**Alabama agricultural and
mechanical university.**
Board of trustees, §16-49-29.

CONFLICTS OF INTEREST
—Cont'd
Alabama state university.
Board of trustees, §16-50-29.
**Alcoholic beverage control
board, §28-3-40.**
Alcoholic beverages.
Interlocking businesses and
interests prohibited,
§28-7-22.
Attorneys at law.
Client security fund.
Committee, ACSF, Rule
13.
**Banks and financial
institutions.**
Directors, officers and
employees.
Receiving commission to
procure loans,
purchases, discounts,
etc., §5-6A-22.
State banking department.
Loans, gifts, etc., from
banks or employees,
§5-3A-9.
Boxing and wrestling.
Athletic commission,
§41-9-90.1.
Bridges.
Construction and
maintenance of roads
and bridges.
Highway department.
Employees and director,
§23-1-58.
Cahaba trace commission,
§41-9-804.
Canons of judicial ethics.
Procedure for determining,
ACJE, Canon 6C.
Coal.
Certain persons not to have
interest in Alabama coal
mines, §25-9-4.
Surface mining commission,
§9-16-76.
Code of ethics.
See PUBLIC OFFICERS
AND EMPLOYEES.
Constitution of Alabama.
Disclosure of personal or
private interest in bills,
etc., by legislators,
Const. Ala., art. IV, §82.
Purchases and supplies.
Stationery, printing, fuel,
etc., Const. Ala., art.
IV, §69.
Contracts.
Public contracts.
General provisions.
See CONTRACTS.
Corporations.
Directors, §10-2A-63.
County commissioners.
Awarding contracts, etc., in
which county interested
to relatives, §11-3-5.
Crime victims compensation.
Failure of commission
member to disclose
conflict of interest.
Penalties, §15-23-19.
Director of finance, §41-4-30.
Education.
Textbooks, §16-36-36.
Environmental management.
Commission, §22-22A-6.

CONFLICTS OF INTEREST
—Cont'd
**Executors and
administrators.**
Enforcement of decree or
judgment when
administrator adversely
interested, §43-2-254.
**Failure to disclose conflicts
by public servant,**
§13A-10-62.
Finance.
Director of finance, §41-4-30.
Grand jury.
Grand juror not to
participate in
deliberations as to
offenses committed
against his person or
property, §12-16-207.
Guardian and ward.
Uniform guardianship and
protective proceedings
act.
Conservators.
Sales, encumbrances, or
transactions,
§26-2A-150.
Harbors and ports.
Director of state docks.
Financial interest in
harbor facilities,
§33-1-3.
Highway department.
Director or employees,
§23-1-58.
Historic Blakeley authority,
§41-10-173.
Horse racing.
Commission members,
§11-65-7.
Hospitals.
County and municipal
hospital authorities,
§22-21-189.
Housing authorities.
Municipal housing
authorities.
Commissioners or
employees, §24-1-26.
Insurance.
Commissioner of insurance,
§27-2-13.
Insurers, §27-27-26.
Judges.
Procedure for determining,
ACJE, Canon 6C.
Labor.
Department of industrial
relations.
Board of appeals, §25-2-12.
Legislature.
Disclosure of personal or
private interest in bills,
etc., by legislators,
Const. Ala., art. IV, §82.
Livingston university.
Board of trustees.
Removal of member
conducting business
with university,
§16-53-3.
Motor vehicle carriers.
Commission members not to
have pecuniary interest,
etc., in carriers or
brokers, §37-3-8.

CONFLICTS OF INTEREST
—Cont'd
Municipal corporations.
Boards of water and sewer commissioners.
Members, agents or employees of board, §11-50-355.
Class 5 municipalities.
Mayor/commission/city manager form of government.
Acceptance of gifts from public utilities, §11-44E-183.
Commission.
Dealings with administrative service, §11-44E-45.
Interference with appointment or removal of officers and employees, §11-44E-45.
Interest of officials or employees in contracts with city or public utilities, §11-44E-183.
Manager.
Political or other improper influences on prohibited, §11-44E-94.
Public service utilities.
Financial interest in, §11-44E-163.
Mayor-council form of government, §11-43C-88.
Commission form of government.
Officers or employees, §§11-44-46 to 11-44-48, 11-44-94, 11-44-138.
Optional form A, §11-44-94.
Optional form B, §11-44-138.
Council-manager form of government.
Mayor and council prohibited from involvement in administrative service, §11-43A-18.
Councilmen, §§11-43-12, 11-43-53.
Aldermen not to vote on certain matters, §11-43-54.
Employees.
Commission form of government, §§11-44-46 to 11-44-48, 11-44-94, 11-44-138.
Generally, §11-43-12.
Mayor/commission/city manager form of government.
Acceptance of gifts, §11-44E-183.
Interest in contracts with city or public utilities, §11-44E-183.

CONFLICTS OF INTEREST
—Cont'd
Municipal corporations
—Cont'd
Mayor/commission/city manager form of government.
Acceptance of gifts from public utilities, §11-44E-183.
Commission.
Dealings with administrative service, §11-44E-45.
Interference in appointment or removal of officers and employees, §11-44E-45.
Interest in contracts with city or public utilities, §11-44E-183.
Manager.
Political or other improper influences on prohibited, §11-44E-94.
Public service utilities.
Financial interest in, §11-44E-163.
Officers.
Commission form of government, §§11-44-46 to 11-44-48, 11-44-94, 11-44-138.
Employment by corporations holding franchises as to use of streets, §11-43-11.
Generally, §11-43-12.
Grounds for impeachment, §11-43-161.
Mayor/commission/city manager form of government.
Acceptance of gifts, §11-44E-183.
Penalty, §11-43-53.
Personal property.
Purchase from elected officials, employees or members of municipal boards, §11-43-12.1.
Services.
Purchase from elected officials, employees or members of municipal boards, §11-43-12.1.
Potential conflicting interest.
Defined, §13A-10-62.
Public defenders.
Division not to exclude alternative appointment in cases of conflict, §15-12-46.
Public disclosure.
Defined, §13A-10-62.
Public servants.
Class A misdemeanor, §13A-10-62.
Purchases and supplies.
Stationery, printing, fuel, etc., Const. Ala., art. IV, §69.
Savings and loan associations.
Commissioner of savings and loan, §5-2A-61.

CONFLICTS OF INTEREST
—Cont'd
Sports.
Agents.
Disclosure of interest in entity giving investment advice required, §8-26-31.
Interest in entity directly involved in same sport. Prohibited, §8-26-30.
Tannehill furnace and foundry commission.
Conflicts of interest of members or employees, §41-9-322.
Textbooks.
Purchase, §16-36-36.
USS Alabama battleship commission.
Conflicts of interest of members or employees, §41-9-341.
Water conservation and irrigation.
Agency.
Officers of corporation, §9-10-12.
Corporations.
Officers, §9-10-45.
Youth services, §44-1-29.

CONGRESS.
Absent members, Const. U. S., Art. I, §5.
Adjournment, Const. U. S., Art. I, §§5, 7; Art. II, §3.
Admiralty, Const. U. S., Art. I, §8.
Age.
Representative in congress, Const. U. S., Art. I, §2.
Senator, Const. U. S., Art. I, §3.
Aliens.
Eligibility to be representative, Const. U. S., Art. I, §2.
Amendments to the constitution, Const. U. S., Art. V.
Ameraport offshore harbor and terminal commission.
When commission ceases to exist.
Authorization of bistate compact by congress, §33-10-26.
Apportionment, Const. U. S., Art. I, §§2, 3; Amendments XIV, XVII.
Division of state into congressional districts, §17-20-1.
Appropriations, Const. U. S., Art. I, §§7, 9.
Approval by president of order, resolution or vote, Const. U. S., Art. I, §7.
Army and navy.
Powers of congress, Const. U. S., Art. I, §8.
Arrest.
Arrest of members, Const. U. S., Art. I, §6.
Privilege from, Const. U. S., Art. I, §6.
Bankruptcy and insolvency.
Powers of congress, Const. U. S., Art. I, §8.

CONGRESS—Cont'd

Borrowing money, Const. U. S., Art. I, §8.

Changing meeting of congress, Const. U. S., Amendment XX.

Commerce, Const. U. S., Art. I, §§8, 9.

Compensation of members, Const. U. S., Art. I, §6.

Consists of senate and house of representatives, Const. U. S., Art. I, §1.

Constitution of the United States, Const. U. S., Art. I, §1.

Absent members, Const. U. S., Art. I, §5.

Adjournment, Const. U. S., Art. I, §§5, 7; Art. II, §3.

Admiralty, Const. U. S., Art. I, §8.

Amendments to the constitution, Const. U. S., Art. V.

Appropriations, Const. U. S., Art. I, §9.

Approval by president of order, resolution or vote, Const. U. S., Art. I, §7.

Army and navy.
Powers of congress, Const. U. S., Art. I, §8.

Arrest, Const. U. S., Art. I, §6.

Bankruptcy.
Powers of congress, Const. U. S., Art. I, §8.

Borrowing money, Const. U. S., Art. I, §8.

Commerce, Const. U. S., Art. I, §§8, 9.

Compensation of members, Const. U. S., Art. I, §6.

Consists of senate and house of representatives, Const. U. S., Art. I, §1.

Copyright, Const. U. S., Art. I, §8.

Counterfeiting.
Powers of congress, Const. U. S., Art. I, §8.

Courts.
Power to constitute tribunals inferior to supreme court, Const. U. S., Art. I, §8.

Debate, Const. U. S., Art. I, §6.

Debt.
Powers of congress, Const. U. S., Art. I, §8.

Declaration of war, Const. U. S., Art. I, §8.

Defense.
Powers of congress, Const. U. S., Art. I, §8.

District of Columbia, Const. U. S., Art. I, §8.

Duties and imposts.
Powers of congress, Const. U. S., Art. I, §8.

Excises.
Powers of congress, Const. U. S., Art. I, §8.

Foreign commerce, Const. U. S., Art. I, §8.

Freedom of speech.
Members of congress, Const. U. S., Art. I, §6.

CONGRESS—Cont'd

Constitution of the United States—Cont'd

Holding other office, Const. U. S., Art. I, §6.

House of representatives, Const. U. S., Art. I, §§1, 2, 4, 5.

Absent members, Const. U. S., Art. I, §5.

Arrest of members, Const. U. S., Art. I, §6.

Compensation of members, Const. U. S., Art. I, §6.

Debate, Const. U. S., Art. I, §6.

Elections.
Election of representatives, Const. U. S., Art. I, §2.

Times, places and manner of holding, Const. U. S., Art. I, §4.

Expulsion of member, Const. U. S., Art. I, §5.

Freedom of speech, Const. U. S., Art. I, §6.

Holding other office, Const. U. S., Art. I, §6.

Impeachment, Const. U. S., Art. I, §2.

Journal, Const. U. S., Art. I, §§5, 7.

Libel and slander.
Privilege of members, Const. U. S., Art. I, §6.

Officers, Const. U. S., Art. I, §2.

Presidential elector.
Representative ineligible, Const. U. S., Art. II, §1.

Punishment of members, Const. U. S., Art. I, §5.

Qualifications.
Electors, Const. U. S., Art. I, §2.

Members, Const. U. S., Art. I, §2.

Judge of qualifications, Const. U. S., Art. I, §5.

Revenue bills, Const. U. S., Art. I, §7.

Rules of procedure, Const. U. S., Art. I, §5.

Speaker, Const. U. S., Art. I, §2.

Term, Const. U. S., Art. I, §2.

Vacancies, Const. U. S., Art. I, §2.

Insurrections, Const. U. S., Art. I, §8.

International law.
Power of congress to punish offenses against, Const. U. S., Art. I, §8.

Interstate commerce, Const. U. S., Art. I, §§8, 9.

Invasions, Const. U. S., Art. I, §8.

Journals, Const. U. S., Art. I, §§5, 7.

Legislative powers vested in congress, Const. U. S., Art. I, §1.

CONGRESS—Cont'd

Constitution of the United States—Cont'd

Letters of marque and reprisal, Const. U. S., Art. I, §8.

Libel and slander.
Privilege of members of congress, Const. U. S., Art. I, §6.

Messages to congress, Const. U. S., Art. II, §3.

Militia.
Powers of congress, Const. U. S., Art. I, §8.

Money.
Powers of congress, Const. U. S., Art. I, §8.

Naturalization, Const. U. S., Art. I, §8.

Navy.
Powers of congress, Const. U. S., Art. I, §8.

Patents, Const. U. S., Art. I, §8.

Piracy.
Powers of congress, Const. U. S., Art. I, §8.

Post offices and post roads, Const. U. S., Art. I, §8.

Powers of congress, Const. U. S., Art. I, §8.

Limitations on powers, Const. U. S., Art. I, §9.

Qualifications of members of congress, Const. U. S., Art. I, §§2, 3, 5.

Rules of procedure, Const. U. S., Art. I, §5.

Senate.
Absent members, Const. U. S., Art. I, §5.

Arrest of members, Const. U. S., Art. I, §6.

Compensation of members, Const. U. S., Art. I, §6.

Debate, Const. U. S., Art. I, §6.

Elections.
Election of senators, Const. U. S., Amendment XVII.

Times, places and manner of holding, Const. U. S., Art. I, §4.

Equal suffrage in senate, Const. U. S., Art. V.

Expulsion of member, Const. U. S., Art. I, §5.

Freedom of speech, Const. U. S., Art. I, §6.

Holding other office, Const. U. S., Art. I, §2.

Impeachment, Const. U. S., Art. I, §3.

Journals, Const. U. S., Art. I, §§5, 7.

Libel and slander.
Privilege of members, Const. U. S., Art. I, §6.

Officers, Const. U. S., Art. I, §3.

President, Const. U. S., Art. I, §3.

Pro tempore, Const. U. S., Art. I, §3.

Presidential elector.
Senator ineligible, Const. U. S., Art. II, §1.

CONGRESS—Cont'd
Constitution of the United States—Cont'd
Senate—Cont'd
Punishment of members, Const. U. S., Art. I, §5.
Qualifications.
Qualifications of electors, Const. U. S., Amendment XVII.
Qualifications of senators, Const. U. S., Art. I, §§3, 5.
Quorum, Const. U. S., Art. I, §5.
Revenue bills, Const. U. S., Art. I, §7.
Rules of procedure, Const. U. S., Art. I, §5.
Vacancies, Const. U. S., Amendment XVII.
Special sessions, Const. U. S., Art. II, §3.
Taxation.
Powers of congress, Const. U. S., Art. I, §8.
Territories, Const. U. S., Art. IV, §3.
War.
Articles of war, Const. U. S., Art. I, §8.
Declaration of war, Const. U. S., Art. I, §8.
Weights and measures, Const. U. S., Art. I, §8.
Welfare.
Power of congress to provide for general welfare, Const. U. S., Art. I, §8.
Copyright, Const. U. S., Art. I, §8.
Counterfeiting.
Powers of congress, Const. U. S., Art. I, §8.
Courts.
Power to constitute tribunals inferior to supreme court, Const. U. S., Art. I, §8.
Death of members.
Notice to governor, §36-9-6.
Debate, Const. U. S., Art. I, §6.
Debts.
Powers of congress, Const. U. S., Art. I, §8.
Declaration of war, Const. U. S., Art. I, §8.
Defense.
Powers of congress, Const. U. S., Art. I, §8.
District of Columbia, Const. U. S., Art. I, §8.
Districts.
Elections.
State divided into congressional districts, §17-20-1.
Duties and imposts.
Powers of congress, Const. U. S., Art. I, §8.
Elections.
Districts.
State divided into congressional districts, §17-20-1.
House of representatives. See within this heading, "House of representatives."

CONGRESS—Cont'd
Elections—Cont'd
Payment of poll tax not required, Const. U. S., Amendment XXIV.
Proclamation by governor of names of members of congress elected.
Judge of elections, returns and qualifications of members, Const. U. S., Art. I, §5.
Senate. See within this heading, "Senate."
Evidence.
Transcripts of congressional acts, §12-21-94.
Excises.
Powers of congress, Const. U. S., Art. I, §8.
Foreign commerce, Const. U. S., Art. I, §8.
Freedom of speech.
Members of congress, Const. U. S., Art. I, §6.
Holding other office, Const. U. S., Art. I, §6.
House of representatives, Const. U. S., Art. I, §2.
Absent members, Const. U. S., Art. I, §5.
Arrest of members, Const. U. S., Art. I, §6.
Compensation of members, Const. U. S., Art. I, §6.
Death of member.
Notice to governor, §36-9-6.
Debate, Const. U. S., Art. I, §6.
Elections, Const. U. S., Art. I, §§2, 4.
Each congressional district entitled to elect one representative, §17-20-2.
General elections.
Offices for which general election held, §17-2-2.
Judge of elections, returns and qualifications of members, Const. U. S., Art. I, §5.
Notice of election.
Governor to give notice, §17-20-4.
Returns.
Board of supervisors to make returns to secretary of state, §17-20-3.
Governor to estimate returns, §17-20-4.
Judge of returns, Const. U. S., Art. I, §5.
Special elections.
Vacancies in office of representative, §17-18-1.
State and county officers elected by the people, §17-2-1.
State divided into congressional districts, §17-20-1.
When congressmen elected, §17-2-10.
Expulsion of member, Const. U. S., Art. I, §5.
Freedom of speech, Const. U. S., Art. I, §6.

CONGRESS—Cont'd
House of representatives —Cont'd
Governor.
Elections.
Returns.
Governor to estimate returns and give notice of election, §17-20-4.
Holding other office, Const. U. S., Art. I, §6.
Impeachment, Const. U. S., Art. I, §2.
Journals, Const. U. S., Art. I, §§5, 7.
Libel and slander.
Privilege of members, Const. U. S., Art. I, §6.
Officers, Const. U. S., Art. I, §2.
Presidential elector.
Representative ineligible, Const. U. S., Art. II, §1.
Punishment of members, Const. U. S., Art. I, §5.
Qualifications.
Electors, Const. U. S., Art. I, §2.
Members, Const. U. S., Art. I, §2.
Judge of qualifications, Const. U. S., Art. I, §5.
Resignation of members, §36-9-12.
Revenue bills, Const. U. S., Art. I, §7.
Rules of procedure, Const. U. S., Art. I, §5.
Speaker, Const. U. S., Art. I, §2.
Term, Const. U. S., Art. I, §2.
Vacancies in office, Const. U. S., Art. I, §2.
Death.
Notice to governor, §36-9-6.
Resignation, §36-9-12.
Vice-president of the United States.
Vacancy in office.
Confirmation on nomination of president, Const. U. S., Amendment XXV, §2.
Insurrections, Const. U. S., Art. I, §8.
International law.
Power to punish offenses against, Const. U. S., Art. I, §8.
Interstate commerce, Const. U. S., Art. I, §§8, 9.
Invasions, Const. U. S., Art. I, §8.
Legislative powers vested in, Const. U. S., Art. I, §1.
Letters of marque and reprisal, Const. U. S., Art. I, §8.
Libel and slander.
Privilege of members of congress, Const. U. S., Art. I, §6.
Messages to congress, Const. U. S., Art. II, §3.

CONGRESS—Cont'd
Militia.
Powers of congress, Const. U.
S., Art. I, §8.
Money.
Powers of congress, Const. U.
S., Art. I, §8.
Naturalization, Const. U. S.,
Art. I, §8.
Navy.
Powers of congress, Const. U.
S., Art. I, §8.
Oath of office, Const. U. S.,
Art. VI.
Patents, Const. U. S., Art. I,
§8.
Piracy.
Powers of congress, Const. U.
S., Art. I, §8.
Post offices and post roads,
Const. U. S., Art. I, §8.
Powers of congress, Const.
U. S., Art. I, §8.
Limitations on powers,
Const. U. S., Art. I, §9.
**President of the United
States.**
Adjourning congress, Const.
U. S., Art. II, §3.
Convening congress, Const.
U. S., Art. II, §3.
Declaration of president's
disability.
Determination of issue,
Const. U. S.,
Amendment XXV, §4.
By two-thirds vote of
both houses, Const.
U. S., Amendment
XXV, §4.
Messages to congress, Const.
U. S., Art. II, §3.
Special sessions of congress,
Const. U. S., Art. II, §3.
**Qualifications of members of
congress,** Const. U. S.,
Art. I, §§2, 3, 5.
Redistricting.
Division of state into
congressional districts,
§17-20-1.
Rules of procedure, Const. U.
S., Art. I, §5.
Senate.
Absent members, Const. U.
S., Art. I, §5.
Adjournment, Const. U. S.,
Art. I, §§5, 7; Art. II, §3.
Arrest of members, Const. U.
S., Art. I, §6.
Compensation of members,
Const. U. S., Art. I, §6.
Death of members.
Notice to governor, §36-9-6.
Debate, Const. U. S., Art. I,
§§4, 6.
Elections.
Electors, Const. U. S.,
Amendments XIV,
XVII.
General elections.
Offices for which general
election held,
§17-2-2.
When senator to be
elected, §17-2-11.
State and county officers
elected by the people,
§17-2-1.
When congressmen elected,
§17-2-10.

CONGRESS—Cont'd
Senate—Cont'd
Equal suffrage in senate,
Const. U. S., Art. V.
Expulsion of member, Const.
U. S., Art. I, §5.
Freedom of speech, Const. U.
S., Art. I, §6.
Holding other office, Const.
U. S., Art. I, §6.
Impeachment, Const. U. S.,
Art. I, §3.
Journals, Const. U. S., Art. I,
§§5, 7.
Libel and slander.
Privilege of members,
Const. U. S., Art. I, §6.
Officers, Const. U. S., Art. I,
§3.
President.
Pro tempore, Const. U. S.,
Art. I, §3.
Presidential elector.
Senator ineligible, Const.
U. S., Art. II, §1.
Punishment of members,
Const. U. S., Art. I, §5.
Qualifications.
Electors, Const. U. S.,
Amendment XVII.
Members, Const. U. S.,
Art. I, §3.
Judge of qualifications,
Const. U. S., Art. I,
§5.
Resignation of members,
§36-9-12.
Revenue bills, Const. U. S.,
Art. I, §7.
Rules of procedure, Const. U.
S., Art. I, §5.
Term of office, §17-2-11.
Vacancies in office.
Death.
Notice to governor,
§36-9-6.
Elections.
Authorization, §36-9-8.
Notice, §36-9-9.
Procedure, §36-9-8.
Resignation, §36-9-12.
Temporary appointment of
senator, §36-9-7.
Vice-president of the United
States.
Vacancy in office.
Confirmation of
nomination of
president, Const. U.
S., Amendment
XXV, §2.
Sessions, Const. U. S., Art. I,
§4; Amendment XX, §2.
Special sessions, Const. U. S.,
Art. II, §3.
Taxation.
Powers of congress, Const. U.
S., Art. I, §8.
Territories, Const. U. S., Art.
IV, §3.
War.
Articles of war, Const. U. S.,
Art. I, §8.
Declaration of war, Const. U.
S., Art. I, §8.
Weights and measures,
Const. U. S., Art. I, §8.
Welfare.
Power of congress to provide
for general welfare,
Const. U. S., Art. I, §8.

CONSENT.
Abortion.
Parental consent to
performing abortions
upon minors, §§26-21-1
to 26-21-8.
See ABORTION.
Adoption.
Parental consent, §26-10-3.
Anatomical gifts, §22-19-142.
Bone marrow donation.
Minors and parents, §22-8-9.
Health services.
Consent for health services,
§§22-8-1 to 22-8-9.
See HEALTH.
Motor vehicles.
Chemical tests for
intoxication, §32-5-192.
Rape.
See RAPE.
Sexual offenses.
Lack of consent, §13A-6-70.
Persons deemed incapable of
consent, §13A-6-70.

**CONSERVATION AND
NATURAL RESOURCES.**
Advisory board, §§9-2-14 to
9-2-15.1.
Airboats.
Prohibition on use of
airboats, §9-2-15.1.
Appointment, §9-2-14.
Chairman, §9-2-14.
Commissioner.
Ex officio secretary,
§9-2-14.
Composition, §9-2-14.
Creation, §9-2-14.
Duties.
General provisions,
§9-2-15.
Ex officio secretary.
Commissioner, §9-2-14.
Expenses.
Reimbursement, §9-2-14.
Meetings, §9-2-14.
Minutes, §9-2-14.
Powers and duties.
General provisions,
§9-2-15.
Rules and regulations.
Promulgation of,
§9-2-15.1.
Penalty for violations,
§9-2-15.1.
Qualifications of members,
§9-2-14.
Rules and regulations.
Promulgation of, §9-2-15.1.
Penalty for violation of
provisions, §9-2-15.1.
Term of office, §9-2-14.
Agriculture.
United States department of
agriculture.
Department to cooperate,
§9-2-26.
Airboats.
Advisory board of
conservation and natural
resources.
Prohibition on use of
airboats, §9-2-15.1.
Air pollution.
See AIR POLLUTION.

CONSERVATION AND NATURAL RESOURCES
—Cont'd
Architects.
Buildings and facilities.
Construction or
modification.
Contracts, §9-2-42.
Bond issues.
Department.
Issuance.
Department to have no
authority to issue,
§9-2-24.
Bonds, surety.
Commissioner, §9-2-5.
Department.
Certain officers and
employees, §9-2-18.
Buildings and facilities,
§§9-2-40 to 9-2-44.
Construction or modification.
Commissioner.
Designated awarding
authority, §9-2-40.
Preparation of plans and
specifications,
§9-2-41.
Contracts.
Advisory engineering or
architectural
services, §9-2-42.
Approval of state
building commission
not required for
certain contracts,
§9-2-44.
Authority of department,
§9-2-43.
Awarding authority.
Commissioner
designated,
§9-2-40.
Procedures, §9-2-43.
State building
commission.
Approval not required
as to certain
contracts, §9-2-44.
Plans and specifications.
Preparation, §9-2-41.
State building code.
Compliance with,
§9-2-44.
Caves.
General provisions, §§9-19-1
to 9-19-5.
Coal.
See COAL.
Coastal areas, §§9-7-1 to
9-7-22, 22-22A-10.
See COASTAL AREAS.
Commissioner.
Advisor to governor and
legislature, §9-2-5.
Appointment, §9-2-5.
Bonds, surety, §9-2-5.
Buildings and facilities.
Construction or
modification, §§9-2-40
to 9-2-44.
Commercial fishing.
See FISH AND GAME.
Department.
Divisions.
Appointment of directors,
§9-2-11.
Creation of additional
divisions, §9-2-11.

CONSERVATION AND NATURAL RESOURCES
—Cont'd
Commissioner—Cont'd
Department—Cont'd
Employees.
Determination of number
of employees needed,
§9-2-17.
Director of game and fish
division.
Appointment, §9-2-64.
Distribution of laws, §9-2-8.
Division of land surveys.
Functions, duties, etc., of
commissioner acting
through chief of
division, §35-2-24.
Division of parks.
Director.
Appointment, §9-2-100.
Duties.
General provisions, §9-2-6.
Field assistant.
Appointment, §9-2-64.
Fish and game.
See FISH AND GAME.
Full time position, §9-2-5.
Governor.
Responsible to governor,
§9-2-5.
Head of department, §9-2-5.
Marine resources.
See MARINE
RESOURCES.
Oaths, §9-2-5.
Peace officer, §9-11-5.
Powers and duties.
Buildings and facilities
generally. See within
this heading,
"Buildings and
facilities."
Fish and game, §9-2-7.
General provisions, §9-2-6.
Marine resources, §9-2-7.
State parks, §9-2-9.
Preservation,
maintenance, etc.,
§9-2-10.
Publication of laws, §9-2-8.
Responsible to governor,
§9-2-5.
Rules and regulations.
Delegation of rule-making
power, §9-2-12.
Importation of fish,
animals, etc., §9-2-13.
Promulgation, §9-2-8.
Administration of
department, §9-2-12.
Salary.
Proration among divisions
of department, §9-2-19.
Salt springs.
Lease of salt springs, etc.,
§35-4-380.
State parks, §§9-2-9, 9-2-10.
Powers and duties, §9-2-9.
Term of office, §9-2-5.
Vacancies in office, §9-2-5.
Conservation officers.
Wardens.
See FISH AND GAME.
Contracts.
Buildings and facilities.
Construction or
modification, §§9-2-40
to 9-2-44.

CONSERVATION AND NATURAL RESOURCES
—Cont'd
Department.
Boats.
See BOATS.
Bond issues.
Issuance.
No authority to issue,
§9-2-24.
Bonds, surety.
Officers and employees,
§9-2-18.
Borrowing money.
Department to have no
authority to borrow,
§9-2-24.
Coastal areas.
Permissible uses, §9-7-13.
Commissioner. See within
this heading,
"Commissioner."
Control.
Commissioner, §9-2-5.
Creation, §9-2-1.
Divisions.
Creation of additional
divisions, §9-2-11.
Directors.
Appointment, §9-2-11.
Game and fish division,
§§9-2-60 to 9-2-65.
Land surveys division,
§§35-2-20 to 35-2-38.
See SURVEYS AND
SURVEYORS.
Marine resources division,
§§9-2-80 to 9-2-89.
See MARINE
RESOURCES.
Parks division, §§9-2-100
to 9-2-108.
See STATE PARKS.
Duties.
General provisions, §9-2-2.
Employees.
Number of employees,
§9-2-17.
Executive and administrative
department, §9-2-1.
Expenses.
Proration among divisions
of department, §9-2-19.
Game and fish division,
§§9-2-60 to 9-2-65.
Land resources information
center.
Created, §9-2-121.
Law enforcement officers or
investigators.
Badge and pistol as part of
retirement benefits,
§36-21-8.
Marine resources. §9-2-4.
Mineral resources
management committee.
Coordination of efforts of
department, §9-5-3.
No authority to borrow
money, §9-2-24.
Powers and duties.
General provisions, §9-2-2.
Parkways, §9-2-3.
State parks, §9-2-3.
Purposes, §9-2-1.
Reports.
Annual report to governor,
§9-2-2.
Rules and regulations.
Administration of
department, §9-2-12.

CONSERVATION AND NATURAL RESOURCES
—Cont'd
Department—Cont'd
Salaries.
Proration among divisions
of department, §9-2-19.
Seal, §9-2-1.
Ships and shipping.
See SHIPS AND
SHIPPING.
State parks.
Division of parks,
§§9-2-100 to 9-2-108.
See STATE PARKS.
Supervision.
Commissioner, §9-2-5.
Surveys and surveyors.
Division of land surveys,
§§35-2-20 to 35-2-38.
See SURVEYS AND
SURVEYORS.
Uniform relocation assistance
and land acquisition
policies act.
Compliance with, §9-2-27.
United States.
Cooperation with federal
agencies, §9-2-26.
Uniform relocation
assistance and land
acquisition policies act.
Compliance with,
§9-2-27.
Drainage.
Water management and
drainage.
General provisions, §§9-9-1
to 9-9-80.
See WATER
MANAGEMENT
AND DRAINAGE.
Education.
Department of conservation
and natural resources.
Powers and duties.
General provisions,
§9-2-2.
**Energy conservation
building code,** §§41-9-170
to 41-9-174.
**Energy management and
conservation.**
General provisions,
§§41-6A-1 to 41-6A-11.
See ENERGY
MANAGEMENT AND
CONSERVATION.
Engineers.
Buildings and facilities.
Construction or
modification.
Contracts for advisory
engineering services,
§9-2-42.
**Environmental improvement
authorities,** §§9-6-1 to
9-6-17.
See ENVIRONMENTAL
CONTROL.
Facilities, §§9-2-40 to 9-2-44.
Fish.
General provisions.
See FISH AND GAME.
Marine resources.
See MARINE
RESOURCES.
Forests and forestry.
See FORESTS AND
FORESTRY.

CONSERVATION AND NATURAL RESOURCES
—Cont'd
Funds.
Game and fish fund, §§9-2-20
to 9-2-23.
Game and fish.
General provisions.
See FISH AND GAME.
Gas.
General provisions, §§9-17-1
to 9-17-88.
See OIL AND GAS.
Liquefied petroleum gas,
§§9-17-101 to 9-17-110.
See LIQUEFIED
PETROLEUM GAS.
Geological survey.
General provisions, §§9-4-1 to
9-4-19.
See GEOLOGICAL
SURVEY.
Governor.
Commissioner.
Advisor of the governor,
§9-2-5.
Responsible to governor,
§9-2-5.
Irrigation.
General provisions, §§9-10-1
to 9-10-47.
See WATER
CONSERVATION
AND IRRIGATION.
Legislature.
Commissioner.
Advisor of the legislature,
§9-2-5.
Department.
Recommendations to
legislature, §9-2-2.
Licenses.
Fees.
Erroneous or excessive
fees.
Refunds, §9-2-25.
Fish and game.
See FISH AND GAME.
Marine resources.
See MARINE
RESOURCES.
Liquefied petroleum gas,
§§9-17-101 to 9-17-110.
See LIQUEFIED
PETROLEUM GAS.
**Marine environmental
sciences consortium,**
§§16-45-1 to 16-45-5.
Marine mammal protection,
§§9-11-390 to 9-11-398.
See MARINE MAMMAL
PROTECTION.
Marine resources.
General provisions, §§9-12-1
to 9-12-184.
See MARINE
RESOURCES.
**Mineral resource
management committee,**
§§9-5-1 to 9-5-3.
Mines and minerals.
See MINES AND
MINERALS.
Oaths.
Commissioner, §9-2-5.
Officers.
Wardens.
See FISH AND GAME.

CONSERVATION AND NATURAL RESOURCES
—Cont'd
Oil and gas.
General provisions, §§9-17-1
to 9-17-88.
See OIL AND GAS.
Parks.
State parks.
General provisions,
§§9-14-1 to 9-14-29.
See STATE PARKS.
Penalties.
Advisory board.
Rules and regulations.
Violation of provisions,
§9-2-15.1.
Violation of title and rules
and regulations, §9-1-4.
Pittman-Robertson act.
Cooperation with federal
agencies, §9-2-26.
Principal and income.
Disposition of natural
resources, §19-3-278.
Public lands.
See PUBLIC LANDS.
Relocation assistance.
Department.
Compliance with uniform
relocation assistance
and land acquisition
policies act, §9-2-27.
Reports.
Department.
Annual report to governor,
§9-2-2.
Rules and regulations.
Advisory board.
Promulgation, §9-2-15.1.
Penalty for violation,
§9-2-15.1.
Commissioner.
Delegation of rule-making
power, §9-2-12.
Importation of birds,
animals, etc., §9-2-13.
Promulgation, §9-2-8.
Department.
Administration of
department, §9-2-12.
Penalties, §9-1-4.
Promulgation and
enforcement.
Advisory board, §9-2-15.1.
Commissioner, §9-2-8.
Publication and distribution,
§9-2-8.
Salaries.
Commissioner.
Proration among divisions
of department, §9-2-19.
Department.
Proration among divisions
of department, §9-2-19.
Seafood.
See MARINE RESOURCES.
**Seals and sealed
instruments.**
Department of conservation
and natural resources,
§9-2-1.
Soil and water conservation.
See SOIL AND WATER
CONSERVATION.
State parks, §§9-2-9, 9-2-10.
Statutes.
Commissioner.
Publication and
distribution, §9-2-8.

**CONSERVATION AND
    NATURAL RESOURCES**
    —Cont'd
Trusts and trustees.
Principal and income.
    Disposition of natural
        resources, §19-3-278.
**Uniform relocation
    assistance and land
    acquisition policies act.**
Compliance with, §9-2-27.
United States.
Department.
    Cooperation with federal
        agencies, §9-2-26.
    Uniform relocation assistance
        and land acquisition
        policies act.
    Compliance with, §9-2-27.
Violation of title.
Penalties, §9-1-4.
**Water conservation and
    irrigation.**
General provisions, §§9-10-1
    to 9-10-47.
    See WATER
        CONSERVATION
        AND IRRIGATION.
**Water conservation and
    natural resources.**
Water resources research
    institution.
    See SOIL AND WATER
        CONSERVATION.
**Water management and
    drainage,** §§9-9-1 to
    9-9-80.
    See WATER
        MANAGEMENT AND
        DRAINAGE.
Water pollution.
General provisions.
    See WATER POLLUTION.
Water pollution control act,
    §§22-22-1 to 22-22-14.
    See WATER POLLUTION
        CONTROL ACT.
**Watershed conservancy
    districts.**
General provisions, §§9-8-50
    to 9-8-67.
    See SOIL AND WATER
        CONSERVATION.

CONSERVATORS.
Accounts and accounting.
Settlements of accounts of
    conservators, §§26-5-1 to
    26-5-54. See within this
    heading, "Settlements of
    accounts."
Appointment.
Court appointment,
    §26-2A-130.
Petition for appointment,
    §26-2A-133.
    Notice, §26-2A-134.
    Procedure, §26-2A-135.
Venue of proceedings,
    §26-2A-132.
Attorneys at law.
Settlements of accounts of
    guardians.
    Fees.
        Determination and
            allowance, §26-5-13.
Audits.
Settlements of accounts of
    guardians.
    Partial settlement, §26-5-4.

CONSERVATORS—Cont'd
Bonds, surety, §26-3-1.
Additional bond.
    Requirement, §26-3-7.
        Failure to give, §26-3-7.
Conditionally executed
    bonds.
    Liability of sureties,
        §26-3-11.
General conservators of
    county, §26-3-5.
Liability of sureties.
    Conditionally executed
        bonds, §26-3-11.
    Discharge from liability.
        Application, §26-3-8.
        New bond required,
            §26-3-9.
Neglect in taking.
    Liability of probate judge,
        §26-3-13.
New bond.
    Application for discharge
        from liability of surety.
        Effect of giving new
            bond, §26-3-9.
        Required, §26-3-8.
            Failure to give,
                §26-3-8.
    Requirement, §26-3-7.
        Failure to give, §26-3-7.
Omission in taking.
    Liability of probate judge,
        §26-3-13.
Recordation, §26-3-12.
Reductions.
    Partial settlement of
        estate, §26-3-14.
Settlement of estate.
    Reduction upon partial
        settlement, §26-3-14.
Settlements of accounts.
    Death of conservator.
        Enforcement of
            judgments against
            sureties, §26-5-54.
        Filing of account and
            vouchers for final
            settlement, §26-5-50.
        Succeeding conservator.
            Requiring sureties to
                make settlement,
                §26-5-52.
Statutory bonds.
    Force and effect of
        statutory bonds given
        bonds of certain
        conservators, §26-3-10.
Testamentary conservators.
    Relief from requirement of
        giving bond, §26-3-3.
    Requirement by probate
        court of bond, §26-3-4.
        Effect of failure to give,
            §26-3-4.
Uniform guardianship and
    protective proceedings
    act, §26-2A-139.
    Terms and requirements,
        §26-2A-140.
Circuit courts.
Removal of conservatorship
    from probate courts,
    §26-2-2.
Compensation.
Settlements of accounts,
    §26-5-16.

CONSERVATORS—Cont'd
Compromise and settlement.
Settlements of accounts of
    conservators, §§26-5-1 to
    26-5-54. See within this
    heading, "Settlements of
    accounts."
Corporations.
Voting of shares, §10-2A-53.
Costs.
Settlements of accounts.
    Compulsion of settlement.
        Partial settlement,
            §26-5-32.
    Settlements of accounts of
        guardians.
        Final settlement.
            Vouchers.
                Contest or rejection,
                    §26-5-10.
        Partial settlement.
            Contest or examination
                where vouchers or
                items rejected,
                §26-5-4.
Counties.
General conservator for
    county.
    Appointment, §26-2-26.
Courts.
Probate court.
    Definition of "court,"
        §26-2A-20.
    Generally. See within this
        heading, "Probate
        courts."
Death.
Settlements of accounts.
    Death of conservator,
        §§26-5-50 to 26-5-54.
Decrees.
Settlements of accounts.
    Enforcement against
        conservators, §26-5-18.
    Settlements of accounts of
        guardians.
        Final settlement, §26-5-11.
        Determination of
            finality, §26-5-15.
Executions.
Settlements of accounts.
    Death of conservator.
        Issuance against surety,
            §26-5-54.
**Executors and
    administrators.**
Settlements of accounts.
    Death of conservator.
        Personal representatives.
            Party to settlement
                proceedings,
                §26-5-51.
    Settlements of accounts of
        guardians.
        Compulsion of settlement.
            Final settlement.
                Authorization and
                    procedure,
                    §26-5-34.
Fees.
Settlements of accounts.
    Determination and
        allowance generally,
        §26-5-13.
    Final settlement, §26-5-14.
Fiduciaries generally.
See FIDUCIARIES.
General conservators.
Appointment, §26-2-26.
    Incapacitated persons,
        §26-2-50.

CONSERVATORS—Cont'd
General conservators
—Cont'd
Bonds, surety, §26-3-5.
Statutory bonds.
Bonds to have force and
effect of statutory
bonds, §26-3-10.
Guardian ad litem.
Settlements of accounts.
Final settlement.
Appointment of guardian
ad litem, §26-5-8.
Partial settlement.
Appointment of guardian
ad litem, §26-5-2.
Guardian and ward.
General provisions.
See GUARDIAN AND
WARD.
Uniform guardianship and
protective proceedings
act, §§26-2A-1 to
26-2A-160.
See GUARDIAN AND
WARD.
Hearings.
Incapacitated persons.
Revocation of
conservatorship.
Application by person
ascertained to be
incapacitated.
Date for hearing,
§26-2-52.
Hearing or trial on
contested
application,
§26-2-53.
Settlements of accounts.
Compulsion of settlement.
Partial settlement,
§26-5-31.
Incapacitated persons.
Appointment of conservators.
General conservators of
counties, §26-2-50.
Inquisition.
Attendance by person
alleged to be
incapacitated,
§26-2-43.
Entry of decree,
§26-2-45.
Guardian ad litem.
Appointment to
represent and
defend persons in
hospital or
asylum, §26-2-46.
Hospitalized persons.
Procedure, §26-2-46.
Jury.
Filling of vacancies,
§26-2-44.
Impaneling, §26-2-44.
Summoning of jurors,
§26-2-43.
Swearing in, §26-2-44.
Persons confined to
hospital or asylum.
Procedure, §26-2-46.
Recordation of
proceedings,
§26-2-45.
Witnesses.
Subpoenas for
witnesses,
§26-2-43.

CONSERVATORS—Cont'd
Incapacitated persons
—Cont'd
Appointment of conservators
—Cont'd
Nonresident incapacitated
persons having
property within state.
Authorization, §26-2-47.
Procedure, §26-2-48.
Sheriff as conservator,
§26-2-50.
Nonresidents.
Appointment of
conservator for
nonresidents having
property within state,
§26-2-47.
Procedure, §26-2-48.
Removal of person or
property of minors and
wards, §§26-8-1 to
26-8-52.
See GUARDIAN AND
WARD.
Revocation of
conservatorship.
Application by conservator,
§26-2-55.
Revocation of guardianship.
Application by persons
ascertained to be
incapacitated,
§26-2-51.
Contents of application,
§26-2-51.
Entry of decree.
Contested applications,
§26-2-54.
Uncontested
applications,
§26-2-53.
Hearings.
Date for hearing,
§26-2-52.
Hearing or trial on
contested
application,
§26-2-53.
Notice to guardian,
§26-2-52.
Uniform guardianship and
protective proceedings
act, §§26-2A-1 to
26-2A-160.
See GUARDIAN AND
WARD.
Investments.
Standards for fiduciary
investment and
management,
§19-3-120.2.
Uniform guardianship and
protective proceedings
act.
Powers in administration,
§26-2A-152.
Judges.
Judge to consider himself the
conservator of estates
under his jurisdiction,
ACJE, Canon 3B.
Jurisdiction.
Appointment by court,
§26-2A-130.
Probate court.
Appointment of
conservator,
§26-2A-130.

CONSERVATORS—Cont'd
Jurisdiction—Cont'd
Probate court—Cont'd
Settlements of accounts,
§26-5-1.
Death of conservator,
§26-5-50.
Settlements of accounts of
guardians.
Compulsion of
settlement, §26-5-30.
Management of property.
Standards for fiduciary
investment and
management,
§19-3-120.2.
Minors.
Appointment of conservators.
General conservators for
county, §26-2-26.
Removal of person or
property of minors and
wards, §§26-8-1 to
26-8-52.
See GUARDIAN AND
WARD.
Uniform guardianship and
protective proceedings
act, §§26-2A-1 to
26-2A-160.
See GUARDIAN AND
WARD.
Notice.
Incapacitated persons.
Revocation of
conservatorship.
Application by person
ascertained to be
incapacitated.
Notice to conservator,
§26-2-52.
Petitions for appointment,
§26-2A-134.
Settlements of accounts of
guardians.
Filing of annual, partial or
final settlement,
§26-5-15.
Final settlement.
Day for settlement,
§26-5-9.
Filing, §26-5-15.
Partial settlement.
Day for settlement,
§26-5-3.
Filing, §26-5-15.
Penalties.
Settlements of accounts.
Compulsion of settlement.
Appearance by
conservator or
representative.
Failure to appear,
§26-5-35.
Petitions.
Appointment, §26-2A-133.
Notice, §26-2A-134.
Procedure, §26-2A-135.
Presumptions.
Settlements of accounts of
guardians.
Partial settlement.
Correctness, §26-5-6.
Probate courts.
Bonds, surety.
Additional bond.
Authority to require,
§26-3-7.
Neglect in taking.
Liability of probate
judge, §26-3-13.

CONSERVATORS—Cont'd
  Probate courts—Cont'd
    Bonds, surety—Cont'd
      New or additional bond.
        Authority to require,
          §26-3-7.
        Omission in taking.
          Liability of probate
            judge, §26-3-13.
        Recordation, §26-3-12.
    Jurisdiction.
      Accounts of conservators.
        Settlements, §26-5-1.
      Appointment of
        conservator,
        §26-2A-130.
      Settlements of accounts.
        Compulsion of
          settlement, §26-5-30.
      Removal of conservatorship
        to circuit courts, §26-2-2.
    Death of conservators.
      Jurisdiction, §26-5-50.
    Final settlement.
      Account and vouchers.
        Examination, §26-5-10.
      Guardian ad litem
        appointed, §26-5-8.
    Settlements of accounts.
      Compulsion of settlement,
        §§26-5-30 to 26-5-39.
        See within this
          heading, "Settlements
          of accounts."
    Settlements of accounts of
      guardians.
      Finality of orders or
        decrees, §26-5-15.
    Final settlement.
      Account and vouchers.
        Filing by conservators,
          §26-5-8.
      Day for settlement,
        §26-5-9.
      Decree, §26-5-11.
      Recordation.
        Decree, §26-5-11.
    Partial settlement.
      Day for settlement,
        §26-5-3.
      Examination of vouchers,
        §26-5-4.
      Recordation.
        Decree as to vouchers
          and accounts,
          §26-5-5.
  Recordation.
    Bonds, surety, §26-3-12.
    Settlements of accounts.
      Final settlement.
        Accounts and vouchers,
          §26-5-11.
        Decree of probate court,
          §26-5-11.
      Settlements of accounts of
        guardians.
        Partial settlement.
          Decree as to vouchers
            and accounts,
            §26-5-5.
  **Removal of person or
    property of minors and
    wards, §§26-8-1 to 26-8-52.**
    See GUARDIAN AND
      WARD.
  **Savings and loan
    associations, §5-16-37.**
  Securities.
    Fiduciary security transfers,
      §§8-6-70 to 8-6-80.
      See SECURITIES.

CONSERVATORS—Cont'd
  Securities—Cont'd
    Uniform fiduciaries act,
      §§19-1-1 to 19-1-13.
      See FIDUCIARIES.
  Service of process.
    Settlements of accounts.
      Compulsion of settlement.
        Final settlement,
          §26-5-33.
        Personal
          representatives of
          conservators,
          §26-5-34.
        Partial settlement,
          §26-5-30.
        Costs, §26-5-32.
        Issuance, §26-5-31.
  Settlements of accounts,
    §§26-5-1 to 26-5-54.
    Appearances.
      Compulsion of settlement.
        Appearance by
          conservator or
          representative,
          §26-5-38.
        Failure to appear,
          §§26-5-35, 26-5-39.
    Attorneys at law.
      Fees.
        Generally, §26-5-13.
    Audits.
      Partial settlement, §26-5-4.
    Bonds, surety.
      Death of conservator.
        Enforcement of
          judgments against
          sureties, §26-5-54.
        Filing of account and
          vouchers for final
          settlement by
          sureties, §26-5-50.
        Succeeding conservator
          requiring sureties to
          make settlement,
          §26-5-52.
    Compensation, §26-5-16.
    Compulsion of settlement.
      Accounts and vouchers.
        Filing, §26-5-38.
        Statement of account by
          court upon failure to
          file, §26-5-36.
      Appearance by conservator
        or representative,
        §26-5-38.
      Failure to appear.
        Penalty, §26-5-35.
        Proceedings, §26-5-39.
      Contests.
        Appearance by
          conservator or
          representative.
          Failure to appear,
            §26-5-39.
      Costs.
        Partial settlement,
          §26-5-32.
      Executors and
        administrators.
        Final settlement.
          Authorization and
            procedure,
            §26-5-34.
      Final settlement.
        Generally, §26-5-33.
        Grounds, §26-5-33.

CONSERVATORS—Cont'd
  Settlements of accounts
    —Cont'd
    Compulsion of settlement
      —Cont'd
      Final settlement—Cont'd
        Personal representatives
          of conservators.
          Authorization and
            procedure,
            §26-5-34.
        Procedure, §26-5-33.
      Compulsion of
        settlement,
        §26-5-34.
      Service of process,
        §26-5-33.
      Personal
        representatives,
        §26-5-34.
    Hearings.
      Partial settlement,
        §26-5-31.
    Jurisdiction.
      Partial settlement,
        §26-5-30.
    Partial settlement.
      Application, §26-5-31.
      Dismissal, §26-5-31.
      Costs, §26-5-32.
      Hearing, §26-5-31.
      Jurisdiction, §26-5-30.
      Service of process,
        §26-5-30.
      Costs, §26-5-32.
      Issuance, §26-5-31.
    Penalties.
      Appearance by
        conservator or
        representative.
        Failure to appear,
          §26-5-35.
      Personal representatives.
        Final settlement.
          Authorization and
            procedure,
            §26-5-34.
    Service of process.
      Final settlement,
        §26-5-33.
      Personal
        representatives of
        conservators,
        §26-5-34.
      Partial settlement,
        §26-5-30.
      Costs, §26-5-32.
      Issuance, §26-5-31.
    Personal representatives
      of conservators.
      Final settlement,
        §26-5-34.
    Statement of account.
      Failure to file accounts
        and vouchers after
        notice, §26-5-36.
    Vouchers.
      Filing, §26-5-38.
      Statement of account by
        court upon failure to
        file, §26-5-36.
    Consent settlement.
      Final consent settlement
        between conservators
        and ward, §26-5-12.
    Costs.
      Final settlement.
        Vouchers.
          Contest or rejection,
            §26-5-10.

CONSERVATORS—Cont'd
Settlements of accounts
—Cont'd
Costs—Cont'd
Partial settlement.
Contest or examination
where vouchers or
items rejected,
§26-5-4.
Death of conservator.
Bond, surety.
Enforcement of
judgments against
sureties, §26-5-54.
Succeeding conservator
requiring sureties to
make settlement,
§26-5-52.
Conclusiveness of
settlement, §26-5-53.
Execution.
Issuance against
sureties, §26-5-54.
Executors and
administrators.
Personal representative
made party to
settlement
proceedings,
§26-5-51.
Finality of settlement,
§26-5-53.
Jurisdiction, §26-5-50.
Personal representative of
conservator.
Party to settlement
proceedings,
§26-5-51.
Succeeding conservators.
Requiring sureties to
make settlement,
§26-5-52.
Sureties on bonds of
conservators.
Filing of account and
vouchers for final
settlement, §26-5-50.
Decrees.
Enforcement against
conservators, §26-5-18.
Finality, §26-5-15.
Execution.
Death of conservator.
Issuance against
sureties, §26-5-54.
Executors and
administrators.
Compulsion of settlement.
Final settlement.
Authorization and
procedure,
§26-5-34.
Death of conservator.
Personal representative
made party,
§26-5-51.
Fees.
Attorney's fees, §26-5-13.
Determination and
allowance generally,
§26-5-13.
Final settlement, §26-5-14.
Final settlement.
Accounts and accounting.
Examination of vouchers
by probate court,
§26-5-10.
Filing of account and
vouchers by
conservators,
§26-5-8.

CONSERVATORS—Cont'd
Settlements of accounts
—Cont'd
Final settlement—Cont'd
Compensation, §26-5-16.
Compulsion of settlement,
Generally, §26-5-33.
Personal representatives.
Authorization and
procedure,
§26-5-34.
Procedure, §26-5-33.
Compulsion of
settlement by
personal
representatives of
conservators,
§26-5-34.
Service of process,
§26-5-33.
Personal
representatives of
conservators,
§26-5-34.
Consent settlement
between conservator
and ward, §26-5-12.
Costs.
Vouchers.
Contest or rejection,
§26-5-10.
Day for settlement.
Established, §26-5-9.
Death of conservators.
Filing of account and
vouchers for final
settlement, §26-5-50.
Decrees of court, §26-5-11.
Enforcement against
conservators,
§26-5-18.
Finality, §26-5-15.
Expenses.
Allowances, §26-5-16.
Fees, §§26-5-13, 26-5-14.
Generally, §26-5-7.
Guardian ad litem.
Appointment, §26-5-8.
Notice.
Day for settlement,
§26-5-9.
Filing, §26-5-15.
Probate court.
Account and vouchers.
Examination, §26-5-10.
Filing by conservators,
§26-5-8.
Consent settlement
between conservator
and ward.
Approval, §26-5-12.
Day for settlement.
Established, §26-5-9.
Notice, §26-5-9.
Decree, §26-5-11.
Finality, §26-5-15.
Guardian ad litem
appointed, §26-5-8.
Recordation.
Decree, §26-5-11.
Vouchers.
Examination, §26-5-10.
Filing by conservators,
§26-5-8.
Recordation.
Accounts and vouchers,
§26-5-11.
Decree of probate court,
§26-5-11.

CONSERVATORS—Cont'd
Settlements of accounts
—Cont'd
Final settlement—Cont'd
Service of process.
Compulsion of settlement
by probate court,
§26-5-33.
Personal
representatives of
conservators,
§26-5-34.
Vouchers.
Examination by court,
§26-5-10.
Filing by conservators,
§26-5-8.
When required, §26-5-7.
Guardian ad litem.
Final settlement.
Appointment, §26-5-8.
Partial settlement.
Appointed, §26-5-2.
Jurisdiction.
Compulsion of settlement.
Partial settlement,
§26-5-30.
Death of conservator,
§26-5-50.
Probate courts, §26-5-1.
Notice.
Filing of annual, partial or
final settlement,
§26-5-15.
Final settlement.
Day for settlement,
§26-5-9.
Filing, §26-5-15.
Partial settlement.
Filing, §26-5-15.
Probate courts.
Day for settlement,
§26-5-3.
Partial settlement.
Audits, §26-5-4.
Contests.
Taxing of costs, §26-5-4.
Correctness presumed,
§26-5-6.
Costs.
Contest or examination
where vouchers or
items rejected,
§26-5-4.
Day for settlement,
§26-5-3.
Decrees of court.
Enforcement against
conservators,
§26-5-18.
Finality, §26-5-15.
Examination of vouchers,
§26-5-4.
Items rejected.
Taxing of costs,
§26-5-4.
Fees, §26-5-13.
Filing of account and
vouchers, §26-5-2.
Guardian ad litem
appointed, §26-5-2.
Notice.
Filing, §26-5-15.
Presumption as to
correctness, §26-5-6.
Probate court.
Day for settlement.
Establishment,
§26-5-3.
Notice, §26-5-3.

CONSERVATORS—Cont'd
Settlements of accounts
—Cont'd
Partial settlement—Cont'd
Probate court—Cont'd
Decree.
Finality, §26-5-15.
Examination of vouchers,
§26-5-4.
Recordation.
Account, §26-5-5.
Decree as to vouchers
and accounts,
§26-5-5.
Vouchers, §26-5-5.
Recordation.
Decree as to vouchers
and accounts,
§26-5-5.
Stating account, §26-5-4.
Vouchers.
Decree as to vouchers
and accounts.
Recordation, §26-5-5.
Examination by probate
court, §26-5-4.
Rejection.
Costs, §26-5-4.
When required, §26-5-2.
Penalties.
Compulsion of settlement.
Appearance by
conservator or
representative.
Failure to appear,
§26-5-35.
Personal representatives.
Compulsion of settlement.
Final settlement.
Authorization and
procedure
generally,
§26-5-34.
Death of conservator.
Party to settlement
proceedings,
§26-5-51.
Presumptions.
Partial settlement.
Correctness, §26-5-6.
Probate court.
Compulsion of settlement,
§§26-5-30 to 26-5-39.
Final settlement.
Account and vouchers.
Examination, §26-5-10.
Filing by conservator,
§26-5-8.
Day for settlement,
§26-5-9.
Decree, §26-5-11.
Determination of
finality, §26-5-15.
Guardian ad litem
appointed, §26-5-8.
Recordation.
Decree, §26-5-11.
Jurisdiction, §26-5-1.
Death of conservator,
§26-5-50.
Partial settlement.
Day for settlement,
§26-5-3.
Examination of vouchers,
§26-5-4.
Recordation.
Decree as to vouchers
and accounts,
§26-5-5.

CONSERVATORS—Cont'd
Settlements of accounts
—Cont'd
Recordation.
Final settlement.
Accounts and vouchers,
§26-5-11.
Decree of probate court,
§26-5-11.
Partial settlement.
Decree as to vouchers
and accounts,
§26-5-5.
Reopening of account,
§26-5-15.
Service of process.
Compulsion of settlement.
Final settlement,
§26-5-33.
Personal
representatives of
conservators,
§26-5-34.
Partial settlement,
§26-5-30.
Sheriffs.
Appointment of sheriff as
conservator.
Incapacitated persons,
§26-2-50.
**Standards for fiduciary
investment and
management,** §19-3-120.2.
Testamentary conservators.
Bonds, surety.
Relief of testamentary
conservators, §26-3-3.
Requirement by probate
court of bond, §26-3-4.
Effect of failure to give,
§26-3-4.
**Uniform guardianship and
protective proceedings
act,** §§26-2A-1 to
26-2A-160.
See GUARDIAN AND
WARD.
Venue.
Proceedings under division,
§26-2A-132.
Veterans.
Incompetent veterans and
dependents, §§26-9-1 to
26-9-19.
See VETERANS.
Wards.
Removal of person or
property of minors and
wards, §§26-8-1 to
26-8-52.
See GUARDIAN AND
WARD.

**CONSOLIDATION OR
MERGER.**
Banks and trust companies.
Dissenting shareholders'
rights, §5-7A-44.
General provisions, §§5-7A-1
to 5-7A-6.
See BANKS AND
FINANCIAL
INSTITUTIONS.
Resulting banks, §5-7A-45.
Corporations.
Generally, §§10-2A-140 to
10-2A-146.
See CORPORATIONS.
Electric cooperatives.
See ELECTRIC
COOPERATIVES.

**CONSOLIDATION OR
MERGER**—Cont'd
Fraternal benefit societies,
§§27-34-48, 27-34-49.
Schools.
Consolidation of schools.
See EDUCATION.

CONSPIRACY.
Attorneys at law.
Practicing law without
license.
Conspiring, aiding or
abetting in violation.
Penalty, §34-3-7.
**Consummation of object
offense not defense to
prosecution,** §13A-4-5.
Corporations.
Conspiracy to interfere with
or hinder business,
§13A-11-122.
Defenses to prosecution,
§13A-4-3.
Consummation of object
offense not defense to
prosecution, §13A-4-5.
Drugs.
Controlled substances.
Criminal conspiracy to
commit controlled
substance crime,
§13A-12-204.
Included offenses,
§13A-12-205.
Elements generally, §13A-4-3.
**Formation in this state to
commit crime elsewhere
indictable here,** §13A-4-4.
Gambling.
Conspiracy to promote
gambling, §13A-12-23.
Indictments.
Form of indictment,
§15-8-150.
**Interference with or
hindering businesses,**
§13A-11-122.
Liability as accomplice,
§13A-4-3.
Marine resources.
Evasion of provisions of
article, §9-12-116.
**Multiple convictions on
basis of same course of
conduct,** §13A-4-5.
Offenses enumerated,
§13A-4-3.
Other states.
Conspiracy formed in this
state to commit crime
elsewhere indictable
here, §13A-4-4.
**Renunciation of criminal
purpose,** §13A-4-3.

CONSTABLES.
Abolition of office.
Authority of counties,
§36-23-1.
Arbitration and award.
Fees and charges, §6-6-10.
Assault upon police officer.
See ASSAULT AND
BATTERY.
Attachments.
Service when office of
constable vacant,
§36-23-8.

CONSTABLES—Cont'd
Attorneys at law.
Attorneys not deemed
sufficient sureties on
official bonds of
constables, §36-5-13.
Bonds, surety, §36-23-4.
Attorneys not deemed
sufficient sureties on
official bonds of
constables, §36-5-13.
Liability of constable and
sureties, §36-23-9.
Circuit courts.
Fees due constables for
services in connection
with circuit court
proceedings, §12-19-94.
Conservators of the peace,
§36-23-5.
Constitution of Alabama.
Fees.
Authorized, Const. Ala.,
amd. 328.
Increase prohibited, Const.
Ala., art. IV, §104.
Impeachments, Const. Ala.,
art. VII, §175.
Restrictions, rights and
limitations, Const. Ala.,
amd. 328.
District courts.
Coroners' fees, §12-19-94.
Duties, §36-23-6.
Election, §36-23-1; Const. Ala.,
art. VI, §168.
Executions.
Collection of commissions on
costs on execution by
constables, §12-19-95.
Duty to execute and return,
§36-23-6.
Service when office of
constable vacant,
§36-23-8.
When constables entitled to
receive full commissions,
§12-19-96.
When constables entitled to
receive only half
commissions, §12-19-97.
Fayette county.
Abolition of office, Const.
Ala., amd. 417.
Fees, §§12-19-92, 12-19-191;
Const. Ala., art. VI, §168.
Authorized, Const. Ala., amd.
328.
Circuit and district court
proceedings.
Fees due constables for
services in connection
with, §12-19-94.
Criminal cases, §12-19-191.
Executions.
Collection of commissions
on costs on execution
by constables,
§12-19-95.
Full commissions.
When constables entitled
to receive full
commissions,
§12-19-96.
Half commissions.
When constables entitled
to receive only half
commissions,
§12-19-97.

CONSTABLES—Cont'd
Fees—Cont'd
Increasing fees of constables.
Special, private or local
laws prohibited, Const.
Ala., art. IV, §104.
**Forcible entry and unlawful
detainer.**
Process.
Neglect or refusal to
execute, §6-6-333.
Forests and forestry.
Wardens.
Designation as forest
wardens, §9-13-5.
Impeachment, Const. Ala.,
art. VII, §175.
Subject to impeachment,
§36-11-1.
Jefferson county.
Fees.
Exception, §12-19-92.
Lamar county.
Abolition of office, Const.
Ala., amd. 419.
Limitation of actions.
Nonfeasance, misfeasance or
malfeasance.
Actions against surety.
Six year limitation,
§6-2-34.
Ten year limitation,
§6-2-33.
Lis pendens.
Liability on bonds, §35-4-139.
Money.
Duty to pay over, §36-23-6.
Number, §36-23-1.
Peace officers generally.
See PEACE OFFICERS.
**Process required of
constables.**
Execution by sheriffs.
Compensation, §36-22-9.
Liability, §36-22-9.
Public officers generally.
See PUBLIC OFFICERS
AND EMPLOYEES.
Resignation, §36-9-13.
Summons and process.
Duty to execute and return,
§36-23-6.
Term of office, §36-23-1.
Vacancies in office.
Filling, §36-23-2.
Notice, §36-23-3.
Removal from election
precinct deemed vacation
of office, §36-23-7.
Resignation, §36-9-13.
Service of executions and
attachments when office
vacant, §36-23-8.

**CONSTITUTION OF
ALABAMA.**
Actions.
Attorney general may be
required to defend
actions against state,
political subdivisions,
officers, etc., Const. Ala.,
amd. 111.
Corporations.
Right to sue and be sued
like natural persons,
Const. Ala., art. XII,
§240.

**CONSTITUTION OF
ALABAMA**—Cont'd
Actions—Cont'd
Removal of cause of action or
defense to suit after
commencement of suit,
Const. Ala., art. IV, §95.
Revival of barred rights or
remedies, Const. Ala.,
art. IV, §95.
Right to prosecute civil
cause, Const. Ala., art. I,
§10.
Adoption.
Probate courts.
Jurisdiction, Const. Ala.,
amd. 364.
Special, private or local laws
prohibited, Const. Ala.,
art. IV, §104.
**Airports and air navigation
facilities.**
Construction, maintenance,
etc., by state, Const.
Ala., amd. 58.
Alabama heritage trust fund,
Const. Ala., amd. 394.
**Alabama Polytechnic
Institute.** See within this
heading, "Auburn
university."
Alabama trust fund, Const.
Ala., amd. 450.
Aliens.
Property rights of aliens,
Const. Ala., art. I, §34.
Amendments.
Addison, municipality of.
Economic development,
Const. Ala., amd. 256.
Adoption.
Proposed amendments
affecting only one
county, Const. Ala.,
amd. 425.
Airports and air navigation
facilities.
Construction, maintenance,
etc., by state, Const.
Ala., amd. 58.
Alabama City.
Property tax, Const. Ala.,
amd. 17.
Alabama Heritage Trust
Fund.
Creation, Const. Ala., amd.
394.
Alabama polytechnic
institute.
Bonds for construction and
improvement purposes,
Const. Ala., amd. 120.
Alabama state house, Const.
Ala., amd. 427.
Alabama trust fund, Const.
Ala., amd. 450.
Alabaster, City of.
Taxation.
Additional ad valorem
tax in city, Const.
Ala., amd. 409.
Albany, municipality of.
Property tax, Const. Ala.,
amd. 13.
Aliceville, municipality of.
Property tax, Const. Ala.,
amd. 8.
Anniston, municipality of.
Cerebral palsy center.
Appropriation for, Const.
Ala., amd. 494.

CONSTITUTION OF ALABAMA—Cont'd
Amendments—Cont'd

Anniston, municipality of —Cont'd
Industrial parks.
Acquisition and development, Const. Ala., amd. 376.
Property tax, Const. Ala., amd. 8.
School tax.
Application of special school taxes, Const. Ala., amd. 281.
Special property tax for educational purposes, Const. Ala., amd. 350.
Special school tax, Const. Ala., amd. 232.
Appropriations.
Paramount duty to make basic appropriations at regular sessions, Const. Ala., amd. 448.
Unpaid appropriations for which money unavailable at end of fiscal year, Const. Ala., amd. 26.
Ashland, municipality of.
Property tax, Const. Ala., amd. 8.
Athens, municipality of.
Property tax, Const. Ala., amd. 8.
Atmore, municipality of.
Property tax, Const. Ala., amd. 8.
Attalla, municipality of.
Property tax, Const. Ala., amd. 31.
Attorney general.
Defense of suits against state, political subdivisions, officers, etc., Const. Ala., amd. 111.
Duties, Const. Ala., amd. 111.
Restrictions on receipt of fees, Const. Ala., amd. 111.
Succession.
One additional term, Const. Ala., amd. 282.
Term of office, Const. Ala., amd. 282.
Auburn, municipality of.
Property tax, Const. Ala., amd. 8.
Recreation.
Special property tax for recreational purposes, Const. Ala., amd. 242.
School tax.
Special property tax for educational purposes, Const. Ala., amd. 148.
Auburn university.
Board of trustees, Const. Ala., amd. 161.
Bonds for construction and improvement purposes, Const. Ala., amd. 120.

CONSTITUTION OF ALABAMA—Cont'd
Amendments—Cont'd

Augusta county.
Probate judge.
Compensation, Const. Ala., amd. 493.
Autauga county.
Economic development, Const. Ala., amd. 183.
Baldwin county.
Court costs and charges, Const. Ala., amd. 229.
Fire protection districts, Const. Ala., amd. 365.
Hospitals.
Special district tax, Const. Ala., amds. 230, 471.
Libraries.
Special property tax for public library purposes, Const. Ala., amd. 319.
Officers.
Compensation of certain officers, Const. Ala., amd. 229.
Roads.
Districts to build and maintain roads, Const. Ala., amd. 15.
School tax.
Additional tax for school purposes, Const. Ala., amd. 162.
Seawalls.
Districts to build and maintain seawalls, Const. Ala., amd. 15.
Barbour county.
Court costs and charges, Const. Ala., amd. 290.
Probate judge.
Compensation, Const. Ala., amd. 290.
Property tax.
Special property tax, Const. Ala., amd. 143.
Sheriff.
Compensation, Const. Ala., amd. 290.
Bayou La Batre, municipality of.
Economic development.
Promotion of industrial, commercial and agricultural development, Const. Ala., amds. 220, 261.
Bear Creek watershed area.
Development, Const. Ala., amd. 247.
Benevolent corporations.
Exemption from franchise taxes, Const. Ala., amd. 27.
Bessemer, municipality of.
Property tax, Const. Ala., amd. 8.
Bibb county.
Court costs and charges, Const. Ala., amds. 306, 332.
Economic development, Const. Ala., amd. 312.
Officers.
Compensation of certain officers, Const. Ala., amd. 332.

CONSTITUTION OF ALABAMA—Cont'd
Amendments—Cont'd

Bibb county—Cont'd
Sheriff.
Compensation of sheriff, Const. Ala., amd. 306.
Birmingham-Jefferson county civic center, Const. Ala., amds. 238, 280.
Birmingham, municipality of.
Circuit court holding at Birmingham.
Vacancies in office of judge, Const. Ala., amd. 83.
Property tax, Const. Ala., amd. 8.
Special ad valorem tax for paying principal and interest on bonds, Const. Ala., amd. 240.
Blind persons.
Exemptions from poll tax, Const. Ala., amd. 109.
Institute for deaf and blind.
Bonds for construction and improvement purposes, Const. Ala., amd. 117.
Blount county.
Consolidation of offices of tax assessor and tax collector, Const. Ala., amd. 430.
Court costs and charges, Const. Ala., amd. 344.
Economic development.
Municipalities in Blount county, Const. Ala., amd. 95.
Officers.
Compensation of certain officers, Const. Ala., amd. 344.
Boll weevil.
Eradication or control of boll weevil in cotton, Const. Ala., amd. 449.
Bond issues.
Alabama state docks department.
Not debt of state, Const. Ala., amd. 446.
Capital costs of public facilities and works or internal improvement, Const. Ala., amd. 395.
Capital improvements in Mobile county, Const. Ala., amd. 193.
Certain county revenue securities not to constitute bonds or indebtedness, Const. Ala., amd. 398.
General obligation bonds of Mobile county, Const. Ala., amd. 447.
Penal and correctional facilities, Const. Ala., amd. 374.
Public corporations, Const. Ala., amd. 108.
Refunding bonds for existing indebtedness, Const. Ala., amd. 26.

CONSTITUTION OF ALABAMA—Cont'd
Amendments—Cont'd
Brewton, municipality of.
Property tax, Const. Ala., amd. 8.
Bridges.
Alabama bridge commission.
Bonds to pay or retire bridge commission bonds, Const. Ala., amd. 42.
Bond issues, Const. Ala., amd. 21.
Bond issue for acquiring in conjunction with United States, Const. Ala., amd. 87.
Construction, maintenance, etc., by state, Const. Ala., amds. 12, 58.
State not to engage in internal improvements or lend money or credit for improvements.
Exception as to bridges, Const. Ala., amd. 1.
Building and loan associations.
Exemption of federal associations from franchise taxes, Const. Ala., amd. 27.
Bullock county.
Economic and industrial development promotion, Const. Ala., amd. 429.
Economic development, Const. Ala., amd. 128.
Officers.
Compensation of certain officers, Const. Ala., amd. 231.
Probate court.
Compensation of judge, Const. Ala., amd. 414.
Judge not to serve on county governing body, Const. Ala., amd. 414.
School tax.
License taxes for school purposes, Const. Ala., amd. 163.
Butler county.
Court costs and charges, Const. Ala., amd. 353.
Officers.
Compensation, Const. Ala., amd. 353.
School tax.
Special property tax for educational purposes, Const. Ala., amd. 131.
Calera, municipality of.
Property tax, Const. Ala., amd. 17.
Calhoun county.
Cerebral palsy center.
Appropriation by city of Anniston, Const. Ala., amd. 494.
Court costs and charges, Const. Ala., amd. 412.

CONSTITUTION OF ALABAMA—Cont'd
Amendments—Cont'd
Calhoun county—Cont'd
Industrial sites and industrial park projects, Const. Ala., amd. 415.
Officers.
Regulation of salaries, etc., of certain public officers, Const. Ala., amd. 33.
School taxes.
Special district school tax, Const. Ala., amd. 335.
Special school tax, Const. Ala., amd. 68.
Special tax in school districts, Const. Ala., amd. 291.
Use of special school tax funds.
Refunding of bonds, etc., Const. Ala., amd. 165.
Camden, municipality of.
Property tax, Const. Ala., amd. 8.
Canals.
Navigable waterway between Demopolis and Tennessee river, Const. Ala., amd. 270.
Navigable waterway between Montgomery and Gadsden and to the Alabama-Georgia boundary, Const. Ala., amd. 287.
Capital punishment.
Authority of governor to grant reprieves and commutations, Const. Ala., amd. 38.
Carbon Hill, municipality of.
Economic development, Const. Ala., amd. 277.
Property tax, Const. Ala., amd. 8.
Carrollton, municipality of.
Property tax, Const. Ala., amd. 8.
Catfish.
Promotion, Const. Ala., amd. 492.
Cattle industry.
Promotion, Const. Ala., amds. 201, 452.
Chambers county.
Court costs and charges, Const. Ala., amd. 103.
Fire and rescue fund, Const. Ala., amd. 476.
Hospitals.
Special tax for hospital and public health purposes.
Use of proceeds of special tax, Const. Ala., amd. 307.
Officers.
Offices, terms and compensation of officers, Const. Ala., amd. 103.

CONSTITUTION OF ALABAMA—Cont'd
Amendments—Cont'd
Chambers county—Cont'd
School tax.
Special ad valorem tax for school purposes on real and tangible personal property, Const. Ala., amd. 102.
Cherokee county.
Officers.
Regulation of salaries, etc., of certain public officers, Const. Ala., amd. 43.
School tax.
Special school district tax, Const. Ala., amd. 78.
Chilton county.
Court costs and charges, Const. Ala., amd. 346.
Economic development.
Special property tax for rural and industrial development, Const. Ala., amd. 166.
Industrial development.
Special property tax, Const. Ala., amd. 166.
Officers.
Compensation of certain officers, Const. Ala., amd. 346.
Rural development.
Special property tax, Const. Ala., amd. 166.
Special property tax, Const. Ala., amd. 402.
Vocational trade school.
Special property tax for acquiring, etc., Const. Ala., amd. 166.
Choctaw county.
Probate judge.
Compensation, Const. Ala., amd. 495.
School tax.
Additional tax for school purposes, Const. Ala., amd. 167.
Circuit courts, Const. Ala., amd. 328.
Circuit solicitors.
Designation as district attorneys, Const. Ala., amd. 226.
Citronelle, municipality of.
Property tax, Const. Ala., amd. 13.
Civic centers.
Bonds for civic centers in certain counties, Const. Ala., amds. 238, 280.
Civil service.
Appointments and promotions, Const. Ala., amd. 88.
Clarke county.
Court costs and charges, Const. Ala., amd. 416.
Economic development, Const. Ala., amd. 217.
Fire districts, Const. Ala., amd. 464.

**CONSTITUTION OF
ALABAMA**—Cont'd
  Amendments—Cont'd
    Clarke county—Cont'd
      Probate judge.
        Compensation, Const.
          Ala., amd. 478.
      School tax.
        Additional tax for school
          purposes, Const.
          Ala., amd. 168.
      Classification of laws, Const.
        Ala., amd. 375.
    Clay county.
      Courts.
        Costs and charges,
          Const. Ala., amd.
          359.
      Officers.
        Compensation, Const.
          Ala., amd. 359.
      School tax.
        Special school tax, Const.
          Ala., amd. 169.
    Clayton, municipality of.
      Property tax, Const. Ala.,
        amd. 17.
    Cleburne county.
      Court costs and charges,
        Const. Ala., amds. 331,
        347.
      Officers.
        Compensation, Const.
          Ala., amds. 331, 347.
      School tax.
        Special school district
          taxes, Const. Ala.,
          amd. 123.
    Clerks of court, Const. Ala.,
      amd. 328.
    Selection of clerks of
      inferior courts, Const.
      Ala., amd. 271.
    Clio, municipality of.
      Property tax, Const. Ala.,
        amd. 17.
    Coffee county.
      Courts.
        Costs and charges,
          Const. Ala., amd.
          360.
      Economic and industrial
        development
        promotion, Const. Ala.,
        amd. 429.
      Officers.
        Compensation, Const.
          Ala., amd. 360.
      Reorganization of offices,
        Const. Ala., amd. 377.
      School tax.
        Additional taxes for
          school purposes,
          Const. Ala., amd.
          206.
        Warrants payable from
          proceeds of special
          school taxes, Const.
          Ala., amd. 216.
      Taxation.
        Establishment of
          consolidated and
          unified tax system,
          Const. Ala., amd.
          377.
    Colbert county.
      Drainage districts, Const.
        Ala., amd. 45.
      Malaria control.
        Drainage districts,
          Const. Ala., amd. 45.

**CONSTITUTION OF
ALABAMA**—Cont'd
  Amendments—Cont'd
    Colbert county—Cont'd
      Officers.
        Compensation,
          allowances, etc.,
          Const. Ala., amd.
          136.
        Laws changing term of
          office, compensation,
          allowances, etc., of
          officers, Const. Ala.,
          amd. 144.
      School taxes.
        Special school tax in
          school districts Nos.
          1 and 2, Const. Ala.,
          amd. 293.
        Special tax by school
          districts, Const. Ala.,
          amd. 130.
    Columbiana, municipality of.
      Property tax, Const. Ala.,
        amd. 8.
    Commissioner of agriculture
      and industries.
      Duties and restrictions on
        receipt of fees, Const.
        Ala., amd. 111.
      Succession.
        One additional term,
          Const. Ala., amd.
          282.
      Term of office, Const. Ala.,
        amd. 282.
    Conecuh county.
      Trucks, trailers, etc.
      Taxation.
        Annual license taxes
          and registration,
          Const. Ala., amd.
          435.
    Conventions.
      Calling, Const. Ala., art.
        XVIII, §§286, 287.
      Repeal of act or
        resolution calling,
        Const. Ala., art.
        XVIII, §286.
      Jurisdiction of convention
        not restricted, Const.
        Ala., art. XVIII, §286.
      Power of convention not
        restricted, Const. Ala.,
        art. XVIII, §286.
    Coosa county.
      Court costs and charges,
        Const. Ala., amd. 345.
      Economic and industrial
        development
        promotion, Const. Ala.,
        amd. 429.
      Officers.
        Compensation of certain
          officers, Const. Ala.,
          amd. 345.
      School tax.
        Special tax in school
          districts, Const. Ala.,
          amd. 145.
    Cordova, municipality of.
      Property tax, Const. Ala.,
        amd. 13.
    Corporations.
      Benevolent corporations.
        Exemption from
          franchise taxes,
          Const. Ala., amd. 27.

**CONSTITUTION OF
ALABAMA**—Cont'd
  Amendments—Cont'd
    Corporations—Cont'd
      Charters.
        General law as to grant
          or amendment,
          Const. Ala., amd. 27.
      Educational corporations.
        Exemption from
          franchise taxes,
          Const. Ala., amd. 27.
      Federal building and loan
        associations.
        Exemption from
          franchise taxes,
          Const. Ala., amd. 27.
      Foreign corporations
        making mortgage
        loans through licensed
        mortgage loan brokers,
        Const. Ala., amd. 154.
      Franchise taxes.
        Exemption, Const. Ala.,
          amd. 27.
        Taxes to be paid, Const.
          Ala., amd. 27.
      Powers.
        Special laws conferring
          corporate powers
          prohibited, Const.
          Ala., amd. 27.
      Religious corporations.
        Exemption from
          franchise taxes,
          Const. Ala., amd. 27.
      State interest in corporate
        enterprises prohibited,
        Const. Ala., amd. 1.
        Exceptions, Const. Ala.,
          amds. 12, 58.
    Cotton.
      Promotion of cotton
        industry, Const. Ala.,
        amd. 388.
    Counties.
      Actions against.
        Attorney general may be
          required to defend,
          Const. Ala., amd.
          111.
      Civic centers.
        Bonds for civic centers in
          certain counties,
          Const. Ala., amds.
          238, 280.
      Debt limit, Const. Ala.,
        amd. 342.
      Expenditure of county
        funds.
        Effectiveness of laws
          providing for, Const.
          Ala., amd. 474.
      Health.
        Special tax for hospital
          and public health
          purposes in counties
          except Mobile,
          Montgomery and
          Jefferson, Const.
          Ala., amd. 72.
      Hospitals.
        Additional county taxes
          for county hospitals,
          Const. Ala., amd. 59.

**CONSTITUTION OF
  ALABAMA**—Cont'd
Amendments—Cont'd
Counties—Cont'd
Hospitals—Cont'd
Special county tax,
    Const. Ala., amd. 76.
Use for care and
    treatment of
    indigent residents,
    Const. Ala., amd.
    125.
Special tax for hospital
    and public health
    purposes in counties
    except Mobile,
    Montgomery and
    Jefferson, Const.
    Ala., amd. 72.
Loans and grants.
Counties not to grant
    public money or lend
    credit to individuals
    or corporations,
    Const. Ala., amd.
    112.
Membership and powers of
    development authority,
    Const. Ala., amd. 431.
Officers.
Salaries.
Increasing or
    decreasing, Const.
    Ala., amd. 92.
Suspension of
    restriction on
    diminishing,
    Const. Ala., amd.
    26A.
Population based acts.
Amendment procedure,
    Const. Ala., amd.
    389.
Validation, Const. Ala.,
    amd. 389.
Roads.
Laws placing
    responsibility for
    county roads in state
    highway
    department, Const.
    Ala., amd. 142.
Taxation.
Limitation on county
    property tax rates,
    Const. Ala., amd.
    208.
Public buildings, bridges
    or roads.
Special tax authorized,
    Const. Ala., amd.
    208.
Tax increment districts,
    Const. Ala., amd.
    475.
Court of civil appeals, Const.
    Ala., amd. 328.
Court of criminal appeals,
    Const. Ala., amd. 328.
Court of the judiciary, Const.
    Ala., amd. 328.
Courts generally.
Abolishing branch
    courthouse or division
    or branch of court of
    record, Const. Ala.,
    amd. 81.
Administration of courts,
    Const. Ala., amd. 328.

**CONSTITUTION OF
  ALABAMA**—Cont'd
Amendments—Cont'd
Courts generally—Cont'd
Counties.
Minimum standards for
    establishment,
    Const. Ala., amd.
    139.
Establishing branch
    courthouse or division
    or branch of court of
    record, Const. Ala.,
    amd. 81.
Covington county.
Compensation of officers,
    Const. Ala., amd. 479.
School tax.
Special school tax in
    school districts Nos.
    1 and 2, Const. Ala.,
    amd. 292.
Crenshaw county.
Probate judge.
Compensation, Const.
    Ala., amd. 496.
Criminal law and procedure.
Grand jury.
Not required in
    misdemeanor cases,
    Const. Ala., amd. 37.
Indictments.
Plea of guilty prior to
    indictment, Const.
    Ala., amd. 37.
Informations.
Proceedings against
    person by
    information, Const.
    Ala., amd. 37.
Cullman county.
Court costs and charges,
    Const. Ala., amd. 137.
Officers.
Fees, allowances, etc.,
    Const. Ala., amd.
    137.
Cullman, municipality of.
School tax.
Special tax for
    educational
    purposes, Const.
    Ala., amd. 52.
Dale county.
Court costs and charges,
    Const. Ala., amd. 326.
Officers.
Consolidation of officers
    and regulation of
    fees, compensation,
    etc., of officers,
    Const. Ala., amd.
    326.
School tax.
Special property tax for
    educational
    purposes, Const.
    Ala., amd. 295.
Dallas county.
Court costs and charges,
    Const. Ala., amd. 233.
Economic and industrial
    development
    promotion, Const. Ala.,
    amd. 429.
Officers.
Fees, allowances, etc.,
    Const. Ala., amd.
    138.

**CONSTITUTION OF
  ALABAMA**—Cont'd
Amendments—Cont'd
Dallas county—Cont'd
Officers—Cont'd
Salaries, etc., of certain
    public officers,
    Const. Ala., amd. 46.
Daniel "Chappie" James
    Aerospace Memorial.
Indebtedness for.
Macon county, Const.
    Ala., amd. 437.
Tuskegee, municipality
    of, Const. Ala., amd.
    438.
Deaf persons.
Exemptions from poll tax,
    Const. Ala., amd. 109.
Institute for deaf and
    blind.
Bonds for construction
    and improvement
    purposes, Const.
    Ala., amd. 117.
Decatur, municipality of.
Economic development.
Promotion of industrial,
    commercial and
    agricultural
    development, Const.
    Ala., amd. 303.
School tax.
Special tax for
    educational
    purposes, Const.
    Ala., amd. 52.
DeKalb county.
Court costs and charges,
    Const. Ala., amd. 134.
Hospitals.
Special tax for hospital
    and public health
    purposes, Const.
    Ala., amd. 65.
Legislation as to DeKalb
    county, Const. Ala.,
    amd. 184.
Officers.
Fees, compensation, etc.,
    Const. Ala., amds.
    134, 337.
Public health.
Special tax for hospital
    and public health
    purposes, Const.
    Ala., amd. 65.
School tax.
Special property tax for
    educational
    purposes, Const.
    Ala., amd. 146.
Warrants payable out of
    proceeds of special
    taxes for educational
    purposes, Const.
    Ala., amd. 210.
Demopolis, municipality of.
Property tax, Const. Ala.,
    amd. 8.
Special property tax,
    Const. Ala., amd.
    385.
District attorneys, Const.
    Ala., amd. 328.
Designation of circuit
    solicitor as district
    attorney, Const. Ala.,
    amd. 226.
District courts, Const. Ala.,
    amd. 328.

CONSTITUTION OF ALABAMA—Cont'd
Amendments—Cont'd
Divorce and alimony.
Cohabitation or remarriage of spouse.
Termination of alimony, Const. Ala., amd. 390.
Docks.
Bonds for state docks facilities, Const. Ala., amds. 213, 222, 273.
Conveyance of state docks property to local authorities, Const. Ala., amds. 443, 454.
Dora, municipality of.
Property tax, Const. Ala., amd. 13.
Double Springs, municipality of.
Economic development, Const. Ala., amd. 104.
Drains and drainage.
Districts, Const. Ala., amds. 15, 22.
Economic and industrial development.
Promotion in certain counties and municipalities, Const. Ala., amd. 429.
Education.
Corporations.
Exemption of educational corporations from franchise taxes, Const. Ala., amd. 27.
Election of certain schools for attendance by parents of minors, Const. Ala., amd. 111.
Escheats.
Estates of persons dying without will or heirs to be applied to furtherance of education, Const. Ala., amd. 111.
Establishment and operation of schools, Const. Ala., amd. 111.
Grant, donation, sale, etc., of funds and property for educational purposes, Const. Ala., amd. 111.
Policy of state, Const. Ala., amd. 256.
Property donated or appropriated for educational purposes to be applied to furtherance of education, Const. Ala., amd. 111.
School boards.
Authority of legislature to constitute members of state, county and city school boards as judicial officers, Const. Ala., amd. 139.
Segregation, Const. Ala., amd. 111.

CONSTITUTION OF ALABAMA—Cont'd
Amendments—Cont'd
Education—Cont'd
State board of education.
Election of members, Const. Ala., amd. 284.
State superintendent of education.
Duties and restrictions on receipt of fees, Const. Ala., amd. 111.
Selection qualifications, powers, duties, etc., Const. Ala., amd. 284.
Succession, Const. Ala., amd. 282.
Term of office, Const. Ala., amd. 282.
Elections.
Duty of legislature to pass laws regulating elections, Const. Ala., amd. 41.
Registration, Const. Ala., amd. 223.
Mail, Const. Ala., amds. 285, 322.
Persons registered under 1901 constitution not required to reregister, Const. Ala., amd. 91.
Qualifications for registration, Const. Ala., amds. 91, 223.
After January 1, 1903, Const. Ala., amd. 55.
Requirements, Const. Ala., amd. 96.
Voters.
Qualifications of voters, Const. Ala., amds. 96, 223.
Residents, Const. Ala., amd. 96.
Voting machines.
Bond issues, Const. Ala., amd. 200.
Provision for use of voting machines, Const. Ala., amd. 41.
Elk river watershed area.
Development, Const. Ala., amd. 243.
Elmore county.
Consolidation of offices, Const. Ala., amd. 356.
Court costs and charges, Const. Ala., amd. 278.
Local service districts, Const. Ala., amd. 466.
Officers.
Compensation of certain officers, Const. Ala., amd. 185.
Enemy attack.
Continuity of legislature in event of enemy attack, Const. Ala., amd. 159.
Escambia county.
Costs, Const. Ala., amd. 391.

CONSTITUTION OF ALABAMA—Cont'd
Amendments—Cont'd
Escambia county—Cont'd
Hospitals.
Special tax for hospital and public health purposes, Const. Ala., amd. 70.
Officers and employees.
Compensation, Const. Ala., amd. 391.
Public health.
Special tax for hospital and public health purposes, Const. Ala., amd. 70.
Estate and inheritance tax, Const. Ala., amd. 23.
Etowah county.
Annexation in county, Const. Ala., amd. 467.
Economic and industrial development promotion, Const. Ala., amd. 429.
Fire protection districts, Const. Ala., amds. 432, 445.
Officers.
Fees, salaries, etc., of certain public officers, Const. Ala., amd. 62.
Regulation of salaries, etc., of certain public officers, Const. Ala., amd. 43.
School tax.
Special property tax for educational purposes, Const. Ala., amd. 296.
Special school tax, Const. Ala., amd. 67.
Trial tax or charge on litigation, Const. Ala., amd. 235.
Evergreen, municipality of.
Economic development.
Promotion of industrial, commercial and agricultural development, Const. Ala., amd. 259.
Property tax, Const. Ala., amd. 17.
Fairfield, municipality of.
Property tax, Const. Ala., amd. 8.
Fairhope, municipality of.
Property tax, Const. Ala., amd. 8.
Fayette county.
Abolition of office of constable, Const. Ala., amd. 417.
Economic development.
Municipalities in Fayette county, Const. Ala., amd. 94.
Fayette, municipality of.
Property tax, Const. Ala., amd. 17.
Fiduciaries.
Restrictions on investment of trust funds by fiduciaries in private corporations, Const. Ala., amd. 40.

CONSTITUTION OF ALABAMA—Cont'd
Amendments—Cont'd
Fires and fire prevention.
Jackson county.
Fire districts and fire prevention services, Const. Ala., amd. 436.
Lee county.
Fire fighting districts and fire protection in Lee county, Const. Ala., amd. 392.
Flomaton, municipality of.
Property tax, Const. Ala., amd. 8.
Flood control projects.
Tributary streams of Tombigbee river, Const. Ala., amd. 270.
Florala, municipality of.
Property tax, Const. Ala., amd. 17.
Florence, municipality of.
Property tax, Const. Ala., amd. 8.
School tax.
Special school tax, Const. Ala., amd. 178.
Foreign corporations.
Doing business in state, Const. Ala., amd. 473.
Fort Payne, municipality of.
School tax.
Special property tax for educational purposes, Const. Ala., amd. 279.
Special school tax, Const. Ala., amd. 234.
Franklin county.
Compensation of judge of probate, Const. Ala., amd. 418.
Court costs and charges, Const. Ala., amd. 418.
Economic development, Const. Ala., amd. 186.
Hospitals.
Tax in districts one, two and three, Const. Ala., amd. 262.
School tax.
Additional tax for school purposes, Const. Ala., amd. 173.
Further provisions as to additional tax for school purposes, Const. Ala., amd. 211.
Game and fish fund, Const. Ala., amd. 272.
Gasoline tax.
Expenditure, Const. Ala., amd. 93.
Geneva county.
County officers, Const. Ala., amd. 372.
Courthouse.
Bond issue for construction and equipment, Const. Ala., amd. 187.
Economic and industrial development promotion, Const. Ala., amd. 429.

CONSTITUTION OF ALABAMA—Cont'd
Amendments—Cont'd
Geneva county—Cont'd
Economic development.
Municipalities in Geneva county, Const. Ala., amd. 263.
Jail.
Bond issue for construction and equipment, Const. Ala., amd. 187.
Probate judge.
Fees, allowances, etc., Const. Ala., amd. 357.
Girard, municipality of.
Property tax, Const. Ala., amds. 8, 13.
Gordo, municipality of.
Property tax, Const. Ala., amd. 8.
Governor.
Death sentence.
Authority to grant reprieves and commutations, Const. Ala., amd. 38.
Succession.
One additional term, Const. Ala., amd. 282.
Term of office, Const. Ala., amd. 282.
Grain industry.
Promotion of, Const. Ala., amd. 453.
Grand jury.
Not required in misdemeanor cases, Const. Ala., amd. 37.
Greene county.
Economic development, Const. Ala., amd. 188.
Officers.
Compensation.
Repeal of amendment, Const. Ala., amd. 433.
Probate judge.
Compensation, Const. Ala., amd. 480.
Greensboro, municipality of.
Property tax, Const. Ala., amd. 17.
Greenville, municipality of.
Property tax, Const. Ala., amd. 17.
Hale county.
Economic development, Const. Ala., amd. 313.
Probate judge.
Compensation, Const. Ala., amd. 481.
Haleyville, municipality of.
Economic development, Const. Ala., amd. 104.
Property tax, Const. Ala., amd. 54.
Harbors and ports.
Construction, maintenance, etc., by state, Const. Ala., amds. 12, 58.
Hartselle, municipality of.
Economic development.
Promotion of industrial, commercial and agricultural development, Const. Ala., amd. 303.

CONSTITUTION OF ALABAMA—Cont'd
Amendments—Cont'd
Hartselle, municipality of —Cont'd
School taxes, Const. Ala., amd. 456.
Health.
Counties.
Special tax for hospital and public health purposes in counties except Mobile, Montgomery and Jefferson, Const. Ala., amd. 72.
Public hospitals and health facilities, Const. Ala., amd. 53.
Heflin, municipality of.
Property tax, Const. Ala., amd. 8.
Henry county.
Courthouse.
Bonds for courthouse, Const. Ala., amd. 230.
Jail.
Bonds for jail, Const. Ala., amd. 237.
Probate judge.
Costs and charges of courts and compensation of probate judge, Const. Ala., amd. 403.
Heritage trust fund.
Creation, Const. Ala., amd. 394.
Highways.
Bond issues, Const. Ala., amds. 11, 21.
Bond issue for acquiring in conjunction with United States, Const. Ala., amd. 87.
Construction, maintenance, etc., by state, Const. Ala., amds. 12, 58.
County roads.
Laws placing responsibility for in state highway department, Const. Ala., amd. 142.
State not to engage in internal improvements or lend money or credit for improvements.
Exception as to highways, Const. Ala., amd. 1.
Homestead exemptions.
Income tax, Const. Ala., amd. 61.
Hospitals.
Bond issues.
Bonds for state board of health hospitals and district tuberculosis sanitoria, Const. Ala., amd. 74.
Construction and equipment of hospitals, Const. Ala., amds. 114, 121, 158.

CONSTITUTION OF
ALABAMA—Cont'd
Amendments—Cont'd
Hospitals—Cont'd
County hospitals.
Additional county taxes
for county hospitals,
Const. Ala., amd. 59.
Special county tax,
Const. Ala., amd. 76.
Use for hospital care
and treatment of
indigent persons,
Const. Ala., amd.
125.
Special tax for hospital
and public health
purposes in counties
except Mobile,
Montgomery and
Jefferson, Const.
Ala., amd. 72.
Public hospitals and health
facilities, Const. Ala.,
amd. 53.
Housing finance authority.
Payment by state of
expenses incurred,
Const. Ala., amd. 396.
Houston county.
Economic and industrial
development
promotion, Const. Ala.,
amd. 429.
Officers.
Fees, salaries, etc., of
certain public
officers, Const. Ala.,
amd. 48.
Huntsville, municipality of.
Economic development.
Promotion of industrial,
commercial and
agricultural
development, Const.
Ala., amds. 191, 245.
Property tax, Const. Ala.,
amd. 8.
School tax.
Special school tax, Const.
Ala., amds. 80, 218,
305.
Amendment of
amendment,
Const. Ala., amd.
407.
Hurtsboro, municipality of.
Property tax, Const. Ala.,
amd. 8.
Income taxes, Const. Ala.,
amd. 25.
Corporations, Const. Ala.,
amd. 212.
Deduction of federal
income tax, Const.
Ala., amd. 225.
Disposition of income tax,
Const. Ala., amd. 61.
Homestead exemptions,
Const. Ala., amd. 61.
Indictments.
Plea of guilty prior to
indictment, Const.
Ala., amd. 37.
Indigent persons.
Hospital care and
treatment.
Use of certain special
county taxes, Const.
Ala., amd. 125.

CONSTITUTION OF
ALABAMA—Cont'd
Amendments—Cont'd
Informations.
Proceeding against person
by information, Const.
Ala., amd. 37.
Inglenook, municipality of.
Property tax, Const. Ala.,
amd. 8.
Internal improvements.
State not to engage in
internal improvements
or lend money or
credit for
improvements, Const.
Ala., amd. 1.
Exceptions, Const. Ala.,
amds. 12, 58.
Irrigation.
Development of irrigation
districts, Const. Ala.,
amd. 227.
Jackson county.
Compensation of certain
officers, Const. Ala.,
amd. 367.
Costs and charges of
courts, Const. Ala.,
amd. 367.
Economic development.
Special property tax for
rural and industrial
development, Const.
Ala., amd. 174.
Fire districts and fire
prevention services,
Const. Ala., amd. 436.
Industrial development.
Special property tax,
Const. Ala., amd.
174.
Rural development.
Special property tax,
Const. Ala., amd.
174.
School tax.
Additional property tax
for educational
purposes, Const.
Ala., amd. 203.
Vocational trade school.
Special property tax for
acquiring, etc.,
Const. Ala., amd.
174.
Jackson, municipality of.
Port authority, Const. Ala.,
amds. 465, 477.
Jacksonville, municipality of.
Property tax, Const. Ala.,
amd. 8.
Jasper, municipality of.
Property tax, Const. Ala.,
amd. 13.
School tax.
Special property tax for
educational
purposes, Const.
Ala., amd. 253.
Jefferson county.
Bingo.
Operation by nonprofit
organizations, Const.
Ala., amd. 386.
Circuit court holding at
Birmingham.
Vacancies in office of
judge, Const. Ala.,
amd. 83.

CONSTITUTION OF
ALABAMA—Cont'd
Amendments—Cont'd
Jefferson county—Cont'd
Circuit court of Jefferson
county.
Filling vacancy in office
of judge, Const. Ala.,
amd. 110.
Economic and industrial
development
promotion, Const. Ala.,
amd. 429.
Fees of officers, Const.
Ala., amd. 2.
Fire protection districts,
Const. Ala., amds. 239,
314.
Amendment of
amendment no. 239,
Const. Ala., amd.
369.
Garbage and trash disposal
districts, Const. Ala.,
amds. 239, 314.
Amendment of
amendment no. 239,
Const. Ala., amd.
369.
Inferior courts established
in lieu of justices of
the peace.
Legislation as to
jurisdiction, Const.
Ala., amds. 258, 283.
Junk.
Prohibition of
accumulation, Const.
Ala., amd. 497.
Probate judgeship.
Additional judgeship for
county, Const. Ala.,
amd. 384.
School tax.
Consolidation school tax
amendment, Const.
Ala., amd. 82.
Special district tax for
furtherance of
education, Const.
Ala., amds. 175, 298.
Special tax in Mountain
Brook school district,
Const. Ala., amd.
316.
Sewer bonds, Const. Ala.,
amd. 73.
Weeds.
Prohibition of
overgrowth, Const.
Ala., amd. 497.
Judges, Const. Ala., amd.
328.
Censure, Const. Ala., amd.
317.
Compensation, Const. Ala.,
amds. 328, 426.
Disqualification, Const.
Ala., amd. 328.
Election, Const. Ala., amd.
328.
Inquiry commission, Const.
Ala., amd. 317.
Powers.
Judicial power, Const.
Ala., amd. 328.
Qualifications, Const. Ala.,
amd. 328.
Removal, Const. Ala., amd.
317.

**CONSTITUTION OF
ALABAMA**—Cont'd
Amendments—Cont'd
Judges—Cont'd
Retirement, Const. Ala.,
amds. 317, 328.
Suspension, Const. Ala.,
amd. 317.
Term of office, Const. Ala.,
amd. 328.
Vacancies in office, Const.
Ala., amd. 328.
Judicial commission, Const.
Ala., amd. 317.
Judicial inquiry commission,
Const. Ala., amd. 328.
Judicial power.
Vesting, Const. Ala., amd.
139.
Justice of the peace.
Abolition of office, Const.
Ala., amd. 323.
Lafayette, municipality of.
Property tax, Const. Ala.,
amd. 8.
Lamar county.
Abolition of office of
constable, Const. Ala.,
amd. 419.
Economic development.
Municipalities in Lamar
county, Const. Ala.,
amd. 189.
School tax.
Additional tax for school
purposes, Const.
Ala., amd. 176.
Lanett, municipality of.
Property tax, Const. Ala.,
amd. 8.
Lauderdale county.
Compensation of certain
officers, Const. Ala.,
amd. 241.
Elk river watershed area.
Development, Const.
Ala., amd. 243.
School district tax, Const.
Ala., amd. 404.
School tax.
Special property tax for
educational
purposes, Const.
Ala., amd. 177.
Special, private or local
laws relating to
Lauderdale county or
municipalities, Const.
Ala., amd. 140.
Tax assessor.
Combination of offices of
tax assessor and tax
collector, Const.
Ala., amd. 405.
Lawrence county.
Bond issues, Const. Ala.,
amd. 30.
Court costs and charges,
Const. Ala., amd. 321.
Economic and industrial
development
promotion, Const. Ala.,
amd. 429.
Economic development,
Const. Ala., amd. 190.
Health.
Special property tax for
general health
purposes, Const.
Ala., amd. 311.

**CONSTITUTION OF
ALABAMA**—Cont'd
Amendments—Cont'd
Lawrence county—Cont'd
Officers.
Fees, compensation, etc.,
of certain officers,
Const. Ala., amd.
321.
School districts.
Authorization of creation
of special school
districts, etc., Const.
Ala., amd. 99.
Change in boundaries of
school districts,
Const. Ala., amd.
294.
Special school district in
Lawrence county,
Const. Ala., amd. 79.
School tax.
Special tax in school
districts, Const. Ala.,
amd. 294.
Tax elections in certain
school districts,
Const. Ala., amds.
20, 32.
Lee county.
Fire fighting districts and
fire protection, Const.
Ala., amd. 392.
Financial charges or
assessments on
property within,
Const. Ala., amd.
498.
Juveniles.
Special tax for improving
enforcement of laws
relative to and
providing facilities
for, Const. Ala.,
amd. 324.
Officers.
Fees and compensation
of elected officials,
Const. Ala., amd.
362.
School tax.
Special property tax for
educational
purposes, Const.
Ala., amd. 147.
Special school district
tax, Const. Ala.,
amd. 309.
Legislature.
Basis of representation in
legislature not to be
changed by
amendment, Const.
Ala., art. XVIII, §284;
amd. 24.
Budgets.
Legislative budget,
Const. Ala., amd.
448.
Compensation of members,
Const. Ala., amds. 39,
57.
Election of president pro
tempore of senate and
speaker of house,
Const. Ala., amds. 39,
57.

**CONSTITUTION OF
ALABAMA**—Cont'd
Amendments—Cont'd
Legislature—Cont'd
Enemy attack.
Continuity of legislature
in event of enemy
attack, Const. Ala.,
amd. 159.
Pardons and paroles.
Regulation of
administration,
Const. Ala., amd. 38.
Probation.
Regulation of
administration of
probation, Const.
Ala., amd. 38.
Remission of fines and
forfeitures, Const. Ala.,
amd. 38.
Sessions.
Annual sessions, Const.
Ala., amd. 339.
Biennial sessions, Const.
Ala., amds. 39, 57.
Maximum length, Const.
Ala., amds. 39, 57.
Organizational sessions,
Const. Ala., amds.
39, 57.
Regular sessions, Const.
Ala., amd. 339.
Special sessions, Const.
Ala., amd. 339.
Time and place of
meetings, Const.
Ala., amds. 39, 57.
Suspension of sentence,
Const. Ala., amd. 38.
Travel allowances of
members, Const. Ala.,
amds. 39, 57.
Vacancies.
Special elections to fill,
Const. Ala., amd. 97.
Lester, municipality of.
Economic development,
Const. Ala., amd. 244.
Libraries.
Special property tax for
library purposes,
Const. Ala., amd. 269.
Lieutenant governor.
Succession.
One additional term,
Const. Ala., amd.
282.
Term of office, Const. Ala.,
amd. 282.
Limestone county.
Commission.
Authority to dispose of
dead farm animals
and excavate human
graves, Const. Ala.,
amd. 482.
Elk river watershed area.
Development, Const.
Ala., amd. 243.
Establishment of fire
districts, Const. Ala.,
amd. 371.
Health.
Special property tax for
general health
purposes, Const.
Ala., amd. 311.
Malaria control.
Tax for malaria control,
Const. Ala., amd. 34.

CONSTITUTION OF ALABAMA—Cont'd
Amendments—Cont'd
Limestone county—Cont'd
Officers.
Fees, salaries, etc., of certain public officers, Const. Ala., amd. 64.
Police jurisdiction of municipalities within, Const. Ala., amd. 499.
Livingston, municipality of.
Economic development, Const. Ala., amd. 251.
Property tax, Const. Ala., amd. 8.
Loans.
Mortgage loans.
Nonresidents making mortgage loans through licensed brokers, Const. Ala., amd. 154.
Local constitutional amendments.
Adoption of proposed constitutional amendment affecting only one county, Const. Ala., amd. 425.
Lowndes county.
Probate judge.
Compensation, Const. Ala., amd. 483.
Lynn, municipality of.
Economic development, Const. Ala., amd. 256.
Macon county.
Boundaries.
Altering boundaries.
Repeal of amendment, Const. Ala., amd. 406.
Daniel "Chappie" James Aerospace Memorial.
Indebtedness for, Const. Ala., amd. 437.
Economic and industrial development promotion, Const. Ala., amd. 429.
Reducing area.
Repeal of amendment, Const. Ala., amd. 406.
School tax.
Additional tax for education purposes, Const. Ala., amd. 420.
Madison county.
Bingo.
Operation by nonprofit organizations, Const. Ala., amd. 387.
Circuit court.
Procedure for filling vacancies in office of judge, Const. Ala., amd. 334.
Court costs and charges, Const. Ala., amd. 105.
Economic and industrial development promotion, Const. Ala., amd. 429.

CONSTITUTION OF ALABAMA—Cont'd
Amendments—Cont'd
Madison county—Cont'd
Economic development.
Promotion of industrial, commercial and agricultural development, Const. Ala., amds. 191, 245.
Establishment of fire districts, Const. Ala., amd. 378.
Judicial commission, Const. Ala., amd. 334.
Officers.
Fees, allowances, etc., of judge of probate and other officers, Const. Ala., amd. 135.
Property tax.
Delinquent tax notices, Const. Ala., amd. 348.
School bonds.
Bonds for school buildings, Const. Ala., amd. 320.
School tax.
Repeal of school tax exemptions, Const. Ala., amd. 455.
Special school tax in school district No. 1, Const. Ala., amds. 149, 304.
Space exhibits.
Bonds for display of certain exhibits, Const. Ala., amd. 224.
Marengo county.
Courthouse.
Bonds for courthouse, Const. Ala., amd. 264.
Economic and industrial development promotion, Const. Ala., amd. 429.
Economic development, Const. Ala., amd. 308.
Industrial development in county, Const. Ala., amd. 468.
Officers.
Compensation of certain officers, Const. Ala., amd. 265.
Marion county.
Bond issues.
Refunding of securities by certain municipalities, Const. Ala., amd. 246.
Economic development.
Municipalities in Marion county, Const. Ala., amd. 84.
Health facilities.
Bonds, etc., for health facilities, Const. Ala., amd. 75.
Hospitals.
Bonds, etc., for hospital purposes, Const. Ala., amd. 75.
Special tax for hospital purposes, Const. Ala., amd. 69.

CONSTITUTION OF ALABAMA—Cont'd
Amendments—Cont'd
Marion county—Cont'd
Refunding of securities by certain municipalities, Const. Ala., amd. 246.
School tax.
Special district tax for Hamilton special school district, Const. Ala., amd. 329.
Special property taxes for school purposes, Const. Ala., amd. 205.
Water authority.
Creation authorized, Const. Ala., amd. 490.
Marshall county.
Annexation, Const. Ala., amd. 469.
Court costs and charges, Const. Ala., amd. 215.
Forest fire protection in, Const. Ala., amd. 439.
Motor fuel.
License tax on selling, etc., Const. Ala., amd. 66.
Officers.
Fees, etc., of officers, Const. Ala., amd. 215.
School tax.
Special property tax for public school buildings, Const. Ala., amd. 101.
Mentally ill.
Bond issues for acquisition, improvement, etc., of mental health facilities, Const. Ala., amds. 266, 340.
Military affairs.
Adjutant general.
Appointment, Const. Ala., amd. 89.
Administration by military department and adjutant general, Const. Ala., amd. 89.
General officers.
Appointment, Const. Ala., amd. 89.
Governor's staff.
Appointment, Const. Ala., amd. 89.
National guard.
Qualifications of personnel, Const. Ala., amd. 89.
Officers.
Appointment, removal, etc., Const. Ala., amd. 89.
State military forces.
Conformance with federal statutes and regulations, Const. Ala., amd. 89.
Milk.
Promotion of milk industry, Const. Ala., amd. 388.
Misdemeanors.
Grand jury not required, Const. Ala., amd. 37.

CONSTITUTION OF ALABAMA—Cont'd
Amendments—Cont'd
Mobile county.
Bingo games in, Const. Ala., amd. 440.
Bond issues, Const. Ala., amds. 29, 193, 447, 463.
Debt limit, Const. Ala., amd. 60.
Extension of debt limit, Const. Ala., amd. 100.
Change in purposes of levy and distribution of special tax, Const. Ala., amd. 301.
General obligation bonds, Const. Ala., amd. 463.
Capital improvements.
Bond issue for capital improvements, Const. Ala., amd. 301.
Debt limit, Const. Ala., amd. 60.
Extension of debt limit, Const. Ala., amd. 301.
Economic and industrial development promotion, Const. Ala., amd. 429.
Education article.
Applicability of article to Mobile county, Const. Ala., amd. 111.
Health.
Special property tax, Const. Ala., amd. 351.
Amount of tax, Const. Ala., amd. 393.
Hospitals.
Bond issues, Const. Ala., amd. 301.
Budget of public hospital board, Const. Ala., amd. 194.
Special tax for public hospital purposes, Const. Ala., amd. 301.
Insurance.
Comprehensive health insurance plan for retired county employees, Const. Ala., amd. 441.
Investment of municipal and county funds, Const. Ala., amd. 500.
Judges.
Procedure for filling vacancies in office, Const. Ala., amd. 408.
Mosquitoes.
Special property tax for control, Const. Ala., amd. 351.
Officers.
Costs, fees, salaries, etc., of certain officers, Const. Ala., amd. 28.

CONSTITUTION OF ALABAMA—Cont'd
Amendments—Cont'd
Mobile county—Cont'd
Officers—Cont'd
Pensions of former officers, Const. Ala., amd. 192.
Pension or retirement system, Const. Ala., amd. 150.
Privilege license taxes.
Levy of certain privilege license taxes by municipalities, Const. Ala., amd. 219.
Public buildings.
Bonds for certain public buildings, Const. Ala., amd. 300.
Retirement.
Comprehensive health insurance plan for retired employees, Const. Ala., amd. 441.
Roads.
Bond issues, Const. Ala., amds. 18, 152.
Amendment to amendment no. 18, Const. Ala., amd. 363.
Change in purposes of levy and distribution of special tax, Const. Ala., amd. 301.
Districts to build and maintain public roads, Const. Ala., amd. 15.
Rodents.
Special property tax for control, Const. Ala., amd. 351.
School bonds.
Bonds for public school buildings, Const. Ala., amds. 122, 151.
Change in purposes of levy and distribution of special tax, Const. Ala., amd. 301.
School lands.
Title to sixteenth section of school lands, Const. Ala., amd. 289.
School tax, Const. Ala., amd. 16.
Special property tax for school capital outlay purposes, Const. Ala., amd. 179.
Seawalls.
Districts to build and maintain seawalls, Const. Ala., amd. 15.
Sheriff.
Fees, commissions, salaries, etc., Const. Ala., amd. 47.
Special tax for public hospital purposes, Const. Ala., amd. 195.
Amendment of amendment, Const. Ala., amd. 248.

CONSTITUTION OF ALABAMA—Cont'd
Amendments—Cont'd
Mobile county—Cont'd
Welfare.
Special property tax, Const. Ala., amd. 351.
Mobile harbor.
Bonds for Theodore ship channel project, Const. Ala., amd. 286.
Development, improvement, etc., of state docks facilities, Const. Ala., amd. 338.
Mode of amending the constitution, Const. Ala., art. XVIII, §§284 to 287.
Monroe county.
Fire protection districts.
Property taxes.
Additional property tax, Const. Ala., amd. 501.
School tax.
Special school tax, Const. Ala., amd. 86.
Monroeville, municipality of.
Property tax, Const. Ala., amd. 8.
Montgomery county.
Bingo.
Operation by nonprofit organizations, Const. Ala., amd. 413.
Court costs and charges, Const. Ala., amd. 139.
Establishment of fire districts, Const. Ala., amd. 379.
Hospitals.
Special tax for hospital and public health purposes, Const. Ala., amd. 63.
Public health.
Special tax for hospital and public health purposes, Const. Ala., amd. 63.
Salaries of officers, Const. Ala., amd. 4.
Morgan county.
Abolition of office of constable, Const. Ala., amd. 368.
Ad valorem tax.
Additional tax, Const. Ala., amd. 484.
Consolidation of offices, Const. Ala., amd. 330.
Economic and industrial development promotion, Const. Ala., amd. 429.
Economic development.
Promotion of industrial, commercial and agricultural development, Const. Ala., amd. 303.
Health.
Special property tax for general health purposes, Const. Ala., amd. 311.
Hospitals.
Special tax for hospital purposes, Const. Ala., amd. 52.

CONSTITUTION OF
    ALABAMA—Cont'd
Amendments—Cont'd
Morgan county—Cont'd
Jail.
    Bonds for erection, etc.,
        of jail, Const. Ala.,
        amd. 36.
Libraries.
    Special property tax for
        library service,
        Const. Ala., amd.
        318.
Officers.
    Regulation of salaries,
        etc., of officers,
        Const. Ala., amd. 44.
Offices.
    Consolidation of offices,
        Const. Ala., amd.
        330.
School tax.
    Additional taxes for
        public school
        purposes, Const.
        Ala., amd. 106.
Sheriff's posse.
    Grant of money to.
        Authorized, Const.
        Ala., amd. 502.
Sheriff's reserve.
    County commission
        authorized to grant
        money to, Const.
        Ala., amd. 457.
Mortgage loans.
    Nonresidents making
        mortgage loans
        through licensed
        brokers, Const. Ala.,
        amd. 154.
Motor vehicles.
    Conecuh county.
        Taxation.
            Annual license taxes
                and registration
                on trucks, trailers,
                etc., Const. Ala.,
                amd. 435.
    Fees or taxes relating to
        use, etc., of vehicles
        and to fuels used for
        vehicles.
        Expenditure, Const. Ala.,
            amd. 93.
Mountain Brook,
    municipality of.
Property tax.
    Additional tax, Const.
        Ala., amds. 209, 336.
Municipal corporations.
    Actions against.
        Attorney general may be
            required to defend,
            Const. Ala., amd.
            111.
    Additional municipal
        taxes, Const. Ala.,
        amd. 56.
    Bond issues.
        Revenue bonds, Const.
            Ala., amd. 107.

CONSTITUTION OF
    ALABAMA—Cont'd
Amendments—Cont'd
Municipal corporations
    —Cont'd
Debt limit, Const. Ala.,
    amd. 268.
Certain obligations of
    municipality having
    less than 6,000
    inhabitants.
    Not indebtedness
        within meaning of
        section 225, Const.
        Ala., amd. 126.
Expenditures.
    Effective date of laws,
        Const. Ala., amd.
        491.
Loans and grants.
    Municipalities not to
        grant public money
        or lend credit to
        individuals or
        corporations, Const.
        Ala., amd. 112.
Manufacturing, industrial
    or commercial projects.
    Bonds for enlargement,
        etc., of municipally-
        owned projects,
        Const. Ala., amd.
        228.
Officers.
    Salaries.
        Suspension of
            restriction on
            diminishing,
            Const. Ala., amd.
            26A.
Population based acts.
    Amendment procedure,
        Const. Ala., amd.
        389.
    Validation of certain
        population based
        acts, Const. Ala.,
        amd. 389.
Revenue securities.
    Issuance, Const. Ala.,
        amd. 107.
Taxation.
    Tax increment districts,
        Const. Ala., amd.
        475.
Municipal courts, Const.
    Ala., amd. 328.
Muscle Shoals, municipality
    of.
School tax.
    Special property tax for
        educational
        purposes, Const.
        Ala., amd. 172.
Music hall of fame board.
    Bond issues, Const. Ala.,
        amd. 489.
National guard.
    Qualifications of personnel,
        Const. Ala., amd. 89.
Navigable waterways.
    Bond issues.
        Navigable waterway
            between Demopolis
            and Tennessee river
            and Tombigbee
            valley projects,
            Const. Ala., amd.
            355.

CONSTITUTION OF
    ALABAMA—Cont'd
Amendments—Cont'd
Notaries public.
    Abolition of office of notary
        public with power and
        jurisdiction of justice of
        the peace, Const. Ala.,
        amd. 323.
Oneonta, municipality of.
    School tax.
        Special school tax, Const.
            Ala., amd. 299.
Opelika, municipality of.
    Property tax, Const. Ala.,
        amd. 8.
    School tax.
        Special property tax for
            educational
            purposes, Const.
            Ala., amd. 147.
Opp, municipality of.
    Property tax, Const. Ala.,
        amd. 17.
Oxford, municipality of.
    Property tax, Const. Ala.,
        amd. 13.
Ozark, municipality of.
    School tax.
        Special property tax for
            educational
            purposes, Const.
            Ala., amds. 295, 462.
Pardons.
    Civil and political
        disabilities.
        Pardon not relieved
            unless specifically
            provided, Const.
            Ala., amd. 38.
    Legislature to regulate,
        Const. Ala., amd. 38.
Parks and recreation.
    Alienation of public parks,
        playgrounds, etc., by
        political subdivisions
        and public bodies,
        Const. Ala., amd. 112.
    Bond issue to acquire,
        develop, etc., state
        parks and facilities,
        Const. Ala., amd. 267.
Paroles.
    Legislature to regulate,
        Const. Ala., amd. 38.
Peanut farmers.
    Indemnification program,
        Const. Ala., amd. 383.
Peanuts.
    Promotion of peanut
        industry, Const. Ala.,
        amd. 388.
Pell City, municipality of.
    Property tax, Const. Ala.,
        amd. 8.
Perry county.
    Probate judge.
        Compensation, Const.
            Ala., amd. 485.
Phoenix, municipality of.
    Property tax, Const. Ala.,
        amd. 8.
Pickens county.
    Consolidation of offices of
        tax assessor and tax
        collector, Const. Ala.,
        amd. 366.
    Municipalities in Pickens
        county, Const. Ala.,
        amd. 302.

CONSTITUTION OF ALABAMA—Cont'd
Amendments—Cont'd
Piedmont, municipality of.
Property tax, Const. Ala., amd. 17.
Pike county.
Compensation of judge of probate, Const. Ala., amd. 421.
Disposition of charges collected by judge of probate, Const. Ala., amd. 421.
Modernization of county government, Const. Ala., amd. 503.
Truck tax, Const. Ala., amd. 458.
Pine Hill, municipality of.
Property tax, Const. Ala., amd. 8.
Pollard, municipality of.
Property tax, Const. Ala., amd. 8.
Poll tax.
Blind persons.
Exemptions from tax, Const. Ala., amd. 109.
Deaf persons.
Exemptions from tax, Const. Ala., amd. 109.
Exemptions.
Blind and deaf persons, Const. Ala., amd. 109.
Veterans, Const. Ala., amds. 7, 10, 14, 49, 90.
Requirements, Const. Ala., amds. 96, 207.
Use for support of public schools, Const. Ala., amd. 111.
Veterans.
Exemptions from tax, Const. Ala., amds. 7, 10, 14, 49, 90.
Poultry.
Promotion of poultry and poultry products, Const. Ala., amds. 214, 428.
Private enterprise.
State interest in private enterprises prohibited, Const. Ala., amd. 1.
Exceptions, Const. Ala., amds. 12, 58.
Probate courts, Const. Ala., amds. 328, 364.
Probation.
Legislature to regulate, Const. Ala., amd. 38.
Promotion of cattle industry, Const. Ala., amds. 201, 452.
Proposing amendments, Const. Ala., art. XVIII, §284; amd. 24.
Public corporations.
Bond issues, Const. Ala., amd. 108.

CONSTITUTION OF ALABAMA—Cont'd
Amendments—Cont'd
Public officers and employees.
Actions against officers.
Attorney general may be required to defend, Const. Ala., amd. 111.
Appointments and promotions in civil service, Const. Ala., amd. 88.
Salaries.
Increasing or decreasing salaries, etc., of state and county officers, Const. Ala., amd. 92.
Suspension of restriction on diminishing, Const. Ala., amd. 26A.
Randolph county.
Funding county facilities.
County facilities building fund, Const. Ala., amd. 444.
Privilege, license, etc., taxes and securities, Const. Ala., amd. 442.
Judge of probate, Const. Ala., amd. 459.
School tax.
Special property tax for educational purposes in school district No. 1, Const. Ala., amd. 156.
Reform, municipality of.
Property tax, Const. Ala., amd. 8.
Religion.
Corporations.
Exemption of religious corporations from franchise taxes, Const. Ala., amd. 27.
Roads.
Bond issues, Const. Ala., amds. 11, 21, 58, 87.
Bond issue for acquiring public roads in conjunction with United States, Const. Ala., amd. 87.
Bonds for construction, Const. Ala., amd. 11.
Construction, maintenance, etc., by state, Const. Ala., amds. 12, 58.
Districts to build and maintain public roads, Const. Ala., amd. 15.
Laws placing responsibility for county roads in state highway department, Const. Ala., amd. 142.
State not to engage in internal improvements or lend money or credit for improvements.
Exception as to public roads, Const. Ala., amd. 1.
Roanoke, municipality of.
Property tax, Const. Ala., amd. 17.

CONSTITUTION OF ALABAMA—Cont'd
Amendments—Cont'd
Russell county.
Fires and fire protection.
Establishment of fire fighting districts, Const. Ala., amd. 381.
Officers and employees.
Compensation, Const. Ala., amd. 380.
Probate court.
Costs and charges, Const. Ala., amd. 380.
School tax.
Special school tax, Const. Ala., amd. 124.
Tax anticipation bonds, Const. Ala., amd. 124.
Russellville, municipality of.
Property tax, Const. Ala., amd. 8.
St. Clair county.
Annexation, Const. Ala., amd. 460.
Courts.
Costs and charges.
Repeal of amendment, Const. Ala., amd. 422.
Economic development, Const. Ala., amd. 197.
Officers.
Compensation.
Repeal of amendment, Const. Ala., amd. 422.
School tax.
Special school tax, Const. Ala., amd. 77.
School taxes.
Additional property tax for county educational purposes, Const. Ala., amd. 202.
Levy and collection of additional tax, Const. Ala., amd. 382.
Special annual tax for schools.
Amendment to section 260, Const. Ala., amd. 111.
Special county school taxes.
Amendment to section 269, Const. Ala., amd. 111.
Special school tax amendment, Const. Ala., amd. 3.
Scottsboro, municipality of.
Property tax, Const. Ala., amd. 8.
Seawalls.
Districts to build and maintain seawalls, Const. Ala., amd. 15.
Secretary of state.
Duties, Const. Ala., amd. 111.
Fees.
Restrictions on receipt of fees, Const. Ala., amd. 111.

CONSTITUTION OF ALABAMA—Cont'd
Amendments—Cont'd

Secretary of state—Cont'd
Succession.
One additional term,
Const. Ala., amd.
282.
Term of office, Const. Ala.,
amd. 282.
Selma, municipality of.
Property tax, Const. Ala.,
amd. 8.
School tax.
Additional school tax,
Const. Ala., amd. 6.
Sheffield, municipality of.
Debt limit, Const. Ala.,
amd. 268.
Property tax, Const. Ala.,
amd. 8.
School tax.
Special property tax for
educational
purposes, Const.
Ala., amd. 171.
Shelby county.
Court costs and charges,
Const. Ala., amd. 249.
Economic and industrial
development
promotion, Const. Ala.,
amd. 429.
Local public service
districts, Const. Ala.,
amd. 370.
Officers.
Compensation, Const.
Ala., amd. 249.
Public service districts.
Local public service
districts, Const. Ala.,
amd. 343.
Sheriffs.
Election, Const. Ala., amd.
35.
Impeachment, Const. Ala.,
amd. 35.
Succession to office, Const.
Ala., amd. 35.
Term of office, Const. Ala.,
amd. 35.
Soil and water conservation
commission, Const. Ala.,
amd. 451.
Soybeans.
Promotion of soybean
industry, Const. Ala.,
amd. 315.
Amendment of
amendment, Const.
Ala., amd. 401.
Special, private or local laws,
Const. Ala., amd. 397.
State auditor.
Annual reports, Const.
Ala., amd. 111.
Duties, Const. Ala., amd.
111.
Fees.
Restrictions on receipt of
fees, Const. Ala.,
amd. 111.
Succession.
One additional term,
Const. Ala., amd.
282.
Term of office, Const. Ala.,
amd. 282.

CONSTITUTION OF ALABAMA—Cont'd
Amendments—Cont'd

State debt.
Creation after ratification
of constitution, Const.
Ala., amd. 26.
Refunding bonds for
existing indebtedness,
Const. Ala., amd. 26.
State parks.
Bond issue to acquire,
develop, etc., Const.
Ala., amd. 267.
State retirement systems.
Use of assets, Const. Ala.,
amd. 472.
State treasurer.
Duties, Const. Ala., amd.
111.
Fees.
Restrictions on receipt of
fees, Const. Ala.,
amd. 111.
Reports, Const. Ala., amd.
111.
Succession.
One additional term,
Const. Ala., amd.
282.
Term of office, Const. Ala.,
amd. 282.
Stevenson, municipality of.
Property tax, Const. Ala.,
amd. 8.
Submission of amendments
to electors, Const. Ala.,
art. XVIII, §284; amd.
24.
Sumter county.
Economic development,
Const. Ala., amd. 250.
Probate judge.
Compensation, Const.
Ala., amd. 486.
Supreme court, Const. Ala.,
amd. 328.
Appointment of clerk,
Const. Ala., amd. 271.
Rules of court, Const. Ala.,
amd. 328.
Suspension of sentence.
Legislature to regulate,
Const. Ala., amd. 38.
Swine and swine products.
Promotion of production,
distribution, research,
etc., of swine and
swine products, Const.
Ala., amds. 327, 400.
Talladega county.
Court costs and charges,
Const. Ala., amd. 85.
Economic and industrial
development
promotion, Const. Ala.,
amd. 429.
Jail.
Construction.
Fee on civil and
criminal cases for,
Const. Ala., amd.
504.
Officers.
Fees, salaries, etc.,
Const. Ala., amd. 85.
Property tax.
Levy and collection of
additional property
taxes, Const. Ala.,
amd. 98.

CONSTITUTION OF ALABAMA—Cont'd
Amendments—Cont'd

Talladega county—Cont'd
School tax.
Special school district
taxes, Const. Ala.,
amd. 310.
Special school tax, Const.
Ala., amd. 181.
Special school tax in
school district No. 1,
Const. Ala., amd.
252.
Talladega, municipality of.
Property tax, Const. Ala.,
amd. 13.
Tallapoosa county.
Hospitals.
Tax and tax anticipation
bonds, Const. Ala.,
amd. 198.
Officers.
Compensation of certain
officers, Const. Ala.,
amd. 297.
School tax.
Additional property
taxes in school
districts, Const. Ala.,
amd. 129.
Taxation.
Ad valorem tax.
Classification of taxable
property, Const.
Ala., amd. 373.
Lid bill.
Ad valorem tax.
Classification of
taxable property,
Const. Ala., amd.
373.
Property tax generally,
Const. Ala., amd. 325.
Tax assessor, tax collector
or license
commissioner.
Abolishment,
combination or
alteration of offices,
Const. Ala., amd.
411.
Thorsby, municipality of.
Property tax, Const. Ala.,
amd. 17.
Trust funds.
Creation of Alabama
Heritage Trust Fund,
Const. Ala., amd. 394.
Investment of certain trust
funds, Const. Ala.,
amd. 488.
Tuberculosis sanitoria.
Bonds for district
tuberculosis sanitoria,
Const. Ala., amd. 74.
Tuscaloosa county.
Bond issues.
Extension of debt limit,
Const. Ala., amd.
115.
Debt limit.
Extension of debt limit,
Const. Ala., amd.
115.
Economic and industrial
development
promotion, Const. Ala.,
amd. 429.

CONSTITUTION OF ALABAMA—Cont'd
Amendments—Cont'd
Tuscaloosa county—Cont'd
Fire protection or garbage and trash disposal districts, Const. Ala., amd. 358.
Officers.
Regulation of salaries, etc., of certain public officers, Const. Ala., amd. 33.
Recreation.
Special property tax for recreational purposes, Const. Ala., amd. 333.
School tax.
Special property tax for educational purposes, Const. Ala., amd. 164.
Special school tax, Const. Ala., amd. 71.
Tuscaloosa, municipality of.
Property tax, Const. Ala., amd. 13.
Tuscumbia, municipality of.
Debt limit, Const. Ala., amd. 268.
Property tax, Const. Ala., amd. 8.
School tax.
Special property tax for educational purposes, Const. Ala., amd. 170.
Tuskegee, municipality of.
Property tax, Const. Ala., amd. 8.
Uniontown, municipality of.
Economic development, Const. Ala., amd. 155.
Universities and colleges.
Issuance of revenue securities, Const. Ala., amd. 160.
University of Alabama.
Board of trustees, Const. Ala., amd. 399.
University of Alabama medical center.
Bond issue for mental hospital, Const. Ala., amd. 141.
Bonds for construction and improvement purposes, Const. Ala., amd. 119.
University of Alabama research institute.
Bonds for construction and improvement purposes, Const. Ala., amd. 157.
Vestavia Hills, municipality of.
Property tax, Const. Ala., amd. 352.
Veterans.
Exemptions from poll tax, Const. Ala., amds. 7, 10, 14, 49, 90.
Walker county.
Court costs and fees, Const. Ala., amd. 127.
Hospitals.
Tax in district two, Const. Ala., amd. 276.

CONSTITUTION OF ALABAMA—Cont'd
Amendments—Cont'd
Walker county—Cont'd
Officers.
Allowances, etc., of officers, Const. Ala., amd. 127.
Fees, salaries, etc., of certain public officers, Const. Ala., amd. 50.
Roads.
Tax.
Special road tax, Const. Ala., amd. 19.
Salaries.
License, excise, etc., taxes on salaries by municipal corporations, Const. Ala., amd. 133.
School tax.
Special school taxes, Const. Ala., amd. 204.
Wages.
License, excise, etc., taxes on wages by municipal corporations, Const. Ala., amd. 133.
Warrants.
Not to be drawn on state treasury unless money available for payment, Const. Ala., amd. 26.
Outstanding and unpaid state warrants.
Payment of interest on, Const. Ala., amd. 26.
Washington county.
Court costs and charges, Const. Ala., amd. 349.
Officers.
Compensation of certain officers, Const. Ala., amd. 349.
Port authority, Const. Ala., amd. 470.
Establishment, Const. Ala., amd. 470.
Public buildings.
Special tax and bond issues for public buildings, Const. Ala., amd. 199.
Roads and bridges.
Indebtedness to improve, Const. Ala., amd. 410.
School tax.
Additional school tax, Const. Ala., amd. 182.
Water management districts, Const. Ala., amd. 257.
Waters and watercourses.
Development of docks and other facilities along inland waterways, Const. Ala., amds. 116, 274, 288.
Navigable waterway between Demopolis and Tennessee river, Const. Ala., amd. 270.

CONSTITUTION OF ALABAMA—Cont'd
Amendments—Cont'd
Waters and watercourses —Cont'd
Navigable waterway between Montgomery and Gadsden and to the Alabama-Georgia boundary, Const. Ala., amd. 287.
Wilcox county.
Additional ad valorem tax, Const. Ala., amd. 461.
Court costs and charges, Const. Ala., amd. 434.
Probate judge.
Compensation, Const. Ala., amd. 487.
Winston county.
County revenue commissioner.
Consolidation of offices of tax assessor and tax collector, Const. Ala., amd. 423.
Court costs and charges, Const. Ala., amd. 424.
Hospitals.
Additional taxes for hospital purposes, Const. Ala., amd. 254.
Legislation as to Winston county, Const. Ala., amd. 255.
School tax.
Special tax for school purposes, Const. Ala., amd. 153.
York, municipality of.
Economic development, Const. Ala., amd. 221.
Annexation.
Acquisition of foreign territory, Const. Ala., art. IV, §90.
Appeals.
Constitutional questions, ARAP, Rule 44.
Criminal cases.
Appeal when statute under which prosecution preferred held unconstitutional, §12-22-91.
Justices of the peace.
Appeals from justices, Const. Ala., art. VI, §168.
Apportionment.
General provisions. See within this heading, "Legislative department."
Legislators, Const. Ala., art. IV, §50.
Appropriations, Const. Ala., art. IV, §§71 to 73.
Arbitration and award.
Adoption of laws to provide for arbitration between parties, Const. Ala., art. IV, §84.
Army.
Military subordinate to civil power, Const. Ala., art. I, §27.
Standing army, Const. Ala., art. I, §27.

CONSTITUTION OF ALABAMA—Cont'd

Arrest, Const. Ala., art. I, §7.
Elections.
Electors attending, going to or returning from elections, Const. Ala., art. VIII, §192.
Militia.
Immunity of members, Const. Ala., art. XV, §275.
Assault.
Assault with intent to ravish.
Exclusion of persons from courtroom, Const. Ala., art. VI, §169.
Assembly.
Right of assembly, Const. Ala., art. I, §25.
Assessments.
Rate, Const. Ala., amd. 325.
Associations.
Regulation of associations, Const. Ala., art. IV, §103.
Attorney general.
Compensation, Const. Ala., art. V, §118.
Duties, Const. Ala., art. V, §137; amd. 111.
Election.
Contested elections, Const. Ala., art. V, §115.
Generally, Const. Ala., art. V, §114.
Returns.
Opening, Const. Ala., art. V, §115.
Duties of speaker and legislature, Const. Ala., art. V, §115.
Publication, Const. Ala., art. V, §115.
Transmission to speaker of house of representatives, Const. Ala., art. V, §115.
Tie votes, Const. Ala., art. V, §115.
Time, Const. Ala., art. V, §114.
Executive department.
Member of department, Const. Ala., art. V, §112.
Fees.
Restrictions on receipt, Const. Ala., art. V, §137; amd. 111.
Impeachment, Const. Ala., art. VII, §173.
Mental unsoundness, Const. Ala., art. V, §136.
Qualifications, Const. Ala., art. V, §132.
Residency requirements, Const. Ala., art. V, §118.
Succession.
Ineligible to succeed self, Const. Ala., art. V, §116.
One additional term, Const. Ala., amd. 282.
Term of office, Const. Ala., art. V, §116; amd. 282.
Vacancy in office, Const. Ala., art. V, §136.

CONSTITUTION OF ALABAMA—Cont'd

Attorney general—Cont'd
Validity of statutes, ordinances, etc., questioned on constitutional grounds.
Notice to attorney general, §6-6-227; ARAP, Rule 44.
Auburn university.
Board of trustees, Const. Ala., art. XIV, §266; amd. 161.
Bonds for construction and improvement purposes, Const. Ala., amd. 120.
Location.
Change, Const. Ala., art. XIV, §267.
Aviation.
Construction, maintenance, etc., of airports and air navigation facilities by state, Const. Ala., amd. 58.
Bail and recognizance.
Excessive bail, Const. Ala., art. I, §16.
Right to bail, Const. Ala., art. I, §16.
Banks and financial institutions.
Applicability of article, Const. Ala., art. XIII, §255.
Bankruptcy and insolvency.
Preference of certain creditors in case of insolvency.
Repeal of section 250, Const. Ala., art. XIII, §250; amd. 5.
Bills or notes issued as money, Const. Ala., art. XIII, §249.
Redeemable in gold or silver, Const. Ala., art. XIII, §249.
Charters.
Renewal of existing charters not required, Const. Ala., amd. 51.
Duration of corporations not limited, Const. Ala., amd. 51.
Examination of banks by public officers, Const. Ala., art. XIII, §254.
General laws, Const. Ala., art. XIII, §248.
Interest.
Maximum rate, Const. Ala., art. XIII, §252.
Legislature.
Authority restricted, Const. Ala., art. XIII, §247.
Reports.
Semiannual reports, Const. Ala., art. XIII, §254.
Specie.
Basis, Const. Ala., art. XIII, §248.
Bills or notes issued as money.
Redeemable in specie, Const. Ala., art. XIII, §249.

CONSTITUTION OF ALABAMA—Cont'd

Banks and financial institutions—Cont'd
Specie—Cont'd
Payments.
Laws not to sanction suspension, Const. Ala., art. XIII, §249.
Stock and stockholders.
State and political subdivisions thereof not to be stockholders, Const. Ala., art. XIII, §253.
Termination of business, Const. Ala., art. XIII, §251.
Duration of corporations not limited, Const. Ala., amd. 51.
Bear Creek watershed area.
Development, Const. Ala., amd. 247.
Bills. See within this heading, "Legislative department."
Bingo.
Charities.
Jefferson county.
Operation by nonprofit organizations, Const. Ala., amd. 386.
Madison county.
Operation by nonprofit organizations, Const. Ala., amd. 387.
Montgomery county.
Operation by nonprofit organizations, Const. Ala., amd. 413.
Birmingham-Jefferson county civic center, Const. Ala., amds. 238, 280.
Blind persons.
Exemptions from poll tax, Const. Ala., amd. 109.
Institute for deaf and blind.
Bonds for construction and improvement purposes, Const. Ala., amd. 117.
Bond issues.
Acts relating to bonded debt of state.
Governor authorized to act thereunder, Const. Ala., art. XVII, §283.
Validation, Const. Ala., art. XVII, §283.
Highways. See within this heading, "Highways."
Hospitals. See within this heading, "Hospitals."
Mental health facilities. See within this heading, "Mentally ill."
Mobile harbor.
Bonds for Theodore ship channel project, Const. Ala., amd. 286.
Municipal corporations.
Issuance, Const. Ala., art. XII, §222; amd. 108.
Revenue bonds, Const. Ala., amd. 107.
Obligations and liabilities of corporations, etc., held or owned by state, counties or municipalities, Const. Ala., art. IV, §100.

CONSTITUTION OF ALABAMA—Cont'd

Bond issues—Cont'd

Public corporations.

Bonds and other securities issued by certain public corporations, Const. Ala., amd. 108.

Refunding bonds for existing indebtedness, Const. Ala., art. XI, §213; amd. 26.

Research institute.

Bonds for construction and improvement purposes at university of Alabama research institute, Const. Ala., amd. 157.

Special, private or local laws prohibited, Const. Ala., art. IV, §104.

University of Alabama, Const. Ala., amds. 141, 157.

Waters and watercourses.

Navigable waterway between Demopolis and Tennessee river and Tombigbee valley projects, Const. Ala., amd. 355.

Booms and bulkheads.

Districts to build and maintain seawalls, Const. Ala., amd. 15.

Boundaries.

County boundaries.

Arrangement, Const. Ala., art. II, §39.

Confirmed, Const. Ala., art. II, §38.

County site.

Removal, Const. Ala., art. II, §41.

Courthouse.

Minimum distance of county boundaries from courthouse, Const. Ala., art. II, §40.

Removal of courthouse, Const. Ala., art. II, §41.

Designation, Const. Ala., art. II, §39.

New counties, Const. Ala., art. II, §39.

Ratified, Const. Ala., art. II, §38.

Removal of courthouse or county site, Const. Ala., art. II, §41.

State boundaries.

Defined, Const. Ala., art. II, §37.

Bribery.

Corrupt solicitation.

Offense of corrupt solicitation to be defined by law, Const. Ala., art. IV, §81.

Offer, gift, etc., of money, etc., to executive or judicial officers or members of legislature to influence official acts, Const. Ala., art. IV, §80.

Solicitation, acceptance, etc., of bribes by legislators, Const. Ala., art. IV, §81.

CONSTITUTION OF ALABAMA—Cont'd

Bridges.

Bond issues, Const. Ala., amd. 21.

Alabama bridge commission.

Bonds to pay or retire Alabama bridge commission bonds, Const. Ala., amd. 42.

Bond issue for acquiring bridges in conjunction with United States, Const. Ala., amd. 87.

Construction, maintenance, etc., of bridges by state, Const. Ala., amds. 12, 58.

State not to engage in internal improvements or lend money or credit for improvements.

Exception as to bridges, Const. Ala., amd. 1.

Budgets.

Legislative budgets, Const. Ala., amd. 448.

Building and loan associations.

Exemption of federal associations from franchise taxes, Const. Ala., amd. 27.

Canals.

Canal companies, Const. Ala., art. XII, §242.

Navigable waterway between Demopolis and Tennessee river, Const. Ala., amd. 270.

Navigable waterway between Montgomery and Gadsden and to the Alabama-Georgia boundary, Const. Ala., amd. 287.

Public highways.

When deemed, Const. Ala., art. XII, §242.

Carriers.

Regulation of common carriers, Const. Ala., art. IV, §103.

Cattle industry.

Promotion, Const. Ala., amds. 201, 452.

Chancery courts.

Appointment of chancellors.

Initial appointment for newly created divisions, Const. Ala., art. VI, §159.

Attendance by chancellors.

Failure of chancellors to attend regular terms of court, Const. Ala., art. VI, §161.

Compensation of chancellors, Const. Ala., art. VI, §150.

Consolidation of courts in counties having two or more courts of record, Const. Ala., art. VI, §148.

Districts within chancery divisions, Const. Ala., art. VI, §145.

CONSTITUTION OF ALABAMA—Cont'd

Chancery courts—Cont'd

Division of state into chancery divisions, Const. Ala., art. VI, §145.

Certain counties need not be included in divisions, Const. Ala., art. VI, §147.

Minimum number of counties in chancery divisions, Const. Ala., art. VI, §147.

Dual office holding by chancellors, Const. Ala., art. VI, §150.

Election of chancellors, Const. Ala., art. VI, §152.

Initial election for newly created divisions, Const. Ala., art. VI, §159.

Establishment.

Authority to establish, Const. Ala., art. VI, §145.

Holding court for each other.

Chancellors may hold court for each other, Const. Ala., art. VI, §146.

Impeachment of chancellors, Const. Ala., art. VII, §174.

Incompetence of chancellor.

Procedure when chancellor incompetent, Const. Ala., art. VI, §160.

Jurisdiction.

Legislature may confer jurisdiction of circuit and chancery court on either court, Const. Ala., art. VI, §148.

Newly created divisions.

Initial appointment or election of chancellors, Const. Ala., art. VI, §159.

Qualifications of chancellors, Const. Ala., art. VI, §154.

Registers in chancery, Const. Ala., art. VI, §§163, 165, 166.

Residency requirements for chancellor, Const. Ala., art. VI, §145.

Terms of chancellors, Const. Ala., art. VI, §155.

Vacancies in office of chancellor, Const. Ala., art. VI, §158.

When and where held, Const. Ala., art. VI, §146.

Charities.

Appropriations to charitable institutions not under absolute control of state, Const. Ala., art. IV, §73.

Bingo.

Jefferson County.

Operation by nonprofit organizations, Const. Ala., amd. 386.

Madison County.

Operation by nonprofit organizations, Const. Ala., amd. 387.

CONSTITUTION OF ALABAMA—Cont'd

Circuit courts, Const. Ala., amd. 328.
Clerks of court, Const. Ala., amd. 328.
Election, Const. Ala., art. VI, §165.
Impeachment, Const. Ala., art. VII, §175.
Registers.
Clerk may serve as register in chancery, Const. Ala., art. VI, §165.
Term of office, Const. Ala., art. VI, §165.
Incumbents.
Terms of incumbents not abridged, Const. Ala., art. VI, §172.
Vacancies.
Filling, Const. Ala., art. VI, §165.
Consolidation of courts in counties having two or more courts of record, Const. Ala., art. VI, §148.
Division of state into circuits, Const. Ala., art. VI, §142; amd. 328.
Certain counties need not be included in circuit divisions, Const. Ala., art. VI, §147.
Minimum number of counties in circuit divisions, Const. Ala., art. VI, §147.
Judges.
Appointment.
Initial appointment for newly created circuits, Const. Ala., art. VI, §159.
Attendance.
Failure of judges to attend regular terms of court, Const. Ala., art. VI, §161.
Compensation, Const. Ala., art. VI, §150.
Dual office holding, Const. Ala., art. VI, §150.
Election, Const. Ala., art. VI, §152.
Holding court for each other, Const. Ala., art. VI, §144.
Impeachment, Const. Ala., art. VII, §174.
Incompetence.
Procedure when judge incompetent, Const. Ala., art. VI, §160.
Injunctions.
Power of circuit judges to issue writs returnable to courts of chancery, Const. Ala., art. VI, §144.
Newly created circuits.
Initial appointment or election of judges, Const. Ala., art. VI, §159.
Number of judges, Const. Ala., amd. 328.

CONSTITUTION OF ALABAMA—Cont'd

Circuit courts—Cont'd
Judges—Cont'd
Qualifications, Const. Ala., art. VI, §154.
Residency requirements, Const. Ala., art. VI, §142.
Salaries, Const. Ala., art. VI, §150.
Terms of office, Const. Ala., art. VI, §155.
Incumbents.
Terms of incumbents not abridged, Const. Ala., art. VI, §172.
Vacancies, Const. Ala., art. VI, §158.
Jurisdiction, Const. Ala., art. VI, §143; amd. 328.
Legislature may confer jurisdiction of circuit and chancery court on either court, Const. Ala., art. VI, §148.
Registers, Const. Ala., amd. 328.
Appointment, Const. Ala., art. VI, §163.
Clerk may serve as register in chancery, Const. Ala., art. VI, §165.
Compensation, Const. Ala., art. VI, §163.
Fees.
Uniformity of fees, Const. Ala., art. VI, §163.
Qualifications, Const. Ala., art. VI, §163.
Removal, Const. Ala., art. VI, §166.
Salaries, Const. Ala., art. VI, §163.
Terms of office, Const. Ala., art. VI, §163.
Incumbents.
Terms of incumbents not abridged, Const. Ala., art. VI, §172.
Salaries.
Judges, Const. Ala., art. VI, §150.
Registers, Const. Ala., art. VI, §163.
Solicitors.
Designation of circuit solicitor as district attorney, Const. Ala., amd. 226.
General provisions, Const. Ala., art. VI, §167.
Impeachment, Const. Ala., art. VII, §174.
When held, Const. Ala., art. VI, §144.
Where held, Const. Ala., art. VI, §144.
Civic centers.
Bonds for civic centers in certain counties, Const. Ala., amds. 238, 280.
Civil duty.
Exemptions from civil duty. Special, private or local laws prohibited, Const. Ala., art. IV, §104.

CONSTITUTION OF ALABAMA—Cont'd

Civil service.
Appointments and promotions, Const. Ala., amd. 88.
Clerks of court.
Circuit courts. See within this heading, "Circuit courts."
Continuation, Const. Ala., amd. 328.
Impeachment, Const. Ala., art. VII, §175.
Selection of clerks of inferior courts, Const. Ala., art. VI, §164; amd. 271.
Supreme court. See within this heading, "Supreme court."
Colbert county.
Form of government.
Laws changing form of government, Const. Ala., amd. 144.
Commissioner of agriculture and industries.
Compensation, Const. Ala., art. V, §118.
Duties, Const. Ala., art. V, §137; amd. 111.
Election.
Contested elections, Const. Ala., art. V, §115.
Generally, Const. Ala., art. V, §§114, 115.
Returns.
Opening, Const. Ala., art. V, §115.
Duties of speaker and legislature, Const. Ala., art. V, §115.
Publication, Const. Ala., art. V, §115.
Transmission to speaker of house, Const. Ala., art. V, §115.
Tie votes, Const. Ala., art. V, §115.
Time, Const. Ala., art. V, §114.
Fees.
Restrictions on receipt, Const. Ala., art. V, §137; amd. 111.
Impeachment, Const. Ala., art. VII, §173.
Mental soundness, Const. Ala., art. V, §136.
Qualifications, Const. Ala., art. V, §132.
Residency requirements, Const. Ala., art. V, §118.
Succession.
Ineligible to succeed self, Const. Ala., art. V, §116.
One additional term, Const. Ala., amd. 282.
Term of office, Const. Ala., art. V, §116; amd. 282.
Vacancy in office, Const. Ala., art. V, §136.
Commissions.
Issuance and execution, Const. Ala., art. V, §135.
Common carriers.
Canals, Const. Ala., art. XII, §242.
Railroads, Const. Ala., art. XII, §242.

CONSTITUTION OF ALABAMA—Cont'd

Conflicts of interest.

Disclosure of personal or private interest in bills, etc., by legislators, Const. Ala., art. IV, §82.

Purchases and supplies.

Stationery, printing, fuel, etc., Const. Ala., art. IV, §69.

Constables.

Election, Const. Ala., art. VI, §168.

Fees, Const. Ala., art. VI, §168.

Authorized, Const. Ala., amd. 328.

Increase prohibited, Const. Ala., art. IV, §104.

Impeachment, Const. Ala., art. VII, §175.

Restrictions, rights and limitations, Const. Ala., amd. 328.

Contracts.

Impairment of obligations of contracts, Const. Ala., art. I, §22; art. IV, §95.

Public contracts.

Extra compensation not to be granted contractor after service rendered or contract made, Const. Ala., art. IV, §68.

Conventions.

Amendments.

Amendments generally. See within this heading, "Amendments."

Calling of conventions, Const. Ala., art. XVIII, §§286, 287.

Coroners.

Impeachment, Const. Ala., art. VII, §175.

Corporations.

Actions.

Right to sue and be sued like natural persons, Const. Ala., art. XII, §240.

Benevolent corporations.

Exemption from franchise taxes, Const. Ala., art. XII, §229; amd. 27.

Building and loan associations.

Exemption of federal building and loan associations from franchise taxes, Const. Ala., amd. 27.

Charters.

Amendment.

General law, Const. Ala., art. XII, §229; amd. 27.

Business authorized by charter.

Restriction to, Const. Ala., art. XII, §233.

Cancellation of certain corporate charters, Const. Ala., art. XII, §230.

CONSTITUTION OF ALABAMA—Cont'd

Corporations—Cont'd

Charters—Cont'd

Forfeiture.

Remitting.

Limitation, Const. Ala., art. XII, §232.

Granting.

General law, Const. Ala., art. XII, §229; amd. 27.

Revocation.

Authority of legislature, Const. Ala., art. XII, §238.

Special, private or local laws prohibited, Const. Ala., art. IV, §104.

Defined, Const. Ala., art. XII, §241.

Doing business in state.

Foreign corporations, Const. Ala., art. XII, §232.

Mortgage loans by nonresident corporation, Const. Ala., amd. 154.

Educational corporations.

Exemption from franchise taxes, Const. Ala., art. XII, §229; amd. 27.

Eminent domain, Const. Ala., art. XII, §235.

Exemption of private corporations from operation of general laws, Const. Ala., art. IV, §108.

Foreign corporations.

Doing business in state, Const. Ala., art. XII, §232; amd. 473.

Mortgage loans by nonresident corporation, Const. Ala., amd. 154.

Venue, Const. Ala., art. XII, §232.

Franchises.

Benevolent corporations.

Exemption, Const. Ala., art. XII, §229; amd. 27.

Building and loan associations.

Exemption of federal building and loan associations, Const. Ala., amd. 27.

Educational corporations.

Exemption, Const. Ala., art. XII, §229; amd. 27.

Religious corporations.

Exemption, Const. Ala., art. XII, §229; amd. 27.

Tax to be paid, Const. Ala., art. XII, §229; amd. 27.

General law as to grant or amendment of corporate charters, Const. Ala., art. XII, §229; amd. 27.

Income tax, Const. Ala., amd. 212.

CONSTITUTION OF ALABAMA—Cont'd

Corporations—Cont'd

Investments.

Authorization of investment of trust funds in private corporations prohibited, Const. Ala., art. IV, §74.

Restrictions on investment of trust funds by executors, trustees, etc., in private corporations, Const. Ala., amd. 40.

Religious corporations.

Exemption from franchise taxes, Const. Ala., art. XII, §229; amd. 27.

Restrictions on donation or sale of state lands to private corporations, Const. Ala., art. IV, §99.

Security for dues, Const. Ala., art. XII, §236.

Special laws conferring corporate powers.

Prohibited, Const. Ala., art. XII, §229; amd. 27.

State interest in corporate enterprises prohibited, Const. Ala., art. IV, §93; amd. 1.

Exceptions, Const. Ala., amds. 12, 58.

Stock and stockholders.

Issuance of corporate stocks and bonds.

Restrictions, Const. Ala., art. XII, §234.

Liability of stockholders, Const. Ala., art. XII, §236.

Preferred stock.

Issuance, Const. Ala., art. XII, §237.

Suspension of general laws for benefit of private corporations, Const. Ala., art. IV, §108.

Telegraph and telephone companies, Const. Ala., art. XII, §239.

Corruption of blood.

Attainder of treason not to work, Const. Ala., art. I, §19.

Corrupt solicitation.

Offense of corrupt solicitation to be defined by law, Const. Ala., art. IV, §81.

Costs.

Uniformity of laws regulating court costs, Const. Ala., art. IV, §96.

Cotton.

Promotion of cotton industry, Const. Ala., amd. 388.

Counties.

Bond issues.

Public corporations, Const. Ala., amd. 108.

Boundaries. See within this heading, "Boundaries."

Civic centers.

Bonds for civic centers in certain counties, Const. Ala., amds. 238, 280.

CONSTITUTION OF ALABAMA—Cont'd
Counties—Cont'd
Courts of general jurisdiction.
Minimum standards for establishment, Const. Ala., art. VI, §139; amd. 111.
Debt.
Limitation on county indebtedness, Const. Ala., art. XII, §224; amd. 342.
Education.
Special county school taxes, Const. Ala., art. XIV, §269.
Expenditure of county funds.
Effectiveness of laws providing for, Const. Ala., amd. 474.
Hospitals.
Additional county taxes for county hospitals, Const. Ala., amd. 59.
Special county tax, Const. Ala., amd. 76.
Use for hospital care and treatment of indigent residents, Const. Ala., amd. 125.
Special tax for hospital and public health purposes in counties except Mobile, Montgomery and Jefferson, Const. Ala., amd. 72.
Loans and grants.
Counties not to grant public money or lend credit to individuals or corporations, Const. Ala., amd. 112.
Local laws. See within this heading, "Special, private or local laws."
Maintenance of poor.
Counties to provide for, Const. Ala., art. IV, §88.
Obligations and liabilities of corporations, etc., held or owned by counties, Const. Ala., art. IV, §100.
Officers and employees.
Impeachment of county officers, Const. Ala., art. VII, §175.
Increase or decrease in salary of county officers, Const. Ala., amd. 92.
Suspension of restriction on diminishing public salaries, Const. Ala., amd. 26A.
Population based acts.
Amendment, Const. Ala., amd. 389.
Validation, Const. Ala., amd. 389.
Roads.
Laws placing responsibility for county roads in state highway department, Const. Ala., amd. 142.

CONSTITUTION OF ALABAMA—Cont'd
Counties—Cont'd
Taxation.
Exemption from payment of charges payable from state treasury, Const. Ala., art. XI, §218.
Rates.
Limitation on county property tax rates, Const. Ala., art. XI, §215; amd. 208.
Special county taxes for public buildings, bridges and roads, Const. Ala., art. XI, §215; amd. 208.
Special school taxes, Const. Ala., art. XIV, §269.
Tax increment districts, Const. Ala., amd. 475.
Voting machines.
Bonds, Const. Ala., amd. 200.
County seats.
Changing or locating.
Special, private or local laws prohibited, Const. Ala., art. IV, §104.
County solicitors.
Appointment or election, Const. Ala., art. VI, §167.
Court of civil appeals, Const. Ala., amd. 328.
Judges, Const. Ala., amd. 328.
Compensation, Const. Ala., art. VI, §150.
Dual office holding, Const. Ala., art. VI, §150.
Impeachment, Const. Ala., art. VII, §174.
Qualifications, Const. Ala., art. VI, §154.
Salaries, Const. Ala., art. VI, §150.
Jurisdiction, Const. Ala., amd. 328.
Salaries.
Judges, Const. Ala., art. VI, §150.
Court of criminal appeals, Const. Ala., amd. 328.
Judges, Const. Ala., amd. 328.
Compensation, Const. Ala., art. VI, §150.
Dual office holding, Const. Ala., art. VI, §150.
Impeachment, Const. Ala., art. VII, §174.
Qualifications, Const. Ala., art. VI, §154.
Salaries, Const. Ala., art. VI, §150.
Jurisdiction, Const. Ala., amd. 328.
Salaries.
Judges, Const. Ala., art. VI, §150.
Court of the judiciary, Const. Ala., amd. 328.

CONSTITUTION OF ALABAMA—Cont'd
Courts.
Abolished courts.
Abolishing branch courthouse or division or branch of court of record, Const. Ala., amd. 81.
Authority of legislature to abolish courts when function conferred upon some other court, Const. Ala., art. VI, §171.
Administration of courts, Const. Ala., amd. 328.
Chancery courts. See within this heading, "Chancery courts."
Circuit courts. See within this heading, "Circuit courts."
Continuation of courts, Const. Ala., amd. 328.
Court of civil appeals. See within this heading, "Court of civil appeals."
Court of criminal appeals. See within this heading, "Court of criminal appeals."
Courts to be open, Const. Ala., art. I, §13.
District courts. See within this heading, "District courts."
Establishment.
Establishing branch courthouse or division or branch of court of record, Const. Ala., amd. 81.
Inferior courts.
Judges.
Election or appointment, Const. Ala., art. VI, §153.
Judicial department. See within this heading, "Judicial department."
Probate courts. See within this heading, "Probate courts."
Revenue, Const. Ala., amd. 328.
Supreme court. See within this heading, "Supreme court."
Criminal law and procedure.
Accusation, Const. Ala., art. I, §7.
Arrest, Const. Ala., art. I, §7.
Change of venue, Const. Ala., art. I, §6.
Cruel and unusual punishment, Const. Ala., art. I, §15.
Detention, Const. Ala., art. I, §7.
Double jeopardy, Const. Ala., art. I, §9.
Due process of law, Const. Ala., art. I, §6.
Ex post facto laws.
Punishment limited to laws established prior to offense, Const. Ala., art. I, §7.

CONSTITUTION OF ALABAMA—Cont'd
Criminal law and procedure —Cont'd
Fines.
Excessive fines, Const. Ala., art. I, §15.
Fixing punishment of crime. Special, private or local laws prohibited, Const. Ala., art. IV, §104.
Grand jury.
Not required in misdemeanor cases, Const. Ala., art. I, §8; amd. 37.
Informations.
Proceeding against person by information, Const. Ala., art. I, §8; amd. 37.
Jury.
Discharge of juries from cases, Const. Ala., art. I, §9.
Right to trial by jury, Const. Ala., art. I, §11.
Public trial, Const. Ala., art. I, §6.
Rights of persons in criminal prosecutions generally, Const. Ala., art. I, §6.
Self-incrimination, Const. Ala., art. I, §6.
Cruel and unusual punishment, Const. Ala., art. I, §15.
Daniel "Chappie" James Aerospace Memorial.
Indebtedness for.
Macon county, Const. Ala., amd. 437.
Tuskegee, municipality of, Const. Ala., amd. 438.
Deaf persons.
Exemptions from poll tax, Const. Ala., amd. 109.
Institute for deaf and blind.
Bonds for construction and improvement purposes, Const. Ala., amd. 117.
Debts.
Imprisonment for debts, Const. Ala., art. I, §20.
Decedents' estates.
Establishing rules of descent or distribution.
Special, private or local laws prohibited, Const. Ala., art. IV, §104.
Declaration of government, Const. Ala., art. I, §35.
Construction of declaration of rights, Const. Ala., art. I, §36.
Declaration of rights, Const. Ala., art. I, §§1 to 36.
Actions.
Right to prosecute civil cause, Const. Ala., art. I, §10.
Aliens.
Property rights of aliens, Const. Ala., art. I, §34.
Assembly, Const. Ala., art. I, §25.
Bail and recognizance, Const. Ala., art. I, §16.

CONSTITUTION OF ALABAMA—Cont'd
Declaration of rights—Cont'd
Contracts.
Impairment of obligations of contracts, Const. Ala., art. I, §22.
Courts to be open, Const. Ala., art. I, §13.
Criminal law and procedure.
Accusation, arrest and detention, Const. Ala., art. I, §7.
Punishment limited to laws established prior to offense, Const. Ala., art. I, §7.
Rights of persons in criminal prosecutions, Const. Ala., art. I, §6.
Cruel or unusual punishment, Const. Ala., art. I, §15.
Debts.
Imprisonment for debts, Const. Ala., art. I, §20.
Double jeopardy, Const. Ala., art. I, §9.
Due process of law, Const. Ala., art. I, §6.
Emigration, Const. Ala., art. I, §30.
Eminent domain, Const. Ala., art. I, §23.
Equality, Const. Ala., art. I, §1.
Excessive fines, Const. Ala., art. I, §15.
Exile, Const. Ala., art. I, §30.
Ex post facto laws, Const. Ala., art. I, §22.
Punishment limited to laws established prior to offense, Const. Ala., art. I, §7.
Grand jury.
Not required in misdemeanor cases, Const. Ala., art. I, §8; amd. 37.
Habeas corpus.
Suspension of habeas corpus, Const. Ala., art. I, §17.
Hereditary distinctions prohibited, Const. Ala., art. I, §29.
Immigration, Const. Ala., art. I, §30.
Immunities.
Irrevocable or exclusive grants of immunities, Const. Ala., art. I, §22.
Impairment of obligations of contracts, Const. Ala., art. I, §22.
Impartiality of justice, Const. Ala., art. I, §13.
Informations.
Proceeding against person by information, Const. Ala., art. I, §8; amd. 37.
Involuntary servitude, Const. Ala., art. I, §32.
Jury.
Discharge of juries from cases, Const. Ala., art. I, §9.
Right to trial by jury, Const. Ala., art. I, §11.

CONSTITUTION OF ALABAMA—Cont'd
Declaration of rights—Cont'd
Libel.
Truth as defense in prosecutions for libel, Const. Ala., art. I, §12.
Military subordinate to civil power, Const. Ala., art. I, §27.
Navigable waters declared free public highways, Const. Ala., art. I, §24.
People source of power, Const. Ala., art. I, §2.
Political power inherent in people, Const. Ala., art. I, §2.
Press.
Freedom of press, Const. Ala., art. I, §4.
Privileges.
Irrevocable or exclusive grants of special privileges, Const. Ala., art. I, §22.
Public officers.
Truth of defense in prosecutions for publication of papers investigating official conduct, Const. Ala., art. I, §12.
Religious freedom, Const. Ala., art. I, §3.
Remedies for all injuries, Const. Ala., art. I, §13.
Residence not forfeited by temporary absence from state, Const. Ala., art. I, §31.
Rights of men, Const. Ala., art. I, §1.
Searches and seizures.
Unreasonable search and seizure, Const. Ala., art. I, §5.
Self-incrimination, Const. Ala., art. I, §6.
Shores.
Taxes, tolls, etc., for use of shores, Const. Ala., art. I, §24.
Slavery prohibited, Const. Ala., art. I, §32.
Sovereign immunity of state, Const. Ala., art. I, §14.
Speech.
Freedom of speech, Const. Ala., art. I, §4.
Standing army, Const. Ala., art. I, §27.
Suffrage.
Protection of suffrage, Const. Ala., art. I, §33.
Suspension of laws, Const. Ala., art. I, §21.
Titles of nobility prohibited, Const. Ala., art. I, §29.
Treason against the state, Const. Ala., art. I, §18.
Bills of attainder of treason by legislature prohibited, Const. Ala., art. I, §19.
Conviction not to work corruption of blood or forfeiture of estate, Const. Ala., art. I, §19.

CONSTITUTION OF ALABAMA—Cont'd

Declaration of rights—Cont'd

Trial.

Right to speedy, public trial, Const. Ala., art. I, §6.

Venue.

Change of venue, Const. Ala., art. I, §6.

Warrants.

Search warrants.

Conditions for issuance, Const. Ala., art. I, §5.

Wharves.

Taxes, tolls, etc., for use of wharves, Const. Ala., art. I, §24.

Deeds.

Invalid deed.

Giving effect to invalid deed.

Special, private or local laws prohibited, Const. Ala., art. IV, §104.

Defenses.

Removal of defense to suit after commencement of suit, Const. Ala., art. IV, §95.

Descent and distribution.

Establishing rules of descent or distribution.

Special, private or local laws prohibited, Const. Ala., art. IV, §104.

District attorneys, Const. Ala., amd. 328.

Continuation, Const. Ala., amd. 328.

Designation of circuit solicitor as district attorney, Const. Ala., amd. 226.

District courts, Const. Ala., amd. 328.

Judges.

Appointment, Const. Ala., art. VI, §153.

Compensation, Const. Ala., art. VI, §150.

Dual office holding, Const. Ala., art. VI, §150.

Election, Const. Ala., art. VI, §152.

Impeachment, Const. Ala., art. VII, §175.

Incompetence.

Procedure when judge incompetent, Const. Ala., art. VI, §160.

Number of judges, Const. Ala., amd. 328.

Qualifications, Const. Ala., art. VI, §154.

Salaries, Const. Ala., art. VI, §150.

Jurisdiction, Const. Ala., amd. 328.

Salaries.

Judges, Const. Ala., art. VI, §150.

Divorce and alimony.

Cohabitation or remarriage of spouse.

Termination of alimony, Const. Ala., amd. 390.

CONSTITUTION OF ALABAMA—Cont'd

Divorce and alimony—Cont'd

Special, private or local laws prohibited, Const. Ala., art. IV, §104.

Docks.

Bonds for state docks facilities, Const. Ala., amds. 213, 222, 273.

Conveyance of state docks property to local authorities, Const. Ala., amds. 443, 454.

Double jeopardy, Const. Ala., art. I, §9.

Drains and drainage.

Districts.

Establishment and maintenance, Const. Ala., amds. 15, 22, 257.

Dueling.

Suppression of dueling, Const. Ala., art. IV, §86.

Due process of law, Const. Ala., art. I, §6.

Economic and industrial development.

Promotion in certain counties and municipalities, Const. Ala., amd. 429.

Education.

Alabama girls industrial school.

Location.

Change, Const. Ala., art. XIV, §267.

Alabama schools for the deaf and blind.

Location.

Change, Const. Ala., art. XIV, §267.

Appropriations to educational institutions not under absolute control of state, Const. Ala., art. IV, §73.

Auburn university. See within this heading, "Auburn university."

Census.

School census, Const. Ala., art. XIV, §268.

Denominational schools.

School funds not to be used for support, Const. Ala., art. XIV, §263.

Election of certain schools for attendance by parents of minors, Const. Ala., amd. 111.

Escheats.

Application of property to furtherance of education, Const. Ala., amd. 111.

Application of property to maintenance of public schools, Const. Ala., art. XIV, §258.

Establishment and operation of schools.

Authority of legislature to provide for or authorize.

Establishment and operation of schools by persons, municipalities, etc., Const. Ala., amd. 111.

CONSTITUTION OF ALABAMA—Cont'd

Education—Cont'd

Franchise taxes.

Exemption of educational corporations, Const. Ala., art. XII, §229; amd. 27.

Funds.

Income.

Certain income to be applied to support and maintenance of public schools, Const. Ala., art. XIV, §260.

Grant, donation, sale, etc., of funds and property for educational purposes, Const. Ala., amd. 111.

Legislature.

Duty to establish and maintain public school system, Const. Ala., art. XIV, §256.

Mobile county.

Applicability of article, Const. Ala., art. XIV, §270.

Amendment to section 270, Const. Ala., amd. 111.

Policy of state, Const. Ala., amd. 111.

Property.

Donation or appropriation for educational purposes.

Application to furtherance of education, Const. Ala., amd. 111.

Application to maintenance of public schools, Const. Ala., art. XIV, §258.

Sale.

Disposition of income therefrom, Const. Ala., art. XIV, §257.

Principal to be preserved, Const. Ala., art. XIV, §257.

Public school funds.

Apportionment, Const. Ala., art. XIV, §256.

Sectarian or denominational schools.

Funds not to be used for support, Const. Ala., art. XIV, §263.

Teachers' salaries.

Percentage of school funds, Const. Ala., art. XIV, §261.

School boards.

State, county and city school boards.

Authority of legislature to constitute members as judicial officers, Const. Ala., amd. 111.

School census, Const. Ala., art. XIV, §268.

Sectarian schools.

School funds not to be used for support, Const. Ala., art. XIV, §263.

CONSTITUTION OF
ALABAMA—Cont'd
Education—Cont'd
Segregation, Const. Ala., art.
 XIV, §256; amd. 111.
Separate school districts.
 Special, private or local
 laws establishing
 prohibited, Const. Ala.,
 art. IV, §104.
State board of education.
 Election of members,
 Const. Ala., amd. 284.
State superintendent of
 education.
 Appointment, Const. Ala.,
 amd. 284.
 Compensation, Const. Ala.,
 amd. 284.
 Duties, Const. Ala., art. V,
 §137; amds. 111, 284.
 Election.
 Contested elections,
 Const. Ala., art. V,
 §115.
 Generally, Const. Ala.,
 art. V, §§114, 115.
 Returns.
 Opening, Const. Ala.,
 art. V, §115.
 Publication, Const.
 Ala., art. V, §115.
 Transmission to
 speaker of house,
 Const. Ala., art. V,
 §115.
 Tie votes, Const. Ala.,
 art. V, §115.
 Time, Const. Ala., art. V,
 §114.
 Fees.
 Restrictions on receipt of
 fees, Const. Ala., art.
 V, §137; amd. 111.
 Impeachment, Const. Ala.,
 art. VII, §173.
 Mental unsoundness,
 Const. Ala., art. V,
 §136.
 Powers, Const. Ala., amd.
 284.
 Qualifications, Const. Ala.,
 art. V, §132; amd. 284.
 Residency requirements,
 Const. Ala., art. V,
 §118.
 Succession.
 Ineligible to succeed self,
 Const. Ala., art. V,
 §116.
 One additional term,
 Const. Ala., amd.
 282.
Supervision of public
 schools, Const. Ala.,
 art. XIV, §262.
Term of office, Const. Ala.,
 art. V, §116; amds.
 282, 284.
Vacancy in office, Const.
 Ala., art. V, §136.
Taxation.
 Additional property tax for
 county educational
 purposes, Const. Ala.,
 amd. 202.
 Local school tax
 amendments. See
 within this heading,
 "Amendments."

CONSTITUTION OF
ALABAMA—Cont'd
Education—Cont'd
Taxation—Cont'd
 Poll taxes.
 Use for support of public
 schools, Const. Ala.,
 art. XIV, §259.
 Amendment to section
 259, Const. Ala.,
 amd. 111.
 Special annual tax for
 schools, Const. Ala.,
 art. XIV, §260.
 Amendment to section
 260, Const. Ala.,
 amd. 111.
 Special county school
 taxes, Const. Ala., art.
 XIV, §269.
 Additional property tax
 for county
 educational
 purposes, Const.
 Ala., amd. 202.
 Amendment to section
 269, Const. Ala.,
 amd. 111.
 Special district school tax.
 Levy and collection of
 additional tax,
 Const. Ala., amd.
 382.
 Special school tax
 amendment, Const.
 Ala., amd. 3.
 Teachers.
 Salaries.
 Percentage of school
 funds, Const. Ala.,
 art. XIV, §261.
 University of Alabama. See
 within this heading,
 "University of Alabama."
Elections.
Alcoholic beverages.
 Protection against evils of
 intoxicating liquors at
 elections, Const. Ala.,
 art. VIII, §191.
Amendments to constitution,
 Const. Ala., amd. 284.
Ballot for constitutional
 amendment, §17-8-22;
 Const. Ala., art. XVIII,
 §285.
Costs, §17-17-5.
 Proclamation of result,
 §17-17-4.
 State comptroller.
 Duty to ascertain
 expenses and file
 same, §17-17-6.
Counting votes, §17-17-1.
 Returns, §17-17-3.
Majority vote required,
 Const. Ala., art. XVIII,
 §285.
Reimbursing counties for
 expenses of certain
 elections.
 Constitutional
 amendments
 affecting state as a
 whole, §17-21-5.
 Constitutional
 amendments in
 general, §17-21-4.

CONSTITUTION OF
ALABAMA—Cont'd
Elections—Cont'd
Amendments to constitution
 —Cont'd
 Results.
 Proclamation of result.
 Expense of publication
 of proclamation,
 §17-17-4.
 Returns, §17-17-1.
 Counting returns,
 §17-17-3.
 Making returns to
 secretary of state,
 §17-17-2.
Applicability of article as to
 elections held after 1902
 general election, Const.
 Ala., art. VIII, §184.
Arrest.
 Electors attending, going
 to or returning from
 elections, Const. Ala.,
 art. VIII, §192.
Attorney general, Const.
 Ala., art. V, §§114, 115.
Challenges.
 Oaths, Const. Ala., art.
 VIII, §185.
Commissioner of agricultural
 and industries, Const.
 Ala., art. V, §§114, 115.
Contests.
 Trial.
 Testimony may be
 required of any
 person other than
 defendant, Const.
 Ala., art. VIII, §189.
Conventions.
 Qualifications to
 participate in party
 conventions, Const.
 Ala., art. VIII, §183.
Convicts.
 Disqualification from
 registration and
 voting, Const. Ala.,
 art. VIII, §182.
Criminal law and procedure.
 Criminal prosecutions
 under election laws,
 Const. Ala., art. VIII,
 §189.
 Disqualification from
 registration and
 voting.
 Convicted persons,
 Const. Ala., art.
 VIII, §182.
 Immunity from prosecution
 due to testimony
 given, Const. Ala., art.
 VIII, §189.
Disqualification from
 registration and voting.
 Certain persons
 disqualified, Const.
 Ala., art. VIII, §182.
Governor, Const. Ala., art. V,
 §§114, 115.
Investigations.
 Proceedings to investigate
 elections under
 election laws, Const.
 Ala., art. VIII, §189.
Legislature. See within this
 heading, "Legislative
 department."

CONSTITUTION OF ALABAMA—Cont'd
Elections—Cont'd
Lieutenant governor, Const.
Ala., art. V, §§114, 115.
Mentally ill.
Disqualification from
registering and voting,
Const. Ala., art. VIII,
§182.
Political parties.
Qualifications as elector
required to participate
in political party
action, Const. Ala., art.
VIII, §183.
Poll tax.
Amount, Const. Ala., art.
VIII, §194.
Collection.
Returns of collections to
be separate from
other collections,
Const. Ala., art.
VIII, §194.
Delinquency, Const. Ala.,
art. VIII, §194.
Education.
Use to support public
schools, Const. Ala.,
art. XIV, §259.
Amendment to section
259, Const. Ala.,
amd. 111.
Exemptions from tax.
Blind and deaf persons,
Const. Ala., amd.
109.
Veterans, Const. Ala.,
amds. 7, 10, 14, 49,
90.
Influencing votes.
Advance of money for
payment in order to
influence vote,
Const. Ala., art.
VIII, §195.
Maximum age for
payment, Const. Ala.,
art. VIII, §194.
Payment of tax of another,
Const. Ala., art. VIII,
§195.
Requirements, Const. Ala.,
art. VIII, §178; amds.
96, 207.
When due and payable,
Const. Ala., art. VIII,
§194.
Primary elections.
Legislature.
Duty of legislature to
pass laws regulating
primary elections,
Const. Ala., art.
VIII, §190; amd. 41.
Voters.
Qualifications of voters,
Const. Ala., art.
VIII, §183.
Protection of suffrage, Const.
Ala., art. I, §33.
Registrars.
List of names registered by
precincts, districts, etc.
County board to furnish
to judges of probate
by February 1, 1903,
Const. Ala., art.
VIII, §187.

CONSTITUTION OF ALABAMA—Cont'd
Elections—Cont'd
Registration, Const. Ala.,
amd. 223.
Certificate of registration.
Change of residence.
Certificate to be
furnished elector
when place of
residence changed,
Const. Ala., art.
VIII, §187.
Disqualification, Const.
Ala., art. VIII, §182.
Information to be furnished
prior to registration,
Const. Ala., art. VIII,
§188.
Legislature to provide for
registration procedure
after January 1, 1903,
Const. Ala., art. VIII,
§186.
Lists of qualified voters,
Const. Ala., art. VIII,
§187.
Purging of registration
lists.
Duty of legislature to
pass laws
regulating, Const.
Ala., art. VIII,
§190; amd. 41.
Mail.
Persons entitled to
register by mail,
Const. Ala., amds.
285, 322.
Persons registered under
1901 constitution not
required to reregister,
Const. Ala., amd. 91.
Procedure for registration
prior to January 1,
1903, Const. Ala., art.
VIII, §186.
Qualifications for
registration, Const.
Ala., art. VIII, §§180,
181; amd. 91.
Persons qualified after
January 1, 1903,
Const. Ala., amd. 55.
Requirements, Const. Ala.,
art. VIII, §178; amd.
96.
Residence.
Certain information to
be furnished prior to
registration, Const.
Ala., art. VIII, §188.
Change of residence.
Certificate of
registration to be
furnished when
place of residence
changed, Const.
Ala., art. VIII,
§187.
Term for which
registration valid,
Const. Ala., art. VIII,
§187.
Reimbursing counties for
expenses of certain
elections.
Constitutional
amendments affecting
state as a whole,
§17-21-5.

CONSTITUTION OF ALABAMA—Cont'd
Elections—Cont'd
Reimbursing counties for
expenses of certain
elections—Cont'd
Constitutional
amendments in
general, §17-21-4.
Results.
Proclamation of results,
§17-17-3; Const. Ala.,
art. XVIII, §284; amd.
284.
Returns.
Secretary of state.
Returns of elections for
certain officials to be
made to secretary of
state, Const. Ala.,
art. VIII, §193.
Secretary of state, Const.
Ala., art. V, §§114, 115.
Severability of article, Const.
Ala., art. VIII, §196.
Special, private or local laws
prohibited, Const. Ala.,
art. IV, §104.
State auditor, Const. Ala.,
art. V, §§114, 115.
State treasurer, Const. Ala.,
art. V, §§114, 115.
Superintendent of education,
Const. Ala., art. V,
§§114, 115.
Voters.
Qualifications of voters.
Generally, Const. Ala.,
art. VIII, §§177, 178;
amds. 96, 223.
Primary elections, Const.
Ala., art. VIII, §183.
Voting.
Method of voting, Const.
Ala., art. VIII, §179.
Voting machines.
Bond issues, Const. Ala.,
amd. 200.
Provision for use of voting
machines, Const. Ala.,
amd. 41.
Elk river development agency.
Authorization, Const. Ala.,
amd. 243.
Emigration, Const. Ala., art. I,
§30.
Eminent domain, Const. Ala.,
art. I, §23.
Municipal and other
corporations.
Taking of property for
public use, Const. Ala.,
art. XII, §235.
Escheats.
Education.
Application of property to
furtherance of
education, Const. Ala.,
amd. 111.
Application of property to
maintenance of public
schools, Const. Ala.,
art. XIV, §258.
Estate and inheritance tax,
Const. Ala., amd. 23.
Repeal of section 219, Const.
Ala., amd. 23.

CONSTITUTION OF ALABAMA—Cont'd

Executions.

Exemption of personal property of value of one thousand dollars, Const. Ala., art. X, §204.

Rules and regulations to ascertain value of property exempted from sale under legal process, Const. Ala., art. IV, §92.

Executive department.

Attorney general.

Member of department, Const. Ala., art. V, §112.

Commissioner of agriculture and industries.

Member of department, Const. Ala., art. V, §112.

Composition, Const. Ala., art. V, §112.

Education.

Superintendent of education.

Member of department, Const. Ala., art. V, §112.

Established, Const. Ala., art. III, §42.

Governor.

Member of department, Const. Ala., art. V, §112.

Lieutenant governor.

Member of department, Const. Ala., art. V, §112.

Officers.

Enumeration, Const. Ala., art. V, §112.

Reports.

Governor may require from officers of department, Const. Ala., art. V, §121.

Secretary of state.

Member of department, Const. Ala., art. V, §112.

Sheriffs.

Members of department, Const. Ala., art. V, §112.

State auditor.

Member of department, Const. Ala., art. V, §112.

State treasurer.

Member of department, Const. Ala., art. V, §112.

Executors and administrators.

Probate courts.

Power to grant letters of administration, Const. Ala., amd. 364.

Exemptions.

Generally, Const. Ala., art. X.

Individuals or private corporations, Const. Ala., art. IV, §108.

Special, private or local laws prohibited, Const. Ala., art. IV, §104.

Waiver of right of exemption, Const. Ala., art. X, §210.

CONSTITUTION OF ALABAMA—Cont'd

Exemptions from levy and sale under process.

Personal property of value of one thousand dollars, Const. Ala., art. X, §204.

Rules and regulations to ascertain value of property exempted from sale under legal process, Const. Ala., art. IV, §92.

Special, private or local laws prohibited, Const. Ala., art. IV, §104.

Waiver of right of exemption, Const. Ala., art. X, §210.

Exemptions from taxation, Const. Ala., art. IV, §91.

Exile, Const. Ala., art. I, §30.

Ex post facto laws, Const. Ala., art. I, §22.

Prohibited, Const. Ala., art. I, §7.

Punishment limited to laws established prior to offense, Const. Ala., art. I, §7.

Fees.

Constables, Const. Ala., art. VI, §168.

Justices of the peace, Const. Ala., art. VI, §168.

Talladega county.

Jail.

Construction.

Fee on civil and criminal cases for, Const. Ala., amd. 504.

Felonies.

Pardons, Const. Ala., art. V, §124.

Fiduciaries.

Authorization of investment in private corporations prohibited, Const. Ala., art. IV, §74.

Restrictions on investment of trust funds by fiduciaries in private corporations, Const. Ala., amd. 40.

Fires and fire prevention.

Clarke county.

Fire districts, Const. Ala., amd. 464.

Jackson county.

Fire districts and fire prevention services, Const. Ala., amd. 436.

Lee county.

Fire fighting districts and protection, Const. Ala., amd. 392.

Financial charges or assessments on property within, Const. Ala., amd. 498.

Marshall county.

Forest fire protection in, Const. Ala., amd. 439.

Monroe county.

Fire protection districts.

Property taxes.

Additional property tax, Const. Ala., amd. 501.

Fish and game.

Fund, Const. Ala., amd. 272.

CONSTITUTION OF ALABAMA—Cont'd

Floods.

Flood control projects on tributary streams of Tombigbee river, Const. Ala., amd. 270.

Foreign corporations.

Doing business in state, Const. Ala., art. XII, §232; amd. 473.

Foreign territory.

Acquisition, Const. Ala., art. IV, §90.

Franchises.

Corporations.

Exemptions from franchise taxes, Const. Ala., art. XII, §229; amd. 27.

Franchise taxes to be paid, Const. Ala., art. XII, §229; amd. 27.

Public utilities.

Maximum term of franchises in cities and towns having population of six thousand or more, Const. Ala., art. XII, §228.

Gasoline.

Tax.

Expenditure of taxes, Const. Ala., amd. 93.

General bills of local application.

Classification of laws, Const. Ala., amd. 375.

General law, local law and special law defined, Const. Ala., amd. 397.

Population based acts.

Validation, Const. Ala., amd. 389.

Gift enterprises.

Prohibited, Const. Ala., art. IV, §65.

Governor.

Absence from state.

Procedure when governor or successor absent from state, Const. Ala., art. V, §127.

Bond issues.

Governor authorized to act under certain acts relating to bonded debt of state, Const. Ala., art. XVII, §283.

Compensation, Const. Ala., art. V, §118.

Acting governor, Const. Ala., art. V, §129.

Increase in salary at session of legislature following ratification of constitution, Const. Ala., art. V, §119.

Death sentence.

Authority to grant reprieves and commutations to persons under sentence of death, Const. Ala., amd. 38.

Duties.

Faithfully execute laws, Const. Ala., art. V, §120.

CONSTITUTION OF
    ALABAMA—Cont'd
Governor—Cont'd
  Election.
    Contested elections, Const.
      Ala., art. V, §115.
    Generally, Const. Ala., art.
      V, §§114, 115.
    Returns.
      Opening, Const. Ala.,
        art. V, §115.
      Publication, Const. Ala.,
        art. V, §115.
      Transmission to speaker
        of house, Const. Ala.,
        art. V, §115.
      Tie votes, Const. Ala., art.
        V, §115.
      Time, Const. Ala., art. V,
        §114.
  Executive department.
    Member of department,
      Const. Ala., art. V,
      §112.
  Fines and forfeitures.
    Authority to remit, Const.
      Ala., art. V, §124.
  Impeachment, Const. Ala.,
    art. VII, §173.
    Procedure when governor
      or successor
      impeached, Const.
      Ala., art. V, §127.
  Legislature.
    Governor authorized to
      convene on
      extraordinary
      occasions, Const. Ala.,
      art. V, §122.
  Mental illness.
    Procedure when governor
      or acting governor
      appears to be of
      unsound mind, Const.
      Ala., art. V, §128.
  Military powers, Const. Ala.,
    art. V, §131.
  Other offices.
    Holding, Const. Ala., art.
      V, §130.
    Ineligible for other state
      office or senate of
      United States during
      term or within one
      year thereafter, Const.
      Ala., art. V, §116.
  Pardons and paroles, Const.
    Ala., art. V, §124.
    Authority to grant
      reprieves and
      commutations to
      persons under sentence
      of death, Const. Ala.,
      amd. 38.
  Powers.
    Supreme executive power
      vested in governor,
      Const. Ala., art. V,
      §113.
  Proclamations.
    State matters on which
      action necessary,
      Const. Ala., art. V,
      §122.
  Qualifications, Const. Ala.,
    art. V, §117.
    Failure of governor-elect to
      qualify, Const. Ala.,
      art. V, §127.

CONSTITUTION OF
    ALABAMA—Cont'd
Governor—Cont'd
  Reports.
    Governor may require from
      officers of executive
      department and
      officers and managers
      of state institutions,
      Const. Ala., art. V,
      §121.
    Reports and information to
      be given legislature,
      Const. Ala., art. V,
      §123.
  Reprieves, Const. Ala., art.
    V, §124; amd. 38.
  Residency requirements,
    Const. Ala., art. V, §118.
  Succession, Const. Ala., art.
    V, §127.
    Ineligible to succeed self,
      Const. Ala., art. V,
      §116.
    One additional term,
      Const. Ala., amd. 282.
  Term of office, Const. Ala.,
    art. V, §116; amd. 282.
  Vacancy in office.
    Filling when offices of
      governor and
      lieutenant governor
      both vacant, Const.
      Ala., art. V, §127.
  Veto power, Const. Ala., art.
    V, §125.
    Item veto.
      Appropriation bills,
        Const. Ala., art. V,
        §126.
Grand jury.
  Misdemeanor cases.
    Grand jury not required in
      misdemeanor cases,
      Const. Ala., art. I, §8;
      amd. 37.
Grants.
  Issuance and execution,
    Const. Ala., art. V, §135.
Guardians.
  Probate courts.
    Powers to grant letters of
      guardianships, Const.
      Ala., amd. 364.
Habeas corpus.
  Supreme court.
    Power to issue writs,
      Const. Ala., art. VI,
      §140.
  Suspension of habeas corpus,
    Const. Ala., art. I, §17.
Harbors and ports.
  Construction, maintenance,
    etc., by state, Const.
    Ala., amds. 12, 58.
Health.
  Counties.
    Special tax for hospital and
      public health purposes
      in counties except
      Mobile, Montgomery
      and Jefferson, Const.
      Ala., amd. 72.
  Public hospitals and health
    facilities, Const. Ala.,
    amd. 53.
Hereditary distinctions, etc.
  Prohibited, Const. Ala., art.
    I, §29.

CONSTITUTION OF
    ALABAMA—Cont'd
Highways.
  Bond issues, Const. Ala.,
    amd. 21.
  Bond issue for acquiring in
    conjunction with
    United States, Const.
    Ala., amd. 87.
  Bonds for construction,
    Const. Ala., amd. 11.
  Chartering or licensing
    roads.
    Special, private or local
      laws prohibited, Const.
      Ala., art. IV, §104.
  Construction, maintenance,
    etc., of highways by
    state, Const. Ala., amds.
    12, 58.
  County roads.
    Laws placing responsibility
      for county roads in
      state highway
      department, Const.
      Ala., amd. 142.
  Navigable waters declared
    free public highways,
    Const. Ala., art. I, §24.
  State not to engage in
    internal improvements
    or lend money or credit
    for improvements, Const.
    Ala., art. IV, §93.
    Exception as to public
      roads, highways and
      bridges, Const. Ala.,
      amd. 1.
Homestead exemptions,
    Const. Ala., art. X, §§205,
    206, 208.
  Income tax, Const. Ala., amd.
    61.
  Laborers' liens and
    mechanics' liens not
    barred by homestead
    exemptions, Const. Ala.,
    art. X, §207.
  Waiver of right of exemption,
    Const. Ala., art. X, §210.
Hospitals.
  Bond issues.
    Bonds for state board of
      health hospitals and
      district tuberculosis
      sanitoria, Const. Ala.,
      amd. 74.
    Building construction and
      improvement at
      Alabama state
      hospitals and Partlow
      state school for mental
      deficients, Const. Ala.,
      amds. 113, 118.
    Construction and
      equipment of hospitals,
      Const. Ala., amds. 114,
      121, 158.
  County hospitals.
    Additional county taxes for
      county hospitals,
      Const. Ala., amd. 59.
  Indigent persons.
    Use of certain special
      county taxes for
      hospital care and
      treatment, Const.
      Ala., amd. 125.

CONSTITUTION OF ALABAMA—Cont'd

Hospitals—Cont'd

County hospitals—Cont'd

Special county tax, Const. Ala., amd. 76.

Use for hospital care and treatment of indigent residents, Const. Ala., amd. 125.

Special tax for hospital and public health purposes in counties except Mobile, Montgomery and Jefferson, Const. Ala., amd. 72.

Public hospitals and health facilities, Const. Ala., amd. 53.

House of representatives.

See within this heading, "Legislative department."

Housing.

Alienation of housing projects by political subdivisions and public bodies, Const. Ala., amd. 112.

Husband and wife.

Divorce and alimony.

Cohabitation or remarriage of spouse.

Termination of alimony, Const. Ala., amd. 390.

Special, private or local laws prohibited, Const. Ala., art. IV, §104.

Property of wife not liable for debts, etc., of husband, Const. Ala., art. X, §209.

Waiver of right of exemption, Const. Ala., art. X, §210.

Immigration, Const. Ala., art. I, §30.

Immunity.

Irrevocable or exclusive grants of special privileges or immunities, Const. Ala., art. I, §22.

Impartiality of justice, Const. Ala., art. I, §13.

Impeachment.

Attorney general, Const. Ala., art. VII, §173.

Chancellors, Const. Ala., art. VII, §174.

Circuit court clerks, Const. Ala., art. VII, §175.

Circuit court judges, Const. Ala., art. VII, §174.

Clerks of court, Const. Ala., art. VII, §175.

Commissioner of agriculture and industries, Const. Ala., art. VII, §173.

Constables, Const. Ala., art. VII, §175.

Coroners, Const. Ala., art. VII, §175.

County officers, Const. Ala., art. VII, §175.

Court of civil appeal judges, Const. Ala., art. VII, §174.

Court of criminal appeal judges, Const. Ala., art. VII, §174.

District court judges, Const. Ala., art. VII, §175.

CONSTITUTION OF ALABAMA—Cont'd

Impeachment—Cont'd

Governor, Const. Ala., art. VII, §173.

Justices of the peace, Const. Ala., art. VII, §175.

Lieutenant governor, Const. Ala., art. VII, §173.

Limitation on impeachment penalties, Const. Ala., art. VII, §176.

Municipal officers, Const. Ala., art. VII, §175.

Notaries public, Const. Ala., art. VII, §175.

Penalties.

Accused person liable to indictment and punishment, Const. Ala., art. VII, §176.

Limitation on impeachment penalties, Const. Ala., art. VII, §176.

Probate judges, Const. Ala., art. VII, §174.

Procedure when governor or successor impeached, Const. Ala., art. V, §127.

Reports.

False reports or failure to file reports constitutes impeachable offense, Const. Ala., art. V, §121.

Secretary of state, Const. Ala., art. VII, §173.

Sheriffs, Const. Ala., art. V, §138; art. VII, §174.

Effect, Const. Ala., art. V, §138.

Solicitors, Const. Ala., art. VII, §174.

State auditor, Const. Ala., art. VII, §173.

State treasurer, Const. Ala., art. VII, §173.

Superintendent of education, Const. Ala., art. VII, §173.

Supreme court justices, Const. Ala., art. VII, §173.

Tax collectors and assessors, Const. Ala., art. VII, §175.

Income tax, Const. Ala., amd. 25.

Corporations, Const. Ala., amd. 212.

Deductions.

Federal income tax.

Deduction from gross income when computing state income tax, Const. Ala., amd. 225.

Disposition of income tax, Const. Ala., amd. 61.

Homestead exemptions, Const. Ala., amd. 61.

Indictments.

Plea of guilty prior to indictment, Const. Ala., amd. 37.

Indigent persons.

Counties to provide for maintenance of the poor, Const. Ala., art. IV, §88.

CONSTITUTION OF ALABAMA—Cont'd

Indigent persons—Cont'd

Hospital care and treatment. Use of certain special county taxes for care and treatment, Const. Ala., amd. 125.

Informations.

Proceedings against person by information, Const. Ala., art. I, §8; amd. 37.

Injunctions.

Power of circuit judges to issue writs of injunction returnable to courts of chancery, Const. Ala., art. VI, §144.

Supreme court.

Power to issue, Const. Ala., art. VI, §140.

Inspections.

State office for inspection or measuring of merchandise, commodities, etc., prohibited, Const. Ala., art. IV, §77.

Interest.

Banks and financial institutions.

Maximum rate, Const. Ala., art. XIII, §252.

Special, private or local laws regulating rate of interest prohibited, Const. Ala., art. IV, §104.

Internal improvements.

State not to engage in or lend money or credit for same, Const. Ala., art. IV, §93; amd. 1.

Exceptions, Const. Ala., amds. 12, 58.

Investments.

Trust funds, Const. Ala., amd. 488.

Involuntary servitude, Const. Ala., art. I, §32.

Irrigation.

Development of irrigation districts, Const. Ala., amd. 227.

Judges.

Circuit courts. See within this heading, "Circuit courts."

Compensation, Const. Ala., amds. 328, 426.

Conservators of the peace, Const. Ala., art. VI, §157.

Court of civil appeals. See within this heading, "Court of civil appeals."

Court of criminal appeals. See within this heading, "Court of criminal appeals."

Disqualification, Const. Ala., amd. 328.

District courts. See within this heading, "District courts."

Election, Const. Ala., amd. 328.

Judicial department generally. See within this heading, "Judicial department."

**CONSTITUTION OF
ALABAMA**—Cont'd
Judges—Cont'd
Judicial inquiry commission,
Const. Ala., amd. 328.
Powers.
Vesting of judicial power,
Const. Ala., amd. 328.
Practice of law.
Judges of courts of record
not to practice law,
Const. Ala., art. VI,
§162.
Probate courts. See within
this heading, "Probate
courts."
Prohibited activities, Const.
Ala., amd. 328.
Qualifications, Const. Ala.,
amd. 328.
Retirement, Const. Ala.,
amd. 328.
Terms of office, Const. Ala.,
amd. 328.
Incumbents.
Terms of incumbents not
abridged, Const.
Ala., art. VI, §172.
Vacancies in office, Const.
Ala., amd. 328.
Judicial department, Const.
Ala., amd. 328.
Abolishing courts.
Authority of legislature
when function
conferred upon some
other court, Const.
Ala., art. VI, §171.
Chancery courts. See within
this heading, "Chancery
courts."
Circuit courts. See within
this heading, "Circuit
courts."
Counties.
Minimum standards for
establishment of courts
of general jurisdiction
in counties, Const.
Ala., art. VI, §139;
amd. 111.
Court of civil appeals. See
within this heading,
"Court of civil appeals."
Court of criminal appeals.
See within this heading,
"Court of criminal
appeals."
District courts. See within
this heading, "District
courts."
Established, Const. Ala., art.
III, §42.
Probate courts. See within
this heading, "Probate
courts."
School boards.
Authority of legislature to
constitute members of
school boards as
judicial officers, Const.
Ala., amd. 111.
Style of all processes, Const.
Ala., art. VI, §170.
Supreme court. See within
this heading, "Supreme
court."
Vesting of judicial power,
Const. Ala., art. VI,
§139; amds. 111, 328.

**CONSTITUTION OF
ALABAMA**—Cont'd
Judicial inquiry commission,
Const. Ala., amd. 328.
Judicial sales.
Rules and regulations to
ascertain value of
property exempted from
sale under legal process,
Const. Ala., art. IV, §92.
Jurisdiction.
Circuit courts, Const. Ala.,
art. VI, §143.
Legislature may confer
jurisdiction of circuit
and chancery court on
either court, Const.
Ala., art. VI, §148.
Justices of the peace, Const.
Ala., art. VI, §168.
Probate courts, Const. Ala.,
amds. 328, 364.
Supreme court, Const. Ala.,
art. VI, §140.
Jury.
Discharge of juries from
cases, Const. Ala., art. I,
§9.
Exemption from jury duty.
Special, private or local
laws prohibited, Const.
Ala., art. IV, §104.
Justices of supreme court.
See within this heading,
"Supreme court."
Justices of the peace.
Abolition of office, Const.
Ala., amd. 323.
Appeals from justices, Const.
Ala., art. VI, §168.
Election, Const. Ala., art. VI,
§168.
Fees, Const. Ala., art. VI,
§168.
Impeachment, Const. Ala.,
art. VII, §175.
Increasing jurisdiction and
fees of justices.
Special, private or local
laws prohibited, Const.
Ala., art. IV, §104.
Jurisdiction, Const. Ala., art.
VI, §168.
Terms of office, Const. Ala.,
art. VI, §168.
Legislative department.
Amendment of laws.
By title only, Const. Ala.,
art. IV, §45.
Amendments to constitution.
Basis of representation in
legislature not to be
changed, Const. Ala.,
art. XVIII, §284; amd.
24.
Apportionment, Const. Ala.,
art. IV, §50.
Census.
Apportionment of house
based on decennial
census of United
States, Const. Ala.,
art. IX, §198.
Duty of legislature to
apportion
representatives, Const.
Ala., art. IX, §199.
Each county entitled to at
least one
representative, Const.
Ala., art. IX, §199.

**CONSTITUTION OF
ALABAMA**—Cont'd
Legislative department
—Cont'd
Apportionment—Cont'd
Enumeration of
inhabitants.
State may provide for
enumeration for
purpose of
apportionment,
Const. Ala., art. IX,
§201.
Equality of senatorial
districts, Const. Ala.,
art. IX, §200.
Initial apportionment of
house of
representatives, Const.
Ala., art. IX, §202.
Initial apportionment of
senatorial districts,
Const. Ala., art. IX,
§203.
Ratio of senators to
representatives, Const.
Ala., art. IX, §197.
Appropriations.
Charitable or educational
institutions.
Appropriations to
institutions not
under absolute
control of state,
Const. Ala., art. IV,
§73.
General appropriation bill.
Restrictions on, Const.
Ala., art. IV, §71.
Payment of money out of
state treasury, Const.
Ala., art. IV, §72.
Restrictions on general
appropriation bill,
Const. Ala., art. IV,
§71.
Unpaid appropriations for
which money
unavailable at end of
fiscal year, Const. Ala.,
amd. 26.
Banks and banking.
Authority of legislature
restricted, Const. Ala.,
art. XIII, §247.
Bills.
Amendments to bills.
Procedure for
amendment, Const.
Ala., art. IV, §64.
Restrictions on
amendments, Const.
Ala., art. IV, §61.
Revenue bills.
Amendments by
senate, Const.
Ala., art. IV, §70.
Committees of conference.
Adoption of reports of
committees, Const.
Ala., art. IV, §64.
General appropriation bill.
Restrictions on, Const.
Ala., art. IV, §71.
Laws to be passed by bills,
Const. Ala., art. IV,
§61.

CONSTITUTION OF ALABAMA—Cont'd
Legislative department
—Cont'd
Bills—Cont'd
Presentation to governor for signature, Const. Ala., art. V, §125.
Effect of failure of governor to sign, Const. Ala., art. V, §125.
Readings.
Number of readings for bills, Const. Ala., art. IV, §63.
Reading of bills at length may be dispensed with, Const. Ala., art. IV, §66.
Referral to standing committees, Const. Ala., art. IV, §62.
Revenue bills.
Amendments to revenue bills by senate, Const. Ala., art. IV, §70.
Preparation of general revenue bill, Const. Ala., art. IV, §70.
Revenue bills to originate in house of representatives, Const. Ala., art. IV, §70.
Time limit for passage, Const. Ala., art. IV, §70.
Signature by presiding officer of each house, Const. Ala., art. IV, §66.
Veto.
Procedure for passage after veto, Const. Ala., art. V, §125.
Votes on bills.
Majority vote required for passage, Const. Ala., art. IV, §63.
Recordation, Const. Ala., art. IV, §63.
Bribery, Const. Ala., art. IV, §§79 to 81.
Budgets.
Legislative budget, Const. Ala., amd. 448.
Compensation of members of legislature, Const. Ala., art. IV, §49; amds. 39, 57.
Composition of legislature, Const. Ala., art. IV, §44.
Conflicts of interest.
Disclosure of personal or private interest in bills, etc., by legislators, Const. Ala., art. IV, §82.
Contempt.
Punishment for contempt, Const. Ala., art. IV, §53.
Not bar to indictment for same offense, Const. Ala., art. IV, §54.

CONSTITUTION OF ALABAMA—Cont'd
Legislative department
—Cont'd
Convening.
Governor authorized to convene on extraordinary occasions, Const. Ala., art. V, §122.
Corporations.
Charters.
Authority of legislature to revoke, Const. Ala., art. XII, §238.
Disorderly behavior.
Punishment for disorderly behavior, Const. Ala., art. IV, §53.
Not bar to indictment for same offense, Const. Ala., art. IV, §54.
Division of laws, Const. Ala., art. IV, §45.
Dual office holding.
Appointment of legislators to other offices during terms for which elected, Const. Ala., art. IV, §59.
Education.
Duty of legislature to establish and maintain public school system, Const. Ala., art. XIV, §256.
Election.
Duty to pass laws regulating, Const. Ala., art. VIII, §190; amd. 41.
Each house judge of election, returns and qualifications of members, Const. Ala., art. IV, §51.
Senators and representatives, Const. Ala., art. IV, §46.
Special elections to fill vacancies, Const. Ala., amd. 97.
Voting in elections by legislature, Const. Ala., art. IV, §83.
Enemy attack.
Continuity of legislature in event of enemy attack, Const. Ala., amd. 159.
Established, Const. Ala., art. III, §42.
Expulsion of members, Const. Ala., art. IV, §53.
Expulsion for corruption bar to further service in legislature, Const. Ala., art. IV, §54.
Gift enterprises.
Prohibited, Const. Ala., art. IV, §65.
House of representatives.
Adjournment.
Without consent of other house, Const. Ala., art. IV, §58.
Admittance to floor.
Restrictions on admittance, Const. Ala., art. IV, §57.
Apportionment, Const. Ala., art. IV, §50.

CONSTITUTION OF ALABAMA—Cont'd
Legislative department
—Cont'd
House of representatives —Cont'd
Change of place of sitting.
Without consent of senate, Const. Ala., art. IV, §58.
Compensation of members, Const. Ala., art. IV, §49; amds. 39, 57.
Conviction of certain crimes bar to eligibility, Const. Ala., art. IV, §60.
Doors of each house to be open, Const. Ala., art. IV, §57.
Employees.
Number, duties and compensation, Const. Ala., art. IV, §67.
Journal of proceedings, Const. Ala., art. IV, §55.
Maximum number of members, Const. Ala., art. IX, §198.
Number of members, Const. Ala., art. IV, §50.
Duty of legislature to fix, Const. Ala., art. IX, §199.
Maximum number, Const. Ala., art. IX, §198.
Officers, Const. Ala., art. IV, §51.
Compensation, Const. Ala., art. IV, §67.
Duties, Const. Ala., art. IV, §67.
Number, Const. Ala., art. IV, §67.
Qualifications of representatives, Const. Ala., art. IV, §47.
Conviction of certain crimes bar to eligibility, Const. Ala., art. IV, §60.
Each house judge of qualifications of members, Const. Ala., art. IV, §51.
Quorum, Const. Ala., art. IV, §52.
Ratio of senators to representatives, Const. Ala., art. IX, §197.
Revenue bills.
Revenue bills to originate in house of representatives, Const. Ala., art. IV, §70.
Rules of proceedings, Const. Ala., art. IV, §53.
Speaker of house.
Election, Const. Ala., art. IV, §51; amds. 39, 57.
Signature of bills, Const. Ala., art. IV, §66.
Temporary speaker, Const. Ala., art. IV, §51.

CONSTITUTION OF ALABAMA—Cont'd
Legislative department —Cont'd
House of representatives —Cont'd
Speaker of house—Cont'd
Term of office, Const. Ala., art. IV, §51.
Terms of representatives, Const. Ala., art. IV, §46.
Travel allowance of members, Const. Ala., amds. 39, 57.
Vacancies in office, Const. Ala., art. IV, §46.
Immunity of legislators, Const. Ala., art. IV, §56.
Journal of proceedings of each house, Const. Ala., art. IV, §55.
Laws to effectuate Constitution.
Duty of legislature to enact, Const. Ala., art. XVII, §282.
Legislative budget, Const. Ala., amd. 448.
Lotteries.
Prohibited, Const. Ala., art. IV, §65.
Meetings of legislature.
Time and place of meetings, Const. Ala., art. IV, §48; amds. 39, 57.
Number of senators and representatives, Const. Ala., art. IV, §50.
Duty of legislature to fix, Const. Ala., art. IX, §§199, 200.
Oath of office, Const. Ala., art. XVI, §279.
Officers of each house, Const. Ala., art. IV, §51.
Process.
Enforcement of process, Const. Ala., art. IV, §53.
Promulgation of laws.
Periodic promulgation, Const. Ala., art. IV, §85.
Protection of members from violence, bribes, etc., Const. Ala., art. IV, §53.
Qualifications of senators and representatives, Const. Ala., art. IV, §47.
Each house judge of qualifications of members, Const. Ala., art. IV, §51.
Quorum in each house, Const. Ala., art. IV, §52.
Railroad companies.
Free passes or discount tickets to members of legislature, Const. Ala., art. XII, §244.
Regulation, Const. Ala., art. XII, §243.
Reports.
Governor to give certain reports and information, Const. Ala., art. V, §123.

CONSTITUTION OF ALABAMA—Cont'd
Legislative department —Cont'd
Restriction of laws to one subject, Const. Ala., art. IV, §45.
Revision of laws.
Periodic revision, Const. Ala., art. IV, §85.
Revival of laws.
By title only, Const. Ala., art. IV, §45.
Rules of proceedings in both houses, Const. Ala., art. IV, §53.
Senate.
Adjournment.
Without consent of other house, Const. Ala., art. IV, §58.
Admittance to floor.
Restrictions, Const. Ala., art. IV, §57.
Change of place of sitting.
Without consent of house of representatives, Const. Ala., art. IV, §58.
Compensation of members, Const. Ala., art. IV, §49; amds. 39, 57.
Conviction of certain crimes bar to eligibility, Const. Ala., art. IV, §60.
Districts.
Change in districts.
Senatorial districts not to be changed until next apportioning session, Const. Ala., art. IX, §200.
Counties.
Counties within senatorial districts to be contiguous, Const. Ala., art. IX, §200.
Division of counties between senatorial districts prohibited, Const. Ala., art. IX, §200.
Duty of legislature to divide state into senatorial districts, Const. Ala., art. IX, §200.
Equality of senatorial districts, Const. Ala., art. IX, §200.
Initial apportionment, Const. Ala., art. IX, §203.
Doors of each house to be open, Const. Ala., art. IV, §57.
Election of senators, Const. Ala., art. IV, §46.
Each house judge of election, returns and qualifications of members, Const. Ala., art. IV, §51.
Special elections to fill vacancies, Const. Ala., amd. 97.

CONSTITUTION OF ALABAMA—Cont'd
Legislative department —Cont'd
Senate—Cont'd
Employees.
Number, duties and compensation, Const. Ala., art. IV, §67.
Journal of proceedings, Const. Ala., art. IV, §55.
Lieutenant governor.
Ex officio president of senate, Const. Ala., art. V, §117.
Number of senators, Const. Ala., art. IV, §50.
Duty of legislature to fix, Const. Ala., art. IX, §200.
Officers, Const. Ala., art. IV, §51.
Compensation, Const. Ala., art. IV, §67.
Duties, Const. Ala., art. IV, §67.
Number, Const. Ala., art. IV, §67.
President pro tem.
Election, Const. Ala., art. IV, §51; amds. 39, 57.
Signature of bills, Const. Ala., art. IV, §66.
Temporary president, Const. Ala., art. IV, §51.
Term of office, Const. Ala., art. IV, §51.
Qualifications of senators, Const. Ala., art. IV, §47.
Conviction of certain crimes bar to eligibility, Const. Ala., art. IV, §60.
Each house judge of qualifications of members, Const. Ala., art. IV, §51.
Quorum, Const. Ala., art. IV, §52.
Ratio of senators to representatives, Const. Ala., art. IX, §197.
Revenue bills.
Amendments to revenue bills by senate, Const. Ala., art. IV, §70.
Rules of proceedings, Const. Ala., art. IV, §53.
Terms of senators, Const. Ala., art. IV, §46.
Travel allowance of members, Const. Ala., amds. 39, 57.
Vacancies in office, Const. Ala., art. IV, §46.
Special elections to fill, Const. Ala., amd. 97.
Sessions of legislature.
Annual sessions, Const. Ala., amd. 339.
Biennial sessions, Const. Ala., amds. 39, 57.

**CONSTITUTION OF
ALABAMA**—Cont'd
Legislative department
—Cont'd
Sessions of legislature
—Cont'd
Maximum length of
sessions, Const. Ala.,
art. IV, §48; amds. 39,
57.
Organizational sessions,
Const. Ala., amds. 39,
57.
Regular sessions, Const.
Ala., amd. 339.
Special sessions, Const.
Ala., amd. 339.
Time and place of
meetings, Const. Ala.,
art. IV, §48; amds. 39,
57.
Special, private or local laws.
See within this heading,
"Special, private or local
laws."
Special sessions, Const. Ala.,
amd. 339.
Duration, Const. Ala., art.
IV, §76.
Restrictions on legislation
at special sessions,
Const. Ala., art. IV,
§76.
Standing committees.
Referral of bills to
standing committees,
Const. Ala., art. IV,
§62.
Style of laws, Const. Ala.,
art. IV, §45.
Suspension of general laws.
For benefit of individuals
or private corporations,
Const. Ala., art. IV,
§108.
Terms of senators and
representatives, Const.
Ala., art. IV, §47.
Travel allowance of
members, Const. Ala.,
amds. 39, 57.
Vacancies in office, Const.
Ala., art. IV, §46.
Special elections to fill,
Const. Ala., amd. 97.
War.
Continuity of legislature in
event of enemy attack,
Const. Ala., amd. 159.
Legislature. See within this
heading, "Legislative
department."
Legitimation.
Special, private or local laws
prohibited, Const. Ala.,
art. IV, §104.
Libel and slander.
Truth as defense in
prosecutions for libel,
Const. Ala., art. I, §12.
Libraries.
Special property tax by
counties or
municipalities for library
purposes, Const. Ala.,
amd. 269.

**CONSTITUTION OF
ALABAMA**—Cont'd
Licenses.
Payment of state license tax
not to excuse payment of
other privilege and
license taxes, Const.
Ala., art. XII, §221.
Liens.
Laborers' liens and
mechanics' liens not
barred by homestead
exemptions, Const. Ala.,
art. X, §207.
Special, private or local laws
creating, extending or
impairing liens
prohibited, Const. Ala.,
art. IV, §104.
Lieutenant governor.
Compensation, Const. Ala.,
art. V, §118.
Election.
Contested election, Const.
Ala., art. V, §115.
Generally, Const. Ala., art.
V, §§114, 115.
Returns.
Opening, Const. Ala.,
art. V, §115.
Publication, Const. Ala.,
art. V, §115.
Transmission to speaker
of house, Const. Ala.,
art. V, §115.
Tie votes, Const. Ala., art.
V, §115.
Time, Const. Ala., art. V,
§114.
Executive department.
Member of department,
Const. Ala., art. V,
§112.
Ex officio president of senate,
Const. Ala., art. V, §117.
Impeachment, Const. Ala.,
art. VII, §173.
Qualifications, Const. Ala.,
art. V, §117.
Failure of lieutenant
governor-elect to
qualify, Const. Ala.,
art. V, §127.
Residency requirements,
Const. Ala., art. V, §118.
Succession.
Ineligible to succeed self,
Const. Ala., art. V,
§116.
One additional term,
Const. Ala., amd. 282.
Term of office, Const. Ala.,
art. V, §116; amd. 282.
Limitation of actions.
Special, private or local laws
prohibited, Const. Ala.,
art. IV, §104.
Livestock.
Establishing separate stock
districts.
Special, private or local
laws prohibited, Const.
Ala., art. IV, §104.
Promotion of cattle industry,
Const. Ala., amds. 201,
452.
Promotion of production,
research, etc., of swine
and swine products,
Const. Ala., amds. 327,
400.

**CONSTITUTION OF
ALABAMA**—Cont'd
Loans.
Mortgage loans.
Nonresidents making
mortgage loans
through licensed
brokers, Const. Ala.,
amd. 154.
Lobbying and lobbyists.
State or county officials.
Lobbying in legislature by
state or county
officials, Const. Ala.,
art. IV, §101.
Local laws. See within this
heading, "Special, private
or local laws."
Lotteries.
Prohibited, Const. Ala., art.
IV, §65.
Marengo county.
Industrial development.
Establishment of industrial
development
corporation, Const.
Ala., amd. 468.
Mechanics' liens.
Homestead exemptions.
Not barred by homestead
exemptions, Const.
Ala., art. X, §207.
Mentally ill.
Bond issues.
Bond issues for acquisition,
improvement, etc., of
mental health
facilities, Const. Ala.,
amds. 266, 340.
Building construction and
improvement purposes
at Alabama state
hospitals and Partlow
state school for mental
deficients, Const. Ala.,
amds. 113, 118.
University of Alabama
medical center.
Bond issue for mental
hospital, Const. Ala.,
amd. 141.
Elections.
Certain persons
disqualified from
registering and voting,
Const. Ala., art. VIII,
§182.
Governor.
Procedure when governor
or acting governor
appears to be of
unsound mind, Const.
Ala., art. V, §128.
Military affairs.
Adjutant general.
Administration of military
affairs, Const. Ala.,
amd. 89.
Appointment, Const. Ala.,
amd. 89.
Administration by military
department and adjutant
general, Const. Ala.,
amd. 89.
Department of defense.
Conformance with
regulations of United
States department of
defense, Const. Ala.,
amd. 89.

**CONSTITUTION OF
ALABAMA**—Cont'd
Military affairs—Cont'd
Governor.
Powers, Const. Ala., art. V,
§131.
Staff, Const. Ala., amd. 89.
Military subordinate to civil
power, Const. Ala., art. I,
§27.
Militia.
Arming.
Safe keeping of arms,
ammunition, etc.,
Const. Ala., art. XV,
§277.
Army, Const. Ala., art.
XV, §271.
Arrest.
Immunity of members,
Const. Ala., art. XV,
§275.
Compensation.
Officers and men not
entitled when not in
active service, Const.
Ala., art. XV, §278.
Composition, Const. Ala.,
art. XV, §271.
Discipline, Const. Ala., art.
XV, §271.
Enlisted personnel.
Compensation.
Not entitled to
compensation
when not in active
service, Const.
Ala., art. XV,
§278.
Governor.
Staff, Const. Ala., art.
XV, §276; amd. 89.
Officers.
Appointment, Const.
Ala., amd. 89.
Company and regimental
officers.
Election or
appointment,
Const. Ala., art.
XV, §273.
Compensation.
Not entitled to
compensation
when not in active
service, Const.
Ala., art. XV,
§278.
Discharge, Const. Ala.,
amd. 89.
General officers.
Appointment, Const.
Ala., art. XV,
§276; amd. 89.
Terms of office, Const.
Ala., art. XV,
§276.
Removal, Const. Ala.,
amd. 89.
Retirement, Const. Ala.,
amd. 89.
Suspension, Const. Ala.,
amd. 89.
Organizing, Const. Ala.,
art. XV, §271.
Records.
Safe keeping, Const.
Ala., art. XV, §277.
Staffs, Const. Ala., art.
XV, §276.

**CONSTITUTION OF
ALABAMA**—Cont'd
Military affairs—Cont'd
Militia—Cont'd
United States Army.
Conformance with
regulations
governing, Const.
Ala., art. XV, §272.
Volunteer organizations,
Const. Ala., art. XV,
§274.
National guard.
Qualifications of personnel,
Const. Ala., amd. 89.
Naval militia.
Authorized, Const. Ala.,
art. XV, §271.
Quartering of soldiers in
houses, Const. Ala., art.
I, §28.
Standing army, Const. Ala.,
art. I, §27.
State military forces.
Conformance with federal
statutes and
regulations, Const.
Ala., amd. 89.
Milk and milk products.
Promotion of industry, Const.
Ala., amd. 388.
Minors.
Relieving minors of
disabilities of nonage.
Special, private or local
laws prohibited, Const.
Ala., art. IV, §104.
Miscegenation laws, Const.
Ala., art. IV, §102.
Mobile harbor.
Bonds for Theodore ship
channel project, Const.
Ala., amd. 286.
Development, improvement,
etc., of state docks
facilities, Const. Ala.,
amd. 338.
**Mode of amending the
constitution,** Const. Ala.,
art. XVIII, §§284 to 287.
Monopolies.
Regulation of monopolies,
Const. Ala., art. IV,
§103.
**Mortgages and deeds of
trust.**
Nonresidents.
Making mortgage loans
through licensed
mortgage loan brokers,
Const. Ala., amd. 154.
Motor vehicles.
Conecuh county.
Taxation.
Annual license taxes and
registration on
trucks, trailers, etc.,
Const. Ala., amd.
435.
Fees or taxes relating to use
of vehicles and to fuels
used for vehicles.
Expenditure, Const. Ala.,
amd. 93.

**CONSTITUTION OF
ALABAMA**—Cont'd
Municipal corporations.
Allegations municipal
ordinance or franchise
unconstitutional,
§6-6-227.
Attorney general.
Entitled to be heard,
§6-6-227.
Served with copy of
proceedings,
§6-6-227.
Persons to be made parties,
§6-6-227.
Rights of persons not
parties, §6-6-227.
Assessments for public
improvements.
Limitation, Const. Ala.,
art. XII, §223.
Bond issues, Const. Ala., art.
XII, §222.
Bonds and other securities
issued by certain
public corporations,
Const. Ala., amd. 108.
Revenue bonds, Const.
Ala., amd. 107.
Charters.
Special, private or local
laws prohibited, Const.
Ala., art. IV, §104.
Conflict of laws.
Municipalities not to pass
laws in conflict with
general laws of state,
Const. Ala., art. IV,
§89.
Debt limit, Const. Ala., art.
XII, §225; amd. 268.
Certain obligations of
municipality having
less than 6,000
inhabitants.
Not indebtedness within
meaning of section
225, Const. Ala.,
amd. 126.
Exception as to Sheffield
and Tuscumbia, Const.
Ala., art. XII, §225;
amd. 268.
Limitation not applicable
to obligations or
indebtedness
exempted by
constitution or
amendments, Const.
Ala., amd. 268.
Municipal corporations
whose present
indebtedness exceeds
constitutional
limitation, Const. Ala.,
art. XII, §226.
Exception as to Sheffield
and Tuscumbia,
Const. Ala., art. XII,
§226.
Eminent domain, Const. Ala.,
art. XII, §235.
Expenditures.
Effective date of laws,
Const. Ala., amd. 491.
Incorporation.
Special, private or local
laws prohibited, Const.
Ala., art. IV, §104.

CONSTITUTION OF ALABAMA—Cont'd
Municipal corporations
—Cont'd
Libraries.
  Special property tax for library purposes, Const. Ala., amd. 269.
Loans and grants.
  Municipalities not to grant public money or lend credit to private persons or corporations, Const. Ala., art. IV, §94; amd. 112.
Local laws. See within this heading, "Special, private or local laws."
Manufacturing, industrial or commercial projects.
  Bonds for enlargement, etc., of municipally-owned projects, Const. Ala., amd. 228.
Obligations and liabilities of corporations, etc., held or owned by municipalities, Const. Ala., art. IV, §100.
Officers and employees.
  Impeachment of municipal officers, Const. Ala., art. VII, §175.
  Suspension of restriction on diminishing public salaries, Const. Ala., amd. 26A.
Population based acts.
  Amendment procedure, Const. Ala., amd. 389.
  Validation of certain population based acts, Const. Ala., amd. 389.
Property.
  Use for public utility or private enterprise purposes.
    Consent prerequisite, Const. Ala., art. XII, §220.
Public improvements.
  Limitation on assessments, Const. Ala., art. XII, §223.
Public utilities.
  Damages to abutting property owners.
    Liability, Const. Ala., art. XII, §227.
  Franchises.
    Maximum term in cities and towns having population of six thousand or more, Const. Ala., art. XII, §228.
  Revenue securities.
    Issuance, Const. Ala., amd. 107.
Taxation. See within this heading, "Taxation."
Tax increment districts, Const. Ala., amd. 475.
Municipal courts, Const. Ala., amd. 328.
Names.
Change of name.
  Special, private or local laws prohibited, Const. Ala., art. IV, §104.

CONSTITUTION OF ALABAMA—Cont'd
National guard.
Qualifications of personnel, Const. Ala., amd. 89.
Notaries public.
Abolition of office of notary public with powers and jurisdiction of justice of the peace, Const. Ala., amd. 323.
Appointment, Const. Ala., art. VI, §168.
Impeachment, Const. Ala., art. VII, §175.
Terms of office, Const. Ala., art. VI, §168.
Oath of office.
Administration, Const. Ala., art. XVI, §279.
Form, Const. Ala., art. XVI, §279.
Required, Const. Ala., art. XVI, §279.
Objective of government, Const. Ala., art. I, §35.
Orphans.
Probate courts.
  General jurisdiction of orphan's business, Const. Ala., amd. 364.
Pardons.
Authority of governor, Const. Ala., art. V, §124.
Felonies and offenses involving moral turpitude, Const. Ala., art. V, §124.
Legislature to regulate, Const. Ala., amd. 38.
Parks and recreation.
Alienation of public parks, playgrounds, etc., by political subdivisions and public bodies, Const. Ala., amd. 112.
Bond issue to acquire, develop, etc., state parks and facilities, Const. Ala., amd. 267.
Parole.
Authority of governor, Const. Ala., art. V, §124.
Board of pardons and parole, Const. Ala., art. V, §124.
Legislature to regulate, Const. Ala., amd. 38.
Partlow state school for mental deficients.
Bond issue for building construction and improvement purposes, Const. Ala., amds. 113, 118.
Partnerships.
Regulation of partnerships, Const. Ala., art. IV, §103.
Peanuts.
Promotion of peanut industry, Const. Ala., amd. 388.
Penalties.
Cruel or unusual punishment, Const. Ala., art. I, §15.
Excessive fines.
  Prohibited, Const. Ala., art. I, §15.
Impeachment, Const. Ala., art. VII, §176.

CONSTITUTION OF ALABAMA—Cont'd
Penalties—Cont'd
Remitting fines, penalties or forfeitures.
  Special, private or local laws prohibited, Const. Ala., art. IV, §104.
  Special, private or local laws fixing punishment prohibited, Const. Ala., art. IV, §104.
Poll tax. See within this heading, "Elections."
Poor persons.
Counties to provide for maintenance of the poor, Const. Ala., art. IV, §88.
Population based acts.
Classification of laws, Const. Ala., amd. 375.
Validation of certain population based acts, Const. Ala., amd. 389.
Poultry.
Promotion of poultry and poultry products, Const. Ala., amds. 214, 428.
Powers of government.
Division of powers of government, Const. Ala., art. III, §42.
Separation of powers, Const. Ala., art. III, §43.
Press.
Freedom of press, Const. Ala., art. I, §4.
Private enterprise.
State interest in private enterprises prohibited, Const. Ala., art. IV, §93; amd. 1.
  Exceptions, Const. Ala., amds. 12, 58.
Private laws. See within this heading, "Special, private or local laws."
Privileges.
Irrevocable or exclusive grants of special privileges, Const. Ala., art. I, §22.
Probate courts, Const. Ala., amds. 328, 364.
Establishment.
  Legislature may establish in each county, Const. Ala., art. VI, §149.
Judges.
  Election, Const. Ala., art. VI, §152.
  Fees, allowances, etc.
    Geneva county, Const. Ala., amd. 357.
  Impeachment, Const. Ala., art. VII, §174.
  Terms of office, Const. Ala., art. VI, §155.
  Incumbents.
    Terms of incumbents not abridged, Const. Ala., art. VI, §172.
Jurisdiction, Const. Ala., amds. 328, 364.
Powers, Const. Ala., art. VI, §149.
Probation.
Legislature to regulate, Const. Ala., amd. 38.

CONSTITUTION OF ALABAMA—Cont'd

Procedure for amending,
Const. Ala., art. XVIII, §§284 to 287.

Process.
Style of all processes, Const. Ala., art. VI, §170.

Property.
Sale of property of any individual or estate.
Special, private or local laws providing for sale prohibited, Const. Ala., art. IV, §104.

Public funds.
Annual statement of receipts and expenditures.
Publication, Const. Ala., art. IV, §72.
Payment of money out of state treasury, Const. Ala., art. IV, §72.

Public lands.
Restrictions on donation or sale of state lands to private corporations or individuals, Const. Ala., art. IV, §99.
Special, private or local laws donating lands owned or under control by state to any person or corporation prohibited, Const. Ala., art. IV, §104.

Public officers and employees.
Charges, fees, commissions and allowances.
Uniformity of laws regulating, Const. Ala., art. IV, §96.
Compensation.
Deductions from compensation for neglect of duty, Const. Ala., art. IV, §87.
Extra compensation not to be granted after service rendered, Const. Ala., art. IV, §68.
Increase or decrease in salary, Const. Ala., art. IV, §68; Const. Ala., amd. 92.
During term for which elected or appointed, Const. Ala., art. XVII, §281.
Payment of salary of deceased officer after date of death, Const. Ala., art. IV, §97.
Suspension of restriction on diminishing public salaries, Const. Ala., amd. 26A.
Conviction of certain crimes bar to eligibility for holding state office of trust or profit, Const. Ala., art. IV, §60.

CONSTITUTION OF ALABAMA—Cont'd

Public officers and employees—Cont'd

Fees.
Creating, increasing or decreasing fees.
Special, private or local laws prohibited, Const. Ala., art. IV, §104.
Restrictions on receipt of fees, Const. Ala., art. V, §137; amd. 111.
Lobbying in legislature by state or county officials, Const. Ala., art. IV, §101.
Merit system.
Appointments and promotions in civil service, Const. Ala., amd. 88.
Multiple office holding, Const. Ala., art. XVII, §280.
Restriction on appointments to office, Const. Ala., art. I, §29.
Retirement.
Payments or grants to retiring officers, Const. Ala., art. IV, §98.
Truth as defense in prosecutions for publication of papers investigating official conduct, Const. Ala., art. I, §12.

Public utilities.
Damages to abutting property owners.
Liability of public utilities in municipal corporations, Const. Ala., art. XII, §227.
Franchises.
Maximum term in cities and towns having population of six thousand or more, Const. Ala., art. XII, §228.

Purchases and supplies.
Stationery, printing, fuel, etc.
Furnishing by lowest responsible bidder, Const. Ala., art. IV, §69.

Quartering of soldiers in houses, Const. Ala., art. I, §28.

Quo warranto.
Supreme court.
Power to issue writs, Const. Ala., art. VI, §140.

Racial minorities.
Miscegenation laws, Const. Ala., art. IV, §102.

Railroads.
Acceptance of article prerequisite to benefits of future legislation, Const. Ala., art. XII, §246.
Bonuses in nature of rebates.
Prohibited, Const. Ala., art. XII, §245.

CONSTITUTION OF ALABAMA—Cont'd

Railroads—Cont'd

Free passes or discount tickets.
Giving to members of legislature or judicial officers, Const. Ala., art. XII, §244.
Grant of easements to railroad companies, Const. Ala., art. IV, §99.
Public highways.
When deemed, Const. Ala., art. XII, §242.
Railroad companies, Const. Ala., art. XII, §242.
Regulation.
Legislature, Const. Ala., art. XII, §243.
Rights.
Generally, Const. Ala., art. XII, §242.
Rates.
Deceiving or misleading public, Const. Ala., art. XII, §245.
Rebates.
Prohibited, Const. Ala., art. XII, §245.

Rape.
Trial.
Exclusion of persons from courtroom, Const. Ala., art. VI, §169.

Rebates.
Railroad companies.
Prohibited, Const. Ala., art. XII, §245.

Redress of grievances.
Right to petition for, Const. Ala., art. I, §25.

Registers in chancery, Const. Ala., art. VI, §§163, 165, 166.

Religious freedom, Const. Ala., art. I, §3.

Religious organizations.
Franchise taxes.
Exemption, Const. Ala., art. XII, §229; amd. 27.

Remedies.
Remedies for all injuries, Const. Ala., art. I, §13.
Revival of barred rights or remedies, Const. Ala., art. IV, §95.

Reports.
Banks and financial institutions.
Semiannual reports, Const. Ala., art. XIII, §254.
Failure to file.
Impeachable offense, Const. Ala., art. V, §121.
False reports.
Impeachable offense, Const. Ala., art. V, §121.
Governor.
Reports and information to be given legislature, Const. Ala., art. V, §123.

Residence.
Not forfeited by temporary absence from state, Const. Ala., art. I, §31.

CONSTITUTION OF ALABAMA—Cont'd

Revenue commissioners.
Salaries, fees, etc., Const. Ala., amd. 411.

Rights.
Declaration of rights, Const. Ala., art. I, §§1 to 36.
See within this heading, "Declaration of rights." Ala., art.

Roads.
Bond issues, Const. Ala., amd. 21.
Bonds for acquiring in conjunction with United States, Const. Ala., amd. 87.
Bonds for construction, Const. Ala., amd. 11.
Construction, maintenance, etc., of public roads, Const. Ala., amds. 12, 58.
Districts to build and maintain public roads, Const. Ala., amd. 15.
State not to engage in internal improvements or lend money or credit for same.
Exception as to public roads, Const. Ala., amd. 1.

Sales tax.
Exemptions.
Gross receipts of businesses which the state is prohibited from taxing, §40-23-4.

Schools. See within this heading, "Education."

Seal.
Great seal of state, Const. Ala., art. V, §133.

Searches and seizures.
Warrants.
Conditions for issuance, Const. Ala., art. I, §5.

Seat of government.
Legislation to change, Const. Ala., art. IV, §78.

Seawalls.
Districts to build and maintain seawalls, Const. Ala., amd. 15.

Secretary of state.
Compensation, Const. Ala., art. V, §118.
Duties, Const. Ala., art. V, §§134, 137; amd. 111.
Election.
Contested elections, Const. Ala., art. V, §115.
Generally, Const. Ala., art. V, §§114, 115.
Returns.
Opening, Const. Ala., art. V, §115.
Publication, Const. Ala., art. V, §115.
Transmission to speaker of house, Const. Ala., art. V, §115.
Tie votes, Const. Ala., art. V, §115.
Time, Const. Ala., art. V, §114.

CONSTITUTION OF ALABAMA—Cont'd

Secretary of state—Cont'd
Fees.
Restrictions on receipt, Const. Ala., art. V, §137; amd. 111.
Impeachment, Const. Ala., art. VII, §173.
Mental unsoundness, Const. Ala., art. V, §136.
Qualifications, Const. Ala., art. V, §132.
Residency requirements, Const. Ala., art. V, §118.
Succession.
Ineligible to succeed self, Const. Ala., art. V, §116.
One additional term, Const. Ala., amd. 282.
Term of office, Const. Ala., art. V, §116; amd. 282.
Vacancy in office, Const. Ala., art. V, §136.

Securities.
Bonds and other securities issued by certain public corporations, Const. Ala., amd. 108.

Self-incrimination, Const. Ala., art. I, §6.

Senate. See within this heading, "Legislative department."

Separation of powers, Const. Ala., art. III, §43.

Sheriffs.
Election, Const. Ala., art. V, §138; amd. 35.
Impeachment, Const. Ala., art. V, §138; art. VII, §174; amd. 35.
Morgan county.
Grant of money to sheriff's posse.
Authorized, Const. Ala., amd. 502.
Succession to office.
Sheriff eligible to succeed self, Const. Ala., amd. 35.
Sheriff not eligible to succeed self, Const. Ala., art. V, §138.
Term of office, Const. Ala., art. V, §138; amd. 35.

Slavery.
Prohibited, Const. Ala., art. I, §32.

Sovereign immunity of state, Const. Ala., art. I, §14.

Soybeans.
Promotion of soybean industry, Const. Ala., amd. 315.
Amendment of amendment, Const. Ala., amd. 401.

Special, private or local laws.
Amendment, Const. Ala., amd. 397.
Amendment of bill introduced as general law so as to become special, private or local on passage, Const. Ala., art. IV, §111.

CONSTITUTION OF ALABAMA—Cont'd

Special, private or local laws —Cont'd
Courts.
Time of holding courts.
Exception as to time of holding courts, Const. Ala., art. IV, §105.
Defined, Const. Ala., art. IV, §110.
Notice of intent to apply for.
Prerequisite to repeal or amendment, Const. Ala., art. IV, §107.
Publication or posting of notice within county or counties affected prior to introduction of bill, Const. Ala., art. IV, §106; amd. 341.
Partial repeal of general laws, Const. Ala., art. IV, §105.
Prohibited in cases provided for by general law, Const. Ala., art. IV, §105.
Prohibited in certain cases, Const. Ala., art. IV, §104.

Speech.
Freedom of speech, Const. Ala., art. I, §4.

Standing army, Const. Ala., art. I, §27.

State.
Boundaries.
Defined, Const. Ala., art. II, §37.
Nobility, title of.
Titles of nobility prohibited, Const. Ala., art. I, §29.
Obligations and liabilities of corporations, etc., held or owned by state, Const. Ala., art. IV, §100.
State not to be made defendant, Const. Ala., art. I, §14.
Treason against the state, Const. Ala., art. I, §18.

State auditor.
Compensation, Const. Ala., art. V, §118.
Duties, Const. Ala., art. V, §137; amd. 111.
Election.
Contested elections, Const. Ala., art. V, §115.
Generally, Const. Ala., art. V, §§114, 115.
Returns.
Opening, Const. Ala., art. V, §115.
Publication, Const. Ala., art. V, §115.
Transmission to speaker of house, Const. Ala., art. V, §115.
Tie votes, Const. Ala., art. V, §115.
Time, Const. Ala., art. V, §114.
Fees.
Restrictions on receipt, Const. Ala., art. V, §137; amd. 111.

CONSTITUTION OF ALABAMA—Cont'd

State auditor—Cont'd

Impeachment, Const. Ala., art. VII, §173.

Mental unsoundness, Const. Ala., art. V, §136.

Qualifications, Const. Ala., art. V, §132.

Reports.

Annual report by state auditor, Const. Ala., art. V, §137; amd. 111.

Residency requirements, Const. Ala., art. V, §118.

Succession.

Ineligible to succeed self, Const. Ala., art. V, §116.

One additional term, Const. Ala., amd. 282.

Term of office, Const. Ala., art. V, §116; amd. 282.

Vacancy in office, Const. Ala., art. V, §136.

State capital.

Legislation to change seat of government of state, Const. Ala., art. IV, §78.

State debts.

Creation after ratification of constitution, Const. Ala., art. XI, §213; amd. 26.

Refunding bonds for existing indebtedness, Const. Ala., art. XI, §213; amd. 26.

Sinking fund for payment of floating indebtedness, Const. Ala., amd. 26.

State parks.

Bond issue to acquire, develop, etc., Const. Ala., amd. 267.

State retirement systems.

Use of assets, Const. Ala., amd. 472.

State superintendent of education. See within this heading, "Education."

State treasurer.

Compensation, Const. Ala., art. V, §118.

Duties, Const. Ala., art. V, §137; amd. 111.

Election.

Contested elections, Const. Ala., art. V, §115.

Generally, Const. Ala., art. V, §§114, 115.

Returns.

Opening, Const. Ala., art. V, §115.

Publication, Const. Ala., art. V, §115.

Transmission to speaker of house, Const. Ala., art. V, §115.

Tie votes, Const. Ala., art. V, §115.

Time, Const. Ala., art. V, §114.

Fees.

Restrictions on receipt of fees, Const. Ala., art. V, §137; amd. 111.

Impeachment, Const. Ala., art. VII, §173.

Mental unsoundness, Const. Ala., art. V, §136.

CONSTITUTION OF ALABAMA—Cont'd

State treasurer—Cont'd

Qualifications, Const. Ala., art. V, §132.

Reports.

Annual report by state treasurer, Const. Ala., art. V, §137; amd. 111.

Residency requirements, Const. Ala., art. V, §118.

Succession.

Ineligible to succeed self, Const. Ala., art. V, §116.

One additional term, Const. Ala., amd. 282.

Term of office, Const. Ala., art. V, §116; amd. 282.

Vacancy in office, Const. Ala., art. V, §136.

Statutes.

Allegations that statute unconstitutional, §6-6-227.

Attorney general.

Entitled to be heard, §6-6-227.

Served with copy of proceedings, §6-6-227.

General laws.

Amendment, Const. Ala., amd. 397.

Defined, Const. Ala., art. IV, §110.

Exemption of individuals or private corporations, Const. Ala., art. IV, §108.

Protection of local or private interests, Const. Ala., art. IV, §109.

Suspension for benefit of individuals or private corporations, Const. Ala., art. IV, §108.

Legislative department generally. See within this heading, "Legislative department."

Special, private or local laws. See within this heading, "Special, private and local laws."

Suspension of laws, Const. Ala., art. I, §21.

Suffrage.

Protection of suffrage, Const. Ala., art. I, §33.

Summons and process.

Style of all processes, Const. Ala., art. VI, §170.

Supreme court, Const. Ala., amd. 328.

Clerk.

Appointment, Const. Ala., art. VI, §164; amd. 271.

Removal, Const. Ala., art. VI, §166.

Term of office, Const. Ala., art. VI, §164.

Composition.

Composition of supreme court, Const. Ala., art. VI, §151.

CONSTITUTION OF ALABAMA—Cont'd

Supreme court—Cont'd

Constitutional questions.

Advisory opinions on constitutional questions.

Effect, §12-2-12.

How opinion obtained, §12-2-10.

Habeas corpus.

Power to issue writs, Const. Ala., art. VI, §140.

Injunctions.

Power to issue writs, Const. Ala., art. VI, §140.

Jurisdiction, Const. Ala., art. VI, §140; amd. 328.

Justices.

Compensation, Const. Ala., art. VI, §150.

Dual office holding, Const. Ala., art. VI, §150.

Election, Const. Ala., art. VI, §152.

Time of holding election, Const. Ala., art. VI, §156.

Impeachment, Const. Ala., art. VII, §173.

Salary, Const. Ala., art. VI, §150.

Terms of office, Const. Ala., art. VI, §155.

Incumbents.

Terms of incumbents not abridged, Const. Ala., art. VI, §172.

Staggered terms of office, Const. Ala., art. VI, §156.

Vacancies, Const. Ala., art. VI, §158.

Original writs.

Power to issue, Const. Ala., art. VI, §140.

Place of holding, Const. Ala., art. VI, §141.

Quo warranto.

Power of supreme court to issue writs, Const. Ala., art. VI, §140.

Remedial writs.

Power of supreme court to issue, Const. Ala., art. VI, §140.

Rules of court, Const. Ala., amd. 328.

Salaries.

Justices, Const. Ala., art. VI, §150.

Suspension of general laws.

For benefit of individuals or private corporations, Const. Ala., art. IV, §108.

Swine and swine products.

Promotion of production, research, etc., of swine and swine products, Const. Ala., amds. 327, 400.

Tax assessors.

Abolishment, combination or alteration of office, Const. Ala., amd. 411.

CONSTITUTION OF ALABAMA—Cont'd

Taxation.

Assessments, Const. Ala., amd. 325.

Property taxes to be assessed in exact proportion to value of property, Const. Ala., art. XI, §211.

Classification of taxable property, Const. Ala., amd. 325.

Counties. See within this heading, "Counties."

Education.

Poll taxes.

Use for support of public schools, Const. Ala., art. XIV, §259.

Special annual tax for schools, Const. Ala., art. XIV, §260.

Estate taxes, Const. Ala., art. XI, §219; amd. 23.

Repeal of section 219, Const. Ala., amd. 23.

Exemptions from taxation.

Special, private or local laws prohibited, Const. Ala., art. IV, §104.

State, county, municipal, cemetery and certain religious, educational and charitable property, Const. Ala., art. IV, §91.

Income tax. See within this heading, "Income tax."

Municipal corporations.

Additional municipal taxes, Const. Ala., amd. 56.

Exemption from payment of charges payable from state treasury, Const. Ala., art. XI, §218.

Rates of taxation.

Additional municipal taxes, Const. Ala., amd. 56.

Limitation on property tax rates, Const. Ala., art. XI, §216.

Poll taxes.

Use for support of public schools, Const. Ala., art. XIV, §259.

Power to levy taxes.

Delegation.

Power not to be levied, Const. Ala., art. XI, §212.

Property tax generally, Const. Ala., amd. 325.

Rate of taxation, Const. Ala., amd. 325.

Limitation on state property tax rate, Const. Ala., art. XI, §214.

CONSTITUTION OF ALABAMA—Cont'd

Taxation—Cont'd

Rate of taxation—Cont'd

Property of private corporations, associations and individuals to be taxed at same rate, Const. Ala., art. XI, §217.

Exception as to religious, educational and charitable property, Const. Ala., art. XI, §217.

Special, private or local laws prohibited, Const. Ala., art. IV, §104.

State debt.

Creation after ratification of constitution, Const. Ala., art. XI, §213; amd. 26.

Refunding bonds for existing indebtedness, Const. Ala., art. XI, §213; amd. 26.

Subjects of taxation, Const. Ala., amd. 325.

Tax assessors.

Abolishment, combination or alteration of office, Const. Ala., amd. 411.

Impeachment, Const. Ala., art. VII, §175.

Tax collectors.

Abolishment, combination or alteration of office, Const. Ala., amd. 411.

Impeachment, Const. Ala., art. VII, §175.

Tax collectors.

Abolishment, combination or alteration or office, Const. Ala., amd. 411.

Telegraph companies, Const. Ala., art. XII, §239.

Grant of easements to, Const. Ala., art. XII, §239.

Telephone companies, Const. Ala., art. XII, §239.

Easements.

Grant of easements to telephone companies, Const. Ala., art. IV, §99.

Titles of nobility.

Prohibited, Const. Ala., art. I, §29.

Treason.

Against the state, Const. Ala., art. I, §18.

Bills of attainder of treason by legislature prohibited, Const. Ala., art. I, §19.

Conviction not to work corruption of blood or forfeiture of estate, Const. Ala., art. I, §19.

Trial.

Right to speedy, public trial, Const. Ala., art. I, §6.

Trusts and trustees.

Regulation of trusts, Const. Ala., art. IV, §103.

Tuberculosis.

District tuberculosis sanatoria.

Bonds, Const. Ala., amd. 74.

CONSTITUTION OF ALABAMA—Cont'd

Universities and colleges.

Revenue securities.

Issuance by institutions of learning, Const. Ala., amd. 160.

University of Alabama.

Board of trustees, Const. Ala., art. XIV, §264.

Amendment, Const. Ala., amd. 399.

Bond issues.

Bonds for construction and improvement purposes, Const. Ala., amd. 157.

Mental hospital at university of Alabama medical center, Const. Ala., amd. 141.

Funds.

Interest.

Annual payment, Const. Ala., art. XIV, §265.

Medical center.

Bonds for construction and improvement purposes, Const. Ala., amd. 119.

Military system at university.

Authority to abolish, Const. Ala., art. XIV, §265.

Venue.

Change of venue, Const. Ala., art. I, §6; art. IV, §75.

Special, private or local laws prohibited, Const. Ala., art. IV, §104.

Veterans.

Exemptions from poll tax, Const. Ala., amds. 7, 10, 14, 49, 90.

War.

Continuity of legislature in event of enemy attack, Const. Ala., amd. 159.

Warrants.

Searches and seizures.

Conditions for issuance, Const. Ala., art. I, §5.

Warrants for the payment of money.

Interest on certain outstanding and unpaid state warrants.

Payment of interest, Const. Ala., amd. 26.

Not to be drawn on state treasury unless money available for payment, Const. Ala., amd. 26.

Water conservation and irrigation.

Development of irrigation districts, Const. Ala., amd. 227.

Water management and drainage.

Districts, Const. Ala., amds. 15, 22, 257.

Waters and watercourses.

Development of docks and other facilities along inland waterways, Const. Ala., amds. 116, 274, 288.

Navigable waters declared free public highways, Const. Ala., art. I, §24.

**CONSTITUTION OF
ALABAMA**—Cont'd
Waters and watercourses
—Cont'd
Navigable waterway between
Demopolis and
Tennessee river and
Tombigbee valley
projects, Const. Ala.,
amd. 270.
Bond issues, Const. Ala.,
amd. 355.
Navigable waterway between
Montgomery and
Gadsden and to the
Alabama-Georgia
boundary, Const. Ala.,
amd. 287.
Weapons.
Right to bear arms, Const.
Ala., art. I, §26.
Weights and measures.
State office for inspection or
measuring of
merchandise,
commodities, etc.,
prohibited, Const. Ala.,
art. IV, §77.
Wharves.
Taxes, tolls, etc., for use of
shores or wharves,
Const. Ala., art. I, §24.
Wills.
Giving effect to invalid will.
Special, private or local
laws prohibited, Const.
Ala., art. IV, §104.
Probate courts.
Power to grant letters
testimentary, Const.
Ala., amd. 364.
Witnesses.
Right to be confronted by
witnesses, Const. Ala.,
art. I, §6.
Women.
Property rights of females,
Const. Ala., art. X, §209.

**CONSTITUTION OF THE
UNITED STATES.**
Absence.
Congress.
Members of congress,
Const. U. S., Art. I, §5.
Vice-president.
Senate to choose president
pro tempore, Const. U.
S., Art. I, §3.
Accounts and accounting.
Receipts and expenditures of
public money.
Publication of statement
and account, Const. U.
S., Art. I, §9.
**Actions to which United
States a party,** Const. U.
S., Art. III, §2.
Admiralty, Const. U. S., Art.
I, §8.
Jurisdiction of courts, Const.
U. S., Art. III, §2.
Age.
Congress.
Representative in congress,
Const. U. S., Art. I, §2.
Senator, Const. U. S., Art.
I, §3.

**CONSTITUTION OF THE
UNITED STATES**—Cont'd
Age—Cont'd
Elections.
Right to vote not to be
abridged on account of
age, Const. U. S.,
Amendment XXVI.
Voting by persons eighteen
years of age, Const. U.
S., Amendment XXVI.
President of the United
States, Const. U. S., Art.
II, §1.
Vice-president, Const. U. S.,
Amendment XII.
Alcoholic liquors, Const. U.
S., Amendments XVIII,
XXI.
Aliens.
Eligibility to be
representative, Const. U.
S., Art. I, §2.
Naturalization, Const. U. S.,
Art. I, §8.
Presidency.
Ineligibility for presidency,
Const. U. S., Art. II,
§1.
Suits against state, Const. U.
S., Amendment XI.
Ambassadors and consuls,
Const. U. S., Art. II, §§2, 3;
Art. III, §2.
Amendments, Const. U. S.,
Art. V.
Bail, Const. U. S.,
Amendment VIII.
Congress.
Sessions, Const. U. S.,
Amendment XX, §2.
Terms of office, Const. U.
S., Amendment XX,
§1.
Time of convening, Const.
U. S., Amendment XX,
§2.
Criminal law, Const. U. S.,
Amendments V, VI.
Due process of law, Const. U.
S., Amendments V, XIV.
Effect of enumeration of
rights, Const. U. S.,
Amendment IX.
Election of senators, Const.
U. S., Amendment
XVIII.
Eminent domain, Const. U.
S., Amendment V.
Freedom of religion, speech
and press, Const. U. S.,
Amendment I.
Guarantees in criminal cases,
Const. U. S.,
Amendments V, VI.
House of representatives.
Terms of representatives,
Const. U. S.,
Amendment XX, §1.
Income tax, Const. U. S.,
Amendment XVI.
Intoxicating liquors, Const.
U. S., Amendments
XVIII, XXI.
Lame duck amendment,
Const. U. S., Amendment
XX.
Manner of making
amendments, Const. U.
S., Art. V.

**CONSTITUTION OF THE
UNITED STATES**—Cont'd
Amendments—Cont'd
Poll tax.
Denial or abridgement of
right to vote upon
failure to pay.
Prohibited, Const. U. S.,
Amendment XXIV.
President.
Death, Const. U. S.,
Amendment XX.
Election, Const. U. S.,
Amendments XII, XX.
Failure to qualify, Const.
U. S., Amendment XX.
Succession upon death,
resignation, or removal
of president, Const. U.
S., Amendment XXV.
Terms of office, Const. U.
S., Amendments XX,
XXII.
Limitation on terms,
Const. U. S.,
Amendment XXII.
Proposal and ratification of
amendments, Const. U.
S., Art. V.
Punishments, Const. U. S.,
Amendment VIII.
Quartering soldiers in
houses, Const. U. S.,
Amendment III.
Ratification of amendment,
Const. U. S., Art. V.
Repeal of the eighteenth
amendment, Const. U.
S., Amendment XXI.
Reservation of powers to
state, Const. U. S.,
Amendment X.
Restriction of judicial power,
Const. U. S., Amendment
XI.
Rights and immunities of
citizens, Const. U. S.,
Amendment XIV.
Right to bear arms, Const. U.
S., Amendment II.
Right to vote, Const. U. S.,
Amendment XV.
Not to be abridged on
account of age, Const.
U. S., Amendment
XXVI.
Searches and seizures, Const.
U. S., Amendment IV.
Self-incrimination, Const. U.
S., Amendment V.
Senate.
Election of senators, Const.
U. S., Amendment
XVII.
Terms of senators, Const.
U. S., Amendment XX,
§1.
Slavery, Const. U. S.,
Amendment XIII.
Suits against state, Const. U.
S., Amendment XI.
Terms of office, Const. U. S.,
Amendment XX, §1.
Limitation on terms of
president, Const. U. S.,
Amendment XXII.
Trial by jury, Const. U. S.,
Amendments VI, VII.
Vice-president.
Death, Const. U. S.,
Amendment XX.

CONSTITUTION OF THE UNITED STATES—Cont'd
Congress—Cont'd
Libel and slander.
Privilege of members of congress, Const. U. S., Art. I, §6.
Messages to congress, Const. U. S., Art. II, §3.
Post office and post roads, Const. U. S., Art. I, §8.
Powers of congress, Const. U. S., Art. I, §8.
Limitations on powers, Const. U. S., Art. I, §9.
President of the United States.
Declaration of president's disability.
Determination of issue, Const. U. S., Amendment XXV, §4.
By two-thirds vote of both houses, Const. U. S., Amendment XXV, §4.
Qualifications of members of congress, Const. U. S., Art. I, §§2, 3, 5.
Rules of procedure, Const. U. S., Art. I, §5.
Senate.
Absent members, Const. U. S., Art. I, §5.
Arrest of members, Const. U. S., Art. I, §6.
Compensation of members, Const. U. S., Art. I, §6.
Debate, Const. U. S., Art. I, §6.
Elections. See within this heading, "Elections."
Equal suffrage in senate, Const. U. S., Art. V.
Expulsion of member, Const. U. S., Art. I, §5.
Freedom of speech, Const. U. S., Art. I, §6.
Holding other office, Const. U. S., Art. I, §6.
Journal, Const. U. S., Art. I, §§5, 7.
Libel and slander.
Privilege of members, Const. U. S., Art. I, §6.
Officers, Const. U. S., Art. I, §3.
President, Const. U. S., Art. I, §3.
Pro tempore, Const. U. S., Art. I, §3.
Presidential elector.
Senator ineligible, Const. U. S., Art. II, §1.
Punishment of members, Const. U. S., Art. I, §5.
Qualifications.
Electors, Const. U. S., Amendment XVII.
Members, Const. U. S., Art. I, §3.
Judge of qualifications, Const. U. S., Art. I, §5.
Quorum, Const. U. S., Art. I, §5.
Revenue bills, Const. U. S., Art. I, §7.

CONSTITUTION OF THE UNITED STATES—Cont'd
Congress—Cont'd
Senate—Cont'd
Rules of procedure, Const. U. S., Art. I, §5.
Vacancies, Const. U. S., Amendment XVII.
Vice-president of the United States.
Vacancy in office.
Confirmation of nomination of president, Const. U. S., Amendment XXV, §2.
Sessions, Const. U. S., Art. I, §4; Amendment XX, §2.
Special sessions, Const. U. S., Art. II, §3.
Taxation.
Powers of congress, Const. U. S., Art. I, §8.
Territories, Const. U. S., Art. IV, §3.
Vice-president.
Vacancy in office.
Nomination by president, Const. U. S., Amendment XXV, §2.
Confirmation by majority of both houses of congress, Const. U. S., Amendment XXV, §2.
War.
Articles of war, Const. U. S., Art. I, §8.
Declaration of war, Const. U. S., Art. I, §8.
Weights and measures, Const. U. S., Art. I, §8.
Welfare.
Power of congress to provide for general welfare, Const. U. S., Art. I, §8.
Construction and interpretation.
Effect of enumeration of rights, Const. U. S., Amendment IX.
Consuls, Const. U. S., Art. II, §§2, 3; Art. III, §2.
Contracts.
Impairment of obligations of contracts, Const. U. S., Art. I, §10.
Copyright, Const. U. S., Art. I, §8.
Corruption of blood.
Attainder of treason not to work, Const. U. S., Art. III, §3.
Counsel for defense, Const. U. S., Amendment VI.
Counterfeiting, Const. U. S., Art. I, §8.
Courts.
Congress.
Power to constitute tribunals inferior to supreme court, Const. U. S., Art. I, §8.
Inferior courts, Const. U. S., Art. III, §1.
Judges.
Compensation, Const. U. S., Art. III, §1.

CONSTITUTION OF THE UNITED STATES—Cont'd
Courts—Cont'd
Judges—Cont'd
Tenure, Const. U. S., Art. III, §1.
Restriction of judicial power, Const. U. S., Amendment XI.
Criminal procedure.
Constitutional provisions, Const. U. S., Amendment VIII.
Cruel and unusual punishment, Const. U. S., Amendment VIII.
Excessive bail, Const. U. S., Amendment VIII.
Extradition, Const. U. S., Art. IV, §2.
Fugitives from justice, Const. U. S., Art. IV, §2.
Guarantees in criminal cases, Const. U. S., Amendments V, VI.
Public trial, Const. U. S., Amendment VI.
Self-incriminations, Const. U. S., Amendment V.
Speedy trial, Const. U. S., Amendment VI.
Cruel and unusual punishment, Const. U. S., Amendment VIII.
Customs.
Congress.
Power to lay and collect, Const. U. S., Art. I, §8.
Exportations from any state.
Duties not to be laid on, Const. U. S., Art. I, §9.
Importation of persons, Const. U. S., Art. I, §9.
State may not impose without consent of congress, Const. U. S., Art. I, §10.
Death.
President and vice-president of the United States.
Duty of congress, Const. U. S., Art. II, §1; Amendment XXV.
President elect.
Provision in case of, Const. U. S., Amendment XX.
Debts.
Aid of rebellion, Const. U. S., Amendment XIV.
Debts and engagements contracted before adoption, Const. U. S., Art. VI.
Not to be questioned, Const. U. S., Amendment XIV.
Powers of congress, Const. U. S., Art. I, §8.
Declaration of rights, Const. U. S., Amendments I to X.
Defense.
Power of congress, Const. U. S., Art. I, §8.
Double jeopardy, Const. U. S., Amendment V.
Due process of law, Const. U. S., Amendments V, XIV.
Duties and imposts.
Duty of tonnage, Const. U. S., Art. I, §10.

CONSTITUTION OF THE UNITED STATES—Cont'd

Duties and imposts—Cont'd
Powers of congress, Const. U. S., Art. I, §8.
States, Const. U. S., Art. I, §§9, 10.
Tonnage, Const. U. S., Art. I, §10.

Education.
Required courses, §16-40-2.

Elections.
Age.
Right to vote not to be abridged on account of age, Const. U. S., Amendment XXVI.
Voting by persons eighteen years of age, Const. U. S., Amendment XXVI.
House of representatives, Const. U. S., Art. I, §2.
Election of members, Const. U. S., Art. I, §2.
Judge of elections, returns and qualifications of members, Const. U. S., Art. I, §5.
Qualifications of electors, Const. U. S., Art. I, §2.
Taxation.
Denial or abridgement of right to vote for failure to pay tax prohibited, Const. U. S., Amendment XXIV.
Times, places and manner of holding, Const. U. S., Art. I, §4.
Race.
Right to vote not to be abridged on account of race, Const. U. S., Amendment XV.
Senate, Const. U. S., Amendment XVII.
Election of members, Const. U. S., Amendment XVII.
Judge of elections, returns and qualifications of members, Const. U. S., Art. I, §5.
Qualifications of electors, Const. U. S., Amendment XVII.
Times, places and manner of holding, Const. U. S., Art. I, §4.
Suffrage, Const. U. S., Amendments XV, XIX.

Eminent domain, Const. U. S., Amendment V.

Emoluments, Const. U. S., Art. I, §9.

Equal protection of the laws, Const. U. S., Amendment XIV.

Equity.
Judicial power to extend to cases in, Const. U. S., Art. III, §2.

Excessive bail, Const. U. S., Amendment VIII.

Excessive fines, Const. U. S., Amendment VIII.

Excises.
Powers of congress, Const. U. S., Art. I, §8.

CONSTITUTION OF THE UNITED STATES—Cont'd

Execution of laws, Const. U. S., Art. II, §3.

Expenditures.
Necessity for appropriations, Const. U. S., Art. I, §9.
Publication of statement, Const. U. S., Art. I, §9.

Exports and imports, Const. U. S., Art. I, §§9, 10.

Ex post facto laws, Const. U. S., Art. I, §§9, 10.

Extradition, Const. U. S., Art. IV, §2.

Fines.
Excessive fines, Const. U. S., Amendment VIII.

Foreign presents, Const. U. S., Art. I, §9.

Former jeopardy, Const. U. S., Amendment V.

Freedom of conscience, Const. U. S., Amendment I.

Freedom of speech, Const. U. S., Amendment I.
Members of congress, Const. U. S., Art. I, §6.

Freedom of the press, Const. U. S., Amendment I.

Fugitives, Const. U. S., Art. IV, §2.

Full faith and credit clause, Const. U. S., Art. IV, §1.

Gifts.
Foreign presents to United States officials, Const. U. S., Art. I, §9.

Grand jury.
Presentments by, Const. U. S., Amendment V.

Habeas corpus, Const. U. S., Art. I, §9.

Immigration, Const. U. S., Art. I, §9.

Immunities, Const. U. S., Art. IV, §2.

Impairment of obligations of contracts, Const. U. S., Art. I, §10.

Impeachment, Const. U. S., Art. I, §§2, 3; Art. II, §4; Art. III, §2.

Imports and exports, Const. U. S., Art. I, §§9, 10.

Income tax, Const. U. S., Amendment XVI.

Indictments, informations and presentments, Const. U. S., Amendment V.

Insurrection or rebellion, Const. U. S., Art. I, §8.

International law.
Power of congress to punish offenses against, Const. U. S., Art. I, §8.

Interstate commerce, Const. U. S., Art. I, §§8, 9.

Intoxicating liquors.
Prohibition, Const. U. S., Amendments XVIII, XXI.
Repeal of the eighteenth amendment, Const. U. S., Amendment XXI.

Invasions, Const. U. S., Art. I, §8.

Involuntary servitude, Const. U. S., Amendment XIII.

CONSTITUTION OF THE UNITED STATES—Cont'd

Jeopardy.
Double jeopardy, Const. U. S., Amendment V.

Journals.
Congress, Const. U. S., Art. I, §§5, 7.

Judges.
Compensation, Const. U. S., Art. III, §1.
Tenure, Const. U. S., Art. III, §1.

Judgments.
Full faith and credit clause, Const. U. S., Art. IV, §1.
Proof, Const. U. S., Art. IV, §1.

Jury.
Jury of vicinage, Const. U. S., Amendment VI.

Lame duck amendment, Const. U. S., Amendment XX.

Legal tender, Const. U. S., Art. I, §10.

Letters of marque and reprisal, Const. U. S., Art. I, §§8, 10.

Libel and slander.
Congress.
Privilege of members of congress, Const. U. S., Art. I, §6.

Limitations on powers of states, Const. U. S., Art. I, §10.

Liquors, Const. U. S., Amendments XVIII, XXI.

Messages to congress, Const. U. S., Art. II, §3.

Militia.
Powers of congress, Const. U. S., Art. I, §8.
Quartering soldiers, Const. U. S., Amendment III.

Ministers.
Jurisdiction of cases affecting, Const. U. S., Art. III, §2.
Receiving, Const. U. S., Art. II, §3.

Money, Const. U. S., Art. I, §§8, 10.
Coinage, Const. U. S., Art. I, §§8, 10.
Counterfeiting, Const. U. S., Art. I, §8.
Powers of congress, Const. U. S., Art. I, §8.

Naturalization, Const. U. S., Art. I, §8.

Navy.
Powers of congress, Const. U. S., Art. I, §8.

New states, Const. U. S., Art. IV, §3.

Nonresidents.
Jurisdiction of suits against state, Const. U. S., Amendment XI.

Pardons, Const. U. S., Art. II, §2.

Patents, Const. U. S., Art. I, §8.

Payments.
Legal tender, Const. U. S., Art. I, §10.

Petitions.
Right of, Const. U. S., Amendment I.

CONSTITUTION OF THE UNITED STATES—Cont'd

Piracy.
Powers of congress, Const. U. S., Art. I, §8.

Poll tax.
Failure to pay poll or other tax.
Denial or abridgement of right to vote.
Prohibited, Const. U. S., Amendment XXIV.

Post offices, Const. U. S., Art. I, §8.

Post roads, Const. U. S., Art. I, §8.

Powers of congress, Const. U. S., Art. I, §8.

Powers reserved to states and people, Const. U. S., Amendment X.

President.
Age, Const. U. S., Art. II, §1.
Ambassadors and consuls, Const. U. S., Art. II, §§2, 3.
Appointment of officers, etc., Const. U. S., Art. II, §2.
Approval of laws by president, Const. U. S., Art. I, §7.
Approval of order, resolution or vote of congress, Const. U. S., Art. I, §7.
Bribery, Const. U. S., Art. II, §4.
Commander-in-chief, Const. U. S., Art. II, §2.
Compensation, Const. U. S., Art. II, §1.
Congress.
Adjourning congress, Const. U. S., Art. II, §3.
Convening congress, Const. U. S., Art. II, §3.
Messages to congress, Const. U. S., Art. II, §3.
Special sessions of congress, Const. U. S., Art. II, §3.
Death, Const. U. S., Art. II, §1; Amendment XX, §3.
Succession upon death, Const. U. S., Amendment XXV, §1.
Disability, Const. U. S., Art. II, §1.
Declaration by president.
Inability to perform duties, Const. U. S., Amendment XXV, §3.
Declaration by vice-president and other officers, Const. U. S., Amendment XXV, §4.
Determination of issue by congress, Const. U. S., Amendment XXV, §4.

CONSTITUTION OF THE UNITED STATES—Cont'd

President—Cont'd
Duties, Const. U. S., Art. II, §3.
Declaration by president of inability to perform duties, Const. U. S., Amendment XXV, §3.
Transmittal to senate and house of representatives, Const. U. S., Amendment XXV, §3.
Electors, Const. U. S., Art. II, §1; Amendments XII, XIV, XXIII.
Eligibility, Const. U. S., Art. II, §1.
Execution of laws, Const. U. S., Art. II, §3.
Executive power, Const. U. S., Art. II, §1.
Failure to qualify, Const. U. S., Amendment XX.
Impeachment, Const. U. S., Art. I, §3; Art. II, §4.
Inability, Const. U. S., Art. II, §1.
Limitation on terms, Const. U. S., Amendment XXII.
Message to congress, Const. U. S., Art. II, §3.
Ministers.
Receiving, Const. U. S., Art. II, §3.
Opinions from principal officers in executive departments, Const. U. S., Art. II, §2.
Pardons, Const. U. S., Art. II, §2.
Powers of president, Const. U. S., Art. II, §§2, 3.
Public officers.
Commissions, Const. U. S., Art. II, §3.
Qualifications, Const. U. S., Art. II, §1.
Removal, Const. U. S., Art. II, §§1, 4.
Succession upon removal, Const. U. S., Amendment XXV, §1.
Resignation, Const. U. S., Art. II, §1.
Succession upon resignation, Const. U. S., Amendment XXV, §1.
Signing of bills, Const. U. S., Art. I, §7.
Statutes.
Veto, Const. U. S., Art. I, §7.
Succession to office, Const. U. S., Art. II, §1; Amendment XX.
Upon death, resignation or removal of president, Const. U. S., Amendment XXV, §2.
Supreme court.
Appointment of justices, Const. U. S., Art. II, §2.

CONSTITUTION OF THE UNITED STATES—Cont'd

President—Cont'd
Terms of office, Const. U. S., Art. II, §1; Amendments XX, XXII.
Limitation on terms, Const. U. S., Amendment XXII.
Time of taking office, Const. U. S., Amendment XX.
Treason, Const. U. S., Art. II, §4.
Treaties, Const. U. S., Art. II, §2.
Vacancy in office, Const. U. S., Art. II, §1; Amendment XX.
During senate recess, Const. U. S., Art. II, §2.
Veto, Const. U. S., Art. I, §7.

Press.
Freedom of the press, Const. U. S., Amendment I.

Privileges.
Privileged from arrest, Const. U. S., Art. I, §6.

Prohibition, Const. U. S., Amendments XVIII, XXI.

Protection and aid of states, Const. U. S., Art. IV, §4.

Public debt, Const. U. S., Art. I, §8.

Public officers and employees.
Appointment, Const. U. S., Art. II, §2.
Senate recess, Const. U. S., Art. II, §2.
Bribery, Const. U. S., Art. II, §4.
Commissions, Const. U. S., Art. II, §3.
Emoluments, Const. U. S., Art. I, §9.
Foreign office or title, Const. U. S., Art. I, §9.
Holding more than one office, Const. U. S., Art. I, §6.
Impeachment, Const. U. S., Art. II, §4.
Ineligibility of members of congress, Const. U. S., Art. I, §6.
Presents from foreign states, Const. U. S., Art. I, §9.
Presidential electors.
Eligibility, Const. U. S., Art. II, §1.
Religious tests, Const. U. S., Art. VI.
Removal, Const. U. S., Art. II, §4.
Treason, Const. U. S., Art. II, §4.
Vacancies during senate recess, Const. U. S., Art. II, §2.

Public trial, Const. U. S., Amendment VI.

Punishment.
Cruel and unusual punishment, Const. U. S., Amendment VIII.

Quartering soldiers in houses, Const. U. S., Amendment III.

Quorum, Const. U. S., Art. I, §5.

CONSTITUTION OF THE UNITED STATES—Cont'd

Racial minorities, Const. U. S., Amendments XIV, XV.

Ratification, Const. U. S., Art. VII.

Records.
Full faith and credit clause, Const. U. S., Art. IV, §1.
Proof, Const. U. S., Art. IV, §1.

Redress of grievances.
Right to petition for, Const. U. S., Amendment I.

Religious test, Const. U. S., Art. VI.

Republican form of government, Const. U. S., Art. IV, §4.

Reservation of rights of the people, Const. U. S., Amendment IX.

Revenue bills, Const. U. S., Art. I, §7.

Right of assembly, Const. U. S., Amendment I.

Right of trial by jury, Const. U. S., Art. III, §2.

Right to bear arms, Const. U. S., Amendment II.

Right to counsel, Const. U. S., Amendment VI.

Right to petition for a redress of grievances, Const. U. S., Amendment I.

Searches and seizures, Const. U. S., Amendment IV.

Self-incrimination, Const. U. S., Amendment V.

Sentence and punishment, Const. U. S., Amendment VIII.
Capital punishment, Const. U. S., Amendment V.

Sessions of congress, Const. U. S., Art. I, §4.
Special sessions, Const. U. S., Art. II, §3.

Slavery, Const. U. S., Amendments XIII, XIV, XV.

Soldiers.
Quartering prohibited, Const. U. S., Amendment III.

Speech.
Freedom of speech, Const. U. S., Amendment I.

Speedy trial, Const. U. S., Amendment VI.

States.
Admission of new states, Const. U. S., Art. IV, §3.
Bill of attainder, Const. U. S., Art. I, §10.
Bills of credit, Const. U. S., Art. I, §10.
Commerce, Const. U. S., Art. I, §§8, 9.
Compacts between the states or with foreign powers, Const. U. S., Art. I, §10.
Contracts.
Impairing obligations of contracts, Const. U. S., Art. I, §10.
Controversies between citizens of different states, Const. U. S., Art. III, §2.

CONSTITUTION OF THE UNITED STATES—Cont'd

States—Cont'd
Controversies between states, Const. U. S., Art. III, §2.
Duties and imposts, Const. U. S., Art. I, §10.
Equal suffrage in senate, Const. U. S., Art. V.
Exports, Const. U. S., Art. I, §§9, 10.
Ex post facto laws, Const. U. S., Art. I, §10.
Full faith and credit clause, Const. U. S., Art. IV, §1.
Gold and silver coin tender in payment of debts, Const. U. S., Art. I, §10.
Impairing obligations of contracts, Const. U. S., Art. I, §10.
Imports and exports, Const. U. S., Art. I, §10.
Invasion.
Protection against, Const. U. S., Art. IV, §4.
Legal tender, Const. U. S., Art. I, §10.
Letters of marque and reprisal, Const. U. S., Art. I, §10.
Limitations on powers of states, Const. U. S., Art. I, §10.
Money.
Coining money, Const. U. S., Art. I, §10.
New states, Const. U. S., Art. IV, §3.
Protection and aid of states, Const. U. S., Art. IV, §4.
Republican form of government guaranteed, Const. U. S., Art. IV, §4.
Reservation of powers to states, Const. U. S., Amendment X.
Right to coin money, Const. U. S., Art. I, §10.
Suits against state, Const. U. S., Amendment XI.
Tender in payment of debts, Const. U. S., Art. I, §10.
Tonnage, Const. U. S., Art. I, §10.
Treaties, Const. U. S., Art. I, §10.
Troops or ships of war in time of peace, Const. U. S., Art. I, §10.
War, Const. U. S., Art. I, §10.

Statutes.
Approval of laws by president, Const. U. S., Art. I, §7.
Ex post facto laws, Const. U. S., Art. I, §§9, 10.
Full faith and credit clause, Const. U. S., Art. IV, §1.
Limitations on legislation, Const. U. S., Art. I, §9.
Proof, Const. U. S., Art. IV, §1.
Revenue bills, Const. U. S., Art. I, §7.
Supreme law of the land, Const. U. S., Art. VI.
Veto, Const. U. S., Art. I, §7.

Suits against state, Const. U. S., Amendment XI.

CONSTITUTION OF THE UNITED STATES—Cont'd

Suits against United States, Const. U. S., Art. III, §2.

Supreme court.
Chief justice presides in impeachment of president, Const. U. S., Art. I, §3.
Jurisdiction, Const. U. S., Art. III, §2.
Justices.
Appointment, Const. U. S., Art. II, §2.
Compensation, Const. U. S., Art. III, §1.
Tenure, Const. U. S., Art. III, §1.

Supreme law of the land, Const. U. S., Art. VI.

Taxation.
Capitation tax, Const. U. S., Art. I, §9.
Elections.
Denial or abridgement of right to vote for failure to pay tax prohibited, Const. U. S., Amendment XXIV.
Excises.
Powers of congress, Const. U. S., Art. I, §8.
Exports, Const. U. S., Art. I, §§9, 10.
Income tax, Const. U. S., Amendment XVI.
Limitations on powers of states, Const. U. S., Art. I, §10.
Powers of congress, Const. U. S., Art. I, §8.
Revenue bills, Const. U. S., Art. I, §7.

Tender, Const. U. S., Art. I, §10.

Territories, Const. U. S., Art. IV, §3.

Time when constitution effective, Const. U. S., Art. VII.

Titles of nobility, Const. U. S., Art. I, §§9, 10.

Tonnage, Const. U. S., Art. I, §10.

Treason, Const. U. S., Art. I, §6; Art. II, §4; Art. III, §3.
Supreme law of the land, Const. U. S., Art. VI.

Trial.
Public trial, Const. U. S., Amendment VI.
Speedy trial, Const. U. S., Amendment VI.

Use tax.
Exemptions.
Property prohibited from being taxed under constitution, §40-23-62.

Vessels and boats.
Bound to and from one state not to be obliged to clear, etc., in another, Const. U. S., Art. I, §9.

Veto, Const. U. S., Art. I, §7.

Vice-president of the United States.
Bribery, Const. U. S., Art. II, §4.
Failure to qualify, Const. U. S., Amendment XX.

CONSTITUTION OF THE UNITED STATES—Cont'd
Vice-president of the United States—Cont'd
Impeachment, Const. U. S., Art. II, §4.
President of senate, Const. U. S., Art. I, §3.
Qualifications, Const. U. S., Amendment XII.
Removal, Const. U. S., Art. II, §4.
Succession to office of president, Const. U. S., Art. II, §1; Amendments XX, XXV.
Upon death, resignation or removal of president, Const. U. S., Amendment XXV, §1.
Treason, Const. U. S., Art. II, §4.
War.
Articles of war, Const. U. S., Art. I, §8.
Declaration by congress, Const. U. S., Art. I, §8.
Grand jury.
Presentment as dispensable in certain cases, Const. U. S., Amendment V.
Quartering of soldiers in times of war, Const. U. S., Amendment III..
State engaging in, Const. U. S., Art. I, §10.
Treason.
Levying against the United States, Const. U. S., Art. III, §3.
Warrants.
Searches and seizures.
Conditions for issuance, Const. U. S., Amendment IV.
Weapons.
Right to bear arms, Const. U. S., Amendment II.
Weights and measures, Const. U. S., Art. I, §8.
Welfare.
General welfare.
Powers of congress, Const. U. S., Art. I, §8.
Witnesses.
Confrontation with witnesses, Const. U. S., Amendment VI.
Process to obtain, Const. U. S., Amendment VI.
Self-incrimination, Const. U. S., Amendment V.
Treason.
Number in treason cases, Const. U. S., Art. III, §3.
Woman suffrage, Const. U. S., Amendment XIX.

CONSTRUCTION AND INTERPRETATION.
Adverse possession.
Time, §6-5-200.
Alcoholic beverages.
Native farm wines, §28-6-6.
Attachment.
Liberal construction of attachment law, §6-6-143.

CONSTRUCTION AND INTERPRETATION
—Cont'd
Banks and financial institutions.
Credit unions.
See CREDIT UNIONS.
Regional reciprocal banking, §§5-13A-9, 5-13A-10.
Child support programs.
Construction of provisions of chapter, §38-10-11.
Department of pensions and security.
Causes of action created, §38-10-11.
Civil defense.
Chapter to be liberally construed, §31-9-23.
Code of Alabama, §§1-1-1 to 1-1-16.
Commercial code.
General provisions.
See COMMERCIAL CODE.
Computation of time, §1-1-4.
Condominiums.
Building or zoning laws, ordinances and regulations, §35-8-21.
Chapter to be liberally construed, §35-8-22.
Constitution of the United States.
Effect of enumeration of rights, Const. U. S., Amendment IX.
Contracts.
Statute of frauds, §8-9-2.
Conveyances.
Words "grant," "bargain," or "sell," §35-4-271.
Corporations.
S corporations.
Due consideration given to federal laws, §40-18-173.
Counties.
County engineers.
Construction of article, §11-6-6.
County industrial development authorities.
Liberal construction of provisions, §11-92A-2.
Industry and trade.
Industrial development boards.
Construction of article, §§11-20-31, 11-20-50.
Projects for promotion.
Construction of chapter, §11-20-13.
Public building authorities.
Construction of chapter, §11-15-19.
Warrants for construction of public buildings, bridges and roads.
Liberal construction of chapter, §11-28-1.
Warrants made in anticipation of ad valorem taxes.
Applicability of chapter provisions, §11-11A-5.
Workmen's compensation self-insurance groups.
Construction of provisions, §11-26-6.

CONSTRUCTION AND INTERPRETATION
—Cont'd
Credit cards.
Construction of act with other laws, §5-20-10.
Credit unions.
Procedure for adopting, amending or repealing interpretations, §5-17-47.
Reliance upon regulations and interpretations, §5-17-46.
Written interpretations of laws and regulations.
Authority of administrator, §5-17-46.
Crime victims' court attendance.
Construction of article, §15-14-51.
Criminal law and procedure.
Culpability.
Construction of statutes with respect to culpability requirements, §13A-2-4.
General rule of construction, §13A-1-6.
Custody and support.
Minors.
Uniform child custody jurisdiction act, §30-3-21.
Declaration of rights, Const. Ala., art. I, §36.
Declaratory judgments, §§6-6-221 to 6-6-224.
See DECLARATORY JUDGMENTS.
Deeds.
Words "grant," "bargain," or "sell," §35-4-271.
Definitions generally.
See DEFINITIONS.
Dental service corporations.
Board of dental examiners not regulated by article, §22-21-384.
Practice of dentistry.
Not regulated or limited by article, §22-21-384.
Disclaimer of interests in property.
Remedy not exclusive, §43-8-296.
Uniformity of application and construction, §43-8-297.
Dogs.
Dogs biting or injuring persons.
Construction of chapter, §3-6-4.
Domestic violence facilities, §30-6-13.
Education.
Public school and college authority, §16-16-2.
Elections.
Fair campaign practices, §17-22A-23.
Enterprise zones.
Complementary to and consistent with federal tax exemptions, §41-23-32.
Superseded when necessary by federal enterprise zone legislation, §41-23-32.

CONSTRUCTION AND INTERPRETATION
—Cont'd

Estates.
Estate taken as fee simple unless expressly limited, §35-4-2.

Fee simple estates.
Estate taken as fee simple unless expressly limited, §35-4-2.

Fraudulent transfers.
Uniformity of application and construction, §8-9A-11.
"Value" contrued, §8-9A-3.

Garnishment.
Applicability of section 6-6-143, §6-6-371.

Gender, §1-1-2.

Guardian and ward.
Curators.
Appointment.
Provisions of chapter deemed cumulative, §26-7A-17.
Uniform guardianship and protective proceedings act.
Construction against implied repeal, §26-2A-5.
Liberally construed, §26-2A-2.
Severability of provisions, §26-2A-4.

Hazardous waste and substances.
Fees for disposal of hazardous waste or substances, §22-30B-18.

Health care authorities, §22-21-311.
Additional powers.
Cumulative effect of provisions, §22-21-356.
Cumulative effect of article, §22-21-343.
Ethics act.
Applicability, §22-21-334.
Exclusivity of provisions, §22-21-342.

Historical preservation authorities.
Generally, §41-10-149.

Indictments.
See INDICTMENTS.

Insurance.
Effect of captions or headings, §27-1-7.
Pharmaceutical insurance coverage.
Pharmaceutical services.
Provisions do not mandate that pharmaceutical services be provided, §27-45-5.
Policies, §27-14-17.
Prevalence of particular over general provisions, §27-1-6.

Interstate compact on child placement, §44-2-20.

Joint authority, §1-1-2.

Judgments.
Foreign judgments.
Construction of article, §6-9-238.

CONSTRUCTION AND INTERPRETATION
—Cont'd

Law-enforcement planning agency.
Construction of chapter, §41-8A-13.

Long term quality health care.
References to federal law, §22-6-22.

Mandatory disposition of detainers.
Construction of article, §15-9-88.

Minors.
Custody and support.
Uniform child custody jurisdiction act, §30-3-21.
Interstate compact on child placement, §44-2-20.

Motor vehicles.
Commercial driver licenses.
Cumulative nature of sanctions and penalties, §32-6-49.2.
Liberal construction of provisions, §32-6-49.2.
Safety-responsibility act.
Uniformity of interpretation, §32-7-42.
Tags and plates.
Retired military.
Provisions cumulative, §32-6-295.

Municipal corporations.
Annexation.
Construction of article, §11-42-24.
Demolition of unsafe structures.
Cumulative nature of provisions, §11-40-36.
Special health care facility authorities.
Construction of chapter, §11-62-21.
Weeds.
Abatement of weeds.
Class 2 municipalities.
Applicability of article, §11-67-1.
Class 5 municipalities.
Applicability of article, §11-67-20.

Obscenity.
Anti-obscenity enforcement act.
Affect on other laws, §13A-12-200.9.

Parole.
Municipal parole boards.
Provisions of article not construed to repeal or supersede inconsistent laws, §15-22-77.

Partnerships.
Construction of chapter, §10-8-6.
"Knowledge" or "notice" of a fact, §10-8-3.
Limited partnerships.
Construction of article, §10-9A-200.

Physicians.
Licenses, §34-24-342.

Pleadings, ARCP, Rule 8 (f).

CONSTRUCTION AND INTERPRETATION
—Cont'd

Plumbing.
Conflicting laws repealed, §34-37-18.

Plural includes singular, §1-1-2.

Posthumous children.
Included in "heirs," "issue" or "children," §35-4-8.

Prison-made goods.
Construction of chapter, §14-7-23.

Public works.
Contracts.
Actions on contracts let in violation of law.
Construction of chapter, §39-5-6.

Real property.
Estate taken as fee simple unless expressly limited, §35-4-2.

Restitution to victims of crimes, §15-18-65.

Rules of civil procedure, ARCP, Rule 1 (c).

Seals and sealed instruments.
Effect of writings importing to be under seal, §35-4-22.

Securities.
Fiduciary security transfers.
Construction of article, §8-6-80.

Shakespeare festival theatre finance authority.
Liberal construction of article, §41-10-215.

Simultaneous death act.
Uniformity of interpretation, §43-7-8.

Singular includes plural, §1-1-2.

Soil classifiers, §34-32-3.

Stores, §40-12-310.

Supercomputer authority.
Construction of article, §41-10-391.

Taxation.
Multistate tax compact, §40-27-1.

Tennessee Valley authority.
Exhibit commission.
Liberal construction of article, §41-9-787.

Tenses, §1-1-2.

Time.
Computation of time, §1-1-4.

Transfers to minors.
Uniformity of application and construction, §35-5A-24.

Trees and timber.
Condemnation of timber theft equipment.
Cumulative nature of provisions, §9-13-227.

Trial.
Crime victims' court attendance.
Construction of article, §15-14-51.

Unclaimed property.
Uniform disposition of unclaimed property act.
Construction of article, §35-12-48.

Uniform child custody jurisdiction act, §30-3-21.

**CONSTRUCTION AND
INTERPRETATION**
—Cont'd
**Uniform disposition of
unclaimed property act,**
§35-12-48.
**Uniform guardianship and
protective proceedings
act.**
Construction against implied
repeal, §26-2A-5.
Liberally construed,
§26-2A-2.
Severability of provisions,
§26-2A-4.
Uniform vehicle code.
Rules of the road act.
Uniformity of
interpretation,
§32-5A-11.
Utility services facilities.
Liberal construction of
chapter, §11-97-27.
Vacation time-sharing plans.
Provisions not construed in
limited manner,
§34-27-62.
Victim counselors.
Confidentiality, §§15-23-44 to
15-23-46.
Wills.
General provisions.
See WILLS.
**Youth services department
district.**
Construction of article,
§44-1-77.

CONSUMER FINANCE,
§§5-19-1 to 5-19-31.
Actions.
Creditors.
Affidavit, §5-19-11.
Administrator.
Cease and desist orders,
§5-19-25.
Defined, §5-19-1.
Orders.
Appeals to circuit court,
§5-19-26.
Appeals from decision of
circuit court,
§5-19-26.
Cease and desist orders,
§5-19-25.
Rules and regulations.
Powers, §5-19-21.
Affidavits.
Actions by creditors.
Affidavit to be filed before
bringing, §5-19-11.
Amendments.
Certain laws not amended,
§5-19-31.
Appeals.
Orders of administrator,
§5-19-26.
Applicability of chapter.
Exceptions, §5-19-31.
Application of payments.
Buyer indebted to same
seller for two or more
sales, §5-19-9.
Assignments.
Assignee of seller or lessor
subject to claims and
defenses of buyer or
lessee, §5-19-8.

CONSUMER FINANCE
—Cont'd
Assignments—Cont'd
Taking assignments of
consumer credit
contracts.
Licenses for business. See
within this heading,
"Licenses."
Attorneys at law.
Contractual provisions for
fees, §5-19-10.
Cease and desist orders,
§5-19-25.
Circuit courts.
Appeals from orders of
administrator, §5-19-26.
Appeals from decision of
circuit court, §5-19-26.
Contracts.
Attorneys' fees, §5-19-10.
Consumer credit contracts.
Business of taking
assignments of
contracts.
Licenses. See within this
heading, "Licenses."
Finance charges.
Inducing obligation on
more than one contract
to obtain higher
finance charge.
Prohibited, §5-19-17.
Minimum finance charge.
Contracting for, §5-19-3.
Statement required, §5-19-6.
Copies of instruments.
Furnishing to debtors,
§5-19-6.
Default.
Additional charges, §5-19-4.
Defenses.
Assignee of seller or lessor
subject to claims and
defenses of buyer or
lessee, §5-19-8.
Deferral.
Additional charges, §5-19-4.
Definitions, §5-19-1.
Discounts.
Inducement for aiding sale or
lease.
Prohibited, §5-19-14.
Fees.
License to engage in business
of making consumer
loans or taking
assignments of consumer
credit contracts,
§5-19-22.
Finance charges.
Defined, §5-19-1.
Excess finance charges.
Liability of creditor,
§5-19-19.
Penalties, §5-19-30.
Maximum finance charges,
§5-19-3.
Minimum finance charges.
Contracting for, §5-19-3.
Garnishment, §5-19-15.
Home solicitation sales.
Buyer's right to cancel,
§5-19-12.
Statement required,
§5-19-12.
Injunctions, §5-19-29.
Installment payments.
Debt of $1,000 or less,
§5-19-18.

CONSUMER FINANCE
—Cont'd
Insurance.
Requirements by creditor,
§5-19-20.
Licenses.
Business of making consumer
loans or taking
assignments of consumer
credit contracts.
Administrator.
Examinations and
investigations of
licensees, §5-19-24.
Application, §5-19-22.
Hearing on
qualifications,
§5-19-22.
Investigation of
applicant, §5-19-22.
Fee, §5-19-22.
Fee.
Investigation of
applicant, §5-19-22.
License fee, §5-19-22.
Penalty for late
payment, §5-19-22.
Form, §5-19-22.
Issuance.
Standards, §5-19-22.
Penalties, §5-19-30.
Late payment of license
fee, §5-19-22.
Posting, §5-19-22.
Required, §5-19-22.
Exceptions, §5-19-22.
Revocation, §5-19-23.
Small loan act.
Effect of holding license,
§5-19-22.
Suspension, §5-19-23.
Transfer.
Nontransferable,
§5-19-22.
Collection agencies,
§40-12-80.
Credit agencies, §40-12-89.
Loans.
Business of making consumer
loans.
Licenses. See within this
heading, "Licenses."
Negotiable instruments.
Acceptance as evidence of
consumer debt, §5-19-5.
Pawnbrokers.
Nonapplicability of chapter,
§5-19-31.
Penalties, §5-19-30.
Points, §5-19-4.
Prepayment, §5-19-4.
Rebates.
Inducement for aiding sale or
lease.
Prohibited, §5-19-14.
Renewal or refinancing,
§5-19-4.
Right to refinance amount of
certain scheduled
payments, §5-19-7.
Repeals.
Certain laws not repealed,
§5-19-31.
Repossession.
Goods priced at $1,000 or
less, §5-19-13.
Unconscionable agreements.
Courts may refuse to enforce,
§5-19-16.

CONSUMER FINANCE
—Cont'd
Violations of chapter.
Cease and desist orders,
§5-19-25.

CONSUMER PROTECTION.
Deceptive trade practices.
General provisions.
See DECEPTIVE TRADE
PRACTICES.

CONTAGIOUS DISEASES.
General provisions.
See DISEASES.
School children.
Immunization, §§16-30-1 to
16-30-5.
Mental and physical
examinations of school
children, §§16-29-1 to
16-29-6, 16-30-1.
See EDUCATION.

CONTAINERS.
Agricultural products.
Standards for containers of
farm products, §§8-16-16,
8-16-17.
Alcoholic beverages.
See ALCOHOLIC
BEVERAGES.
Beverage containers.
Alcoholic beverages.
See ALCOHOLIC
BEVERAGES.
Generally, §§8-12-20 to
8-12-23.
Milk and milk products.
Marked containers,
§§8-12-40 to 8-12-44,
8-16-95 to 8-16-97.
See MILK AND MILK
PRODUCTS.
Destruction.
Nuisances menacing public
health.
Summary destruction
without compensation,
§22-10-3.
Farm products.
Standards for containers of
farm products, §§8-16-16,
8-16-17.
Health.
Nuisances menacing public
health, §§22-10-1 to
22-10-3.
Honeybees and apiaries.
Shipment or movement of
honeybees into state.
Packaging requirements,
§2-14-4.
Linseed oil, §8-17-42.
Meat and meat products.
Labeling, §2-17-10.
Mellorine.
When container deemed
misbranded, §20-1-135.
Milk and milk products.
Marked containers, §§8-12-40
to 8-12-44, 8-16-95 to
8-16-97.
See MILK AND MILK
PRODUCTS.
**Nuisances menacing public
health,** §§22-10-1 to
22-10-3.
See HEALTH.
Nuts.
Requirements as to labeling,
§20-1-92.

CONTAINERS—Cont'd
Petroleum products,
§8-17-136.
See OIL AND GAS.
Poultry products.
Labeling of cans, pots, tins,
etc., §2-17-10.
Recorded devices.
Manufacturer's name
required on packages,
§13A-8-83.

CONTEMPT.
Appeals.
By attorney or officer,
§12-1-11.
Rules of appellate procedure.
Contempt as penalty for
willful noncompliance
with rules, ARAP,
Rule 48.
Attachments.
Cases in which courts may
issue attachments for
contempt, §12-1-8.
Attorneys at law.
Appeal to appellate court by
attorney from judgment
for contempt, §12-1-11.
Circuit courts.
Jurisdiction, §12-11-30.
Coal.
Mine safety.
Contempt proceedings,
§25-9-23.
Counties.
County commissions.
Powers and duties of
county commissions,
§11-3-11.
Court of civil appeals.
Punishment for contempt,
§12-3-11.
Court of criminal appeals.
Punishment for contempt,
§12-3-11.
District courts.
Powers as to punishment for
contempt, §12-12-6.
Elections.
Contests.
State officers.
Commission.
Power to punish,
§17-15-57.
Guardian and ward.
Uniform guardianship and
protective proceedings
act.
Incapacitated persons.
Termination of
incapacity.
Knowingly interfering
with transmission
of request for
order, §26-2A-110.
Habeas corpus.
Court not to inquire into
contempt commitment,
§15-21-23.
Failure to obey writ,
§15-21-30.
Income tax.
Books and papers.
Failure to produce before
department, §40-18-56.
Inquiries.
Conduct of inquiries as to
violations of section
12-1-8, §12-1-9.

CONTEMPT—Cont'd
**Interfering with judicial
proceedings,** §13A-10-130.
Jails.
Commitment of prisoners.
Nearest sufficient jail to
insure safekeeping,
§14-6-6.
Persons committed for
contempt.
Who may be confined in
county jail, §14-6-3.
Judicial inquiry commission.
Power to punish for
contempt, AJICR, Rule
8.
Juvenile proceedings.
Punishment for contempt of
persons disobeying
orders of court,
§12-15-12.
Legislature.
Punishment for contempt or
disorderly behavior,
Const. Ala., art. IV, §53.
Not bar to indictment for
same offense, Const.
Ala., art. IV, §54.
Nuisances.
Lewdness, assignation or
prostitution, §§6-5-145,
6-5-154.
Powers of courts, §12-1-7.
Probate courts.
Powers of courts as to
punishment for
contempt, §12-13-9.
Public service commission.
Compliance with commission
orders.
Power of circuit court,
§37-1-104.
Punishment, §12-1-10.
Courts of appeals, §12-3-11.
District courts.
Powers as to punishment,
§12-12-6.
Probate courts, §12-13-9.
Summary punishment.
Cases in which courts may
inflict, §12-1-8.
Conduct of inquiries as to
violations of section
12-1-8, §12-1-9.
**Restitution to victims of
crimes.**
Employment income
withholding order.
Violations of provisions,
§15-18-143.
**Rules of appellate
procedure.**
Contempt as penalty for
willful noncompliance
with rules, ARAP, Rule
48.
**Rules of judicial
administration.**
Willful noncompliance,
ARJA, Rule 34.
Sentencing.
Article not to deprive court
of authority to cite for
contempt, §13A-5-2.
Subpoenas.
Failure to obey subpoena,
ARCP, Rule 45 (f).
Summary punishment.
Cases in which courts may
inflict, §12-1-8.

CONTEMPT—Cont'd
Summary punishment —Cont'd
Conduct of inquiries, etc., as to violations of section 12-1-8, §12-1-9.
Supreme court.
Powers of court, §12-2-7.

CONTINGENT INTEREST.
See REMAINDERS, REVERSIONS AND EXECUTORY INTERESTS.

CONTINUOUS TRESPASS.
Trespass.
Damages, §6-5-217.

CONTRACTORS, §§34-8-1 to 34-8-27.
Accounts and accounting.
State licensing board, §34-8-25.
Appeals.
Decisions of state licensing board, §34-8-27.
Asbestos contractors accreditation.
General provisions, §§22-39-1 to 22-39-5.
See ASBESTOS.
Board, §§34-8-20 to 34-8-27.
See within this heading, "State licensing board."
Building permits.
Issuance of permits, §34-8-9.
Certificate of authority, §34-8-2.
Effect of issuance, §34-8-5.
Classification of contractors, §34-8-2.
Complaints.
Investigation and report by secretary-treasurer of board, §34-8-26.
Copy of chapter to be included in plans of architects and engineers, §34-8-8.
Definitions.
General contractor, §34-8-1.
Electrical contractors, §§34-36-1 to 34-36-17.
See ELECTRICAL CONTRACTORS.
Examinations.
Generally, §34-8-2.
Method of examinations, §34-8-3.
Exemptions from chapter, §34-8-7.
Fees.
Licenses, §34-8-2.
Fire protection sprinkler systems, §§34-33-1 to 34-33-12.
See FIRES AND FIRE PREVENTION.
General contractor.
Defined, §34-8-1.
Governor.
State licensing board.
Annual report to governor, §34-8-26.
Hearings.
Revocation of licenses, §34-8-4.

CONTRACTORS—Cont'd
Heating and air conditioning contractors.
General provisions, §§34-31-18 to 34-31-34.
See HEATING AND AIR CONDITIONING CONTRACTORS.
Indictment or complaint.
Sufficiency of allegations, §34-8-10.
Licenses.
Application, §34-8-2.
Register of applicants, §34-8-26.
Building permits.
Proof of license required before issuance of permits, §34-8-9.
Classification of licensees, §34-8-2.
Construction companies or contractors, §40-12-84.
Effect of issuance of certificate of license, §34-8-5.
Examinations. See within this heading, "Examinations."
Falsification of information, §34-8-6.
Fees, §34-8-2.
Hearings.
Lost licenses, §34-8-4.
Revocation of license, §34-8-4.
Issuance.
Effect of issuance, §34-8-5.
Limited licenses for particular projects, §34-8-2.
Register of applicants, §34-8-26.
Renewal, §34-8-2.
Revocation.
Charges, §34-8-4.
Grounds, §34-8-4.
Hearings, §34-8-4.
Reissuance of revoked license, §34-8-4.
Liens.
Improvements on public streets, etc., §§35-11-410 to 35-11-417.
See HIGHWAYS.
Mechanics' and materialmen's liens, §§35-11-218, 35-11-219, 35-11-227, 35-11-228.
See MECHANICS' AND MATERIALMEN'S LIENS.
Nonresidents.
Public works.
Out-of-state contractors.
Preference to resident contractors in letting of certain contracts, §39-3-5.
Oaths.
State licensing board.
Oath of board, §34-8-21.
Penalties.
Indictment or complaint, §34-8-10.
Violations of chapter, §34-8-6.

CONTRACTORS—Cont'd
Plans.
Copy of chapter to be included in plans of architects and engineers, §34-8-8.
Prohibited acts, §34-8-6.
Indictment or complaint, §34-8-10.
Records.
State licensing board, §34-8-25.
Reports.
State licensing board.
Annual report, §34-8-26.
Sales tax.
Street and highway contractors, §40-23-50.
State licensing board, §§34-8-20 to 34-8-27.
Accounts, §34-8-25.
Appeals from decisions of board, §34-8-27.
Appointment of members, §34-8-20.
Bonds, surety.
Treasurer to give bond, §34-8-22.
Compensation of members, §34-8-22.
Complaints.
Investigation and report by secretary-treasurer, §34-8-26.
Composition of board, §34-8-20.
Creation, §34-8-20.
Expenses of members, §34-8-22.
Funds.
Receipt, disposition and accounting of funds, §34-8-25.
Hearings.
Revocation of licenses, §34-8-4.
Meetings.
Generally, §34-8-24.
Oath of board, §34-8-21.
Officers, §34-8-22.
Qualifications of members, §34-8-20.
Quorum, §34-8-24.
Records.
Secretary-treasurer to keep record of proceedings, §34-8-25.
Register of applicants for licenses, §34-8-26.
Removal of members, §34-8-20.
Reports.
Annual report, §34-8-26.
Roster of contractors, §34-8-26.
Rules and regulations.
Promulgation by board, §34-8-22.
Seal, §34-8-23.
Terms of office, §34-8-20.
Treasurer.
Records and accounts, §34-8-25.
Vacancies.
Filling vacancies, §34-8-20.
Taxation.
Sales tax on street and highway contractors, §40-23-50.

CONTRACTORS—Cont'd
Water management and drainage.
Districts.
Construction and improvements, §§9-9-42 to 9-9-45.

CONTRACTS.
Abandonment.
When recorded contract presumed abandoned, §35-4-75.
Accord and satisfaction.
Consideration.
Accepting accord consideration deemed satisfaction, §8-1-22.
Obligation extinguished by new consideration, §8-1-23.
Definitions.
Accord, §8-1-20.
Execution.
Obligation not extinguished by accord until executed, §8-1-21.
Writing.
Obligation extinguished by writing, §8-1-23.
Actions.
Breach of contract. See within this heading, "Breach of contract."
Defenses.
Contracts for payment of money, §6-5-286.
Foreign causes of action.
Jurisdiction of defendant can be obtained in this state, §6-5-430.
Joint obligations and promises, §6-5-283.
Agriculture.
Incorporated marketing associations.
Marketing contracts, §2-10-65.
Marketing contracts.
Incorporated marketing associations, §2-10-65.
Airport authorities.
Exemption from state contracting restrictions, §4-3-10.
Alternate procedure for incorporation, §4-3-60.
Airports.
Acquisition, construction, etc., §4-2-43.
Contracts made during flight, §4-2-5.
Law governing contracts for acquisition, construction, etc., §4-2-43.
Ameraport.
Offshore harbor and terminal commission.
See AMERAPORT.
Arbitration.
Specific performance.
Agreement to arbitrate cannot be specifically enforced, §8-1-41.
Assignments.
Assignable by endorsement, §8-5-20.
Notice of assignment.
Subject to payments, setoffs and discounts prior to, §8-5-25.

CONTRACTS—Cont'd
Attachment.
Issuance to recovery damages for breach, §6-6-41.
Awards.
Public contracts, §§41-16-27, 41-16-30.
Banks and financial institutions.
Receiver.
Assumption or rejection of executory contracts, §5-8A-35.
Savings and loan associations.
See SAVINGS AND LOAN ASSOCIATIONS.
Bear Creek development authority.
Authority may enter into contracts, §33-15-6.
Bond issues.
Contracts to secure bonds and other obligations, §33-15-9.
Bids and bidding.
Public contracts.
Competitive bidding, §§41-16-20 to 41-16-63.
See within this heading, "Public contracts."
Breach of contract.
Attachments.
Issuance to recovery damages for breach, §6-6-41.
Commercial code.
See COMMERCIAL CODE.
Contract to marry.
Exemptions from liability, §6-5-330.
Interest.
Accrual on breach, §8-8-8.
Limitation on actions, §6-5-280.
Ratable compensation for services, §6-5-282.
Successive actions, §6-5-281.
Bridges.
See BRIDGES.
Civil defense.
Insurance.
Compensation insurance for civil defense workers and trainees, §31-9-21.
Claims against state.
See CLAIMS AGAINST STATE.
Collateral.
Receipt or acknowledgment.
Required, §8-1-3.
Commercial code.
See COMMERCIAL CODE.
Conditional sales.
Evidence.
When conditional sales contract received in evidence, §35-4-98.
Secured transactions, §§7-9-101 to 7-9-507.
See COMMERCIAL CODE.
Conservation and natural resources.
Buildings and facilities.
Construction or modification.
See CONSERVATION AND NATURAL RESOURCES.

CONTRACTS—Cont'd
Consideration,
action." §§8-1-22, 8-1-23.
Constitution of Alabama.
Impairment of obligations of contracts, Const. Ala., art. I, §22; art. IV, §95.
Public contracts.
Extra compensation not to be granted contractor after service rendered or contract made, Const. Ala., art. IV, §68.
Constitution of the United States.
Impairment of obligations of contracts, Const. U. S., Art. I, §10.
Consumer finance.
See CONSUMER FINANCE.
Conveyances.
Abandonment.
When recorded contract presumed abandoned, §35-4-75.
Breach of agreement to transfer.
Pecuniary compensation presumed inadequate, §8-1-47.
Death of person contracting to sell real property.
Conveyances by executors and administrators.
See EXECUTORS AND ADMINISTRATORS.
Judgment for specific performance, §35-4-33.
Specific performance, §§8-1-46, 8-1-47, 35-4-33.
Coosa valley development authority.
Power to enter into certain contracts, §33-16-8.
Corporations.
See CORPORATIONS.
Counties.
General provisions.
See COUNTIES.
Public contracts generally.
See within this heading, "Public contracts."
Covenants not to compete, §8-1-1.
Criminal law and procedure.
Offering a false instrument for recording, §13A-9-12.
Death.
Conveyances by executors and administrators, §§35-4-320 to 35-4-323.
Declaratory judgments.
Questions of construction or validity, §6-6-223.
Construction before or after breach, §6-6-224.
Definitions.
Accord, §8-1-20.
Future delivery, §8-1-120.
Delivery.
Future delivery, §§8-1-120 to 8-1-131. See within this heading, "Future delivery."
Dental service corporations.
See DENTAL SERVICE CORPORATIONS.

CONTRACTS—Cont'd

Destroyed papers or records.
Substitution in civil cases, §12-20-30.

Detinue.
Conditional sales contracts.
Actions by vendor or against vendee, §6-6-259.

Downtown redevelopment authorities.
Exemption from competitive bid laws, §11-54A-17.

Education.
See EDUCATION.

Electric cooperatives.
Power to make contracts necessary or convenient, §37-6-3.

Elk river development agency.
Power to enter into contracts, §33-12-5.

Employers and employees.
Covenants not to compete, §8-1-1.

Energy management and conservation.
Department of energy.
Assumption of contract, §41-6A-10.
Contracts with other agencies, departments, etc., §41-6A-7.

Enterprise zones.
Preference and priority to state manufacturers, suppliers, contractors and labor, §41-23-30.
Tax exemptions, §41-23-30.
Wage subsidies, §41-23-30.

Environmental improvement authorities.
Bond issues.
Security for payment, §9-6-10.
Power to contract, §9-6-8.

Evidence.
Future delivery. See within this heading, "Future delivery."
Market value testimony, §12-21-114.
Parol evidence generally.
See EVIDENCE.
Sales contracts.
Parol or extrinsic evidence, §7-2-202.
Written contract as evidence of debt or duty, §12-21-112.

Failure of consideration.
Affirmative defense, ARCP, Rule 8 (c).

Ferries.
Construction, maintenance and beautification.
Contracts relative to federal assistance, §23-1-1.

Forgery and counterfeiting.
Second degree forgery, §13A-9-3.

Fraud.
Agreement to forfeit right of action for not presenting damage claim void, §8-9-10.
Exceptions, §8-9-10.

CONTRACTS—Cont'd

Fraud—Cont'd

Specific performance.
Cases in which specific performance not enforced, §8-1-40.
Written contract not expressing parties' intent may be revised, §8-1-2.

Future delivery, §§8-1-120 to 8-1-131.
Actual delivery not intended.
Contracts made in another state, §8-1-127.
Making or assisting in making contract.
Price based on bona fide sales without making execution on exchange or board of trade,
Profit intended to be paid in money on day of delivery, §8-1-125.
Commodities information.
Establishment of place to publish.
Proof prima facie evidence of guilt, §8-1-129.
Cotton.
Contracts for future delivery not made subject to federal statutes.
Prima facie evidence of void contract, §8-1-124.
Definitions, §8-1-120.
Deposit of margins.
Failure to deliver after deposit prima facie evidence of void contract, §8-1-123.
Evidence.
Cotton.
Contracts for future delivery not made subject to federal statutes.
Prima facie evidence of void contract, §8-1-124.
Deposit of margins.
Failure to deliver after deposit prima facie evidence of void contract, §8-1-123.
Establishment of place to publish commodities information.
Proof prima facie evidence of guilt, §8-1-129.
Participation in futures contracts prima facie evidence of guilt, §8-1-130.
Statement on future delivery.
Failure to furnish prima facie evidence of illegal contract, §8-1-122.
Not excused from testifying, §8-1-130.
Office to engage in business of futures.
Establishing, §8-1-128.

CONTRACTS—Cont'd

Future delivery—Cont'd

Persons involved in futures contracts.
Participation prima facie evidence of guilt, §8-1-130.
Statement on future delivery.
Failure to furnish prima facie evidence of illegal contract, §8-1-122.
Void contracts.
Certain contracts for future delivery void, §8-1-121.
Exceptions, §8-1-121.
Cotton.
Contracts for future delivery not made subject to federal statutes.
Prima facie evidence of void contract, §8-1-124.
Deposit of margins.
Failure to deliver after deposit prima facie evidence of void contract, §8-1-123.
Money paid on illegal contract may be recovered, §8-1-131.
Statement on future delivery.
Failure to furnish prima facie evidence of void contract, §8-1-122.
Witnesses.
Person involved in futures contracts not excused from testifying, §8-1-130.

Gambling, §§8-1-150 to 8-1-152.
See GAMBLING.

Garbage and trash.
Disposal.
Authority of localities to enter into mutual contracts, §22-27-5.
Department approval, §22-27-5.

Geological survey.
Research and experiments.
Retention of faculty members and students, §§9-4-15, 9-4-16.

Guardian and ward.
Uniform guardianship and protective proceedings act.
Conservators.
Personal liability, §26-2A-157.

Handicapped persons.
Rehabilitation program for the homebound.
Contracts with state agencies and private organizations, §21-6-1.

Harbors and ports.
Docks department.
Authority to contract with federal government, §33-1-36.

Health.
Medicaid program.
Eyewear.
Procurement of prescription eyewear for recipients, §22-6-7.1.

CONTRACTS—Cont'd
Health—Cont'd
  Medicaid programs.
    Authority to contract with
      intermediaries for
      purpose of receiving,
      processing and paying
      claims, §22-6-7.
Health care authorities.
  Powers of authority,
    §22-21-318.
  Public contracts.
    Competitive bidding.
      Applicability of
        competitive bidding
        laws, §22-21-335.
Health care service plans.
  Contracts with public,
    §10-4-106.
**Health maintenance
organizations.**
  Reinsurance.
    Filing, §27-21A-2.
Health studio services,
  §§8-23-4 to 8-23-9.
  See HEALTH STUDIO
    SERVICES.
Highways.
  See HIGHWAYS.
Hirings.
  Duty of care.
    Ordinary care, §8-1-61.
  Injuries.
    Lessee to repair, §8-1-62.
    Lessor may reclaim
      before end of term
      on failure to repair,
      §8-1-63.
  Ordinary care.
    Lessee to use, §8-1-61.
  Purpose.
    Thing let for particular
      purpose to be so used,
      §8-1-60.
    Lessor may reclaim
      before end of term
      on use contrary to
      agreement, §8-1-63.
  Termination.
    When lessor may reclaim
      before end of term,
      §8-1-63.
History and archives.
  Alabama historical
    commission.
    Archaeological treasures.
      Contracts for recovery or
      salvage, §41-9-249.1.
Horse racing.
  Racetracks.
    Operators.
      Restricting competition,
      §11-65-20.
      Restricting competition,
      §11-65-17.
**Hotels, inns and other
transient lodging places.**
  Special contract between
    hotel and guest,
    §34-15-11.
Husband and wife.
  See HUSBAND AND WIFE.
Illegality.
  Affirmative defense, ARCP,
    Rule 8 (c).
**Impairment of obligations of
contracts.**
  Constitution of Alabama,
    Const. Ala., art. I, §22;
    art. IV, §95.

CONTRACTS—Cont'd
**Impairment of obligations of
contracts**—Cont'd
  Constitution of the United
    States, Const. U. S., Art.
    I, §10.
**Industrial access roads and
bridges.**
  Construction, §23-6-9.
**Industrial development
corporations.**
  Powers of corporation,
    §10-4-133.
**Insane persons, §§8-1-170 to
8-1-172.**
Insurance contracts.
  General provisions, §§27-14-1
    to 27-14-32.
  See INSURANCE.
Interest.
  Accrual on breach, §8-8-8.
  Enforcement of usurious
    contracts, §8-8-12.
**Joint purchasing
agreements, §41-16-21.1.**
Junior colleges.
  Competitive bidding,
    §16-60-89.
Legislature.
  Contract review permanent
    legislature oversight
    committee, §§29-2-40,
    29-2-41.
Licenses.
  Dealers in conditional sales
    contracts, drafts,
    acceptances, etc.,
    §40-12-83.
Limitation of actions.
  See LIMITATION OF
    ACTIONS.
Liquidated damages.
  Insurance.
    See INSURANCE.
  Specific performance.
    Liquidation of damages
      does not bar specific
      performance, §8-1-45.
Livestock.
  Department of agriculture
    and industries.
    Inspection or testing
      services, §2-15-1.
Loans.
  Small loans, §§5-18-15,
    5-18-16.
Lost papers or records.
  Substitution in civil cases,
    §12-20-30.
Market value.
  Testimony as to market
    value.
    Use in evidence,
      §12-21-114.
Marriage.
  Breach of contract to marry.
    Exemptions from liability,
      §6-5-330.
**Mental health finance
authority.**
  Obligations of state.
    Contracts do not create,
      §41-10-366.
  Power to contract,
    §41-10-356.
**Mentally ill, §§8-1-170 to
8-1-172.**

CONTRACTS—Cont'd
Military affairs.
  Veterans.
    Minor veterans empowered
      to contract liability for
      repayment of certain
      loans, §31-1-2.
Minors.
  Age of majority.
    Contracting for educational
      loans for college level
      education and above,
      §26-1-5.
Mistake.
  Specific performance.
    Cases in which specific
      performance not
      enforced, §8-1-40.
  Written contract not
    expressing parties' intent
    may be revised, §8-1-2.
Motor fuels.
  Marketing.
    Violations of chapter.
      Void and unenforceable
      contracts, §8-22-14.
Motor vehicle carriers.
  See MOTOR VEHICLE
    CARRIERS.
Motor vehicles.
  Drivers' licenses.
    Contracts for lease or
      purchase of equipment,
      §32-6-20.
**Mowa Choctaw housing
authority.**
  Contract with government
    for loans and
    contributions, §24-7-6.
Municipal corporations.
  General provisions.
    See MUNICIPAL
      CORPORATIONS.
  Public contracts generally.
    See within this heading,
      "Public contracts."
Noncompetition clause.
  Covenants not to compete,
    §8-1-1.
Oil and gas.
  Geological survey.
    Retention of faculty
      members and students
      for research, §§9-4-15,
      9-4-16.
Parol evidence.
  See EVIDENCE.
Partnerships.
  Dissolution.
    Covenants not to compete,
      §8-1-1.
  Fraud.
    Rights where contracts
      rescinded for fraud,
      §10-8-44.
  Misrepresentation.
    Rights where contract
      rescinded for
      misrepresentation,
      §10-8-44.
Power districts.
  Power to make and enter
    into, §37-5-3.
Presumptions.
  Abandonment.
    When recorded contract
      presumed abandoned,
      §35-4-75.
  Specific performance.
    Availability as remedy,
      §8-1-47.

CONTRACTS—Cont'd
Printing.
Public printing and binding.
See PRINTING.
Public contracts.
Assignment, §41-16-29.
Bond for faithful
performance.
Advertisement for bids.
Emergencies.
Letting of contracts
without
advertisement,
§41-16-23.
Conflict of law.
Provisions in invitations
for bids and contract
documents in conflict
with article,
§41-16-82.
Conflicts of interest.
Public officers or
employees not to
require procurement
of surety bond from
particular company,
§41-16-80.
Execution.
Approval of manner of
execution of surety
bonds furnished by
surety company
selected by bidder,
§41-16-81.
Form.
Approval of form of
surety bonds,
§41-16-81.
Required, §41-16-28.
Selection of surety
company by bidder,
§§41-16-80, 41-16-81.
Sufficiency of surety bonds.
Approval of sufficiency,
§41-16-81.
Competitive bidding,
§§41-16-20 to 41-16-63.
Advanced disclosure of
terms of bid.
Effect of advance
disclosure,
§41-16-26.
Advertisement for bids,
§41-16-24.
Agreements among
bidders.
Effect of agreements in
restraint of
competition,
§41-16-25.
Assignment of contracts,
§41-16-29.
Award of contracts.
Awarding in violation of
article, §41-16-30.
Manner of awarding,
§41-16-27.
Negotiated contracts,
§41-16-27.
Records as to awarding
to be open to public
inspection,
§41-16-27.
Bond for faithful
performance.
Required, §41-16-28.
Collusion among bidders.
Effect of collusion in
restraint of
competition,
§41-16-25.

CONTRACTS—Cont'd
Public contracts—Cont'd
Competitive bidding—Cont'd
Conflicts of interest of
purchasing agents,
assistants, etc.,
§41-16-30.
Contracts for which
competitive bidding
required, §41-16-20.
Contracts for which
competitive bidding
not required,
§§41-16-21, 41-16-22.
Contracts of certain state
and local agencies.
Advanced disclosure of
terms of bid.
Effect, §41-16-56.
Advertising for bids,
§41-16-54.
Letting of contracts
without public
advertisement,
§41-16-53.
Agreements among
bidders.
Effect of agreements in
restraint of
competition,
§41-16-55.
Applicability of article.
Provisions not
applicable to
certain municipal
contracts,
§41-16-62.
Assignment of contracts,
§41-16-59.
Awarding contracts,
§41-16-57.
Manner of awarding,
§41-16-50.
Resident bidders,
§41-16-50.
Violations of article,
§41-16-60.
Bond for faithful
performance of
contract, §41-16-58.
When required,
§41-16-50.
Collusion among bidders.
Effect of collusion in
restraint of
competition,
§41-16-55.
Conflicts of interest,
§41-16-60.
Construction equipment.
Expenditures for
repair or lease,
§41-16-52.
Duration of contracts.
Purchase of personal
property or
contractual
services,
§41-16-57.
Emergencies.
Letting of contracts
without public
advertisement,
§41-16-53.
Exemptions from
competitive bidding
requirements,
§41-16-51.

CONTRACTS—Cont'd
Public contracts—Cont'd
Competitive bidding—Cont'd
Contracts of certain state
and local agencies
—Cont'd
Injunctions.
Institution of actions
to enjoin execution
of contracts,
§41-16-61.
Inspections.
Public inspection of
bids, §41-16-54.
Records to be open to
public inspection,
§41-16-57.
Joint contracts,
§41-16-50.
Negotiation of contracts,
§41-16-50.
Opening of bids,
§41-16-54.
Open market.
When purchases or
contracts may be
made in open
market, §41-16-54.
Partial contracts.
Certain partial
contracts declared
void, §41-16-54.
Preference to Alabama
commodities, firms,
etc., §41-16-57.
Procedures for
competitive bidding,
§41-16-51.
Provisions of article
cumulative,
§41-16-63.
Public inspection of bids,
§41-16-54.
Purchasing facilities,
§41-16-51.
Records to be open to
public inspection,
§41-16-57.
Rejection of bids,
§41-16-57.
Required.
Contracts for which
not required,
§§41-16-51,
41-16-52.
Contracts for which
required,
§41-16-50.
Resident bidders.
Award of contracts to
resident bidders,
§41-16-50.
Retention of bids,
§41-16-54.
Sealing of bids,
§41-16-54.
Solicitation of bids,
§41-16-54.
Splitting contracts.
Not to be split to avoid
requirements of
article, §41-16-54.
Terms of bid.
Effect of advanced
disclosure,
§41-16-56.
Violations of article.
Contracts void,
§41-16-51.

CONTRACTS—Cont'd
Public contracts—Cont'd
Competitive bidding—Cont'd
Contracts of certain state
and local agencies
—Cont'd
Violations of article
—Cont'd
Institution of actions
to enjoin execution
of contracts,
§41-16-61.
Making of purchases
or awarding of
contracts in
violation of article,
§41-16-60.
Void contracts.
Certain partial
contracts declared
void, §41-16-54.
Contracts entered into
in violation of
article void,
§41-16-51.
When competitive
bidding not required,
§§41-16-51, 41-16-52.
When competitive
bidding required,
§41-16-50.
Exception, §41-16-50.
County industrial
development boards.
Corporation exempt from
competitive bid laws,
§11-20-49.
Emergency affecting public
health, safety, etc.
Letting of contracts
without public
advertisement
authorized in case of
such emergencies,
§41-16-23.
Exemptions from article,
§41-16-21.
Emergencies.
Letting of contracts
without public
advertisement,
§41-16-23.
Shakespeare festival
theatre finance
authority,
§41-10-212.
State and local
government,
§41-16-51.
Utility services facilities,
§11-97-20.
Facilities necessary for
competitive bidding.
Establishment,
maintenance, etc.,
§41-16-21.
Federal government.
Not required on
purchases from
federal government,
§41-16-22.
Honorariums.
Exemption of certain
departments or
agencies,
§41-16-21.2.
Injunctions.
Institution of actions to
enjoin execution of
contracts, §41-16-31.

CONTRACTS—Cont'd
Public contracts—Cont'd
Competitive bidding—Cont'd
Medicaid contracts,
§41-16-27.
Negotiated contracts.
Award, §41-16-27.
Opening of bids, §41-16-24.
Partial contracts.
Certain partial contracts
declared void,
§41-16-24.
Provisions of article
cumulative, §41-16-32.
Public inspection of bids,
§41-16-24.
Records.
Open to public
inspection,
§41-16-27.
Repeal of other provisions
of law, §41-16-32.
Retention of bids,
§41-16-24.
Sealing of bids required,
§41-16-24.
Solicitation of bids,
§41-16-24.
Solid waste disposal
authorities.
Exemption from
competitive bid laws,
§11-89A-18.
Splitting of contracts.
Contracts not to be split,
§41-16-24.
Violations of article.
Contracts, §41-16-21.
Institution of actions to
enjoin execution of
contracts, §41-16-31.
Limitation on actions,
§41-16-2.
Making of purchase or
awarding of
contracts in violation
of article, §41-16-30.
Void contracts.
Certain partial contracts,
§41-16-24.
Contracts entered into in
violation of article,
§41-16-21.
When not required,
§41-16-22.
When required, §41-16-20.
Duration.
Contracts for purchase of
personal property or
contractual services,
§41-16-27.
Execution.
Timely execution required,
§41-16-3.
Extra compensation not to be
granted contractor after
service rendered or
contract made, Const.
Ala., art. IV, §68.
Insurance.
Conflicts of interest.
Requiring for
procurement of
insurance from
particular company,
etc., §41-16-80.
Conflicts witht article.
Provisions declared void
and unenforceable,
§41-16-82.

CONTRACTS—Cont'd
Public contracts—Cont'd
Insurance—Cont'd
Execution of insurance
contracts.
Approval of manner of
execution, §41-16-81.
Form of insurance
contracts.
Approval of form,
§41-16-81.
Selection of insurance
company by bidder,
§§41-16-80, 41-16-81.
Sufficiency of insurance
contracts.
Approval of sufficiency,
§41-16-81.
Joint purchasing agreements,
§41-16-21.1.
Limits under contract.
Withdrawal by contractor
of amounts retained
from payments,
§41-16-1.
Negotiated contracts.
Award, §41-16-27.
Payments by state.
Timely state payments
required, §41-16-3.
Preference to be given to
Alabama commodities,
firms, etc., §41-16-27.
Shakespeare festival theatre
finance authority.
Exemption from
competitive bid laws,
§41-10-212.
Splitting of contracts.
Not to be split, §41-16-24.
Void contracts.
Advertisement for bids,
§41-16-24.
Certain partial contracts
declared void,
§41-16-24.
Contracts in violation of
competitive bidding
requirements,
§41-16-21.
Opening of bids, §41-16-24.
Partial contracts.
Certain partial contracts
declared void,
§41-16-24.
Public inspection of bids,
§41-16-24.
Retention of bids,
§41-16-24.
Sealing of bids required,
§41-16-24.
Solicitation of bids,
§41-16-24.
Splitting of contracts.
Contracts not to be split,
§41-16-24.
Withdrawal by contractor of
amounts retained from
payments under contract,
§41-16-1.
**Public improvement
contracts.**
See PUBLIC WORKS.
Public lands.
See PUBLIC LANDS.
**Public officers and
employees.**
Code of ethics.
Entering into contracts
with state agencies,
§36-25-11.

CONTRACTS—Cont'd
Public officers and
    employees—Cont'd
  Code of ethics—Cont'd
    Former officials or
      employees.
      Notice required,
        §36-25-13.
    Reports by persons related
      to state officials or
      employees who
      contract with state,
      §36-25-16.
  Insurance.
    State employees' health
      insurance plan.
      See PUBLIC OFFICERS
        AND EMPLOYEES.
Public utilities.
  Ameraport offshore harbor
    and terminal
    commission.
    Contracts for public
      utilities, §33-10-21.
  Municipal corporations.
    Rates and service
      regulations established
      by contract, §37-4-22.
    Submission to commission,
      §37-4-22.
Public works.
  See PUBLIC WORKS.
Railroad authorities.
  Construction and purchasing
    contracts.
    Exemption from certain
      provisions, §37-13-20.
  Power to execute contracts,
    §37-13-7.
Real estate brokers.
  Commission authorized to
    contract for educational
    services, §34-27-6.
Real property.
  Sale of real property. See
    within this heading,
    "Conveyances."
Recordation.
  See RECORDATION.
Redevelopment projects.
  Powers of housing authorities
    or municipalities,
    §24-2-3.
Reformation.
  Deeds, mortgages and
    conveyances.
    See CONVEYANCES.
  Written contract not
    expressing parties'
    intent, §8-1-2.
Releases.
  Consideration.
    Required, §8-1-23.
  Written release.
    No consideration required,
      §8-1-23.
Rent.
  Hirings. See within this
    heading, "Hirings."
Rental-purchase agreements,
  §§8-25-1 to 8-25-6.
  See RENTAL-PURCHASE
    AGREEMENTS.
Restraint of trade.
  Contracts restraining
    business void, §8-1-1.
    Exceptions, §8-1-1.
Revision.
  Written contract not
    expressing parties'
    intent, §8-1-2.

CONTRACTS—Cont'd
Sales.
  Commercial code, §§7-2-101
    to 7-2-725.
    See COMMERCIAL CODE.
  Conditional sales contract.
    Evidence, §35-4-98.
    Secured transactions,
      §§7-9-101 to 7-9-507.
      See SECURED
        TRANSACTIONS.
  Public lands.
    Bids under agreement to
      transfer prohibited.
    Contracts in violation
      void, §8-1-102.
  Public sales.
    Bidding.
      Consideration for bidding
        or not bidding
        prohibited.
        Contracts in violation
          void, §8-1-102.
  Real property. See within
    this heading,
    "Conveyances."
Sales representative's
  commission contracts,
  §§8-24-1 to 8-24-5.
Satisfaction.
  Accord and satisfaction. See
    within this heading,
    "Accord and
    satisfaction."
Savings and loan
  associations.
  Operating or management
    contracts, §5-16-42.
  Power to enter into contracts,
    §5-16-51.
  State associations may make
    contracts available to
    federal associations,
    §5-16-52.
Seals and sealed
  instruments.
  Commercial code.
    Sales contracts.
      Seals inoperative,
        §7-2-203.
Secured transactions,
  §§7-9-101 to 7-9-507.
  See COMMERCIAL CODE.
Shakespeare festival theatre
  finance authority.
  Exemption from competitive
    bid laws, §41-10-212.
Small loans.
  Preexisting contracts.
    Revocation, suspension or
      surrender of licenses
      not to impair
      preexisting contracts,
      §5-18-9.
Soil and water conservation.
  Districts.
    Effect of discontinuance of
      district, §9-8-31.
    Powers of district, §9-8-25.
  Watershed conservancy
    districts.
    Powers of board, §9-8-61.
Southeast interstate low-
  level radioactive waste
  management compact.
  Bonds, surety, §22-32-5.
  Operation and disposal of
    waste, §22-32-4.
Specific performance.
  See SPECIFIC
    PERFORMANCE.

CONTRACTS—Cont'd
Sports.
  Agents.
    Generally, §§8-26-1 to
      8-26-41.
    See SPORTS.
State.
  Impairing obligations of
    contracts, Const. U. S.,
    Art. I, §10.
State departments and
  agencies.
  Public improvement
    contracts.
    General provisions.
      See PUBLIC WORKS.
State parks.
  Maintenance and operation
    of concessions within
    state park areas.
    See STATE PARKS.
Statute of frauds.
  Certain agreements void
    unless in writing, §8-9-2.
  Sales contracts, §7-2-202.
    Modification of sales
      contracts, §7-2-209.
Supercomputer authority.
  Liability upon contract,
    §41-10-402.
  Requirements.
    Contractual agreements
      with supercomputer
      services, §41-10-399.
Surveys and surveyors.
  Division of land surveys,
    §35-2-36.
Synfuels development
  authority.
  Aggregation monetary
    obligation, §9-6A-8.
  Competitive bidding,
    §9-6A-8.
  Highways, roads and bridges.
    Supervision or performance
      by highway
      department, §9-6A-8.
Teachers.
  Employment.
    See EDUCATION.
Tennessee Valley Authority.
  Exhibit commission.
    Powers, §41-9-782.
Textbooks.
  Adoption of textbooks.
    See EDUCATION.
Tombigbee Valley
  development authority.
  United States.
    Power to enter into
      contracts with United
      States, §33-17-8.
Trade schools.
  Competitive bidding,
    §16-60-89.
Tunnels.
  Construction.
    Federal assistance, §23-1-1.
Uniform commercial code.
  See COMMERCIAL CODE.
Universities and colleges.
  Age of majority.
    Contracting for educational
      loans for college level
      education and above,
      §26-1-5.
  Prepaid tuition contracts,
    §§16-33C-7, 16-33C-8.
Usury.
  Enforcement of usurious
    contracts, §8-8-12.

CONTRACTS—Cont'd

Vacation time-sharing plans generally, §§34-27-50 to 34-27-69.
See VACATION TIME-SHARING PLANS.
Venue, §§6-3-2, 6-3-3.
Veterans.
Loans.
Minor veterans empowered to contract liability for repayment of certain loans, §31-1-2.
State veterans' homes.
Operation of homes.
Award of contract, §31-5A-4.
Veterans' organizations.
Assistance in processing claims, §31-5-5.
Void contracts.
Contracts restraining business, §8-1-1.
Exceptions, §8-1-1.
Future delivery. See within this heading, "Future delivery."
Gambling contracts.
See GAMBLING.
Insane persons, §§8-1-170 to 8-1-172.
Public lands.
Sales.
Bids under agreement to transfer prohibited.
Contracts in violation void, §8-1-102.
Public sales.
Consideration for bidding or not bidding prohibited.
Contract in violation void, §8-1-102.
Wagering, §§8-1-150 to 8-1-152.
Water conservation and irrigation.
Agency.
Construction work, §9-10-7.
Officers of corporation not to be interested, §9-10-12.
Powers of agency, §9-10-5.
Purchases of materials, §9-10-7.
Corporations.
See WATER CONSERVATION AND IRRIGATION.
Water management and drainage.
Board of water management commissioners.
Powers to contract, §9-9-15.
Districts.
Construction of improvements, §9-9-42.
Waters and watercourses.
Opening and cleaning navigable streams.
County commission authorized to make contracts, §33-7-2.
Water supply and waterworks.
Water distribution facilities.
Conveyance of facilities without commission approval, §37-4-45.

CONTRACTS—Cont'd

Weights and measures.
Construction according to standards ascertained by congress, §8-16-4.
Wills.
Concerning making or not revoking a will or devise.
Establishment, §43-8-250.
Youth services.
Competitive bids, §44-1-29.
Conflicts of interest, §44-1-29.

CONTRIBUTING TO DELINQUENCY OF MINORS, §12-15-13.

CONTRIBUTORY NEGLIGENCE.

Affirmative defense, ARCP, Rule 8 (c).
Motor vehicles.
Child passenger restraints.
Failure to wear restraint devices.
Contributory negligence not imputed, §32-5-222.

CONTROLLED SUBSTANCES.
See DRUGS.

CONVENTION FACILITIES.

Appropriations.
Source of appropriations, §11-100-7.
State assistance payments, §11-100-4.
Bond issues.
Faith and credit of state not pledged, §11-100-7.
Refunding or refinancing of bonds.
Application of payments and credits, §11-100-8.
Citation of act.
Short title, §11-100-1.
Definitions, §11-100-3.
Findings of legislature, §11-100-2.
Funds.
Alabama convention facilities fund, §11-100-5.
Legislative declaration, §11-100-2.
Short title of act, §11-100-1.
State assistance payments, §11-100-4.
Alabama convention facilities fund, §11-100-5.
Applications, §§11-100-4, 11-100-5.
Appropriations, §11-100-4.
Quarterly requests, §11-100-4.
Termination, §11-100-6.
Return of moneys held, §11-100-6.
Title of act.
Short title, §11-100-1.

CONVENTIONS.

Churches.
State conventions or associations of churches, §§10-4-60 to 10-4-63.
Constitution of Alabama,
Const. Ala., art. XVIII, §§286, 287.
Political parties.
See ELECTIONS.

CONVEYANCES.

Acknowledgments.
Appointment of commissioners in other states, §36-1-1.
Disqualification of corporate officers or shareholders, §35-4-25.
Forms, §§35-4-29, 35-4-68.
Improperly acknowledged instruments as evidence, §35-4-72.
Officers authorized to take.
In other states or foreign countries, §35-4-26.
In this state, §35-4-24.
Officers holding stock in certain corporations, §35-4-25.
Official seal.
Proof of official seal, §35-4-27.
Powers of attorney, etc., §35-4-28.
Proof of official seal, §35-4-27.
Seals.
Proof of official seal, §35-4-27.
Witness requirements.
Acknowledgments operate as compliance with witness requirements, §35-4-23.
Actions.
Reformation of deeds, mortgages and conveyances, §§35-4-150 to 35-4-153.
Administrators.
Conveyances by executors and administrators, §§35-4-303, 35-4-320 to 35-4-323.
Affidavits.
By whom made, §35-4-69.
Evidence.
Admissibility as evidence, §35-4-70.
Filing by probate judge, §35-4-71.
Notice.
Record as notice of facts recited, §35-4-69.
Recordation.
By probate judge, §35-4-71.
Record as notice of facts recited, §35-4-69.
Associations.
Literary or social societies, §§35-4-340 to 35-4-344.
Attestation by witnesses, §35-4-20.
Attornment.
Attornment of tenant unnecessary, §35-4-32.
"Bargain."
Construction of word, §35-4-271.
Capacity.
Who may convey lands by deed or will, §35-4-1.
Cemeteries.
Charitable trusts.
Burial societies, cemeteries, etc., §11-17-14.

CONVEYANCES—Cont'd
  Cemeteries—Cont'd
    Charitable trusts—Cont'd
      Conveyances, devises, etc.,
        for preservation,
        repair, etc., of public
        or private burial
        places, etc., §11-17-13.
      Perpetual trusts,
        §11-17-15.
      Validation, etc., of prior
        conveyances,
        §11-17-16.
  Condominiums.
    Common and limited
      common elements.
      Conveyance includes
        undivided interest in,
        §35-8-6.
  Consideration.
    Recitation unnecessary,
      §35-4-34.
  **Construction and
    interpretation.**
    Words "grant," "bargain," or
      "sell," §35-4-271.
  Contracts.
    Abandonment.
      When recorded contract
        presumed abandoned,
        §35-4-75.
    Death of person contracting
      to sell real property.
      Conveyances by executors
        and administrators.
      See EXECUTORS AND
        ADMINISTRATORS.
    Judgment for specific
      performance, §35-4-33.
    Recitation of consideration
      unnecessary, §35-4-34.
  Corporations.
    Acknowledgments.
      Disqualification of
        corporate officers or
        shareholders, §35-4-25.
    Proof of conveyances
      executed in name of
      corporation, §35-4-67.
  Counties.
    County industrial
      development authorities.
      Transfer of funds and
        assets to authority,
        §11-92A-21.
    County property generally,
      §11-14-2.
    Effect of conveyances to
      officers, etc., for use of
      county, §11-14-1.
    Public building authorities.
      Conveyance of property to
        corporation by county,
        §11-15-16.
    Waterworks plants and
      distribution systems.
      Conveyance to municipal
        corporations, §11-14-3.
  Covenants of warranty.
    When implied, §35-4-271.
  Death.
    Contract to convey real
      property.
      Conveyances by executors
        and administrators,
        §§35-4-303, 35-4-320 to
        35-4-323.

CONVEYANCES—Cont'd
  Death—Cont'd
    Powers of disposition.
      Death of trustee with right
        of selection.
      Execution of power upon
        death, §35-4-298.
  Debtors and creditors.
    Powers of disposition.
      Special and beneficial
        powers liable to claims
        of creditors, §35-4-305.
  Decedents' estates.
    Conveyances by executors
      and administrators,
      §§35-4-303, 35-4-320 to
      35-4-323.
  Deeds.
    See DEEDS.
  Delivery of deed.
    Time for delivery of deed,
      §35-4-75.
  **Destroyed papers or
    records.**
    Substitution in civil cases,
      §12-20-30.
  Dower.
    See DOWER.
  Evidence.
    Affidavits.
      Admissibility as evidence,
        §35-4-70.
    Improperly acknowledged or
      recorded instruments as
      evidence, §35-4-72.
    When conveyance receivable
      in evidence, §35-4-65.
  Execution, §35-4-20.
    Execution sales.
      See EXECUTIONS.
  **Executors and
    administrators.**
    Conveyances by executors
      and administrators,
      §§35-4-303, 35-4-320 to
      35-4-323.
  Foreclosure of mortgage.
    See MORTGAGES AND
      DEEDS OF TRUST.
  Forms.
    Acknowledgments, §35-4-29.
    Probate of conveyance,
      §35-4-30.
  Fraud.
    General provisions, §§8-9A-1
      to 8-9A-12.
    See FRAUDULENT
      TRANSFERS.
  **Governor or state agency or
    institution, §§35-4-380 to
    35-4-391.**
    Adverse possession.
      Conveyances in cases of
        adverse possession,
        §35-4-391.
    Contingent interests.
      Sale of contingent interests
        by state institutions,
        §35-4-384.
    Decedents' estates.
      Public land patents.
        Patent to decedent vests
        title in his
        successors,
        §35-4-386.
    Educational institutions.
      Sale of contingent interests
        by state institutions,
        §35-4-384.

CONVEYANCES—Cont'd
  **Governor or state agency or
    institution**—Cont'd
    Leases.
      Salt springs, etc.,
        §35-4-380.
      Validity of leases, etc., by
        state agencies,
        §35-4-383.
    Limestone and clay.
      Sale of right to quarry
        limestone and clay,
        §35-4-381.
    Lost deeds.
      Conveyances in cases of
        lost deeds, §35-4-391.
    Minerals.
      Lease of salt springs, etc.,
        §35-4-380.
    Oil and gas.
      Lease of salt springs, etc.,
        §35-4-380.
    Prior conveyances.
      Ratified and confirmed,
        §35-4-390.
    Public lands.
      Conveyance of lands owned
        by state, §35-4-385.
      Lease of salt springs, etc.,
        §35-4-380.
    Patents.
      Decedent's estates.
        Patent to decedent
        vests title in his
        successors,
        §35-4-386.
      Recordation, §35-4-387.
      Swamp and overflowed
        lands, §35-4-389.
      When purchaser entitled
        to receive patent,
        §35-4-388.
    Quarries.
      Sale of right to quarry
        limestone and clay,
        §35-4-381.
    Recordation.
      Public land patents,
        §35-4-387.
    Salt springs.
      Lease of salt springs, etc.,
        §35-4-380.
    Universities and colleges.
      Sale of contingent interests
        by state institutions,
        §35-4-384.
    Validity of conveyances by
      state agencies, §35-4-382.
    Validity of leases, etc., by
      state agencies, §35-4-383.
  "Grant."
    Construction of word,
      §35-4-271.
  Homesteads, §6-10-3.
    Deed to husband or wife,
      §6-10-6.
  Housing projects.
    Alienation of certain public
      improvements by
      political subdivisions,
      §§35-4-410 to 35-4-412.
  Husband and wife.
    Conveyances by spouse of
      insane person, §§30-4-30
      to 30-4-37.
    See HUSBAND AND
      WIFE.

CONVEYANCES—Cont'd
Husband and wife—Cont'd
Conveyances by spouse of
prisoner, person non
compos mentis or by
abandoning spouse,
§30-4-12.
Judgment creditors.
Recordation necessary as to
judgment creditors.
Generally, §§35-4-390 to
35-4-397.
See RECORDATION.
Judgments.
Specific performance.
Judgment for specific
performance, §35-4-33.
Landlord and tenant.
Attornment of tenant
unnecessary, §35-4-32.
Conveyance of greater estate
by tenant for life or
years passes his estate,
§35-4-232.
Payment of rent without
notice of conveyance,
§35-4-32.
Life estates.
Conveyance of greater estate
by tenant for life or
years passes his estate,
§35-4-232.
Literary or social societies,
§§35-4-340 to 35-4-344.
Applicability of article.
Article not exclusive,
§35-4-344.
Property subject to
provisions of article,
§35-4-342.
Vendor's liens and
mortgages, §35-4-343.
Article not exclusive,
§35-4-344.
Execution of deed, §35-4-341.
Meeting of trustees,
§35-4-341.
Mortgages.
Societies not prevented
from taking
mortgages, §35-4-343.
Property subject to provisions
of article, §35-4-342.
Trustees.
Meeting of trustees,
§35-4-341.
Who may convey title,
§35-4-340.
Vendor's liens.
Societies not prevented
from retaining
vendor's lien,
§35-4-343.
Who may convey title,
§35-4-340.
Livery of seisin.
Unnecessary, §35-4-31.
Lost papers or records.
Substitution in civil cases,
§12-20-30.
Maps and plats.
Town surveys, plats or maps.
Certification,
acknowledgment, etc.,
held to be conveyance,
§35-2-51.

CONVEYANCES—Cont'd
Marriage.
Personal property conveyed
in consideration of
marriage.
Necessary recordation,
§35-4-93.
Recitation of marital status
of grantor or vendor
required, §35-4-73.
Mentally ill.
Husband and wife.
Conveyances by spouse of
insane person.
See HUSBAND AND
WIFE.
Void contracts.
Conveyance of real estate
not void if made in
good faith, §8-1-171.
Minors.
Powers of disposition.
Disposition to or among
children, §35-4-300.
Mistake.
Reformation, §35-4-153.
**Mortgages and deeds of
trust.**
See MORTGAGES AND
DEEDS OF TRUST.
Municipal corporations.
Town surveys, plats or maps.
Certification,
acknowledgment, etc.,
held to be conveyance,
§35-2-51.
Notice.
Acknowledgments.
Disqualification of
corporate officers or
shareholders, §35-4-25.
Purchasers, mortgagees or
judgment creditors.
Notice of conveyances,
§35-4-90.
Option to purchase land.
Limitations on duration of
option, §35-4-76.
Parks and recreation.
Alienation of certain public
improvements by
political subdivisions of
state, §§35-4-410 to
35-4-412.
Parties.
Reformation.
Grantors, etc., may be
made parties
defendant, §35-4-152.
Partition.
Sale of land of minors and
insane persons for
distribution among joint
owners, §§35-6-80 to
35-6-91.
See PARTITION.
Partnerships.
Real property, §10-8-73.
Personal property.
Minors.
Conveyances of personalty
to minors, §35-4-96.
Recordation.
See RECORDATION.
Power districts.
Power to make and enter,
§37-5-3.

CONVEYANCES—Cont'd
Powers of disposition,
§§35-4-290 to 35-4-306.
Absolute powers.
Effect of grant of absolute
power, §35-4-292.
Powers deemed absolute,
§35-4-291.
Applicability of article.
Power of attorney.
Article not extended to
simple power of
attorney, §35-4-306.
Beneficial powers.
Liable to claims of
creditors, §35-4-305.
Children.
Disposition to or among
children, §35-4-300.
Construction and
interpretation.
Powers deemed absolute,
§35-4-291.
Creditors.
Special and beneficial
powers liable to claims
of creditors, §35-4-305.
Death of trustee.
Execution of power upon
death of trustee with
right of selection,
§35-4-298.
Devises.
Requirements for
disposition by devise,
§35-4-295.
Donees.
Execution of power by
surviving donee,
§35-4-304.
Execution of power.
Cases where instrument
specified is
insufficient, §35-4-296.
Consent of third persons,
§35-4-299.
Surviving donee,
§35-4-304.
Surviving or acting
executors, §35-4-303.
Upon death of trustee with
right of selection,
§35-4-298.
Executors.
Execution of power by
surviving or acting
executors, §35-4-303.
Presumption that power
not personal,
§35-4-303.
Extent of power.
Dispositions valid to extent
of power, §35-4-293.
Grantor.
Reservation of power,
§35-4-290.
Insufficient instrument.
Execution in cases where
instrument specified is
insufficient, §35-4-296.
Irrevocability.
Powers irrevocable unless
otherwise indicated,
§35-4-301.
Minors.
Disposition to or among
children, §35-4-300.
Personal power.
Presumption that power
not personal,
§35-4-303.

CONVEYANCES—Cont'd
Powers of disposition
—Cont'd
Power of attorney.
Article not extended to
simple power of
attorney, §35-4-306.
Presumption that power not
personal, §35-4-303.
Real property.
Power disposing of real
estate required to be
in writing, §35-4-294.
Release of powers, §35-4-302.
Requirements.
Disposition by devise or
will, §35-4-295.
Execution in cases where
instrument specified is
insufficient, §35-4-296.
Power disposing of real
estate required to be
in writing, §35-4-294.
Reservation of power by
grantor, §35-4-290.
Several persons.
Disposition by, between or
among several persons,
§35-4-297.
Special powers.
Liable to claims of
creditors, §35-4-305.
Surviving donee.
Execution of power by
surviving donee,
§35-4-304.
Third persons.
Consent of third persons to
execution of power,
§35-4-299.
Validity.
Dispositions valid to extent
of power, §35-4-293.
Wills.
Requirements for
disposition by devise or
will, §35-4-295.
Writing.
Power disposing of real
estate required to be
in writing, §35-4-294.
**Preparer of instruments
conveying real property.**
Statement of name and
address of preparer of
certain instruments,
§§35-4-110 to 35-4-112.
Presumptions.
Powers of disposition.
Presumption that power
not personal,
§35-4-303.
Probate of conveyance.
Form of probate, §35-4-30.
Proof.
Appointment of
commissioners in other
states or territories to
take proof of conveyances
of property within state,
§36-1-1.
Public lands.
Conveyances by governor or
state agency or
institution, §§35-4-380 to
35-4-391. See within this
heading, "Governor or
state agency or
institution."

CONVEYANCES—Cont'd
Purchasers.
Recordation necessary as to
purchasers.
See RECORDATION.
Recordation tax.
See RECORDATION.
**Reformation of deeds,
mortgages and
conveyances,** §§35-4-150
to 35-4-153.
Actions.
Civil action for reformation
of conveyances
containing erroneous
description, §35-4-150.
Defendants.
Grantors, etc., may be
made parties
defendant,
§35-4-152.
Error in any description
sufficient to maintain
action, §35-4-151.
Defendants.
Grantors, etc., may be
made parties
defendant, §35-4-152.
Erroneous descriptions.
Civil action for reformation
of conveyances
containing erroneous
description, §35-4-150.
Error in any description
sufficient to maintain
civil action, §35-4-151.
Fraud, §35-4-153.
Grantors.
May be made parties
defendant, §35-4-152.
Mistake, §35-4-153.
Parties.
Grantors, etc., may be
made parties
defendant, §35-4-152.
Rule against perpetuities.
Conveyance to avoid
perpetuities, §35-4-5.
Generally, §35-4-4.
Seal unnecessary, §35-4-21.
"Sell."
Construction of word,
§35-4-271.
Signature, §35-4-20.
Societies.
Literary or social societies,
§§35-4-340 to 35-4-344.
Specific performance,
§§8-1-46, 8-1-47.
Judgment for specific
performance, §35-4-33.
Standing timber.
Conveyances of standing
timber.
Generally, §§35-4-360 to
35-4-363.
**State agencies or
institutions,** §§35-4-380 to
35-4-391. See within this
heading, "Governor or
state agency or
institution."
Support and maintenance.
Voiding of conveyances based
on consideration of
support, §8-9-12.
Tenant for life or years.
Conveyance of greater estate
by tenant for life or
years passes his estate,
§35-4-232.

CONVEYANCES—Cont'd
**Town surveys, plats or
maps.**
Certification,
acknowledgment, etc.,
held to be conveyance,
§35-2-51.
Trees and timber.
Conveyances of standing
timber.
Generally, §§35-4-360 to
35-4-363.
Transfers of standing timber,
trees and cutting rights.
Void and inoperative
without notice or prior
recordation, §35-4-92.
Trusts and trustees.
Powers of disposition,
§§35-4-290 to 35-4-306.
See within this heading,
"Powers of disposition."
**Unincorporated professional
associations,** §10-10-9.
Warranties.
When covenants of warranty
implied, §35-4-271.
Words "grant," "bargain," or
"sell," §35-4-271.
**Water supply and
waterworks.**
Water distribution facilities.
Conveyance without
commission approval,
§37-4-45.
Witnesses.
Acknowledgments.
Operate as compliance
with witness
requirements,
§35-4-23.
Attestation by witnesses,
§35-4-20.
Form of proof of conveyances,
§35-4-68.
Writing.
Required to be in writing,
§35-4-20.

CONVICTS.
See PRISONS AND
PRISONERS.

**COOPERATIVE
ASSOCIATIONS.**
Agriculture.
See AGRICULTURE.
Condominiums.
See CONDOMINIUMS.
Electric cooperatives,
§§37-6-1 to 37-6-49.
See ELECTRIC
COOPERATIVES.
Motor vehicle carriers.
Vehicles controlled and
operated by cooperative
associations.
Exemptions from chapter,
§37-3-4.

COORDINATE SYSTEM.
Alabama coordinate system,
§§35-2-1 to 35-2-9.
See SURVEYS AND
SURVEYORS.

COOSA COUNTY.
Court costs and charges,
Const. Ala., amd. 345.
Economic and industrial
development promotion,
Const. Ala., amd. 429.

COOSA COUNTY—Cont'd
Officers.
Compensation of certain
officers, Const. Ala.,
amd. 345.
School tax.
Special tax in school
districts, Const. Ala.,
amd. 145.

**COOSA VALLEY
DEVELOPMENT
AUTHORITY, §§33-16-1 to
33-16-15.**
Actions.
Power to sue and be sued,
§33-16-8.
Bond issues.
Authority to issue, §33-16-12.
Dates, §33-16-12.
Delivery, §33-16-12.
Execution, §33-16-12.
Full faith and credit of state
pledged for payment,
§33-16-12.
Governor.
Approval of terms and
conditions, §33-16-12.
Installments, §33-16-12.
Interest.
Rates of interest,
§33-16-12.
State treasurer to pay
interest, §33-16-14.
Legislative intent, §33-16-2.
Maximum principal,
§33-16-12.
Payment.
Full faith and credit of
state pledged for
payment, §33-16-12.
Principal.
Maximum amount,
§33-16-12.
State treasurer to pay
principal, §33-16-14.
Proceeds.
Disposition, §33-16-13.
Records.
Payment of principal and
interest by state
treasurer, §33-16-14.
Refunding bonds.
Proceeds from sale,
§33-16-13.
Sale.
Approval of directors,
§33-16-12.
Notice of sale, §33-16-12.
Sale for less than face
value, §33-16-12.
State treasurer.
Payment of principal and
interest, §33-16-14.
Bridges.
Contracts for construction,
reconstruction, etc.,
§33-16-9.
Duties and obligations in
regard to, §33-16-7.
Construction of chapter,
§33-16-2.
Contracts.
Approval by board, §33-16-9.
Between authority and
United States, §33-16-9.
Maximum obligation that
authority may incur,
§33-16-9.
Power to enter into certain
contracts, §33-16-8.

**COOSA VALLEY
DEVELOPMENT
AUTHORITY**—Cont'd
Counties.
Cooperation with counties,
§33-16-2.
Definitions, §33-16-1.
Directors, §33-16-6.
Compensation, §33-16-6.
Contracts.
Approval by directors,
§33-16-9.
Records of proceedings,
§33-16-6.
Dissolution of authority,
§33-16-15.
Duties.
Delegation of duties to other
public corporations,
agencies and
departments of state,
§33-16-10.
Generally, §33-16-7.
Eminent domain.
Exercise of power, §33-16-8.
Evidence.
Records of proceedings.
Prima facie evidence,
§33-16-6.
Fees.
Incorporation.
No fees to be paid to
secretary of state,
§33-16-5.
Governor.
President of authority,
§33-16-6.
Public corporation, §33-16-3.
Highways.
Contracts, §33-16-9.
Incorporation.
Application.
Contents, §33-16-4.
Presentation to secretary of
state, §33-16-4.
Signatures, §33-16-4.
Authorization to form public
corporation, §33-16-3.
Certificate of incorporation.
Issuance, §33-16-5.
Procedure, §33-16-4.
Interest.
Bond issues, §§33-16-12,
33-16-14.
Legislature.
Legislative intent, §33-16-2.
Members, §33-16-6.
Compensation, §33-16-6.
Municipal corporations.
Cooperation with
municipalities, §33-16-2.
Navigation.
Authority, §33-16-11.
Obligations.
Generally, §33-16-7.
Officers, §33-16-6.
Compensation, §33-16-6.
Powers.
Enumerated, §33-16-8.
Public corporation.
Authorization to form,
§33-16-3.
Real property.
Dissolution of authority.
Disposition of real property
upon dissolution,
§33-16-15.
Power to receive, take and
hold, §33-16-8.

**COOSA VALLEY
DEVELOPMENT
AUTHORITY**—Cont'd
Records.
Proceedings of board of
directors, §33-16-6.
River and canal terminals.
Duties and obligations with
respect to, §33-16-7.
Seal, §33-16-5.
Secretary of state.
Application for incorporation.
Presentation to secretary,
§33-16-4.
Certificate of incorporation.
Issuance, §33-16-5.
Dissolution of authority.
Application for dissolution.
Filing with secretary,
§33-16-15.
Fees.
No fees to be paid to
secretary of state,
§33-16-5.
Sewers.
Duties and obligations with
respect to, §33-16-7.
**State departments and
agencies.**
Cooperation with, §33-16-2.
Delegation of duties,
§33-16-10.
State treasurer.
Bond issues.
Payment of principal and
interest, §33-16-14.
Custodian of funds, §33-16-6.
Treasurer of authority,
§33-16-6.
Taxation.
Bond issues.
Exemption from taxation,
§33-16-12.
United States.
Cooperation with United
States, §33-16-2.
**Water supply and
waterworks.**
Duties and obligations with
respect to, §33-16-7.

COPYRIGHTS.
Authors.
Protection of rights, Const.
U. S., Art. I, §8.
Governor.
Reports and statutes,
§36-13-5.
Principal and income act.
Generally, §§19-3-270 to
19-3-282.
See TRUSTS AND
TRUSTEES.

CORAM NOBIS.
Rules of civil procedure.
Writ abolished, ARCP, Rule
60 (b).

CORAM VOBIS.
Rules of civil procedure.
Writ abolished, ARCP, Rule
60 (b).

**CORDOVA, MUNICIPALITY
OF.**
Property tax, Const. Ala.,
amd. 13.

CORN.
See GRAIN.

CORNMEAL.
General provisions, §§20-1-70 to 21-1-78.
See BREAD, FLOUR, CORNMEAL AND GRITS.
Weights and measures, §8-16-102.

CORONERS, §§11-5-1 to 11-5-13.
Absence.
Appointment of special coroners, §11-5-10.
Applicability of provisions of chapter, §11-5-13.
Attorneys at law.
Attorneys not deemed sufficient sureties on coroners' bonds, §36-5-13.
Blood and urine samples from certain dead bodies.
Authority, §22-19-80.
Exemption from civil and criminal liability, §22-19-82.
Bonds, surety, §11-5-3.
Additional bond.
Effect of failure to give, §11-5-9.
When required, §11-5-9.
Attorneys not deemed sufficient sureties on coroners' bonds, §36-5-13.
When to give additional bond.
Effect, §11-5-9.
Corrections.
Board of corrections.
Appointment of special coroner.
Request of board, §14-6-99.
Duties.
Generally, §11-5-4.
Sheriff's duties.
Liability for wrongful acts while discharging duties of sheriff, §11-5-12.
When coroner to discharge duties of sheriff, §11-5-5.
Special coroners, §11-5-11.
Elections, §11-5-1.
General elections.
Offices for which general election held, §17-2-2.
Time, §17-2-3.
State and county officers elected by the people, §17-2-1.
Executions.
Collection, etc., of commissions on costs on execution by coroners, §12-19-95.
Execution by coroner or special coroner, §6-9-25.
When coroners entitled to receive full commissions, §12-19-96.
When coroners entitled to receive only half commissions, §12-19-97.

CORONERS—Cont'd
Fees, §§12-19-192, 12-19-193.
Circuit and district court proceedings.
Fees due coroners for services in connection with, §12-19-94.
Criminal cases, §12-19-192.
Executions.
Collection of commissions on costs on execution, §12-19-95.
When coroners entitled to receive full commissions, §12-19-96.
When coroners entitled to receive only half commissions, §12-19-97.
Inquest, §§12-19-192, 12-19-193.
Postmortem examinations, §12-19-193.
Physician's fee for postmortem examination, §15-4-11.
Recovery of costs by county against estate, §15-4-11.
Sheriffs.
Payment of fees to coroners for services rendered in discharging duties of sheriff, §§12-19-192, 12-19-193.
Impeachment.
General provisions.
See IMPEACHMENT.
Subject to impeachment, §36-11-1; Const. Ala., art. VII, §175.
Imprisonment.
Appointment of special coroners, §11-5-10.
Inquest, §§15-4-1 to 15-4-11.
Arrest.
Issuance and execution of warrant for accused, §15-4-9.
Duty to hold inquests, §11-5-4.
Evidence.
Defaulting witnesses.
Endorsement as presumptive evidence of default, §15-4-4.
Examination of body, §15-4-2.
Fees, §§12-19-192, 12-19-193.
Physician's fee for postmortem examinations, §15-4-11.
Inquisition.
Certification by inquisition, §15-4-7.
Contents, §15-4-7.
Return, §15-4-8.
Jury.
Compensation of jurors, §15-4-1.
Direction to summon jury, §15-4-1.
Oath of jurors, §15-4-1.
Rendition of verdict, §15-4-7.
Service of jurors, §15-4-1.
Oaths.
Jurors, §15-4-1.

CORONERS—Cont'd
Inquest—Cont'd
Oaths—Cont'd
Right of coroner to administer, §15-4-6.
Physician or surgeon.
Fees for postmortem examinations, §15-4-11.
Recovery of costs by county against estate, §15-4-11.
Postmortem examination of body, §15-4-2.
Property of deceased.
Delivery to county treasurer, §15-4-10.
Disposition, §15-4-10.
Refusal to answer questions, §15-4-5.
Reports, §15-4-2.
Return of inquisition and preliminary investigation to circuit court, §15-4-8.
Subpoenas.
Service, §15-4-4.
Sworn statement.
Duty of coroner to take on death, §15-4-1.
Warrants.
Issuance and execution of arrest warrant for accused, §15-4-9.
Witnesses.
Examination, §15-4-3.
Proceedings against defaulting witnesses, §15-4-4.
Subpoenas, §15-4-3.
Service, §15-4-4.
Summoning, §15-4-3.
Undertaking of witnesses to appear in court, §15-4-8.
Jails.
When coroner to act as keeper of jail, §11-5-6.
Jury.
Coroner's inquest, §§15-4-1 to 15-4-11. See within this heading, "Inquest."
Liability.
Wrongful acts, etc., while discharging duties of sheriff, §11-5-12.
Limitation of actions.
Actions for nonfeasance, misfeasance or malfeasance.
Actions against surety.
Six year limitation, §6-2-34.
Ten year limitation, §6-2-33.
Motor vehicle accidents.
Reporting requirements, §§32-10-5, 32-10-9.
Negligence.
Liability of coroner or special coroner for wrongful acts while discharging duties of sheriff, §11-5-12.
Postmortem examinations.
Fees, §12-19-193.
Samples.
Blood and urine samples from certain dead bodies, §§22-19-80, 22-19-82.

CORONERS—Cont'd
Sheriffs.
Fees.
Payment of fees to coroners
for services rendered
in discharging duties
of sheriff, §12-19-193.
Liability for wrongful acts
while discharging duties
of sheriff, §11-5-12.
Official acts valid through
process directed to
sheriff, etc., §11-5-8.
When coroner to discharge
duties of sheriff, §11-5-5.
Special coroners.
Appointment, §11-5-10.
Request of board of
corrections, §14-6-99.
Duties, §11-5-11.
Liability for wrongful acts,
etc., while discharging
duties of sheriff,
§11-5-12.
State toxicologist.
See STATE
TOXICOLOGIST.
**Summary proceedings
involving officials.**
General provisions.
See PUBLIC OFFICERS
AND EMPLOYEES.
Summons and process.
Execution, §6-4-3.
When coroner to execute
summons, §11-5-7.
Term of office, §11-5-1.
Vacancies.
Appointment of special
coroners, §11-5-10.
Filling, §11-5-2.
Validity of acts, §11-5-8.
Witnesses.
Coroner's inquest. See within
this heading, "Inquest."
Writs.
When coroners to execute
writs, §11-5-7.
Wrongful acts.
Liability for wrongful acts,
etc., while discharging
duties of sheriff,
§11-5-12.

CORPORATIONS.
Acknowledgments.
Forms, §35-4-29.
Actions.
Derivative actions by
shareholders, ARCP,
Rule 23.1.
Form of complaint, ARCP,
Form 25.
Dissolution.
Creditor's action for
dissolution or
liquidation,
§10-2A-195.
Stockholder's suit for
dissolution or
liquidation,
§10-2A-195.
Indemnification of directors,
officers, employees and
agents, §10-2A-21.
Nonprofit corporations.
Officers.
Liability, §§10-11-1 to
10-11-5.
Powers of corporations,
§10-2A-20.

CORPORATIONS—Cont'd
Actions—Cont'd
Right to sue and be sued,
Const. Ala., art. XII,
§240.
Agents.
Change bills.
Emitting as money,
§13A-9-19.
Employment.
Powers of corporations,
§10-2A-20.
Generally, §§10-2A-29 to
10-2A-31.
Indemnification, §10-2A-21.
Insurance.
Liability insurance,
§10-2A-21.
Nonprofit corporations,
§§10-2A-23 to 10-2A-25,
10-2A-176, 10-2A-177.
Rebates.
Taking by agent of
railroad,
manufacturing or
mining corporation,
§8-11-4.
Registered agents,
§§10-2A-29 to 10-2A-31.
Foreign corporations,
§§10-2A-235 to
10-2A-237, 10-2A-244.
Removal, §10-2A-78.
Service of process.
How process served,
§10-2A-31.
Agriculture.
Acts or omissions of officers
or agents, §2-1-2.
Agricultural markets and
coliseum corporation,
§§2-6-70 to 2-6-86.
See AGRICULTURE.
**Alabama agricultural
markets and coliseum
corporation.**
See AGRICULTURE.
**Alabama business
corporation act.**
General provisions,
§§10-2A-1 to 10-2A-339.
Title of chapter, §10-2A-1.
**Alabama corrections
institution finance
authority.**
See CORRECTIONS.
**Alabama highway finance
corporation.**
See HIGHWAYS.
**Alabama public school
corporation.**
See EDUCATION.
Annual report. See within
this heading, "Reports."
Annulling existence.
Quo warranto.
Right of action and venue,
§6-6-590.
Appeals.
Taxation.
Corporate shares of stock.
Assessment, §40-14-71.
Applicability of provisions.
Existing corporation,
§10-2A-334.
Foreign and interstate
commerce, §10-2A-337.
Generally, §10-2A-336.

CORPORATIONS—Cont'd
Architects.
Certificate of authorization,
§34-2-35.
Renewal.
Fee, §34-2-35.
Art.
Society for promoting art.
See within this heading,
"Public societies."
Articles of dissolution,
§§10-2A-190, 10-2A-191.
Articles of incorporation.
Amendments.
Certificate of amendment.
Effect, §10-2A-115.
Change of name,
§10-2A-110.
Class voting on
amendment,
§10-2A-112.
Contents and execution of
articles of amendment,
§10-2A-113.
Election to become close
corporation,
§10-2A-303.
Filing of articles of
amendment,
§10-2A-114.
Procedure to amend
articles of
incorporation,
§10-2A-111.
Reorganization
proceedings,
§10-2A-117.
Restated articles of
incorporation,
§10-2A-116.
Right to amend articles,
§10-2A-110.
Certificate of incorporation.
See within this heading,
"Certificate of
incorporation."
Change of name.
Right to amend articles of
incorporation,
§10-2A-110.
Class voting on amendments,
§10-2A-112.
Close corporations. See
within this heading,
"Close corporations."
Consolidation or merger,
§10-2A-143.
Contents, §10-2A-91.
Correction of errors or
omissions, §10-2A-95.
Relation back of correction,
§10-2A-95.
Defined, §10-2A-2.
Effect of filing articles,
§10-2A-94.
Filing, §10-2A-92.
Amendment of articles,
§10-2A-114.
Correction of errors or
omissions, §10-2A-95.
Effect of filing, §10-2A-94.
Forfeiture by probate judge
for failure to comply
with section,
§10-2A-92.
Probate judge or secretary
of state, §10-2A-93.
Relation back of correction,
§10-2A-95.
Foreign corporations,
§§10-2A-239, 10-2A-244.

CORPORATIONS—Cont'd
Articles of incorporation
—Cont'd
Names.
Change of name.
Right to amend articles,
§10-2A-110.
Nonprofit corporations. See
within this heading,
"Nonprofit corporations."
Recordation.
Probate judge or secretary
of state generally,
§10-2A-93.
Reorganization.
Amendment of articles in
reorganization
proceedings,
§10-2A-117.
Restated articles of
incorporation,
§10-2A-116.
Stock and stockholders.
Class voting on
amendments,
§10-2A-112.
Issuance of stock.
Powers of corporation
stated in certificate,
§10-2A-32.
Assets.
Net assets.
Defined, §10-2A-2.
Nonprofit corporations. See
within this heading,
"Nonprofit corporations."
Sale, lease, exchange, etc., of
corporate property and
assets.
In course of business by
directors, §10-2A-160.
Nonprofit corporations,
§10-3A-120.
Attachment.
See ATTACHMENTS.
Auctions and auctioneers.
Effect of license issued to
corporation, §34-4-28.
Authorized shares.
Defined, §10-2A-2.
Bankruptcy and insolvency.
Close corporations.
Receiver appointed,
§10-2A-309.
Definitions, §10-2A-2.
**Banks and financial
institutions.**
Applicability of corporations
provisions, §10-2A-336.
General provisions, §§5-1A-1
to 5-21-11.
See BANKS AND
FINANCIAL
INSTITUTIONS.
Benevolent societies.
Public societies. See within
this heading, "Public
societies."
Bishop of diocese, §§10-4-1 to
10-4-9.
See BISHOP OF DIOCESE.
Blacklists, §13A-11-123.
Board of directors. See
within this heading,
"Directors."
Bond issues.
Depreciating bonds of
corporation with intent
to buy, §10-2A-71.

CORPORATIONS—Cont'd
Bond issues—Cont'd
Directors.
Depreciating bonds with
intent to buy,
§10-2A-71.
Officers.
Depreciating bonds of
corporation with intent
to buy, §10-2A-71.
Bonds, surety.
Liquidation.
Receivers, §10-2A-197.
Books.
Inspections, §10-2A-79.
Rights of inspection,
§10-2A-79.
Bridges.
Toll road, bridge and tunnel
authority.
See TOLL ROAD, BRIDGE
AND TUNNEL
AUTHORITY.
**Building and loan
associations.**
Franchise taxes.
Exemption of federal
associations, Const.
Ala., amd. 27.
Bulk transfers.
Exception of sales on
dissolution or
reorganization, §7-6-103.
Burial societies, §§10-4-20 to
10-4-28.
See CEMETERIES.
Business corporations.
Alabama business
corporation act,
§§10-2A-1 to 10-2A-339.
Bylaws.
Adoption, §10-2A-45.
Alteration, §10-2A-45.
Amendment, §10-2A-45.
Contents, §10-2A-45.
Emergencies, §10-2A-46.
Nonprofit corporation,
§10-3A-27.
Powers of corporations,
§10-2A-20.
Repeal, §10-2A-45.
Capacity.
Nonprofit corporations.
When lack of capacity may
be asserted, §10-3A-21.
Powers of corporations,
§10-2A-20.
Capital.
Stated capital.
Deduction, §10-2A-121.
Defined, §10-2A-2.
Determination of amount,
§10-2A-38.
Surplus.
Capital surplus, §§10-2A-2,
10-2A-38.
Defined, §10-2A-2.
Cemeteries.
Burial societies, §§10-4-20 to
10-4-28.
See CEMETERIES.
Certificate of authority.
Foreign corporations.
Amended certificate.
Grounds for obtaining,
§10-2A-241.
Procedure for obtaining,
§10-2A-241.
Application for certificate.
Contents, §10-2A-232.
Execution, §10-2A-232.

CORPORATIONS—Cont'd
Certificate of authority
—Cont'd
Foreign corporations—Cont'd
Application for certificate
—Cont'd
Filing, §10-2A-233.
Effect, §10-2A-234.
Issuance, §10-2A-233.
Requirement of certificate
to transact business in
state, §10-2A-226.
Revocation.
Grounds, §10-2A-244.
Issuance, §10-2A-245.
Procedural requirements,
§10-2A-244.
Suspension.
Change of name to name
not usable in state,
§10-2A-231.
Transacting business
without certificate.
Contracts voidable,
§10-2A-247.
Effects, §10-2A-247.
Liability to state for tax,
fees, etc.,
§10-2A-247.
Voidability of contracts,
§10-2A-247.
Certificate of incorporation.
Alabama corrections
institution finance
authority, §14-2-5.
Churches, §10-4-20.
Corporation not of business
character.
Issuance, §10-1-3.
Graveyard owners, §10-4-20.
Issuance, §10-2A-94.
Corporations not of
business character,
§10-1-3.
Public societies, §10-4-20.
Change bills.
Circulating, §13A-9-20.
Emitting as money,
§13A-9-19.
Change of name. See within
this heading, "Names."
Charters.
Alteration.
Corporation not of business
character, §10-1-3.
Amendment.
Corporations not of
business character,
§10-1-3.
General law, Const. Ala.,
art. XII, §229; amd.
27.
Business authorized by
charter.
Restriction to, Const. Ala.,
art. XII, §233.
Cancellation of certain
corporate charters,
Const. Ala., art. XII,
§230.
Educational institutions.
Amendment, §10-4-80.
Forfeiture.
Remitting.
Limitation, Const. Ala.,
art. XII, §231.
Granting.
General law, Const. Ala.,
art. XII, §229; amd.
27.

CORPORATIONS—Cont'd
Charters—Cont'd
Granting—Cont'd
Special, private or local
laws prohibited, Const.
Ala., art. IV, §104.
Revocation.
Authority of legislature,
Const. Ala., art. XII,
§238.
Vacating.
Quo warranto.
Right of action and
venue, §6-6-590.
Churches.
Bishop of diocese, §§10-4-1 to
10-4-9.
See BISHOP OF
DIOCESE.
Borrowing money, §10-4-24.
Effect of recital in minutes
on proceedings,
§10-4-26.
Certificate of incorporation,
§10-4-20.
Conference of ministers,
§§10-4-40 to 10-4-43.
Franchise taxes.
Exemptions, Const. Ala.,
art. XII, §229; amd.
27.
Incorporation, §10-4-20.
Loans.
Borrowing money,
§10-4-24.
Effect of recital in minutes
on proceedings,
§10-4-26.
Mortgages and deeds of
trust.
Securing loans by,
§10-4-24.
Nonprofit corporations. See
within this heading,
"Nonprofit corporations."
Powers of corporation,
§10-4-21.
Property.
Conveyance, §10-4-25.
Effect of recital in
minutes on
proceedings,
§10-4-26.
Independence of church
corporations in control
of real property,
§10-4-22.
Sale, §10-4-26.
Real property.
Independence of church
corporations in control
of real property,
§10-4-22.
Sale and conveyance,
§10-4-26.
Service of process.
Validity of sevice of
process on trustee,
§10-4-23.
State conventions or
associations of churches.
See CHURCHES.
Citation of chapter.
Alabama business
corporation act,
§10-2A-1.
Clergymen.
Conference of ministers,
§§10-4-40 to 10-4-43.

CORPORATIONS—Cont'd
Close corporations.
Applicable law, §10-2A-300.
Articles of incorporation.
Amendment to voluntarily
terminate status,
§10-2A-304.
Contents, §10-2A-301.
Provisions for management
by shareholders,
§10-2A-308.
Requirements, §10-2A-302.
Bankruptcy and insolvency.
Receivers, §10-2A-309.
Breach of qualifying
conditions.
Issuance or transfer of
shares, §10-2A-305.
Conflict of laws, §10-2A-313.
Custodians.
Appointment, §10-2A-309.
Grounds, §10-2A-309.
Powers, §10-2A-309.
Deadlock.
Appointment of provisional
director, §10-2A-310.
Custodian appointed,
§10-2A-309.
Defined, §10-2A-301.
Directors.
Agreements restricting
discretion, §10-2A-307.
Provisional director,
§10-2A-310.
Dissolution.
Stockholders' option,
§10-2A-312.
Effect of provisions on other
laws, §10-2A-313.
Election of existing
corporation to become
close corporation,
§10-2A-303.
Formation, §10-2A-302.
Law applicable to close
corporations, §10-2A-300.
Receivers.
Appointment, §10-2A-309.
Grounds for appointment,
§10-2A-309.
Stock and stockholders.
Agreements with
stockholders.
Restrictions, §10-2A-311.
Dissolution of corporation.
Option of stockholder,
§10-2A-312.
Issuance or transfer of
shares in breach of
conditions, §10-2A-305.
Management by
stockholders,
§10-2A-308.
Number of stockholders,
§10-2A-301.
Restrictions on transfer.
Corporate option where
restriction held
invalid, §10-2A-306.
Termination of status,
§10-2A-304.
Commercial code.
Bulk transfers.
Exception of sales on
dissolution or
reorganization,
§7-6-103.

CORPORATIONS—Cont'd
Commercial code—Cont'd
Commercial paper.
Corporation exceeding
powers.
Negotiation effective
although subject to
rescission, §7-3-207.
Payee described as agent
or officer, §7-3-117.
Signature by authorized
representative,
§7-3-403.
Investment securities,
§§7-8-101 to 7-8-406.
See COMMERCIAL CODE.
Secured transactions.
Filing.
Applicability of filing
provisions, §7-9-302.
Commissioner of revenue.
Foreign corporations.
Acting in fiduciary
capacity.
Filing verified statement
with commissioner
prior to acting as
fiduciary,
§10-2A-222.
Conference of ministers.
Changing of corporate name,
§10-4-42.
Fees, §10-4-40.
Formation of ministers into
body corporate, §10-4-40.
Incorporation, §10-4-40.
Defectively incorporated
conference.
Incorporation by
successor, §10-4-43.
Unincorporated conference.
Incorporation by
successor, §10-4-43.
Name.
Changing of corporate
name, §10-4-42.
Powers of corporations,
§10-4-41.
Conflict of laws.
Close corporations,
§10-2A-313.
Conflicts of interest.
Directors, §10-2A-63.
Conservators.
Voting of shares, §10-2A-53.
Consolidation or merger.
Abandonment of merger or
consolidation pursuant to
plan, §10-2A-142.
Articles of merger or
consolidation,
§10-2A-143.
Domestic corporations with
foreign corporations.
Resulting or surviving
corporation,
§10-2A-146.
Effect, §10-2A-145.
Foreign corporations.
Domestic corporations with
foreign corporations.
Resulting or surviving
corporation,
§10-2A-146.
Failure to file articles of
merger grounds for
revocation of
certificate of authority,
§10-2A-244.

CORPORATIONS—Cont'd
Consolidation or merger
—Cont'd
Foreign corporations—Cont'd
Merger of foreign
corporation authorized
to transact business in
state.
Effect, §10-2A-240.
Nonprofit corporations,
§§10-2A-100 to
10-2A-105, 10-2A-180.
Notice, §10-2A-142.
Plan.
Abandonment, §10-2A-142.
Two or more domestic
corporations,
§§10-2A-140,
10-2A-141.
Powers of corporations,
§10-2A-20.
Resulting or surviving
corporation,
§10-2A-145.
Procedure, §§10-2A-140,
10-2A-141.
Resulting or surviving
corporation, §10-2A-146.
Filings required,
§10-2A-335.
Stock and stockholders.
Articles of merger or
consolidation,
§10-2A-143.
Two or more domestic
corporations.
Approval by
shareholders,
§10-2A-142.
Subsidiary corporations,
§10-2A-144.
Two or more domestic
corporations.
Plan.
Abandonment,
§10-2A-142.
Procedure generally,
§§10-2A-140,
10-2A-141.
**Conspiracy to interfere with
or hinder business,**
§13A-11-122.
Constitution of Alabama.
See CONSTITUTION OF
ALABAMA.
Contracts.
Foreign corporations.
Nonqualified corporations.
Contracts of nonqualified
corporations deemed
void, §40-14-4.
Transacting business
without certificate of
authority.
Voidability of contracts,
§10-2A-247.
Powers of corporations,
§10-2A-20.
Conveyances.
Acknowledgments.
Disqualifications from
acknowledging
conveyances, §35-4-25.
Proof of conveyances
executed in name of
corporation, §35-4-67.

CORPORATIONS—Cont'd
Copies.
Certified copies and
certificates to be received
in evidence by probate
judge or secretary of
state, §10-2A-332.
Corrections.
Alabama corrections
institution finance
authority, §§14-2-1 to
14-2-36.
See CORRECTIONS.
Counties.
Counties not to grant public
money or lend credit to
individuals or
corporations, Const. Ala.,
amd. 112.
County declared a body
corporate, §11-1-2.
Industrial development
boards, §§11-20-30 to
11-20-50.
See COUNTIES.
Obligations of corporations,
etc., held by counties,
Const. Ala., art. IV,
§100.
Courts.
Jurisdiction.
Granting of relief not
impaired, §10-2A-76.
**Creation by active
legislature.**
Filings for such corporations,
§10-2A-335.
Creditors.
Liability of stockholders and
subscribers to creditors
of corporation,
§10-2A-43.
Credit unions.
Applicability of Alabama
business corporation act,
§5-17-59.
General provisions, §§5-17-1
to 5-17-59.
See CREDIT UNIONS.
Criminal law and procedure.
Business records.
Falsifying, §13A-9-45.
Change bills, §§13A-9-19,
13A-9-20.
Criminal liability of
individuals for corporate
conduct, §13A-2-26.
Evidence.
When proof of
incorporation
necessary, §12-21-201.
Prosecution of corporations.
See within this heading,
"Prosecution of
corporations."
Deadlock.
Dissolution upon,
§10-2A-195.
Debtors and creditors.
Creditors of corporation.
Liability of stockholders
and subscribers to
creditors, §10-2A-43.
Debts.
Powers of corporations,
§10-2A-20.
Deeds.
Proof of conveyances
executed in name of
corporation, §35-4-67.

CORPORATIONS—Cont'd
Defenses.
Ultra vires, §10-2A-24.
Definitions, Const. Ala., art.
XII, §241.
Close corporations,
§10-2A-301.
Foreign corporations,
§10-2A-220.
Nonprofit corporations,
§§10-3A-2, 10-11-2.
S corporations. See within
this heading, "S
corporations."
Dental service corporations,
§§22-21-360 to 22-21-391.
See DENTAL SERVICE
CORPORATIONS.
**Derivative actions by
shareholders,** ARCP, Rule
23.1.
Form of complaint, ARCP,
Form 25.
Directors.
Action without meeting,
§10-2A-66.
Bond issues.
Depreciating bonds with
intent to buy,
§10-2A-71.
Classification, §10-2A-59.
Close corporations.
Agreements restricting
discretion of directors,
§10-2A-307.
Provisional director,
§10-2A-310.
Committees, §10-2A-64.
Compensation, §10-2A-57.
Conflicts of interest,
§10-2A-63.
Contribution from certain
shareholders, §10-2A-75.
Criminal law and procedure.
Criminal liability of
individuals for
corporate conduct,
§13A-2-26.
Deadlock.
Stockholder's action for
dissolution or
liquidation,
§10-2A-195.
Dissent of director to action
of board, §10-2A-72.
Dividends.
Declaration, §10-2A-67.
Duties, §10-2A-57.
Generally, §10-2A-74.
Election, §10-2A-58.
Filling vacancies,
§10-2A-60.
Voting of stock, §10-2A-53.
Fiduciary obligations.
Not impaired by chapter,
§10-2A-76.
Indemnification, §10-2A-21.
Insurance.
Liability insurance,
§10-2A-21.
Liability insurance,
§10-2A-21.
Liability of directors in
certain cases, §10-2A-75.
Loans, §10-2A-69.
Meetings, §10-2A-65.
Notice of meetings,
§10-2A-65.
Organization meeting,
§10-2A-96.
Quorum, §10-2A-62.

CORPORATIONS—Cont'd
Directors—Cont'd
Misdemeanors, §10-2A-284.
Nonprofit corporations. See
within this heading,
"Nonprofit corporations."
Notice.
Meetings, §10-2A-65.
Number, §10-2A-58.
Organization meeting,
§10-2A-96.
Penalties, §10-2A-284.
Qualifications, §10-2A-57.
Quorum to transact business,
§10-2A-62.
Records.
Protection of director
relying upon certain
records or reports,
§10-2A-73.
Removal, §10-2A-61.
Reports.
Protection of director
relying upon certain
reports and records,
§10-2A-73.
Residence, §10-2A-57.
Sale, mortgage or pledge of
assets, §10-2A-160.
Disposition in course of
business, §10-2A-160.
Stock and stockholders.
Depreciating stock with
intent to buy,
§10-2A-71.
Election of directors.
Voting of shares,
§10-2A-53.
Surplus.
Distributions from capital
surplus, §10-2A-68.
Terms, §10-2A-58.
Vacancies, §10-2A-60.
Dissolution.
Articles of dissolution.
Execution and contents,
§10-2A-190.
Filing, §10-2A-191.
Certificate of dissolution.
Issuance, §10-2A-191.
Close corporations.
Stockholders' option to
dissolve, §10-2A-312.
Deposit with commissioner of
revenue of amount due
certain shareholders,
§10-2A-202.
Filing of statement of intent
to dissolve, §10-2A-183.
Effect, §10-2A-184.
Procedure after filing,
§10-2A-185.
Involuntary dissolution,
§10-2A-192.
Abatement of action,
§10-2A-193.
Deposit with commissioner
of revenue of amount
due certain
shareholders,
§10-2A-202.
Grounds, §10-2A-192.
Initiation of action,
§10-2A-193.
Notification of causes for
dissolution,
§10-2A-193.
Service of process,
§10-2A-194.
Venue, §10-2A-194.

CORPORATIONS—Cont'd
Dissolution—Cont'd
Judgments.
Quo warranto.
Judgment dissolving
corporation,
§6-6-599.
Nonprofit corporations. See
within this heading,
"Nonprofit corporations."
Order of dissolution.
Entering of order by court,
§10-2A-200.
Filing of order, §10-2A-201.
Powers of corporations,
§10-2A-20.
Quo warranto.
Judgment dissolving
corporation, §6-6-599.
Recordation.
Statement of name and
address of preparer of
instruments,
§§35-4-110 to 35-4-112.
Remedies.
Survival of remedy after
dissolution,
§10-2A-203.
Revocation of proceedings.
Act of corporation,
§10-2A-187.
Consent of shareholders,
§10-2A-186.
Filing of statement of
revocation,
§10-2A-188.
Effect, §10-2A-189.
Service of process.
Involuntary dissolution,
§10-2A-194.
Statement of intent to
dissolve.
Effect, §10-2A-184.
Filing, §10-2A-183.
Procedure after,
§10-2A-185.
Stock and stockholders.
Action for dissolution or
liquidation,
§10-2A-195.
Deposit with commissioner
of revenue of amount
due certain
shareholders,
§10-2A-202.
Voluntary dissolution.
Consent of shareholders,
§10-2A-181.
Revocation of
proceedings by
consent of
shareholders,
§10-2A-186.
Effect of statement,
§10-2A-189.
Filing of statement,
§10-2A-188.
Venue.
Involuntary dissolution,
§10-2A-194.
Voluntary dissolution.
Act of corporation,
§10-2A-182.
Articles of dissolution.
Execution and contents,
§10-2A-190.
Subsidiary corporation,
§10-2A-181.1.
Consent of stockholders,
§10-2A-181.

CORPORATIONS—Cont'd
Dissolution—Cont'd
Voluntary dissolution
—Cont'd
Deposit with commissioner
of revenue of amount
due certain
shareholders,
§10-2A-202.
Incorporators, §10-2A-180.
Nonprofit corporations. See
within this heading,
"Nonprofit
corporations."
Revocation of proceedings
by act of corporation,
§10-2A-187.
Filing of statement,
§10-2A-188.
Revocation of proceedings
by consent of
shareholders,
§10-2A-186.
Effect of statement,
§10-2A-189.
Filing of statement,
§10-2A-188.
Subsidiary corporation,
§10-2A-181.1.
Dividends. See within this
heading, "Stock and
stockholders."
Dockets.
Prosecution of corporations.
Docketing notice of
indictment, §10-7-1.
Doing business in state.
Foreign corporations, Const.
Ala., art. XII, §232; amd.
473.
Mortgage loans by
nonresident
corporations not
constituting doing
business in state,
Const. Ala., amd. 154.
Earned surplus.
Defined, §10-2A-2.
Educational institutions.
Ceasing business.
Distribution of proceeds,
§§10-4-81, 10-4-82.
Charters.
Amendment, §10-4-80.
Fees.
Filing charter amendment,
§10-4-80.
Franchise taxes.
Exemptions, Const. Ala.,
art. XII, §229; amd.
27.
Stock and stockholders.
Distribution of proceeds
when corporation
ceases business,
§10-4-81.
Where stockholders are
unknown or number
of shares unknown,
§10-4-82.
Elections.
Coercion of employees of
corporations, §17-23-11.
Directors, §10-2A-58.
Vacancies, §10-2A-60.
Voting of stock, §10-2A-53.
Fair campaign practices.
Political committees
established by
corporation,
§17-22A-14.

CORPORATIONS—Cont'd
Elections—Cont'd
Political funds.
Segregated, separate
political funds, §10-1-2.
Political parties or
candidates.
Giving aid or contributions
to, §10-2A-70.
Exceptions for voluntary
separate political
funds, §10-2A-70.
Legislative intent,
§10-2A-70.2.
Limitation on amount of
political
contributions,
§10-2A-70.1.
Penalty, §10-2A-70.
Repealing provisions,
§10-2A-70.2.
Supplemental provisions,
§10-2A-70.1.
Electric cooperatives.
Conversion of existing
corporation into
cooperative.
See ELECTRIC
COOPERATIVES.
Electricity.
Foreign corporations.
Extension of lines into
state, §10-2A-229.
Electric membership
corporations, §§37-7-1 to
37-7-21.
See ELECTRIC
MEMBERSHIP
CORPORATIONS.
Emergencies.
Bylaws, §10-2A-46.
Eminent domain, Const. Ala.,
art. XII, §235.
Foreign corporations,
§10-2A-228.
Employees.
Criminal liability of
individuals for corporate
conduct, §13A-2-26.
Defined, §10-2A-2.
Fiduciary obligations.
Not impaired by chapter,
§10-2A-76.
Indemnification, §10-2A-21.
Insurance.
Liability insurance,
§10-2A-21.
Liability insurance,
§10-2A-21.
Loans, §10-2A-69.
Employment agencies,
§§34-10-1 to 34-10-5.
Engineers.
Certificate of authorization,
§34-11-9.
Disciplinary action,
§34-11-11.
Practice of engineering,
§34-11-9.
Evidence.
Criminal cases.
When proof of
incorporation
necessary, §12-21-201.
Nonprofit corporations.
Certificates and certified
copies to be received in
evidence, §10-3A-222.

CORPORATIONS—Cont'd
Evidence—Cont'd
Probate judge.
Certificates and certified
copies to be received in
evidence, §10-2A-332.
Secretary of state.
Certificates and certified
copies to be received in
evidence, §10-2A-332.
Executions.
Prosecution of corporations.
Execution on judgment,
§10-7-4.
Executors and
administrators.
Bonds, surety.
Testator may preclude
corporate surety,
§43-8-256.
Foreign corporations.
Acting in fiduciary
capacity, §§10-2A-221
to 10-2A-224.1.
Voting of shares, §10-2A-53.
Fees.
Certificates.
Schedule of fees for issuing
certificates,
§10-2A-281.
Collection.
Probate judge, §10-2A-280.
Secretary of state,
§10-2A-280.
Conference of ministers,
§10-4-40.
Educational institutions.
Filing charter amendment,
§10-4-80.
Filing documents.
Schedule, §10-2A-281.
Foreign corporations.
Failure to pay grounds for
revocation of
certificate of authority,
§10-2A-244.
Transacting business
without certificate.
Liability of corporation
to state, §10-2A-247.
Issuing certificates.
Schedule, §10-2A-281.
Miscellaneous charges,
§10-2A-282.
Nonprofit corporations,
§§10-3A-200, 10-3A-201.
Reports.
Annual report.
Filing fee, §§10-2A-260,
10-2A-261,
10-2A-281.
Secretary of state.
Collection, §10-2A-280.
Fiduciaries.
Foreign corporations.
Acting in fiduciary
capacity, §§10-2A-221
to 10-2A-224.1.
Officers, directors', etc.,
duties not diminished,
§10-2A-76.
Securities.
Registration of securities
held by corporate
fiduciary in name of
nominee, §19-3-7.

CORPORATIONS—Cont'd
Fish and game.
Violations of fish and game
laws.
Warrants.
Service and return of
warrant, §9-11-9.
Foreign corporations.
Acting in fiduciary capacity.
Authority of corporations
to act, §10-2A-221.
Deemed not doing business
in state, §10-2A-223.
Filing verified statement
with commissioner of
revenue prior to,
§10-2A-222.
Previously acting
corporations.
Effect of provisions,
§10-2A-224.
Service of process on
corporation,
§10-2A-224.1.
Admission of foreign
corporations, §10-2A-226.
Contracts.
When void, §40-14-4.
Qualification to do
business in state.
Contracts, §40-14-4.
Tax, §40-14-1.
Statements.
Filing with department
of revenue, §40-14-2.
Tax, §40-14-1.
Single payment,
§40-14-3.
Applicability of provisions to
heretofore authorized
corporations, §10-2A-246.
Articles of incorporation.
Amendment.
Failure to file grounds
for revocation of
certificate of
authority,
§10-2A-244.
Requirements,
§10-2A-239.
Certificate of authority.
Amended certificate.
Grounds for obtaining,
§10-2A-241.
Procedure for obtaining,
§10-2A-241.
Application for certificate.
Contents, §10-2A-232.
Execution, §10-2A-232.
Filing, §10-2A-233.
Effect, §10-2A-234.
Issuance, §10-2A-233.
Required to transact
business in state,
§10-2A-226.
Revocation.
Grounds, §10-2A-244.
Issuance, §10-2A-245.
Procedural requirements,
§10-2A-244.
Suspension.
Change of name to name
not usable in state,
§10-2A-231.
Transacting business
without certificate.
Contracts voidable,
§10-2A-247.
Effects, §10-2A-247.

CORPORATIONS—Cont'd
Foreign corporations—Cont'd
Certificate of authority
—Cont'd
Transacting business
without certificate
—Cont'd
Liability to state for
taxes, fees, etc.,
§10-2A-247.
Voidability of contracts,
§10-2A-247.
Commissioner of revenue.
Acting in fiduciary
capacity.
Filing verified statement
with commissioner
prior to, §10-2A-222.
Consolidation or merger.
Domestic corporations with
foreign corporations.
Resulting or surviving
corporation,
§10-2A-146.
Effect of merger,
§10-2A-240.
Failure to file articles of
merger, §10-2A-244.
Contracts.
Nonqualified corporations.
Contracts, etc., of
nonqualified
corporations deemed
void, §40-14-4.
Transacting business
without certificate of
authority.
Voidability of contracts,
§10-2A-247.
Defined, §10-2A-220.
Doing business act,
§§10-2A-235 to
10-2A-237.
Doing business in state,
Const. Ala., art. XII,
§232; amd. 473.
Fiduciary capacity.
Corporation acting as
fiduciary not deemed
doing business in
state, §10-2A-223.
Mortgage loans as not
doing business in
state, Const. Ala.,
amd. 154.
Electric cooperatives,
§37-6-26.
Electric lines.
Extension into state,
§10-2A-229.
Electric membership
corporations, §37-7-20.
Eminent domain,
§10-2A-228.
Fees.
Failure to pay grounds for
revocation of
certificate of authority,
§10-2A-244.
Transacting business
without certificate of
authority.
Liability of corporation
to state, §10-2A-247.
Fiduciaries.
Acting in fiduciary
capacity, §§10-2A-221
to 10-2A-224.1.
Franchise tax. See within
this heading, "Franchise
tax."

CORPORATIONS—Cont'd
Foreign corporations—Cont'd
Lines.
Extension of lines into
state, §10-2A-229.
Misrepresentation.
Grounds for revocation of
certificate of authority,
§10-2A-244.
Mortgage loans by
nonresident corporation.
Not doing business in
state, Const. Ala.,
amd. 154.
Name, §10-2A-230.
Change of name to name
not usable in state.
Suspension of certificate
of authority,
§10-2A-231.
Exceptions to requirement,
§10-2A-230.
Nonprofit corporations. See
within this heading,
"Nonprofit corporations."
Out-of-state business,
property, etc.
Regulation or control by
state.
Not subject to control or
regulation.
Exception, §10-2A-225.
Penalties.
Failure to pay is grounds
for revocation of
certificate of authority,
§10-2A-244.
Transacting business
without certificate of
authority.
Liability of corporation
for penalties
imposed, §10-2A-247.
Powers, §10-2A-227.
Presently authorized
corporations.
Applicability of chapter,
§10-2A-246.
Registered agents.
Change of registered agent.
Procedure, §10-2A-236.
Doing business act,
§§10-2A-235 to
10-2A-237.
Failure to appoint and
maintain as grounds
for revocation of
certificate of authority,
§10-2A-244.
Maintenance by
corporation,
§10-2A-235.
Service of process on
registered agent,
§10-2A-237.
Registered office.
Change.
Failure to file statement
grounds for
revocation of
certificate of
authority,
§10-2A-244.
Procedure, §10-2A-236.
Doing business act,
§§10-2A-235 to
10-2A-237.
Maintenance by foreign
corporation,
§10-2A-235.

CORPORATIONS—Cont'd
Foreign corporations—Cont'd
Reports.
Contents of annual report,
§10-2A-260.
Correction of annual
report, §10-2A-261.
Execution of annual report,
§10-2A-260.
Acceptance of public
record information
in lieu thereof,
§10-2A-260.
Filing of annual report,
§10-2A-261.
Failure to file annual
report grounds for
revocation of
certificate of
authority,
§10-2A-244.
Public record
information in lieu
thereof, §10-2A-261.
Penalty for failure or
refusal to file,
§10-2A-283.
Saving clause, §10-2A-246.
Service of process.
Acting in fiduciary
capacity, §10-2A-224.1.
Doing business act,
§§10-2A-235 to
10-2A-237.
Registered agent to receive
service, §10-2A-237.
Taxation.
Franchise tax. See within
this heading,
"Franchise tax."
Transacting business
without certificate of
authority.
Liability of corporation
for taxes,
§10-2A-247.
Tracks.
Extension of tracks into
state, §10-2A-229.
Venue, Const. Ala., art. XII,
§232.
Withdrawal.
Application, §10-2A-242.
Filing, §10-2A-243.
Certificate of withdrawal.
Issuance, §10-2A-243.
Works.
Extension of works into
state, §10-2A-225.
Foresters.
Corporations not to be
licensed under chapter,
§34-12-10.
Forms.
Secretary of state to furnish,
§10-2A-333.
Foundations.
Private foundations,
§§19-3-300 to 19-3-303.
Franchises.
Incorporation by purchasers
of property or franchise
of corporation,
§10-2A-97.
Franchise tax, Const. Ala.,
art. XII, §229.
Additional annual franchise
tax on corporations,
§40-14-41.1.

CORPORATIONS—Cont'd
Franchise tax—Cont'd
Air carriers.
Foreign corporations.
Exclusions and
deductions,
§40-14-41.
Assessment.
Foreign corporations,
§40-14-50.
Benevolent corporations.
Exemption from franchise
taxes, §40-14-40;
Const. Ala., art. XII,
§229; amd. 27.
Building and loan
associations.
Exemption of federal
associations, Const.
Ala., amd. 27.
Calender year tax, §40-14-47.
Consolidation or merger,
§40-14-42.
Dissolution, §40-14-49.
Educational corporations.
Exemption, §40-14-40;
Const. Ala., art. XII,
§229; amd. 27.
Foreign corporations.
Assessment, §40-14-50.
Exclusions and deductions,
§40-14-41.
Failure to pay grounds for
revocation of
certificate of authority,
§10-2A-244.
Levy, §40-14-41.
Report when qualified,
§40-14-54.
Forms.
Blank forms, §40-14-48.
Half-year tax, §40-14-46.
Levy.
Domestic corporations,
§40-14-40.
Foreign corporations,
§40-14-41.
License or privilege tax.
Payment does not affect,
§40-14-52.
Money collected.
Payment into treasury,
§40-14-55.
Notices, §40-14-48.
Receivership or trusteeship,
§40-14-56.
Records.
Custody, §40-14-57.
Religious corporations.
Exemption, §40-14-40;
Const. Ala., art. XII,
§229; amd. 27.
Remittance, §40-14-43.
Report to department of
revenue, §40-14-53.
Custody of reports,
§40-14-57.
Failure to make, §40-14-45.
Filing, §40-14-44.
Returns, §40-14-43.
Custody, §40-14-57.
Witnesses.
Summoning, §40-14-51.
Fraternal orders.
See FRATERNAL ORDERS.
Funds.
Secretary of state
corporations fund,
§10-2A-281.
Funeral establishments.
See FUNERALS.

CORPORATIONS—Cont'd
Garbage and trash.
Disposal.
Licensing of corporate
agencies, §22-27-5.
Garnishment.
Answer of garnishee.
Answers on behalf of
corporations, §6-6-451.
Graveyard owners, §§10-4-20
to 10-4-28.
See CEMETERIES.
Guardian and ward.
Foreign corporations.
Acting in fiduciary
capacity, §§10-2A-221
to 10-2A-224.1.
Voting of shares by
guardian, §10-2A-53.
Health.
Municipal special health care
facility authorities.
See MUNICIPAL
CORPORATIONS.
Health care service plans,
§§10-4-100 to 10-4-115.
See HEALTH CARE
SERVICE PLANS.
Highways.
Alabama highway authority,
§§23-1-150 to 23-1-160.
See HIGHWAYS.
Alabama highway finance
corporation, §§23-1-170
to 23-1-181.
See HIGHWAYS.
Horse racing.
Commission.
Incorporation of
commission, §11-65-6.
Hospitals.
County hospital corporations,
§§22-21-100 to 22-21-112.
See HOSPITALS.
General provisions,
§§22-21-5, 22-21-6.
Immunity.
Nonprofit corporations.
Officers.
Liability, §§10-11-1 to
10-11-5.
Income tax.
See INCOME TAX.
Incorporation.
Certificate of incorporation.
See within this heading,
"Certificate of
incorporation."
Churches, §10-4-20.
Conference of ministers,
§10-4-40.
Defectively incorporated
conference.
Incorporation by
successor, §10-4-43.
Successor of
unincorporated or
defectively
incorporated
conference, §10-4-43.
Unincorporated conference.
Incorporation by
successor, §10-4-43.
Criminal cases.
When proof of
incorporation
necessary, §12-21-201.
Dissolution. See within this
heading, "Dissolution."

CORPORATIONS—Cont'd
Incorporation—Cont'd
Extension of corporate
existence.
Powers of corporations,
§10-2A-20.
Graveyard owners, §10-4-20.
Incorporators.
Minimum number,
§10-2A-90.
Nonprofit corporations,
§§10-3A-4, 10-3A-60.
Number of incorporators.
Minimum number,
§10-2A-90.
Public societies, §10-4-20.
Purchasers of property or
franchise of corporation,
§10-2A-97.
Renewal of corporate
existence.
Powers of corporations,
§10-2A-20.
Stock and stockholders.
Expenses of organization,
§10-2A-39.
Indemnification.
Directors, officers, employees
and agents, §10-2A-21.
Indictments.
Prosecution of corporations.
Notice of indictment,
§§10-7-1, 10-7-2.
**Industrial access roads and
bridges,** §§23-6-1 to
23-6-12.
See INDUSTRIAL ACCESS
ROADS AND BRIDGES.
**Industrial development
boards.**
Counties, §§11-20-30 to
11-20-50.
See COUNTIES.
**Industrial development
corporations,** §§10-4-130
to 10-4-152.
See INDUSTRIAL
DEVELOPMENT
CORPORATIONS.
Infant stockholders, §§10-6-1
to 10-6-4.
Insolvency. See within this
heading, "Bankruptcy and
insolvency."
Inspections.
Books and records,
§10-2A-79.
Nonprofit corporations,
§10-3A-43.
Nonprofit corporations.
Books and records,
§10-3A-43.
Reports, §10-2A-79.
Insurance.
Insurance companies.
Application of corporations
provisions, §10-2A-336.
Liability insurance,
§10-2A-21.
Interest.
Maximum rates of interest.
Credit sales or loans to
corporations, §8-8-5.
Interstate commerce.
Application of corporations
provisions, §10-2A-337.
Investments.
Restrictions on investment of
trust funds in private
corporations, Const. Ala.,
amd. 40.

CORPORATIONS—Cont'd
Investment securities,
§§7-8-101 to 7-8-406.
Involuntary dissolution. See
within this heading,
"Dissolution."
Issuance of stock. See within
this heading, "Stock and
stockholders."
Judgments.
Prosecution of corporations.
Execution on judgment,
§10-7-4.
Jurisdiction.
Courts.
Granting of relief not
impaired, §10-2A-76.
Liquidation.
Assets and business of
corporation,
§10-2A-195.
Nonprofit corporations.
Liquidation, §10-3A-149.
Landscape architects.
See LANDSCAPE
ARCHITECTS.
Land surveyors.
See SURVEYS AND
SURVEYORS.
Legislature.
Charters.
Authority of legislature to
revoke, Const. Ala.,
art. XII, §238.
Reservation of power,
§10-2A-338.
Letters of credit as security.
Authority of public
corporations, §11-80-7.
Liability insurance,
§10-2A-21.
Licenses.
Exemptions from licenses.
Disabled veterans.
Inapplicability to
corporations,
§40-12-348.
Veterans of World War II.
Inapplicability to
corporations,
§40-12-375.
Liens.
Stock.
Lien on shares by
corporation, §10-2A-43.
Liquidation.
Bond, surety.
Receivers, §10-2A-197.
Claims.
Filing of claims,
§10-2A-198.
Court.
Order of dissolution of
corporation,
§§10-2A-200,
10-2A-201.
Powers of court,
§10-2A-196.
Discontinuance of liquidation
proceedings, §10-2A-199.
Dissolution. See within this
heading, "Dissolution."
Filing of claims, §10-2A-198.
Income tax.
See INCOME TAX.
Jurisdiction, §10-2A-195.
Nonprofit corporations. See
within this heading,
"Nonprofit corporations."

CORPORATIONS—Cont'd
Liquidation—Cont'd
Order of dissolution.
Entering of order by court,
§10-2A-200.
Filing of order, §10-2A-201.
Powers of court, §10-2A-196.
Procedure and liquidation of
corporation by court,
§10-2A-196.
Receivers, §§10-2A-196,
10-2A-197.
List of corporations.
Maintenance by secretary of
state, §10-2A-29.
Literary clubs.
See SOCIAL AND
LITERARY CLUBS.
Loans.
Churches, §10-4-24.
Effect of recital in minutes
on proceedings,
§10-4-26.
Directors, §10-2A-69.
Employees, §10-2A-69.
Graveyard owners, §10-4-26.
Nonprofit corporations.
Loans to directors and
officers prohibited,
§10-3A-45.
Public societies, §10-4-24.
Effect of recital in minutes
on proceedings,
§10-4-26.
Meetings.
Directors, §§10-2A-62,
10-2A-65, 10-2A-96.
Nonprofit corporations. See
within this heading,
"Nonprofit corporations."
Stockholders' meetings. See
within this heading,
"Stock and stockholders."
**Mental health programs and
facilities.**
See MENTALLY ILL.
Merger. See within this
heading, "Consolidation or
merger."
Ministers.
Conference of ministers,
§§10-4-40 to 10-4-43.
Minors.
Stockholders. See within this
heading, "Stock and
stockholders."
Transfers to minors,
§§35-5A-1 to 35-5A-24.
See TRANSFERS TO
MINORS.
Misdemeanors.
Directors, §10-2A-284.
Officers, §10-2A-284.
Misrepresentation.
Foreign corporations.
Grounds for revocation of
certificate of authority,
§10-2A-244.
Monopolies.
See MONOPOLIES.
Monument societies. See
within this heading,
"Public societies."
**Mortgages and deeds of
trust.**
Churches.
Securing loans by
mortgage or deed of
trust, §10-4-24.

CORPORATIONS—Cont'd
**Mortgages and deeds of
trust**—Cont'd
Foreign corporations.
Mortgage loans by
nonresident
corporation.
Not constituting doing
business in state,
Const. Ala., amd.
154.
Graveyard owners.
Securing loans by
mortgage or deed of
trust, §10-4-24.
Effect of recital in
minutes on
proceedings,
§10-4-26.
Powers of corporations,
§10-4-20.
Proof of conveyances
executed in name of
corporation, §35-4-67.
Property.
Sale and conveyance,
§10-4-25.
Public societies.
Securing loans by
mortgage or deed of
trust, §10-4-26.
Municipal corporations.
Corporate obligations held by
municipalities, Const.
Ala., art. IV, §100.
General provisions.
See MUNICIPAL
CORPORATIONS.
Municipalities not to grant
public money or lend
credit to private
corporations, Const. Ala.,
art. IV, §94; amd. 112.
Names.
Change of name, §10-2A-110.
Business corporations,
§10-2A-110.
Conference of ministers,
§10-4-42.
Foreign corporations.
Change of name to name
not usable in state.
Suspension of
certificate of
authority,
§10-2A-231.
Right to amend articles of
incorporation,
§10-2A-110.
Special, private or local
laws prohibited, Const.
Ala., art. IV, §104.
Contents, §10-2A-25.
Foreign corporations,
§10-2A-230.
Change of name to name
not usable in state.
Suspension of certificate
of authority,
§10-2A-231.
Registered name, §10-2A-27.
Renewal, §10-2A-28.
Reserved name, §10-2A-26.
Use of word "trust" in
corporate or partnership
name, §§5-11A-1,
5-11A-4.
Nature study societies. See
within this heading,
"Public societies."

CORPORATIONS—Cont'd
Negligence.
Nonprofit corporations.
Officers.
Liability, §§10-11-1 to
10-11-5.
Nonnegotiable instruments.
Change bills, etc.
Issuance prohibited, §8-5-2.
Nonprofit corporations.
Administration of chapter.
Powers of probate judge
and secretary of state,
§10-3A-220.
Agent.
Change in registered
agent, §10-3A-24.
Foreign corporation,
§10-3A-177.
Foreign corporations,
§10-3A-176.
Change in registered
agent, §10-3A-177.
Requirement of registered
agent, §10-3A-23.
Service of process,
§10-3A-25.
Appeal from probate judge or
secretary of state,
§10-3A-221.
Applicability of chapter,
§10-3A-3.
Articles of incorporation.
Amendment.
Articles of amendment,
§§10-3A-82,
10-3A-83.
Foreign corporation,
§10-3A-179.
Procedure, §10-3A-81.
Right of corporation to
amend, §10-3A-80.
Contents, §10-3A-61.
Filing, §10-3A-62.
Effect of filing,
§10-3A-63.
Restated articles,
§10-3A-84.
Voting provisions.
Effect of greater voting
provisions in articles
of incorporation,
§10-3A-33.
Assets.
Deposit with state
treasurer upon
dissolution,
§10-3A-156.
Distribution upon
dissolution or
liquidation, §10-3A-44.
Sale, lease, exchange, etc.,
§10-3A-120.
Books.
Duty to keep book,
§10-3A-43.
Burial societies.
See CEMETERIES.
Bylaws, §10-3A-27.
Voting provisions.
Effect of greater voting
provisions and
bylaws, §10-3A-33.
Capacity.
When lack of capacity may
be asserted, §10-3A-21.
Certificates of incorporation.
Conclusive evidence of
incorporation,
§10-3A-63.
Issuance, §10-3A-62.

CORPORATIONS—Cont'd
Nonprofit corporations
—Cont'd
Certificates of membership,
§10-3A-26.
Churches.
Bishop of diocese, §§10-4-1
to 10-4-9.
See BISHOP OF
DIOCESE.
General provisions. See
within this heading,
"Churches."
Conference of ministers,
§§10-4-40 to 10-4-43.
Consolidation or merger.
Abandonment, §10-3A-102.
Approval, §10-3A-102.
Articles of merger or
consolidation,
§10-3A-103.
Domestic and foreign
corporations,
§10-3A-105.
Effect, §10-3A-104.
Foreign corporation,
§10-3A-180.
Procedure, §§10-3A-100,
10-3A-101.
Definitions, §10-3A-2.
Liability of officers of
nonprofit
organizations,
§10-11-2.
Directors.
Action by directors without
meeting, §10-3A-40.
Appointment, §10-3A-35.
Books.
Inspection of books of
corporation,
§10-3A-43.
Committees, §10-3A-38.
Meetings, §10-3A-39.
Minutes, §10-3A-43.
Compensation for services
rendered, §10-3A-44.
Duties, §10-3A-34.
Election, §10-3A-35.
Exceeding authority,
§10-3A-21.
False statement.
Penalties, §10-3A-202.
Inspection of books and
records, §10-3A-43.
Loans to directors
prohibited, §10-3A-45.
Majority vote required for
approval, §10-3A-37.
Meetings.
Action without meeting,
§10-3A-40.
Minutes, §10-3A-43.
Notice, §10-3A-39.
Waiver, §10-3A-30.
Organization meetings,
§10-3A-64.
Place of meetings,
§10-3A-39.
Regular meeting,
§10-3A-39.
Special meeting,
§10-3A-39.
Notice of meetings,
§10-3A-39.
Waiver of notice,
§10-3A-30.
Number, §10-3A-35.
Organization meetings,
§10-3A-64.
Qualifications, §10-3A-34.

CORPORATIONS—Cont'd
Nonprofit corporations
—Cont'd
Directors—Cont'd
Quorum, §10-3A-37.
Records.
Inspection of records of
corporation,
§10-3A-43.
Removal, §10-3A-35.
Terms, §10-3A-35.
Vacancies, §10-3A-36.
Voting.
Effect of greater voting
provisions in articles
or bylaws,
§10-3A-33.
Waiver of notice,
§10-3A-30.
Dissolution.
Deposit of assets with state
treasurer, §10-3A-156.
Distributions upon
dissolution, §10-3A-44.
Effect on remedies, rights
and claims,
§10-3A-157.
Involuntary dissolution,
§10-3A-146.
Certification of
corporation as
having giving cause
for dissolution,
§10-3A-147.
Deposit of assets with
state treasurer,
§10-3A-156.
Notification of attorney
general, §10-3A-147.
Service of process,
§10-3A-148.
Venue, §10-3A-148.
Liquidation.
Order dissolving
corporation,
§10-3A-154.
Filing order,
§10-3A-155.
Order dissolving
corporation,
§10-3A-154.
Filing order, §10-3A-155.
Survival of remedies after
dissolution,
§10-3A-157.
Voluntary dissolution.
Articles of dissolution,
§10-3A-144.
Filing, §10-3A-145.
Deposit of assets with
state treasurer,
§10-3A-156.
Distribution of assets,
§§10-3A-141,
10-3A-142.
Procedure, §10-3A-140.
Revocation of
proceedings,
§10-3A-143.
Statement of intent to
dissolve, §10-3A-140.
Dividends.
Prohibited, §10-3A-44.
Effect of repeal of prior act,
§10-3A-225.
Evidence.
Certificates and certified
copies to be received in
evidence, §10-3A-222.
Fees, §§10-3A-200,
10-3A-201.

CORPORATIONS—Cont'd
Nonprofit corporations
—Cont'd
Foreign corporations.
Admission, §10-3A-170.
Articles of incorporation.
Amendment, §10-3A-179.
Certificate of authority,
§10-3A-170.
Amendment, §10-3A-181.
Application, §10-3A-173.
Filing, §10-3A-174.
Conducting affairs
without certificate,
§10-3A-186.
Effect, §10-3A-175.
Revocation, §10-3A-184.
Issuance of certificate
of revocation,
§10-3A-185.
Certificate of withdrawal,
§10-3A-182.
Corporate name,
§10-3A-172.
Merger, §10-3A-180.
Name, §10-3A-172.
Powers, §10-3A-171.
Registered agent,
§10-3A-176.
Registered office,
§10-3A-176.
Service of process,
§10-3A-178.
Withdrawal, §10-3A-182.
Filing of application,
§10-3A-183.
Fraternal orders.
See FRATERNAL
ORDERS.
Fraud.
Liability of officers of
nonprofit
organizations.
Exception to immunity
from suit, §10-11-3.
Incorporation.
Purposes, §10-3A-4.
Who may incorporate,
§10-3A-60.
Inspections.
Books and records,
§10-3A-43.
Jefferson County.
Bingo games.
Operation of bingo
games by nonprofit
organizations, Const.
Ala., amd. 386.
Jurisdiction.
Liquidation, §10-3A-149.
Liability.
Officers, §§10-11-1 to
10-11-5.
Licenses.
Exemptions, §§40-9-2,
40-9-13, 40-9-18.
Liquidation.
Claims.
Filing of claim,
§10-3A-152.
Deposit of assets with state
treasurer, §10-3A-156.
Discontinuance of
proceedings,
§10-3A-153.
Distribution of assets,
§10-3A-150.
Filing of claim,
§10-3A-152.
Jurisdiction, §10-3A-149.

CORPORATIONS—Cont'd
Nonprofit corporations
—Cont'd
Liquidation—Cont'd
Order dissolving
corporation,
§10-3A-154.
Filing order, §10-3A-155.
Parties, §10-3A-149.
Proceedings, §10-3A-150.
Discontinuance,
§10-3A-153.
Receivers, §10-3A-150.
Qualification of
receivers,
§10-3A-151.
Venue, §10-3A-149.
Loans.
Prohibited to directors and
officers, §10-3A-45.
Madison County.
Bingo.
Operation of bingo
games by nonprofit
organizations, Const.
Ala., amd. 387.
Members.
Action without meeting,
§10-3A-40.
Books.
Inspection of books of
corporation,
§10-3A-43.
Certificates of membership,
§10-3A-26.
Classes of members,
§10-3A-26.
Compensation for services
rendered, §10-3A-44.
Inspection of books and
records, §10-3A-43.
Meetings.
Action without meetings,
§10-3A-40.
Annual meeting,
§10-3A-28.
First meeting of
members, §10-3A-64.
Minutes, §10-3A-43.
Notice, §10-3A-29.
Waiver, §10-3A-30.
Special meetings,
§10-3A-28.
Where held, §10-3A-28.
Notice of meetings,
§10-3A-29.
Waiver, §10-3A-30.
Not required, §10-3A-26.
Quorum, §10-3A-32.
Records.
Inspection of records of
corporation,
§10-3A-43.
Voting.
Cumulative voting,
§10-3A-31.
Effect of greater voting
provisions in articles
or bylaws,
§10-3A-33.
Eligibility to vote,
§10-3A-31.
Majority vote required
for approval,
§10-3A-32.
Proxy, §10-3A-31.
Waiver of notice,
§10-3A-30.

CORPORATIONS—Cont'd
Nonprofit corporations
—Cont'd
Mental health finance
authority.
Status as nonprofit
corporation,
§41-10-368.
Name.
Foreign corporations,
§10-3A-172.
Restrictions on corporate
name, §10-3A-22.
Style, §10-3A-22.
Negligence.
Liability of officers.
Gross negligence as
exception to
immunity from suit,
§10-11-3.
Notice.
Directors' meetings,
§10-3A-39.
Members' meetings,
§10-3A-29.
Officers.
Appointment, §10-3A-41.
Compensation for services
rendered, §10-3A-44.
Election, §10-3A-41.
Enumeration, §10-3A-41.
Exceeding authority,
§10-3A-21.
False statements.
Penalties, §10-3A-202.
Liability.
Applicability of
provisions.
Exceptions, §§10-11-4,
10-11-5.
Declaration of
legislature, §10-11-1.
Definitions, §10-11-2.
Fraud.
Exception to immunity
from suit,
§10-11-3.
Gross negligence.
Exception to immunity
from suit,
§10-11-3.
Immunity from suit,
§10-11-3.
Legislative intent,
§10-11-1.
Scope of provisions.
Exceptions, §§10-11-4,
10-11-5.
Subsidiaries.
For-profit subsidiary
not immune,
§10-11-3.
Willful misconduct.
Exception to immunity
from suit,
§10-11-3.
Loans to officers
prohibited, §10-3A-45.
Records.
Inspection of records of
corporation,
§10-3A-43.
Removal, §10-3A-42.
Terms, §10-3A-41.
Penalties.
False statements by
directors and officers,
§10-3A-202.

CORPORATIONS—Cont'd
Nonprofit corporations
—Cont'd
Powers of corporations,
§10-3A-20.
Foreign corporations,
§10-3A-171.
When lack of power may
be asserted, §10-3A-21.
Private colleges and
universities facilities
authority.
See EDUCATION.
Probate judge.
Appeal from judge,
§10-3A-221.
Powers, §10-3A-220.
Property.
Sale, lease, exchange, etc.,
of corporate property,
§10-3A-120.
Transfer of real property,
§10-3A-21.
Public societies. See within
this heading, "Public
societies."
Purposes of corporations,
§10-3A-4.
Records.
Duty to keep record,
§10-3A-43.
Registered office.
Change, §10-3A-24.
Foreign corporations,
§10-3A-177.
Foreign corporations,
§10-3A-176.
Change of office,
§10-3A-177.
Requirement of registered
office, §10-3A-23.
Repeal of prior act.
Effect of, §10-3A-225.
Sale, lease, etc., of property
and assets, §10-3A-120.
Secretary of state.
Appeal, §10-3A-221.
Powers, §10-3A-220.
Service of process, §10-3A-25.
Foreign corporations,
§10-3A-178.
Short title of chapter,
§10-3A-1.
Stock and stockholders.
Issuance of stock
prohibited, §10-3A-44.
Taxation.
Exemptions, §§40-9-12,
40-9-13, 40-9-16,
40-9-18.
Corporations organized
for purpose of aiding
retired teachers,
§40-9-18.
Property used in
connection with
college or
university,
§40-9-16.
Venue.
Involuntary dissolution,
§10-3A-148.
Liquidation, §10-3A-149.
Voting.
Majority vote required for
approval, §10-3A-37.
Waiver of notice, §10-3A-30.
Notice.
Consolidation or merger,
§10-2A-142.

CORPORATIONS—Cont'd
Notice—Cont'd
Directors.
Meetings, §10-2A-65.
Dissolution.
Involuntary dissolution.
Causes for dissolution,
§10-2A-193.
Franchise tax, §40-14-48.
Nonprofit corporations.
Directors' meetings,
§10-3A-39.
Members' meetings,
§10-3A-29.
Waiver of notice of
meetings, §10-3A-30.
Stockholders.
Meetings, §10-2A-48.
Waiver of notice,
§10-2A-49.
Waiver of notice of meetings,
§10-3A-30.
Nonprofit corporations,
§10-3A-30.
Officers.
Appointment, §10-2A-77.
Powers of corporations,
§10-2A-20.
Bond issues.
Depreciating bonds of
corporation with intent
to buy, §10-2A-71.
Criminal liability of
individuals for corporate
conduct, §13A-2-26.
Directors. See within this
heading, "Directors."
Duties.
Generally, §10-2A-77.
Enumeration, §10-2A-77.
Fiduciary obligations.
Not impaired by chapter,
§10-2A-76.
Indemnification, §10-2A-21.
Insurance.
Liability insurance,
§10-2A-21.
Liability insurance,
§10-2A-21.
Misdemeanors, §10-2A-284.
Nonprofit corporations. See
within this heading,
"Nonprofit corporations."
Penalties, §10-2A-284.
Quo warranto.
Usurpation of office.
Right of action and
venue, §6-6-591.
Rebates.
Taking by officer of certain
corporations, §8-11-4.
Removal, §10-2A-78.
Stock and stockholders.
Depreciating stock with
intent to buy,
§10-2A-71.
Usurpation of office.
Quo warranto.
Right of action and
venue, §6-6-591.
Organization.
Incorporation. See within
this heading,
"Incorporation."
Statement of name and
address of preparer of
instruments relating to
organization, §§35-4-110
to 35-4-113.

CORPORATIONS—Cont'd
Parks and recreation.
Societies for establishing
parks, etc. See within
this heading, "Public
societies."
Partnerships.
Participation in partnerships,
§10-2A-23.
Patriotic societies. See within
this heading, "Public
societies."
Penalties.
Collection.
Probate judge, §10-2A-280.
Secretary of state,
§10-2A-280.
Directors, §10-2A-284.
Foreign corporations.
Failure to pay grounds for
revocation of
certificate of authority,
§10-2A-244.
Transacting business
without certificate of
authority.
Liability of corporation
for penalties
imposed, §10-2A-247.
Nonprofit corporations.
False statements by
directors and officers,
§10-3A-202.
Officers, §10-2A-284.
Reports.
Failure or refusal to file,
§10-2A-283.
Secretary of state.
Collection, §10-2A-280.
Permits.
Domestic corporations,
§40-14-22.
Foreign corporations,
§40-14-21.
Reports of resident
stockholders.
Filing, §40-14-20.
Statements.
How made, §40-14-23.
Pipelines.
Foreign corporations.
Extension of pipelines into
state, §10-2A-225.
Political contributions,
§§10-2A-70 to 10-2A-70.2.
Political funds.
Segregated, separate political
funds, §10-1-2.
Powers of corporations.
Churches, §10-4-21.
Conference of ministers,
§10-4-41.
Consolidation or merger.
Resulting or surviving
corporation,
§10-2A-145.
Generally, §10-2A-20.
Graveyard owners, §10-4-21.
Nonprofit corporations,
§10-3A-20.
When lack of power may
be asserted, §10-3A-21.
Public societies, §10-4-21.
Stock and stockholders.
Issuance of stock,
§10-2A-32.
**Presently existing
corporations.**
Applicability of chapter,
§10-2A-334.

CORPORATIONS—Cont'd
Probate judge.
Evidence.
Certificates and certified
copies to be received in
evidence, §10-2A-332.
Professional corporations,
§§10-4-380 to 10-4-406.
See PROFESSIONAL
CORPORATIONS.
Property.
Churches.
Conveyance, §10-4-25.
Effect of recital in
minutes on
proceedings,
§10-4-26.
Independence of church
corporations in control
of real property,
§10-4-22.
Sale and conveyance of
property, §10-4-25.
Graveyard owners.
Sale and conveyance,
§10-4-25.
Incorporation by purchasers
of property or franchise
of corporation,
§10-2A-97.
Mortgages and deeds of trust.
Sale and conveyance,
§10-4-25.
Nonprofit corporations.
Sale, lease, exchange, etc.,
of corporate property,
§10-3A-120.
Transfer of real or personal
property, §10-3A-21.
Powers of corporations,
§10-2A-20.
Public societies.
Sale and conveyance,
§10-4-25.
Sale and conveyance of
property, §10-4-25.
Effect of recital in minutes
on proceedings,
§10-4-26.
Sale, lease, etc., of property
and assets.
In course of business,
§10-2A-160.
Nonprofit corporations,
§10-3A-120.
Prosecution of corporations.
Conviction.
Execution on judgment
upon conviction,
§10-7-4.
Docketing notice of
indictment, §10-7-1.
Evidence.
When proof of
incorporation
necessary, §12-21-201.
Failing to appear.
Entry of not guilty plea for
corporation failing to
appear, etc., §10-7-3.
Judgments.
Execution on judgment,
§10-7-4.
Not guilty plea.
Entry for corporation
failing to appear, etc.,
§10-7-3.
Notice of indictment, §10-7-1.
Service of notice and copy,
§10-7-2.

CORPORATIONS—Cont'd
Prosecution of corporations
—Cont'd
Pleas.
Not guilty plea.
Entry for corporation
failing to appear,
etc., §10-7-3.
Service of process.
Notice of indictment,
§10-7-2.
Stay of execution on
judgment, §10-7-4.
Trial.
Failure to appear.
Entry of not guilty plea
for corporation
failing to appear,
§10-7-3.
When case stands for trial,
§10-7-2.
When case stands for trial,
§10-7-2.
Proxies.
Fiduciaries.
Execution of proxies by
fiduciary holding
corporate stocks,
§19-3-8.
Voting by proxy, §10-2A-53.
Public school corporation,
§§16-14-1 to 16-14-19.
See EDUCATION.
Public societies, §§10-4-20 to
10-4-28.
Borrowing money, §10-4-24.
Effect of recital in minutes
on proceedings,
§10-4-26.
Certificate of incorporation,
§10-4-20.
Incorporation, §10-4-20.
Loans, §10-4-24.
Effect of recital in minutes
on proceedings,
§10-4-26.
Mortgages and deeds of trust.
Securing loans by,
§10-4-24.
Effect of recital in
minutes on
proceedings,
§10-4-26.
Powers of corporations,
§10-4-21.
Property.
Sale and conveyance,
§10-4-26.
Service of process.
Validity of service on
trustee, §10-4-23.
Trustees, §10-4-20.
Validity of service of
process on trustee,
§10-4-23.
Public utilities.
Application of corporations
provisions, §10-2A-336.
Elections.
Political parties or
candidates.
Giving aid or
contributions to,
§§10-2A-70.1,
10-2A-70.2.
Eminent domain.
Power of public utilities,
§10-5-1.
General provisions.
See PUBLIC UTILITIES.
Purposes, §10-2A-1.

CORPORATIONS—Cont'd
Quo warranto, §§6-6-590 to
6-6-604.
See QUO WARRANTO.
Railroad authorities.
General provisions, §§37-13-1
to 37-13-21.
See RAILROAD
AUTHORITIES.
Railroads.
Application of corporations
provisions, §10-2A-336.
Foreign corporations.
Extension of tracks into
state, §10-2A-225.
Real estate brokers.
See REAL ESTATE
BROKERS.
Rebates.
Officer, agent, etc., of certain
corporation taking
rebate, §8-11-4.
Receivers.
Close corporations.
Appointment, §10-2A-309.
Grounds, §10-2A-309.
General provisions.
See RECEIVERS.
Liquidation. See within this
heading, "Liquidation."
Voting of shares, §10-2A-53.
Recordation.
Filing and recording by
probate judge or
secretary of state.
Generally, §10-2A-93.
Statement of name and
address of preparer of
instructions relating to
organization, etc.,
§§35-4-110 to 35-4-113.
Records.
Directors.
Protecition of director
relying upon certain
records, §10-2A-73.
Falsifying business records,
§13A-9-45.
Inspections, §10-2A-79.
Nonprofit corporations.
Duty to keep record,
§10-3A-43.
Registered agents, §10-2A-29.
Change, §10-2A-30.
Foreign corporations,
§§10-2A-235 to
10-2A-237, 10-2A-244.
Resignation, §10-2A-30.
Service of process.
How corporation served,
§10-2A-31.
Registered name, §10-2A-27.
Renewal, §10-2A-28.
Registered offices, §10-2A-29.
Change, §10-2A-30.
Foreign corporations,
§§10-2A-235 to
10-2A-237, 10-2A-244.
Nonprofit corporations. See
within this heading,
"Nonprofit corporations."
Religious societies. See
within this heading,
"Churches."
Remedies.
Dissolution.
Survival of remedy after
dissolution,
§10-2A-203.

CORPORATIONS—Cont'd
Reorganization.
Articles of incorporation.
Amendment in
reorganization
proceedings,
§10-2A-117.
Statement of name and
address of preparer of
instruments relating to
reorganization,
§§35-4-110 to 35-4-113.
Stock and stockholders.
Expenses of reorganization,
§10-2A-39.
Repeal of prior acts.
Effect, §10-2A-339.
Reports.
Contents of annual report,
§10-2A-260.
Correction of annual report,
§10-2A-261.
Directors.
Protection of director
relying upon certain
reports, §10-2A-73.
Execution of annual report,
§10-2A-260.
Fee for filing annual report,
§§10-2A-260, 10-2A-261,
10-2A-281.
Filing of annual report,
§10-2A-261.
Financial reports.
Inspection, §10-2A-79.
Foreign corporations.
Contents of annual report,
§10-2A-260.
Correction of annual
report, §10-2A-261.
Execution of annual report,
§10-2A-260.
Failure to file annual
report, §10-2A-244.
Filing of annual report,
§10-2A-261.
Penalty for failure or
refusal to file,
§10-2A-283.
Public record information.
Acceptance in lieu of
annual report,
§10-2A-261.
Franchise tax.
Report to department of
revenue. See within
this heading,
"Franchise tax."
Inspections, §10-2A-79.
List of corporations,
§10-2A-29.
Penalties.
Failure or refusal to file,
§10-2A-283.
Permits.
Filing of reports of resident
stockholders,
§40-14-20.
Taxation of corporate shares
of stock, §40-14-72.
**Reservation of power by
legislature,** §10-2A-338.
Reserved name, §10-2A-26.
Reserves.
Special provisions relating to
surplus and reserves,
§10-2A-122.
Restated articles.
Execution, §10-3A-84.

CORPORATIONS—Cont'd
**Restitution to victims of
crimes.**
Default by corporation.
Forfeiture of right to do
business, §15-18-73.
Requirements, §15-18-73.
**Restraint of trade or
production.**
Entering combination to fix
price, etc., §8-10-2.
**Retail merchants
associations,** §10-4-260.
Rules and regulations.
Powers of corporations,
§10-2A-20.
**Sale, lease, etc., of property
and assets.**
In course of business.
Directors, §10-2A-160.
Nonprofit corporations.
§10-3A-120.
Not in course of business.
Rights of dissenting
stockholders,
§§10-2A-162,
10-2A-163.
Stockholders'
authorization,
§10-2A-161.
**Savings and loan
associations.**
Application of corporations
provisions, §10-2A-336.
General provisions, §§5-16-1
to 5-16-53.
See SAVINGS AND LOAN
ASSOCIATIONS.
Schools.
Alabama public school
corporation, §§16-14-1 to
16-14-19.
See EDUCATION.
Educational institutions. See
within this heading,
"Educational
institutions."
Scientific research societies.
See within this heading,
"Public societies."
S corporations.
Accumulated adjustments
account.
Applicability, §40-18-166.
Defined, §40-18-166.
Adjustments to earnings and
profits, §40-18-169.
Affected shareholder.
Defined, §40-18-166.
Built-in gains.
Tax imposed on,
§40-18-174.
Capital furnished.
Adjustments for,
§40-18-163.
Carryforward and carryback
provisions, §40-18-168.
Construction and
interpretation.
Due consideration to be
given to federal laws,
§40-18-173.
Definitions, §40-18-160.
Accumulated adjustments
account, §40-18-166.
Affected shareholder,
§40-18-166.
Post-termination transition
period, §40-18-172.
S period, §40-18-166.

CORPORATIONS—Cont'd
S corporations—Cont'd
Definitions—Cont'd
Two-percent shareholder,
§40-18-170.
Determination, §40-18-172.
Defined, §40-18-172.
Distribution of property,
§40-18-165.
Exemptions, §40-18-166.
Exemption from certain tax,
§40-18-160.
Individual.
When corporation may be
considered individual,
§40-18-167.
Partnerships.
Circumstances under
which corporation
treated as, §40-18-170.
Two-percent shareholder.
Considered as partner,
§40-18-170.
Passive investment income.
Tax imposed, §40-18-175.
Post-termination transition
period.
Defined, §40-18-172.
Services rendered.
Adjustments for,
§40-18-163.
Shareholders.
Affected shareholder.
Defined, §40-18-166.
Basis of stock.
Increase or decrease,
§40-18-164.
Capital furnished by
spouse, etc., of
shareholder.
Adjustments for,
§40-18-163.
Determination of pro rata
share, §40-18-171.
Services rendered by
spouse, etc., of
shareholder.
Adjustments for,
§40-18-163.
Taxation.
Determination of tax of
shareholder,
§40-18-162.
Two-percent shareholder.
Defined, §40-18-170.
S period.
Defined, §40-18-166.
Taxation.
Adjustments to earnings
and profits,
§40-18-169.
Built-in gains, §40-18-174.
Carryforward and
carryback provisions,
§40-18-168.
Deductions.
Certain deductions not
allowed, §40-18-161.
Income tax.
Applicability of chapter
18, Title 40,
§40-18-167.
Passive investment income.
Tax imposed when profit
exceeds certain
amount, §40-18-175.
Returns.
Nonresident shareholder
composite returns,
§40-18-176.

CORPORATIONS—Cont'd
S corporations—Cont'd
Taxation—Cont'd
Shareholders.
Determination of tax of
shareholder,
§40-18-162.
Taxable income.
Determination,
§40-18-161.
**Seals and sealed
instruments.**
Corporate seal, §10-2A-20.
Secretary of state.
Corporations fund,
§10-2A-281.
Evidence.
Certificates and certified
copies to be received in
evidence, §10-2A-332.
Fees.
Collection, §10-2A-280.
Forms to be furnished,
§10-2A-333.
List of corporations.
Maintenance by secretary
of state, §10-2A-29.
Penalties.
Collection, §10-2A-280.
Secured transactions.
Filing.
Applicability of filing
provisions, §7-9-302.
Securities.
General provisions. See
within this heading,
"Stock and stockholders."
Regulation, §§8-6-1 to
8-6-122.
See SECURITIES.
Security for dues, Const.
Ala., art. XII, §236.
Sentencing.
Article not to deprive court
of authority to dissolve
corporation, §13A-5-2.
Service of process.
Agents.
How process served,
§10-2A-31.
Churches.
Validity of service of
process on trustee,
§10-4-23.
Dissolution.
Involuntary dissolution,
§10-2A-194.
Foreign corporations.
Acting in fiduciary
capacity, §10-2A-224.1.
Registered agent to receive
service, §10-2A-237.
Graveyard owners.
Validity of service of
process on trustee,
§10-4-23.
How corporation served,
ARCP, Rule 4 (c).
Nonprofit corporations,
§10-3A-25.
Prosecution of corporations.
Notice of indictment,
§10-7-2.
Public societies.
Validity of service on
trustee, §10-4-23.
Registered agents, §10-2A-31.
Foreign corporations,
§10-2A-237.

CORPORATIONS—Cont'd
Shares and shareholders.
See within this heading,
"Stock and stockholders."
Sheriffs.
Creditors' actions.
Subjecting unpaid
subscriptions to satisfy
payment of judgment,
§6-6-187.
Short title.
Alabama business
corporation act,
§10-2A-1.
**Single-tax and other mutual
economic associations,**
§§10-4-190 to 10-4-194.
Soil classifiers.
Practice through corporations
not prohibited, §34-32-4.
**Special laws conferring
corporate powers.**
Prohibited, Const. Ala., art.
XII, §229; amd. 27.
State.
Obligations held by state,
Const. Ala., art. IV,
§100.
State interest in corporate
enterprises prohibited,
Const. Ala., art. IV, §93;
amd. 1.
Exceptions, Const. Ala.,
amds. 12, 58.
**State bar building
foundation,** §§34-3-101 to
34-3-108.
See ATTORNEYS AT LAW.
Stay of proceedings.
Prosecution of corporations.
Stay of execution on
judgment, §10-7-4.
Stock and stockholders.
Acquisition of own shares,
§10-2A-22.
Action by shareholders
without a meeting,
§10-2A-56.
Actions.
Derivative actions by
shareholders, ARCP,
Rule 23.1.
Form of complaint,
ARCP, Form 25.
Articles of incorporation.
Class voting by
shareholders on
amendments,
§10-2A-112.
Issuance of stock.
Powers stated in
certificate,
§10-2A-32.
Assets.
Sale, mortgage, etc., of
assets not in course of
business.
Rights of dissenting
stockholders,
§§10-2A-162,
10-2A-163.
Cancellation of shares.
Reacquired shares,
§10-2A-120.
Redeemable shares.
Cancellation by
redemption or
purchase,
§10-2A-119.

CORPORATIONS—Cont'd
Stock and stockholders
—Cont'd
Capital stock.
Power to increase or
decrease, §10-2A-20.
Reduction of stated capital
in certain cases,
§10-2A-121.
Certificates representing
shares, §10-2A-40.
Contents, §10-2A-40.
Classes of shares.
Power to issue classes
stated in articles,
§10-2A-32.
Preferred or special classes,
§10-2A-32.
Issuance, §10-2A-33.
Close corporations.
Agreement with
stockholders.
Restrictions, §10-2A-311.
Dissolution of corporation.
Option of stockholders,
§10-2A-312.
Issuance or transfer of
shares in breach of
conditions, §10-2A-305.
Management by
stockholders,
§10-2A-308.
Number of stockholders,
§10-2A-301.
Restrictions on transfer.
Corporate option where
restriction held
invalid, §10-2A-306.
Commercial code.
Investment securities,
§§7-8-101 to 7-8-406.
See COMMERCIAL
CODE.
Consideration for shares,
§10-2A-35.
Determination of amount
of stated capital,
§10-2A-38.
Payment for shares,
§10-2A-36.
Consolidation or merger.
Articles of merger or
consolidation,
§10-2A-143.
Two or more domestic
corporations.
Approval by
shareholders,
§10-2A-142.
Corporate shares.
Taxation of corporate
shares of stock,
§§40-14-70 to 40-14-74.
Creditors of corporation.
Liability of subscribers and
shareholders,
§10-2A-43.
Deadlock.
Action for dissolution or
liquidation,
10-2A-195.
Definitions, §10-2A-2.
Depreciating stock with
intent to buy, §10-2A-71.
Derivative actions by
shareholders, ARCP,
Rule 23.1.
Form of complaint, ARCP,
Form 25.

CORPORATIONS—Cont'd
Stock and stockholders
—Cont'd
Directors.
Depreciating stock with
intent to buy,
§10-2A-71.
Disposal of own shares.
Right of corporation to
dispose of its own
shares, §10-2A-22.
Dissenting stockholders.
Rights, §§10-2A-162,
10-2A-163.
Dissolution.
Action by stockholders for
dissolution or
liquidation,
§10-2A-195.
Deposit with commissioner
of revenue of amount
due certain
shareholders,
§10-2A-202.
Voluntary dissolution.
Consent of shareholders,
§10-2A-181.
Revocation of
proceedings by
consent of
shareholders,
§10-2A-186.
Effect of statement of
revocation,
§10-2A-189.
Filing of statement,
§10-2A-188.
Dividends.
Declaration of dividends,
§10-2A-67.
Directors may declare,
§10-2A-67.
Minors.
Right of infant to receive
dividends in own
name, §10-6-3.
Nonprofit corporations.
Dividends prohibited,
§10-3A-44.
Educational institutions.
Distribution of proceeds
from issuance of stock
when corporation
ceases business,
§§10-4-81, 10-4-82.
Electric cooperatives.
Conversion of existing
corporation into
cooperative.
Approval of stockholders
required, §37-6-16.
Exchange of stock.
Approval of shareholders
required, §10-2A-171.
Dissent from exchange,
§10-2A-171.
Procedure, §10-2A-170.
Voluntary exchange with
shareholders.
Section does not limit
power to secure,
§10-2A-170.
Execution sales.
Purchaser becomes owner
of stock, §6-9-144.
Fiduciaries.
Execution of proxies by
fiduciary holding
corporate stocks,
§19-3-8.

CORPORATIONS—Cont'd
Stock and stockholders
—Cont'd
Forms.
Stockholder's derivative
action, ARCP, Form
25.
Fractional shares.
Issuance, §10-2A-42.
Incorporation.
Expenses of incorporation,
§10-2A-39.
Industrial development
corporations, §§10-4-130
to 10-4-152.
See INDUSTRIAL
DEVELOPMENT
CORPORATIONS.
Issuance of stock.
Articles of incorporation.
Power to issue number
and classes of shares
stated in articles,
§10-2A-32.
Certificates representing
shares, §10-2A-40.
Classes of shares.
Power to issue classes of
shares stated in
articles, §10-2A-32.
Preferred or special
classes, §§10-2A-32,
10-2A-33.
Fractional shares.
Issuance of certificates
for fractional shares,
§10-2A-42.
Number of shares.
Power to issue number of
shares stated in
articles, §10-2A-32.
Power to issue number and
classes of shares stated
in articles, §10-2A-32.
Preemptive rights to
purchase issuance,
§10-2A-44.
Preferred or special class
in series, §10-2A-33.
Restrictions, Const. Ala.,
art. XII, §224.
Liability of stockholders,
Const. Ala., art. XII,
§236.
Liability to corporation or
its creditors,
§10-2A-43.
Liens.
Lien on shares by
corporation, §10-2A-43.
Meetings of stockholders.
Action by shareholders
without a meeting,
§10-2A-56.
Annual meetings,
§10-2A-47.
Fixing of record date,
§10-2A-50.
Notice of meetings,
§10-2A-48.
Waiver of notice,
§10-2A-49.
Place, §10-2A-47.
Powers of corporations,
§10-2A-20.
Quorum, §10-2A-52.
Record date.
Fixing record date,
§10-2A-50.
Special meetings,
§10-2A-47.

CORPORATIONS—Cont'd
Stock and stockholders
—Cont'd
Meetings of stockholders
—Cont'd
Voting record, §10-2A-51.
Minors.
Dividends.
Right of infant to receive
dividends in own
name, §10-6-3.
Effect of chapter on gifts to
minors act, §10-6-4.
Notice of infancy.
Treating infant as adult,
§10-6-1.
When required, §10-6-2.
Transfer of shares.
When corporation may
treat infant as
having capacity,
§10-6-1.
Transfers to minors.
Effect of chapter on
transfers to minors
act, §10-6-4.
General provisions,
§§35-5A-1 to
35-5A-24.
See TRANSFERS TO
MINORS.
Voting.
When corporation may
treat infant as
having capacity to
vote, §10-6-1.
Nonprofit corporations.
Issuance of stock
prohibited, §10-3A-44.
Notice.
Meetings, §10-2A-48.
Waiver of notice,
§10-2A-49.
Officers.
Depreciating stock with
intent to buy,
§10-2A-71.
Options, §10-2A-37.
Other corporations.
Power to acquire stocks
and bonds of other
corporations,
§10-2A-20.
Own shares.
Right of corporation to
acquire and dispose of,
§10-2A-22.
Payment for shares,
§10-2A-36.
Powers of corporation.
Issuance of stock,
§10-2A-32.
Preemptive rights.
Stockholders' preemptive
right to purchase,
§10-2A-44.
Preferred stock.
Issuance, §10-2A-33; Const.
Ala., art. XII, §237.
Property.
Sale, mortgage or pledge of
assets not in course of
business.
Rights of dissenting
stockholders,
§§10-2A-162,
10-2A-163.

CORPORATIONS—Cont'd
Stock and stockholders
—Cont'd
Proxies.
Fiduciaries.
Execution of proxies by
fiduciary holding
corporate stocks,
§19-3-8.
Purchase of stock.
Preemptive right of
stockholder to
purchase issuance of
stock, §10-2A-44.
Record date.
Fixing, §10-2A-50.
Redeemable shares.
Cancellation by redemption
or purchase,
§10-2A-119.
Restriction on redemption,
§10-2A-118.
Redemption or purchase of
redeemable shares.
Cancellation of shares by
redemption or
purchase, §10-2A-119.
Restriction upon,
§10-2A-118.
Regulation of securities.
See SECURITIES.
Reorganization.
Expenses of reorganization,
§10-2A-39.
Restriction on transfer,
§§7-8-204, 10-2A-41.
Rights of stockholders.
Dissenting stockholders,
§§10-2A-162,
10-2A-163.
Preemptive right to
purchase issuance of
stock, §10-2A-44.
Rights or options, §10-2A-37.
Sale, mortgage or pledge of
assets.
Authorization when not in
course of business,
§10-2A-161.
Rights of dissenting
stockholders,
§§10-2A-162,
10-2A-163.
Securities regulation.
See SECURITIES.
Series.
Preferred or special class
in series.
Issuance of shares,
§10-2A-33.
Stockholder obligations not
impaired by chapter,
§10-2A-76.
Subscription for shares.
Garnishment.
Unpaid subscription,
§6-6-414.
Irrevocability of
subscription,
§10-2A-34.
Liability of subscribers to
corporation or its
creditors, §10-2A-43.
Taxation of corporate shares,
§§40-7-70 to 40-7-74.
Transfer books.
Closing, §10-2A-50.
Voting record, §10-2A-51.
Transfer of shares.
Closing of stock transfer
books, §10-2A-50.

CORPORATIONS—Cont'd
Stock and stockholders
—Cont'd
Transfer of shares—Cont'd
Commercial code,
§§7-8-101 to 7-8-406.
See COMMERCIAL
CODE.
Fixing of record date,
§10-2A-50.
Minors.
Notice of infancy,
§§10-6-1, 10-6-2.
Restrictions on, §§7-8-204,
10-2A-41.
Treasury shares.
Right of corporation to
acquire and dispose of
its own shares,
§10-2A-22.
Trustees.
Registration of securities
held by corporate
fiduciary in name of
nominee, §19-3-7.
Trusts.
Voting trusts and
agreements among
shareholders,
§10-2A-55.
Voting of shares, §10-2A-53.
Action by shareholders
without a meeting,
§10-2A-56.
Greater voting
requirements,
§10-2A-54.
Minors.
Notice of infancy.
Effect, §§10-6-1,
10-6-2.
Trusts.
Voting trusts and
agreements,
§10-2A-55.
Voting record, §10-2A-51.
Voting trusts.
Creation by stockholders,
§10-2A-55.
Subsidiary corporations.
Consolidation or merger,
§10-2A-144.
Surplus.
Capital surplus.
Defined, §10-2A-2.
Determination of amount
of stated capital,
§10-2A-38.
Defined, §10-2A-2.
Directors.
Distributions from capital
surplus, §10-2A-68.
Dividends.
Declaration and payment
of dividends,
§10-2A-67.
Earned surplus.
Defined, §10-2A-2.
Special provisions relating to
surplus and reserves,
§10-2A-122.
Surveys and surveyors.
See SURVEYS AND
SURVEYORS.
Taxation.
Assessments.
By whom property should
be listed, §40-7-17.
Corporate shares of stock.
Appeals.
Assessment, §40-14-71.

CORPORATIONS—Cont'd
Taxation—Cont'd
Corporate shares of stock
—Cont'd
Assessment, §40-14-70.
Appeal, §40-14-71.
Collection, §40-14-70.
Exempted corporations.
Provisions not
applicable,
§40-14-74.
List of shareholders.
Corporations paying tax
need not file,
§40-14-73.
Reports.
Failure to make.
Effect, §40-14-72.
How made, §40-14-72.
Exemptions.
Mental health.
Corporations organized
to establish regional
mental health
programs, §40-9-23.
Foreign corporations.
Transacting business
without certificate of
authority.
Liability of corporation
for taxes,
§10-2A-247.
Franchise tax. See within
this heading, "Franchise
tax."
Income tax.
See INCOME TAX.
Nonprofit corporations. See
within this heading,
"Nonprofit corporations."
S corporations. See within
this heading, "S
corporations."
Telephones.
Foreign corporations.
Extension of lines into
state, §10-2A-225.
Title of chapter.
Alabama business
corporation act,
§10-2A-1.
**Toll road, bridge and tunnel
authority.**
See TOLL ROAD, BRIDGE
AND TUNNEL
AUTHORITY.
Torts.
Nonprofit corporations.
Officers.
Liability, §§10-11-1 to
10-11-5.
Treasury shares.
Defined, §10-2A-2.
Trial.
Prosecution of corporations.
When case stands for trial,
§10-7-2.
Trusts and trustees.
Application of corporations
provisions, §10-2A-336.
Conversion, etc., of securities
upon merger,
consolidation, etc.,
§19-3-10.
Foreign corporations.
Acting in fiduciary
capacity, §§10-2A-221
to 10-2A-224.1.

CORPORATIONS—Cont'd
Trusts and trustees—Cont'd
Proxies.
Execution by fiduciary
holding corporate
stocks, §19-3-8.
Securities.
Registration of securities
held by corporate
fiduciary in name of
nominee, §19-3-7.
Stock.
Execution of proxies by
fiduciary holding
corporate stocks,
§19-3-8.
Voting of shares by trustee,
§10-2A-53.
Voting trusts.
Creation by stockholders,
§10-2A-55.
Ultra vires.
Defense of ultra vires,
§10-2A-24.
Utility services facilities,
§§11-97-1 to 11-97-27.
See UTILITY SERVICES
FACILITIES.
Venue.
Actions against corporations,
§6-3-7.
Insurers, §6-3-5.
Dissolution.
Involuntary dissolution.
Actions for, §10-2A-194.
Foreign corporations, Const.
Ala., art. XII, §232.
Nonprofit corporations.
Involuntary dissolution,
§10-3A-148.
Liquidation, §10-3A-149.
Quo warranto, §§6-6-590,
6-6-591.
Voluntary dissolution.
General provisions. See
within this heading,
"Dissolution."
Nonprofit corporations. See
within this heading,
"Nonprofit corporations."
Voting.
Stock and stockholders. See
within this heading,
"Stock and stockholders."
**Water conservation and
irrigation corporations,**
§§9-10-30 to 9-10-47.
See WATER
CONSERVATION AND
IRRIGATION.
Water power companies.
See DAMS.
**Water system assistance
authority.**
Application to become
corporation, §22-23A-5.
Incorporation of authority.
Proceedings, notice or
approval not required,
§22-23A-15.
**Wholesale merchants
associations.**
Incorporation, §10-4-280.
Witnesses.
Franchise tax.
Summons of witnesses,
§40-14-51.

CORPSES.
General provisions, §§22-19-1
to 22-19-144.
See DEAD BODIES.

CORRECTIONS.
Actions.
Institution finance authority.
Application, §14-2-4.
Bond issues.
Contest of authorizing
resolution, §14-2-15.
Power to maintain,
§14-2-8.
Venue, §14-2-33.
Judgments against board.
Payment by board of
adjustment, §41-9-74.
**Administrative procedure
act.**
Inmate community
reintegration under SIR
act.
Exemption of program
from administrative
procedure act,
§15-18-122.
Board of corrections.
Abolished, §14-1-16.
Bonds, surety.
Officers and employees,
§14-1-5.
Capital outlay oversight
commission, §14-1-18.
Commissioner of corrections.
Institution finance
authority.
Vice-chairman, §14-2-6.
Coroners.
Special coroners.
Appointment at request
of board, §14-6-99.
Corrections revolving fund,
§14-1-14.
Correspondence.
Preservation of official
correspondence,
§14-3-6.
County commission.
Ordering or calling a
special session,
§14-6-102.
Courts.
Cooperation with, §14-1-8.
Department of pensions and
security.
Cooperation with
department, §14-1-8.
Cooperation with state
board of corrections.
Investigations of families
or dependents of
prisoners, §38-2-6.
Deputy commissioners.
Term of office, §14-1-4.
Divisions.
Authority to create,
§14-1-7.
Chiefs of divisions.
Appointment, §14-1-7.
Full-time position,
§14-1-7.
Oath of office, §14-1-7.
Salaries, §14-1-7.
Duties.
Advisor to governor and
legislature, §14-1-9.
Exercise, §14-1-10.
General provisions,
§§14-1-8, 14-3-1.
Restrictions, §14-1-10.

CORRECTIONS—Cont'd
Board of corrections—Cont'd
Duties—Cont'd
Transferral of duties to
governor, §§14-1-15,
14-1-16.
Employees.
Appointment, §14-1-4.
Bonds, surety, §14-1-5.
Fiscal year, §14-1-13.
Functions.
Advisor to governor and
legislature, §14-1-9.
Exercise, §14-1-10.
General provisions,
§14-1-8.
Restrictions, §14-1-10.
Governor.
Administrative functions of
department, §14-1-17.
Advisor to the governor,
§14-1-9.
Duties, authority, property,
rights, etc., vested in
governor, §§14-1-15,
14-1-16.
Notice prior to decision on
construction of
permanent facilities,
§14-1-9.
Reports.
Annual report to
governor, §14-1-13.
Hospitals.
Prisoners needing long-
time hospitalization.
Treatment, care and
segregation,
§14-1-12.
Inspections.
Authority, §14-6-106.
Effect of orders of board,
§14-6-107.
Jails.
See JAILS.
Outside of state, §14-6-108.
Penitentiary.
See PENITENTIARY.
Jails.
See JAILS.
Judgments.
Payment by board of
adjustment, §41-9-74.
Legislative committee for
evaluation of board,
§§29-2-20 to 29-2-22.
Legislature.
Advisor to the legislature,
§14-1-9.
Notice prior to decision on
construction of
permanent facilities,
§14-1-9.
Periodic recommendations,
§14-1-13.
Litigation.
Judgments.
Payment by board of
adjustment,
§41-9-74.
Merit system.
Officers and employees,
§14-1-4.
Notice prior to decision on
construction of
permanent facilities,
§14-1-9.

CORRECTIONS—Cont'd
  Board of corrections—Cont'd
    Oaths.
      Divisions.
        Chiefs of divisions.
          Constitutional oath of
            office, §14-1-7.
      Officers, §14-1-4.
    Bonds, surety, §14-1-5.
    Powers and duties.
      Advisor to governor and
        legislature, §14-1-9.
      Exercise, §14-1-10.
      General provisions,
        §14-1-8.
      Restrictions, §14-1-10.
      Tubercular prisoners,
        §14-1-12.
      Vested in governor,
        §§14-1-15, 14-1-16.
    Prisons and prisoners.
      General provisions.
        See PRISONS AND
          PRISONERS.
    Property vested in governor,
      §§14-1-15, 14-1-16.
    Public documents.
      Official correspondence,
        §14-3-6.
    Records.
      Convicts, §14-3-7.
      Official correspondence,
        §14-3-6.
      Public documents, §14-3-6.
    Reports.
      Annual report to governor,
        §14-1-13.
      Transmission to
        legislature, §14-3-11.
    Rules and regulations.
      Prisons and prisoners.
        Promulgation, §14-1-8.
      Promulgation, §14-1-11.
    State personnel
      department.
      Exemptions, §14-1-4.
    Salaries.
      Chiefs of divisions, §14-1-7.
    Statistics.
      Duty to collect, §14-1-8.
    Tubercular prisoners.
      Powers and duties,
        §14-1-12.
    Visiting of places outside of
      state, §14-6-108.
    Work release program.
      Inmate not deemed agent
        of board of corrections,
        §14-8-5.
  Bond issues.
    Institution finance authority.
      See within this heading,
      "Institution finance
      authority."
    Penal and correctional
      facilities, Const. Ala.,
      amd. 374.
  Bonds, surety.
    Board of corrections.
      Officers and employees,
        §14-1-5.
    Commissioner of corrections,
      §14-1-1.4.
    Inmate community
      reintegration under SIR
      act, §§15-18-111,
      15-18-120.
  Commissioner of
    corrections.
    Appointment, §14-1-1.3.
    Bonds, surety, §14-1-1.4.

CORRECTIONS—Cont'd
  Commissioner of corrections
    —Cont'd
    Deputy commissioners,
      §14-1-1.5.
    Head of department of
      corrections, §14-1-1.3.
    Institution finance authority.
      Vice-chairman, §14-2-6.
    Oath of office, §14-1-1.4.
    Powers and duties, §14-1-1.3.
    Qualifications, §14-1-1.4.
    Salary, §14-1-1.3.
  Compacts.
    Interstate corrections
      compact, §§14-13-1 to
      14-13-3.
  Contracts.
    Institution finance authority.
      Construction of facilities,
        §14-2-28.
      Property.
        Sale or lease, §14-2-26.
  Convict labor.
    See PRISONS AND
      PRISONERS.
  Correctional investigative
    services officers, §14-3-9.
  Corrections revolving fund,
    §14-1-14.
  Counties.
    Commission.
      Special session of county
        commission.
        Authority of board of
          corrections to order,
          §14-6-102.
    Institution finance authority.
      Leasing of facilities,
        §14-2-30.
    Jails.
      General provisions.
        See JAILS.
  Definitions.
    Inmate community
      reintegration under SIR
      act, §15-18-111.
    Institution finance authority,
      §14-2-1.
  Department of corrections.
    Administrative department,
      §14-1-1.2.
    Commissioner of corrections.
      General provisions. See
        within this heading,
        "Commissioner of
        corrections."
    Head of department,
      §14-1-1.3.
    Control over penal and
      corrections institutions,
      §14-1-1.2.
    Created, §14-1-1.1.
    Established, §14-1-1.1.
    Inmate community
      reintegration under SIR
      act, §§15-18-110 to
      15-18-123. See within
      this heading, "Inmate
      community reintegration
      under SIR act."
    Powers and duties, §14-1-1.1.
  Deposits.
    Institution finance authority.
      Bond issues.
        Security for deposit of
          governmental funds,
          §14-2-18.

CORRECTIONS—Cont'd
  Detainers.
    Mandatory disposition of
      detainers, §§15-9-88.
    See DETAINERS.
  Education.
    Schools at correctional units,
      §§14-12-1 to 14-12-4.
  Eminent domain.
    Institution finance authority,
      §14-2-9.
  Federal government.
    Institution finance authority.
      Leasing of facilities,
        §14-2-30.
  Fees.
    Secretary of state.
      Institution finance
        authority.
        Incorporation or
          dissolution of
          authority, §14-2-35.
  Finance authority. See within
    this heading, "Institution
    finance authority."
  Funds.
    Corrections revolving fund,
      §14-1-14.
  Governor.
    Board of corrections.
      Abolition.
        Exercise of
          administrative
          functions, §14-1-17.
      Advisor to the governor,
        §14-1-9.
      Duties, authority, property,
        rights, etc., vested in
        governor, §§14-1-15,
        14-1-16.
      Notice prior to decision on
        construction of
        permanent facilities,
        §14-1-9.
      Reports to governor,
        §14-1-13.
  Inmate community
    reintegration under SIR
    act.
    Administrative procedure
      act.
      Exemption from,
        §15-18-122.
    Annual report required,
      §15-18-119.
    Charge for supervision costs,
      §15-18-117.
    Commissioner.
      Defined, §15-18-111.
      Promoting public
        understanding of
        program, §15-18-120.
    Definitions, §15-18-111.
    Department.
      Defined, §15-18-111.
      Investigation regarding
        inmate suitability,
        §15-18-114.
    Legal status of inmate
      involved in free
      community, etc.,
      §15-18-118.
    Disposition of unclaimed,
      etc., funds, §15-18-115.
    Eligibility of inmates,
      §15-18-113.
    Exemption of program from
      administrative procedure
      act, §15-18-122.

CORRECTIONS—Cont'd
**Inmate community
reintegration under SIR
act**—Cont'd
Extension of limits of
confinement authorized,
§15-18-112.
Failure to remain within
limits of confinement,
etc.
Penalty for failure,
§15-18-121.
Forty-hour workweek
required, §15-18-116.
Investigation of inmate
suitability, §15-18-114.
Legal status of inmate
involved in free
community, etc.,
§15-18-118.
Legislative review
authorized, §15-18-123.
Minimum security risks.
Eligibility of inmates
classified as,
§15-18-113.
Notice.
Investigation by
department regarding
inmate suitability,
§15-18-114.
Oversight committee.
Legislative review
authorized, §15-18-123.
Penalties.
Failure to remain within
limits of confinement,
etc., §15-18-121.
Program.
Defined, §15-18-111.
Promoting public
understanding of
program.
Commissioner required to
promote, §15-18-120.
Recommendations of
oversight committee,
§15-18-123.
Reports.
Annual report, §15-18-119.
Review and recommendations
of oversight committee,
§15-18-123.
Schedule of payment of
restitution, §15-18-115.
Short title, §15-18-110.
State correctional institution.
Defined, §15-18-111.
Supervision charge
authorized, §15-18-117.
Title of article, §15-18-110.
Workweek required,
§15-18-116.
Institution finance authority.
Actions.
Application, §14-2-4.
Bond issues.
Contest of authorizing
resolution, §14-2-15.
Power to maintain,
§14-2-8.
Venue, §14-2-33.
Board of directors.
Governing body of
authority, §14-2-6.
Membership, §14-2-6.
Proceedings.
Recording, §14-2-7.
Quorum, §14-2-6.

CORRECTIONS—Cont'd
Institution finance authority
—Cont'd
Board of directors—Cont'd
Resolutions.
Actions of authority,
§14-2-7.
Salaries, §14-2-6.
Successors in office,
§14-2-6.
Vacancies, §14-2-6.
Bond issues.
Actions.
Contest of authorizing
resolution, §14-2-15.
Amount.
Aggregate amount,
§14-2-12.
Authorization, §14-2-12.
Contents, §14-2-14.
Contest.
Authorizing resolutions,
§14-2-15.
Default.
Enforcement upon
default, §14-2-22.
Deposits.
Security for deposit of
governmental funds,
§14-2-18.
Enforcement.
Default, §14-2-22.
Execution, §14-2-11.
Interest.
Security, §14-2-21.
Investment of funds,
§14-2-17.
Proceeds of sale,
§14-2-20.
Issuance.
Authorization, §14-2-12.
Refunding bonds,
§14-2-13.
Temporary loans in
anticipation,
§14-2-10.
Maturity date, §14-2-14.
Negotiable instruments,
§14-2-23.
Not debt of state, §14-2-24.
Notice.
Authorizing resolutions,
§14-2-15.
Sale, §14-2-16.
Payment.
Dissolution of authority
on payment,
§14-2-34.
Precedence, §14-2-14.
Priority of pledges,
§14-2-14.
Purposes, §14-2-12.
Recitals.
Authorizing resolutions,
§14-2-15.
Refunding bonds.
Issuance, §14-2-13.
Sale, §14-2-13.
Disposition of proceeds,
§14-2-19.
Resolutions, §14-2-15.
Sale.
Notice, §14-2-16.
Price, §14-2-16.
Procedure, §14-2-16.
Proceeds.
Disposition, §14-2-19.
Investment, §14-2-20.

CORRECTIONS—Cont'd
Institution finance authority
—Cont'd
Bond issues—Cont'd
Sale—Cont'd
Refunding bonds,
§14-2-13.
Disposition of proceeds,
§14-2-19.
Terms and commissions,
§14-2-16.
Seals, §14-2-11.
Security.
Deposit of governmental
funds, §14-2-18.
Principal or interest on
bonds, §14-2-21.
Signatures, §14-2-11.
Special funds, §14-2-31.
Specifications, §14-2-14.
Taxation.
Exemptions, §14-2-32.
Temporary loans in
anticipation of
issuance, §14-2-10.
Trusts and trustees.
Investment of trust
funds, §14-2-17.
Construction of chapter,
§14-2-2.
Construction of facilities.
Contracts, §14-2-28.
Convict labor.
Use, §14-2-28.
Plan specifications.
Approval, §14-2-28.
Definitions, §14-2-1.
Dissolution.
Fees of secretary of state,
§14-2-35.
Procedure, §14-2-34.
When authorized, §14-2-34.
Eminent domain.
Powers, §14-2-9.
Employees.
Authority to appoint and
employ, §14-2-8.
Fiscal year, §14-2-8.
Funds.
Special funds, §14-2-31.
Incorporation.
Application.
Filing, §14-2-4.
Authority, §14-2-3.
Certificate of incorporation,
§14-2-5.
Fees of secretary of state,
§14-2-35.
Recordation, §14-2-3.
Intent of chapter, §14-2-2.
Interest.
Loans.
Temporary loans in
anticipation of
issuance of bonds,
§14-2-10.
Investments.
Bond issues, §14-2-17.
Proceeds of sale,
§14-2-20.
Kilby property.
Consideration for transfer
by state, §14-2-25.
Conveyance to authority,
§14-2-25.
Defined, §14-2-1.
Lease.
Anticipation of rent,
§14-2-8.

CORRECTIONS—Cont'd
Institution finance authority
—Cont'd
Kilby property—Cont'd
Lease—Cont'd
Assignability.
Security for bonds,
§14-2-21.
Pleasure rents and
revenues, §14-2-8.
Power of authority,
§14-2-26.
Proceeds.
Disposition, §14-2-26.
United States
environmental
protection agency,
§14-2-27.
Possession.
Right to possession,
§14-2-25.
Sale, §14-2-26.
Transfer by state.
Consideration, §14-2-25.
Leasing of facilities.
Competitive bid laws.
Exemption from,
§14-2-36.
Counties, §14-2-30.
Federal government,
§14-2-30.
Municipal corporations,
§14-2-30.
State or agency thereof,
§14-2-29.
Taxation.
Exemptions from
taxation, §14-2-32.
Loans.
Temporary loans.
Anticipation of issuance
of bonds, §14-2-10.
Members, §14-2-6.
Notes.
Execution, §14-2-11.
Not debt of state, §14-2-24.
Temporary loans in
anticipation of
issuance of bonds,
§14-2-10.
Notice.
Bond issues.
Authorizing resolutions,
§14-2-15.
Sale, §14-2-16.
Kilby property.
Sale or lease, §14-2-26.
Possession.
Power of authority,
§14-2-26.
Right to possession,
§14-2-25.
Powers.
Eminent domain, §14-2-9.
General provisions,
§14-2-8.
President.
Governor, §14-2-6.
Proceeds.
Disposition, §14-2-26.
Property.
Acquisition and holding
title to, §14-2-8.
Construction of facilities,
§14-2-8.
Conveyance of property by
state, §14-2-25.
Eminent domain.
Powers, §14-2-9.
Taxation.
Exemptions, §14-2-32.

CORRECTIONS—Cont'd
Institution finance authority
—Cont'd
Purpose of chapter, §14-2-2.
Recordation.
Incorporation, §14-2-4.
Sale, §14-2-26.
Seal.
Corporate seal, §14-2-8.
Execution of bonds and
notes, §14-2-11.
Secretary.
Director of finance,
§14-2-6.
Signatures.
Execution of bonds and
notes, §14-2-11.
Taxation.
Exemption from taxation,
§14-2-32.
Treasurer.
State treasurer, §14-2-6.
United States
environmental
protection agency,
§14-2-27.
Venue.
Actions, §14-2-33.
Vice-president.
Commissioner of
corrections, §14-2-6.
Interest.
Institution finance authority.
Bond issues.
Security, §14-2-21.
Temporary loans in
anticipation of
issuance of bonds,
§14-2-10.
**Interstate corrections
compact.**
Adoption, §14-13-2.
Citation of chapter, §14-13-1.
Commissioner.
Authority to carry out
compact, §14-13-3.
Contracts.
With other member states,
§14-13-3.
Short title of chapter,
§14-13-1.
Text, §14-13-2.
Investigations.
Inmate community
reintegration under SIR
act.
Suitability of inmate
program, §15-18-114.
Investments.
Institution finance authority.
Bond issues, §14-2-17.
Proceeds of sale,
§14-2-20.
Jails.
Generally.
See JAILS.
Kilby property. See within
this heading, "Institution
finance authority."
Leases.
Institution finance authority.
See within this heading,
"Institution finance
authority."
Legislature.
Board of corrections.
Advisor to the legislature,
§14-1-9.

CORRECTIONS—Cont'd
Legislature—Cont'd
Board of corrections—Cont'd
Notice prior to decision on
construction of
permanent facilities,
§14-1-9.
Periodic recommendations,
§14-1-13.
Loans.
Institution finance authority.
Temporary loans in
anticipation of
issuance of bonds,
§14-2-10.
**Mandatory disposition of
detainers,** §§15-9-80 to
15-9-88.
See DETAINERS.
Municipal corporations.
Institution finance authority.
Leasing of facilities,
§14-2-30.
Notice.
Inmate community
reintegration under SIR
act.
Investigation of inmate
suitability, §15-18-114.
Institution finance authority.
Bond issues.
Authorizing resolutions,
§14-2-15.
Sale, §14-2-16.
Kilby property.
Sale or lease, §14-2-26.
Possession.
Power of authority,
§14-2-26.
Right to possession,
§14-2-25.
Oaths.
Board of corrections.
Chiefs of divisions, §14-1-7.
Commissioner of corrections,
§14-1-1.4.
Penalties.
Inmate community
reintegration under SIR
act.
Failure to remain within
limits of confinement,
etc., §15-18-121.
Penitentiary, §§14-3-30 to
14-3-60.
See PENITENTIARY.
Prisons and prisoners.
See PRISONS AND
PRISONERS.
Recordation.
Institution finance authority.
Incorporation, §14-2-4.
Sale, §14-2-26.
Records.
Board of corrections,
§§14-3-6, 14-3-7.
**Reintegration of inmate into
society.**
Inmate community
reintegration under SIR
act, §§15-18-110 to
15-18-123. See within
this heading, "Inmate
community reintegration
under SIR act."
Reports.
Board of corrections.
Annual report, §14-1-13.

CORRECTIONS—Cont'd
Reports—Cont'd
Inmate community
reintegration under SIR
act.
Annual report required,
§15-18-119.
Revolving fund, §14-1-14.
Rules and regulations.
Board of corrections.
Prisons and prisoners.
Promulgation, §14-1-8.
Promulgation, §14-1-11.
State personnel
department.
Exemptions, §14-1-4.
Inmate community
reintegration under SIR
act.
Extension of limits of
confinement
authorized, §15-18-112.
Salaries.
Board of corrections.
Chiefs of divisions, §14-1-7.
Commissioner of corrections,
§14-1-1.3.
Deputy commissioners,
§14-1-1.5.
Institution finance authority.
Board of directors, §14-2-6.
Sales.
Institution finance authority.
Bond issues. See within
this heading,
"Institution finance
authority."
Recordation, §14-2-26.
**Schools at correctional
units.**
Attendance.
Eligibility to attend,
§14-12-3.
Minimum number of hours,
§14-12-2.
Eligibility to attend,
§14-12-3.
Establishment, §14-12-1.
Operation, §14-12-1.
Costs, §14-12-4.
Professional units to be
provided.
Determination of number,
§14-12-2.
Studies.
Establishment and
operation of schools,
§14-12-1.
Teachers.
Qualifications, §14-12-2.
Salaries, §14-12-2.
Secretary of state.
Institution finance authority.
Fees for incorporation or
dissolution, §14-2-35.
State.
Institution finance authority.
Leasing of facilities,
§14-2-29.
**Supervised intensive
restitution,** §§15-18-110 to
15-18-123. See within this
heading, "Inmate
community reintegration
under SIR act."
Taxation.
Institution finance authority.
Exemption from taxation,
§14-2-32.

CORRECTIONS—Cont'd
Trusts and trustees.
Institution finance authority.
Bond issues.
Investment of trust
funds, §14-2-17.
**Uniform mandatory
disposition of detainers
act,** §§15-9-80 to 15-9-88.
See DETAINERS.
Venue.
Institution finance authority.
Actions, §14-2-33.

**CORRESPONDENCE
SCHOOLS.**
Unaccredited schools,
§§16-46-1 to 16-46-10.
See EDUCATION.

CORROBORATION.
Perjury.
Required for perjury
conviction, §13A-10-105.

CORROSIVE SUBSTANCES.
General provisions, §§8-17-20
to 8-17-24.

CORRUPTION.
Bribery.
See BRIBERY.
Code of ethics, §§36-25-1 to
36-25-30.
See PUBLIC OFFICERS
AND EMPLOYEES.
Impeachment.
Grounds, §36-11-1.
Investigations, §36-11-3.
Legislature.
Expulsion for corruption bar
to further service, Const.
Ala., art. IV, §54.

CORRUPTION OF BLOOD.
Constitution of Alabama.
Attainder of treason not to
work, Const. Ala., art. I,
§19.
**Constitution of the United
States.**
Attainder of treason not to
work, Const. U. S., Art.
III, §3.

COSMETICS.
Administration of chapter.
Applicability of
administrative provisions
of Title 2, §20-1-1.
**Adulteration and
misbranding.**
Construction of division,
§20-1-56.
Dealers.
Exemption from
prosecution of dealers,
§20-1-55.
Definitions, §20-1-50.
Exemption from prosecution
of dealers, §20-1-55.
Manufacturers.
Possession of adulterated
or misbranded
cosmetics, §20-1-54.
Standards of purity and
quality, §20-1-57.
When deemed adulterated,
§20-1-51.
When deemed misbranded,
§20-1-52.

COSMETICS—Cont'd
**Board of agriculture and
industries.**
Rules and regulations.
Adoption, §20-1-2.
Brands and marks.
Adulteration and
misbranding. See within
this heading,
"Adulteration and
misbranding."
**Commissioner of agriculture
and industries.**
Enforcement of chapter,
§20-1-1.
Right of entry by
commissioner and
agents, §20-1-3.
Cosmetologists.
General provisions.
See COSMETOLOGISTS.
Definitions.
Adulteration and
misbranding, §20-1-50.
**Department of agriculture
and industries.**
Enforcement of chapter,
§20-1-1.
Enforcement of chapter,
§20-1-1.
Applicability of enforcement
provisions of Title 2,
§20-1-1.
Manufacturers.
Adulteration and
misbranding.
Possession by
manufacturer of
adulterated or
misbranded cosmetics,
§20-1-54.
Misbranding. See within this
heading, "Adulteration and
misbranding."
Penalties.
Violations of chapter or
orders, rules or
regulations, §20-1-5.
Records.
Investigation, §20-1-3.
Right of entry.
Commissioner of agriculture
and industries, §20-1-3.
Rules and regulations.
Adoption, §20-1-2.
Penalty for violations,
§20-1-5.
Sales.
Suspension from sale of
articles sold in violation
of chapter, §20-1-4.
Samples.
Commissioner of agriculture
and industries.
Authority to take samples,
§20-1-3.
**Standards of purity and
quality,** §20-1-57.
Storage.
Suspension from sale, seizure
and condemnation of
articles stored in
violation of chapter,
§20-1-4.
Violations of chapter.
Penalty, §20-1-5.
Suspension from sale, seizure
and condemnation of
articles, §20-1-4.

COSMETOLOGISTS, §§34-7-1 to 34-7-47.
Alum.
Use of alum, §22-17-7.
Appeals.
Board of cosmetology.
Appeals from, §34-7-47.
Applicability of chapter.
Exemptions, §34-7-24.
Apprentice.
Beauty shops.
Acceptance of apprentices, §34-7-5.
Defined, §34-7-1.
Licenses.
Qualifications of applicants, §34-7-4.
Beauty shops.
Apprentices.
Acceptance of apprentices, §34-7-5.
Defined, §34-7-1.
Duty of manager as to maintenance, §22-17-3.
Fees.
Registration fees, §34-7-11.
Health regulations. See within this heading, "Health regulations."
Licenses, §40-12-61.
Operation without certificate of registration, §34-7-3.
Practice of cosmetology permitted, §34-7-16.
Registration of beauty shops, §34-7-5.
Use as dormitory, §22-17-11.
Board of cosmetology, §§34-7-40 to 34-7-47.
Appeals from finding or ruling of board, §34-7-47.
Appointment of members, §34-7-40.
Bonds, surety.
Treasurer and members, §34-7-41.
Compensation of members, §34-7-42.
Composition of board, §34-7-40.
Counsel.
Authority to employ, §34-7-45.
Created, §34-7-40.
Defined, §34-7-1.
Election of officers, §34-7-41.
Evidence.
Books and records of board, §34-7-44.
Proceedings before board, §34-7-21.
Expenses of members, §34-7-42.
Fees.
Compensation and expenses of board members, §34-7-42.
Funds.
Use of funds, §34-7-42.
Hearings.
Appeals from finding or ruling of board, §34-7-47.
Conduct by four members of board, §34-7-46.
Revocation or suspension of licenses and certificates, §34-7-21.
Inspectors.
Authority to employ, §34-7-45.

COSMETOLOGISTS—Cont'd
Board of cosmetology —Cont'd
Investigations, §34-7-46.
Meetings, §34-7-43.
Officers and employees.
Bonds, surety, §34-7-41.
Employment of inspectors, counsel and clerks, §34-7-45.
Generally, §34-7-41.
President.
Election, §34-7-41.
Qualifications of members, §34-7-40.
Quorum, §34-7-43.
Records.
Permanent records of proceedings to be kept, §34-7-44.
Removal of members, §34-7-40.
Rules and regulations.
Promulgation by board, §34-7-40.
Seal, §34-7-43.
Secretary.
Payment and disposition of fees, §34-7-15.
Terms of office, §34-7-40.
Treasurer.
Bond, §34-7-41.
Election, §34-7-41.
Vacancies, §34-7-40.
Certificates of registration.
Application, §34-7-7.
Display, §34-7-18.
Fees, §§34-7-11, 34-7-19.
Payment and disposition of fees, §34-7-15.
Issuance, §34-7-10.
Operation of beauty shop or school of cosmetology without certificate, §34-7-3.
Picture of licensee, §34-7-18.
Refusal, revocation or suspension, §34-7-21.
Renewal, §34-7-19.
Restoration, §34-7-19.
Cleansing of hands, §22-17-5.
Cosmetics generally.
See COSMETICS.
Cosmetic studio.
Defined, §34-7-1.
Definitions, §§22-17-1, 34-7-1.
Demonstrator.
Defined, §34-7-1.
Diseases.
Service by persons having skin or venereal disease, §22-17-8.
Service of persons having inflamed, etc., skin, §22-17-9.
Treatment of skin diseases or infections prohibited, §22-17-10.
Dormitories.
Use of shop or parlor as dormitory, §22-17-11.
Equipment.
Duty of manager as to maintenance, §22-17-3.
Reuse of certain materials prohibited, §22-17-7.
Esthetician.
Apprentice esthetician.
Defined, §34-7-1.
Defined, §34-7-1.

COSMETOLOGISTS—Cont'd
Esthetician—Cont'd
Esthetician instructor.
Defined, §34-7-1.
Licenses, §34-7-4.
Esthetician student instructor.
Defined, §34-7-1.
Licenses, §34-7-4.
Fees, §34-7-11.
Qualifications of applicants, §34-7-4.
Managing esthetician.
Defined, §34-7-1.
Licenses, §34-7-4.
Student esthetician.
Defined, §34-7-1.
Licenses, §34-7-4.
Esthetician salons.
Defined, §34-7-1.
Practice of cosmetology in, §34-7-16.
Evidence.
Board of cosmetology.
Books and records of board, §34-7-44.
Proceedings before board, §34-7-21.
Examinations.
Application for examination, §34-7-7.
Conduct and contents generally, §34-7-9.
Failure of examination.
Additional training required after second failure, §34-7-9.
Temporary permits after first failure, §34-7-9.
Fees, §34-7-11.
Payment and disposition of fees, §34-7-15.
Passing examination prerequisite to issuance of license, §34-7-10.
Physical examination of applicants, §34-7-7.
Qualifications of applicants, §34-7-4.
Subjects covered, §34-7-9.
Exemptions from provisions of chapter, §34-7-24.
Fees.
Certificates of registration. See within this heading, "Certificates of registration."
Disposition of fees, §34-7-15.
Licenses. See within this heading, "Licenses."
Payment of fees, §34-7-15.
Schedule, §34-7-11.
Witnesses.
Proceedings before board of cosmetology, §34-7-21.
Hands.
Cleansing of hands, §22-17-5.
Headrests, §22-17-6.
Health regulations.
Alum.
Use of alum, §22-17-7.
Applicability of chapter, §22-17-2.
Certificate of health, §34-7-7.
Cleansing of hands, §22-17-5.
Definitions, §22-17-1.
Dormitories.
Use of shop or parlor as dormitory, §22-17-11.

COSMETOLOGISTS—Cont'd
Health regulations—Cont'd
Equipment.
Duty of manager as to
maintenance, §22-17-3.
Reuse of certain materials
prohibited, §22-17-7.
Hands.
Cleansing of hands,
§22-17-5.
Headrests, §22-17-6.
Infections.
Treatment prohibited,
§22-17-10.
Maintenance of shop and
equipment.
Duty of manager, §22-17-3.
Manager.
Duties, §22-17-3.
Reuse of certain materials
prohibited, §22-17-7.
Shops.
Duty of manager as to
maintenance, §22-17-3.
Use as dormitory,
§22-17-11.
Skin diseases.
Service by persons having
skin disease, §22-17-8.
Service of persons having
inflamed, etc., skin,
§22-17-9.
Treatment of skin diseases
prohibited, §22-17-10.
Treatment of skin diseases or
infections prohibited,
§22-17-10.
Venereal diseases.
Service by persons having
venereal disease,
§22-17-8.
Waste disposal, §22-17-4.
Water connections, §22-17-4.
Hearings.
Board of cosmetology. See
within this heading,
"Board of cosmetology."
Infections.
Treatment of infections
prohibited, §22-17-10.
Inspectors.
Employment by board,
§34-7-45.
Instructors.
Defined, §34-7-1.
Fees.
License fees, §34-7-11.
Student instructor
registration fee,
§34-7-11.
Licenses, §34-7-4.
Qualifications of instructors,
§34-7-4.
Student instructor.
Defined, §34-7-1.
Qualifications, §34-7-4.
Registration fees, §34-7-11.
Investigations.
Board of cosmetology,
§34-7-46.
Licenses, §40-12-124.
Application, §34-7-7.
Register of applicants,
§34-7-44.
Apprentices, §34-7-4.
Beauty parlors, §40-12-61.
Display, §34-7-18.
Esthetician, §34-7-4.
Fees, §34-7-11.

COSMETOLOGISTS—Cont'd
Licenses—Cont'd
Examinations. See within
this heading,
"Examinations."
Expiration, §34-7-19.
Fees, §§34-7-11, 34-7-19.
Payment and disposition of
fees, §34-7-15.
Hairdressers, §40-12-124.
Health of applicants.
Certificate of health,
§34-7-7.
Instructors, §34-7-4.
Issuance, §34-7-10.
Lost license.
Fee for reissuance,
§34-7-11.
Manicurists, §§34-7-4,
34-7-11, 40-12-124.
Nonresidents, §34-7-12.
Picture of licensee, §34-7-18.
Practicing without license,
§34-7-2.
Qualifications of applicants,
§34-7-4.
Refusal, revocation or
suspension, §34-7-21.
Register of applicants,
§34-7-44.
Renewal, §34-7-19.
Fees, §34-7-11.
Penalty fee for late
renewal, §34-7-11.
Restoration, §34-7-19.
Temporary licenses, §34-7-17.
Managing cosmetologist.
Defined, §34-7-1.
Fees.
License fees, §34-7-11.
Health regulations.
Duties as to, §22-17-3.
Licenses.
Qualifications of
applicants, §34-7-4.
Manicurists.
Defined, §34-7-1.
Fees.
License fees, §34-7-11.
Health regulations. See
within this heading,
"Health regulations."
Licenses, §40-12-124.
Fees, §34-7-11.
Qualifications of
applicants, §34-7-4.
Master cosmetologists.
Defined, §34-7-1.
Nonresidents.
Registration or licensing of
nonresidents, §34-7-12.
Penalties.
Violations of chapter,
§34-7-25.
Permits.
Temporary permits after first
failure of examination,
§34-7-9.
Physicians.
Examination and
certification of
applicants, §34-7-7.
Place of cosmetology.
Defined, §34-7-1.
Practice of cosmetology.
Defined, §34-7-1.
Qualifications, §34-7-4.
Instructors, §34-7-4.
School of cosmetology,
§34-7-6.
Shampoo assistant, §34-7-5.

COSMETOLOGISTS—Cont'd
Registration.
Beauty shops, §34-7-5.
Certificates of registration.
See within this heading,
"Certificates of
registration."
Fees, §34-7-11.
Nonresidents, §34-7-12.
Schools of cosmetology,
§34-7-5.
Fees, §34-7-11.
Qualifications, §34-7-6.
School of cosmetology.
Defined, §34-7-1.
Fees.
Registration fees, §34-7-11.
Instructors. See within this
heading, "Instructors."
Operation without certificate
of registration, §34-7-3.
Practice of cosmetology
permitted, §34-7-16.
Registration, §34-7-5.
Fees, §34-7-11.
Qualifications, §34-7-6.
Sewers.
Waste disposal, §22-17-4.
Shampoo assistant.
Authority to employ, §34-7-5.
Defined, §34-7-1.
Qualifications, §34-7-5.
Shops. See within this
heading, "Beauty shops."
Skin diseases.
Service by persons having
skin disease, §22-17-8.
Service of persons having
inflamed, etc., skin,
§22-17-9.
Treatment of skin diseases
prohibited, §22-17-10.
Students, §34-7-4.
Defined, §34-7-1.
Qualifications of students,
§34-7-4.
Registration of students,
§34-7-4.
Subpoenas.
Board of cosmetology.
Subpoena power of board,
§34-7-21.
Time.
Duration of certificates and
licenses, §34-7-19.
**Unlawful practice of
cosmetology.**
Practice prohibited except in
established beauty shop
or school, §34-7-16.
Venereal diseases.
Service by persons having,
§22-17-8.
Violations of chapter.
Penalties for violations,
§34-7-25.
Waste disposal, §22-17-4.
Water connections, §22-17-4.
Witnesses.
Board of cosmetology.
Proceedings before board,
§34-7-21.

COSTS.
Abortion.
Parental consent to abortion
for minors.
No fees or costs required of
minors, §26-21-4.

COSTS—Cont'd

Administrative director of courts.
Court fees.
Procedures for collection and distribution, §12-19-21.
Advance.
Payment in advance, §12-19-70.
Affidavit of hardship, §12-19-70.
Appeals.
Costs on appeal.
See APPEALS.
Attorneys' fees.
See ATTORNEYS' FEES.
Banks and financial institutions.
Permits, §5-5A-1.
Bonds, surety.
Costs on appeal.
See APPEALS.
Boundaries.
Determination of boundaries in pending actions, §35-3-22.
Deposit of costs, §35-3-23.
Chiropractors.
Licenses.
Refusal, revocation or suspension, §34-24-170.
Circuit courts.
Municipal corporations.
Docket fees, fines, etc., collected in ordinance cases.
Inapplicability of provisions, §12-19-155.
Prescribed costs for circuit courts to be exclusive, §12-19-156.
Transfer of certain costs to circuit clerk, §12-19-22.
Civil cases.
Advance payment, §12-19-70.
Affidavit of hardship, §12-19-70.
Appeals from district courts to circuit courts.
Final assessment of costs in circuit court, §12-19-51.
Assessment of costs, §12-19-22.
Appeals from district courts to circuit courts.
Final assessment of costs in circuit court upon appeals, §12-19-51.
Prepaid fees.
Assessment as costs against defendant, §12-19-49.
Attachment.
Circuit and district court fees, §12-19-75.
Bills for fees or costs.
Preparation.
Officers' fees, §§12-19-41, 12-19-42.
Submission by district court clerk, §12-19-51.
Defendant.
Circuit and district court defendant service fees, §12-19-73.

COSTS—Cont'd

Civil cases—Cont'd
Defendant—Cont'd
Prepaid fees.
Assessment as costs against defendant, §12-19-49.
Recovery of full costs upon showing of usurious interest, §12-19-52.
Exclusiveness of prescribed fees, §12-19-20.
Executions.
Circuit and district court fees, §12-19-75.
Ex officio services.
Allowances for, §12-19-44.
Garnishment.
Circuit and district court fees, §12-19-75.
Hardship affidavits, §12-19-70.
Interest.
Usurious interest, §12-19-52.
Jurors' fees.
See JURY.
Motor vehicles.
Filing report of sale of abandoned motor vehicle, §12-19-76.
Officers' fees generally, §§12-19-90 to 12-19-98.
Ex officio services, §12-19-44.
Liability for receiving unauthorized fees, §§12-19-46, 12-19-47.
Preparation of bills for fees or costs, §12-19-41.
Unauthorized fees.
Liability for receiving, §§12-19-46, 12-19-47.
Unpaid fees.
When execution issued against plaintiff, §12-19-49.
Plaintiffs.
Issuance of execution against for own costs, §12-19-50.
Nominal plaintiffs.
Entry of judgment for costs against, §12-19-53.
Previously dismissed actions, ARCP, Rule 41 (d).
Uniformity of court fees in circuit and district courts, §12-19-20.
Usury.
Recovery by defendant upon showing of, §12-19-52.
Witnesses' fees, §§12-19-130 to 12-19-138.
See WITNESSES.
Witness subpoenas.
Circuit and district court fee for issuance, §12-19-74.
Collection.
Administrative director of courts to prescribe procedures, §12-19-21.
Computers.
Dissemination of computer-based court information, ARJA, Rule 33.

COSTS—Cont'd

Conservators.
Settlements of accounts of conservators.
Compulsion of settlement by probate court.
Partial settlement, §26-5-32.
Final settlement.
Vouchers.
Contest or rejection, §26-5-10.
Partial settlement.
Contest or examination where vouchers or items rejected, §26-5-4.
Constitution of Alabama.
Uniformity of laws regulating court costs, Const. Ala., art. IV, §96.
Counties.
Bond issues.
Validation proceedings, §6-6-757.
Law libraries.
Court cost disbursed to county law libraries, §11-25-9.
Crime victims compensation.
Assessment of additional costs and penalties, §15-23-17.
Criminal cases.
Applicability of provisions, §12-19-25.
Assessment of costs, §12-19-150.
Legislative intent, §12-19-150.
Bill for costs.
Appeals to circuit court, §12-19-150.
Confession of judgment by prosecutor for costs, §15-18-61.
Continuation of district court case to permit payment, §12-12-5.
Exclusiveness of prescribed fees, §12-19-20.
Failure to pay fine for costs, §15-18-62.
Imposition of additional hard labor to pay costs, §15-18-63.
Municipal courts.
Imposition of court costs, §12-19-153.
Municipal ordinance cases in district and circuit courts.
Docket fees, fines, etc.
Distribution, §12-19-154.
Inapplicability of provisions, §12-19-155.
Uniformity of court fees in circuit and district courts, §12-19-20.
Data.
Dissemination of computer-based court information, ARJA, Rule 33.
Declaratory judgments.
Awarding, §6-6-231.
Depositions.
Taxation of costs, §12-21-144.
Dismissal of actions.
Previously dismissed actions, ARCP, Rule 41 (d).

COSTS—Cont'd

Distribution, §12-19-22.
Procedures for distribution of court fees, §12-19-21.

District attorneys.
When prosecutor liable for cost, §15-18-60.

District courts.
Exclusiveness of prescribed fees, §12-19-156.
Municipal corporations.
Docket fees, fines, etc., collected in ordinance cases.
Inapplicability of provisions, §12-19-155.

Docket fees, §§12-19-170 to 12-19-179.
See DOCKETS.

Dower interests.
Ascertainment and payment, §35-4-191.

Eminent domain.
See EMINENT DOMAIN.

Escambia county.
Court costs and charges, Const. Ala., amd. 390.

Exclusiveness of prescribed fees, §§12-19-20, 12-19-156.

Executions, §§6-9-26, 6-9-27.

Exemptions from administration and payment of debts.
Report of appraisers or commissioners.
Exceptions.
Taxation of cost on filing, §6-10-90.

Extradition.
Return of prisoner to Alabama.
Expenses, §§15-9-62, 15-9-65.

Fair trial tax.
Additional fee, §§12-19-250, 12-19-250.1.
Assessment, §12-19-250.
Charge, §12-19-250.
Collection, §12-19-250.
Retention of tax by municipalities collected in municipal court, §12-19-251.1.
Disposition of proceeds by municipalities, §12-19-251.1.
Disposition of unexpended and unencumbered funds, §12-19-254.
Expenditures from fund, §12-19-252.
Subject to control and approval of governor, §12-19-253.
Fund.
Additional fee.
Remittance into fair trial tax fund, §12-19-250.
Balance in fund at close of fiscal year.
Disposition, §12-19-254.
Expenditures from fund subject to control and approval of governor, §12-19-253.
Indigent defense.
Appropriation from fund, §12-19-252.

COSTS—Cont'd

Fair trial tax—Cont'd
Fund—Cont'd
Indigent defense—Cont'd
Withdrawals to pay administration expenses, §15-12-24.1.
Remittance into fair trial tax fund, §12-19-251.
Withdrawals to pay expenses, §15-12-24.1.
Imposition on every case, §12-19-250.
Indigent defense.
Annual appropriation from fund for payment of expenses, §12-19-252.
Withdrawal from fund, §15-12-24.1.
Municipal courts.
Retention and disposition of tax by municipalities collected in municipal court, §12-19-251.1.
Public defender offices.
County payment of share of cost of maintaining, §12-19-252.
Remittance into fair trial tax fund, §12-19-251.

Fences.
Partition fences.
Action to recover costs and expenses, §35-7-7.

Filing of papers.
Fees for miscellaneous filings, ARJA, Rule 7.

Garnishment.
Payment to garnishee upon discharge, §6-6-462.

Generally, ARCP, Rule 54 (d).

Guardian and ward.
Removal of person or property of minors and wards.
Hearings, §26-8-22.

Habeas corpus.
Guards to convey prisoner, §15-21-34.
Taxation and collection of witness costs, §15-21-33.

Hardship affidavit, §12-19-70.

Hazardous substances.
Cleanup fund.
Liability for hazardous substance sites, §22-30A-8.

Health.
Council on health costs, administration and organization, §§22-2-9, 22-2-10.
State health department.
How costs to be paid, §22-2-12.

Highways.
Closing and vacating streets, alleys and highways.
Hearings, §23-4-4.

Impeachment.
See IMPEACHMENT.

Interest.
Civil cases.
Usurious interest, §12-19-52.

Judgments, ARCP, Rule 54 (d).

Judicial sales.
Abstracts of title, §6-8-30.

COSTS—Cont'd

Judicial sales—Cont'd
Notices.
Publication, §§6-8-64, 6-8-65.

Jurors' fees, §§12-19-110 to 12-19-113, 12-19-210, 12-19-211.
See JURY.

Juvenile proceedings, §§12-15-10, 12-15-11; ARJP, Rule 26.

Law libraries.
Court cost disbursed to county law libraries, §11-25-9.

Life interests.
Ascertainment and payment, §35-4-191.

Mentally ill.
Moving of insane prisoners.
Recovery of costs by state, §15-16-3.
State to pay, §15-16-3.

Motor vehicles.
Uniform traffic infractions.
Costs paid to clerk of court, ARJA, Rule 19.

Municipal corporations.
Bond issues.
Validation proceedings, §§6-6-757, 11-81-226.
Demolition of unsafe structures, §§11-40-33 to 11-40-35.

Municipal courts.
See MUNICIPAL COURTS.

New trial, §15-17-5.

Nuisances.
Lewdness, assignation or prostitution.
Action to abate and perpetually enjoin, §6-5-149.

Officers' fees generally.
Civil cases. See within this heading, "Civil cases."

Parole.
Community residential facilities.
Charging parolees room and board, §15-22-30.
Retaking of parolee.
Fees for execution of warrant, §15-22-31.

Partition.
Crops, §35-6-123.
Fences.
Action for costs, §35-7-7.
Probate courts, §35-6-54.

Payment in advance, §12-19-70.

Peace bonds.
Appeals, §15-6-42.
Execution for collection, §15-6-26.
Prosecution costs, §15-6-26.
When paid by complainant, §15-6-23.

Personal property.
Trial of right of property.
Execution for amount of costs, §6-6-163.

Previously dismissed action, ARCP, Rule 41 (d).

Prisons and prisoners.
County convicts.
Sentencing of convicts.
Cost of conviction, §14-4-10.

COSTS—Cont'd
Prisons and prisoners
—Cont'd
Insane prisoners.
Moving costs, §15-16-3.
Probate courts.
See PROBATE COURTS.
Probation.
Assessment and payment of
termination costs,
§15-22-55.
Contributions by
probationers toward
certain costs, §15-22-2.
Misdemeanant required to
pay costs of incarceration
as condition, §14-6-22.
Quieting title.
In personam proceedings,
§6-6-545.
In rem proceedings.
Assessment of cost,
§6-6-571.
Quo warranto, §§6-6-601,
6-6-602.
Sheriffs.
Creditors' actions.
Discovery of assets.
Taxation of costs,
§6-6-203.
Failure to return, levy or
collect execution.
Issuance of execution
against sheriff upon,
§12-19-50.
**Substitution of lost or
destroyed records or
papers,** §12-20-1.
Taxation.
Sale of land for taxes not due
at time of sale.
Warrant for costs,
§40-10-105.
Taxation of costs, ARCP,
Rule 54 (d).
Payment of court costs taxed
against estate, §40-1-14.
Transitional provisions,
§12-19-22.
Uniformity.
Court fees to be uniform,
§§12-19-20; Const. Ala.,
art. IV, §96.
Usury.
Recovery of full costs by
defendant, §12-19-52.
Waiver, §12-19-70.
Wills.
Contesting validity of wills,
§43-8-196.
Change of venue,
§43-8-197.
Witnesses.
Fees.
See WITNESSES.
Workmen's compensation.
Proceedings for disputed
claims, §25-5-89.

COTTON.
Agents.
Appropriation of cotton from
bale by agent having
custody, §2-19-4.
Attachment.
Liens of owners of cotton
gins, §35-11-291.
Baled cotton.
Appropriation of cotton from
bale, §2-19-4.

COTTON—Cont'd
Baled cotton—Cont'd
Dealers.
Records, §2-19-2.
Fraudulent baling, §2-19-11.
Ginner's tag.
Removal from bale of
cotton, §2-19-14.
Opening without consent of
owner, consignee, etc.,
§2-19-8.
Records, §2-19-2.
Sampling.
Removal of cotton from
bale for sampling,
§2-19-20.
Without consent of owner,
consignee, etc.,
§2-19-8.
Taking cotton from bale
without consent, §2-19-5.
Buying or receiving cotton
so taken, §2-19-7.
Weighing.
Deductions from actual
weight.
Persons buying or selling
baled cotton, §2-19-1.
Records, §2-19-2.
Boll weevil eradication,
Const. Ala., amd. 449.
Assessment of cotton
growers.
Failure to pay assessment,
§2-19-135.
Generally, §2-19-132.
Referendum, §2-19-132.
Conduct, §2-19-133.
Subsequent referendum,
§2-19-134.
Commissioner.
Duties, §2-19-122.
Entry of premises,
§2-19-123.
Cooperative programs.
Authorized, §2-19-122.
Cotton growers' organization.
Certification, §§2-19-130,
2-19-131.
Definitions, §2-19-121.
Elimination zones.
Authority to designate,
§2-19-126.
Compensation.
When compensation
payable, §2-19-127.
Destruction of cotton in
elimination zones,
§2-19-127.
Treatment of cotton in
zones, §2-19-127.
Entry of premises, §2-19-123.
Eradication activities,
§2-19-123.
Authority to require
participation in,
§2-19-126.
Inspection, §2-19-123.
Legislative findings,
§2-19-120.
Misdemeanors.
Class C misdemeanors.
Violations of provisions,
§2-19-129.
Penalties.
Violations of provisions,
§2-19-129.
Prohibition against planting
of cotton.
Authority to prohibit,
§2-19-126.

COTTON—Cont'd
Boll weevil eradication
—Cont'd
Purpose of article, §2-19-120.
Quarantine, §2-19-125.
Reports.
Cotton growers, §2-19-124.
Rules and regulations,
§2-19-128.
Bonds, surety.
Promotion of cotton products.
Treasurer of commission,
§2-8-204.
Brands and marks.
Ginners, §2-19-16.
Mutilation, etc., by ginners,
warehouse proprietors,
etc., §2-19-3.
Brokers. See within this
heading, "Buyers."
Buyers.
Defined, §2-19-100.
Failure to pay for cotton
purchased and disposed
of, §2-19-10.
Registration. See within this
heading, "Registration of
cotton buyers."
Rejection by buyers.
Replacement of cotton
removed from
warehouse upon
rejection, §2-19-19.
Classification.
Certificate of classification.
Admissibility in evidence,
§2-19-83.
Cotton to be classed on
request of storer,
§2-19-82.
Evidence.
Admissibility of certificate
of classification,
§2-19-83.
Grade indications, §2-19-81.
Violation of laws as to
classification, §2-19-18.
Commission merchants.
Appropriation of cotton from
bale, §2-19-4.
Cotton gins. See within this
heading, "Gins."
Dams.
Erection of dams for gins,
§§18-2-1 to 18-2-21.
See DAMS.
Definitions.
Boll weevil eradication,
§2-19-121.
Registration of cotton buyers,
§2-19-100.
Evidence.
Classification.
Admissibility in evidence
of certificate of
classification of cotton,
§2-19-83.
Factors.
Appropriation of cotton from
bale by factor having
custody, §2-19-4.
Fees.
Gins.
Permit fee, §2-19-61.
Registration of cotton buyers.
Application fee, §2-19-102.
Fraud.
Packing or baling, §2-19-11.

COTTON—Cont'd
Garnishment.
Liens of owners of cotton
gins.
Enforcement of lien,
§35-11-291.
Gins.
Commissioner of agriculture
and industries.
Rules and regulations,
§2-19-62.
Concealment of cotton by
ginners, §2-19-3.
Cotton seed.
Ginneries to keep separate
upon request of
owners, §§2-19-23 to
2-19-25.
Dams.
Erection of dams for gins,
§§18-2-1 to 18-2-21.
See DAMS.
Fees.
Permit fee, §2-19-61.
Liens of owners.
Attachment, §35-11-291.
Declaration, §35-11-290.
Enforcement, §35-11-291.
Garnishment, §35-11-291.
Liens generally.
See LIENS.
Priority, §35-11-290.
Sale of cotton, §35-11-291.
Lint cotton.
Ginneries to keep separate
upon request of
owners, §§2-19-23 to
2-19-25.
Lots of cotton.
Ginneries to keep separate
upon request of
owners, §§2-19-23 to
2-19-25.
Mutilation of marks, brands,
etc., on cotton by
ginners, §2-19-3.
Operation of gin without
permit, §2-19-64.
Permits.
Application, §2-19-61.
Denial, §2-19-63.
Fee, §2-19-61.
Issuance, §2-19-61.
Operation of gin without
permit, §2-19-64.
Required, §2-19-61.
Revocation, §2-19-63.
Price for ginning.
Charging different price for
ginning to persons
selling seed to ginner,
§2-19-17.
Rebates, §2-19-17.
Public gins.
Purpose of article,
§2-19-60.
Rules and regulations.
Enforcement, §2-19-63.
Promulgation by
commissioner,
§2-19-62.
Registers of cotton ginned,
§2-19-15.
Rules and regulations.
Enforcement, §2-19-63.
Promulgation by
commissioner,
§2-19-62.
Separation of cotton.
Applicability of provisions,
§2-19-25.

COTTON—Cont'd
Gins—Cont'd
Separation of cotton—Cont'd
Duty, §2-19-23.
Liability for
noncompliance,
§2-19-24.
Tags.
Removal from bale of
cotton of ginner's tag,
§2-19-14.
Required, §2-19-16.
Grade.
Classification. See within
this heading,
"Classification."
Implied warranties.
Packing of cotton, §2-19-22.
Injunctions.
Promotion of cotton products.
Violations of provisions,
§2-8-211.
Inspections.
Applicability of laws relative
to inspection, §2-19-26.
Boll weevil eradication,
§2-19-123.
Licenses.
Buyers, §40-12-85.
Compresses, §40-12-86.
Factories, §40-12-87.
Mills, §40-12-87.
Cotton seed oil mills,
§40-12-87.
Warehouses, §40-12-88.
Liens.
Boll weevil eradication.
Assessment of cotton
growers.
Failure to pay,
§2-19-135.
Gins, §§35-11-290, 35-11-291.
Removal from state of cotton
subject to purchase
money lien, §2-19-13.
Lint cotton.
Separation in ginneries upon
request of owners,
§§2-19-23 to 2-19-25.
Lots of cotton.
Separation in ginneries upon
request of owners,
§§2-19-23 to 2-19-25.
Misdemeanors.
Boll weevil eradication.
Violations of provisions,
§2-19-129.
Motor vehicle carriers.
Vehicles hauling cotton.
Exemptions, §37-3-4.
Motor vehicles.
Cotton wagons.
Towing cotton wagons,
§32-9-2.
Loads which must be
fastened, §32-5-75.
Notice.
Promotion of cotton products.
Assessments.
Referendum to levy
assessment,
§2-8-196.
Packing.
Fraudulent packing,
§2-19-11.
Implied warranty as to
packing, §2-19-22.
Penalties.
Promotion of cotton products.
Violations of provisions,
§2-8-211.

COTTON—Cont'd
Permits.
Gins. See within this
heading, "Gins."
**Promotion of cotton
products.**
Assessments.
Amount, §2-8-199.
Collection, §2-8-201.
Expenditure, §2-8-205.
Ginners.
Remittance of
assessments by,
§2-8-201.
Referendum to levy
assessment.
Application to conduct,
§2-8-193.
Action by board of
agriculture on,
§2-8-194.
Authority of certified
commission to
conduct, §2-8-195.
Canvass of results,
§2-8-199.
Conduct, §2-8-197.
Declared in public
interest, §2-8-192.
Eligibility to vote,
§2-8-199.
Secret ballot, §2-8-198.
Expenses, §2-8-197.
Majority vote required,
§2-8-199.
Notice, §2-8-196.
Secret ballot, §2-8-198.
Subsequent referendums,
§2-8-200.
Voting, §2-8-198.
Refunds, §2-8-203.
Bonds, surety.
Treasurer of commission,
§2-8-204.
Certified commissions.
Audits.
Annual audit, §2-8-207.
Examination by
department of
examiners of public
accounts, §2-8-207.
Remittance to treasurer of
commission, §2-8-202.
Revocation of certification,
§2-8-209.
Treasurers.
Bonds, surety, §2-8-204.
Constitution of Alabama,
Const. Ala., amd. 388.
Enforcement of provisions,
§2-8-209.
Ginners.
Books and records.
Inspection, §2-8-201.
Compliance with provisions
prerequisite for
holding ginner's
permit, §2-8-210.
Defined, §2-8-201.
Remittance of assessments
by, §2-8-201.
Injunctions.
Violations of provisions,
§2-8-211.
Joint programs with other
states, §2-8-206.
Legislative intent, §2-8-190.
Notice.
Referendum on assessment,
§2-8-196.

COTTON—Cont'd
Promotion of cotton products—Cont'd
Penalties.
Violations of provisions, §2-8-211.
Purpose of provisions, §2-8-190.
Restraint of trade.
Authorized activities not in restraint of trade, §2-8-191.
Rules and regulations, §2-8-208.
Public cotton gins. See within this heading, "Gins."
Purchasers.
Buyers. See within this heading, "Buyers."
Records.
Failure of purchaser to maintain record as to name of seller, etc., §2-19-9.
Rejection by purchaser.
Replacement of cotton removed from warehouse upon rejection, §2-19-19.
Quarantine.
Boll weevil eradication, §2-19-125.
Referendum.
Boll weevil eradication.
Assessment of cotton growers, §§2-19-132 to 2-19-134.
Promotion of cotton products.
Assessments.
Referendum to levy assessment. See within this heading, "Promotion of cotton products."
Registration of cotton buyers, §2-19-103.
Application, §2-19-102.
Commissioner of agriculture and industries.
List of registered cotton buyers.
Publication, §2-19-105.
Registration of applicant, §2-19-103.
Definitions, §2-19-100.
Disposition of funds collected under article, §2-19-106.
Duration of registration, §2-19-104.
Fee.
Application fee, §2-19-102.
Funds collected under article.
Disposition, §2-19-106.
List of registered buyers.
Publication, §2-19-105.
Required, §2-19-101.
Reports.
Boll weevil eradication.
Cotton growers, §2-19-124.
Rules and regulations.
Boll weevil eradication, §2-19-128.
Promotion of cotton products, §2-8-208.
Sales.
Liens of owners of cotton gins, §35-11-291.
Samples.
Conversion or refusal to deliver samples, §2-19-6.

COTTON—Cont'd
Samples—Cont'd
Exhibition of false samples, §2-19-12.
False samples.
Exhibition, §2-19-12.
Removal of cotton from bale for sampling, §2-19-20.
Resampling.
Replacement of cotton removed from warehouse upon rejection, §2-19-19.
Sampling bale of cotton without consent of owner, consignee, etc., §2-19-8.
Violation of laws as to sampling, §2-19-18.
Seed cotton.
Cotton seed hulls.
See GRAIN.
Sales tax.
Exemptions, §40-23-4.
Separation in ginneries upon request of owners, §§2-19-23 to 2-19-25.
Traffic in seed cotton, §§2-19-40 to 2-19-43.
Seizure.
Applicability of laws relative to seizure, §2-19-26.
Sellers.
Records.
Failure of purchaser to maintain record of name of seller, §2-19-9.
Standards.
Grade indications, §2-19-81.
United States standards.
Adoption, §2-19-80.
Stapling.
Violation of laws as to stapling, §2-19-18.
Storage.
Baled cotton.
Records, §2-19-2.
Classification.
Request of storer, §2-19-82.
Suspension from sale.
Applicable provisions, §2-19-26.
Traffic in seed cotton.
Purchase from person other than owner of land on which grown, §2-19-43.
Record book as to purchases, etc.
Effect of failure to maintain, §2-19-42.
Exceptions, §2-19-41.
Required, §2-19-40.
United States.
Standards.
United States standards adopted, §2-19-80.
Wagons.
Towing cotton wagons, §32-9-2.
Warehouses.
Classification.
Request of warehouseman, §2-19-82.
Concealment of cotton by proprietors, §2-19-3.
Mutilation of marks, brands, etc., on cotton, §2-19-3.
Replacement of cotton removed from warehouse upon rejection by purchaser, §2-19-19.

COTTON—Cont'd
Warranty.
Implied warranty as to packing, §2-19-22.
Weighing.
Deductions from actual weight.
Persons buying or selling baled cotton, §2-19-1.
Removal from place where sold prior to weighing without consent, §2-19-21.
Reweighing.
Replacement of cotton removed from warehouse upon rejection, §2-19-19.
Untested weights.
Use of untested weights in weighing cotton, §2-19-1.

COUNCIL OF STATE GOVERNMENTS.
Sales and use taxes.
Exemptions, §40-23-5.

COUNCIL ON THE ARTS AND HUMANITIES.
See ART.

COUNSELORS.
Activities exempt from chapter, §34-8A-3.
Appeal.
Refusal, revocation or suspension, §34-8A-16.
Application.
Acceptance.
Notice required, §34-8A-9.
Fees, §34-8A-6.
Investigations, §34-8A-9.
Out-of-state applicants, §34-8A-15.
Qualifications of applicants, §§34-8A-7, 34-8A-8.
Rejection.
Notice required, §34-8A-9.
Board of examiners.
Appointment, §34-8A-4.
Attorney general.
Attorney for board, §34-8A-18.
Chairman, §34-8A-5.
Compensation of members, §34-8A-5.
Composition, §34-8A-1.
Created, §34-8A-1.
Expenses of members, §34-8A-5.
Grants.
Board empowered to accept grants, §34-8A-5.
Immunity from civil liability, §34-8A-4.
Licensure.
All qualified applicants, §34-8A-20.
Meetings, §34-8A-5.
Organization of boards, §34-8A-5.
Powers and duties, §34-8A-1.
Qualifications of members, §34-8A-4.
Quasi-judicial authority, §34-8A-19.
Rules and regulations, §34-8A-5.
Seal of board, §34-8A-5.
Terms of office, §34-8A-4.
Vacancies.
Filling, §34-8A-4.

COUNSELORS—Cont'd
Board of examiners—Cont'd
Vice-chairman, §34-8A-5.
Certificates.
Applicants qualified out of
state, §34-8A-15.
Applications, §34-8A-6.
Fees, §34-8A-6.
Qualifications of applicants,
§34-8A-7.
Recertification, §34-8A-14.
Reinstatement, §34-8A-16.
Renewal, §34-8A-6.
Code of ethics, §34-8A-22.
Continuing education,
§34-8A-14.
Definitions, §34-8A-2.
Ethics, §34-8A-22.
Examination.
Focus, §34-8A-11.
Grading, §34-8A-12.
Anonymity, §34-8A-12.
Place, §34-8A-10.
Preservation, §34-8A-13.
Reexamination, §34-8A-12.
Time, §34-8A-10.
Fees, §34-8A-6.
Hearing.
Refusal, revocation or
suspension, §34-8A-16.
Injunction, §34-8A-17.
Licenses.
Applicants qualified out of
state, §34-8A-15.
Application, §34-8A-6.
Fees, §34-8A-6.
Qualifications of applicants,
§34-8A-7.
Reinstatement, §34-8A-16.
Relicensing, §34-8A-14.
Renewal, §34-8A-6.
Revocation, suspension or
refusal, §§34-8A-16.
Waiver of requirement,
§34-8A-23.
Mandamus, §34-8A-17.
Out-of-state applicants,
§34-8A-15.
Penalties.
Violations of chapter,
§34-8A-18.
Privileged communications,
§34-8A-21.
Victim counselors.
Confidentiality generally,
§§15-23-40 to 15-23-46.
See VICTIM
COUNSELORS.
Relicensing, §34-8A-14.
Restrictions and limitations,
§34-8A-3.
Victim counselors.
Confidentiality, §§15-23-40 to
15-23-46.
See VICTIM
COUNSELORS.
Violations of chapter,
§34-8A-18.
Waiver of licensure
requirements, §34-8A-23.

COUNSELORS AT LAW.
See ATTORNEYS AT LAW.

COUNTERCLAIMS.
Appealed actions, ARCP,
Rule 13 (j).
Compulsory counterclaims,
ARCP, Rule 13 (a).
Judgment for defendant,
§6-8-86.

COUNTERCLAIMS—Cont'd
Debt or liquidated demand
due comaker or
principal, §6-8-81.
Default judgments, ARCP,
Rule 55 (d).
Dismissal, ARCP, Rule 41 (c).
District courts.
Appeals from district court,
ARCP, Rule 13 (j).
Exceeding opposing claim,
ARCP, Rule 13 (c).
Exemptions.
Negotiated commercial
paper, §6-8-83.
Wages of head of family,
§6-8-82.
Joinder of additional
parties, ARCP, Rule 13
(h).
Judgments, §6-8-80.
Judgment for defendant.
Compulsory counterclaims,
§6-8-86.
Permissive counterclaims,
§6-8-85.
Separate judgments, ARCP,
Rule 13 (i).
Limitation of actions.
Effect of statute of
limitations, §6-8-84.
Negotiable instruments.
Exemptions.
Negotiated commercial
paper, §6-8-83.
Omitted counterclaim, ARCP,
Rule 13 (f).
Permissive counterclaims,
ARCP, Rule 13 (b).
Judgment for defendant,
§6-8-85.
Rules of civil procedure.
See RULES OF CIVIL
PROCEDURE.
Small claims.
Forms, ASCR, Form 4.
State.
Counterclaim against the
state of Alabama, ARCP,
Rule 13 (d).
Supplemental pleadings,
ARCP, Rule 13 (e).
Suretyship.
Debt or liquidated demand
due principal, §6-8-81.
Trial.
Separate trials, ARCP, Rule
13 (i).
Wages.
Exemption of wages of head
of family, §6-8-82.

COUNTERFEITING.
General provisions,
§§13A-9-1 to 13A-9-92.
See FORGERY AND
COUNTERFEITING.

COUNTIES.
Accounts and accounting.
County commissions.
Powers and duties,
§11-3-11.
Depositories, §§11-4-40 to
11-4-50.
Opening of accounts,
§11-4-46.
Treasurers.
Annual account.
Recordation and posting
of copy, §11-4-28.

COUNTIES—Cont'd
Actions.
Attorney general.
Defending actions against
political subdivisions,
Const. Ala., amd. 111.
Claims against county.
Presentment to county
commission, §6-5-20.
Depositories.
Civil actions and
proceedings by and
against depositories,
§11-4-47.
Property.
Actions for recovery.
No limitation of time for
bringing, §6-2-31.
Adjoining counties.
Public roads, bridges and
ferries, §§23-1-87 to
23-1-89, 23-1-91.
Administrators.
Claims and demands against
counties.
Verification of claims by
executors and
administrators,
§11-12-6.
General administrators,
§§43-2-170 to 43-2-175.
Advertising.
Public roads, bridges and
ferries.
Contract bids, §§23-1-92,
23-1-93.
Aged persons.
Programs to provide
assistance to the aged.
Authority to participate in
programs, §38-1-6.
Planning, establishment,
etc., §11-80-5.
Agriculture.
Acquisition of lands for
public purposes.
Use of land for betterment
and improvement of
agriculture, §11-18-2.
Agricultural extension work.
County appropriations for
extension work.
Payment of
appropriations,
§2-30-4.
Exhibit of agricultural
resources of county,
§11-3-11.
Farmers' market authority.
Local appropriations
authorized, §2-5-17.
Promotion of agriculture,
§11-3-11.
Air pollution.
Local air pollution control
programs, §22-28-23.
Airports.
Authorities.
Assistance and cooperation
by counties, §4-3-13.
Alternate procedure for
incorporation,
§4-3-49.
Investment of county funds
in bonds of authority,
§4-3-20.
Alternate procedure for
incorporation,
§4-3-57.

COUNTIES—Cont'd

Airports—Cont'd

Bond issues.

Authority to issue bonds, §4-1-1.

Public improvement bonds. See within this heading, "Bond issues."

Warrants and certificates of indebtedness for airport purposes.

Applicability of chapter, §4-5-1.

Conflicts of law.

Provisions of chapter control, §4-5-5.

Denominations, §4-5-2.

Disposition of proceeds of sale, §4-5-2.

Form, §4-5-2.

Issuance, §4-5-2.

Applicable provisions, §4-5-5.

Pledge of special taxes, §4-5-3.

Proceeds of sale.

Disposition, §4-5-2.

Purpose of chapter, §4-5-1.

Sale, §4-5-2.

Disposition of proceeds of sale, §4-5-2.

Taxation.

Pledge of special taxes, §4-5-3.

Terms, §4-5-2.

Zoning, §§4-6-1 to 4-6-15.

See AVIATION.

Alcoholic beverages.

Dry counties, §§28-4-1 to 28-4-326.

See ALCOHOLIC BEVERAGES.

Elections.

Sale and distribution. See ALCOHOLIC BEVERAGES.

Privilege or license taxes.

Authorized, §28-3A-21.

Wet counties, §§28-3-1 to 28-3-286.

See ALCOHOLIC BEVERAGES.

Ambulance service.

Appropriations, §11-87-2.

Chapter cumulative, §11-87-5.

Contracts for services, §11-87-3.

Creation.

Authorized, §11-87-1.

Establishment.

Authorized, §11-87-1.

Fees, §11-87-4.

Joint operation with municipalities, §11-87-1.

Rules and regulations.

Promulgation, §11-87-1.

Animals.

Acquisition of lands for public purposes.

Betterment of animal life, §11-18-2.

Prevention of cruelty to animals.

Employment of enforcement staff, §3-1-16.

COUNTIES—Cont'd

Appeals.

Bond issues.

Validation.

Judgment of circuit court, §6-6-754.

Cemeteries.

Appeals from assessment of damages, §§11-17-7 to 11-17-11.

Public roads, bridges and ferries.

Eminent domain, §23-1-82.

Appropriations.

Agriculture.

Farmers' markets.

Local appropriations authorized, §2-5-17.

Capital improvements, §11-29-5.

County commissions.

Appropriation of funds for payment of actual expenses, §11-3-13.

Hospitals.

Service program for indigents.

Source, §22-21-223.

Jails, §§11-14-19 to 11-14-21.

Payment of actual expenses, §11-3-13.

State parks.

Improvement, operation, etc., of state park system, §9-14-6.

Welfare, §38-2-9.

Armories.

Acquisition of lands for state armories, §11-18-2.

Cooperation of counties for acquisition of buildings, §31-4-9.

Public improvement bonds. See within this heading, "Bond issues."

Sale of real estate and buildings suitable for use as armories, §31-4-9.

Sites.

Conveyance of public lands for use as, §31-4-11.

Arrest in other counties, §§15-10-70 to 15-10-74.

Art galleries.

Acquisition of lands for, §11-18-2.

Powers as to, §11-47-16.

Assessments.

Cemeteries.

Damages from taking of property, etc., §11-17-7.

Appeals from assessments, §§11-17-7 to 11-17-11.

Property not deemed dedicated until damages and costs paid, §11-17-12.

Forest fire protection, §§19-13-180 to 19-13-187.

See FORESTS AND FORESTRY.

Maps and plats.

Preparation, etc., §11-1-12.

COUNTIES—Cont'd

Assessments—Cont'd

Water, sewer and fire protection authorities.

See WATER, SEWER AND FIRE PROTECTION AUTHORITIES.

Atomic energy.

Radiation.

Effect of chapter on local ordinances, §22-14-15.

Attorney general.

Defense of actions against political subdivisions, Const. Ala., amd. 111.

Duty to give opinions to county officers, §36-15-18.

Certificate of officer, §36-15-20.

Moot or private questions not to be submitted, §36-15-20.

Written opinion protects officer, governing body, etc., §36-15-19.

Auctions and auctioneers.

Limitations on authority of political subdivisions to tax auctioneers, §34-4-6.

Audits.

Claims and demands against counties.

Auditing claims, §11-12-4.

County commissions.

Powers and duties of county commissions, §11-3-11.

Department of examiners of public accounts.

Periodic audits of county offices, departments, boards, etc., §41-5-14.

Warrants for construction of public buildings, bridges and roads.

Issuance of warrants deemed to constitute audit in allowance of claim, §11-28-6.

Waterworks systems warrants.

Issuance of warrants deemed to constitute audit and allowance of claim, §11-9-26.

Authorities.

Housing authorities, §§24-1-60 to 24-1-84.

See HOUSING AUTHORITIES.

Improvement authorities, §§39-7-1 to 39-7-34.

See PUBLIC WORKS.

Public building authorities, §§11-15-1 to 11-15-19.

See within this heading, "Public building authorities."

Water, sewer and fire protection authorities, §§11-88-1 to 11-88-111.

See WATER, SEWER AND FIRE PROTECTION AUTHORITIES.

Bands.

Appropriations for bands, §11-80-4.

COUNTIES—Cont'd
Banks and financial institutions.
Deposit of county funds.
Pledge of assets as security, §5-5A-28.
Depositories. See within this heading, "Depositories."
Industrial development corporations.
Occupational license tax, §10-4-144.
Industry and trade.
Projects for promotion.
Investment in bonds by savings banks, §11-20-10.
Barbers.
Chapter not applicable to certain counties, §34-5-15.
Bear creek development authority.
Monetary contributions by certain counties, §33-15-13.
Beats.
Lines.
Alteration, etc., of beat lines, §11-1-13.
Provision of voting places where beat lines altered, §11-1-14.
Billiard rooms.
Commercial operation of tables.
Authorized in certain areas, §34-6-8.1.
License.
Required, §34-6-8.1.
Minors.
Playing billiards permitted in certain counties, §34-6-9.
Operating tables outside incorporated cities or towns, §34-6-8.
Blind persons.
Employment by counties, §21-7-8.
Board of human resources, §38-2-7.
See WELFARE.
Boards of education, §§16-8-1 to 16-8-43.
See EDUCATION.
Boards of health, §§22-3-1 to 22-3-3.
Boats.
Local regulation, §33-5-31.
Numbering.
Exemption from numbering provisions.
Boats owned by counties, §33-5-19.
Body corporate.
County declared a body corporate, §11-1-2.
Bond issues.
Airports.
Issuance for acquisition, improvement, etc., §4-1-1.
Anticipation notes, §11-81-28.
Applicability of provisions pertaining to municipal bonds, §11-81-97.

COUNTIES—Cont'd
Bond issues—Cont'd
Authorization of issuance.
Powers of counties, §11-81-3.
Claims and demands against counties.
Requirements as to bonds, §11-12-4.
Commercial paper, §11-81-30.
Definitions.
Public improvement bonds, §11-81-140.
Securities issued in anticipation of grants, §11-11B-1.
Validation, §6-6-750.
Validation of bonds prior to issuance, §11-81-220.
Delivery, §11-81-92.
Validity of delivery.
Limitation of actions to contest, §11-81-14.
Presumption, §11-81-14.
Destroyed bonds.
Issuance of duplicates, §11-81-32.
Disposition of proceeds from sale, §11-81-13.
Duplicate bonds.
Issuance for lost, mutilated or destroyed bonds, §11-81-32.
Elections.
Applicability of provisions as general election laws, §11-81-96.
Ballots, §11-81-83.
Canvassers.
Board of canvassers, §11-81-86.
Clerks.
Appointment, §11-81-84.
Compensation, §11-81-85.
Conduct of election, §11-81-84.
Contest.
Authorized, §11-81-88.
Bonds required, §11-81-88.
Hearing, §11-81-89.
Limitation of actions, §11-81-90.
Notice, §11-81-89.
Representation of county, §11-81-89.
Directory provisions of article, §11-81-96.
Expenses, §11-81-85.
General election laws.
Applicability of provisions, §11-81-96.
Limitation of actions.
Contest, §11-81-90.
Managers.
Appointment, §11-81-84.
Compensation, §11-81-85.
Mandatory provisions of article, §11-81-96.
Notice of election, §11-81-82.
Ordering of election for determination as to issuance, §11-81-81.
Ratification of certain irregular elections, §11-81-31.

COUNTIES—Cont'd
Bond issues—Cont'd
Elections—Cont'd
Recordation of results, §11-81-87.
Results.
Recordation, §11-81-87.
Returning officers.
Appointment, §11-81-84.
Compensation, §11-81-85.
Electricity.
Alternate borrowing for electric systems, §§11-81-200 to 11-81-206. See within this heading, "Electricity."
Public improvement bonds, §§11-81-140 to 11-81-150.
Revenue bonds, §§11-81-160 to 11-81-190. See within this heading, "Public utilities."
Security for bonds and indebtedness, §11-81-1.
Engraved signature.
Execution of bonds with, §11-81-33.
Exchange, §11-81-11.
Refunding bonds, §11-81-11.
Execution, §11-81-92.
Engraved or otherwise reproduced facsimile of signature or seal, §11-81-33.
Public improvement bonds, §11-81-144.
Validity of execution.
Limitation of actions to contest, §11-81-14.
Presumption, §11-81-14.
Exemption from taxation, §11-81-29.
Exemption from usury and interest statutes, §11-14-18.
Facsimile signature, §11-81-33.
Finance chapter.
Applicability of provisions, §11-8-16.
Form, §11-81-9.
Public improvement bonds, §11-81-144.
Gas.
Revenue bonds, §§11-81-160 to 11-81-190. See within this heading, "Public utilities."
Security for bonds and indebtedness, §11-81-1.
Improvement for which bonds issued.
Estimate as to period of usefulness of improvement, §11-81-8.
Industry and trade.
Industrial development boards. See within this heading, "Industrial development boards."
Projects for promotion. See within this heading, "Industry and trade."

COUNTIES—Cont'd
Bond issues—Cont'd
Interest.
　Exemption, §§8-8-7,
　　11-14-18.
Interest coupons.
　Exempt from taxation,
　　§11-81-29.
Irregular elections for
　issuance.
　Ratification of certain
　　irregular elections,
　　§11-81-31.
Irregularities in proceedings
　for issuance not to affect
　validity, §11-81-30.
Issuance.
　Duplicates.
　　Issuance for lost,
　　　mutilated or
　　　destroyed bonds,
　　　§11-81-32.
　Generally, §11-81-91.
　Irregularities not to affect
　　validity, §11-81-30.
　Purposes for which bonds
　　may be issued,
　　§11-81-80.
　Refunding bonds,
　　§11-81-93.
Letters of credit.
　Security for bonds, notes,
　　etc., §11-80-7.
Licenses.
　Pledge of revenues for
　　payment on bonds,
　　§11-81-18.
Limitation of actions.
　Election contest, §11-81-90.
　Validity of issuance, sale,
　　etc.
　　Limitation of actions to
　　　contest, §11-81-14.
Lost bonds.
　Issuance of duplicates,
　　§11-81-32.
Maturity, §11-81-6.
　Bonds issued and sold in
　　series, §11-81-7.
Mortgages and deeds of trust.
　Execution upon property
　　acquired with proceeds
　　of bond issues,
　　§11-81-2.
　Recordation, §11-81-2.
Municipal bonds.
　Applicability of provisions
　　pertaining to,
　　§11-81-97.
Mutilated bonds.
　Issuance of duplicates,
　　§11-81-32.
Parks and recreation.
　General provisions. See
　　within this heading,
　　"Parks and
　　recreation."
Payment, §11-81-6.
　Bonds issued and sold in
　　series, §11-81-7.
　Disposition of funds from
　　special tax levy,
　　§11-3-15.
　Places of payment,
　　§11-81-5.
　Pledge of revenues,
　　§§11-81-16 to 11-81-18.
　Sinking fund for payment.
　　See within this
　　heading, "Sinking
　　funds."

COUNTIES—Cont'd
Bond issues—Cont'd
Payment—Cont'd
　Tax for payment.
　　Collection of special tax,
　　　§11-81-15.
　　Disposition of special
　　　tax, §11-81-15.
　　Levy of special tax,
　　　§11-81-15.
　　Mandamus proceedings,
　　　§11-81-26.
　　Refunding bonds,
　　　§11-81-95.
　Waterworks system.
　　Pledge of revenues from
　　　waterworks system
　　　to secure payment,
　　　§§11-81-16, 11-81-17.
Period of usefulness of
　improvement or property
　for which bonds issued.
　Estimate as to period,
　　§11-81-8.
Pledge of revenues,
　§§11-81-16 to 11-81-18.
Price.
　Sale price, §11-81-10.
Proceeds from sale.
　Disposition, §11-81-13.
　Execution of mortgages or
　　deeds of trust upon
　　property acquired
　　with, §11-81-2.
Projects for promotion of
　industry and trade. See
　within this heading,
　"Industry and trade."
Property for which bonds
　issued.
　Estimate as to period of
　　usefulness of property,
　　§11-81-8.
Public corporations, Const.
　Ala., amd. 108.
Public improvement bonds.
　Acquisition, construction,
　　etc., of undertakings.
　　Authorization,
　　　§11-81-142.
　　Determination of costs,
　　　§11-81-141.
　Adjoining counties.
　　Public roads, bridges and
　　　ferries.
　　　Establishment of
　　　　facilities between
　　　　counties, §23-1-87.
　Definitions, §11-81-140.
　Delivery of bonds,
　　§11-81-144.
　Denominations of bonds,
　　§11-81-144.
　Enforcement of provisions
　　of division and bond
　　resolutions,
　　§11-81-143.
　Evidence of validity of
　　bonds, §11-81-145.
　Execution of bonds,
　　§11-81-144.
　Exemption from taxation of
　　undertakings, bonds,
　　etc., §11-81-149.
　Form of bonds, §11-81-144.
　Liability of counties on
　　bonds, §11-81-147.

COUNTIES—Cont'd
Bond issues—Cont'd
Public improvement bonds
　—Cont'd
　Lien of bonds, §11-81-146.
　Provisions in
　　instruments creating
　　liens for payment of
　　bonds, §11-81-141.
　Maturity of bonds,
　　§11-81-144.
　Mortgages and deeds of
　　trust.
　　Security for payment of
　　　bonds, §11-81-141.
　Payment of bonds.
　　Exercise of county taxing
　　　power for payment,
　　　§11-81-148.
　　Security for payment of
　　　bonds, §11-81-141.
　Pledges.
　　Security for payment of
　　　bonds, §11-81-141.
　Powers of counties,
　　§11-81-141.
　Rates and fees, §11-81-150.
　Refunding bonds.
　　Issuance, §11-81-144.
　Resolutions.
　　Authorization of issuance
　　　of bonds, §11-81-142.
　　Covenants in bond
　　　authorization
　　　resolutions,
　　　§11-81-143.
　　Enforcement of bond
　　　resolutions,
　　　§11-81-143.
　Sale of bonds, §11-81-144.
　Taxation.
　　Exemption from
　　　taxation, §11-81-149.
　　Exercise of county taxing
　　　power for payment of
　　　bonds, §11-81-148.
　Terms of bonds,
　　§11-81-144.
　Validity of bonds.
　　Evidence, §11-81-145.
Public utilities.
　Alternate borrowing for
　　electric systems,
　　§§11-81-200 to
　　11-81-206. See within
　　this heading,
　　"Electricity."
　Revenue bonds for
　　waterworks, gas, sewer
　　or electric systems,
　　§§11-81-160 to
　　11-81-190. See within
　　this heading, "Public
　　utilities."
Purposes for which bonds
　may be issued,
　§11-81-80.
Redemption of securities. See
　within this heading,
　"Redemption of
　securities."
Refunding bonds.
　Exchange, §11-81-11.
　Issuance.
　　Authority for issuance,
　　　§11-81-93.
　Payment.
　　Special tax levy for
　　　payment of principal
　　　and interest,
　　　§11-81-95.

COUNTIES—Cont'd
  Bond issues—Cont'd
    Refunding bonds—Cont'd
      Powers of counties
        authorizing issuance,
        §11-81-3.
      Sale, §11-81-11.
      Security, §11-81-94.
      Sinking funds. See within
        this heading, "Sinking
        funds."
    Registration.
      Appointment of registrar,
        §11-81-9.
      Provision for registration
        and transfer, §11-81-9.
    Revenue bonds for
      waterworks, gas, sewer
      or electric systems,
      §§11-81-160 to 11-81-190.
      See within this heading,
      "Public utilities."
    Sale, §11-81-11.
      Bids, §11-81-11.
        Determination of highest
          bidder, §11-81-12.
      Disposition of proceeds
        from sale, §11-81-13.
      Price, §11-81-10.
      Proceeds from sale.
        Disposition, §11-81-13.
        Mortgages or deeds of
          trust upon property
          acquired with,
          §11-81-2.
      Refunding bonds,
        §11-81-11.
      Validity of sale.
        Limitation period for
          actions to contest
          validity, §11-81-14.
        Presumption as to
          validity, §11-81-14.
    School buildings.
      Security for bonds,
        §11-81-1.
    Securities issued in
      anticipation of grants.
      Additional nature of
        provisions, §11-11B-8.
      Amount.
        Total principal amount,
          §11-11B-4.
      Construction and
        interpretation.
        Other laws not repealed,
          restricted or
          modified, §11-11B-8.
      Definitions, §11-11B-1.
      Denominations, §11-11B-4.
      Execution, §11-11B-4.
      Grantees.
        Defined, §11-11B-1.
        Powers, §11-11B-2.
      Interest.
        Coupons for interest,
          §11-11B-4.
      Investments.
        Legal investment status
          of securities,
          §11-11B-6.
      Maturity of securities,
        §11-11B-4.
      Power and authority of
        counties and public
        corporations,
        §11-11B-3.
      Power and authority of
        grantees, §11-11B-2.
      Public corporations.
        Defined, §11-11B-1.

COUNTIES—Cont'd
  Bond issues—Cont'd
    Securities issued in
      anticipation of grants
      —Cont'd
      Public corporations
        —Cont'd
        Powers, §11-11B-3.
        Supervision and control.
          Exemption of securities,
            §11-11B-7.
        Taxation.
          Exemption of securities,
            §11-11B-5.
    Series bonds.
      Bonds for installments on
        serial bonds
        outstanding.
        Authority for issuance,
          §11-81-93.
        Security, §11-81-94.
        Special tax levy for
          payment, §11-81-95.
      Maturity of bonds issued
        and sold in series,
        §11-81-7.
      Payment of bonds issued
        and sold in series,
        §11-81-7.
    Sewers.
      Revenue bonds,
        §§11-81-160 to
        11-81-190. See within
        this heading, "Public
        utilities."
    Sinking funds. See within
      this heading, "Sinking
      funds."
    Special, private or local laws
      prohibited, Const. Ala.,
      art. IV, §104.
    Taxation.
      Exemption from taxation,
        §§11-81-29, 40-9-1.
      Public improvement
        bonds, §11-81-149.
      Pledge of revenues from
        certain taxes,
        §§11-81-16 to 11-81-18.
      Refunding bonds.
        Special tax levy for
          payment of principal
          and interest,
          §11-81-95.
      Securities issued in
        anticipation of grants.
        Exemption from
          taxation, §11-11B-5.
      Special tax levy for
        payment of principal
        and interest on bonds.
        Collection, §11-81-15.
        Disposition, §11-81-15.
        Levy, §11-81-15.
        Mandamus proceedings,
          §11-81-26.
        Refunding bonds,
          §11-81-95.
      State-wide property
        reappraisal.
        County bonds for purpose
          of paying costs.
          See TAXATION.
    Transfer.
      Provision for transfer,
        §11-81-9.
    Trusts and trustees.
      Counties.
        Tax anticipation bonds,
          etc., of certain
          counties, §19-3-126.

COUNTIES—Cont'd
  Bond issues—Cont'd
    Trusts and trustees—Cont'd
      Investment of trust estate
        in tax anticipation
        bonds, §19-3-126.
    Usury.
      Exemption from usury
        statutes, §11-14-18.
    Validation of bonds prior to
      issuance.
      Appeals from judgment of
        circuit court,
        §11-81-223.
      Applicability of article,
        §11-81-227.
      Complaint for
        determination as to
        legality of proposed
        issuance.
        Contents, §11-81-222.
        Filing, §11-81-221.
      Costs of proceedings,
        §11-81-226.
      Definitions, §11-81-220.
      Hearing to show cause why
        obligations not valid,
        §11-81-223.
      Notice, §11-81-222.
      Order, §11-81-222.
      Judgment as to validity.
        Appeals from,
          §11-81-223.
        Entry, §11-81-223.
        When judgment final
          and conclusive,
          §11-81-224.
      Legend to appear on
        validated obligations,
        §11-81-225.
      Validated obligations.
        Legend to appear on
          validated
          obligations,
          §11-81-225.
    Validation of county
      obligations.
      Appeals.
        Judgment of circuit
          court, §6-6-754.
      Costs, §6-6-757.
      Definitions, §6-6-750.
      District attorney.
        Defined, §6-6-750.
        Service of petition and
          order on, §6-6-752.
      Hearing and
        determination,
        §6-6-753.
      Judgment.
        Appeal, §6-6-754.
        Conclusiveness, §6-6-755.
        Contents, §6-6-753.
      Marking of validated
        obligations, §6-6-756.
      Notice of hearing.
        Publication, §6-6-752.
        Order to show cause,
          §6-6-752.
        Service on district
          attorney, §6-6-752.
      Petition.
        Contents, §6-6-752.
        Right to file, §6-6-751.
        Service on district
          attorney, §6-6-752.
    Validity.
      Irregularities in
        proceedings not to
        affect, §11-81-30.

COUNTIES—Cont'd
Bond issues—Cont'd
Validity—Cont'd
Limitation of actions to contest, §11-81-14.
Presumption, §11-81-14.
Public improvement bonds.
Evidence of validity, §11-81-145.
Warrants.
Redemption of securities. See within this heading, "Redemption of securities."
Water supply and waterworks.
Revenue bonds, §§11-81-160 to 11-81-190. See within this heading, "Public utilities."
Security for bonds and indebtedness, §11-81-1.
Bonds, surety.
Cemeteries.
Appeals from assessment of damages, §11-17-8.
County commissions.
Commissioners' bonds, §11-3-3.
Depositories, §11-4-42.
Banks holding deposit of funds from special tax levy, §11-3-14.
Grand juries.
Examination of bonds of county officers, §12-16-192.
Official bonds.
Additional bonds.
Coroners, §11-5-9.
Requirement of additional bonds, §§11-2-20 to 11-2-29.
Conditions of bonds, §11-2-2.
Coroners, §11-5-3.
Additional bonds, §11-5-9.
County commissioners, §11-3-3.
Discharge of sureties, §11-2-7.
Effect of new bond, §11-2-7.
Execution.
Failure of officer to timely execute new bond, §11-2-34.
Filing, §11-2-3.
Guaranty companies.
Bonds to be made by guaranty companies, §11-2-6.
Liability for collecting and paying out money under void, etc., law, §36-5-24.
Minimum amount, §11-1-7.
New bonds.
Proceedings as to sufficiency of bonds of certain officers, §§11-2-30 to 11-2-34.
Premiums on bonds.
Payment, §11-2-4.
Refund upon reduction of bonds, §11-2-5.

COUNTIES—Cont'd
Bonds, surety—Cont'd
Official bonds—Cont'd
Proceedings as to sufficiency of bonds of certain county officers.
Application by county freeholders for order requiring new bond, §11-2-30.
Bond of applicants, §11-2-31.
Filing, §11-2-33.
Hearing of application, §11-2-32.
Execution of new bond.
Entry of order requiring, §11-2-32.
Minutes of proceedings, §11-2-33.
Oath of applicants for order requiring new bond, §11-2-31.
Order of proceedings, §11-2-33.
Provisions governing bonds, §11-2-2.
Recordation, §36-5-3.
Reduction of bonds, §11-2-5.
Required bonds, §11-2-1.
Requirement of additional bonds.
Authority, §11-2-20.
County officers whose terms extended.
Amount, §11-2-22.
Authority, §11-2-22.
Conditions of bond, §§11-2-22, 11-2-26.
Contents of requisition for bond, §11-2-23.
Effect of additional bond, §11-2-27.
Effect of bonds, §11-2-22.
Effect of execution of additional bond, §11-2-28.
Failure to give bond, §11-2-24.
Failure to timely file, §11-2-25.
Form of requisition for bond, §11-2-23.
Penalty of bond, §11-2-26.
Remedies on additional bond, §11-2-27.
Requisition for bond, §11-2-23.
Service of requisition for bond, §11-2-23.
Sureties' rights and remedies among themselves, §11-2-29.
When bond to be given, §11-2-24.
Failure to give bond within prescribed time, §11-2-21.
Procedure, §11-2-21.
Proceeding upon failure to give bond within prescribed time, §11-2-21.

COUNTIES—Cont'd
Bonds, surety—Cont'd
Official bonds—Cont'd
Surety companies.
Bonds to be made by surety companies, §11-2-6.
Surveyors, §11-7-2.
Liability for damages, §11-7-9.
Treasurers, §11-4-22.
Borrowing money.
Warrants for borrowing purposes, §11-1-17.
Execution, §11-1-16.
Boundaries.
Arrangement, Const. Ala., art. II, §39.
Beats.
Alteration, etc., §11-1-13.
Cemeteries.
Duty of commission to mark boundaries, §11-17-1.
Establishment, §11-17-3.
Marking, §11-17-3.
Confirmed, Const. Ala., art. II, §38.
Courthouses.
Minimum distance of county boundaries from courthouse, Const. Ala., art. II, §40.
Criminal law and procedure.
Venue when offense committed on or near boundary, §15-2-7.
Designation, Const. Ala., art. II, §39.
New counties, Const. Ala., art. II, §39.
Precincts.
Alteration, etc., §11-1-13.
Ratified, Const. Ala., art. II, §38.
Venue.
Offense committed on or near county boundary, §15-2-7.
Bridges.
Construction or maintenance of state bridges.
Application by counties for construction or maintenance, §23-1-48.
Navigable, etc., streams.
Expenditure of county funds, §11-3-15.
Joint operation by several counties, §11-3-16.
Public improvement bonds, §§11-81-140 to 11-81-150. See within this heading, "Bond issues."
Public roads, bridges and ferries. See within this heading, "Public roads, bridges and ferries."
Warrant for construction of public buildings, bridges and roads, §§11-28-1 to 11-28-7. See within this heading, "Warrants."
Budgets.
Adoption of budget system for county, §11-3-13.
Annual budget.
Generally, §11-8-3.

COUNTIES—Cont'd
Budgets—Cont'd
Annual budget—Cont'd
Principal and interest on
refunding warrants as
part of annual
operating budget,
§11-8-4.
Temporary loans to
constitute part of
annual county
operating revenue and
expenses, §11-8-5.
County commissions.
Adoption of budget system
for county, §11-3-13.
Buildings.
Construction.
Duty of county commission
to erect, §11-14-10.
Proposed construction to be
submitted for approval
of regional planning
commission, §11-85-7.
Special tax authorized,
§11-14-11.
Contracts between counties
and municipalities.
Use and occupation of
public buildings
located in
municipalities,
§11-80-3.
County commissions.
Duty to erect, §11-14-10.
Courthouses. See within this
heading, "Courthouses."
Eminent domain.
Condemnation of lands for
public building sites,
§11-80-1.
Furnishing.
Special tax authorized,
§11-14-11.
Insurance.
Powers and duties of
county commissions,
§11-3-11.
Jails. See within this
heading, "Jails."
Maintenance, §11-14-4.
Special tax authorized,
§11-14-11.
Minimum building standards
code.
Adoption by counties,
§41-9-166.
Municipal corporations.
Contracts between counties
and municipalities.
Use and occupation of
public buildings
located in
municipalities,
§11-80-3.
Payment for improvements
benefitting county
buildings,
Appropriations for cost of
improvements,
§11-14-7.
Authorized, §11-14-6.
Liability for prior
payments, §11-14-8.
Public building authorities.
See within this heading,
"Public building
authorities."
Public improvement bonds.
See within this heading,
"Bond issues."

COUNTIES—Cont'd
Buildings—Cont'd
Taxation.
Levy of special taxes,
§11-14-17.
Cable television.
Community antenna
television facilities
generally, §§11-27-1 to
11-27-3, 23-1-59.
Cancer.
Lurleen B. Wallace memorial
cancer hospital fund.
Appropriations by counties,
§11-8-12.
Capital improvements,
§11-29-3.
Allocation of funds.
Distribution, §11-29-7.
Payment, §11-29-7.
Appropriations, §11-29-5.
Citation of chapter, §11-29-1.
Declaration of purpose,
§11-29-2.
Definitions, §11-29-3.
Fund.
Allocation of funds,
§11-29-7.
Creation, §11-29-4.
Distribution of fund
capital, §11-29-6.
Purposes, §11-29-4.
Legislative findings,
§11-29-2.
Purposes for which counties
may use funds, §11-29-6.
Short title of chapter,
§11-29-1.
Cattle.
Dipping of cattle.
Indemnification of owners
for injuries, etc.,
§§11-12-1 to 11-12-3.
Cemeteries, §§11-17-1 to
11-17-16.
Appeals from assessment of
damages.
Authorized, §11-17-7.
Bond, §11-17-8.
Costs.
Entry of judgment for
damages and costs,
§11-17-11.
Entry of judgment for
damages and costs,
§11-17-11.
Hearings.
Conduct of hearing,
§11-17-10.
Establishment of date for
hearing, §11-17-9.
Notice of hearing,
§11-17-9.
Summoning and
empaneling of jurors,
§11-17-9.
Judgments.
Entry of judgment for
damages and costs,
§11-17-11.
Jury.
Establishment of
damages by jury,
§11-17-10.
Summoning and
empaneling of jurors,
§11-17-9.
Notice of hearing, §11-17-9.

COUNTIES—Cont'd
Cemeteries—Cont'd
Assessments.
Damages from taking of
property, etc.,
§11-17-7.
Property not deemed
dedicated until
damages and costs
paid, §11-17-12.
Bonds, surety.
Appeals from assessment of
damages, §11-17-8.
Boundaries.
Duties of commission,
§11-17-1.
Charities.
Trusts and trustees.
Perpetual trusts,
§11-17-15.
Powers, §§11-17-13,
11-17-14.
Validation of prior
conveyances,
bequests, etc.,
§11-17-16.
Commission, §§11-17-1 to
11-17-4.
Appointment, §11-17-2.
Notice, §11-17-2.
Petition, §11-17-1.
Assessments.
Damages from taking of
property, etc.,
§11-17-4.
Boundaries.
Duties of commission,
§11-17-1.
Establishment, §11-17-3.
Marking, §11-17-3.
Duties, §11-17-1.
Issuance of commission to
members, §11-17-2.
Notice of appointment,
§11-17-2.
Reports.
Damages from taking of
property, etc.,
§11-17-4.
Preparation and filing,
§11-17-3.
Conveyances.
Perpetual trusts,
§11-17-15.
Powers of burial societies,
cemeteries, etc.,
§11-17-14.
Validation of prior
conveyances, etc.,
§11-17-16.
Costs.
Damages from taking of
property, etc.
Appeals from assessment
of damages.
Entry of judgment for
costs, §11-17-7.
Entry of judgment for
costs, §11-17-11.
Appeal from
assessment of
damages, §11-17-7.
Property not deemed
dedicated until
damages and costs
paid, §11-17-12.
Recordation of
proceedings upon
payment of costs,
§11-17-5.

COUNTIES—Cont'd
Cemeteries—Cont'd
Damages from taking of
property, etc.
Appeals from assessment of
damages.
Authorized, §11-17-7.
Bond, §11-17-8.
Costs.
Entry of judgment for
damages and costs,
§11-17-11.
Hearings.
Conduct, §11-17-10.
Establishment of date,
§11-17-9.
Notice, §11-17-9.
Summoning and
impaneling jurors,
§11-17-9.
Judgments.
Entry of judgment for
damages and costs,
§11-17-11.
Jury.
Establishment of
damages,
§11-17-10.
Summoning and
impaneling jurors,
§11-17-9.
Notice of hearing,
§11-17-9.
Assessment of damages,
§11-17-4.
Appeals, §§11-17-7 to
11-17-11.
Costs.
Entry of judgment for
costs, §11-17-11.
Property not deemed
dedicated until
damages and costs
paid, §11-17-12.
Dedication of property.
Property not deemed
dedicated until
damages and costs
paid, §11-17-12.
Establishment of damages
by jury, §11-17-10.
Jury.
Establishment of
damages, §11-17-10.
Summoning and
impaneling of jurors,
§11-17-9.
Payment of damages.
Recordation of
proceedings upon,
§11-17-5.
Dedication to public,
§11-17-6.
Property not deemed
dedicated until
damages and costs
paid, §11-17-12.
Enlargement.
Duties of commission,
§11-17-1.
Hearings.
Appeals from assessment of
damages, §§11-17-9,
11-17-10.
Indigent persons.
Burial of persons dying
with no estate, §38-8-2.

COUNTIES—Cont'd
Cemeteries—Cont'd
Judgments.
Appeals from assessment of
damages.
Entry of judgment for
damages and costs,
§11-17-11.
Jury.
Appeals from assessment of
damages.
Establishment of
damages by jury,
§11-17-10.
Summoning and
impaneling of jurors,
§11-17-9.
Location.
Duties of commission,
§11-17-1.
Petitions.
Appointment of
commission, §11-17-1.
Recordation.
Damages from taking of
property, etc.
Recordation of
proceedings upon
payment, §11-17-5.
Reports.
Commission.
Damages from taking of
property, etc.,
§11-17-4.
Filing of reports,
§11-17-3.
Preparation of reports,
§11-17-3.
Damages from taking of
property, etc.
Report of damages,
§11-17-4.
Trusts and trustees.
Burial societies,
cemeteries, etc.,
empowered to act as
trustees, §11-17-14.
Charitable trusts.
Validation of prior
conveyances,
§11-17-16.
When created, §11-17-13.
Perpetual trusts,
§11-17-15.
Use of burial place, §11-17-6.
**Chairman of county
commission.**
Appointment of special clerk
to attend meetings in
absence of chairman,
§11-3-19.
Determination of certain
matters by chairman,
§11-3-20.
Inspection of county jails,
§11-14-22.
Charities.
Cemeteries.
Preservation, repair, etc.,
of public or private
burial places as
charitable purpose,
§11-17-13.
Checks.
Issuance of orders for checks
by officers authorized to
pay claims not first
approved by county
commission, §11-8-9.

COUNTIES—Cont'd
Checks—Cont'd
Persons authorized to draw
checks on county
treasury or depository,
§11-8-9.
Circuit clerks.
Membership fees in state
organizations, etc.
Payment by county
commissions, §11-1-11.
Circuit courts.
Circuit court in every county,
§12-11-1.
Telephones.
Offices, §11-3-11.
Utilities for courthouse
offices, §11-12-13.
Civic centers.
Bonds for, Const. Ala., amds.
238, 280.
Civil defense.
Employees.
Powers and duties of
employees rendering
outside aid, §31-9-11.
Immunity from liability for
torts, §31-9-16.
Officers.
Military service in time of
war or national
emergency.
See PUBLIC OFFICERS
AND EMPLOYEES.
Powers with respect to civil
defense generally,
§31-9-10.
State grants to political
subdivisions, §31-9-24.
Civil service.
Engineers.
Effect of county civil
service law, §11-6-5.
**Claims and demands against
counties.**
Actions against counties.
Presentment of claim to
county commission,
§6-5-20.
Administrators.
Verification of claims,
§11-12-6.
Approval of claims.
Liability for approval of
claims not legally
chargeable to or
payable from public
funds, §11-12-12.
Auditing, §11-12-4.
Bond issues.
Requirements as to bonds,
§11-12-4.
County commissions.
Payment of claims
presented by chairman
of commission.
Review as to authority
for payment,
§11-12-10.
Powers and duties of
county commissions,
§11-3-11.
Presentment of claim to
county commission,
§6-5-20.
Equitable claims.
Payment, §11-12-16.
Executors.
Verification of claims,
§11-12-6.

COUNTIES—Cont'd
Claims and demands against counties—Cont'd
Fiduciaries.
Verification of claims, §11-12-6.
Filing.
Claims to be filed, §11-12-5.
Guardians.
Verification of claims, §11-12-6.
Indemnification for injuries, etc., caused by dipping of cattle.
Authorized, §11-12-1.
Carelessness, etc., of owners or agents, §11-12-2.
Inspectors.
Absence of inspector.
Limitations of liability, §11-12-3.
Limitations of liability, §11-12-3.
Carelessness, etc., of owners or agents, §11-12-2.
Interest.
Requirements as to interest coupons, §11-12-4.
Itemization.
Claims to be itemized, §11-12-5.
Liability for approval of claims not legally chargeable, §11-12-12.
Liability upon claims.
Determination as to legal liability upon claims, §11-12-11.
Limitation period for presentation, §11-12-8.
Moral claims.
Payment, §11-12-16.
Officers.
Books, stationery, telephones, etc., for certain officers, §11-12-14.
Payment, §11-12-4.
Equitable claims, §11-12-16.
Moral claims, §11-12-16.
Preferred claims, §11-12-15.
Review as to authority for payment, §11-12-10.
Preferred claims, §11-12-15.
Presentation.
Limitation period for presentation, §11-12-8.
Priorities.
Preferred claims, §11-12-15.
Probate judges.
Books, stationery, telephones, etc., for, §11-12-14.
Registration, §11-12-4.
Claims to be registered, §11-12-5.
Destruction of county records by fire.
Claims to be registered upon, §11-12-9.
Rejection of claims, §11-12-11.

COUNTIES—Cont'd
Claims and demands against counties—Cont'd
Sheriffs.
Books, stationery, telephones, etc., for sheriffs, §11-12-14.
Deputy sheriffs.
Claims for compensation for services performed.
Preferred claims against counties, §36-22-4.
Tax assessors.
Books, stationery, telephones, etc., for tax assessors, §11-12-14.
Tax collectors.
Books, stationery, telephones, etc., for tax collectors, §11-12-14.
Torts.
Definitions, §11-93-1.
Liability of counties not extended, §11-93-3.
Maximum amount of damages recoverable, §11-93-2.
Settlements or compromises, §11-93-2.
Treasurers.
Books, stationery, telephones, etc., for treasurers, §11-12-14.
When claim to be paid though prior claims outstanding, §11-4-26.
Trustees.
Verification of claims, §11-12-6.
Verification of claims.
Executors, trustees, etc., §11-12-6.
Withdrawal, §11-12-7.
Coal.
Severance tax.
Political subdivisions of state prohibited from levying, §40-13-9.
Codification of laws, §11-13-1.
Commissioners. See within this heading, "County commissions."
Community action agencies.
Appropriations to agencies, §11-80-4.1.
Contributions to agencies, §11-80-4.1.
Community antenna television facilities, §§11-27-1 to 11-27-3, 23-1-59.
Concert halls.
Establishment, acquisition, administration, etc., §11-47-16.
Condemnation.
Eminent domain. See within this heading, "Eminent domain."
Conflict of laws.
Land-use management in flood-prone areas, §11-19-23.

COUNTIES—Cont'd
Conflicts of interest.
County commissions.
Awarding contracts, etc., in which county interested to relatives, §11-3-5.
Conservators.
General conservator for county.
Appointment, §26-2-26.
Constables generally.
See CONSTABLES.
Constitution of Alabama.
See CONSTITUTION OF ALABAMA.
Construction and interpretation.
County engineers.
Construction of article, §11-6-6.
Industrial development boards.
Construction of article, §§11-20-31, 11-20-50.
Industry and trade.
Projects for promotion.
Construction of chapter, §11-20-13.
Public building authorities.
Construction of chapter, §11-15-19.
Warrants for construction of public buildings, bridges and roads.
Liberal construction of chapter, §11-28-1.
Workmen's compensation self-insurance groups.
Construction of provisions, §11-26-6.
Contempt.
County commissions.
Powers and duties of county commissions, §11-3-11.
Contracts.
Ambulance service.
Contracts for services, §11-87-3.
County commissions.
Awarding of contracts, etc., in which county interested to relatives, §11-3-5.
Federal government.
Contracts with federal government, §11-1-10.
Joint purchasing agreements, §41-16-21.1.
Other county governments.
Contracts with other county governments, §11-1-10.
Publication of legislative laws of local nature.
Contracts for publication, §11-13-3.
Public contracts generally, §§41-16-1 to 41-16-125.
See CONTRACTS.
Public roads, bridges and ferries. See within this heading, "Public roads, bridges and ferries."
State government.
Contracts with state government, §11-1-10.
Conveyances.
County property generally, §11-14-2.

COUNTIES—Cont'd
  Conveyances—Cont'd
    Effect of conveyances to
      officers, etc., for use of
      county, §11-14-1.
    Public building authorities.
      Conveyance of property to
        corporation by county,
        §11-15-16.
    Waterworks plants and
      distribution systems.
      Conveyance to municipal
        corporations, §11-14-3.
  Convicts, §§14-4-1 to 14-4-14.
    See PRISONS AND
      PRISONERS.
  Coosa valley development
    authority.
    Cooperation with counties,
      §33-16-2.
  Coroners, §§11-5-1 to 11-5-13.
    See CORONERS.
  Corporations.
    Counties not to grant public
      money or lend credit to
      individuals or
      corporations, Const. Ala.,
      amd. 112.
    County declared a body
      corporate, §11-1-2.
    Industrial development
      boards, §§11-20-30 to
      11-20-50. See within this
      heading, "Industrial
      development boards."
    Obligations and liabilities of
      corporations, etc., held or
      owned by counties,
      Const. Ala., art. IV,
      §100.
  Corrections.
    County convicts, §§14-4-1 to
      14-4-14.
      See PRISONS AND
        PRISONERS.
    Institution finance authority.
      Leasing of facilities,
        §14-2-30.
    Jails.
      General provisions.
        See JAILS.
    Special session of county
      commission.
      Authority of board of
        corrections to order,
        §14-6-102.
  Costs.
    Bond issues.
      Validation proceedings,
        §6-6-757.
    Cemeteries.
      Damages from taking of
        property, etc. See
        within this heading,
        "Cemeteries."
  County commissions.
    Accounts and accounting.
      Powers, §11-3-11.
    Agriculture.
      Promotion of agriculture,
        §11-3-11.
    Appropriations.
      Payment of actual
        expenses, §11-3-13.
    Audits.
      Powers and duties,
        §11-3-11.
    Bonds, surety.
      Commissioners' bonds,
        §11-3-3.

COUNTIES—Cont'd
  County commissions—Cont'd
    Bridges.
      Authority, §11-3-10.
      Operation, etc., of bridges
        over navigable, etc.,
        streams, §§11-3-15 to
        11-3-17.
    Budgets.
      Adoption of budget system
        for county, §11-3-13.
      Duty to prepare and adopt
        annual budget,
        §11-8-3.
    Buildings.
      Duty to erect, §11-14-10.
    Insurance.
      Powers and duties of
        county commissions,
        §11-3-11.
    Chairman.
      Appointment of special
        clerk to attend
        meetings in absence of
        chairman, §11-3-19.
      Determination of certain
        matters, §11-3-20.
    Claims and demands against
      counties.
      Payment of claims
        presented by chairman
        of commission.
      Review as to authority
        for payment,
        §11-12-10.
      Powers and duties of
        county commissions,
        §11-3-11.
    Clerk.
      Special clerk to attend
        meetings in absence of
        probate judge,
        §11-3-19.
    Community antenna
      television facilities.
      Generally, §§11-27-1 to
        11-27-3, 23-1-59.
    Compensation of
      commissioners, §11-3-4.
      Applicability of provisions,
        §11-3-4.1.
      Effective date of increases,
        §11-3-4.1.
      Expense and travel
        allowances, §11-3-4.
      Minimum compensation,
        §11-3-4.1.
    Composition, §11-3-1.
    Conflicts of interest.
      Awarding contracts, etc., in
        which county
        interested to relatives,
        §11-3-5.
    Contempt.
      Powers of county
        commissions, §11-3-11.
    Contracts.
      Conflicts of interest,
        §11-3-5.
      Opening and cleaning
        navigable streams,
        §33-7-2.
    Courthouses.
      Custody of courthouse,
        §11-14-9.
      Duty to erect, §11-14-10.
      Utilities for offices,
        §11-12-13.
    Created, §11-3-1.

COUNTIES—Cont'd
  County commissions—Cont'd
    Debts.
      Powers and duties,
        §11-3-11.
    Depositories.
      General provisions. See
        within this heading,
        "Depositories."
    Designation.
      Uniform designation for
        county governing
        bodies, §11-1-5.
    Dual office holding, §11-3-2.
    Duties.
      Generally, §11-3-11.
    Election, §11-3-1.
    Eligibility for other public
      offices, §11-3-2.
    Expenditures.
      Semiannual publication of
        county receipts and
        expenditures,
        §§11-3-21 to 11-3-23.
    Expenses of commissioners,
      §11-3-4.
    Ferries.
      Authority as to
        establishment, etc.,
        §11-3-10.
    Health.
      Powers and duties,
        §11-3-11.
    Historic Blakeley authority.
      Powers as to, §41-10-178.
    Hospitals.
      Duty to erect, §11-14-10.
    Indigent persons.
      Powers and duties of
        county commissions,
        §11-3-11.
    Insurance.
      Powers and duties of
        county commissions,
        §11-3-11.
    Jails.
      Duty to erect, §11-14-10.
      Special meeting to make
        special appropriations
        for jail.
        Appropriation of funds,
          §11-14-20.
        Designation of meeting
          date, §11-14-19.
        Issuance of warrant to
          sheriff, §11-14-20.
        Notice of meeting,
          §11-14-19.
    Maps and plats.
      Powers and duties of
        county commissions,
        §11-3-11.
    Meetings.
      Election of members.
        Meeting following
          election, §11-3-1.
      Jails.
        Special meeting to make
          special
          appropriations for
          jail, §§11-14-19,
          11-14-20.
      Proceedings at meetings of
        county commissions.
        Chairman.
          Determination of
            certain matters,
            §11-3-20.
        Clerk.
          Appointment of special
            clerk, §11-3-19.

COUNTIES—Cont'd
  County commissions—Cont'd
    Meetings—Cont'd
      Proceedings at meetings of
        county commissions
        —Cont'd
        Orders.
          Issuance of orders,
            §11-3-18.
        Process.
          Issuance of process,
            §11-3-18.
        Record.
          Preparation of record,
            §11-3-18.
        Quorum, §11-3-7.
        Regular meetings, §11-3-8.
        When regular meeting
          falls on holiday,
          §11-3-8.1.
        Special meetings, §11-3-9.
        Authority of board of
          corrections to order,
          §14-6-102.
        Judge of probate.
          Calling at request of
            board of
            corrections,
            §14-6-102.
    National association of
      county commissions.
      Authority to join, §11-1-15.
    Navigable streams.
      Opening and cleaning.
        County commission
          authorized to make
          contracts, §33-7-2.
    Nepotism.
      Awarding contracts, etc., in
        which county
        interested to relatives,
        §11-3-5.
    Notice.
      Sewers.
        Requiring property
          owner to connect
          disposal facility to
          county sewer system,
          §11-3-11.
    Penalties.
      Semiannual publication of
        county receipts and
        expenditures.
        Failure to publish.
          Penalty for failure to
            publish, §11-3-23.
      Voting against
        publication.
        Penalty for voting
          against
          publication,
          §11-3-22.
    Powers.
      Generally, §11-3-11.
    Probate judges.
      Chairman of county
        commissions, §11-3-1.
      Special clerk to attend
        meetings in absence of
        judge, §11-3-19.
    Property.
      Powers and duties of
        county commissions,
        §11-3-11.
      Requiring property owner
        to connect disposal
        facility to sewer
        system, §11-3-11.

COUNTIES—Cont'd
  County commissions—Cont'd
    Public roads, bridges and
      ferries. See within this
      heading, "Public roads,
      bridges and ferries."
    Quarantine.
      Powers and duties,
        §11-3-11.
    Quorum, §11-3-7.
    Record of proceedings.
      Preparation of records,
        §11-3-18.
    Records commission.
      Local government records
        commission,
        §§41-13-22 to 41-13-25.
    Roads.
      Private roads.
        Establishment,
          §23-1-130.
      Public roads, bridges and
        ferries. See within this
        heading, "Public roads,
        bridges and ferries."
      Semiannual publication of
        county receipts and
        expenditures,
        §§11-3-21 to 11-3-23.
    Sewers.
      Powers and duties,
        §11-3-11.
      Requiring property owner
        to connect disposal
        facility to county sewer
        system, §11-3-11.
        Limitations, §11-3-11.
    Sheriffs.
      Furnishing of necessary
        quarters, equipment,
        etc., §36-22-18.
    Special meetings, §11-3-9.
    State association of county
      commissions.
      Authority to join, §11-1-15.
    Subdivisions.
      Powers and duties,
        §11-3-11.
    Subpoenas.
      Powers, §11-3-11.
    Supernumerary county
      commissioners.
      Establishment of office,
        §11-3-26.
      Qualifications, §11-3-26.
    Surveys.
      Acquisition, etc., of copies
        of field notes of
        original government
        survey of county lands,
        §11-3-25.
    Taxation.
      Powers and duties,
        §11-3-11.
      Ratification of certain
        actions of county
        governing bodies,
        §11-3-11.1.
    Terms of commissioners,
      §11-3-1.
    Treasurers.
      Settlement with county
        commission prior to
        leaving office,
        §11-4-30.
    Uniform designation for
      county governing bodies,
      §11-1-5.
    Utilities.
      Courthouse offices,
        §11-12-13.

COUNTIES—Cont'd
  County commissions—Cont'd
    Vacancies, §11-3-6.
    Waters and watercourses.
      Opening and cleaning
        navigable streams.
      County commission
        authorized to make
        contracts, §33-7-2.
    Welfare.
      Powers and duties,
        §11-3-11.
    Witnesses.
      Powers, §11-3-11.
  County seats.
    Constitution of Alabama.
      Changing or locating.
        Special, private or local
          laws prohibited,
          Const. Ala., art. IV,
          §104.
    Relocation of county seats.
      Acquisition of lands for
        new county seat,
        §11-16-28.
      Commissioners.
        Appointment, §11-16-2.
          Notice, §11-16-2.
        Chairman, §11-16-3.
        Commission, §11-16-5.
        Designation of chairman,
          §11-16-3.
        Majority may act,
          §11-16-26.
        Notice of appointment,
          §11-16-2.
        Oath, §11-16-4.
        Qualifications, §11-16-2.
        Removal, §11-16-7.
        Vacancies, §11-16-6.
      Constitution of Alabama.
        Special, private or local
          laws prohibited,
          Const. Ala., art. IV,
          §104.
      Court of record.
        Holding of court of
          record, §11-16-30.
      Courts.
        To remain at old county
          seat until buildings
          provided at new site,
          §11-16-31.
      Declaration of new county
        seat, §11-16-27.
      Duties required by chapter.
        Penalties for failure to
          perform, §11-16-40.
      Elections.
        Ballots.
          Form of ballot,
            §11-16-19.
          Numbering of ballots,
            §11-16-20.
          Opening of polls to be
            proclaimed prior to
            receipt of ballots,
            §11-16-18.
        Clerks.
          Appointment,
            §§11-16-11,
            11-16-12, 11-16-17.
          Compensation,
            §11-16-15.
          Notice of appointment,
            §11-16-12.
          Oath, §11-16-13.
          Opening of polls,
            §11-16-16.

COUNTIES—Cont'd
County seats—Cont'd
Relocation of county seats
—Cont'd
Elections—Cont'd
Clerks—Cont'd
Penalty for failure to
perform duties,
§11-16-40.
Polls, attendance at
and opening of,
§11-16-16.
Counting votes,
§11-16-23.
Date of election.
Order establishing
date, §§11-16-8,
11-16-9.
Declaration of result,
§11-16-23.
Erection of new
courthouse.
Ballots, §11-16-36.
Laws governing
elections,
§11-16-37.
Managers, §11-16-37.
Notice of election,
§11-16-35.
Ordering of election for
determination as
to erection,
§11-16-34.
Returning officers,
§11-16-37.
Subsequent elections,
§11-16-39.
Form of ballot,
§11-16-19.
Inspectors.
Appointment,
§§11-16-11,
11-16-17.
Attendance at polls,
§11-16-16.
Compensation,
§11-16-15.
Lists of registered
voters provided
for, §11-16-21.
Majority may act,
§11-16-26.
Notice of appointment,
§11-16-12.
Oath, §11-16-13.
Opening of polls,
§11-16-16.
Penalty for failure to
perform duties,
§11-16-40.
Polls, attendance at
and opening of,
§11-16-16.
Lists.
Disposition of poll
lists, §11-16-22.
Preparation of poll
lists, §§11-16-20,
11-16-22.
Provision of certified
lists of registered
voters for
inspectors,
§11-16-21.
Notice of election,
§11-16-10.
Order establishing date
for election.
Form, §11-16-9.
Issuance, §11-16-8.

COUNTIES—Cont'd
County seats—Cont'd
Relocation of county seats
—Cont'd
Elections—Cont'd
Penalties for failure to
perform duties
required by chapter,
§11-16-40.
Petition of qualified
electors for election,
§11-16-1.
Poll lists.
Disposition, §11-16-22.
Preparation,
§§11-16-20,
11-16-22.
Polls.
Attendance at polls by
inspectors, clerks
and returning
officers, §11-16-16.
Disposition of poll
lists, §11-16-22.
Opening of polls,
§11-16-16.
Opening of polls to be
proclaimed prior to
receipt of ballots,
§11-16-18.
Preparation of poll
lists, §11-16-22.
Qualifications for voting,
§11-16-21.
Receipts of returns,
§11-16-23.
Recordation of certified
copy of election
result, §11-16-25.
Result.
Certified copy of
election result,
§11-16-25.
Declaration of result,
§11-16-23.
Filing of certified copy,
§11-16-25.
Preparation of certified
copy, §11-16-25.
Publication of certified
copy, §11-16-25.
Recordation of certified
copy, §11-16-25.
Returning officers.
Appointment,
§§11-16-11,
11-16-17.
Attendance at polls,
§11-16-16.
Compensation,
§11-16-15.
Duties, §11-16-14.
Notice of appointment,
§11-16-12.
Oath, §11-16-13.
Opening of polls,
§11-16-16.
Penalty for failure to
perform duties,
§11-16-40.
Polls, attendance at
and opening of,
§11-16-16.
Powers, §11-16-14.
Returns.
Delay, proceedings
upon, §11-16-24.
Destruction,
proceedings upon,
§11-16-24.

COUNTIES—Cont'd
County seats—Cont'd
Relocation of county seats
—Cont'd
Elections—Cont'd
Returns—Cont'd
Proceedings when
returns withheld,
§11-16-24.
Receipt, §11-16-23.
Statements of votes.
Preparation and
disposition,
§11-16-22.
Votes.
Certified statements of
votes, §11-16-22.
Counting, §11-16-23.
Erection of new
courthouse, §11-16-38.
Court of record.
Holding of court of
record, §11-16-30.
Election.
Ballots, §11-16-36.
Form of ballots,
§11-16-36.
Laws governing
elections,
§11-16-37.
Managers, §11-16-37.
Marking of ballots,
§11-16-36.
Notice, §11-16-35.
Ordering, §11-16-34.
Penalties for failure to
perform duties
required by
chapter, §11-16-40.
Preparation of ballots,
§11-16-36.
Returning officers,
§11-16-37.
Subsequent elections,
§11-16-39.
Holding of court of
record, §11-16-30.
Notice of election,
§11-16-35.
Offices.
Removal to new
courthouse,
§11-16-29.
Penalties for failure to
perform duties
required by chapter,
§11-16-40.
Records.
Removal to new
courthouse,
§11-16-29.
Removal of county offices
and records to new
courthouse,
§11-16-29.
Resolution of county
commission for
erection, §11-16-33.
Erection of new jail,
§11-16-28.
Prisoners.
Removal to new jail,
§11-16-29.
Removal of prisoners to
new jail, §11-16-29.
Governor.
Petitions for removal.
Discretion of governor
as to petitions,
§11-16-32.

COUNTIES—Cont'd

County seats—Cont'd

Relocation of county seats —Cont'd

New county seat.

Acquisition of lands, §11-16-28.

Declaration, §11-16-27.

Notice of election, §11-16-10.

Offices.

Removal of offices to new courthouse and jail, §11-16-29.

To remain at old county seat until buildings provided at new site, §11-16-31.

Penalties.

Failure to perform duties required by chapter, §11-16-40.

Petitions.

Discretion of governor as to petitions for removal, §11-16-32.

Proceedings as to two or more petitions, §11-16-32.

Qualified electors may petition for election to change county seat, §11-16-1.

Prisoners.

Removal to new jail, §11-16-29.

Recordation.

Election result.

Certified copy of election result, §11-16-25.

Records.

Removal of records to new courthouse and jail, §11-16-29.

County treasuries.

Depositories. See within this heading, "Depositories."

Error.

Transfer of money erroneously paid into county treasury, §11-1-6.

Grand juries.

Examination of county treasury by grand jury, §12-16-192.

Warrants.

Persons authorized to issue, §11-8-9.

Courthouses.

Buildings generally. See within this heading, "Buildings."

County commissions.

Custody of courthouse, §11-14-9.

Duty to erect, §11-14-10.

Custody, §11-14-9.

Damage.

Location of courts and offices when courthouse damaged, §11-14-12.

Destruction.

Location of courts and offices when courthouse destroyed, §11-14-12.

COUNTIES—Cont'd

Courthouses—Cont'd

Erection.

Duty of county commission to erect, §11-14-10.

Relocated county seats, §§11-16-28, 11-16-38.

Courts to remain at old county seat until replacement provided, §11-16-31.

Election.

Ballots, §11-16-36.

Form of ballots, §11-16-36.

Laws governing elections, §11-16-37.

Managers, §11-16-37.

Notice, §11-16-35.

Ordering, §11-16-34.

Returning officers, §11-16-37.

Notice of election, §11-16-35.

Penalties for failure to perform duties required by chapter, §11-16-40.

Resolution of county commission, §11-16-33.

Subsequent elections, §11-16-39.

Janitor.

County commission to provide, §11-3-11.

Located in municipalities.

Payment of costs of certain improvements, §11-14-5.

Municipal corporations.

Contracts as to use and occupation of courthouses located in, §11-80-3.

Removal of courthouse, Const. Ala., art. II, §41.

Repairs.

Location of courts and offices when courthouse undergoing repair, §11-14-12.

Sheriffs.

Prevention of trespassing, §11-14-9.

Taxation.

Special tax for courthouse or jail, §11-14-16.

Telephones.

Designation of courthouse offices for installation of telephones, §11-3-12.

Installation of telephones, §11-3-11.

Utilities for offices, §11-12-13.

Court of civil appeals.

Offices and other physical facilities.

Appellate courts authorized to contract with localities for, §12-1-20.

Court of criminal appeals.

Offices and other physical facilities.

Authorization to contract for counties for, §12-1-20.

COUNTIES—Cont'd

Criminal law and procedure.

General provisions.

See CRIMINAL LAW AND PROCEDURE.

Venue.

See VENUE.

Cruelty to animals.

Prevention of cruelty to animals.

Employment of enforcement staff, §3-1-16.

Cultural facilities.

Establishment, acquisition, administration, etc., §11-47-16.

Damages.

Cemeteries.

Appeals from assessment of damages, §§11-17-7 to 11-17-11. See within this heading, "Cemeteries."

Assessment of damages from taking of property, etc., §11-17-4.

Property not deemed dedicated until damages and costs paid, §11-17-12.

Costs, §11-17-5.

Payment of damages.

Recordation of proceedings upon payment of damages and costs, §11-17-5.

Reports of damages from taking of property, etc., §11-17-4.

Claims and demands against counties, §§11-12-1 to 11-12-16.

Surveyors.

Liability for damages, §11-7-9.

Death.

Treasurers.

Proceedings upon death for treasurer, §11-4-29.

Debts.

Claims and demands against counties, §§11-12-1 to 11-12-16.

County commissions.

Powers and duties, §11-3-11.

Limitation on, Const. Ala., art. XII, §224; amd. 342.

Decedents' estates.

General administrators, §§43-2-170 to 43-2-175.

See EXECUTORS AND ADMINISTRATORS.

Deeds.

Effect of deeds to officers, etc., for use of county, §11-14-1.

Definitions.

Bond issues. See within this heading, "Bond issues."

Capital improvements, §11-29-3.

Captive counties, §23-1-100.

Claims and demands against counties.

Torts, §11-93-1.

Fiscal year, §11-8-1.

COUNTIES—Cont'd
 Definitions—Cont'd
  Gasoline taxes.
   Issuing of warrants in
    anticipation of gasoline
    taxes, §11-11-1.
  Industrial development
   boards, §11-20-30.
  Industry and trade.
   Projects for promotion,
    §11-20-1.
  Land-use management in
   flood-prone areas,
   §11-19-1.
  Liability self-insurance
   funds, §11-30-1.
  Parks and recreation.
   Acquisition of lands for,
    §11-18-20.
  Public park and recreation
   boards, §11-22-1.
  Public building authorities,
   §11-15-1.
  Warrants.
   Construction of public
    buildings, bridges and
    roads, §11-28-1.1.
   Waterworks systems
    warrants, §11-9-20.
   Waterworks systems
    warrants, §11-9-20.
 Demands against counties.
  See within this heading,
   "Claims and demands
   against counties."
 **Department of examiners of
  public accounts.**
  Periodic examinations and
   audits, §41-5-14.
 **Departments of human
  resources,** §§38-2-6 to
  38-2-10, 38-4-6, 38-4-10.
  See WELFARE.
 Depositories, §§11-4-40 to
  11-4-50.
  Accounts.
   Opening of accounts,
    §11-4-46.
  Actions by and against,
   §11-4-47.
  Applicability of provisions of
   chapter, §11-4-1.
  Appointment of county
   depositories, §11-1-7.
  Bonds, surety, §11-4-42.
   Banks holding deposit of
    funds from special tax
    levy, §11-3-14.
  Checks.
   Persons authorized to draw
    checks on county
    depository, §11-8-9.
  Civil actions and proceedings
   by and against, §11-4-47.
  Compensation of banks,
   §11-4-44.
  Duties, §11-4-43.
   Performance of duties
    other than receipt and
    disbursement of funds,
    §11-4-50.
  Establishment in lieu of
   treasurer, §11-4-40.
  Expenditures.
   Disbursement of funds,
    etc., §11-4-46.
   Performance of duties
    other than receipt and
    disbursement of funds,
    §11-4-50.

COUNTIES—Cont'd
 Depositories—Cont'd
  Expenditures—Cont'd
   Statement of disbursement,
    §11-4-46.
  Liabilities, §11-4-43.
   Loss of funds, §11-1-7.
  Loss of funds.
   Liability, etc., §11-1-7.
  Opening of accounts,
   §11-4-46.
  Payment of moneys into
   depository, §11-4-45.
  Receipts.
   Performance of duties
    other than receipt and
    disbursement of funds,
    §11-4-50.
   Statement of receipts,
    §11-4-46.
  Reports, §11-4-45.
  Security, §11-4-42.
  Selection, §11-4-41.
  Settlements, §11-4-45.
  Statement of receipts and
   disbursements, §11-4-46.
  Tax collectors.
   Distributions, remittances,
    etc., of funds deposited,
    §11-1-7.
  Treasurer appointed when no
   depository designated,
   §11-4-49.
  Warrants.
   Execution, §11-4-48.
   Liability upon warrant,
    §11-4-48.
   Persons authorized to issue
    warrants or draw
    checks on depository,
    §11-8-9.
 Development.
  Regional planning and
   development, §§11-85-1
   to 11-85-73.
  See PLANNING.
 Disasters.
  Financial measures,
   §11-8-15.
 District attorneys.
  Bond issues.
   Validation, §§6-6-750,
    6-6-752.
 District courts.
  County personnel serving
   court to become state
   employees, §12-17-1.
 Ditches.
  Acquisition of lands for
   drainage ditches,
   §11-14-23.
  Conduct of condemnation
   proceedings, §11-14-24.
 Dogs.
  Running at large.
   Permitting dogs to run at
    large, §3-1-5.
 Drainage ditches.
  Acquisition of lands for
   drainage ditches,
   §11-14-23.
  Conduct of condemnation
   proceedings, §11-14-24.
 Dry counties, §§28-4-1 to
  28-4-326.
  See ALCOHOLIC
   BEVERAGES.

COUNTIES—Cont'd
 Dual office holding.
  County commissions.
   Eligibility of
    commissioners for
    other public offices,
    §11-3-2.
 Education.
  County boards of education,
   §§16-8-1 to 16-8-43.
  See EDUCATION.
  County license tax for school
   purposes, §§40-12-4 to
   40-12-7.
  Local aid to state educational
   institutions, §§16-19-1 to
   16-19-8.
  See UNIVERSITIES AND
   COLLEGES.
 Elections.
  Alcoholic beverages.
   Elections as to sale and
    distribution of
    alcoholic beverages.
   See ALCOHOLIC
    BEVERAGES.
  Bond issues. See within this
   heading, "Bond issues."
  County commissions, §11-3-1.
   See ELECTIONS.
  County seats.
   Relocation. See within this
    heading, "County
    seats."
  General provisions.
   See ELECTIONS.
  Relocation of county seats.
   See within this heading,
    "County seats."
  Treasurers, §11-4-20.
 Electricity.
  Acquisition of light and
   power plants.
   Security for bonds and
    indebtedness incurred
    in acquisition,
    §11-81-1.
  Acquisition of systems.
   Authorized, §11-81-200.
   Estimate of costs,
    §11-81-162.
  Alternate borrowing for
   electric systems.
   Acquisition of systems.
    Authorized, §11-81-200.
   Borrowing money for
    acquisition
    authorized,
    §11-81-202.
   Authorization of
    borrowing, §11-81-202.
  Charges for energy and
   service.
   Limitation as to charges
    by counties,
    §11-81-204.
  Construction of article,
   §11-81-206.
  Contracts for security of
   lender, §11-81-204.
  Election as to proposed
   undertaking,
   §11-81-201.
  Extension of systems.
   Authorized, §11-81-200.
   Borrowing money for
    extension
    authorized,
    §11-81-202.

COUNTIES—Cont'd
  Electricity—Cont'd
    Alternate borrowing for
      electric systems—Cont'd
      Form of instrument
        evidencing loan,
        §11-81-205.
      Limitations on borrowing,
        §11-81-202.
      Maturity of instrument
        evidencing loan,
        §11-81-205.
      Operation of systems.
        Authorized, §11-81-200.
      Borrowing money for
        operation authorized,
        §11-81-202.
      Pledges of plants as
        security for repayment,
        §11-81-203.
      Rights of way.
        Acquisition, §11-81-200.
      Security for repayment of
        money borrowed.
        Contracts for security of
          lender, §11-81-204.
        Pledges of plants as
          security, §11-81-203.
      Terms of instrument
        evidencing loan,
        §11-81-205.
    Bond issues.
      Public improvement bonds.
        See within this
        heading, "Bond
        issues."
      Revenue bonds. See within
        this heading, "Public
        utilities."
      Security for bonds and
        indebtedness, §11-81-1.
    Calendar basis.
      Determination as to
        operation of system
        upon, §11-81-187.
    Consolidation of systems.
      Authorized, §11-81-161.
      Estimate of costs,
        §11-81-162.
    Construction of light and
      power plants.
      Security for bonds and
        indebtedness incurred
        in construction,
        §11-81-1.
    Depository for revenues,
      §11-81-183.
    Expenses of operation or
      maintenance of systems.
      Payment out of general
        funds, §11-81-182.
    Extension of systems.
      Authorized, §11-81-161.
      Estimate of costs,
        §11-81-162.
    Financial condition of
      systems.
      Books of record and
        accounts, etc.,
        §11-81-188.
    Fiscal year basis.
      Determination as to
        operation of system
        upon fiscal year basis,
        §11-81-187.
    Highways.
      Rights of way.
        Construction of facilities,
        §23-1-85.

COUNTIES—Cont'd
  Electricity—Cont'd
    Improvement authorities,
      §§39-7-1 to 39-7-34.
      See PUBLIC WORKS.
    Maintenance of systems.
      Expenses.
        Payment out of general
          funds, §11-81-182.
    Operation of systems.
      Authorized, §11-81-200.
      Determination as to
        operation upon
        calendar or fiscal year
        basis, §11-81-187.
      Expenses.
        Payment out of general
          funds, §11-81-182.
    Payment by counties for
      services furnished by
      system, §11-81-186.
    Properties of system.
      Books of record and
        accounts, etc.,
        §11-81-188.
    Public improvement bonds.
      See within this heading,
      "Bond issues."
    Purchase of light and power
      plants.
      Security for bonds and
        indebtedness incurred
        in construction,
        §11-81-1.
    Rates.
      Establishment, §11-81-184.
      Limitation as to charges
        for electric energy and
        service by counties,
        §11-81-204.
      State supervision or
        regulation.
        Not subject to,
          §11-81-185.
    Repair of systems.
      Authorized, §11-81-161.
      Estimate of costs,
        §11-81-162.
    Revenue bonds. See within
      this heading, "Public
      utilities."
    Revenues.
      Depository.
        Designation of
        depository,
        §11-81-183.
        Disposition and
        disbursement of
        gross revenue
        account and special
        funds, §11-81-183.
      Disposition of gross
        revenues, §11-81-181.
      Gross revenues.
        Disposition and
        disbursement,
        §§11-81-181,
        11-81-183.
      Pledge of revenues for
        payment of bonds,
        §§11-81-16, 11-18-181.
  **Elk river development
    agency.**
    Contributions to work of
      agency by certain
      counties, §33-12-6.
    Taxation.
      Levy by governing bodies,
        §33-12-6.

COUNTIES—Cont'd
  Emergencies.
    Ambulance service, §§11-87-1
      to 11-87-5. See within
      this heading,
      "Ambulance service."
    Financial provisions for
      emergencies, §11-8-15.
    Military service by county
      officers in time of
      national emergency,
      §§36-8-1 to 36-8-6.
      See PUBLIC OFFICERS
      AND EMPLOYEES.
  Eminent domain.
    Acquisition of lands for
      drainage ditches, lime
      and stone quarries, etc.,
      §11-14-23.
    Conduct of condemnation
      proceedings, §11-14-24.
    General provisions.
      See EMINENT DOMAIN.
    Public parks or recreational
      purposes.
      Acquisition of land.
        Authority, §11-18-21.
    Public roads, bridges and
      ferries, §§11-80-1,
      23-1-82.
    Public utilities.
      Land-use management in
        flood-prone areas,
        §11-19-24.
    Relocation assistance,
      §11-80-2.
  Employees.
    Accident insurance.
      Group insurance for
        officers and employees,
        §§11-91-1 to 11-91-8.
        See within this
        heading, "Insurance."
    Appointment, §11-8-14.
    Bonds, surety.
      Official bonds. See within
        this heading, "Bonds,
        surety."
    Code of ethics.
      See PUBLIC OFFICERS
      AND EMPLOYEES.
    Insurance.
      Group insurance for
        officers and employees,
        §§11-91-1 to 11-91-7.
        See within this
        heading, "Insurance."
    Pension and retirement
      plans. See within this
      heading, "Pension and
      retirement plans."
    Social security.
      See SOCIAL SECURITY.
    State employees' retirement
      system.
      Participation of county
        employees, §36-27-6.
  Engineers.
    Appointment, §11-6-1.
    Construction of article,
      §11-6-6.
    Contract of employment,
      §11-6-1.
    County civil service laws.
      Effect, §11-6-5.
    Duties, §11-6-3.
    Full-time employment,
      §11-6-1.
    Merit system laws.
      Effect, §11-6-5.

COUNTIES—Cont'd
Engineers—Cont'd
Public works.
Supervision and
preparation by
professional engineers,
§34-11-10.
Qualifications, §11-6-2.
Salary, §11-6-1.
State participation in
salary, §11-6-4.
Engineer trainees,
§11-6-23.
State employees' retirement
system.
See PUBLIC OFFICERS
AND EMPLOYEES.
Trainees.
Appointment, §11-6-20.
Considered county
employee, §11-6-24.
Duties, §11-6-22.
Full-time office, §11-6-20.
Provisions of article
cumulative, §11-6-25.
Qualifications, §11-6-21.
Salary.
State participation in
salary, §11-6-23.
Enterprise zones, §§41-23-20
to 41-23-32.
See ENTERPRISE ZONES.
**Environmental improvement
authorities.**
Aid and cooperation of
counties, §9-6-13.
Evidence.
Public building authorities.
Records of proceedings,
§11-15-6.
Surveyors.
When survey or plat
evidence of facts
stated, §11-7-8.
**Executors and
administrators.**
Claims and demands against
counties.
Verification, §11-12-6.
General administrators,
§§43-2-170 to 43-2-175.
See EXECUTORS AND
ADMINISTRATORS.
Warrants for construction of
public buildings, bridges
and roads.
Deemed legal investments
for trust funds,
§11-28-5.
**Exemptions from levy and
sale under process.**
County property, §6-10-10.
Expenditures.
Depositories.
Disbursement of funds,
etc., §11-4-46.
Performance of duties
other than receipt and
disbursement of funds,
§11-4-50.
Statement of disbursement,
§11-4-46.
Semiannual publication of
county receipts and
expenditures, §§11-3-21
to 11-3-23.
Factories.
Promotion, §11-3-11.
Farmers' markets.
Local appropriations
authorized, §2-5-17.

COUNTIES—Cont'd
Fees.
Fees of certain county
officials to be paid into
local treasury, §1-3-6.
Land-use management in
flood-prone areas.
Construction and
development permit
fees, §11-19-7.
Officers.
Ex officio fees, §11-8-13.
Surveyors.
Court ordered surveys.
Fees taxed as costs,
§11-7-6.
Ferries.
Establishment and
maintenance on river
between two counties,
§§11-49-20 to 11-49-23.
Public improvement bonds.
See within this heading,
"Bond issues."
Public roads, bridges and
ferries, §§23-1-80 to
23-1-95. See within this
heading, "Public roads,
bridges and ferries."
Fiduciaries.
Claims and demands against
counties.
Verification, §11-12-6.
Warrants for construction of
public buildings, bridges
and roads.
Warrants deemed legal
investments for trust
funds, §11-28-5.
Finance.
Applicability of provisions of
chapter, §§11-8-16,
11-8-17.
Bond issues. See within this
heading, "Bond issues."
Budgets. See within this
heading, "Budgets."
Depositories. See within this
heading, "Depositories."
Emergencies.
Financial provisions for
emergencies, §11-8-15.
Fiscal year.
Defined, §11-8-1.
Loans. See within this
heading, "Loans."
Purpose of chapter, §11-8-2.
Record of financial status.
Contents, §11-8-7.
Examination.
Public examination,
§11-8-7.
Keeping record, §11-8-8.
Maintenance, §11-8-8.
Public examination,
§11-8-7.
Required, §11-8-7.
Semiannual publication of
county receipts and
expenditures, §§11-3-21
to 11-3-23.
Surplus funds.
Investment in United
States securities,
§11-8-11.
Treasurers. See within this
heading, "Treasurers."
Unexpended balances.
Disposition, §11-8-6.
Warrants. See within this
heading, "Warrants."

COUNTIES—Cont'd
Fine and forfeiture fund.
Transfer of balance to
general fund, etc.,
§11-4-25.
Fires and fire prevention.
Assessments.
County taxes and
assessments for forest
and forest fire
protection, §§9-13-160
to 9-13-187.
See FORESTS AND
FORESTRY.
Firemen.
Personnel standards and
education.
Appropriations and
grants to fund
authorized,
§36-32-10.
Sprinkler systems.
Power of county to
regulate work of
contractors, §34-33-9.
Volunteer fire departments.
Donations by county,
§9-3-18.
Water, sewer and fire
protection authorities,
§§11-88-1 to 11-88-111.
See WATER, SEWER AND
FIRE PROTECTION
AUTHORITIES.
Water, sewer and fire
protection districts,
§§11-89-1 to 11-89-19.
See WATER, SEWER AND
FIRE PROTECTION
DISTRICTS.
Fiscal year.
Defined, §11-8-1.
Fish and game.
Acquisition of lands for
public purposes.
Use of land for betterment
of fish and game,
§11-18-2.
Licenses.
Hunting license, §9-11-44.
Flood-prone areas.
Land-use management.
Board of adjustment.
Appeals from final
judgment of board,
§11-19-20.
Appeals to board,
§11-19-19.
Appointment, §11-19-19.
Chairman, §11-19-19.
Composition, §11-19-19.
Duties, §11-19-19.
Final judgment of board.
Appeals from final
judgment,
§11-19-20.
Meetings, §11-19-19.
Powers, §11-19-19.
Removal of members,
§11-19-19.
Rules, §11-19-19.
Terms of members,
§11-19-19.
Vacancies, §11-19-19.
Building codes, §11-19-6.
Adoption for flood-prone
areas outside
municipalities,
§11-19-3.

COUNTIES—Cont'd
  Flood-prone areas—Cont'd
    Land-use management
      —Cont'd
      Buildings.
        Conflict of laws,
          §11-19-23.
        Unauthorized
          construction of
          buildings.
          Institution of actions
            to prevent, correct,
            etc., §11-19-21.
      Conflict of laws, §11-19-23.
      Construction and
        development.
        Fees for permits,
          §11-19-7.
        Permits.
          Fees, §11-19-7.
          Issuance of permits,
            §11-19-7.
        Plans.
          Submission of plans,
            §11-19-7.
        Specifications.
          Submission of
            specifications,
            §11-19-7.
        Submission of plans and
          specifications,
          §11-19-7.
        Unauthorized
          construction.
          Institution of actions
            to prevent, correct,
            etc., §11-19-21.
      Construction of chapter.
        Not to impair right of
          eminent domain,
          etc., granted to
          utilities, §11-19-24.
      Control measures,
        §11-19-4.
      County commissions.
        Zoning powers.
          Grant of zoning
            powers, §11-19-16.
      Definitions, §11-19-1.
      Eminent domain.
        Construction of chapter
          not to impair,
          §11-19-24.
      Fees.
        Construction and
          development.
          Permits, §11-19-7.
      Health regulations,
        §11-19-6.
      Map.
        Zoning map.
          Procedure for
            preparation,
            adoption,
            amendment, etc.,
            §11-19-18.
      Ordinances.
        Conflict of laws,
          §11-19-23.
        Violations.
          Penalties, §11-19-22.
        Zoning ordinance.
          Procedure for
            preparation,
            adoption,
            amendment, etc.,
            §11-19-18.
      Penalties, §11-19-22.

COUNTIES—Cont'd
  Flood-prone areas—Cont'd
    Land-use management
      —Cont'd
      Permits.
        Construction and
          development,
          §11-19-7.
      Planning commissions.
        Appointment of
          members, §11-19-8.
        Bylaws.
          Adoption, §11-19-9.
        Compensation of
          members, §11-19-8.
        Composition, §11-19-8.
        Creation, §11-19-8.
        Duties, §11-19-10.
        Employees.
          Appointment, §11-19-9.
        Examinations.
          Right of entry upon
            lands for
            preparation of
            examinations,
            §11-19-10.
        Expenditure of funds,
          §11-19-9.
        Funds.
          Acceptance and
            expenditure,
            §11-19-9.
        Meetings, §11-19-9.
        Officers, §11-19-9.
        Powers, §11-19-10.
        Qualifications, §11-19-8.
        Record of transactions,
          etc.
          Maintenance, §11-19-9.
        Removal of members,
          §11-19-8.
        Right of entry upon
          lands for preparation
          of examinations and
          surveys, §11-19-10.
        Staff.
          Appointment, §11-19-9.
        Studies.
          Special studies,
           §11-19-10.
        Surveys.
          Right of entry upon
           lands for,
           §11-19-10.
          Special surveys,
           §11-19-10.
        Terms of members,
          §11-19-8.
        Vacancies, §11-19-8.
        Zoning.
          Manner in which
           territory is zoned,
           §11-19-17.
      Plats.
        Subdivisions.
          Approval of plats
           before recordation,
           §§11-19-13,
           11-19-14.
          Transferring, sale, etc.,
           of lands in
           subdivision prior
           to approval of plat,
           §11-19-15.
      Public utilities.
        Chapter not to impair
          right of eminent
          domain, etc.,
          §11-19-24.
      Purpose of chapter,
        §11-19-2.

COUNTIES—Cont'd
  Flood-prone areas—Cont'd
    Land-use management
      —Cont'd
      Restrictions.
        Land-use and control
          measures, §11-19-4.
        Right of entry upon lands
          for preparation of
          examinations and
          surveys, §11-19-10.
        Subdivision regulations.
          Adoption, §11-9-11.
          Certification of adopted
           regulations to
           probate judge,
           §11-19-11.
          Contents, §11-19-12.
          Conveyance of land in
           subdivisions prior to
           approval of plat,
           §11-19-15.
          Generally, §11-19-5.
          Plats.
           Approval of plats
            before recordation,
            §§11-19-13,
            11-19-14.
           Sale or transfer of
            lands in
            subdivision prior
            to approval,
            §11-19-15.
          Probate judge.
           Certification of
            adopted
            regulations to,
            §11-19-11.
          Procedure for adoption,
           §11-19-11.
          Sale of lands in
           subdivision prior to
           approval of plat,
           §11-19-15.
          Scope, §11-19-12.
          Unauthorized
           establishment of
           subdivisions.
           Institution of actions
            to prevent, correct,
            etc., §11-19-21.
        Surveys.
          Powers and duties of
           planning
           commission,
           §11-19-10.
          Right of entry upon
           lands for preparation
           of surveys,
           §11-19-10.
          Special surveys by
           planning
           commission,
           §11-19-10.
        Unauthorized construction
          of buildings,
          subdivision or use of
          lands, etc.
          Institution of actions to
           prevent, correct, etc.,
           §11-19-21.
        Use of lands.
          Unauthorized use.
           Institution of actions
            to prevent, correct,
            etc., §11-19-21.
        Utilities.
          Chapter not to impair
           right of eminent
           domain, etc.,
           §11-19-24.

COUNTIES—Cont'd
Flood-prone areas—Cont'd
Land-use management
  —Cont'd
  Violations of provisions of
    chapter, ordinances,
    etc.
    Penalties, §11-19-22.
  Zoning.
    Adoption of zoning
      ordinance, §11-19-18.
    Flood-prone areas
      outside
      municipalities,
      §11-19-3.
    Amendment of zoning
      ordinance, §11-19-18.
    Appeals from board of
      adjustment,
      §11-19-20.
    Appeals to board of
      adjustment,
      §11-19-19.
    Board of adjustment,
      §11-19-19.
    County commissions.
      Grant of zoning powers
        to, §11-19-16.
    Grant of zoning powers
      to county
      commissions,
      §11-19-16.
    Manner in which
      territory zoned,
      §11-19-17.
    Map.
      Procedure for
        preparation,
        adoption,
        amendment, etc.,
        §11-19-18.
    Ordinance.
      Procedure for
        preparation,
        adoption,
        amendment, etc.,
        §11-19-18.
    Powers.
      Grant to county
        commissions,
        §11-19-16.
      Scope, §11-19-16.
    Unauthorized use of
      lands.
      Institution of actions
        to prevent, correct,
        etc., §11-19-21.
Forests and forestry.
Acquisition and
    administration of forest
    lands.
    Authorized, §11-84-1.
    Seedlings.
      Provision, §11-84-2.
    Technical assistance.
      Provision, §11-84-2.
    Transplants.
      Provision, §11-84-2.
County taxes and
    assessments for forest
    and forest fire protection,
    §§9-13-180 to 9-13-187.
    See FORESTS AND
      FORESTRY.
Forest products.
    Privilege and severance
      taxes.
      Payment by counties
        purchasing forest
        products, §9-13-106.

COUNTIES—Cont'd
Forests and forestry—Cont'd
National forests.
  Receipts from national
    forests.
    Distribution and
      expenditure, §9-13-2.
  Research and educational
    programs.
    Appropriation of funds by
      counties, §2-30-23.
    Receipt of donations from
      counties, §2-30-23.
Full faith and credit.
Warrants for construction of
  public buildings, bridges
  and roads, §11-28-2.
Funds.
Capital improvement,
  §§11-29-1 to 11-29-7.
Fine and forfeiture fund.
  Transfer of balance by
    treasurer to general
    fund, etc., §11-4-25.
General funds.
  Surplus.
    Transfer to road fund,
      §23-1-83.
  Investments.
    Sinking funds, §§11-81-19
      to 11-81-21.
  Oil and gas.
    Severance tax trust funds,
      §40-20-50.
Public building authorities.
  Investment of county funds
    in warrants, §11-15-15.
Road fund, §23-1-83.
Sinking funds. See within
  this heading, "Sinking
  funds."
Surplus funds.
  Investment in United
    States securities,
    §11-8-11.
Treasurers. See within this
  heading, "Treasurers."
Unexpended balances.
  Disposition at end of fiscal
    year, §11-8-6.
Garbage and refuse.
Solid waste management
  plan, §§22-27-40 to
  22-27-49.
  See SOLID WASTE.
Gas.
Acquisition of gas plants.
  Security for bonds and
    indebtedness incurred
    in acquisition,
    §11-81-1.
Acquisition of systems.
  Authorized, §11-81-161.
  Estimate of costs,
    §11-81-162.
Bond issues.
  Revenue bonds. See within
    this heading, "Public
    utilities."
Calendar basis.
  Determination as to
    operation of system
    upon, §11-81-187.
Consolidation of systems.
  Authorized, §11-81-161.
  Estimate of costs,
    §11-81-162.

COUNTIES—Cont'd
Gas—Cont'd
Construction of gas plants.
  Security for bonds and
    indebtedness incurred
    in construction,
    §11-81-1.
Depository for revenues,
  §11-81-183.
Expenses of operation or
  maintenance of systems.
  Payment out of general
    funds, §11-81-182.
Extension of systems.
  Authorized, §11-81-161.
  Estimate of costs,
    §11-81-162.
Financial condition of
  system.
  Books of record and
    accounts, etc.,
    §11-81-188.
Fiscal year basis.
  Determination as to
    operation of system
    upon, §11-81-187.
Improvement authorities,
  §§39-7-1 to 39-7-34.
  See PUBLIC WORKS.
Maintenance of system.
  Expenses.
    Payment out of general
      funds, §11-81-182.
Operation of system.
  Determination as to basis,
    §11-81-187.
  Expenses.
    Payment out of general
      funds, §11-81-182.
Payment by counties for
  services furnished by
  system, §11-81-186.
Properties of system.
  Books of record and
    accounts, etc.,
    §11-81-188.
Purchase of gas plants.
  Security for bonds and
    indebtedness incurred
    in purchase, §11-81-1.
Rates.
  Establishment, §11-81-184.
  State supervision or
    regulation.
    Rates not subject to,
      §11-81-185.
Repair of systems.
  Authorization, §11-81-161.
  Estimate of costs,
    §11-81-162.
Revenue bonds. See within
  this heading, "Public
  utilities."
Revenues.
  Depository.
    Designation, §11-81-183.
  Disposition and
    disbursement of
    gross revenue
    account and special
    funds, §11-81-183.
  Disposition of gross
    revenues, §11-81-181.
  Gross revenues.
    Disposition and
      disbursement,
      §§11-81-181,
      11-81-183.
  Pledge of revenues for
    payment of revenue
    bonds, §11-81-181.

COUNTIES—Cont'd
  Gasoline.
    Issuing warrants in
      anticipation of gasoline
      taxes.
      Applicability of chapter.
        Counties to which
          chapter applicable,
          §11-11-2.
        Issuance of warrants by
          counties not subject
          to chapter, §11-11-7.
        Issuance of warrants by
          counties subject to
          chapter, §11-11-7.
      Authority for issuance,
        §11-11-3.
      Definitions, §11-11-1.
      Denominations of
        warrants, §11-11-3.
      Disposition of proceeds
        from sale of warrants,
        §11-11-5.
      Exemption from usury and
        interest statutes,
        §11-11-8.
      Form of warrants,
        §11-11-3.
      Gasoline tax.
        Assignment and pledge
          of proceeds of share
          of tax for payment,
          §11-11-4.
      Interest on warrants,
        §11-11-3.
        Assignment and pledge
          of proceeds of share
          of highway gasoline
          tax for payment,
          §11-11-4.
        Exemption from interest
          statutes, §11-11-8.
        Security for payment of
          principal and
          interest, §11-11-3.
      Issuance by counties not
        subject to chapter,
        §11-11-7.
      Maturity of warrant,
        §11-11-3.
      Payment.
        Assignment and pledge
          of proceeds of share
          of highway gasoline
          tax for payment,
          §11-11-4.
        Security for payment of
          principal and
          interest, §11-11-3.
      Proceeds from sale of
        warrants.
        Disposition, §11-11-5.
      Refunding warrants.
        Issuance, §11-11-6.
      Retirement of warrants,
        §11-11-3.
      Sale of warrants.
        Disposition of proceeds
          from sale, §11-11-5.
      Terms of warrants,
        §11-11-3.
      Usury statutes.
        Exemptions from usury
          statutes, §11-11-8.
    Taxation.
      Public roads, bridges and
        ferries.
        Expenditure of funds
          derived from fees
          levied on fuels,
          §23-1-84.

COUNTIES—Cont'd
  General administrators,
    §§43-2-170 to 43-2-175.
    See EXECUTORS AND
      ADMINISTRATORS.
  Golf.
    Public improvement bonds.
      See within this heading,
      "Bond issues."
  Governing bodies.
    Uniform designation for
      county governing bodies,
      §11-1-5.
  Governor.
    Relocation of county seats.
      Petitions for removal.
        Discretion of governor as
          to petitions,
          §11-16-32.
  Granaries.
    Public improvement bonds.
      See within this heading,
      "Bond issues."
  Grants.
    Effect of grants to officers,
      etc., for use of county,
      §11-14-1.
    Securities.
      Issuance of securities in
        anticipation of receipt
        of grants, §§11-81A-1
        to 11-81A-7.
      See GRANTS.
  Gravel pits.
    Acquisition of lands for
      gravel pits, §11-14-23.
    Conduct of condemnation
      proceedings, §11-14-24.
  Graveyards. See within this
    heading, "Cemeteries."
  Guardian and ward.
    Claims and demands against
      counties.
      Verification of claims,
        §11-12-6.
    Removal of personal property
      of minors and wards,
      §§26-8-40 to 26-8-52.
      See GUARDIAN AND
        WARD.
  Handicapped persons.
    Employment by counties,
      §21-7-8.
  Harbors and ports.
    Public improvement bonds.
      See within this heading,
      "Bond issues."
  Hazardous substances.
    Fees for disposal of
      hazardous waste or
      substances.
      Additional fee collected by
        counties, §22-30B-4.
      Cooperation with county
        officials, §22-30B-17.
  Hazardous waste.
    Commercial treatment
      facilities or disposal
      sites.
      Restriction on number per
        county, §22-30-5.1.
      Construction of
        provisions,
        §22-30-5.2.
    Fees for disposal of
      hazardous waste or
      substances.
      Additional fee collected by
        counties, §22-30B-4.
      Cooperation with county
        officials, §22-30B-17.

COUNTIES—Cont'd
  Health.
    Certain county and local
      laws unaffected by title,
      §22-1-9.
    County boards of health,
      §§22-3-1 to 22-3-3.
    County commissions.
      Powers and duties of
        county commissions,
        §11-3-11.
    County health officers,
      §§22-3-4 to 22-3-7.
    Indigent persons.
      Responsibility for health
        care.
        See HEALTH.
    Officers, §§22-3-4 to 22-3-7.
    Special tax for hospital and
      public health purposes in
      certain counties, Const.
      Ala., amd. 72.
    State health department.
      Payment of health
        department claims out
        of county budgets,
        §22-3-12.
  Health care authorities,
    §§22-21-310 to 22-21-356.
    See HEALTH CARE
      AUTHORITIES.
  Health care service plan.
    License, privilege or other
      taxes prohibited,
      §10-4-107.
  Hearings.
    Bond issues.
      Validation, §6-6-753.
  Highways.
    Closing and vacating streets,
      alleys and highways,
      §§23-4-1 to 23-4-6.
      See HIGHWAYS.
    Construction or maintenance
      of state roads or bridges.
      Application by counties for,
        §23-1-48.
    Interstate highway system.
      Controlled access facilities.
        Agreements with
          counties, §23-3-8.
    Public roads, bridges and
      ferries. See within this
      heading, "Public roads,
      bridges and ferries."
    Rights of way.
      Acquisition.
        When deemed necessary
          by director of
          highways, §23-1-45.
    Transferred county roads and
      bridges.
      Employees used on.
        Residents of county,
          §23-1-36.
  **Historical preservation
    authorities.**
    Loans, sales, grants, etc., of
      money, property, etc., by
      counties, §41-10-146.
  Historical research.
    Authorization to undertake
      research into history,
      §16-42-1.
    Contracts between counties
      and historical
      corporations, etc.,
      authorized, §16-42-3.
    Funds.
      Use of county funds,
        §16-42-2.

COUNTIES—Cont'd
Historic Blakeley authority.
County commission.
Powers as to, §41-10-178.
Hospitals.
Acquisition of lands for
hospitals, §11-18-2.
Appropriations.
Service program for
indigents, §22-21-223.
Assets.
Transfer of assets to
hospital authorities by
counties, §22-21-181.
Authorities.
County and municipal
hospital authorities,
§§22-21-170 to
22-21-191.
See HOSPITALS.
Boards of health.
Duties, §22-3-2.
Bond issues.
Hospital boards, §22-21-78.
Public improvement bonds.
Certain revenue
producing
undertakings. See
within this heading,
"Bond issues."
County commissions.
Duty to erect, §11-14-10.
Erection.
Duty of county commission
to erect, §11-14-10.
Establishment, §22-21-1.
Funds.
Transfer of funds to
hospital authorities,
§22-21-181.
Transfer of funds to
hospital corporations,
§22-21-81.
General provisions.
See HOSPITALS.
Hospital boards, §§22-21-70
to 22-21-83.
See HOSPITALS.
Hospital corporations,
§§22-21-100 to 22-21-112.
See HOSPITALS.
Public hospital associations.
Appropriations, §22-21-56.
Public hospitals, §§11-95-1 to
11-95-21.
See HOSPITALS.
Housing authorities,
§§24-1-60 to 24-1-84.
See HOUSING
AUTHORITIES.
Housing projects.
Alienation of certain public
improvements,
§§35-4-410 to 35-4-412.
Improvement authorities.
See PUBLIC WORKS.
Indigent persons.
Counties to provide for
maintenance of the poor,
Const. Ala., art. IV, §88.
County commissions.
Powers and duties of
county commissions,
§11-3-11.
County departments of
human resources,
§§38-2-6 to 38-2-10,
38-4-6, 38-4-10.
See WELFARE.

COUNTIES—Cont'd
Indigent persons—Cont'd
Hospital care and treatment.
Use of certain special
county taxes for,
Const. Ala., amd. 125.
Hospital service program for
indigents, §§22-21-210 to
22-21-227.
See HOSPITALS.
Occupational license tax,
§10-4-144.
Relief and support by
counties, §§38-8-1 to
38-8-3.
**Industrial development
authorities,** §§11-92A-1 to
11-92A-22.
See COUNTY INDUSTRIAL
DEVELOPMENT
AUTHORITIES.
**Industrial development
boards,** §§11-20-30 to
11-20-50.
Board of directors, §11-20-36.
Bond issues.
Delivery, §11-20-38.
Denominations, §11-20-38.
Execution, §11-20-38.
Exemptions from taxation,
§11-20-47.
Form, §11-20-38.
Liability of county,
§11-20-42.
Limitation of actions to
contest, §11-20-40.
Notice of resolution
authorizing issuance,
§11-20-40.
Redemption, §11-20-38.
Refunding of bonds,
§11-20-38.
Remedies upon default,
§11-20-39.
Sale, §11-20-38.
Security for payment,
§11-20-39.
Temporary revenue bonds,
etc., §11-20-41.
Terms, §11-20-38.
Borrowing money for
temporary use,
§11-20-41.
Issuance of temporary
revenue bonds or
notes, §11-20-41.
Competitive bid laws.
Exemptions, §11-20-49.
Construction of article,
§§11-20-31, 11-20-50.
Contracts.
Exemption from
competitive bid laws,
§11-20-49.
Conveyances, etc., of assets
to corporations by other
public corporations,
§11-20-44.
Assumption of obligations
or indebtedness of
corporations making
conveyances, etc.,
§11-20-44.
Definitions, §11-20-30.
Dissolution of corporations.
Authority, §11-20-45.
Certificate of dissolution.
Filing, §11-20-46.
Disposition of funds and
properties upon
dissolution, §11-20-45.

COUNTIES—Cont'd
**Industrial development
boards**—Cont'd
Dissolution of corporations
—Cont'd
Procedure, §11-20-45.
Documents of corporations.
Filing for record without
payment of taxes or
certain fees, §11-20-46.
Earnings.
Disposition of net earnings,
§11-20-43.
Exemptions of corporations.
Competitive bid laws,
§11-20-49.
Interest rate laws,
§11-20-48.
Taxation, §11-20-47.
Usury laws, §11-20-48.
Incorporation.
Application for authority,
§11-20-32.
Certificate of incorporation.
Acknowledgment,
§11-20-33.
Amendment, §11-20-35.
Contents, §11-20-33.
Execution, §11-20-33.
Filing, §11-20-34.
May be filed for record
without payment of
taxes or certain fees,
§11-20-46.
Recordation, §11-20-34.
More than one corporation,
§11-20-32.
Resolution authorizing
incorporation,
§11-20-32.
Interest rates.
Exemptions of
corporations,
§11-20-48.
Legislative intent, §11-20-31.
Liability of county.
Bonds, obligations,
agreements, etc., of
corporations,
§11-20-42.
Powers of corporation,
§11-20-37.
Projects.
Defined, §11-20-30.
Location, §11-20-37.
Operation, §11-20-37.
Taxation.
Exemptions of
corporations,
§11-20-47.
Usury laws.
Exemptions of
corporations,
§11-20-48.
Industrial parks, §§11-23-1 to
11-23-8.
Abolition of park, §11-23-7.
Bylaws, §11-23-5.
County commissions.
Authority to establish
industrial park,
§11-23-1.
Resolution of designation
by county commission,
§11-23-3.
Designation as industrial
park.
Hearings.
Public hearing, §11-23-3.
Petition for, §11-23-1.

COUNTIES—Cont'd
　Industrial parks—Cont'd
　　Designation as industrial
　　　park—Cont'd
　　　Resolution of designation
　　　　by county commission,
　　　　§11-23-3.
　　Enforcement of land
　　　restrictions, §11-23-4.
　　Establishment.
　　　Autohrity of county
　　　　commissions, §11-23-1.
　　　Rights and responsibilities
　　　　of county not limited
　　　　by creation, §11-23-8.
　　Hearings.
　　　Public hearing, §11-23-3.
　　Includable land, §11-23-2.
　　Jurisdiction.
　　　County sheriff and courts,
　　　　§11-23-6.
　　Landowners.
　　　Written approval required,
　　　　§11-23-1.
　　Land which may be included,
　　　§11-23-2.
　　Maps and descriptive matter.
　　　Filing, §11-23-3.
　　Municipalities.
　　　Contracts for services,
　　　　§11-23-6.
　　　Parks not subject to
　　　　annexation or police
　　　　jurisdiction, §11-23-6.
　　Petition for designation,
　　　§11-23-1.
　　Powers of counties, §11-92-3.
　　Removal of territory from
　　　park, §11-23-7.
　　Restrictions on use of land
　　　following designation,
　　　§11-23-4.
　　Rights and responsibilities of
　　　county.
　　　Not limited by creation of
　　　　industrial park,
　　　　§11-23-8.
　　Roads.
　　　Public road access
　　　　required, §11-23-6.
　　Services within industrial
　　　parks.
　　　Bylaws listing facilities to
　　　　be furnished by
　　　　governing body of
　　　　park, §11-23-5.
　　　Certain services to be
　　　　provided by industries
　　　　within park, §11-23-6.
　　　Contracts with county or
　　　　municipalities for
　　　　services, §11-23-6.
　Industry and trade.
　　Industrial development
　　　boards, §§11-20-30 to
　　　11-20-50. See within this
　　　heading, "Industrial
　　　development boards."
　　Projects for promotion.
　　　Acquisition of projects.
　　　　County not to contribute
　　　　　costs or county
　　　　　lands, §11-20-11.
　　　　Powers of counties,
　　　　　§11-20-3.
　　　Bond issues.
　　　　Default.
　　　　　Remedies upon default,
　　　　　　§11-20-6.
　　　　Delivery, §11-20-5.
　　　　Denominations, §11-20-5.

COUNTIES—Cont'd
　Industry and trade—Cont'd
　　Projects for promotion
　　　—Cont'd
　　　Bond issues—Cont'd
　　　　Election not required,
　　　　　§11-20-13.
　　　　Execution, §11-20-5.
　　　　Exemption from
　　　　　taxation, §11-20-12.
　　　　Form, §11-20-5.
　　　　Interest, §11-20-5.
　　　　　Applicability of usury
　　　　　　laws, §11-20-5.
　　　　　Security for payment,
　　　　　　§11-20-6.
　　　　Investment in bonds by
　　　　　savings banks and
　　　　　insurance
　　　　　companies,
　　　　　§11-20-10.
　　　　Issuance.
　　　　　Powers of counties,
　　　　　　§11-20-3.
　　　　　Requirements,
　　　　　　§11-20-9.
　　　　Negotiability, §11-20-5.
　　　　Payment of principal and
　　　　　interest.
　　　　　Pledge of revenues,
　　　　　　§11-20-6.
　　　　　Security for payment,
　　　　　　§11-20-6.
　　　　Preissuance procedure
　　　　　for industrial
　　　　　revenue bonds,
　　　　　§§8-6-110 to 8-6-122.
　　　　　See INDUSTRIAL
　　　　　　REVENUE
　　　　　　BONDS.
　　　　Proceeds from sale.
　　　　　Disposition, §11-20-7.
　　　　Redemption, §11-20-5.
　　　　Refunding bonds,
　　　　　§11-20-8.
　　　　Remedies upon default,
　　　　　§11-20-6.
　　　　Sale, §11-20-5.
　　　　　Disposition of proceeds
　　　　　　from sale,
　　　　　　§11-20-7.
　　　　　Requirements,
　　　　　　§11-20-9.
　　　　Security for payment of
　　　　　principal and
　　　　　interest, §11-20-6.
　　　　Terms, §11-20-5.
　　　　Usury.
　　　　　Applicability of usury
　　　　　　laws, §11-20-5.
　　　Construction of chapter,
　　　　§§11-20-2, 11-20-13.
　　　Contributions by county.
　　　　Counties not to
　　　　　contribute costs of
　　　　　acquisition of
　　　　　projects or county
　　　　　lands, §11-20-11.
　　　Costs of acquisition of
　　　　projects.
　　　　Counties not to
　　　　　contribute,
　　　　　§11-20-11.
　　　County lands.
　　　　Not to be contributed,
　　　　　§11-20-11.
　　　Definitions, §11-20-1.
　　　Exemption from taxation of
　　　　projects, bonds, etc.,
　　　　§11-20-12.

COUNTIES—Cont'd
　Industry and trade—Cont'd
　　Projects for promotion
　　　—Cont'd
　　　Insurance companies.
　　　　Investment in bonds by,
　　　　　§11-20-10.
　　　Investments.
　　　　Savings banks and
　　　　　insurance companies
　　　　　may invest in bonds,
　　　　　§11-20-10.
　　　Leasing of projects.
　　　　Powers of counties,
　　　　　§11-20-3.
　　　　Requirements as to
　　　　　leasing, §11-20-4.
　　　Legislative intent,
　　　　§11-20-2.
　　　Mortgages and deeds of
　　　　trust.
　　　　Executions, §11-20-9.
　　　　Exemption from
　　　　　taxation, §11-20-12.
　　　　Remedies upon default of
　　　　　bonds, §11-20-6.
　　　　Security for payment of
　　　　　bonds, §11-20-6.
　　　Powers of counties.
　　　　Acquisition, leasing, etc.,
　　　　　of projects, §11-20-3.
　　　　Issuance of revenue
　　　　　bonds, §11-20-3.
　　　Savings banks.
　　　　Investment in bonds by
　　　　　savings banks,
　　　　　§11-20-10.
　　　Taxation.
　　　　Exemption from taxation
　　　　　of projects, bonds,
　　　　　etc., §11-20-12.
　Insurance.
　　County commissions.
　　　Powers and duties of
　　　　county commissions,
　　　　§11-3-11.
　　Group insurance for officers
　　　and employees.
　　　Amounts of insurance
　　　　under policies.
　　　　Determination, §11-91-3.
　　　　Requirements, §11-91-2.
　　　Appropriation of funds.
　　　　Implementation of
　　　　　provisions, §11-91-6.
　　　Authorization, §11-91-1.
　　　Contracting for policies,
　　　　§11-91-2.
　　　Coverage of policies.
　　　　Requirements, §11-91-2.
　　　Funds for implementation
　　　　of chapter.
　　　　Appropriation, §11-91-6.
　　　Implementation of chapter.
　　　　Appropriation of funds
　　　　　for, §11-91-6.
　　　Kind of insurance.
　　　　Determination, §11-91-3.
　　　Provision of health or
　　　　medical insurance
　　　　for retired
　　　　employees, §11-91-8.
　　　Nature of insurance.
　　　　Determination, §11-91-3.
　　　Payment of premiums,
　　　　§11-91-4.
　　　　Manner of paying,
　　　　　§11-91-3.
　　　Persons to be insured.
　　　　Determination, §11-91-3.

COUNTIES—Cont'd
Insurance—Cont'd
Group insurance for officers
and employees—Cont'd
Policies.
Amounts of insurance
under policies.
Requirements,
§11-91-2.
Contracting for policies,
§11-91-2.
Coverage.
Requirements,
§11-91-2.
Purchase of policies,
§11-91-2.
Validation of policies
issued prior to
August 16, 1947,
§11-91-7.
Premiums.
Payment, §11-91-4.
Manner of paying,
§11-91-3.
Validation of
premiums paid in
accordance with
certain policies,
§11-91-7.
Return of premiums,
§11-91-5.
Provision by governing
bodies authorized,
§11-91-1.
Purchase of policies,
§11-91-2.
Retired employees.
Provision for health or
medical insurance
for, §11-91-8.
Return of premiums,
§11-91-5.
Validation of policies, etc.,
§11-91-7.
Health and accident self-
insurance groups.
Appropriations, §11-26-2.
Attorneys and employees,
§11-26-4.
Authorized, §11-26-2.
Bylaws, §11-26-4.
Filing, §11-26-5.
Collection of charges,
§11-26-4.
Collection of funds,
§11-26-2.
Contracts with solvent
insurance companies,
§11-26-4.
Establishment, §11-26-2.
Exempt from insurance
premium tax, §11-26-5.
Exempt from regulation by
department of
insurance, §11-26-5.
Governing body of trustees.
Establishment, §11-26-4.
Management and
consultant contracts,
§11-26-4.
Officers.
Liability of officers of
nonprofit
associations,
§§10-11-1 to 10-11-5.
Powers, §11-26-4.
Purpose, §11-26-2.
Schedule of benefits,
§11-26-4.
Filing, §11-26-5.

COUNTIES—Cont'd
Insurance—Cont'd
Health and accident self-
insurance groups
—Cont'd
Schedule of charges,
§11-26-4.
Filing, §11-26-5.
Industry and trade.
Projects for promotion.
Investment in bonds by
insurance
companies,
§11-20-10.
Liability self-insurance
funds.
Appropriation of funds,
§11-30-2.
Bylaws.
Filing with state
insurance
commissioner,
§11-30-4.
Chapter not to impose tort
liability where not
already existing,
§11-30-6.
Claims against county.
Fund not subject to suit
by third party based
on, §11-30-7.
Coverage, §11-30-5.
Definitions, §11-30-1.
Establishment by two or
more counties,
§11-30-2.
Exemption from
regulation, §11-30-4.
Powers, §11-30-3.
Premium tax.
Exemption from,
§11-30-4.
Purposes, §11-30-2.
Schedule of benefits and
charges.
Filing, §11-30-4.
Scope of liability, §11-30-7.
Tort liability.
Chapter not to impose
where not already
existing by law,
§11-30-6.
Taxation.
Counties not permitted to
tax insurers, §27-4-9.
Interest.
Bond issues. See within this
heading, "Bond issues."
Claims and demands against
counties.
Requirements as to
interest coupons,
§11-12-4.
Industrial development
boards.
Exemption of corporation
from interest laws,
§11-20-48.
Maximum rates of interest.
Exemption of bonds, notes,
etc., of counties, §8-8-7.
Investments.
Public building authorities.
Investment of county funds
in warrants, §11-15-15.
Securities issued in
anticipation of grants.
Legal investment status,
§11-11B-6.
Sinking funds, §§11-81-19 to
11-81-21.

COUNTIES—Cont'd
Investments—Cont'd
Surplus funds.
Investment in United
States securities,
§11-8-11.
Warrants. See within this
heading, "Warrants."
Irrigation.
Water conservation and
irrigation. See within
this heading, "Water
conservation and
irrigation."
Jails.
Appropriations.
Expenditure of funds by
sheriff, §11-14-21.
Special meeting to make
special appropriations,
§§11-14-19, 11-14-20.
Arrangement, §11-14-13.
Buildings generally. See
within this heading,
"Buildings."
Construction, §11-14-13.
County commissions.
Duty to erect, §11-14-10.
Special meeting to make
special appropriations,
§§11-14-19, 11-14-20.
Deductions from sentence.
Computation of incentive
time deductions,
§14-9-41.
Good conduct time
previously earned.
Applicability of article,
§14-9-43.
Habitual offender laws.
Effect of article,
§14-9-44.
Nonretroactive effect of
article, §14-9-44.
Parole.
Effect of deductions on
parole, §14-9-42.
Erection.
Duty of county commission
to erect, §11-14-10.
Failure to levy tax for
erection when
necessary, §11-14-15.
Tax.
Levy of tax for erection,
§11-14-14.
Erection at relocated county
seats.
Removal of county
prisoners to new jail,
§11-16-29.
Examination of jail,
§11-14-22.
Health and sanitation.
County boards of health.
Duties, §22-3-2.
County health officers.
Duties, §22-3-5.
Examination of jail,
§11-14-22.
Sheriffs.
Duties, §11-14-21.
Municipal corporations.
Contracts with
municipalities as to
use of jails in
municipalities,
§11-80-3.

COUNTIES—Cont'd
Jails—Cont'd
Repair.
Failure to levy tax for
repair when necessary,
§11-14-15.
Levy of tax for repair,
§11-14-14.
Sheriffs.
Expenditure of
appropriations by
sheriff, §11-14-21.
Taxation.
Levy of tax for erection,
etc.
Failure to levy tax when
necessary, §11-14-15.
Special tax for jail,
§11-14-16.
Telephones.
Procuring and providing
telephones for jailers,
§11-3-11.
Judgments.
Bond issues.
Validation, §§6-6-753 to
6-6-755.
Cemeteries.
Appeals from assessment of
damages.
Entry of judgment for
damages and costs,
§11-17-11.
Jurisdiction.
Industrial parks, §11-23-6.
Navigable streams not
within limits of any
county, §11-1-3.
Jury.
Cemeteries.
Appeals from assessment of
damages.
Establishment of
damages by jury,
§11-17-10.
Summoning and
impaneling of jurors,
§11-17-9.
Jury commissions, §§12-16-30
to 12-16-51.
See JURY.
Juvenile proceedings.
Liability for costs, attorney's
fees, etc., §12-15-10.
Repeal of attorney fees
provisions, §12-15-10.1.
Labor.
Developing, advertising and
promoting labor
resources, §11-3-11.
Land-use management.
Flood-prone areas. See within
this heading, "Flood-
prone areas."
Law enforcement officers.
Overtime, §36-21-4.1.
Salaries.
Minimum starting salary,
§36-21-10.
Laws.
Codification of county laws,
§11-13-1.
Furnishing copies to
county officials,
§11-13-1.
Local bill introduced in
legislature.
Payment of cost of
advertising, §11-13-6.

COUNTIES—Cont'd
Laws—Cont'd
Publication of legislative
laws of local nature.
Authorized, §11-13-2.
Contracts for publication,
§11-13-3.
Copies.
Furnishing copies to
county and precinct
officers, §11-13-5.
Recordation, §11-13-5.
Costs, §11-13-4.
Recordation of copies,
§11-13-5.
Legislative reference service.
See LEGISLATURE.
Legislature.
Local bill introduced in
legislature.
Payment of cost of
advertising, §11-13-6.
Local laws.
Publication, §§11-13-2 to
11-13-5.
Letters of credit.
Security for bonds, notes,
etc., §11-80-7.
Liability.
Claims and demands against
counties. See within this
heading, "Claims and
demands against
counties."
Liability self-insurance
funds, §§11-30-1 to
11-30-7. See within this
heading, "Insurance."
Parks and recreation.
Bonds issued by public
park and recreation
boards, §11-22-14.
Libraries.
Boards.
Library boards, §§11-90-2,
11-90-3.
Establishment of free public
libraries.
Powers of counties as to
establishment,
§11-90-1.
Interstate library compact.
Restrictions as to
agreements, §41-8-23.
Joint library service.
Establishment and
maintenance, §11-90-4.
Law libraries, §§11-25-1 to
11-25-12.
See LIBRARIES.
Maintenance of free public
libraries.
Powers of counties as to
maintenance, §11-90-1.
Powers of counties as to,
§11-90-1.
Special property tax for
library purposes, Const.
Ala., amd. 269.
Licenses.
Bond issues.
Pledge of revenues from
licenses, §11-81-16.
County license tax for school
purposes.
Administration, §40-12-6.
Authority to levy, §40-12-4.
Collection, §§40-12-5,
40-12-6.
Charge for collecting,
§40-12-7.

COUNTIES—Cont'd
Licenses—Cont'd
County license tax for school
purposes—Cont'd
Collection—Cont'd
Disposition of funds
collected, §40-12-7.
Enforcement, §40-12-5.
Funds collected.
Disposition, §40-12-7.
Exemptions from licenses.
Disabled veterans,
§40-12-342.
Veterans of World War II,
§40-12-372.
Fish and game.
See FISH AND GAME.
Health care service plans.
License taxes by counties
prohibited, §10-4-107.
Industrial development
corporations, §10-4-144.
Levy of county tax, §40-12-2.
Collection and distribution
where state and county
tax levied, §40-12-3.
Requirement.
Who must procure county
licenses, §40-12-40.
Veterans.
Exemptions from licenses.
Disabled veterans,
§40-12-342.
Veterans of World War
II, §40-12-372.
Lime.
Acquisition of lands for lime
quarries, §11-14-23.
Conduct of condemnation
proceedings, §11-14-24.
Limitation of actions.
See LIMITATION OF
ACTIONS.
Livestock.
Appropriations to pay
premiums on livestock
exhibited, §11-3-11.
Dipping of cattle.
Indemnification of owners
for injuries, §§11-12-1
to 11-12-3.
Running at large.
Refunding of counties
where livestock kept
and fed in county
pounds, §3-5-11.
Loans.
Making loans in anticipation
of taxes.
Amount of loans, §11-10-2.
Authorized, §11-10-1.
Certificates evidencing
loans.
Cancellation, §11-10-4.
Exempt from taxation,
§11-10-5.
Issuance, §11-10-1.
Payment, §11-10-3.
Registration, §11-10-3.
Disposition of proceeds,
§11-10-2.
Exemption of certificates
from taxation,
§11-10-5.
Interest, §11-10-2.
Maturity, §11-10-2.
Pledge of uncollected taxes
to secure repayment,
§11-10-1.
Proceeds.
Disposition, §11-10-2.

COUNTIES—Cont'd

Loans—Cont'd

Making loans in anticipation of taxes—Cont'd

Refunding, §11-10-2.

Registration.

Certificates evidencing loans, §11-10-3.

Renewal, §11-10-2.

Repayment.

Pledge of uncollected taxes to secure, §11-10-1.

State and local fiscal assistance act of 1972, §11-10-6.

Exemption of certificates from taxation, §11-10-6.

No grant of public money or credit to individuals or corporations, Const. Ala., amd. 112.

State and local fiscal assistance act of 1972.

Making loans in anticipation of receipt of payment.

Exemption of certificates from taxation, §11-10-6.

Temporary loans.

Payment, §11-8-5.

To constitute part of annual county operating budget, §11-8-5.

Local laws.

Public roads, bridges and ferries.

Construction of article.

Not to conflict with local or special laws, §23-1-94.

Lost or unclaimed property.

Bond issues.

Issuance of duplicates for lost bonds, §11-81-32.

Lurleen B. Wallace memorial cancer hospital fund.

Appropriations by counties, §11-8-12.

Mandamus.

Special tax for payment of principal and interest on bonds and sinking fund payments.

Mandamus proceedings, §11-81-26.

Manufacturers.

Promotion of manufacturing plant, §11-3-11.

Maps and plats.

Assessment maps and plats.

Preparation, etc., §11-1-12.

County commissions.

Powers and duties, §11-3-11.

Flood-prone areas.

Land-use management in flood-prone areas. See within this heading, "Flood-prone areas."

Industrial parks.

Filing of maps, etc., §11-23-3.

Public lands.

Preparation of maps, §9-15-11.

COUNTIES—Cont'd

Maps and plats—Cont'd

Surveyors. See within this heading, "Surveys and surveyors."

Markets.

Public improvement bonds.

See within this heading, "Bond issues."

Mentally ill.

Regional mental health programs and facilities, §§22-51-1 to 22-51-14.

See MENTALLY ILL.

Merit system.

County engineers.

Effect of merit system laws, §11-6-5.

Engineers.

Effect of merit system laws, §11-6-5.

Military affairs.

Appropriations, §31-2-129.

Armories.

Acquisition of land for, §11-18-2.

Cooperation of counties, §31-4-9.

Public improvement bonds.

See within this heading, "Bond issues."

Armory commission.

Buildings.

Cooperation of counties for acquisition, §31-4-9.

Conveyance of public lands to commission, §31-4-11.

Donations for aid of local national guard or naval militia, §31-4-17.

Military service by county officers in time of national emergency, §§36-8-1 to 36-8-6.

See PUBLIC OFFICERS AND EMPLOYEES.

Real property.

Sale of real estate and buildings to local national guard units, §31-2-130.

Reversion of donations, §31-4-18.

Mines and minerals.

Acquisition of lands for public purposes.

Collection and exhibit of minerals, §11-18-2.

Developing, advertising and promoting mineral resources, §11-3-11.

Exhibit of mineral resources of county, §11-3-11.

Mistake.

Money erroneously paid into county treasury, etc.

Transfer to state treasury, §11-1-6.

Mortgages and deeds of trust.

Bond issues.

Execution upon property acquired with proceeds, §11-81-2.

Recordation, §11-81-2.

COUNTIES—Cont'd

Mortgages and deeds of trust—Cont'd

Industry and trade.

Projects for promotion. See within this heading, "Industry and trade."

Public property.

Mortgage for payment of debts, §11-81-27.

Sale under power.

Lands situated in two or more counties, §35-10-4.

Where held, §35-10-7.

Motor fuel.

Excise tax.

Exemptions, §40-17-220.

Taxation.

Public roads, bridges and ferries.

Expenditure of funds derived from taxes levied on fuels, §23-1-84.

Motor sports hall of fame commission.

Bonds not obligation of counties, §41-9-475.

Motor vehicle carriers.

Fees.

Public roads, bridges and ferries.

Expenditure of funds derived from fees levied on vehicles, §23-1-84.

Highway and traffic safety coordination act.

Powers of counties, §32-4-7.

Highway patrol.

Fees and costs.

When not to be paid by county, §32-2-25.

Powers generally, §32-5-1.

Tags.

County vehicles, §40-12-250.

Vehicles owned and operated by counties.

Exemptions from chapter, §37-3-4.

Motor vehicles.

Arrest made by county officers.

Disposition of fines and forfeitures, §32-5A-10.

Municipal corporations.

County buildings.

Improvements to sidewalks and streets adjoining.

Appropriations, §11-14-7.

Authorized, §11-14-6.

Ratification of and discharge from liability for prior payments, §11-14-8.

Courthouses located in municipalities.

Improvements which benefit property of county, §11-14-5.

Fire departments.

Contracts with counties, §11-43-142.

Hospitals, poorhouses, etc.

Establishment, aid, etc., §11-47-134.

COUNTIES—Cont'd
  Municipal corporations
    —Cont'd
    Public roads, bridges and
      ferries.
      Access roads or bridges to
        certain facilities.
      Aid for development by
        municipalities,
        §23-1-91.
      Establishment within
        municipalities,
        §23-1-86.
      Extension of aid by
        benefited
        municipalities,
        §23-1-90.
      Operation, etc., of bridges
        over navigable, etc.,
        streams.
        Bridges in incorporated
          cities, towns or
          municipalities,
          §11-3-17.
    Streets.
      Assumption of authority
        over streets controlled
        by counties,
        §§11-49-80, 11-49-81.
      Costs of streets
        constructed, improved,
        etc., by county, state
        or federal government,
        §§11-49-60 to 11-49-63.
    Subdivisions, §§11-52-30 to
      11-52-54.
      See MUNICIPAL
        CORPORATIONS.
    Waterworks plants and
      distribution systems.
      Conveyance to municipal
        corporations, §11-14-3.
  Museums.
    Powers of counties,
      §§11-18-2, 11-47-16.
  Music.
    Bands.
      Appropriations for bands,
        §11-80-4.
    Establishment, etc., of
      concert halls, §11-47-16.
  Names, §11-1-1.
  Navigation.
    Opening and cleaning
      navigable streams.
      County commission
        authorized to make
        contracts, §33-7-2.
  Notes.
    Bond issues.
      Anticipation notes.
        Negotiable notes in
          anticipation of sale
          of bonds, §11-81-28.
    Engraved signature.
      Execution with facsimile of
        signature, seal, etc.,
        §11-81-33.
    Execution.
      Anticipation notes,
        §11-81-28.
      Facsimile of signature,
        seal, etc., §11-81-33.
    Facsimile signature,
      §11-81-33.
    Issuance.
      Anticipation notes,
        §11-81-28.
    Maturity.
      Anticipation notes,
        §11-81-28.

COUNTIES—Cont'd
  Notes—Cont'd
    Redemption of securities
      generally. See within
      this heading,
      "Redemption of
      securities."
    Sale.
      Anticipation notes,
        §11-81-28. §11-3-11.
  Number of counties, §11-1-1.
  Officers.
    Accident insurance.
      Group insurance for
        officers and employees.
        See within this
        heading, "Insurance."
    Actions against county
      officials.
      Payment of costs of
        defense, §11-1-9.
    Appointment, §11-8-14.
    Bonds, surety.
      Official bond. See within
        this heading, "Bonds,
        surety."
    Claims and demands against
      counties.
      Office supplies for,
        §11-12-14.
    Code of ethics.
      See PUBLIC OFFICERS
        AND EMPLOYEES.
    Codification of county laws.
      Furnishing copies to
        county officials,
        §11-13-1.
    Conveyances to officers for
      use of county.
      Effect, §11-14-1.
    Coroners.
      See CORONERS.
    Deeds to officers for use of
      county.
      Effect, §11-14-1.
    Defense of lawsuits against
      county officials.
      Payment of costs, §11-1-9.
    Elections.
      List of officers elected by
        the people, §17-2-1.
      When officers elected,
        §17-2-4.
    Engineers. See within this
      heading, "Engineers."
    Ex officio fees, §11-8-13.
    Grand juries.
      Examination of bonds of
        county officers by
        grand jury, §12-16-192.
    Grants to officers for use of
      county.
      Effect, §11-14-1.
    Impeachment, Const. Ala.,
      art. VII, §175.
    Insurance.
      Group insurance for
        officers and employees,
        §§11-91-1 to 11-91-7.
        See within this
        heading, "Insurance."
    Lawsuits against county
      officials.
      Payment of costs of
        defense, §11-1-9.
    Oaths.
      Filing, §36-4-4.
    Offices.
      Closing one weekday each
        week, §11-1-8.
      Supplies, §11-8-13.

COUNTIES—Cont'd
  Officers—Cont'd
    Official bonds. See within
      this heading, "Bonds,
      surety."
    Pension and retirement
      plans. See within this
      heading, "Pension and
      retirement plans."
    Publication of legislative
      laws of local nature.
      Furnishing copies to
        county and precinct
        officers, §11-13-5.
    Salaries.
      Increase or decrease in
        salaries, Const. Ala.,
        amd. 92.
      Suspension of restriction
        on diminishing public
        salaries, Const. Ala.,
        amd. 26A.
    Supplies, §11-8-13.
      Office supplies, §11-8-13.
    Surveyors. See within this
      heading, "Surveys and
      surveyors."
    Terms of office.
      Commencement, §36-2-10.
      County tax assessors,
        §36-3-5.
      County tax collectors,
        §36-3-6.
      Generally, §36-3-4.
    Traveling expenses.
      Advancement.
        Resolution.
          Adoption by governing
            body prior to
            travel, §36-7-3.
      Reimbursement.
        Approval, §§36-7-1,
          36-7-2.
        Disallowance, §36-7-2.
        Statement of expenses.
          Presentation, §§36-7-1,
            36-7-2.
      Statement of expenses.
        Approval, §36-7-4.
        Effect of failure to
          present and secure
          approval, §36-7-4.
        Presentation, §36-7-4.
      Warrant on treasury in
        violation of provisions,
        §36-7-5.
    Treasurers. See within this
      heading, "Treasurers."
    Vacancies in office.
      Filling.
        Generally, §36-9-17.
  Offices.
    Closing of offices of county
      officials one weekday
      each week, §11-1-8.
    Records and papers in county
      offices.
      District attorney and grand
        jury entitled to
        examine, §12-16-196.
    Relocation of county seats.
      Removal of county offices
        to new courthouse,
        §11-16-29.
      Timing, §11-16-31.
  Official bonds. See within
    this heading, "Bonds,
    surety."

COUNTIES—Cont'd
Oil and gas.
Funds.
Severance tax trust funds, §40-20-50.
Petroleum products.
Use of fees, §8-17-91.
Privilege tax on production.
Allocation and distribution of net taxes collected to counties, §40-20-8.
Exemption from ad valorem tax levied by counties, §40-20-12.
Funds.
Severance tax trust funds, §40-20-50.
Levy of taxes by counties, §40-20-2.
Severance tax trust funds, §40-20-50.
Parks and recreation.
Acquisition of lands for public parks or recreational purposes.
Adjoining counties.
Acquisition of lands in adjoining counties, §11-18-22.
Appropriation of funds, §11-18-23.
Authorized, §11-18-21.
Cooperation by counties, §11-18-24.
Definitions, §11-18-20.
Expenditure of funds, §11-18-23.
Alienation of certain public improvements by political subdivisions, §§35-4-410 to 35-4-412.
Boards.
Construction of chapter, §11-22-18.
Definitions, §11-22-1.
Directors.
Board of directors, §11-22-7.
Disposition of surplus revenue, §11-22-15.
Dissolution, §11-22-16.
Incorporation.
Application for authority to incorporate, §11-22-3.
Approval.
Resolution of approval, §11-22-3.
Certificate of incorporation.
Amendments, §11-22-6.
Contents, §11-22-4.
Execution, §11-22-4.
Filing, §11-22-5.
Recording, §11-22-5.
Defective incorporation, §11-22-6.
More than one corporation, §11-22-3.
Resolution of approval, §11-22-3.
Intent of legislature, §11-22-2.
Nonprofit status, §11-22-15.
Powers.
Generally, §11-22-8.

COUNTIES—Cont'd
Parks and recreation—Cont'd
Boards—Cont'd
Projects.
Partially within county, §11-22-8.
Recordation of instrument, §11-22-17.
Recreation boards.
See PARKS AND RECREATION.
Surplus revenue.
Disposition, §11-22-15.
Transfer of assets from other public corporations, §11-22-19.
Bond issues.
Authorization of issuance.
Notice of authorization, §11-22-11.
Boards.
Borrowing money.
Temporary borrowing, §11-22-12.
Tax exemptions, §11-22-13.
Temporary borrowing, §11-22-12.
Construction of chapter, §11-22-18.
Default, §11-22-10.
Execution, §11-22-9.
Exemptions from taxation, §11-22-13.
Form, §11-22-9.
Funds for payment, §11-22-9.
Issuance.
Notice of authorization of issuance, §11-22-11.
Liability of county, §11-22-14.
Mortgages and deeds of trust.
Securing principal and interest, §11-22-10.
Negotiability, §11-22-9.
Notice of authorization of issuance, §11-22-11.
Payment.
Funds for payment, §11-22-9.
Liability of county, §11-22-14.
Securing of principal and interest, §11-22-10.
Public improvement bonds.
See within this heading, "Bond issues."
Redemption, §11-22-9.
Refunding, §11-22-9.
Sale, §11-22-9.
Securing of principal and interest, §11-22-10.
Surplus revenue.
Disposition, §11-22-15.
Tax exemptions, §11-22-13.
Establishment of parks.
Appropriation and expenditure of funds, §11-18-23.
Maintenance of parks.
Appropriation and expenditure of funds, §11-18-23.
Recreation boards, §§11-86-1 to 11-86-6.
See PARKS AND RECREATION.

COUNTIES—Cont'd
Partition.
Probate courts.
Partition of land lying partly in different counties, §35-6-41.
Unclaimed money.
Deposit in county treasury, §35-6-1.
Peace officers' standards and training commission.
Appropriations by counties, §36-21-48.
Penalties.
Fine and forfeiture fund.
Transfer of balance to general fund, §11-4-25.
Land-use management in flood-prone areas.
Penalties for violations of provisions, §11-19-22.
Public roads, bridges and ferries.
Rules and regulations.
Violations, §23-5-14.
Relocation of county seats.
Penalties for failure to perform duties, §11-16-40.
Semiannual publication of county receipts and expenditures.
Failure to publish, §11-3-23.
Voting against publication, §11-3-22.
Surveyors.
Obstruction of surveyor, §11-7-5.
Pension and retirement plans.
Administration of funds.
Applicability of chapter, §36-31-3.
Trustees.
Compensation, §36-31-2.
Designation, §36-31-1.
Powers and duties.
Prescription, §36-31-1.
Board of human resources.
See WELFARE.
Department of human resources.
See WELFARE.
State employees' retirement system.
Participation of county employees, §36-27-6.
Permits.
Land-use management in flood-prone areas.
Construction and development, §11-19-7.
Petitions.
Cemeteries.
Petition for appointment of commission, §11-17-1.
Relocation of county seats.
See within this heading, "County seats."
Planning commissions.
Comprehensive advisory planning and research.
Powers of local planning commissions, §11-85-40.

COUNTIES—Cont'd
Planning commissions
—Cont'd
Flood-prone areas.
Land-use management in
flood-prone areas,
§§11-19-8 to 11-19-10,
11-19-17.
Record of transactions,
etc., §11-19-9.
Plats.
Maps and plats. See within
this heading, "Maps and
plats."
**Pledge and collateral
security.**
Depositories, §11-4-42.
Poor persons.
Relief and support by
counties.
See INDIGENT PERSONS.
Precincts.
Alteration, etc., of precinct
lines, §11-1-13.
Provision of voting places,
§11-1-14.
New precincts.
Creation, §11-1-13.
Provision of voting places,
§11-1-14.
Priorities.
Claims and demands against
counties.
Preferred claims and order
of their priority,
§11-12-15.
Prisons and prisoners.
County convicts, §§14-4-1 to
14-4-14.
See PRISONS AND
PRISONERS.
Jails.
See JAILS.
Work release, §§14-8-30 to
14-8-44.
See PRISONS AND
PRISONERS.
Private roads.
See ROADS.
Probate judges.
Bonds, surety.
General provisions. See
within this heading,
"Bonds, surety."
Proceedings as to
sufficiency of bonds,
§§11-2-30 to 11-2-34.
Books.
Claims against counties for
books, §11-12-14.
Claims and demands against
counties.
Books, stationery,
telephones, etc., for
probate judge,
§11-12-14.
County commissions.
Chairman of county
commissions, §11-3-1.
Special clerk to attend
meetings in absence of
probate judge,
§11-3-19.
Inspection of county jails,
§11-14-22.
Jefferson county.
Additional judgeship for
county, Const. Ala.,
amd. 384.

COUNTIES—Cont'd
Probate judges—Cont'd
Stamps.
Claims against counties for
postage stamps,
§11-12-14.
Stationery.
Claims against counties for
stationery, §11-12-14.
Telephones.
Claims against counties for
telephones, §11-12-14.
Procuring and providing
telephones for offices,
§11-3-11.
Property.
Acquisition of lands for
public purposes.
Authorized, §11-18-1.
Board of trustees, §11-18-3.
Contributions by county,
state, etc., §11-18-3.
Drainage ditches.
Lime and stone quarries,
etc., §11-14-23.
Parks and recreation. See
within this heading,
"Parks and
recreation."
Trust fund, §11-18-3.
Uses of lands, §11-18-2.
Actions for recovery.
No limitation, §6-2-31.
Conveyances.
Generally, §11-14-2.
Public building authorities.
Conveyance of property
to corporation by
county, §11-15-16.
Waterworks plants and
distribution systems.
Conveyance to municipal
corporations,
§11-14-3.
County commissions.
Powers and duties of
county commissions,
§11-3-11.
Custody, §11-14-2.
Deeds, grants, etc., to
officers, etc., for use of
county.
Effect, §11-14-1.
Parks and recreation.
Acquisition of lands for
public purposes. See
within this heading,
"Parks and
recreation."
Public building authorities.
Conveyance of property to
corporation by county,
§11-15-16.
Powers of authority,
§11-15-7.
Publication.
Laws, §§11-13-2 to 11-13-5.
Semiannual publication of
county receipts and
expenditures, §§11-3-19
to 11-3-21.
Public building authorities.
Board of directors.
Defined, §11-15-1.
Generally, §11-15-6.
Construction of chapter,
§11-15-2.
Conveyance of property to
corporation by county,
§11-15-16.

COUNTIES—Cont'd
Public building authorities
—Cont'd
Corporation.
Defined, §11-15-1.
County funds.
Investment in warrants,
§11-15-15.
Coupons.
Defined, §11-15-1.
Definitions, §11-15-1.
Dissolution, §11-15-18.
Evidence.
Records of proceedings,
§11-15-6.
Exemption from taxation.
Projects.
Income from leases,
warrants, etc.,
§11-15-17.
Governing bodies.
Defined, §11-15-1.
Income from leases,
warrants, etc.
Exemption from taxation,
§11-15-17.
Incorporation.
Authorized, §11-15-3.
Certificate of incorporation,
§§11-15-4, 11-15-5.
§11-15-4.
Recordation, §11-15-5.
Procedure, §11-15-3.
Investments.
County funds may be
invested in warrants,
§11-15-15.
Leases,
Income from leases.
Exemption from
taxation, §11-15-17.
Legislative intent, §11-15-2.
Mortgages and deeds of
trusts.
Defined, §11-15-1.
Officers of corporation.
Execution of warrants,
§11-15-11.
Generally, §11-15-6.
Powers.
Generally, §11-15-7.
Projects.
Defined, §11-15-1.
Exemption from taxation,
§11-15-17.
Leasing to counties,
§11-15-8.
Property.
Conveyance to corporation
by county, §11-15-16.
Powers of authority,
§11-15-7.
Recordation.
Certificate of incorporation,
§11-15-5.
Records of proceedings,
§11-15-6.
Refunding warrants,
§11-15-14.
Resolutions.
Notice of warrant
resolution, §11-15-10.
Warrants.
Actions to question
proceedings for
issuance, §11-15-10.
Authorized, §11-15-9.
County funds.
Investment in warrants,
§11-15-15.
Default, §11-15-12.

COUNTIES—Cont'd
Public building authorities
—Cont'd
Warrants—Cont'd
Defined, §11-15-1.
Delivery, §11-15-11.
Denominations, §11-15-9.
Disposition of proceeds
from sale, §11-15-13.
Dissolution of corporation,
§11-15-18.
Execution, §11-15-11.
Exemption from taxation,
§11-15-17.
Form, §11-15-9.
For sale.
Proceeds.
Disposition of proceeds,
§11-15-13.
Interest, §11-15-9.
Security for payment,
§11-15-12.
Invalidation, §11-15-10.
Investment of county funds
in warrants, §11-15-15.
Issuance.
Actions to question
proceedings for
issuance, §11-15-10.
Authority for issuance,
§11-15-9.
Maturity, §11-15-9.
Notice of warrant
resolution, §11-15-10.
Payment of principal and
interest.
Security for payment,
§11-15-12.
Powers of authority,
§11-15-6.
Proceeds from sale.
Disposition, §11-15-13.
Redemption, §11-15-9.
Refunding warrants,
§11-15-14.
Resolutions.
Notice, §11-15-10.
Sale, §11-15-9.
Security for payment of
principal and interest,
§11-15-12.
Terms, §11-15-9.
Public buildings. See within
this heading, "Buildings."
Public contracts.
General provisions, §§41-16-1
to 41-16-125.
See CONTRACTS.
Public improvements.
Bond issues, §§11-81-140 to
11-81-150. See within
this heading, "Bond
issues."
Housing projects.
Alienation of certain public
improvements,
§§35-4-410 to 35-4-412.
Improvement authorities,
§§39-7-1 to 39-7-34.
See PUBLIC WORKS.
Parks and recreation.
Alienation of certain public
improvements,
§§35-4-410 to 35-4-412.
Public lands.
Effect of article.
Local laws governing
ownership, §9-15-19.

COUNTIES—Cont'd
Public lands—Cont'd
Maps.
Ownership and location of
public lands.
Preparation of county
maps, §9-15-11.
Tax assessors.
Lists of used and unused
lands.
Preparation for county
assessor, §9-15-12.
Notice of acquisition or
disposition of lands,
§9-15-12.
**Public roads, bridges and
ferries.**
Adjoining counties.
Access roads or bridges to
certain facilities.
Aid for development,
§23-1-91.
Establishment of facilities
between counties.
Authority of counties,
§23-1-88.
Expenses.
Extension of aid by
other counties,
§23-1-89.
Payment by bond
issue, §23-1-87.
Proration, §23-1-87.
Extension of aid by other
counties, §23-1-89.
Bond issues.
Adjoining counties.
Establishment of
facilities between
counties, §23-1-87.
Public improvement bonds.
See within this
heading, "Bond
issues."
Captive counties.
Contracts.
Existing contracts,
§23-1-105.
County commissions.
Powers and duties,
§23-1-101.
Defined, §23-1-100.
Disposition of funds
received by state from
counties, §23-1-106.
Effective date of article,
§23-1-107.
Effect of article upon
outstanding financial
obligations, §23-1-106.
Employees, §23-1-104.
Federal aid accruals.
Payment to counties,
§23-1-102.
Highway department
facilities and
properties.
Transferred to counties,
§23-1-103.
Taxation.
Payment to counties of
proceeds, §23-1-102.
Unexpended funds
maintained by state
highway department.
Transferred to counties,
§23-1-102.
Change.
Authority of county
commissions, §11-3-10.

COUNTIES—Cont'd
**Public roads, bridges and
ferries**—Cont'd
Closing and vacating streets,
alleys and highways.
Authority of county
commissions, §11-3-10.
General provisions,
§§23-4-1 to 23-4-20.
See HIGHWAYS.
Construction.
Captive counties.
County commissions.
Powers and duties,
§23-1-101.
Effect of article on
existing contracts,
§23-1-105.
County commissions.
Powers and duties,
§23-1-80.
Captive counties,
§23-1-101.
Highway department.
Consultation with
department,
§23-1-40.
Planning commission
approval, §11-85-7.
Special tax authorized,
§11-14-11.
Construction of article.
Not to conflict with local or
special laws, §23-1-94.
Contracts.
Advertising for bids.
Requirements, §23-1-92.
Exceptions, §23-1-93.
Bid guaranty, §23-1-2.
Captive counties.
Effect of article upon
contracts, §23-1-105.
County commissions.
Powers, §23-1-80.
Emergency repairs.
Exceptions to advertising
for bids, §23-1-93.
Convicts.
Work on public roads.
See PRISONS AND
PRISONERS.
County buildings.
Payment for improvements
benefiting county
buildings, §§11-14-6 to
11-14-8.
County commissions.
Authority as to
establishment, etc.,
§11-3-10.
Captive counties,
§23-1-101.
Eminent domain.
Authority of county
commissions,
§23-1-82.
Powers and duties.
Captive counties,
§23-1-101.
Establishment of bridges,
ferries and
causeways, §23-1-81.
General provisions,
§23-1-80.
Purchase of bridges,
ferries and
causeways, §23-1-81.
Discontinuance.
Authority of county
commissions, §11-3-10.

COUNTIES—Cont'd
Public roads, bridges and ferries—Cont'd
Drainage ditches.
Acquisition of lands for drainage ditches, §§11-14-23, 11-14-24.
Eminent domain.
Appeals, §23-1-82.
Authority of county commissions, §23-1-82.
Condemnation of lands, §11-80-1.
Erection.
Special tax authorized, §11-14-11.
Establishment.
Authority of county commissions, §11-3-10.
Bridges, ferries and causeways, §23-1-81.
Facilities and properties for construction and maintenance.
Transfer to counties by highway department, §23-1-103.
Forests and forestry.
National forests.
Distribution and expenditure of receipts from, §9-13-2.
Funds.
Captive counties.
Disposition of funds received by state from counties, §23-1-106.
Transfer to counties of unexpended funds, §23-1-102.
Fees levied on vehicles and fuels.
Expenditure, §23-1-84.
Road fund.
Transfer of general fund surplus, §23-1-83.
Gravel and gravel pits.
Acquisition of lands, §§11-14-23, 11-14-24.
Highways.
See HIGHWAYS.
Hunting from or near roads, §9-11-257.
Industrial parks.
Public road.
Access required, §11-23-6.
Interstate highway system.
See HIGHWAYS.
Littering.
See HIGHWAYS.
Local laws.
Construction of article.
Not to conflict with local or special laws, §23-1-94.
Maintenance.
Captive counties.
County commissions.
Powers and duties, §23-1-101.
Effect of article upon existing contracts, §23-1-105.
County commissions.
Powers and duties, §23-1-80.
Captive counties, §23-1-101.

COUNTIES—Cont'd
Public roads, bridges and ferries—Cont'd
Maintenance—Cont'd
Special tax authorized, §11-14-11.
Motor fuels.
Fees and taxes.
Expenditure of funds derived from, §23-1-84.
Motor vehicles.
Fees and taxes.
Expenditure of funds derived from, §23-1-84.
Municipal corporations.
Access roads or bridges to certain facilities.
Aid for development by municipalities, §23-1-91.
Assumption of authority over streets controlled by counties, §§11-49-80, 11-49-81.
Establishment within municipalities, §23-1-86.
Extension of aid by benefited municipalities, §23-1-90.
Operation, etc., of bridges over navigable streams.
Authority where bridges in municipal corporations, §11-3-17.
Operation, etc., of bridges over navigable, etc., streams.
Authorized, §§11-3-15, 11-3-17.
Expenditure of county funds, §11-3-15.
Joint operation by several counties, §11-3-16.
Municipal corporations.
Location in, §11-3-17.
Public utilities.
Contracting for use of public roads, §10-5-14.
Purchase.
Bridges, ferries and causeways.
Authority of county commissions, §23-1-81.
Quarries.
Acquisition of lands for lime and stone quarries, §§11-14-23, 11-14-24.
Rights of way.
Public utilities.
Construction of facilities, §23-1-85.
Road fund.
Transfer of general fund surplus, §23-1-83.
Rules and regulations.
County commissions.
Promulgation, §23-1-80.
Penalties.
Violations, §23-5-14.
Promulgation.
County commissions, §23-1-80.

COUNTIES—Cont'd
Public roads, bridges and ferries—Cont'd
Rules and regulations —Cont'd
Violations, §23-1-95.
Penalties, §23-5-14.
Sand and sand pits.
Acquisition of lands for, §§11-14-23, 11-14-24.
State highway department.
Responsibility for county roads in state highway department, Const. Ala., amd. 142.
Taxation.
Apportionment between counties and municipalities.
Maintenance of municipal streets declared county matter, §11-83-1.
One half of road tax collected in county to be paid to municipalities, §11-83-2.
Use of taxes paid over to municipalities, §11-83-3.
Special tax authorized, §11-14-11; Const. Ala., art. XI, §215; amd. 208.
Disposition of excess proceeds, §11-14-11.
Transferred to state highway department.
Employees used on.
Residents of county, §23-1-36.
Responsibility for county roads in state highway department, Const. Ala., amd. 142.
Warrants for construction of public buildings, bridges and roads, §§11-28-1 to 11-28-7. See within this heading, "Warrants."
Public school funds.
Applicability of finance chapter, §11-8-17.
General provisions.
See EDUCATION.
Public utilities.
Bond issues.
Alternate borrowing for electric systems, §§11-81-200 to 11-81-206. See within this heading, "Electricity."
Public improvement bonds, §§11-81-140 to 11-81-150. See within this heading, "Bond issues."
Construction.
Planning commission approval, §11-85-7.
Definitions.
Revenue bonds for waterworks, gas, sewer or electric systems, §11-81-160.

COUNTIES—Cont'd
Public utilities—Cont'd
Electricity.
Alternate borrowing for
electric systems,
§§11-81-200 to
11-81-206. See within
this heading,
"Electricity."
General provisions. See
within this heading,
"Electricity."
Improvement authorities,
§§39-7-1 to 39-7-34.
See PUBLIC WORKS.
Public improvement bonds,
§§11-81-140 to
11-81-150. See within
this heading, "Bond
issues."
Eminent domain.
Land-use management in
flood-prone areas,
§11-19-24.
Fees.
Inspection and supervision
fees.
Assessment by counties
prohibited, §37-4-23.
Franchises and intangibles.
Local taxes on, §40-21-26.
Apportionment of local
taxes, §40-21-27.
Entry and collection,
§40-21-28.
Gas.
General provisions. See
within this heading,
"Gas."
Improvement authorities,
§§39-7-1 to 39-7-34.
See PUBLIC WORKS.
Improvement authorities,
§§39-7-1 to 39-7-34.
See PUBLIC WORKS.
Inspection and supervision
fees.
Assessment by counties
prohibited, §37-4-23.
Public roads, bridges and
ferries.
Contracts for use of public
roads and places by
public utility
corporations, §10-5-14.
Rights of way.
Construction of facilities,
§23-1-85.
Revenue bonds for
waterworks, gas, sewer
or electric systems,
§§11-81-160 to 11-81-190.
Acquisition, etc., of
systems.
Authorized, §11-81-161.
Estimate of costs,
§11-81-162.
Alternate borrowing for
electric systems. See
within this heading,
"Electricity."
Anticipatory borrowing,
§11-81-165.
Construction of article,
§11-81-190.
Contracts.
Impairment of valid
contracts not
authorized by
article, §11-81-189.

COUNTIES—Cont'd
Public utilities—Cont'd
Revenue bonds for
waterworks, gas, sewer
or electric systems
—Cont'd
Default in payment.
Appointment and powers
of receiver upon
default, §11-81-180.
Delivery of bonds,
§11-81-166.
Denominations of bonds,
§11-81-166.
Disposition of proceeds
from sale, §§11-81-169,
11-81-170.
Elections.
Not required for issuance
and sale of bonds,
§11-81-176.
Execution of bonds,
§11-81-166.
Executors and
administrators.
Investment in bonds,
§11-81-177.
Exemption from taxation,
§11-81-172.
Fiduciaries.
Investment in bonds,
§11-81-177.
Form of bonds,
§11-81-166.
Insurance companies.
Investment in bonds,
§11-81-177.
Investment in bonds.
Generally, §11-81-177.
Issuance of bonds.
Authorization
proceedings,
§11-81-166.
Limitation period for
actions to set
aside, §11-81-164.
Notice of adoption,
§11-81-164.
Borrowing in
anticipation of
issuance,
§11-81-165.
Elections.
Not required for
issuance,
§11-81-176.
Ordinances.
Adoption, amendment,
recordation, etc.,
§11-81-163.
Publication not
required for
issuance and sale,
§11-81-176.
Resolutions.
Adoption, amendment,
recordation, etc.,
§11-81-163.
Publication not
required for
issuance,
§11-81-176.
Restraining issuance.
Limitation period for
actions to restrain
issuance,
§11-81-164.

COUNTIES—Cont'd
Public utilities—Cont'd
Revenue bonds for
waterworks, gas, sewer
or electric systems
—Cont'd
Liens.
Impairment, etc., of valid
liens not authorized
by article,
§11-81-189.
Statutory mortgage lien
of bondholders,
§§11-81-178,
11-81-179.
Limitation of actions.
Actions to set aside
authorization
proceedings or
restrain issuance of
bonds, §11-81-164.
Limitations in certain
other provisions of
chapter as to bonds.
Applicability of
limitations,
§11-81-175.
Maturity of bonds,
§11-81-166.
Negotiability, §11-81-168.
Ordinances, §11-81-163.
Publication not required
for issuance and sale
of bonds, §11-81-176.
Payment of bonds,
§11-81-166.
Default in payment.
Appointment of
receiver upon
default,
§11-81-180.
Powers of receiver
upon default,
§11-81-180.
Pledge of revenues from
systems for payment,
§11-81-181.
Pledge of revenues from
systems for payment of
bonds, §11-81-181.
Proceeds from sale of
bonds.
Disposition, §§11-81-169,
11-81-170.
Receivers.
Default in payment.
Appointment and
powers of receiver,
§11-81-180.
Redemption, §11-81-171.
Refunding bonds,
§11-81-172.1.
Resolutions.
Issuance of bonds, etc.
Adoption, amendment,
recordation, etc.,
§11-81-163.
Publication not required
for issuance and sale
of bonds, §11-81-176.
Restraining issuance.
Limitation period for
actions to restrain
issuance, §11-81-164.
Sale of bonds, §11-81-166.
Borrowing in
anticipation of sale,
§11-81-165.

COUNTIES—Cont'd
Public utilities—Cont'd
Revenue bonds for
waterworks, gas, sewer
or electric systems
—Cont'd
Sale of bonds—Cont'd
Disposition of proceeds
from sale,
§§11-81-169,
11-81-170.
Elections.
Not required for sale,
§11-81-176.
Ordinances.
Publication not
required for sale,
§11-81-176.
Proceeds from sale.
Disposition,
§11-81-169.
Excess proceeds,
§11-81-170.
Use, §11-81-170.
Resolutions.
Publication not
required for sale,
§11-81-176.
Savings banks.
Investment in bonds,
§11-81-177.
Segregation of revenues.
Ordinances or
resolutions,
§11-81-163.
Statutory mortgage lien of
bondholders.
Creation, §11-81-178.
Duration, §11-81-179.
Enforcement, §11-81-179.
Filing of notice,
§11-81-178.
Notice of lien,
§11-81-178.
Taxation.
Exemption from
taxation, §11-81-172.
Terms of bonds,
§11-81-166.
Trustees.
Investment in bonds,
§11-81-177.
Trust indentures,
§11-81-166.
Revenues.
Pledge of revenues from
utilities, §11-81-16.
Sewers.
General provisions. See
within this heading,
"Sewers."
Improvement authorities,
§§39-7-1 to 39-7-34.
See PUBLIC WORKS.
Taxation.
Franchises and intangibles.
Local taxes on,
§§40-21-26 to
40-21-28.
Water, sewer and fire
protection authorities,
§§11-88-1 to 11-88-111.
See WATER, SEWER AND
FIRE PROTECTION
AUTHORITIES.
Water, sewer and fire
protection districts,
§§11-89-1 to 11-89-19.
See WATER, SEWER AND
FIRE PROTECTION
DISTRICTS.

COUNTIES—Cont'd
Public utilities—Cont'd
Water supply and
waterworks.
General provisions. See
within this heading,
"Water supply and
waterworks."
Improvement authorities,
§§39-7-1 to 39-7-34.
See PUBLIC WORKS.
Public works.
Radioactive fallout
protection.
Requirement in new public
buildings or structures
and additions, §39-6-2.
Water, sewer and fire
protection authorities,
§§11-88-1 to 11-88-111.
See WATER, SEWER AND
FIRE PROTECTION
AUTHORITIES.
Water, sewer and fire
protection districts,
§§11-89-1 to 11-89-19.
See WATER, SEWER AND
FIRE PROTECTION
DISTRICTS.
Purchases.
Joint purchasing agreements,
§41-16-21.1.
Public roads, bridges and
ferries.
Bridges, ferries and
causeways.
Authority of county
commission,
§23-1-81.
Quarantine.
County commissions.
Powers and duties,
§11-3-11.
County quarantine officers,
§22-3-8.
Enforcement.
Local quarantine,
§22-12-13.
Expense, §22-12-16.
Quarantine of infected
portions of county,
§22-12-15.
General provisions.
See QUARANTINE.
Infected portions of county.
Enforcement, §22-12-15.
Establishment of
quarantine, §22-12-14.
Proclamation in counties,
§22-12-12.
Report of local quarantine to
state, §22-12-17.
Quarries.
Lime and stone quarries.
Acquisition of lands for
lime and stone
quarries, §11-14-23.
Conduct of condemnation
proceedings,
§11-14-24.
Radiation.
Effect of chapter on local
ordinances, §22-14-15.
Radio utilities.
Inspection and supervision
fees.
Prohibited, §37-4-116.
Railroad authorities.
Cooperation by counties,
§37-13-9.

COUNTIES—Cont'd
Railroads.
Rights-of-way.
Abandoned rights of way.
Authorized to transfer to
county commission,
§10-5-2.1.
Real property.
Warrants for construction of
public buildings, bridges
and roads.
Generally, §§11-28-1 to
11-28-7. See within
this heading,
"Warrants."
Receipts.
Depositories.
Performance of duties
other than receipt and
disbursement of funds,
§11-4-50.
Statement of receipts,
§11-4-46.
Forests and forestry.
National forests.
Distribution and
expenditure of
receipts from
national forests,
§9-13-2.
Semiannual publication of
county receipts and
expenditures, §§11-3-19
to 11-3-21.
Recordation.
Cemeteries.
Damages from taking of
property, etc.
Recordation of
proceedings upon
payment of costs,
§11-17-5.
Conveyances recorded in
county where property
situated, §35-4-62.
Official bonds, §11-2-3.
Publication of legislative
laws of local nature.
Recordation of copies,
§11-13-5.
Public building authorities.
Certificate of incorporation,
§11-15-5.
Relocation of county seats.
Recordation of certified
copy of election result,
§11-16-25.
Treasurers.
Annual account.
Recordation and posting
of copy, §11-4-28.
Records.
County commissions.
Preparation of record of
proceedings, §11-3-18.
Destroyed records.
Claims against counties to
be registered when
county records
destroyed by fire,
§11-12-9.
Establishment or
restoration, §12-20-50.
Replacement of destroyed
record books, §11-3-24.
District attorney entitled to
examine, §12-16-196.
Examinations.
District attorney and grand
jury entitled to
examine, §12-16-196.

COUNTIES—Cont'd
Records—Cont'd
Financial status. See within this heading, "Finance."
Fire.
Claims against counties to be registered when county records destroyed by fire, §11-12-9.
Grand jury entitled to examine, §12-16-196.
Local government records commission, §§41-13-22 to 41-13-25.
Lost records.
Establishment or restoration, §12-20-50.
Photographing or microphotographing.
Appropriation of funds, §41-13-43.
Planning commissions.
Land-use management in flood-prone areas.
Record of transactions, etc., §11-19-9.
Public building authorities.
Records of proceedings, §11-15-6.
Relocation of county seats.
Removal of records to new courthouse, §11-16-29.
Replacement of destroyed record books, §11-3-24.
Semiannual publication of county receipts and expenditures, §§11-3-21 to 11-3-23.
Recreation. See within this heading, "Parks and recreation."
Redemption of securities.
Applicability of provisions of chapter, §11-82-6.
Definitions, §11-82-1.
Limitation on redemption prices, §11-82-4.
Option to redeem.
Defined, §11-82-1.
Retention of option, §§11-82-2, 11-82-3.
To be provided in proceedings for issuance of securities, §11-82-5.
Prices.
Limitation on redemption prices, §11-82-4.
Retention of option to redeem, §11-82-2.
Securities maturing more than 10 years after date, §11-82-3.
Validation of certain proceedings, §11-82-7.
Regional planning and development.
See PLANNING.
Registers.
Membership fees in state organizations, etc.
Payment by county commissions, §11-1-11.
Registration.
Bond issues. See within this heading, "Bond issues."
Claims and demands against counties.
Claims to be registered, §11-12-5.

COUNTIES—Cont'd
Registration—Cont'd
Claims and demands against counties—Cont'd
Destruction of county records by fire.
Claims to be registered when county records destroyed by fire, §11-12-9.
Registration of claims, §11-12-4.
Relocation assistance, §11-80-2.
Relocation of county seats.
See within this heading, "County seats."
Removal of courthouse or county site, Const. Ala., art. II, §41.
Reports.
Cemeteries.
Commission.
Damages from taking of property, etc., §11-17-4.
Filing of reports, §11-17-3.
Preparation of reports, §11-17-3.
Damages from taking of property, etc.
Report of damages, §11-17-4.
Depositories, §11-4-45.
Semiannual publication of county receipts and expenditures, §§11-3-19 to 11-3-21.
Treasurers, §11-4-23.
Proceedings upon resignation, removal, death, etc., of treasurer, §11-4-29.
Resorts.
Construction of sewage treatment or disposal plants in resort areas, §§11-88-40 to 11-88-111.
See WATER, SEWER AND FIRE PROTECTION AUTHORITIES.
Restitution to victims of crimes.
Restitution centers.
Cooperation of counties and municipalities, §15-18-76.
Powers of counties, §15-18-77.
Retirement.
Pension and retirement plans. See within this heading, "Pension and retirement plans."
Right of entry.
Land-use management in flood-prone areas.
Right of entry upon lands for preparation of examinations and surveys, §11-19-10.
Surveyors, §§11-7-5, 11-7-11.
Rights of way.
Public roads, bridges and ferries.
Public utilities.
Construction of facilities, §23-1-85.

COUNTIES—Cont'd
Rights of way—Cont'd
Railroads.
Abandoned rights-of-way.
Authorized to transfer to county commission, §10-5-2.1.
Roads.
Closing and vacating streets, alleys and highways.
See HIGHWAYS.
Fund. See within this heading, "Public roads, bridges and ferries."
Oil and gas.
Petroleum products.
Use of fees, §8-17-91.
Private roads.
See ROADS.
Public roads, bridges and ferries. See within this heading, "Public roads, bridges and ferries."
Secondary road committee.
Appointment, §8-17-91.
Composition, §8-17-91.
Creation, §8-17-91.
Duties, §8-17-91.
Warrants for construction of public buildings, bridges and roads, §§11-28-1 to 11-28-7. See within this heading, "Warrants."
Rules and regulations.
Public roads, bridges and ferries.
County commissions.
Promulgation, §23-1-80.
Penalties.
Violations, §23-5-14.
Violations, §23-1-95.
Penalties, §23-5-14.
St. Stephens historical commission.
Appropriations.
Authorized, §41-9-336.
Public facilities and improvements on commission land.
Powers as to, §41-9-336.
Salaries.
Engineers, §11-6-1.
State participation in salary, §11-6-4.
Trainees.
State participation in salary, §11-6-23.
Increase or decrease in salaries of county officers, Const. Ala., amd. 92.
Law enforcement officers.
Minimum starting salary, §36-21-10.
Surveyors, §11-7-12.
Suspension of restriction on diminishing public salaries, Const. Ala., amd. 26A.
Treasurers, §11-4-24.
Sales tax.
Collection of tax on same sale.
Only one county sales or use tax collectible, §40-23-2.1.
County tax for school purposes, §§40-12-4, 40-12-4.1.

COUNTIES—Cont'd
Sales tax—Cont'd
Exemptions, §40-23-5.
Gross proceeds of sales of
tangible personal
property to counties,
§40-23-4.
Sand pits.
Acquisition of lands for sand
pits, §11-14-23.
Conduct of condemnation
proceedings, §11-14-24.
Sanitation.
Duties of county health
officers, §22-3-5.
Schools.
General provisions.
See EDUCATION.
Licenses.
County license tax for
school purposes. See
within this heading,
"Licenses."
Secondary road committee.
Generally, §8-17-91.
Securities.
Bond issues. See within this
heading, "Bond issues."
Exemption from usury and
interest statutes,
§11-14-18.
Redemption of securities,
§§11-82-1 to 11-82-7. See
within this heading,
"Redemption of
securities."
Warrants. See within this
heading, "Warrants."
**Semiannual publication of
county receipts and
expenditures.**
Compensation paid for
publication, §11-3-21.
Contents, §11-3-21.
Failure to publish.
Penalty for failure to
publish, §11-3-23.
Penalties.
Failure to publish,
§11-3-23.
Voting against publication,
§11-3-22.
Required, §11-3-21.
Voting against publication.
Penalty for voting against
publication, §11-3-22.
Senior citizens.
Recreational, social and
cultural facilities.
Planning, establishment,
etc., §11-80-5.
Service commissioners,
§§31-5-9 to 31-5-11,
31-5-14.
Service of process.
How county served, ARCP,
Rule 4 (c).
Severance taxes.
Oil and gas.
Severance tax trust funds,
§40-20-50.
Sewers.
Acquisition of systems.
Authorization, §11-81-161.
Estimate of costs,
§11-81-162.
Authorities.
Improvement authorities,
§§39-7-1 to 39-7-4.

COUNTIES—Cont'd
Sewers—Cont'd
Authorities—Cont'd
Water, sewer and fire
protection authorities,
§§11-88-1 to 11-88-111.
See WATER, SEWER
AND FIRE
PROTECTION
AUTHORITIES.
Calendar basis.
Determination as to
operation of system
upon, §11-81-187.
Consolidation of systems.
Authorization, §11-81-161.
Estimate of costs,
§11-81-162.
County commissions.
Connections required,
§11-3-11.
Powers and duties of
county commissions,
§11-3-11.
Depository for revenues,
§11-81-183.
Expenses of operation or
maintenance of system.
Payment out of general
funds, §11-81-182.
Extension of systems.
Authorization, §11-81-161.
Estimate of costs,
§11-81-162.
Financial condition of
system.
Books of record and
accounts, etc.,
§11-81-188.
Fiscal year basis.
Determination as to
operation of system
upon, §11-81-187.
Improvement authorities,
§§39-7-1 to 39-7-34.
See PUBLIC WORKS.
Maintenance of systems.
Expenses.
Payment out of general
funds, §11-81-182.
Operation of systems.
Determination as to basis,
§11-81-187.
Expenses.
Payment out of general
funds, §11-81-182.
State board of health.
Supervision of operation,
§11-81-185.
Supervision by state board
of health, §11-81-185.
Payment by counties for
services furnished by
system, §11-81-186.
Properties of system.
Books of record and
accounts, etc.,
§11-81-188.
Rates.
Establishment, §11-81-184.
State supervision or
regulation.
Rates not subject to,
§11-81-185.
Repair of systems.
Authorization, §11-81-161.
Estimate of costs,
§11-81-162.

COUNTIES—Cont'd
Sewers—Cont'd
Resort areas.
Construction of sewage
treatment or disposal
plants in resort areas,
§§11-88-40 to
11-88-111.
See WATER, SEWER
AND FIRE
PROTECTION
AUTHORITIES.
Revenue bonds. See within
this heading, "Public
utilities."
Revenues.
Depository.
Designation of
depository,
§11-81-183.
Disposition and
disbursement of
gross revenue
account and special
funds, §11-81-183.
Gross revenue account.
Disposition and
disbursement,
§11-81-183.
Gross revenues.
Disposition, §11-81-181.
Pledge of revenues,
§§11-81-16, 11-81-181.
State board of health.
Supervision of operation,
§11-81-185.
Warrants or certificates of
indebtedness.
Applicability of provisions
of article, §11-9-1.
Denominations, §11-9-2.
Disposition of proceeds,
§11-9-2.
Form, §11-9-2.
Interest, §11-9-2.
Investment of trust funds
in warrants or
certificates, §11-9-4.
Issuance.
Authority for issuance,
§11-9-2.
Maturity, §11-9-2.
Payment.
Pledge for payment of
principal and
interest, §11-9-2.
Pledges of special
sanitary tax,
§11-9-3.
Where payable, §11-9-2.
Pledge for payment,
§11-9-2.
Special sanitary tax.
Pledges of special
sanitary tax,
§11-9-3.
Proceeds.
Disposition of proceeds,
§11-9-2.
Refunding warrants and
certificates.
Issuance, §11-9-5.
Sale, §11-9-2.
Special sanitary tax.
Defined, §11-9-1.
Pledge for payments of
principal and
interest, §11-9-3.
Terms, §11-9-2.

COUNTIES—Cont'd
  Sewers—Cont'd
    Warrants or certificates of
      indebtedness—Cont'd
    Trust funds.
      Investment in warrants
        or certificates of
        indebtedness,
        §11-9-4.
      Where payable, §11-9-2.
    Water, sewer and fire
      protection districts,
      §§11-89-1 to 11-89-19.
      See WATER, SEWER AND
        FIRE PROTECTION
        DISTRICTS.
  Sheriffs.
    Bonds, surety.
      General provisions. See
        within this heading,
        "Bonds, surety."
      Proceedings as to
        sufficiency of bonds,
        §§11-2-30 to 11-2-34.
    Books.
      Claims against counties for
        books, §11-12-14.
    Claims and demands against
      counties.
      Books, stationery,
        telephones, etc., for
        sheriffs, §11-12-14.
    Coroners.
      Discharge of duties of
        sheriff, §11-5-5.
    County commissions.
      Furnishing of necessary
        quarters, equipment,
        etc., §36-22-18.
    Courthouses.
      Prevention of trespasses,
        §11-14-9.
    Deputies.
      Employment by municipal
        corporations as police,
        §11-43-16.
      Overtime compensation,
        §36-21-4.1.
      General provisions.
      See SHERIFFS.
    Industrial parks.
      Jurisdiction of county
        sheriff, §11-23-6.
    Jails.
      Expenditure of
        appropriations by
        sheriff, §11-14-21.
    Membership fees in state
      organizations, etc.
      Payment by county
        commissions, §11-1-11.
    Overtime compensation,
      §36-21-4.1.
    Stamps.
      Claims against counties for
        postage stamps,
        §11-12-14.
    Stationery.
      Claims against counties for
        stationery, §11-12-14.
    Telephones.
      Claims against counties for
        telephones, §11-12-14.
      Procuring and providing
        for offices, §11-3-11.
  Ships and shipping.
    Local regulation, §33-5-31.

COUNTIES—Cont'd
  Ships and shipping—Cont'd
    Numbering provisions.
      Exemption from
        numbering provisions.
      Vessels owned by
        municipalities,
        §33-5-19.
  Sinking funds.
    Bond issues, §11-3-11.
      Designation, §11-81-23.
      Disposition, §11-81-23.
      Duties of trustee of sinking
        fund, §11-81-24.
      Execution, §11-81-22.
      Interest, §11-81-23.
      Issuance, §11-81-22.
      Maturity, §11-81-23.
      Powers of trustee of
        sinking fund,
        §11-81-25.
    Creation, §11-81-24.
    Deposit.
      Reports as to deposit,
        §11-81-19.
    Establishment, §11-81-24.
    Funds received to credit of
      sinking fund.
      Investment, §11-81-20.
    Investment.
      Funds received to credit of
        sinking fund,
        §11-81-20.
      Generally, §11-81-19.
      Municipal or county funds.
        Investment in
          obligations in which
          sinking funds may
          be invested,
          §11-81-21.
      Reports as to investment,
        §11-81-19.
    Payments.
      Special tax for payments,
        §11-81-15.
      Mandamus proceedings,
        §11-81-26.
    Reports.
      Investment or deposit.
        Reports as to investment
          or deposit, §11-81-19.
    Savings certificates.
      Contracts for purchase of
        savings certificates,
        §11-81-19.
    Taxation.
      Special tax for sinking
        fund payments,
        §§11-81-15, 11-81-26.
    Trustee of sinking fund.
      Duties, §11-81-24.
      Employment, §11-81-24.
      Powers, §11-81-25.
  Social security.
    Public employees.
      See SOCIAL SECURITY.
  Solid waste.
    Management plan.
      General provisins,
        §§22-27-40 to 22-27-49.
      See SOLID WASTE.
  Southeast interstate low-
    level radioactive waste
    management compact.
    Cooperation with
      commission, §22-32-7.
  Stadiums.
    Public improvement bonds,
      §§11-81-140 to 11-81-150.
      See within this heading,
        "Bond issues."

COUNTIES—Cont'd
  Stamps.
    Claims against counties for
      stamps for officers,
      §11-12-14.
  State.
    Contracts with state
      government, §11-1-10.
  State parks.
    Appropriations, §9-14-6.
    Grants of lands to state park
      system, §9-14-6.
  State products mart and
    coliseum authority.
    Investment of surplus county
      funds in bonds of
      corporation, §41-10-101.
  Stone.
    Acquisition of lands for stone
      quarries, §11-14-23.
    Conduct of condemnation
      proceedings, §11-14-24.
  Streams.
    Navigable steams.
      Jurisdiction over, §11-1-3.
      Not within limits of any
        county.
        Execution of process on
          streams, §11-1-3.
      Operation, etc., of bridges
        over navigable, etc.,
        streams, §§11-3-15 to
        11-3-17.
  Subdivisions.
    Bonds, surety.
      Developers, §11-24-2.
    Buildings.
      Southern standard building
        code.
        Compliance with code
          required, §11-24-1.
    Codes.
      Southern standard building
        code.
        Compliance required,
          §11-24-1.
    Compliance with chapter.
      Developer to comply with
        chapter provisions,
        §11-24-2.
    Violations.
      County to institute
        appropriate action,
        §11-24-3.
    County commissions.
      Powers and duties,
        §11-3-11.
    Cumulative provisions.
      Local laws not repealed,
        §11-24-7.
    Drains and sewers.
      Regulation by counties,
        §11-24-1.
    Eminent domain.
      Exemptions, §11-24-4.
    Exemptions.
      Eminent domain, §11-24-4.
      Existing structures in
        violation of chapter,
        §11-24-3.
    Existing facilities.
      Exempt violations,
        §11-24-3.
    Federal laws and regulations.
      Consistency with
        requirements,
        §11-24-1.

COUNTIES—Cont'd
  Subdivisions—Cont'd
    Flood-prone areas.
      Land-use management in
        flood-prone areas. See
        within this heading,
        "Flood-prone areas."
    Jurisdiction.
      Agreements with
        municipalities on
        scope, §11-24-6.
      No jurisdiction within that
        of municipal planning
        commissions, §11-24-5.
    Lots.
      Regulation by counties,
        §11-24-1.
    Municipal corporations.
      General provisions,
        §§11-52-30 to 11-52-54.
      See MUNICIPAL
        CORPORATIONS.
    Jurisdiction.
      Agreements with
        counties on scope,
        §11-24-6.
      Planning commissions.
        County jurisdiction
        restricted,
        §11-24-5.
    Planning.
      General provisions.
      See PLANNING.
      Municipal planning
        commissions.
        Jurisdiction.
          Restrictions on county
            jurisdiction,
            §11-24-5.
    Plat of proposed subdivisions.
      Generally, §11-24-2.
    Provisions of chapter deemed
      cumulative, §11-24-7.
    Repealed.
      Local laws not repealed,
        §11-24-7.
    State laws and regulations.
      Consistency with
        requirements,
        §11-24-1.
    Streets and sidewalks.
      Regulation by counties,
        §11-24-1.
    Utility fixtures and systems.
      Authority of counties to
        regulate, §11-24-1.
      Uneconomically situated
        facilities.
        Reimbursement of
          utilities by
          developers, §11-24-1.
  Subpoenas.
    County commissions.
      Powers and duties,
        §11-3-11.
  Summons and process.
    Adjoining county.
      Execution, §6-4-2.
    Navigable streams not
      within limits of any
      county.
      Execution of process on
        said streams, §11-1-3.
  Sunshine law.
    County commissions.
      Executive or secret
        sessions prohibited,
        §13A-14-2.

COUNTIES—Cont'd
  Surveys and surveyors.
    Buildings.
      Rights as to buildings not
        lost by straightening
        or location of section
        lines, §11-7-10.
    Chain bearers.
      Compensation, §11-7-12.
      Oaths, §11-7-7.
    County surveyors.
      Appointment, §11-7-1.
      Bonds, surety, §11-7-2.
        Liability for damages,
          §11-7-9.
      Compensation, §11-7-12.
      Damages.
        Liability for damages,
          §11-7-9.
      Duties.
        Generally, §11-7-4.
      Fees.
        Court ordered surveys.
          Fees taxed as costs,
            §11-7-6.
      Liability for damages,
        §11-7-9.
      Number of surveyors,
        §11-7-1.
      Obstruction.
        Penalty for obstruction of
          surveyor, §11-7-5.
      Plats.
        Preparation, §11-7-7.
      Qualifications, §11-7-1.
      Removal, §11-7-3.
      Right of entry, §§11-7-5,
        11-7-11.
      Term of office, §11-7-1.
    Court ordered surveys.
      Fees taxed as costs,
        §11-7-6.
      Penalty for obstruction of
        surveyor, §11-7-5.
      Right of entry upon lands
        for execution, §11-7-5.
    Evidence.
      Survey or plat, §11-7-8.
    Fences.
      Rights as to fences not lost
        by straightening or
        location of section, etc.,
        lines, §11-7-10.
    Flood-prone areas.
      Land-use management in
        flood-prone areas. See
        within this heading,
        "Flood-prone areas."
    Markers.
      Compensation, §11-7-12.
    Original government survey
      of county lands.
      Acquisition, etc., of copies
        of field notes, §11-3-25.
    Penalties.
      Obstruction of surveyor,
        §11-7-5.
    Plats.
      Contents, §11-7-7.
      Evidence.
        When survey or plat
          evidence of facts
          stated, §11-7-8.
      Preparation, §11-7-7.
  Swimming pools.
    Public improvement bonds,
      §§11-81-140 to 11-81-150.
    See within this heading,
      "Bond issues."

COUNTIES—Cont'd
  **Tannerhill furnace and
    foundry commission.**
    Appropriations by counties,
      §41-9-328.
  Tax assessors.
    Bonds, surety, §11-51-73.
      General provisions. See
        within this heading,
        "Bonds, surety."
      Proceedings as to
        sufficiency of bonds,
        §§11-2-30 to 11-2-34.
    Books.
      Claims against counties for
        books, §11-12-14.
    Claims and demands against
      counties.
      Books, stationery,
        telephones, etc., for tax
        assessors, §11-12-14.
    Membership fees in state
      organizations, etc.
      Payment by county
        commissions, §11-1-11.
    Municipal corporations.
      Optional method for levy
        and collection of
        property taxes,
        §§11-51-40 to 11-51-74.
      See MUNICIPAL
        CORPORATIONS.
    Stamps.
      Claims against counties for
        postage stamps,
        §11-12-14.
    Stationery.
      Claims against counties for
        stationery, §11-12-14.
    Telephones.
      Claims against counties for
        telephones, §11-12-14.
      Procuring and providing
        for offices of tax
        assessor, §11-3-11.
  Taxation, Const. Ala., amd.
    325.
    Ad valorem tax.
      Tax anticipation warrants,
        §§11-11A-1 to
        11-11A-5.
    Airports.
      Certificates of
        indebtedness.
        Warrants and certificates
          of indebtedness for
          airport purposes.
          Pledge of special taxes,
            §4-5-3.
    Boards of equalization.
      County boards, §§40-3-1 to
        40-3-26.
      See TAXATION.
    Bond issues.
      Exemption from taxation,
        §§11-81-29, 40-9-1.
      Public improvement
        bonds, §11-81-149.
      Pledge of revenues from
        certain taxes for
        payment, §11-81-16.
      Public improvement bonds.
        Exemption from
          taxation, §11-81-149.
      Exercise of county taxing
        power for payment,
        §11-81-148.
      Refunding bonds.
        Special tax levy for
          payment, §11-81-95.

COUNTIES—Cont'd
Taxation—Cont'd
Bond issues—Cont'd
Securities issued in
anticipation of grants.
Exemption from
taxation, §11-11B-5.
Special tax for payment of
bonds. See within this
heading, "Bond
issues."
Bridges.
Special tax for erection,
etc., §11-14-11.
Buildings.
Levy of special taxes,
§11-14-17.
Special tax for erection,
etc., §11-14-11.
Charges payable from state
treasury.
Counties exempt from
payment, Const. Ala.,
art. XI, §218.
County boards of
equalization, §§40-3-1 to
40-3-26.
See TAXATION.
County commissions.
Powers and duties,
§11-3-11.
Ratification of certain
actions of county
governing bodies,
§11-3-11.1.
County license tax for school
purposes.
Authority to levy, §40-12-4.
County tax for education,
§40-12-4.
Courthouses.
Special tax for courthouse,
§11-14-16.
Education.
See EDUCATION.
Elimination of small
payments to
municipalities,
§40-1-31.2.
Equalization.
County boards of
equalization, §§40-3-1
to 40-3-26.
See TAXATION.
Exemption from taxation.
Bond issues, §11-81-29.
Factories, industries and
plants.
Application, §40-9-41.
Cessation of exemption,
§40-9-42.
Generally, §40-9-40.
Inapplicability to taxes
to which factories,
plants, etc., already
subject, §40-9-46.
New or extended
factories, industries
and plants,
§§40-9-47, 40-9-49.
Health and accident self-
insurance groups.
Exemption from
insurance premium
tax, §11-26-5.
Industrial development
boards.
Corporations exempt,
§11-20-47.
Law library fund, §11-25-7.

COUNTIES—Cont'd
Taxation—Cont'd
Exemption from taxation
—Cont'd
Parks and recreation.
Exemption of public
parks and recreation
boards, §11-22-13.
Projects for promotion of
industry and trade.
Exemption from taxation
of projects, bonds,
etc., §11-20-12.
Property, §40-9-1.
Public building authorities,
§11-15-17.
Forest protection.
Special taxes for forest
protection, §§9-13-160
to 9-13-167.
See FORESTS AND
FORESTRY.
Gasoline taxes.
Issuing warrants in
anticipation of gasoline
taxes. See within this
heading, "Gasoline."
Health.
County health officer and
health department.
Tax to establish and
maintain, §22-3-10.
Health care service plans.
County taxes prohibited,
§10-4-107.
Hospitals.
Special county tax.
See HOSPITALS.
Jails.
Levy of tax for erection,
etc., §11-14-14.
Failure to levy tax when
necessary, §11-14-15.
Special tax for jail,
§11-14-16.
Loans.
Making loans in
anticipation of taxes.
See within this
heading, "Loans."
Motor fuels.
Additional excise tax on
gasoline, motor fuel
and lubricating oil.
Exemptions, §40-17-220.
Parks and recreation.
Tax exemptions, §11-22-13.
Pledge of revenues for bond
payments, §§11-81-16,
11-81-18.
Public building authorities.
Exemptions, §11-15-17.
Public roads, bridges and
ferries. See within this
heading, "Public roads,
bridges and ferries."
Rates of taxation.
Limitation on county
property tax rates,
Const. Ala., art. XI,
§215; amd. 208.
Revenues.
Pledge of revenues for
bond payments,
§11-81-18.
Road and bridge taxes. See
within this heading,
"Public roads, bridges
and ferries."

COUNTIES—Cont'd
Taxation—Cont'd
Schools.
License taxes. See within
this heading,
"Licenses."
School taxes.
See EDUCATION.
Sinking funds.
Special tax for sinking
fund payments,
§11-81-15.
Mandamus proceedings,
§11-81-26.
Special sanitary tax,
§§11-9-1, 11-9-3.
Special taxes.
Exemption of securities
from usury and
interest statutes,
§11-14-18.
Hospitals.
See HOSPITALS.
Levy, §11-14-17.
Disposition of funds from
levies, §11-3-14.
Surety bond of
depositary bank,
§11-3-14.
Public roads, bridges and
ferries.
Authorized, §11-14-11;
Const. Ala., art. XI,
§215; amd. 208.
Disposition of excess
proceeds,
§11-14-11.
Sinking funds.
Special tax for sinking
fund payments,
§11-81-15.
Mandamus
proceedings,
§11-81-26.
State-wide property
reappraisal.
County bonds for purpose
of paying costs of
reappraisal, §§40-7-90
to 40-7-100.
See TAXATION.
Tax increment districts,
Const. Ala., amd. 475.
Tax collectors.
Bonds, surety, §11-51-73.
Proceedings as to
sufficiency of bonds,
§§11-2-30 to 11-2-34.
Books.
Claims against counties for
books, §11-12-14.
Claims and demands against
counties.
Books, stationery,
telephones, etc., for tax
collectors, §11-12-14.
Membership fees in state
organizations, etc.
Payment by county
commissions, §11-1-11.
Municipal corporations.
Optional method for levy
and collection of
property taxes,
§§11-51-40 to 11-51-74.
See MUNICIPAL
CORPORATIONS.
Remittances of funds
deposited, §11-1-7.

COUNTIES—Cont'd
  Tax collectors—Cont'd
    Stamps.
      Claims against counties for
        postage stamps,
        §11-12-14.
    Stationery.
      Claims against counties for
        stationery, §11-12-14.
    Telephones.
      Claims against counties for
        telephones, §11-12-14.
      Procuring and providing
        telephones for offices of
        tax collectors,
        §11-3-11.
  Tax increment districts,
    §§11-99-1 to 11-99-10.
    See TAX INCREMENT
      DISTRICTS.
  Telephones.
    Claims and demands against
      counties.
      Telephones for probate
        judge, tax assessor,
        sheriff, etc., §11-12-14.
    Courthouses.
      Designation of courthouse
        offices for installation
        of telephones, §11-3-12.
    Powers and duties of
      county commissions,
      §11-3-11.
    Procuring and providing for
      offices, §11-3-11.
  Television.
    Community antenna
      television facilities,
      §§11-27-1 to 11-27-3,
      23-1-59.
  Tennis courts.
    Public improvement bonds.
      See within this heading,
      "Bond issues."
  Tobacco.
    Sales tax.
      Basis of tax levy,
      §40-25-29.
  Tombigbee Valley
    development authority.
    Contracts.
      Power to contract with
      counties, §33-17-8.
  Torts.
    Claims and demands against
      counties. See within this
      heading, "Claims and
      demands against
      counties."
  Trade and commerce.
    Projects for promotion of
      industry and trade. See
      within this heading,
      "Industry and trade."
  Treasurers.
    Annual account.
      Posting of copy, §11-4-28.
      Recordation, §11-4-28.
    Applicability of provisions,
      §11-4-1.
    Appointment.
      When no depository
        designated, §11-4-49.
    Bonds, surety, §11-4-22.
      Official bonds generally.
        See within this
        heading, "Bonds,
        surety."
    Books.
      Claims against counties for
        books, §11-12-14.

COUNTIES—Cont'd
  Treasurers—Cont'd
    Books—Cont'd
      Provided at expense of
        county, §11-4-27.
    Claims and demands against
      counties.
      Books, stationery,
        telephones, etc., for
        treasurers, §11-12-14.
      When claim to be paid
        though prior claims
        outstanding, §11-4-26.
    Compensation, §11-4-24.
    County commissions.
      Settlement with county
        commission prior to
        leaving office,
        §11-4-30.
    Death.
      Proceedings upon death of
        treasurer, §11-4-29.
    Depositories.
      Appointment of treasurer
        when no depository
        designated, §11-4-49.
      General provisions. See
        within this heading,
        "Depositories."
    District attorney entitled to
      free access to office of
      county treasurer,
      §12-16-196.
    Duties.
      Generally, §11-4-23.
    Elections, §11-4-20.
      Failure to elect successor
        vacates office, §36-9-5.
      General elections.
        Offices for which general
          election held,
          §17-2-2.
      State and county officers
        elected by the people,
        §17-2-1.
    Fine and forfeiture fund.
      Transfer of balance,
        §11-4-25.
    Grand jury entitled to free
      access to office,
      §12-16-196.
    Impeachment.
      General provisions.
        See IMPEACHMENT.
      Subject to impeachment,
        §36-11-1.
    Leaving office.
      Proceedings upon
        resignation, removal,
        death, etc., of
        treasurer, §11-4-29.
      Settlement with county
        commission, §11-4-30.
    Money erroneously paid into
      county treasury, etc.
      Transfer to state treasury,
        §11-1-6.
    Offices.
      Location, §11-4-23.
    Payment of claims.
      When claim to be paid
        though prior claims
        outstanding, §11-4-26.
    Removal.
      Proceedings upon removal,
        §11-4-29.
    Reports, §11-4-23.
    Proceedings upon
      resignation, removal,
      death, etc., of
      treasurer, §11-4-29.

COUNTIES—Cont'd
  Treasurers—Cont'd
    Resignation.
      Proceedings upon,
        §11-4-29.
    Stamps.
      Claims against counties
        for, §11-12-14.
    Stationery.
      Claims against counties
        for, §11-12-14.
    Summary proceedings
      involving officials,
      §§6-6-660 to 6-6-740.
      See PUBLIC OFFICERS
        AND EMPLOYEES.
    Telephones.
      Claims against counties
        for, §11-12-14.
    Terms of office, §11-4-20.
    Transfer of funds.
      Fine and forfeiture fund,
        §11-4-25.
    Vacancies in office, §11-4-21.
      Failure to elect successor,
        §36-9-5.
      Proceedings upon
        resignation, removal,
        death, etc., of
        treasurer, §11-4-29.
    Warrants.
      Resisting payment of
        warrant, §11-3-11.
  Trees and timber.
    Developing, advertising and
      promoting timber
      resources, §11-3-11.
  Trusts and trustees.
    Acquisition of land for public
      purposes.
      Trust fund, §11-18-3.
    Charitable trusts.
      Cemeteries.
        Conveyances, etc., to
          benefit as, §11-17-13.
    Claims and demands against
      counties.
      Verification of claims by
        trustees, §11-12-6.
    Sinking funds.
      Trustee of sinking fund,
        §§11-81-24, 11-81-25.
    Warrants for construction of
      public buildings, bridges
      and roads.
      Deemed legal investments
        for trust funds,
        §11-28-5.
  Tunnels.
    Public improvement bonds.
      See within this heading,
      "Bond issues."
  Unemployment
    compensation.
    Coverage.
      Election of coverage under
        chapter, §25-4-131.
  United States.
    Contracts with federal
      government, §11-1-10.
    Surplus funds.
      Investment in United
        States securities,
        §11-8-11.
  Universities and colleges.
    Local aid to state educational
      institutions, §§16-19-1 to
      16-19-8.
      See UNIVERSITIES AND
        COLLEGES.

COUNTIES—Cont'd
Usefulness of improvement or property for which bonds issued.
Estimate as to period of usefulness, §11-81-8.
Use tax.
Collection of tax on same sale.
Only one county sales or use tax collectible, §40-23-2.1.
Exemptions, §40-23-62.
USS Alabama battleship commission.
Appropriations by counties, §41-9-356.
Usury.
Industrial development boards.
Exemption of corporations from usury and interest laws, §11-20-48.
Securities.
Exemption from usury and interest statutes, §11-14-18.
Warrants in anticipation of gasoline taxes.
Exemptions from usury statutes, §11-11-8.
Waterworks systems warrants.
Exemptions from usury statutes, §11-9-27.
Utility services facilities, §§11-97-1 to 11-97-27.
See UTILITY SERVICES FACILITIES.
Validation of obligations. See within this heading, "Bond issues."
Venue.
Damages for personal injury, death or property damage, §6-3-11.
Local laws in counties having two courthouses unaffected, §6-3-10.
Veterans.
County service commissioners.
Counties to furnish offices, §31-5-14.
District service commissioners.
Counties to furnish offices, §31-5-14.
Voting machines.
Bonds for voting machines, Const. Ala., amd. 200.
War.
Financial provisions, §11-8-15.
Military service by officers in time of national emergency, §§36-8-1 to 36-8-6.
See PUBLIC OFFICERS AND EMPLOYEES.
Warehouses.
Public improvement bonds.
See within this heading, "Bond issues."
Warrants.
Airports, §§4-5-1 to 4-5-5.
Availability of funds.
Warrants issued only upon, §11-8-10.

COUNTIES—Cont'd
Warrants—Cont'd
Bond issues.
Redemption of securities.
See within this heading, "Bond issues."
Borrowing money.
Warrants for borrowing purposes, §§11-1-16, 11-1-17.
Buildings.
Public building authorities.
See within this heading, "Public building authorities."
Construction of public buildings, bridges and roads.
Applicability of section 11-8-10, §11-28-7.
Authorized, §11-28-2.
Claims.
Issuance of warrants as allowance of claim, §11-28-6.
Definitions, §11-28-1.1.
Denomination, §11-28-2.
Fiduciaries.
Warrants deemed legal investments for trust funds, §11-28-5.
Full faith and credit, §11-28-2.
Inconsistent provisions.
Section controls over inconsistent statutes, §11-28-7.
Intent of legislature, §11-28-1.
Interest, §11-28-2.
Investments.
Warrants deemed legal investments for trust funds, §11-28-5.
Issuance.
Deemed to constitute audit and allowance of claim, §11-28-6.
Refunding warrants, §11-28-4.
Legal investments for trust funds, §11-28-5.
Legislative intent, §11-28-1.
Liberal construction of chapter, §11-28-1.
Maturity, §11-28-2.
Pledges.
Special pledges, §11-28-3.
Real property.
Acquisition of land within scope of chapter, §11-28-1.
Refunding warrants.
Issuance, §11-28-4.
Special pledges, §11-28-3.
Terms, §11-28-3.
Trust funds.
Warrants deemed legal investments, §11-28-5.
Definitions.
Waterworks systems warrants, §11-9-20.
Depositories.
Execution, §11-4-48.
Liability upon warrant, §11-4-48.

COUNTIES—Cont'd
Warrants—Cont'd
Depositories—Cont'd
Persons authorized to issue warrants on depository, §11-8-9.
Education.
Local aid to state educational institutions, §§16-19-3 to 16-19-5, 16-19-7.
Execution of warrants.
Depositories, §11-4-48.
Garbage and trash.
Financing collection and disposal facilities, §§22-27-22 to 22-27-27.
See GARBAGE AND TRASH.
Gasoline taxes.
Issuing warrants in anticipation of gasoline taxes. See within this heading, "Gasoline."
Industrial parks, §§11-92-6 to 11-92-10.
Investment of trust funds in warrants.
Sanitary sewer system warrants, §11-9-4.
Waterworks system warrants, §11-9-25.
Issuance.
Availability of funds prerequisite, §11-8-10.
Persons authorized to issue, §11-8-9.
Liability upon warrants.
Depositories, §11-4-48.
Made in anticipation of ad valorem taxes, §§11-11A-1 to 11-11A-5.
Persons authorized to issue, §11-8-9.
Public building authorities.
See within this heading, "Public building authorities."
Redemption of securities generally. See within this heading, "Redemption of securities."
Refunding warrants.
Principal and interest.
Part of annual county operating budget, §11-8-4.
Payment, §11-8-4.
Resisting payment of warrants, §11-3-11.
Sanitary sewer systems. See within this heading, "Sewers."
Tax anticipation warrants, §§11-11A-1 to 11-11A-5.
Anticipation of longer-term warrants, §11-11A-1.
Applicability of chapter, §11-11A-5.
Authorized, §11-11A-1.
Construction and interpretation of chapter provisions, §11-11A-5.
Denominations, §11-11A-1.
Interest, §11-11A-1.
Assignment and pledge of tax proceeds for payment, §11-11A-2.

COUNTIES—Cont'd
Warrants—Cont'd
Tax anticipation warrants
—Cont'd
Interest—Cont'd
Exemption from state
limits, §11-11A-4.
Maturity, §11-11A-1.
Price.
Term.
Anticipation of longer-
term warrants,
§11-11A-1.
Redemption.
Assignment and pledge
of tax proceeds for
payment, §11-11A-2.
Refunding warrants.
Issuance, §11-11A-3.
Scope of chapter,
§11-11A-5.
Usury.
Exemption from state
usury statutes,
§11-11A-4.
Treasurers.
Persons authorized to issue
warrants, §11-8-9.
Resisting payment of
warrant, §11-3-11.
Universities and colleges.
Local aid to state
educational
institutions, §§16-19-3
to 16-19-5, 16-19-7.
Waterworks systems
warrants, §§11-9-20 to
11-9-28. See within this
heading, "Water supply
and waterworks."
**Water conservation and
irrigation.**
Agency.
Contributing money for
work of agency,
§9-10-9.
Taxation.
Collection of taxes for
work of agency,
§9-10-9.
Corporations.
Bond issues.
Not obligations of
counties, §9-10-40.
Property.
Lease or conveyance of
real property,
§9-10-42.
General provisions.
See WATER
CONSERVATION
AND IRRIGATION.
**Water management and
drainage.**
Drainage subdistricts.
See WATER
MANAGEMENT AND
DRAINAGE.
Waters and watercourses.
Acquisition of lands for
public purposes.
Use of land for creation
and maintenance,
§11-18-2.
County commission.
Opening and cleaning
navigable streams.
Contracts, §33-7-2.
Developing, advertising and
promoting water
resources, §11-3-11.

COUNTIES—Cont'd
Waters and watercourses
—Cont'd
Navigable streams.
Execution of process on
streams, §11-1-3.
Not within limits of any
county.
Jurisdiction over,
§11-1-3.
Operation, etc., of bridges
over navigable, etc.,
streams, §§11-3-15 to
11-3-17.
**Water, sewer and fire
protection authorities,**
§§11-88-1 to 11-88-111.
See WATER, SEWER AND
FIRE PROTECTION
AUTHORITIES.
**Water, sewer and fire
protection distircts,**
§§11-89-1 to 11-89-19.
See WATER, SEWER AND
FIRE PROTECTION
DISTRICTS.
**Water supply and
waterworks.**
Acquisition of waterworks
plants or distribution
systems.
Election.
No election required,
§11-21-4.
Municipal corporations.
Power of municipalities
to sell, §11-21-2.
Publication of notice of
sale, transfer or
conveyance,
§11-21-3.
Power of counties to
purchase, §11-21-1.
Power of municipalities to
sell, §11-21-2.
Purchase.
Power of counties to
purchase, §11-21-1.
Sale by municipalities.
Power of municipalities
to sell, §11-21-2.
Publication of notice,
§11-21-3.
Security for bonds and
indebtedness incurred
in acquisition,
§11-81-1.
Authorities.
Improvement authorities.
See PUBLIC WORKS.
Bond issues.
Revenue bonds. See within
this heading, "Public
utilities."
Calendar basis.
Determination as to
operation of system
upon calendar basis,
§11-81-187.
Construction of waterworks.
Security for bonds and
indebtedness incurred
in construction,
§11-81-1.
Conveyance of plants, etc., to
municipal corporations,
§11-14-3.
Definitions.
Waterworks systems
warrants, §11-9-20.

COUNTIES—Cont'd
**Water supply and
waterworks**—Cont'd
Depository for revenues,
§11-81-183.
Expenses of operation or
maintenance of system.
Payment out of general
funds, §11-81-182.
Financial condition of
system.
Books of record and
accounts, etc.,
§11-81-188.
Fiscal year basis.
Determination as to
operation of system
upon, §11-81-187.
Maintenance of system.
Expenses, §11-81-182.
Municipal corporations.
Conveyance of plants, etc.,
to municipal
corporations, §11-14-3.
Operation of system.
Accounting year,
§11-81-187.
Expenses.
Payment out of general
funds, §11-81-182.
Payment by counties for
services furnished by
system, §11-81-186.
Properties of system.
Books of record and
accounts, etc.,
§11-81-188.
Purchase of waterworks.
Security for bonds and
indebtedness incurred
in purchase, §11-81-1.
Rates.
Establishment, §11-81-184.
State supervision or
regulation.
Rates not subject to,
§11-81-185.
Revenue bonds. See within
this heading, "Public
utilities."
Revenues.
Depository.
Designation, §11-81-183.
Gross revenue account.
Disposition and
disbursement,
§11-81-183.
Gross revenues.
Disposition, §11-81-181.
Pledge of revenues from
waterworks,
§§11-81-16, 11-81-17,
11-81-181.
Water, sewer and fire
protection authorities,
§§11-88-1 to 11-88-111.
See WATER, SEWER AND
FIRE PROTECTION
AUTHORITIES.
Water, sewer and fire
protection districts,
§§11-89-1 to 11-89-19.
See WATER, SEWER AND
FIRE PROTECTION
DISTRICTS.
Waterworks systems
warrants.
Applicability of provisions
of section 11-8-10,
§11-9-28.

COUNTIES—Cont'd

Water supply and waterworks—Cont'd

Waterworks systems warrants—Cont'd

Audits.

Issuance of warrants deemed to constitute audit and allowance of claim, §11-9-26.

Construction of article, §11-9-21.

Definitions, §11-9-20.

Denominations, §11-9-22.

Disposition of proceeds, §11-9-22.

Exemptions from usury statutes, §11-9-27.

Form, §11-9-22.

Interest, §11-9-22.

Exemptions from interest rate statutes, §11-9-27.

Pledge for payment, §§11-9-22, 11-9-23.

Investment of trust funds in warrants, §11-9-25.

Issuance.

Authority for issuance, §11-9-22.

Deemed to constitute audit and allowance of claim, §11-9-26.

Legislative intent, §11-9-21.

Maturity.

Date of maturity, §11-9-22.

Pledge for payment, §11-9-22.

Special pledges, §11-9-23.

Proceeds.

Disposition of proceeds, §11-9-22.

Provisions of article controlling, §11-9-28.

Rate of interest, §11-9-22.

Refunding warrants.

Issuance, §11-9-24.

Sale, §11-9-22.

Tax.

Special pledges for payment, §11-9-23.

Terms, §11-9-22.

Trust funds.

Investment in warrants, §11-9-25.

Usury.

Exemptions from usury statutes, §11-9-27.

Water system assistance authority.

Investments in bonds of authority, §22-23A-12.

Weights and measures.

Local sealers.

See WEIGHTS AND MEASURES.

Welfare.

Allocation of funds.

Department of human resources, §38-2-5.

Appropriations, §38-2-9.

County commissions.

Powers and duties of county commissions, §11-3-11.

COUNTIES—Cont'd

Welfare—Cont'd

County departments of human resources, §§38-2-6 to 38-2-10, 38-4-6, 38-4-10.

See WELFARE.

Relief and support of poor persons by counties, §§38-8-1 to 38-8-3.

Wet counties, §§28-3-1 to 28-3-286.

See ALCOHOLIC BEVERAGES.

Wharves.

Public improvement bonds.

See within this heading, "Bond issues."

Wildlife.

Acquisition of lands for public purposes.

Use of land for betterment of wildlife, §11-18-2.

Witnesses.

County commissions.

Powers of county commissions, §11-3-11.

Workmen's compensation.

Applicability of chapter to counties, §25-5-13.

Workmen's compensation self-insurance group.

Attorneys and employees, §11-26-3.

Authorized, §11-26-1.

Bylaws.

Establishment, §11-26-3.

Construction of provisions, §11-26-6.

Contract with solvent insurance companies, §11-26-3.

Establishment, §11-26-1.

Governing body of trustees.

Establishment, §11-26-3.

Management and consultant contracts, §11-26-3.

Officers.

Liability of officers of nonprofit associations, §§10-11-1 to 10-11-5.

Powers generally, §11-26-3.

Providing of workmen's compensation benefits, §11-26-1.

Purpose, §11-26-1.

Qualification as self-insurers, §11-26-1.

Schedule of charges.

Establishment, §11-26-3.

Zoning.

Airports, §§4-6-1 to 4-6-15.

See AVIATION.

Flood-prone areas.

Land-use management in flood-prone areas. See within this heading, "Flood-prone areas."

COUNTY ADMINISTRATORS,

§§43-2-170 to 43-2-175.

See EXECUTORS AND ADMINISTRATORS.

COUNTY COURTS.

Judges.

Retirement.

Transitional provisions, §§12-18-51, 12-18-55.

COUNTY INDUSTRIAL DEVELOPMENT AUTHORITIES.

Agents.

Liability.

Limitation, §11-92A-12.

Amendment of articles, §11-92A-11.

Articles.

Amendment, §11-92A-11.

Contents, §11-92A-5.

Filing, §§11-92A-5, 11-92A-8.

Probate judges.

Recordation of articles, §11-92A-8.

Recordation, §11-92A-8.

Signing, §11-92A-5.

Bids and bidding.

Exemption from competitive bid laws, §11-92A-19.

Boards of directors.

Bylaws.

Adoption, §11-92A-9.

Composition, §11-92A-10.

Dissolution of authority.

Resolution of board, §11-92A-22.

Generally, §11-92A-9.

Liability of directors.

Limitation, §11-92A-12.

Meetings, §11-92A-10.

Notice, §11-92A-9.

Proceedings.

Evidence.

Admissibility as evidence, §11-92A-9.

Recordation, §11-92A-9.

Qualifications of members, §11-92A-10.

Quorum, §11-92A-10.

Removal of members, §11-92A-10.

Terms of directors, §11-92A-10.

Bond issues, §11-92A-14.

Investments.

Authorized investments, §11-92A-16.

Refunding bonds, §11-92A-14.

Sale of bonds, §11-92A-14.

Application of proceeds, §11-92A-16.

Security for bonds, §§11-92A-15, 11-92A-16.

Taxation.

Exemption, §§11-92A-16, 11-92A-19.

Validation of bonds, §11-92A-14.

Construction and interpretation.

Liberal construction, §11-92A-2.

Conveyances.

Transfer of funds and assets to authority, §11-92A-21.

Damages.

Limitation on liability of authority, §11-92A-20.

Definitions, §11-92A-1.

Dissolution, §11-92A-22.

Evidence.

Boards of directors.

Proceedings.

Admissibility, §11-92A-9.

Existing authorities.

Reincorporation of existing authorities and boards, §§11-92A-6, 11-92A-7.

COUNTY INDUSTRIAL DEVELOPMENT AUTHORITIES—Cont'd

Incorporation.
Applications, §11-92A-4.
  Filing, §§11-92A-3, 11-92A-4.
Articles, §11-92A-5.
  §§11-92A-8, 11-92A-11.
Authorized, §11-92A-3.
Procedure, §§11-92A-3, 11-92A-4.
Reincorporation of existing authorities, §§11-92A-6, 11-92A-7.

Interest.
Exemption from usury and interest laws, §11-92A-17.

Investments.
Bond issues.
  Authorized investments, §11-92A-16.

Legislative declaration, §11-92A-2.

Liability.
Limitations on liability, §§11-92A-12, 11-92A-20.

Notice.
Boards of directors.
  Meetings, §11-92A-9.

Officers, §11-92A-9.
Liability.
  Limitation, §11-92A-12.

Powers, §11-92A-12.

Probate judges.
Articles.
  Recordation of articles, §11-92A-8.
Fees.
  No fees allowed, §11-92A-8.

Property.
Dissolution of authority.
  Vesting of title to property, §11-92A-22.

Recordation.
Articles, §11-92A-8.
Boards of directors.
  Proceedings, §11-92A-9.

Taxation.
Exemptions from taxation, §11-92A-18.
Bond issues, §§11-92A-16, 11-92A-18.

Transfer of funds and assets to authority, §11-92A-21.

COUNTY SEATS.

Constitution of Alabama.
Changing or locating.
  Special, private or local laws prohibited, Const. Ala., art. IV, §104.

Relocation, §§11-16-1 to 11-16-40.
See COUNTIES.

COUNTY SOLICITORS.

Appointment or election, Const. Ala., art. VI, §167.

COURSE OF DEALING.

Commercial code, §§7-1-205, 7-2-202, 7-2-314.

COURTHOUSES.

County boards of health.
Duties, §22-3-2.

County courthouses.
General provisions.
  See COUNTIES.

COURTHOUSES—Cont'd

County courthouses—Cont'd
Law libraries, §§11-25-1 to 11-25-12.
  See LIBRARIES.

Elections.
See ELECTIONS.

State board of health.
Authority and jurisdiction, §22-2-2.

COURT OF CIVIL APPEALS.

Attorney general.
Attending civil suits in courts in which state a party, §12-3-32.

Bonds, surety.
Clerk of court, §12-3-24.

Certiorari.
Powers of judges as to issuance of writs, §12-3-8.

Clerk of court.
Appointment, §12-3-23.
Bond, surety, §12-3-24.
Clerks generally.
  See CLERKS OF COURT.
Compensation, §12-3-23.
Duties, §12-3-26; ARAP, Rule 17.
Fees, §12-19-91.
Office hours, §12-3-25.
Powers, §12-3-26.
Removal, §12-3-23.

Composition, §12-3-1; Const. Ala., amd. 328.

Constitution of Alabama, Const. Ala., amd. 328.

Contempt.
Punishment for contempt, §12-3-11.

Costs.
Substitution of appellate court records, §12-20-1.

Counties.
Offices for courts.
  Contracting with localities for, §12-1-20.

Courts generally.
See COURTS.

Created, §12-3-1.

Decisions.
Absence of judge or judges, §12-3-17.
Decisions of supreme court to govern, §12-3-16.
Disqualification of judge or judges, §12-3-17.
Reporter of decisions.
  See REPORTER OF DECISIONS OF SUPREME COURT AND COURTS OF APPEALS.
Reporting, §12-3-18.
Subject to general superintendence and control of supreme court, §12-3-16.

Divisions.
Court sitting in divisions, ARAP, Rule 16 (d).

Elections.
Judges, §12-3-3.
  Contested elections.
  State officers generally, §§17-15-50 to 17-15-63.
  See ELECTIONS.

COURT OF CIVIL APPEALS —Cont'd

Elections—Cont'd
Judges—Cont'd
  General elections.
    Offices for which general election held, §17-2-2.
    State and county officers elected by the people, §17-2-1.
  Two or more justices running at the same time.
    Designating justices by number, §17-7-20.
  When judges to be elected, §17-2-7.

Employees.
Payment of salaries, §12-3-30.

Extraodinary writs.
Review in supreme court of decisions of courts of appeals.
  Rules of appellate procedure, ARAP, Rule 21.

Facilities.
Contracts for, §12-1-20.

Fees.
Clerk of court, §12-19-91.
Substitution of appellate court records, §12-20-1.

Furniture.
Furnishing, §12-3-31.

Habeas corpus.
Authority to issue writs, §12-3-11.

Holdings.
Decisions of supreme court to govern, §12-3-16.

Illegitimacy.
Determination of paternity.
  See ILLEGITIMACY.

Improperly submitted cases.
Transfer, §12-1-4.

Injunctions.
Judges may grant, §§6-6-500, 12-3-8, 12-3-11.

Judges.
Absence.
  Decision of cases, §12-3-17.
Appointment, §12-3-3.
Canons of judicial ethics.
  See CANONS OF JUDICIAL ETHICS.
Certiorari.
  Powers of judges as to issuance of writs, §12-3-8.
Clerks.
  Law clerks. See within this heading, "Law clerks."
Colleges.
  Reimbursement of travel expenses of judges attending judicial colleges, §12-1-17.
Compensation, §12-3-6; Const. Ala., art. VI, §150.
  Retired judges on active duty status, §12-18-10.
Composition of court, §12-3-1; Const. Ala., amd. 328.
Conferences.
  Reimbursement of travel expenses, §12-1-17.
Confidential secretaries, §12-3-23.

COURT OF CIVIL APPEALS
—Cont'd

Judges—Cont'd

Death.
Payment of retirement
benefits to spouses
upon, §12-18-10.
Disability benefits,
§12-18-10.
Disqualification.
Decision of qualification of
judge, §12-3-17.
Grounds, §12-1-13.
District attorneys.
Time of service as full-time
state prosecutor.
Crediting with judicial
retirement system,
§12-18-8.1.
Dual office holding, Const.
Ala., art. VI, §150.
Duties.
Retired judges, §12-18-7.
Active duty status,
§12-18-10.
Election, §12-3-3.
Contested elections.
State officers generally,
§§17-15-50 to
17-15-63.
See ELECTIONS.
General elections.
Offices for which general
election held,
§17-2-2.
State and county officers
elected by the people,
§17-2-1.
Two or more judges at the
same election.
Designating by number,
§17-7-20.
When judges to be elected,
§17-2-7.
Expenses.
Reimbursement of travel
expenses, §12-1-17.
General provisions.
See JUDGES.
Impeachment.
General provisions.
See IMPEACHMENT.
Subject to impeachment,
§36-11-1; Const. Ala.,
art. VII, §174.
Injunctions.
Powers of judges as to
granting, §§6-6-500,
12-3-8, 12-3-11.
Law clerks, §§12-3-27 to
12-3-29.
Montgomery.
Judges to reside in
Montgomery during
terms of court, §12-3-5.
Number of judges, Const.
Ala., amd. 328.
Oath of office.
Retired judges, §12-18-7.
Powers.
Retired judges, §12-18-7.
Retired judges on active
duty status,
§12-18-10.
Presiding judge, §12-3-4.
Qualifications, §12-3-1;
Const. Ala., art. VI,
§154.

COURT OF CIVIL APPEALS
—Cont'd

Judges—Cont'd

Residence.
Judges to reside in
Montgomery during
terms of court, §12-3-5.
Retirement.
Active duty status,
§12-18-10.
Applicability of article,
§§12-18-5, 12-18-12.
Benefits, §12-18-10.
Death.
Payment of benefits to
spouses upon
death of judges,
§12-18-10.
Forfeiture, §12-18-7.
Payment to spouses upon
death of judges,
§12-18-10.
Spouses.
Payment of benefits to
spouses upon
death of judges,
§12-18-10.
Compensation of retired
judges on active duty
status, §12-18-10.
Construction of article,
§12-18-13.
Contributions made to
employees' retirement
system.
Transfer into judicial
retirement fund,
§12-18-8.
Contributions to
retirement fund by
judges, §12-18-5.
Refund upon termination
prior to eligibility,
§12-18-8.
Credit for time of service
as full-time state
prosecutor, §12-18-8.1.
Death.
Payment of benefits to
spouses upon death
of judges, §12-18-10.
Declaration as to intention
to retire, §12-18-7.
Duties of retired judges,
§12-18-7.
Retired judges on active
duty status,
§12-18-10.
Eligibility for retirement,
§12-18-6.
Entitlement to retirement
and receipt of pension,
§12-18-4.
Forfeiture of benefits,
§12-18-7.
Intention to retire.
Declaration as to
intention, §12-18-7.
Judicial retirement fund.
See JUDGES.
Military service.
Granting of credit for
military service,
§12-18-5.
Oath of retired judges,
§12-18-7.
Powers of retired judges,
§12-18-7.
Retired judges on active
duty status,
§12-18-10.

COURT OF CIVIL APPEALS
—Cont'd

Judges—Cont'd

Retirement—Cont'd
Prior service.
Credit for service under
employees'
retirement system,
§12-18-8.
Prior to eligibility for
benefits.
Refund of contributions
to judicial
retirement fund,
§12-18-8.
Retirement order, §12-18-4.
Secretaries.
Retired judges
performing active
duty, §12-5-21.
Spouses.
Payment of benefits to
spouses upon death
of judges, §12-18-10.
State and local governing
bodies authorized to
pick up contributions
to retirement fund,
§12-18-5.
Time of service as full-time
state prosecutor,
§12-18-8.1.
Vacancies in office,
§12-18-9.
Salaries, §12-3-6; Const. Ala.,
art. VI, §150.
Retired judges on active
duty status, §12-18-10.
Secretaries.
Confidential secretaries,
§12-3-23.
Retired judges
performing active
duty, §12-5-21.
Seminars.
Reimbursement of travel
expenses of judges
attending judicial
seminars, §12-1-17.
Stay of proceedings.
Powers of judges as to
issuance of stays,
§12-3-8.
Supernumerary judges.
Continuation of laws
concerning, §12-3-7.
Travel expenses.
Reimbursement for
attending judicial
colleges, etc., §12-1-17.
Vacancies, §12-18-9.
Filling, §12-3-3.
Jurisdiction, Const. Ala., amd.
328.
Appellate jurisdiction,
§12-3-10.
Original jurisdiction,
§12-3-11.
Law clerks.
Appointment, §12-3-27.
Successors, §12-3-28.
Clerk to serve appointing
judge, §12-3-28.
Dismissal, §12-3-28.
Salaries, §12-3-29.
Successors.
Appointment, §12-3-28.
Librarian, §12-3-19.
Mandamus.
Original jurisdiction of court,
§12-3-11.

COURT OF CIVIL APPEALS —Cont'd

Mandamus—Cont'd
Review in supreme court of decisions of courts of appeals.
Rules of appellate procedure, ARAP, Rule 21.
Marshal, §12-3-19.
Montgomery.
Judges to reside in Montgomery during terms of court, §12-3-5.
Municipal corporations.
Offices and other physical facilities for courts.
Contracts with municipalities, §12-1-20.
Prosecution assistance by municipality, ARJA, Rule 17.
Notice of appeal.
Form, ARAP, Form 1.
Notice of orders, ARAP, Rule 17 (a).
Officers.
Travel expenses.
Reimbursement for attending conferences, etc., §12-1-17.
Offices.
Contracting with localities for, §12-1-20.
Opinions.
Reporting, §12-3-18.
Orders of court.
Notice of orders, ARAP, Rule 17 (a).
Presiding judge, §12-3-4.
Prohibition, writ of.
Review in supreme court of decisions of.
Rules of appellate procedure, ARAP, Rule 21.
Quarters, §12-3-13.
Quo warranto.
Original jurisdiction of court, §12-3-11.
Records.
Binding.
Payment of costs, §12-3-31.
Destroyed records.
Substitution, §12-20-32.
Furnishing of record books, §12-3-31.
Lost records.
Substitution, §12-20-32.
Costs and fees, §12-20-1.
Substitution of appellate court records, §12-20-32.
Costs and fees of substitution, §12-20-1.
Reporter of decisions, §§12-4-1 to 12-4-4.
Reporting opinions and decisions, §12-3-18.
Review of decisions, ARAP, Rule 39.
Rules of appellate procedure.
See APPEALS.
Salaries.
Clerk of court, §12-3-23.
Judges, §12-3-6; Const. Ala., art. VI, §150.
Retired judges on active duty status, §12-18-10.
Law clerks, §12-3-29.

COURT OF CIVIL APPEALS —Cont'd

Salaries—Cont'd
Payment of salaries of employees of courts, §12-3-30.
Secretaries.
Confidential secretaries, §12-3-23.
Retired judges performing active duty, §12-5-21.
Special terms.
Applicability of provisions of section 12-2-9, §12-3-33.
State.
Attorney general to attend civil suits in courts in which state a party, §12-3-32.
Stationery.
Furnishing, §12-3-31.
Stay of proceedings.
Powers of judges as to issuance of stays, §12-3-8.
Supreme court.
Authority over appeals court, §12-3-16.
Review of decisions, ARAP, Rule 39.
Transfer of cases to supreme court, §12-3-15.
Terms of court.
Regular term, §12-3-12.
Special terms.
Applicability of provisions of section 12-2-9, §12-3-33.
Transfer of cases.
Improperly submitted cases, §12-1-4.
Transfer of cases to supreme court, §12-3-15.
Writs.
Remedial and original writs.
Powers of court as to issuance, §12-3-11.

COURT OF CRIMINAL APPEALS.

Appeals to court of criminal appeals.
Charges to jury.
Presumption that written charges asked before jury retired, §12-22-132.
Judgment of conviction, §12-22-130.
Jurisdiction.
Decision where conflict over jurisdiction, §12-22-131.
Retention of jurisdiction by trial court, §12-22-133.
Questions of law.
Reserving questions of law, §12-22-132.
Review in court of criminal appeals, §12-22-131.
Wrong court.
When appeal taken to wrong court, §12-22-131.
Attorney general.
Attending criminal cases in courts in which state a party, §12-3-32.
Attorneys at law.
Staff attorneys, §12-3-35.
Appointment, §12-3-34.

COURT OF CRIMINAL APPEALS—Cont'd

Attorneys at law—Cont'd
Staff attorneys—Cont'd
Stenographers, §12-3-34.
Bonds, surety.
Clerk of court, §12-3-21.
Certiorari.
Powers of judges as to issuance of writs, §12-3-8.
Clerks of court.
Appointment, §12-3-20.
Assistant clerk, §12-3-20.
Bond, surety, §12-3-21.
Clerks generally.
See CLERKS OF COURT.
Compensation, §12-3-20.
Confidential assistant, §12-3-36.
Dockets clerk, §12-3-22.
Duties, ARAP, Rule 17.
Executions clerk, §12-3-20.
Fees, §12-19-91.
Office hours, §12-3-25.
Powers, §12-3-26.
Composition, §12-3-1; Const. Ala., amd. 328.
Constitution of Alabama, Const. Ala., amd. 328.
Contempt.
Punishment for contempt, §12-3-11.
Costs.
Substitution of appellate court records, §12-20-1.
Counties.
Offices and other physical facilities.
Contracts with counties for, §12-1-20.
Courts generally.
See COURTS.
Created, §12-3-1.
Criminal cases.
Consideration by court, §12-22-240.
Decisions.
Absence of judge or judges, §12-3-17.
Decisions of supreme court to govern, §12-3-16.
Disqualification of judge or judges, §12-3-17.
Reporter of decisions, §§12-4-1 to 12-4-4.
Reporting, §12-3-18.
Subject to superintendence and control of supreme court, §12-3-16.
Divisions.
Court sitting in divisions, ARAP, Rule 16 (d).
Dockets clerk, §12-3-22.
Elections.
Judges, §12-3-2.
Contests, §§17-15-50 to 17-15-63.
See ELECTIONS.
Two or more justices running at the same time.
Designation by number, §17-7-20.
Employees.
Confidential assistant, §12-3-36.
Travel expenses.
Reimbursement for attending conferences, etc., §12-1-17.

COURT OF CRIMINAL APPEALS—Cont'd

Executions clerk, §12-3-20.

Extraordinary writs.
Review in supreme court, ARAP, Rule 21.

Fees.
Attorney general's fee, §12-19-190.
Clerk of court, §12-19-91.
Substitution of appellate court records, §12-20-1.

Furniture.
Furnishing, §12-3-31.

Habeas corpus.
Authority to issue writs, §12-3-11.

Holdings.
Decisions of supreme court to govern, §12-3-16.

Improperly submitted cases.
Transfer, §12-1-4.

Injunctions.
Judges may grant, §§6-6-500, 12-3-8, 12-3-11.

Judges.
Absence.
Decision of cases in event of absence, §12-3-17.
Appointment, §12-3-2.
Canons of judicial ethics.
See CANONS OF JUDICIAL ETHICS.
Certiorari.
Powers of judges as to issuance of writs, §12-3-8.
Clerks.
Law clerks, §§12-3-27 to 12-3-29.
Colleges.
Reimbursement of travel expenses for attending judicial colleges, §12-1-17.
Compensation, §12-3-6; Const. Ala., art. VI, §150.
Retired judges on active duty status, §12-18-10.
Composition of court, §12-3-1; Const. Ala., amd. 328.
Conferences.
Reimbursement of travel expenses for attending conferences, §12-1-17.
Confidential secretaries, §12-3-20.
Death.
Payment of retirement benefits to spouses upon, §12-18-10.
Disability benefits, §12-18-10.
Disqualification.
Decision of cases in event of disqualification, §12-3-17.
Grounds, §12-1-13.
District attorneys.
Time of service by judge as full-time state prosecutor, §12-18-8.1.
Dual office holding, Const. Ala., art. VI, §150.
Duties.
Retired judges, §12-18-7.
Retired judges on active duty status, §12-18-10.

COURT OF CRIMINAL APPEALS—Cont'd

Judges—Cont'd
Election, §12-3-2.
Contests, §§17-15-50 to 17-15-63.
See ELECTIONS.
General elections.
Offices for which general election held, §17-2-2.
State and county officers elected by the people, §17-2-1.
Two or more judges running at the same time.
Designating by number, §17-7-20.
When judges to be elected, §17-2-7.
General provisions.
See JUDGES.
Impeachment.
General provisions, §§36-11-1 to 36-11-25; Const. Ala., art. VII, §§173 to 176.
See IMPEACHMENT.
Subject to impeachment, §36-11-1; Const. Ala., art. VII, §174.
Injunctions.
Powers as to granting of injunctions, §§6-6-500, 12-3-8, 12-3-11.
Law clerks, §§12-3-27 to 12-3-29.
Montgomery.
Judges to reside in Montgomery during terms of court, §12-3-5.
Number of judges, Const. Ala., amd. 328.
Oath of office.
Retired judges, §12-18-7.
Panels.
Designation of panels to decide cases, §12-3-2.
Powers.
Retired judges, §12-18-7.
Retired judges on active duty status, §12-18-10.
Presiding judge, §12-3-4.
Qualifications, §12-3-1; Const. Ala., art. VI, §154.
Residence.
Judges to reside in Montgomery during term of court, §12-3-5.
Retirement.
Active duty status, §12-18-10.
Applicability of article.
Future additional state judicial officers, §12-18-12.
Judges elected or appointed to office after September 18, 1973, §12-18-5.
Benefits, §12-18-10.
Death of judges.
Payment of benefits to spouses upon, §12-18-10.
Forfeiture, §12-18-7.

COURT OF CRIMINAL APPEALS—Cont'd

Judges—Cont'd
Retirement—Cont'd
Benefits—Cont'd
Payment to spouses upon death of judges, §12-18-10.
Spouses.
Payment of benefits to spouses upon death of judges, §12-18-10.
Compensation.
Retired judges on active duty status, §12-18-10.
Confidential secretaries.
Retired judges performing active duty, §12-5-21.
Construction of article, §12-18-13.
Contributions by state and local governing bodies, §12-18-5.
Contributions made to employees retirement system,
Transfer into judicial retirement fund, §12-18-8.
Contributions to retirement fund by judges, §12-18-5.
Refund upon termination of service, §12-18-8.
Death.
Payment of benefits to spouses upon death of judges, §12-18-10.
Declaration as to intention to retire, §12-18-7.
Duties of retired judges, §12-18-7.
Retired judges on active duty status, §12-18-10.
Eligibility for retirement, §12-18-6.
Entitlement to retirement and receipt of pension, §12-18-4.
Forfeiture of benefits, §12-18-7.
Intention to retire.
Declaration as to intention, §12-18-7.
Judicial retirement fund.
See JUDGES.
Military service.
Granting of service for military service, §12-18-5.
Oath of retired judges, §12-18-7.
Powers of retired judges, §12-18-7.
Retired judges on active duty status, §12-18-10.
Prior service.
Credit for service un employees retirement system, §12-18-8.
Retirement order, §12-18-4.
Spouses.
Payment of benefits to spouses upon death of judges, §12-18-10.

COURT OF CRIMINAL APPEALS—Cont'd

Judges—Cont'd

Retirement—Cont'd

Time of service as full-time state prosecutor, §12-18-8.1.

Transitional provisions, §12-18-5.

Vacancies in office, §12-18-9.

Salaries, §12-3-6; Const. Ala., art. VI, §150.

Retired judges on active duty status, §12-18-10.

Secretaries.

Confidential secretaries, §12-3-20.

Retired judges performing active duty, §12-5-21.

Seminars.

Reimbursement of travel expenses of judges attending, §12-1-17.

Stay of proceedings.

Powers of judges as to issuance of stays, §12-3-8.

Supernumerary judges.

Continuation of laws concerning duties, benefits, etc., §12-3-7.

Travel expenses.

Reimbursement for judges attending judicial colleges, seminars, etc., §12-1-17.

Vacancies, §12-18-9.

Filling, §12-3-2.

Jurisdiction, Const. Ala., amd. 328.

Appellate jurisdiction, §12-3-9.

Original jurisdiction, §12-3-11.

Law clerks.

Appointment, §12-3-27.

Successors, §12-3-28.

Clerk to serve appointing judge, §12-3-28.

Dismissal, §12-3-28.

Salaries, §12-3-29.

Successors.

Appointment, §12-3-28.

Librarian, §12-3-19.

Mandamus.

Original jurisdiction of court, §12-3-11.

Review in supreme court of decisions of courts of appeals.

Rules of appellate procedure, ARAP, Rule 21.

Marshal, §12-3-19.

Montgomery.

Judges to reside in Montgomery during terms of court, §12-3-5.

Municipal corporations.

Offices and other physical facilities.

Authorization to contract with municipalities for, §12-1-20.

Prosecution assistance by municipality, ARJA, Rule 17.

Notice of appeal.

Form, ARAP, Form 11.

COURT OF CRIMINAL APPEALS—Cont'd

Notice of orders, ARAP, Rule 17 (a).

Officers.

Travel expenses.

Reimbursement for attending conferences, etc., §12-1-17.

Offices.

Contracting with localities for, §12-1-20.

Opinions.

Reporting, §12-3-18.

Orders of court.

Notice of orders, ARAP, Rule 17 (a).

Post-conviction remedies.

Court to which appeal taken, ARCrP, Rule 20.10 (a).

Presiding judge, §12-3-4.

Prohibition, writ of.

Review in supreme court of decisions of.

Rules of appellate procedure, ARAP, Rule 21.

Quarters, §12-3-13.

Quo warranto.

Original jurisdiction of court, §12-3-11.

Records.

Binding.

Payment of cost of binding, §12-3-31.

Destroyed records.

Substitution, §12-20-32.

Furnishing of record books, §12-3-31.

Lost records.

Substitution, §12-20-32.

Costs and fees of substitution, §12-20-1.

Substitution of appellate court records, §12-20-32.

Costs and fees of substitution, §12-20-1.

Reporter of decisions.

See REPORTER OF DECISIONS OF SUPREME COURT AND COURTS OF APPEALS.

Reporting of opinions and decisions, §12-3-18.

Retirement.

Judges. See within this heading, "Judges."

Review of decisions, ARAP, Rule 39.

Rules of appellate procedure.

See APPEALS.

Salaries.

Clerk of court, §12-3-20.

Judges, §12-3-6; Const. Ala., art. VI, §150.

Retired judges on active duty status, §12-18-10.

Law clerks, §12-3-29.

Payment of salaries of employees of courts, §12-3-30.

Staff attorneys, §12-3-35.

Secretaries, §12-3-20.

Retired judges performing active duty, §12-5-21.

Special terms.

Applicability of provisions of section 12-2-9, §12-3-33.

COURT OF CRIMINAL APPEALS—Cont'd

Staff attorneys, §12-3-35.

Appointment and compensation, §12-3-34.

Stenographers, §12-3-34.

State as party.

Attorney general to attend, §12-3-32.

Stationery.

Furnishing, §12-3-31.

Stay of proceedings.

Powers of judges as to issuance of stays, §12-3-8.

Supreme court.

Authority over appeals courts, §12-3-16.

Review of decisions, ARAP, Rule 39.

Transfer of cases in court of criminal appeals to supreme court, §12-3-14.

Terms of court.

Regular term, §12-3-12.

Special terms.

Applicability of provisions of section 12-2-9, §12-3-33.

Transfer of cases.

Improperly submitted cases, §12-1-4.

Transfer of cases to supreme court, §12-3-14.

Writs.

Powers of courts as to issuance of remedial and original writs, §12-3-11.

COURT OF THE JUDICIARY.

Appeals.

Costs.

Security, ARAJC, Rule B.

Filing record with supreme court, ARAJC, Rule C.

Notice, ARAJC, Rule A.

Rules of procedure, ARAJC, Rule D.

Construction and application, ARAJC, Rule E.

Security for costs, ARAJC, Rule B.

Appearance.

Court to proceed where no appearance made, ARJC, Rule 11.

Assisting and aiding court.

Obligation to assist or aid, ARJC, Rule 15.

Attorneys at law.

Appointment of counsel, ARJC, Rule 12.

Bailiff.

Designation, ARJC, Rule 17.

Complaints.

Contents, ARJC, Rule 3.

Filing, ARJC, Rule 3.

Notice.

Right to notice, ARJC, Rule 3.

Service, ARJC, Rule 4.

Conflicts of interest.

When court members not to participate, ARJC, Rule 6.

Constitution of Alabama, Const. Ala., amd. 328.

Contempt.

Punishment, ARJC, Rule 17.

Court reporter, §12-7-2.

COURT OF THE JUDICIARY
—Cont'd
Decisions.
Finality, ARJC, Rule 16.
Definitions, ARJC, Rule 1.
Dilatory actions disfavored,
ARJC, Rule 7.
Evidence.
Rules of evidence, ARJC,
Rule 10.
Expenses of members.
Reimbursement, §12-7-1.
Fees.
Witnesses, ARJC, Rule 22.
Hearings.
Date of hearing, ARJC, Rule
8.
Nature of hearing, ARJC,
Rule 9.
Place of hearing, ARJC, Rule
19. ARJC, Rule 8.
Judges.
Alternate judges, ARJC, Rule
26.
Presiding judge, ARJC, Rule
24.
Judicial inquiry commission.
Prosecution of charges before
court of the judiciary,
AJICR, Rule 15.
Judicial notice.
Right to take, ARJC, Rule
18.
Notice.
Appeals, ARAJC, Rule A.
Complaints.
Right to notice, ARJC,
Rule 3.
Service, ARJC, Rule 4.
Orders.
Entering, ARJC, Rule 16.
Form, ARJC, Rule 20.
Parties.
Interested party.
Persons designated as,
ARJC, Rule 13.
Pleadings.
Court to proceed where no
pleadings filed, ARJC,
Rule 11.
Responsive pleadings.
Filing, ARJC, Rule 5.
Rights, ARJC, Rule 3.
Presiding judge, ARJC, Rule
24.
Reporter.
Court reporter, §12-7-2.
Rules of civil procedure.
Applicability, ARJC, Rule 10.
Rules of procedure.
Appeals, ARAJC, Rules D, E.
Copies, ARJC, Rule 23.
Effective date, ARJC, Rule
25.
Secretary.
Clerk of court of civil
appeals, ARJC, Rule 2.
Subpoenas.
Issuance, ARJC, Rule 22.
Supreme court.
Appeals.
Filing record with supreme
court, ARAJC, Rule C.
Transcript of proceedings.
Keeping, ARJC, Rule 21.
Witnesses, ARJC, Rule 14.
Fees, ARJC, Rule 22.

COURTS.
Abolished courts.
Abolishing branch
courthouse or division or
branch of court of record,
Const. Ala., amd. 81.
Courts not authorized by
constitution, §12-12-1.
Courts of record.
Appeal from judgments or
decrees, §12-22-3.
Inferior courts of record.
Preserving judgment
records, §12-20-23.
Transfer of pending actions
and preservation and
enforcement of
judgments, §12-12-1.
Abuse of process, §12-1-8.
Administration of courts,
Const. Ala., amd. 328.
Chief justice of supreme
court.
Powers and duties,
§12-2-30.
Rules of judicial
administration. See
within this heading,
"Rules of judicial
administration."
**Administrative director of
courts.**
Administrative decisions.
Review by supreme court
justices, §12-5-20.
Administrative office of
courts.
Director head of office,
§12-5-8.
Appointment, Const. Ala.,
amd. 328.
Appropriations.
Expenditure of
appropriations,
§12-5-13.
Chief justice.
Assisting chief justice,
§12-5-9.
Delegation to
administrative
director.
Authority to act for chief
justice, §12-5-15.
Confidential secretaries.
Retired justices or judges
performing active
duty, §12-5-21.
Consultants.
Employment, §12-5-14.
Coordination of functions and
duties of local personnel,
§12-5-13.
Court services, ARJA, Rule
3.
Decisions.
Administrative decisions.
Review by supreme court
justices, §12-5-20.
Department of court
management.
Ex officio head of
department, §12-5-8.
Duties, §12-5-10.
Assisting chief justice,
§12-5-9.
Expenditures, §12-5-13.
Local legislation.
Procedure when local
legislation affecting
judiciary introduced,
§12-1-6.

COURTS—Cont'd
**Administrative director of
courts**—Cont'd
Physical facilities, ARJA,
Rule 3.
Powers, §12-5-10.
Retired justices or judges
performing active duty.
Confidential secretaries,
§12-5-21.
**Administrative office of
courts.**
Administrative director of
courts.
Director head of office,
§12-5-8.
Conferences or meetings
sponsored by.
Payment of expenses,
§12-5-19.
Confidential secretaries.
Retired justices or judges
performing active
duty, §12-5-21.
Created, §12-5-1.
Grants.
Service as agency for
application for and
receipt of, §12-5-2.
Officers and employees,
§12-5-2.
Colleges, conferences, etc.,
pertaining to
administration of
courts, §12-5-17.
Insurance, retirement and
other state employees'
benefits, §12-5-7.
Organizations devoted to
improvement of justice,
etc.
Membership authorized,
§12-5-16.
Offices, etc., for courts.
Contracting for, §12-1-20.
Studies, etc., as to
improvement of
administration of justice.
Coordination of studies,
etc., §12-5-2.
Appellate courts.
Court of civil appeals.
See COURT OF CIVIL
APPEALS.
Court of criminal appeals.
See COURT OF
CRIMINAL APPEALS.
Arbitration and award.
Duty to encourage settlement
of controversies, §6-6-1.
Associations.
State membership in certain
national associations,
§12-5-16.
Attendance.
Crime victims' court
attendance, §§15-14-50 to
15-14-57.
See TRIAL.
Attorneys at law.
Litigation accountability.
Fees.
Attorneys' fees
negotiated in
private, §12-19-274.
Court may approve
stipulations,
§12-19-274.
Bailiffs, §§12-17-310,
12-17-311; ARJA, Rule 11.

COURTS—Cont'd

Bonds, surety.
Officials and employees of unified judicial system.
Bonding of court officials and employees, ARJA, Rule 1.

Branch courthouse or branch of court of record.
Establishing or abolishing, Const. Ala., amd. 81.

Capital punishment.
Authority of court following review, §13A-5-53.
Specific determinations to be made by court, §13A-5-53.

Chancery courts.
Constitution of Alabama.
See CONSTITUTION OF ALABAMA.

Chancery powers.
Elections.
Jurisdiction denied courts exercising chancery powers in election contests, §17-15-6.

Circuit courts, §§12-11-1 to 12-11-61.
See CIRCUIT COURTS.

Clerks of court.
See CLERKS OF COURT.

Compromise and settlement.
Duty to encourage, §6-6-1.

Congress.
Power to constitute tribunals inferior to supreme court, Const. U. S., Art. I, §8.

Constitution of Alabama, Const. Ala., art. VI, §§139 to 172.
See CONSTITUTION OF ALABAMA.

Constitution of the United States.
Congress.
Power to constitute tribunals inferior to supreme court, Const. U. S., Art. I, §8.
Inferior courts, Const. U. S., Art. III, §1.
Judges.
Compensation, Const. U. S., Art. III, §1.
Tenure, Const. U. S., Art. III, §1.
Restriction of judicial power, Const. U. S., Amendment XI.

Contempt.
See CONTEMPT.

Corporations.
Jurisdiction of courts to grant relief not impaired by chapter, §10-2A-76.

Corrections.
Board of corrections.
Cooperation with courts, §14-1-8.

Costs.
General provisions.
See COSTS.

Court of civil appeals.
See COURT OF CIVIL APPEALS.

Court of criminal appeals.
See COURT OF CRIMINAL APPEALS.

COURTS—Cont'd

Court of the judiciary, §§12-7-1, 12-7-2.

Crime victims' court attendance, §§15-14-50 to 15-14-57.
See TRIAL.

Criminal jurisdiction.
Vesting, §12-1-3.

Declaratory judgments, §§6-6-220 to 6-6-232.
See DECLARATORY JUDGMENTS.

Definitions.
Litigation accountability, §12-19-271.

Department of court management.
Administrative director of courts.
Ex officio head of department, §12-5-8.
Appointment, §12-5-4.
Assistant court administrator, §12-5-4.
Conferences or meetings sponsored by.
Payment of expenses, §12-5-19.
Court administrator.
Chief justice.
Delegation to court administrator of authority to act for, §12-5-15.
Duties, §12-5-4.
Duties, §12-5-3.
Employees.
Appointment, §12-5-4.
Colleges, conferences, etc., pertaining to administration of courts, §12-5-17.
Compensation, §12-5-4.
Entitlement to state employees' benefits, §12-5-7.
Organizations and associations devoted to improvement of justice.
Membership authorized, §12-5-16.
State merit system.
Applicability, §12-5-5.
Established, §12-5-3.
Offices and other physical facilities for courts.
Contracts for, §12-1-20.
Powers, §12-5-3.
Responsibility for trial court administration, §12-5-6.
Trial court administration.
Department to be responsible for, §12-5-6.

Deposit in court, ARCP, Rule 67.

Director.
Admininstrative director of courts. See within this heading, "Administrative director of courts."

District attorneys.
See DISTRICT ATTORNEYS.

District courts, §§12-12-1 to 12-12-73.
See DISTRICT COURTS.

Disturbances, §12-1-8.

COURTS—Cont'd

Disturbing the peace.
Interference with judicial proceedings, §13A-10-130.

Employees.
Benefits.
Employment benefits, §12-1-15.
Voluntary diminishment, §12-1-16.
Certain statutes relative to court personnel continued in effect, §12-1-22.
Compensation.
Voluntary diminishment, §12-1-16.
Department of court management. See within this heading, "Department of court management."
Salaries, §12-1-21.

Enforcement of judgments.
Powers, §12-1-7.

Enumeration, §12-1-2.

Equipment.
County-owned equipment.
Transfer to state, §§12-19-8, 12-19-9.
Inventory, §12-19-8.
Local purchasing procedures, §12-19-10.

Establishing.
Branch courthouse or division or branch of court of record, Const. Ala., amd. 81.

Expenditures, §12-1-2.

Expenses.
Budget estimates.
Preparation as to state expenditures for trial courts, §12-19-5.
Counties.
Continuation of financial support by counties from January 16, 1977 through September 30, 1977, §12-19-2.
Supplementation of state expenditures by counties, §12-19-1.
Payment by state, §12-19-6.
Salaries.
Payment by state, §12-19-6.
State responsibility for operating expenses of unified judicial system, §12-19-1.
Phasing of state assumption of financial responsibility, §12-19-3.
Preparation of budget estimates for trial courts, §12-19-5.

Facilities.
Offices, etc., for courts.
Contracting for, §12-1-20.

Federal grants, §12-5-12.

Fees.
Costs.
See COSTS.
Docket fees.
See DOCKETS.
Miscellaneous filings, ARJA, Rule 7.

COURTS—Cont'd
Fees—Cont'd
Records.
Copies and certification,
ARJA, Rule 30.
Findings by court.
Stay on motion for
amendment to or
addition to findings,
ARCP, Rule 62 (b).
Foundations.
Powers of courts not
impaired, §10-4-210.
Frivolous actions. See within
this heading, "Litigation
accountability."
Funds.
Federal funds, §12-5-12.
Furniture.
County-owned furniture.
Transfer to state,
§§12-19-8, 12-19-9.
Inventory, §12-19-8.
Local purchasing procedures,
§12-19-10.
Grants.
Federal grants, §12-5-12.
Holidays.
Clerks of court and registers.
Office hours, ARJA, Rule
5.
**Interference with judicial
proceedings,** §13A-10-130.
Judges.
General provisions.
See JUDGES.
Judicial conference, §§12-8-1
to 12-8-5.
See JUDICIAL
CONFERENCE.
**Judicial system study
commission,** §§12-9-1 to
12-9-9.
See JUDICIAL SYSTEM
STUDY COMMISSION.
Judiciary.
Court of the judiciary.
See COURT OF THE
JUDICIARY.
Jurisdiction.
Chancery powers.
Election contests, §17-15-6.
Criminal jurisdiction.
Vesting, §12-1-3.
Jury.
General provisions.
See JURY.
When words "jury" or
"juries" include court or
judge, §12-16-1.
Juvenile proceedings,
§§12-15-1 to 12-15-120.
See JUVENILE
PROCEEDINGS.
Libraries.
Law libraries.
Counties, §§11-25-1 to
11-25-12.
See LIBRARIES.
Litigation accountability.
Application of provisions,
§12-19-275.
Attorneys' fees.
Assessment, §12-19-272.
Negotiated in private,
§12-19-274.
Stipulations.
Court may approve,
§12-19-274.

COURTS—Cont'd
Litigation accountability
—Cont'd
Awards.
Factors to be considered,
§12-19-273.
Citation of act, §12-19-270.
Costs, §12-19-272.
Definitions, §12-19-271.
Dismissal.
Voluntary dismissal,
§12-19-272.
Provisions applicable to,
§12-19-275.
Provisions cumulative,
§12-19-276.
Short title, §12-19-270.
Title of act, §12-19-270.
Local legislation.
Procedure to introduce in
legislature, §12-1-6.
Lost papers, records, etc.
Substitution. See within this
heading, "Records."
Management.
Department of court
management. See within
this heading,
"Department of court
management."
Masters, ARCP, Rule 53.
Military courts.
See MILITARY AFFAIRS.
Municipal courts, §§12-14-1
to 12-14-71.
See MUNICIPAL COURTS.
Oath.
Powers of courts, §12-1-7.
Officers.
Bail and recognizance.
Signature, §36-10-11.
Benefits.
Employment benefits,
§12-1-15.
Voluntary diminishment,
§12-1-16.
Compensation.
Voluntary diminishment,
§12-1-16.
Contempt.
Appeal to appellate court
by officer from
judgment of contempt,
§12-1-11.
Employment benefits,
§12-1-15.
Fees.
Payment of uncollected
fees from fine and
forfeiture fund.
See PENALTIES.
Misbehavior, §12-1-8.
Salaries, §12-1-21.
Saving provision, §12-1-22.
Offices.
Contracting for, §12-1-20.
Organizations.
State membership and
certain national
organizations, §12-5-16.
Papers.
Removal of court papers,
§12-20-24.
Substitution of lost or
destroyed papers or
records in civil cases. See
within this heading,
"Records."
Personnel system.
Establishment, ARJA, Rule
9.

COURTS—Cont'd
Physical facilities, ARJA,
Rule 3.
Powers.
Vesting of judicial power of
state, §12-1-2.
Preservation of order.
Cases in which courts may
inflict summary
punishment for
contempt, §12-1-8.
Powers of courts, §12-1-7.
Probate courts, §§12-13-1 to
12-13-70.
See PROBATE COURTS.
Purchases.
Local purchasing procedures,
§12-19-10.
Quo warranto.
Court always open, §6-6-593.
Trial by court, §6-6-593.
Radio.
When broadcasting in
courtroom permitted,
ACJE, Canon 3A.
Records.
Certification.
Fees, ARJA, Rule 30.
Copies.
Fees, ARJA, Rule 30.
Damaged or destroyed
records.
Disposal of remains of
records, ARJA, Rule
31.
Disposal, §41-13-21.
After microfilming, ARJA,
Rule 31.
Damaged or destroyed
records.
Disposal of remains,
ARJA, Rule 31.
Method, ARJA, Rule 31.
Fees.
Copies and certification,
ARJA, Rule 30.
Juvenile records, ARJA, Rule
31.
Microfilming.
Disposal after
microfilming, ARJA,
Rule 31.
Orders, judgments and
decrees.
Copying into final record
not required,
§12-20-21.
Removal, §12-20-24.
Retention schedule.
Adoption, ARJA, Rule 31.
Amendments and
additions.
Procedure, ARJA, Rule
31.
Description, ARJA, Rule
31.
Juvenile records.
Inapplicability to, ARJA,
Rule 31.
Substitution of lost or
destroyed papers or
records.
After determination of
action or proceeding,
§12-20-29.
Appeal from court order or
decree granting or
denying, §12-20-31.
Appellate court records,
§12-20-32.
Costs, §12-20-1.

COURTS—Cont'd
Records—Cont'd
Substitution of lost or
destroyed papers or
records—Cont'd
Deeds, contracts, etc.,
§12-20-30.
Fees, §12-20-1.
Generally, §12-20-27.
Pending action or
proceeding, §12-20-28.
Power of courts, §12-20-26.
Reporters.
Circuit courts.
See CIRCUIT COURTS.
Decisions of supreme court
and courts of appeals,
§§12-4-1 to 12-4-4.
District courts.
See DISTRICT COURTS.
Duties, ARCrP, Rule 21.
Fees.
Transcripts.
Preparation, ARJA, Rule
29.
Official court reporters,
ARJA, Rule 12.
Roving reporters.
Special roving reporters,
ARJA, Rule 12.
Rules of criminal procedure.
Duties, ARCrP, Rule 21.
Special court reporters.
Request for, ARJA, Rule
12.
Roving reporters, ARJA,
Rule 12.
State employees' retirement
system.
Participation, §36-27-52.
Supernumerary court
reporters.
State employees'
retirement system.
Effect of participation on
supernumerary
status, §36-27-52.
Transcripts.
Fees, ARJA, Rule 29.
Revenue, Const. Ala., amd.
328.
**Rules for mandatory
continuing legal
education.**
See ATTORNEYS AT LAW.
Rules of civil procedure.
See RULES OF CIVIL
PROCEDURE.
**Rules of judicial
administration.**
Amendments to rules.
Procedure, ARJA, Rule 25.
Arrest.
Warrant of arrest twice
returned not found.
Indictments withdrawn,
ARJA, Rule 16.
Assignment of judges.
Temporary assignments,
ARJA, Rule 13.
Bail and recognizance.
Discretionary bail
schedule, ARJA, Rule
2.
Factors considered for
setting bail, ARJA,
Rule 2.
Personal recognizance,
ARJA, Rule 2.

COURTS—Cont'd
**Rules of judicial
administration**—Cont'd
Bail and recognizance
—Cont'd
Schedule.
Discretionary bail
schedule, ARJA,
Rule 2.
Setting bail.
Factors considered,
ARJA, Rule 2.
Bailiffs, ARJA, Rule 11.
Temporary assignment,
ARJA, Rule 13.
Bonds, surety.
Officials and employees of
unified judicial system,
ARJA, Rule 1.
Calendar management,
ARJA, Rule 16.
Child support expedited
process.
hearings, ARJA, Rule 35.
Monitors.
Appointment, ARJA,
Rule 35.
Referees.
Appointment, ARJA,
Rule 35.
Hearings before, ARJA,
Rule 35.
Rehearings before courts,
ARJA, Rule 35.
Scope, ARJA, Rule 35.
Child support guidelines.
Basic child support
obligations.
Determination, ARJA,
Rule 32.
Schedule, ARJA, Rule
32.
Review and update,
ARJA, Rule 32.
Computation of child
support, ARJA, Rule
32.
Definitions, ARJA, Rule
32.
Effective date, ARJA, Rule
32.
Established, ARJA, Rule
32.
Forms.
Standardized child
support guideline
form and income
statement form,
ARJA, Rule 32.
Income statements, ARJA,
Rule 32.
Forms, ARJA, Rule 32.
Payment of support to
court, ARJA, Rule 32.
Clerks of court.
Circuit courts.
Secretarial services,
ARJA, Rule 15.
District courts.
Appointment, ARJA,
Rule 27.
Establishment of office,
ARJA, Rule 27.
Factors in determining
need, ARJA, Rule
27.
Nomination, ARJA, Rule
27.
Duties, ARJA, Rule 4.

COURTS—Cont'd
**Rules of judicial
administration**—Cont'd
Clerks of court—Cont'd
Financial systems account
for funds.
Assistance in
development, ARJA,
Rule 28.
Office hours.
Closing offices.
Effect on computation
of time periods,
ARJA, Rule 5.
Routine work days,
ARJA, Rule 5.
Saturdays, Sundays and
other holidays,
ARJA, Rule 5.
Conflicting state and
county holidays,
ARJA, Rule 5.
Severe weather,
hazardous or other
emergency
conditions, ARJA,
Rule 5.
Commissions.
Cases filed prior to
January 16, 1977,
ARJA, Rule 23.
Committee.
Standing committee.
Amendments and
proposals.
Procedure, ARJA, Rule
25.
Established, ARJA, Rule
25.
Computer-based court
information.
Dissemination.
Applications, ARJA,
Rule 33.
Costs, ARJA, Rule 33.
Forms, ARJA, Rule 33.
Policies and procedures,
ARJA, Rule 33.
Release of data, ARJA,
Rule 33.
Contempt.
Willful noncompliance with
rules, ARJA, Rule 34.
Costs.
Dissemination of computer-
based court
information, ARJA,
Rule 33.
Court services, ARJA, Rule
3.
Definitions.
Child support guidelines,
ARJA, Rule 32.
District courts.
Clerks of court.
Appointment, ARJA,
Rule 27.
Establishment of office,
ARJA, Rule 27.
Nomination, ARJA, Rule
27.
Municipal corporations.
Prosecution assistance,
ARJA, Rule 17.
Prosecutorial services.
Assistance by
municipality, ARJA,
Rule 17.
Dockets.
Call of cases, ARJA, Rule
16.

COURTS—Cont'd
  **Rules of judicial
    administration**—Cont'd
  Expedited process for child
    support, ARJA, Rule 35.
  Fees.
    Cases filed prior to
      January 16, 1977,
      ARJA, Rule 23.
    Miscellaneous filings,
      ARJA, Rule 7.
    Records.
      Copies and certification,
        ARJA, Rule 30.
      Transcripts, ARJA, Rule
        29.
      Transfer of cases, ARJA,
        Rule 26.
  Filing papers.
    Fees for miscellaneous
      filings, ARJA, Rule 7.
  Fiscal procedures, ARJA,
    Rule 28.
  Forms.
    Child support guidelines.
      Standardized child
        support guideline
        form and income
        statement form,
        ARJA, Rule 32.
    Dissemination of computer-
      based court
      information, ARJA,
      Rule 33.
    Plea of guilty, ARJA, Rule
      20.
  Hearings.
    Child support.
      Expedited process for
        child support, ARJA,
        Rule 35.
  Holidays.
    Clerks of court and
      registers.
      Office hours. ARJA, Rule
        5.
  Indigent defense services,
    ARJA, Rule 8.
  Judges.
    Assignment of judges.
      Temporary assignments,
        ARJA, Rule 13.
    Presiding judges.
      Selection, ARJA, Rule 6.
    Robes.
      Wearing suitable black
        judicial robe, ARJA,
        Rule 22.
    Secretarial services, ARJA,
      Rule 10.
    Special judges.
      Compensation, ARJA,
        Rule 14.
  Law students.
    Legal internship by, ARJA,
      Appx. A.
  Magistrates.
    Administrative agency,
      ARJA, Rule 18.
    Appointment, ARJA, Rule
      18.
    Financial systems to
      account for funds.
      Assistance in
        development, ARJA,
        Rule 28.
    Notice.
      Appointment, ARJA,
        Rule 18.
    Oath of office, ARJA, Rule
      18.

COURTS—Cont'd
  **Rules of judicial
    administration**—Cont'd
  Magistrates—Cont'd
    Qualifications for
      appointment, ARJA,
      Rule 18.
  Monitors.
    Child support.
      Express process
        monitors.
        Appointment, ARJA,
          Rule 35.
  Municipal corporations.
    Circuit courts.
      Prosecution assistance by
        municipality, ARJA,
        Rule 17.
    Court of civil appeals.
      Prosecution assistance by
        municipality, ARJA,
        Rule 17.
    Court of criminal appeals.
      Prosecution assistance by
        municipality, ARJA,
        Rule 17.
    District courts.
      Prosecution assistance by
        municipality, ARJA,
        Rule 17.
    Prosecution assistance by
      municipality, ARJA,
      Rule 17.
    Prosecutorial services.
      Assistance by
        municipality, ARJA,
        Rule 17.
  Noncompliance with rules.
    Willful noncompliance.
      Contempt, ARJA, Rule
        34.
  Penalties.
    Schedule of fines, ARJA,
      Rule 20.
  Personnel system.
    Establishment, ARJA,
      Rule 9.
  Physical facilities, ARJA,
    Rule 3.
  Pleas.
    Forms.
      Plea of guilty, ARJA,
        Rule 20.
  Presiding judges.
    Secretarial services, ARJA,
      Rule 10.
    Selection, ARJA, Rule 6.
    Temporary assignment of
      judges and other court
      personnel, ARJA, Rule
      13.
  Prosecution assistance by
    municipality, ARJA,
    Rule 17.
  Records.
    Certification.
      Fees, ARJA, Rule 30.
    Copies.
      Fees, ARJA, Rule 30.
    Damaged or destroyed
      records.
      Disposal, ARJA, Rule 31.
    Disposal.
      After microfilming,
        ARJA, Rule 31.
      Damaged or destroyed
        records, ARJA, Rule
        31.
      Method, ARJA, Rule 31.

COURTS—Cont'd
  **Rules of judicial
    administration**—Cont'd
  Records—Cont'd
    Fees.
      Certification, ARJA,
        Rule 30.
      Copies, ARJA, Rule 30.
    Juvenile records.
      Inapplicability of
        retention schedule,
        ARJA, Rule 31.
    Microfilming.
      Disposal after, ARJA,
        Rule 31.
    Retention schedule.
      Adoption, ARJA, Rule
        31.
      Amendments and
        additions, ARJA,
        Rule 31.
      Description, ARJA, Rule
        31.
      Juvenile records.
        Inapplicability to,
          ARJA, Rule 31.
    Transfer of cases, ARJA,
      Rule 26.
  Referees.
    Child support.
      Expedited process for
        child support.
        Appointment of
          referees, ARJA,
          Rule 35.
        Hearings before
          referees, ARJA,
          Rule 35.
  Registers.
    Duties, ARJA, Rule 4.
    Financial systems for
      receipt, deposit and
      disbursement of funds.
      Assistance in
        development, ARJA,
        Rule 28.
    Office hours.
      Closing offices.
        Effect on computation
          of time periods,
          ARJA, Rule 5.
      Routine work days,
        ARJA, Rule 5.
      Saturdays, Sundays and
        other holidays,
        ARJA, Rule 5.
      Severe weather,
        hazardous or other
        emergency
        conditions, ARJA,
        Rule 5.
  Reporters.
    Official court reporters,
      ARJA, Rule 12.
    Roving reporters.
      Special roving reporters,
        ARJA, Rule 12.
    Special court reporters.
      Requests for, ARJA,
        Rule 12.
      Roving reporters, ARJA,
        Rule 12.
    Temporary assignment,
      ARJA, Rule 13.
    Transcripts.
      Fees, ARJA, Rule 29.
  Seal of court, ARJA, Rule 24.

COURTS—Cont'd
Rules of judicial administration—Cont'd
Secretarial services, ARJA, Rule 10.
Clerks of court.
Circuit courts, ARJA, Rule 15.
Judges, ARJA, Rule 10.
Temporary assignment of secretaries, ARJA, Rule 13.
Small claims.
Forms.
Proceedings in small claims court, ARJA, Rule 21.
Instructions.
Using small claims court.
Publication, ARJA, Rule 21.
Sessions of small claims courts.
Regularly held, ARJA, Rule 21.
Special judges.
Compensation, ARJA, Rule 14.
Standing committee.
Amendments and proposals.
Procedure, ARJA, Rule 25.
Established, ARJA, Rule 25.
Sundays.
Clerks of court and registers.
Office hours, ARJA, Rule 5.
Traffic offenses.
Schedule of fines, ARJA, Rule 20.
Uniform traffic infractions, ARJA, Rule 19.
Transcripts.
Fees, ARJA, Rule 29.
Preparation.
Requirements, ARJA, Rule 29.
Transfer of cases, ARJA, Rule 26.
Uniform traffic infractions.
Accountability for tickets, ARJA, Rule 19.
Appearance.
Defendant's appearance, ARJA, Rule 19.
Failure of defendant to appear, ARJA, Rule 19.
Bail.
Failure of defendant to appear.
Forfeiture of bail according to law, ARJA, Rule 19.
Clerks of court.
Fines and court costs paid to, ARJA, Rule 19.
Complaint and summons.
Forms.
Uniform traffic ticket and complaint, ARJA, Rule 19.
Costs.
Paid to clerks of court, ARJA, Rule 19.

COURTS—Cont'd
Rules of judicial administration—Cont'd
Uniform traffic infractions —Cont'd
Fines.
Paid to clerks of court, ARJA, Rule 19.
Forms, ARJA, Rule 19.
Complaint and summons, ARJA, Rule 19.
Law enforcement officers.
Issuance of tickets to, ARJA, Rule 19.
Municipal parking offenses, ARJA, Rule 19.
Notice.
Failure of defendant to appear.
Issuance of additional notice, ARJA, Rule 19.
Parking.
Municipal parking offenses, ARJA, Rule 19.
Pleas, ARJA, Rule 19.
Procedures.
Generally, ARJA, Rule 19.
Summons.
Failure of defendant to appear.
Issuance of supplemental summons, ARJA, Rule 19.
Trial.
Waiver, ARJA, Rule 19.
Uniform traffic ticket and complaint.
Declaration of approval, ARJA, Rule 19.
Form of traffic complaint and summons, ARJA, Rule 19.
Use of ticket, ARJA, Rule 19.
Warrant.
Failure of defendant to appear.
Issuance, ARJA, Rule 19.
Weighted caseload system, ARJA, Appx. B.
Willful noncompliance with rules.
Contempt, ARJA, Rule 34.
Rules of supreme court.
Effect, §12-1-1.
Salaries, §12-1-21.
Secretaries.
Circuit courts.
See CIRCUIT COURTS.
Confidential secretaries.
Retired justices or judges performing active duty, §12-5-21.
District courts.
See DISTRICT COURTS.
Supreme court.
See SUPREME COURT.
Services, ARJA, Rule 3.
Settlements.
Pro tanto settlements, §12-21-109.
Special sessions.
Ordering by chief justice, §12-2-33.

COURTS—Cont'd
State.
State not to be made defendant, Const. Ala., art. I, §14.
Statistics, §12-8-7.
Statutes.
Repeal.
Practice and procedure in certain courts not affected, §6-1-1.
Studies, projects, etc., to improve administration of justice, §12-5-18.
Sundays.
Clerks of court and registers.
Office hours.
Saturdays, Sundays and other holidays, ARJA, Rule 5.
Supervision of courts.
Chief justice of supreme court.
Powers and duties, §12-2-30.
Supplies.
County-owned supplies.
Transfer to state, §§12-19-8, 12-19-9.
Inventory, §12-19-8.
Local purchasing procedures, §12-19-10.
Supreme court, §§12-2-1 to 12-2-160.
See SUPREME COURT.
Taxation.
Costs.
See COSTS.
Television.
When broadcasting in courtroom permitted, ACJE, Canon 3A.
Trial.
See TRIAL.
United States.
Certified questions from federal courts, ARAP, Rule 18.
Constitution of the United States.
See CONSTITUTION OF THE UNITED STATES.

COURTS-MARTIAL.
See MILITARY AFFAIRS.

COVENANTS NOT TO COMPETE, §8-1-1.

COVINGTON COUNTY.
Counties generally.
See COUNTIES.
Officers.
Compensation, Const. Ala., amd. 479.
School tax.
Special school tax in school districts Nos. 1 and 2, Const. Ala., amd. 292.

COWS.
Animals generally.
See ANIMALS.
Estrays, §§3-2-1 to 3-2-23.
See ESTRAYS.
Livestock.
See LIVESTOCK.
Milk and milk products, §§2-13-1 to 2-13-94.
See MILK AND MILK PRODUCTS.

CRABS.
Reciprocal agreements as to commercial seafood fishing, §§9-12-160 to 9-12-162.

CREAM.
See MILK AND MILK PRODUCTS.

CREDIT.
Bills of credit.
Constitutional provisions, Const. U. S., Art. I, §10.
Cards, §§5-20-2 to 5-20-10, 13A-9-14, 13A-9-15.
See CREDIT CARDS.
Consumer finance, §§5-19-1 to 5-19-31.
See CONSUMER FINANCE.
Credit unions, §§5-17-1 to 5-17-59.
See CREDIT UNIONS.
Debtors and creditors.
See DEBTORS AND CREDITORS.
Fraud.
Representation or assurance of another's credit to be in writing, §8-9-5.
Insurance premium finance companies, §§27-40-1 to 27-40-18.
See INSURANCE.
Letters of credit.
Commercial code, §§7-5-101 to 7-5-117.
See COMMERCIAL CODE.
Savings and loan associations, §§5-16-1 to 5-16-53.
See SAVINGS AND LOAN ASSOCIATIONS.
Secured transactions, §§7-9-101 to 7-9-507.
See COMMERCIAL CODE.
Suretyship.
See SURETYSHIP.

CREDIT AGENCIES.
Licenses, §40-12-87.

CREDIT CARDS.
Banking laws.
Applicability to credit card banks, §5-20-8.
Charges, §5-20-5.
Citation of act.
Short title, §5-20-2.
Conflict of laws.
Repeal of conflicting laws, §5-20-10.
Construction and interpretation, §§5-20-9, 5-20-10.
Credit card banks.
Acquisition, §5-20-4.
Applications, §5-20-6.
Filing fee, §§5-20-4, 5-20-6.
Applicable law, §5-20-8.
Defined, §5-20-3.
Establishment, §5-20-4.
Applications, §5-20-6.
Filing fee, §§5-20-4, 5-20-6.
Severability of provisions, §5-20-9.
Supervision, §5-20-7.
Criminal law and procedure.
Fraudulent use, §13A-9-14.
Illegal possession, §13A-9-14.
Definitions, §5-20-3.

CREDIT CARDS—Cont'd
Fees, §5-20-5.
Credit card banks.
Establishment or acquisition.
Applications.
Filing fee, §§5-20-4, 5-20-6.
Felonies.
Fraud by persons authorized to provide goods and services.
Class B felony, §13A-9-14.1.
Fraud.
Fraud by persons authorized to provide goods and services, §13A-9-14.1.
Fraudulent use of credit card, §13A-9-14.
Illegal possession, §13A-9-14.
Lost, stolen or mislaid credit cards.
False reports, §13A-9-15.
Penalties.
Cease and desist orders.
Violation by credit card banks, §5-20-7.
Rates, §5-20-5.
Reports.
False reporting of lost, stolen or mislaid credit cards, §13A-9-15.
Rules and regulations.
Superintendent of banks, §5-20-7.
Short title of act, §5-20-2.
Superintendent of banks.
Cease and desist orders, §5-20-7.
Definition of "superintendent," §5-20-3.
Enforcement powers, §5-20-7.
Rules and regulations, §5-20-7.
Supervision of credit card banks, §5-20-7.
Theft.
Second degree theft of property, §13A-8-4.
Title of act.
Short title, §5-20-2.

CREDITORS.
See DEBTORS AND CREDITORS.

CREDIT UNIONS.
Actions.
Rules and regulations.
Determination of validity or applicability, §5-17-47.
Activities not restricted, §5-1A-7.
Administration. See within this heading, "Credit union administration."
Administrator.
Credit union administration. See within this heading, "Credit union administration."
Alabama credit union administration. See within this heading, "Credit union administration."

CREDIT UNIONS—Cont'd
Alabama credit union league.
Dues.
Advance payment of dues, §5-17-25.
Amortization of credit represented by certificate, §5-17-27.
Issuance of certificates, §5-17-26.
Redemption and purchase of certificate upon dissolution, §5-17-28.
Appeals.
Board.
Actions of administrator, §5-17-55.
Suspension of director, officer, etc., §5-17-8.
Attorneys at law.
Credit union administration.
Administrator.
Employment of attorneys, §5-17-50.
Audits.
Supervisory committee.
Powers and duties, §5-17-13.
Board.
Appeals from actions of administrator, §5-17-55.
Compensation of members, §5-17-58.
Composition, §5-17-55.
Creation, §5-17-55.
Expenses of members, §5-17-58.
Immunity from personal liability, §5-17-51.
Meetings.
How often held, §5-17-56.
Location, §5-17-56.
Notice, §5-17-56.
Quorum, §5-17-57.
Membership, §5-17-55.
Quorum, §5-17-57.
Removal of member, §5-17-44.
Terms of members, §5-17-55.
Vacancies, §5-17-55.
Bonds, surety.
Bureau of credit unions.
Supervisor, §5-2A-100.
Credit union administration.
Administrator, §5-17-42.
Examiners and office assistants, §5-17-54.
Borrowing money.
Power to borrow money, §5-17-4.
Bureau of credit unions, §§5-2A-100 to 5-2A-103.
Created, §5-2A-100.
Credit union administration.
See within this heading, "Credit union administration."
Credit union board. See within this heading, "Board."
Employees.
Appointment, §5-2A-100.
Examinations, §5-2A-102.
Expenses.
Payment of operating expenses, §5-2A-103.
Inspections, §5-2A-102.
Operating expenses.
Payment, §5-2A-103.

CREDIT UNIONS—Cont'd

Bureau of credit unions
—Cont'd
Records.
Open to public inspection,
§5-2A-100.
Reports.
Open to public inspection,
§5-2A-100.
Supervision, §5-2A-102.
Supervisor.
Administrator of credit
union administration.
General provisions. See
within this heading,
"Credit union
administration."
Appointment, §5-2A-100.
Bonds, surety, §5-2A-100.
Duties, §5-2A-100.
Examinations of credit
unions, §5-2A-102.
Inspection of credit unions,
§5-2A-102.
Investigations,
§5-2A-100.
Oath, §5-2A-100.
Qualifications, §5-2A-101.
Transfer of jurisdiction,
authority, powers and
duties, §5-17-7.
Transfer of duties to credit
union administration,
§5-17-7.
Bylaws, §5-17-2.
Amendment, §5-17-9.
Capital.
Composition, §5-17-14.
Commercial code.
Secured transactions.
Transfer of accounts
excluded from
provisions of article,
§7-9-104.
**Construction and
interpretation.**
Reliance upon regulations
and interpretations,
§5-17-46.
Written interpretations of
laws and regulations.
Adoption, amending or
repealing
interpretations,
§5-17-47.
Authority of administrator,
§5-17-46.
Conversion.
Procedures, §5-17-22.
Corporations.
Applicability of Alabama
business corporation act,
§5-17-59.
Credit committee.
Compensation of members,
§5-17-11.
Duties, §5-17-12.
Election, §5-17-10.
Powers, §5-17-12.
Credit union administration.
Administrator.
Appeals to board from
actions of
administrator,
§5-17-55.
Appointment, §5-17-41.
Assistants, §5-17-50.
Attorneys at law,
§5-17-50.

CREDIT UNIONS—Cont'd

Credit union administration
—Cont'd
Administrator—Cont'd
Authority to expand
powers of credit
unions.
Legislative findings,
§5-17-45.
Bonds, surety, §5-17-42.
Certificate of approval,
§5-17-2.
Revocation of certificate,
§5-17-8.
Eligibility, §5-17-41.
Employees, §5-17-50.
Immunity from personal
liability, §5-17-51.
Examiners, §§5-17-52 to
5-17-54.
Immunity from personal
liability, §5-17-51.
Interpretations of laws and
regulations, §5-17-46.
Adopting, amending or
repealing, §5-17-47.
Contesting regulation
for failure to
comply with
procedure,
§5-17-47.
Oaths, §5-17-42.
Removal from office,
§5-17-44.
Reports.
Annual report, §5-17-48.
Public distribution of
report and other
material, §5-17-48.
Reports to administrator,
§5-17-8.
Revocation of certificate of
approval, §5-17-8.
Rules and regulations.
Procedure for adopting,
amending or
repealing, §5-17-47.
Contesting regulation
for noncompliance
with procedure,
§5-17-47.
Promulgation, §5-17-46.
Seal, §5-17-43.
Special counsel, §5-17-50.
Vacancy, §5-17-41.
Violations of credit union
laws.
Submission to grand
jury, §5-17-49.
Creation, §5-17-40.
Functions, §5-17-40.
State banking department.
Transfer of authority
previously vested in
department, §5-17-40.
Credit union board. See
within this heading,
"Board."
Death.
Deposits in names of two
persons, §5-17-15.
Disposition of shares or
deposit account of
deceased person,
§5-17-16.
Trustees.
Deposits for trust
beneficiaries, §5-17-15.

CREDIT UNIONS—Cont'd

Decedents' estates.
Disposition of shares or
deposit account of
deceased person,
§5-17-16.
Defined, §5-17-1.
Deposits.
Death.
Deposits in names of two
persons, §5-17-15.
Disposition of deposit
account of deceased
person, §5-17-16.
Trustees, §5-17-15.
Joint deposits, §5-17-15.
Lien on deposits, §5-17-14.
Minors, §5-17-15.
Powers as to, §5-17-4.
Trust beneficiaries, §5-17-15.
Directors.
Compensation, §5-17-11.
Duties, §5-17-11.
Election of board of directors,
§5-17-10.
Loans to directors, §5-17-17.
Suspension, §5-17-8.
Dissolution.
Alabama credit union league.
Redemption and purchase
of advance dues
certificate, §5-17-28.
Voluntary dissolution,
§5-17-21.
Dividends, §5-17-20.
Elections.
Directors and committees,
§5-17-10.
Officers, §5-17-11.
Entrance fee, §5-17-14.
Evidence.
Credit union administration.
Administrator.
Seal.
Evidentiary effect,
§5-17-43.
Examinations, §5-17-8.
Examiners, §§5-17-52 to
5-17-54.
Supervisory committee.
Powers and duties of
supervisory committee,
§5-17-13.
Examiners.
Bonds, surety, §5-17-54.
Commissioning examiners.
Exhibit of commission to
credit union upon
making examination,
§5-17-53.
Furnishing commission to
examiner, §5-17-53.
Duties, §5-17-52.
Oaths, §5-17-52.
Office assistants.
Bonds, surety, §5-17-54.
**Expanding powers of credit
unions.**
Authority of administrator,
§5-17-45.
Federally chartered credit
unions, §5-17-45.
Legislative findings,
§5-17-45.
Out-of-state credit unions
doing business in state,
§5-17-45.
**Federally chartered credit
unions.**
Expanding powers of credit
unions, §5-17-45.

CREDIT UNIONS—Cont'd
Fees.
Certificate of organization.
Fee filed with certificate,
§5-17-7.
Entrance fee, §5-17-14.
Membership fee, §§5-17-5,
5-17-14.
Operating fee, §5-17-7.
Fiduciaries.
Power to accept deposit of
fiduciary funds, §5-17-4.
Fiscal year, §5-17-9.
Grand jury.
Violations of credit union
laws.
Administrator to submit to
grand jury, §5-17-49.
Hearings.
Revocation of certificates,
§5-17-8.
Immunity.
Administrator, board
members or employees,
§5-17-51.
Incorporation.
Procedure, §5-17-2.
Injunctions.
Cease and desist orders,
§5-17-8.
Insurance.
Requirements for obtaining
insurance, §5-17-19.
Interest.
Loans.
Interest rates on loans,
§5-17-18.
Investigations.
Supervision of bureau.
Generally, §5-2A-100.
Investments.
Powers as to, §5-17-4.
**Joint tenants and tenants in
common.**
Deposits in names of two
persons, §5-17-15.
League.
Alabama credit union league,
§§5-17-25 to 5-17-28.
Liability.
Immunity from personal
liability.
Administrator, board
members or employees,
§5-17-51.
Liens.
Lien on shares and deposits
of members, §5-17-14.
Liquidation.
Alabama credit union league.
Redemption and purchase
of advance dues
certificate, §5-17-28.
Voluntary dissolution,
§5-17-21.
Loans.
Credit committee.
Powers and duties,
§5-17-12.
Directors.
Loans to, §5-17-17.
Generally, §5-17-17.
Interest rates, §5-17-18.
Members.
Loans to, §5-17-17.
Officers.
Loans to, §5-17-17.
Penalties.
Commission received for
procuring loans,
§5-17-30.

CREDIT UNIONS—Cont'd
Loans—Cont'd
Penalties—Cont'd
Concealment of loans,
§5-17-29.
Powers of credit unions,
§5-17-4.
Meetings of members,
§5-17-9.
Membership.
Composition, §5-17-5.
Eligibility, §5-17-5.
Expulsion of members,
§5-17-6.
Fee, §§5-17-5, 5-17-14.
Loans to members, §5-17-17.
Meetings of members,
§5-17-9.
Withdrawal of members,
§5-17-6.
Merger.
Procedures, §5-17-22.
Minors.
Deposits, §5-17-15.
Names.
Use of words "credit union"
in name or title, §5-17-3.
Notice.
Board.
Meetings, §5-17-56.
Oaths.
Bureau of credit unions.
Supervisor, §5-2A-100.
Credit union administration.
Administrator, §5-17-42.
Examiners, §5-17-52.
Officers.
Duties, §5-17-11.
Election, §5-17-11.
Loans to officers, §5-17-17.
Suspension, §5-17-8.
Operating fees, §5-17-7.
Organization.
Certificate of organization,
§5-17-2.
Fee filed with certificate,
§5-17-7.
Procedure, §5-17-2.
**Out-of-state credit unions
doing business in state.**
Expanding powers of credit
unions, §5-17-45.
Overdraws.
Penalty, §5-17-30.
Penalties.
Concealment of discounts or
loans, §5-17-29.
False or omitted entries,
§5-17-32.
Overdraws, §5-17-30.
Receipt of commission, etc.,
for procuring loans,
§5-17-30.
Receipt of property other
than in payment for just
demand, §5-17-31.
Place of business.
Change of place of business,
§5-17-23.
Powers.
Expanding powers of credit
unions, §5-17-45.
Generally, §5-17-4.
Property.
Powers of credit unions,
§5-17-4.
Recordation.
Credit union administration.
Administrator.
Seal, §5-17-43.

CREDIT UNIONS—Cont'd
Reports.
Administrator.
Annual report, §5-17-48.
Duty to report to
administrator, §5-17-8.
Public distribution of
report, §5-17-48.
Reserves.
Regular and special,
§5-17-19.
Rules and regulations.
Procedure for adopting,
amending or repealing,
§5-17-47.
Promulgation, §5-17-46.
Reliance on regulations and
interpretations, §5-17-46.
Savings.
Power to receive, §5-17-4.
Seals.
Credit union administration,
§5-17-43.
Secured transactions.
Transfer of accounts excluded
from provisions of
article, §7-9-104.
Shares.
Death.
Disposition of shares of
deceased person,
§5-17-16.
Lien on shares of members,
§5-17-14.
Supervisory committee.
Compensation of members,
§5-17-11.
Duties, §5-17-13.
Election, §5-17-10.
Powers, §5-17-13.
Suspension of operation,
§5-17-8.
Taxation.
General provisions, §5-17-24.
Trusts and trustees.
Deposits for trust
beneficiaries, §5-17-15.
Violations.
Administrator to submit to
grand jury, §5-17-49.
Revocation of certificate of
approval, §5-17-8.
Suspension of operation,
§5-17-8.
Voluntary dissolution,
§5-17-21.
Alabama credit union league.
Redemption and purchase
of advance dues
certificate, §5-17-28.

CREEKS.
General provisions.
See WATERS AND
WATERCOURSES.

CREMATION.
**Body removed from state to
be cremated,** §22-19-2.
**Receipts for disposition of
dead bodies,** §22-9-73.

CRENSHAW COUNTY.
Probate judge.
Compensation, Const. Ala.,
amd. 496.

CREOSOTING.
Licenses, §40-12-90.

CRIMES AND OFFENSES.
General provisions.
See CRIMINAL LAW AND
PROCEDURE.

CRIME VICTIMS COMPENSATION,
§§15-23-1 to 15-23-23.
Additional assessments.
Collection and disposition,
§15-23-17.
Additional costs and penalties.
Assessment of, §15-23-17.
Amount of compensation,
§15-23-15.
Audits.
Financial affairs of
commission, §15-23-7.
Bonds, surety.
Members and employees of
commission, §15-23-4.
Bribery.
Penalties for influence
peddling, §15-23-18.
Certain persons deemed ineligible for compensation, §15-23-23.
Citation of act, §15-23-1.
Claimant.
Defined, §15-23-3.
Physician-patient privilege.
Filing claim under chapter
as waiver of privilege,
§15-23-11.
Where claimant was
offender, accomplice, etc.
No award of compensation,
§15-23-12.
Collateral source.
Defined, §15-23-3.
Economic loss resulting from
criminal conduct.
Contribution not required,
§15-23-9.
Recovery held in trust for
commission, §15-23-14.
Subrogation for commission,
§15-23-14.
Commission.
Annual report, §15-23-6.
Audit of financial affairs.
Authorized, §15-23-7.
Bond, §15-23-4.
Collateral source.
Recovery held in trust for
commission, §15-23-14.
Compensation, §15-23-4.
Composition, §15-23-4.
Conflicts of interest.
Failure of member to
disclose, §15-23-19.
Creation, §15-23-4.
Defined, §15-23-3.
Duties, §15-23-5.
Financial affairs.
Audit authorized, §15-23-7.
Funds.
Administration crime
victims compensation
fund, §15-23-16.
Money or securities.
Unauthorized control.
Penalties, §15-23-22.
Officers, §15-23-4.
Place of meeting, §15-23-4.
Powers and duties, §15-23-5.
Qualifications, §15-23-4.
Quorum, §15-23-4.
Record of proceedings,
§15-23-4.
Records.
Alteration of records.
Penalties, §15-23-20.
Reports.
Annual report, §15-23-6.

CRIME VICTIMS COMPENSATION—Cont'd
Commission—Cont'd
Terms, §15-23-4.
Unauthorized control over
money or securities.
Penalties, §15-23-22.
Conflicts of interest.
Nondisclosure.
Penalties, §15-23-19.
Contingency of award.
Prosecution or conviction of
offender, §15-23-13.
Conviction of offender.
Award not contingent on,
§15-23-13.
Costs.
Assessment of additional
costs, §15-23-17.
Criminally injurious conduct.
Defined, §15-23-3.
Economic loss.
Authorized compensation,
§15-23-8.
Collateral source
contribution not
required, §15-23-9.
Hearing required
generally, §15-23-10.
Procedure for
compensation,
§15-23-8.
Procedure in contested
cases, §15-23-10.
Settlement by consent
orders, etc., §15-23-10.
Damages.
Notice of action to recover
damages, §15-23-14.
Definitions, §15-23-3.
Allowance expense, §15-23-3.
Claimant, §15-23-3.
Collateral source, §15-23-3.
Commission, §15-23-3.
Criminally injurious conduct,
§15-23-3.
Dependent, §15-23-3.
Economic loss, §15-23-3.
Economic loss of a
dependent, §15-23-3.
Replacement services loss,
§15-23-3.
Replacement services loss of
dependent, §15-23-3.
Victim, §15-23-3.
Work loss, §15-23-3.
Denial of compensation,
§15-23-12.
Diminution of compensation,
§15-23-12.
Economic loss.
Criminally injurious conduct.
Authorized compensation,
§15-23-8.
Collateral source
contribution not
required, §15-23-9.
Hearing required
generally, §15-23-10.
Procedure for
compensation,
§15-23-8.
Procedure in contested
cases, §15-23-10.
Settlement by consent
orders, etc., §15-23-10.
Defined, §15-23-3.
Future economic loss
generally, §15-23-15.

CRIME VICTIMS COMPENSATION—Cont'd
Eligibility for compensation.
Certain persons deemed
ineligible, §15-23-23.
False information.
Furnishing false information.
Penalties, §15-23-21.
Funds.
Crime victims compensation
fund, §15-23-16.
Future economic loss.
Generally, §15-23-15.
Ineligibility for compensation.
Certain persons deemed
ineligible, §15-23-23.
Influence peddling.
Penalties, §15-23-18.
Legislative findings, determinations and declarations, §15-23-2.
Material fact.
Failure to omit or disclose
material fact.
Penalties, §15-23-21.
Method of compensation,
§15-23-15.
Notice.
Action to recover damages,
§15-23-14.
Penalties.
Alteration of commission
records, §15-23-20.
Assessment of additional
costs and penalties,
§15-23-17.
Failure of commission
members to disclose
conflict of interest,
§15-23-19.
Failure to omit or disclose
material fact, etc.,
§15-23-21.
Furnishing false information,
§15-23-21.
Influence peddling,
§15-23-18.
Money or securities of
commission.
Unauthorized control,
§15-23-22.
Physician-patient privilege.
Filing claim under chapter
constitutes waiver of
privilege, §15-23-11.
Policy of state, §15-23-2.
Proof of conviction.
Effect of proof, §15-23-13.
Prosecution or conviction of offender.
Award not contingent on,
§15-23-13.
Public policy of state,
§15-23-2.
Reconsideration of award,
§15-23-12.
Records.
Alteration of commission
records.
Penalties, §15-23-20.
Reducing award of compensation, §15-23-12.
Reports.
Annual report of commission
required, §15-23-6.
Restitution hearings,
§15-23-14.
Short title, §15-23-1.

CRIME VICTIMS COMPENSATION—Cont'd

Subrogation.
Collateral source.
Award subrogates commission, §15-23-14.
Suspension of proceedings under chapter, §15-23-13.
Taxation.
Exemption from state or local taxes, etc., §15-23-15.
Title of chapter, §15-23-1.
Trusts and trustees.
Collateral source.
Funds recovered from collateral source held in trust for commission, §15-23-14.
Disposition of trust funds, §15-23-14.
Withdrawal or reduction of award of compensation, §15-23-12.

CRIME VICTIMS' COURT ATTENDANCE, §§15-14-50 to 15-14-57.
See TRIAL.

CRIMINAL CONVERSATION.
Actions.
Age limitation, §6-5-331.

CRIMINAL JUSTICE ADVISORY COMMISSION, §§41-9-570 to 41-9-574.

CRIMINAL JUSTICE INFORMATION CENTER, §§41-9-590 to 41-9-648.
See CRIMINAL LAW AND PROCEDURE.

CRIMINAL LAW AND PROCEDURE.
Abortion.
Inducing or attempting to induce, §13A-13-7.
Abuse of public office, §§13A-10-80, 13A-10-82.
Accomplices and accessories.
Accessories after the fact, §§13A-10-42 to 13A-10-45.
General provisions.
See ACCOMPLICES AND ACCESSORIES.
Accountants.
Unlawful practice, §§34-1-16 to 34-1-20.
Acquittal for mental illness.
Ordering to state hospital, §15-16-43.
Hearing.
Final hearing, §15-16-42.
When required, §15-16-41.
Actions.
Justification and excuse.
Civil remedy unimpaired, §13A-3-21.
Adulteration.
Selling adulterated commodities, §13A-9-41.
Age.
Immaturity as defense, §13A-3-3.
Agents.
Commercial bribery, §13A-11-120.

CRIMINAL LAW AND PROCEDURE—Cont'd

Agriculture.
Vehicles transporting farm or commercial products.
Hindering transportation of commodities, §13A-11-221.
Aiding and abetting.
General provisions.
See AIDING AND ABETTING.
Alcoholic beverages.
Intoxication as defense, §13A-3-2.
Animals.
Cruelty to animals.
See CRUELTY TO ANIMALS.
Antiques.
Criminal simulation, §13A-9-10.
Appeals.
Court of criminal appeals.
See COURT OF CRIMINAL APPEALS.
General provisions.
See APPEALS.
Arrests.
General provisions.
See ARREST.
Records. See within this heading, "Criminal justice information center."
Arson, §§13A-7-41 to 13A-7-43.
Art.
Criminal simulation, §13A-9-10.
Assault and battery, §§13A-6-20 to 13A-6-25.
See ASSAULT AND BATTERY.
Assembly.
Unlawful assembly, §13A-11-5.
Attempts, §§13A-4-2, 13A-12-203, 13A-12-205.
Attorney general.
Direction of prosecution, §36-15-14.
Attorneys at law.
Counsel for accused, Const. U. S., Amendment VI.
Aviation.
Jurisdiction of crimes, §4-2-4.
Bad checks, §§13A-9-13.1 to 13A-9-13.3.
Enforcement, §12-17-224.
Negotiating worthless instruments, §§13A-9-13.1 to 13A-9-13.3.
Bail and recognizance, §§15-13-1 to 15-13-82.
See BAIL AND RECOGNIZANCE.
Bait advertising, §§13A-9-43, 13A-9-44.
Bankruptcy and insolvency.
Financial statements.
Issuing false statements, §13A-9-49.
Fraud in insolvency, §13A-9-48.
Banks and financial institutions.
Failing financial institutions.
Receiving deposits in, §13A-9-50.

CRIMINAL LAW AND PROCEDURE—Cont'd

Battery, §§13A-6-20 to 13A-6-25.
See ASSAULT AND BATTERY.
Beggars.
Loitering for purpose of begging, §13A-11-9.
Maiming one's self to obtain alms, §13A-14-1.
Betting.
General provisions.
See GAMBLING.
Bigamy, §13A-13-1.
Blacklists.
Maintaining, §13A-11-123.
Boards and commissions.
Executive or secret sessions of certain boards, §13A-14-2.
Bonds, surety.
Peace bonds, §§15-6-1 to 15-6-61.
See PEACE BONDS.
Bookmaking.
Defined, §13A-12-20.
Gambling generally.
See GAMBLING.
Boundaries.
Offense committed on or near county boundary.
Venue, §15-2-7.
Brass knuckles.
Prohibited, §13A-11-53.
Bribery.
Compounding, §13A-10-7.
General provisions.
See BRIBERY.
Buildings.
Defined, §13A-3-20.
Burden of proof.
Where offense was committed.
Proving at trial, §15-8-31.
Burglary.
See BURGLARY.
Business records.
Falsifying, §13A-9-45.
Capital offenses, §§13A-5-40 to 13A-5-59.
See CAPITAL OFFENSES.
Capital punishment.
See CAPITAL PUNISHMENT.
Carnal knowledge.
Rape generally, §§13A-6-61, 13A-6-62.
Carriers.
Force.
Use by persons keeping order in contract carriers, §13A-3-24.
Hindering transportation of commodities, §13A-11-221.
Carrying concealed weapons, §§13A-11-50, 13A-11-51, 13A-11-55.
Cattle rustling, §§2-15-40 to 2-15-48.
Cemeteries.
Desecration of venerated objects, §13A-11-12.
Cesspools.
Creating hazards, §13A-11-220.
Change bills, §§13A-9-19, 13A-9-20.

CRIMINAL LAW AND PROCEDURE—Cont'd

Change of venue, §§15-2-20 to 15-2-27.
See VENUE.
Checks.
Negotiating worthless instruments, §§13A-9-13.1 to 13A-9-13.4.
Enforcement, §12-17-224.
Cigarettes.
Selling cigarettes to minors, §13A-12-3.
Citation of criminal code, §13A-1-1.
Civil actions.
Effect of title on civil actions, §13A-1-8.
Classification of offenses, §13A-5-3.
Clergymen.
Fraudulently pretending to be clergymen, §13A-14-4.
Coal.
Deceptive sales, §13A-9-52.
Cockfights.
Keeping cockpit, §13A-12-4.
Prohibited, §13A-12-4.
Compensation.
Crime victims compensation, §§15-23-1 to 15-23-23.
See CRIME VICTIMS COMPENSATION.
Complaints, §§15-7-1 to 15-7-22.
See COMPLAINTS.
Compounding, §13A-10-7.
Computer crimes act, §§13A-8-100 to 13A-8-103.
Concealed weapons, §§13A-11-50, 13A-11-51, 13A-11-55.
Confession of judgment.
See JUDGMENTS.
Conflicts of interest.
Public servants, §13A-10-62.
Consent.
Ineffective consent, §13A-2-7.
When consent defense, §13A-2-7.
Conspiracy.
See CONSPIRACY.
Constitution of Alabama.
Accusation, Const. Ala., art. I, §7.
Arrest, Const. Ala., art. I, §7.
Change of venue, Const. Ala., art. I, §6.
Cruel and unusual punishment, Const. Ala., art. I, §15.
Detention, Const. Ala., art. I, §7.
Double jeopardy, Const. Ala., art. I, §9.
Due process of law, Const. Ala., art. I, §6.
Ex post facto laws, Const. Ala., art. I, §7.
Fines.
Excessive fines, Const. Ala., art. I, §15.
Fixing punishment of crime. Special, private or local laws prohibited, Const. Ala., art. IV, §104.

CRIMINAL LAW AND PROCEDURE—Cont'd

Constitution of Alabama —Cont'd
Grand jury.
Not required in misdemeanor cases, Const. Ala., art. I, §8; amd. 37.
Informations.
Proceeding against person by information, Const. Ala., art. I, §8.
Jury.
Discharge of juries, Const. Ala., art. I, §9.
Right to trial by jury, Const. Ala., art. I, §11.
Public trial, Const. Ala., art. I, §6.
Rights of persons in criminal prosecutions, Const. Ala., art. I, §6.
Self-incrimination, Const. Ala., art. I, §6.
Constitution of the United States, Const. U. S., Amendment VIII.
Cruel and unusual punishment, Const. U. S., Amendment VIII.
Excessive bail, Const. U. S., Amendment VIII.
Extradition, Const. U. S., Art. IV, §2.
Fugitives from justice, Const. U. S., Art. IV, §2.
Guarantees in criminal cases, Const. U. S., Amendments V, VI.
Public trial, Const. U. S., Amendment VI.
Self-incriminations, Const. U. S., Amendment V.
Speedy trial, Const. U. S., Amendment VI.
Construction and interpretation.
Culpability, §13A-2-4.
General rule of construction, §13A-1-6.
Contempt.
General provisions.
See CONTEMPT.
Contests.
Marathon contests prohibited, §13A-14-3.
Contraband.
Prison contraband, §§13A-10-36 to 13A-10-38.
Contracts.
Offering a false instrument for recording, §13A-9-12.
Controlled substances.
Crimes amendment act, §§13A-12-210 to 13A-12-216.
See DRUGS.
Inchoate offenses, §§13A-12-201 to 13A-12-205.
Convictions.
Post-conviction remedies, ARCrP, Rule 20.
Records. See within this heading, "Criminal justice information center."

CRIMINAL LAW AND PROCEDURE—Cont'd

Copying and sale of recorded devices, §§13A-8-80 to 13A-8-86.
See RECORDED DEVICES.
Coroners' inquests, §§15-4-1 to 15-4-11.
See CORONERS.
Corporations.
Change bills, §§13A-9-19, 13A-9-20.
Criminal liability of individuals for corporate conduct, §13A-2-26.
Evidence.
When proof of incorporation necessary, §12-21-201.
Prosecution of corporations.
See CORPORATIONS.
Corpses.
Abuse, §13A-11-13.
Corrections.
General provisions.
See CORRECTIONS.
Jails.
See JAILS.
Penitentiary, §§14-3-30 to 14-3-60.
See PENITENTIARY.
Prisons and prisoners.
See PRISONS AND PRISONERS.
Corrupt influence.
Bribery.
See BRIBERY.
Costs in criminal cases.
See COSTS.
Counterfeiting, §§13A-9-1 to 13A-9-92.
See FORGERY AND COUNTERFEITING.
Court of criminal appeals.
See COURT OF CRIMINAL APPEALS.
Courts.
Crime victims' court attendance, §§15-14-50 to 15-14-57.
See TRIAL.
General provisions.
See COURTS.
Courts-martial.
See MILITARY AFFAIRS.
Credit cards.
Fraud by persons authorized to provide goods and services, §13A-9-14.1.
Fraudulent use, §13A-9-14.
Illegal possession, §13A-9-14.
Crime victims compensation, §§15-23-1 to 15-23-23.
See CRIME VICTIMS COMPENSATION.
Crime victims' court attendance, §§15-14-50 to 15-14-57.
See TRIAL.
Criminal assistance.
Defined, §13A-10-42.
Criminal damage to property, §§13A-7-20 to 13A-7-26.
See PROPERTY.
Criminal justice advisory commission.
Composition, §41-9-570.
Created, §41-9-570.
Expenses of members, §41-9-574.

CRIMINAL LAW AND
PROCEDURE—Cont'd
Criminal justice advisory
commission—Cont'd
Function, §41-9-572.
Meetings, §41-9-571.
Officers, §41-9-571.
Reports, §41-9-573.
Criminal justice information
center.
Administration of center.
Responsibility of
commission, §41-9-591.
Appropriations, §41-9-599.
Arrests.
Criminal record of persons
arrested.
Compilation, §41-9-624.
Fingerprints, photographs,
etc., of persons
arrested.
Submission to
department of public
safety, §41-9-623.
Information collected and
disseminated,
§41-9-622.
Notice where warrants
subsequently served or
withdrawn, §41-9-627.
Outstanding warrants.
Confirmation of warrants
remaining
outstanding,
§41-9-627.
Release without charge or
cleared of offense,
§41-9-625.
Warrants which cannot be
served.
Forwarding to
department of public
safety, §41-9-627.
Collection.
Corpses.
Unidentified human
corpses found in
state, §41-9-638.
Criminal justice agencies
outside state.
Dissemination of
information to,
§41-9-641.
Dissemination of
information, §41-9-622.
Criminal histories.
Log of disseminations,
§41-9-640.
Establishment of policies,
safeguards, etc.,
§41-9-594.
Grounds for collecting,
§41-9-622.
Inspection fees, §41-9-644.
Limitations upon provision
of information, §41-9-636.
Outside state.
Dissemination of
information to
agencies outside
state, §41-9-641.
Powers and duties of
commission, §41-9-621.
Prisons.
Persons confined to jails,
workhouses, etc.,
§41-9-637.
To whom information may
be disclosed, §41-9-642.

CRIMINAL LAW AND
PROCEDURE—Cont'd
Criminal justice information
center—Cont'd
Collection—Cont'd
Violations as to data
reporting or
dissemination,
§41-9-647.
Commission.
Administration of center.
Responsibility of
commission,
§41-9-591.
Advisory section.
Composition, §41-9-592.
Appropriations, §41-9-599.
Budget, §41-9-599.
Chairman, §41-9-593.
Compensation of members,
§41-9-593.
Composition, §41-9-592.
Creation, §41-9-591.
Definitions, §41-9-590.
Development of center.
Responsibility of
commission,
§41-9-591.
Duties, §41-9-621.
Functions, §41-9-591.
Funds.
Annual request for
funds, §41-9-599.
Meetings, §41-9-593.
Policies.
Establishment by
commission,
§41-9-594.
Powers, §41-9-621.
Quorum, §41-9-593.
Record of transactions
discussed or voted
upon, §41-9-593.
Rules and regulations.
Appeals from rules and
regulations
promulgated by
commission,
§41-9-598.
Establishment by
commission,
§41-9-594.
Terms of members,
§41-9-592.
Vice-chairman, §41-9-593.
Voting section.
Composition, §41-9-592.
Communication of
information in violation
of article, §41-9-602.
Conflict of laws, §41-9-603.
Convictions.
Collection of information
pertaining to convicts,
§41-9-622.
Corpses.
Unidentified human
corpses.
Collection and
dissemination of
information on
corpses, §41-9-638.
Fingerprints,
photographs, etc.
Obtaining by law
enforcement and
correction
agencies,
§41-9-625.

CRIMINAL LAW AND
PROCEDURE—Cont'd
Criminal justice information
center—Cont'd
Criminal histories.
Disclosure.
To whom information
may be disclosed,
§41-9-642.
Disseminations.
Log of disseminations,
§41-9-640.
Information which may be
included in, §41-9-639.
Log of disseminations,
§41-9-640.
Criminal identification files.
Furnishing of information
in files, §41-9-630.
Criminal justice agencies
outside state.
Dissemination of
information to,
§41-9-641.
Definitions, §41-9-590.
Delinquent parolees.
Supplying of information
by probation and
parole officers,
§41-9-635.
Department of public safety.
Forwarding of data to
center, §41-9-629.
Deputy director.
Appointment, §41-9-595.
Duties, §41-9-595.
Qualifications, §41-9-595.
Development of center.
Responsibility of
commission, §41-9-591.
Director.
Appointment, §41-9-595.
Duties, §41-9-595.
Qualifications, §41-9-595.
Disposition of criminal cases.
Information and statistics
pertaining to,
§41-9-648.
Expungement of records,
§§41-9-645, 41-9-646.
False pretenses.
Obtaining information
under false pretenses,
§41-9-601.
Fingerprints.
Corpses.
Unidentified human
corpses.
Obtaining by law
enforcement and
correction
agencies,
§41-9-625.
Forwarding, §41-9-626.
Department of public
safety to forward,
§41-9-629.
Fugitives.
Obtaining fingerprints
by law enforcement
and correction
agencies, §41-9-625.
Prisons.
Obtaining and
forwarding to
department of public
safety by prisons,
§41-9-628.

CRIMINAL LAW AND
PROCEDURE—Cont'd
Criminal justice information
center—Cont'd
Fingerprints—Cont'd
Submission to department
of public safety by
criminal justice
agencies, §41-9-623.
Fugitives from justice.
Apprehension.
Notification of center of
apprehension,
§41-9-634.
Fingerprints, photographs,
etc.
Obtaining by law
enforcement and
correction agencies,
§41-9-625.
Notification of center of
apprehension,
§41-9-634.
Reporting by criminal
justice agencies of
persons wanted,
§41-9-633.
Furnishing of identifying
data to center by
criminal justice agencies,
§41-9-630.
Inspection of one's own
criminal records,
§§41-9-643, 41-9-644.
Invasions of privacy.
Unconstitutional invasions
not authorized by
article, §41-9-642.
Jails.
Collection and
dissemination of
information on persons
jailed, §41-9-637.
Fingerprints, photographs,
etc.
Obtaining and
forwarding to
department of public
safety, §41-9-628.
Limitations upon provision of
information, §41-9-636.
Modification of records,
§§41-9-645, 41-9-646.
Obtaining information under
false pretenses,
§41-9-601.
Office of state planning and
federal programs.
Inapplicability of
provisions to center,
§41-9-214.
Parole and probation officers.
Duty to furnish data to
center, §41-9-623.
Photographs.
Corpses.
Unidentified human
corpses.
Obtaining
photographs,
§41-9-625.
Forwarding, §41-9-626.
Department of public
safety to forward,
§41-9-629.
Fugitives.
Obtaining photographs,
§41-9-625.

CRIMINAL LAW AND
PROCEDURE—Cont'd
Criminal justice information
center—Cont'd
Photographs—Cont'd
Prisons.
Obtaining and
forwarding to
department of public
safety, §41-9-628.
Submission to department
of public safety,
§41-9-623.
Policies.
Establishment by
commission, §41-9-594.
Prisons.
Collection and
dissemination of
information on
prisoners, §41-9-637.
Fingerprints, photographs,
etc., of prisoners.
Obtaining and
forwarding to
department of public
safety, §41-9-628.
Privacy.
Invasions of privacy.
Unconstitutional
invasions not
authorized by
article, §41-9-642.
Privacy and security
committee.
Establishment, §41-9-594.
Purging of records,
§§41-9-645, 41-9-646.
Reports.
Failure of officer or official
to make report,
§41-9-600.
Required acts.
Failure of officer or official
to do act required by
article, §41-9-600.
Rules and regulations.
Appeals from, §41-9-598.
Establishment by
commission, §41-9-594.
Sheriffs.
Duty to furnish data to
center, §41-9-623.
Staff.
Applicability of state
personnel merit
system, §41-9-597.
Maintenance of staff,
§41-9-596.
Stolen property.
Notification of center of
recovery of property,
§41-9-634.
Recovery.
Notification of center,
§41-9-634.
Reporting by criminal
justice agencies,
§41-9-633.
Supplementation of records,
§§41-9-645, 41-9-646.
Support services.
Maintenance, §41-9-596.
Uniform crime reports.
Commission to provide for,
§41-9-620.
Contents, §41-9-631.
Submission by criminal
justice agencies,
§41-9-631.

CRIMINAL LAW AND
PROCEDURE—Cont'd
Criminal justice information
center—Cont'd
Uniform crime reports
—Cont'd
Submission by other
governmental
agencies, §41-9-632.
Use of information
contained in,
§41-9-632.
Violations as to data
reporting or
dissemination, §41-9-647.
Violations of article.
Communication of
information in
violation of article,
§41-9-602.
Criminal pleading, §§15-15-1
to 15-15-44.
See PLEADINGS.
Cruelty to animals.
See CRUELTY TO
ANIMALS.
Culpability.
Act.
Defined, §13A-2-1.
Causal relationship between
conduct and results,
§13A-2-5.
Conduct.
Defined, §13A-2-1.
Consent, §13A-2-7.
Ineffective consent,
§13A-2-7.
Construction of statutes with
respect to, §13A-2-4.
Culpable mental state.
Defined, §§13A-2-1,
13A-2-2.
Definitions, §13A-2-1.
Ignorance.
Effect, §13A-2-6.
Mistake.
Effect, §13A-2-6.
Omission.
Defined, §13A-2-1.
Recklessness.
Defined, §13A-2-2.
Requirements for criminal
liability, §13A-2-3.
Voluntary act.
Defined, §13A-2-1.
Damages.
Civil actions.
Effect of title on, §13A-1-8.
Restitution to victims of
crimes, §§15-18-65 to
15-18-78, 15-18-140 to
15-18-151.
See RESTITUTION TO
VICTIMS OF
CRIMES.
Damages to property.
Criminal damage to property,
§§13A-7-20 to 13A-7-26.
See PROPERTY.
Dance contests.
Prohibited, §13A-14-3.
Dead bodies.
Abuse of corpses, §13A-11-13.
Death penalty, §§13A-5-39 to
13A-5-59, 15-18-80 to
15-18-86.
See CAPITAL
PUNISHMENT.

CRIMINAL LAW AND PROCEDURE—Cont'd

Debit cards.
Illegal possession or fraudulent use, §13A-9-14.

Debtors and creditors.
Judgment creditors.
Defrauding, §13A-9-47.
Secured creditors.
Defrauding, §13A-9-46.

Decency.
Offenses against public order and decency. See within this heading, "Offenses against public order and decency."

Defamation.
See LIBEL AND SLANDER.

Defense of indigents.
General provisions, §§15-12-1 to 15-12-25.
See INDIGENT PERSONS.
Public defenders.
See PUBLIC DEFENDERS.

Defenses.
Age, §13A-3-3.
Bail jumping, §§13A-10-39, 13A-10-40.
Compounding, §13A-10-7.
Consent.
When defense, §13A-2-7.
Conspiracy.
Consummation of object offense not defense to prosecution, §13A-4-5.
Culpability generally. See within this heading, "Culpability."
Duress, §13A-3-30.
Eavesdropping prosecutions, §13A-11-36.
Entrapment, §13A-3-31.
Excuse. See within this heading, "Justification and excuse."
False advertising, §13A-9-42.
Gambling.
Possession of gambling records, §13A-12-26.
Immaturity, §13A-3-3.
Intoxication, §13A-3-2.
Justification and excuse. See within this heading, "Justification and excuse."
Mental disease or defect, §13A-3-1.
Solicitation.
Consummation of object offense not defense to prosecution, §13A-4-5.

Definitions, §13A-1-2.
Bribery, §13A-10-60.
Burden of injecting the issue, §13A-1-2.
Crime, §13A-1-2.
Criminal assistance, §13A-10-42.
Culpability, §13A-2-1.
Dangerous instrument, §13A-1-2.
Deadly physical force, §13A-1-2.
Deadly weapon, §13A-1-2.
Eavesdropping, §13A-11-30.
Escape, §13A-10-30.
Felony, §13A-1-2.
Gambling, §13A-12-20.
Intoxication, §13A-3-2.

CRIMINAL LAW AND PROCEDURE—Cont'd

Definitions—Cont'd
Justification and excuse, §13A-3-20.
Mentally retarded defendants, §15-24-2.
Misdemeanor, §13A-1-2.
Negligence.
Criminal negligence, §13A-2-2.
Obscenity, §13A-12-130.
Obstructing governmental operations, §13A-10-1.
Offense, §13A-1-2.
Offenses against public order and decency, §13A-11-1.
Person, §13A-1-2.
Physical injury, §13A-1-2.
Possess, §13A-1-2.
Prostitution, §13A-12-110.
Vehicle, §13A-1-2.
Violations, §13A-1-2.
Voluntary intoxication, §13A-3-2.

Depositions, §§12-21-260 to 12-21-263, 15-7-2.

Desecration of venerated objects, §13A-11-12.

Desertion and nonsupport, §§30-4-50 to 30-4-65.
See DESERTION AND NONSUPPORT.

Detainers.
Mandatory disposition of detainers, §§15-9-80 to 15-9-88.
See DETAINERS.

Disabled persons.
Maiming one's self to escape duty or obtain alms, §13A-14-1.

Disorderly conduct, §13A-11-7; Const. Ala., art. IV, §§53, 54.

District attorneys, §§12-17-180 to 12-17-224.
See DISTRICT ATTORNEYS.

District courts.
District attorneys.
Administrative responsibility for district court prosecutions, §12-12-8.
Jurisdiction, §12-12-32.
Vesting, §12-1-3.
Powers as to disposition of criminal cases, §12-12-4.

Dogs.
Killing dogs used by peace officers, §13A-11-15.

Double jeopardy, Const. Ala., art. I, §9.
Constitution of the United States, Const. U. S., Amendment V.

Drugs.
Controlled substances.
Crimes amendment act, §§13A-12-210 to 13A-12-216.
See DRUGS.
Inchoate offenses, §§13A-12-201 to 13A-12-205.

Duress.
Defense to prosecution, §13A-3-30.

CRIMINAL LAW AND PROCEDURE—Cont'd

Eavesdropping, §§31A-11-30 to 31A-11-37.
See EAVESDROPPING.

Education.
See EDUCATION.

Effective date of title, §13A-1-11.

Elections.
Criminal prosecutions under election laws, Const. Ala., art. VIII, §189.
Disqualification from registration and voting.
Convicted persons, Const. Ala., art. VIII, §182.
Restoration of right to vote by pardon, §17-3-10.
Immunity from prosecution due to testimony given, Const. Ala., art. VIII, §189.
Lists of qualified voters.
Purging.
Registrars to receive information of convictions, §17-4-131.

Embezzlement.
See EMBEZZLEMENT.

Employers and employees.
Bribery.
Commercial bribery, §13A-11-120.

Enactment of title.
Applicability to offenses committed before and after enactment, §13A-1-7.

Entrapment.
When entrapment defense, §13A-3-31.

Escape.
See ESCAPE.

Evidence.
General provisions.
See EVIDENCE.

Excuse. See within this heading, "Justification and excuse."

Executors and administrators.
Commercial bribery, §13A-11-120.

Extortion, §§13A-8-13 to 13A-8-15.

Extradition, §§15-9-20 to 15-9-65.
See EXTRADITION.

Failure to disperse, §13A-11-6.

False advertising, §§13A-9-42, 13A-9-44.

False alarms.
Rendering false alarms, §13A-10-8.

False pretenses.
Bringing into state property obtained by false pretense elsewhere, §13A-8-21.

Farm products.
Hindering transportation, §13A-11-221.

Felonies.
General provisions.
See FELONIES.
Profits from crime, §§41-9-80 to 41-9-84.

CRIMINAL LAW AND PROCEDURE—Cont'd

Fences.
Common fences.
Allowing stock to run at large under common fence, §13A-7-61.

Fiduciaries.
Commercial bribery, §13A-11-120.
Embezzlement.
See EMBEZZLEMENT.
Misapplication of property, §31A-9-51.

Fighting.
Disorderly conduct, §13A-11-7.
Firearms.
Use, §13A-11-56.

Financial institutions.
Receiving deposits in failing institutions, §13A-9-50.

Fines.
See PENALTIES.

Fingerprints.
Criminal justice information center. See within this heading, "Criminal justice information center."
Persons taken into custody, §§15-10-90, 15-10-91.

Firearms.
See WEAPONS.

Fires and fire prevention.
Arson, §§13A-3-25, 13A-7-40 to 13A-7-43, 15-8-150.
See ARSON.
False alarms, §13A-10-8.
Refusing to assist in fire control, §13A-10-6.
Reports.
Falsely reporting occurrence of fire, §13A-11-11.

Flags.
Desecration, §13A-11-12.

Food stamps.
Illegal possession of food stamps.
Generally, §§13A-9-90 to 13A-9-92.

Force.
Arrest.
Resisting arrest.
Use of force, §13A-3-28.
Use of force in making arrest, §13A-3-27.
Carriers.
Use of force by persons keeping order, §13A-3-24.
Deadly physical force.
Arson.
Prevention of arson, §13A-3-25.
Defined, §13A-3-20.
Use in defense of persons, §13A-3-23.
Defined, §13A-3-20.
Escape.
Use of force in escape, §13A-10-31.
Use of force in preventing escape, §13A-3-27.
Guardian and ward.
Use of force by persons with custodial responsibilities, §13A-3-24.

CRIMINAL LAW AND PROCEDURE—Cont'd

Force—Cont'd
Guards.
When use of force justified, §13A-3-27.
Jails.
Wardens.
Use of force, §13A-3-24.
Justification and excuse. See within this heading, "Justification and excuse."
Minors.
Use of force by persons with parental, custodial or special responsibilities, §13A-3-24.
Parent and child.
Use of force by persons with parental responsibilities, §13A-3-24.
Peace officers.
When use by peace officers justified, §13A-3-27.
Physicians.
Use to administer treatment, §13A-3-24.
Police.
When use of force by police justified, §13A-3-27.
Premises.
Defense of premises, §13A-3-25.
Prisons and prisoners.
Wardens.
Use of force, §13A-3-24.
Robbery.
Use of force against person.
Third degree robbery, §13A-8-43.
Suicide.
Use of force to thwart suicide, §13A-3-24.
Weapons.
Committing crime when armed, §13A-11-71.

Forgery.
See FORGERY AND COUNTERFEITING.

Fraud by persons authorized to provide goods and services, §13A-9-14.1.

Freezers.
Creating hazards, §13A-11-220.

Fugitives from justice.
Criminal justice information center. See within this heading, "Criminal justice information center."
Extradition, §§15-9-20 to 15-9-65.
See EXTRADITION.
Rewards, §§15-9-1 to 15-9-4.

Gambling.
General provisions.
See GAMBLING.
Lotteries.
See LOTTERIES.

Governmental operations.
Obstruction, §§13A-10-1, 13A-10-2.

Grand jury, §§12-16-190 to 12-16-211.
See GRAND JURY.

CRIMINAL LAW AND PROCEDURE—Cont'd

Guardian and ward.
Interference with custody, §13A-6-45.
Use of force by persons with custodial responsibilities, §13A-3-24.

Guilty pleas, §§15-15-20 to 15-15-26.
See PLEADINGS.

Gunpowder.
Storing in city or town, §13A-11-224.

Guns.
See WEAPONS.

Habeas corpus, §§15-21-1 to 15-21-34.
See HABEAS CORPUS.

Habitual felony offenders.
See FELONIES.

Harassment, §13A-11-8.

Hazardous substances and waste.
Fees for disposal.
Violations of chapter.
Institution of prosecution, §22-30B-12.

Hazards.
Creating hazards.
Elements of crime, §13A-11-220.

Hindering prosecution or apprehension, §§13A-10-42 to 13A-10-44.

Homicide, §§13A-6-1 to 13A-6-4.

Hotels, inns and other transient lodging places.
Theft of services, §13A-8-10.

Iceboxes.
Creating hazards, §13A-11-220.

Identification.
Fingerprinting of persons taken into custody, §§15-10-90, 15-10-91.

Identity.
Assuming false identity, §13A-9-18.

Ignorance.
Effect upon criminal liability, §13A-2-6.

Impersonation.
Criminal impersonation, §13A-9-18.
Impersonating peace officers, §13A-10-11.
Impersonating public servants, §13A-10-10.

Incest, §§13A-13-3, 15-8-150.

Inchoate offenses.
Attempts, §§13A-4-2, 13A-12-203, 13A-12-205.
Conspiracy.
See CONSPIRACY.
Controlled substances.
General provisions, §§13A-12-201 to 13A-12-205.
Criminal solicitation, §§13A-4-1, 13A-4-5.

Inciting to riot, §13A-11-4.

Indictments, §§15-8-1 to 15-8-150.
See INDICTMENTS.

CRIMINAL LAW AND PROCEDURE—Cont'd
Indigent persons.
Appeals.
Providing records on appeals for indigents, §§12-22-190 to 12-22-201.
See APPEALS.
Defense of indigents.
General provisions, §§15-12-1 to 15-12-25; ARJA, Rule 8.
See INDIGENT PERSONS.
Public defenders, §§15-12-40 to 15-12-46.
See PUBLIC DEFENDERS.
Information.
Guilty plea to information, §§15-15-20 to 15-15-26.
Appeals.
No right of appeal, §15-15-26.
Date to formally make and interplea, §15-15-22.
Degree of offense.
Determination, §15-15-24.
Entry of judgment, §15-15-23.
Felony cases, §15-15-20.
Filing information, §15-15-21.
Hearing, §15-15-23.
Jury.
When impaneled, §15-15-24.
Preferring information against defendant, §15-15-21.
Receiving plea, §15-15-23.
Refusal of plea, §15-15-25.
Sentencing, §15-15-23.
Fixing punishment, §15-15-24.
Jury.
When impaneled, §15-15-24.
Service of notice of plea, §15-15-22.
When plea not accepted, §15-15-25.
Information center.
Criminal justice information center. See within this heading, "Criminal justice information center."
Inquests.
Coroners' inquests, §§15-4-1 to 15-4-11.
See CORONERS.
Insanity.
Defense of insanity, §13A-3-1.
General provisions, §§15-16-1 to 15-16-71.
See MENTALLY ILL.
Prisons and prisoners.
Mentally ill prisoners, §§15-16-20 to 15-16-24, 15-16-60 to 15-16-71.
See PRISONS AND PRISONERS.
Inspections.
Refusing public servant authority to inspect property, §13A-10-3.

CRIMINAL LAW AND PROCEDURE—Cont'd
Insurance.
Holding companies.
Criminal proceedings against, §27-29-10.
Intent.
Defined, §13A-2-2.
Intimidating jurors, §13A-10-127.
Intimidating witnesses, §13A-10-123.
Intoxication.
Defense to criminal charge, §13A-3-2.
Jails, §§14-6-1 to 14-6-109.
See JAILS.
Judgment creditors.
Defrauding, §13A-9-47.
Judgments.
Judgment creditors.
Defrauding, §13A-9-47.
Judicial proceedings.
Interference with, §13A-10-130.
Jurisdiction, §15-2-1.
All persons liable for offenses committed in Alabama, §15-2-1.
Vesting of criminal jurisdiction, §12-1-3.
Jury.
Grand jury, §§12-16-190 to 12-16-211.
See GRAND JURY.
Tampering with jury, §13A-10-128.
Verdict, §§15-16-24, 15-17-2 to 15-17-4.
Justification and excuse.
Actions.
Civil remedy unimpaired, §13A-3-21.
Arrest.
Resisting arrest.
Use of force, §13A-3-28.
Use of force in making arrest, §13A-3-27.
Arson.
General provisions, §§13A-7-40 to 13A-7-43, 15-8-150.
Use of deadly physical force to prevent, §13A-3-25.
Basis for defense generally, §13A-3-21.
Building.
Defined, §13A-3-20.
Burglary.
When deadly physical force justified, §13A-3-23.
Carriers.
Use of force by persons keeping order, §13A-3-24.
Deadly physical force.
Defined, §13A-3-20.
Duress, §13A-3-30.
Dwelling.
Defined, §13A-3-20.
Entrapment, §13A-3-31.
Escape.
Use of force in preventing escape, §13A-3-27.
Force.
Arrest.
Resisting arrest.
Use of force, §13A-3-28.

CRIMINAL LAW AND PROCEDURE—Cont'd
Justification and excuse —Cont'd
Force—Cont'd
Arrest—Cont'd
Use of force in making arrest, §13A-3-27.
Danger to innocent persons.
Injuries caused by reckless or negligent use of force, §13A-3-21.
Deadly physical force, §13A-3-20.
Defense of persons, §13A-3-23.
Defense of premises, §13A-3-25.
Peace officers.
When use justified, §13A-3-27.
Retreating from use, §13A-3-23.
Defense of persons, §13A-3-23.
Defense of property other than premises, §13A-3-26.
Defined, §13A-3-20.
Escape.
Use of force to prevent escape, §13A-3-27.
Persons with parental, custodial or special responsibilities, §13A-3-24.
Guardian and ward.
Use of force by persons with custodial responsibilities, §13A-3-24.
Jails.
Guards.
When use of force justified, §13A-3-27.
Wardens.
Use of force, §13A-3-24.
Kidnapping.
When use of deadly physical force justified, §13A-3-23.
Minors.
Use of force by persons with parental, custodial or special responsibilities, §13A-3-24.
Parent and child.
Use of force by persons with parental responsibilities, §13A-3-24.
Physicians.
Use of force to administer treatment, §13A-3-24.
Police.
When use of force by police justified, §13A-3-27.
Premises.
Defined, §13A-3-20.
Use of force in defense, §13A-3-25.
Prisons and prisoners.
Guards.
Use of force, §13A-3-27.
Wardens.
Use of force, §13A-3-24.
Public duty.
Execution, §13A-3-22.

**CRIMINAL LAW AND
PROCEDURE**—Cont'd
Justification and excuse
—Cont'd
Rape.
When use of deadly
physical force justified,
§13A-3-23.
Remedies.
Civil remedy unimpaired,
§13A-3-21.
Retreat.
Use of deadly physical
force, §13A-3-23.
Robbery.
When use of deadly
physical force justified,
§13A-3-23.
Suicide.
Use of force to thwart
suicide, §13A-3-24.
Trespass.
Force in defense of
premises, §13A-3-25.
Wardens.
Use of force, §13A-3-24.
Juvenile offenders.
Youthful offenders, §§15-19-1
to 15-19-7.
See YOUTHFUL
OFFENDERS.
Juvenile proceedings.
General provisions, §§12-15-1
to 12-15-120.
See JUVENILE
PROCEEDINGS.
Transfer of cases from
juvenile court to criminal
court, §12-15-34.
Kidnapping, §§13A-6-40 to
13A-6-45.
See KIDNAPPING.
Labels.
Selling mislabeled
commodities, §13A-9-41.
Larceny.
Theft generally, §§13A-8-1 to
13A-8-144.
See THEFT.
**Law enforcement planning
agency,** §§41-8A-1 to
41-8A-13.
See LAW ENFORCEMENT
PLANNING AGENCY.
Lesser included offenses,
§13A-1-9.
Charges to the jury,
§13A-1-9.
Lewdness.
Obscenity generally,
§§13A-12-130 to
13A-12-200.10.
See OBSCENITY.
Prostitution, §§13A-12-110 to
13A-12-113.
Liability.
Generally. See within this
heading, "Culpability."
Libel, §§13A-11-160 to
13A-11-164.
Liens.
Defrauding secured creditors,
§13A-9-46.
Limitations on prosecution.
Arson, §15-3-5.
Capital offenses, §15-3-5.
Commencement of
prosecution, §15-3-7.
Conversion of public
revenues, §15-3-3.
Counterfeiting, §15-3-5.

**CRIMINAL LAW AND
PROCEDURE**—Cont'd
Limitations on prosecution
—Cont'd
Crimes punishable under
different provisions,
§15-3-8.
Drugs.
Trafficking in drugs,
§15-3-5.
Felonies, §15-3-1.
Offenses having no
limitations, §15-3-5.
Forgery, §15-3-5.
Misdemeanors, §15-3-2.
Offenses having no
limitations, §15-3-5.
Sexual offenses, §15-3-5.
Time between first charge
and indictment.
When deducted from time
limitation, §15-3-6.
Unlawful taking or
temporarily using
property, §15-3-4.
Littering.
Criminal littering.
Class C misdemeanor,
§13A-7-29.
Generally, §13A-7-29.
Livestock.
Allowing stock to run at
large under common
fence, §13A-7-61.
Cattle rustling, §§2-15-40 to
2-15-48.
Loans.
Pistols.
Loans secured by deposit of
pistol, §13A-11-80.
Loitering, §13A-11-9.
Lost or unclaimed property.
Theft, §§13A-8-6 to 13A-8-9,
13A-8-12.
Lotteries.
See LOTTERIES.
**Maiming one's self to escape
duty or obtain alms,**
§13A-14-1.
**Mandatory disposition of
detainers,** §§15-9-80 to
15-9-88.
See DETAINERS.
Manslaughter, §§13A-6-3,
15-3-5.
Menacing, §13A-6-23.
Mentally ill.
Defenses.
Mental disease or defect as
defense, §13A-3-1.
General provisions, §§15-16-1
to 15-16-71.
See MENTALLY ILL.
Mentally retarded
defendants. See within
this heading, "Mentally
retarded defendants."
Prisons and prisoners.
Mentally ill prisoners,
§§15-16-20 to 15-16-24,
15-16-60 to 15-16-71.
See PRISONS AND
PRISONERS.
Release of criminal
psychopaths, §§15-16-60
to 15-16-71.
See MENTALLY ILL.
**Mentally retarded
defendants.**
Affidavits.
Filing, §15-24-3.

**CRIMINAL LAW AND
PROCEDURE**—Cont'd
**Mentally retarded
defendants**—Cont'd
Affidavits—Cont'd
Part of court record,
§15-24-6.
To whom furnished,
§15-24-4.
Use, §§15-24-4, 15-24-6.
Citation of chapter, §15-24-1.
Definitions, §15-24-2.
Finding, §15-24-5.
Information gained under
chapter.
Inadmissible on issue of
guilt, §15-24-7.
Proceedings upon finding,
§15-24-5.
Short title of chapter,
§15-24-1.
Meters.
Gas and electric meters,
§37-8-6.
Minors.
Abandonment of child,
§13A-13-5.
Child care and treatment.
Criminal conviction
information on
applicants for
employment, §26-1-4.
Endangering welfare of child,
§13A-13-6.
Force.
Use of force by persons
with parental,
custodial or special
responsibilities,
§13A-3-24.
Hazards.
Creating hazards,
§13A-11-220.
Immaturity as defense to
criminal liability,
§13A-3-3.
Juvenile proceedings,
§§12-15-1 to 12-15-120.
See JUVENILE
PROCEEDINGS.
Youthful offenders, §§15-19-1
to 15-19-7.
See YOUTHFUL
OFFENDERS.
Misapplication of property,
§13A-9-51.
Miscarriage.
Inducing or attempting to
induce, §13A-13-7.
Misdemeanors.
General provisions.
See MISDEMEANORS.
Mistake.
Culpability.
Generally. See within this
heading, "Culpability."
Effect upon criminal liability,
§13A-2-6.
Money.
Change bills, §§13A-9-19,
13A-9-20.
Monuments and markers.
Desecration, §13A-11-12.
Motor vehicles.
Disorderly conduct.
Obstructing traffic,
§13A-11-7.
General provisions.
See MOTOR VEHICLES.

CRIMINAL LAW AND PROCEDURE—Cont'd

Motor vehicles—Cont'd

Hindering transportation of commodities, §13A-11-221.

Lotteries.
Transportation of lottery paraphernalia, §§13A-12-70 to 13A-12-75.
See LOTTERIES.

Municipal corporations.
Election offenses generally.
See MUNICIPAL CORPORATIONS.

Murder, §13A-6-2.
See HOMICIDE.

Negligence.
Creating hazards, §13A-11-220.
Criminal negligence.
Defined, §13A-2-2.
Homicide.
Criminally negligent homicide, §13A-6-4.
See HOMICIDE.

Negotiable instruments.
Negotiating worthless instruments.
Conduct constituting, §13A-9-13.1.
Evidence.
Prima facie evidence.
Identity, §13A-9-13.3.
Identity.
Prima facie evidence, §13A-9-13.3.
Notice of refusal of payment, §13A-9-13.2.
Prima facie evidence, §13A-9-13.1.
Identity, §13A-9-13.3.
Worthless check unit of special services division of district attorney, §12-17-224.

Noise.
Making unreasonable noise.
Disorderly conduct, §13A-11-7.

Nonresidents.
Liability for offenses committed in Alabama, §15-2-1.

Nonsupport, §§30-4-50 to 30-4-65.
See DESERTION AND NONSUPPORT.

Noxious substances.
Criminal possession of, §13A-7-28.
Criminal use of, §13A-7-27.

Nudity.
Indecent exposure, §§13A-6-68, 13A-6-69, 13A-12-130.

Oaths.
Perjury, §§13A-10-100 to 13A-10-109.
See PERJURY.
Unsworn falsification to authorities, §13A-10-109.

Obscenity.
General provisions, §§13A-12-130 to 13A-12-200.10.
See OBSCENITY.

Obstructing governmental operations, §§13A-10-1, 13A-10-2.

CRIMINAL LAW AND PROCEDURE—Cont'd

Offenses.

Classification, §13A-5-3.
Designation of offenses, §13A-5-4.

Offenses against public order and decency.
Cruelty to animals.
See CRUELTY TO ANIMALS.
Definitions, §13A-11-1.
Disorderly conduct, §13A-11-7; Const. Ala., art. IV, §§53, 54.
Harassment, §13A-11-8.
Loitering, §13A-11-9.
Public intoxication, §13A-11-10.
Riots.
See RIOTS.
Treason, §13A-11-2; Const. Ala., art. I, §§18, 19.
Unlawful assembly, §§13A-11-5, 13A-11-6.

Offering a false instrument for recording, §13A-9-12.

Office of prosecution services, §§12-17-230 to 12-17-234.

Omissions.
Defined, §13A-2-1.
When omission constitutes crime, §13A-1-4.

Pardons.
See PARDONS.

Parent and child.
Immaturity as bar to criminal liability, §13A-3-3.
Interference with custody, §13A-6-45.
Justification and excuse.
Use of force by persons with parental responsibilities, §13A-3-24.
Minors. See within this heading, "Minors."

Parole.
See PAROLE.

Parties.
Corporations.
Liability of individuals for corporate conduct, §13A-2-26.
Liability based upon behavior of another, §13A-2-20.
Accountability imposed by statute, §13A-2-21.
Certain defenses not available, §13A-2-25.
Complicity, §13A-2-23.
Exceptions, §13A-2-24.
Innocent person, §13A-2-22.

Party lines.
Falsely requesting use for emergency, §13A-11-223.
Unlawfully refusing to yield, §13A-11-222.

Peace bonds, §§15-6-1 to 15-6-61.
See PEACE BONDS.

Peace officers.
See PEACE OFFICERS.

Penal acts.
When penal acts take effect, §1-1-8.

CRIMINAL LAW AND PROCEDURE—Cont'd

Penalties.
See PENALTIES.

Pending proceedings.
Rights and liabilities not affected, §13A-1-10.

Phonograph records.
Copying and sale of recorded devices, §§13A-8-80 to 13A-8-85.
See RECORDED DEVICES.

Photographs.
Criminal justice information center. See within this heading, "Criminal justice information center."

Physicians.
Force.
Use of force for certain treatment, §13A-3-24.

Pistols.
General provisions, §§13A-11-70 to 13A-11-84.
See WEAPONS.
Sheriffs.
Who may carry pistol, §13A-11-52.

Pleading, §§15-15-1 to 15-15-44.
See PLEADINGS.

Pleas in abatement, §§15-15-40 to 15-15-44.

Police.
Attempting to elude officer.
Bail jumping, §§13A-10-39, 13A-10-40.
Escape generally, §§13A-10-31 to 13A-10-35.
Hindering prosecution or apprehension, §§13A-10-42 to 13A-10-45.
Motor vehicle cases, §32-5A-193.
Resisting arrest, §13A-10-41.
Fleeing officer.
Bail jumping, §§13A-10-39, 13A-10-40.
Escape generally, §§13A-10-31 to 13A-10-35.
Hindering prosecution or apprehension, §§13A-10-42 to 13A-10-45.
Motor vehicle cases, §32-5A-193.
Resisting arrest, §13A-10-41.

Post-conviction remedies, ARCrP, Rule 20.

Pregnant women.
Inducing or attempting to induce abortion, etc., §13A-13-7.

Preliminary hearings, §§15-11-1 to 15-11-15.
See PRELIMINARY HEARINGS.

Presumptions.
Persons over 14 presumed responsible for acts, §15-16-2.

CRIMINAL LAW AND PROCEDURE—Cont'd

Prisons and prisoners.
See PRISONS AND PRISONERS.

Privacy.
Offenses against privacy, §§13A-11-30 to 13A-11-37.
See EAVESDROPPING.

Probation, §§15-22-50 to 15-22-55.
See PROBATION.

Profits from crime, §§41-9-80 to 41-9-84.

Property.
Criminal damage to property, §§13A-7-20 to 13A-7-26.
See PROPERTY.
Inspections.
Public officers.
Refusal to permit inspection, §13A-10-3.
Misapplication of property, §13A-9-51.
Public officers and employees.
Acquisition through misuse of confidential information, §13A-10-82.
Receiving stolen property, §§13A-8-16 to 13A-8-19.

Prosecution.
Hindering prosecution or apprehension, §§13A-10-42 to 13A-10-44.
Limitations on prosecutions.
See within this heading, "Limitations on prosecution."
Office of prosecution services, §§12-17-230 to 12-17-234.

Prostitution, §§13A-12-110 to 13A-12-113.

Psychopaths.
Mentally ill prisoners generally, §§15-16-1 to 15-16-71.
See PRISONS AND PRISONERS.
Release of criminal psychopaths, §§15-16-60 to 15-16-71.
See MENTALLY ILL.

Public defenders, §§15-12-40 to 15-12-46.
See PUBLIC DEFENDERS.

Public duty.
Execution of public duty.
Justification or excuse of criminal conduct, §13A-3-22.

Public offenses.
Certain acts or omissions not public offenses, §1-1-6.

Public officers and employees.
Abuse of public office, §§13A-10-80, 13A-10-82.
Bribery generally.
See BRIBERY.
Code of ethics.
Chapter not to repeal any criminal law, §36-25-27.
Conflicts of interest, §13A-10-62.
Impersonating, §13A-10-10.

CRIMINAL LAW AND PROCEDURE—Cont'd

Public officers and employees—Cont'd
Inspections.
Refusal to permit, §13A-10-3.
Obstructing governmental operations, §§13A-10-1, 13A-10-2.
Reports.
Failing to file, §13A-10-4.
Sentencing.
Article not to deprive court of authority to remove person from office, §13A-5-2.
Trading in public office, §13A-10-63.

Public order and decency.
Offenses against. See within this heading, "Offenses against public order and decency."

Punishment.
See PENALTIES.

Purposes of title, §13A-1-3.

Railroads.
Force.
Use by persons keeping order, §13A-3-24.

Rape.
See RAPE.

Real property.
Dispossession under legal process.
Disobeying process, §13A-7-60.
Trespass.
See TRESPASS.

Receiving stolen property, §§13A-8-16 to 13A-8-19.

Reckless endangerment, §13A-6-24.

Recklessness.
Defined, §13A-2-2.

Recognizance, §§15-13-1 to 15-13-82.
See BAIL AND RECOGNIZANCE.

Recorded devices.
Copying and sale, §§13A-8-80 to 13A-8-86.
See RECORDED DEVICES.

Records.
Arrest records. See within this heading, "Criminal justice information center."
Business records.
Falsifying, §13A-9-45.
Criminal justice information center. See within this heading, "Criminal justice information center."
Gambling.
Possession of gambling records, §§13A-12-24 to 13A-12-26.
Indictments.
See INDICTMENTS.
Phonograph records.
Copying and sale of recorded devices, §§13A-8-80 to 13A-8-86.
See RECORDED DEVICES.

CRIMINAL LAW AND PROCEDURE—Cont'd

Records—Cont'd
Tampering with governmental records, §13A-10-12.
Unsworn falsification to authorities, §13A-10-109.

Refrigerators.
Creating hazards, §13A-11-220.

Registration.
Felons, §§13A-11-180 to 13A-11-186.
See FELONIES.
Sex offenders, §§13A-11-200 to 13A-11-203.

Religion.
Desecration of venerated objects, §13A-11-12.
Endangering welfare of child.
Spiritual treatment, §13A-13-6.

Reports.
Criminal justice advisory commission, §41-9-573.
Failing to file required reports, §13A-10-4.
Falsely reporting an incident, §13A-11-11.
False reporting to law enforcement authorities, §13A-10-9.
Uniform crime reports, §§41-9-620, 41-9-631, 41-9-632.
Unsworn falsification to authorities, §13A-10-109.

Resisting arrest, §13A-10-41.

Responsibility.
Justification and excuse. See within this heading, "Justification and excuse."

Restaurants.
Theft of services, §13A-8-10.

Restitution to victims of crimes, §§15-18-65 to 15-18-78, 15-18-140 to 15-18-151.
See RESTITUTION TO VICTIMS OF CRIMES.

Retreat.
Use of force in defense of person, §13A-3-23.

Rewards.
Arrest and conviction of fugitives from justice, §§15-9-1 to 15-9-4.

Riots.
See RIOTS.

Robbery, §§13A-8-40 to 13A-8-52.
See ROBBERY.

Rules of court.
Effect of rules of supreme court on title, §15-1-1.

Rules of criminal procedure.
See RULES OF CRIMINAL PROCEDURE.

Rumors.
Falsely reporting incidents, §13A-11-11.

Searches and seizures, §§15-5-1 to 15-5-31.
See SEARCHES AND SEIZURES.

Secret sessions of certain boards, §13A-14-2.

Secured creditors.
Defrauding, §13A-9-46.

CRIMINAL LAW AND PROCEDURE—Cont'd

Security to keep the peace,
§§15-6-1 to 15-6-61.
See PEACE BONDS.

Self-defense.
Use of physical force,
§13A-3-23.

Sentencing.
See SENTENCING.

Sexual offenses.
Abortion.
Inducing or attempting to
induce, §13A-13-7.
Adultery, §13A-13-2.
General provisions.
See SEXUAL OFFENSES.
Incest, §13A-13-3.
Indecent exposure,
§§13A-6-68, 13A-6-69,
13A-12-130.
Prostitution, §§13A-12-110 to
13A-12-113.
Rape.
See RAPE.
Registration of sexual
offenders, §§13A-11-200
to 13A-11-203.
Sodomy, §§13A-6-63,
13A-6-64.

Sheriffs.
Pistols.
Who may carry pistol,
§13A-11-52.

Shopping carts, §§13A-8-60 to
13A-8-64.

Signatures.
Obtaining by deception,
§13A-9-11.

Simulation.
Criminal simulation,
§13A-9-10.

Slander, §§13A-11-160 to
13A-11-164.

Slingshots.
Prohibited, §13A-11-53.

Slot machines.
Gambling devices generally.
See GAMBLING.
Possession, §13A-12-27.

Slugs.
Unlawful use of slugs.
See VENDING
MACHINES.

Sodomy, §§13A-6-63,
13A-6-64.

Solicitation.
Criminal solicitation,
§§13A-4-1, 13A-4-5.

Sports.
Bribery, §§13A-11-140 to
13A-11-142.
Tampering with sports
contest, §13A-11-143.

**State departments and
agencies.**
Obstructing governmental
operations, §§13A-10-1,
13A-10-2.

Statute of limitations.
Limitations on prosecution.
See within this heading,
"Limitations on
prosecution."

Stays pending appeal,
§§12-22-170 to 12-22-173.

Stink bombs.
Criminal possession,
§13A-7-28.
Criminal use, §13A-7-27.

CRIMINAL LAW AND PROCEDURE—Cont'd

Stolen property.
General provisions.
See STOLEN PROPERTY.
Receiving stolen property,
§§13A-8-16 to 13A-8-19.

Strict liability.
Requirements for criminal
liability for offenses,
§13A-2-3.

Suicide.
Force.
Use of force to thwart,
§13A-3-24.

Summons and process.
Dispossession under legal
process.
Disobeying process,
§13A-7-60.
Simulating legal process,
§13A-10-131.

Sunshine law.
Boards and commissions.
Executive or secret
sessions of certain
boards, §13A-14-2.

Supermarkets.
Shopping carts, §§13A-8-60
to 13A-8-64.

Support and maintenance.
Nonsupport, §§30-4-50 to
30-4-65.
See DESERTION AND
NONSUPPORT.

Supreme court of Alabama.
Effect of court rules on title,
§15-1-1.

Surveillance.
Criminal surveillance,
§13A-11-32.

Tampering.
Governmental records,
§13A-10-12.
Jury, §13A-10-128.
Witnesses, §13A-10-124.

Tapes.
Copying and sale of recorded
devices, §§13A-8-80 to
13A-8-86.
See RECORDED
DEVICES.

Taxation.
Financial statements.
Issuing false statements,
§13A-9-49.
Gambling.
Federal wagering
occupational tax
stamp, §§13A-12-90 to
13A-12-92.
Limitation of actions,
§40-29-119.

Telephones.
Harassment, §13A-11-8.
Party lines.
Falsely requesting use for
emergency,
§13A-11-223.
Unlawfully refusing to
yield, §13A-11-222.

Theft.
Embezzlement.
See EMBEZZLEMENT.
General provisions,
§§13A-8-1 to 13A-8-144.
See THEFT.
Receiving stolen property,
§§13A-8-16 to 13A-8-19.
Robbery, §§13A-8-40 to
13A-8-44.

CRIMINAL LAW AND PROCEDURE—Cont'd

Theft—Cont'd
Shopping carts, §§13A-8-60
to 13A-8-64.

Threats.
Extortion, §§13A-8-13 to
13A-8-15.

Time.
Effective date of title,
§13A-1-11.
Transitional provisions,
§13A-1-7.

Title of criminal code,
§13A-1-1.

**Transportation of
commodities.**
Hindering, §13A-11-221.

Treason, §13A-11-2; Const.
Ala., art. I, §§18, 19.

Trespass.
See TRESPASS.

Trial.
Crime victims' court
attendance, §§15-14-50 to
15-14-57.
See TRIAL.
General provisions, §§15-14-1
to 15-14-30.
See TRIAL.
Verdict, §§15-17-2 to 15-17-5.

**Uniform certificate of title
and antitheft act,**
§§32-8-1 to 32-8-88.
See MOTOR VEHICLES.

**Uniform mandatory
disposition of detainers
act,** §§15-9-80 to 15-9-88.
See DETAINERS.

United States.
Gambling.
Federal wagering
occupational tax
stamp, §§13A-12-90 to
13A-12-92.
Marshals.
Pistols.
Carrying, §13A-11-52.

Unlawful assembly,
§13A-11-5.

Unlawful imprisonment.
General provisions,
§§13A-6-40 to 13A-6-45.
See KIDNAPPING.

Vending machines.
Slugs.
Unlawful use, §§13A-9-16,
13A-9-17.

Venerated objects.
Desecration, §13A-11-12.

Venue, §§15-2-1 to 15-2-27.
See VENUE.

Verdict, §§15-17-2 to 15-17-5.

Victims of crimes.
Crime victims compensation,
§§15-23-1 to 15-23-23.
See CRIME VICTIMS
COMPENSATION.
Crime victims' court
attendance, §§15-14-50 to
15-14-57.
See TRIAL.
Restitution.
Escrow account for profits
from crime.
See PROFITS FROM
CRIME.
General provisions.
See RESTITUTION TO
VICTIMS OF
CRIMES.

CRIMINAL LAW AND PROCEDURE—Cont'd

Victims of crimes—Cont'd
Victim counselors.
Confidentiality, §§15-23-40 to 15-23-46.
See VICTIM COUNSELORS.

Video cassettes.
Copying and sale of recorded devices, §§13A-8-80 to 13A-8-86.
See RECORDED DEVICES.

Warrants.
Arrests.
See ARREST.
Search warrants, §§15-5-1 to 15-5-19.
See SEARCHES AND SEIZURES.

Weapons.
General provisions.
See WEAPONS.

Wells.
Abandoned wells.
Creating hazards, §13A-11-220.

Witnesses.
General provisions.
See WITNESSES.

Worthless checks.
Negotiating worthless instruments, §§13A-9-13.1 to 13A-9-13.3.
Enforcement, §12-17-224.

Youthful offenders, §§15-19-1 to 15-19-7.
See YOUTHFUL OFFENDERS.

CRIMINAL SOLICITATION, §§13A-4-1, 13A-4-5.

CRIMINAL SURVEILLANCE, §13A-11-32.

CRIPPLED PERSONS.

Handicapped persons generally.
See HANDICAPPED PERSONS.

CROPS.

Advances.
Maturity of advances, §35-9-31.

Agriculture generally.
See AGRICULTURE.

Assignments.
Partition of crops.
Article applicable to assignees, §35-6-126.
Right to assign interest in crops, §8-5-22.

Attachment.
Landlord and tenant.
Liens for advances and rent of lands, §§35-9-34 to 35-9-36, 35-9-39, 35-9-41.
See LANDLORD AND TENANT.
Liens of agricultural superintendents and laborers, §§35-11-92 to 35-11-94.
Liens of tenants in common, §35-11-351.

CROPS—Cont'd

Commercial code.
Sales.
Definition of goods, §7-2-105.
Goods to be severed from realty, §7-2-107.
Identification of goods, §7-2-501.
Secured transactions.
Classification of goods, §7-9-109.
Description of land, §7-9-203.
Financing statement, §7-9-402.
Place of filing, §7-9-401.
When security interest attaches, §7-9-204.
Warehouse receipts.
Storage under government bond, §7-7-201.

Ejectment.
Retention of possession for one year where crop planted or growing.
Bond, §6-6-294.

Emblements.
When tenant at will entitled to emblements, §35-9-2.

Executions.
Growing or ungathered crops.
Property subject to execution, §6-9-41.

Executors and administrators.
Completion, gathering and sale of crops commenced by decedent, §43-2-418.

Fertilizer, §§2-22-1 to 2-22-23.
See FERTILIZER.

Joint tenants and tenants in common.
Liens of tenants in common, §§35-11-350, 35-11-351.
Partition of crops, §§35-6-110 to 35-6-126.
See PARTITION.

Landlord and tenant.
Emblements.
When tenant at will entitled to, §35-9-2.
Failure or refusal of tenant to plant crop, §35-9-38.
Levy upon crop of subtenant, §35-9-39.
Liens of landlord.
Advances and rent of lands, §§35-9-30 to 35-9-42.
See LANDLORD AND TENANT.
Seizure upon abandonment of premises, §35-9-12.

Liens.
Agricultural superintendents and laborers, §§35-11-90 to 35-11-97.
See AGRICULTURE.
Landlord and tenant.
Advances and rent of lands, §§35-9-30 to 35-9-42.
See LANDLORD AND TENANT.
Partition of crops.
Effect on existing liens, §35-6-115.

CROPS—Cont'd

Liens—Cont'd
Rent or advances.
Failure to apply farm produce to payment of lien for, §2-1-4.
Tenants in common, §§35-11-350, 35-11-351.
Partition, §§35-6-110 to 35-6-126.
See PARTITION.

Searches and seizures.
Landlord and tenant.
Seizure of crops upon abandonment of premises, §35-9-12.
Partition of crops.
Seizure of crops to be divided, §35-6-117.

Secured transactions.
Classification of goods, §7-9-109.
Description of land, §7-9-203.
Financing statement, §7-9-402.
Place of filing, §7-9-401.

Sharecroppers.
Liens of tenants in common, §§35-11-350, 35-11-351.

Warehouse receipts.
Storage under government bond, §7-7-201.

CROSS-CLAIMS.

Against co-party, ARCP, Rule 13 (g).
Appealed actions, ARCP, Rule 13 (j).
Default judgments, ARCP, Rule 55 (d).
Dismissal, ARCP, Rule 41 (c).
Joinder of additional parties, ARCP, Rule 13 (h).
Judgments.
Separate judgments, ARCP, Rule 13 (i).
Pleadings generally.
See PLEADINGS.
Separate trials, ARCP, Rule 13 (i).

CROSS-EXAMINATION.

Depositions.
Oral deposition, ARCP, Rule 30 (c).
Witnesses, §§12-21-137, 12-21-138; ARCP, Rule 43 (b).

CROSSWALKS, §§32-5A-210 to 32-5A-214.

CROWS.

Hunting.
Unprotected birds, §9-11-233.

CRUELTY TO ANIMALS.

Baby rabbits, chicks, ducklings, etc.
Sale, etc., as pets or novelties, §3-1-15.
Class B misdemeanor, §13A-11-14.
Counties.
Prevention of cruelty to animals.
Employment of persons to enforce laws, §3-1-16.
Education.
Humane treatment of animals taught, §16-40-4.
Elements, §13A-11-14.

CRUELTY TO ANIMALS
—Cont'd
Enforcement of laws for prevention of cruelty.
Employment by county commissions of persons to enforce, §3-1-16.
Income tax.
Deductions.
Gifts to institutions for the prevention of cruelty, §40-18-15.
Killing or injuring without good cause animals belonging to another, §13A-11-14.
Livestock.
Handling of livestock in markets and in transit, §§2-15-110 to 2-15-114.
Societies for prevention of cruelty to animals.
Care and keeping of neglected or abused animals, §3-1-13.
Destruction of certain abandoned animals, §3-1-8.

CULLMAN COUNTY.
Counties generally.
See COUNTIES.
Court costs and charges, Const. Ala., amd. 137.
Officers.
Fees, allowances, etc., Const. Ala., amd. 137.

CULLMAN, MUNICIPALITY OF.
School tax.
Special tax, Const. Ala., amd. 52.

CULPABILITY.
Criminal culpability.
General provisions, §§13A-2-1 to 13A-2-7.
See CRIMINAL LAW AND PROCEDURE.

CURATORS.
General provisions, §§26-7A-1 to 26-7A-17.
See GUARDIAN AND WARD.
Securities.
Fiduciary security transfers, §§8-6-70 to 8-6-80.
See SECURITIES.

CURTESY.
Partnerships.
Property not subject to curtesy, §10-8-72.
Probate code.
Abolished, §43-8-57.

CURVE ACT.
Railroad crossings.
Warning devices.
Duty of engineer, §§37-2-81, 37-2-83.

CUSTODIANS.
Executors and administrators.
General provisions.
See EXECUTORS AND ADMINISTRATORS.
Fiduciaries generally.
See FIDUCIARIES.

CUSTODIANS—Cont'd
Gifts to minors, §§35-5A-1 to 35-5A-24.
See TRANSFERS TO MINORS.
Guardian and ward.
General provisions.
See GUARDIAN AND WARD.
Partition.
Sale of land of minors and insane persons.
Contest by custodian, §35-6-84.
Securities.
Fiduciary security transfers, §§8-6-70 to 8-6-80.
See SECURITIES.

CUSTODY.
Child custody and support.
Child support programs, §§38-10-1 to 38-10-33.
See CHILD SUPPORT PROGRAMS.
Generally, §§30-3-1 to 30-3-99.
See MINORS.
Uniform child custody jurisdiction act, §§30-3-20 to 30-3-44.
See MINORS.
Interference with custody, §13A-6-45.
Minors.
Child custody and support, §§30-3-1 to 30-3-99.
See MINORS.
Parent and child.
Termination of parental rights.
Transfer of custody, §26-18-8.
Uniform child custody jurisdiction act, §§30-3-20 to 30-3-44.
See MINORS.

CY PRES ACT, §35-4-251.

D

DAGGERS.
General provisions.
See WEAPONS.

DAIRY PRODUCTS.
General provisions.
See MILK AND MILK PRODUCTS.

DALE COUNTY.
Court costs and charges, Const. Ala., amd. 326.
Offices.
Consolidation, Const. Ala., amd. 326.
School tax.
Special property tax, Const. Ala., amd. 295.

DALLAS COUNTY.
Court costs and charges, Const. Ala., amd. 233.
Economic and industrial development promotion, Const. Ala., amd. 429.
Officers.
Fees, allowances, etc., Const. Ala., amd. 138.
Salaries, Const. Ala., amd. 46.

DAMAGES.
Alcoholic beverages.
Beer.
Business relations between wholesalers and suppliers.
Violations of provisions, §28-9-11.
Appeals.
Frivolous appeal, ARAP, Rule 38.
Attachment.
Issuance when action sounds in damages merely, §6-6-41.
Bills of exchange, §§8-4-1 to 8-4-4.
Bills of lading.
Limitation of liability, §7-7-309.
Blind persons.
Liability for damages caused by guide dogs, §21-7-4.
Carriers.
Limitation of liability.
Carrier issuing bill of lading, §7-7-309.
Cemeteries.
County cemeteries, §§11-17-1 to 11-17-16.
See COUNTIES.
Claims against state.
See CLAIMS AGAINST STATE.
Coal.
Unauthorized removal, §9-1-6.
Coal mine safety.
Correction, §25-9-90.
Commercial code.
See COMMERCIAL CODE.
Counties.
Cemeteries.
Damages from taking of property, etc.
See COUNTIES.
County industrial development authorities.
Limitation on liability, §11-92A-20.
Crime victims compensation.
Notice of action to recover damages, §15-23-14.
Criminal law and procedure.
Civil actions.
Effect of title on damages in civil actions, §13A-1-8.
Restitution to victims of crimes.
See RESTITUTION TO VICTIMS OF CRIMES.
Dams.
Erection of dams for mills, gins, factories or electric generators.
See DAMS.
Definitions.
Punitive damages, §6-11-20.
Structured damages, §6-11-2.
Education.
Reports of property damage, §16-1-24.
Teachers.
Breach of employment contract, §16-24-10.
Ejectment.
See EJECTMENT.

DAMAGES—Cont'd
Electricity.
Service territories for electric
suppliers.
1984 act violations,
§37-14-9.
1985 act violations,
§37-14-37.
Eminent domain.
See EMINENT DOMAIN.
Forest products.
Unauthorized cutting,
§9-13-62.
Unauthorized purchases,
§9-13-62.
Fraud.
Punitive damages.
Definition of fraud,
§6-11-20.
Frivolous appeal, ARAP,
Rule 38.
Future damages.
Structured damages, §§6-11-1
to 6-11-3. See within this
heading, "Structured
damages."
Habeas corpus.
Unlawful detention or arrest
after discharge order,
§15-21-27.
Highways.
See HIGHWAYS.
Installment payments.
Malpractice.
Future damages, §6-5-543.
Structured damages.
Future damages, §6-11-3.
Landlord and tenant.
Reasonable satisfaction for
use and occupation of
land, §35-9-100.
Libel and slander.
Actions, §§6-5-183 to 6-5-186.
Liquidated damages.
Specific performance of
contracts not barred,
§8-1-45.
Malpractice, §§6-5-542 to
6-5-544.
Meat and meat products.
Evidence of violations,
Admissibility, §2-17-31.
Military affairs.
Payment for damages caused
by national guard
members acting in line
of duty, §31-2-86.
**Motion picture fair
competition.**
Award of damages in civil
actions, §8-18-6.
Motor fuels.
Marketing.
Violation of chapter,
§8-22-17.
Motor vehicles.
Safety-responsibility act.
Inadmissible evidence in
civil actions, §32-7-12.
Navigation.
Diverting streams.
Damages for diversion,
§33-7-4.
Nuisances.
Special damage to individual
by public nuisance,
§6-5-123.

DAMAGES—Cont'd
Past damages.
Structured damages, §§6-11-1
to 6-11-7. See within this
heading "Structured
damages."
Periodic payments.
Malpractice.
Future damages, §6-5-543.
Personal property.
Trial of right of property.
Execution for amount of
damages, §6-6-163.
Pleadings.
Special damage, ARCP, Rule
9 (g).
Poultry.
Evidence of violations of
chapter or regulations,
§2-17-31.
Products liability, §§6-5-520,
6-5-522.
Punitive damages.
Award.
Court to independently
reassess award,
§6-11-23.
Cause of action.
No cause of action created,
§6-11-28.
Damages not to exceed
$250,000.
Exceptions, §6-11-21.
Mistrial.
Limitation mentioned in
presence of jury,
§6-11-22.
Definitions, §6-11-20.
Effective date of article,
§6-11-30.
Evidence, §§6-11-20, 6-11-23.
Fraud.
Defined, §6-11-20.
Hearings, §6-11-23.
Presumption of correctness.
No presumption, §6-11-23.
Appeals, §6-11-24.
Principal, master, etc., not
liable for damages for
conduct of agent,
servant, etc., §6-11-27.
Setting aside damages.
Ability of court not
limited, §6-11-25.
State or agency thereof.
No punitive damages
awarded against,
§6-11-26.
Structured damages, §§6-11-1
to 6-11-7. See within this
heading, "Structured
damages."
Wrongful death.
Action not affected,
§6-11-29.
Recorded devices.
Civil actions, §13A-8-85.
Roads.
Private roads.
Damages caused by road,
§23-1-131.
Soil and water conservation.
Districts.
Land-use regulations.
Violations, §9-8-27.
Sports agents.
Registration.
Damages not limited to
amount of bond,
§8-26-15.

DAMAGES—Cont'd
State.
Claims against state.
See CLAIMS AGAINST
STATE.
Structured damages.
Damages not affected,
§6-11-6.
Definitions, §6-11-2.
Evidence, §6-11-5.
Future damages.
Damages greater than
$150,000, §6-11-3.
Defined, §6-11-2.
Evidence of financial
ability to make
payments, §6-11-3.
Installment payments,
§6-11-3.
Not to be reduced to
present value, §6-11-1.
Periodic payments over
period of years,
§6-11-3.
Present value.
Evidence of inadmissible,
§6-11-3.
Hearings.
Court to conduct, §6-11-5.
Installment payments.
Future damages, §6-11-3.
Itemization, §6-11-1.
Past damages.
Defined, §6-11-2.
Prior rights not affected,
§6-11-7.
Requirements when
judgment structured,
§6-11-4.
Termination, §6-11-4.
Surveys and surveyors.
Division of land surveys.
Liability for damages to
private property,
§35-2-32.
Teachers.
Breach of employment
contract, §16-24-10.
**Trademarks and service
marks.**
Fraudulent filing or
registration, §8-12-15.
Trade secrets.
Misappropriation, §8-27-3.
Transportation companies.
Loss, injury or delay in
delivery, §§37-2-60 to
37-2-62.
Trees and timber.
Destruction, injury or
removal of trees,
§§35-14-1 to 35-14-3.
Uniform commercial code.
See COMMERCIAL CODE.
Utility services actions.
Effect of criminal conviction,
§6-5-603.
Estimated lost revenue.
Determination, §6-5-604.
Treble damages, §6-5-602.
**Water conservation and
irrigation.**
Corporations.
Entry on property,
§9-10-46.
**Water management and
drainage.**
Board's entry on lands to
make surveys, §9-9-22.

DAMAGES—Cont'd

Water management and drainage—Cont'd

Districts.

Damages to improvements, §9-9-48.

Drainage subdistricts.

Eminent domain, §9-9-78.

Waters and watercourses.

Diverting streams, §33-7-4.

DAMS.

Affidavits.

Erection of dams for mills, gins, factories or electric generators.

Application to erect, §18-2-2.

Appeals.

Erection of dams for mills, gins, factories or electric generators.

Assessment of damages, §18-2-19.

Assessments.

Erection of dams for mills, gins, factories or electric generators.

Assessment of lands. See within this heading, "Erection of dams for mills, gins, factories or electric generators."

Canals.

Erection of dams for mills, gins, factories or electric generators.

Construction of canal through adjoining lands, §18-2-16.

Condemnation.

Eminent domain generally. See within this heading, "Eminent domain."

Erection of dams for mills, gins, factories or electric generators generally, §§18-2-1 to 18-2-21. See within this heading, "Erection of dams for mills, gins, factories or electric generators."

Construction.

Condemnation of ways and rights of way by companies constructing internal improvements, §10-5-4.

Cotton gins.

Erection of dams for gins, §§18-2-1 to 18-2-21. See within this heading, "Erection of dams for mills, gins, factories or electric generators."

Damages.

Erection of dams for mills, gins, factories or electric generators. See within this heading, "Erection of dams for mills, gins, factories or electric generators."

Ditches.

Erection of dams for mills, gins, factories or electric generators.

Construction through adjoining lands, §18-2-16.

DAMS—Cont'd

Electric generators.

Erection of dams for electric generators, §§18-2-1 to 18-2-21. See within this heading, "Erection of dams for mills, gins, factories or electric generators."

Eminent domain.

Authorization for dams, §10-4-323.

Companies constructing, operating or maintaining, §10-5-3.

Condemnation of ways and rights of way, §10-5-4.

Dams on navigable rivers, §33-7-31.

Erection of dams for mills, gins, factories or electric generators generally, §§18-2-1 to 18-2-21. See within this heading, "Erection of dams for mills, gins, factories or electric generators."

Legislature.

Authorization for dams, §10-4-323.

Power of eminent domain, §10-5-1.

Procedure for condemnation, §10-4-322.

Routes and sites.

Rights of condemning corporations in selection of routes and sites, §10-5-8.

Erection of dams for mills, gins, factories or electric generators, §§18-2-1 to 18-2-21.

Appeals.

Assessment of damages, §18-2-19.

Application for erection.

Affidavit, §18-2-2.

Contents, §18-2-3.

Contest of application.

Persons permitted to contest, §18-2-11.

Denial, §18-2-12.

Filing.

Issuance of writ upon filing, §18-2-5.

Probate court, §18-2-2.

Grant of application, §18-2-12.

Notice.

Owner of land on opposite side of stream, §18-2-4.

Procedure, §18-2-17.

Show cause against grant.

Notice of hearing to show cause, §18-2-10.

Summons to landowners to appear, §18-2-9.

Writ.

Issuance, §18-2-5.

Assessment of lands.

Appeals, §18-2-19.

Payment.

Failure to make payment, §18-2-13.

Time for payment, §18-2-13.

DAMS—Cont'd

Erection of dams for mills, gins, factories or electric generators—Cont'd

Assessment of lands—Cont'd

When applicant not owner of land on both sides, §18-2-7.

Canals.

Construction through adjoining lands.

Proceedings, §18-2-16.

Commencement of construction, §18-2-14.

Completion of construction, §18-2-14.

Damages.

Appeals.

Assessment of damages, §18-2-19.

Building or raising dam without authority, §18-2-18.

Ditches.

Construction through adjoining lands.

Proceedings when construction necessary, §18-2-16.

Estate in fee in acre of land.

Reversion of estate, §18-2-15.

Vesting of estate.

Compliance with certain conditions, §18-2-14.

Effect of noncompliance, §18-2-15.

Gristmills.

Order of grinding of grain, §18-2-21.

Rate of toll.

Applicability of provisions of code, §18-2-21.

Guardian ad litem.

Appointment, §18-2-4.

Hearings.

Notice, §18-2-10.

Jury, §§18-2-5 to 18-2-8.

Assessment of value of property.

When applicant not owner of land on both sides of stream, §18-2-7.

Attendance, §18-2-6.

Charge by sheriff, §18-2-6.

Duties generally, §18-2-6.

Inquest.

Delivery to sheriff, §18-2-8.

Execution, §18-2-8.

Return by sheriff to probate court, §18-2-8.

Summoning, §18-2-5.

Liabilities.

Building or raising dam without authority, §18-2-18.

Mentally ill.

Guardian ad litem.

Appointment, §18-2-4.

Minors.

Guardian ad litem.

Appointment, §18-2-4.

Nuisances.

Building or raising dam without authority, §18-2-18.

DAMS—Cont'd
Erection of dams for mills, gins, factories or electric generators—Cont'd
Parties.
  Persons permitted to contest application, §18-2-11.
Property owners.
  Notice of owner of land on opposite side of stream, §18-2-4.
  Right to erect dam, §18-2-1.
  Summons, §18-2-9.
Repairs.
  Time limitation, §18-2-14.
Right of property owner to erect dam, §18-2-1.
Sheriffs.
  Appearance on date designated for inquest, §18-2-6.
  Deputies, §18-2-20.
  Inquest of jury.
    Delivery to sheriff, §18-2-8.
    Return by sheriff to probate court, §18-2-8.
  Jury.
    Summoning of jurors, §18-2-5.
Factories.
Erection of dams for factories, §§18-2-1 to 18-2-21. See within this heading, "Erection of dams for mills, gins, factories or electric generators."
Fees.
Ad quod damnum proceedings.
  Jurors' fees, §12-19-112.
Fish and game.
Commercial fishing.
  Public impounded waters and navigable streams. See FISH AND GAME.
Generators.
Erection of dams for electric generators, §§18-2-1 to 18-2-21. See within this heading, "Erection of dams for mills, gins, factories or electric generators."
Gins.
Erection of dams for gins, §§18-2-1 to 18-2-21. See within this heading, "Erection of dams for mills, gins, factories or electric generators."
Guardian ad litem.
Erection of dams for mills, gins, factories or electric generators.
  Minors or mentally ill persons, §18-2-4.
Hearings.
Erection of dams for mills, gins, factories or electric generators, §§18-2-10, 18-2-11.
Hydroelectric power companies. See within this heading, "Water power companies."

DAMS—Cont'd
Jury.
Erection of dams for mills, gins, factories or electric generators, §§18-2-5 to 18-2-8.
Legislature.
Dams considered as authorized by legislature, §10-4-323.
Mentally ill.
Erection of dams for mills, gins, factories or electric generators.
  Guardian ad litem, §18-2-4.
Mills.
Erection of dams for mills, §§18-2-1 to 18-2-21. See within this heading, "Erection of dams for mills, gins, factories or electric generators."
Mines and minerals.
Surface mining reclamation.
  Construction of dams, §9-16-7.
Minors.
Erection of dams for mills, gins, factories or electric generators.
  Guardian ad litem, §18-2-4.
Navigable rivers.
Consent of federal government, §33-7-31.
Construction across.
  Right to, §33-7-30.
Easements across.
  Right of, §33-7-30.
Eminent domain, §33-7-31.
Foreign corporations.
  Acquisition of rights granted under article, §33-7-31.
Improvement of navigation, §33-7-31.
Prior rights, §33-7-32.
United States.
  Consent, §33-7-31.
Notice.
Erection of dams for mills, gins, factories or electric generators.
  Application to erect.
    Owner of land on opposite side of stream, §18-2-4.
  Hearing to show cause against grant of application, §18-2-10.
Nuisances.
Erection of dams for mills, gins, factories or electric generators.
  Building or raising dam without authority, §18-2-18.
Operation.
Condemnation of ways and rights of way by companies operating internal improvement, §10-5-4.
Probate courts.
Ad quod damnum proceedings.
  Jurors' fees, §12-19-112.

DAMS—Cont'd
Raising of dams.
Erection of dams for mills, gins, factories or electric generators, §§18-2-1 to 18-2-21. See within this heading, "Erection of dams for mills, gins, factories or electric generators."
Sheriffs.
Erection of dams for mills, gins, factories or electric generators. See within this heading, "Erection of dams for mills, gins, factories or electric generators."
United States.
Consent to dams on navigable rivers, §33-7-31.
Water power companies.
Authority, §10-4-320.
Condemnation.
  Procedure, §10-4-322.
Conforming dams considered authorized by legislature, §10-4-323.
Duty to serve public, §10-4-321.
Easements.
  Condemnation, §10-5-3.
Eminent domain.
  Companies constructing, operating or maintaining public utility, §10-5-4.
  Condemnation for rights of way or easements by power companies, §10-5-3.
  Power of eminent domain, §10-5-1.
  Rights of condemning corporations in selection of routes and sites, §10-5-8.
Powers, §10-4-320.
Public service.
  Duty to serve public, §10-4-321.
Rights, §10-4-320.
Rights of way.
  Condemnation, §10-5-3.

DANGEROUS WEAPONS.
General provisions.
See WEAPONS.

DANIEL "CHAPPIE" JAMES AEROSPACE MEMORIAL.
Macon county.
Indebtedness for, Const. Ala., amd. 437.
Tuskegee, municipality of.
Indebtedness for, Const. Ala., amd. 438.

DATA.
Dissemination of computer-based court information,
ARJA, Rule 33.
Applications, ARJA, Rule 33.
Costs, ARJA, Rule 33.
Criteria to determine release, ARJA, Rule 33.
Forms, ARJA, Rule 33.
Information for release, ARJA, Rule 33.
Policies and procedures, ARJA, Rule 33.

DATA—Cont'd
  **Dissemination of computer-
  based court information**
  —Cont'd
    Release of data, ARJA, Rule
    33.
  **Division of data systems
  management.**
    Advisory committee,
    §41-4-224.
    Created, §41-4-220.
    Director, §41-4-222.
    Duties, §41-4-221.
    Employees, §41-4-223.
  **Obtaining from court
  officials,** §12-8-7.

**DAUGHTERS OF THE
AMERICAN
REVOLUTION.**
  Licenses.
    Exemptions, §40-9-13.
  Taxation.
    Exemptions, §40-9-13.

DAY CARE CENTERS.
  Child care facilities.
    See WELFARE.
  Diseases.
    Notifiable diseases.
      General provisions.
      See DISEASES.
      Persons responsible for
      reporting diseases,
      §22-11A-2.

DEAD BODIES.
  Abandonment, §§22-19-20 to
  22-19-30.
  Anatomical gifts.
    General provisions.
    See ANATOMICAL
      GIFTS.
    Licenses.
      Donor eye enucleation
      licenses, §§34-13-150
      to 34-13-152.
      See FUNERALS.
  Blood and urine samples,
  §§22-19-80 to 22-19-82.
    Coroners.
      Authority, §22-19-80.
    Deputy coroners.
      Authority, §22-19-80.
      Exemption from civil and
      criminal liability,
      §22-19-82.
    Exemption from civil and
      criminal liability,
      §22-19-82.
    Law enforcement officers.
      Authority, §22-19-80.
    Persons who may be directed
      to withdraw samples,
      §22-19-81.
    Exemptions from civil and
      criminal liability,
      §22-19-82.
    Purpose, §22-19-80.
    State toxicologists.
      Authority, §22-19-80.
      Exemption from civil and
      criminal liability,
      §22-19-82.
  Burial.
    Cemeteries.
      County cemeteries
      generally, §§11-17-1 to
      11-17-16.
      See COUNTIES.
      General provisions.
      See CEMETERIES.

DEAD BODIES—Cont'd
  Burial—Cont'd
    Cemeteries—Cont'd
      Municipal cemeteries
      generally, §§11-47-40
      to 11-47-74.
      See MUNICIPAL
        CORPORATIONS.
    General provisions.
      See BURIAL.
    Indian burial grounds.
      Aboriginal mounds,
      earthworks and other
      antiquities, §§41-3-1 to
      41-3-6.
      See HISTORY AND
        ARCHIVES.
  Cemeteries.
    County cemeteries, §§11-17-1
    to 11-17-16.
    See COUNTIES.
    General provisions.
    See CEMETERIES.
    Municipal cemeteries,
    §§11-47-40 to 11-47-74.
    See MUNICIPAL
      CORPORATIONS.
  Certificates of death.
    Crimes and offenses,
    §22-19-3.
  Coroners.
    See CORONERS.
  Cremation.
    Body removed from state,
    §22-19-2.
  Criminal law and procedure.
    Abuse of corpses, §13A-11-13.
  Death penalty.
    Costs of transportation of
    body after execution,
    §15-18-85.
  Disposition.
    Receipts for burial, removal
    or other disposition,
    §22-9-73.
    Wording of receipt for in-
    state interment,
    §22-9-74.
  Embalmers.
    See FUNERALS.
  Embalming.
    Body removed from state,
    §22-19-2.
  Funerals.
    See FUNERALS.
  Indictments.
    Removing body from grave
    for purposes of sale, etc.
    Form of indictment,
    §15-8-150.
  Morgues.
    Municipal corporations,
    §11-47-7.
  Morticians.
    See FUNERALS.
  Penalties.
    Distribution of unclaimed
    bodies for scientific
    study.
      Violations, §22-19-30.
  Permits.
    Burial permits.
      See BURIAL.
    Regulation of transportation
    of dead bodies, §22-19-1.
    Removal permits. See within
    this heading, "Removal."

DEAD BODIES—Cont'd
  Physicians.
    Blood and urine samples
    from certain dead bodies.
    Exemption from civil and
    criminal liability,
    §22-19-82.
    May be directed to
    withdraw samples,
    §22-19-81.
  **Receipts for burial, removal
  or other disposition,**
  §22-9-73.
    Wording of receipt for in-
    state interment,
    §22-9-74.
  Records.
    Unclaimed bodies.
      Distribution for scientific
      study, §22-19-21.
  Removal.
    Body removed from state to
    be embalmed or
    cremated, §22-19-2.
    Permits.
      Disposal of body without
      permit, §22-19-3.
      Ministers at funerals to
      ascertain if permit has
      been secured, §22-19-4.
      Out-of-state burials,
      §22-9-75.
    Receipts for removal or other
    disposition, §22-9-73.
    Wording of receipt for in-
    state interment,
    §22-9-74.
    Regulation of transportation,
    §22-19-1.
  State toxicologist.
    See STATE
      TOXICOLOGIST.
  Transportation.
    Regulation of transportation,
    §22-19-1.
  Unclaimed bodies, §§22-19-20
  to 22-19-30.
    Authority to solicit dead
    bodies for scientific
    studies, §22-19-22.
    Delivery of bodies to board
    for distribution and
    delivery, §22-19-22.
    When prohibited,
    §22-19-23.
    Distribution for scientific
    study, §§22-19-20 to
    22-19-30.
      Authority to solicit dead
      bodies from counties,
      §22-19-22.
      Board for distribution and
      delivery.
        Composition, §22-19-20.
        Delivery of bodies to
        board, §22-19-22.
        Notice to board of bodies
        required to be buried
        at public expense,
        §22-19-22.
        Powers, §22-19-21.
        Records, §22-19-21.
        Secretary, §22-19-20.
      Carriers for conveyance of
      bodies, §22-19-28.
      Claims for bodies.
        Preservation of bodies for
        60 days by schools
        pending claims,
        §22-19-26.

DEAD BODIES—Cont'd
Unclaimed bodies—Cont'd
Distribution for scientific
study—Cont'd
Conveyance of bodies.
Carriers for conveyance,
§22-19-28.
Delivery of bodies to board,
§22-19-22.
When bodies not to be
delivered to board,
§22-19-23.
Disposal of bodies after use
by schools, §22-19-27.
Expenses.
Payment, §22-19-29.
Holding period, §22-19-24.
Notice of death, §22-19-24.
Payment of expenses,
§22-19-29.
Penalty, §22-19-30.
Preservation of bodies for
60 days by schools
pending claims,
§22-19-26.
Receipts for bodies,
§22-19-28.
Records, §22-19-21.
Schools.
Disposal of bodies after
use by schools,
§22-19-27.
Distribution to schools,
§22-19-25.
Preservation of bodies for
60 days by schools
pending claims,
§22-19-26.
Transportation of bodies,
§22-19-28.
Violations of article,
§22-19-30.
Notice of death, §22-19-24.
Notice to board of bodies
required to be buried at
public expense,
§22-19-22.
Surrender to relatives,
§22-19-23.
Uniform anatomical gift act.
Generally, §§22-19-40 to
22-19-47.
See ANATOMICAL
GIFTS.
Urine samples, §§22-19-80 to
22-19-82.

DEADLY WEAPONS.
General provisions.
See WEAPONS.

DEAD MAN'S STATUTE,
§12-21-163.

DEAF PERSONS.
**Alabama institute for deaf
and blind,** §§21-1-1 to
21-1-26.
See HANDICAPPED
PERSONS.
Audiologists.
General provisions,
§§34-28A-1 to 34-28A-44.
See SPEECH
PATHOLOGISTS AND
AUDIOLOGISTS.
Buildings.
Accessibility to and use of
public buildings and
facilities by physically
handicapped persons,
§§21-4-1 to 21-4-7.
See PUBLIC BUILDINGS.

DEAF PERSONS—Cont'd
Constitution of Alabama.
Exemptions from poll tax,
Const. Ala., amd. 109.
Institute for deaf and blind.
Bonds for construction and
improvement purposes,
Const. Ala., amd. 117.
Dogs.
Guide dog for hearing-
impaired persons,
§21-7-4.
Education.
Exceptional children,
§§16-39-1 to 16-39-12.
See EDUCATION.
Institute for deaf and blind,
§§21-1-1 to 21-1-26.
See HANDICAPPED
PERSONS.
Elections.
Accessibility to registration
and polling places by
handicapped persons,
§§21-4-20 to 21-4-24.
**Hearing aid dealers and
fitters,** §§34-14-1 to
34-14-33.
See HEARING AID
DEALERS AND
FITTERS.
Hearing dogs.
Right to be accompanied by,
§21-7-4.
Home industries, §§21-2-1 to
21-2-4.
Institute for deaf and blind,
§§21-1-1 to 21-1-26.
See HANDICAPPED
PERSONS.
Interpreters.
Handicapped witnesses,
§§12-21-131 to 12-21-134.
Libraries.
Operation of library service
by department of adult
blind and deaf, §21-1-15.
Poll tax.
Exemptions, Const. Ala.,
amd. 109.
Public buildings.
Accessibility to and use of
public buildings and
facilities by physically
handicapped persons,
§§21-4-1 to 21-4-7.
See PUBLIC BUILDINGS.
**Speech pathologists and
audiologists.**
General provisions,
§§34-28A-1 to 34-28A-44.
See SPEECH
PATHOLOGISTS AND
AUDIOLOGISTS.
Telephones.
Surcharge, §37-1-80.2.
Witnesses.
Interpreters, §§12-21-131 to
12-21-134.
**Workshops, home industries,
etc.,** §§21-2-1 to 21-2-4.

DEATH.
Actions.
Abatement of actions.
See ABATEMENT,
REVIVAL AND
SURVIVAL OF
ACTIONS.
Wrongful death.
See WRONGFUL DEATH.

DEATH—Cont'd
Anatomical gifts.
See ANATOMICAL GIFTS.
**Annuity and mortality
tables.**
See ANNUITY AND
MORTALITY TABLES.
Appeals.
Death sentence.
See APPEALS.
Substitution of parties,
ARAP, Rule 43 (a).
Attorneys at law.
Appointment of counsel to
protect client's interests,
ARDE, Rule 21.
**Banks and financial
institutions.**
Death of depositor or trustee,
§§5-5A-38 to 5-5A-41.
Boat accidents.
Report required, §33-5-25.
Brain death act, §§22-31-1 to
22-31-4.
Burial generally.
See BURIAL.
Capital punishment.
See CAPITAL
PUNISHMENT.
Cemeteries.
County cemeteries, §§11-17-1
to 11-17-16.
See COUNTIES.
General provisions.
See CEMETERIES.
Municipal cemeteries,
§§11-47-40 to 11-47-74.
See MUNICIPAL
CORPORATIONS.
Certificates.
General provisions.
See VITAL STATISTICS.
Claims against state.
Wrongful death, §§41-9-64,
41-9-70.
Commercial code.
Bank deposits and
collections.
Death of customer.
Authority of payor or
collecting bank,
§7-4-405.
Conservators.
Settlements of accounts of
conservators.
Death of conservator,
§§26-5-50 to 26-5-54.
**Constitution of the United
States.**
President and vice-president
of the United States.
Duty of congress, Const. U.
S., Art. II, §1;
Amendment XXV.
President-elect.
Provision in case of,
Const. U. S.,
Amendment XX.
Conveyances.
Conveyances by executors
and administrators.
See EXECUTORS AND
ADMINISTRATORS.
Powers of disposition.
Death of trustee with right
of selection.
Execution of power upon
death, §35-4-298.
Coroners generally.
See CORONERS.

DEATH—Cont'd
Corpses.
See DEAD BODIES.
Counties.
Indigent persons.
Burial of persons dying
with no estate, §38-8-2.
County treasurers.
Proceedings upon death,
§11-4-29.
Credit unions.
Deposits in names of two
persons, §5-17-15.
Disposition of shares or
deposit account of
deceased person,
§5-17-16.
Trustees.
Deposits for trust
beneficiaries, §5-17-15.
Dead bodies.
See DEAD BODIES.
Determination of death,
§§22-31-1 to 22-31-4.
Liability for acts, §22-31-4.
Medically and legally dead.
When person considered,
§22-31-1.
Procedures, §22-31-1.
Use of other methods,
§22-31-2.
When part of body to be
used for
transplantation,
§22-31-3.
Standards, §22-31-1.
Use of other methods,
§22-31-2.
Transplantation.
Procedures for parts of
body to be used,
§22-31-3.
Diseases.
Vital statistics.
Proceedings when death
due to infectious, etc.,
disease, §22-9-7.
Elections.
Abatement of contests.
Legislature, judicial or
county officers,
§17-15-33.
Lists of qualified voters.
Purging of registration
lists, §17-4-131.
Embalmers generally.
See FUNERALS.
Evidence.
Ancient rights.
Declarations of deceased
persons, §12-21-30.
Armed forces death.
Official notice, §12-21-90.
Certified registers of death,
§12-21-101.
Executions.
Death of defendant or
plaintiff.
See EXECUTIONS.
**Executors and
administrators.**
See EXECUTORS AND
ADMINISTRATORS.
Explosives.
Death occurring during
transportation of
explosives.
Penalty, §37-8-184.

DEATH—Cont'd
Firefighters.
Compensation for death,
§§36-30-1 to 36-30-7.
See FIRES AND FIRE
PREVENTION.
Survivor's education
assistance act,
§§36-21-100 to 36-21-105.
Fish and game.
Hunting deaths.
Investigation by grand
jury, §9-11-21.
Reporting of accidents,
§9-11-21.
Funerals generally.
See FUNERALS.
Governor.
Notice to lieutenant
governor, §36-9-6.
Guardian and ward.
Books of account kept by
deceased guardian.
Evidence, §12-21-32.
Uniform guardianship and
protective proceedings
act.
Conservators.
Appointment of
successor,
§26-2A-143.
Incapacitated persons.
Termination of
guardianship,
§26-2A-109.
Minors.
Termination of
guardianship,
§26-2A-79.
Homicide.
See HOMICIDE.
Income tax.
Gain or loss.
Property transmitted at
death, §40-18-6.
Inquests.
Coroners' inquests.
See CORONERS.
Jails.
Delivery of jail upon death of
sheriff, §14-6-2.
Life estates.
See LIFE ESTATES.
Manslaughter, §§13A-6-3,
15-3-5.
Homicide generally.
See HOMICIDE.
**Mechanics' and
materialmen's liens.**
Personal representatives.
Actions against,
§35-11-230.
Actions by, §35-11-229.
Midwives.
Failure of midwife to report
death, §22-9-78.
Military affairs.
Compensation for death of
national guardsmen,
§§31-3-1 to 31-3-7.
See MILITARY AFFAIRS.
Evidence of armed forces
death.
Official notice, §12-21-90.
Mortality tables.
See ANNUITY AND
MORTALITY TABLES.
Morticians generally.
See FUNERALS.
Motor vehicle accidents.
See MOTOR VEHICLES.

DEATH—Cont'd
Motor vehicles.
Homicide by vehicle,
§32-5A-192.
Municipal corporations.
Commissioners.
Filling of vacancies caused
by death, §§11-44-12,
11-44-77.
Murder, §13A-6-2.
Homicide generally.
See HOMICIDE.
National guardsmen.
Compensation for death of
national guardsmen,
§§31-3-1 to 31-3-7.
See MILITARY AFFAIRS.
Natural death act, §§22-8A-1
to 22-8A-10.
See NATURAL DEATH
ACT.
Nursing homes.
Replacement of
administrators, §34-20-2.
Parties.
Abatement, revival and
survival of actions
generally.
See ABATEMENT,
REVIVAL AND
SURVIVAL OF
ACTIONS.
Substitution of parties,
ARCP, Rule 25 (a), (d).
Partition.
Circuit courts.
Judgment not affected by
death of defendant,
§35-6-25.
Probate courts.
Applicability of article to
executors or
administrators,
§35-6-65.
Completion of partition by
substitute
commissioner,
§35-6-52.
Sale instead of partition.
Completion of sale by
substitute
commissioner,
§35-6-64.
Partnerships.
Disposition of partner's
interest, §10-8-72.
Dissolution.
Death of partner, §10-8-91.
Liability of deceased
partners, §10-8-101.
Duty of partners to render
information to legal
representative of
deceased partner,
§10-8-46.
Liability of deceased partners
upon dissolution,
§10-8-101.
Limited partnerships.
Death of general partner,
§10-9A-61.
Powers of successors in
interest, §10-9A-124.
Rights of estate of deceased
partners, §10-8-103.
Peace officers.
Annuity and benefit fund,
§§36-21-60 to 36-21-78.
See PEACE OFFICERS.

DEATH—Cont'd
　Peace officers—Cont'd
　　Badges.
　　　Providing badge for
　　　　survivor of officer
　　　　killed or disabled in
　　　　line of duty,
　　　　§36-21-8.1.
　　Compensation for death,
　　　§§36-30-1 to 36-30-7.
　　　See PEACE OFFICERS.
　　Survivor's education
　　　assistance act,
　　　§§36-21-100 to 36-21-105.
　Penalty of death.
　　See CAPITAL
　　　PUNISHMENT.
　Penitentiary.
　　Convicts.
　　　Disposition of effects,
　　　　§14-3-36.
　Permits.
　　Burial permits.
　　　See BURIAL.
　Police.
　　Municipal police.
　　　Compensation for death or
　　　　disability from
　　　　occupational diseases,
　　　　§§36-30-20 to 36-30-23.
　　Peace officers generally.
　　　See PEACE OFFICERS.
　　State police.
　　　Occupational diseases.
　　　　Compensation for death
　　　　　or disability,
　　　　　§§36-30-20 to
　　　　　36-30-23.
　Poultry.
　　Poultry waste, dead poultry
　　　and unhatched or unused
　　　eggs, §§2-16-40 to
　　　2-16-42.
　**President of the United
　　States.**
　　Duty of congress, Const. U.
　　　S., Art. II, §1.
　　President-elect.
　　　Provision in case of, Const.
　　　　U. S., Amendment XX.
　　Succession upon death,
　　　Const. U. S., Amendment
　　　XXV, §1.
　Presumption of death.
　　Executors and
　　　administrators.
　　　Persons presumed dead,
　　　　§§43-2-230 to 43-2-238.
　　　See EXECUTORS AND
　　　　ADMINISTRATORS.
　　Generally, §43-8-6.
　Professional corporations.
　　Transfer of shares upon
　　　death of shareholder,
　　　§10-4-389.
　**Public officers and
　　employees.**
　　Notice, §36-9-6.
　　Payment of salary of
　　　deceased officer after
　　　date of death, Const.
　　　Ala., art. IV, §97.
　　Preretirement death benefit
　　　program, §§36-27B-1 to
　　　36-27B-5.
　　Public property, papers, etc.
　　　Recovery of papers,
　　　　property, etc., by
　　　　successor to office upon
　　　　death of incumbent,
　　　　§36-12-26.

DEATH—Cont'd
　**Public officers and
　　employees**—Cont'd
　　Vacation of office, §36-9-1.
　Real estate brokers.
　　Effect of death of licensed
　　　broker on company,
　　　§34-27-32.
　Real property.
　　Person contracting to sell
　　　real property.
　　　Conveyances by executors
　　　　and administrators
　　　　generally, §§35-4-320
　　　　to 35-4-323.
　Registers of death.
　　Evidence.
　　　Certified registers,
　　　　§12-21-101.
　Revival of actions.
　　General provisions.
　　　See ABATEMENT,
　　　　REVIVAL AND
　　　　SURVIVAL OF
　　　　ACTIONS.
　Salvage.
　　Applicability of chapter to
　　　taker's personal
　　　representative,
　　　§35-13-10.
　**Savings and loan
　　associations.**
　　Accounts.
　　　Disposition of account of
　　　　deceased person,
　　　　§5-16-46.
　　Deposit in names of two
　　　persons payable to either
　　　or survivor, §§15-16-44,
　　　15-16-45.
　　Trustee's death.
　　　Disposition of deposit,
　　　　§5-16-47.
　Sheriffs.
　　Jails.
　　　Delivery upon death of
　　　　sheriff, §14-6-2.
　　Retirement system.
　　　Refunds of salary
　　　　deductions, §36-22-42.
　Simultaneous death act,
　　§§43-7-1 to 43-7-8.
　　See SIMULTANEOUS
　　　DEATH ACT.
　State police.
　　Occupational diseases.
　　　Compensation for death or
　　　　disability, §§36-30-20
　　　　to 36-30-23.
　　Peace officers generally.
　　　See PEACE OFFICERS.
　State toxicologist.
　　See STATE
　　　TOXICOLOGIST.
　Survival of actions.
　　See ABATEMENT,
　　　REVIVAL AND
　　　SURVIVAL OF
　　　ACTIONS.
　Tables.
　　Annuity tables.
　　　See ANNUITY AND
　　　　MORTALITY
　　　　TABLES.
　　Mortality tables.
　　　See ANNUITY AND
　　　　MORTALITY
　　　　TABLES.

DEATH—Cont'd
　**Termination of life-support
　　procedures,** §§22-8A-1 to
　　22-8A-10.
　　See NATURAL DEATH
　　　ACT.
　Trusts and trustees.
　　Books of account kept by
　　　deceased trustee.
　　　Evidence, §12-21-32.
　　Powers of disposition.
　　　Execution of power upon
　　　　death of trustee with
　　　　right of selection,
　　　　§35-4-298.
　　Representative of deceased
　　　sole trustee to settle
　　　with succeeding trustee,
　　　§19-3-253.
　　Survivorship between
　　　cotrustees, §19-3-252.
　　Trust estate not descendible
　　　upon death of trustee,
　　　§35-4-258.
　　Trusts for employees or self-
　　　employed persons.
　　　Death benefit plans,
　　　　§35-4-259.
　**Uniform simultaneous death
　　act,** §§43-7-1 to 43-7-8.
　　See SIMULTANEOUS
　　　DEATH ACT.
　Vice-president, Const. U. S.,
　　Art. II, §1.
　Vital statistics.
　　General provisions.
　　　See VITAL STATISTICS.
　Welfare.
　　Payment of assistance after
　　　death, §38-4-3.
　Wills generally.
　　See WILLS.
　Witnesses.
　　Proof of execution of
　　　documents when
　　　subscribing witnesses
　　　dead, §12-21-62.
　Workmen's compensation.
　　See WORKMEN'S
　　　COMPENSATION.
　Wrongful death.
　　See WRONGFUL DEATH.

DEATH PENALTY.
　General provisions.
　　See CAPITAL
　　　PUNISHMENT.
　Jury.
　　See JURY.

DEBENTURES.
　**Industrial development
　　corporations.**
　　Evidencing loans by
　　　members, §10-4-140.
　Investment securities,
　　§§7-8-101 to 7-8-406.
　　See COMMERCIAL CODE.
　Public utilities.
　　Receiver's certificate or
　　　debentures.
　　　Issuance, §37-4-14.

DEBIT CARDS.
　**Fraudulent use of debit
　　cards,** §13A-9-14.
　Illegal possession, §13A-9-14.
　Theft.
　　Second degree theft of
　　　property, §13A-8-4.

DEBTORS AND CREDITORS.
Actions.
Creditors' actions. See within this heading, "Creditors' actions."
Administration of debts.
Exemptions from administration and payment of debts.
See EXEMPTIONS FROM ADMINISTRATION AND PAYMENT OF DEBTS.
Assets.
Discovery of assets, §§6-6-180 to 6-6-185, 6-6-187. See within this heading, "Creditors' actions."
Assignments for benefit of creditors.
See ASSIGNMENTS FOR BENEFIT OF CREDITORS.
Conveyances.
Powers of disposition.
Special and beneficial powers liable to claims of creditors, §35-4-305.
Corporations.
Liability of stockholders and subscribers to creditors, §10-2A-43.
Counterclaims.
Debt or liquidated demand due comaker or principal, §6-8-81.
Creditors' actions.
Corporations.
Subjecting unpaid subscriptions to satisfy judgment against corporation, §6-6-187.
Discovery of assets.
Complaint.
Answer of debtor, §6-6-183.
Creditor without lien or judgment, §§6-6-182, 6-6-183.
Evidence.
Answer to charge of fraud, §6-6-181.
Execution for money not satisfied, §6-6-180.
Execution returned "no property found," §6-6-183.
Intent to hinder, delay or defraud creditors, §6-6-181.
Answer to charge of fraud, §6-6-181.
Joinder of parties, §6-6-184.
Orders or judgments, §6-6-185.
Receiver.
Appointment, §6-6-185.
Costs, §6-6-203.
Remedy deemed cumulative, §6-6-204.
Statement of assets.
Contents, §6-6-200.
Notice to debtor to file, §6-6-200.
Oral examination.
Order to appear before court for, §6-6-201.
Refusal to submit, §6-6-202.

DEBTORS AND CREDITORS
—Cont'd
Creditors' actions—Cont'd
Discovery of assets—Cont'd
Statement of assets —Cont'd
Production of papers, §6-6-201.
Refusal to file, §6-6-202.
Criminal law and procedure.
Judgment creditors.
Defrauding, §13A-9-47.
Secured creditors.
Defrauding, §13A-9-46.
Debts generally.
See DEBTS.
Discovery of assets, §§6-6-180 to 6-6-185, 6-6-187. See within this heading, "Creditors' actions."
Electric cooperatives.
Consolidation or merger, §37-6-15.
Evidence.
Complaint for discovery of assets.
Answer to charge of fraud, §6-6-181.
Examination of debtor as to his property, §6-6-186.
Executors and administrators.
Appointment of debtor as executor, §43-8-254.
Exemptions from administration and payment of debts.
See EXEMPTIONS FROM ADMINISTRATION AND PAYMENT OF DEBTS.
Extradition.
Constraint on use for collection of debt, demand or claim, §15-9-48.
Interest.
General provisions.
See INTEREST.
Judgment creditors.
Recordation necessary as to judgment creditors, §§35-4-90 to 35-4-97.
See RECORDATION.
Life tenants.
Recordation necessary as to creditors of life tenants, §35-4-91.
Limited partnerships.
See PARTNERSHIPS.
Loans generally.
See LOANS.
Mortgages and deeds of trust generally.
See MORTGAGES AND DEEDS OF TRUST.
Partnerships.
Rights of judgment creditors of partners, §10-9A-122.
Payment of debts.
Exemptions from administration and payment of debts.
See EXEMPTIONS FROM ADMINISTRATION AND PAYMENT OF DEBTS.

DEBTORS AND CREDITORS
—Cont'd
Powers of disposition.
Special and beneficial powers liable to claims of creditors, §35-4-305.
Complaint for discovery of assets, §§6-6-180 to 6-6-185.
Recordation.
Necessary as to judgment creditors, §§35-4-90 to 35-4-97.
See RECORDATION.
Remainders, reversions and executory interests.
Recordation necessary as to creditors of life tenants, §35-4-91.
Secured transactions.
General provisions, §§7-9-101 to 7-9-507.
See COMMERCIAL CODE.
Self-service storage facilities.
Effect of laws governing rights of creditors, §8-15-37.
Small loans generally.
See SMALL LOANS.
Suretyship.
General provisions.
See SURETYSHIP.
Wills.
Appointment of debtor as executor, §43-8-254.

DEBTS.
Administration.
Exemptions from administration and payment of debts.
See EXEMPTIONS FROM ADMINISTRATION AND PAYMENT OF DEBTS.
Administration of estates.
See EXECUTORS AND ADMINISTRATORS.
Attachment.
Issuance to enforce collections, §6-6-41.
Claims against state.
See CLAIMS AGAINST STATE.
Congress.
Powers of congress, Const. U. S., Art. I, §8.
Constitution of Alabama.
Imprisonment for debts, Const. Ala., art. I, §20.
Constitution of the United States.
Aid of rebellion, Const. U. S., Amendment XIV.
Debts and engagements contracted before adoption, Const. U. S., Art. VI.
Not to be questioned, Const. U. S., Amendment XIV.
Powers of congress, Const. U. S., Art. I, §8.
Consumer finance.
General provisions, §§5-19-1 to 5-19-31.
See CONSUMER FINANCE.
Counties.
General provisions.
See COUNTIES.

DEBTS—Cont'd
Debtors and creditors.
General provisions.
See DEBTORS AND
CREDITORS.
Decedents' estates.
Executors and
administrators.
See EXECUTORS AND
ADMINISTRATORS.
Evidence.
Composition of debts.
Written settlements for
composition of debts,
§12-21-31.
Effect of written receipts,
releases and discharges,
§12-21-109.
Written contract as evidence
of debt, §12-21-112.
**Executors and
administrators.**
See EXECUTORS AND
ADMINISTRATORS.
**Exemptions from
administration and
payment of debts.**
See EXEMPTIONS FROM
ADMINISTRATION
AND PAYMENT OF
DEBTS.
Garnishment, §6-6-410.
Husband and wife.
Property of wife not liable for
debts, etc., of husband,
Const. Ala., art. X, §209.
Imprisonment for debts,
Const. Ala., art. I, §20.
Income tax.
Deductions.
Losses from debts,
§40-18-15.
Worthless debts owing to
corporations,
§40-18-35.
Interest.
General provisions.
See INTEREST.
Loans generally.
See LOANS.
**Mental health finance
authority.**
Bond issues and contracts.
Debts of state not created,
§41-10-366.
Minors.
Exemptions from
administration and
payment generally.
See EXEMPTIONS FROM
ADMINISTRATION
AND PAYMENT OF
DEBTS.
**Mortgages and deeds of
trust generally.**
See MORTGAGES AND
DEEDS OF TRUST.
Motor vehicle carriers.
Mileage tax, §40-19-3.
Municipal corporations.
See MUNICIPAL
CORPORATIONS.
Salaries.
Intestate former employee
owed wages.
Discharge of debtor,
§43-8-115.
Sales tax.
Tax levied, §40-23-21.

DEBTS—Cont'd
Secured transactions,
§§7-9-101 to 7-9-507.
See COMMERCIAL CODE.
Settlements.
Evidence.
Written settlements for
composition of debts,
§12-21-31.
Small loans generally.
See SMALL LOANS.
Snead Junior College.
Outstanding indebtedness,
§16-60-151.
**Space science exhibit
finance authority.**
Bond issues.
Not debt of state,
§41-10-321.
State debt.
Constitution of Alabama,
Const. Ala., art. XI,
§213; amd. 26.
Suretyship.
General provisions.
See SURETYSHIP.
Transfers to minors.
Person holding property or
owing liquidated debt to
minor, §35-5A-8.
Trusts and trustees.
Express trust for payment or
security of debts,
§§19-3-20 to 19-3-41.
See TRUSTS AND
TRUSTEES.
Wages.
Intestate former employee
owed wages.
Discharge of debtor,
§43-8-115.
Wills.
Intestate succession.
Debts owed to decedent
against whom debts
charged, §43-8-55.
Women.
Property of wife not liable for
debts, etc., of husband,
Const. Ala., art. X, §209.

**DECATUR, MUNICIPALITY
OF.**
Economic development.
Promotion of industrial,
commercial and
agricultural
development, Const.
Ala., amd. 303.
School tax.
Special tax for educational
purposes, Const. Ala.,
amd. 52.

DECEDENTS' ESTATES,
§§43-2-1 to 43-8-298.
Actions.
Against executor or
administrator for waste,
trespass, etc., §6-5-90.
Administration of estates.
See EXECUTORS AND
ADMINISTRATORS.
Adoption.
Adults for purposes of
inheritance, §§43-4-1 to
43-4-4.
Advancements.
Ademption by satisfaction,
§43-8-231.
Considered part of estate,
§43-8-49.

DECEDENTS' ESTATES
—Cont'd
Advancements—Cont'd
Controversy as to
advancements.
Consequence of failure to
answer, §43-8-54.
Contest of answer,
§43-8-53.
Death of distributee.
Proceedings and answer
upon death of
distributee, §43-8-52.
Discovery of advancements,
§43-8-51.
How issue made up and
tried, §43-8-50.
Valuation, §43-8-49.
Appeals.
Appeals from probate court,
§§12-22-20 to 12-22-27.
See PROBATE COURTS.
Judgment on partial or
annual settlement of
estate, §12-22-4.
**Arbitration on settlement of
estates,** §§43-2-600 to
43-2-607.
See EXECUTORS AND
ADMINISTRATORS.
Bankruptcy and insolvency.
Insolvent estates, §§43-2-700
to 43-2-813.
See EXECUTORS AND
ADMINISTRATORS.
**Banks and financial
institutions.**
Credit unions.
Disposition of shares or
deposit account of
decedent, §5-17-16.
Disposition of decedents'
deposits, §5-5A-38.
Time for payment,
§5-5A-39.
Payment of deposit,
§5-5A-41.
Savings and loan
associations.
Disposition of decedents'
accounts, §5-16-46.
Circuit courts.
Administration of estates in
circuit court.
Proceedings on
administration,
§12-11-40.
Removal of administration
from probate court,
§12-11-41.
Settlements of estates.
Correction of errors in
probate court,
§12-11-60.
Claims and debts.
General provisions,
§§43-2-350 to 43-2-394.
See EXECUTORS AND
ADMINISTRATORS.
Compromise and settlement.
Sale or division of land
received on compromise,
§§43-2-468.
Settlements and
distributions, §§43-2-500
to 43-2-696.
See EXECUTORS AND
ADMINISTRATORS.

DECEDENTS' ESTATES
—Cont'd
Credit unions.
  Disposition of shares or
    deposit account of
    deceased person,
    §5-17-16.
Curtesy.
  Abolished, §43-8-57.
Debts.
  Executors and
    administrators.
  Claims and debts,
    §§43-2-350 to 43-2-394.
  See EXECUTORS AND
    ADMINISTRATORS.
  Insolvent estates,
    §§43-2-700 to 43-2-813.
  See EXECUTORS AND
    ADMINISTRATORS.
Declaratory judgments.
  Questions on administration,
    §6-6-225.
**Disclaimer of interests in
  property,** §§43-8-290 to
  43-8-298.
  See DISCLAIMER OF
    INTERESTS IN
    PROPERTY.
Dower.
  Abolished, §43-8-57.
Escheats, §§43-6-2 to 43-6-9.
  See ESCHEATS.
Estate and inheritance tax,
  §§40-15-1 to 40-15-21.
  See ESTATE AND
    INHERITANCE TAX.
**Executors and
  administrators.**
  See EXECUTORS AND
    ADMINISTRATORS.
**Exemptions from
  administration and
  payment of debts.**
  General provisions.
  See EXEMPTIONS FROM
    ADMINISTRATION
    AND PAYMENT OF
    DEBTS.
Inheritance tax, §§40-15-1 to
  40-15-21.
  See ESTATE AND
    INHERITANCE TAX.
Insolvent estates, §§43-2-700
  to 43-2-813.
  See EXECUTORS AND
    ADMINISTRATORS.
Intestate succession.
  Administrators.
    Authorization to sell
      realty, §43-2-442.
    Letters of administration.
    See EXECUTORS AND
      ADMINISTRATORS.
  General provisions, §§43-8-40
    to 43-8-58.
  See WILLS.
Inventories.
  See EXECUTORS AND
    ADMINISTRATORS.
**Joint tenants and tenants in
  common.**
  Survivorship, §35-4-7.
Jurisdiction.
  Probate courts, §12-13-1.
Land patents.
  Public lands.
    Patent to decedent vests
      title in his successors,
      §35-4-386.

DECEDENTS' ESTATES
—Cont'd
Limitation of actions.
  Claims to charge real estate
    with debts and
    obligations of decedent,
    §6-2-41.
  Suspension of limitation.
    Claims against estates,
      §6-2-9.
Mentally ill.
  Claims and debts.
    Time and manner of filing
      claims by persons of
      unsound mind,
      §43-2-351.
Minors.
  Claims and debts.
    Time and manner of filing
      claims, §43-2-351.
Partnerships.
  Disposition of partner's
    interest, §10-8-72.
  Rights of estate of deceased
    partner, §10-8-103.
Patents.
  Public land patents,
    §35-4-386.
Posthumous children.
  Included in terms "heirs,"
    "issue" and "children,"
    §35-4-8.
Presumptions.
  Persons presumed to be dead,
    §§43-2-230 to 43-2-238.
  See EXECUTORS AND
    ADMINISTRATORS.
  Settlements and
    distributions.
    Presumption of settlement
      after twenty years,
      §§43-2-660 to 43-2-664.
Public land patents,
  §35-4-386.
**Removal of administration
  from probate court,**
  §12-11-41.
Sales.
  Personal property.
    See EXECUTORS AND
      ADMINISTRATORS.
  Real property.
    See EXECUTORS AND
      ADMINISTRATORS.
**Savings and loan
  associations.**
  Disposition of account of
    deceased person,
    §5-16-46.
Settlement of estates.
  Correction of errors in
    probate court, §12-11-60.
  Executors and
    administrators.
    Settlements and
      distributions,
      §§43-2-500 to 43-2-696.
    See EXECUTORS AND
      ADMINISTRATORS.
Simultaneous death act,
  §§43-7-1 to 43-7-8.
  See SIMULTANEOUS
    DEATH ACT.
Small estates, §§43-2-690 to
  43-2-696.
  See EXECUTORS AND
    ADMINISTRATORS.

DECEDENTS' ESTATES
—Cont'd
Taxation.
  Estate and inheritance tax,
    §§40-15-1 to 40-15-21.
  See ESTATE AND
    INHERITANCE TAX.
Trespass.
  Right of action against
    executor or
    administrator, §6-5-90.
Trusts and trustees.
  Death of trustee, §35-4-258.
**Uniform simultaneous death
  act,** §§43-7-1 to 43-7-8.
  See SIMULTANEOUS
    DEATH ACT.
United States.
  Persons in federal service.
    Jurisdiction of probate
      courts, §12-13-2.
Waste generally.
  See WASTE.
Wills.
  General provisions.
  See WILLS.

DECEIT.
  Actions, §§6-5-103, 6-5-104.
  Fraud generally.
    See FRAUD.
  Podiatrists.
    Revocation or suspension of
      license, §34-24-276.

**DECEPTIVE TRADE
  PRACTICES.**
  Attorney general.
    Powers and duties, §8-19-4.
  Citation of chapter, §8-19-1.
  Consumer finance.
    General provisions, §§5-19-1
      to 5-19-31.
    See CONSUMER
      FINANCE.
  Defenses, §8-19-13.
  Definitions, §8-19-3.
  Discovery of information,
    §8-19-9.
  District attorneys.
    Powers and duties, §8-19-4.
  Exemptions, §8-19-7.
  Injunctions, §8-19-8.
  Interpretation of provisions,
    §8-19-6.
  Legislative intent, §8-19-2.
  Limitation of actions,
    §8-19-14.
  Misdemeanors, §8-19-12.
  Motor vehicles.
    Manufacturers.
      Dealings by manufacturers
        with dealers, §§8-20-1
        to 8-20-12.
      See MOTOR VEHICLES.
  Penalties, §§8-19-11, 8-19-12.
  **Practices declared to be
    unlawful,** §8-19-5.
  Private right of actions,
    §8-19-10.
  Restraining orders, §8-19-8.
  Savings clause, §8-19-15.
  Short title, §8-19-1.
  Unlawful trade practices,
    §8-19-5.
  Violations.
    Penalties, §§8-19-11, 8-19-12.

DECLARATION OF RIGHTS,
  Const. Ala., art. I, §§1 to 36.
  See CONSTITUTION OF
    ALABAMA.

DECLARATION OF WAR.
Powers of congress, Const.
U. S., Art. I, §8.

DECLARATORY
JUDGMENTS, §§6-6-220 to
6-6-232.
Administration of article,
§6-6-221.
Administrative procedure
act.
Validity of agency rules,
§41-22-10.
Alcoholic beverages.
Beer.
Business relations between
wholesalers and
suppliers.
Actions for declaratory
judgments, §28-9-11.
Construction.
Contracts, §§6-6-223, 6-6-224.
Deeds, §6-6-223.
Liberal construction,
§6-6-221.
Ordinances, §6-6-223.
Statutes, §6-6-223.
Wills, §6-6-223.
Contracts.
Construction or validity,
§§6-6-223, 6-6-224.
Costs, §6-6-231.
Courts of record.
Powers, §6-6-222.
Enumeration not exclusive,
§6-6-226.
Decedents' estates.
Questions on administration,
§6-6-225.
Deeds.
Questions of construction or
validity, §6-6-223.
Definitions.
"Person," §6-6-220.
Effect, §6-6-222.
Persons not parties, §6-6-227.
Executors and
administrators.
Questions on administration,
§6-6-225.
Form of declarations,
§6-6-222.
Franchises.
Questions of construction or
validity, §6-6-223.
Fraternal orders, §10-4-177.
Further relief.
Application, §6-6-230.
Granting, §6-6-230.
Order to show cause,
§6-6-230.
Issues of fact.
Determination, §6-6-228.
Municipal ordinances.
Questions of construction or
validity, §6-6-223.
Parties.
Persons to be made parties,
§6-6-227.
Persons not parties.
Rights, §6-6-227.
Procedure, ARCP, Rule 57.
Purpose of article, §6-6-221.
Refusal to enter.
When proper, §6-6-229.
Review, §6-6-232.
Rules of civil procedure,
ARCP, Rule 57.
Statutes.
Questions of construction or
validity, §6-6-223.

DECLARATORY
JUDGMENTS—Cont'd
Trusts and trustees.
Questions on administration
of trust, §6-6-225.
Use tax.
Fixing tax liability,
§40-23-87.
Wills.
Questions of construction or
validity, §6-6-223.

DECREES.
Bankruptcy and insolvency.
Recordation of decree,
§35-4-52.
Conservators.
Settlements of accounts of
conservators.
Enforcement against
conservators, §26-5-18.
Settlements of accounts of
guardians.
Final settlement, §26-5-11.
Determination of
finality, §26-5-15.
Executors and
administrators.
Compelling of conveyances
by, §35-4-322.
Guardian and ward.
Curators.
Appointment, §26-7A-4.
Effect of decree,
§26-7A-7.
Settlement of accounts.
Final settlement, §26-5-11.
Determination of
finality, §26-5-15.
Judgments.
See JUDGMENTS.
Juvenile proceedings.
Consent to supervision,
ARJP, Rule 16.
Entry in separate minute
book, §12-15-2.
Modification, ARJP, Rule 27.
Limitation of actions.
Enforcement of judgment,
§6-2-32.
Municipal corporations.
Charter.
Forfeiture of charter,
§§11-41-24 to 11-41-26,
11-41-28.
Dissolution, §§11-41-23,
11-41-26.
Orders of court.
See ORDERS OF COURT.
Partition.
See PARTITION.
Recordation.
Statement of name and
address of preparer,
§35-4-112.
Records.
Copying of decrees into final
record, §12-20-21.
Reversal.
Procedure upon, §12-22-70.

DEEDS.
Acknowledgments.
Conveyances generally.
See CONVEYANCES.
Actions.
Reformation of deeds,
§§35-4-150 to 35-4-153.
Affidavits.
Conveyances generally,
§§35-4-69 to 35-4-71.

DEEDS—Cont'd
Assignment for benefit of
creditors.
Recordation of deeds of
assignment, §35-4-57.
"Bargain."
Construction of word,
§35-4-271.
Capacity.
Who may convey lands by
deed, §35-4-1.
Condominiums.
Recordation, §35-8-11.
Units, §35-8-8.
Consideration.
Recitation of consideration
unnecessary, §35-4-34.
Constitution of Alabama.
Invalid deed.
Giving effect to invalid
deed.
Special, private or local
laws prohibited,
Const. Ala., art. IV,
§104.
Construction and
interpretation.
Words "grant," "bargain," or
"sell," §35-4-271.
Conveyances.
See CONVEYANCES.
Corporations.
Proof of conveyances
executed in name of
corporation, §35-4-67.
Counties.
Effect of deeds to officers,
etc., for use of county,
§11-14-1.
Covenants.
When covenants of warranty
implied, §35-4-271.
Declaratory judgments.
Questions of construction or
validity, §6-6-223.
Deeds in lieu of foreclosure.
Definitions, §35-10-50.
Effect, §35-10-51.
Deeds of trust.
See MORTGAGES AND
DEEDS OF TRUST.
Definitions.
Deeds in lieu of foreclosure,
§35-10-50.
Delivery.
Time for delivery, §35-4-75.
Description of land.
Erroneous description.
Reformation, §§35-4-150,
35-4-151.
Destroyed papers or
records.
Substitution in civil cases,
§12-20-30.
Erroneous descriptions.
Reformation, §§35-4-150,
35-4-151.
Evidence.
Land office deeds or written
instruments for
conveyance or sale of
land, §12-21-66.
Executions, §35-4-20.
Execution and delivery of
deed to real estate sold
by sheriff, §6-9-149.
Fees.
Probate courts, §12-19-90.
Fish and game.
State game lands, §9-11-3.

DEEDS—Cont'd
Foreclosure deeds.
General provisions.
See MORTGAGES AND
DEEDS OF TRUST.
Forgery and counterfeiting.
Second degree forgery,
§13A-9-3.
Fraud.
Reformation, §35-4-153.
Fraudulent transfers.
See FRAUDULENT
TRANSFERS.
"Grant."
Construction of word,
§35-4-271.
Homesteads, §6-10-6.
Husband and wife.
Conveyances by spouse of
prisoner, person non
compos mentis or who
has abandoned spouse,
§30-4-12.
Literary or social societies.
Conveyances, §§35-4-340 to
35-4-344.
Lost papers or records.
Substitution in civil cases,
§12-20-30.
Marital status.
Recitation of marital status
of grantor or vendor
required, §35-4-73.
Mistake.
Reformation, §35-4-153.
**Mortgages and deeds of
trust.**
Foreclosure deeds generally.
See MORTGAGES AND
DEEDS OF TRUST.
Municipal corporations.
Mayors.
Execution, etc., §11-43-83.
Oil and gas.
Mineral documentary tax
generally, §§40-20-30 to
40-20-37.
See OIL AND GAS.
**Ownership of title
instruments,** §35-4-9.
Parties.
Reformation of deeds.
Grantors, etc., may be
made parties
defendant, §35-4-152.
Powers of disposition.
Conveyances generally,
§§35-4-290 to 35-4-306.
See CONVEYANCES.
Probate courts.
Fees, §12-19-90.
Public lands.
Conveyances by governor or
state agency or
institution, §§35-4-380 to
35-4-391.
See CONVEYANCES.
Public utilities.
Purchase of property by
municipality or
governmental agency.
Forced sales.
Tender of deed, §37-4-64.
Recordation tax.
See RECORDATION.
Reformation, §§35-4-150 to
35-4-153.
Seals.
Unnecessary, §35-4-21.

DEEDS—Cont'd
"Sell."
Construction of word,
§35-4-271.
Sheriff's deed.
Evidence, §12-21-99.
Signature, §35-4-20.
Specific performance,
§35-4-33.
Taxation.
Recordation tax.
See RECORDATION.
Trees and timber.
Conveyances of standing
timber, §§35-4-92,
35-4-360 to 35-4-363.
Warranties.
When covenants of warranty
implied, §35-4-271.
**Who may convey lands by
deed,** §35-4-1.
Witnesses.
Attestation by witnesses,
§35-4-20.
Form of proof of conveyances,
§35-4-68.
Writing.
Required to be in writing,
§35-4-20.

**DEEDS IN LIEU OF
FORECLOSURE.**
Definitions, §35-10-50.
Equity of redemption.
Defined, §35-10-50.
Effect of deed in lieu of
foreclosure, §35-10-51.
Mortgaged property.
Defined, §35-10-50.
Mortgagees.
Defined, §35-10-50.
Mortgages.
Defined, §35-10-50.
Mortgagors.
Defined, §35-10-50.
Redemption.
Effect of deed in lieu of
foreclosure, §35-10-51.
Equity of redemption,
§35-10-50.
Effect of deed in lieu of
foreclosure, §35-10-51.

DEEDS OF TRUST.
See MORTGAGES AND
DEEDS OF TRUST.

DEER.
Game laws.
See FISH AND GAME.
Hunting.
See FISH AND GAME.

DEFAMATION.
See LIBEL AND SLANDER.

DEFAULTS.
**Banks and financial
institutions.**
Proceedings by
superintendent before
banking board, §5-8A-20.
Consumer finance.
Additional charges, §5-19-4.
Indigent persons.
Reimbursement of court
appointed attorneys,
§15-12-25.
Judgments.
Default judgments.
See JUDGMENTS.
Leases.
Notice to quit for default of
terms of lease, §35-9-6.

DEFAULTS—Cont'd
Secured transactions,
§§7-9-501 to 7-9-507.
See COMMERCIAL CODE.
Small loans.
Charges, §5-18-15.

DEFENSE.
Civil defense.
General provisions, §§31-9-1
to 31-9-24.
See CIVIL DEFENSE.
Military service in time of
national emergency or
war.
County officers.
See COUNTIES.
Municipal officers.
See MUNICIPAL
CORPORATIONS.
Public officers and
employees generally,
§§36-8-1 to 36-8-6.
See PUBLIC OFFICERS
AND EMPLOYEES.
Congress.
Powers of congress, Const. U.
S., Art. I, §8.
Military affairs.
See MILITARY AFFAIRS.

DEFENSES.
Affirmative defenses, ARCP,
Rule 8 (c).
Alternative defenses, ARCP,
Rule 8 (e).
Appeals.
Litigation on merits after
loss on certain defenses
not to bar raising of
same defenses on appeal,
§6-8-101.
Code of Alabama.
Existing defenses preserved,
§1-1-9.
Consolidation in motion,
ARCP, Rule 12 (g).
Constitution of Alabama.
Removal of defense to suit
after commencement of
suit, Const. Ala., art. IV,
§95.
Consumer finance.
Assignee of seller or lessor
subject to claims and
defenses of buyer or
lessee, §5-19-8.
Corporations.
Ultra vires, §10-2A-24.
Criminal law and procedure.
General provisions.
See CRIMINAL LAW AND
PROCEDURE.
Deceptive trade practices,
§8-19-13.
Denials.
Effect of failure to deny,
ARCP, Rule 8 (d).
Form of denials, ARCP, Rule
8 (b).
Ejectment.
Disclaimer of possession,
§6-6-284.
Estoppel.
Affirmative defense, ARCP,
Rule 8 (c).
**Executors and
administrators.**
Resignation as defense,
§43-2-114.

DEFENSES—Cont'd
Failure to join a party under Rule 19, ARCP, Rule 12 (b), (h).
Failure to state a claim, ARCP, Rule 12 (b), (h).
Forms, ARCP, Forms 26, 27.
Denials, ARCP, Rule 8 (b).
Fraud.
Affirmative defense, ARCP, Rule 8 (c).
Fraudulent transfers, §8-9A-8.
Frivolous defenses.
Litigation accountability, §§12-19-270 to 12-19-276.
See COURTS.
How presented, ARCP, Rule 12 (b).
Improper venue, ARCP, Rule 12 (b), (h).
Insufficiency of process, ARCP, Rule 12 (b), (h).
Jurisdiction.
Lack of jurisdiction, ARCP, Rule 12 (b), (h).
Litigation on merits after loss on defense not bar to raising of same defense on appeal, §6-8-101.
Laches.
Affirmative defense, ARCP, Rule 8 (c).
Limitation of actions.
Affirmative defenses, ARCP, Rule 8 (c).
Litigation accountability.
General provisions, §§12-19-270 to 12-19-276.
See COURTS.
Military affairs.
Actions against present or former members of national guard, §31-2-89.
At state expense, §31-2-89.
Motions.
Consolidation of defenses in motion, ARCP, Rule 12 (g).
Defenses which may be made by motion, ARCP, Rule 12 (b).
Forms, ARCP, Form 26.
Obscenity.
Displaying materials harmful to minors.
Affirmative defenses, §13A-12-200.5.
Disseminating obscene materials.
Affirmative defenses, §13A-12-200.4.
Distributing obscene materials.
Affirmative defenses, §13A-12-200.4.
Producing obscene materials.
Affirmative defenses, §13A-12-200.4.
Preservation of certain defenses, ARCP, Rule 12 (h).
Removal of defense to suit after commencement of suit, Const. Ala., art. IV, §95.
Rules of civil procedure.
See RULES OF CIVIL PROCEDURE.

DEFENSES—Cont'd
Rules of criminal procedure, ARCrP, Rule 16.2.
See RULES OF CRIMINAL PROCEDURE.
Summons and process.
Insufficiency of process.
Litigation on merits after loss on defense not bar to raising of same defense on appeal, §6-8-101.
Venue.
Improper venue.
Litigation on merits after loss on defense not bar to raising of same defense on appeal, §6-8-101.
Waiver of certain defenses, ARCP, Rule 12 (h).
When presented, ARCP, Rule 12 (a).

DEFINITIONS.
Abortion.
Parental consent to performing abortions upon minors, §26-21-2.
Accountants, §34-1-2.
Administrative procedure act, §41-22-3.
Adoption.
Subsidized adoption.
Child, §26-10-22.
Adult protective services, §38-9-2.
Advertising.
Outdoor advertising, §23-1-271.
Aged persons.
Medical assistance, §38-6-2.
Agriculture.
See AGRICULTURE.
Air commerce.
See AIR COMMERCE.
Air pollution, §22-28-2.
Airport authorities.
Alternate procedure for incorporation, §4-3-40.
Alcoholic beverages, §28-3-1.
Beer, §28-3-1.
Business relations between wholesalers and suppliers, §28-9-2.
Native farm wine.
Regulation of production, sale, etc., §28-6-1.
Sales.
Exclusive sales territories, §28-8-7.
Taxation.
Malt or brewed beverages.
Excise tax, §28-3-183.
Alcoholism.
Treatment.
Group plans, §27-20A-1.
Alligator farms, §9-12-200.
Ambulances, §22-18-1.
Ameraport.
Deep draft harbor and terminal contract, §33-9-1.
Offshore harbor and terminal commission, §33-10-1.
Anatomical gifts, §22-19-41.
Acquisition and transportation of donor organs, bones and tissues, §22-19-121.

DEFINITIONS—Cont'd
Anatomical gifts—Cont'd
Lifesaving organ procurement act, §22-19-141.
Animals, §3-5-1.
Appeals.
Automatic appeal from death sentence, §12-22-150.
Rules of appellate procedure, ARAP, Rule 51.
Architects.
Practicing architects, §34-2-30.
Associations.
Officers.
Liability of officers of nonprofit organizations, §10-11-2.
Athlete agents, §8-26-2.
Atomic energy.
Radiation, §22-14-1.
Attorneys at law.
Legal services liability, §6-5-572.
Practice of law, §34-3-6.
Auctions and auctioneers, §34-4-2.
Automobile clubs and associations, §27-39-1.
Aviation, §4-2-3.
Airports, §4-6-2.
Airport authorities, §4-3-1.
Municipal airports, §4-4-1.
Bail and recognizance, §15-13-1.
Banks and financial institutions.
See BANKS AND FINANCIAL INSTITUTIONS.
Barbers, §22-17-1.
Practice of barbering, §34-5-1.
Bear Creek development authority, §33-15-1.
Bench warrants, §15-10-60.
Billiard rooms, §34-6-1.
Black archives, research center and museum, §16-49-51.
Black Heritage Museum of West Alabama, §16-62-2.
Blind persons, §1-1-3.
Blind-made products or services, §21-1-60.
Operation of vending stands by blind persons, §21-1-40.
Boats, §33-5-3.
Discharge of litter and sewage from watercraft, §33-6-1.
Bond issues.
Private activity bonds.
State ceiling, §41-10-36.
Brake fluid, §8-17-1.
Brands and marks.
Adoption of regulations defining commercial fertilizers, §2-22-16.
Bread, flour, cornmeal and grits, §20-1-71.
Buildings.
Energy conservation building code, §41-9-170.
Minimum building standards code, §41-9-160.
Capital development assistance fund, §9-7A-2.

DEFINITIONS—Cont'd

Capital offenses, §13A-5-39.

Capital punishment.

Automatic appeal from death sentence, §12-22-150.

Catfish.

Marketing of catfish, §2-11-31.

Caustic or corrosive substances, §8-17-20.

Caves, §9-19-1.

Cemeteries, §34-13-1.

Charitable fraud, §13A-9-70.

Checks.

Sale of checks, §8-7-2.

Chick dealers, §2-16-1.

Child placement.

Interstate compact on child placement, §44-2-20.

Child support.

Interstate income withholding act, §30-3-91.

Withholding orders, §30-3-60.

Child support programs, §38-10-2.

Right of department to support owed by parents to child, §38-10-30.

Chiropractic, §34-24-120.

Cigarettes.

Tax on gummed cigarette papers, §40-25A-1.

Circuit, §1-1-1.

Civil defense, §31-9-3.

Coal.

Abandoned mine reclamation, §9-16-121.

Mine safety, §25-9-2.

Severance tax, §40-13-1.

Severance tax of 1977, §40-13-30.

Surface mining control and reclamation, §9-16-72.

Coastal areas, §9-7-10.

Code of Alabama, §1-1-1.

Codicils.

Inclusion of term "codicil" within term "will," §43-8-1.

Commercial code.

See COMMERCIAL CODE.

Commission merchants.

Sale of farm produce, §2-29-1.

Commission on higher education, §16-5-1.

Community services grants, §41-24-1.

Complaints, §15-7-1.

Warrant of arrest, §15-7-4.

Computer crimes, §13A-8-101.

Condominiums, §35-8-2.

Confession of judgment, §12-22-1.

Consumer finance, §5-19-1.

Contractors.

General contractor, §34-8-1.

Contracts.

Accord, §8-1-20.

Future delivery, §8-1-120.

Convention facilities, §11-100-3.

Coosa Valley development authority, §33-16-1.

Cornmeal, §20-1-71.

Corporations.

See CORPORATIONS.

DEFINITIONS—Cont'd

Corrections.

Inmate community reintegration under SIR act, §15-18-111.

Institution finance authority, §14-2-1.

Cosmetics.

Adulteration and misbranding, §20-1-50.

Cosmetologists, §22-17-1.

Cotton.

Boll weevil eradication, §2-19-121.

Registration of cotton buyers, §2-19-100.

Counselors, §34-8A-2.

Counties.

See COUNTIES.

County industrial development authorities, §11-92A-1.

Court of the judiciary, ARJC, Rule 1.

Courts.

Litigation accountability, §12-19-271.

Credit cards, §5-20-3.

Credit unions, §5-17-1.

Crime victims compensation, §15-23-3.

Criminal law and procedure.

General provisions.

See CRIMINAL LAW AND PROCEDURE.

Mentally retarded defendants, §15-24-2.

Damages.

Punitive damages, §6-11-20.

Structured damages, §6-11-2.

Deceptive trade practices, §8-19-3.

Declaratory judgments.

"Person," §6-6-220.

Deeds.

Deeds in lieu of foreclosure, §35-10-50.

Deeds in lieu of foreclosure, §35-10-50.

Dental service corporations, §22-21-361.

Dentists.

Impaired professionals, §34-38-1.

Dentists and dental hygienists.

See DENTISTS.

Development.

Office of state planning and federal programs, §41-9-205.

Dietitians and nutritionists, §34-34A-3.

Dog racing.

Pari-mutuel pool tax, §40-26A-1.

Domestic relations.

Domestic violence facilities, §30-6-1.

Protection from abuse, §30-5-2.

Domestic violence facilities, §30-6-1.

Downtown redevelopment authorities, §11-54A-2.

Use of phrases, §11-54A-3.

Drinking water.

Safe drinking water act, §22-23-31.

Drugs.

See DRUGS.

DEFINITIONS—Cont'd

Education.

General provisions.

See EDUCATION.

Eggs and egg products, §2-12-1.

Elections.

See ELECTIONS.

Electrical contractors, §34-36-3.

Electric cooperatives, §37-6-1.

Gas districts, §37-6-30.

Rural electric cooperatives, §37-6-30.

Electricity.

General provisions.

See ELECTRICITY.

Electric membership corporations, §37-7-1.

Eminent domain, §18-1A-3.

Fair market value, §18-1A-172.

Uneconomic remnant, §18-1A-27.

Energy conservation building code, §41-9-170.

Engineers, §34-11-1.

Enterprise zones, §41-23-21.

Environmental improvement authorities, §9-6-2.

Environmental management, §22-22A-3.

Environmental management department, §22-22-1.

Estate and inheritance tax, §40-15-1.

Evidence.

Substantial evidence, §12-21-12.

Executory interests, §35-4-210.

Extradition, §15-9-20.

False imprisonment, §6-5-170.

Farm equipment.

Repurchase of inventory from farm equipment retailers, §8-21-1.

Feeds.

Commercial feed law of 1978, §2-21-17.

Fences.

Partition fences, §35-7-1.

Fertilizer, §2-22-2.

Fiduciaries.

Fiduciaries in war service, §19-2-1.

Securities held by fiduciaries, §§19-4-1, 19-4-20, 19-4-40.

Uniform fiduciaries act, §19-1-2.

Finance.

General provisions.

See FINANCE.

State funds.

Linked deposits, §5-21-3.

Fire protection sprinkler systems, §34-33-1.

Fires and fire prevention.

Firemen.

Compensation for death, §36-30-1.

Personnel standards and education commission, §36-32-1.

Forest fires.

Assessments for protection, §9-13-180.

Sprinkler systems, §34-33-1.

DEFINITIONS—Cont'd

Fires and fire prevention —Cont'd
Survivor's education assistance act, §36-21-101.
Fireworks, §8-17-210.
Fish and game.
See FISH AND GAME.
Flour, §20-1-71.
Food.
Adulteration and misbranding, §20-1-20.
Food stamps.
Illegal possession of food stamps, §13A-9-90.
Forcible entry and unlawful detainer, §6-6-310.
Foreclosure.
Deeds in lieu of foreclosure, §35-10-50.
Forests and forestry.
See FORESTS AND FORESTRY.
Fraternal benefit societies, §27-34-1.
Fraternal orders, §10-4-170.
Fraud.
Charitable fraud, §13A-9-70.
Fraudulent transfers, §8-9A-1.
Fruits and vegetables.
Grading and standards, §2-11-70.
Funeral services, §34-13-1.
Garbage and trash, §22-27-2.
Financing collection and disposal facilities, §22-27-20.
Garnishment, §6-6-370.
Salaries of public officers and employees, §6-6-480.
Gas fitters.
Plumbers and gas fitters generally, §34-37-1.
Gasoline tax, §40-17-30.
Distribution and use of proceeds, §40-17-70.
Gasoline used for agricultural purposes, §40-17-100.
Gasoline used for static testing of engine, §40-17-120.
General laws, Const. Ala., amd. 375.
Ginseng, §9-13-241.
Grain dealers, §2-31-1.
Grants.
Securities.
Issuance of securities in anticipation of receipt of grants, §11-81A-1.
Grits, §20-1-71.
Guardian and ward.
Uniform guardianship and protective proceedings act, §26-2A-20.
Handicapped persons.
Accessibility to and use of public buildings and facilities by physically handicapped persons, §21-4-2.
Harbors and ports.
Docks.
Bonds for state docks facilities, §33-2-180.
Port authority, §11-94-1.
Hazardous substances.
Cleanup fund, §22-30A-2.

DEFINITIONS—Cont'd

Hazardous substances —Cont'd
Fees for disposal of hazardous waste or substances, §22-30B-1.
Hazardous waste, §§6-5-332.1, 22-30-3, 22-30-11.
Fees for disposal of hazardous waste or substances, §22-30B-1.
Health.
Physical fitness, §22-5-1.
Responsibility for health care, §22-21-292.
State health department, §22-1-1.
State health planning and development, §22-4-2.
Health care authorities, §22-21-311.
Additional powers, §22-21-350.
Health maintenance organizations, §27-21A-1.
Health studio services, §8-23-2.
Hearing aid dealers and fitters, §34-14-1.
Heating and air conditioning contractors, §34-31-18.
Hemophilia treatment, §21-8-1.
Highways, §23-1-21.1.
Department.
Road machinery and equipment management program, §23-1-50.1.
Federal aid highway finance authority, §23-1-301.
Interstate highway system. Controlled access facilities, §23-3-1.
Historical preservation authorities, §41-10-136.
History and archives.
State black archives, research center and museum, §16-49-51.
Honey, §2-11-120.
Honeybees and apiaries, §2-14-1.
Horse racing, §11-65-2.
Hospitals.
See HOSPITALS.
Hotels, inns and other transient lodging places, §34-15-1.
Baggage, §34-15-15.
Housing authorities.
See HOUSING AUTHORITIES.
Ice cream, §2-13-11.
Income tax.
See INCOME TAX.
Indictment, §15-8-1.
Indigent persons.
Defense of indigents, §15-12-1.
Industrial access roads and bridges, §23-6-1.
Industrial alcohol, §28-5-1.
Industrial development authority, §41-10-20.
Industrial development corporations, §10-4-130.
Industrial parks, §11-92-1.
Industrial revenue bonds, §8-6-110.

DEFINITIONS—Cont'd

Insane, §1-1-1.
Insurance.
See INSURANCE.
Interior designers, §34-15A-1.
Joint authority, §1-1-2.
Judgments, ARCP, Rule 54 (a).
Confession of judgment, §12-22-1.
Foreign judgments, §6-9-231.
Judicial building authority, §41-10-260.
Junior colleges.
Management and control, §16-60-110.
Trade school and junior college authority, §16-60-81.
Junkyard control, §23-1-241.
Jury, §1-1-1.
Juvenile proceedings, §12-15-1.
Regional custody and care of youths under jurisdiction of juvenile court, §44-3-1.
Labor.
Unemployment compensation, §§25-4-1 to 25-4-17.
See UNEMPLOYMENT COMPENSATION.
Unions and labor relations, §25-7-2.
Landscape architects, §34-17-1.
Landscaping.
Horticulture and floriculture work, §2-28-1.
Law enforcement planning agency, §41-8A-1.
Lead, §22-37-2.
Libraries.
Interstate library compact. State library agency defined, §41-8-20.
Registration records, §41-8-9.
Lime, §2-23-2.
Liquefied petroleum gas, §9-17-100.
Livestock.
See LIVESTOCK.
Local law, Const. Ala., amd. 375.
Long term quality health care.
Facilities, §22-6-23.
Long-term residential health care recipient ombudsmen, §22-5A-2.
Lubricating oils and greases.
Tax, §40-17-170.
Lunatics, §1-1-1.
Malpractice, §§6-5-481, 6-5-542.
Manufactured buildings, §24-4A-2.
Marine mammal protection, §9-11-391.
Marine resources.
See MARINE RESOURCES.
Meat and meat products, §2-17-1.
Mechanics' and materialmen's liens.
Owner or proprietor, §35-11-232.
Medical technicians, §34-18-1.
Registered medical technician, §34-18-20.

DEFINITIONS—Cont'd

Mellorine, §§20-1-130, 20-1-132.
Mental health finance authority, §41-10-351.
Mentally ill.
See MENTALLY ILL.
Midwives, §34-19-2.
Military affairs, §31-2-1.
Compensation for death of national guardsmen, §31-3-1.
National guard educational assistance, §31-10-2.
Milk and milk products.
Ice cream, §2-13-11.
Imitation butter and imitation cheese, §2-13-16.
Mines and minerals.
Surface mining reclamation, §9-16-2.
Minors.
See MINORS.
Missing persons, §26-19-1.
Mobile homes, §24-5-2.
Anchoring, §24-5-31.
Molds, dyes or patterns.
Disposal, §8-28-1.
Month, §1-1-1.
Mortgages and deeds of trust.
Foreclosure.
Deeds in lieu of foreclosure, §35-10-50.
Power of sale, §35-10-11.
Motion pictures.
Fair competition, §8-18-2.
Motorcycles, §32-1-1.1.
Motor fuels.
Diesel fuel tax.
"Motor fuel" defined, §40-17-1.
Distributors of motor fuels.
Licenses, §40-12-190.
Marketing, §8-22-4.
Motor vehicle carriers, §§37-3-2, 40-19-1.
Fuel tax, §40-17-140.
Motor vehicles.
See MOTOR VEHICLES.
Mowa Choctaw housing authority, §24-7-1.
Municipal corporations.
See MUNICIPAL CORPORATIONS.
Museums.
State Black archives, research center and museum, §16-49-51.
Natural death act, §22-8A-3.
Non compos mentis, §1-1-1.
Nuisances, §6-5-120.
Lewdness, assignation or prostitution, §6-5-140.
Nurses, §34-21-1.
Nursing homes.
Administrators, §34-20-1.
Oaths, §1-1-1.
Obscenity, §13A-12-200.1.
Obscene materials containing visual reproduction of children, §13A-12-190.
Oil and gas.
See OIL AND GAS.
Optometrists, §34-22-1.
Outdoor advertising, §23-1-271.
Oysters.
Natural oyster reef, §9-12-21.

DEFINITIONS—Cont'd

Parent and child.
Parent and child relationship, §26-17-2.
Termination of parental rights, §26-18-3.
Parks and recreation.
Capital development assistance fund, §9-7A-2.
Parole.
Board of pardons and paroles.
Due notice, §15-22-23.
Partition fences, §35-7-1.
Partnerships, §§10-8-2, 10-8-3.
Dissolution, 10-8-90.
Limited partnerships, §10-9A-1.
Peace officers.
See PEACE OFFICERS.
Person, §1-1-1.
Personal property, §1-1-1.
Leasing or renting.
Licenses, §40-12-220.
Pest control, §2-28-1.
Pesticides, §2-27-2.
Application, §2-27-50.
Petroleum products, §8-17-80.
Posting price and tax.
"Motor vehicle" defined, §8-17-150.
Reclaimed or re-refined oil, §8-17-110.
Pharmacists and pharmacies, §34-23-1.
Impaired professionals, §34-38-1.
Physical fitness, §22-5-1.
Physical therapists, §34-24-191.
Physicians.
Assistants to physicians, §34-24-290.
Practice of medicine or osteopathy, §34-24-50.
Pipelines.
See PIPELINES.
Planning.
See PLANNING.
Plant pathology, §2-28-1.
Plumbing, §34-37-1.
Podiatrists, §34-24-230.
Unprofessional conduct, §34-24-276.
Poison, §34-23-1.
Polygraph examiners, §34-25-2.
Port authorities, §11-94-1.
Poultry, §§2-16-1, 2-17-1.
Power districts, §37-5-1.
Prisons and prisoners.
See PRISONS AND PRISONERS.
Product liability actions, §§6-5-501, 6-5-521.
Products marts.
Southern products mart authority, §41-10-51.
State products mart and coliseum authority, §41-10-81.
Professional corporations, §§6-5-481, 10-4-382.
Property, §1-1-1.
Public lands.
Unused public lands, §9-15-1.
Public officers and employees.
See PUBLIC OFFICERS AND EMPLOYEES.

DEFINITIONS—Cont'd

Public service commission.
Utility, §37-1-30.
Public works.
Contracts, §39-2-1.
Improvement authorities, §39-7-1.
Radioactive fallout protection, §39-6-1.
Rabies, §3-7-1.
Radiation, §22-14-1.
Railroad authorities, §37-13-1.
Railroads.
Authorities, §37-13-1.
Preservation, §37-10-2.
Real estate brokers, §34-27-2.
Real property, §1-1-1.
Redemption, §6-5-247.
Recorded devices.
Owners, §13A-8-80.
Records.
Public records, §41-13-1.
Remainders, reversions and executory interests, §§35-4-210, 35-4-211.
Rental-purchase agreements, §8-25-1.
Research centers.
State Black archives, research center and museums, §16-49-51.
Restitution to victims of crimes, §15-18-66.
Withholding act, §15-18-142.
Rules of appellate procedure, ARAP, Rule 51.
Rules of civil procedure.
Judgments, ARCP, Rule 54 (a).
Rules of criminal procedure, ARCrP, Rules 1, 15.1.
Rural telephone service, §37-6-40.
Safe drinking water act, §22-23-31.
Sales.
Commercial code, §§7-2-103 to 7-2-106.
Going out of business or distress merchandise sales, §8-13-1.
Sales representative's commission contracts, §8-24-1.
Sales tax, §40-23-1.
Gross receipts, §§40-23-1, 40-23-50.
Savings and loan associations, §5-16-2.
Regional reciprocal savings institutions, §5-14A-2.
Seafood, §9-2-80.
Search warrant, §15-5-1.
Secured transactions.
See COMMERCIAL CODE.
Securities.
See SECURITIES.
Seeds, §2-26-1.
Self-service storage facilities, §8-15-31.
Sex offenses.
Sexual perversion, §15-20-1.
Shakespeare Festival Theatre Finance Authority, §41-10-201.
Ships and shipping, §33-5-3.
Sidewalks, §32-1-1.1.
Signatures, §1-1-1.

DEFINITIONS—Cont'd
Small business assistance, §25-10-3.
Small business office of advocacy, §41-9-761.
Small claims.
Rules of procedure, ASCR, Rule B.
Small loans, §5-18-3.
Social security.
Public employees, §36-28-1.
Social workers, §34-30-1.
Soil and water conservation.
Cost-share grants, §9-8A-1.
Soil classifiers, §34-32-2.
Solid waste.
Management plan, §22-27-43.
Solid waste disposal authorities, §11-89A-2.
Southern products mart authority, §41-10-51.
Space science exhibit finance authority, §41-10-300.
Special health care facility authorities, §11-62-1.
Special or private laws, Const. Ala., amd. 375.
Speech pathologists and audiologists, §34-28A-1.
Sports.
Agents, §8-26-2.
State Black archives, research center and museum, §16-49-51.
State parks, §9-14-1.
State police.
Occupational diseases.
Compensation for death or disability, §36-30-20.
State products mart and coliseum authority, §41-10-81.
Stores, §40-12-310.
Student loan program, §16-33B-1.
Subscription, §1-1-1.
Surveys and surveyors, §34-11-1.
Synfuels development authority, §9-6A-1.
Taxation, §40-1-1.
Assessments.
Statewide property reappraisal.
County bonds for purpose of paying costs of reappraisal, §40-7-90.
Multistate tax compact, §40-27-1.
Tax increment districts, §11-99-2.
Telephones.
See TELEPHONES.
Television.
Community antenna television facilities, §11-27-1.
Theft.
Theft of trademarks or trade secrets, §13A-8-10.4.
Time, §1-1-1.
Tobacco.
Sales tax, §40-25-1.
Use tax, §40-25-40.
Tombigbee valley development authority, §33-17-1.
Toxic substances in the workplace, §22-33-2.

DEFINITIONS—Cont'd
Trademarks.
Registration of trademarks and service marks, §8-12-6.
Theft of trademarks, §13A-8-10.4.
Trade school and junior college authority, §16-60-81.
Trade schools.
Management and control, §16-60-110.
Trade secrets, §8-27-2.
Theft of trade secrets, §13A-8-10.4.
Transfers to minors, §35-5A-2.
Transient merchants, §34-35-1.
Transportation companies, §37-2-1.
Tree surgery, §2-28-1.
Trial.
Crime victims' court attendance, §15-14-52.
Trusts and trustees.
Generation-skipping tax, §19-5-1.
Generation-skipping transfer, §40-15A-1.
Principal and income, §19-3-270.
Unclaimed property.
Uniform disposition of unclaimed property act, §35-12-21.
Underground storage tanks, §22-35-3.
Tank and wellhead protection, §22-36-2.
Unemployment compensation, §§25-4-1 to 25-4-17.
See UNEMPLOYMENT COMPENSATION.
Uniform commercial code.
See COMMERCIAL CODE.
Uniform guardianship and protective proceedings act, §26-2A-20.
Unincorporated professional associations, §10-10-1.
Universities and colleges.
Commission on higher education, §16-5-1.
Local aid to state educational institutions, §16-19-1.
Prepaid tuition, §16-33C-3.
Use tax, §40-23-60.
Utility services actions, §6-5-600.
Utility services facilities, §11-97-2.
Vacation time-sharing plans, §34-27-50.
Veterans, §31-5-1.
Educational benefits, §31-6-2.
State veterans' homes, §31-5A-2.
Veterinarians, §34-29-61.
Victim counselors, §15-23-41.
Vital statistics, §22-9-1.
Warehouses, §8-15-1.
Self-service storage facilities, §8-15-31.
Warrant.
Search warrant, §15-5-1.
Waste.
Solid waste disposal authorities, §11-89A-2.

DEFINITIONS—Cont'd
Water and wastewater systems and treatment plants, §22-25-1.
Water pollution.
Agricultural nonpoint source pollution, §22-38-2.
Pollution control finance authority, §22-29-1.
Water pollution control authority, §22-34-1.
Waters and watercourses.
Development of docks and other facilities along inland waterways.
See WATERS AND WATERCOURSES.
Water supply and waterworks.
Safe drinking water act, §22-23-31.
Wells, §22-24-1.
Water system assistance authority, §22-23A-1.
Weights and measures, §8-16-1.
Coal, coke or charcoal.
"Ton" defined, §8-16-98.
Welfare.
Child care facilities, §38-7-2.
Public welfare, §38-1-1.
Wills.
Codicils.
Inclusion of term "codicil" within term "will," §43-8-1.
Probate code, §43-8-1.
Witnesses.
Criminal cases.
Attendance of out-of-state witnesses.
Securing of attendance, §12-21-281.
Securing attendance of out-of-state witnesses, §12-21-281.
Workmen's compensation.
See WORKMEN'S COMPENSATION.
Writing, §1-1-1.
Year, §1-1-1.
Youth services, §44-1-2.

DEKALB COUNTY.
Court costs and charges, Const. Ala., amd. 134.
Hospitals.
Special tax, Const. Ala., amd. 65.
Junior college for DeKalb county, §§16-60-50 to 16-60-67.
See JUNIOR COLLEGES.
Legislation as to DeKalb county, Const. Ala., amd. 184.
Officers.
Fees, compensation, etc., Const. Ala., amds. 134, 337.
Public health.
Special tax, Const. Ala., amd. 65.
School tax.
Special property tax for educational purposes, Const. Ala., amd. 146.
Warrants payable out of proceeds of special taxes for educational purposes, Const. Ala., amd. 210.

DEKALB COUNTY—Cont'd
Special, private or local laws, Const. Ala., amd. 184.

DELICATESSENS.
Licenses, §40-12-91.

DELINQUENCY.
Causing, etc., §12-15-13.
Juvenile proceedings.
See JUVENILE PROCEEDINGS.
Parole.
Delinquent parolees, §§15-22-32, 41-9-635.
Youthful offenders generally.
See YOUTHFUL OFFENDERS.
Youth services.
See YOUTH SERVICES.

DEMOPOLIS, MUNICIPALITY OF.
Property tax, Const. Ala., amd. 8.
Special property tax, Const. Ala., amd. 385.

DEMURRERS.
Abolished, ARCP, Rule 7 (c).

DENATURED ALCOHOL.
General provisions, §§28-5-1 to 28-5-14.
See INDUSTRIAL ALCOHOL.

DENGUE.
Notifiable diseases, §§22-11A-1 to 22-11A-38.
See DISEASES.

DENTAL CARE SERVICES.
Insurance, §§27-19A-1 to 27-19A-11.
See INSURANCE.

DENTAL COLLEGE OF ALABAMA.
Established, §16-47-50.
General provisions, §§16-47-76 to 16-47-81.
See UNIVERSITY OF ALABAMA.
Teaching permits, §34-9-8.

DENTAL HYGIENISTS.
See DENTISTS.

DENTAL SERVICE CORPORATIONS, §§22-21-360 to 22-21-391.
Accounts and accounting.
Sales representatives.
Funds received, §22-21-378.
Amendments, §22-21-385.
Blanket contracts.
Authorized, §22-21-371.
Board of dental examiners.
Not regulated or limited by article, §22-21-384.
Bonds, surety.
Hearings, §22-21-370.
Modification orders, §22-21-370.
Noncompliance.
Effect, §22-21-370.
Release, §22-21-370.
Requirements, §22-21-370.

DENTAL SERVICE CORPORATIONS—Cont'd
Bylaws.
Amendments, §22-21-385.
Certificate of authority.
Applications, §22-21-363.
Criteria for issuance, §22-21-364.
Certificate of incorporation.
Amendments, §22-21-385.
Charter.
Amendments, §22-21-385.
Commissioner.
Consent of commissioner, §22-21-365.
Citation, §22-21-360.
Commissioner.
Charter.
Consent, §22-21-365.
Contracting sales representatives.
Registration with commissioner, §22-21-377.
Defined, §22-21-361.
Reports to commissioner, §22-21-373.
Rulemaking power, §22-21-391.
Subscribers.
Filing and approval of rates, §22-21-372.
Complaints against corporation.
Review of mediation procedures, §22-21-375.
Construction and interpretation.
Board of dental examiners not regulated by article, §22-21-384.
Practice of dentistry.
Not regulated or limited by article, §22-21-384.
Contracts.
Amendments, §22-21-385.
Dentists and other service providers.
Filing and approval of amendments, §22-21-373.
Filing and approval of contracts, §22-21-373.
Individual, group, blanket or franchise contracts, §22-21-371.
Issuance to subscribers.
Contents of proposed contracts, §22-21-368.
License prerequisite, §22-21-367.
Proposed contracts.
Contents, §22-21-369.
Provisions in contract, §22-21-366.
Sales representatives, §§22-21-377 to 22-21-382.
Solicitation.
Who may solicit, §22-21-376.
Definitions, §22-21-361.
Dental service plan.
Use of phrase by nonlicensed entities, §22-21-387.
Department.
Amendments to charter, certificate of incorporation, etc.
Approval of department required, §22-21-385.

DENTAL SERVICE CORPORATIONS—Cont'd
Department—Cont'd
Defined, §22-21-361.
Deposit of moneys received pursuant to article, §22-21-383.
Dissolution or liquidation of corporation.
Supervision by department, §22-21-388.
Subscribers.
Rates for subscribers subject to approval of department, §22-21-366.
Directors, §22-21-362.
Dissolution.
Department supervised, §22-21-388.
Evidence.
Contracting sales representatives.
Denial, suspension, revocation or refusal to renew registration, §22-21-381.
Examinations, §22-21-386.
Existing corporations.
Saving clause for existing nonprofit corporations, §22-21-389.
Fees.
Contracting sales representatives.
Registration with commissioner.
Filing fee, §22-21-377.
Required fees, §22-21-374.
Franchise contracts.
Authorized, §22-21-371.
Funds.
Examiners' revolving fund of the department of insurance, §22-21-383.
Group contracts.
Authorized, §22-21-371.
Hearings.
Bonds, surety or securities to be posted, §22-21-370.
Contracting sales representatives.
Denial, suspension, revocation or refusal to renew registration, §22-21-381.
Incorporation.
Certificate of authority.
Applications, §22-21-363.
Criteria for issuance, §22-21-364.
Certificate of incorporation.
Amendments, §22-21-385.
Commissioner's consent, §22-21-365.
Generally, §22-21-362.
Individual contracts.
Authorized, §22-21-371.
Injunctions.
Violations of article, §22-21-390.
Insurance.
Applicable insurance laws, §22-21-374.
Licenses.
Certificate of incorporation, §§22-21-363, 22-21-364.

DENTAL SERVICE CORPORATIONS—Cont'd
Licenses—Cont'd
Complaints.
Procedures for review mediation, §22-21-375.
Defined, §22-21-361.
Issuance, §22-21-375.
Revocation, §22-21-375.
Subscribers.
Contracts with subscribers, §22-21-367.
Use of phrase "dental service plan" by nonlicensed entity, §22-21-387.
Liquidation.
Department supervised, §22-21-388.
Nonprofit corporations.
Existing corporations.
Saving clause, §22-21-389.
Notice.
Termination of contracting sales representatives, §22-21-377.
Penalties.
Contracting sales representatives.
Administrative penalty in lieu of discretionary suspension, revocation, etc., of registration, §22-21-382.
Diversion or appropriation of funds, §22-21-378.
Violations of article, §22-21-390.
Plans.
Defined, §22-21-361.
Practice of dentistry.
Not regulated or limited by article, §22-21-384.
Rates.
Amendments, §22-21-385.
Registration.
Contracting sales representatives. See within this heading, "Sales representatives."
Reports.
Annual report to commissioner, §22-21-373.
Rules and regulations.
Commissioner to promulgate, §22-21-391.
Sales representatives.
Accounting for funds received, §22-21-378.
Contracting sales representatives, §§22-21-377 to 22-21-382.
Denial, suspension, revocation or refusal to renew registration.
Discretionary basis.
Grounds, §22-21-380.
Penalty in lieu of discretionary suspension, §22-21-382.
Evidence and investigation, §22-21-381.
Hearings, §22-21-381.
Violation of article.
Immediate revocation upon conviction, §22-21-381.

DENTAL SERVICE CORPORATIONS—Cont'd
Sales representatives—Cont'd
Contracting sales representatives—Cont'd
Hearings.
Denial, suspension, revocation or refusal to renew registration, §22-21-381.
Penalties.
Administrative penalty in lieu of discretionary suspension, revocation, denial or refusal to renew registration, §22-21-382.
Registration with commissioner, §22-21-377.
Denial, suspension, revocation or refusal to renew.
Discretionary basis, §22-21-380.
Evidence and investigation, §22-21-381.
Grounds, §22-21-379.
Hearing, §22-21-381.
Penalty in lieu of discretionary suspension, §22-21-382.
Violation of article, §22-21-381.
Fees.
Filing fee, §22-21-377.
Termination.
Notice, §22-21-377.
Diversion or appropriation of funds.
Penalties, §22-21-378.
Penalties.
Diversion or appropriation of funds, §22-21-378.
Securities.
Custody of securities, §22-21-370.
Hearings on posting, §22-21-370.
Modification orders, §22-21-370.
Noncompliance.
Effect, §22-21-370.
Posting, §22-21-370.
Release of securities, §22-21-370.
Short title, §22-21-360.
Solicitation of contracts.
Who may solicit, §22-21-376.
Subpoenas.
Examination and investigation of corporations, §22-21-386.
Subscribers.
Commissioner.
Filing and approval of rates, §22-21-372.
Contracts.
Contents of proposed contracts, §22-21-368.
Defined, §22-21-361.
Department.
Rates for subscribers subject to approval of department, §22-21-366.

DENTAL SERVICE CORPORATIONS—Cont'd
Subscribers—Cont'd
Filing and approval of subscription rates.
Criteria, §22-21-372.
Relevant information to be submitted, §22-21-372.
Licenses.
Contracts with subscribers.
Requirement of license, §22-21-367.
Taxation.
Exemption from taxation, §22-21-370.
Required taxes, §22-21-374.
Title of article, §22-21-360.
Witnesses.
Examination and investigation of corporations, §22-21-386.

DENTISTS, §§34-9-1 to 34-9-65.
Address.
Change of address.
Notice, §34-9-14.
Advertising, §34-9-19.
Unauthorized advertising, §34-9-20.
Alcoholic beverages.
Acquisition, dispensing, etc., for medicinal, scientific, etc., purposes, §28-3-15.
Anesthesia, §§34-9-60 to 34-9-65.
General anesthesia.
Cardiopulmonary resuscitation.
Certification in, §34-9-62.
Fees.
Permits, §34-9-60.
Renewal, §34-9-61.
Intravenous sedation.
Permit, §34-9-63.
Renewal, §34-9-64.
Mortalities.
Reports, §34-9-65.
Permits.
Annual review, §34-9-61.
Application, §34-9-60.
Fees, §34-9-60.
Renewal fee, §34-9-61.
Intravenous sedation, §34-9-63.
Renewal, §34-9-64.
Qualifications of applicant, §34-9-60.
Re-evaluation of credentials and facility, §34-9-61.
Renewal, §34-9-61.
Required, §34-9-60.
Reports.
Mortalities and other incidents, §34-9-65.
Local anesthesia.
Use, §34-9-60.
Appeals.
Board of dental examiners.
Judicial review of orders, §34-9-25.
Applicability of chapter, §§34-9-6, 34-9-7.
Associations.
Professional corporations generally, §§10-4-380 to 10-4-406.
See PROFESSIONAL CORPORATIONS.

DENTISTS—Cont'd
Associations—Cont'd
Unincorporated professional
associations generally,
§§10-10-1 to 10-10-16.
See UNINCORPORATED
PROFESSIONAL
ASSOCIATIONS.
Audits.
Board of dental examiners.
Annual audit, §34-9-42.
Board of dental examiners.
American association of
dental examiners.
Board may affiliate with
association, §34-9-42.
Appeals.
Judicial review of orders of
board, §34-9-25.
Audit.
Annual audit, §34-9-42.
Compensation of members,
§34-9-41.
Composition, §34-9-40.
Creation, §34-9-40.
Defined, §34-9-1.
Depositions, §34-9-47.
Elections, §34-9-40.
Enforcement of chapter,
§34-9-45.
Evidence.
Board records, §34-9-44.
Expenses of members,
§34-9-41.
Fees.
Receipt and disposition by
secretary-treasurer,
§34-9-41.
Injunctions.
Board may enjoin
violations of chapter,
§34-9-29.
Licenses. See within this
heading, "Licenses."
Meetings, §34-9-41.
Record of minutes to be
kept, §34-9-44.
Officers of board, §34-9-41.
Powers and duties.
Generally, §34-9-43.
Qualifications of members,
§34-9-40.
Quorum, §34-9-41.
Records, §34-9-44.
Removal of members,
§34-9-40.
Reports.
Annual report, §34-9-42.
Revocation or suspension of
licenses. See within this
heading, "Licenses."
Rulemaking power, §34-9-43.
Seal of board, §34-9-41.
Secretary-treasurer.
Bond, §34-9-42.
Compensation, §34-9-41.
Notification of change of
address, §34-9-14.
Receipt and disposition of
fees, §34-9-41.
Recordkeeping duties,
§34-9-44.
Subpoena power, §34-9-46.
Teaching permits.
Issuance, §34-9-8.
Terms of office, §34-9-40.
Vacancies.
Filling vacancies, §34-9-40.
Witnesses.
Power to compel
attendance, §34-9-46.

DENTISTS—Cont'd
Bonds, surety.
Secretary-treasurer of board,
§34-9-42.
Certificates.
License certificate. See
within this heading,
"Licenses."
Registration certificates. See
within this heading,
"Registration."
**Commercial dental
laboratory.**
Defined, §34-9-1.
Employing services of
laboratory, §34-9-21.
Construction of chapter,
§34-9-2.
**Continuing education
requirements,** §34-9-15.
Controlled substances.
Prescription, administration,
etc., by dentists for
persons not under
treatment in regular
practice of profession,
§20-2-74.
Corporations.
Dental service corporations,
§§22-21-360 to 22-21-391.
See DENTAL SERVICE
CORPORATIONS.
Professional corporations
generally, §§10-4-380 to
10-4-406.
See PROFESSIONAL
CORPORATIONS.
Council on dental health,
§§22-2-9, 22-2-10.
Definitions, §§6-5-481, 34-9-1.
Advertising, §34-9-19.
Impaired professionals,
§34-38-1.
Practice of dentistry, §34-9-6.
Dental care services,
§§27-19A-1 to 27-19A-11.
See INSURANCE.
Dental college of Alabama.
General provisions,
§§16-47-76 to 16-47-81.
See UNIVERSITY OF
ALABAMA.
Teaching certificates.
Issuance by board, §34-9-8.
Dental hygienists. See within
this heading, "Hygienists."
Dental service corporations,
§§22-21-360 to 22-21-391.
See DENTAL SERVICE
CORPORATIONS.
Depositions.
Proceedings before board,
§34-9-47.
Diploma.
Alteration or unauthorized
procurement, §34-9-22.
Selling diploma prohibited,
§34-9-22.
Disciplinary actions.
Grounds, §34-9-18.
Diseases.
Notifiable diseases.
General provisions.
See DISEASES.
Persons responsible for
reporting diseases,
§22-11A-2.

DENTISTS—Cont'd
Drugs.
Prescription, administration,
etc., by dentists for
persons not under
treatment in regular
practice of profession,
§20-2-74.
Education.
Continuing education
requirements, §34-9-15.
Employees.
Employment of dentists who
treat employees, §34-9-9.
Enforcement of chapter,
§34-9-45.
Evidence.
Board of dental examiners.
Records, §34-9-44.
Examinations.
Applicants for licenses,
§34-9-11.
Board of dental examiners
generally. See within
this heading, "Board of
dental examiners."
Conduct, §34-9-11.
Dental hygienists, §34-9-26.
Fees, §34-9-16.
Exemptions from chapter,
§34-9-7.
Fees.
Hygienists.
License fees, §34-9-26.
Reinstatement of license,
§34-9-28.
Receipt and disposition,
§34-9-41.
Registration.
Certificate fee, §34-9-16.
Waiver of fees, §34-9-15.
Schedule of fees, §34-9-16.
Teaching permits, §§34-9-8,
34-9-16.
Fraud.
Alteration or procurement of
diploma or certificate,
§34-9-22.
Grounds for disciplinary
action, §34-9-18.
Health.
Council on dental health,
§§22-2-9, 22-2-10.
Salary of public health
dentists, §22-1-5.
Hygienists.
Address.
Notice of change, §34-9-28.
Arrangements with
unlicensed persons.
License revocation or
suspension, §34-9-9.
Employment and supervision
of hygienists, §34-9-27.
Examination, §34-9-26.
Fees.
License and registration
fees, §34-9-26.
Reinstatement of license,
§34-9-28.
Insurance.
"Physicians" under health
and accident policies,
§27-1-11.
Penalties.
Practicing without license,
§34-9-5.
Practice of dental hygiene,
§34-9-27.
Qualifications, licensing, etc.,
of hygienists, §34-9-26.

DENTISTS—Cont'd
Hygienists—Cont'd
Registration.
Annual registration,
§34-9-28.
Unlawful to practice without
license, §34-9-4.
Penalty, §34-9-5.
Impaired professionals,
§§34-38-1 to 34-38-8.
Definitions, §34-38-1.
Illness, inebriation, etc.
Confidentiality of
information, records,
etc., §34-38-6.
Disclosure and joint review
of information,
§34-38-4.
Evaluation of professional
who is believed to be
impaired, §34-38-8.
Impaired professionals
committee, §34-38-2.
Annual report, §34-38-7.
Contracts, §34-38-3.
Nonliability of personnel,
§34-38-5.
Promotion of early
treatment, etc.,
§34-38-2.
Reports.
Procedure for reporting
impaired
professional program
activity, §34-38-4.
Indictments.
Practice of dentistry without
license, §15-8-150.
Injunctions, §34-9-29.
Unauthorized advertising,
selling or offering of
dental services and
appliances, §34-9-20.
Insurance.
Dental care services,
§§27-19A-1 to 27-19A-11.
See INSURANCE.
Medical liability insurance,
§§27-26-1 to 27-26-43.
See INSURANCE.
"Physicians" under health or
accident insurance
policies, §27-1-11.
Leases.
Certain employment,
ownership and lease
arrangements with
unlicensed persons
prohibited, §34-9-9.
Liability insurance.
Medical liability insurance,
§§27-26-1 to 27-26-43.
See INSURANCE.
Licenses, §40-12-92.
Appeals.
Orders of board, §34-9-25.
Applications, §34-9-10.
Certificate.
Alteration or unauthorized
procurement, §34-9-22.
Defined, §34-9-1.
Fraudulently obtaining,
§34-9-22.
Issuance, §34-9-11.
Recording, §34-9-12.
Register, §34-9-44.
Sale prohibited, §34-9-22.
To be kept in office of
practitioner, §34-9-13.
Change of address, §34-9-14.

DENTISTS—Cont'd
Licenses—Cont'd
Continuing education
requirements, §34-9-15.
Defined, §34-9-1.
Disciplinary actions.
Grounds, §34-9-18.
Fraudulently obtaining,
§34-9-22.
Hygienists.
Qualifications, §34-9-26.
Required, §34-9-4.
Issuance, §34-9-11.
Nonresidents, §34-9-10.
Practicing without license.
Penalty, §34-9-5.
Prohibited, §§34-9-3,
34-9-4.
Qualifications of applicants,
§34-9-10.
Recording of license
certificate, §34-9-12.
Refusal to license.
Grounds, §34-9-18.
Required, §34-9-3.
Revocation or suspension.
Advertising.
Violations, §34-9-19.
Arrangements with
unlicensed persons as
grounds, §34-9-9.
Failure to renew
registration, §34-9-15.
Grounds for revocation or
suspension, §34-9-18.
Improper use of names,
§34-9-17.
Notice of hearing, §34-9-24.
Statement of charges,
§34-9-24.
Malpractice.
General provisions.
See MALPRACTICE.
Medical liability insurance,
§§27-26-1 to 27-26-43.
See INSURANCE.
Medical liability insurance,
§§27-26-1 to 27-26-43.
See INSURANCE.
Names.
Use of name in practice of
dentistry, §34-9-17.
Nonresidents.
Reciprocity, §34-9-10.
Peer review committees.
Exemption from liability,
§6-5-333.
Penalties.
Alteration or procurement of
diploma or certificate,
§34-9-22.
Hygienists.
Violations of licensing
provisions, §34-9-26.
Practicing without license,
§34-9-5.
Sale of diploma or certificate,
§34-9-22.
Unauthorized advertising,
selling or offering of
dental services and
appliances, §34-9-20.
Violations, §34-9-5.
Permits.
Anesthesia.
Use of general anesthesia.
See within this
heading, "Anesthesia."
Teaching permits, §34-9-8.

DENTISTS—Cont'd
**Pharmacists and
pharmacies.**
Exemption of dentists from
provisions of chapter,
§34-23-11.
General provisions.
See PHARMACISTS AND
PHARMACIES.
Policy of state, §34-9-2.
Practice of dentistry.
Advertising, §§34-9-19,
34-9-20.
Certificates to be kept in
office of practitioner,
§34-9-13.
Declaration of policy,
§34-9-2.
Defined, §34-9-6.
Exemption of certain
practices from provisions
of chapter, §34-9-7.
Licenses. See within this
heading, "Licenses."
Name.
Use of names, §34-9-17.
Penalties.
Practicing without license,
§34-9-5.
Title and letters signifying
degree, §34-9-23.
Unlawful to practice without
license, §34-9-3.
Penalty, §34-9-5.
What constitutes practice of
dentistry, §34-9-6.
Exemption of certain
practices and
operations, §34-9-7.
Private technicians.
Defined, §34-9-1.
Employing services of private
technicians, §34-9-21.
**Professional advertising
generally.** See within this
heading, "Advertising."
**Professional corporations
generally,** §§10-4-380 to
10-4-406.
See PROFESSIONAL
CORPORATIONS.
**Professional standards
review committees.**
Exemption of dentist
members from liability,
§6-5-333.
Public health dentists.
Salaries, §22-1-5.
Records, §34-9-44.
Registration.
Annual registration,
§34-9-15.
Defined, §34-9-1.
Certificate.
Alteration or unauthorized
procurement, §34-9-22.
Fees, §34-9-16.
Fraudulently obtaining,
§34-9-22.
Sale prohibited, §34-9-22.
To be kept in office of
practitioner, §34-9-13.
Fees, §34-9-16.
Waiver, §34-9-15.
Hygienists.
Annual registration,
§34-9-28.
Renewal.
Suspension of license for
failure to renew,
§34-9-15.

DENTISTS—Cont'd

Revocation or suspension of licenses. See within this heading, "Licenses."

Rules and regulations.
Board of dental examiners.
Promulgation by board, §34-9-43.
Penalty for violations, §34-9-5.

Salaries.
Public health dentists, §22-1-5.

Subpoenas.
Power of board, §34-9-46.

Title and letters signifying degree.
Hygienists, §34-9-27.
Use by graduates of dental school, §34-9-23.
Use of title and letters constitutes practice of dentistry, §34-9-6.

Unincorporated professional associations generally, §§10-10-1 to 10-10-16.
See UNINCORPORATED PROFESSIONAL ASSOCIATIONS.

University of Alabama.
Dental college of Alabama.
General provisions, §§16-47-76 to 16-47-81.
See UNIVERSITY OF ALABAMA.
Teaching certificates.
Issuance by board, §34-9-8.

Utilization review and quality control committees.
Immunity, §6-5-333.

Witnesses.
Power of board to compel attendance, §34-9-46.

DEPARTMENTS OF STATE.
See STATE DEPARTMENTS AND AGENCIES.

DEPOSITARIES.
State depositaries, §§41-14-1 to 41-14-16.
See FINANCE.

DEPOSITIONS.
Accounts and accounting.
Department of examiners of public accounts.
Authority to take, §41-5-15.

Attendance.
Failure of party to attend at own deposition, ARCP, Rule 37 (d).

Attorneys at law.
Disciplinary proceedings, ARDE, Rule 13.

Commissioners.
Appointment in other states or territories, §36-1-1.

Costs, §12-21-144.

Criminal cases.
Complainant's deposition, §15-7-2.
Convict in penitentiary, §12-21-263.
Defendants, §12-21-260.
Exclusion at trial, §12-21-262.
Manner of taking.
By defendant, §12-21-260.
By state, §12-21-261.

DEPOSITIONS—Cont'd

Criminal cases—Cont'd
Rules governing use, §12-21-262.
State.
Causes and manner of taking, §12-21-261.
Trial.
Exclusion at trial, §12-21-262.
When may be taken.
By defendant, §12-21-260.
By state, §12-21-261.

Cross-examination.
Depositions upon oral examination, ARCP, Rule 30 (c).

Dentists.
Proceedings before board, §34-9-47.

Department of examiners of public accounts.
Authority to take depositions, §41-5-15.

Depositions upon oral examination. See within this heading, "Oral examination."

Depositions upon written questions. See within this heading, "Written questions."

Discovery generally.
See DISCOVERY.

District courts.
Persons before whom depositions taken.
Applicability of rules to district courts, ARCP, Rule 28 (dc).

Effect of taking, ARCP, Rule 32 (c).

Elections.
Contests, §§17-15-28, 17-16-84.

Errors.
Effect, ARCP, Rule 32 (d).

Evidentiary objections, ARCP, Rule 32 (b).

Executors and administrators.
Sale of real property for payment of debts and for division, §43-2-452.

Failure of party to attend at own deposition, ARCP, Rule 37 (d).

Forms, ARCP, Forms 41 to 46, 62, 67.

Hearing aid dealers and fitters.
Depositions in proceedings before board, §34-14-9.

Irregularities.
Effect, ARCP, Rule 32 (d).

Motions.
Depositions upon oral examination.
Motion to terminate or limit examination, ARCP, Rule 30 (d).
Form, ARCP, Form 44.
Forms, ARCP, Forms 42 to 46, 62, 67.

Notice.
Depositions upon oral examination. See within this heading, "Oral examination."

DEPOSITIONS—Cont'd

Notice—Cont'd
Effect of errors and irregularities, ARCP, Rule 32 (d).

Objections.
Depositions upon oral examination, ARCP, Rule 30 (c).
Evidentiary objections, ARCP, Rule 32 (b).

Oral examination, ARCP, Rule 30 (c).
Certification by officer, ARCP, Rule 30 (f).
Changes, ARCP, Rule 30 (e).
Copies, ARCP, Rule 30 (f).
Cross-examination, ARCP, Rule 30 (c).
Exhibits, ARCP, Rule 30 (f).
Failure to attend or to serve subpoena, ARCP, Rule 30 (g).
Filing by officer, ARCP, Rule 30 (f).
Motions.
Termination or limitation of examination, ARCP, Rule 30 (d).
Form, ARCP, Form 44.
Notice of examination, ARCP, Rule 30 (b).
Forms, ARCP, Forms 41, 42.
Notice of filing, ARCP, Rule 30 (f).
Oath, ARCP, Rule 30 (c).
Objections, ARCP, Rule 30 (c).
Procurement of documents and things, ARCP, Rule 30 (b).
Record of examination, ARCP, Rule 30 (c).
Signing, ARCP, Rule 30 (e).
Submission to witness, ARCP, Rule 30 (e).
Termination of examination, ARCP, Rule 30 (d).
When depositions may be taken, ARCP, Rule 30 (a).

Penitentiary.
Convict in penitentiary, §12-21-263.

Perpetuation of testimony, ARCP, Rule 27.

Persons before whom depositions taken.
Compensation, §12-21-144.
Depositions to be used in state.
Taken in foreign countries, ARCP, Rule 28 (b).
Taken within United States, ARCP, Rule 28 (a).
Depositions to be used outside state.
Taken within state, ARCP, Rule 28 (c).
Disqualification for interest, ARCP, Rule 28 (d).
Objections to deposition, ARCP, Rule 32 (d).
District courts.
Applicability of rule in district courts, ARCP, Rule 28 (dc).
Stipulations as to persons, ARCP, Rule 29.

DEPOSITIONS—Cont'd
Physicians.
Revocation or suspension of
licenses, §34-24-365.
Place of examination, ARCP,
Rule 45 (d).
Prisoners.
Convict in penitentiary,
§12-21-263.
Form of motion for leave to
take deposition, ARCP,
Form 45.
Public service commission.
Hearings on rate and other
regulations.
Depositions of witnesses,
§37-1-92.
Records.
Depositions upon oral
examination, ARCP,
Rule 30 (c).
Depositions upon written
questions, ARCP, Rule
31 (b).
Rules and regulations.
Criminal cases.
Rules governing use,
§12-21-262.
Rules of civil procedure.
See RULES OF CIVIL
PROCEDURE.
Subpoenas.
Form, ARCP, Form 75.
Taking of depositions, ARCP,
Rule 45 (d).
**Supplementation of
responses,** ARCP, Rule 45
(d).
Use at trial, ARCP, Rule 32.
Criminal cases.
Exclusion at trial,
§12-21-262.
Rules governing use,
ARCP, Rule 32 (a).
Effect of using depositions,
ARCP, Rule 32 (c).
Wills.
Witnesses, §43-8-168.
Contesting validity of
wills, §43-8-194.
Written questions.
Filing.
Notice, ARCP, Rule 31 (c).
Forms.
Notice of taking deposition,
ARCP, Form 46.
Notice, ARCP, Rule 31 (a).
Form of notice, ARCP,
Form 46.
Officer to take responses and
prepare record, ARCP,
Rule 31 (b).
Record, ARCP, Rule 31 (b).
Service of questions, ARCP,
Rule 31 (a).

DEPOSITORIES.
County depositories.
See COUNTIES.

DEPOSITS.
Bail and recognizance.
Cash deposit.
See BAIL AND
RECOGNIZANCE.
**Banks and financial
institutions.**
Commercial code.
General provisions,
§§7-4-101 to 7-4-504.
See COMMERCIAL
CODE.

DEPOSITS—Cont'd
**Banks and financial
institutions—Cont'd**
General provisions.
See BANKS AND
FINANCIAL
INSTITUTIONS.
Certificates of deposit.
Securities regulation.
See SECURITIES.
Corrections.
Institution finance authority.
Bond issues.
Security for deposit of
governmental funds,
§14-2-18.
Counties.
Depositories.
See COUNTIES.
Credit unions.
See CREDIT UNIONS.
Fiduciaries.
Uniform fiduciaries act,
§§19-1-7 to 19-1-10.
**Hazardous waste or
substances.**
Fees for disposal of
hazardous waste or
substances.
Fees paid by operators,
§22-30B-3.
**Hotels, inns and other
transient lodging places.**
Safe depository.
Defined, §34-15-1.
Generally, §§34-15-12 to
34-15-14.
Insurers, §§27-6-1 to 27-6-16.
See INSURANCE.
**Long term quality health
care.**
Funds received pursuant to
act, §22-6-24.
Resident protection trust
fund.
Deposit of civil penalties
collected, §22-6-27.
Mutual aid associations,
§§27-30-18, 27-30-19.
Rules of civil procedure.
Deposits in court, ARCP,
Rule 67.
**Savings and loan
associations,** §§5-14A-2,
5-16-23.
State funds.
General provisions,
§§41-14-30 to 41-14-38.
See FINANCE.
Linked deposits, §§5-21-1 to
5-21-11.
See FINANCE.
Uniform fiduciaries act,
§§19-1-7 to 19-1-10.
**Water system assistance
authority.**
Water supply assistance
fund, §22-23A-4.

DEPRESSANTS.
**Controlled substances
generally.**
See DRUGS.

**DESCENT AND
DISTRIBUTION.**
Constitution of Alabama.
Establishing rules of descent
or distribution.
Special, private or local
laws prohibited, Const.
Ala., art. IV, §104.

**DESCENT AND
DISTRIBUTION—Cont'd**
Decedents' estates.
General provisions, §§43-2-1
to 43-8-298.
See DECEDENTS'
ESTATES.
Escheats.
See ESCHEATS.
Estate and inheritance tax.
Constitutional provisions,
Const. Ala., art. XI,
§219; amd. 23.
General provisions, §§40-15-1
to 40-15-21.
See ESTATE AND
INHERITANCE TAX.
**Executors and
administrators.**
See EXECUTORS AND
ADMINISTRATORS.
Intestate succession.
General provisions, §§43-8-40
to 43-8-58.
See WILLS.
Salaries.
Debt for wages owed to
intestate former
employee.
Discharge of debtor,
§43-8-115.
Simultaneous death act,
§§43-7-1 to 43-7-8.
See SIMULTANEOUS
DEATH ACT.
Trusts and trustees.
Trust estate not descendible
upon death of trustee,
§35-4-258.
Wages.
Debt for wages owed to
intestate former
employee.
Discharge of debtor,
§43-8-115.
Wills.
See WILLS.

**DESERTION AND
NONSUPPORT,** §§30-4-50
to 30-4-65.
Actions.
Enforcement of support.
Payment of overdue
support, §30-3-6.
Arraignment.
Representation of defendants
prior to arraignment,
§15-12-20.
Bonds, surety.
Payment of overdue support,
§30-3-6.
Child support.
General provisions.
See CHILD SUPPORT.
Criminal proceedings.
Appeals.
Conviction on appeal.
Probation, §30-4-62.
Right to appeal, §30-4-61.
Temporary support order
pending appeal,
§30-4-58.
Definitions, §30-4-50.
District courts.
Jurisdiction, §30-4-55.
Evidence.
Proof of marriage and
parenthood, §30-4-57.
Willful abandonment or
desertion, §30-4-57.

**DESERTION AND
NONSUPPORT**—Cont'd
Criminal proceedings
—Cont'd
Extradition, §30-4-56.
Institution of proceedings.
Child, §30-4-53.
Probation officer,
§§30-4-54, 30-4-64.
Wife, §30-4-53.
Jurisdiction, §§30-4-55,
30-4-56.
Juvenile courts.
Jurisdiction, §30-4-55.
Marriage.
Privileged communications.
Privilege shall not apply,
§30-4-57.
Proof of marriage,
§30-4-57.
Orders of court.
Probation, §30-4-59.
Bond, §30-4-59.
Sentences.
Suspension of sentence,
§30-4-59.
After portion served,
§30-4-60.
Support orders, §30-4-59.
Temporary support
orders, §30-4-58.
Violations of terms,
§30-4-63.
Temporary support orders,
§30-4-58.
Parents.
Defined, §30-4-50.
Probation, §30-4-52.
Conviction on appeal,
§30-4-62.
Proof of parenthood,
§30-4-57.
Sentence.
Suspension of sentence,
§30-4-59.
After portion served,
§30-4-60.
Probation, §30-4-52.
Bond, §30-4-59.
Officers.
Appointment, §30-4-64.
Duties, §§30-4-64,
30-4-65.
Institution of
proceedings.
Duty of probation
officer, §§30-4-54,
30-4-64.
Reports, §§30-4-64,
30-4-65.
Release of defendant on
probation, §30-4-59.
Conviction on appeal,
§30-4-62.
Sentences.
Suspension of sentence,
§30-4-59.
After portion served,
§30-4-60.
Violation of probation.
Proceedings, §30-4-63.
Reports, §30-4-65.
Service of process.
Generally, §30-4-64.
Sheriff.
Service of process,
§30-4-64.
**Elements of crime of
nonsupport,** §13A-13-4.

**DESERTION AND
NONSUPPORT**—Cont'd
**Enforcement of duty to
support,** §§30-4-80 to
30-4-98. See within this
heading, "Reciprocal state
enforcement of duty to
support."
Hearings.
Payment of overdue support.
Bond, security or other
guarantee to secure,
§30-3-6.
Indigent persons.
Representation of defendants
prior to arraignment,
§15-12-20.
Notice.
Payment of overdue support.
Bond, security or other
guarantee to secure.
Petition or original
pleading to clearly
notify obligor,
§30-3-6.
Overdue support.
Bond, security or other
guarantee to secure
payment, §30-3-6.
**Reciprocal state
enforcement of duty to
support,** §§30-4-80 to
30-4-98.
Choice of laws.
Generally, §30-4-84.
In state obligors, §30-4-83.
Presence of obligor.
Presumptions, §30-4-84.
Court.
Defined, §30-4-81.
Definitions, §30-4-81.
Department of pensions and
security.
Duties, §30-4-82.
Information agency for
state, §30-4-82.
Depositions, §30-4-88.
District attorney.
May represent plaintiff,
§30-4-88.
Duty of support.
Defined, §30-4-81.
Extradition.
Generally, §30-4-86.
Relief from extradition,
§30-4-87.
Husband and wife.
Privileged communications,
§30-4-90.
Information agency for state,
§30-4-82.
Initiating state.
Defined, §30-4-81.
Findings.
Transmission to court in
responding state,
§30-4-91.
Powers and duties.
Generally, §30-4-91.
Receipt and
disbursement of
payments from
defendants in
responding state,
§30-4-92.
Procedure.
Generally, §30-4-91.
Interrogatories, §30-4-88.
Jurisdiction, §30-4-88.
Law.
Defined, §30-4-81.

**DESERTION AND
NONSUPPORT**—Cont'd
**Reciprocal state
enforcement of duty to
support**—Cont'd
Obligee.
Defined, §30-4-81.
Obligor.
Defined, §30-4-81.
Payments.
Receipt and disbursement.
Initiating state, §30-4-92.
Remedies cumulative,
§30-4-98.
Transmittal to court of
initiating state,
§30-4-97.
Petition, §§30-4-88, 30-4-89.
Privileged communications.
Husband and wife,
§30-4-90.
Public assistance.
Reimbursement.
State or political
subdivisions rights
against obligor,
§30-4-85.
Purposes of article, §30-4-80.
Remedies cumulative,
§30-4-98.
Responding state.
Defined, §30-4-81.
Enforcement of orders,
§30-4-96.
Order of support.
Issuance, §30-4-94.
Transmittal to court of
initiating state,
§30-4-95.
Payments.
Costs and fees, §30-4-96.
Transmittal to court of
initiating state,
§30-4-97.
Powers and duties.
Generally, §30-4-93.
State.
Defined, §30-4-81.
Welfare.
Reimbursement.
State or political
subdivisions rights
against obligor,
§30-4-85.
Support.
Defined, §13A-13-4.
**Unemployment
compensation.**
Deduction of child support
obligations, §25-4-152.
**Uniform reciprocal
enforcement of support
act.**
Generally, §§30-4-80 to
30-4-98. See within this
heading, "Reciprocal
state enforcement of duty
to support."
Witnesses.
Competency of wife against
husband in abandonment
cases, §12-21-226.

DETAINERS.
**Forcible entry and unlawful
detainer.**
See FORCIBLE ENTRY
AND UNLAWFUL
DETAINER.

DETAINERS—Cont'd
Habeas corpus.
General provisions.
See HABEAS CORPUS.
Jails.
See JAILS.
Mandatory disposition of detainers.
Adoption of agreement on detainers, §15-9-81.
Citation of article, §15-9-80.
Construction of article, §15-9-88.
Continuances, §15-9-84.
Escape.
After request for final determination filed, §15-9-83.
Final disposition of untried indictments, etc.
Request for final determination.
Action by official having custody upon receipt of request, §15-9-83.
Escape by prisoner after request filed, §15-9-85.
Right of prisoner, §15-9-82.
Notice to prisoners.
Duty of official having custody to give notice of untried indictments, etc., §15-9-82.
Failure to notify of filing of detainers, §15-9-82.
Provisions of article.
Notice of provisions, §15-9-87.
Officials having custody.
Action upon receipt of request for final determination, §15-9-83.
Duty of official to notify prisoner of untried indictments, etc., §15-9-82.
Short title of article, §15-9-80.
Text of agreement on detainers, §15-9-81.
Time within which indictment, etc., to be brought to trial, §15-9-84.
Untried indictments, etc.
Duty of official having custody to inform prisoners, §15-9-82.
Penitentiary.
See PENITENTIARY.
Prisons and prisoners.
See PRISONS AND PRISONERS.
Stop and frisk law, §§15-5-30, 15-5-31.

DETECTIVE AGENCIES.
Licenses, §40-12-93.

DETINUE, §§6-6-250 to 6-6-264.
Alcoholic beverages.
Dry counties.
Beverages seized not to be recovered by detinue during pendency of proceedings under article, §28-4-265.
Assessment of value and damages.
Dismissal of action, §6-6-257.

DETINUE—Cont'd
Assessment of value and damages—Cont'd
Failure of defendant to appear and plead, §6-6-258.
Jury to assess, §6-6-256.
Attorneys at law.
Recovery of attorney's fee by person claiming to be owner of lost or stolen property, §6-6-260.
Bonds, surety.
Execution, garnishment or other process on bond, §6-6-262.
Failure of defendant to give bond.
Disposition of property, §6-6-250.
Duty of clerk to require taking of property by sheriff, §6-6-250.
Interpleader by defendant of adverse claimant of property.
Force and effect of bonds, §6-6-253.
Return.
Compelling, §6-6-254.
Liability of sheriff for failure, §6-6-254.
Claimants of property.
Interpleader by defendant, §6-6-253.
Bonds, surety.
Force and effect, §6-6-253.
Intervention, §6-6-252.
Commercial code.
Investment securities.
Action against purchaser based upon wrongful transfer, §7-8-315.
Contracts.
Conditional sales contracts.
Actions by vendor or against vendee, §6-6-259.
Interpleader.
Adverse claimant of property, §6-6-253.
Intervention.
Claimant of property, §6-6-252.
Judgments.
Assessment of value and damages. See within this heading, "Assessment of value and damages."
Execution upon, §6-6-261.
Mortgages.
Actions by mortgagee or against mortgagor, §6-6-259.
Proceedings on failure of officer to find and take property, §6-6-255.
Restoration of property.
Compelling by execution or attachment, §6-6-263.
Rules of civil procedure.
Seizure of personal property, ARCP, Rule 64 (b).
Sales.
Conditional sales contracts.
Actions by vendor or against vendee, §6-6-259.

DETINUE—Cont'd
Securities.
Action against purchaser based upon wrongful transfer, §7-8-315.
Seizure of personal property, ARCP, Rule 64 (b).
Service of process.
Action for recovery of household furniture and equipment, §6-6-251.
Writs.
Form, §6-6-263.
Issuance until judgment satisfied, §6-6-264.

DETOURS.
Highways, §23-5-2.

DEVELOPMENT.
Appropriations.
Office of state planning and federal programs.
Transfer to office, §41-9-212.
State development office.
Transfer, §41-9-204.
Bear Creek development authority, §§33-15-1 to 33-15-19.
See BEAR CREEK DEVELOPMENT AUTHORITY.
Coastal area board.
Office of state planning and federal programs.
Transfer of functions, personnel, etc., from board to office, §22-22A-10.
Coosa Valley development authority, §§33-16-1 to 33-16-15.
See COOSA VALLEY DEVELOPMENT AUTHORITY.
Counties.
Regional planning and development generally, §§11-85-1 to 11-85-73.
See PLANNING.
Definitions.
Office of state planning and federal programs, §41-9-205.
Downtown redevelopment authorities, §§11-54A-1 to 11-54A-24.
See DOWNTOWN REDEVELOPMENT AUTHORITIES.
Elk river development agency, §§33-12-1 to 33-12-10.
See ELK RIVER DEVELOPMENT AGENCY.
Enterprise zones, §§41-23-20 to 41-23-32.
See ENTERPRISE ZONES.
Federal programs, §§41-9-205 to 41-9-214. See within this heading, "Office of state planning and federal programs."
Health.
State health planning and development, §§22-4-1 to 22-4-17.
See HEALTH.

DEVELOPMENT—Cont'd
Industrial development authority.
General provisions, §§41-10-20 to 41-10-32.
See INDUSTRIAL DEVELOPMENT AUTHORITY.
Industrial development board.
Advisory board, §§41-9-185 to 41-9-188.
Counties, §§11-20-30 to 11-20-50.
See COUNTIES.
Generally.
See INDUSTRIAL DEVELOPMENT BOARD.
Municipal corporations, §§11-54-80 to 11-54-101.
See MUNICIPAL CORPORATIONS.
Industrial development corporations, §§10-4-130 to 10-4-152.
See INDUSTRIAL DEVELOPMENT CORPORATIONS.
Law enforcement planning agency.
Office of state planning and federal programs.
Inapplicability of provisions to law enforcement planning agency, §41-9-214.
Municipal corporations.
Industrial development boards, §§11-54-80 to 11-54-101.
See MUNICIPAL CORPORATIONS.
Regional planning and development generally, §§11-85-1 to 11-85-73.
See PLANNING.
Office of state planning and federal programs, §§41-9-205 to 41-9-214.
Advisory committees or councils, §41-9-209.
Applicability of provisions, §41-9-214.
Appropriations.
Transfer, §41-9-212.
Coastal area board.
Transfer of functions, personnel, etc., from board to office, §22-22A-10.
Comprehensive planning.
Encouraged, §41-9-208.
Cooperation of other agencies, §41-9-208.
Creation, §41-9-208.
Criminal justice information center.
Inapplicability of article, §41-9-214.
Definitions, §41-9-205.
Director.
Employment of one unclassified employee, §41-9-213.
Duties and goals of agency, §41-9-207.
Duties of office, §§41-9-210, 41-9-211.
Employees, §41-9-213.

DEVELOPMENT—Cont'd
Office of state planning and federal programs—Cont'd
Federal programs.
Office to succeed state development office, §41-9-210.
Law enforcement planning agency.
Inapplicability of article, §41-9-214.
Legislative findings and declarations, §41-9-207.
Powers of office, §41-9-211.
Purpose of article, §41-9-207.
Purpose of office, §41-9-210.
Responsibilities of office, §41-9-210.
Planning generally.
See PLANNING.
Redevelopment projects.
General provisions, §§24-2-1 to 24-2-10.
See REDEVELOPMENT PROJECTS.
Regional planning and development, §§11-85-1 to 11-85-73.
See PLANNING.
Southern growth policies agreement, §§41-18-1 to 41-18-3.
State development office.
Advisory committees or councils, §41-9-203.
Appropriations.
Consolidation and transfer to development office, §41-9-204.
Chief administrative officer, §41-9-201.
Composition, §41-9-201.
Comprehensive advisory planning and research.
Powers of office, §11-85-40.
Creation, §41-9-201.
Duties, §41-9-202.
Encouragement by governor of comprehensive and coordinated planning and programming of state governmental affairs, §41-9-201.
Equipment.
Furnishing to office by departments or agencies, §41-9-201.
Federal programs.
Succession of office of state planning and federal programs, §41-9-210.
Functions, §41-9-202.
Furnishing of personnel, equipment, etc., to office by departments or agencies, §41-9-201.
Legislative findings, §41-9-200.
Office of state planning and federal programs.
Federal programs.
Office to succeed state development office, §41-9-210.
Powers, duties, etc., of state development office retained except as to federal programs, §41-9-206.

DEVELOPMENT—Cont'd
State development office—Cont'd
Personnel.
Furnishing by departments or agencies, §41-9-201.
Powers, §41-9-202.
Purpose of article, §41-9-200.
Small business office of advocacy, §§41-9-760 to 41-9-767.
See SMALL BUSINESS OFFICE OF ADVOCACY.
State planning office, §§41-9-205 to 41-9-214. See within this heading, "Office of state planning and federal programs."
Tombigbee Valley development authority, §§33-17-1 to 33-17-15.
See TOMBIGBEE VALLEY DEVELOPMENT AUTHORITY.
United States.
Federal programs, §§41-9-205 to 41-9-214. See within this heading, " Office of state planning and federal programs."
Urban renewal projects, §§24-3-1 to 24-3-9.
See URBAN RENEWAL PROJECTS.
Waters and watercourses.
Development of docks along inland waterways, §§33-2-1 to 33-2-196.
See WATERS AND WATERCOURSES.

DIABETES TRUST FUND, INC.
Exemption from sale and use taxes, §40-23-5.

DICTAPHONES.
Licenses.
Sales, §40-12-127.

DIESEL FUELS.
Diesel fuel tax, §§40-17-1 to 40-17-21.
See MOTOR FUELS.
General provisions.
See MOTOR FUELS.

DIETITIANS AND NUTRITIONISTS.
Definitions.
Practice act, §34-34A-3.
Examinations.
Practice act.
Licensure, §34-34A-7.
Waiver of examination requirement, §34-34A-12.
False representation.
Penalties, §34-34-3.
Funds.
Practice act.
Special revenue trust fund, §34-34A-8.
Licenses.
Practice act.
Examinations, §34-34A-7.
Waiver, §34-34A-12.
Expiration of license, §34-34A-13.
Qualification for license, §34-34A-7.

DIETITIANS AND NUTRITIONISTS—Cont'd
Licenses—Cont'd
Practice act—Cont'd
Reciprocity, §34-34A-11.
Refusal, revocation or suspension, §34-34A-14.
Reinstatement of license, §34-34A-14.
Renewal of license, §34-34A-13.
Temporary license, §34-34A-9.
Qualification for license, §34-34A-7.
Penalties.
False representation, §34-34-3.
Practice act.
Violations, §34-34A-15.
Practice act, §§34-34A-1 to 34-34A-10.
Board of examiners for dietitics/nutrition practice, §34-34A-6.
Citation of act.
Short title, §34-34A-1.
Definitions, §34-34A-3.
Dietitic practice, §34-34A-4.
Examinations.
Licensure, §34-34A-7.
Waiver of examination requirement, §34-34A-12.
Exceptions, §34-34A-10.
Funds.
Special revenue trust fund, §34-34A-8.
Legislative declaration.
Purpose of chapter, §34-34A-2.
Licenses.
Examination, §34-34A-7.
Waiver, §34-34A-12.
Expiration, §34-34A-13.
Reciprocity, §34-34A-11.
Refusal, revocation or suspension, §34-34A-14.
Reinstatement, §34-34A-14.
Renewal, §34-34A-13.
Temporary license, §34-34A-9.
Penalties.
Violations of act, §34-34A-15.
Persons authorized to practice, §34-34A-5.
Purpose of chapter, §34-34A-2.
Purpose of dietitic practice, §34-34A-4.
Reciprocity, §34-34A-11.
Special revenue trust fund, §34-34A-8.
Title of act.
Short title, §34-34A-1.
Violations, §34-34A-15.
Qualifications, §34-34-1.
Reciprocity.
Practice act, §34-34A-11.
Rights generally, §34-34-2.
Unqualified persons.
Authority to represent themselves as dietitians or nutritionists, §34-34-4.

DIKES.
Inland waterways.
Development of docks along inland waterways, §§33-2-1 to 33-2-196.
See WATERS AND WATERCOURSES.
Municipal corporations.
Assessments for public improvements.
Manner of assessments, §11-48-16.

DILATORY PLEADINGS,
ARCP, Rule 11.
Court of the judiciary, ARJC, Rule 7.

DIPHTHERIA.
Notifiable diseases generally, §§22-11A-1 to 22-11A-38.
See DISEASES.

DIRECTED VERDICT.
See VERDICT.

DIRKS.
Weapons generally.
See WEAPONS.

DISABILITY INSURANCE.
General provisions.
See INSURANCE.
Life and disability insurance guaranty association, §§27-44-1 to 27-44-21.
See INSURANCE.

DISABLED AMERICAN VETERANS.
Exemption from sales and use taxes, §40-23-5.

DISABLED PERSONS.
Blind persons.
See BLIND PERSONS.
Cancer.
Examinations, §22-13-9.
Children.
Crippled and disabled children, §§21-3-1 to 21-3-8.
See HANDICAPPED PERSONS.
Consent for health services, §§22-8-1 to 22-8-9.
See HEALTH.
Deaf persons.
See DEAF PERSONS.
Education.
Exceptional children, §§16-39-1 to 16-39-12.
See EDUCATION.
Fishing licenses.
Special annual fishing license, §9-11-54.
Guardian and ward.
Uniform guardianship and protective proceedings act, §§26-2A-1 to 26-2A-160.
See GUARDIAN AND WARD.
Handicapped persons.
General provisions.
See HANDICAPPED PERSONS.
Insurance.
Disability insurance.
General provisions.
See INSURANCE.

DISABLED PERSONS—Cont'd
Insurance—Cont'd
Disability insurance—Cont'd
Life and disability insurance guaranty association, §§27-44-1 to 27-44-21.
See INSURANCE.
Maiming one's self to escape duty or obtain alms, §13A-14-1.
Mentally ill.
General provisions.
See MENTALLY ILL.
Minors.
Crippled and disabled children, §§21-3-1 to 21-3-8.
See HANDICAPPED PERSONS.
Peace officers.
Annuity and benefit fund, §§36-21-60 to 36-21-78.
See PEACE OFFICERS.
Police.
State or municipal police.
Occupational diseases.
Compensation for death or disability, §§36-30-20 to 36-30-23.
Public buildings.
Accessibility to and use of public buildings and facilities by handicapped persons.
See PUBLIC BUILDINGS.
Uniform guardianship and protective proceedings act, §§26-2A-1 to 26-2A-160.
See GUARDIAN AND WARD.
Veterans.
Educational benefits, §§31-6-1 to 31-6-17.
See VETERANS.
Exemptions from licenses.
See LICENSES.
Incompetent veterans and dependents, §§26-9-1 to 26-9-19.
See VETERANS.
Motor vehicles.
See MOTOR VEHICLES.
Welfare generally.
See WELFARE.
Workmen's compensation.
See WORKMEN'S COMPENSATION.

DISABLED VEHICLES.
Stopping on highways, §32-5A-136.

DISASTERS.
Civil defense.
General provisions, §§31-9-1 to 31-9-24.
See CIVIL DEFENSE.
Military service in time of national emergency or war.
County officers.
See COUNTIES.
Municipal officers.
See MUNICIPAL CORPORATIONS.

DISASTERS—Cont'd
Civil defense—Cont'd
Military service in time of
national emergency or
war—Cont'd
Public officers and
employees generally,
§§36-8-1 to 36-8-6.
See PUBLIC OFFICERS
AND EMPLOYEES.
Coal mine safety, §25-9-63.
Counties.
Financial measures,
§11-8-15.
Land-use management in
flood-prone areas,
§§11-19-1 to 11-19-24.
See COUNTIES.
Emergencies generally.
See EMERGENCIES.

**DISCLAIMER OF
INTERESTS IN
PROPERTY,** §§43-8-290 to
43-8-298.
Applicability of provisions,
§43-8-298.
Citation of act, §43-8-290.
**Construction and
interpretation.**
Remedy not exclusive,
§43-8-296.
Uniformity of application and
construction, §43-8-297.
**Delivery of copy of
disclaimer,** §43-8-292.
Effect, §43-8-294.
Eminent domain, §§18-1A-90,
18-1A-92.
Filing, §43-8-292.
Forms, §43-8-293.
Persons who may disclaim,
§43-8-291.
Relation back, §43-8-294.
Remedy not exclusive,
§43-8-296.
Right to disclaim, §§43-8-291,
43-8-298.
Bar, §43-8-295.
Waiver, §43-8-295.
Signing, §43-8-293.
Title of act.
Short title, §43-8-290.
Waiver of right to disclaim,
§43-8-295.

DISCOVERY.
Admissions.
Requests for admission. See
within this heading,
"Requests for admission."
Advancements, §43-8-51.
Appeals.
Discovery pending appeal,
ARCP, Rule 27 (b).
Attorneys at law.
Disciplinary proceedings,
ARDE, Rule 13.
**Banks and financial
institutions.**
Examination of banks,
§5-3A-6.
Before action, ARCP, Rule 27
(a).
Compelling discovery.
Order compelling discovery.
Failure to comply with
order, ARCP, Rule 37
(b).

DISCOVERY—Cont'd
Compelling discovery
—Cont'd
Order compelling discovery
—Cont'd
Motion for order, ARCP,
Rule 37 (a).
Forms, ARCP, Forms 62
to 67.
Debtors and creditors.
Discovery of assets, §§6-6-180
to 6-6-185, 6-6-187.
See DEBTORS AND
CREDITORS.
Deceptive trade practices,
§8-19-9.
Depositions.
See DEPOSITIONS.
**Entry upon land for
inspection and other
purposes,** ARCP, Rule 34.
Failure of party to respond to
request for inspection,
ARCP, Rule 37 (d).
Failure to make discovery,
ARCP, Rule 37.
Insurance agreements,
ARCP, Rule 26 (b).
Interest.
Generally, §18-1A-130.
Interrogatories.
See INTERROGATORIES.
**Mental examination of
persons.** See within this
heading, "Physical and
mental examination of
persons."
Methods, ARCP, Rule 26 (a).
Pending appeal, ARCP, Rule
27 (b).
**Perpetuation of testimony
by action,** ARCP, Rule 27
(c).
**Physical and mental
examination of persons.**
Form of motion for physical
examination, ARCP,
Form 53.
Order for examination,
ARCP, Rule 35 (a).
Report of examining
physician, ARCP, Rule
35 (b).
**Production of documents
and things.**
Banks and financial
institutions.
Examination of banks,
§5-3A-6.
Depositions upon oral
examination.
Request for documents and
things accompanying
notice of examination,
ARCP, Rule 30 (b).
Forms, ARCP, Forms 50 to
52.
Procedure, ARCP, Rule 34
(b).
Scope, ARCP, Rule 34 (a).
Protective orders, ARCP,
Rule 26 (c).
Requests for admission,
ARCP, Rule 36.
Failure to admit.
Expenses on failure,
ARCP, Rule 37 (c).
Forms, ARCP, Forms 54 to
61A.
Rules of criminal procedure,
ARCrP, Rules 18.1 to 18.5.

DISCOVERY—Cont'd
Sanctions.
Failure to make discovery,
ARCP, Rule 37.
Scope of discovery, ARCP,
Rule 26 (b).
Sequence, ARCP, Rule 26 (d).
Small claims.
Exchange of information in
advance of trial, ASCR,
Rule G.
**Stipulations regarding
discovery procedure,**
ARCP, Rule 29.
**Supplementation of
responses,** ARCP, Rule 26
(e).
Timing, ARCP, Rule 26 (d).

DISCRIMINATION.
Alcoholic beverages,
§28-3-13.
Constitution of Alabama.
Miscegenation laws, Const.
Ala., art. IV, §102.
**Constitution of the United
States,** Const. U. S.,
Amendments XIV, XV.
Elections.
Fair campaign practices,
§17-22A-20.
Fraternal benefit societies,
§27-34-46.
Housing.
Zoning regulations,
§11-52-75.
Insurance.
Insurers.
Protection of state insurers
against foreign
discriminatory or
onerous requirements,
§27-3-29.
Life, annuity and disability
insurance.
Exceptions to
discrimination,
§27-12-13.
Unfair discrimination in
rates, §27-12-11.
Jury.
Prohibited in selection of
jury, §12-16-56.
Military affairs.
Discrimination against
person wearing uniform,
§31-2-21.
Motor vehicle carriers.
Charging or collecting higher
than lawful rate,
§37-8-23.
Violation of statutes relating
to unjust
discriminations,
§37-8-20.
Municipal corporations.
Council-manager form of
government.
Prohibition, §11-43A-45.
Housing.
Zoning regulations,
§11-52-75.
Pilots and pilotage.
Pay of pilots, §33-4-51.
Public utilities.
Accepting rebates,
concessions or
discrimination, §37-8-25.

DISCRIMINATION—Cont'd
Railroads.
Charging or collecting higher than lawful rate, §37-8-23.
Violation of statutes relating to unjust discriminations, §37-8-20.
Transportation companies.
See TRANSPORTATION COMPANIES.

DISEASES.
Actinomycosis.
Notifiable diseases. See within this heading, "Notifiable diseases."
AIDS.
Sexually transmitted diseases.
Notifiable diseases generally. See within this heading, "Notifiable diseases."
Animals.
Nuisances menacing public health, §§22-10-1 to 22-10-3.
See HEALTH.
Anthrax.
Notifiable diseases. See within this heading, "Notifiable diseases."
Appeals.
Notifiable diseases.
Commitment orders, §22-11A-36.
Attorneys at law.
Notifiable diseases.
Commitment of afflicted persons.
Appointment of attorney, §22-11A-29.
Attorneys and expert fees, §22-11A-35.
Bang's disease, §§2-15-190 to 2-15-197.
See LIVESTOCK.
Barbers and cosmetologists.
Service by persons having skin or venereal disease, §22-17-8.
Service of persons having inflamed, etc., skin, §22-17-9.
Treatment of skin diseases prohibited, §22-17-10.
Brucellosis, §§2-15-190 to 2-15-197.
See LIVESTOCK.
Cancer.
General provisions, §§22-13-1 to 22-13-13.
See CANCER.
Chancroid.
Notifiable diseases. See within this heading, "Notifiable diseases."
Chicken pox.
Notifiable diseases. See within this heading, "Notifiable diseases."
Child care facilities.
Notifiable diseases.
Director responsible for reporting disease, §22-11A-2.
Generally. See within this heading, "Notifiable diseases."

DISEASES—Cont'd
Cholera.
Notifiable diseases. See within this heading, "Notifiable diseases."
Confidentiality of information.
Notifiable diseases, §22-11A-38.
Contagious diseases.
Notifiable diseases. See within this heading, "Notifiable diseases."
Penitentiary.
Removal of prisoners, §14-3-43.
Tuberculosis, §14-3-41.
School children.
Immunization, §§16-30-1 to 16-30-5.
See EDUCATION.
Mental and physical examinations of school children, §§16-29-1 to 16-29-6, 16-30-1.
See EDUCATION.
Council on prevention of disease and medical care, §§22-2-9, 22-2-10.
Counties.
Boards of health.
Duties, §22-3-2.
Health officers.
Duties, §22-3-5.
Day care center directors.
Notifiable diseases.
Generally. See within this heading, "Notifiable diseases."
Persons responsible for reporting disease, §22-11A-2.
Death.
Vital statistics.
Proceedings when death due to infectious, etc., disease, §22-9-7.
Dengue.
Notifiable diseases. See within this heading, "Notifiable diseases."
Dentists.
Notifiable diseases.
Generally. See within this heading, "Notifiable diseases."
Persons responsible for reporting disease, §22-11A-2.
Diphtheria.
Notifiable diseases. See within this heading, "Notifiable diseases."
Dispensaries.
Public dispensaries treating communicable diseases, §22-1-6.
Dysentery.
Notifiable diseases. See within this heading, "Notifiable diseases."
Education.
Immunization of school children, §§16-30-1 to 16-30-5.
Mental and physical examinations of school children, §§16-29-1 to 16-29-6.
See EDUCATION.

DISEASES—Cont'd
Education—Cont'd
Notifiable diseases.
Superintendent of education.
Notification, §22-11A-38.
School principals.
Notifiable diseases.
Generally. See within this heading, "Notifiable diseases."
Persons responsible for reporting disease, §22-11A-2.
Testing children for certain diseases, §16-30-1.
Emergency medical personnel.
Notifiable diseases.
Notification of patient's contagious condition, §22-11A-38.
Encephalitis.
Notifiable diseases. See within this heading, "Notifiable diseases."
Epidemics.
Notifiable diseases. See within this heading, "Notifiable diseases."
Faith healing.
Tuberculosis.
Preservation of religious freedom, §22-11A-10.
Favus.
Notifiable diseases. See within this heading, "Notifiable diseases."
Firemen.
Compensation for death or disability from occupational diseases, §11-43-144.
Diseases without known cure.
Preference given to police officers and fire fighters in admission to research programs, §36-21-11.
Foot and mouth disease.
See LIVESTOCK.
Forests and forestry.
Protection of forest trees from tree disease infection, §§9-13-120 to 9-13-126.
See FORESTS AND FORESTRY.
German measles.
Notifiable diseases. See within this heading, "Notifiable diseases."
Glanders.
Notifiable diseases. See within this heading, "Notifiable diseases."
Gonorrhea.
Notifiable diseases. See within this heading, "Notifiable diseases."
Venereal diseases generally.
See VENEREAL DISEASES.
Granuloma venereum.
Notifiable diseases. See within this heading, "Notifiable diseases."

DISEASES—Cont'd
Guardian ad litem.
Notifiable diseases.
Commitment petition.
Appointment of guardian
ad litem,
§22-11A-29.
Hemophilia treatment,
§§21-8-1 to 21-8-5.
Hog cholera, §§2-15-230 to
2-15-274.
See LIVESTOCK.
Honeybees and apiaries,
§§2-14-9 to 2-14-12.
Hospital administrators.
Notifiable diseases.
Generally. See within this
heading, "Notifiable
diseases."
Persons responsible for
reporting disease,
§22-11A-2.
Hypothyroidism.
Testing of infants, §22-20-3.
Immunity.
Notifiable diseases.
Third parties, §22-11A-38.
Immunization.
School children, §§16-30-1 to
16-30-5.
Infectious diseases.
Notifiable diseases. See
within this heading,
"Notifiable diseases."
Jails.
Contagious diseases.
See JAILS.
Notifiable diseases.
Petition for testing and
treatment of inmate of
correctional facility,
§22-11A-37.
Sexually transmitted
diseases.
Prisoner testing
generally,
§22-11A-17.
Jurisdiction.
Notifiable diseases.
Commitment of persons,
§22-11A-33.
Jury.
Qualifications of jurors,
§12-16-60.
Laboratory directors.
Notifiable diseases.
Generally. See within this
heading, "Notifiable
diseases."
Persons responsible for
reporting disease,
§22-11A-2.
Leprosy.
Notifiable diseases. See
within this heading,
"Notifiable diseases."
Livestock.
General provisions.
See LIVESTOCK.
Meat and meat products.
See MEAT AND MEAT
PRODUCTS.
Malaria.
Notifiable diseases. See
within this heading,
"Notifiable diseases."
Measles.
Notifiable diseases. See
within this heading,
"Notifiable diseases."

DISEASES—Cont'd
Meat and meat products.
See MEAT AND MEAT
PRODUCTS.
Medical examiners.
Notifiable diseases.
Generally. See within this
heading, "Notifiable
diseases."
Persons responsible for
reporting disease,
§22-11A-2.
Medical records.
Sexually transmitted
diseases, §22-11A-22.
Meningitis.
Notifiable diseases. See
within this heading,
"Notifiable diseases."
Milk from diseased cows,
§2-13-7.
Minors.
Consent for health services.
Consent of any minor as to
reportable diseases,
§22-8-6.
Notifiable diseases.
Sexually transmitted
diseases.
Consent may be given by
minor for medical
treatment,
§22-11A-19.
Informing parent or
guardian.
Authority of medical
care provider,
§22-11A-19.
Mumps.
Notifiable diseases. See
within this heading,
"Notifiable diseases."
Municipal corporations.
Contagious, etc., diseases.
Removal and detention of
persons with
contagious, etc.,
diseases, §11-47-134.
Fire departments.
Compensation for death or
disability of fire
fighters from
occupational diseases,
§11-43-144.
Vaccination.
Provision for system of
compulsory
vaccination,
§11-47-132.
Notifiable diseases,
§§22-11A-1 to 22-11A-38.
Afflicted persons.
Commitment.
Grounds, §22-11A-24.
Petition, §22-11A-25.
Obedience to directions of
health officials
required, §22-11A-7.
Quarantine or isolation,
§22-11A-3.
Testing of persons exposed
to diseases,
§22-11A-23.
Appeals.
Commitment orders,
§22-11A-36.
Cancer generally.
See CANCER.

DISEASES—Cont'd
Notifiable diseases—Cont'd
Chronic lung diseases.
Contract hospitals to admit
indigent patients,
§22-11A-11.
Costs, §22-11A-11.
Commitment, §§22-11A-24 to
22-11A-38.
Appeal of commitment
order, §22-11A-36.
Limitation upon liberty
of person pending
appeal, §22-11A-36.
Notice of appeal,
§22-11A-36.
Attorneys' fees,
§22-11A-35.
Confinement when no
treatment available,
§22-11A-32.
Custody of committed
person, §22-11A-34.
Exposure to disease.
Commitment of persons.
Grounds, §22-11A-24.
Petition, §22-11A-25.
Grounds for commitment,
§22-11A-24.
Jurisdiction over person
committed.
Probate court to retain,
§22-11A-33.
Petition, §22-11A-25.
Attorney to be appointed,
§22-11A-29.
Contents, §22-11A-25.
Dismissal, §22-11A-26.
Guardian ad litem to be
appointed,
§22-11A-29.
Hearings.
Confinement when no
treatment
available,
§22-11A-32.
Findings, §22-11A-32.
Order to appear,
§22-11A-30.
Rehearing,
§22-11A-32.
Rules of procedure to
apply, §22-11A-31.
Liberty of person
pending appeal,
§22-11A-36.
Liberty of person
pending outcome of
petition, §22-11A-28.
Order to appear for
hearing and
examination by
physician,
§22-11A-30.
Probate judge may take
sworn testimony of
petitioner,
§22-11A-26.
Service of notice of
petition, §22-11A-27.
Reports on progress of
committed persons,
§22-11A-34.
Witnesses.
Expert witness fees,
§22-11A-35.

DISEASES—Cont'd
  Notifiable diseases—Cont'd
    Complaints.
      Health officers to
        investigate complaints
        of diseases, §22-11A-8.
      Afflicted person to be
        moved to suitable
        place, §22-11A-8.
      Expenses of removal,
        §22-11A-8.
    Confidentiality of
      information.
      Notice to third parties of
        diseases, §22-11A-38.
    Consent for health services.
      Consent of any minor as to
        reportable diseases,
        §22-8-6.
    Education.
      Superintendent of
        education.
        Notification that student
          or employee as
          contagious disease,
          §22-11A-38.
    Emergency medical
      personnel.
      Notification of patient's
        contagious condition,
        §22-11A-38.
    Exposure to disease.
      Commitment of persons,
        §§22-11A-24 to
        22-11A-38.
      Testing of persons exposed
        to diseases,
        §22-11A-23.
    Hospitals.
      Third parties.
        Notification of diseases,
          §22-11A-38.
    Immunity.
      Notification of third parties
        of diseases,
        §22-11A-38.
    Investigations.
      Health officers to
        investigate complaints
        of diseases, §22-11A-8.
      Tuberculosis.
        State board of health to
          investigate reported
          cases of tuberculosis,
          §22-11A-10.
        When state board of health
          to take charge of
          investigation,
          §22-11A-5.
    Isolation of afflicted persons,
      §22-11A-3.
    Jails.
      Sexually transmitted
        diseases.
        Prisoner testing
          generally,
          §22-11A-17.
    Limitation of liberty of
      person, §§22-11A-28,
      22-11A-36.
    Penalties.
      Failure to make report,
        §22-11A-6.
    Physicians.
      Persons responsible for
        reporting diseases,
        §22-11A-2.
      Third parties.
        Notification of diseases,
          §22-11A-38.

DISEASES—Cont'd
  Notifiable diseases—Cont'd
    Pre-hospital transport
      agencies.
      Notification of patient's
        contagious condition,
        §22-11A-38.
    Prisoner testing.
      Petition, §22-11A-37.
      Sexually transmitted
        diseases, §22-11A-17.
    Quarantine of afflicted
      persons, §22-11A-3.
      Sexually transmitted
        diseases, §22-11A-18.
      Tuberculosis, §22-11A-10.
    Records.
      Physician, hospital, etc.,
        records available to
        health officer,
        §22-11A-4.
    Reports.
      Failure to report.
        Penalty, §22-11A-6.
      Person responsible for
        reporting disease,
        §22-11A-2.
      Tuberculosis cases to be
        reported, §22-11A-9.
    Sexually transmitted
      diseases.
      Afflicted persons.
        Confidentiality of
          medical records.
          Penalty for release,
            §22-11A-22.
        Isolation of person
          believed to have
          sexually transmitted
          disease, §22-11A-18.
      Medical records.
        Confidentiality,
          §22-11A-22.
        Penalty for transmitting
          disease to another
          person, §22-11A-21.
      Cure.
        Physicians to instruct
          person on prevention
          and cure,
          §22-11A-20.
      Generally, §22-11A-13.
      Instructions.
        Physicians to instruct
          person on prevention
          and cure,
          §22-11A-20.
      Isolation of person believed
        to have sexually
        transmitted disease,
        §22-11A-18.
      Compulsory treatment
        and quarantine,
        §22-11A-18.
      Person required to report
        for treatment,
        §22-11A-18.
      Costs, §22-11A-18.
      Measures for protection of
        others.
        Authority of county or
          state health officer
          as to, §22-11A-14.
      Medical records.
        Confidentiality,
          §22-11A-22.
        Penalty for release,
          §22-11A-22.

DISEASES—Cont'd
  Notifiable diseases—Cont'd
    Sexually transmitted
      diseases—Cont'd
      Minors.
        Consent may be given by
          minor for medical
          treatment,
          §22-11A-19.
        Medical care provider
          may inform parent
          or guardian,
          §22-11A-19.
        Physicians to instruct
          person on prevention
          and cure, §22-11A-20.
        Prisoner testing,
          §22-11A-17.
      Quackery.
        Penalties for treating or
          preparing medicine
          without a license,
          §22-11A-21.
      Reports, §22-11A-14.
      State board of health.
        Powers and duties as to,
          §22-11A-13.
      Syphilis.
        Marriage license
          examinations,
          §22-11A-15.
        Newborns.
          Blood tests for syphilis
            required upon
            pregnant women
            and newborns,
            §22-11A-16.
        Pregnant women.
          Blood tests for syphilis
            required upon
            pregnant women
            and newborns,
            §22-11A-16.
      Transmitting disease to
        another person.
        Penalty, §22-11A-21.
      Treating or preparing
        medicine without a
        license.
        Penalties, §22-11A-21.
    State board of health.
      Designation of notifiable
        diseases and health
        conditions, §22-11A-1.
      Investigation of complaints
        of diseases, §22-11A-8.
      Tuberculosis cases,
        §22-11A-10.
      When state board of
        health to take
        charge of
        investigation,
        §22-11A-5.
      Sexually transmitted
        diseases.
        Powers and duties as to,
          §22-11A-13.
      Statewide outpatient
        clinics, §22-11A-12.
      Tuberculosis cases.
        Investigation,
          §22-11A-10.
    Statewide outpatient clinics,
      §22-11A-12.
    Superintendent of education.
      Notification that student or
        employee has
        contagious disease,
        §22-11A-38.

DISEASES—Cont'd
  Notifiable diseases—Cont'd
    Syphilis.
      Marriage licenses.
        Examination for syphilis
          as prerequisite for
          marriage license,
          §22-11A-15.
      Pregnant women.
        Serologic tests for
          syphilis required
          upon pregnant
          women, §22-11A-16.
    Testing of persons exposed to
      diseases, §22-11A-23.
    Third parties.
      Notification of third parties
        of diseases,
        §22-11A-38.
    Transportation of dead
      bodies, §22-19-1.
    Treatment.
      Compulsory treatment.
        Commitment to
          department of public
          health.
          Grounds, §22-11A-24.
      Persons believed afflicted
        with diseases to seek
        and accept treatment,
        §22-11A-23.
    Tuberculosis.
      Compulsory treatment and
        quarantine,
        §22-11A-10.
      Faith healing, treatment
        by prayer or spiritual
        means.
        Preservation of religious
          freedom, §22-11A-10.
      Reporting tuberculosis
        cases, §22-11A-9.
      State board of health to
        investigate reported
        cases of tuberculosis,
        §22-11A-10.
      Statewide outpatient
        clinics, §22-11A-12.
      Voluntary treatment,
        §22-11A-10.
  **Nuisances menacing public
    health,** §§22-10-1 to
    22-10-3.
    See HEALTH.
  Nurseries.
    Insect and disease control,
      §§2-25-1 to 2-25-22.
    See NURSERIES.
  Nurses.
    Notifiable diseases.
      Generally. See within this
        heading, "Notifiable
        diseases."
      Persons responsible for
        reporting disease,
        §22-11A-2.
  **Nursing home
    administrators.**
    Notifiable diseases.
      Generally. See within this
        heading, "Notifiable
        diseases."
      Persons responsible for
        reporting disease,
        §22-11A-2.
  Occupational diseases.
    Compensation for
      occupational diseases.
    See WORKMEN'S
      COMPENSATION.

DISEASES—Cont'd
  Occupational diseases
    —Cont'd
    Fire fighters.
      Compensation for death or
        disability, §11-43-144.
      Notifiable diseases. See
        within this heading,
        "Notifiable diseases."
    Police.
      State or municipal police.
        Compensation for death
          or disability from
          occupational
          diseases, §§36-30-20
          to 36-30-23.
  Ophthalmia neonatorum.
    Notifiable diseases. See
      within this heading,
      "Notifiable diseases."
  Parent and child.
    Notifiable diseases.
      Sexually transmitted
        diseases.
        Treatment of minor,
          §22-11A-19.
  Peace officers.
    Unknown cure.
      Preference given to police
        officers and fire
        fighters suffering from
        diseases without
        known cure in
        admission to research
        programs, §36-21-11.
  Pellagra.
    Notifiable diseases. See
      within this heading,
      "Notifiable diseases."
  Penalties.
    Notifiable diseases.
      Reports.
        Failure to make report,
          §22-11A-6.
  Penitentiary.
    Contagious diseases.
      Removal of convicts,
        §14-3-43.
    Notifiable diseases.
      Petition for testing and
        treatment of inmate of
        correctional facility,
        §22-11A-37.
      Sexually transmitted
        diseases.
        Prisoner testing,
          §22-11A-17.
    Tuberculosis.
      Convicts suffering from,
        §14-3-41.
  Petitions.
    Notifiable diseases. See
      within this heading,
      "Notifiable diseases."
    Prisoner testing.
      Petition for testing and
        treatment of inmate
        of correctional
        facility, §22-11A-37.
  Phenylketonuria.
    Testing infants for
      phenylketonuria,
      §22-20-3.
  Physicians.
    Notifiable diseases.
      Generally. See within this
        heading, "Notifiable
        diseases."
      Persons responsible for
        reporting disease,
        §22-11A-2.

DISEASES—Cont'd
  Plague.
    Notifiable diseases. See
      within this heading,
      "Notifiable diseases."
  Plants.
    Nurseries.
      Insect and disease control,
        §§2-25-1 to 2-25-22.
      See NURSERIES.
    Pathologists, §§2-28-1 to
      2-28-12.
    See PLANTS.
  Pneumoconiosis.
    Evidence of pneumoconiosis,
      §25-5-174.
    Workmen's compensation,
      §§25-5-140 to 25-5-180.
    See WORKMEN'S
      COMPENSATION.
  Pneumonia.
    Notifiable diseases. See
      within this heading,
      "Notifiable diseases."
  Poisons.
    Notifiable diseases. See
      within this heading,
      "Notifiable diseases."
  Police.
    Diseases without known
      cure.
      Preference given to police
        officers and fire
        fighters in admission
        to research programs,
        §36-21-11.
    State or municipal police.
      Occupational diseases.
        Compensation for death
          or disability,
          §§36-30-20 to
          36-30-23.
  Polio.
    Notifiable diseases. See
      within this heading,
      "Notifiable diseases."
  Poultry.
    See POULTRY.
  Prisons and prisoners.
    Notifiable diseases.
      Petition for testing and
        treatment of inmate of
        correctional facility,
        §22-11A-37.
      Sexually transmitted
        diseases.
        Prisoner testing,
          §22-11A-17.
    Tubercular prisoners.
      General provisions.
        See PRISONS AND
          PRISONERS.
    Jails.
      See JAILS.
  Privileges.
    Notifiable diseases.
      Confidentiality of
        information.
        Notification of third
          parties, §22-11A-38.
  Public dispensaries.
    Conduct and maintenance of
      public dispensaries
      treating communicable
      diseases, §22-1-6.
  Quarantine.
    General provisions.
      See QUARANTINE.
    Notifiable diseases.
      Afflicted persons,
        §22-11A-3.

DISEASES—Cont'd
  Quarantine—Cont'd
    Notifiable diseases—Cont'd
      Sexually transmitted
        diseases, §22-11A-18.
      Tuberculosis.
        Compulsory treatment
          and quarantine,
          §22-11A-10.
        Cost of treatment,
          §22-11A-10.
  Rabbit fever.
    Notifiable diseases. See
      within this heading,
      "Notifiable diseases."
  Rabies, §§3-7-1 to 3-7-13.
    See RABIES.
  Radiation generally.
    See ATOMIC ENERGY.
  Records.
    Sexually transmitted
      diseases, §22-11A-22.
  Reports.
    Notifiable diseases. See
      within this heading,
      "Notifiable diseases."
  Research programs.
    Diseases without known
      cure.
      Preference given to police
        officers and fire
        fighters in admission
        to research programs,
        §36-21-11.
  **Rocky mountain spotted
    fever.**
    Notifiable diseases. See
      within this heading,
      "Notifiable diseases."
  Scarlet fever.
    Notifiable diseases. See
      within this heading,
      "Notifiable diseases."
  School children.
    Immunization, §§16-30-1 to
      16-30-5.
    Mental and physical
      examinations of school
      children, §§16-29-1 to
      16-29-6, 16-30-1.
    See EDUCATION.
  Scurvy.
    Notifiable diseases. See
      within this heading,
      "Notifiable diseases."
  Service of process.
    Notifiable diseases.
      Commitment petition.
        Notice of petition to be
          served, §22-11A-27.
  **Sexually transmitted
    diseases.**
    Notifiable diseases generally.
      See within this heading,
      "Notifiable diseases."
    Venereal diseases.
      Barbers and
        cosmetologists.
        Service by persons
          having venereal
          disease, §22-17-8.
      Marriage licenses.
        Syphilis examination,
          §22-11A-15.
  Sickle cell anemia.
    Testing of infants, §22-20-3.
    Trait.
      Testing of infants,
        §22-20-3.

DISEASES—Cont'd
  Skin diseases.
    Barbers and cosmetologists.
      Service by persons having
        skin disease, §22-17-8.
      Service of persons having
        inflamed, etc., skin,
        §22-17-9.
      Treatment of skin diseases
        prohibited, §22-17-10.
  Sleeping sickness.
    Notifiable diseases. See
      within this heading,
      "Notifiable diseases."
  Smallpox.
    Notifiable diseases. See
      within this heading,
      "Notifiable diseases."
  Spinal meningitis.
    Notifiable diseases. See
      within this heading,
      "Notifiable diseases."
  State board of health.
    Authority and jurisdiction,
      §22-2-2.
    Notifiable diseases. See
      within this heading,
      "Notifiable diseases."
  State health officer.
    Powers and duties of officer,
      §22-2-8.
  State police.
    Occupational diseases.
      Compensation for death or
        disability, §§36-30-20
        to 36-30-23.
  Swine diseases.
    See LIVESTOCK.
  Syphilis.
    Notifiable diseases. See
      within this heading,
      "Notifiable diseases."
    Venereal diseases generally.
      See VENEREAL
        DISEASES.
  Tetanus.
    Notifiable diseases. See
      within this heading,
      "Notifiable diseases."
  Tick fever.
    Notifiable diseases. See
      within this heading,
      "Notifiable diseases."
  Trachoma.
    Notifiable diseases. See
      within this heading,
      "Notifiable diseases."
  **Transportation of dead
    bodies.**
    Regulation, §22-19-1.
  Trees.
    Forests and forestry.
      Insect infestation or tree
        disease infection,
        §§9-13-120 to
        9-13-126.
      See FORESTS AND
        FORESTRY.
    Nurseries generally.
      See NURSERIES.
    Tree surgery, §§2-28-1 to
      2-28-11.
      See TREES AND TIMBER.
  Trichinosis.
    Notifiable diseases. See
      within this heading,
      "Notifiable diseases."
  Tuberculosis.
    General provisions.
      See TUBERCULOSIS.

DISEASES—Cont'd
  Tuberculosis—Cont'd
    Notifiable diseases. See
      within this heading,
      "Notifiable diseases."
    Prisons and prisoners.
      General provisions.
        See PRISONS AND
          PRISONERS.
    Jails.
      See JAILS.
  Tularemia.
    Notifiable diseases. See
      within this heading,
      "Notifiable diseases."
  Typhoid fever.
    Notifiable diseases. See
      within this heading,
      "Notifiable diseases."
  Typhus.
    Notifiable diseases. See
      within this heading,
      "Notifiable diseases."
  Undulant fever.
    Notifiable diseases. See
      within this heading,
      "Notifiable diseases."
  Venereal diseases.
    Barbers and cosmetologists.
      Service by persons having
        venereal disease,
        §22-17-8.
    Marriage licenses.
      Syphilis examination,
        §22-11A-15.
    Notifiable diseases. See
      within this heading,
      "Notifiable diseases."
  Whooping cough.
    Notifiable diseases. See
      within this heading,
      "Notifiable diseases."
  Workmen's compensation.
    Compensation for
      occupational diseases.
      See WORKMEN'S
        COMPENSATION.
  Yellow fever.
    Notifiable diseases. See
      within this heading,
      "Notifiable diseases."

DISMISSAL OF ACTIONS.
  Appeals.
    See APPEALS.
  Class actions, ARCP, Rule 23
    (e).
  Costs.
    Previously dismissed action,
      ARCP, Rule 41 (d).
  Counterclaims, ARCP, Rule
    41 (c).
  Cross-claims, ARCP, Rule 41
    (c).
  Forms, ARCP, Forms 70, 71.
  Garnishment.
    Applicability of section
      6-6-143, §6-6-371.
  Indictments.
    Dismissal of indictments.
      See INDICTMENTS.
  Involuntary dismissal, ARCP,
    Rule 41 (b).
  Notice of dismissal, ARCP,
    Rule 41 (a).
    Form of notice, ARCP, Form
      70.
  Stipulation for dismissal,
    ARCP, Rule 41 (a).
    Form of stipulation, ARCP,
      Form 71.

DISMISSAL OF ACTIONS
—Cont'd
Third-party claim, ARCP,
Rule 41 (c).
Voluntary dismissal, ARCP,
Rule 41 (a).

DISORDERLY CONDUCT.
Class C misdemeanor,
§13A-11-7.
Elements of crime, §13A-11-7.
Intent required, §13A-11-7.
Legislature.
Punishment for disorderly
behavior, Const. Ala.,
art. IV, §53.
Not bar to indictment for
same offense, Const.
Ala., art. IV, §54.
Motor vehicles.
Obstructing vehicular or
pedestrian traffic,
§13A-11-7.
Noise.
Making unreasonable noise,
§13A-11-7.
Obscenity.
Using abusive or obscene
language or making
obscene gestures,
§13A-11-7.
Police.
Orders to disperse.
Failure to comply with
lawful order,
§13A-11-7.
Riots.
See RIOTS.
Unlawful assembly.
See ASSEMBLY.

DISORDERLY HOUSES.
General provisions,
§§13A-12-110 to
13A-12-113.
**Loitering for purposes of
prostitution,** §13A-11-9.
Nuisances.
Actions for nuisances,
§§6-5-140 to 6-5-154.
See NUISANCES.

DISPENSARIES.
Hospitals generally.
See HOSPITALS.
**Pharmacists and pharmacies
generally.**
See PHARMACISTS AND
PHARMACIES.
**Public dispensaries treating
communicable diseases,**
§22-1-6.

DISPLACED HOMEMAKERS
PROGRAMS, §§16-60-240
to 16-60-243.

DISSOLUTION.
Corporations.
See CORPORATIONS.
Credit unions.
Alabama credit union league.
Redemption and purchase
of advance dues
certificate upon
dissolution, etc., of
member credit union,
§5-17-28.
Voluntary dissolution,
§5-17-21.
Dental service corporations.
Department supervised,
§22-21-388.

DISSOLUTION—Cont'd
Health care authorities.
Grounds, §22-21-339.
Procedure, §22-21-339.
Municipal corporations.
Consolidation of
noncontiguous
municipalities,
§§11-42-166, 11-42-167.
General provisions,
§§11-41-20 to 11-41-28.
See MUNICIPAL
CORPORATIONS.
Partnerships.
Contracts.
Convenants not to compete,
§8-1-1.
General provisions, §§10-8-90
to 10-8-103.
See PARTNERSHIPS.
**Savings and loan
associations.**
See SAVINGS AND LOAN
ASSOCIATIONS.
**Tombigbee valley
development authority,**
§33-17-15.
Application.
Filing with secretary of
state, §33-17-15.
**Unincorporated professional
associations.**
See UNINCORPORATED
PROFESSIONAL
ASSOCIATIONS.

DISTILLERS.
**Alcoholic beverages
generally.**
See ALCOHOLIC
BEVERAGES.

DISTRESS MERCHANDISE
SALES, §§8-13-1 to 8-13-23.
See SALES.

DISTRICT ATTORNEYS,
§§12-17-180 to 12-17-224.
Absence.
Appointment of attorney to
act for district attorney,
§12-17-186.
Affidavits.
Commencing prosecution on
own affidavit,
§12-17-194.
Agriculture.
Duties, §2-3-6.
Alcoholic beverages.
Dry counties.
Enforcement of chapter,
§§28-4-314, 28-4-315.
Appointment.
Appointment of attorney to
act for district attorney
when office vacant, etc.,
§12-17-186.
District attorney pro tem,
§12-17-189.
Assistant district attorneys.
Appointment, §12-17-198.
Circuit solicitors.
Election by solicitors
serving terms to which
elected prior to
January 16, 1977,
§12-12-9.
Performance of functions of
circuit solicitors,
§12-12-9.
Compensation, §12-17-198.
Supplementation,
§12-17-220.

DISTRICT ATTORNEYS
—Cont'd
Assistant district attorneys
—Cont'd
Construction of division,
§12-17-223.
Entitlement of elected
assistant district
attorneys to entitlements
in article, §12-17-199.
Number, §12-17-198.
Representation of defendants
charged with criminal
offenses, §12-17-195.
Retirement.
Election by former
assistant district
attorneys serving as
circuit judges on
January 16, 1977 to
come under provisions
of article 1 of chapter,
§12-18-55.
Tenth judicial circuit.
Applicability of division,
§12-17-222.
Attendance at court,
§12-17-185.
Outside home county.
Allowance for attendance,
§12-17-191.
Attorney general.
Authority, §36-15-15.
Attorneys at law.
Partner of district attorney
prohibited from
defending certain cases,
§34-3-12.
**Banks and financial
institutions.**
Superintendent of banks.
Representation in civil
actions, §5-2A-23.
Budgets.
Procedure, §12-17-221.
Checks.
Special services division.
Worthless check unit,
§12-17-224.
Circuit courts.
Special sessions, §§12-2-34,
12-2-35, 12-2-37.
**Commencing prosecution on
own affidavit,** §12-17-194.
Compensation, §12-17-182.
Additional allowance in
circuits having four or
more counties,
§12-17-192.
Allowance for attendance
outside home county,
§12-17-191.
Assistant district attorneys,
§12-17-198.
District attorney pro tem,
§12-17-189.
Compounding, §13A-10-7.
Constitution of Alabama,
Const. Ala., amd. 328.
Continuation, Const. Ala.,
amd. 328.
Designation of circuit
solicitor as district
attorney, Const. Ala.,
amd. 226.
Costs.
When prosecutor liable,
§15-18-60.

DISTRICT ATTORNEYS
—Cont'd

Counties.
Bond issues.
Validation, §§6-6-750,
6-6-752.
County offices.
Examination of records and
papers in county offices,
§12-16-196.
County treasurers.
Free access to office of county
treasurer, §12-16-196.
Deceptive trade practices.
Authority, §8-19-4.
**Department of examiners of
public accounts.**
Legal assistance, §41-5-11.
Disqualification.
Appointment of attorney to
act for district attorney
when district attorney
disqualified, §12-17-186.
**District attorneys' spouses
fund,** §§12-17-201 to
12-17-207.
Administration, §12-17-202.
Benefits, §12-17-206.
Contributions, §12-17-204.
Coverage, §12-17-204.
Creation, §12-17-201.
Credit for prior service,
§12-17-205.
Disbursements, §12-17-202.
Eligibility, §12-17-203.
Establishment, §12-17-201.
Prior service credit,
§12-17-205.
Sources of funds, §12-17-201.
Supernumerary status.
Termination of service
prior to assumption of
status, §12-17-207.
Termination of service prior
to assumption of
supernumerary status,
§12-17-207.
District courts.
Charged with administrative
responsibility for district
court prosecutions,
§12-12-8.
Domestic violence facilities.
Duties, §30-6-4.
Inspection, §30-6-3.
Reports to office, §30-6-5.
Duties, §12-17-184.
Attendance at court,
§12-17-185.
Education.
County superintendents of
education.
Examination of books and
papers of county
superintendent,
§12-16-195.
Elections, Const. Ala., amd.
328.
General elections.
Offices for which general
election held, §17-2-2.
Registration.
Appeals from refusal of
registration, §17-4-124.
State and county officers
elected by the people,
§17-2-1.
Terms of office, §17-2-9.
When elected, §§12-17-180,
17-2-9.

DISTRICT ATTORNEYS
—Cont'd

Expenses.
Estimates, §12-17-221.
Payment, §36-15-16.
Fees.
Fish and game.
Violations of laws.
Prosecution, §9-11-7.
Marine resources.
Violation of chapter,
§9-12-6.
Payment into state treasury,
§12-17-193.
Special services division.
Worthless check unit,
§12-17-224.
Fire marshal.
Assistance in investigations,
§36-19-16.
Fish and game.
Violation of laws, §9-11-7.
Forests and forestry.
Violation of chapter.
Duty to prosecute,
§9-13-22.
Forfeitures.
Supreme court.
Failure to perform duties
required by certain
sections, §12-2-38.
Fraud.
Charitable fraud.
Enforcement of provisions,
§13A-9-76.
Funds, §12-17-197.
District attorneys' spouses
fund, §§12-17-201 to
12-17-207. See within
this heading, "District
attorneys' spouses fund."
Funerals.
Enforcement of chapter,
§34-13-5.
Gambling places.
Complaints filed on certain
information, §13A-12-51.
Grain dealers.
Prosecution of violations,
§2-31-18.
Grand jury.
Attendance and duties
before, §12-16-209.
Habeas corpus.
Notice of writ, §15-21-13.
Impeachment.
Duty to institute and
prosecute proceedings,
§36-11-4.
General provisions.
See IMPEACHMENT.
Subject to impeachment,
§36-11-1.
Supernumerary district
attorneys, §12-17-215.
Indictments.
Disclosure prior to arrest of
person indicted,
§12-16-210.
General provisions.
See INDICTMENTS.
Insurance code.
Enforcement, §27-2-19.
Investigators.
Employment, §12-17-220.
Salaries, §12-17-220.
Jails.
Free access to county jail,
§12-16-196.

DISTRICT ATTORNEYS
—Cont'd

Judicial retirement fund.
Time of service by judge as
full-time state
prosecutor.
Credit for time, §12-18-8.1.
Juvenile proceedings,
§12-15-5.
Labor.
Enforcement of laws,
§25-2-24.
Law partners.
Restrictions as to defending
criminal cases,
§12-17-196.
Marine resources.
Violation of chapter.
Fee, §9-12-6.
Marriage offenses.
Probate judge to notify
district attorney,
§30-1-18.
Municipal corporations.
Bond issues.
Validation, §§6-60-750,
6-60-752.
Negotiable instruments.
Special services division.
Worthless check unit,
§12-17-224.
Nonresidents.
Vacation of office for
nonresidency,
§12-17-183.
**Office of prosecution
services,** §§12-17-230 to
12-17-234.
Partners.
Restrictions as to defending
criminal cases,
§12-17-196.
Powers, §12-17-184.
Probate judges.
Examination of fee book of
probate judge,
§12-16-194.
**Public officers and
employees.**
Bonds, surety.
Notification of district
attorney of failure of
public officer to file
bond, §36-5-16.
Failure to give notice,
§36-5-17.
Expenses.
Submission of estimate,
§12-17-221.
Qualifications, Const. Ala.,
amd. 328.
Railroads.
Noncompliance with
commission order to
erect depot or provide
conveniences for
travelers.
Failure of commission to
notify district attorney,
§37-8-111.
Passengers.
Failure of companies to
comply with orders in
regard to passenger
accommodations.
District attorney to bring
civil action,
§37-2-113.
Residence requirements,
§12-17-183.

DISTRICT ATTORNEYS
—Cont'd
Restitution to victims of crime.
Special services division.
Worthless check unit, §12-17-224.
Retirement.
Election by former district attorneys serving as circuit judges on January 16, 1977 to come under provisions of article 1 of chapter, §12-18-55.
Salaries, §12-17-182.
Supplements, §12-17-30.
Assistant district attorneys, §12-17-220.
Special services division.
Authority of district attorney to establish, §12-17-224.
Worthless check unit, §12-17-224.
Special sessions of court, §§12-2-34 to 12-2-37.
Subpoenas.
Authority to issue, §§12-16-198, 12-17-184, 12-21-245.
Superintendent of banks.
Representation in civil actions, §5-2A-23.
Supernumerary district attorneys, §§12-17-210 to 12-17-216.
Commission.
Issuance, §12-17-214.
Compensation, §12-17-215.
Duties, §12-17-216.
Filling of vacancies in office of district attorney, §12-17-214.
Funds.
District attorneys' spouses fund generally, §§12-17-201 to 12-17-207. See within this heading, "District attorneys' spouses fund."
Impeachment, §12-17-215.
Issuance of commission, §12-17-214.
Oath of office, §12-17-216.
Powers, §12-17-216.
Qualifications for supernumerary status.
Eighteen years of service as district attorney, judge, county solicitor, etc., with minimum of 15½ years service as district attorney, §12-17-213.
Elected district attorney, §12-17-210.
Fifteen years of service and not less than 70 years of age, §12-17-211.
Sixty years of age and 18 years of service as district attorney, judge, county solicitor, etc., with minimum of 10 years service as district attorney, §12-17-213.
Twelve years service and total disability, §12-17-212.

DISTRICT ATTORNEYS
—Cont'd
Supernumerary district attorneys—Cont'd
Qualifications for supernumerary status —Cont'd
Twenty-five years continuous service, §12-17-212.
Twenty years service as judge and district attorney, §12-17-212.
Term of office, §12-17-215.
Suspension from office.
Appointment of district attorney pro tem, §12-17-189.
Compensation of district attorney pro tem, §12-17-189.
District attorney pro tem.
Appointment and compensation, §12-17-189.
Indictment pending, §12-17-188.
When order of suspension set aside, §12-17-190.
Term of office, §§12-17-180, 17-2-9, 36-3-3; Const. Ala., amd. 328.
Trees and timber.
Condemnation of timber theft equipment.
See TREES AND TIMBER.
Vacancies.
Appointment of attorney to act for district attorney when office vacant, §12-17-186.
Filling, §12-17-181; Const. Ala., amd. 328.
Supernumerary district attorneys.
Filling of vacancies in office of district attorney, §12-17-214.
Welfare.
Child care facilities.
Duty to enforce chapter or prosecute violations, §38-7-17.
Worthless checks.
Special services division.
Worthless check unit, §12-17-224.

DISTRICT COURTS, §§12-12-1 to 12-12-73.
Administration.
Rules of judicial administration.
See COURTS.
Administrative agency.
Created, §12-17-250.
Duties, §12-17-250.
Officials of agency, §§12-17-250, 12-17-251.
Powers, §12-17-250.
Rules of administration for agency.
Supreme court to provide, §12-17-252.
Administrative fee for periodic payments, §12-19-26.
Administrative personnel.
Coordination of functions and duties, §12-5-13.

DISTRICT COURTS—Cont'd
Adoption proceedings, §12-12-35.
Appeals.
Appeals from district court, §§12-12-70 to 12-12-73.
Bonds on appeals, §12-12-73.
Circuit courts generally, §12-12-71.
Counterclaims.
Statement of compulsory counterclaim as amendment to proceedings, ARCP, Rule 13 (j).
Dismissal for failure to appear, §12-12-70.
Jurisdictional amount.
Counterclaims heard on trial de novo, ARCP, Rule 13 (j).
Jury trial.
Right upon appeals to circuit courts, §12-12-71.
Procedure, §12-12-70.
Right of appeal, §12-12-70.
When appeals may be taken directly to appellate courts, §12-12-72.
When taken to circuit courts, §12-12-71.
Costs of appeals to circuit courts, §12-19-150.
Attachment.
Fees, §12-19-75.
Issuance, §6-6-43.
Bailiffs, ARJA, Rule 11.
Boats.
Jurisdiction of offenses, §33-5-32.
Bonds, surety.
Appeals bond, §12-12-73.
Boundaries of districts, §12-17-60.
Change in boundaries.
Procedure when bill introduced in legislature, §12-1-5.
Calendars.
Management, ARJA, Rule 16.
Circuit courts.
Appeals from district courts.
See within this heading, "Appeals."
Superintendence of district courts, §12-11-30.
Supervision of district courts, §12-12-10.
Transfer of cases between circuit and district court, §12-11-9.
Clerks of court.
Abolition of separate office, §12-17-161.
Appointment, §12-17-161; ARJA, Rule 27.
Circuit court clerk ex officio clerk of district court, §12-17-160.
Clerks generally.
See CLERKS OF COURT.
Duties, ARJA, Rule 4.
Employees.
District court clerk employees component of office of clerk, §12-17-162.

DISTRICT COURTS—Cont'd
Clerks of court—Cont'd
Establishment of office,
ARJA, Rule 27.
Fees collected.
Monthly reports, §12-1-19.
Fines collected.
Monthly reports, §12-1-19.
Nomination, ARJA, Rule 27.
Office hours.
Closing offices.
Effect on computation of
time periods, ARJA,
Rule 5.
Routine work days, ARJA,
Rule 5.
Saturdays, Sundays and
other holidays, ARJA,
Rule 5.
Conflicting state and
county holidays,
ARJA, Rule 5.
Severe weather, hazardous
or other emergency
conditions, ARJA, Rule
5.
Removal, §12-17-161.
Reports.
Fines, fees, etc., §12-1-19.
Rules of judicial
administration.
See COURTS.
Secretaries for clerks,
§12-17-341.
Separate office of clerk of
district court may be
established, §12-17-161.
Constables.
Coroners' fees, §12-19-94.
Constitution of Alabama.
District court judges.
See CONSTITUTION OF
ALABAMA.
Contempt powers, §12-12-6.
Continuances.
Fines and costs.
Payment, §12-12-5.
Costs.
General provisions.
See COSTS.
Municipal corporations.
Docket fees, fines, etc.,
collected in municipal
ordinance cases,
§12-19-155.
Prescribed costs for district
courts to be exclusive,
§12-19-156.
Counterclaims.
Appeals from district court.
Compulsory counterclaims,
ARCP, Rule 13 (j).
County court personnel.
Employees of state, §12-17-1.
Court of record, §12-12-2.
Court reporters. See within
this heading, "Reporters."
Courts generally.
See COURTS.
Creation, §12-12-1.
Criminal law and procedure.
District attorneys.
Charged with
administrative
responsibility for
district court
prosecutions, §12-12-8.
Jurisdiction, §12-12-32.
Vesting, §12-1-3.

DISTRICT COURTS—Cont'd
Criminal law and procedure
—Cont'd
Powers of court as to
disposition of criminal
cases, §12-12-4.
Traffic offenses. See within
this heading, "Traffic
offenses."
Depositions.
Persons before whom
depositions taken, ARCP,
Rule 28 (dc).
Designation, §12-12-1.
District attorneys.
Administrative responsibility
prosecutions, §12-12-8.
**District court administrative
agency.** See within this
heading, "Administrative
agency."
Divorce and alimony.
Judges.
Designation of judge in
districts having more
than one judge,
§12-17-70.
Dockets.
Fees.
See DOCKETS.
Establishment, §12-12-1.
Executions.
Fees, §12-19-75.
Extradition proceedings,
§12-12-33.
Fees.
Administrative fee for
periodic payments,
§12-19-26.
Applicability of provisions,
§12-19-25.
Attachment fees, §12-19-75.
Clerks of court.
Monthly report as to fees
collected, §12-1-19.
Coroners' fees, §12-19-94.
Costs generally.
See COSTS.
Defendant service fees,
§12-19-73.
Docket fees.
See DOCKETS.
Execution fees, §12-19-75.
Garnishment fees, §12-19-75.
Prescribed fees for district
courts to be exclusive,
§12-19-156.
Subpoenas, §12-19-74.
Witnesses' fees.
See WITNESSES.
Felonies.
Jurisdiction, §12-12-32.
Fines.
Continuation of cases to
permit payment,
§12-12-5.
General provisions.
See PENALTIES.
Schedule of fines, §12-12-55;
ARJA, Rule 20.
Traffic offenses.
Schedule, §12-12-55;
ARJA, Rule 20.
Fish and game laws.
Jurisdiction over
violations, §9-11-6.
**Forcible entry and unlawful
detainer.**
See FORCIBLE ENTRY
AND UNLAWFUL
DETAINER.

DISTRICT COURTS—Cont'd
Forests and forestry.
Jurisdiction of prosecutions,
§9-13-23.
Frivolous actions.
Litigation accountability,
§§12-19-270 to 12-19-276.
See COURTS.
Garnishment.
Fees, §12-19-75.
Holidays.
Clerks of court.
Office hours, ARJA, Rule
5.
Indigent persons.
Defense of indigents.
See INDIGENT PERSONS.
Judges, §§12-17-60 to
12-17-70.
Additional judges, §12-17-66.
Appointment, Const. Ala.,
art. VI, §153.
Assignment.
Temporary assignments,
ARJA, Rule 13.
Attachments.
Issuance, §6-6-43.
Canons of judicial ethics.
See CANONS OF
JUDICIAL ETHICS.
Commissioned judges,
§12-17-66.
Compensation, §12-17-68;
Const. Ala., art. VI,
§150.
Retired judges on active
duty, §12-18-61.
Special judges, ARJA, Rule
14.
Conferences, seminars, etc.
Attendance, §12-1-18.
Constitution of Alabama.
See CONSTITUTION OF
ALABAMA.
County law libraries.
Appointment of libraries
and custodians,
§11-25-5.
Death.
Retirement benefits,
§§12-18-54, 12-18-60.
Disability benefits,
§12-18-59.
Domestic relations cases.
Designation of judge to
handle in districts
having more than one
judge, §12-17-70.
Dual office holding, Const.
Ala., art. VI, §150.
Duty to serve districts for
which elected, §12-17-69.
Election, Const. Ala., art. VI,
§152.
Ballots.
Districts in which more
than one judge
elected, §§12-17-62,
17-7-20.
Boundaries of election
districts, §12-17-60.
Contests.
Legislative, judicial or
county offices,
§§17-15-20 to
17-15-35.
See ELECTIONS.
General elections.
Offices for which held,
§17-2-2.

DISTRICT COURTS—Cont'd
Judges—Cont'd
Election—Cont'd
Manner of election,
§12-17-61.
State and county officers
elected by the people,
§17-2-1.
Two or more judges at
same election.
Designating by number,
§§12-17-62, 17-7-20.
When judges to be elected,
§17-2-7.
Expenses.
Travel expenses for
attending conferences,
seminars, etc.,
§12-1-18.
Family law.
Designation of judge to
handle in districts
having more than one
judge, §12-17-70.
Impeachment.
General provisions.
See IMPEACHMENT.
Subject to impeachment,
§36-11-1; Const. Ala.,
art. VII, §175.
Incompetence.
Procedure when judge
incompetent, Const.
Ala., art. VI, §160.
Number of judges, Const.
Ala., amd. 328.
Number per district,
§12-17-61.
Procedure when bill to
increase or decrease
introduced in
legislature, §12-1-5.
Oaths.
Filing, §36-4-4.
Presiding judges.
Selection, ARJA, Rule 6.
Temporary assignment,
ARJA, Rule 13.
Qualifications, §12-17-63;
Const. Ala., art. VI,
§154.
Residence requirements,
§12-17-64.
Retirement, §§12-18-50 to
12-18-61.
Active duty status,
§12-18-61.
Applicability of provisions.
Effective date, §12-18-91.
Article 1 of chapter.
Applicability to judges
elected or appointed
to office after
October 10, 1975,
§12-18-51.
Benefits, §12-18-58.
Age sixty, §12-18-40.
Applicability of
provisions,
§12-18-58.1.
Death.
Payment of benefits,
§§12-18-60,
12-18-60.1.
Disability benefits,
§12-18-59.
Entitlement to receipt of
pension, §12-18-50.

DISTRICT COURTS—Cont'd
Judges—Cont'd
Retirement—Cont'd
Benefits—Cont'd
Spouses.
Payment of benefits
upon death of
judges, §12-18-60.
Certificate of time of
service accumulated
toward retirement,
§12-18-54.
Compensation of retired
judges on active duty,
§12-18-61.
Contributions to
retirement fund,
§12-18-52.
Creditable service as
district or county court
judge, §12-18-41.
Crediting previous
payments by counties
or municipalities,
§12-18-53.
Death.
Certificate of time of
service accumulated
toward retirement,
§12-18-54.
Payment of benefits to
spouse, §12-18-60.
Applicability of
provisions,
§12-18-60.1.
Disability benefits,
§12-18-59.
Effective date of article,
§12-18-91.
Election by judges entitled
to receive commissions
as district judges to
come under article,
§12-18-51.
Eligibility, §12-18-55.
Applicability of
provisions,
§12-18-58.1.
Entitlement to retirement
and receipt of pension,
§12-18-50.
Intention to retire.
Notice, §12-18-56.
Money previously paid into
retirement funds by
counties or
municipalities.
Payment into judicial
retirement fund,
§12-18-53.
Notice of intention to
retire, §12-18-56.
Retirement order,
§12-18-50.
Spouses.
Payment of benefits to
spouse upon death of
judge, §12-18-60.
Applicability of
provisions,
§12-18-60.1.
Termination of service of
judge prior to
eligibility for
retirement benefits.
Election for withdrawal
and refund,
§12-18-54.

DISTRICT COURTS—Cont'd
Judges—Cont'd
Retirement—Cont'd
Transfer of contributions
and creditable service
to judicial retirement
fund, §§12-18-110 to
12-18-114.
Vacancies in office of
judge, §12-18-57.
Salaries, §12-17-68; Const.
Ala., art. VI, §150.
Retired judges on active
duty, §12-18-61.
Secretarial services,
§12-17-340; ARJA, Rule
10.
Special judges.
Appointment, §12-1-14.
Compensation, ARJA, Rule
14.
Oath of office, §12-1-14.
Powers, §12-1-14.
Qualifications, §12-1-14.
Temporary assignments,
ARJA, Rule 13.
Terms of office, §12-17-65.
Travel expenses.
Reimbursement of judges
attending conferences,
seminars, etc.,
§12-1-18.
Vacancies, §12-18-57.
Filling, §12-17-67.
Jurisdiction, Const. Ala., amd.
328.
Adoption proceedings,
§12-12-35.
Civil jurisdiction, §12-12-30.
Criminal jurisdiction,
§12-12-32.
Vesting, §12-1-3.
Extradition proceedings,
§12-12-33.
Fish and game laws.
Violations, §9-11-6.
Forcible entry and unlawful
detainer, §6-6-330.
Juvenile proceedings,
§§12-12-34, 12-15-2.
Small claims actions,
§12-12-31.
Traffic infractions.
Misdemeanor prosecutions,
§12-12-51.
Juvenile proceedings.
Jurisdiction, §§12-12-34,
12-15-2.
Litigation accountability.
General provisions,
§§12-19-270 to 12-19-276.
See COURTS.
Location.
Designation of additional
locations for court sites,
§12-12-36.
Sessions of court, §12-12-1.
Magistrates.
Administrative agency.
Appointment, §12-17-251.
Deemed chief officers of
agency, §12-17-251.
District court magistrates
agency division, ARJA,
Rule 18.
Authority, ARJA, Rule
18.
Selection, ARJA, Rule
18.
Powers, §12-17-251.

DISTRICT COURTS—Cont'd
Magistrates—Cont'd
Inferior court judges whose positions were abolished by constitution, §12-17-253.
Supernumerary magistrates.
Death benefits, §12-17-265.
Eligibility, §12-17-260.
Filing of written declaration, §12-17-261.
Issuance of commission, §12-17-261.
Notice of intent to become, §12-17-263.
Oath of office, §12-17-263.
Prior service credit, §12-17-264.
Salaries, §12-17-262.
Payment of percentage earned as judge or magistrate, §12-17-263.
Term of office, §12-17-262.
Who may become, §12-17-260.
Traffic offenses.
Receipt of guilty pleas, §12-12-52.
Marine resources.
Violation of chapter.
Jurisdiction, §9-12-4.
Minors.
Juvenile jurisdiction, §§12-12-34, 12-15-2.
Juvenile proceedings.
See JUVENILE PROCEEDINGS.
Misdemeanors.
Jurisdiction, §12-12-32.
Motor vehicles.
Traffic offenses. See within this heading, "Traffic offenses."
Municipal corporations.
Costs.
Docket fees, fines, etc., collected in municipal ordinance cases.
Distribution, §12-19-154.
Inapplicability of provisions, §12-19-155.
Courtrooms and judicial and clerical facilities, §12-19-4.
Notice.
Administrative fee for periodic payments, §12-19-26.
Officers and employees.
Benefits.
State assumption of retirement and other employee benefits, §12-17-4.
Compensation.
Establishment of rates, §12-17-2.
Conferences, seminars, etc., §12-1-18.
Controversies as to composition of court personnel.
Determination, §12-17-1.
County personnel serving district courts to become employees of state, §12-17-1.

DISTRICT COURTS—Cont'd
Officers and employees —Cont'd
Expenses.
Reimbursement for expenses incurred at locations other than principal court site, §12-17-3.
Reimbursement of travel expenses for attending conferences, seminars, etc., §12-1-18.
Job descriptions.
Establishment, §12-17-2.
Merit system, §12-17-1.
Retirement system, §12-17-1.
State assumption of retirement and other employee benefits, §12-17-4.
State employee personnel system.
Court personnel included in, §12-17-2.
Papers.
Substitution of lost or destroyed papers or records in civil cases, §§12-20-26 to 12-20-31.
See COURTS.
Pensions.
Judges.
Retirement generally, §§12-18-50 to 12-18-61.
See within this heading, "Judges."
Transfer of contributions and creditable service to judicial retirement fund, §§12-18-110 to 12-18-114.
Probate courts.
Adoption proceedings in.
Transfer to district court, §12-12-35.
Property.
Seizure, ARCP, Rule 64 (b).
Records.
Maintenance, §12-12-2.
Preparation, §12-12-2.
Reporters.
Employment, §12-12-2.
Substitution of lost or destroyed records in civil cases, §§12-20-26 to 12-20-31.
Traffic tickets, §12-12-54.
Transcripts, §12-12-2.
Referees.
Juvenile cases, §12-17-330.
Reporters.
Employment, §12-12-2.
Official court reporters, ARJA, Rule 12.
State employees' retirement system.
Election of coverage, §36-27-52.
Roving reporters, ARJA, Rule 12.
Special court reporters.
Request for, ARJA, Rule 12.
Roving reporters, ARJA, Rule 12.
Reports.
Monthly reports as to fines, fees, etc., §12-1-19.

DISTRICT COURTS—Cont'd
Retirement.
Judges.
Generally, §§12-18-50 to 12-18-61. See within this heading, "Judges."
Transfer of contributions and creditable service to judicial retirement fund, §§12-18-110 to 12-18-114.
Officers and employees, §§12-17-1, 12-17-4.
Rules of civil procedure.
Applicability of Alabama rules of civil procedure, §12-12-11.
Depositions.
Persons before whom depositions taken, ARCP, Rule 28 (dc).
Local court rules and administrative orders.
Applicability to district courts, ARCP, Rule 83 (dc).
Seizure of property, ARCP, Rule 64 (b).
Rules of judicial administration.
See COURTS.
Salaries.
Court personnel, §12-17-2.
Judges. See within this heading, "Judges."
Salvage.
Exhibition of property to district court, §35-13-2.
Seal of court, ARJA, Rule 24.
Secretaries.
Clerks of court.
Secretaries for clerks, §12-17-341.
Judicial secretaries, §12-17-340.
Seizure of property, ARCP, Rule 64 (b).
Service of process.
Defendant service fees, §12-19-73.
Witness subpoenas.
Fee, §12-19-74.
Sessions of court.
Location, §12-12-1.
Ships and shipping.
Jurisdiction of offenses, §§33-5-32.
Small claims.
Jurisdiction, §12-12-31.
Sundays.
Clerks of court.
Office hours, ARJA, Rule 5.
Supervision by presiding circuit judges, §12-12-10.
Traffic offenses.
Definition of traffic infraction, §12-12-50.
Docket fees.
Distribution of docket fees, §12-19-179.
Provisions not to increase municipal share of docket fees, §12-19-155.
Fines, ARJA, Rule 20.
Provisions not to increase municipal share of docket fees, §12-19-155.

DISTRICT COURTS—Cont'd
Traffic offenses—Cont'd
Fines—Cont'd
Schedules, §12-12-55;
ARJA, Rule 20.
Guilty pleas.
Receipt by magistrates,
§12-12-52.
Jurisdiction.
Misdemeanor prosecutions,
§12-12-51.
Magistrates.
Receipt of guilty pleas,
§12-12-52.
Records.
Traffic tickets, §12-12-54.
Tickets.
Records and reports,
§12-12-54.
Uniform traffic ticket and
complaint, §§12-12-53,
12-12-54, 12-12-56.
Transcripts, §12-12-2.
Transfer of actions.
Improperly located actions,
§12-12-36.
Trial.
Generally, §12-12-3.
Venue, §12-12-36.
Writs.
Issuance, §12-12-7.

DISTRICT OF COLUMBIA.
Constitutional provisions,
Const. U. S., Art. I, §8.

DISTRICTS.
Congress.
State divided into
congressional districts,
§17-20-1.
Drainage subdistricts,
§§9-9-70 to 9-9-80.
See WATER
MANAGEMENT AND
DRAINAGE.
Education.
See EDUCATION.
Elections.
See ELECTIONS.
Firefighting districts.
Lee County, Const. Ala.,
amd. 392.
Funerals.
Board of funeral service.
Membership districts,
§34-13-20.
Gas districts, §§11-50-390 to
11-50-417.
See MUNICIPAL
CORPORATIONS.
Independent school districts.
Boards of education,
§§16-1-6, 16-3-27.
Legislative districts.
See LEGISLATURE.
Libraries.
Interstate library districts,
§§41-8-21, 41-8-24.
Municipal corporations.
See MUNICIPAL
CORPORATIONS.
Power districts, §§37-5-1 to
37-5-9.
See POWER DISTRICTS.
Schools.
Independent school districts.
Boards of education,
§§16-1-6, 16-3-27.

DISTRICTS—Cont'd
Soil and water conservation,
§§9-8-20 to 9-8-32.
See SOIL AND WATER
CONSERVATION.
Tax increment districts,
§§11-99-1 to 11-99-10.
See TAX INCREMENT
DISTRICTS.
Telephones.
Emergency telephone service.
Communications districts,
§§11-98-2, 11-98-4.
Water management districts,
§§9-9-1 to 9-9-58; Const.
Ala., amd. 257.
See WATER
MANAGEMENT AND
DRAINAGE.
**Water, sewer and fire
protection districts,**
§§11-89-1 to 11-89-19.
See WATER, SEWER AND
FIRE PROTECTION
DISTRICTS.
**Watershed conservancy
districts,** §§9-8-50 to
9-8-67.
See SOIL AND WATER
CONSERVATION.
Youth services.
Department of youth
services, §§44-1-20 to
44-1-40.
See YOUTH SERVICES.
Zoning.
Municipal corporations.
See MUNICIPAL
CORPORATIONS.

DISTURBING THE PEACE.
Courts, §12-1-8.
Interference with judicial
proceedings,
§13A-10-130.

DITCHES.
Counties.
Acquisition of lands for
drainage ditches,
§11-14-23.
Conduct of condemnation
proceedings, §11-14-24.
Dams.
Erection of dams for mills,
gins, factories or electric
generators.
Construction of ditches
through adjoining
lands, §18-2-16.
**Drains and drainage
generally.**
See DRAINS AND
DRAINAGE.

DIVIDENDS.
**Banks and financial
institutions.**
See BANKS AND
FINANCIAL
INSTITUTIONS.
Corporations.
See CORPORATIONS.
Credit unions, §5-17-20.
**Savings and loan
associations.**
See SAVINGS AND LOAN
ASSOCIATIONS.

DIVORCE AND ALIMONY.
Alimony and support,
§§30-2-50 to 30-2-55.
Action for divorce pending,
§30-2-50.
Attorneys' fees, §30-2-54.
Child custody and support.
See MINORS.
Cohabitation of spouse.
Termination of alimony
upon, §30-2-55; Const.
Ala., amd. 390.
Desertion and nonsupport.
See DESERTION AND
NONSUPPORT.
Divorce a mensa et thoro,
§30-2-31.
Grant of divorce.
Generally, §30-2-51.
Misconduct of spouse,
§30-2-52.
Misconduct of spouse,
§30-2-52.
Nonsupport.
See DESERTION AND
NONSUPPORT.
Pending in action for divorce,
§30-2-50.
Remarriage of spouse.
Termination of alimony,
§30-2-55; Const. Ala.,
amd. 390.
Termination of alimony.
Upon remarriage or
cohabitation with
member of opposite
sex, §30-2-55; Const.
Ala., amd. 390.
A mensa et thoro, §§30-2-30,
30-2-31.
Alimony, §30-2-31.
Child support, §30-2-31.
Custody of children, §30-2-31.
Grounds, §30-2-30.
Proceedings.
Generally, §30-2-31.
A vinculo, §§30-2-1 to 30-2-12.
A mensa et thoro.
In effect for more than two
years, §30-2-2.
Answer.
Effect, §30-2-7.
Not required to be sworn,
§30-2-7.
Collusion.
Judgment of divorce not to
be rendered, §30-2-3.
Complaint.
Place of filing, §30-2-4.
Condonation.
Judgment of divorce not to
be rendered, §30-2-3.
Filing.
Complaint.
Place of filing, §30-2-4.
Grounds, §30-2-1.
Pregnancy of wife at time
of marriage.
Issue deemed
illegitimate,
§30-2-12.
Injunctions.
Wife may be enjoined from
use of given name or
initials of divorced
husband, §30-2-11.
Judgment.
Awarded to both parties,
§30-2-1.

DIVORCE AND ALIMONY
—Cont'd
A vinculo—Cont'd
Judgment—Cont'd
Refusal.
Collusion between
parties, §30-2-3.
Condonation, §30-2-3.
Jurisdiction, §30-2-1.
Minors.
When husband or wife may
sue or defend in own
name, §30-2-6.
Name.
Wife may be enjoined from
use of given name of
divorced husband,
§30-2-11.
Nonresidents.
Complaint.
Place of filing, §30-2-4.
Residency requirement,
§30-2-5.
Proceedings.
Generally, §30-2-8.
Remarriage.
Restrictions.
Appeal of divorce,
§30-2-10.
Sixty-day restrictions,
§30-2-10.
Validation of remarriage
not specifically
prohibited, §30-2-9.
Venue, §30-2-4.
Certificates.
General provisions.
See VITAL STATISTICS.
Child custody and support.
See MINORS.
**Cohabitation with member
of the opposite sex.**
Termination of alimony,
§30-2-55; Const. Ala.,
amd. 390.
Constitution of Alabama.
Special, private or local laws
prohibited, Const. Ala.,
art. IV, §104.
Custody.
Child custody and support.
See MINORS.
Default judgments.
Proof required despite
default, ARCP, Rule 55
(e).
District court judges.
Designation to handle cases
in districts having more
than one judge,
§12-17-70.
**Divorce from bed and
board.** See within this
heading, "A mensa et
thoro."
**Divorce from bonds of
matrimony,** §§30-2-1 to
30-2-12. See within this
heading, "A vinculo."
Evidence.
Exclusion of audience where
evidence vulgar, etc.,
§12-21-9.
Fees.
Department of human
resources.
Investigation services fees,
§30-3-7.
Grandparents.
Visitation rights, §30-3-4.

DIVORCE AND ALIMONY
—Cont'd
Investigations.
Department of human
resources.
Fees, §30-3-7.
Minors.
Child custody and support,
§30-3-1.
Award of visitation rights
to grandparents,
§30-3-4.
Venue of proceedings
seeking modification of
child custody,
visitation rights or
child support, §30-3-5.
Nonsupport.
See DESERTION AND
NONSUPPORT.
Remarriage.
Restrictions.
Appeal of divorce, §30-2-10.
Sixty-day restrictions,
§30-2-10.
Termination of alimony,
§30-2-55.
Validation of remarriage not
specifically prohibited,
§30-2-9.
Separation.
Bed and board, §§30-2-2,
30-2-30.
Support.
Generally, §§30-2-50 to
30-2-55.
Venue.
A vinculo, §30-2-4.
Visitation.
Generally, §§30-3-4 to 30-3-6.
Vital statistics.
See VITAL STATISTICS.
Wills.
Effect of divorce, §43-8-252.
Revocation of will by divorce,
§43-8-137.

DOCKETS.
Appeals.
Docket fee, ARAP, Rule 12
(a).
Docketing appeals, ARAP,
Rule 12 (a).
Call of cases, ARJA, Rule 16.
Circuit courts.
Civil docket, ARCP, Rule 79
(a).
Fees.
Civil cases. See within this
heading, "Fees."
Criminal cases. See within
this heading, "Fees."
Corporations.
Prosecution of corporations.
Docketing notice of
indictment, §10-7-1.
District courts.
Fees.
Civil cases. See within this
heading, "Fees."
Criminal cases. See within
this heading, "Fees."
**Executors and
administrators.**
Insolvent estates.
Claims against insolvent
estates.
Claims docket,
§43-2-745.
Fees.
Appeals, ARAP, Rule 12 (a).

DOCKETS—Cont'd
Fees—Cont'd
Civil cases.
Circuit and district court
docket fee.
Amount, §12-19-71.
Applicability of
provisions,
§12-19-25.
Collection, §12-19-70.
Creation, §12-19-70.
Distribution, §12-19-72.
Payment of circuit court
docket fee upon
appeals from district
courts to circuit
courts, §12-19-51.
Taxation as costs at
conclusion of case,
§12-19-70.
Waiver and taxation as
costs at conclusion of
case, §12-19-70.
Criminal cases.
Amount of docket fees.
Circuit and district
courts, §12-19-171.
Circuit courts generally,
§12-19-171.
Collection of docket fees
and fines where
defendants convicted of
misdemeanors confess
judgment for fees and
fines, §12-19-151.
Conservation cases,
§12-19-170.
Distribution of docket fees.
Circuit court felony
cases, §12-19-174.
Circuit court
misdemeanor cases,
§12-19-175.
District court felony
guilty pleas,
§12-19-176.
District court
misdemeanor cases,
§12-19-178.
District court
preliminary
hearings,
§12-19-177.
District court traffic
infractions,
§12-19-179.
Felony cases in circuit
court, §12-19-174.
Felony guilty pleas in
district court,
§12-19-176.
Forfeiture of bond.
District and circuit
court cases,
§12-19-173.
Misdemeanor cases in
circuit court,
§12-19-175.
Misdemeanor cases in
district court,
§12-19-178.
Municipal ordinance
cases.
Fees collected in
district and circuit
courts, §12-19-154.
Inapplicability of
provisions,
§12-19-155.

DOCKETS—Cont'd
Fees—Cont'd
Criminal cases—Cont'd
Distribution of docket fees —Cont'd
Preliminary hearings in district court, §12-19-177.
Traffic violations in district court, §12-19-179.
District courts generally, §12-19-171.
Juvenile courts, §12-19-171.
Municipal ordinance cases, §12-19-154.
Amounts of docket fees in circuit and district courts, §12-19-172.
Uniformity of docket fees, §12-19-170.
Municipal ordinance cases.
Inapplicability of provisions, §12-19-155.
Probate judges, §12-19-90.
Juvenile proceedings.
Inspection of court dockets, §12-15-100.
Separate docket, §12-15-2.

DOCKS.
Booms and bulkheads.
See BOOMS AND BULKHEADS.
Constitution of Alabama.
Conveyance of state docks property to local authorities, Const. Ala., amds. 443, 454.
General provisions.
See HARBORS AND PORTS.
Inland waterways.
Development of docks along inland waterways, §§33-2-1 to 33-2-196; Const. Ala., amds. 116, 274, 288.
See WATERS AND WATERCOURSES.
State docks department.
See HARBORS AND PORTS.
State docks property.
Conveyance to local authorities, Const. Ala., amd. 443.

DOG RACING.
Definitions.
Pari-mutuel pool tax, §40-26A-1.
Pari-mutuel betting.
Legalized betting not affected by gambling article, §13A-12-31.
Pari-mutuel pool tax.
Administration and enforcement of chapter.
Appropriations, §40-26A-17.
Amount, §40-26A-2.
Assessment.
Appeals, §40-26A-10.
Hearings, §40-26A-9.
Notice, §40-26A-9.
When department to make assessment, §40-26A-7.
Collection.
Civil actions, §40-26A-13.
Debt due state, §40-26A-13.

DOG RACING—Cont'd
Pari-mutuel pool tax—Cont'd
Deficiencies.
Collection, §40-26A-8.
Definitions, §40-26A-1.
Effect on other licenses and taxes, §40-26A-11.
Enforcement of chapter, §40-26A-16.
Appropriation, §40-26A-17.
Injunctions.
Violators restrained from continuing in business, §40-26A-14.
Writ of injunction authorized, §40-26A-15.
Levy, §40-26A-2.
Licenses.
Effect on other licenses and taxes, §40-26A-11.
Limitation of action.
Collection of tax, §40-26A-13.
Payment.
Failure to pay when due.
Penalty, §40-26A-6.
When due and payable, §40-26A-3.
Penalties.
Execution, levy and sale of property, §40-26A-12.
Failure to pay tax when due, §40-26A-6.
Proceeds.
Disposition, §40-26A-17.
Property.
Execution, levy and sale, §40-26A-12.
Records.
Audits, §40-26A-8.
Examination, §40-26A-4.
Maintaining, §40-26A-4.
Refunds, §40-26A-8.
Reports.
Failure to make, §40-26A-5.
Monthly report, §40-26A-3.
Returns.
When department to make returns, §40-26A-7.
Rules and regulations.
Promulgation, §40-26A-16.
Sale of property, §40-26A-12.
Violations.
Restrain from continuing in business, §40-26A-14.
Writ of injunction authorized, §40-26A-15.
Sales tax.
Admissions to track or handle.
Sales tax exemption, §40-11-5.
Taxation.
Exemptions.
Admissions and handle.
Sales tax exemption, §40-11-5.
Validity of prior exemptions, §40-11-5.
Imposition on dog tracks, §40-11-5.
Payment of taxes.
Taxes required to be paid, §40-11-5.

DOG RACING—Cont'd
Taxation—Cont'd
Track pari-mutuel pool tax, §§40-26A-1 to 40-26A-17.
See within this heading, "Pari-mutuel pool tax."

DOGS.
Abandonment.
Destruction of certain abandoned animals, §3-1-8.
Animals generally.
See ANIMALS.
Assembly.
Killing dogs used by peace officers.
Persons violating provisions of section during course of orderly demonstrations.
Inapplicability of section, §13A-11-15.
Biting or injuring persons, §§3-6-1 to 3-6-4.
Construction of chapter, §3-6-4.
Damages.
Mitigation, §3-6-3.
Liability of owner.
Person bitten or injured while upon property owned or controlled by owner, §3-6-1.
Mitigation of damages, §3-6-3.
Rabies.
General provisions, §§3-7-1 to 3-7-13.
See RABIES.
Liability of owner for injuries caused by rabid dog, §3-1-2.
When person deemed lawfully on property of owner of dog, §3-6-2.
Blind persons.
Guide dogs.
See BLIND PERSONS.
Construction and interpretation.
Dogs biting or injuring persons.
Construction of chapter, §3-6-4.
Contraband.
Fighting dogs.
Confiscation, §3-1-29.
Counties.
Permitting dogs to run at large, §3-1-5.
Criminal law and procedure.
Killing dogs used by peace officers, §13A-11-15.
Destruction.
Abandoned animals, §3-1-8.
Fees.
Trainers' licenses, §9-11-52.
Felonies.
Killing dogs used by peace officers.
Class C felony, §13A-11-15.
Fighting of dogs.
Prohibited, §3-1-29.
Fish and game.
See FISH AND GAME.
Guide dogs.
Blind persons.
See BLIND PERSONS.

DOGS—Cont'd
Impoundment.
Rabies.
Dogs running at large,
§§3-7-7, 3-7-8.
Wildlife management areas,
§9-11-306.
Injuring persons, §§3-6-1 to
3-6-4.
Inoculation.
Rabies, §§3-7-2, 3-7-3.
**Killing dogs used by peace
officers,** §13A-11-15.
Licenses.
Shows, §40-12-111.
Trainers, §9-11-52.
Livestock.
Killing or injuring livestock.
Keeping of dog known to
kill, etc., prohibited,
§3-1-1.
Liability of owners, §3-1-1.
Injuries to livestock
caused by dog while
off premises of
owner, §§3-1-1,
3-1-6.
Permitting dog known to
kill or injure to run at
large, §3-1-4.
Rabid dogs.
Liability of owner for
injuries caused by
rabid dog, §3-1-2.
Municipal corporations.
Canine leash ordinances.
Procedure for adoption or
repeal, §11-45-10.
Dogs running at large,
§11-47-110.
Notice.
Wildlife management areas.
Impoundment of dogs,
§9-11-306.
Peace officers.
Killing dogs used by peace
officers, §13A-11-15.
Penalties.
Fighting of dogs, §3-1-29.
Trainers.
Training without license,
§9-11-52.
Rabies.
General provisions, §§3-7-1 to
3-7-13.
See RABIES.
Liability of owner for injuries
caused by rabid dog,
§3-1-2.
Race tracks.
Generally.
See DOG RACING.
Running at large.
Impoundment of dogs
running at large.
Rabies, §§3-7-7, 3-7-8.
Liability of owner for injuries
to livestock, etc., caused
by dog while off premises
of owner, §3-1-6.
Municipal corporations.
Canine leash ordinances,
§11-45-10.
Impoundment and
destruction,
§11-47-110.

DOGS—Cont'd
Running at large—Cont'd
Permitting dogs to run at
large, §3-1-5.
Applicability of provisions
of section in counties
and certain cities or
towns, §3-1-5.
Dog known to kill or injure
livestock, §3-1-4.
Wildlife management areas.
Impoundment, §9-11-306.
Liability of owners,
§9-11-305.
Seeing eye dogs.
Guide dogs.
See BLIND PERSONS.
**Societies for prevention of
cruelty to animals.**
Destruction of certain
abandoned animals,
§3-1-8.
Tags.
Rabies, §§3-7-4 to 3-7-6.
Trainers.
Licenses.
Fees, §9-11-52.
Required, §9-11-52.
Training without license,
§9-11-52.
Veterinarians.
See VETERINARIANS.
Wildlife management areas.
Impoundment, §9-11-306.
Running at large.
Liability of owners,
§9-11-305.
When dogs permitted in
areas, §9-11-305.

DOLPHINS.
Marine mammal protection,
§§9-11-390 to 9-11-398.
See MARINE MAMMAL
PROTECTION.

DOMESTIC RELATIONS.
Abuse.
Domestic violence facilities,
§§30-6-1 to 30-6-13.
See DOMESTIC
VIOLENCE
FACILITIES.
Investigative reports,
§15-22-31.
Protection from abuse
generally, §§30-5-1 to
30-5-11. See within this
heading, "Protection
from abuse."
Adoption.
See ADOPTION.
Alimony.
See DIVORCE AND
ALIMONY.
Attorneys at law.
Protection from abuse
hearings.
Right to counsel, §30-5-6.
Bastards.
See ILLEGITIMACY.
Child support.
Withholding orders.
General provisions,
§§30-3-60 to 30-3-71.
Interstate income
withholding, §§30-3-90
to 30-3-99.
See CHILD SUPPORT.
Definitions.
Domestic violence facilities,
§30-6-1.

DOMESTIC RELATIONS
—Cont'd
Definitions—Cont'd
Protection from abuse,
§30-5-2.
Desertion and nonsupport.
See DESERTION AND
NONSUPPORT.
Divorce and alimony.
See DIVORCE AND
ALIMONY.
Domestic violence facilities,
§§30-6-1 to 30-6-13.
See DOMESTIC VIOLENCE
FACILITIES.
Husband and wife.
See HUSBAND AND WIFE.
Illegitimacy.
See ILLEGITIMACY.
Jurisdiction.
Protection from abuse cases,
§30-5-3.
Legitimation of children.
Fees.
Probate judges' fees,
§12-19-90.
General provisions, §§26-11-1
to 26-11-3.
Special, private or local laws
prohibited, Const. Ala.,
art. IV, §104.
Marriage.
See MARRIAGE.
Parent and child.
See PARENT AND CHILD.
Protection from abuse,
§§30-5-1 to 30-5-11.
Agreements.
Violation.
Contempt, §30-5-10.
Attorneys at law.
Right to counsel, §30-5-6.
Citation of act.
Short title, §30-5-1.
Construction and
intrepretation, §30-5-11.
Contempt.
Violation of protection
order or agreement,
§30-5-10.
Definitions, §30-5-2.
Domestic violence facilities.
General provisions,
§§30-6-1 to 30-6-13.
See DOMESTIC
VIOLENCE
FACILITIES.
Hearings.
Petition for relief.
Hearing on, §30-5-6.
Petition filed where
court unavailable,
§30-5-9.
Jurisdiction, §30-5-3.
Leaving household.
Right to relief not affected
by, §30-5-4.
Orders of court.
Copies.
Issuance, §30-5-8.
Protection orders, §30-5-7.
Amendment, §30-5-7.
Violation.
Contempt, §30-5-10.
Temporary orders, §30-5-6.
Petition for relief, §30-5-5.
Court unavailable.
Filing petition, §30-5-9.
Hearing on, §30-5-6.
Rules of civil procedure.
Applicability, §30-5-10.

DOMESTIC RELATIONS
—Cont'd
Protection from abuse
—Cont'd
Title of act.
Short title, §30-5-1.
Service by publication,
ARCP, Rule 4.3 (e).
Support and maintenance.
Divorce and alimony.
See DIVORCE AND
ALIMONY.
**Withholding for child
support.**
General provisions, §§30-3-60
to 30-3-71.
See CHILD SUPPORT.
Interstate income
withholding, §§30-3-90 to
30-3-99.
See CHILD SUPPORT.

**DOMESTIC VIOLENCE
FACILITIES,** §§30-6-1 to
30-6-13.
Boards.
Composition, §30-6-6.
Budgets.
Submission to office, §30-6-6.
Certification of facilities.
Requirements, §30-6-6.
Civil liability.
Immunity from, §30-6-12.
**Confidentiality of
information,** §30-6-8.
**Construction and
interpretation,** §30-6-13.
Definitions, §30-6-1.
District attorneys.
Duties, §30-6-4.
Inspection of facilities,
§30-6-3.
Reports to office, §30-6-5.
Establishment, §30-6-6.
Fees, §30-6-11.
Funding of facilities.
Distribution of funds,
§30-6-11.
Limitation on appropriation
and expenditure of funds,
§30-6-7.
Maximum amount, §30-6-6.
Requirements, §30-6-6.
Use of unspent funds,
§30-6-11.
Immunity.
Civil liability, §30-6-12.
Inspections, §30-6-3.
Law enforcement officers.
Advising persons of available
facilities, §30-6-9.
Legislative declaration,
§30-6-2.
**Office of prosecution
services.**
Definition of "office," §30-6-1.
Duties, §30-6-3.
Inspection of facilities,
§30-6-3.
Reports to legislature,
§30-6-5.
Rules and regulations,
§30-6-10.
Reports.
District attorneys.
Reports to office, §30-6-5.
Office of prosecution services.
Reports to legislature,
§30-6-5.
Rules and regulations,
§30-6-10.

DORA, MUNICIPALITY OF.
Property tax, Const. Ala.,
amd. 13.

DORMITORIES.
**Barbers, beauticians or
cosmetologists.**
Use of shop or parlor as
dormitory, §22-17-11.

DOUBLE JEOPARDY.
Constitution of Alabama,
Const. Ala., art. I, §9.
**Constitution of the United
States,** Const. U. S.,
Amendment V.
Juvenile proceedings,
§12-15-66.
Rules of criminal procedure,
ARCrP, Rules 15.3 (f), 15.4
(g).

**DOUBLE SPRINGS,
MUNICIPALITY OF.**
Economic development,
Const. Ala., amd. 104.

DOWER.
Abolished, §43-8-57.
Appeals.
Ascertainment and payment
of dower interests,
§35-4-192.
**Ascertainment and payment
of dower interests,**
§§35-4-190 to 35-4-192.
Appeals, §35-4-192.
Application, §35-4-191.
Costs, §35-4-191.
Guardian ad litem.
Appointment, §35-4-191.
Hearing, §35-4-191.
Mentally ill.
Appointment of guardian
ad litem, §35-4-191.
Minors.
Appointment of guardian
ad litem, §35-4-191.
Notice, §35-4-191.
Present value.
Duty of court to ascertain,
§35-4-190.
Value.
Duty of court to ascertain
present value,
§35-4-190.
Witnesses, §35-4-191.
Costs.
Ascertainment and payment
of interest, §35-4-191.
Fees.
Probate judges' fees,
§12-19-90.
Forests and forestry.
Auxiliary state forests.
Designation of lands.
Release of dower,
§9-13-42.
Guardian ad litem.
Ascertainment and payment
of dower interests.
Appointment, §35-4-191.
Hearings.
Ascertainment and payment
of dower interests,
§35-4-191.
**Jurisdiction of probate
courts,** §12-13-1.
Notice.
Ascertainment and payment,
§35-4-191.

DOWER—Cont'd
Partnerships.
Property not subject to
dower, §10-8-72.
Payment of dower interests,
§§35-4-109 to 35-4-192.
Probate code.
Abolished, §43-8-57.
Probate courts.
Jurisdiction, §12-13-1.
Value of dower interests,
§§35-4-190 to 35-4-192.
Witnesses.
Ascertainment and payment,
§35-4-191.

**DOWNTOWN
REDEVELOPMENT
AUTHORITIES,** §§11-54A-1
to 11-54A-24.
Board of directors,
§11-54A-7.
Bond issues, §§11-54A-10 to
11-54A-15.
Execution, §11-54A-10.
Form, §11-54A-10.
Interest, §11-54A-10.
Investments.
Eligibility, §11-54A-10.
Liability of city, §11-54A-15.
Maturity, §11-54A-10.
Nature of obligation,
§11-54A-10.
Negotiability, §11-54A-10.
Notice.
Bond resolution,
§11-54A-13.
Payment.
Source of, §11-54A-10.
Pledge of revenues, receipts
and other security,
§11-54A-10.
Refunding bonds,
§11-54A-12.
Sale, §11-54A-10.
Proceeds, §11-54A-11.
Tax exempt, §11-54A-14.
Validity.
Time to bring action to
question validity,
§11-54A-13.
Bonds, surety.
Treasurer, §11-54A-8.
Certificate of incorporation,
§§11-54A-5, 11-54A-6.
Contracts.
Exemption from competitive
bid laws, §11-54A-17.
Definitions, §11-54A-2.
Use of phrases, §11-54A-3.
Dissolution, §11-54A-20.
Vesting of title to property in
city, §11-54A-20.
Earnings.
Disposition, §11-54A-19.
Existing authorities,
§11-54A-24.
**Freedom from state
supervision and control,**
§11-54A-18.
Incorporation.
Application, §11-54A-4.
Authorization, §11-54A-4.
Certificate of incorporation,
§§11-54A-5, 11-54A-6.
Existence of authority to
prevent incorporation of
another, §11-54A-21.
Procedure.
Generally, §11-54A-5.

DOWNTOWN REDEVELOPMENT AUTHORITIES—Cont'd
Interest.
Bond issues, §11-54A-10.
Exemption from usury and interest laws, §11-54A-16.
Investments.
Bond issues.
Eligibility for investments, §11-54A-10.
Legislative intent, §11-54A-1.
Liability of city.
Bond issues, §11-54A-15.
Loans.
To authorities by counties, municipalities, etc., §11-54A-22.
Nonprofit corporations, §11-54A-19.
Notice.
Bond resolution, §11-54A-13.
Officers, §11-54A-8.
Pledges.
Revenues, receipts and other security, §11-54A-10.
Powers.
Generally, §11-54A-9.
Prior law.
Authorities organized under, §11-54A-24.
Projects.
Location, §11-54A-9.
Provisions of chapter cumulative, §11-54A-23.
Purpose of chapter, §11-54A-1.
Refunding bonds, §11-54A-12.
Sales.
Bond issues, §11-54A-10.
Proceeds from sale, §11-54A-11.
State supervision and control.
Freedom from, §11-54A-18.
Taxation.
Exemption from taxation, §11-54A-14.
Use of phrases, §11-54A-3.

DRAFTS.
Banks and financial institutions.
Checks.
See BANKS AND FINANCIAL INSTITUTIONS.
Commercial paper, §§7-3-101 to 7-3-805.
See COMMERCIAL CODE.
General provisions.
See CHECKS.
Negotiable instruments generally.
See NEGOTIABLE INSTRUMENTS.
Sale of checks, §§8-7-1 to 8-7-15.
See CHECKS.
Worthless checks.
Negotiating worthless checks, §§13A-9-13.1 to 13A-9-13.3.

DRAINS AND DRAINAGE.
Constitution of Alabama.
Establishment and maintenance of drainage systems, Const. Ala., amds. 15, 22.

DRAINS AND DRAINAGE —Cont'd
Construction works.
Duty to drain areas in, §22-20-10.
Counties.
Acquisition of lands for drainage ditches, §11-14-23.
Conduct of condemnation proceedings, §11-14-24.
Subdivisions.
Regulation by counties, §11-24-1.
Districts.
Establishment and maintenance of drainage systems, Const. Ala., amds. 15, 22.
Municipal corporations.
Connections to drains.
Regulation, installation, etc., §§11-50-53, 11-50-54.
Construction and maintenance of drains, §11-50-50.
Regulation, installation, etc., of drains, §11-50-54.
Prisons and prisoners.
Convict labor.
County convicts, §§14-5-6, 14-5-8.
State convicts, §§14-5-7, 14-5-9.
Subdistricts, §§9-9-70 to 9-9-80.
See WATER MANAGEMENT AND DRAINAGE.
Subdivisions.
County regulation, §11-24-1.
Water management and drainage, §§9-9-1 to 9-9-58; Const. Ala., amd. 257.
See WATER MANAGEMENT AND DRAINAGE.

DRAM SHOP ACT, §6-5-71.

DRAWBRIDGES.
Bridges generally.
See BRIDGES.
Railroad drawbridges.
Steamboats passing through, §37-2-88.

DREDGES AND DREDGING.
Marine resources.
See MARINE RESOURCES.
Riparian owners.
Dredging or cleaning creeks, etc., running through property, §33-7-54.
Limitations on right, §33-7-54.

DRINKING CUPS.
Public places.
Use prohibited, §22-20-1.

DRINKING WATER.
Safe drinking water act, §§22-23-30 to 22-23-53.
See WATER SUPPLY AND WATERWORKS.

DRIVER EDUCATION.
Driver training schools.
See MOTOR VEHICLES.
General provisions, §§16-40-5.1 to 16-40-5.4.

DRIVERS' LICENSES.
See MOTOR VEHICLES.

DRIVER TRAINING SCHOOLS.
See MOTOR VEHICLES.

DRIVING UNDER THE INFLUENCE.
See MOTOR VEHICLES.

DROUGHT.
Fires and fire prevention.
Emergency drought conditions, §§9-13-140 to 9-13-142.

DRUGGISTS AND DRUGSTORES.
See PHARMACISTS AND PHARMACIES.

DRUGS.
Addicts.
Curators.
Appointment, §§26-7A-1 to 26-7A-17.
See GUARDIAN AND WARD.
Uniform guardianship and protective proceedings act, §§26-2A-1 to 26-2A-160.
See GUARDIAN AND WARD.
Administration of chapter, applicability of administrative provisions of Title 2, §20-1-1.
Adulteration and misbranding.
Dealers.
Exemption from prosecution, §20-1-32.
Definitions, §20-1-20.
Manufacturers.
Effect of possession by manufacturer, §20-1-31.
Pharmacists and pharmacies.
See PHARMACISTS AND PHARMACIES.
Purpose of division, §20-1-21.
Sales, §20-1-27.
Standards of purity.
Board of agriculture and industries to fix, §20-1-21.
When drugs deemed adulterated, §20-1-24.
When drugs deemed misbranded, §20-1-26.
Advertising.
Imitation controlled substances, §20-2-143.
Aged persons.
Sales tax exemption, §40-23-4.
Amphetamines.
Controlled substances generally, §§20-2-1 to 20-2-144. See within this heading, "Controlled substances."
Appeals.
Controlled substances.
Manufacturers and distributors.
Denial, refusal, revocation or suspension, §20-2-53.

DRUGS—Cont'd
Attempts.
Controlled substances.
Attempt to commit controlled substance crime, §13A-12-203.
Included offenses, §13A-12-205.
Auctions.
Notice of sale, §34-23-6.
Bail and recognizance.
Municipal ordinance violations.
Discretionary bail schedule, ARJA, Rule 2.
Bankruptcy.
Notice of bankruptcy sale of drugs and medicines, §34-23-6.
Barbituates.
Controlled substances generally, §§20-2-1 to 20-2-144. See within this heading, "Controlled substances."
Board of agriculture and industries.
Rulemaking power, §20-1-2.
Standards of purity.
Board to fix, §20-1-21.
Boats.
Prohibited operations, §33-5-24.
Brands and marks.
Adulteration and misbranding. See within this heading, "Adulteration and misbranding."
Pharmacists and pharmacies. See PHARMACISTS AND PHARMACIES.
Cannabis.
Therapeutic research, §§20-2-110 to 20-2-120.
See within this heading, "Therapeutic research."
Capsules.
Marking or imprinting required, §20-1-150.
Circuit courts.
Controlled substances.
Manufacturers and distributors.
Review in circuit court of Montgomery county for denial, nonrenewal, suspension or revocation of registration, §20-2-53.
Commissioner of agriculture and industries.
Enforcement of chapter, §20-1-1.
Right of entry by commissioner and agents, §20-1-3.
Conspiracy.
Controlled substances.
Criminal conspiracy to commit controlled substance crime, §13A-12-204.
Included offenses, §13A-12-205.

DRUGS—Cont'd
Contracts.
Therapeutic research.
Contracts for receipt of cannabis, §20-2-117.
Controlled substances, §§20-2-1 to 20-2-144.
Administration of chapter, §20-2-20.
Attempt to commit controlled substance crime, §13A-12-203.
Included offenses, §13A-12-205.
Board of dental examiners.
Enforcement of chapter, §20-2-90.
Board of health.
Enforcement of chapter, §20-2-90.
Board of medical examiners.
Enforcement of chapter, §20-2-90.
Board of pharmacy.
Enforcement of chapter, §20-2-90.
Certifying boards.
Fees.
Power to charge, §20-2-50.
Rulemaking power, §20-2-50.
Consent for health services.
Consent of any minor as to drug dependency, §22-8-6.
Conspiracy to commit controlled substance crime.
Criminal conspiracy, §13A-12-204.
Included offenses, §13A-12-205.
Crimes amendment act, §§13A-12-210 to 13A-12-216.
Criminal code.
Provisions of drug trafficking act included in, §13A-12-216.
Distribution of controlled substances.
Unlawful distribution.
Conduct constituting, §13A-12-211.
Felony, §13A-12-211.
Marijuana.
Possession in first degree.
Conduct constituting, §13A-12-213.
Felony, §13A-12-213.
Possession in second degree.
Conduct constituting, §13A-12-213.
Misdemeanor, §13A-12-214.
Minors.
Sale, furnishing, etc., of controlled substances to minors, §13A-12-215.
Possession.
Unlawful possession.
Conduct constituting, §13A-12-212.
Felony, §13A-12-212.

DRUGS—Cont'd
Controlled substances —Cont'd
Crimes amendment act —Cont'd
Receipt of controlled substances.
Unlawful receipt.
Conduct constituting, §13A-12-212.
Felony, §13A-12-212.
Schedules of controlled substances, §13A-12-215.
Short title, §13A-12-210.
Criminal code.
Provisions of drug trafficking act included in, §13A-12-216.
Criminal offenses.
Inchoate offenses.
Attempt to commit controlled substance crime, §13A-12-203.
Included offenses, §13A-12-205.
Conspiracy to commit controlled substance crime, §13A-12-204.
Included offenses, §13A-12-205.
Drug predator control act of 1987.
Short title, §13A-12-201.
Included offenses, §13A-12-205.
Solicitation to commit controlled substance crimes, §13A-12-202.
Included offenses, §13A-12-205.
Definitions, §20-2-2.
Drug paraphernalia, §13A-12-260.
Imitation controlled substances, §20-2-141.
Therapeutic research, §20-2-112.
Dentists.
Prescription, administration, etc., of controlled substances by dentists for persons not under treatment in regular practice, §20-2-74.
Department of public safety.
Enforcement of chapter, §20-2-90.
Distribution.
Unlawful distribution.
Criminal offense, §13A-12-211.
Driving under the influence.
See MOTOR VEHICLES.
Drug kingpen's enforcement act, §§13A-12-231, 13A-12-232.
Drug paraphernalia, §13A-12-260.
Drug predator control act of 1987, §§13A-12-201 to 13A-12-205.
Attempt to commit controlled substance crime, §13A-12-203.
Included offenses, §13A-12-205.

DRUGS—Cont'd
  Controlled substances
    —Cont'd
  Drug predator control act of
      1987—Cont'd
    Conspiracy to commit
        controlled substance
        crime.
      Criminal conspiracy,
          §13A-12-204.
      Included offenses,
          §13A-12-205.
    Included offenses,
        §13A-12-205.
    Short title, §13A-12-201.
    Solicitation to commit
        controlled substance
        crime.
      Criminal solicitation,
          §13A-12-202.
      Included offenses,
          §13A-12-205.
  Enforcement of chapter,
      §§20-2-90 to 20-2-93.
  Forfeitures, §20-2-93.
  Imitation controlled
      substances, §§20-2-140 to
      20-2-144.
  Immunity of persons
      reporting suspected use
      of controlled substance
      by minor child, §20-2-3.
  Included offenses, §20-2-164.
  Injunctions, §20-2-92.
  Inspections.
    Stocks of controlled
        substances and
        prescriptions, orders,
        etc., required by
        chapter, §20-2-91.
  Inventories.
    Manufacturers and
        distributors.
      Maintenance of
          inventories,
          §20-2-56.
      Registered pharmacies,
          §20-2-58.
  Mandatory minimum terms
      of imprisonment,
      §13A-12-231.
  Reduction, suspension, etc.,
      of sentence,
      §13A-12-232.
  Sentence not to be
      suspended, deferred,
      etc., §13A-12-232.
  Manufacturers and
      distributors.
    Administrative fines,
        §34-24-380.
    Disposition, §34-24-382.
    Certifying boards.
      Fees.
        Power to charge,
            §20-2-50.
        Rulemaking power,
            §20-2-50.
    Distribution of certain
        substances by one
        registrant to another,
        §20-2-57.
    Penalties for prohibited
        acts, §20-2-72.
    Inventories.
      Maintenance, §20-2-56.
      Registered pharmacies,
          §20-2-58.
    Penalties.
      Administrative fines,
          §34-24-380.

DRUGS—Cont'd
  Controlled substances
    —Cont'd
  Manufacturers and
      distributors—Cont'd
    Penalties—Cont'd
      Further prohibited acts,
          §20-2-72.
    Records, §20-2-56.
      Maintenance by
          registrants, §20-2-56.
      Registered pharmacies,
          §20-2-58.
    Registration.
      Appeal from denial,
          refusal, revocation or
          suspension, §20-2-53.
      Circuit court of
          Montgomery county.
        Appeal from denial,
            refusal to renew,
            revocation or
            suspension,
            §20-2-53.
      Denial, §20-2-53.
      Federal registration.
        Effect, §20-2-52.
      Fees, §20-2-50.
      General requirements,
          §20-2-51.
      Penalties for prohibited
          acts, §20-2-71.
      Refusal of renewal,
          §20-2-53.
      Requirements generally,
          §20-2-51.
      Research.
        Requirements as to
            practitioners
            conducting
            research, §20-2-52.
      Revocation or
          suspension.
        Generally, §20-2-53.
        Grounds, §20-2-54.
        Procedure, §20-2-54.
        Suspension without
            prior order to show
            cause, §20-2-55.
      Rules and regulations,
          §20-2-54.1.
        Promulgation,
            §20-2-50.
        Standards, §20-2-52.
      Supreme court.
        Appeal of denial,
            refusal to renew,
            revocation or
            suspension of
            registration,
            §20-2-53.
    Schedule II substances.
      Dispensing, §20-2-58.
      Standards, §20-2-52.
  Marijuana.
    Defined, §20-2-2.
    Possession of marijuana.
      First degree possession.
        Conduct constituting,
            §13A-12-213.
        Felony, §13A-12-213.
      Second degree
          possession.
        Conduct constituting,
            §13A-12-214.
        Misdemeanor,
            §13A-12-214.

DRUGS—Cont'd
  Controlled substances
    —Cont'd
  Minors.
    Consent for health
        services.
      Consent of any minor as
          to drug dependency,
          §22-8-6.
    Immunity of persons
        reporting suspected
        use, etc., of controlled
        substance by minor
        child, §20-2-3.
    Sale, furnishing, etc., of
        controlled substances
        to minors, §13A-2-215.
  Money.
    Forfeiture in controlled
        substance violation,
        §20-2-93.
  Motor vehicles.
    Driving under the
        influence.
      See MOTOR VEHICLES.
    Forfeiture in controlled
        substance violation,
        §20-2-93.
  Names.
    Nomenclature of controlled
        substances in
        schedules, §20-2-21.
  Paraphernalia, §13A-12-260.
  Penalties.
    Additional penalty if
        unlawful sale on or
        near school campus,
        §13A-12-250.
    Manufacturers and
        distributors, §§20-2-71,
        20-2-72.
    Minors.
      Sale, furnishing, etc., to
          minor, §13A-2-215.
    Penalties imposed by
        chapter in addition to
        other penalties,
        §20-2-78.
  Pharmacies.
    General provisions.
      See PHARMACISTS
          AND
          PHARMACIES.
    Maintenance of records and
        inventories by
        registered pharmacies,
        §20-2-58.
  Possession.
    Unlawful possession.
      Criminal offense,
          §13A-12-212.
  Predators.
    Drug predator control act
        of 1987.
      Generally, §§13A-12-201
          to 13A-12-205.
  Prescriptions, orders, etc.
    Disclosure of information
        as to prescriptions,
        orders, etc., by
        enforcement personnel,
        §20-2-91.
    Inspections, §20-2-91.
  Receipt of controlled
      substances.
    Unlawful receipt.
      Criminal offense,
          §13A-12-212.

DRUGS—Cont'd
Controlled substances
—Cont'd
Records.
Manufacturers and
distributors.
Maintenance of records,
§20-2-56.
Registered pharmacies,
§20-2-58.
Research.
Therapeutic research,
§§20-2-110 to 20-2-120.
See within this
heading, "Therapeutic
research."
Rules and regulations.
Promulgation, §20-2-54.1.
Schedules.
Addition of substances to
schedules, §20-2-20.
Crime amendments act.
References to schedule,
§13A-12-215.
Deletion of substances from
schedules, §20-2-20.
Nomenclature of controlled
substances in
schedules, §20-2-21.
Republication, §20-2-32.
Rescheduling of
substances, §20-2-20.
Revision, §20-2-32.
Schedule I.
Listing of controlled
substances, §20-2-23.
Standards for
compilation,
§20-2-22.
Schedule II.
Dispensing of controlled
substances in
schedule II, §20-2-58.
Listing of controlled
substances, §20-2-25.
Standards for
compilation,
§20-2-24.
Schedule III.
Listing of controlled
substances, §20-2-27.
Standards for
compilation,
§20-2-26.
Schedule IV.
Listing of controlled
substances, §20-2-29.
Standards for
compilation,
§20-2-28.
Schedule V.
Listing of controlled
substances, §20-2-31.
Standards for
compilation,
§20-2-30.
Schools.
Additional penalty if
unlawful sale on or
near school campus,
§13A-12-250.
Seizures, §20-2-93.
Short title of chapter,
§20-2-1.
Solicitation to commit
controlled substance
crime.
Criminal solicitation,
§13A-12-202.
Included offenses,
§13A-12-205.

DRUGS—Cont'd
Controlled substances
—Cont'd
Taxation.
Administration of chapter,
§40-17A-2.
Amount, §40-17A-8.
Assessments.
Injunction prohibited,
§40-17A-12.
Jeopardy assessment,
§40-17A-12.
Presumption,
§40-17A-12.
Calculation, §40-17A-4.
Collection, §40-17A-2.
Confidentiality of
information,
§40-17A-13.
Definitions, §40-17A-1.
Examination of books,
records, etc.,
§40-17A-14.
Exemptions, §40-17A-6.
Forfeiture laws.
Applicability,
§40-17A-13.
Immunity.
Effect of chapter on
immunity,
§40-17A-5.
Intent of chapter,
§40-17A-16.
Jeopardy assessment or
collection, §40-17A-12.
Limitation of actions,
§40-17A-9.
Payment.
Manner of payment,
§40-17A-2.
Restrictions imposed if
tax not paid,
§40-17A-4.
When due, §40-17A-11.
Penalties.
Violation of chapter,
§40-17A-9.
Proceeds.
Disposition, §40-17A-15.
Rates, §40-17A-8.
Rules and regulations.
Promulgation,
§40-17A-3.
Stamps, §40-17A-3.
Affixing, §40-17A-11.
Production, §40-17A-10.
Purchase, §40-17A-10.
Violation of chapter.
Penalties, §40-17A-9.
Therapeutic research,
§§20-2-110 to 20-2-120.
See within this heading,
"Therapeutic research."
Trafficking in cannabis,
§13A-12-231.
Mandatory minimum
terms of imprisonment,
§13A-12-231.
Habitual felony offender
act.
Applicability,
§13A-12-231.
Suspension, deferral,
etc., of sentence,
§13A-12-232.

DRUGS—Cont'd
Controlled substances
—Cont'd
Trafficking in cocaine,
§13A-12-231.
Mandatory minimum
terms of imprisonment,
§13A-12-231.
Habitual felony offender
act.
Applicability,
§13A-12-231.
Suspension, deferral,
etc., of sentence,
§13A-12-232.
Trafficking in illegal drugs,
§§13A-12-231,
13A-12-232.
Drug kingpen's
enforcement act,
§§13A-12-231,
13A-12-232.
Mandatory minimum
terms of imprisonment,
§13A-12-231.
Habitual felony offender
act.
Applicability,
§13A-12-231.
Suspension, deferral,
etc., of sentence,
§13A-12-232.
Veterinarians.
Prescription,
administration, etc., of
controlled substances
by practitioners of
veterinary medicine
for use of human
beings, §20-2-74.
Criminal law and procedure.
See within this heading,
"Controlled substances."
Definitions, §34-23-1.
Adulteration and
misbranding, §20-1-20.
Controlled substances,
§20-2-2.
Drug paraphernalia,
§13A-12-260.
Taxation, §40-17A-1.
Therapeutic research,
§20-2-112.
Drug paraphernalia,
§13A-12-260.
Imitation controlled
substances, §20-2-141.
Dentists.
Controlled substances.
Prescription,
administration, etc., by
dentists for persons not
under treatment in
regular practice of
profession, §20-2-74.
**Department of agriculture
and industries.**
Enforcement of chapter,
§20-1-1.
Destruction.
Nuisances menacing public
health.
Summary destruction
without compensation,
§22-10-3.
Distributors.
Controlled substances. See
within this heading,
"Controlled substances."
Driving under the influence.
See MOTOR VEHICLES.

DRUGS—Cont'd
Drug abuse education,
  §§16-41-1 to 16-41-10.
Administration of chapter,
  §16-41-4.
Administrators.
  Exclusion of administrators
    employed by nonpublic
    schools prohibited,
    §16-41-5.
Alcoholic beverages.
  Citation of chapter,
    §16-41-1.
  Definition of drugs,
    §16-41-2.
Denominational schools.
  Exclusion of teacher or
    administrator
    prohibited, §16-41-5.
  Exemption of children by
    parents, §16-41-6.
Funds.
  Combining of funds from
    various sources,
    §16-41-9.
Implementation of
  program.
  Priorities, §16-41-4.
Instructions as to,
  §16-41-4.
Private schools.
  Exclusion of teacher or
    administrator
    prohibited, §16-41-5.
Purpose of chapter,
  §16-41-3.
Religious objections.
  Exemption of children by
    parents, §16-41-6.
Reports.
  State superintendent of
    education to report
    status of program,
    §16-41-10.
Teachers.
  Exclusion of teacher
    employed by
    nonpublic school
    prohibited, §16-41-5.
Citation of chapter, §16-41-1.
Definition of drug, §16-41-2.
Denominational schools.
  Exclusion of teacher or
    administrator
    prohibited, §16-41-5.
  Exemption of children by
    parents, §16-41-6.
Funds.
  Combining of funds from
    various sources,
    §16-41-9.
Implementation of program.
  Priorities for
    implementation,
    §16-41-4.
Legislative intent, §16-41-3.
Parochial schools.
  Exclusion of teacher or
    administrator
    prohibited, §16-41-5.
Private schools.
  Exclusion of teacher or
    administrator
    prohibited, §16-41-5.
Program.
  Report of status of
    program, §16-41-10.
Purpose of chapter, §16-41-3.
Religious objection.
  Exemption of children by
    parents, §16-41-6.

DRUGS—Cont'd
Drug abuse education
  —Cont'd
Reports.
  Status of program,
    §16-41-10.
Rules and regulations.
  Adoption by state board,
    §16-41-7.
Scheduling of courses,
  §16-41-7.
Sex education.
  Teaching of sex education
    not authorized,
    §16-41-8.
Short title of chapter,
  §16-41-1.
State board of education.
  Rulemaking power,
    §16-41-7.
State superintendent of
  education.
  Administration of chapter,
    §16-41-4.
  Report of status of
    program, §16-41-10.
Teachers.
  Exclusion of teacher
    employed by nonpublic
    school prohibited,
    §16-41-5.
Education.
Controlled substances.
  School campus.
    Additional penalty if
      unlawful sale on or
      near school campus,
      §13A-12-250.
Drug abuse education,
  §§16-41-1 to 16-41-10.
  See within this heading,
    "Drug abuse education."
Exemptions, §40-23-4.
Enforcement of chapter,
  §20-1-1.
Applicability of enforcement
  provisions of Title 2,
  §20-1-1.
Felonies.
Controlled substances.
  Dentistry and veterinary
    related penalties,
    §20-2-74.
  Manufacturers and
    distributors, §§20-2-71,
    20-2-72.
  Sale, furnishing to minor,
    §13A-12-215.
  Trafficking offenses.
    Habitual felony offender
      act.
      Applicability,
        §13A-12-231.
    Mandatory minimum
      terms of
      imprisonment,
      §13A-12-231.
Generic drugs, §34-23-8.
Guardian and ward.
Addicts.
  Uniform guardianship and
    protective proceedings
    act, §§26-2A-1 to
    26-2A-160.
    See GUARDIAN AND
      WARD.

DRUGS—Cont'd
Hallucinogenic drugs.
Controlled substances
  generally, §§20-2-1 to
  20-2-144. See within this
  heading, "Controlled
  substances."
Health.
Nuisances menacing public
  health, §§22-10-1 to
  22-10-3.
Heroin.
Controlled substances
  generally, §§20-2-1 to
  20-2-144. See within this
  heading, "Controlled
  substances."
Horse racing.
Possession of certain drugs
  prohibited, §11-65-41.
Tampering with horses,
  §11-65-39.
Identification of drug
  products.
Descriptive material.
  Furnishing upon request,
    §20-1-151.
Exemptions for drugs
  compounded by a
  pharmacist, §20-1-154.
Exemptions from
  requirement, §20-1-153.
Marking or imprinting
  required, §20-1-150.
  Exemptions from
    requirement,
    §20-1-153.
Oral dosage forms.
  Marking or imprinting
    required, §20-1-150.
Rules.
  State board of health to
    promulgate, §20-1-152.
Imitation controlled
  substances, §§20-2-140 to
  20-2-144.
Advertising prohibited,
  §20-2-143.
Applicability of article.
  Exceptions, §20-2-144.
Citation, §20-2-140.
Definitions, §20-2-141.
Exceptions to article,
  §20-2-144.
Immunity from liability of
  certain persons,
  §20-2-143.
Legislative intent, §20-2-142.
Manufacture, distribution,
  possession or advertising
  prohibited, §20-2-143.
Penalties, §20-2-143.
Short title, §20-2-140.
Immunity.
Controlled substances.
  Imitation controlled
    substances, §20-2-143.
  Minors.
    Immunity of persons
      reporting suspected
      use, etc., of
      controlled substance
      by minor child,
      §20-2-3.
Impeachment.
Intemperance as ground for
  impeachment, §36-11-1.

DRUGS—Cont'd
Inciting to crime.
Controlled substances.
Criminal solicitation to commit controlled substance crime, §13A-12-202.
Included offenses, §13A-12-205.
Income tax.
Deductions.
Expenses for medicine and drugs, §40-18-15.
Inspectors.
State drug inspectors, §34-23-3.
Insurance.
Disability insurance.
Optional policy provision as to narcotics, §27-19-26.
Pharmaceutical insurance coverage, §§27-45-1 to 27-45-9.
See INSURANCE.
Jails.
Medicines.
Furnishing to prisoners, §14-6-19.
Labels.
Identification of drug products, §§20-1-150 to 20-1-153.
Loitering.
Loitering for purposes of using or possessing drugs, §13A-11-9.
Manufacturers.
Adulterated or misbranded drugs.
Effect of possession by manufacturer, §20-1-31.
Controlled substances. See within this heading, "Controlled substances."
Defined, §34-23-1.
Permits, §34-23-32.
Marijuana.
Controlled substances generally, §§20-2-1 to 20-2-144. See within this heading, "Controlled substances."
Medicaid program.
Copayments, §22-6-4.2.
Minors.
Consent for health services.
Drug dependency, §22-8-6.
Controlled substances.
Immunity of persons reporting suspected use, etc., of controlled substance by minor child, §20-2-3.
Sale, furnishing, etc., of controlled substances by persons over age 18 to persons under age 18, §13A-2-215.
Penalties, §13A-2-215.
Misbranding. See within this heading, "Adulteration and misbranding."
Misdemeanors.
Controlled substances.
Manufacturers and distributors, §§20-2-71, 20-2-72.

DRUGS—Cont'd
Motor vehicles.
Controlled substances.
Forfeiture of vehicle in controlled substance violation, §20-2-93.
Drivers' licenses.
Grounds for revocation, §32-5A-195.
Driving under the influence of narcotic drugs.
See MOTOR VEHICLES.
Names.
Controlled substances.
Nomenclature of controlled substances in schedules, §20-2-21.
Narcotics.
Controlled substances generally, §§20-2-1 to 20-2-144. See within this heading, "Controlled substances."
Driving under the influence.
See MOTOR VEHICLES.
Education, §§16-41-1 to 16-41-10.
See EDUCATION.
Nuisances menacing public health, §§22-10-1 to 22-10-3.
Oral dosage.
Marking or imprinting required, §20-1-150.
Paraphernalia.
Controlled substances, §13A-12-260.
Penalties.
Controlled substances.
Manufacturers and distributors, §§20-2-71, 20-2-72.
Minors.
Sale, furnishing, etc., to minor, §13A-2-215.
Penalties imposed by chapter in addition to other penalties, §20-2-78.
Schools.
Additional penalty if unlawful sale on or near school campus, §13A-12-250.
Imitation controlled substances.
Manufacture, distribution, possession or advertisement, §20-2-143.
Therapeutic research.
Violation of article, §20-2-120.
Violations of chapter or orders, rules or regulations, §20-1-5.
Pharmacists and pharmacies.
Controlled substances. See within this heading, "Controlled substances."
General provisions.
See PHARMACISTS AND PHARMACIES.
Pistols, §§13A-11-72, 13A-11-76.

DRUGS—Cont'd
Pregnant women.
Inducing or attempting to induce abortion, miscarriage or premature delivery by administering drugs, §13A-13-7.
Prescriptions.
Controlled substances. See within this heading, "Controlled substances."
Pharmacists and pharmacies.
See PHARMACISTS AND PHARMACIES.
Prisons and prisoners.
Providing drugs to prisoners.
See PRISONS AND PRISONERS.
Public intoxication, §13A-11-10.
Records.
Investigation, §20-1-3.
Registration.
Controlled substances.
Manufacturers and distributors. See within this heading, "Controlled substances."
Religion.
Exemption of children from drug abuse education, §16-41-6.
Reports.
Therapeutic research.
Annual reports to governor and legislature, §20-2-118.
Research.
Controlled substances.
Therapeutic research. See within this heading, "Therapeutic research."
Right of entry.
Commissioner of agriculture and industry, §20-1-3.
Rules and regulations.
Adoption, §20-1-2.
Controlled substances.
Promulgation, §20-2-54.1.
Identification of drug products.
State board of health to promulgate, §20-1-152.
Penalties for violations, §20-1-5.
Therapeutic research.
Promulgation, §20-2-113.
Sales.
Controlled substances.
Persons over age eighteen selling controlled substances to minors.
Penalties, §13A-2-215.
Suspension from sale of articles sold in violation of article, §20-1-4.
Sales tax.
Exemptions, §§40-23-4, 40-23-4.1.
Samples.
Commissioner of agriculture and industries.
Authority to take samples, §20-1-3.
Searches and seizures.
Controlled substances, §20-2-93.

DRUGS—Cont'd
Sentencing.
Controlled substances.
Trafficking offenses.
Habitual felony offender
act.
Applicability,
§13A-12-231.
Mandatory minimum
terms of
imprisonment,
§13A-12-231.
Suspension, deferral,
etc., of sentence,
§13A-12-232.
Standards of purity.
Board of agriculture and
industries to fix,
§20-1-21.
State toxicologist.
See STATE
TOXICOLOGIST.
Storage.
Suspension from sale, seizure
and condemnation of
articles stored in
violation of chapter,
§20-1-4.
Supreme court.
Controlled substances.
Manufacturers and
distributors.
Appeal from denial,
refusal to renew,
revocation or
suspension, §20-2-53.
Tablets.
Marking or imprinting
required, §20-1-150.
Taxation.
Controlled substances excise
tax, §§40-17A-1 to
40-17A-16. See within
this heading, "Controlled
substances."
**Theft of controlled
substances.**
Second degree theft of
property, §13A-8-4.
Therapeutic research,
§§20-2-110 to 20-2-120.
Annual reports to governor
and legislature,
§20-2-118.
Cancer chemotherapy.
Limitation of program,
§20-2-114.
Cannabis, §20-2-117.
Citation of article, §20-2-110.
Contracts.
Receipt of cannabis,
§20-2-117.
Definitions, §20-2-112.
Glaucoma.
Limitation of program,
§20-2-114.
Legislative findings,
§20-2-111.
Patients.
Certification by authorized
practitioner, §20-2-114.
Limitation on patients,
§20-2-114.
Penalties, §20-2-120.
Physicians.
Certification, §20-2-116.
Recertification,
§20-2-116.
Qualifications, §20-2-116.
Program.
Administration, §20-2-113.

DRUGS—Cont'd
Therapeutic research
—Cont'd
Program—Cont'd
Established, §20-2-113.
Limitations on scope,
§20-2-114.
Reports.
Annual reports to governor
and legislature,
§20-2-118.
Review committee.
Administration of program,
§20-2-113.
Composition, §20-2-115.
Rules and regulations.
Promulgation, §20-2-113.
Schedule I or II substance.
Enumeration inapplicable,
§20-2-119.
Short title of article,
§20-2-110.
Violations.
Penalties, §20-2-120.
Use tax.
Exemptions, §40-23-62.
Veterinarians.
Controlled substances.
Prescription,
administration, etc., of
controlled substances
by veterinarians for
use of human beings,
§20-2-74.
Victim counselors.
Prescribing drugs.
Confidentiality provisions
not to authorize,
§15-23-46.
Violations of chapter.
Penalties, §20-1-5.
Suspension from sale, seizure
and condemnation of
articles sold, stored, etc.,
in violation of chapter,
§20-1-4.
Weapons.
Delivery of pistols to drug
addicts, §13A-11-76.
Drug addicts forbidden to
possess pistol,
§13A-11-72.

DRUNKENNESS.
**Alcoholic beverages
generally.**
See ALCOHOLIC
BEVERAGES.
Alcoholism.
See ALCOHOLISM.
Blood tests.
Chemical tests for
intoxication, §§32-5-190
to 32-5-194.
Coal.
Mine safety.
Entry into mine while
intoxicated, §25-9-27.
Driving under the influence,
§§32-5-171 to 32-5-194.
See MOTOR VEHICLES.
Elections.
Alcoholic beverages.
See ELECTIONS.
Estates.
Preservation of inebriate's
estate, §§6-6-520 to
6-6-527.
See WASTE.

DRUNKENNESS—Cont'd
Indictments.
Form of indictment for public
drunkenness, §15-8-150.
Judges.
Maintenance of temperance
at all times, ACJE,
Canon 2B.
Military affairs.
Authority of commanders to
detain persons
interfering with troops
engaged in drilling,
§31-2-126.
Motor vehicles.
Chemical tests for
intoxication, §§32-5-190
to 32-5-194.
Driving under the influence,
§§32-5-171 to 32-5-194.
See MOTOR VEHICLES.
Municipal corporations.
Elections.
Drunkenness at or about
polling place during
election day,
§§11-46-68, 11-46-139.
Railroads.
Public drinking on railway
passenger cars or in
waiting rooms,
§37-8-160.
Temperance.
Judges.
Maintenance at all times,
ACJE, Canon 2B.
Municipal corporations.
Promotion of temperance,
§11-47-112.
Waste.
Remedies to preserve
inebriate's estates,
§§6-6-520 to 6-6-527.
See WASTE.
Weapons.
Delivery of pistols to
drunkards, §13A-11-76.
Habitual drunkards
forbidden to possess
pistols, §13A-11-72.
Witnesses.
Incompetent witnesses,
§12-21-165.
Workmen's compensation.
Grounds for denial of
compensation, §25-5-51.

DRY COUNTIES, §§28-4-1 to
28-4-326.
See ALCOHOLIC
BEVERAGES.

DUCKS.
Hunting game generally.
See FISH AND GAME.
Poultry generally.
See POULTRY.

DUELING.
Suppression of dueling,
Const. Ala., art. IV, §86.

DUE PROCESS.
Constitution of Alabama,
Const. Ala., art. I, §6.
**Constitution of the United
States,** Const. U. S.,
Amendments V, XIV.

DUMPS.
Financing collection and disposal facilities,
§§22-27-20 to 22-27-26.
See GARBAGE AND TRASH.
Unauthorized dumps,
§22-27-4.

DUPLICATING MACHINES.
Licenses.
Sales, §40-12-127.

DURABLE POWER OF ATTORNEY, §26-1-2.

DURESS.
Affirmative defense, ARCP, Rule 8 (c).
Commercial code.
Commercial paper.
Defenses against holder in due course, §7-3-305.
Negotiation effective although subject to rescission, §7-3-207.
Criminal law and procedure.
When defense to criminal liability, §13A-3-30.

DUST.
Coal mine safety, §§25-9-110, 25-9-111.

DWELLINGS.
Buildings generally.
See BUILDINGS.
Housing generally.
See HOUSING.

DYNAMITE.
General provisions.
See EXPLOSIVES AND EXPLOSIONS.

DYSENTERY.
Notifiable diseases generally, §§22-11A-1 to 22-11A-38.
See DISEASES.

E

EAGLES CLUB.
Taxation.
Property exempt, §40-9-1.

EARS.
Deaf persons.
See DEAF PERSONS.
Hearing aid dealers and fitters, §§34-14-1 to 34-14-33.
See HEARING AID DEALERS AND FITTERS.

EARTHQUAKES.
Civil defense generally, §§31-9-1 to 31-9-24.
See CIVIL DEFENSE.
Emergencies generally.
See EMERGENCIES.

EASEMENTS.
Airports.
Acquisition of easements, §4-6-13.
State airports, §4-2-91.
Cemeteries.
Rights of way.
Private parties, §§18-3-20 to 18-3-22.

EASEMENTS—Cont'd
Dams.
Navigable rivers.
Right of easement, §33-7-30.
Electricity.
Transmission lines.
Acquisition of rights of way or easements, §37-4-130.
Eminent domain.
General provisions.
See EMINENT DOMAIN.
Graveyards.
Rights of way.
Private parties.
See EMINENT DOMAIN.
Highways.
Rights of way.
Eminent domain.
Private parties, §§18-3-1 to 18-3-3.
Industrial companies.
Condemnation, §10-5-3.
Manufacturers.
Condemnation, §10-5-3.
Mines and minerals.
Condemnation by mining companies, §10-5-3.
Municipal corporations.
See MUNICIPAL CORPORATIONS.
Quarries.
Condemnation by quarrying companies, §10-5-3.
Railroads.
See RAILROADS.
Rights of way.
Eminent domain, §§18-3-1 to 18-3-3, 18-3-20 to 18-3-22.
See EMINENT DOMAIN.
Roads.
Rights of way.
Eminent domain.
Private parties, §§18-3-1 to 18-3-3.
Telegraph companies.
Eminent domain.
Foreign companies.
Acquisition of easements for connecting lines, §18-1A-272.
Telephone companies.
Eminent domain.
See EMINENT DOMAIN.
Venue.
Actions for breach of easement contracts, §6-3-3.

EAST ALABAMA SERVICES FOR THE ELDERLY, INC.
Taxation.
Exemption from taxation, §40-9-26.

EASTERN STAR.
Grand chapter of all orders of the Eastern Star.
Exemption from sales and use taxes, §40-23-5.

EAST PRESBYTERIAN APARTMENTS.
Taxation.
Exemption from taxation, §40-9-26.

EAVESDROPPING,
§§13A-11-30 to 13A-11-37.
Criminal eavesdropping.
Class A misdemeanor, §13A-11-31.
Elements of crime, §13A-11-31.
Criminal surveillance,
§13A-11-32.
Defenses to prosecution,
§13A-11-36.
Definitions, §13A-11-30.
Devices.
Criminal possession of devices, §13A-11-34.
Forfeiture, §13A-11-37.
Installing, §13A-11-33.
Divulging illegally obtained information, §13A-11-35.
Installing eavesdropping device, §13A-11-33.
Private place.
Defined, §13A-11-30.
Surveillance.
Criminal surveillance, §13A-11-32.
Defined, §13A-11-30.

ECOLOGY.
Air pollution.
See AIR POLLUTION.
Conservation and natural resources.
See CONSERVATION AND NATURAL RESOURCES.
Environmental control.
See ENVIRONMENTAL CONTROL.
Environmental improvement authorities, §§9-6-1 to 9-6-17.
See ENVIRONMENTAL IMPROVEMENT AUTHORITIES.
Municipal corporations.
Promotion of pollution control, §§11-54-1 to 11-54-33.
See MUNICIPAL CORPORATIONS.
Pollution generally.
See POLLUTION.
Water pollution.
See WATER POLLUTION.
Water pollution control act,
§§22-22-1 to 22-22-14.
See WATER POLLUTION CONTROL ACT.
Water pollution control authority, §§22-34-1 to 22-34-17.
See WATER POLLUTION CONTROL AUTHORITY.

ECONOMIC AND COMMUNITY AFFAIRS,
§§41-23-1 to 41-23-32.
Department.
Aims of department, §41-23-4.
Appropriations.
Transfer of appropriations to department, §41-23-3.
Composition, §41-23-1.
Creation, §41-23-1.
Director. See within this heading, "Director."

**ECONOMIC AND
    COMMUNITY AFFAIRS**
    —Cont'd
Department—Cont'd
  Divisions.
    Chiefs.
      Appointment, §41-23-5.
      Establishment, §41-23-5.
    Employees in classified
        service.
      Implementation of duties
          and functions,
          §41-23-2.
      Salary, §41-23-2.
    Implementation of duties and
        functions, §41-23-2.
    Legislative oversight
        commission, §41-23-7.
    Purposes of chapter,
        §41-23-5.
    Transfer of functions to
        department, §41-23-1.
  Director.
    Appointment, §41-23-4.
    Qualifications, §41-23-4.
    Rules and regulations.
      Promulgation, §41-23-6.
    Salary, §41-23-4.
    Term of office, §41-23-4.
  Enterprise zones, §§41-23-20
      to 41-23-32.
    See ENTERPRISE ZONES.
  Rules and regulations.
    Director.
      Promulgation, §41-23-6.

EDUCATION.
  Absence.
    Must be explained,
        §16-28-15.
  Accountants.
    Permits.
      Continuing education
          requirements,
          §34-1-11.
    Qualifications of certified
        public accountants,
        §34-1-4.
  Accreditation.
    High schools, §16-26-1.
    Unaccredited schools,
        §§16-46-1 to 16-46-10.
      See within this heading,
          "Unaccredited schools."
  Actions.
    County boards of education.
      Right to sue, §16-8-40.
  Admission to public schools.
    City boards of education.
      Eligibility for admission to
          public schools,
          §16-11-16.
    County superintendents of
        education.
      Conditions of admittance to
          high schools, §16-9-19.
      Eligibility for admission,
          §16-11-16.
    High schools.
      Conditions of admittance to
          high schools, §16-9-19.
  Adult education.
    Appropriations.
      Legislative appropriation
          for adult education
          programs and classes,
          §16-34-4.
    Classes.
      Legislative appropriation,
          §16-34-4.

EDUCATION—Cont'd
  Adult education—Cont'd
    Programs.
      Legislative appropriation,
          §16-34-4.
  Age.
    Attendance. See within this
        heading, "Attendance."
    Majority.
      Contracting for educational
          loans for college level
          education and above,
          §26-1-5.
  Aid to education.
    Federal financial assistance.
      See within this heading,
          "Federal grants."
    Local aid to state educational
        institutions, §§16-19-1 to
        16-19-8.
  **Alabama agricultural and
      mechanical university,**
      §§16-49-1 to 16-49-30.
    See ALABAMA
        AGRICULTURAL AND
        MECHANICAL
        UNIVERSITY.
  **Alabama educational
      television commission,**
      §§16-17-1 to 16-17-6. See
      within this heading,
      "Educational television
      commission."
  **Alabama education
      authority.**
    Bond issues.
      Conditions of bonds,
          §16-15-9.
      Disposition of proceeds,
          §16-15-10.
      Execution, §16-15-9.
      Exemption from taxation,
          §16-15-9.
      Form, §16-15-9.
      Investments.
        Bonds legal investments,
            §16-15-9.
      Issuance, §16-15-8.
      Negotiability, §16-15-9.
      Payment, §16-15-12.
        Pledge of revenues for
            payment, §16-15-11.
        Security for payment,
            §16-15-9.
      Pledge of revenues for
          payment, §16-15-11.
      Proceeds.
        Disposition, §16-15-10.
      Refunding bonds, §16-15-9.
      Sale, §§16-15-8, 16-15-9.
      Security for payment,
          §16-15-9.
      Terms, §16-15-9.
    Certificate of incorporation.
      Issuance and recording,
          §16-15-5.
    Contracts, §16-15-8.
    Definitions, §16-15-1.
    Directors, §16-15-6.
    Dissolution, §16-15-13.
      Fees.
        No fees to be paid,
            §16-15-5.
    Fees.
      Incorporation or
          dissolution.
        No fees to be paid,
            §16-15-5.
    Findings of fact.
      Legislative findings of fact,
          §16-15-2.

EDUCATION—Cont'd
  **Alabama education
      authority**—Cont'd
    Incorporation.
      Application for
          incorporation,
          §16-15-4.
      Authorized, §16-15-3.
      Certificate of incorporation.
        Issuance and recording,
            §16-15-5.
      Fees.
        No fees to be paid,
            §16-15-5.
      Intent.
        Declaration of legislative
            intent, §16-15-2.
      Legislative findings of fact
          and declaration of intent,
          §16-15-2.
      Members, §16-15-6.
      Officers, §16-15-6.
      Powers.
        Generally, §16-15-7.
      Purchases, §16-15-8.
      Record of proceedings,
          §16-15-6.
  **Alabama education study
      commission,** §§16-6-1 to
      16-6-6. See within this
      heading, "Study
      commission."
  **Alabama high school of
      mathematics and
      science,** §§16-26A-1 to
      16-26A-7.
  **Alabama public school
      corporation,** §§16-14-1 to
      16-14-19. See within this
      heading, "Public school
      corporation."
  Alabama state university,
      §§16-50-1 to 16-50-30.
    See ALABAMA STATE
        UNIVERSITY.
  Alcoholic beverages.
    Drug abuse education.
      General provisions,
          §§16-41-1 to 16-41-10.
        See DRUGS.
    Keeping on school premises,
        §16-1-10.
    Selling, etc., to school
        children, §16-1-10.
  Animals.
    Humane treatment of
        animals taught,
        §16-40-4.
  Annexation.
    Territory embracing schools.
      Agreements and
          arbitration.
        Appointment of board of
            arbitration, §16-8-21.
        Hearing by board of
            arbitration, §16-8-22.
        Retention of control by
            county boards
            pending agreements,
            §16-8-20.
        When arbitration
            required, §16-8-21.
  Annuities.
    Tax sheltered annuities.
      Salary deductions,
          §16-22-6.
  Appeals.
    Nonteacher, nonclassified,
        etc., employees.
      Dismissal procedure.
        Termination, §36-26-105.

EDUCATION—Cont'd
Appeals—Cont'd
Nonteacher, nonclassified,
etc., employees—Cont'd
Dismissal procedure
—Cont'd
Transfers, §36-26-107.
Teachers.
Cancellation of contract of
employment,
§16-24-10.
State tenure commission,
§§16-24-36 to 16-24-38.
Transfers, §16-24-7.
Appointments.
City boards of education,
§16-11-3.
Appropriations.
Educational institutions not
under absolute control of
state, Const. Ala., art.
IV, §73.
Educational reform.
Commission, §16-6A-5.
Public school funds
generally. See within
this heading, "Public
school funds."
Teachers.
Employment of teacher
aides, §16-1-1.1.
Transfer of appropriated
funds among line items,
§16-13-40.
Arbitration.
Annexing to city territory
embracing schools.
Appointment of board of
arbitration, §16-8-21.
Hearing by board of
arbitration, §16-8-22.
When arbitration of
agreement required,
§16-8-21.
Arrest.
Truancy, §16-28-17.
Assault.
Reports of physical assaults
on students and school
personnel, §16-1-24.
**Association of school board
members.**
Dues, §16-1-6.
Expenses, §16-1-6.
Recognition, §16-1-6.
Teachers' retirement system.
Eligibility of executive
officers and employees,
§16-25-10.1.
Training program.
Cooperation of boards and
officials, §16-1-6.
Attendance.
Absence.
Must be explained,
§16-28-15.
Age.
Ages of children required
to attend school,
§16-28-3.
Children exempt from
attending public
school, §16-28-6.
Minimum age at which
child may enter,
§16-28-4.
Burden of proof on person in
loco parentis, §16-28-13.
Church schools, §16-28-3.
Compulsory attendance,
§16-28-3.

EDUCATION—Cont'd
Attendance—Cont'd
Compulsory attendance.
Ages of children required
to attend school,
§16-28-3.
Church schools, §16-28-3.
Enforcement of attendance
laws, §16-9-30.
Exemptions, §16-28-6.
Institute for deaf and
blind, §§21-1-10 to
21-1-13.
See HANDICAPPED
PERSONS.
Compulsory school
attendance districts,
§16-8-34.
Appointment of attendance
officers, §16-28-19.
Arrangement, §16-28-19.
Boundaries, §16-9-17.
Recommendation by county
superintendents as to
kind, location, etc.,
§16-9-14.
County superintendents of
education.
Enforcement of attendance
laws, §16-9-30.
Definitions, §16-28-1.
Enforcement of attendance
laws, §16-12-18.
County superintendents of
education, §16-9-30.
Enrollment.
Cases of nonenrollment,
§16-28-16.
Report of enrollment,
§16-28-7.
Comparing report of
enrollment with list
of children who
should attend school,
§16-28-9.
Evidence.
Burden of proof on person
in loco parentis,
§16-28-13.
Register and rules and
regulations as
evidence, §16-28-23.
Exemptions.
Children exempt from
attending public
school, §16-28-6.
Explanation of absence,
§16-28-15.
Handicapped persons.
Children exempt from
attending public
school, §16-28-6.
Institute for deaf and
blind, §§21-1-10 to
21-1-13.
Jurisdiction.
Juvenile court jurisdiction,
§16-28-21.
Juvenile court jurisdiction,
§16-28-21.
List of children who should
attend school.
Comparing list with
enrollment report,
§16-28-11.
Contents of list, §16-28-9.
Enrollment report.
Comparing list with
enrollment report,
§16-28-11.

EDUCATION—Cont'd
Attendance—Cont'd
List of children who should
attend school—Cont'd
Preparation.
How lists prepared,
§§16-28-9, 16-28-10.
Required, §16-28-9.
Minimum age, §16-28-4.
Officers.
Appointment, §16-28-19.
Certificates required,
§16-23-1.
Compensation, §16-28-20.
Employment by city
superintendent,
§16-12-18.
Record kept by attendance
officer, §16-28-18.
Persons in loco parentis.
Burden of proof on person
in loco parentis,
§16-28-13.
Responsible for child's
attendance, §16-28-12.
Private schools.
Defined, §16-28-1.
Private tutors, §16-28-5.
Prosecutions, §16-28-22.
Purposes of chapter,
§16-28-2.
Records.
Attendance officer,
§16-28-18.
Register.
Use as evidence, §16-28-23.
Reports.
Enrollment.
Report of enrollment,
§16-28-7.
Comparing with list of
children who
should attend
school, §16-28-9.
Required reports must be
furnished, §16-28-8.
Responsibility for child's
attendance.
Burden of proof on person
in loco parentis,
§16-28-13.
Persons in loco parentis
responsible, §16-28-12.
Rules and regulations.
Use as evidence, §16-28-23.
Truancy.
Arrest, §16-28-17.
Cases of nonattendance,
§16-28-16.
Evidence.
Attendance register and
rules and
regulations,
§16-28-23.
Habitual truant, §16-28-14.
Jurisdiction of juvenile
court, §16-28-21.
Prosecutions, §16-28-22.
When child may be taken
into custody,
§16-28-17.
Auburn university, §§16-48-1
to 16-48-12.
See AUBURN
UNIVERSITY.
Audits.
City boards of education.
Audit of accounts,
§16-11-22.

EDUCATION—Cont'd
Audits—Cont'd
Department of examiners of
public accounts.
Audits of certain
institutions authorized,
§16-1-22.
Insurance.
Risk management
cooperatives.
Filing certified financial
audit, §16-8-42.1.
Textbooks.
Accounting books and
records, §16-36-31.
Authorities.
Alabama education
authority, §§16-15-1 to
16-15-13. See within this
heading, "Alabama
education authority."
Educational building
authorities, §§16-17-1 to
16-17-19. See within this
heading, "Educational
building authorities."
Public educational building
authorities, §§16-18-1 to
16-18-21. See within this
heading, "Educational
building authorities."
Public school and college
authority, §§16-16-1 to
16-16-13. See within this
heading, "Public school
and college authority."
Aviation.
Air schools, §§4-2-72, 4-2-77,
4-2-79.
**Banks and financial
institutions.**
Public school funds.
Pledge of assets as security
for deposit, §5-5A-28.
Barber colleges.
See BARBERS.
Beautification of schools.
Powers and duties of county
commissions, §11-3-11.
Blind persons.
Alabama institute for deaf
and blind, §§21-1-1 to
21-1-26.
See HANDICAPPED
PERSONS.
Benefits for dependents of
blind parents, §§16-33-1
to 16-33-12.
See UNIVERSITIES AND
COLLEGES.
Employment by public
schools, §21-7-8.
Exceptional children,
§§16-39-1 to 16-39-12.
See within this heading,
"Exceptional children."
Boards of education.
Association of school board
members, §16-1-6.
City boards of education,
§§16-11-1 to 16-11-27.
See within this heading,
"City boards of
education."
County boards of education,
§§16-8-1 to 16-8-43. See
within this heading,
"County boards of
education."

EDUCATION—Cont'd
Boards of education—Cont'd
Electronic pagers or
communication devices.
When board to prohibit
pupils from carrying,
§16-1-27.
Employees.
Rewards for suggestions,
§16-1-21.
Gasoline tax.
City and county boards of
education.
Exemptions, §40-17-31.
Independent school districts,
§16-3-27.
Insurance.
Group insurance.
Authority to form groups
for purpose of
obtaining, §16-22-5.
Payment of premiums,
§16-22-5.
Lubricating oils and greases.
Tax.
City and county boards
of education.
Exemption,
§40-17-171.
Members.
Association of school board
members, §16-1-6.
Motor fuels.
Additional excise tax on
gasoline, motor fuel
and lubricating oil.
City and county boards
of education.
Exemptions,
§40-17-220.
State board of education,
§§16-3-1 to 16-3-37. See
within this heading,
"State board of
education."
Boards of school trustees.
Bond issues.
Authority to issue,
§16-3-28.
Borrowing money.
From federal agencies or
others, §16-3-28.
Buildings.
School building controlled
by trustees, §16-10-8.
Use of schoolhouse for civic
purposes, §16-10-11.
Chairman, §16-10-2.
Civic use of schoolhouse,
§16-10-11.
Dismissal of pupils, §16-10-5.
Duties of trustees, §16-10-1.
Elementary schools.
Incidental fees, §16-10-6.
Meetings, §16-10-2.
Notes.
Authority to issue,
§16-3-28.
Principals.
Secretary of board,
§16-10-3.
Pupils.
Dismissal of pupils,
§16-10-5.
Qualification of trustees,
§16-10-1.
Sanitary conditions
maintained by trustees,
§16-10-10.
Secretary, §16-10-3.

EDUCATION—Cont'd
Boards of school trustees
—Cont'd
Securities.
Authority to issue,
§16-3-28.
Selection of trustees,
§16-10-1.
Teachers.
Charges against teachers
may be filed by
trustees, §16-10-9.
Dismissal of pupils,
§16-10-5.
Refusal by trustees,
§16-10-4.
Terms of office, §16-10-1.
Use of schoolhouse for civic
purposes, §16-10-11.
Visitation of schools,
§16-10-7.
Bond issues.
Alabama education
authority, §§16-15-8 to
16-15-12.
Authority to issue, §16-3-28.
City boards of education,
§16-11-19.
Indebtedness where county
unit system adopted,
§16-11-8.
Counties.
Security for indebtedness
incurred in purchase,
construction, etc., of
school buildings,
§11-81-1.
Educational building
authorities, §§16-17-10 to
16-17-14, 16-17-17,
16-17-18.
Issuance.
Authority to issue,
§16-3-28.
Municipal corporations.
Security for indebtedness
incurred in purchase,
construction, etc., of
school buildings,
§11-81-1.
Public school and college
authority, §§16-16-8 to
16-16-12.
State board of education.
Authority to issue,
§16-3-28.
Bonds, surety.
City superintendents of
schools, §16-11-7.
County superintendents of
education, §16-9-3.
Secretary of county boards
of education, §16-8-7.
Generally, §16-22-4.
Public school funds.
Bonding of persons
handling, §§16-13-8,
16-13-9.
State superintendent of
education, §16-4-3.
Treasurer of city school
boards, §16-11-7.
Books.
Textbooks, §§16-36-1 to
16-36-39. See within this
heading, "Textbooks."
Borrowing money.
Budgets.
Against revenues of
current year,
§16-13-145.

EDUCATION—Cont'd

Borrowing money—Cont'd
Public school corporation,
§16-14-6.
State board of education.
From federal agencies or
others, §16-3-28.
Boundaries.
Compulsory school
attendance districts,
§16-9-17.
Public school funds.
Apportionment of funds
when boundaries
changed, §16-13-35.
School tax district.
Boundaries fixed by county
board, §16-13-191.
Duration of boundaries,
§16-13-192.
Budgets.
Borrowing money.
Against revenues of
current year,
§16-13-145.
Changes in budget,
§16-13-143.
Establishment.
For county and city school
systems, §16-13-140.
Estimate of funds.
Certification of estimated
funds available,
§16-13-142.
Comptroller, §16-13-141.
State superintendent,
§16-13-141.
Exceeding budget.
Penalty for exceeding
budget, §16-13-144.
Faculty.
Opportunity to develop
budget, §16-13-13.
Form of annual budget
required, §16-13-140.
Interest rate on current
loans, §16-13-146.
Overspending.
Penalty for exceeding
budget, §16-13-144.
Penalty for exceeding budget,
§16-13-144.
Receipt of funds.
Approval of school board
budget prerequisite to
receipt of funds,
§16-13-143.
State board of education,
§16-4-19.
State comptroller.
Estimate of funds,
§16-13-141.
State superintendent of
education, §16-13-141.
Teachers' salaries.
Approval of funds for,
§16-13-143.
Payment when due,
§16-13-147.
When budget official,
§16-13-143.
Building authorities,
§§16-17-1 to 16-18-21. See
within this heading,
"Educational building
authorities."
Buildings.
Authorities, §§16-17-1 to
16-18-21. See within this
heading, "Educational
building authorities."

EDUCATION—Cont'd

Buildings—Cont'd
Boards of school trustees.
School building controlled
by trustees, §16-10-8.
Use of schoolhouse for civic
purposes, §16-10-11.
City boards of education.
Insurance, §16-11-27.
City superintendents of
schools.
Building program for city
schools, §16-12-6.
Generally, §16-12-7.
Civic purposes.
Use of schoolhouse for civic
purposes, §16-10-11.
Condemnation, §16-9-18.
Construction.
Acceptance of completed
construction, §16-1-2.
Contracts.
Forms for construction
contract, §16-1-2.
Forms for construction
contract, §16-1-2.
Inspection.
During and after
construction,
§16-1-2.
Rules for construction,
§16-4-10.
Contracts.
Construction contract.
Form, §16-1-2.
County superintendents of
education.
Building program,
§16-9-17.
Condemnation, §16-9-18.
Improvements, §16-9-18.
Educational building
authorities, §§16-17-1 to
16-17-19. See within this
heading, "Educational
building authorities."
High schools, §16-26-1.
Improvement, §16-9-18.
Inspection.
During and after
construction, §16-1-2.
Insurance, §16-8-42.
City boards of education,
§16-11-27.
Inventory, §16-4-21.
Minimum building standards
code, §§41-9-160 to
41-9-166.
See BUILDINGS.
Municipal corporations.
Erection of school
buildings, §11-47-13.
Burden of proof.
Attendance.
Burden of proof on person
in loco parentis,
§16-28-13.
Buses.
School buses. See within this
heading, "School buses."
Bylaws.
Insurance.
Risk management
cooperatives.
Filing.
Bylaws, §16-8-42.1.

EDUCATION—Cont'd

Cafeteria workers.
Lunchroom managers and
assistants.
Membership in teachers'
retirement system,
§16-25-8.
Personal leave, §16-8-26.1.
Personal leave, §16-8-26.1.
Cancer, §§22-13-3, 22-13-4.
**Cardiopulmonary
resuscitation.**
Instruction and techniques,
§16-40-8.
**Caustic or explosive
substances.**
Eye protective devices for
pupils and teachers,
§16-1-7.
Census.
County boards of education.
Census enumerators,
§16-8-32.
Quadrennial school census,
§16-8-31.
County superintendents of
education.
Quadrennial school census,
§16-9-29.
Decennial school census,
§16-4-15.
Enumerators, §16-8-32.
Municipal census.
Cities, §16-11-10.
City superintendents of
schools, §16-12-13.
County boards of
education, §§16-8-31,
16-8-32.
County superintendents of
education, §16-9-29.
Effect as to conduct of
school census,
§11-47-91.
Quadrennial census,
§16-8-31.
School census, §16-4-15;
Const. Ala., art. XIV,
§268.
Charities.
State board of education.
Supervision of educational
work of special
institutions, §16-3-20.
Checkoffs.
Salary deductions.
Purposes for which
deductions made,
§16-22-6.
Child care.
State board of education.
Supervision of educational
work of special
institutions, §16-3-20.
**Child nutrition food
program.**
Storage and distribution.
Department of education
authorized to contract
for, §16-2-8.
Church schools.
See CHURCHES.
City boards of education,
§§16-11-1 to 16-11-27.
Admission to public schools.
Eligibility for admission,
§16-11-16.

EDUCATION—Cont'd
City boards of education
—Cont'd
Annexing territory
embracing schools.
Arbitration.
Appointment of board,
§16-8-21.
Hearing by board,
§16-8-22.
When arbitration
required, §16-8-21.
Retention of control by
county boards pending
agreements, §16-8-20.
Appointment, §16-11-3.
Association of school board
members, §16-1-6.
Audits.
Audit of accounts,
§16-11-22.
Bond issues, §16-11-19.
Indebtedness where county
unit system adopted,
§16-11-8.
Buildings.
Insurance, §16-11-27.
Census.
Quadrennial census for
city, §16-11-10.
City superintendents of
schools.
Nomination, removal, etc.,
of employees,
§16-12-16.
Supervision of employees,
§16-12-15.
Compensation of members,
§§16-1-26, 16-11-2.
Composition, §16-11-2.
Consolidation of
noncontiguous
municipalities.
Continuation in office of
boards, §11-42-159.
Election of boards,
§11-42-159.
Consolidation of schools.
County and city systems,
§16-8-17.
Cooperative agreements with
city council or
commission.
Authority to enter into,
§§16-8-12.1, 16-11-9.1.
County unit system.
Indebtedness where county
unit system adopted,
§16-11-8.
Courses of study, §16-11-20.
Custodian of school funds,
§16-11-6.
Definition of city, §16-11-1.
Educational policy for city,
§16-11-18.
Election, §16-11-3.
Consolidated
noncontiguous
municipalities,
§11-42-159.
Electronic pagers or
communication devices.
When boards to prohibit
pupils from carrying,
§16-1-27.
Elementary schools.
Incidental fees in city
elementary schools,
§16-11-26.
Eminent domain, §16-11-13.

EDUCATION—Cont'd
City boards of education
—Cont'd
Employees.
Dismissal, §16-11-17.
Expenses for participation
in conferences, etc.
Advancement of and
accounting for
expenses, §16-13-14.
Forms of contracts, §16-4-9.
Leaves of absence,
§16-12-21.
Personal leave.
Support personnel,
§16-8-26.1.
Support personnel.
Personal leave,
§16-8-26.1.
Nomination, removal, etc.,
by city
superintendents,
§16-12-16.
Reports.
Forms for reports of
employees,
§16-12-12.
Rewards for suggestions,
§16-1-21.
Salaries, §16-11-17.
Supervision by city
superintendents,
§16-12-15.
Vacations, §16-12-21.
Expenses of members for
participation in
conferences, meetings,
etc.
Advances of and
accounting for
expenses, §16-13-14.
Forms for reports, §16-11-21.
Funds.
Allocation of funds,
§16-13-13.
Custodian of school funds,
§16-11-6.
Minimum program funds.
Direct payment of funds
to independent city
boards of education,
§16-13-59.
Suggestion saving funds.
Rewards, §16-1-21.
Gasoline tax.
Exemptions, §40-17-31.
Grading schools, §16-11-20.
Handicapped persons.
Institute for deaf and
blind.
Cooperation by city
boards, §21-1-8.
High schools.
System of high schools,
§16-26-2.
Illiteracy.
Federal government.
Authority to cooperate
with federal
government,
§16-34-3.
State board of education.
Cooperation with state
board, §16-34-2.
Indebtedness where county
unit system adopted,
§16-11-8.
Institute for deaf and blind.
Cooperation by city boards,
§21-1-8.

EDUCATION—Cont'd
City boards of education
—Cont'd
Insurance.
Group insurance, §16-22-5.
Insuring school buildings,
property, etc., in fund,
§16-11-27.
Risk management
cooperatives,
§16-8-42.1.
Judicial officers.
Authority of legislature to
constitute members as
judicial officers, Const.
Ala., amd. 111.
Kindergartens, §16-11-16.
Leaves of absence, §16-12-21.
Libraries.
Establishment and
maintenance,
§16-11-23.
Licenses.
Allocation of revenue from
licenses, §16-11-25.
Lubricating oils and greases.
Tax exemption, §40-17-171.
Majority vote, §16-11-5.
Meetings, §16-11-5.
Minimum program funds.
Direct payment of funds to
certain independent
city boards of
education, §16-13-59.
Motor fuels.
Additional excise tax on
gasoline, motor fuel
and lubricating oil.
Exemptions, §40-17-220.
Notes.
Anticipation of warrants,
§§19-13-210 to
19-13-217.
Officers, §16-11-5.
Offices, §16-11-4.
Playgrounds, §16-11-16.
Policy.
Educational policy for city,
§16-11-18.
Powers.
Generally, §16-11-9.
Tax anticipation warrants
in cities and counties.
Effect of article on
existing powers of
boards of education,
§16-13-77.
Principals.
Suspension or dismissal,
§16-11-17.
Property.
Acquisition, maintenance,
etc.
Condemnation,
§16-11-13.
Generally, §16-11-12.
Condemnation, §16-11-13.
Insurance, §16-11-27.
School property vested in
board, §16-11-11.
Qualifications of members,
§16-11-2.
Rehabilitation and crippled
children service.
Cooperation in
rehabilitation work,
§16-38-7.
Reports.
Annual report.
Publication, §16-11-24.

EDUCATION—Cont'd
City boards of education
—Cont'd
Reports—Cont'd
Audit of accounts,
§16-11-22.
Forms for reports,
§16-11-21.
Employees of city boards,
§16-12-12.
Publication of annual
report, §16-11-24.
Reports to state board,
§16-11-22.
Revenue from licenses and
taxes.
Allocation, §16-11-25.
Review of local actions by
state superintendent,
§§16-3-27, 16-4-8.
Rules of procedure, §16-11-5.
Salaries.
Establishment of salaries,
§16-11-17.
Sales tax.
Exemptions.
Gross proceeds of sale of
tangible personal
property, §40-23-4.
School buses.
Liability of school board
members, §16-11-15.
Operation, §16-11-15.
Purchase, §16-11-14.
Special schools.
Establishment and
maintenance,
§16-11-23.
Standardizing schools,
§16-11-20.
State board of education.
Illiteracy.
Cooperation with state
board, §16-34-2.
Reports of city board to
state board, §16-11-22.
State superintendent of
education.
Conferences, §16-4-6.
Review of local actions,
§§16-3-27, 16-4-8.
Suggestions.
Saving funds.
Rewards, §16-1-21.
Tax anticipation warrants in
cities and counties.
Effect of article on existing
powers of boards of
education, §16-13-77.
Taxation.
Allocation of revenue from
licenses and taxes,
§16-11-25.
Exemptions.
Notes refunding
warrants,
§16-13-216.
Teachers.
Dismissal or suspension,
§16-11-17.
Leaves of absence,
§16-12-21.
Personal leave for
teachers during time
schools are in
session, §16-8-26.

EDUCATION—Cont'd
City boards of education
—Cont'd
Teachers—Cont'd
Substitute teachers
replacing teachers
absent on sick leave.
Reimbursing local boards
for payments to
substitutes, §16-3-36.
Vacations, §16-12-21.
Terms of office, §16-11-3.
Textbooks.
Filing of school board
policies with
superintendent of
education, §16-36-4.
Local appropriations,
§16-36-20.
Treasurer.
Bonds, surety, §16-11-7.
Designation, §16-11-6.
Duties, §16-11-6.
Use tax.
Exemptions, §40-23-62.
Vacancies, §16-11-3.
Vacations, §16-12-21.
Vocational education.
Authorized to operate
vocational high schools
jointly with county
boards, §16-37-8.
Cooperation with state
board, §16-37-5.
Voting.
Majority vote, §16-11-5.
Warrants.
Investment of trust estate
in interest-bearing
warrants, §19-3-121.
Notes in anticipation.
Authorized, §16-13-211.
Board of education.
Defined, §16-13-210.
Definitions, §16-13-210.
Extension, §16-13-213.
Investments by
fiduciaries,
§16-13-217.
Issuance, §16-13-211.
Approval by state
superintendent,
§16-13-215.
Obligations.
Notes deemed not
general obligation,
§16-13-212.
Pledge of tax proceeds.
Authority of board,
§16-13-212.
Refunding, §16-13-213.
Sales.
Public or private sale,
§16-13-214.
State superintendent.
Approval of issuance,
§16-13-215.
Taxation.
Exemption,
§16-13-216.
Warrants.
Defined, §16-13-210.
**City superintendents of
schools.**
Administration of office,
§16-12-15.
Appointment, §16-12-1.

EDUCATION—Cont'd
**City superintendents of
schools**—Cont'd
Assistants.
Employment of
professional, clerical,
etc., assistants,
§16-12-19.
Attendance.
Enforcement of attendance
laws, §16-12-18.
Attendance officers.
Employment, §16-12-18.
Bonds, surety, §16-11-7.
Buildings.
Building program for city
schools, §16-12-6.
Generally, §16-12-7.
Census.
Quadrennial census,
§16-12-13.
Certificates.
Required, §16-23-1.
City boards of education.
Nomination, removal, etc.,
of employees,
§16-12-16.
Supervision of employees,
§16-12-15.
Clerical assistants.
Employment, §16-12-19.
Compensation, §16-12-1.
Compulsory attendance.
Enforcement of attendance
laws, §16-12-18.
Contracts.
Approval, §16-12-7.
Courses of study, §16-12-9.
Duties.
Generally, §16-12-3.
Educational benefits for
dependents of blind
parents.
Duties of city
superintendents,
§16-33-8.
Educational policy.
Recommendations,
§16-12-5.
Employees.
Supervision, §16-12-15.
Establishment of schools,
§16-12-4.
Grading schools, §16-12-8.
Grounds.
School grounds, §16-12-7.
Institutes organized by city
superintendent,
§16-12-10.
Leaves of absence, §16-12-21.
Maintenance of schools,
§16-12-4.
Payroll, §16-12-17.
Policy.
Recommendations of
educational policy,
§16-12-5.
Principals.
Nomination, removal, etc.,
§16-12-16.
Professional assistants.
Employment, §16-12-19.
Qualifications, §16-12-2.
Recommendations of
educational policy,
§16-12-5.
Records.
Textbooks.
Duty to maintain
records, §16-36-34.
Removal, §16-12-1.

EDUCATION—Cont'd
City superintendents of schools—Cont'd
Reports.
Forms for reports of employees of city boards, §16-12-12.
Required by state board, §16-12-14.
Retirement system. See within this heading, "Teachers."
Review of local actions by state superintendent, §§16-3-27, 16-4-8.
Rules and regulations, §16-12-5.
Standardizing schools, §16-12-8.
State superintendent of education.
Conferences, §16-4-6.
Review of local actions, §§16-3-27, 16-4-8.
Supervision of employees, §16-12-15.
Teachers.
Full-time employment of teachers authorized, §16-12-20.
Nomination of teachers, §16-12-16.
Payroll of city superintendent, §16-12-17.
Removal, §16-12-16.
Teachers' retirement system.
Eligibility of elected superintendent to participate in, §16-25-10.6.
Textbooks.
Approval of invoices, §16-36-18.
Inventory.
Duty to maintain, §16-36-34.
Number of textbooks.
Annual reports on number of books, §16-36-27.
Estimates.
Duty of local superintendent to furnish estimates of textbooks needed, §16-36-34.
Records.
Duty to maintain, §16-36-34.
Reports, §16-36-6.
Storage.
Duty to provide for storage, §16-36-34.
Vacations, §16-12-21.
Veterans.
Educational benefits.
City superintendent to inform veterans' dependents of benefits provided, §31-6-14.
Visitation of schools, §16-12-11.
Colleges.
See UNIVERSITIES AND COLLEGES.

EDUCATION—Cont'd
Commission on higher education.
General provisions, §§16-5-1 to 16-5-10.
See UNIVERSITIES AND COLLEGES.
Communism.
Instruction in history, doctrines, etc., of communism, §16-40-3.
Textbooks.
Contract to exclude communist authors, §16-36-10.
Compact for education.
Alabama education council.
Generally, §16-44-2.
Bylaws of commission, §16-44-3.
Entry into compact.
Governor authorized to enter into compact, §16-44-1.
Form, §16-44-1.
Governor authorized to enter, §16-44-1.
Provisions of compact, §16-44-1.
Secretary of state.
Bylaws of commission and amendments to be filed with secretary of state, §16-44-3.
Compacts.
Compact for education, §§16-44-1 to 16-44-3.
Interstate agreement on qualifications of educational personnel, §§16-23A-1 to 16-23A-44.
Compulsory school attendance. See within this heading, "Attendance."
Conferences.
County superintendents of education, §16-9-16.
State superintendent of education, §16-4-6.
Teachers, §16-23-12.
Textbooks, §16-36-36.
Conservation and natural resources.
Department.
Powers and duties.
General provisions, §9-2-2.
Consolidation of schools.
Authority, §16-8-13.
In two counties, §16-8-14.
County and city systems.
Generally, §16-8-17.
County superintendents of education.
Plans for consolidated schools, §16-9-20.
In two counties.
Apportionment of funds, §16-8-16.
Authority, §16-8-14.
Control, §16-8-15.
Plans for consolidated schools, §16-9-20.
Teachers.
Effect of consolidation on tenure, §16-24-2.
Constitution of Alabama.
See CONSTITUTION OF ALABAMA.

EDUCATION—Cont'd
Constitution of United States.
Required courses, §16-40-2.
Construction and interpretation.
Public school and college authority, §16-16-2.
Contingent interests.
Sale by state institutions, §35-4-384.
Contracts.
Age of majority.
Contracting for educational loans for college level education and above, §26-1-5.
Alabama education authority, §16-15-8.
Building.
Construction contract.
Forms, §16-1-2.
Child nutrition food program.
Storage and distribution.
Department of education authorized to contract for, §16-2-8.
City superintendents of schools.
Approval of contracts, §16-12-7.
Construction contract.
Form, §16-1-2.
County boards of education.
Right to contract, §16-8-40.
County superintendents of education.
Approval of contracts, §16-9-18.
Department of education.
Child nutrition food program.
Storage and distribution.
Department authorized to contract for, §16-2-8.
Educational building authorities.
Contracts to secure bonds and assumed obligations, §§16-17-11, 16-18-12.
Educational television commission, §16-7-6.
Employment contracts.
Forms, §16-4-9.
Federal food programs.
Storage and distribution.
Department of education authorized to contract for, §16-2-8.
Forms, §16-4-9.
Construction contracts, §16-1-2.
Interstate agreement on qualifications of educational personnel, §§16-23A-2, 16-23A-3.
Loans.
Age of majority.
Contracting for educational loans for college level education and above, §26-1-5.
Teachers.
Employment, §§16-24-8 to 16-24-11.

EDUCATION—Cont'd
  Contracts—Cont'd
    Textbooks.
      Adoption of textbooks,
        §§16-36-10 to 16-36-13,
        16-36-36, 16-36-38. See
        within this heading,
        "Textbooks."
  Contributions.
    Voluntary contributions.
      Salary deductions,
      §16-22-6.
  Corporations.
    Educational institutions,
      §§10-4-80 to 10-4-82;
      Const. Ala., art. XII,
      §229; amd. 27.
      See CORPORATIONS.
    Nonprofit corporations.
      General provisions,
        §§10-3A-1 to
        10-3A-225.
      See CORPORATIONS.
    Public school corporation,
      §§16-14-1 to 16-14-19.
      See within this heading,
      "Public school
      corporation."
  Corrections.
    Schools at correctional units,
      §§14-12-1 to 14-12-4.
      See CORRECTIONS.
  Correspondence schools.
    Regulations, §§16-46-1 to
      16-46-10. See within this
      heading, "Unaccredited
      schools."
  Cosmetology.
    School of cosmetology,
      §§34-7-3 to 34-7-5,
      34-7-11, 34-7-16.
      See COSMETOLOGISTS.
  **Council for school
    administration and
    supervision.**
    Teachers' retirement system.
      Eligibility of executive
        officers and employees,
        §16-25-10.2.
  Counseling of pupils,
    §16-1-16.
  Counties.
    Acquisition of lands for
      school building, §11-18-2.
    Appropriation of funds out of
      county treasury,
      §16-13-36.
    Boards of education, §§16-8-1
      to 16-8-43. See within
      this heading, "County
      boards of education."
    Boards of school trustees,
      §§16-10-1 to 16-10-11.
      See within this heading,
      "Boards of school
      trustees."
    Bond issues.
      Security for indebtedness
        incurred in purchase,
        construction, etc., of
        school buildings,
        §11-81-1.
    Budget system, §§16-13-140
      to 16-13-147. See within
      this heading, "Budgets."
    Custodian of county school
      funds, §16-8-33.
    Financial ability of counties.
      Minimum school program
        fund, §§16-13-53 to
        16-13-55.

EDUCATION—Cont'd
  Counties—Cont'd
    Forests and forestry.
      National forests.
        Distribution and
          expenditure of
          receipts from,
          §9-13-2.
      Improvement, beautification
        or decoration of schools,
        §11-3-11.
    Licenses.
      County license tax for
        school purposes.
        See COUNTIES.
    Local aid to state educational
      institutions, §§16-19-1 to
      16-19-8.
      See UNIVERSITIES AND
        COLLEGES.
    Minimum school program
      fund.
      Financial ability of
        counties, §§16-13-53 to
        16-13-55.
    One-mill county school tax,
      §§16-13-160 to 16-13-166.
      See within this heading,
      "Taxation."
    Policy.
      Educational policy of
        county, §16-8-10.
    Public school funds.
      County custodian of school
        funds, §§16-8-33,
        16-13-10 to 16-13-12.
    Taxation. See within this
      heading, "Taxation."
    Textbooks.
      Local textbooks selection
        committee, §§16-36-4
        to 16-36-6.
    Trustees.
      Boards of school trustees,
        §§16-10-1 to 16-10-11.
        See within this
        heading, "Boards of
        school trustees."
  County boards of education,
    §§16-8-1 to 16-8-43.
    Actions.
      Right to sue, §16-8-40.
    Administration of schools.
      Generally, §16-8-8.
    Annexing to city territory
      embracing schools.
      Arbitration.
        Appointment of board,
          §16-8-21.
        Hearing by board,
          §16-8-22.
        When arbitration
          required, §16-8-21.
      Retention of control by
        county boards pending
        agreements, §16-8-20.
    Association of school board
      members, §16-1-6.
    Attendance.
      Compulsory school
        attendance districts,
        §16-8-31.
      Boundaries, §16-9-17.
      Recommendations as to
        kind, location, etc.,
        §16-9-14.
    Boards of school trustees,
      §§16-10-1 to 16-10-11.
      See within this heading,
      "Boards of school
      trustees."

EDUCATION—Cont'd
  County boards of education
    —Cont'd
    Capacity.
      To sue and contract,
        §16-8-40.
    Census.
      Enumerators, §16-8-32.
      Quadrennial school census,
        §16-8-31.
    Chief executive of board.
      County superintendent of
        education, §16-9-1.
    Compensation of members,
      §§16-1-26, 16-8-5.
    Composition, §16-8-1.
    Compulsory school
      attendance districts,
      §16-8-34.
      Boundaries, §16-9-17.
      Recommendations as to
        kind, location, etc.,
        §16-9-14.
    Contracts.
      Right to contract, §16-8-40.
    Cooperative agreements with
      county commission.
      Authority to enter into,
        §§16-8-12.1, 16-11-9.1.
    County superintendents of
      education.
      Chief executive of board,
        §16-9-1.
      Nomination, assignment,
        removal, etc., of
        employees, §16-9-23.
      Secretary of board, §16-9-1.
      Duties and bond of
        superintendent as
        secretary, §16-8-7.
      Selection of
        superintendent.
        Term of office when
          county board selects
          superintendent,
          §16-9-9.
    Courses of study, §16-8-28.
    Custodian of county school
      funds, §16-8-33.
    Districts.
      Compulsory school
        attendance districts,
        §16-8-34.
      Boundaries, §16-9-17.
      Recommendations as to
        kind, location, etc.,
        §16-9-14.
    Duties.
      As executive officer of
        board, §16-9-13.
    Educational policy of county,
      §16-8-10.
    Election of members, §16-8-1.
      General elections, §17-2-5.
      Single member election
        districts.
        Apportionment, §16-8-1.
        Boundaries.
          Determined by
            majority vote of
            county board of
            education, §16-8-1.
        Establishment.
          Provisions of
            subsection used to
            establish, §16-8-1.
        Number of districts,
          §16-8-1.
        Qualifications of
          members so elected,
          §16-8-1.

EDUCATION—Cont'd
County boards of education
—Cont'd
Election of members—Cont'd
When members to be
elected, §§16-8-2,
17-2-5.
Electronic pagers or
communication devices.
When boards to prohibit
pupils from carrying,
§16-1-27.
Employees.
Expenses for participation
in conferences, etc.
Advancement of and
acccounting for
expenses, §16-13-14.
Forms of contracts, §16-4-9.
Leaves of absence,
§16-8-25.
Personal leave.
Support personnel,
§16-8-26.1.
Support personnel.
Personal leave,
§16-8-26.1.
Nomination, assignment,
removal, etc., by
county superintendent,
§16-9-23.
Payrolls.
Approval by county
superintendents,
§16-9-33.
Preparation by county
superintendent,
§16-9-32.
Rewards for suggestions,
§16-1-21.
Transportation, §16-8-27.
Vacations, §16-8-25.
Execution of process,
§16-8-40.
Executive officer of board,
§16-9-1.
Powers and duties of
executive officer,
§16-9-13.
Expenses for participation in
conferences, meetings,
etc.
Advances of and
accounting for,
§16-13-14.
Funds.
Allocation, §16-13-13.
Custodian of county school
funds, §16-8-33.
Suggestions saving funds.
Rewards, §16-1-21.
Gasoline tax.
Exemptions, §40-17-31.
Grades included in public
schools, §16-8-36.
Grading schools, §16-8-29.
Handicapped persons.
Institute for deaf and
blind.
Cooperation by county
boards, §21-1-8.
High schools.
System of high schools,
§16-26-2.
Illiteracy.
Cooperation with state
board, §16-34-2.

EDUCATION—Cont'd
County boards of education
—Cont'd
Illiteracy—Cont'd
Federal government.
Authority to cooperate
with federal
government,
§16-34-3.
Institute for deaf and blind.
Cooperation by county
boards, §21-1-8.
Insurance.
Group insurance.
Authority of to form
groups for purpose of
obtaining, §16-22-5.
Payment of premiums,
§16-22-5.
Insurance on schools,
§16-8-42.
Risk management
cooperatives,
§16-8-42.1.
Joint maintenance of schools.
Attendance by pupils near
county lines, §16-8-18.
Between counties,
§16-8-18.
State-line schools,
§16-8-19.
Judicial officers.
Authority of legislature to
constitute members of
county boards as
judicial officers, Const.
Ala., amd. 111.
Kindergartens, §16-8-41.
Leaves of absence, §16-8-25.
Personal leave for teachers
during time schools
are in session,
§16-8-26.
Lubricating oils and greases.
Tax exemption, §40-17-171.
Majority vote, §16-8-4.
Meetings.
Annual public meetings,
§16-8-3.
Notice, §§16-8-3, 16-8-4.
Organizational meetings,
§16-8-4.
Regular meetings, §16-8-4.
Special annual public
meetings, §16-8-3.
Special meetings, §16-8-4.
Motor fuels.
Additional excise tax on
gasoline, motor fuel
and lubricating oil.
Exemptions, §40-17-220.
Municipality may remain
under county board of
education, §16-13-199.
Oaths of members, §16-8-2.
Opening date of schools.
Uniform opening date,
§16-8-30.
Playgrounds.
Condemnation, §16-9-18.
Establishment, §16-8-41.
Improvements, §16-9-18.
Maintenance, §16-8-41.
Policy.
Educational policy of
county, §16-8-10.
Powers.
Tax anticipation warrants.
Effect of article on
existing powers,
§16-13-77.

EDUCATION—Cont'd
County boards of education
—Cont'd
Process.
Execution of process,
§16-8-40.
Promotion of pupils.
Conditions of promotion,
§16-8-35.
Property.
Acquisition of property,
§16-8-40.
Property vested in county
board, §16-8-12.
Qualifications, §16-8-1.
Rehabilitation and crippled
children service.
Cooperation in
rehabilitation work,
§16-38-7.
Reports.
Annual report published,
§16-8-37.
Forms of reports required
by boards, §§16-8-38,
16-9-27.
Publication of annual
reports, §16-8-37.
Reports to state board,
§16-8-39.
Restrooms.
Sanitary restrooms,
§16-8-43.
Review of local actions by
state superintendent,
§§16-3-27, 16-4-8.
Rules of procedure, §16-8-4.
Sales tax.
Exemptions.
Gross proceeds of sale of
tangible personal
property to county
school boards,
§40-23-4.
Secretary of board.
Appointment, duties and
bond of superintendent
as secretary of board,
§16-8-7.
County superintendents of
schools, §16-9-1.
Special annual public
meetings, §16-8-3.
Notice, §16-8-3.
Standardizing schools,
§16-8-29.
State board of education.
Reports by county board to
state board, §16-8-39.
State superintendent of
education.
Conferences, §16-4-6.
Review of local actions by
state superintendent,
§§16-3-27, 16-4-8.
Supervision of schools.
Exercise of supervision,
§16-8-9.
Generally, §16-8-8.
Tax anticipation warrants in
cities and counties.
Effect of article on existing
powers of boards of
education, §16-13-77.
Taxation.
Exemptions.
Notes in anticipation of
warrants,
§16-13-216.
Teachers.
Appointment, §16-8-23.

EDUCATION—Cont'd
County boards of education
—Cont'd
Teachers—Cont'd
Full-time employment by
county board, §16-8-24.
Leaves of absence,
§16-8-25.
Personal leave for
teachers during time
schools are in
session, §16-8-26.
Removal, §16-8-23.
Substitute teachers
replacing teachers
absent on sick leave.
Reimbursing local boards
for payments to
substitutes, §16-3-36.
Vacations, §16-8-25.
Terms of members, §§16-8-2,
17-2-5.
Textbooks.
Filing of school board
policies with state
superintendent of
education, §16-36-4.
Local appropriations,
§16-36-20.
Transportation of employees,
§16-8-27.
Trustees.
Boards of school trustees,
§§16-10-1 to 16-10-11.
See within this
heading, "Boards of
school trustees."
Uniform system of schools.
Maintenance, §16-8-11.
Use tax.
Exemptions, §40-23-62.
Vacancies, §16-8-6.
Vocational education.
Authorized to operate
vocational high schools
jointly with city
boards, §16-37-8.
Cooperation with state
board, §16-37-5.
Voting.
Majority vote, §16-8-4.
Warrants, §§16-13-210 to
16-13-270.
Defined, §16-13-210.
Investment of trust estate
in interest-bearing
warrants, §19-3-121.
Notes in anticipation.
Authorized, §16-13-211.
Definitions, §16-13-210.
Extension, §16-13-213.
Investment by
fiduciaries,
§16-13-217.
Issuance, §16-13-211.
Approval by state
superintendent,
§16-13-215.
Obligations.
Notes deemed not
general obligation,
§16-13-212.
Refunding, §16-13-213.
Sales.
Public or private sales,
§16-13-214.
Taxation.
Exemption from
taxation,
§16-13-216.

EDUCATION—Cont'd
County boards of education
—Cont'd
Warrants—Cont'd
Notes in anticipation
—Cont'd
Tax proceeds.
Authority of board to
pledge, §16-13-212.
County boards of health.
Duties, §22-3-2.
County health officers.
Duties, §22-3-5.
Mental and physical
examinations of school
children.
Equipment, §16-29-4.
**County superintendents of
education.**
Accounts.
Examination by state
superintendent,
§16-9-31.
Admittance to high schools.
Conditions of admittance,
§16-9-19.
Assignment, §16-9-23.
Assistants, §16-9-24.
Attendance.
Compulsory school
attendance districts.
Boundaries, §16-9-17.
Recommendations as to
kind, location, etc.,
§16-9-14.
Enforcement of attendance
laws, §16-9-30.
Bonds, surety, §16-9-3.
Bond of superintendent as
secretary of county
board, §16-8-7.
Books and papers.
Examination by district
attorney and grand
jury, §12-16-195.
Examination by state
superintendent,
§16-9-31.
Buildings.
Building program,
§16-9-17.
Condemnation, §16-9-18.
Improvements, §16-9-18.
Census.
Quadrennial school census,
§16-9-29.
Certificate of administration
and supervision,
§16-9-10.
Misdemeanor to print
name of person
without certificate on
ballot, §16-9-4.
Qualifications of
superintendent,
§16-9-2.
Required, §16-23-1.
Clerical assistants, §16-9-24.
Committee, §§16-31-1 to
16-31-5.
Compulsory school
attendance.
Enforcement of attendance
laws, §16-9-30.
Compulsory school
attendance districts.
Boundaries, §16-9-17.
Recommendations as to
kind, location, etc.,
§16-9-14.
Conferences, §16-9-16.

EDUCATION—Cont'd
**County superintendents of
education**—Cont'd
Consolidation of schools.
Plans for consolidated
schools, §16-9-20.
Contracts.
Approval of contracts,
§16-9-18.
County boards of education.
Chief executive of board,
§16-9-1.
Nomination, assignment,
removal, etc., of
employees, §16-9-23.
Secretary of board, §16-9-1.
Duties and bond of
superintendent as
secretary, §16-8-7.
Selection of
superintendent.
Term of office when
county board selects
superintendent,
§16-9-9.
Courses of study, §16-9-21.
Disbursements.
Annual statement of
disbursements,
§16-9-28.
District attorneys.
Examination of books and
papers of county
superintendent by
district attorney and
grand jury, §12-16-195.
Districts.
Compulsory school
attendance districts.
Boundaries, §16-9-17.
Recommendations as to
kind, location, etc.,
§16-9-14.
Educational benefits for
dependents of blind
parents.
Duties of county
superintendents,
§16-33-8.
Educational policies,
§16-9-15.
Elections, §§16-9-4 to 16-9-8.
Ballots.
Instructions on ballot,
§16-9-7.
Misdemeanor to print
name of person
without certificate
on ballot, §16-9-4.
Candidates, §16-9-4.
Death or resignation of
successful candidate
prior to taking office.
Procedure, §16-9-8.
Instructions on ballot,
§16-9-7.
Nominations.
By political party,
§16-9-5.
Primary elections,
§16-9-6.
Primary elections, §16-9-6.
Taking office on July 1
following election,
§16-9-8.
Employees.
Nomination, assignment,
removal, etc., §16-9-23.
Equipment, §16-9-24.

EDUCATION—Cont'd
  **County superintendents of
    education**—Cont'd
  Examination of books,
    accounts, etc., by state
    superintendent, §16-9-31.
  Expenses.
    Traveling expenses,
      §16-9-12.
  Forms.
    Report forms, §16-9-27.
  Full-time office, §16-9-12.
  Grading schools, §16-9-22.
  Grand jury.
    Examination of books and
      papers of by district
      attorney and grand
      jury, §12-16-195.
  Institutes organized by
    superintendents,
    §16-9-25.
  Nomination, assignment,
    removal, etc., §16-9-23.
  Offices.
    Maintenance at county
      seat, §16-9-24.
  Payrolls.
    Approval, §16-9-33.
    Preparation, §16-9-32.
  Playgrounds.
    Condemnation, §16-9-18.
    Improvements, §16-9-18.
  Policies.
    Educational policies,
      §16-9-15.
  Powers as executive officer of
    board, §16-9-13.
  Principals.
    Conferences, §16-9-16.
  Qualifications of
    superintendent, §16-9-2.
  Receipts.
    Annual statement of
      receipts, §16-9-28.
  Recommendations as to kind,
    location, etc., of schools
    and compulsory school
    attendance districts,
    §16-9-14.
  Records.
    Textbooks.
      Duty to maintain
        records, §16-36-34.
  Reports.
    Annual statement of
      receipts and
      disbursements,
      §16-9-28.
    Forms.
      Superintendents to
        prepare, §16-9-27.
    Preparation of reports,
      §16-9-30.
    State superintendent of
      education.
      Report on schools to
        state superintendent,
        §16-9-31.
  Review of local actions by
    state superintendent,
    §§16-3-27, 16-4-8.
  Salary, §16-9-12.
  Schools.
    Recommendations as to
      kind, location, etc.,
      §16-9-14.
  Standardizing schools,
    §16-9-22.
  State superintendent of
    education.
    Conferences, §16-4-6.

EDUCATION—Cont'd
  **County superintendents of
    education**—Cont'd
  State superintendent of
    education—Cont'd
    Examination of books,
      accounts, etc., by state
      superintendent,
      §16-9-31.
    Report on schools to state
      superintendent,
      §16-9-31.
    Review of local actions by
      state superintendent,
      §§16-3-27, 16-4-8.
  Supervisors, §16-9-24.
  Taking office on July 1,
    following election,
    §16-9-8.
  Teachers.
    Conferences, §16-9-16.
    Nomination, §16-9-23.
    Payrolls.
      Approval, §16-9-33.
      Preparation, §16-9-32.
    Promotion, §16-9-23.
    Removal, §16-9-23.
    Suspension, §16-9-23.
  Teachers' retirement system.
    Eligibility of elected
      superintendent to
      participate in,
      §16-25-10.6.
  Terms of office.
    When county board selects
      superintendent,
      §16-9-9.
  Textbooks.
    Approval of invoices,
      §16-36-18.
    Inventory.
      Duty to maintain,
        §16-36-34.
    Number of textbooks.
      Annual reports on
        number of books,
        §16-36-27.
    Estimates.
      Duty of local
        superintendent to
        furnish estimates
        of textbooks
        needed, §16-36-34.
    Records.
      Duty to maintain,
        §16-36-34.
    Reports, §16-36-6.
      Annual reports on
        number of books,
        §16-36-27.
    Storage of books.
      Duty to provide for
        storage, §16-36-34.
  Traveling expenses, §16-9-12.
  Vacancy in office, §16-9-11.
  Veterans.
    Educational benefits.
      Superintendent to inform
        dependents of
        benefits provided,
        §31-6-14.
  Visitation of schools,
    §16-9-26.
  Courses of study.
  Cardiopulmonary
    resuscitation, §16-40-8.
  City boards of education,
    §16-11-20.
  City superintendents of
    schools, §16-12-9.

EDUCATION—Cont'd
  Courses of study—Cont'd
  Communism.
    Instruction in history,
      doctrines, etc., of
      communism, §16-40-3.
  Constitution of United
    States.
    Required, §16-40-2.
  Content of courses.
    Minimum content,
      §16-35-4.
  County boards of education,
    §16-8-28.
  County superintendents of
    education, §16-9-21.
  Driver education, §§16-40-5.1
    to 16-40-5.4.
  Drug abuse education,
    §§16-41-1 to 16-41-10.
    See DRUGS.
  Elementary schools.
    Studies required to be
      taught in elementary
      schools, §16-35-5.
  Generally, §16-3-15.
  Health education.
    Comprehensive health
      education, §16-40-7.
  High schools, §16-26-1.
  Humane treatment of
    animals, §16-40-4.
  Maximum number of courses,
    §16-35-4.
  Minimum contents,
    §§16-3-15, 16-35-4.
  Number of courses.
    Maximum number,
      §16-35-4.
  Patriotism, §16-40-6.
  Physical education.
    Required, §16-40-1.
  Regulation of certain schools
    and courses of
    instruction, §§16-46-1 to
    16-46-10. See within this
    heading, "Unaccredited
    schools."
  Sex education.
    Teaching not authorized,
      §16-41-8.
  Special courses, §16-1-16.
  State board of education,
    §16-3-15.
  State committee.
    Appointment of members,
      §16-35-1.
    Compensation of members,
      §16-35-2.
    Composition, §16-35-1.
    Content of courses.
      Minimum content,
        §16-35-4.
    Duties.
      Generally, §16-35-3.
    Elementary school.
      Studies required to be
        taught in
        elementary school,
        §16-35-5.
    Expenses of members,
      §16-35-2.
    Maximum number of
      courses, §16-35-4.
    Minimum course contents,
      §16-35-4.
    Number of courses.
      Maximum number,
        §16-35-4.
    Oath of members, §16-35-2.

EDUCATION—Cont'd
Courses of study—Cont'd
State committee—Cont'd
Qualifications of members,
§16-35-1.
Terms of members,
§16-35-1.
Textbooks. See within this
heading, "Textbooks."
Unaccredited schools.
Regulation of certain
schools and courses of
instruction, §§16-46-1
to 16-46-10. See within
this heading,
"Unaccredited schools."
CPR.
Instruction and techniques of
cardiopulmonary
resuscitation, §16-40-8.
Criminal law.
Alcoholic beverages.
Keeping on school
premises, §16-1-10.
Selling, etc., to school
children, §16-1-10.
Diversion of funds by
officials.
Penalty, §16-13-4.
Textbooks.
Charging more than
contract price,
§16-36-38.
Conflicts of interest,
§16-36-36.
Use of other than contract
books in public schools,
§16-36-37.
Cruelty to animals.
Humane treatment of
animals taught,
§16-40-4.
Damages.
Property damage.
Reports of property
damage, §16-1-24.
Teachers.
Breach of employment
contract, §16-24-10.
Day.
Scholastic day.
Defined, §16-1-1.
Deaf persons.
Alabama institute for deaf
and blind, §§21-1-1 to
21-1-26.
See HANDICAPPED
PERSONS.
Exceptional children,
§§16-39-1 to 16-39-12.
See within this heading,
"Exceptional children."
Decoration of schools.
Powers and duties of county
commissions, §11-3-11.
Definitions.
Alabama education
authority, §16-15-1.
Attendance, §16-28-1.
Church schools, §16-28-1.
Day.
Scholastic day, §16-1-1.
Denominational schools,
§16-28-1.
Displaced homemakers,
§16-60-240.
Educational building
authorities, §16-17-1.
Educational reform,
§16-6A-2.
Fiscal year, §16-1-1.

EDUCATION—Cont'd
Definitions—Cont'd
Generally, §16-1-1.
Hazing, §16-1-23.
Mathematics and science
high school, §16-26A-2.
Month.
Scholastic month, §16-1-1.
Nonteacher, nonclassified,
etc., employees,
§36-26-100.
Public education employees'
health insurance,
§16-25A-1.
Public school and college
authority, §16-16-1.
Risk management
cooperatives, §16-8-42.1.
School buses, §32-1-1.1.
Support personnel or
employee, §16-25-1.
Teachers, §16-25-1.
Teachers' retirement system,
§16-25-1.
Time, §16-1-1.
Unaccredited schools,
§16-46-1.
Week.
Scholastic week, §16-1-1.
Year.
Fiscal year, §16-1-1.
Scholastic year, §16-1-1.
Denominational schools.
Drug abuse education.
Exclusion of teacher or
administrator from
participation
prohibited, §16-41-5.
Establishment, §10-4-61.
School funds not to be used
for support, Const. Ala.,
art. XIV, §263.
Dentists.
Continuing education
requirements, §34-9-15.
Department of education.
Administration, §16-4-11.
Assistants.
Clerical assistants,
§16-4-12.
Professional assistants,
§16-4-12.
Assistant state
superintendent of
education.
Duties, §16-2-1.
Child nutrition food program.
Storage and distribution.
Department authorized
to contract for,
§16-2-8.
Clerical assistants, §16-4-12.
Contracts.
Child nutrition food
program.
Department authorized
to contract for
storage and
distribution of,
§16-2-8.
Creation, §16-2-1.
Division directors.
Appointment, §16-2-7.
Compensation, §16-2-7.
Continuance under merit
system law, §16-2-7.
Duties, §16-2-2.

EDUCATION—Cont'd
Department of education
—Cont'd
Educational benefits for
dependents of blind
parents.
Application to be made to
state department of
education, §16-33-6.
Duties of state department,
§16-33-7.
Employees.
Clerical assistants,
§16-4-12.
Nomination, §16-4-11.
Professional assistants,
§16-4-12.
Supervision, §16-4-11.
Expenses, §16-2-5.
Federal food programs.
Storage and distribution of.
Department authorized
to contract for,
§16-2-8.
Kindergarten.
Public kindergarten pilot
programs, §16-2-6.
Mathematics and science
high school.
Coordination of programs
and curriculum with
department,
§16-26A-3.
Definition of department,
§16-26A-2.
Organization, §16-2-3.
Professional assistants,
§16-4-12.
Publications by department,
§16-2-4.
State superintendent of
education.
Administration of
department, §16-4-11.
Director of department of
education, §16-2-1.
Supervision and
nomination of
employees of
department, §16-4-11.
Unaccredited schools.
Hearing, §16-46-9.
Petition for review of
actions by department,
§16-46-9.
Disability.
Exceptional children,
§§16-39-1 to 16-39-12.
See within this heading,
"Exceptional children."
Disciplinary problem.
Removal, separation or
grouping of pupils
creating disciplinary
problems, §16-1-14.
Diseases.
Immunization of school
children, §§16-30-1 to
16-30-5.
Mental and physical
examinations of school
children, §§16-29-1 to
16-29-6. See within this
heading, "Mental and
physical examinations of
school children."
Notifiable diseases.
General provisions.
See DISEASES.

EDUCATION—Cont'd
Diseases—Cont'd
Notifiable diseases—Cont'd
Principals.
Persons responsible for
reporting diseases,
§22-11A-2.
Superintendent of
education.
Notification that student
or employee has
contagious disease,
§22-11A-38.
Testing children for certain
diseases, §16-30-1.
Dismissal procedure.
Nonteacher, nonclassified,
etc., employees,
§§36-26-100 to 36-26-108.
**Displaced homemakers
programs.**
Contents, §16-60-242.
Defined, §16-60-240.
Director.
Appointment, §16-60-242.
Establishment, §16-60-241.
Reports.
Annual report to
chancellor, §16-60-243.
Display of flags, §§16-43-1 to
16-43-4.
District attorneys.
Examination of books and
papers of county
superintendents,
§12-16-195.
Districts.
Compulsory school
attendance districts,
§16-8-34.
Boundaries, §16-9-17.
Recommendation by county
superintendents as to
kind, location, etc.,
§16-9-14.
Independent school districts.
Boards of education.
Association of school
board members,
§16-1-6.
Review of local actions
by state
superintendent,
§16-3-27.
State superintendent of
education.
Review of local actions
by state
superintendent,
§16-3-27.
School tax district.
County and district three-
mill school tax,
§§16-13-180 to
16-13-199. See within
this heading,
"Taxation."
Warrants for special county
and district taxes,
§§16-13-90 to 16-13-109.
See within this heading,
"Taxation."
Donations.
Administration of donations,
§16-3-30.
Held for schools, §16-3-29.
Driver education, §§16-40-5.1
to 16-40-5.4.
See MOTOR VEHICLES.
Driver training schools.
See MOTOR VEHICLES.

EDUCATION—Cont'd
Drugs.
See DRUGS.
Dues.
Membership dues.
Salary deductions,
§16-22-6.
**Educational building
authorities.**
Ancillary improvements.
Defined, §16-17-1.
Location, §16-17-8.
Powers of authority,
§16-17-7.
Public educational building
authorities, §§16-18-7
to 16-18-9.
Applicant.
Defined, §16-17-1.
Assumed obligations.
Contracts to secure,
§16-17-11.
Public educational
building authorities,
§16-18-12.
Board of directors, §16-17-5.
Bond issues.
Contracts to secure bonds
and assumed
obligations, §16-17-11.
Defined, §16-17-1.
Exemption from taxation,
§16-17-14.
Generally, §16-17-10.
Investments in bonds of
authority, §16-17-17.
Notice of bond resolution,
§16-17-18.
Proceeds from sale,
§16-17-13.
Resolution.
Notice of bond
resolution,
§16-17-18.
Sale.
Proceeds from sale,
§16-17-13.
Statutory mortgage lien,
§16-17-12.
Construction.
Defined, §16-17-1.
Contracts.
To secure bonds and
assumed obligations,
§16-17-11.
Public educational
building authorities,
§16-18-12.
Definitions, §16-17-1.
Public educational building
authorities, §16-18-1.
Determining municipality.
Defined, §16-17-1.
Dissolution, §16-17-19.
Public educational building
authorities, §16-18-21.
Vesting of title to property,
§16-17-19.
Earnings of authority,
§16-17-16.
Public educational building
authorities, §16-18-18.
Educational institutions.
Defined, §16-17-1.
Exemption from taxation,
§16-17-14.
Public educational building
authorities, §16-18-16.
Freedom of authority from
state supervision and
control, §16-18-17.

EDUCATION—Cont'd
**Educational building
authorities**—Cont'd
Governing body.
Defined, §16-17-1.
Incorporation.
Amendments to certificate
of incorporation,
§16-17-4.
Certificate of incorporation,
§16-17-3.
Amendments, §16-17-4.
Definition of incorporators,
§16-17-1.
Procedure to incorporate,
§16-17-3.
Incorporators.
Defined, §16-17-1.
Investments in bonds of
authority, §16-17-17.
Public educational building
authorities, §16-18-19.
Lease agreements.
Powers of authority,
§16-17-7.
Remedies under lease
agreements, §16-17-9.
Legislative intent, §16-17-2.
Public educational building
authorities, §16-18-2.
Liens.
Statutory mortgage lien,
§16-17-12.
Public educational
building authorities,
§16-18-13.
Mortgages and deeds of trust.
Statutory mortgage lien,
§16-18-3.
Officers, §16-17-6.
Public educational building
authorities, §16-18-6.
Powers, §16-17-7.
Public educational building
authorities, §16-18-7.
Public educational building
authorities, §§16-18-1,
16-18-3, 16-18-4.
Aid from other public
bodies, §16-18-15.
Ancillary improvements.
Defined, §16-18-1.
Lease by educational
institutions,
§16-18-9.
Location, §16-18-8.
Powers of authority,
§16-18-7.
Applicants, §16-18-3.
Defined, §16-18-1.
Assumed obligations.
Contracts to secure,
§16-18-12.
Board of directors,
§16-18-5.
Bond issues.
Contracts to secure
bonds, §16-18-12.
Defined, §16-18-1.
Exemption from
taxation, §16-18-16.
Generally, §16-18-11.
Investments in bonds of
authority, §16-18-19.
Notice of bond
resolution,
§16-18-20.
Powers of authority,
§16-18-7.
Proceeds from sale,
§16-18-14.

EDUCATION—Cont'd
Educational building authorities—Cont'd
Public educational building authorities—Cont'd
Bond issues—Cont'd
Sale proceeds, §16-18-14.
Securities, §16-18-12.
Statutory mortgage lien, §16-18-13.
Construction.
Defined, §16-18-1.
Contracts.
Securing bonds and assumed obligations, §16-18-12.
Cooperation with other public bodies, §16-18-15.
Definitions, §16-18-1.
Determining municipality.
Defined, §16-18-1.
Dissolution, §16-18-21.
Earnings of authority, §16-18-18.
Educational institutions.
Defined, §16-18-1.
Lease of ancillary improvements, §16-18-9.
Exemption from taxation, §16-18-16.
Freedom from state supervision and control, §16-18-17.
Governing body.
Defined, §16-18-2.
Incorporation.
Certificate of incorporation, §16-18-3.
Amendments, §16-18-4.
Definition of incorporators, §16-18-1.
Procedure to incorporate, §16-18-3.
Investments in bonds of authority, §16-18-19.
Leases.
Ancillary improvements, §16-18-9.
Powers of authority, §16-18-7.
Remedies under lease agreements, §16-18-10.
Legislative intent, §16-18-2.
Liens.
Statutory mortgage lien, §16-18-13.
Mortgages.
Statutory mortgage lien, §16-18-13.
Officers, §16-18-6.
Powers, §16-18-7.
Property.
Vesting of title upon dissolution, §16-18-21.
Remedies under lease agreements, §16-18-10.
State supervision and control.
Freedom of authority, §16-18-17.
Taxation.
Exemption from taxation, §16-18-16.

EDUCATION—Cont'd
Educational building authorities—Cont'd
Remedies under lease agreements, §16-17-9.
Public educational building authorities, §16-18-10.
State educational institutions.
Defined, §16-17-1.
State supervision and control.
Freedom of authority from state supervision and control, §16-17-15.
Public educational building authorities, §16-18-17.
Taxation.
Exemption from taxation, §16-18-16.
Educational reform.
Citation of chapter, §16-6A-1.
Commission, §§16-6A-5 to 16-6A-8.
Appointment, §16-6A-5.
Appropriations, §16-6A-5.
Chairperson, §16-6A-6.
Composition, §16-6A-5.
Creation, §16-6A-5.
Dissolution, §16-6A-7.
Duties, §16-6A-7.
Additional duties, §16-6A-8.
Expenses, §16-6A-6.
Meetings, §16-6A-6.
Not to duplicate responsibilities of state board of education, §16-6A-7.
Reports.
Annual report to governor and legislature, §16-6A-7.
Staff, §16-6A-6.
Contracts.
Employment contracts with certified professionals, §16-6A-17.
Critical needs areas.
Comprehensive plan for improving courses.
Contents, §16-6A-9.
Development, §16-6A-9.
Development of plans for improving courses, §16-6A-9.
In-service education centers, §16-6A-16.
Provisionally certified teachers.
Employment, §16-6A-10.
Scholarship loans for teacher education programs.
Administration, §16-6A-11.
Agreements with Alabama commission on higher education, §16-6A-13.
Amount, §16-6A-13.
Duration of loan, §16-6A-13.
Eligibility for loans, §16-6A-12.
Established, §16-6A-11.
Proceedings to recover, §16-6A-13.

EDUCATION—Cont'd
Educational reform—Cont'd
Critical needs areas—Cont'd
Scholarship loans for teacher education programs—Cont'd
Repayment, §16-6A-13.
Disposition of repayments, §16-6A-13.
Rules and regulations, §16-6A-14.
Tuition grant program for certified teachers, §16-6A-15.
Definitions, §16-6A-2.
Governor's educational reform commission, §§16-6A-5 to 16-6A-8.
Governor's program for improving education.
Contents, §16-6A-4.
Implementation, §16-6A-4.
In-service and professional development activities.
Number of days to be used for, §16-6A-17.
In-service education centers.
Critical needs areas, §16-6A-16.
Legislative intent, §16-6A-3.
Short title of chapter, §16-6A-1.
Tuition grant program for certified teachers, §16-6A-15.
Educational television commission, §§16-7-1 to 16-7-6.
Agents, §16-7-4.
Appointment of members, §16-7-2.
Composition, §16-7-2.
Conflicts of interest.
Members not to have financial interest in facilities, §16-7-3.
Contracts, §16-7-6.
Creation, §16-7-1.
Duties, §16-7-5.
Delegation, §16-7-4.
Educational television foundation authority.
Governing body, §16-7A-7.
Expenses of members, §16-7-2.
Gifts.
Acceptance of gifts, §16-7-6.
Governing body of public network, §16-7A-7.
Membership, §16-7-2.
Officers, §16-7-4.
Organization, §16-7-4.
Per diem, §16-7-2.
Powers.
Delegation, §16-7-4.
Removal of members, §16-7-3.
Rules and regulations, §16-7-4.
Terms of members, §16-7-2.
Vacancies, §16-7-2.

EDUCATION—Cont'd
Educational television foundation authority,
§§16-7A-1 to 16-7A-8.
See EDUCATIONAL TELEVISION FOUNDATION AUTHORITY.
Education authority,
§§16-15-1 to 16-15-13. See within this heading, "Alabama education authority."
Education study commission, §§16-6-1 to 16-6-6. See within this heading, "Study commission."
Ejectment.
Recovery of lands by or in name of state for schools, §6-6-281.
Elections.
City boards of education, §16-11-3.
Consolidated noncontiguous municipalities, §11-42-159.
County boards of education, §16-8-1.
General elections, §17-2-5.
Single member election districts.
Apportionment, §16-8-1.
Boundaries.
Determined by majority vote of county board of education, §16-8-1.
Establishment.
Provisions of subsection used to establish, §16-8-1.
Number of districts allowed, §16-8-1.
Qualifications of members so elected, §16-8-1.
When members elected, §§16-8-2, 17-2-5.
County superintendent of education, §§16-9-4 to 16-9-8.
State superintendent of education, Const. Ala., art. V, §§114, 115.
Taxation.
Contest of certain elections, §16-1-17.
County and district three-mill school taxes, §§16-13-180 to 16-13-190. See within this heading, "Taxation."
One-mill county school tax, §§16-13-160 to 16-13-164.
Warrants for special county and district taxes, §16-13-108.
Electronic pagers.
When pupils prohibited from carrying, §16-1-27.
Elementary schools.
City boards of education.
Incidental fees in city elementary schools, §16-11-26.

EDUCATION—Cont'd
Elementary schools—Cont'd
Courses of study.
Studies required to be taught in elementary school, §16-35-5.
Fees.
Incidental fees, §§16-10-6, 16-11-26.
High schools.
May be placed under same principal, §16-26-3.
Incidental fees, §§16-10-6, 16-11-26.
Principals.
Elementary and high school may be placed under same principal, §16-26-3.
Required studies, §16-35-5.
Teachers.
Scholarship fund, §16-23-17.
Emergency secondary education scholarship fund, §§16-23-18 to 16-23-23.
Eminent domain.
City boards of education, §16-11-13.
Eminent scholars trust fund, §§16-61-1 to 16-61-10.
See UNIVERSITIES AND COLLEGES.
Employees.
Annuities.
Tax sheltered annuities.
Salary deductions, §16-22-6.
Checkoffs.
Salary deductions.
Purposes for which deductions made, §16-22-6.
Contributions.
Voluntary contributions.
Salary deductions, §16-22-6.
Dues.
Membership dues.
Salary deductions, §16-22-6.
Insurance.
Salary deductions.
Group insurance premiums, §16-22-6.
Membership dues.
Salary deductions, §16-22-6.
Nonteacher, nonclassified employees, §§36-26-101 to 36-26-107.
Public employees' individual retirement account fund.
Salary deductions, §16-22-6.
Retirement system, §§16-25-1 to 16-25-47. See within this heading, "Teachers."
Salaries.
Annuities.
Tax sheltered annuities.
Salary deductions, §16-22-6.
Checkoffs.
Salary deductions, §16-22-6.
Contributions.
Voluntary contributions.
Salary deductions, §16-22-6.

EDUCATION—Cont'd
Employees—Cont'd
Salaries—Cont'd
Deductions.
Annuities.
Tax sheltered annuities, §16-22-6.
Insurance.
Group insurance premiums, §16-22-6.
Membership dues, §16-22-6.
Policies as to salary deductions, §16-22-6.
Public employees' individual retirement account, §16-22-6.
Purposes for which deductions made, §16-22-6.
Voluntary contributions, §16-22-6.
Dues.
Membership dues.
Salary deductions, §16-22-6.
Insurance.
Group insurance premiums.
Salary deductions, §16-22-6.
Membership dues.
Salary deductions, §16-22-6.
Public employees' individual retirement account fund.
Salary deductions, §16-22-6.
Voluntary contributions.
Salary deductions, §16-22-6.
Suggestions from employees.
Payments as reward, §16-1-21.
Support personnel.
Defined, §16-25-1.
Personal leave.
Authorized, §16-8-26.1.
Unemployment compensation.
Appropriation of funds for payment of benefits of local school systems, §25-4-150.
Voluntary contributions.
Salary deductions, §16-22-6.
Endowment funds.
Investment of endowment funds held by state board of education and trustees of state institutions, §16-13-2.
Energy management and conservation.
Public awareness and education programs.
Objectives, §41-6A-5.
Enrollment.
Cases of nonenrollment, §16-28-16.
Church schools.
Report of enrollment, §16-28-7.

EDUCATION—Cont'd
Enrollment—Cont'd
Report of enrollment,
§16-28-7.
Comparing report with list
of children who should
attend school,
§16-28-9.
Escheats.
Application of property to
furtherance of education,
Const. Ala., amd. 111.
Application of property to
maintenance of public
schools, Const. Ala., art.
XIV, §258.
Evidence.
Attendance register and
rules and regulations.
Use as evidence, §16-28-23.
Copies of proceedings as
evidence, §16-16-6.
Public school corporation.
Records or certificates as
evidence, §16-14-16.
Examinations.
Mental and physical
examinations of school
children, §§16-29-1 to
16-29-6. See within this
heading, "Mental and
physical examinations of
school children."
**Excellence in local
education act.**
Local funding of school
programs, §§16-13-60 to
16-13-65.
Exceptional children,
§§16-39-1 to 16-39-12.
Case history.
Record of case history,
§16-39-8.
Classification of child,
§16-39-8.
Definitions, §16-39-2.
Funds.
Source of funds, §16-39-3.
Hearing impaired.
Textbooks, equipment, etc.,
for vision or hearing
impaired, §16-39-10.
Implementation of program,
§16-39-4.
Learning disabilities.
Textbooks, equipment, etc.,
for those having
special learning
disabilities, §16-39-10.
Placement committee.
Defined, §16-39-2.
Placement of child, §16-39-8.
Plans.
School board plan,
§§16-39-4, 16-39-6.
Program.
Implementation of
program, §16-39-4.
Records.
Case history, §16-39-8.
Reports, §16-39-9.
Required education for
exceptional children,
§16-39-3.
Retarded.
Defined, §16-39-2.
Rules and regulations.
Responsibilities of state
board of education,
§16-39-5.

EDUCATION—Cont'd
Exceptional children—Cont'd
Scholarships.
Special teachers, §16-39-12.
School buses, §16-39-11.
Short title of chapter,
§16-39-1.
Source of funds, §16-39-3.
Specialist.
Defined, §16-39-2.
Special services.
Defined, §16-39-2.
State board of education.
Responsibilities, §16-39-5.
Teachers.
Scholarships for special
teachers, §16-39-12.
Teacher units, §16-39-7.
Textbooks.
Vision or hearing
impaired, §16-39-10.
Transportation, §16-39-11.
Units.
Teacher units, §16-39-7.
Vision impaired.
Textbooks, equipment, etc.,
for vision impaired,
§16-39-10.
Excise taxes.
Warrants for special license,
privilege or excise taxes,
§§16-13-120 to 16-13-122.
Expenditures.
State superintendent of
education.
Examination of
expenditures, §16-4-7.
Explosives.
Eye protective devices for
pupils and teachers
participating in certain
courses, §16-1-7.
Eye protective devices.
Pupils and teachers
participating in certain
courses, §16-1-7.
Faculty.
Development of budget.
Faculty to have
opportunity to develop,
§16-13-13.
Federal grants, §§16-13-5 to
16-13-7.
Acceptance, §16-13-5.
Administration.
State board of education
designated state
agency in
administration,
§16-13-6.
Minimum program fund.
Appropriation to minimum
program fund,
§16-13-7.
State board of education.
Designated state agency in
administration,
§16-13-6.
State superintendent of
education, §16-4-21.
Fees.
Alabama education
authority.
Incorporation or
dissolution.
No fees to be paid,
§16-15-5.
Elementary schools.
Incidental fees, §§16-10-6,
16-11-26.

EDUCATION—Cont'd
Fees—Cont'd
High schools.
Matriculation fee may be
charged, §16-26-4.
Matriculation fees.
Distribution of for
purchase of supplies
and maintenance of
property, §16-13-38.
High schools.
Matriculation fee may be
charged, §16-26-4.
Public school and college
authority.
Incorporation and
dissolution.
No fees to be paid,
§16-16-5.
Public school corporation.
No fees for incorporation or
dissolution, §16-14-14.
State superintendent of
education.
Restrictions on receipt of
fees, Const. Ala., art.
V, §137; amd. 111.
Teachers.
Applicants for certificates,
§16-23-4.
Fiduciaries.
Public school and college
authority.
Bond issues.
Investment of fiduciary
funds, §16-16-9.
Tax anticipation warrants in
cities and counties.
Warrants legal
investments for
fiduciaries, §16-13-74.
Finance.
Borrowing money.
Funds may be borrowed
against revenues of
current year,
§16-13-145.
Budgets, §§16-13-140 to
16-13-146. See within
this heading, "Budgets."
Department of finance.
Powers and duties of
department as to
educational
institutions, §41-4-8.
Fiscal year, §16-13-1.
Defined, §16-1-1.
Funds.
General provisions. See
within this heading,
"Funds."
Public school funds. See
within this heading,
"Public school funds."
Loans.
Interest rate on current
loans, §16-13-146.
Public school funds. See
within this heading,
"Public school funds."
Taxation. See within this
heading, "Taxation."
Firemen.
General provisions.
See FIRES AND FIRE
PREVENTION.
Fires and fire prevention.
Fire marshal.
Regulation of fire drills,
doors and exits,
§36-19-10.

EDUCATION—Cont'd
Fires and fire prevention
—Cont'd
Firemen.
See FIRES AND FIRE
PREVENTION.
Fiscal year, §16-13-1.
Defined, §16-1-1.
Flags.
United States flag and state
flag, §§16-43-1 to
16-43-5.
Display.
Flags must be displayed
daily, §16-43-1.
Teachers not displaying
flag not allowed
public funds,
§16-43-3.
Teacher's report on
display, §16-43-2.
Purchase of flags, §16-43-4.
Report on display by
teachers, §16-43-2.
Teachers.
Not displaying flag not
allowed public funds,
§16-43-3.
Report on display,
§16-43-2.
Voluntary recital of pledge
of allegiance, §16-43-5.
Food.
Child nutrition food program.
Storage and distribution.
Department of education
authorized to
contract for, §16-2-8.
Food handlers.
Employment of food handlers
with tuberculosis,
§16-22-3.
Forests and forestry.
Forest research and
educational programs,
§§2-30-20 to 2-30-24.
State forestry commission.
Program of education,
§9-3-4.
Forms.
Contracts, §16-4-9.
Construction contracts,
§16-1-2.
County superintendents of
education.
Report forms, §16-9-27.
State superintendent of
education to prepare,
§16-4-16.
Textbooks.
Records of textbooks
delivered to local
superintendents,
§16-36-31.
Fraternal benefit societies.
Creation, etc., of educational
institutions, §27-34-20.
Fraud.
Insurance.
Risk management
cooperatives.
Actions brought directly
against cooperative
or agents not
prohibited,
§16-8-42.1.
Unaccredited schools,
§16-46-4.

EDUCATION—Cont'd
Funds.
Allocation.
Local boards of education,
§16-13-13.
Depositories.
Bonds, surety required of
officers, §11-1-7.
Emergency secondary
education scholarship
fund, §§16-23-18 to
16-23-23.
Endowment funds.
Investment of endowment
funds held by state
board of education and
trustees of state
institutions, §16-13-2.
Income.
Certain income to be
applied to support and
maintenance of public
schools, Const. Ala.,
art. XIV, §260.
Local funding of school
programs, §§16-13-60 to
16-13-65.
Minimum program fund,
§§16-13-50 to 16-13-59.
See within this heading,
"Public school funds."
Public school funds,
§§16-13-30 to 16-13-38.
See within this heading,
"Public school funds."
Saving funds through
suggestions.
Rewards to employees,
§16-1-21.
Special educational trust
fund.
Personal leave.
Funding for support
personnel,
§16-8-26.1.
Public school corporation.
Borrowing in
anticipation of
appropriation fund,
§16-14-10.
Setting up account,
§40-1-32.
Source of revenue,
§40-1-31.
State board of education.
Endowment funds held by
state board.
Investment, §16-13-2.
Teachers.
Elementary teachers'
scholarship fund,
§16-23-17.
Textbooks. See within this
heading, "Textbooks."
Transfer of appropriated
funds among line items,
§16-13-40.
Gifted children.
Exceptional children
generally, §§16-39-1 to
16-39-12. See within this
heading, "Exceptional
children."
Gifts.
Administration of gifts,
§16-3-30.
Alabama education study
commission.
Acceptance of gifts, etc.,
§16-6-6.
Conditional gifts, §16-3-31.

EDUCATION—Cont'd
Gifts—Cont'd
Educational television
commission.
Acceptance of gifts,
§16-7-6.
May be accepted on
conditions, §16-3-31.
Governor.
Compact for education.
Governor authorized to
enter, §16-44-1.
Governor's educational
reform commission,
§§16-6A-5 to 16-6A-8.
State board of education.
Governor to president of
board, §16-3-2.
Vocational education.
Annual report to governor,
§16-37-6.
Grades.
What grades included in
county schools, §16-8-36.
Grading schools.
City boards of education,
§16-11-20.
City superintendents of
schools, §16-12-8.
County boards of education,
§16-8-29.
County superintendents of
education, §16-9-22.
State board of education,
§16-3-14.
State superintendent of
education, §16-4-14.
Graduate instruction.
Providing instruction not
available at state-
supported institutions,
§16-3-32.
Habitual truant, §16-28-14.
Handicapped persons.
Children exempt from
attending public school,
§16-28-6.
Employment by public
schools, §21-7-8.
Exceptional children,
§§16-39-1 to 16-39-12.
See within this heading,
"Exceptional children."
Institute for deaf and blind,
§§21-1-1 to 21-1-26.
See HANDICAPPED
PERSONS.
Rehabilitation and crippled
children's service,
§§16-38-1 to 16-38-9.
See HANDICAPPED
PERSONS.
Hazing.
Prohibited, §16-1-23.
Health.
Authority and jurisdiction of
state board of health,
§22-2-2.
Boards of school trustees.
Sanitary conditions
maintained by
trustees, §16-10-10.
Comprehensive health
education.
Courses of study in public
school, §16-40-7.
County boards of health.
Duties, §22-3-2.
County health officers.
Duties, §22-3-5.

EDUCATION—Cont'd
Health—Cont'd
Drug abuse education,
§§16-41-1 to 16-41-10.
See DRUGS.
Immunization of school
children, §§16-30-1 to
16-30-5.
Mental and physical
examinations of school
children, §§16-29-1 to
16-29-6. See within this
heading, "Mental and
physical examinations of
school children."
Rules for protection of
health, §16-4-13.
Sanitary rest rooms,
§16-8-43.
Health care authorities.
Powers of authority,
§22-21-318.
**Hearing aid dealers and
fitters.**
Continuing education
requirements, §34-14-6.
Hearings.
Nonteacher, nonclassified,
etc., employees.
Termination, §36-26-106.
Unaccredited schools.
Review of actions by state
department of
education, §16-46-9.
High schools, §§16-26-1 to
16-26-4.
Accreditment, §16-26-1.
Administration of high school
affairs, §16-26-1.
Admittance.
Conditions of admittance to
high schools, §16-9-19.
Alabama high school athletic
association.
Membership of certain
employees in teachers'
retirement system,
§16-25-7.
Buildings, §16-26-1.
City boards of education.
System of high schools,
§16-26-2.
County boards of education.
System of high schools,
§16-26-2.
Courses of study, §16-26-1.
Elementary schools.
May be placed under same
principal, §16-26-3.
Establishments, §16-26-1.
Fees.
Matriculation fee may be
charged, §16-26-4.
High school system, §16-26-2.
Mathematics and science,
§§16-26A-1 to 16-26A-7.
Matriculation fee may be
charged, §16-26-4.
Operation, §16-26-1.
Principals, §16-26-1.
Elementary and high
school may be placed
under same principal,
§16-26-3.
System of high schools,
§16-26-2.
Teachers, §16-26-1.

EDUCATION—Cont'd
High schools—Cont'd
Vocational education.
City and county boards of
education authorized
to operate vocational
high schools jointly,
§16-37-8.
Historical research.
Contracts between counties
or cities and historical
corporations, etc.,
authorized, §16-42-3.
Counties and cities
authorized to undertake
research into history of
state, §16-42-1.
Funds.
Use of county and
municipal funds,
§16-42-2.
Holidays.
Enumerated, §1-3-8.
Home study schools.
Unaccredited schools
generally, §§16-46-1 to
16-46-10. See within this
heading, "Unaccredited
schools."
Hospitals.
Classes and schools operated
under Alabama state
hospitals.
Textbooks.
Purchase and furnishing
of state-owned
textbooks, §16-36-23.
Illiteracy, §§16-34-1 to
16-34-4.
Adult education programs
and classes.
Legislative appropriation,
§16-34-4.
Appropriations.
Legislative appropriation
for illiteracy and adult
education programs
and classes, §16-34-4.
City boards of education.
Cooperation with federal
government, §16-34-3.
Cooperation with state
board, §16-34-2.
Cooperation of county and
city boards with state
board, §16-34-2.
Cooperation with federal
government.
Authority to cooperate,
§16-34-3.
County boards of education.
Cooperation with federal
government, §16-34-3.
Cooperation with state
board, §16-34-2.
Federal government.
Authority of state, county
and city boards to
cooperate with federal
government, §16-34-3.
State board of education.
County and city boards to
cooperate with state
board, §16-34-2.
Duty to remove illiteracy,
§16-34-1.
Federal government.
Authority to cooperate
with federal
government,
§16-34-3.

EDUCATION—Cont'd
Illiteracy—Cont'd
State board of education
—Cont'd
Removal of illiteracy duty
of state board,
§16-34-1.
**Immunization of school
children,** §§16-30-1 to
16-30-5.
Certificate of immunization,
§16-30-3.
Presentation of certificate
upon initial entrance
into school, §16-30-4.
Designation of diseases,
§16-30-1.
Exceptions to chapter,
§16-30-3.
Initial entrance into school.
Presentation of certificate
upon initial entrance,
§16-30-4.
Matriculation.
Presentation of certificate
upon initial entrance
into school, §16-30-4.
Parents.
Responsibilities of parents,
§16-30-2.
Responsibilities of parents,
§16-30-2.
Rules and regulations.
State health officer to
promulgate, §16-30-5.
Testing for certain diseases,
§16-30-1.
Certificate of testing,
§16-30-3.
Presentation of
certificate upon
initial entrance into
school, §16-30-4.
Improvement of schools.
Powers and duties of county
commissions, §11-3-11.
Income tax.
Corporations.
Deductions.
Contributions or gifts to
educational
institutions,
§§40-18-15, 40-18-35.
Industrial arts.
Eye protective devices.
Pupils and teachers
participating in certain
courses, §16-1-7.
Injuries.
Industrial injuries.
Rehabilitation and crippled
children's service,
§§16-38-1 to 16-38-9.
See HANDICAPPED
PERSONS.
Inspections.
Building.
During and after
construction, §16-1-2.
School buses.
Safety inspections,
§§16-27-3, 16-27-5.
Institute for deaf and blind,
§§21-1-1 to 21-1-26.
See HANDICAPPED
PERSONS.
Insurance.
Buildings.
City boards of education,
§16-11-27.

EDUCATION—Cont'd
  Insurance—Cont'd
    City boards of education,
      §§16-8-42.1, 16-22-5.
    County boards of education.
    Insurance on schools,
      §16-8-42.
    Dental insurance, §16-22-8.
    Group insurance.
      Authority of school boards
        to form groups for
        purpose of obtaining,
        §16-22-5.
      Payment of premiums,
        §16-22-5.
      Presumption as to
        payments and
        deductions, §16-22-7.
    Life insurers organized to aid
      nonprofit educational
      and scientific
      institutions.
      Annual license fee, §27-4-8.
    Public education employees'
      health insurance,
      §§16-25A-1 to 16-25A-7.
      See within this heading,
        "Public education
        employees' health
        insurance."
    Risk management
      cooperatives.
      Audits.
        Filing certified financial
          audit, §16-8-42.1.
      Benefits and charges.
        Filing schedule,
          §16-8-42.1.
      Boards of education.
        Authority to establish,
          §16-8-42.1.
        Liability for tort claims,
          §16-8-42.1.
        Liability to third parties,
          §16-8-42.1.
      Bylaws.
        Filing, §16-8-42.1.
      Definitions, §16-8-42.1.
      Fraud.
        Actions brought directly
          against cooperative
          or agents not
          prohibited,
          §16-8-42.1.
      Powers and authority,
        §16-8-42.1.
      Premium taxes.
        Exemption, §16-8-42.1.
      Public education employees
        health insurance plan.
        Providing coverage or
          benefits as
          authorized under.
          Prohibited, §16-8-42.1.
      State insurance fund.
        Providing coverage or
          benefits as
          authorized under.
          Prohibited, §16-8-42.1.
      Torts.
        Boards of education.
          Liability for tort
            claims, §16-8-42.1.
    Salary deductions.
      Group insurance
        premiums, §16-22-6.
    School buses.
      Vehicle liability insurance
        for drivers, §16-27-7.

EDUCATION—Cont'd
  Interest.
    Loans of $100,000 or more to
      state board of education
      and trustees of state
      educational institutions.
      Maximum rates, §8-8-4.
    Teachers' retirement system.
      Regular interest.
        Defined, §16-25-1.
    Warrants for special county
      and district taxes.
      Interest rates, §16-13-95.
    Warrants for special license,
      privilege or excise taxes.
      Interest rates, §16-13-120.
  **Interstate agreement on
    qualifications of
    educational personnel,**
    §§16-23A-1 to 16-23A-3.
  Investigations.
    State board of education.
      Educational needs
        investigated, §16-3-17.
  Investments.
    Alabama education
      authority.
      Bond issues.
        Bonds legal investments,
          §16-15-9.
    Educational building
      authorities.
      Bond issues, §16-17-17.
      Public educational
        building authorities,
        §16-18-19.
    Endowment funds.
      State board of education
        and trustees of state
        institutions, §16-13-2.
    Public school and college
      authority.
      Bond issues.
        Investment of fiduciary
          funds, §16-16-9.
    Tax anticipation warrants.
      Warrants legal
        investments for
        fiduciaries, §16-13-74.
    Warrants for special county
      and district taxes.
      Investment of unused
        proceeds in
        government securities,
        §16-13-109.
  **Jacksonville state
    university,** §§16-52-1 to
    16-52-15.
    See JACKSONVILLE
      STATE UNIVERSITY.
  Janitors.
    Retirement system.
      General provisions,
        §§16-25-1 to 16-25-28.
        See within this
        heading, "Teachers."
      Transfer of membership,
        §16-25-5.
    Tuberculosis.
      Employment of janitors
        with tuberculosis,
        §16-22-3.
  **Joint maintenance of
    schools.**
    Attendance by pupils near
      county lines, §16-8-18.
    Between counties, §16-8-18.
    State-line schools, §16-8-19.

EDUCATION—Cont'd
  Junior colleges.
    General provisions, §§16-60-1
      to 16-60-270.
    See JUNIOR COLLEGES.
  Jurisdiction.
    Truancy.
      Juvenile court jurisdiction,
        §16-28-21.
  Juvenile proceedings.
    Truancy.
      Jurisdiction of juvenile
        court, §16-28-21.
  Kindergartens.
    Age limits of children
      admitted, §16-8-41.
    City boards of education.
      Maintenance of
        kindergartens,
        §16-11-16.
    County boards of education.
      Age limits of children
        admitted, §16-8-41.
      Establishment, §16-8-41.
      Maintenance, §16-8-41.
    Establishment.
      City boards, §16-11-16.
      County boards, §16-8-41.
    Maintenance.
      City boards, §16-11-16.
      County boards, §16-8-41.
    Pilot programs.
      Public pilot programs,
        §16-2-6.
    Teachers.
      Kindergarten program.
        Additional teacher units
          earned.
          Allocated for
            employment of
            classroom
            teachers,
            §16-13-52.1.
        Funding to reduce pupil
          teacher ratio,
          §16-13-52.1.
        Teacher units allowed for
          specified number of
          pupils and average
          daily attendance,
          §16-13-52.1.
  Laboratories.
    Eye protective devices.
      Pupils and teachers
        participating in certain
        courses, §16-1-7.
  Lands.
    School lands.
      General provisions,
        §§9-15-36 to 9-15-44,
        9-15-49 to 9-15-51,
        16-20-1 to 16-20-9.
      See PUBLIC LANDS.
  Learning disabilities.
    Exceptional children,
      §§16-39-1 to 16-39-12.
      See within this heading,
        "Exceptional children."
  Legislation.
    Recommendation by state
      board of education,
      §16-3-22.
    State superintendent of
      education.
      Duties, §16-4-20.
  Legislature.
    Alabama education study
      commission.
      Reports to legislature,
        §16-6-4.

EDUCATION—Cont'd
Legislature—Cont'd
Duty to establish and
maintain public school
system, Const. Ala., art.
XIV, §256.
Teachers.
Retirement system.
Legislative service as
full-time employee.
Use in determining
creditable service,
§16-25-11.2.
Libraries.
Appropriation of funds.
Counties may appropriate
funds for school
libraries, §16-21-1.
Books, §16-21-2.
Circulating libraries,
§16-21-3.
City boards of education.
Establishment and
maintenance,
§16-11-23.
Counties.
Appropriation of funds for
school libraries,
§16-21-1.
Equipment, §16-21-2.
Establishment, §16-11-23.
Maintenance, §16-11-23.
Scholarships and grants in
field of library service.
Licenses.
City boards of education.
Allocation of revenue from
licenses, §16-11-25.
Teachers.
Exemptions from licenses.
Corporation organized
for purpose of aiding
retired teachers,
§40-9-18.
Warrants for special license,
privilege or exicse taxes,
§§16-13-120 to 16-13-122.
Livingston university,
§§16-53-1 to 16-53-12.
See LIVINGSTON
UNIVERSITY.
Loans.
Age of majority.
Contracting for educational
loans for college level
education and above,
§26-1-5.
Contracts.
Age of majority.
Contracting for
educational loans for
college level
education and above,
§26-1-5.
Interest rate on current
loans, §16-13-146.
**Local funding of school
programs,** §§16-13-60 to
16-13-65.
Allocations.
Minimum program fund.
Reduction in fund
allocation for
noncompliance,
§16-13-64.
Amount of local taxes to be
received by school
systems, §16-13-62.
Determination of
compliance, §16-13-62.
Citation of article, §16-13-60.

EDUCATION—Cont'd
**Local funding of school
programs**—Cont'd
Counties.
City school system's share
of county-wide tax,
§16-13-63.
Legislative findings,
§16-13-61.
Minimum program fund.
Reduction in allocation for
noncompliance,
§16-13-64.
Noncompliance.
Penalties, §16-13-65.
Reduction in minimum
program fund
allocation, §16-13-64.
Penalties.
Noncompliance.
Applicability of penalty
for noncompliance,
§16-13-65.
Short title, §16-13-60.
Taxation.
Amount of local taxes to be
received by school
systems, §16-13-62.
Determination of
compliance,
§16-13-62.
City school system's share
of county-wide tax,
§16-13-63.
**Lunchroom managers and
assistants.**
Membership in teachers'
retirement system,
§16-25-8.
Maids.
Retirement system.
General provisions,
§§16-25-1 to 16-25-28.
See within this
heading, "Teachers."
Transfer of membership,
§16-25-5.
Mail order schools.
Regulations. See within this
heading, "Unaccredited
schools."
Maintenance workers.
Teachers' retirement system.
Membership, §16-25-9.
Persons previously under
employees' retirement
system of Alabama,
§16-25-10.
Majority.
Age of majority.
Contracting for educational
loans for college level
education and above,
§26-1-5.
Maps and plats.
School tax district,
§§16-13-192, 16-13-193.
**Mathematics and science
high school.**
Admission.
Early admission,
§16-26A-7.
Eligibility, §16-26A-7.
Board of directors.
Compensation, §16-26A-4.
Composition, §16-26A-4.
Duties, §16-26A-4.
Governance of school,
§16-26A-3.
Powers, §16-26A-4.
Terms, §16-26A-4.

EDUCATION—Cont'd
**Mathematics and science
high school**—Cont'd
Definitions, §16-26A-2.
Department of education.
Coordination of programs
and curriculum with
department,
§16-26A-3.
Definition of department,
§16-26A-2.
Early admission, §16-26A-7.
Established, §16-26A-3.
Extension courses and
campuses, §16-26A-5.
Extracurricular activities,
§16-26A-6.
Mobile county school
system.
Participation in
activities where
school unable to
provide, §16-26A-6.
Intent of legislature,
§16-26A-1.
Legislative intent, §16-26A-1.
Operation in school year
basis, §16-26A-5.
School.
Defined, §16-26A-2.
Short courses, §16-26A-5.
State board of education.
Definition of state board,
§16-26A-2.
State superintendent of
education.
Definition of state
superintendent,
§16-26A-2.
Summer school, §16-26A-5.
Matriculation.
Fees.
Distribution of funds for
purchase of supplies
and maintenance of
property, §16-13-38.
High schools, §16-26-4.
Immunization of school
children.
Presentation of certificate
upon initial entrance
into school, §16-30-4.
Mechanics.
Teachers' retirement system.
Membership, §16-25-9.
Persons previously under
employees' retirement
system of Alabama,
§16-25-10.
Medical technicians.
Educational prerequisites of
applicants for
registration, §34-18-21.
Training schools, §34-18-2.
Meditation.
Period of silence for
meditation at beginning
of first class in public
schools, §§16-1-20,
16-1-20.1.
School prayer, §16-1-20.2.
Membership dues.
Salary deductions, §16-22-6.
**Mental and physical
examinations of school
children,** §§16-29-1 to
16-29-6.
Certificate of examination.
Furnished to pupils,
§16-29-3.

EDUCATION—Cont'd
Mental and physical examinations of school children—Cont'd
Cooperation of county board of health, §16-29-6.
County board of health.
Cooperation, §16-29-6.
County health officers.
Furnished with certain equipment, §16-29-4.
Equipment.
County health officers furnished with certain equipment, §16-29-4.
Infected child.
Suspension of infected child, §16-29-1.
Laboratory tests, §16-29-5.
Required, §16-29-1.
Scope, §16-29-1.
Suspension of infected child, §16-29-1.
Testing for certain diseases, §16-30-1.
Tests.
Laboratory tests, §16-29-5.
When examination made, §16-29-2.
Mental retardation.
Exceptional children, §§16-39-1 to 16-39-12.
See within this heading, "Exceptional children."
Merit system.
Compensation of employees subject to merit system, §16-3-10.
Microphotographing records, §§16-1-3, 16-1-4.
Military affairs.
Military recruiting representatives.
Access to school facilities, §16-1-25.
National guard educational assistance, §§31-10-1 to 31-10-4.
See MILITARY AFFAIRS.
Minimum program fund, §§16-13-50 to 16-13-59. See within this heading, "Public school funds."
Mining.
Alabama mining academy, §§16-60-260 to 16-60-264.
See MINES AND MINERALS.
Mobile county.
Constitution of Alabama.
Applicability of education article, Const. Ala., art. XIV, §270.
Amendment to section 270, Const. Ala., amd. 111.
Month.
Scholastic month.
Defined, §16-1-1.
Motor vehicles.
Driver training schools, §§32-14-1 to 32-14-24.
See MOTOR VEHICLES.
Eye protective devices for pupils and teachers participating in certain courses, §16-1-7.
School buses, §§16-27-1 to 16-27-7. See within this heading, "School buses."

EDUCATION—Cont'd
Municipal corporations.
Annexation.
Territory exempt from taxation.
Right of children to attend public schools, §11-42-85.
Boards of education, §§16-11-1 to 16-11-27.
See within this heading, "City boards of education."
Bond issues.
Security for indebtedness incurred in purchase, construction, etc., of school buildings, §11-81-1.
City boards of education. See within this heading, "City boards of education."
Consolidation of noncontiguous municipalities.
Boards of education.
Continuation in office, §11-42-159.
Election, §11-42-159.
County boards of education.
Municipality may remain under county board, §16-13-199.
Erection of school buildings, §11-47-13.
Independent cities.
Apportionment of state and county funds to independent cities, §16-13-34.
Levy of tax for school buildings, §11-47-13.
Local aid to state educational institutions.
See UNIVERSITIES AND COLLEGES.
Police jurisdiction over schoolhouses, §11-47-22.
Purchase of school property, §11-47-13.
Superintendents of schools, §§16-12-1 to 16-12-21.
See within this heading, "City superintendents of schools."
Textbooks.
Local textbook selection committee, §§16-36-4 to 16-36-6.
Narcotics.
Drug abuse education, §§16-41-1 to 16-41-10.
See DRUGS.
National guard.
Educational assistance, §§31-10-1 to 31-10-4.
See MILITARY AFFAIRS.
Negotiable instruments.
Public school and college authority.
Bonds as negotiable instruments, §16-16-9.
Nonprofit corporations.
General provisions.
See CORPORATIONS.

EDUCATION—Cont'd
Nonteacher, nonclassified, etc., employees, §§36-26-101 to 36-26-107.
Dismissal procedure.
Appeals.
Termination, §36-26-105.
Transfer, §36-26-107.
Definitions, §36-26-100.
Discipline.
Authority to, §36-26-108.
Right to contest, §36-26-108.
Employee review panel.
Termination, §36-26-105.
Hearings.
Termination, §36-26-106.
Nonprobationary status, §36-26-102.
Notice.
Termination, §§36-26-101, 36-26-104.
Probationary period, §36-26-101.
Suspension with pay, §36-26-104.
Termination.
Appeals, §36-26-105.
Causes, §36-26-102.
Contest.
Notice of intention to contest, §36-26-104.
Employee review panel, §36-26-105.
Hearing process, §36-26-106.
Notice, §§36-26-101, 36-26-104.
Procedure, §36-26-103.
Transfer.
Appeal of decision, §36-26-107.
Authority to transfer, §36-26-107.
Personal leave.
Support personnel.
Authorized, §16-8-26.1.
Notes.
Public school corporation.
Securities, §§16-14-6, 16-14-7, 16-14-17 to 16-14-19. See within this heading, "Public school corporation."
Notice.
County boards of education.
Meetings, §§16-8-3, 16-8-4.
Nonteacher, nonclassified, etc., employees.
Termination, §§36-26-101, 36-26-104.
One-mill county school tax.
Election, §16-13-161.
Textbooks.
Public meetings to consider adoption, §16-36-9.
Nurses.
Continuing education, §34-21-23.
General provisions, §§34-21-5, 34-21-7, 34-21-40 to 34-21-43.
See NURSES.
University of Alabama school of nursing, §§16-47-130 to 16-47-137, 16-47-150 to 16-47-152.
See UNIVERSITY OF ALABAMA.

EDUCATION—Cont'd
Nursing homes.
  Administrators.
    Continuing education,
      §34-20-13.
Oaths.
  State board of education.
    Authority to administer
      oaths, §16-3-24.
    Oath of members, §16-3-6.
  State superintendent of
    education.
    Oath of office, §16-4-2.
Obscenity.
  Public school or college or
    university libraries.
    Inapplicability of criminal
      provisions to,
      §13A-12-200.10.
Officers and employees.
  Attendance officers,
    §§16-28-18 to 16-28-20.
  Bonds, surety. See within
    this heading, "Bonds,
    surety."
  Insurance. See within this
    heading, "Insurance."
  Principals. See within this
    heading, "Principals."
  Retirement system, §§16-25-1
    to 16-25-28. See within
    this heading, "Teachers."
  Salaries. See within this
    heading, "Salaries."
  Teachers. See within this
    heading, "Teachers."
One-mill county school tax,
  §§16-13-160 to 16-13-166.
  See within this heading,
  "Taxation."
Opening date of schools.
  County boards of education.
    Uniform opening date,
      §16-8-30.
  Uniform opening date,
    §16-8-30.
Optometrists.
  Board of optometrists.
    Authority to establish
      standards, §34-22-42.
  Continuing education
    requirements, §34-22-22.
  Limited teaching licenses,
    §34-22-5.
  Qualifications of applicants,
    §34-22-20.
Pagers.
  When pupils prohibited from
    carrying, §16-1-27.
Patriotism.
  Courses of study, §16-40-6.
Peace officers.
  Minimum educational
    standards, §36-21-46.
Penalties.
  Diversion of funds by
    officials, §16-13-4.
  Exceeding budget,
    §16-13-144.
  Unaccredited schools.
    Violation of provisions of
      chapters, §16-46-10.
Pensions.
  Teachers' retirement system.
    See within this heading,
    "Teachers."
Personal leave.
  Support personnel.
    Funding, §16-8-26.1.

EDUCATION—Cont'd
Pharmacists and
  pharmacies.
  General provisions.
    See PHARMACISTS AND
      PHARMACIES.
Photography.
  Records.
    Photographing or
      microphotographing.
      See within this
      heading, "Records."
Physical education.
  Required, §16-40-1.
Physical examinations of
  school children, §§16-29-1
  to 16-29-6. See within this
  heading, "Mental and
  physical examinations of
  school children."
Physical therapists.
  Continuing education,
    §34-24-216.
Physicians.
  Foreign medical school
    graduates.
    Off-shore medical schools,
      §§34-24-79 to 34-24-84.
    See PHYSICIANS.
Playgrounds.
  City boards of education.
    Duties, §16-11-16.
  Condemnation, §16-9-18.
  County boards of education.
    See within this heading,
    "County boards of
    education."
  County superintendents of
    education.
    Condemnation, §16-9-18.
    Improvements, §16-9-18.
  Establishment, §16-8-41.
    By city boards, §16-11-16.
  Improvements, §16-9-18.
  Maintenance, §16-11-16.
Pledge and collateral
  security.
  Tax anticipation warrants in
    cities and counties.
    Public school funds and
      minimum school
      program fund moneys
      not to be pledged,
      §16-13-76.
Pledge of allegiance.
  Voluntary recital of pledge of
    allegiance to United
    States flag, §16-43-5.
Policy of state, Const. Ala.,
  amd. 111.
Poll taxes.
  Use for support of public
    schools, Const. Ala., art.
    XIV, §259.
  Amendment of section 259,
    Const. Ala., amd. 111.
Prayer.
  School prayer, §16-1-20.2.
Principals.
  Boards of school trustees.
    Secretary of board,
      §16-10-3.
  Certificates.
    Required, §16-23-1.
  City boards of education.
    Suspension or dismissal,
      §16-11-17.
  City superintendents of
    schools.
    Nomination, removal, etc.,
      §16-12-16.

EDUCATION—Cont'd
Principals—Cont'd
  Conferences.
    County superintendents of
      education, §16-9-16.
  County superintendents of
    education.
    Conferences, §16-9-16.
  Diseases.
    Notifiable diseases.
      Persons responsible for
      reporting diseases,
      §22-11A-2.
  Dismissal.
    By city boards, §16-11-17.
  Elementary schools.
    Elementary and high
      school may be placed
      under same principal,
      §16-26-3.
  High schools, §16-26-3.
  Property damage or assaults
    on students and school
    personnel.
    Reports of principal,
      §16-1-24.
  Reports.
    Forms, §16-12-12.
  Retirement system, §§16-25-1
    to 16-25-28. See within
    this heading, "Teachers."
  Salaries, §16-11-17.
  State superintendent of
    education.
    Conferences, §16-4-6.
  Suspension.
    By city boards, §16-11-17.
  Tenure, §§16-24-8 to
    16-24-38. See within this
    heading, "Teachers."
Prisons and prisoners.
  Release for educational
    purposes, §§14-8-60 to
    14-8-67.
    See PRISONS AND
      PRISONERS.
  Schools at correctional units,
    §§14-12-1 to 14-12-4.
  State board of education.
    Supervision of educational
      work of special
      institutions, §16-3-20.
Private schools.
  Defined, §16-28-1.
  Drug abuse education.
    Exclusion of teacher or
      administrator
      employed by nonpublic
      school from
      participation
      prohibited, §16-41-5.
  Gasoline tax.
    Exemptions, §40-17-31.
  Lubricating oils and greases.
    Tax exemption, §40-17-171.
  Motor fuels.
    Additional excise tax on
      gasoline, motor fuel
      and lubricating oil.
    Exemptions, §40-17-220.
  Registration, §16-1-11.
  Regulation of certain schools
    and courses of
    instruction, §§16-46-1 to
    16-46-10. See within this
    heading, "Unaccredited
    schools."
  Reports, §16-1-11.
Private tutors, §16-28-5.

EDUCATION—Cont'd

Privilege taxes.
Warrants for special license, privilege or excise taxes, §§16-13-120 to 16-13-122.
Professional instruction.
Providing instruction not available at state-supported institutions, §16-3-32.
Propaganda.
Instruction in history, doctrines, etc., of communism, §16-40-3.
Property.
Buildings. See within this heading, "Buildings."
City boards of education. See within this heading, "City boards of education."
County boards of education.
Acquisition of property, §16-8-40.
Donation or appropriation for educational purposes.
Application to furtherance of education, Const. Ala., amd. 111.
Application to maintenance of public schools, Const. Ala., art. XIV, §258.
Maintenance.
Distribution of funds from matriculation fees and local fees for maintenance of school property, §16-13-38.
Municipal corporations.
Purchase of school property, §11-47-13.
School lands.
General provisions.
See PUBLIC LANDS.
Public educational building authorities, §§16-18-1 to 16-18-21. See within this heading, "Educational building authorities."
Public education employees' health insurance, §§16-25A-1 to 16-25A-17.
Administration.
Board to contract for, §16-25A-7.
Advisory committee, §16-25A-13.
Authorization for plan, §16-25A-5.
Benefits.
Board to contract for, §16-25A-7.
Relationship between benefits and expenses, §16-25A-4.
Board.
Compensation, §16-25A-2.
Composition, §16-25A-2.
Employees not liable for good faith performance, §16-25A-3.
Liability for good faith in performance, §16-25A-3.
Oath of office, §16-25A-2.
Officers, §16-25A-2.
Rules and regulations.
Promulgation, §16-25A-15.

EDUCATION—Cont'd

Public education employees' health insurance—Cont'd
Claims.
Denial.
Notice, §16-25A-7.
Committees.
Advisory committee, §16-25A-13.
Contracts, §16-25A-7.
Coordination with state employees' health insurance board, §16-25A-16.
Costs.
Payment by employees, §16-25A-8.
Coverage.
Eligible employees covered, §16-25A-9.
Deductions.
Companies presently providing coverage to have access to, §16-25A-14.
Definitions, §16-25A-1.
Dependents.
Coverage, §16-25A-8.
Election for optional coverage, §16-25A-5.
Election not to participate, §16-25A-12.
Subsequent election to participate, §16-25A-12.
Eligibility.
Coverage of employees, §16-25A-9.
Employees in teachers' retirement system.
Election to be covered, §16-25A-11.
Exclusions, §16-25A-6.
Expenses.
Relationship between benefits and expenses, §16-25A-4.
Fund.
Creation, §16-25A-8.
Funding of plan, §16-25A-8.
Hospitals.
Payment to, §16-25A-10.
Notice.
Denial of claim, §16-25A-7.
Optional coverage.
Election, §16-25A-5.
Partial funding for retired employees, §16-25A-17.
Payments.
Physicians, hospitals, etc., §16-25A-10.
Payroll deductions.
Companies presently providing coverage to have access to, §16-25A-14.
Physicians.
Payment to, §16-25A-10.
Reinsurance, §16-25A-7.
Reports.
Reports to legislature, §16-25A-8.
Retired employees.
Partial funding of coverage, §16-25A-17.
Rules and regulations.
Board.
Promulgation, §16-25A-15.

EDUCATION—Cont'd

Public education employees' health insurance—Cont'd
State employees' health insurance board.
Coordination with, §16-25A-16.
Supplemental coverage.
Companies presently providing.
Access to payroll deduction, §16-25A-14.
Teachers' retirement system.
Election to be covered, §16-25A-11.
Public employees' individual retirement account fund.
Salary deductions, §16-22-6.
Public officers and employees.
Diversion of funds by officials.
Penalty, §16-13-4.
Public school and college authority.
Bond issues, §§16-16-8 to 16-16-12.
Conditions, §16-16-9.
Disposition of proceeds, §16-16-10.
Execution, §16-16-9.
Exemption from taxation, §16-16-9.
Form, §16-16-9.
Interest.
Payment, §16-16-12.
Investment of fiduciary funds, §16-16-9.
Issuance.
Power to issue, §16-16-8.
Limited obligations, §16-16-9.
Negotiability, §16-16-9.
Payment.
Pledge of revenues for payment, §16-16-11.
Principal and interest on bonds, §16-16-12.
Security for payment, §16-16-9.
Pledge of revenues for payment, §16-16-11.
Power to sell and issue, §16-16-8.
Proceeds.
Disposition of proceeds, §16-16-10.
Refunding bonds, §16-16-9.
Sales, §16-16-9.
Power to sell, §16-16-8.
Security for deposits, §16-16-9.
Security for payment, §16-16-9.
Terms, §16-16-9.
Certificate of incorporation.
Issuance and recording, §16-16-5.
Construction of chapter.
Liberal construction, §16-16-2.
Contracts.
Procedure for letting, §16-16-8.
Death of members, officers or directors.
Effect, §16-16-6.
Definitions, §16-16-1.

EDUCATION—Cont'd
Public school and college authority—Cont'd
Directors, §16-16-6.
  Effect of death, resignation or expiration of term, §16-16-6.
Dissolution, §16-16-13.
Fees.
  No fees to be paid, §16-16-5.
Evidence.
  Copies of proceedings as evidence, §16-16-6.
Fees.
  Dissolution.
    No fees to be paid, §16-16-5.
  Incorporation.
    No fees to be paid, §16-16-5.
Incorporation.
  Application for incorporation, §16-16-4.
  Authorized, §16-16-3.
  Certificate of incorporation.
    Issuance and recording, §16-16-5.
  Fees.
    No fees to be paid, §16-16-5.
Interest.
  Payment of interest on bonds, §16-16-12.
Legislative findings of fact and declaration of intent, §16-16-2.
Members, §16-16-6.
  Effect of death, resignation or expiration of term, §16-16-6.
Officers, §16-16-6.
Powers.
  Generally, §16-16-7.
Quorum, §16-16-6.
Record of proceedings, §16-16-6.
Resignation of members, officers or directors.
  Effect, §16-16-6.
Salaries, §16-16-6.
Terms of office.
  Expiration.
    Effect, §16-16-6.
Public school corporation.
Borrowing money, §16-14-6.
  Borrowing in anticipation of appropriation from Alabama special educational trust fund, §16-14-10.
  Monthly estimate of amounts to be borrowed, §16-14-8.
Certificate of incorporation, §16-14-3.
  Evidence, §16-14-16.
Debt.
  Issuing evidence of debt, §16-14-6.
  Payable from proceeds of minimum fund appropriation, §16-14-7.
  Securities not debt of state, §16-14-18.
Dissolution, §16-14-15.
Evidence.
  Records or certificates, §16-14-16.

EDUCATION—Cont'd
Public school corporation—Cont'd
Incorporation.
  Certificate of incorporation, §16-14-3.
  Method of becoming corporation, §16-14-2.
  Who may become corporation, §16-14-1.
Minimum program fund.
  Debt payable from proceeds of minimum program fund appropriation, §16-14-7.
  Pledging proceeds of appropriation, §16-14-6.
  Procedure in disbursing, §16-14-9.
  Notes, §§16-14-6, 16-14-7, 16-14-17 to 16-14-19.
Officers, §16-14-11.
Pledging proceeds of minimum program fund appropriation, §16-14-6.
Powers, §16-14-4.
Purpose, §16-14-5.
Records.
  Evidence, §16-14-16.
Securities.
  Execution, §16-14-19.
  Generally, §16-14-17.
  Issuance, §16-14-6.
  Not debt of state, §16-14-18.
  Principal and interest payable from proceeds of minimum program fund appropriation, §16-14-7.
Special educational trust fund.
  Borrowing in anticipation of appropriation, §16-14-10.
Vacancy in membership of corporation, §16-14-13.
Warrants, §§16-14-6, 16-14-7, 16-14-17 to 16-14-19.
Who may become corporation, §16-14-1.
Public school funds.
Allocation.
  Boards of education, §16-13-13.
Apportionment, §16-4-5; Const. Ala., art. XIV, §256.
  Boundaries.
    When boundaries have been changed, §16-13-35.
  How made, §16-13-30.
  Independent cities, §16-13-34.
Appropriation of funds out of county treasury, §16-13-36.
Bonding of persons handling public school funds.
  Authority to require, §16-13-8.
  Payment of premiums, §16-13-9.
Boundaries.
  Change in boundaries.
    Apportionment of county funds, §16-13-35.

EDUCATION—Cont'd
Public school funds—Cont'd
County commissions.
  Appropriation of funds out of county treasury, §16-13-36.
County custodian, §16-8-33.
Payment of payrolls, §16-13-10.
Removal, §16-13-12.
Vouchers required, §16-13-11.
County finances.
  Applicability of provisions of chapter, §11-8-17.
Determining number of teacher units for purpose of apportioning.
  Funding to reduce teacher pupil ratio, §16-13-52.1.
Disbursements.
  Expenditure of local school funds, §16-13-32.
  Record of disbursements, §16-13-31.
Diversion of funds by officials.
  Penalty, §16-13-4.
Divided townships.
  Funds of townships divided by state or county lines, §16-13-33.
Expenditure of local school funds, §16-13-32.
Independent cities.
  Apportionment of funds to, §16-13-34.
Junior college for Franklin, Marion and Winston counties.
  Use of funds, §16-60-26.
Junior college for Jackson and DeKalb counties.
  Use of funds, §16-60-56.
Local fees.
  Distribution of funds for purchase of supplies and maintenance of property, §16-13-38.
  Effect of collecting prior to and after November 18, 1975, §16-13-39.
Matriculation fees.
  Distribution of funds for purchase of supplies and maintenance of property, §16-13-38.
Minimum program fund, §§16-13-50 to 16-13-59.
  Amount of fund needed by each county, §16-13-58.
  Apportionment, §§16-13-52, 16-13-52.1.
  Appropriation to minimum program fund, §16-13-7.
  City boards of education.
    Direct payment to certain independent city boards of education, §16-13-59.
  Composition, §16-13-50.
  Costs of established minimum program.
    Determining cost, §16-13-51.
  Determining funds available to provide program, §16-13-51.

EDUCATION—Cont'd
Public school funds—Cont'd
Minimum program fund
—Cont'd
Determining funds needed
by for established
minimum term,
§16-13-51.
Direct payment to certain
independent city
boards of education,
§16-13-59.
Disbursement.
Procedure in disbursing,
§16-14-9.
Establishment, §16-13-50.
Federal grants.
Appropriation to
minimum program
fund, §16-13-7.
Index of financial ability of
counties, §16-13-53.
Assessed valuation
index, §16-13-54.
Average index,
§16-13-55.
Participation in fund.
Requirements for
participation,
§16-13-51.
Percentage allotments.
State board to determine,
§16-13-51.
Plan of apportionment,
§16-13-51.
Pledging proceeds of
appropriation,
§16-14-6.
Public school corporation.
Debt payable from
appropriation,
§16-14-7.
Pledging proceeds of
appropriation,
§16-14-6.
Procedure in disbursing
fund, §16-14-9.
Purposes, §16-13-51.
Requirements for
participation,
§16-13-51.
Salary deductions and
insurance payments.
Eligibility for foundation
program not
affected, §16-22-7.
Tax anticipation warrants.
Moneys allocated under
article 3 not to be
pledged, §16-13-76.
Teacher units.
Determining number for
purpose of
apportioning
program, §16-13-52.
Total local funds for state,
§16-13-56.
Total local funds in each
county, §16-13-57.
Minimum school funds.
Transportation of pupils.
Formula for determining
allowance not to
include certain
pupils, §16-13-51.
Payrolls.
Payment of payrolls,
§16-13-10.

EDUCATION—Cont'd
Public school funds—Cont'd
Property.
Distribution of
matriculation fees and
local fees for
maintenance of,
§16-13-38.
Receipts.
Record of receipts,
§16-13-31.
Sales and use tax funds.
Use of county sales and
use tax funds for
general educational
purposes, §16-13-37.
Sectarian or denominational
schools.
Funds not to be used for
support, Const. Ala.,
art. XIV, §263.
Supplies.
Allocation to city and
county boards of
education.
Funds appropriated to
state board of
education, §16-13-39.
Distribution of
matriculation fees and
local fees for purchase,
§16-13-38.
Tax anticipation warrants.
Public school funds
allocated under article
2 not to be pledged,
§16-13-76.
Teachers' salaries.
Percentage of school funds,
Const. Ala., art. XIV,
§261.
Townships divided by state
or county line, §16-13-33.
Vouchers.
Required, §16-13-11.
Pupils.
Ability.
Teaching pupils of
disparate ability,
§16-1-13.
Achievement.
Teaching pupils of
disparate achievement,
§16-1-13.
Alcoholic beverages.
Selling, etc., alcoholic
beverages to school
children, §16-1-10.
Assaults on pupils.
Reports, §16-1-24.
Attendance, §§16-28-1 to
16-28-24. See within this
heading, "Attendance."
Background.
Teaching pupils of
disparate background,
§16-1-13.
Boards of school trustees.
Dismissal of pupils,
§16-10-5.
Classification, §§16-1-13 to
16-1-16.
Compulsory attendance,
§§16-28-1 to 16-28-24.
See within this heading,
"Attendance."
Counseling, §16-1-16.

EDUCATION—Cont'd
Pupils—Cont'd
Disciplinary problems.
Removal, separation or
grouping of pupils
creating disciplinary
problems, §16-1-14.
Dismissal.
Consent of board of school
trustees required,
§16-10-5.
Electronic pagers or
communication devices
in school.
When prohibited, §16-1-27.
Eye protective devices.
Pupils participating in
certain courses,
§16-1-7.
Grouping.
Generally, §§16-1-13 to
16-1-16.
Health.
Rules for protection of
health, §16-4-13.
Immunization, §§16-30-1 to
16-30-5.
Mental and physical
examinations of school
children, §§16-29-1 to
16-29-6. See within this
heading, "Mental and
physical examinations of
school children."
Promotion of pupils.
Conditions of promotion,
§16-8-35.
Social attitudes.
Classification and grouping
of pupils, §16-1-15.
Special courses, §16-1-16.
Suspension.
Infected children, §16-29-1.
Textbooks, §§16-36-1 to
16-36-39. See within this
heading, "Textbooks."
Transportation. See within
this heading, "School
buses."
Truancy. See within this
heading, "Attendance."
Tutoring, §16-1-16.
Real estate brokers.
See REAL ESTATE
BROKERS.
Real property.
Federal grants.
Principal to be preserved,
Const. Ala., art. XIV,
§257.
School lands.
General provisions,
§§9-15-36 to 9-15-44,
9-15-49 to 9-15-51,
16-20-1 to 16-20-9.
See PUBLIC LANDS.
Records.
Alabama education
authority.
Record of proceedings,
§16-15-6.
Attendance.
Attendance officer,
§16-28-18.
Bond issues, §16-18A-7.
City superintendents of
schools.
Textbooks.
Duty to maintain
records, §16-36-34.

EDUCATION—Cont'd
  Records—Cont'd
  County superintendents of
    education.
  Textbooks.
    Duty to maintain
      records, §16-36-34.
  Exceptional children.
    Case history, §16-39-8.
  Forms and blanks, §16-4-16.
  Record of textbooks
    delivered to local
    superintendents,
    §16-36-31.
  Photographing or
    microphotographing.
    Authorized, §16-1-3.
    Destruction, §16-1-4.
    Effect, §16-1-3.
    Force and effect, §16-1-3.
    Retention, §16-1-4.
  Public school and college
    authority.
    Record of proceedings,
      §16-16-6.
  Public school corporation.
    Records as evidence,
      §16-14-16.
  Public school funds.
    Receipts and
      disbursements,
      §16-13-31.
  School buses.
    Inspections and corrections,
      §16-27-3.
  Study commission.
    Authority to require
      production and
      examine, §16-6-5.
  Taxation.
    Warrants for special
      county and district
      taxes, §16-13-106.
  Teachers' retirement system.
    Admissibility in evidence
      of photo-reproduced
      copies of records or
      documents maintained
      by system,
      §16-25-27.
  Textbooks.
    Audit of accounting books
      and records,
      §16-36-31.
    Blanks and forms,
      §16-36-31.
    Duty of local
      superintendent to
      maintain, §16-36-34.
    Textbooks delivered to
      local superintendents,
      §16-36-31.
  Warrants for special county
    and district taxes,
    §16-13-106.
Reformatories.
  Supervision of educational
    work, §16-3-20.
Registration.
  Private schools, §16-1-11.
**Regulation of certain
  schools and courses of
  instructions,** §§16-46-1 to
    16-46-10. See within this
    heading, "Unaccredited
    schools."
**Rehabilitation and crippled
  children's service,**
    §§16-38-1 to 16-38-9.
  See HANDICAPPED
    PERSONS.

EDUCATION—Cont'd
  Religion.
  Drug abuse education.
  Religious objection.
    Exemption of child by
      parents, §16-41-6.
  Parochial schools. See within
    this heading, "Parochial
    schools."
Reports.
  Attendance.
    Enrollment.
      Church schools, §16-28-7.
      Report of enrollment,
        §16-28-7.
      Comparing report with
        list of children
        who should attend
        school, §16-28-9.
    Required reports must be
      furnished, §16-28-8.
  City boards of education.
    Annual report.
      Publication, §16-11-24.
    Audit of accounts,
      §16-11-22.
    Forms for reports,
      §16-11-21.
    Employees of city boards,
      §16-12-12.
    Publication of annual
      report, §16-11-24.
    Reports to state board,
      §16-11-22.
  City superintendents of
    schools.
    Forms for reports of
      employees of city
      boards, §16-12-12.
    Required by state board,
      §16-12-14.
  County boards of education.
    Annual report published,
      §16-8-37.
    Forms of reports required
      by boards, §§16-8-38,
      16-9-27.
    Publication of annual
      reports, §16-8-37.
    Reports to state board,
      §16-8-39.
  County superintendents of
    education.
    Annual statement of
      receipts and
      disbursements,
      §16-9-28.
    Forms.
      Superintendents to
        prepare, §16-9-27.
      Preparation of reports,
        §16-9-30.
    State superintendent of
      education.
      Report on schools to
        state superintendent,
        §16-9-31.
  Displaced homemakers
    programs.
    Annual report to
      chancellor, §16-60-243.
  Drug abuse education.
    State superintendent of
      education to report
      status of program,
      §16-41-10.

EDUCATION—Cont'd
  Reports—Cont'd
  Educational reform.
    Commission.
      Annual reports to
        governor and
        legislature,
        §16-6A-7.
  Enrollment, §16-28-7.
    Comparing report of
      enrollment with list of
      children who should
      attend school,
      §16-28-9.
  Exceptional children,
    §16-39-9.
  Physical assaults on students
    and school personnel,
    §16-1-24.
  Principals.
    Forms, §16-12-12.
  Private schools, §16-1-11.
  School buses.
    Inspections and corrections,
      §16-27-3.
  State board of education.
    Annual report, §16-3-21.
    State superintendent of
      education to prepare,
      §16-4-18.
    Vocational education.
      Annual report to
        governor, §16-37-6.
  State superintendent of
    education.
    Annual report of state
      board of education,
      §16-4-18.
    Drug abuse education.
      Report of status of
        program, §16-41-10.
    Examination of reports,
      §16-4-7.
    Forms and blanks,
      §16-4-16.
  Study commission.
    Reports to legislature,
      §16-6-4.
  Teachers.
    Forms, §16-12-12.
  Textbooks.
    Local superintendents,
      §16-36-6.
    Number of textbooks,
      §16-36-27.
  Vocational education.
    Annual report to governor,
      §16-37-6.
Rest rooms.
  Sanitary rest rooms.
    Duty of board of school
      trustees, §16-10-10.
    Duty of county boards,
      §16-8-43.
Retarded children.
  Exceptional children,
    §§16-39-1 to 16-39-12.
  See within this heading,
    "Exceptional children."
Retirement.
  Teachers' retirement system,
    §§16-25-1 to 16-25-47.
  See within this heading,
    "Teachers."
Rules and regulations.
  Attendance.
    Use as evidence, §16-28-23.
  City superintendents of
    schools, §16-12-5.

EDUCATION—Cont'd
Rules and regulations
—Cont'd
Drug abuse education.
Adoption of regulations by
state board, §16-41-7.
Educational television
commission, §16-7-4.
Exceptional children.
Responsibilities of state
board of education,
§16-39-5.
Health, §16-4-13.
Immunization of school
children.
State health officer to
promulgate, §16-30-5.
School buses.
State board of education to
prescribe, §16-27-1.
State board of education. See
within this heading,
"State board of
education."
Teachers.
Certificates.
Issuance.
State board of
education,
§16-3-16.
State tenure commission,
§16-24-35.
Training, §16-23-16.
Textbooks.
Care of and accounting for
textbooks, §16-36-26.
Unaccredited schools.
Adoption, §16-46-7.
Vocational education,
§16-37-3.
Safety.
School buses.
Inspections, §16-27-3.
Monthly safety
inspections,
§16-27-5.
Seat belts, §16-27-6.
Salaries.
Annuities.
Tax sheltered annuities.
Salary deductions,
§16-22-6.
Checkoffs.
Salary deductions,
§16-22-6.
Contributions.
Voluntary contributions.
Salary deductions,
§16-22-6.
County superintendents of
education, §16-9-12.
Deductions.
Annuities.
Tax sheltered annuities,
§16-22-6.
Insurance.
Group insurance
premiums,
§§16-22-5, 16-22-6.
Membership dues,
§16-22-6.
Policies as to salary
deductions, §16-22-6.
Presumption as to
payments and
deductions, §16-22-7.
Public employees'
individual retirement
account fund, §16-22-6.

EDUCATION—Cont'd
Salaries—Cont'd
Deductions—Cont'd
Purposes for which
deductions made,
§16-22-6.
Voluntary contributions,
§16-22-6.
Dues.
Membership dues.
Salary deductions,
§16-22-6.
Insurance.
Group insurance
premiums.
Salary deductions,
§16-22-6.
Membership dues.
Salary deductions,
§16-22-6.
No additional salary
permitted, §16-14-12.
Principals, §16-11-17.
Public employees' individual
retirement account fund.
Salary deductions,
§16-22-6.
Public school and college
authority, §16-16-6.
State superintendent of
education, §16-4-1;
Const. Ala., art. V, §118.
Teachers. See within this
heading, "Teachers."
Voluntary contributions.
Salary deductions,
§16-22-6.
Sale.
School lands, §§9-15-41 to
9-15-43.
Sales tax.
Exemptions.
County, city and
independent school
boards.
Gross proceeds of sale of
tangible personal
property, §40-23-4.
Tax levied on gross receipts
of educational
institutions, §40-23-2.
Use of county sales and use
tax funds for general
educational purposes,
§16-13-37.
Scholarships.
General provisions.
See SCHOLARSHIPS.
School attendance, §§16-28-1
to 16-28-24. See within
this heading, "Attendance."
School boards.
Tort liability.
Limitations, §11-93-2.
School buses.
Approaching school bus or
vehicle, §32-5A-154.
City boards of education.
Liability of school board
members, §16-11-15.
Operation, §16-11-15.
Purchase, §16-11-14.
Community colleges.
Transportation of students
on public school buses,
§16-27-2.
Death.
Claims against state.
See CLAIMS AGAINST
STATE.

EDUCATION—Cont'd
School buses—Cont'd
Deficiencies.
Reporting and remedying,
§16-27-3.
Defined, §32-1-1.1.
Drivers.
Examination, §16-27-4.
Licensing of drivers,
§16-27-4.
Membership in teachers'
retirement system,
§16-25-9.
Personal leave.
Funding, §16-8-26.1.
Support personnel
entitled to personal
leave, §16-8-26.1.
Sick leave.
Payment, §16-1-18.
Substitutes.
Reimbursement of
local boards of
education,
§16-1-18.
Substitutes.
Reimbursement of local
boards of education,
§16-1-18.
Teachers' retirement
system.
Persons previously under
employees'
retirement system of
Alabama, §16-25-10.
Tuberculosis.
Employment of bus
drivers with
tuberculosis,
§16-22-3.
Vehicle liability insurance,
§16-27-7.
Exceptional children,
§16-39-11.
Expenditures for
transportation.
From what receipts
expenditures for
transportation paid,
§16-13-3.
Identifying marking,
§32-5A-154.
Injuries.
Claims against state.
See CLAIMS AGAINST
STATE.
Inspections.
Safety inspections,
§§16-27-3, 16-27-5.
Inspectors.
Safety inspections by state
school bus inspectors,
§16-27-3.
Insurance.
Liability insurance for
drivers, §16-27-7.
Junior colleges.
Transportation of students
on public school buses,
§16-27-2.
Liability of school board
members, §16-11-15.
Motor vehicle carriers.
Exemptions from chapter,
§37-3-4.
Operation, §32-5-8.

EDUCATION—Cont'd
School buses—Cont'd
  Pupils living less than two
      miles from school.
    Minimum program fund
        allowance for pupil
        transportation not to
        provide for, §16-13-51.
  Purchase by school boards,
      §16-11-14.
  Records.
    Inspections and corrections,
        §16-27-3.
  Reports.
    Inspections and corrections,
        §16-27-3.
  Rules and regulations.
    State board of education to
        prescribe, §16-27-1.
  Safety.
    Inspections, §16-27-3.
      Monthly safety
          inspections,
          §16-27-5.
    Seat belts, §16-27-6.
  Seat belts, §16-27-6.
  Signal lights, §32-5A-154.
  Specifications, §32-5-8.
  State board of education.
    Rules and regulations.
      State board to prescribe,
          §16-27-1.
  Stopping when approaching
      school bus, §32-5A-154.
  Technical colleges.
    Transportation of students
        on public school buses,
        §16-27-2.
  Tuberculosis.
    Employment of bus drivers
        with tuberculosis,
        §16-22-3.
School census. See within
    this heading, "Census."
School districts.
  Establishing separate school
      districts.
    Special, private or local
        laws prohibited, Const.
        Ala., art. IV, §104.
School lands.
  General provisions, §§9-15-36
      to 9-15-44, 9-15-49 to
      9-15-51, 16-20-1 to
      16-20-9.
  See PUBLIC LANDS.
School libraries, §§16-21-1 to
    16-21-3.
School prayer, §16-1-20.2.
School tax district.
  Boundaries.
    Duration, §16-13-192.
    Fixed by county boards,
        §16-13-191.
  City school tax district.
    Consolidation with other
        territory, §16-13-195.
    Map not required,
        §16-13-193.
  Consolidation.
    City district with other
        territory, §16-13-195.
    Effect, §16-13-196.
    Generally, §16-13-194.
  County and district three-
      mill school taxes,
      §§16-13-180 to 16-13-190.
    See within this heading,
        "Taxation."

EDUCATION—Cont'd
School tax district—Cont'd
  Map.
    Not required of city school
        tax district,
        §16-13-193.
    Required, §16-13-192.
  Use of district funds,
      §16-13-198.
Science.
  High school of mathematics
      and science, §§16-26A-1
      to 16-26A-7.
Secretary of state.
  Compact for education.
    Bylaws of commission and
        amendments to be filed
        with secretary of state,
        §16-44-3.
Securities.
  Public school corporation,
      §§16-14-6, 16-14-7,
      16-14-17 to 16-14-19. See
      within this heading,
      "Public school
      corporation."
Segregation, Const. Ala., art.
    XIV, §256; amd. 111.
Separation of schools.
  Teachers.
    Effect of separation on
        tenure, §16-24-2.
Sex education.
  Teaching not authorized,
      §16-41-8.
Shop classes.
  Eye protective devices.
    Pupils and teachers,
        §16-1-7.
Sick leave.
  Bank plans.
    Establishment, §16-22-9.
  Noncertificated educational
      employees, §16-1-18.
  School bus drivers, §16-1-18.
  Teachers, §16-3-36.
    Accrued sick leave.
      Use in determining
          creditable service in
          retirement system,
          §16-25-11.1.
    Bank plan, §16-22-9.
Silence.
  Period of silence for
      meditation at beginning
      of first class in public
      schools, §§16-1-20,
      16-1-20.1.
Societies.
  Public societies, §§10-4-20 to
      10-4-26.
  See CORPORATIONS.
Soil classifiers.
  Qualifications for
      registration, §34-32-9.
**Special educational trust
    fund.**
  Personal leave.
    Educational support
        personnel.
      Funding, §16-8-26.1.
  Public school corporation.
    Borrowing in anticipation
        of appropriation from,
        §16-14-10.
  Setting up account, §40-1-32.
  Source of revenue, §40-1-31.
**Speech pathologists and
    audiologists.**
  Continuing education,
      §34-28A-25.

EDUCATION—Cont'd
Standardizing schools.
  City boards of education,
      §16-11-20.
  City superintendents of
      schools, §16-12-8.
  County boards of education,
      §16-8-29.
  County superintendents of
      education, §16-9-22.
  State board of education,
      §16-3-14.
  State superintendent of
      education, §16-4-14.
State board of education,
    §§16-3-1 to 16-3-37.
  Alabama school of trades.
    Board of control,
        §16-60-216.
  Appointees.
    Filling of vacancies in
        office of appointees,
        §16-3-25.
    Removal of appointees,
        §16-3-25.
  Association of school board
      members, §16-1-6.
  Bond issues.
    Authority to issue,
        §16-3-28.
    Letters of credit as security
        for bonds, notes, etc.,
        §11-80-7.
  Borrowing money.
    Authority to borrow from
        federal agencies or
        others, §16-3-28.
  Budget, §16-4-19.
  Charitable institutions.
    Supervision of educational
        work, §16-3-20.
  Child care institutions.
    Supervision of educational
        work, §16-3-20.
  City boards of education.
    Reports of city board to
        state board, §16-11-22.
  Compensation of employees.
    Subject to merit system,
        §16-3-10.
  Compensation of members,
      §16-3-8.
  Composition, §16-3-1.
  County boards of education.
    Reports by county board to
        state board, §16-8-39.
  Courses of study, §16-3-15.
  Crippled and disabled
      children, §§21-3-1 to
      21-3-8.
    See HANDICAPPED
        PERSONS.
  Designating institutions of
      higher learning,
      §16-3-37.
  Drug abuse education.
    Adoption of regulations,
        §16-41-7.
  Election of members, §16-3-1;
      Const. Ala., amd. 284.
  Employees.
    Compensation of employees
        subject to merit
        system, §16-3-10.
    Forms of contracts, §16-4-9.
  Endowment funds.
    Investment of funds held
        by state board,
        §16-13-2.

EDUCATION—Cont'd
State board of education
—Cont'd
Exceptional children.
Responsibilities of state board of education, §16-39-5.
Executive officer.
State superintendent to be executive officer, §16-3-2.
Expense allowance for members, §16-3-9.
Federal grants.
Acceptance by board, §16-3-19.
Designated state agency in administration, §16-13-6.
Funds.
Endowment funds held by state board.
Investment, §16-13-2.
Governor.
President of board, §16-3-2.
Grading schools, §16-3-14.
Handicapped persons.
Crippled and disabled children, §§21-3-1 to 21-3-8.
See HANDICAPPED PERSONS.
Institute for deaf and blind.
Cooperation by state board, §21-1-8.
Illiteracy.
County and city boards to cooperate with state board, §16-34-2.
Duty to remove, §16-34-1.
Federal government.
Authority to cooperate with, §16-34-3.
Removal.
Duty of state board, §16-34-1.
Institute for deaf and blind.
Cooperation by state board, §21-1-8.
Investigations.
Educational needs investigated, §16-3-17.
Judicial officers.
Authority of legislature to constitute members of state board as judicial officers, Const. Ala., amd. 139.
Junior colleges.
Management and control, §§16-60-110 to 16-60-113.
Legislation.
Recommendation of legislation, §16-3-22.
Letters of credit.
Letters of credit as security for bonds, notes, etc., §11-80-7.
Local actions.
Review by state superintendent, §16-3-27.
Mathematics and science high school.
Definition of state board, §16-26A-2.
Meetings, §16-3-7.

EDUCATION—Cont'd
State board of education
—Cont'd
Meharry Medical College.
Contracts for education of Alabama students, §16-3-35.
Merit system.
Compensation of employees subject to merit system, §16-3-10.
Naming institutions of higher learning, §16-3-37.
Notes.
Authority to issue, §16-3-28.
Oaths.
Authority to administer oaths, §16-3-24.
Oaths of members, §16-3-6.
Officers, §16-3-2.
Penal institutions.
Supervision of educational work, §16-3-20.
Powers, §16-60-111.4.
Generally, §16-3-11.
President.
Governor to be president of board, §16-3-2.
Property control, §16-3-26.
Providing instruction not available at state-supported institutions.
College or university instruction, §16-3-33.
Graduate and professional instruction, §16-3-32.
Qualifications of members, §16-3-3.
Rehabilitation and crippled children service.
Annual report to governor on rehabilitation, §16-38-9.
Federal rehabilitation agency.
State board of education's authority to cooperate with, §16-38-6.
Removal of members, §16-3-4.
Reports.
Annual report, §16-3-21.
State superintendent of education to prepare, §16-4-18.
Vocational education.
Annual report to governor, §16-37-6.
Rules and regulations.
Generally, §16-3-12.
Grading and standardizing schools, §16-3-14.
Necessary to make effective the law's purpose, §16-3-13.
School buses.
State board to prescribe, §16-27-1.
School buses.
Rules and regulations.
State board to prescribe, §16-27-1.
Seal.
Official seal, §16-3-23.
Secretary.
State superintendent to be secretary, §16-3-2.

EDUCATION—Cont'd
State board of education
—Cont'd
Securities.
Authority to issue, §16-3-28.
Special institutions.
Supervision of educational work of special institutions, §16-3-20.
Standardizing schools, §16-3-14.
State superintendent of education.
Secretary and executive officer of board, §16-3-2.
Teachers.
Sick leave.
Establishment of sick leave plan, §16-3-36.
Reimbursing local boards for payment to substitute teachers, §16-3-36.
Training and certification of teachers, §16-3-16.
Terms of members, §16-3-1.
Textbooks.
Authority to contract for furnishing, storing or delivering, §16-36-14.
Conflicts of interest, §16-36-36.
Sufficiency of textbooks.
Duty of state board to provide sufficient textbooks, §16-36-27.
Trade schools.
Management and control, §§16-60-110 to 16-60-113.
Regional, vocational and trade schools, §§16-60-190 to 16-60-198.
See TRADE SCHOOLS.
Tuskegee Institute.
Contracts for education of Alabama students, §16-3-35.
Universities and colleges.
Naming or designating, §16-3-37.
Vacancies, §16-3-5.
Vocational education.
Annual report to governor, §16-37-6.
Authority of as to vocational education, §16-37-4.
City and county boards may cooperate with state board, §16-37-5.
Cooperation with federal board, §16-3-18.
Vocational schools, §§16-60-190 to 16-60-198.
See TRADE SCHOOLS.
Witnesses.
Examination of witnesses, §16-3-24.
Youth services.
Department of youth services district.
Relationship of district and state board, §44-1-70.
State board of health.
Authority and jurisdiction, §22-2-2.

EDUCATION—Cont'd
State comptroller.
Budget system.
Estimate of funds,
§16-13-141.
**State department of
education,** §§16-2-1 to
16-2-8. See within this
heading, "Department of
education."
State-line schools, §16-8-19.
**State superintendent of
education.**
Agricultural and industrial
exhibit commission.
Member of commission,
§2-7-1.
Alabama school of trades.
Ex officio member of board
of trustees, §16-60-213.
Appointment, Const. Ala.,
amd. 284.
Apportionment of school
funds, §16-4-5.
Assistant state
superintendent.
Appointment, §16-2-7.
Compensation, §16-2-7.
Continuation of coverage
by merit system law,
§16-2-7.
Department of education.
Duties of assistant state
superintendent,
§16-2-1.
Bond, surety, §16-4-3.
Budgets, §16-4-19.
Estimate of funds,
§16-13-141.
Preparing for state board
of education, §16-4-19.
Buildings.
Condemnation, §16-4-10.
Inventory, §16-4-21.
Rules for construction,
§16-4-10.
Census for schools, §16-4-16.
City boards of education.
Conferences, §16-4-6.
Review of action by city
boards, §§16-3-27,
16-4-8.
City superintendents of
schools.
Conferences, §16-4-6.
Review of actions,
§§16-3-27, 16-4-8.
Compensation, §16-4-1.
Conferences, §16-4-6.
Constitution of Alabama.
Duties, Const. Ala., art. V,
§137; amds. 111, 284.
Election.
Generally, Const. Ala.,
art. V, §§114, 115.
Executive department.
Member of department,
Const. Ala., art. V,
§112.
Fees.
Restrictions on receipt,
Const. Ala., art. V,
§137; amd. 111.
Mental unsoundness,
Const. Ala., art. V,
§136.
Powers, Const. Ala., amd.
284.
Qualifications, Const. Ala.,
art. V, §132; amd. 284.

EDUCATION—Cont'd
**State superintendent of
education**—Cont'd
Constitution of Alabama
—Cont'd
Residency requirements,
Const. Ala., art. V,
§118.
Succession.
Ineligible to succeed self,
Const. Ala., art. V,
§116.
One additional term,
Const. Ala., amd.
282.
Term of office, Const. Ala.,
art. V, §116; amds.
282, 284.
Vacancy in office, Const.
Ala., art. V, §136.
Contract.
Forms of contract, §16-4-9.
County boards of education.
Conferences, §16-4-6.
Review of action of county
boards, §§16-3-27,
16-4-8.
County superintendents of
education.
Conferences, §16-4-6.
Examination of books,
accounts, etc., by state
superintendent,
§16-9-31.
Report on schools to state
superintendent,
§16-9-31.
Review of actions,
§§16-3-27, 16-4-8.
Department of education.
Administration of
department, §16-4-11.
Director of department of
education, §16-2-1.
Supervision and
nomination of
employees of
department, §16-4-11.
Drug abuse education.
Administration of chapter,
§16-41-4.
Report of status of
program, §16-41-10.
Duties, Const. Ala., amds.
111, 284.
Generally, §16-4-4; Const.
Ala., art. V, §137.
Educational benefits for
dependents of blind
parents.
Duties of state
superintendent,
§16-33-7.
Educational policy.
Execution, §16-4-6.
Election.
Constitutional provisions,
Const. Ala., art. V,
§§114, 115.
Employment contracts.
Forms, §16-4-9.
Execution of educational
policy, §16-4-6.
Executive department.
Member of department,
Const. Ala., art. V,
§112.
Expenditures.
Examination of
expenditures, §16-4-7.
Federal grants, §16-4-21.

EDUCATION—Cont'd
**State superintendent of
education**—Cont'd
Fees.
Restrictions on receipt of
fees, Const. Ala., amd.
111.
Forms and blanks, §16-4-16.
Funds.
Apportionment of school
funds, §16-4-5.
Grading schools, §16-4-14.
Health.
Rules for protection of
health, §16-4-13.
Impeachment, Const. Ala.,
art. VII, §173.
General provisions.
See IMPEACHMENT.
Inventory of buildings and
sites, §16-4-21.
Junior college for Franklin,
Marion and Winston
counties.
Member of board of
trustees, §16-60-20.
Junior college for Jackson
and DeKalb counties.
Member of board of
trustees, §16-60-50.
Legislation, §16-4-20.
Local actions.
Review by state
superintendent,
§16-3-27.
Mathematics and science
high school.
Definition of state
superintendent,
§16-26A-2.
Mental unsoundness, Const.
Ala., art. V, §136.
Oath of office, §16-4-2.
Powers, Const. Ala., amd.
284.
Principals.
Conferences, §16-4-6.
Publications of laws, rules,
etc., §16-4-7.
Qualifications, §16-4-1;
Const. Ala., art. V, §132;
amd. 284.
Rehabilitation and crippled
children service.
Duties of superintendent as
to rehabilitation work,
§16-38-5.
Reports.
Annual report of state
board of education,
§16-4-18.
Drug abuse education.
Report of status of
program, §16-41-10.
Examination of reports,
§16-4-7.
Forms and blanks,
§16-4-16.
Residency requirements,
Const. Ala., art. V, §118.
Salary, §16-4-1; Const. Ala.,
art. V, §118.
Authority of board to
establish salary,
§16-60-111.3.
Standardizing schools,
§16-4-14.
State board of education.
Secretary and executive
officer of board,
§16-3-2.

EDUCATION—Cont'd

State superintendent of education—Cont'd

Study commission.
Cooperation, §16-6-5.
Succession.
Ineligible to succeed self,
Const. Ala., art. V,
§116.
One additional term,
Const. Ala., amd. 282.
Supervision of public schools,
Const. Ala., art. XIV,
§262.
Tax anticipation warrants in
cities and counties.
Approval of issue by state
superintendent,
§16-13-73.
Teachers.
Conferences, §16-4-6.
Teachers' retirement system.
Eligibility of elected
superintendent to
participate in,
§16-25-10.6.
Term of office, Const. Ala.,
art. V, §116; amds. 282,
284.
Textbooks.
Action upon receipt of
requisitions, §16-36-17.
Conflicts of interest,
§16-36-36.
Members of local selection
committees.
Filing of names with
state superintendent,
§16-36-4.
School board policies.
Filing with state
superintendent,
§16-36-4.
Troy State University.
Ex officio member of board
of trustees, §16-56-3.
University of Alabama.
Member of board of
trustees, §16-47-30.
University of Montevallo.
Member of board of
trustees, §16-54-2.
University of South
Alabama.
Member of board of
trustees, §16-55-2.
Vacancy in office, Const.
Ala., art. V, §136.
Vocational education.
In charge of vocational
education, §16-37-3.
Plans and rules and
regulations, §16-4-17.
Youth services board.
Member of board, §44-1-51.

State treasurer.

Vocational education.
Treasurer custodian of
federal funds, §16-37-2.

**Stonewall Jackson memorial
fund,** §§16-32-1 to 16-32-3.

Student grant program,
§§16-33A-1 to 16-33A-11.
See STUDENT GRANT
PROGRAM.

Student loan program,
§§16-33B-1 to 16-33B-7.
See STUDENT LOAN
PROGRAM.

Students. See within this
heading, "Pupils."

EDUCATION—Cont'd

Study commission, §§16-6-1
to 16-6-6.
Appointment, §16-6-1.
Compensation of members,
§16-6-1.
Contracts for services,
§16-6-3.
Cooperation of state
superintendent and other
agencies, §16-6-5.
Created, §16-6-1.
Employees, §16-6-3.
Gifts.
Acceptance of gifts, etc.,
§16-6-6.
Majority vote, §16-6-2.
Membership, §16-6-1.
Organization, §16-6-2.
Other agencies.
Cooperation, §16-6-5.
Use of facilities, etc., of
other agencies,
§16-6-5.
Public officers.
Authority to summon and
examine, §16-6-5.
Quorum, §16-6-2.
Records.
Authority to summon and
examine, §16-6-5.
Reports.
Reports to legislature,
§16-6-4.
Services.
Contracts for services,
§16-6-3.
State superintendent of
education.
Cooperation, §16-6-5.
Terms of members, §16-6-1.
Vacancies, §16-6-1.
Voting.
Majority vote, §16-6-2.
Witnesses.
Authority to summon and
examine officials and
records, §16-6-5.

Suggestions.

Payments to employees,
§16-1-21.

Summons and process.

County boards of education.
Execution of process,
§16-8-40.

**Superintendents of
education.**

City superintendents,
§§16-12-1 to 16-12-21.
See within this heading,
"City superintendents of
schools."
County superintendents of
education, §§16-9-1 to
16-9-34. See within this
heading, "County
superintendents of
education."
Diseases.
Notifiable diseases.
Notification that
students or
employees have
contagious disease,
§22-11A-38.
State superintendent,
§§16-4-1 to 16-4-21. See
within this heading,
"State superintendent of
education."

EDUCATION—Cont'd

**Superintendents of
education**—Cont'd

Teachers' retirement system.
Eligibility of elected
superintendent to
participate in,
§16-25-10.6.

Supervisors.

Certificates.
Required, §16-23-1.
Tenure. See within this
heading, "Teachers."

Supplies.

Purchase.
Allocation to city and
county boards of
education.
Funds appropriated to
state board of
education, §16-13-39.
Distribution of
matriculation fees and
local fees for purchase,
§16-13-38.

Support personnel.

Defined, §16-25-1.
Nonteacher, nonclassified,
etc., employees
generally, §§36-26-100 to
36-26-108. See within
this heading,
"Nonteacher,
nonclassified, etc.,
employees."
Personal leave.
Authorized, §16-8-26.1.
Funding, §16-8-26.1.

**Sylacauga nurses' training
school,** §§16-58-1 to
16-58-3.
See SYLACAUGA NURSES'
TRAINING SCHOOL.

Taxation.

Additional property tax for
county educational
purposes, Const. Ala.,
amd. 202.
Alabama special educational
trust funds surplus
account, §40-1-32.
City boards of education.
Allocation of revenue from
licenses and taxes,
§16-11-25.
Constitution of Alabama.
See CONSTITUTION OF
ALABAMA.
Counties.
County license tax for
school purposes,
§40-12-4.
Licenses.
County license tax for
school purposes,
§§40-12-4 to 40-12-7.
See COUNTIES.
Special county school
taxes, Const. Ala., art.
XIV, §269.
Additional property tax
for educational
purposes, Const.
Ala., amd. 202.
Amendment to section
269, Const. Ala.,
amd. 111.
Tax for education,
§40-12-4.

EDUCATION—Cont'd
Taxation—Cont'd
County and district three-
mill school taxes,
§§16-13-180 to 16-13-199.
Amount of tax, §16-13-188.
Collection of tax,
§16-13-197.
Disposition of tax.
When city assumed
control of schools,
§16-13-199.
Duration of tax,
§16-13-188.
Elections.
Ballots, §16-13-187.
Calling of election,
§16-13-180.
Conduct of election,
§16-13-184.
Electors, §16-13-189.
Expenses, §16-13-185.
Notice, §16-13-183.
Officers, §16-13-184.
Petition for election,
§16-13-180.
Request by board of
education for
election, §16-13-181.
Result, §16-13-188.
Supplies, §16-13-186.
Validation of elections,
§16-13-190.
When district tax cannot
be levied,
§16-13-182.
Electors, §16-13-189.
Levy, §16-13-188.
When district tax cannot
to levied, §16-13-182.
Limitation on use of
proceeds, §16-13-188.
Municipality may remain
under county board of
education, §16-13-199.
Petition for election,
§16-13-180.
Proceeds.
Limitation on use,
§16-13-188.
School tax district.
Boundaries.
Duration of
boundaries,
§16-13-192.
Fixed by county board,
§16-13-191.
City school tax district.
Consolidation with
other territory,
§16-13-195.
Map not required,
§16-13-193.
Consolidation.
City district with other
territory,
§16-13-195.
Effect, §16-13-196.
Generally, §16-13-194.
Map.
Duration of
boundaries,
§16-13-192.
Not required of city
school tax district,
§§16-13-192,
16-13-193.
Use of district funds,
§16-13-198.
Use of district funds,
§16-13-198.

EDUCATION—Cont'd
Taxation—Cont'd
County and district three-
mill school taxes—Cont'd
Validation of elections,
§16-13-190.
When district tax cannot
be levied, §16-13-182.
Elections.
Contest of certain
elections, §16-1-17.
Warrants for special
county and district
taxes, §16-13-108.
Excise taxes.
Warrants for special
license, privilege or
excise taxes,
§§16-13-120 to
16-13-122.
Exemption from taxation,
§40-9-1.
Franchise taxes.
Exemption of educational
corporations, Const.
Ala., art. XII, §229.
Notes in anticipation of
warrants in cities and
counties, §16-13-216.
Private colleges and
universities facilities
authority.
Bond issues, §16-18A-9.
Sales tax.
Gross proceeds of sale of
tangible personal
property to school
boards, §40-23-4.
Tax anticipation warrants
in cities and counties,
§16-13-75.
Franchise taxes.
Exemption of educational
corporations, Const.
Ala., art. XII, §229.
Income tax.
Deductions.
Contributions to
educational
institutions,
§40-18-15.
Licenses.
Warrants for special
license, privilege or
excise taxes,
§§16-13-120 to
16-13-122.
Local funding of school
programs, §§16-13-60 to
16-13-65.
One-mill county school tax,
§§16-13-160 to 16-13-166.
Assessment, §16-13-165.
Collection, §16-13-166.
Election.
Ballot, §16-13-164.
Calling of election,
§16-13-160.
Conduct of election,
§16-13-162.
Electors, §16-13-163.
Notice, §16-13-161.
Officers, §16-13-162.
Petition for election,
§16-13-160.
Supplies, §16-13-164.
Levy, §16-13-165.
Petition for election,
§16-13-160.

EDUCATION—Cont'd
Taxation—Cont'd
Poll taxes.
Use for support of public
schools, Const. Ala.,
art. XIV, §259.
Amendment to section
259, Const. Ala.,
amd. 111.
Privilege taxes.
Warrants for special
license, privilege or
excise taxes,
§§16-13-120 to
16-13-122.
Property exempt, §40-9-1.
Records.
Warrants for special
county and district
taxes, §16-13-106.
Sales tax. See within this
heading, "Sales tax."
School tax district,
§§16-13-191 to 16-13-196.
See within this heading,
"School tax district."
Special annual tax for
schools, Const. Ala., art.
XIV, §260.
Amendment to section 260,
Const. Ala., amd. 111.
Special district school tax.
Levy and collection of
additional tax, Const.
Ala., amd. 382.
Special school tax
amendment, Const. Ala.,
amd. 3.
Teachers.
Exemptions from taxation.
Corporation organized
for purpose of aiding
retired teachers.
Property exempt,
§40-9-18.
Use tax.
Use of county sales and
use taxes for general
educational purposes,
§16-13-37.
Warrants.
Special county and district
taxes.
Approval of issuance,
§16-13-91.
Care of fund, §16-13-98.
Delivery of refunding
warrants,
§16-13-102.
Elections, §16-13-108.
Exchange of refunding
warrants,
§16-13-102.
Exclusiveness of article,
§16-13-107.
Execution, §16-13-92.
Exemption from
taxation, §16-13-104.
Form, §16-13-93.
Interest rate, §16-13-95.
Investment of unused
proceeds in
government
securities,
§16-13-109.
Issuance.
Approval of issuance,
§16-13-91.
Purposes for which
warrants issued,
§16-13-90.

EDUCATION—Cont'd
  Taxation—Cont'd
    Warrants—Cont'd
      Special county and district
        taxes—Cont'd
        Maturity, §16-13-94.
        Redemption of
          warrants prior to
          maturity,
          §16-13-101.
        Payment, §§16-13-94,
          16-13-98.
        Method, §16-13-99.
        Place, §16-13-99.
        Preference, §16-13-98.
        Price, §16-13-97.
        Purposes for which
          warrants issued,
          §16-13-90.
        Records, §16-13-106.
        Refunding warrants.
          Exchange and
            delivery,
            §16-13-102.
        Sale.
          Generally, §16-13-96.
          Price, §16-13-97.
        Validity, §16-13-103.
        Warrants may be
          validated,
          §16-13-105.
      Special license, privilege or
        excise taxes.
      Approval of issue by
        state superintendent,
        §16-13-121.
      Interest.
        Rate, §16-13-120.
      Issuance.
        Approval of issue by
          state
          superintendent,
          §16-13-121.
        Authority, §16-13-120.
      Proceeds.
        Use of proceeds,
          §16-13-120.
      Provisions of article
        cumulative,
        §16-13-122.
      Refunding warrants,
        §16-13-120.
      Terms, §16-13-120.
    Tax anticipation warrants
      in cities and counties.
      Boards of education.
      Effect of article on
        existing powers,
        §16-13-77.
      Conditions, §16-13-71.
      Effect of article on
        existing powers of
        boards of education,
        §16-13-77.
      Exemption from
        taxation, §16-13-75.
      Fiduciaries.
        Warrants legal
          investments for
          fiduciaries,
          §16-13-74.
      Investments.
        Warrants legal
          investments for
          fiduciaries,
          §16-13-74.

EDUCATION—Cont'd
  Taxation—Cont'd
    Warrants—Cont'd
      Tax anticipation warrants
        in cities and counties
        —Cont'd
      Issuance authorized,
        §16-13-70.
      Approval of issue by
        state
        superintendent of
        education,
        §16-13-73.
      Minimum school
        program fund.
      Moneys allocated
        under article 3 not
        to be pledged,
        §16-13-76.
      Pledge and collateral
        security.
        Public school funds
          and minimum
          school program
          fund not to be
          pledged, §16-13-76.
      Proceeds.
        Use of proceeds,
          §16-13-71.
      Public school funds.
        Moneys allocated
          under article 2 not
          to be pledged,
          §16-13-76.
      Purposes, §16-13-70.
      Refunding warrants,
        §16-13-72.
      Sale, §16-13-71.
      Source of payment,
        §16-13-70.
      State superintendent of
        education.
        Approval of issue by
          state
          superintendent,
          §16-13-73.
      Terms, §16-13-71.
      Use of proceeds,
        §16-13-71.
    Warrants for special county
      and district taxes,
      §§16-13-90 to 16-13-109.
  Teachers.
    Aides.
      Employment, §16-1-1.1.
    Annuities.
      Tax sheltered annuities.
      Salary deductions,
        §16-22-6.
    Appeals.
      Cancellation of
        employment contract,
        §16-24-10.
      Transfers, §16-24-7.
    Appointment.
      County boards of
        education, §16-8-23.
    Assault.
      Reports of assaults on
        teachers, §16-1-24.
    Assignment.
      City superintendents,
        §16-12-16.
      County superintendents,
        §16-9-23.
      Refusal by board of school
        trustees, §16-10-4.
    Boards of school trustees.
      Charges against teachers
        may be filed by
        trustees, §16-10-9.

EDUCATION—Cont'd
  Teachers—Cont'd
    Boards of school trustees
      —Cont'd
      Dismissal of pupils,
        §16-10-5.
      Refusal of teachers,
        §16-10-4.
    Budget.
      Faculty to have
        opportunity to develop,
        §16-13-13.
    Cancellation of contracts,
      §§16-24-8 to 16-24-11.
    Certificates.
      Applicant's fee, §16-23-4.
      Extension, §16-23-2.
      Fees.
        Applicant's fee, §16-23-4.
      Issuance, §16-23-2.
        Rules and regulations,
        §16-3-16.
      Provisional certificates,
        §16-23-3.
      Renewal, §16-23-2.
      Required, §16-23-1.
      Revocation, §16-23-5.
      State board of education.
        Rules and regulations
          governing issuance,
          §16-3-16.
    Charges against teachers.
      May be filed by boards of
        school trustees,
        §16-10-9.
    Checkoffs.
      Salary deductions.
        Purposes for which
          deductions made,
          §16-22-6.
    Child abuse or neglect.
      See MINORS.
    City boards of education.
      Dismissal or suspension,
        §16-11-17.
      Leaves of absence,
        §16-12-21.
      Personal leave for
        teachers during time
        schools are in
        session, §16-8-26.
      Substitute teachers
        replacing teachers
        absent on sick leave.
        Reimbursing local boards
          for payments to
          substitutes, §16-3-36.
      Vacations, §16-12-21.
    City superintendents of
      schools.
      Full-time employment of
        teachers authorized,
        §16-12-20.
      Nomination of teachers,
        §16-12-16.
      Payroll of city
        superintendent,
        §16-12-17.
      Removal, §16-12-16.
    Colleges.
      State teachers colleges.
        See UNIVERSITIES
          AND COLLEGES.
    Conferences, §16-23-12.
      County superintendents of
        education, §16-9-16.
    Consolidation or separation
      of schools.
      Effect, §16-24-2.
    Continuing service status,
      §§16-24-2, 16-24-13.

EDUCATION—Cont'd
Teachers—Cont'd
Contracts.
Employment, §§16-24-8 to
16-24-11.
Contributions.
Voluntary contributions.
Salary deductions,
§16-22-6.
County boards of education.
Appointment and removal
of teachers, §16-8-23.
Full-time employment by
county board, §16-8-24.
Leaves of absence,
§16-8-25.
Personal leave for
teachers during time
schools are in
session, §16-8-26.
Removal of teachers,
§16-8-23.
Substitute teachers
replacing teachers
absent on sick leave.
Reimbursement of local
boards for payments,
§16-3-36.
Vacations, §16-8-25.
County superintendents of
education.
Conferences, §16-9-16.
Nomination, §16-9-23.
Payrolls.
Approval, §16-9-33.
Preparation, §16-9-32.
Promotion, §16-9-23.
Removal, §16-9-23.
Suspension, §16-9-23.
Damages.
Breach of employment
contract, §16-24-10.
Defined, §§16-24-1, 16-25-1.
Dismissal.
City boards, §16-11-17.
City superintendents,
§16-12-16.
County superintendent,
§16-9-23.
Drug abuse education.
Exclusion of teacher
employed by nonpublic
school, §16-41-5.
Dues.
Membership dues.
Salary deductions,
§16-22-6.
Educational benefits for
dependents of blind
parents.
Duties of teachers,
§16-33-8.
Elementary teachers.
Scholarship fund,
§16-23-17.
Employment.
Aides, §16-1-1.1.
Contract of employment.
Breach.
Damages, §16-24-10.
Cancellation.
Appeals, §16-24-10.
By teacher, §16-24-11.
Damages for breach of
contract,
§16-24-10.
Finality of action of
employing board,
§16-24-10.
Grounds, §16-24-8.
Hearings, §16-24-9.

EDUCATION—Cont'd
Teachers—Cont'd
Employment—Cont'd
Contract of employment
—Cont'd
Cancellation—Cont'd
Procedure, §16-24-9.
Damages for breach of
contract, §16-24-10.
Effective until
superseded or
cancelled, §16-24-3.
Forms of contracts,
§16-4-9.
Exceptional children.
Scholarships for special
teachers, §16-39-12.
Teacher units, §16-39-7.
Eye protective devices.
Teachers participating in
certain courses,
§16-1-7.
Flags.
Teachers not displaying
flag not allowed public
funds, §16-43-3.
Teacher's report on display,
§16-43-2.
Full-time employment.
Authorized, §16-12-20.
County board, §16-8-24.
Retired teachers.
Prohibited, §16-25-26.
Funds.
Elementary teachers'
scholarship fund,
§16-23-17.
High schools, §16-26-1.
Insurance.
Dental insurance, §16-22-8.
Group insurance.
Authority of school
boards to form
groups for purpose of
obtaining, §16-22-5.
Payment of premiums,
§16-22-5.
Presumption as to
payments and
deductions, §16-22-7.
Salary deductions.
Group insurance
premiums, §16-22-6.
Kindergarten programs,
§16-13-52.1.
Leaves of absence, §§16-8-25,
16-12-21.
Effect on continuing
service status,
§16-24-13.
Personal leave for teachers
during time schools
are in session,
§16-8-26.
Licenses.
Exemptions from licenses.
Corporation organized
for purpose of aiding
retired teachers,
§40-9-18.
Membership dues.
Salary deductions,
§16-22-6.
Minimum school program
fund.
Determining number of
teacher units for
purpose of
apportioning,
§§16-13-52, 16-13-52.1.

EDUCATION—Cont'd
Teachers—Cont'd
Nomination.
By city superintendents,
§16-12-16.
By county superintendents,
§16-9-23.
Payrolls.
Approval, §16-9-33.
City superintendents,
§16-12-17.
Preparation, §16-9-32.
Placement bureau, §16-23-6.
Promotion.
By county superintendents,
§16-9-23.
Public employees' individual
retirement account fund.
Salary deductions,
§16-22-6.
Refusal by board of school
trustees, §16-10-4.
Removal.
City superintendents,
§16-12-16.
County boards of
education, §16-8-23.
County superintendents,
§16-9-23.
Reports.
Assault on teachers,
§16-1-24.
Child abuse or neglect.
Mandatory reporting,
§26-14-3.
Forms, §16-12-12.
Retirement system.
Acting president of
university of Alabama.
Retired teacher who
subsequently
becomes.
Election to resume
participation in
system,
§16-25-26.1.
Actuarial equivalent.
Defined, §16-25-1.
Administration.
Board of control,
§16-28-19.
Agricultural experiment
station of Auburn
university.
Membership of
employees, §16-25-6.
Alabama association of
school boards.
Executive officers and
employees.
Membership,
§16-25-10.1.
Alabama congress of
parents and teachers.
Executive officers and
employees,
§16-25-10.4.
Alabama council for school
administration and
supervision.
Executive officers and
employees,
§16-25-10.2.
Alabama opportunities
industrialization
center.
Executive officers and
employees,
§16-25-10.5.
Annuities.
Defined, §16-25-1.

EDUCATION—Cont'd
  Teachers—Cont'd
   Retirement system—Cont'd
    Annuities—Cont'd
     Exemptions from
       execution, §16-25-23.
     Funds, §16-25-21.
     Generally, §16-25-14.
    Annuity reserve.
     Defined, §16-25-1.
    Athens State College.
     Purchase of credit for
       total years of
       service, §16-25-13.1.
    Beneficiaries.
     Defined, §16-25-1.
    Benefits.
     Additional costs of
       benefits, §§16-25-31,
       36-27-16.3.
     Continuation of
       retirement benefits,
       §16-25-26.
     Cost of living increase.
       Additional adjustment,
         §16-25-41.
       Adjustment of
         survivor's
         allowance,
         §16-25-44.
       Appropriations,
         §16-25-45.
       Impairment of
         eligibility under
         medicaid program,
         §16-25-46.
       Persons whose date of
         retirement is prior
         to October 1, 1987,
         §16-25-40.
       Provisions of article
         supplemental,
         §16-25-47.
     Deferred benefits,
       §16-25-3.
     Effective date,
       §§16-25-31,
       36-27-16.3.
     Exemptions from
       execution, §16-25-23.
     Generally, §16-25-14.
     Increase.
       Additional five
         percent, §16-25-16.
       Cost of living increase
         for certain
         persons, §16-25-17.
       Persons whose date of
         retirement is prior
         to October 1, 1987,
         §16-25-40.
       Ten percent, §16-25-15.
     Nomination of recipient
       of surviving spouse
       benefits prior to date
       of retirement,
       §36-27-16.2.
     Redetermination of
       allowances of certain
       retired members,
       §16-25-18.
     Surviving spouse.
       Nomination of
         recipient of
         surviving spouse
         benefits prior to
         date of retirement,
         §36-27-16.2.

EDUCATION—Cont'd
  Teachers—Cont'd
   Retirement system—Cont'd
    Board of control.
     Actuary.
       Designated by board of
         control, §16-25-19.
       Duties, §16-25-19.
     Administration and
       responsibility for
       operation of system
       vested in, §16-25-19.
     Attorney general.
       Legal adviser of board,
         §16-25-19.
     Chairman.
       Election, §16-25-19.
     Compensation.
       Service without
         compensation,
         §16-25-19.
     Composition, §16-25-19.
     Defined, §16-25-1.
     Expenses.
       Reimbursed for
         expenses,
         §16-25-19.
     Management of funds,
       §16-25-20.
     Medical board.
       Designated by board of
         control, §16-25-19.
     Mortality, service and
       other tables.
       Adoption, §16-25-19.
     Number of members,
       §16-25-19.
     Oaths, §16-25-19.
     Records.
       Open to public
         inspection,
         §16-25-19.
     Rules and regulations.
       Board to establish,
         §16-25-19.
     Secretary-treasurer.
       Chief executive officer,
         §16-25-19.
     Vacancies.
       Filling vacancies,
         §16-25-19.
     Votes.
       Votes necessary for
         decision,
         §16-25-19.
    Cafeteria workers.
     Membership in system,
       §16-25-8.
     Transfer, §16-25-5.
     Transfer of membership,
       §16-25-5.
    Compensation.
     Average final
       compensation.
       Defined, §16-25-1.
     Earnable compensation.
       Defined, §16-25-1.
     Maximum compensation,
       §16-25-26.
    Contributions.
     Accumulated
       contributions.
       Defined, §16-25-1.
     Collection, §16-25-21.
     Employee's
       contributions,
       §16-25-21.
       Payment, §16-25-13.
     Employer's contributions,
       §16-25-21.

EDUCATION—Cont'd
  Teachers—Cont'd
   Retirement system—Cont'd
    Contributions—Cont'd
     Normal contribution.
       Defined, §16-25-1.
     Creditable service.
       Out-of-state public
         employment,
         §36-27-15.2.
     Date of establishment,
       §16-25-2.
     Deductions, §16-25-21.
     Definitions, §16-25-1.
     Employees' retirement
       system of Alabama.
       Transfer of membership,
         §§16-25-4, 16-25-5.
     Enumeration of funds,
       §16-25-21.
     Equipment, etc., §16-25-22.
     Errors.
       Correction of errors,
         §16-25-24.
     Establishment.
       Date of establishment,
         §16-25-2.
     Evidence.
       Photo-reproduced copies
         of records or
         documents.
         Admissibility in
           evidence,
           §16-25-27.
     Executions.
       Exemptions from
         execution, §16-25-23.
     False statements,
       §16-25-24.
     Financing.
       Method of financing,
         §16-25-21.
     Full-time employment.
       Prohibited, §16-25-26.
     Funds.
       Enumeration, §16-25-21.
       Management, §16-25-20.
       Method of financing,
         §16-25-21.
       Transfer of contributions
         and creditable
         service to judicial
         retirement fund.
         See JUDGES.
     Interest.
       Regular interest.
         Defined, §16-25-1.
     Janitors.
       Transfer of membership,
         §16-25-5.
     Junior colleges.
       Purchases of service
         credits by employees.
         Leave of absence time,
           §16-25-11.3.
         Total years of service,
           §16-25-13.1.
     Legislation.
       Proposed legislation to
         be accompanied by
         estimate of cost,
         §16-25-28.
     Legislative service.
       Creditable service,
         §16-25-11.2.
     Limitation on membership,
       §16-25-25.
     Maids.
       Transfer of membership,
         §16-25-5.

EDUCATION—Cont'd
  Teachers—Cont'd
    Retirement system—Cont'd
      Maintenance workers.
        Membership, §16-25-9.
        Persons previously under
          employees'
          retirement system,
          §16-25-10.
      Management of funds,
        §16-25-20.
      Maximum compensation,
        §16-25-26.
      Mechanics.
        Membership, §16-25-9.
        Persons previously under
          employees'
          retirement system of
          Alabama, §16-25-10.
      Medical board.
        Defined, §16-25-1.
      Membership.
        Agricultural experiment
          station of Auburn
          university.
          Employees to be
            members,
            §16-25-6.
        Alabama association of
          school boards.
          Executive officers and
            employees,
            §16-25-10.1.
        Alabama congress of
          parents and
          teachers.
          Executive officers and
            employees,
            §16-25-10.4.
        Alabama council for
          school
          administration and
          supervision.
          Executive officers and
            employees,
            §16-25-10.2.
        Alabama high school
          athletic association.
          Certain persons
            employed by,
            §16-25-7.
        Alabama opportunities
          industrialization
          center.
          Executive officers and
            employees,
            §16-25-10.5.
        Cafeteria workers,
          §16-25-8.
        Generally, §16-25-3.
        Limitation on
          membership,
          §16-25-25.
        Retired state employees'
          association,
          §16-25-32.
        School bus drivers,
          mechanics and
          maintenance
          workers, §16-25-9.
        Persons previously
          under employees'
          retirement system,
          §16-25-10.
        School lunchroom
          managers and
          assistants, §16-25-8.
        State employees'
          association,
          §16-25-32.

EDUCATION—Cont'd
  Teachers—Cont'd
    Retirement system—Cont'd
      Membership—Cont'd
        State employees' credit
          union, §16-25-32.
        Transfer of membership
          from employees'
          retirement system,
          §§16-25-4, 16-25-5.
      Military service.
        Membership credit for
          service in armed
          forces, §16-25-3.
        Prior service credit for
          military service
          during World War I,
          §16-25-12.
        Redetermination of
          allowances of certain
          retired members,
          §16-25-18.
      Name, §16-25-2.
      Nomination of recipient of
        surviving spouse
        benefits prior to date
        of retirement,
        §36-27-16.2.
      Pensions.
        Defined, §16-25-1.
        Exemptions from
          execution, §16-25-23.
        Funds, §16-25-21.
        Generally, §16-25-14.
        Increases, §§16-25-15 to
          16-25-17.
      Public school.
        Defined, §16-25-1.
      Purchase of service credit.
        Clerks of circuit court.
          Full time employment
            in office of clerk,
            §16-25-11.4.
        Junior college employees,
          §§16-25-11.3,
          16-25-13.1.
      Real property.
        Purchase, sale, etc., of
          interests or estates,
          §16-25-22.
      Records.
        Admissibility in evidence
          of photo-reproduced
          copies, §16-25-27.
      Reserves.
        Annuity reserve.
          Defined, §16-25-1.
        Pension reserve.
          Defined, §16-25-1.
      Retired state employees'
        association.
        Membership in system,
          §16-25-32.
      Retired teachers serving as
        substitute teachers,
        §16-25-26.
      Retirement allowance,
        §16-25-14.
        Defined, §16-25-1.
        Exemptions from
          execution, §16-25-23.
        Increases.
          Additional five
            percent, §16-25-16.
          Cost of living increase,
            §16-25-17.
          Ten percent, §16-25-15.
        Redetermination of
          allowances,
          §16-25-18.

EDUCATION—Cont'd
  Teachers—Cont'd
    Retirement system—Cont'd
      Retirement of members,
        §16-25-14.
      School bus drivers.
        Membership, §16-25-9.
        Persons previously under
          employees'
          retirement system,
          §16-25-10.
      Service.
        Creditable service,
          §16-25-11.
          Accrued sick leave
            used in
            determining,
            §16-25-11.1.
          Defined, §16-25-1.
          Elected official of state
            or department
            head, §16-25-13.
          Employees of Athens
            State College,
            §16-25-13.1.
          Employment in office
            of clerk of circuit
            court, §16-25-11.4.
          Employment while
            student at public
            institution of
            higher learning,
            §16-25-29.
          Legislative service as
            full-time
            employee,
            §16-25-11.2.
          Military service during
            World War I,
            §16-25-12.
          Purchase by junior
            college employees,
            §§16-25-11.3,
            16-25-13.1.
          Purchase by members
            over sixty upon
            employment,
            §16-25-3.1.
          Students whose
            employment is
            incidental to
            status as student,
            §16-25-30.
        Defined, §16-25-1.
        Membership credit for
          service in armed
          forces, §16-25-3.
        Membership service.
          Defined, §16-25-1.
        Military service.
          Defined, §16-25-1.
          Prior service credit for
            military service
            during World War
            I, §16-25-12.
        Purchase of credit for
          service by members
          over age sixty at
          time of employment,
          §16-25-3.1.
      Sick leave.
        Conversion of unused
          leave into
          membership service,
          §36-26-36.1.
        Use of accrued sick leave
          in determining
          creditable service,
          §16-25-11.1.

EDUCATION—Cont'd
Teachers—Cont'd
Retirement system—Cont'd
State employees'
association.
Membership in system,
§16-25-32.
State employees' credit
union.
Membership in system,
§16-25-32.
State employees'
retirement system.
Transfer of service
credits from
teachers' retirement
system, §36-27-12.
Substitute teachers.
Retired teachers serving
as substitute
teachers, §16-25-26.
Superintendents of
education.
Eligibility of elected
superintendent to
participate in
system, §16-25-10.6.
Support personnel or
employee.
Defined, §16-25-1.
Surviving spouse.
Nomination of recipient
of surviving spouse
benefits prior to date
of retirement,
§36-27-16.2.
Teachers.
Defined, §16-25-1.
Transfer of membership
from employees'
retirement system,
§§16-25-4, 16-25-5.
Janitors, maids, cafeteria
workers, etc.,
§16-25-5.
Trustees.
Defined, §16-25-1.
Designated as board of
control.
General
administration
and responsibility,
§16-25-19.
Management of funds,
§16-25-20.
Vocational association.
Election for participation
in teachers'
retirement system,
§16-25-10.3.
Rules and regulations.
Certificates.
Issuance.
State board of
education,
§16-3-16.
State tenure commission,
§16-24-35.
Training, §16-23-16.
Salaries, §16-11-17.
Annuities.
Tax sheltered annuities.
Salary deductions,
§16-22-6.
Approval of funds for
teachers' salaries,
§16-13-143.
Budget system.
Approval of funds for
teachers' salaries,
§16-13-143.

EDUCATION—Cont'd
Teachers—Cont'd
Salaries—Cont'd
Change of compensation
for succeeding year,
§16-24-4.
Checkoffs.
Salary deductions,
§16-22-6.
Contributions.
Voluntary contributions.
Salary deductions,
§16-22-6.
Deductions.
Annuities.
Tax sheltered
annuities,
§16-22-6.
Insurance.
Group insurance
premiums,
§16-22-6.
Payment of insurance
premiums,
§16-22-5.
Membership dues,
§16-22-6.
Policies as to salary
deductions, §16-22-6.
Presumption as to
payments and
deductions, §16-22-7.
Public employees'
individual
retirement account
fund, §16-22-6.
Purposes for which
deductions made,
§16-22-6.
Teachers' retirement
system, §16-25-21.
Voluntary contributions,
§16-22-6.
Dues.
Membership dues.
Salary deductions,
§16-22-6.
Expenditures for teachers'
salaries.
From what receipts
expenditures paid,
§16-13-3.
Insurance.
Group insurance
premiums.
Salary deductions,
§16-22-6.
Membership dues.
Salary deductions,
§16-22-6.
Payment when due,
§16-13-147.
Percentage of school funds,
Const. Ala., art. XIV,
§261.
Public employees'
individual retirement
account fund.
Salary deductions,
§16-22-6.
Voluntary contributions.
Salary deductions,
§16-22-6.
Scholarships.
Elementary teachers'
scholarship fund,
§16-23-17.
Exceptional children.
Scholarships for special
teachers, §16-39-12.

EDUCATION—Cont'd
Teachers—Cont'd
Sick leave.
Accrued sick leave.
Use in determining
creditable service in
retirement system,
§16-25-11.1.
Bank plan, §16-22-9.
Establishment of sick leave
plan, §16-3-36.
Substitute teachers
replacing teachers
absent on sick leave.
Reimbursing local boards
for payments to
substitutes, §16-3-36.
Special teachers.
Scholarships for special
teachers, §16-39-12.
State board of education.
Training and certification
of teachers, §16-3-16.
State superintendent of
education.
Conferences, §16-4-6.
State tenure commission,
§§16-24-30 to 16-24-38.
Actions.
Finality of action,
§16-24-38.
Review, §16-24-38.
Appeals.
Direct appeal by certain
teachers denied
hearing before local
boards, §16-24-37.
Generally, §16-24-36.
Review of action of
commission,
§16-24-38.
Appointment of members,
§16-24-31.
Appropriations, §16-24-34.
Chairman, §16-24-33.
Compensation of members,
§16-24-34.
Composition, §16-24-30.
Creation, §16-24-30.
Expenses of members,
§16-24-34.
Finality of action,
§16-24-38.
Legal adviser, §16-24-30.
Meetings, §16-24-32.
Organization meetings,
§16-24-33.
Orders, §16-24-35.
Organization meetings,
§16-24-33.
Qualifications of members,
§16-24-31.
Quorum, §16-24-32.
Rules and regulations,
§16-24-35.
Secretary, §16-24-30.
Teacher's tenure not
affected by
membership,
§16-24-31.
Terms of members,
§16-24-31.
Vacancies, §16-24-31.
Vice-chairman, §16-24-33.
Substitute teachers.
Reimbursing local boards
for payments to
substitute teachers
replacing teachers
absent on sick leave,
§16-3-36.

EDUCATION—Cont'd
Teachers—Cont'd
Substitute teachers—Cont'd
Teachers' retirement
system.
Retired teachers serving
as substitute
teachers, §16-25-26.
Summer school for teachers.
Establishment, §16-47-15.
Maintenance, §16-47-16.
Suspension.
City boards, §16-11-17.
City superintendents,
§16-12-16.
County superintendents,
§16-9-23.
Taxation.
Exemptions from taxation.
Corporation organized
for purpose of aiding
retired teachers.
Property exempt,
§40-9-18.
Tenure.
Commission, §§16-24-30 to
16-24-38.
Compensation.
Change of compensation
for succeeding year,
§16-24-4.
Continuing service status.
Criteria, §16-24-2.
Effect of leave of absence
on continuing
service status,
§16-24-13.
List of persons
recommended for
continuing status,
§16-24-2.
Contract of employment.
Breach.
Damages, §16-24-10.
Cancellation.
Appeals, §16-24-10.
By teacher, §16-24-11.
Damages for breach of
contract,
§16-24-10.
Finality of action of
employing board,
§16-24-10.
Grounds, §16-24-8.
Hearings, §16-24-9.
Procedure, §16-24-9.
Damages for breach of
contract, §16-24-10.
Effective until
superseded or
cancelled, §16-24-3.
Criteria for continuing
service status,
§16-24-2.
Definition of teacher,
§16-24-1.
Leaves of absence.
Effect on continuing
service status,
§16-24-13.
Notice.
Teacher deemed
reemployed for
succeeding school
year unless notified,
§16-24-12.

EDUCATION—Cont'd
Teachers—Cont'd
Tenure—Cont'd
Reemployment.
Teacher deemed
reemployed for
succeeding year
unless notified,
§16-24-12.
State tenure commission,
§§16-24-30 to 16-24-38.
Tenure commission,
§§16-24-30 to 16-24-38.
Training.
Advisory council,
§16-23-15.
Conferences, §16-23-12.
Institutes.
Attendance required,
§16-23-8.
Excuses for
nonattendance,
§16-23-9.
List of persons subject
to attendance,
§16-23-10.
Persons not attending
not placed on
payroll, §16-23-11.
Character of instruction,
§16-23-7.
Conduct, §16-23-7.
Duration, §16-23-7.
Penalty for failure to
attend, §16-23-8.
Institutions.
Supervision of teacher-
training institutions,
§16-23-15.
Minimum requirements,
§16-23-14.
Requirements.
Minimum requirements,
§16-23-14.
Rules and regulations,
§16-23-16.
Standards, §16-23-14.
State board of education,
§16-3-16.
Training-in-service work,
§16-23-13.
Transfer.
Appeals, §16-24-7.
Authorized, §16-24-5.
City superintendents,
§16-12-16.
Conditions, §16-24-5.
Contesting, §16-24-6.
Hearing, §16-24-6.
Notice, §16-24-5.
Tuberculosis.
Employment of teachers
with tuberculosis,
§16-22-3.
University of Alabama.
Summer school for
teachers.
Establishment,
§16-47-15.
Maintenance, §16-47-16.
Vacations, §§16-8-25,
16-12-21.
Voluntary contributions.
Salary deductions,
§16-22-6.

EDUCATION—Cont'd
Television.
Educational television
commission, §§16-7-1 to
16-7-6, 16-7A-7. See
within this heading,
"Educational television
commission."
Educational television
foundation authority,
§§16-7A-1 to 16-7A-8.
See EDUCATIONAL
TELEVISION
FOUNDATION
AUTHORITY.
Tenure.
Teachers, §§16-24-1 to
16-24-38. See within this
heading, "Teachers."
Textbooks.
Abuse.
Free textbooks, §16-36-32.
Liability for abuse,
§16-36-35.
Accounting books and
records.
Audits, §16-36-31.
Regulations for accounting,
§16-36-26.
Administration of chapter.
Subject to specific
appropriations,
§16-36-39.
Adoption of textbooks.
Bills, §§16-36-17, 16-36-18.
Communist authors.
Contract to exclude
communist authors,
§16-36-10.
Consideration.
When textbooks
considered or
reconsidered,
§16-36-7.
Contracts.
Action for losses,
§16-36-13.
Bids.
Annual advertisement
for sealed bids,
§16-36-11.
Deposit required with
bids, §16-36-12.
Opening of bids,
§16-36-12.
Specimen copies to
accompany bids,
§16-36-11.
Exclusion of communist
authors, §16-36-10.
Expiration of contracts to
be stabilized,
§16-36-10.
Forfeiture of contract
and damages,
§16-36-13.
Interest in contracts,
etc., prohibited,
§16-36-36.
Price.
Charging more than
contract price,
§16-36-38.
Contract provisions as
to price, §16-36-13.
Credit for existing
inventories of
textbooks purchased
with local funds,
§16-36-33.

EDUCATION—Cont'd
Textbooks—Cont'd
Adoption of textbooks
—Cont'd
Existing adoptions,
§16-36-7.
Issuance of purchase
orders, §16-36-15.
Local selection committees,
§16-36-5.
Made at public meeting,
§16-36-9.
New adoptions.
When new adoptions to
be used, §16-36-7.
Period of adoption,
§§16-36-6, 16-36-10.
Public meetings.
Adoption to be made at,
§16-36-9.
Reconsideration.
When textbooks
reconsidered,
§16-36-7.
Reports, §16-36-6.
Shipment by publisher,
§16-36-15.
Substitutions in certain
cities and counties,
§16-36-22.
When textbooks considered
or reconsidered,
§16-36-7.
Appropriations.
Administration of chapter
subject to specific
appropriations,
§16-36-39.
Chapter not to be
construed as
appropriation of funds,
§16-36-39.
Local appropriations,
§16-36-20.
Audits.
Accounting books and
records, §16-36-31.
Bills.
Approval by local
superintendents,
§16-36-18.
Payment, §16-36-18.
Preparation and mailing,
§16-36-17.
Blind persons, §16-39-10.
Care of textbooks.
Regulations for care,
§16-36-26.
Censorship.
Contract to exclude
communist authors,
§16-36-10.
City boards of education.
Filing of school board
policies with
superintendent of
education, §16-36-4.
Local appropriations,
§16-36-20.
City superintendents of
schools.
Approval of invoices,
§16-36-18.
Inventory.
Duty to maintain,
§16-36-34.
Number of textbooks.
Annual reports,
§16-36-27.

EDUCATION—Cont'd
Textbooks—Cont'd
City superintendents of
schools—Cont'd
Number of textbooks
—Cont'd
Estimates.
Duty of local
superintendent to
furnish, §16-36-34.
Records.
Duty to maintain,
§16-36-34.
Reports, §§16-36-6,
16-36-27.
Storage.
Duty to provide for
storage, §16-36-34.
Committees.
Local textbook selection
committees, §§16-36-4
to 16-36-6.
State textbook committee,
§§16-36-1 to 16-36-3.
Communism.
Contract to exclude
communist authors,
§16-36-10.
Instruction in history,
doctrines, etc., of
communism, §16-40-3.
Conflicts of interest.
Purchase of textbooks,
§16-36-36.
County boards of education.
Filing of school board
policies with state
superintendent,
§16-36-4.
Local appropriations,
§16-36-20.
County superintendents of
education.
Approval of invoices,
§16-36-18.
Inventory.
Duty to maintain,
§16-36-34.
Number of textbooks.
Annual reports,
§16-36-27.
Estimates.
Duty of local
superintendent to
furnish, §16-36-34.
Records.
Duty to maintain,
§16-36-34.
Reports, §16-36-6.
Annual reports on
number of books,
§16-36-27.
Storage of books.
Duty to provide for
storage, §16-36-34.
Courses of study.
Minimum number of
adoptions for each
course, §16-36-9.
Criminal law.
Charging more than
contract price,
§16-36-38.
Conflicts of interest,
§16-36-36.
Use of other than contract
books in public schools,
§16-36-37.
Defective books.
Replacement, §16-36-16.

EDUCATION—Cont'd
Textbooks—Cont'd
Delivering textbooks,
§16-36-16.
Authority of state board to
contract for delivering,
§16-36-14.
Record of textbooks
delivered to local
superintendents,
§16-36-31.
Distribution of textbooks,
§16-36-30.
Dropping of textbooks,
§16-36-21.
Exceptional children.
Vision or hearing
impaired, §16-39-10.
Exchange of textbooks,
§16-36-30.
Free textbooks.
Issuance.
Receipt required upon
issuance, §16-36-32.
Loss, abuse, etc., §16-36-32.
Period of use by pupils,
§16-36-32.
Receipt required upon
issuance, §16-36-32.
To remain property of state
or local school system,
§16-36-32.
Fumigation of used
textbooks, §16-36-30.
Funds.
Appropriation of funds.
Chapter not to be
construed as
appropriation of
funds, §16-36-39.
Expenditure.
Manner of expenditure,
§16-36-26.
Local revolving funds,
§16-36-20.
Local school system's pro
rata share of state
textbook fund,
§16-36-28.
Manner of expenditure,
§16-36-26.
State textbook fund.
Local school system's pro
rata share,
§16-36-28.
Furnishing.
Authority of state board to
contract for furnishing,
§16-36-14.
Failure of contractor to
furnish, §16-36-21.
State-owned textbooks for
classes and schools.
Alabama institute for
deaf and blind,
§16-36-24.
Boys' industrial schools,
§16-36-25.
Hospital schools,
§16-36-23.
Industrial school at Mt.
Meigs, §16-36-25.
State training school for
girls, §16-36-25.
Hospitals.
Purchase and furnishing of
state-owned textbooks
for classes and schools.
Operated under state
hospitals, §16-36-23.

EDUCATION—Cont'd
Textbooks—Cont'd
Inventory.
Certification of required
inventory, §16-36-31.
Credit for existing
inventories of state-
adopted or approved
textbooks purchased
with local funds,
§16-36-33.
Duty of local
superintendent to
maintain inventory,
§16-36-34.
Issuance.
Free textbooks, §16-36-32.
Local selection committees.
Adoption of textbooks,
§16-36-5.
Affidavits of members,
§16-36-4.
Appointment of members,
§16-36-4.
Filing of school board
policies and names of
members, §16-36-4.
Names of members.
Filing, §16-36-4.
Period of adoption,
§16-36-6.
Qualifying affidavits of
members, §16-36-4.
Replacement.
Limitation on textbook
replacement,
§16-36-6.
Samples.
Furnishing and
dispositions,
§16-36-5.
Selection of textbooks,
§16-36-5.
Terms of members,
§16-36-4.
Use of textbooks not on
state list, §16-36-5.
Loss.
Free textbooks, §16-36-32.
Liability of pupils for loss,
etc., §16-36-35.
Minimum number of
adoptions for each
course, §16-36-9.
Notice.
Public meeting to adopt
textbooks, §16-36-9.
Number of adoptions.
Minimum number for each
course, §16-36-9.
Number of textbooks.
Deficiencies in number.
Remedying deficiencies,
§16-36-27.
Duty of state board to
provide sufficient
textbooks, §16-36-27.
Estimates of textbooks
needed.
Duty of local
superintendent to
furnish, §16-36-34.
Remedying deficiencies in
number of books,
§16-36-27.
Reports.
Annual reports by local
superintendents,
§16-36-27.

EDUCATION—Cont'd
Textbooks—Cont'd
Price.
Contract provisions as to
price, §16-36-13.
Maxmium price for books,
§16-36-13.
Publishers.
Shipment of books by
publisher, §16-36-15.
Purchase.
Secondhand textbooks,
§16-36-29.
State-owned textbooks for
certain classes and
schools, §§16-36-23 to
16-36-25.
Recommendations by state
committees, §16-36-8.
Records.
Audit of accounting books
and records, §16-36-31.
Blanks and forms,
§16-36-31.
Duty of local
superintendent to
maintain, §16-36-34.
Textbooks delivered to
local superintendents,
§16-36-31.
Repair of used textbooks,
§16-36-30.
Replacement.
Defective or substandard
books, §16-36-16.
Limitation on replacement,
§16-36-6.
Reports.
Local superintendents,
§16-36-6.
Number of textbooks.
Annual reports,
§16-36-27.
Requisitions.
Actions of state
superintendent upon
receipt of requisitions,
§16-36-17.
Rules and regulations.
Care of and accounting for
textbooks, §16-36-26.
Sale to pupils, §16-36-35.
Samples.
Furnishing and disposition
of samples, §16-36-11.
Local selection committees.
Furnishing and
disposition of
samples, §16-36-5.
Secondhand textbooks.
Purchase, §16-36-29.
Repair and fumigation of
used textbooks,
§16-36-30.
Use, §16-36-29.
Selection committees,
§§16-36-4 to 16-36-6.
Shipment.
Books to be shipped upon
purchase orders of
state purchasing
agent, §16-36-17.
By publisher, §16-36-15.
Special textbooks, §16-36-19.
State-adopted textbooks.
Credit for existing
inventories of
textbooks purchased
with local funds,
§16-36-33.

EDUCATION—Cont'd
Textbooks—Cont'd
State-adopted textbooks
—Cont'd
Substitutions for,
§16-36-22.
State board of education.
Authority to contract for
furnishing, storing, or
delivering, §16-36-14.
Conflicts of interest,
§16-36-36.
Sufficiency of textbooks.
Duty of state board to
provide sufficient
textbooks, §16-36-27.
State committee.
Affidavits.
Qualifying affidavits of
members, §16-36-2.
Appointment of members,
§16-36-2.
Chairman.
Election, §16-36-3.
Compensation of members,
§16-36-3.
Composition, §16-36-2.
Creation, §16-36-1.
Duties, §16-36-1.
Election of chairman and
secretary, §16-36-3.
Expenses of members,
§16-36-3.
Meetings, §16-36-3.
Qualifying affidavits of
members, §16-36-2.
Recommendations of
textbooks, §16-36-8.
Secretary.
Election, §16-36-3.
Terms of members,
§16-36-2.
Vacancies, §16-36-2.
State-owned textbooks.
Free textbooks, §16-36-32.
Purchase and furnishing
for classes and schools.
Boys' industrial schools,
§16-36-25.
Industrial school at Mt.
Meigs, §16-36-23.
Institute for deaf and
blind, §16-36-24.
Operated under state
hospitals, §16-36-23.
State training school for
girls, §16-36-25.
State purchasing agent.
Books to be shipped upon
purchase orders of,
§16-36-17.
State superintendent of
education.
Action upon receipt of
requisitions, §16-36-17.
Conflicts of interest,
§16-36-36.
Members of local selection
committees.
Filing of names with
state superintendent,
§16-36-4.
School board policies.
Filing with state
superintendent,
§16-36-4.
Storing textbooks, §16-36-30.
Authority of state board to
contract for storing,
§16-36-14.

EDUCATION—Cont'd
  Textbooks—Cont'd
    Storing textbooks—Cont'd
      Duty of local
          superintendent to
          provide for storage,
          §16-36-34.
    Substandard books.
        Replacement, §16-36-16.
    Substitutions.
        State-adopted books,
            §16-36-22.
    Used textbooks.
        Purchase and use,
            §16-36-29.
        Repair and fumigation,
            §16-36-30.
    Use of other than contract
        books in public schools,
        §16-36-37.
    Use of textbooks not on state
        list, §16-36-5.
  Time.
    Definitions, §16-1-1.
  Torts.
    Insurance.
        Risk management
            cooperatives.
          Boards of education.
            Liability for tort
                claims, §16-8-42.1.
  Trade schools.
    General provisions.
        See TRADE SCHOOLS.
    Vocational education,
        §§16-37-1 to 16-37-8. See
        within this heading,
        "Vocational education."
  Transportation of pupils.
    Pupils living less than two
        miles from school.
      Minimum program fund
          not to provide for,
          §16-13-51.
    School buses, §§16-27-1 to
        16-27-7. See within this
        heading, "School buses."
  Trespass.
    Reports of property damage
        and physical assaults on
        students and school
        personnel, §16-1-24.
  Troy state university,
      §§16-56-1 to 16-56-15.
    See TROY STATE
        UNIVERSITY.
  Truancy.
    General provisions. See
        within this heading,
        "Attendance."
    Juvenile proceedings,
        §§16-28-21 to 16-28-23.
      See JUVENILE
          PROCEEDINGS.
  Trusts and trustees.
    Boards of school trustees,
        §§16-10-1 to 16-10-11.
      See within this heading,
          "Boards of school
          trustees."
    Support and maintenance of
        relatives.
      Express trust for support
          and maintenance,
          §19-3-1.
  Tuberculosis.
    Employment of teachers,
        janitors, food handlers or
        bus drivers with
        tuberculosis, §16-22-3.

EDUCATION—Cont'd
  Tuskegee institute, §§16-57-1
      to 16-57-4.
  Tutoring, §16-1-16.
  Unaccredited schools.
    Advisory committee,
        §16-46-7.
    Declaration of policy,
        §16-46-2.
    Definitions, §16-46-1.
    Department of education.
      Hearing, §16-46-9.
      Petition for review of
          actions by department,
          §16-46-9.
    Employment.
      Promises of employment,
          §16-46-4.
    Enforcement proceedings,
        §16-46-8.
    Exemptions from chapter,
        §16-46-3.
    False statements, §16-46-4.
    Fraud, §16-46-4.
    Hearing by department of
        education, §16-46-9.
    Inapplicability of chapter,
        §16-46-3.
    Licenses.
      Operation of school,
          §16-46-5.
      Review of actions,
          §16-46-9.
      Solicitation of students,
          §16-46-6.
    Montgomery county.
      Review of actions by
          circuit court of
          Montgomery county,
          §16-46-9.
    Operation of school.
      License for operation,
          §16-46-5.
    Penalties for violation of
        chapters, §16-46-10.
    Permits.
      Solicitation of students,
          §16-46-6.
    Petition for review of actions
        by state department of
        education, §16-46-9.
    Promises of employment,
        §16-46-4.
    Records.
      Private schools ceasing
          operations, §16-46-3.
    Review of actions by circuit
        court of Montgomery
        county, §16-46-9.
    Review of actions by state
        department of education,
        §16-46-9.
    Rules and regulations.
      Adoption, §16-46-7.
    Schools to which chapter not
        applicable, §16-46-3.
    Solicitation of students.
      Permit, §16-46-6.
    Violation of provisions of
        chapter, §16-46-10.
  **Unemployment
      compensation.**
    Benefits for employees of
        local school systems.
    Appropriation of funds for
        payment, §25-4-150.
  United States.
    Federal financial assistance,
        §§16-13-5 to 16-13-7.
    Flags, §§16-43-1 to 16-43-5.

EDUCATION—Cont'd
  United States—Cont'd
    Illiteracy.
      Authority of state and
          local boards to
          cooperate with federal
          government, §16-34-3.
  Universities and colleges.
    See UNIVERSITIES AND
        COLLEGES.
  University of Alabama,
      §§16-47-1 to 16-47-204.
    See UNIVERSITY OF
        ALABAMA.
  University of Montevallo,
      §§16-54-1 to 16-54-18.
    See UNIVERSITY OF
        MONTEVALLO.
  **University of North
      Alabama,** §§16-51-1 to
      16-51-15.
    See UNIVERSITY OF
        NORTH ALABAMA.
  **University of South
      Alabama,** §§16-55-1 to
      16-55-9.
    See UNIVERSITY OF
        SOUTH ALABAMA.
  Use tax.
    Use of county funds for
        general educational
        purposes, §16-13-37.
  Vaccination.
    Immunization of school
        children, §§16-30-1 to
        16-30-5.
  Vandalism.
    Reports, §16-1-24.
  Veterans.
    Benefits.
      Veterans' and dependents'
          educational benefits,
          §§31-6-1 to 31-6-17.
        See VETERANS.
  Visitation of schools.
    Boards of school trustees,
        §16-10-7.
    City superintendents of
        schools, §16-12-11.
    County superintendents of
        education, §16-9-26.
  **Visually handicapped
      children.**
    Exceptional children,
        §§16-39-1 to 16-39-12.
      See within this heading,
          "Exceptional children."
  Vocational education.
    Acceptance of provisions of
        federal act, §16-37-1.
    Administration of chapter,
        §16-37-3.
    Appropriations.
      County may make
          appropriations for
          Smith-Hughes type of
          vocational training,
          §16-37-7.
    City boards of education.
      Authorized to operate
          vocational high schools
          jointly with county
          boards, §16-37-8.
      Cooperation with state
          board, §16-37-5.
    Counties.
      May make appropriation
          for Smith-Hughes type
          of vocational training,
          §16-37-7.

EDUCATION—Cont'd
Vocational education—Cont'd
County boards of education.
Authorized to operate
vocational high schools
jointly with city
boards, §16-37-8.
Cooperation with state
board, §16-37-5.
Eye protective devices.
Pupils and teachers
participating in certain
courses, §16-1-7.
Federal act.
Acceptance of provisions of
federal act, §16-37-1.
Federal funds.
Treasurer custodian of
federal funds, §16-37-2.
Governor.
Annual report to governor
by state board,
§16-37-6.
High schools.
City and county boards of
education authorized
to operate vocational
high schools jointly,
§16-37-8.
Junior college for Jackson
and DeKalb counties,
§16-60-57.
Regional vocational and
trade schools act,
§§16-60-190 to 16-60-198.
See TRADE SCHOOLS.
Reports.
Annual report to governor,
§16-37-6.
Retirement.
Participation in teachers'
retirement system,
§16-25-10.3.
Rules and regulations,
§16-37-3.
Smith-Hughes type of
vocational training.
County may make
appropriation for,
§16-37-7.
State board of education.
Annual report to governor,
§16-37-6.
Authority of as to
vocational education,
§16-37-4.
City and county boards
may cooperate with
state board, §16-37-5.
Cooperation with federal
board, §16-3-18.
State funds.
Disbursement, §16-37-2.
State superintendent of
education.
In charge of vocational
education, §16-37-3.
Plans and rules and
regulations, §16-4-17.
State treasurer.
Custodian of federal funds,
§16-37-2.
Trade schools.
General provisions.
See TRADE SCHOOLS.
Voluntary contributions.
Salary deductions, §16-22-6.
Warrants.
Local aid to state educational
institutions, §§16-19-3 to
16-19-5, 16-19-7.

EDUCATION—Cont'd
Warrants—Cont'd
Public school corporation.
Evidence of debt payable
from proceeds of
minimum program
fund appropriation,
§16-14-7.
Execution, §16-14-19.
Generally, §16-14-17.
Issuing evidence of debt,
§16-14-6.
Securities not debt of state,
§16-14-18.
Tax warrants, §§16-13-90 to
16-13-109. See within
this heading, "Taxation."
§16-14-7.
Week.
Scholastic week.
Defined, §16-1-1.
Welding.
Eye protective devices for
pupils and teachers,
§16-1-7.
Witnesses.
State board of education.
Examination of witnesses,
§16-3-24.
Study commission.
Authority to summon and
examine, §16-6-5.
Workmen's compensation.
Rehabilitation and crippled
children's service,
§§16-38-1 to 16-38-9.
See HANDICAPPED
PERSONS.
Year.
Fiscal year.
Defined, §16-1-1.
Scholastic year.
Defined, §16-1-1.
Youth services, §§44-1-1 to
44-3-12.
See YOUTH SERVICES.

**EDUCATIONAL TELEVISION
COMMISSION,** §§16-7-1 to
16-7-6, 16-7A-7.
See EDUCATION.

**EDUCATIONAL TELEVISION
FOUNDATION
AUTHORITY.**
**Alabama educational
television commission.**
Governing body, §16-7A-7.
Appointment, §§16-7A-1,
16-7A-2.
Assets.
Disposition upon dissolution,
§16-7A-6.
Audits, §16-7A-4.
Chapter cumulative,
§16-7A-8.
Compensation, §16-7A-1.
Composition, §16-7A-1.
Creation, §16-7A-1.
Dissolution.
Disposition of assets,
§16-7A-6.
Elections.
Political activities prohibited,
§16-7A-5.
Governing body.
Alabama educational
television commission,
§16-7A-7.
Meetings, §16-7A-3.
Officers.
Election, §16-7A-3.

**EDUCATIONAL TELEVISION
FOUNDATION
AUTHORITY**—Cont'd
Political campaigns.
Prohibited, §16-7A-5.
Prohibited activities,
§16-7A-5.
Propaganda.
Activities prohibited,
§16-7A-5.
Purpose.
Generally, §16-7A-4.
Salary, §16-7A-1.
Taxation.
Exemption from taxation,
§16-7A-4.
Terms of office, §16-7A-2.

EGGS AND EGG PRODUCTS.
Administration of chapter,
§2-12-8.
Appeals.
Revocation of permits for
sale, §2-12-4.
Associations of producers.
Promotion of industry
generally, §§2-8-150 to
2-8-171. See within this
heading, "Promotion of
industry."
Audits.
Promotion of industry.
Annual audit of growers'
association, §2-8-166.
Bonds, surety.
Promotion of industry.
Treasurer of growers'
association, §2-8-163.
Buildings.
Inspection of buildings,
§2-12-10.
Bulk sales, §2-12-2.
**Commissioner of agriculture
and industries.**
Administration and
enforcement of chapter,
§2-12-8.
Definitions, §2-12-1.
Disposition of fines, §2-12-11.
Elections.
Promotion of industry.
Referendum. See within
this heading,
"Promotion of
industry."
Enforcement of chapter,
§2-12-8.
Exemptions from chapter,
§2-12-6.
Fees.
Penalty for failure to pay
inspection fee, §2-12-10.
Permits for sale, §2-12-4.
Fines.
Disposition, §2-12-11.
Food generally.
See FOOD.
Funds.
Egg inspection fund, §2-9-40.
Grading and standards.
Classifications, §2-12-3.
Suspension from sale.
Grading and suspension,
§2-12-9.
Injunctions.
Violations of chapter,
§2-12-12.
Inspections.
Buildings, vehicles, records,
etc., §2-12-10.
Costs of inspection, §2-12-9.

EGGS AND EGG PRODUCTS —Cont'd

Inspections—Cont'd

Egg inspection fund, §2-9-40.

Fees.

Penalty for failure to pay inspection fee, §2-12-10.

Invoices.

Furnishing duplicate copies to department of agriculture and industries, §2-12-7.

Labels, §2-12-2.

Penalty for failure to affix labels, §2-12-10.

Motor vehicles.

Inspection of vehicles, §2-12-10.

Notice.

Promotion of industry.

Referendum of assessments, §2-8-156.

Offenses, §2-12-11.

Packers.

Name and address to be on egg cartons, §2-12-2.

Penalties.

Delinquency in payment of permit fee, §2-12-4.

Failure to pay inspection fee or affix labels, §2-12-10.

Promotion of industry.

Failure to deduct and pay over assessments, §2-8-171.

Permits.

Permits for sale.

Fee, §2-12-4.

Required, §2-12-4.

Revocation, §2-12-4.

Promotion of industry.

Sellers of hens, §2-8-170.

Promotion of industry.

Assessments.

Amount, §2-8-159.

Collection, §2-8-161.

Deductions for expenses, §2-8-161.

Expenditure, §2-8-164.

Penalty for failure to deduct and pay over assessments, §2-8-171.

Period during which assessments levied, §2-8-158.

Referendum.

Application for approval to conduct.

Action by board, §2-8-154.

Generally, §2-8-153.

Authority of certified association to conduct, §2-8-155.

Canvass of results, §2-8-159.

Conduct, §2-8-157.

Declared to be in public interest, §2-8-152.

Eligibility to vote, §2-8-158.

Expense.

Payment, §2-8-157.

Notice, §2-8-156.

Question to be voted on, §2-8-158.

Subsequent referendums, §2-8-160.

EGGS AND EGG PRODUCTS —Cont'd

Promotion of industry —Cont'd

Assessments—Cont'd

Referendum—Cont'd

Two-thirds vote required for approval of assessment, §2-8-159.

Refund, §2-8-169.

Remittances to treasurer of growers' association, §2-8-162.

Audit of growers' association.

Annual audit, §2-8-166.

Authorized activities.

Not illegal or in restraint of trade, §2-8-151.

Board of agriculture and industries.

Application for certification of producers' association and approval to conduct referendum.

Action by board on application, §2-8-154.

Rules and regulations, §2-8-167.

Bonds, surety.

Treasurer of growers' association, §2-8-163.

Certification of growers' association.

Application for certification.

Action by board, §2-8-154.

Generally, §2-8-153.

Revocation of certification, §2-8-168.

Commissioner of agriculture and industries.

Enforcement duties of commissioner, §2-8-168.

Enforcement duties of commissioner, §2-8-168.

Examination of growers' association by department of examiners of public accounts, §2-8-166.

Joint programs with other states, §2-8-165.

Legislative purpose and intent, §2-8-150.

Penalty for failure to deduct and pay over assessment, §2-8-171.

Permit required of sellers of hens, §2-8-170.

Rules and regulations, §2-8-167.

Sellers.

Inspection of books and records, §2-8-171.

Statements of grower's associations.

Publications, §2-8-166.

Treasurer of growers' association.

Bond of treasurer, §2-8-163.

Remittances to treasurer, §2-8-162.

Records.

Inspection of records, §2-12-10.

EGGS AND EGG PRODUCTS —Cont'd

Referendum.

Promotion of industry, §§2-8-152 to 2-8-160. See within this heading, "Promotion of industry."

Requirements for sale, §2-12-2.

Rules and regulations, §2-12-8.

Promotion of industry, §2-8-167.

Sale.

Bulk sales, §2-12-2.

Invoices.

Furnishing duplicate copies, §2-12-7.

Permits, §2-12-4.

Requirements, §2-12-2.

Suspension from sale for violation of chapter, §2-12-9.

Wholesale dealers.

Sales between wholesale dealers, §2-12-5.

Seizures, §2-12-9.

Unhatched or unused eggs, §§2-16-40 to 2-16-42.

Violations of chapter.

Injunctions, §2-12-12.

Offenses, §2-12-11.

Suspension from sale and seizure for violations, §2-12-9.

Weight classes, §2-12-3.

Wholesale dealers.

Sales between wholesale dealers, §2-12-5.

EJECTMENT.

Abstract of title.

Demanding when relied on for recovery or defense, §6-6-283.

Failure to furnish.

Proceedings upon, §6-6-283.

Action of ejectment.

Election to proceed by action of ejectment or action in nature of ejectment, §6-6-280.

Proceedings upon, §6-6-280.

Adverse possession.

Proceedings upon defendant's suggestion, §6-6-286.

Auburn University.

Recovery of lands by or in name of state for university, §6-6-281.

Bonds, surety.

Retention of possession for one year by defendant if crop planted or growing.

Force and effect of bond, §6-6-294.

Color of title.

Person holding possession under.

Liability, §6-6-289.

Crops.

Retention of possession for one year by defendant if crop planted or growing.

Filing of bond, §6-6-294.

Force and effect of bond, §6-6-294.

Damages.

Assessment in severalty, §6-6-295.

EJECTMENT—Cont'd
Damages—Cont'd
Exemplary or punitive,
§6-6-296.
Judgment for damages only,
§6-6-292.
Defenses.
Disclaimer of possession,
§6-6-284.
Disputed boundary lines.
Proceedings upon defendant's
suggestion, §6-6-285.
Judgments.
Damages only, §6-6-292.
Default judgment.
Effect, §6-6-290.
Rent of premises after
judgment and before
possession, §6-6-293.
Two judgments in
defendant's favor bar
further action, §6-6-298.
Writs.
Issuance before judgment
satisfied, §6-6-297.
Landlord and tenant.
Joinder of landlord as party
defendant, §6-6-287.
Continuation of action
against tenant,
§6-6-287.
Liability.
Tenant in possession,
§6-6-288.
Possession wrongfully
withheld.
See LANDLORD AND
TENANT.
Mortgages.
Actions by mortgagee against
mortgagor, §6-6-282.
Schools.
Recovery of lands by or in
name of state for schools,
§6-6-281.
State.
Recovery of lands by or in
name of state for
educational or
governmental
institutions, §6-6-281.
Title.
Abstract of title.
Demanding when relied on
for recovery or defense,
§6-6-283.
Failure to furnish.
Proceedings upon,
§6-6-283.
Color of title.
Liability of person holding
possession under color
of title, §6-6-289.
University of Alabama.
Recovery of lands by or in
name of state for
university, §6-6-281.
Verdicts.
What verdict for plaintiff to
specify, §6-6-291.
Writs.
Issuance before judgment
satisfied, §6-6-297.

ELDERLY PERSONS.
See AGED PERSONS.

ELECTIONS.
Absentee voting.
Affidavit.
Form, §§17-10-7, 17-10-8.

ELECTIONS—Cont'd
Absentee voting—Cont'd
Application.
Applicant for primary
ballot may make
application for general
election, §17-10-5.
Contents, §17-10-4.
Filing, §17-10-4.
Form, §17-10-4.
Military personnel.
Postcard applications,
§17-10-3.
Physician's certificate.
When required, §17-10-4.
Postcard application for
certain military
personnel and wives,
§17-10-3.
Signature, §17-10-4.
Time for filing, §17-10-3.
Assistance to voters.
Unauthorized assistance,
§17-10-17.
Ballots.
Applicant for primary
ballot may make
application for general
election, §17-10-5.
Changing ballots,
§17-10-17.
Counting, §17-10-10.
Officials for counting,
§17-10-11.
Delivery to manager,
§§17-10-9, 17-10-12.
Endorsement, §17-10-9.
Envelopes.
Delivery to manager,
§17-10-12.
Furnished with ballot,
§17-10-9.
Form, §17-10-6.
Oaths.
Ballots to be sworn to
before notary public,
§17-10-6.
Persons obtaining absentee
ballots not to vote at
polling place, §17-10-5.
Probate judges.
Volunteering suggestions
as to ballots for
absent voters,
§17-10-20.
Procedure upon receipt of
ballot by manager,
§17-10-10.
Receipt.
Procedure by manager,
§17-10-10.
Sealing, §17-10-9.
Unlawful use of absentee
ballot, §17-10-17.
Candidates.
Appointment of manager
when clerk, register or
register in chancery is
candidate for office,
§17-10-13.
Manager.
Procedure when manager
is candidate,
§17-10-12.
Clerk of circuit court.
Application.
Filing with clerk,
§17-10-4.
Ballots.
Delivery to clerk,
§17-10-12.

ELECTIONS—Cont'd
Absentee voting—Cont'd
Clerk of circuit court—Cont'd
Ballots—Cont'd
Procedure upon receipt,
§17-10-10.
Candidate in election.
Appointment of manager
when clerk is
candidate, §17-10-13.
Procedure, §17-10-12.
Compensation, §17-10-14.
Designated absentee
election manager,
§17-10-2.
Disqualification, §17-10-13.
Duties.
Refusing to perform
duties, §17-10-18.
List of qualified voters.
Furnishing to clerk,
§17-10-5.
Municipal elections.
Designation of person to
perform duties of
clerk, §17-10-15.
Costs and expenses,
§17-10-16.
Definitions.
Register or register in
chancery, §17-10-1.
Election officials.
Ballots.
Counting ballots,
§17-10-11.
Duties.
Refusing to perform
duties, §17-10-18.
Eligibility.
Persons eligible to vote
absentee ballot,
§17-10-3.
Expenses, §17-10-16.
Forms.
Affidavits, §§17-10-7,
17-10-8.
Application, §17-10-4.
Ballots, §17-10-6.
General elections.
Clerk or register in
municipal elections
held at time different
from, §17-10-15.
Handicapped persons.
Physician's certificate.
When required, §17-10-4.
List of qualified voters.
Destruction of list after
election, §17-10-5.
Furnishing to manager,
§17-10-5.
Notation of absentee voters
on list, §17-10-5.
Managers.
Application.
Filing with manager,
§17-10-4.
Appointment if register
and clerk decline
duties, §17-10-2.
Appointment when clerk,
register or register in
chancery is candidate
for office, §17-10-13.
Ballots.
Delivery to manager,
§17-10-12.
Procedure upon receipt,
§17-10-10.

ELECTIONS—Cont'd
Absentee voting—Cont'd
Managers—Cont'd
Candidate in election.
Procedure when manager
is candidate,
§17-10-12.
Compensation, §17-10-14.
Counting ballots,
§17-10-11.
Duties, §17-10-2.
Lists of qualified voters.
Furnishing to manager,
§17-10-5.
Qualifications, §17-10-2.
Register or clerk
designated absentee
election manager,
§17-10-2.
Term of office, §17-10-2.
Military personnel.
Postcard applications,
§17-10-3.
Municipal elections.
Clerk or register in
municipal elections
held at time different
from primary or
general election,
§17-10-15.
Oaths.
Ballots to be sworn to
before notary public,
§17-10-6.
Persons eligible to vote by
absentee ballot, §17-10-3.
Physicians.
When physician's
certificate required,
§17-10-4.
Polling places.
Persons obtaining absentee
ballots not to vote at
polling place, §17-10-5.
Primary elections.
Clerk or register in
municipal elections
held at time different
from primary,
Probate judges.
Ballots.
Volunteering suggestions
as to ballots for
absent voters,
§17-10-20.
Register.
Application.
Filing with register,
§17-10-4.
Ballots.
Delivery to register,
§17-10-12.
Procedure upon receipt,
§17-10-10.
Candidate in election,
§17-10-12.
Appointment of manager
when register is
candidate, §17-10-13.
Compensation, §17-10-14.
Defined, §17-10-1.
Designated absentee
election manager,
§17-10-2.
Disqualification, §17-10-13.
Duties.
Refusing to perform
duties as to absentee
voters, §17-10-18.

ELECTIONS—Cont'd
Absentee voting—Cont'd
Register—Cont'd
List of qualified voters.
Furnishing to register,
§17-10-5.
Municipal elections.
Designation of person to
perform duties,
§17-10-15.
Register in chancery.
Defined, §17-10-1.
Registration of absentee
voters, §17-4-134; Const.
Ala., amd. 55.
Time.
Applications.
Time for filing, §17-10-3.
Unlawfully voting absentee
ballot, §17-10-17.
Violations.
Assistance to voter.
Unauthorized assistance,
§17-10-17.
Ballots.
Changing ballots,
§17-10-17.
Probate judges
volunteering
suggestions as to
ballots for absent
voters, §17-10-20.
Unlawful use, §17-10-17.
Probate judges.
Volunteering suggestions
as to ballots for
absent voters,
§17-10-20.
Willfully refusing to
perform duties,
§17-10-18.
Voting machines.
Absentee ballots, §17-9-27.
**Accepting payment for
votes,** §17-22A-17.
Adjournment.
No adjournment after polls
opened, §17-7-7.
Advertising.
Fair campaign practices.
Cards, pamphlets, etc., to
contain identification,
§17-22A-13.
Identification as paid
political
advertisement,
§17-22A-12.
Affidavits.
Absentee voting, §§17-10-7,
17-10-8.
Age.
Persons eighteen years of
age, Const. U. S.,
Amendment XXVI.
Qualifications of voters,
Const. Ala., art. VIII,
§177.
Right to vote not to be
abridged on account of
age, Const. U. S.,
Amendment XXVI.
Aged persons.
Accessibility to registration
and polling places,
§§21-4-20 to 21-4-24.
Agriculture.
Commissioner of agriculture
and industries.
Constitutional provisions,
Const. Ala., art. V,
§§114, 115.

ELECTIONS—Cont'd
Agriculture—Cont'd
Commissioner of agriculture
and industries—Cont'd
Contested elections,
State officers generally,
§§17-15-50 to
17-15-63. See within
this heading,
"Contests."
General elections.
Offices for which general
election held,
§17-2-2.
Time of general election,
§17-2-3.
State officers elected by
the people, §17-2-1.
Alcoholic beverages.
Election officers.
Officers consuming
alcoholic beverages
during election,
§17-6-16.
Municipal elections,
§11-46-132.
Inspectors.
Consuming during election,
§17-6-16.
Municipal elections.
Drinking of intoxicating
liquors by watcher,
§11-46-65.
Drunkenness at or about
polling place during
election day,
§§11-46-68, 11-46-139.
Officers of election.
Drinking while election
being held,
§11-46-132.
Polling places.
Intoxication at polling
place.
Municipal elections,
§§11-46-68,
11-46-139.
Primary elections,
§17-16-47.
Poll watchers.
Consuming during election,
§17-6-16.
Municipal elections,
§11-46-65.
Protection against evils of
intoxicating liquors at
elections, Const. Ala.,
art. VIII, §191.
Returning officer.
Consuming during election,
§17-6-16.
Sale and distribution.
See ALCOHOLIC
BEVERAGES.
Amendments.
Constitution of Alabama,
§§17-17-1 to 17-17-6;
Const. Ala., art. XVIII,
§§284, 285.
See CONSTITUTION OF
ALABAMA.
Annulment of election.
When election not annulled,
§17-15-2.
Appeals.
Contests, §§17-15-34,
17-15-35.
Purging of registration lists,
§17-4-132.
Registration, §§17-4-124,
17-4-132.

ELECTIONS—Cont'd
Applicability of title to primary elections and county or municipal elections, §17-1-1.
Arrest.
Electors attending, going to or returning from elections, §17-1-6; Const. Ala., art. VIII, §192.
Assessments.
Primary elections.
Candidates.
Assessments and other qualifications for candidates, §17-16-15.
Assistance to voters.
Absentee voting.
Unauthorized assistance, §17-10-17.
Ballots.
Assistance in casting ballots, §17-8-29.
Blind persons, §17-8-29.
Candidates.
Prohibited from assisting, §17-8-29.
Handicapped persons. See within this heading, "Handicapped persons."
Instruction cards, §§17-8-23, 17-8-43.
Length of time elector and assistant may stay in polling place, §17-8-29.
Primary elections, §§17-16-26 to 17-16-29.
Voting machines, §17-9-25.
Attorney general.
Canvass of election returns.
Opening of returns in presence of attorney general, §17-14-20.
Constitutional provisions, Const. Ala., art. V, §§114, 115.
Contested elections, State officers generally, §§17-15-50 to 17-15-63. See within this heading, "Contests."
Fair campaign practices.
Prosecution of violations, §17-22A-22.
General elections.
Offices for which general election held, §17-2-2.
Time of general election, §17-2-3.
State officers elected by the people, §17-2-1.
Attorneys at law.
Board of commissioners, §34-3-41.
Ballot boxes.
Congestion at polling places.
Use of ballot boxes to avoid congestion, §17-9-28.
Number, §17-8-14.
Precincts.
Installation of voting boxes or machines, §17-5A-5.
Provided by whom, §17-8-14.
Ballots.
Absentee voting. See within this heading, "Absentee voting."
Assistance in casting, §17-8-29.
Binding, §17-8-24.

ELECTIONS—Cont'd
Ballots—Cont'd
Blank forms, §17-8-44.
Blind persons.
Assistance in casting, §17-8-29.
Candidates.
Independent candidates, §17-8-5.
List of candidates.
Printing, §17-8-4.
Names of candidates, §17-8-2.
Withdrawal of name, §17-8-2.
Classification.
Designation of different offices of same classification, §17-8-10.
Constitution of Alabama.
Amendments, §17-8-22; Const. Ala., art. XVIII, §285.
Contents, §17-8-2.
Costs.
Counties and cities to pay, §17-8-23.
Counting votes, §§17-13-3 to 17-13-5, 17-10-10, 17-10-11. See within this heading, "Counting votes."
Delivery to voter, §17-8-27.
Deposit, §17-8-39.
More than one ballot, §17-23-1.
Design, §17-8-4.
Disclosing ballot, §17-8-41.
Emblems, §§17-8-6 to 17-8-9.
Examination by persons involved in contests.
Authorization, §17-8-45.
Bonds, surety, §17-8-46.
Procedure, §17-8-46.
Folding after voting, §17-8-34.
Form, §§17-8-3, 17-8-5.
Handicapped persons.
Assistance in casting, §17-8-29.
Inspectors.
Deceiving elector in preparation of ballot, §17-8-31.
Deposit of ballot, §17-8-39.
Numbering, §17-8-13.
Receiving folded ballots, §17-8-34.
Lists of qualified voters.
Voting in precinct where elector's name not on official list.
Ballots cast declared illegal, §17-4-127.
Municipal elections.
See MUNICIPAL CORPORATIONS.
Names of candidates, §17-8-2.
Withdrawal of name, §17-8-2.
Nomination.
Persons entitled to have names printed on ballots, §17-7-1.
Numbering, §17-8-35.
Inspectors to number, §17-8-13.
Number of ballots per voter, §17-8-25.
Official ballot, §17-8-1.

ELECTIONS—Cont'd
Ballots—Cont'd
Persons entitled to have names printed on ballots, §17-7-1.
Failure of secretary of state to certify, §17-7-1.
Political parties.
Including parties on ballot, §17-8-2.1.
Poll list.
Comparing ballot with poll list, §17-8-42.
Poll watchers.
Watchers permitted to see ballots, §17-6-8.
Presidential and vice-presidential elections, §17-19-3; Const. U. S., Amendment XII.
Primary elections. See within this heading, "Primary elections."
Printing, §17-8-4.
Removing ballot from polling place, §17-8-41.
Seals.
Applicability of sections 17-8-35 through 17-8-37, §17-8-38.
Placing seal on ballot, §17-8-35.
Removal or breaking of seals, §17-8-36.
When removing or breaking allowed, §17-8-36.
Secret ballot, §17-8-11.
Spoiled ballots, §17-8-33.
Straight party ticket, §17-8-15.
Tickets.
Candidates not on party ticket, §17-8-16.
Split tickets, §17-8-18.
Straight party ticket.
Procedure when straight ticket does not contain names of all officers, §17-8-19.
Voting straight party ticket, §17-8-15.
Two or more candidates on different tickets, §17-8-17.
Voting blank for any officer on ticket, §17-8-21.
Voting for person whose name not on ballot, §17-8-20.
Voting machines. See within this heading, "Voting machines."
Write-in votes, §17-8-20.
Blind persons.
Accessibility to registration and polling places, §§21-4-20 to 21-4-24.
Ballots.
Assistance in casting, §17-8-29.
Municipal elections.
Assistance to disabled voters, §§11-46-40, 11-46-111, 11-46-112, 11-46-138.
Deception of disabled voters by marker, etc., §§11-46-64, 11-46-135.

ELECTIONS—Cont'd
Blind persons—Cont'd
Municipal elections—Cont'd
False declaration
requesting assistance,
§11-46-138.
Mayor-council form of
government.
Assistance of disabled
voters, §11-46-40.
Voting machines,
§11-46-51.
Voting machines.
Assistance at polls,
§17-9-25.
Boards of registrars. See
within this heading,
"Registrars."
Bond issues.
County bonds, §§11-81-81 to
11-81-90.
See COUNTIES.
Municipal bonds, §§11-81-52
to 11-81-61.
See MUNICIPAL
CORPORATIONS.
Voting machines.
Payment for machines,
§17-9-8.
Bonds, surety.
Examination of ballots,
voting machines, etc., by
persons involved in
contests, §17-8-46.
Booths.
Generally, §§17-7-8, 17-8-41.
Voting machines, §§17-9-1,
17-9-23.
Boundaries.
Districts. See within this
heading, "Districts."
Bribery.
Bribing or attempting to
influence voter, §17-23-3.
Candidates.
Barred by bribery,
§17-23-6.
Contests.
Grounds of contest,
§17-15-1.
Municipal elections,
§§11-46-67, 11-46-68.
Buying votes, §§17-22A-17,
17-23-4.
Campaign expenditures. See
within this heading, "Fair
campaign practices."
Campaign, §§17-22A-1 to
17-22A-23. See within this
heading, "Fair campaign
practices."
Candidates.
Absentee voting. See within
this heading, "Absentee
voting."
Announcements to contain
number of office sought,
§17-7-21.
Assistance to voters.
Prohibited, §17-8-29.
Ballots. See within this
heading, "Ballots."
Bribery.
Candidate barred by
bribery, §17-23-6.
Campaign expenditures. See
within this heading,
"Fair campaign
practices.",
Certificates of nomination,
§§17-7-2, 17-16-46.

ELECTIONS—Cont'd
Candidates—Cont'd
Clerk of circuit court.
When clerk not eligible for
appointing board,
§17-6-3.
Corrupt practices. See within
this heading, "Corrupt
practices."
Declaration of intention to
become candidate.
Name of candidate not to
be certified or placed
on ballot unless
declaration filed,
§17-7-21.
When filing required,
§17-7-21.
Fair campaign practices.
Definition of candidate,
§17-22A-2.
Independent candidates.
Ballots, §17-8-5.
Nominations. See within this
heading, "Nomination."
Presidential and vice-
presidential elections,
§§17-19-2, 17-19-3.
Primary elections.
General provisions. See
within this heading,
"Primary elections."
Probate judges.
When judge not eligible for
appointing board,
§17-6-3.
Sheriffs.
When sheriff not eligible
for appointing board,
§17-6-3.
Straight party ticket.
Procedure to vote,
§17-8-15.
Vote blanks for any officer
on ticket, §17-8-21.
Voting machines. See within
this heading, "Voting
machines."
Write-in votes, §17-8-20.
Canvassing votes.
County elections.
Declaration of results,
§17-14-2.
Election officials, §17-14-1.
Time of canvassing,
§17-14-1.
Declaration of election
results.
County elections, §17-14-2.
Evidence.
Prima facie evidence of
result, §17-14-2.
State elections.
Proclamation by
governor, §17-14-21.
Evidence.
Declaration of county
election results.
Prima facie evidence of
result, §17-14-2.
Manner of canvassing.
County elections, §17-14-1.
Primary elections. See within
this heading, "Primary
elections."
State elections.
Canvass of returns by state
officials, §17-14-20.

ELECTIONS—Cont'd
Canvassing votes—Cont'd
State elections—Cont'd
Certificates of elections.
Members of congress and
legislature,
§17-14-24.
Governor.
Proclaiming result of
certain elections,
§17-14-21.
Inspections.
List of registered voters,
§17-14-23.
List of registered voters.
Inspection, §17-14-23.
Opening of returns in
presence of state
officials, §17-14-20.
Returns of election of state
officers, §17-14-22.
Time of canvassing.
County elections, §17-14-1.
Voting machines, §§17-9-33
to 17-9-35, 17-9-38.
Catfish.
Promotion of industry.
Assessments.
Referendum on
assessment,
§§2-8-272 to 2-8-280.
Certificates of election.
Canvassing votes.
Secretary of state to
furnish members of
congress and
legislators, §17-14-24.
Forwarding to speaker of the
house, §17-14-22.
Withholding or revocation
upon failure to file
reports, etc., §17-22A-21.
Certificates of nomination,
§§17-7-1, 17-16-46.
Challenges.
Communicating challenge to
inspectors, §17-12-1.
Duties of challenger,
§17-12-2.
Excluding or receiving votes
unlawfully, §17-12-7.
Identity of voter.
Oath to establish, §17-12-4.
Inspectors.
Allowing unlawful vote,
§17-12-8.
Communicating challenge
to inspector, §17-12-1.
Excluding or receiving
votes unlawfully,
§17-12-7.
Primary elections.
Duty when voter's name
not on official list,
§17-16-23.
Selection as challenger,
§17-12-2.
Oaths, Const. Ala., art. VIII,
§185.
Challenged voters,
§17-12-3.
Establishment of identity
of voter, §17-12-4.
False oath, §17-12-6.
Refusal to take oath.
Vote rejected, §17-12-5.
Rejection of vote if voter
refuses to take oath,
§17-12-5.
Primary elections,
§§17-16-23, 17-16-24.

ELECTIONS—Cont'd
  Challenges—Cont'd
    Rejection of vote if voter
      refuses to take oath,
      §17-12-5.
    Right to challenge, §17-12-1.
    Selection of challenger,
      §17-12-2.
    Sheriff.
      Communicating challenge
        to inspector, §17-12-1.
    Voting machines, §17-9-23.
    Who may challenge,
      §17-12-1.
  **Chief justice of the supreme
    court.**
    General elections.
      Offices for which general
        election held, §17-2-2.
    State and county officers
      elected by the people,
      §17-2-1.
    When chief justice to be
      elected, §17-2-6.
  Circuit courts.
    Clerk of court.
      Absentee voting. See
        within this heading,
        "Absentee voting."
      Deputy circuit clerks in
        counties having more
        than five circuit
        judges, §17-2-8.
      Election officials. See
        within this heading,
        "Election officials."
      General elections.
        Offices for which general
          election held,
          §17-2-2.
        State and county officers
          elected by the people,
          §17-2-1.
    Judges generally. See within
      this heading, "Judges."
    Registration.
      Appeals from refusal of
        registration, §17-4-124.
  **Commissioner of agriculture
    and industries.** See
    within this heading,
    "Agriculture."
  Congress, §§17-20-1 to
    17-20-4.
    See CONGRESS.
  Constables, §36-23-1; Const.
    Ala., art. VI, §168.
    Contests.
      Notice.
        Failure to serve,
          §17-15-5.
  Constitution of Alabama,
    Const. Ala., art. I, §22.
    Amendments, §§17-17-1 to
      17-17-6; Const. Ala., art.
      XVIII, §§284, 285.
      See CONSTITUTION OF
        ALABAMA.
    General provisions.
      See CONSTITUTION OF
        ALABAMA.
  **Constitution of the United
    States.**
    Age.
      Right to vote not to be
        abridged on account of
        age, Const. U. S.,
        Amendment XXVI.
      Voting by persons eighteen
        years of age, Const. U.
        S., Amendment XXVI.

ELECTIONS—Cont'd
  **Constitution of the United
    States**—Cont'd
    House of representatives,
      Const. U. S., Art. I, §2.
    Election of members,
      Const. U. S., Art. I, §2.
    Judge of elections, returns
      and qualifications of
      members, Const. U. S.,
      Art. I, §5.
    Qualifications of electors,
      Const. U. S., Art. I, §2.
    Times, places and manner
      of holding, Const. U.
      S., Art. I, §4.
    Racial minorities, Const. U.
      S., Amendment XV.
    Senate, Const. U. S.,
      Amendment XVII.
    Election of members,
      Const. U. S.,
      Amendment XVII.
    Judge of elections, returns
      and qualifications of
      members, Const. U. S.,
      Art. I, §5.
    Qualifications of electors,
      Const. U. S.,
      Amendment XVII.
    Times, places and manner
      of holding, Const. U.
      S., Art. I, §4.
    Suffrage, Const. U. S.,
      Amendments XV, XIX.
  **Construction and
    interpretation.**
    Fair campaign practices,
      §17-22A-23.
  Contempt.
    Contests.
      Primary elections,
        §17-16-84.
      State officers.
        Commission.
          Power to punish for
            contempt,
            §17-15-57.
  Contests.
    Abatement.
      Legislature, judicial or
        county officers.
        Death of contestant.
          Contest not abated,
            §17-15-33.
    Affidavits.
      Legislature, judicial or
        county offices.
        Verification of statement
          of grounds by
          affidavit, §17-15-20.
    Annulment of election.
      When election not
        annulled, §17-15-2.
    Appeals.
      Legislature, judicial or
        county officers.
        Bond, §17-15-35.
        Costs of appeal,
          §17-15-35.
        Generally, §17-15-34.
        When appeal made,
          §17-15-34.
    Attorney general, Const.
      Ala., art. V, §115.
      State officers generally,
        §§17-15-50 to 17-15-63.

ELECTIONS—Cont'd
  Contests—Cont'd
    Ballots.
      Examination of ballots,
        §17-15-31.
      Certain persons may
        examine, §17-8-45.
      Procedure for
        examination,
        §17-8-46.
    Bribery.
      Annulment of election.
        When election not
          annulled, §17-15-2.
      Grounds of contest,
        §17-15-1.
    Circuit court judges,
      §§17-15-20 to 17-15-35.
    Commissioner of agriculture
      and industries, Const.
      Ala., art. V, §115.
      State officers generally,
        §§17-15-50 to 17-15-63.
    Constables.
      Notice.
        Failure to serve notice,
          §17-15-5.
    Constitutional provisions,
      Const. Ala., art. V, §115.
    Contempt.
      Primary elections,
        §17-16-84.
      State officers.
        Commission.
          Power to punish for
            contempt,
            §17-15-57.
    Corruption.
      Grounds of contest,
        §17-15-1.
    Costs.
      Legislature, county or
        judicial offices,
        §§17-15-20 to 17-15-35.
      Primary elections,
        §17-16-84.
      State officers.
        Execution for costs,
          §17-15-63.
    County offices, §§17-15-20 to
      17-15-35.
    Court of appeals judges.
      State officers generally,
        §§17-15-50 to 17-15-63.
    Courts.
      Chancery powers of courts.
        Jurisdiction denied
          courts exercising in
          election contests,
          §17-15-6.
    Death.
      Contest not abated by
        death of contestant,
        §17-15-33.
    Depositions.
      Circuit court judges,
        §17-15-28.
      District court judges,
        §17-15-28.
      Primary elections,
        §17-16-84.
    District court judges,
      §§17-15-20 to 17-15-35.
    Fraud.
      Annulment of election.
        When election not
          annulled, §17-15-2.
      Grounds of contest,
        §17-15-1.

ELECTIONS—Cont'd
　Contests—Cont'd
　　Governor, Const. Ala., art. V,
　　　§115.
　　　State officers generally,
　　　　§§17-15-50 to 17-15-63.
　　Grounds of contest, §17-15-1.
　　　Legislature, judicial or
　　　　county offices.
　　　　Statement of grounds,
　　　　　§17-15-20.
　　Illegal votes.
　　　Grounds of contest,
　　　　§17-15-1.
　　　Legislature, judicial or
　　　　county offices.
　　　　Judgment of court,
　　　　　§17-15-32.
　　　　Notice of nature of
　　　　　evidence, §17-15-21.
　　Injunctions.
　　　Chancery powers of judges
　　　　or courts.
　　　　Jurisdiction denied
　　　　　judges or courts
　　　　　exercising in election
　　　　　contests, §17-15-6.
　　Inspectors.
　　　Fraud or corruption on
　　　　part of inspector.
　　　　Grounds of contest,
　　　　　§17-15-1.
　　Judgment of court.
　　　Legislature, judicial or
　　　　county officers,
　　　　§17-15-32.
　　Jury trial.
　　　Legislature, judicial or
　　　　county offices,
　　　　§§17-15-28, 17-15-29.
　　Justices of the supreme
　　　court, §§17-15-50 to
　　　17-15-63.
　　Legislature, judicial or
　　　county offices, §§17-15-20
　　　to 17-15-35.
　　　Affidavits.
　　　　Statement of grounds,
　　　　　§17-15-20.
　　　Certification of results.
　　　　Presiding officer of
　　　　　legislative branch,
　　　　　§17-15-26.
　　　Circuit court judges.
　　　　Depositions, §17-15-28.
　　　　Jury.
　　　　　Hearing without jury,
　　　　　　§17-15-28.
　　　　Procedure.
　　　　　Generally, §17-15-27.
　　　　Security for costs,
　　　　　§17-15-27.
　　　　　Affidavit, §17-15-27.
　　　　　Filing, §17-15-27.
　　　　Summons.
　　　　　Notice of trial,
　　　　　　§17-15-27.
　　　　When trial to be held,
　　　　　§17-15-27.
　　　　Witnesses.
　　　　　Depositions, §17-15-28.
　　　　　Testimony, §17-15-28.
　　Commencement of contest.
　　　When contest
　　　　commenced,
　　　　§17-15-22.

ELECTIONS—Cont'd
　Contests—Cont'd
　　Legislature, judicial or
　　　county offices—Cont'd
　　Costs.
　　　Security for costs,
　　　　§17-15-22.
　　　Contest of senator or
　　　　representative,
　　　　§17-15-23.
　　　Taxation of costs.
　　　　Contest of senator or
　　　　　representative,
　　　　　§17-15-26.
　　District court judges.
　　　Appointment of day for
　　　　trial, §17-15-27.
　　　Depositions, §17-15-28.
　　　Jury trial, §17-15-28.
　　　Security for costs,
　　　　§17-15-27.
　　　Statement of grounds,
　　　　§17-15-27.
　　　Filing, §17-15-31.
　　　Witnesses, §17-15-28.
　　Evidence.
　　　Contest of senator or
　　　　representative.
　　　　Mailing to presiding
　　　　　officer of
　　　　　legislative branch,
　　　　　§17-15-25.
　　　Notice of nature of
　　　　evidence, §17-15-21.
　　Grounds of contest,
　　　§17-15-20.
　　Jury trial.
　　　Circuit court judges,
　　　　§17-15-28.
　　　District court judges,
　　　　§17-15-28.
　　　Probate court judges,
　　　　§17-15-29.
　　Presiding officer of
　　　legislative branch.
　　　Contest of senator or
　　　　representative.
　　　　Certification of results
　　　　　of contests,
　　　　　§17-15-26.
　　　　Mailing of evidential
　　　　　package,
　　　　　§17-15-25.
　　　　Opening of evidential
　　　　　package,
　　　　　§17-15-26.
　　Probate judges and other
　　　county officers.
　　　Circuit court to be open
　　　　at all times,
　　　　§17-15-30.
　　　Heard without jury,
　　　　§17-15-29.
　　　Statement of grounds.
　　　　Filing, §17-15-29.
　　　　Witnesses, §17-15-29.
　　　Security for costs,
　　　　§17-15-22.
　　　Contest of senator or
　　　　representative,
　　　　§17-15-23.
　　Senators and
　　　representatives in
　　　legislature.
　　　Costs.
　　　　Security, §17-15-23.
　　　　Taxation, §17-15-26.
　　　Depositions, §17-15-24.
　　　Return of depositions,
　　　　§17-15-25.

ELECTIONS—Cont'd
　Contests—Cont'd
　　Legislature, judicial or
　　　county offices—Cont'd
　　Senators and
　　　representatives in
　　　legislature—Cont'd
　　　Execution.
　　　　Issuance, §17-15-26.
　　　Filing required,
　　　　§17-15-23.
　　　Security for costs,
　　　　§17-15-23.
　　　Statement of grounds,
　　　　§17-15-20.
　　　Testimony, §17-15-24.
　　　Witnesses.
　　　　Testimony, §17-15-24.
　　　Statement of grounds,
　　　　§17-15-20.
　　　　Affidavit, §17-15-20.
　　　When contest commenced,
　　　　§17-15-22.
　　Municipal corporations.
　　　See MUNICIPAL
　　　　CORPORATIONS.
　　Notice.
　　　Failure of officer to serve
　　　　notice, §17-15-5.
　　　Primary elections.
　　　　Contestant to notify
　　　　　contestee of votes
　　　　　sought to be proved
　　　　　illegal, §17-16-79.
　　　Sheriff.
　　　　Failure to serve notice,
　　　　　§17-15-5.
　　Poll lists.
　　　Either party may have
　　　　copy, §17-15-4.
　　Primary elections, §§17-16-70
　　　to 17-16-89. See within
　　　this heading, "Primary
　　　elections."
　　Qualifications of voters.
　　　Voter must answer to
　　　　qualifications,
　　　　§17-15-3.
　　Registration lists.
　　　Either party may have
　　　　copy, §17-15-4.
　　Rejection of legal votes.
　　　Grounds of contest,
　　　　§17-15-1.
　　　Judgment of court,
　　　　§17-15-32.
　　　Legislature, judicial or
　　　　county offices.
　　　　Notice of nature of
　　　　　evidence, §17-15-21.
　　Representatives, §§17-15-50
　　　to 17-15-35.
　　Seals.
　　　Removal or breaking of
　　　　seals.
　　　　When removal or
　　　　　breaking allowed,
　　　　　§17-8-36.
　　Secretary of state, Const.
　　　Ala., art. V, §115.
　　　State officers generally,
　　　　§§17-15-50 to 17-15-63.
　　Self-incrimination, §17-15-3.
　　Senators, §§17-15-20 to
　　　17-15-35.
　　Service of process.
　　　Primary elections,
　　　　§17-16-84.
　　Sheriffs.
　　　Service of notice in
　　　　contests, §17-15-5.

ELECTIONS—Cont'd
 Contests—Cont'd
  State auditor, Const. Ala.,
    art. V, §115.
  State officers generally,
    §§17-15-50 to 17-15-63.
  State officers.
   Allegations.
    Evidence confined to
      allegations,
      §17-15-58.
   Bond, §17-15-50.
   Commission.
    Appeals from judgment
      of commission,
      §17-15-54.
    Contempt, §17-15-57.
    Election by joint
      convention,
      §17-15-53.
    Evidence.
     Report of evidence,
       §17-15-60.
    Expenses, §17-15-54.
    Members, §17-15-53.
    Per diem, §17-15-54.
    Presiding officer,
      §17-15-54.
    Reports, §17-15-60.
    Sheriffs to serve writs,
      §17-15-62.
    Sitting of commission,
      §17-15-54.
    Taking of testimony,
      §17-15-55.
    Warrants.
     Power to issue,
       §17-15-55.
    Witnesses.
     Parties to apply to
       commission to
       examine
       witnesses,
       §17-15-56.
     Power to send for
       witnesses,
       §17-15-55.
    Writs.
     Sheriffs to serve writs,
       §17-15-62.
   Contempt.
    Commission.
     Power to punish for
       contempt,
       §17-15-57.
   Costs.
    Execution for costs,
      §17-15-63.
   Evidence.
    Confined to allegations,
      §17-15-58.
   Execution for costs,
     §17-15-63.
   Joint convention of house
     and senate.
    Commission.
     Election by joint
       convention,
       §17-15-53.
     Judgments rendered by,
       §17-15-52.
     Officers tried by,
       §17-15-52.
     To constitute tribunal,
       §17-15-52.
   Notice.
    Adverse parties,
      §17-15-56.
   Parties entitled to be
     present, §17-15-59.

ELECTIONS—Cont'd
 Contests—Cont'd
  State officers—Cont'd
   Statement of grounds.
    Amendments,
      §§17-15-51, 17-15-58.
    Contents, §17-15-51.
    Evidence confined to
      allegations in
      statement,
      §17-15-58.
    Filing, §17-15-50.
    Service of copies,
      §17-15-51.
    Verification, §17-15-51.
   Trial.
    Joint convention of house
      and senate,
      §17-15-52.
   When contest made,
     §17-15-50.
   Witnesses.
    Compensation,
      §17-15-61.
  State treasurer, Const. Ala.,
    art. V, §115.
  State officers generally,
    §§17-15-50 to 17-15-63.
  Subpoenas.
   Primary elections,
     §17-16-84.
  Supreme court justices.
   State officers generally,
     §§17-15-50 to 17-15-63.
  Trial.
   State officers.
    Joint convention of house
      and senate,
      §17-15-52.
   Testimony may be required
     of any person other
     than defendant, Const.
     Ala., art. VIII, §189.
  Voting machines.
   Examination by persons
     involved in contests.
    Authorization, §17-8-45.
    Procedure, §17-8-46.
  Witnesses.
   Circuit court judges.
    Depositions, §17-15-28.
    Testimony, §17-15-28.
   Primary elections. See
     within this heading,
     "Primary elections."
   Probate judges and other
     county officers,
     §17-15-29.
   Self-incrimination of
     witnesses, §17-15-3.
   State officers.
    Compensation of
      witnesses, §17-15-61.
   Voter must answer as to
     his qualifications,
     §17-15-3.
 Contributions.
  Corporate contributions,
    §§10-2A-70 to
    10-2A-70.2.
 Conventions, §17-16-42.
  Certificate of nomination by
    convention, §17-16-46.
  Delegates, §17-16-42.
   Nominating or selecting at
     mass meetings,
     §17-16-43.
  Mass meetings of parties.
   Selecting delegates to
     conventions, §17-16-43.

ELECTIONS—Cont'd
 Conventions—Cont'd
  National conventions.
   Selection of delegates,
     §17-16-7.
  Qualifications to participate
    in, Const. Ala., art. VIII,
    §183.
  State executive committee.
   Committee may provide,
     §17-16-42.
 Coroners, §11-5-1.
  General elections.
   Offices for which general
     election held, §17-2-2.
   Time, §17-2-3.
  State and county officers
    elected by the people,
    §17-2-1.
 Corporations.
  Coercion of employees,
    §17-23-11.
  Directors, §10-2A-59.
   Vacancies, §10-2A-60.
  Fair campaign practices.
   Political committees
     established by
     corporation,
     §17-22A-14.
  Political funds.
   Segregated, separate
     political funds, §10-1-2.
  Political parties or
    candidates.
   Giving aid or contributions
     to, §10-2A-70.
   Exceptions for voluntary
     separate political
     funds, §10-2A-70.
   Legislative intent,
     §10-2A-70.2.
   Limitation on amount of
     political
     contributions,
     §10-2A-70.1.
   Penalty, §10-2A-70.
   Repealing provisions,
     §10-2A-70.2.
   Supplemental provisions,
     §10-2A-70.1.
 Corruption.
  Fair campaign practices,
    §§17-22A-1 to 17-22A-23.
   See within this heading,
     "Fair campaign
     practices."
 Counters.
  Voting machines. See within
    this heading, "Voting
    machines."
 Counties.
  Applicability of title to
    county elections, §17-1-1.
  Ballots.
   Counties to pay for ballots,
     §17-8-23.
  Bond issues, §§11-81-81 to
    11-81-90.
   See COUNTIES.
  Canvassing votes, §§17-14-1,
    17-14-2.
  Contests.
   Legislature, judicial or
     county offices,
     §§17-15-20 to 17-15-35.
    See within this
      heading, "Contests."
  County boards of education.
   When members to be
     elected, §17-2-5.

ELECTIONS—Cont'd
  Counties—Cont'd
    County commission, §11-3-1.
      Identification of voters.
        Authority to require
          identification,
          §17-11-1.
      Voting machines. See
        within this heading,
        "Voting machines."
    County seats.
      Relocation.
        See COUNTIES.
    Courthouses.
      Erection of new
        courthouses,
        §§11-16-34 to 11-16-37.
      See COUNTIES.
    Detached territories.
      Lists of qualified voters.
        Changing list when
          territory detached
          from one county and
          added to another,
          §17-4-128.
    Elector must vote in county
      and precinct of residence,
      §17-7-13.
    Expenses.
      Reimbursing counties for
        expenses of certain
        elections, §§17-21-1 to
        17-21-6.
    Instruction cards.
      Payment by counties,
        §17-8-23.
    Lists of qualified voters.
      Changing list when
        territory detached from
        one county and added
        to another, §17-4-128.
    Officers.
      List of officers elected by
        the people, §17-2-1.
    Political parties.
      County executive
        committees.
        Primary elections. See
          within this heading,
          "Primary elections."
    Precincts. See within this
      heading, "Precincts."
    Qualifications of voters.
      Liners between counties or
        precincts, §17-3-13.
      Residence in two or more
        counties or precincts,
        §17-3-12.
    Registration. See within this
      heading, "Registration."
    Reimbursing counties for
      expenses of certain
      elections.
      Appropriations.
        Carrying out provisions
          of chapter, §17-21-6.
      Constitutional
        amendments.
        Affecting state as a
          whole, §17-21-5.
        Generally, §17-21-4.
      County offices.
        Both federal, state and
          county offices,
          §17-21-2.
      Definitions.
        Expenses, §17-21-1.
      Expenses.
        Defined, §17-21-1.

ELECTIONS—Cont'd
  Counties—Cont'd
    Reimbursing counties for
      expenses of certain
      elections—Cont'd
      Federal offices.
        Both federal or state and
          county offices,
          §17-21-2.
        Only federal offices,
          §17-21-3.
      State offices.
        Both federal or state and
          county offices,
          §17-21-2.
        Only state offices,
          §17-21-3.
    Relocation of county seats.
      See COUNTIES.
    Special elections.
      Vacancies occurring in
        county offices,
        §17-18-1.
    Time.
      When county officers
        elected, §17-2-4.
    Treasurers, §11-4-20.
      Failure to elect successor
        vacates office, §36-9-5.
    General elections.
      Offices for which general
        election held,
        §17-2-2.
      State and county officers
        elected by the people,
        §17-2-1.
    Voting machines.
      Applicability of laws to use
        of voting machines,
        §17-9-39.
      County commissions. See
        within this heading,
        "Voting machines."
    When county officers elected,
      §17-2-4.
  Counting votes.
    Absentee votes, §§17-10-10,
      17-10-11.
    Ballot boxes.
      Total votes received by
        each candidate,
        §17-13-3.
    Ballots.
      Counting, §17-13-4.
        Absentee ballots,
          §§17-10-10, 17-10-11.
      Delivery to returning
        officer, §17-13-4.
      Improperly marked ballots,
        §17-13-2.
      Labeling, §17-13-4.
      Sealing, §17-13-4.
      Sheriff.
        Keeping ballots six
          months after
          election, §17-13-5.
    Candidates.
      Paper showing total votes
        received by each
        candidate to be
        attached to ballot box,
        §17-13-3.
    Close of polls.
      Counting upon close,
        §17-13-1.
    Improperly marked ballots,
      §17-13-2.
    Inspectors.
      Ascertaining number of
        votes received for each
        person, §17-13-6.

ELECTIONS—Cont'd
  Counting votes—Cont'd
    Inspectors—Cont'd
      Certification of poll list,
        §17-13-6.
      Labeling ballots, §17-13-4.
      Procedure for counting
        votes, §17-13-2.
      When inspectors to count
        votes, §17-13-1.
    Primary elections.
      Counting at close of
        election at each polling
        place, §17-16-31.
    Probate judge.
      Certificate of votes
        delivered to probate
        judge to be forwarded,
        §17-13-7.
    Procedure, §17-13-2.
    Returning officer.
      Ballots to be counted,
        labeled, sealed and
        delivered to returning
        officer, §17-13-4.
      Statement of votes.
        Delivery to returning
          officer, §17-13-6.
    Sheriff.
      Ballots.
        Sheriff to keep ballots
          six months after
          election, §17-13-5.
      Statement of votes.
        Delivery to returning
          officer, §17-13-6.
        Forwarding by probate
          judge, §17-13-7.
      When votes to be counted,
        §17-13-1.
  **County executive
    committees.** See within
    this heading, "Primary
    elections."
  **County superintendents of
    education,** §§16-9-4 to
    16-9-8.
    See EDUCATION.
  Courthouses.
    Counties.
      Erection of new
        courthouses,
        §§11-16-34 to 11-16-37.
      See COUNTIES.
    Registration.
      Time and place of
        registration in counties
        with two or more
        courthouses, §17-4-157.
  Court of civil appeals.
    Judges, §12-3-3.
      Contested elections.
        State officers generally,
          §§17-15-50 to
          17-15-63. See within
          this heading,
          "Contests."
      General elections.
        Offices for which general
          election held,
          §17-2-2.
        State and county officers
          elected by the people,
          §17-2-1.
      Two or more justices
        running at the same
        time.
        Designating justices by
          number, §17-7-20.
      When judges to be elected,
        §17-2-7.

ELECTIONS—Cont'd
Court of criminal appeals.
Judges, §12-3-2.
Contested elections.
State officers generally,
§§17-15-50 to
17-15-63. See within
this heading,
"Contests."
General elections.
Offices for which general
election held,
§17-2-2.
State and county officers
elected by the people,
§17-2-1.
Two or more justices
running at the same
time.
Designation by number,
§17-7-20.
When judges to be elected,
§17-2-7.
Credit unions.
Board of directors, credit
committee and
supervisory committee,
§5-17-10.
Officers, §5-17-11.
Criminal law and procedure.
Criminal prosecutions under
election laws, Const.
Ala., art. VIII, §189.
Disqualification from
registration and voting.
Convicted persons, Const.
Ala., art. VIII, §182.
Restoration of right to
vote by pardon,
§17-3-10.
Immunity from prosecution
due to testimony given,
Const. Ala., art. VIII,
§189.
Lists of qualified voters.
Purging of registration
lists.
Registrars to receive
information of
convictions,
§17-4-131.
Death.
Contests.
Legislature, judicial or
county officers.
Contest not abated by
death of contestant,
§17-15-33.
Lists of qualified voters.
Purging of registration
lists.
Registrars to receive
information of
deaths, §17-4-131.
**Declaration of intention to
become candidate,**
§17-7-21.
Definitions.
Absentee voting.
Register, §17-10-1.
Electronic voting systems,
§17-24-2.
Fair campaign practices,
§17-22A-2.
Handicapped persons.
Accessibility to registration
and polling places,
§21-4-21.
Precincts, §17-5A-2.
Primary elections, §17-16-1.

ELECTIONS—Cont'd
Definitions—Cont'd
Reimbursing counties for
expenses of certain
elections.
Expenses defined, §17-21-1.
Voting machines, §17-9-1.
Depositions.
Contests, §17-15-28.
Detached territories.
Lists of qualified voters.
Changing list when
territory detached from
one county and added
to another, §17-4-128.
Disclosing votes, §17-8-12.
Discrimination.
Fair campaign practices.
Solicitation of money by
job discrimination,
§17-22A-20.
**Disqualification from
registration and voting.**
Convicted persons, Const.
Ala., art. VIII, §182.
Restoration of right to vote
by pardon, §17-3-10.
Generally, Const. Ala., art.
VIII, §182.
Mentally ill persons, Const.
Ala., art. VIII, §182.
Pardons.
Restoration of right to vote
by pardon, §17-3-10.
District attorneys.
General elections.
Offices for which general
election held, §17-2-2.
Registration.
Appeals from refusal of
registration.
District attorney to
represent state,
§17-4-124.
State and county officers
elected by the people,
§17-2-1.
Terms of office, §17-2-9.
When elected, §§12-17-180,
17-2-9.
District courts.
Judges, Const. Ala., art. VI,
§152.
Ballots.
Numbering and
designation of
positions on ballots
in districts in which
more than one judge
elected, §§12-17-62,
17-7-20.
Boundaries of districts for
election of judges,
§12-17-60.
Contests.
Legislature, judicial or
county officers,
§§17-15-20 to
17-15-35. See within
this heading,
"Contests."
General elections.
Offices for which general
election held,
§17-2-2.
Manner of election,
§12-17-61.
State and county officers
elected by the people,
§17-2-1.

ELECTIONS—Cont'd
District courts—Cont'd
Judges—Cont'd
Two or more judges at
same election.
Designating by number,
§§12-17-62, 17-7-20.
When judges to be elected,
§17-2-7.
Districts.
Boundaries.
Districts for election of
district court judges,
§12-17-60.
Congressional districts.
State divided into
congressional districts,
§17-20-1.
Precincts. See within this
heading, "Precincts."
Voting districts, §§17-5A-4,
17-5A-5.
Drunkenness. See within this
heading, "Alcoholic
beverages."
Education.
See EDUCATION.
**Educational television
foundation authority.**
Political activities prohibited,
§16-7A-5.
Electioneering.
Proximity of persons to
polling place, §17-7-18.
Election officials.
Absentee voting. See within
this heading, "Absentee
voting."
Alcoholic beverages.
Officers consuming
intoxicating liquors
during election,
§17-6-16.
Appointment.
Appointing board, §17-6-1.
Compensation, §17-6-4.
Replacement of ineligible
members, §17-6-4.
When county officers not
eligible, §17-6-3.
Notice of ineligibility,
§17-6-3.
Replacement of
ineligible member
of appointing
board, §17-6-4.
Serving on board when
ineligible, §17-6-3.
Notice of appointment,
§17-6-2.
Political parties.
Parties to furnish lists
from which
appointments are
made, §17-6-6.
Who appoints, §17-6-1.
Clerk of the circuit court.
Appointing board.
When clerk not eligible,
§17-6-3.
Appointment of officials,
§17-6-1.
Proceedings when clerk
disqualified, §17-6-5.
Clerks.
Alcoholic beverages.
Consuming during
election, §17-6-16.
Appointment, §17-6-9.
Compensation, §17-6-13.
Corrupt conduct, §17-6-14.

ELECTIONS—Cont'd
Election officials—Cont'd
Clerks—Cont'd
Disclosing votes, §17-8-12.
Duty.
Failure to perform duty,
§17-6-14.
Oaths, §17-6-10.
Time and place of holding
elections, §17-7-6.
Compensation, §17-6-13.
Counties where
compensation
prescribed by other
provisions, §17-6-13.
Corrupt conduct, §17-6-14.
Counties.
Compensation in counties
where compensation
prescribed by other
provisions, §17-6-13.
Disclosing votes, §17-8-12.
Duty.
Failure to perform duty,
§17-6-14.
Failure to attend, §17-6-7.
Identification of voters,
§§7-11-1 to 7-11-3.
Inspectors. See within this
heading, "Inspectors."
Managers.
Absentee voting. See
within this heading,
"Absentee voting."
Municipal corporations.
Officers of election.
See MUNICIPAL
CORPORATIONS.
Notice of appointment,
§17-6-2.
Number, §17-6-1.
Oaths, §17-6-10.
Poll list.
Unlawful use, §17-7-17.
Poll watchers.
Alcoholic beverages.
Consuming during
election, §17-6-16.
Allowed at polling place,
§17-6-8.
Ballots.
Watchers permitted to
see ballots, §17-6-8.
Municipal officer or
employee acting as poll
watcher, §17-6-15.
Primary elections,
§§17-16-26, 17-16-49.
Right to observe conduct of
election, §17-9-29.
Voting machines,
§§17-9-18, 17-9-29.
Primary elections. See within
this heading, "Primary
elections."
Probate judges.
Appointing board.
When judges not eligible,
§17-6-3.
Appointment of officials,
§17-6-1.
Registrars. See within this
heading, "Registrars."
Returning officers. See
within this heading,
"Sheriffs."
Sheriffs.
Appointing board.
When sheriff not eligible,
§17-6-3.

ELECTIONS—Cont'd
Election officials—Cont'd
Sheriffs—Cont'd
Appointment of officials,
§17-6-1.
Returning officer. See
within this heading,
"Sheriffs."
Time and place of holding
elections, §17-7-6.
Voting machines, §§17-9-18
to 17-9-23, 17-9-40. See
within this heading,
"Voting machines."
Electors.
Presidential electors. See
within this heading,
"Presidential and vice-
presidential elections."
Voters. See within this
heading, "Voters."
Electronic voting systems,
§§17-24-1 to 17-24-11.
Applicability of other
provisions of law,
§17-24-7.
Approval.
Requirements, §17-24-3.
Certification of equipment,
§17-24-5.
Report, §17-24-6.
Citation of chapter, §17-24-1.
Committee.
Authority.
Limitation, §17-24-11.
Compensation, §17-24-4.
Creation, §17-24-4.
Limitation on authority,
§17-24-11.
Membership, §17-24-4.
Cumulative provisions,
§17-24-10.
Definitions, §17-24-2.
Examination of equipment,
§17-24-5.
Implementation of chapter.
Procedure, §17-24-7.
Instructions to voters,
§17-24-8.
Precincts.
Definition of electronic
vote counting statutes,
§17-5A-2.
Provisions cumulative,
§17-24-10.
Rejection of equipment.
Report to be issued,
§17-24-6.
Reports.
Certification or rejection of
equipment, §17-24-6.
Requirements for approval of
system, §17-24-3.
Short title of chapter,
§17-24-1.
Testing of equipment,
§17-24-9.
Emblems.
Approval, §17-8-6.
Certification to probate
judge, §17-8-7.
Probate judges.
Certification of emblem,
§17-8-7.
Prohibited designs, §17-8-8.
Submission, §17-8-6.
Use when party is divided,
§17-8-9.

ELECTIONS—Cont'd
Employers and employees.
Corporations.
Coercion of employees,
§17-23-11.
Employer intimidating
employee, §17-23-10.
Fair campaign practices.
Job discrimination to
solicit money,
§17-22A-20.
Public employees.
Improper use of position to
influence votes or
political activities,
§17-1-7.
Right to participate,
§17-1-7.
English language.
Voters unable to write
English.
Assistance in casting votes,
§17-8-29.
Evidence.
County elections.
Declaration of election
results.
Prima facie evidence of
result, §17-14-2.
Expenses.
Absentee voting, §17-10-16.
Amendments to state
constitution.
See CONSTITUTION OF
ALABAMA.
Campaign expenditures. See
within this heading,
"Fair campaign
practices."
Counties.
Reimbursing counties for
expenses of certain
elections. See within
this heading,
"Counties."
Fair campaign practices,
§§17-22A-1 to 17-22A-23.
Accepting payment for votes,
§17-22A-17.
Advertising.
Cards, pamphlets, etc., to
contain identification,
§17-22A-13.
Identification as paid
advertisement,
§17-22A-12.
Attorney general to prosecute
violations, §17-22A-22.
Buying votes, §17-22A-17.
Candidates.
Definition of candidate,
§17-22A-2.
Reports of contributions
and expenditures,
§17-22A-8.
Certificates withheld or
revoked upon failure to
file under chapter,
§17-22A-21.
Citation of chapter, §17-22A-1.
Construction and
interpretation of chapter,
§17-22A-23.
Contributions.
Accepting in name of
another.
When prohibited,
§17-22A-18.
Definitions, §17-22A-2.

ELECTIONS—Cont'd
Fair campaign practices
—Cont'd
Contributions—Cont'd
Making in name of
another.
When prohibited,
§17-22A-18.
Reports, §17-22A-8.
Definitions, §17-22A-2.
Expenditures.
Defined, §17-22A-2.
Political committees.
Checking accounts to be
maintained,
§17-22A-6.
Principal campaign
committees to control,
§17-22A-4.
Reports, §17-22A-8.
Filing.
Reports of contributions
and expenditures to be
filed, §17-22A-8.
Fraudulent
misrepresentation of
affiliation with
candidate, §17-22A-19.
Identification.
Advertisements to be
identified as such,
§17-22A-13.
Cards, pamphlets, etc.,
§17-22A-13.
Defined, §17-22A-2.
Inspection of reports and
statements by public,
§17-22A-10.
Job discrimination to solicit
money, §17-22A-20.
Loans.
Defined, §17-22A-2.
Local offices.
Defined, §17-22A-2.
Misdemeanor for violation,
§17-22A-22.
Misrepresentation of
affiliation with
candidate, §17-22A-19.
Obstruction of voting rights.
Prohibited, §17-22A-16.
Penalties, §17-22A-22.
Persons.
Defined, §17-22A-2.
Political committees.
Accounting and reporting
of funds, §17-22A-3.
Checking accounts to be
maintained, §17-22A-6.
Commingling of funds.
Prohibition, §17-22A-3.
Corporation may establish,
§17-22A-14.
Defined, §17-22A-2.
Officers, §17-22A-3.
Report filed under federal
provisions.
Secretary of state to
receive copy,
§17-22A-15.
Reports of contributions
and expenditures,
§17-22A-8.
Statement of organization,
§17-22A-5.
Report of material
changes, §17-22A-5.
Termination or dissolution.
Notice, §17-22A-5.

ELECTIONS—Cont'd
Fair campaign practices
—Cont'd
Principal campaign
committees.
Candidate acting as own
committee, §17-22A-4.
Defined, §17-22A-2.
Excess money received by
committee.
Use, §17-22A-7.
Expenditures controlled by
committee, §17-22A-4.
Filing statement showing
committees, §17-22A-4.
Reports of contributions
and expenditures,
§17-22A-8.
Probate judges.
Duties of probate judge,
§17-22A-11.
Propositions. §17-22A-2.
Reports.
Certificates withheld or
revoked upon failure to
file, §17-22A-21.
Reports of contributions and
expenditures.
Filing, §17-22A-8.
Procedure, §17-22A-9.
Inspection by public,
§17-22A-10.
Secretary of state.
Duties, §17-22A-11.
Political committees.
Filing copy of federal
report with
secretary,
§17-22A-15.
Short title, §17-22A-1.
Solicitation by force, job
discrimination, etc.,
§17-22A-20.
State.
Defined, §17-22A-2.
State office.
Defined, §17-22A-2.
Threats to solicit money,
§17-22A-20.
Title of chapter.
Short title, §17-22A-1.
Forgery and counterfeiting.
Ballots.
Forging inspector's name
on ballot, §11-46-68.
Forms.
Absentee voting. See within
this heading, "Absentee
voting."
Ballots, §§17-8-3, 17-8-5.
Blank forms, §17-8-44.
Certificates of results.
Blank forms, §17-8-44.
Fraud.
Altering or changing vote of
elector, §17-23-7.
Contests, §§17-15-1, 17-15-2.
Misrepresentation of
affiliation with
candidate, §17-22A-19.
Primary elections.
Ballots.
Fraudulently changing,
§17-16-48.
Returns, §17-16-48.
General elections.
County boards of education,
§17-2-5.
Holding of general elections,
§17-2-2.

ELECTIONS—Cont'd
General elections—Cont'd
Offices for which general
election held, §17-2-2.
Time, §17-2-3.
General provisions. See
within this heading, "Fair
campaign practices."
Governor.
Canvass of election returns.
Opening of returns in
presence of governor,
§17-14-20.
Congressional elections.
Notice of election.
Governor to give notice,
§17-20-4.
Returns.
Governor to estimate,
§17-20-4.
Constitution of Alabama.
Amendments to
constitution.
Governor's proclamation,
§17-17-3.
Contests. See within this
heading, "Contests."
General elections.
Offices for which general
election held, §17-2-2.
Time of general election,
§17-2-3.
Gubernatorial elections.
Constitutional provisions,
Const. Ala., art. V,
§§114, 115.
Contested elections.
State officers generally,
§§17-15-50 to
17-15-63. See within
this heading,
"Contests."
State officers elected by
the people, §17-2-1.
Presidential and vice-
presidential elections.
See within this heading,
"Presidential and vice-
presidential elections."
Results.
Proclamation of result,
§17-14-21.
Special elections,
§17-18-3.
Grand jury.
Ballots.
Seals.
When breaking of seals
allowed, §17-8-36.
Handicapped persons.
Absentee voting.
Physician's certificate.
When required, §17-10-4.
Accessibility to registration
and polling places,
§§21-4-20 to 21-4-24.
Definitions, §21-4-21.
Enforcement of article,
§21-4-24.
Guidelines, §21-4-22.
Injunctions.
Enforcement of article,
§21-4-24.
Legislative intent,
§21-4-20.
Promulgation of guidelines,
§21-4-22.
Purpose, §21-4-20.
Registration and voting
aids, §21-4-23.

ELECTIONS—Cont'd
Handicapped persons
—Cont'd
Assistance in casting votes,
§17-8-29.
Municipal elections,
§§11-46-40, 11-46-51,
11-46-111, 11-46-122.
Primary elections,
§17-16-27.
Municipal elections.
Assistance to disabled
voters, §§11-46-40,
11-46-51, 11-46-111,
11-46-122.
Deception of disabled
voters by marker, etc.,
§§11-46-64, 11-46-135.
False declaration
requesting assistance,
§11-46-138.
Mayor-council form of
government.
Assistance of disabled
voters, §11-46-40.
Voting machines,
§11-46-51.
Voting machines.
Assistance at polls,
§17-9-25.
Municipal elections.
Mayor-council form of
government,
§11-46-51.
Holidays.
Municipal elections.
Commission form.
Effect of legal holidays
or closing days,
§11-46-91.
Mayor-council form.
Effect of legal holidays
or closing days,
§11-46-20.
Horse racing.
Pari-mutuel betting.
County-wide referendum to
approve, §11-65-46.
Referendum to approve
commission, §11-65-4.
House of representatives.
See CONGRESS.
Identification of voters,
§§17-11-1 to 17-11-4.
Illegal voting.
Contests.
Grounds of contest,
§17-15-1.
Depositing more than one
ballot, §17-23-1.
Indictment.
Form, §15-8-150.
Municipal elections, §17-23-2.
Voting more than once at
any election, §17-23-1.
Improvement authorities,
§§37-7-3 to 37-7-9, 37-7-31.
See PUBLIC WORKS.
Indictments.
Betting on elections.
Form of indictment,
§15-8-150.
Illegal voting.
Form of indictment,
§15-8-150.

ELECTIONS—Cont'd
Injunctions.
Contests.
Chancery powers of judges
or courts.
Jurisdiction denied
judges or courts
exercising chancery
powers in election
contests, §17-15-6.
Inspections.
List of registered voters.
Open to inspection,
§17-14-23.
Inspectors.
Alcoholic beverages.
Consuming during election,
§17-6-16.
Appointment, §17-6-9.
Ballots.
Deceiving elector in
preparation of ballot,
§17-8-31.
Deposit of ballot, §17-8-39.
Numbering, §17-8-13.
Receiving folded ballots,
§17-8-34.
Calling name of voter after
casting ballot, §17-8-34.
Challenging votes. See
within this heading,
"Challenges."
Compensation, §17-6-13.
Corrupt conduct, §17-6-14.
Counting votes. See within
this heading, "Counting
votes."
Disclosing votes, §17-8-12.
Duty.
Failure to perform,
§17-6-14.
Failure to attend, §17-6-7.
Failure to perform duty,
§17-6-14.
Markers.
Inspector refusing to
appoint, §17-8-32.
Oaths, §17-6-10.
Primary elections. See within
this heading, "Primary
elections."
Proclaiming polls open,
§17-7-11.
Registration, §17-4-130.
Time and place of holding
elections, §17-7-6.
Voting machines. See within
this heading, "Voting
machines."
Instruction cards.
Counties and cities to pay for
instruction cards,
§17-8-23.
Polling places.
Placement of cards in
polling places,
§17-8-43.
Probate judge to have
printed, §17-8-43.
Investigations.
Proceedings to investigate
elections under election
laws, Const. Ala., art.
VIII, §189.
Judges, Const. Ala., amd. 328.
Canons of judicial ethics.
See CANONS OF
JUDICIAL ETHICS.
Circuit courts, Const. Ala.,
art. VI, §152.

ELECTIONS—Cont'd
Judges—Cont'd
Contests. See within this
heading, "Contests."
General elections.
Offices for which general
election held, §17-2-2.
Inferior courts, Const. Ala.,
art. VI, §153.
Initial election of judges for
newly created circuits,
Const. Ala., art. VI,
§159.
Probate judges.
Failure to perform.
Duties to devolve upon
circuit court,
§17-1-4.
Misdemeanor, §17-1-5.
Penalty, §17-1-5.
State and county officers
elected by the people,
§17-2-1.
Supreme court justices. See
within this heading,
"Supreme court."
Two or more judges running
at the same time.
Designation by number,
§17-7-20.
When circuit court judges to
be elected, §17-2-7.
Judgments.
Contests, §17-15-32.
Void elections.
Certification of judgment
declaring election void,
§36-9-15.
Jurisdiction.
Contests.
Judges or courts exercising
chancery powers.
Jurisdiction denied,
§17-15-6.
Jury.
Contests, §17-15-28.
Justices of the peace, Const.
Ala., art. VI, §168.
Labor.
Fair campaign practices.
Job discrimination to
solicit money,
§17-22A-20.
Legislature.
Duty of legislature to pass
laws regulating
elections, Const. Ala.,
art. VIII, §190; amd. 41.
Elections by legislature.
Voting, Const. Ala., art.
IV, §83.
Senators and representatives,
Const. Ala., art. IV, §46.
Certificates of election.
Members of assembly to
receive, §17-14-24.
Contests, §§17-15-20 to
17-15-31. See within
this heading,
"Contests."
General elections.
Time, §17-2-3.
Special elections.
Vacancies in office of
senator or
representative,
§17-18-1.
State and county officers
elected by the people,
§17-2-1.

ELECTIONS—Cont'd

Legislature—Cont'd

Tie votes.

Duty of legislature upon
tie vote, §17-14-25.

Libraries.

Public library service.

Executive board.

Election of officers,
§41-8-3.

Lieutenant governor.

Constitutional provisions,
Const. Ala., art. V,
§§114, 115.

General elections.

Offices for which general
election held, §17-2-2.

Time of general election,
§17-2-3.

State officers elected by the
people, §17-2-1.

Limitation of actions.

Action to test validity of
municipal election for
bond issues or tax levies.

Six month limitation,
§6-2-40.

Liners.

Persons declared to be liners
between counties or
precincts, §17-3-13.

Lists.

Absentee voters.

List of qualified voters,
§17-10-5.

Electors.

Registration. See within
this heading,
"Registration."

Primary elections. See within
this heading, "Primary
elections."

Purging of registration lists.
See within this heading,
"Registration."

Qualified voters. See within
this heading,
"Registration."

Registration. See within this
heading, "Registration."

Loitering.

Polling places, §17-7-19.

Machines.

Voting machines, §§17-9-1 to
17-9-41. See within this
heading, "Voting
machines."

Mail.

Absentee voting generally,
§§17-10-1 to 17-10-20.
See within this heading,
"Absentee voting."

Registration of absentee
electors.

Persons entitled to register
by mail, §17-4-134.

Managers.

Absentee voting. See within
this heading, "Absentee
voting."

Markers.

Inspector refusing to appoint
markers, §17-8-32.

Mentally ill.

Disqualification from
registering and voting,
Const. Ala., art. VIII,
§182.

ELECTIONS—Cont'd

Mentally ill—Cont'd

Lists of qualified voters.

Purging of registration
lists.

Registrars to receive
information of
incompetency,
§17-4-131.

Military affairs.

Absentee voting.

Application.

Postcard application for
certain military
personnel and wives,
§17-10-3.

Residence of voters.

No loss or acquisition of
residence by military
service, §17-3-11.

Misdemeanors.

Fair campaign practices,
§17-22A-22.

Precincts.

Task force.

Failure to cooperate with
task force, §17-5A-9.

Municipal corporations,
§§11-46-1 to 11-46-144.

See MUNICIPAL
CORPORATIONS.

Names.

Ballots, §17-8-2.

Poll list.

Voter to sign name,
§17-7-15.

Nomination.

Ballots.

Persons entitled to have
names printed on
ballots, §17-7-1.

Certificate of nomination.

Certificate of nomination
by convention, mass
meeting, etc.,
§17-16-46.

Preservation by probate
judge, §17-7-2.

Mass meetings for purpose of
nominating candidates,
§§17-16-43 to 17-16-46.

Suppressing nomination,
§17-7-4.

Nominations.

Certification of nomination.

Withholding or revocation
upon failure to file
reports, etc.,
§17-22A-21.

Notice.

Appointing board.

Notice of ineligibility,
§17-6-3.

Contests, §§17-15-5, 17-16-79.

Publication in newspaper,
§17-7-5.

Returns.

Failure to make return,
§17-14-27.

Sheriff to give notice,
§17-7-5.

Special elections, §§17-18-4
to 17-18-6.

Oaths.

Absentee voting.

Ballots.

Swearing to ballots
before notary public,
§17-10-6.

Blank forms, §17-8-44.

ELECTIONS—Cont'd

Oaths—Cont'd

Challenges, Const. Ala., art.
VIII, §185.

Clerks, §17-6-10.

Contests.

Primary elections.

Witnesses, §17-16-76.

Election officers, §17-6-10.

Inspectors, §17-6-10.

Primary elections.

Contests.

Witnesses, §17-16-76.

Registration.

Applicants for registration,
§17-4-122.

Voting machines.

Assistance at polls.

Oath of voter requiring
assistance, §17-9-25.

Voting without taking oath,
§17-7-12.

Obstruction of voting rights,
§17-22A-16.

Offenses.

Municipal elections.

See MUNICIPAL
CORPORATIONS.

Officials.

Election officials, §§17-6-1 to
17-6-16. See within this
heading, "Election
officials."

Parties.

Political parties. See within
this heading, "Political
parties."

Penalties.

Ballots.

Seals.

Removing or breaking of
seals, §17-8-37.

Fair campaign practices,
§17-22A-22.

Petitions.

Presidential and vice-
presidential elections.

Nominating petitions,
§17-19-2.

Presidential preference
primary, §§17-16A-3,
17-16A-4.

Photography.

Voting machines.

Photographing name of
candidates or question
together with total
vote cast, §17-9-34.

Physicians.

Absentee voting.

Physician's certificate.

When required, §17-10-4.

Political parties.

Ballots.

Parties may be included on
ballots, §17-8-2.1.

Conventions.

General provisions. See
within this heading,
"Conventions."

Corporations.

Giving aid or contribution
to political party,
§10-2A-70.

Legislative intent,
§10-2A-70.2.

Limitation on amount of
political
contribution,
§10-2A-70.1.

ELECTIONS—Cont'd
Political parties—Cont'd
Corporations—Cont'd
Giving aid or contribution
to political party
—Cont'd
Repealing provisions,
§10-2A-70.2.
Supplemental provisions,
§10-2A-70.1.
County executive
committees. See within
this heading, "Primary
elections."
Election officials.
Appointment.
Parties to furnish lists
from which
appointments are
made, §17-6-6.
Emblems, §§17-8-6 to 17-8-9.
Mass meetings.
Applicability of provisions,
§17-16-45.
Certificate of nomination
by mass meeting,
§17-16-46.
Conventions.
Selecting delegates to
conventions,
§17-16-43.
Holding or participating in
illegal meetings,
§17-16-44.
Illegal meetings.
Holding or participating
in, §17-16-44.
Municipal elections.
Applicability to,
§17-16-45.
Notice of holding,
§17-16-43.
Other violations of chapter
relative to meetings,
§17-16-44.
Place of holding, §17-16-43.
Right of public to attend,
§17-16-43.
Special elections.
Applicability to,
§17-16-45.
Time, §17-16-43.
Municipal corporations.
Primary elections by
political parties
abolished in certain
municipalities,
§11-46-3.
National conventions.
Selection of delegates,
§17-16-7.
Presidential and vice-
presidential elections,
§§17-19-2, 17-19-3.
Primary elections, §§17-16-1
to 17-16-89. See within
this heading, "Primary
elections."
Procedure to vote for one
candidate not on party
ticket, §17-8-16.
Qualifications as elector
required to participate in
political party action,
Const. Ala., art. VIII,
§183.
Registration.
Voter registration
information.
Political parties may
obtain, §17-4-122.

ELECTIONS—Cont'd
Political parties—Cont'd
Selection of delegates to
national conventions,
§17-16-7.
State conventions. See within
this heading,
"Conventions."
State executive committees.
See within this heading,
"Primary elections."
State party chairman.
Primary elections. See
within this heading,
"Primary elections."
Tickets.
Procedure to vote for one
candidate not on party
ticket, §17-8-16.
Procedure to vote straight
party ticket, §17-8-15.
Procedure when straight
ticket does not contain
names of all officers,
§17-8-19.
Split tickets, §17-8-18.
Two or more candidates on
different tickets,
§17-8-17.
Voting straight party
ticket, §17-8-15.
Voter registration
information.
Political parties may
obtain, §17-4-122.
Polling places, §17-7-6.
Absentee voting.
Persons obtaining absentee
ballots not to vote at
polling place, §17-10-5.
Accessibility to handicapped
persons, §§21-4-20 to
21-4-24.
Ballots.
Removing from polling
place, §17-8-41.
Booths.
Expenses, §17-7-8.
Providing booths, §17-7-8.
Remaining in booth,
§17-8-41.
Compartments.
Providing compartments,
§17-7-8.
Counting votes.
Counting upon close of
polls, §17-13-1.
Delivery of ballot to voter
upon entering polling
place, §17-8-27.
Discouraging qualified
electors from entering
voting place, §17-7-19.
Electioneering.
Proximity of persons to
polling place, §17-7-18.
Handicapped persons.
Accessibility, §§21-4-20 to
21-4-24.
Hours polls to be open,
§17-7-5.1.
Instruction cards.
Placement of cards in
polling places,
§17-8-43.
Length of time elector may
stay in polling place,
§17-8-29.
Loitering about polling place,
§17-7-19.

ELECTIONS—Cont'd
Polling places—Cont'd
Municipal corporations.
See MUNICIPAL
CORPORATIONS.
Number of electors in polling
place, §17-8-29.
Poll list.
Blank forms, §17-8-44.
Certification of upon
counting of votes,
§17-13-6.
Comparing ballot with poll
list, §17-8-42.
Contests.
Either party may have
copy of poll list,
§17-15-4.
Delivery by probate judge
to inspectors,
§17-4-130.
Preparation, §17-4-130.
Primary elections. See
within this heading,
"Primary elections."
Sealing, §§17-7-16, 17-13-6.
Signing name of another
person, §17-7-15.
Taking down of name after
voting, §17-8-34.
Unlawful use, §17-7-17.
Voter to sign name,
§17-7-15.
Precincts.
Designation of voting
places, §17-5A-5.
List of voters for each
voting place, §17-5A-6.
Notice of location, etc., of
voting places,
§17-5A-5.
Primary elections. See within
this heading, "Primary
elections."
Proclaiming polls open,
§17-7-11.
Proximity of persons to
polling place, §17-7-18.
Standing in line of voters
after having voted,
§17-7-19.
Watchers. See within this
heading, "Election
officials."
Poll tax.
Amount, Const. Ala., art.
VIII, §194.
Collection.
Returns of collections to be
separate from other
collections, Const. Ala.,
art. VIII, §194.
Deaf persons.
Exemptions from tax,
Const. Ala., amd. 109.
Delinquency, Const. Ala., art.
VIII, §194.
Education.
Use to support public
schools, Const. Ala.,
art. XIV, §259.
Exemptions.
Blind and deaf persons,
Const. Ala., amd. 109.
Veterans, Const. Ala.,
amds. 7, 10, 14, 49, 90.

ELECTIONS—Cont'd
Poll tax—Cont'd
Failure to pay poll or other tax.
Denial or abridgement of right to vote by reason of failure to vote prohibited, Const. U. S., Amendment XXIV.
Influencing votes.
Advance of money for payment in order to influence vote, Const. Ala., art. VIII, §195.
Maximum age for payment, Const. Ala., art. VIII, §194.
Payment of tax of another, Const. Ala., art. VIII, §195.
Requirements, Const. Ala., art. VIII, §178; amds. 96, 207.
Veterans.
Exemptions, Const. Ala., amds. 7, 10, 14, 49, 90.
When due and payable, Const. Ala., art. VIII, §194.
Poll watchers. See within this heading, "Election officials."
Precincts.
Ballot boxes.
Installation of voting boxes or machines, §17-5A-5.
Boundaries, §17-5A-3.
Changing, §17-5A-7.
Census bureau.
Defined, §17-5A-2.
Task force serving as liaison with, §17-5A-8.
Changing.
Procedure, §17-5A-7.
Definitions, §17-5A-2.
Elector must vote in precinct of residence, §17-7-13.
Electronic voting systems.
Definition of electronic vote counting statutes, §17-5A-2.
Establishment, §17-5A-3.
Legislative intent, §17-5A-1.
List of voters for each voting place, §17-5A-6.
Map, §17-5A-3.
Municipal elections.
Inapplicability of provisions to municipal elections, §17-5A-10.
Polling places.
Designation of voting places, §17-5A-5.
List of voters for each voting place, §17-5A-6.
Notice of location, etc., of voting places, §17-5A-5.
Purpose of provisions, §17-5A-1.
Qualifications of voters.
Liners between counties or precincts, §17-3-13.
Residence in two or more counties or precincts, §17-3-12.
Registration. See within this heading, "Registration."
Requirements of precincts, §17-5A-3.

ELECTIONS—Cont'd
Precincts—Cont'd
Task force.
Defined, §17-5A-2.
Establishment of precincts.
Coordination with task force to establish, §17-5A-3.
Misdemeanor for failure to cooperate with, §17-5A-9.
Service as liaison with census bureau, §17-5A-8.
State and local officials to cooperate with task force, §17-5A-9.
Voting districts.
Boundaries to be filed, §17-5A-4.
Division of precincts into, §17-5A-4.
Name, §17-5A-4.
Voting only in appropriate district, §17-5A-5.
Voting machines.
Installation of voting boxes or machines, §17-5A-5.
Voting places.
Designation, §17-5A-5.
Preservation of order.
Duty of sheriff to preserve, §17-1-2.
Presidential and vice-presidential elections.
Ballots.
Electors to vote by ballot, Const. U. S., Amendment XII.
Names of candidates for president and vice-president on ballots, §17-19-3.
Candidates.
Ballots.
Names on ballots, §17-19-3.
Certification of names of candidates, §17-19-2.
Nominating petitions, §17-19-2.
Vote for candidate counted as vote for designated electors, §17-19-3.
Electors.
Appointment, Const. U. S., Art. II, §1.
Congress may appoint time of choosing electors, Const. U. S., Art. II, §1.
Ballot.
Vote to be by ballot, Const. U. S., Amendment XII.
Compensation, §17-19-8.
Electoral meetings, §17-19-7.
Execution of statement by electors, §17-19-2.
General elections.
Offices for which general election held, §17-2-2.
Majority vote is necessary to elect president or vice-president, Const. U. S., Amendment XII.
Meetings, §17-19-7.
Names of electors, §17-19-2.

ELECTIONS—Cont'd
Presidential and vice-presidential elections—Cont'd
Electors—Cont'd
Number, §17-19-1.
State and county officers elected by the people, §17-2-1.
Vacancies.
Filling, §17-19-7.
Vote.
How given and transmitted, Const. U. S., Amendment XII.
Vote for candidate counted as vote for designated electors, §17-19-3.
When presidential electors elected, §17-2-10.
Governor.
Notice of election, §17-19-5.
Returns.
Governor to estimate returns, §17-19-5.
Tie votes.
Governor to decide, §17-19-6.
Notice.
Governor to give notice of election, §17-19-5.
Petitions.
Nominating petitions, §17-19-2.
Political parties.
Emblems.
Names of candidates to appear on ballot under emblem of respective party, §17-19-3.
Nominating petitions, §17-19-2.
Poll tax.
Payment not required, Const. U. S., Amendment XXIV.
Presidential preference primary.
General provisions, §§17-16A-2 to 17-16A-5.
Primary elections. See within this heading, "Primary elections."
Returns.
Governor to estimate returns, §17-19-5.
Making returns to secretary of state, §17-19-4.
Proclamation by governor, §17-19-5.
Secretary of state.
Returns.
Making returns to secretary of state, §17-19-4.
Tie votes.
Governor to decide, §17-19-6.
Vacancies.
Filling of presidential elector vacancies, §17-19-7.
Presumptions.
Primary elections.
Presumption of acceptance of chapter, §17-16-5.

ELECTIONS—Cont'd
Primary elections.
Acceptance of chapter.
Presumption of acceptance,
§17-16-5.
Affidavits.
Challenge of voters not on
official list, §17-16-23.
Alcoholic beverages.
Intoxication at polling
place, §17-16-47.
Appeals.
Primary elections.
Contest of nomination to
county office.
Appeals from decision
of county
executive
committee,
§17-16-82.
Applicability of chapter,
§17-16-4.
Election by political party
whether to come under
provisions of chapter,
§17-16-5.
Applicability of title, §17-1-1.
Assistance to voters.
Elector receiving
unauthorized
assistance, §17-16-29.
Illiterate or disabled
voters, §17-16-27.
Poll watchers not to assist,
§17-16-26.
Unauthorized assistance to
voter in preparation of
ballot, §17-16-28.
Ballot boxes.
Canvass of vote.
Disposition of box after
canvass, §17-16-33.
County governing body to
furnish, §17-16-19.
Marking, §17-16-19.
Returning officers.
Duties as to, §17-16-30.
When ballot box may be
opened by chairman of
county executive
committee, §17-16-33.
Ballots.
Assistance to voters.
Unauthorized assistance
to voter in
preparation of ballot,
§17-16-28.
Candidates.
Failure to place name on
ballot, §17-16-53.
Only qualified
candidates to be
listed on ballots,
§17-16-12.
Order of listing on
ballots, §17-16-20.
Challenged ballots.
Marking, §17-16-24.
Change, mutilation, etc.
Effect, §17-16-18.
Falsely or fraudulently
changing ballots,
§17-16-48.
Colors.
Different color for each
political party,
§17-16-18.
Counting ballots.
Procedure, §17-16-32.

ELECTIONS—Cont'd
Primary elections—Cont'd
Ballots—Cont'd
Failure to place candidate's
name on ballot,
§17-16-53.
Falsely or fraudulently
changing ballots,
§17-16-48.
Furnishing, §17-16-18.
Inspectors.
Marking ballots,
§17-16-55.
Procedure for handling
ballots, §17-16-25.
Mutilation.
Effect, §17-16-18.
Order of listing of
candidates on ballots,
§17-16-20.
Poll list.
Comparing with ballot,
§17-16-49.
Preparation, §17-16-11.
Presidential preference
primary.
Appearance on first or
top position on
ballot, §17-16-7.
Printing, §17-16-18.
Probate judges.
Preparation of ballot by
judge, §17-16-11.
Secrecy.
Keeping ballots secret
and inviolate,
§17-16-25.
Unopposed candidates.
Not listed on ballots,
§17-16-11.
Candidates.
Assessments for
candidates, §17-16-15.
Certification of names of
candidates, §17-16-11.
Certification of nominees
after second primary,
§17-16-40.
Death, resignation or
revocation.
Filling of vacancies in
nominations,
§17-16-41.
Declarations of candidacy.
Filing, §17-16-11.
State executive
committees,
§17-16-9.
Election officers.
Candidates to present
names of election
officers, §17-16-17.
Fees.
Assessment of
unauthorized fees
against candidates,
§17-16-16.
Majority vote.
Candidate receiving
majority vote
nominee of party,
§17-16-36.
Determination,
§17-16-38.
Numbering of places when
candidates for two or
more state offices of
same classification to
be nominated,
§17-16-21.

ELECTIONS—Cont'd
Primary elections—Cont'd
Candidates—Cont'd
Second primary to be held
if no candidate
receives majority vote,
§17-16-36.
Two or more state offices of
same classification.
Numbering of places,
§17-16-21.
Unopposed candidates.
Not listed on ballots,
§17-16-11.
Vacancies in nominations.
Filling of vacancies by
state executive
committee,
§17-16-41.
Canvass of vote.
County executive
committees, §17-16-35.
Disposition of ballot box
after canvass,
§17-16-33.
Disposition of returns,
certificates and lists of
voters after canvass,
§17-16-19.
Second primary, §17-16-36.
Challenge of voters.
Affidavit by voter,
§17-16-23.
Disposition, §17-16-24.
Certificate from probate
judge entitles voter to
vote without challenge,
§17-16-23.
Disposition of affidavits of
challenged voters,
§17-16-24.
Inspectors.
Duty when voter's name
not on official list,
§17-16-23.
Marking of challenged
ballots, §17-16-24.
Chief of police.
Additional duties,
§17-16-56.
Contests.
Ballot box, §17-16-33.
Bribery.
Grounds for contest,
§17-16-71.
Commencement.
Manner.
County office
nominations,
§17-16-80.
Nomination to office
other than county
office, §17-16-83.
Time.
County office
nominations,
§17-16-80.
Contempt, §17-16-84.
Costs, §17-16-84.
County office nominations.
Appeals.
Decisions of county
executive
committee,
§17-16-82.
Commencement.
Time and manner,
§17-16-80.

ELECTIONS—Cont'd
  Primary elections—Cont'd
    Contests—Cont'd
      County office nominations
        —Cont'd
        County executive
          committee.
          Appeals from
            decisions,
            §17-16-82.
          Duty of chairman,
            §17-16-81.
      Declaration of result,
        §17-16-86.
      Depositions, §17-16-84.
      Documents.
        Production, §17-16-74.
      Effect.
        Certification of
          candidate, §17-16-73.
        Declared nomination,
          §17-16-72.
      Fraud.
        Grounds for contest,
          §17-16-71.
      Grounds, §17-16-71.
      Hearing, §17-16-70.
      Illegality.
        Contestant to notify
          contestee of votes
          sought to be proved
          illegal, §17-16-79.
        Grounds for contest,
          §17-16-71.
      Mistake.
        Grounds for contest,
          §17-16-71.
      New primary in case
        contest cannot be
        decided, §17-16-87.
      Notice.
        Contestant to notify
          contestee of votes
          sought to be proved
          illegal, §17-16-79.
      Registration lists.
        Furnishing, §17-16-77.
      Result.
        Declaration, §17-16-86.
      Service of process,
        §17-16-84.
      State executive committee.
        Meeting, §17-16-85.
        Power to provide rules of
          party procedure,
          §17-16-88.
      Statement by elector
        contesting, §17-16-78.
      Statement of contest.
        Filing, §17-16-84.
      Subpoenas, §17-16-84.
      Time for contesting,
        §17-16-70.
      Witnesses.
        Fees, §17-16-76.
        Mileage allowances,
          §17-16-76.
        Oath, §17-16-76.
        Summoning, §17-16-74.
          Deposits by persons
            summoning,
            §17-16-76.
        Testimony.
          Commissioners to take,
            §17-16-89.
          Testifying as to vote,
            §17-16-75.
    Conventions. See within this
      heading, "Conventions."

ELECTIONS—Cont'd
  Primary elections—Cont'd
    Counting of votes at close of
      election at each polling
      place, §17-16-31.
    County executive
      committees.
      Ballot boxes.
        When boxes may be
          opened by chairman,
          §17-16-33.
        Canvass, tabulation and
          declaration of results
          by committee,
          §17-16-35.
      Chairman.
        Certification and return
          of results to
          chairman, §17-16-35.
        Comparing poll list with
          ballot, §17-16-49.
      Sealed records.
        Delivery to chairman,
          §17-16-25.
      Second primary, §17-16-36.
    Definitions, §17-16-1.
    Electioneering, §17-16-55.
    Election officers.
      Compensation, §17-16-10.
      Failure to appear at
        polling place,
        §17-16-17.
      Failure to serve, §17-16-54.
      Poll lists.
        Comparing poll list with
          ballot, §17-16-49.
      Poll watchers.
        Watchers not to be
          officers, §17-16-26.
      Selection and appointment,
        §17-16-17.
    Expenses, §17-16-10.
    Fees.
      Candidates.
        Assessment of
          unauthorized fees
          against candidates,
          §17-16-16.
    Fraud.
      Ballots.
        Fraudulently changing,
          §17-16-48.
      Returns, §17-16-48.
    General election laws.
      Applicability to primary
        elections, §17-16-4.
    Hearings.
      Contests, §17-16-70.
    Inspectors.
      Ballots.
        Marking ballots,
          §17-16-55.
        Procedure for handling,
          §17-16-25.
      Challenge of voters not on
        official list.
        Duty of inspector,
          §17-16-23.
      Counting of votes,
        §17-16-31.
      Divulging how elector
        voted, §17-16-55.
      Electioneering, §17-16-55.
    Legislature.
      Duty of legislature to pass
        laws regulating, Const.
        Ala., art. VIII, §190.
    Majority vote.
      Candidate receiving
        majority vote nominee
        of party, §17-16-36.

ELECTIONS—Cont'd
  Primary elections—Cont'd
    Majority vote—Cont'd
      Determination of majority
        of votes cast,
        §17-16-38.
      Second primary.
        Holding of second
          primary if no
          candidate receives
          majority vote,
          §17-16-36.
    Municipal corporations.
      Abolished in certain
        municipalities,
        §11-46-3.
    Nominee of party.
      Candidate receiving
        majority vote,
        §17-16-36.
    Notice.
      Governing body of political
        party to give notice of
        desire to enter
        primary, §17-16-13.
      Presidential preference
        primary, §17-16-7.
      Notice to candidate of
        qualification,
        §17-16A-5.
    Optional, §17-16-5.
    Penalties.
      Violations of chapter,
        §17-16-57.
    Place for holding, §17-16-6.
    Second primary, §17-16-6.
    Political parties.
      Candidate receiving
        majority vote nominee
        of party, §17-16-36.
      Conventions. See within
        this heading,
        "Conventions."
      Defined, §17-16-2.
      Election by party whether
        to come under
        provisions of chapter,
        §17-16-5.
      Failure to place candidate's
        name on ballot,
        §17-16-53.
      Filing resolution with
        secretary of state,
        §17-16A-6.
      Indication of party
        preference on poll lists,
        §17-16-14.
      Mass meetings. See within
        this heading, "Political
        parties."
      National conventions.
        Selection of delegates,
          §17-16-7.
      Notice by governing body
        of political party of
        desire to enter
        primary, §17-16-13.
      Obligation to hold primary
        election, §17-16-4.
      Pledge of party support.
        Voters to sign on poll
          lists, §17-16-14.
      Selection of delegates to
        national conventions,
        §17-16-7.
      State party chairman.
        Certification of
          candidates to
          secretary of state,
          §17-16-11.

ELECTIONS—Cont'd
Primary elections—Cont'd
Political parties—Cont'd
State party chairman
—Cont'd
Declaration of candidacy.
Filing with chairman,
§17-16-11.
Total vote.
Determination, §17-16-3.
Polling places.
Certificate of results.
Posting, §17-16-32.
Close of polling place.
Votes to be counted at
close, §17-16-31.
Intoxication at polling
place, §17-16-47.
Removing copy of returns
posted at polling place,
§17-16-52.
Watchers allowed at
polling place,
§17-16-26.
Poll lists.
Comparing poll list with
ballot, §17-16-49.
Disposition after canvass of
votes, §17-16-19.
Indication of party
preference, §17-16-14.
Opening, §17-16-50.
Pledge of party support.
Voters to sign on poll
lists, §17-16-14.
Voter's name not on
official list.
Challenge of voters not
on list.
Duty of inspectors,
§17-16-23.
Poll watchers.
Appointment by
candidates, §17-16-26.
Assistance to voters
prohibited, §17-16-26.
Comparing poll list with
ballot, §17-16-49.
Impersonating a poll
watcher, §17-16-26.
Not to act as election
officer, §17-16-26.
Polling places.
Watchers allowed at
polling place,
§17-16-26.
Returning officer not to be
poll watcher,
§17-16-26.
Violations, §17-16-26.
Presidential preference
primary.
Applicability of section
17-7-1 and chapter 16,
§17-16A-2.
Ballots.
Appearance in first or
top position,
§17-16-7.
Delegates.
Slate of proposed
delegates to be filed
with petition,
§17-16A-3.
Fees.
Filing fee for petition,
§17-16A-4.
Notice of primary,
§17-16-7.

ELECTIONS—Cont'd
Primary elections—Cont'd
Presidential preference
primary—Cont'd
Notice to candidate of
qualification,
§17-16A-5.
Petitions.
Fee.
Filing fee, §17-16A-4.
Filing, §17-16A-3.
Fee, §17-16A-4.
Form, §17-16A-3.
Number of signatures
required, §17-16A-3.
Proposed delegates.
Filing slate with
petition,
§17-16A-3.
Regulatory.
Decision of secretary of
state final,
§17-16A-3.
Qualification of candidate.
Notice, §17-16A-5.
Withdrawal by candidate,
§17-16A-5.
Presumption of acceptance of
chapter, §17-16-5.
Probate judges.
Ballots.
Preparation by judge,
§17-16-12.
Candidates.
Certification of
candidates to
probate judge,
§17-16-11.
Challenge of voters.
Certificate from probate
judge entitles voter
to vote without
challenge, §17-16-23.
Nominees.
Certification by secretary
of state to probate
judge after second
primary, §17-16-40.
Supplies.
Duty to furnish,
§17-16-22.
Qualifications of voters,
Const. Ala., art. VIII,
§183.
Records.
Delivery of sealed records
to chairman of county
executive committee,
§17-16-25.
Restrictions on opening of
sealed records,
§17-16-25.
When sealed records to be
destroyed, §17-16-25.
Results.
Certificate of results.
Distribution, §17-16-34.
Posting at polling place,
§17-16-32.
County executive
committees.
Tabulation and
declaration of
results, §17-16-35.
Determination of majority
of votes cast,
§17-16-38.
Falsely or fraudulently
changing results,
§17-16-48.

ELECTIONS—Cont'd
Primary elections—Cont'd
Results—Cont'd
Public proclamation of
results, §17-16-34.
Returning results.
Procedure, §17-16-32.
Second primary.
Determining results,
§17-16-36.
Secretary of state to
receive, §17-16-35.
Second primary,
§17-16-36.
State executive committee.
Tabulation and
declaration of
results, §17-16-35.
Tie votes, §17-16-39.
Returning officers.
Comparing poll list with
ballot, §17-16-49.
Duties, §17-16-30.
Poll watchers.
Returning officer not to
be poll watcher,
§17-16-26.
Returns.
Duties as to, §17-16-30.
Sheriff to perform duty of
returning officer,
§17-16-30.
Returns.
Changing or altering,
§17-16-52.
Disposition, §17-16-19.
False or fraudulent
returns, §17-16-48.
Removing copy of returns
posted at polling place,
§17-16-52.
Second primary, §17-16-36.
Second primary.
Canvass of vote, §17-16-36.
Certification of nominees
after second primary,
§17-16-40.
County executive
committees, §17-16-36.
No candidate receiving
majority vote,
§17-16-36.
Persons eligible, §17-16-36.
Place for holding, §17-16-6.
Procedure for conducting,
§17-16-36.
Procedure when one
candidate declines to
enter, §17-16-37.
Refusal by one candidate
to enter.
Procedure, §17-16-37.
Results.
Determining results,
§17-16-36.
Secretary of state to
receive, §17-16-36.
Returns, §17-16-36.
State executive committee.
Refusal by one candidate
to enter second
primary.
Certification to
chairman of
committee,
§17-16-37.
Time, §17-16-6.

ELECTIONS—Cont'd
Primary elections—Cont'd
Secretary of state.
  Candidates.
    Certification of names of
      candidates to
      secretary of state,
      §17-16-11.
  Nominees.
    Certification to probate
      judge after second
      primary, §17-16-40.
  Results to be received by
    secretary, §§17-16-35,
    17-16-36.
Sheriff.
  Duties.
    Additional duties,
      §17-16-56.
    Preservation of order,
      §17-16-56.
    Returning officer,
      §17-16-30.
  Supplies.
    Duties as to, §17-16-22.
State executive committees.
  Authorized, §17-16-8.
  Canvass, tabulation and
    declaration of results
    by committee,
    §17-16-35.
  Chairman.
    Comparing poll list with
      ballot, §17-16-49.
  Declaration of candidacy,
    §17-16-9.
  Provision for election of
    members, §17-16-9.
  Second primary.
    Refusal by one candidate
      to enter second
      primary.
      Certification to
        chairman of
        committee,
        §17-16-37.
  Tie votes.
    Deciding tie vote by
      chairman, §17-16-39.
  Vacancies in nominations.
    Filling, §17-16-41.
  Vested with party powers
    when local committees
    not established,
    §17-16-8.
Stationery, §17-16-18.
Supplies, §17-16-18.
  Delivery, §17-16-22.
  Probate judge.
    Duty to furnish,
      §17-16-22.
  Sheriff.
    Duties as to, §17-16-22.
Tie votes, §17-16-39.
Time, §17-16-6.
  Presidential preference
    primaries, §17-16A-1.
  Second primary, §17-16-6.
Vacancies in nominations.
  Filling by state executive
    committee, §17-16-41.
Violations.
  Penalty for violation of
    chapter, §17-16-57.
Voters.
  Disabled voters.
    Assistance to disabled
      voters, §17-16-27.
  Divulging how elector
    voted, §17-16-55.

ELECTIONS—Cont'd
Primary elections—Cont'd
Voters—Cont'd
  Electioneering with voter,
    §17-16-55.
  Establishment of
    qualifications,
    §17-16-14.
  Illiterate voters.
    Assistance to illiterate
      voters, §17-16-27.
  Persons eligible to vote,
    §17-16-14.
  Pledge of party support in
    general election.
    Voters to sign pledge on
      poll list, §17-16-14.
  Qualifications of voters,
    Const. Ala., art. VIII,
    §183.
  Voting more than once,
    §17-16-51.
Voting machines.
  County governing body to
    furnish, §17-16-19.
  Use of machines in
    primary elections,
    §17-9-6.
Voting more than once,
  §17-16-51.
When held, §17-16-6.
  Presidential preference
    primaries, §17-16A-1.
Probate judges.
Absentee voting.
  Volunteering suggestions
    as to ballots for absent
    voters, §17-10-20.
Ballot boxes.
  Provided by whom,
    §17-8-14.
Candidates.
  Ineligibility for appointing
    board, §17-6-3.
Certificate of nomination.
  Preservation by probate
    judge, §17-7-2.
Contests. See within this
  heading, "Contests."
Election officials. See within
  this heading, "Election
  officials."
Emblems.
  Certification to probate
    judge, §17-8-7.
Failure to perform.
  Duties to devolve upon
    circuit court, §17-1-4.
  Misdemeanor, §17-1-5.
  Penalty, §17-1-5.
Fair campaign practices.
  Duties of probate judge,
    §17-22A-11.
General elections.
  Offices for which general
    election held, §17-2-2.
Instruction cards.
  Probate judge to have
    printed, §17-8-43.
Primary elections. See within
  this heading, "Primary
  elections."
Registration. See within this
  heading, "Registration."
Special elections.
  Sheriff must notify probate
    judge, §17-18-6.
State and county officers
  elected by the people,
  §17-2-1.

ELECTIONS—Cont'd
Probate judges—Cont'd
Voting machines. See within
  this heading, "Voting
  machines."
When judges to be elected,
  §17-2-7.
Public employees.
Participation in political
  activities, §17-1-7.
Public officers.
List of state and county
  officers elected by the
  people, §17-2-1.
Public service commission.
Candidates.
  Public utility corporations.
    Giving aid or
      contributions to
      candidates,
      §§10-2A-70.1,
      10-2A-70.2.
General elections.
  Offices for which general
    election held, §17-2-2.
  Time, §17-2-3.
State officers elected by the
  people, §17-2-1.
Two or more members at
  same election.
  Designating by number,
    §17-7-20.
Public works.
Improvement authorities.
  See PUBLIC WORKS.
Purging of registration lists.
See within this heading,
  "Registration."
**Qualifications for
  registration.** See within
  this heading,
  "Registration."
Qualifications of voters. See
  within this heading,
  "Voters."
Quo warranto.
Validity of election not
  triable, §6-6-598.
Recess.
No recess after polls opened,
  §17-7-7.
Referendum.
Alcoholic beverages.
  Elections as to sale and
    distribution.
    See ALCOHOLIC
      BEVERAGES.
Voting machines.
  Referendum on adoption,
    §17-9-3.
Registers.
Absentee voting. See within
  this heading, "Absentee
  voting."
Registrars.
Allowances, §17-4-153.
Applications for registration.
  Electors previously
    registered in another
    county or state,
    §17-4-135.
  Examination of applicants,
    §17-4-122.
  Refusal of application for
    registration, §17-4-123.
    Appeals from denial,
      §17-4-124.
    Registrars not to be
      made parties in
      appeal, §17-4-124.
Appointment, §17-4-150.

ELECTIONS—Cont'd
Registrars—Cont'd
Board of registrars génerally,
§17-4-150.
Chairman, §17-4-150.
Clerical assistants and help,
§17-4-138.
Compensation, §17-4-159.
Expenditure of county
funds for, §17-4-159.
Compensation, §§17-4-153,
17-4-188.
Deputy registrars,
§§17-4-158, 17-4-189.
Equipment.
County commission to
furnish, §17-4-190.
Examination of applicants for
registration, §17-4-122.
Electors previously
registered in another
county or state,
§17-4-135.
Expenses, §17-4-153.
Forms.
Preparation and
furnishing, §17-4-126.
Secretary of state to
furnish to boards,
§17-4-137.
Judicial officers.
Designated as judicial
officers, §17-4-154.
List of names registered by
precincts, districts, etc.
County board to furnish to
judges of probate by
February 1, 1903,
Const. Ala., art. VIII,
§187.
Purging of registration
lists. See within this
heading,
"Registration."
Majority of board to pass
upon person's
qualifications, §17-4-136.
Notice.
Preparation and furnishing
of notices, §17-4-126.
Number of members of
board, §17-4-150.
Oaths.
Oath of office, §17-4-154.
Office space, §17-4-138.
Expenditure of county
funds for, §17-4-159.
Purging of registration lists.
See within this heading,
"Registration."
Qualifications, §17-4-150.
Quorum, §17-4-155.
Removal from office,
§17-4-151.
Rules and regulations,
§17-4-136.
Sessions.
Time and place of meeting
in counties with two or
more courthouses,
§17-4-157.
Statewide registration.
Duties as to, §17-4-214.
Supplies.
Expenditure of county
funds for, §17-4-159.
Purging of registration
lists.
County commission to
furnish supplies,
§17-4-190.

ELECTIONS—Cont'd
Registrars—Cont'd
Supplies—Cont'd
Secretary of state to
furnish to boards,
§17-4-137.
Terms of office, §17-4-151.
Universities and colleges.
Duty to visit for purpose of
registering voters,
§17-4-160.
Registration of electors
attending, §17-4-134.
Unlawful registration,
§17-4-139.
Vacancies.
Filling vacancies,
§§17-4-152, 17-4-188.
Working days, §17-4-156.
Special registration
sessions, §17-4-156.
Registration, Const. Ala.,
amd. 223.
Absentee voters.
After January 1, 1903,
Const. Ala., amd. 55.
Application, §17-4-134.
Electors attending
institutions of higher
learning, §17-4-134.
Mail.
Certain persons entitled
to register by mail,
§17-4-134.
Electors temporarily out
of county may
register, §17-4-134.
Place of registration,
§17-4-134."
Students.
Electors attending
institutions of higher
learning.
Registration by mail,
§17-4-134.
Accessibility of places of
registration to the
handicapped, §§21-4-20
to 21-4-24.
Appeals.
Purging of registration
lists, §17-4-132.
Refusal of registration,
§17-4-124.
Applications, §17-4-122.
Absentee electors,
§17-4-134.
Electors previously
registered in another
county or state,
§17-4-135.
Examination of applicants,
§17-4-122.
Oath of applicants,
§17-4-122.
Refusal of application for
registration, §17-4-123.
Appeal from refusal of
registration,
§17-4-124.
Boards of registrars. See
within this heading,
"Registrars."
Certificate of registration.
Change of residence.
Certificate to be
furnished elector
when place of
residence changed,
Const. Ala., art.
VIII, §187.

ELECTIONS—Cont'd
Registration—Cont'd
Certificate of registration
—Cont'd
Issuance, §17-4-121.
When not required,
§17-7-14.
Clerical assistants.
Probate judge may employ
assistants and clerical
help, §17-4-138.
Convictions.
Purging of registration
lists.
Registrars to receive
information of
convictions,
§17-4-131.
Counties.
Courthouses.
Time and place of
registration in
counties with two or
more courthouses,
§17-4-157.
Detached territories.
Lists of qualified voters.
Changing list when
territory detached
from one county
and added to
another,
§17-4-128.
Electors previously
registered in another
county or state,
§17-4-135.
Lists of qualified voters.
Changing list when
territory detached
from one county and
added to another,
§17-4-128.
Courthouses.
Time and place of
registration in counties
with two or more
courthouses, §17-4-157.
Criminal law and procedure.
Purging of registration
lists.
Registrars to receive
information of
convictions,
§17-4-131.
Deadline, §17-4-120.
Death.
Purging of registration
lists.
Registrars to receive
information of
deaths, §17-4-131.
Department of finance.
Forms and notices.
Preparation and
furnishing,
§17-4-126.
Detached territories.
Lists of qualified voters.
Changing list when
territory detached
from one county and
added to another,
§17-4-128.
Disqualification from
registration and voting,
§17-3-10; Const. Ala.,
art. VIII, §182.

ELECTIONS—Cont'd
Registration—Cont'd
Examination of applicants,
§17-4-122.
Electors previously
registered in another
county or state,
§17-4-135.
Forms.
Preparation and
furnishing, §17-4-126.
Secretary of state to
furnish to registrars,
§17-4-137.
Handicapped persons.
Accessibility of places of
registration, §§17-4-20
to 17-4-24.
Information to be furnished
prior to registration,
Const. Ala., art. VIII,
§188.
Inspectors.
Alphabetical lists of
electors registered by
precincts, districts or
other subdivisions.
Delivery of list by
probate judge,
§17-4-130.
Legislature to provide for
registration procedure
after January 1, 1903,
Const. Ala., art. VIII,
§186.
List of qualified voters,
Const. Ala., art. VIII,
§187.
Alphabetical lists of
electors registered by
precincts, districts or
other subdivisions.
Additions to list,
§17-4-129.
Copies.
Delivery to inspectors,
§17-4-130.
Delivery to inspectors in
each precinct, ward,
etc., §17-4-130.
Preparation by probate
judge, §17-4-129.
Publication, §17-4-129.
Board of registrars.
Maintenance of
permanent list of
electors, §17-4-187.
Changing list when
territory detached from
one county and added
to another, §17-4-128.
Contests.
Either party may have
copy of registration
list, §17-15-4.
Counties.
Changing list when
territory detached
from one county and
added to another,
§17-4-128.
County board of registrars.
Per diem for meetings,
§17-4-188.
Entering names upon
registration list
without registration,
§17-4-139.
Filing of lists in office of
probate judge,
§17-14-23.

ELECTIONS—Cont'd
Registration—Cont'd
List of qualified voters
—Cont'd
Inspections.
List open to inspection,
§17-14-23.
Previous registration in
another county or
state.
Notice to be given,
§17-4-135.
Purging of registration
lists.
Appeals, §17-4-132.
Appointment of deputy
registrar, §17-4-189.
Board of registrars to
meet in August to
purge lists,
§17-4-181.
Convictions.
Registrars to receive
information of
convictions,
§17-4-131.
County board of
registrars,
§17-4-180.
Appointments to fill
vacancies,
§17-4-188.
Death.
Registrars to receive
information of
deaths, §17-4-131.
Failure to perform,
§17-4-132.
Incompetency.
Registrars to receive
information of
incompetency,
§17-4-131.
Information of death,
incompetency and
convictions.
Registrars to receive,
§17-4-131.
Legislature.
Duty to pass laws
regulating, Const.
Ala., art. VIII,
§190; amd.
41.
Penalties for making
false statements to
board, §17-4-191.
Previous registration in
another county or
state, §17-4-135.
Publication of names to
be struck,
§17-4-183.
Reason for striking name
to be recorded,
§17-4-133.
Reidentification of
electors.
Electors to reidentify
themselves,
§17-4-182.
Failure to reidentify
not permanent
disqualification,
§17-4-185.
Notice of
reidentification,
§17-4-182.
Required, §17-4-180.

ELECTIONS—Cont'd
Registration—Cont'd
List of qualified voters
—Cont'd
Purging of registration
lists—Cont'd
Restoration of name to
list.
Procedure, §17-4-186.
Statewide registration.
Completion of purge as
prerequisite,
§17-4-210.
Time for purging,
§17-4-132.
Transfer of names to
precinct to which
elector has moved,
§17-4-132.
When purging to occur,
§17-4-181.
Who to be purged,
§17-4-184.
Reidentification of electors.
Only electors not
reidentified to be
removed, §17-4-184.
Unlawful to vote in
precinct, etc., where
elector's name not on
official list, §17-4-127.
Mail.
Absentee registration.
Persons entitled to
register by mail,
Const. Ala., amds.
285, 322.
Mentally ill.
Purging of registration
lists.
Registrars to receive
information of
incompetency,
§17-4-131.
Municipal elections.
Registering or attempting
to register a second
time, §17-23-2.
Notice.
Preparation and furnishing
of notices, §17-4-126.
Refusal of registration.
Required notice,
§17-4-123.
Oath of applicants,
§17-4-122.
Pardons.
Reregistration when
pardoned from
conviction, §17-4-125.
Perjury.
Persons registered under
1901 constitution not
required to reregister,
Const. Ala., amd. 91.
Places of registration.
Accessibility to
handicapped and
elderly persons,
§§17-4-20 to 17-4-24.
Counties with two or more
courthouses, §17-4-157.
Political parties.
Voter registration
information.
Permitted to obtain,
§17-4-122.

ELECTIONS—Cont'd
　Registration—Cont'd
　　Probate judges.
　　　Alphabetical lists of
　　　　electors registered by
　　　　precincts, districts or
　　　　other subdivisions.
　　　　Delivery of lists to
　　　　　inspectors,
　　　　　§17-4-130.
　　　　Preparation of lists,
　　　　　§17-4-129.
　　　Clerical assistants and
　　　　help, §17-4-138.
　　　Mentally ill.
　　　　Judges to furnish
　　　　　registrars lists of
　　　　　residents declared
　　　　　incompetent,
　　　　　§17-4-131.
　　Procedure for registration
　　　prior to January 1, 1903,
　　　Const. Ala., art. VIII,
　　　§186.
　　Qualifications for
　　　registration, Const. Ala.,
　　　art. VIII, §§180, 181;
　　　amds. 91, 96, 223.
　　Refusal of registration.
　　　Appeals, §17-4-124.
　　　Authorized, §17-4-123.
　　　Notice required, §17-4-123.
　　Registrars.
　　　Applications for
　　　　registration.
　　　　Rules and regulations by
　　　　　registrars, §17-4-136.
　　　Deputies.
　　　　Appointment, §17-4-189.
　　　General provisions. See
　　　　within this heading,
　　　　"Registrars."
　　Removal of disability.
　　　Reregistration required
　　　　when disability
　　　　removed, §17-4-125.
　　Required only once,
　　　§17-4-125.
　　　Exceptions, §17-4-125.
　　Requirements, Const. Ala.,
　　　art. VIII, §178.
　　Reregistration.
　　　Persons registered under
　　　　1901 constitution not
　　　　required to reregister,
　　　　Const. Ala., amd. 91.
　　　When required, §17-4-125.
　　Residence.
　　　Certain information to be
　　　　furnished prior to
　　　　registration, Const.
　　　　Ala., art. VIII, §188.
　　　Change of residence.
　　　　Certificate of registration
　　　　　to be furnished when
　　　　　place of residence
　　　　　changed, Const. Ala.,
　　　　　art. VIII, §187.
　　　　Transfer of names to
　　　　　precinct to which
　　　　　elector has moved,
　　　　　§17-4-132.
　　　Lists of qualified voters.
　　　　Changing list when
　　　　　territory detached
　　　　　from one county and
　　　　　added to another,
　　　　　§17-4-128.

ELECTIONS—Cont'd
　Registration—Cont'd
　　Residence—Cont'd
　　　Lists of qualified voters
　　　　—Cont'd
　　　　Transfer of names to
　　　　　precinct to which
　　　　　elector has moved,
　　　　　§17-4-132.
　　　Notice of previous
　　　　registration in another
　　　　county or state,
　　　　§17-4-135.
　　　Reregistration required
　　　　when county of
　　　　residence changed,
　　　　§17-4-125.
　　Restoration of right to vote.
　　　Pardon, §17-3-10.
　　Special registration sessions,
　　　§17-4-156.
　　Statewide registration,
　　　§§17-4-210 to 17-4-215.
　　　Boards of registrars.
　　　　Duties as to statewide
　　　　　file, §17-4-214.
　　　Director of voter
　　　　registration.
　　　　Appointment, §17-4-211.
　　　　Compensation,
　　　　　§17-4-211.
　　　　Duties, §17-4-211.
　　　　Information provided to
　　　　　director, §17-4-212.
　　　　Removal from office,
　　　　　§17-4-211.
　　　File.
　　　　Boards of registrars.
　　　　　Duties, §17-4-214.
　　　　Contents, §17-4-210.
　　　　Inactive list, §17-4-213.
　　　　Procedure for voter
　　　　　reidentification,
　　　　　§17-4-215.
　　　　Procedure for registration,
　　　　　§17-4-215.
　　　　Purge of local list.
　　　　　Completion as
　　　　　　prerequisite,
　　　　　　§17-4-210.
　　　　Purging of statewide file.
　　　　　Procedure, §17-4-215.
　　　　Striking voters from list.
　　　　　Grounds, §17-4-213.
　　　　　Procedure, §17-4-213.
　　　　Vital statistics.
　　　　　Information provided to
　　　　　　director, §17-4-212.
　　　Voter registration advisory
　　　　board.
　　　　Composition, §17-4-210.
　　　　Created, §17-4-210.
　　　　Duties, §17-4-210.
　　Students.
　　　Duty of registrars to visit
　　　　universities and
　　　　colleges for purpose of
　　　　registering voters,
　　　　§17-4-160.
　　　Registration by mail when
　　　　absent at institution of
　　　　higher learning,
　　　　§17-4-134.
　　Supplies.
　　　Expenditure of county
　　　　funds for, §17-4-159.
　　　Secretary of state to
　　　　furnish to registrars,
　　　　§17-4-137.

ELECTIONS—Cont'd
　Registration—Cont'd
　　Term for which registration
　　　valid, Const. Ala., art.
　　　VIII, §187.
　　Time for registration.
　　　Counties with two or more
　　　　courthouses, §17-4-157.
　　　No person to be registered
　　　　within ten days before
　　　　election, §17-4-120.
　　Universities and colleges.
　　　Duty of registrars to visit
　　　　for purpose of
　　　　registering voters,
　　　　§17-4-160.
　　　Registration by mail when
　　　　absent at institution of
　　　　higher learning,
　　　　§17-4-134.
　　Unlawful registration,
　　　§17-4-139.
　　Voter registration
　　　information.
　　　Political parties may
　　　　obtain, §17-4-122.
　　Voting without registration,
　　　§17-7-12.
　Rejection of legal votes.
　　Annulment of election.
　　　When election not
　　　　annulled, §17-15-2.
　Reports.
　　Fair campaign practices.
　　　Contributions and
　　　　expenditures,
　　　　§§17-22A-8 to
　　　　17-22A-10.
　Residency.
　　Absentee voting. See within
　　　this heading, "Absentee
　　　voting."
　　Elector must vote in county
　　　and precinct of residence,
　　　§17-7-13.
　　Qualifications of voters. See
　　　within this heading,
　　　"Voters."
　　Registration. See within this
　　　heading, "Registration."
　Results.
　　Amendments to constitution.
　　　See within this heading,
　　　"Constitution of
　　　Alabama."
　　Certificate of result.
　　　Blank forms, §17-8-44.
　　　Posting, §17-13-8.
　　　Primary elections. See
　　　　within this heading,
　　　　"Primary elections."
　　　Signature by inspector,
　　　　§17-13-10.
　　Posting certificate of result,
　　　§17-13-8.
　　Primary elections. See within
　　　this heading, "Primary
　　　elections."
　　Returns. See within this
　　　heading, "Returns."
　　State officers, §17-14-25.
　　Tie votes.
　　　Resolution, §17-14-25.
　　Voting machines.
　　　Seals.
　　　　Breaking seal to obtain
　　　　　result, §17-9-31.
　Returning officer. See within
　　this heading, "Sheriffs."

ELECTIONS—Cont'd
Returns.
Canvass of votes. See within this heading, "Canvassing votes."
Certificates of election. See within this heading, "Certificates of election."
Congressional elections.
Governor to estimate returns, §17-20-4.
Constitutional provisions, Const. Ala., art. V, §115.
Copies.
Delivery to probate judge, §17-13-11.
Failure to make returns.
Notice of failure, §17-14-27.
Penalty, §17-14-26.
How made, §17-13-10.
Inspectors.
Signature by inspectors, §17-13-10.
Municipal corporations.
See MUNICIPAL CORPORATIONS.
Opening of returns in presence of state officials, §17-14-20.
Presidential and vice-presidential elections.
See within this heading, "Presidential and vice-presidential elections."
Primary elections. See within this heading, "Primary elections."
Probate judge.
Duty, §17-13-10.
Sealing in envelope, §17-13-10.
Secretary of state.
Returns of elections for certain officials to be made to secretary of state, Const. Ala., art. VIII, §193.
Special elections, §17-18-7.
Right to vote.
Constitutional provisions, Const. U. S., Amendments XIV, XIX, XXVI.
Disqualification from registration and voting. See within this heading, "Disqualification from registration and voting."
Interfering with free exercise of right of suffrage, §17-23-3.
Restoration of right to vote.
Special, private or local laws prohibited, Const. Ala., art. IV, §104.
Riots.
Sheriffs.
Duty to preserve order at elections, §17-1-2.
Salaries.
Election officers, §17-6-13.
Registrars, §17-4-153.
School tax.
See EDUCATION.
Seals and sealed instruments.
Ballots. See within this heading, "Ballots."

ELECTIONS—Cont'd
Secretary of state.
Amendments to constitution.
Returns made to secretary of state, §17-17-2.
Canvass of election returns.
Opening in presence of secretary of state, §17-14-20.
Congressional elections.
Returns.
Board of supervisors to make returns to secretary of state, §17-20-3.
Constitutional provisions, Const. Ala., art. V, §§114, 115.
Contested elections, Const. Ala., art. V, §115.
State officers generally, §§17-15-50 to 17-15-63.
See within this heading, "Contests."
Contests. See within this heading, "Contests."
Fair campaign practices.
Duties of secretary, §17-22A-11.
Political committees.
Filing copy of federal report with secretary, §17-22A-15.
Forms.
Furnishing to registrars, §17-4-137.
General elections.
Certification of nomination.
Failure to certify, §17-7-1.
Offices for which general election held, §17-2-2.
Time of general election, §17-2-3.
Presidential and vice-presidential elections.
Returns.
Making returns to secretary of state, §17-19-4.
Primary elections. See within this heading, "Primary elections."
Registrars.
Furnishing forms and supplies to registrars, §17-4-137.
Returns.
Opening, Const. Ala., art. V, §115.
Publication, Const. Ala., art. V, §115.
Returns of elections for certain officials to be made to secretary of state, Const. Ala., art. VIII, §193.
Transmission to speaker of house, Const. Ala., art. V, §115.
State officers elected by the people, §17-2-1.
Supplies.
Furnishing to registrars, §17-4-137.
Tie votes, Const. Ala., art. V, §115.
Time, Const. Ala., art. V, §114.

ELECTIONS—Cont'd
Selling votes, §17-23-5.
Senate.
See CONGRESS.
Service of process.
Contests.
Notice of contest.
Failure of officer to serve notice, §17-15-5.
Sheriffs.
Arrest.
Electors attending, going to or returning from elections, §17-1-6.
Ballot boxes.
Providing, §17-8-14.
Ballots.
Keeping six months after election, §17-13-5.
Candidates.
Ineligibility for appointing board, §17-6-3.
Challenges.
Communicating challenge to inspectors, §17-12-1.
Election officials.
Appointing board.
When sheriff not eligible, §17-6-3.
Appointment of officials, §17-6-1.
Election of sheriff, Const. Ala., art. V, §138; amd. 35.
General elections.
Offices for which general election held, §17-2-2.
Time, §17-2-3.
State and county officers elected by the people, §17-2-1.
Failure to perform duty, §17-1-2.
Notice of election, §17-7-5.
Order at elections.
Duty of sheriff to preserve order, §17-1-2.
Primary elections. See within this heading, "Primary elections."
Returning officer.
Acting returning officer.
Appointment in absence of regular officer, §17-6-12.
Alcoholic beverages.
Consuming during election, §17-6-16.
Compensation, §17-6-13.
Counting votes, §17-13-2.
Municipal officer or employee acting as returning officer, §17-6-15.
Primary elections. See within this heading, "Primary elections."
Sheriff designated, §17-6-11.
Time and place of holding elections, §17-7-6.
Special elections. See within this heading, "Special elections."
Tie vote.
How tie vote decided, §17-1-3.

ELECTIONS—Cont'd

Soil and water conservation.
Districts.
Discontinuance of district, §9-8-31.
Incorporation of districts, §9-8-23.
Land-use regulations, §9-8-26.
Watershed conservancy districts.
Board of directors, §9-8-59.
Referendum upon creation, §§9-8-56 to 9-8-58.
See SOIL AND WATER CONSERVATION.

Solicitation.
Fair campaign practices.
Force, threats, etc., to solicit money, §17-22A-20.

Special elections.
Absentee voting. See within this heading, "Absentee voting."
Certificates, §17-18-7.
Clerk of circuit court.
Sheriff to notify clerk, §17-18-6.
Congress.
Special elections for representatives in congress.
Governor to give notice, §17-18-4.
Counties.
Sheriff to give notice of elections in his county, §17-18-5.
Day for holding special elections, §17-18-2.
Governor.
Special elections ordered by governor, §17-18-3.
Writs of election.
Issuance, §17-18-3.
How conducted, §17-18-7.
Improvement authorities, §§39-7-1 to 39-7-11.
See PUBLIC WORKS.
Notice.
Probate judges.
Sheriff to notify probate judge, §17-18-6.
Representatives in congress.
Governor to give notice, §17-18-4.
Sheriff to give notice of elections in his county, §17-18-5.
Offices.
For what offices held, §17-18-1.
Returns, §17-18-7.
Sheriff.
Notice.
Probate judge, §17-18-6.
Sheriff to give notice of elections in his county, §17-18-5.
Probate judges.
Sheriff to notify probate judge and clerk, §17-18-6.
Writs of election.
Issuance by governor, §17-18-3.
Voting machines.
Use of machines in special elections, §17-9-6.

ELECTIONS—Cont'd

Special elections—Cont'd
When held, §17-18-1.
State auditor.
Constitutional provisions, Const. Ala., art. V, §§114, 115.
Contested elections.
State officers generally, §§17-15-50 to 17-15-63. See within this heading, "Contests."
General elections.
Offices for which general election held, §17-2-2.
Time of general election, §17-2-3.
State officers elected by the people, §17-2-1.
State comptroller.
Amendments to constitution of Alabama.
Duty of comptroller to ascertain expenses and file same, §17-17-6.
State executive committees.
See within this heading, "Primary elections."
Statement of campaign expenditures. See within this heading, "Campaign expenditures."
State treasurer.
Constitutional provisions, Const. Ala., art. V, §§114, 115.
Contested elections.
State officers generally, §§17-15-50 to 17-15-63. See within this heading, "Contests."
General elections.
Offices for which general election held, §17-2-2.
Time of general election, §17-2-3.
State officers elected by the people, §17-2-1.
Statewide registration, §§17-4-210 to 17-4-215.
Stationery, §17-8-44.
Students.
Registration.
Duty of registrars to visit colleges and universities for purpose of registering voters, §17-4-160.
Registration by mail when absent at institution of higher learning, §17-4-134.
Suffrage.
Constitutional provisions, Const. U. S., Amendments XV, XIX.
Right to vote generally. See within this heading, "Right to vote."
Supplies.
Voting machines, §17-9-16.
Supreme court.
Chief justice. See within this heading, "Chief justice of the supreme court."
Contests. See within this heading, "Contests."

ELECTIONS—Cont'd

Supreme court—Cont'd
Justices, §12-2-1; Const. Ala., art. VI, §152.
Contested elections.
State officers generally, §§17-15-50 to 17-15-63. See within this heading, "Contests."
General elections.
Offices for which general election held, §17-2-2.
Justices elected by the people, §§12-2-1, 17-2-1.
Time of holding election, Const. Ala., art. VI, §156.
Two or more justices to be elected at same time.
Designation by number, §17-7-20.
When justices to be elected, §17-2-6.
Taxation.
Denial or abridgement of right to vote.
Failure to pay poll or other tax, Const. U. S., Amendment XXIV.
Education.
See EDUCATION.
Special taxes.
Ratification of certain municipal and county elections as to levy, §40-1-37.
Tax assessors.
General elections.
Offices for which general election held, §17-2-2.
Time, §17-2-3.
State and county officers elected by the people, §17-2-1.
Tax collectors.
General elections.
Offices for which general election held, §17-2-2.
Time, §17-2-3.
State and county officers elected by the people, §17-2-1.
Threats.
Fair campaign practices.
Solicitation of money by threats, §17-22A-20.
Tie votes.
Constitutional provisions, Const. Ala., art. V, §115.
How tie vote decided, §17-1-3; Const. Ala., art. V, §115.
Presidential and vice-presidential elections.
Governor to decide, §17-19-6.
Primary elections, §17-16-39.
Resolution, §17-14-25.
Time, §17-7-6.
Absentee voting.
Time for filing applications, §17-10-3.

ELECTIONS—Cont'd
Time—Cont'd
Candidates.
Declaration of intention to
become candidate.
When filing required,
§17-7-21.
Circuit court judges, §17-2-7.
Congressmen, §17-2-10.
Counties.
When county officers
elected, §17-2-4.
Counting votes.
When votes to be counted,
§17-13-1.
County boards of education.
When members to be
elected, §17-2-5.
District attorneys, §17-2-9.
General elections, §17-2-3.
Judges of circuit, district and
probate courts, §17-2-7.
Judges of courts of appeals,
§17-2-7.
Mass meetings.
Political parties, §17-16-43.
Polling places.
Hours of operation,
§17-7-5.1.
Length of time elector may
stay in polling place,
§17-8-29.
Presidential electors,
§17-2-10.
Primary elections, §17-16-6.
Probate judges, §17-2-7.
Registration. See within this
heading, "Registration."
Supreme court justices,
§17-2-6.
Universities and colleges.
Registrars.
Duty to visit for purpose of
registering voters,
§17-4-160.
Registration by mail when
absent at institution of
higher learning,
§17-4-134.
University of Alabama.
Board of trustees, §16-47-30.
Vital statistics.
Registration.
Statewide registration.
Information provided to
director of voter
registration,
§17-4-212.
Void elections.
Declaration vacates office,
§36-9-1.
Judgment declaring election
void.
Certification, §36-9-15.
Voters.
Absentee voters.
General provisions,
§§17-10-1 to 17-10-20.
See within this
heading, "Absentee
voting."
Registration. See within
this heading,
"Registration."
Age.
Persons eighteen years of
age, Const. U. S.,
Amendment XXVI.
Qualifications of voters,
Const. Ala., art. VIII,
§177.

ELECTIONS—Cont'd
Voters—Cont'd
Age—Cont'd
Right to vote not to be
abridged on account of
age, Const. U. S.,
Amendment XXVI.
Altering or changing vote of
elector, §17-23-7.
Arrest.
Voters attending, going to
or returning from
elections, §17-1-6.
Assistance to voters.
General provisions. See
within this heading,
"Assistance to voters."
Instruction cards. See
within this heading,
"Instruction cards."
Ballots.
Delivery of ballot to voter,
§17-8-27.
Number of ballots per
voter, §17-8-25.
Bribing or attempting to
influence voter, §17-23-3.
Challenging voters, §§17-12-1
to 17-12-8. See within
this heading,
"Challenges."
Constitutional provisions,
Const. U. S.,
Amendments XIV, XV,
XIX, XXVI.
Disqualification from
registration and voting.
See within this heading,
"Disqualification from
registration and voting."
Disturbing voter on election
day, §17-23-8.
Employers intimidating
employees, §17-23-10.
Identification of voters.
Authority to require
identification.
County commission
authorized, §17-11-1.
Costs, §17-11-2.
County commission.
Authority to require
identification,
§17-11-1.
Election officials.
Corrupt conduct,
§17-11-4.
Failure to perform duty.
Penalties, §17-11-4.
Supplying of marking
substances, §17-11-2.
When person deemed
official, §17-11-4.
Hands.
Marking and
examination of
voter's hand,
§§17-11-1 to 17-11-3.
Marking of voter's hands,
§17-11-1.
Invisible marking
substance, §17-11-1.
Person refusing to have
hand examined not
permitted to vote,
§17-11-3.
Procurement of marking
substances,
applicators and
inspection devices,
§17-11-2.

ELECTIONS—Cont'd
Voters—Cont'd
Identification of voters
—Cont'd
Marking of voter's hands
—Cont'd
Supplying of marking
substances to
election officials,
§17-11-2.
Influencing voters, §§17-8-41,
17-23-3.
Instruction cards, §§17-8-23,
17-8-43.
Interference with voters,
§17-8-41.
Duty of sheriff to preserve
order, §17-1-2.
Standing in line of voters
after having voted,
§17-7-19.
List of electors.
Registration. See within
this heading,
"Registration."
Primary elections. See within
this heading, "Primary
elections."
Qualifications of voters,
§17-3-9.
Disqualification from
registration and
voting.
Generally, Const. Ala.,
art. VIII, §§177, 178,
182; amds. 96, 223.
Persons eighteen years of
age, Const. U. S.,
Amendment XXVI.
Primary elections, Const.
Ala., art. VIII, §183.
Registration. See within
this heading,
"Registration."
Residence, Const. Ala., art.
VIII, §178; amd. 96.
Liners between counties,
districts or precincts,
§17-3-13.
Loss of residence,
§17-3-11.
Military service.
Residence not acquired
or lost by military
service, §17-3-11.
Selection of precinct or
residence when
located in two or
more counties,
districts or precincts,
§17-3-12.
Two or more counties or
precincts, §17-3-12.
Registration. See within this
heading, "Registration."
Voting.
Absentee voting, §§17-10-1 to
17-10-20. See within this
heading, "Absentee
voting."
Accepting payment for votes,
§17-22A-17.
Ballots. See within this
heading, "Ballots."
Blank votes for any officer on
ticket, §17-8-21.
Buying votes, §17-22A-17.
Disqualification from voting.
See within this heading,
"Disqualification from
registration and voting."

ELECTIONS—Cont'd
Voting—Cont'd
Hours of voting, §17-7-5.1.
Illegal voting. See within
  this heading, "Illegal
  voting."
Lists of qualified voters.
  Unlawful to vote in
    precinct, etc., where
    elector's name not on
    official list, §17-4-127.
Machines, §§17-9-1 to
  17-9-41. See within this
  heading, "Voting
  machines."
Method of voting, Const.
  Ala., art. VIII, §179.
Municipal corporations.
  See MUNICIPAL
  CORPORATIONS.
Obstruction of voting rights,
  §17-22A-16.
Persons eighteen years of
  age, Const. U. S.,
  Amendment XXVI.
Places of voting.
  Accessibility to
    handicapped. See
    within this heading,
    "Handicapped
    persons."
Polling places. See within
  this heading, "Polling
  places."
Procedure to vote for one
  candidate not on party
  ticket, §17-8-16.
Qualifications of voters. See
  within this heading,
  "Voters."
Right to vote. See within this
  heading, "Right to vote."
Split tickets, §17-8-18.
Straight party ticket.
  Procedure to vote straight
    party ticket, §17-8-15.
Two or more candidates on
  different tickets,
  §17-8-17.
Voting blank for any officer
  on ticket, §17-8-21.
Voting machines, §§17-9-1 to
  17-9-41. See within this
  heading, "Voting
  machines."
Write-in votes, §17-8-20.
Voting districts, §§17-5A-4,
  17-5A-5.
Voting machines.
Absentee ballots, §17-9-27.
Adoption.
  Referendum on adoption,
    §17-9-3.
Applicability of other laws,
  §17-9-41.
Assistance at polls, §17-9-25.
  Blind persons, §17-9-25.
  Disabled persons, §17-9-25.
  Forms for receiving
    assistance, §17-9-25.
  Oath of voters, §17-9-25.
Authorization, §17-9-2.
Ballots.
  Absentee ballots, §17-9-27.
  Diagram of ballots.
    Defined, §17-9-1.
  Irregular ballots, §17-9-1.
    Voting by irregular
      ballot, §17-9-26.
  Labels.
    Defined, §17-9-1.

ELECTIONS—Cont'd
Voting machines—Cont'd
Ballots—Cont'd
  Labels—Cont'd
    Duties of probate judges,
      §17-9-17.
  Official ballot.
    Defined, §17-9-1.
  Paper ballots.
    Use of paper ballots
      instead or to avoid
      congestion, §17-9-28.
  Preservation, §17-9-35.
  Sample ballots, §17-9-18.
    Delivery to election
      officers, §17-9-22.
Blind persons.
  Assistance at polls,
    §17-9-25.
Bond issues, Const. Ala.,
  amd. 200.
  Payment for machines,
    §17-9-8.
Booths.
  Defined, §17-9-1.
  Length of time elector may
    remain in booth,
    §17-9-23.
  Refusal to leave booth
    after reasonable time,
    §17-9-23.
Breaking seal of machine,
  §17-9-31.
Candidates.
  Counters.
    Defined, §17-9-1.
  Photographing name of
    candidate with total
    vote cast, §17-9-34.
Canvass of vote.
  Canvassing board.
    Records taken from
      machines, §17-9-35.
  Generally, §17-9-33.
  Recanvass of votes,
    §17-9-38.
  Statements of canvass,
    §17-9-34.
Challenging voters, §17-9-23.
  Applicability of laws,
    §17-9-23.
City clerks.
  Duties, §17-9-17.
Clerks.
  Duties.
    City clerks, §17-9-17.
    Generally, §17-9-23.
Closing polls.
  Keys.
    Delivery of keys after
      closing, §17-9-32.
  Locking machines,
    §17-9-33.
Congestion at polling places.
  Use of paper ballots to
    avoid congestion,
    §17-9-28.
Counters.
  Candidate counter.
    Defined, §17-9-1.
  Canvass of vote and
    proclamation of result,
    §17-9-33.
  Examination by election
    officials, §17-9-18.
  Inspectors.
    Counter compartments.
      Duties of inspectors as
        to, §17-9-23.
  Probate judges.
    Duty of judges, §17-9-17.

ELECTIONS—Cont'd
Voting machines—Cont'd
Counters—Cont'd
  Protective counter.
    Defined, §17-9-1.
  Public counter.
    Defined, §17-9-1.
Counties.
  Applicability of laws to use
    of voting machines,
    §17-9-39.
County commission.
  Authority to adopt,
    §17-9-2.
  Election not to install
    voting machines in
    certain wards or
    precincts, §17-9-4.
  Referendum on adoption.
    Submission to voters,
      §17-9-3.
Custodians.
  Compensation, §17-9-37.
  Defined, §17-9-1.
  Expenses, §17-9-37.
  Storage of machines when
    not in use, §17-9-36.
Custody, §17-9-36.
Definitions, §17-9-1.
Demonstrations, §17-9-15.
Diagrams.
  Defined, §17-9-1.
Discontinuance of use,
  §17-9-5.
  Submission of question of
    discontinuance to
    voters, §17-9-5.
Election officials.
  Challenging voters,
    §17-9-23.
  Compensation, §17-9-20.
  Duties.
    Generally, §17-9-23.
    Enumerated, §17-9-23.
  Excuses from service,
    §17-9-21.
  Failure to serve, §17-9-21.
    Excuses, §17-9-21.
  Instruction and assistance
    at polls, §17-9-25.
  Instruction of officials,
    §17-9-19.
  Preliminaries of opening
    polls, §17-9-18.
  Supplies.
    Delivery of supplies to
      officials, §17-9-22.
  Vacancies.
    Filling vacancy when
      person excused,
      §17-9-21.
  Violations of chapter,
    §17-9-40.
Electronic voting systems,
  §§17-24-1 to 17-24-11.
  See within this heading,
  "Electronic voting
  systems."
Examination.
  Probate judges to examine,
    §17-9-17.
Examination by persons
  involved in contests.
  Authorization, §17-8-45.
  Bonds, surety, §17-8-46.
  Procedure, §17-8-46.
Expenses.
  Transportation and
    operation, §17-9-37.
Formal declaration of poll
  opening, §17-9-18.

ELECTIONS—Cont'd
  Voting machines—Cont'd
  General elections.
    Use of machines in all
      elections, §17-9-6.
  Handicapped persons.
    Assistance at polls,
      §17-9-25.
    Municipal elections.
      Mayor-council form of
        government,
        §11-46-51.
  Injuring, §17-9-40.
  Inspectors.
    Assistance at polls,
      §17-9-25.
    Canvass of vote and
      proclamation of result,
      §17-9-33.
    Counter compartments.
      Duties as to, §17-9-23.
    Duties.
      Generally, §17-9-23.
    Keys.
      Delivery to inspector,
        §17-9-18.
    Installation, §17-9-4.
      Authority to install,
        §17-9-2.
      Requirements, §17-9-7.
    Instruction of voters.
      At polls, §17-9-25.
      Before election, §17-9-24.
    Keys.
      Certificate that keys were
        delivered, §17-9-18.
      Closing of polls.
        Delivery of keys to
          authorities after
          closing, §17-9-32.
      Custody, §17-9-36.
      Delivery to inspector,
        §17-9-18.
      Envelope for return of
        keys, §17-9-22.
      Unauthorized person in
        possession of keys,
        §17-9-40.
    Length of time elector may
      remain in booth,
      §17-9-23.
    Lighting facilities, §17-9-22.
    Locking machines, §17-9-35.
      Officials to lock machines
        after poll closes,
        §17-9-33.
      Probate judges.
        Duty of judges, §17-9-17.
    Model.
      Defined, §17-9-1.
    Municipal corporations.
      See MUNICIPAL
        CORPORATIONS.
    Number of voters per
      machine, §17-9-4.
    Oaths.
      Assistance at polls.
        Oath of voter needing
          assistance, §17-9-25.
    Opening polls.
      Poll watchers.
        Right to observe opening,
          §17-9-29.
    Payment for machines,
      §17-9-8.
    Photographing name of
      candidate or question,
      §17-9-34.
    Placement, §17-9-18.

ELECTIONS—Cont'd
  Voting machines—Cont'd
  Poll lists.
    Chief clerk to mark off
      from poll list, §17-9-23.
  Poll watchers.
    Observing preliminaries of
      opening polls,
      §17-9-29.
    Preliminaries of opening
      polls, §17-9-18.
  Precincts.
    Installation of voting boxes
      or machines, §17-5A-5.
  Preparation.
    Duty of probate judge,
      §17-9-17.
  Primary elections.
    Irregular ballots, §17-9-26.
    Use in all elections,
      §17-9-6.
  Probate judges, §17-9-17.
  Proclamation of result of
    votes.
    Inspector to proclaim
      results, §17-9-33.
  Provision for use of voting
    machines, Const. Ala.,
    amd. 41.
  Public exhibition.
    Instruction of voters before
      election, §17-9-24.
  Purchase.
    Joint purchase agreements,
      §17-9-9.
  Questions.
    Defined, §17-9-1.
    Photographing question
      with total vote cast,
      §17-9-34.
  Records, §17-9-35.
    Preservation of records,
      §17-9-35.
  Referendum on adoption,
    §17-9-3.
    Demonstration before
      referendum, §17-9-15.
  Renting or leasing.
    Persons owning machines
      to give guarantee of
      compliance with
      regulations, §17-9-7.
    Rental and joint purchase
      agreements, §17-9-9.
  Repairs, §17-9-28.
  Requirements, §17-9-7.
  Results of election.
    Breaking seal to obtain
      result, §17-9-31.
    Proclamation of result,
      §17-9-33.
  Seals.
    Breaking seal, §17-9-31.
    Defined, §17-9-1.
    Delivery to election
      officers, §17-9-22.
    Inspectors.
      Breaking of seals by
        inspector, §17-9-18.
    Probate judges.
      Duty of judges, §17-9-17.
    Recanvass of votes.
      Breaking seals for
        recanvassing,
        §17-9-38.
  Special elections.
    Use in special elections,
      §17-9-6.
  Specifications, §17-9-7.
  Storage when not in use,
    §17-9-36.

ELECTIONS—Cont'd
  Voting machines—Cont'd
  Substitution, §17-9-28.
  Supplies, §17-9-16.
    Election officials.
      Delivery of supplies to
        officials, §17-9-22.
  Tampering with, §17-9-40.
  Time.
    Length of time voters
      allowed in booth,
      §17-9-23.
  Transportation.
    Expenses, §17-9-37.
  Use.
    All elections, §17-9-6.
    Authority to use, §17-9-2.
    Discontinuance of use,
      §17-9-5.
  Violations of chapter,
    §17-9-40.
  Warrants or certificates for
    purchase.
    Applicability, §17-9-14.
    Form, §17-9-10.
    Inconsistent laws.
      Sections 17-9-10 through
        17-9-14 control
        inconsistent laws,
        §17-9-13.
    Interest, §17-9-10.
    Issuance, §17-9-10.
    Payment.
      Pledge of general ad
        valorem tax for
        payment, §17-9-11.
    Proceeds, §17-9-10.
    Refunding.
      Authorized, §17-9-12.
    Taxation.
      Pledge of general ad
        valorem tax for
        payment, §17-9-11.
Voting places. See within this
  heading, "Polling places."
Wards.
  Municipal corporations.
    See MUNICIPAL
      CORPORATIONS.
Warrants.
  Voting machines.
    Warrants or certificates for
      purchase of machines,
      §§17-9-10 to 17-9-14.
Watchers.
  Poll watchers. See within
    this heading, "Election
    officials."
Witnesses.
  Contests. See within this
    heading, "Contests."
Women.
  Woman suffrage, Const. U.
    S., Amendment XIX.

**ELECTRICAL
  CONTRACTORS, §§34-36-1
  to 34-36-17.**
**Board of electrical
  contractors.**
  Appointment, §34-36-4.
  Compensation, §34-36-5.
  Creation, §34-36-4.
  Duties.
    Generally, §34-36-6.
  Executive secretary,
    §34-36-4.
  Expenses, §34-36-5.
  Fund.
    Creation, §34-36-17.
    Expenditures, §34-36-17.

ELECTRICAL CONTRACTORS—Cont'd

Board of electrical contractors—Cont'd
Meetings, §34-36-4.
Powers and duties.
Generally, §34-36-6.
Qualifications of members, §34-36-4.
Rules and regulations, §34-36-4.
Seal, §34-36-4.
Terms of office, §34-36-4.
Citation of chapter, §34-36-1.
Declaration of purpose, §34-36-2.
Definitions, §34-36-3.
Electrical appeals and advisory board.
Appointment, §34-36-14.
Compensation, §34-36-14.
Composition, §34-36-14.
Examinations.
Conduct, §34-36-7.
Fees, §34-36-11.
Passing grade, §34-36-7.
Required, §34-36-13.
Injunctions.
Unauthorized practice, §34-36-15.
Licenses.
Display, §34-36-12.
Exemption, §34-36-13.
Expiration, §34-36-8.
Restoration, §34-36-9.
Suspended license, §34-36-10.
Fees, §34-36-11.
Renewal, §34-36-8.
Required, §34-36-13.
Suspension.
Expiration of suspended license, §34-36-10.
Penalties.
Violations of chapter, §34-36-16.
Purpose of chapter, §34-36-2.
Short title of chapter, §34-36-1.
Violation of chapter.
Penalties, §34-36-16.

ELECTRIC COOPERATIVES, §§37-6-1 to 37-6-49.

Acknowledgments.
Persons authorized to take acknowledgments.
Not disqualified by reason of being officer, director or member, §37-6-25.
Actions.
Right to sue and be sued, §37-6-3.
Amendments.
Articles of incorporation, §37-6-7.
Filing of amendments, §37-6-19.
Bylaws, §37-6-8.
Articles of incorporation.
Amendment, §37-6-19.
Contents.
Generally, §37-6-6.
Filing, §§37-6-6, 37-6-19.
Generally, §37-6-6.
Name, §37-6-6.
Notice.
Waiver of provisions requiring notice, §37-6-24.

ELECTRIC COOPERATIVES —Cont'd

Articles of incorporation —Cont'd
Signature of incorporators, §37-6-6.
Assets.
Dissolution.
Distribution of assets, §37-6-18.
Board of trustees.
Articles of incorporation.
Amendments.
Approval of board, §37-6-7.
Bylaws.
Adoption by board, §37-6-8.
Consolidation.
Approval of board required, §37-6-13.
Conversion of existing corporations into cooperatives.
Approval by board required, §37-6-16.
Dissolution.
Power of trustees to wind up and settle affairs of cooperative, §37-6-18.
District or area meetings.
Elections at, §37-6-11.
Division into classes, §37-6-10.
Duties generally, §37-6-10.
Election.
District or area meeting.
Election of trustees at district or area meetings, §37-6-11.
Voting districts.
Election of trustees from voting districts, §37-6-11.
Husband and wife.
Election to board at same time, §37-6-10.
Initiative by members.
Approval not required, §37-6-17.
Merger.
Approval by board, §37-6-14.
Number, §37-6-10.
Officers.
Election or appointment of certain other officers, §37-6-12.
Powers.
Generally, §37-6-10.
Qualifications, §37-6-10.
Quorum, §37-6-10.
Removal, §37-6-10.
Salaries, §37-6-10.
Term of office, §37-6-10.
Voting districts.
Election of trustees from voting districts, §37-6-11.
Bond issues.
Department of finance.
Consent required, §37-6-28.
Issuance.
Consent of department of finance, §37-6-28.
Securities law.
Exemptions from provisions, §37-6-29.
Bylaws.
Adoption by board of trustees, §37-6-8.

ELECTRIC COOPERATIVES —Cont'd

Bylaws—Cont'd
Adoption by members, §37-6-8.
Amendment.
Members to adopt, amend or repeal, §37-6-8.
Annual meeting, §37-6-9.
Contents, §37-6-8.
Notice.
Waiver of provisions requiring notice, §37-6-24.
Repeal by members, §37-6-8.
Voting districts, §37-6-11.
Consolidation.
Articles of consolidation.
Contents, §37-6-13.
Filing, §37-6-19.
Board of trustees.
Approval required, §37-6-13.
Creditors.
Impairing rights of creditors, §37-6-15.
Effect, §37-6-15.
Generally, §37-6-13.
Requirements, §37-6-13.
Rights, privileges, immunities and powers of new or surviving cooperative, §37-6-15.
Submission to vote of members, §37-6-13.
Contracts.
Power to make contracts necessary or convenient for full purpose of powers and chapter, §37-6-3.
Conversion of existing corporation into cooperative, §37-6-16.
Articles of conversion.
Contents, §37-6-16.
Filing, §37-6-19.
Board of trustees.
Approval, §37-6-16.
Requirements, §37-6-16.
Rural telephone service.
Duplication of telephone service, §37-6-42.
Stockholder approval, §37-6-16.
Corporations.
Conversion of existing corporation into cooperative. See within this heading, "Conversion of existing corporation into cooperative."
Foreign corporations, §37-6-26.
Creditors.
Consolidation or merger.
Impairing rights of creditors, §37-6-15.
Debts.
Collection of debts owed cooperative, §37-6-18.
Consolidation or merger.
Effect on rights of creditors, §37-6-15.
Nonliability of members for debts, §37-6-22.
Definitions, §37-6-1.
Gas districts, §37-6-30.
Rural electric cooperatives, §37-6-30.

ELECTRIC COOPERATIVES
—Cont'd
Dissolution.
Articles of dissolution.
Affidavit, §37-6-18.
Contents, §37-6-18.
Execution, §37-6-18.
Filing, §§37-6-18, 37-6-19.
Assets.
Distribution, §37-6-18.
Debts owed to cooperative.
Collection by board of
trustees, §37-6-18.
Generally, §37-6-18.
Property.
Distribution, §37-6-18.
Voluntary dissolution,
§37-6-18.
Electricity generally.
See ELECTRICITY.
Eminent domain.
Power to exercise, §37-6-3.
Excess revenues.
Disposition, §37-6-20.
Existing corporations.
Conversion into cooperative.
See within this heading,
"Conversion of existing
corporation into
cooperative."
Foreign corporations,
§37-6-26.
Gas districts.
Defined, §37-6-30.
Terminating or declining
services.
Applicants or customers
indebted to district for
services at present or
former location,
§37-6-30.
Husband and wife.
Board of trustees.
Membership on board at
same time, §37-6-10.
Incorporators.
Articles of incorporation.
Signature of incorporators
required, §37-6-6.
Number, §37-6-5.
Indemnification.
Power of cooperative, §37-6-3.
Initiative by members,
§37-6-17.
Board of trustees.
Approval not required,
§37-6-17.
Leases.
Lease of property.
Approval of members
required, §37-6-21.
Liens.
Mortgages or deeds of trust
creating liens, §37-6-23.
Loans.
Power to make loans to
certain persons, §37-6-3.
Lost or unclaimed property.
Uniform disposition of
unclaimed property act.
Exemption from act,
§35-12-24.1.
Meetings, §37-6-9.
Area meetings, §37-6-9.
Election of board of
trustees at district or
area meetings,
§37-6-11.
Board of trustees.
Election at district or area
meetings, §37-6-11.

ELECTRIC COOPERATIVES
—Cont'd
Meetings—Cont'd
Central annual meetings,
§37-6-9.
Definitions.
Gas districts, §37-6-30.
Rural electric cooperatives,
§37-6-30.
Gas districts.
Defined, §37-6-30.
Determinating or declining
services.
Applicants or customers
indebted to district
for services at
present or former
location, §37-6-30.
Notice.
Waiver of notice by
attending meetings,
§37-6-24.
Quorum, §37-6-9.
Rural electric cooperatives.
Defined, §37-6-30.
Special meetings, §37-6-9.
Members.
Acknowledgment of
instruments.
Persons authorized not
disqualified by reason
of being member,
§37-6-25.
Bylaws.
Adoption, amendment or
repeal by members,
§37-6-8.
Consolidation.
Vote of members, §37-6-13.
Debts of cooperative.
Nonliability of members,
§37-6-22.
Defined, §37-6-1.
Division into voting districts,
§37-6-11.
Initiative by members,
§37-6-17.
Liability.
Debts of cooperative,
§37-6-22.
Meetings, §37-6-9.
Merger.
Vote of members, §37-6-14.
Private property of members.
Exempt from execution for
debts of cooperative,
§37-6-22.
Property.
Sale, lease or encumbrance
of property.
Approval of members
required, §37-6-21.
Qualifications for
membership, §37-6-9.
Transfer of membership,
§37-6-9.
Voting, §37-6-9.
Merger.
Articles of merger.
Contents, §37-6-14.
Filing, §37-6-19.
Board of trustees.
Approval by board,
§37-6-14.
Creditors.
Impairing rights of
creditors, §37-6-15.
Effect, §37-6-15.
Generally, §37-6-14.
Requirements, §37-6-14.

ELECTRIC COOPERATIVES
—Cont'd
Merger—Cont'd
Rights, privileges,
immunities and powers
of new or surviving
cooperative, §37-6-15.
Vote of members, §37-6-14.
**Mortgages and deeds of
trust.**
Board of trustees.
Powers as to, §37-6-21.
Encumbrance of property.
Approval of members
required, §37-6-21.
Liens.
Instruments creating liens,
§37-6-23.
Name.
Articles of incorporation.
Name to be included in
articles, §37-6-6.
Use of words electric, power
or cooperative in
cooperative's name,
§37-6-4.
Notice.
Articles of incorporation.
Waiver of provisions
requiring notice,
§37-6-24.
Bylaws.
Waiver of provisions
requiring notice,
§37-6-24.
Meetings.
Attendance at meetings as
waiver of notice,
§37-6-24.
Office.
Location of principal office.
Change of location,
§37-6-7.
Officers, §37-6-12.
Acknowledgment of
instruments.
Persons authorized to take
acknowledgments not
disqualified by reason
of being officer,
§37-6-25.
Board of trustees.
Election or appointment of
certain other officers,
§37-6-12.
Election, §37-6-12.
Removal, §37-6-12.
Organization, §37-6-2.
Incorporators.
Number, §37-6-5.
Perpetual existence, §37-6-3.
Petitions.
Initiative by members,
§37-6-17.
Powers.
Enumerated powers, §37-6-3.
Probate judges.
Articles.
Transmission of copies of
articles to probate
judge, §37-6-19.
Property.
Dissolution.
Distribution of property
upon dissolution,
§37-6-18.
Encumbrance of property.
Approval of members
required, §37-6-21.

ELECTRIC COOPERATIVES —Cont'd

Property—Cont'd
Leases.
Approval of members required, §37-6-21.
Mortgages or deeds of trust creating liens, §37-6-23.
Sale.
Approval of members required, §37-6-21.
Public service commission.
Exemption from jurisdiction of commission, §37-6-27.
Purpose, §37-6-2.
Quorum.
Board of trustees, §37-6-10.
Meetings, §37-6-9.
Revenue.
Disposition of excess revenue, §37-6-20.
Rural electric cooperatives.
Defined, §37-6-30.
Terminating or declining services.
Applicants or customers indebted to cooperative for services at present or former location, §37-6-30.
Rural telephone service, §§37-6-40 to 37-6-49.
See TELEPHONES.
Seal.
Adoption of corporate seal, §37-6-3.
Secretary of state.
Filing of articles, §37-6-19.
Securities.
Bond issues.
Exemption from provisions of securities law, §37-6-29.
Spouses.
Board of trustees.
Membership on board at same time, §37-6-10.
Telephone service.
Rural telephone service, §§37-6-40 to 37-6-49.
See TELEPHONES.
Terminating or declining services.
Rural electric cooperatives and gas districts.
Applicants or customers indebted to cooperative or district for services at present or former locations, §37-6-30.
Voting, §37-6-9.
Proxy votes, §37-6-9.
Voting by mail, §37-6-9.
Voting districts.
Bylaws to provide, §37-6-11.

ELECTRICITY.

Actions.
Service territories for electric suppliers.
1984 act.
Violations of provisions.
Action for injunction or damages, §37-14-9.
1985 act.
Violation of provisions.
Action for injunction or damages, §37-14-37.

ELECTRICITY—Cont'd

Appeals.
Service territories for electric suppliers.
1984 act.
Judicial determination of legality and validity of provisions, §37-14-13.
1985 act.
Judicial determination of legality and validity of provisions, §37-14-38.
Authorities.
Improvement authorities, §§39-7-1 to 39-7-34.
See PUBLIC WORKS.
Municipal electric authority, §§11-50A-1 to 11-50A-33.
See MUNICIPAL CORPORATIONS.
Coal mine safety.
Electrical equipment, §§25-9-170 to 25-9-176, 25-9-230, 25-9-250, 25-9-274.
See COAL.
Commercial code.
Secured transactions.
Applicability of filing provisions, §7-9-302.
Condemnation by electric utilities.
Procedure for condemnation, §37-4-131.
Right to condemn, §37-4-130.
Transmission lines.
Acquisition of rights of way or easements for erection of lines, §37-4-130.
Trees and timber.
Right to clear, §37-4-130.
Ways and rights of way by companies operating public utilities, §10-5-4.
Construction.
Condemnation of ways and rights of way by companies constructing public utilities, §10-5-4.
Cooperatives, §§37-6-1 to 37-6-49.
See ELECTRIC COOPERATIVES.
Corporations.
Electric membership corporations, §§37-7-1 to 37-7-21.
See ELECTRIC MEMBERSHIP CORPORATIONS.
Foreign corporations.
Extension of lines into state, §10-2A-225.
Counties.
See COUNTIES.
Criminal law and procedure.
Meters.
Furnishing, §37-8-6.
Inspections.
Open for inspection, §37-8-6.
Damages.
Service territories for electric suppliers.
1984 act.
Violations of provisions, §37-14-9.

ELECTRICITY—Cont'd

Damages—Cont'd
Service territories for electric suppliers—Cont'd
1985 act.
Violations of provisions, §37-14-37.
Dams.
Erection of dams for electric generators, §§18-2-1 to 18-2-21.
See DAMS.
Definitions.
Operations in proximity to high voltage overhead conductors, §37-8-52.
Service territories for electric suppliers.
1984 act, §37-14-2.
Distribution facilities, §37-14-5.
1985 act, §37-14-31.
Distribution facility, §37-14-33.
Districts.
Power districts, §§37-5-1 to 37-5-9.
See POWER DISTRICTS.
Duplication of facilities.
Avoidance.
General provisions, §§37-14-1 to 37-14-17, 37-14-30 to 37-14-40.
See within this heading, "Service territories for electric suppliers."
Easements.
Transmission lines.
Acquisition of rights of way or easements for erection of transmission lines, §37-4-130.
Electric cooperatives, §§37-6-1 to 37-6-49.
See ELECTRIC COOPERATIVES.
Electric membership corporations, §§37-7-1 to 37-7-21.
See ELECTRIC MEMBERSHIP CORPORATIONS.
Eminent domain.
Companies constructing, operating or maintaining public utility.
Condemnation of ways and rights of ways, §10-5-4.
Dams.
Erection of dams for mills, gins, factories or electric generators, §§18-2-1 to 18-2-21.
See DAMS.
Electric utilities.
Condemnation by electric utilities, §§37-4-130, 37-4-131.
Power of public utility corporations, §10-5-1.
Routes and sites.
Rights of condemning corporations in selection of routes and sites, §10-5-8.
Fishing.
Catching or killing of fish by electrical devices, §9-11-94.

ELECTRICITY—Cont'd
Generators.
  Dams.
    Erection of dams for
      electric generators,
      §§18-2-1 to 18-2-21.
      See DAMS.
**High voltage overhead
  conductors.**
  Operators in proximity to,
    §§37-8-52 to 37-8-55.
Highways.
  Contracting with local
    authorities on use of
    public roads by public
    utility corporations,
    §10-5-14.
Hydroelectric power.
  Water power companies,
    §§10-4-320 to 10-4-323.
Improvement authorities,
    §§39-7-1 to 39-7-34.
  See PUBLIC WORKS.
Injunctions.
  Service territories for electric
    suppliers.
    1984 act.
    Violations of provisions,
      §37-14-9.
    1985 act.
    Violations of provisions,
      §37-14-37.
Judgments.
  Service territories for electric
    suppliers.
    1984 act.
    Judicial determination of
      legality and validity
      of provisions,
      §§37-14-13, 37-14-14.
    1985 act.
    Judicial determination of
      legality and validity
      of provisions,
      §37-14-38.
Meters.
  Criminal law and procedure.
    Furnishing, §37-8-6.
    Inspection, §37-8-6.
Municipal corporations.
  See MUNICIPAL
    CORPORATIONS.
Municipal electric authority,
    §§11-50A-1 to 11-50A-33.
  See MUNICIPAL
    CORPORATIONS.
Notice.
  1985 act.
    Judicial determination of
      legality and validity of
      provisions.
    Complaint.
      Contents, §37-14-38.
    Hearing.
      Notice, §37-14-38.
    Show cause order,
      §37-14-38.
    Notice.
      Hearing, §37-14-38.
  Service territories for electric
    suppliers.
    1984 act.
    Judicial determination of
      legality and validity
      of provisions.
      Hearing, §37-14-12.
    1985 act.
    Judicial determination of
      legality and validity
      of provisions.
      Hearing, §37-14-38.

ELECTRICITY—Cont'd
**Operations in proximity to
  high voltage overhead
  conductors.**
  Definitions, §37-8-52.
  Exemptions, §37-8-54.
  Generally, §37-8-52.
  High voltage.
    Defined, §37-8-52.
  Overhead conductor.
    Defined, §37-8-52.
  Railway equipment.
    Exemptions, §37-8-54.
  Safeguards against danger of
    accidental contact,
    §37-8-52.
  Signs.
    Warning signs, §37-8-53.
  Utility companies.
    Civil liability, §37-8-55.
  Violation of section, §37-8-52.
  Warning signs, §37-8-53.
Overhead conductors.
  Operations in proximity to
    high voltage overhead
    conductors, §§37-8-52 to
    37-8-55.
Power districts, §§37-5-1 to
    37-5-9.
  See POWER DISTRICTS.
Public service commission.
  General provisions, §§37-1-1
    to 37-1-157.
Public utilities. See within
    this heading, "Utilities."
Railroads.
  Overhead conductors.
    Operations in proximity to
      high voltage overhead
      conductors.
    Exemption from
      provision of sections,
      §37-8-54.
Rates.
  General provisions.
    See PUBLIC UTILITIES.
Safety.
  Operations in proximity to
    high voltage overhead
    conductors, §§37-8-52 to
    37-8-55.
Sales tax.
  Exemptions.
    Gross proceeds from the
      sale of electric power
      or energy, §40-23-4.
Secured transactions.
  Applicability of filing
    provisions, §7-9-302.
**Service territories for
  electric suppliers.**
  1984 act.
    Actions.
      Violations of provisions.
      Action for injunction
        or damages,
        §37-14-9.
    Agreements between
      electric suppliers.
      Applicability, §37-14-8.
      Enumerated, §37-14-8.
    Damages.
      Violations of provisions,
        §37-14-9.
    Definitions, §37-14-2.
    Distribution facilities,
      §37-14-5.
    Distribution facilities.
      Defined, §37-14-5.

ELECTRICITY—Cont'd
**Service territories for
  electric suppliers**—Cont'd
  1984 act—Cont'd
    Distribution facilities
      —Cont'd
      Purchase by primary
        supplier.
        Applicability of certain
          provisions,
          §37-14-7.
      Option to acquire
        facilities within
        existing municipal
        limits, §37-14-4.
      Resolution of disputes
        regarding,
        §37-14-6.
    Distribution lines.
      Defined, §37-14-2.
      Restrictions.
        Electric service outside
          existing municipal
          limits, §37-14-3.
    Exemptions from
      provisions, §37-14-8.
    Existing municipal limits.
      Acquisition of facilities
        within.
        Primary supplier's
          option, §37-14-4.
      Defined, §37-14-2.
      Electric service outside,
        §37-14-3.
    Industrial customers.
      Defined, §37-14-2.
    Injunctions.
      Violations of provisions,
        §37-14-9.
    Judicial determination of
      legality and validity of
      provisions.
      Appeals, §37-14-13.
      Authorized, §37-14-10.
      Complaint.
        Content, §37-14-12.
        Filing, §37-14-11.
      Costs, §37-14-15.
      Finality of judgment,
        §37-14-14.
      Hearing, §37-14-13.
        Notice, §37-14-12.
      Intervention, §37-14-12.
      Judgments.
        Entry, §37-14-13.
        Finality, §37-14-14.
      Notice.
        Hearing, §37-14-12.
      Pending actions or
        proceedings.
        Effect on applicability
          of provisions,
          §37-14-16.
      Show cause orders,
        §37-14-12.
    Legislative declaration,
      §37-14-1.
    Primary electric supplier.
      Defined, §37-14-2.
      Facilities within existing
        municipal limits.
        Option to acquire,
          §37-14-4.
      Option to acquire
        facilities within
        existing municipal
        limits, §37-14-4.
    Secondary electric supplier.
      Defined, §37-14-2.
    Severability of provisions,
      §37-14-17.

ELECTRICITY—Cont'd
Service territories for electric suppliers—Cont'd
1984 act—Cont'd
Violations of provisions.
Action for injunction or damages, §37-14-9.
1985 act.
Actions.
Action taken pursuant to inconsistent provisions, §37-14-40.
Violation of provisions.
Action for injunctions or damages, §37-14-37.
Agreements between electric suppliers.
Applicability, §37-14-36.
Enumerated, §37-14-36.
Damages.
Violations of provisions, §37-14-37.
Definitions, §37-14-31.
Distribution facility, §37-14-33.
Distribution facilities.
Defined, §37-14-33.
Purchase by primary supplier.
Applicability of certain provisions, §37-14-35.
Option to acquire facilities within existing municipal limits, §37-14-33.
Resolution of disputes regarding, §37-14-34.
Distribution lines.
Defined, §37-14-31.
Restrictions.
Electric service outside existing municipal limits, §37-14-32.
Exemptions from provisions, §37-14-36.
Existing municipal limits.
Acquisition of facilities within.
Primary supplier's option, §37-14-33.
Defined, §37-14-31.
Electric service outside, §37-14-32.
Industrial customers.
Defined, §37-14-31.
Injunctions.
Violations of provisions, §37-14-37.
Judgments.
Entry, §37-14-38.
Judicial determination of legality and validity of provisions.
Appeal, §37-14-38.
Authorized, §37-14-38.
Complaint.
Filing, §37-14-38.
Costs, §37-14-38.
Finality of judgment, §37-14-38.
Hearing, §37-14-38.
Judgments.
Finality, §37-14-38.

ELECTRICITY—Cont'd
Service territories for electric suppliers—Cont'd
1985 act—Cont'd
Judicial determination of legality and validity of provisions—Cont'd
Pending actions or proceedings.
Effect on applicability of provisions, §37-14-38.
Legislative declaration, §37-14-30.
Primary electric supplier.
Defined, §37-14-31.
Facilities within existing municipal limits.
Option to acquire, §37-14-33.
Option to acquire facilities within existing municipal limits, §37-14-33.
Relationship to 1984 act, §37-14-30.
Repealer, §37-14-40.
Secondary electric supplier.
Defined, §37-14-31.
Severability of provisions, §37-14-39.
Violations of provisions.
Action for injunction or damages, §37-14-37.
Signs.
Operations in proximity to high voltage overhead conductors.
Warning signs, §37-8-53.
Taxation.
General provisions.
See PUBLIC UTILITIES.
Theft.
Acts which make electricity unlawfully available, §13A-8-23.
Transmission lines.
Condemnation by electric utilities.
Erection of transmission lines, §37-4-130.
Operations in proximity to high voltage overhead conductors, §§37-8-52 to 37-8-55.
Trees and timber.
Condemnation by electric utilities.
Right to remove timber and other growth, §37-4-130.
Utilities.
Condemnation by electric utilities, §§37-4-130, 37-4-131.
Electric cooperatives, §§37-6-1 to 37-6-49.
See ELECTRIC COOPERATIVES.
Municipal corporations.
See MUNICIPAL CORPORATIONS.
Operations in proximity to high voltage overhead conductors of electricity.
Civil liability of utility companies, §37-8-55.
Public utilities generally.
See PUBLIC UTILITIES.
Water power companies.
See DAMS.

ELECTRIC MEMBERSHIP CORPORATIONS, §§37-7-1 to 37-7-20.
Actions.
Power to sue and be sued, §37-7-10.
Assets.
Dissolution.
Liquidation of assets upon dissolution, §37-7-19.
Board of directors.
Appointment of agents and employees, §37-7-6.
Bylaws.
Power to adopt and amend, §37-7-6.
Compensation, §37-7-5.
Election, §37-7-5.
Expenses.
Reimbursement, §37-7-5.
Governing body, §37-7-5.
Powers.
Generally, §37-7-6.
President.
Election, §37-7-5.
Reducing number of directors.
Amendment of certificate of incorporation, §37-7-21.
Secretary, §37-7-5.
Body corporate, §37-7-4.
Bond issues.
Covenants or agreements, §37-7-14.
Defined, §37-7-1.
Department of finance.
Consent for issuance, §37-7-12.
Petition, §37-7-12.
Execution, §37-7-13.
Interest, §37-7-13.
Issuance.
Consent of department of finance, §37-7-12.
Manner of issuance, §37-7-13.
Maturity, §37-7-13.
Payment, §37-7-13.
Proceeds.
Use of proceeds, §37-7-12.
Purchase of own obligations.
Cancellation of obligations so purchased, §37-7-15.
Price, §37-7-15.
Sale.
Manner of sale, §37-7-13.
Bylaws.
Board of directors.
Power to adopt and amend, §37-7-6.
Members.
Provisions regulating admission, withdrawal, suspension or expulsion of members, §37-7-6.
Certificate of incorporation.
Acknowledgment, §37-7-4.
Amendment, §37-7-21.
Certificate of amendment, §37-7-21.
Contents, §37-7-3.
Filing, §37-7-4.
Form, §37-7-3.
Persons executing, §37-7-4.
Charges.
Services rendered, §37-7-18.
Consolidation.
Agreement to consolidate, §37-7-16.

ELECTRIC MEMBERSHIP CORPORATIONS—Cont'd

Consolidation—Cont'd
Certificate of consolidation, §37-7-16.

Corporate purpose, §37-7-8.
Vesting of powers for accomplishment, §37-7-9.

Debts.
Dissolution.
Satisfaction of debt, §37-7-19.

Definitions, §37-7-1.

Directors. See within this heading, "Board of directors."

Dissolution.
Assets.
Liquidation of assets, §37-7-19.
Certificate of dissolution.
Contents, §37-7-19.
Filing in office of secretary of state, §37-7-19.

Employees.
Appointment by board of directors, §37-7-6.

Energy.
Defined, §37-7-1.

Extension of territory, §37-7-17.
Certificate, §37-7-17.
Construction of extensions, §37-7-17.

Fees.
Membership fees, §37-7-8.
Power to charge reasonable fees, §37-7-18.

Foreign corporations, §37-7-20.

Formation, §37-7-2.
Number of persons necessary, §37-7-2.

Incorporation.
Certificate of incorporation. See within this heading, "Certificate of incorporation."

Interest.
Bond issues, §37-7-13.

Leases.
Power to lease property, §37-7-11.

Members.
Bylaws.
Provisions regulating admission, withdrawal, suspension or expulsion of members, §37-7-6.
Certificates of membership.
Issuance, §37-7-7.
Consolidation.
Approval of members, §37-7-16.
Defined, §37-7-1.
Encumbering or disposing of property.
Approval of members required, §37-7-11.
Fees, §37-7-8.
Nonmembers.
Service to nonmembers, §37-7-8.
Termination of membership.
Bylaw provisions, §37-7-6.
Transfer of membership.
Bylaw provisions, §37-7-6.
Voting.
Members entitled to only one vote, §37-7-7.

ELECTRIC MEMBERSHIP CORPORATIONS—Cont'd

Mortgages and deeds of trust.
Encumbering property, §37-7-11.

Out-of-state service, §37-7-8.

Powers.
Enumerated powers, §37-7-10.
Vesting of powers for accomplishment of corporate purpose, §37-7-9.

Property.
Encumbering or disposing of property, §37-7-11.
Power to acquire, hold and dispose of property, §37-7-10.
Sale, §37-7-11.

Purpose, §37-7-2.
Corporate purpose, §37-7-8.
Vesting of powers for accomplishment, §37-7-9.

Seal, §37-7-10.

Service.
Charges for services rendered, §37-7-18.
Nonmembers, §37-7-8.
Outside state, §37-7-8.

System.
Defined, §37-7-1.

Winding up business and affairs, §37-7-19.

ELECTROCUTION.
Death penalty, §§15-18-1, 15-18-82.

ELECTRONIC PAGERS.
Education.
When pupils prohibited from carrying, §16-1-27.

ELECTRONIC SURVEILLANCE.
General provisions, §§13A-11-30 to 13A-11-37.
See EAVESDROPPING.

ELECTRONIC VOTING SYSTEMS, §§17-24-1 to 17-24-11.
See ELECTIONS.

ELEMENTARY SCHOOLS.
See EDUCATION.

ELEVATORS.
Coal mine safety.
Hoisting and haulage, §§25-9-210 to 25-9-216.
See COAL.
Insurance.
Casualty insurance generally.
See INSURANCE.
Waters and watercourses.
Development of docks and other facilities along inland waterways.
See WATERS AND WATERCOURSES.

ELK RIVER DEVELOPMENT AGENCY, §§33-12-1 to 33-12-10.
Advisory board.
Establishment by directors, §33-12-9.
Bond issues.
Exemption from taxation, §33-12-5.

ELK RIVER DEVELOPMENT AGENCY—Cont'd

Bylaws, §33-12-5.
Construction of chapter, §33-12-10.
Contracts.
Power to enter into contracts, §33-12-5.
Contributions to work of agency.
Certain counties, §33-12-6.
Cooperation and assistance of other agencies, §33-12-8.
Corporate name, §33-12-3.
Perpetual succession, §33-12-5.
Counties.
Contributions to work of agency by certain counties, §33-12-6.
Taxation.
Levy by governing bodies, §33-12-6.
Development plans.
Formulation and execution, §33-12-5.
Directors.
Advisory board.
Establishment by directors, §33-12-9.
Appointment, §33-12-2.
Compensation, §33-12-4.
Expenses, §33-12-4.
Incorporation.
Application, §33-12-3.
Qualifications, §33-12-2.
Reports.
Annual report to governor, §33-12-7.
Terms, §33-12-2.
Vacancies, §33-12-2.
Duties.
Generally, §33-12-5.
Establishment, §33-12-1.
Financing, §33-12-5.
Financial receipts.
Annual report to governor, §33-12-7.
Functions.
Generally, §33-12-5.
Incorporation.
Application, §33-12-3.
Corporate name, §33-12-3.
Procedure, §33-12-3.
Instrumentality of state, §33-12-1.
Land acquisition, §33-12-5.
Management and operation, §33-12-5.
Meetings.
Time and place, §33-12-4.
Municipal corporations.
Contributions to work of agency by certain municipalities, §33-12-6.
Officers.
Election, §33-12-4.
Organization, §33-12-2.
Other agencies.
Cooperation and assistance, §33-12-8.
Powers.
Generally, §33-12-5.
Reports.
Annual reports.
Directors to report annually to governor, §33-12-7.

**ELK RIVER DEVELOPMENT
AGENCY**—Cont'd
Secretary of state.
Incorporation.
Application for
incorporation.
Duties as to, §33-12-3.
Taxation.
Counties.
Levy by governing bodies,
§33-12-6.
Exemption from taxation,
§33-12-5.
Municipal corporations.
Levy by governing bodies,
§33-12-6.

ELKS CLUB.
Licenses.
Exemptions.
Elks memorial center,
§40-9-12.
Taxation.
Exemptions from taxation.
Elks memorial center,
§40-9-12.
Property, §40-9-1.

ELMORE COUNTY.
Court costs and charges,
Const. Ala., amd. 278.
Local service districts, Const.
Ala., amd. 466.
Officers.
Compensation of certain
officers, Const. Ala.,
amd. 185.
Consolidation of offices,
Const. Ala., amd. 356.

**EMANCIPATION OF
MINORS.**
**Relief from disabilities of
nonage,** §§26-13-1 to
26-13-8; Const. Ala., art.
IV, §104.
See MINORS.

EMBALMERS.
General provisions,
§§34-13-90 to 34-13-94.

EMBEZZLEMENT.
Elements of crime, §13A-9-51.
**Executors and
administrators.**
Grounds for removal,
§43-2-290.
Fiduciaries.
Defined, §13A-9-51.
General provisions.
See THEFT.
Indictments.
Form of indictment,
§15-8-150.
Insurance.
Property, casualty and surety
insurance
representatives.
Diversion or appropriation
of trust funds,
§27-7-36.
Misapplication of property,
§13A-9-51.
Class A misdemeanor,
§13A-9-51.
Motor vehicles.
Renting and hiring.
Embezzlement of vehicle
subject to larceny,
§32-15-7.

EMBLEMENTS.
**When tenant at will entitled
to emblements,** §35-9-2.

EMBLEMS.
Political parties, §§17-8-6 to
17-8-9.

EMERGENCIES.
Abortion.
Parental consent to
performing abortion
upon minors.
Medical emergencies.
Chapter inapplicable to,
§26-21-5.
Air pollution, §22-28-21.
Alcoholic beverages.
Temporary closings of
licensed places in
municipalities during
emergencies, §28-3-47.
Ambulances.
General provisions, §§22-18-1
to 22-18-7.
See AMBULANCES.
Appropriations, §41-4-94.
Banking emergencies,
§§5-10A-1 to 5-10A-17.
See BANKS AND
FINANCIAL
INSTITUTIONS.
Civil defense, §§31-9-1 to
31-9-24.
See CIVIL DEFENSE.
Consent for health services,
§§22-8-1 to 22-8-9.
See HEALTH.
Counties.
Ambulance service, §§11-87-1
to 11-87-5.
Financial provisions for
emergencies, §11-8-15.
Drought.
Fire prevention in emergency
drought conditions,
§§9-13-140 to 9-13-142.
Emergency management act,
§§31-9-1 to 31-9-24.
See CIVIL DEFENSE.
Good Samaritan Act.
Doctors, nurses, policemen,
firemen, rescue squad
members, etc., rendering
first aid or emergency
care at scene of accident.
Exemption from liability,
§6-5-332.
Health services.
Consent for health services,
§§22-8-1 to 22-8-9.
See HEALTH.
Legislature.
Emergency interim
succession, §§29-3-1 to
29-3-16.
See LEGISLATURE.
Management.
Civil defense, §§31-9-1 to
31-9-24.
See CIVIL DEFENSE.
Municipal corporations.
See MUNICIPAL
CORPORATIONS.
Nurses.
Exemptions from licensing
provisions, §34-21-6.
Physicians.
Emergency services exempt
from provisions of
chapter, §34-24-55.

EMERGENCIES—Cont'd
**Public officers and
employees.**
Military service in time of
national emergency.
General provisions,
§§36-8-1 to 36-8-6.
See PUBLIC OFFICERS
AND EMPLOYEES.
Rescue squads, §§32-11-1 to
32-11-4.
See RESCUE SQUADS.
Telephones.
Party lines.
Failure to relinquish party
line for emergency
call, §37-8-213.
Falsely requesting party
line for emergency,
§37-8-213.

**EMERGENCY INTERIM
SUCCESSION ACT,**
§§29-3-1 to 29-3-16.
See LEGISLATURE.

**EMERGENCY
MANAGEMENT ACT.**
Civil defense, §§31-9-1 to
31-9-24.
See CIVIL DEFENSE.

**EMERGENCY MEDICAL
PERSONNEL.**
Diseases.
Notifiable diseases.
Notification of patient's
contagious condition,
§22-11A-38.

**EMERGENCY TELEPHONE
SERVICE,** §§11-98-1 to
11-98-7.
See TELEPHONES.

EMIGRATION.
Constitution of Alabama,
Const. Ala., art. I, §30.

EMINENT DOMAIN.
Abandonment of acquisition.
Arbitration and award,
§18-1A-256.
**Acquisition of
improvements.**
Improvements to be removed
or adversely affected,
§18-1A-28.
Actions.
Answers, §§18-1A-90,
18-1A-91, 18-1A-92.
Authority to bring action.
Direction of governor to
attorney of record,
§18-1A-270.
Commencement, §18-1A-71.
Complaint. See within this
heading, "Complaints."
Condemnation action
required, §18-1A-32.
Dismissal.
Damages, §18-1A-233.
Involuntary dismissal,
§18-1A-230.
Litigation expenses.
Award to defendant,
§18-1A-232.
Notice, §18-1A-75.
Restitution of property,
§18-1A-233.
Voluntary dismissal,
§18-1A-231.

EMINENT DOMAIN—Cont'd
Actions—Cont'd
Inverse condemnation.
Awarding plaintiff's
litigation expenses,
§18-1A-32.
Notice of pending action.
Recordation, §18-1A-75.
Prerequisites.
Offer to purchase,
§18-1A-55.
Procedure.
Generally, §18-1A-70.
Universities and colleges.
Use of condemnation
proceedings,
§18-1A-295.
Venue, §18-1A-71.
Affidavits.
Proceedings without
affidavit, §18-1A-270.
Agriculture.
Farmers' market authority.
No right of eminent
domain, §2-5-6.
Airports.
Municipal airports.
Acquisition of lands,
§4-4-6.
State airports.
Abandonment of
proceedings, §4-2-93.
Exercise of power in name
of state, §4-2-93.
Power of condemnation,
§4-2-90.
Answers.
Contents, §18-1A-91.
Preliminary objection,
§18-1A-91.
Hearing, §18-1A-93.
When answer required,
§18-1A-90.
Appeals.
Appeal of final judgment in
ad quod damnum
proceedings, §12-22-5.
Application to condemnation.
Denial, §18-1A-286.
Bonds.
Separate bonds.
Joint appeal, §18-1A-285.
Suspension of judgment.
Judgment not suspended
if bond given,
§18-1A-284.
Circuit court.
Assessment of damages
and compensation,
§18-1A-286.
Final judgment of circuit
court, §18-1A-288.
Compensation.
Assessment upon appeal,
§18-1A-286.
Costs.
Payment of costs on
appeal.
Issuance of order of
condemnation,
§18-1A-287.
Counties.
Public roads, bridges and
ferries, §23-1-82.
Damages.
Assessment upon appeal,
§18-1A-286.
Deposit into court.
Judgment not suspended
by appeal,
§18-1A-284.

EMINENT DOMAIN—Cont'd
Appeals—Cont'd
Damages—Cont'd
Deposit into court—Cont'd
Right of entry,
§18-1A-289.
Payment of damages.
Issuance of order of
condemnation on
appeal, §18-1A-287.
Joint appeals.
Separate bond, §18-1A-285.
Notice of appeal, §18-1A-283.
Orders of court.
Effect of appeal,
§18-1A-289.
Issuance upon payment of
damages upon appeal,
§18-1A-287.
Right of appeal, §18-1A-283.
Right of entry.
Effect of appeal,
§18-1A-284.
Pending appeal.
Deposit into court of
damages and
compensation,
§18-1A-289.
Suspension of judgment.
When not suspended,
§18-1A-284.
Trial, §18-1A-283.
Applicability of chapter,
§18-1A-311.
Appraisals.
Basis.
Written statement of basis
for amount of
compensation,
§18-1A-22.
Changes in fair market value
caused by project to be
disregarded, §18-1A-22.
Offer to purchase at full
appraised value,
§18-1A-22.
Owner may accompany
appraiser, §18-1A-21.
Reduction in compensation
based on benefits,
§18-1A-22.
Required, §18-1A-21.
Arbitration and award.
Abandonment of acquisition,
§18-1A-256.
Absence of concurrent
condemnation action,
§18-1A-254.
Authorized, §18-1A-250.
Effect of pending
condemnation action,
§18-1A-253.
Effect on right to commence
action, §18-1A-252.
Enforceability of agreement,
§18-1A-251.
Noncompliance with articles
2 and 3, §18-1A-250.
Procedure, §18-1A-255.
Recordation of agreement,
§18-1A-257.
When agreement may be
made, §18-1A-252.
Assessments.
Costs, §18-1A-293.
Atomic energy.
Disposal of nuclear waste.
Non-consent of state to
acquisition of land by
federal government,
§22-14-16.

EMINENT DOMAIN—Cont'd
Aviation.
Aircraft control and warning
stations.
City may pay awards and
costs of condemnation
proceedings by federal
government, §4-7-2.
Airport authorities.
Alternate procedure for
incorporation.
Powers, §4-3-47.
Airports.
Municipal airports.
Acquisition of lands by,
§4-4-6.
State airports.
Abandonment of
proceedings, §4-2-93.
Exercise of power in
name of state,
§4-2-93.
Power of condemnation,
§4-2-90.
**Bear Creek development
authority.**
Acquisition of certain
property or rights not
authorized, §33-15-5.
Bonds, surety.
Counties.
Proceedings without bond,
§18-1A-270.
Entry upon property,
§18-1A-52.
State.
Proceedings without bond,
§18-1A-270.
Bridges.
Power in internal
improvement
corporations, §10-5-1.
Burden of proof.
Amount of compensation,
§18-1A-153.
Hearings.
Preliminary objections,
§18-1A-94.
Canals.
Condemnation of ways and
rights of way, §10-5-4.
Power of internal
improvement
corporations, §10-5-1.
Cemeteries.
Rights of way.
Private parties, §§18-3-20
to 18-3-22.
Citation of chapter, §18-1A-1.
Coercion.
Actions prohibited,
§18-1A-26.
Commissioners.
Appointment, §18-1A-279.
Notice.
Service of notice,
§18-1A-280.
Assessments, §18-1A-281.
Reports, §18-1A-282.
Compensation.
Assessments, §18-1A-281.
Investment.
Report, §18-1A-282.
Damages.
Assessment, §18-1A-282.
Evidence.
Damages.
Receiving all evidence,
§18-1A-281.
Qualifications, §18-1A-279.

EMINENT DOMAIN—Cont'd
Commissioners—Cont'd
Reports.
Assessment, §18-1A-282.
Vacancy, §18-1A-279.
View of land, §18-1A-281.
Compensation.
Appeals.
Assessment upon appeal, §18-1A-286.
Deposit into court.
Right of entry, §18-1A-289.
Apportionment.
Separation of issues of compensation and apportionment, §18-1A-154.
Arbitration of compensation, §§18-1A-250 to 18-1A-257. See within this heading, "Arbitration and award."
Assessment.
Appeal to circuit court, §18-1A-286.
Commissioner, §18-1A-281.
Burden of proof, §18-1A-153.
Commissioners.
Assessments.
Reports, §18-1A-282.
Evidence.
Receiving of evidence, §18-1A-281.
Decrease in value due to owner's neglect, §18-1A-173.
Distribution among property owners.
Claims.
Adverse claim or title.
Assertion, §18-1A-292.
Court doubtful as to proper distribution.
Proceedings, §18-1A-292.
Determination by court, §18-1A-291.
Filing, §18-1A-291.
Proceedings when claims not filed, §18-1A-292.
Title to land.
Assertion of adverse claim or title, §18-1A-292.
Effect of condemnation action on value, §18-1A-173.
Evidence.
General provisions. See within this heading, "Evidence."
Fair market value.
Defined, §18-1A-172.
Highest and best use.
Jury issue, §18-1A-174.
Interest, §18-1A-211.
Opinion evidence as to value. See within this heading, "Evidence."
Partial taking, §18-1A-170.
Payment.
After judgment from funds deposited with court, §18-1A-216.
Failure to pay.
Effect, §18-1A-290.
Issuance for order of condemnation, §18-1A-282.

EMINENT DOMAIN—Cont'd
Compensation—Cont'd
Payment—Cont'd
Time for payment, §18-1A-290.
Performance of work to reduce amount of award, §18-1A-213.
Reduction of costs of incidental benefits from taking.
Prohibited, §18-1A-171.
Separation of issues of compensation and apportionment, §18-1A-154.
Standards.
Generally, §18-1A-170.
Taxation.
Deduction of taxes from award, §18-1A-214.
Valuation of second taking, §18-1A-173.
Complaints.
Amendment.
After notice of pending action filed, §18-1A-75.
Contents, §18-1A-72.
Costs, §18-1A-293.
Filing.
Commencement of condemnation actions, §18-1A-71.
Joinder of lands in same county, §18-1A-73.
Separate hearing for each owner, §18-1A-73.
Map or diagram to accompany, §18-1A-72.
Orders of court.
Order granting or refusing complaint, §18-1A-276.
Probate courts.
Deemed opened at all times, §18-1A-294.
Property already subject to public use, §18-1A-72.
Railroads.
Easement to cross line of another railroad, §18-1A-72.
Compromise and settlement, §18-1A-4.
Conflicting provisions, §18-1A-2.
Constitution of Alabama, Const. Ala., art. I, §23.
Municipal and other corporations.
Taking of property for public use, Const. Ala., art. XII, §235.
Constitution of the United States, Const. U. S., Amendment V.
Coosa Valley development authority.
Exercise of power, §33-16-8.
Corporations.
Constitutional provisions, Const. Ala., art. XII, §235.
Foreign corporations, §10-2A-228.
Corrections.
Institution finance authority.
Powers of eminent domain, §14-2-9.

EMINENT DOMAIN—Cont'd
Costs.
Appeals.
Payment of costs on appeal.
Issuance of order of condemnation, §18-1A-287.
Right of entry pending appeal, §18-1A-289.
Assessment, §18-1A-293.
Hearings.
Guardian ad litem.
Compensation, §18-1A-275.
Payment.
Issuance of order of condemnation, §18-1A-287.
Counties.
See COUNTIES.
Damages.
Assessments.
Appeal to circuit court, §18-1A-286.
Commissioner, §18-1A-281.
Award upon dismissal of actions, §18-1A-233.
Commissioners.
Assessments.
Reports, §18-1A-282.
Distribution among property owners, §§18-1A-291, 18-1A-292.
Entry upon property.
Bonds, surety, §18-1A-52.
Payment of damages, §18-1A-54.
Proceeding or action to recover damages, §18-1A-54.
Payment.
Appeals.
Issuance of order of condemnation on appeal, §18-1A-287.
Failure to pay.
Effect, §18-1A-290.
Issuance of order of condemnation on appeal, §§18-1A-275, 18-1A-287.
Suspension of judgment.
Judgment not suspended if damages paid, §18-1A-284.
Time for payment, §18-1A-290.
Rights of way.
Private parties, §18-3-2.
Cemeteries or graveyards, §18-3-21.
Dams.
Authorization for dams.
Dams considered as authorized by legislature, §10-4-323.
Companies constructing, operating or maintaining.
Condemnation of ways and rights of way, §10-5-4.
Dams on navigable rivers, §33-7-31.
Erection of dams for mills, factories, etc., §§18-2-1 to 18-2-21.
See DAMS.
Procedure for condemnation, §10-4-322.

EMINENT DOMAIN—Cont'd
Dams—Cont'd
Routes and sites.
Rights of condemning
corporations in
selection, §10-5-8.
Definitions, §18-1A-3.
Fair market value,
§18-1A-172.
Uneconomic remnant,
§18-1A-27.
Deposit of funds.
Commissioners.
Issuance of order of
condemnation,
§18-1A-282.
Interest.
Allocation, §18-1A-111.
Investment, §18-1A-111.
Payment after judgment from
funds deposited with
court, §18-1A-216.
Withdrawal of funds.
Crediting amounts paid or
withdrawn from
deposited funds,
§18-1A-212.
Withdrawal before
judgment.
Motion, §18-1A-110.
Disclaimer.
Filing, §18-1A-92.
Generally, §18-1A-92.
Where no interest claimed,
§18-1A-90.
Discovery, §18-1A-130.
Dower.
Ascertainment and payment
of dower interest,
§§35-4-190 to 35-4-192.
Easements.
Railroads.
Crossings.
Acquisition of easement,
§18-1A-273.
Easement to cross line of
another railroad,
§18-1A-72.
Rights of way generally,
§§18-3-1 to 18-3-3.
Telegraph companies.
Foreign companies.
Acquisition of easements
for connecting lines,
§18-1A-272.
Telephone companies. See
within this heading,
"Telephone companies."
Education.
City boards of education,
§16-11-13.
Electric cooperatives.
Power to exercise, §37-6-3.
Electricity.
Companies constructing,
operating or maintaining
public utility.
Condemnation of ways and
rights of way, §10-5-4.
Dams.
Erection of dams for
electric generators,
§§18-2-1 to 18-2-21.
See DAMS.
Electric utilities.
Condemnation by electric
utilities, §§37-4-130,
37-4-131.
Power in public utility
corporations, §10-5-1.

EMINENT DOMAIN—Cont'd
Electricity—Cont'd
Routes and sites.
Rights of condemning
corporations in
selection, §10-5-8.
Entry upon property.
Authorized, §18-1A-50.
Bonds, surety, §18-1A-52.
Damages.
Bonds, surety, §18-1A-52.
Payment, §18-1A-54.
Proceeding or action to
recover, §18-1A-54.
Orders of court, §18-1A-51.
Modification, §18-1A-53.
Scope, §18-1A-50.
Suitability studies,
§18-1A-50.
Environmental control.
Environmental improvement
authorities.
Powers of authority, §9-6-8.
Evidence.
Admissibility, §18-1A-131.
Commissioners.
Damages.
Receiving all evidence
touching damages,
§18-1A-281.
Compensation.
Commissioners.
Receiving of evidence,
§18-1A-281.
Hearings.
Consideration of evidence,
§18-1A-276.
Procedure, §18-1A-277.
Opinion evidence as to value.
Basis, §18-1A-196.
Factors upon which
opinion may not be
based, §18-1A-197.
Evidence supporting
opinion, §18-1A-193.
Factors upon which opinion
may not be based,
§18-1A-197.
Owner's opinion,
§18-1A-195.
When authorized,
§18-1A-192.
Who may give, §18-1A-192.
Order of presentation,
§18-1A-152.
Partial taking.
Evidence supporting
opinion as to
remainder value,
§18-1A-194.
Scope of article, §18-1A-190.
View of property taken,
§18-1A-191.
Expenses.
Incidental to transfer of title,
§18-1A-30.
Fair market value.
Defined, §18-1A-172.
General provisions. See
within this heading,
"Compensation."
Federal aid.
Compliance with
requirements for,
§18-1A-5.
Construction of article,
§18-1A-33.

EMINENT DOMAIN—Cont'd
Forests and forestry.
Experimental work in
forestry.
Authorization and
procedure for
condemnation of lands,
§2-30-24.
State forestry commission.
Powers of commission,
§9-13-3.
Funds.
Deposit of funds. See within
this heading, "Deposit of
funds."
Gas.
Companies constructing,
operating or maintaining
public utility, §10-5-4.
Power in public utility
corporations, §10-5-1.
Routes and sites.
Rights of condemning
corporations in
selection, §10-5-8.
Governor.
Actions.
Direction of governor to
attorney of record.
Authority for bringing
action, §18-1A-270.
Graveyards.
Rights of way.
Private parties, §§18-3-20
to 18-3-22.
Guardian ad litem.
Hearings.
Appointment of guardians.
Infants or incompetents,
§18-1A-275.
Harbors and ports.
Acquisition of property and
rights of way by
purchase or eminent
domain proceedings,
§33-1-22.
Limitation on power of
eminent domain,
§33-1-12.
Privately-owned facilities.
Limitation on power of
eminent domain,
§33-1-12.
To what property eminent
domain applicable,
§33-1-23.
Hearings.
Appearance.
Attorneys, §18-1A-278.
Parties, §18-1A-278.
Cost.
Guardian ad litem.
Compensation,
§18-1A-275.
Evidence.
Consideration of evidence,
§18-1A-276.
Procedure, §18-1A-277.
Joinder of lands in same
county.
Separate hearing for each
owner, §18-1A-73.
Mentally ill.
Guardian ad litem.
Appointment,
§18-1A-275.
Minors.
Guardian ad litem.
Appointment,
§18-1A-275.

EMINENT DOMAIN—Cont'd
Hearings—Cont'd
Orders of court.
Entry of order, §18-1A-276.
Preliminary objections,
§18-1A-93.
Burden of proof, §18-1A-94.
Highest and best use.
Jury issue, §18-1A-174.
Highways.
General provisions.
See HIGHWAYS.
Rights of way.
Authority of department to
condemn, §23-1-45.
Private parties, §§18-3-1 to
18-3-3.
Hospitals.
County and municipal
hospital authorities,
§22-21-180.
Municipal hospital building
authorities.
Power of eminent domain,
§22-21-138.
Public hospitals, §11-95-14.
Housing authorities.
County housing authorities.
Acquisition of property by
eminent domain,
§24-1-67.
Municipal housing
authorities.
Acquisition of property by
eminent domain,
§24-1-28.
Improvements.
Acquisition.
Improvements to be
removed or adversely
affected, §18-1A-28.
Tenant-owned improvements.
Compensation for,
§18-1A-29.
Inconsistent provisions,
§18-1A-310.
Industrial companies.
Condemnation for rights of
way or easements,
§10-5-3.
Interest.
Award.
Interest on award,
§18-1A-30.
Compensation, §18-1A-211.
Deposit of funds.
Allocation, §18-1A-111.
Inverse condemnation.
Actions.
Awarding plaintiff's
litigation expenses,
§18-1A-32.
Investments.
Deposit of funds, §18-1A-111.
Judgments.
Circuit court.
Appeal, §18-1A-288.
Contents, §18-1A-210.
Crediting amounts paid or
withdrawn from
deposited funds,
§18-1A-212.
Failure to pay.
Effect, §18-1A-215.
Interest on compensation
awarded, §18-1A-211.
Payment.
Effect of failure to pay,
§18-1A-215.

EMINENT DOMAIN—Cont'd
Judgments—Cont'd
Payment—Cont'd
Payment after judgment
from funds deposited
with court,
§18-1A-216.
Payment by plaintiffs,
§18-1A-214.
Performance of work to
reduce amount of award,
§18-1A-213.
Taxation.
Deduction of taxes from
award, §18-1A-214.
Junkyard control.
Acquisition of land.
Authority of director,
§23-1-248.
Jury.
Demand for trial by jury,
§18-1A-151.
Highest and best use.
Jury issue, §18-1A-174.
Procedures.
Generally, §18-1A-151.
Waiver, §18-1A-151.
Leases.
Rental to former owner or
tenant.
Amount of rent, §18-1A-25.
Life estates.
Ascertainment and payment
of life interest,
§§35-4-190 to 35-4-192.
Manufacturers.
Condemnation for rights of
way or easements by
manufacturing
companies, §10-5-3.
Routes and sites.
Rights of condemning
corporations in
selection, §10-5-8.
Maps.
Accompanying complaint,
§18-1A-72.
Mentally ill.
Hearings.
Guardian ad litem.
Appointment,
§18-1A-275.
Military affairs.
Armory commission.
Exercise of power of
condemnation,
§31-4-10.
Mines and minerals.
Condemnation for rights of
way or easements by
mining companies,
§10-5-3.
Routes and sites.
Rights of condemning
corporations in
selection, §10-5-8.
Minors.
Hearings.
Guardian ad litem.
Appointment,
§18-1A-275.
Motions.
Withdrawal of deposited
funds before judgment,
§18-1A-110.
Municipal corporations.
See MUNICIPAL
CORPORATIONS.

EMINENT DOMAIN—Cont'd
Notice.
Appeals.
Notice of appeal,
§18-1A-283.
Commissioners.
Appointment.
Service of notice,
§18-1A-280.
Dismissal of action,
§18-1A-75.
Pending action.
Recordation, §18-1A-75.
Termination of occupancy,
§18-1A-24.
Offer to purchase.
Prerequisite to condemnation
action, §18-1A-55.
**Opinion evidence as to
value,** §§18-1A-192 to
18-1A-197.
Orders of court.
Complaints.
Order granting or refusing,
§18-1A-276.
Effect of order, §18-1A-289.
Entry upon property.
Court order permitting,
§18-1A-51.
Modification, §18-1A-53.
Issuance.
Appeals.
When damages paid on
appeal, §18-1A-287.
Deposit of damages or
compensation in court,
§18-1A-282.
Effect of order of
condemnation,
§18-1A-289.
Suspension.
Effect of appeal,
§18-1A-284.
Partial taking.
Compensation, §18-1A-170.
Evidence.
Remainder value in partial
taking, §18-1A-194.
Payment of purchase price.
Prerequisite to surrender of
property, §18-1A-23.
Penitentiary.
Acquisition of land, etc.,
§18-1A-271.
Piers.
Power of eminent domain in
internal improvement
corporations, §10-5-1.
Pipelines.
Companies constructing,
operating or maintaining
internal improvement.
Condemnation of ways and
rights of way, §10-5-4.
Power of eminent domain in
internal improvement
corporations, §10-5-1.
Routes and sites.
Rights of condemning
corporations in
selection, §10-5-8.
**Policies governing land
acquisition.**
Application of article,
§18-1A-20.
Construction of article,
§18-1A-33.
Noncompliance with article.
Not to affect validity of
condemnor's interest,
§18-1A-33.

EMINENT DOMAIN—Cont'd
Possession of property.
Prerequisites to surrender of
possession, §18-1A-23.
Termination of occupancy.
Notice, §18-1A-24.
Power districts.
District to have power,
§37-5-3.
Rights of way.
Private parties.
Cemeteries or
graveyards.
Application to probate
court, §18-3-22.
Public roads or
highways.
Application to probate
court, §18-3-3.
Preliminary objections.
Award of litigation expenses
to defendant, §18-1A-95.
Disposition, §18-1A-95.
Generally, §18-1A-91.
Hearings, §18-1A-93.
Burden of proof, §18-1A-94.
Prisons and prisoners.
Acquisition of land, etc.,
§18-1A-271.
Probate courts.
Application.
Who may apply,
§18-1A-270.
Deemed opened at all times,
§18-1A-294.
Procedure.
Generally, §18-1A-70.
**Property already subject to
public use,** §18-1A-72.
Public utilities.
Companies constructing,
operating or maintaining
public utility, §10-5-4.
Power of eminent domain,
§10-5-1.
Radio utility systems.
Antennas and towers,
§37-4-113.
Public works.
Improvement authorities.
Powers, §39-7-22.
Quarries.
Condemnation for rights of
way or easements by
quarrying companies,
§10-5-3.
Sites.
Rights of condemning
corporations in
selection, §10-5-8.
Radio.
Radio utility systems.
Right of eminent domain,
§37-4-113.
Railroad authorities.
Powers of authorities,
§37-13-7.
Railroads.
Condemnation for ways and
rights of way, §§10-5-2,
10-5-4.
Crossings.
Easements.
Acquisition, §18-1A-273.
Depots, yards and tracks.
Condemnation of lands for,
§10-5-7.
Easements.
Crossings.
Acquisition, §18-1A-273.

EMINENT DOMAIN—Cont'd
Railroads—Cont'd
Easements—Cont'd
Easement to cross line of
another railroad,
§18-1A-72.
Power of eminent domain in
internal improvement
corporations, §10-5-1.
Routes and sites.
Rights of condemning
corporations in
selection, §10-5-8.
Subways.
Municipal corporations.
Acquisition of land,
§18-1A-274.
Viaducts.
Municipal corporations.
Acquisition of land,
§18-1A-274.
Recordation.
Arbitration agreement,
§18-1A-257.
Notice of pending action,
§18-1A-75.
Redevelopment projects.
Powers of housing authorities
or municipalities,
§24-2-3.
**Rental to former owner or
tenant.**
Amount of rent, §18-1A-25.
Reports.
Commissioners.
Assessments, §18-1A-282.
Restitution of property.
Dismissal of action,
§18-1A-233.
**Right of entry upon
property.**
Appeals.
Effect of appeal,
§18-1A-284.
Pending appeals.
Deposit into court of
damages and
compensation,
§18-1A-289.
Rights of way.
Private parties.
Cemeteries or graveyards,
§§18-3-20 to 18-3-22.
Acquisition, §18-3-20.
Application to probate
court, §18-3-22.
Compensation.
Payment, §18-3-21.
Damages.
Payment, §18-3-21.
Probate court.
Application to probate
court, §18-3-22.
Width, §18-3-20.
Yards, gardens, orchards,
etc.
Rights of way through,
§18-3-21.
Compensation.
Payment, §18-3-2.
Public roads or highways.
Acquisition, §18-3-1.
Application to probate
court, §18-3-3.
Damages.
Payment, §18-3-2.
Width, §18-3-1.
Roads.
Rights of way.
Private parties, §§18-3-1 to
18-3-3.

EMINENT DOMAIN—Cont'd
Rules of civil procedure.
Governing of procedure for
condemnation of
property, §18-1A-70.
Scope of chapter, §18-1A-2.
Service of process, §18-1A-74.
Sewers.
Routes and sites.
Rights of condemning
corporations in
selection of routes and
sites, §10-5-8.
Short title of chapter,
§18-1A-1.
Soil and water conservation.
Watershed conservancy
districts.
Powers of board of
directors, §9-8-61.
**Solid waste disposal
authorities.**
Power of eminent domain,
§11-89A-14.
**Southeast interstate low-
level radioactive waste
management compact.**
Acquisition of disposal sites,
§22-32-3.
**Southern products mart
authority.**
Acquisition of real property
or rights owned by
railroads or utilities not
authorized, §41-10-54.
**State products mart and
coliseum authority.**
Powers of corporation,
§41-10-92.
Subways.
Municipal corporations.
Acquisition of land,
§18-1A-274.
Suitability studies.
Entry upon property,
§18-1A-50.
Taxation.
Deduction of taxes from
award, §18-1A-214.
Telegraph companies.
Foreign companies.
Acquisition of easements,
§18-1A-272.
Telephone companies.
Condemnation of ways and
rights of way by
companies constructing,
operating or maintaining
public utility, §10-5-4.
Foreign companies.
Acquisition of easements
for connecting lines,
§18-1A-272.
Power of eminent domain,
§10-5-1.
Routes and sites.
Rights of condemning
corporations in
selection, §10-5-8.
Tenants.
Improvements.
Compensation for tenant-
owned improvements,
§18-1A-29.
Termination of occupancy.
Notice, §18-1A-24.
Title.
Adverse claim or title.
Distribution of award
among property
owners, §18-1A-292.

EMINENT DOMAIN—Cont'd
Title—Cont'd
Transfer of title.
Expenses incidental to,
§18-1A-30.
**Tombigbee Valley
development authority.**
Exercise of power, §33-17-8.
Trial.
Appeals, §18-1A-283.
Arguments.
Order of argument,
§18-1A-152.
Burden of proof, §18-1A-153.
Evidence.
Order of presentation,
§18-1A-152.
Juries.
Demand for trial by jury,
§18-1A-151.
Procedure, §18-1A-151.
Separate trial of nonjury
issues, §18-1A-150.
Setting for trial, §18-1A-150.
Uneconomic remnant.
Defined, §18-1A-27.
Offer to acquire, §18-1A-27.
United States.
Condemnation of land or
rights of way, §§42-2-1 to
42-2-12.
See UNITED STATES.
Universities and colleges.
Use of condemnation
proceedings, §18-1A-295.
University of Montevallo.
Lands may be condemned,
§16-54-15.
Utilities. See within this
heading, "Public utilities."
Utility services facilities.
Powers of corporation,
§11-97-14.
Venue.
Actions, §18-1A-71.
Viaducts.
Municipal corporations.
Acquisition of land,
§18-1A-274.
Power of eminent domain in
internal improvement
corporations, §10-5-1.
**View of land or property
taken,** §18-1A-191.
Commissioners, §18-1A-281.
Waiver.
Failure to comply with
sections 18-1A-20 to
18-1A-30, §18-1A-31.
**Water conservation and
irrigation.**
Agency.
Powers of corporation,
§9-10-5.
Corporations.
Right of eminent domain,
§9-10-34.
**Water management and
drainage.**
Districts.
Powers of eminent domain,
§9-9-21.
Drainage subdistricts.
Damages, §9-9-78.
Right of condemnation,
§9-9-78.
Waters and watercourses.
See WATERS AND
WATERCOURSES.

EMINENT DOMAIN—Cont'd
**Water supply and
waterworks.**
Companies constructing,
operating or maintaining
public utility, §10-5-4.
Power of eminent domain,
§10-5-1.
Routes and sites.
Rights of condemning
corporations in
selection, §10-5-8.
Water sources, riparian
rights and necessary
lands.
Condemnation, §10-5-6.
Wharves.
Power of eminent domain in
internal improvement
corporations, §10-5-1.

**EMPLOYERS AND
EMPLOYEES.**
Agencies.
Employment agencies,
§§34-10-1 to 34-10-5.
Blacklists.
Maintaining blacklists,
§13A-11-123.
Blind persons.
Employment by state,
political subdivisions,
public schools, etc.,
§21-7-8.
Bribery.
Commercial bribery,
§13A-11-120.
Child labor, §§25-8-1 to
25-8-31.
See LABOR.
Commercial bribery,
§13A-11-120.
Contracts.
Covenants not to compete,
§8-1-1.
Convict labor, §§14-5-1 to
14-5-11.
See PRISONS AND
PRISONERS.
Corporations.
See CORPORATIONS.
Covenants not to compete,
§8-1-1.
Criminal law and procedure.
Bribery.
Commercial bribery,
§13A-11-120.
Death.
Employer's liability for
certain injuries, §§25-6-1
to 25-6-4.
Workmen's compensation,
§§25-5-1 to 25-5-231.
See WORKMEN'S
COMPENSATION.
Elections.
Corporations.
Coercion of employees,
§17-23-11.
Employer intimidating
employee, §17-23-10.
Fair campaign practices.
Job discrimination to
solicit money,
§17-22A-20.
**Employer's liability for
certain injuries.**
Applicability of sections
25-5-31 and 25-5-32 to
other claims for personal
injury or death, §25-5-33.

**EMPLOYERS AND
EMPLOYEES**—Cont'd
**Employer's liability for
certain injuries**—Cont'd
Damages recovered not
subject to debts of
employee, §25-6-2.
Death.
Maintenance of action by
personal
representative,
§25-6-3.
Debts of employee.
Damages recovered not
subject to debts,
§25-6-2.
Defect causing injury.
Effect of employee's
knowledge of defect,
§25-6-1.
Defenses.
Excluded defenses,
§25-5-32.
Disposition of damages
recovered, §25-6-3.
Effect of employee's
knowledge of defect or
negligence, §25-6-1.
Generally, §25-6-1.
Insurance benefits, etc.
Acceptance not to bar
action, §25-6-4.
Negligence causing injury.
Effect of employee's
knowledge, §25-6-1.
Personal representatives.
Maintenance of action by,
§25-6-3.
Right of action for damages
for injuries or death of
employee, §25-5-31.
Second injury trust fund.
Escheat of judgments
under employer's
liability act, §25-5-71.
Setoff of contributions to
insurance, §25-6-4.
Employment agencies,
§§34-10-1 to 34-10-5.
**Governor's committee on
employment of the
handicapped,** §§21-5-1 to
21-5-10.
See HANDICAPPED
PERSONS.
Handicapped persons.
Governor's committee on
employment of the
handicapped, §§21-5-1 to
21-5-10.
See HANDICAPPED
PERSONS.
Historic Blakeley authority.
Insurance programs provided
for state employees.
Participation of authority
employees, §41-10-180.
Income tax.
Deductions.
Contributions paid by
employer under stock
bonus, pension, profit-
sharing or annuity
plan, §40-18-15.
Trusts.
Contributions to trust
made by employer,
§40-18-25.
Withholding tax, §§40-18-70
to 40-18-80.
See INCOME TAX.

EMPLOYERS AND EMPLOYEES—Cont'd

Injuries.

Employer's liability for certain injuries, §§25-6-1 to 25-6-4.

Workmen's compensation, §§25-5-1 to 25-5-231.

See WORKMEN'S COMPENSATION.

Injury by fellow servant.

Affirmative defense, ARCP, Rule 8 (c).

Involuntary servitude.

Constitution of Alabama, Const. Ala., art. I, §32.

Constitution of the United States, Const. U. S., Amendments XIII, XV.

Jury.

Compensation to which employees entitled during jury service, §12-16-8.

Discharge of employee on jury duty.

Employee's cause of action upon discharge, §12-16-8.1.

Forbidden, §12-16-8.1.

Employee's cause of action upon discharge.

Damages, §12-16-8.1.

Provision supplemental to other law, §12-16-8.1.

Excusing of employees for jury service, §12-16-8.

When employee must return to work, §12-16-8.1.

Labor.

General provisions.

See LABOR.

Liens for wages.

Agricultural laborers, §§35-11-91 to 35-11-97.

Lumber employees or laborers, §§35-11-270 to 35-11-273.

See LUMBER.

Railroad employees, §§35-11-91 to 35-11-97.

Sawmill employees or laborers, §§35-11-270 to 35-11-273.

Timber employees or laborers, §§35-11-270 to 35-11-273.

Motor vehicles.

Safety-responsibility act.

Employment of necessary employees by director of public safety, §32-7-38.

Proof of financial responsibility.

Owner may give proof for employees, §32-7-28.

Noncompetitive clause.

Covenants not to compete, §8-1-1.

Prisons and prisoners.

Convict labor, §§14-5-1 to 14-5-11.

See PRISONS AND PRISONERS.

EMPLOYERS AND EMPLOYEES—Cont'd

Public officers and employees.

See PUBLIC OFFICERS AND EMPLOYEES.

Right to work law, §§25-7-30 to 25-7-36.

See LABOR.

Toxic substances in the workplace, §§22-33-1 to 22-33-15.

See TOXIC SUBSTANCES IN THE WORKPLACE.

Trusts and trustees.

Trusts for employees or self-employed persons, §35-4-259.

Unemployment compensation, §§25-4-1 to 25-4-152.

See UNEMPLOYMENT COMPENSATION.

Unions, §§25-7-1 to 25-7-54.

See LABOR.

Wages.

See WAGES.

Withholding tax, §§40-18-70 to 40-18-80.

See INCOME TAX.

Workmen's compensation, §§25-5-1 to 25-5-231.

See WORKMEN'S COMPENSATION.

EMPLOYMENT AGENCIES, §§34-10-1 to 34-10-5.

Licenses.

Application, §34-10-2.

Renewal application, §34-10-3.

Change of names of persons on license, §34-10-3.

Contents, §34-10-3.

Corporations.

Effect of changes in corporation, §34-10-4.

Expiration, §34-10-3.

Fees.

Annual license fee, §34-10-5.

Operation or maintenance of employment agency.

Prohibited without license, §34-10-1.

Partnerships.

Admission of partners to business, §34-10-4.

Qualifications of applicants, §34-10-1.

Renewal, §34-10-3.

Required, §34-10-1.

Term, §34-10-3.

Transferability, §34-10-4.

EMPLOYMENT SECURITY.

General provisions, §§25-4-1 to 25-4-152.

See UNEMPLOYMENT COMPENSATION.

ENCEPHALITIS.

Notifiable diseases, §§22-11A-1 to 22-11A-38.

See DISEASES.

ENCUMBRANCES.

Liens.

General provisions.

See LIENS.

ENCUMBRANCES—Cont'd

Liens—Cont'd

Mechanics' and materialmen's liens.

See MECHANICS' AND MATERIALMEN'S LIENS.

Mortgages and deeds of trust.

See MORTGAGES AND DEEDS OF TRUST.

Secured transactions, §§7-9-101 to 7-9-507.

See COMMERCIAL CODE.

ENDORSEMENTS.

Assignments.

Action to charge endorser or assignor on contracts assigned by writing and not covered by uniform commercial code, §§8-5-26 to 8-5-30.

Bonds.

Assignable by endorsement, §8-5-20.

Contracts.

Assignable by endorsement, §8-5-20.

Commercial code.

Indorsements.

See COMMERCIAL CODE.

Hospitals.

Liens of hospitals.

Verified statement, §35-11-371.

Lis pendens.

Notices in record to be endorsed on original, §35-4-133.

Mechanics' and materialmen's liens.

Verified statement.

Endorsement by probate judge, §35-11-216.

Uniform commercial code.

Indorsements.

See COMMERCIAL CODE.

ENEMY ATTACK.

Civil defense, §§31-9-1 to 31-9-24.

See CIVIL DEFENSE.

Emergency interim succession, §§29-3-1 to 29-3-16.

See LEGISLATURE.

ENERGY.

Atomic energy.

See ATOMIC ENERGY.

Cogeneration facilities, §§37-12-1 to 37-12-5.

Citation of act, §37-12-1.

Coal.

Purchase of coal produced in Alabama, §37-12-5.

Declaration of public policy, §37-12-2.

Federal rules and regulations.

Incorporation by reference, §37-12-3.

Implementation of chapter.

Public service commission, §37-12-4.

Policy.

Declaration of public policy, §37-12-2.

Public service commission.

Implementation of chapter, §37-12-4.

ENERGY—Cont'd
Cogeneration facilities
—Cont'd
Rules and regulations.
Promulgation, §37-12-3.
Short title of act, §37-12-1.
Conservation.
Energy conservation building
code, §§41-9-170 to
41-9-174.
See BUILDINGS.
Management, §§41-6A-1 to
41-6A-11.
See ENERGY
MANAGEMENT AND
CONSERVATION.
Department of energy.
See ENERGY
MANAGEMENT AND
CONSERVATION.
Electricity.
See ELECTRICITY.
Gas.
See GAS.
Management.
Conservation, §§41-6A-1 to
41-6A-11.
See ENERGY
MANAGEMENT AND
CONSERVATION.
**Southern states energy
compact,** §§9-18A-1 to
9-18A-4.
**Synfuels development
authority,** §§9-6A-1 to
9-6A-10.
See SYNFUELS
DEVELOPMENT
AUTHORITY.
Water power companies.
See DAMS.

**ENERGY MANAGEMENT
AND CONSERVATION,**
§§41-6A-1 to 41-6A-11.
Advisory council.
Compensation of members,
§41-6A-8.
Composition of members,
§41-6A-8.
Creation, §41-6A-8.
Duties, §41-6A-9.
Functions, §41-6A-9.
Meetings, §41-6A-8.
Officers, §41-6A-8.
Terms of members, §41-6A-8.
Appropriations.
Operation of department of
energy, §41-6A-10.
Awareness programs.
Public awareness and
education programs.
Objectives, §41-6A-5.
**Confidentiality of proprietor
information,** §41-6A-11.
Contracts.
Department of energy.
Assumption of contract,
§41-6A-10.
Contracts with other
agencies, departments,
etc., §41-6A-7.
Data.
Clearinghouse for energy
data.
Function of department,
§41-6A-4.
Department of energy.
Abstract of proposal sent to
department, §41-6A-7.

**ENERGY MANAGEMENT
AND CONSERVATION**
—Cont'd
Department of energy
—Cont'd
Administration of chapter,
§41-6A-7.
Agencies, departments, etc.,
affecting chapter to
report to department,
§41-6A-7.
Appropriations by
legislature, §41-6A-10.
Contracts.
Assumption of contracts of
energy management
board, §41-6A-10.
Contracts with other
agencies, departments,
etc., §41-6A-7.
Creation, §41-6A-3.
Data.
Clearinghouse for energy
data, §41-6A-4.
Department of economic and
community affairs.
Transfer of functions,
§41-23-1.
Director.
Administration of
department, §41-6A-3.
Appointment, §41-6A-3.
Synfuels development
authority.
Individuals who may
become public
corporation, §9-6A-3.
Duties of officers, §41-6A-3.
Education.
Public awareness and
education programs.
Objectives of programs,
§41-6A-5.
Employees of department,
§41-6A-3.
Functions of department,
§41-6A-4.
Grants.
Abstracts of grant
proposals sent to
department, §41-6A-7.
Organization, §41-6A-3.
Rules and regulations.
Authority of department,
§41-6A-6.
Scope of rules, §41-6A-6.
State departments and
agencies.
Other agencies,
departments, etc.,
affecting chapter to
report to department of
energy, §41-6A-7.
Education.
Public awareness and
education programs.
Objectives, §41-6A-5.
Energy management board.
Department of energy to
assume appropriations
and contracts of former
board, §41-6A-10.
Grants.
Abstract of proposal sent to
department, §41-6A-7.
Legislative intent, §41-6A-2.
Proprietary information.
Confidentiality to be
maintained by
department employees,
§41-6A-11.

**ENERGY MANAGEMENT
AND CONSERVATION**
—Cont'd
**Public awareness and
education programs.**
Objectives, §41-6A-5.
Rules and regulations.
Authority of department of
energy, §41-6A-6.
Scope of rules, §41-6A-6.
Short title of act, §41-6A-1.
**State departments and
agencies.**
Agencies, departments, etc.,
affecting chapter to
report to department of
energy, §41-6A-7.
Title of act, §41-6A-1.

ENGINEERS.
Appeals.
Board of registration.
Appeals from decisions of
board, §34-11-13.
Architects.
Interprofessional privileges
between architects and
professional engineers,
§34-2-32.
Associations.
Unincorporated professional
associations, §§10-10-1 to
10-10-16.
See UNINCORPORATED
PROFESSIONAL
ASSOCIATIONS.
Board of registration.
Appeals from decisions of
board, §34-11-13.
Appointment of members,
§34-11-30.
Compensation of members,
§34-11-32.
Composition, §34-11-30.
Creation, §34-11-30.
Defined, §34-11-1.
Disciplinary action,
§34-11-11.
Enforcement of chapter.
Powers and duties of
board, §34-11-35.
Examinations.
Authority of board,
§34-11-6.
Expenses of members,
§34-11-32.
Funds.
Receipts and
disbursements by
secretary of board,
§34-11-36.
Governor.
Annual report to governor,
§34-11-37.
Filling vacancies on board,
§34-11-33.
Removal of board
members, §34-11-33.
Immunity of board for good
faith actions, §34-11-35.
Legal office of board,
§34-11-34.
Meetings, §34-11-34.
Oaths.
Member's oath of office,
§34-11-30.
Power of members to
administer, §34-11-35.
Office.
Legal office of board,
§34-11-34.

ENGINEERS—Cont'd
Board of registration—Cont'd
Officers of board, §34-11-34.
Powers, §34-11-35.
Qualifications of members,
§34-11-31.
Quorum, §34-11-34.
Records, §34-11-37.
Reissuance of revoked
certificates, §34-11-12.
Removal of members,
§34-11-33.
Reports.
Annual report to governor,
§34-11-37.
Revocation or suspension of
registration certificate,
§34-11-11.
Rules and regulations.
Promulgation by board,
§34-11-35.
Rules of professional conduct.
Adoption, §34-11-35.
Seals.
Official seal of board,
§34-11-35.
Secretary.
Receipt and disbursement
of funds, §34-11-36.
Roster of registrants,
§34-11-3.
Subpoena power of board,
§34-11-35.
Terms of office,
§34-11-30.
Vacancies.
Filling vacancies,
§34-11-33.
Witnesses.
Power to compel
attendance of
witnesses, §34-11-35.
Certification.
Examinations, §§34-11-4,
34-11-6.
General requirements for
certification, §34-11-4.
Registration. See within this
heading, "Registration."
Coal mine safety.
Hoist engineers, §25-9-210.
**Conservation and natural
resources.**
Buildings and facilities.
Construction or
modification.
Contracts for advisory
engineering services,
§9-2-42.
Corporations.
Certificate of authorization,
§34-11-9.
Practice of engineering,
§34-11-9.
County engineers, §§11-6-1 to
11-6-25.
See COUNTIES.
Definitions, §34-11-1.
Enforcement of chapter.
Penalties for violations,
§34-11-15.
Engineer-in-training.
Defined, §34-11-1.
Fees, §34-11-5.
General certification
requirements, §34-11-4.
Issuance of certificate,
§34-11-7.

ENGINEERS—Cont'd
Evidence.
Board of registration.
Admissibility of board
records, §34-11-37.
Examinations, §§34-11-4,
34-11-6.
Exemptions from chapter,
§34-11-14.
Fees.
Duplicate certificates,
§34-11-12.
Examinations, §34-11-6.
Registration, §34-11-5.
Funds.
Board of registration.
Secretary to receive and
account for all funds,
§34-11-36.
Governor.
Board of registration. See
within this heading,
"Board of registration."
Harbors and ports.
Acquisition and operation of
wharves, docks and
warehouses by state.
Consultation with
engineers, §33-1-12.
Director of state docks.
Appointment of engineers
by director, §33-1-5.
Highways.
See HIGHWAYS.
Injunctions.
Board of registration.
Authority of board to seek
injunctions, §34-11-35.
Landscape architects.
Engineers exempt from
licensing requirements,
§34-17-27.
General provisions, §§34-17-1
to 34-17-27.
See LANDSCAPE
ARCHITECTS.
Licenses, §40-12-99.
Municipal corporations,
§§11-48-10, 11-48-12.
Partnerships.
Certificate of authorization,
§34-11-9.
Practice of engineering,
§34-11-9.
Disciplinary action,
§34-11-11.
Penalties.
Violations of chapter,
§34-11-15.
Policy.
Public policy regarding
regulation of
engineering, §34-11-2.
Practice of engineering.
Corporate practice, §34-11-9.
Defined, §34-11-1.
Exemptions from
requirements of chapter,
§34-11-14.
Partnership practice,
§34-11-9.
Regulation of practice,
§34-11-2.
Public work.
Services of professional
engineer required,
§34-11-10.

ENGINEERS—Cont'd
Registration.
Applications, §§34-11-5,
34-11-15.
Record of applicants to be
kept by board,
§34-11-37.
Board of registration,
§§34-11-30 to 34-11-37.
See within this heading,
"Board of registration."
Certificate.
Duplicate certificate,
§34-11-12.
Expiration, §34-11-8.
Issuance of certificate,
§34-11-7.
Renewal, §34-11-8.
Corporations.
Registration of corporation
prohibited, §34-11-9.
Examinations, §§34-11-4,
34-11-6.
Fees, §34-11-5.
General requirements for
registration, §34-11-4.
Issuance of certificate,
§34-11-7.
Partnerships.
Registration of partnership
prohibited, §34-11-9.
Policy regarding registration
requirements, §34-11-2.
Revocation or suspension of
certificate.
Appeals from decisions of
board, §34-11-13.
Grounds, §34-11-11.
Power of board, §34-11-11.
Reissuance of revoked
certificate,
§34-11-12.
Roster of registrants,
§34-11-3.
Seal, §34-11-7.
Responsible charge.
Defined, §34-11-1.
**Rules of professional
conduct.**
Adoption, §34-11-35.
Seals.
Board of registration.
Official seal, §34-11-35.
Registered professional
engineer, §34-11-7.
Subpoenas.
Board of registration.
Subpoena power of board,
§34-11-35.
**Unincorporated professional
associations,** §§10-10-1 to
10-10-16.
See UNINCORPORATED
PROFESSIONAL
ASSOCIATIONS.
**Water management and
drainage.**
Districts.
See WATER
MANAGEMENT AND
DRAINAGE.
Witnesses.
Board of registration.
Power to compel
attendance of
witnesses, §34-11-35.

ENGLISH COMMON LAW.
Adopted, §1-3-1.

ENGLISH SPARROWS.
  Hunting.
    Unprotected birds, §9-11-233.

ENTERPRISE ZONES,
  §§41-23-20 to 41-23-32.
  Additional requirements for business to receive benefits, §41-23-26.
  Advisory council.
    Appointment of members, §41-23-23.
    Composition, §41-23-23.
    Definition of council, §41-23-21.
    Implementation of law, §41-23-23.
    Selection of zones.
      Input from council, §41-23-23.
  Applications.
    Processing, §41-23-23.
  Citation of act, §41-23-20.
  Construction and interpretation.
    Complementary to and consistent with federal tax exemptions, §41-23-32.
    Superseded when necessary by federal enterprise zone legislation, §41-23-32.
  Contracts.
    Preference and priority to state manufacturers, suppliers, contractors and labor, §41-23-30.
    Tax exemptions, §41-23-30.
    Wage subsidies, §41-23-30.
  Cooperation of state agencies and departments, §41-23-31.
  Creation within Class 1 cities, §11-40-16.
    See MUNICIPAL CORPORATIONS.
  Definitions, §41-23-21.
  Department of economic and community affairs.
    Department defined, §41-23-21.
    Duties.
      Generally, §41-23-29.
    Powers.
      Generally, §41-23-29.
    Reports.
      Annual reports, §41-23-27.
  Duration of enterprise zones, §41-23-22.
  Employee training and technical assistance.
    Nontax incentives, §41-23-25.
  Federal enterprise zone legislation.
    Superseded when necessary by, §41-23-32.
  Governing authorities.
    Agreements.
      Required agreements by appropriate governing authorities, §41-23-28.
    Defined, §41-23-21.
  Governor.
    Advisory council.
      Appointment of members, §41-23-23.
  Guidelines for implementation of provisions of article.
    Generally, §41-23-23.

ENTERPRISE ZONES—Cont'd
  Incentives.
    Nontax incentives, §41-23-25.
    Tax incentives, §41-23-24.
  Increased or specialized services provided by local governments.
    Nontax incentives, §41-23-25.
  Legislative findings, §41-23-20.
  Legislative oversight committee.
    Appointment of members, §41-23-23.
    Composition, §41-23-23.
  Notice.
    Agreement by appropriate governing authorities, §41-23-28.
  Number of enterprise zones, §41-23-22.
  Preferences.
    State manufacturers, suppliers, contractors and laborers, §41-23-30.
  Priorities.
    Manufacturers, suppliers, contractors and laborers, §41-23-30.
  Purposes of act, §41-23-20.
  Qualifications of enterprise zones.
    Criteria established, §41-23-22.
  Reports.
    Department of economic and community affairs.
    Annual report, §41-23-27.
  Requirements.
    Additional requirements for business to receive benefits, §41-23-26.
  Residents.
    Certification that percentage of employees residents of zone, §41-23-30.
  Rules and regulations.
    Authority to formulate, §41-23-31.
    Exemption from local regulations.
      Nontax incentives, §41-23-25.
    Tax credits or incentives.
      Rules to implement, §41-23-24.
  Rural enterprise zones.
    Defined, §41-23-21.
  Selection of zones.
    Generally, §41-23-23.
  Size of enterprise zones, §41-23-22.
  Taxation.
    Credits, §41-23-24.
      In addition to credits for income taxes, §41-23-24.
      Maximum amount per new permanent employee, §41-23-24.
      No credits for taxes to other states, §41-23-24.
    Exemptions.
      Contracts with eligible businesses to provide for, §41-23-30.
      Federal tax exemptions.
        Complimentary to and consistent with, §41-23-32.
    Incentives, §41-23-24.

ENTERPRISE ZONES—Cont'd
  Taxation—Cont'd
    Rules and regulations.
      Incentives, §41-23-24.
  Title of act, §41-23-20.
  Urban enterprise zones.
    Defined, §41-23-21.
  Wages.
    Subsidies.
      Agreements with employers to receive, §41-23-30.

ENTOMOLOGY.
  Pest control.
    See PEST CONTROL.

ENTRAPMENT.
  Criminal law and procedure.
    When entrapment defense, §13A-3-31.

ENTRY.
  Forcible entry and unlawful detainer, §§6-6-310 to 6-6-353.
    See FORCIBLE ENTRY AND UNLAWFUL DETAINER.
  Right of entry.
    General provisions.
      See RIGHT OF ENTRY.

ENUCLEATION.
  Donor eye enucleation licenses, §§34-13-150 to 34-13-152.

ENVIRONMENTAL CONTROL.
  Air pollution, §§22-28-1 to 22-28-23.
    See AIR POLLUTION.
  Authorities.
    Environmental improvement authorities, §§9-6-1 to 9-6-17.
      See ENVIRONMENTAL IMPROVEMENT AUTHORITIES.
    Pollution control finance authority, §§22-29-1 to 22-29-23.
      See WATER POLLUTION.
  Coal.
    Surface mining control and reclamation, §§9-16-70 to 9-16-107.
      See COAL.
  Conservation and natural resources.
    See CONSERVATION AND NATURAL RESOURCES.
  Council on animal and environmental health, §§22-2-9, 22-2-10.
  Environmental improvement authorities, §§9-6-1 to 9-6-17.
    See ENVIRONMENTAL IMPROVEMENT AUTHORITIES.
  Health.
    Council on animal and environmental health, §§22-2-9, 22-2-10.
  Improvement authorities, §§9-6-1 to 9-6-17.
    See ENVIRONMENTAL IMPROVEMENT AUTHORITIES.
  Lime.
    See LIME.

ENVIRONMENTAL
CONTROL—Cont'd
Management, §§22-22A-1 to
22-22A-16.
See ENVIRONMENTAL
MANAGEMENT.
Marine environmental
sciences consortium,
§§16-45-1 to 16-45-5.
See MARINE
ENVIRONMENTAL
SCIENCES
CONSORTIUM.
Pesticides.
General provisions, §§2-27-1
to 2-27-63.
See PESTICIDES.
Pollution control finance
authority, §§22-29-1 to
22-29-23.
See WATER POLLUTION.
Water pollution.
General provisions.
See WATER POLLUTION.
Water pollution control act.
See WATER POLLUTION
CONTROL ACT.

ENVIRONMENTAL
IMPROVEMENT
AUTHORITIES, §§9-6-1 to
9-6-17.
Actions.
Maintaining of civil actions,
§9-6-8.
Advisory committee.
Appointment, §9-6-7.
Composition, §9-6-7.
Creation.
When to be created, §9-6-7.
Meetings, §9-6-7.
Purposes of committee,
§9-6-7.
Qualifications of members,
§9-6-7.
Terms of office, §9-6-7.
Application for
incorporation.
Contents, §9-6-4.
Denial.
Grounds, §9-6-4.
Filing, §9-6-4.
Issuance.
Executive order, §9-6-4.
Presumption that facts are
true, §9-6-4.
Area of operation.
Defined, §9-6-2.
Described in application,
§9-6-4.
Board of directors.
Appointment, §9-6-6.
Composition, §9-6-6.
Exercise of powers of
corporation, §9-6-6.
Expenses, §9-6-6.
Governing of authority,
§9-6-6.
Qualifications of members,
§9-6-6.
Removal from office, §9-6-6.
Salaries, §9-6-6.
Terms of office, §9-6-6.
Vacancies in office, §9-6-6.
Bond issues.
Chapter provisions exclusive,
§9-6-17.
Execution, §9-6-9.
Form, §9-6-9.
Issuance.
Power to issue, §9-6-8.

ENVIRONMENTAL
IMPROVEMENT
AUTHORITIES—Cont'd
Bond issues—Cont'd
Liens.
Creation of statutory
mortgage lien, §9-6-11.
Mortgage lien.
Creation of statutory
mortgage lien, §9-6-11.
Negotiable instruments,
§9-6-9.
Payment, §9-6-9.
Contracts.
Security for payment,
§9-6-10.
Pledge for payment.
Sources of pledge, §9-6-9.
Refunding bonds, §9-6-9.
Sale, §9-6-9.
Use of proceeds, §9-6-12.
Signatures, §9-6-9.
Taxation.
Exemptions from taxation,
§9-6-15.
Borrowing of money.
Powers of authority, §9-6-8.
Bylaws.
Adoption and alteration,
§9-6-8.
Certificate of incorporation,
§§9-6-5, 9-6-8.
Citation of chapter, §9-6-1.
Contracts.
Bond issues.
Security for payment,
§9-6-10.
Power to contract, §9-6-8.
Counties.
Aid and cooperation of
counties, §9-6-13.
Cumulative provisions,
§9-6-17.
Definitions, §9-6-2.
Directors, §9-6-6.
Duties.
General provisions, §9-6-8.
Eminent domain.
Powers of authority, §9-6-8.
Employees.
Powers to appoint, employ,
etc., §9-6-8.
Exclusive provisions of
chapter, §9-6-17.
Fees.
Payment of fees to secretary
of state.
Exemptions, §9-6-15.
Governor.
Application to incorporate.
Issuance of executive
orders, §9-6-4.
Notification that authority
has been formed, §9-6-5.
Review of application to
incorporate, §9-6-4.
Incorporation.
Applications, §§9-6-3, 9-6-4.
Certificate of incorporation.
Acknowledgment, §9-6-5.
Amendment, §9-6-8.
Contents, §9-6-5.
Execution, §9-6-5.
Filing, §9-6-5.
Signatures, §9-6-5.
Chapter provisions exclusive,
§9-6-17.
Fees.
Exemptions from fees,
§9-6-15.

ENVIRONMENTAL
IMPROVEMENT
AUTHORITIES—Cont'd
Incorporation—Cont'd
Procedure.
General provisions, §9-6-5.
Insurance.
Power to provide, §9-6-8.
Investments.
Powers of authority, §9-6-8.
Leases.
Power to lease, §9-6-8.
Liens.
Bond issues.
Creation of statutory
mortgage lien, §9-6-11.
Mortgages and deeds of
trust.
Bond issues.
Creation of statutory
mortgage lien, §9-6-11.
Municipal corporations.
Aid and cooperation of
municipal corporations,
§9-6-13.
Notice.
Governor.
Formation of authority,
§9-6-5.
Payments.
Security for payment.
Contracts, §9-6-10.
Powers and duties.
General provisions, §9-6-8.
Property.
Acquisition, §9-6-8.
Purposes of authority, §9-6-3.
Governmental function,
§9-6-14.
Reports.
Annual report to governor,
§9-6-16.
Special interim reports,
§9-6-16.
Review by governor, §9-6-4.
Salaries.
Board of directors, §9-6-6.
Seal.
Adoption and use, §9-6-8.
Signatures.
Bond issues, §9-6-9.
State.
Aid and cooperation of state,
§9-6-13.
Taxation.
Exemptions from taxation,
§9-6-15.
Title of chapter, §9-6-1.
Torts.
Immunity from tort liability,
§9-6-14.
United States.
Cooperation with, §9-6-8.

ENVIRONMENTAL
MANAGEMENT,
§§22-22A-1 to 22-22A-16.
Administrative actions.
Commission.
Hearings and procedures
before commission.
Stay of administrative
action, §22-22A-7.
Defined, §22-22A-3.
Appeals.
Commission.
Hearings and procedures
before commission,
§22-22A-7.

ENVIRONMENTAL MANAGEMENT—Cont'd

Asbestos.

Contractors accreditation, §§22-39-1 to 22-39-5.

See ASBESTOS.

Attorney general.

Effect of chapter on powers, §22-22A-13.

Environmental management department.

Representation of department in legal actions, §22-22A-5.

Bacteriological analyses.

Department.

Contract with for routine analyses, §22-22A-4.

Citation, §22-22A-1.

Coastal area board.

Transfer of functions, personnel, etc., to office of state planning and federal programs, §22-22A-10.

Coastal resources advisory committee.

Chairman, §22-22A-12.

Composition, §22-22A-12.

Meetings, §22-22A-12.

Office of state planning and federal programs.

Advice to office, §22-22A-12.

Terms of members, §22-22A-12.

Commission, §§22-22A-6 to 22-22A-8.

Administrative actions.

Hearings and procedures before commission.

Stay of administrative action, §22-22A-7.

Appointments, §22-22A-6.

Chairman, §22-22A-6.

Compensation of members, §22-22A-6.

Composition, §22-22A-6.

Conflicts of interest, §22-22A-6.

Defined, §22-22A-3.

Duties, §22-22A-6.

Ethics, §22-22A-6.

Expenses, §22-22A-6.

Hazardous substances.

Cleanup fund.

General provisions, §§22-30A-1 to 22-30A-11.

See HAZARDOUS SUBSTANCES.

Hearings and procedures before commission.

Administrative actions.

Stay, §22-22A-7.

Appeals, §22-22A-7.

Evidence, §22-22A-7.

Hearing officers, §22-22A-7.

Notice of hearing, §22-22A-7.

Orders.

Issuance of orders, §22-22A-7.

Record of proceedings, §22-22A-7.

Request for hearing, §22-22A-7.

Right to hearing, §22-22A-7.

ENVIRONMENTAL MANAGEMENT—Cont'd

Commission—Cont'd

Hearings and procedures before commission —Cont'd

Time of hearing, §22-22A-7.

Meetings.

Attendance.

Effect of failure to attend three consecutive meetings, §22-22A-6.

Regular and special meetings, §22-22A-6.

Powers, §22-22A-6.

Qualifications of members, §22-22A-6.

Quorum, §22-22A-6.

Record of proceedings, §22-22A-6.

Rules and regulations.

Adoption, §22-22A-8.

Terms of members, §22-22A-6.

Vacancies, §22-22A-6.

Conflicts of interest.

Commission, §22-22A-6.

Definitions, §§22-22-1, 22-22A-3.

Department.

Air pollution.

See AIR POLLUTION.

Attorney general.

Representation of department in legal actions, §22-22A-5.

Bacteriological analyses.

Contract for routine analyses, §22-22A-4.

Citation of chapter, §22-22A-1.

Created, §22-22A-4.

Definitions, §§22-22-1, 22-22A-3.

Designation as state environmental control agency, §22-22A-4.

Director.

Defined, §22-22A-3.

Deputy director, §22-22A-4.

Rules and regulations.

Review by director, §22-22A-8.

Divisions, §22-22A-4.

Chiefs, §22-22A-4.

Functions, §22-22A-5.

Transfer to department, §22-22A-9.

Funds.

Alabama department of environmental management fund, §22-22A-11.

Transfer to department, §22-22A-9.

Hazardous substances.

Cleanup fund.

General provisions, §§22-30A-1 to 22-30A-11.

See HAZARDOUS SUBSTANCES.

Hazardous waste.

General provisions, §§22-30-1 to 22-30-20.

See HAZARDOUS WASTE.

ENVIRONMENTAL MANAGEMENT—Cont'd

Department—Cont'd

Health department.

Contract with for routine bacteriological analyses, §22-22A-4.

Personnel.

Transfer of functions, personnel, equipment, etc., to department, §22-22A-9.

Pollution.

Water pollution control act, §§22-22-1 to 22-22-14.

See WATER POLLUTION CONTROL ACT.

Powers, §22-22A-5.

Principal office, §22-22A-4.

Safe drinking water act, §§22-23-30 to 22-23-53.

See WATER SUPPLY AND WATERWORKS.

Solid wastes.

See GARBAGE AND TRASH.

Transfer of functions, §22-22A-4.

Water and wastewater systems, §§22-25-1 to 22-25-15.

See WATER AND WASTEWATER SYSTEMS AND TREATMENT PLANTS.

Water pollution control act, §§22-22-1 to 22-22-14.

See WATER POLLUTION CONTROL ACT.

Water pollution control authority, §§22-34-1 to 22-34-17.

See WATER POLLUTION CONTROL AUTHORITY.

Fees.

Hazardous waste or substances.

Fees for disposal of, §§22-30B-1 to 22-30B-18.

See HAZARDOUS WASTE.

Funds.

Hazardous substances.

Cleanup fund, §§22-30A-1 to 22-30A-11.

See HAZARDOUS SUBSTANCES.

Pollution control grant fund, §22-22A-16.

Hazardous substances.

Cleanup fund.

General provisions, §§22-30A-1 to 22-30A-11.

See HAZARDOUS SUBSTANCES.

Fees for disposal of.

General provisions, §§22-30B-1 to 22-30B-18.

See HAZARDOUS WASTE.

Hazardous waste.

Fees for disposal of, §§22-30B-1 to 22-30B-18.

See HAZARDOUS WASTE.

ENVIRONMENTAL MANAGEMENT—Cont'd
Hazardous waste—Cont'd
General provisions, §§22-30-1 to 22-30-20.
See HAZARDOUS WASTE.
Pollution control grant fund, §22-22A-16.
Repeal of provisions.
Chapter does not repeal section 22-30-5.1, §22-22A-15.
Water pollution control act, §§22-22-1 to 22-22-14.
See WATER POLLUTION CONTROL ACT.

EPIDEMICS.
General provisions.
See DISEASES.
Quarantine, §22-12-1.

EPISCOPAL FOUNDATION OF JEFFERSON COUNTY.
Licenses.
Exemptions, §40-9-13.
Taxation.
Exemptions, §40-9-13.

EQUALIZATION.
County boards of equalization, §§40-3-1 to 40-3-26.
See TAXATION.

EQUITABLE REMEDIES.
See REMEDIES.

ERROR.
Appeals.
Assignment of error not required, ARAP, Rule 20.
Error without injury, ARAP, Rule 45.
Writs of error.
Criminal cases, §§12-22-220, 12-22-222.
Conveyances.
Reformation, §§35-4-150 to 35-4-153.
Deeds.
Reformation, §§35-4-150 to 35-4-153.
Harmless error, ARCP, Rule 61.
Mortgages and deeds of trust.
Reformation, §§35-4-150 to 35-4-153.
New trial.
Error of law grounds for new trial, §15-17-5.
Writs of error.
Criminal cases, §§12-22-220, 12-22-222.

ESCAMBIA COUNTY.
Costs.
Court costs and charges, Const. Ala., amd. 390.
Hospitals.
Special tax for hospital and public health purposes, Const. Ala., amd. 70.
Officers of county.
Compensation, Const. Ala., amd. 391.

ESCAMBIA COUNTY—Cont'd
Public health.
Special tax for hospital and public health purposes, Const. Ala., amd. 70.
Salaries.
Officers of county, Const. Ala., amd. 391.

ESCAPE.
Arrest, §14-3-15.
Rearrest after escape or rescue, §15-10-9.
Bail and recognizance.
Bail jumping, §§13A-10-39, 13A-10-40.
Discretionary bail schedule, ARJA, Rule 2.
Contraband.
Promoting prison contraband, §§13A-10-36 to 13A-10-38.
Credit towards sentence for time spent incarcerated.
Time between recapture and return to penal system, §15-18-6.
Applicability to prisoners presently incarcerated, §15-18-7.
Custody.
Defined, §13A-10-30.
Escaping from custody.
Third degree escape, §13A-10-30.
Death penalty.
Rearrest and execution of person escaping before execution, §15-18-84.
Definitions, §13A-10-30.
Detention facility.
Defined, §13A-10-30.
Educational release.
City jails.
Failure to return deemed escape, §15-22-74.
First degree escape.
Class B felony, §13A-10-31.
Elements, §13A-10-31.
Permitting or facilitating, §13A-10-34.
Force.
First degree escape, §13A-10-31.
Use of force to prevent escape, §13A-3-27.
Fugitives from justice.
Rewards, §§15-9-1 to 15-9-65.
See FUGITIVES FROM JUSTICE.
Guards.
Summoning jail guards to prevent escape, §14-6-11.
Hindering apprehension of escapee, §13A-10-45.
Jails.
Guards.
Summoning to prevent escape, §14-6-11.
Mandatory disposition of detainers.
Request for final determination of untried indictments, etc.
Escape by prisoner after request filed, §15-9-85.
Penal facility.
Defined, §13A-10-30.
Penitentiary.
Duty of board of corrections, §14-3-58.

ESCAPE—Cont'd
Penitentiary—Cont'd
Posting of code provisions, §14-3-59.
Proceedings upon escape, §14-3-58.
Reward, §14-3-58.
Permitting or facilitating escape.
First degree, §13A-10-34.
Second degree, §13A-10-35.
Physical injury.
Use in escape.
First degree escape, §13A-10-31.
Pursuit of escaped convicts, §14-3-15.
Quarantine.
Escapes from detention, §22-12-20.
Rewards.
Information leading to arrest and conviction, §§15-9-1 to 15-9-4.
Second degree escape.
Class C felony, §13A-10-32.
Elements, §13A-10-32.
Permitting or facilitating, §13A-10-35.
Third degree escape.
Class C felony, §13A-10-33.
Elements, §13A-10-33.
Work release.
Municipal jails.
Failure to return deemed escape, §15-22-74.
Youth services.
Detention without order or warrant of escaped youths, §44-1-9.

ESCHEATS.
Constitution of Alabama.
Application of property to furtherance of education, Const. Ala., amd. 111.
Education.
Application of property to maintenance of public schools, Const. Ala., art. XIV, §258.
Education.
Application of property to furtherance of education, Const. Ala., amd. 111.
Application of property to maintenance of public schools, Const. Ala., art. XIV, §258.
Executors and administrators.
Failure to pay over proceeds.
Decree against personal representative for failure to pay over, §43-6-6.
Notice by personal representative, §43-6-2.
Contents, §43-6-3.
Fees.
Probate judges' fees, §12-19-90.
Interest of state.
Duty of probate judge to attend to interest of state, §43-6-9.
Notice by personal representative.
Contents, §43-6-3.

ESCHEATS—Cont'd
Personal property.
Action by state to recover personal property distributed without authority, §43-6-8.
Disposition of personalty when no heir appears, §43-6-4.
Probate judges.
Decree against personal representative for failure to pay over proceeds, §43-6-6.
Duty to attend to interest of state, §43-6-9.
Payment of receipts to state treasurer, §43-6-7.
Real property.
Disposition of real estate when no heir appears, §43-6-5.
Receipts.
Payment to state treasurer, §43-6-7.
State treasurer.
Payment of receipts to state treasurer, §43-6-7.
Unclaimed property.
Property presumed abandoned or escheated under laws of another state, §35-12-47.
Reciprocity for property abandoned or escheated under laws of another state, §35-12-30.
Uniform disposition of unclaimed property act, §§35-12-21 to 35-12-48.
See LOST OR UNCLAIMED PROPERTY.

E.S.P.N.
Community antenna television facilities generally, §§11-27-1 to 11-27-3, 23-1-59.

ESSAY CONTESTS.
Stonewall Jackson memorial fund, §§16-32-1 to 16-32-3.

ESTATE AND INHERITANCE TAX, §§40-15-1 to 40-15-21.
Administration of chapter, §40-15-19.
Amount, §40-15-2.
Appeals, §40-15-20.
Assessment.
Final assessment, §40-15-15.
Limitation of time, §40-15-6.
Computation.
Department of revenue, §40-15-3.
Constitutional provisions, Const. Ala., art. XI, §219; amd. 23.
Repeal of section 219, Const. Ala., amd. 23.
Definitions.
Administrator, §40-15-1.
Executors, §40-15-1.
Legal representative, §40-15-1.
Estate property.
Payment out of, §40-15-18.
Execution for tax, §40-15-11.

ESTATE AND INHERITANCE TAX—Cont'd
Federal tax.
Determination.
Extension of payment time until determination of federal tax, §40-15-14.
Returns.
Amended return showing change, §40-15-5.
Duplicate filed by executor, §40-15-3.
Interest.
Delinquent payments, §40-15-16.
Lien of state, §40-15-13.
Location of property for purposes of death taxation, §40-15-8.
Effect of unconstitutionality of reciprocity provision, §40-15-9.
Nonresident decedents, §40-15-7.
Payment.
Delinquent payments.
Interest, §40-15-16.
Estate property.
Payment from, §40-15-18.
Time, §40-15-4.
Extension, §40-15-4.
Extension of payment until determination of federal tax, §40-15-14.
Proceeds.
Disposition, §40-15-12.
Property outside of state, §40-15-17.
Reciprocity, §40-15-9.
Unconstitutionality of provision.
Effect, §40-15-9.
Refunds, §40-15-21.
Reports.
Failure to make.
Appraisement, §40-15-10.
Returns.
Federal tax. See within this heading, "Federal tax."

ESTATES.
Administration of estates, §§43-2-1 to 43-2-813.
See EXECUTORS AND ADMINISTRATORS.
Construction and interpretation.
Estate taken as fee simple unless expressly limited, §35-4-2.
Decedents' estates.
See DECEDENTS' ESTATES.
Estate and inheritance tax.
See ESTATE AND INHERITANCE TAX.
Estates pur autre vie.
Character, §35-4-231.
Executors and administrators.
Administration of estates.
See EXECUTORS AND ADMINISTRATORS.
Fee simple estates.
Estate taken as fee simple unless expressly limited, §35-4-2.
Fee tail converted into fee simple, §35-4-3.

ESTATES—Cont'd
Fee tail estates.
Converted into fee simple, §35-4-3.
Forcible entry and unlawful detainer, §§6-6-311, 6-6-312.
Future interests.
See FUTURE INTERESTS.
Leaseholder estates.
See LEASES.
Life estates.
General provisions, §§35-4-170 to 35-4-192.
See LIFE ESTATES.
Small estates, §§43-2-690 to 43-2-696.
See EXECUTORS AND ADMINISTRATORS.
Trusts and trustees.
See TRUSTS AND TRUSTEES.
Waste.
See WASTE.

ESTATES PUR AUTRE VIE.
Character, §35-4-231.

ESTOPPEL.
Affirmative defense, ARCP, Rule 8 (c).
Landlord and tenant.
Tenant estopped to deny landlord's title, §35-9-1.
Partnerships.
Liability of partner by estoppel, §10-8-55.

ESTRAYS.
Department of agriculture and industries.
Determination of ownership and furnishing information to interested persons, §2-15-25.
Fees.
Highways.
Taking up and impounding of animals running at large, §§3-2-21, 3-2-23.
Highways.
Duty of director of public safety, §3-2-20.
Fees, §3-2-21.
Disposition of fees collected under article, §3-2-23.
Notification of owner of animal taken up and impounded, §3-2-21.
Recovery of animal by owner.
Procedure, §3-2-21.
Sale of animals taken up and impounded, §3-2-22.
Where owner cannot be located.
Filing of notice with probate judge, §3-2-21.
Liens.
Costs of keeping animal, etc., §3-2-2.
Notice.
Publication and posting of notice as to estrayed animal where owner not located, §3-2-4.
Seizure.
Notice to department of agriculture, §3-2-2.

ESTRAYS—Cont'd
Register of brands.
Department to determine
ownership of estrayed
livestock and furnish
information to interested
persons, §2-15-25.
Return of animal.
Generally, §3-2-4.
Highways.
Taking up and impounding
of animals running at
large.
Procedure for recovery of
animal, §3-2-21.
Where owner located.
Procedure, §3-2-3.
Sale, §3-2-4.
Highways.
Animals running at large
on state and federal
aid highways, §3-2-22.
Seizure, §3-2-1.
Investigation by department
of agriculture and
industries, §3-2-3.
Notice of department of
agriculture and
industries as to seizure,
§3-2-2.
Unclaimed estrays.
Procedure for sale, §3-2-4.
Publication and posting of
notice, §3-2-4.

ETHICS.
Attorneys at law.
Disciplinary proceedings,
§§34-3-80 to 34-3-89;
ARDE, Rules 1 to 24.
See ATTORNEYS AT
LAW.
Code of ethics, §§36-25-1 to
36-25-30.
See PUBLIC OFFICERS
AND EMPLOYEES.
Environmental management.
Commission, §22-22A-6.
Judges.
Canons of judicial ethics,
ACJE, Canons 1 to 7C.
See CANONS OF
JUDICIAL ETHICS.
**Public officers and
employees.**
Code of ethics, §§36-25-1 to
36-25-30.
See PUBLIC OFFICERS
AND EMPLOYEES.

ETOWAH COUNTY.
Annexation, Const. Ala., amd.
467.
**Economic and industrial
development promotion,**
Const. Ala., amd. 429.
Fire protection districts,
Const. Ala., amds. 19, 432.
Officers.
Fees, salaries, etc., of certain
public officers, Const.
Ala., amds. 43, 62.
Regulation of salaries, etc., of
certain public officers,
Const. Ala., amd. 43.
School tax.
Special property tax for
educational purposes,
Const. Ala., amd. 296.
Special school tax, Const.
Ala., amd. 67.

ETOWAH COUNTY—Cont'd
**Trial tax or charge on
litigation,** Const. Ala.,
amd. 235.

EUTHANASIA.
Natural death act.
Provisions of chapter not an
approval of mercy
killing, §22-8A-10.

**EVERGREEN,
MUNICIPALITY OF.**
Economic development.
Promotion of industrial,
commercial and
agricultural
development, Const.
Ala., amd. 259.
Property tax, Const. Ala.,
amd. 17.

EVICTION.
Landlord's remedies, §35-9-6.

EVIDENCE.
Accomplices.
Testimony for felony
conviction, §12-21-222.
Accountants.
See ACCOUNTANTS.
Accounts and accounting.
Books of account as proof of
accounts, §12-21-42.
Verified itemized statement
as evidence of account's
correctness, §12-21-111.
Acknowledgments.
Improperly acknowledged
instruments as evidence,
§35-4-72.
Administration of estates.
See within this heading,
"Executors and
administrators."
**Administrative procedure
act.**
Rules of evidence in
contested cases,
§41-22-13.
Admissibility, ARCP, Rule 43
(a).
Applicability of provisions
regulating admissibility,
§12-21-11.
Expenses.
Hospital or medical
expenses.
Evidence that expenses
to be paid or
reimbursed.
Admissible, §12-21-45.
Juvenile proceedings.
Sexual offenses.
Minors, §12-15-65.
Affidavits.
Admissibility as evidence,
§35-4-70.
Agents.
Missing persons.
Presumption of signer's
authority, §12-21-91.
Agriculture.
Analysis of products.
Certificate of analysis
admissible as evidence,
§2-2-35.
Marketing of agricultural
products.
Certificate of inspection or
classification as
evidence, §2-11-7.
Notices, §2-2-17.

EVIDENCE—Cont'd
Agriculture—Cont'd
Prima facie evidence of
possession with intent to
sell, §2-1-3.
Rules and regulations,
§2-2-17.
Alcoholic beverages.
General provisions.
See ALCOHOLIC
BEVERAGES.
Ancient rights.
Declarations of deceased
persons as to ancient
rights, §12-21-30.
Annuity tables, §35-16-2.
Appeals.
Criminal cases.
Appeals to circuit courts.
Rules as to evidence
governing appeals,
§12-22-114.
Art.
Books of art as evidence of
facts of general notoriety
and interest, §12-21-108;
ARCP, Rule 44 (g).
Assault.
Exclusion of audience where
evidence vulgar,
§§12-21-9, 12-21-202.
Attorneys at law, §§34-3-23,
34-3-82, 34-3-83.
Appearance without
authority, §34-3-23.
Disciplinary proceedings.
Right of accused to
introduce evidence,
§34-3-83.
Subpoenas, §34-3-82;
ARDE, Rule 13.
Privileges, §12-21-161.
Auctions and auctioneers.
Board of auctioneers.
Copies of records and
papers as evidence,
§34-4-50.
**Authentication of
documents,** ARCP, Rule
44 (a).
Additional or alternative
mode of proof of certain
official documents,
§12-21-73.
Alteration in writing.
Accounting for alteration
in writing introduced
as genuine, §12-21-63.
Bureau heads, §12-21-72.
Department heads,
§12-21-72.
Division cumulative as to
proof of documents or
records, §12-21-10.
Executive acts, §12-21-73.
Foreign countries, ARCP,
Rule 44 (a).
Legislative acts, §12-21-70.
Public records or books,
§12-21-71.
Lack of record, ARCP, Rule
44 (b).
Land office deeds or written
instruments for
conveyance or sale of
land, §12-21-66.
Legislative proceedings,
§12-21-73.
Municipal acts, §12-21-73.
Original documents, ARCP,
Rule 44 (d).

EVIDENCE—Cont'd
Authentication of documents
—Cont'd
Other state or territory.
Legislative acts, §12-21-70.
Public records or books,
§12-21-71.
Proof of execution.
By maker, §12-21-60.
Subscribing witnesses.
Proof of execution when
dead, etc., §12-21-62.
When must be produced,
§12-21-61.
Public offices.
Proof of exemplifications or
copies of records, etc.,
kept in public office,
§12-21-67.
Recordation.
Documents recorded under
recording act, ARCP,
Rule 44 (e).
Beverage containers.
Presumptive evidence of
unlawful use or
purchase, §8-12-22.
Bishop of diocese.
Records and certificates
prima facie evidence,
§10-4-9.
Blind persons.
How blindness proved,
§1-1-3.
Boats.
Accident reports.
Use as evidence in trials,
§33-5-25.
Rules and regulations of
commissioner.
Admissibility as evidence,
§33-5-30.
Bonds, surety.
Official bonds.
Copies of required official
bonds, §12-21-104.
Proof of bonds or
recognizances,
§36-5-21.
Books.
Production of books, etc. See
within this heading,
"Production of books,
etc."
Bureaus.
Authentication of paper or
document by bureau
head, §12-21-72.
Business records, ARCP,
Rule 44 (h).
Books of account as proof of
accounts, §12-21-42.
Writings or records made in
regular course of
business, §§12-21-43,
12-21-44.
Bylaws.
Municipal bylaws, §12-21-95.
Canons of judicial ethics.
Electronic presentation.
Discretion of trial judge,
ACJE, Canon 3A.
Personal knowledge of
disputed evidentiary
facts.
Disqualification, ACJE,
Canon 3C.
Photographic presentation.
Discretion of trial judge or
appellate court, ACJE,
Canon 3A.

EVIDENCE—Cont'd
Capital offenses.
Sentence hearing.
Admissibility of evidence
in sentence hearing,
§13A-5-45.
Child abuse or neglect.
Privileged communications
not grounds for exclusion
of evidence, §26-14-10.
Child labor.
Evidence of employment,
§25-8-4.
Child pornography.
Obscene materials containing
visual reproduction of
children, §§13A-12-192
to 13A-12-195.
Chiropractors.
Licenses.
Refusal, revocation or
suspension.
Rules of evidence,
§34-24-173.
Claims by and against state.
Board of adjustment may
adopt rules of evidence,
§41-9-66.
Commercial code.
See COMMERCIAL CODE.
Commercial list, §12-21-113.
Common law.
Proof of common law of other
states and territories,
§12-21-65.
Compromise and settlement.
Admissibility of for
composition of debts,
§12-21-31.
Conditional sales.
When conditional sales
contract received in
evidence, §35-4-98.
Congress.
Transcripts of congressional
acts, §12-21-94.
Contracts.
Future delivery, §§8-1-20 to
8-1-30.
See CONTRACTS.
Market value testimony,
§12-21-114.
Sales contracts.
Parol or extrinsic evidence,
§7-2-202.
Statute of frauds, §8-9-2.
Written contract as evidence
of debt or duty,
§12-21-112.
Conveyances.
Affidavits.
Admissibility as evidence,
§35-4-70.
Improperly acknowledged or
recorded instruments as
evidence, §35-4-72.
When conveyance receivable
in evidence, §35-4-65.
**Coosa Valley development
authority.**
Records of proceedings.
Prima facie evidence,
§33-16-6.
Copies.
When certified copy good
secondary evidence,
§12-21-107.

EVIDENCE—Cont'd
Corporations.
Criminal cases.
When proof of
incorporation
necessary, §12-21-201.
Nonprofit corporations.
Certificates and certified
copies to be received in
evidence, §10-3A-222.
Probate judge.
Certificates and certified
copies to be received in
evidence, §10-2A-332.
Secretary of state.
Certificates and certified
copies to be received in
evidence, §10-2A-332.
Cosmetology.
Board of cosmetology.
Books and records of board,
§34-7-44.
Proceedings before board,
§34-7-21.
Cotton.
Classification.
Admissibility in evidence
of certificate of
classification of cotton,
§2-19-83.
Counties.
Public building authorities.
Records of proceedings,
§11-15-6.
Surveyors.
When survey or plat
evidence of facts
stated, §11-7-8.
**County industrial
development authorities.**
Boards of directors.
Admissibility of board
proceedings,
§11-92A-9.
Creditors' actions.
Complaint for discovery of
assets.
Answer to charge of fraud
as evidence on fraud
indictment, §6-6-181.
Credit unions.
Seal.
Evidentiary effect of
official seal, §5-17-43.
Criminal cases.
Appeals to circuit courts.
Rules as to evidence
governing appeals,
§12-22-114.
Case action summary sheets.
Admissibility into
evidence.
Rules of criminal
procedure, ARCrP,
Rule 22.
Incorporation.
When proof necessary,
§12-21-201.
Intent to injure, defraud or
cheat.
Proof of intent, §12-21-200.
Sexual conduct.
Admissibility of evidence
relating to past sexual
behavior, §12-21-203.
Vulgarity.
Exclusion of audience
where evidence vulgar,
etc., §12-21-202.
Dead man's statute,
§12-21-163.

EVIDENCE—Cont'd
Death.
Ancient rights.
Declarations of deceased
persons as to ancient
rights, §12-21-30.
Armed forces death.
Official notice.
Prima facie evidence of
death, §12-21-90.
Certified registers of death,
§12-21-101.
Rules of evidence, §43-8-6.
Debts.
Composition of debts,
§12-21-31.
Effect of written receipts,
releases and discharges,
§12-21-109.
Written contract as evidence
of debt, §12-21-112.
Deeds.
Land office deeds or written
instruments for
conveyance or sale of
land.
Proof, §12-21-66.
Definitions.
Substantial evidence,
§12-21-12.
Dental service corporations.
Sales representatives.
Contracting sales
representatives.
Denial, suspension,
revocation or refusal
to renew
registration,
§22-21-381.
Dentists.
Board of dental examiners.
Admissibility of board
records, §34-9-44.
Depositions.
Objections to admissibility,
ARCP, Rule 32 (b).
Destruction of evidence.
Class A misdemeanor,
§13A-10-129.
Discharges.
Effect of written discharges,
§12-21-109.
Divorce and alimony.
Exclusion of audience where
evidence vulgar, etc.,
§12-21-9.
Documents.
Copies.
When certified copy good
secondary evidence,
§12-21-107.
Production of books, etc.,
§§12-21-1 to 12-21-3.
Proof of documents, ARCP,
Rule 44.
Registration.
Official entry on paper as
evidence of registry,
§12-21-106.
Secondary evidence.
When certified copy good
secondary evidence,
§12-21-107.
Education.
Attendance register and
rules and regulations.
Use as evidence, §16-28-23.
Public school and college
authority.
Copies of proceedings as
evidence, §16-16-6.

EVIDENCE—Cont'd
Education—Cont'd
Public school corporation.
Records or certificates as
evidence, §16-14-16.
Elections.
County elections.
Declaration of election
results.
Prima facie evidence of
result, §17-14-2.
Embezzlement.
See EMBEZZLEMENT.
Eminent domain.
General provisions.
See EMINENT DOMAIN.
Engineers.
Board of registration.
Admissibility of board
records, §34-11-37.
Environmental management.
Commission.
Hearings and procedures
before commission,
§22-22A-7.
Excluded evidence.
Record of excluded evidence,
ARCP, Rule 43 (c).
Exclusionary rule.
Alcoholic beverages.
Admissibility of evidence
obtained by illegal
searches, §28-1-2.
Execution of documents.
Proof of execution. See
within this heading,
"Authentication of
documents."
**Executors and
administrators.**
Books of account kept by
deceased executor or
administrator.
Admissibility in evidence,
§12-21-32.
Inventory as evidence,
§43-2-139.
Letters testamentary and of
administration.
Copies of letters,
§12-21-102.
Transcripts of records of
letters and bonds,
§43-2-1.
**Exemptions from levy and
sale under process.**
Declaration of claimed
exemptions.
Effect as evidence,
§6-10-23.
Exhibits.
Destruction of exhibits
offered and received in
evidence, §12-21-8.
Felonies.
Habitual felony offenders.
Proof of prior convictions,
§13A-5-10.1.
**Fingerprinting of persons
taken into custody.**
General provisions,
§§15-10-90, 15-10-91.
See FINGERPRINTS.
Fires and fire prevention.
Firemen.
Compensation for death.
Determination of claims.
Adoption of rules of
evidence, §36-30-5.

EVIDENCE—Cont'd
Fish and game.
Spearfishing.
Possession of spear,
§9-11-175.
Food.
Obtaining food by fraud or
misrepresentation.
Prima facie evidence of
offense, §34-15-19.
Foreign countries.
Legislative acts.
Authentication of foreign
country's legislative
acts, §12-21-70.
Proof of certain official
documents, §12-21-73.
Proof of laws of foreign
countries, §12-21-64.
Public records or books.
Authentication of foreign
country's public
records or books,
§12-21-70.
Foreign law.
Determination of foreign law,
ARCP, Rule 44.1.
Form, ARCP, Rule 43 (a).
Fraternal benefit societies.
Licenses, §27-34-6.
Fraud.
Proof of intent to defraud or
cheat, §12-21-200.
Funerals.
Board of funeral service.
Evidentiary effect of board
documents, §34-13-8.
Gambling.
Electric bells or warning
devices.
Presence prima facie
evidence, §13A-12-58.
Federal wagering
occupational tax stamp.
Possession of stamp prima
facie evidence of
gambling violation,
§13A-12-90.
Newspapers.
Published reports of
occurrence of sporting
events, §13A-12-28.
Prima facie proof of
gambling offense,
§13A-12-28.
Grand jury.
Evidence which may be
received by grand jury,
§12-16-200.
Guardian and ward.
Books of account kept by
deceased guardian.
Admissibility in evidence,
§12-21-32.
Curators.
Appointment, §26-7A-4.
Evidentiary standard of
hearings, §26-7A-4.
Letters of guardianship.
Copies of letters,
§12-21-102.
Uniform guardianship and
protective proceedings
act.
Conservators.
Letters of
conservatorship,
§26-2A-149.
Orders termining
conservatorships,
§26-2A-149.

EVIDENCE—Cont'd
Habitual felony act.
Proof of prior convictions,
§13A-5-10.1.
Handwriting. See within this
heading, "Writing."
Health care authorities.
Board.
Meetings.
Record of proceedings,
§22-21-316.
Hearsay.
Ancient rights.
Declarations of deceased
persons as to ancient
rights, §12-21-30.
Business records.
Writings or records made
in regular course of
business.
Admissibility in
evidence, §§12-21-43,
12-21-44.
Deceased persons.
Declarations of deceased
persons as to ancient
rights, §12-21-30.
Exceptions to hearsay rule.
Ancient rights.
Declarations of deceased
persons as to ancient
rights, §12-21-30.
Business records,
§§12-21-43, 12-21-44.
Highways.
Department.
Records, §23-1-34.
Historical works.
Prima facie evidence of facts
of general notoriety and
interest, §12-21-108;
ARCP, Rule 44 (g).
Hospitals.
Expenses.
Hospital or medical
expenses to be paid or
reimbursed admissible
as competent evidence,
§12-21-45.
Records.
Copy of hospital records.
Admissibility, §12-21-5.
Certificate of custodian,
§§12-21-6, 12-21-7.
Costs, §12-21-6.
Form, §12-21-6.
Inspection, §12-21-6.
Subpoena duces tecum,
§12-21-6.
**Hotels, inns and other
transient lodging places.**
Obtaining accommodations
by fraud or
misrepresentation.
Prima facie evidence,
§34-15-19.
Illegitimacy.
Determination of paternity.
See PARENT AND
CHILD.
Impeachment.
Matters as to which evidence
may be introduced,
§36-11-20.
Written contracts,
§12-21-112.
Incest.
Corroboration requirement,
§13A-13-3.

EVIDENCE—Cont'd
**Industrial development
authority.**
Proceedings of board of
directors.
Admissibility in evidence,
§41-10-25.
Insurance.
Commissioner of insurance.
Examinations, §27-2-26.
Compelling production of
documents, §27-2-27.
Hearings, §27-2-27.
Investigations, §27-2-27.
Records, documents and
files.
Use as evidence,
§27-2-15.
Policies.
Application for policy.
Admissibility into
evidence, §27-14-6.
Records, documents and files.
Use as evidence, §27-2-15.
Reports.
Examinations by
commissioner,
§27-2-24.
Surplus line insurance,
§27-10-27.
Interest.
Foreign interest rates.
Secretary of state's
publication of foreign
interest rates,
§12-21-92.
Judges.
Canons of judicial ethics,
ACJE, Canons 3A, 3C.
Judgments, §12-21-100.
Admissibility, ARCP, Rule
44 (f).
Pro tanto settlements.
Effect, §12-21-109.
Judicial sales.
Notices.
Newspapers as evidence of
publication, §6-8-67.
Jury.
Taking of written evidence
by jury on retirement,
§12-16-14.
Justices of the peace.
Foreign justices.
Copies of proceedings and
judgments.
Admissibility in
evidence, §12-21-38.
Juvenile proceedings,
§12-15-65.
Evidence given in hearings
and disposition of child.
Admissibility in evidence
against child of
evidence given in
hearings and
disposition, §12-15-72.
Extrajudicial statements,
§12-15-66.
Illegally seized or obtained
evidence, §12-15-66.
Sexual offenses.
Minors.
Admissibility, §12-15-65.
Conduct of hearings,
§12-15-65.
Disposition of cases
generally, §12-15-65.
Statement by child.
Admissibility, ARJP, Rule
21.

EVIDENCE—Cont'd
Labor.
Child labor.
Evidence of employment,
§25-8-4.
Land patents, §12-21-96.
Legislature.
Nonprofit corporations.
Reservation of power in
legislature,
§10-3A-224.
Libel and slander.
Truth or circumstances,
§6-5-183.
Livestock.
Brands.
Admissibility of certificate
of registration of
brands in civil actions
or criminal
proceedings as to title
or right of possession,
§2-15-22.
Malpractice.
Admissibility.
Evidence that medical
expenses will be
reimbursed, §6-5-545.
No evidence admitted of
medical liability
insurance, §6-5-548.
Burden of proof, §6-5-548.
Rules of evidence in civil
actions preserved,
§6-5-488.
Scintilla rule of evidence
abolished, §6-5-549.
Substantial evidence.
Defined, §6-5-542.
Standard of proof shall be
proof by substantial
evidence, §6-5-549.
Maps and plats.
Prima facie evidence of facts
of general notoriety and
interest, §12-21-108;
ARCP, Rule 44 (g).
Surveyor general of the
United States.
Admissibility of certified
copies of surveyor
general's books, maps
and field notes,
§12-21-36.
Town surveys, plats or maps.
Certification,
acknowledgment and
recordation of plat or
map.
Copies as evidence,
§35-2-51.
Market value.
Commercial code, §§7-2-723,
7-2-724.
Testimony as to market
value, §12-21-114.
Marriage.
See MARRIAGE.
Meat and meat products.
Mutilation, alteration, etc., of
documentary evidence,
§2-17-34.
Violations of chapter or
regulations.
Admissibility of evidence of
violations in civil
actions for damages,
§2-17-31.

EVIDENCE—Cont'd

Medical expenses.
Medical or hospital expenses
to be paid or reimbursed.
Admissible as competent
evidence, §12-21-45.

**Mental health finance
authority.**
Record of proceedings,
§41-10-355.

Microphotographs.
Records.
Admissibility in evidence,
§41-13-40.

Military affairs.
Armed forces death.
Official notice.
Prima facie evidence of
death, §12-21-90.
Compensation for death of
national guardsmen.
Rules of evidence for
determination of
claims, §31-3-5.
Courts-martial, §31-2-98.
Missing persons.
Official report of person
missing, §12-21-91.

Milk and milk products.
Marked containers.
Possession by secondhand
or junk dealer prima
facie evidence of
violation, §8-12-42.

Missing persons.
Official report of person
missing, etc., §12-21-91.

Mortality tables, §35-16-4.

Motions.
Evidence on motions, ARCP,
Rule 43 (e).

Motor vehicles.
Accident report, §32-10-11.
Certificate of title.
Prima facie evidence of
facts appearing on it,
§32-8-39.
Chemical tests for
intoxication, §32-5A-194.
Safety-responsibility act.
Matters not to be evidence
in civil actions,
§32-7-12.
Size and weight of vehicles.
Scales.
Certificate of approval.
Prima facie evidence of
accuracy, §32-9-32.

Municipal corporations.
Ordinances, bylaws and
resolutions, §12-21-95.
Proof of certain official
documents, §12-21-73.
Reduction of corporate limits.
Map or plat.
Evidence of municipal
boundaries,
§11-42-211.

Negotiable instruments.
Certificate of notary, etc., as
to presentment for
acceptance, etc., of
instrument governed by
commercial law,
§12-21-105.
Instrument lost or destroyed
by theft, etc.
Evidence of loss,
destruction and
contents, §6-5-284.

EVIDENCE—Cont'd

Newly discovered evidence.
Grounds for new trial,
§15-17-5.
Relief from judgment or
order, ARCP, Rule 60
(b).

Newspapers.
Proof of publication of notice,
§12-21-68.
Protection of sources,
§12-21-142.

New trial.
Newly discovered evidence.
Grounds for new trial,
§15-17-5.

Nonprofit corporations.
Acting as corporation
without authority.
Liability of person so
acting, §10-3A-223.
Legislature.
Reservation of power in
legislature,
§10-3A-224.
Liability of persons acting as
corporation without
authority, §10-3A-223.
Reservation of power in
legislature, §10-3A-224.

Notaries public.
Certificate of notary as to
presentment for
acceptance, etc., of
instrument governed by
commercial law,
§12-21-105.

Notice.
Posting of notice.
Proof of posting, §12-21-69.
Publication of notice.
Proof of publication,
§12-21-68.

Nuisances.
Lewdness, assignation or
prostitution.
Action to abate and
perpetually enjoin,
§6-5-149.

Nurseries.
Insect and disease control.
Rules and regulations.
Admissibility in
evidence, §2-25-20.

Objections.
Disclosure of evidence sought
by objected to question,
§12-21-139.

Obscenity.
Exclusion of audience where
evidence vulgar, obscene,
etc., §§12-21-9,
12-21-202.
Obscene materials containing
visual reproduction of
children.
See OBSCENITY.

Omission in testimony.
Court may allow introduction
before argument
concluded, §15-14-4.

Optometrists.
Board of optometry.
Admissibility of copies of
board records,
§34-22-43.

Ordinances.
Municipal ordinances,
§12-21-95.

EVIDENCE—Cont'd

Other states and territories.
Authentication of foreign
state or territory's
legislative acts,
§12-21-70.
Proof of certain official
documents, §12-21-73.
Proof of unwritten or
common law, §12-21-65.
Public records or books.
Authentication, §12-21-71.
Statutes, §12-21-93.
Transcripts of foreign
statutes, §12-21-94.

Parent and child.
Presumption of paternity.
Rebuttal, §26-17-5.

Parol evidence.
Commercial code.
Sales contracts.
Parol or extrinsic
evidence, §7-2-202.
Foreign countries.
Proof of laws of foreign
countries, §12-21-64.
Production of books, etc.
Parol in lieu of production,
§12-21-3.
Receipts for money,
§12-21-110.
Sales contracts.
Parol or extrinsic evidence,
§7-2-202.
Void writing.
Admissibility of parol
evidence to show
writing void,
§12-21-33.

Partition.
Probate courts.
Record of application as
evidence, §35-6-49.
Sale instead of partition,
§35-6-61.

Partnerships.
Admission or representation
of partner as evidence
against partnership,
§10-8-50.

Patents.
Land patents, §12-21-96.

Peace officers.
Compensation for death.
Determination of claims.
Adoption of rules of
evidence, §36-30-5.

Penitentiary.
Commission of offense during
incarceration.
Fact of confinement in
penitentiary, §14-3-57.

**Pharmacists and
pharmacies.**
Board of pharmacy.
Furnishing evidence to
prosecuting officers,
§34-23-93.
Records and books as
evidence, §34-23-91.

Photographs.
Records.
Photographed records,
§41-13-40.

Physical evidence.
Defined, §13A-10-129.
Tampering with physical
evidence, §13A-10-129.

EVIDENCE—Cont'd
Pilots and pilotage.
Physical and mental fitness
of pilots.
State pilotage commission.
Authority to require
evidence, §33-4-11.
Pneumoconiosis, §25-5-174.
Polygraph examiners,
§§34-25-5, 34-25-6,
34-25-34.
Posting of notice.
Proof of posting, §12-21-69.
Poultry.
Mutilation, alteration, etc., of
documentary evidence,
§2-17-34.
Violations of chapter or
regulations.
Admissibility of evidence of
violations in civil
actions for damages,
§2-17-31.
Price current, §12-21-113.
Private documents.
Proof of private documents,
ARCP, Rule 44 (i).
Private legislative acts.
Admissibility in evidence,
§12-21-37.
Privileges.
Attorney-client privilege,
§12-21-161.
Clergy-patient privilege,
§12-21-166.
Counselors, §34-8A-21.
News-gatherers, §12-21-142.
Professional corporations,
§12-4-391.
Psychiatrist-patient
privilege, §34-26-2.
Criminal psychopath
conditional releases,
§15-16-69.
Psychologist-patient
privilege, §34-26-2.
Criminal psychopath
conditional releases,
§15-16-69.
Victim counselors.
Confidentiality, §§15-23-40
to 15-23-46.
See VICTIM
COUNSELORS.
Probate courts.
Applicability of provisions
pertaining to evidence in
circuit courts, §12-13-12.
Production of books, etc.
Compelling books, etc., to be
produced, §12-21-3.
Failure to comply.
Parties, §12-21-1.
Resident nonparties,
§12-21-2.
Nonparties.
Resident nonparties,
§12-21-2.
Parol evidence in lieu of
production, §12-21-3.
Parties, §12-21-1.
Products liability, §§6-5-522
to 6-5-524.
Proof of facts generally.
Applicability of provisions
regulating proof of facts,
§12-21-11.
**Psychiatrist-patient
privilege.**
Privileges, §34-26-2.

EVIDENCE—Cont'd
**Psychologist-patient
privilege.**
Privileges, §34-26-2.
Publication of notice.
Proof of publication,
§12-21-68.
Public lands.
Sale or transfer of state
lands.
Pre-1879 documents or
certified copies
executed by governor
as evidence of sale or
transfer of state lands,
§12-21-97.
**Public officers and
employees.**
Bonds, surety.
Proof of bonds or
recognizances,
§36-5-21.
Copies of required official
bonds, etc., and
transcripts, §12-21-104.
Exemplifications or copies of
records, etc., kept in
public office.
Proof, §12-21-67.
State employees' retirement
system.
Photo-reproduced copies of
records or documents.
Admissibility, §36-27-29.
Summary proceedings
involving officials.
Sheriffs, coroners, etc.
Copy of execution and
certification of clerk
as evidence,
§6-6-682.
Public service commission.
Injunctions or restraining
orders.
Bonds.
Receipt in evidence,
§37-1-156.
Rate hearings.
See PUBLIC SERVICE
COMMISSION.
Rates and orders of
commission.
Deemed prima facie
reasonable and valid,
§37-1-99.
Quieting title.
In rem proceedings,
§§6-6-566, 6-6-567.
Rape.
Exclusion of audience where
evidence vulgar, etc.,
§§12-21-9, 12-21-202.
Past sexual behavior of
complaining witness.
Admissibility of evidence,
§12-21-203.
Rape shield law, §12-21-203.
Rape shield law, §12-21-203.
Real estate brokers.
Disciplinary actions.
Authority of commission to
compel production,
§34-27-37.
Real property.
Title to lands.
Admissibility of evidence of
title to lands,
§12-21-41.
Receipts.
Effect of written receipts,
§12-21-109.

EVIDENCE—Cont'd
Receipts—Cont'd
Receipts for money,
§12-21-110.
Recordation.
Improperly recorded
instruments as evidence,
§35-4-72.
Proof of documents recorded
under recording act,
ARCP, Rule 44 (e).
When conveyance receivable
in evidence, §35-4-65.
Records.
Authentication of documents.
See within this heading,
"Authentication of
documents."
Business records, ARCP,
Rule 44 (h).
Writings or records made
in regular course of
business.
Copies, §12-21-44.
Originals, §12-21-43.
Copies.
Admissibility, §36-12-41.
Excluded evidence, ARCP,
Rule 43 (c).
Governmental books and
papers.
Duty to furnish, §12-21-35.
Transcripts.
Admissibility of certified
transcripts of official
government books
and papers,
§12-21-35.
Honorable discharges,
§31-1-1.
Hospital records.
Copy of hospital records,
§§12-21-5, 12-21-6.
Lack of record, ARCP, Rule
44 (b).
Nonexistence of record.
Certificate of public officer
on nonexistence of
record, §12-21-34.
Photographed or
microphotographed
records.
Admissibility in evidence,
§41-13-40.
Proof of documents or
records.
Division cumulative as to
proof of documents or
records, §12-21-10.
Public building authorities.
Records of proceedings,
§11-15-6.
Transcribed records,
§12-21-103.
Welfare.
Photographic
reproductions,
§38-2-11.
Registration.
Copies.
When certified copy good
secondary evidence,
§12-21-107.
Official entry on paper as
evidence of registry,
§12-21-106.
Releases.
Effect of written releases,
§12-21-109.

EVIDENCE—Cont'd

Requests for admission.
Rules of civil procedure.
See RULES OF CIVIL
PROCEDURE.

Resolutions.
Municipal resolutions,
§12-21-95.

Restaurants.
Obtaining food by fraud or
misrepresentation.
Prima facie evidence of
offense, §34-15-19.

Rules of civil procedure.
See RULES OF CIVIL
PROCEDURE.

Rules of criminal procedure.
See RULES OF CRIMINAL
PROCEDURE.

Sales.
Contracts.
Parol or extrinsic evidence,
§7-2-202.

Science.
Books of science prima facie
evidence of facts of
general notoriety and
interest, §12-21-108;
ARCP, Rule 44 (g).

Scintilla rule.
Abolished, §12-21-12.

Secondary evidence.
When certified copy good
secondary evidence,
§12-21-107.

Securities.
Copies of register entries or
documents.
Certified copy deemed
prima facie evidence,
§8-6-28.
Fiduciary security transfers.
Evidence of appointment or
incumbency, §8-6-76.

Sentencing.
Habitual felony offenders.
Proof of prior convictions,
§13A-5-10.1.

Settlements.
Pro tanto settlements,
§12-21-109.

Sexual conduct.
Past sexual behavior of
complaining witness.
Admissibility of evidence,
§12-21-203.

Sexual offenses.
Rape shield law, §12-21-203.

Sheriffs.
Deeds.
Recitals in sheriff's deed,
§12-21-99.

Ships and shipping.
Rules and regulations of
commissioner.
Admissibility as evidence,
§33-5-30.

Simultaneous death act.
No sufficient evidence of
survivorship, §43-7-2.

**Speech pathologists and
audiologists.**
Board of examiners.
Admissibility of board
records, etc.,
§34-28A-44.
Authority to compel
production of
documents,
§34-28A-43.

EVIDENCE—Cont'd

**State departments and
agencies.**
Authentication of paper or
documents by
department head,
§12-21-72.

**State products mart and
coliseum authority.**
Admissibility in evidence of
proceedings of board of
directors, §41-10-87.

Statutes.
Other states and territories,
§12-21-93.
Transcripts of foreign
statutes, §12-21-94.
Private legislative acts.
Admissibility in evidence,
§12-21-37.

Stenographic reports.
Admissibility of
stenographically reported
testimony, ARCP, Rule
80.

Subpoenas.
General provisions.
See SUBPOENAS.

Substantial evidence.
Defined, §12-21-12.
Malpractice.
Definition of substantial
evidence, §6-5-542.
Standard of proof, §6-5-549.
Proof by substantial
evidence.
Required, §12-21-12.

Suretyship.
Parol evidence.
Proof of suretyship, §8-3-6.

**Surveyor general of the
United States.**
Books, maps and field notes.
Admissibility of certified
copies, §12-21-36.

Surveys and surveyors.
Board of registration.
Admissibility of board
records, §34-11-37.
Division of land surveys.
Admissibility of division
records in court
proceedings, §35-2-33.

**Tampering with physical
evidence,** §13A-10-129.

Taxation.
See TAXATION.

Teachers' retirement system.
Admissibility in evidence of
photo-reproduced copies
of records or documents
maintained by system,
§16-25-27.

Title.
Admissibility of evidence of
title to lands, §12-21-41.
Certificate and transcripts as
evidence of land title and
facts, §12-21-98.

**Town surveys, plats or
maps.**
Certification,
acknowledgment and
recordation of plat or
map.
Copies as evidence,
§35-2-51.

Trade and commerce.
Market value testimony,
§12-21-114.

EVIDENCE—Cont'd

Trade and commerce—Cont'd
Negotiable instruments.
Certificate of notary as to
presentment for
acceptance, etc., of
instrument governed
by commercial law,
§12-21-105.
Price current and commercial
lists, §12-21-113.

Transcripts.
Admissibility, ARCP, Rule
80.

Trusts and trustees.
Books of accounts kept by
deceased trustee.
Admissibility in evidence,
§12-21-32.

Uniform commercial code.
See COMMERCIAL CODE.

United States.
Authentication of certain
official documents,
§12-21-73.
Land office deeds or written
instruments for
conveyance or sale of
land.
Proof of deeds, §12-21-66.

Valuation.
Market value testimony,
§12-21-114.

Vital statistics.
Certified registers of
marriages, births and
deaths, §12-21-101.

Vulgarity.
Exclusion of audience where
evidence vulgar,
§§12-21-9, 12-21-202.

Weapons.
Committing crime when
armed.
Evidence of intent,
§13A-11-71.

**Weight and sufficiency
generally,** §§12-21-90 to
12-21-114.

Weights and measures.
Altered weight, measure or
device.
Possession prima facie
evidence of guilt,
§8-16-12.
Incorrect, false or unsealed
weight, measure, device,
package or commodity.
Seizure for evidence,
§8-16-10.
Weight certificate.
Prima facie evidence of
weight, §8-16-56.

Welfare.
Records.
Photographic
reproductions,
§38-2-11.

Wills.
Admission of will in
evidence, §43-8-171.
Probate code.
Death or status, §43-8-6.
Rules of evidence, §43-8-6.

Witnesses generally,
§§12-21-130 to 12-21-184,
12-21-220 to 12-21-263.
See WITNESSES.

Workmen's compensation.
Pneumoconiosis, §25-5-174.

EVIDENCE—Cont'd

Writing.
　Alteration in writing.
　　Accounting for alteration
　　　in writing introduced
　　　as genuine, §12-21-63.
　Authentication of documents.
　　See within this heading,
　　　"Authentication of
　　　documents."
　Execution.
　　Proof of execution. See
　　　within this heading,
　　　"Authentication of
　　　documents."
　Handwriting.
　　Admissibility of evidence
　　　for comparison,
　　　§12-21-39.
　　Comparison of disputed
　　　writing with genuine,
　　　§12-21-40.
　　Proof of execution when
　　　subscribing witnesses
　　　dead, etc., §12-21-62.
　　Proof of handwriting,
　　　ARCP, Rule 44 (j).
　Parol evidence. See within
　　this heading, "Parol
　　evidence."
　Production of books, etc.,
　　§§12-21-1 to 12-21-3.
　Proof of handwriting, ARCP,
　　Rule 44 (j).
　Void writing.
　　Parol evidence.
　　　Admissibility of parol
　　　evidence to show
　　　writing void,
　　　§12-21-33.

EXAMINATIONS.

Accountants, §§34-1-4, 34-1-8.
Attorneys at law.
　Board of examiners, §34-3-2.
　Certified graduates of certain
　　law schools.
　　Authority to take bar
　　　exam, §34-3-2.1.
Auctioneers.
　License examination,
　　§34-4-21.
Audiologists, §§34-28A-21 to
　34-28A-24.
　See SPEECH
　　PATHOLOGISTS AND
　　AUDIOLOGISTS.
Banks.
　General provisions, §§5-3A-1
　　to 5-3A-11.
　See BANKS AND
　　FINANCIAL
　　INSTITUTIONS.
Barbers.
　License examinations,
　　§34-5-2.
　See BARBERS.
Blind persons.
　Assistance to needy blind
　　persons.
　　Freedom of choice in
　　　selection of specialists
　　　to make examinations,
　　　§38-1-2.
Cancer, §§22-13-6 to 22-13-11.
　See CANCER.
Chiropractors.
　Licensure, §34-24-161.
Coal mine safety, §§25-9-86,
　25-9-87.
Contractors, §§34-8-2, 34-8-3.

EXAMINATIONS—Cont'd

Coroners' inquests, §§15-4-1
　to 15-4-11.
　See CORONERS.
Cosmetologists.
　General provisions.
　　See COSMETOLOGISTS.
Credit unions.
　Generally, §5-17-8.
Dental service corporations.
　Investigation and
　　examination of
　　corporations, §22-21-386.
**Dentists and dental
　hygienists.**
　License examinations,
　　§34-9-11.
**Department of examiners of
　public accounts,** §§41-5-1
　to 41-5-24.
　See ACCOUNTS AND
　　ACCOUNTING.
Dietitians and nutritionists.
　Practice act.
　　Licensure, §34-34A-7.
　　Waiver of examination
　　　requirement,
　　　§34-34A-12.
Drivers' licenses, §§32-6-3,
　32-6-8.
Education.
　Mental and physical
　　examinations of school
　　children, §§16-29-1 to
　　16-29-6.
　See EDUCATION.
Electrical contractors,
　§34-36-7.
　Fees, §34-36-11.
Embalmers, §§34-13-91,
　34-13-93, 34-13-94.
Engineers, §§34-11-4, 34-11-6.
Finance companies.
　Small loans.
　　Annual examination of
　　　licensees, §5-18-10.
Foresters, §34-12-6.
Fraternal benefit societies,
　§27-34-39.
Funeral directors, §§34-13-70,
　34-13-72, 34-13-73.
Gas fitters.
　Certification of plumbers and
　　gas fitters, §§34-37-6,
　　34-37-7.
Grain dealers.
　Books and records.
　　Power of commissioner,
　　　§2-31-10.
Habeas corpus.
　Disposition of detainee on
　　adjournment, §15-21-20.
　Inquiry into imprisonment or
　　detention, §15-21-20.
Handicapped persons.
　Crippled and disabled
　　children.
　　Physical examination of
　　　children having
　　　malformations or
　　　disabilities, §§21-3-5 to
　　　21-3-7.
Health care service plans.
　Power of commissioner of
　　insurance, §10-4-110.
**Health maintenance
　organizations,**
　§27-21A-16.
**Hearing aid dealers and
　fitters,** §§34-14-4, 34-14-5.

EXAMINATIONS—Cont'd

**Heating and air conditioning
　contractors.**
　Applications.
　　Form, §34-31-27.
　　Content, §34-31-29.
　　Exemption of certain persons,
　　　§34-31-28.
　　Notice, §34-31-29.
　　Time and place, §34-31-29.
　　Written or oral
　　　examinations, §34-31-28.
Horse racing.
　Stewards, §11-65-27.
**Industrial development
　corporations.**
　Annual examination,
　　§10-4-147.
Inspections generally.
　See INSPECTIONS.
Insurance.
　Insurance guaranty
　　association, §§27-42-13,
　　27-42-14.
　Reports.
　　Examination by
　　　commissioner,
　　　§27-2-24.
Interior designers,
　§§34-15A-3, 34-15A-4.
Juvenile proceedings,
　§§12-15-69, 12-15-70.
Landscape architects,
　§§34-17-21 to 34-17-25.
Land surveyors, §§34-11-4,
　34-11-6.
Medical technicians,
　§§34-18-21, 34-18-22.
Mentally ill.
　See MENTALLY ILL.
Motor vehicles.
　Drivers' licenses, §§32-6-3,
　　32-6-8.
Municipal corporations.
　See MUNICIPAL
　　CORPORATIONS.
Nurses, §§34-21-21, 34-21-22.
**Nursing home
　administrators,** §§34-20-9
　to 34-20-11.
Optometrists.
　See OPTOMETRISTS.
Osteopaths, §§34-24-70 to
　34-24-78.
　See PHYSICIANS.
Pest control, §§2-28-2, 2-28-4,
　2-28-6.
**Pharmacists and
　pharmacies,** §34-23-51.
Physical therapists,
　§§34-24-212 to 34-24-214.
Physicians, §§34-24-70 to
　34-24-78.
　See PHYSICIANS.
Pilots, §§33-4-30, 33-4-35,
　33-4-36.
Plumbing.
　Certification of plumbers and
　　gas fitters, §§34-37-6,
　　34-37-7.
Podiatrists, §§34-24-255 to
　34-24-257.
**Polygraph examiners
　generally.**
　See POLYGRAPH
　　EXAMINERS.
Psychologists, §§34-26-43 to
　34-26-45.

EXAMINATIONS—Cont'd
Public accounts.
Department of examiners of
public accounts, §§41-5-1
to 41-5-24.
See ACCOUNTS AND
ACCOUNTING.
Real estate brokers,
§34-27-33.
Rules of civil procedure.
Physical and mental
examination of persons,
ARCP, Rule 35.
Form of motion for
physical examination,
ARCP, Form 53.
Savings and loan
associations, §5-16-36.
School bus drivers, §16-27-4.
School children.
Mental and physical
examinations, §§16-29-1
to 16-29-6.
See EDUCATION.
Small loans.
Annual examination of
licenses, §5-18-10.
Speech pathologists and
audiologists, §§34-28A-21
to 34-28A-24.
Surveyors, §§34-11-4, 34-11-6.
Vacation time-sharing plans.
Persons desiring to act as
sellers, §34-27-66.
Applications, §34-27-66.
Fees, §34-27-66.
Issuance and renewal of
license, §34-27-66.
Qualifications, §34-27-66.
Required, §34-27-66.
Youthful offenders,
§§15-19-1, 15-19-5.

EXCEPTIONAL CHILD
EDUCATION ACT,
§§16-39-1 to 16-39-12.
See EDUCATION.

EXCEPTIONS.
Rules of civil procedure.
Unnecessary, ARCP, Rule 46.

EXCISE TAXES.
Alcoholic beverages.
General provisions.
See ALCOHOLIC
BEVERAGES.
Gasoline.
Additional excise tax on
gasoline, motor fuel and
lubricating oil,
§§40-17-220 to 40-17-225.

EXCLUSIONARY RULE.
Alcoholic beverages.
Admissibility of evidence
obtained by illegal
searches, §28-1-2.

EXECUTIONS.
Adjoining counties.
Execution of writs,
attachments and other
process, §15-10-45.
Appeals.
Execution upon dismissal of
appeal or affirmation of
judgment, §12-22-75.
Unpaid costs.
Execution by lower courts
for unpaid costs,
§12-22-76.

EXECUTIONS—Cont'd
Arbitration on settlement,
§§43-2-600 to 43-2-607. See
within this heading,
"Settlements and
distributions."
Arrest writs, §§15-10-44,
15-10-45.
Assignment of judgments.
Right of assignee to have
execution, §6-9-196.
Attachments.
See ATTACHMENTS.
Bills of lading.
Lien on goods covered by
negotiable document,
§7-7-602.
Bonds, surety.
Forthcoming bonds,
§§6-9-160, 6-9-161.
Indemnity bond, §6-9-81.
Lien of execution.
Destruction upon execution
of bond for appeal, etc.,
§6-9-61.
Bulk transfers.
Limitation of levies,
§7-6-111.
Sales excepted from article,
§7-6-103.
Business trusts.
Property subject to execution,
§19-3-66.
Cigarettes.
Tax on gummed cigarette
papers.
Execution on final
assessment,
§40-25A-13.
Circuit courts.
Fees, §12-19-75.
Commercial code.
Bank deposits and
collections.
When items subject to
legal process, §7-4-303.
Bulk transfers.
Limitation of levies,
§7-6-111.
Sales excepted from article,
§7-6-103.
Documents of title.
Lien on goods covered by
negotiable document,
§7-7-602.
Investment securities.
Levy upon security,
§7-8-317.
Secured transactions.
Debtor's rights in
collateral, §7-9-311.
Priority over unperfected
security interests,
§7-9-301.
Conservators.
Settlements of accounts of
conservators.
Death of conservator.
Issuance against surety,
§26-5-54.
Constables.
Collection of commissions on
costs on execution by
constables, §12-19-95.
Duty to execute and return,
§36-23-6.
Service of executions when
office of constable
vacant, §36-23-8.

EXECUTIONS—Cont'd
Constables—Cont'd
When constables entitled to
receive full commissions,
§12-19-96.
When constables entitled to
receive only half
commissions, §12-19-97.
Constitution of Alabama.
Exemption of personal
property of value of one
thousand dollars, Const.
Ala., art. X, §204.
Rules and regulations to
ascertain value of
property exempted from
sale under legal process,
Const. Ala., art. IV, §92.
Conveyances, §35-4-20.
Execution sales. See within
this heading, "Execution
sales."
General provisions.
See CONVEYANCES.
Coroners.
Collection, etc., of
commissions on costs on
execution by coroners,
§12-19-95.
Execution by coroner or
special coroner, §6-9-25.
When coroners entitled to
receive full commissions,
§12-19-96.
When coroners entitled to
receive only half
commissions, §12-19-97.
Corporations.
Prosecution of corporations.
Execution on judgment,
§10-7-4.
Costs.
Certification of total court
costs to accompany
execution, §6-9-26.
Execution against plaintiff
for costs, §6-9-27.
Crops.
Growing or ungathered crops.
Property subject to
execution, §6-9-41.
Death of defendant.
Execution where defendant
dead, §6-9-63.
Issuance of execution.
Death of party after
issuance, §6-9-94.
Levy of execution after,
§6-9-62.
Death of plaintiff.
Execution in favor of
surviving plaintiffs,
§6-9-195.
Issuance of execution.
Death of party after
issuance, §6-9-94.
Deeds, §35-4-20.
Execution sales.
Execution and delivery of
deed to real estate sold
by sheriff, §6-9-149.
District courts.
Fees, §12-19-75.
Endorsements on execution
writs.
Execution sales.
Description of land sold
and price, §6-9-100.
Levy.
Date, §6-9-99.

EXECUTIONS—Cont'd
  Endorsements on execution writs—Cont'd
    Levy—Cont'd
      Description of property levied, §6-9-99.
      Money collected.
        Amount, §6-9-101.
        Receipt for defendant, §6-9-101.
      Order of receipt, §6-9-98.
      Time of receipt, §6-9-98.
  Equities of redemption.
    Property subject to execution, §6-9-40.
  Estate and inheritance tax.
    Execution for tax, §40-15-11.
  Execution sales.
    Caveat emptor, §6-9-142.
    Continuances, §6-9-86.
    Conveyance of title, §6-9-140.
      Covenants running with land.
        Enforcement, §6-9-145.
      Fraud binds officer personally, §6-9-142.
      Lands sold by predecessor.
        Conveyance by sheriff, §6-9-150.
    Deeds.
      Execution and delivery of deed to real estate sold by sheriff, §6-9-149.
    Endorsements on execution writs, §§6-9-98 to 6-9-101.
    Excess proceeds.
      Payment to debtor, §6-9-93.
    Exemptions from levy and sale under process.
      See EXEMPTIONS FROM LEVY AND SALE UNDER PROCESS.
    Hours of sale, §6-8-41.
    Judicial sales generally.
      See JUDICIAL SALES.
    Livestock.
      Levying officer to provide sustenance for unsold livestock, §6-9-95.
    Noncompliance with terms of sale.
      Liability of purchaser, §6-9-143.
        Form of action, §6-9-143.
    Notice, §6-9-87.
      Notice to plaintiff of money made, §6-9-92.
    Perishable goods and chattels.
      Generally, §6-9-88.
      Strawberries, §6-9-89.
    Place, §6-9-86.
    Redemption, §§6-5-247 to 6-5-257.
      See REAL PROPERTY.
    Rights of debtor.
      Designation of property to be sold first, §6-9-90.
      Substitution of other property, §6-9-91.
    Setting aside by courts, §6-9-147.
    Stock.
      Purchaser owner of stock sold, §6-9-144.
    Strawberries, §6-9-89.
    Time, §6-9-86.
    Undivided interest in property, §6-9-85.

EXECUTIONS—Cont'd
  Execution sales—Cont'd
    Void sales.
      Mortgage foreclosure.
        Purchaser at void or irregular sale under foreclosure succeeds to all interest of mortgagee, §6-9-146.
      When debtor bound, §6-9-148.
      Writing unnecessary, §6-9-141.
  Executors and administrators.
    See EXECUTORS AND ADMINISTRATORS.
  Exemptions from levy and sale under process.
    See EXEMPTIONS FROM LEVY AND SALE UNDER PROCESS.
  Fees.
    Certification of fees to accompany execution, §6-9-26.
    Circuit and district court execution fees, §12-19-75.
  Forms, §6-9-1.
    Venditioni exponas, §6-9-120.
  Forthcoming bonds.
    Forfeiture of bond.
      Execution upon, §6-9-160.
      Exceptions, §6-9-160.
    Restoration of property to debtor.
      Execution of bond, §6-9-160.
    Value of restored property.
      Tendering by bond obligors where same dead or destroyed, §6-9-161.
  Fraternal benefit societies.
    Exemption of benefits, etc., from attachment, garnishment or other process, §27-34-27.
  Fraud.
    Fraudulent disposal or removal of property by defendant.
      When execution to issue, §6-9-23.
  Garnishment generally.
    See GARNISHMENT.
  Gasoline.
    Gasoline tax.
      Delinquents, §40-17-4.
  Hotels, inns and other transient lodging places.
    Transient occupancy tax, §40-26-15.
  Indictments.
    Resisting officer in executing process.
      Form of indictment, §15-8-150.
  Insolvent estates.
    Decree on insolvency.
      Effect on pending suits, §§43-2-810 to 43-2-813.
    Report of insolvency.
      Pending suits.
        Effect on pending suits, §§43-2-810 to 43-2-813.
  Insurance.
    Insurers.
      Delinquency proceedings, §27-32-21.

EXECUTIONS—Cont'd
  Investment securities.
    Levy upon security, §7-8-317.
  Issuance.
    Alias writs, §6-9-24.
    Death of party after issuance, §6-9-94.
    Executors and administrators.
      Issuance in favor of personal representative or successor without revival of judgment, §6-9-193.
    When execution to issue.
      Fraudulent disposal or removal of property by defendant, §6-9-23.
      Generally, §6-9-21.
      Prior to time prescribed, §6-9-22.
    Who may issue, §6-9-20.
  Judges.
    Issuance, §6-9-20.
  Judgments and decrees against personal representatives.
    Garnishment to enforce, §§43-2-150 to 43-2-155.
  Judicial sales generally.
    See JUDICIAL SALES.
  Levy.
    Death of defendant.
      Levy of execution after, §6-9-62.
    Endorsements on execution writs, §§6-9-98 to 6-9-101.
    Exemptions from levy and sale under process.
      See EXEMPTIONS FROM LEVY AND SALE UNDER PROCESS.
    Livestock.
      Levying officer to provide sustenance for unsold livestock, §6-9-95.
    Real property.
      Notice where levy on real estate, §6-9-82.
    Suretyship.
      Levy on property of principal first if execution against sureties, §6-9-83.
    Undivided interest in property, §6-9-85.
  Lien of execution.
    Bonds, surety.
      Destruction of lien upon execution of bond for appeal, etc., §6-9-61.
    Subjected property sold by debtor.
      Charging, §6-9-84.
    Writ of execution.
      When becomes lien, §6-9-60.
  Livestock.
    Sustenance.
      Levying officer to provide sustenance for unsold livestock, §6-9-95.
  Military affairs.
    Arms and equipment.
      Personally owned arms of officers and enlisted men.
        Exempt from sale under execution, §31-2-78.

EXECUTIONS—Cont'd
Military affairs—Cont'd
Uniforms.
Personally owned uniforms
of officers and enlisted
men.
Exempt from sale under
execution, §31-2-78.
**Mortgages and deeds of
trust.**
Void or irregular sale under
foreclosure.
Purchaser succeeds to
interest of mortgagee,
§6-9-146.
Motor fuels.
Diesel fuel tax.
Delinquents, §40-17-15.
Motor vehicle carriers.
Mileage tax.
Execution against property
of delinquent taxpayer,
§40-19-10.
Notices.
Execution sales, §6-9-87.
Notice to plaintiff of money
made, §6-9-92.
Levy on real estate, §6-9-82.
Parole.
Retaking of parolee.
Warrant, §15-22-31.
Peace bonds.
Collection of costs, §15-6-26.
Personal property.
Property subject to execution,
§6-9-40.
Equity of redemption,
§6-9-40.
**Public officers and
employees.**
Summary proceedings
involving officials.
Judgment against clerk,
register or their
sureties, §6-6-700.
Judgment against sheriff
or coroner, §§6-6-681,
6-6-682.
Real property.
Levy.
Notice, §6-9-82.
Property subject to execution,
§6-9-40.
Equity of redemption,
§6-9-40.
Redemption, §§6-5-247 to
6-5-257.
See REAL PROPERTY.
Return.
Sheriff of another county,
§6-9-97.
Time, §6-9-80.
Writs.
Unexecuted writ, §6-9-96.
Revival of judgments.
Judgment of district or
circuit court on which
execution did not issue
within 10 years,
§6-9-192.
Rules of civil procedure,
ARCP, Rule 69.
Forms.
Notice of right to claim
exemption, ARCP,
Form 92.
Sales. See within this heading,
"Execution sales."
Sales tax.
Failure to pay tax, §40-23-20.

EXECUTIONS—Cont'd
Searches and seizures.
Execution of search
warrants, §§15-5-7 to
15-5-9, 15-5-12.
See SEARCHES AND
SEIZURES.
Secured transactions.
Debtor's rights in collateral,
§7-9-311.
Priority over unperfected
security interests,
§7-9-301.
**Settlements and
distributions.**
Accounts.
Compelling settlement by
existing executor or
administrator,
§§43-2-550 to 43-2-564.
Legacies.
Compelling payment,
§§43-2-580 to 43-2-586.
Payment of legacies.
Compelling, §§43-2-580 to
43-2-586.
Removal or resignation of
executor or
administrator.
Compelling settlement of
executor or
administrator whose
authority has ceased,
§§43-2-550 to 43-2-564.
Sheriffs.
Deeds.
Execution and delivery of
deed to real estate
sold, §6-9-149.
Evidence.
Recitals in sheriff's deed,
§12-21-99.
Failure to return, levy or
collect execution.
Issuance of execution
against sheriff upon,
§12-19-50.
Lands sold by predecessor.
Conveyance by sheriff,
§6-9-150.
Stock and stockholders.
Execution sales.
Purchaser owner of stock,
§6-9-144.
**Summary distribution of
small estates,** §§43-2-690
to 43-2-696.
Suretyship.
Levy on property of principal
first if execution against
sureties, §6-9-83.
Right of surety paying
execution, §6-9-2.
Teachers' retirement system.
Benefits exempt from
execution, §16-25-23.
Testamentary letters,
§§43-2-20 to 43-2-29. See
within this heading,
"Letters testamentary."
Title.
Conveyance by sale under
judicial process, §6-9-140.
Caveat emptor, §6-9-142.
Tobacco.
Sales tax.
Unpaid taxes or penalties,
§40-25-21.
Use tax, §40-25-44.

EXECUTIONS—Cont'd
Transfer of judgment.
Right of assignee to have
execution, §6-9-196.
**Unemployment
compensation.**
Benefits.
Exemption, §25-4-140.
Venditioni exponas.
Form, §6-9-120.
Issuance, §6-9-120.
Death of levying officer
prior to sale, §6-9-121.
Proceedings if property
not delivered by
representatives of
deceased officer,
§6-9-121.
Return showing goods
levied on unsold,
§6-9-120.
Warehouse receipts.
Lien on goods covered by
negotiable document,
§7-7-602.
Warrants.
Execution of search
warrants, §§15-5-7 to
15-5-9, 15-5-12.
Workmen's compensation.
Pneumoconiosis.
Coal miners.
Exemption of benefits,
§25-5-179.
Writs.
Alias writs.
Issuance, §6-9-24.
Endorsements, §§6-9-98 to
6-9-101.
Forms, §6-9-1.
Venditioni exponas,
§6-9-120.
Lien of execution.
When writ becomes lien,
§6-9-60.
Seizure and delivery of
specific property.
Form, §6-9-1.
Time for execution and
return, §6-9-80.
Venditioni exponas,
§§6-9-120, 6-9-121.
Writ of execution.
Form, §6-9-1.
Writ of possession and
execution.
Form, §6-9-1.

EXECUTIVE MANSION.
Advisory board, §§41-9-530 to
41-9-532.

**EXECUTORS AND
ADMINISTRATORS.**
Abatement, revival and
survival.
Personal representatives,
§6-5-462.
Accounts and accounting.
Assignment or transfer,
§43-2-420.
Death.
Books of account kept by
deceased executor or
administrator.
Use as evidence,
§12-21-32.
Evidence.
Books of account kept by
deceased executor or
administrator.
Admissibility, §12-21-32.

EXECUTORS AND ADMINISTRATORS
—Cont'd

Accounts and accounting
—Cont'd

Exemption from filing inventory or making report or final settlement.

Testator may exempt executor, §43-2-311.

Settlements and distributions, §§43-2-500 to 43-2-696. See within this heading, "Settlements and distributions."

Actions by and against.

Bonds, surety.
Action on bond, §43-2-137.

Damages to realty.
Survival of actions, §43-2-136.

Enforcement of judgment and decrees against personal representatives, §§43-2-150 to 43-2-155.

Evidence.
Inventory, §43-2-139.

Foreign executors and administrators.
Action not affected by grant of letters of administration in state, §43-2-212.

Compliance with section 43-2-211 to be proved, §43-2-213.

Right of intervention by administrator appointed in state, §43-2-212.

Right to maintain actions, §43-2-211.

Inventory as evidence, §43-2-139.

Judgments and decrees against personal representatives, §§43-2-134, 43-2-150 to 43-2-155. See within this heading, "Judgments and decrees against personal representatives."

Legatees.
Action to recover legacy, §43-2-138.

Limitation on actions, §43-2-131.

Nonresident executors and administrators.
Liability to actions, §43-2-197.

Right to maintain actions, §43-2-196.

Real property.
Damages to realty.
Survival of actions, §43-2-136.

Service of summons, §43-2-130.

Special administrators.
Actions begun by special administrator not abated, §43-2-132.

Succeeding executors or administrators.
To be made party to civil actions, §43-2-133.

EXECUTORS AND ADMINISTRATORS
—Cont'd

Actions by and against
—Cont'd

Survival of actions.
Damages to realty, §43-2-136.

Survivor of two or more executors or administrators.
Actions against, §43-2-135.

Trespass.
Right of action against executor or administrator, §6-5-90.

Venue, §43-2-130.
Nonresident executors and administrators, §43-2-197.

Waste.
Right of action against executor or administrator, §6-5-90.

Ad colligendum.
Special administrator ad colligendum, §43-2-47.

Ad litem.
Administrator ad litem, §§43-2-250 to 43-2-256. See within this heading, "Administrators ad litem."

Administration of estates of persons presumed dead, §§43-2-230 to 43-2-238. See within this heading, "Persons presumed dead."

Administrators ad litem.
Appointment, §43-2-250.
Compensation, §43-2-256.
Decree in favor of administrator ad litem, §43-2-251.

Enforcement of decree for recovery of property, §43-2-253.

Enforcement of decree when administrator adversely interested, §43-2-254.

Execution on money decree or judgment, §43-2-252.

Judgments.
Enforcement of judgment for recovery of property, §43-2-253.

Enforcement of judgment when administrator adversely interested, §43-2-254.

Execution on judgments, §43-2-252.

Payment of judgment or decree.
Duty of judge, clerk or register to make payment, §43-2-255.

Personal property.
Enforcement of decree or judgment for recovery of property, §43-2-253.

Administrators de bonis non.
Judgments against administrators in chief.
Revived against administrators de bonis non, §43-2-134.

EXECUTORS AND ADMINISTRATORS
—Cont'd

Administrators in chief.
Judgments against administrators in chief.
Revived against administrators de bonis non, §43-2-134.

Administrators with will annexed.
Powers same as those of executors, §43-8-255.

Advertising.
Distribution or division on final settlement.
Sale of property, §43-2-624.

Sale of real property for payment of debts and for division, §43-2-455.

Aliens.
Foreign executors and administrators, §§43-2-210 to 43-2-214. See within this heading, "Foreign executors and administrators."

Appeals.
Appeals from probate court, §§12-22-20 to 12-22-27. See PROBATE COURTS.

Bond on appeal of order removing executor or administrator, §12-22-24.

Conveyances by executors and administrators.
Application to compel conveyance, §35-4-321.

Judgment on partial or annual settlement of estate, §12-22-4.

Appointment.
Administrators ad litem, §43-2-250.

Circuit court, §12-11-40.

Final settlement.
Administrator appointed after, §43-2-274.

Notice of appointment.
Failure to give notice.
Penalty, §43-2-62.
Generally, §43-2-60.
Manner, §43-2-61.
Penalty for failure to give notice, §43-2-62.

Persons presumed dead.
Appointment of personal representative, §43-2-231.

Renouncing appointment.
Issuance of letters to others named in will upon renunciation, §43-2-26.

Letters of administration granted in stated order.
The following executors named to renounce, §43-2-27.

Procedure, §43-2-25.

Attachment.
Judgments.
Suspending entry of judgment against executor or administrator, §6-6-144.

Right to commence action, §6-6-47.

EXECUTORS AND
ADMINISTRATORS
—Cont'd
Attachment—Cont'd
Settlements and
distributions.
Compelling settlement of
executor or
administrator whose
authority has ceased,
§43-2-555.
Attorneys' fees.
Court may allow up to time
of settlement, §43-2-682.
Audits.
Settlements and
distributions.
Auditing of account,
§43-2-507.
Compelling settlement
by existing executor
or administrator.
When court required to
audit account,
§43-2-531.
Compelling settlement of
executor or
administrator whose
authority has ceased.
When court required to
audit account,
§43-2-556.
Bankruptcy and insolvency.
Insolvent estates, §§43-2-700
to 43-2-813. See within
this heading, "Insolvent
estates."
Banks and financial
institutions.
Accounts, §5-16-43.
Conversion of state banks
into or consolidation
with national banks.
Continuation of obligations
of state bank,
§5-7A-43.
Disposition of deposits of
deceased persons,
§5-5A-38.
Time for payment,
§5-5A-39.
Powers of banks, §5-5A-18.
Bonds, surety.
Action on bond, §43-2-137.
Additional bond.
Application for, §43-2-293.
Notice of application by
publication,
§43-2-295.
Service of citation,
§43-2-294.
Continuation of force and
obligations of former
bonds, §43-2-89.
Costs, §43-2-297.
Default.
Removal for, §43-2-292.
Force and obligations of
former bonds
continued, §43-2-89.
General administrator,
§43-2-86.
May be required,
§43-2-292.
Motion of court.
Additional bond on,
§43-2-299.
Order to give additional
bond, §43-2-298.

EXECUTORS AND
ADMINISTRATORS
—Cont'd
Bonds, surety—Cont'd
Additional bond—Cont'd
Removal of executor or
administrator,
§43-2-292.
Service of citation,
§43-2-294.
Sheriff, §43-2-87.
When sureties discharged
by, §43-2-88.
Amount, §43-2-80.
Approval by probate judge,
§43-2-80.
Conditional execution or
delivery, §43-2-92.
Corporations.
Testator may preclude
corporation from
becoming surety on
bond, §43-8-256.
Default.
Additional bond.
Removal for default of,
§43-2-292.
Delivery.
Conditional delivery,
§43-2-92.
Discharge of sureties,
§43-2-83.
When discharged by
additional bond,
§43-2-88.
Execution.
Conditional execution,
§43-2-92.
Enforcement of judgments
and decrees against
personal
representatives.
Liability of sureties,
§43-2-151.
Exemptions.
Express provision in will,
§43-2-81.
Trust companies, etc.,
acting as
administrators,
§5-11A-9.
Foreign executors and
administrators,
§43-2-210.
Former bonds.
Force and obligations
continued, §43-2-89.
General administrators,
§43-2-85.
Additional bond, §43-2-86.
Bond of third party
applicant when
administration
committed to general
administrator,
§43-2-84.
Liability of probate judge in
taking bond, §43-2-82.
Liability of sureties,
§43-2-151.
New bond after discharge of
surety, §43-2-83.
Persons required to give
bond, §43-2-80.
Probate judges.
Approval by, §43-2-80.
Liability of judge in taking
bond, §43-2-82.
Recordation, §43-2-1.
Reducing amount of bond,
§43-2-93.

EXECUTORS AND
ADMINISTRATORS
—Cont'd
Bonds, surety—Cont'd
Removal of executor or
administrator.
New or additional bond,
§43-2-292.
Rights of sureties among
themselves, §43-2-90.
Sheriffs.
Bond of third party
applicant when
administration
committed to, §43-2-84.
Statutory bonds.
Valid and operative as
statutory bonds,
§43-2-91.
Sureties required, §43-2-80.
Third party applicants.
Bond of applicant when
administration
committed to general
administrator or
sheriff, §43-2-84.
Validity.
Bonds valid and operative
as statutory bonds,
§43-2-91.
Who required to give,
§43-2-80.
Wills.
Exemption of executor by
express provision in
will, §43-2-81.
Bribery.
Commercial bribery,
§13A-11-120.
Bulk transfers.
Transfers excepted from
article, §7-6-103.
Circuit courts.
Appointment of personal
representatives,
§12-11-40.
Proceedings on
administration of estates
in, §12-11-40.
Removal of administration of
estates from probate
court, §12-11-41.
Claims and debts.
Appeals, §43-2-354.
Bonds, surety.
When executor or
administrator may
give bond to extend or
settle debt, §43-2-393.
Costs, §43-2-354.
Debts not due.
Payment, §43-2-375.
Discharge of debtor,
§43-2-394.
Extension.
When executor or
administrator may
give note, etc., to
extend or settle debt,
§43-2-393.
Filing.
Time and manner of filing.
Exception as to minors
or persons of
unsound mind,
§43-2-351.
Generally, §43-2-350.
Hearing, §43-2-354.
Sale, compromise and
settlement, §43-2-391.

EXECUTORS AND ADMINISTRATORS —Cont'd

Claims and debts—Cont'd
Insolvent estates, §§43-2-740 to 43-2-751. See within this heading, "Insolvent estates."
Judgment, §43-2-354.
Limitation of actions.
Payment of claims barred by, §43-2-373.
Manner of filing.
Exception as to minors or persons of unsound mind, §43-2-351.
Generally, §43-2-350.
Mentally ill.
Time and manner of filing claims.
Exception, §43-2-351.
Minors.
Time and manner of filing claims, §43-2-351.
Notes.
When executor or administrator may give note, etc., to extend or settle debt, §43-2-393.
Notice, §43-2-354.
Sale, compromise and settlement, §43-2-391.
Order of preference, §43-2-371.
Payment.
Claims barred by statute of limitations, §43-2-373.
Debts not due, §43-2-375.
Property charged with payment, §43-2-370.
When executor or administrator protected in payment of debts, §43-2-374.
Pending action.
Revival of considered as presentation, §43-2-353.
Preferences.
Debts of same class.
No preference among, §43-2-372.
Order of preference, §43-2-371.
Property.
Property charged with payment of debts, §43-2-370.
Reports.
Sale, compromise and settlement, §43-2-392.
Revival of pending action considered as presentation, §43-2-353.
Sale, compromise and settlement.
Authorization, §43-2-390.
Compounding with and discharge of debtor, §43-2-394.
Discharge of debtor, §43-2-394.
Hearing, §43-2-391.
Notes.
When executor or administrator may give note, etc., to extend or settle debt, §43-2-393.
Notice, §43-2-391.

EXECUTORS AND ADMINISTRATORS —Cont'd

Claims and debts—Cont'd
Sale, compromise and settlement—Cont'd
Report, §43-2-392.
Sale or division of land received on compromise, §43-2-468.
Sale of real property for payment of debts and for division, §§43-2-440 to 43-2-468. See within this heading, "Real property."
Statute of limitations.
Payment of claims barred by, §43-2-373.
Time of filing.
Exception as to minors or persons of unsound mind, §43-2-351.
Generally, §43-2-350.
Verification of claims, §43-2-352.
Claims by and against state.
Claims against state for death to be made by personal representative, §41-9-64.
Commercial code.
Bulk transfers.
Transfers excepted from article, §7-6-103.
Investment securities, §§7-8-101 to 7-8-406.
See COMMERCIAL CODE.
Representative defined, §7-1-201.
Commissions on money or property sold or distributed, §43-2-681.
Compensation.
Court may allow up to time of settlement, §43-2-682.
Executors and administrators may be allowed fair compensation, etc., §43-2-680.
Compromise and settlement.
Claims and debts, §§43-2-390 to 43-2-394.
Sale or division of land received on compromise, §43-2-468.
Settlements and distributions, §§43-2-500 to 43-2-696. See within this heading, "Settlements and distributions."
Condition of estate.
Exhibit showing, §43-2-318.
Conflicts of interest.
Enforcement of decree or judgment when administrator adversely interested, §43-2-254.
Conservators.
Settlements of accounts of conservators.
Compulsion of settlement by probate court.
Final settlement.
Authorization and procedure, §26-5-34.

EXECUTORS AND ADMINISTRATORS —Cont'd

Conservators—Cont'd
Settlements of accounts of conservators—Cont'd
Death of conservator.
Personal representatives.
Party to settlement proceedings, §26-5-51.
Constitution of Alabama.
Probate courts.
Power to grant letters of administration, Const. Ala., amd. 364.
Conveyances by executors and administrators, §§35-4-320 to 35-4-323.
Authorization, §35-4-320.
Compelling conveyance.
Application to compel.
Appeals, §35-4-322.
Contents, §35-4-322.
Decree, §35-4-322.
Generally, §35-4-321.
Minors.
Notice to guardians of minor heirs, §35-4-323.
Notice, §35-4-322.
To guardians of minor heirs, §35-4-323.
Contracts for conveyance.
Personal representative authorized to make conveyance, §35-4-320.
Powers of disposition.
Execution of power by surviving or acting executors, §35-4-303.
Corporations.
Bonds, surety.
Testator may preclude corporation from becoming surety on bond of executor or administrator, §43-8-256.
Foreign corporations.
Acting in fiduciary capacity, §§10-2A-221 to 10-2A-224.1.
See CORPORATIONS.
Voting of shares, §10-2A-53.
Counties.
Claims and demands against counties.
Verification of claims by executors or administrators, §11-12-6.
General administrators, §§43-2-170 to 43-2-175.
Warrants for construction of public buildings, bridges and roads.
Legal investments for trust funds, §11-28-5.
County administrators, §§43-2-170 to 43-2-175.
Criminal law and procedure.
Commercial bribery, §13A-11-120.
Crops.
Completion, gathering and sale of crops commenced by decedent, §43-2-418.

EXECUTORS AND ADMINISTRATORS
—Cont'd

Curators.
Fiduciary security transfers, §§8-6-70 to 8-6-80.
See SECURITIES.
General provisions, §§26-7A-1 to 26-7A-17.
See GUARDIAN AND WARD.

Damages.
Liability, §§43-2-110 to 43-2-114.

Death.
Administration of estates of persons presumed dead, §§43-2-230 to 43-2-238.
See within this heading, "Persons presumed dead."
Books of account kept by deceased executor or administrator.
Admissibility in evidence, §12-21-32.
Letters of administration.
Duty of probate court to grant letters upon vacancy, §43-2-272.
Settlements and distributions.
Compelling settlement of executor or administrator whose authority has ceased, §§43-2-550 to 43-2-564.
See within this heading, "Settlements and distributions."
Sole executor, §43-2-28.
Surviving executor or administrator, §43-2-28.
Removal.
Grounds, §43-2-290.
When survivor continues to act, §43-2-273.

Debtor of testator.
Appointment of debtor as executor, §43-8-254.

Debts and claims.
Generally, §§43-2-350 to 43-2-394. See within this heading, "Claims and debts."
Insolvent estates, §§43-2-740 to 43-2-751. See within this heading, "Insolvent estates."

Declaratory judgments.
Questions on administration, §6-6-225.

Decrees.
Conveyances by executors and administrators.
Applications to compel conveyance, §35-4-322.

Defenses.
Resignation as defense, §43-2-114.

Definitions.
Small estates.
Summary distribution, §43-2-691.

Delivery of will, §43-8-270.

EXECUTORS AND ADMINISTRATORS
—Cont'd

Depositions.
Sale of real property for payment of debts and for division.
Order of sale.
When depositions required, §43-2-452.

Discharge from liability, §43-2-628.

Disqualifications.
Certain persons disqualified to serve, §43-2-22.

Distributions. See within this heading, "Settlements and distributions."

Dockets.
Insolvent estates.
Claims against.
Claims docket, §43-2-745.

Embezzlement.
Grounds for removal, §43-2-290.

Escheats.
Failure to pay over proceeds.
Decree against personal representative for, §43-6-6.
Notice by personal representative, §43-6-2.
Contents, §43-6-3.

Evidence.
Books of account kept by deceased executor or administrator.
Admissibility, §12-21-32.
Inventory, §43-2-139.
Letters testamentary and of administration.
Copies of letters, §12-21-102.
Transcripts of records of letters and bonds, §43-2-1.

Executions.
Administrators ad litem.
Execution on money decree or judgment, §43-2-252.
Enforcement of judgments and decrees against personal representatives, §§43-2-150 to 43-2-155.
Issuance in favor of personal representative or successor without revival of judgment, §6-9-193.

Executor de son tort, §43-2-113.

Exhibit showing condition of estate, §43-2-318.

Fees.
General provisions, §§43-2-680 to 43-2-682.
Previous fees considered upon final settlement, §43-2-683.
Probate judges' fees, §12-19-90.

Fiduciaries generally.
See FIDUCIARIES.

Foreign decedents.
Disposition of personal estate, §43-2-629.

EXECUTORS AND ADMINISTRATORS
—Cont'd

Foreign executors and administrators.
Actions.
Compliance with section 43-2-211 to be proved, §43-2-213.
Not affected by grant of letters of administration in state, §43-2-212.
Right of intervention of administrator appointed in state, §43-2-212.
Right to maintain actions and recover or receive property in state, §43-2-211.
Bonds, surety, §43-2-210.
Judgments.
Protection afforded by recovery of judgment, §43-2-214.
Letters of administration.
Actions not affected by grant of letters of administration in state, §43-2-212.
Property.
Protection afforded by delivery, §43-2-214.
Right to recover or receive property in state, §43-2-211.

Forms.
Letters testamentary, §43-2-21.

Fraud.
Certain agreements void unless in writing, §8-9-2.

Garnishment.
Enforcement of judgments and decrees against personal representatives, §§43-2-150 to 43-2-155.
What may be garnished, §6-6-411.

General administrators.
Appointment, §43-2-170.
Bonds, surety, §43-2-85.
Bond of third party applicant when administration committed to general administrator, §43-2-84.
Delay for committing administration of estate, §43-2-171.
Duties, §43-2-170.
Record of official acts, §43-2-175.
Resignation and removal.
Appointment of successor, §43-2-174.
Generally, §43-2-173.
Successors.
Appointment, §43-2-174.
Term of office, §43-2-170.

Guardian ad litem.
Sale of real property for payment of debts and for division.
Appointment, §43-2-445.
Compensation, §43-2-448.
Duties, §43-2-448.

EXECUTORS AND ADMINISTRATORS
—Cont'd

Guardian ad litem—Cont'd
Settlements and distributions.
Appointment, §43-2-504.

Guardian and ward.
Settlements and distributions.
Arbitration on settlement of estates.
Consent by guardian, §43-2-601.
Special guardians, §43-2-517.

Imprisonment.
Grounds for removal, §43-2-290.
Rights terminated by sentence of imprisonment, §43-2-291.

Income tax.
Assessment.
Request for prompt assessment, §40-18-45.
Declaration of estimated tax.
Not required, §40-18-85.
Defined, §40-18-1.

Insolvent estates, §§43-2-700 to 43-2-813.
Action by creditor to recover dividend, §43-2-751.
Appeals, §43-2-709.
Appointment of administrator, §43-2-723.
Former letters revoked upon, §43-2-724.
Claims against insolvent estates.
Action by creditor to recover dividend, §43-2-751.
Allowing claims.
Due part of claim, §43-2-748.
Objections, §43-2-747.
Partial distribution.
Claim allowed after, §43-2-750.
When claim allowed without further proof, §43-2-746.
Debt not due, §43-2-749.
Docket.
Claims docket, §43-2-745.
Endorsement by judge, §43-2-744.
Filing.
Claims verified in another state, §43-2-742.
Claims verified in foreign country, §43-2-743.
Time and manner of filing, §43-2-740.
Minors and persons of unsound mind, §43-2-741.
Mentally ill.
Time allowed for filing, §43-2-741.
Minors.
Time allowed for filing, §43-2-741.
Objections to allowance of claims, §43-2-747.
Receipt for claim, §43-2-744.

EXECUTORS AND ADMINISTRATORS
—Cont'd

Insolvent estates—Cont'd
Claims against insolvent estates—Cont'd
Time of filing, §§43-2-740, 43-2-741.
Costs.
Payment, §43-2-706.
Declaration of insolvency, §43-2-707.
Second declaration by succeeding administrator not necessary, §43-2-708.
Distribution.
Claim allowed after partial distribution, §43-2-750.
Election of administrators.
Discretion of court upon failure of creditors to attend, §43-2-723.
Person receiving plurality appointed, §43-2-722.
Voting procedure, §43-2-721.
Hearings.
Notice, §43-2-704.
Time, §43-2-704.
Jury trial.
Trial of issue of insolvency, §43-2-705.
Letters of administration.
Former letters revoked upon appointment, §43-2-724.
Nomination of administrators.
When creditors may make nomination, §43-2-720.
Who may be nominated, §43-2-720.
Order of payment of debts, §43-2-700.
Payment of debts.
Order, §43-2-700.
Preference, §43-2-700.
Pending suits.
Report or decree of insolvency as effecting, §§43-2-810 to 43-2-813.
Continuance upon showing of insolvency, §43-2-810.
Effect of order or decree of insolvency certified to other courts after judgment or decree rendered, §43-2-813.
Judgment certified to probate court, §43-2-812.
Special plea of insolvency, §43-2-811.
Preference of payment of debts, §43-2-700.
Property vested in administrator, §43-2-724.
Real property.
Action by administrator for recovery, §43-2-792.
Sale of lands of insolvent estates.
Application for order of sale, §43-2-790.
Contents, §43-2-791.
Form, §43-2-791.

EXECUTORS AND ADMINISTRATORS
—Cont'd

Insolvent estates—Cont'd
Real property—Cont'd
Sale of lands of insolvent estates—Cont'd
Application for order of sale—Cont'd
Notice to heirs and devisees, §43-2-791.
Verification, §43-2-791.
Report of insolvency.
Affidavit accompanying report, §43-2-703.
Generally, §43-2-701.
Statement to be filed with report, §43-2-702.
Settlement.
Decree, §43-2-771.
When settlement must be made, §43-2-770.
Succeeding administrator.
Second declaration by succeeding administrator not necessary, §43-2-708.
Trial of issue of insolvency to be by jury, §43-2-705.
Vacancies, §43-2-725.

Interest.
Liability of executor or administrator for interest, §43-2-509.

Intestate succession.
Authorization to sell real property, §43-2-442.
General provisions, §§43-8-40 to 43-8-58.
See WILLS.
Letters of administration, §§43-2-40 to 43-2-48. See within this heading, "Letters of administration."

Inventories.
Contents, §43-2-312.
Duty of executor or administrator to make, §43-2-310.
Evidence.
Inventory as evidence in action against executor or administrator, §43-2-139.
Exemption of executor from filing.
Testator may exempt executor, §43-2-311.
Failure to make and return.
Grounds for removal, §43-2-290.
Oath upon return of inventory, §43-2-313.
Return of inventory.
Oath, §43-2-313.
Time, §43-2-315.
Supplemental inventories, §43-2-316.
Time for returning, §43-2-315.

Investments.
Authorization of investment of trust funds in bonds or stock of private corporations prohibited, Const. Ala., art. IV, §74.

EXECUTORS AND ADMINISTRATORS —Cont'd

Investments—Cont'd
Restrictions on investment of trust funds in private corporations, Const. Ala., amd. 40.
Standards for fiduciary investment, §19-3-120.2.
Investment securities, §§7-8-101 to 7-8-406.
See COMMERCIAL CODE.
Joint tenants and tenants in common.
Partition in probate courts.
Article applicable to executors or administrators of deceased parties, §35-6-65.
Judgments and decrees against personal representatives.
Administrators de bonis non.
Judgments against administrators in chief revived against administrators de bonis non, §43-2-134.
Administrators in chief.
Judgments against administrators in chief revived against administrators de bonis non, §43-2-134.
Enforcement.
Execution and garnishment, §§43-2-150 to 43-2-155.
Execution and garnishment to enforce, §§43-2-150 to 43-2-155.
Circuit court judgment, §43-2-153.
Generally, §43-2-150.
Judgment rendered against decedent before his death, §43-2-152.
Liability of sureties, §43-2-151.
Purchase of property sold under execution, §43-2-154.
Sale of property under execution, §43-2-154.
Purchase of property sold, §43-2-154.
Succeeding representative.
Right to execution, §43-2-155.
Revival.
Judgments against administrators in chief revived against administrators de bonis non, §43-2-134.
Judgments in favor of decedent.
Revival.
Issuance of execution in favor of personal representative or successor without revival, §6-9-193.
Revival in favor of personal representative, §6-9-194.

EXECUTORS AND ADMINISTRATORS —Cont'd

Judicial sales.
Notice to executors and administrators in probate court, §6-8-68.
Jurisdiction.
Probate courts, §12-13-1.
Jury.
Insolvent estates.
Trial of issue of insolvency, §43-2-705.
Removal.
When entitled to jury trial, §43-2-296.
Keeping estates together.
Annual settlements, §43-2-338.
Authorization by probate court, §43-2-330.
Certain rights not affected by provisions, §43-2-339.
Conflict with will.
Sections not to be construed as to conflict with will, §43-2-337.
Cultivation under direction of executor or administrator, §43-2-336.
Distributed shares.
When distributed share kept and worked with undivided portion of estate, §43-2-332.
Extension of time, §43-2-331.
Laborers.
Order authorizing hiring, §43-2-334.
Hearing, §43-2-335.
Notice, §43-2-335.
Petition, §43-2-335.
Profits.
Payment to share owners, §43-2-333.
Settlements.
Annual settlements, §43-2-338.
Share owners.
Payment of profits to, §43-2-333.
Term, §43-2-330.
Extension of time, §43-2-331.
Landlord and tenant.
Renting of lands for payment of debts and for division, §43-2-440.
Legatees.
Action to recover legacy, §43-2-138.
Letters of administration, §§43-2-40 to 43-2-48.
Administrator ad colligendum.
Special administrator ad colligendum, §43-2-47.
Appeals.
Postponing issuance of letters during time for appeal, §43-2-46.
Applicants.
Examination, §43-2-45.
Conclusiveness of letters, §43-2-48.
Death of sole or surviving executor, §43-2-28.
Evidence.
Copies of letters, §12-21-102.

EXECUTORS AND ADMINISTRATORS —Cont'd

Letters of administration —Cont'd
Examination of applicants and witnesses, §43-2-45.
Failure to apply for letters testamentary.
Letters of administration granted in stated order on, §43-2-27.
Fees.
Probate judges, §12-19-90.
Form, §43-2-41.
Grant generally, §43-2-40.
Half blood.
Preference of whole blood over, §43-2-44.
Intestate succession generally, §§43-8-40 to 43-8-58.
See WILLS.
Issuance generally, §43-2-40.
Jurisdiction of probate courts, §12-13-1.
Limitation of actions.
Computation of time as to granting, §6-2-14.
More than one person entitled.
Grant of administration, §43-2-44.
Order of grant, §43-2-42.
Postponing issuance of letters during time for appeal, §43-2-46.
Preference of whole blood over half blood, §43-2-44.
Probate courts.
Jurisdiction, §12-13-1; Const. Ala., amd. 364.
Proof of will.
Revocation of letters of administration and grant of letters testamentary, §43-2-29.
Recordation, §43-2-1.
Removal.
Duty of probate court to grant letters upon vacancy, §43-2-272.
Renunciation of appointment.
Letters of administration granted in stated order on, §43-2-27.
Renunciation or relinquishment of right to administration, §43-2-43.
Resignation.
Duty of probate court to grant letters upon vacancy, §43-2-272.
Revocation.
Grant of letters testamentary after, §43-2-29.
Special administrator ad colligendum, §43-2-47.
When granted.
Letters not granted until five days after intestate's death, §43-2-45.
Whole blood.
Preference over half blood, §43-2-44.
Witnesses.
Examination, §43-2-45.

EXECUTORS AND ADMINISTRATORS —Cont'd

Letters testamentary,
§§43-2-20 to 43-2-29.
Conclusiveness of letters,
§43-2-48.
Death of sole or surviving
executor, §43-2-28.
Disqualification of certain
persons, §43-2-22.
Evidence.
Copies of letters,
§12-21-102.
Execution, §12-13-5.
Failure to apply for letters.
Fees.
Probate judges, §12-19-90.
Form, §§12-13-5, 43-2-21.
Grant generally, §43-2-20.
Issuance, §43-2-20.
Issuance of letters to others
named in will upon,
§43-2-26.
Letters of administration
granted in stated order
on, §43-2-27.
Jurisdiction of probate
courts, §12-13-1.
Limitation of actions.
Computation of time as to
granting, §6-2-14.
Married women.
Issuance of letters,
§43-2-23.
Supplemental letters upon
removal of disability,
§43-2-24.
Minors.
Supplemental letters upon
removal of disability,
§43-2-24.
Probate courts.
Jurisdiction, §12-13-1.
Process, §12-13-5.
When courts deemed open
for granting, §12-13-3.
Recordation, §43-2-1.
Renouncing appointment.
Issuance of letters to
others named in will
upon, §43-2-26.
Letters of administration
granted in stated order
on, §43-2-27.
Procedure, §43-2-25.
Return, §12-13-5.
Revocation of letters of
administration.
Grant of letters
testamentary after,
§43-2-29.
Sole or surviving executor.
Death, §43-2-28.
Supplemental letters.
Minors and married
women upon removal
of disability, §43-2-24.
Women.
Issuance of letters to
married women,
§43-2-23.
Supplemental letters for
married women upon
removal of disability,
§43-2-24.

EXECUTORS AND ADMINISTRATORS —Cont'd

Liability.
Conversion.
Executor or administrator
of decedent who
converted another
decedent's assets,
§43-2-112.
Discharge of from liability,
§43-2-628.
Executor de son tort,
§43-2-113.
Liability for damages
recovered under certain
sections, §43-2-111.
Limits of liability, §43-2-110.
Resignation.
Liability for assets upon
resignation, §43-2-271.
Resignation as defense,
§43-2-114.
Waste.
Executor or administrator
of decedent who
wasted another
decedent's assets,
§43-2-112.
**Liens for improvements on
public streets, etc.**
Actions against personal
representatives,
§35-11-415.
Life estates.
Recovery of rent upon death
of life tenant who has
demised estate, §35-9-13.
Limitation of actions.
Against executor or
administrator, §43-2-131.
Nonfeasance, misfeasance or
malfeasance.
Actions against surety,
§6-2-34.
Limits of liability, §43-2-110.
Management.
Standards for fiduciary
management,
§19-3-120.2.
Married women.
Letters testamentary.
Issuance to, §43-2-23.
Supplemental letters upon
removal of disability,
§43-2-24.
**Mechanics' and
materialmen's liens.**
Actions against personal
representatives,
§35-11-230.
Actions by personal
representatives,
§35-11-229.
Mentally ill.
Claims and debts.
Time and manner of filing
claims, §43-2-351.
Grounds for removal,
§43-2-290.
Insolvent estates.
Claims against insolvent
estates.
Time allowed persons of
unsound mind for
filing, §43-2-741.

EXECUTORS AND ADMINISTRATORS —Cont'd

Mentally ill—Cont'd
Real property.
Sale for payment of debts
and for division.
Guardian ad litem.
Appointment,
§43-2-445.
Compensation,
§43-2-448.
Duties, §43-2-448.
Order of sale.
When depositions
required,
§43-2-452.
Settlements and
distributions.
Appointment of guardian
ad litem, §43-2-504.
Arbitration on settlement
of estates.
Consent by guardian,
§43-2-601.
Special guardians,
§43-2-517.
Merchants.
Stock in trade.
Sale, §43-2-421.
Minors.
Claims and debts.
Time and manner of filing,
§43-2-351.
Conveyances by executors
and administrators.
Application to compel
conveyance.
Notice to guardians of
minor heirs,
§35-4-323.
Insolvent estates.
Claims against insolvent
estates.
Time allowed for filing,
§43-2-741.
Letters testamentary.
Supplemental letters upon
removal of disability,
§43-2-24.
Real property.
Sale for payment of debts
and for division.
Guardian ad litem,
§43-2-445.
Appointment,
§43-2-445.
Compensation,
§43-2-448.
Duties, §43-2-448.
Order of sale.
When depositions
required,
§43-2-452.
Settlements and
distributions.
Appointment of guardian
ad litem, §43-2-504.
Arbitration on settlement
of estates.
Consent by guardian,
§43-2-601.
Expenses.
Credit for expenses of
minor distributees,
§43-2-510.
Special guardians,
§43-2-517.

EXECUTORS AND ADMINISTRATORS
—Cont'd

Mortgages and deeds of trust.
Assignment or transfer, §43-2-420.
Releases.
Execution, §35-10-25.
Nonresidents, §§43-2-190 to 43-2-200.
Actions.
Liability to actions, §43-2-197.
Right to maintain actions, §43-2-196.
Venue, §43-2-197.
Applications for letters testamentary or of administration, §43-2-190.
Appointment of nonresident administrator, §43-2-193.
Appointment of nonresident executor, §43-2-191.
Bonds, surety, §43-2-192.
Liability of sureties to execution, §43-2-200.
Debts.
Collection, §43-2-195.
Deposits.
Collection, §43-2-195.
Disqualification of certain persons to serve, §43-2-22.
Filing copies of will and letters testamentary, §43-2-192.
Letters of administration.
Applications for, §43-2-190.
Letters testamentary.
Applications for, §43-2-190.
Filing copies, §43-2-192.
Liability to actions, §43-2-197.
Manner of administering and settling estate, §43-2-194.
Notice.
Service, §43-2-199.
Service of process.
Citations or notices, §43-2-199.
Generally, §43-2-198.
Return of process, §43-2-199.
Venue, §43-2-197.
Wills.
Filing copies, §43-2-192.
Notice.
Appointment, §§43-2-60 to 43-2-62.
Conveyances by executors and administrators.
Application to compel, §§35-4-322, 35-4-323.
Removal.
Notice by publication, §43-2-295.
Settlements and distributions. See within this heading, "Settlements and distributions."
Partition.
Partition in probate courts.
Article applicable to executors or administrators of deceased parties, §35-6-65.

EXECUTORS AND ADMINISTRATORS
—Cont'd

Penalties.
Notice of appointment.
Failure to give notice, §43-2-62.
Personal property.
Collection.
Duty of to collect, §43-2-310.
Crops.
Completion, gathering and sale of crops commenced by decedent, §43-2-418.
Foreign decedents.
Disposition of personal estate of foreign decedent, §43-2-629.
Inventory, §§43-2-310 to 43-2-316. See within this heading, "Inventories."
Notice.
Sale, §43-2-413.
Notice of application, §43-2-411.
Sale, §§43-2-410 to 43-2-422.
Accounts.
Assignment or transfer, §43-2-420.
Returns, §43-2-422.
Application, §43-2-410.
Contesting application, §43-2-412.
Notice, §43-2-411.
Contesting application, §43-2-412.
Crops.
Completion, gathering and sale of crops commenced by decedent, §43-2-418.
Failure of purchaser to comply with terms.
Liability for deficiency, §43-2-417.
Resale upon, §43-2-417.
Hours of sale, §43-2-414.
Mortgages.
Assignment or transfer, §43-2-420.
Notes.
Assignment or transfer, §43-2-420.
Notice of application, §43-2-411.
Notice of sale, §43-2-413.
Postponing sale, §43-2-416.
Power of sale conferred, §43-2-410.
Rejection of bid, §43-2-416.
Resale upon failure of purchaser to comply with terms, §43-2-417.
Returns of accounts of sales, §43-2-422.
Stock in trade, §43-2-421.
Terms of sale, §43-2-415.
Persons presumed dead, §§43-2-230 to 43-2-238.
Applicability of other laws relating to administration of decedents' estates, §43-2-238.
Appointment of personal representative, §43-2-231.
Costs, §43-2-237.
Hearing, §43-2-232.

EXECUTORS AND ADMINISTRATORS
—Cont'd

Persons presumed dead
—Cont'd
Issuance of letters of administration, §43-2-234.
Letters of administration.
Applications for letters of administration, §43-2-230.
Costs, §43-2-237.
Issuance, §43-2-234.
Revocation of letters upon proof that supposed decedent is alive.
Distribution of assets, §43-2-235.
Reopening judgments, §43-2-235.
Substitution of parties, §43-2-236.
Notice.
Publication of notice of presumption of death, §43-2-233.
Revocation of letters upon proof that supposed decedent is alive.
Distribution of assets, §43-2-235.
Reopening judgments, §43-2-236.
Substitution of parties, §43-2-236.
Preferences and priorities.
Claims and debts, §§43-2-371, 43-2-372. See within this heading, "Claims and debts."
Letters of administration, §43-2-44.
Presumptions.
Death.
Administration of estates of persons presumed dead, §§43-2-230 to 43-2-238. See within this heading, "Persons presumed dead."
Settlements and distributions.
Presumption of settlement after twenty years, §§43-2-660 to 43-2-664.
Probate courts.
Correction of errors, §12-11-60.
Jurisdiction, §12-13-1.
Removal of administration from, §12-11-41.
Profits.
Liability for, §43-2-509.
Property.
Personal property. See within this heading, "Personal property."
Real property. See within this heading, "Real property."
Real property.
Conveyances, §§35-4-320 to 35-4-323.
Damages to realty.
Survival of actions for, §43-2-136.
Division.
Sale of land for payment of debts and for division, §§43-2-440 to 43-2-468.

EXECUTORS AND ADMINISTRATORS
—Cont'd
Real property—Cont'd
Insolvent estates, §§43-2-790 to 43-2-792.
Redemption of real property, §6-5-249.
Renting of lands for payment of debts and for division, §43-2-440.
Sale for payment of debts and for division, §§43-2-440 to 43-2-468.
Advertisement of sale, §43-2-455.
Application for sale, §43-2-444.
Dismissal upon failure of proof, §43-2-454.
Hearing, §43-2-445.
Notice of hearing, §43-2-445.
Nonresidents, §43-2-446.
Unknown parties, §43-2-447.
Proof of facts on application to sell for division, §43-2-451.
Authorization to sell.
In case of intestacy, §43-2-442.
Sale for division, §43-2-443.
Where will exists, §43-2-441.
Compromise.
Sale or division of land received on, §43-2-468.
Confirmation of sale, §43-2-462.
Conveyance, §43-2-464.
Depositions.
When depositions required, §43-2-452.
Description of lands sold.
Correction of mistake, §43-2-467.
Evidence of title, §43-2-453.
Failure of purchaser to comply with terms.
Resale upon, §43-2-456.
Guardian ad litem.
Appointment, §43-2-445.
Compensation, §43-2-448.
Duties, §43-2-448.
Hours of sale, §43-2-456.
Mentally ill.
Guardian ad litem, §43-2-445.
Appointment, §43-2-445.
Compensation, §43-2-448.
Duties, §43-2-448.
Order of sale.
When depositions required, §43-2-452.
Minors.
Guardian ad litem, §43-2-445.
Appointment, §43-2-445.
Compensation, §43-2-448.
Duties, §43-2-448.

EXECUTORS AND ADMINISTRATORS
—Cont'd
Real property—Cont'd
Sale for payment of debts and for division—Cont'd
Minors—Cont'd
Order of sale.
When depositions required, §43-2-452.
Mistake in description of lands sold.
Correction of mistake, §43-2-467.
Nonresidents.
Notice to nonresidents of hearing on application, §43-2-446.
Notice of hearing on application, §43-2-445.
Nonresidents, §43-2-446.
Unknown parties, §43-2-447.
Order of sale for division, §43-2-451.
Depositions, §43-2-452.
Order of sale for payment of debts, §43-2-450.
Place of sale, §43-2-458.
Postponing sale.
When bid rejected and sale postponed, §43-2-456.
Purchase money.
How secured, §43-2-457.
Report of payment, §43-2-463.
Purchaser.
Resale upon failure of purchaser to comply with terms, §43-2-456.
Right to cite executor or administrator to report sale, §43-2-465.
Rejection of bid.
When bid rejected and sale postponed, §43-2-456.
Report and examination of sale, §43-2-459.
Hearing, §43-2-460.
Notice, §43-2-460.
Right of purchaser to cite executor or administrator to report sale, §43-2-465.
Report of payment of purchase money, §43-2-463.
Resale upon failure of purchaser to comply with terms, §43-2-456.
Security for purchase money.
How secured, §43-2-457.
Setting aside sale, §43-2-461.
Special guardian for unknown parties, §§43-2-447, 43-2-448.
Title.
Evidence of title, §43-2-453.
Unknown parties.
Disposition of shares, §43-2-447.

EXECUTORS AND ADMINISTRATORS
—Cont'd
Real property—Cont'd
Sale for payment of debts and for division—Cont'd
Unknown parties—Cont'd
Notice of hearing on application, §43-2-447.
Special guardian.
Appointment, §43-2-447.
Compensation, §43-2-448.
Sale of land for payment of legacies, §§43-2-480 to 43-2-482.
Application for sale, §43-2-481.
Authorization to sell, §43-2-480.
Notice of application, §43-2-482.
Order of sale, §43-2-482.
Proceedings, §43-2-482.
Recordation.
Bonds, surety, §43-2-1.
Letters, §43-2-1.
Resignation, §43-2-270.
Records.
General administrators, §43-2-175.
Redemption of real property, §6-5-249.
Removal.
Application for, §43-2-293.
Notice by publication, §43-2-295.
Service of citation, §43-2-294.
Bonds, surety.
Additional bond.
May be required, §43-2-292.
Appeal of order removing executor or administrator, §12-22-24.
Default.
Removal for default, §43-2-292.
Citation.
Service, §43-2-294.
Costs, §43-2-297.
Embezzlement.
Grounds for removal, §43-2-290.
General administrators, §43-2-173.
Appointment of successor, §43-2-174.
Imprisonment.
Grounds for removal, §43-2-290.
Rights terminated by sentence of imprisonment, §43-2-291.
Inventories.
Failure to make and return.
Grounds for removal, §43-2-290.
Jury trial.
When entitled to jury trial, §43-2-296.
Mentally ill.
Grounds for removal, §43-2-290.

EXECUTORS AND ADMINISTRATORS
—Cont'd

Removal—Cont'd

Motion of court.
Removal on, §43-2-299.
Notice by publication, §43-2-295.
Probate court.
Removal of administration from probate court, §12-11-41.
Resident executor removed from state, §43-2-275.
Service of citation, §43-2-294.
Settlements and distributions.
Compelling settlement of executor or administrator whose authority has ceased, §§43-2-550 to 43-2-564. See within this heading, "Settlements and distributions."
State.
Resident executor removed from state, §43-2-275.
Surviving executor and administrator.
Grounds for removal, §43-2-290.
Trial, §43-2-296.
Use of funds for own benefit.
Grounds for removal, §43-2-290.
Waste.
Grounds for removal, §43-2-290.
When survivor continues to act, §43-2-273.

Renouncing appointment, §§43-2-25 to 43-2-27.
Issuance of letters to others named in will upon renunciation, §43-2-26.
Letters of administration granted in stated order upon renunciation by all named in will, §43-2-27.
Procedure, §43-2-25.

Rent.
Recovery of rent upon death of life tenant who has demised estate, §35-9-13.

Reports.
Exemption from making.
Testator may exempt executor, §43-2-311.
Insolvency, §§43-2-701 to 43-2-703.
Effect of report of insolvency on pending suits, §§43-2-810 to 43-2-813.
Sale of real property for payment of debts and for division.
Report and examination of sale, §§43-2-459, 43-2-460.
Report of payment of purchase money, §43-2-463.
Right of purchaser to cite executor or administrator to report sale, §43-2-465.

EXECUTORS AND ADMINISTRATORS
—Cont'd

Resignation.

Defenses.
Resignation as defense, §43-2-114.
Filing, §43-2-270.
General administrators, §43-2-173.
Appointment of successor, §43-2-174.
Liability for assets upon resignation, §43-2-271.
Recordation, §43-2-270.
Settlements and distributions.
Compelling settlement of executor or administrator whose authority has ceased, §§43-2-550 to 43-2-564. See within this heading, "Settlements and distributions."
Surviving executor and administrator.
Grounds for removal, §43-2-290.
When survivor continues to act, §43-2-273.

Revocation of letters of administration after proof of will, §43-2-29.

Sales.
Claims and debts, §§43-2-390 to 43-2-394. See within this heading, "Claims and debts."
Going-out-of-business or distressed merchandise sales, §§8-13-1 to 8-13-23.
See SALES.
Personal property, §§43-2-410 to 43-2-422. See within this heading, "Personal property."
Real property, §§43-2-440 to 43-2-482. See within this heading, "Real property."

Salvage.
Taker of property.
Applicability of chapter to taker's personal representative, §35-13-10.

Savings and loan associations.
Accounts, §5-16-43.

Securities.
Fiduciary security transfers, §§8-6-70 to 8-6-80.
See SECURITIES.
Securities held by fiduciaries, §§19-4-1 to 19-4-42.
See FIDUCIARIES.

Service of process.
Actions by and against.
Summons, §43-2-130.
Nonresident executors and administrators, §§43-2-198, 43-2-199.
Removal.
Citation, §43-2-294.

Setoffs.
Distribution or division on final settlement.
Setting off indebtedness of distributee or legatee, §43-2-627.

EXECUTORS AND ADMINISTRATORS
—Cont'd

Settlements and distributions.

Accounts.
Auditing, §43-2-507.
Contest of account, §§43-2-511 to 43-2-515.
Decree passing account as stated, §43-2-516.
Filing, §§43-2-502, 43-2-503.
Proof of credit, §43-2-507.
Reopening, §43-2-519.
Annual settlement.
Notice, §43-2-519.
When required, §43-2-500.
Arbitration on settlement of estates, §§43-2-600 to 43-2-607.
Applicability of certain sections in Title 6, §43-2-607.
Appointment of arbitrators, §43-2-602.
Award, §43-2-603.
Effect, §43-2-604.
Execution, §43-2-604.
Force, §43-2-604.
Objections, §43-2-606.
Second reference of matters to arbitrators, §43-2-605.
Setting aside, §43-2-605.
Consent by guardian, §43-2-601.
Mentally ill.
Consent by guardian, §43-2-601.
Minors.
Consent by guardian, §43-2-601.
When matters of controversy may be referred to arbitration, §43-2-600.
Attorney's fees.
Court may allow up to time of settlement, §43-2-682.
Auditing of account, §43-2-507.
Compelling settlement by existing executor or administrator.
When court required to audit account, §43-2-531.
Compelling settlement of executor or administrator whose authority has ceased.
When court required to audit account, §43-2-556.
Claims.
Satisfaction of claims, §43-2-508.
Commissions on money or property sold or distributed, §43-2-681.
Compelling payment of legacies, §§43-2-580 to 43-2-586.
Applicability to widow, §43-2-586.
Application, §43-2-581.
Enforcement of payment or delivery, §43-2-585.

**EXECUTORS AND
ADMINISTRATORS**
—Cont'd
**Settlements and
distributions**—Cont'd
Compelling payment of
legacies—Cont'd
Hearings.
Conduct, §43-2-583.
Time, §43-2-582.
Notice to executor or
administrator of
hearing, §43-2-582.
Refunding bond, §43-2-584.
Time for hearing,
§43-2-582.
When legatee or widow
entitled to compel
payment, §43-2-580.
When payment or delivery
directed, §43-2-583.
Widows.
Applicability to widow,
§43-2-586.
Compelling settlement of
executor or
administrator whose
authority has ceased,
§§43-2-550 to 43-2-564.
Attachment.
Compelling settlement
by, §43-2-555.
Audit of account.
When court required to
audit, §43-2-556.
Deceased executor or
administrator.
Execution against
sureties, §43-2-564.
Settlement by sureties.
Conclusiveness,
§43-2-563.
Filing account and
vouchers,
§43-2-560.
Making representative
of deceased
executor or
administrator
party to,
§43-2-561.
Petition for order
requiring,
§43-2-562.
Decree for balance.
Decree in favor of
outgoing executor or
administrator,
§43-2-553.
Generally, §43-2-552.
Insolvent estates,
§43-2-553.
Setting aside decree,
§43-2-558.
Staying execution on
decree, §43-2-554.
Examination of account.
When court required to
examine, §43-2-556.
Final settlement.
Proceedings on final,
§43-2-557.
Insolvent estates.
Decree for balance,
§43-2-553.
Issuance of citation,
§43-2-556.
Notice, §43-2-556.
Other actions not barred,
§43-2-559.

**EXECUTORS AND
ADMINISTRATORS**
—Cont'd
**Settlements and
distributions**—Cont'd
Compelling settlement of
executor or
administrator whose
authority has ceased
—Cont'd
Required.
Final settlement
required following
death, removal or
resignation,
§43-2-550.
Restating account.
When court required to
restate account,
§43-2-556.
Setting aside decree,
§43-2-558.
Stating account, §43-2-555.
Succeeding executor or
administrator.
Making party to
settlement,
§43-2-551.
Compelling settlements by
existing executor or
administrator,
§§43-2-530 to 43-2-533.
Account.
Audit.
When court required to
audit, §43-2-531.
Examination.
When court required to
examine,
§43-2-531.
Proceedings on
settlement of
account, §43-2-532.
Restating account.
When court required to
restate, §43-2-531.
Audit of account.
When court required to
audit, §43-2-531.
Authorization to compel
settlement, §43-2-530.
Issuance of citation,
§43-2-531.
Notice, §43-2-531.
Setting aside decree,
§43-2-533.
Compensation.
Court may allow up to
time of settlement,
§43-2-682.
Executors and
administrators may be
allowed fair
compensation, etc.,
§43-2-680.
Confirming distribution.
Distribution on final
settlement, §43-2-623.
Consent.
Settlement by consent
without notice,
§43-2-506.
Contest of account.
Disallowance of item,
§43-2-514.
Examination of witnesses,
§43-2-513.
Failure to discharge trust.
Showing of failure,
§43-2-512.
Generally, §43-2-511.

**EXECUTORS AND
ADMINISTRATORS**
—Cont'd
**Settlements and
distributions**—Cont'd
Contest of account—Cont'd
Reduction of item,
§43-2-514.
Withdrawal of item,
§43-2-515.
Witnesses.
Examination, §43-2-513.
Credits.
Proof of credit, §43-2-507.
Death of executor or
administrator.
Decrees.
Conclusiveness of order
or decree, §43-2-519.
Discharge of executor or
administrator from
liability, §43-2-628.
Distribution before
settlement, §§43-2-640 to
43-2-649.
Application.
Contents, §43-2-642.
Notice, §43-2-643.
Time for hearing,
§43-2-643.
Authorization to make
distribution.
Distribution by court
after six months
from grant of letters,
§43-2-641.
Distribution by executor
or administrator,
§43-2-640.
Costs, §43-2-649.
Limit on amount,
§43-2-644.
Refunding bonds.
Action on bond,
§43-2-647.
Conditions, §43-2-645.
Recordation, §43-2-646.
Required, §43-2-645.
Rights of parties among
themselves,
§43-2-648.
Security.
Bond stands as
security,
§43-2-647.
Terms, §43-2-645.
When distribution made,
§43-2-644.
Distribution or division on
final settlement,
§§43-2-620 to 43-2-629.
Confirming distribution,
§43-2-623.
Delivery of property
upon, §43-2-625.
Delivery of property after
confirmation,
§43-2-625.
Discharge of executor or
administrator from
liability, §43-2-628.
Foreign decedents.
Disposition of personal
estate, §43-2-629.
How sale advertised and
made, §43-2-624.
Judgments or claims.
Division, sale or
assignment,
§43-2-626.

EXECUTORS AND ADMINISTRATORS —Cont'd

Settlements and distributions—Cont'd
Distribution or division on final settlement—Cont'd
Orders of distribution.
Contents, §43-2-621.
Exceptions to report, §43-2-622.
Generally, §43-2-620.
Oath, §43-2-622.
Return, §43-2-622.
To whom directed, §43-2-621.
Sale of property.
Advertising, §43-2-624.
When sale may be directed, §43-2-623.
Setting aside distribution, §43-2-623.
Setting off indebtedness of distributee or legatee, §43-2-627.
Exemption of executor from making report or final settlement,
Testator may exempt executor, §43-2-311.
Fees.
Previous fees considered upon final settlement, §43-2-683.
Filing of account, etc.
Generally, §43-2-502.
Liability for failure to file statement, §43-2-503.
Final settlements.
Death of executor or administrator.
Final settlement required, §43-2-550.
Discharge of executor or administrator from liability, §43-2-628.
Exemption of executor from making.
Testator may exempt executor, §43-2-311.
Fees.
Previous fees considered upon final settlement, §43-2-683.
Proceedings on, §43-2-557.
Removal of executor or administrator.
Required following removal, §43-2-550.
Resignation of executor or administrator.
Required after resignation, §43-2-550.
When final settlement may be made, §43-2-501.
Guardian ad litem.
Appointment, §43-2-504.
Guardian and ward.
Arbitration on settlement of estates.
Consent by guardian, §43-2-601.
Special guardians.
Appointment and compensation, §43-2-517.
Insolvent estates.
Decree, §43-2-771.

EXECUTORS AND ADMINISTRATORS —Cont'd

Settlements and distributions—Cont'd
Insolvent estates—Cont'd
Partial distribution.
Claim allowed after, §43-2-750.
When settlement must be made, §43-2-770.
Interest.
Liability of executor or administrator for interest, §43-2-509.
Keeping estates together.
Annual settlements, §43-2-338.
When distributed share kept and worked with undivided portion of estate, §43-2-332.
Liability of executor or administrator for interest or profits, §43-2-509.
Mentally ill.
Appointment of guardian ad litem, §43-2-504.
Arbitration on settlement of estates.
Consent by guardian, §43-2-601.
Special guardians, §43-2-517.
Minors.
Appointment of guardian ad litem, §43-2-504.
Arbitration on settlement of estates.
Consent by guardian, §43-2-601.
Expenses.
Credit for expenses of minor distributees, §43-2-510.
Special guardians, §43-2-517.
Notice, §43-2-505.
Annual settlement, §43-2-519.
Compelling payment of legacies.
Hearing on application, §43-2-582.
Compelling settlement by existing executor or administrator, §43-2-531.
Compelling settlement of executor or administrator whose authority has ceased, §43-2-556.
Partial settlement, §43-2-519.
Settlement by consent without notice, §43-2-506.
Orders.
Conclusiveness, §43-2-519.
Distribution or division on final settlement, §§43-2-620 to 43-2-622.
Partial settlement.
Notice, §43-2-519.
When required, §43-2-500.

EXECUTORS AND ADMINISTRATORS —Cont'd

Settlements and distributions—Cont'd
Payment to probate judge of money due on decree upon settlement, §12-13-48.
Duty of judge as to payment of money to person entitled and liability for failure to perform duty, §12-13-48.
Payment of probate judge for receipt of money under section 12-13-48, §12-13-49.
Presumption of settlement after twenty years, §§43-2-660 to 43-2-664.
Contest of petition to establish presumption, §43-2-663.
Order after hearing, §43-2-664.
Petition to establish presumption, §43-2-661.
Contest of petition, §43-2-663.
Notice of hearing on petition, §43-2-662.
Order after hearing on petition, §43-2-664.
When presumption arises, §43-2-660.
Previous settlements.
Reexamination of items included in, §43-2-518.
Profits.
Liability of executor or administrator for profits, §43-2-509.
Reexamination of items included in previous settlements, §43-2-518.
Reopening account, §43-2-519.
Satisfaction of claims, §43-2-508.
Setting aside distribution.
Distribution on final settlement, §43-2-623.
Small estates.
Summary distribution of small estates, §§43-2-690 to 43-2-696.
Special guardians.
Appointment and compensation, §43-2-517.
Summary distribution of small estates, §§43-2-690 to 43-2-696. See within this heading, "Small estates."
Time for settlement, §43-2-505.
Witnesses.
Contest of account.
Examination, §43-2-513.

Sewers.
Liens for improvements.
Actions against personal representatives, §35-11-415.

EXECUTORS AND ADMINISTRATORS
—Cont'd
Sheriffs.
Bonds, surety.
Additional bond of sheriff, §43-2-87.
Third party applicant when administration committed to sheriff, §43-2-84.
Commitment of administration to sheriff, §43-2-172.
Delay for committing administration of estate, §43-2-171.
Small estates.
Summary distribution, §§43-2-690 to 43-2-696.
Assets.
Delivery by probate judge, §43-2-693.
Probate judge to take possession of assets of estate, §43-2-692.
Release by probate judge, §43-2-693.
Defeasible rights of surviving spouse or distributees.
Limitation, §43-2-695.
Definitions, §43-2-691.
Limitation on defeasible rights of surviving spouse or distributees, §43-2-695.
Order directing summary distribution.
Entry, §43-2-693.
Petition for summary distribution, §43-2-692.
Short title, §43-2-690.
Transfer of property to surviving spouse or distributees, §43-2-694.
Transfer pursuant to affidavit.
Effect, §43-2-696.
Special administrator ad colligendum, §43-2-47.
Standards for fiduciary investment and management, §19-3-120.2.
Streets.
Liens for improvements.
Actions against personal representatives, §35-11-415.
Succeeding executors and administrators.
General administrators.
Appointment of successor, §43-2-174.
Insolvent estates.
Second declaration by succeeding administrator not necessary, §43-2-708.
Judgments and decrees against former representatives.
Right of succeeding representative to execution, §43-2-155.
Settlements and distributions.
Making succeeding executor or administrator party to settlement, §43-2-551.

EXECUTORS AND ADMINISTRATORS
—Cont'd
Summons and process.
Actions by and against.
Service of summons, §43-2-130.
Suretyship.
Provisions of chapter insue to benefit of personal representatives, §8-3-14.
Surviving executors and administrators.
Grounds for removal, §43-2-290.
Taxation.
Assessments.
By whom property should be listed, §40-7-17.
Returns.
Separate returns in individual and fiduciary capacity, §40-7-20.
Tax assessors.
Notification of appointment of fiduciaries, §40-7-30.
Trespass.
Right of action against executor or administrator, §6-5-90.
Trial.
Insolvent estates.
Trial of issue of insolvency to be by jury, §43-2-705.
Removal, §43-2-296.
Uniform fiduciaries act, §§19-1-1 to 19-1-13.
See FIDUCIARIES.
Vacancies.
Circuit court appointment to fill, §12-11-40.
Letters of administration.
Duty of probate court to grant upon vacancy, §43-2-272.
Venue.
Actions by and against, §43-2-130.
Nonresident executors and administrators, §43-2-197.
Waste.
Grounds for removal, §43-2-290.
Right of action against executor or administrator, §6-5-90.
Water system assistance authority.
Investments in bonds of authority, §22-23A-12.
Widows.
Compelling payment of legacies.
Applicability to dissenting widow, §43-2-586.
Witnesses.
Letters of administration.
Examination of witnesses, §43-2-45.
Women.
Letters testamentary.
Issuance of letters to married women, §43-2-23.
Supplemental letters for married women upon removal of disability, §43-2-24.

EXECUTORS AND ADMINISTRATORS
—Cont'd
Wrongful death.
Right of action, §6-5-410.

EXECUTORY INTERESTS.
See REMAINDERS, REVERSIONS AND EXECUTORY INTERESTS.

EXEMPTIONS FROM ADMINISTRATION AND PAYMENT OF DEBTS.
Actions.
Actions on property before set apart.
Right to commence or defend, §6-10-67.
Appeals.
Report of appraisers or commissioners.
Exceptions.
Appeal from decree on exceptions, §6-10-91.
Appraisers, §§6-10-80 to 6-10-93.
Commission.
Issuance, §6-10-80.
Failure to set apart exemptions or appraise homestead.
Proceedings upon, §6-10-84.
Personal property.
Duty to set apart, §6-10-81.
Report.
Confirmation when no exceptions filed, §6-10-93.
Exceptions, §6-10-86.
Appeal from decree, §6-10-91.
Cost.
Taxation, §6-10-90.
Hearing, §6-10-88.
Notice, §6-10-86.
Report that homestead does not exceed allowance, §6-10-92.
Excessive or insufficient exemption of personalty.
Proceedings, §6-10-88.
Hearing of report.
Notice, §6-10-87.
Homestead appraisement, §6-10-82.
Return, §6-10-81.
Setting aside.
Proceedings upon, §6-10-89.
Commissioners.
Compensation, §6-10-104.
Oath, §6-10-103.
Qualifications, §6-10-103.
Report.
Exceptions, §6-10-86.
Appeal from decree, §6-10-91.
Cost.
Taxation, §6-10-90.
Hearing, §6-10-88.
Notice, §6-10-86.
Excessive or insufficient exemption of personalty.
Proceedings, §6-10-88.
Hearing of report.
Notice, §6-10-87.

EXEMPTIONS FROM ADMINISTRATION AND PAYMENT OF DEBTS —Cont'd

Commissioners—Cont'd
Report—Cont'd
Setting aside.
Proceedings upon,
§6-10-89.
Costs.
Report of appraisers or
commissioners.
Exceptions.
Taxation of costs,
§6-10-90.
Family allowance, §43-8-112.
Fees.
Homestead exemption.
Recordation of judgments
allotting, §6-10-105.
Hearings.
Report of appraisers or
commissioners.
Hearing on exceptions,
§§6-10-86, 6-10-88.
Notice, §§6-10-86,
6-10-87.
Homestead exemption.
Amount, §43-8-110.
Appraisement.
Proceedings on failure of
appraisers to appraise,
§6-10-84.
Report, §6-10-82.
Exemption in lieu of.
How claimed and set apart,
§6-10-85.
Judgments allotting.
Recordation, §6-10-105.
Fee, §6-10-105.
Payment by devisees to clear
property of homestead
right, §6-10-99.
Petition for relief of personal
representative or
interested person,
§43-8-113.
Reduced homestead incapable
of allotment.
Notice, §6-10-96.
Order, §6-10-96.
Proceeds.
Application, §6-10-96.
Sale.
Bids.
Proceedings when no
bid in excess of
$6,000 received,
§6-10-97.
Possession by surviving
spouse and minor
children until sold,
§6-10-94.
Proof of facts, §6-10-96.
Purchase by persons
entitled to
homestead
exemption, §6-10-98.
When allowed, §6-10-95.
Terms, §6-10-96.
Removal from homestead.
Effect, §6-10-102.
Setting apart.
Proceedings when
homestead exceeds
value allowed,
§6-10-83.
Source, determination and
documentation of
exemption, §43-8-113.

EXEMPTIONS FROM ADMINISTRATION AND PAYMENT OF DEBTS —Cont'd

Husband and wife.
Husband or wife absent
seven years and
residence not
ascertainable.
Proceedings to set aside
exemptions,
§§6-10-106, 6-10-107.
Notices.
Homestead exemption.
Reduced homestead
incapable of allotment.
Sale, §6-10-96.
Report of appraisers or
commissioners.
Hearing of report,
§6-10-87.
Hearing on exceptions,
§6-10-86.
Oaths.
Commissioners, §6-10-103.
Parent and child.
Parent absent seven years
and residence not
ascertainable.
Proceedings to set aside
exemptions,
§§6-10-106, 6-10-107.
Personal property.
Petition for relief for
personal representative
or interested persons,
§43-8-113.
Source, determination and
documentation of exempt
property, §43-8-113.
Specific personal property,
§43-8-111.
Reports.
Appraisers, §§6-10-80 to
6-10-93. See within this
heading, "Appraisers."
Commissioners. See within
this heading,
"Commissioners."
Setting apart.
Administration not granted
within 60 days after
death.
Generally, §6-10-100.
Title to real property,
§6-10-101.
Appraisers, §§6-10-80 to
6-10-93. See within this
heading, "Appraisers."
Homestead. See within this
heading, "Homestead
exemption."
Right to use property before
such set apart, §6-10-67.
Title.
Administration not granted
within 60 days after
death.
Vesting of title to real
property, §6-10-101.
Husband, wife or parent
absent seven years and
residence not
ascertainable.
Vesting for life in deserted
spouse or minors,
§6-10-107.

EXEMPTIONS FROM ADMINISTRATION AND PAYMENT OF DEBTS —Cont'd

Waiver, §§6-10-120 to
6-10-126.
Attachment.
Endorsement on writ,
§6-10-124.
Proceedings when waiver
not sustained,
§6-10-125.
Enforcement in action,
§6-10-123.
Exceptions, §6-10-126.
Homestead exemption.
How made, §6-10-122.
Personal property.
How made, §6-10-121.
Right to waive, §6-10-120.

EXEMPTIONS FROM LEVY AND SALE UNDER PROCESS.

Bankruptcy.
Federal bankruptcy,
§6-10-11.
Bonds, surety.
Contest of exemption claim.
See within this heading,
"Contest of exemption
claim."
Burial place, §6-10-5.
Cemeteries.
Burial place, §6-10-5.
Churches.
Church pew or seat, §6-10-5.
Claim.
Between levy and sale,
§6-10-26.
Contest, §§6-10-26 to 6-10-37.
See within this heading,
"Contest of exemption
claim."
Declaration, §§6-10-20 to
6-10-25.
Constitution of Alabama.
Personal property of value of
one thousand dollars,
Const. Ala., art. X, §204.
Rules and regulations to
ascertain value of
exempted property,
Const. Ala., art. IV, §92.
Special, private or local laws
prohibited, Const. Ala.,
art. IV, §104.
Waiver of right, Const. Ala.,
art. X, §210.
Contest of exemption claim,
§§6-10-26 to 6-10-37.
Bonds, surety.
Damages resulting from
detention on bond.
Assessment, §6-10-36.
Delivery of personalty to
defendant upon
execution, §6-10-27.
Judgment and execution
on, §6-10-36.
Proceedings when not
forthcoming, §6-10-27.
Claim of exemption after
levy and prior to sale,
§6-10-26.
Declaration of claimed
exemptions, §§6-10-20 to
6-10-25.

EXEMPTIONS FROM LEVY AND SALE UNDER PROCESS—Cont'd

Contest of exemption claim —Cont'd

Excessive claims.
  Proceedings when claim of personalty found excessive, §6-10-33.

Garnishment.
  Money, choses in action or personal property, §6-10-37.

Inventory.
  Effect of failure to file, §6-10-29.
  Filing by defendant, §6-10-29.
  Personalty not embraced by claim of exemption.
  Proceedings when inventory discloses, §6-10-34.
  Tender of issue by plaintiff on inventory, §6-10-35.

Judgment, §6-10-32.
Jury trial, §6-10-31.

Lien on property.
  Effect of contest, §6-10-43.

Probate court.
  Trial by jury, §6-10-31.

Return of levying officer, §6-10-28.

Sale of property.
  Effect of contest, §6-10-43.

Tender of issue on inventory.
  Determination, §6-10-35.

Trial, §6-10-30.
  Jury trial in probate court, §6-10-31.

Value of property.
  Assessment, §6-10-36.

Counties.
County property, §6-10-10.

Declaration of claimed exemptions, §§6-10-20 to 6-10-25.

Contest, §6-10-25.
Effect, §6-10-24.

Copies.
  Certified copies, §6-10-21.

Evidence.
  Effect as, §6-10-23.

Fees, §6-10-22.
Filing, §6-10-20.
Making, §6-10-20.

Notice.
  Effect as notice, §6-10-23.

Receipt, §6-10-21.
Recordation, §6-10-21.

Waiver.
  Effect, §6-10-24.

Evidence.
Declaration of claimed exemptions.
  Effect as evidence, §6-10-23.

Federal bankruptcy, §6-10-11.

Fees.
Declaration of claimed exemptions, §6-10-22.

Garnishment.
Contest of exemption claim, §6-10-37.

Homestead exemption.
Alienation by married person, §6-10-3.
Amount, §6-10-2.
Area, §6-10-2.

EXEMPTIONS FROM LEVY AND SALE UNDER PROCESS—Cont'd

Homestead exemption —Cont'd

Contest of exemption claim.
  Defense by wife or minor children, §6-10-39.
  Proceedings when homestead found to exceed value or area allowed, §6-10-38.
  Interposition by spouse or minor children, §6-10-39.

Lease of homestead.
  Effect, §6-10-41.

Leaving homestead temporarily.
  Effect, §6-10-41.

Liens not affected, §6-10-4.

Mobile homes or similar dwellings, §6-10-2.

Sale of land and separation of homestead interest from that of alienee, §6-10-40.

Separate claim by husband and wife owning jointly, §6-10-2.

Husband and wife.
Homestead exemption.
  Alienation by married person, §6-10-3.
  Interposition of claim or defense of contest by spouse, §6-10-39.

Insurance.
Rights of beneficiaries and assignees under life insurance policies, §6-10-8.

Judgments.
Contest of exemption claim, §6-10-32.
Bonds, surety.
  Judgment on bond, §6-10-36.

Jury.
Contest of exemption claim.
  Trial by jury in probate court, §6-10-31.

Law governing, §6-10-1.

Levy on exempt property.
When no action lies against officer levying, §6-10-42.

Liens.
Contest of exemption claim.
  Effect, §6-10-43.
Homestead exemption.
  Liens not affected, §6-10-4.
When no action lies against officer levying, §6-10-42.

Municipal corporations.
Municipal property, §6-10-10.

Notice.
Declaration of claimed exemptions.
  Effect as notice, §6-10-23.

Parent and child.
Homestead exemption.
  Interposition of claim or defense of contest by minor children, §6-10-39.

Partnerships.
Partnership property, §§6-10-9, 10-8-72.

EXEMPTIONS FROM LEVY AND SALE UNDER PROCESS—Cont'd

Personal property, §6-10-6; Const. Ala., art. X, §204.

Contest of exemption claim.
  Delivery of personalty to defendant upon executing bond, §6-10-27.
  Proceedings when claim of personalty found excessive, §6-10-33.
  Proceedings when inventory discloses personalty not embraced by claim, §6-10-34.

Waiver.
  How made, §6-10-121.

Probate courts.
Contest of exemption claim.
  Trial by jury, §6-10-31.

Teachers' retirement system.
Benefits, §16-25-23.

Trial.
Contest of exemption claim, §§6-10-26 to 6-10-37. See within this heading, "Contest of exemption claim."

Valuation of property.
Rules and regulations to ascertain, Const. Ala., art. IV, §92.

Wages.
Personal services, §6-10-7.

Waiver, Const. Ala., art. X, §210.

Attachment.
  Endorsement on writ, §6-10-124.
  Proceedings when waiver not sustained, §6-10-125.

Enforcement in action, §6-10-123.

Exceptions, §6-10-126.

Homestead exemption.
  How made, §6-10-122.

Personal property.
  How made, §6-10-121.

Right to waive, §6-10-120.

Welfare.
Assistance grants, §38-4-8.

EXEMPTIONS FROM TAXATION, §11-89-16; Const. Ala., art. IV, §91.

EXHIBITIONS.

Agricultural fairs and exhibits, §§2-7-1 to 2-7-53.
See AGRICULTURE.

Armories.
Kinds of exhibitions held in armories, §31-2-56.
Revenues derived from exhibitions, §31-2-56.

Boats.
Protection from marine traffic interference and hazards, §33-5-27.

Municipal corporations.
Provision of music and other exhibitions, §11-47-19.

Wildlife.
Possession for public exhibition purposes, §§9-11-320 to 9-11-328.
See FISH AND GAME.

EXHIBITS.

Appeals.

Appendix to briefs.

Reproduction of exhibits, ARAP, Rule 30 (f).

Form of request for original to be filed, ARAP, Form 20.

Record on appeal.

Custody of exhibits, ARAP, Rule 11 (e).

Use of physical exhibits at oral argument, ARAP, Rule 34 (e).

Evidence.

Destruction of exhibits offered and received in evidence, §12-21-8.

Pleadings, ARCP, Rule 10 (c).

EXILE.

Constitution of Alabama, Const. Ala., art. I, §30.

EXPERT WITNESSES.

See WITNESSES.

EXPLOSIVES AND EXPLOSIONS.

Arson.

General provisions, §§13A-7-40 to 13A-7-43.

Bombs.

See BOMBS.

Brands and marks.

Transportation of explosives.

Marking of packages containing explosives, §37-8-182.

Carriers.

Transportation of explosives, §§37-8-180 to 37-8-184.

Coal.

Mine safety.

Explosives and blasting, §§25-9-130 to 25-9-137.

See COAL.

Reports.

Premature explosions, §25-9-137.

Criminal law and procedure.

Falsely reporting occurrence of explosion, §13A-11-11.

Death.

Transportation of explosives.

Death occurring during.

Penalty, §37-8-184.

Definitions, §13A-7-40.

Education.

Eye protective devices.

Pupils and teachers participating in certain courses, §16-1-7.

Fire marshal.

Regulations for keeping, storing, etc.

Promulgation, §36-19-9.

Fireworks.

See FIREWORKS.

Fish and game.

Fishing.

Catching or killing of fish, §9-11-93.

Private ponds, lakes, pools or reservoirs, §9-11-91.

Hunting.

Taking of protected birds or animals by use of explosives, §9-11-245.

Penalties, §9-11-246.

Gun powder.

Provision of building for storage, §11-47-12.

EXPLOSIVES AND EXPLOSIONS—Cont'd

Indictments.

Unlawfully setting off explosives.

Form, §15-8-150.

Military affairs.

National guard.

Commanders of national guard troops may order closing of certain places and forbid sale of explosives, §31-2-124.

Transportation of explosives.

Exception as to transportation of military or land forces, §37-8-180.

Motor vehicles.

Decal, plate or placard.

Vehicles transporting.

Prominent display required, §32-5A-171.

Defined, §32-1-1.1.

Equipment required of vehicles transporting, §32-5-74.

Flammable liquid.

Defined, §32-1-1.1.

Vehicles transporting.

Decal, plate or placard.

Prominent display required, §32-5A-171.

Maximum speed, §32-5A-171.

Flares.

Vehicle carrying explosives, §32-5-220.

Marking of vehicles transporting, §32-5-74.

Speed.

Vehicles transporting.

Maximum speed, §32-5A-171.

Transportation of explosives.

General provisions, §§37-8-180 to 37-8-184.

Municipal corporations.

Regulation of storage, use, etc., §11-43-60.

Storage.

Provisions of building for, §11-47-12.

Regulation, §11-43-60.

Possession, §13A-7-44.

Class C felony, §13A-7-44.

Public service commission.

Transportation of explosives, §§37-8-180 to 37-8-184.

Transportation of explosives, §§37-8-180 to 37-8-184.

Death resulting from.

Penalty, §37-8-184.

Marking of packages containing explosives, §37-8-182.

False or deceptive marking, §37-8-182.

Military or naval forces.

Exceptions to prohibition, §37-8-180.

Nitroglycerine or other like explosives.

Transportation by common carrier prohibited, §37-8-181.

EXPLOSIVES AND EXPLOSIONS—Cont'd

Transportation of explosives —Cont'd

Packages.

Marking of packages containing explosives, §37-8-182.

False or deceptive marking, §37-8-182.

Passenger conveyances.

Exceptions, §37-8-180.

Prohibited, §37-8-180.

Penalties.

Violations, §37-8-184.

Public service commission.

Regulations for safe transportation.

Formulation, §37-8-183.

Violation.

Penalty, §37-8-184.

Safe transportation.

Public service commission to formulate regulations, §37-8-183.

Vehicles transporting, §32-5-74.

Decal, plate or placard.

Prominent display required, §32-5A-171.

Flares required, §32-5-220.

Marking, §32-5-74.

Maximum speed, §32-5A-171.

Violations.

Penalties, §37-8-184.

EXPORTS AND IMPORTS.

Constitution of the United States, Const. U. S., Art. I, §§9, 10.

EX POST FACTO LAWS.

Constitution of Alabama, Const. Ala., art. I, §§7, 22.

Constitution of the United States, Const. U. S., Art. I, §§9, 10.

EXPRESS COMPANIES.

Bills of lading.

Documents of title, §§7-7-101 to 7-7-603.

See COMMERCIAL CODE.

General provisions.

See TRANSPORTATION COMPANIES.

Licenses.

Municipal license schedule, §11-51-126.

Municipal corporations.

License schedules, §11-51-126.

Taxation.

General provisions.

See PUBLIC UTILITIES.

EXPUNGEMENT.

Attorneys at law.

Disciplinary proceedings.

Complaint or grievance dismissed without discipline, ARDE, Rule 8.

Criminal justice information center.

Purging of records, §§41-9-645, 41-9-646.

Juvenile proceedings.

Destruction of records generally, §12-15-103.

EXTERMINATORS.
See PEST CONTROL.

EXTORTION.
Class B felony, §13A-8-14.
Definition, §13A-8-13.
First degree extortion.
Elements of crime,
§13A-8-14.
Restitution.
Honest claims of property of
restitution or
indemnification.
When persons not liable
for threat, §13A-8-15.
Second degree extortion.
Claims of restitution or
indemnification.
When persons not liable
for threat, §13A-8-15.
Class C felony, §13A-8-15.
Elements of crime,
§13A-8-15.

EXTRADITION, §§15-9-20 to
15-9-65.
Arrest.
Extradition from Alabama,
§§15-9-30 to 15-9-49. See
within this heading,
"From Alabama."
Bail.
Arrest without warrant,
§§15-9-41 to 15-9-45.
Extradition from Alabama.
See within this
heading, "From
Alabama."
**Commission of act in
Alabama resulting in
crime in another state.**
Surrender of person by
governor, §15-9-34.
**Constitution of the United
States,** Const. U. S., Art.
IV, §2.
Costs.
Return of prisoner to
Alabama.
Expenses when accused
returns without
requisition, §15-9-65.
Debtors and creditors.
Constraint on use for
collection of debt,
demand or claim,
§15-9-48.
Definitions, §15-9-20.
Detainers.
Mandatory disposition of
detainers, §§15-9-80 to
15-9-88.
See DETAINERS.
District courts.
Jurisdiction, §12-12-33.
Executive authority.
Defined, §15-9-20.
From Alabama, §§15-9-30 to
15-9-49.
Arrest warrant.
Arresting officer.
Authority to command
assistance, §15-9-37.
Authorization to,
§15-9-36.
Arrest prior to requisition,
§15-9-40.
Authorization to arresting
officer, §15-9-36.
Contents, §15-9-35.
Issuance, §§15-9-35,
15-9-40.

EXTRADITION—Cont'd
From Alabama—Cont'd
Arrest warrant—Cont'd
Recall of warrant,
§15-9-49.
Reissuance, §15-9-49.
Arrest without warrant.
Appearance before judge,
§15-9-41.
Bail.
Admission to bail,
§§15-9-42, 15-9-43.
Conditions, §15-9-43.
Forfeiture, §15-9-45.
Commitment of accused to
jail, §15-9-42.
Persons authorized to
make arrest, §15-9-41.
Time.
Failure to arrest accused
on warrant within
time specified,
§15-9-44.
When authorized, §15-9-41.
Commission of act in state
resulting in crime in
another state.
Surrender of person by
governor, §15-9-34.
Confinement of prisoners,
§15-9-39.
Debts.
Constraint on use for
collection, §15-9-48.
Form of demand, §15-9-31.
Governor.
Duty of arrest and delivery
of foreign fugitives,
§15-9-30.
Habeas corpus.
Application for writ,
§15-9-38.
Inquiry into guilt or
innocence, §15-9-47.
Investigation of demand,
§15-9-32.
Notice.
Right of arrestee to be
informed, §15-9-38.
Prosecution already
instituted in Alabama,
§15-9-46.
Supporting documents.
Contents, §15-9-33.
Fugitive from justice.
Constitutional provisions,
Const. U. S., Art. IV, §2.
Habeas corpus.
Right of prisoner to apply for
writ, §15-9-38.
Jails.
Temporary confinement of
prisoner, §15-9-39.
**Mandatory disposition of
detainers,** §§15-9-80 to
15-9-88.
See DETAINERS.
Obscenity.
Anti-obscenity enforcement
act.
Persons in violation of,
§13A-12-200.6.
Penalties.
Failure to inform arrestee of
rights, §15-9-38.
Habeas corpus.
Failure to allow prisoner to
apply, §15-9-38.

EXTRADITION—Cont'd
Service of process.
Return of accused to
Alabama.
Exemption from civil
process upon return,
§15-9-63.
To Alabama.
Exemption from civil process.
Upon return, §15-9-63.
Expenses.
Fees and expenses of
officers, §15-9-62.
Payment of expenses for
returning accused,
§15-9-62.
When accused returns
without requisition,
§15-9-65.
Trial for crimes other than
those specified in
requisition, §15-9-64.
Warrant.
Application by district
attorney for issuance,
§15-9-61.
Filing, §15-9-61.
Forwarding of papers and
requisition, §15-9-61.
Fugitives from Alabama,
§15-9-60.
**Uniform mandatory
disposition of detainers
act,** §§15-9-80 to 15-9-88.
See DETAINERS.
Warrants.
Extradition from Alabama.
See within this heading,
"From Alabama."
Extradition to Alabama,
§§15-9-60, 15-9-61.

EXTRAORDINARY.
Appeals.
Review in supreme court of
decisions of courts of
appeals.
Rules of appellate
procedure, ARAP, Rule
21.
Certiorari.
See CERTIORARI.
Court of civil appeals.
Review in supreme court of
decisions of courts of
appeals.
Rules of appellate
procedure, ARAP, Rule
21.
Court of criminal appeals.
Review in supreme court of
decisions of courts of
appeals.
Rules of appellate
procedure, ARAP, Rule
21.
Habeas corpus, §§15-21-1 to
15-21-34.
See HABEAS CORPUS.
Mandamus.
See MANDAMUS.
Petitions, ARAP, Rule 21.
Prohibition, writ of.
See PROHIBITION, WRIT
OF.
Quo warranto.
See QUO WARRANTO.
**Rules of appellate
procedure,** ARAP, Rule
21.

EXTRAORDINARY—Cont'd
Service of process.
Petitions.
Rules of appellate
procedure, ARAP, Rule
21.
Supreme court.
Review in supreme court of
decisions of courts of
appeals.
Rules of appellate
procedure, ARAP, Rule
21.

EYE FOUNDATION, INC.
Sales and use taxes.
Exemption, §40-23-5.

EYEGLASSES.
Health.
Medicaid program.
Prescription eyewear for
recipients, §22-6-7.1.
Licenses.
Sales, §40-12-161.
Opticians.
Licenses, §40-12-135.
Optometrists.
See OPTOMETRISTS.

EYES.
Anatomical gifts.
See ANATOMICAL GIFTS.
Blind persons.
See BLIND PERSONS.
Donor eye enucleation
licenses, §§34-13-150 to
34-13-152.
Education.
Eye protective devices.
Pupils and teachers
participating in certain
courses, §16-1-7.
Optometrists.
See OPTOMETRISTS.
Protective devices.
Pupils and teachers
participating in certain
courses, §16-1-7.

F

FACTORIES.
Counties.
Promotion, §11-3-11.
Dams.
Erection of dams for
factories, §§18-2-1 to
18-2-21.
See DAMS.
Fires and fire prevention.
Fire marshal.
Regulation of doors and
exits, §36-19-10.
Nuisances.
Agricultural, manufacturing
and industrial plants.
Facilities not nuisances
after operating one
year.
Effect of section on
municipal
ordinances, §6-5-127.

FACTORS.
Commercial code.
Factor's lien.
Secured transactions,
§§7-9-101 to 7-9-507.
See COMMERCIAL
CODE.

FACTORS—Cont'd
Commission merchants,
§§2-29-1 to 2-29-11.
See COMMISSION
MERCHANTS.
Cotton.
Appropriation from bale by
factor having custody,
§2-19-4.
Liens.
Secured transactions,
§§7-9-101 to 7-9-507.
See COMMERCIAL CODE.
Rebates, §8-11-5.

FACTORY-BUILT HOUSING,
§§24-4A-1 to 24-4A-7.
See HOUSING.

FAIRFIELD, MUNICIPALITY
OF.
Property tax, Const. Ala.,
amd. 8.

FAIRHOPE, MUNICIPALITY
OF.
Property tax, Const. Ala.,
amd. 8.

FAIRS.
Agricultural fairs, §§2-7-20 to
2-7-32.
See AGRICULTURE.
Alabama state fair and
exhibit association.
Licenses and taxation.
Exemptions, §40-9-15.
Alcoholic beverages.
Licenses.
Special retail license for
fair authority,
§28-3A-19.
Horse shows.
State championship horse
show.
Designation, §1-2-22.
Renaissance faires.
State renaissance faire.
Designation, §1-2-21.
Street fairs.
Licenses, §40-12-163.
Transportation companies.
Free transportation or
reduced rates to or from
fairs and expositions,
§37-2-40.

FAIR TRADE.
Insurance.
Trade practices law,
§§27-12-1 to 27-12-24.
See INSURANCE.
Monopolies.
See MONOPOLIES.
Motion picture fair
competition, §§8-18-1 to
8-18-6.
See MOTION PICTURES.
Restraint of trade, §§8-10-1 to
8-10-3.
See TRADE AND
COMMERCE.

FAIR TRIAL TAX, §§12-19-250
to 12-19-254.

FAITH HEALING.
Tuberculosis.
Treatment by prayer or
spiritual means,
§22-11A-10.

FALLOUT SHELTERS.
Income tax.
Deductions, §40-18-15.

FALLOUT SHELTERS—Cont'd
Public buildings.
Construction with radioactive
fallout protection,
§§39-6-1, 39-6-2.

FALSE ALARMS.
Rendering false alarms,
§13A-10-8.

FALSE IMPRISONMENT.
Defined, §6-5-170.
Limitation of actions.
Six year limitation, §6-2-34.
Pleadings.
Form of complaint, ARCP,
Form 18.

FALSE PRETENSES.
Bringing into state property
obtained by, §13A-8-21.
Fraud.
Generally.
See FRAUD.
Theft generally, §§13A-8-1 to
13A-8-23.
See THEFT.

FAMILY.
Adoption procedure,
§§26-10-1 to 26-10-30.
See ADOPTION.
Marriage.
See MARRIAGE.

FAMILY PURPOSE
DOCTRINE.
Property damage by minor.
Liability of parents, §6-5-380.

FARM CRISIS AND
TRANSITION PROGRAM,
§§2-6A-1 to 2-6A-6.
See AGRICULTURE.

FARM EQUIPMENT.
Liens.
Owners of hay baling
machines or presses,
§§35-11-290, 35-11-291.
Repurchase of inventory
from retailers, §§8-21-1 to
8-21-14.
Actions.
Accrual, §8-21-14.
Audits.
Time limitation, §8-21-9.
Bulk sales law.
Applicability, §8-21-8.
Death or incapacity.
Effect, §8-21-7.
Debts.
Outstanding debts to
wholesaler, §8-21-2.
Definitions, §8-21-1.
Fees.
Payment, §8-21-3.
Franchises.
Termination, etc., without
good cause, §8-21-10.
Indemnification by
wholesaler.
Retailer's losses, §8-21-12.
Inspections.
Representative of retailers,
§8-21-8.
Items not subject to
repurchase, §8-21-5.
Limitation of actions,
§8-21-14.
Records.
Time limitation for
auditing records,
§8-21-9.
Remedies, §8-21-13.

FARM EQUIPMENT—Cont'd
Repurchase of inventory from retailers—Cont'd
Security interest.
Effect of chapter on, §8-21-8.
Title.
Transfer to wholesaler, §8-21-4.
Warranties.
Payment of claims made by retailer to wholesaler, §8-21-11.
Wholesalers.
Amount of payment by wholesaler for repurchase, §8-21-3.
Civil liability for refusal to repurchase, §8-21-6.
Effect of chapter on security interest of wholesalers, §8-21-8.
Indemnification by wholesaler for retailer's losses, §8-21-12.
Procedure where retailer has outstanding debt to wholesaler, §8-21-2.
Transfer of title and right of possession to wholesaler, §8-21-4.
Wholesaler.
Repurchase of inventory from retailers, §§8-21-1 to 8-21-14. See within this heading, "Repurchase of inventory from retailers."

FARM PRODUCTS.
Agriculture generally.
See AGRICULTURE.
Bushels and barrels.
Weight established by custom of market place, §8-16-94.
Cotton.
General provisions, §§2-19-1 to 2-19-135.
See COTTON.
Promotion, §§2-8-190 to 2-8-211.
See COTTON.
Crops.
See CROPS.
Eggs and egg products.
General provisions, §§2-9-40, 2-12-1 to 2-12-12.
See EGGS AND EGG PRODUCTS.
Promotion, §§2-8-150 to 2-8-171.
See EGGS AND EGG PRODUCTS.
Feeds, §§2-21-16 to 2-21-34, 40-23-4.
See FEEDS.
Fruits and vegetables.
General provisions.
See FRUITS AND VEGETABLES.
Promotion, §§2-8-120 to 2-8-137.
See FRUITS AND VEGETABLES.
Grain.
General provisions.
See GRAIN.

FARM PRODUCTS—Cont'd
Grain—Cont'd
Promotion, §§2-8-230 to 2-8-252.
See GRAIN.
Hay.
Liens, §§35-11-290, 35-11-291.
Loads to be fastened, §32-5-75.
Honeybees and apiaries, §§2-14-1 to 2-14-15.
See HONEYBEES AND APIARIES.
Livestock.
General provisions, §§2-15-1 to 2-15-317.
See LIVESTOCK.
Milk and milk products, §§2-13-1 to 2-13-94.
See MILK AND MILK PRODUCTS.
Nuts.
General provisions, §§1-2-19, 2-25-15, 20-1-90 to 20-1-93, 40-9-3.
See NUTS.
Promotion, §§2-8-120 to 2-8-137.
See NUTS.
Peanuts.
Liens, §§35-11-290, 35-11-291.
Motor carriers, §37-3-4.
Tax, §40-9-3.
Poultry, §§2-16-1 to 2-17-38.
See POULTRY.
Soybeans, §§2-8-80 to 2-8-103.
See SOYBEANS.

FARMS.
Agriculture generally.
See AGRICULTURE.
Alligator farms, §§9-12-200 to 9-12-214.
See ALLIGATOR FARMS.
Surface mining control and reclamation.
Issuance of permits to mine on prime farm land, §9-16-85.

FAVUS.
Notifiable diseases, §§22-11A-1 to 22-11A-38.
See DISEASES.

FAYETTE COUNTY.
Constable.
Abolition of office, Const. Ala., amd. 417.
Economic development.
Municipalities in Fayette county, Const. Ala., amd. 94.

FAYETTE, MUNICIPALITY OF.
Property tax, Const. Ala., amd. 17.

FEDERAL AID HIGHWAY FINANCE AUTHORITY, §§23-1-300 to 23-1-317.
See HIGHWAYS.

FEDERAL DEPOSIT INSURANCE CORPORATION, §§5-5A-12, 5-8A-31, 5-8A-34.

FEDERAL GOVERNMENT.
See UNITED STATES.

FEDERAL HOME LOAN BANK.
Savings and loan associations.
Power to qualify as member, §5-16-24.

FEDERAL SAVINGS AND LOAN INSURANCE CORPORATION.
See SAVINGS AND LOAN ASSOCIATIONS.

FEEDS.
Commercial feed law of 1978, §§2-21-1 to 2-21-34.
Adulteration, §2-21-22.
Analysis, §2-21-26.
Board.
Defined, §2-21-17.
Brand name.
Defined, §2-21-17.
Commercial feed.
Defined, §2-21-17.
Commissioner to enforce, §2-21-18.
Condemnation, §2-21-27.
Confidentiality of information.
Protection of trade secrets, §2-21-32.
Container.
Defined, §2-21-17.
Contract feeder.
Defined, §2-21-17.
Cooperation with governmental agencies, §2-21-33.
Customer-buyer.
Defined, §2-21-17.
Customer-formula feed.
Defined, §2-21-17.
Definitions, §2-21-17.
Distribute.
Defined, §2-21-17.
Distributor.
Defined, §2-21-17.
Drug.
Defined, §2-21-17.
Feed ingredient.
Defined, §2-21-17.
Injunctions, §2-21-31.
Inspections.
Fees, §2-21-24.
Procedure, §2-21-26.
Reports, §2-21-24.
Label, §2-21-20.
Defined, §2-21-17.
Labeling.
Defined, §2-21-17.
Licenses, §2-21-19.
Manufacture.
Defined, §2-21-17.
Mineral feed.
Defined, §2-21-17.
Misbranding, §2-21-21.
Notices.
Warning notices concerning violations, §2-21-31.
Official sample.
Defined, §2-21-17.
Penalties, §§2-21-29 to 2-21-31.
Deficiency in feed, §2-21-29.
Recovery, §2-21-30.
Rules and regulations.
Violations, §2-21-31.
Violations of chapter provisions, §2-21-31.

FEEDS—Cont'd
Commercial feed law of 1978
—Cont'd
Percent.
Defined, §2-21-17.
Percentages.
Defined, §2-21-17.
Permitted analytical
variation.
Defined, §2-21-17.
Person.
Defined, §2-21-17.
Pet.
Defined, §2-21-17.
Pet food.
Defined, §2-21-17.
Product name.
Defined, §2-21-17.
Prohibited acts, §2-21-23.
Publication of information.
Authority of commissioner,
§2-21-34.
Purchaser.
Defined, §2-21-17.
Reports.
Inspections, §2-21-24.
Rules and regulations.
Penalties for violations,
§2-21-31.
Promulgation by
commissioner,
§2-21-25.
Sales.
Stop sale order, §2-21-27.
Sampling, §2-21-26.
Seizure, §2-21-27.
Short title, §2-21-16.
Short weight, §2-21-28.
Specialty pet.
Defined, §2-21-17.
Specialty pet food.
Defined, §2-21-17.
Ton.
Defined, §2-21-17.
Trade secrets.
Protection, §2-21-32.
Vertical-integrater feed.
Defined, §2-21-17.
Weight.
Short weight, §2-21-28.
Definitions.
Commercial feed law of 1978,
§2-21-17.
Inspections.
Commercial feed law of 1978.
Fees, §2-21-24.
Procedure, §2-21-26.
Labels, §§2-21-17, 2-21-20.
Penalties.
Commercial feed law of 1978,
§§2-21-29 to 2-21-31.
Rules and regulations.
Commercial feed law of 1978.
Penalties for violations,
§2-21-31.
Promulgation by
commissioner,
§2-21-25.
Sales tax.
Exemption of gross proceeds,
§40-23-4.

FEES.
Accountants.
See ACCOUNTANTS.
Adoption.
Investigation services,
§26-10-4.1.
Probate judges' fees,
§12-19-90.

FEES—Cont'd
Affidavits.
Probate judges' fees,
§12-19-90.
Agriculture.
See AGRICULTURE.
Air commerce.
Certificates and permits,
§37-9-25.
Alcoholic beverages.
See ALCOHOLIC
BEVERAGES.
Alligator farms.
See ALLIGATOR FARMS.
Ambulances.
Licenses, §22-18-4.
Appeals.
Docket fee, ARAP, Rule 12
(a).
Arbitration and award,
§§6-6-10, 6-6-11.
Architects, §34-2-33.
Atomic energy.
Search of criminal records
of employees,
§22-14-31.
Attachments, §12-19-75.
Attorney general.
Criminal cases, §12-19-190.
Payment into state treasury,
§36-15-4.
Restrictions on receipt of
fees, Const. Ala., art. V,
§137; amd. 111.
Attorneys at law.
See ATTORNEYS' FEES.
Auctions and auctioneers,
§§34-4-5, 34-4-21.
Audiologists, §§34-28A-22,
34-28A-25, 34-28A-27.
**Banks and financial
institutions,** §§5-2A-20,
5-5A-1, 5-5A-13.
Barbers, §§34-5-8 to 34-5-10.
Bishop of diocese, §10-4-8.
Boards and commissions.
Disposition, §41-4-92.
Boats.
See BOATS.
Boxing and wrestling.
Collection of license and
permit fees, §41-9-96.
Change of name, §12-19-90.
Checks.
Sale of checks, §§8-7-1 to
8-7-15.
See CHECKS.
Chiropractors.
See CHIROPRACTORS.
Circuit courts.
Docket fees.
See DOCKETS.
General provisions.
See CIRCUIT COURTS.
Coal, §25-9-10.
Commercial code.
Secured transactions.
Filing.
Central filing system.
Implementation,
§7-9-410.
Commission merchants.
Sale of farm produce,
§2-29-2.
**Conservation and natural
resources.**
Licenses.
Refunds on erroneous or
excessive fees, §9-2-25.

FEES—Cont'd
Conservators.
Settlements of accounts of
conservators, §§26-5-13,
26-5-14.
Constables.
See CONSTABLES.
Constitution of Alabama.
Talladega county.
Jail.
Construction.
Fee on civil and
criminal cases for,
Const. Ala., amd.
504.
Consumer finance, §5-19-22.
Contractors.
Licenses, §34-8-2.
Coroners.
See CORONERS.
Corporations.
See CORPORATIONS.
Cosmetologists, §§34-7-11,
34-7-15, 34-7-21.
Costs.
Civil cases, §§12-19-40 to
12-19-138.
See COSTS.
Criminal cases, §§12-19-150
to 15-19-211.
See COSTS.
Cotton.
Gins.
Permit fee, §2-19-61.
Registration of cotton buyers.
Application fee, §2-19-102.
Counties.
See COUNTIES.
Court of civil appeals,
§§12-19-91, 12-20-1.
Court of criminal appeals,
§§12-19-91, 12-19-190,
12-20-1.
Copies and certification,
ARJA, Rule 30.
Credit cards, §5-20-5.
Credit card banks.
Establishment or
acquisition.
Applications, §§5-20-4,
5-20-6.
Credit unions, §§5-17-7,
5-17-14.
Criminal cases.
Applicability of provisions,
§12-19-25.
Dams.
Ad quod damnum
proceedings.
Jurors' fees, §12-19-112.
Dental service corporations.
Required fees, §22-21-374.
Sales representatives.
Contracting sales
representatives.
Registration with
commissioner,
§22-21-377.
**Dentists and dental
hygienists.**
See DENTISTS.
District attorneys.
See DISTRICT
ATTORNEYS.
District courts.
Docket fees.
See DOCKETS.
General provisions.
See DISTRICT COURTS.

FEES—Cont'd
Divorce and alimony.
Department of human
resources.
Investigation services fees,
§30-3-7.
Docket fees.
See DOCKETS.
Dogs.
Trainers.
License fees, §9-11-52.
Domestic violence facilities,
§30-6-11.
Dower.
Probate judges' fees,
§12-19-90.
Education.
See EDUCATION.
Eggs and egg products.
Failure to pay inspection fee,
§2-12-10.
Permits for sale, §2-12-4.
**Electric membership
corporations,** §§37-7-8 to
37-7-18.
See ELECTRIC
MEMBERSHIP
CORPORATIONS.
Employment agencies.
Annual license fee, §34-10-5.
Engineers, §§34-11-5, 34-11-6,
34-11-12.
**Environmental improvement
authorities.**
Exemptions from payment of
fees, §9-6-15.
Environmental management.
Hazardous waste or
substances.
Fees for disposal of
hazardous waste or
substances, §§22-30B-1
to 22-30B-18.
See HAZARDOUS
WASTE.
Escheats.
Probate judges' fees,
§12-19-90.
Estrays.
Highways.
Animals running at large
on state and federal
aid highways,
§§3-2-21, 3-2-23.
Executions, §§6-9-26,
12-19-75.
**Executors and
administrators.**
See EXECUTORS AND
ADMINISTRATORS.
**Exemptions from
administration and
payment of debts.**
Homestead exemption.
Recordation of judgments
allotting, §6-10-105.
**Exemptions from levy and
sale under process.**
Declaration of claimed
exemptions, §6-10-22.
Farm equipment.
Repurchase of inventory from
retailers.
Payment of fee for
handling, §8-21-3.
Feeds.
Inspections, §2-21-24.
Fences.
Partition fences.
Orders of court, §35-7-5.

FEES—Cont'd
Fertilizer.
Inspections, §2-22-9.
Filing of papers.
Fees for miscellaneous
filings, ARJA, Rule 7.
Fires and fire prevention.
Fire marshal.
Assistants.
Payment to local
assistants,
§36-19-23.
Disposition, §36-19-29.
Fees of witnesses and
officers serving
subpoenas, §36-19-22.
Sprinkler systems.
Certified fire protection
sprinkler contractors.
Local license fees,
§34-33-8.
State fire marshal's permit.
Application fees,
§34-33-4.
Fish and game.
Commercial fee fishing
ponds, §§9-11-450 to
9-11-457.
See FISH AND GAME.
Licenses.
See FISH AND GAME.
Forests and forestry.
See FORESTS AND
FORESTRY.
Fraternal benefit societies.
Licenses, §27-34-6.
Fruits and vegetables.
Grading and standards,
§2-11-76.
**Funerals and funeral
services.**
See FUNERALS.
Garbage and trash.
See GARBAGE AND
TRASH.
Garnishment, §12-19-75.
Gins.
Cotton gins.
Permit fee, §2-19-102.
Ginseng.
Registration.
Dealers, growers and
collectors, §9-13-243.
Grain.
Grading and standards.
Disposition of fees,
§2-11-101.
Grain dealers.
Licenses.
Filing fee to accompany
application, §2-31-3.
Grand jury.
Jurors' fees in criminal cases,
§12-19-210.
Guardian ad litem,
§§12-19-90, 35-4-191.
Guardian and ward.
Conservators.
Settlements of accounts of,
§§26-5-13, 26-5-14.
Probate judges' fees,
§12-19-90.
Harbors and ports, §§33-1-26,
33-3-3.

FEES—Cont'd
**Hazardous substances and
waste.**
Fees for disposal of
hazardous waste or
substances.
General provisions,
§§22-30B-1 to
22-30B-18.
See HAZARDOUS
WASTE.
Health.
Home health services,
§§22-7-1 to 22-7-6.
Health care service plan.
Certificates of authority,
§10-4-106.
**Health maintenance
organizations,**
§27-21A-21.
**Hearing aid dealers and
fitters,** §§34-14-3, 34-14-6,
34-14-7.
**Heating and air conditioning
contractors.**
Application and renewal fees,
§34-31-25.
Homestead exemption.
Probate judges' fees,
§12-19-90.
Honeybees and apiaries,
§2-14-3.
Horse racing.
See HORSE RACING.
Hospitals.
Licenses, §22-21-24.
Illegitimacy.
Probate judges' fees,
§12-19-90.
Impeachment, §§36-11-17,
36-11-21.
Indexes.
Circuit courts.
Fees for keeping indexes
not allowed, §12-19-98.
Indictments.
Receipt of unauthorized
official fees.
Form of indictment,
§15-8-150.
Industrial alcohol.
Generally, §28-5-11.
**Industrial development
authority.**
Incorporation and
dissolution.
Secretary of state to
receive no fees,
§41-10-24.
**Industrial development
corporations.**
Incorporation, §10-4-131.
Inquests, §§12-19-192,
12-19-193.
Insurance.
See INSURANCE.
Interior designers.
Examination fees, §34-15A-4.
Jefferson county.
Constables.
Exception, §12-19-92.
Judgments.
Foreign judgments.
Filing fee, §6-9-235.
Judicial sales, §12-19-23.
**Junior college for Franklin,
Marion and Winston
counties.**
Matriculation, library and
laboratory fees,
§16-60-34.

FEES—Cont'd

Junior college for Jackson and DeKalb counties.
Matriculation, library and laboratory fees, §16-60-64.

Junkyard control.
Licenses, §23-1-244.

Jurors.
See JURY.

Justices of the peace, Const. Ala., art. VI, §168.
Increasing fees.
Special, private or local laws prohibited, Const. Ala., art. IV, §104.

Landlord and tenant.
Possession wrongfully withheld, §35-9-88.

Landscape architects, §§34-17-20 to 34-17-26.

Landscaping.
Horticulture and floriculture work.
Permit fees, §2-28-4.

Land surveyors, §§34-11-5, 34-11-6, 34-11-12.

Leases.
Probate judges' fees, §12-19-90.

Lime.
Inspection fee, §2-23-5.
Permits.
Application fees, §2-23-3.
Disposition of fees, §2-23-5.

Limitation of actions.
Actions for recovery of fees.
Two year limitation, §6-2-38.

Liquefied petroleum gas.
Assessment, §§9-17-106, 9-17-109, 9-17-110.
Failure to report and remit.
Penalties, §9-17-109.
Permit fees, §9-17-106.
Assessment, §§9-17-106, 9-17-109, 9-17-110.

Lis pendens.
Recording notice, §35-4-138.

Livestock.
See LIVESTOCK.

Manufactured buildings.
Defined, §24-4A-2.
Schedule of fees, §24-4A-3.

Maps and plats.
Probate judges' fees, §12-19-90.

Marine resources.
See MARINE RESOURCES.

Marriage.
Performance of marriages, §30-1-8.
Probate judges' fees, §12-19-90.

Mechanics' and materialmen's liens, §35-11-216.

Medical technicians.
See MEDICAL TECHNICIANS.

Mellorine.
Permit fee, §20-1-133.

Mentally ill.
Department of mental health and mental retardation.
Disposition of fees, §22-50-3.
Probate judges' fees, §12-19-90.

FEES—Cont'd

Mentally ill—Cont'd
Proceedings to pass upon soundness of mind of person.
Probate court jurors' fees, §12-19-113.
Witness fees in probate court, §12-19-135.

Midwives.
Licenses.
Issuance and renewal, §34-19-5.

Milk and milk products, §2-13-8.

Mines and minerals.
Surface mining reclamation, §§9-16-6, 9-16-12.

Mobile homes.
Licenses, §§24-5-6, 24-5-10.
Seals, §24-5-10.

Mortgages and deeds of trust.
Probate judges' fees, §12-19-90.

Motor fuels.
Distributors of motor fuels.
Filing fee for license application, §40-12-193.

Motor vehicle carriers, §37-3-32.

Motor vehicles.
See MOTOR VEHICLES.

Municipal corporations.
See MUNICIPAL CORPORATIONS.

Names.
Change of name, §12-19-90.

Notaries public, §36-20-6.
Notaries public for state at large.
Fee for issuance of notary commission, §36-20-30.
Probate judges, §12-19-90.
For issuance of commission, §36-20-1.

Nurseries.
Insect and disease control.
Inspection certificates, §2-25-6.
Registration of agents or salesmen, §2-25-7.

Nurses, §§34-21-24, 34-21-25.
Licenses, §34-21-24.

Nursing home administrators.
License fees.
General provisions, §§34-20-1 to 34-20-15.
See NURSING HOMES.

Optometrists, §§32-22-5, 32-22-20 to 32-22-24.

Partition.
See PARTITION.

Peace bonds.
When paid by complainant, §15-6-23.

Peace officers' annuity and benefit fund.
Membership fees, §36-21-68.
Refunds, §36-21-74.

Pest control.
Permit fees, §2-28-4.

Pesticides.
Application.
License fee, §2-27-53.

Petroleum products, §§8-17-85, 8-17-87, 8-17-91.

FEES—Cont'd

Pharmacists and pharmacies, §§34-23-30, 34-23-32, 34-23-50 to 34-23-52.

Physicians.
See PHYSICIANS.

Pilots and pilotage.
See PILOTS AND PILOTAGE.

Pipelines.
Safety inspection fees, §37-4-88.

Plant pathology.
Permit fees, §2-28-4.

Plumbing.
Certification of plumbers and gas fitters.
Board to set fees, §34-37-9.

Podiatrists.
See PODIATRISTS.

Polygraph examiners, §§34-25-5, 34-25-22 to 34-25-26.

Poultry, §§2-18-3, 2-18-8.

Probate courts.
See PROBATE COURTS.

Probation.
Intensive supervision program, §15-22-56.

Psychologists, §§34-26-22, 34-26-43.

Public officers and employees.
See PUBLIC OFFICERS AND EMPLOYEES.

Public service commission, §37-1-93.

Public utilities, §§37-4-23, 37-4-24.

Public works.
Contracts.
Fees to be paid awarding authorities, §39-2-3.

Rabies.
Inoculation fee, §3-7-3.

Real estate brokers, §§34-27-4, 34-27-33 to 34-27-35.

Recordation, §35-4-58.

Records.
Copies.
Certified copies of writings upon payment of fees, §36-12-41.
Court records.
Copies and certification, ARJA, Rule 30.
Substitution of lost or destroyed records or papers, §12-20-1.

Rules of judicial administration.
Cases filed prior to January 16, 1977.
Fees and commissions, ARJA, Rule 23.
Transfer of cases, ARJA, Rule 26.

Sale of checks, §§8-7-6, 8-7-9.

Sales.
Going out of business or distress merchandise sales.
License, §§8-13-6, 8-13-8.

Salvage.
Appraisers, §35-13-6.

Savings and loan associations.
Assessment fees, §5-16-38.1.

FEES—Cont'd

Searches and seizures.
Search warrants.
Payment of fees, §15-5-18.
Secretary of state.
See SECRETARY OF
STATE.
Securities.
Registration of securities.
Filing and registration
fees, §8-6-8.
Seeds.
Permits for sale, §2-26-5.
Service of process,
§§12-19-73, 12-19-74,
12-19-171.
Sheriffs.
See SHERIFFS.
Small loans.
Examination, §5-2A-24.
Recording fees, §5-18-13.
Social workers, §§34-30-6,
34-30-23, 34-30-25.
Soil classifiers.
Registration, §34-32-12.
**Southeast interstate low-
level radioactive waste
management compact,**
§22-32-5.
**Speech pathologists and
audiologists,** §§34-28A-22,
34-28A-25, 34-28A-27.
Sports.
Agents.
Changes in schedule of
fees, §8-26-24.
Filing of schedule,
§8-26-24.
Limitation, §8-26-24.
Where athlete fails to
procure or be paid
for employment,
§8-26-35.
Registration, §§8-26-12,
8-26-13.
Renewal, §8-26-9.
State.
Disposition, §41-4-92.
State auditor, §36-16-5.
Restrictions on receipt of
fees, Const. Ala., art. V,
§137; amd. 111.
State treasurer.
Restrictions on receipt of
fees, Const. Ala., art. V,
§137; amd. 111.
Stores.
Licenses, §§40-12-315,
40-12-316.
Supreme court.
See SUPREME COURT.
Surveyors, §§34-11-5, 34-11-6,
34-11-12.
Taxation.
See TAXATION.
Trademarks.
Registration of trademarks
and service marks,
§§8-12-8, 8-12-10,
8-12-11.
Transcripts, ARJA, Rule 29.
Court reporters.
Preparation of original and
providing copies,
ARJA, Rule 29.
Transfer of cases, ARJA,
Rule 26.
Transient merchants.
Licenses, §34-35-7.
Transportation companies,
§37-2-41.

FEES—Cont'd

Trees and timber.
Arrest by forest officers,
§§9-13-24.
Tree surgery.
Permit fees, §2-28-4.
Trusts and trustees, §§19-3-6,
19-3-234, 34-3-60.
**Unemployment
compensation.**
Arrest fee, §25-4-147.
Attorneys' fees, §25-4-139.
Generally, §25-4-139.
**Uniformity of laws
regulating fees of public
officers,** Const. Ala., art.
IV, §96.
Vacation time-sharing plans,
§34-27-66.
Violations of article.
Assessment of
investigation costs,
§34-27-64.
Vital statistics, §§22-9-8,
22-9-10.
Warehouses, §§8-15-3,
8-15-13.
Weights and measures.
See WEIGHTS AND
MEASURES.
Wills.
Probate judges' fees,
§12-19-90.
Witnesses.
Civil cases, §§12-19-130 to
12-19-138.
Criminal cases.
See WITNESSES.
Workmen's compensation.
Proceedings for
determination of
disputed claims for
compensation, §25-5-89.

FEE SIMPLE ESTATES.

**Construction of words
"grant," "bargain," or
"sell,"** §35-4-271.
**Estate taken as fee simple
unless expressly limited,**
§35-4-2.
**Fee tail converted into fee
simple,** §35-4-3.
Life estates.
Effect of grant of absolute
power, §35-4-292.
Powers of disposition.
Effect of grant of absolute
power, §35-4-292.

FEET.

Podiatrists, §§34-24-230 to
34-24-276.
See PODIATRISTS.

FEE TAIL ESTATES.

Converted into fee simple,
§35-4-3.

FELONIES.

**Actions for felonious
injuries.**
Without criminal
prosecution, §6-5-370.
Appeals.
Bonds, §12-22-170.
Arson.
General provisions,
§§13A-7-40 to 13A-7-44.
Assault and battery.
General provisions,
§§13A-6-20 to 13A-6-25.

FELONIES—Cont'd

Attorneys at law.
Conviction grounds for
removal, §34-3-86.
Bail and recognizance.
Discretionary schedule,
ARJA, Rule 2.
Fixing of bail, §15-13-6.
Bribery.
See BRIBERY.
Burglary.
General provisions,
§§13A-7-1 to 13A-7-8.
See BURGLARY.
Capital offenses.
See CAPITAL OFFENSES.
Capital punishment.
See CAPITAL
PUNISHMENT.
Class A felony.
Arson.
First degree arson,
§13A-7-41.
Burglary, §13A-7-5.
Fines.
Limitation, §13A-5-11.
Kidnapping.
First degree, §13A-6-43.
Rape.
First degree, §13A-6-61.
Robbery.
First degree, §13A-8-41.
Sentence of imprisonment,
§13A-5-6.
Sexual abuse.
First degree, §13A-6-66.
Sodomy.
First degree, §13A-6-63.
Treason, §13A-11-2.
Weapons.
Use of firearm or deadly
weapon, §13A-5-6.
Class B felony.
Credit cards.
Fraud by persons providing
goods and services,
§13A-9-14.1.
Class C felony.
Arson.
Second degree, §13A-7-42.
Assault.
Second degree, §13A-6-21.
Bail jumping.
First degree, §13A-10-39.
Bigamy, §13A-13-1.
Bribery.
Jurors, §13A-10-125.
Receiving bribes,
§13A-10-126.
Public servants,
§13A-10-61.
Witnesses, §13A-10-121.
Receiving bribe,
§13A-10-122.
Burglary, §§13A-7-6 to
13A-7-8.
Possession of tools,
§13A-7-8.
Second degree, §13A-7-6.
Third degree, §13A-7-7.
Contraband.
Promoting prison
contraband in first
degree, §13A-10-36.
Promoting prison
contraband in second
degree, §13A-10-37.
Credit cards.
Fraudulent use of,
§13A-9-14.

FELONIES—Cont'd
Class C felony—Cont'd
Credit cards—Cont'd
Illegal possession,
§13A-9-14.
Criminal mischief.
First degree, §13A-7-21.
Criminal tampering.
First degree, §13A-7-25.
Debit card.
Illegal possession or
fraudulent use,
§13A-9-14.
Dogs.
Killing dogs used by peace
officers, §13A-11-15.
Drugs, §§13A-12-211 to
13A-12-213.
Marihuana.
Unlawful possession in
first degree,
§13A-12-213.
Unlawful distribution,
§13A-12-211.
Unlawful possession or
receipt, §13A-12-212.
Eavesdropping.
Installing devices,
§13A-11-33.
Escape, §§13A-10-31 to
13A-10-34.
First degree, §13A-10-31.
Permitting or
facilitating,
§13A-10-34.
Second degree, §13A-10-32.
Third degree, §13A-10-33.
Explosives.
Criminal possession,
§13A-7-44.
Extortion.
First degree, §13A-8-14.
Second degree, §13A-8-15.
False alarms, §13A-10-8.
Fines.
Limitation, §13A-5-11.
First degree assault,
§13A-6-20.
Forgery.
First degree, §13A-9-2.
Possession.
Devices, §13A-9-9.
Instruments.
First degree, §13A-9-5.
Second degree,
§13A-9-6.
Second degree, §13A-9-3.
Hindering of prosecution.
First degree, §13A-10-43.
Homicide.
Criminally negligent
homicide.
Driving under influence,
§13A-6-4.
Impersonating peace officers,
§13A-10-11.
Incest, §13A-13-3.
Jury, §§13A-10-125 to
13A-10-127.
Bribing a juror,
§13A-10-125.
Receiving bribe,
§13A-10-126.
Intimidating jurors,
§13A-10-127.
Kidnapping.
Interference with custody,
§13A-6-45.
Second degree, §13A-6-44.
Manslaughter, §13A-6-3.

FELONIES—Cont'd
Class C felony—Cont'd
Motor vehicles.
Breaking and entering,
§13A-8-11.
Embezzlement, conversion,
etc., §32-15-7.
False representation.
Obtaining possession by,
§32-15-4.
Hiring.
Failure to redeliver,
§32-15-6.
Intent to defraud,
§32-15-5.
Obscuring identity,
§13A-8-22.
Obscenity.
Producing obscene
materials,
§13A-12-200.2.
Peace officers.
Impersonating, §13A-10-11.
Perjury.
First degree, §13A-10-101.
Prostitution.
Promoting first degree,
§13A-12-111.
Promoting second degree,
§13A-12-112.
Rape.
Second degree, §13A-6-62.
Receiving stolen property.
First degree, §13A-8-17.
Second degree, §13A-8-18.
Robbery.
Second degree, §13A-8-42.
Third degree, §13A-8-43.
Sentence of imprisonment,
§13A-5-6.
Sodomy.
Second degree, §13A-6-64.
Theft of property.
First degree, §13A-8-3.
Lost property.
First degree, §13A-8-7.
Second degree, §13A-8-8.
Second degree, §13A-8-4.
Theft of services.
First degree, §13A-8-10.1.
Second degree,
§13A-8-10.2.
Theft of trademarks or trade
secrets, §13A-8-10.4.
Weapons.
Use of firearm or deadly
weapon, §13A-5-6.
Witnesses.
Bribing, §13A-10-121.
Receiving bribe,
§13A-10-122.
Intimidating, §13A-10-123.
Classification, §13A-5-3.
Conspiracy.
See CONSPIRACY.
Constitution of Alabama.
Pardons, Const. Ala., art. V,
§124.
Contraband.
Prison contraband,
§§13A-10-30, 13A-10-36
to 13A-10-38.
Credit cards.
Fraud by persons providing
goods and services.
Class B felony,
§13A-9-14.1.
Criminal law and procedure.
General provisions.
See CRIMINAL LAW AND
PROCEDURE.

FELONIES—Cont'd
Designation of offenses,
§13A-5-4.
District courts.
Jurisdiction, §12-12-32.
Dogs.
Killing dogs used by peace
officers.
Class C felony, §13A-11-15.
Drugs.
Controlled substances.
Dentistry and veterinary
related penalties,
§20-2-74.
Furnishing to minor,
§13A-2-215.
Manufacturers and
distributors, §§20-2-71,
20-2-72.
Trafficking offenses.
Habitual felony offender
act, §13A-12-231.
Mandatory minimum
terms of
imprisonment,
§13A-12-231.
Embezzlement, §13A-9-51.
Escape, §§13A-10-31 to
13A-10-33.
Evidence.
Habitual felony offenders.
Prior convictions,
§13A-5-10.1.
Extortion, §§13A-8-13 to
13A-8-15.
Felons.
Profits from crime, §§41-9-80
to 41-9-84.
See PROFITS FROM
CRIME.
Registration, §§13A-11-180 to
13A-11-186. See within
this heading,
"Registration of felons."
Fines.
Authorized, §13A-5-2.
Distribution, §12-19-152.
Generally, §13A-5-11.
Food stamps.
Class B felony.
First degree illegal
possession, §13A-9-91.
Class C felony.
Second degree illegal
possession,
§13A-9-91.
Forgery, §§13A-9-1 to 13A-9-7.
See FORGERY AND
COUNTERFEITING.
Fraud.
Charitable fraud.
First degree.
Class B felony,
§13A-9-73.
Second degree.
Class C felony,
§13A-9-74.
Credit cards.
Fraud by persons providing
goods and services.
Class B felony,
§13A-9-14.1.
Gambling.
General provisions.
See GAMBLING.
Lotteries.
See LOTTERIES.
Habitual felony offenders.
Additional penalties,
§13A-5-9.

FELONIES—Cont'd
Habitual felony offenders
    —Cont'd
Bail and recognizance.
Controlled substances.
    Trafficking offenses.
        Applicability of act,
            §13A-12-231.
    Discretionary bail
        schedule, ARJA, Rule
        2.
Evidence of prior convictions,
    §13A-5-10.1.
Hearings, §13A-5-10.
Parole, §15-22-27.1.
    Life imprisonment upon
        second conviction of
        class A felonies,
        §15-22-27.2.
Penalties.
    Correctional incentive
        time.
        Deductions from
            sentences, §14-9-44.
    Persons previously
        convicted of felonies,
        §15-18-9.
    Restriction on imposition of
        penalty, §13A-5-10.
Hard labor.
Sentences to include,
    §13A-5-6.
Homicide, §§13A-6-1 to
    13A-6-4.
Criminally negligent
    homicide.
    Motor vehicles.
        Driving under the
            influence, §13A-6-4.
Imprisonment.
Limitation on term,
    §13A-5-6.
Place, §13A-5-8.
Indictments.
Offenses which are
    indictable, §15-8-2.
Investigations.
Presentence investigation,
    §13A-5-5.
Kidnapping, §§13A-6-40 to
    13A-6-45.
Larceny.
See THEFT.
Limitations on prosecution.
Generally, §15-3-1.
Offenses having no
    limitations, §15-3-5.
Manslaughter, §§13A-6-3,
    15-3-5.
Motor vehicles.
Breaking and entering,
    §13A-8-11.
Drivers' licenses.
    Use of motor vehicle in
        commission of felony.
        Grounds for revocation,
            §32-5A-195.
    Embezzlement, conversion,
        etc., §32-15-7.
    False representation.
        Obtaining possession,
            §32-15-4.
    Hiring.
        Failure to redeliver,
            §32-15-6.
        Intent to defraud, §32-15-5.
Homicide.
    Criminally negligent
        homicide.
        Driving under influence,
            §13A-6-4.

FELONIES—Cont'd
Motor vehicles—Cont'd
Obscuring identity,
    §13A-8-22.
Murder, §13A-6-2.
Parole.
Repeat offenders,
    §15-22-27.1.
    Life imprisonment upon
        second conviction of
        class A felonies,
        §15-22-27.2.
Perjury.
See PERJURY.
Physical therapists.
Revocation or suspension of
    licenses, §34-24-217.
Pleading.
Criminal pleading generally.
    See PLEADINGS.
Polygraph examiners.
Refusal, suspension or
    revocation of licenses,
    §34-25-32.
Preliminary hearings,
    §15-11-1.
Presentence investigation,
    §13A-5-5.
Probation.
Authorized, §13A-5-2.
Profits from crime, §§41-9-80
    to 41-9-84.
Property.
Criminal damage to property.
    See PROPERTY.
Prostitution, §§13A-12-110 to
    13A-12-112.
Rape, §§13A-6-61 to 13A-6-62.
Receiving stolen property,
    §§13A-8-17, 13A-8-18.
Registration of felons,
    §§13A-11-180 to
    13A-11-186.
Address.
    Notice of change,
        §13A-11-183.
Cards.
    Carrying cards,
        §13A-11-182.
Counties.
    Registration in county of
        residence,
        §13A-11-181.
Definitions, §13A-11-180.
Duty to register,
    §13A-11-181.
Exemptions, §13A-11-184.
Notice.
    Change of address or place
        of residence,
        §13A-11-183.
Penalties, §13A-11-186.
Place of residence.
    Notice of change,
        §13A-11-183.
Registration book.
    Access to book,
        §13A-11-185.
Resides.
    Defined, §13A-11-180.
Sheriff.
    Access to registration book,
        §13A-11-185.
    Informing of address or
        residence change,
        §13A-11-183.
    Registration with sheriff of
        county of residence,
        §13A-11-181.
Violations of article,
    §13A-11-186.

FELONIES—Cont'd
Repeat offenders. See within
    this heading, "Habitual
    felony offenders."
Reports.
Presentence investigation,
    §13A-5-5.
Robbery, §§13A-8-41 to
    13A-8-43.
Searches and seizures.
Search warrants.
    Commission of felony as
        grounds for issuance,
        §15-5-2.
**Second or subsequent
    offense.** See within this
    heading, "Habitual felony
    offenders."
Sentencing.
Capital offenses.
    See CAPITAL OFFENSES.
Capital punishment.
    See CAPITAL
        PUNISHMENT.
Definite term, §13A-5-6.
    Place of imprisonment,
        §13A-5-8.
Hard labor, §13A-5-6.
Limitation on term,
    §13A-5-6.
Presentence investigation,
    §13A-5-5.
Previous convictions,
    §15-18-9.
Sodomy, §§13A-6-63,
    13A-6-64.
**Speech pathologists and
    audiologists.**
Revocation or suspension of
    licenses, §34-28A-26.
Stolen property.
Receiving stolen property,
    §§13A-8-17, 13A-8-18.
Term of imprisonment.
Authorized disposition,
    §13A-5-2.
Theft.
Embezzlement.
    See EMBEZZLEMENT.
General provisions.
    See THEFT.
Treason, §13A-11-2.
Weapons.
Delivery of pistols to
    convicted felons,
    §13A-11-76.
Youthful offenders, §15-19-6.

FEMALES.
See WOMEN.

FENCES.
Abutting landowners.
Partition fences, §§35-7-1 to
    35-7-7.
See PARTITION.
Actions.
Partition fences, §35-7-7.
Animals, §§3-4-1 to 3-4-7.
See LIVESTOCK.
Barbed wire fences, §§3-4-1
    to 3-4-7.
See LIVESTOCK.
Common fences.
Allowing stock to run at
    large under, §13A-7-61.
Costs.
Partition fences.
    Action to recover, §35-7-7.
Definitions.
Partition fences, §35-7-1.

FENCES—Cont'd

Fees.
Partition fences.
Orders of court, §35-7-5.

Highways.
Detour fences.
Driving around, §23-5-2.

Joint tenants and tenants in common.
Partition fences, §§35-7-1 to 35-7-7.
See PARTITION.

Livestock, §§3-4-1 to 3-4-7.
See LIVESTOCK.

Oaths.
Partition fences.
Fence viewers, §35-7-6.

Orders of court.
Partition fences, §35-7-4.

Partition, §§35-7-1 to 35-7-7.
See PARTITION.

Railroads.
Cattle guards, §37-2-137.
Failure to fence railroads.
Liability for injury to stock, §37-2-89.
Notification of persons operating, §37-2-89.

Surveys and surveyors.
County surveyors.
Rights as to fences, §11-7-10.

Viewers.
Partition fences, §35-7-6.

FERRIES.

Beautification.
Federal assistance, §23-1-1.

Charter.
Special, private or local laws prohibited, Const. Ala., art. IV, §104.

Construction.
Federal assistance, §23-1-1.

Contracts.
Construction, etc.
Federal assistance, §23-1-1.

Counties.
Establishment and operation on rivers between two counties, §§11-49-20 to 11-49-23.
Licenses.
Annulment, §11-49-23.
Applications.
Notice, §11-49-22.
Procedure, §11-49-21.
Crossings.
Public road crossings, §11-49-23.
Granting, §§11-49-21, 11-49-22.
Nonconforming licenses, §11-49-23.
Notice of application, §11-49-22.
Rights of municipalities, §11-49-20.
Public roads, bridges and ferries, §§23-1-80 to 23-1-95.
See COUNTIES.

Licenses.
Establishment of ferries on rivers between two counties, §§11-49-20 to 11-49-23.
Special, private or local laws prohibited, Const. Ala., art. IV, §104.

FERRIES—Cont'd

Maintenance.
Federal assistance, §23-1-1.

Public roads, bridges and ferries, §§23-1-80 to 23-1-95.
See COUNTIES.

Rivers between two counties.
Establishment and operation, §§11-49-20 to 11-49-23.

Rules and regulations.
Federal assistance, §23-1-1.

FERTILIZER, §§2-22-1 to 2-22-23.

Administration of chapter, §2-22-3.

Adulteration, §2-22-17.

Analysis.
Commissioner of agriculture and industries, §2-22-11.
Results.
Furnishing results to licensees where fertilizers found subject to penalty or legal action, §2-22-11.

Brands and marks.
Misbranding, §2-22-16.

Classification standards.
Establishment, §2-22-15.
Plant nutrients.
Establishment of standards and minimum guarantees, §2-22-15.
Specialty fertilizers.
Adoption, §2-22-15.

Commercial fertilizers.
Licenses for sale. See within this heading, "Licenses."

Commissioner of agriculture and industries.
Administration of chapter, §2-22-3.
Annual publications, §2-22-19.
Sampling, §2-22-11.

Condemnation.
Noncomplying fertilizers, §2-22-21.

Contents.
Classification standards, §2-22-15.
Deficiency in guaranteed primary plant nutrients, §§2-22-12, 2-22-13.
Fair market values.
Ascertainment and publication, §2-22-14.

Dealers.
Permits, §2-22-4.
Licensees not required, §2-22-4.

Deficiency in guaranteed primary plant nutrients.
Proceedings upon determination, §2-22-12.
Recovery of penalty, §2-22-13.

Definitions, §2-22-2.
Adoption of regulations defining, §2-22-16.

Distributors.
Defined, §2-22-2.

Factories.
Licenses, §40-12-100.

Fees.
Inspections, §2-22-9.

FERTILIZER—Cont'd

Ingredients.
Classification standards, §2-22-15.
Fair market values.
Ascertainment and publication, §2-22-14.

Injunctions, §2-22-22.

Inspections, §2-22-11.
Fees, §2-22-9.
Results.
Furnishing of results to licensees where fertilizers found subject to penalty or legal action, §2-22-11.

Labels.
Defined, §2-22-2.
Generally, §2-22-7.
Soil conditioners and soil amendments.
Requirements, §2-22-8.

Licenses.
Applications, §2-22-5.
Cancellation, §2-22-6.
Fees, §2-22-5.
Refusal, §2-22-6.
Soil conditioners and soil amendments, §2-22-8.
Transfer, §2-22-5.

Manufacturers.
Penalty for fertilizer short in weight, §2-22-18.
Sales or exchanges between manufacturers, processors, etc., §2-22-23.

Misbranding, §2-22-16.

Motor vehicle carriers.
Vehicles hauling fertilizer.
Exemptions from chapter, §37-3-4.

Nitrogen, §§2-22-12 to 2-22-16.
Classification standards, §2-22-15.
Deficiency in guaranteed primary plant nutrients, §§2-22-12, 2-22-13.
Fair market values.
Ascertainment and publication, §2-22-14.
Regulation defining, §2-22-16.

Nutrients, §§2-22-12 to 2-22-16.
Deficiency in guaranteed primary plant nutrients, §§2-22-12, 2-22-13.
Fair market values of nitrogen, available phosphorus and soluble potassium.
Ascertainment and publication, §2-22-14.
Rules and regulations, §2-22-16.
Standards and minimum guarantees.
Establishment, §2-22-15.

Penalties.
Manufacture short in weight, §2-22-18.

Permits.
Dealers, §2-22-4.

Phosphorus, §§2-22-12 to 2-22-16.
Classification standards, §2-22-15.
Deficiency in guaranteed primary plant nutrients, §§2-22-12, 2-22-13.

FERTILIZER—Cont'd
Phosphorus—Cont'd
Fair market values.
Ascertainment and
publication, §2-22-14.
Regulations defining,
§2-22-16.
**Plant nutrients, §§2-22-12 to
2-22-16.**
**Potassium, §§2-22-12 to
2-22-16.**
Classification standards,
§2-22-15.
Deficiency in guaranteed
primary plant nutrients,
§§2-22-12, 2-22-13.
Fair market values.
Ascertainment and
publication, §2-22-14.
Regulations defining,
§2-22-16.
Processors.
Chapter not to restrict or
avoid sales or exchanges
between manufacturers,
processors, etc., §2-22-23.
Reports.
Tonnage reports, §§2-22-9,
2-22-10.
Rules and regulations.
Board of agriculture and
industries, §2-22-20.
Definition of commercial
fertilizer.
Adoption of regulations
defining, §2-22-16.
Noncompliance with rules
and regulations,
§2-22-21.
Promulgation, §2-22-20.
Violations.
Injunctions, §2-22-22.
Misdemeanors, §2-22-22.
Seizure and condemnation,
§2-22-21.
Suspension from sale,
§2-22-21.
Sales tax.
Exemptions, §40-23-4.
Samples.
Commissioner of agriculture
and industries, §2-22-11.
Official sample.
Defined, §2-22-2.
Results of sampling.
Furnishing results to
licensees, §2-22-11.
Seizure.
Noncomplying fertilizers,
§2-22-21.
Short title of chapter,
§2-22-1.
**Soil conditioners and soil
amendments.**
Licensing and labeling
requirements, §2-22-8.
Standards.
Classification standards,
§2-22-15.
Suspension from sale.
Noncomplying fertilizers,
§2-22-21.
Testing.
Commissioner of agriculture
and industries, §2-22-11.
Results.
Furnishing results to
licensees, §2-22-11.
Use tax.
Exemptions, §40-23-62.

FERTILIZER—Cont'd
Violations of chapter.
Injunctions, §2-22-22.
Misdemeanors, §2-22-22.
Seizure and condemnation,
§2-22-21.
Suspension from sale,
§2-22-21.
Weights and measures.
Short weight.
Penalty, §2-22-18.

FIDUCIARIES.
Administrators.
See EXECUTORS AND
ADMINISTRATORS.
**Banks and financial
institutions.**
Common trust funds,
§5-12A-8.
Conversion into or
consolidation with
national banks.
Continuation of
obligations, §5-7A-43.
Credit unions.
Deposits of fiduciary funds,
§5-17-4.
Fiduciary accounts.
Transfers, §§5-11A-30 to
5-11A-37.
See BANKS AND
FINANCIAL
INSTITUTIONS.
Savings and loan
associations, §5-16-43.
Trust companies purchasing
own securities in
fiduciary capacity,
§5-11A-12.
Bonds, surety.
Fiduciaries in war service,
§19-2-5.
Bribery.
Commercial bribery,
§13A-11-120.
Bulk transfers.
Excepted from article,
§7-6-103.
Canons of judicial ethics.
Fiduciary interest of judge.
Disqualifications, ACJE,
Canon 3C.
Permitted fiduciary
activities, ACJE, Canon
5D.
Restriction of fiduciary
activities, ACJE, Canon
5D.
Checks.
Drawn by and payable to
fiduciary, §19-1-6.
Third persons.
Drawn by fiduciary
payable to, §19-1-5.
Clerks of court.
Fiduciary funds in hands of
officials, §§19-2-80 to
19-2-83.
Commercial bribery,
§13A-11-120.
Commercial code.
See COMMERCIAL CODE.
Corporations.
Directors, officers, etc.
Fiduciary obligations,
§10-2A-76.

FIDUCIARIES—Cont'd
Counties.
Claims and demands against
counties.
Verification by fiduciaries,
§11-12-6.
County warrants.
Investment of trust funds.
Indebtedness for sanitary
sewer systems, §11-9-4.
Warrants for construction,
§11-28-5.
Waterworks systems
warrants, §11-9-25.
Credit unions.
Deposits of fiduciary funds,
§5-17-4.
Curators.
General provisions,
§§26-7A-1 to 26-7A-17.
See GUARDIAN AND
WARD.
Securities.
Fiduciary security
transfers, §§8-6-70 to
8-6-80.
See SECURITIES.
Definitions.
Fiduciaries in war service,
§19-2-1.
Securities held by fiduciaries,
§§19-4-1, 19-4-20,
19-4-40.
Uniform fiduciaries act,
§19-1-2.
Deposits.
Uniform fiduciaries act,
§§19-1-1 to 19-1-13. See
within this heading,
"Uniform fiduciaries
act."
Education.
Public school and college
authority.
Bond issues.
Investment of fiduciary
funds, §16-16-9.
Tax anticipation warrants in
cities and counties.
Investments for fiduciaries,
§16-13-74.
Embezzlement, §13A-9-51.
Executors.
See EXECUTORS AND
ADMINISTRATORS.
**Fiduciaries in war service,
§§19-2-1 to 19-2-5.**
Bonds, surety, §19-2-5.
Definitions, §19-2-1.
Removal, §19-2-2.
Notice of petition, §19-2-4.
Petition, §19-2-2.
Notice, §19-2-4.
Reappointment of removed
fiduciary, §19-2-3.
Representation by
attorney, §19-2-4.
Successors, §19-2-2.
**Fiduciary funds in hands of
officials, §§19-3-80 to
19-3-87. See within this
heading, "Public officers."**
Good faith.
Reliance on express
provisions of governing
instrument, §19-3-120.2.
Guardian ad litem.
See GUARDIAN AD LITEM.

FIDUCIARIES—Cont'd
Guardian and ward, §§26-2-1
to 26-5-54, 26-8-1 to
26-9-19.
See GUARDIAN AND
WARD.
**Health maintenance
organizations.**
Responsibilities of directors,
officers, etc., §27-21A-1.
Income tax.
Assessment.
Prompt assessment,
§40-18-45.
Declaration of estimated tax,
§40-18-85.
Defined, §40-18-1.
Payment, §40-18-25.
Installments, §40-18-42.
Time, §40-18-42.
Report from source.
Defined, §40-18-1.
Returns, §40-18-29.
Certification of knowledge
of affairs, §40-18-29.
Responsibility of fiduciary,
§40-18-25.
Investments.
Private corporations.
Authorization prohibited,
Const. Ala., art. IV,
§74.
Restrictions, Const. Ala.,
amd. 40.
Standards, §19-3-120.2.
Judges.
Canons of judicial ethics. See
within this heading,
"Canons of judicial
ethics."
Management of property.
Standards, §19-3-120.2.
Military affairs.
Fiduciaries in war service,
§§19-2-1 to 19-2-5.
Misapplication of property,
§13A-9-51.
Negotiable instruments.
Uniform fiduciaries act.
Transfer, §19-1-4.
Partnerships.
Definition of fiduciary,
§19-3-150.
Liability of, §19-3-151.
Liability of partnership for
breach, §10-8-54.
Limitation of liability,
§19-3-152.
Partner accountable,
§10-8-48.
Right to participate,
§19-3-151.
Probate judges.
Fiduciary funds in hands of
officials, §§19-3-81 to
19-3-85.
Property.
Management.
Standards, §19-3-120.2.
Public officers.
Fiduciary funds in hands of
officials, §§19-3-80 to
19-3-87.
Clerks, §§19-3-80 to
19-3-82.
Reports, §19-3-81.
Filing, §19-3-82.
Definition, §19-3-80.
Enforcement, §19-3-86.

FIDUCIARIES—Cont'd
Public officers—Cont'd
Fiduciary funds in hands of
officials—Cont'd
Probate judge.
Reports, §19-3-81.
Filing and recording,
§19-3-85.
Registers.
Reports, §19-3-81.
Filing, §19-3-82.
Reports, §§19-3-82 to
19-3-85.
Clerk, §19-3-82.
Filing, §§19-3-82,
19-3-83, 19-3-85.
Open to public, §19-3-84.
Probate judge, §19-3-85.
Register, §19-3-82.
Required, §19-3-81.
Sheriff, §19-3-83.
Sheriffs.
Reports, §19-3-81.
Filing, §19-3-83.
Unclaimed funds, §19-3-87.
**Public school and college
authority.**
Bond issues.
Investment, §16-16-9.
Public utilities.
Officers and directors,
§37-4-3.
Receivers.
General provisions, §§6-6-620
to 6-6-628.
See RECEIVERS.
Registers.
Fiduciary funds in hands of
officials, §§19-8-81,
19-8-82.
Removal.
Fiduciaries in war service,
§§19-2-2 to 19-2-4.
Sales.
Going out of business or
distress merchandise
sales, §§8-13-1 to
8-13-23.
See SALES.
**Savings and loan
associations.**
Accounts, §5-16-43.
Investments, §5-16-43.
**Securities held by
fiduciaries,** §§19-4-1 to
19-4-3, 19-4-20 to 19-4-22,
19-4-40 to 19-4-42.
Banks holding securities in
bulk, §§19-4-20 to
19-4-22.
Applicability of article,
§19-4-22.
Authorization, §19-4-21.
Certification, §19-4-21.
Definitions, §19-4-20.
Records, §19-4-21.
Registration, §19-4-21.
Rules and regulations,
§19-4-21.
Scope of article, §19-4-22.
Banks holding treasury
securities, §§19-4-40 to
19-4-42.
Applicability of article,
§19-4-42.
Authorization, §19-4-41.
Certification, §19-4-41.
Definitions, §19-4-40.
Records, §19-4-41.
Rules and regulations,
§19-4-41.

FIDUCIARIES—Cont'd
**Securities held by
fiduciaries**—Cont'd
Banks holding treasury
securities—Cont'd
Scope of article, §19-4-42.
Transfer, §19-4-41.
Definitions, §§19-4-1,
19-4-20, 19-4-40.
Deposit in closing
corporations, §§19-4-1 to
19-4-3.
Applicability of article,
§19-4-3.
Authorized, §19-4-2.
Certification, §19-4-2.
"Closing corporation"
defined, §19-4-1.
Definitions, §19-4-1.
Records, §19-4-2.
Rules and regulations,
§19-4-2.
Scope of article, §19-4-3.
Transfer, §19-4-2.
Deposit in federal reserve
banks.
Authorized, §19-4-41.
Security transfers, §§8-6-70 to
8-6-80.
See SECURITIES.
Sheriffs.
Fiduciary funds in hands of
officials, §§19-2-81,
19-2-83.
**Standards for investment
and management,**
§19-3-120.2.
Trusts and trustees, §§19-3-1
to 19-3-303.
See TRUSTS AND
TRUSTEES.
Unclaimed property.
Presumption of
abandonment.
Intangible property held by
fiduciaries, §35-12-27.
Uniform commercial code.
See COMMERCIAL CODE.
Uniform fiduciaries act,
§§19-1-1 to 19-1-13.
Application of payments,
§19-1-3.
Cases not provided for in
chapter, §19-1-12.
Chapter not retroactive,
§19-1-11.
Checks.
Drawn by and payable to
fiduciary, §19-1-6.
Payable to third person,
§19-1-5.
Definitions, §19-1-2.
Deposits, §§19-1-7 to 19-1-10.
In fiduciary's personal
account, §19-1-9.
In name of fiduciary as
such, §19-1-7.
In name of principal,
§19-1-8.
In names of two or more
fiduciaries, §19-1-10.
Interpretation.
Uniformity of
interpretation,
§19-1-13.
Negotiable instruments.
Transfer by fiduciary,
§19-1-4.
Payments.
Application, §19-1-3.

FIDUCIARIES—Cont'd
　Uniform fiduciaries act
　　—Cont'd
　　Short title of chapter,
　　　§19-1-1.
　USS Alabama battleship
　　commission.
　　Bond issues.
　　　Investments, §41-9-353.
　War service.
　　Fiduciaries in war service,
　　　§§19-2-1 to 19-2-5.
　Water system assistance
　　authority.
　　Investments, §22-23A-12.

FIGHTING.
　Boxing and wrestling,
　　§§40-23-2, 41-9-90.1 to
　　41-9-96.
　　See BOXING AND
　　　WRESTLING.
　Disorderly conduct,
　　§13A-11-7.

FILBERTS.
　Importation, §2-25-15.
　Promotion of industry
　　generally, §§2-8-120 to
　　2-8-137.
　　See NUTS.
　Sale or offer for sale,
　　§20-1-90.

FINANCE.
　Accounts and accounting.
　　Department of examiners of
　　　public accounts, §§41-5-1
　　　to 41-5-24.
　　See ACCOUNTS AND
　　　ACCOUNTING.
　　Division of control and
　　　accounts, §§41-4-50,
　　　41-4-54.
　　Inspection and production,
　　　§41-4-36.
　　Legislative committee on
　　　public accounts,
　　　§§41-5-18 to 41-5-20.
　Alabama building finance
　　authority, §41-10-2.
　Appropriations, §§41-4-90 to
　　41-4-97.
　　See LEGISLATURE.
　Banks and financial
　　institutions.
　　General provisions, §§5-1A-1
　　　to 5-13A-20.
　　See BANKS AND
　　　FINANCIAL
　　　INSTITUTIONS.
　Bond issues.
　　See BOND ISSUES.
　Bonds, surety.
　　Department of finance.
　　　Officers and chiefs of
　　　　divisions, §41-4-7.
　　Director of finance, §41-4-31.
　Budgets management,
　　§§41-19-1 to 41-19-12.
　　See BUDGETS.
　Buildings.
　　Alabama building finance
　　　authority, §41-10-2.
　　Department of finance.
　　　Rent charged for use,
　　　　§41-4-17.
　Claims based on void
　　warrants, §41-4-60.
　Companies.
　　Finance companies generally,
　　　§§5-18-1 to 5-18-24.
　　See SMALL LOANS.

FINANCE—Cont'd
　Companies—Cont'd
　　Insurance premium finance
　　　companies, §§27-40-1 to
　　　27-40-18.
　　See INSURANCE.
　Comptroller.
　　General provisions.
　　　See COMPTROLLER.
　Conflicts of interest.
　　Director of finance, §41-4-30.
　Constitution of Alabama.
　　Annual statement of receipts
　　　and expenditures.
　　　Publication, Const. Ala.,
　　　　art. IV, §72.
　　Payment of money out of
　　　state treasury, Const.
　　　Ala., art. IV, §72.
　Consumer finance, §§5-19-1
　　to 5-19-31.
　　See CONSUMER FINANCE.
　Contingent funds.
　　Evidence required for
　　　payment from, §41-4-56.
　Corrections.
　　Alabama corrections
　　　institution finance
　　　authority, §§14-2-1 to
　　　14-2-35.
　　See CORRECTIONS.
　　Capital outlay oversight
　　　commission, §14-1-18.
　Correctness of claim.
　　Proof, §41-4-61.
　Counties, §§11-8-1 to 11-8-17.
　　See COUNTIES.
　Data systems management.
　　Division of data systems
　　　management, §§41-4-220
　　　to 41-4-224.
　Definitions.
　　Department of finance,
　　　§41-4-1.
　　State funds.
　　　Linked deposits, §5-21-3.
　Department of finance.
　　Appropriations, §41-4-4.
　　　Estimates submitted,
　　　　§41-4-84.
　　Budget management act.
　　　See BUDGETS.
　　Buildings.
　　　Rent charged for use,
　　　　§41-4-17.
　　Chiefs of divisions, §§41-4-5
　　　to 41-4-7.
　　　Bonds, surety, §41-4-7.
　　　Full time service, §41-4-6.
　　　Merit system, §41-4-5.
　　　Oath of office, §41-4-6.
　　Comptroller.
　　　General provisions.
　　　　See COMPTROLLER.
　　Data systems management.
　　　Division of data systems
　　　　management.
　　　See DATA.
　　Definitions, §41-4-1.
　　Director of finance, §§41-4-30
　　　to 41-4-37. See within
　　　this heading, "Director of
　　　finance."
　　District electric corporations.
　　　Bond issues, §11-50-527.
　　Division of control and
　　　accounts.
　　　Comptroller.
　　　　See COMPTROLLER.
　　　Established, duties and
　　　　functions, §41-4-50.

FINANCE—Cont'd
　Department of finance
　　—Cont'd
　　Division of control and
　　　accounts—Cont'd
　　　Itemization of accounts
　　　　against state, §41-4-54.
　　Division of data systems
　　　management, §§41-4-220
　　　to 41-4-224.
　　Division of service.
　　　Chief of service, §41-4-181.
　　　Bond, surety, §41-4-7.
　　　Full time service,
　　　　§41-4-6.
　　　Oath of office, §41-4-6.
　　　Duties, §41-4-180.
　　　Established, §41-4-180.
　　　Police officers.
　　　　Employment, §41-4-182.
　　Division of the budget,
　　　§§41-4-80 to 41-4-96.
　　　See BUDGETS.
　　Divisions.
　　　Additional divisions,
　　　　§41-4-37.
　　　Assignment of duties,
　　　　§41-4-37.
　　　Division of control and
　　　　accounts, §41-4-50.
　　　Division of data systems
　　　　management,
　　　　§§41-4-220 to 41-4-224.
　　　See DATA.
　　　Division of purchasing,
　　　　§§41-4-110 to 41-4-115.
　　　See PURCHASES AND
　　　　STORES.
　　　Division of the budget,
　　　　§§41-4-80 to 41-4-96.
　　　See BUDGETS.
　　Duties.
　　　Director of finance,
　　　　§41-4-32.
　　　Generally, §41-4-3.
　　Educational and
　　　eleemosynary
　　　institutions.
　　　Powers and duties, §41-4-8.
　　Employees.
　　　Appointment, §41-4-5.
　　　Merit system, §41-4-5.
　　Estimates of income.
　　　Preparation, §41-4-85.
　　Expenditures, §41-4-4.
　　Federal grants, §41-4-9.
　　Head of department,
　　　§41-4-30.
　　Issuance of securities by
　　　state commissions,
　　　authorities, etc.,
　　　§41-4-16.
　　Legal division, §§41-4-200 to
　　　41-4-204.
　　　Chief of division,
　　　　§§41-4-201 to 41-4-204.
　　　Advice, §41-4-203.
　　　Appearance in financial
　　　　litigation, §41-4-203.
　　　Assistant attorney
　　　　general, §41-4-202.
　　　Bond, surety, §41-4-7.
　　　Duties, §41-4-202.
　　　Full time service,
　　　　§41-4-6.
　　　Head of division,
　　　　§41-4-201.
　　　Oath of office, §§41-4-6,
　　　　41-4-202.
　　　Opinions, §41-4-203.

FINANCE—Cont'd
Department of finance
—Cont'd
Legal division—Cont'd
Chief of division—Cont'd
Representation of state
board of adjustment,
§41-4-204.
Subject to merit system,
§41-4-5.
Vacancies in office,
§41-4-201.
Established, §41-4-200.
Licenses.
Small loans, §§5-18-1 to
5-18-9.
See SMALL LOANS.
Oaths of office.
Officers and chiefs of
divisions, §§41-4-6,
41-4-202.
Office of space management,
§§41-4-260 to 41-4-263.
Additional employees,
§41-4-263.
Director, §41-4-262.
Duties, §41-4-261.
Established, §41-4-260.
Officers, §§41-4-5 to 41-4-7.
Bonds, surety, §41-4-7.
Full time service, §41-4-6.
Oath of office, §41-4-6.
Subject to merit system,
§41-4-5.
Printing and publications.
Manager, §§41-4-240 to
41-4-242.
Purchases and stores.
Division of purchasing,
§§41-4-110 to 41-4-161.
See PURCHASES AND
STORES.
Purpose of department,
§41-4-2.
Seal, §41-4-2.
Voluntary nonprofit
ambulance service.
Transfer of surplus lands,
§41-4-33.2.
Voluntary nonprofit rescue
squads.
Transfer of surplus lands,
§41-4-33.2.
Volunteer fire departments.
Transfer of surplus lands,
§41-4-33.1.
White House of the
Confederacy.
Maintenance of building,
§41-12-2.
Depositaries.
State depositaries, §§41-14-1
to 41-14-16. See within
this heading, "State
funds."
Deposits.
State funds.
General provisions,
§§41-14-30 to 41-14-38.
See within this
heading, "State funds."
Linked deposits, §§5-21-1
to 5-21-11. See within
this heading, "State
funds."

FINANCE—Cont'd
Director of finance, §§41-4-30
to 41-4-37.
Alabama corrections
institution finance
authority.
Secretary of authority,
§14-2-6.
Appointment, §41-4-30.
Bond, surety, §41-4-31.
Additional bond, §§36-5-40,
36-5-41.
Capitol.
Duties, §41-4-34.
Chief financial officer,
§41-4-30.
Conflicts of interest,
§41-4-30.
Department of finance.
Assignment of duties,
§41-4-37.
Creation of additional
divisions, §41-4-37.
Divisions of department.
Assignment of duties,
§41-4-37.
Creation of additional
divisions, §41-4-37.
Duties of department,
§41-4-32.
Head of department,
§41-4-30.
Full time position, §41-4-30.
Governor.
Advisor to governor,
§41-4-30.
Head of department,
§41-4-30.
Highways.
Authority.
President of corporation,
§23-1-154.
Finance corporation.
Treasurer of corporation,
§23-1-174.
Inspections, §41-4-36.
Legislature.
Advisor to legislature,
§41-4-30.
Oath of office, §41-4-30.
Offices.
Duties, §41-4-34.
Police officers.
Employment at Capitol
and other state
buildings, §41-4-182.
Public lands.
Surplus lands, §41-4-33.
Records, §41-4-36.
Rules and regulations,
§41-4-36.
Secretary of state.
Disposal of certain books,
acts, codes, etc.
Returns and payments to
director, §36-14-7.
Surplus lands.
Sale, §41-4-33.
Synfuels development
authority.
Individuals who may
become public
corporation, §9-6A-3.
Term of office, §41-4-30.
Vacancies, §41-4-30.
Witnesses.
Examination, §41-4-36.

FINANCE—Cont'd
**Division of control and
accounts.**
Comptroller.
General provisions.
See COMPTROLLER.
Duties, §41-4-50.
Established, §41-4-50.
Functions, §41-4-50.
Itemization of accounts
against state, §41-4-54.
Division of purchasing.
General provisions,
§§41-4-110 to 41-4-161.
See PURCHASES AND
STORES.
Printing.
Public printing and
binding.
See PRINTING.
Division of the budget,
§§41-4-80 to 41-4-96.
See BUDGETS.
Education.
See EDUCATION.
Fiscal year of state, §1-3-4.
Funds.
Inactive funds.
Closing out, §41-4-64.
State funds, §§41-14-1 to
41-14-38. See within this
heading, "State funds."
State sinking fund, §§41-4-10
to 41-4-15. See within
this heading, "Sinking
fund."
**George Wallace, Jr., plan for
linked deposits of 1988.**
State funds.
Linked deposits, §§5-21-1
to 5-21-11. See within
this heading, "State
funds."
Governor.
Approval of vouchers or
accounts, §41-4-55.
Highways.
Alabama highway finance
corporation, §§23-1-170
to 23-1-181.
See HIGHWAYS.
Federal aid highway finance
authority, §§23-1-300 to
23-1-318.
See HIGHWAYS.
Inspections, §41-4-36.
**Insurance premium finance
companies,** §§27-40-1 to
27-40-18.
See INSURANCE.
Interest.
State funds.
Linked deposits, §5-21-7.
Investments.
State funds.
Bonds and notes of United
States or federal
agencies, §41-14-30.
Funds in treasury 30 days
or less, §41-14-32.
Itemization of accounts.
Accounts against state,
§41-4-54.
Legislative fiscal office,
§§29-5-1 to 29-5-10.
See LEGISLATURE.
Lost or unclaimed property.
Warrants.
Issuance of duplicates,
§41-4-58.

FINANCE—Cont'd
Mental health finance authority.
General provisions,
§§41-10-350 to 41-10-371.
See MENTAL HEALTH
FINANCE
AUTHORITY.
Printing.
Public printing and binding,
§§41-4-130 to 41-4-161.
See PRINTING.
Public accounts.
Department of examiners of
public accounts, §§41-5-1
to 41-5-24.
See ACCOUNTS AND
ACCOUNTING.
Legislative committee on
public accounts,
§§41-5-18 to 41-5-20.
Public money.
State funds, §§41-14-1 to
41-14-38. See within this
heading, "State funds."
**Public officers and
employees.**
Statement of expenses filed
with comptroller,
§41-4-57.
Records, §41-4-36.
Sinking fund, §41-4-14.
Reports.
State funds.
Linked deposits.
Annual report by
treasurer, §5-21-10.
Rules and regulations,
§41-4-35.
Sinking fund, §§41-4-10 to
41-4-15.
State treasurer.
Special trustee of state
sinking funds,
§36-17-17.
Use of funds in sinking fund,
§§41-4-10 to 41-4-15.
Deposit in savings banks,
§41-4-13.
Diversion of sinking fund,
§41-4-15.
Records, §41-4-14.
Reinvestment, §41-4-11.
Savings banks.
Deposits, §41-4-13.
State bonds, §§41-4-10 to
41-4-12.
Cancellation of paid
bonds, §41-4-11.
Purchase and holding in
trust, §41-4-10.
Purchase in lieu of use of
sinking fund,
§41-4-12.
Sale of bonds, §41-4-11.
State funds, §§5-21-1 to
5-21-11, 41-14-1 to
41-14-16, 41-14-30 to
41-14-36.
Actions, §6-5-4.
Conversion of public
revenues.
Limitation of prosecution,
§15-3-3.
Deposit.
Applicability of article,
§41-14-38.
Current operational
expenses, §41-14-31.
Daily expenditures,
§41-14-32.

FINANCE—Cont'd
State funds—Cont'd
Deposit—Cont'd
Demand deposits.
Apportionment among
state depositaries,
§41-14-31.
Current operational
expenses, §41-14-31.
Projected daily
expenditures,
§41-14-32.
Receipt of fee,
compensation, etc.,
for placement in,
§41-14-36.
Security for state money,
§41-14-35.
Fees, compensation, etc.
Placement in deposits,
§41-14-36.
Linked deposits, §§5-21-1
to 5-21-11.
Mental health finance
authority.
Bond issues.
Use of bonds as
security,
§41-10-362.
Monthly expenditures.
Determination,
§41-14-32.
Section 36-17-18 not
affected by article,
§41-14-37.
Security for state money,
§41-14-35.
Mental health finance
authority.
Bonds of authority,
§41-10-362.
Time deposits, open
account, §§41-14-32 to
41-14-36.
Contracts with state
depositories,
§41-14-33.
Emergency withdrawal,
§41-14-34.
Excess funds, §41-14-32.
Fee, compensation, etc.,
for placement in,
§41-14-36.
Interest.
Calculation, §41-14-34.
Payment, §41-14-34.
Rate, §41-14-33.
Projection of income
furnished to director,
§41-14-32.
Security for state money,
§41-14-35.
Withdrawal of funds.
Early withdrawal,
§41-14-33.
Emergency
withdrawal,
§41-14-34.
Treasurer.
Authority, §41-14-30.
Depositaries, §§41-14-1 to
41-14-16.
Application for
designation.
Filing, §41-14-2.
Certification, §41-14-3.
Statement as to assets,
etc., §41-14-2.
Bonds or securities.
Deposit, §§41-14-2,
41-14-3.

FINANCE—Cont'd
State funds—Cont'd
Depositaries—Cont'd
Bonds or securities—Cont'd
Registration, §41-14-10.
Sale of bonds, etc.,
deposited as security
upon failure of
depositary to pay
check of treasurer or
account for state
funds, §41-14-9.
Sale passes title,
§41-14-10.
Withdrawal when
ceasing to act as,
§41-14-12.
Collection methods,
§41-14-15.
Daily deposits, §41-14-8.
Designation.
Application, §§41-14-2,
41-14-3.
Governor may designate,
§41-14-1.
Revocation, §41-14-6.
Surrender.
Notice, §41-14-11.
Withdrawal of bonds
or securities,
§41-14-12.
Maximum amount
received, §41-14-5.
Remittance of excess
funds, §41-14-6.
Order declaring state
depositary.
Promulgation, §41-14-3.
Penalties, §41-14-16.
Public officers.
Deposit by state or
county officers,
§§41-14-5, 41-14-13,
41-14-14.
Receipts, §41-14-7.
Regulations, §41-14-15.
Removal of state funds.
Without cost, expense or
risk to state,
§41-14-4.
Reports, §41-14-8.
Statements of balance,
§41-14-8.
Surrender of designation.
Notice, §41-14-11.
Transfers.
Without cost, expense or
risk to state,
§41-14-4.
Violations of article,
§41-14-16.
Withdrawal of funds,
§41-14-6.
Investments.
Funds in treasury 30 days
or less, §41-14-32.
Notes and bonds of United
States or federal
agencies, §41-14-30.
Linked deposits, §§5-21-1 to
5-21-11.
Agreements between state
and eligible lending
institutions, §5-21-8.
Agricultural operations
loans, §5-21-5.
Eligible operation.
Defined, §5-21-3.
Authorized, §5-21-4.

FINANCE—Cont'd
State funds—Cont'd
Linked deposits—Cont'd
Business operations loans, §5-21-5.
Eligible operation.
Defined, §5-21-3.
Citation of plan.
Short title, §5-21-1.
Creation of plan, §5-21-4.
Definitions, §5-21-3.
Effective date, §5-21-11.
Forms.
Loan application forms, §5-21-9.
Interest, §5-21-7.
Legislative declaration, §5-21-2.
Lenders.
Agreements between state and eligible lending institutions, §5-21-8.
Defined, §5-21-3.
Discount points.
Lenders not entitled to charge, §5-21-6.
Fees, §5-21-6.
Participation in plan.
Procedures and requirements, §5-21-9.
Purpose of plan, §5-21-2.
Reports, §5-21-10.
Security of funds, §5-21-9.
Short title of plan, §5-21-1.
Termination date, §5-21-11.
Title of plan.
Short title, §5-21-1.
Treasurer.
Defined, §5-21-3.
Forms.
Providing, §5-21-9.
Reports, §5-21-10.
Sinking fund, §§41-4-10 to 41-4-15. See within this heading, "Sinking fund."
State treasurer.
See STATE TREASURER.
Taxation.
See TAXATION.
Vouchers.
Method of indicating governor's approval, §41-4-55.
Warrants.
Duplicate warrants.
Issuance, §41-4-58.
Execution, §41-4-59.
Expenses of state officers and employees.
Statement of expenses before warrant issued, §41-4-57.
Late presentation, §41-4-60.
Lost warrants.
Issuance of duplicates, §41-4-58.
Not to be drawn on treasury unless money available for payment, Const. Ala., amd. 26.
Outstanding and unpaid state warrants.
Interest, Const. Ala., amd. 26.
Void warrants, §41-4-60.
Witnesses.
Examination, §41-4-36.

FINANCE COMPANIES.
Insurance premium finance companies, §§27-40-1 to 27-40-18.
See INSURANCE.
Small loans, §§5-18-1 to 5-18-24.
See SMALL LOANS.

FINANCIAL INSTITUTIONS.
Banks, §§5-1A-1 to 5-13A-10.
See BANKS AND FINANCIAL INSTITUTIONS.
Credit unions, §§5-17-1 to 5-17-28.
See CREDIT UNIONS.
Industrial development corporations.
General provisions, §§10-4-130 to 10-4-152.
See INDUSTRIAL DEVELOPMENT CORPORATIONS.
Savings and loan associations, §§5-16-1 to 5-16-53.
See SAVINGS AND LOAN ASSOCIATIONS.
Trust companies, §§5-11A-1 to 5-11A-12.
See BANKS AND FINANCIAL INSTITUTIONS.

FINANCIAL RESPONSIBILITY.
Motor vehicle safety-responsibility act, §§32-7-1 to 32-7-42.
See MOTOR VEHICLES.

FINES.
See PENALTIES.

FINGERPRINTS.
Atomic energy.
Employees.
Electric generating facilities, §§22-14-31, 22-14-32.
Cards.
Furnishing sheriffs, §15-10-93.
Central state assembling agency, §15-10-91.
Criminal justice information center.
See CRIMINAL LAW AND PROCEDURE.
Envelopes.
Furnishing sheriffs, §15-10-93.
Equipment.
Cards and envelopes, §15-10-93.
Furnishing, §15-10-92.
Juvenile proceedings.
Taking and disposition, §12-15-102.
Persons taken into custody.
Copies.
Disposition, §15-10-90.
Duty of sheriff, §15-10-90.
Records.
Central state assembling agency, §15-10-91.
Youthful offenders.
Confidentiality of records, §15-19-7.

FIREARMS.
Weapons offenses generally, §§13A-11-50 to 13A-11-84.
See WEAPONS.

FIRE BOMBS.
Motor vehicles.
Throwing fire bombs into occupied vehicle, §32-5-11.

FIRE DEPARTMENTS.
General provisions.
See FIRES AND FIRE PREVENTION.
Municipal corporations, §§11-43-140 to 11-43-144.
Volunteer fire departments.
See FIRES AND FIRE PREVENTION.

FIRE INSURANCE.
See INSURANCE.

FIRE MARSHAL.
General provisions, §§36-19-1 to 36-19-29.
See FIRES AND FIRE PREVENTION.

FIRE PROTECTION SPRINKLER SYSTEMS, §§34-33-1 to 34-33-12.
See FIRES AND FIRE PREVENTION.

FIRE SALES.
Going out of business or distress merchandise sales, §§8-13-1 to 8-13-23.
See SALES.

FIRES AND FIRE PREVENTION.
Appeals.
Orders of fire marshal.
Appeal to circuit court, §36-19-12.
Appeals from, §36-19-13.
Appropriations.
Survivor's education assistance act, §36-21-105.
Arson, §§13A-7-40 to 13A-7-44.
Authorities.
Water, sewer and fire protection authorities, §§11-88-1 to 11-88-111.
See WATER, SEWER AND FIRE PROTECTION AUTHORITIES.
Bids and bidding.
Sprinkler systems.
Copies of chapter furnished, §34-33-10.
Civil defense.
General provisions, §§31-9-1 to 31-9-24.
See CIVIL DEFENSE.
Clarke county.
Fire districts, Const. Ala., amd. 464.
Coal mine safety, §§25-9-1 to 25-9-370.
See COAL.
Compacts.
Southeastern interstate forest fire protection compact, §§9-13-200, 9-13-201.
Constitution of Alabama.
Clarke county.
Fire districts, Const. Ala., amd. 464.

FIRES AND FIRE PREVENTION—Cont'd
Constitution of Alabama —Cont'd
Jackson county.
Fire districts and fire prevention services, Const. Ala., amd. 436.
Lee county.
Fire fighting districts, Const. Ala., amd. 498.
Marshall county.
Forest fire protection in, Const. Ala., amd. 439.
Monroe county.
Fire protection districts. Property taxes, Const. Ala., amd. 501.
Contractors.
Sprinkler systems generally, §§34-33-1 to 34-33-12. See within this heading, "Sprinkler systems."
Counties.
Fire fighters.
Personnel standards and education, §36-32-10.
Sprinkler systems.
Power of county to regulate work, §34-33-9.
Volunteer fire departments.
Donation of money, property, etc., §9-3-18.
Criminal law and procedure.
Arson, §§13A-7-40 to 13A-7-44.
False alarms, §13A-10-8.
Refusing to assist in fire control, §13A-10-6.
Reports.
Falsely reporting, §13A-11-11.
Death.
Fire fighters.
Compensation for death, §§36-30-1 to 36-30-7. See within this heading, "Fire fighters."
Tuition.
Survivor's education assistance act, §§36-21-100 to 36-21-105. See within this heading, "Survivor's education assistance act."
Definitions.
Fire fighters.
Compensation for death, §36-30-1.
Personnel standards and education commission, §36-32-1.
Insurer, §36-19-40.
Sprinkler systems, §34-33-1.
Survivor's education assistance act, §36-21-101.
Diseases.
Fire fighters.
Unknown cure for disease. Preference given in admission to research programs, §36-21-11.
Explosives.
See EXPLOSIVES AND EXPLOSIONS.

FIRES AND FIRE PREVENTION—Cont'd
Factories.
Fire marshal.
Regulation of doors and exits, §36-19-10.
False alarms, §13A-10-8.
Fees.
Fire marshal. See within this heading, "Fire marshal."
Sprinkler systems.
Certified fire protection sprinkler contractors. Payment of local license fees, §34-33-8.
State fire marshal's permit. Application fees, §34-33-4.
Fire departments.
Fire fighters. See within this heading, "Fire fighters."
Municipal corporations, §§11-43-140 to 11-43-144. See MUNICIPAL CORPORATIONS.
Strikes.
Municipal or state fire fighters, §11-43-143.
Unions.
Right to join, §11-43-143.
Volunteer fire departments.
Certification, §9-3-17.
Definition of volunteer fire fighters, §36-32-1.
Donation of money, property, etc.
Authority of governmental entities, §9-3-18.
Legislative intent, §9-3-18.
Liability.
Preserving and protecting burning buildings, etc.
Exemption from liability, §6-5-335.
Licenses.
Exemptions, §40-9-13.
Surplus lands.
Transfer, §41-4-33.1.
Taxation.
Exemptions, §40-9-13.
Training requirements, §36-32-7.
Fire fighters.
Benefits.
Compensation for death, §§36-30-1 to 36-30-7.
Compensation for death, §§36-30-1 to 36-30-7.
Amount, §36-30-2.
Awarding authority.
Decision final, §36-30-7.
Defined, §36-30-1.
Entry of judgment and order for payment, §36-30-6.
Hearing and determination of claims, §36-30-6.
Claims.
Determination, §36-30-5.
Hearing, §36-30-6.
Presentation, §36-30-5.
Construction of article, §36-30-7.
Death from occupational disease, §11-43-144.
Deaths deemed compensable, §36-30-2.

FIRES AND FIRE PREVENTION—Cont'd
Fire fighters—Cont'd
Compensation for death —Cont'd
Definitions, §§36-30-1, 36-32-1.
Dependents.
Persons deemed, §36-30-1.
Evidence.
Determination of claims, §36-30-5.
Payment, §36-30-3.
Order, §36-30-6.
United States residents only, §36-30-4.
Death.
Compensation for death, §§36-30-1 to 36-30-7.
Survivor's education assistance act, §§36-21-100 to 36-21-105. See within this heading, "Survivor's education assistance act."
Diseases.
Unknown cure for disease. Preference given in admission to research programs, §36-21-11.
Education.
Personnel standards and education, §§36-32-1 to 36-32-12.
Survivor's education assistance act, §§36-21-100 to 36-21-105. See within this heading, "Survivor's education assistance act."
Good Samaritan act, §6-5-332.
Payrolls.
Deduction, §36-1-4.2.
Personnel standards and education, §§36-32-1 to 36-32-12.
Character, §36-32-7.
Clerical assistants, §36-32-3.
Commission.
Appointment of members, §36-32-2.
Bylaws.
Adoption, §36-32-2.
Inspection, §36-32-6.
Keeping current, §36-32-6.
Composition, §36-32-2.
Creation, §36-32-2.
Defined, §36-32-1.
Duties, §36-32-5.
Functions, §36-32-5.
Meetings, §36-32-4.
Mutual assistance agreements, §36-32-11.
Qualifications of members, §36-32-2.
Quorum, §36-32-4.
Regulations, §36-32-6.
Seal, §36-32-4.
Terms of office, §36-32-2.
Compensation of members, §36-32-3.

**FIRES AND FIRE
PREVENTION**—Cont'd
Fire fighters—Cont'd
Personnel standards and
education—Cont'd
Counties.
Appropriations and
grants, §36-32-10.
Curriculum requirements,
§36-32-5.
Definitions, §36-32-1.
Executor director, §36-32-3.
Fund.
Appropriations.
Acceptance and
disposition,
§36-32-9.
Municipalities and
counties,
§36-32-10.
Creation, §36-32-9.
Defined, §36-32-1.
Grants.
Acceptance and
disposition,
§36-32-9.
Municipalities and
counties,
§36-32-10.
Minimum standards,
§36-32-7.
Penalty for failing to
meet, §36-32-8.
Municipal corporations.
Appropriations and
grants, §36-32-10.
Powers and duties,
§36-32-12.
Officers, §36-32-3.
Physical qualifications,
§36-32-7.
Trainees.
Defined, §36-32-1.
Minimum standards,
§36-32-7.
Training.
Minimum standards,
§36-32-7.
Volunteer fire fighters.
Defined, §36-32-1.
Training requirements,
§36-32-7.
Salaries.
Deductions, §36-1-4.2.
Survivor's education
assistance act,
§§36-21-100 to 36-21-105.
See within this heading,
"Survivor's education
assistance act."
Training.
Minimum standards,
§36-32-7.
Fire marshal, §§36-19-1 to
36-19-29.
Appeals.
Orders, §§36-19-12,
36-19-13.
Appointment, §27-2-10.
Arrest.
Power, §36-19-18.
Arson.
Insurers.
Suspecting.
Notice to, §36-19-42.
Assistants.
Appointment, §27-2-10.
Fees.
Payment to local
assistants,
§36-19-23.

**FIRES AND FIRE
PREVENTION**—Cont'd
Fire marshal—Cont'd
Assistants—Cont'd
Inspections, §36-19-11.
Investigation of fires,
§36-19-5.
Persons deemed assistants,
§36-19-3.
Police powers, §36-19-1.
Powers and duties,
§§36-19-2, 36-19-3.
Reporting of fires,
§§36-19-5, 36-19-6.
Bonds, surety, §27-2-10.
Books.
Production, §36-19-19.
Buildings.
Inspection, §36-19-11.
Regulations for protection,
§36-19-9.
Repair upon failure of
party to obey order of
court, §36-19-14.
Lien for expenses,
§36-19-15.
Combustible matter.
Removal, §§36-9-11 to
36-9-13.
Commissioner of insurance.
Appointment, etc., of state
fire marshal, §27-2-10.
Compensation, §27-2-10.
Deputies.
Inspections, §36-19-11.
Police powers, §36-19-1.
Powers and duties
generally, §36-19-2.
Deputy inspectors, §36-19-7.
District attorneys.
Furnishing of information,
§36-19-18.
Duties, §27-2-10.
Generally, §36-19-2.
Expenses of department,
§36-19-8.
Explosives.
Regulations for keeping,
storing, etc., §36-19-9.
Fees.
Assistants.
Payment to local
assistants,
§36-19-23.
Disposition, §36-19-29.
Witnesses and officers
serving subpoenas,
§36-19-22.
Fire drills, §36-19-10.
Fireworks.
Enforcement of article,
§8-17-211.
Searches and seizures,
§§8-17-221, 8-17-225.
Forfeitures.
Disposition, §36-19-29.
Inspections.
Buildings, §36-19-11.
Right of entry, §36-19-4.
Investigations.
Assistants, §36-19-5.
District attorneys.
Assistance to fire
marshal, §36-19-16.
Insurer must release
relevant information,
§36-19-41.
Insurer to cooperate with
law enforcement
agency, §36-19-41.

**FIRES AND FIRE
PREVENTION**—Cont'd
Fire marshal—Cont'd
Investigations—Cont'd
Noncompliance by insurers
with disclosure
provisions.
Penalties, §36-19-44.
Right of entry, §36-19-4.
Taking of testimony,
§36-19-17.
Mobile homes.
See MOBILE HOMES.
Orders, §§36-19-11 to
36-19-13.
Appeal to circuit court,
§36-19-12.
Appeal from, §36-19-13.
Issuance, §36-19-11.
Penalties.
Disposition, §36-19-29.
Failure to comply with
requirements of fire
marshal, §36-19-27.
Powers.
Generally, §36-19-2.
Police powers, §36-19-1.
Qualifications, §27-2-10.
Records, §36-19-25.
Removal, §27-2-10.
Reports.
Annual report, §36-19-26.
Assistants reporting fires,
§§36-19-5, 36-19-6.
Insurance companies.
Confidentiality of,
§36-19-43.
Fire losses, §36-19-24.
Nonliability for reports
made without fraud
or malice, §36-19-43.
Right of entry, §36-19-4.
Rules and regulations,
§36-19-9.
Schools.
Regulation of fire drills,
doors and exits,
§36-19-10.
Sprinkler systems.
Administration of chapter,
§34-33-2.
Permits.
State fire marshal's
permit, §§34-33-4 to
34-33-8.
Subpoenas.
Fees of officers serving,
§36-19-22.
Testimony.
Taking during
investigations,
§36-19-17.
Witnesses.
Fees, §36-19-22.
Imprisonment for
contempt, §36-19-21.
Subpoenas.
Fees of officers serving,
§36-19-22.
Summoning, §36-19-19.
**Fire protection sprinkler
systems,** §§34-33-1 to
34-33-12. See within this
heading, "Sprinkler
systems."
Fireworks, §§8-17-210 to
8-17-226.
See FIREWORKS.
Forest fires.
See FORESTS AND
FORESTRY.

FIRES AND FIRE PREVENTION—Cont'd

Gifts.
Sprinkler systems.
Grants and donations allowed, §34-33-11.

Good Samaritan act.
Firemen rendering first aid or emergency care, §6-5-332.

Hospitals.
Fire marshal.
Regulation of doors and exits, §36-19-10.

Insurance.
Fire insurance.
See INSURANCE.

Investigations.
Fire marshal. See within this heading, "Fire marshal."

Jackson county.
Fire districts and fire prevention services, Const. Ala., amd. 436.

Jails, §§14-6-8, 14-6-103.

Lee county.
Fire fighting districts, Const. Ala., amd. 498.
Financial charges or assessments, Const. Ala., amd. 498.

License plates.
Fire fighters.
Special plates, §§40-12-270 to 40-12-274.

Limestone county.
Establishment of fire districts, Const. Ala., amd. 371.

Madison county.
Establishment of fire districts, Const. Ala., amd. 378.

Marshal.
State fire marshal, §§36-19-1 to 36-19-29. See within this heading, "Fire marshal."

Marshall county.
Forest fire protection, Const. Ala., amd. 439.

Misdemeanors.
Sprinkler systems.
Violations of provisions, §34-33-12.

Monroe county.
Fire protection districts.
Property tax, Const. Ala., amd. 501.

Montgomery county.
Establishment of fire districts, Const. Ala., amd. 379.

Motor vehicles.
Fire fighters.
Special plates or tags, §§40-12-270 to 40-12-274.
Flammable liquid.
Defined, §32-1-1.1.
Sirens and warning devices, §32-5-213.
Speed limits.
When speed limit not applicable, §32-5A-7.
Stopping, standing and parking.
Privileges, §32-5A-7.
Stop signals and stop signs.
Proceeding through, §32-5A-7.

FIRES AND FIRE PREVENTION—Cont'd

Municipal corporations.
Class 1 municipalities.
Firemen's pensions and relief plans.
Benefits, §11-40-18.
Codes.
Adoption, §11-45-8.
Fire departments, §§11-43-140 to 11-43-144.
Fire fighters' personnel standards and education.
Appropriations and grants, §36-32-10.
Powers and duties, §36-32-12.
Fire limits, §11-43-59.
Sprinkler systems.
Power to regulate contractors, §34-33-9.

Peace officers.
Assistance in fire control, §13A-10-6.

Penalties.
Fire fighters.
Personnel standards and education.
Failure to meet standards, §36-32-8.
Fire marshal, §§36-19-27, 36-19-29.
Sprinkler systems, §34-33-12.

Permits.
Sprinkler systems.
State fire marshal's permit, §§34-33-4 to 34-33-8.

Police.
Assistance in fire control, §13A-10-6.

Public lands.
Enforcement of state fire laws, §9-15-34.

Railroad locomotives.
Devices to prevent escape of fire, §9-13-14.

Reciprocity.
Sprinkler systems.
State fire marshal's permit, §34-33-4.

Reports.
Fire marshal. See within this heading, "Fire marshal."

Rules and regulations.
Fire fighters' personnel standards and education commission, §36-32-6.
Promulgation by fire marshal, §36-19-9.

Russell county.
Establishment of fire fighting districts, Const. Ala., amd. 381.

Schools.
Lands.
Enforcement of fire laws, §9-15-34.

Southeastern interstate forest fire protection compact, §§9-13-200, 9-13-201.

Sprinkler systems, §§34-33-1 to 34-33-12.
Administration of chapter, §34-33-2.
Application of chapter, §34-33-10.
Bids and bidding.
Copies of chapter furnished to invited bidders, §34-33-10.

FIRES AND FIRE PREVENTION—Cont'd

Sprinkler systems—Cont'd
Compliance with chapter.
Installation or repair, §34-33-3.
Required before contract awarded, §34-33-10.
Contracts.
Compliance with chapter, §34-33-10.
Definitions, §34-33-1.
Disposition of funds collected, §34-33-11.
Donations allowed, §34-33-11.
Fees.
Certified fire protection sprinkler contractors.
Local license fees, §34-33-8.
State fire marshal's permit.
Application fees, §34-33-4.
Fire marshal.
Administration of chapter, §34-33-2.
State fire marshal's permit, §§34-33-4 to 34-33-8.
Gifts.
Grants and donations allowed, §34-33-11.
Grants and donations allowed, §34-33-11.
Installation, repair, maintenance or inspection.
Application for state fire marshal's permit, §34-33-4.
Conformity with chapter, §34-33-3.
Misdemeanors, §34-33-12.
Municipal corporations.
Regulation of contractors.
Chapter imposes no limitation on power, §34-33-9.
Penalties, §34-33-12.
Permits.
State fire marshal's permit, §§34-33-4 to 34-33-8.
Reciprocity.
State fire marshal's permit, §34-33-4.
State fire marshal.
Administration of chapter, §34-33-2.
Permit, §§34-33-4 to 34-33-8.
State fire marshal's permit.
Applications, §34-33-4.
Competency test, §34-33-4.
Copy to accompany bid, §34-33-10.
Disposition of funds, §34-33-11.
Expiration, §34-33-7.
Fees.
Application, §34-33-4.
Local license fees, §34-33-8.
Issuance, §34-33-5.
Limitations upon permit holder, §34-33-6.
Local license fees, §34-33-8.
Names noted on certificate, §34-33-5.
Presentation to local building official, §34-33-8.

**FIRES AND FIRE
PREVENTION**—Cont'd
Sprinkler systems—Cont'd
State fire marshal's permit
—Cont'd
Reciprocity, §34-33-4.
Renewal, §34-33-7.
Restrictions upon permit
holder, §34-33-6.
Status of applicant,
§34-33-4.
Terms, §34-33-7.
Violations of chapter,
§34-33-11.
State.
Volunteer fire departments.
Donation of money,
property, etc.
Authority of state to
donate, §9-3-18.
State fire marshal.
General provisions, §§36-19-1
to 36-19-29. See within
this heading, "Fire
marshal."
**Survivor's education
assistance act,**
§§36-21-100 to 36-21-105.
Applications, §36-21-103.
Appropriations, §36-21-105.
Assistance authorized,
§36-21-102.
Board, §36-21-104.
Citation of act, §36-21-100.
Definitions, §36-21-101.
Eligibility for benefits,
§36-21-102.
Eligible programs.
Defined, §36-21-101.
Forms, §36-21-103.
Title of act.
Short title, §36-21-100.
Tuition.
Defined, §36-21-101.
Training of fire fighters.
Minimum standards,
§36-32-7.
Tuition.
Survivor's education
assistance act,
§§36-21-100 to 36-21-105.
See within this heading,
"Survivor's education
assistance act."
Volunteer fire departments.
See within this heading,
"Fire departments."
**Water, sewer and fire
protection authorities,**
§§11-88-1 to 11-88-111.
See WATER, SEWER AND
FIRE PROTECTION
AUTHORITIES.
**Water, sewer and fire
protection districts,**
§§11-89-1 to 11-89-19.
See WATER, SEWER AND
FIRE PROTECTION
DISTRICTS.
Witnesses.
Fire marshal. See within this
heading, "Fire marshal."

FIREWORKS, §§8-17-210 to
8-17-226.
Applicability of article,
§8-17-223.
Definitions, §8-17-210.
Display.
Requirements generally,
§8-17-221.

FIREWORKS—Cont'd
Distributors.
Defined, §8-17-210.
Fees.
Permits, §8-17-211.
Fire marshal.
Enforcement of article,
§8-17-211.
Searches and seizures.
Authority, §§8-17-221,
8-17-225.
**Identification marks on
items.**
Requirements generally,
§8-17-219.
Incapacitated persons.
Sales, §8-17-222.
Inspections.
Permits.
Renewal at same location,
§8-17-221.
State fire marshal may
inspect, §8-17-221.
Licenses.
Dealers, §40-12-102.
**Local acts or city
ordinances.**
Effect of article, §8-17-226.
Manufacturers.
Defined, §8-17-210.
Minors.
Sales, §8-17-222.
Mobile buildings.
Sales from, §8-17-221.
Modular buildings.
Sales from, §8-17-221.
Motor vehicles.
Sales from motor vehicles,
§8-17-221.
Ordinances.
Effect of article on validity,
§8-17-226.
Penalties, §8-17-224.
Permissible items, §8-17-217.
Conformance to
nomenclauture,
§8-17-219.
Sales.
Authorization for retail
sales, §8-17-220.
Permits, §§8-17-210 to
8-17-216.
Age restrictions, §8-17-211.
Applications, §8-17-211.
Authority conferred by
permit, §8-17-211.
Defined, §8-17-210.
Display, §8-17-211.
Duration of permits,
§8-17-211.
Enforcement of article,
§8-17-211.
Fees, §8-17-211.
Inspections.
Renewal at same location,
§8-17-221.
Issuance, §8-17-211.
License requirements.
Effect of article on,
§8-17-215.
Numbers.
Assignment and
utilization, §8-17-212.
Record of sales, §8-17-211.
Keeping of records,
§8-17-213.
Requirements generally,
§8-17-211.
Revocation, §8-17-214.
Rules and regulations,
§8-17-211.

FIREWORKS—Cont'd
Permits—Cont'd
Sales, §8-17-213.
Special fireworks, §8-17-216.
Taxation.
Valid sales tax number,
§8-17-215.
Transfer, §8-17-211.
Records.
Keeping of records by permit
holders, §8-17-213.
Sales, §8-17-211.
Retailers.
Defined, §8-17-210.
Sales.
Defined, §8-17-210.
Incapacitated persons,
§8-17-222.
Mail orders.
Prohibited, §8-17-211.
Minors, §8-17-222.
Mobile buildings.
Sales from, §8-17-221.
Modular buildings.
Sales from, §8-17-221.
Motor vehicles.
Sales from, §8-17-221.
Permissible items.
Retail sales, §8-17-220.
Permits.
Consignees to produce
permit prior to
delivery or sale,
§8-17-213.
Purchasers to obtain proof
of permit, §8-17-213.
Required, §8-17-211.
Record of sales, §8-17-211.
Special fireworks.
Class B commercial type
ground salutes,
§8-17-218.
Items for which permit not
required, §8-17-220.
Tents.
Retail sales from tents,
§8-17-221.
Searches and seizures.
Authority of state fire
marshal, §§8-17-221,
8-17-225.
Special fireworks.
Class B commercial type
ground salutes.
Sale or use, §8-17-218.
Defined, §8-17-210.
Permits, §8-17-216.
Sales.
Class B commercial type
ground salutes,
§8-17-218.
Items for which permit not
required, §8-17-220.
Storage, §8-17-221.
Taxation.
Permits.
Valid sales tax number,
§8-17-215.
Tents.
Retail sales from tents,
§8-17-221.
Violations of provisions,
§8-17-224.
Wholesalers.
Defined, §8-17-210.

FISCAL YEAR OF STATE,
§1-3-4.

FISH AND GAME.
  Accidents.
    Hunting deaths.
      Reporting of accidents,
        §9-11-21.
  Agents.
    Special agents.
      Licenses. See within this
        heading, "Licenses."
  Amusements.
    Possession of wildlife for
      public exhibition
      purposes, §§9-11-320 to
      9-11-328. See within this
      heading, "Exhibitions."
  Appeals, §§9-11-14, 9-11-15.
  Arrest.
    Violations of fish and game
      laws.
      Arrest without warrant,
        §9-11-8.
      Fees of arresting officers,
        §9-11-12.
  Aviation.
    Use of aircraft for hunting,
      etc., prohibited, §4-2-9.
  Bait.
    Game fish.
      Use for bait generally,
        §9-11-89.
      Sunfish, §9-11-90.
    Hunting.
      Taking of protected birds
        or animals by means
        of bait, §9-11-244.
      Penalties, §9-11-246.
    Shrimp.
      See MARINE
        RESOURCES.
  Baskets.
    Catching of nongame fish
      with wire baskets,
      §§9-11-190 to 9-11-198.
      See within this heading,
      "Wire baskets."
  Bass.
    Largemouth bass.
      State fresh water fish,
        §1-2-9.
  Beaver.
    Hunting, §9-11-262.
  Birds.
    Commercial fowl hunting
      preserves, §§9-11-410 to
      9-11-419. See within this
      heading, "Commercial
      fowl hunting preserves."
    Enumeration of birds not
      protected, §9-11-233.
    Hunting, §§9-11-232,
      9-11-233.
    Migratory birds, §9-11-263.
    Migratory water fowl,
      §§9-11-430 to 9-11-434.
    Nests.
      Destruction, §9-11-232.
    Protected wild birds,
      §§9-11-232, 9-11-233.
    Quail.
      Commercial quail
        breeding, §§9-11-340 to
        9-11-351. See within
        this heading, "Quail."
  Bonds, surety.
    Fur dealers.
      Nonresidents, §9-11-253.
    Game and fish division.
      Director, §9-2-63.
    Licenses.
      Special agents, §§9-11-39,
        9-11-40.

FISH AND GAME—Cont'd
  Bonds, surety—Cont'd
    Wardens, §9-2-64.
  Boundaries.
    Wildlife management areas,
      §9-11-301.
  Bounties.
    Beavers.
      Killing of beavers,
        §9-11-262.
  Breeders.
    Licenses, §§9-11-30, 9-11-31.
    Propagation. See within this
      heading, "Propagation."
    Quail.
      Commercial quail
        breeding, §§9-11-340 to
        9-11-351. See within
        this heading, "Quail."
    Sales.
      Procedures, §9-11-31.
  Buildings.
    Propagation of fish and
      game.
      Erection or purchase of
        buildings, §9-11-2.
  **Butchering, etc., of legally
    taken wild animals,**
    §22-20-6.
  Catfish.
    Generally, §§2-8-270 to
      2-8-291.
      See CATFISH.
    Marketing, §§2-11-30 to
      2-11-40.
      See CATFISH.
    Promotion, Const. Ala., amd.
      492.
  Commercial code.
    Secured transactions.
      When security interest
        attaches, §7-9-204.
  **Commercial fee fishing
    ponds.**
    Compliance with provisions,
      §§9-11-450 to 9-11-457.
      Required, §9-11-450.
    Creel limits, §9-11-455.
    Farm or hatchery produced
      fish.
      Ponds to be stocked with,
        §9-11-452.
    Fines.
      Violations of provisions,
        §9-11-457.
    Fishing license.
      Not required, §9-11-454.
    Limits on taking of fish.
      Creel limits, §9-11-455.
    Penalties.
      Fine for violations,
        §9-11-457.
    Permits.
      Applications, §9-11-453.
      Display of letter permit,
        §9-11-454.
      Issuance, §9-11-453.
      Required, §9-11-450.
    Selling of fish caught,
      §9-11-456.
    Signs.
      Entrance to be marked,
        §9-11-451.
    Sites, §9-11-451.
      Marking of entrance with
        sign, §9-11-451.
    Stocking of ponds.
      Farm or hatchery produced
        fish, §9-11-452.
    Violations of provisions.
      Fine, §9-11-457.

FISH AND GAME—Cont'd
  Commercial fishing.
    Baskets.
      Catching of nongame fish
        with wire baskets,
        §§9-11-190 to 9-11-198.
        See within this
        heading, "Wire
        baskets."
    Fees.
      Commercial fee fishing
        ponds, §§9-11-450 to
        9-11-457. See within
        this heading,
        "Commercial fee
        fishing ponds."
    Freshwater nongame fish
      dealers, §§9-11-153,
      9-11-154.
    Licenses.
      General provisions. See
        within this heading,
        "Licenses."
    Public impounded waters
      and navigable streams,
      §§9-11-141 to 9-11-146.
    Navigable streams,
      §§9-11-141 to 9-11-146.
    Public impounded waters and
      navigable streams.
      Applicability of article,
        §9-11-155.
      Boats and motors.
        Violations of article.
          Seizures, §9-11-156.
      Dams or locks.
        Use of fishing gear
          within one-half mile
          below lock or dam,
          §9-11-149.
      Disposition of proceeds,
        §9-11-146.
      Exemptions from article,
        §9-11-155.
      Fishing gear.
        Confiscation.
          Violation of article,
            §9-11-151.
        Identification, §9-11-147.
        Location.
          Marking location of,
            §9-11-147.
        Seizure.
          Violation of article,
            §9-11-151.
        Use within one-half mile
          below lock or dam,
          §9-11-149.
        Use within 100 yards of
          mouths of streams
          emptying into salt
          waters or bays,
          §9-11-150.
        Violations of article.
          Seizures, §9-11-156.
      Game fish, §9-11-148.
      How permitted, §9-11-140.
      Licenses.
        Expiration, §9-11-144.
        Fees, §9-11-143.
          Disposition,
            §§9-11-143,
            9-11-146.
        Forfeiture.
          Violation of article,
            §9-11-145.
        Individual licenses
          required, §9-11-142.
        Issuance, §9-11-143.
        Qualifications of
          applicant, §9-11-143.

FISH AND GAME—Cont'd
Commercial fishing—Cont'd
Public impounded waters and
navigable streams
—Cont'd
Licenses—Cont'd
Records, §9-11-143.
Reports, §9-11-143.
Required, §9-11-141.
Individual licenses
required,
§9-11-142.
Term, §9-11-144.
Penalties.
Violations of article,
§9-11-156.
Salt waters or bays.
Use of fishing gear
within 100 yards of
mouths of streams
emptying into salt
waters or bays,
§9-11-150.
Searches and seizures.
Fish illegally transported
or shipped,
§9-11-152.
Fishing gear.
Used in violation of
article, §9-11-151.
Violations of article,
§9-11-156.
Transportation of fish.
Violation of article,
§9-11-152.
Violations of article.
Licenses.
Forfeiture, §9-11-145.
Penalties, §9-11-156.
Seizure, confiscation and
disposition of fishing
gear, §9-11-151.
Shipment or
transportation of fish
taken in violation of
article, §9-11-152.
When permitted,
§9-11-140.
Where permitted,
§9-11-140.
Marking location of
fishing gear,
§9-11-147.
Salt water fishing.
See MARINE
RESOURCES.
Spearfishing, §§9-11-170 to
9-11-176. See within this
heading, "Spearfishing."
Violations of fish and game
laws, §§9-11-6 to 9-11-15.
See within this heading,
"Violations of fish and
game laws."
**Commercial fowl hunting
preserves,** §§9-11-410 to
9-11-419.
Area.
Restrictions, §9-11-411.
Bob-white quail.
Hunting on preserve
authorized, §9-11-412.
Tagging, §9-11-415.
Boundaries.
Marking, §9-11-411.
Chuckar partridge.
Hunting on preserve
authorized, §9-11-412.

FISH AND GAME—Cont'd
**Commercial fowl hunting
preserves**—Cont'd
Commissioner of
conservation and natural
resources.
Operators to cooperate
with, §9-11-415.
Enforcement of game and
fish laws, §9-11-418.
Fowl to be hunted, §9-11-412.
Harvest.
Limits, §9-11-414.
Inspection, §9-11-418.
Licenses.
Applications, §9-11-413.
Fee, §9-11-413.
Disposition of fees,
§9-11-413.
Hunting licenses.
Operators as agent
vendors, §9-11-417.
Required of patrons,
§9-11-417.
Required, §9-11-410.
Revocation.
Violations of provisions,
§9-11-419.
Pen-raised birds.
Exception to harvest
limits, §9-11-414.
Hunting period, §9-11-414.
Pheasants.
Hunting on preserve
authorized, §9-11-412.
Proximity to other preserves
or management areas,
§9-11-411.
Records, §9-11-416.
Rules and regulations.
Compliance required,
§9-11-410.
Signs.
Marking of boundaries,
§9-11-411.
Stock released for hunting.
Requirements, §9-11-412.
Tags.
Bob-white quail, §9-11-415.
Turkey shooting prohibited,
§9-11-411.
Violations of provisions,
§9-11-419.
Commercial fur catchers. See
within this heading, "Fur
catchers."
Commercial quail breeding,
§§9-11-340 to 9-11-351. See
within this heading,
"Quail."
**Commissioner of
conservation and
natural resources.**
Peace officer.
Commissioner constituted
peace officer, §9-11-5.
Powers and duties, §9-2-7.
Propagation. See within this
heading, "Propagation."
Rules and regulations.
Promulgation, §9-2-8.
Common carriers.
Transporting protected birds
or game.
Liabilities, §9-11-256.
Conservation officers.
General provisions. See
within this heading,
"Wardens."
Title defined, §9-2-28.

FISH AND GAME—Cont'd
Constitution of Alabama.
Fund, Const. Ala., amd. 272.
Coon on the log contests,
§§9-11-247 to 9-11-249.
Corporations.
Violations of fish and game
laws.
Warrants.
Service and return of
warrant, §9-11-9.
Counties.
Acquisition of lands for
public purposes.
Use of land for betterment
of fish and game,
§11-18-2.
Licenses.
Hunting license, §9-11-44.
Crows.
Hunting.
Unprotected birds,
§9-11-233.
Dealers.
Freshwater nongame fish
dealers.
Licenses, §9-11-153.
Records.
Inspection, §9-11-154.
Maintenance, §9-11-154.
Fur dealers. See within this
heading, "Fur dealers."
Live fish and minnow
dealers.
Nonresidents.
Licenses.
Fees, §9-11-58.
Required, §9-11-58.
Death.
Hunting deaths, §9-11-21.
Deeds.
State game lands, §9-11-3.
Deer.
Hunting.
General provisions. See
within this heading,
"Hunting."
Licenses. See within this
heading, "Licenses."
Definitions, §9-11-1.
Exhibitions.
Possession of wildlife for
public exhibition
purposes, §9-11-320.
Fur dealers, §9-11-62.
Migratory water fowl,
§9-11-430.
Public and private waters,
§9-11-80.
Quail.
Commercial quail
breeding, §9-11-340.
Spearfishing, §9-11-170.
**Department of conservation
and natural resources.**
Division of game and fish,
§§9-2-60 to 9-2-65. See
within this heading,
"Division."
Powers and duties.
General provisions, §9-2-2.
Disabled persons.
Licenses.
Fishing licenses.
Special annual fishing
license, §9-11-54.
District attorneys.
Violations of fish and game
laws.
Prosecution, §9-11-7.

FISH AND GAME—Cont'd
District courts.
Violations of fish and game
laws.
Jurisdiction, §9-11-6.
Division, §§9-2-60 to 9-2-65.
Control.
Director, §9-2-61.
Creation, §9-2-60.
Director, §§9-2-61 to 9-2-65.
Appointment, §9-2-64.
Bonds, surety, §9-2-63.
Full-time position, §9-2-62.
Oath of office, §9-2-62.
Powers and duties.
Game and fish wardens,
§9-2-65.
Expenses.
Game and fish fund.
Payment from fund,
§9-2-22.
Personnel, §9-2-61.
Powers and duties.
General provisions,
§9-2-61.
Supervision.
Director, §9-2-61.
Dogs.
Hunting wild turkeys,
§9-11-238.
Trainers.
Licenses, §9-11-52.
Wildlife management areas.
Impoundment.
Procedure, §9-11-306.
Redemption or
destruction of
impounded dogs,
§9-11-306.
Running at large.
Liability of owners,
§9-11-305.
When dogs permitted,
§9-11-305.
**Duty of care owed persons
on premises for sporting
or recreational purposes,**
§§35-15-1 to 35-15-5.
Education.
Exemptions.
Gross proceeds from the
sales of certain fish
feeds, §40-23-4.
Electricity.
Fishing.
Catching or killing of fish
by electrical devices,
§9-11-94.
Endowment fund, §9-2-20.1.
English sparrows.
Hunting.
Unprotected birds,
§9-11-233.
Evidence.
Spearfishing.
Possession of spear,
§9-11-175.
Exhibitions.
Possession of wildlife for
public exhibition
purposes, §§9-11-320 to
9-11-328.
Applicability of article,
§9-11-328.
Compliance with article,
§9-11-321.
Definitions, §9-11-320.
Enforcement of article,
§9-11-326.
Exemptions from article,
§9-11-328.

FISH AND GAME—Cont'd
Exhibitions—Cont'd
Possession of wildlife for
public exhibition
purposes—Cont'd
Inspection of facilities.
Condition in permit,
§9-11-325.
Penalties.
Violations, §9-11-327.
Permits, §§9-11-324 to
9-11-327.
Applications, §9-11-324.
Conditions.
Inspections, §9-11-325.
Enforcement of
conditions,
§9-11-326.
Fees, §9-11-324.
Inspection of facilities.
Condition in permit,
§9-11-325.
Issuance, §9-11-324.
Violations.
Penalties, §9-11-327.
Standards for care and
treatment.
Appointment of
committee to study
and recommend,
§9-11-322.
Committee.
Appointment of
committee to study
and recommend,
§9-11-322.
Compliance with,
§9-11-321.
Enforcement, §9-11-326.
Promulgation of
regulations,
§9-11-323.
Regulations.
Promulgation,
§9-11-323.
Violations.
Penalties, §9-11-327.
Violations, §§9-11-325,
9-11-327.
Explosives.
Fishing.
Catching or killing of fish,
§9-11-93.
Private ponds, lakes, pools
or reservoirs, §9-11-91.
Hunting.
Taking of protected birds
or animals by use of
explosives, §9-11-245.
Penalties, §9-11-246.
Fees.
Commercial fee fishing
ponds, §§9-11-450 to
9-11-457.
Licenses. See within this
heading, "Licenses."
Field assistant.
Appointment.
Commissioner of
conservation and
natural resources,
§9-2-64.
Firearms.
Wildlife management areas.
Carrying or possession of
firearms, §9-11-304.
Fishing.
Bait.
Game fish.
Sunfish, §9-11-90.
Use generally, §9-11-89.

FISH AND GAME—Cont'd
Fishing—Cont'd
Baskets.
Catching of nongame fish
with wire baskets,
§§9-11-190 to 9-11-198.
See within this
heading, "Wire
baskets."
Commercial fee fishing
ponds, §§9-11-450 to
9-11-457.
Commercial fishing,
§§9-11-140 to 9-11-156.
See within this heading,
"Commercial fishing."
Definitions.
Public and private waters,
§9-11-80.
Duty of care owed persons on
premises for sporting or
recreational purposes,
§§35-15-1 to 35-15-5.
Electrical devices, §9-11-94.
Explosives.
Catching or killing of fish,
§9-11-93.
Private ponds, lakes, etc.,
§9-11-91.
Fish farms.
Unauthorized fishing from
farm prohibited,
§9-11-91.1.
Freshwater nongame fish
dealers, §§9-11-153,
9-11-154.
Game fish.
Bait.
Use for bait, §9-11-90.
Commercial fishing.
General provisions,
§§9-11-140 to
9-11-156. See within
this heading,
"Commercial
fishing."
Designation, §9-11-82.
Means of catching,
§9-11-87.
Nets.
Use of gill, trammel,
etc., nets, §9-11-88.
Sale.
Restrictions, §9-11-84.
Searches and seizures.
Confiscation of game fish
taken or transported
illegally, §9-11-85.
Transportation, §§9-11-84
to 9-11-86.
Beyond boundaries of
state, §9-11-86.
Confiscation of fish
transported illegally,
§9-11-85.
Fish to be transported
openly, §9-11-85.
Outside of state,
§9-11-86.
Penalties, §9-11-85.
Purposes of sale,
§9-11-84.
Wire baskets.
Return of game fish
taken to waters,
§9-11-196.
Garfish.
Killing before returning to
waters, §9-12-112.
Licenses. See within this
heading, "Licenses."

FISH AND GAME—Cont'd
Fishing—Cont'd
Marine resources, §§9-12-1 to
9-12-184.
See MARINE
RESOURCES.
Means of catching fish.
Electrical devices,
§9-11-94.
Explosives, §9-11-93.
Game fish, §9-11-87.
Gill, trammel, etc., nets,
§9-11-88.
Means not expressly
allowed, §9-11-94.
Nets, §9-11-88.
Poisons and poisoning,
§9-11-93.
Nets, §9-11-88.
Private ponds, lakes, etc.,
§9-11-91.
Nongame fish.
Catching with wire
baskets, §§9-11-190 to
9-11-198. See within
this heading, "Wire
baskets."
Dealers, §§9-11-153,
9-11-154.
Designation, §9-11-83.
Nets.
Use of gill, trammel,
etc., nets, §9-11-88.
Penalties.
Disposition of fines,
§9-11-95.
Fish farms.
Unauthorized fishing
from farm.
Violations of
provisions,
§9-11-91.1.
Game fish.
Catching by unlawful
means, §9-11-87.
Sale, §9-11-84.
Transportation, §9-11-84.
Beyond boundaries of
state, §9-11-86.
Fish to be transported
openly, §9-11-85.
Private ponds, lakes, pools
or reservoirs.
Catching of fish,
§9-11-91.
Pike county public lake.
Fishing without paying
admission fee,
§9-11-66.
Poisons.
Killing of fish, §9-11-93.
Private ponds, lakes, etc.,
§9-11-91.
Private ponds and lakes.
Catching of fish, §9-11-91.
Private waters.
Defined, §9-11-80.
Public waters.
Defined, §9-11-80.
Real property.
Recreational or sporting
premises liability,
§§35-15-1 to 35-15-28.
See REAL PROPERTY.
Reciprocal agreements as to
freshwater fishing,
§§9-11-210 to 9-11-213.
Rights and privileges
exercised in accordance
with Alabama laws,
§9-11-213.

FISH AND GAME—Cont'd
Fishing—Cont'd
Reciprocal agreements as to
freshwater fishing
—Cont'd
Waters lying between
Alabama and adjoining
states.
Agreements as to fishing
in waters, §9-11-211.
Agreements to apply
separately to waters
lying between
Alabama and each
agreeing bordering
state, §9-11-212.
Waters of Alabama and of
bordering states.
Agreements as to
fishing, §9-11-210.
Reservoirs.
Catching of fish, §9-11-91.
Saltwater fishing, §§9-12-1 to
9-12-184.
See MARINE
RESOURCES.
Shellfish, §§9-12-1 to
9-12-184.
See MARINE
RESOURCES.
Spearfishing, §§9-11-170 to
9-11-174.
Title.
Freshwater fish, §9-11-81.
Traps.
Passage of fish up rivers or
creeks.
Preventing, §9-11-92.
Violations of fish and game
laws, §§9-11-6 to 9-11-15.
See within this heading,
"Violations of fish and
game laws."
Wildlife management areas.
Closing of land or water in
areas to fishing,
§9-11-302.
Wire baskets.
Catching of nongame fish
with wire baskets,
§§9-11-190 to 9-11-198.
See within this
heading, "Wire
baskets."
Fishing ponds.
Commercial fee fishing
ponds, §§9-11-450 to
9-11-457. See within this
heading, "Commercial
fee fishing ponds."
**Fish restoration and
management projects.**
Assent to federal act,
§9-11-19.
Establishment, §9-11-19.
Flattened musk turtle.
Protection, §9-11-269.
Forests and forestry.
National forests.
Shooting preserves, game
refuges, etc.
Establishment, §9-11-4.
Forfeitures.
Prohibited devices used in
hunting, fishing or
trapping, §9-11-16.
Free fishing day, §9-11-56.2.
Fund, §§9-2-20 to 9-2-23;
Const. Ala., amd. 272.
Composition, §9-2-20.
Creation, §9-2-20.

FISH AND GAME—Cont'd
Fund—Cont'd
Credit of fund.
Remission of collections to
state treasurer,
§9-2-21.
Disbursements, §9-2-22.
Diversion of funds from
particular purposes,
§9-2-23.
Endowment fund.
Created, §9-2-20.1.
Purposes, §9-2-22.
Diversion of funds from
particular purpose,
§9-2-23.
Remittance of collections.
Credit of fund, §9-2-21.
Fur catchers.
Licenses.
Fees, §9-11-59.
Disposition of proceeds,
§9-11-60.
Penalties, §9-11-59.
Qualification of applicant,
§9-11-59.
Reports of license issued,
§9-11-60.
Required, §9-11-59.
Transporting furs, skins
or pelts, §9-11-61.
Transporting furs, skins or
pelts, §9-11-61.
Penalties.
Licenses.
Violation of provisions,
§9-11-59.
Transporting furs without
license, §9-11-61.
Traps.
Limitation as to number,
§9-11-254.
Violations of provisions,
§9-11-268.
Sales.
Licensed fur dealers,
§9-11-237.
Transporting furs, skins or
pelts.
Licenses, §9-11-61.
Traps.
Bait.
Hanging or suspending
over or within 25
feet of steel trap,
§9-11-266.
Penalty, §9-11-268.
Checking, §9-11-266.
Penalty for violations,
§9-11-268.
Highways.
Trapping on or from
right-of-way of state
highway, §9-11-265.
Applicability in
Limestone county,
§9-11-265.1.
Exemption of
Lawrence county,
§9-11-265.
Penalties, §9-11-268.
Liability for injury or
damage to persons or
domestic animals,
§9-11-264.
Applicability of sections
in Limestone county,
§9-11-265.1.
Exemption of Lawrence
county, §9-11-264.

FISH AND GAME—Cont'd
Fur catchers—Cont'd
Traps—Cont'd
Number of traps.
Limitation, §9-11-254.
Penalties for violations,
§9-11-268.
Reports required,
§9-11-267.
Penalty for violations,
§9-11-268.
Fur dealers.
Bonds, surety.
Nonresidents, §9-11-253.
Defined, §9-11-62.
Inspections.
Books and records,
§9-11-64.
Licenses, §9-11-63.
Nonresidents.
Bonds, surety, §9-11-253.
License fee, §9-11-63.
Presumptions as to
dealership, §9-11-62.
Records.
Inspection, §9-11-64.
Reports.
Animals trapped,
purchased, etc.,
§9-11-267.
Penalty for violations,
§9-11-268.
Sales.
Furs to fur dealers,
§9-11-237.
Furs.
Catchers.
General provisions. See
within this heading,
"Fur catchers."
Dealers.
General provisions. See
within this heading,
"Fur dealers."
Sales.
Dealers.
Sales to licensed dealers,
§9-11-237.
Transportation.
Taxation.
Shipment without
payment of state tax,
§9-11-253.
Game lands of state,
§§9-11-2, 9-11-3.
Garfish.
Killing before returning to
waters, §9-12-112.
Grading and standards of
farm products and fish,
§§2-11-50 to 2-11-59.
See AGRICULTURE.
Grand jury.
Hunting deaths.
Investigation, §9-11-21.
Health.
Nuisances menacing public
health, §§22-10-1 to
22-10-3.
Hides, etc..
Sales, §9-11-237.
Highways.
Hunting or discharge of
firearm from, upon or
across highways,
§9-11-257.
Hunting within one hundred
yards of public roads or
highways, §9-11-257.

FISH AND GAME—Cont'd
Hunting.
Accidents.
Deaths.
Reporting of accidents,
§9-11-21.
Aircraft.
Use of aircraft for hunting,
etc., prohibited, §4-2-9.
Bait.
Taking of protected birds
or animals by means
of bait, §9-11-244.
Penalties, §9-11-246.
Beavers.
Bounty, §9-11-262.
Season.
Opening or closing of
season, §9-11-262.
Birds.
Commercial fowl hunting
preserves, §§9-11-410
to 9-11-419. See within
this heading,
"Commercial fowl
hunting preserves."
Crows.
Unprotected birds,
§9-11-233.
English sparrows.
Unprotected birds,
§9-11-233.
Enumeration of birds not
protected, §9-11-233.
Migratory water fowl,
§§9-11-430 to 9-11-434.
Protected wild birds.
Possession, sale,
purchase, etc,
§9-11-232.
Starlings.
Unprotected birds,
§9-11-233.
Bounties.
Beavers, §9-11-262.
Collection for scientific
purposes.
Permits, §9-11-231.
Commercial fowl hunting
preserves, §§9-11-410 to
9-11-419. See within this
heading, "Commercial
fowl hunting preserves."
Deaths, §9-11-21.
Deer.
Female deer, §9-11-239.
Opening of season,
§9-11-240.
Nighttime, §9-11-251.
Liability for killing
stock, §9-11-258.
Penalties, §9-11-252.
Vehicles, weapons and
equipment used in
nighttime deer
hunting.
Seizure, §9-11-252.1.
Public waters, §9-11-252.
Unantlered male deer,
§9-11-239.
Opening of season,
§9-11-240.
Waters and watercourses.
Taking of deer from
public waters,
§9-11-250.
Penalties, §9-11-252.
Wildlife management
areas.
Licenses, §9-11-45.

FISH AND GAME—Cont'd
Hunting—Cont'd
Dogs.
Hunting wild turkeys,
§9-11-238.
Explosives.
Taking of protected birds
or animals by use of
explosives, §9-11-245.
Penalties, §9-11-246.
Foxes.
Nighttime, §9-11-235.
Fur catchers. See within this
heading, "Fur catchers."
Highways.
Hunting or discharge of
firearm from, upon or
across highways,
§9-11-257.
Lands of another.
Daytime.
Hunting or trapping
without permission,
§9-11-241.
Nighttime.
Hunting or trapping
without permission,
§9-11-242.
Within ten feet of banks of
water.
Hunting or trapping of
fur-bearing animals
without permission,
§9-11-243.
Without permission.
Daytime, §9-11-241.
Fur-bearing animals
within ten feet of
banks of water,
§9-11-243.
Nighttime, §9-11-242.
Licenses. See within this
heading, "Licenses."
Livestock.
Deer.
Persons hunting deer at
night.
Liable for killing
stock, §9-11-258.
Migratory water fowl,
§§9-11-430 to 9-11-434.
Nets.
Taking of protected birds
or animals by use of
nets, §9-11-245.
Penalties, §9-11-246.
Nighttime.
Deer, §9-11-251.
Liability for killing
stock, §9-11-258.
Penalties, §9-11-252.
Vehicles, weapons and
equipment used in
nighttime deer
hunting.
Condemnation and
forfeiture,
§9-11-252.1.
Contraband,
§9-11-252.1.
Seizure, §9-11-252.1.
Foxes, §9-11-235.
Lands of another.
Hunting or trapping
without permission,
§9-11-242.
Opossums, §9-11-235.
Weapons used,
§9-11-235.1.

FISH AND GAME—Cont'd
  Hunting—Cont'd
    Nighttime—Cont'd
      Raccoons, §9-11-235.
        Weapons used,
          §9-11-235.1.
        Taking of protected birds
          or animals, §9-11-235.
      Opossums.
        Nighttime, §9-11-235.
          Weapons used,
            §9-11-235.1.
    Penalties.
      Deer.
        Female deer and
          unantlered male
          deer, §9-11-239.
        Nighttime.
          Taking of protected birds
            or animals,
            §9-11-235.
      Seasons.
        Hunting of or possession
          of protected birds or
          animals during
          closed season,
          §9-11-236.
      Wild turkeys.
        Hens, §9-11-239.
        Hunting with dogs,
          §9-11-238.
    Permits.
      Collection for scientific
        purposes, §9-11-231.
    Poisons.
      Taking of protected birds
        or animals by use of
        poisons, §9-11-245.
        Penalties, §9-11-246.
    Preserves.
      Commercial fowl hunting
        preserves, §§9-11-410
        to 9-11-419. See within
        this heading,
        "Commercial fowl
        hunting preserves."
    Public roads.
      Hunting or discharge of
        firearm from, upon or
        across public roads,
        §9-11-257.
      Within one hundred yards
        of public roads or
        highways, §9-11-257.
    Raccoons.
      Coon on the log contests,
        §§9-11-247 to 9-11-249.
      Nighttime, §9-11-235.
        Weapons used,
          §9-11-235.1.
    Railroads.
      Hunting or discharge of
        firearm from, upon or
        across railroads,
        §9-11-257.
    Real property.
      Recreational or sporting
        premises liability,
        §§35-15-1 to 35-15-28.
        See REAL PROPERTY.
    Reciprocal agreements as to
      waterfowl hunting,
      §§9-11-280 to 9-11-283.
      Exercise of rights and
        agreements in
        accordance with
        Alabama law,
        §9-11-283.

FISH AND GAME—Cont'd
  Hunting—Cont'd
    Reciprocal agreements as to
      waterfowl hunting
      —Cont'd
      Waters lying between
        Alabama and adjoining
        states, §9-11-281.
      Agreements to apply
        separately,
        §9-11-282.
      Waters of Alabama and of
        bordering states,
        §9-11-280.
    Refuges, §§9-11-4, 9-11-234.
    Sales.
      Game birds or game
        animals, §9-11-237.
    Scaffolds.
      Use for hunting, §9-11-245.
    Seasons.
      Beavers, §9-11-262.
      Closed season.
        Hunting of or possession
          of protected birds or
          animals, §9-11-236.
      Deer.
        Female deer and
          unantlered male
          deer.
        Opening of season,
          §9-11-240.
      During closed season,
        §9-11-236.
      Nonresidents.
        Reciprocity, §9-11-49.1.
    Shooting preserves.
      Federal lands, §9-11-4.
    Spotlighting, §32-5-17.
    Sundays.
      Prohibited, §13A-12-1.
    Title to wild birds and
      animals.
      Vested in state, §9-11-230.
    Turkeys.
      Wild turkeys, §§9-11-238,
        9-11-239.
    Violations of fish and game
      laws. See within this
      heading, "Violations of
      fish and game laws."
    Waters and watercourses.
      Ten feet of banks of water.
        Property of another
          without permission,
          §9-11-243.
    Wildlife management areas,
      §§9-11-301 to 9-11-307.
      See within this heading,
      "Wildlife management
      areas."
    Wild turkeys.
      Dogs.
        Hunting with dogs,
          §9-11-238.
      Hens, §9-11-239.
    Wildlife management
      areas.
      Licenses, §9-11-45.
  Importation.
    Rules and regulations.
      Penalties.
        Violations, §9-2-13.
        Promulgation, §9-2-13.
  **Impounded waters and
    navigable streams.**
    Commercial fishing,
      §§9-11-140 to 9-11-156.
      See within this heading,
      "Commercial fishing."

FISH AND GAME—Cont'd
  Income tax.
    Voluntary check-off
      designations on state
      income tax returns.
      Alabama nongame wildlife
        program, §§40-18-143
        to 40-18-145.
  Inspections.
    Dealers.
      Freshwater nongame fish
        dealers.
        Records, §9-11-154.
    Exhibitions.
      Possession of wildlife for
        public exhibition
        purposes.
        Condition in permits to
          allow inspections,
          §9-11-325.
    Fur dealers.
      Books and records,
        §9-11-64.
    Quail.
      Commercial quail
        breeding.
        Records and premises,
          §9-11-349.
    Spearfishing.
      Licenses, §9-11-172.
  Investigations.
    Hunting deaths.
      Grand jury, §9-11-21.
  Judgments.
    Violations of fish and game
      laws.
      Appeals.
        Judgment on appeal,
          §9-11-15.
  Lands.
    State game lands.
      Acquisition of land.
        Authority of
          commissioner,
          §9-11-2.
  Largemouth bass.
    State fresh water fish, §1-2-9.
  Licenses.
    Applications.
      False statements, §9-1-1.
    Blank licenses.
      Delivery to issuing
        authorities, §9-11-41.
      Furnishing to issuing
        authorities, §9-11-33.
      Return of unused licenses,
        §9-11-33.
    Borrowing, §9-1-3.
    Breeders, §§9-11-30, 9-11-31.
    Cards.
      Printing on cards of
        distinctive and
        different colors,
        §9-11-34.
    Commercial fishing,
      §§9-11-141 to 9-11-146.
      See within this heading,
      "Commercial fishing."
    Commercial fowl hunting
      preserves. See within
      this heading,
      "Commercial fowl
      hunting preserves."
    Commissioner.
      Responsibility of license
        commissioner as to
        licenses, §9-11-43.
    Dealers.
      Freshwater nongame fish
        dealers, §§9-11-153,
        9-11-154.

FISH AND GAME—Cont'd
Licenses—Cont'd
Dealers—Cont'd
Fur dealers. See within
this heading, "Fur
dealers."
Dogs.
Trainers, §9-11-52.
Duration, §9-11-32.
Exemptions.
Military affairs.
Members of armed forces
during war,
§9-11-35.
Fees.
Commercial fishing.
Public impounded waters
and navigable
streams, §9-11-143.
Dealers.
Freshwater nongame fish
dealers, §9-11-153.
Fur dealers, §9-11-63.
Live fish and minnow
dealers.
Nonresidents,
§9-11-58.
Erroneous or excessive
fees.
Refunds, §9-2-25.
Fishing licenses, §9-11-53.
Disabled persons,
§9-11-54.
Disposition of revenue,
§9-11-53.
Exemptions, §9-11-53.
Lifetime resident
hunting, fishing and
combination licenses,
§9-11-65.
Nonresidents.
Annual license,
§9-11-55.
Commercial license,
§9-11-56.1.
Trip license, §9-11-56.
Fur catchers, §9-11-59.
Fur dealers, §9-11-63.
Game breeder's license,
§9-11-30.
Hunting licenses, §9-11-44.
Disposition, §9-11-44.
Exemptions, §9-11-44.
Lifetime resident
hunting, fishing and
combination licenses,
§9-11-65.
Issuance on
combination basis,
§9-11-65.1.
Nonresidents, §9-11-49.1.
All game, §9-11-47.
Exemptions, §9-11-44.
Reciprocity, §9-11-49.1.
Small game only,
§9-11-46.
Trip all game,
§9-11-49.
Trip small game,
§9-11-48.
Wildlife management
areas.
Deer or wild turkey,
§9-11-45.
Issuance fees, §9-11-37.
Remittance, §9-11-37.
Lifetime resident hunting,
fishing and
combination licenses.
Issuance on combination
basis, §9-11-65.1.

FISH AND GAME—Cont'd
Licenses—Cont'd
Fees—Cont'd
Quail.
Commercial quail
breeding, §9-11-342.
Refunds.
Erroneous or excessive
fees, §9-2-25.
Special agents.
Remittance of fees
collected, §9-11-42.
Wire baskets.
Catching of nongame
fish with wire
baskets, §9-11-191.
Fishing licenses.
Borrowing, §9-11-53.
Commercial fee fishing
ponds.
Fishing license not
required, §9-11-454.
Commercial fishing,
§§9-11-141 to 9-11-146.
See within this
heading, "Commercial
fishing."
Disabled persons.
Special license, §9-11-54.
Exemptions, §9-11-53.
Annual free fishing day,
§9-11-56.2.
Fees, §9-11-53.
Disabled persons,
§9-11-54.
Disposition of revenue,
§9-11-53.
Exemptions, §9-11-53.
Nonresidents.
Annual license,
§9-11-55.
Commercial license,
§9-11-56.1.
Trip license, §9-11-56.
Hook and line license,
§9-11-53.
Lifetime resident hunting,
fishing and
combination licenses,
§9-11-65.
Issuance on combination
basis, §9-11-65.1.
Nonresidency.
Effect, §9-11-65.
Nonresidents, §§9-11-55 to
9-11-56.1.
Annual license, §9-11-55.
Commercial license,
§9-11-56.1.
Fees.
Annual license,
§9-11-55.
Commercial license,
§9-11-56.1.
Trip license, §9-11-56.
Penalties.
Violations of
provisions,
§§9-11-55, 9-11-56.
Trip license, §9-11-56.
Nontransferable, §9-11-53.
Penalties, §9-11-53.
Fishing without license,
§9-11-57.
Nonresidents.
Violations of
provisions,
§§9-11-55, 9-11-56.
Reciprocal agreement with
Florida, §9-11-53.

FISH AND GAME—Cont'd
Licenses—Cont'd
Fishing licenses—Cont'd
Required, §9-11-53.
Commercial fee fishing
ponds.
Exception to
requirement,
§9-11-454.
Fishing without license.
Penalties, §9-11-57.
Fur catchers, §§9-11-59 to
9-11-61.
Fur dealers, §9-11-63.
Hunting licenses, §§9-11-48
to 9-11-51.
Application, §9-11-44.
County license, §9-11-44.
Deer.
Wildlife management
areas, §9-11-45.
Duplicate license, §9-11-44.
Exemptions, §9-11-44.
Persons under 16 years
of age, §9-11-50.
Hunting without license,
§9-11-51.
Lifetime resident hunting,
fishing and
combination licenses,
§9-11-65.
Issuance on combination
basis, §9-11-65.1.
Nonresidency.
Effect, §9-11-65.
Minors.
Exemptions of persons
under 16 years of
age, §9-11-50.
Nonresidents, §§9-11-46 to
9-11-51.
All game, §9-11-47.
Hunting without license,
§9-11-51.
Payment of property
taxes, §9-11-49.2.
Reciprocity, §9-11-49.1.
Small game only,
§9-11-46.
Trip all game, §9-11-49.
Trip small game,
§9-11-48.
Penalties.
Hunting without license,
§9-11-51.
Required, §9-11-51.
Wildlife management
areas.
Deer or wild turkey,
§9-11-45.
Issuance.
False statement to officer
issuing, §9-1-1.
Fees, §9-11-37.
Persons authorized,
§9-11-36.
Records, §9-11-36.
Reports, §9-11-37.
Stubs.
Return of stubs,
§9-11-33.
Lending, §9-1-3.
Minors.
Fishing licenses.
Persons under 16 years
of age, §9-11-53.
Hunting licenses.
Persons under 16 years
of age, §9-11-50.

FISH AND GAME—Cont'd
  Licenses—Cont'd
    Nonresidents.
      Fishing licenses, §§9-11-55
        to 9-11-56.1.
      Payment of ad valorem
        property taxes.
        Treatment as Alabama
          resident, §9-11-49.2.
    Numbering, §9-11-33.
    Penalties.
      Dealers.
        Live fish and minnow
          dealers.
          Nonresidents,
            §9-11-58.
      Dogs.
        Trainers.
          Training without
            license, §9-11-52.
      False statements, §9-1-1.
    Fees.
      Charging an amount in
        excess of fee
        provided, §9-11-37.
      Fishing licenses, §9-11-53.
      Fishing without license,
        §9-11-57.
      Nonresidents.
        Violations of
          provisions,
          §§9-11-55, 9-11-56.
      Fur catchers, §9-11-59.
        Transporting furs
          without license,
          §9-11-61.
      Hunting without license,
        §9-11-51.
      Lending, borrowing, etc.,
        §9-1-3.
      Nonresidents.
        Hunting without license,
          §9-11-51.
      Violation of article,
        §9-11-63.
    Persons under 16 years of
      age.
      Exemptions, §9-11-50.
    Probate judge.
      Responsibility as to
        licenses, §9-11-43.
    Quail.
      Commercial quail
        breeding, §§9-11-342,
        9-11-349.
    Records.
      Issuance of licenses,
        §9-11-36.
    Reports.
      Issuance of licenses,
        §9-11-37.
    Retail freshwater nongame
      fish dealers, §9-11-153.
    Spearfishing. See within this
      heading, "Spearfishing."
    Special agents.
      Appointment, §9-11-39.
      Application, §9-11-38.
      Authority, §9-11-38.
      Blank licenses.
        Furnishing to agents,
          §9-11-41.
      Bonds, surety, §9-11-39.
        Payable to probate judge
          or license
          commissioner,
          §9-11-40.
      Duties.
        General provisions,
          §9-11-42.

FISH AND GAME—Cont'd
  Licenses—Cont'd
    Special agents—Cont'd
      Fees.
        Catching of nongame
          fish with wire
          baskets, §9-11-191.
        Commercial fishing.
          Public impounded
            waters and
            navigable streams,
            §9-11-143.
        Disabled persons,
          §9-11-54.
        Fishing licenses,
          §9-11-53.
        Hunting license,
          §9-11-44.
        Remittance of fees
          collected, §9-11-42.
        Wildlife management
          areas.
          License to hunt deer or
            wild turkey,
            §9-11-45.
      Furnishing blank licenses,
        §9-11-33.
      Hunting licenses.
        Fee for issuing, §9-11-44.
        Responsibility for licenses,
          §9-11-41.
      Stubs.
        Return of stubs, §9-11-33.
      Term, §9-11-32.
      Transportation.
        Prerequisites to
          transporting protected
          birds or game,
          §9-11-255.
      Use by another, §9-1-3.
      Wholesale freshwater
        nongame fish dealers,
        §9-11-153.
      Wire baskets.
        Catching of nongame fish
          with wire baskets,
          §§9-11-190 to 9-11-198.
        See within this
          heading, "Wire
          baskets."
  Livestock.
    Persons hunting deer at
      night.
      Liable for killing stock,
        §9-11-258.
  Management.
    Wildlife management areas,
      §§9-11-300 to 9-11-307.
      See within this heading,
        "Wildlife management
        areas."
  **Marine environmental
    sciences consortium,**
    §§16-45-1 to 16-45-5.
    See MARINE
      ENVIRONMENTAL
      SCIENCES
      CONSORTIUM.
  Marine mammal protection,
    §§9-11-390 to 9-11-398.
    See MARINE MAMMAL
      PROTECTION.
  Marine resources, §§9-12-1 to
    9-12-184.
    See MARINE RESOURCES.
  Migratory birds.
    Reservations, §9-11-263.
  Migratory water fowl,
    §§9-11-430 to 9-11-435.
    Definitions, §9-11-430.

FISH AND GAME—Cont'd
  Migratory water fowl
    —Cont'd
    Purpose of provisions,
      §9-11-431.
    Stamp.
      Defined, §9-11-430.
      Form, §9-11-432.
      Issuance, §§9-11-432,
        9-11-433.
        Fees, §9-11-433.
        Revenue used in
          preservation of
          wetlands,
          §9-11-434.
      Required for hunting,
        §9-11-432.
      Wetland preservation.
        Projects outside United
          States.
          Contracts with nonprofit
            organizations for,
            §9-11-434.
          Requirements for
            approval, §9-11-435.
        Revenue used for,
          §9-11-434.
  Military affairs.
    Licenses.
      Members of armed forces
        during war, §9-11-35.
  Minnows.
    Dealers, §9-11-58.
  Minors.
    Licenses.
      Fishing licenses.
        Persons under 16 years
          of age, §9-11-53.
      Hunting license.
        Persons under 16 years
          of age, §9-11-50.
  Mollusks.
    General provisions, §§9-12-1
      to 9-12-184.
    See MARINE
      RESOURCES.
  Navigable streams.
    Commercial fishing in
      impounded waters and
      navigable streams,
      §§9-11-140 to 9-11-156.
      See within this heading,
        "Commercial fishing."
  Nets.
    Fishing, §9-11-88.
      Private ponds, lakes,
        reservoirs, etc.,
        §9-11-91.
    Hunting.
      Taking of protected birds
        or animals by use of
        nets, §9-11-245.
      Penalties, §9-11-246.
    Wire baskets.
      Catching of nongame fish
        with wire baskets,
        §§9-11-190 to 9-11-198.
        See within this
          heading, "Wire
          baskets."
  Nonresidents.
    Bag limits.
      Establishment, §9-11-49.1.
    Fishing licenses, §§9-11-55 to
      9-11-56.1.
    Fur dealers.
      Bonds, surety, §9-11-253.
    Hunting licenses, §§9-11-46
      to 9-11-51. See within
      this heading, "Licenses."

FISH AND GAME—Cont'd
Nonresidents—Cont'd
Length of seasons,
§9-11-49.1.
Property taxes.
Treated as resident upon
payment, §9-11-49.2.
Reciprocal agreements as to
freshwater fishing,
§§9-11-210 to 9-11-213.
Waterfowl hunting.
Reciprocal agreements as
to waterfowl hunting,
§§9-11-280 to 9-11-283.
Notice.
Exhibitions.
Possession of wildlife for
public exhibition
purposes.
Notice of violations,
§9-11-325.
Spearfishing.
Competitive events,
§9-11-170.
Wildlife management areas.
Dogs.
Impoundment, §9-11-306.
Nuisances.
Nuisances menacing public
health, §§22-10-1 to
22-10-3.
Prohibited devices used in
hunting, fishing or
trapping, §9-11-16.
Oaths.
Game and fish division.
Director, §9-2-62.
Wardens, §9-2-64.
Oysters, §§9-12-1 to 9-12-184.
See MARINE RESOURCES.
Parks.
Possession of wildlife for
public exhibition
purposes, §§9-11-320 to
9-11-328. See within this
heading, "Exhibitions."
Penalties.
Bait.
Taking of protected birds
or animals by means
of bait, §9-11-244.
Birds.
Nests.
Destruction, §9-11-232.
Protected wild birds.
Possession or sale,
§9-11-232.
Commercial fee fishing
ponds.
Fines for violations,
§9-11-457.
Commercial fishing.
Public impounded waters
and navigable streams.
Violations of article,
§9-11-156.
Dealers.
Licenses.
Nonresidents.
Live fish and minnow
dealers, §9-11-58.
Dogs.
Trainers.
Training without license,
§9-11-52.
Exhibitions.
Possession of wildlife for
public exhibition
purposes, §9-11-327.

FISH AND GAME—Cont'd
Penalties—Cont'd
Explosives.
Catching or killing of fish,
§9-11-93.
Fishing.
Disposition of fines,
§9-11-95.
Electricity.
Catching or killing of
fish by electrical
devices, §9-11-94.
Fish farms.
Unauthorized fishing
from farm.
Violations of
provisions,
§9-11-91.1.
Game fish.
Means of catching
generally, §9-11-87.
Transportation.
Beyond boundaries of
state, §9-11-86.
Fish to be transported
openly, §9-11-85.
Private ponds, lakes, pools
or reservoirs.
Catching of fish,
§9-11-91.
Sale of game fish, §9-11-84.
Transportation of game
fish, §9-11-84.
Flattened musk turtle.
Protection.
Violations of provisions,
§9-11-269.
Fur catchers.
Licenses.
Transporting furs
without license,
§9-11-61.
Violation of provisions,
§9-11-59.
Transporting furs without
license, §9-11-61.
Traps.
Limitation as to number
of traps, §9-11-254.
Hunting.
Deer.
Female deer and
unantlered male
deer, §9-11-239.
Nighttime, §9-11-252.
Waters and
watercourses.
Taking of deer from
public waters,
§9-11-250.
Discharging firearm from,
upon or across public
roads, etc., §9-11-257.
Lands of another.
Without permission,
§§9-11-241 to
9-11-243.
Daytime, §9-11-241.
Fur-bearing animals
within ten feet of
banks of water,
§9-11-243.
Nighttime, §9-11-242.
Nighttime.
Taking of protected birds
or animals,
§9-11-235.

FISH AND GAME—Cont'd
Penalties—Cont'd
Hunting—Cont'd
Seasons.
Hunting of or possession
of protected birds or
animals during
closed season,
§9-11-236.
Wild turkeys.
Hens, §9-11-239.
Hunting with dogs,
§9-11-238.
Within one hundred yards
of public roads,
highways or railroads,
§9-11-257.
Importation.
Rules and regulations.
Violations, §9-2-13.
Licenses. See within this
heading, "Licenses."
Poisons and poisoning.
Catching or killing of fish,
§9-11-93.
Propagation.
Private purposes.
Violation of permit,
§9-11-261.
Quail.
Commercial quail
breeding.
Violations of article,
§9-11-351.
Raccoons.
Coon on the log contests,
§9-11-249.
Refuges.
Hunting.
Protected birds or
animals, §9-11-234.
Sales.
Game birds or animals,
§9-11-237.
Spearfishing.
Violation of article,
§9-11-176.
Transportation.
Common carriers.
Liability, §9-11-256.
Failure to transport
openly, §9-11-259.
Restrictions on
transporting protected
birds or game,
§9-11-255.
Turkeys.
Release into wild areas of
state, §9-11-20.
Violations of fish and game
laws.
Disposition of fines and
forfeitures, §9-11-6.
Waters and watercourses.
Preventing passage of fish
up rivers, §9-11-92.
Wildlife management areas.
Violations of article,
§9-11-307.
Wire baskets.
Catching of nongame fish
with wire baskets.
Violations of article,
§9-11-198.
Permits.
Collection of wild animals
and birds for scientific
purposes, §9-11-231.
Commercial fee fishing
ponds.
Applications, §9-11-453.

FISH AND GAME—Cont'd
Permits—Cont'd
Commercial fee fishing ponds
—Cont'd
Display of letter permit,
§9-11-454.
Issuance, §9-11-453.
Required, §9-11-450.
Coon on the log contests,
§§9-11-248, 9-11-249.
Exhibitions.
Possession of wildlife for
public exhibition
purposes, §§9-11-324 to
9-11-327.
Propagation.
Game birds or animals.
Private purposes,
§9-11-261.
Pike county public lake.
Fishing without paying
admission fee, §9-11-66.
Poisons and poisoning.
Fishing.
Catching or killing of fish,
§9-11-93.
Private ponds, lakes, pools
or reservoirs, §9-11-91.
Hunting.
Taking of protected birds
or animals by use of
poisons, §9-11-245.
Penalties, §9-11-246.
Ponds.
Commercial fee fishing
ponds, §§9-11-450 to
9-11-457.
Presumptions.
Fur dealers.
Presumptions as to
dealership, §9-11-62.
Probate judge.
Licenses, §9-11-43.
**Prohibited devices used in
hunting, fishing or
trapping.**
Seizure, forfeiture and
disposal, §9-11-16.
Propagation.
Acquisition of land.
Commissioner of
conservation and
natural resourses,
§9-11-260.
Buildings.
Purchase or erection,
§9-11-2.
Commissioner of
conservation and natural
resources.
Authority, §9-11-260.
Private purposes.
Permits, §9-11-261.
Quail.
Commercial quail
breeding. See within
this heading, "Quail."
State game refuges or
sanctuaries, §9-11-4.
Use of state game lands,
§9-11-2.
Public exhibitions, §§9-11-320
to 9-11-328. See within
this heading,
"Exhibitions."
Public roads.
Hunting.
Hunting or discharge of
firearm from, upon or
across public roads,
§9-11-257.

FISH AND GAME—Cont'd
Public waters.
Commercial fishing,
§§9-11-140 to 9-11-156.
See within this heading,
"Commercial fishing."
Quail.
Commercial quail breeding,
§§9-11-340 to 9-11-351.
Applicability of article.
Persons shipping quail
into state, §9-11-350.
Authority to propagate,
§9-11-341.
Carcasses to be marked
before sale, §9-11-344.
Definitions, §9-11-340.
Disposition by other than
retail vendors,
§9-11-348.
Inspections.
Records and premises,
§9-11-349.
Invoices.
Attached to packages of
carcasses, §9-11-345.
Killing of quail.
Otherwise than by
shooting, §9-11-344.
Licenses, §9-11-342.
Records, §9-11-349.
Markers or marking
devices.
Carcasses to be marked
before sale,
§9-11-344.
Licensees to obtain,
§9-11-343.
Packages of carcasses.
Invoices
Attached to packages,
§9-11-346.
Kept attached during
storage, §9-11-347.
Shipped with invoices
attached, §9-11-346.
Storage.
Invoices to be kept
attached during
storage, §9-11-347.
Penalties.
Violations of article,
§9-11-351.
Pen-raised quail.
Defined, §9-11-340.
Persons authorized to
engage in propagation,
§9-11-341.
Records of licensees.
Inspection, §9-11-349.
Maintaining, §9-11-349.
Resale by persons other
than retail vendors,
§9-11-348.
Retail vendors.
Resale or disposition of
quail by other than
retail vendors,
§9-11-348.
Sales.
Resale by persons other
than retail vendors,
§9-11-348.
Violations of article.
Penalties, §9-11-351.
Raccoons.
Coon on the log contests,
§§9-11-247 to 9-11-249.
Keeping of raccoons for
use, §9-11-247.
Penalties, §9-11-249.

FISH AND GAME—Cont'd
Raccoons—Cont'd
Coon on the log contests
—Cont'd
Permits, §9-11-248.
Penalties, §9-11-249.
Taking raccoons for use in,
§9-11-247.
Hunting, §§9-11-235,
9-11-235.1.
Railroads.
Hunting or discharge of
firearm from, upon or
across railroads,
§9-11-257.
Hunting within one hundred
yards of railroads,
§9-11-257.
Real property.
Recreational or sporting
premises liability,
§§35-15-1 to 35-15-28.
See REAL PROPERTY.
Reciprocity.
Freshwater fishing.
Reciprocal agreements as
to freshwater fishing,
§§9-11-210 to 9-11-213.
Licenses.
Fishing licenses.
Reciprocal agreement
with Florida,
§9-11-53.
Waterfowl hunting.
Reciprocal agreements as
to waterfowl hunting,
§§9-11-280 to 9-11-283.
Records.
Commercial fishing.
Public impounded waters
and navigable streams.
Licenses, §9-11-143.
Commercial fowl hunting
preserves, §9-11-416.
Dealers.
Freshwater nongame fish
dealers, §9-11-154.
Fur dealers.
Inspection of books and
records, §9-11-64.
Licenses.
Issuance of licenses,
§9-11-36.
Quail.
Commercial quail
breeding.
Licensees, §9-11-349.
Refuges.
Establishment, §9-11-4.
Federal lands, §9-11-4.
Hunting.
Protected birds or animals,
§9-11-234.
Maintenance, §9-11-4.
Migratory bird reservations,
§9-11-263.
Penalties.
Hunting.
Protected birds or
animals, §9-11-234.
Reports.
Commercial fishing.
Public impounded waters
and navigable streams.
Licenses, §9-11-143.
Fur catchers.
Licenses, §9-11-60.
Hunting deaths.
Accident reports, §9-11-21.
Licenses.
Fur catchers, §9-11-60.

FISH AND GAME—Cont'd
  Reports—Cont'd
    Licenses—Cont'd
      Issuance, §9-11-37.
    Violations of fish and game
      laws.
      Convictions, §9-11-6.
      Results of prosecutions,
        §9-11-10.
  Reservoirs.
    Fishing.
      Catching of fish, §9-11-91.
  Retail freshwater nongame
    fish dealers, §§9-11-153,
    9-11-154.
  Rules and regulations.
    Beavers.
      Killing of beavers,
        §9-11-262.
    Commercial fowl hunting
      preserves, §9-11-410.
    Commissioner.
      Promulgation, §9-2-8.
    Exhibitions.
      Possession of wildlife for
        public exhibition
        purposes, §9-11-323.
    Importations, §9-2-13.
    Publication and distribution,
      §9-2-8.
    Violations, §§9-11-6 to
      9-11-15.
    Wildlife management areas.
      Establishment, §9-11-301.
    Wire baskets.
      Catching of nongame fish,
        §9-11-190.
  Sales.
    Birds.
      Protected wild birds,
        §9-11-232.
    Breeders.
      Purposes of sale, §9-11-31.
      Restrictions, §9-11-31.
    Commercial fee fishing
      ponds.
      Selling of fish caught,
        §9-11-456.
    Finished products, §9-11-237.
    Fishing.
      Commercial fee fishing
        ponds.
        Selling of fish caught,
          §9-11-456.
      Game fish.
        Restrictions, §9-11-84.
    Furs.
      Sales to licensed dealers,
        §9-11-237.
    Game birds or animals,
      §9-11-237.
    Grading and standards of
      farm products and fish,
      §§2-11-50 to 2-11-59.
      See AGRICULTURE.
    Hides, etc., §9-11-237.
    Wire baskets.
      Catching of nongame fish.
      Sale of fish by licensees,
        §9-11-192.
  Salt water fishing, §§9-12-1 to
    9-12-184.
    See MARINE RESOURCES.
  Sanctuaries.
    State game refuges or
      sanctuaries, §§9-11-4,
      9-11-234.

FISH AND GAME—Cont'd
  Science.
    Collection of animals and
      birds for scientific
      purposes.
      Permits, §9-11-231.
  Searches and seizures.
    Boats and motors.
      Violations of article,
        §9-11-156.
    Commercial fishing.
      Public impounded waters
        and navigable streams.
      Boats and motors.
        Violations of article,
          §9-11-156.
      Fish illegally
        transported or
        shipped, §9-11-152.
      Fishing gear.
        Seizure and
          confiscation of
          gear used in
          violation of article,
          §9-11-151.
      Violations of article,
        §9-11-156.
    Fish farm.
      Unauthorized fishing from.
      Seizure and disposal of
        fishing equipment,
        §9-11-91.1.
    Game fish.
      Confiscation of fish taken
        or transported
        illegally, §9-11-85.
    Prohibited devices used in
      hunting, fishing or
      trapping.
      Seizure, §9-11-16.
    Transportation.
      Animals or birds illegally
        transported or taken,
        §9-11-259.
    Wardens.
      Powers and duties, §9-2-65.
    Wildlife management areas.
      Authority, §9-11-301.
  Seasons.
    Hunting. See within this
      heading, "Hunting."
  Secured transactions.
    When security interest
      attaches, §7-9-204.
  Shellfish, §§9-12-1 to 9-12-184.
    See MARINE RESOURCES.
  Sheriffs.
    Violations of fish and game
      laws.
      Deputy sheriffs.
        Enforcement officers to
          have powers of
          deputy sheriff,
          §9-11-8.
  Shipments. See within this
    heading, "Transportation."
  Shooting preserves.
    Federal lands, §9-11-4.
  Shrimp, §§9-12-1 to 9-12-184.
    See MARINE RESOURCES.
  Spearfishing, §§9-11-170 to
    9-11-176.
    Competitive events.
      Notice, §9-11-170.
    Compliance with water
      safety laws, §9-11-174.
    Definitions, §9-11-170.
    Evidence.
      Possession of spear,
        §9-11-175.

FISH AND GAME—Cont'd
  Spearfishing—Cont'd
    Flags.
      Display of diver's flag,
        §9-11-174.
    Hours of spearfishing.
      Regulation, §9-11-173.
    How permitted, §9-11-170.
    Licenses.
      Display, §9-11-172.
      Fees, §9-11-171.
      Inspection, §9-11-172.
      Required, §9-11-171.
    Notice.
      Competitive events,
        §9-11-170.
    Penalties.
      Violation of article,
        §9-11-176.
    Possession of spear.
      Evidence of spearfishing,
        §9-11-175.
    Seasons.
      Regulation of seasons,
        §9-11-173.
    Skin divers.
      Compliance with water
        safety laws, §9-11-174.
    Violation of article.
      Penalties, §9-11-176.
    Water safety laws.
      Compliance with laws,
        §9-11-174.
    When permitted, §9-11-170.
    Where permitted, §9-11-170.
  Special agents.
    Licenses. See within this
      heading, "Licenses."
  Spotlighting, §32-5-17.
  Standards.
    Grading and standards of
      farm products and fish,
      §§2-11-50 to 2-11-59.
      See AGRICULTURE.
  Starlings.
    Hunting.
      Unprotected birds,
        §9-11-233.
  State fresh water fish, §1-2-9.
  State game lands.
    Deeds, §9-11-3.
    Purposes, §9-11-2.
    Supervision.
      Commissioner of
        conservation and
        natural resources,
        §9-11-3.
    Title to land, §9-11-3.
  State saltwater fish, §1-2-8.
  Subpoenas.
    Wardens.
      Service, §9-2-65.
  Sunday hunting prohibited,
    §13A-12-1.
  Tarpon.
    State saltwater fish, §1-2-8.
  Taxation.
    Furs.
      Shipment of furs without
        tax, §9-11-253.
    Nonresidents.
      Payment of ad valorem
        property taxes.
        Treatment as Alabama
          resident, §9-11-49.2.
  Title.
    Fresh water fish.
      Vesting in state, §9-11-81.
    State game lands, §9-11-3.
    Wild birds and animals.
      Vested in state, §9-11-230.

FISH AND GAME—Cont'd
Torts.
Duty of care owed persons on premises for sporting or recreational purposes, §§35-15-1 to 35-15-5.
Trainers.
Dogs, §9-11-52.
Transportation.
Commercial fishing, §9-11-152.
Common carriers.
Liability, §9-11-256.
Confiscation.
Illegally transported game or birds, §9-11-259.
Furs, §9-11-237.
Game fish. See within this heading, "Fishing."
Licenses.
Hunting license required, §9-11-255.
Open transportation, §9-11-259.
Restrictions, §9-11-255.
Searches and seizures.
Birds or animals illegally taken or transported, §9-11-259.
Two-days bag limit, §9-11-255.
Trapping.
Fur catchers. See within this heading, "Fur catchers."
Fur dealers. See within this heading, "Fur dealers."
General provisions. See within this heading, "Hunting."
Turkeys.
Hunting, §§9-11-45, 9-11-238, 9-11-239.
Release into wild areas of state prohibited, §9-11-20.
Exception, §9-11-20.
Penalty, §9-11-20.
Turtles.
Flattened musk turtle.
Protection, §9-11-269.
United States.
Fish restoration and management projects.
Assent to federal act relating to, §9-11-19.
Migratory birds.
Reservations.
Acquisition of lands, §9-11-263.
Shooting preserves.
Federal lands, §9-11-4.
Violations of fish and game laws, §§9-11-6 to 9-11-15.
Appeals.
Judgment on appeal, §9-11-15.
Procedure, §9-11-14.
Arrest.
Fees of arresting officers, §9-11-12.
Without warrant, §9-11-8.
Charging of several offenses, §9-11-11.
Complaints.
Two or more offenses charged in same complaint, §9-11-11.
Corporations.
Warrants.
Service and return of warrant, §9-11-9.

FISH AND GAME—Cont'd
Violations of fish and game laws—Cont'd
District attorney.
Duty to prosecute, §9-11-7.
Fees, §9-11-7.
District courts.
Jurisdiction, §9-11-6.
Enforcement officers.
Authority generally, §9-11-8.
Fees.
Arresting officers, §9-11-12.
District attorney, §9-11-7.
Judgments.
Appeals.
Judgment on appeal, §9-11-15.
Jurisdiction.
District courts, §9-11-6.
Penalties.
Disposition.
Reports, §9-11-10.
Fines and forfeitures, §9-11-6.
Prosecutions.
Duties of district attorney, §9-11-7.
Report of results, §9-11-10.
Style of proceedings, §9-11-13.
Reports.
Convictions, §9-11-6.
Results of prosecutions, §9-11-10.
Separate offenses for each bird, animal or fish, §9-11-11.
Sheriffs.
Deputy sheriffs.
Authority of enforcement officers, §9-11-8.
Style of proceedings, §9-11-13.
Wardens.
Authority of enforcement officers generally, §9-11-8.
Warrants.
Arrest without warrant, §9-11-8.
Return.
Firms or corporations, §9-11-9.
Service.
Firms or corporations, §9-11-9.
Wardens.
Appointment.
Commissioner of conservation and natural resources, §9-2-64.
Bonds, surety, §9-2-64.
Deputy wardens, §9-11-17.
Defined, §9-11-1.
Deputy wardens.
Appointment, §9-11-17.
Authority, §9-11-17.
Bonds, surety, §9-11-17.
Compensation, §9-11-17.
Duties.
General provisions, §9-11-17.
Status, §9-11-17.
Superintendent of private hunting and fishing clubs, §9-2-64.

FISH AND GAME—Cont'd
Wardens—Cont'd
Director.
Powers and duties with respect to wardens, §9-2-65.
Duties.
General provisions, §9-2-65.
Equipment.
Furnishing of necessary equipment, §9-11-18.
Purchases of equipment, §9-11-18.
Expenses.
Reimbursement, §9-2-64.
Firearms.
Carrying of firearms, §9-2-65.
Jurisdiction.
General provisions, §9-11-5.
Number of wardens, §9-2-64.
Oath of office, §9-2-64.
Peace officers.
Constituted peace officer of the state, §9-11-5.
Powers and duties.
General provisions, §9-2-65.
Right of entry, §9-2-65.
Searches and seizures.
Powers and duties, §9-2-65.
Warrants.
Execution, §9-2-65.
Subpoenas.
Service, §9-2-65.
Title defined, §9-2-28.
Violations of fish and game laws.
Authority of enforcement officers generally, §9-11-8.
Warrants.
Search warrants.
Wardens.
Execution, §9-2-65.
Violations of fish and game laws.
Arrest without warrant, §9-11-8.
Corporations.
Service and return of warrant, §9-11-9.
Waterfowl.
Migratory water fowl, §§9-11-230 to 9-11-234.
Waters and watercourses.
Commercial fishing, §§9-11-140 to 9-11-156.
See within this heading, "Commercial fishing."
Hunting.
Deer.
Taking of deer from public waters, §9-11-250.
Penalties, §9-11-252.
Passage of fish.
Preventing passage up rivers or creeks, §9-11-92.
Weapons.
Wardens.
Carrying of firearms, §9-2-65.
Wildlife management areas.
Firearms.
Carrying or possession of firearms, §9-11-304.

FISH AND GAME—Cont'd
Wholesale fresh water
　nongame fish dealers,
　§§9-11-153, 9-11-154.
Wildlife management areas,
　§§9-11-300 to 9-11-306.
　Boundaries.
　　Establishment, §9-11-301.
　Deer.
　　Hunting.
　　　Licenses, §9-11-45.
　Dogs.
　　Impoundment.
　　　Procedure, §9-11-306.
　　　Redemption or
　　　　destruction of
　　　　impounded dogs,
　　　　§9-11-306.
　　Running at large.
　　　Impoundment, §9-11-306.
　　　Liability of owners,
　　　　§9-11-305.
　　When permitted in areas,
　　　§9-11-305.
　Establishment.
　　Agreements, §9-11-300.
　　Authority, §9-11-300.
　Firearms.
　　Carrying or possession,
　　　§9-11-304.
　Fishing.
　　Closing of land or water in
　　　areas to fishing,
　　　§9-11-302.
　Hunting.
　　Closing of land or water in
　　　areas to hunting,
　　　§9-11-302.
　Licenses.
　　Deer or wild turkey,
　　　§9-11-45.
　Licenses.
　　Hunting license.
　　　Deer or wild turkey,
　　　　§9-11-45.
　Management.
　　Rules and regulations,
　　　§9-11-301.
　Notice.
　　Dogs.
　　　Impoundment, §9-11-306.
　Penalties.
　　Violations of article,
　　　§9-11-307.
　Rules and regulations.
　　Promulgation, §9-11-301.
　Searches and seizures.
　　Authority, §9-11-303.
　Violations of article.
　　Penalties, §9-11-307.
　Weapons.
　　Firearms.
　　　Carrying or possession of
　　　　firearms, §9-11-304.
　Wild turkeys.
　　Hunting.
　　　Licenses, §9-11-45.
Wild turkeys.
　Hunting, §§9-11-45, 9-11-238,
　　9-11-239.
　State game bird, §1-2-17.
Wire baskets.
　Catching of nongame fish
　　with wire baskets,
　　§§9-11-190 to 9-11-198.
　Commercial fishing.
　　Prohibited, §9-11-192.
　Game fish.
　　Return of fish to waters,
　　　§9-11-196.
　How permitted, §9-11-190.

FISH AND GAME—Cont'd
Wire baskets—Cont'd
　Catching of nongame fish
　　with wire baskets
　　—Cont'd
　　Identification of baskets,
　　　§9-11-194.
　　Destruction of unmarked
　　　baskets, §9-11-195.
　　Inspection of baskets by
　　　unlicensed persons,
　　　§9-11-197.
　　Licenses.
　　　Fees, §9-11-191.
　　　　Disposition, §9-11-191.
　　　Issuance, §9-11-191.
　　　　Not to be issued to
　　　　　persons holding
　　　　　commercial fishing
　　　　　license, §9-11-192.
　　　Obtaining more than
　　　　four licenses
　　　　prohibited,
　　　　§9-11-193.
　　　Required, §9-11-191.
　　　Revocation.
　　　　Violations of article,
　　　　　§9-11-198.
　　　Separate license for each
　　　　basket, §9-11-191.
　　Marking of baskets,
　　　§9-11-194.
　　Destruction of unmarked
　　　baskets, §9-11-195.
　　Nongame fish only to be
　　　taken, §9-11-196.
　　Number of baskets.
　　　Restriction, §9-11-193.
　　Penalties.
　　　Violations of article,
　　　　§9-11-198.
　　Personal consumption,
　　　§9-11-192.
　　Petition.
　　　Establishment of rules
　　　　and regulations,
　　　　§9-11-190.
　　Raising of basket by
　　　unlicensed persons,
　　　§9-11-197.
　　Rules and regulations.
　　　Promulgation, §9-11-190.
　　Sale of fish.
　　　Prohibited, §9-11-192.
　　Taking of fish by
　　　unlicensed persons,
　　　§9-11-197.
　　Use of more than four
　　　baskets, §9-11-193.
　　Violations of article.
　　　Penalties, §9-11-198.
　　　Revocation of license,
　　　　§9-11-198.
　　When permitted,
　　　§9-11-190.
　　Where permitted,
　　　§9-11-190.
Zoos.
　Possession of wildlife for
　　public exhibition
　　purposes, §§9-11-320 to
　　9-11-328. See within this
　　heading, "Exhibitions."

FISHING.
General provisions.
　See FISH AND GAME.

FISHING PONDS.
Commercial fee fishing
　ponds, §§9-11-450 to
　9-11-457.
　See FISH AND GAME.

FIVE-GALLON ACT, §28-4-115.
Alcoholic beverages.
　Dry counties.
　　Transportation, §28-4-115.

FIXTURES.
Secured transactions.
　Financing statement,
　　§7-9-402.
　Place of filing, §7-9-401.
　Priority of security interests
　　in fixtures, §7-9-313.

FLAGS.
Boats.
　Airboats.
　　Flag required, §33-5-22.
　Diver's flag, §33-5-22.
Criminal law and procedure.
　Desecration, §13A-11-12.
Desecration, §13A-11-12.
Distress flag for
　handicapped or
　paraplegic drivers,
　§§32-5-12 to 32-5-14.
Education.
　United States flag and state
　　flag, §§16-43-1 to
　　16-43-5.
Governor.
　Military flag of governor,
　　§31-2-54.
Harbors and ports.
　Mobile harbor.
　　Ships entering or leaving
　　　port, §33-1-34.
Military affairs.
　Governor's flag, §31-2-54.
Motor vehicles.
　Handicapped persons.
　　Distress flag, §§32-5-12 to
　　　32-5-14.
　Loads.
　　Flag or light at end of
　　　load, §32-5-211.
Ships and shipping.
　Mobile harbor.
　　Ships entering or leaving
　　　port, §33-1-34.
State flag.
　Description, §1-2-5.
　Display.
　　General provisions, §1-2-6.
　　Schools, §§16-43-1 to
　　　16-43-3.
　Education.
　　United States flag and
　　　state flag, §§16-43-1 to
　　　16-43-5.
United States flag.
　Education.
　　United States flag and
　　　state flag, §§16-43-1 to
　　　16-43-5.

FLARES.
Motor vehicles, §§32-5-220,
　32-5-221.

FLATTENED MUSK TURTLE.
Protection, §9-11-269.

FLIGHT.
Police.
　Bail jumping, §§13A-10-39,
　　13A-10-40.

FLIGHT—Cont'd

Police—Cont'd
Escape generally,
§§13A-10-31 to
13A-10-35.
Fleeing officer.
Motor vehicle cases,
§32-5A-193.
Hindering prosecution or
apprehension,
§§13A-10-42 to
13A-10-45.
Resisting arrest, §13A-10-41.

FLOMATON, MUNICIPALITY OF.

Property tax, Const. Ala.,
amd. 8.

FLOODS.

Civil defense, §§31-9-1 to
31-9-24.
See CIVIL DEFENSE.
Constitution of Alabama.
Flood control projects on
tributary streams of
Tombigbee river, Const.
Ala., amd. 270.
Counties.
Land-use management in
flood-prone areas,
§§11-19-1 to 11-19-24.
See COUNTIES.
Land-use management.
Counties.
Land-use management in
flood-prone areas,
§§11-19-1 to 11-19-24.
See COUNTIES.
Municipal corporations.
Assessments for public
improvements.
Manner of assessment of
costs of seawalls,
levees, etc., §11-48-16.

FLORALA, MUNICIPALITY OF.

Property tax, Const. Ala.,
amd. 17.

FLORENCE, MUNICIPALITY OF.

Property tax, Const. Ala.,
amd. 8.
School tax.
Special school tax, Const.
Ala., amd. 178.

FLORIDA.

**Boundary between Alabama
and Florida.**
Generally, §41-2-3.
Precise location at mouth of
Perdido river and
surrounding area,
§41-2-4.

FLOUR, §§20-1-70 to 20-1-78.

See BREAD, FLOUR,
CORNMEAL AND GRITS.

FLOWERS.

Camellia.
State flower, §1-2-11.
Forests and forestry.
Removal from bushes and
shrubs.
See FORESTS AND
FORESTRY.
State flower, §1-2-11.

FLU.

Notifiable diseases,
§§22-11A-1 to 22-11A-38.
See DISEASES.

FOOD.

Administration of chapter.
Applicability of
administrative provisions
of Title 2, §20-1-1.
**Adulteration and
misbranding.**
Board of agriculture and
industries.
Standards of purity.
Board to fix, §20-1-21.
Dealers.
Exemption from
prosecution of dealers,
§20-1-32.
Definitions, §20-1-20.
Inspections.
Municipal corporations,
§11-47-136.
Manufacture for sale,
§20-1-27.
Manufacturers.
Effect of possession by
manufacturer, etc.,
§20-1-31.
Municipal corporations.
Prohibition of sale, etc., of
impure, adulterated,
etc., food, §11-47-136.
Provision for inspections,
§11-47-136.
Potatoes.
Artificially colored
potatoes.
Sale, offer for sale, etc.,
§20-1-30.
Purpose of division, §20-1-21.
Sales.
Prohibition of sale,
§20-1-27.
Municipal corporations,
§11-47-136.
Standards of purity.
Board of agriculture and
industries to fix,
§20-1-21.
When food deemed
adulterated, §20-1-22.
Confectionery, §20-1-23.
When food deemed
misbranded, §20-1-25.
**Board of agriculture and
industries.**
Rules and regulations,
§20-1-2.
Standards of purity.
Board to fix standards,
§20-1-21.
Brands and marks.
Adulteration and
misbranding, §§20-1-20
to 20-1-32. See within
this heading,
"Adulteration and
misbranding."
Bread.
Manufacture and sale,
§§20-1-70 to 20-1-78.
See BREAD, FLOUR,
CORNMEAL AND
GRITS.
Charities.
Nonliability of good faith
donors and distributors
of food, §20-1-6.

FOOD—Cont'd

Commercial code.
Sales.
Implied warranty of
merchantability,
§7-2-314.
**Commissioner of agriculture
and industries.**
Enforcement of chapter,
§20-1-1.
Right of entry by
commissioner and
agents, §20-1-3.
Contaminated food.
Nuisances menacing public
health, §§22-10-1 to
22-10-3.
Cornmeal.
Manufacture and sale,
§§20-1-70 to 20-1-78.
See BREAD, FLOUR,
CORNMEAL AND
GRITS.
Dairy products, §§2-13-1 to
2-13-94.
See MILK AND MILK
PRODUCTS.
Dealers.
Adulteration and
misbranding.
Exemption from
prosecution, §20-1-32.
Decayed food.
Nuisances menacing public
health, §§22-10-1 to
22-10-3.
Definitions.
Adulteration and
misbranding, §20-1-20.
**Department of agriculture
and industries.**
Enforcement of chapter,
§20-1-1.
Destruction.
Nuisances menacing public
health.
Destruction without
compensation,
§22-10-3.
Donors.
Nonliability of good faith
donors and distributors
of food, §20-1-6.
Eggs and egg products,
§§2-12-1 to 2-12-12.
See EGGS AND EGG
PRODUCTS.
Enforcement of chapter,
§20-1-1.
Applicability of enforcement
provisions of Title 2,
§20-1-1.
Flour.
Manufacture and sale,
§§20-1-70 to 20-1-78.
See BREAD, FLOUR,
CORNMEAL AND
GRITS.
Food stamps, §§13A-9-90 to
13A-9-92, 38-2-6.
Fraud.
Obtaining food by fraud or
misrepresentation.
Posting of law, §34-15-20.
Prima facie evidence of
offense, §34-15-19.
Frozen food.
Mellorine.
Manufacture and sale,
§§20-1-130 to 20-1-137.
See MELLORINE.

FOOD—Cont'd
Fruit, §§2-11-70 to 2-11-79.
  See FRUITS AND
    VEGETABLES.
Gifts.
  Nonliability of good faith
    donors and distributors
    of food, §20-1-6.
Grits, §§20-1-70 to 20-1-78.
  Nuisances menacing public
    health, §§22-10-1 to
    22-10-3.
Health.
  Regulations for
    establishments handling
    food, §22-20-5.
Inspections.
  Municipal corporations,
    §11-47-136.
Jails.
  Feeding of prisoners,
    §§14-6-40 to 14-6-50.
  See JAILS.
Manufacturers.
  Adulteration and
    misbranding.
  Effect of possession by
    manufacturers,
    §20-1-31.
Margarine, §§20-1-110 to
  20-1-113.
Mellorine.
  Manufacture and sale,
    §§20-1-130 to 20-1-137.
  See MELLORINE.
Milk and milk products,
  §§2-13-1 to 2-13-94.
  See MILK AND MILK
    PRODUCTS.
Misbranding, §§20-1-20 to
  20-1-32. See within this
  heading, "Adulteration and
  misbranding."
Municipal corporations.
  Impure, adulterated, etc.
    food.
  Inspections, §11-47-136.
  Prohibition of sale, etc.,
    §11-47-136.
  Inspection, §11-47-136.
  Charges for inspection,
    §11-43-59.
  Markets and marketing of
    food products.
  Regulation, etc.,
    §11-47-137.
  Regulation of sales,
    §11-47-137.
**Nuisances menacing public
  health,** §§22-10-1 to
  22-10-3.
Nuts.
  General provisions, §§1-2-19,
    2-25-15, 20-1-90 to
    20-1-93, 40-9-3.
  See NUTS.
  Promotion, §§2-8-120 to
    2-8-137.
  See NUTS.
**Obtaining food by fraud or
  misrepresentation,**
  §§34-15-19, 34-15-20.
Oleomargarine, §§20-1-110 to
  20-1-113.
Penalties.
  Violations of chapter or
    orders, rules or
    regulations, §20-1-5.

FOOD—Cont'd
Prisons and prisoners.
  Jails.
  Feeding of prisoners,
    §§14-6-40 to 14-6-50.
  See JAILS.
Records.
  Investigation, §20-1-3.
Restaurants.
  See RESTAURANTS.
Rules and regulations.
  Adoption, §20-1-2.
  Violations.
    Penalty for violations,
      §20-1-5.
Sales.
  Adulterated or misbranded
    food, §20-1-27.
  Implied warranty of
    merchantability,
    §7-2-314.
  Seizure and condemnation of
    articles sold in violation
    of chapter, §20-1-4.
Sales tax.
  Selling food through coin-
    operated dispensing
    machines.
  Tax levied on gross
    receipts, §40-23-2.
Samples.
  Commissioner of agriculture
    and industries.
  Authority to take samples,
    §20-1-3.
Seafood.
  General provisions.
  See MARINE
    RESOURCES.
Seizure.
  Articles sold, stored, etc., in
    violation of chapter,
    §20-1-4.
Stamps.
  See FOOD STAMPS.
Storage.
  Seizure and condemnation of
    food stored in violation
    of chapter, §20-1-4.
Vegetables, §§2-11-70 to
  2-11-79.
  See FRUITS AND
    VEGETABLES.
Violations of chapter.
  Penalties, §20-1-5.
  Suspension from sale, seizure
    and condemnation of
    articles sold, stored, etc.,
    in violation, §20-1-4.
Warranties.
  Implied warranty of
    merchantability,
    §7-2-314.

FOOD STAMPS.
Alcoholic beverages.
  Licenses.
  Revocation.
    Illegal possession of food
      stamps, §13A-9-92.
Definitions.
  Illegal possession of food
    stamps, §13A-9-90.
**Department of pensions and
  security.**
  Responsibility for program,
    §38-2-6.

FOOD STAMPS—Cont'd
Felonies.
  Class B felony.
    First degree illegal
      possession of food
      stamps, §13A-9-91.
  Class C felony.
    Second degree illegal
      possession of food
      stamps, §13A-9-91.
**Illegal possession of food
  stamps,** §§13A-9-90 to
  13A-9-92.
  Alcoholic beverages.
    Revocation of liquor license
      for illegal possession,
      §13A-9-92.
  Authorization cards.
    Food stamp authorization
      cards.
    Defined, §13A-9-90.
  Coupons.
    Food stamp coupon.
    Defined, §13A-9-90.
  First degree illegal
    possession.
    Class B felony, §13A-9-91.
    Elements of crime,
      §13A-9-91.
  Second degree illegal
    possession.
    Class C felony, §13A-9-91.
    Elements of crime,
      §13A-9-91.
  Third degree illegal
    possession.
    Class A misdemeanor,
      §13A-9-91.
    Elements of crime,
      §13A-9-91.
Misdemeanors.
  Class A misdemeanor.
  Third degree illegal
    possession of food
    stamps, §13A-9-91.
Sales tax.
  Exemptions, §40-23-4.2.

**FOOT AND MOUTH
  DISEASE.**
Livestock diseases,
  §§2-15-150 to 2-15-274.
  See LIVESTOCK.

FOOTBALL.
Agents.
  Generally, §§8-26-1 to
    8-26-41.
  See SPORTS.

FORCED SHARE ACT,
  §43-8-70.

**FORCIBLE ENTRY AND
  UNLAWFUL DETAINER,**
  §§6-6-310 to 6-6-353.
Absence.
  Effect of temporary absence,
    §6-6-313.
Appeals, §§6-6-350 to 6-6-353.
  Bonds, surety.
    Suspension of writ of
      restitution or
      possession upon
      posting by defendant,
      §6-6-351.
  Circuit courts.
    Appeal from district court,
      §6-6-350.
    Issuance of writ of
      restitution or
      possession, §6-6-351.

FORCIBLE ENTRY AND UNLAWFUL DETAINER —Cont'd

Appeals—Cont'd
Proceedings when determination is against appellant, §6-6-353.
Writs of restitution or possession.
Issuance by appellate court, §6-6-352.
Suspension upon posting of bond by defendant, §6-6-351.
Appearance.
Proceedings when parties appear or defendant fails to do so, §6-6-335.
Bonds, surety.
Appeals.
Suspension of writ of restitution or possession upon posting of bond by defendant, §6-6-351.
Circuit courts.
Appeal from district court, §6-6-350.
Issuance of writ of restitution or possession, §6-6-352.
Constables.
Process.
Neglect or refusal to execute, §6-6-333.
Definitions, §6-6-310.
District courts.
Appeals to circuit courts, §6-6-350.
Courts deemed always open, §6-6-318.
Jurisdiction, §6-6-330.
Estates.
Applicability to all estates, §6-6-311.
Joint estates.
Commencement of action where property held jointly, §6-6-312.
Extent of inquiry, §6-6-336.
Forms, §6-6-319.
Process.
Notice, §6-6-332.
Holding over.
Liability of lessee, §6-6-314.
How recovered, §6-6-314.
Joint estates.
Commencement of action where property held jointly, §6-6-312.
Judgments.
Form, §6-6-319.
Jurisdiction.
District courts, §6-6-330.
Limitation of actions.
Uninterrupted occupation for three years bars action, §6-6-315.
Notice or demand, §6-6-317.
Process. See within this heading, "Process."
Proceedings.
Appeals.
Proceedings when determination is against appellant, §6-6-353.
Appearance.
Proceedings when parties appear or defendant fails to do so, §6-6-335.

FORCIBLE ENTRY AND UNLAWFUL DETAINER —Cont'd

Proceedings—Cont'd
Determination for either plaintiff or defendant, §6-6-337.
Process.
Execution.
Neglect or failure to execute by sheriff or constable, §6-6-333.
Notice, §6-6-332.
Sheriffs.
Process.
Neglect or refusal to execute, §6-6-333.
Title.
Limitations on inquiry into, §6-6-336.
Trespass.
Action of trespass not precluded, §6-6-316.
Venue, §6-6-331.
Witnesses.
Failure to attend or refusal to testify, §6-6-334.
Writ of restitution or possession.
Appeals. See within this heading, "Appeals."
Form, §6-6-319.

FORECLOSURE.
Deeds.
Foreclosure deeds.
Deeds in lieu of foreclosure, §§35-10-50, 35-10-51.
Generally, §§35-10-1, 35-10-5.
Definitions.
Deeds in lieu of foreclosure, §35-10-50.
Judicial sales.
General provisions.
See JUDICIAL SALES.

FOREIGN CORPORATIONS.
Banks and financial institutions, §§5-3A-5, 5-3A-6.
Fraternal benefit societies.
Foreign societies, §§27-34-1 to 27-34-54.
See FRATERNAL BENEFIT SOCIETIES.
General provisions, §§10-2A-220 to 10-2A-247, 10-3A-170 to 10-3A-186.
See CORPORATIONS.
Insurers.
Foreign insurers.
See INSURANCE.
Savings and loan associations.
Foreign corporations not to transact business in state, §5-16-39.

FOREIGN COUNTRIES.
Acknowledgments.
Officers authorized to take in foreign countries, §35-4-26.
Evidence.
Legislative acts.
Authentication of foreign country's legislative acts, §12-21-70.
Proof of certain official documents, §12-21-73.

FOREIGN COUNTRIES —Cont'd

Evidence—Cont'd
Proof of laws of foreign countries, §12-21-64.
Public records or books.
Authentication of foreign country's public records or books, §12-21-70.
Parol evidence.
Production of books, etc. Parol in lieu of, §12-21-3.
Proof of laws of foreign countries, §12-21-64.
Receipt of money, §12-21-110.
Void writing.
Admissibility of parol evidence to show writing void, §12-21-33.

FOREIGN EXECUTORS AND ADMINISTRATORS, §§43-2-210 to 43-2-214.
See EXECUTORS AND ADMINISTRATORS.

FOREIGN JUDGMENTS.
Uniform enforcement of foreign judgments act, §§6-9-230 to 6-9-238.
See JUDGMENTS.

FOREIGN TRADE AND RELATIONS COMMISSION, §§41-9-660 to 41-9-664.
Appointment, §41-9-660.
Assistance of officers, departments and agencies of state, §41-9-663.
Compensation of members, §41-9-662.
Composition, §41-9-660.
Consultants.
Compensation, §41-9-662.
Cooperation of officers, departments and agencies of state, §41-9-663.
Creation, §41-9-660.
Duties, §41-9-661.
Expenses.
Payment of clerical expenses, §41-9-663.
Filling of vacancies, §41-9-660.
Gifts, §41-9-664.
Governor.
Annual report to governor, §41-9-662.
Legislature.
Annual report to legislature, §41-9-662.
Officers.
Compensation, §41-9-662.
Powers, §41-9-661.
Qualifications of members, §41-9-660.
Quorum, §41-9-660.
Reports.
Annual report to governor and legislature, §41-9-662.
Taxation.
Gifts, §41-9-664.
Terms of office, §41-9-660.
Vacancies.
Filling, §41-9-660.

FORENSIC SCIENCES,
§§36-18-1 to 36-18-5.
Director.
Appointment, §36-18-1.
Assistants.
Police authority, §36-18-2.
Duties.
Generally, §36-18-2.
Employees.
Office of state toxicologist.
Continued employment
of certain employees,
§36-18-5.
Expenses, §36-18-4.
Investigations.
Reports, §36-18-2.
Laboratories, §36-18-3.
Offices, §36-18-3.
Police authority, §36-18-2.
Removal, §36-18-1.
Salary, §36-18-4.

FORESTS AND FORESTRY.
Actions.
Forest products.
Privilege and severance
taxes.
Collection of delinquent
taxes, §9-13-101.
Appeals.
Forest products.
Privilege and severance
taxes, §§9-13-96,
9-13-98.
Appropriations.
Forest products.
Privilege and severance
taxes.
Appropriation of tax
receipts, §9-13-84.
Arrests.
Fees, §9-13-24.
**Assessments for forest fire
protection.**
Participation by counties in
fire prevention program,
§§9-13-180 to 9-13-187.
See within this heading,
"Fires and fire
prevention."
State assessments,
§§9-13-189 to 9-13-198.
See within this heading,
"Fires and fire
prevention."
Attorney general.
State forests.
Gifts of land.
Duties, §9-13-1.
Auxiliary state forests,
§§9-13-40 to 9-13-50. See
within this heading, "State
forests."
**Board of registration for
foresters,** §§34-12-30 to
34-12-37. See within this
heading, "Foresters."
Bonds, surety.
Board of registration for
foresters.
Bond of secretary,
§34-12-36.
State forester, §9-3-5.
Campfires.
Fires and fire prevention.
Emergency drought
conditions.
Building of campfires,
§9-13-141.

FORESTS AND FORESTRY
—Cont'd
Commission.
State forestry commission,
§§9-3-1 to 9-3-17. See
within this heading,
"State forestry
commission."
Compacts.
Southeastern interstate
forest fire protection
compact, §§9-13-200,
9-13-201.
Condemnation.
Timber theft equipment,
§§9-13-220 to 9-13-227.
See TREES AND TIMBER.
Constables.
Wardens.
Designation as forest
wardens, §9-13-5.
Contracts.
State forests.
Auxiliary state forests.
Designation of lands,
§§9-13-43 to 9-13-45.
Counties.
Acquisition and
administration of forest
lands, §§11-84-1, 11-84-2.
Assessments for forest fire
protection, §§9-13-180 to
9-13-187. See within this
heading, "Fires and fire
prevention."
Forest products.
Privilege and severance
taxes.
Payment by counties
purchasing forest
products, §9-13-106.
National forests.
Receipts from national
forests.
Distribution and
expenditure, §9-13-2.
Research and educational
programs.
Appropriation of funds by
counties, §2-30-23.
Special taxes for forest
protection, §§9-13-160 to
9-13-166. See within this
heading, "Taxation."
Damages.
Forest products.
Cutting.
Unauthorized cutting,
§9-13-62.
Purchases.
Unauthorized purchases.
Liability of violators to
owners, §9-13-62.
Definitions.
Fires and fire prevention.
Assessments for forest fire
protection, §9-13-180.
Foresters, §34-12-1.
Forest products.
Privilege and severance
taxes, §9-13-80.
Insect infestation or tree
disease infection.
Protection of forest trees,
§9-13-120.
Taxation.
Special county taxes for
forest protection,
§9-13-160.

FORESTS AND FORESTRY
—Cont'd
Diseases.
Protection of forest trees
from tree disease
infection, §§9-13-120 to
9-13-126. See within this
heading, "Insect
infestation or tree
disease infection."
District attorneys.
Violation of chapter.
Prosecution, §9-13-22.
District courts.
Violation of chapter.
Jurisdiction of
prosecutions, §9-13-23.
Dower.
State forests.
Auxiliary state forests.
Designation of lands.
Release of dower,
§9-13-42.
Drought.
Fire prevention in emergency
drought conditions,
§§9-13-140 to 9-13-142.
Educational programs.
Research and educational
programs, §§2-30-20 to
2-30-24.
State forestry commission.
Program of education and
public enlightenment.
Authority to conduct,
§9-3-4.
Emergencies.
Fire prevention in emergency
drought conditions,
§§9-13-140 to 9-13-142.
Eminent domain.
Experimental work in
forestry.
Authorization and
procedure for
condemnation of lands,
§2-30-24.
State forestry commission.
Powers of commission,
§9-3-3.
Examinations.
Foresters, §34-12-6.
Experimental forestry units.
Disposition of revenues from
units, §2-30-22.
Experimental work.
Research and educational
programs, §§2-30-20 to
2-30-24.
Fees.
Arrests.
Arresting officers,
§9-13-24.
Foresters. See within this
heading, "Foresters."
Informers' fees, §9-13-24.
Fires and fire prevention.
Assessments for forest fire
protection.
Definitions, §9-13-180.
State assessment,
§9-13-189.

FORESTS AND FORESTRY
—Cont'd
Fires and fire prevention
—Cont'd
Assessments for forest fire
protection—Cont'd
Participation by counties
in fire protection
program.
Assessments against
owners of forest
lands for costs,
§§9-13-180 to
9-13-187.
Amount,
establishment,
§9-13-182.
Authorized, §9-13-182.
Compensation of
officials,
§9-13-186.
Determination of need,
§9-13-183.
Discontinuance of
assessment,
§9-13-187.
Disposition of revenue,
§9-13-185.
Expenditures,
§9-13-185.
Liens for payment,
§9-13-184.
Limitations, §9-13-182.
Payment, §9-13-184.
Rate, §9-13-182.
Removal of
assessment,
§9-13-187.
Reports by tax
assessor,
§9-13-184.
Authorized, §9-13-181.
State assessment,
§§9-13-189 to 9-13-198.
Administration,
§9-13-190.
Amount, §9-13-193.
Change or modification,
§9-13-197.
Collection.
Manner of collection,
§9-13-192.
Definitions, §9-13-189.
Disposition of proceeds,
§9-13-191.
Distribution of revenue
collected, §9-13-192.
Established, §9-13-191.
Intent of legislature,
§9-13-188.
Levy, §9-13-191.
Lien on property.
Failure to pay
assessment,
§9-13-196.
Notice.
Referendum,
§9-13-193.
Payment, §9-13-193.
Failure to pay
assessment,
§9-13-196.
Penalties.
Failure to pay
assessment,
§9-13-196.
Referendum, §§9-13-193
to 9-13-195.
Authorized, §9-13-193.
Management,
§9-13-194.

FORESTS AND FORESTRY
—Cont'd
Fires and fire prevention
—Cont'd
Assessments for forest fire
protection—Cont'd
State assessment—Cont'd
Referendum—Cont'd
Notice, §9-13-193.
Referendum after
failed referendum,
§9-13-195.
Remission, §9-13-193.
Rules and regulations,
§9-13-190.
Status as tax.
Not a tax, §9-13-198.
Campfires.
Emergency drought
conditions, §9-13-141.
Costs.
Uncontrolled fires.
Controlling by fire
suppression force,
§9-13-12.
Counties.
Assessments for forest fire
protection. §§9-13-180
to 9-13-187.
Emergency drought
conditions, §§9-13-140 to
9-13-142.
Backfires, §9-13-141.
Burning of trash,
§9-13-141.
Campfires, §9-13-141.
Declaration of conditions,
§9-13-140.
Penalties.
Violation of article,
§9-13-142.
Setting of fires, §9-13-141.
Violations of article.
Penalties, §9-13-142.
Emergency forest fire, insect
and disease fund,
§9-3-10.1.
Engines and boilers.
Equipping with appliances
to prevent escape of
fire, §9-13-14.
Equipment.
Issuance and use, §9-13-8.
Escape of fire.
Allowing fires to escape,
§9-13-11.
Fire lanes.
Construction.
Right of entry, §9-13-7.
Forest fire warden, §§9-13-6
to 9-13-9.
Fund.
Emergency forest fire,
insect and disease
fund, §9-3-10.1.
Garbage and trash.
Emergency drought
conditions.
Burning of trash,
§9-13-141.
Notice.
Assessments for forest fire
protection.
State assessment.
Referendum,
§9-13-193.
Setting of fires.
Written notice to
adjacent landowners,
§9-13-13.

FORESTS AND FORESTRY
—Cont'd
Fires and fire prevention
—Cont'd
Nuisances.
Uncontrolled fires,
§9-13-12.
Organized forest fire
protection areas.
Placement of lands in
areas, §9-13-11.
Penalties.
Allowing fires to escape,
§9-13-11.
Assessments for forest fire
protection.
State assessment.
Failure to pay,
§9-13-196.
Organized forest fire
protection areas.
Setting of fires in areas,
§9-13-11.
Setting of fires.
Willful, malicious or
intentional setting of
fires, §9-13-11.
Permits.
Issuance of burning
permits, §9-13-11.
Railroads.
Locomotives.
Equipping with
appliances to
prevent escape of
fire, §9-13-14.
Setting of fires.
Burning permits, §9-13-11.
Emergency drought
conditions, §9-13-141.
Failing to protect property,
§9-13-11.
Notice.
Adjacent landowners,
§9-13-13.
Organized forest fire
protection areas.
Setting of fires in areas,
§9-13-11.
Willful, malicious or
intentional setting on
fire of woods, §9-13-11.
Southeastern interstate
forest fire protection
compact.
Advisory committee.
Expenses in attending
meetings, §9-13-201.
Authorized, §9-13-200.
Contents, §9-13-200.
Expenses of advisory
committee.
Payment in attending
meetings, §9-13-201.
Form, §9-13-200.
State forestry commission.
Assistance in control and
suppression of
wildfires by other state
agencies, §9-13-10.1.
Powers generally, §9-13-3.
Prevention and suppression
of forest fires,
§9-13-10.

FORESTS AND FORESTRY
—Cont'd
Fires and fire prevention
—Cont'd
Steering committee for rural
community fire
departments.
State forestry commission,
§§9-3-11 to 9-3-16. See
within this heading,
"State forestry
commission."
Uncontrolled fires.
Costs.
Controlling by organized
fire suppression
forces, §9-13-12.
Nuisances, §9-13-12.
Refusal or neglect to
control or extinguish.
Liability, §9-13-12.
Wardens, §§9-13-6 to 9-13-9.
Appointment, §9-13-6.
Commission, §9-13-6.
Compensation, §9-13-9.
Duties.
Generally, §9-13-6.
Expenses, §9-13-9.
Fire-fighting equipment.
Issuance and use,
§9-13-8.
Right of entry.
Construction of fire lanes
or fire breaks,
§9-13-7.
Warning signs.
Injuring, defacing, etc.,
§9-13-11.
Fish and game.
Shooting preserves, game
refuges, etc.
Establishment in national
forests, §9-11-4.
Foresters, §§34-12-1 to
34-12-37.
Board of registration,
§§34-12-30 to 34-12-37.
Appointment of members,
§34-12-30.
Compensation of members,
§34-12-32.
Composition, §34-12-30.
Creation, §34-12-30.
Defined, §34-12-1.
Employees, §34-12-36.
Expenses of members,
§34-12-32.
Gifts.
Board authorized to
accept gifts and
donations, §34-12-36.
Governor.
Annual report to
governor, §34-12-37.
Appointment of board
members, §34-12-30.
Appointment of initial
board, §34-12-34.
Immunity of board for good
faith actions,
§34-12-35.
Meetings.
Generally, §34-12-34.
Oath of office, §34-12-30.
Officers, §34-12-34.
Powers.
Generally, §34-12-35.
Qualifications of members,
§34-12-31.
Quorum, §34-12-34.
Records, §34-12-37.

FORESTS AND FORESTRY
—Cont'd
Foresters—Cont'd
Board of registration—Cont'd
Removal of members,
§34-12-33.
Reports.
Annual report to
governor, §34-12-37.
Revocation or suspension of
licenses, §34-12-9.
Rules and regulations.
Promulgation by board,
§34-12-35.
Secretary, §34-12-36.
Subpoena power of board,
§34-12-35.
Terms of office, §34-12-30.
Vacancies.
Filling vacancies,
§34-12-33.
Witnesses.
Compelling attendance
at board proceedings,
§34-12-35.
Corporations.
Not to be licensed under
chapter, §34-12-10.
Definitions, §34-12-1.
Examinations, §34-12-6.
Fees.
Examination fees,
§34-12-6.
Licenses.
Renewal fee, §34-12-8.
Replacement of lost
license, §34-12-9.
Reciprocity card, §34-12-11.
Registration fees, §34-12-5.
Firms.
Not to be licensed under
chapter, §34-12-10.
Landscape architects.
Foresters exempt from
licensing
requirements,
§34-17-27.
Licenses, §§34-12-7 to
34-12-10.
Contents, §34-12-7.
Expiration, §34-12-8.
Fees, §§9-12-8, 9-12-9.
Firms, partnerships and
corporations not to be
licensed, §34-12-10.
Issuance, §34-12-7.
Lost licenses, §34-12-9.
Number.
Use of license number,
§34-12-7.
Reissuance, §34-12-9.
Renewal, §34-12-8.
Replacement of lost
licenses, §34-12-9.
Revocation, §34-12-9.
Nonresidents.
Reciprocity, §34-12-11.
Partnerships.
Not to be licensed under
chapter, §34-12-10.
Penalties.
Disposition of fines in
professional foresters
fund, §34-12-12.
Violations of chapter,
§34-12-12.
Plans, maps, specifications,
etc.
Endorsement with name
and license number,
§34-12-7.

FORESTS AND FORESTRY
—Cont'd
Foresters—Cont'd
Practice of forestry.
Defined, §34-12-1.
Reciprocity.
Qualification of
nonresidents as
foresters, §34-12-11.
Records.
Board of registration to
keep certain records,
§34-12-37.
Registration, §§34-12-2 to
34-12-5.
Applications, §34-12-5.
Board of registration,
§§9-12-30 to 9-12-37.
Exceptions to registration
requirements,
§34-12-2.
Fees, §34-12-5.
Qualifications of
applicants, §34-12-4.
Required, §34-12-2.
Roster of registered
foresters, §34-12-3.
Roster of registered foresters,
§34-12-3.
Forest products.
Chips.
Privilege and severance
taxes, §9-13-82.
Cutting, §§9-13-60 to 9-13-65.
Damages.
Unauthorized cutting,
§9-13-62.
Unauthorized cutting,
removal or
transporting, §9-13-60.
Charges in affidavits,
informations or
indictments,
§9-13-61.
Damages, §9-13-62.
Enforcement of article,
§9-13-64.
Indictments, §9-13-61.
Liability of violators to
owners, §9-13-62.
Penalties, §9-13-60.
Disposition of fines,
§9-13-65.
Proof of title, §9-13-61.
Title.
Proof of title, §9-13-61.
Definitions.
Privilege and severance
taxes, §9-13-80.
Liens.
Privilege and severance
taxes.
Payment of tax, interest
and penalties,
§§9-13-81, 9-13-99.
Manufacturers using forest
products.
Taxation, §§9-13-82,
9-13-88.
Privilege and severance
taxes, §§9-13-80 to
9-13-108.
Actions.
Collection of delinquent
taxes, §9-13-101.
Appeals.
Assessment of taxes by
department,
§9-13-96.
Final assessment,
§9-13-98.

FORESTS AND FORESTRY
—Cont'd
Forest products—Cont'd
Privilege and severance taxes
—Cont'd
Applicability of article,
§9-13-107.
Appropriation of receipts
for use of state forestry
commission, §9-13-84.
Assessment of taxes by
department.
Appeals, §9-13-98.
Final assessment,
§9-13-97.
Appeals, §9-13-98.
Hearings, §9-13-97.
Interest, §9-13-95.
Notice, §9-13-97.
Penalties, §9-13-95.
Preparation of returns
for delinquent
taxpayers, §9-13-95.
Concealment of property.
Proceedings as to persons
designing to conceal,
§9-13-103.
Concentration yards.
Failure to collect tax
from seller, §9-13-86.
Payment of tax,
§9-13-86.
Records.
Maintenance and
inspection,
§9-13-88.
Refund of taxes,
§9-13-86.
Counties.
Payment of taxes by
counties purchasing
forest products,
§9-13-106.
Debt due state, §9-13-101.
Deficiency in taxes paid,
§9-13-92.
Definitions, §9-13-80.
Delinquent taxes.
Collection.
Civil action, §9-13-101.
Levy and execution,
§9-13-100.
Sale of property,
§9-13-100.
Debt due state,
§9-13-101.
Interest, §9-13-94.
Penalty, §9-13-94.
Preparation of returns by
department,
§9-13-95.
When taxes delinquent,
§9-13-93.
Exemptions from taxes,
§9-13-83.
Forest protection.
Expenditures for
protection, §9-13-85.
Imposition of tax, §9-13-81.
Applicability of article,
§9-13-107.
Interest.
Assessment of taxes by
department,
§9-13-95.
Deficiency in taxes paid,
§9-13-92.
Deficient payment of tax,
§9-13-96.
Delinquent taxes,
§9-13-94.

FORESTS AND FORESTRY
—Cont'd
Forest products—Cont'd
Privilege and severance taxes
—Cont'd
Interest—Cont'd
Lien upon property for
payment, §9-13-99.
Levy.
Applicability of article,
§9-13-107.
Delinquent taxes,
§9-13-100.
Privilege tax against
processor, §9-13-82.
Severance tax, §9-13-81.
Liens.
Payment of taxes,
interest and
penalties, §§9-13-81,
9-13-99.
Local laws.
Levy by local law
prohibited,
§9-13-108.
Manufacturers of products.
Privilege tax, §9-13-82.
Records.
Maintenance and
inspection,
§9-13-88.
Municipal corporations.
Payment of taxes by
municipalities
purchasing forest
products, §9-13-106.
Notices.
Assessment of taxes by
department,
§9-13-97.
Deficiency in taxes paid,
§9-13-92.
Failure to make returns,
§9-13-95.
Payment of taxes.
Ascertainment of taxes
due, §9-13-92.
Counties.
Purchasing forest
products,
§9-13-106.
Deficiency of payment,
§9-13-96.
Disposition of proceeds,
§9-13-84.
Forest protection,
§9-13-85.
Lien, §§9-13-81, 9-13-99.
Municipal corporations.
Purchasing forest
products,
§9-13-106.
Notice of deficiency,
§9-13-92.
Refunds, §9-13-92.
Excess taxes paid,
§9-13-96.
Shipment of products out
of state in
unmanufactured
condition, §9-13-87.
When due and payable,
§9-13-86.
Penalties.
Assessment of taxes by
department,
§9-13-95.
Deficient payment,
§§9-13-92, 9-13-96.
Delinquent taxes,
§9-13-94.

FORESTS AND FORESTRY
—Cont'd
Forest products—Cont'd
Privilege and severance taxes
—Cont'd
Penalties—Cont'd
Failure to pay or report
tax, §9-13-86.
Lien upon property for
payment, §9-13-99.
Political subdivisions.
Levy of tax.
Prohibited, §9-13-108.
Proceedings as to persons
removing or concealing
property, §9-13-103.
Processors of products.
Privilege tax, §9-13-82.
Producers of products.
Records.
Maintenance and
inspection,
§9-13-88.
Rates, §9-13-82.
Records.
Failure to produce,
§9-13-102.
Maintenance, §9-13-88.
Production and
examination,
§9-13-102.
Refunds, §9-13-92.
Excess taxes paid,
§9-13-96.
Removal of property.
Proceedings as to persons
designing to remove,
§9-13-103.
Reports.
Concentration yards,
§9-13-86.
Examination of reports,
§9-13-92.
Failure to make reports,
§9-13-90.
Manufacturers of
products, §9-13-86.
Notice of failure to make
returns, §9-13-95.
Preparation for
delinquent taxpayers
by department,
§9-13-95.
Producers of forest
products.
Shipping products out
of state in
unmanufactured
condition,
§9-13-87.
Shipping of products out
of state in
unmanufactured
condition, §9-13-87.
Transporters of forest
products.
Failure to make
report, §9-13-105.
Required, §9-13-104.
Round wood pulpwood.
Conversion into chips,
§9-13-82.
Special state forestry fund,
§9-13-84.
State forestry commission.
Appropriation of receipts
for use of, §9-13-84.

FORESTS AND FORESTRY
—Cont'd
Forest products—Cont'd
Privilege and severance taxes
—Cont'd
Statewide tax.
Levy of tax by local laws
or political
subdivisions.
Prohibited, §9-13-108.
Transporters of forest
products.
Reports, §§9-13-104,
9-13-105.
Witnesses.
Power to summon,
§9-13-102.
Processors of forest products.
Taxation, §9-13-82.
Purchases, §§9-13-60 to
9-13-65.
Manufactured or
semimanufactured
products.
Record of purchases,
§9-13-63.
Providing false information
to purchasers,
§9-13-63.
Unauthorized purchases,
§9-13-60.
Damages, §9-13-62.
Enforcement of article,
§9-13-64.
Indictments, §9-13-62.
Liability of violators,
§9-13-62.
Penalties, §9-13-60.
Disposition of fines,
§9-13-65.
Proof of title, §9-13-61.
Records.
Privilege and severance
taxes, §§9-13-88,
9-13-102.
Purchases.
Manufactured or
semimanufactured
products, §9-13-63.
Removal, §§9-13-60 to
9-13-65.
Severance taxes, §§9-13-80 to
9-13-109.
Transportation, §§9-13-60 to
9-13-65.
Forest protection.
Taxation.
Special county taxes for
forest protection,
§§9-13-160 to 9-13-167.
See within this
heading, "Taxation."
Forestry study committee.
Appointment of members,
§9-13-25.
Chairman.
Election, §9-13-25.
Composition, §9-13-25.
Duties, §9-13-25.
Employees, §9-13-25.
Established, §9-13-25.
Expenses of members.
Travel expenses, §9-13-25.
Meetings, §9-13-25.
Organizational meeting,
§9-13-25.
Number of members,
§9-13-25.
Per diem of members,
§9-13-25.
Reports, §9-13-25.

FORESTS AND FORESTRY
—Cont'd
Funds.
Alabama forestry commission
fund, §§9-3-10, 9-13-4.
Control of forest tree insects
and diseases fund,
§9-13-126.
Emergency forest fire, insect
and disease fund,
§9-3-10.1.
Forest products.
Privilege and severance
taxes.
Special state forestry
fund, §9-13-84.
Forest protection fund,
§9-13-166.
Professional foresters fund,
§34-12-36.
Disposition of fines in
fund, §34-12-12.
Garbage and trash.
Fires and fire prevention.
Emergency drought
conditions.
Burning of trash,
§9-13-141.
Geological survey.
General provisions, §§9-4-1 to
9-4-19.
See GEOLOGICAL
SURVEY.
Gifts.
State forests.
Gifts of lands, §9-13-1.
Ginseng regulation.
General provisions,
§§9-13-240 to 9-13-250.
See GINSENG.
Homestead rights.
State forests.
Auxiliary state forests.
Designation of lands.
Release of homestead
rights, §9-13-42.
Indictments.
Forest products.
Unauthorized cutting.
Charges in affidavits,
informations or
indictments,
§9-13-61.
Informers.
Violation of chapter.
Fees, §9-13-24.
**Insect infestation or tree
disease infection.**
Protection of forest trees,
§§9-13-120 to 9-13-126.
Control of forest tree
insects and diseases
fund, §9-13-126.
Control zones, §§9-13-122
to 9-13-124.
Boundaries.
Establishment,
§9-13-122.
Declaration of existence,
§9-13-122.
Dissolution, §9-13-124.
Establishment.
Declaration of
existence,
§9-13-122.
Notice to landowners,
§9-13-123.

FORESTS AND FORESTRY
—Cont'd
**Insect infestation or tree
disease infection**—Cont'd
Protection of forest trees
—Cont'd
Cooperative agreements.
Federal government,
public or private
agencies and
landowners,
§9-13-125.
Definitions, §9-13-120.
Existence of infestations or
infections.
Control measures,
§9-13-121.
Failure or refusal of
landowner to
initiate, §9-13-123.
Investigations,
§9-13-121.
Notice to landowners,
§9-13-121.
Recommended control
measures, §9-13-121.
Funds.
Control of forest tree
insects and diseases
fund, §9-13-126.
Investigations.
Existence of infestations
or infections,
§9-13-121.
Notice.
Control zones.
Establishment,
§9-13-123.
Existence of infestations
or infections,
§9-13-121.
Special county taxes for
forest protection,
§§9-13-160 to 9-13-167.
See within this
heading, "Taxation."
United States.
Cooperative agreements,
§9-13-125.
Special county taxes for
forest protection,
§§9-13-160 to 9-13-167.
See within this heading,
"Taxation."
Inspections.
State forests.
Auxiliary state forests.
Designation of lands,
§9-13-43.
Interest.
Forest products.
Privilege and severance
taxes.
Assessment of taxes.
Due by department,
§9-13-95.
Deficiency in taxes paid,
§9-13-92.
Deficient payment of tax,
§9-13-96.
Delinquent taxes,
§9-13-94.
Lien upon property for
payment, §9-13-99.
Legislature.
State forestry commission.
Recommendations to
legislature, §9-3-4.
Licenses.
Foresters, §§34-12-7 to
34-12-10.

FORESTS AND FORESTRY
—Cont'd
Liens.
Fires and fire prevention.
Assessments for forest fire
protection.
Lien on property for
payment, §9-13-184.
State assessment.
Failure to pay
assessment,
§9-13-196.
Forest products.
Payment of taxes, interest
and penalties,
§§9-13-81, 9-13-99.
Marshals.
Wardens.
Designation as forest
wardens, §9-13-5.
Municipal corporations.
Acquisition and
administration of forest
lands, §§11-84-1, 11-84-2.
Forest products.
Privilege and severance
taxes.
Payments by
municipalities
purchasing forest
products, §9-13-106.
Research and educational
programs.
Appropriation of funds by
municipalities,
§2-30-23.
Receipt of donations from
municipalities,
§2-30-23.
National forests.
Consent to acquisition of
lands needed for
consolidation and
administration, §42-1-2.
Counties.
Receipts from national
forests.
Distribution and
expenditure, §9-13-2.
Receipts.
Distribution and
expenditure of receipts,
§9-13-2.
Shooting preserves, game
refuges, etc.
Establishment, §9-11-4.
Notice.
Fires and fire prevention.
Assessments for forest fire
protection.
State assessment.
Referendum,
§9-13-193.
Setting of fires.
Written notice to
adjacent landowners,
§9-13-13.
Forest products.
Privilege and severance
taxes.
Assessment of taxes by
department,
§9-13-97.
Deficiency in taxes paid,
§9-13-92.
Failure to make returns,
§9-13-95.

FORESTS AND FORESTRY
—Cont'd
Notice—Cont'd
Insect infestation or tree
disease infection.
Protection of forest trees,
§§9-13-120 to 9-13-126.
See within this
heading, "Insect
infestation or tree
disease infection."
Oaths.
State forester, §9-3-5.
Paper.
Forest products. See within
this heading, "Forest
products."
Penalties.
Fires and fire prevention.
Assessments for forest fire
protection.
State assessment.
Failure to pay,
§9-13-196.
Emergency drought
conditions.
Violation of article,
§9-13-142.
Escape of fires, §9-13-11.
Organized forest fire
protection areas.
Setting of fires in areas,
§9-13-11.
Setting of fires, §9-13-11.
Foresters.
Violations of chapter,
§34-12-12.
Forest products.
Cutting.
Unauthorized cutting,
§9-13-60.
Disposition of fines,
§9-13-65.
Privilege and severance
taxes. See within this
heading, "Forest
products."
Purchases.
Records.
Failure to maintain,
§9-13-63.
Providing false
information to
purchasers,
§9-13-63.
Unauthorized purchases.
Disposition of fines,
§9-13-65.
Records.
Disposition of fines,
§9-13-65.
Petitions.
Taxation.
Special county taxes for
forest protection,
§9-13-163.
Pine tar.
Forest products. See within
this heading, "Forest
products."
Property.
Gifts of lands.
State forestry, §9-13-1.
State forestry commission.
Powers and duties.
General provisions,
§9-13-3.

FORESTS AND FORESTRY
—Cont'd
Protection of forests.
Special county taxes for
forest protection,
§§9-13-160 to 9-13-167.
See within this heading,
"Taxation."
Public lands.
General provisions.
See PUBLIC LANDS.
Practice of forestry.
School lands, §9-15-34.
Swamp and overflowed
lands, §§9-15-30,
9-15-35.
Unused public lands.
Use as state forests,
§9-15-3.
Public utilities.
Municipal corporations.
Attachment of wires to
trees in towns or
cities, §9-13-15.
Pulp.
Forest products. See within
this heading, "Forest
products."
Purchases.
Forest products, §§9-13-60 to
9-13-65. See within this
heading, "Forest
products."
Railroads.
Fires and fire prevention.
Locomotives.
Equipping with
appliances to
prevent escape of
fire, §9-13-14.
Records.
Board of registration for
foresters.
Board to keep certain
records, §34-12-37.
Foresters.
Board of registration to
keep certain records,
§34-12-37.
Forest products.
Privilege and severance
taxes, §§9-13-88,
9-13-102.
Purchases.
Manufactured or
semimanufactured
products, §9-13-63.
State forestry commission.
Proceedings of commission,
§9-3-2.
State forests.
Auxiliary state forests.
Maintenance of records,
§9-13-50.
Referendums.
Fires and fire prevention.
Assessments for forest fire
protection.
State assessment,
§§9-13-193 to
9-13-195.
Registration.
Foresters, §§34-12-1 to
34-12-37. See within this
heading, "Foresters."
Reports.
Fires and fire prevention.
Assessments for forest fire
protection.
Tax assessor, §9-13-184.

FORESTS AND FORESTRY
—Cont'd
Reports—Cont'd
Forest products.
Privilege and severance
taxes. See within this
heading, "Forest
products."
State forestry commission.
Annual report to governor,
§9-3-4.
**Research and educational
programs,** §§2-30-20 to
2-30-24.
Appropriation of funds by
counties and
municipalities, §2-30-23.
Condemnation of lands for
experimental work,
§2-30-24.
Control of research work,
§2-30-21.
Counties.
Appropriation of funds by
counties, §2-30-23.
Donations.
Receipt from counties,
municipalities,
individuals, etc.,
§2-30-23.
Establishment, §2-30-20.
Experimental forestry units.
Disposition of revenues
from units, §2-30-22.
Experimental work.
Authorization and
procedure for
condemnation of lands
for experimental work,
§2-30-24.
Forest ranger courses.
Establishment, §2-30-20.
Gifts.
Receipt of donations from
counties,
municipalities,
individuals, etc.,
§2-30-23.
Maintenance, §2-30-20.
Municipal corporations.
Appropriation of funds by
municipalities,
§2-30-23.
Receipt of donations from
municipalities,
§2-30-23.
Revenues from sale of timber
or forest products.
Disposition, §2-30-22.
Supervision of research work,
§2-30-21.
Training in forestry.
Expansion of facilities for
training, §2-30-20.
Resin.
Forest products. See within
this heading, 'Forest
products."
Rules and regulations.
Fires and fire prevention.
Assessments for forest fire
protection.
State assessment,
§9-13-190.
State forestry commission.
Promulgation and
enforcement, §9-3-9.
Salaries.
State forester, §9-3-5.
Assistant state forester,
§9-3-6.

FORESTS AND FORESTRY
—Cont'd
Salaries—Cont'd
State forestry commission,
§9-3-2.
Searches and seizures.
Timber theft equipment.
Condemnation, §§9-13-220
to 9-13-227.
See TREES AND
TIMBER.
Severance taxes.
Forest products, §§9-13-80 to
9-13-108. See within this
heading, "Forest
products."
Sheriffs.
Designation as forest warden,
§9-13-5.
**Southeastern interstate
forest fire protection
compact,** §§9-13-200,
9-13-201.
Standing timber.
Taxation.
Exemption of standing
timber from taxes,
§40-11-1.
State.
Sale of timber or forest
products.
Disposition of revenues,
§2-30-22.
State forester.
Appointment, §9-3-5.
Assistant state forester.
Appointment, §9-3-6.
Expenses, §9-3-6.
Qualifications, §9-3-6.
Salary, §9-3-6.
Bond, surety, §9-3-5.
Expenses, §9-3-5.
Full-time position, §9-3-5.
Oath of office, §9-3-5.
Qualifications, §9-3-5.
Salary, §9-3-5.
State forestry commission.
Members not eligible for
appointment, §9-3-8.
Steering committee to
represent rural
community fire
departments.
Provisions generally,
§§9-3-11 to 9-3-16.
Term of office, §9-3-5.
State forestry commission,
§§9-13-1 to 9-13-17.
Acquisition of lands, §9-13-3.
Gifts of lands for state
forests, §9-13-1.
Appointment, §9-3-1.
Assistance by other state
agencies.
Control and suppression of
wildfires, §9-13-10.1.
Compensation of members,
§9-3-2.
Composition, §9-3-1.
Creation, §9-3-1.
Disposition of land.
Powers of commission,
§9-13-3.
Duties.
Generally, §§9-3-4, 9-13-3.
Education.
Conduct of program of
education, §9-3-4.
Eminent domain.
Powers of commission,
§9-13-3.

FORESTS AND FORESTRY
—Cont'd
State forestry commission
—Cont'd
Employment.
Members eligibility, §9-3-8.
Expenses of members, §9-3-2.
Payment from fund,
§9-13-4.
Forest fires.
General provisions. See
within this heading,
"Fires and fire
prevention."
Forest law enforcement
officers.
Powers and duties,
§9-13-10.
Forest products.
Privilege and severance
taxes.
Appropriation of receipts
for use of
commission,
§9-13-84.
Fund, §§9-3-10, 9-13-4.
Legislature.
Recommendations to
legislature, §9-3-4.
Location of offices, §9-3-7.
Management of land.
Powers of commission,
§9-13-3.
Meetings, §9-3-2.
Officers.
Election, §9-3-2.
Executive secretary.
State forester, §9-3-5.
Offices.
Location, §9-3-7.
Personnel.
Employment, §9-13-3.
Enforcement of laws,
§9-13-10.
Prevention and suppression
of forest fires,
§9-13-10.
Supervision and
management, §9-3-4.
Powers and duties.
Enforcement of laws,
§9-13-10.
Generally, §§9-3-4, 9-13-3.
Prevention and suppression
of forest fires,
§9-13-10.
Private land owners.
Assistance, §9-13-3.
Qualifications of members,
§9-3-1.
Quorum, §9-3-2.
Records.
Auxiliary state forests.
Maintenance of records,
§9-13-50.
Proceedings of commission,
§9-3-2.
Removal from office.
Failure to attend meetings,
§9-3-3.
Reports.
Annual report to governor,
§9-3-4.
Rules and regulations.
Promulgation and
enforcement, §9-3-9.
Salaries, §9-3-2.
State forester. See within
this heading, "State
forester."

FORESTS AND FORESTRY
—Cont'd

State forestry commission
—Cont'd

Steering committee, §§9-3-11
to 9-3-16.
Advisory committee on
general forestry
matters, §9-3-16.
Appointments, §9-3-12.
Compensation of members,
§9-3-15.
Created to represent rural
community fire
department, §9-3-11.
Expenses of members,
§9-3-15.
Meetings, §9-3-14.
Membership, §9-3-12.
Purpose of committee,
§9-3-11.
Qualifications of members,
§9-3-12.
Quorum, §9-3-14.
Recommendations to state
forester, §9-3-13.
Terms of members, §9-3-12.
Vacancies, §9-3-12.
Terms of office, §9-3-1.
United States.
Cooperative agreements,
§9-3-4.
Sole cooperating agency in
joint work, §9-13-3.
Vacancies in office.
Filling, §9-3-1.
Removal from office for
failure to attend
meetings, §9-3-3.
Volunteer fire departments,
§9-3-17.
State forests.
Attorney general.
Gifts of land.
Duties, §9-13-1.
Auxiliary state forests,
§§9-13-40 to 9-13-50.
Abstract of title.
When required, §9-13-42.
Declaration of public
policy, §9-13-40.
Designation of lands.
Application, §9-13-41.
Contracts.
Abrogation of
contracts,
§9-13-45.
Contents, §9-13-44.
Drafting and
execution,
§9-13-43.
Dower.
Release, §9-13-42.
Homestead rights.
Release, §9-13-42.
Inspection of lands,
§9-13-43.
Release of dower or
homestead rights,
§9-13-42.
Title.
When abstract of title
required, §9-13-42.
Policies.
Declaration of public
policy, §9-13-40.
Records.
Maintenance, §9-13-50.

FORESTS AND FORESTRY
—Cont'd

State forests—Cont'd

Auxiliary state forests
—Cont'd
Taxation of timber.
Abrogation of contracts.
Tax becomes due and
payable, §9-13-45.
Collection of other taxes,
§9-13-48.
Deferred taxation
authorized, §9-13-40.
Disposition of taxes,
§9-13-49.
Lien on timber for
payment, §9-13-48.
Withdrawing of lands or
harvesting of timber.
Appraisal of timber,
§9-13-47.
Lien on timber for
payment, §9-13-48.
Payment of privilege
tax generally,
§9-13-47.
Rate of taxation,
§9-13-47.
Withdrawing of lands.
Application, §9-13-46.
Harvesting or use of
timber without
withdrawing of
lands, §9-13-46.
Gifts of land.
Acceptance, §9-13-1.
Unused public lands.
Use as state forests,
§9-15-3.
Steering committee.
State forestry commission,
§§9-3-11 to 9-3-16. See
within this heading,
"State forestry
commission."
Taxation.
Assessments for forest fire
protection.
Participation by counties
in fire prevention
program, §§9-13-180 to
9-13-187. See within
this heading, "Fires
and fire prevention."
State assessment,
§§9-13-189 to 9-13-198.
See within this
heading, "Fires and
fire prevention."
Auxiliary state forests.
Taxation of timber. See
within this heading,
"State forests."
Forest products.
Privilege and severance
taxes, §§9-13-80 to
9-13-108. See within
this heading, "Forest
products."
Special county taxes for
forest protection,
§§9-13-160 to 9-13-166.
Assessments.
Petition of freeholders,
§9-13-163.
Requirements prior to
assessment,
§9-13-165.
Authorized, §9-13-161.
Collection of tax,
§9-13-166.

FORESTS AND FORESTRY
—Cont'd

Taxation—Cont'd

Special county taxes for
forest protection—Cont'd
Definitions, §9-13-160.
Designation of forest
protection areas,
§9-13-162.
Discontinuance of tax.
Petition of freeholders or
state forestry
commission,
§9-13-167.
Disposition of proceeds,
§9-13-166.
Expenditure of revenue,
§9-13-166.
Forest protection areas.
Designation, §9-13-162.
List of landowners,
§9-13-164.
Forest protection fund,
§9-13-166.
Inspection of property.
Prior to assessment and
levy, §9-13-165.
Levy, §9-13-163.
Requirements prior to
levy, §9-13-165.
List of landowners.
Within forest protection
areas, §9-13-164.
Petition.
Request for assessment,
§9-13-163.
Purposes, §9-13-161.
Rate, §9-13-161.
Change upon petition,
§9-13-167.
Standing timber.
Exemption of standing
timber from taxes,
§40-11-1.
State forests.
Auxiliary state forests.
Taxation of timber. See
within this heading,
"State forests."
Theft.
Timber theft equipment.
Condemnation, §§9-13-220
to 9-13-227.
See TREES AND
TIMBER.
Timber.
Forest products generally.
See within this heading,
"Forest products."
Taxation.
Auxiliary state forests. See
within this heading,
"State forests."
Trees and timber generally.
See TREES AND
TIMBER.
Title.
Forest products.
Cutting.
Unauthorized cutting.
Proof of title, §9-13-61.
State forests.
Auxiliary state forests.
Designation of lands.
When abstract of title
required, §9-13-42.
Training in forestry.
Research and educational
programs.
Expansion of facilities,
§2-30-20.

FORESTS AND FORESTRY
—Cont'd
Transportation.
Forest products, §§9-13-60 to
9-13-65.
Trees and timber.
General provisions.
See TREES AND TIMBER.
United States.
Insect infestation or tree
disease infection.
Protection of forest trees.
Cooperative agreements,
§9-13-125.
National forests. See within
this heading, "National
forests."
State forestry commission.
Cooperative agreements
and stipulations.
Authority to enter into,
§9-3-4.
Violation of chapter,
§§9-13-22 to 9-13-24.
District attorneys.
Prosecution, §9-13-22.
District courts.
Jurisdiction of
prosecutions, §9-13-23.
Informers.
Fees, §9-13-24.
Jurisdiction of prosecutions,
§9-13-23.
Prosecution.
District attorneys,
§9-13-22.
Duty to prosecute,
§9-13-22.
Jurisdiction, §9-13-23.
Wardens, §9-13-5.
Forest fire wardens, §§9-13-6
to 9-13-9.
Witnesses.
Board of registration for
foresters.
Authority to compel
attendance, §34-12-35.
Forest products.
Privilege and severance
taxes.
Power of department as
to witnesses,
§9-13-102.

FORFEITURES.
Alcoholic beverages.
Dry counties.
Forfeiture and
condemnation.
See ALCOHOLIC
BEVERAGES.
Wet counties.
Contraband.
Confiscation generally.
See ALCOHOLIC
BEVERAGES.
Alligator farms.
Violations of chapter.
Parts, skins, etc., forfeited,
§9-12-214.
Bail.
See BAIL AND
RECOGNIZANCE.
Controlled substances,
§20-2-93.
District attorneys.
Supreme court.
Failure to perform duties
required by certain
sections, §12-2-38.

FORFEITURES—Cont'd
Drugs.
Controlled substances,
§20-2-93.
Eavesdropping devices,
§13A-11-37.
Fish and game.
Prohibited devices used in
fishing, hunting or
trapping, §9-11-16.
General provisions.
See PENALTIES.
Livestock theft.
Vehicles, etc., used in theft,
§2-2-14.2.
Lotteries.
Forfeiture of vehicles used to
transport lottery
paraphernalia.
See LOTTERIES.
Motor vehicles.
Controlled substance
violations, §20-2-93.
Obscenity.
Minors.
Materials containing visual
reproduction of
children.
Forfeiture of equipment,
materials, etc.,
§13A-12-198.
Property subject to forfeiture,
§13A-12-200.8.
Recorded devices.
Nonconforming recordings,
equipment and
components.
Confiscation, §13A-8-84.
Persons convicted of offenses
under article.
Disposition of infringing
recordings and
equipment and
components,
§13A-8-86.
Weapons.
Seizure of pistols involved in
violations of certain
sections, §13A-11-84.

**FORGERY AND
COUNTERFEITING.**
Alcoholic beverages.
Stamps, crowns or lids,
§28-3-228.
Antiques.
Criminal simulation,
§13A-9-10.
Art.
Criminal simulation,
§13A-9-10.
Assignment.
Second degree forgery,
§13A-9-3.
Ballots.
Forging inspector's name on
ballot, §11-46-68.
Change bills.
Corporations, §§13A-9-19,
13A-9-20.
Coal mine safety.
Certificates of competency for
fire bosses and mine
foreman, §25-9-14.
Codicil.
Second degree forgery,
§13A-9-3.

**FORGERY AND
COUNTERFEITING**
—Cont'd
Commercial code.
Bank deposits and collection.
Customer's duty to discover
and report
unauthorized
signature, §7-4-406.
Commercial paper.
Conversion of instrument,
§7-3-419.
Notice of claim or defense
to purchaser, §7-3-304.
Unauthorized signatures,
§7-3-404.
Negligence contributing
to unauthorized
signature, §7-3-406.
Investment securities.
Effect of unauthorized
indorsement,
§§7-8-311, 7-8-315.
Effect of unauthorized
signature on issue,
§7-8-205.
Unauthorized signature
includes forgery,
§7-1-201.
**Constitution of the United
States,** Const. U. S., Art. I,
§8.
Contracts.
Second degree forgery,
§13A-9-3.
Corporations.
Change bills, §§13A-9-19,
13A-9-20.
Criminal simulation.
Class A misdemeanor,
§13A-9-10.
Elements of crime,
§13A-9-10.
Deeds.
Second degree forgery,
§13A-9-3.
Definitions, §13A-9-1.
Elections.
Ballots.
Forging inspector's name
on ballot, §11-46-68.
First degree forgery.
Class B felony, §13A-9-2.
Elements of crime, §13A-9-2.
Forged instrument.
Defined, §13A-9-1.
Forgery devices.
Criminal possession of
devices, §13A-9-9.
Indictments.
Form of indictment,
§15-8-150.
Industrial alcohol.
Permits, §28-5-12.
Intent to defraud.
Defined, §13A-9-1.
Investment securities.
Effect of unauthorized
indorsement, §§7-8-311,
7-8-315.
Effect of unauthorized
signature on issue,
§7-8-205.
**Limitation on criminal
liability for forgery,**
§13A-9-8.
Limitations on prosecution,
§15-3-5.
Meat and meat products.
Official marks, §2-17-14.

FORGERY AND COUNTERFEITING —Cont'd

Nurseries.
Insect and disease control.
Forgery of inspection
certificates, §2-25-22.
Offering a false instrument for recording, §13A-9-12.
Possession of forged instruments, §§13A-9-5 to 13A-9-8.
First degree.
Class B felony, §13A-9-5.
Elements of crime, §13A-9-5.
Limitation on criminal
liability, §13A-9-8.
Second degree.
Class C felony, §13A-9-6.
Elements of crime, §13A-9-6.
Third degree.
Class A misdemeanor, §13A-9-7.
Elements of crime, §13A-9-7.
Poultry.
Official marks, §2-17-14.
Public records.
Second degree forgery, §13A-9-3.
Second degree forgery.
Class C felony, §13A-9-3.
Elements of crime, §13A-9-3.
Securities.
Government securities.
First degree forgery, §13A-9-2.
Signatures.
Obtaining signature by
deception, §13A-9-11.
Third degree forgery.
Class A misdemeanor, §13A-9-4.
Elements of crime, §13A-9-4.
Tobacco.
Sales tax.
Counterfeit stamps, §40-25-6.
Wills.
Second degree forgery, §13A-9-3.
Written instrument.
Defined, §13A-9-1.

FORMER JEOPARDY.

Constitution of Alabama, Const. Ala., art. I, §9.
Constitution of the United States, Const. U. S., Amendment V.
Juvenile proceedings, §12-15-66.
Rules of criminal procedure, ARCrP, Rules 15.3 (f), 15.4 (g).

FORMS.

Acknowledgments, §35-4-29.
Alligator farms.
Parts transaction form, §9-12-207.
Appeals.
Rules of appellate procedure.
See APPEALS.
Bail and recognizance.
Bail not taken in open court, §15-13-21.
Bail taken in open court, §15-13-20.

FORMS—Cont'd

Bail and recognizance —Cont'd
Conditional judgment, §15-13-81.
Ballots, §§17-8-3, 17-8-5.
Certiorari.
Petition for writ of certiorari
to a court of appeals,
ARAP, Form 22.
Claims against state.
Board of adjustment.
Board may prescribe forms, §41-9-66.
Class actions.
Form of complaint, ARCP, Form 24.
Computers.
Dissemination of computer-
based court information,
ARJA, Rule 33.
Consolidation.
Motion to consolidate, ARCP, Form 72.
Conveyances.
Acknowledgments, §35-4-29.
Probate of conveyance, §35-4-30.
Corporations.
Secretary of state to furnish, §10-2A-333.
Data.
Dissemination of computer-
based court information,
ARJA, Rule 33.
Default judgments, ARCP, Forms 79 to 83.
Defenses, ARCP, Forms 26, 27.
Denials, ARCP, Rule 8 (b).
Depositions, ARCP, Forms 41 to 46, 62, 67.
Disclaimer of interests in property, §43-8-293.
Dismissal of actions, ARCP, Forms 70, 71.
Education.
See EDUCATION.
Elections, §§17-8-3, 17-8-5, 17-8-44.
Absentee voting, §§17-10-4, 17-10-6 to 17-10-8.
Executions, §§6-9-1, 6-9-120.
Forcible entry and unlawful detainer, §6-6-319.
Process.
Notice, §6-6-332.
Fraud.
Complaint for fraud, ARCP, Form 20.
Habeas corpus.
Form of writ, §15-21-9.
Writ not to be disobeyed
for want of form, §15-21-10.
Return, §15-21-17.
Indictments, §§15-8-23, 15-8-150.
Injunctions, ARCP, Rule 65 (d).
Insurance.
Existing forms, §27-1-13.
Health insurance claims, §27-1-16.
Interpleader, ARCP, Form 38.
Interrogatories, ARCP, Forms 47 to 49, 63, 64.
Intervention.
Motion to intervene, ARCP, Form 32.

FORMS—Cont'd

Jails.
Feeding of prisoners.
Records and statements, §14-6-47.
Joinder, ARCP, Forms 32 to 37.
Judgments, ARCP, Rule 54 (a).
Jury.
Demand for trial by jury, ARCP, Form 68.
Motion for trial by advisory
jury, ARCP, Form 69.
Landlord and tenant.
Notice to quit for breach or
default of terms of lease, §35-9-6.
Leases.
Notice to quit for breach or
default of terms of lease, §35-9-6.
Licenses, §40-12-2.
Department of finance.
Duty to prepare, §40-12-19.
Transient merchants, §34-35-5.
Magistrates, ARJA, Rule 18.
Mandamus.
Petition for writ of
mandamus, ARAP, Form 19.
Mechanics' and materialmen's liens.
Verified statement, §35-11-213.
Mentally ill, §22-50-20.
Mistake.
Form of complaint for money
paid by mistake, ARCP, Form 10.
Motor vehicles.
Uniform certificate of title
and antitheft act.
Department to provide, §32-8-9.
Uniform traffic infractions, ARJA, Rule 19.
Municipal corporations.
Class 5 municipalities.
Mayor/commission/city
manager form of
government.
Elections.
Statement of
candidacy, §§11-44E-41, 11-44E-71.
Recall of elected officials, §11-44E-168.
Natural death act.
Declaration for withdrawal of
life-support procedures, §22-8A-4.
Negotiable instruments.
Complaint on a promissory
note, ARCP, Form 2.
New trial.
Motion for new trial, ARCP, Form 78.
Offer of judgment, ARCP, Forms 86, 87.
Physical examination of persons.
Form of motion for physical
examination, ARCP, Form 53.
Pleading, ARCP, Rule 10;
ARCP, Forms 2 to 29.
Criminal pleading, §15-15-4.

FORMS—Cont'd
**Production of documents
    and things,** ARCP, Forms
    50 to 52.
Recordation.
  Statement of name and
      address of preparer of
      certain instruments,
      §35-4-113.
Requests for admission,
    ARCP, Forms 54 to 61A.
**Rules of appellate
    procedure.**
  See APPEALS.
Rules of civil procedure.
  See RULES OF CIVIL
      PROCEDURE.
Rules of criminal procedure.
  Post-conviction remedies.
    Petitions, ARCrP, Rule 20.
**Savings and loan
    associations.**
  Generally, §5-16-49.
Securities.
  Liability for acts or
      omissions in good faith
      under forms, §8-6-24.
**Seizure of person or
    property,** ARCP, Forms
    88 to 91.
Small claims, ASCR, Forms 1
    to 5.
  Promulgation of forms,
      ARJA, Rule 21.
**Stockholder's derivative
    action,** ARCP, Form 25.
Subpoenas, ARCP, Rule 45
    (a); ARCP, Forms 73 to 75.
Substitution of parties,
    ARCP, Forms 39, 40.
Summary judgment.
  Motion for summary
      judgment, ARCP, Forms
      84, 85.
Summons and process,
    ARCP, Rule 4 (a).
Transient merchants.
  Licenses, §34-35-5.
Verdict.
  Majority verdict.
    Stipulation for majority
        verdict, ARCP, Form
        76.
  Motion for directed verdict,
      ARCP, Form 77.
  Motion for judgment
      notwithstanding verdict,
      ARCP, Form 78.
Vital statistics.
  Certificates, §§22-9-6,
      22-9-31.
**Water management and
    drainage.**
  Districts.
    Tax records, §§9-9-31,
        9-9-32.
Wills.
  Self-proving wills, §43-8-132.

**FORTHCOMING AND
    DELIVERY BONDS.**
Executions, §§6-9-160,
    6-9-161.
Partition.
  Crops.
    Forthcoming bond,
        §35-6-114.
Surety bonds generally.
  See BONDS, SURETY.

**FORT LOUIS DE LA
    MOBILE.**
Monument.
  Maintenance, §9-14-3.

**FORT PAYNE,
    MUNICIPALITY OF.**
School tax.
  Special property tax for
      educational purposes,
      Const. Ala., amd. 279.
  Special school tax, Const.
      Ala., amd. 234.

**FORT TOMBECKBEE
    HISTORICAL ADVISORY
    BOARD,** §41-9-262.

FORTUNETELLERS.
Licenses.
  Fee, §40-12-104.

FOSSILS.
State fossil.
  Designation, §1-2-20.

FOSTER CARE FACILITIES.
Inspection, §44-1-27.

FOUNDATIONS.
Attorney general.
  Powers of attorney general
      not impaired, §10-4-210.
Attorneys at law.
  State bar building
      foundation, §§34-3-100 to
      34-3-108.
    See ATTORNEYS AT
        LAW.
Charities.
  Generally.
    See CHARITIES.
Courts.
  Powers of courts not
      impaired, §10-4-210.
**Private foundations,
    charitable trusts and
    split interest trusts,**
    §§19-3-300 to 19-3-303.
**Restrictions on private
    foundations,** §10-4-210.
**State bar building
    foundation,** §§34-3-100 to
    34-3-108.
  See ATTORNEYS AT LAW.

FOUNDLINGS.
Vital statistics.
  Registration of foundlings,
      §22-9-33.

FOWL.
Animals generally.
  See ANIMALS.
Aviation.
  Domestic fowl on airports or
      other aeronautical
      facilities, §4-2-6.
Eggs and egg products.
  General provisions, §§2-9-40,
      2-12-1 to 2-12-12.
    See EGGS AND EGG
        PRODUCTS.
  Promotion, §§2-8-150 to
      2-8-171.
    See EGGS AND EGG
        PRODUCTS.
Poultry, §§2-16-1 to 2-17-38,
    2-18-1 to 2-18-3.
  See POULTRY.
Waterfowl.
  Game laws, §§9-11-140 to
      9-11-156, 9-11-230 to
      9-11-234.

FOWL—Cont'd
Waters and watercourses.
  Depositing dead fowl in
      running streams,
      §22-20-9.

FRANCHISES.
Alcoholic beverages.
  Special retail license,
      §28-3A-19.
**Community antenna
    television facilities
    generally,** §§11-27-1 to
    11-27-3, 23-1-59.
Constitution of Alabama.
  Corporations.
    Franchise taxes to be paid,
        Const. Ala., art. XII,
        §229; amd. 27.
    Exemption of benevolent,
        educational or
        religious
        corporations, Const.
        Ala., art. XII, §229.
  Public utilities.
    Maximum term of public
        utility franchises in
        cities and towns
        having population of
        six thousand or more,
        Const. Ala., art. XII,
        §228.
Corporations, §10-2A-97.
  Franchise tax, §§40-14-40 to
      40-14-57; Const. Ala.,
      art. XII, §229; amd. 27.
  See CORPORATIONS.
Declaratory judgments.
  Questions of construction or
      validity, §6-6-223.
Farm equipment.
  Repurchase of inventory from
      retailers.
    Effect of termination,
        cancellation or
        nonrenewal of
        franchise without good
        cause, §8-21-10.
Limitation of actions.
  Actions by state or political
      subdivision for franchise
      tax.
    Five year limitation,
        §6-2-35.
Motor vehicle franchise act.
  Dealings by manufacturers
      with dealers, §§8-20-1 to
      8-20-12.
  See MOTOR VEHICLES.
Municipal corporations.
  See MUNICIPAL
      CORPORATIONS.
Public utilities.
  See PUBLIC UTILITIES.
Public works.
  Improvement authorities.
    Chapter exclusive,
        §39-7-33.
Quo warranto.
  Judgments.
    Excluding defendant from
        franchise, §6-6-600.
  Usurpation.
    Right of action and venue,
        §6-6-591.
Railroads.
  Conveyance to another
      railroad corporation,
      §10-5-10.

FRANCHISES—Cont'd
Streets.
Municipal corporations.
See MUNICIPAL
CORPORATIONS.
Taxation, §§40-14-40 to
40-14-57; Const. Ala., art.
XII, §229; amd. 27.
See CORPORATIONS.
Television.
Community antenna
television facilities,
§§11-27-1 to 11-27-3,
23-1-59.
University of Alabama.
Previous franchises retained,
§16-47-6.

FRANK LEE YOUTH
CENTER.
Trade school, §§16-60-170 to
16-60-173.

FRANKLIN COUNTY.
Court costs and charges,
Const. Ala., amd. 418.
Economic development,
Const. Ala., amd. 186.
Hospitals.
Tax in districts one, two and
three, Const. Ala., amd.
262.
Junior college for Franklin
county, §§16-60-20 to
16-60-40.
See JUNIOR COLLEGES.
Probate judge.
Compensation, Const. Ala.,
amd. 418.
School tax.
Additional tax for school
purposes, Const. Ala.,
amd. 173.
Further provisions as to
additional tax for school
purposes, Const. Ala.,
amd. 211.
Trade schools.
Conversion of junior college
for Franklin, Marion and
Winston counties to
trade school and junior
college, §§16-60-38 to
16-60-40.

FRATERNAL BENEFIT
SOCIETIES, §§27-34-1 to
27-34-54.
Accident insurance
contracts, §27-34-32.
Actions.
Conversion into stock or
mutual life insurance
company.
Pending actions, §27-35-10.
Age.
Members, §27-34-21.
Agents.
Licenses, §27-34-43.
Solicitation without license,
§27-34-44.
Alien societies.
Examinations, §27-34-40.
Licenses, §§27-34-7, 27-34-8.
Annual statements,
§§27-34-36 to 27-34-38.
Valuation of certificates,
§27-34-37.
Appeals.
Review of decisions and
findings of commissioner
of insurance, §27-34-52.

FRATERNAL BENEFIT
SOCIETIES—Cont'd
Applicability of chapter,
§§27-34-4, 27-34-5.
Exceptions, §27-34-5.
Generally, §27-34-4.
Applicability of other
provisions of title,
§27-34-54.
Articles of incorporation.
Amendment, §27-34-17.
Conversion into stock or
mutual life insurance
company, §§27-35-4,
27-35-5.
Bonds, surety, §27-34-10.
Contents, §27-34-9.
Conversion into stock or
mutual life insurance
company.
Ratification or amendment.
Filing, §27-35-5.
Generally, §27-35-4.
Filing with other documents,
§27-34-10.
Assets, §27-34-34.
Attachment.
Exemption of benefits, etc.,
from attachment,
§27-34-27.
Beneficiaries.
Generally, §27-34-26.
Benefits.
Attachment.
Exemption from
attachment, §27-34-27.
Cash surrender values,
§27-34-25.
Certificates.
Life benefit certificates,
§§27-34-30, 27-34-31.
Executions.
Exemption from execution,
§27-34-27.
Exemption from attachment,
garnishment or other
process, §27-34-27.
Garnishment.
Exemption from
garnishment,
§27-34-27.
Generally, §27-34-23.
Liability for payment.
Personal liability,
§27-34-28.
Life benefit certificate,
§§27-34-30, 27-34-31.
Lives of children, §27-34-24.
Misrepresentations,
§27-34-25.
Nonforfeiture benefits.
Paid-up nonforfeiture
benefits, §27-34-25.
Payment.
Personal liability for
payment, §27-34-28.
Benevolent institutions.
Creation, etc., §27-34-20.
Bonds, surety.
Articles of incorporation,
§27-34-10.
Branches.
Conversion into stock or
mutual life insurance
company.
Notice to subordinate
lodges or branches,
§27-35-3.
Cash surrender values,
§27-34-25.

FRATERNAL BENEFIT
SOCIETIES—Cont'd
Certificates.
Cash surrender values,
§27-34-25.
Compliance.
Preliminary certificate,
§§27-34-10 to 27-34-12.
Initial solicitations and
qualifications,
§27-34-12.
Issuance, §27-34-10.
Qualifications, §27-34-12.
Time to complete
organization,
§27-34-11.
Validity.
Time to complete
organization,
§27-34-11.
Conversion into stock or
mutual life insurance
company.
Obligation to holders of
certificates, §27-35-10.
Provision for certificate
holders to subscribe to
stock, §27-35-7.
Death or disability of
certificate holder.
False statements as to
death or disability,
§27-34-53.
Issuance to each benefit
member, §27-34-29.
Life benefit certificate,
§§27-34-30, 27-34-31.
Loans.
Surrender values.
Cash surrender values,
§27-34-25.
Valuation of certificates.
Annual statements,
§27-34-37.
Charitable institutions.
Creation, etc., §27-34-20.
Children.
Benefits.
Lives of children,
§27-34-24.
Commissioner of insurance.
Review of decisions and
findings of commissioner,
§27-34-52.
Compliance with chapter.
Certificate of compliance,
§§27-34-10 to 27-34-13.
Consolidation or merger,
§§27-34-48, 27-34-49.
Constitution, §27-34-14.
Amendment, §27-34-17.
Waiver, §27-34-18.
Contracts.
Misrepresentations,
§27-34-45.
Conversion into stock or
mutual life insurance
company, §§27-35-1 to
27-35-11.
Actions.
Pending actions, §27-35-10.
Approval of plan of
conversion, §27-35-2.
Articles of incorporation.
Ratification or amendment.
Filing, §27-35-5.
Generally, §27-35-4.
Authority, §27-35-1.
Branches.
Notice to subordinate
branches, §27-35-3.

FRATERNAL BENEFIT SOCIETIES—Cont'd

Conversion into stock or mutual life insurance company—Cont'd
Certificates of incorporation and authority, §27-35-6.
Obligation to holders of certificates, §27-35-10.
Provision for certificate holders to subscribe to stock, §27-35-7.
Completion of conversion, §27-35-8.
Debts.
Preservation of debts, §27-35-9.
Disapproval of plan of conversion, §27-35-2.
Duties.
Preservation, §27-35-9.
Effect of conversion, §27-35-8.
How effected, §27-35-1.
Incorporation.
Articles of incorporation.
Ratification or amendment, §§27-35-4, 27-35-5.
Certificates of incorporation and authority.
Obligation to holders of certificates, §27-35-10.
Provision for certificate holders to subscribe to stock, §27-35-7.
Liabilities.
Preservation, §27-35-9.
Lodges.
Notice to subordinate lodges, §27-35-3.
Notice to subordinate lodges or branches, §27-35-3.
Pending actions, §27-35-10.
Plan of conversion, §27-35-2.
Policies.
Obligation to holders of policies, §27-35-10.
Premiums, §27-35-11.
Exemption from premium taxes, §27-35-22.
Separate record of premiums, §27-35-11.
Records.
Separate record of premiums, §27-35-11.
Subordinate lodges or branches.
Notice to subordinate lodges or branches, §27-35-3.
Subscription to stock.
Provision for certificate holders to subscribe to stock, §27-35-7.
Taxation.
Exemption from premium taxes, §27-35-11.
Debts.
Conversion into stock or mutual insurance company.
Preservation of debts, §27-35-9.
Deficiencies.
Members.
Payment of equitable part of deficiency by member, §27-34-22.

FRATERNAL BENEFIT SOCIETIES—Cont'd

Definitions, §27-34-1.
Disability insurance.
Total or permanent disability insurance contracts, §27-34-32.
Discrimination, §27-34-46.
Duties.
Conversion into stock or mutual life insurance company.
Preservation, §27-35-9.
Educational institutions.
Creation, etc., §27-34-20.
Evidence.
Licenses, §27-34-6.
Examinations, §27-34-39.
Alien societies, §27-34-40.
Foreign societies, §27-34-40.
Publication of financial statement, report or finding, §27-34-41.
Exceptions to chapter, §27-34-5.
Executions.
Exemption of benefits, etc., from attachment, garnishment or other process, §27-34-27.
Exemption from taxation, §27-34-42.
Exemptions, §27-34-34.
Existing incorporated societies, §27-34-15.
Existing unincorporated domestic voluntary associations.
Incorporation, §27-34-16.
False statements, §27-34-53.
Fees.
Licenses, §27-34-6.
Financial statement.
Publication, §27-34-41.
Foreign societies.
Examinations, §27-34-40.
Licenses, §§27-34-7, 27-34-8.
Fraud, §27-34-50.
Funds, §27-34-34.
Garnishment.
Exemption of benefits, etc., from garnishment, §27-34-27.
Meetings of governing body, §27-34-19.
When society deemed as having representative form of government, §27-34-3.
Health insurance.
Contract, §27-34-32.
Income tax.
Exemptions of certain fraternal beneficiary societies, §40-18-32.
Incorporation.
Articles of incorporation. See within this heading, "Articles of incorporation."
Conversion into stock or mutual life insurance company.
Articles of incorporation. Ratification or amendment, §§27-35-4, 27-35-5.

FRATERNAL BENEFIT SOCIETIES—Cont'd

Incorporation—Cont'd
Conversion into stock or mutual life insurance company—Cont'd
Certificates of incorporation and authority, §27-35-6.
Obligation to holders of certificates, §27-35-10.
Provisions for holders to subscribe to stock, §27-35-7.
Existing incorporated societies, §27-34-15.
Existing unincorporated domestic voluntary associations, §27-34-16.
Inducements, §27-34-46.
Injunctions, §§27-34-50, 27-34-51.
Actions to enjoin, §27-34-50.
Applications for injunctions, §27-34-51.
Investments, §27-34-35.
Laws, §27-34-14.
Amendment, §27-34-17.
Waiver, §27-34-18.
Liabilities.
Conversion into stock or mutual life insurance company.
Preservation, §27-35-9.
Licenses.
Agents, §27-34-43.
Alien societies, §§27-34-7, 27-34-8.
Applications.
Foreign or alien societies, §27-34-7.
Evidence, §27-34-6.
Fee, §27-34-6.
Foreign societies, §§27-34-7, 27-34-8.
Qualifications.
Foreign or alien societies, §27-34-7.
Refusal.
Foreign or alien societies, §27-34-8.
Renewal, §27-34-6.
Requirement,
Revocation.
Foreign or alien societies, §27-34-8.
Suspension.
Foreign or alien societies, §27-34-8.
Life benefit certificate, §§27-34-30, 27-34-31.
Life insurance.
Conversion into stock or mutual life insurance company, §§27-35-1 to 27-35-11. See within this heading, "Conversion into stock or mutual life insurance company."
Liquidation, §27-34-50.
Loans.
Certificate loans, §27-34-25.
Lodge system.
Conversion of society into stock or mutual life insurance company.
Notice to subordinate lodges or branches, §27-35-3.

FRATERNAL BENEFIT SOCIETIES—Cont'd

Lodge system—Cont'd
Societies deemed operating on lodge system, §27-34-2.

Members.
Age, §27-34-21.
Certificates.
Issuance to each benefit member, §27-34-29.
Deficiencies.
Payment of equitable part of deficiency by member, §27-34-22.
Qualification for membership, §27-34-21.

Merger, §§27-34-48, 27-34-49.
Effect, §27-34-49.
Procedure, §27-34-48.

Minors.
Benefits.
Lives of children, §27-34-24.

Misrepresentations, §27-34-45.

Nonforfeiture benefits.
Paid-up nonforfeiture benefits, §27-34-45.

Notice.
Conversion into stock or mutual life insurance company.
Notice to subordinate lodges or branches, §27-35-3.

Office.
Principal office, §27-34-19.

Penalties.
Failure to file annual statements, §27-34-38.
Misrepresentations, §27-34-45.

Perjury, §27-34-53.

Policies.
Conversion into stock or mutual life insurance company.
Obligation to holders of policies, §27-35-10.

Powers, §27-34-14.

Preliminary certificate.
Compliance, §§27-34-10 to 27-34-12.

Premiums.
Conversion into stock or mutual life insurance company, §27-35-11.
Exemption from premium taxes, §27-35-11.
Separate record of premiums, §27-35-11.
Defined, §27-34-1.

Quo warranto.
Actions in quo warranto, §27-34-50.

Rebates, §27-34-46.

Receivership, §27-34-50.

Records.
Conversion into stock or mutual life insurance company.
Separate record of premiums, §27-35-11.
Minutes of governing body, §27-34-19.

Reinsurance, §27-34-33.

Reports.
Annual statements, §27-34-36.
Failure to file, §27-34-38.

FRATERNAL BENEFIT SOCIETIES—Cont'd

Reports—Cont'd
Publication of report of examinations, §27-34-41.
Requirements, §27-34-36.
Reserves, §27-34-37.
Valuation of certificates, §27-34-37.

Representative form of government.
When society deemed to have, §27-34-3.

Reserves.
Annual statements, §27-34-37.

Service of process, §27-34-37.

Solicitation of members.
Agents.
Solicitation without license, §27-34-44.
Initial solicitations, §27-34-12.

Statements.
Annual statements, §§27-34-36 to 27-34-38.
Failure to file, §27-34-38.
Requirements, §27-34-36.
Reserves, §27-34-37.
Valuation of certificates, §27-34-37.

Subordinate lodges or branches.
Conversion into stock or mutual life insurance company.
Notice to subordinate lodges or branches, §27-35-3.

Taxation.
Conversion into stock or mutual life insurance company.
Exemption from premium taxes, §27-35-11.
Exemption from taxation, §27-34-42.
Premium taxes.
Conversion into stock or mutual life insurance company, §27-35-11.
Property exempt, §40-9-1.

Waiver of laws and constitutions, §27-34-18.

FRATERNAL ORDERS, §§10-4-170 to 10-4-179.

Declaratory actions, §§10-4-174 to 10-4-178.
Averments as to loans from parent organization, §10-4-178.
Averments of plaintiff, §10-4-176.
Institution of action, §10-4-174.
Judgment, §10-4-177.
Service of process, §10-4-175.

Definitions, §10-4-170.

Judgments.
Declaratory actions, §10-4-177.
Repayment and lien for unsecured loans from parent organization, §10-4-178.

Liens.
Effect of article on existing liens, §10-4-179.

FRATERNAL ORDERS —Cont'd

Liens—Cont'd
Judgment to provide liens for unsecured loans from parent organization, §10-4-178.

Loans.
From parent organization, §10-4-178.

Majority group of local organization.
Right in fraternal property, §10-4-171.

Mortgages and deeds of trust.
Effect of article on existing mortgages, §10-4-179.

Parent organization.
Loans from parent organization.
Averments as to loans, §10-4-178.
Judgment to provide for repayment and lien for unsecured loans, §10-4-178.
Rights to set up unit independent of parent corporation, §10-4-173.
Withdrawal from parent organization, §10-4-172.

Property.
Right of majority group of local organization in fraternal property, §10-4-171.
Use of fraternal property free from trust clause, §10-4-172.

Service of process.
Declaratory actions, §10-4-175.

Withdrawal from parent organization, §10-4-172.

FRAUD.

Actions.
Deceit, §§6-5-103, 6-5-104.
Right of action, §§6-5-100 to 6-5-102.
Generally, §6-5-100.
Misrepresentation of material facts, §6-5-101.
Suppression of material facts, §6-5-102.

Adulteration.
Deceptive business practices.
Selling adulterated commodities, §13A-9-41.

Advertising.
Bait advertising, §§13A-9-43, 13A-9-44.
False advertising, §§13A-9-42, 13A-9-44.

Aged persons.
Medical assistance to elderly persons.
False representations. Penalty, §38-6-8.

Antiques.
Criminal simulation, §13A-9-10.

Art.
Criminal simulation, §13A-9-10.

FRAUD—Cont'd
Attorney general.
Charitable fraud.
Enforcement of provisions,
§13A-9-76.
Auctions and auctioneers.
Memorandum of auctioneer.
Sufficiency as note of
contract, §8-9-3.
Bait advertising, §§13A-9-43,
13A-9-44.
Bankruptcy and insolvency.
Fraud in insolvency,
§13A-9-48.
**Banks and financial
institutions,** §§5-6A-23 to
5-6A-25.
Business fraud.
Deceptive business practices,
§13A-9-41.
Definitions, §13A-9-40.
Financial statements.
Issuing false statements,
§13A-9-49.
Charitable fraud, §§13A-9-70
to 13A-9-76.
Attorney general.
Enforcement of provisions,
§13A-9-76.
Charitable organizations.
Consent necessary to use
name of, §13A-9-71.
Defined, §13A-9-70.
Charitable purposes.
Defined, §13A-9-70.
Consent necessary to use
name of charitable
organization, §13A-9-71.
Violations, §13A-9-71.
Defense, §13A-9-71.
Contributions.
Defined, §13A-9-70.
Definitions, §13A-9-70.
Disclosures by solicitors.
Violations, §13A-9-71.
Defense, §13A-9-71.
District attorneys.
Enforcement of provisions,
§13A-9-76.
Elements of crime,
§13A-9-75.
Enforcement of provisions by
injunction, mandamus,
etc., §13A-9-76.
First degree charitable fraud.
Class B felony, §13A-9-73.
Elements of crime,
§13A-9-73.
Injunctions to enforce
provisions, §13A-9-76.
Mandamus to enforce
provisions, §13A-9-76.
Misdemeanors.
Class A misdemeanor,
§13A-9-75.
Class C misdemeanors,
§13A-9-71.
Persons.
Defined, §13A-9-70.
Professional fundraisers.
Defined, §13A-9-70.
Professional solicitors.
Defined, §13A-9-70.
Remedies, §13A-9-76.
Reporting names of
contributors.
Violations, §13A-9-71.
Defense, §13A-9-71.
Second degree charitable
fraud.
Class C felony, §13A-9-74.

FRAUD—Cont'd
Charitable fraud—Cont'd
Second degree charitable
fraud—Cont'd
Elements of crime,
§13A-9-74.
Chiropractors.
Refusal, revocation or
suspension of licenses.
Fraud as grounds,
§34-24-166.
Clergy.
Fraudulently pretending to
be clergymen, §13A-14-4.
Commercial code.
See COMMERCIAL CODE.
Contracts.
Agreement to forfeit right of
action for not presenting
damage claim void,
§8-9-10.
Certain agreements void
unless in writing, §8-9-2.
Public works.
Certificates of compliance.
Issuance of fraudulent
certificate, §39-5-2.
Specific performance.
Cases in which specific
performance not
enforced, §8-1-40.
Written contract not
expressing parties' intent
may be revised, §8-1-2.
Conveyances.
Contracts for sale of lands
void unless in writing,
§8-9-2.
Fraudulent transfers,
§§8-9A-1 to 8-9A-12.
See FRAUDULENT
TRANSFERS.
Realty conveyance wherein
grantee agrees to support
grantor during life
voidable, §8-9-12.
Reformation, §35-4-153.
Cotton.
Packing or baling.
Fraudulent packing or
baling, §2-19-11.
Credit, §8-9-5.
Credit cards.
Fraud by persons authorized
to provide goods and
services, §13A-9-14.1.
Fraudulent use of credit
card, §13A-9-14.
Damages.
Punitive damages.
Definition of fraud,
§6-11-20.
Debit cards.
Fraudulent use of debit
cards, §13A-9-14.
Debtors and creditors.
Secured creditors.
Defrauding, §13A-9-46.
Deceit.
Actions for deceit, §§6-5-103,
6-5-104.
Deceptive trade practices,
§§8-19-1 to 8-19-15.
See DECEPTIVE TRADE
PRACTICES.
Deeds.
Reformation, §35-4-153.
Defenses.
Affirmative defense, ARCP,
Rule 8 (c).

FRAUD—Cont'd
Definitions.
Charitable fraud, §13A-9-70.
Dentists, §§34-9-18 to 34-9-22.
District attorneys.
Charitable fraud.
Enforcement of provisions,
§13A-9-76.
Education.
Insurance.
Risk management
cooperatives.
Actions brought directly
against, §16-8-42.1.
Unaccredited schools,
§16-46-4.
Elections, §§17-15-2, 17-16-48,
17-23-7.
Evidence.
Proof of intent to defraud or
cheat, §12-21-200.
Executions.
Fraudulent disposal or
removal of property by
defendant.
When execution to issue,
§6-9-23.
**Executors and
administrators.**
Certain agreements void
unless in writing, §8-9-2.
False advertising, §§13A-9-42,
13A-9-44.
Felonies.
Charitable fraud.
First degree charitable
fraud.
Class B felony,
§13A-9-73.
Second degree charitable
fraud.
Class C felony,
§13A-9-74.
Credit cards.
Fraud by persons
authorized to provide
goods and services.
Class B felony,
§13A-9-14.1.
Financial statements.
Issuing false statements,
§13A-9-49.
Food.
Obtaining food by fraud or
misrepresentation,
§§34-15-19, 34-15-20.
Forgery and counterfeiting,
§§13A-9-1 to 13A-9-9.
See FORGERY AND
COUNTERFEITING.
Forms.
Complaint for fraud, ARCP,
Form 20.
Fraternal benefit societies,
§27-34-50.
Gasoline tax.
Refund on gasoline used for
agricultural purposes.
False or fraudulent claims,
§40-17-108.
Refund on gasoline used for
static testing of engine.
False or fraudulent claims,
§40-17-124.
Goods and services.
Fraud by persons authorized
to provide, §13A-9-14.1.

FRAUD—Cont'd

Hazardous substances and waste.
Fees for disposal of hazardous waste or substances.
False or fraudulent reports. Penalties, §22-30B-7.
Perjury in making, §22-30B-10.
Records of hazardous substances received for disposal.
False or fraudulent statements.
Class C misdemeanor, §22-30B-11.

Health.
False statements and claim or application for payments or medical benefits, §22-1-11.
Medicaid agency.
Revocation of eligibility upon determination of fraud, §22-6-8.

Hearing aid dealers and fitters.
Grounds for revocation or suspension of license, §34-14-9.
Prohibited acts relating to licenses, §34-14-12.

Hotels, inns and other transient lodging places.
Obtaining accommodations by fraud or misrepresentation, §§34-15-19, 34-15-20.

Income tax.
Collection of tax without assessment, §40-18-46.
Penalty for fraud, §40-18-49.
Withholding tax.
Employee statements, §40-18-80.

Indictments.
Form of indictment, §15-8-150.
General allegation of intent to defraud, §15-8-29.

Injunctions.
Charitable fraud.
Enforcement of provisions, §13A-9-76.

Insurance.
Policies.
Application for policy, §27-14-7.

Judgment creditors.
Defrauding, §13A-9-47.

Judgments.
Agreements to confess judgment before commencement of action void, §8-9-11.
Annulment of illegal judgments, §8-9-11.
Relief from judgment, ARCP, Rule 60 (b).

Judicial sales.
Report of officer making sale. Sufficiency as note of contract, §8-9-4.

Jury.
Objections to venire, §12-16-80.

FRAUD—Cont'd

Labels.
Deceptive business practices. Selling mislabeled commodities, §13A-9-41.

Landscape architects.
Grounds for disciplinary actions, §34-17-5.

Land surveyors.
Grounds for disciplinary actions, §34-17-5.

Liens.
Judgment creditors.
Defrauding judgment creditors, §13A-9-47.
Secured creditors.
Defrauding secured creditors, §13A-9-46.

Limitation of actions.
Accrual of cause of action, §6-2-3.
Probate code, §43-8-5.

Livestock.
Altering appearance of horse or mule by burning, cauterizing, etc., teeth, §3-1-23.
Branding or marking or altering mark or brand, §3-1-27.
Pedigrees, §§2-15-317, 3-1-23, 3-1-27.

Mandamus.
Charitable fraud.
Enforcement of provisions, §13A-9-76.

Marriage.
Agreements upon consideration of marriage void unless in writing, §8-9-2.

Material facts.
Suppression of material facts, §6-5-102.

Medicaid agency.
False statements in claim or application, §22-1-11.

Medical technicians.
False representation in obtaining certificate, §34-18-3.

Misdemeanors.
Charitable fraud.
Class A misdemeanors, §13A-9-75.
Class C misdemeanor, §13A-9-71.

Misrepresentation.
Right of action.
Misrepresentation of material facts, §6-5-101.

Mortgages and deeds of trust.
Mortgage of personalty, §8-9-1.
Reformation, §35-4-153.

Motor vehicle carriers.
Mileage tax.
Making false or erroneous statements, reports or representations, §40-19-14.

Motor vehicles.
Certificate of title.
Refusal to issue certificate, §32-8-42.

FRAUD—Cont'd

Motor vehicles—Cont'd
Certificate of title—Cont'd
Suspension or revocation of certificate.
Grounds for suspension or revocation, §32-8-49.
Renting and hiring, §§32-5-1 to 32-5-5.
See MOTOR VEHICLES.

Nonprofit organizations.
Charitable fraud, §§13A-9-70 to 13A-9-76. See within this heading, "Charitable fraud."
Officers.
Liability of officers of nonprofit organizations.
Exception to immunity from suit, §10-11-3.

Nurseries, §§2-25-40 to 2-25-42.

Nurses.
Denial, revocation or suspension of license, §34-21-25.
Obtaining or furnishing license or diploma, §34-21-7.

Offering a false instrument for recording, §13A-9-12.

Oil and gas.
Fraud and deceit in sale of petroleum products, §§8-17-130 to 8-17-139.
See OIL AND GAS.

Optometrists.
Grounds for revocation or suspension of license, §34-22-23.
Penalty for fraudulently obtaining license, §34-22-6.

Orders of court.
Relief from order, ARCP, Rule 60 (b).

Partnerships.
Rights where contract rescinded for fraud, §10-8-44.

Pedigrees.
Livestock, §§2-15-317, 3-1-23, 3-1-27.

Personal property.
Fraudulent leasing or rental of property, §§13A-8-140 to 13A-8-144.
Mortgage of personalty, §8-9-1.

Petroleum products.
Fraud and deceit in sales, §§8-17-130 to 8-17-139.
See OIL AND GAS.

Pharmacists and pharmacies.
Grounds for revocation or suspension of licenses or permits, §34-23-33.

Physical therapists.
False statement in registration application. Penalty, §34-24-196.
Revocation or suspension of licenses.
Fraud as grounds, §34-24-217.

Plants.
Sales, §§2-25-40 to 2-25-42.

FRAUD—Cont'd

Pleadings, ARCP, Rule 9 (b).
Form of complaint for fraud, ARCP, Form 20.

Podiatrists.
Revocation or suspension of license, §34-24-276.

Polygraph examiners.
Grounds for refusal, suspension or revocation of license, §34-25-32.

Psychologists.
Refusal, suspension or revocation of licenses.
Fraud as grounds, §34-26-46.

Public officers and employees.
State employees' retirement system.
False statements for purpose of defrauding system, §36-27-27.

Public works.
Contracts.
Certificates of compliance.
Issuance of fraudulent certificate, §39-5-2.

Punitive damages.
Definition of fraud, §6-11-20.

Real estate brokers.
Disciplinary actions.
Fraud as grounds, §34-27-36.

Real property.
Contracts for sale of lands void unless in writing, §8-9-2.
Realty conveyance wherein grantee agrees to support grantor during life voidable, §8-9-12.

Receivers.
Fraud in insolvency, §13A-9-48.

Recordation.
Offering a false instrument for recording, §13A-9-12.

Relief from judgment or order, ARCP, Rule 60 (b).

Remedies.
Charitable fraud.
Enforcement of provisions, §13A-9-76.

Restaurants, §§34-15-19, 34-15-20.

Sales tax.
Reports, §40-23-10.
Returns, §40-23-88.

Seeds.
Sale, etc., of falsely named seeds, §2-25-42.

Signatures.
Obtaining signature by deception, §13A-9-11.

Speech pathologists and audiologists.
Penalty, §34-28A-4.
Revocation or suspension of licenses.
Fraud as grounds, §34-28A-26.

Statute of frauds, §8-9-2.
Commercial code.
Investment securities, §7-8-319.
Personal property not otherwise covered, §7-1-200.
Sales contracts, §§7-2-201, 7-2-209.

FRAUD—Cont'd

Student loan program.
False statements or misrepresentations, §16-33B-6.

Suppression of material facts, §6-5-102.

Surveys and surveyors.
Disciplinary action.
Grounds, §34-11-11.

Taxation.
See TAXATION.

Theft.
Charitable fraud.
Theft of property by charitable fraud, §13A-9-72.

Tobacco.
Sales tax.
Fraud in use or reuse of stamps, §40-25-6.

Transfers.
General provisions, §§8-9A-1 to 8-9A-12.
See FRAUDULENT TRANSFERS.

Trees and timber.
Fruit trees.
Delivery of fruit trees of different kind, variety, etc., than sold, §2-25-40.
Limitation period for prosecutions, §2-25-41.
Sale, etc., of falsely named trees, §2-25-42.

Unemployment compensation.
Arrest fee, §25-4-147.
Enforcement of fraud provisions of chapter.
Employees of department constituted peace officers, §25-4-146.

Uniform commercial code.
See COMMERCIAL CODE.

Use tax.
Penalty for fraud, §40-23-80.

Vacation time-sharing plans.
Violations of article, §§34-27-56, 34-27-60.

Veterans.
Pensions for widows of Confederate veterans.
Persons placed on pension roll through fraud, §31-8-18.

Weights and measures.
Deceptive business practices.
Using false weights or measures, §13A-9-41.

Wills.
Probate code.
Relief against fraud, §43-8-5.

Worthless checks.
See BAD CHECKS.

FRAUDS, STATUTE OF, §8-9-2.

Commercial code.
Investment securities, §7-8-319.
Personal property not otherwise covered, §7-1-206.
Sales contracts, §§7-2-201, 7-2-209.

FRAUDULENT TRANSFERS, §§8-9A-1 to 8-9A-12.

Application of provisions.
Uniformity of application, §8-9A-11.

Assigning or conveying property by debtor to benefit creditors equally, §8-9-8.

Attachment.
Issuance of attachment, §6-6-42.

Bankruptcy and insolvency.
When debtor deemed to be insolvent, §8-9A-2.

Bulk transfers, §§7-6-101 to 7-6-111.
See COMMERCIAL CODE.

Citation of act.
Short title, §8-9A-12.

Claim for relief.
Extinguishment, §8-9A-9.

Commercial code.
Bulk transfers, §§7-6-101 to 7-6-111.
See COMMERCIAL CODE.
Rights of seller's creditors against sold goods, §7-2-402.

Construction and interpretation.
Uniformity of application and construction, §8-9A-11.
"Value" construed, §8-9A-3.

Contracts for sale of lands void unless in writing, §8-9-2.

Defenses, §8-9A-8.

Definitions, §8-9A-1.

Joinder of remedies, ARCP, Rule 18 (b).

Liability, §8-9A-8.

Present and future creditors.
Transfers fraudulent as to, §8-9A-4.

Present creditors.
Transfers fraudulent as to, §8-9A-5.

Protection of transferee, §8-9A-8.

Realty conveyance wherein grantee agrees to support grantor during life voidable, §8-9-12.
Exceptions, §8-9-12.

Reformation, §35-4-153.

Remedies.
Creditors' remedies, §8-9A-7.

Supplementary provisions, §8-9A-10.

Title of act.
Short title, §8-9A-12.

Value.
Construed, §8-9A-3.

When transfers made, §8-9A-6.

FREEDOMS.

Press, Const. Ala., art. I, §4; Const. U. S., Amendment I.

Religious freedom, Const. Ala., art. I, §3; Const. U. S., Amendment I.

Speech, Const. Ala., art. I, §4; Const. U. S., Amendment I.
Members of congress, Const. U. S., Art. I, §6.

FREE TEXTBOOK ACT,
§§16-36-1 to 16-36-39.
See EDUCATION.

**FREEWILL BAPTIST
CHILDREN'S HOME.**
Licenses.
Exemptions, §40-9-12.
Taxation.
Exemptions, §40-9-12.

FREIGHT.
Licenses.
Transfer of freight,
§40-12-171.
Railroads.
See RAILROADS.
Transportation companies.
See TRANSPORTATION
COMPANIES.

FRESH PURSUIT ACT,
§15-10-74.

FRISKS.
Stop and frisk law, §§15-5-30,
15-5-31.

FRIVOLOUS ACTIONS.
Litigation accountability,
§§12-19-270 to 12-19-276.
See COURTS.

FRIVOLOUS APPEAL.
Damages, ARAP, Rule 38.

FRIVOLOUS PLEADINGS,
ARCP, Rule 11.
Court of the judiciary, ARJC,
Rule 7.

FROZEN FOOD.
Mellorine.
Manufacture and sale,
§§20-1-130 to 20-1-137.
See MELLORINE.

FRUITS AND VEGETABLES.
Assessments.
Promotion of industry,
§§2-8-120 to 2-8-137. See
within this heading,
"Promotion of industry."
Citrus fruits.
Shipment, offer for shipment
or sale of certain citrus
fruits, §20-1-29.
**Decayed fruits and
vegetables.**
Inspections.
Provision for inspections by
municipal
corporations,
§11-47-136.
Sale.
Prohibition by municipal
corporations,
§11-47-136.
Definitions.
Grading and standards,
§2-11-70.
Destruction.
Nuisances menacing public
health.
Summary destruction of
property without
compensation,
§22-10-3.
Diseased fruits, etc.
Importation, §2-25-15.
Fees.
Grading and standards,
§2-11-76.
Food generally.
See FOOD.

FRUITS AND VEGETABLES
—Cont'd
Grading and standards,
§§2-11-70 to 2-11-79.
Administration of article,
§2-11-76.
Certificates of inspection,
§§2-11-72, 2-11-74.
Commissioner of agriculture
and industries.
Powers of commissioner,
§2-11-76.
Rules and regulations,
§2-11-77.
Declaration of purpose,
§2-11-71.
Definitions, §2-11-70.
Enforcement of article,
§2-11-76.
Fees, §2-11-76.
Injunctions.
Violations of article,
§2-11-79.
Inspections.
Compulsory inspection in
certain areas, §2-11-75.
Issuance of certificates of
inspection, §2-11-72.
Requirement of certificate
of inspection, §2-11-74.
Labeling.
Compulsory labeling in
certain areas, §2-11-75.
Requirements, §2-11-73.
Official grades, §2-11-72.
Penalties.
Violations of article or
rules and regulations,
§2-11-78.
Rules and regulations,
§2-11-77.
Penalty for violations,
§2-11-78.
Violations of article.
Injunctions, §2-11-79.
Penalty for violations,
§2-11-78.
Grain.
Grading and standards,
§§2-11-90 to 2-11-103.
See GRAIN.
Promotion, §§2-8-230 to
2-8-252.
See GRAIN.
Sales regulations, §§2-20-1 to
2-20-5.
See GRAIN.
Importation.
Infested, infected fruits, etc.,
§2-25-15.
Infested, infected fruits, etc.
Importation, §2-25-15.
Injunctions.
Grading and standards.
Violations of article,
§2-11-79.
Inspections.
Grading and standards. See
within this heading,
"Grading and standards."
Municipal corporations,
§11-47-136.
Labels.
Grading and standards.
Cumpulsory labeling in
certain areas, §2-11-75.
Labeling requirements,
§2-11-73.
Licenses.
Fruit dealers, §40-12-105.

FRUITS AND VEGETABLES
—Cont'd
Municipal corporations.
Decayed fruits and
vegetables.
Sales.
Prohibition, §11-47-136.
Inspections.
Provision for inspections,
§11-47-136.
Regulation of sales,
§11-47-137.
**Nuisances menacing public
health,** §§22-10-1 to
22-10-3.
Nurseries.
Fruit trees, §§2-25-40,
2-25-41.
Penalties.
Grading and standards.
Penalty for violation of
article or rules and
regulations, §2-11-78.
Promotion of industry,
§§2-8-120 to 2-8-137.
Assessments.
Collection, §2-8-133.
Disposition, §2-8-133.
Maximum assessment,
§2-8-126.
Referendum, §§2-8-123 to
2-8-135.
Affirmative vote,
§2-8-130.
Subsequent
referendum after
affirmative vote,
§2-8-135.
Application for approval
to conduct,
§§2-8-123, 2-8-124.
Authority of certified
organization to
conduct referendum,
§2-8-125.
Ballot, §2-8-132.
Canvass of results,
§2-8-132.
Conduct, §2-8-127.
Declared to be in public
interest, §2-8-122.
Eligibility to vote,
§2-8-128.
Hours, §2-8-131.
Negative vote, §2-8-129.
Subsequent
referendum after
negative vote,
§2-8-134.
Notice, §2-8-126.
Payment of expense,
§2-8-127.
Poll holders, §2-8-132.
Question to be voted on,
§2-8-128.
Rules and regulations,
§2-8-131.
Subsequent referendum.
After affirmative vote,
§2-8-135.
After negative vote,
§2-8-134.
Voting places, §2-8-131.
Refund, §2-8-136.
Authorized activities.
Not illegal or in restraint
of trade, §2-8-121.
Bonds, surety.
Treasurer of growers'
organization, §2-8-137.

FRUITS AND VEGETABLES
—Cont'd
Promotion of industry
—Cont'd
Certification of growers'
association.
Application for
certification.
Action by board on
application,
§2-8-124.
Generally, §2-8-123.
Declaration of policy,
§2-8-120.
Notice.
Assessments.
Notice of referendum,
§2-8-126.
Reports.
Annual statements by
treasurer of
organization, §2-8-137.
Treasurer of growers'
organization.
Annual statements,
§2-8-137.
Bond, §2-8-137.
Reports.
Promotion of industry.
Annual statement by
treasurer of
organization, §2-8-137.
Rules and regulations.
Grading and standards,
§2-11-77.
Penalty for violation,
§2-11-78.
Sales tax.
Tomatoes.
Exemptions.
Certain items used in
production of
tomatoes, §40-23-4.
Soybeans, §§2-8-80 to 2-8-103.
See SOYBEANS.
Standards.
Grading and standards,
§§2-11-70 to 2-11-79. See
within this heading,
"Grading and standards."
Tomatoes.
Sales tax.
Exemptions.
Certain items used in
production of
tomatoes, §40-23-4.
Trees.
Fruit trees.
Nurseries, §§2-25-40,
2-25-41.
General provisions.
See TREES AND TIMBER.
**Weight of bushels and
barrels.**
Established by custom of
market place, §8-16-94.
Weights and measures.
Sale by avoirdupois weight
or numerical count,
§8-16-101.

FUEL.
Gasoline.
See GASOLINE.
Motor fuels.
See MOTOR FUELS.
**Petroleum products
generally.**
See OIL AND GAS.

FUGITIVES FROM JUSTICE.
Bail jumping, §§13A-10-39,
13A-10-40; ARJA, Rule 2.
Capital offenses.
Reward for information
leading to arrest and
conviction, §15-9-1.
Escape, §§13A-10-30 to
13A-10-45.
See ESCAPE.
Extradition, §§15-9-20 to
15-9-65.
See EXTRADITION.
Governor.
Authority to offer reward for
apprehension of felons,
§15-9-3.
Life imprisonment.
Rewards for information
leading to arrest and
conviction, §15-9-1.
Municipal corporations.
Rewards when high crime or
misdemeanor committed
in municipality, §15-9-2.
Rewards, §§15-9-1 to 15-9-4.
Capital offenses.
Information leading to
arrest and conviction,
§15-9-1.
Claims.
Court to decide claim to
reward, §15-9-4.
Felonies.
Authority of governor to
authorize reward,
§15-9-3.
Governor.
Authority to offer reward
for apprehension of
felon, §15-9-3.
High crime or misdemeanor
committed in
municipality, §15-9-2.
Life imprisonment.
Information leading to
arrest and conviction,
§15-9-1.

FUGITIVE SPOUSE'S LAW,
§§30-4-80 to 30-4-98.

FULL FAITH AND CREDIT,
Const. U. S., Art. IV, §1.
Counties.
Warrants for construction of
public buildings, bridges
and roads, §11-28-2.

FUNDS.
Accountants, §34-1-22.
Agriculture.
Agricultural center fund,
§2-6-53.
Agricultural fund, §§2-9-1 to
2-9-5.
Egg inspection fund, §2-9-40.
Shipping point inspection
fund, §§2-9-20 to 2-9-22.
Attorneys at law.
Client security fund, ACSF,
Rules 1 to 10.
See ATTORNEYS AT
LAW.
Auburn University.
Interest on federal fund paid
by state, §16-48-3.
Aviation.
Helicopter pilots association.
Education and instruction
fund, §4-9-4.
State airport development
fund, §4-2-42.

FUNDS—Cont'd
**Breeding and development
fund,** §11-65-34.
Cahaba trace fund,
§41-9-805.
**Capital development
assistance fund,** §§9-7A-1
to 9-7A-17.
See PARKS AND
RECREATION.
Coal.
Abandoned mine
reclamation, §9-16-122.
Priority of expenditures of
monies from fund,
§9-16-123.
Special abandoned mine
reclamation trust fund,
§9-16-135.
Surface mining control and
reclamation.
Alabama surface mining
fund, §9-16-103.
Convention facilities.
Alabama convention facilities
fund, §11-100-5.
Corporations.
Secretary of state
corporations fund,
§10-2A-281.
Corrections revolving fund,
§14-1-14.
Counties.
See COUNTIES.
Crime victims compensation.
Establishment of special
fund, §15-23-16.
Dietitians and nutritionists.
Practice act.
Special revenue trust fund,
§34-34A-8.
**District attorneys' spouses
fund,** §§12-17-201 to
12-17-207.
See DISTRICT
ATTORNEYS.
Education.
Public school funds,
§§16-13-30 to 16-13-38.
See EDUCATION.
Special educational trust
fund, §§16-8-26.1,
16-14-10, 40-1-31,
40-1-32.
Egg inspection fund, §2-9-40.
Engineers.
Board of registration.
Secretary to receive and
account for all funds,
§34-11-36.
Environmental management.
Alabama department of
environmental
management fund,
§22-22A-11.
Hazardous substances.
Cleanup fund, §§22-30A-1
to 22-30A-11.
See HAZARDOUS
SUBSTANCES.
Pollution control grant fund,
§22-22A-16.
**Fire fighters' personnel
standards and education
fund,** §§36-32-9, 36-32-10.
Fish and game fund, §§9-2-20
to 9-2-23.
Forests and forestry.
Alabama forestry commission
fund, §§9-3-10, 9-13-4.

FUNDS—Cont'd
  Forests and forestry—Cont'd
    Control of forest tree insects
      and diseases fund,
      §9-13-126.
    Emergency forest fire, insect
      and disease fund,
      §9-3-10.1.
    Forest products.
      Privilege and severance
        taxes.
      Special state forestry
        fund, §9-13-84.
    Forest protection fund,
      §9-13-166.
    Professional foresters fund,
      §34-12-36.
  Funerals.
    State funeral directors and
      embalmers fund,
      §34-13-23.
  Game and fish fund, §§9-2-20
    to 9-2-23.
  Governor.
    Contingency fund, §§36-13-30
      to 36-13-33.
  Governor's mansion fund,
    §36-13-6.
  Harbors and ports.
    State docks facilities reserve
      fund, §33-13-10.
    State docks facilities trust
      fund, §§33-2-210 to
      33-2-213.
  Hazardous substances.
    Cleanup fund, §§22-30A-1 to
      22-30A-11.
    See HAZARDOUS
      SUBSTANCES.
  Health.
    Perinatal health.
      Mothers and babies
        indigent care trust
        fund, §§22-12B-1 to
        22-12B-4.
  Highway funds.
    State highway fund,
      §§23-1-61, 23-1-62.
  History and archives.
    Alabama state historic
      preservation fund,
      §41-9-255.
    Department of archives and
      history.
      Endowment fund,
        §§41-6-30 to 41-6-33.
      Memorial fund, §§41-6-50
        to 41-6-53.
  Horse racing.
    Breeding and development
      fund, §11-65-34.
  Insurance.
    State insurance fund,
      §§41-15-1 to 41-15-13.
    See INSURANCE.
  Judicial retirement fund,
    §§12-18-1 to 12-18-13.
    See JUDGES.
  Landscape architect's fund.
    Generally, §34-17-6.
  Liquefied petroleum gas.
    Liquefied petroleum gas
      board fund, §9-17-104.
    Liquefied petroleum gas
      board personal bond
      fund, §9-17-105.
  **Long term quality health
    care.**
    Resident protection trust
      fund, §22-6-27.
  Mansion fund, §36-13-6.

FUNDS—Cont'd
  Marine resources.
    Seafoods fund, §§9-2-87 to
      9-2-89.
  **Mental health finance
    authority.**
    Mental health facilities
      building fund,
      §41-10-364.
    Sinking fund for payment of
      principal and interest on
      bonds, §41-10-365.
  Military affairs.
    Revolving fund, §§31-1-3,
      31-2-131.
  Mines and minerals.
    Surface mining reclamation,
      §9-16-12.
  Minors.
    Children's trust fund,
      §§26-16-30 to 26-16-33.
  **Mothers and babies indigent
    care trust fund.**
    Perinatal health, §§22-12B-1
      to 22-12B-4.
  Municipal corporations.
    Capital improvements,
      §§11-66-3 to 11-66-6.
  Oil and gas.
    Counties.
      Severance tax trust funds,
        §40-20-50.
  **Peace officers' annuity and
    benefit fund,** §§36-21-60
    to 36-21-78.
    See PEACE OFFICERS.
  **Peace officers' standards
    and training fund,**
    §36-21-47.
    Court costs.
      Remittance to fund,
        §36-21-47.1.
  Penny trust fund, §§41-15A-1
    to 41-15A-5.
    See PENNY TRUST FUND.
  Perinatal health.
    Mothers and babies indigent
      care trust fund,
      §§22-12B-1 to 22-12B-4.
  Physical therapist fund,
    §34-24-195.
  Public lands.
    Unused public lands.
      Management of unused
        lands, §9-15-17.
  **Public officers and
    employees.**
    State employees' retirement
      system, §§36-27-24,
      36-27-25.
  Public service commission.
    Consumer's utility rate
      hearing fund, §37-1-18.
  Real estate brokers.
    Real estate commission fund,
      §34-27-4.
    Recovery fund, §34-27-31.
  Recreation.
    Capital development
      assistance fund, §§9-7A-1
      to 9-7A-17.
    See PARKS AND
      RECREATION.
  Scholarships.
    Elementary teachers'
      scholarship fund,
      §16-23-17.

FUNDS—Cont'd
  Scholarships—Cont'd
    Emergency secondary
      education scholarship
      fund, §§16-23-18 to
      16-23-23.
    See SCHOLARSHIPS.
  Seafoods fund, §§9-2-87 to
    9-2-89.
  **Secretary of state
    corporations fund,**
    §10-2A-281.
  Sinking funds.
    Counties.
      See COUNTIES.
    Municipal corporations.
      See MUNICIPAL
        CORPORATIONS.
    State sinking fund, §§41-4-10
      to 41-4-15.
      See FINANCE.
  Social security.
    Public employees.
      Contribution fund,
        §36-28-8.
  Social workers, §34-30-6.
  **Southeast interstate low-
    level radioactive waste
    management compact,**
    §22-32-5.
  Sports hall of fame board.
    Solicitation and acceptance,
      §41-9-453.
  State highway fund,
    §§23-1-61, 23-1-62.
  State parks, §§9-2-105 to
    9-2-107.
  **State public welfare trust
    fund,** §38-4-13.
  State sinking fund, §§41-4-10
    to 41-4-15.
    See FINANCE.
  **Stonewall Jackson memorial
    fund,** §§16-32-1 to 16-32-3.
  **Underground storage tank
    trust fund,** §§22-35-1 to
    22-35-13.
    See UNDERGROUND
      STORAGE TANKS.
  **Unemployment
    compensation trust fund,**
    §§25-4-30 to 25-4-32.
  **Uniform commercial code
    and farm products
    central index system
    fund,** §7-9-307.
  Universities and colleges.
    Eminent scholars trust fund,
      §§16-61-1 to 16-61-10.
    See UNIVERSITIES AND
      COLLEGES.
  University of Alabama.
    Museum, §16-47-203.
    University fund, §16-47-4.
  Veterans.
    Educational benefits.
      Special educational trust
        fund.
        Reimbursement of
          institutions
          providing benefits,
          §31-6-15.
    State veterans' home trust
      fund, §31-5A-7.
  **Water pollution control
    authority.**
    Water pollution control
      revolving loan fund.
      Generally, §22-34-3.

FUNDS—Cont'd

Water system assistance authority.
Water supply assistance fund.
Established, §22-23A-4.

Welfare.
State public welfare trust fund, §38-4-13.

FUNERALS.

Age.
Embalmers.
Licenses.
Qualifications of applicants, §34-13-92.

Alabama board of funeral service. See within this heading, "Board of funeral service."

American board of funeral service education.
Defined, §34-13-1.

Appeals.
Board of funeral service.
Decisions of board may be appealed, §34-13-6.
Procedure, §34-13-31.

Applicability of chapter, §34-13-3.

Apprentices, §§34-13-130 to 34-13-134.
Certificates.
Annual renewal of certificate, §34-13-131.
Application for issuance, §34-13-130.
Renewal, §34-13-131.
Revocation or suspension.
Grounds, §34-13-134.
Reregistration when certificate has lapsed or is revoked, §34-13-134.
Fees.
Application fee, §34-13-130.
Renewal of certificate, §34-13-131.
Fraud.
Grounds for revocation or suspension of certificate, §34-13-134.
Leaves of absence, §34-13-133.
Reports.
Annual report of apprentices, §34-13-132.
Term of apprenticeship, §34-13-130.

Audits.
Board of funeral service.
Examiner of public accounts to audit board, §34-13-29.

Board of embalming.
Abolition of board, §34-13-20.

Board of funeral service.
Abolition of board of embalming, §34-13-20.
Appeals, §§34-13-6, 34-13-31.
Appointment of members, §34-13-20.
Audits, §34-13-29.
Board of embalming.
Abolition of board, §34-13-20.
Chairman, §34-13-23.

FUNERALS—Cont'd

Board of funeral service —Cont'd
Challenging decisions of board, §34-13-6.
Compensation of members, §34-13-23.
Composition, §34-13-20.
Created, §34-13-20.
Defined, §34-13-1.
Donor eye enucleation licenses, §§34-13-150 to 34-13-152.
Employment of staff and assistants, §34-13-23.
Enforcement of chapter.
Injunctions may be sought by board, §34-13-26.
Evidentiary effect of official documents, §34-13-8.
Executive secretary, §34-13-23.
Examination notices to be mailed by secretary, §34-13-57.
Issuance of apprentice certificates, §34-13-130.
Fees.
Disposition of fees, §34-13-23.
Funds.
Creation of state funeral directors and embalmers fund, §34-13-23.
Deposit of fees collected pursuant to chapter, §34-13-23.
Embezzlement or misuse of board funds, §34-13-7.
Hearings.
Appeals.
Decisions may be appealed, §34-13-6.
Procedure, §34-13-31.
Authority to hold hearings, §34-13-26.
Discussion of proposed rules and regulations, §34-13-26.
Public hearings required, §34-13-25.
Record of proceedings, §34-13-25.
Injunctions.
Power of board to seek injunctions, §34-13-26.
Meetings, §34-13-22.
Membership districts, §34-13-21.
Oath of members, §34-13-24.
Office.
Authority to establish and equip, §34-13-23.
Officers, §34-13-23.
Qualifications of members, §34-13-20.
Quorum, §34-13-22.
Records.
Distribution of list of licensed persons and establishments, §34-13-4.
Proceedings before board to be recorded, §34-13-25.
Reports.
Annual report of apprentices, §34-13-132.

FUNERALS—Cont'd

Board of funeral service —Cont'd
Reports—Cont'd
Annual report to governor and legislature, §34-13-28.
Rules and regulations.
Certified copies, §34-13-8.
Challenging unreasonable rules and regulations, §34-13-6.
Distribution by board, §34-13-4.
Procedural rules and regulations of board, §34-13-23.
Promulgation by board, §34-13-26.
Scope of rules and regulations, §34-13-27.
School or college of mortuary science.
Recognition by board, §34-13-50.
Seal of board, §34-13-27.
Selection of original board, §34-13-20.
Statutes.
Distribution by board, §34-13-4.
Subpoena power of board, §34-13-26.
Terms of office, §34-13-20.
Treasurer.
Bond, §34-13-23.
Witnesses.
Power to compel attendance, §34-13-26.

Bonds, surety.
Board of funeral service.
Bond of treasurer, §34-13-23.

Bribery.
Obtaining licenses by bribery, §34-13-7.

Caskets.
Sales, §22-9-77.

Cemeteries.
General provisions.
See CEMETERIES.

Clergymen.
Burial permits.
Ministers at funerals to ascertain if permit has been secured, §22-19-4.

Copies.
Obtaining certified copies of official documents, §34-13-8.

Cremation.
Body removed from state to be cremated, §22-19-2.

Definitions.
Funeral services, §34-13-1.

Directors. See within this heading, "Funeral directors."

District attorneys.
Enforcement of chapter.
District attorney authorized to institute prosecutions, §34-13-5.

Districts.
Board of funeral service.
Membership districts, §34-13-21.

Donor eye enucleation licenses, §§34-13-150 to 34-13-152.

FUNERALS—Cont'd

Embalmers.

Abolition of board of embalming, §34-13-20.

Age.

Licenses.

Qualifications of applicants, §34-13-92.

Apprentice embalmer.

Apprentices generally, §§34-13-130 to 34-13-134.

Defined, §34-13-1.

Blood and urine samples from certain dead bodies.

Exemption from civil and criminal liability, §22-19-82.

May be directed to withdraw samples, §22-19-81.

Board of embalming.

Abolition of board, §34-13-20.

Body removed from state to be embalmed, §22-19-2.

Defined, §34-13-1.

Examinations.

Application for examination, §34-13-91.

Grades, §34-13-94.

Notice of examination, §§34-13-57, 34-13-93.

Scope and conduct, §34-13-94.

Subjects examined, §34-13-94.

Time and place, §34-13-93.

Funeral establishments, §§34-13-110, 34-13-112.

Licenses, §40-12-98.

Age of applicants, §34-13-92.

Fee, §34-13-90.

Qualifications of applicants, §34-13-92.

Required, §34-13-90.

Practical embalmer.

Defined, §34-13-1.

Enforcement of chapter, §34-13-5.

Penalties. See within this heading, "Penalties."

Evidence.

Board of funeral service.

Evidentiary effect of board documents, §34-13-8.

Examinations.

Embalmers. See within this heading, "Embalmers."

Funeral directors. See within this heading, "Funeral directors."

Exemptions from provisions of chapter, §34-13-3.

Eye enucleation.

Donor eye enucleation licenses, §§34-13-150 to 34-13-152.

Fees.

Apprentices, §§34-13-130, 34-13-131.

Disposition of fees collected pursuant to chapter, §34-13-23.

Embalmers.

License fee, §34-13-90.

FUNERALS—Cont'd

Fees—Cont'd

Funeral directors.

Application for license, §34-13-70.

Funeral establishments.

Inspections, §34-13-111.

Reciprocal licenses, §34-13-51.

Renewal of licenses, §34-13-53.

Funds.

Funeral directors and embalmers fund, §34-13-23.

Funeral directors.

Apprentice funeral director.

Apprentices generally. See within this heading, "Apprentices."

Defined, §34-13-1.

Death certificates.

See VITAL STATISTICS.

Death of funeral director.

Application for license by survivors, §34-13-74.

Operation of business under special permit, §34-13-74.

Defined, §34-13-1.

Examinations.

Notice of examination, §34-13-57.

Preparation and grading by board, §34-13-73.

Qualifications of applicants for examination, §34-13-72.

Scope of examination, §34-13-73.

Subjects examined, §34-13-73.

Time and place of examination, §34-13-70.

Fees.

Application fee, §34-13-70.

Funeral establishments, §§34-13-110, 34-13-112.

Licenses.

Application, §§34-13-70, 34-13-71.

Contents, §34-13-71.

Fee, §34-13-70.

Filing, §34-13-70.

Form, §34-13-71.

Fees.

Application fee, §34-13-70.

Required, §34-13-70.

Surviving spouse.

Application for license upon death of funeral director, §34-13-74.

Qualifications of applicants for examination, §34-13-72.

Surviving spouse.

Application for license upon death of funeral director, §34-13-74.

Funeral establishments.

Corporations.

Change of name, §34-13-110.

Operation of establishments through licensed director or embalmer, §34-13-110.

FUNERALS—Cont'd

Funeral establishments —Cont'd

Corporations—Cont'd

Penalty for failure to register, §34-13-116.

Defined, §34-13-1.

Embalmers.

Employment by other establishments prohibited, §34-13-112.

Legislative declaration as to supervision and control of establishments, §34-13-112.

Licensing of establishment not to license embalmer, §34-13-112.

Operation of establishment through embalmer, §34-13-110.

Fees.

Inspection fees, §34-13-111.

Funeral directors.

Employment of director by other establishments prohibited, §34-13-112.

Legislative declaration as to supervision and control of establishments, §34-13-112.

Licensing of establishment not to license director, §34-13-112.

Operation of establishment through director, §34-13-110.

Inspections, §34-13-111.

Board to inspect establishment upon receipt of application, §34-13-113.

Fees, §34-13-111.

Licenses.

Application, §34-13-113.

Establishment license not to license embalmer or director, §34-13-112.

General provisions. See within this heading, "Licenses."

Inspection of establishment by board, §34-13-113.

Issuance, §34-13-113.

Reissuance when name changed, §34-13-114.

Renewal.

Refusal to renew, §34-13-115.

Required, §34-13-111.

Revocation or suspension, §34-13-115.

Transfer, §34-13-111.

Name.

Change of name, §34-13-110.

Reissuance of license when name changed, §34-13-114.

Partnerships.

Change of name, §34-13-110.

Operation of establishments through licensed director or embalmer, §34-13-110.

Penalty for failure to register, §34-13-116.

FUNERALS—Cont'd
Funeral establishments
  —Cont'd
  Penalties.
    Failure to register
      establishment,
      §34-13-116.
    Revocation or suspension of
      license, §34-13-115.
  Supervision.
    Declaration of legislative
      intent, §34-13-112.
    Licensed director or
      embalmer required,
      §34-13-110.
  Hearings.
    Board of funeral service. See
      within this heading,
      "Board of funeral
      service."
  Injunctions.
    Board of funeral service.
      Power to seek injunctions,
      §34-13-26.
  Inspections.
    Board of funeral service.
      Right of entry for purposes
      of inspection,
      §34-13-23.
    Funeral establishments,
      §§34-13-111, 34-13-113.
  Insurance.
    Insurers.
      Assets.
        Funeral supplies and
          equipment.
          Valuation, §27-37-8.
  Jurisdiction.
    Court jurisdiction in
      prosecutions under
      chapter, §34-13-5.
  Licenses.
    Annual renewal, §34-13-53.
    Bribery to obtain license,
      §34-13-7.
    Certified copies, §34-13-8.
    Change of status, §34-13-53.
    Display, §34-13-52.
    Distribution of list of
      licensed persons and
      establishments, §34-13-4.
    Donor eye enucleation
      licenses.
      Applications, §34-13-150.
      Compliance with uniform
        anatomical gift act,
        §34-13-152.
      Issuance, §34-13-150.
      Qualifications of applicant,
        §34-13-150.
      Rules and regulations.
        Promulgation,
        §34-13-151.
      Uniform anatomical gift
        act.
        Compliance by licensee,
          §34-13-152.
    Embalmers, §§34-13-90,
      34-13-92, 34-13-98.
    Execution, §34-13-52.
    Expiration, §34-13-53.
    Fees, §§34-13-51, 34-13-53.
    Funeral directors,
      §§31-13-70, 31-13-71,
      31-13-74.
    Funeral establishments,
      §§34-13-111 to 34-13-115.
    Issuance.
      Grounds for refusal to
      issue, §34-13-56.

FUNERALS—Cont'd
Licenses—Cont'd
  Lapsed licenses.
    Reinstatement, §34-13-55.
  Reciprocity, §34-13-51.
  Reinstatement of lapsed
    licenses, §34-13-55.
  Renewal, §34-13-53.
    Grounds for refusal to
      renew, §34-13-56.
  Revocation or suspension.
    Authority of board,
      §34-13-56.
    Funeral establishments,
      §34-13-115.
    Grounds, §34-13-56.
  School or college of mortuary
    science.
    Certificate of graduation
      prerequisite to license,
      §34-13-50.
  Transferability, §34-13-54.
  Mortuary science.
    Defined, §34-13-1.
  Penalties.
    Bribery to obtain license,
      §34-13-7.
    Embezzlement or misuse of
      board funds, §34-13-7.
    Funeral establishments.
      Failure to register
        establishment,
        §34-13-116.
    Violations of chapter,
      §34-13-10.
  Prices.
    Requirements and methods of
      quoting prices, §34-13-9.
  Purpose of chapter, §34-13-2.
  Records, §22-9-77.
    Board of funeral service,
      §§34-13-4, 34-13-25.
  Removal from state.
    Body removed from state to
      be embalmed or
      cremated, §22-19-2.
  Reports, §22-9-77.
    Board of funeral service,
      §§34-13-28, 34-13-132.
  Rules and regulations.
    Board of funeral service. See
      within this heading,
      "Board of funeral
      service."
  **School or college of
    mortuary science.**
    Board of funeral service.
      Recognition by board,
      §34-13-50.
    Defined, §34-13-1.
    Licenses.
      Certificate of graduation
        prerequisite to license,
        §34-13-50.
  Statutes.
    Board to distribute relevant
      statutes on request,
      §34-13-4.
  Subpoenas.
    Board of funeral service.
      Power of board, §34-13-26.
  Violations of chapter.
    Penalties, §34-13-10.
    Restraining, §34-13-26.
  Vital statistics.
    Record and report of casket
      sales or funerals,
      §22-9-77.

FUNERALS—Cont'd
  Witnesses.
    Board of funeral service.
      Power to compel
      attendance, §34-13-26.

FUNGI.
  Elimination from seed,
    §§2-26-30 to 2-26-32.

FUR CATCHERS.
  See FISH AND GAME.

FURNITURE.
  Health.
    Nuisances menacing public
      health, §§22-10-1 to
      22-10-3.

FURS.
  Catchers.
    See FISH AND GAME.
  Dealers.
    General provisions.
      See FISH AND GAME.
    Licenses, §40-12-110.

FUTURE DELIVERY.
  Contracts, §§8-1-120 to
    8-1-131.
    See CONTRACTS.

FUTURE INTERESTS.
  **Depending on death of
    person without heirs,
    issue or children.**
    Defeated by birth of
      posthumous child,
      §35-4-8.
  Life estates.
    See LIFE ESTATES.
  Posthumous children.
    Included in "heirs," "issue"
      or "children," §35-4-8.
  **Remainders, reversions and
    executory interests.**
    See REMAINDERS,
      REVERSIONS AND
      EXECUTORY
      INTERESTS.
  Rule against perpetuities,
    §§35-4-4, 35-4-5.
  Rule in Shelly's case.
    Abolished, §35-4-230.

FUTURES.
  Contracts.
    Future delivery, §§8-1-120 to
      8-1-131.
    See CONTRACTS.

G

**GADSDEN STATE
  COMMUNITY COLLEGE.**
  Merger of institutions.
    Educational institution
      resulting from,
      §16-60-270.
    New college designated
      and named,
      §16-60-270.

**GADSDEN STATE JUNIOR
  COLLEGE.**
  Merger of institutions,
    §16-60-270.
    New college designated and
      named, §16-60-270.

**GADSDEN STATE
  TECHNICAL INSTITUTE.**
Merger of institutions,
   §16-60-270.
   New college designated and
     named, §16-60-270.

GAMBLING.
Advance gambling activity.
   Defined, §13A-12-20.
Affidavits.
   Gambling places.
     Court to examine affiant
       under oath,
       §13A-12-54.
Arrests.
   Gambling places.
     Arrest of occupants of
       house, §13A-12-56.
   Municipal corporations,
     §11-47-111.
Billiard rooms, §§34-6-12 to
   34-6-14.
Bingo.
   See BINGO.
Bookmaking.
   Defined, §13A-12-20.
Conspiracy.
   Conspiracy to promote
     gambling, §13A-12-23.
Contests of chance.
   Defined, §13A-12-20.
Contracts.
   Creditor of losing party may
     garnish winner,
     §8-1-151.
   Criminal prosecutions.
     Answers in actions under
       article not to be used,
       §8-1-152.
   Void contracts, §8-1-150.
   Recovery of money or
     things of value,
     §8-1-150.
Defenses.
   Possession of gambling
     records defense to
     prosecution, §13A-12-26.
Definitions, §13A-12-20.
Devices. See within this
   heading, "Gambling
   devices."
District attorneys.
   Gambling places.
     Complaints filed on certain
       information,
       §13A-12-51.
Dog racing.
   See DOG RACING.
Electric bells.
   Gambling places. See within
     this heading, "Gambling
     places."
Elevators or dumbwaiters.
   Maintenance in gambling
     places prohibited,
     §13A-12-50.
Evidence.
   Electric bells or warning
     devices.
     Presence prima facie
       evidence, §13A-12-58.
   Federal wagering
     occupational tax stamp.
     Possession of stamp prima
       facie evidence of
       gambling violation,
       §13A-12-90.

GAMBLING—Cont'd
Evidence—Cont'd
   Newspapers.
     Published reports of
       occurrence of sporting
       events, §13A-12-28.
**Federal wagering
   occupational tax stamp,**
   §§13A-12-90 to 13A-12-92.
Forfeitures.
   Gambling devices and
     proceeds, §13A-12-30.
Gambling devices.
   Defined, §13A-12-20.
   Evidence.
     Possession of gambling
       device prima facie
       proof of gambling
       offense, §13A-12-28.
   Exhibiting in barred house
     or where speaking tubes
     or electric signals are
     used, §13A-12-52.
   Forfeiture, §13A-12-30.
   Manufacture, sale, etc.,
     §13A-12-27.
   Possession, §13A-12-27.
Gambling places, §§13A-12-50
   to 13A-12-58.
   Affidavits.
     Court to examine affiant
       under oath,
       §13A-12-54.
   Arrest of occupants,
     §13A-12-56.
   Breaking into and entering
     houses.
     Duty of officers,
       §13A-12-55.
   Defendants bound over for
     trial, §13A-12-57.
   District attorneys.
     Complaints filed on certain
       information,
       §13A-12-51.
   Electric bells.
     Exhibiting gambling
       devices where electric
       signals are used,
       §13A-12-52.
     Maintenance prohibited,
       §13A-12-50.
     Permitting person to equip
       any room with
       warning devices,
       §13A-12-53.
     Presence prima facie
       evidence, §13A-12-58.
   Elevators or dumbwaiters.
     Maintenance prohibited,
       §13A-12-50.
   Evidence.
     Electric bells or warning
       devices.
       Presence prima facie
         evidence,
         §13A-12-58.
   Exhibiting gambling devices
     in barred house or where
     speaking tubes or
     electric signals are used,
     §13A-12-52.
   Preliminary examinations of
     defendants, §13A-12-57.
   Seizure of gambling
     instruments, §13A-12-55.
   Warrants.
     Duty of officer to break
       into and enter house,
       §13A-12-55.

GAMBLING—Cont'd
Grand jury.
   Witnesses.
     Examinations, §12-16-212.
     Refusal to testify,
       §12-16-213.
Hearings.
   Preliminary hearings.
     Gambling places.
       Court to hear evidence
         and bind parties
         over for trial,
         §13A-12-57.
Horse racing, §§11-65-1 to
   11-65-47.
   See HORSE RACING.
Income tax.
   Wager winnings withholding
     tax, §§40-18-90,
     40-18-91.
Indictments.
   Federal wagering
     occupational tax stamp.
     Production of stamp
       warrants indictment or
       information,
       §13A-12-91.
   Form of indictment,
     §15-8-150.
Licenses.
   Playing cards, §40-12-144.
Loitering.
   Loitering for purpose of
     gambling, §13A-11-9.
Lotteries, §§13A-12-70 to
   13A-12-75.
   See LOTTERIES.
Misdemeanors.
   Class A misdemeanor,
     §§13A-12-23 to
     13A-12-25, 13A-12-27.
**Money used as bets or
   stakes in gambling
   activity.**
   Forfeiture, §13A-12-30.
Motor vehicles.
   Forfeiture of vehicle used in
     violation of article,
     §13A-12-30.
   Transportation of lottery
     paraphernalia,
     §§13A-12-70 to
     13A-12-75.
   See LOTTERIES.
Municipal corporations.
   Prohibition of gaming and
     gambling houses, etc.,
     §11-47-111.
Newspapers.
   Evidence.
     Published reports of
       occurrence of sporting
       events, §13A-12-28.
Numbers.
   See LOTTERIES.
Paraphernalia.
   Transportation of lottery
     paraphernalia,
     §§13A-12-70 to
     13A-12-75.
   See LOTTERIES.
Pari-mutuel betting.
   Legalized betting not
     affected, §13A-12-31.
Peace officers.
   Gambling places.
     Duty of officer to break
       into and enter house,
       §13A-12-55.
Player.
   Defined, §13A-12-20.

GAMBLING—Cont'd
  Police.
    Gambling places.
      Duty of officer to break
        into and enter house,
        §13A-12-55.
  Preliminary hearings.
    Gambling places.
      Court to hear evidence and
        bind parties over for
        trial, §13A-12-57.
  Proceeds.
    Forfeiture of proceeds to
      state, §13A-12-30.
  Promoting gambling,
    §13A-12-22.
    Conspiracy to promote,
      §13A-12-23.
  Records.
    Forfeiture of gambling
      records, §13A-12-30.
    Possession of gambling
      records.
      Defense to prosecution,
        §13A-12-26.
      First degree possession,
        §13A-12-24.
      Second degree possession,
        §13A-12-25.
  Searches and seizures.
    Forfeiture of gambling
      devices and proceeds,
      §13A-12-30.
    Municipal corporations,
      §11-47-111.
  Simple gambling.
    Class C misdemeanor,
      §13A-12-21.
    Elements of crime,
      §13A-12-21.
  Slot machines.
    Defined, §13A-12-20.
    Possession, §13A-12-27.
  Sports.
    Evidence.
      Newspaper reports of
        sporting events,
        §13A-12-28.
  Taxation.
    Federal wagering
      occupational tax stamp,
      §§13A-12-90 to
      13A-12-92.
    Evidence.
      Possession of stamp.
        Prima facie evidence of
          violation of
          gambling laws,
          §13A-12-90.
      Proof of ownership,
        §13A-12-92.
    Indictments.
      Production of stamp
        warrants indictment
        or information,
        §13A-12-91.
    Ownership.
      Proof of ownership of
        stamp, §13A-12-92.
    Possession of stamp.
      Prima facie evidence of
        violations,
        §13A-12-90.
    Witnesses.
      Proof of ownership of
        stamp, §13A-12-92.
  Transportation of lottery
    paraphernalia,
    §§13A-12-70 to 13A-12-75.
    See LOTTERIES.

GAMBLING—Cont'd
  Warning devices.
    Suppression of gambling
      places, §§13A-12-50 to
      13A-12-58. See within
      this heading, "Gambling
      places."
  Witnesses.
    Grand jury. See within this
      heading, "Grand jury."

GAME LAWS, §§9-11-1 to
  9-11-457.
  See FISH AND GAME.

GAMING.
  General provisions,
    §§13A-12-20 to 13A-12-57.
    See GAMBLING.
  Horse racing, §§11-65-1 to
    11-65-47.
    See HORSE RACING.
  Lotteries, §§13A-12-70 to
    13A-12-75.
    See LOTTERIES.

GARAGES.
  See MOTOR VEHICLES.

GARBAGE AND TRASH.
  Agreements.
    Mutual agreements,
      §22-27-5.
  Authorities.
    Solid waste.
      Disposal authorities,
        §§11-89A-1 to
        11-89A-25.
        See SOLID WASTE.
  Boats.
    Discharge of litter and
      sewage from watercraft,
      §§33-6-1 to 33-6-12.
      See BOATS.
  Burning, §22-27-3.
  Charges.
    Authority of localities to
      establish, §22-27-5.
    Noncompliance.
      Remedies, §22-27-6.
    Periodic payment system,
      §22-27-6.
  Collection.
    Authority of local governing
      bodies as to methods of
      collections, §22-27-3.
    Department approval,
      §22-27-3.
    Financing collection and
      disposal facilities,
      §§22-27-20 to 22-27-26.
  Compliance with article.
    Time for compliance,
      §22-27-6.
  Contracts.
    Mutual contracts.
      Authority of localities to
        enter into mutual
        contracts, §22-27-5.
      Department approval,
        §22-27-5.
  Corporate agencies.
    Licensing, §22-27-5.
  Dangerous waste, §22-27-4.
  Definitions, §22-27-2.
    Financing collection and
      disposal facilities,
      §22-27-20.
  Disposal, §§22-27-3 to 22-27-7.
    Authority of local governing
      bodies as to methods of
      disposal, §22-27-3.

GARBAGE AND TRASH
  —Cont'd
  Disposal—Cont'd
    Compliance with article.
      Time for compliance,
        §22-27-6.
    Department approval,
      §22-27-3.
    Fees and charges, §22-27-5.
    Financing collection and
      disposal facilities,
      §§22-27-20 to 22-27-26.
    Hazardous waste, §22-27-4.
    Licensing of private or
      corporate agencies,
      §22-27-5.
    Municipal corporations,
      §11-47-135.
    Penalty for violation of
      article, §22-27-7.
    Rules and regulations,
      §22-27-7.
    Supervision, §22-27-7.
    Unauthorized dumps,
      §22-27-4.
    Violation of article.
      Penalty for violation,
        §22-27-7.
  Dumps.
    Financing solid waste
      collection and disposal
      facilities, §§22-27-20 to
      22-27-26. See within this
      heading, "Financing
      collection and disposal
      facilities."
    Unauthorized dumps,
      §22-27-4.
  Environmental management.
    Department.
      Supervision of regulatory
        control, §22-27-7.
  Fees.
    Authority of localities to
      establish, §22-27-5.
    Department approval,
      §22-27-5.
    Municipal corporations,
      §11-47-135.
    Nonpayment, §22-27-5.
    Periodic payment system,
      §22-27-6.
  Financing collection and
    disposal facilities,
    §§22-27-20 to 22-27-26.
    Conflicts of the law,
      §22-27-27.
    Construction of article,
      §22-27-21.
    Counties.
      Authority to issue and sell
        warrants, §22-27-22.
    Definitions, §22-27-20.
    Purpose of article, §22-27-21.
    Warrants, §§22-27-22 to
      22-27-27.
      Authority of counties to
        issue and sell
        warrants, §22-27-22.
      Claims against county,
        §22-27-26.
      Investment of trust funds
        in warrants, §22-27-25.
      Issuance, §22-27-22.
      Payment.
        Full faith and credit of
          county pledged to
          payment, §22-27-22.
        Special pledges for
          payment, §22-27-23.

GARBAGE AND TRASH
—Cont'd
Financing collection and disposal facilities—Cont'd
Warrants—Cont'd
Refunding warrants, §22-27-24.
Restrictions on use of proceeds, §22-27-22.
Sale, §22-27-22.
Section 11-8-10 not applicable to warrants issued, §22-27-27.
Forests and forestry.
Fires and fire prevention.
Emergency drought conditions.
Burning of trash, §9-13-141.
Hauling, §22-27-3.
Municipal corporations, §11-47-135.
Hazardous waste, §§22-30-1 to 22-30-24.
See HAZARDOUS WASTE.
Landfills.
Financing solid waste collection and disposal facilities, §§22-27-20 to 22-27-26. See within this heading, "Financing collection and disposal facilities."
Licenses.
Collection and disposal.
Private or corporate agencies, §22-27-5.
Littering upon public thoroughfare.
See HIGHWAYS.
Management plan.
Solid waste, §§22-27-40 to 22-27-49.
See SOLID WASTE.
Marinas.
On-shore trash receptacles at marinas, §33-6-7.
Motor vehicles.
Spilling loads or litter, §32-5-76.
Throwing of litter onto highway, §32-5A-60.
Municipal corporations.
Disposal, §11-47-135.
Fees, §11-47-135.
Hauling, §11-47-135.
Incinerators.
Establishment, §11-47-135.
Nonresidents.
Out-of-state transporters.
Permits.
Issuance, §22-27-5.
Out-of-state transporters.
Permits.
Issuance, §22-27-5.
Penalties.
Violation of article, §22-27-7.
Permits, §22-27-3.
Out-of-state transporters, §22-27-5.
Pest control, §22-27-4.
Pilots and pilotage.
Unlawful discharge of ballast, sweepings, rubbish, etc., in bay.
Report by pilot, §33-4-57.
Private agencies.
Licensing, §22-27-5.
Rules and regulations, §22-27-7.

GARBAGE AND TRASH
—Cont'd
Ships and shipping.
Discharge of litter and sewage from watercraft, §§33-6-1 to 33-6-12.
See BOATS.
Solid waste.
Disposal authorities, §§11-89A-1 to 11-89A-25.
See SOLID WASTE.
Management plan, §§22-27-40 to 22-27-49.
See SOLID WASTE.
Solid waste disposal act, §§22-27-1 to 22-27-7.
Short title, §22-27-1.
Supervision, §22-27-7.
Swine.
Feeding garbage to swine, §2-15-211.
Unauthorized dumps, §22-27-4.
Violations of article.
Penalty, §22-27-7.
Warrants.
Financing collection and disposal facilities, §§22-27-22 to 22-27-27.
See within this heading, "Financing collection and disposal facilities."
Watercraft.
Discharge of litter and sewage from watercraft, §§33-6-1 to 33-6-12.
See BOATS.

GARFISH.
Killing before returning to Alabama waters, §9-12-112.

GARNISHMENT, §§6-6-370 to 6-6-484.
Abatement, revival and survival of actions.
Death of garnishee or contestant, §6-6-395.
Affidavits.
Amount due plaintiff, §6-6-391.
Agricultural superintendents and laborers.
Liens.
Property or proceeds subject to garnishment, §35-11-95.
Amendments.
Applicability of section 6-6-143, §6-6-371.
Answer of garnishee, §§6-6-450 to 6-6-460.
Contest by defendant, §6-6-459.
Judgment when issue found against garnishee, §6-6-460.
Controverting by plaintiff, §6-6-458.
Corporations, §6-6-451.
Defendant's money.
Payment into court if garnishee admits possession thereof, §6-6-452.
Effects subject to levy and sale.
Judgment and proceedings if possession admitted, §6-6-456.

GARNISHMENT—Cont'd
Answer of garnishee—Cont'd
Failure to appear and answer.
Proceedings on, §6-6-457.
Filing, §6-6-450.
Indebtedness or liability.
Judgment where answer admits indebtedness to defendant, §6-6-454.
Payment to clerk if admitted, §6-6-453.
Effect, §6-6-453.
Notice, §6-6-450.
Oral examination.
Demand by plaintiff after filing, §6-6-450.
Personal property.
Proceedings when garnishee liable for delivery, §6-6-455.
Appeals, §6-6-464.
Attachment.
Garnishees, §§6-6-70, 6-6-71.
Attorneys at law.
Money in hands of attorney, §6-6-412.
Bonds, surety.
Discharge of garnishee, §6-6-430.
Discharge of money or property from garnishment, §6-6-430.
Double amount.
Dissolution of garnishment and discharge of all garnishees, §6-6-431.
Filing, §6-6-430.
Garnishment in aid of pending action.
Requirement, §6-6-392.
Proceedings as if bonds not executed, §6-6-430.
Bulk transfers.
Limitation of levies, §7-6-111.
Child support.
Withholding orders for child support.
Priority over garnishments, §30-3-67.
Circuit courts.
Fees, §12-19-75.
Claims of other persons suggested by garnishee.
Disposition, §6-6-463.
Commercial code.
Bank deposits and collections.
When items subject to legal process, §7-4-303.
Bulk transfers.
Limitation of levies, §7-6-111.
Secured transactions.
Debtor's rights in collateral, §7-9-311.
Construction and interpretation.
Applicability of section 6-6-143, §6-6-371.
Consumer finance, §5-19-15.
Corporations.
Answer of garnishee.
Answers on behalf of corporations, §6-6-451.
Costs.
Payment to garnishee upon discharge, §6-6-462.

GARNISHMENT—Cont'd

Cotton gins.
Liens of owners, §35-11-291.

Death of garnishee or contestant.
Revival of actions, §6-6-395.

Debts.
Debt or demand on which action pending may be garnished, §6-6-410.

Definitions, §6-6-370.
Salaries of public officers and employees, §6-6-480.

Dismissal.
Applicability of section 6-6-143, §6-6-371.

District courts.
Fees, §12-19-75.

Enforcement.
Probate courts, §12-13-7.

Executors and administrators.
Enforcement of judgment against personal representative, §§43-2-150 to 43-2-155.
See EXECUTORS AND ADMINISTRATORS.

Exemptions from levy and sale under process, §§5-19-15, 6-10-7, 6-10-37.

Fees.
Circuit and district court garnishment fees, §12-19-75.

Fraternal benefit societies.
Exemption of benefits, etc., from garnishment, §27-34-27.

Hay.
Liens of owners of baling machines or presses.
Enforcement of lien, §35-11-291.

Insurance.
Insurers.
Delinquency proceedings, §27-32-21.

Issuance.
Probate courts, §12-13-7.

Judgments.
Contest of answer by defendant.
Judgment when issue found against garnishee, §6-6-460.
Effect of judgment for plaintiff as between garnishee and defendant, §6-6-461.
Effects subject to levy and sale.
Judgment if possession admitted, §6-6-456.
Indebtedness to defendant.
Judgment where answer admits, §6-6-454.

Minors.
Child support.
Withholding orders for child support.
Priority over garnishments, §30-3-67.

Motor vehicle carriers.
Mileage tax.
Execution against property of delinquent taxpayer, §40-19-10.

GARNISHMENT—Cont'd

Municipal corporations.
Taxation.
Collection of taxes.
Garnishment for collection in anticipation of nonpayment, §§11-51-8, 11-51-26.

Notices.
Answer of garnishee, §6-6-450.
Notice to defendant, §6-6-394.

Oral examination.
Demand after filing of answer by garnishee, §6-6-450.

Peace officers' annuity and benefit fund.
Benefits, annuities, etc., not subject, §36-21-77.

Peanuts.
Liens of owners of peanut machines or pickers.
Enforcement of lien, §35-11-291.

Personal property.
Proceedings when garnishee liable for delivery, §6-6-455.

Probate courts.
Applicability of provisions pertaining to garnishments in circuit courts, §12-13-8.
Enforcement, §12-13-7.
Issuance, §12-13-7.

Process.
Issuance, §6-6-393.
Service, §6-6-393.
When obtainable, §6-6-390.

Public officers and employees.
Money in hands of officer, §6-6-412.
Salaries, §§6-6-480 to 6-6-484.
Defined, §6-6-480.
Final judgments.
Answer of state official garnished to show assent to judgment, §6-6-483.
Writ to issue only after final judgments on actions ex contractu, §6-6-482.
How garnishment effected, §6-6-481.
Warrant or check for money due as salary.
Drawing, §6-6-484.
Who may be garnished, §6-6-481.

Railroad laborers' and employees' liens.
Property or proceeds subject to garnishment, §35-11-95.

Revival of actions.
Death of garnishee or contestant, §6-6-395.

Salaries.
Public officers and employees, §§6-6-480 to 6-6-484.

Secured transactions.
Debtor's rights in collateral, §7-9-311.

GARNISHMENT—Cont'd

Seeds.
Liens of owners of plants for drying or processing planting seeds.
Garnishment to enforce lien, §35-11-291.

Service of process, §6-6-393.

Sheriffs.
Money in hands of sheriff, §6-6-412.

Stock and stockholders.
Unpaid subscription of stock, §6-6-414.

Taxation.
Delinquent taxpayers, §§40-5-20 to 40-5-22.

Tobacco.
Use tax, §40-25-44.

Trusts and trustees.
Money or effects in hands of trustee, §6-6-413.
Exception, §6-6-413.

Unemployment compensation.
Benefits.
Exemption from garnishment, §25-4-140.

Wages.
Amount subject to garnishment, §§5-19-15, 6-10-7.
Exemptions from levy and sale under process, §§5-19-15, 6-10-7, 6-10-37.
Salaries of public officers and employees, §§6-6-480 to 6-6-484.

Workmen's compensation.
Exemption of claims from garnishment, §25-5-86.
Pneumoconiosis.
Coal miners.
Benefits exempt from garnishment, §25-5-179.

GARRISONS.

Enforcement of sanitation laws in garrisons, §31-2-40.

GAS.

Authorities.
Improvement authorities, §§39-7-1 to 39-7-34.
See PUBLIC WORKS.

Coal mine safety.
See COAL.

Conservation and regulation of production, §§9-17-1 to 9-17-32.
See OIL AND GAS.

Construction.
Condemnation of ways and rights of way by companies constructing public utility, §10-5-4.

Counties.
Bond issues for, §§11-81-1, 11-81-160 to 11-81-190.
See COUNTIES.

Criminal law and procedure.
Meters.
Furnishing, §37-8-6.
Inspections.
Open for inspection, §37-8-6.

GAS—Cont'd
Eminent domain.
Companies constructing, operating or maintaining public utility, §10-5-4.
Power of eminent domain in public utility corporations, §10-5-1.
Routes and sites.
Rights of condemning corporations in selection of routes and sites, §10-5-8.
Flat fee, §40-17-160.
Remittance, §40-17-160.
Highways.
Contracting with local authorities on use of public roads by public utility corporations, §10-5-14.
Improvement authorities, §§39-7-1 to 39-7-34.
See PUBLIC WORKS.
Leases.
Oil and gas leases, §§9-17-50 to 9-17-69.
See OIL AND GAS.
Liquefied petroleum gas.
Fuel tax, §§40-17-160 to 40-17-165.
General provisions, §§9-17-100 to 9-17-110.
See LIQUEFIED PETROLEUM GAS.
Meters.
Criminal law and procedure, §37-8-6.
Municipal corporations.
See MUNICIPAL CORPORATIONS.
Oil and gas board.
See OIL AND GAS.
Operation of utility.
Condemnation of ways and rights of way by companies operating public utility, §10-5-4.
Municipal corporations.
See MUNICIPAL CORPORATIONS.
Pipelines, §§37-4-80 to 37-4-88.
See PIPELINES.
Production.
Conservation and regulation of production, §§9-17-1 to 9-17-32.
See OIL AND GAS.
Privilege tax on production, §§40-20-1 to 40-20-13.
See OIL AND GAS.
Public service commission, §§37-1-1 to 37-1-157.
See PUBLIC SERVICE COMMISSION.
Public utilities generally.
See PUBLIC UTILITIES.
Taxation.
Privilege tax on production, §§40-20-1 to 40-20-13.
See OIL AND GAS.
Public utility taxes, §§40-21-1 to 40-21-107.
See PUBLIC UTILITIES.
Theft.
Acts which make gas unlawfully available, §13A-8-23.

GAS FITTERS.
Plumbers and gas fitters generally, §§34-37-1 to 34-37-18.
See PLUMBING.

GASOLINE.
Agricultural purposes.
Refunds of tax on gasoline used for agricultural purposes, §§40-17-100 to 40-17-107. See within this heading, "Tax."
Air commerce.
Tax.
Air carriers.
Exemptions from tax, §40-17-31.
Constitution of Alabama.
Tax.
Expenditure of taxes, Const. Ala., amd. 93.
Counties.
Issuing warrants in anticipation of gasoline taxes, §§11-11-1 to 11-11-8.
See COUNTIES.
Definitions.
Gasoline tax, §40-17-30.
Distribution and use of proceeds, §40-17-70.
Gasoline used for agricultural purposes, §40-17-100.
Gasoline used for static testing of engine, §40-17-120.
Distributors of motor fuels, §§40-12-190 to 40-12-206.
See MOTOR FUELS.
Education.
Boards of education.
Tax.
City and county boards of education.
Exemption, §40-17-31.
Church schools.
Tax.
Exemption, §40-17-31.
Private schools.
Tax exemption, §40-17-31.
Excise taxes.
Additional excise tax on gasoline, motor fuel and lubricating oil, §§40-17-220 to 40-17-225.
See TAXATION.
Executions.
Gasoline tax.
Delinquents, §40-17-4.
Fraud.
Gasoline tax.
Refund on gasoline used for agricultural purposes.
False or fraudulent claims, §40-17-108.
Refund on gasoline used for static testing of engine.
False or fraudulent claims, §40-17-124.
Gasoline tax, §§40-17-30 to 40-17-124. See within this heading, "Tax."
Institute for deaf and blind.
Tax.
Exemptions from tax, §40-17-31.

GASOLINE—Cont'd
Licenses.
Stations and pumps, §40-12-106.
Liens.
Gasoline tax.
Delinquents, §40-17-46.
Military affairs.
Taxation.
Exemption of certain post exchanges and canteens from gasoline taxes, §31-2-81.
Notice.
Gasoline tax.
Delinquents.
Notice to show cause, §40-17-46.
Penalties.
Tax, §40-17-37.
Petroleum products generally.
See OIL AND GAS.
Refunds.
Tax refunds, §§40-17-100 to 40-17-124. See within this heading, "Tax."
Reports.
Tax. See within this heading, "Tax."
Sales tax. See within this heading, "Tax."
Service stations.
Highways.
Interstate highway system. Controlled access facilities, §23-3-4.
Sheriffs.
Gasoline tax.
Delinquents.
Collection of taxes and penalties, §40-17-47.
Tax, §§40-17-30 to 40-17-124.
Acceptance of money on recovery of balance. Effect, §40-17-40.
Actions by state.
Limitation, §40-17-41.
Applicability to all other excise taxes on motor fuels, §40-17-42.
Additional excise tax on gasoline, motor fuel and lubricating oil, §§40-17-220 to 40-17-225.
Air carriers.
Exemptions from tax, §40-17-31.
Allocation.
Method, §40-17-31.
Amount, §40-17-31.
Aviation fuel.
New or additional tax.
Cities and towns prohibited from levying, §40-17-50.
Church schools.
Exemption from tax, §40-17-31.
Collection.
By whom collected and paid over, §40-17-32.
Delinquents, §40-17-47.
Commissioner of revenue.
Refund on gasoline used for agricultural purposes.
Powers of commissioner, §40-17-106.

GASOLINE—Cont'd
Tax—Cont'd
Counties.
  Issuing warrants in
    anticipation of gasoline
    taxes, §§11-11-1 to
    11-11-8.
    See COUNTIES.
  Provision that local tax be
    born by consumer and
    paid to county but
    once, §40-17-51.
Dealers.
  Adding tax to price,
    §40-17-31.
  Retail dealers.
    Defined, §40-17-31.
Definitions, §40-17-30.
Distribution and use of
  proceeds, §40-17-70.
Gasoline used for
  agricultural purposes,
  §40-17-100.
Gasoline used for static
  testing of engine,
  §40-17-120.
Delinquents, §§40-17-46 to
  40-17-48.
  Claims, §40-17-48.
  Collection of taxes and
    penalties by sheriff,
    §40-17-47.
  Execution, §40-17-46.
  Liens, §40-17-46.
  Notification to show cause,
    §40-17-46.
  Sheriff.
    Collection of taxes and
      penalties, §40-17-47.
Department of revenue.
  Duty of enforcement,
    §40-17-39.
  Forms.
    Department to prescribe
      form of statements
      and reports,
      §40-17-43.
Diesel fuel tax.
  Effect on provisions of
    gasoline tax,
    §40-17-19.
Discount.
  Distributors, etc., licensed
    under section
    40-12-194, §40-17-38.
Distribution and use of
  proceeds, §40-17-31;
  Const. Ala., amd. 93.
  Census.
    Effective date, §40-17-77.
  Counties, §§40-17-73 to
    40-17-76.
    County and municipal
      highway purposes.
      Fifty-five percent of
        net proceeds,
        §40-17-73.
    County governing bodies.
      Payment of
        compensation of
        clerks, §40-17-76.
      Payment of salaries of
        members,
        §40-17-75.
    Disposition of sums
      allocated and
      apportioned to
      counties, §40-17-74.
    Definitions, §40-17-70.

GASOLINE—Cont'd
Tax—Cont'd
Distribution and use of
  proceeds—Cont'd
Highway purposes.
  County and municipal
    highway purposes.
    Construction and
      maintenance of
      streets in
      municipalities,
      §40-17-79.
    Fifty-five percent of
      net proceeds,
      §40-17-73.
  Generally, §40-17-78.
  Highways and traffic
    control areas on
    school property.
    Construction and
      maintenance,
      §40-17-80.
  State highway purposes.
    Forty-five percent of
      net proceeds,
      §40-17-72.
Legislative intent,
  §40-17-71.
Method, §40-17-31.
Municipal corporations.
  County and municipal
    highway purposes.
    Fifty-five percent of
      net proceeds,
      §40-17-73.
Prior pledges.
  Preservations, §40-17-82.
State highway purposes.
  Forty-five percent of net
    proceeds, §40-17-72.
State treasurer.
  Allocations and
    distributions,
    §40-17-81.
Distributors.
  Adding tax to price,
    §40-17-31.
  Address.
    Report, §40-17-36.
  Defined, §40-17-31.
  Discount allowed to
    distributor licensed
    under section
    40-12-194, §40-17-38.
Education.
  Exemptions from tax,
    §40-17-31.
Enforcement.
  Duty of department of
    revenue, §40-17-39.
Executions.
  Delinquents, §40-17-46.
Expenditure of taxes, Const.
  Ala., amd. 354.
Fraud.
  Refund on gasoline used
    for agricultural
    purposes.
    False or fraudulent
      claims, §40-17-108.
  Refund on gasoline used
    for static testing of
    engine.
    False or fraudulent
      claims, §40-17-124.
Institute for deaf and blind.
  Exemptions from tax,
    §40-17-31.
Interstate sales.
  Adjustment of taxes,
    §40-17-52.

GASOLINE—Cont'd
Tax—Cont'd
Levy, §40-17-31.
Liens.
  Delinquents, §40-17-46.
Limitation of actions,
  §40-17-41.
  Applicability to all other
    excise taxes on motor
    fuels, §40-17-42.
Military affairs.
  Exemption of certain post
    exchanges and
    canteens, §31-2-81.
Motor carrier fuel tax.
  Credit of payment of
    gasoline tax,
    §40-17-142.
Motor fuel upon which tax
  has not been paid.
  Use, §40-17-45.
Municipal corporations.
  New or additional tax on
    aviation fuel.
    Prohibited from levying,
      §40-17-50.
  Provision that local tax be
    borne by consumer and
    paid to municipality
    but once, §40-17-51.
Penalties.
  Records.
    Failure to keep,
      §40-17-37.
  Reports.
    Failure to make,
      §40-17-37.
Price of gasoline.
  Tax to be added to,
    §40-17-31.
Private schools.
  Exemptions from tax,
    §40-17-31.
Proceeds.
  Distribution and use,
    §40-17-31; Const. Ala.,
    amd. 93.
Records, §§40-17-35,
  40-17-37.
Refiners.
  Address.
    Report, §40-17-36.
  Defined, §40-17-30.
Refunds, §§40-17-100 to
  40-17-124.
  Gasoline used for
    agricultural purposes.
    Amount of refund,
      §40-17-102.
    Claim for refund.
      Filing, §§40-17-103,
        40-17-104.
      Form, §40-17-103.
      Time for filing,
        §40-17-104.
    Commissioner of
      revenue.
      Powers, §40-17-106.
    Defined, §40-17-100.
    Eligibility for refund,
      §40-17-102.
    False or fraudulent
      claims, §40-17-108.
    Payment of refund,
      §40-17-105.
    Appropriations,
      §40-17-105.
    Purpose of division,
      §40-17-101.

GASOLINE—Cont'd
Tax—Cont'd
Refunds—Cont'd
Gasoline used for
agricultural purposes
—Cont'd
Tractors owned by
applicant.
Assessment for ad
valorem tax,
§40-17-107.
Gasoline used for static
testing of engine.
Amount of refund,
§40-17-122.
Defined, §40-17-120.
Eligibility for refund,
§40-17-122.
False or fraudulent
claims, §40-17-124.
How refund made,
§40-17-123.
Purpose of division,
§40-17-121.
Reports.
Address.
Report by distributor,
refiner, storer, etc.,
§40-17-36.
Carriers.
Information not public,
§40-17-202.
Penalty for failure to
comply, §40-17-203.
When report to be made
by carriers,
§40-17-200.
Failure to make.
Penalty, §40-17-37.
Forms.
Department of revenue
to prescribe,
§40-17-43.
Sales, §40-17-33.
Warehouses.
Information not public,
§40-17-202.
Penalty for failure to
comply, §40-17-203.
When reports to be made
by warehousemen
and transfer
companies,
§40-17-201.
Withdrawals, §40-17-33.
Returns.
Monthly returns.
Failure to make,
§40-17-44.
Sales.
Exemptions, §40-23-4.
Record, §40-17-35.
Report, §40-17-33.
Sheriffs.
Delinquents.
Collection of taxes and
penalties, §40-17-47.
Statements.
Forms.
Department of revenue
to prescribe,
§40-17-43.
Monthly statements.
Sworn to, §40-17-34.
Storers.
Address.
Report, §40-17-36.
Defined, §40-17-30.
Violations.
Restraint of violators,
§40-17-49.

GASOLINE—Cont'd
Tax—Cont'd
Withdrawals.
Record, §40-17-35.
Report, §40-17-33.
Youth services.
Department of youth
services.
School districts.
Exemptions from tax,
§40-17-31.
Warrants.
Counties.
Issuing warrants in
anticipation of gasoline
taxes, §§11-11-1 to
11-11-8.
See COUNTIES.
Youth services.
Tax.
Department of youth
services.
School districts.
Exemption, §40-17-31.

GEESE.
Hunting.
See FISH AND GAME.
Poultry.
See POULTRY.

GENDER.
Masculine includes feminine
and neuter, §1-1-2.

GENERAL
ADMINISTRATORS,
§§43-2-84, 43-2-85, 43-2-170
to 43-2-175.
See EXECUTORS AND
ADMINISTRATORS.

GENERATION-SKIPPING
TAX.
General provisions, §§19-5-1
to 19-5-12.
See TRUSTS AND
TRUSTEES.
Levy, §§40-15A-1 to 40-15A-14.
See TRUSTS AND
TRUSTEES.

GENERIC DRUGS.
General provisions, §34-23-8.

GENETIC SERVICE,
§§22-10A-1 to 22-10A-3.
Counseling, §22-10A-2.
Declaration of policy,
§22-10A-1.
Diagnostic facilities,
§22-10A-2.
Participation by individuals
voluntary, §22-10A-3.
Prenatal testing, §22-10A-2.
University of Alabama in
Birmingham.
Diagnostic facilities, genetic
counseling and prenatal
testing, §22-10A-2.
University of South
Alabama.
Diagnostic facilities, genetic
counseling and prenatal
testing, §22-10A-2.
Voluntary participation,
§22-10-3.

GENEVA COUNTY.
County officers.
Compensation, Const. Ala.,
amd. 372.
County offices.
Restructuring or abolition,
Const. Ala., amd. 372.

GENEVA COUNTY—Cont'd
Courthouse.
Bond issue for construction
and equipment, Const.
Ala., amd. 187.
Economic and industrial
development promotion,
Const. Ala., amd. 429.
Economic development.
Municipalities in Geneva
county, Const. Ala., amd.
263.
Jail.
Bond issue for construction
and equipment, Const.
Ala., amd. 187.
Probate court.
Fees, allowances, etc., of
judge, Const. Ala., amd.
357.

GEOLOGICAL SURVEY,
§§9-4-1 to 9-4-19.
Appropriations.
Expenditures from annual
appropriation, §9-4-8.
Approval, §9-4-9.
Procedure, §9-4-9.
Bench marks.
Establishment of permanent
bench marks along
highways, etc., §9-4-11.
Coal.
General provisions.
See COAL.
Legislature.
State geologist.
Reports to legislature,
§9-4-2.
Mineral resources
management committee,
§§9-5-1 to 9-5-3.
Reports.
State geologist.
Legislature.
Reports to legislature,
§9-4-2.
Procedure for publication,
§9-4-10.
Special reports, §9-4-2.
Research and experiments.
Retention of faculty members
and students.
Authority of survey and oil
and gas board, §9-4-14.
Compensation, §9-4-19.
Contracts, §§9-4-15, 9-4-16.
Interference with ordinary
duties.
Retention not to
interfere with,
§9-4-17.
Merit system act.
Persons not subject to,
§9-4-18.
Not to interfere with
ordinary duties,
§9-4-17.
Salaries, §9-4-19.
Salaries.
Research and experiments.
Retention of faculty
members and students,
§9-4-19.
State geologist.
Appointment, §9-4-1.
Assistants.
Appointment, §9-4-3.
Full-time employees,
§9-4-3.
Qualifications, §9-4-3.

GEOLOGICAL SURVEY
—Cont'd
State geologist—Cont'd
Assistants—Cont'd
University of Alabama.
Teaching, §9-4-4.
Compensation for
teaching, §9-4-6.
Limitations, §9-4-5.
Not to participate in
retirement system,
§9-4-7.
Collections of specimens,
§9-4-2.
Duties.
General provisions, §9-4-2.
Full-time position, §9-4-2.
Qualifications, §9-4-1.
Reports.
Annual report to
legislature, §9-4-2.
Preparation, §9-4-2.
Procedure for publication,
§9-4-10.
Retirement.
Teachers' retirement
system.
State geologist and
assistants not to
participate, §9-4-7.
Surveys.
Duties, §9-4-2.
Term of office, §9-4-1.
University of Alabama.
President.
Appointment, §9-4-1.
Teaching.
Authority to teach,
§9-4-4.
Compensation, §9-4-6.
Limitations, §9-4-5.
Retirement system.
Not to participate in
teachers'
retirement system,
§9-4-7.
Vacancies in office.
Filling, §9-4-1.
Topographic surveys,
§§9-4-11 to 9-4-13.
Bench marks.
Establishment of
permanent marks
along highways, etc.,
§9-4-11.
Contents, §9-4-11.
Execution, §9-4-11.
Expenses.
Agreements as to payment,
§9-4-12.
Right of entry.
Preparation of surveys,
§9-4-13.
United States.
Agreements as to payment
of expenses of field
surveys, §9-4-12.
Cooperation with United
States geological
survey, §9-4-11.
United States.
Cooperation with United
States geological survey,
§9-4-11.
Topographic survey.
Agreements as to payment
of expenses, §9-4-12.

GEOLOGICAL SURVEY
—Cont'd
Universities and colleges.
Research and experiments.
Retention of faculty
members and students,
§§9-4-14 to 9-4-19.
University of Alabama.
State geologist. See within
this heading, "State
geologist."
**Water resources research
institute.**
Article supplementary,
§9-8-4.
General provisions.
See SOIL AND WATER
CONSERVATION.

**GEORGE WALLACE, JR.
PLAN FOR LINKED
DEPOSITS OF 1988.**
State funds.
Linked deposits, §§5-21-1 to
5-21-11.
See FINANCE.

GEORGIA.
**Boundary between Alabama
and Georgia,** §41-2-2.

GERMAN MEASLES.
Notifiable diseases,
§§22-11A-1 to 22-11A-38.
See DISEASES.

GERRYMANDERING.
Legislature.
Senatorial districts, Const.
Ala., art. IX, §200.

GIFTED CHILDREN.
Education.
Exceptional children,
§§16-39-1 to 16-39-12.
See EDUCATION.

GIFTS.
Advancements, §§43-8-49 to
43-8-54, 43-8-231.
See DECEDENTS'
ESTATES.
Aged persons.
Commission on the aging.
Authority to receive,
§38-3-6.
**Alabama Agricultural and
Mechanical University.**
Not to fail because of
misnomer, etc., §16-49-3.
Alabama school of trades.
Acceptance by board of
control, §16-60-217.
Powers of board, §16-60-215.
Alabama State University.
Not to fail because of
misnomer, etc., §16-50-3.
Recommendation of programs
to state agencies in order
to qualify for federal,
etc., of funds, §16-50-1.
Anatomical gifts, §§22-19-40
to 22-19-61.
See ANATOMICAL GIFTS.
Assets.
Inter vivos gifts of assets.
Void if donor left without
means of support,
§35-1-2.
Auburn University.
Preserved, §16-48-10.

GIFTS—Cont'd
**Banks and financial
institutions.**
Directors, officers and
employees.
Receipt of gifts to procure
loans, purchases,
discounts, etc.,
§5-6A-22.
Canons of judicial ethics.
Prohibited if gift reflects
expectation of judicial
favor, ACJE, Canon 5C.
Civil defense.
Acceptance by governor of
gifts from private
persons, §31-9-18.
**Constitution of the United
States.**
Foreign presents to United
States officials, Const. U.
S., Art. I, §9.
Education.
See EDUCATION.
Fires and fire prevention.
Sprinkler systems.
Grants and donations
allowed, §34-33-11.
Food.
Nonliability of good faith
donors and distributors
of canned or perishable
food, §20-1-6.
**Foreign presents to United
States officials,** Const. U.
S., Art. I, §9.
**Foreign trade and relations
commission.**
Gifts deemed gifts to state,
§41-9-664.
Taxation, §41-9-664.
Forests and forestry.
State forests.
Gifts of land, §9-13-1.
**Governor's mansion
advisory board,**
§41-9-532.
Health care authorities.
Powers of authority,
§22-21-318.
Highways.
Authority.
Acceptance, §23-1-175.
Finance corporation.
Acceptance, §23-1-175.
Interstate highway system.
Controlled access facilities.
Acquisition of property
and property rights,
§23-3-5.
Scenic enhancement.
Acquisition of land,
§23-1-223.
Income tax.
Corporations.
Deductions allowed
corporations,
§40-18-35.
Deductions.
Corporations, §40-18-35.
Gifts for public purposes,
§40-18-15.
Gain or loss.
Basis of property.
Gift or transfer in trust,
§40-18-6.
Gifts to religious, charitable,
scientific or educational
institutions, §40-18-15.

GIFTS—Cont'd
Indigent persons.
Inter vivos gifts of assets.
Void if donor left without
means of support,
§35-1-2.
Inter vivos gifts.
Donor left without means of
support.
Gift void, §35-1-2.
**Jacksonville State
University.**
Not to fail for informality,
§16-52-11.
Judges.
Prohibited if gift reflects
expectation of judicial
favor, ACJE, Canon 5C.
**Junior college for Franklin,
Marion and Winston
counties, §16-60-24.**
**Junior college for Jackson
and DeKalb counties,**
§16-60-54.
Livingston University.
Not to fail for informality,
§16-53-11.
Men's hall of fame.
Donations, contributions and
gifts.
Exemption from taxation,
§41-9-853.
Military affairs.
City and county donations,
§31-4-17.
Reversion of donations,
§31-4-18.
Minors.
Uniform transfers to minors
act, §§35-5A-1 to
35-5A-24.
See TRANSFERS TO
MINORS.
Music.
Hall of fame board.
Solicitation and
acceptance, §41-9-683.
Taxation, §41-9-683.
**Parol gifts of personal
property.**
Effect of parol gifts, §35-4-97.
Peace officers.
Hall of fame.
Donations, contributions
and gifts.
Exemption from
taxation, §41-9-872.
Soil and water conservation.
Districts.
Acceptance, §9-8-25.
Watershed conservancy
districts.
Acceptance, §9-8-61.
Sports hall of fame board.
Solicitation and acceptance,
§41-9-453.
Sprinkler systems.
Fires and fire prevention.
Grants and donations
allowed, §34-33-11.
Tennessee Valley Authority.
Exhibit commission.
Power to accept public or
private gifts, grants
and donations,
§41-9-782.
Troy State University.
Not to fail for informality,
§16-56-11.

GIFTS—Cont'd
Trusts and trustees.
Satisfaction of pecuniary
gifts by distribution of
property in kind, §19-3-9.
**Uniform transfers to minors
act, §§35-5A-1 to 35-5A-24.**
See TRANSFERS TO
MINORS.
United States.
Foreign presents to United
States officials, Const. U.
S., Art. I, §9.
University of Alabama.
Preserved, §16-47-5.
**University of North
Alabama.**
Not to fail for informality,
§16-51-11.
**Unsolicited goods delivered
by mail or common
carrier.**
Deemed gift to recipient,
§35-1-3.
**Water conservation and
irrigation.**
Agency.
Power to accept, §9-10-5.
Corporations.
Acceptance, §9-10-34.
Welfare.
Department of human
resources.
Authority to receive,
§38-2-6.
Women's hall of fame board,
§41-9-554.

GINS.
**Cotton generally, §§2-19-1 to
2-19-106.**
See COTTON.
Dams.
Erection of dams for gins,
§§18-2-1 to 18-2-21.
See DAMS.

**GINSENG, §§9-13-240 to
9-13-250.**
Appeals.
Refusal or recall of permits
or certificates, §9-13-249.
Arrest.
Enforcement of provisions,
§9-13-250.
Collection.
Prohibited acts, §9-13-242.
Quotas.
Establishment, §9-13-242.
Season for legal collection,
§9-13-242.
Collectors.
Defined, §9-13-241.
Records, §9-13-244.
Registration, §9-13-243.
Commissioner of agriculture.
Appeals from commissioner.
Refusal or recall of permits
or certificates,
§9-13-249.
Definition of "commissioner,"
§9-13-241.
Enforcement of provisions,
§9-13-250.
Monitoring program,
§9-13-247.
Powers.
Refusal or recall of permits
or certificates,
§9-13-249.
Right of entry, §9-13-248.

GINSENG—Cont'd
Commissioner of agriculture
—Cont'd
Rules and regulations,
§9-13-246.
Dealers.
Defined, §9-13-241.
Records, §9-13-244.
Registration, §9-13-243.
Definitions, §9-13-241.
Enforcement of provisions,
§9-13-250.
Export.
Defined, §9-13-241.
Permit, §9-13-245.
Fees.
Registration.
Dealers, growers and
collectors, §9-13-243.
Growers.
Defined, §9-13-241.
Records, §9-13-244.
Registration, §9-13-243.
Legislative findings,
§9-13-240.
Misdemeanors.
Violations of provisions,
§9-13-250.
Monitoring program.
Commissioner of agriculture,
§9-13-247.
Permits.
Exportation of ginseng,
§9-13-245.
Refusal or recall of permits.
Powers of commissioner,
§9-13-249.
Purpose of provisions,
§9-13-240.
Records.
Collectors, dealers and
growers, §9-13-244.
Registration.
Dealers, growers and
collectors, §9-13-243.
Right of entry.
Commission of agriculture,
§9-13-248.
Rules and regulations,
§9-13-246.

**GIRARD, MUNICIPALITY
OF.**
Property tax, Const. Ala.,
amds. 8, 13.

GIRL SCOUTS OF AMERICA.
Licenses.
Exemptions, §40-9-12.
Taxation.
Exemptions, §40-9-12.

GLANDERS.
Notifiable diseases,
§§22-11A-1 to 22-11A-38.
See DISEASES.
**Sale or exchange of horse or
mule affected with
glanders, §3-1-21.**

GLASS.
Insurance.
Casualty insurance
generally.
See INSURANCE.
Licenses.
Selling, §40-12-107.
Motor vehicles.
Glass on highways,
§32-5A-60.
Safety glazing material,
§32-5-218.
Tinting, §32-5-215.

GLASS—Cont'd
Motor vehicles—Cont'd
Windshields, §32-5-215.

GLASSES.
Eyeglasses.
Licenses for sale, §40-12-161.
Medicaid program.
Procurement of
prescription eyewear
for recipients,
§22-6-7.1.
Optometrists, §§34-22-1 to
34-22-64.
See OPTOMETRISTS.

GOATS.
Estrays, §§3-2-1 to 3-2-23.
See ESTRAYS.
Livestock generally, §§2-8-1
to 2-8-62, 2-15-1 to
2-15-317, 3-3-1 to 3-5-14.
See LIVESTOCK.

**GOING OUT OF BUSINESS
SALES,** §§8-13-1 to 8-13-23.
See SALES.

GOLD.
Auction sales.
See AUCTIONS AND
AUCTIONEERS.

GOLF.
Bond issues.
Counties.
Public improvement bonds,
§§11-81-140 to
11-81-150.
See COUNTIES.
Municipal corporations.
Public improvement bonds,
§§11-81-110 to
11-81-150.
See COUNTIES.
Licenses.
Golf or miniature golf
courses, §40-12-108.
Public athletic boards,
§§11-59-1 to 11-59-17.
See MUNICIPAL
CORPORATIONS.

GONORRHEA.
Notifiable diseases,
§§22-11A-1 to 22-11A-38.
See DISEASES.

GOOD FAITH.
Commercial code, §§7-1-203,
7-1-208, 7-2-103.
Fiduciaries.
Reliance on express
provisions of governing
instrument.
Liability to persons whose
interest arise from
instrument,
§19-3-120.2.

GOOD SAMARITAN ACT.
Mines and minerals.
Mine rescue planning and
recovery operations.
Qualified persons,
§6-5-332.
**Persons exempt from
liability,** §6-5-332.

GOOD TIME ACT.
Prisons and prisoners.
Deductions from sentence,
§§14-9-40 to 14-9-44.

GOOD TIME LAW, §§14-9-40 to
14-9-44.

GOODWILL INDUSTRIES.
**Exemption from sales and
use taxes,** §40-23-5.

GORDO, MUNICIPALITY OF.
Property tax, Const. Ala.,
amd. 8.

**GORGAS MEMORIAL
BOARD.**
Generally, §41-9-220.

GOVERNOR.
Absence from state.
Procedure when governor or
successor absent from
state, Const. Ala., art. V,
§127.
Acting governor.
Compensation, Const. Ala.,
art. V, §129.
Mental illness.
Procedure when acting
governor appears to be
of unsound mind,
Const. Ala., art. V,
§128.
Actions.
Defense of certain civil
actions against state to
recover lands, §36-13-3.
Eminent domain.
Direction of governor to
attorney of record.
Authority for bringing
action, §18-1A-270.
Administrative assistants.
Employment, §36-13-2.
Agriculture.
Agricultural center
corporation.
Member of corporation,
§2-6-24.
Board of agriculture and
industries.
Appointment of farmer and
industry members,
§2-3-2.
Ex officio chairman of
board, §2-3-1.
Ameraport.
Deep draft harbor and
terminal contract.
Authority of governor to
execute, §33-9-2.
Offshore harbor and terminal
commission.
Appointment of
commissioners,
§33-10-3.
Ex officio member,
§33-10-3.
Appropriations.
Restriction of allotments by
governor, §41-4-90.
Armories.
Designation by governor,
§31-2-15.
Atomic energy.
Radiation.
Agreements with federal
government, §22-14-9.
**Banks and financial
institutions.**
Banking board.
Appointment of members,
§5-2A-40.
Superintendent of banks.
Annual report to governor,
§5-2A-13.

GOVERNOR—Cont'd
Bond issues.
Governor authorized to act
under certain acts
relating to bonded debt
of state, Const. Ala., art.
XVII, §283.
Tombigbee Valley
development authority.
Approval of terms and
condition, §33-17-12.
Civil defense.
See CIVIL DEFENSE.
Clay.
Sale of right to quarry clay,
§35-4-381.
Coastal areas.
Coastal area management
program.
Approval, §9-7-17.
Commander-in-chief.
General provisions.
See MILITARY AFFAIRS.
Compensation, Const. Ala.,
art. V, §118.
Acting governor, Const. Ala.,
art. V, §129.
Increase in salary at session
of legislature following
ratification of
constitution, Const. Ala.,
art. V, §119.
**Conservation and natural
resources.**
Commissioner.
Advisor of the governor,
§9-2-5.
Responsible to governor,
§9-2-5.
Constables.
Vacancies in office.
Filling, §36-23-2.
Constitution of Alabama.
See CONSTITUTION OF
ALABAMA.
Contingency fund, §§36-13-30
to 36-13-33.
Creation, §36-13-30.
Expenditures, §36-13-31.
Limitation, §36-13-33.
Reports, §36-13-30.
Uses, §36-13-31.
Withdrawals.
Method of withdrawal,
§36-13-32.
Conveyances by governor,
§§35-4-380 to 35-4-391.
See CONVEYANCES.
**Coosa Valley development
authority.**
President of authority,
§33-16-6.
Public corporation, §33-16-3.
Copyright.
Reports and statutes,
§36-13-5.
Corrections.
Board of corrections.
Advisor to the governor,
§14-1-9.
Duties, authority, property,
rights, etc., of board
vested in governor,
§14-1-15.
Notice prior to decision on
construction of
permanent facilities,
§14-1-9.
Reports.
Annual report to
governor, §14-1-13.

GOVERNOR—Cont'd

Councillor.

Office created, §36-13-13.

Counsel.

Employment, §36-13-2.

Counties.

Relocation of county seats.

Petitions for removal.

Discretion of governor as to petitions, §11-16-32.

Death.

Notice to lieutenant governor, §36-9-6.

Disability.

Procedure when governor or successor disabled, Const. Ala., art. V, §127.

Duties.

Faithfully execute laws, Const. Ala., art. V, §120.

Economic and community affairs.

Department.

Transfer of functions to department, §41-23-1.

Education.

Compact for education.

Governor authorized to enter, §16-44-1.

State board of education.

Governor to president of board, §16-3-2.

Vocational education.

Annual report to governor, §16-37-6.

Election, Const. Ala., art. V, §§114, 115.

General provisions.

See ELECTIONS.

Emergency interim succession, §§29-3-1 to 29-3-16; Const. Ala., amd. 159.

See LEGISLATURE.

Eminent domain.

Actions.

Direction of governor to attorney of record.

Authority for bringing action, §18-1A-270.

Employees.

Removal, §36-13-7.

Enterprise zones.

Advisory council.

Appointment of members, §41-23-23.

Environmental control.

Environmental improvement authorities.

Application to incorporate.

Issuance of executive orders, §9-6-4.

Notice of formation, §9-6-5.

Executive department.

Member of department, Const. Ala., art. V, §112.

Executive mansion, §§41-9-530 to 41-9-532.

Executive orders.

Environmental control.

Environmental improvement authorities.

Application to incorporate, §9-6-4.

GOVERNOR—Cont'd

Executive secretary.

Highways.

Authority.

Vice-president of corporation, §23-1-154.

Extradition, §§15-9-20 to 15-9-65.

See EXTRADITION.

Federal grants and advances.

Acceptance, §36-13-8.

Conditions.

Requiring state agencies to meet, §36-13-8.

Finance.

Approval of vouchers or accounts.

Method of indicating where required, §41-4-55.

Fines and forfeitures.

Authority to remit, Const. Ala., art. V, §124.

Flags.

Military flag of governor, §31-2-54.

Foreign trade and relations commission.

Annual report to governor, §41-9-662.

Former governors.

Protection and security.

Provision of personnel to provide, §36-13-14.

Retirement allowance, §36-13-11.

Fugitives from justice.

Authority to offer reward for apprehension of felons, §15-9-3.

Funds.

Contingency fund, §§36-13-30 to 36-13-33.

Mansion fund, §36-13-6.

Handicapped persons.

Governor's committee on employment of handicapped persons, §§21-5-1 to 21-5-10.

See HANDICAPPED PERSONS.

Rehabilitation and crippled children's service.

Annual report to governor on rehabilitation, §16-38-9.

Harbors and ports.

Advisory committee.

Ex officio member of committee, §33-1-8.

Appraisal of real property.

Prerequisite to approval by governor, §33-1-14.

Certificates of approval, §33-1-27.

Exercise and evidence of authority of governor, §33-1-27.

Investigations.

Acquisition of facilities by state.

Governor may make additional investigations, §33-1-13.

Plans.

Submission of certain plans to governor, §33-1-12.

GOVERNOR—Cont'd

Harbors and ports—Cont'd

Real property.

Appraisal.

Prerequisite to approval of purchase, §33-1-14.

Health.

State board of health.

Annual report to governor, §22-2-3.

Highway and traffic safety coordination act.

Authority of governor, §32-4-2.

Cooperation with and participation in programs of federal and other agencies, §32-4-6.

Highways.

Department.

Annual report to governor, §23-1-35.

Executive secretary.

Authority.

Vice-president of corporation, §23-1-154.

Obligations, encumbrances or commitments.

Limitation on amount.

Inauguration date of incoming governor, §23-1-63.

Impeachment, Const. Ala., art. VII, §173.

Procedure when governor or successor impeached, Const. Ala., art. V, §127.

Industrial alcohol.

Enforcement of chapter, §28-5-9.

Notice of changes in officers, directors, etc., of permittees, §28-5-11.

Insurance.

Commissioner of insurance.

Annual report to governor, §27-2-9.

Appointment of commissioner, §27-2-2.

Interstate compact on juveniles.

Execution of compact, §44-2-7.

Junior college for Franklin, Marion and Winston counties.

Board of trustees.

Ex officio chairman, §16-60-21.

Junior college for Jackson and DeKalb counties.

Board of trustees.

Ex officio chairman, §16-60-51.

Juveniles.

Interstate compact.

Execution, §44-2-7.

Law enforcement planning agency.

Request for funds by governor in appropriation bill, §41-8A-12.

Submission of annual budget and request for funds to governor, §41-8A-12.

GOVERNOR—Cont'd
Leases.
Conveyances by governor or
state agency or
institution, §§35-4-380 to
35-4-391.
See CONVEYANCES.
Legislative reference service.
General provisions, §§29-7-1
to 29-7-7.
See LEGISLATURE.
Legislature.
Convening.
Governor authorized to
convene on
extraordinary
occasions, Const. Ala.,
art. V, §122.
Emergency interim
succession, §§29-3-1 to
29-3-16; Const. Ala.,
amd. 159.
See LEGISLATURE.
Reports.
Governor to give certain
information and
reports to legislature,
Const. Ala., art. V,
§123.
Lieutenant governor.
See LIEUTENANT
GOVERNOR.
Limestone.
Sale of right to quarry
limestone, §35-4-381.
Loans.
Temporary loans to meet
deficiencies in treasury.
Negotiation, §36-13-4.
Mansion.
Advisory board, §§41-9-530 to
41-9-532.
Accounts and accounting.
Maintenance of account
of receipts and
expenditures,
§41-9-532.
Appointment of members,
§41-9-530.
Chairman.
Election, §41-9-530.
Compensation.
Members to serve
without
compensation,
§41-9-530.
Composition, §41-9-530.
Contributions, §41-9-532.
Creation, §41-9-530.
Election of chairman and
secretary, §41-9-530.
Expenditure of funds,
§41-9-532.
Gifts, §41-9-532.
Inventory of gifts.
Maintenance, §41-9-532.
Purpose of board,
§41-9-531.
Secretary.
Election, §41-9-530.
Terms of members,
§41-9-530.
Mental illness.
Procedure when governor
appears to be of unsound
mind, Const. Ala., art. V,
§128.

GOVERNOR—Cont'd
Military affairs.
Annual encampments or
cruises.
Governor may order,
§31-2-37.
Armed forces organizations.
Leaving state without
permission, §31-2-82.
Armory commission.
See MILITARY AFFAIRS.
Commander-in-chief.
General provisions.
See MILITARY
AFFAIRS.
Courts-martial.
Execution of sentence.
Approval of governor
prerequisite,
§31-2-103.
General courts-martial for
national guard.
Governor to convene,
§31-2-93.
Review of sentence by
governor, §31-2-103.
Emergency officers.
Appointment in state
militia, §31-2-47.
Flag, §31-2-54.
Ordering out of troops.
See MILITARY AFFAIRS.
Personal military staff of
governor, §31-2-53.
Powers of governor, Const.
Ala., art. V, §131.
Reports.
Adjutant general.
Annual report to
governor, §31-2-67.
Staff, Const. Ala., art. XV,
§276.
State defense force.
Organization of state
defense force by
governor, §31-2-8.
Powers of governor with
respect to state defense
force, §31-2-9.
Unorganized militia.
Ordering out of
unorganized militia,
§§31-2-46, 31-2-48.
Minors.
Interstate compact on
juveniles.
Execution, §44-2-7.
Motor vehicles.
Highway and traffic safety
coordination act.
Authority of governor,
§32-4-2.
Cooperation with and
participation in
programs of federal
and other agencies,
§32-4-6.
Safety coordinating
committee.
Chairman of committee,
§32-3-1.
Speed zones.
Establishment of state
speed zones,
§32-5A-172.
Municipal corporations.
Failure of municipal official
to comply with order of
governor, §15-6-4.

GOVERNOR—Cont'd
Municipal corporations
—Cont'd
Police.
Employment within state
by governor during
riots, etc., §§36-21-20
to 36-21-24.
Oath of office, §36-13-1.
Obscenity.
Extradition of persons in
violation of anti-
obscenity enforcement
act, §13A-12-200.6.
Other offices.
Holding, Const. Ala., art. V,
§130.
Ineligible for other state
office or senate of United
States during term or
within one year
thereafter, Const. Ala.,
art. V, §116.
Pardons and paroles, Const.
Ala., art. V, §124.
Authority, Const. Ala., art.
V, §124.
Pensions.
Widows or widowers of
governors, §36-13-12.
Powers.
Military powers, Const. Ala.,
art. V, §131.
Supreme executive power
vested in governor,
Const. Ala., art. V, §113.
Press secretary.
Employment, §36-13-2.
Printing.
Public printing and binding.
Approval of contract and
bond, §41-4-136.
Proclamations.
Quarantine, §22-12-4.
State matters on which
action necessary, Const.
Ala., art. V, §122.
Property.
Control of state property,
§36-13-10.
Exceptions, §36-13-10.
Protection.
Former governors.
Provision of personnel to
provide protection and
security for, §36-13-14.
General provisions, §§36-33-1
to 36-33-4.
Public lands.
Conveyances by governor,
§§35-4-380 to 35-4-391.
See CONVEYANCES.
Public officers generally.
See PUBLIC OFFICERS
AND EMPLOYEES.
Qualifications, Const. Ala.,
art. V, §117.
Failure of governor-elect to
qualify, Const. Ala., art.
V, §127.
Quarantine.
Proclamation of quarantine
by governor, §22-12-4.
Quarries.
Sale of right to quarry
limestone or clay,
§35-4-381.
Radiation.
Agreements with federal
government, §22-14-9.

GOVERNOR—Cont'd

Real estate commission.
Appointment of
commissioners, §34-27-7.

**Rehabilitation and crippled
children's service.**
Annual report to governor,
§16-38-9.

Reports.
Adjutant general.
Annual report to governor,
§31-2-67.
Copyright, §36-13-5.
Governor may require from
officers, Const. Ala., art.
V, §121.
Legislature.
Governor to give certain
information and
reports to legislature,
Const. Ala., art. V,
§123.

Reprieves, Const. Ala., art. V,
§124.
Authority to grant, Const.
Ala., art. V, §124; amd.
38.

Residency requirements,
Const. Ala., art. V, §118.

Resignation, §36-9-11.

Retirement.
Allowance for former
governors, §36-13-11.

Rewards.
Apprehension or rearrest of
felons, §15-9-3.

Riots.
Municipal police.
Employment within state
by governor during
riots, etc., §§36-21-20
to 36-21-24.
Ordering out of troops.
See MILITARY AFFAIRS.

**Safety coordinating
committee.**
Chairman of committee,
§32-3-1.

Salaries.
Councillor, §36-13-13.

Sales tax.
Allowance by governor,
§40-23-36.

Savings and loan board.
Appointment of members,
§5-2A-63.

Secretaries.
Employment, §36-13-2.

Secretary of state.
Disposal of certain books,
acts, codes, etc.
List of books to be filed
with governor,
§36-14-7.

Security.
Former governors.
Provision of personnel to
provide security,
§36-13-14.

Snead Junior College.
Authorized to accept property
and provide for operation
and maintenance,
§16-60-150.

Southern Union College.
Acceptance of facilities by
governor, §16-60-130.

Special investigator.
Employment, §36-13-2.

GOVERNOR—Cont'd

State agencies.
Federal grants and advances.
Requiring state agencies to
meet conditions,
§36-13-8.
Federal laws, regulations,
etc.
Authority to give state
agencies powers and
duties required to
implement, §36-13-9.

State authority.
Maintenance and defense,
§41-1-2.

State board of education.
Governor to be president of
board, §16-3-2.

State property.
Control, §36-13-10.
Exceptions, §36-13-10.

Statutes.
Copyright, §36-13-5.

Stenographers.
Employment, §36-13-2.

Succession, Const. Ala., art.
V, §127; amd. 282.
Emergency interim
succession.
See LEGISLATURE.
Ineligible to succeed self,
Const. Ala., art. V, §116.

Superintendent of banks.
Annual report to governor,
§5-2A-13.

**Synfuels development
authority.**
Individuals who may become
public corporation,
§9-6A-3.

Term of office, §36-3-1; Const.
Ala., art. V, §116; amd.
282.

**Tombigbee-Tennessee
waterway development
compact.**
See TOMBIGBEE-
TENNESSEE
WATERWAY
DEVELOPMENT
COMPACT.

**Tombigbee valley
development authority.**
Bond issues.
Approval of terms and
condition, §33-17-12.
President of authority,
§33-17-6.
Public corporation, §33-17-3.

Troy State University.
Board of trustees.
Ex officio president of
board, §16-56-3.

Tuskegee Institute.
Appointment of
commissioner, §16-57-1.

United States.
Cession of land by state to
United States.
Authority of governor to
cede jurisdiction,
§42-3-1.

University of Alabama.
Museum.
Governor may convey
interest of state in
museum lands to
university, §16-47-204.

GOVERNOR—Cont'd

University of Montevallo.
Board of trustees.
Ex officio president,
§16-54-2.

**University of South
Alabama.**
Board of trustees.
Ex officio president of
board, §16-55-2.

Vacancies in office.
Constables.
Filling, §36-23-2.
Death.
Notice to lieutenant
governor, §36-9-6.
Filling when offices of
governor and lieutenant
governor both vacant,
Const. Ala., art. V, §127.
Resignation, §36-9-11.

Veto power, Const. Ala., art.
V, §125.
Item veto.
Appropriation bills, Const.
Ala., art. V, §126.

**Water system assistance
authority.**
President of authority,
§22-23A-5.
Reports.
Annual report, §22-23A-6.

**Widows or widowers of
governors.**
Pension, §36-13-12.

Youth services board.
Annual report to governor,
§44-1-55.

GRAFT.

Bribery.
See BRIBERY.

GRAIN.

Adulteration, §2-20-4.

Appeals.
Grading and standards.
Appeal from grading,
§2-11-97.

Assessments.
Promotion of grain industry.
See within this heading,
"Promotion of grain
industry."

Audits.
Promotion of grain industry.
Certified associations.
Annual audit, §2-8-248.

Bags.
Sale in quantities other than
prescribed by section
2-20-1, §2-20-2.
Size, marking, etc., §2-20-1.

Bonds, surety.
Promotion of grain industry.
Treasurer of association,
§2-8-245.

Brands and marks.
Sacks, bags, etc.
Marking, §2-20-1.

**Bread, flour, cornmeal and
grits,** §§20-1-70 to 20-1-78.
See BREAD, FLOUR,
CORNMEAL AND
GRITS.

Bulk sales, §2-20-3.

Dams.
Erection of dams for mills,
gins, factories or electric
generators, §§18-2-1 to
18-2-21.
See DAMS.

GRAIN—Cont'd
Dealers, §§2-31-1 to 2-31-19.
See GRAIN DEALERS.
Fees.
Grading and standards.
Disposition of fees,
§2-11-101.
Flour, §§20-1-70 to 20-1-78.
See BREAD, FLOUR,
CORNMEAL AND
GRITS.
Grading and standards,
§§2-11-90 to 2-11-102.
Apparatus for testing and
grading, §2-11-99.
Appeal from grading,
§2-11-97.
Board of agriculture and
industries.
Powers of board, §2-11-91.
Certificates.
Grade certificates,
§2-11-92.
Sale without certificate
of grade, §2-11-95.
Inspectors.
Certificate of authority,
§2-11-94.
Commissioner of agriculture
and industries.
Duties of commissioner,
§2-11-90.
Fees.
Disposition of fees,
§2-11-101.
Inspections, §2-11-100.
Applicability of laws
relative to inspection,
§2-11-102.
Stations for inspection,
§2-11-92.
Inspectors.
Certificate of authority,
§2-11-94.
Designation, §2-11-93.
Interest in grain
warehouse or elevator
prohibited, §2-11-93.
Publication of grain
standards, §2-11-98.
Samples.
Grading by samples,
§2-11-96.
Seizure.
Applicability of laws,
§2-11-102.
Stations for inspection,
§2-11-92.
Suspension from sale.
Applicability of laws,
§2-11-102.
Testing.
Apparatus for testing and
grading, §2-11-99.
Violations of article,
§2-11-103.
Growers.
Sale by growers, §2-20-3.
Injunctions.
Promotion of grain industry.
Violation of provisions,
§2-8-252.
Inspections.
Applicability of laws relative
to inspection, §2-20-6.
Grading and standards. See
within this heading,
"Grading and standards."
Mill oats.
Sale of mill oats, §2-20-4.

GRAIN—Cont'd
Notice.
Promotion of grain industry.
Assessments.
Referendum to levy
assessment,
§2-8-236.
Penalties.
Promotion of grain industry.
Violation of provisions,
§2-8-252.
Permits.
Promotion of grain industry.
Purchasers to obtain,
§2-8-251.
Producers.
Sale by producers, §2-20-3.
Promotion of grain industry,
§§2-8-230 to 2-8-252;
Const. Ala., amd. 453.
Applicability of provisions.
Inapplicable to certain
purchases, §2-8-243.
Assessments.
Amount, §2-8-239.
Books and records.
Inspection, §2-8-241.
Collection, §2-8-241.
Deductions for expenses,
§2-8-241.
Deduction by first
purchaser, §2-8-241.
Expenditures, §2-8-246.
Referendum to levy
assessment, §§2-8-232
to 2-8-240.
Application to conduct
referendum,
§2-8-233.
Action by board of
agriculture on
application,
§2-8-234.
Approval of assessment,
§2-8-239.
Authority of certified
association to
conduct referendum,
§2-8-235.
Canvass of results,
§2-8-239.
Conduct of referendum,
§2-8-237.
Declared in public
interest, §2-8-232.
Eligibility to vote,
§2-8-238.
Expenses, §2-8-237.
Majority vote required,
§2-8-239.
Notice, §2-8-236.
Question to be voted on,
§2-8-238.
Subsequent referendums,
§2-8-240.
Refunds, §2-8-244.
Remittance to
commissioner,
§2-8-241.
Audits.
Certified associations.
Annual audit, §2-8-248.
Bonds, surety.
Treasurer of association,
§2-8-245.
Certified associations.
Audits.
Annual audit, §2-8-248.

GRAIN—Cont'd
Promotion of grain industry
—Cont'd
Certified associations
—Cont'd
Examination by
department of
examiners of public
accounts, §2-8-248.
Remittance by
commissioner of
agriculture and
industries to treasurer
of association,
§2-8-242.
Revocation of certification,
§2-8-250.
Treasurers.
Bonds, surety, §2-8-245.
Enforcement of provisions,
§2-8-250.
Injunctions.
Violation of provisions,
§2-8-252.
Joint programs with other
states, §2-8-247.
Legislative intent, §2-8-230.
Notice.
Referendum on assessment,
§2-8-236.
Penalties.
Violation of provisions,
§2-8-252.
Permits.
Purchasers to obtain,
§2-8-251.
Provisions not applicable to
certain purchasers,
§2-8-243.
Purpose of provisions,
§2-8-230.
Refunds.
Assessments, §2-8-244.
Restraint of trade.
Authorized activities not in
restraint of trade,
§2-8-231.
Rules and regulations,
§2-8-249.
Rules and regulations.
Promotion of grain industry,
§2-8-249.
Sacks.
Sale in quantities other than
prescribed by section
2-20-1, §2-20-2.
Size, marking, etc., §2-20-1.
Seeds.
See SEEDS.
Seizure, §2-20-6.
Adulterated grain, §2-20-4.
Grading and standards.
Applicability of laws
relative to seizure,
§2-11-102.
Grain bleached with sulphur
fumes, §2-20-5.
Sulphur.
Sale of grain bleached with
sulphur fumes, §2-20-5.
Suspension from sale,
§2-20-6.

GRAIN DEALERS, §§2-31-1 to
2-31-19.
Appeals.
Judicial review of rulings of
commissioner, §2-31-15.
Appeal from circuit court,
§2-31-15.

GRAIN DEALERS—Cont'd
Applicability of provisions.
  Exceptions, §2-31-2.
Bonds, surety, §§2-31-4,
  2-31-5.
  Default.
    Action by commissioner
      upon default, §2-31-8.
  Suspension or revocation of
    license for failure to
    keep bond, §2-31-7.
  Trust fund agreement in lieu
    of bond requirements,
    §2-31-5.
Commissioner of agriculture.
  Default.
    Action by commissioner
      upon default, §2-31-8.
  Definition of "commissioner,"
    §2-31-1.
  Hearings.
    Refusal, suspension or
      revocation of license,
      §§2-31-12, 2-31-13.
  Injunctions.
    Violations of provisions,
      §2-31-19.
  Inspections, §2-31-10.
  Judicial review of rulings,
    §2-31-15.
  Licenses. See within this
    heading, "Licenses."
  Rules and regulations,
    §2-31-16.
  Subpoenas.
    Power to issue, §2-31-14.
  Witnesses.
    Powers as to, §2-31-14.
Default.
  Action by commissioner
    upon, §2-31-8.
Definitions, §2-31-1.
District attorneys.
  Prosecution of violations,
    §2-31-18.
Examinations.
  Books and records.
    Power of commissioner,
      §2-31-10.
Exemptions from provisions,
  §2-31-2.
Fees.
  Licenses.
    Filing fee to accompany
      application, §2-31-3.
Hearings.
  Refusal, suspension or
    revocation of license,
    §§2-31-12, 2-31-13.
Injunctions.
  Violations of provisions,
    §2-31-19.
Inspections.
  Commissioner of agriculture,
    §2-31-10.
Insurance.
  Fire and extended coverage
    insurance required,
    §2-31-6.
  Suspension or revocation of
    license for failure to
    maintain insurance,
    §2-31-7.
Licenses.
  Applications, §2-31-3.
  Bonds, surety, §§2-31-4,
    2-31-5.
  Default.
    Action by commissioner
      upon default,
      §2-31-8.

GRAIN DEALERS—Cont'd
Licenses—Cont'd
  Bonds, surety—Cont'd
    Suspension or revocation of
      license for failure to
      keep bond, §2-31-7.
    Trust fund agreement in
      lieu of bond
      requirements, §2-31-5.
  Fees.
    Filing fee to accompany
      application, §2-31-3.
  Insurance.
    Requirements, §2-31-6.
    Suspension or revocation of
      license for failure to
      maintain insurance,
      §2-31-7.
  Issuance, §2-31-9.
  Posting of license and
    certificate, §2-31-9.
  Refusal.
    Contesting, §2-31-12.
    Hearing, §§2-31-12,
      2-31-13.
    Notice, §2-31-11.
  Renewal, §2-31-3.
  Required, §2-31-3.
  Suspension or revocation,
    §2-31-7.
    Contesting, §2-31-12.
    Hearing, §§2-31-12,
      2-31-13.
    Notice, §2-31-11.
Notice.
  Refusal, suspension or
    revocation of license,
    §2-31-11.
Penalties.
  Violations of provisions,
    §2-31-17.
Reports, §2-31-10.
Rules and regulations.
  Commissioner of agriculture,
    §2-31-16.
Subpoenas.
  Commissioner of agriculture.
    Power to issue subpoenas,
      §2-31-14.
Violations of provisions.
  Injunctions, §2-31-19.
  Penalty, §2-31-17.
  Prosecution.
    Duty of district attorney,
      §2-31-18.
Witnesses.
  Powers of commissioner of
    agriculture as to,
    §2-31-14.

GRAND JURY.
Alcoholic beverages.
  Dry counties.
    Enforcement of chapter.
      See ALCOHOLIC
      BEVERAGES.
Attorney general.
  Appearance before grand
    juries, §36-15-13.
Banks and financial
  institutions.
  Credit unions.
    Violations of credit union
      laws.
      Administrator to submit
        to grand jury,
        §5-17-49.
  Superintendent of banks.
    Reports of criminal
      violations to grand
      juries, §5-2A-14.

GRAND JURY—Cont'd
Bill of impeachment,
  §12-16-223.
Bonds, surety.
  County officers.
    Examination of bonds of
      county officers,
      §12-16-192.
Charging of grand jury,
  §12-16-202.
Conflicts of interest.
  Grand juror not to
    participate in
    deliberations as to
    offenses committed
    against his person or
    property, §12-16-207.
Constitution of Alabama.
  Misdemeanor cases.
    Grand jury not required in
      misdemeanor cases,
      Const. Ala., art. I, §8.
Constitution of the United
  States, Const. U. S.,
  Amendment V.
Counsel.
  Right of witness or defendant
    to counsel.
    Unaffected by division,
      §12-16-222.
County offices.
  Examination of records and
    papers in county offices,
    §12-16-196.
County treasury.
  Examination, §12-16-192.
  Free access to office of county
    treasurer, §12-16-196.
Credit unions.
  Violations of credit union
    laws.
    Administrator to submit to
      grand jury, §5-17-49.
Defendant.
  Counsel.
    Right to counsel unaffected
      by secrecy
      requirements,
      §12-16-222.
Deficiency in number of
  grand jurors, §12-16-207.
Disclosure.
  District attorneys.
    Evidence, §§12-16-220,
      12-16-221.
  Testimony of witnesses.
    Disclosure to district
      attorney's staff,
      §12-16-220.
District attorneys.
  Attendance before grand
    jury, §12-16-209.
  Disclosure.
    Evidence, §§12-16-220,
      12-16-221.
  Duties of district attorney
    before grand jury,
    §12-16-209.
  Not to be present at
    expression of opinions or
    giving of votes by grand
    jury, §12-16-209.
Drawing of names for grand
  jury, §12-16-74.
  Destruction, etc., of jury box,
    §12-16-83.
  Fair drawing.
    Performance of act with
      intent to affect fair
      drawing by officer,
      §12-16-86.

GRAND JURY—Cont'd
Drawing of names for grand jury—Cont'd
Forwarding names drawn to clerk of court, §12-16-70.
Influence.
Attempting to influence jury commissioner or other officer drawing jurors, §12-16-85.
Judge.
Drawing for first week of next session of court, §12-16-70.
Lists of names drawn. Preparation, §12-16-70.
Next session of court, §12-16-70.
When juries for next session drawn by presiding judge, §12-16-72.
Powers of jurors drawn, §12-16-90.
Presiding judge.
When juries for next session of court drawn by presiding judge, §12-16-72.
Provisions of article as to drawing jurors directory, §12-16-90.
Sealing of names drawn, §12-16-70.
Unlawfully placing in or withdrawing names from jury box, §12-16-83.
Duty of grand juror to disclose to fellow jurors public offense of which he has knowledge, §12-16-206.
Education.
County superintendents of education.
Examination of books and papers of county superintendent, §12-16-195.
Elections.
Ballots.
Seals.
When breaking of seals allowed, §17-8-36.
Empaneling, §§12-16-74, 12-16-190.
Influence.
Attempting to influence officer empaneling jurors, §12-16-85.
Powers of jurors empaneled, §12-16-90.
Evidence.
Evidence which may be received by grand jury, §12-16-200.
Examination of witnesses, §12-16-200.
Excusing from jury service.
Hearing of excuses, §12-16-74.
Exemption from jury service.
Hearing of claims of exemption, §12-16-74.
Fees.
Jurors' fees in criminal cases, §12-19-210.
Witnesses.
See WITNESSES.

GRAND JURY—Cont'd
Fish and game.
Hunting deaths.
Investigation, §9-11-21.
Foreman.
Discharge of foreman. Replacement, §12-16-208.
Excuse of foreman. Replacement, §12-16-208.
Lists of witnesses summoned before and attending grand jury.
Preparation and disposition by foreman of book and list of witnesses, §12-16-199.
Oath, §12-16-171.
Replacement of foreman, §12-16-208.
Gambling, §§12-16-212, 12-16-213.
Hunting deaths.
Investigation, §9-11-21.
Impeachment.
See IMPEACHMENT.
Indictments.
Concurrence of 12 jurors required, §12-16-204.
Disclosure by grand juror prior to arrest of person indicted, §12-16-210.
Endorsement, §12-16-204.
Prosecutor's name on indictment, §12-16-205.
Where no prosecutor appears, §12-16-205.
Misdemeanors.
Finding of indictment for misdemeanors, §12-16-203.
Presentation of indictment to court, §15-8-70.
Signature of indictment, §12-16-204.
Injuring property or person of participant, §12-16-218.
Inquiry into indictable offenses committed or triable within county, §12-16-192.
Insufficiency of jurors, §12-16-76.
Jails.
Feeding of prisoners.
Sheriff to deliver book of accounts to grand jury for examination as to correctness,
Free access to county jail, §12-16-196.
Inspection of jails.
County jail, §12-16-191.
Reports.
Furnishing to grand jury, §14-6-91.
Probate judge to furnish grand jury report to board, §14-6-100.
Judges.
Secrecy.
Powers generally, §12-16-226.
Juries generally.
See JURY.
Libel and slander.
Reports.
Privileged information, §13A-11-161.

GRAND JURY—Cont'd
Lotteries.
See LOTTERIES.
Misdemeanors.
Indictments.
Finding of indictment for misdemeanors, §12-16-203.
Not required in misdemeanor cases, Const. Ala., art. I, §8; amd. 37.
Names.
Drawing of names. See within this heading, "Drawing of names for grand jury."
News-gathering persons.
Exemption from disclosing sources, §12-21-142.
Number of grand jurors.
Deficiency in number, §12-16-207.
Oaths of jurors, §12-16-172.
Defect in administration of oath.
Reversal of criminal cases appealed to court of criminal appeals on ground of defect, §12-16-173.
Foreman, §12-16-171.
Swearing of grand jurors, §12-16-74.
Offenses committed against grand juror's person or property.
Jury not to participate in deliberations, §§12-16-207, 12-16-208.
Opinions.
District attorney not to be present at expression of opinions, §12-16-209.
Personal knowledge of public offense.
Duty of grand jury to disclose to fellow jurors, §12-16-206.
Pleas in abatement.
Objection to formation of grand jury, §15-15-40.
When plea on ground grand jurors improperly drawn to be filed, §15-15-44.
Powers of jurors selected, drawn, summoned, etc., §12-16-90.
Probate judges.
Examination of fee book of probate judge, §12-16-194.
Public officers and employees.
Bonds of county officers. Examination, §12-16-192.
Public service commission.
Witnesses.
Requiring witnesses to testify, §37-8-4.
Railroads.
Signs resembling railroad signs.
Erection or maintenance of signs.
Sheriff to report violations to grand jury, §37-8-200.
Reassembling, §12-16-190.
Recessing, §12-16-190.

GRAND JURY—Cont'd
Reporters.
Exemption from disclosing
sources, §12-21-142.
Reports, §12-16-224.
Impeachment.
Investigations of alleged
misconduct or
incompetency.
Disposition of grand jury
reports, §36-11-3.
Jails.
Inspection of jails. See
within this heading,
"Jails."
Libel and slander.
Privileged information,
§13A-11-161.
Secrecy.
Prohibited where no
indictment,
§12-16-223.
Secrecy.
Confidential nature of
testimony, §§12-16-215,
12-16-216.
Exceptions, §12-16-216.
Conflicting laws repealed,
§12-16-226.
Desirability, §12-16-214.
Judges.
Powers generally,
§12-16-226.
Oath of secrecy.
Witnesses, §12-16-219.
Purpose of division,
§12-16-214.
Reports.
Prohibited where no
indictment,
§12-16-223.
Right of witnesses and
defendant to confer with
council.
Effect of secrecy
requirements,
§12-16-222.
Violations.
Penalties, §12-16-225.
Cumulative affect,
§12-16-226.
Sheriffs.
Summoning jurors. See
within this heading,
"Summoning jurors."
State prosecutions.
Exceptions to secrecy
requirements,
§12-16-216.
Subpoenas, §12-21-243.
Witnesses.
Issuance of subpoenas for
witnesses, §12-16-197.
District attorneys,
§12-16-198.
Summoning jurors.
Execution of order to
summon jurors by
sheriff, §12-16-73.
Failure of juror summoned to
attend.
Effect, §12-16-82.
Not grounds for quashing
venire, §12-16-81.
Failure of sheriff to summon
juror drawn.
Negligent failure,
§12-16-89.
Not grounds for quashing
venire, §12-16-81.

GRAND JURY—Cont'd
Summoning jurors—Cont'd
Influence.
Attempting to influence
jury commissioner or
other officer
summoning jurors,
§12-16-85.
Negligent failure of sheriff or
deputy to summon juror,
§12-16-89.
Powers of jurors summoned,
§12-16-90.
Provisions of article as to
summoning jurors
directory, §12-16-90.
Return of order to summon
jurors by sheriff,
§12-16-73.
Superintendent of banks.
Reports of criminal violations
to grand juries, §5-2A-14.
Venire.
Issuance of venire to sheriff
by clerk, §12-16-70.
Objections which may be
taken to venire of jurors,
§12-16-80.
Quashing venire.
Failure of sheriff to
summon juror drawn
or failure of juror
summoned to attend
not grounds for
quashing venire,
§12-16-81.
Veterans.
Pensions for widows of
Confederate veterans.
Investigations of county
pension list, §31-8-29.
Votes.
District attorney not to be
present at giving of votes
by grand jury,
§12-16-209.
Welfare, §38-2-6.
Witnesses.
Certificates.
Issuance of certificates to
witnesses by foreman,
§12-16-199.
Counsel.
Right to counsel unaffected
by secrecy
requirements,
§12-16-222.
Disclosure of testimony.
By witness prior to arrest
of person indicted,
§12-16-211.
When grand jurors may be
required to disclose
testimony of witnesses,
§12-16-201.
Examination, etc.,
§12-16-200.
Gaming and lottery cases,
§12-16-212.
Failure to attend.
Proceedings upon failure of
witnesses summoned
to attend, §12-16-197.
False testimony, §12-16-217.
Fees.
See WITNESSES.
Injuring property or person
of witness, §12-16-218.

GRAND JURY—Cont'd
Witnesses—Cont'd
Lists of witnesses summoned
before and attending
grand jury.
Preparation and disposition
by foreman,
§12-16-199.
Oaths.
Administration of oath to
witnesses, §12-16-199.
Secrecy, §12-16-219.
Prevention of testimony,
§12-16-217.
Public service commission.
Requiring witnesses to
testify, §37-8-4.
Subpoenas.
Issuance of subpoenas for
witnesses, §12-16-197.
District attorneys,
§12-16-198.

GRANDPARENTS.
Visitation rights of
grandparents, §30-3-4.

GRANTS.
Alabama Agricultural and
Mechanical University.
Not to fail because of
misnomer, etc., §16-49-3.
Alabama State University.
Not to fail because of
misnomer, etc., §16-50-3.
Recommendation of programs
to state agencies in order
to qualify for federal,
etc., of funds, §16-50-1.
Application for grants for
conference, §12-8-8.
Black Heritage Museum of
West Alabama.
Acceptance, §16-62-6.
Community services grants
program, §§41-24-1 to
41-24-5.
See COMMUNITY
SERVICES GRANTS.
Constitution of Alabama.
Issuance and execution,
Const. Ala., art. V, §135.
Counties.
Effect of grants to officers,
etc., for use of county,
§11-14-1.
Industrial development
authority.
Terms and conditions of
grants, §41-10-27.
Jacksonville State
University.
Not to fail for informality,
§16-52-11.
Library science and library
education.
See LIBRARIES.
Livingston University.
Not to fail for informality,
§16-53-11.
Railroad authorities.
Power to receive and accept,
§§37-13-7, 37-13-8.
Securities.
Issuance of securities in
anticipation of receipt of
grants, §§11-81A-1 to
11-81A-7.
Authorization of securities.
Limitations and
amplification,
§11-81A-4.

GRANTS—Cont'd
Securities—Cont'd
Issuance of securities in
anticipation of receipt of
grants—Cont'd
Counties.
Power and authority,
§11-81A-3.
Definitions, §11-81A-1.
Effect of chapter,
§11-81A-7.
Exemption of securities
from taxation,
§11-81A-5.
Grantees.
Power and authority,
§11-81A-2.
Investments.
Legal investment status
of securities,
§11-81A-6.
Legal investment status of
securities, §11-81A-6.
Limitations and
amplifications of
securities
authorization,
§11-81A-4.
Municipalities.
General provisions,
§§11-64-1 to 11-64-7.
See MUNICIPAL
CORPORATIONS.
Power and authority,
§11-81A-3.
Public corporations.
Power and authority,
§11-81A-3.
Taxation.
Exemption of securities,
§11-81A-5.
Soil and water conservation.
Cost-share grants, §§9-8A-1
to 9-8A-16.
See SOIL AND WATER
CONSERVATION.
Tennessee Valley Authority.
Exhibit commission.
Power to accept public or
private gifts, grants
and donations,
§41-9-782.
Troy State University.
Not to fail for informality,
§16-56-11.
University of Alabama.
Preserved, §16-47-5.
University of Montevallo.
Federal grants.
Lease or disposal of lands
received by federal
grant, §16-54-16.
Preserved, §16-54-14.
**University of North
Alabama.**
Not to fail for informality,
§16-51-11.
Welfare.
See WELFARE.

GRANULOMA VENEREUM.
Notifiable diseases,
§§22-11A-1 to 22-11A-38.
See DISEASES.

GRAVEL.
Counties.
Acquisition of lands for
gravel pits, §11-14-23.
Conduct of condemnation
proceedings, §11-14-24.

GRAVEL—Cont'd
Motor vehicles.
Spilling loads, §32-5-76.
Public lands.
Sale or leasing of gravel,
§§9-15-52, 9-15-53.

GRAVEYARDS.
Cemeteries generally.
See CEMETERIES.
County cemeteries, §§11-17-1
to 11-17-16.
See COUNTIES.
Eminent domain.
Rights of way.
Private parties, §§18-3-20
to 18-3-22.
Funerals.
General provisions.
See FUNERALS.
Municipal cemeteries,
§§11-47-40 to 11-47-74.
See MUNICIPAL
CORPORATIONS.

GREASE.
Lubricating oils and greases,
§§40-17-170 to 40-17-186.
See LUBRICATING OILS
AND GREASES.

GREENE COUNTY.
Economic development,
Const. Ala., amd. 188.
Officers.
Compensation.
Repeal of amendment,
Const. Ala., amd. 433.
Probate judge.
Compensation, Const. Ala.,
amd. 480.

**GREENSBORO,
MUNICIPALITY OF.**
Property tax, Const. Ala.,
amd. 17.

**GREENVILLE,
MUNICIPALITY OF.**
Property tax, Const. Ala.,
amd. 17.

GRISTMILLS.
Dams.
Erection of dams for mills,
gins, factories or electric
generators, §§18-2-1 to
18-2-21.
See DAMS.

GRITS.
General provisions, §§20-1-70
to 20-1-78.
See BREAD, FLOUR,
CORNMEAL AND
GRITS.
Weights and measures,
§8-16-102.

GROCERY STORES.
County health officers.
Duties, §22-3-5.

GROSS RECEIPTS TAX.
Public utilities, §§40-21-80 to
40-21-87.
See PUBLIC UTILITIES.

GROUP INSURANCE.
**Alcoholism treatment in
group plans,** §§27-20A-1
to 27-20A-4.

GROUP INSURANCE—Cont'd
**County officers and
employees.**
Group insurance for officers
and employees, §§11-91-1
to 11-91-8.
See COUNTIES.
Self-insurance groups,
§§11-26-2 to 11-26-5.
Disabilities insurance,
§§27-20-1 to 27-20-3.
Life insurance, §§27-18-1 to
27-18-16.
See INSURANCE.
**Municipal officers and
employees,** §§11-91-1 to
11-91-8.
See MUNICIPAL
CORPORATIONS.

**GUARANTEED STUDENT
LOAN PROGRAM,**
§§16-33B-1 to 16-33B-8.
See STUDENT LOAN
PROGRAM.

GUARANTY.
Commercial code.
Commercial paper, §7-3-416.
Investment securities,
§§7-8-308, 7-8-312.
Warranties.
See WARRANTY.

GUARANTY ASSOCIATIONS.
**Life and disability insurance
guaranty association,**
§§27-44-1 to 27-44-21.
See INSURANCE.

GUARDIAN AD LITEM.
Actions.
Improper appointment,
§6-7-103.
Appeals.
Probate courts.
Appeals by guardians of
minors or persons of
unsound mind from
probate courts,
§12-22-26.
Appointment, ARCP, Rule 17
(c).
Action for improper
appointment, §6-7-103.
Attorneys at law.
Appointment by court,
§15-12-21.
Commitment of mentally ill.
Involuntary commitment.
Appointment of guardian
ad litem for persons
sought to be
committed, §22-52-4.
Compensation, ARCP, Rule
17 (d).
Decedents' estates.
Sale of real property for
payment of debts and
for division, §43-2-448.
Conservators.
Settlements of accounts of
conservators.
Final settlement.
Appointment of guardian
ad litem, §26-5-8.
Partial settlement.
Appointment of guardian
ad litem, §26-5-2.

GUARDIAN AD LITEM
—Cont'd

Curators of mentally or physically incapacitated persons.
Appointment at hearings, §26-7A-5.

Dams.
Erection of dams for mills, gins, factories or electric generators.
Minors or mentally ill persons.
Appointment, §18-2-4.

Developmentally disabled persons.
Probate courts.
Appointment of guardian for, §12-13-21.

Diseases.
Notifiable diseases.
Commitment petition.
Appointment of guardian ad litem, §22-11A-29.

Dower interests.
Ascertainment and payment.
Appointment of guardian ad litem, §35-4-191.

Eminent domain.
Hearings.
Appointment.
Infants or incompetents, §18-1A-275.

Executors and administrators.
Sale of real property for payment of debts and for division.
Appointment of guardian ad litem, §43-2-445.
Compensation of guardian ad litem, §43-2-448.
Duties of guardian ad litem, §43-2-448.
Settlements and distributions.
Appointment of guardian ad litem, §43-2-504.

Fees.
Life or dower interests.
Ascertainment and payment of life or dower interests, §35-4-191.
Probate judges' fees, §12-19-90.

Fiduciaries generally.
See FIDUCIARIES.

Guardian and ward.
Curators.
Appointment at hearings, §26-7A-5.
Removal of person or property of minors and wards.
Removal to another county.
Appointment, §26-8-21.
Uniform guardianship and protective proceedings act.
Appointment to represent interest of minors or other persons, §26-2A-52.

How chosen, ARCP, Rule 17 (d).

Juvenile proceedings.
Appointment by courts, §12-15-8.

GUARDIAN AD LITEM
—Cont'd

Life interests.
Ascertainment and payment.
Appointment of guardian ad litem, §35-4-191.

Limitation of actions.
Action for improper appointment, §6-7-103.

Partition.
Circuit courts.
Appointment of guardian ad litem, §35-6-25.
Crops.
Appointment of guardian ad litem for partition of crops, §35-6-112.
Probate courts.
Appointment of guardian ad litem, §35-6-43.
Sale instead of partition, §35-6-60.
Sale of land of minors and insane persons for distribution among joint owners.
Appointment of guardian ad litem, §35-6-83.

Probate courts.
Developmentally disabled persons.
Appointment of guardian for, §12-13-21.

Probate judges.
Appeals by guardian of minors or persons of unsound mind, §12-22-26.
Fees, §12-19-90.

Quieting title.
In rem proceedings.
Appointment of guardian ad litem, §6-6-562.

Uniform fiduciaries act,
§§19-1-1 to 19-1-13.
See FIDUCIARIES.

United States.
Condemnation of land or rights of way.
Appointment of guardian ad litem for infants and persons of unsound mind, §42-2-4.

GUARDIAN AND WARD.
Abortion.
Parental consent to performing abortions upon minors, §§26-21-1 to 26-21-8.
See ABORTION.

Accounts and accounting.
Curators.
Audit and examination of accounts, §26-7A-12.
Confirmation of curator's account, §26-7A-11.
Final records, §26-7A-13.
Deceased guardian.
Books of account kept by deceased guardian.
Admissibility in evidence, §12-21-32.
Settlement of conservators' accounts, §§26-5-1 to 26-5-54.
See CONSERVATORS.

GUARDIAN AND WARD
—Cont'd

Accounts and accounting
—Cont'd
Uniform guardianship and protective proceedings act.
Conservators.
Accounting to court, §26-2A-147.

Adoption.
General provisions, §§26-10-1 to 26-10-10.
See ADOPTION.
Uniform guardianship and protective proceedings act.
Minors.
Termination of appointment of guardians, §26-2A-79.

Aged persons.
Curators.
Appointment, §§26-7A-1 to 26-7A-17. See within this heading, "Curators."
Uniform guardianship and protective proceedings act, §§26-2A-1 to 26-2A-160. See within this heading, "Uniform guardianship and protective proceedings act."

Age of majority.
Uniform guardianship and protective proceedings act.
Termination of appointment of guardian upon minor obtaining, §26-2A-79.

Alcoholism.
Generally.
Uniform guardianship and protective proceedings act, §§26-2A-1 to 26-2A-160. See within this heading, "Uniform guardianship and protective proceedings act."

Appeals.
Curators.
Appointment, §26-7A-16.
Probate courts.
Appeals by guardians of minors or persons of unsound mind from probate courts, §12-22-26.
Uniform guardianship and protective proceedings act, §26-2A-36.

Appointment of guardians,
§26-2A-70.
Circuit courts.
Protective services, §38-9-6.
Court appointment, §26-2A-73.
Best interest served by appointment, §26-2A-76.
Procedure, §§26-2A-75, 26-2A-102.
Qualifications of guardian, §26-2A-76.

GUARDIAN AND WARD
—Cont'd
Appointment of guardians
—Cont'd
Court appointment—Cont'd
Service of process.
Consent to service by
acceptance of
appointment,
§26-2A-77.
Venue, §26-2A-74.
Curators.
Appointment, §§26-7A-1 to
26-7A-17. See within
this heading,
"Curators."
Emergency appointment,
§26-2A-107.
Findings, §26-2A-105.
Incapacitated persons,
§§26-2A-100, 26-2A-111.
Jurisdiction.
Acceptance of appointment
as consent to
jurisdiction,
§26-2A-106.
Minors, §§26-2A-70 to
26-2A-81.
Notice, §26-2A-103.
Order of appointment,
§26-2A-105.
Emergency appointment,
§26-2A-107.
Parental appointment.
Objections by minors to
appointment,
§26-2A-72.
Service of process.
Consent to service by
acceptance of
appointment,
§26-2A-77.
Wills, §§26-2A-71,
26-2A-100.
Powers and duties,
§26-2A-108.
Proceedings subsequent to
appointment,
§§26-2A-80, 26-2A-111.
Resignation, removal, etc.,
§§26-2A-81, 26-2A-110.
Venue, §§26-2A-80,
26-2A-111.
Qualifications, §§26-2A-76,
26-2A-104.
Resignation, removal, etc.,
§§26-2A-81, 26-2A-110.
Service of process.
Consent to service by
acceptance of
appointment,
§26-2A-77.
Temporary guardian,
§26-2A-107.
Termination of appointment,
§§26-2A-79, 26-2A-109.
Venue, §§26-2A-74,
26-2A-101.
Proceedings subsequent to
appointment,
§§26-2A-80, 26-2A-111.
Veterans.
Incompetent veterans and
dependents, §§26-9-1 to
26-9-19.
See VETERANS.

GUARDIAN AND WARD
—Cont'd
Appointment of guardians
—Cont'd
Veterans—Cont'd
Probate judges.
Copies of decrees.
Furnishing to
veterans'
administration,
§12-13-42.
Wills.
Incapacitated persons
appointed by will,
§26-2A-100.
Wills as method of
parental appointment,
§§26-2A-71, 26-2A-100.
Audits.
Curators.
Accounts of curators,
§26-7A-12.
**Banks and financial
institutions.**
Administration of common
trust funds, §§5-12A-1 to
5-12A-17.
See BANKS AND
FINANCIAL
INSTITUTIONS.
Powers of banks, §5-5A-18.
Bicycles.
Violations of regulations.
Guardians not to authorize
or permit, §32-5A-266.
Bonds, surety.
Curators.
Appointment, §26-7A-8.
Uniform guardianship and
protective proceedings
act.
Conservators, §26-2A-139.
Foreign conservators,
§26-2A-160.
Terms and requirements,
§26-2A-140.
Circuit courts.
Removal of guardianship
from probate courts,
§26-2-2.
Clerks of court.
Uniform guardianship and
protective proceedings
act.
Records and certified
copies.
Duties, §26-2A-34.
Compromise and settlement.
Settlements of accounts of
conservators, §§26-5-1 to
26-5-54.
See CONSERVATORS.
Uniform guardianship and
protective proceedings
act.
Conservators.
Final consent
settlements,
§26-2A-158.
Conflicts of interest.
Uniform guardianship and
protective proceedings
act.
Conservators.
Sales, encumbrances, or
transactions,
§26-2A-150.
Consent for health services,
§§22-8-1 to 22-8-9.
See HEALTH.

GUARDIAN AND WARD
—Cont'd
Conservators.
General provisions.
See CONSERVATORS.
Removal of person or
property of minors and
wards, §§26-8-1 to
26-8-52. See within this
heading, "Removal of
person or property of
minors and wards."
Uniform guardianship and
protective proceedings
act, §§26-2A-1 to
26-2A-160. See within
this heading, "Uniform
guardianship and
protective proceedings
act."
Constitution of Alabama.
Probate courts.
Powers to grant letters of
guardianships, Const.
Ala., amd. 364.
**Construction and
interpretation.**
Uniform guardianship and
protective proceedings
act.
Construction against
implied repeal,
§26-2A-5.
Liberally construed,
§26-2A-2.
Severability of provisions,
§26-2A-4.
Contempt.
Uniform guardianship and
protective proceedings
act.
Incapacitated persons.
Termination of
incapacity.
Knowingly interfering
with transmission
of request for
order, §26-2A-110.
Contracts.
Uniform guardianship and
protective proceedings
act.
Conservators.
Personal liability,
§26-2A-157.
Corporations.
Voting of shares by
guardian, §10-2A-53.
Costs.
Removal of person or
property of minors and
wards.
Removal to another county.
Hearings, §26-8-22.
Counties.
Claims and demands against
counties.
Verification of claims by
guardians, §11-12-6.
Removal of person or
property of minors and
wards.
Removal to another county,
§§26-8-20 to 26-8-25.
See within this
heading, "Removal of
persons or property of
minors and wards."

GUARDIAN AND WARD
—Cont'd
Criminal law and procedure.
Force.
Use by persons with
parental, custodial or
special responsibilities,
§13A-3-24.
Use of force by persons with
custodial responsibilities,
§13A-3-24.
Curators.
Accounts and accounting,
§§26-7A-11 to 26-7A-13.
Appeals, §26-7A-16.
Appointment, §§26-7A-1 to
26-7A-17.
Accounts and accounting.
Audit and examination
of accounts,
§26-7A-12.
Curator's account,
§26-7A-11.
Final records, §26-7A-13.
Appeals, §26-7A-16.
Bonds, surety, §26-7A-8.
Citation, §26-7A-3.
Committee of inquiry.
Appointment and
assistance to court,
§26-7A-6.
Construction and
interpretation.
Provisions of chapter
deemed cumulative,
§26-7A-17.
Decrees.
Effect, §26-7A-7.
Estate of ward.
Powers of court,
§26-7A-9.
Grounds for appointment,
§26-7A-1.
Guardian ad litem,
§26-7A-5.
Hearing.
Accounts and accounting.
Confirmation of
curator's account,
§26-7A-11.
Conduct of hearing,
§26-7A-4.
Decree, §26-7A-4.
Evidentiary standard,
§26-7A-4.
Notice, §26-7A-3.
Recovery of ward.
Discharge, §26-7A-14.
Venue, §26-7A-2.
Notice.
Hearing, §26-7A-3.
Parties.
Appeals, §26-7A-16.
Petitions.
Authority to file,
§26-7A-2.
Contents, §26-7A-2.
Venue, §26-7A-2.
Powers.
Deemed equivalent to
powers of guardian
and court,
§26-7A-15.
Probate court.
Estate of ward,
§26-7A-9.
Special curator,
§26-7A-10.
Probate court.
Authority to appoint,
§26-7A-1.

GUARDIAN AND WARD
—Cont'd
Curators—Cont'd
Appointment—Cont'd
Probate court—Cont'd
Powers.
Estate of ward,
§26-7A-9.
Procedure.
Jurisdiction of probate
court, §26-7A-1.
Recovery of ward,
§26-7A-14.
Reports.
Accounts and accounting.
Filing in office of
probate judge,
§26-7A-13.
Service of process,
§26-7A-3.
Special curator, §26-7A-10.
Venue.
Hearing, §26-7A-2.
Ward.
Recovery, §26-7A-14.
Audits.
Accounts of curators,
§26-7A-12.
Bonds, surety.
Appointment, §26-7A-8.
Committee of inquiry.
Appointment and
assistance to court,
§26-7A-6.
Decrees.
Appointment, §26-7A-4.
Effect, §26-7A-7.
Discharge.
Recovery of ward,
§26-7A-14.
Evidence.
Hearings on appointment.
Evidentiary standards,
§26-7A-4.
Guardian ad litem.
Hearings.
Appointment, §26-7A-5.
Hearings.
Accounts and accounting.
Confirmation of curator's
account, §26-7A-11.
Appointment.
Conduct of hearings,
§26-7A-4.
Venue, §26-7A-2.
Guardian ad litem
appointed, §26-7A-5.
Recovery of ward.
Discharge, §26-7A-14.
Parties.
Appeals, §26-7A-16.
Petitions.
Appointment, §26-7A-2.
Powers.
Deemed equivalent to
powers of guardian
and court, §26-7A-15.
Recovery of ward, §26-7A-14.
Reports.
Accounts and accounting.
Filing in office of probate
judge, §26-7A-13.
Service of process.
Filing of petition,
§26-7A-3.
Venue.
Appointment.
Hearing, §26-7A-2.

GUARDIAN AND WARD
—Cont'd
Curators—Cont'd
Ward.
Recovery.
Discharge of curator,
§26-7A-14.
Death.
Books of account kept by
deceased guardian.
Admissibility in evidence,
§12-21-32.
Uniform guardianship and
protective proceedings
act.
Conservators.
Appointment of
successor,
§26-2A-143.
Incapacitated persons.
Termination of
guardianship,
§26-2A-109.
Minors.
Termination of
appointment of
guardian, §26-2A-79.
Decrees.
Curators.
Appointment, §26-7A-4.
Effect of decree,
§26-7A-7.
Definitions.
Uniform guardianship and
protective proceedings
act, §26-2A-20.
Disabled persons.
Probate courts.
Appointment of guardian,
§12-13-21.
Uniform guardianship and
protective proceedings
act, §§26-2A-1 to
26-2A-160. See within
this heading, "Uniform
guardianship and
protective proceedings
act."
Drugs.
Addicts.
Generally.
Uniform guardianship
and protective
proceedings act,
§§26-2A-1 to
26-2A-160. See
within this heading,
"Uniform
guardianship and
protective
proceedings act."
Evidence.
Books of account kept by
deceased guardian.
Admissibility in evidence,
§12-21-32.
Curators.
Appointment.
Evidentiary standard of
hearings, §26-7A-4.
Letters of guardianship.
Copies of letters,
§12-21-102.
Uniform guardianship and
protective proceedings
act.
Conservators, §26-2A-149.

GUARDIAN AND WARD
—Cont'd
Executors and administrators.
Settlements and distributions.
Arbitration on settlement of estates.
Consent by guardian, §43-2-601.
Special guardians, §43-2-517.
Fees.
Probate judges' fees, §12-19-90.
Fiduciaries generally.
See FIDUCIARIES.
Guardian ad litem.
Curators of mentally or physically incapacitated persons.
Appointment, §26-7A-5.
Removal of person or property of minors and wards.
Removal to another county.
Appointment, §26-8-21.
Uniform guardianship and protective proceedings act.
Appointment to represent interest of minors or other persons, §26-2A-52.
Handicapped persons.
Curators.
Appointment, §§26-7A-1 to 26-7A-17. See within this heading, "Curators."
Uniform guardianship and protective proceedings act, §§26-2A-1 to 26-2A-160. See within this heading, "Uniform guardianship and protective proceedings act."
Health services.
Consent for health services, §§22-8-1 to 22-8-7.
See HEALTH.
Hearings.
Curators.
Accounts and accounting.
Confirmation of curator's account, §26-7A-11.
Appointment.
Conduct of hearings, §26-7A-4.
Venue, §26-7A-2.
Guardian ad litem appointed, §26-7A-5.
Recovery of ward.
Discharge, §26-7A-14.
Incapacitated persons.
Revocation of guardianship.
Application of person ascertained to be incapacitated.
Date for hearing, §26-2-52.
Hearing or trial on contested applications, §26-2-53.

GUARDIAN AND WARD
—Cont'd
Hearings—Cont'd
Removal of person or property of minors and wards.
Removal to another county, §§26-8-21, 26-8-22.
Uniform guardianship and protective proceedings act.
Appointment of conservators or other protective orders.
Procedure concerning hearing on original petition, §26-2A-135.
Incapacitated persons.
Court appointment of guardian, §26-2A-102.
Rights of persons alleged to be incapacitated, §26-2A-102.
Guardians.
Removal or permission to resign, §26-2A-110.
Minors.
Court-appointment of guardians for minors, §26-2A-75.
Petitions for removal of guardian or for permission to resign, §26-2A-81.
Protective proceedings.
Appointment of conservators or other protective orders, §26-2A-130.
Incapacitated persons.
Removal of person or property of minors and wards, §§26-8-1 to 26-8-52. See within this heading, "Removal of person or property of minors and wards."
Revocation of guardianship, §§26-2-51 to 26-2-54.
Application by guardian, §26-2-55.
Application by person ascertained to be incapacitated, §26-2-51.
Contents of application, §26-2-51.
Entry of decree.
Contested applications, §26-2-54.
Uncontested applications, §26-2-53.
Hearings.
Date for hearing, §26-2-52.
Hearing or trial on contested application, §26-2-53.
Notice to guardian, §26-2-52.

GUARDIAN AND WARD
—Cont'd
Incapacitated persons
—Cont'd
Uniform guardianship and protective proceedings act, §§26-2A-1 to 26-2A-160. See within this heading, "Uniform guardianship and protective proceedings act."
Insane persons.
Actions against guardians, §6-7-102.
Curators.
Appointment, §§26-7A-1 to 26-7A-17. See within this heading, "Curators."
Interference with custody, §13-6-45.
Inventories.
Uniform guardianship and protective proceedings act.
Conservators.
Preparation and filing complete inventory of estate.
Duties, §26-2A-146.
Investments.
Authorization of investment of trust funds in bonds or stock of private corporations prohibited, Const. Ala., art. IV, §74.
Restrictions on investment of trust funds by guardians in private corporations, Const. Ala., amd. 40.
Standards for fiduciary investment and management, §19-3-120.2.
Uniform guardianship and protective proceedings act.
Conservators.
Powers in administration, §26-2A-152.
Joint tenants and tenants in common.
Sale of land of minors and insane persons for distribution among joint owners, §§35-6-80 to 35-6-91.
See PARTITION.
Judicial sales.
Notice to guardians in probate court, §6-8-68.
Jurisdiction.
Probate court, §12-13-1.
Uniform guardianship and protective proceedings act.
Conservators.
Submission to personal jurisdiction of court by accepting appointment, §26-2A-141.
Incapacitated persons.
Guardians.
Concurrent jurisdiction of court at place where ward resides, §26-2A-111.

GUARDIAN AND WARD
—Cont'd
Jurisdiction—Cont'd
Uniform guardianship and
protective proceedings
act—Cont'd
Incapacitated persons
—Cont'd
Guardians—Cont'd
Submission personally
to jurisdiction of
court upon
accepting
appointment,
§26-2A-106.
Minors.
Guardians.
Proceedings
subsequent to
appointment,
§26-2A-80.
Submission personally
to jurisdiction of
court upon
acceptance of
appointment,
§26-2A-77.
Probate court.
Subject matter
jurisdiction,
§26-2A-31.
Protective proceedings.
Business affairs of
protected persons,
§26-2A-131.
Jury.
Uniform guardianship and
protective proceedings
act.
Trial by jury, §26-2A-35.
Juvenile proceedings.
Appointment of guardians by
court, §12-15-8.
Attorneys at law.
Notification of guardians of
right to counsel,
§12-15-63.
Kidnapping.
Interference with custody,
§13-6-45.
Letters of guardianship.
Evidence.
Copies of letters,
§12-21-102.
Fees.
Probate judges' fees,
§12-19-90.
Limitation of actions.
Nonfeasance, misfeasance
and malfeasance.
Actions against surety,
§6-2-34.
Maintenance and education.
Veterans.
See VETERANS.
Majority.
Age of majority.
Uniform guardianship and
protective proceedings
act.
Termination of
appointment of
guardian upon minor
reaching majority,
§26-2A-79.
Management of property.
Standards for fiduciary
investment and
management,
§19-3-120.2.

GUARDIAN AND WARD
—Cont'd
Marriage.
Uniform guardianship and
protective proceedings
act.
Minors.
Termination of
appointment of
guardians,
§26-2A-79.
Mentally ill.
Curators.
Appointment, §§26-7A-1 to
26-7A-17. See within
this heading,
"Curators."
Minors.
Removal of person or
property of minors and
wards, §§26-8-1 to
26-8-52. See within this
heading, "Removal of
person or property of
minors and wards."
Sheriffs.
When sheriff to be
appointed guardian,
§26-2-27.
Uniform guardianship and
protective proceedings
act, §§26-2A-1 to
26-2A-160. See within
this heading, "Uniform
guardianship and
protective proceedings
act."
Motorcycles.
Authorizing or permitting
violations, §32-12-20.
Notice.
Incapacitated persons.
Revocation of
guardianship.
Application by persons
ascertained to be
incapacitated.
Notice to guardian,
§26-2-52.
Removal of person or
property of minors and
wards.
Removal to another county.
Hearings, §26-8-21.
Uniform guardianship and
protective proceedings
act.
Conservators.
Service of notice on,
§26-2A-141.
Court appointment of
guardians for minors.
Hearings, §26-2A-75.
Generally, §26-2A-50.
Incapacitated persons.
Guardians.
Service of notice,
§26-2A-106.
Guardianship
proceedings,
§26-2A-103.
Interested persons.
Requests for notice,
§26-2A-53.
Method of giving,
§26-2A-50.

GUARDIAN AND WARD
—Cont'd
Notice—Cont'd
Uniform guardianship and
protective proceedings
act—Cont'd
Minors.
Guardians.
Hearing on petition for
order subsequent
to appointment,
§26-2A-81.
Petitions for removal
or for permission
to resign,
§26-2A-81.
Service of notice,
§26-2A-77.
Parental appointment of
guardians.
Acceptance of
appointment,
§26-2A-71.
Protective proceedings.
Appointment of
conservators or other
protective orders,
§26-2A-130.
Generally, §26-2A-134.
Request for notice.
Interested persons,
§26-2A-53.
Time of giving, §26-2A-50.
Waiver, §26-2A-51.
Obscenity.
Obscene materials containing
visual reproduction of
children.
Parents or guardians
permitting children to
engage in production
of, §13A-12-196.
Orders of court.
Removal of person or
property of minors and
wards to another county,
§26-8-22.
Removal of person or
property of minors and
wards to another state.
Application for order,
§26-8-41.
Conservatorship.
Settlement of
conservatorship of
conservator within
state, §26-8-43.
Entry of order, §26-8-42.
Nonresidents.
Removal of property or
money when minor
or ward and
conservator
nonresidents,
§§26-8-44 to 26-8-47.
Settlement of
conservatorship of
conservator within
state, §26-8-43.
Uniform guardianship and
protective proceedings
act.
Appointment of
conservators or other
protective orders.
Permissible court orders,
§26-2A-136.

GUARDIAN AND WARD
—Cont'd
Orders of court—Cont'd
Uniform guardianship and
protective proceedings
act—Cont'd
Appointment of
conservators or other
protective orders
—Cont'd
Petitions for orders
subsequent to
appointment of
conservators,
§26-2A-144.
Procedure concerning
order on original
petition, §26-2A-135.
Termination of
conservatorship.
Evidence and
recordation,
§26-2A-149.
Incapacitated persons.
Court appointment of
guardian.
Order of appointment,
§26-2A-105.
Termination of
incapacity.
Request for order,
§26-2A-110.
Protective orders. See
within this heading,
"Uniform guardianship
and protective
proceedings act."
Parental appointment,
§§26-2A-71, 26-2A-100.
Wills, §§26-2A-71, 26-2A-100.
Parties.
Curators.
Appeals, §26-7A-16.
Infants and incompetents.
Actions against guardians,
§6-7-102.
Substitution of guardian
for next friend pending
action, §6-7-100.
Partition.
Sale of land of minors and
insane persons for
distribution among joint
owners, §§35-6-80 to
35-6-91.
See PARTITION.
Personal property.
Removal of person or
property of minors and
wards, §§26-8-1 to
26-8-52. See within this
heading, "Removal of
person or property of
minors and wards."
Persons of unsound mind.
Actions against guardians,
§6-7-102.
Curators.
Appointment, §§26-7A-1 to
26-7A-17. See within
this heading,
"Curators."
Petitions.
Curators.
Appointment, §26-7A-2.

GUARDIAN AND WARD
—Cont'd
Petitions—Cont'd
Uniform guardianship and
protective proceedings
act.
Appointment of
conservators or other
protective orders.
Petitions for orders
subsequent to
appointment of
conservators,
§26-2A-144.
Procedure concerning
hearing and order on
original petition,
§26-2A-135.
Resignation or removal
of conservators,
§26-2A-143.
Termination of
conservatorships,
§26-2A-158.
Court appointment of
guardians for minors,
§26-2A-75.
Incapacitated persons.
Court appointment of
guardian,
§26-2A-102.
Removal of guardian or
permission to resign,
§26-2A-110.
Temporary guardians,
§26-2A-107.
Termination of
incapacity,
§26-2A-110.
Minors.
Court appointment of
guardians,
§26-2A-75.
Removal of guardian or
permission to resign,
§26-2A-81.
Protective proceedings.
Appointment of
conservators or other
protective orders,
§26-2A-130.
Original petition,
§26-2A-133.
Powers of attorney.
Uniform guardianship and
protective proceedings
act.
Delegation of powers.
Parents or guardians,
§26-2A-7.
Priorities.
Uniform guardianship and
protective proceedings
act.
Conservators.
Appointment,
§26-2A-138.
Probate courts.
Appeals by guardians of
minors and persons of
unsound mind,
§12-22-26.
Developmentally disabled
persons.
Appointment of guardian
for, §12-13-21.
Jurisdiction, §12-13-1.
Removal of guardianship to
circuit courts, §26-2-2.

GUARDIAN AND WARD
—Cont'd
Probate courts—Cont'd
Uniform guardianship and
protective proceedings
act.
Clerks of court.
Records and certified
copies.
Duties, §26-2A-34.
Jurisdiction.
Subject matter
jurisdiction,
§26-2A-31.
Welfare.
Legal representatives for
handling public
assistance payments,
§38-1-3.
Property of ward.
Curator.
Appointment, §§26-7A-1 to
26-7A-17. See within
this heading,
"Curators."
Records.
Removal of person or
property of minors and
wards.
Removal to another county.
Record of proceedings,
§26-8-23.
Uniform guardianship and
protective proceedings
act.
Clerks of court.
Duties, §26-2A-34.
Conservators, §26-2A-146.
**Removal of person or
property of minors and
wards,** §§26-8-1 to 26-8-52.
Applicability of chapter,
§26-8-1.
Authorization.
Removal to another county,
§26-8-20.
Costs.
Removal to another county.
Hearings, §26-8-22.
Guardian ad litem.
Removal to another county.
Appointment, §26-8-21.
Hearings.
Removal to another county,
§26-8-21.
Orders of court. See within
this heading, "Orders of
court."
Records.
Removal to another county.
Record of proceedings,
§26-8-23.
Filed in county in
which removal to
be made, §26-8-23.
Removal to another county,
§§26-8-20 to 26-8-25.
Applications, §26-8-21.
Authorization, §26-8-20.
Conservatorship.
Grant of conservatorship,
§26-8-23.
Settlement of former
conservators,
§26-8-24.
Grant of guardianship,
§26-8-23.
Guardian ad litem.
Appointment, §26-8-21.
Hearing.
Costs, §26-8-22.

GUARDIAN AND WARD
—Cont'd
Removal of person or property of minors and wards—Cont'd
Removal to another county —Cont'd
Hearing—Cont'd
Guardian ad litem.
Appointment, §26-8-21.
Notice, §26-8-21.
Order of court, §26-8-22.
Jurisdiction.
Removal of property only, §26-8-25.
Powers of guardians or conservators.
Recovery, receipt of property, §26-8-23.
Records.
Record of proceedings.
Certification, §26-8-23.
Filed in county in which removal is to be made, §26-8-23.
Removal of property only.
Jurisdiction not affected, §26-8-25.
Settlement of conservator, §26-8-24.
Removal to another state, §§26-8-48 to 26-8-52.
Applications, §26-8-41.
Authorization, §26-8-40.
Foreign conservators.
Removal of property or money.
Receipt, §26-8-52.
Orders of court. See within this heading, "Orders of court."
Receipts.
Foreign conservators, §26-8-52.
Sale of property, §§26-8-48 to 26-8-51.
Application, §26-8-49.
Authorization, §26-8-48.
Commissioner for conduct of sale.
Appointment, §26-8-50.
Compensation, §26-8-51.
Powers and duties, §26-8-50.
Disposition of proceeds from sale, §26-8-51.
Sale of property.
Removal to another state, §§26-8-48 to 26-8-51.
Application, §26-8-49.
Authorization, §26-8-48.
Commissioner for conduct of sale.
Appointment, §26-8-50.
Compensation, §26-8-51.
Powers and duties, §26-8-50.
Disposition of proceeds from sale, §26-8-51.
Service of process.
Removal to another county, §26-8-21.
Reports.
Curators.
Accounts and accounting.
Filing in office of probate judge, §26-7A-13.

GUARDIAN AND WARD
—Cont'd
Rules of civil procedure.
Uniform guardianship and protective proceedings act.
Rules govern proceedings under chapter, §26-2A-33.
Sales.
Removal of person or property of minors and wards.
Sale of property.
Removal to another state, §§26-8-48 to 26-8-51.
Uniform guardianship and protective due proceedings act.
Conservators.
Conflicts of interest, §26-2A-150.
Savings and loan associations.
Accounts, §5-16-43.
Securities.
Fiduciary security transfers, §§8-6-70 to 8-6-80.
See SECURITIES.
Service of process.
Curators.
Appointment.
Filing of petition, §26-7A-2.
Uniform guardianship and protective proceedings act.
Conservators.
Submission personally to jurisdiction of court by accepting appointment, §26-2A-141.
Incapacitated persons.
Guardians.
Acceptance of appointment constitutes consent to jurisdiction, §26-2A-106.
Minors.
Guardians.
Consent to service by acceptance of appointment, §26-2A-77.
Settlements of accounts of guardians.
Compulsion of settlement by probate court.
Public assistance payments of incompetents, §38-1-3.
Conservators' accounts, §§26-5-1 to 26-5-54.
See CONSERVATORS.
Fees.
Probate judges' fees, §12-19-90.
Payment to probate judge of money due on decree upon settlement, §12-13-48.
Payment of probate judge for receipt of money under section 12-13-48, §12-13-49.
Veterans, §§26-9-14 to 26-9-18.

GUARDIAN AND WARD
—Cont'd
Sheriffs.
Appointment of sheriff as guardian.
Minors, §26-2-27.
Standards for fiduciary investment and management, §19-3-120.2.
Taxation.
Assessments.
By whom property should be listed, §40-7-17.
Returns.
Separate returns in individual and fiduciary capacity, §40-7-20.
Tax assessors.
Notification of appointment of fiduciaries, §40-7-30.
Title.
Uniform guardianship and protective proceedings act.
Conservators.
Title by appointment.
Appointment of conservator vests in conservator title as trustee, §26-2A-148.
Torts.
Uniform guardianship and protective proceedings act.
Conservators.
Personal liability, §26-2A-157.
Trial.
Uniform guardianship and protective proceedings act.
Jury trial, §26-2A-35.
Uniform fiduciaries act, §§19-1-1 to 19-1-13.
See FIDUCIARIES.
Uniform guardianship and protective proceedings act, §§26-2A-1 to 26-2A-160.
Accounts and accounting.
Conservators.
Accounting to court, §26-2A-147.
Adoption.
Minors.
Termination of appointment of guardians, §26-2A-79.
Age.
Majority.
Termination of appointment of guardian upon obtaining age of majority, §26-2A-79.
Appeals, §26-2A-36.
Applicability of chapter.
Existing relationships, §26-2A-8.
Territorial application, §26-2A-30.
Bonds, surety.
Conservators, §26-2A-139.
Foreign conservators, §26-2A-160.
Terms and requirements, §26-2A-140.

GUARDIAN AND WARD
—Cont'd
Uniform guardianship and protective proceedings act—Cont'd
Citation of chapter.
　Short title, §26-2A-1.
Claims against protected
　persons.
　Conservators.
　　Paying or securing,
　　　§26-2A-156.
　　Exhaustion before existing
　　　claims paid.
　　Payment of unsecured
　　　claims, §26-2A-156.
　　Preferences, §26-2A-156.
　　Presentation, §26-2A-156.
　　Priorities, §26-2A-156.
Clerks of court.
　Duties.
　　Records and certified
　　　copies, §26-2A-34.
Compensation.
　Conservators, §26-2A-142.
Compromise and settlement.
　Conservators.
　　Final consent
　　　settlements,
　　　§26-2A-158.
Conflicts of interest.
　Conservators.
　　Sales, encumbrances or
　　　transactions,
　　　§26-2A-150.
Conservators, §§26-2A-130 to
　26-2A-160.
　Accounts and accounting.
　　Accounting to court,
　　　§26-2A-147.
　Administration.
　　Powers, §26-2A-152.
　　　Acts without court
　　　　authorization or
　　　　confirmation,
　　　　§26-2A-152.
　　　Acts with prior court
　　　　authorization,
　　　　§26-2A-152.
　Appointment.
　　Acceptance.
　　　Effect, §26-2A-141.
　　Priorities, §26-2A-138.
　　Protective proceedings,
　　　§26-2A-130.
　　Title vested in
　　　conservator as
　　　trustee, §26-2A-148.
　　Who may be appointed,
　　　§26-2A-138.
　Bonds, surety, §26-2A-139.
　　Foreign conservators,
　　　§26-2A-160.
　　Terms and requirements,
　　　§26-2A-140.
　Business affairs of
　　protected persons.
　　Jurisdiction of court in
　　　which petition filed,
　　　§26-2A-131.
　Care.
　　Standard of care and
　　　performance,
　　　§26-2A-145.
　Claims against protected
　　persons.
　　Enforcement,
　　　§26-2A-156.
　Compensation, §26-2A-142.

GUARDIAN AND WARD
—Cont'd
Uniform guardianship and protective proceedings act—Cont'd
Conservators—Cont'd
　Compromise and
　　settlement.
　　Final consent
　　　settlements,
　　　§26-2A-158.
　Conflicts of interest.
　　Sales, encumbrances or
　　　transactions,
　　　§26-2A-150.
　Contracts.
　　Personal liability,
　　　§26-2A-157.
　Death.
　　Appointment of
　　　successor,
　　　§26-2A-143.
　Debts.
　　Payment to foreign
　　　conservators without
　　　local proceedings,
　　　§26-2A-159.
　Distribution.
　　Duties and powers,
　　　§26-2A-153.
　Effect of acceptance of
　　appointment,
　　§26-2A-141.
　Encumbrances.
　　Conflicts of interest,
　　　§26-2A-150.
　Enlargement of powers,
　　§26-2A-154.
　Estate plan of protected
　　persons.
　　Preservation,
　　　§26-2A-155.
　Foreign conservators.
　　Bond, surety,
　　　§26-2A-160.
　　Payment of debt and
　　　delivery of property,
　　　§26-2A-159.
　　Powers, §26-2A-160.
　　Proof of authority,
　　　§26-2A-160.
　Grounds for appointment,
　　§26-2A-130.
　Hearings.
　　Appointment,
　　　§26-2A-130.
　　Procedure on original
　　　petition, §26-2A-135.
　Inventory.
　　Preparation and filing.
　　　Duties, §26-2A-146.
　Jurisdiction.
　　Acceptance of
　　　appointment.
　　　Submission personally
　　　　to jurisdiction of
　　　　court, §26-2A-141.
　　Jurisdiction of court in
　　　which petition filed,
　　　Business affairs of
　　　　protected persons,
　　　　§26-2A-131.
　Letters of conservatorship.
　　Evidence, §26-2A-149.
　　Recordation, §26-2A-149.
　Liability.
　　Personal liability,
　　　§26-2A-157.
　Limitation of powers,
　　§26-2A-154.

GUARDIAN AND WARD
—Cont'd
Uniform guardianship and protective proceedings act—Cont'd
Conservators—Cont'd
　Notice.
　　Appointment,
　　　§26-2A-130.
　　Generally, §26-2A-134.
　　Methods of service,
　　　§26-2A-141.
　　Persons required to be
　　　given notice,
　　　§26-2A-134.
　　Publication, §26-2A-134.
　Orders.
　　Permissible court orders,
　　　§26-2A-136.
　　Petitions for orders
　　　subsequent to
　　　appointment,
　　　§26-2A-144.
　　Procedure concerning
　　　orders on original
　　　petition, §26-2A-135.
　　Termination of
　　　conservatorships.
　　　Evidence, §26-2A-149.
　　　Recordation,
　　　　§26-2A-149.
　Performance.
　　Standard of care and
　　　performance,
　　　§26-2A-145.
　Persons dealing with
　　conservators.
　　Protection, §26-2A-151.
　Petitions.
　　Appointment,
　　　§26-2A-130.
　　Contents, §26-2A-133.
　　Final consent
　　　settlements,
　　　§26-2A-158.
　　Orders subsequent to
　　　appointment,
　　　§26-2A-144.
　　Procedure concerning
　　　hearing and order on
　　　original petition,
　　　§26-2A-135.
　　Removal or resignation,
　　　§26-2A-143.
　　Termination of
　　　conservatorship,
　　　§26-2A-158.
　　Who may petition for
　　　appointment,
　　　§26-2A-133.
　Powers.
　　Administration,
　　　§26-2A-152.
　　Distributive duties and
　　　powers, §26-2A-153.
　　Enlargement,
　　　§26-2A-154.
　　Foreign conservators,
　　　§26-2A-160.
　　Limitation, §26-2A-154.
　Priorities.
　　Appointment,
　　　§26-2A-138.
　Property.
　　Delivery to foreign
　　　conservators without
　　　local proceedings,
　　　§26-2A-159.
　Protection of persons
　　dealing with,
　　§26-2A-151.

GUARDIAN AND WARD
—Cont'd
Uniform guardianship and protective proceedings act—Cont'd
Conservators—Cont'd
Protective arrangements and transactions authorized, §26-2A-137.
Prudent man rule.
Standard of care and performance, §26-2A-145.
Publication.
Notice, §26-2A-134.
Recordation.
Letters of conservatorship, §26-2A-149.
Orders terminating conservatorships, §26-2A-149.
Records, §26-2A-146.
Removal, §26-2A-143.
Resignation, §26-2A-143.
Sales.
Conflicts of interest, §26-2A-150.
Service of process.
Acceptance of appointment.
Submission personally to jurisdiction of court, §26-2A-141.
Special skills.
Standard of care and performance, §26-2A-145.
Standard of care and performance, §26-2A-145.
Successor conservators.
Appointment, §26-2A-143.
Termination of conservatorships.
Orders,
Proceedings, §26-2A-158.
Third persons.
Protection of persons dealing with conservators, §26-2A-151.
Title by appointment.
Appointment vests in conservator title as trustee, §26-2A-148.
Torts.
Personal liability, §26-2A-157.
Transactions.
Conflicts of interest, §26-2A-150.
Persons dealing with conservators.
Protection, §26-2A-151.
Venue.
Proceedings for appointment, §26-2A-132.
Who may be appointed, §26-2A-138.
Wills of protected persons.
Examination, §26-2A-155.
Construction and interpretation.
Construction against implied repeal, §26-2A-5.

GUARDIAN AND WARD
—Cont'd
Uniform guardianship and protective proceedings act—Cont'd
Construction and interpretation—Cont'd
Liberally construed, §26-2A-2.
Severability of provisions, §26-2A-4.
Contracts.
Conservators.
Personal liability, §26-2A-157.
Court appointment of guardians.
Authorized, §26-2A-70.
Conditions for appointment, §26-2A-73.
Hearings, §26-2A-75.
Incapacitated persons.
Orders, §26-2A-105.
Procedure, §26-2A-102.
Jurisdiction.
Proceedings subsequent to appointment, §26-2A-80.
Notice.
Hearings, §26-2A-75.
Persons nominated by minors, §26-2A-76.
Petitions, §26-2A-75.
Procedure, §26-2A-75.
Proceedings subsequent to appointment.
Jurisdiction, §26-2A-80.
Qualifications of guardian, §26-2A-76.
Temporary guardians, §26-2A-73.
Venue, §26-2A-74.
Proceedings subsequent to appointment, §26-2A-80.
Death.
Conservators.
Appointment of successor, §26-2A-143.
Incapacitated persons.
Termination of guardianship, §26-2A-109.
Minors.
Termination of appointment of guardian, §26-2A-79.
Definitions, §26-2A-20.
Delivery of money or personal property.
Persons to whom money or personal property may be delivered, §26-2A-6.
Estate plan.
Conservators.
Preservation of estate plan of protected persons, §26-2A-155.
Evidence.
Conservators.
Letters of conservatorship, §26-2A-149.
Orders terminating conservatorships, §26-2A-149.
Existing relationships.
Applicability of chapter to, §26-2A-8.

GUARDIAN AND WARD
—Cont'd
Uniform guardianship and protective proceedings act—Cont'd
Guardian ad litem.
Appointment ot represent interest of minors or other persons, §26-2A-52.
Guardians.
Delegation of powers, §26-2A-7.
Existing relationships.
Applicability of chapter to, §26-2A-8.
Incapacitated persons, §§26-2A-100 to 26-2A-111.
Minors, §§26-2A-70 to 26-2A-81.
Hearings.
Appointment of conservators or other protective orders.
Procedure concerning hearing on original petition, §26-2A-135.
Incapacitated persons.
Court appointment of guardians, §26-2A-102.
Removal of guardian or permission to resign, §26-2A-110.
Minors.
Court-appointment of guardian, §26-2A-75.
Petitions for removal of guardian or for permission to resign, §26-2A-81.
Protective proceedings.
Appointment of conservators or other protective orders, §26-2A-130.
Incapacitated persons.
Appointment of guardian.
Court appointment, §26-2A-102.
Orders, §26-2A-105.
Conservators, §§26-2A-130 to 26-2A-160. See within this heading, "Conservators."
Court appointment of guardians, §26-2A-102.
Orders, §26-2A-105.
Death.
Termination of guardianship, §26-2A-109.
Guardians, §§26-2A-100 to 26-2A-111.
Appointment, §26-2A-100.
Acceptance as consent to jurisdiction, §26-2A-106.
Court appointment, §§26-2A-102, 26-2A-105.
Method of appointment, §26-2A-100.
Objections, §26-2A-100.
Order of appointment, §26-2A-105.
Parents, §26-2A-100.

GUARDIAN AND WARD
—Cont'd
**Uniform guardianship and
protective proceedings
act**—Cont'd
Incapacitated persons
—Cont'd
Guardians—Cont'd
Appointment—Cont'd
Spouse, §26-2A-100.
Temporary guardians,
§26-2A-107.
Court appointment.
Orders, §26-2A-105.
Procedure, §26-2A-102.
Death.
Termination of
guardianship,
§26-2A-109.
Duties.
Generally, §26-2A-108.
Hearings.
Court appointment,
§26-2A-102.
Removal or permission
to resign,
§26-2A-110.
Ineffective performance
of duties.
Temporary guardian
appointed,
§26-2A-107.
Jurisdiction.
Concurrent jurisdiction
of court at place
where ward
resides,
§26-2A-111.
Submission personally
to jurisdiction of
court upon
accepting
appointment,
§26-2A-106.
Notice, §26-2A-103.
Service, §26-2A-106.
Objections.
Appointment,
§26-2A-100.
Orders.
Court appointment,
§26-2A-105.
Parents.
Appointment of
guardian,
§26-2A-100.
Petitions.
Court appointment,
§26-2A-102.
Removal of guardian
or permission to
resign,
§26-2A-110.
Temporary guardians,
§26-2A-107.
Powers.
Generally, §26-2A-108.
Priorities.
Who may be guardian,
§26-2A-104.
Qualifications,
§26-2A-104.
Removal.
Hearings, §26-2A-110.
Petitions, §26-2A-110.
Temporary guardians,
§26-2A-107.
Termination of
guardianship,
§26-2A-109.

GUARDIAN AND WARD
—Cont'd
**Uniform guardianship and
protective proceedings
act**—Cont'd
Incapacitated persons
—Cont'd
Guardians—Cont'd
Resignation.
Hearings, §26-2A-110.
Petitions, §26-2A-110.
Termination of
guardianship,
§26-2A-109.
Service of process.
Consent to jurisdiction
upon acceptance of
appointment,
§26-2A-106.
Spouse.
Appointment of
guardian,
§26-2A-100.
Successor guardians.
Appointment,
§26-2A-110.
Temporary guardians,
§26-2A-107.
Termination of
guardianship,
§26-2A-109.
Venue, §26-2A-101.
Proceedings
subsequent to
appointment,
§26-2A-111.
Who may be guardian,
§26-2A-104.
Priorities, §26-2A-104.
Hearings.
Court appointment of
guardians,
§26-2A-102.
Rights of persons
alleged to be
incapacitated,
§26-2A-102.
Notice.
Guardianship
proceedings,
§26-2A-103.
Protective orders,
§§26-2A-130 to
26-2A-137.
Termination of incapacity.
Contempt.
Knowingly interfering
with transmission
of request for
order, §26-2A-110.
Petitions, §26-2A-110.
Request for order,
§26-2A-110.
Termination of
guardianship,
§26-2A-109.
Interested persons.
Notice.
Request for notice,
§26-2A-53.
Inventories.
Conservators.
Preparation and filing
complete inventory
of estate.
Duties, §26-2A-146.
Investments.
Conservators.
Powers in
administration,
§26-2A-152.

GUARDIAN AND WARD
—Cont'd
**Uniform guardianship and
protective proceedings
act**—Cont'd
Jurisdiction.
Conservators.
Submission personally to
jurisdiction of court
by accepting
appointment,
§26-2A-141.
Incapacitated persons.
Guardians.
Concurrent jurisdiction
of court at place
where ward
resides,
§26-2A-111.
Submission personally
to jurisdiction of
court upon
accepting
appointment,
§26-2A-106.
Minors.
Guardians.
Proceedings
subsequent to
appointment,
§26-2A-80.
Submission personally
to jurisdiction of
court upon
acceptance of
appointment,
§26-2A-77.
Probate courts.
Subject matter
jurisdiction,
§26-2A-31.
Protective proceedings.
Business affairs of
protected persons,
§26-2A-131.
Jury.
Trial by jury, §26-2A-35.
Liability.
Conservators.
Personal liability,
§26-2A-157.
Majority.
Age of majority.
Termination of
appointment of
guardian, §26-2A-79.
Marriage.
Minors.
Termination of
appointment of
guardians,
§26-2A-79.
Minors.
Adoption.
Termination of
appointment of
guardians,
§26-2A-79.
Age of majority.
Termination of
appointment of
guardian, §26-2A-79.
Appointment of guardians.
Court appointment of
guardian,
§§26-7A-70 to
26-7A-80.
Parental appointment of
guardians,
§§26-7A-70 to
26-7A-72, 26-7A-80.

GUARDIAN AND WARD
—Cont'd
Uniform guardianship and protective proceedings act—Cont'd
Minors—Cont'd
Conservators generally, §§26-2A-130 to 26-2A-160.
Court appointment of guardians, §§26-7A-70 to 26-7A-80.
Death.
Termination of appointment of guardians, §26-2A-79.
Delivery of money or personal property to.
Persons to whom delivery may be made, §26-2A-6.
Guardians, §§26-2A-70 to 26-2A-81.
Appointment, §26-2A-70.
Court appointment, §§26-7A-70 to 26-7A-80.
Parental appointment, §§26-7A-70 to 26-7A-72, 26-7A-80.
Termination, §26-2A-79.
Compensation for services, §26-2A-78.
Death.
Termination of appointment, §26-2A-79.
Duties.
Generally, §26-2A-78.
Expenses of ward.
Liability, §26-2A-78.
Hearings.
Court appointment of guardians, §26-2A-75.
Petition for removal of guardian, §26-2A-81.
Jurisdiction.
Proceedings subsequent to appointment, §26-2A-80.
Submission personally to jurisdiction of court upon acceptance of appointment, §26-2A-77.
Letters of guardianship.
Method of appointment required to be indicated, §26-2A-77.
Liability.
Expenses of ward, §26-2A-78.
Third persons by reason of relationship for acts of ward, §26-2A-78.
Notice.
Court appointment of guardians, §26-2A-75.

GUARDIAN AND WARD
—Cont'd
Uniform guardianship and protective proceedings act—Cont'd
Minors—Cont'd
Guardians—Cont'd
Notice—Cont'd
Hearing on petition for order subsequent to appointment, §26-2A-81.
Petition for removal of guardian, §26-2A-81.
Service of notice, §26-2A-77.
Petitions.
Court appointment of guardians, §26-2A-75.
Removal of guardian or permission to resign, §26-2A-81.
Post-appointment proceedings, §26-2A-81.
Powers.
Generally, §26-2A-78.
Limitations in interest of developing self reliance on part of ward, §26-2A-78.
Proceedings subsequent to appointment, §26-2A-80.
Jurisdiction, §26-2A-80.
Venue, §26-2A-80.
Removal.
Petitions, §26-2A-81.
Termination of appointment, §26-2A-79.
Resignation.
Petition for permission to resign, §26-2A-81.
Termination of appointment, §26-2A-79.
Service of process.
Consent to service by acceptance of appointment, §26-2A-77.
Status of guardian.
Continues until terminated, §26-2A-70.
Temporary guardians.
Court appointment, §26-2A-73.
Termination of appointment, §26-2A-79.
Third persons.
Liability by reason of relationship for acts of ward, §26-2A-78.
Venue.
Court appointment of guardians, §26-2A-74.
Proceedings subsequent to appointment, §26-2A-80.

GUARDIAN AND WARD
—Cont'd
Uniform guardianship and protective proceedings act—Cont'd
Minors—Cont'd
Majority.
Termination of appointment of guardian upon minor obtaining, §26-2A-79.
Marriage.
Termination of appointment of guardians, §26-2A-79.
Payment of money or personal property to.
Persons to whom payment may be made, §26-2A-6.
Protective orders generally, §§26-2A-130 to 26-2A-137.
Multiple proceedings, §26-2A-32.
Notice, §26-2A-50.
Conservators.
Service of notice on, §26-2A-141.
Court appointment of guardians for minors.
Hearings, §26-2A-75.
Incapacitated persons.
Guardianship proceedings, §26-2A-103.
Service of notice, §26-2A-106.
Interested persons.
Request for notice, §26-2A-53.
Method of giving, §26-2A-50.
Minors.
Guardians.
Court appointment hearings, §26-2A-75.
Hearing on petition for order subsequent to appointment, §26-2A-81.
Petitions for removal of guardian or permission to resign, §26-2A-81.
Service of notice upon, §26-2A-77.
Parental appointment of guardians.
Acceptance of appointment, §26-2A-71.
Protective proceedings.
Appointment of conservators or other protective orders, §26-2A-130.
Generally, §26-2A-134.
Request for notice.
Interested persons, §26-2A-53.
Time of giving, §26-2A-50.
Waiver, §26-2A-51.

GUARDIAN AND WARD
—Cont'd
Uniform guardianship and
protective proceedings
act—Cont'd
Orders.
  Appointment of
    conservators or other
    protective orders.
    Permissible court orders,
      §26-2A-136.
    Petitions for orders
      subsequent to
      appointment of
      conservators,
      §26-2A-144.
    Procedure concerning
      orders on original
      petition, §26-2A-135.
    Termination of
      conservatorships.
      Evidence and
        recordation,
        §26-2A-149.
  Incapacitated persons.
    Court appointment of
      guardian,
      §26-2A-105.
    Termination of
      incapacity.
      Request for order,
        §26-2A-110.
  Protective orders,
    §§26-2A-130 to
    26-2A-137.
Parental appointment of
  guardians, §§26-7A-70 to
  26-7A-72, 26-7A-80.
Acceptance of appointment,
  §26-2A-71.
Authorized, §26-2A-70.
Generally, §26-2A-71.
Incapacitated persons,
  §26-2A-100.
Jurisdiction.
  Proceedings subsequent
    to appointment,
    §26-2A-80.
Method of appointment,
  §26-2A-71.
Minors of fourteen or older.
  Objections, §26-2A-72.
Notice.
  Acceptance of
    appointment,
    §26-2A-71.
Objections.
  Minors of fourteen or
    older, §26-2A-72.
Priority.
  Two or more
    appointments made,
    §26-2A-71.
Proceedings subsequent to
  appointment.
  Jurisdiction, §26-2A-80.
  Venue, §26-2A-80.
Two or more appointments
  made.
  Priority, §26-2A-71.
Venue.
  Proceedings subsequent
    to appointment,
    §26-2A-80.
Will to appoint,
  §§26-2A-71, 26-2A-100.
Parental authority, §26-2A-7.

GUARDIAN AND WARD
—Cont'd
Uniform guardianship and
protective proceedings
act—Cont'd
Payment of money or
  personal property.
  Persons to whom payment
    may be made,
    §26-2A-6.
Petitions.
  Appointment of
    conservators or other
    protective orders.
    Orders subsequent to
      appointment of
      conservators,
      §26-2A-144.
    Procedure concerning
      hearing and order on
      original petition,
      §26-2A-135.
    Termination of
      conservatorships,
      §26-2A-158.
Conservators.
  Removal or resignation,
    §26-2A-143.
Court appointment of
  guardians for minors,
  §26-2A-75.
Incapacitated persons.
  Court appointment of
    guardians,
    §26-2A-102.
  Guardians.
    Removal or permission
      to resign,
      §26-2A-110.
    Temporary guardians,
      §26-2A-107.
  Termination of
    incapacity,
    §26-2A-110.
Minors.
  Guardians.
    Court appointment,
      §26-2A-75.
    Removal or permission
      to resign,
      §26-2A-81.
  Protective proceedings.
    Appointment of
      conservators or other
      protective orders,
      §26-2A-130.
    Original petition,
      §26-2A-133.
Powers.
  Delegation.
    Parents or guardians,
      §26-2A-7.
Powers of attorney.
  Parents or guardians.
    Delegation of powers,
      §26-2A-7.
Principles of law and equity.
  Supplement provisions of
    chapter, §26-2A-3.
Priorities.
  Appointment of
    conservators,
    §26-2A-138.
Probate courts.
  Jurisdiction.
    Subject matter
      jurisdiction,
      §26-2A-31.

GUARDIAN AND WARD
—Cont'd
Uniform guardianship and
protective proceedings
act—Cont'd
Protective orders,
  §§26-2A-130 to
  26-2A-137.
  Arrangements and
    transactions
    authorized,
    §26-2A-137.
  Business affairs of
    protected persons.
    Jurisdiction of court in
      which petition filed,
      §26-2A-131.
  Grounds for making,
    §26-2A-130.
  Hearings.
    Petitions, §26-2A-130.
    Procedure concerning
      hearing on original
      petition, §26-2A-135.
  Jurisdiction of court in
    which petition filed.
    Business affairs of
      protected persons,
      §26-2A-131.
  Notice.
    Generally, §26-2A-134.
    Petitions, §26-2A-130.
    Publication, §26-2A-134.
  Permissible court orders,
    §26-2A-136.
  Petitions, §26-2A-130.
    Contents, §26-2A-133.
    Procedure concerning
      hearing and order on
      original petition,
      §26-2A-135.
    Who may petition,
      §26-2A-133.
  Procedure concerning
    hearing and order on
    original petition,
    §26-2A-135.
  Publication.
    Notice, §26-2A-134.
    Venue, §26-2A-132.
  Protective proceedings.
    Conservators generally,
      §§26-2A-130 to
      26-2A-160. See within
      this heading,
      "Conservators."
  Protective orders,
    §§26-2A-130 to
    26-2A-137.
  Publication.
    Protective proceedings.
      Notice.
        When notice required
          to be given by
          publication,
          §26-2A-134.
  Purposes and policies of
    chapter, §26-2A-2.
  Recordation.
    Conservators.
      Letters of
        conservatorship,
        §26-2A-149.
      Orders terminating
        conservatorships,
        §26-2A-149.
  Records.
    Clerks of court.
      Duties, §26-2A-34.
    Conservators, §26-2A-146.

GUARDIAN AND WARD
—Cont'd

Uniform guardianship and protective proceedings act—Cont'd

Repeal.
Implied repeal.
Construction against, §26-2A-5.
Rules of civil procedure.
Rules govern proceedings under chapter, §26-2A-33.
Sales.
Conservators.
Conflicts of interest, §26-2A-150.
Service of process.
Conservators.
Submission personally to jurisdiction of a court by accepting appointment, §26-2A-141.
Incapacitated persons.
Guardians.
Consent to jurisdiction, §26-2A-106.
Minors.
Guardians.
Consent to service by acceptance of appointment, §26-2A-77.
Settlements.
Conservators.
Final consent settlements, §26-2A-158.
Severability of provisions, §26-2A-4.
Supplement provisions of chapter.
Principles of law and equity, §26-2A-3.
Territorial application of chapter, §26-2A-30.
Title.
Conservators.
Title by appointment.
Appointment vests in conservator title as trustee, §26-2A-148.
Title of chapter.
Short title, §26-2A-1.
Torts.
Conservators.
Personal liability, §26-2A-157.
Transfer of proceedings, §26-2A-32.
Trial.
Jury trial, §26-2A-35.
Venue.
Court appointment of guardians for minors, §26-2A-74.
Incapacitated persons.
Guardianship proceedings, §26-2A-101.
Minors.
Guardians.
Proceedings subsequent to appointment, §26-2A-80.
Multiple proceedings, §26-2A-32.

GUARDIAN AND WARD
—Cont'd

Uniform guardianship and protective proceedings act—Cont'd

Venue—Cont'd
Protective proceedings, §26-2A-132.
Wills.
Conservators.
Examination of will of protected persons, §26-2A-155.
Parental appointment by will, §§26-2A-71, 26-2A-100.
Venue.
Curators.
Appointment, §26-7A-2.
Uniform guardianship and protective proceedings act.
Court appointment of guardians for minors, §26-2A-74.
Incapacitated persons.
Guardianship proceedings, §26-2A-101.
Subsequent to appointment, §26-2A-111.
Minors.
Guardians.
Proceedings subsequent to appointment, §26-2A-80.
Multiple proceedings, §26-2A-32.
Protective proceedings, §26-2A-132.
Veterans.
Incompetent veterans and dependents, §§26-9-1 to 26-9-19.
See VETERANS.
Probate judges.
Copies of decrees.
Furnishing to veterans administration, §12-13-42.
Welfare.
Legal representatives for handling public assistance payments, §38-1-3.
Wills.
Parental appointment of guardians, §§26-2A-71, 26-2A-100.
Uniform guardianship and protective proceedings act.
Conservators.
Examination of will of protected persons, §26-2A-155.
Youth services.
Custody of department.
Guardianship of youth in custody of department, §44-1-31.

GUARDS.
Habeas corpus.
Summoning and compensation of guards to convey prisoner, §15-21-34.

GUARDS—Cont'd
Jails, §§13A-3-27, 14-6-10, 14-6-11.
Penitentiary, §§14-3-49, 14-3-54, 14-3-55.
Prisons and prisoners.
See PRISONS AND PRISONERS.

GUESTS.
Duty of care owed persons on premises for sporting or recreational purposes, §§35-15-1 to 35-15-5.
See PARKS AND RECREATION.
Hotels, inns and other transient lodging places, §§34-15-1 to 34-15-20.
See HOTELS, INNS AND OTHER TRANSIENT LODGING PLACES.
State visitors.
Protection of certain state officers and visitors, §§36-33-1 to 36-33-4.

GUEST STATUTE.
Motor vehicles.
Liability for injury or death of guest, §32-1-2.

GUIDE DOGS.
See BLIND PERSONS.

GUILTY PLEAS.
General provisions, §§13A-5-42, 15-15-20 to 15-15-26.
See PLEADINGS.

GULF OF MEXICO.
Marine resources. §§9-12-1 to 9-12-184.
See MARINE RESOURCES.
Motor vehicles.
Operation of vehicles on beaches and sand dunes of Gulf of Mexico.
Prohibited, §32-1-7.

GULF STATES MARINE FISHERIES COMPACT, §§9-12-180 to 9-12-184.

GUNPOWDER.
Storage.
Provision of building for storage, §11-47-12.
Storing in city or town, §13A-11-224.

GUNS.
Weapons offenses, §§13A-11-50 to 13A-11-84.
See WEAPONS.

H

HABEAS CORPUS.
Address.
To whom petition addressed, §15-21-6.
When petition may be addressed to another judge, §15-21-7.
Writ presumed addressed to recipient, §15-21-10.
Appeals, ARAP, Rule 22.
Application.
Petition, §15-21-4.
Attachment.
Compelling obedience of writ, §15-21-30.

HABEAS CORPUS—Cont'd
Bail and recognizance.
Failure to appear at
examination, §15-21-20.
Forfeiture of bail, §15-21-22.
Persons entitled to prosecute
writ.
Persons confined for failure
to enter into
undertaking to keep
the peace, §15-21-2.
Transmission of bail to clerk
of court, §15-21-22.
Without notice, §15-21-13.
Constitution of Alabama.
Power of supreme court to
issue writs, Const. Ala.,
art. VI, §140.
Suspension of habeas corpus,
Const. Ala., art. I, §17.
**Constitution of the United
States.**
Habeas corpus not to be
suspended, Const. U. S.,
Art. I, §9.
Contempt.
Court not to inquire into
contempt commitment,
§15-21-23.
Failure to obey writ,
§15-21-30.
Costs.
Guards to convey prisoner,
§15-21-34.
Taxation and collection of
witness costs, §15-21-33.
Court of civil appeals.
Authority to issue writs,
§12-3-11.
Court of criminal appeals.
Authority to issue writs,
§12-3-11.
Damages.
Unlawful detention or arrest
after discharge order,
§15-21-27.
Delay.
To whom writ returnable,
§15-21-8.
Writ to be granted without
delay, §15-21-8.
Discharge.
Grounds for discharge under
process legally issued,
§15-21-24.
Reimprisonment for same
cause after discharge,
§15-21-26.
Unlawful detention or arrest
after discharge order,
§15-21-27.
When party to be discharged,
§15-21-21.
District attorneys.
Notice of writ, §15-21-13.
Examinations.
Disposition of detainee on
adjournment, §15-21-20.
Inquiry into imprisonment or
detention, §15-21-20.
Extradition.
Right of prisoner to apply for
writ, §15-9-38.
Form, §15-21-9.
Return, §15-21-17.
Writ not be disobeyed for
want of form or
misdescription,
§15-21-10.

HABEAS CORPUS—Cont'd
Guards.
Summoning and
compensation of guards
to convey prisoner,
§15-21-34.
Indigent persons.
Appointment and
compensation of counsel,
§§15-12-23, 15-12-24.
Infirmity.
Proceedings when person not
produced on account of
infirmity, §15-21-19.
Interested parties.
Notice to any other person
interested, §15-21-12.
Investigations.
Inquiry into imprisonment or
detention, §§15-21-17,
15-21-20.
Judgments.
Court not to inquire into
legal judgment,
§15-21-23.
Jurisdiction.
Ouster of jurisdiction of
nearest judge, §15-21-7.
Mentally ill.
Persons confined as insane
entitled to prosecute
writ, §15-21-3.
Misdescription.
Writ not be disobeyed due to
misdescription,
§15-21-10.
Notice.
Bail without notice,
§15-21-13.
District attorney, prosecutor
or arrestor, §15-21-13.
Other interested parties,
§15-21-12.
Penalties.
Refusal or neglect to deliver
true copy of detention
order, §15-21-28.
Transferring custody so as to
elude service or effect of
writ, §15-21-31.
Unlawful detention or arrest
after discharge,
§15-21-27.
**Persons entitled to
prosecute writ.**
Generally, §15-21-1.
Persons confined as insane,
§15-21-3.
Persons confined for failure
to enter into undertaking
to keep the peace,
§15-21-2.
Petition.
Application to be made by
petitions, §15-21-4.
Contents, §15-21-4.
Description of party if name
uncertain or unknown,
§15-21-5.
To whom petition addressed,
§15-21-6.
When petition may be
addressed to another
judge, §15-21-7.
Precept.
Execution by sheriff or
constable, §15-21-14.
Issuance, §15-21-14.
**Reimprisonment for same
cause after discharge,**
§15-21-26.

HABEAS CORPUS—Cont'd
Remand.
Guilty party irregularly
committed, §15-21-25.
When party to be remanded,
§15-21-21.
Return.
Contesting, §15-21-20.
Form and contents,
§15-21-17.
Person and original
detaining warrant to be
produced with return,
§15-21-18.
Service of process, §15-21-16.
Sickness.
Proceedings when person not
produced on account of
sickness, §15-21-19.
Subpoenas.
Witnesses, §15-21-15.
Supreme court.
Powers of court, §12-2-7;
Const. Ala., art. VI,
§140.
Suspension.
Prohibited, Const. Ala., art.
I, §17; Const. U. S., Art.
I, §9.
Transportation.
Summoning and
compensation of guards
to convey prisoners,
§15-21-34.
Unknown persons.
Description of party if name
uncertain or unknown,
§15-21-5.
Witnesses.
Proceedings against
defaulting witnesses,
§15-21-32.
Subpoenas for witnesses,
§15-21-15.
Taxation and collection of
costs, §15-21-33.

HABITUAL FELONY ACT.
Additional penalties,
§13A-5-9.
**Determination of whether
defendant repeat or
habitual offender,**
§13A-5-10.
Proof of prior convictions,
§13A-5-10.1.

HALE COUNTY.
Economic development,
Const. Ala., amd. 313.
Probate judge.
Compensation, Const. Ala.,
amd. 481.

**HALE MEMORIAL
HOSPITAL.**
Employees.
Merit system.
Employees governed by
merit system,
§36-26-64.

**HALEYVILLE,
MUNICIPALITY OF.**
Economic development,
Const. Ala., amd. 104.
Property tax, Const. Ala.,
amd. 54.

HALL OF FAME.
Academy of honor, §§41-11-1
to 41-11-6.
See ACADEMY OF HONOR.

HALL OF FAME—Cont'd
Aviation hall of fame board,
§§41-9-720 to 41-9-722.
**Chiropractors' hall of fame
board,** §§41-9-880 to
41-9-883.
See CHIROPRACTORS.
Men's hall of fame,
§§41-9-850 to 41-9-853.
**Motor sports hall of fame
commission,** §§41-9-470 to
41-9-478.
See MOTOR SPORTS HALL
OF FAME
COMMISSION.
Peace officers, §§41-9-870 to
41-9-873.
Senior citizens hall of fame,
§§41-9-740 to 41-9-745.
See AGED PERSONS.
Sports hall of fame board,
§§41-9-450 to 41-9-454.
Turkey hunters hall of fame,
§§41-9-830 to 41-9-833.
Women's hall of fame,
§§41-9-550 to 41-9-554.

HALLUCINOGENIC DRUGS.
Controlled substances,
§§20-2-1 to 20-2-144.
See DRUGS.

HAM RADIO OPERATORS.
**Motor vehicle tags and
plates.**
Amateur radio operators
licensed by civil air
patrol, §§32-6-90 to
32-6-93.
General provisions, §§32-6-70
to 32-6-73.

HANDGUNS.
See WEAPONS.

HANDICAPPED PERSONS,
§§21-1-1 to 21-8-5.
Adult protective services,
§§38-9-1 to 38-9-11.
See ADULT PROTECTIVE
SERVICES.
**Agreements with public and
private clinics and
agencies,** §21-3-1.
**Alabama institute for deaf
and blind,** §§21-1-1 to
21-1-26. See within this
heading, "Institute for deaf
and blind."
Amusements.
Right to use of places of
public amusement,
§21-7-3.
Audiologists, §§34-28A-1 to
34-28A-44.
See SPEECH
PATHOLOGISTS AND
AUDIOLOGISTS.
Aviation.
Right to use of public
conveyances and
transportation facilities,
§21-7-3.
Blind persons.
General provisions, §§21-1-1
to 21-1-62.
See BLIND PERSONS.
Institute for deaf and blind,
§§21-1-1 to 21-1-26. See
within this heading,
"Institute for deaf and
blind."

HANDICAPPED PERSONS
—Cont'd
Blind persons—Cont'd
Rights of blind persons,
§§21-7-1 to 21-7-10.
Boats.
Right to use of public
conveyances and
transportation facilities,
§21-7-3.
Buildings.
Accessibility to and use of
public buildings and
facilities by handicapped
persons, §§21-4-1 to
21-4-24.
See PUBLIC BUILDINGS.
Buses.
Right to use of public
conveyances and
transportation facilities,
§21-7-3.
Children.
Crippled and disabled
children, §§21-3-1 to
21-3-8. See within this
heading, "Crippled and
disabled children."
Crippled children's service,
§§16-38-1 to 16-38-9. See
within this heading,
"Rehabilitation and
crippled children's
service."
Education.
Children exempt from
attending public
school, §16-28-6.
Employment by public
schools, §21-7-8.
Exceptional children,
§§16-39-1 to 16-39-12.
See EDUCATION.
Institute for deaf and
blind, §§21-1-1 to
21-1-26. See within
this heading, "Institute
for deaf and blind."
Committees.
Governor's committee on
employment, §§21-5-1 to
21-5-10. See within this
heading, "Governor's
committee on
employment."
Common carriers.
Right to use of public
conveyances and
transportation facilities,
§21-7-3.
Consent for health services,
§§22-8-1 to 22-8-9.
See HEALTH.
Contracts.
Examinations.
Physical examination of
children having
malformations or
disabilities, §§21-3-5 to
21-3-7.
Rehabilitation program for
the homebound.
Contracts with state
agencies and private
organizations, §21-6-1.
Counties.
Employment by counties,
§21-7-8.

HANDICAPPED PERSONS
—Cont'd
**Crippled and disabled
children,** §§21-3-1 to
21-3-8.
Administration of chapter,
§21-3-1.
Crippled children's service,
§§16-38-1 to 16-38-9. See
within this heading,
"Rehabilitation and
crippled children's
service."
Disabilities.
Physical examination of
children having
disabilities, §§21-3-5 to
21-3-7.
Donations.
Expenditure of donations,
§21-3-1.
Education of exceptional
children, §§16-39-1 to
16-39-12.
See EDUCATION.
Funds.
Disbursement of funds,
§21-3-3.
Use of funds appropriated
for physical restoration
of crippled children,
§21-3-2.
Gifts.
Acceptance and
expenditure, §21-3-1.
Lists of children having
malformations.
Compilation of lists,
§21-3-4.
Malformations.
Compilation of lists of
children having
malformations,
§21-3-4.
Physical examination of
children having
malformations,
§§21-3-5 to 21-3-7.
Reports.
Disposition, §21-3-8.
Forms for reporting,
§21-3-8.
Physical examination of
children having
malformations or
disabilities.
Information to be given
parents, §21-3-7.
Report of findings, §21-3-6.
Required, §21-3-5.
Reports.
Disposition of reports,
§21-3-8.
Forms for reporting
malformations and
disabilities, §21-3-8.
Physical examination of
children having
malformations or
disabilities.
Report of findings,
§21-3-6.
Crippled children's service,
§§16-38-1 to 16-38-9. See
within this heading,
"Rehabilitation and
crippled children's service."

HANDICAPPED PERSONS
—Cont'd
Curators.
Appointment, §§26-7A-1 to
26-7A-17.
See GUARDIAN AND
WARD.
Deaf persons.
General provisions, §§21-1-1
to 21-1-62.
See DEAF PERSONS.
Definitions.
Accessibility to and use of
public buildings and
facilities by physically
handicapped persons,
§21-4-2.
Motor vehicles, §32-6-230.
**Department of adult blind
and deaf,** §§21-1-15,
21-1-17.
Disabled children, §§21-3-1 to
21-3-8.
Generally. See within this
heading, "Crippled and
disabled children."
Education.
Children exempt from
attending public school,
§16-28-6.
Employment by public
schools, §21-7-8.
Exceptional children,
§§16-39-1 to 16-39-12.
See EDUCATION.
Institute for deaf and blind,
§§21-1-1 to 21-1-26. See
within this heading,
"Institute for deaf and
blind."
Rehabilitation and crippled
children's service,
§§16-38-1 to 16-38-9.
Elections.
Absentee voting.
Physician's certificate.
When required, §17-10-4.
Accessibility to registration
and polling places by
handicapped and elderly
persons, §§21-4-20 to
21-4-24.
See ELECTIONS.
Assistance in casting votes,
§17-8-29.
Municipal elections,
§§11-46-40, 11-46-51,
11-46-111, 11-46-122.
Primary elections,
§17-16-27.
Municipal elections.
Assistance to disabled
voters, §§11-46-40,
11-46-51, 11-46-111,
11-46-122.
Deception of disabled voter
by marker, etc.,
§§11-46-64, 11-46-135.
False declaration
requesting assistance,
§11-46-138.
Mayor-council form of
government.
Assistance to disabled
voters, §11-46-40.
Voting machines,
§11-46-51.

HANDICAPPED PERSONS
—Cont'd
Elections—Cont'd
Voting machines.
Assistance at polls,
§17-9-25.
Municipal elections.
Mayor-council form,
§11-46-51.
Employment.
By state, political
subdivisions of state,
public schools, etc.,
§21-7-8.
Governor's committee on
employment, §§21-5-1 to
21-5-10. See within this
heading, "Governor's
committee on
employment."
**Employ the handicapped
week.**
Designation, §21-5-2.
Examinations.
Crippled and disabled
children.
Physical examination of
children having
malformations or
disabilities, §§21-3-5 to
21-3-7.
Facilities.
Special health care facility
authorities, §§11-62-1 to
11-62-21.
See MUNICIPAL
CORPORATIONS.
Governor.
Rehabilitation and crippled
children's service.
Annual report to governor
on rehabilitation,
§16-38-9.
**Governor's committee on
employment,** §§21-5-1 to
21-5-10.
Advisory council, §21-5-6.
Annual report and
evaluation, §21-5-10.
Appointment of members,
§21-5-4.
Chairman.
Appointment, §21-5-5.
Term, §21-5-5.
Compensation of members,
§21-5-4.
Composition, §21-5-4.
Created, §21-5-1.
Duties, §21-5-1.
Employ the handicapped
week.
Designation, §21-5-2.
Executive committee.
Election, §21-5-5.
Executive secretary, §21-5-8.
Expenses.
Payment, §21-5-8.
Funds.
Trust fund, §21-5-9.
Liaison group.
Employment of
handicapped liaison
group, §21-5-7.
Meetings, §21-5-5.
Nonpartisan.
Committee to be
nonpartisan, §21-5-3.
Nonprofit.
Committee to be nonprofit,
§21-5-3.
Personnel, §21-5-8.

HANDICAPPED PERSONS
—Cont'd
**Governor's committee on
employment**—Cont'd
Rules and regulations.
Promulgation, §21-5-1.
Salaries.
Payment, §21-5-8.
Secretary-treasurer.
Election, §21-5-5.
Trust fund, §21-5-9.
Guardian and ward.
Uniform guardianship and
protective proceedings
act, §§26-2A-1 to
26-2A-160.
See GUARDIAN AND
WARD.
Hemophilia treatment,
§§21-8-1 to 21-8-5.
See HEMOPHILIA
TREATMENT.
Homebound persons.
Rehabilitation program for
the homebound, §§21-6-1
to 21-6-5.
Home industries, §§21-2-1 to
21-2-4.
**Hotels, inns and other
transient lodging places.**
Right to use of public lodging
places, §21-7-3.
Housing.
Right to housing
accommodations, §21-7-9.
Income tax.
Deductions.
Removal of any
architectural or
transportation barriers
from property.
Actual expenses
incurred, §40-18-15.
Institute for deaf and blind,
§§21-1-1 to 21-1-26.
Admissions to school,
§21-1-8.
Adults.
Department of adult blind
and deaf, §§21-1-15,
21-1-17.
Attendance of blind, deaf or
mute children between
seven and sixteen years
of age.
Enforcement of attendance
of children eligible for
benefits of school,
§21-1-12.
Exemptions, §21-1-11.
Failure of minors to
attend.
Prosecutions for failure
to attend, §21-1-13.
Prosecutions for failure of
minors to attend,
§21-1-13.
Required, §21-1-10.
Board of trustees, §§21-1-2 to
21-1-7.
Appointment of members,
§21-1-2.
Chairman, §21-1-5.
Compensation, §21-1-5.
Composition, §21-1-2.
Executive committee,
§21-1-4.

HANDICAPPED PERSONS
—Cont'd
Institute for deaf and blind
—Cont'd
Board of trustees—Cont'd
Expenses of members for
participation in
conferences, etc.
Advancement of and
accounting for,
§16-13-14.
Insurance of state property,
§21-1-6.
Maintenance of state
property, §21-1-6.
President of institute.
Appointment by board,
§21-1-5.
Qualifications of members,
§21-1-2.
Quorum, §21-1-3.
Secretary, §21-1-3.
Compensation, §21-1-5.
State property.
Insurance, §21-1-6.
Maintenance, §21-1-6.
Terms of members, §21-1-2.
Treasurer, §21-1-3.
Compensation, §21-1-5.
Reports, §21-1-7.
Bond issues.
Construction and
improvement purposes,
Const. Ala., amd. 117.
Bureau of information for aid
of blind or deaf,
§21-1-17.
Competitive bid law.
Expenditures for services,
supplies, etc., subject
to provisions of state
competitive bid law,
§21-1-18.
County school boards.
Cooperation by, §21-1-8.
Created, §21-1-1.
Department of adult blind
and deaf.
Appropriations, §21-1-15.
Establishment, §21-1-15.
Library service.
Operation, §21-1-15.
Policies.
Development of policies,
etc., §21-1-17.
Powers and duties of
department as to
training, etc., §21-1-17.
Workshops, home
industries, etc.
Powers of department as
to, §21-2-1.
Employees.
Expenses for participation
in conferences, etc.
Advancement of and
accounting for
expenses, §16-13-14.
Personal leave.
Support personnel,
§16-8-26.1.
Expenditures for services,
supplies, etc.
Subject to provisions of
state competitive bid
law, §21-1-18.
Funds.
Disbursement, §21-1-7.
Gasoline tax.
Exemptions, §40-17-31.

HANDICAPPED PERSONS
—Cont'd
Institute for deaf and blind
—Cont'd
Information.
Bureau of information for
aid of blind or deaf,
§21-1-17.
Junior college levels.
Education and training at
junior college levels,
§21-1-9.
Library service.
Operation by department
of adult blind and
deaf, §21-1-15.
Lists of deaf and blind
children within counties,
§21-1-12.
Loans.
Negotiation of temporary
loans, §21-1-19.
Local school boards.
Cooperation by, §21-1-8.
Location, §21-1-1.
Change, Const. Ala., art.
XIV, §267.
Lubricating oils and greases.
Tax exemptions,
§40-17-171.
Minors.
Attendance, §§21-1-10 to
21-1-13.
Municipal school boards.
Cooperation by, §21-1-8.
Nonresident handicapped
persons.
Education and training,
§21-1-14.
Police officers.
Employment, §16-22-1.
Jurisdiction.
Extension of jurisdiction,
§16-22-2.
Powers and duties,
§16-22-1.
Powers, §21-1-1.
Preschool levels.
Education and training at
preschool levels,
§21-1-9.
President of institute.
Appointment by board of
trustees, §21-1-5.
Assistants.
Appointment by board of
trustees, §21-1-5.
Privileges, §21-1-1.
Programs.
Institute official state
agency to conduct state
educational and
training programs,
§21-1-23.
Residential education and
training programs,
§21-1-8.
Property.
Insurance of state property,
§21-1-6.
Maintenance of state
property, §21-1-6.
Register of blind persons.
Maintenance, §21-1-16.
Preparation, §21-1-16.
Reports.
Treasurer's reports,
§21-1-7.
Residential education and
training programs,
§21-1-8.

HANDICAPPED PERSONS
—Cont'd
Institute for deaf and blind
—Cont'd
Rights, §21-1-1.
State board of education.
Cooperation by, §21-1-8.
Teachers.
Compensation, §21-1-5.
Personal leave, §21-1-22.
Sick leave, §21-1-21.
Substitute teachers.
Reimbursement of
institute for
payments to
substitute teachers,
§21-1-20.
Textbooks.
Approval of book
shipments, §21-1-26.
Braille materials, §21-1-25.
Large print materials,
§21-1-25.
Payment for shipment,
§21-1-26.
Purchase and furnishing of
state-owned textbooks,
§16-36-23.
Use of material other than
prescribed by state
board of education,
§21-1-24.
Trustees.
Board of trustees, §§21-1-2
to 21-1-7.
Junior colleges.
Institute for deaf and blind.
Education and training of
handicapped persons at
junior college levels,
§21-1-9.
Jury.
Qualifications of jurors,
§12-16-60.
Libraries.
Operation of library service
by department of adult
blind and deaf, §21-1-15.
Lodging places.
Right to use of public lodging
places, §21-7-3.
Markets.
Products produced by
handicapped.
Powers of department of
adult blind and deaf as
to marketing of
products, §21-2-1.
Motor vehicles.
Blind persons, §§21-7-3,
21-7-6, 21-7-7,
32-5A-220.
Definitions, §32-6-230.
Distress flag for handicapped
or paraplegic drivers,
§§32-5-12 to 32-5-14.
Drivers' licenses.
Persons to whom license
not to be issued,
§32-6-7.
License plates.
Distinctive decal,
§32-6-231.
False representations to
obtain, §32-6-233.
Temporary identification
placard, §32-6-231.
Unlimited parking
periods, §32-6-232.
Distinctive license plates.
Applications, §40-12-300.

HANDICAPPED PERSONS
—Cont'd

Motor vehicles—Cont'd
License plates—Cont'd
Distinctive license plates
—Cont'd
Design, §40-12-302.
Fees, §40-12-300.
Issuance, §40-12-300.
Standard license plates.
Issuance to motor
vehicles previously
issued distinctive
license plates,
§40-12-301.
Transfer, §40-12-301.
Misuse of privileges,
§32-6-233.
Parking.
Agreements with other
states as to parking
privileges, §32-6-234.
Unauthorized use of
handicapped parking
place, §32-6-233.1.
Unlimited parking periods,
§32-6-232.
Pedestrians, §32-5A-220.
Reciprocity.
Agreements concerning
parking privileges,
§32-6-234.
Right to use of public
conveyances and
transportation facilities,
§21-7-3.
Municipal corporations.
Elections.
Assistance to disabled
voters, §§11-46-40,
11-46-51, 11-46-111,
11-46-122.
Deception of disabled
voters by marker, etc.,
§§11-46-64, 11-46-135.
False declaration
requesting assistance,
§11-46-138.
Mayor-council form.
Assistance of disabled
electors, §11-46-40.
Voting machines,
§11-46-51.
Employment by
municipalities, §21-7-8.
Facilities.
Special health care facility
authorities, §§11-62-1
to 11-62-21.
See MUNICIPAL
CORPORATIONS.
Nonresidents.
Institute for deaf and blind.
Education and training of
nonresident
handicapped persons,
§21-1-14.
Penalties.
Rights of blind or other
physically disabled
persons.
Penalty for denial of or
interference with
enumerated rights,
§21-7-5.
**Physical therapists
generally,** §§34-24-190 to
34-24-217.
See PHYSICAL
THERAPISTS.

HANDICAPPED PERSONS
—Cont'd

Public accommodations.
Right to use of places of
public accommodations,
§21-7-3.
Public buildings.
Accessibility to and use of
public buildings and
facilities by handicapped
persons, §§21-4-1 to
21-4-7.
See PUBLIC BUILDINGS.
**Public officers and
employees.**
Merit system.
Certification for
employment,
§36-26-16.
Railroads.
Right to use of, §21-7-3.
**Rehabilitation and crippled
children's service,**
§§16-38-1 to 16-38-9.
City boards of education.
Cooperation in
rehabilitation work,
§16-38-7.
County boards of education.
Cooperation in
rehabilitation work,
§16-38-7.
Federal funds.
Reimbursements, §16-38-8.
Treasurer custodian,
§16-38-4.
Use of funds, §16-38-8.
Federal rehabilitation act.
Acceptance of provisions,
§16-38-1.
Federal rehabilitation
agency.
State board of education's
authority to cooperate
with, §16-38-6.
Governor.
Annual report to governor
on rehabilitation,
§16-38-9.
Industry.
Rehabilitation of persons
disabled in industry or
otherwise, §16-38-2.
Reimbursements.
Use of reimbursements,
§16-38-8.
Reports.
Annual report to governor
on rehabilitation,
§16-38-9.
Restoration of crippled
children, §16-38-3.
State board of education.
Annual report to governor
on rehabilitation,
§16-38-9.
Authority to cooperate
with federal
rehabilitation agency,
§16-38-6.
State funds.
Reimbursements, §16-38-8.
Use of funds, §16-38-8.
State superintendent of
education.
Duties as to rehabilitation
work, §16-38-5.
State treasurer.
Custodian of federal funds
for rehabilitation,
§16-38-4.

HANDICAPPED PERSONS
—Cont'd

**Rehabilitation and crippled
children's service**
—Cont'd
Universities and colleges.
Cooperation in
rehabilitation work,
§16-38-7.
**Rehabilitation program for
the homebound.**
Attendant care, §21-6-4.
Authorized, §21-6-1.
Care.
Attendant care, §21-6-4.
Committees.
Regional rehabilitation
committees, §21-6-5.
Contracts with state agencies
and private
organizations, §21-6-1.
Eligible persons.
Requirements for
eligibility, §21-6-3.
Services available to
eligible persons,
§21-6-2.
Establishment.
Authorized, §21-6-1.
Regional rehabilitation
committees, §21-6-5.
Requirements for eligibility,
§21-6-3.
Services available to eligible
persons, §21-6-2.
State agencies.
Contracts with state
agencies, §21-6-1.
Reports.
Crippled and disabled
children.
Disposition of reports,
§21-3-8.
Forms for reporting
malformations and
disabilities, §21-3-8.
Physical examination of
children having
malformations or
disabilities.
Report of findings,
§21-3-6.
Rehabilitation and crippled
children service.
Annual report to governor
on rehabilitation,
§16-38-9.
Resorts.
Right to use of public resorts,
§21-7-3.
**Rights of blind and other
physcially disabled
persons,** §§21-7-1 to
21-7-10.
Airplanes.
Right to use of public
conveyances and
transportation
facilities, §21-7-3.
Amusements.
Right to use of public
amusements, §21-7-3.
Boats.
Right to use of public
conveyances and
transportation
facilities, §21-7-3.

HANDICAPPED PERSONS
—Cont'd
Rights of blind and other physcially disabled persons—Cont'd
Buses.
  Right to use of public conveyances and transportation facilities, §21-7-3.
Canes.
  Duties of drivers to blind or partially blind pedestrians carrying cane, §21-7-6.
  Rights of blind persons not using cane, §21-7-7.
Common carriers.
  Right to use of common carriers, §21-7-3.
Counties.
  Employment by counties, §21-7-8.
Declaration of policy, §21-7-1.
Denial of enumerated rights.
  Penalty for denial, §21-7-5.
Employment by state, political subdivisions of state, public schools, etc., §21-7-8.
Guide dogs.
  Duty of drivers to blind or partially blind pedestrians using guide dogs, §21-7-6.
  Housing accommodations, §21-7-9.
  Liability for damages done by guide dogs, §21-7-4.
  Right of blind or partially blind persons to be accompanied by guide dog, §21-7-4.
  Rights of blind persons not using guide dogs, §21-7-7.
Hearing dogs, §21-7-4.
Hotels.
  Right to use of public lodging places, §21-7-3.
Housing accommodations.
  Right to housing accommodations, §21-7-9.
Interference with enumerated rights.
  Penalty for interference, §21-7-5.
Lodging places.
  Right to use of public lodging places, §21-7-3.
Motor vehicles.
  Right to use of public conveyances and transportation facilities, §21-7-3.
Municipal corporations.
  Employment by municipalities, §21-7-8.
Penalty for denial or interference with enumerated rights, §21-7-5.
Public accommodations.
  Right to use of places of public accommodations, §21-7-3.
Public buildings and facilities.
  Right to full use, §21-7-2.

HANDICAPPED PERSONS
—Cont'd
Rights of blind and other physcially disabled persons—Cont'd
Railroads.
  Right to use of public conveyances and transportation facilities, §21-7-3.
Resorts.
  Right to use of public resorts, §21-7-3.
Schools.
  Employment in public schools, §21-7-8.
Sidewalks.
  Right to full use of sidewalks, §21-7-2.
State.
  Employment by state, §21-7-8.
Streetcars.
  Right to use of public conveyances and transportation facilities, §21-7-3.
Streets.
  Right to full use of streets, §21-7-2.
Transportation.
  Right to use of public conveyances and transportation facilities, §21-7-3.
White canes.
  Duties of drivers to blind or partially blind pedestrians carrying cane, §21-7-6.
  Failure to use cane not evidence of contributory negligence, §21-7-7.
  Rights of blind persons not using cane, §21-7-7.
White cane safety day.
  Annual proclamation, §21-7-10.
Scholarships.
  Special teachers, §16-39-12.
Ships and shipping.
  Right to use of public conveyances and transportation facilities, §21-7-3.
Sidewalks.
  Right to full use of sidewalks, §21-7-2.
Speech pathologists and audiologists generally, §§34-28A-1 to 34-28A-44.
  See SPEECH PATHOLOGISTS AND AUDIOLOGISTS.
State.
  Employment by state, §21-7-8.
State board of education.
  Acceptance of donations, etc., §21-3-1.
  Administration of chapter, §21-3-1.

HANDICAPPED PERSONS
—Cont'd
State board of education
—Cont'd
Crippled and disabled children.
  Crippled children's service, §§16-38-1 to 16-38-9. See within this heading, "Rehabilitation and crippled children's service."
  Education of exceptional children, §§16-39-1 to 16-39-12. See EDUCATION.
  Expenditure of donations, etc., §21-3-1.
State treasurer.
  Rehabilitation and crippled children service.
  Federal funds for rehabilitation.
  Treasurer custodian, §16-38-4.
Streets.
  Right to full use of streets, §21-7-2.
Taxation.
  Exemptions.
    Principal residence of totally disabled persons, §40-9-21.
    Verification of eligibility by mail, §40-9-21.1.
    Property, §40-9-1.
  Income tax deductions.
    Removal of any architectural or transportation barriers from property, §40-18-15.
Therapy.
  Physical therapists generally, §§34-24-190 to 34-24-217. See PHYSICAL THERAPISTS.
Transportation.
  Right to use of public conveyances and transportation facilities, §21-7-3.
Uniform guardianship and protective proceedings act, §§26-2A-1 to 26-2A-160.
  See GUARDIAN AND WARD.
Voting.
  Accessibility to registration and polling places by handicapped and elderly persons, §§21-4-20 to 21-4-24.
  See ELECTIONS.
  General provisions. See within this heading, "Elections."
Witnesses.
  Interpreters, §§12-21-130 to 12-21-134.
Workshops, home industries, etc., §§21-2-1 to 21-2-4.
  Board to fix price of products offered for sale, etc., §21-2-3.

HANDICAPPED PERSONS
—Cont'd
Workshops, home industries, etc.—Cont'd
Department of adult blind and deaf.
Powers as to development of workshops, marketing of products, etc., §21-2-1.
Preference in purchase of products made under supervision of department by state departments, etc., and political subdivisions, §21-2-2.
Development.
Powers of department of adult blind and deaf as to development, §21-2-1.
Evasion of article, §21-2-3.
Marketing of products.
Powers of department of adult blind and deaf as to marketing, §21-2-1.
Preference in purchase of products by state departments, etc., and political subdivisions, §21-2-2.
Price of products offered for sale, etc.
Board to fix price, §21-2-3.
State departments.
Preference in purchase of products by state departments, §21-2-2.
Violations of section 21-2-3.
Effect of violations, §21-2-4.

HANDWRITING.
Evidence.
Admissibility of evidence for comparison, §12-21-39.
Comparison of disputed writing with genuine, §12-21-40.
Proof of execution when subscribing witnesses dead, etc., §12-21-62.
Proof of handwriting, ARCP, Rule 44 (j).

HARASSMENT.
Class C misdemeanor, §13A-11-8.
Elements of crime, §13A-11-8.

HARBORS AND PORTS.
Accounts and accounting.
Certain expenditures, §33-1-1.
Acquisition of facilities by state.
Architects.
Consultation with architects prior to acquisition, §33-1-12.
Eminent domain.
Limitation on power, §33-1-12.
Engineers.
Consultation with engineers prior to acquisition, §33-1-12.

HARBORS AND PORTS
—Cont'd
Acquisition of facilities by state—Cont'd
Governor.
Investigations.
Governor may make additional investigations relative to acquisition, §33-1-13.
Investigations.
Governor may make additional investigations relative to acquisition, §33-1-13.
Power to acquire, §33-1-12.
Railroads.
State may acquire, operate, etc., terminal railroads, §33-1-16.
Wharves, docks and warehouses.
Power of state to acquire and operate, §33-1-12.
Actions.
Docks department.
Department may prosecute necessary actions, §33-1-21.
Advisory committee.
Acting in advisory capacity only, §33-1-10.
Appointment by governor, §33-1-8.
Compensation, §33-1-8.
Composition, §33-1-8.
Expenses.
Travel expenses of members, §33-1-8.
Governor.
Ex officio member of committee, §33-1-8.
Meetings, §33-1-9.
Qualifications, §33-1-8.
Quorum, §33-1-9.
Records, §33-1-9.
Secretary, §33-1-9.
Terms of office, §33-1-8.
Vacancies.
Filling vacancies, §33-1-8.
Vice-chairman, §33-1-9.
Alabama port authority, §§33-13-1 to 33-13-13. See within this heading, "Port authorities."
Ameraport.
Deep draft harbor and terminal compact, §§33-9-1, 33-9-2.
Offshore harbor and terminal commission, §§33-10-1 to 33-10-26.
See AMERAPORT.
Anchorage.
Harbor masters.
Powers to regulate, §33-3-2.
State docks department.
Powers to regulate, §33-3-2.
Architects.
Acquisition, operation, etc., of wharves, docks and warehouses by state.
Consultation with architects, §33-1-12.
Director of state docks.
Appointment of architects by director, §33-1-5.

HARBORS AND PORTS
—Cont'd
Audits.
Certain expenditures, §33-1-1.
Authorities. See within this heading, "Port authorities."
Beacon lights.
Mobile harbor.
Fastening collection of logs, lumber or timber to beacon lights, §33-7-10.
Injuring, §33-7-11.
Boarding vessels.
Harbor masters and deputies, §33-3-5.
Bond issues.
Counties.
Public improvement bonds, §§11-81-110 to 11-81-123.
See COUNTIES.
Docks.
State docks facilities. See within this heading, "Docks."
Municipal corporations.
Public improvement bonds, §§11-81-110 to 11-81-123.
See MUNICIPAL CORPORATIONS.
Port authorities. See within this heading, "Port authorities."
Bonds, surety.
Director of state docks.
Bond required, §33-1-3.
Docks department.
Bonds required of certain employees, §33-1-6.
Harbor masters and deputies, §33-3-5.
Secretary-treasurer of docks department, §33-1-7.
Booms and bulkheads.
General provisions, §§35-11-310, 35-11-311.
Buildings.
Displaced persons.
Payment of relocation expenses of persons displaced by projects, §33-1-36.
Exchange of property and relocation of buildings by department, §33-1-20.
Insurance.
State docks department.
Authority to carry insurance, §33-1-25.
Charges, §§33-3-3, 33-1-26.
Conflicts of interest.
Director of state docks.
Financial interest in harbor facilities, §33-1-3.
Constitution of Alabama.
Construction, maintenance, etc., by state, Const. Ala., amds. 12, 58.
Construction.
State.
Promotion of construction, §33-1-1.

HARBORS AND PORTS
—Cont'd
Contracts.
Docks department.
Authority of department to
contract with federal
government for
purpose of receiving
funds, supplies and
facilities, §33-1-36.
Counties.
Bond issues.
Public improvement bonds,
§§11-81-110 to
11-81-123.
See COUNTIES.
Customers.
Expenditure of funds to
entertain customers,
§33-1-1.
Dangerous vessels.
Failure to remove on order of
department, §33-1-33.
Definitions.
Docks.
Bonds for state docks
facilities, §33-2-180.
Deputy harbor masters,
§§33-3-4 to 33-3-6.
Director of state docks.
Advisory committee.
Director to serve as secretary
of committee, §33-1-9.
Appointment by governor,
§33-1-3.
Architects.
Appointment by director,
§33-1-5.
Assistant directors, §33-1-4.
Bonds.
Required, §33-1-3.
Conflicts of interest.
Financial interest in
harbor facilities,
§33-1-3.
Engineers.
Appointment by director,
§33-1-5.
Orders.
Violation of orders of
director, §33-1-32.
Plans.
Submission of plans by
director to governor,
§33-1-12.
Powers.
Generally, §33-1-3.
Qualifications, §33-1-3.
Salary, §33-1-3.
Submerged lands and lands
lying under or abutting
tidal waters.
Sale, §33-1-18.
Term of office, §33-1-3.
Displaced persons.
Payment of relocation
expenses of persons
displaced by projects,
§33-1-36.
Docks, §§33-2-180 to 33-2-196.
Acquisition of property and
rights of way by
purchase or eminent
domain, §33-1-22.

HARBORS AND PORTS
—Cont'd
Docks—Cont'd
Bonds for state docks
facilities, §§33-2-180 to
33-2-196; Const. Ala.,
amds. 213, 222, 273.
Authorization to issue,
§33-2-181.
Refunding bonds,
§33-2-182.
Continuation of special
charges, §33-2-191.
Covenant by department to
maintain charges and
fees, §33-2-194.
Defeasance, §33-2-190.
Definitions, §33-2-180.
Disposition of proceeds,
§33-2-189.
Docks facilities debt
service fund,
§33-2-195.
Execution, §33-2-184.
Generally, §33-2-183.
Investments, §33-2-187.
Issuance.
Refunding bonds,
§33-2-182.
Negotiable instruments,
§33-2-186.
Pledge.
Constitutes sinking fund,
§33-2-192.
Nature of pledge,
§33-2-186.
Preservation of
outstanding
appropriations, pledges
and covenants,
§33-2-193.
Proceeds.
Disposition, §33-2-189.
Refunding bonds.
Authorization to issue,
§33-2-182.
Continuation of special
charges, §33-2-191.
Covenant by department
to maintain charges
and fees, §33-2-194.
Defeasance, §33-2-190.
Disposition of proceeds,
§33-2-188.
Execution, §33-2-184.
Generally, §33-2-183.
Investments, §33-2-187.
Negotiable instruments,
§33-2-186.
Pledge.
Constitutes sinking
fund, §33-2-192.
Nature of pledge,
§33-2-186.
Preservation of
outstanding
appropriations,
pledges and
covenants,
§33-2-193.
Proceeds.
Disposition, §33-2-188.
Sale, §33-2-185.
Security.
Use to secure deposit,
§33-2-187.
Taxation.
Exemption, §33-2-187.
Reserve funds for
outstanding bonds,
§33-2-196.

HARBORS AND PORTS
—Cont'd
Docks—Cont'd
Bonds for state docks
facilities—Cont'd
Sale, §33-2-185.
Security.
Use to secure deposit,
§33-2-187.
Taxation.
Exemption, §33-2-187.
Funds.
State docks facilities
contingency trust fund.
Creation, §33-2-210.
Deficiency.
Adjustment of amount
previously
transferred,
§33-2-212.
Notice of expected
deficiency,
§33-2-211.
Report attesting to
actual deficiency,
§33-2-212.
Funding, §33-2-210.
Notice.
Director of department
to give notice of
expected
deficiency,
§33-2-211.
Reports.
Report attesting to
actual deficiency,
§33-2-212.
Use of amounts of funds
transferred,
§33-2-213.
Liens on watercraft for
dockage, §35-11-60.
Power of state to acquire and
operate, §33-1-12.
State docks facilities
contingency trust fund,
§§33-2-210 to 33-2-213.
Taxation.
Subjects of taxation,
§40-11-1.
Docks department, §§33-1-1
to 33-1-36.
Actions.
Department may prosecute
necessary actions,
§33-1-21.
Advisory committee, §§33-1-8
to 33-1-10.
Anchorage.
Powers to regulate,
§33-3-2.
Bond issues.
Not debt of state, Const.
Ala., amd. 446.
Bonds, surety.
Certain employees, §33-1-6.
Secretary-treasurer,
§33-1-7.
Buildings.
Relocation of buildings by
department, §33-1-20.
Charges.
Use of state facilities,
§33-1-26.
Conduct of operation of
harbors, ports, facilities
by department, §33-1-24.
Created, §33-1-2.

HARBORS AND PORTS
—Cont'd
Docks department—Cont'd
Dangerous vessels.
  Failure to remove upon
    order of department,
    §33-1-33.
Director of state docks,
  §33-1-3.
Eminent domain.
  Limitation on power,
    §33-1-12.
Employees.
  Bonds required, §33-1-6.
  Generally, §33-1-5.
  Life and health insurance
    for certain salaried
    officers and employees,
    §33-1-5.2.
  Retirement plans,
    §33-1-5.1.
Exercise and evidence of
  authority of department,
  §33-1-27.
Fees and charges.
  Fixing and determining by
    department, §33-3-3.
Functions, §33-1-2.
Funds.
  Authority to expend funds,
    §33-1-1.
Harbor lines.
  Establishment by
    department, §33-1-28.
Harbor masters, §§33-3-1 to
  33-3-6. See within this
  heading, "Masters."
Insurance.
  Authority to carry fire and
    casualty and public
    liability insurance,
    §33-1-25.
Jurisdiction, §33-1-11.
Officers.
  Generally, §33-1-5.
Orders.
  Dangerous vessels.
    Failure to remove upon
      order of department,
      §33-1-33.
Plans.
  Amendment of plans,
    §33-1-15.
Police and supervisory duties
  of department, §33-3-1.
Port authorities, §§11-94-1 to
  11-94-24. See within this
  heading, "Port
  authorities."
Protection of ship while in
  harbor, §33-3-1.
Real property.
  Exchange of property and
    relocation of buildings
    by department,
    §33-1-20.
Rules and regulations.
  Adoption of rules for
    regulating, controlling
    and conducting
    operation of harbors,
    §33-1-24.
  Enforcement by harbor
    masters, §33-3-4.
  Penalties for violation of
    regulations, §33-1-31.
  Promulgation of
    regulations by
    department, §33-1-31.

HARBORS AND PORTS
—Cont'd
Docks department—Cont'd
Secretary-treasurer.
  Appointment by director of
    state docks, §33-1-5.
  Functions, §33-1-7.
State may engage in
  promoting, constructing
  and operating harbors
  and ports through
  department, §33-1-1.
Tombigbee valley
  development authority.
  River and canal terminals.
    Authority of department
      to provide and
      maintain, §33-17-11.
United States.
  Authority of department to
    contract with federal
    government for
    purpose of receiving
    funds, supplies and
    facilities, §33-1-36.
Eminent domain.
Acquisition of property and
  rights of way by
  purchase or eminent
  domain proceedings,
  §33-1-22.
Limitation on power of
  eminent domain,
  §33-1-12.
Privately-owned facilities.
  Limitation on power of
    eminent domain,
    §33-1-12.
Real property.
  Acquisition by eminent
    domain proceedings,
    §33-1-22.
To what property eminent
  domain applicable,
  §33-1-23.
Engineers.
Acquisition and operation of
  wharves, docks and
  warehouses by state.
  Consultation with
    engineers, §33-1-12.
Director of state docks.
  Appointment of engineers
    by director, §33-1-5.
Fees and charges.
Harbor masters.
  Collection, §33-3-3.
  Power of state docks
    department, §33-3-3.
  Raising and lowering,
    §33-3-3.
Private facilities, §33-1-26.
Schedules of rates.
  Filing with state public
    service commission,
    §33-1-26.
State docks department.
  Harbor masters.
    Power to raise and
      lower, §33-3-3.
  Power to fix charges for
    use of state facilities,
    §33-1-26.
Flags.
Mobile harbor.
  Ships entering or leaving
    harbor to fly flag of
    country of registry,
    §33-1-34.
Foreign trade zones.
Establishment, §33-1-30.

HARBORS AND PORTS
—Cont'd
Funds.
Docks department.
  Authority of department to
    contract with federal
    government for
    purpose of receiving
    funds, §33-1-36.
  Authority to expend funds,
    §33-1-1.
State docks facilities
  contingency trust fund,
  §§33-2-210 to 33-2-213.
State docks facilities reserve
  fund.
  Creation, §33-13-10.
General provisions, §§33-1-1
  to 33-1-36.
Governor.
Advisory committee.
  Ex officio member of
    committee, §33-1-8.
Appraisal of real property.
  Prerequisite to approval by
    governor, §33-1-14.
Certificates of approval,
  §33-1-27.
Exercise and evidence of
  authority of governor,
  §33-1-27.
Investigations.
  Acquisition of facilities by
    state.
    Governor may make
      additional
      investigations,
      §33-1-13.
Plans.
  Submission of certain plans
    to governor, §33-1-12.
Real property.
  Appraisal.
    Prerequisite to approval
      of purchase,
      §33-1-14.
Harbor lines.
Establishment, §33-1-28.
Harbor masters, §§33-3-1 to
  33-3-6. See within this
  heading, "Masters."
Insurance.
Docks department.
  Authority to carry fire and
    casualty and public
    liability insurance,
    §33-1-25.
  Life and health insurance
    for certain salaried
    officers and employees,
    §33-1-5.2.
Investigations.
Acquisition of facilities by
  state.
  Governor may make
    additional
    investigations relative
    to acquisition,
    §33-1-13.
Jackson, municipality of.
Port authority, Const. Ala.,
  amd. 465.
Jurisdiction.
State docks department,
  §33-1-11.
Leases.
Real property, §33-1-17.
Taxation.
  Exemption of leases from
    taxation, §33-1-19.

HARBORS AND PORTS
—Cont'd

Legislature.
Port authority.
Legislative intent,
§33-13-2.

Licenses.
Construction of wharves, etc.,
§33-1-28.
Harbor masters, §33-3-5.
Upland owners.
Revocation or suspension,
§33-1-29.

Marine police, §§33-5-4 to
33-5-6.

Marine resources.
General provisions, §§9-12-1
to 9-12-184.
See MARINE
RESOURCES.

Masters, §§33-3-1 to 33-3-6.
Anchorage, berthage and
moorage.
Powers to regulate,
§33-3-2.
Appointment, §33-3-4.
Boarding vessels, §33-3-5.
Bond.
Required, §33-3-5.
Deputies.
Additional deputies,
§33-3-5.
Appointment, §33-3-4.
Bond, §33-3-5.
Duties.
Generally, §33-3-4.
Person other than deputy
performing duties,
§33-3-6.
Probation period, §33-3-5.
Qualifications, §33-3-5.
Records, §33-3-5.
Vacancies.
Filling, §33-3-5.
Duties.
Generally, §33-3-4.
Examinations.
Written examination as to
qualifications, §33-3-5.
Fees and charges, §33-3-3.
Licenses.
Federal pilot license for
Mobile Bay required,
§33-3-5.
State pilot license required,
§33-3-5.
Persons other than harbor
master or deputy
performing duties,
§33-3-6.
Probation period, §33-3-5.
Qualifications, §33-3-5.
Persons other than
qualified master or
deputy performing
duties, §33-3-6.
Records, §33-3-5.
Removal, §33-3-5.
Rules and regulations.
Enforcement, §33-3-4.
State pilotage commission.
Jurisdiction over harbor
masters, §33-4-10.
Vacancies.
Filling by director, §33-3-5.

Mobile harbor.
Bonds for Theodore ship
channel project, Const.
Ala., amd. 286.

HARBORS AND PORTS
—Cont'd

Mobile harbor—Cont'd
Channels.
Injuring ship channels,
§33-7-11.
Obstructing channel in
bay, §33-7-10.
Development of docks and
other facilities along
inland waterways,
§§33-2-1 to 33-2-196.
See WATERS AND
WATERCOURSES.
Docks department.
Police and supervisory
duties, §33-3-1.
Fastening vessels, rafts, etc.,
§33-7-10.
Flags.
Ships entering or leaving
port of Mobile to fly
flag of country of
registry, §33-1-34.
Injuring ship channel, beacon
light, etc., §33-7-11.
Masters.
Vessels drawing more than
12 feet.
Passing channel without
permit, §33-7-12.
Obstructing channel in
Mobile bay, §33-7-10.
Permits.
Vessels drawing more than
12 feet passing
channel without
permit, §33-7-12.
Ships entering or leaving
port.
Flag of country of registry
to be flown, §33-1-34.
State docks facilities.
Development,
improvement, etc.,
Const. Ala., amd. 338.
Trees and timber.
Fastening collection of
logs, lumber or timber
to beacon lights or
pilings, §33-7-10.
Vessels drawing more than
12 feet.
Passing channel without
permit, §33-7-12.

Municipal corporations.
Alteration of channel of
watercourse, §11-47-15.
Bond issues.
Public improvement bonds,
§§11-81-110 to
11-81-123.
See MUNICIPAL
CORPORATIONS.
Channel of watercourse.
Alteration of channel,
§11-47-15.
Construction, maintenance,
etc., of wharves and
buildings, §11-47-15.
Construction of port facilities
by class I municipalities,
§11-47-14.1.
Improvement of waterfronts,
§11-47-14.
Provision of wharves and
landings, §11-47-14.

Navigation.
General provisions, §§33-1-1
to 33-17-15.
See NAVIGATION.

HARBORS AND PORTS
—Cont'd

Notice.
Docks.
State docks facilities
contingency trust fund.
Director of department to
give notice of
expected deficiency,
§33-2-211.

Operation.
Conduct of operation of
harbors, ports, facilities,
etc., by department,
§33-1-24.
Rules and regulations of
department.
Adoption, §33-1-24.
State may engage in
operation, §33-1-1.

Oysters.
Ports of entry, §9-12-28.

Penalties.
Rules and regulations of
department.
Penalties for violation of
regulations, §33-1-31.

Piers.
Docks, §§33-2-180 to
33-2-196. See within this
heading, "Docks."
Wharves. See within this
heading, "Wharves."

Pilots and pilotage, §§33-4-1
to 33-4-57.
See PILOTS AND
PILOTAGE.

Plans.
Amendment of plans,
§33-1-15.
Submission of certain plans
to governor, §33-1-12.

Police.
Marine police, §§33-5-4 to
33-5-6.
State docks department.
Police duties of state docks
department, §33-3-1.

Port authorities, §§11-94-1 to
11-94-25.
Actions by authorizing
subdivisions to attain
objectives of chapter,
§11-94-15.
Agreements of authority,
§11-94-15.
Alabama port authority,
§§33-13-1 to 33-13-13.
Actions.
Power to sue and be
sued, §33-13-7.
Bond issues.
Execution, §33-13-9.
Exemption from
taxation, §33-13-10.
Interest, §33-13-13.
Investment of proceeds,
§33-13-9.
Maximum amount,
§33-13-9.
Power to issue, §33-13-7.
Principal, §33-13-13.
Proceeds, §33-13-12.
Purpose, §33-13-9.
Refunding bonds,
§33-13-11.
Sale, §33-13-9.
Terms and conditions,
§33-13-9.
Definitions, §33-13-1.

HARBORS AND PORTS
—Cont'd
Port authorities—Cont'd
Alabama port authority
—Cont'd
Director of docks
department.
Member, §33-13-6.
Fees.
No fees to be paid to
secretary of state,
§33-13-5.
Fiscal year, §33-13-8.
Funds.
State docks facilities
reserve fund.
Creation, §33-13-10.
Governor.
Member, §33-13-6.
Public corporation,
§33-13-3.
Incorporation.
Authorization to form
public corporation,
§33-13-3.
Certificate of
incorporation.
Issuance by secretary
of state, §33-13-5.
Procedure, §33-13-4.
Investments.
Bond issues.
Proceeds, §33-13-12.
Legislative intent,
§33-13-2.
Meetings, §33-13-6.
Members, §33-13-6.
Compensation, §33-13-6.
Powers, §33-13-7.
Public corporation.
Authorization to form,
§33-13-3.
Recommendations,
§33-13-8.
Records.
Proceedings, §33-13-6.
Refunding bonds,
§33-13-11.
Reports.
Submission of report to
legislature, §33-13-8.
Seal.
Corporate seal, §33-13-7.
Secretary of state.
Application for
incorporation,
§33-13-4.
Certificate of
incorporation.
Issuance, §33-13-5.
Fees.
No fees to be paid to
secretary,
§33-13-5.
Speaker of the house.
Public corporation.
Appointment of one
member, §33-13-3.
State docks department.
Director.
Public corporation,
§33-13-3.
Treasurer, §33-13-6.
State docks facilities.
Defined, §33-13-1.
Studies and analyses.
Power to make, §33-13-7.

HARBORS AND PORTS
—Cont'd
Port authorities—Cont'd
Alabama port authority
—Cont'd
Taxation.
Bond issues.
Exemption from
taxation,
§33-13-10.
Treasurer.
Director of state docks
department,
§33-13-6.
Applicability of article 5 of
chapter 6 of title 8,
§11-94-22.
Application for incorporation,
§11-94-3.
Approval by local
governing bodies and
state docks
department, §11-94-3.
Board of directors.
Election, §11-94-7.
Expenses, §11-94-7.
Impeachment, §11-94-7.
Proceedings, §11-94-7.
Qualifications, §11-94-7.
Quorum, §11-94-7.
Report.
Annual report, §11-94-7.
Terms of office, §11-94-7.
Vacancies, §11-94-7.
Bond issues.
Alabama port authority,
§§11-13-9 to 11-13-13.
Denomination, §11-94-10.
Execution, §11-94-11.
Form, §11-94-10.
Indenture, §11-94-12.
Legal investments,
§11-94-17.
Liability of authorizing
subdivisions,
§11-94-15.
Lien, §11-94-12.
Negotiability, §11-94-10.
Proceeds.
Application of, §11-94-13.
Redemption, §11-94-10.
Refunding bonds,
§11-94-14.
Remedies of bondholders,
§11-94-12.
Revenues to be used for
paying bonds of
authorities, §11-94-25.
Sale, §11-94-10.
Source payable from,
§11-94-10.
Subsequent issues,
§11-94-10.
Terms, §11-94-10.
Certificate of incorporation,
§§11-94-4 to 11-94-6.
Acknowledgment, §11-94-4.
Amendments.
Procedure, §11-94-6.
Approval by probate judge,
§11-94-5.
Contents, §11-94-4.
Examination by probate
judge, §11-94-5.
Execution, §11-94-4.
Filing with probate judge,
§11-94-5.
Recordation, §11-94-5.
Amendment as
conclusive evidence,
§11-94-6.

HARBORS AND PORTS
—Cont'd
Port authorities—Cont'd
Certificate of incorporation
—Cont'd
Recordation—Cont'd
Conclusive evidence as,
§11-94-5.
Construction of chapter,
§11-94-21.
Correction of errors or
omissions in
incorporation, §11-94-23.
Director of finance.
Member, §33-13-6.
Public corporation,
§33-13-3.
Dissolution, §11-94-18.
Vesting of title to funds
and property of
authority, §11-94-18.
Docks department.
Application for
incorporation of
authority.
Approval by department,
§11-94-3.
Exemptions.
Fees, §11-94-19.
Taxation, §11-94-19.
Usury and interest laws,
§11-94-20.
Fees.
Exemption, §11-94-19.
Incorporation of authority.
Application, §11-94-3.
Certificate, §11-94-4.
Acknowledgment,
§11-94-4.
Amendments, §11-94-6.
Contents, §11-94-4.
Examination by probate
judge, §11-94-5.
Execution, §11-94-4.
Filing with probate
judge, §11-94-5.
Recordation, §11-94-5.
Amendment as
conclusive
evidence, §11-94-6.
Conclusive evidence
as, §11-94-5.
Correction of errors or
omissions, §11-94-23.
Invalid incorporations,
§11-94-24.
Validation of incorporation
of certain authorities,
§11-94-24.
Investments.
Bonds of authority as legal
investments,
§11-94-17.
Legislative intent, §11-94-2.
Liberal construction of
chapter, §11-94-2.
Location of projects, §11-94-9.
Net earnings.
Disposition of, §11-94-16.
Obligations of authority,
§11-94-15.
Officers of authority,
§11-94-8.
Powers, §11-48-9.
Projects.
Location of, §11-94-9.
Refunding bonds, §11-94-14.
Revenues.
Used for paying bonds of
authorities, §11-94-25.

HARBORS AND PORTS
—Cont'd
Port authorities—Cont'd
Taxation.
Exemption, §11-94-19.
Usury and interest laws.
Exemption, §11-94-20.
Ports of entry.
Oysters, §9-12-28.
Shrimp, §9-12-28.
Privately-owned facilities.
Charges.
Use of private facilities,
§33-1-26.
Eminent domain.
Limitation on power,
§33-1-12.
To what property eminent
domain applicable,
§33-1-23.
Projects.
Displaced persons.
Payment of relocation
expenses, §33-1-36.
Real property.
Appraisal of real property
prerequisite to
approval by governor,
§33-1-14.
Regulation and promotion of
projects, §33-1-36.
Promotion.
State may promote harbors
and ports, §33-1-1.
Railroads.
Acquisition of property and
rights of way necessary
by purchase or eminent
domain, §33-1-22.
Terminal railroads.
State may acquire, operate,
etc., §33-1-16.
Real property.
Appraisal of real estate,
§33-1-14.
Eminent domain.
Acquisition by eminent
domain proceedings,
§33-1-22.
Exchange of property by
department, §33-1-20.
Insurance.
Authority of department to
carry insurance,
§33-1-25.
Leases.
Exemptions from taxation,
§33-1-19.
Generally, §33-1-17.
Sales.
Generally, §33-1-17.
Submerged lands and lands
lying under or
abutting tidal waters,
§33-1-18.
Title to property acquired
under chapter vests in
state, §33-1-17.
Records.
Advisory committee, §33-1-9.
Harbor masters, §33-3-5.
Retirement.
Docks department.
Retirement plans for
employees of state
docks department,
§33-1-5.1.
Rights of way.
Acquisition by purchase or
eminent domain
proceedings, §33-1-22.

HARBORS AND PORTS
—Cont'd
Riparian owners, §§33-7-50 to
33-7-54.
Rules and regulations.
State docks department.
Adoption of rules for
regulating, controlling
and conducting
operation of harbors,
§33-1-24.
Enforcement by harbor
masters, §33-3-4.
Promulgation, §33-1-31.
Safety.
State docks department.
Powers as to safety,
§§33-3-1, 33-3-2.
Sales.
Real property, §33-1-17.
Submerged lands and lands
lying under or abutting
tidal waters, §33-1-18.
**Secretary-treasurer of docks
department.**
Appointment by director of
state docks, §33-1-5.
Functions, §33-1-7.
Shrimp.
Ports of entry, §9-12-28.
State.
Acquisition of facilities by
state, §§33-1-12, 33-1-13.
Actions.
Department may prosecute
necessary actions to
enforce rights of state,
§33-1-21.
Enforcement of rights of
state.
Docks department to
prosecute necessary
actions, §33-1-21.
Promoting, constructing and
operating harbors and
ports.
State may engage in,
§33-1-1.
State docks department,
§§33-1-1 to 33-1-36. See
within this heading,
"Docks department."
**State docks facilities
contingency trust fund,**
§§33-2-210 to 33-2-213.
State docks facilities,
§§33-2-180 to 33-2-196. See
within this heading,
"Docks."
State treasurer.
Alabama port authority.
Bond issues.
State treasurer to pay
principal and
interest of bonds,
§33-13-13.
Submerged lands.
Sale, §33-1-18.
Taxation.
Leases.
Exemption from taxation,
§33-1-19.
Subjects of taxation,
§40-11-1.
Terminals.
Ameraport.
Deep draft harbor and
terminal contract,
§§33-9-1, 33-9-2.

HARBORS AND PORTS
—Cont'd
Terminals—Cont'd
Ameraport—Cont'd
Offshore harbor and
terminal commission,
§§33-10-1 to 33-10-26.
See AMERAPORT.
Tidal waters.
Lands lying under or
abutting tidal waters.
Sales, §33-1-18.
Trade and commerce.
Foreign trade zones.
Establishment, §33-1-30.
**Transportation companies
generally.**
See TRANSPORTATION
COMPANIES.
Trees and timber.
Mobile harbor.
Fastening collection of
logs, lumber or timber
to beacon lights or
pilings, §33-7-10.
United States.
Foreign trade zones.
Establishment, §33-1-30.
State docks department.
Authority to contract with
federal government for
purpose of receiving
funds, supplies and
facilities, §33-1-36.
Upland owners.
Licenses.
Revocation or suspension,
§33-1-29.
Warehouses.
Acquisition of necessary
property and rights of
way by purchase or
eminent domain,
§33-1-22.
Power of state to acquire and
operate, §33-1-12.
Waterbottoms.
Ameraport offshore harbor
and terminal
commission.
See AMERAPORT.
Waters and watercourses.
General provisions, §§33-1-1
to 33-17-15.
See WATERS AND
WATERCOURSES.
State docks department.
Jurisdiction of department,
§33-1-11.
Wharves.
Acquisition of necessary
property by purchase or
eminent domain
proceedings, §33-1-22.
Bond issues.
County public
improvement bonds,
§§11-81-110 to
11-81-123.
See COUNTIES.
Municipal public
improvement bonds,
§§11-81-110 to
11-81-123.
See MUNICIPAL
CORPORATIONS.
Constitution of Alabama.
Taxes, tolls, etc., for use,
Const. Ala., art. I, §24.

HARBORS AND PORTS
—Cont'd
Wharves—Cont'd
Eminent domain.
Power in internal
improvement
corporations, §10-5-1.
Licenses for construction,
§33-1-28.
Liens on watercraft for
wharfage, §35-11-60.
Municipal corporations.
Bond issues.
Construction of port
facilities by class 1
municipalities,
§11-47-14.1.
Operation of wharves,
§11-47-15.
Power of state to acquire and
operate, §33-1-12.

HARD LABOR.
**Imposition of additional
hard labor to pay costs,**
§15-18-63.
**Permissible legal
punishments,** §15-81-1.

HARMLESS ERROR.
Appeals.
Error without injury, ARAP,
Rule 45.
Rules of civil procedure,
ARCP, Rule 61.

**HARTSELLE,
MUNICIPALITY OF.**
Economic development.
Promotion of industrial,
commercial and
agricultural
development, Const.
Ala., amd. 303.
School taxes, Const. Ala.,
amd. 456.

HASHISH.
Controlled substances,
§§20-2-1 to 20-2-144.
See DRUGS.

HATCHERIES.
Poultry, §§2-16-1 to 2-16-9.
See POULTRY.

HAY.
Attachment.
Liens of owners of baling
machines or presses,
§35-11-291.
Garnishment.
Liens of owners of baling
machines or presses.
Enforcement of lien,
§35-11-291.
Liens.
Owners of hay baling
machines or presses,
§§35-11-290, 35-11-291.
Liens generally.
See LIENS.
Motor vehicles.
Loads which must be
fastened by cables or
chains, §32-5-75.
Presses.
Liens of owners, §§35-11-290,
35-11-291.
Sales.
Liens of owners of baling
machines or presses.
Sale to enforce lien,
§35-11-291.

**HAZARDOUS LIQUID
PIPELINE FACILITIES,**
§§37-4-90 to 37-4-97.
See PIPELINES.

HAZARDOUS SUBSTANCES.
Actions.
Cleanup fund.
Actions for costs of
cleanup, §§22-30A-5,
22-30A-8.
Fees for disposal of
hazardous waste or
substances.
Time limitations under
chapter, §22-30B-14.
Appropriations.
Cleanup fund, §22-30A-3.
Cleanup fund, §§22-30A-1 to
22-30A-11.
Actions.
Orders to implement
cleanup plans.
Recovery of expenses,
§22-30A-5.
Recovery of expenses for
cleanup of hazardous
substance sites,
§22-30A-8.
Appeals.
Orders to implement
cleanup plans,
§20-30A-5.
Appropriations, §22-30A-3.
Attorney general.
Actions for recovery of
expenses for cleanup,
§22-30A-8.
Cleanup.
Defined, §22-30A-2.
Contracts.
Powers of department of
environmental
management,
§22-30A-4.
Costs of cleanup.
Liability, §22-30A-8.
Definitions, §22-30A-2.
Department of environmental
management.
Actions for recovery of
expenses for cleanup,
§22-30A-8.
Definition of "department,"
§22-30A-2.
Director.
Defined, §22-30A-2.
Identification of inactive
or abandoned
hazardous substance
sites, §22-30A-5.
Liable parties.
Identification,
§22-30A-5.
Reports.
Annual report,
§22-30A-7.
Right to enter property,
§22-30A-10.
Scope of cleanup plan.
Factors considered,
§22-30A-6.
Immunity.
Liability for actions
taken or omitted
under chapter,
§22-30A-9.
Liability for actions taken
or omitted under
chapter, §22-30A-9.
Powers, §22-30A-4.

HAZARDOUS SUBSTANCES
—Cont'd
Cleanup fund—Cont'd
Environmental management
commission.
Commission defined,
§22-30A-2.
Established, §22-30A-3.
Immunity.
Liability for actions taken
or omitted under
chapter, §22-30A-9.
Intent of chapter, §22-30A-1.
Legislative findings,
§22-30A-1.
Liability for actions taken or
omitted under chapter,
§22-30A-9.
Liability for hazardous
substance sites,
§22-30A-8.
Notice.
Identification of inactive or
abandoned sites.
Notice to liable parties
to develop cleanup
plans, §22-30A-5.
Operators.
Defined, §22-30A-2.
Orders to implement cleanup
plans, §22-30A-5.
Parties.
Liable parties.
Annual reports
transmitted to,
§22-30A-7.
Defined, §22-30A-2.
Identification, §22-30A-5.
Liability for hazardous
substance sites,
§22-30A-8.
Orders to implement
cleanup plans,
§22-30A-5.
Penalties.
Orders to implement
cleanup plans.
Failure to comply with
provisions of orders,
§22-30A-5.
Violations of chapter.
Civil penalties,
§22-30A-11.
Purposes of chapter,
§22-30A-1.
Releases.
Defined, §22-30A-2.
Reports.
Annual report, §22-30A-7.
Right to enter property,
§22-30A-10.
Scope of cleanup plan.
Factors considered,
§22-30A-6.
Sites.
Defined, §22-30A-2.
Inactive or abandoned
hazardous substance
sites.
Defined, §22-30A-2.
Identification, §22-30A-5.
Liability for hazardous
sites, §22-30A-8.
Uses of fund, §22-30A-4.
Violations of chapter,
§22-30A-11.
Civil penalties,
§22-30A-11.

HAZARDOUS SUBSTANCES
—Cont'd
Confidentiality of
information.
Fees for disposal of
hazardous waste or
substances.
Confidentiality of fee
reports, §22-30B-15.
Construction and
interpretation.
Fees for disposal of
hazardous waste or
substances, §22-30B-18.
Contracts.
Cleanup fund.
Department of
environmental
management.
Powers, §22-30A-4.
Costs.
Cleanup fund.
Liability for hazardous
substance sites,
§22-30A-8.
Counties.
Fees for disposal of
hazardous waste or
substances.
Additional fees collected by
counties, §22-30B-4.
Cooperation by
commissioner of
revenue with county
officials, §22-30B-17.
Criminal law and procedure.
Fees for disposal of
hazardous waste or
substances.
Violations of chapter.
Institution of
prosecution,
§22-30B-12.
Definitions.
Cleanup fund, §22-30A-2.
Fees for disposal of
hazardous waste or
substances, §22-30B-1.
Department of
environmental
management.
Cleanup fund, §§22-30A-1 to
22-30A-11. See within
this heading, "Cleanup
fund."
Deposits.
Fees for disposal of
hazardous waste or
substances.
Fees paid by operators,
§22-30B-3.
Disposal.
Fees for disposal of
hazardous waste or
substances.
General provisions,
§§22-30B-1 to
22-30B-18.
See HAZARDOUS
WASTE.
Environmental management
commission.
Cleanup fund.
Commission defined,
§22-30A-2.

HAZARDOUS SUBSTANCES
—Cont'd
Fees for disposal of
hazardous waste or
substances.
General provisions,
§§22-30B-1 to 22-30B-18.
See HAZARDOUS
WASTE.
Fraud.
Fees for disposal of
hazardous waste or
substances.
False or fraudulent reports.
Penalties, §22-30B-7.
Perjury in making,
§22-30B-10.
Records of hazardous
substances received for
disposal.
False or fraudulent
statements.
Class C misdemeanor,
§22-30B-11.
Immunity.
Cleanup fund.
Liability for actions taken
or omitted under
chapter, §22-30A-9.
Injunctions.
Fees for disposal of
hazardous waste or
substances.
Violations of chapter.
Restraint from
continuing in
business,
§22-30B-12.
Interest.
Fees for disposal of
hazardous waste or
substances.
Time for payment of fees.
Failure to pay within
time required,
§22-30B-5.
Liens.
Fees for disposal of
hazardous waste or
substances.
Lien upon property of
operators, §22-30B-9.
Limitation of actions.
Fees for disposal of
hazardous waste or
substances.
Time limits for actions
under chapter,
§22-30B-14.
Misdemeanors.
Fees for disposal of
hazardous waste or
substances.
Assistants or agents of
department of revenue.
Refusal to perform
duties, §22-30B-15.
Confidentiality of fee
reports.
Violation of section,
§22-30B-15.
Records of hazardous
substances received for
disposal.
Violations of section.
Class C misdemeanor,
§22-30B-11.

HAZARDOUS SUBSTANCES
—Cont'd
Notice.
Cleanup fund.
Orders to implement
cleanup plans.
Notice to liable parties,
§22-30A-5.
Fees for disposal of
hazardous waste or
substances.
Monthly reports.
Notice of failure to
make, §22-30B-8.
Oaths.
Fees for disposal of
hazardous waste or
substances.
Monthly reports to be
sworn, §22-30B-10.
Penalties.
Cleanup fund.
Orders to implement
cleanup plans.
Failure to comply,
§22-30A-5.
Violations of chapter.
Civil penalties,
§22-30A-11.
Fees for disposal of
hazardous waste or
substances.
Failure to make monthly
reports, §22-30B-6.
Waiver of penalties for
good cause,
§22-30B-8.
False or fraudulent reports,
§22-30B-7.
Time for payment of fees.
Failure to pay within
time required,
§22-30B-5.
Perjury.
Fees for disposal of
hazardous waste or
substances.
Monthly reports to be
sworn.
Perjury in making
reports, §22-30B-10.
Privileges.
Fees for disposal of
hazardous waste or
substances.
Confidentiality of fee
reports, §22-30B-15.
Records.
Fees for disposal of
hazardous waste or
substances.
Location of records,
§22-30B-16.
Records of hazardous
substances received for
disposal, §22-30B-11.
Reports.
Cleanup fund.
Annual reports, §22-30A-7.
Fees for disposal of
hazardous waste or
substances.
Confidentiality,
§22-30B-15.
Failure to make monthly
reports.
Notice of failure,
§22-30B-8.
Penalty, §22-30B-6.
False or fraudulent reports.
Penalties, §22-30B-7.

HAZARDOUS SUBSTANCES
—Cont'd
Reports—Cont'd
Fees for disposal of
hazardous waste or
substances—Cont'd
Location of reports,
§22-30B-16.
Oaths, §22-30B-10.
Right of entry.
Cleanup fund.
Department of
environmental
management.
Director, §22-30A-10.
Rules and regulations.
Fees for disposal of
hazardous waste or
substances.
Adoption, §22-30B-17.
**Southeast interstate low-
level radioactive waste
management compact.**
Fees for disposal of
hazardous waste or
substances.
Effect of chapter on
compact, §22-30B-18.

HAZARDOUS WASTE,
§§22-30-1 to 22-30-24.
Actions.
Fees for disposal of
hazardous waste or
substances.
Time limit for actions
under chapter,
§22-30B-14.
Administration of chapter,
§22-30-20.
Environmental management
department.
Powers and duties towards
administering chapter,
§22-30-20.
**Capacity assurance
programs.**
Contracting with states other
than Alabama in order
to satisfy, §22-30-11.
Chapter supplemental,
§22-30-24.
**Commercial treatment
facilities or disposal
sites.**
Defined, §22-30-11.
Fees for disposal of
hazardous waste or
substances.
Commercial sites for
disposal of hazardous
waste or hazardous
substances. See within
this heading, "Fees for
disposal of hazardous
waste or hazardous
substances."
Legislative approval,
§22-30-5.1.
Construction of provisions,
§22-30-5.2.
Monitoring, §22-30-4.
Operators.
Defined, §22-30-11.
Commission.
Defined, §22-30-3.

HAZARDOUS WASTE—Cont'd
**Confidentiality of
information.**
Fees for disposal of
hazardous waste or
substances.
Confidentiality of fee
reports, §22-30B-15.
**Construction and
interpretation.**
Fees for disposal of
hazardous waste or
substances, §22-30B-18.
Counties.
Commercial treatment
facilities or disposal
sites.
Restriction on number per
county, §22-30-5.1.
Construction of
provisions,
§22-30-5.2.
Fees for disposal of
hazardous waste or
substances.
Additional fees collected by
counties, §22-30B-4.
Cooperation of
commissioner of
revenue with county
officials, §22-30B-17.
Criminal law and procedure.
Fees for disposal of
hazardous waste or
substances.
Violations of chapter.
Institution of
prosecution,
§22-30B-12.
**Criteria for determining
hazardous waste.**
Adoption.
Environmental
management
department, §22-30-11.
Development and revision.
Environmental
management
department, §22-30-10.
Definitions, §§6-5-332.1,
22-30-3, 22-30-11.
Fees for disposal of
hazardous waste or
substances, §22-30B-1.
Deposits.
Fees for disposal of
hazardous waste or
substances.
Fees paid by operators,
§22-30B-3.
Director.
Defined, §22-30-3.
Discharge.
Defined, §6-5-332.1.
Mitigation of effects.
Immunity of persons
assisting or advising
as to, §6-5-332.1.
Disposal.
Defined, §22-30-3.
Fees for disposal of
hazardous waste or
substances.
Generally, §§22-30B-1 to
22-30B-18. See within
this heading, "Fees for
disposal of hazardous
waste or substances."
General provisions. See
within this heading,
"Storage and disposal."

HAZARDOUS WASTE—Cont'd
Disposal—Cont'd
Site.
Defined, §22-30-3.
Waste generated in state
outside of state of
Alabama, §22-30-11.
**Environmental management
department.**
Administration of chapter.
Powers and duties towards
administering chapter,
§22-30-20.
Criteria for determining
hazardous waste.
Adoption, §22-30-11.
Development and revision,
§22-30-10.
Defined, §22-30-3.
General responsibilities,
§22-30-9.
Generators.
Powers and duties of
department as to,
§22-30-14.
Guidelines, criteria and
standards.
Adoption, §22-30-11.
Inspections.
Enforcement of provisions,
§22-30-19.
Investigative authority,
§22-30-4.
Manifest.
Development and
promulgation,
§22-30-17.
Permit program.
Powers and duties as to,
§22-30-12.
Regulatory authority,
§22-30-4.
Responsibilities.
General responsibilities,
§22-30-9.
Right of entry, §22-30-19.
Rules and regulations.
Adoption, §22-30-11.
Generally, §22-30-9.
Storage and disposal sites.
Operators.
Powers and duties of
department as to,
§22-30-16.
Regulation and
supervision, §22-30-6.
Transporters.
Powers and duties of
department as to,
§22-30-15.
Treatment facilities.
Operators.
Powers and duties of
department as to,
§22-30-16.
Violations.
Orders requiring
compliance, §22-30-19.
**Exemptions from
applicability of chapter,**
§22-30-21.
**Fees for disposal of
hazardous waste or
substances,** §§22-30B-1 to
22-30B-18.
Actions.
Time limit for actions
under chapter,
§22-30B-14.

HAZARDOUS WASTE—Cont'd
Fees for disposal of hazardous waste or substances—Cont'd
Additional fees collected by counties, §22-30B-4.
Cooperation with county officials, §22-30B-17.
Commercial sites for disposal of hazardous waste or hazardous substances.
Defined, §22-30B-1.
Fees paid by operators, §22-30B-2.
    Additional fees collected by counties, §22-30B-4.
    Deposit, §22-30B-3.
    Liens upon property of operators, §22-30B-9.
    Refund of overpayment of fees, §22-30B-13.
    Time for payment of fees, §22-30B-5.
Records of hazardous waste or substances received for disposal, §22-30B-11.
Reports.
    Confidentiality of fee reports, §22-30B-15.
    Failure to make monthly reports.
        Notice, §22-30B-8.
        Penalty, §22-30B-6.
    False or fraudulent reports.
        Penalties, §22-30B-7.
    Monthly reports to be sworn, §22-30B-10.
    Perjury in making false or fraudulent statements, §22-30B-10.
    Violations of chapter.
        Institution of prosecution, §22-30B-12.
        Restraint from continuing in business, §22-30B-12.
Confidentiality of fee reports, §22-30B-15.
Construction of chapter, §22-30B-18.
Counties.
    Additional fees collected by, §22-30B-4.
    Cooperation with county officials, §22-30B-17.
Criminal law and procedure.
    Violations of chapter.
        Institution of prosecution, §22-30B-12.
Definitions, §22-30B-1.
Department of revenue.
    Assistants or agents.
        Misdemeanor for refusal to perform duties, §22-30B-15.
Deposit of fees paid by operators, §22-30B-3.
Disposal.
    Defined, §22-30B-1.

HAZARDOUS WASTE—Cont'd
Fees for disposal of hazardous waste or substances—Cont'd
Fraud.
    Records of hazardous waste or substances received for disposal.
        False or fraudulent statements.
            Class C misdemeanor, §22-30B-11.
    Reports.
        Penalties, §22-30B-7.
Hazardous substances.
    Defined, §22-30B-1.
Hazardous waste.
    Defined, §22-30B-1.
Injunctions.
    Violations of chapter.
        Restraint from continuing in business, §22-30B-12.
Interest.
    Time for payment of fees.
        Failure to pay fees within time required, §22-30B-5.
Liens upon property of operators, §22-30B-9.
Limitation of actions.
    Time limit for actions under chapter, §22-30B-14.
Misdemeanors.
    Assistants or agents of department of revenue.
        Refusal to perform duties, §22-30B-15.
    Confidentiality of fee reports.
        Violation of section, §22-30B-15.
Notice of failure to make monthly reports, §22-30B-8.
Oaths.
    Monthly reports to be sworn, §22-30B-10.
Operators.
    Defined, §22-30B-1.
    Fees paid by operators, §22-30B-2.
        Additional fees collected by counties, §22-30B-4.
        Deposit, §22-30B-3.
        Liens upon property of operators, §22-30B-9.
        Refund of overpayment of fees, §22-30B-13.
        Time for payment of fees, §22-30B-5.
    Records of hazardous waste or substances received for disposal, §22-30B-11.
    Reports.
        Confidentiality of fee reports, §22-30B-15.
        Failure to make monthly reports.
            Notice, §22-30B-8.
            Penalty, §22-30B-6.
        False or fraudulent reports.
            Penalties, §22-30B-7.
        Monthly reports to be sworn, §22-30B-10.

HAZARDOUS WASTE—Cont'd
Fees for disposal of hazardous waste or substances—Cont'd
Operators—Cont'd
    Reports—Cont'd
        Perjury in making false or fraudulent statements, §22-30B-10.
        Violations of chapter.
            Institution of prosecution, §22-30B-12.
            Restraint from continuing in business, §22-30B-12.
    Overpayment of fees.
        Refunds, §22-30B-13.
    Penalties.
        False or fraudulent reports, §22-30B-7.
        Reports.
            Failure to make monthly reports, §22-30B-6.
            Waiver of penalties for good cause, §22-30B-8.
        Time for payment of fees.
            Failure to pay within time required, §22-30B-5.
        Perjury in making false or fraudulent statements in monthly reports, §22-30B-10.
    Records of hazardous waste or substances received for disposal, §22-30B-11.
        Location of records, §22-30B-16.
        Maintenance, §22-30B-11.
    Misdemeanors.
        False or fraudulent statements.
            Class C misdemeanor, §22-30B-11.
    Refunds for overpayment of fees, §22-30B-13.
    Reports.
        Confidentiality of fee reports, §22-30B-15.
        Failure to make monthly reports.
            Notice, §22-30B-8.
            Penalties, §22-30B-6.
            Remission for good cause, §22-30B-6.
            Waiver of penalties for good cause, §22-30B-8.
        False or fraudulent reports.
            Penalties, §22-30B-7.
        Location, §22-30B-16.
        Monthly reports to be sworn, §22-30B-10.
        Perjury in making false or fraudulent statements, §22-30B-10.
    Restraint from continuing in business.
        Violations of chapter, §22-30B-12.
    Rules and regulations.
        Promulgation, §22-30B-17.
    Southeast interstate low-level radioactive waste management compact.
        Effect of chapter on, §22-30B-18.

HAZARDOUS WASTE—Cont'd
Fees for disposal of hazardous waste or substances—Cont'd
Time for payment of fees, §22-30B-5.
Tons.
Defined, §22-30B-1.
Violations of chapter, §22-30B-12.
Fraud.
Fees for disposal of hazardous waste or substances.
False or fraudulent reports.
Penalties, §22-30B-7.
Records of hazardous waste received for disposal.
False or fraudulent statements.
Class C misdemeanor, §22-30B-11.
Funds.
Hazardous substance cleanup fund, §§22-30A-1 to 22-30A-11.
See HAZARDOUS SUBSTANCES.
Generation.
State of generation.
Defined, §22-30-11.
Generator.
Defined, §22-30-3.
Environmental management department.
Powers and duties of department as to generators, §22-30-14.
Permits.
Exemption, §22-30-12.
Records, §22-30-18.
Reports, §22-30-18.
Responsibilities, §22-30-14.
Guidelines, criteria and standards.
Environmental management department.
Adoption, §22-30-11.
Hazardous waste generation.
Defined, §22-30-3.
Hazardous waste management.
Defined, §22-30-3.
Hearings.
Environmental management department.
Authority, §22-30-4.
Immunity.
Mitigation of effects of discharge.
Persons assisting or advising as to, §6-5-332.1.
Injunctions.
Fees for disposal of hazardous waste or substances.
Violations of chapter.
Restraint from continuing in business, §22-30B-12.
Inspections.
Environmental management department.
Enforcement of provisions, §22-30-19.
Intent of chapter, §22-30-2.

HAZARDOUS WASTE—Cont'd
Interest.
Fees for disposal of hazardous waste or substances.
Time for payment of fees.
Failure to pay within time required, §22-30B-5.
Investigative authority.
Environmental management department, §22-30-4.
Legislative findings, §22-30-2.
Liens.
Fees for disposal of hazardous waste or substances.
Liens upon property of operators, §22-30B-9.
Limitation of actions.
Fees for disposal of hazardous waste or substances.
Time limit for actions under chapter, §22-30B-14.
Management.
Rules and regulations.
Duty of environmental management department, §22-30-11.
Management and minimization act.
Short title, §22-30-1.
Manifest.
Copy to environmental management department, §22-30-17.
Defined, §22-30-3.
Development and promulgation, §22-30-17.
Technical advisory committee.
Review and recommendations, §22-30-17.
Misdemeanors.
Fees for disposal of hazardous waste or substances.
Assistants or agents of department of revenue.
Refusal to perform duties, §22-30B-15.
Confidentiality of fee reports.
Violation of section, §22-30B-15.
Records of hazardous waste received for disposal.
False or fraudulent statements.
Class C misdemeanor, §22-30B-11.
Mitigation of effects of discharge.
Immunity of persons assisting or advising as to, §6-5-332.1.
Monitoring.
Commercial disposal sites, §22-30-4.
Notice.
Fees for disposal of hazardous waste or substances.
Failure to make monthly reports, §22-30B-8.

HAZARDOUS WASTE—Cont'd
Oaths.
Fees for disposal of hazardous waste or substances.
Monthly reports to be sworn, §22-30B-10.
Ownership.
Transfer, §22-30-12.
Penalties.
Fees for disposal of hazardous waste or substances.
Failure to make monthly reports, §22-30B-6.
Waiver of penalties for good cause, §22-30B-8.
False or fraudulent reports, §22-30B-7.
Time for payment of fees.
Failure to pay within time required, §22-30B-5.
Safety regulations.
Violations of provisions, §22-30-15.1.
Violations, §22-30-19.
Hazardous materials regulations, §22-30-15.1.
Perjury.
Fees for disposal of hazardous waste or substances.
Monthly reports to be sworn.
Perjury in making false or fraudulent statements, §22-30B-10.
Permits.
Applications.
Approval.
Time limits, §22-30-12.
Bond, surety.
Required, §22-30-12.
Disapproval.
Time limit, §22-30-12.
Investigations.
Authority, §22-30-12.
Expenses, §22-30-12.
Notice, §22-30-12.
Required, §22-30-12.
Revocation, §22-30-12.
Storage and disposal sites.
Applications.
Approval.
Time limit, §22-30-12.
Bond, surety.
Required, §22-30-12.
Disapproval.
Time limit, §22-30-12.
Investigations.
Authority, §22-30-12.
Expenses, §22-30-12.
Notice, §22-30-12.
Existing permits.
Continuation, §22-30-12.
Existing sites.
Permit variances, §22-30-12.
Issuance, §22-30-12.
Required, §22-30-12.
Revocation, §22-30-12.
Transportation.
Issuance, §22-30-12.
Previously issued permits.
Continuance, §22-30-12.
Treatment facilities.
Applications, §22-30-12.

HAZARDOUS WASTE—Cont'd
Permits—Cont'd
Treatment facilities—Cont'd
Existing permits.
Continuation, §22-30-12.
Issuance, §22-30-12.
Required, §22-30-12.
Revocation, §22-30-12.
Perpetuity.
Defined, §22-30-3.
Person.
Defined, §22-30-3.
Privileges.
Fees for disposal of
hazardous waste or
substances.
Confidentiality of fee
reports, §22-30B-15.
Purpose of chapter, §22-30-2.
RCRA.
Defined, §22-30-3.
Records.
Fees for disposal of
hazardous waste or
substances.
Records of hazardous waste
or substances received
for disposal,
§22-30B-11.
Location, §22-30B-16.
Generators, §22-30-18.
Regional.
Defined, §22-30-11.
Regulatory authority.
Environmental management
department, §22-30-4.
Reports.
Fees for disposal of
hazardous waste or
substances.
Confidentiality of fee
reports, §22-30B-15.
Failure to make monthly
reports.
Notice, §22-30B-8.
Penalties, §22-30B-6.
Waiver, §22-30B-8.
False or fraudulent reports.
Penalties, §22-30B-7.
Location of reports,
§22-30B-16.
Monthly reports to be
sworn, §22-30B-10.
Perjury in making false or
fraudulent statements,
§22-30B-10.
Generators, §22-30-18.
Trade secrets, §22-30-18.
Transporters, §22-30-18.
Rules and regulations.
Environmental management
department.
Adoption of regulations,
§22-30-11.
Powers and duties of
department.
Generally, §22-30-9.
Fees for disposal of
hazardous waste or
substances.
Adoption, §22-30B-17.
Generators.
Powers and duties of
environmental
management
department, §22-30-14.
Management.
Duties of environmental
management
department, §22-30-11.

HAZARDOUS WASTE—Cont'd
Rules and regulations
—Cont'd
Permit program.
Duties of environmental
management
department, §22-30-12.
Storage and disposal site
operators.
Authority of environmental
management
department as to,
§22-30-16.
Transporters.
Authority of department,
§22-30-15.
Penalty for violation of
safety and hazardous
materials regulations,
§22-30-15.1.
Treatment facility operators.
Powers and duties of
department as to,
§22-30-16.
Short titles, §22-30-1.
Solid waste.
Defined, §22-30-3.
**Southeast interstate low-
level radioactive waste
management compact.**
Fees for disposal of
hazardous waste or
substances.
Effect of chapter on
compact, §22-30B-18.
Storage and disposal.
Defined, §22-30-3.
Fees for disposal of
hazardous waste or
substances.
Generally, §§22-30B-1 to
22-30B-18. See within
this heading, "Fees for
disposal of hazardous
waste or substances."
Sites.
Construction.
Private enterprise and
investment capital.
Use encouraged,
§22-30-12.
Defined, §22-30-3.
Operators.
Responsibilities,
§22-30-16.
Permits, §22-30-12.
Regulation and
supervision.
Environmental
management
department,
§22-30-6.
**Supplemental nature of
chapter,** §22-30-24.
**Technical advisory
committee.**
Defined, §22-30-3.
Manifest.
Review and
recommendations,
§22-30-17.
**Toxic substances in the
workplace,** §§22-33-1 to
22-33-15.
See TOXIC SUBSTANCES
IN THE WORKPLACE.
Trade secrets.
Defined, §22-30-3.

HAZARDOUS WASTE—Cont'd
Trade secrets—Cont'd
Generators.
Reports.
When reports deemed
trade secrets,
§22-30-18.
Inspections by environmental
management
department.
Applicability of provisions,
§22-30-19.
Records.
Generators, §22-30-18.
Transportation.
Certain transporters
exempted from
applicability of chapter,
§22-30-21.
Defined, §22-30-3.
Facility or site which does
not have permit.
Transporting to.
Prohibited, §22-30-19.
Permits, §22-30-12.
Regulations as to
transporters, §22-30-15.
Transporters.
Applicability of chapter,
§22-30-21.
Defined, §22-30-3.
Environmental management
department.
Powers and duties of
department.
Generally, §22-30-15.
Regulations as to
transporters, §22-30-15.
Reports, §22-30-18.
Treatment.
Defined, §22-30-3.
Waste generated in state
outside state of Alabama,
§22-30-11.
Treatment facilities.
Construction.
Private enterprise and
investment capital.
Use encouraged,
§22-30-12.
Defined, §22-30-3.
Existing facilities.
Permit variances,
§22-30-12.
Operators.
Responsibilities, §22-30-16.
Permits, §22-30-12.
Violations.
Environmental management
department.
Orders requiring
compliance, §22-30-19.
Penalties, §22-30-19.
Prohibited acts, §22-30-19.
Wastes.
Defined, §22-30-3.

HAZING.
Prohibited, §16-1-23.

HEALTH.
Administration.
Council on health costs,
administration and
organization, §§22-2-9,
22-2-10.

HEALTH—Cont'd

Aged persons.

Long term quality health care, §§22-6-20 to 22-6-27.

See LONG TERM QUALITY HEALTH CARE.

Medicaid program, §§22-6-1 to 22-6-9. See within this heading, "Medicaid program."

Medical assistance to elderly persons, §§38-6-1 to 38-6-9.

See AGED PERSONS.

Alabama health care plan, §§27-21-1 to 27-21-6.

See INSURANCE.

Animals.

Council on animal and environmental health, §§22-2-9, 22-2-10.

Nuisances menacing public health, §§22-10-1 to 22-10-3.

Appeals.

State health planning and development.

Appeal from rules, regulations, standards, etc., by state board of health, §22-4-5.

Appropriations.

Municipal corporations.

Appropriations by municipalities for public health work, §22-3-11.

Authorities.

Health care authorities, §§22-21-310 to 22-21-356.

See HEALTH CARE AUTHORITIES.

Banks and financial institutions.

Authority and jurisdiction of state board of health, §22-2-2.

Duties of county boards of health, §22-3-2.

Barbers.

Health regulations, §§22-17-1 to 22-17-11.

See BARBERS.

Beauty shops.

Health regulations, §§22-17-1 to 22-17-11.

See COSMETOLOGISTS.

Beverages.

Nuisances menacing public health, §§22-10-1 to 22-10-3.

Bids and bidding.

Medicaid program.

Eyewear.

Procurement of prescription eyewear for recipients, §22-6-7.1.

Billiard rooms.

Compliance with health and sanitation ordinances and regulations, §34-6-5.

Blind persons.

General provisions.

See BLIND PERSONS.

Prevention of infantile blindness, §22-20-2.

HEALTH—Cont'd

Boards of health.

County boards of health, §§22-3-1 to 22-3-3.

State board of health, §§22-2-1 to 22-2-3.

Boats.

Discharge of litter and sewage from watercraft, §§33-6-1 to 33-6-12.

See BOATS.

Bonds, surety.

County health officers, §22-3-7.

State health officer, §22-2-8.

Buildings.

Nuisances menacing public health, §§22-10-1 to 22-10-3.

Cancer, §§22-13-1 to 22-13-13.

See CANCER.

Certificates of need for health facilities, §§22-21-260 to 22-21-276.

See HOSPITALS.

Child abuse or neglect, §§26-14-1 to 26-14-13.

See MINORS.

Child care, §§38-7-1 to 38-7-18.

See WELFARE.

Child support, §§38-10-1 to 38-10-33.

See CHILD SUPPORT PROGRAMS.

Churches.

Authority and jurisdiction of state board of health, §22-2-2.

Duties of county boards of health, §22-3-2.

Committee.

State committee of public health, §§22-2-4 to 22-2-7.

Conflicts of law.

Municipal and general health laws.

Conflicts between municipal and general health laws, §22-1-2.

Consent for health services, §§22-8-1 to 22-8-9.

Alcoholism.

Consent of any minor as to alcohol toxicity, §22-8-6.

Authorized consent deemed cumulative, §22-8-8.

Bone marrow donation, §22-8-9.

Drug dependency.

Consent of any minor as to drug dependency, §22-8-6.

Inability to consent.

Persons physically or mentally unable to consent, §22-8-1.

Liability of physicians, etc., §22-8-7.

Minors.

Alcoholism.

Consent of any minor as to alcohol toxicity, §22-8-6.

Bone marrow donation, §22-8-9.

Consent of minor for self and child, §22-8-5.

HEALTH—Cont'd

Consent for health services —Cont'd

Minors—Cont'd

Effect of minor's consent, §22-8-7.

Pregnancy.

Consent of any minor as to pregnancy, §22-8-6.

Reportable diseases.

Consent of any minor as to reportable diseases, §22-8-6.

Venereal disease.

Consent of any minor as to venereal disease, §22-8-6.

When minor may give consent, §22-8-4.

When physician may proceed without consent of parent, §22-8-3.

Missing spouse.

When consent of missing spouse not required, §22-8-2.

Parents.

Bone marrow donation, §22-8-9.

When physician may proceed without consent of parent, §22-8-3.

Physicians.

Liability, §22-8-7.

Pregnancy.

Consent of any minor as to pregnancy, §22-8-6.

Venereal disease.

Consent of any minor as to venereal disease, §22-8-6.

Waiver of rights or causes of action, §22-8-7.

Constitution of Alabama.

Counties.

Special tax for hospital and public health purposes in counties except Mobile, Montgomery and Jefferson, Const. Ala., amd. 72.

Public hospitals and health facilities, Const. Ala., amd. 53.

Containers.

Nuisances menacing public health, §§22-10-1 to 22-10-3.

Contracts.

Medicaid program.

Authority to contract with intermediaries for purpose of receiving, processing and paying claims, §22-6-7.

Eyewear.

Procurement of prescription eyewear for recipients, §22-6-7.1.

Control of public health work.

County and state boards of health, §22-1-3.

Coordinating council.

Statewide coordinating council, §§22-4-7, 22-4-8.

HEALTH—Cont'd
  Corporations.
    Health care service plans,
      §§10-4-100 to 10-4-115.
    See HEALTH CARE
      SERVICE PLANS.
  Cosmetologists.
    Health regulations for beauty
      shops, §§22-17-1 to
      22-17-11.
    See COSMETOLOGISTS.
  Costs.
    Council on health costs,
      administration and
      organization, §§22-2-9,
      22-2-10.
    State health department.
      How costs to be paid,
      §22-2-12.
  Council on animal and
    environmental health.
    Appointment of members,
      §22-2-9.
    Chairman, §22-2-10.
    Composition, §22-2-9.
    Creation, §22-2-9.
    Duties, §22-2-9.
    Meetings, §22-2-10.
    Terms of members, §22-2-9.
    Vacancies, §22-2-10.
  Council on dental health.
    Appointment of members,
      §22-2-9.
    Chairman, §22-2-10.
    Composition, §22-2-9.
    Creation, §22-2-9.
    Duties, §22-2-9.
    Meetings, §22-2-10.
    Quorum, §22-2-10.
    Terms of members, §22-2-9.
    Vacancies, §22-2-10.
  Council on health costs,
    administration and
    organization.
    Appointment of members,
      §22-2-9.
    Chairman, §22-2-10.
    Composition, §22-2-9.
    Creation, §22-2-9.
    Duties, §22-2-9.
    Meetings, §22-2-10.
    Quorum, §22-2-10.
    Terms of members, §22-2-9.
    Vacancies, §22-2-10.
  Council on prevention of
    disease and medical
    care, §§22-2-9, 22-2-10.
  Counties.
    Certain county and local
      laws unaffected by title,
      §22-1-9.
    County commissions.
      Powers and duties of
        county commissions,
        §11-3-11.
    Indigent persons.
      Responsibility for health
        care, §§22-21-290 to
        22-21-297. See within
        this heading,
        "Responsibility for
        health care."
    Special tax for hospital and
      public health purposes in
      counties except Mobile,
      Montgomery and
      Jefferson, Const. Ala.,
      amd. 72.

HEALTH—Cont'd
  Counties—Cont'd
    State health department.
      Payment of health
        department claims out
        of county budgets,
        §22-3-12.
  County and district health
    departments.
    Creation of district health
      departments, §22-3-2.
    Home health services,
      §§22-7-1 to 22-7-6. See
      within this heading,
      "Home health services."
    Public officers and
      employees.
      Merit system, §§36-26-80
        to 36-26-83.
    Tax to establish and
      maintain, §22-3-10.
  County boards of health,
    §§22-3-1 to 22-3-3.
    Composition, §22-3-1.
    Control of public health work
      under county and state
      boards of health, §22-1-3.
    Control over county boards.
      State board of health,
        §22-2-2.
      State health officer,
        §22-2-8.
    Duties, §22-3-2.
    Inspections, §22-3-2.
    Money.
      Authority to receive, hold,
        etc., §22-3-3.
    Presiding officer, §22-3-1.
    Real estate.
      Authority to receive, hold,
        etc., §22-3-3.
    State board of health.
      Supervision and control
        over county boards,
        §22-2-2.
    State health officer.
      Supervision and control of
        county boards, §22-2-8.
    Supervision of county boards.
      State board of health,
        §22-2-2.
      State health officer,
        §22-2-8.
  County health officers,
    §§22-3-4 to 22-3-7.
    Absence, §22-3-5.
    Approval by state committee
      of public health, §22-3-2.
    Assistants, §22-3-4.
    Bonds, surety, §22-3-7.
    Control over county officers.
      State board of health,
        §22-2-2.
      State health officer,
        §22-2-8.
    Duties, §22-3-5.
    Education.
      See EDUCATION.
    Election by county boards of
      health, §22-3-2.
    Employees, §22-3-4.
    Expenses.
      Recovery of expenses by
        health officer,
        §22-2-13.
    Inspections, §22-3-5.
    Powers, §22-3-4.
    Records, §22-3-5.
    Removal by state health
      officer, §22-3-2.
    Reports, §22-3-5.

HEALTH—Cont'd
  County health officers
    —Cont'd
    Resisting officers.
      Procedure when county
        health officer resisted,
        §22-1-7.
    Salary, §22-3-6.
    State board of health.
      Supervision and control
        over officers, §22-2-2.
    State committee of public
      health.
      Approval of county health
        officers, §22-3-2.
    State health officer.
      Removal of county health
        officers, §22-3-2.
      Supervision and control of
        county officers,
        §22-2-8.
    Subordinate officers and
      employees.
      Appointment, §22-1-4.
    Supervision of county
      officers.
      State board of health,
        §22-2-2.
      State health officer,
        §22-2-8.
    Tax to establish and
      maintain, §22-3-10.
  Definitions.
    Physical fitness, §22-5-1.
    Responsibility for health
      care, §22-21-292.
    State health department,
      §22-1-1.
    State health planning and
      development, §22-4-2.
  Dental hygienists.
    General provisions, §§34-9-1
      to 34-9-47.
    See DENTISTS.
  Dentists.
    Council on dental health,
      §§22-2-9, 22-2-10.
    General provisions, §§34-9-1
      to 34-9-47.
    See DENTISTS.
    Salary of public health
      dentists, §22-1-5.
  Departments.
    County and district health
      departments.
      Creation of district health
        departments, §22-3-2.
      Home health services,
        §§22-7-1 to 22-7-6. See
        within this heading,
        "Home health
        services."
      Public officers and
        employees.
        Merit system, §§36-26-80
          to 36-26-83.
      Tax to establish and
        maintain, §22-3-10.
    State health department. See
      within this heading,
      "State health
      department."
  Development.
    State health planning and
      development, §§22-4-1 to
      22-4-17. See within this
      heading, "State health
      planning and
      development."

HEALTH—Cont'd
Diseases.
Generally.
See DISEASES.
Notifiable diseases.
General provisions,
§§22-11A-1 to
22-11A-38.
See DISEASES.
Workmen's compensation.
Occupational diseases,
§§25-5-110 to 25-5-123.
See WORKMEN'S
COMPENSATION.
Occupational
pneumoconiosis,
§§25-5-140 to 25-5-152.
See WORKMEN'S
COMPENSATION.
Pneumoconiosis of coal
miners, §§25-5-170 to
25-5-180.
See WORKMEN'S
COMPENSATION.
Dispensaries.
Public dispensaries treating
communicable diseases,
§22-1-6.
District health departments.
Creation, §22-3-2.
Home health services,
§§22-7-1 to 22-7-6. See
within this heading,
"Home health services."
Public officers and
employees.
Merit system, §§36-26-80
to 36-26-83.
Tax to establish and
maintain, §2-3-10.
District health officers,
§22-3-2.
Dogs.
Rabies.
General provisions, §§3-7-1
to 3-7-13.
See RABIES.
Domestic health remedies.
Exemption from provisions
relating to physicians,
§34-24-55.
Drinking cups.
Use of common drinking cups
in public places
prohibited, §22-20-1.
Drugs.
General provisions.
See DRUGS.
Nuisances menacing public
health, §§22-10-1 to
22-10-3.
Education.
Authority and jurisdiction of
state board of health,
§22-2-2.
Boards of school trustees.
Sanitary conditions
maintained by
trustees, §16-10-10.
Comprehensive health
education.
Courses of study in public
school, §16-40-7.
County boards of health.
Duties, §22-3-2.
County health officers.
Duties, §22-3-5.
Drug abuse education,
§§16-41-1 to 16-41-10.
See EDUCATION.

HEALTH—Cont'd
Education—Cont'd
Immunization of school
children, §§16-30-1 to
16-30-5.
Mental and physical
examinations of school
children, §§16-29-1 to
16-29-6.
See EDUCATION.
Rules for protection of
health, §16-4-13.
Sanitary rest rooms,
§16-8-43.
Emergencies.
Consent for health services,
§§22-8-1 to 22-8-9. See
within this heading,
"Consent for health
services."
Enforcement of laws.
Authority and jurisdiction of
state board of health,
§22-2-2.
Environmental control.
General provisions.
See ENVIRONMENTAL
CONTROL.
**Environmental management
department.**
State health department.
Contracts with health
department for routine
bacteriological
analyses, §22-22A-4.
Transfer of certain
functions of state
health department,
§22-22A-4.
Expenditures.
Control of expenditures,
§22-1-4.
Expenses.
County health officers.
Recovery of expenses by
health officer,
§22-2-13.
Sheriffs.
Recovery of expenses by
sheriff, §22-2-13.
State health department.
How expenses to be paid,
§22-2-12.
State health officer.
Recovery of expenses by
health officer,
§22-2-13.
Eyeglasses.
Medicaid program, §22-6-7.1.
Fees.
Home health services,
§§22-7-1 to 22-7-6. See
within this heading,
"Home health services."
Fish and game.
Nuisances menacing public
health, §§22-10-1 to
22-10-3.
Food.
Nuisances menacing public
health, §§22-10-1 to
22-10-3.
Regulations for
establishments handling
food, §22-20-5.
Fraud.
False statements and claim
or application for
payments or medical
benefits, §22-1-11.

HEALTH—Cont'd
Fraud—Cont'd
Medicaid agency.
Revocation of eligibility of
recipient upon
determination of
abuse, fraud or misuse
of benefits, §22-6-8.
Restoration of eligibility,
§22-6-8.
Restricted status.
Placing pregnant
recipients on,
§22-6-8.
Fruits and vegetables.
Nuisances menacing public
health, §§22-10-1 to
22-10-3.
Funds.
Perinatal health.
Mothers and babies
indigent care trust
fund, §§22-12B-1 to
22-12B-4.
Funerals.
General provisions, §§34-13-1
to 34-13-152.
See FUNERALS.
Garbage and trash.
General provisions, §§22-27-1
to 22-27-27.
See GARBAGE AND
TRASH.
Hazardous waste, §§22-30-1
to 22-30-24.
See HAZARDOUS
WASTE.
Glasses.
Medicaid program.
Procurement of
prescription eyewear
for recipients,
§22-6-7.1.
Governor.
State board of health.
Annual report to governor,
§22-2-3.
Hazardous waste, §§22-30-1
to 22-30-24.
See HAZARDOUS WASTE.
Health care service plans,
§§10-4-100 to 10-4-115.
See HEALTH CARE
SERVICE PLANS.
Health officers.
County health officers,
§§22-3-4 to 22-3-7.
State health officer, §22-2-8.
**Hearing aid dealers and
fitters.**
General provisions, §§34-14-1
to 34-14-33.
See HEARING AID
DEALERS AND
FITTERS.
Home health services,
§§22-7-1 to 22-7-6.
Fees.
Appropriation of receipts,
§22-7-5.
Authority to charge and
collect, §22-7-1.
Collected fees.
Payment into home
health service fund,
§22-7-4.
Expenditure of receipts,
§22-7-5.
Rules and regulations,
§22-7-6.
Schedule of fees, §22-7-2.

HEALTH—Cont'd
Home health services
—Cont'd
Fees—Cont'd
Waiver of payment,
§22-7-3.
Fund.
Payment of collected fees
into home health
service fund, §22-7-4.
Rules and regulations,
§22-7-6.
Hospitals.
General provisions, §§22-21-1
to 22-21-391.
See HOSPITALS.
Regional referral hospitals.
Responsibility for health
care, §§22-21-292 to
22-21-296.
Hotels, inns and other
transient lodging places.
Authority and jurisdiction of
state board of health,
§22-2-2.
Duties of county boards of
health, §22-3-2.
Duties of county health
officers, §22-3-5.
Duties of hotel owners, etc.,
§34-15-4.
Operation of chapter in
conjunction with health
rules and regulations,
§34-15-2.
Regulations, §22-20-5.
Immunization.
School children, §§16-30-1 to
16-30-5.
See EDUCATION.
Indigent persons.
Responsibility for health
care, §§22-21-290 to
22-21-296. See within
this heading,
"Responsibility for
health care."
Inspections.
County boards of health,
§22-3-2.
County health officers,
§22-3-5.
State board of health.
Authority and jurisdiction
of state board, §22-2-2.
Insurance.
Alabama health care plan,
§§27-21-1 to 27-21-6.
See INSURANCE.
General provisions.
See INSURANCE.
Jails.
Authority and jurisdiction of
state board of health,
§22-2-2.
Duties of county boards,
§22-3-2.
Duties of county health
officers, §22-3-5.
Expenses.
Payment, §14-6-104.
Inspection of jails.
See JAILS.
Tubercular prisoners,
§§14-6-60 to 14-6-62.
See JAILS.
Jurisdiction.
State board of health,
§22-2-2.

HEALTH—Cont'd
Legislature.
Annual report to legislature
by state committee of
public health, §22-2-7.
Requests for information,
§22-2-7.
Long term quality health
care.
General provisions, §§22-6-20
to 22-6-27.
See LONG TERM
QUALITY HEALTH
CARE.
Manicurists.
Health regulations, §§22-17-1
to 22-17-11.
See COSMETOLOGISTS.
Manufacturers.
Authority and jurisdiction of
state board of health,
§22-2-2.
Duties of county boards of
health, §22-3-2.
Marine resources.
Shrimp.
Unfit for human
consumption.
Condemnation,
disposition, etc.,
§9-12-47.
Markets.
Duties of county boards of
health, §22-3-2.
Mattresses.
Nuisances menacing public
health, §§22-10-1 to
22-10-3.
Meat and meat products.
General provisions, §§2-17-1
to 2-17-38.
See MEAT AND MEAT
PRODUCTS.
Nuisances menacing public
health, §§22-10-1 to
22-10-3.
Medicaid agency.
False statements in claim or
application for payments
or benefits from,
§22-1-11.
Kickbacks, bribes, etc.,
§22-1-11.
Medicaid program, §§22-6-1
to 22-6-9.
Appropriations, §22-6-1.
Assignment to state of
recipient's rights to
payments for medical
care, §22-6-6.1.
Authorization to release
needed information,
§22-6-6.1.
Awarding of medicaid
contracts.
Competitive bidding
required, §41-16-27.
Bids.
Eyewear.
Procurement of
prescription eyewear
for recipients of
medicaid program,
§22-6-7.1.
Claims.
Contracts for purposes of
receiving, processing
and paying claims,
§22-6-7.

HEALTH—Cont'd
Medicaid program—Cont'd
Competitive bidding in
award of contracts,
§41-16-27.
Confidentiality.
Recipients of medicaid
identification cards,
§22-6-9.
Contract adjustments.
Payment, §22-6-2.
Contracts.
Authority to contract with
intermediaries for
purposes of receiving,
processing and paying
claims, §22-6-7.
Eyewear.
Procurement of
prescription eyewear
for recipients of
medicaid program,
§22-6-7.1.
Copayments by persons
receiving medical
services from physicians
or other medical
practitioners under
program, §§22-6-4,
22-6-4.1.
Prescription drugs,
§22-6-4.2.
Eyewear.
Procurement of
prescription eyewear
for recipients of
medicaid program,
§22-6-7.1.
Fraud.
Revocation of eligibility,
§22-6-8.
Restoration of eligibility,
§22-6-8.
Restricted status.
Placing pregnant
recipients on,
§22-6-8.
Fund balances.
Disposition, §22-6-3.
Glasses.
Procurement of
prescription eyewear
for recipients of
medicaid program,
§22-6-7.1.
Insurance.
Denial or reduction of
benefits due to
medicaid eligibility,
§27-14-11.1.
Long term quality health
care, §§22-6-20 to
22-6-27.
See LONG TERM
QUALITY HEALTH
CARE.
Medicaid identification card,
§22-6-9.
Confidentiality of recipient,
§22-6-9.
Issuance, §22-6-9.
Uses, §22-6-9.
Nursing home patients,
§22-6-5.1.
State employees
investigating and
bringing charges against
doctors relating to abuse
of.
Exemption from liability,
§6-5-334.

HEALTH—Cont'd
Medicaid program—Cont'd
Subrogation of state to rights
of recipients, §22-6-6.
Medical care.
Council on prevention of
disease and medical care,
§§22-2-9, 22-2-10.
See DISEASES.
Medical technicians,
§§34-18-1 to 34-18-47.
See MEDICAL
TECHNICIANS.
Mental health, §§22-50-1 to
22-55-4.
See MENTALLY ILL.
Midwives, §§34-19-2 to
34-19-10.
See MIDWIVES.
Military affairs.
Abatement of menaces to
health, §31-2-126.
Milk and milk products.
General provisions, §§2-13-80
to 2-13-94.
See MILK AND MILK
PRODUCTS.
Minors.
Consent for health services,
§§22-8-1 to 22-8-9. See
within this heading,
"Consent for health
services."
Prevention of infantile
blindness, §22-20-2.
**Mothers and babies indigent
care trust fund,**
§§22-12B-1 to 22-12B-4.
Municipal corporations.
Appropriations by
municipalities for public
health work, §22-3-11.
Cemeteries, §§11-47-40 to
11-47-74.
See MUNICIPAL
CORPORATIONS.
Certain county and local
laws unaffected by title,
§22-1-9.
Codes.
Adoption of technical codes
by reference, §11-45-8.
Conflicts between municipal
and general health laws,
§22-1-2.
Maintenance of health,
§11-47-130.
Medical clinic boards,
§§11-58-1 to 11-58-15.
See MUNICIPAL
CORPORATIONS.
Powers as to health,
§11-47-131.
Sanitary regulations.
Territorial operation of
ordinances for
enforcement,
§11-40-10.
State health department.
Payment of health
department claims out
of municipal budgets,
§22-3-12.
Nitrate of silver.
Prevention of infantile
blindness, §22-20-2.
Notifiable diseases,
§§22-11A-1 to 22-11A-38.
See DISEASES.

HEALTH—Cont'd
**Nuisances menacing public
health.**
Abatement.
How and by whom
nuisances to be abated,
§22-10-2.
By whom nuisances to be
abated, §22-10-2.
Destruction of property.
Summary destruction
without compensation,
§22-10-3.
Enumeration, §22-10-1.
How nuisances to be abated,
§22-10-2.
Nurses, §§34-21-1 to 34-21-63.
See NURSES.
**Nursing home
administrators,** §§34-20-1
to 34-20-16.
See NURSING HOMES.
Officers and employees.
Appointment of subordinate
officers and employees,
§22-1-4.
Compensation of state health
department personnel,
§22-2-11.
How salaries to be paid,
§22-2-12.
County health officers,
§§22-3-4 to 22-3-7.
Sanitary officers.
Appointment, §22-3-9.
State employees' health
insurance plan,
§§36-29-1 to 36-29-13.
See PUBLIC OFFICERS
AND EMPLOYEES.
State health officers, §22-2-8.
Subordinate officers and
employees.
Appointment, §22-1-4.
Organization.
Council on health costs,
administration and
organization, §§22-2-9,
22-2-10.
Penalties.
Violation of health or
quarantine law, §22-1-8.
Violation of state board of
health rules or
regulations, §22-2-14.
Penny trust fund, §§41-15A-1
to 41-15A-5.
See PENNY TRUST FUND.
Perinatal health, §§22-12A-1
to 22-12A-6.
Bureau of maternal and child
health.
Annual report, §22-12A-5.
Development of priorities,
guidelines and
procedures, §22-12A-4.
Plan to reduce infant
mortality and
handicapping
conditions, §22-12A-3.
Citation, §22-12A-1.
Definitions, §22-12A-2.
Funds.
Restrictions, §22-12A-5.
Use of funds generally,
§22-12A-6.
Legislative intent, §22-12A-2.
Mothers and babies indigent
care trust fund.
Board, §22-12B-2.

HEALTH—Cont'd
Perinatal health—Cont'd
Mothers and babies indigent
care trust fund—Cont'd
Disbursement of funds,
§22-12B-4.
Establishment, §22-12B-1.
Purpose, §22-12B-1.
Sources of funding,
§22-12B-3.
Unobligated fund balance
shall automatically
carry forward into
succeeding fiscal year,
§22-12B-4.
Plan to reduce infant
mortality and
handicapping conditions,
§22-12A-3.
Contents, §22-12A-3.
Procedure, §22-12A-3.
Title.
Short title, §22-12A-1.
Pests.
Nuisances menacing public
health, §§22-10-1 to
22-10-3.
**Pharmacists and
pharmacies.**
General provisions, §§34-23-1
to 34-23-94.
See PHARMACISTS AND
PHARMACIES.
Physical fitness commission,
§§22-5-1 to 22-5-9.
Acceptance of gifts or grants,
§22-5-9.
Appointment of members,
§22-5-3.
Compensation of members,
§22-5-3.
Creation, §22-5-2.
Definition of physical fitness,
§22-5-1.
Duties, §22-5-5.
Employees.
Application of merit
system, §22-5-6.
Executive director, §22-5-6.
Gifts.
Acceptance of gifts,
§22-5-9.
Grants.
Acceptance of grants,
§22-5-9.
Meetings, §22-5-4.
Merit system.
Application to employees,
§22-5-6.
Personnel, §22-5-7.
Purpose, §22-5-2.
Qualifications of members,
§22-5-3.
Quorum, §22-5-4.
Reports.
Annual report, §22-5-8.
Rules and regulations.
Adoption, §22-5-4.
Terms of members, §22-5-3.
Vacancies, §22-5-3.
Physicians.
General provisions, §§34-24-1
to 34-24-384.
See PHYSICIANS.
Planning.
State health planning and
development, §§22-4-1 to
22-4-17. See within this
heading, "State health
planning and
development."

HEALTH—Cont'd
Poultry.
Regulations for
establishments handling
food, §22-20-5.
Prisons.
Duties of county boards of
health, §22-3-2.
Public buildings.
Authority and jurisdiction of
state board of health,
§22-2-2.
Duties of county boards of
health, §22-3-2.
Duties of county health
officers, §22-3-5.
Public dispensaries.
Treating communicable
diseases, §22-1-6.
**Public officers and
employees.**
State employees' health
insurance plan,
§§36-29-1 to 36-29-13.
See PUBLIC OFFICERS
AND EMPLOYEES.
Quarantine.
General provisions, §§22-12-1
to 22-12-29.
See QUARANTINE.
Rabies, §§3-7-1 to 3-7-13.
See RABIES.
Radiation, §§22-14-1 to
22-14-35.
See ATOMIC ENERGY.
Railroads.
Authority and jurisdiction of
state board of health,
§22-2-2.
Duties of county boards of
health, §22-3-2.
Records.
County health officers,
§22-3-5.
Reports.
County health officers,
§22-3-5.
Physical fitness commission.
Annual report, §22-5-8.
State board of health.
Annual report to governor,
§22-2-3.
Annual report to
legislature, §22-2-7.
State committee of public
health.
Annual report to
legislature, §22-2-7.
**Responsibility for health
care,** §§22-21-290 to
22-21-296.
Certification of indigency,
§22-21-294.
Required for treatment,
§22-21-297.
Citation of article,
§22-21-290.
Definitions, §22-21-292.
Legislative intent,
§22-21-291.
Out-of-county indigent
patients.
Treatment at regional
referral hospitals,
§22-21-293.
Regional referral hospitals.
Defined, §22-21-292.
Obligation to admit for
treatment, §22-21-295.
Out-of-county indigent
patients, §22-21-293.

HEALTH—Cont'd
**Responsibility for health
care**—Cont'd
Regional referral hospitals
—Cont'd
Procedure for settlement of
disputes between
county and hospital,
§22-21-296.
Short title of article,
§22-21-290.
Restaurants.
Duties of county health
officers, §22-3-5.
Regulations, §22-20-5.
Rules and regulations.
Home health services,
§22-7-6.
Penalty for violation,
§22-2-14.
Physical fitness commission.
Adoption, §22-5-4.
State board of health,
§22-2-2.
Home health services,
§22-7-6.
State health planning and
development.
Adoption, revision, etc.,
of rules and
regulations, §22-4-5.
Violations.
Penalty for violation,
§22-2-14.
Violations.
Penalty for violation,
§22-2-14.
Salaries.
Compensation of state health
department personnel,
§22-2-11.
Dentists.
Public health dentists,
§22-1-5.
How salaries to be paid,
§22-2-12.
Sanitarians.
General provisions.
See SANITARIANS.
Sanitary officers.
Appointment, §22-3-9.
Sewers.
Insanitary sewage facilities
menacing public health,
§22-26-1.
Sheriffs.
Expenses.
Recovery of expenses by
sheriff, §22-2-13.
Shrimp.
Unfit for human
consumption.
Condemnation, disposal,
etc., §9-12-47.
Silver nitrate.
Prevention of infantile
blindness, §22-20-2.
State board of health,
§§22-2-1 to 22-2-3.
Authority, §22-2-2.
Boards for operation of
water, sewer, gas and
electric systems.
Jurisdiction, etc., of state
board of health,
§11-50-323.
Boats.
Discharge of litter and
sewage from
watercraft.
See BOATS.

HEALTH—Cont'd
State board of health—Cont'd
Compensation of personnel,
§22-2-11.
Controlled substances.
Enforcement of chapter,
§20-2-90.
Control of public health work
under county and state
boards of health, §22-1-3.
County boards of health.
Supervision and control
over county boards,
§22-2-2.
County health officers.
Supervision and control
over officers, §22-2-2.
Development.
State health planning and
development, §§22-4-2
to 22-4-6.
Discharge of litter and
sewage from watercraft,
§§33-6-1 to 33-6-12.
See BOATS.
Drinking water.
General provisions.
See WATER SUPPLY
AND
WATERWORKS.
Safety drinking water act,
§§22-23-30 to 22-23-53.
See WATER SUPPLY
AND
WATERWORKS.
Governor.
Annual report to governor,
§22-2-3.
Health care facilities.
Designation of board as
state agency, §22-4-15.
Land, buildings, etc.
Acquisition, sale, etc., for
carrying out health
care facility
construction and
operation program,
§22-4-16.
Health centers.
Construction, operation,
etc., §22-4-14.
Hearing aid dealers and
fitters.
Powers and duties of
board, §34-14-11.
Hospitals.
See HOSPITALS.
How constituted, §22-2-1.
Inspections.
Authority and jurisdiction,
§22-2-2.
Jails.
Authority and jurisdiction,
§22-2-2.
Jurisdiction, §22-2-2.
Legislature.
Annual report to
legislature, §22-2-7.
Medical association of state.
Constitutes state board of
health, §22-2-1.
Notifiable diseases.
General provisions,
§§22-11A-1 to
22-11A-38.
See DISEASES.
Tuberculosis, §§22-11A-9,
22-11A-10, 22-11A-12.
See DISEASES.
Personnel.
Compensation, §22-2-11.

HEALTH—Cont'd
　State board of health—Cont'd
　　Planning.
　　　State health planning and
　　　　development, §§22-4-2
　　　　to 22-4-6.
　　Powers, §22-2-2.
　　Radiation.
　　　State radiation control
　　　　agency.
　　　　Board of health
　　　　　designated state
　　　　　radiation control
　　　　　agency, §22-14-4.
　　Reports.
　　　Annual report to governor,
　　　　§22-2-3.
　　　Annual report to
　　　　legislature, §22-2-7.
　　Rules and regulations,
　　　§22-2-2.
　　　Home health services,
　　　　§22-7-6.
　　　Safe drinking water act,
　　　　§§22-23-32 to 22-23-35.
　　　State health planning and
　　　　development.
　　　　Adoption, revision, etc.,
　　　　　of rules and
　　　　　regulations, §22-4-5.
　　　Violations.
　　　　Penalty for violation,
　　　　　§22-2-14.
　　Sewers.
　　　Operation of sanitary
　　　　sewer systems by
　　　　public water
　　　　corporations.
　　　　Rights and powers of
　　　　　board not impaired
　　　　　by article,
　　　　　§11-50-372.
　　State committee of public
　　　health, §§22-2-4 to
　　　22-2-7.
　　State health planning and
　　　development, §§22-4-2 to
　　　22-4-6.
　　Tuberculosis.
　　　Notifiable diseases,
　　　　§§22-11A-9, 22-11A-10,
　　　　22-11A-12.
　　Vital statistics, §§22-9-1 to
　　　22-9-79.
　　　See VITAL STATISTICS.
　　Water and wastewater
　　　systems and treatment
　　　plants, §§22-25-1 to
　　　22-25-15.
　　　See WATER AND
　　　　WASTEWATER
　　　　SYSTEMS AND
　　　　TREATMENT
　　　　PLANTS.
　　Water, sewer and fire
　　　protection districts.
　　　Jurisdiction over and
　　　　regulation of district
　　　　by state board of
　　　　health, §11-89-19.
　　Water supply and
　　　waterworks.
　　　Safe drinking water act,
　　　　§§22-23-1 to 22-23-53.
　　　See WATER SUPPLY
　　　　AND
　　　　WATERWORKS.

HEALTH—Cont'd
　State board of health—Cont'd
　　Waterworks and sewer
　　　boards.
　　　Jurisdiction, etc., of state
　　　　board of health,
　　　　§11-50-241.
　　　Management and operation
　　　　of sanitary sewer
　　　　systems as agents of
　　　　municipalities.
　　　　Rights and powers of
　　　　　state board of health
　　　　　not impaired by
　　　　　division, §11-50-291.
　**State commission on
　　physical fitness,** §§22-5-1
　　to 22-5-9. See within this
　　heading, "Physical fitness
　　commission."
　**State committee of public
　　health.**
　　Chairman, §22-2-4.
　　Compensation, §22-2-4.
　　Composition, §22-2-4.
　　County health officers.
　　　Approval of county health
　　　　officers, §22-3-2.
　　Duties, §22-2-5.
　　How constituted, §22-2-4.
　　Legislature.
　　　Annual report to
　　　　legislature, §22-2-7.
　　　Request for information by
　　　　general assembly,
　　　　§22-2-7.
　　Meetings, §22-2-6.
　　Per diem of members,
　　　§22-2-4.
　　Personnel.
　　　Compensation, §22-2-11.
　　Powers, §22-2-5.
　　Prerogatives, §22-2-5.
　　Reports.
　　　Annual report to
　　　　legislature, §22-2-7.
　　Secretary of committee,
　　　§22-2-4.
　　Selection of members,
　　　§22-2-4.
　　State board of health,
　　　§§22-2-1 to 22-2-3.
　　State health officer.
　　　Election of state health
　　　　officer, §22-2-8.
　　　Ex officio secretary of
　　　　committee, §22-2-4.
　　Tuberculosis.
　　　See TUBERCULOSIS.
　　Vice-chairman, §22-2-4.
　　Voting, §22-2-4.
　　When committee to act for
　　　state board, §22-2-6.
　State health department.
　　Barbers.
　　　Cooperation with board of
　　　　barber examiners,
　　　　§34-5-13.
　　Claims, etc.
　　　Payment out of county or
　　　　municipal budgets,
　　　　§22-3-12.
　　Compensation of personnel,
　　　§22-2-11.
　　How salaries to be paid,
　　　§22-2-12.
　　Costs.
　　　How costs to be paid,
　　　　§22-2-12.

HEALTH—Cont'd
　State health department
　　—Cont'd
　　Counties.
　　　Payment of health
　　　　department claims out
　　　　of county or municipal
　　　　budgets, §22-3-12.
　　Defined, §22-1-1.
　　Environmental management
　　　department.
　　　Contracts with health
　　　　department for routine
　　　　bacteriological
　　　　analyses, §22-22A-4.
　　　Transfer of certain
　　　　functions of state
　　　　health department,
　　　　§22-22A-4.
　　Expenses.
　　　How expenses to be paid,
　　　　§22-2-12.
　　Home health services,
　　　§§22-7-1 to 22-7-6. See
　　　within this heading,
　　　"Home health services."
　　Municipal corporations.
　　　Payment of health
　　　　department claims out
　　　　of municipal budgets,
　　　　§22-3-12.
　　State board of health,
　　　§§22-2-1 to 22-2-3.
　　State committee of public
　　　health, §§22-2-4 to
　　　22-2-7.
　State health officer, §22-2-8.
　　Bonds, surety, §22-2-8.
　　County boards of health.
　　　Supervision and control of
　　　　county boards, §22-2-8.
　　County health officers.
　　　Removal of county health
　　　　officers, §22-3-2.
　　　Supervision and control of
　　　　county officers,
　　　　§22-2-8.
　　Diseases.
　　　Powers and duties of state
　　　　health officer, §22-2-8.
　　Duties, §22-2-8.
　　Election by state committee
　　　of public health, §22-2-8.
　　Expenses.
　　　Recovery of expenses by
　　　　health officer,
　　　　§22-2-13.
　　Powers, §22-2-8.
　　Qualifications, §22-2-8.
　　Recommendations, §22-2-8.
　　Salary, §22-2-8.
　　State committee of public
　　　health.
　　　Election of state health
　　　　officer, §22-2-8.
　　　Ex officio secretary of
　　　　committee, §22-2-4.
　　State radiation control
　　　agency.
　　　State health officer to be
　　　　director of agency,
　　　　§22-14-4.
　　Subordinate officers and
　　　employees.
　　　Appointment, §22-1-4.
　　Term of office, §22-2-8.

HEALTH—Cont'd
State health officer—Cont'd
Water and waste water
systems and treatment
plants.
Certification of operators.
Duty of state health
officer, §22-25-7.
Youth services board.
Member of board, §44-1-51.
**State health planning and
development,** §§22-4-1 to
22-4-17.
Administration of state
health plan.
Designation of state board
of health as agency for
receipt,
administration, etc., of
funds for
administration of plan,
§22-4-12.
Appeals.
From rules, regulations,
standards, etc., by
state board of health,
§22-4-5.
Appropriations to state board
of health, §22-4-6.
Bureaus.
Establishment of internal
bureaus by state board
of health, §22-4-4.
Construction of chapter,
§22-4-17.
Definitions, §22-4-2.
Divisions.
Establishment of internal
divisions by state
board of health,
§22-4-4.
Health care facilities.
Defined, §22-4-2.
Designation of state board
of health as state
agency, §22-4-15.
Land, buildings, etc.
Acquisition, purchase,
sale, etc., by state
board of health,
§22-4-16.
Health centers.
Construction, operation,
etc., by state board of
health, §22-4-14.
Health service areas.
Defined, §22-4-2.
Health system agencies.
Defined, §22-4-2.
Hospitals.
Construction, operation,
etc., of public hospitals
by state board of
health, §22-4-14.
Implementation of provisions
of chapter, §22-4-17.
Medical facilities plan.
Defined, §22-4-2.
Preparation, publication,
etc., §22-4-13.
Preliminary state health
plan.
Preparation, §22-4-11.
Visual care.
Provision in plan for
visual care, §22-4-11.

HEALTH—Cont'd
**State health planning and
development**—Cont'd
Preparation of state health
plan.
Designation of state board
of health as agency for
receipt,
administration, etc., of
funds for preparation,
§22-4-12.
Professional staff, §22-4-4.
Rules and regulations.
Adoption, revision, etc., by
state board of health,
§22-4-5.
Short title of chapter,
§22-4-1.
Standards.
Adoption, revision, etc., by
state board of health,
§22-4-5.
State board of health,
§§22-4-2 to 22-4-6.
Administration of funds.
Board not to
discriminate among
branches of healing
arts in
administration,
§22-4-5.
Construction,
maintenance, etc., of
public health care
facilities, §22-4-15.
Designation of state
board of health as
state agency for
administration of
funds for
preparation,
administration, etc.,
of state health plan,
§22-4-12.
Appropriations to state
board, §22-4-6.
Bureaus.
Establishment of
internal bureaus,
§22-4-4.
Defined, §22-4-2.
Designated as state health
planning and
development agency,
§22-4-3.
Divisions.
Establishment of
internal divisions,
§22-4-4.
Duties, §22-4-3.
Federal government.
Power to cooperate and
enter into contracts
with federal
government in
construction and
operation of
hospitals, health
centers, etc.,
§22-4-14.
Health care facilities.
Acquisition, sale, etc., of
land, buildings, etc.,
for carrying out
health care facility
construction and
operation program,
§22-4-16.

HEALTH—Cont'd
**State health planning and
development**—Cont'd
State board of health—Cont'd
Health care facilities
—Cont'd
Designation of state
board as state
agency for receipt
and administration
of funds for
construction,
maintenance, etc.,
§22-4-15.
Powers, §22-4-3.
Professional staff, §22-4-4.
Rules and regulations.
Adoption, revision, etc.,
by state board,
§22-4-5.
State health plan.
Administration.
Designation of state
board of health as
state agency for
receipt,
administration, etc.,
of funds for
administration of
plan, §22-4-12.
Defined, §22-4-2.
State board of health.
Designation as state
agency for receipt,
administration, etc.,
of funds for
preparation,
administration, etc.,
of plan, §22-4-12.
Statewide health
coordinating council.
Appointment of members,
§22-4-7.
Composition, §22-4-7.
Defined, §22-4-2.
Establishment, §22-4-7.
Functions, §22-4-8.
Meetings, §22-4-7.
Officers, §22-4-7.
Qualifications of members,
§22-4-7.
Terms of members, §22-4-7.
Visual care.
Provision in state health
plan for visual care,
§22-4-11.
Statistics.
Vital statistics, §§22-9-1 to
22-9-79.
See VITAL STATISTICS.
Subrogation.
Medicaid program.
Subrogation of state to
rights of recipients,
§22-6-6.
Taxation.
County health officer and
health department.
Tax to establish and
maintain, §22-3-10.
Theaters.
Authority and jurisdiction of
state board of health,
§22-2-2.
Duties of county boards of
health, §22-3-2.
Towels.
Use of common towels in
public places prohibited,
§22-20-1.

HEALTH—Cont'd
Toxic substances in the workplace, §§22-33-1 to 22-33-15.
See TOXIC SUBSTANCES IN THE WORKPLACE.
Tuberculosis.
Notifiable diseases, §§22-11A-9, 22-11A-10, 22-11A-12.
Veterinarians, §§34-29-60 to 34-29-94.
See VETERINARIANS.
Violations of health laws.
Duties of county health officers, §22-3-5.
Penalty, §22-1-8.
Vital statistics, §§22-9-1 to 22-9-79.
See VITAL STATISTICS.
Water and wastewater systems and treatment plants, §§22-25-1 to 22-25-15.
See WATER AND WASTEWATER SYSTEMS AND TREATMENT PLANTS.
Watercraft.
Discharge of litter and sewage from watercraft, §§33-6-1 to 33-6-12.
See BOATS.
Water pollution.
See WATER POLLUTION.
Waters and watercourses.
Nuisances menacing public health, §§22-10-1 to 22-10-3.
Water supply and waterworks.
Authority and jurisdiction of state board of health, §22-2-2.
Duties of county boards of health, §22-3-2.
Duties of county health officers, §22-3-5.
Nuisances menacing public health, §§22-10-1 to 22-10-3.

HEALTH CARE AUTHORITIES, §§22-21-310 to 22-21-356.
Actions.
Powers of authority, §22-21-318.
Additional powers, §§22-21-350 to 22-21-356.
Authority.
Definition of authority, §22-21-350.
Authorizing resolution.
Definition of authorizing resolution, §22-21-350.
Authorizing subdivision.
Definition of authorizing subdivision, §22-21-350.
Board.
Definition of board, §22-21-350.
Credit rating agencies.
Nationally recognized credit rating agencies.
Defined, §22-21-350.
Cumulative nature of provisions, §22-21-356.
Declarations of legislature, §22-21-351.

HEALTH CARE AUTHORITIES—Cont'd
Additional powers—Cont'd
Director.
Definition of director, §22-21-350.
Enabling statute.
Definition of enabling statute, §22-21-350.
Incorporation of authority.
Certificate of incorporation.
Amendments, §22-21-352.
Investments, §22-21-355.
Legislative findings, §22-21-351.
Office space of nonhospital based physicians, dentists, etc., for use in private practice, §22-21-354.
Reincorporation of existing corporations, §22-21-352.
Securities.
Defined, §22-21-350.
Federal securities.
Defined, §22-21-350.
General obligations of the authority, §22-21-353.
Applicants.
Defined, §22-21-311.
Application for incorporation of authority.
Contents, §22-21-313.
Filing, §22-21-313.
Assets.
Transfer of assets to authority, §22-21-336.
Authority.
Defined, §§22-21-311, 22-21-350.
Authorizing resolution.
Defined, §§22-21-311, 22-21-350.
Authorizing subdivision.
Defined, §§22-21-311, 22-21-350.
Bids and bidding.
Competitive bidding laws.
Applicability, §22-21-335.
Board, §§22-21-316, 22-21-350.
Additional powers.
Definition of board, §22-21-350.
Appointment, §22-21-316.
Compensation, §22-21-316.
Defined, §§22-21-311, 22-21-350.
Election or appointment, §22-21-316.
Meetings, §22-21-316.
Qualifications, §22-21-316.
Quorum, §22-21-316.
Terms of members, §22-21-316.
Vacancies, §22-21-316.
Borrowing money.
Powers of authority, §22-21-318.
Bylaws.
Powers of authority, §22-21-318.
Certificate of incorporation.
Amendment.
Application for amendment, §22-21-315.
Approving resolution, §22-21-315.

HEALTH CARE AUTHORITIES—Cont'd
Certificate of incorporation—Cont'd
Amendment—Cont'd
Filing of amended certificate, §22-21-315.
Recordation, §22-21-315.
Extraordinary power of authority §22-21-319.
Filing, form and contents, §22-21-314.
Recordation, §22-21-314.
Charges for services.
Powers of authority, §22-21-318.
Citation, §22-21-310.
Code of ethics for public officers and employees.
Applicability, §22-21-334.
Construction and interpretation, §22-21-311.
Additional powers.
Cumulative effect of provisions, §22-21-356.
Cumulative effect of article, §22-21-343.
Ethics act.
Applicability, §22-21-334.
Exclusivity of provisions, §22-21-342.
Contracts.
Powers of authority, §22-21-318.
Public contracts.
Competitive bidding.
Applicability of competitive bidding laws, §22-21-335.
Corporation of authority.
Multiple corporations permitted, §22-21-340.
Reincorporation of existing corporations, §22-21-341.
Counties.
Defined, §22-21-311.
Securities not obligation of counties, §22-21-325.
County hospital corporations.
Designation of authority as agency for purposes of chapter, §22-21-338.
Coupons.
Defined, §22-21-311.
Negotiability, §22-21-327.
Credit rating agencies.
Additional powers.
Nationally recognized credit rating agencies.
Defined, §22-21-350.
Cumulative effect of article, §22-21-343.
Definitions, §22-21-311.
Additional powers, §22-21-350.
Directors.
Board of directors, §22-21-316.
Defined, §§22-21-311, 22-21-350.
Disposition of earnings of authority, §22-21-337.
Dissolution.
Grounds, §22-21-339.
Procedure, §22-21-339.
Earnings of authority.
Disposition, §22-21-337.

HEALTH CARE AUTHORITIES—Cont'd
Education.
Powers of authority,
§22-21-318.
Employees.
Powers of authority,
§22-21-318.
Enabling statute.
Additional powers.
Definition of enabling
statute, §22-21-350.
Ethics.
Code of ethics for public
officers and employees.
Applicability, §22-21-334.
Evidence.
Board.
Meetings.
Record of proceedings.
Use as evidence,
§22-21-316.
Exclusivity of provisions,
§22-21-342.
Expenditures.
Powers of authority,
§22-21-318.
Extraordinary power of
authority, §22-21-319.
Federal securities.
Defined, §22-21-311.
Findings.
Legislative findings,
§22-21-312.
Fiscal year.
Defined, §22-21-311.
Funds.
Transfer of funds to
authority, §22-21-336.
Gifts.
Powers of authority,
§22-21-318.
Governing body.
Defined, §22-21-311.
Health care facilities.
Defined, §22-21-311.
Powers of authority,
§22-21-318.
Hospital taxes.
Defined, §22-21-311.
Proceeds.
Use, §22-21-344.
Incorporation of authority,
§§22-21-313 to 22-21-315.
Application.
Contents, §22-21-313.
Filing, §22-21-313.
Certificate of incorporation.
Amendment.
Additional powers,
§22-21-352.
Application, §22-21-315.
Approving resolution,
§22-21-315.
Recordation of amended
certificate,
§22-21-315.
Contents, §22-21-314.
Extraordinary power of
authority, §22-21-319.
Filing, §22-21-314.
Filing amended certificate,
§22-21-315.
Form, §22-21-314.
Recordation, §22-21-314.
Incorporators.
Defined, §22-21-311.
Indenture.
Defined, §22-21-311.

HEALTH CARE AUTHORITIES—Cont'd
Indenture—Cont'd
Securities.
Source of payment,
§22-21-323.
Indigent persons.
Powers of authority,
§22-21-318.
Intent of legislature,
§22-21-312.
Interest.
Exemption of authorities
from usury interest
provisions, §22-21-328.
Securities of authority,
§22-21-320.
Investments.
Funds of authority,
§22-21-332.
Additional powers,
§22-21-355.
Powers of authority,
§22-21-318.
Securities issued under
article deemed legal
investments, §22-21-326.
Leases.
Agreements with authorizing
subdivisions.
Authorized, §22-21-330.
Options.
Renewal options,
§22-21-330.
Remedies for default in
performance of lease
agreement, §22-21-331.
Security for payment of
rental.
Special pledge as
security, §22-21-330.
Terms, §22-21-330.
Vacant space.
Use, §22-21-330.
Legislative findings,
§22-21-312.
Legislative intent, §22-21-312.
Legislature.
Defined, §22-21-311.
Limitation of actions.
Securities.
Limitation of actions to
contest validity,
§22-21-329.
Mortgages and deeds of
trust.
Powers of authority,
§22-21-318.
Multiple corporations.
Permitted, §22-21-340.
Municipal corporations.
Defined, §22-21-311.
Securities not obligations of
municipality, §22-21-325.
Names.
Powers of authority,
§22-21-318.
Negotiable instruments.
Securities and coupons as
negotiable instruments,
§22-21-327.
Notice.
Board meetings.
Waiver, §22-21-316.
Securities.
Issuance, §22-21-329.
Officers, §22-21-317.

HEALTH CARE AUTHORITIES—Cont'd
Office space.
Additional powers.
Nonhospital based
physicians, dentists,
etc., using office space
for private practice.
Financial effect of
arrangement,
§22-21-354.
Personal property.
Powers of authority,
§22-21-318.
Powers.
Additional powers,
§§22-21-350 to 22-21-356.
See within this heading,
"Additional powers."
Extraordinary power of
authority, §22-21-319.
Generally, §22-21-318.
Principal office.
Defined, §22-21-311.
Public hospital corporation.
Defined, §22-21-311.
Public officers and
employees.
Code of ethics.
Applicability of ethics act,
§22-21-334.
Real property.
Powers of authority,
§22-21-318.
Recordation.
Certificate of incorporation,
§22-21-314.
Amended certificate,
§22-21-315.
Records.
Board.
Meetings, §22-21-316.
Refunding securities,
§22-21-321.
Reincorporation of existing
corporations, §22-21-341.
Additional powers,
§22-21-352.
Remedies.
Lease agreements.
Default, §22-21-331.
Rules and regulations.
Powers of authority,
§22-21-318.
Scholarships.
Powers of authority,
§22-21-318.
Seals and sealed
instruments.
Powers of authority,
§22-21-318.
Securities, §§22-21-320 to
22-21-331.
Additional powers.
Definition of "securities,"
§22-21-350.
Federal securities.
Defined, §22-21-350.
General obligations
securities, §22-21-353.
Conditions, §22-21-320.
Defined, §§22-21-311,
22-21-350.
Execution and delivery,
§22-21-320.
Conditions for execution,
§22-21-322.
Indenture.
Source of payment,
§22-21-323.

HEALTH CARE
    AUTHORITIES—Cont'd
Securities—Cont'd
  Interest, §22-21-320.
    Exemption from usury and
      interest provisions,
      §22-21-328.
  Legal investments.
    Status of securities issued
      under article,
      §22-21-326.
  Limitation of actions to
    contest validity,
    §22-21-329.
  Negotiability, §22-21-327.
  Notice of issuance,
    §22-21-329.
  Payment.
    Remedies for default in
      payment, §22-21-331.
    Source of payment,
      §22-21-323.
  Powers of authority,
    §22-21-318.
  Proceeds.
    Use of proceeds,
      §22-21-324.
  Refunding securities,
    §22-21-321.
  Specific obligation securities,
    §22-21-323.
  State, counties or
    municipalities not
    indebted, §22-21-325.
  Terms, §22-21-320.
  Usury.
    Exemption from usury and
      interest provisions,
      §22-21-328.
  Validity.
    Limitation on actions to
      contest, §22-21-329.
Short title, §22-21-31.
Staff.
  Powers of authority,
    §22-21-318.
State.
  Defined, §22-21-311.
  Securities not obligation of
    state, §22-21-325.
Taxation.
  Exemptions from taxation,
    §22-21-333.
  Hospital tax.
    Defined, §22-21-311.
    Proceeds.
      Use, §22-21-344.
Title of act, §22-21-310.
Usury.
  Exemption from usury and
    interest provisions,
    §22-21-328.

HEALTH CARE SERVICE
    PLANS, §§10-4-100 to
  10-4-115.
Agents.
  Certificates for agents,
    §10-4-111.
Alabama health care plan,
  §§27-21-1 to 27-21-6.
  See INSURANCE.
Applicability of article,
  §10-4-100.
Board of directors, §10-4-103.
Bylaws, §10-4-104.
Certificate of incorporation,
  §10-4-101.
Certificates of authority.
  Agents, §10-4-111.
  Fee, §10-4-106.

HEALTH CARE SERVICE
    PLANS—Cont'd
Charges.
  Regulation of rates, charges,
    etc., §10-4-109.
Charter, §10-4-105.
Commissioner of insurance.
  Certificates of authority,
    §10-4-106.
  Examination power,
    §10-4-110.
  Filing health service
    certificates with
    commissioner, §10-4-111.
  Review of decisions by
    commissioner, §10-4-114.
Contracts.
  Contracts with public,
    §10-4-106.
Counties.
  License, privilege or other
    taxes prohibited,
    §10-4-107.
Deposit of securities with
    state treasurer, §10-4-112.
Directors.
  Board of directors, §10-4-103.
Examinations.
  Power of commissioner of
    insurance, §10-4-110.
Facilities.
  Health care facilities,
    §§10-4-102, 10-4-108.
Fees.
  Certificates of authority,
    §10-4-106.
Health care facilities.
  Eligibility for participation,
    §10-4-102.
  Selection by certificate
    holders, §10-4-108.
Health service certificates.
  Deposit of securities with
    state treasurer,
    §10-4-112.
  Filing, §10-4-111.
  Issuance, §10-4-111.
Incorporation, §10-4-101.
Insurance.
  Applicability of insurance
    laws, §10-4-115.
  Commissioner of insurance,
    §10-4-110.
Licenses.
  License taxes by
    municipalities or
    counties prohibited,
    §10-4-107.
Municipal corporations.
  License, privilege or other
    taxes by municipalities
    prohibited, §10-4-107.
Names.
  Change of corporate name,
    §10-4-105.
Participation.
  Health care facilities which
    may participate,
    §10-4-102.
Pharmacists and
    pharmacies.
  Prescriptions.
    Third party prescription
      program.
      Provisions inapplicable
        to corporations
        organized for
        establishment and
        operation of plans,
        §34-23-116.

HEALTH CARE SERVICE
    PLANS—Cont'd
Rates and charges.
  Filing of annual statement,
    §10-4-113.
  Regulation, §10-4-109.
Regulation of rates, charges,
    etc., §10-4-109.
Securities.
  Deposit with state treasurer,
    §10-4-112.
Statements.
  Filing annual statements,
    §10-4-113.
State treasurer.
  Deposit of securities with
    state treasurer,
    §10-4-112.
Taxation.
  License, privilege or other
    taxes by municipalities
    or counties prohibited,
    §10-4-107.

HEALTH MAINTENANCE
    ORGANIZATIONS,
  §§27-21A-1 to 27-21A-32.
Advertising.
  Untrue or misleading
    advertising, §27-21A-13.
Advisory council, §27-21A-31.
Agents.
  Licenses, §27-21A-14.
  Regulation of agent,
    §27-21A-14.
Bankruptcy.
  Protection against
    insolvency, §27-21A-12.
Benefits.
  Coordination, §27-21A-30.
Certificate of authority.
  Application, §27-21A-2.
  Contents, §27-21A-2.
  Filing fee, §27-21A-21.
  Denial.
    Administrative procedure,
      §27-21A-20.
  Existing organizations,
    §27-21A-29.
  Issuance, §27-21A-3.
  Required, §27-21A-2.
  Suspension or revocation.
    Administrative procedure,
      §27-21A-20.
    Grounds, §27-21A-17.
Charges for services.
  Schedule, §27-21A-7.
Commissioner.
  Contracts.
    Consultant contract,
      §27-21A-26.
Complaint systems.
  Establishment, §27-21A-10.
  Reports.
    Annual report, §27-21A-10.
Confidentiality of
    information.
  Medical information,
    §27-21A-25.
Conservation, §27-21A-18.
Construction of chapter with
    other statutes and laws,
  §27-21A-23.
Contracts.
  Consultant contracts,
    §27-21A-26.
  Reinsurance.
    Filing, §27-21A-2.
Control.
  Acquisition, §27-21A-27.

HEALTH MAINTENANCE ORGANIZATIONS—Cont'd

Coordination of benefit, §27-21A-30.

Definitions, §27-21A-1.

Deposits.
Annual deposit requirement, §27-21A-12.

Enrollment requirement, §27-21A-32.

Evidence of coverage.
Deceptive evidence, §27-21A-13.
Enrollee entitled to, §27-21A-7.

Examinations, §27-21A-16.

Existing organizations.
Certificate of authority, §27-21A-29.

Fees, §27-21A-21.

Fiduciaries.
Responsibilities of directors, officers, employees and partners, §27-21A-6.

Foreign corporations.
Qualifying under chapter, §27-21A-2.

Governing body, §27-21A-5.

Health care service plans.
General provisions, §§10-4-100 to 10-4-115.
Powers, §27-21A-15.

Information to enrollees, §27-21A-9.

Injunctions.
Violations of chapter, §27-21A-22.

Insolvency.
Protection against, §27-21A-12.

Insurers.
Powers, §27-21A-15.

Investments, §27-21A-11.

Licenses.
Agents, §27-21A-14.

Liquidation, §27-21A-18.

Material change in operation.
Information to enrollees, §27-21A-9.

Merger, §27-21A-27.

Modification of operation.
Notice, §27-21A-2.

Officers and employees.
Fiduciary responsibilities, §27-21A-6.

Penalties.
Violation of chapter.
Administrative penalties, §27-21A-22.

Powers.
Generally, §27-21A-4.

Prohibited practices, §27-21A-13.

Records.
Examination, §27-21A-16.

Rehabilitation of organization, §27-21A-18.

Reinsurance.
Contracts.
Filing, §27-21A-2.

Reports.
Annual report, §27-21A-8.
Complaint system, §27-21A-10.
Public documents, §27-21A-24.

Rules and regulations.
Promulgation, §27-21A-16.

HEALTH MAINTENANCE ORGANIZATIONS—Cont'd

Solicitations.
Untrue or misleading solicitations, §27-21A-13.

State health officer.
Contracts.
Consultant contract, §27-21A-26.

Taxation, §27-21A-28.

Violations of chapter.
Cease and desist orders, §27-21A-22.
Injunctions, §27-21A-32.
Penalties.
Administrative penalties, §27-21A-22.

HEALTH STUDIO SERVICES, §§8-23-1 to 8-23-13.

Applicability of chapter, §8-23-6.

Bonds, surety, §8-23-3.

Chapter not exclusive, §8-23-12.

Contracts, §§8-23-4 to 8-23-9.
Applicability of chapter, §8-23-6.
Assignment.
Effect on right of action or defense, §8-23-7.
Notice, §8-23-7.
Cancellation, §8-23-4.
Contents, §8-23-4.
Effect of noncompliance with chapter, §8-23-9.
Noncompliance with chapter.
Void and unenforceable, §8-23-9.
Rescission, §8-23-4.
Restriction on right of action of buyer prohibited, §8-23-8.
Term, §8-23-4.
Written contracts required, §8-23-5.

Declaration of legislature, §8-23-1.

Definitions, §8-23-2.

Enforcement of chapter, §8-23-10.

Findings of legislature, §8-23-1.

Legislative findings and declaration, §8-23-1.

Noncompliance with chapter.
Unfair trade practice, §8-23-13.

Notice.
Assignment of contract, §8-23-7.

Penalties.
Violation of chapter, §8-23-11.

Registered agent, §8-23-3.

Registration.
Salespersons, §8-23-3.

Supervision of chapter, §8-23-10.

Unfair or deceptive trade practice.
Failure to comply with chapter, §8-23-13.

Violation of chapter.
Penalty, §8-23-11.

HEARING AID DEALERS AND FITTERS, §§34-14-1 to 34-14-33.

Address.
Notice to board of business address, §34-14-8.
Notice to licensee sent to business address, §34-14-8.
Record of business addresses, §34-14-8.

Advertising.
False advertising.
Grounds for suspension or revocation of license, §34-14-9.

Appeals.
Suspension or revocation of license, §34-14-9.

Applicability of chapter.
Chapter not applicable with certain persons and practices, §34-14-13.

Board of hearing aid dealers, §§34-14-30 to 34-14-33.
Accounts.
Hearing aid account, §34-14-33.
Address.
Licensees to notify board of address, §34-14-8.
Notice from board sent to licensee's business address, §34-14-8.
Appointment of members, §34-14-30.
Compensation of members, §34-14-30.
Complaints against licensees, §34-14-9.
Composition, §34-14-30.
Defined, §34-14-1.
Duties, §34-14-31.
Enforcement of chapter, §34-14-9.
Established, §34-14-30.
Examinations.
Duties of board, §34-14-31.
Expenses of members, §34-14-30.
Meetings, §34-14-32.
Receipts.
Disposition of receipts, §34-14-33.
Revocation or suspension of licenses.
General procedure, §34-14-9.
Terms of office, §34-14-30.
Vacancies.
Filling vacancies, §34-14-30.

Bonds, surety.
Temporary licenses, §34-14-7.

Complaints against licensees, §34-14-9.

Definitions, §34-14-1.

Depositions.
Board of hearing aid dealers and fitters.
Depositions in proceedings before board, §34-14-9.

Education.
Continuing education requirements, §34-14-6.

Enforcement of chapter, §34-14-9.

Examinations.
Licenses. See within this heading, "Licenses."

HEARING AID DEALERS AND FITTERS—Cont'd

Exemptions from provisions of chapter, §34-14-13.

Fees.
License fees, §34-14-3.
Renewal of license, §34-14-6.
Temporary permits, §34-14-7.

Fraud.
Grounds for revocation or suspension of license, §34-14-9.
Prohibited acts relating to licenses, §34-14-12.

Hearings.
Board of hearing aid dealers.
Complaints against licensees, §34-14-9.

Licenses, §§34-14-1 to 34-14-6.
Alteration of licenses prohibited, §34-14-12.
Certificates of endorsement, §34-14-3.
Corporations.
Compliance with licensing provisions, §34-14-2.
Defined, §34-14-1.
Display, §34-14-2.
Duplicates, §34-14-2.
Education.
Continuing education requirements, §34-14-6.
Examinations.
Qualifications of applicants, §34-14-4.
Scope of examination, §34-14-5.
Fees, §34-14-3.
Renewal, §34-14-6.
Fines.
Administrative fines.
Disciplining of licensees, §34-14-9.
Fraud.
Grounds for revocation or suspension of license, §34-14-9.
Prohibited acts, §34-14-12.
Issuance, §34-14-3.
Powers and duties of state board of health, §34-14-11.
Nonresidents.
Reciprocity, §34-14-3.
Partnerships.
Compliance with licensing provisions, §34-14-2.
Powers and duties of state board of health, §34-14-11.
Prohibited acts and practices, §34-14-12.
Qualifications of applicants, §34-14-4.
Reciprocity, §34-14-3.
Renewal, §34-14-6.
Powers and duties of state board of health, §34-14-11.
Required, §34-14-2.
Revocation or suspension, §34-14-9.
Sale or barter of license prohibited, §34-14-12.
Temporary permits, §34-14-1.

Nonresidents.
License reciprocity requirements, §34-14-3.

HEARING AID DEALERS AND FITTERS—Cont'd

Notice.
Business address of licensee, §34-14-8.

Penalties.
Administrative fines.
Disciplining of licensees, §34-14-9.
Violations of chapter, §34-14-14.

Permits.
Temporary permits.
Defined, §34-14-1.
Fees, §34-14-7.

Practice of fitting and dealing in hearing aids.
Applicability of chapter, §34-14-13.
Defined, §34-14-1.
Exemptions from provisions of chapter, §34-14-13.
Prohibited acts and practices, §34-14-12.
Receipt to persons supplied with hearing aid, §34-14-10.

Receipts.
Furnishing to persons supplied with hearing aid, §34-14-10.

Reciprocity.
Licenses, §34-14-3.

Speech pathologists and audiologists.
Exemptions from provisions of chapter, §34-28A-3.
General provisions, §§34-28A-1 to 34-28A-44.
See SPEECH PATHOLOGISTS AND AUDIOLOGISTS.

State board of health.
Powers and duties, §34-14-11.

Subpoenas.
Board of hearing aid dealers and fitters.
Subpoena power of board, §34-14-9.

Witnesses.
Board of hearing aid dealers and fitters.
Compelling attendance of witnesses, §34-14-9.

HEARINGS.

Abortion.
Parental consent to performing abortion upon minors.
Waiver of written consent requirements, §26-21-4.

Accountants.
Proceedings before board of public accountancy, §31-1-14.

Adoption.
Petitions, §26-10-2.
Subsidized adoptions, §26-10-29.

Adult protective services.
Emergency protective services, §38-9-5.
Protective placement, §38-9-6.

Aged persons.
Medical assistance to elderly persons.
Applicants or recipients, §38-6-7.

HEARINGS—Cont'd

Air pollution.
Rules and regulations, §22-28-15.

Attachment.
Sale of property levied on.
Order for receipt of sale proceeds by plaintiff pending action.
Hearing on motion, §6-6-78.
Seizure of person or property.
Rules of civil procedure.
Procedure for seizure of property, ARCP, Rule 64 (b).

Attorneys at law.
Disciplinary proceedings.
Rules of disciplinary enforcement, ARDE, Rule 8.

Aviation.
Aeronautics commission, §4-2-48.
Reports, §4-2-49.

Banks and financial institutions.
Fiduciary accounts.
Transfers.
Objections, §5-11A-33.

Budgets.
Tentative budget, §41-4-87.

Canons of judicial ethics.
Adjudicative responsibilities.
Standards of performance, ACJE, Canon 3A.

Cemeteries.
County cemeteries.
Appeals from assessment of damages, §§11-17-9, 11-17-10.

Child care facilities.
Revocation or refusal to renew licenses, §38-7-9.

Chiropractors.
Certificates of qualification.
See CHIROPRACTORS.

Circuit courts.
Conduct in open court, ARCP, Rule 77 (b).

Coal.
Surface mining control and reclamation.
Designation of areas unsuitable for surface coal mining.
Review and public hearing, §9-16-96.
Division of hearings and appeals, §9-16-77.
Hearing officers, §9-16-78.
Permits.
Suspension or revocation of permit, §9-16-93.
Procedure for hearings, §9-16-79.

Conservators.
Incapacitated persons.
Revocation of conservatorship.
Application by person ascertained to be incapacitated, §§26-2-52, 26-2-53.
Settlements of accounts of conservators.
Compulsion of settlement by probate court.
Partial settlement, §26-5-31.

HEARINGS—Cont'd
Coroners' inquests, §§15-4-1 to 15-4-11.
See CORONERS.
Cosmetology.
Proceedings before board of cosmetology, §§34-7-46, 34-7-47.
Counties.
Bond issues.
Validation, §6-6-753.
Court of the judiciary.
Place of hearing, ARJC, Rule 19.
Credit unions.
Revocation of certificate of authority, §5-17-8.
Dams.
Erection of dams for mills, gins, factories or electric generators, §§18-2-1 to 18-2-21.
See DAMS.
Dental service corporations.
Bonds, surety or securities to be posted, §22-21-370.
Sales representatives.
Contracting sales representatives.
Denial, suspension, revocation or refusal to renew registration, §22-21-381.
Desertion and nonsupport.
Payment of overdue support.
Bond, security, or other guarantee to secure.
Obligor to have opportunity to be heard on matter, §30-3-6.
Domestic relations.
Protection from abuse.
See DOMESTIC RELATIONS.
Dower interests.
Ascertainment and payment, §35-4-191.
Education.
Nonteacher, nonclassified, etc., employees.
Termination, §36-26-106.
Elections.
Contesting elections generally, §§17-15-1 to 17-15-63.
See ELECTIONS.
Eminent domain, §§18-1A-275 to 18-1A-278.
Environmental management.
Commission, §22-22A-7.
Rules and regulations.
Adoption of rules, regulations and standards, §22-22A-8.
Exemptions from administration and payment of debts, §§6-10-86 to 6-10-88.
Fires and fire prevention.
Firemen.
Compensation for death.
Claims, §36-30-6.
Funerals.
Board of funeral service.
See FUNERALS.
Grain dealers.
Refusal, suspension or revocation of license, §§2-31-12, 2-31-13.

HEARINGS—Cont'd
Guardian and ward.
Conservators, §§26-2-52, 26-2-53, 26-5-31.
Removal of person or property of minors and wards.
Removal to another county, §§26-8-21, 26-8-22.
Habitual felony act.
Determination of whether defendant repeat or habitual offender, §13A-5-10.
Hearing aid dealers and fitters.
Complaints against licensees, §34-14-9.
Highways.
Closing and vacating streets, alleys and highways, §23-4-2.
Hotels, inns and other transient lodging places.
Transient occupancy tax.
Assessment, §40-26-13.
Income tax.
Assessments.
Hearing by department of revenue on taxpayer protest, §40-18-40.
Setoff debt collection, §§40-18-103, 40-18-104.
Insurance.
Commissioner of insurance, §§27-2-26 to 27-2-32.
See INSURANCE.
Generally.
See INSURANCE.
Juvenile proceedings, §12-15-65; ARJP, Rules 23, 24.
See JUVENILE PROCEEDINGS.
Life interests.
Ascertainment and payment, §35-4-191.
Liquefied petroleum gas.
Assessment, §9-17-109.
Authority of board, §9-17-108.
Marine resources.
General provisions.
See MARINE RESOURCES.
Violations of chapter, §9-12-5.
Mentally ill.
Criminal law and procedure.
Release of criminal psychopaths, §15-16-64.
Conditional releases, §§15-16-70, 15-16-71.
Failure to hold hearing, §15-16-66.
Mines and minerals.
Mineral resources management committee.
Conduct of hearing, §9-5-3.
Surface mining reclamation.
Violation of article, §9-16-10.
Minors.
Custody and support.
Expedited process for child support, ARJA, Rule 35.

HEARINGS—Cont'd
Minors—Cont'd
Withholding orders for child support.
Obligor to be served notice and given opportunity for hearing, §30-3-62.
Motor vehicle carriers.
Examiners, §§37-3-9, 37-3-28.
Public service commission, §§37-3-7, 37-3-9, 37-3-19.
Motor vehicles.
Abandoned vehicles.
Hearing to determine whether vehicle abandoned, §32-13-4.
Automotive dismantlers and parts recyclers.
License.
Refusal, cancellation or revocation, §40-12-417.
Drivers' licenses.
Cancellation, suspension or revocation.
Right to file petitions, §32-5A-195.
Uniform certificate of title and antitheft act.
Protesting actions of department, §32-8-4.
Municipal corporations.
See MUNICIPAL CORPORATIONS.
National guard.
Compensation for death of national guardsman.
Hearing by board of adjustment, §31-3-6.
Obscenity.
Anti-obscenity enforcement act.
Forfeitures of property, §13A-12-200.8.
Preliminary injunctions for violations, §13A-12-200.7.
Oil and gas board, §9-17-3.
Rules of procedure, §9-17-7.
Optometrists.
Disciplinary action, §34-22-8.
Parole.
Court to be held upon return of prisoner, §15-22-32.
Partition.
Crops.
Notice, §35-6-113.
Time, §35-6-112.
Probate courts, §35-6-43.
Sale instead of partition.
Notice, §35-6-60.
Time, §35-6-59.
Sale of land of insane persons for distribution among joint owners.
Conduct of hearings, §35-6-85.
Notice of hearing, §35-6-82.
Time for hearing, §35-6-82.
Peace bonds, §15-6-22.
Peace officers.
Compensation for death.
Claims, §36-30-6.
Penitentiary.
Management and treatment of convicts, §14-3-54.
Physicians.
Licenses.
Suspension or revocation.
See PHYSICIANS.

HEARINGS—Cont'd

Pilots.
Revocation or suspension of
licenses, §33-4-45.

Plumbing.
Certification of plumbers and
gas fitters.
Revocation of certificate,
§34-37-12.

Post-conviction remedies,
ARCrP, Rule 20.9 (a).

Preliminary hearings,
§§15-11-1 to 15-11-15.
See PRELIMINARY
HEARINGS.

**Public officers and
employees.**
Merit system.
Investigations and
hearings.
Buildings.
Use of state, county,
etc., buildings,
§36-26-43.
Generally, §36-26-40.
Witnesses, §36-26-41.
Public property, papers, etc.
Recovery of papers,
property, etc., by
successors to office,
§36-12-22.
Summary proceedings
involving officials,
§6-6-663.

Public service commission.
Generally.
See PUBLIC SERVICE
COMMISSION.
Rate and other regulations,
§§37-1-85 to 37-1-105.
See PUBLIC SERVICE
COMMISSION.

Real estate brokers.
Disciplinary actions,
§34-27-37.
Rehearings, §34-27-37.

**Restitution to victims of
crimes.**
Findings.
Statement of findings,
§15-18-69.
Objections to order,
§15-18-69.
Persons entitled to be heard,
§15-18-67.
Restitution hearing,
§15-18-67.
Statement of findings,
§15-18-69.

Rules of civil procedure.
Seizure of person or property.
Procedure for seizure of
property, ARCP, Rule
64 (b).

Rules of criminal procedure.
Post-conviction remedies,
ARCrP, Rule 20.9.

Sales.
Going-out-of business or
distress merchandise
sales.
License.
Public hearing on
application, §8-13-5.
Costs, §8-13-8.

Sales tax.
Assessments, §40-23-17.

Searches and seizures.
Search warrants.
Challenging warrant,
§15-5-15.

HEARINGS—Cont'd

Searches and seizures
—Cont'd
Seizure of person or property.
Rules of civil procedure.
Procedure for seizure of
property, ARCP,
Rule 64 (b).

Securities.
Orders of commission.
Hearing by commission on
order or failure to
make order, §8-6-32.
Private hearings.
Request for, §8-6-25.
Public hearings, §8-6-25.

Sentencing.
Generally, ARCrP, Rule 6.
Habitual felony offenders.
Hearing to determine
whether defendant is
repeat or habitual
offender, §13A-5-10.
Presence of defendant,
ARCrP, Rule 7.

Social workers.
Disciplinary proceedings,
§34-30-5.

Soil and water conservation.
Districts.
Discontinuance of district,
§9-8-31.
Incorporation, §9-8-23.
Land-use regulations,
§9-8-26.
Watershed conservancy
districts, §§9-8-55, 9-8-62
to 9-8-65.

Soil classifiers.
Powers of board generally,
§34-32-8.

Sports.
Agents.
Registration.
Refusal.
Procedure, §8-26-7.

**State departments and
agencies.**
Sunset law, §§41-20-1 to
41-20-16.
See STATE
DEPARTMENTS AND
AGENCIES.

Subpoenas, ARCP, Rule 45
(e).

Sunset law, §§41-20-1 to
41-20-16.
See STATE DEPARTMENTS
AND AGENCIES.

Support and maintenance.
Payment of overdue support.
Bond, security, or other
guarantee to secure.
Obligor to have
opportunity to be
heard on matter,
§30-3-6.

Taxation.
Department of revenue.
Notice of hearing, §40-2-5.
Hotels, inns and other
transient lodging places.
Transient occupancy tax.
Assessment, §40-26-13.
Income tax.
Assessments.
Taxpayers' protest,
§40-18-40.
Setoff debt collection,
§§40-18-103,
40-18-104.

HEARINGS—Cont'd

Taxation—Cont'd
Public utilities.
Incorrect valuations,
§40-21-24.
Sales tax.
Assessments, §40-23-17.
Use tax.
Redeterminations,
§40-23-73.

Transportation companies.
Abandonment of service.
Application for permit to
abandon, §37-2-6.

Use tax.
Redeterminations, §40-23-73.

Vacation time-sharing plans.
Violation of article,
§34-27-61.

Veterinarians, §34-29-79.

Visitation of children.
Compliance with visitation
order.
Bond, security, or other
guarantee to secure.
Obligor to have
opportunity to be
heard on matter,
§30-3-6.

Warehouses, §8-15-13.

**Water management and
drainage.**
Districts.
Annexation of land to
district, §9-9-50.
Board of viewers.
Hearing upon exceptions
and report, §9-9-29.
Reports.
Notice of hearing,
§9-9-28.
Establishment of districts.
Notice, §9-9-9.
Opinion of representative
of state committee,
§9-9-10.
Procedure, §9-9-11.
Drainage subdistricts.
Establishment, §9-9-75.

**Water supply and
waterworks.**
See WATER SUPPLY AND
WATERWORKS.

Welfare.
Child care facilities.
Revocation or refusal to
renew licenses,
§38-7-9.

HEARSAY.
General provisions,
§§12-21-30, 12-21-43,
12-21-44.

HEARSES.
License taxes and
registration fees,
§40-12-247.

HEART ASSOCIATION.
Licenses.
Exemptions, §40-9-13.
Taxation.
Exemptions, §40-9-13.

HEART BALM ACT.
Seduction, §§6-5-330, 6-5-331.

HEART OF DIXIE.
Motor vehicle tags, §32-6-54.

HEART TRANSPLANTS.
Anatomical gifts, §§22-19-40 to 22-19-47.
See ANATOMICAL GIFTS.

HEATERS.
Licenses.
Dealers, §40-12-97.

HEATING AND AIR CONDITIONING CONTRACTORS, §§34-31-1 to 34-31-34.
Administrative procedure.
Procedures of board to follow Alabama administrative procedures law, §34-31-33.
Advertisements.
Only certified contractors to advertise, §34-31-24.
Appeals, §34-31-34.
Board, §§34-31-20 to 34-31-23.
Appointment of members, §34-31-20.
Bonds, surety, §34-31-21.
Chairman and secretary, §34-31-21.
Created, §34-31-20.
Defined, §34-31-18.
Duties, §34-31-21.
Expenses of members, §34-31-22.
Meetings.
Regular meetings, §34-31-23.
Mileage and expenses of members, §34-31-22.
Minimum repair and service standards.
Adoption, §34-31-21.
Property.
Transfer, §34-31-20.
Quorum, §34-31-21.
Terms of members, §34-31-20.
Withdrawal of funds, §34-31-21.
Bonds, surety.
Performance bonds, §34-31-28.
Requirement of bond authorized, §34-31-30.
Certificates.
Annual renewal, §34-31-26.
Applications.
Form, §34-31-27.
Removal of certification, §34-31-32.
Renewal certificates.
Form, §34-31-27.
Suspension or revocation, §34-31-32.
Certified contractors.
Defined, §34-31-18.
Only certified contractors to advertise, etc., §34-31-24.
Definitions, §34-31-18.
Disciplinary actions, §34-31-32.
Examinations, §§34-31-27 to 34-31-29.
Applications.
Form, §34-31-27.
Content, §34-31-29.
Exemption of certain persons, §34-31-28.
Notice, §34-31-29.
Time and place, §34-31-29.
Written or oral examinations, §34-31-28.

HEATING AND AIR CONDITIONING CONTRACTORS—Cont'd
Fees.
Application and renewal fees, §34-31-25.
Late fees, §34-31-32.
Licenses.
Annual renewal, §34-31-26.
Certificate of qualification required, §34-31-24.
Fees.
Application and renewal fees, §34-31-25.
List of certified contractors.
Publication and mailing, §34-31-31.
Notice.
Examinations, §34-31-29.
Penalties.
Use of penalties collected, §34-31-25.
Violations of chapter, §34-31-32.
Publication.
List of certified contractors, §34-31-31.
Purpose of chapter, §34-31-19.
Qualifications.
Certificate of qualification required for license, §34-31-24.
Violations.
Penalty, §34-31-32.

HEFLIN, MUNICIPALITY OF.
Property tax, Const. Ala., amd. 8.

HEIRS.
Adoption of adults for purposes of inheritance, §§43-4-1 to 43-4-4.
Decedents' estates.
See DECEDENTS' ESTATES.
Limitation of actions.
Exceptions to applicability of chapter, §6-2-2.
Posthumous children included in "heirs," §35-4-8.
Remainders, reversions and executory interests.
Remainder limited after death without heirs or issue.
Construction of words "heirs" or "issue," §35-4-213.
Wills.
Generally.
See WILLS.
Probate code, §§43-8-1 to 43-8-298.
See WILLS.

HELMETS.
Motorcycles, §§32-5A-245, 32-12-41, 32-12-42, 32-12-44.

HELPING HAND CLUB OF ANNISTON.
Licenses.
Exemptions, §40-9-12.
Taxation.
Exemptions, §40-9-12.

HEMATITE.
Official mineral of state, §1-2-13.

HEMOPHILIA TREATMENT, §§21-8-1 to 21-8-5.
Advisory committee, §21-8-4.
Definitions, §21-8-1.
Division of vocational rehabilitation and crippled children service.
Duties, §21-8-5.
Legislative intent, §21-8-2.
Treatment program, §21-8-3.

HENRY COUNTY.
Constitution of Alabama.
Amendments.
Probate judge.
Costs and charges of courts and compensation of probate judge, Const. Ala., amd. 403.
Courthouse.
Bonds for courthouse, Const. Ala., amd. 237.
Jail.
Bonds for jail, Const. Ala., amd. 237.

HERALDRY.
State code of arms.
Description in heraldic terms, §1-2-2.

HEROIN.
Controlled substances.
See DRUGS.

HIDE.
Licenses.
Dealers, §40-12-110.

HIGH SCHOOLS.
General provisions.
See EDUCATION.
Mathematics and science high school, §§16-26A-1 to 16-26A-7.
See EDUCATION.

HIGHWAY PATROL.
General provisions, §§32-2-20 to 32-2-26.
See MOTOR VEHICLES.

HIGHWAYS.
Abandonment.
Closing and vacating streets, alleys and highways, §§23-4-1 to 23-4-20. See within this heading, "Closing and vacating streets, alleys and highways."
Abutting landowners.
Closing and vacating streets, alleys and highways.
Notice, §23-4-2.
Vacating street or alleys, §23-4-20.
Liens.
Improvements on public streets, etc.
Generally, §§35-11-410 to 35-11-417. See within this heading, "Liens."
Accidents, §§32-10-1 to 32-10-12.
See MOTOR VEHICLES.
Actions.
Authority.
Maintaining and defending, §23-1-175.
Damages to highways, §32-5-9.

HIGHWAYS—Cont'd
  Actions—Cont'd
    Finance corporation.
      Maintaining and
        defending, §23-1-175.
  **Additions to state road
    system.**
    Conformative to federal aid
      laws, §23-1-46.
  Advertising.
    Outdoor advertising,
      §§23-1-270 to 23-1-288.
    See ADVERTISING.
    Rights of way.
      Prohibited on highway
        rights of way, §23-1-6.
  Affidavits.
    Department.
      Power to take affidavits,
        §23-1-39.
  Agriculture.
    Experiment station system.
      Construction and
        maintenance.
      State highway
        department,
        §23-1-43.
  Airports.
    Tax or license for use of
      public streets, etc.,
      leading to or from
      airport prohibited,
      §4-3-9.
  Alabama highway authority,
    §§23-1-150 to 23-1-160. See
    within this heading,
    "Authority."
  **Alabama highway finance
    corporation,** §§23-1-170 to
    23-1-181. See within this
    heading, "Finance
    corporation."
  Alleys.
    Closing and vacating streets,
      alleys and highways,
      §§23-4-1 to 23-4-20. See
      within this heading,
      "Closing and vacating
      streets, alleys and
      highways."
  Animals.
    Estrays, §§3-2-20 to 3-2-23.
  Appeals.
    Closing and vacating streets,
      alleys and highways,
      §23-4-5.
  Attorney general.
    Department.
      Chief and assistant
        counsels.
        Commissioned as
          assistant attorneys
          general, §23-1-26.
    Finance corporation.
      Vice-president of
        corporation, §23-1-174.
  Attorneys at law.
    Legal division of highway
      department, §§23-1-25 to
      23-1-31. See within this
      heading, "Department."
  Authority, §§23-1-150 to
    23-1-160.
    Actions.
      Maintaining and
        defending, §23-1-175.
    Board of directors.
      Members of corporation,
        §23-1-154.
      Quorum, §23-1-154.

HIGHWAYS—Cont'd
  Authority—Cont'd
    Board of directors—Cont'd
      Vacancies in office,
        §23-1-154.
    Bond issues, §§23-1-157 to
      23-1-159.
      Amount, §23-1-177.
      Execution, §23-1-157.
      Interest, §23-1-157.
      Issuance.
        Authority to issue,
          §23-1-155.
        Procedure, §23-1-157.
      Maturity date, §23-1-157.
      Payment.
        State treasurer,
          §23-1-159.
      Proceeds.
        Disposition, §23-1-158.
      Sale, §23-1-157.
        Proceeds.
          Disposition, §23-1-158.
      Seal, §23-1-157.
      Signatures, §23-1-157.
      State treasurer.
        Payments by treasurer,
          §23-1-159.
    Certificate of incorporation.
      Issuance, §23-1-153.
    Composition, §§23-1-151,
      23-1-154.
    Construction of article,
      §23-1-150.
    Contracts.
      Procedure, §23-1-156.
    Dissolution.
      Application for dissolution,
        §23-1-160.
      Procedure, §23-1-160.
    Eminent domain.
      Powers, §23-1-155.
    Federal aid highway finance
      authority, §§23-1-300 to
      23-1-318. See within this
      heading, "Federal aid
      highway finance
      authority."
    Gifts.
      Acceptance, §23-1-175.
    Incorporation.
      Application, §23-1-152.
      Authorization, §23-1-151.
      Certificate of incorporation.
        Issuance, §23-1-153.
    Intent of article, §23-1-150.
    Officers, §23-1-154.
    Personnel.
      Employment, §23-1-155.
    Powers.
      General provisions,
        §23-1-155.
    President.
      Director of finance,
        §23-1-154.
    Property.
      Acquisition, §23-1-155.
      Conveyance to state,
        §23-1-156.
    Purpose of article, §23-1-150.
    Records.
      Proceedings, §23-1-154.
    Rules and regulations.
      Promulgation, §23-1-156.
    Salaries, §23-1-154.
    Seal, §23-1-155.
      Bond issues, §23-1-157.
    Secretary.
      Highway director,
        §23-1-154.

HIGHWAYS—Cont'd
  Authority—Cont'd
    Secretary of state.
      Application for
        incorporation,
        §23-1-152.
      Fees.
        Not to be paid for in
          connection with
          incorporation or
          dissolution,
          §23-1-153.
    State treasurer.
      Bond issues.
        Payments by, §23-1-159.
      Treasurer of corporation,
        §23-1-154.
    Taxation.
      Bond issues.
        Exemptions, §23-1-157.
    Vice-president.
      Executive secretary to the
        governor, §23-1-154.
  Barricades.
    Detours, §23-5-2.
  **Bear Creek development
    authority.**
    Use of public roads,
      §§33-15-16.
  Beautification.
    Contracts.
      Federal assistance, §23-1-1.
    Junkyard control, §§23-1-240
      to 23-1-251.
      See JUNKYARD
        CONTROL.
    Outdoor advertising,
      §§23-1-270 to 23-1-288.
    See ADVERTISING.
    Rules and regulations.
      Federal assistance.
        Promulgation and
          enforcement,
          §23-1-1.
    Scenic enhancement,
      §§23-1-220 to 23-1-223.
  Beautification board.
    General provisions,
      §§41-9-490 to 41-9-498.
    See BEAUTIFICATION.
  Bench marks.
    Establishment of permanent
      bench marks, §9-4-11.
  Bicycles.
    General provisions,
      §§32-5A-260 to
      32-5A-266.
    See BICYCLES.
  Billboards.
    Outdoor advertising,
      §§23-1-270 to 23-1-288.
    See ADVERTISING.
  Blue reflective markers.
    Fire/water hydrants,
      §23-1-10.
  Bond issues, Const. Ala.,
    amds. 11, 21.
    Alabama highway authority,
      §§23-1-157 to 23-1-159.
    Alabama highway finance
      corporation, §§23-1-177
      to 23-1-179.
    Federal aid highway finance
      authority, §§23-1-306 to
      23-1-316. See within this
      heading, "Federal aid
      highway finance
      authority."
    Finance corporation,
      §§23-1-177 to 23-1-179.

HIGHWAYS—Cont'd

Bond issues—Cont'd

Highway authority,
§§23-1-157 to 23-1-159.
United States.
Bond issue for acquiring
public roads in
conjunction with
United States, Const.
Ala., amd. 87.

Bonds, surety.

Contracts.
Bid guaranty, §23-1-2.
Department.
Chief engineer, §23-1-22.
Director, §23-1-21.
Utilities.
Digging up of roads.
Restoration of road,
§23-1-4.

Borrow pits.

Acquisition of land, §23-1-3.

Bridges.

Department.
Rules and regulations.
Promulgation, §23-1-59.
General provisions.
See BRIDGES.

Changes of state road system.

Conformative to federal aid
law, §23-1-46.

Chief counsel.

Legal division, §§23-1-25,
23-1-26.

Chief engineer, §§23-1-22 to 23-1-24.

Closing and vacating streets, alleys and highways, §§23-4-1 to 23-4-20.

Abutting landowners.
Notice, §23-4-2.
Vacation of street or alley.
Procedure, §23-4-20.
Appeals, §23-4-5.
Application of governing
body, §23-4-1.
Approval, §23-4-3.
Assessments.
Damages.
Commissioners, §23-4-3.
Authority, §23-1-3.
Commissioners.
Appointment, §23-4-3.
Assessment of damages,
§23-4-3.
Reports.
Filing, §23-4-3.
Recordation, §23-4-4.
Salaries, §23-4-3.
Contest by interested
persons, §23-4-3.
Counties and municipalities.
Authority, §23-1-3.
Detour roads, §23-1-3.
Cumulative provisions,
§23-4-6.
Damages.
Commissioners.
Assessment, §23-4-3.
Payment, §23-4-3.
Detour roads, §23-1-3.
Hearings, §23-4-2.
Contest by interested
persons, §23-4-3.
Cost, §23-4-4.
Interstate highway system.
Controlled access facilities.
Authority of highway
director, §23-3-3.
Notice, §23-4-2.

HIGHWAYS—Cont'd

Closing and vacating streets, alleys and highways —Cont'd

Petitions, §§23-4-2, 23-4-3.
Procedure.
Application of governing
body, §23-4-1.
General provisions,
§23-4-2.
Resolution.
Adoption, §23-4-2.
State trooper may close
highways, §32-5-16.
Surveys, plats or maps.
Vacation and annulment
by circuit court,
§§35-2-58 to 35-2-62.
See MUNICIPAL
CORPORATIONS.

Committees.

Permanent joint highway
committee, §§29-2-1 to
29-2-8.
See LEGISLATURE.

Condemnation. See within this heading, "Eminent domain."

Conflicts of interest.

Director or employees of
highway department,
§23-1-58.

Constitution of Alabama.

Bond issues, Const. Ala.,
amd. 21.
Bonds for construction,
Const. Ala., amd. 11.
United States.
Bond issue for acquiring
in conjunction with
United States,
Const. Ala., amd. 87.
Chartering or licensing
roads.
Special, private or local
laws prohibited, Const.
Ala., art. IV, §104.
Construction, maintenance,
etc., of highways by
state, Const. Ala., amds.
12, 58.
County roads.
Laws placing responsibility
for county roads in
state highway
department, Const.
Ala., amd. 142.
Distribution of proceeds of
vehicle related taxes,
Const. Ala., amds. 93,
354.
Navigable waters declared
free public highways,
Const. Ala., art. I, §24.
State not to engage in
internal improvements
or lend money or credit
for improvements, Const.
Ala., art. IV, §93.
Exception as to public
roads, highways and
bridges, Const. Ala.,
amd. 1.

Construction.

Agricultural experiment
station.
State highway department,
§23-1-43.

HIGHWAYS—Cont'd

Construction—Cont'd

Character of work.
Alteration.
Authority of highway
director, §23-1-60.
Conflicts of interest.
Director or employees of
department, §23-1-58.
Contracts, §§23-1-53 to
23-1-57.
Counties.
Application by counties for
construction of state
roads, §23-1-48.
Department.
Conflicts of interest,
§23-1-58.
Drainage.
Ditches.
Acquisition of land,
§23-1-3.
Duty to drain areas in
construction works,
§22-20-10.
Engineers.
Competent engineers.
Department to furnish,
§23-1-49.
Extra work.
Determination of need.
Authority of highway
director, §23-1-60.
Supplemental agreement
or force account order,
§23-1-60.
Plans and specifications.
Alteration.
Authority of highway
director, §23-1-60.
Character of work.
Alteration by highway
director, §23-1-60.
Quarries.
Acquisition of land,
§23-1-3.
Rules and regulations.
Promulgation, §23-1-59.
Speed limits.
Speed limit between
working signs,
§32-5-93.
Supervision.
Engineers.
Competent engineers,
§23-1-49.
Highway department,
§23-1-40.
Universities and colleges.
State highway department,
§23-1-42.
Utilities.
Relocation of utility
facilities.
Payment of cost, §23-1-5.
Working signs.
Speed limit between
working signs,
§32-5-93.

Contractors.

Liens.
Improvements on public
streets, etc.,
§§35-11-410 to
35-11-417. See within
this heading, "Liens."
Sales tax.
Street and highway
contractors, §40-23-50.

Contracts.

Approval, §§23-1-54, 23-1-55.

HIGHWAYS—Cont'd
  Contracts—Cont'd
    Authority of department to
        contract, §23-1-53.
    Beautification of highways.
      Federal assistance, §23-1-1.
      General provisions. See
          within this heading,
          "Beautification."
    Bids.
      Bid guaranty, §23-1-2.
      Qualification of bidders,
          §23-1-56.
    Community antenna
        television systems.
      Operating in rights of way.
        Authority of department
            to enter, §23-1-59.
    Conflicts of interest.
      Director or employees of
          highway department,
          §23-1-58.
    Extra work.
      Supplemental agreements,
          §23-1-60.
    Federal assistance.
      Authority to enter into
          necessary contracts,
          §23-1-1.
      Federal aid highway
          finance authority,
          §23-1-317.
    Filing, §23-1-55.
    Finance corporation.
      Approval, §23-1-176.
      Authority of corporation,
          §23-1-175.
      Procedure, §23-1-176.
    Force account basis.
      Extra work, §23-1-60.
    Guaranty.
      Bid guaranty, §23-1-2.
    Highway authority.
      Procedure, §23-1-156.
    Maintenance of highways.
      Federal assistance, §23-1-1.
    Name of state, §23-1-54.
    Penalties.
      Qualification of bidders.
        False representations,
            §23-1-56.
    Pipelines.
      Operating in rights of way.
        Authority of department
            to enter, §23-1-59.
    Preconditions, §23-1-55.
    Prisons and prisoners.
      Convict labor.
        Use on public roads and
            bridges, §23-1-37.
    Public utilities.
      Relocation of utility
          facilities.
        Payment of cost, §23-1-5.
    Qualification of bidders.
      Appeals, §23-1-56.
      Application of contractor,
          §23-1-56.
      Certificate of qualification.
        Issuance, §23-1-56.
      Financial position.
        False representations,
            §23-1-56.
      Forms, §23-1-56.
      Prequalification of
          contractors, §23-1-56.
      Procedure, §23-1-56.
      Rules and regulations,
          §23-1-56.
      Unqualified bidders,
          §23-1-56.

HIGHWAYS—Cont'd
  Contracts—Cont'd
    Rights of way.
      Procurement prerequisite
          to contract, §23-1-55.
    Supplemental agreements.
      Extra work, §23-1-60.
    Telegraph companies.
      Operating in rights of way.
        Authority of department
            to enter into
            contract, §23-1-59.
    Telephone companies.
      Operating in rights of way.
        Authority of highway
            department to enter,
            §23-1-59.
    Television.
      Community antenna
          television systems.
        Rights of way.
          Contracts with
              highway
              department,
              §23-1-59.
    United States.
      Rivers forming boundaries
          between states.
        Agreements and
            contracts with
            adjoining states and
            federal government
            relative to bridges,
            §23-1-57.
  Controlled access facilities,
      §§23-3-1 to 23-3-8. See
      within this heading,
      "Interstate highway
      systems."
  Convict labor.
    Use on public roads and
        bridges, §23-1-37.
  Coosa Valley development
      authority.
    Contracts, §33-16-9.
  Corporations.
    Alabama highway finance
        corporation, §§23-1-170
        to 23-1-181. See within
        this heading, "Finance
        corporation."
  Cost.
    Closing and vacating streets,
        alleys and highways.
      Hearings.
        Payment, §23-4-4.
  Counties.
    Closing and vacating streets,
        alleys and highways,
        §§23-4-1 to 23-4-6. See
        within this heading,
        "Closing and vacating
        streets, alleys and
        highways."
    Construction or maintenance
        of state roads or bridges.
      Application by counties for
          construction or
          maintenance, §23-1-48.
    Interstate highway system.
      Controlled access facilities.
        Agreements with
            counties, §23-3-8.
    Public roads, bridges and
        ferries, §§23-1-80 to
        23-1-95.
      See COUNTIES.

HIGHWAYS—Cont'd
  Counties—Cont'd
    Rights of way.
      Acquisition.
        When deemed necessary
            by director of
            highways, §23-1-45.
      Transferred county roads and
          bridges.
        Employees used on.
          Residents of county,
              §23-1-36.
        Laws placing responsibility
            for county roads in
            state highway
            department, Const.
            Ala., amd. 142.
  Crossing highways.
    Use of white cane or guide
        dogs, §32-5A-220.
  Damages.
    Closing and vacating streets,
        alleys and highways,
        §§23-4-3, 23-4-4.
    Liability for damage to
        highway, §32-5-9.
  Dangerous conditions.
    Closing highways.
      State trooper may close,
          §32-5-16.
  Debris.
    Littering, §§23-5-6, 23-5-9.
  Definitions, §23-1-21.1.
    Department.
      Road machinery and
          equipment
          management program,
          §23-1-50.1.
    Federal aid highway finance
        authority, §23-1-301.
    Interstate highway system.
      Controlled access facilities,
          §23-3-1.
  Department, §§23-1-20 to
      23-1-63.
    Affidavits.
      Power to take affidavits,
          §23-1-39.
    Bonds, surety.
      Chief engineer, §23-1-22.
      Highway director,
          §23-1-21.
    Bridges.
      General provisions.
        See BRIDGES.
    Chief council, §§23-1-25,
        23-1-26.
    Chief engineer, §§23-1-22 to
        23-1-24.
    Chief executive officer.
      Highway director,
          §23-1-21.
    Conflicts of interest.
      Construction of roads and
          bridges, §23-1-58.
    Counties.
      Laws placing responsibility
          for county roads in
          state highway
          department, Const.
          Ala., amd. 142.
    Creation, §23-1-20.
    Definitions, §23-1-21.1.
    Director.
      Appointment, §23-1-21.
      Bonds, surety, §23-1-21.
      Chief executive officer,
          §23-1-21.
      Defined, §23-1-21.1.

HIGHWAYS—Cont'd
Department—Cont'd
Director—Cont'd
Finance corporation.
President of corporation,
§23-1-174.
Full-time position,
§23-1-32.
Highway authority.
Secretary of corporation,
§23-1-154.
Outstanding or authorized
obligations.
Limitation on
inauguration date of
incoming governor,
§23-1-63.
Public transportation.
Authority with regard to,
§23-1-21.2.
Cooperation with federal,
state and local
entities in
administration of
programs,
§23-1-21.3.
Safety coordinating
committee.
Member of committee,
§32-3-1.
Scenic enhancement,
§§23-1-220 to 23-1-223.
Speed zones.
Establishment of state
speed zones,
§32-5A-172.
Terms of office, §23-1-21.
Divisions.
Legal division, §§23-1-25 to
23-1-31.
Duties.
Exercise.
Highway director,
§23-1-21.
General provisions,
§23-1-40.
Engineers.
Expenses.
Payment, §23-1-50.
Equipment and machinery.
Equipment management
surplus reserve
account, §23-1-50.1.
Road machinery and
equipment
management program,
§23-1-50.1.
Expenses.
Nonemployees.
Paying expenses of
nonemployee
prohibited, §23-1-38.
Payment, §23-1-50.
Interstate and intrastate
highways.
Authority to classify,
designate, etc.,
§32-5A-30.
Legal division, §§23-1-25 to
23-1-31.
Appointments.
Assistant counsel,
§23-1-26.
Chief counsel, §23-1-25.
Assistant counsel.
Appointment, §23-1-26.
Assistant attorney
general, §23-1-26.
Oath as assistant
attorney general,
§23-1-26.

HIGHWAYS—Cont'd
Department—Cont'd
Legal division—Cont'd
Assistant counsel—Cont'd
Private practice
prohibited, §23-1-31.
Salaries, §23-1-27.
Charging of salary,
§23-1-29.
Chief counsel.
Appointment, §23-1-25.
Assistant attorney
general, §23-1-26.
Merit system employee,
§23-1-25.
Oath as assistant
attorney general,
§23-1-26.
Private practice
prohibited, §23-1-31.
Salary, §23-1-29.
Clerical personnel,
§23-1-28.
Composition, §23-1-26.
Control, §23-1-25.
Creation, §23-1-25.
Duties.
General provisions,
§23-1-30.
Expenses.
Charging of expenses,
§23-1-29.
Functions.
General provisions,
§23-1-30.
Offices, §23-1-28.
Legislature.
Recommendations for
legislation, §23-1-35.
Licenses.
Motor vehicles.
Exemptions, §23-1-52.
Maintenance.
Supervision by department,
§23-1-40.
Maps.
Preparation, §23-1-40.
Motor fuels.
Purchases, §23-1-51.
Motor vehicles.
Licenses.
Exemptions, §23-1-52.
Load and weight
restrictions.
When highway
department may
prescribe load and
weight restrictions,
§32-1-3.
Municipal corporations.
Municipal connecting link
roads.
Maintenance and repair.
Responsibility,
§23-1-112.
Streets.
Authority to maintain,
§23-1-47.
Contract for paving city
streets, §23-1-40.
Nonemployees.
Paying expenses of
nonemployees
prohibited, §23-1-38.
Oaths.
Power to administer,
§23-1-39.

HIGHWAYS—Cont'd
Department—Cont'd
Obligations, encumbrances or
commitments.
Limitation on amount.
Inauguration date of
incoming governor,
§23-1-63.
Offices, §23-1-32.
Personnel.
Appointment, §23-1-33.
Expenses.
Payment, §23-1-50.
Merit system, §23-1-33.
Transferred county roads
and bridges.
Employees to be
residents of county,
§23-1-36.
Plans and specifications.
Copies.
Keeping on file in office,
§23-1-34.
Powers and duties.
Exercise.
Highway director,
§23-1-21.
General provisions,
§23-1-40.
Prisons and prisoners.
Convict labor.
Use on public roads and
bridges, §23-1-37.
Purchases.
Equipment and supplies.
Authority, §23-1-50.
Motor fuels, oils, etc.,
§23-1-51.
Railroad preservation,
§§37-10-1 to 37-10-7.
See RAILROADS.
Railroads.
Rights-of-way.
Railroads authorized to
transfer abandoned
rights-of-way to,
§10-5-2.1.
Recommendations for
legislation, §23-1-35.
Records.
Evidence, §23-1-34.
Inspection, §23-1-34.
Maintaining of official
records, §23-1-33.
Reports.
Annual report to governor,
§23-1-35.
Right of entry.
Soil samples, §23-1-44.
Surveys, §23-1-44.
Rights-of-way.
Abandoned rights-of-way.
Railroads authorized to
transfer to,
§10-5-2.1.
Rules and regulations.
Penalties.
Violations, §23-5-13.
Promulgation, §23-1-59.
Scope, §23-1-59.
Salaries.
Chief engineer, §23-1-22.
Legal division.
Charging of salary,
§23-1-29.
Chief counsel and
assistant counsel,
§23-1-27.
Personnel, §23-1-33.
Seal, §23-1-39.

HIGHWAYS—Cont'd
  Department—Cont'd
    Soil samples.
      Right of entry for purposes
        of taking, §23-1-44.
    State employees' retirement
      system.
      County engineers.
        Payment of member's
          and employer's
          contributions by
          highway
          department,
          §36-27-9.
    Statistics.
      Preparation, §23-1-40.
    Surveys.
      Right of entry for purposes
        of making, §23-1-44.
    Synfuels development
      authority.
      Contracts for construction,
        reconstruction, etc., of
        highways, roads and
        bridges.
        Supervision or
          performance by
          highway
          department, §9-6A-8.
  Detours.
    Barricades.
      Destroying, injuring, etc.,
        §23-5-2.
      Driving around, §23-5-2.
    Signs.
      Definitions, §23-5-2.
      Driving around, §23-5-2.
      Injuring, removing, etc.,
        §23-5-2.
  **Director of state highway
    department.** See within
    this heading,
    "Department."
  Drainage.
    Ditches.
      Acquisition of land,
        §23-1-3.
  Electricity.
    Contracting with local
      authorities on use of
      public roads by public
      utility corporations,
      §10-5-14.
  Eminent domain.
    Borrow pits.
      Acquisition of land,
        §23-1-3.
    Drainage ditches.
      Acquisition of land,
        §23-1-3.
    Federal aid highway finance
      authority.
      Power of eminent domain,
        §23-1-306.
    Finance corporation.
      Powers, §23-1-175.
    Highway authority.
      Powers, §23-1-155.
    Interstate highway system.
      Controlled access facility.
        Acquisition of property
          and property rights,
          §23-3-5.
    Pits.
      Sand, gravel, etc.
        Acquisition of land,
          §23-1-3.
    Quarries.
      Acquisition of land,
        §23-1-3.

HIGHWAYS—Cont'd
  Eminent domain—Cont'd
    Rights of way.
      Authority of department to
        condemn, §23-1-45.
      Private parties, §§18-3-1 to
        18-3-3.
    Scenic enhancement.
      Acquisition of land,
        §23-1-223.
  Engineers.
    Chief engineer, §§23-1-22 to
      23-1-24.
    Competent engineers.
      Department to furnish,
        §23-1-49.
    Expenses.
      Payment, §23-1-50.
  Estrays, §§3-2-20 to 3-2-23.
  Evidence.
    Department.
      Records, §23-1-34.
  Federal aid.
    Contracts and regulations
      relative to federal
      assistance, §23-1-1.
    State road system.
      Changes or additions to
        system.
        Conformative to federal
          aid law, §23-1-46.
  **Federal aid highway finance
    authority,** §§23-1-300 to
    23-1-318.
    Bonds and notes, §§23-1-306
      to 23-1-316.
      Defined, §23-1-301.
      Denominations, §23-1-308.
      Disposition of proceeds,
        §23-1-313.
      Eligibility as investments
        for fiduciary funds,
        §23-1-312.
      Execution, §23-1-309.
      Form, §23-1-308.
      Investments.
        Eligibility as investment
          for fiduciary funds,
          §23-1-312.
        Interest.
          Pledge of interest from
            investments,
            §23-1-315.
        Sinking fund, §23-1-315.
      Issuance, §23-1-310.
        Authorization, §23-1-307.
        Power to issue
          obligations,
          §23-1-306.
      Negotiability, §23-1-311.
      Payment, §23-1-311.
        Appropriations,
          §23-1-314.
        Pledge of funds,
          §23-1-311.
        Pledge of revenue,
          §23-1-314.
        Principal and interest.
          Payment by state
            treasurer,
            §23-1-316.
        Records.
          Maintenance of
            records, §23-1-316.
        Pledge of funds for
          payment, §23-1-311.
        Redemption, §23-1-308.
      Sale, §23-1-310.
        Disposition of proceeds,
          §23-1-313.

HIGHWAYS—Cont'd
  **Federal aid highway finance
    authority**—Cont'd
    Bonds and notes—Cont'd
      Security.
        Use of security for
          deposits, §23-1-312.
      Sinking fund, §23-1-314.
      Taxation.
        Exemption from
          taxation, §23-1-312.
      Terms, §23-1-308.
    Certificate of incorporation,
      §23-1-304.
    Compensation of members,
      §23-1-305.
    Construction of article,
      §23-1-300.
    Contracts, §23-1-317.
    Definitions, §23-1-301.
    Directors, §23-1-305.
    Dissolution, §23-1-318.
    Eminent domain.
      Power of eminent domain,
        §23-1-306.
    Expenditure of federal aid
      directed by state
      highway department.
      Authorization, §23-1-317.
    Filling of vacancies,
      §23-1-305.
    Highway constructed deemed
      part of public highway
      system, §23-1-317.
    Incorporation.
      Application, §23-1-303.
      Authorization, §23-1-302.
      Certificate, §23-1-304.
    Interest.
      Bonds and notes.
        Appropriations and
          pledges for payment,
          §23-1-314.
    Investments.
      Bonds and notes.
        Eligibility as investment
          for fiduciary funds,
          §23-1-312.
        Investment of proceeds
          and sinking fund,
          §23-1-315.
        Pledge of interest from
          investments,
          §23-1-315.
    Membership, §23-1-305.
    Notes, §§23-1-307 to
      23-1-316.
    Officers, §23-1-305.
    Performance of construction
      by authority without
      award of contract,
      §23-1-317.
    Pledge of revenue for
      payment, §23-1-314.
    Powers, §23-1-306.
    Property.
      Conveyance to state,
        §23-1-317.
    Purpose of article, §23-1-300.
    Quorum, §23-1-305.
    Records, §23-1-305.
      Bonds and notes.
        Payment by state
          treasurer, §23-1-316.
    Rules and regulations,
      §23-1-317.
    Secretary of state.
      Application for
        incorporation,
        §23-1-303.

HIGHWAYS—Cont'd

Federal aid highway finance authority—Cont'd
Taxation.
Bonds and notes.
Exemption from taxation, §23-1-312.
Fences.
Detour fences.
Driving around, §23-5-2.
Finance corporation,
§§23-1-170 to 23-1-181.
Actions.
Maintaining and defending, §23-1-175.
Board of directors, §23-1-174.
Bond issues, §§23-1-177 to 23-1-179.
Amount, §23-1-177.
Appropriations for payment of principal and interest, §23-1-181.
Disposition of proceeds, §23-1-178.
Execution, §23-1-177.
Issuance.
Authority, §23-1-175.
Procedure, §23-1-177.
Payments.
Appropriations and pledges of revenue for payment, §23-1-181.
State treasurer, §23-1-179.
Pledges of revenue for payment of principal and interest, §23-1-181.
Proceeds.
Disposition, §23-1-178.
Sale, §23-1-177.
Proceeds.
Disposition, §23-1-178.
Signatures, §23-1-177.
Sinking fund, §23-1-181.
State treasurer.
Payments by treasurer, §23-1-179.
Taxation.
Exemption from taxation, §23-1-177.
Certificate of incorporation, §23-1-173.
Composition, §23-1-174.
Construction of article, §23-1-170.
Contracts.
Approval, §23-1-176.
Authority of corporation, §23-1-175.
Procedure, §23-1-176.
Dissolution.
Application for dissolution, §23-1-180.
Procedure, §23-1-180.
Eminent domain.
Powers, §23-1-175.
Gifts.
Acceptance, §23-1-175.
Incorporation.
Application, §23-1-172.
Authorization, §23-1-171.
Certificate of incorporation, §23-1-173.
Intent of article, §23-1-170.
Membership, §23-1-174.
Powers.
General provisions, §23-1-175.

HIGHWAYS—Cont'd

Finance corporation—Cont'd
President.
Of highway director, §23-1-174.
Proceedings.
Records, §23-1-174.
Property.
Conveyance to state, §23-1-176.
Powers generally, §23-1-175.
Purposes of article, §23-1-170.
Records.
Proceedings, §23-1-174.
Seal, §23-1-175.
Secretary.
Director of finance, §23-1-174.
Sinking fund, §23-1-181.
State treasurer.
Bond issues.
Payments by treasurer, §23-1-179.
Treasurer of corporation, §23-1-174.
Taxation.
Bond issues.
Exemptions, §23-1-177.
Vice-president.
Attorney general, §23-1-174.
Fire/water hydrants.
Blue reflective markers, §23-1-10.
Fish and game.
Highways.
Hunting within one hundred yards of public roads or highways, §9-11-257.
Hunting or discharge of firearm from, upon or across highways, §9-11-257.
Funds.
State highway fund, §§23-1-61, 23-1-62.
Gas.
Contracting with local authorities on use of public roads by public utility corporations, §10-5-14.
Gasoline tax.
Distribution and use of proceeds.
Highway purposes, §§40-17-72, 40-17-73, 40-17-78 to 40-17-80.
See GASOLINE.
Gifts.
Finance corporation.
Acceptance, §23-1-175.
Highway authority.
Acceptance, §23-1-175.
Interstate highway system.
Controlled access facilities.
Acquisition of property and property rights, §23-3-5.
Scenic enhancement.
Acquisition of land, §23-1-223.
Glass.
Littering.
Criminal littering, §13A-7-29.
Generally, §§23-5-6 to 23-5-9.

HIGHWAYS—Cont'd

Glass—Cont'd
Littering—Cont'd
Vehicle loaded with gravel, rock, sawdust, wood, etc.
Restriction on and penalty for spilling loads, §32-5-76.
Governor.
Department.
Annual report to governor, §23-1-35.
Obligations, encumbrances or commitments.
Inauguration date of incoming governor.
Limitation of outstanding obligations, §23-1-63.
Grade crossings, §§23-1-9, 37-2-84.
Hearings.
Closing and vacating streets, alleys and highways, §23-4-2.
Contest by interested persons, §23-4-3.
Costs, §23-4-4.
Highway authority, §§23-1-150 to 23-1-160. See within this heading, "Authority."
Highway department, §§23-1-20 to 23-1-63. See within this heading, "Department."
Highway finance corporation, §§23-1-170 to 23-1-181. See within this heading, "Finance corporation."
Highway patrol.
General provisions, §§32-2-20 to 32-2-26.
See MOTOR VEHICLES.
Hotels, inns and other transient lodging places.
General provisions, §§34-15-1 to 34-15-20.
See HOTELS, INNS AND OTHER TRANSIENT LODGING PLACES.
Hunting.
Hunting or discharge of firearm from, upon or across highways, §9-11-257.
Hunting within one hundred yards of public roads or highways, §9-11-257.
Improvements on public streets, etc.
Liens, §§35-11-410 to 35-11-417. See within this heading, "Liens."
Industrial access roads and bridges, §§23-6-1 to 23-6-12.
See INDUSTRIAL ACCESS ROADS AND BRIDGES.
Injuries.
Rules and regulations.
Prevention of unnecessary injuries.
Promulgation by highway department, §23-1-59.

HIGHWAYS—Cont'd
Inspections.
Department.
Records, §23-1-34.
Insurance.
Highway department.
Self-insurance program for
employees, §23-1-41.
Interest.
Federal aid highway finance
authority.
Bills and notes, §§23-1-311,
23-1-315.
Highway authority.
Bond issues, §23-1-157.
Intersections.
Grade separations.
Controlled access facilities.
Elimination of
intersections at
grade, §23-3-6.
Interstate highway system.
Construction.
Utilities.
Relocation of utilities.
Payment of cost,
§23-1-5.
Controlled access facilities,
§§23-3-1 to 23-3-8.
Abutting property.
Right of ingress or
egress, §23-3-4.
Counties.
Agreements with county
governments,
§23-3-8.
Declaration of policy,
§23-3-2.
Definitions, §23-3-1.
Designation.
Authority of highway
director, §§23-3-3,
23-3-4.
Eminent domain.
Acquisition of property
and property rights,
§23-3-5.
Establishment.
Authority of highway
director, §23-3-3.
Gasoline service stations,
§23-3-4.
Grade separations, §23-3-6.
Highway director.
Powers generally,
§23-3-3.
Intersections.
Elimination of
intersections at
grade, §23-3-6.
Local service roads and
streets, §23-3-7.
Maintenance.
Authority of highway
director, §23-3-3.
Marking of roadways,
§23-3-4.
Motor vehicles.
Restrictions on use by
various classes of
vehicles, §23-3-3.
Municipal corporations.
Agreements with
municipal
corporations,
§23-3-8.
Policy.
Declaration of policy,
§23-3-2.

HIGHWAYS—Cont'd
Interstate highway system
—Cont'd
Controlled access facilities
—Cont'd
Property.
Acquisition of property
and property rights,
§23-3-5.
Gifts.
Acceptance, §23-3-5.
Rights of way.
Ingress or egress,
§23-3-4.
Service roads and streets,
§23-3-7.
Signs, §23-3-4.
United States.
Agreements with federal
government, §23-3-8.
Vacation.
Authority of highway
director, §23-3-3.
Definitions.
Controlled access facilities,
§23-3-1.
Designation.
Authority of highway
department to classify,
designate and mark,
§32-5A-30.
Junkyard control, §§23-1-240
to 23-1-251.
See JUNKYARD
CONTROL.
Outdoor advertising,
§§23-1-270 to 23-1-288.
See ADVERTISING.
Toll bridges, §§23-2-121,
23-2-122.
Toll tunnels, §§23-2-121,
23-2-122.
Intrastate highways.
Classification, designation,
etc.
Authority of highway
department,
§32-5A-30.
Investments.
Federal aid highway finance
authority, §§23-1-312,
23-1-315.
Junkyard control.
General provisions,
§§23-1-240 to 23-1-251.
See JUNKYARD
CONTROL.
Legal division, §§23-1-25 to
23-1-31. See within this
heading, "Department."
Legislature.
Department.
Recommendations for
legislation, §23-1-35.
Permanent joint highway
committee, §§29-2-1 to
29-2-8.
See LEGISLATURE.
Licenses.
Motor vehicles.
Highway department.
Exemptions, §23-1-52.
Liens.
Improvements on public
streets, etc., §§35-11-410
to 35-11-417.
Acknowledgment of
satisfaction,
§35-11-416.
Assignment of claims,
§35-11-417.

HIGHWAYS—Cont'd
Liens—Cont'd
Improvements on public
streets, etc.—Cont'd
Commencement of action
for enforcement,
§35-11-413.
Enforcement of lien.
Commencement of
action, §35-11-413.
Judgment, §35-11-414.
Jurisdiction, §35-11-413.
Personal representatives.
Actions against
personal
representatives,
§35-11-415.
Judgment, §35-11-414.
Jurisdiction, §35-11-413.
Limitation of actions,
§35-11-412.
Perfection.
Filing of verified
statement,
§35-11-412.
Priority of lien, §35-11-411.
Satisfaction of lien.
Acknowledgment,
§35-11-416.
Verified statement.
Filing, §35-11-412.
Form, §35-11-412.
Limitation of obligations.
Outstanding or authorized
obligations.
Inauguration date of
incoming governor,
§23-1-63.
Littering, §§23-5-6 to 23-5-9.
Criminal littering,
§13A-7-29.
Cumulative provisions,
§23-5-9.
Enforcement, §23-5-8.
Driver presumed offender,
§23-5-6.
Enforcement of provisions,
§23-5-8.
Motor vehicles.
Spilling loads or litter,
§32-5-76.
Throwing of litter onto
highway, §32-5A-60.
Presumptions.
Driver presumed offender,
§23-5-6.
Provisions deemed
cumulative, §23-5-9.
Signs.
Erection, §23-5-7.
Livestock.
Estrays, §§3-2-20 to 3-2-23.
Markets.
Purchase of livestock on
public highway within
2,500 feet of public
livestock market,
§2-15-71.
Running at large.
Liability of owner of
livestock for collision
with motor vehicle,
§3-5-3.
Staking, pasturing, etc., of
animals upon highway
rights of way, §§3-3-1 to
3-3-3.

HIGHWAYS—Cont'd
Maintenance.
Conflicts of interest.
Department.
Employees and director
of department,
§23-1-58.
Contracts.
Federal assistance, §23-1-1.
Generally. See within this
heading, "Contracts."
Counties.
Application by counties for
maintenance of state
roads, §23-1-48.
Drainage ditches.
Acquisition of land,
§23-1-3.
Engineers.
Competent engineers.
Department to furnish,
§23-1-49.
Interstate highways.
Authority of highway
director, §23-3-3.
Controlled access facilities.
Quarries.
Acquisition of land,
§23-1-3.
Rules and regulations.
Federal assistance.
Promulgation and
enforcement,
§23-1-1.
Promulgation, §23-1-59.
Standards.
Establishment, §23-1-40.
Supervision.
Engineers.
Competent engineers,
§23-1-49.
Highway department,
§23-1-40.
Universities and colleges.
Highway department,
§23-1-42.
Manufacturers.
Connections to public ways.
Construction and operation
of connections by
manufacturing
corporations, §10-5-13.
Map.
Preparation.
Highway department,
§23-1-40.
Military affairs.
Right of troops to use
highways, §31-2-84.
Mines and minerals.
Connections to public ways.
Construction and operation
by mining
corporations, §10-5-13.
Motor fuels.
Purchases.
Highway department,
§23-1-51.
Motor vehicle carriers.
General provisions.
See MOTOR VEHICLE
CARRIERS.
Motor vehicles.
General provisions.
See MOTOR VEHICLES.
**Municipal connecting link
roads,** §§23-1-110 to
23-1-113.
See MUNICIPAL
CORPORATIONS.

HIGHWAYS—Cont'd
Municipal corporations.
Architectural review boards.
Applicability of provisions
to highways, streets
and bridges, §11-68-15.
Closing and vacating streets,
alleys and highways,
§§23-4-1 to 23-4-20. See
within this heading,
"Closing and vacating
streets, alleys and
highways."
Historic preservation
commission.
Applicability of provisions
to highways, streets
and bridges, §11-68-15.
Interstate highway system.
Controlled access facilities.
Agreements with
municipalities,
§23-3-8.
Municipal connecting link
roads, §§23-1-110 to
23-1-113.
See MUNICIPAL
CORPORATIONS.
Rights of way.
When acquisition deemed
necessary by state
highway department,
§23-1-45.
Streets.
Contracts.
Paving of streets.
Highway department,
§23-1-40.
Designation as part of
state highway system
by department,
§23-1-40.
General provisions.
See MUNICIPAL
CORPORATIONS.
Maintenance.
Authority of highway
department,
§23-1-47.
Names.
Designation, §23-1-8.
Signs.
Designation on directional
signs, §23-1-8.
Expenditure of state funds
for erection and
maintenance.
Signs designating roads
in honor or memory
of individuals,
§23-1-8.1.
**National highway safety act
of 1966.**
Highway and traffic safety
coordination act.
Participation in benefits of
national act, §32-4-5.
Notice.
Closing and vacating streets,
alleys and highways,
§23-4-2.
Numbers.
Designation, §23-1-8.
Signs.
Designation on directional
signs, §23-1-8.
Oaths.
Department.
Power to administer oaths,
§23-1-39.

HIGHWAYS—Cont'd
Obstructions.
Removal by highway
director, §32-5-5.
Parking lots.
Construction and
maintenance.
State highway department,
§23-1-42.
Parking on highways,
§32-5A-136.
Pedestrians, §§32-5A-210 to
32-5A-222.
Penalties.
Contracts.
Qualification of bidders.
False representations,
§23-1-56.
Department.
Rules and regulations.
Violations, §23-5-13.
Detours.
Signs.
Driving around,
destruction, etc.,
§23-5-2.
Permits.
Movement of oversized
vehicles or loads.
General provisions,
§32-9-29.
Special permits for
movement of certain site-
built buildings,
§32-9-29.1.
Utilities.
Digging up of roads,
§23-1-4.
Petitions.
Closing and vacating streets,
alleys and highways,
§23-4-2.
Pipelines.
Digging up of roads, §23-1-4.
Pits.
Sand, gravel, etc.
Acquisition, §23-1-3.
Police.
Highway patrol, §§32-2-20 to
32-2-26.
See MOTOR VEHICLES.
Political signs.
Outdoor advertising
generally, §§23-1-270 to
23-1-288.
See ADVERTISING.
Power districts.
Right to use and occupy
highways, §37-5-3.
Presumptions.
Littering.
Driver presumed offender,
§23-5-6.
Prisons and prisoners.
Convict labor, §23-1-37.
Private roads, §§23-1-130,
23-1-131.
Property.
Finance corporation.
Conveyance to state,
§23-1-176.
Powers generally,
§23-1-175.
Highway authority.
Acquisition, §23-1-155.
Conveyance to state,
§23-1-156.
**Public roads, bridges and
ferries,** §§23-2-120 to
23-2-161.
See COUNTIES.

HIGHWAYS—Cont'd
　Public transportation.
　　Defined, §23-1-21.1.
　　Director.
　　　Authority with regard to
　　　　public transportation,
　　　　§23-1-21.2.
　　　Cooperation with federal,
　　　　state and local entities
　　　　in administration of
　　　　programs, §23-1-21.3.
　Public utilities.
　　Construction of highways.
　　　Relocation of facilities.
　　　　Payment of cost, §23-1-5.
　　Contracting with local
　　　authorities on use of
　　　public roads and places
　　　by public utility
　　　corporations, §10-5-14.
　　Digging up of roads, §23-1-4.
　　Relocation of facilities.
　　　Construction of highways.
　　　　Payment of cost, §23-1-5.
　　Rights of way.
　　　Operating within rights of
　　　　way.
　　　　Contracts.
　　　　　Authority of
　　　　　　department to
　　　　　　enter, §23-1-59.
　　　　Rules and regulations.
　　　　　Promulgation by
　　　　　　department,
　　　　　　§23-1-59.
　Purchases.
　　Department.
　　　Equipment.
　　　　Authority to procure,
　　　　　§23-1-50.
　　　Motor fuels, oils, etc.,
　　　　§23-1-51.
　　　Scenic enhancement.
　　　　Acquisition of land,
　　　　　§23-1-223.
　Quarries.
　　Connections to public ways.
　　　Construction and operation
　　　　of connections by
　　　　quarrying
　　　　corporations, §10-5-13.
　　Lime and stone quarries.
　　　Acquisition, §23-1-3.
　Railroads.
　　Accidents.
　　　Failure to use proper
　　　　precautions to prevent
　　　　accidents, §37-8-118.
　　Digging up of roads, §23-1-4.
　　Grade crossings.
　　　Abandonment and
　　　　discontinuance,
　　　　§37-2-84.
　　　Elimination.
　　　　Authority of highway
　　　　　department, §23-1-9.
　　　　Cost.
　　　　　Apportionment,
　　　　　　§23-1-9.
　　　　　Collection by state,
　　　　　　§23-1-9.
　　　　Failure of railroad to
　　　　　eliminate.
　　　　　Work by highway
　　　　　　department,
　　　　　　§23-1-9.
　　Obstructing streets, etc.
　　　Crew members acting on
　　　　instructions not
　　　　responsible for
　　　　obstruction, §37-8-115.

HIGHWAYS—Cont'd
　Railroads—Cont'd
　　Signs.
　　　Erection or maintenance of
　　　　advertising signs
　　　　resembling railroad
　　　　signs near public roads
　　　　or streets, §37-8-200.
　　　Erection where highway
　　　　crosses tracks,
　　　　§37-2-80.
　　　Liability for failure to
　　　　comply, §37-2-83.
　Recordation.
　　Closing and vacating streets,
　　　alleys and highways.
　　　Reports by commissioners,
　　　　§23-4-4.
　Records.
　　Department.
　　　Evidence, §23-1-34.
　　　Inspection, §23-1-34.
　　　Maintaining of official
　　　　records, §23-1-33.
　　Finance corporation.
　　　Proceedings, §23-1-174.
　　Highway authority.
　　　Proceedings, §23-1-154.
　Refuse, §§23-5-6 to 23-5-9.
　Relocation assistance.
　　Authorization to provide,
　　　§23-1-210.
　　Conservation and natural
　　　resources.
　　　Compliance by department
　　　　with uniform
　　　　relocation assistance
　　　　and land acquisition
　　　　policies act, §9-2-27.
　　Payments.
　　　Authority to provide,
　　　　§23-1-210.
　　　Not deemed compensation
　　　　for real property,
　　　　§23-1-211.
　　Purposes, §23-1-211.
　　Rules and regulations.
　　　Administrative procedure
　　　　act.
　　　　Regulations and
　　　　　procedures not
　　　　　subject to, §23-1-212.
　　　Issuance, §23-1-212.
　Repairs. See within this
　　heading, "Maintenance."
　Reports.
　　Closing and vacating streets,
　　　alleys and highways,
　　　Commissioners, §§23-4-3,
　　　23-4-4.
　　Department.
　　　Annual report to governor,
　　　　§23-1-35.
　Resolutions.
　　Closing and vacating streets,
　　　alleys and highways,
　　　§23-4-2.
　Rights of way.
　　Acquisition.
　　　Authority of department,
　　　　§23-1-45.
　　　Counties.
　　　　When deemed necessary
　　　　　by state director of
　　　　　highways, §23-1-45.
　　　Methods of acquisition,
　　　　§23-1-45.
　　　Municipal corporations.
　　　　When deemed necessary
　　　　　by state director of
　　　　　highways, §23-1-45.

HIGHWAYS—Cont'd
　Rights of way—Cont'd
　　Advertising.
　　　Prohibited, §23-1-6.
　　Eminent domain.
　　　Authority of department to
　　　　condemn, §23-1-45.
　　　Private parties, §§18-3-1 to
　　　　18-3-3.
　　Public utilities.
　　　Operating in rights of way.
　　　　Authority of department
　　　　　to enter into
　　　　　contracts with,
　　　　　§23-1-59.
　　　Rules and regulations.
　　　　Promulgation by
　　　　　department,
　　　　　§23-1-59.
　　Railroads.
　　　Abandoned rights-of-way
　　　　authorized to transfer
　　　　to department,
　　　　§10-5-2.1.
　　Signs.
　　　Restrictions, §23-1-6.
　　Trespass.
　　　Promulgation by highway
　　　　department, §23-1-59.
　Rules and regulations.
　　Contracts.
　　　Qualification of bidders,
　　　　§23-1-56.
　　Department.
　　　Penalties.
　　　　Violations, §23-5-13.
　　　Promulgation, §23-1-59.
　　Federal assistance.
　　　Adoption of regulations
　　　　relative to, §23-1-1.
　　Highway authority.
　　　Promulgation, §23-1-156.
　　Motor vehicles.
　　　Weight restrictions.
　　　　Promulgation by
　　　　　highway
　　　　　department,
　　　　　§23-1-59.
　Rules of the road act,
　　§§32-5A-1 to 32-5A-266.
　　See MOTOR VEHICLES.
　Safety.
　　Highway and traffic safety
　　　coordination act,
　　　§§32-4-1 to 32-4-7.
　　See MOTOR VEHICLES.
　　Safety coordinating
　　　committee, §§32-3-1 to
　　　32-3-7.
　　See MOTOR VEHICLES.
　Salaries.
　　Closing and vacating streets,
　　　alleys and highways.
　　　Commissioners, §23-4-3.
　　Department.
　　　Chief engineer, §23-1-22.
　　　Legal division.
　　　　Charging of salary,
　　　　　§23-1-29.
　　　　Chief counsel and
　　　　　assistant counsel,
　　　　　§23-1-27.
　　　Personnel, §23-1-33.
　　Finance corporation,
　　　§23-1-174.
　　Highway authority,
　　　§23-1-154.
　Sales.
　　Finance corporation.
　　　Bond issues, §23-1-177.

HIGHWAYS—Cont'd
Sales—Cont'd
Highway authority.
Bond issues, §23-1-157.
Scenic enhancement,
§§23-1-220 to 23-1-223.
Acquisition of land.
Authority of highway
director, §23-1-222.
Eminent domain,
§23-1-223.
Interest in acquired land,
§23-1-223.
Manner of acquisition,
§23-1-223.
Citation of division,
§23-1-220.
Eminent domain.
Acquisition of land,
§23-1-223.
Gifts.
Acquisition of land,
§23-1-223.
Highway director.
Acquisition of land,
§23-1-222.
Purchases.
Acquisition of land,
§23-1-223.
Purpose of division,
§23-1-221.
Short title of division,
§23-1-220.
Seals and sealed
instruments.
Authority, §23-1-175.
Bond issues, §23-1-157.
Department.
Seal of department,
§23-1-39.
Finance corporation,
§23-1-175.
Secondary road committee,
§40-12-270.
Sewers.
Digging up of roads, §23-1-4.
Signatures.
Authority.
Bond issues, §23-1-157.
Finance corporation.
Bond issues, §23-1-177.
Signs, §§23-1-6 to 23-1-8.
Detours, §23-5-2.
Interstate highway system.
Controlled access facilities,
§23-3-4.
Littering.
Erection of signs, §23-5-7.
Markers.
Tourist attractions,
§23-1-7.
Names of highways.
Designation on directional
signs, §23-1-8.
Expenditure of state funds.
Erection and
maintenance of
signs.
Designating road in
honor or memory
of individual,
§23-1-8.1.
Numbers of highways.
Designation on signs,
§23-1-8.
Outdoor advertising.
Erection and maintenance
of signs, §§23-1-273 to
23-1-277.

HIGHWAYS—Cont'd
Signs—Cont'd
Outdoor advertising—Cont'd
Nonconforming signs,
§§23-1-279 to 23-1-283.
See ADVERTISING.
Rights of way.
Restrictions, §23-1-6.
Tourist attractions, §23-1-7.
Traffic signs, §§32-5A-30 to
32-5A-37.
See MOTOR VEHICLES.
Soil.
Samples.
Department.
Right of entry for
purpose of taking,
§23-1-44.
Spotlighting, §32-5-17.
State highway fund,
§§23-1-61, 23-1-62.
Statistics.
Department.
Preparation, §23-1-40.
Stopping on highways,
§32-5A-136.
Streets.
Construction.
State highway department,
§23-1-42.
General provisions.
See MUNICIPAL
CORPORATIONS.
Maintenance.
State highway department,
§23-1-42.
Vacation, §§23-4-1 to 23-4-20.
See within this heading,
"Closing and vacating
streets, alleys and
highways."
Surveys.
Department.
Right of entry for purposes
of making surveys,
§23-1-44.
System.
Changes or additions.
Conformative to federal aid
law, §23-1-46.
Taxation.
Contractors.
Sales tax on street and
highway contractors,
§40-23-50.
See SALES TAX.
Federal aid highway finance
authority.
Bonds and notes.
Exemption from
taxation, §23-1-312.
Finance corporation.
Bond issues.
Exemptions, §23-1-177.
Highway authority.
Bond issues.
Exemption from
taxation, §23-1-157.
Toll road, bridge and tunnel
authority, §§23-2-140 to
23-2-161.
See TOLL ROAD, BRIDGE
AND TUNNEL
AUTHORITY.
Tombigbee Valley
development authority.
Duties and obligations as to
highway relocation,
§33-17-7.

HIGHWAYS—Cont'd
Tourists.
Signs and markers.
Indications of tourist
attractions, §23-1-7.
Traffic control devices.
Signs, signals and markers,
§§32-5A-30 to 32-5A-37.
See MOTOR VEHICLES.
Traffic regulations.
See MOTOR VEHICLES.
Trash.
Littering, §§23-5-6 to 23-5-9.
Trespass.
Rules and regulations.
Promulgation by highway
department, §23-1-59.
Trial.
Closing and vacating streets,
alleys and highways.
Appeals, §23-4-5.
United States.
Bond issue for acquiring
highways in conjunction
with United States,
Const. Ala., amd. 87.
Federal aid, §§23-1-1,
23-1-46.
National highway safety act
of 1966.
Participation in benefits,
§32-4-5.
Rivers forming boundaries
between states.
Agreements and contracts
with adjoining states
and federal
government relative to
bridges, §23-1-57.
Universities and colleges.
Construction and
maintenance.
State highway department,
§23-1-42.
Part of state highway
system, §23-1-42.
Utilities, §§23-1-4, 23-1-5,
23-1-59.
Vacating streets and
highways, §§23-4-1 to
23-4-20. See within this
heading, "Closing and
vacating streets, alleys and
highways."
Water management and
drainage.
Districts.
Construction of
improvements.
Cost of bridges and
culverts when ditch,
drain or watercourse
crosses public
highway, §9-9-46.
Waters and watercourses.
Navigable waters declared
free public highways,
Const. Ala., art. I, §24.
Water supply and
waterworks.
Contracting with local
authorities on use of
public roads by public
utility corporations,
§10-5-14.

HIKING.
Duty of care owed persons
on premises for sporting
or recreational purposes,
§§35-15-1 to 35-15-5.

HINDERING PROSECUTION OR APPREHENSION, §§13A-10-42 to 13A-10-45.
Criminal assistance.
Defined, §13A-10-42.
Definitions, §13A-10-42.
Escapes.
Hindering apprehension of escapee, §13A-10-45.
First degree hindering prosecution, §13A-10-43.
Second degree hindering prosecution, §13A-10-44.

HIRING VEHICLES, §§32-7-36, 32-15-1 to 32-15-8.
See MOTOR VEHICLES.

HISTORICAL PRESERVATION AUTHORITIES, §§41-10-135 to 41-10-154.
Acquisition of property or facilities.
Loans, sales, grants, etc., to authority by counties, municipal corporations, etc., §41-10-146.
Provisions of article as to acquisition exclusive, §41-10-149.
Applicability of provisions.
Retrospective validation not intended, §41-10-154.
Applicant.
Defined, §41-10-136.
Area of operation.
Defined, §41-10-136.
Board of directors, §41-10-140.
Defined, §41-10-136.
Bond issues, §§41-10-142 to 41-10-145.
Contracts to secure payments, §41-10-143.
Defined, §41-10-136.
Denominations, §41-10-142.
Disposition of proceeds from sale, §41-10-145.
Exemption from taxation, §41-10-147.
Form, §41-10-142.
Interest, §41-10-142.
Issuance, §41-10-142.
Liability on bonds, §41-10-142.
Payment.
Contracts to secure payment, §41-10-143.
Security for payment, §41-10-142.
Statutory mortgage lien to secure payment, §41-10-144.
Proceeds from sale.
Disposition, §41-10-145.
Refunding bonds, §41-10-142.
Sale, §41-10-142.
Disposition of proceeds from sale, §41-10-145.
Security for payment, §41-10-142.
Contracts to secure, §41-10-143.
Statutory mortgage lien to secure, §41-10-144.
Statutory mortgage lien to secure payment, §41-10-144.
Terms, §41-10-142.
Certificate of incorporation.
Contents, §41-10-139.

HISTORICAL PRESERVATION AUTHORITIES—Cont'd
Certificate of incorporation —Cont'd
Execution and filing with secretary of state, §41-10-139.
Recordation, §41-10-139.
Citation of article, §41-10-135.
Construction and interpretation.
Generally, §41-10-149.
Counties.
Defined, §41-10-136.
Loans, sales, grants, etc., of money, property, etc., by counties, §41-10-146.
Definitions, §41-10-136.
Director.
Defined, §41-10-136.
Dissolution of authority.
Title to property deemed vested in state, §41-10-150.
Distribution of net earnings, §41-10-152.
Earnings.
Distribution of net earnings, §41-10-152.
Exemption from taxation.
Bonds, §41-10-147.
Governor.
Issuance of resolution denying or approving application, §41-10-138.
Reports by authority to governor, §41-10-148.
Improvements.
Vicinity improvements. Defined, §41-10-136.
Incorporation of authorities.
Applications, §41-10-138.
Certificate of incorporation.
Contents, §41-10-139.
Execution and filing with secretary of state, §41-10-139.
Recordation, §41-10-139.
Multiple county authorities.
Notification by governor to respective county governing bodies, §41-10-138.
Payment of fees, taxes or costs to secretary of state or probate judge, §41-10-147.
Provisions of article as to incorporation exclusive, §41-10-149.
Review of applications, §41-10-138.
Incorporators.
Defined, §41-10-136.
Interest.
Usury.
Exemption from usury or other interest limiting laws, §41-10-153.
Licenses.
Imposition of license tax on authority, §41-10-147.
Municipal corporations.
Defined, §41-10-136.
Loans, sales, etc., of money, property, etc., by municipal corporations, §41-10-146.

HISTORICAL PRESERVATION AUTHORITIES—Cont'd
National register of historic places, §41-10-136.
Nonprofit nature of organization, §41-10-152.
Notice.
Incorporation in multiple county area.
Governor to notify respective county governing bodies, §41-10-138.
Organization as nonprofit corporation, §41-10-152.
Person.
Defined, §41-10-136.
Powers and duties.
Generally, §41-10-141.
Prior law.
Authorities organized under former law deemed valid, §41-10-151.
Probate judges.
Payment of fees, taxes or costs for incorporation, etc. to probate judge, §41-10-147.
Property.
Defined, §41-10-136.
Purposes for which authorities may be incorporated, §41-10-137.
Recordation.
Certificate of incorporation, §41-10-139.
Reports.
Reports by authority to governor, §41-10-148.
Secretary of state.
Certificate of incorporation.
Filing with secretary, §41-10-139.
Recordation by secretary, §41-10-139.
Fees, taxes or costs for incorporation, etc.
Payment to secretary of state, §41-10-147.
Short title, §41-10-135.
State.
Defined, §41-10-136.
Taxation.
Exemption from taxation, §41-10-147.
Incorporation.
Payment to secretary of state or probate judge, §41-10-147.
License or excise tax.
Imposition on authority, §41-10-147.
Usury.
Exemption from usury or other interest limiting laws, §41-10-153.
Vicinity improvements.
Defined, §41-10-136.

HISTORIC BLAKELEY AUTHORITY, §§41-10-170 to 41-10-182.
Acceptance of gratuity services.
Authorized, §41-10-177.
Admission charges.
Authorized, §41-10-177.

HISTORIC BLAKELEY AUTHORITY—Cont'd

Agreements with groups relative to management of the park.
Authorized, §41-10-177.

Appointment, §41-10-171.

Bond issues.
Authorized, §41-10-176.

Bonds, surety.
Treasurer, §41-10-174.

Chairman, §41-10-174.

Composition, §41-10-171.

Conflicts of interest, §41-10-173.

Control over Blakeley site, §41-10-181.

Counties.
County commission.
Appropriation of public funds for authority.
Authorized, §41-10-178.
Construction and maintenance of roads and other public facilities for authority.
Authorized, §41-10-178.

Creation, §41-10-170.

Designation as state agency, §41-10-181.

Duties.
Exhibition of facilities to public, §41-10-177.

Emoluments, §41-10-172.

Employers and employees.
Insurance programs provided for state employees.
Participation of employees of the authority, §41-10-180.

Expenses, §41-10-172.

Fees.
Charging, receiving or obtaining prohibited.
Penalty, §41-10-173.

Insurance.
Program provided for state employees.
Participation of employees of the authority, §41-10-180.

Meetings, §41-10-174.

Municipal corporations.
Appropriation of public funds for authority.
Authorized, §41-10-178.
Construction and maintenance of roads and other public facilities.
Authorized, §41-10-178.

Organization, §41-10-174.

Penalties, fines and forfeitures.
Charging, receiving or obtaining of fees, §41-10-173.
Rules and regulations.
Violations, §41-10-181.

Police.
Deputy police officers.
Designation, §41-10-181.
Powers, §41-10-181.

Powers, §41-10-175.
Acquisition of property within Blakeley national register site, §41-10-176.
Borrowing money, §41-10-176.
Issuance of revenue bonds, §41-10-176.

HISTORIC BLAKELEY AUTHORITY—Cont'd

Powers—Cont'd
Pledging security, §41-10-176.
Police powers, §41-10-181.

Procedure, §41-10-174.

Purpose, §41-10-170.

Quorum, §41-10-174.

Rules and regulations.
Promulgation and alteration, §41-10-181.
Violation.
Penalty, §41-10-181.

Salary, §41-10-172.

Seals and sealed instruments.
Official seal, §41-10-174.

Secretary.
Election, §41-10-174.
Term, §41-10-174.

Taxation.
Exemption from taxation, §41-10-179.

Term, §41-10-171.
Chairman, §41-10-174.
Vice-chairman, §41-10-174.
Secretary, §41-10-174.
Treasurer, §41-10-174.
Vice-chairman, §41-10-174.

Town of Blakeley.
Authority as governing body, §41-10-182.
Boundaries, §41-10-182.
Charter.
Reaffirmation, §41-10-182.
Recognition as municipality, §41-10-182.

Treasurer.
Election, §41-10-174.
Requirement of bond, §41-10-174.
Term, §41-10-174.

Vacancies, §41-10-171.

Vice-chairman.
Election, §41-10-174.
Term, §41-10-174.

HISTORY AND ARCHIVES.

Aboriginal mounds, earthworks and other antiquities, §§41-3-1 to 41-3-6.
Contracts for recovery or salvage of archaeological treasures, §41-9-249.1.
Exclusive right and privilege of state to explore, excavate or survey.
Reservation of exclusive right, §41-3-1.
Explorations, excavations, etc.
Consent of landowner required, §41-3-3.
Destroying, defacing, etc., remains, §41-3-4.
Illegal exploration or excavation, §41-3-6.
Injury to crops, houses, etc., prohibited, §41-3-3.
Nonresidents not to explore or excavate, §41-3-2.
Reservation of exclusive right and privilege of state to explore, excavate or survey, §41-3-1.

HISTORY AND ARCHIVES—Cont'd

Aboriginal mounds, earthworks and other antiquities—Cont'd
Explorations, excavations, etc —Cont'd
Restoration of remains after explorations or excavations, §41-3-4.
Injury to crops, houses, etc.
Prohibited, §41-3-3.
Landowners.
Consent of landowners required for exploration or excavation of remains, §41-3-3.
Nonresidents.
Not to explore or excavate remains or carry away from state objects discovered, §41-3-2.
Objects found.
Disposition of objects taken from remains, §41-3-5.
Nonresidents not to carry away from state objects discovered, §41-3-2.
State ownership declared, §41-3-1.
Restoration of remains after explorations or excavations, §41-3-4.

Alabama Agricultural and Mechanical University.
State Black archives, research center and museum, §§16-49-50 to 16-49-55. See within this heading, "State Black archives, research center and museum."

Alabama historical commission, §§41-9-240 to 41-9-262.
Appointment of members, §41-9-243.
Archaeological treasures.
Contract for recovery or salvage, §41-9-249.1.
Board of advisors, §41-9-246.
Cahaba historical site, §§41-9-251 to 41-9-253.
Capitol.
Restoration and preservation.
Designation of commission as agency responsible, §41-9-261.
Compensation.
Members to serve without pay, §41-9-244.
Composition, §41-9-243.
Contracts.
Recovery or salvage of archaeological treasures, etc., §41-9-249.1.
Council on historic pilgrimages, §§41-9-257, 41-9-258.
Creation, §41-9-240.
Duties, §41-9-249.
Employees, §41-9-248.
Executive director, §41-9-247.
Exemption from taxation, §41-9-256.

HISTORY AND ARCHIVES
—Cont'd
**Alabama historical
    commission**—Cont'd
Expenses of members,
    §41-9-244.
Fort Morgan historical
    commission.
Transfer of powers,
    authority and
    jurisdiction, §41-9-260.
Fort Morgan military
    reservation.
Department of
    conservation and
    natural resources.
Operation of portion of
    reservation,
    §41-9-260.
Development and
    restoration, §41-9-260.
Transfer to commission of
    certain parts,
    §41-9-260.
Historical quarterly.
Commission not to engage
    in publishing or
    printing, §41-9-254.
Hobson memorial board.
Transfer of powers from
    board to commission,
    §41-9-222.
Legislative findings,
    §41-9-240.
Libraries.
Acquisition, operation, etc.,
    by commission,
    §41-9-254.
Meetings, §41-9-245.
Museums.
Acquisition, operation, etc.,
    by commission,
    §41-9-254.
Officers, §41-9-245.
Organizations, §41-9-245.
Powers, §41-9-249.
Cahaba historical site,
    §41-9-253.
Preservation, operation, etc.,
    of certain historical
    properties and sites by
    commission, §41-9-250.
Procedure, §41-9-245.
Public body corporate,
    §41-9-241.
Purpose of commission,
    §41-9-242.
Purpose of division,
    §41-9-240.
Qualifications of members,
    §41-9-243.
Quarterlies.
Historical quarterlies.
Commission not to
    engage in publishing
    or printing,
    §41-9-254.
Quorum, §41-9-245.
Removal of members,
    §41-9-243.
Salvage.
Contracts for recovery or
    salvage of
    archaeological
    treasures, etc.,
    §41-9-249.1.

HISTORY AND ARCHIVES
—Cont'd
**Alabama historical
    commission**—Cont'd
State capitol.
Restoration and
    preservation.
Designation of
    commission as
    agency responsible,
    §41-9-261.
Taxation.
Exemption from taxation of
    commission and
    properties, income,
    etc., §41-9-256.
Terms of members,
    §41-9-243.
Vacancies, §41-9-243.
Alabama historical society.
Funds.
Alabama state historic
    preservation fund,
    §41-9-255.
**Alabama state historic
    preservation fund,**
    §41-9-255.
Archaeological treasures.
Alabama historical
    commission.
Contract for recovery or
    salvage, §41-9-249.1.
**Archives and history
    department, §§41-6-1 to**
    41-6-53. See within this
    heading, "Department of
    archives and history."
Authorities.
Historical preservation
    authorities, §§41-10-135
    to 41-10-154.
See HISTORICAL
    PRESERVATION
    AUTHORITIES.
**Black archives, research
    center and museum,**
    §§16-49-50 to 16-49-55. See
    within this heading, "State
    Black archives, research
    center and museum."
Cahaba historical site,
    §§41-9-251 to 41-9-253.
Advisory committee,
    §41-9-252.
Expenses.
Payment of expenses,
    §41-9-253.
Powers of commission,
    §41-9-253.
Preservation, operation, etc.,
    by commission,
    §41-9-251.
Capitol.
Alabama historical
    commission.
Restoration and
    preservation of capitol.
Designation of
    commission as
    agency, §41-9-261.
Generally.
See CAPITOL.
Cemeteries.
Aboriginal mounds,
    earthworks and other
    antiquities, §§41-3-1 to
    41-3-6. See within this
    heading, "Aboriginal
    mounds, earthworks and
    other antiquities."

HISTORY AND ARCHIVES
—Cont'd
Contracts.
Alabama historical
    commission.
Archaeological treasures.
Contracts for recovery or
    salvage, §41-9-249.1.
**Council on historic
    pilgrimages.**
Appointment of members,
    §41-9-259.
Composition, §41-9-258.
Created, §41-9-257.
Duties, §41-9-259.
Purpose, §41-9-257.
Terms of members,
    §41-9-259.
Counties.
Historical research.
Authorized to undertake
    research into history,
    §16-42-1.
Contracts between counties
    and historical
    corporations, etc.,
    authorized, §16-42-3.
Funds.
Use of county funds,
    §16-42-2.
Definitions.
State Black archives,
    research center and
    museum, §16-49-51.
**Department of archives and
    history.**
Assistants.
Clerical assistants in
    department, §41-6-9.
Board of trustees of
    department, §§41-6-3,
    41-6-4.
Books, records, etc.
Copies.
Provision of certified
    copies of books,
    records, etc.,
    surrendered to
    department,
    §41-6-11.
Surrender by state, county,
    etc., officials of books,
    records, etc., not in
    current use, §41-6-10.
Clerical assistants in
    department, §41-6-9.
Confederate soldiers.
Collection of data as to
    Alabama soldiers in
    war between states,
    §41-6-13.
Director.
Commission.
Director to be
    commissioned,
    §41-6-6.
Duties, §41-6-8.
Election, §41-6-5.
Functions, §41-6-8.
Local government records
    commission.
Chairman of commission,
    §41-13-22.
Oath of office, §41-6-6.
Powers, §41-6-8.
Salary, §41-6-7.
State records commission.
Chairman of commission,
    §41-13-20.
Term of office, §41-6-5.

HISTORY AND ARCHIVES
—Cont'd
Department of archives and history—Cont'd
Endowment fund, §§41-6-30 to 41-6-34.
Composition, §41-6-31.
Deposit of gifts or donations in state treasury to credit of department, §41-6-30.
Donations.
Deposit in state treasury to credit of department, §41-6-30.
Perpetuation or memorialization of names of certain donors, §41-6-34.
Real property, §41-6-33.
Established, §41-6-31.
Expenditures, §41-6-31.
Investment, §41-6-31.
Real property.
Disposition of proceeds from sale or rent, §41-6-33.
Lease, sale, etc., of gifts or donations of real property authorized, §41-6-33.
Established, §41-6-1.
Funds.
Endowment fund, §§41-6-30 to 41-6-34.
Memorial fund, §§41-6-50 to 41-6-53.
Gifts.
Endowment fund.
Donations, §§41-6-30 to 41-6-34.
Memorial fund.
Donations, §§41-6-50 to 41-6-53.
Historical quarterly, §41-6-15.
Income tax.
Deduction of amount of gift for income tax purposes, §41-6-53.
Interest.
Appropriated to department, §41-6-32.
Expenditure, §41-6-32.
Location, §41-6-1.
Memorial fund, §§41-6-50 to 41-6-53.
Deposit of gifts or donations in state treasury in memorial fund, §41-6-50.
Disposition, §41-6-51.
Donations.
Deemed gifts to state, §41-6-53.
Deposit in state treasury in memorial fund, §41-6-50.
Income tax.
Deduction of gifts, §41-6-53.
Establishment, §41-6-50.
Expenditure, §§41-6-51, 41-6-52.
Gifts deemed gifts to state, §41-6-53.

HISTORY AND ARCHIVES
—Cont'd
Department of archives and history—Cont'd
Memorial fund—Cont'd
Identification of item or purpose for which gift expended where gift designated in memory of specified person, §41-6-52.
Income tax.
Deduction of amount of gift for income tax purposes, §41-6-53.
Objects of department, §41-6-2.
Official publications of commissions, bureaus, boards, etc.
Disposition, §41-6-12.
Provision to department, §41-6-12.
Public officers.
Books, records, etc.
Copies.
Provision of certified copies of books, records, etc., surrendered to department, §41-6-11.
Surrender by state, county, etc., officials of books, records, etc., not in current use to department for permanent preservation, §41-6-10.
Public records.
Assistance of public officials in preserving, filing, etc., §41-13-4.
Photographing or microphotographing, §41-13-41.
Purposes of department, §41-6-2.
Quarterly.
Historical quarterly, §41-6-15.
Real property.
Endowment fund.
Disposition of proceeds from sale or rent, §41-6-33.
Lease, sale, etc., of gifts or donations of real property authorized, §41-6-33.
Statistical register, §41-6-14.
Trustees.
Board of trustees of department, §§41-6-3, 41-6-4.
Education.
Historical research, §§16-42-1 to 16-42-3.
Endowment fund, §§41-6-30 to 41-6-34.
Evidence.
Historical works prima facie evidence of facts of general notoriety and interest, §12-21-108; ARCP, Rule 44 (g).
Fort Louis de la Mobile.
Monument.
Maintenance, §9-14-3.

HISTORY AND ARCHIVES
—Cont'd
Fort Morgan historical commission.
Jurisdiction.
Transfer to Alabama historical commission, §41-9-260.
Transfer of powers, authority and jurisdiction to Alabama historical commission, §41-9-260.
Fort Tombeckbee historical advisory board, §41-9-262.
Funds.
Alabama state historic preservation fund, §41-9-255.
Department of archives and history.
Endowment fund, §§41-6-30 to 41-6-34.
Memorial fund, §§41-6-50 to 41-6-53.
Gifts.
Department of archives and history.
Endowment fund, §§41-6-30 to 41-6-34.
Memorial fund, §§41-6-50 to 41-6-53.
Historical preservation authorities, §§41-10-135 to 41-10-154.
See HISTORICAL PRESERVATION AUTHORITIES.
Historical quarterly, §41-6-15.
Alabama historical commission.
Commission not to engage in publishing or printing, §41-9-254.
Historical sites.
State parks.
Confederate memorials, §§9-2-104, 9-2-105.
See CONFEDERACY.
Generally, §§9-14-1 to 9-14-3.
See STATE PARKS.
Historic Blakeley authority, §§41-10-170 to 41-10-182.
See HISTORIC BLAKELEY AUTHORITY.
Historic Chattahoochee compact, §41-9-311.
Hobson memorial board.
Alabama historical commission.
Transfer of powers from board to commission, §41-9-222.
Indians.
Aboriginal mounds, earthworks and other antiquities, §§41-3-1 to 41-3-6. See within this heading, "Aboriginal mounds, earthworks and other antiquities."
Jurisdiction.
Tannehill furnace and foundry commission, §41-9-325.
LaGrange historical commission, §41-9-270.

HISTORY AND ARCHIVES
—Cont'd
LaGrange historical site.
Transferred to state
commission, §41-9-271.
Libraries.
Alabama historical
commission.
Acquisition, operation, etc.,
of libraries by
commission, §41-9-254.
Memorial fund, §§41-6-50 to
41-6-54.
Municipal corporations.
Historical research.
Authorization to undertake
research into history,
§16-42-1.
Contracts between counties
or cities and historical
corporations, etc.,
authorized, §16-42-3.
Funds.
Use of municipal funds,
§16-42-2.
Museums.
Alabama historical
commission.
Acquisition, operation, etc.,
of museums by
commission, §41-9-254.
Pilgrimages.
Council on historic
pilgrimages, §§41-9-257
to 41-9-259.
Quarterly.
Historical quarterly,
§41-6-15.
Alabama historical
commission.
Not to engage in
publishing or
printing, §41-9-254.
Registers.
Statistical register, §41-6-14.
Research.
Historical research, §§16-42-1
to 16-42-3.
**St. Stephens historical
commission,** §§41-9-335 to
41-9-337.
Salvage.
Contracts for recovery or
salvage of archaeological
treasure, etc.,
§41-9-249.1.
Shipwrecks.
Contracts for recovery or
salvage of archaeological
treasure, §41-9-249.1.
State.
Historical research.
Contracts between counties
or cities and historical
corporations, etc.,
authorized, §16-42-3.
Counties and cities
authorized to
undertake research
into history of state,
§16-42-1.
Funds.
Use of county and
municipal funds,
§16-42-2.
**State Black archives,
research center and
museum,** §§16-49-50 to
16-49-55.
Afro-American.
Defined, §16-49-51.

HISTORY AND ARCHIVES
—Cont'd
**State Black archives,
research center and
museum**—Cont'd
Alabama Agricultural and
Mechanical University.
Funds, grants, services,
etc.
Authority to accept,
§16-49-55.
President.
Appointment of curator,
§16-49-53.
Citation of act.
Short title, §16-49-50.
Curator, §16-49-53.
Definitions, §16-49-51.
Funds, grants, services, etc.
Alabama Agricultural and
Mechanical University.
Authority to accept,
§16-49-55.
Purposes, §16-49-52.
Repository.
Defined, §16-49-51.
Duties and services of,
§16-49-54.
Source materials.
Defined, §16-49-51.
Title.
Short title, §16-49-50.
State capitol.
Alabama historical
commission.
Responsibility for
restoration and
preservation,
§41-9-261.
Generally.
See CAPITOL.
Statistical register, §41-6-14.
**Tannehill furnace and
foundry commission,**
§§41-9-320 to 41-9-330.
Acquisition of property,
§41-9-326.
Appointment of members,
§41-9-321.
Appropriations by counties
and municipalities,
§41-9-328.
Arrest.
Powers of arrest,
§41-9-325.
Bond issues.
Issuance of revenue bonds,
§41-9-326.
Bonds, surety.
Requirement of bond from
treasurer, §41-9-323.
Borrowing money, §41-9-326.
Civic organizations.
Entry into agreement with
civic organizations,
§41-9-327.
Compensation of members,
§41-9-322.
Composition, §41-9-321.
Conflicts of interest of
members or employees of
commission, §41-9-322.
Corporation.
Commission a body
corporate, §41-9-324.
Counties.
Appropriations by counties,
§41-9-328.
Creation, §41-9-320.

HISTORY AND ARCHIVES
—Cont'd
**Tannehill furnace and
foundry commission**
—Cont'd
Employees.
Conflicts of interest,
§41-9-322.
Hostesses, guards, etc.,
§41-9-327.
Insurance programs for
employees, §41-9-330.
Exemption from taxation,
§41-9-329.
Expenses of members,
§41-9-322.
Gratuitous services.
Acceptance, §41-9-327.
Guards.
Employment of guards,
§41-9-327.
Hostesses.
Employment, §41-9-327.
Insurance programs for
employees, §41-9-330.
Jurisdiction of commission,
§41-9-325.
Meetings, §41-9-323.
Municipal corporations.
Appropriations by
municipalities,
§41-9-328.
Officers, §41-9-323.
Operation, etc., of park or
historic site, §41-9-327.
Organization, §41-9-323.
Police powers, §41-9-325.
Powers, §41-9-325.
Procedure, §41-9-323.
Property.
Acquisition of property,
§41-9-326.
Exemption from taxation,
§41-9-329.
Purpose, §41-9-320.
Quorum, §41-9-323.
Rules and regulations.
Power to promulgate,
§41-9-325.
Seal, §41-9-323.
State agency.
Commission a state
agency, §41-9-325.
Taxation.
Exemption from taxation,
§41-9-329.
Terms of members,
§41-9-321.
Vacancies, §41-9-321.
Taxation.
Alabama historical
commission.
Exemption from taxation,
§41-9-256.
Tannehill furnace and
foundry commission.
Exemption from taxation,
§41-9-329.
**USS Alabama battleship
commission,** §§41-9-340 to
41-9-358.
See USS ALABAMA
BATTLESHIP
COMMISSION.

HIT AND RUN ACT.
Motor vehicles.
Accidents, §§32-10-1 to
32-10-12.
See MOTOR VEHICLES.

HITCHHIKING.
  Motor vehicles.
    Prohibition against
      hitchhiking, §32-5A-216.

**HOBSON MEMORIAL
  BOARD.**
  Abolished, §41-9-222.
  **Transfer of powers to
    historical commission,**
    §41-9-222.

HOCKEY.
  Agents.
    Generally, §§8-26-1 to
      8-26-41.
    See SPORTS.

HOG CHOLERA, §§2-15-230 to
  2-15-274.
  See LIVESTOCK.

HOGS.
  Estrays.
    General provisions, §§3-2-1 to
      3-2-23.
    See ESTRAYS.
  Livestock.
    Swine.
      Hog cholera, §§2-15-230 to
        2-15-274.
      See LIVESTOCK.
      Promotion of swine
        industry, §§2-8-40 to
        2-8-62.
      See LIVESTOCK.
  Running at large, §§3-2-1 to
    3-2-23.
    See ESTRAYS.

HOLDING COMPANIES.
  Insurance, §§27-28-1 to
    27-29-14.
    See INSURANCE.

HOLIDAYS.
  Appeals.
    Rules of appellate procedure,
      ARAP, Rule 26 (a).
  **Banks and financial
    institutions.**
    Closing of banks, §1-3-8.
    One business day of each
      week, §5-5A-32.
    Emergencies.
      Declaration of banking
        holidays, §5-10A-3.
      Extension of banking
        holidays, §5-10A-4.
    Transaction of business on
      legal holidays, §5-5A-30.
    Liability for transaction,
      §5-5A-31.
  Circuit courts.
    Clerks of court and registers.
      Office hours, ARJA, Rule
        5.
  County commissions.
    Meetings.
      When regular meeting falls
        on holiday, §11-3-8.1.
  Courts.
    Clerks of court and registers.
      Office hours, ARJA, Rule
        5.
  Dates, §1-3-8.
  District courts.
    Clerks of court.
      Office hours, ARJA, Rule
        5.
  Education.
    Holidays enumerated, §1-3-8.

HOLIDAYS—Cont'd
  Elections.
    Municipal elections.
      Commission form.
        Effect of legal holidays
          or closing days,
          §11-46-91.
      Mayor-council form.
        Effect of legal holidays
          or closing days,
          §11-46-20.
  Enumerated, §1-3-8.
  Legal holidays, §1-3-8.
  Municipal corporations.
    Elections.
      Commission form.
        Effect of legal holidays
          or closing days,
          §11-46-91.
      Mayor-council form.
        Effect of legal holidays
          or closing days,
          §11-46-20.
  Penitentiary.
    Convict labor, §14-3-48.
  **Public officers and
    employees.**
    Compensatory leave.
      When holiday worked,
        §1-3-8.
  Schools.
    Holidays enumerated, §1-3-8.
  State, §1-3-8.
  **State departments and
    agencies.**
    When state offices may be
      open on holidays, §1-3-8.
  Sundays.
    General provisions.
      See SUNDAYS.

**HOLY COMFORTER HOUSE,
  INC., OF GADSDEN.**
  Licenses.
    Exemptions, §40-9-12.
  Taxation.
    Exemptions, §40-9-12.

HOME BOX OFFICE.
  **Community antenna
    television facilities
    generally,** §§11-27-1 to
    11-27-3, 23-1-59.

HOMESTEAD EXEMPTION.
  **Alienation by married
    persons,** §6-10-3.
  Amount.
    Exemptions from levy and
      sale under process,
      §6-10-2.
  Appraisement of homestead.
    Exemptions from
      administration and
      payment of debts.
      Proceedings upon failure to
        appraise, §6-10-84.
      Report, §6-10-82.
  Assignment.
    Dwelling, etc.
      Surviving spouse may
        retain dwelling, etc.,
        until assignment,
        §43-8-114.
  Constitution of Alabama,
    Const. Ala., art. X, §§205,
    206, 208.
    Income tax, Const. Ala., amd.
    61.

HOMESTEAD EXEMPTION
  —Cont'd
  Constitution of Alabama
    —Cont'd
    Laborers' liens and
      mechanics' liens not
      barred by homestead
      exemptions, Const. Ala.,
      art. X, §207.
    Waiver of right of exemption,
      §43-8-72; Const. Ala.,
      art. X, §210.
  **Contested claim of
    exemption.**
    Exemptions from levy and
      sale under process.
      Defense by wife or minor
        children, §6-10-39.
      Proceedings when
        homestead found
        excessive, §6-10-38.
  Enumeration, Const. Ala., art.
    X, §§205, 206, 208.
  **Exemptions from
    administration and
    payment of debts.**
    Appraisement of homestead.
      Proceedings upon failure to
        appraise, §6-10-84.
      Report, §6-10-82.
    Exemptions in lieu of
      homestead.
      Claiming and setting
        apart, §6-10-85.
    Judgments alloting.
      Recordation, §6-10-105.
      Fee, §6-10-105.
    Payment by devisees to clear
      property of homestead
      right, §6-10-99.
    Reduced homestead incapable
      of allotment.
      Application of proceeds,
        §6-10-96.
      Notice, §6-10-96.
      Order, §6-10-96.
      Sale.
        Bid, §6-10-97.
        Possession by surviving
          spouse and minor
          children until sold,
          §6-10-94.
        Proof of facts, §6-10-96.
        Purchase by persons
          entitled to
          exemption, §6-10-98.
        When allowed, §6-10-95.
    Removal from homestead.
      Effect, §6-10-102.
    Setting apart.
      Proceeding when
        homestead exceeds
        value allowed,
        §16-10-83.
    Source, determination and
      documentation,
      §43-8-113.
    Wills.
      Amount of exemption,
        §43-8-110.
  **Exemptions from levy and
    sale under process.**
    Alienation by married
      person, §6-10-3.
    Amount, §6-10-2.
    Area, §6-10-2.
    Contested claim of
      exemption.
      Defense by wife or minor
        children, §6-10-39.

HOMESTEAD EXEMPTION
—Cont'd
Exemptions from levy and sale under process
—Cont'd
Contested claim of exemption
—Cont'd
Proceedings when homestead found excessive, §6-10-38.
Interposition by spouse or minor children, §6-10-39.
Lease of homestead.
Effect, §6-10-41.
Leasing homestead temporarily.
Effect, §6-10-41.
Liens.
Effect on liens, §6-10-4.
Mobile homes.
Inclusion, §6-10-2.
Sale of land and separation of homestead interest from that of alienee, §6-10-40.
Separate claim of husband and wife, §6-10-2.
Exemptions in lieu of homestead.
Exemptions from administration and payment of debts.
Claiming and setting apart, §6-10-85.
Fees.
Probate judges' fees, §12-19-90.
Forests and forestry.
State forests.
Auxiliary state forests.
Designation of lands.
Release of homestead rights, §9-13-42.
Husband and wife.
Alienation by married persons, §6-10-3.
Income tax, Const. Ala., amd. 61.
Appropriations.
Replacement of revenues lost by reason of exemption of homesteads, §40-18-58.
Lease of homestead.
Exemptions from levy and sale under process.
Effect, §6-10-41.
Liens.
Exemptions from levy and sale under process.
Effect on liens, §6-10-4.
Laborers' liens and mechanics' liens not barred by homestead exemptions, Const. Ala., art. X, §207.
Mobile homes.
Exemptions from levy and sale under process.
Inclusion, §6-10-2.
Partnerships.
Property not subject to homestead rights, §10-8-72.
Reduced homestead incapable of allotment.
Exemptions from administration and payment of debts.
Application of proceeds, §6-10-96.

HOMESTEAD EXEMPTION
—Cont'd
Reduced homestead incapable of allotment
—Cont'd
Exemptions from administration and payment of debts
—Cont'd
Notice, §6-10-96.
Order, §6-10-96.
Sale.
Bid, §6-10-97.
Possession by surviving spouse and minor children until sold, §6-10-94.
Proof of facts, §6-10-96.
Purchase by persons entitled to exemption, §6-10-98.
When allowed, §6-10-95.
Removal from homestead.
Exemptions from administration and payment of debts.
Effect, §6-10-102.
Setting apart.
Exemptions from administration and payment of debts.
Proceeding when homestead exceeds value allowed, §16-10-83.
Taxation, §§40-7-9.1, 40-9-19.
Waiver, §43-8-72; Const. Ala., art. X, §210.
How made, §6-10-122.
Wills.
Elective share of surviving spouse.
Surviving spouse entitled to certain benefits regardless of election, §43-8-74.
Exemptions from administration and payment of debts.
Amount of exemption, §43-8-110.

HOMESTEADS.
Conveyance, §6-10-3.
Deed to husband or wife, §6-10-6.

HOME STUDY SCHOOLS.
Unaccredited schools, §§16-46-1 to 16-46-10.
See EDUCATION.

HOMICIDE.
Bail and recognizance.
Discretionary bail schedule.
Murder, ARJA, Rule 2.
Criminal homicide.
Defined, §13A-6-1.
Criminally negligent homicide, §13A-6-4.
Definitions, §13A-6-1.
Indictments.
Form of indictment, §15-8-150.
Insurance.
Life insurance.
Effect of, §43-8-253.
Slayer act, §43-8-253.
Manslaughter.
Class B felony, §13A-6-3.
Elements of crime, §13A-6-3.

HOMICIDE—Cont'd
Manslaughter—Cont'd
Limitations on prosecution.
First degree manslaughter, §15-3-5.
Misdemeanors.
Criminally negligent homicide.
Class A misdemeanor, §13A-6-4.
Motor vehicles.
Criminally negligent homicide.
Drivers of motor vehicles driving under influence.
Class C felony, §13A-6-4.
Homicide by vehicle, §32-5A-192.
Murder.
Elements of crime, §13A-6-2.
Killing under legal provocation.
Burden remains on defendant, §13A-6-2.
Penalty, §13A-6-2.
Negligence.
Criminally negligent homicide.
Class A misdemeanor, §13A-6-4.
Elements, §13A-6-4.
Jury may consider statutes and ordinances, §13A-6-4.
Penalties.
Capital punishment.
General provisions.
See CAPITAL PUNISHMENT.
Life imprisonment without parole.
Attorneys at law.
Appointment of experienced counsel for indigent defendants, §13A-5-2.
Manslaughter, §§13A-6-3, 15-3-5.
Murder, §13A-6-2.
Person.
Defined, §13A-6-1.
Sentencing.
Authorized disposition, §13A-5-2.
Wills.
Effect on, §43-8-253.
Intestate succession.
Effect on, §43-8-253.
Slayer act, §43-8-253.
Wrongful death, §§6-5-410, 6-5-411.

HONEY, §§2-11-120 to 2-11-123.
Definitions, §2-11-120.
Labels.
Requirements, §2-11-121.
Violations of provisions.
Penalty, §2-11-123.
Words "imitation" and "honey,"
Use, §2-11-122.
Penalties.
Labeling.
Violations of provisions, §2-11-123.

HONEYBEES AND APIARIES, §§2-14-1 to 2-14-15.
Beekeeping equipment.
Diseases.
Destruction of diseased bees, supplies or equipment, §2-14-11.
Order of commissioner.
Enforcement, §2-14-12.
Failure of owner to destroy upon notification by commissioner, §2-14-12.
Hearing for review of order, §2-14-12.
Moving of quarantined bees, supplies or equipment, §2-14-10.
Quarantine.
Moving of quarantined bees, supplies or equipment, §2-14-10.
Used equipment.
Shipment, movement, etc., into state, §2-14-5.
Shipment, movement, etc., without permit from commissioner of agriculture and industries, §2-14-6.
Bee yards.
Registration, §2-14-3.
Brands and marks.
Hive-bodies and supers.
Owners, etc., to mark, §2-14-7.
Colonies.
Registration, §2-14-3.
Commissioner of agriculture and industries.
Diseases.
Control.
Powers of commissioner, §2-14-9.
Order of commissioner to treat or destroy diseased bees.
Failure of owner to destroy bees, equipment, etc., upon notification by commissioner, §2-14-12.
Hearing for review, §2-14-12.
Rules and regulations.
Promulgation of rules and regulations for implementation of chapter, §2-14-13.
Definitions, §2-14-1.
Diseases, §§2-14-9 to 2-14-12.
Commissioner of agriculture and industries.
Order of commissioner to treat or destroy diseased bees.
Enforcement, §2-14-12.
Control.
Powers of commissioner of agriculture and industries, state apiarist, etc., §2-14-9.
Destruction of diseased bees, supplies or equipment, §2-14-11.
Order of commissioner to destroy diseased bees, §2-14-12.

HONEYBEES AND APIARIES —Cont'd
Diseases—Cont'd
Eradication.
Powers of commissioner of agriculture and industries, state apiarist, etc., §2-14-9.
Inspection of combs, hives, etc., §2-14-9.
Ordering of transfer of honeybees to hives with movable frames, §2-14-9.
Quarantine, §2-14-10.
Moving of quarantined bees, supplies or equipment, §2-14-10.
Right of entry, §2-14-9.
Treatment.
Order of commissioner to treat, §2-14-12.
Fees.
Registration fee, §2-14-3.
Hive-bodies.
Owners to mark, §2-14-7.
Inspections.
Diseases, §2-14-9.
Shipment or movement of honeybees into state.
Certificate of inspection, §2-14-4.
Maps.
Apiary locations.
Preparation and maintenance of county maps, §2-14-8.
Packages.
Shipment or movement of honeybees into state.
Packaging requirements, §2-14-4.
Penalties.
Violations of article or rules and regulations, §2-14-15.
Permits.
Used beekeeping equipment.
Shipment, movement, etc., without permit from commissioner of agriculture and industries, §2-14-6.
Purpose of chapter, §2-14-2.
Quarantine.
Diseased apiary or colony, §2-14-10.
Registration.
Annual registration, §2-14-3.
Disposition of registration fees and fines, §2-14-3.
Fee, §2-14-3.
Owners, etc., to register colonies, bee yards and apiaries annually, §2-14-3.
Transfer of registration, §2-14-3.
Rules and regulations.
Penalties for violations, §2-14-15.
Promulgation of rules and regulations for implementation of chapter, §2-14-13.
State apiarist.
Designation, §2-14-14.
Diseases.
Control.
Powers, §2-14-9.
Marks, etc., to be approved by, §2-14-7.

HONEYBEES AND APIARIES —Cont'd
State apiarist—Cont'd
Powers, §2-14-14.
Supers.
Owners to mark, §2-14-7.
Transportation.
Beekeeping equipment.
Shipment, movement, etc., of used beekeeping equipment, §2-14-5.
Into state, §2-14-5.
Without penalty, §2-14-6.
Shipment or movement of honeybees into state, §2-14-4.
Violations of article.
Penalties for violations, §2-14-15.

HONORARIUMS.
State departments and agencies.
Competitive bid laws.
Exemption of certain departments and agencies whose principal business is honorariums, §41-16-21.2.

HORIZONTAL PROPERTY.
Condominiums, §§35-8-1 to 35-8-22.
See CONDOMINIUMS.

HORNS.
Motor vehicles, §§32-5-213, 32-5A-213.
Railroads, §§37-8-112 to 37-8-114.
See RAILROADS.

HORSE RACING, §§11-65-1 to 11-65-47.
Agents.
Permits, §§11-65-23 to 11-65-26, 11-65-42.
Appeals.
Commission.
Review of commission actions, §11-65-12.
Applicability of chapter, §11-65-47.
Bonds, surety.
Racetracks.
Operators, §11-65-20.
Owners, §11-65-17.
Breeding and development fund, §11-65-34.
Commission, §§11-65-3 to 11-65-12.
Appeals.
Review of commission actions, §11-65-12.
Approval, §11-65-5.
Referendum to approve, §11-65-4.
Authority to create, §11-65-3.
Commission wagering fee, §11-65-30.
Compensation, §11-65-7.
Composition, §11-65-5.
Conflicts of interest, §11-65-7.
Corporations.
Incorporation of commission, §11-65-6.
Employees.
Qualifications, §11-65-11.
Exemption from jurisdiction of state racing commission, §11-65-45.

HORSE RACING—Cont'd
  Commission—Cont'd
    Expenses.
      Reimbursement, §11-65-7.
    Fees.
      Disposition, §11-65-3.
    Incorporation, §11-65-6.
    Investments.
      Funds not needed to
        discharge obligations,
        §11-65-9.
    Name, §11-65-3.
    Officers, §11-65-8.
      Qualifications, §11-65-11.
    Powers and duties.
      Generally, §§11-65-3,
        11-65-10.
    Qualifications of employees,
      §11-65-11.
    Qualifications of members,
      §11-65-5.
    Quorum, §11-65-7.
    Referendum to approve,
      §11-65-4.
    Removal of members,
      §11-65-5.
    Status, §11-65-3.
    Terms of office, §11-65-5.
    Treasurer, §11-65-9.
    Vacancies in office, §11-65-5.
  Concessionaires.
    Conditions for operation,
      §11-65-23.
    Permits, §§11-65-23 to
      11-65-26.
  Conflicts of interest.
    Commission members,
      §11-65-7.
  Contracts.
    Racetracks.
      Operators.
        Restricting competition,
          §11-65-20.
      Restricting competition,
        §11-65-17.
  Corporations.
    Commission.
      Incorporation of
        commission, §11-65-6.
  Declarations of legislature,
    §11-65-1.
  Definitions, §11-65-2.
  Development fund, §11-65-34.
  Drugs.
    Possession of certain drugs
      prohibited, §11-65-41.
    Tampering with horses,
      §11-65-39.
  Elections.
    Approval of pari-mutuel
      betting.
      County-wide referendum,
        §11-65-46.
    Referendum to approve
      commission, §11-65-4.
  Examinations.
    Stewards, §11-65-27.
  Exercise boys.
    Permits, §§11-65-23 to
      11-65-26.
  Fees.
    Application of net revenues,
      §11-65-36.
    Breeding and development
      fund, §11-65-34.
    Commission wagering fee,
      §11-65-30.
    Disposition, §11-65-3.
    Permits, §11-65-24.
    Racetracks.
      Admission fees, §11-65-33.

HORSE RACING—Cont'd
  Fees—Cont'd
    Racetracks—Cont'd
      Operators.
        Licenses.
          Application fee,
            §11-65-18.
      Owners.
        Licenses, §11-65-17.
    State wagering fee,
      §11-65-29.
  Findings of legislature,
    §11-65-1.
  Funds.
    Breeding and development
      fund, §11-65-34.
  Gambling, §§11-65-28 to
    11-65-31.
  Grooms.
    Permits, §§11-65-23 to
      11-65-26.
  Horse owners.
    Permits, §§11-65-23 to
      11-65-26.
  Horses.
    Racing under unregistered
      name, §11-65-43.
    Tampering with prohibited,
      §11-65-39.
  **Host county house or senate
    delegation.**
    Meetings, §11-65-5.
  Injunctions.
    Violation of law or rule or
      regulation, §11-65-13.
  Investments.
    Commission.
      Funds not needed to
        discharge obligations,
        §11-65-9.
  **Involvement in racing
    activities.**
    Disqualification due to
      gambling activities,
      §11-65-38.
  Jockeys.
    Permits, §§11-65-23 to
      11-65-26.
  **Legislative declarations and
    findings,** §11-65-1.
  Licenses.
    Conducting race without
      license, §11-65-37.
    Misuse, §11-65-42.
    Racetracks.
      Operators, §§11-65-14,
        11-65-18 to 11-65-22.
        See within this
        heading, "Racetracks."
      Owners, §§11-65-14 to
        11-65-17, 11-65-38.
    Stewards, §11-65-27.
  Municipal corporations.
    Racetrack admission fee,
      §11-65-33.
  Net revenues.
    Applications, §11-65-36.
  Pari-mutuel betting.
    Commission wagering fee,
      §11-65-30.
    Conduct, §11-65-28.
    County-wide referendum to
      approve, §11-65-46.
    Legalized betting not
      affected, §13A-12-31.
    Pool, §11-65-28.
    State wagering fee,
      §11-65-29.

HORSE RACING—Cont'd
  Pari-mutuel betting—Cont'd
    Twenty-one years of age or
      older.
    Wagering by underage
      persons prohibited,
      §11-65-44.
    Unlicensed race.
      Wagering on, §11-65-37.
  Pari-mutuel employees.
    Permits. See within this
      heading, "Permits."
  Permits, §§11-65-23 to
    11-65-26.
    Application, §11-65-24.
      Review, §11-65-25.
    Fees, §11-65-24.
    Fines.
      Holder of permit,
        §11-65-26.
    Misuse, §11-65-42.
    Nontransferable, §11-65-23.
    Suspension or revocation,
      §11-65-26.
    Term, §11-65-25.
  Purses.
    Allocation of purse moneys,
      §11-65-31.
    Estimates, §11-65-31.
  Racetracks.
    Admission fees, §11-65-33.
    Bonds, surety.
      Operators, §11-65-20.
      Owners, §11-65-17.
    Contracts.
      Restricting competition,
        §11-65-17.
    Employees.
      Permits, §§11-65-23 to
        11-65-26.
    Operators.
      Application to acquire
        interest in, §11-65-22.
      Bonds, surety, §11-65-20.
      Contracts.
        Restricting competition,
          §11-65-20.
      Fines, §11-65-21.
      Licenses.
        Application, §11-65-18.
          Review, §11-65-19.
        Conducting race without
          license, §11-65-37.
        Disqualification due to
          gambling activities,
          §11-65-38.
        Required, §11-65-14.
        Review of application,
          §11-65-19.
        Suspension or revocation,
          §11-65-21.
        Term, §11-65-20.
        Transferability,
          §11-65-14.
    Owners.
      Fines, §11-65-21.
      Licenses.
        Application, §11-65-15.
          Review, §11-65-16.
        Bonds, surety, §11-65-17.
        Disqualification due to
          gambling activities,
          §11-65-38.
        Fees, §11-65-15.
        Required, §11-65-14.
        Review of application,
          §11-65-16.
        Suspension or revocation,
          §11-65-21.
        Term, §11-65-17.

HORSE RACING—Cont'd
  Racetracks—Cont'd
    Owners—Cont'd
      Licenses—Cont'd
        Transferability,
          §11-65-14.
      State wagering fee,
        §11-65-29.
  Racing information.
    Transmission, §11-65-40.
  Radio.
    Transmission of racing
      events, §11-65-32.
  Referendum.
    Pari-mutuel betting.
      County-wide referendum,
        §11-65-46.
  Revenues.
    Application of net revenues,
      §11-65-36.
  Sales tax.
    Tax levied on gross receipts,
      §40-23-2.
  Stable foremen.
    Permits, §§11-65-23 to
      11-65-26.
  State racing commission.
    Exemption from jurisdiction,
      §11-65-45.
  Stewards, §11-65-27.
  Tampering with horses,
    §11-65-39.
  Taxation.
    Exemption from certain
      taxes, §11-65-35.
  Television.
    Transmission of racing
      events, §11-65-32.
  Trainers.
    Permits, §§11-65-23 to
      11-65-26.
  Valets.
    Permits, §§11-65-23 to
      11-65-26.
  Veterinarians.
    Permits, §§11-65-23 to
      11-65-26.
  Wagering, §§11-65-28 to
    11-65-31.

HORSES.
  Estrays, §§3-2-1 to 3-2-23.
    See ESTRAYS.
  General provisions, §§3-1-21
    to 3-1-26.
    See LIVESTOCK.
  Horse shows.
    State championship horse
      show.
      Designation, §1-2-22.
  Licenses.
    Dealers, §40-12-112.
    Shows, §40-12-111.
  Liens.
    Owners of stallions, jacks,
      bulls, etc., §§35-11-330,
      35-11-331.
  Livery stables.
    See LIVERY STABLES.
  Livestock generally, §§3-1-21
    to 3-1-26.
    See LIVESTOCK.
  Racing, §§11-65-1 to 11-65-47.
    See HORSE RACING.
  Racking horse.
    State horse, §1-2-10.
  Running at large, §§3-2-1 to
    3-2-4, 3-2-20 to 3-2-23.
    See ESTRAYS.

HORSES—Cont'd
  Stallions.
    Liens of owners, §§35-11-330,
      35-11-331.
  **State championship horse
    show.**
    Designation, §1-2-22.
  State horse, §1-2-10.

HOSPITALS.
  Accreditation.
    Confidentiality of
      information, §22-21-8.
    Hospitals, §22-21-24.
  Adoption.
    Child placing, §22-21-31.
  Ambulances, §§22-18-1 to
    22-18-7.
    See AMBULANCES.
  Anatomical gifts.
    Generally.
      See ANATOMICAL
        GIFTS.
    Uniform anatomical gift act,
      §§22-19-40 to 22-19-47.
      See ANATOMICAL
        GIFTS.
  Appeals.
    Licenses.
      Judicial review of
        suspension or
        revocation, §22-21-26.
    Liens of hospitals,
      §35-11-373.
  Appropriations.
    Indigent persons.
      Appropriations for indigent
        persons in hospitals,
        §22-21-2.
    Public hospital associations.
      Local political subdivisions,
        §22-21-56.
    Service program for
      indigents.
      Apportionment of
        appropriated funds to
        counties, §22-21-220.
      Proceeds of special county
        tax or funds in county
        treasury, §22-21-223.
  Associations.
    Public hospital associations,
      §§22-21-50 to 22-21-57.
      See within this heading,
        "Public hospital
        associations."
  Audits.
    Publicly-owned medical
      institutions.
      Annual audit of books and
        records, §22-21-4.
  Authorities.
    Building authorities.
      Municipal hospital
        building authorities,
        §§22-21-130 to
        22-21-156. See within
        this heading,
        "Municipal
        corporations."
    County and municipal
      hospital authorities,
      §§22-21-170 to 22-21-191.
      Assets.
        Transfer of assets by
          counties and
          municipalities,
          §22-21-181.
      Board of directors,
        §22-21-175.

HOSPITALS—Cont'd
  Authorities—Cont'd
    County and municipal
      hospital authorities
      —Cont'd
      Bond issues, §§8-6-110 to
        8-6-122.
        See INDUSTRIAL
          REVENUE BONDS.
      Borrowing, §22-21-182.
        Disposition of proceeds
          from borrowing,
          §22-21-183.
      Certificate of incorporation,
        §§22-21-173,
        22-21-174.
      Competitive bidding.
        Applicability of state
          competitive bid law,
          §22-21-190.
      Conflicts of interest,
        §22-21-189.
      Construction of article,
        §22-21-171.
      Contracts.
        Applicability of state
          competitive bid law,
          §22-21-190.
      Definitions, §22-21-170.
      Directors, §22-21-175.
      Dissolution of corporation,
        §22-21-191.
      Eminent domain,
        §22-21-180.
      Ethics.
        Applicability of
          provisions of state
          law as to ethics of
          public officials, etc.,
          §22-21-189.
      Exemptions from taxation,
        §§22-21-182,
        22-21-186.
      Financial statement.
        Publication, §22-21-187.
      Formation of other
        corporations,
        §22-21-177.
      Funds.
        Transfer of funds by
          counties and
          municipalities,
          §22-21-181.
      Immunity.
        Governmental immunity,
          §22-21-178.
      Incorporation, §22-21-5.
        Authority, §22-21-172.
        Certificate of
          incorporation.
          Acknowledgment,
            §22-21-173.
          Amendment,
            §22-21-174.
          Contents, §22-21-173.
          Filing, §22-21-173.
        Formation of other
          corporations,
          §22-21-177.
      Interest.
        Exemption from interest
          rate limitation laws,
          §22-21-6.
      Investment in securities of
        authorities,
        §22-21-185.
      Officers, §22-21-176.
      Personnel, §22-21-176.
      Powers, §§22-21-5,
        22-21-179.

HOSPITALS—Cont'd
  Authorities—Cont'd
    County and municipal
    hospital authorities
    —Cont'd
    Provisions exclusive,
      §22-21-188.
    Purchases.
      Applicability of state
        competitive bid law,
        §22-21-190.
    Purpose of article,
      §22-21-171.
    Refunding securities,
      §22-21-184.
    Securities.
      Banks.
        Investment in
          securities,
          §22-21-185.
      Borrowing, §22-21-182.
      Disposition of proceeds
        from borrowing,
        §22-21-183.
      Investment by
        fiduciaries,
        §22-21-185.
      Issuance, §22-21-182.
      Refunding securities,
        §22-21-184.
      Sale, §22-21-182.
      Tax exemptions,
        §22-21-182.
    Sovereignty.
      Governmental
        sovereignty,
        §22-21-178.
    Tax exemptions,
      §§22-21-182,
      22-21-186.
    Transfer of funds and
      assets by counties and
      municipalities,
      §22-21-181.
    Usury.
      Exemption from usury
        laws, §22-21-6.
    Municipal hospital building
      authorities, §§22-21-130
      to 22-21-156. See within
      this heading, "Municipal
      corporations."
  Blind persons.
    Assistance to needy blind
      persons.
    Cost of hospitalization.
      Not to constitute lien on
        property, §38-5-5.
      Relatives not legally
        liable, §38-5-6.
  Boards.
    Hospital boards.
      County hospital boards,
        §§22-21-70 to 22-21-83.
        See within this
        heading, "Counties."
      State board of health. See
        within this heading,
        "State board of
        health."
  Bond issues.
    Constitutional bonds.
      Bonds for state board of
        health hospitals and
        district tuberculosis
        sanitoria, Const. Ala.,
        amd. 74.

HOSPITALS—Cont'd
  Bond issues—Cont'd
    Constitutional bonds—Cont'd
      Building, construction and
        improvement at
        Alabama state
        hospitals and Partlow
        state school for mental
        deficients, Const. Ala.,
        amds. 113, 118.
      Construction and
        equipment of hospitals,
        Const. Ala., amds. 114,
        121, 158.
    Counties.
      Public improvement bonds,
        §§11-81-140 to
        11-18-150.
      See COUNTIES.
    County hospital boards,
      §22-21-78.
    Municipal corporations.
      Hospital building
        authorities,
        §§22-21-141 to
        22-21-150. See within
        this heading,
        "Municipal
        corporations."
      Public improvement bonds,
        §§11-81-140 to
        11-81-150.
      See COUNTIES.
    Public hospitals, §§11-95-8 to
      11-95-11.
  Building authorities.
    Municipal hospital building
      authorities, §§22-21-130
      to 22-21-156. See within
      this heading, "Municipal
      corporations."
  Cancer.
    Standards.
      Establishment and
        designation of
        standard requirements
        for cancer units,
        §22-13-1.
  Certificates of need,
    §§22-21-265 to 22-21-272.
    Applications, §22-21-267.
      Contracts for review and
        recommendations,
        §22-21-272.
      Fees, §22-21-271.
        Disposition, §22-21-271.
      Review, §§22-21-272 to
        22-21-275.
    Appropriations, §22-21-271.
    Cumulative provisions,
      §22-21-277.
    Definitions, §22-21-260.
    Emergency certificate prior
      to hearing, §22-21-268.
    Extension of certificate,
      §22-21-270.
      Application, §22-21-267.
    Health systems agencies.
      Contracts for review and
        recommendations
        concerning
        applications,
        §22-21-272.
    Injunctions.
      Violations of articles,
        §22-21-276.
    In-patient facilities.
      Required findings,
        §22-21-266.
    Legislative findings,
      §22-21-261.

HOSPITALS—Cont'd
  Certificates of need—Cont'd
    Modification of certificate.
      Application, §22-21-267.
      Requirement of certificate
        of need, §22-21-265.
      Subject to review,
        §22-21-263.
    New institutional health
      services.
      Requirement of certificate
        of need, §22-21-265.
      Subject to review,
        §22-21-263.
    Period for which valid,
      §22-21-270.
    Planning.
      Certificate of need for
        planning, §22-21-269.
    Purpose of article,
      §22-21-261.
    Repeal of conflicting laws,
      §22-21-277.
    Required.
      New institutional health
        services, §22-21-265.
    Review.
      Contracts with health
        systems agencies,
        §22-21-272.
      Criteria, §22-21-264.
        Adoption and public
          notice, §22-21-274.
      New institutional health
        services subject to,
        §22-21-263.
      Procedures, §22-21-275.
        Adoption and public
          notice, §22-21-274.
    Termination, §22-21-270.
    Transfer.
      Nontransferable,
        §22-21-270.
    Violations of article,
      §22-21-276.
      Injunctive relief,
        §22-21-276.
  Child abuse or neglect.
    Reporting child abuse or
      neglect.
      General provisions,
        §§26-14-1 to 26-14-13.
      See MINORS.
      Mandatory reporting,
        §26-14-3.
  Child placing, §22-21-31.
  Churches.
    Conventions or associations
      of churches.
      Establishment of hospitals
        by state, sectional or
        national conventions
        or associations,
        §10-4-61.
  Claims against hospitals.
    Trusts for payment,
      §§22-21-240 to 22-21-243.
  Commitment.
    Veterans.
      Incompetent veterans.
        Commitment to veterans'
          hospital, §26-9-13.
  Conflicts of interest.
    County and municipal
      hospital authorities,
      §22-21-189.
  Consent for health services,
    §§22-8-1 to 22-8-9.
    See HEALTH.

HOSPITALS—Cont'd
Constitution of Alabama.
Bond issues.
Bonds for state board of
health hospitals and
district tuberculosis
sanitoria, Const. Ala.,
amd. 74.
Building construction and
improvement at
Alabama state
hospitals and Partlow
state school for mental
deficients, Const. Ala.,
amds. 113, 118.
Construction and
equipment of hospitals,
Const. Ala., amds. 114,
121, 158.
County hospitals.
Additional county taxes for
county hospitals,
Const. Ala., amd. 59.
Indigent persons.
Use of certain special
county taxes for
hospital care and
treatment of
indigent residents,
Const. Ala., amd.
125.
Special county tax, Const.
Ala., amd. 76.
Use of special county
taxes for hospital
care and treatment
of indigent residents,
Const. Ala., amd.
125.
Special tax for hospital and
public health purposes
in counties except
Mobile, Montgomery
and Jefferson, Const.
Ala., amd. 72.
Public hospitals and health
facilities, Const. Ala.,
amd. 53.
Corporations.
County hospital corporations,
§§22-21-100 to 22-21-112.
See within this heading,
"Counties."
Incorporations, §22-21-5.
Usury.
Certain public hospital
corporations exempted
from usury laws,
§22-21-6.
Corrections.
Board of corrections.
Prisoners needing long-
time hospitalization.
Treatment, care and
segregation,
§14-1-12.
Counties, §§22-21-70 to
22-21-112.
Acquisition of lands for
hospitals, §11-18-2.
Appropriations.
Service program for
indigents.
Appropriation of
proceeds of special
county tax or funds
in county treasury,
§22-21-223.

HOSPITALS—Cont'd
Counties—Cont'd
Assets.
Transfer of assets to
hospital authorities by
counties, §22-21-181.
Authorities.
County and municipal
hospital authorities,
§§22-21-170 to
22-21-191. See within
this heading,
"Authorities."
Boards of health.
Duties, §22-3-2.
Bond issues.
Hospital boards, §22-21-78.
Corporations, §§22-21-100 to
22-21-112.
Erection.
Duty of county commission
to erect, §11-14-10.
Establishment, §22-21-1.
Funds.
Transfer of funds to
hospital authorities,
§22-21-181.
Transfer of funds to
hospital corporations,
§22-21-81.
Hospital boards, §§22-21-70
to 22-21-83.
Board of directors,
§22-21-76.
Bond issues, §22-21-78.
Investment of trust funds
in corporation's
securities, §22-21-79.
Borrowing by corporation,
§22-21-78.
Certificates of
incorporation,
§§22-21-73, 22-21-74.
Construction of division,
§22-21-71.
Cumulative nature of
division, §22-21-83.
Definitions, §22-21-70.
Directors, §22-21-76.
Dissolution of corporation,
§22-21-82.
Division cumulative,
§22-21-83.
Exemption from taxation,
§22-21-80.
Incorporation, §22-21-5.
Application, §22-21-72.
Certificate of
incorporation,
§§22-21-73, 22-21-74.
Noncomplying
corporations.
Validation, §22-21-75.
Validation of
noncomplying
corporations,
§22-21-75.
Interest.
Exemption from interest
rate limitation laws,
§22-21-6.
Investment of trust funds
in corporation's
securities, §22-21-79.
Noncomplying
corporations,
§22-21-75.
Powers, §§22-21-5,
22-21-77.
Purpose of division,
§22-21-71.

HOSPITALS—Cont'd
Counties—Cont'd
Hospital boards—Cont'd
Securities, §22-21-78.
Investment of trust funds
in corporation's
securities, §22-21-79.
Taxation exemptions,
§22-21-80.
Transfer of hospitals and
funds by counties or
municipalities,
§22-21-81.
Usury.
Exemption from usury
laws, §22-21-6.
Validation of noncomplying
corporations,
§22-21-75.
Hospital corporations,
§§22-21-100 to 22-21-112.
Definitions, §22-21-100.
Designation as agency to
operate, etc., public
hospital facilities,
§22-21-101.
Elections.
Validation of elections,
§22-21-105.
Health care authorities.
Designation of
authorities as
agencies for purposes
of chapter,
§22-21-338.
Incorporation, §22-21-5.
Interest.
Exemption from interest
rate limitation laws,
§22-21-6.
Securities, §22-21-108.
Investment of trust funds
and securities,
§22-21-110.
Validation.
Prior to issuance,
§22-21-112.
Validity, §22-21-111.
Powers, §22-21-5.
Securities, §§22-21-106 to
22-21-110.
Conditions, §22-21-107.
Delivery, §22-21-108.
Execution, §22-21-108.
Expenses, §22-21-109.
Funds from which
payable, §22-21-106.
Interest, §22-21-108.
Investment of trust
funds, §22-21-110.
Issuance in anticipation
of tax, §22-21-106.
Nature of obligation,
§22-21-106.
Payment, §22-21-108.
Security for payment,
§22-21-107.
Pledge of revenues,
§22-21-107.
Refunding, §22-21-108.
Sale, §22-21-109.
Security for payment,
§22-21-107.
Status, §22-21-108.
Tax exemption,
§22-21-108.
Terms, §22-21-107.

HOSPITALS—Cont'd
  Counties—Cont'd
    Hospital corporations
        —Cont'd
      Special county tax.
        Elections.
          Validation of elections,
              §§22-21-103,
              22-21-104.
          Issuance of securities in
              anticipation of tax,
              §22-21-106.
          Payment to hospital
              corporations,
              §22-21-102.
          Validation of elections,
              §§22-21-103,
              22-21-104.
      Usury.
        Exemption from usury
            laws, §22-21-6.
    Indigent persons.
      Service program for
          indigents, §§22-21-210
          to 22-21-227. See
          within this heading,
          "Service program for
          indigents."
    Public hospital associations.
      Appropriations, §22-21-56.
    Public hospitals, §§11-95-1 to
        11-95-21. See within this
        heading, "Public
        hospitals."
    Service program for
        indigents, §§22-21-210 to
        22-21-227. See within
        this heading, "Service
        program for indigents."
    Special county tax, Const.
        Ala., amds. 59, 72, 76.
      County hospital
          corporations,
          §§22-21-100 to
          22-21-112.
      Service program for
          indigents.
        Appropriation of
            proceeds of special
            county tax,
            §22-21-223.
      Use for hospital care and
          treatment of indigent
          residents, Const. Ala.,
          amd. 125.
    Transfer of hospitals and
        funds by counties,
        §22-21-81.
  County boards of health.
    Duties, §22-3-2.
  Definitions, §34-23-1.
    Authorities, §22-21-170.
    Certificates of need,
        §22-21-260.
    County and municipal
        hospital authorities,
        §22-21-170.
    County hospital boards,
        §22-21-70.
    County hospital corporations,
        §22-21-100.
    Licenses, §22-21-20.
    Municipal hospital building
        authorities, §22-21-130.
    Public hospitals, §11-95-2.
    Service program for
        indigents, §22-21-210.
  Diseases.
    Notifiable diseases,
        §§22-11A-1 to 22-11A-38.
      See DISEASES.

HOSPITALS—Cont'd
  Education.
    Classes and schools operated
        under Alabama state
        hospitals.
      Textbooks.
        Purchase and furnishing
            of state-owned
            textbooks, §16-36-23.
    Public education employees'
        health insurance.
      Payment to hospital,
          §16-25A-10.
  Eminent domain.
    County and municipal
        hospital authorities,
        §22-21-180.
    Municipal hospital building
        authorities.
      Power of eminent domain,
          §22-21-138.
    Public hospitals, §11-95-14.
  Erection of hospitals.
    Counties.
      Duty of county commission,
          §11-14-10.
  Establishment.
    Local authorities, §22-21-1.
  Evidence.
    Expenses.
      Hospital or medical
          expenses to be paid or
          reimbursed admissible
          as competent evidence,
          §12-21-45.
    Records, §§12-21-5 to 12-21-7.
      Copy of hospital records,
          §§12-21-5 to 12-21-7.
      Admissibility, §12-21-5.
      Certificate, §12-21-6.
      Certificate of custodian,
          §12-21-7.
      Costs, §12-21-6.
      Form, §12-21-6.
      Inspection, §12-21-6.
      Subpoena duces tecum,
          §12-21-6.
  Expenses.
    Evidence, §12-21-45.
    Itemized statement of
        expenses to be provided
        upon request, §22-21-7.
  Fees.
    Licenses, §22-21-24.
  Fires and fire prevention.
    Fire marshal.
      Regulation of doors and
          exits, §36-19-10.
  Health care authorities,
      §§22-21-310 to 22-21-356.
    See HEALTH CARE
        AUTHORITIES.
  Health care service plans,
      §§10-4-100 to 10-4-107.
    See HEALTH CARE
        SERVICE PLANS.
  Incorporation.
    Public bodies created under
        chapter, §22-21-5.
  Indigent persons.
    Appropriations for indigent
        persons in hospitals,
        §22-21-2.
    Regional referral hospitals.
      Responsibility for health
          care, §§22-21-290 to
          22-21-296.
        See HEALTH.

HOSPITALS—Cont'd
  Indigent persons—Cont'd
    Service program for
        indigents, §§22-21-210 to
        22-21-227. See within
        this heading, "Service
        program for indigents."
    Use of certain special county
        taxes for hospital care
        and treatment of
        indigent residents,
        Const. Ala., amd. 125.
  Indorsements.
    Liens of hospitals.
      Verified statement,
          §35-11-371.
  Injunctions.
    Certificates of need.
      Violations of article,
          §22-21-276.
  Inspections, §22-21-29.
    Disclosure of information,
        §22-21-30.
  Insurance.
    Medical liability insurance,
        §§27-26-1 to 27-26-43.
      See INSURANCE.
    Payment of claims by
        insurance companies,
        §22-21-7.
  Interest.
    Public hospital corporations.
      Certain corporations
          exempted from interest
          rate limitation laws,
          §22-21-6.
  Investments.
    Public hospitals.
      Powers of corporation,
          §11-95-7.
  Jails.
    Removal of prisoners.
      Ill health of prisoners,
          §14-6-9.
  Jurisdiction.
    Liens of hospitals.
      Jurisdiction to determine
          matters connected with
          lien, §35-11-373.
  Liability insurance.
    Medical liability insurance,
        §§27-26-1 to 27-26-43.
      See INSURANCE.
  Licenses, §§22-21-20 to
      22-21-31.
    Accreditation, §22-21-24.
    Advisory board, §22-21-27.
    Appeals.
      Judicial review of
          suspension or
          revocation, §22-21-26.
    Applications, §22-21-23.
      New applications after
          revocation, §22-21-25.
    Definitions, §22-21-20.
    Disclosure of information,
        §22-21-30.
    Exceptions to requirements,
        §22-21-22.
    Expiration date, §22-21-24.
    Fees, §22-21-24.
    Form, §22-21-24.
    Inspections, §22-21-29.
    Issuance, §22-21-25.
    Penalty for violation of
        article, §22-21-33.
    Posting, §22-21-24.
    Purpose of article, §22-21-21.
    Renewal, §22-21-24.
    Required, §22-21-22.

HOSPITALS—Cont'd
  Licenses—Cont'd
    Revocation, §22-21-25.
      Judicial review of
        revocation, §22-21-26.
      New applications after
        revocation, §22-21-25.
    Rules and regulations,
      §22-21-28.
    Suspension, §22-21-25.
      Judicial review of
        suspension, §22-21-26.
    Term, §22-21-24.
    Transferability, §22-21-24.
    Violation of article.
      Penalty, §22-21-33.
  Liens, §§35-11-370 to
    35-11-375.
    Appeals, §35-11-373.
    Commencement of action for
      enforcement, §35-11-372.
    Declaration of lien,
      §35-11-370.
    Enforcement of lien,
      §35-11-372.
    Filing.
      Verified statement,
        §35-11-371.
    Impairment of lien,
      §35-11-372.
    Jurisdiction to determine
      matters connected with
      lien, §35-11-373.
    Liability for injuries.
      Hospital not given
        independent right to
        determine liability for
        injuries, §35-11-375.
    Liens generally.
      See LIENS.
    Perfection of lien, §35-11-371.
    Recordation.
      Verified statement,
        §35-11-371.
    Release, §35-11-372.
    Satisfaction, §35-11-372.
    Verified statement.
      Generally, §35-11-371.
    Workmen's compensation.
      Division not applicable to
        moneys due under
        workmen's
        compensation act,
        §35-11-374.
  Malpractice.
    General provisions, §§6-5-480
      to 6-5-488, 6-5-540 to
      6-5-552.
    See MALPRACTICE.
    Medical liability insurance,
      §§27-26-1 to 27-26-43.
    See INSURANCE.
  Medical clinic boards.
    Municipal corporations,
      §§11-58-1 to 11-58-15.
    See MUNICIPAL
      CORPORATIONS.
  Medical technicians,
    §§34-18-1 to 34-18-47.
    See MEDICAL
      TECHNICIANS.
  Memorial hospitals.
    Stringfellow memorial
      hospital nonprofit realty
      company.
      Exemption from state,
        county and municipal
        ad valorem taxation,
        §40-9-1.1.

HOSPITALS—Cont'd
  Memorial hospitals—Cont'd
    Susie Parker Stringfellow
      Memorial Hospital.
      Exemption from state,
        county and municipal
        ad valorem taxation,
        §40-9-1.1.
  Mentally ill.
    Commitment, §§22-52-1 to
      22-52-72.
    See MENTALLY ILL.
    Facilities.
      General provisions.
        See MENTALLY ILL.
      Regional mental health
        programs and
        facilities, §§22-51-1 to
        22-51-14.
        See MENTALLY ILL.
      Security medical facility,
        §§22-54-1 to 22-54-5.
    Support of persons in state
      mental institutions,
      §§22-53-1 to 22-53-26.
      See MENTALLY ILL.
    Mental health capital outlay
      oversight commission,
      §22-50-25.
  Municipal corporations.
    Assets.
      Transfer of assets to
        hospital authorities,
        §22-21-181.
    Authorities.
      Building authorities,
        §§22-21-130 to
        22-21-156.
      County and municipal
        hospital authorities,
        §§22-21-170 to
        22-21-191. See within
        this heading,
        "Authorities."
    Building authorities,
      §§22-21-130 to 22-21-156.
    Board of directors,
      §22-21-135.
    Bond issues.
      Authority to issue,
        §22-21-141.
      Contesting.
        Limitation on actions
          to contest,
          §22-21-145.
      Default in payment,
        §22-21-150.
      Execution, §22-21-143.
      Exemption from
        taxation, §22-21-153.
      Insurers.
        Investment in bonds,
          §22-21-146.
      Interest, §22-21-141.
      Investment in bonds,
        §§22-21-146,
        22-21-147.
      Limitation on actions to
        contest, §22-21-145.
      Maturity, §22-21-141.
      Negotiable instruments,
        §22-21-148.
      Notice of issuance,
        §22-21-145.
      Obligations not debt of
        state or
        municipality,
        §22-21-151.
      Payment, §22-21-141.
      Default in payment,
        §22-21-150.

HOSPITALS—Cont'd
  Municipal corporations
    —Cont'd
    Building authorities—Cont'd
      Bond issues—Cont'd
        Payment—Cont'd
          Security for payment,
            §22-21-144.
        Proceeds of sale.
          Use of proceeds,
            §22-21-149.
        Refunding bonds,
          §22-21-142.
        Sale, §22-21-141.
          Refunding bonds,
            §22-21-142.
          Use of proceeds,
            §22-21-149.
        Security for payment,
          §22-21-144.
        Tax exemption,
          §22-21-153.
        Validity.
          Limitation on actions
            to contest,
            §22-21-145.
    Certificate of incorporation,
      §§22-21-132,
      22-21-134.
    Construction of article,
      §22-21-131.
    Conveyance of property by
      municipalities,
      §22-21-139.
    Cumulative nature of
      article, §22-21-155.
    Definitions, §22-21-130.
    Directors, §22-21-135.
    Dissolution, §22-21-154.
    Eminent domain.
      Power of eminent
        domain, §22-21-138.
    Exemption from taxation,
      §22-21-153.
    Funds.
      Investment of funds,
        §22-21-152.
    Incorporation, §22-21-5.
      Application, §22-21-132.
      Certificate of
        incorporation.
        Amendment,
          §22-21-133.
        Contents, §22-21-133.
        Filing, §22-21-134.
        Resolution, §22-21-132.
    Interest.
      Exemption from interest
        rate limitation laws,
        §22-21-6.
    Investment in bonds,
      §§22-21-146,
      22-21-147.
    Investment of funds,
      §22-21-152.
    Lease agreements with
      municipality,
      §22-21-140.
    Lease of hospitals,
      buildings or facilities
      to public or nonprofit
      corporations,
      §22-21-156.
    Obligations not debt of
      state or municipality,
      §22-21-151.
    Officers, §22-21-136.

HOSPITALS—Cont'd
Municipal corporations
—Cont'd
Building authorities—Cont'd
Powers, §§22-21-5,
22-21-137, 22-21-138.
Lease of hospitals,
buildings or facilities
to public or nonprofit
corporations,
§22-21-156.
Purpose of article,
§22-21-131.
Usury.
Exemption from usury
laws, §22-21-6.
Conveyance of property to
building authorities,
§22-21-139.
Counties.
Establishment, aid, etc., of
hospitals in counties,
§11-47-134.
Establishment, §§11-47-134,
22-21-1.
Funds.
Transfer of funds to
hospital authorities,
§22-21-181.
Transfer of funds to
hospital corporations,
§22-21-81.
Indigent persons.
Appropriation of funds for
care of certain sick
and wounded persons
in municipal hospitals,
§11-47-133.
Lease agreements with
building authorities,
§22-21-140.
Maintenance, §11-47-7.
Medical clinic boards,
§§11-58-1 to 11-58-15.
See MUNICIPAL
CORPORATIONS.
Police jurisdiction over
hospitals, §11-47-22.
Public hospital associations,
§§22-21-50 to 22-21-57.
See within this heading,
"Public hospital
associations."
Public hospitals, §§11-95-1 to
11-95-21. See within this
heading, "Public
hospitals."
Regulation, §11-47-7.
Transfer of hospitals and
funds by municipalities,
§22-21-81.
Natural death act.
Liability of participating
facility, §22-8A-7.
Nurses.
General provisions, §§34-21-1
to 34-21-63.
See NURSES.
Nursing homes.
General provisions, §§34-20-1
to 34-20-16.
See NURSING HOMES.
Ombudsmen.
Long-term residential health
care recipient
ombudsmen, §§22-5A-1
to 22-5A-7.
See NURSING HOMES.
Penalties.
Violation of licensing article,
§22-21-33.

HOSPITALS—Cont'd
Penitentiary, §§14-3-41 to
14-3-43.
**Pharmacists and
pharmacies,** §34-23-74.
Defined, §34-23-1.
Permits, §§34-23-30 to
34-23-34.
Powers.
Public bodies created under
chapter, §22-21-5.
Prisons and prisoners.
Prisoners needing long-time
hospitalization.
Treatment, care and
segregation, §14-1-12.
Property.
Public hospitals.
Dissolution of corporation.
Passage of title to
property of
corporation,
§11-95-19.
Powers of corporations as
to, §11-95-19.
Public hospital associations,
§§22-21-50 to 22-21-57.
Appropriations.
Local political subdivisions,
§22-21-56.
Bylaws, §22-21-52.
Constitution, §22-21-52.
Counties.
Appropriations, §22-21-56.
Directors, §§22-21-51,
22-21-52.
Dissolution, §22-21-55.
Effect of article on local
executive committees,
§22-21-57.
Establishment.
Proceedings to establish,
§22-21-50.
Executive committee,
§22-21-52.
Effect of article on local
executive committees,
§22-21-57.
Incorporation, §22-21-5.
Interest rate limitation laws.
Exemption, §22-21-6.
Municipal corporations.
Appropriations, §22-21-56.
Noncomplying associations.
Validation, §22-21-54.
Powers, §§22-21-5, 22-21-53.
Usury laws.
Exemption, §22-21-6.
Validation of noncomplying
associations, §22-21-54.
Public hospitals, §§11-95-1 to
11-95-21.
Actions.
Power of corporation to sue
and be sued, §11-95-7.
Authorizing subdivisions.
Defined, §11-95-2.
Liability, §11-95-12.
Board of directors.
Composition, §11-95-6.
Expenses of directors,
§11-95-6.
Impeachment and removal
from office, §11-95-6.
Number of members,
§11-95-6.
Qualifications of members,
§11-95-6.
Terms of members,
§11-95-6.
Vacancies, §11-95-6.

HOSPITALS—Cont'd
Public hospitals—Cont'd
Bond issues, §§11-95-8 to
11-95-11.
Execution of bonds,
§11-95-8.
Interest, §11-95-8.
Investments.
Eligibility for
investment,
§11-95-8.
Maturity of bonds,
§11-95-8.
Negotiable instruments,
§11-95-8.
Pledge of revenues and
other security,
§11-95-8.
Refunding bonds,
§11-95-10.
Sale of bonds, §11-95-9.
Source of payment,
§11-95-8.
Taxation.
Exemption, §11-95-11.
Certificates of incorporation,
§§11-95-4, 11-95-5.
Construction and
interpretation.
Cumulative effect of
provisions, §11-95-21.
Liberal construction of
provisions, §11-95-1.
Construction, operation, etc.,
by state board of health,
§22-4-14.
Definitions, §11-95-2.
Dissolution of corporation,
§11-95-19.
Eminent domain, §11-95-14.
Funds.
Powers of corporation as
to, §11-95-7.
Transfer of funds to
corporation, §11-95-17.
Governing bodies.
Applications for
incorporation.
Action on, §11-95-3.
Defined, §11-95-2.
Governmental entities.
Corporations to constitute
for certain purposes,
§11-95-16.
Incorporation, §§11-95-3 to
11-95-5.
Application for, §11-95-3.
Certificate of incorporation,
§11-95-4.
Amendment, §11-95-5.
Contents, §11-95-4.
Filing, §11-95-4.
Number of incorporators,
§11-95-3.
Indigent patients.
Rules and regulations for
treatment.
Power of corporation to
make and alter,
§11-95-7.
Interest.
Bond issues, §11-95-8.
Exemption from interest
laws, §11-95-13.
Investments.
Powers of corporation,
§11-95-7.
Legislative declaration,
§11-95-1.
Multiple corporations
authorized, §11-95-20.

HOSPITALS—Cont'd
Public hospitals—Cont'd
Nonprofit corporations,
§11-95-18.
Powers of corporation,
§11-95-7.
Eminent domain,
§11-95-14.
Property.
Dissolution of corporation.
Passage of title to
property of
corporation,
§11-95-19.
Powers of corporation as
to, §11-95-7.
Seals and sealed
instruments.
Corporate seal, §11-95-7.
Taxation.
Exemption of corporations,
§11-95-11.
Special hospital taxes.
Applicability of certain
provisions,
§11-95-15.
Usury.
Exemption from usury
laws, §11-95-13.
Purchases and stores.
County and municipal
hospital authorities.
Applicability of state
competitive bid law,
§22-21-190.
**Quality assurance
credentials.**
Confidentiality, §22-21-8.
Recordation.
Liens of hospitals,
§35-11-371.
Records.
Evidence.
Admissibility of copy of
hospital records in
evidence, §12-21-5.
Certificate, §12-21-6.
Costs, §12-21-6.
Form, §12-21-6.
Inspection of copy of
hospital records,
§12-21-6.
Subpoena duces tecum,
§12-21-6.
Publicly-owned medical
institutions.
Annual audit of books and
records, §22-21-4.
Regional referral hospitals.
Indigent persons.
Responsibility for health
care, §§22-21-290 to
22-21-296.
See HEALTH.
Reports.
Child abuse or neglect.
General provisions,
§§26-14-1 to 26-14-13.
See MINORS.
Mandatory reporting,
§26-14-3.
Rules and regulations.
Licenses, §22-21-28.
Service program for
indigents, §22-21-212.
Sales tax.
Exemptions.
Gross proceeds received
from sales by hospital
canteens, §40-23-4.

HOSPITALS—Cont'd
Sanatoria.
Tuberculosis.
District tuberculosis
sanitaria.
Bonds, Const. Ala., amd.
74.
Generally.
See TUBERCULOSIS.
Scholarships.
Professional and technical
personnel at public
hospitals, §22-21-3.
Schools.
Textbooks.
Purchase and furnishing of
state-owned textbooks
for classes and schools
operated under
Alabama state
hospitals, §16-36-23.
**Service program for
indigents,** §§22-21-210 to
22-21-227.
Administration of program,
§22-21-212.
Appropriations.
Apportionment of
appropriated funds to
counties, §22-21-220.
Proceeds of special county
tax or funds in county
treasury, §22-21-223.
Assisting person in
hospitalization.
Charging, etc., for
assistance, §22-21-227.
Charging, etc., for assisting
person in hospitalization,
§22-21-227.
Collection of costs from
indigent patient,
§22-21-219.
Costs.
Collection of costs, etc.,
from indigent patient,
§22-21-219.
County admissions
committees, §§22-21-214,
22-21-215.
Definitions, §22-21-210.
Determination of need for
indigents'
hospitalization,
§22-21-216.
Disposition of unexpended
funds.
Counties, §22-21-222.
State board of health,
§22-21-221.
Expenses.
State board of health,
§22-21-224.
Federal funds, §22-21-225.
Funds in county treasury.
Appropriation, §22-21-223.
Inadequate facilities.
Admittance in other county
when local facilities
deemed inadequate,
§22-21-218.
Need for indigents'
hospitalization.
Determination of need,
§22-21-216.
Participation by counties
having no hospital,
§22-21-217.

HOSPITALS—Cont'd
**Service program for
indigents**—Cont'd
Physicians.
Payment of public funds to
physicians prohibited,
§22-21-219.
Purpose of article,
§22-21-211.
Rules and regulations,
§22-21-212.
Special county tax.
Appropriation of proceeds,
§22-21-223.
State board of health.
Disposition of unexpended
funds, §22-21-221.
Expenses, §22-21-224.
Taxation.
Appropriation of proceeds
of special county tax,
§22-21-223.
Unexpended funds.
Disposition, §§22-21-221,
22-21-222.
Services rendered.
Itemized statement to be
furnished upon request,
§22-21-7.
State board of health.
Authority and jurisdiction,
§22-2-2.
Bonds for state board of
health hospitals, Const.
Ala., amd. 74.
Construction, operation, etc.,
of public hospitals,
§22-4-14.
Service program for
indigents.
Disposition of unexpended
funds, §22-21-221.
Expenses, §22-21-224.
State institutions.
Public hospital associations,
§§22-21-50 to 22-21-57.
See within this heading,
"Public hospital
associations."
Tuberculosis.
Generally.
See TUBERCULOSIS.
Sanitoria.
District tuberculosis
sanitaria.
Bonds, Const. Ala.,
amd. 74.
**Statement of services
rendered.**
Itemized statement to be
furnished upon request,
§22-21-7.
**Stringfellow Memorial
Hospital Nonprofit
Realty Company.**
Exemption from state, county
and municipal ad
valorem taxation,
§40-9-1.1.
Surgery.
Consent for health services,
§§22-8-1 to 22-8-9.
See HEALTH.
**Susie Parker Stringfellow
Memorial Hospital.**
Exemption from state, county
and municipal ad
valorem taxation,
§40-9-1.1.

HOSPITALS—Cont'd
  Taxation.
    Counties.
      Special county tax.
        Generally. See within
          this heading,
          "Counties."
      Hospital corporations,
        §§22-21-102 to
        22-21-106.
    Exemptions.
      County and municipal
        hospital authorities,
        §§22-21-182,
        22-21-186.
      County hospital boards,
        §22-21-80.
      County hospital
        corporations,
        §22-21-108.
      Municipal hospital
        building authorities,
        §22-21-153.
      Property, §40-9-1.
      Stock of hospital
        corporations, §40-9-1.
      Stringfellow memorial
        hospital nonprofit
        realty company,
        §40-9-1.1.
      Susie Parker Stringfellow
        memorial hospital,
        §40-9-1.1.
    Public hospitals.
      Exemption of corporations
        from taxation,
        §11-95-11.
      Special hospital taxes.
        Applicability of certain
          provisions,
          §11-95-15.
    Service program for
      indigents.
      Appropriation of proceeds
        of special county tax,
        §22-21-223.
  **Trusts for payment of
    liability claims against
    hospitals,** §§22-21-240 to
    22-21-243.
    Administration.
      Authorized, §22-21-240.
    Establishment.
      Authorized, §22-21-240.
    Liabilities.
      Hospitals not liable as
        participants in trust,
        §22-21-242.
      Trustees, §22-21-241.
    Rights, privileges,
      immunities, etc.,
      conferred by article,
      §22-21-243.
    Terms and conditions.
      Specifications, §22-21-240.
    Trustees.
      Liabilities, §22-21-241.
      Powers, §22-21-241.
  Tuberculosis.
    Generally.
      See TUBERCULOSIS.
    Sanitoria.
      District tuberculosis
        sanitoria.
        Bonds, Const. Ala., amd.
          74.
  Usury.
    Public hospital corporations.
      Certain corporations
        exempted from usury
        laws, §22-21-6.

HOSPITALS—Cont'd
  Venereal disease.
    Notifiable diseases.
      General provisions,
        §§22-11A-1 to
        22-11A-38.
      See DISEASES.
  Veterans.
    Commitment of incompetent
      veterans to veterans'
      hospital, §26-9-13.
  Vital statistics.
    Births and deaths.
      Records and reports,
        §22-9-11.
  Welfare.
    Incapacitated applicants and
      recipients.
      Hospitalization, §38-4-9.
  Workmen's compensation.
    Liens of hospitals.
      Division not applicable to
        moneys due under
        workmen's
        compensation act,
        §35-11-374.

**HOTELS, INNS AND OTHER
TRANSIENT LODGING
PLACES,** §§34-15-1 to
34-15-20.
  Accommodations.
    Obtaining accommodations
      by fraud or
      misrepresentation,
      §§34-15-19, 34-15-20.
  Alcoholic beverages.
    Defined, §28-3-1.
    Licenses.
      General provisions,
        §§28-3A-1 to 28-3A-26.
  Appeals.
    Transient occupancy tax.
      Assessment, §40-26-13.
  Baggage.
    Defined, §34-15-15.
    Liability for loss, §34-15-15.
    Liens of hotel keepers,
      §§34-15-130, 34-15-131.
  Blind persons.
    Right to use of public lodging
      places, §21-7-3.
  Building code.
    Minimum building standards
      code, §§41-9-160 to
      41-9-166.
    See BUILDINGS.
  Certificate of inspection,
    §34-15-8.
  Closure of hotels.
    Flagrant or continued
      violation of rules and
      regulations, §34-15-10.
  Contracts.
    Special contract between
      hotel and guest,
      §34-15-11.
  County boards of health.
    Duties, §22-3-2.
  County health officers.
    Duties, §22-3-5.
  Definitions, §34-15-1.
    Baggage, §34-15-15.
  Drinking cups.
    Use of common drinking cups
      prohibited, §22-20-1.

**HOTELS, INNS AND OTHER
TRANSIENT LODGING
PLACES**—Cont'd
  Evidence.
    Obtaining accommodations
      by fraud or
      misrepresentation.
      Prima facie evidence,
        §34-15-19.
  Executions.
    Transient occupancy tax,
      §40-26-15.
  Fraud.
    Obtaining accommodations
      by fraud or
      misrepresentation.
      Posting of law in hotel or
        inn, §34-15-20.
      Prima facie evidence,
        §34-15-19.
  Guests.
    Goods of customers.
      Liens of hotel keepers,
        §§34-15-130,
        34-15-131.
    Liabilities to guests,
      §§34-15-11 to 34-15-15.
    Obtaining accommodations
      by fraud or
      misrepresentation.
      Posting of law, §34-15-20.
      Prima facie evidence of
        offense, §34-15-19.
    Removal of undesirable
      guests, §34-15-17.
    Special contract between
      hotel and guest,
      §34-15-11.
  Handicapped persons.
    Right to use public lodging
      places, §21-7-3.
  Health.
    Authority and jurisdiction of
      state board of health,
      §22-2-2.
    Duties of county boards of
      health, §22-3-2.
    Duties of county health
      officers, §22-3-5.
    Duties of hotel owners, etc.,
      §34-15-4.
    Regulations, §22-20-5.
  Hearings.
    Transient occupancy tax.
      Assessment, §40-26-13.
  **Industrial development
    boards.**
    Ad valorem taxes.
      Hotels and motor inns
        built under act not
        exempt from,
        §11-54-96.1.
  Inspectors.
    Assistants, §34-15-5.
    Certificate of inspection.
      Issuance by inspectors,
        §34-15-8.
    Compliance with rules and
      regulations.
      Inspector to give notice of
        noncompliance,
        §34-15-9.
    Police power, §34-15-6.
    Right of entry, §34-15-6.
    State health officer ex offico
      hotel inspector, §34-15-5.
  Keepers.
    Liens, §§34-15-130,
      34-15-131.

HOTELS, INNS AND OTHER TRANSIENT LODGING PLACES—Cont'd

Liability.
Baggage.
Loss of baggage, §34-15-15.
Safe depository.
Conditional liability, §34-15-13.
Limitation of liability, §§34-15-13, 34-15-14.
Maximum liability, §34-15-13.
Posting notice of limitations of liability, §34-15-12.
Special contract to limit liability, §34-15-11.
Licenses, §40-12-115.
Alcoholic beverage licenses.
General provisions, §§28-3A-1 to 28-3A-26.
See ALCOHOLIC BEVERAGES.
Liens.
Hotel keepers.
Declaration of lien, §35-11-130.
Enforcement of lien, §35-11-131.
Transient occupancy tax.
Lien of tax, §40-26-14.
Locks.
Failure or neglect to provide sufficient locks, §34-15-16.
Misrepresentation.
Obtaining accommodations by misrepresentation, §§34-15-19, 34-15-20.
Motor vehicle carriers.
Exemptions from chapter, §37-3-4.
Municipal corporations.
Acquisition, etc., of projects for promotion of hotel services in certain municipalities, §§11-54-140 to 11-54-152.
See MUNICIPAL CORPORATIONS.
Industrial development boards.
Ad valorem taxes.
Hotels and motor inns built under act not exempt from, §11-54-96.1.
Operation of hotels and related facilities.
Class 1 municipalities and certain public corporations, §11-40-19.
Hotel management contracts, §11-40-20.
Notice.
Obtaining accommodations by fraud or misrepresentation.
Posting of law in hotel or inn, §34-15-20.
Posting notice of safe depository, §34-15-12.
Removal of undesirable guests.
Oral notice required, §34-15-17.
Transient occupancy tax.
Assessment, §40-26-13.

HOTELS, INNS AND OTHER TRANSIENT LODGING PLACES—Cont'd

Owners.
Authority to remove undesirable guests, §34-15-17.
Duties relating to health and sanitation, §34-15-4.
Penalties.
Closure of hotels for flagrant or continued violations, §34-15-10.
Failure or neglect to provide sufficient locks, etc., §34-15-16.
Noncompliance with rules and regulations, §34-15-9.
Undesirable guests.
Refusal of guests to depart, §34-15-17.
Records.
Transient occupancy tax, §§40-26-6, 40-26-8, 40-26-9.
Refunds.
Transient occupancy tax, §40-26-12.
Refund or absorption of tax by taxpayer prohibited, §40-26-16.
Removal of undesirable guests, §34-15-17.
Reports.
Transient occupancy tax, §§40-26-3, 40-26-7 to 40-26-9.
Right of entry.
Police power of hotel inspectors, §34-15-6.
Rules and regulations.
Closure of hotels for flagrant or continued violations, §34-15-10.
Duties of hotel owners, etc., §34-15-4.
Failure to comply with rules and regulations, §34-15-9.
Operation of chapter in conjunction with health rules and regulations, §34-15-2.
Penalty, §34-15-9.
Promulgation, §34-15-3.
Transient occupancy tax, §40-26-19.
Safe depository.
Defined, §34-15-1.
Liability, §§34-15-11 to 34-15-14.
Required, §34-15-12.
Searches and seizures.
Lien of hotel keepers.
Seizure and sale of baggage and goods, §35-11-131.
Services.
Special contract between hotel and guest, §34-15-11.
Smoke detectors.
Duty of owners and operators, §34-15-4.
State board of health.
Authority and jurisdiction, §22-2-2.
Inspectors, §§34-15-5 to 34-15-9.

HOTELS, INNS AND OTHER TRANSIENT LODGING PLACES—Cont'd

State board of health—Cont'd
Operation of chapter in conjunction with board rules, §34-15-2.
Taxation.
Industrial development boards.
Ad valorem taxes.
Hotels and motor inns built under act not exempt from, §11-54-96.1.
Transient occupancy tax, §§40-26-1 to 40-26-21.
See within this heading, "Transient occupancy tax."
Theft.
Theft of services, §13A-8-10.
Towels.
Use of common towels prohibited, §22-20-1.
Transient occupancy tax, §§40-26-1 to 40-26-21.
Adding tax to price of service.
Failure to add, §40-26-16.
Administration of chapter, §40-26-18.
Appeals.
Assessment, §40-26-13.
Assessments.
Appeals, §40-26-13.
When department to assess tax and penalty, §40-26-11.
Cash and credit businesses, §40-26-4.
Deficiencies.
Collection, §40-26-12.
Department of revenue.
Administration of chapter, §40-26-18.
Assessment.
When department to assess tax and penalty, §40-26-11.
Discount of taxes.
Allowance, §40-26-21.
Due date, §40-26-3.
Failure to pay when due, §40-26-10.
Execution, §40-26-15.
Exemptions, §40-26-1.
Hearings.
Assessment, §40-26-13.
Highways.
Markers for tourist attractions.
Payment of expenses from proceeds of tax, §23-1-7.
Imposed, §40-26-1.
Levy, §40-26-15.
Lien of tax, §40-26-14.
Municipal privilege license taxes.
Exclusion in computation of tax, §40-26-2.
Notices.
Assessment, §40-26-13.
Payment.
Annual payment, §40-26-5.
Failure to pay when due, §40-26-10.
Monthly payments, §40-26-3.

HOTELS, INNS AND OTHER TRANSIENT LODGING PLACES—Cont'd
Transient occupancy tax —Cont'd
Proceeds.
Disposition, §40-26-20.
Records.
Duty to keep, §40-26-6.
Failure to keep, §40-26-8.
Willful refusal to permit examination, §40-26-9.
Refunds, §40-26-12.
Refund or absorption of tax by taxpayer prohibited, §40-26-16.
Reports.
Failure to make, §40-26-8.
Monthly reports, §40-26-3.
Verification, §40-26-7.
Willful refusal to make, §40-26-9.
Returns.
Annual return, §40-26-5.
When department to make return, §40-26-11.
Rules and regulations, §40-26-19.
Sale under process, §40-26-15.
Tourists.
Payment of expenses of markers for tourist attractions, §23-1-7.
Vacation time-sharing plans.
Proceeds from sale or resale of lease plans exempt, §34-27-65.
Violations of chapter.
Violators restrained from continuing in business, §40-26-17.
Vacation time-sharing plans, §§34-27-50 to 34-27-69.
See VACATION TIME-SHARING PLANS.
Valuables or valuable articles.
Defined, §34-15-1.
Liability, §§34-15-11 to 34-15-14.
Required, §34-15-12.
Safe depository.
Defined, §34-15-1.

HOT PURSUIT ACT, §15-10-74.

HOURS OF SALE.
Alcoholic beverages, §28-3A-25.
Continuance.
Notice requirements, §6-8-69.
Execution sales, §6-8-41.
Continuances, §6-8-69.
Postponement, §6-8-69.
Judicial sales, §6-8-41.
Legal sales, §6-8-41.
Continuances, §6-8-69.
Postponement, §6-8-69.
Mortgage foreclosures, §6-8-41.
Postponement.
Notice requirements, §6-8-69.
Public sales, §6-8-41.
Continuances, §6-8-69.
Postponement, §6-8-69.

HOUSE OF REPRESENTATIVES.
Legislature, Const. Ala., art. IV, §§44 to 111.
See LEGISLATURE.

HOUSE OF REPRESENTATIVES —Cont'd
United States House of Representatives, Const. Ala., art. IV, §§44 to 111.
See CONGRESS.

HOUSES OF ILL FAME.
Prostitution.
Nuisances.
Actions for nuisances, §§6-5-140 to 6-5-154.
See NUISANCES.
Promoting prostitution, §§13A-12-110 to 13A-12-113.
See PROSTITUTION.

HOUSE TRAILERS.
Mobile homes, §§24-5-1 to 24-5-34.
See MOBILE HOMES.

HOUSING, §§24-1-1 to 24-7-6.
Authorities, §§24-1-1 to 24-1-134.
See HOUSING AUTHORITIES.
Banks and financial institutions.
Investments and loans with respect to housing, §5-5A-23.
Blind persons.
Right to housing accommodations, §21-7-9.
Canals.
Construction through curtilage of house without consent, §10-5-5.
Condominiums, §§35-8-1 to 35-8-22.
See CONDOMINIUMS.
Constitution of Alabama.
Alienation of housing projects by political subdivisions and public bodies, Const. Ala., amd. 112.
Conveyances.
Alienation of certain public improvements by political subdivisions of state, §§35-4-410 to 35-4-412.
Counties.
Alienation of certain public improvements by political subdivisions, §§35-4-410 to 35-4-412.
Authorities, §§24-1-60 to 24-1-84.
See HOUSING AUTHORITIES.
Discrimination.
Municipal corporations.
Zoning regulations.
Discrimination prohibited, §11-52-75.
Factory-built housing.
Manufactured buildings generally, §§24-4A-1 to 24-4A-7.
See MANUFACTURED BUILDINGS.
Finance authority, §§24-1A-1 to 24-1A-21.
See HOUSING FINANCE AUTHORITY.

HOUSING—Cont'd
Handicapped persons.
Right to housing accommodations, §21-7-9.
Highways.
Relocation assistance, §§23-1-210 to 23-1-212.
Hotels, inns and other transient lodging places.
General provisions, §§34-15-1 to 34-15-20.
See HOTELS, INNS AND OTHER TRANSIENT LODGING PLACES.
Housing authorities, §§24-1-1 to 24-1-134.
See HOUSING AUTHORITIES.
Insurance.
Investments and loans with respect to housing by insurance companies, §5-5A-23.
Interest.
Maximum rates of interest.
Exemption of debts incurred pursuant to national housing act, §8-8-6.
Landlord and tenant.
General provisions, §§35-9-1 to 35-9-100.
See LANDLORD AND TENANT.
Manufactured buildings.
General provisions, §§24-4A-1 to 24-4A-7.
See MANUFACTURED BUILDINGS.
Mobile homes, §§24-5-1 to 24-5-34.
See MOBILE HOMES.
Municipal corporations.
Alienation of certain public improvements by political subdivisions, §§35-4-410 to 35-4-412.
Authorities, §§24-1-20 to 24-1-45.
See HOUSING AUTHORITIES.
Codes.
Adoption of technical codes by reference, §11-45-8.
Discrimination by zoning regulation.
Prohibited, §11-52-75.
Redevelopment projects, §§24-2-1 to 24-2-10.
See REDEVELOPMENT PROJECTS.
Standards, §§11-53-1 to 11-53-4.
Urban renewal projects, §§24-3-1 to 24-3-9.
See URBAN RENEWAL PROJECTS.
Zoning, §11-52-75.
Nuisances.
Municipal corporations.
Minimum housing standards and regulation of unsafe buildings.
Generally, §§11-53-1 to 11-53-4.
Pipelines.
Construction through curtilage of house without consent, §10-5-5.

HOUSING—Cont'd
  Projects.
    Alienation of certain public
      improvements by
      political subdivisions.
    Authorization, §35-4-410.
    Referendum.
      Authorization to alienate
        public housing
        projects, §35-4-410.
      Election, §35-4-412.
      Resolution describing
        proposed conveyance,
        §35-4-411.
    Housing authorities.
      County housing
        authorities, §§24-1-68,
        24-1-69, 24-1-73,
        24-1-81.
      See HOUSING
        AUTHORITIES.
      Low rent projects, §§24-1-1,
        24-1-6.
      See HOUSING
        AUTHORITIES.
      Municipal housing
        authorities, §§24-1-29,
        24-1-30, 24-1-34.
      Redevelopment projects,
        §§24-2-1 to 24-2-10.
      See REDEVELOPMENT
        PROJECTS.
      Rural housing projects,
        §24-1-3.
      County housing
        authorities, §24-1-81.
      Urban renewal projects,
        §§24-3-1 to 24-3-9.
      See URBAN RENEWAL
        PROJECTS.
  Public housing.
    Housing authorities,
      §24-1-10.
    See HOUSING
      AUTHORITIES.
  Public improvements.
    Alienation of certain public
      improvements by
      political subdivisions,
      §§35-4-410 to 35-4-412.
  Public works.
    General provisions, §§39-1-1
      to 39-7-34.
    See PUBLIC WORKS.
  Railroads.
    Construction through
      curtilage of house
      without consent, §10-5-5.
  Redevelopment projects,
    §§24-2-1 to 24-2-10.
    See REDEVELOPMENT
      PROJECTS.
  Referendum.
    Alienation of certain public
      improvements by
      political subdivisions,
      §§35-4-410, 35-4-412.
  Relocation assistance.
    Highways, §§23-1-210 to
      23-1-212.
  Rural housing projects,
    §24-1-3.
    County housing authorities,
      §24-1-81.
  Savings and loans
    associations.
    Investments and loans with
      respect to housing,
      §5-5A-23.

HOUSING—Cont'd
  Standards.
    Municipal corporations,
      §§11-53-1 to 11-53-4.
  Subdivisions.
    County regulation of
      subdivisions, §§11-24-1
      to 11-24-7.
    See COUNTIES.
    Generally.
    See SUBDIVISIONS.
  Telephones.
    Construction of line through
      curtilage of house
      without consent, §10-5-5.
  Trusts and trustees.
    National housing act.
      Investment of trust estate
        in debts incurred
        under national housing
        act, §19-3-128.
  Tunnels.
    Construction through
      curtilage of house
      without consent, §10-5-5.
  Urban renewal projects,
    §§24-3-1 to 24-3-9.
    See URBAN RENEWAL
      PROJECTS.
  Vacation time-sharing plans,
    §§34-27-50 to 34-27-69.
    See VACATION TIME-
      SHARING PLANS.

HOUSING AUTHORITIES,
  §§24-1-1 to 24-1-134.
  Agreements.
    Certain agreements
      validated, §24-1-8.
  Alabama housing finance
    authority, §§24-1A-1 to
    24-1A-21.
    See HOUSING FINANCE
      AUTHORITY.
  Bond issues.
    Certain obligations validated,
      §24-1-8.
    County housing authorities,
      §§24-1-70 to 24-1-72.
    Issuance.
      Validated, §24-1-9.
    Municipal housing
      authorities, §§24-1-31 to
      24-1-36. See within this
      heading, "Municipal
      housing authorities."
    Redevelopment projects,
      §24-2-3.
      Investment by public
        bodies, etc., in bonds,
        etc., issued by housing
        authorities, §24-2-9.
    Regional and consolidated
      housing authorities.
      Legal investments,
        §24-1-114.
    Validation.
      Certain obligations
        validated, §24-1-8.
      Issuance of notes and
        bonds validated,
        §24-1-9.
  Boundaries.
    County housing authorities,
      §24-1-62.
    Municipal housing
      authorities, §24-1-23.

HOUSING AUTHORITIES
  —Cont'd
  Boundaries—Cont'd
    Regional and consolidated
      housing authorities,
      §24-1-103.
      Application to secretary of
        state.
        Required for change in
          area of operation,
          §24-1-106.
      Decrease of area of
        operation.
        Procedure for decrease,
          §24-1-105.
      Hearings.
        Public hearings required
          for change in area of
          operation, §24-1-106.
      Increase of area of
        operation.
        Procedure for increase,
          §24-1-104.
      Operation of authorities in
        municipality outside
        area of operation,
        §24-1-111.
  Commissioners.
    County housing authorities,
      §§24-1-63, 24-1-64.
    Municipal housing
      authorities, §§24-1-24 to
      24-1-26.
    Regional and consolidated
      housing authorities,
      §§24-1-107 to 24-1-109.
  Conflict of laws.
    County housing authorities,
      §24-1-84.
    Municipal housing
      authorities, §24-1-45.
  Conflicts of interest.
    Municipal housing
      authorities.
      Commissioners or
        employees, §24-1-26.
  Consolidated housing
    authorities.
    Regional and consolidated
      housing authorities,
      §§24-1-100 to 24-1-117.
    See within this heading,
      "Regional and
      consolidated housing
      authorities."
  Cooperation of cities,
    counties, etc., with
    housing authorities,
    §§24-1-130 to 24-1-134.
    Definitions, §24-1-131.
    Legislative findings and
      declaration of necessity,
      §24-1-130.
    Loans.
      City or town may lend
        money to housing
        authority, §24-1-134.
    Powers of municipalities,
      counties, etc., to aid
      housing authorities,
      §24-1-132.
    Resolution authorizing
      exercise of powers
      granted, §24-1-133.
    Reimbursement of cities or
      towns for loans or
      donations, §24-1-134.
    Resolution authorizing
      exercise of powers
      granted, §24-1-133.

HOUSING AUTHORITIES
—Cont'd
Counties.
Cooperation of cities,
counties, etc., with
housing authorities,
§§24-1-130 to 24-1-134.
County housing authorities,
§§24-1-60 to 24-1-84.
Acquisition of property.
Eminent domain, §24-1-67.
For government housing
projects, §24-1-68.
Agreements.
Title acquired by
purchasers at sale of
authority property
subject to agreements
with government,
§24-1-79.
Bond issues, §§24-1-70 to
24-1-72.
Form of bonds, §24-1-71.
Interest, §24-1-71.
Interim certificates.
Issuance, §24-1-71.
Issuance, §24-1-70.
Liability on bonds,
§24-1-70.
Maturity, §24-1-71.
Power to issue, §24-1-70.
Sale.
Procedure for sale of
bonds, §24-1-71.
Security for bonds,
§24-1-70.
Security for payment.
Powers of authority to
secure payment,
§24-1-72.
Signatures of former
officers on bonds,
§24-1-71.
Terms of bonds, §24-1-71.
Types of bonds, §24-1-70.
Boundaries, §24-1-62.
Building laws.
Authority projects subject
to local building laws,
§24-1-69.
Commissioners, §§24-1-63,
24-1-64.
Appointment, §24-1-63.
Compensation, §24-1-63.
Qualifications, §24-1-63.
Removal, §24-1-64.
Term of office, §24-1-63.
Composition, §24-1-63.
Conflicting provisions,
§24-1-84.
Construction of projects.
Contracts with federal
government for
construction, §24-1-73.
Contracts.
Competitive bidding
required on certain
contracts, §24-1-83.
Enforcement of contracts,
§24-1-83.
Federal government.
Contracts with federal
government for
construction of
projects, §24-1-73.
Cooperation of cities,
counties, etc., with
housing authorities,
§§24-1-130 to 24-1-134.
Definitions, §24-1-61.

HOUSING AUTHORITIES
—Cont'd
County housing authorities
—Cont'd
Deposits.
Security for funds
deposited by
authorities in banks
and trust companies,
§24-1-80.
Duties, §24-1-66.
Delegation of duties by
authority, §24-1-63.
Enforcement of article and
contracts of authority,
§24-1-83.
Eminent domain.
Acquisition of property by
eminent domain,
§24-1-67.
Enforcement of article and
contracts, §24-1-83.
Execution.
Exemption of authority
property from levy and
execution, §24-1-78.
Federal contributions.
Agreements to secure,
§24-1-4.
Federal government.
Contracts with federal
government for
construction of
projects, §§24-1-34,
24-1-73.
Funds.
Security for funds
deposited by
authorities in banks
and trust companies,
§24-1-80.
Incorporation.
Denial of petition for
incorporation,
§24-1-62.
Resubmission of petition,
§24-1-62.
Procedure for
incorporation,
§24-1-62.
Judgment liens.
Exemption of authority
property from
judgment liens,
§24-1-78.
Legislative findings and
declaration of necessity,
§24-1-60.
Levy and execution.
Exemption of authority
property from levy and
execution, §24-1-78.
Liens.
Exemption of authority
property from
judgment liens,
§24-1-78.
Low income housing in rural
areas, §24-1-81.
Mortgages.
Bond issues.
Powers of authority to
secure payment of
bonds, §24-1-72.
Exemption of authority
property from
mortgage foreclosures,
§24-1-78.

HOUSING AUTHORITIES
—Cont'd
County housing authorities
—Cont'd
Mortgages—Cont'd
Mortgages of authority
property in connection
with government
financed projects,
§24-1-74.
Remedies conferrable upon
obligees of authority
by mortgage, §24-1-76.
Municipal corporations.
Cooperation of cities,
counties, etc., with
housing authorities,
§§24-1-130 to 24-1-134.
Officers, §24-1-63.
Petition for incorporation,
§24-1-62.
Planning laws.
Authority projects subject
to local planning laws,
§24-1-69.
Powers, §24-1-66.
Delegation of powers by
authority, §24-1-63.
Projects.
Acquisition of property for
government housing
projects, §24-1-68.
Building laws.
Authority projects
subject to local
building laws,
§24-1-69.
Contracts with federal
government for
construction of
projects, §24-1-73.
Low income housing in
rural areas, §24-1-81.
Planning laws.
Authority projects
subject to local
planning laws,
§24-1-69.
Rural areas.
Low income housing in
rural areas,
§24-1-81.
Sanitary laws.
Authority projects
subject to local
sanitary laws,
§24-1-69.
Zoning laws.
Authority projects
subject to local
zoning laws,
§24-1-69.
Recommendations.
Annual recommendations
of authority, §24-1-82.
Remedies.
Conferrable upon obligees
of authority by trust
indenture, mortgages,
etc., §24-1-76.
Cumulative, §24-1-77.
Generally, §24-1-75.
Reports.
Annual report, §24-1-82.
Sale of authority property.
Title acquired by
purchasers at sale
subject to agreements
with government,
§24-1-79.

HOUSING AUTHORITIES
—Cont'd
County housing authorities
—Cont'd
Sanitary laws.
Authority projects subject
to local sanitary laws,
§24-1-69.
Trust indenture.
Remedies conferrable upon
obligees of authority
by trust indenture,
§§24-1-38, 24-1-76.
Zoning laws.
Authority projects subject
to local zoning laws,
§24-1-69.
Creation.
Validation of creation of
certain housing
authorities, §24-1-7.
Definitions.
Cooperation of cities,
counties, etc., with
housing authorities,
§24-1-131.
County housing authorities,
§24-1-61.
Municipal housing
authorities, §24-1-22.
Regional and consolidated
housing authorities,
§24-1-101.
Eminent domain.
County housing authorities.
Acquisition of property by
eminent domain,
§24-1-67.
Municipal housing
authorities.
Acquisition of property by
eminent domain,
§24-1-28.
Establishment.
Validation of establishment
of certain housing
authorities, §24-1-7.
Federal contributions.
Agreements of municipal,
county or regional
housing authorities to
secure federal
contributions, §24-1-4.
Federal government.
Contracts with federal
government for
construction of projects,
§§24-1-34, 24-1-73.
Housing finance authority,
§§24-1A-1 to 24-1A-21.
See HOUSING FINANCE
AUTHORITY.
Low rent projects, §§24-1-1,
24-1-6.
Counties.
Payments to counties for
maintenance, §24-1-1.
Maintenance.
Payments to cities,
counties etc., for
maintenance, §24-1-1.
Municipal corporations.
Payments to cities for
maintenance, §24-1-1.
Rentals.
Establishment of rentals,
§24-1-6.
Tenant selection.
Establishment, §24-1-6.

HOUSING AUTHORITIES
—Cont'd
**Mortgages and deeds of
trust.**
County housing authorities,
§§24-1-72 to 24-1-76.
Municipal housing
authorities, §§24-1-35,
24-1-38, 24-1-140.
**Mowa Choctaw housing
authority,** §§24-7-1 to
24-7-6.
See MOWA CHOCTAW
HOUSING
AUTHORITY.
Municipal coprorations.
Cooperation of cities,
counties, etc., with
housing authorities,
§§24-1-130 to 24-1-134.
**Municipal housing
authorities,** §§24-1-20 to
24-1-45.
Acquisition of property.
Eminent domain, §24-1-28.
For government projects,
§24-1-29.
Agreements.
Title acquired by
purchasers at sale of
authority property
subject to agreements
with government,
§24-1-41.
Bond issues, §§24-1-31 to
24-1-36.
Denominations of bonds,
§24-1-32.
Federal government.
Contracts with federal
government for
construction of
projects, §24-1-34.
Form of bonds, §24-1-32.
Interest, §24-1-32.
Interim certificates.
Issuance, §24-1-32.
Investment by state,
fiduciaries, banks, etc.,
in bonds issued by
authorities, §24-1-36.
Issuance, §24-1-31.
Liability on bonds,
§24-1-31.
Maturity, §24-1-32.
Payment, §24-1-32.
Powers of authority to
secure payment,
§24-1-33.
Sale.
Procedure for sale,
§24-1-32.
Security for bonds,
§24-1-31.
Terms of bonds, §24-1-32.
Types of bonds, §24-1-31.
Boundaries, §24-1-23.
Building laws.
Authority projects subject
to local building laws,
§24-1-30.
Commissioners.
Appointment, §24-1-24.
Conflicts of interest,
§24-1-26.
Qualifications, §24-1-24.
Composition, §24-1-24.
Conflicting provisions,
§24-1-45.

HOUSING AUTHORITIES
—Cont'd
**Municipal housing
authorities**—Cont'd
Conflicts of interest.
Commissioners or
employees, §24-1-26.
Construction of projects.
Contracts with federal
government for
construction, §24-1-34.
Contracts.
Enforcement of contracts,
§24-1-44.
Counties.
Cooperation of cities,
counties, etc., with
housing authorities,
§§24-1-130 to 24-1-134.
Definitions, §24-1-22.
Deposits.
Security for funds
deposited by
authorities in banks
and trust companies,
§24-1-42.
Duties, §24-1-27.
Delegation of duties by
authority, §24-1-24.
Eminent domain.
Acquisition of property by
eminent domain,
§24-1-28.
Employees, §24-1-24.
Conflicts of interest,
§24-1-26.
Enforcement of article and
contracts of authority,
§24-1-44.
Executions.
Exemption of authority
property from levy and
execution, §24-1-40.
Exemption of authority
property from mortgage
foreclosures, levy and
execution and judgment
liens, §24-1-40.
Federal contributions.
Agreements to secure,
§24-1-4.
Funds.
Security for funds
deposited by
authorities in banks
and trust companies,
§24-1-42.
Incorporations.
Procedure for
incorporation,
§24-1-23.
Investment in bonds of
authorities, §24-1-36.
Judgment liens.
Exemption of authority
property from
judgment liens,
§24-1-40.
Legislative findings and
declaration of necessity,
§24-1-21.
Liens.
Exemption of authority
property from
judgment liens,
§24-1-40.
Mortgages and deeds of trust.
Exemption of authority
property from
mortgage foreclosures,
§24-1-40.

HOUSING AUTHORITIES
—Cont'd
**Municipal housing
authorities**—Cont'd
Mortgages and deeds of trust
—Cont'd
Mortgages of authority
property in connection
with government
financed projects,
§24-1-35.
Remedies conferrable upon
obligees of authority
by trust indenture,
mortgage, etc.,
§24-1-38.
Obligee of authority.
Remedies of obligee,
§24-1-37.
Officers, §24-1-24.
Petition for incorporations,
§24-1-23.
Planning laws.
Authority projects subject
to local planning laws,
§24-1-30.
Powers, §24-1-27.
Delegation of powers by
authority, §24-1-24.
Projects.
Acquisition of property for
government housing
projects, §24-1-29.
Building laws.
Authority projects
subject to local
building laws,
§24-1-30.
Construction.
Contracts with federal
government for
construction,
§24-1-34.
Planning laws.
Authority projects
subject to local
planning laws,
§24-1-30.
Zoning laws.
Authority projects
subject to local
zoning laws,
§24-1-30.
Recommendations.
Annual recommendations,
§24-1-43.
Regional and consolidated
authorities generally.
See within this heading,
"Regional and
consolidated authorities."
Remedies.
Conferrable upon obligees
of authority by trust
indenture, mortgage,
etc., §24-1-38.
Cumulative, §24-1-39.
Obligee of authority
generally, §24-1-37.
Reports.
Annual report of authority,
§24-1-43.
Sale of authority property.
Title acquired by
purchasers at sale
subject to agreements
with government,
§24-1-41.

HOUSING AUTHORITIES
—Cont'd
**Municipal housing
authorities**—Cont'd
Sanitary laws.
Authority projects subject
to local sanitary laws,
§24-1-30.
Short title of article, §24-1-20.
Zoning laws.
Authority projects subject
to local zoning laws,
§24-1-30.
Notes.
Issuance validated, §24-1-9.
Obligations.
Certain obligations validated,
§24-1-8.
Obligee of authority.
Remedies.
Generally, §24-1-75.
Remedies conferrable upon
obligees of authority
by trust indenture,
mortgages, etc.,
§§24-1-38, 24-1-76,
24-1-77.
Organization.
Validation of organization of
certain housing
authorities, §24-1-7.
Planning.
County housing authorities.
Authority projects subject
to local planning laws,
§24-1-69.
Municipal housing
authorities.
Authority projects subject
to local planning laws,
§24-1-30.
**Powers conferred by
sections 24-1-1 through
24-1-4 supplemental,**
§24-1-5.
Projects.
County housing authorities,
§§24-1-68, 24-1-69,
24-1-73, 24-1-81.
Low rent projects, §§24-1-1,
24-1-6.
Municipal housing
authorities, §§24-1-29,
24-1-30, 24-1-34.
Redevelopment projects.
Powers of housing
authorities, §§24-2-2,
24-2-3.
Rural housing projects,
§24-1-3.
County housing
authorities, §24-1-81.
Urban renewal projects.
See URBAN RENEWAL
PROJECTS.
Public housing.
Defined, §24-1-10.
Establishing eligibility by
fraudulent means,
§24-1-10.
Misdemeanor, §24-1-10.
Notice requirement,
§24-1-10.
Penalty, §24-1-10.
Redevelopment projects.
Powers of housing
authorities, §§24-2-2,
24-2-3.

HOUSING AUTHORITIES
—Cont'd
**Regional and consolidated
housing authorities,**
§§24-1-100 to 24-1-117.
Agreements.
Agreements to secure
federal contributions
and loans, §24-1-113.
Area of operation, §24-1-103.
Application to secretary of
state.
Required for change in
area of operation,
§24-1-106.
Decrease of area of
operation.
Procedure for decrease,
§24-1-105.
Hearings.
Public hearings required
for change in area of
operation, §24-1-106.
Increase of area.
Procedure for increase,
§24-1-104.
Operation of authorities in
municipality outside
area of operation,
§24-1-111.
Assistance by municipalities,
counties, etc., §24-1-115.
Bond issues.
Legal investments,
§24-1-114.
Boundaries, §24-1-103.
Application to secretary of
state.
Required for change in
area of operation,
§24-1-106.
Decrease of area of
operation.
Procedure for decrease,
§24-1-105.
Hearings.
Public hearings required
for change in area of
operation, §24-1-106.
Increase.
Procedure for increase of
area of operation,
§24-1-104.
Outside area of operation.
Operation of authorities
in municipality
outside area,
§24-1-111.
Commissioners.
Appointment, §24-1-107.
Duties, §24-1-107.
Meetings, §24-1-108.
Officers, §24-1-107.
Powers, §§24-1-107,
24-1-109.
Quorum, §24-1-107.
Removal, §24-1-107.
Rights, §24-1-109.
Consolidated housing
authorities generally,
§24-1-110.
Cooperation by
municipalities, counties,
etc., §24-1-115.
General provisions,
§§24-1-130 to 24-1-134.
Cooperation of authorities,
§24-1-116.

HOUSING AUTHORITIES
—Cont'd
Regional and consolidated housing authorities
—Cont'd
Counties.
Assistance and cooperation by counties, §24-1-115.
General provisions, §§24-1-130 to 24-1-134.
Definitions, §24-1-101.
Employees, §24-1-107.
Federal contributions and loans.
Agreements to secure, §§24-1-4, 24-1-113.
Incorporation.
Procedure for incorporation, §24-1-102.
Municipal corporations.
Assistance and cooperation by municipalities, §24-1-115.
Obligations of authorities.
Legal investments, §24-1-114.
Officers, §24-1-107.
Powers, §24-1-109.
Powers conferred by article supplemental, §24-1-117.
Resolution authorizing operation of housing authorities in municipality.
Procedure for adoption of resolution, §24-1-112.
Rights of authority, §24-1-109.
Short title of article, §24-1-100.
Reports.
County housing authorities.
Annual report, §24-1-82.
Municipal housing authorities.
Annual report, §24-1-43.
Research.
Housing research and studies, §24-1-2.
Rural housing projects, §24-1-3.
County housing authorities, §24-1-81.
Studies.
Housing research and studies, §24-1-2.
Supplemental housing authorities law, §§24-1-100 to 24-1-117. See within this heading, "Regional and consolidated housing authorities."
Supplemental powers.
Powers conferred by sections 24-1-1 through 24-1-4 supplemental, §24-1-5.
Trust indenture.
Remedies conferrable upon obligees of authority by trust indenture, §§24-1-38, 24-1-76.
United States.
Contracts with federal government for construction of projects, §§24-1-34, 24-1-73.

HOUSING AUTHORITIES
—Cont'd
United States—Cont'd
Federal contributions.
Agreements of municipal, county or regional housing authorities to secure federal contributions, §24-1-4.
Urban renewal projects, §§24-3-1 to 24-3-9.
See URBAN RENEWAL PROJECTS.
Validation.
Certain agreements and obligations of housing authorities validated, §24-1-8.
Creation, etc., of certain housing authorities validated, §24-1-7.
Notes and bonds.
Issuance, etc., validated, §24-1-9.
Zoning.
County housing authorities.
Authority projects subject to local zoning laws, §24-1-69.
Municipal housing authorities.
Authority projects subject to local zoning laws, §24-1-30.

HOUSING FINANCE AUTHORITY, §§24-1A-1 to 24-1A-21.
Authorized investments.
Defined, §24-1A-2.
Board.
Appointment of members, §24-1A-4.
Composition, §24-1A-4.
Directors, §24-1A-4.
Expenses of members, §24-1A-4.
Liability, §24-1A-4.
Meetings, §24-1A-4.
Members, §24-1A-4.
Minutes, §24-1A-4.
Officers, §24-1A-4.
Records, §24-1A-4.
Maintenance, §24-1A-4.
Removal from office, §24-1A-4.
Salaries, §24-1A-4.
Terms of office, §24-1A-4.
Bond issues, §§24-1A-2, 24-1A-6 to 24-1A-10.
Defined, §24-1A-2.
Distribution percentages, §24-1A-7.
Eligible for investment by state and local governments, §24-1A-10.
Execution, §24-1A-6.
Exemption from interest laws, §24-1A-14.
Exemption from usury laws, §24-1A-14.
Form.
General provisions, §24-1A-6.
Generally, §24-1A-6.
Interest rate, §24-1A-6.
Issuance.
Limitation, §24-1A-9.
Procedures, §24-1A-7.

HOUSING FINANCE AUTHORITY—Cont'd
Bond issues—Cont'd
Legal investment by executors, trustees, etc., §24-1A-10.
Limitation on issuance, §24-1A-9.
Maturities, §24-1A-6.
No state debt or obligation, §24-1A-6.
Pledge of revenues and other security, §24-1A-6.
Proceeds from sale, §24-1A-7.
Single family mortgage loans.
Allocation of proceeds available for, §24-1A-7.
Use, §24-1A-7.
Refunding bonds, §24-1A-8.
Sale and negotiability, §24-1A-6.
Sources of payment, §24-1A-6.
Conflicts of interest, §24-1A-19.
Rules governing, §24-1A-19.
Constitution of Alabama.
Payment by state of expenses incurred by authority, Const. Ala., amd. 396.
Construction and interpretation.
Liberal construction, §24-1A-21.
Definitions, §24-1A-2.
Department of finance.
Utilization of services, §24-1A-18.
Dissolution.
Procedure, §24-1A-17.
Vesting title to property in state, §24-1A-17.
Eligible housing units.
Defined, §24-1A-2.
Exemption from taxation, §24-1A-12.
Exemptions from interest laws, §24-1A-14.
Exemptions from usury laws, §24-1A-14.
Income.
Earnings of authority, §24-1A-16.
Excess paid to state, §24-1A-16.
Profits.
Nonprofit corporations, §24-1A-16.
Incorporation.
Application, §24-1A-3.
Contents, §24-1A-4.
Authorized, §24-1A-3.
Fees, §24-1A-3.
Investments.
Authorized investments.
Defined, §24-1A-2.
Bonds, §24-1A-10.
Legislative findings, §24-1A-1.
Legislative oversight committee.
Appointment, §24-1A-4.
Composition, §24-1A-4.
Established, §24-1A-4.
Expenses, §24-1A-4.
Liability of state, §24-1A-13.
Loans.
Mortgage loans.
Defined, §24-1A-2.

**HOUSING FINANCE
   AUTHORITY**—Cont'd
Loans—Cont'd
Multi-family mortgage loans.
   Defined, §24-1A-2.
Single family mortgage
   loans.
   Defined, §24-1A-2.
**Low and moderate income
   families.**
   Defined, §24-1A-2.
Mortgaged property.
   Defined, §24-1A-2.
Mortgage lenders.
   Defined, §24-1A-2.
Mortgage loans.
   Defined, §24-1A-2.
Mortgages.
   Defined, §24-1A-2.
Multi-family mortgage loans.
   Defined, §24-1A-2.
Nonprofit corporations,
   §24-1A-16.
Powers.
Authority deemed
   independent
   instrumentality,
   §24-1A-15.
Generally, §24-1A-5.
Purpose of chapter, §24-1A-1.
Refinancing.
Chapter not to aid in
   refinancing, §24-1A-20.
Rules and regulations.
Conflicts of interest,
   §24-1A-19.
**Single family mortgage
   loans.**
   Defined, §24-1A-2.
Taxation.
Exemption from taxation,
   §24-1A-12.
Uniform commercial code.
Applicability of certain
   provisions, §24-1A-11.

HOUSTON COUNTY.
**Economic and industrial
   development promotion,**
   Const. Ala., amd. 429.
Officers.
Fees, salaries, etc., of certain
   public officers, Const.
   Ala., amd. 48.

HUMANE SOCIETIES, §§3-1-8,
   3-1-13.

HUNTING.
**Duty of care owed persons
   on premises for sporting
   or recreational purposes,**
   §§35-15-1 to 35-15-5.
Fish and game.
See FISH AND GAME.
General provisions, §§9-11-1
   to 9-11-245.
See FISH AND GAME.
Torts.
Duty of care owed persons on
   premises for sporting or
   recreational purposes,
   §§35-15-1 to 35-15-5.

HUNTINGDON COLLEGE.
**Marine environmental
   sciences consortium,**
   §§16-45-1 to 16-45-5.

**HUNTSVILLE,
   MUNICIPALITY OF.**
Economic development.
Promotion of industrial,
   commercial and
   agricultural
   development, Const.
   Ala., amds. 191, 245.
Property tax, Const. Ala.,
   amd. 8.
School tax.
Special school tax, Const.
   Ala., amds. 80, 218, 305.
Amendment of
   amendment, Const.
   Ala., amd. 407.
**University of Alabama,
   Huntsville,** §§16-47-150 to
   16-47-152.

**HURTSBORO,
   MUNICIPALITY OF.**
Property tax, Const. Ala.,
   amd. 8.

HUSBAND AND WIFE,
   §§30-4-1 to 30-4-98.
Actions.
Alienation of affections.
   Abolished for female
      persons 19 years of age
      or over, §6-5-331.
Prosecution or defense of
   actions in name of
   husband by wife, §6-7-1.
Torts.
   Wife's torts.
      To sue and be sued alone
         upon torts, §30-4-11.
Alimony, §§30-2-50 to 30-2-54.
Anatomical gifts, §§22-19-40
   to 22-19-47.
See ANATOMICAL GIFTS.
Consent for health services,
   §§22-8-1 to 22-8-9.
See HEALTH.
Constitution of Alabama.
Property of wife not liable for
   debts, etc., of husband,
   Const. Ala., art. X, §209.
Waiver of right of exemption,
   Const. Ala., art. X, §210.
Contracts, §§30-4-6 to 30-4-13.
Actions.
   Wife's contracts.
      To sue and be sued alone
         upon contracts,
         §30-4-11.
Antenuptial contracts.
   Husband not liable,
      §30-4-6.
Between husband and wife.
   Capacity of husband and
      wife to contract with
      each other, §30-4-9.
Capacity.
   Between husband and wife,
      §30-4-9.
   Wife's capacity to contract,
      §30-4-8.
Nonresidents.
   Wife's contracts as to
      property situated
      within state, §30-4-13.
Postnuptial contracts.
   Husband not liable,
      §30-4-7.

HUSBAND AND WIFE—Cont'd
**Conveyances by spouse of
   insane person,** §§30-4-30
   to 30-4-37.
Real property, §30-4-12.
   Authorization.
      Circuit court, §30-4-32.
      Effect of article,
         §30-4-37.
      Guardian ad litem
         appointed, §30-4-33.
      Hearing, §30-4-33.
      Judgment.
         Effect, §30-4-36.
         Entry, §30-4-34.
         Filing, §30-4-35.
      Mode not exclusive,
         §30-4-37.
      Motion, §30-4-33.
      Notice, §30-4-33.
      Records.
         Filing of judgment,
            §30-4-35.
   Husband of insane wife.
      Conveyance to be
         accompanied by
         judgment or
         certification of wife's
         insanity, §30-4-31.
      Conclusiveness of
         judgment or
         certificate,
         §30-4-31.
      Powers of husband,
         §30-4-30.
      Exception as to
         homestead,
         §30-4-30.
   Jurisdiction.
      Circuit court, §30-4-32.
**Conveyances by spouse who
   is imprisoned or who
   has abandoned other
   spouse, §30-4-12.**
Debts.
Property of wife not liable for
   debts, etc., of husband,
   Const. Ala., art. X, §209.
Deeds.
Conveyances by wife of
   husband who is
   imprisoned, non compos
   mentis or has abandoned
   her, §30-4-12.
Homestead deeds, §6-10-6.
Desertion and nonsupport,
   §§30-4-30 to 30-4-37.
See DESERTION AND
   NONSUPPORT.
**District attorneys' spouses
   fund,** §§12-17-201 to
   12-17-207.
See DISTRICT
   ATTORNEYS.
Divorce and alimony,
   §§30-2-1 to 30-2-54.
See DIVORCE AND
   ALIMONY.
Domestic violence facilities.
General provisions, §§30-6-1
   to 30-6-13.
See DOMESTIC
   VIOLENCE
   FACILITIES.
Dower.
Ascertainment and payment
   of dower interests,
   §§35-4-190 to 35-4-192.
See DOWER.

HUSBAND AND WIFE—Cont'd
Electric cooperatives.
Board of trustees.
Membership on board at
same time, §37-6-10.
**Exemptions from
administration and
payment of debts,**
§§6-10-106, 6-10-107.
**Exemptions from levy and
sale under process,**
§§6-10-3, 6-10-39.
Health services.
Consent for health services,
§§22-8-1 to 22-8-9.
See HEALTH.
Homestead.
Conveyance of, §6-10-6.
Homestead exemptions.
Alienation by married
persons, §6-10-3.
Income tax.
Exemptions.
Personal exemptions,
§40-18-19.
Joint returns.
Joint and several liability
of husband and wife,
§40-18-27.
Insurance.
Policy designating wife as
beneficiary.
Assignment as security for
indebtedness.
Exempted from
prohibition against
contracts of
suretyship by wife,
§30-4-10.
Marriage, §§30-1-3 to 30-1-18.
See MARRIAGE.
Mentally ill.
Conveyances by spouse of
insane person, §§30-4-30
to 30-4-37. See within
this heading,
"Conveyances by spouse
of insane person."
Support of persons in state
mental institutions.
Generally, §§22-53-1 to
22-53-26.
See MENTALLY ILL.
Minors.
Husbands and widowers.
Relieved of disabilities of
minority, §30-4-16.
Wives and widows.
Relieved of disabilities of
minority, §30-4-15.
Motor vehicles.
Safety-responsibility act.
Proof of financial
responsibility.
Owner may give proof
for member of
immediate family,
§32-7-28.
Nonsupport.
General provisions, §§30-4-50
to 30-4-65.
See DESERTION AND
NONSUPPORT.
Parties.
Prosecution or defense of
actions in name of
husband by wife, §6-7-1.
Personal property.
Property generally. See
within this heading,
"Property."

HUSBAND AND WIFE—Cont'd
Property.
Dower.
Generally, §§35-4-190 to
35-4-192.
See DOWER.
Homestead exemptions.
Alienation by married
persons, §6-10-3.
Liability for debts.
Property of wife not liable
for debts, etc., of
husband, Const. Ala.,
art. X, §209.
Mentally ill.
Conveyances by spouse of
insane person,
§§30-4-30 to 30-4-37.
See within this
heading, "Conveyances
by spouse of insane
person."
Nonresidents.
Wife's contracts as to
property situated
within state, §30-4-13.
Real property, §§6-10-3,
30-4-12.
Wife's property.
Acquired after marriage,
§30-4-1.
Alienation or mortgage of
lands by wife.
Consent of husband,
§30-4-12.
Clothing, §30-4-3.
Damages recovered for
injuries to person or
reputation, §30-4-4.
Earnings, §30-4-2.
Held prior to marriage,
§30-4-1.
Leases.
Consent of husband not
required, §30-4-12.
Liabilities of husband.
Not subject to liabilities
of husband, §30-4-1.
Nonresidents.
Contracts as to property
situated within
state, §30-4-13.
Subject to chapter, §30-4-5.
Wills.
Disposition of separate
estates by will,
§30-4-14.
Protection from abuse.
General provisions, §§30-5-1
to 30-5-11.
See DOMESTIC
RELATIONS.
Real property.
Alienation by wife.
Consent of husband,
§30-4-12.
Dower.
See DOWER.
Homestead exemption.
Alienation by married
person, §6-10-3.
Mortgage by wife.
Consent of husband,
§30-4-12.
Property generally. See
within this heading,
"Property."
Sale by wife.
Consent of husband,
§30-4-12.

HUSBAND AND WIFE—Cont'd
Separation.
Bed and board, §§30-2-2,
30-2-30.
Support and maintenance.
Desertion and nonsupport,
§§30-4-50 to 30-4-65.
See DESERTION AND
NONSUPPORT.
Divorce and alimony,
§§30-2-1 to 30-2-54.
See DIVORCE AND
ALIMONY.
Nonsupport, §§30-4-50 to
30-4-65.
See DESERTION AND
NONSUPPORT.
Suretyship.
Insurance policy designating
wife as beneficiary.
Assignment as security for
indebtedness.
Exemption from
prohibition against
contracts
suretyship of wife,
§30-4-10.
Taxation.
Assessments.
By whom property should
be listed, §40-7-17.
Returns.
Separate returns in
individual and
fiduciary capacity,
§40-7-20.
Torts.
Antenuptial torts.
Husband not liable for
antenuptial torts of
wife, §30-4-6.
Postnuptial torts.
Husband not liable for
torts of wife, §30-4-7.
Veterans.
Educational benefits,
§§31-6-1 to 31-6-17.
See VETERANS.
**Waiver of right of
exemption,** Const. Ala.,
art. X, §210.
Wills and estates.
Wives may dispose of
separate estates by will,
§30-4-14.
Witnesses.
Criminal cases.
Competency of witnesses,
§§12-21-226,
12-21-227.

HYDRO-ELECTRIC POWER.
Water power companies,
§§10-4-320 to 10-4-323.

HYDROPHOBIA, §§3-7-1 to
3-7-13.
See RABIES.

HYGIENISTS.
Dental hygienists, §§34-9-26
to 34-9-28.

HYPOTHYROIDISM.
Testing of infants, §22-20-3.

I

ICE.
Factories.
Licenses, §40-12-114.

ICE—Cont'd
Weights and measures.
Sale regulated, §8-16-104.

ICEBOXES.
Creating hazards,
§13A-11-220.

ICE CREAM.
Adulteration, §2-13-12.
Brands and marks.
Misbranded ice cream,
§2-13-13.
Defined, §2-13-11.
Licenses, §40-12-113.
Misbranded ice cream,
§2-13-13.
Standardized, §2-13-11.

ICE FACTORIES.
Licenses, §40-12-114.

IDENTIFICATION.
**Application for license or
identification card,**
§32-6-4.
Department of public safety.
Issuance of identification
cards by department,
§32-6-1.
Drug products, §§20-1-150 to
20-1-154.
**Issuance of identification
cards for nondrivers,**
§32-6-1.
Mentally ill.
Nondriver identification
cards for retarded
persons, §32-6-4.1.

ILLEGITIMACY.
Determination of paternity.
Jurisdiction of juvenile court,
§12-15-31.
Fees.
Probate judges' fees,
§12-19-90.
Incestuous marriages.
Issue not deemed
illegitimate, §30-1-3.
Intestate succession.
Illegitimate child, §43-8-48.
Legitimation of children.
Fees.
Probate judges' fees,
§12-19-90.
Marriage of parents,
§26-11-1.
Name change, §26-11-3.
Probate court.
Written declaration by
father, §26-11-2.
Recognition.
Appointment of guardian
ad litem, §26-11-2.
By father.
Marriage of parents,
§26-11-1.
Written declaration,
§26-11-2.
Certification of minutes of
court to bureau of vital
statistics, §26-11-2.
Filing of response,
§26-11-2.
Hearing, §26-11-2.
Issuance of order by court,
§26-11-2.
Notification of mother,
§26-11-2.
Procedure generally,
§26-11-2.

ILLEGITIMACY—Cont'd
Legitimation of children
—Cont'd
Records.
Written declaration by
father, §26-11-2.
Special, private or local laws
prohibited, Const. Ala.,
art. IV, §104.
Name change, §26-11-3.
Paternity.
Determination of paternity,
§§26-17-1 to 26-17-21.
See PARENT AND
CHILD.
Wills.
Intestate succession.
Illegitimate child, §43-8-48.

ILLITERACY, §§16-34-1 to
16-34-4.

**IMITATION CONTROLLED
SUBSTANCES,** §§20-2-140
to 20-2-144.

IMMIGRATION.
Constitution of Alabama,
Const. Ala., art. I, §30.
**Constitution of the United
States,** Const. U. S., Art. I,
§9.

IMMUNITY.
Associations.
Officers.
Liability of officers of
nonprofit associations,
§§10-11-1 to 10-11-5.
Attorneys at law.
Client security fund.
Committee.
Immunity from civil
liability, ACSF, Rule
14.
Disciplinary proceedings,
ARDE, Rule 9.
Authorities.
Officers.
Liability of officers of
nonprofit
organizations,
§§10-11-1 to 10-11-5.
Boards and commissions.
Officers.
Liability of officers of
nonprofit
organizations,
§§10-11-1 to 10-11-5.
Child abuse or neglect.
Reporting.
Actions under chapter
immune from liability,
§26-14-9.
Constitution of Alabama.
Irrevocable or exclusive
grants of special
privileges or immunities,
Const. Ala., art. I, §22.
**Constitution of the United
States,** Const. U. S., Art.
IV, §2.
Corporations.
Nonprofit corporations.
Officers.
Liability, §§10-11-1 to
10-11-5.
Liability of officers of
nonprofit
corporations,
§§10-11-1 to 10-11-5.

IMMUNITY—Cont'd
Credit unions.
Administrator, board
members and employees
immune from personal
liability, §5-17-51.
Diseases.
Notifiable diseases.
Third parties.
Notification of diseases,
§22-11A-38.
Domestic violence facilities.
Civil liability, §30-6-12.
Drugs.
Controlled substances.
Minors.
Immunity of persons
reporting suspected
use, etc., of
controlled substance
by minor child,
§20-2-3.
General assembly.
Legislators, Const. Ala., art.
IV, §56.
Hazardous substances.
Cleanup fund.
Liability for actions taken
or omitted under
chapter, §22-30A-9.
Hazardous wastes.
Mitigation of effects of
discharge.
Persons assisting or
advising as to,
§6-5-332.1.
Legislators.
Privilege from arrest and
civil process, §29-1-7;
Const. Ala., art. IV, §56.
Mentally ill.
Regional mental health
programs and facilities.
Officers.
Liability of officers of
nonprofit
organizations,
§§10-11-1 to 10-11-5.
Municipal corporations.
Airports.
Municipal immunity from
liability for negligence,
§4-4-4.
Civil defense activities.
Municipal immunity from
liability for negligence,
§31-9-16.
Fire departments.
Operation beyond corporate
limits and police
jurisdiction,
§11-43-141.
Nonprofit corporations.
Officers.
Liability of officers of
nonprofit
organizations,
§§10-11-1 to 10-11-5.
Nurses.
Board of nursing.
Members immune from
individual civil
liability, §34-21-2.
Persons reporting violations
of provisions, §34-21-25.
State trooper reserves,
§32-2-41.

IMMUNIZATION.
  Hog cholera vaccine,
    §§2-15-250 to 2-15-274.
    See LIVESTOCK.
  Rabies, §§3-7-1 to 3-7-13.
    See RABIES.
  School children, §§16-30-1 to
    16-30-5.

IMPEACHMENT.
  Alcoholic beverages.
    Intemperance in use as
      grounds for
      impeachment, §36-11-1.
  Amendments.
    Allowance, §36-11-20.
  Appeals to supreme court.
    Authorization, §36-11-15.
    Costs, §36-11-16.
    Effect as to judgment of
      conviction, §36-11-16.
    Procedure, §36-11-15.
    Security for costs.
      Required, §36-11-16.
  Attorney general, Const. Ala.,
    art. VII, §173.
    Duty to institute and
      prosecute proceedings,
      §36-11-4.
  Bill of impeachment,
    §12-16-223.
  Chancellors, Const. Ala., art.
    VII, §174.
  Circuit courts.
    Clerks, Const. Ala., art. VII,
      §175.
    Judges, Const. Ala., art. VII,
      §174.
    Proceedings in circuit court,
      §§36-11-13, 36-11-14.
  Clerks of court, Const. Ala.,
    art. VII, §175.
  **Commissioner of agriculture
    and industries,** Const.
    Ala., art. VII, §173.
  Constables.
    Subject to impeachment,
      §36-11-1; Const. Ala.,
      art. VII, §175.
  Constitution of Alabama,
    Const. Ala., art. VII, §§173
    to 176.
    See CONSTITUTION OF
      ALABAMA.
  **Constitution of the United
    States,** Const. U. S., Art. I,
    §§2, 3; Art. II, §4; Art. III,
    §2.
  Coroners.
    Subject to impeachment,
      §36-11-1; Const. Ala.,
      art. VII, §175.
  Corruption.
    Grounds for impeachment,
      §36-11-1.
    Investigations of alleged
      misconduct, §36-11-3.
  Costs.
    Appeals to supreme court.
      Requirement of security for
      costs, §36-11-16.
    Generally, §36-11-8.
    Payment, §36-11-17.
  County officers, Const. Ala.,
    art. VII, §175.
  Court of civil appeal judges.
    Subject to impeachment,
      §36-11-1; Const. Ala.,
      art. VII, §174.

IMPEACHMENT—Cont'd
  **Court of criminal appeal
    judges.**
    Subject to impeachment,
      §36-11-1; Const. Ala.,
      art. VII, §174.
  **Disqualification from
    holding office.**
    Grounds for impeachment,
      §36-11-2.
  District attorneys.
    Duty to institute and
      prosecute proceedings,
      §36-11-4.
    Subject to impeachment,
      §36-11-1.
    Supernumerary district
      attorneys, §12-17-215.
  District court judges.
    Subject to impeachment,
      §36-11-1; Const. Ala.,
      art. VII, §175.
  Evidence.
    Matters as to which evidence
      may be introduced,
      §36-11-20.
    Written contracts,
      §12-21-112.
  Fees.
    Payment, §36-11-17.
    Sheriffs.
      Service of process,
        §36-11-17.
    Witnesses, §36-11-21.
  Governor, Const. Ala., art.
    VII, §173.
    Procedure when governor or
      successor impeached,
      Const. Ala., art. V, §127.
  Grand juries, §36-11-3.
  Grounds.
    Disqualification from holding
      office, §36-11-2.
    Generally, §36-11-1.
  Incompetency.
    Grounds for impeachment,
      §36-11-1.
    Investigations of alleged
      incompetency, §36-11-3.
  Indictment of accused,
    §36-11-24.
  Information.
    Contents, §36-11-7.
    Execution, §36-11-7.
    Filing by taxpayers.
      Verification, §36-11-8.
  Institution of proceedings.
    Duty of attorney general and
      district attorneys,
      §36-11-4.
    Manner, §36-11-5.
    Proceedings in name of state,
      §36-11-5.
    Taxpayers.
      Five resident taxpayers
        may institute,
        §36-11-6.
  Intoxicating liquors.
    Intemperance in use.
      Grounds for impeachment,
        §36-11-1.
  Investigations.
    Grand juries.
      Investigations of alleged
        misconduct or
        incompetency,
        §36-11-3.

IMPEACHMENT—Cont'd
  Judges.
    Which judges subject to
      impeachment, §36-11-1;
      Const. Ala., art. VII,
      §§174, 175.
  Judgment of conviction.
    Appeal to supreme court.
      Effect, §36-11-16.
    Effect, §36-11-24.
    Vacancy in office.
      Certification upon final
        judgment of conviction,
        §36-11-23.
  Jury.
    Drawing where member of
      county commission
      subject to impeachment
      proceedings, §36-11-19.
    Right to jury trial in circuit
      court, §36-11-14.
  Justices of the peace, Const.
    Ala., art. VII, §175.
  Lieutenant governor, Const.
    Ala., art. VII, §173.
  Limitation of actions.
    Proceedings not to be barred,
      §36-11-24.
  **Limitation on impeachment
    penalties,** Const. Ala., art.
    VII, §176.
  Municipal officers, Const.
    Ala., art. VII, §175.
    General provisions,
      §§11-43-160 to 11-43-163.
  Narcotics.
    Intemperance in use.
      Grounds for impeachment,
        §36-11-1.
  Neglect of duty.
    Willful neglect grounds for
      impeachment, §36-11-1.
  Notaries public.
    Subject to impeachment,
      §36-11-1; Const. Ala.,
      art. VII, §175.
  Penalties.
    Accused person liable to
      indictment and
      punishment, Const. Ala.,
      art. VII, §176.
    Limitation on impeachment
      penalties, Const. Ala.,
      art. VII, §176.
  Persons subject, §36-11-1.
  President, Const. U. S., Art.
    II, §4.
  Probate judges.
    Subject to impeachment,
      §36-11-1; Const. Ala.,
      art. VII, §174.
  Proceedings in circuit court.
    Appeals to supreme court
      from judgment of circuit
      court, §§36-11-15,
      36-11-6.
    Conduct of trial.
      Generally, §36-11-14.
    Continuances.
      Granting, §36-11-13.
    Information, §36-11-13.
    Jury trial.
      Right of defendant,
        §36-11-14.
    Order to appear and answer
      information.
      Issuance and service,
        §36-11-13.
    Summons, §36-11-13.
    Trial date.
      Setting, §36-11-13.

IMPEACHMENT—Cont'd
Proceedings in circuit court
    —Cont'd
    Trial date—Cont'd
        When case stands for trial,
            §36-11-14.
**Proceedings in supreme
    court.**
    Conduct of trial, §36-11-10.
    Continuances.
        Granting, §36-11-9.
    Examiners.
        Appointment, §36-11-10.
        Compensation, §36-11-17.
        Duties, §36-11-10.
        Powers as to witnesses,
            §36-11-11.
        Rights of parties as to
            proceedings before,
            §36-11-12.
        Statement as to fees and
            compensation to which
            witnesses entitled.
            Filing by examiner,
                §36-11-21.
    Information, §36-11-9.
    Order to appear and answer
        information.
        Issuance and service,
            §36-11-9.
    Parties.
        Rights as to proceedings
            before examiners,
            §36-11-12.
    Summons, §36-11-9.
    Trial date.
        Setting, §36-11-9.
    Witnesses.
        Examination, §36-11-10.
        Fees and compensation,
            §36-11-21.
        Powers of examiners as to,
            §36-11-11.
        Summoning, §36-11-10.
**Proceedings where
    defendant has removed,
    absconded or secreted
    himself,** §36-11-25.
Prosecution.
    Duty of attorney general and
        district attorneys,
        §36-11-4.
Records.
    Final record of impeachment
        proceedings.
        Preparation, §36-11-22.
Reports.
    Grand juries.
        Disposition of reports,
            §36-11-3.
Residence requirements.
    Failure to reside in
        Montgomery county
        deemed ground for
        impeachment of state
        officers, §36-2-5.
Secretary of state, Const.
    Ala., art. VII, §173.
Service of process.
    Duties, liabilities and fees of
        sheriffs, §36-11-17.
    Proceedings where defendant
        has removed, absconded
        or secreted himself,
        §36-11-25.
    Sheriff or clerk of court
        subject to impeachment
        proceedings, §36-11-18.
Sheriffs.
    Effect, Const. Ala., art. V,
        §138.

IMPEACHMENT—Cont'd
Sheriffs—Cont'd
    Execution of process where
        sheriff subject to
        impeachment
        proceedings, §36-11-18.
    Service of process.
        Duties, liabilities and fees
            of sheriffs, §36-11-17.
    Subject to impeachment,
        §§36-11-1, 36-11-18;
        Const. Ala., art. VII,
        §174.
Solicitors, Const. Ala., art.
    VII, §174.
State auditor, Const. Ala., art.
    VII, §173.
State treasurer, Const. Ala.,
    art. VII, §173.
Superintendent of education,
    Const. Ala., art. VII, §173.
Supreme court.
    Appeals to supreme court,
        §§36-11-15, 36-11-16.
    Proceedings in supreme
        court, §§36-11-9 to
        36-11-12.
Supreme court justices,
    Const. Ala., art. VII, §173.
Tax collectors and assessors,
    §36-11-1; Const. Ala., art.
    VII, §175.
Vacancies in office.
    Certification upon final
        judgment of conviction,
        §36-11-23.
Vice-president, Const. U. S.,
    Art. II, §4.
Witnesses.
    Fees.
        Generally, §36-11-21.
        Payment to state witnesses
            before supreme court
            when proceedings
            instituted on
            information of attorney
            general, §36-11-21.
        Statement as to fees and
            compensation to which
            witnesses entitled.
            Filed by examiner,
                §36-11-21.
    Rules of civil procedure,
        ARCP, Rule 43 (b).

IMPLIED CONSENT.
Motor vehicles.
    Chemical test for
        intoxication.
        General provisions,
            §§32-5-190 to 32-5-194.

IMPORTS.
Alcoholic beverages.
    Importers' licenses,
        §§28-3A-7, 28-3A-21,
        28-7-10.
**Constitution of the United
    States,** Const. U. S., Art. I,
    §§9, 10.
Fish and game.
    Rules and regulations.
        Penalties.
            Violations, §9-2-13.
        Promulgation, §9-2-13.
Petroleum products.
    Notification of importation,
        §8-17-89.

IMPOTENCY.
Advertising.
    Advertisements concerning
        impotency, §22-20-12.

IMPRISONMENT.
False imprisonment.
    See FALSE
        IMPRISONMENT.
Generally.
    See PENALTIES.
Jails.
    See JAILS.
Penalties.
    See PENALTIES.
Penitentiary.
    See PENITENTIARY.
Prisons and prisoners.
    See PRISONS AND
        PRISONERS.

**IMPROVEMENT
    AUTHORITIES.**
General provisions, §§39-7-1
    to 39-7-34.
    See PUBLIC WORKS.

IMPROVEMENTS.
Municipal corporations.
    Class 5 municipalities.
        Mayor/commission/city
            manager form of
            government.
            Commission.
                Power to impose and
                    collect local
                    improvement
                    assessments,
                    §11-44E-44.
            Succession of
                government.
                Continuance of public
                    improvements,
                    §11-44E-145.
**Municipal government
    capital improvement,**
    §§11-66-1 to 11-66-7.
    See MUNICIPAL
        CORPORATIONS.

INCEST.
Elements of crime, §13A-13-3.
Evidence.
    Corroboration requirement,
        §13A-13-3.
Incestuous marriages,
    §§30-1-3, 30-1-6.
Indictments.
    Form of indictment,
        §15-8-150.
Marriage.
    Incestuous marriages,
        §§30-1-3, 30-1-6.

INCHOATE OFFENSES.
**Accomplices and
    accessories.**
    See ACCOMPLICES AND
        ACCESSORIES.
Conspiracy.
    See CONSPIRACY.
Criminal solicitation.
    See INCITING TO CRIME.
Inciting to crime.
    See INCITING TO CRIME.
Solicitation.
    See INCITING TO CRIME.

INCITING TO CRIME.
Criminal solicitation.
    Consummation of object
        offense not defense to
        prosecution, §13A-4-5.
    Elements of crime, §13A-4-1.
    Evidence.
        Corroboration required,
            §13A-4-1.

INCITING TO CRIME—Cont'd
Criminal solicitation—Cont'd
Multiple convictions on basis
of same course of
conduct, §13A-4-5.
Renunciation of criminal
intent, §13A-4-1.
Specific offenses enumerated,
§13A-4-1.
Drugs.
Controlled substances.
Criminal solicitation to
commit controlled
substance crime,
§13A-12-202.
Included offenses,
§13A-12-205.
Riots.
Inciting a riot, §13A-11-4.

INCOME TAX.
Accounts and accounting.
Inventory.
Use of inventories to
determine income of
taxpayer, §40-18-11.
Net income of individuals.
Computation, §40-18-13.
Returns.
Changes of accounting
period, §40-18-30.
Rules and regulations.
Promulgation by
department of revenue,
§40-18-57.
Unnecessary examination or
investigation of
taxpayer's books or
accounts, §40-18-56.
Actions.
Exemptions.
Damages received in civil
actions, §40-18-14.
Limitation upon civil actions
by taxpayer, §40-18-47.
Mistake or error.
Refunds.
Failure or refusal of
department of
revenue to make
refund, §40-18-43.
Adjusted gross income.
Defined, §40-18-84.
Advance payment.
Voluntary advance payment,
§40-18-42.
Affidavits.
Making false affidavits,
§40-18-52.
Aged persons.
Voluntary check-off
designations on returns.
Designated contribution by
taxpayer filing state
income tax returns,
§40-18-147.
Disposition of
contributions,
§40-18-147.
Agriculture.
Declaration of estimated tax.
Farmer's declaration,
§40-18-83.
Exemption of certain
agricultural
organizations, §40-18-32.
Air pollution.
Corporations.
Deductions allowed
corporations,
§40-18-35.

INCOME TAX—Cont'd
Animals.
Corporations.
Deductions allowed
corporations.
Contributions or gifts to
institutions for the
prevention of cruelty
to animals,
§40-18-35.
Deductions.
Contributions or gifts made
to institutions for the
prevention of cruelty
to animals, §§40-18-15,
40-18-35.
Appeals.
Assessments, §40-18-40.
Setoff debt collection,
§40-18-104.
Withholding tax.
Appeals of employer,
§40-18-74.
Appropriations.
Homestead exemptions.
Replacement of revenues
lost by reason of
exemption of
homesteads, §40-18-58.
Art.
Art development fund.
Voluntary check-off
designations on state
income tax returns,
§§40-18-140,
40-18-141.
Assessment.
Appeals, §40-18-40.
Blanks, §40-18-40.
Collection after assessment,
§40-18-46.
Corporations.
Request for prompt
assessment, §40-18-45.
Defined, §40-18-40.
Department of revenue.
Duties and responsibilities
as to, §40-18-40.
Executors and
administrators.
Request for prompt
assessment, §40-18-45.
Failure to make return.
Collection of tax without
assessment, §40-18-46.
False return.
Collection of tax without
assessment, §40-18-46.
Fiduciary.
Request for prompt
assessment, §40-18-45.
Generally, §40-18-40.
Involuntary conversion,
§40-18-45.
Jeopardy assessment,
§40-29-90.
Limitation of action,
§40-18-45.
Notice of assessment.
Mailing of tax blank to be
only notice, §40-18-40.
Period of limitation upon
assessment and
collection, §40-18-45.
Suspension, §40-29-50.
Protest of taxpayer.
Hearing on protest,
§40-18-40.
Qualified stock acquisition,
§40-18-45.

INCOME TAX—Cont'd
Assessment—Cont'd
Request for prompt
assessment, §40-18-45.
Supervision of assessment.
Department of revenue to
supervise, §40-18-54.
Waiver, §40-18-46.
Banks and banking.
Corporations.
Deductions allowed
corporations.
Amounts received as
dividends from
national banks,
§40-18-38.
Exemptions.
Federal land banks,
§40-18-32.
Bond issues.
Exemptions.
Interest on obligations of
the state of Alabama,
§40-18-14.
United States.
Interest or other income
received from
obligations of United
States, §40-18-4.
Books and papers.
Examination.
Failure to produce before
department, §40-18-56.
Contempt, §40-18-56.
Unnecessary examination
or investigation,
§40-18-56.
Capital gain or loss,
§§40-18-6 to 40-18-9.
Cash.
Defined, §40-18-1.
Charities.
Corporations.
Deductions allowed
corporations.
Contributions or gifts to
charitable
institutions,
§40-18-35.
Deductions.
Contributions or gifts made
to charitable
institutions.
Corporations, §40-18-35.
Individuals, §40-18-15.
**Check-off designations on
state income tax returns,**
§§40-18-140 to 40-18-148.
See within this heading,
"Returns."
Collection.
Assessment.
Collection after
assessment, §40-18-46.
Delinquency.
Collection prior to
delinquency,
§40-18-51.
Disposition, §40-18-51.
Period of limitation upon
collection, §40-18-45.
Suspension, §40-29-50.
Supervision of collection.
Department of revenue to
supervise, §40-18-54.
Compacts.
Multistate tax compact.
Allocation and
apportionment of
deduction and
exemptions, §40-18-22.

INCOME TAX—Cont'd

Computation.
 Corporations, §40-18-31.
 Deductions, §40-18-15.
 Estates or trusts.
  Computation of net income, §40-18-25.
 Gain or loss, §40-18-7.
 Generally, §40-18-5.
 Individuals.
  Net income of individuals, §40-18-13.
 Inventory.
  Use of inventories to determine income of taxpayer, §40-18-11.
 Partnerships.
  Net income of partnership, §40-18-24.

Constitution of Alabama,
 Const. Ala., amd. 25.
 Corporations, Const. Ala., amd. 212.
 Deductions.
  Federal income tax.
   Deduction of federal income tax from gross income when computing state income tax, Const. Ala., amd. 225.
  Disposition of income tax, Const. Ala., amd. 61.
  Homestead exemptions, Const. Ala., amd. 61.

Constitution of the United States, Const. U. S., Amendment XVI.

Contempt.
 Books and papers.
  Failure to produce before department, §40-18-56.

Conversion.
 Gain or loss.
  Basis of property.
   Involuntary conversion, §40-18-6.
  Involuntary conversion, §40-18-8.

Corporations, Const. Ala., amd. 212.
 Air pollution.
  Deductions allowed corporations.
   Amounts invested in control of air pollution, §40-18-35.
 Annuity plans.
  Deductions allowed corporations.
   Contributions made by employer deductible, §40-18-35.
 Assessment.
  Request for prompt assessment, §40-18-45.
 Charities.
  Deductions allowed, §40-18-35.
 Declaration of estimated tax, §§40-18-82, 40-18-83.1.
  Effective date of provisions, §40-18-83.1.
  Payment, §§40-18-83, 40-18-83.1.
 Deductions.
  Additional deductions allowed, §40-18-38.

INCOME TAX—Cont'd

Corporations—Cont'd
 Deductions—Cont'd
  Air pollution.
   Amounts invested in control of air pollution, §40-18-35.
  Carry forward of net operating losses, §40-18-35.1.
  Contributions or gifts to religious, charitable, scientific or educational institutions, §40-18-35.
  Debts.
   Losses from worthless debts, §40-18-35.
  Dividends.
   Deductions allowed corporations, §40-18-35.
  Employers and employees.
   Contributions paid by employer to stock bonus, pension, profit-sharing or annuity plan, §40-18-35.
  Generally, §40-18-35.
  Handicapped persons.
   Removal of architectural or transportation barriers, §40-18-35.
  Insurance.
   Deductions allowed certain insurance companies, §40-18-35.
  Interest.
   Deductions allowed corporations, §40-18-35.
   Obligations of the United States and bonds issued by the war finance corporation, §40-18-38.
  Items not deductible by corporations, §40-18-37.
  Losses.
   Uninsured losses, §40-18-35.
  Mines.
   Allowance for depletion, §40-18-35.
  National banks.
   Amounts received as dividends from national banks, §40-18-38.
  Net operating losses.
   Carrying forward, §40-18-35.1.
  Property.
   Allowance for exhaustion, wear and tear of property, §40-18-35.
  Stock bonus plans.
   Contributions paid by employer deductible, §40-18-35.
  Taxes imposed by authority of United States, §40-18-35.

INCOME TAX—Cont'd

Corporations—Cont'd
 Deductions—Cont'd
  Taxpayers engaged in multistate business.
   Allocation and apportionment of deductions, §40-18-22.
  Water pollution.
   Amounts invested in control of water pollution, §40-18-35.
 Definitions, §40-18-1.
  Dividend, §40-18-36.
  Gross income of corporations, §40-18-34.
  Net income of corporations, §40-18-33.
  Partial liquidation, §40-18-36.
  Stock dividends, §40-18-36.
 Distribution by corporations, §40-18-36.
 Dividends.
  Deductions allowed corporations.
   Dividends from subsidiary corporations, §40-18-35.
  Defined, §40-18-36.
  Stock dividends.
   Defined, §40-18-36.
 Educational institutions.
  Gifts or contributions deductible, §40-18-35.
 Employers and employees.
  Deductions allowed corporations.
   Contributions paid by employer to or under stock bonus, pension, profit-sharing or annuity plan, §40-18-35.
 Estimated tax.
  Additional amount where 80 percent of tax exceeds estimated tax, §40-18-80.
  Declaration of estimated tax, §§40-18-82, 40-18-83.1.
  Effective date of provisions, §40-18-83.1.
  Payment, §§40-18-83, 40-18-83.1.
 Exemptions.
  Taxpayers engaged in multistate business.
   Allocation and apportionment of exemptions, §40-18-22.
 Gain or loss.
  Basis of stock after stock dividend, §40-18-6.
  Liquidations.
   Basis of property, §40-18-6.
  Property acquired on liquidation of subsidiary, §40-18-6.
  Recognition, §40-18-8.
  Transfers to corporation.
   Basis of property, §40-18-6.

INCOME TAX—Cont'd
  Corporations—Cont'd
    Gifts.
      Deductions allowed
        corporations,
        §40-18-35.
    Gross income of corporations.
      Defined, §40-18-34.
    Imposition of tax on
      corporations, §40-18-31.
    Information from source of
      income.
    Report to department of
      revenue, §40-18-26.
    Insurance.
      Deductions allowed certain
        insurance companies,
        §40-18-35.
    Liquidation.
      Distributions in
        liquidation, §40-18-36.
      Partial liquidation.
        Defined, §40-18-36.
    Minors.
      Deductions allowed
        corporations.
        Contributions or gifts to
          institutions for the
          prevention of cruelty
          to children,
          §40-18-35.
    Net income of corporations.
      Defined, §40-18-33.
    Payment.
      Installment payments,
        §40-18-42.
      Time of payment,
        §40-18-42.
    Persons and subjects taxable,
      §40-18-2.
    Property.
      Deductions allowed
        corporations.
        Allowance for
          exhaustion, wear
          and tear of property,
          §40-18-35.
    Redemption of stock,
      §40-18-36.
    Religious institutions.
      Contributions or gifts
        deductible, §40-18-35.
    Report from source.
      Defined, §40-18-1.
    Returns.
      Contents, §40-18-39.
      Custody, §40-18-48.
      Extension of time for
        filing, §40-18-39.
      Failure to make return.
        Penalty, §40-18-49.
      Inspection of returns by
        federal or foreign state
        agents, §40-18-53.
      Not public documents,
        §40-18-52.
      Required, §40-18-39.
      Signature of officers
        required, §40-18-39.
      When made, §40-18-39.
    Scientific institutions.
      Gifts or contributions
        deductible, §40-18-35.
    S corporations, §§40-18-160
      to 40-18-173.
    See CORPORATIONS.
    Statement to be furnished,
      §40-18-55.
    Stock and stockholders.
      Redemption of stock,
        §40-18-36.

INCOME TAX—Cont'd
  Corporations—Cont'd
    Subsidiary corporations.
      Deductions allowed
        corporations.
        Dividends from
          subsidiaries,
          §40-18-35.
    Taxpayers engaged in
      multistate business.
      Allocation and
        apportionment of
        deductions and
        exemptions, §40-18-22.
    Time of payment, §40-18-42.
    Water pollution.
      Deductions allowed
        corporations.
        Amounts invested in
          control of water
          pollution, §40-18-35.
  Credit.
    Solar energy tax credits,
      §§40-18-120, 40-18-121.
    Taxes paid on income from
      sources without the
      state, §40-18-21.
      Certificate showing
        amount required,
        §40-18-21.
      Taxpayers engaged in
        multistate business,
        §40-18-22.
    Withholding tax.
      Credit for tax withheld,
        §40-18-78.
  Death.
    Gain or loss.
      Basis of property.
        Property transmitted at
        death, §40-18-6.
  Debts.
    Corporations.
      Deductions allowed
        corporations.
        Worthless debts,
        §40-18-35.
    Deductions.
      Losses from debts,
        §§40-18-15, 40-18-35.
  Declaration of estimated tax.
    Agriculture.
      Farmer's declaration,
        §40-18-83.
    Amendments, §40-18-82.
    Contents, §40-18-82.
    Corporations, §§40-18-82,
      40-18-83.1.
      Effective date of provisions,
        §40-18-83.1.
      Payment, §§40-18-83,
        40-18-83.1.
    Executors and
      administrators.
      Declaration not required,
        §40-18-85.
    Extensions of time for filing,
      §40-18-82.
    Failure to file.
      Penalty, §40-18-80.
    Farmer's declaration,
      §40-18-83.
    Fiduciaries.
      Declaration not required to
        be filed, §40-18-85.
    Payment.
      Generally, §40-18-83.
      Installment payments,
        §40-18-83.
    Persons unable to make own
      declaration, §40-18-82.

INCOME TAX—Cont'd
  Declaration of estimated tax
    —Cont'd
    Required, §40-18-82.
    When filed, §40-18-82.
    Who must file, §40-18-82.
  Deductions.
    Amortization of war or
      emergency facilities,
      §40-18-18.
    Animals.
      Gifts or contributions to
        institutions for the
        prevention of cruelty
        to animals, §40-18-15.
    Annuity plans.
      Contributions paid by
        employer, §40-18-15.
    Charitable institutions,
      §40-18-15.
    Children's trust fund.
      Refund designation,
      §26-16-31.
    Conversion of residences
      from gas or electricity to
      wood, §40-18-15.
    Corporations, §§40-18-35,
      40-18-37, 40-18-38.
    Debts.
      Worthless debts,
        §§40-18-15, 40-18-35.
    Deducting the same item
      more than once,
      §40-18-84.
    Department of archives and
      history.
      Deduction of amount of gift
        to department for
        income tax purposes,
        §41-6-53.
    Depletion.
      Basis for depletion,
        §40-18-16.
      Mines.
        Oil and gas wells and
          other natural
          deposits, §40-18-15.
    Depreciation.
      Basis for depreciation,
        §40-18-16.
    Drugs.
      Expenses for medicine and
        drugs, §40-18-15.
    Educational institutions.
      Gifts or contributions made
        to, §40-18-15.
    Emergency facilities.
      Amortization of war or
        emergency facilities,
        §40-18-18.
    Employers and employees.
      Contributions paid by
        employer to stock
        bonus, pension, profit-
        sharing or annuity
        plan, §40-18-15.
    Federal income tax.
      Deduction of federal tax
        when computing state
        tax, Const. Ala., amd.
        225.
    Gifts, §40-18-15.
    Handicapped persons.
      Removal from property any
        architectural or
        transportation barriers
        to.
      Expenses actually
        incurred, §40-18-15.

INCOME TAX—Cont'd
  Deductions—Cont'd
    Insurance.
      Accident and health
        insurance, §40-18-15.
      Items not deductible,
        §40-18-17.
    Losses, §40-18-15.
    Medical and dental expenses,
      §40-18-15.
    Mines and minerals.
      Basis for depletion.
        Discovery value,
          §40-18-16.
        Depletion allowance,
          §40-18-15.
    Minors.
      Contributions or gifts made
        to institutions for the
        prevention of cruelty
        to children, §40-18-15.
    Net operating loss carry-
      overs, §40-18-15.
    Oil and gas.
      Basis for depletion.
        Discovery value,
          §40-18-16.
        Depletion allowance,
          §40-18-15.
    Pension plans.
      Contributions paid by
        employer, §40-18-15.
    Production or collection of
      income, §40-18-15.
    Returns.
      Return required to claim
        deduction, §40-18-27.
    Stock bonus.
      Contributions paid by
        employer, §40-18-15.
    Taxpayers engaged in
      multistate business.
      Allocation and
        apportionment of
        deductions, §40-18-22.
    Trees and timber.
      Depletion allowance,
        §40-18-15.
    United States.
      Taxes paid imposed by
        United States,
        §40-18-15.
  Definitions, §40-18-1.
    Adjusted gross income,
      §40-18-84.
    Assessment, §40-18-40.
    Corporations, §40-18-1.
    Dependents, §40-18-19.
    Depletion, §40-18-16.
    Depreciation, §40-18-16.
    Gross income of individuals,
      §40-18-14.
    Net income of individuals,
      §40-18-12.
    Political parties, §40-18-146.
    Setoff debt collection,
      §40-18-100.
    Solar energy tax credits,
      §§40-18-120, 40-18-121.
    Withholding tax, §40-18-70.
    Wager winnings,
      §40-18-90.
  Dental expenses.
    Deductions for dental
      expenses, §40-18-15.
  **Department of archives and
    history.**
    Deduction of amount of gift
      to department, §41-6-53.

INCOME TAX—Cont'd
  Department of revenue.
    Assessment of taxes.
      Duties and responsibilities
        as to, §40-18-40.
      Hearing on taxpayer
        protest, §40-18-40.
    Corporations.
      Corporate statements to be
        furnished, §40-18-55.
    Failure of agent to perform
      duty, §40-18-52.
    Inspections, §40-18-56.
    Investigations.
      Written notice of
        additional inspections,
        §40-18-56.
    Refunds.
      Mandamus action to
        enforce refunds,
        §40-18-43.
    Reports.
      Source of income,
        §40-18-26.
    Returns.
      Federal returns.
        Furnishing to
          department,
          §40-18-56.
    Rules and regulations.
      Promulgation by
        department, §40-18-57.
    Supervision of assessment
      and collection by
      department, §40-18-54.
    Witnesses.
      Failure to appear before
        department as witness,
        §40-18-56.
  Dependents, §40-18-19.
  Depletion.
    Basis for depletion,
      §40-18-16.
    Deductions.
      Reasonable allowance for
        depletion, §40-18-15.
  Depreciation.
    Amortization of war or
      emergency facilities,
      §40-18-18.
    Basis for depreciation,
      §40-18-16.
    Corporations.
      Deductions allowed
        corporations,
        §40-18-35.
  Disposition, Const. Ala., amd.
    61.
  Dividends.
    Corporations.
      Deductions allowed
        corporations.
        Dividends from
          subsidiary
          corporations,
          §40-18-35.
  Drugs.
    Deductions.
      Expenses for medicine and
        drugs, §40-18-15.
  Education.
    Corporations.
      Deductions allowed
        corporations,
        §40-18-35.
    Deductions.
      Contributions or gifts made
        to educational
        institutions,
        §§40-18-15, 40-18-35.

INCOME TAX—Cont'd
  Employers and employees.
    Deductions.
      Contributions paid by
        employer under stock
        bonus, pension, profit-
        sharing or annuity
        plan, §40-18-15.
    Trusts.
      Contributions to trust
        made by employer,
        §40-18-25.
    Withholding tax, §§40-18-70
      to 40-18-80. See within
      this heading,
      "Withholding tax."
  Estates and trusts, §40-18-25.
  Estimated tax.
    Declaration of estimated tax,
      §§40-18-82 to 40-18-83.1.
  **Executors and
    administrators.**
    Assessment.
      Request for prompt
        assessment, §40-18-45.
    Declaration of estimated tax.
      Not required, §40-18-85.
    Defined, §40-18-1.
  Exemptions.
    Actions.
      Damages received in civil
        actions, §40-18-14.
    Agricultural organizations,
      §40-18-32.
    Banks.
      Federal land banks,
        §40-18-32.
    Dependents, §40-18-19.
    Foreign missionaries.
      Income exempt, §40-18-2.1.
    Fraternal benefit societies,
      §40-18-32.
    Generally, §§40-18-14,
      40-18-19.
    Homestead exemptions,
      §40-18-58; Const. Ala.,
      amd. 61.
    Husband and wife.
      Personal exemptions,
        §40-18-19.
    Insurance.
      Items exempt from income
        tax, §40-18-14.
    Labor organizations,
      §40-18-32.
    Military retirement benefits,
      §40-18-20.
    Nonresident taxpayers,
      §40-18-19.
    Organizations exempt from
      taxation, §40-18-32.
    Pensions, §40-18-19.
    Personal exemptions,
      §40-18-19.
    Retirement allowances,
      §40-18-19.
    Savings and loan
      associations, §40-18-32.
    Taxpayers engaged in
      multistate business.
      Allocation and
        apportionment,
        §40-18-22.
    Trusts and trustees.
      Trust income exempt from
        taxation, §40-18-25.
    United States.
      Interest upon obligations of
        the United States,
        §40-18-14.

INCOME TAX—Cont'd
  Exemptions—Cont'd
    Unrelated business taxable
      income, §40-18-32.
    Workmen's compensation,
      §40-18-14.
  Fallout shelters.
    Deductions, §40-18-15.
  Federal income tax.
    Deduction from gross income
      when computing state
      income tax, Const. Ala.,
      amd. 225.
  Fiduciaries.
    Assessment.
      Request for prompt
        assessment, §40-18-45.
    Declaration of estimated tax.
      Not required, §40-18-85.
    Defined, §40-18-1.
    Payment, §40-18-25.
      Installment payments,
        §40-18-42.
      Time of payment,
        §40-18-42.
    Report from source.
      Defined, §40-18-1.
    Returns, §40-18-29.
      Certification of knowledge
        of affairs of individual,
        estate or trust,
        §40-18-29.
      Responsibility of fiduciary
        for making return,
        §40-18-25.
    Time of payment, §40-18-42.
  Fiscal year.
    Defined, §40-18-1.
    Net income of individuals.
      Computation of income
        based on taxpayer's
        fiscal year, §40-18-13.
    Returns.
      Changes in accounting
        period, §40-18-30.
      Returns made on the basis
        of fiscal year,
        §40-18-27.
  Foreign missionaries.
    Income exempt, §40-18-2.1.
  Fraternal benefit societies.
    Exemptions of certain
      fraternal beneficiary
      societies, §40-18-32.
  Fraud.
    Collection of tax without
      assessment, §40-18-46.
    Penalty for fraud, §40-18-49.
    Withholding tax.
      Employee statements,
        §40-18-80.
  Gain or loss.
    Adjusted basis, §40-18-6.
    Amount realized.
      Defined, §40-18-7.
    Basis of property, §40-18-6.
    Conversion.
      Basis of property.
        Involuntary conversion,
        §40-18-6.
    Corporations.
      Basis of property.
        Liquidation, §40-18-6.
        Property acquired on
          liquidation of
          subsidiary, §40-18-6.
        Stock after stock
          dividend, §40-18-6.
        Transfers to corporation,
          §40-18-6.
      Recognition, §40-18-8.

INCOME TAX—Cont'd
  Gain or loss—Cont'd
    Corporations—Cont'd
      Transfers to corporation.
        Basis of property,
          §40-18-6.
    Death.
      Property transmitted at
        death.
      Basis of property,
        §40-18-6.
    Depreciation.
      Basis for depreciation,
        §40-18-16.
    Determination of amount,
      §40-18-7.
    Gift or transfer in trust.
      Basis of property,
        §40-18-6.
    Installment method.
      Gain or loss upon
        disposition of
        installment
        obligations, §40-18-44.
    Installment sales, §40-18-7.
    Inventory value.
      Basis of property,
        §40-18-6.
    Recognition of gain or loss,
      §§40-18-7, 40-18-8.
    Rollover of gain on sale of
      principal residence,
      §40-18-6.
    Securities.
      Optional method for
        returning as income
        decreases in
        redemption value of
        securities purchased at
        a discount, §40-18-9.
  Game and fish.
    Voluntary check-off
      designations on state
      income tax returns.
      Alabama nongame wildlife
        program, §§40-18-143
        to 40-18-145.
  Gifts.
    Corporations.
      Deductions allowed
        corporations,
        §40-18-35.
    Deductions.
      Corporations, §40-18-35.
      Gifts for public purposes,
        §40-18-15.
      Gifts to religious,
        charitable, scientific or
        educational
        institutions, §40-18-15.
    Gain or loss.
      Basis of property.
        Gift or transfer in trust,
          §40-18-6.
  Gross income of individuals.
    Adjusted gross income.
      Defined, §40-18-84.
    Defined, §40-18-14.
  Handicapped persons.
    Deductions.
      Removal of barriers.
        Actual expenses
          incurred, §40-18-15.
  Hearings.
    Assessments.
      Hearing by department of
        revenue on taxpayer
        protest, §40-18-40.
    Setoff debt collection.
      Application for, §40-18-103.
      Procedure, §40-18-104.

INCOME TAX—Cont'd
  Homestead exemptions,
    Const. Ala., amd. 61.
    Appropriations.
      Replacement of revenues
        lost by reason of
        exemption of
        homesteads, §40-18-58.
  Husband and wife.
    Exemptions.
      Personal exemptions,
        §40-18-19.
    Joint returns.
      Joint and several liability
        of husband and wife,
        §40-18-27.
      Innocent spouse,
        §40-18-27.
  Imposition, §40-18-2.
    Corporations, §40-18-31.
  Individuals.
    Definitions, §40-18-1.
    Gross income of individuals.
      Adjusted gross income.
        Defined, §40-18-84.
      Defined, §40-18-14.
    Net income of individuals.
      Computation, §40-18-13.
      Defined, §40-18-12.
    Persons and subjects taxable,
      §40-18-2.
    Returns, §40-18-27.
    Tax on individuals, §40-18-5.
    Time of payment, §40-18-42.
  **Information from source of
    income,** §40-18-26.
  Insurance.
    Corporations.
      Deductions allowed certain
        insurance companies,
        §40-18-35.
    Deductions.
      Accident and health
        insurance.
        Amounts paid for,
          §40-18-15.
      Corporations, §40-18-35.
      Items not deductible,
        §40-18-17.
    Exemptions.
      Items exempt from income
        tax, §40-18-14.
    Insurers.
      Exemption from income
        tax, §27-4-10.
  Interest.
    Bond issues.
      Interest or other income
        received from
        obligations of United
        States, §40-18-4.
    Corporations.
      Deductions allowed
        corporations generally,
        §40-18-35.
    Deductions, §§40-18-15,
      40-18-35.
    Exemptions.
      Interest upon obligations of
        the United States,
        §40-18-4.
    United States.
      Interest received from
        obligations of United
        States, §40-18-4.
  Inventory.
    Use of inventories to
      determine income of
      taxpayer, §40-18-11.

INCOME TAX—Cont'd
  Investigations.
    Unnecessary examination or
        investigations, §40-18-56.
  Involuntary conversion.
    Assessments.
      Limitation of actions,
          §40-18-45.
  Jeopardy assessment,
        §40-29-27.
  Labor.
    Exemption of certain labor
        organizations, §40-18-32.
  Levied and imposed,
        §40-18-2.
    Corporations, §40-18-31.
    Individuals, §40-18-5.
  Liens.
    Applicability of lien
        provisions.
      Generally, §40-18-51.
    Withholding tax.
      Property of employer who
          fails to withhold or
          pay over subject to
          lien, §40-18-74.
  Limitation of actions.
    Civil actions and proceedings
        by taxpayer, §40-18-47.
    Involuntary conversion,
        §40-18-45.
    Period of limitation upon
        assessment and
        collection, §40-18-45.
    Suspension, §40-29-50.
    Qualified stock acquisition,
        §40-18-45.
  Loss.
    Capital gain or loss,
        §§40-18-6 to 40-18-9.
    Deductions, §40-18-15.
  Mandamus.
    Taxes paid through mistake
        or error.
      Failure or refusal of
          department of revenue
          to refund, §40-18-43.
  Military affairs.
    Deductions.
      Amortization of war or
          emergency facilities,
          §40-18-18.
    Exemptions.
      Military retirement
          benefits, §40-18-20.
    Members of armed forces of
        United States.
      Liability for state income
          tax, §40-18-3.
  Mines and minerals.
    Basis for depletion.
      Discovery value, §40-18-16.
    Corporations.
      Deductions allowed
          corporations.
        Depletion of mines,
            §40-18-35.
    Deductions.
      Depletion allowance,
          §§40-18-15, 40-18-35.
  Minors.
    Children's trust fund.
      State income tax refund
          designation, §26-16-31.

INCOME TAX—Cont'd
  Minors—Cont'd
    Corporations.
      Deductions allowed
          corporations.
        Contributions or gifts to
            institutions for the
            prevention of cruelty
            to children,
            §40-18-35.
    Deductions.
      Contributions or gifts made
          to institutions for the
          prevention of cruelty
          to children, §§40-18-15,
          40-18-35.
  Mistakes.
    Mandamus.
      Refusal or failure of
          department of revenue
          to refund, §40-18-43.
    Tax paid through mistake or
        error, §40-18-43.
  Net income of individual.
    Deductions, §40-18-15.
  Nonresidents.
    Computation of tax, §40-18-5.
    Exemptions.
      Personal exemptions
          allowed, §40-18-19.
    Persons and subjects taxable,
        §40-18-2.
    Presumptions of residents,
        §40-18-2.
  Notice.
    Assessment.
      Mailing of tax blank to be
          only notice required,
          §40-18-40.
      Setoff debt collection,
          §40-18-105.
      Taxpayer to be notified,
          §40-18-103.
  Oaths.
    Corporations.
      Statement furnished to
          department of revenue,
          §40-18-55.
  Oil and gas.
    Basis for depletion.
      Discovery value, §40-18-16.
    Corporations.
      Deductions allowed
          corporations.
        Allowance for depletion,
            §40-18-35.
    Deductions.
      Depletion allowance,
          §§40-18-15, 40-18-35.
  Ophthalmic materials.
    Dispensing or transferring
        not deemed to constitute
        sale subject to state sales
        tax, §40-23-1.
  Optional short form tax,
        §40-18-81.
  Other states.
    Credit for taxes paid on
        income from sources
        without the state,
        §40-18-21.
    Option of certain taxpayers
        to report and pay tax on
        basis of percentage of
        volume, §40-18-23.
    Returns.
      Inspection of returns by
          foreign state agents,
          §40-18-53.
  Partnerships.
    Generally, §40-18-24.

INCOME TAX—Cont'd
  Partnerships—Cont'd
    Net income of partnership.
      Computation, §40-18-24.
    Returns, §40-18-28.
    Tax liability for individual
        partners, §40-18-24.
  Payment.
    Computation of tax.
      Generally, §40-18-5.
      Corporations, §40-18-31.
    Defined, §40-18-1.
    Extension of time for
        payment, §40-18-42.
    Methods of payment,
        §40-18-42.
    Mistake or error.
      Tax paid through mistake
          or error, §40-18-43.
    Option of certain taxpayers
        to pay tax upon basis of
        percentage of volume,
        §40-18-23.
    Time and method of
        payment, §40-18-42.
    Voluntary advance payment,
        §40-18-42.
  Penalties.
    Declaration of estimated tax.
      Failure to file, §40-18-80.
    Fraudulent return,
        §40-18-49.
    Returns.
      Failure to make return,
          §§40-18-49, 40-18-50.
    Withholding tax.
      False information.
        Civil penalties,
            §40-29-75.
      Fraudulent withholding
          exemption certificate,
          §40-29-114.
  Penny trust fund.
    Refunds, §41-15A-4.
  Pensions.
    Corporations.
      Deductions allowed
          corporations.
        Contributions paid by
            employer to pension
            plans, §40-18-35.
    Deductions.
      Contributions paid by
          employer to pension
          plans, §§40-18-15,
          40-18-35.
    Exemptions, §40-18-19.
  Perjury.
    Affidavits.
      Making false affidavits,
          §40-18-52.
    Returns, §40-18-27.
  Personal exemptions,
        §40-18-19.
  Personal property.
    Installment method.
      Dealers in personal
          property, §40-18-44.
      Gain or loss upon
          disposition of
          installment
          obligations, §40-18-44.
  Political parties.
    Voluntary check off
        designations on returns,
        §40-18-146.
  Presumptions.
    Nonresidents, §40-18-5.
    Presumption of residents for
        income tax liability,
        §40-18-2.

INCOME TAX—Cont'd
Real property.
Amortization of ad valorem
tax, §40-18-41.
Basis of property.
Gain or loss, §40-18-6.
Deductions.
Gifts of real property for
public purposes,
§40-18-15.
Gain or loss, §§40-18-6 to
40-18-9.
Records.
Custody of records,
§40-18-48.
Setoff debt collection.
Confidentiality of
taxpayer's records,
§40-18-107.
Refunds.
Limitation on civil actions by
taxpayer, §40-18-47.
Mandamus.
Failure of department of
revenue to refund,
§40-18-43.
Mistake or error.
Refund of tax paid through
mistake or error,
§40-18-43.
Penny trust fund, §41-15A-4.
Setoff debt collection.
General provisions,
§§40-18-100 to
40-18-109. See within
this heading, "Setoff
debt collection."
Warrants.
Refund of tax paid through
mistake or error,
§40-18-43.
Withholding tax.
Refund to employer,
§40-18-77.
Religion.
Corporations.
Deductions allowed
corporations.
Contributions or gifts to
religious
institutions,
§40-18-35.
Deductions.
Contributions or gifts made
to religious
institutions.
Corporations, §40-18-35.
Individuals, §40-18-15.
Reports.
Information from source of
income.
Report to department of
revenue, §40-18-26.
Report from source.
Defined, §40-18-1.
Retirement.
Exemptions.
Military retirement
benefits, §40-18-20.
Retirement allowances,
§40-18-19.
Returns.
Accounts and accounting.
Return when accounting
period changes,
§40-18-30.
Check-off designations,
§§40-18-140 to 40-18-148.
Confidentiality, §40-18-52.
Contents, §40-18-27.
Corporations, §40-18-39.

INCOME TAX—Cont'd
Returns—Cont'd
Custody, §40-18-48.
Deductions.
Return required to claim
deduction, §40-18-27.
Divulging contents,
§40-18-52.
Extensions.
Department may grant
reasonable extension,
§40-18-27.
Failure to make.
Assessment of tax and
penalties, §40-18-49.
Collection of tax without
assessment, §40-18-46.
Penalties, §§40-18-49,
40-18-50.
False returns.
Collection of tax without
assessment, §40-18-46.
Federal returns.
Furnishing federal returns
to department,
§40-18-56.
Fiduciary returns, §40-18-29.
Fraud.
Collection of tax without
assessment, §40-18-46.
Individual taxpayer's
returns, §40-18-27.
Inspection of returns by
federal or foreign state
agents, §40-18-53.
Joint returns.
Joint and several liability
of husband and wife,
§40-18-27.
Innocent spouse,
§40-18-27.
Not public document,
§40-18-52.
Partnership returns.
Generally, §40-18-28.
Penalties.
Failure to make return,
§40-18-49.
Perjury, §40-18-27.
Preparers.
Name and address
required, §40-18-27.
Taxpayers unable to make
return, §40-18-27.
Trusts and trustees.
Responsibility of
fiduciaries to make
return, §40-18-25.
Voluntary check-off
designations.
Aged persons, §40-18-147.
Alabama nongame wildlife
program.
Appropriation,
§40-18-144.
Contribution designation
form, §40-18-143.
Legislative declarations
and intent,
§40-18-142.
Arts development fund.
Appropriation,
§40-18-141.
Contribution
designation,
§40-18-140.
Distribution of funds,
§40-18-141.
Established, §40-18-141.

INCOME TAX—Cont'd
Returns—Cont'd
Voluntary check-off
designations—Cont'd
Department of
conservation and
natural resources.
Construction of article,
§40-18-145.
Implementation,
§40-18-145.
Political parties.
Designated contribution
by individuals filing
state income tax
returns, §40-18-146.
Definition of political
party, §40-18-146.
Disposition of
contributions,
§40-18-146.
Veterans' home program.
Designation form,
§40-18-148.
Legislative intent,
§40-18-148.
When made, §40-18-27.
Failure to make return
within time specified,
§40-18-50.
Who must file return,
§40-18-27.
Rules and regulations.
Department of revenue to
promulgate, §40-18-57.
Salaries.
Withholding tax, §§40-18-70
to 40-18-80. See within
this heading,
"Withholding tax."
Sales.
Payment of tax on basis of
percentage of sales.
Option of taxpayers,
§40-18-23.
**Savings and loan
associations.**
Exemptions of certain
organizations, §40-18-32.
S corporations, §§40-18-160 to
40-18-176.
See CORPORATIONS.
Securities.
Deductions.
Stock bonus plans.
Contributions paid by
employer to or under
stock bonus plan,
§40-18-15.
Gain or loss.
Interest or other income
received from obligations
of United States,
§40-18-4.
Optional method for
returning as income
increases in redemption
value of securities
purchased at a discount,
§40-18-9.
Setoff debt collection.
Additional nature of remedy,
§40-18-101.
Appeals, §40-18-104.
Authorized, §40-18-102.
Claimant agency.
Defined, §40-18-100.
Confidentiality of
information.
Taxpayer records,
§40-18-107.

INCOME TAX—Cont'd
Setoff debt collection—Cont'd
Debts.
Defined, §40-18-100.
Minimum amount,
§40-18-102.
Definitions, §40-18-100.
Finalization of setoff,
§40-18-105.
Hearings.
Application for, §40-18-103.
Procedure, §40-18-104.
Notice, §40-18-105.
Taxpayer to be notified,
§40-18-103.
Priority of department over
claimant agencies,
§40-18-106.
Procedure, §40-18-103.
Hearings, §40-18-104.
Records.
Confidentiality of
taxpayer's records,
§40-18-107.
Refund.
Defined, §40-18-100.
Effect of setoff on refund,
§40-18-108.
Warrants.
Issuance by state treasurer
of separate warrants,
§40-18-109.
Short form, §40-18-81.
Solar energy tax credits.
Active solar energy tax
credits, §40-18-120.
Definitions.
Active solar energy tax
credits, §40-18-120.
Passive solar energy tax
credits, §40-18-121.
Passive solar energy tax
credits, §40-18-121.
State treasurer.
Disposition of collections,
§40-18-51.
**Surplus from proceeds of
tax.**
Reduction of ad valorem
state tax on real and
personal property,
§40-18-41.
Tables.
Optional short form tax,
§40-18-81.
Taxable year.
Defined, §40-18-1.
**Tax enforcement and
compliance act,** §§40-29-1
to 40-29-120.
See TAXATION.
Time.
Corporate returns.
When filed, §40-18-39.
Extension of time for
payment, §40-18-42.
Fiscal year.
Defined, §40-18-1.
Payment of tax.
Generally, §40-18-42.
Period of limitation upon
assessment and
collection, §40-18-45.
Returns.
Failure to make return
within time specified,
§40-18-50.
When made, §40-18-27.
Taxable year.
Defined, §40-18-1.

INCOME TAX—Cont'd
Trees and timber.
Corporations.
Deductions allowed
corporations.
Allowance for depletion,
§40-18-35.
Deductions.
Depletion allowance.
Corporations, §40-18-35.
Individuals, §40-18-15.
Trusts and trustees.
Application of tax, §40-18-25.
Computation of net income of
estate or trust,
§40-18-25.
Employers and employees.
Contributions to trust
made by employer,
§40-18-25.
Exemptions.
Trust income exempt from
taxation, §40-18-25.
Gain or loss.
Basis of property.
Gift or transfer in trust,
§40-18-6.
Payment of tax by fiduciary,
§40-18-25.
Penny trust fund.
Refunds, §41-15A-4.
Returns.
Responsibility of fiduciary
for making return,
§40-18-25.
United States.
Armed forces.
Persons and subjects
taxable, §40-18-3.
Bond issues.
Interest or other income
received from
obligations of United
States, §40-18-4.
Corporations.
Deductions allowed
corporations.
Taxes paid or accrued
imposed by authority
of United States,
§40-18-35.
Deductions.
Corporations, §40-18-35.
Individuals, §40-18-15.
Exemptions.
Interest upon obligations of
the United States,
§40-18-14.
Income of officers or agents,
§40-18-3.
Interest.
Interest received from
obligations of United
States, §40-18-4.
Persons and subjects taxable,
§40-18-3.
Returns.
Inspection of returns by
federal agents,
§40-18-53.
Securities.
Interest or other income
received from
obligations of United
States, §40-18-4.
United States code.
Meaning of specific
references to, §40-18-1.1.

INCOME TAX—Cont'd
**Voluntary check-off
designations on returns,**
§§40-18-140 to 40-18-148.
See within this heading,
"Returns."
**Wager winnings withholding
tax,** §§40-18-90, 40-18-91.
Wages.
Withholding tax, §§40-18-70
to 40-18-80. See within
this heading,
"Withholding tax."
Waiver.
Assessment.
When assessment made,
§40-18-46.
Warrants.
Mistake or error.
Taxes paid through
mistake or error.
Warrant for refund,
§40-18-43.
Water pollution.
Corporations.
Deductions allowed
corporations.
Amounts invested in
water pollution
control, §40-18-35.
Withholding tax, §§40-18-70
to 40-18-80.
Appeals.
Appeals by employer,
§40-18-74.
Certificates, §40-18-73.
False information.
Civil penalty, §40-29-75.
Number of withholding
exemptions claimed,
§40-18-73.
Computing taxable income,
§40-18-71.
Credit for tax withheld,
§40-18-78.
Declaration of estimated tax,
§§40-18-82 to 40-18-83.1.
Definitions, §40-18-70.
Employer.
Appeals, §40-18-74.
Defined, §40-18-70.
Duty of employer,
§40-18-71.
Estimation of wages,
§40-18-71.
Failure to make payments,
§40-18-74.
Liability for tax withheld,
§40-18-76.
Liens.
Property of employer
failing to withhold
or pay over subject
to lien, §40-18-74.
Refund to employer,
§40-18-77.
Estimated tax.
Declaration of estimated
tax, §§40-18-82 to
40-18-83.1.
Estimated wages.
Department may authorize
employers, §40-18-71.
Excluded and included
wages, §40-18-72.
Exemption certificates.
Employee to furnish
employer, §40-18-73.
Fraud.
False or fraudulent
statements, §40-18-80.

INCOME TAX—Cont'd
Withholding tax—Cont'd
Fraudulent withholding
exemption certificate.
Penalties, §40-29-114.
Included and excluded wages,
§40-18-72.
Liability of employer for tax
withheld, §40-18-76.
Liens.
Property of employer who
fails to withhold or
pay subject to lien,
§40-18-74.
Overpayment.
Crediting overpayments,
§40-18-79.
Payment.
Credit for overpayment,
§40-18-79.
Employer required to make
return and pay over to
department of revenue,
§40-18-74.
Failure of employer to
withhold or pay,
§40-18-74.
Penalties.
Generally, §40-18-80.
Refunds to employer,
§40-18-77.
Statement for employees,
§40-18-75.
Failure to furnish
statement, §40-18-80.
False or fraudulent
statements, §40-18-80.
Tables.
Preparation and furnishing
by commissioner of
revenue, §40-18-71.
Wager winnings.
Amount, §40-18-91.
Definitions, §40-18-90.
Failure to withhold,
§40-18-91.
Witnesses.
Failure to appear before the
department of revenue as
witness, §40-18-56.
Workmen's compensation.
Exemptions, §40-18-14.

INCOMPETENTS.
Curators, §§26-7A-1 to
26-7A-17.
See GUARDIAN AND
WARD.
Guardian and ward.
See GUARDIAN AND
WARD.
Mentally ill.
See MENTALLY ILL.
Minors.
See MINORS.
Veterans.
Guardianship and
commitment.
See VETERANS.

INCORPORATION.
General provisions.
See CORPORATIONS.
Municipal corporations.
See MUNICIPAL
CORPORATIONS.

INDECENCY.
General provisions.
See OBSCENITY.

INDECENT EXPOSURE.
Class A misdemeanor,
§13A-6-68.
Elements of crime, §13A-6-68.
Public lewdness,
§13A-12-130.

INDEPENDENT SCHOOL
DISTRICTS, §§16-1-6,
16-3-27.

INDEXES.
Circuit courts.
Fees for keeping indexes not
allowed, §12-19-98.
Fees.
Circuit courts.
Fees for keeping indexes
not allowed, §12-19-98.
General direct and reverse
indexes.
Maintenance by probate
judge for instruments
filed for record,
§12-13-43.
Registers.
General direct and reverse
indexes, §12-17-117.

INDIANS.
Aboriginal mounds,
earthworks and other
antiquities, §§41-3-1 to
41-3-6.
See HISTORY AND
ARCHIVES.
Indian affairs commission,
§§41-9-708 to 41-9-717.
Administration, §41-9-708.
Appointment, §41-9-708.
Appropriations.
Perpetual appropriation,
§41-9-715.
Audits.
Annual audit, §41-9-717.
Bonds, surety, §41-9-717.
Chairman, §41-9-708.
Compensation, §41-9-711.
Composition, §41-9-708.
Created, §41-9-708.
Duties, §41-9-710.
Established, §41-9-708.
Executive director, §41-9-713.
Fiscal record, §41-9-717.
Gifts.
Authority to receive,
§41-9-714.
Meetings, §41-9-712.
Powers and duties, §41-9-710.
Purpose, §41-9-709.
Quorum, §41-9-712.
Recognition of additional
Indian tribes, bands and
groups.
Power of commission,
§41-9-708.
Report.
Annual report, §41-9-716.
Terms of office, §41-9-708.
Vacancies in office,
§41-9-708.
Voting, §41-9-712.
Mowa Choctaw housing
authority, §§24-7-1 to
24-7-6.
See MOWA CHOCTAW
HOUSING
AUTHORITY.
Taxation.
Constitutional provisions,
Const. U. S., Art. I, §2;
Amendment XIV.

INDICES, §§12-13-43, 12-17-117,
12-19-98.

INDICTMENTS.
Advertising.
Unregistered securities.
Form of indictment,
§15-8-150.
Affrays.
Form of indictment,
§15-8-150.
Alcoholic beverages.
See ALCOHOLIC
BEVERAGES.
Alternative averments.
Different means or intents,
§15-8-50.
Different results of same act,
§15-8-51.
Joinder of offenses in same
count, §15-8-52.
Amendments.
Consent.
Dismissal of prosecution
for lack of consent,
§15-8-91.
Required, §15-8-90.
When allowed, §15-8-90.
Animals.
Cruelty to animals,
§15-8-150.
Offenses concerning animals.
Description of animal in
indictment, §15-8-34.
Wanton, malicious, etc.,
destruction of animals,
§15-8-150.
Arrest.
Arrest before indictment,
§§15-10-1 to 15-10-14.
See ARREST.
Arrest of judgment.
Preferring of new
indictments, §15-8-131.
Arrest without process when
defendant present after
indictment, §15-10-30.
Warrant of arrest twice
returned not found.
Withdrawal and filing of
indictment, ARJA,
Rule 16.
Arson.
Form of indictment,
§15-8-150.
Assault and battery.
Form of indictment,
§15-8-150.
Bigamy.
Form of indictment,
§15-8-150.
Bombs.
Setting off explosives near
dwellings.
Form of indictment,
§15-8-150.
Brands and marks.
Alterating, etc., brands and
marks.
Form of indictment,
§15-8-150.
Bribery.
Form of indictment,
§15-8-150.
Burglary.
Form of indictment,
§15-8-150.
Common law.
Offenses charged or described
as at common law,
§15-8-20.

INDICTMENTS—Cont'd

Conspiracy.
Form of indictment,
§15-8-150.

Constitution of Alabama.
Plea of guilty prior to
indictment, Const. Ala.,
amd. 37.
Proceeding against person by
information, Const. Ala.,
art. I, §8.

**Constitution of the United
States,** Const. U. S.,
Amendment V.

**Construction of words used
in indictment,** §15-8-5.
General terms used for
special statutory terms,
§15-8-22.
Statutory language
unnecessary, §15-8-21.

Contents, §15-8-3.
Allegation of unknown
means, §15-8-27.
Alternative averments,
§§15-8-50 to 15-8-52.
Animals.
Description of animal in
indictment, §15-8-34.
Charging of unknown facts,
§15-8-26.
Construction of words used,
§15-8-5.
Formal defects not fatal,
§15-8-4.
Forms, §15-8-150.
General terms used for
special statutory terms,
§15-8-22.
Intent to injure or defraud.
General allegation,
§15-8-29.
Judicial notice.
Matters not needing
statements, §15-8-32.
Legal presumptions need not
be stated, §15-8-32.
Manner of stating act
constituting offense,
§15-8-23.
Name of defendant unknown,
§15-8-28.
Offenses charged or described
as at common law,
§15-8-20.
Ownership of property.
How alleged, §15-8-33.
Statement of facts
constituting offense,
§15-8-25.
Statutory language
unnecessary, §15-8-21.
Time.
Statement of time,
§15-8-30.
Venue allegation
unnecessary, §15-8-31.

Contractors.
Violations of chapter.
Sufficiency of allegations,
§34-8-10.

Corporations.
Prosecution of corporations.
Docketing notice of
indictment, §10-7-1.
Issuance of notice of
indictment, §10-7-1.
Service of notice of
indictment, §10-7-2.

INDICTMENTS—Cont'd

Dead bodies.
Removing body from grave
for purposes of sale, etc.
Form of indictment,
§15-8-150.

Defects.
Formal defects in indictment
not fatal, §15-8-4.

Defined, §15-8-1.

Dentists.
Practice of dentistry without
license.
Form of indictment,
§15-8-150.

**Disclosure by district
attorney, grand juror,
etc., prior to arrest,**
§12-16-210.

Dismissal.
Amendment without consent
of defendant, §15-8-91.
Court permission required,
§15-8-130.
New indictments, §15-8-91.

District attorney.
Disclosure of indictments by
district attorney prior to
arrest of person indicted,
§12-16-210.

Drunkenness.
Form of indictment for public
drunkenness, §15-8-150.

Elections.
Betting on elections.
Form of indictment,
§15-8-150.
Illegal voting.
Form of indictment,
§15-8-150.

Embezzlement.
Form of indictment,
§15-8-150.

Endorsement, §§12-16-204,
15-8-70.
Prosecutor's name,
§12-16-205.
Where no prosecutor appears,
§12-16-205.

Executions.
Resisting officer in executing
process.
Form of indictment,
§15-8-150.

Explosives.
Unlawfully setting off
explosives.
Form of indictment,
§15-8-150.

Facts constituting offense.
How stated, §15-8-25.

Fees.
Receipt of unauthorized
official fees.
Form of indictment,
§15-8-150.

Felonies.
Indictable offenses, §15-8-2.

Filing.
Endorsements, §15-8-70.
Leave to reinstate, §15-8-71.
Withdrawal, §15-8-71.

Forests and forestry.
Unauthorized cutting,
§9-13-61.
Unauthorized purchases,
§9-13-61.

Forgery and counterfeiting.
Form of indictment,
§15-8-150.

INDICTMENTS—Cont'd

Forgery and counterfeiting
—Cont'd
Instrument destroyed or
withheld, §15-8-35.

Forms.
Enumerated, §15-8-150.
Generally, §15-8-150.
Manner of stating act
constituting offense,
§15-8-23.
Sufficiency, §15-8-150.
Use of analogous forms,
§15-8-150.

Fraud.
Form of indictment,
§15-8-150.
General allegation of intent
to defraud, §15-8-29.

Gambling.
Federal wagering
occupational tax stamp.
Production of stamp
warrants indictment or
information,
§13A-12-91.
Form of indictment,
§15-8-150.

Grand jury, §§12-16-203 to
12-16-205, 12-16-210.
See GRAND JURY.

Guilty plea.
Prior to indictment, Const.
Ala., amd. 37.

Homicide.
Form of indictment,
§15-8-150.

Impeachment.
Indictment of accused,
§36-11-24.

Incest.
Form of indictment,
§15-8-150.

Injury.
General allegation of intent
to injure, §15-8-29.

Inspections.
Limitations on inspection
before defendant
arrested, §15-8-70.

Intent.
General allegation of intent
to injure or defraud,
§15-8-29.

Judicial notice.
Matters not needing
statement in indictment,
§15-8-32.

Kidnapping.
Form of indictment,
§15-8-150.

Larceny.
Form of indictment,
§15-8-150.

Legal presumptions.
Unnecessary to state in
indictment, §15-8-32.

Libel.
Form of indictment,
§15-8-150.
Indictment for libel.
Contents, §13A-11-162.
Reports of return of
indictments.
Privileged information,
§13A-11-161.

Livestock.
Cattle theft.
Form of indictment,
§15-8-150.

INDICTMENTS—Cont'd
Lost, mislaid, mutilated or destroyed indictments.
Form of entry of record, §15-8-110.
Preferring of new indictments, §15-8-110.
Utilization of record copy, §15-8-111.
Lotteries.
Form of indictment for carrying on illegal lottery, §15-8-150.
Mayhem.
Form of indictment, §15-8-150.
Military affairs.
Right of national guard members under indictment to change of venue of trial, §31-2-118.
Misdemeanors.
Findings of indictments for misdemeanors, §12-16-203.
Indictable offenses, §15-8-2.
Names.
Amendment of incorrect names, §15-8-90.
When defendant's name unknown, §15-8-28.
Necessity, Const. U. S., Amendment V.
Offenses which are indictable, §15-8-2.
Ownership.
Alleging ownership of property, §15-8-33.
Perjury.
Allegations requiring, §15-8-36.
Form of indictment, §15-8-150.
Inconsistent statements.
Single count indictment, §13A-10-104.
Physicians.
Practice of medicine without license.
Form of indictment, §15-8-150.
Plea of guilty.
Prior to indictment, Const. Ala., amd. 37.
Pleas in abatement.
Objection to indictment, §15-15-40.
Presentation.
Grand jury to present to court, §15-8-70.
Presumptions.
Legal presumption need not be stated, §15-8-32.
Property.
Alleging ownership of property, §15-8-33.
Public place.
Alleging act done in public place, §15-8-24.
Quashing.
Court permission required, §15-8-130.
Preferring of new indictments, §15-8-131.
Rape.
Form of indictment, §15-8-150.
Receiving stolen property.
Form of indictment, §15-8-150.

INDICTMENTS—Cont'd
Records.
Arrest of judgment.
Preferring of new indictments, §15-8-131.
Clerk to record returned indictments, §15-8-72.
Lost, mislaid, mutilated or destroyed indictments, §15-8-110.
Utilization of record copy, §15-8-111.
Photographing or photostating indictments, §15-8-72.
Quashing indictment.
Preferring of new indictments, §15-8-131.
Return.
Recording and safekeeping, §15-8-72.
Robbery.
Form of indictment, §15-8-150.
Rules of criminal procedure, ARCrP Rules 15.1 to 15.5.
Securities.
Advertising unregistered securities.
Form of indictment, §15-8-150.
Seduction.
Form of indictment, §15-8-150.
Service of process.
Resisting officer in executing process.
Form of indictment, §15-8-150.
Signature.
Grand jury foreman to sign, §12-16-204.
Obtaining signature by false pretenses.
Form of indictment, §15-8-150.
Slander.
Form of indictment, §15-8-150.
Subornation of perjury.
Allegations required, §15-8-36.
Time.
Statement of time, §15-8-30.
Trespass.
Unlawful entry after warning.
Form of indictment, §15-8-150.
Unknown facts.
Charging unknown facts, §15-8-26.
Unknown means.
Allegation of unknown means, §15-8-27.
Venue.
Allegation of venue unnecessary, §15-8-31.
Warrant of arrest returned not found.
Withdrawal and filing, ARJA, Rule 16.
Weapons.
Carrying weapons unlawfully, §13A-11-55.
Unlawful sale of weapons.
Form of indictment, §15-8-150.
Unlawful use of weapons.
Form of indictment, §15-8-150.

INDICTMENTS—Cont'd
Where offense committed.
Allegation unnecessary, §15-8-31.
Withdrawal, §15-8-71.
Warrant of arrest twice returned not found.
Withdrawal and filing of indictment, ARJA, Rule 16.
Words.
Construction of words used, §15-8-5.
General terms used for specific statutory terms, §15-8-22.
Public place.
Alleging act done in public place, §15-8-24.
Statutory language unnecessary, §15-8-21.

INDIGENT PERSONS.
Appeals.
Appointment and compensation of counsel, §15-12-22.
Calculation of rates, §15-12-24.
Criminal cases.
Providing record on appeal, §§12-22-190 to 12-22-201.
See APPEALS.
In forma pauperis proceedings, ARAP, Rule 24.
Forms, ARAP, Form 15.
Arraignment.
Matters affecting representation to be ascertained before arraignment, §15-12-20.
Attorneys at law.
Defense of indigents, §§15-12-20 to 15-12-25.
Public defenders, §§15-12-40 to 15-12-46.
See PUBLIC DEFENDERS.
Blind persons.
Assistance to needy blind persons, §§38-5-1 to 38-5-7.
See BLIND PERSONS.
Burial.
Counties.
Burial of persons dying with no estate, §38-8-2.
Cancer.
Financial aid for indigents, §22-13-2.
Free examinations, §22-13-8.
Plan for care of indigents, §22-13-1.
Capital punishment.
Appointment of experienced counsel to represent indigent defendants, §13A-5-54.
Common carriers.
Free tickets, §37-1-15.
Community action agencies, §§11-96-1 to 11-96-6.
See COMMUNITY ACTION AGENCIES.
Constitution of Alabama.
Counties to provide for maintenance of the poor, Const. Ala., art. IV, §88.

INDIGENT PERSONS—Cont'd
Constitution of Alabama
　—Cont'd
　Hospital care and treatment.
　　Use of certain special
　　　county taxes, Const.
　　　Ala., amd. 125.
Counties.
　Counties to provide for
　　maintenance of the poor,
　　Const. Ala., art. IV, §88.
　County commissions.
　　Powers and duties of
　　　county commissions,
　　　§11-3-11.
　Departments and boards of
　　human resources,
　　§§38-2-1 to 38-2-13.
　　See WELFARE.
　Hospital care and treatment.
　　Use of certain special
　　　county taxes, Const.
　　　Ala., amd. 125.
　Hospital service program for
　　indigents, §§22-21-210 to
　　22-21-227.
　　See HOSPITALS.
　Relief and support.
　　Actions.
　　　Persons owning property
　　　　and supported at
　　　　public charge,
　　　　§38-1-5.
　　Burials.
　　　Persons dying with no
　　　　estate, etc., §38-8-2.
　　County commission.
　　　Powers generally,
　　　　§§38-8-1, 38-8-3.
　　Death.
　　　Burial of persons dying
　　　　with no estate,
　　　　§38-8-2.
　　Disbursement of funds,
　　　§38-8-3.
　　Persons owning property
　　　and supported at
　　　public charge.
　　　Civil actions, §38-1-5.
　　Powers of county
　　　commission, §§38-8-1,
　　　38-8-3.
Criminal law and procedure.
　Appeals.
　　Providing records on
　　　appeals for indigents,
　　　§§12-22-190 to
　　　12-22-201.
　　See APPEALS.
　Defense of indigents.
　　General provisions,
　　　§§15-12-1 to 15-12-46.
　　See within this
　　　heading, "Defense of
　　　indigents."
　　Public defenders,
　　　§§15-12-40 to 15-12-46.
　　See PUBLIC
　　　DEFENDERS.
Default.
　Reimbursement of court
　　appointed attorneys,
　　§15-12-25.
Defense of indigents, ARJA,
　Rule 8.
　Annual appropriation from
　　fair trial tax fund for
　　payment of expenses,
　　§12-19-252.

INDIGENT PERSONS—Cont'd
Defense of indigents—Cont'd
　Appointed counsel.
　　Appeals.
　　　Appointment and
　　　　compensation,
　　　　§15-12-22.
　　　Calculation of rates,
　　　　§15-12-24.
　　Appointment.
　　　Appeals, §15-12-22.
　　　Determination of
　　　　indigency, §15-12-4.
　　　Matters to be ascertained
　　　　prior to
　　　　arraignment,
　　　　§15-12-20.
　　　Postconviction
　　　　proceedings,
　　　　§15-12-23.
　　　Trial court, §15-12-21.
　　Compensation.
　　　Appeals, §15-12-22.
　　　Calculation of rates,
　　　　§15-12-24.
　　　Criminal psychopath
　　　　release proceedings,
　　　　§15-16-65.
　　　Generally, §15-12-6.
　　　Postconviction
　　　　proceedings,
　　　　§15-12-23.
　　　Reimbursement by
　　　　defendant,
　　　　§15-12-25.
　　　Default, §15-12-25.
　　　Trial court, §15-12-21.
　　Defined, §15-12-1.
　　Postconviction proceedings.
　　　Appointment and
　　　　compensation,
　　　　§15-12-23.
　　Public defenders.
　　　Division not to exclude
　　　　establishment of
　　　　parallel appointed
　　　　counsel system,
　　　　§15-12-46.
　　Trial court.
　　　Appointment and
　　　　compensation,
　　　　§15-12-21.
　Capital punishment cases.
　　Appointment of
　　　experienced counsel,
　　　§13A-5-54.
　Circuit indigent defense
　　commissions, §15-12-4.
　Criminal psychopath release
　　proceedings, §15-16-65.
　Definitions, §15-12-1.
　Determination of indigency,
　　§15-12-5.
　Fair trial tax fund.
　　Annual appropriation from
　　　fund, §12-19-252.
　　Withdrawals to pay
　　　expenses of
　　　administering chapter,
　　　§15-12-24.1.
　Indigent defendant.
　　Defined, §15-12-1.
　Indigent defense system.
　　Defined, §15-12-1.
　　Determination as to
　　　systems for various
　　　courts, §15-12-2.
　　Presiding circuit judges to
　　　administer system
　　　within circuits,
　　　§15-12-3.

INDIGENT PERSONS—Cont'd
Defense of indigents—Cont'd
　Indigent defense system
　　—Cont'd
　　Rules and regulations,
　　　§15-12-3.
　　Investigation of indigency,
　　　§15-12-5.
　　Affidavit of substantial
　　　hardship, §15-12-5.
　Juveniles.
　　Appointed counsel.
　　　Child court, §15-12-21.
　　　Postconviction
　　　　proceedings,
　　　　§15-12-23.
　　Compensation.
　　　Calculation of rates,
　　　　§15-12-24.
　　　Postconviction
　　　　proceedings,
　　　　§15-12-23.
　Public defender.
　　Defined, §15-12-1.
　　General provisions,
　　　§§15-12-40 to 15-12-46.
　　See PUBLIC
　　　DEFENDERS.
　System, §§15-12-1 to 15-12-3.
Definitions.
　Defense of indigents,
　　§15-12-1.
　Indigent defendant, §15-12-1.
Desertion and nonsupport.
　Representation of defendants
　　prior to arraignment.
　　Matters to be ascertained
　　　by trial judges,
　　　§15-12-20.
Gifts.
　Inter vivos gifts of assets.
　　Void if donor left without
　　　means of support,
　　　§35-1-2.
Habeas corpus.
　Appointment and
　　compensation of counsel,
　　§15-12-23.
　Calculation of rates,
　　§15-12-24.
Health.
　Responsibility for health
　　care, §§22-21-290 to
　　22-21-297.
　See HEALTH.
Health care authorities.
　Powers of authority,
　　§22-21-318.
Hospitals.
　Appropriations for indigent
　　persons in hospitals,
　　§22-21-2.
　Service program for
　　indigents, §§22-21-210 to
　　22-21-227.
　　See HOSPITALS.
　Use of certain special county
　　taxes, Const. Ala., amd.
　　125.
Investigations.
　Defense of indigents.
　　Investigation of indigency,
　　　§15-12-5.
Life sentence without parole.
　Appointment of experienced
　　counsel, §13A-5-54.
Mentally ill.
　Release of criminal
　　psychopaths.
　　Appointment of counsel,
　　　§15-16-65.

INDIGENT PERSONS—Cont'd

Municipal corporations.
Counties.
Establishment, aid, etc., of poorhouses, etc., in counties, §11-47-134.
Hospitals.
Appropriation of funds, §11-47-133.
Municipal courts.
Defense services.
Provision of indigent defense services, §12-14-9.
Paternity.
Representation of defendants prior to arraignment.
Matters to be ascertained by trial judges, §15-12-20.
Public defenders, §§15-12-40 to 15-12-46.
See PUBLIC DEFENDERS.
Public welfare, §§38-1-1 to 38-8-3.
See WELFARE.
Railroads.
Free tickets, §37-1-15.
Relief.
Counties, §§38-8-1 to 38-8-3.
General provisions.
See WELFARE.
Rules and regulations.
Indigent defense systems, §15-12-1.
Support.
Counties, §§38-8-1 to 38-8-3.
General provisions.
See WELFARE.
Welfare.
Counties.
Relief and support of poor persons by counties, §§38-8-1 to 38-8-3.
General provisions.
See WELFARE.

INDORSEMENTS.
See ENDORSEMENTS.

INDUSTRIAL ACCESS ROADS AND BRIDGES.
Authority to incorporate, §23-6-3.
Bond issues.
Disposition, §23-6-9.
Generally, §23-6-8.
Refunding bonds, §23-6-9.
Construction.
Account, §23-6-9.
Authority of state highway department, §23-6-2.
Contracts, §23-6-9.
Contracts.
Construction, §23-6-9.
Corporation.
Authority to incorporate, §23-6-3.
Bond issues, §23-6-8.
Disposition, §23-6-9.
Certificate of incorporation, §23-6-5.
Corporate powers, §23-6-7.
Dissolution, §23-6-12.
Members, §23-6-6.
Officers and directors, §23-6-6.
Powers.
Generally, §23-6-7.
Proceeding to incorporate, §23-6-4.
Revenues, §23-6-10.

INDUSTRIAL ACCESS ROADS AND BRIDGES—Cont'd
Definitions, §23-6-1.
Legislative intent, §23-6-2.
Revenues, §23-6-10.
Disbursement, §23-6-11.
State highway department.
Authority, §23-6-2.
State treasurer.
Disbursement of funds, §23-6-11.

INDUSTRIAL ALCOHOL.
Analysis.
Taking of samples for chemical analysis, §28-5-10.
Beverages.
Removal of denatured alcohol from industrial alcohol plant for purpose of recovering alcohol for beverage purposes, §28-5-8.
Sale, transportation, etc., of denatured alcohol rendered unfit for beverage use, §28-5-7.
Bonds, surety.
Collection of penalties on bonds, §28-5-9.
Permittees, §28-5-4.
Definitions, §28-5-1.
Denaturing plants.
Permits, §§28-5-2 to 28-5-13.
Distilleries, §§28-5-2 to 28-5-13.
Enforcement of chapter.
Burden of proof as to existence of federal permit, §28-5-13.
Government to supervise, §28-5-9.
Obstruction of enforcement, §28-5-12.
Penalties for violations, §28-5-14.
Examinations, §28-5-10.
Fees.
Generally, §28-5-11.
Forgery of permits, §28-5-12.
Governor.
Enforcement of chapter, §28-5-9.
Notice of changes in officers, directors, etc., of permittees, §28-5-11.
Inspections, §28-5-10.
Fees, §28-5-11.
Manufacture, §28-5-5.
Transportation of industrial alcohol manufactured and sold, §28-5-6.
Notice.
Permittees to notify governor of changes in officers, directors, etc., §28-5-11.
Obstruction of enforcement of chapter, §28-5-12.
Penalties.
Violations of chapter, §28-5-14.
Permits for operation of distilleries and denaturing plants.
Abatement of plant operating without permit, §28-5-9.
Applicants.
Documents to be filed by applicants, §28-5-3.

INDUSTRIAL ALCOHOL—Cont'd
Permits for operation of distilleries and denaturing plants—Cont'd
Applicants—Cont'd
False statements in applications, §28-5-12.
Authorization, §28-5-2.
Bonds of permittees, §28-5-4.
Collection of penalties on bonds by governor, §28-5-9.
Documents to be filed by applicants, §28-5-3.
False statements in applications, §28-5-12.
Federal permits.
Burden of proof as to existence of federal permit, §28-5-13.
Forgery, §28-5-12.
Procedure for granting, §28-5-2.
Suspension or revocation, §28-5-9.
Violation of terms of permits, §28-5-12.
Recovering alcohol for beverage purposes, §28-5-8.
Regulations.
Promulgation, §28-5-9.
Reports.
Requirements, §28-5-9.
Sales, §28-5-5.
Alcohol not authorized by federal or state permit, §28-5-7.
Denatured alcohol rendered unfit for beverage use, §28-5-7.
Transportation of industrial alcohol sold, §28-5-6.
Samples.
Taking of samples for chemical analysis, §28-5-10.
Transportation.
Alcohol not authorized by federal or state permit, §28-5-7.
Denatured alcohol rendered unfit for beverage use, §28-5-7.
Unfit for beverage use.
Sale, transportation, etc., of denatured alcohol rendered unfit for beverage use, §28-5-7.
Violations of chapter, §§28-5-9 to 28-5-14. See within this heading, "Enforcement of chapter."

INDUSTRIAL DEVELOPMENT ADVISORY BOARD.
Bureau of publicity and information.
Cooperation of director of bureau with board, §41-9-188.
Compensation for expenses, §41-9-185.
Composition of members, §41-9-185.
Duties, §41-9-186.
Established, §41-9-185.

INDUSTRIAL DEVELOPMENT ADVISORY BOARD —Cont'd

Expenses.
Reimbursement, §41-9-185.
Industrial development board.
Transfer of powers, functions, etc., of industrial development board, §41-9-187.
Meetings, §41-9-185.
Members and officers.
Generally, §41-9-185.
Oaths.
Members' oath, §41-9-185.
Officers, §41-9-185.
Publicity.
Bureau of publicity and information.
Cooperation of director of bureau with board, §41-9-188.
Quorum, §41-9-185.
Removal of members, §41-9-185.
Rules and regulations, §41-9-185.
Seals and sealed instruments, §41-9-185.
Terms of members, §41-9-185.
Transfer of powers, functions, etc., of industrial development board, §41-9-187.

INDUSTRIAL DEVELOPMENT AUTHORITY.

Airport facilities.
Exercise of powers granted to airport authorities, §41-10-26.1.
Board of directors, §41-10-25.
Bond issues, §§41-10-27 to 41-10-31.
Authorization for issuance and sale, §41-10-27.
Denominations, §41-10-28.
Disposition of proceeds from sale, §41-10-29.
Execution, §41-10-28.
Exemption from taxation, §41-10-28.
Form, §41-10-28.
Investments in bonds, §41-10-28.
Liability upon bonds, §41-10-28.
Negotiability, §41-10-28.
Payment, §41-10-31.
Pledge of tax receipts for payment, §41-10-30.
Pledges of certain funds as security for payment, §41-10-28.
Private activity bonds.
State ceiling, §§41-10-35 to 41-10-43.
See BOND ISSUES.
Public hearing of consent of department of finance, etc., not prerequisite to issuance, §41-10-28.
Records.
Payment of bonds, §41-10-31.
Refunding bonds, §41-10-28.
Disposition of proceeds from sale, §41-10-29.

INDUSTRIAL DEVELOPMENT AUTHORITY—Cont'd

Bond issues—Cont'd
Sale, §41-10-28.
Authorized, §41-10-27.
Disposition of proceeds from sale, §41-10-29.
Security for deposits.
Use as security for deposits of funds of state, §41-10-28.
Taxation.
Exemption from taxation, §41-10-28.
Terms, §41-10-28.
Construction of article, §41-10-21.
County industrial development authorities, §§11-92A-1 to 11-92A-22.
See COUNTY INDUSTRIAL DEVELOPMENT AUTHORITIES.
Definitions, §41-10-20.
Directors, §41-10-25.
Dissolution, §41-10-32.
Fees.
Secretary of state to receive no fees, §41-10-24.
Title to property of authority to vest in state upon dissolution, §41-10-32.
Evidence.
Proceedings of board of directors.
Admissibility in evidence, §41-10-25.
Fees.
Dissolution.
Secretary of state to receive no fees, §41-10-24.
Incorporation.
Secretary of state to receive no fees, §41-10-24.
Grants.
Terms and conditions of grants, §41-10-27.
Incorporation.
Application for incorporation, §41-10-23.
Authorization for incorporation, §41-10-22.
Certificate of incorporation.
Issuance, §41-10-24.
Recordation, §41-10-24.
Fees.
Secretary of state to receive no fees, §41-10-24.
Procedure for incorporation, §41-10-22.
Secretary of state.
Application for incorporation, §41-10-23.
Certificate of incorporation, §41-10-24.
Fees.
Prohibited, §41-10-24.
Legislative findings of fact and declaration of intent, §41-10-21.
Members, §41-10-25.
Officers, §41-10-25.

INDUSTRIAL DEVELOPMENT AUTHORITY—Cont'd

Powers.
Airport facilities.
Exercise of powers granted to airport authorities, §41-10-26.1.
Generally, §41-10-26.
Property.
Dissolution of authority.
Title to property to vest in state, §41-10-32.
Recordation.
Application for incorporation, §41-10-23.
Certificate of incorporation, §41-10-24.
Records.
Payment of bonds, §41-10-31.
Secretary of state.
Incorporation, §§41-10-23, 41-10-24.
Sinking fund.
Payment of bonds.
Pledge and appropriation of certain tax receipts, §41-10-30.
Taxation.
Bond issues.
Exemption from taxation, §41-10-28.

INDUSTRIAL DEVELOPMENT BOARD.

Ancillary facilities, §§11-54-120 to 11-54-123.
County boards, §§11-20-30 to 11-20-50.
See COUNTIES.
Industrial development advisory board.
General provisions, §§41-9-185 to 41-9-188.
Municipal boards, §§11-54-80 to 11-54-101.
See MUNICIPAL CORPORATIONS.
Transfer of powers, functions, etc., §41-9-187.

INDUSTRIAL DEVELOPMENT CORPORATIONS, §§10-4-130 to 10-4-152.

Agents.
Appointment, §10-4-136.
Powers of corporation, §10-4-133.
Articles of incorporation, §10-4-131.
Amendment, §10-4-149.
Bond issues.
Evidencing loans to corporation by members, §10-4-140.
Interest, §10-4-140.
Rights to bonds, §10-4-139.
Bylaws.
Adoption, §10-4-132.
Contracts.
Powers of corporation, §10-4-133.
Counties.
Occupational license tax, §10-4-144.
Credit of state.
Not to be pledged, §10-4-141.
Debentures.
Evidencing loans to corporation by members, §10-4-140.

INDUSTRIAL DEVELOPMENT CORPORATIONS—Cont'd

Definitions, §10-4-130.
Depositories.
Deposit of funds in designated depository, §10-4-146.
Directors.
Addresses, §10-4-131.
Duties, §10-4-136.
Election, §10-4-136.
Losses.
Responsibility for losses, §10-4-136.
Members.
Election of directors by members, §10-4-136.
Number, §10-4-136.
Original directors, §10-4-131.
Powers, §10-4-136.
Responsibility for losses, §10-4-136.
Stock and stockholders.
Election of directors, §10-4-136.
Term, §10-4-136.
Vacancies, §10-4-136.
Voting.
Cumulative voting prohibited, §10-4-131.
Dissolution, §10-4-151.
Duration of corporation, §10-4-150.
Employees.
Powers of corporation, §10-4-133.
Examinations.
Annual examination, §10-4-147.
Fees.
Incorporation, §10-4-131.
Fiscal year, §10-4-148.
Funds.
Deposit in designated depository, §10-4-146.
Incorporation.
Articles of incorporation, §10-4-131.
Authority to incorporate, §10-4-131.
Fees, §10-4-131.
First meeting, §10-4-132.
Generally, §10-4-131.
Licenses.
Occupational license taxes, §10-4-144.
Loans.
Members.
Loan limits, §10-4-140.
Loans to corporation by members, §10-4-140.
When not obligated to make loans to corporation, §10-4-135.
Powers of corporations, §10-4-133.
Losses.
Responsibility of officers and directors, §10-4-136.
Marengo county.
Establishment of industrial development corporation, Const. Ala., amd. 468.
Meetings.
Annual meeting, §10-4-136.
First meeting, §10-4-132.
Members.
Application for membership, §10-4-134.

INDUSTRIAL DEVELOPMENT CORPORATIONS—Cont'd

Members—Cont'd
Directors.
Election of directors by members, §10-4-136.
Loans.
Loan limits, §10-4-140.
Loans to corporation by members, §10-4-140.
When not obligated to make loans to corporation, §10-4-135.
Meetings, §§10-4-132, 10-4-136.
Notice of withdrawal, §10-4-135.
Powers, §10-4-138.
Rights to shares, bonds, securities, etc., §10-4-139.
Stock and stockholders.
Amount of capital stock.
Members authorized to acquire, §10-4-139.
Voting, §10-4-138.
When membership effective, §10-4-134.
Withdrawal, §10-4-135.
Mortgages and deeds of trusts.
Powers of corporations, §10-4-133.
Taking of security by mortgage, §10-4-142.
Municipal corporations.
Occupational license taxes, §10-4-144.
Notes.
Evidencing loans to corporation by members, §10-4-130.
Office.
Location of principal office, §10-4-131.
Officers.
Appointment, §10-4-136.
Duties, §10-4-136.
Enumeration, §10-4-136.
Powers of corporation, §10-4-133.
Responsibility for losses, §10-4-136.
Organization, §10-4-132.
Powers of corporation, §10-4-133.
Property.
Powers of corporations, §10-4-133.
Security.
Taking of security by mortgage or otherwise, §10-4-142.
Proxies.
Stock and stockholders, §10-4-138.
Purpose of corporation, §10-4-131.
Records.
First meeting, §10-4-132.
Reports.
Annual reports, §10-4-147.
Secretary of state.
Approval of articles of corporation, §10-4-131.
Securities.
Applicability of laws regulating securities, §10-4-152.

INDUSTRIAL DEVELOPMENT CORPORATIONS—Cont'd

State.
Credit of state not to be pledged, §10-4-141.
State development company.
Corporation to be state development company, §10-4-137.
Stock and stockholders.
Applicability of laws regulating securities, §10-4-152.
Articles of incorporation.
Provisions in articles pertaining to stock, §10-4-131.
Directors.
Election of directors by stockholders, §10-4-136.
Members.
Amount of capital stock.
Members authorized to acquire, §10-4-139.
Powers of corporations, §10-4-133.
Powers of stockholders, §10-4-138.
Proxies, §10-4-138.
Rights to shares, §10-4-139.
Voting, §10-4-138.
Surplus.
Earned surplus.
Setting apart of earned surplus, §10-4-145.
Taxation.
Credits, §10-4-143.
Exemptions, §10-4-143.
Occupational license taxes, §10-4-144.
Privileges, §10-4-143.

INDUSTRIAL PARKS,
§§11-92-1 to 11-92-11.
Acquisition.
Powers of counties and municipalities, §11-92-3.
Procedures, §11-92-4.
Applicability of other law, §11-92-11.
Construction of chapter, §11-92-2.
Counties.
General provisions, §§11-23-1 to 11-23-8.
See COUNTIES.
Powers of counties, §11-92-3.
Definitions, §11-92-1.
Development.
Powers of counties and municipalities, §11-92-3.
Procedures, §11-92-4.
Effect of other law, §11-92-11.
Intent of legislature, §11-92-2.
Investments.
Warrants.
Fiduciaries, §11-92-9.
Municipal corporations.
Acquisition and development of lands for industrial parks, §§11-54-1 to 11-54-4.
Powers generally, §11-92-3.

INDUSTRIAL PARKS—Cont'd
Property.
　Acquisition and development.
　　Powers of counties and
　　　municipalities,
　　　§11-92-3.
　Sale price, §11-92-5.
　Transfer of by municipalities
　　or counties, §11-92-5.
Resolutions.
　Acquisition and development
　　of parks, §11-92-4.
Sales.
　Property.
　　Municipalities or counties,
　　　§11-92-5.
Warrants, §§11-92-6 to
　11-92-10.
　Denominations, §11-92-6.
　Disposition of proceeds,
　　§11-92-6.
　Form, §11-92-6.
　Interest.
　　Amount, §11-92-6.
　　Payment.
　　　Security, §11-92-7.
　Investments.
　　Fiduciaries, §11-92-9.
　Issuance.
　　Deemed audit and
　　　allowance of claims,
　　　§11-92-10.
　　Effect, §11-92-10.
　Liability of counties or
　　municipalities, §11-92-6.
　Payment of principal and
　　interest.
　　Security, §11-92-7.
　Proceeds.
　　Disposition, §11-92-6.
　Refunding warrants,
　　§11-92-8.
　Security.
　　Payment of principal and
　　　interest, §11-92-7.
　Terms, §11-92-6.

INDUSTRIAL RELATIONS.
Department.
　General provisions, §§25-2-1
　　to 25-2-26.
　See LABOR.

**INDUSTRIAL REVENUE
　BONDS,** §§8-6-110 to
　8-6-122.
Advisory council, §8-6-114.
Appeals.
　Appeals to securities
　　commission, §8-6-117.
Approval.
　Director of securities
　　commission, §8-6-116.
　Judicial validation
　　proceedings, §8-6-119.
　Representation that bonds
　　have been approved
　　prohibited, §8-6-120.
　Securities commission,
　　§8-6-118.
Article remedial, §8-6-122.
Certificate of notification,
　§8-6-120.
Definitions, §8-6-110.
**Director of securities
　commission.**
　Action by director upon
　　receipt of notification,
　　§8-6-116.
　Powers, §8-6-112.
　Stop orders, §8-6-116.

**INDUSTRIAL REVENUE
　BONDS**—Cont'd
Intent to issue bonds.
　Notifications of intent,
　　§8-6-115.
Legislative findings, §8-6-111.
Notice.
　Action by director upon
　　receipt of notification,
　　§8-6-116.
　Certificate of notification,
　　§8-6-120.
　Intent to issue bonds.
　　Notifications of intent,
　　　§8-6-115.
Penalties.
　Criminal penalties, §8-6-121.
Purpose of article, §8-6-111.
Repeals.
　Certain statutes not
　　repealed, §8-6-122.
Securities commission.
　Appeals or references to
　　securities commission,
　　§8-6-117.
　Powers, §8-6-113.
　Proceedings before
　　commission, §8-6-118.
Stop orders, §8-6-116.
　Appeals or references to
　　securities commission,
　　§8-6-117.
Validation.
　Judicial validation
　　proceedings, §8-6-119.
Violations.
　Criminal penalties, §8-6-121.

INDUSTRIAL SCHOOLS.
**Alabama boys' industrial
　school, Alabama training
　school for girls and
　Alabama industrial
　school,** §§44-1-3 to 44-1-7.
　See YOUTH SERVICES.

INEBRIATES.
General provisions.
　See DRUNKENNESS.
Waste of estate.
　General provisions, §§6-6-520
　　to 6-6-527.
　See WASTE.

INFANTILE BLINDNESS.
Notifiable diseases,
　§§22-11A-1 to 22-11A-38.
　See DISEASES.

INFANTS.
　See MINORS.

INFECTIOUS DISEASES.
**Notifiable diseases
　generally,** §§22-11A-1 to
　22-11A-38.
　See DISEASES.
Quarantine.
　See QUARANTINE.

INFLUENZA.
Notifiable diseases,
　§§22-11A-1 to 22-11A-38.
　See DISEASES.

INFORMATIONS.
Constitution of Alabama.
　Proceedings against person
　　by information, Const.
　　Ala., art. I, §8; amd. 37.
Guilty plea to information,
　§§15-15-20 to 15-15-26.
　See CRIMINAL LAW AND
　　PROCEDURE.

INFORMATIONS—Cont'd
Impeachment, §§36-11-7,
　36-11-8.

INFORMERS.
Abatement of actions,
　§6-5-461.
Forests and forestry.
　Violation of chapter.
　　Fees, §9-13-24.
Limitation of actions.
　Actions qui tam. §6-2-38.

**INGLENOOK,
　MUNICIPALITY OF.**
Property tax, Const. Ala.,
　amd. 8.

INHERITANCES.
Wills, §§43-8-1 to 43-8-298.
　See WILLS.

INHERITANCE TAX, §§40-15-1
　to 40-15-21.
　See ESTATE AND
　　INHERITANCE TAX.

**INITIATIVE AND
　REFERENDUM.**
　See REFERENDUM.

INJUNCTIONS.
Accountants.
　Unlawful practice, §34-1-18.
Air pollution, §22-28-22.
Alcoholic beverages.
　Beer.
　　Business relations between
　　　wholesalers and
　　　suppliers.
　　　Violations of provisions,
　　　　§28-9-11.
　Dry counties.
　　Abatement of liquor
　　　nuisances.
　　　Persons who may be
　　　　enjoined, §28-4-230.
　　　Preliminary injunctions,
　　　　§§28-4-223, 28-4-224.
　Enforcement of chapter.
　　Issuance of injunctions,
　　　§28-4-324.
Appeals.
　Injunction pending appeal,
　　ARCP, Rule 62 (c).
　Judgments on applications
　　for remedial writs,
　　§12-22-6.
　Temporary restraining
　　orders.
　　Applications for, §12-22-7.
**Banks and financial
　institutions.**
　Liquidation of insolvent
　　banks.
　　Application by bank for
　　　injunction against
　　　acquisition or
　　　possession of business
　　　and property by
　　　receiver or
　　　superintendent,
　　　§5-8A-27.
Bills of lading.
　Enjoining negotiation of
　　document, §7-7-602.
Blind persons.
　Assistance to needy blind
　　persons.
　　Freedom of choice in
　　　selection of specialists
　　　to make examinations.
　　　Enforcement of section,
　　　§38-1-2.

INJUNCTIONS—Cont'd

Bonds, surety, ARCP, Rule 65 (c).

Circuit courts.
Power of judges, §6-6-500; Const. Ala., art. VI, §144.

Coal.
Abandoned mine reclamation, §9-16-132.
Mine safety.
Enforcement of chapter, §25-9-368.
Surface mining control and reclamation.
Suspension or revocation of permits.
Actions by attorney general, §9-16-93.

Commercial code.
Documents of title.
Enjoining negotiation of document, §7-7-602.
Investment securities.
Enjoining transfer, §§7-8-315, 7-8-317.

Constitution of Alabama.
Power of circuit judges to issue writs of injunction returnable to courts of chancery, Const. Ala., art. VI, §144.
Power of supreme court to issue writs, Const. Ala., art. VI, §140.

Consumer finance, §5-19-29.

Cotton.
Promotion of cotton products.
Violations of provisions, §2-8-211.

Court of civil appeals.
Judges may grant, §§6-6-500, 12-3-8, 12-3-11.

Court of criminal appeals.
Judges may grant, §§6-6-500, 12-3-8, 12-3-11.

Credit unions.
Cease and desist orders, §5-17-8.

Deceptive trade practices, §8-19-8.

Dentists and dental hygienists.
See DENTISTS.

Dissolution.
Preliminary injunction, §6-6-501.

Eggs and egg products.
Violations of chapter, §2-12-12.

Elections.
Chancery powers of judges or courts.
Jurisdiction denied judges or courts exercising chancery powers in election contests, §17-15-6.

Electrical contractors.
Unauthorized practice, §34-36-15.

Electricity.
Service territories for electric suppliers.
1984 act.
Violations of provisions, §37-14-9.
1985 act.
Violations of provisions, §37-14-37.

INJUNCTIONS—Cont'd

Engineers.
Board of registration.
Authority of board to seek injunctions, §34-11-35.

Fertilizer.
Proceedings to restrain violations of chapter or rules or regulations, §2-22-22.

Form, ARCP, Rule 65 (d).

Fraternal benefit societies.
Actions to enjoin, §27-34-50.
Applications for injunctions, §27-34-51.

Fraud.
Charitable fraud.
Enforcement of provisions, §13A-9-76.

Fruits and vegetables.
Grading and standards.
Violations of article, §2-11-79.

Funerals.
Board of funeral service.
Power to seek injunction, §34-13-26.

Grain.
Promotion of grain industry.
Violation of provisions, §2-8-252.

Grain dealers.
Violations of provisions, §2-31-19.

Granting.
Who may grant, §6-6-500.

Hazardous waste.
Fees for disposal of hazardous waste or substances.
Violations of chapter.
Restraint from continuing in business, §22-30B-12.

Health maintenance organizations.
Violations of chapter, §27-21A-22.

Horse racing.
Violation of provisions, §11-65-13.

Hospitals.
Certificates of need.
Violations of article, §22-21-276.

Insurance.
Holding companies, §27-29-9.
Insurers, §27-32-5.

Investment securities.
Enjoining transfer, §§7-8-315, 7-8-317.

Landscaping.
Proceedings to restrain performance of professional work or services without permit, §2-28-11.

Liquefied petroleum gas, §9-17-108.

Livestock.
Proceedings to restrain operation of livestock market in violation of provisions of division, §2-15-70.

Manufactured buildings.
Violations of provisions, §24-4A-5.

INJUNCTIONS—Cont'd

Meat and meat products.
Jurisdiction and prosecution of injunctive proceedings under chapter or regulations, §2-17-30.

Mines and minerals.
Surface mining reclamation.
Violation of article, §9-16-11.

Motion picture fair competition.
Enforcement of chapter, §8-18-6.

Motor fuels.
Distributors of motor fuels.
Restraining and enjoining violations of article, §40-12-204.
Marketing.
Violation of chapter, §8-22-17.

Motor vehicles.
Automotive dismantlers and parts recyclers.
Violations of article, §40-12-425.

Municipal corporations.
Enjoining or restraining enforcement of ordinance, §6-6-502.
Nuisances.
Public nuisances.
Right of action to enjoin, §§6-5-122, 11-47-118.

Nuisances.
Injunction before completion, §6-5-125.
Lewdness, assignation or prostitution, §§6-5-142 to 6-5-146, 6-5-150.
See NUISANCES.
Public nuisances.
Municipal corporations.
Right of action to enjoin, §6-5-122.

Nurses.
Practicing nursing without license, §34-21-26.

Obscenity.
Anti-obscenity enforcement act.
Attorney general may initiate, §13A-12-200.7.

Oil and gas.
Conservation and regulation of production.
See OIL AND GAS.
Violations of article, §40-20-11.

Optometrists.
Board may enjoin violations of chapter, §34-22-7.

Ordinances.
Enjoining or restraining enforcement, §6-6-502.

Partnerships.
Foreign limited partnerships.
Transaction of business in violation of provisions, §10-9A-167.

Pest control.
Proceedings to restrain performance of professional work or services without permit, §2-28-11.

Pesticides.
Application, §2-27-62.

INJUNCTIONS—Cont'd

Pesticides—Cont'd

Violations of article, §2-27-16.

Petroleum products.

See OIL AND GAS.

Pharmacists and pharmacies.

Board may enjoin violations of chapter, §34-23-12.

Physicians.

Assistants to physicians.

Enjoining violations of article, §34-24-294.

Unlawful practice of medicine.

See PHYSICIANS.

Unlicensed practice, §34-24-341.

Pipelines.

Gas pipeline systems.

Jurisdiction of circuit court to restrain violations, §37-4-86.

Plant pathologists.

Restraining performance of professional work or services without permit, §2-28-11.

Polygraph examiners board.

Enforcement of chapter, §34-25-7.

Poultry.

Jurisdiction and prosecution of injunctive proceedings under chapter or regulations, §2-17-30.

Power districts.

Bond issues.

Rights and remedies of bondholders, §37-5-8.

Preliminary injunctions, ARCP, Rule 65 (a).

Dissolution, §6-6-501.

Professions and occupations.

Enjoining unauthorized or unlawful practice, §6-6-503.

Public contracts.

Competitive bidding.

Institution of actions to enjoin execution of contracts entered into violation of article, §41-16-31.

Public service commission.

See PUBLIC SERVICE COMMISSION.

Public works.

Contract to let in violation of law.

Actions to enjoin, §39-5-4.

Radio.

Certificate of public convenience and necessity.

Persons operating without certificate, §37-4-115.

Registers, §12-17-116.

Rules of civil procedure, ARCP Rules 62 (c), 65 (a) to (d).

See RULES OF CIVIL PROCEDURE.

Sales tax.

Violations.

Restraining violators from continuing in business, §40-23-27.

Scope, ARCP, Rule 65 (d).

INJUNCTIONS—Cont'd

Securities.

Rules of civil procedure, ARCP, Rule 65 (c).

Violations of article, §8-6-16.

Seeds.

Injunctive proceedings to restrain persons selling, etc., §2-26-6.

Small loans.

Violations of small loan act, §5-18-10.

Injunctive relief as to violations, §5-2A-81.

Social workers.

Violation of chapter, §34-30-5.

Soil classifiers.

Power of board, §34-32-8.

Speech pathologists and audiologists.

Board of examiners, §34-28A-43.

Proceedings to enjoin violations of chapter, §34-28A-5.

Supreme court.

Granting.

Powers of court, §12-2-7; Const. Ala., art. VI, §140.

Powers of justices, §§6-6-500, 12-2-2.

Surveys and surveyors.

Board of registration.

Authority of board to seek injunctions, §34-11-35.

Temporary restraining orders, ARCP, Rule 65 (b).

Applications, §12-22-7.

Applications to supreme court, §12-22-8.

Renewal of applications, §12-22-7.

Duration, ARCP, Rule 65 (b).

Form, ARCP, Rule 65 (d).

Hearing, ARCP, Rule 65 (b).

Notice, ARCP, Rule 65 (b).

Scope, ARCP, Rule 65 (d).

Toxic substances in the workplace.

Violation of chapter, §22-33-13.

Trademarks and service marks.

Registration of.

Grounds for injunctive relief, §8-12-17.

Tree surgery.

Proceedings to restrain performance of professional work or services without permit, §2-28-11.

Use tax.

Injunctions against collection of tax prohibited, §40-23-87.

Vacation time-sharing plans.

Enjoining violations of article, §34-27-68.

Venue.

Action to enjoin proceedings or judgments in other courts, §6-3-2.

Veterinarians.

Unauthorized practice of veterinary medicine, §34-29-78.

INJUNCTIONS—Cont'd

Warehouse receipts.

Enjoining negotiation of document, §7-7-602.

INJURIES.

Assault.

General provisions.

See ASSAULT AND BATTERY.

Boats.

Accidents involving injuries.

Report required, §33-5-25.

Rules and regulations.

Prevention of unnecessary injuries.

Highway department, §23-1-59.

Cattle.

Counties.

Indemnification of owners for injuries, etc., caused by dipping of cattle, §§11-12-1 to 11-12-3.

Caves.

Cave related activities.

Liability for injury while engaged in, §9-19-2.

Claims against the state.

See CLAIMS AGAINST STATE.

Damages.

See DAMAGES.

Dogs injuring persons.

Liability of owner.

See DOGS.

Domestic remedies.

Exemption from provisions relating to physicians, §34-24-55.

Emergency services.

Exemption from requirements relating to physicians, §34-24-55.

Employer's liability for certain injuries, §§25-6-1 to 25-6-4.

Fellow servant.

Affirmative defense, ARCP, Rule 8 (c).

Felonious injuries.

Actions.

Civil action without criminal prosecution, §6-5-370.

Highways.

Prevention of unnecessary injuries.

Promulgation of rules and regulations by highway department, §23-1-59.

Indictments.

General allegation of intent to injure, §15-8-29.

Livestock.

Counties.

Indemnification of owners for injuries, etc., caused by dipping of cattle, §§11-12-1 to 11-12-3.

Minors.

Injury to minor child.

Right of action of parents, §6-5-390.

Motor vehicle accidents.

Reports required following accident involving personal injury, §32-7-5.

INJURIES—Cont'd
  Municipal corporations.
    Liability for negligence of
        agents, etc.
      Manner of injury,
        §11-47-192.
  Physicians.
    Emergency services exempt
        from provisions of
        chapter, §34-24-55.
    Malpractice.
      See PHYSICIANS.
  Torts generally.
    See TORTS.
  Transportation companies.
    Loss, injury or delay in
        delivery, §§37-2-60 to
        37-2-62.
  Trees and timber.
    Damages for destruction,
        injury or removal of
        trees, §§35-14-1 to
        35-14-3.
  **Water management and
      drainage.**
    Districts.
      Improvements.
        Injuries to
            improvements,
            §9-9-48.
  Workmen's compensation.
    Occupational diseases
        generally, §§25-5-110 to
        25-5-123.
      See WORKMEN'S
          COMPENSATION.
    Pneumoconiosis, §§25-5-140
        to 25-5-180.
      See WORKMEN'S
          COMPENSATION.
  Wrongful death, §§6-5-410,
      6-5-411.

INLAND WATERWAYS.
  General provisions, §§33-2-1
      to 33-2-213.
    See WATERS AND
        WATERCOURSES.

INMATE COMMUNITY
    REINTEGRATION
    UNDER SIR ACT.
  Corrections, §§15-18-110 to
      15-18-123.
    See CORRECTIONS.

INNS.
  See HOTELS, INNS AND
      OTHER TRANSIENT
      LODGING PLACES.

INOCULATIONS.
  Rabies, §§3-7-2, 3-7-3.
  School children.
    Immunization, §§16-30-1 to
        16-30-5.
      See EDUCATION.

INQUESTS.
  Coroners' inquests.
    See CORONERS.

INSANE PERSONS.
  Defined, §1-1-1.
  General provisions.
    See MENTALLY ILL.

INSECTICIDES, §§2-27-1 to
    2-27-63.
  See PESTICIDES.

INSECTS.
  Boll weevils.
    Eradication in cotton,
        §§2-19-120 to 2-19-135.
      See COTTON.
  Exterminators, §§2-28-1 to
      2-28-12.
    See PEST CONTROL.
  Forest trees.
    Protection from insect
        infestation, §§9-13-120 to
        9-13-126.
      See FORESTS AND
          FORESTRY.
  Honeybees and apiaries,
      §§2-14-1 to 2-14-15.
    See HONEYBEES AND
        APIARIES.
  Municipal corporations.
    Control of conditions
        favorable to harboring
        insects, §11-47-140.
  Nurseries.
    Insect and disease control,
        §§2-25-1 to 2-25-22.
      See NURSERIES.
  Nuts.
    Infested nuts.
      Importation, §2-25-15.
      Sale or offer for sale,
          §20-1-90.
  Pest control, §§2-28-1 to
      2-28-12.
    See PEST CONTROL.
  Pesticides, §§2-27-1 to 2-27-63.
    See PESTICIDES.
  Plants.
    Control of insects and
        disease, §§2-25-1 to
        2-25-22.
      See NURSERIES.
  State insect, §1-2-25.
  Structural pest control,
      §§2-28-1 to 2-28-12.
    See PEST CONTROL.
  Termites.
    Pest control, §§2-28-1 to
        2-28-12.
      See PEST CONTROL.
  Ticks.
    Eradication, §§2-15-290 to
        2-15-299.
      See LIVESTOCK.
  Trees.
    Control of insects, §§2-25-1 to
        2-25-22.
      See NURSERIES.
    Forest trees.
      Protection from insect
          infestation, §§9-13-120
          to 9-13-126.
        See FORESTS AND
            FORESTRY.
    Tree surgery, §§2-28-1 to
        2-28-12.
      See TREES AND TIMBER.

INSOLVENCY.
  See BANKRUPTCY AND
      INSOLVENCY.

INSPECTIONS.
  Agriculture, §2-2-37.
    See AGRICULTURE.
  Air pollution.
    Right of entry for inspection,
        §22-28-19.
  Alcoholic beverages,
      §28-3-50.
  Armories.
    State building commission to
        inspect, §31-4-13.

INSPECTIONS—Cont'd
  Aviation.
    Airports.
      Authority of aeronautics
          commission to inspect,
          §4-2-50.
  **Banks and financial
      institutions.**
    Examination of banks,
        §§5-3A-1 to 5-3A-17;
        Const. Ala., art. XIII,
        §254.
  Beverages.
    Municipal corporations,
        §11-47-136.
  Billiard rooms, §34-6-2.
  Boats, §§3-5-11, 3-5-21.
  Brake fluid, §8-17-8.
  Catfish.
    Seller's inspection of books
        and records of seller,
        §2-8-291.
  Child labor.
    Establishments where minors
        employed, §25-8-22.
    Inspection and correction of
        insanitary or unhealthful
        conditions, §25-8-25.
  Coal.
    Mine safety, §§25-9-4, 25-9-5.
  Commercial code.
    Sales, §§7-2-512, 7-2-513,
        7-2-515.
  Constitution of Alabama.
    State office for inspection or
        measuring of
        merchandise,
        commodities, etc.,
        prohibited, Const. Ala.,
        art. IV, §77.
  Corporations, §10-2A-79.
  Cotton.
    Applicability of laws relative
        to inspection, §2-19-26.
    Boll weevil eradication,
        §2-19-123.
  Discovery, ARCP, Rules 34,
      37 (d).
  Domestic violence facilities,
      §30-6-3.
  Drugs.
    Pharmacists and pharmacies.
      State drug inspectors,
          §34-23-3.
  Education.
    Buildings, §16-1-2.
    School buses, §§16-27-3,
        16-27-5.
  Eggs and egg products,
      §§2-12-9, 2-12-10.
  Elections.
    Inspectors.
      See ELECTIONS.
  Examinations.
    See EXAMINATIONS.
  Feeds, §§2-21-24, 2-21-26.
  Fertilizer, §2-22-11.
    Fees, §2-22-9.
  Finance, §41-4-36.
  Fish and game.
    See FISH AND GAME.
  Food.
    Municipal corporations,
        §11-47-136.
  Forests and forestry.
    Auxiliary state forests.
      Designation of lands,
          §9-13-43.

INSPECTIONS—Cont'd
　Fruits and vegetables,
　　§§2-11-70 to 2-11-79.
　　See FRUITS AND
　　　VEGETABLES.
　Funerals.
　　Board of funeral service.
　　　Right of entry of members
　　　　for inspection
　　　　purposes, §34-13-23.
　　Funeral establishments,
　　　§34-13-111.
　Grain.
　　Applicability of laws relative
　　　to inspection, §2-20-6.
　　Grading and standards,
　　　§§2-11-90 to 2-11-103.
　　See GRAIN.
　Grain dealers.
　　Commissioner of agriculture,
　　　§2-31-10.
　Hazardous waste.
　　Environmental management
　　　department.
　　　Enforcement of provisions,
　　　　§22-30-19.
　Health, §§22-3-2, 22-3-5.
　　State board of health,
　　　§22-2-2.
　Highway department.
　　Records, §23-1-34.
　Honeybees and apiaries,
　　§2-14-9.
　　Shipment into state.
　　　Certification of inspection,
　　　　§2-14-4.
　Hospitals, §22-21-29.
　　Disclosure of information,
　　　§22-21-30.
　Hotels, inns and other
　　transient lodging places.
　　Inspectors, §§34-15-5 to
　　　34-15-9.
　　See HOTELS, INNS AND
　　　OTHER TRANSIENT
　　　LODGING PLACES.
　Indictments.
　　Limitations on inspection
　　　before defendant
　　　arrested, §15-8-70.
　Industrial alcohol, §28-5-10.
　　Fees, §28-5-11.
　Insect and disease control.
　　Nurseries, §§2-25-6, 2-25-8,
　　　2-25-22.
　Insurance, §§27-2-14,
　　27-10-36.
　Jails, §§14-6-80 to 14-6-105.
　　See JAILS.
　Lime, §§2-23-5, 2-23-6.
　Liquefied petroleum gas.
　　System, §9-17-103.
　Livestock.
　　Meat and meat products,
　　　§§2-17-1 to 2-17-38.
　　See MEAT AND MEAT
　　　PRODUCTS.
　　State livestock inspectors,
　　　§§2-4-2, 2-4-3.
　Marine resources, §§9-12-31,
　　9-12-116.
　　Oyster beds, §9-12-126.
　Meat and meat products,
　　§§2-17-1 to 2-17-38.
　　See MEAT AND MEAT
　　　PRODUCTS.
　Mental hospitals.
　　State mental institutions,
　　　§§14-6-106, 14-6-107.

INSPECTIONS—Cont'd
　Mines and minerals.
　　Coal mines safety, §§25-9-4,
　　　25-9-5.
　　General provisions, §§9-16-8,
　　　9-16-9.
　Mobile homes, §§24-5-4,
　　24-5-9, 24-5-13.
　Motor vehicles.
　　Municipal testing stations,
　　　§§32-18-1 to 32-18-8.
　　See MOTOR VEHICLES.
　　Uniform certificate of title
　　　and antitheft act,
　　　§32-8-8.
　Municipal corporations,
　　§11-43-59.
　　Dairies, §11-47-139.
　　Food.
　　　Impure, adulterated, etc.,
　　　　food, §11-47-136.
　　Jails, §§14-6-80 to 14-6-105.
　　　See JAILS.
　　Motor vehicles.
　　　Municipal testing stations,
　　　　§§32-18-1 to 32-18-8.
　　　See MOTOR VEHICLES.
　Nurseries.
　　Insect and disease control,
　　　§§2-25-6, 2-25-8, 2-25-22.
　Oysters, §9-12-27.
　Partnerships.
　　Partnership books, §10-8-45.
　Penitentiary, §§14-6-106,
　　14-6-107.
　Pesticides, §2-27-12.
　　Application of pesticides,
　　　§2-27-61.
　Petroleum products.
　　Fees, §8-17-87.
　　　Disposition, §8-17-91.
　　Overpayments.
　　　Refund, §8-17-91.
　Pharmacists and
　　pharmacies, §34-23-3.
　Pipelines.
　　Safety inspection fees,
　　　§37-4-88.
　Poultry, §§2-17-1 to 2-17-38.
　　See POULTRY.
　Public officers and
　　employees.
　　Refusal to permit inspections,
　　　§13A-10-3.
　Public service commission,
　　§§37-1-13, 37-1-53, 37-1-82.
　Rabies, §3-7-10.
　Radiation, §§22-14-7,
　　22-14-10.
　Records.
　　Public records, §36-12-40.
　Rules of civil procedure.
　　Entry upon land for
　　　inspection and other
　　　purposes, ARCP, Rule
　　　34.
　　Failure of party to respond
　　　to request for
　　　inspection, ARCP,
　　　Rule 37 (d).
　Sales.
　　Commercial code, §§7-2-512,
　　　7-2-513, 7-2-515.
　Sales tax.
　　Department of revenue.
　　　Authority to inspect books
　　　　and records of
　　　　taxpayer, §40-23-22.
　School buildings, §16-1-2.
　School buses.
　　Generally, §16-27-3.

INSPECTIONS—Cont'd
　School buses—Cont'd
　　Monthly safety inspections,
　　　§16-27-5.
　Ships and shipping.
　　Certificates of registration
　　　and numbering.
　　　Availability for inspection,
　　　　§33-5-11.
　Shrimp, §9-12-27.
　Southeast interstate low-
　　level radioactive waste
　　management compact.
　　Delegation of authority to
　　　inspect and enforce
　　　regulations, §22-32-6.
　State drug inspectors.
　　Pharmacists and pharmacies,
　　　§34-23-3.
　State office for inspection or
　　measuring of
　　merchandise,
　　commodities, etc.,
　　prohibited, Const. Ala.,
　　　art. IV, §77.
　Tobacco.
　　Sales tax, §40-25-12.
　Transportation companies,
　　§37-2-41.
　Uniform commercial code.
　　Sales, §§7-2-512, 7-2-513,
　　　7-2-515.
　Warehouses.
　　Commissioner and agents,
　　　§§8-15-11.
　Welfare.
　　Child care facilities,
　　　§38-7-11.
　　Department of human
　　　resources.
　　　Powers and duties, §38-2-6.
　　Reports.
　　　Name of recipients of
　　　　public assistance,
　　　　§38-1-4.
　Youth services.
　　Detention facilities, §44-1-27.
　　Foster care facilities,
　　　§44-1-27.

INSTITUTE FOR DEAF AND
　BLIND, §§21-1-1 to 21-1-26.
See HANDICAPPED
　PERSONS.

INSTITUTE OF AVIATION
　TECHNOLOGY AT
　OZARK.
　Vocational trade school.
　　To be operated as additional
　　　vocational trade school,
　　　§16-60-198.

INSURANCE, §§27-1-1 to
　27-45-9.
　Accident insurance.
　　County officers and
　　　employees, §§11-91-1 to
　　　11-91-8.
　　See COUNTIES.
　　Dentists and dental
　　　hygienists.
　　　"Physicians" under
　　　　accident insurance
　　　　policies, §27-1-11.
　　Fraternal benefit societies.
　　　Accident insurance
　　　　contracts, §27-34-32.
　　Interest.
　　　Limitation period for
　　　　payment of claims.
　　　　Payment of interest,
　　　　§27-1-17.

INSURANCE—Cont'd
  Accident insurance—Cont'd
    Municipal officers and
      employees.
    See MUNICIPAL
      CORPORATIONS.
  Accounts and accounting.
    Insurance guaranty
      association, §§27-42-5,
      27-42-6.
    Mutual aid associations,
      §27-30-21.
    Duty of officers and agents,
      §27-30-23.
  Actions.
    Disability insurance.
      Provision in policy as to
        legal actions,
        §27-19-14.
    Enforcement of insurance
      code, §27-2-19.
    Insurers.
      Time to answer or plead,
        §27-3-25.
    Mail order insurance,
      §§27-11-4, 27-11-6.
    Reciprocal insurers, §27-31-4.
    Unauthorized insurers,
      §27-10-3.
  Adjusters, §§27-9-1 to 27-9-8.
    Age, §27-9-3.
    Authority to act as adjuster
      without license, §27-9-4.
    Corporations.
      Licenses, §27-9-2.
    Defined, §27-9-1.
    Examinations.
      Commissioner of insurance,
        §§27-2-20 to 27-2-27.
        See within this
        heading,
        "Commissioner of
        insurance."
    Fees.
      Licenses, §§27-4-2, 27-9-2.
    Licenses, §§27-9-2 to 27-9-8.
      Affidavit in lieu of return
        to commissioner,
        §27-9-7.
      Application, §27-9-2.
      Authority to act as
        adjuster without
        license, §27-9-4.
      Continuation, §27-9-5.
      Refusal to continue,
        §27-9-6.
      Return to
        commissioner upon
        refusal, §27-9-7.
      Corporations, §27-9-2.
      Expiration, §27-9-5.
      Fees, §§27-4-2, 27-9-2.
      Issuance, §27-9-2.
      Qualifications, §27-9-3.
      Required, §27-9-2.
      Return to commissioner,
        §27-9-7.
      Revocation, §27-9-6.
      Suspension, §27-9-6.
    Office, §27-9-8.
    Qualifications for licenses,
      §27-9-3.
    Records, §27-9-8.
    Unauthorized insurers.
      Liability of adjusters,
        §27-10-2.
  Advisory organizations,
    §§27-13-100 to 27-13-105.
    See within this heading,
    "Rates and rating
    organizations."

INSURANCE—Cont'd
  African development bank.
    Investments of life, disability
      and burial insurance
      companies.
      Obligations of African
        development bank,
        §27-41-14.
  Age.
    Adjusters, §27-9-3.
    Annuity contracts.
      Misstatement of age,
        §27-15-20.
    Casualty insurance
      representatives, §§27-7-1
      to 27-7-38.
    Disability insurance.
      Age limit, §27-19-36.
      Provision in policy as to
        misstatement of age,
        §27-19-18.
    Disability insurance
      representatives, §§27-8-1
      to 27-8-28.
    Industrial life insurance.
      Misstatement of age in
        policy, §27-16-7.
    Life insurance.
      Misstatement of age in
        policies, §27-15-6.
    Pure endowment contracts.
      Misstatement of age,
        §27-15-20.
  Agents.
    Appeals.
      Life and disability
        insurance
        representatives.
        Appeal of order refusing
          to renew or continue
          or suspending or
          revoking license,
          §27-8-16.
    Automobile clubs and
      associations, §27-39-7.
    Commissioner of insurance.
      Property, casualty and
        surety insurance
        representatives.
        Filing of agent's
          appointment by
          insurer with
          commissioner,
          §27-7-30.
    Countersigning resident
      agents.
      Execution of contracts
        through
        countersigning
        resident agent,
        §27-3-28.
    Definitions.
      Life and disability
        insurance
        representatives.
        Agent defined, §27-8-1.
      Property, casualty and
        surety insurance
        representatives,
        §27-7-1.
    Directory of agents.
      Annual publication by
        commissioner,
        §27-2-16.
    Examinations.
      Commissioner of insurance,
        §§27-2-20 to 27-2-27.
        See within this
        heading,
        "Commissioner of
        insurance."

INSURANCE—Cont'd
  Agents—Cont'd
    Exceptions to requirement of
      agents, §27-3-27.
    Execution of contracts.
      Execution through
        countersigning
        resident agent,
        §27-3-28.
    Fair trade, §§27-12-1 to
      27-12-24. See within this
      heading, "Trade practices
      law."
    False statements, etc., in
      insurance application,
      §27-12-23.
    Fees.
      License fee, §27-4-2.
    Fraternal benefit societies,
      §§27-34-1 to 27-34-54.
    See FRATERNAL
      BENEFIT SOCIETIES.
    Insurers to do business
      through licensed agents,
      §27-3-27.
    Legal expense insurance.
      Sales agents, §§27-43-15 to
      27-43-19.
    Licenses.
      Examinations.
        Fees, §27-4-2.
    Life and disability insurance
      representatives, §§27-8-1
      to 27-8-28.
    Address.
      Notice of business
        address change,
        §27-8-26.
    Affidavit in lieu of return
      for cancellation,
      §27-8-19.
    Appeals.
      Order refusing to renew
        or continue or
        suspending or
        revoking license,
        §27-8-16.
    Applicability of chapter,
      §27-8-2.
    Appointment.
      Termination of agency
        appointment by
        insurer, §27-8-24.
    Bond, surety, §27-8-5.
    Commissions.
      Payment to unlicensed
        persons. §27-8-27.
    Credit facilities.
      Use of credit facilities,
        §27-8-23.
    Definition of agent,
      §27-8-1.
    Examinations for licenses,
      §§27-8-6 to 27-8-11.
    Excess risk.
      Placement of excess risk
        by unlicensed agent,
        §27-8-25.
    Licenses, §§27-8-3 to
      27-8-21.
      Additional licenses.
        Issuance, §27-8-14.
      Annual statements.
        Filing, §27-8-15.
      Appeal of order refusing
        to renew or continue
        or suspending or
        revoking license,
        §27-8-16.
      Applications, §27-8-5.
      Fees, §§27-4-2, 27-8-5.

INSURANCE—Cont'd
  Agents—Cont'd
    Life and disability insurance
      representatives—Cont'd
      Licenses—Cont'd
        Bond, surety, §27-8-5.
        Cancellation.
          Return for
            cancellation,
            §27-8-19.
        Certificate of insurer,
          §27-8-5.
        Content, §27-8-13.
        Continuation, §27-8-15.
          Appeal of order
            refusing
            continuation,
            §27-8-17.
          Grounds for refusal to
            continue, §27-8-16.
          Hearing on refusal to
            continue,
            §§27-8-17, 27-8-18.
          Procedure of refusal to
            continue, §27-8-17.
          Refusal to continue,
            §§27-8-16 to
            27-8-19.
          Return for cancellation
            upon refusal to
            continue, §27-8-19.
        Denial, §27-8-12.
        Educational
          requirements,
          §27-8-6.
        Examination, §§27-8-6 to
          27-8-11.
          Agency advisory board,
            §27-8-11.
          Assistance of state
            personnel
            department,
            §27-8-7.
          Exemption, §27-8-6.
          Fee, §27-8-10.
          Manuals, §27-8-8.
          Materials, §27-8-8.
          Nonresident agents,
            §27-8-22.
          Preparation, §27-8-7.
          Publication of booklet
            by commissioner,
            §27-2-16.
          Reexamination,
            §27-8-10.
          Requirements, §27-8-6.
          Rules and regulations,
            §27-8-7.
          Testing institutions,
            §27-8-7.
          Textbooks, §27-8-8.
         Expiration, §27-8-15.
          Return for
            cancellation,
            §27-8-19.
        Fees, §27-4-2.
          Examination, §27-8-10.
          Filing of annual
            statements and
            fees, §27-8-15.
        Forms, §27-8-3.
        Grounds for refusal to
          renew or continue or
          for suspension or
          revocation, §27-8-16.
        Issuance, §27-8-12.
          Additional licenses,
            §27-8-14.
          Refusal to issue,
            §27-8-12.

INSURANCE—Cont'd
  Agents—Cont'd
    Life and disability insurance
      representatives—Cont'd
      Licenses—Cont'd
        Nonresident agents,
          §27-8-22.
        Number, §27-8-13.
        Qualifications, §27-8-4.
        Refusal, §27-8-12.
        Relicensing after
          revocation, §27-8-20.
        Renewal.
          Appeal of order
            refusing, §27-8-17.
          Grounds for refusal,
            §27-8-16.
          Hearing on refusal,
            §§27-8-17, 27-8-18.
          Proceedings for
            refusal, §27-8-17.
          Refusal to renew,
            §§27-8-16 to
            27-8-19.
          Return for cancellation
            upon refusal,
            §27-8-19.
        Reports.
          Filing of annual
            statements,
            §27-8-15.
        Requirement, §27-8-3.
        Return for cancellation,
          §27-8-19.
        Revocation, §§27-8-16 to
          27-8-20.
        Suspension or revocation.
          Appeal of order,
            §27-8-17.
          Grounds, §27-8-16.
          Hearing, §§27-8-17,
            27-8-18.
          Privileged information,
            §27-8-18.
          Proceedings, §27-8-17.
          Relicensing after
            revocation,
            §27-8-20.
          Return for
            cancellation,
            §27-8-19.
        Temporary licenses,
          §27-8-21.
        Unlicensed agents.
          Placement of excess or
            rejected risk by
            unlicensed agent,
            §27-8-25.
        Unlicensed persons.
          Payment of
            commission to,
            §27-8-27.
      Mutual aid associations.
        Applicability of chapter
          eight to associations,
          §27-30-32.
      Nonresident agents,
        §27-8-22.
      Notice.
        Business address change,
          §27-8-26.
      Office.
        Notice of business
          address change,
          §27-8-26.
      Premiums.
        Accounting for and
          payment of trust
          funds by licensees,
          §27-8-28.

INSURANCE—Cont'd
  Agents—Cont'd
    Life and disability insurance
      representatives—Cont'd
      Qualifications for licenses,
        §27-8-4.
      Rejected risks.
        Placement by unlicensed
          agent, §27-8-25.
      Reports.
        Filing of annual
          statements, §27-8-15.
      Temporary licenses,
        §27-8-21.
      Termination of agency
        appointment by
        insurer, §27-8-24.
      Trust funds.
        Accounting for and
          payment of trust
          funds by licensees,
          §27-8-28.
      Vending machines,
        §27-8-23.
    Mutual aid associations,
      §27-30-23.
    Nonresidents.
      Life and disability
        insurance
        representatives,
        §27-8-22.
      Property, casualty and
        surety insurance
        representatives,
        §§27-7-28, 27-7-29.
    Notices.
      Property, casualty and
        surety insurance
        representatives.
        Appointment.
          Notice to agent of
            appointment or
            renewal, §27-7-30.
    Property, casualty and surety
      insurance
      representatives, §§27-7-1
      to 27-7-38.
      Applicability of chapter,
        §27-7-2.
      Appointment.
        Filing of agent's
          appointment by
          insurer with
          commissioner,
          §27-7-30.
        Notice to agent of
          appointment or
          renewal, §27-7-30.
        Placing of insurance by
          agent not appointed,
          §27-7-34.
        Termination of agent's
          appointment,
          §27-7-30.
        Rights of agent
          following
          termination,
          §27-7-31.
      Commissioner of insurance.
        Filing of agent's
          appointment by
          insurer with
          commissioner,
          §27-7-30.
      Commissions.
        Division of commissions
          by licensees,
          §27-7-35.
        Nonresident agents or
          brokers, §27-7-28.

INSURANCE—Cont'd
  Agents—Cont'd
    Property, casualty and surety
      insurance
      representatives—Cont'd
    Commissions—Cont'd
      Sharing of commissions
        by licensees,
        §27-7-35.
    Complaints against
      licensees, §27-7-37.
    Privileged information,
      §27-7-38.
    Definitions, §27-7-1.
    Display of license,
      §27-7-32.
    Embezzlement.
      Diversion of trust funds,
        §27-7-36.
    Examinations, §§27-7-10 to
      27-7-14.
    Hearing of complaints
      against licensees,
      §27-7-37.
    Privileged information,
      §27-7-38.
    Licenses, §§27-7-4 to
      27-7-26.
      Applications.
        Fees, §§27-4-2, 27-7-7,
          27-7-16.
        Generally, §27-7-7.
        Reapplication upon
          denial, §27-7-16.
      Statement of
        appointing agent
        or broker for
        solicitor, §27-7-9.
      Statement of
        appointing insurer
        for agent, §27-7-8.
    Cancellation.
      Return for
        cancellation,
        §27-7-22.
    Contents, §27-7-17.
    Continuation, §27-7-18.
      Examinations,
        §27-7-12.
      Grounds for refusing to
        continue, §27-7-19.
      Notice of refusal to
        continue, §27-7-21.
      Return for cancellation
        upon refusal to
        continue, §27-7-22.
    Corporations, §27-7-6.
      Applications, §27-7-7.
      Examination, §27-7-10.
      Suspension, revocation
        or refusal of
        license, §27-7-19.
    Denial, §27-7-15.
      Reapplication or
        reexamination
        upon denial,
        §27-7-16.
    Destroyed licenses.
      Affidavit in lieu of
        return for
        cancellation,
        §27-7-22.
    Display, §27-7-32.
    Examinations, §§27-7-10
      to 27-10-14.
      Conduct, §27-7-11.
      Consultations with
        experienced
        persons, §27-7-14.
      Contents, §27-7-11.

INSURANCE—Cont'd
  Agents—Cont'd
    Property, casualty and surety
      insurance
      representatives—Cont'd
    Licenses—Cont'd
      Examinations—Cont'd
        Continuation of
          licenses, §27-7-12.
        Exemptions, §27-7-13.
        Fees, §§27-7-7, 27-7-16.
        Grading, §27-7-11.
        Notifications, §27-7-10.
        Publication of booklet
          by commissioner,
          §27-2-16.
        Reexamination upon
          denial, §27-7-16.
        Renewal of license,
          §27-7-12.
        Scope, §27-7-10.
        Study materials,
          §27-7-11.
        Temporary license
          pending
          examination,
          §27-7-24.
        When given, §27-7-10.
      Expiration, §27-7-18.
      Fees, §§27-4-2, 27-7-7,
        27-7-16.
      Forms, §27-7-4.
      Grounds for refusing to
        renew or continue or
        to suspend or revoke,
        §27-7-19.
      Issuance, §27-7-15.
      Lost licenses.
        Affidavit in lieu of
          return for
          cancellation,
          §27-7-22.
      Nonresident agents or
        brokers, §27-7-28.
      Notice of refusal to
        renew or of
        suspension or
        revocation, §27-7-21.
      Partnerships, §27-7-6.
        Applications, §27-7-7.
        Examination, §27-7-10.
        Suspension, revocation
          or refusal of
          license, §27-7-19.
      Placing of insurance by
        agent not appointed
        or licensed, §27-7-34.
      Qualifications, §27-7-5.
      Refusal, §27-7-15.
        Reapplication or
          reexamination
          upon denial,
          §27-7-16.
      Renewal, §27-7-18.
        Examinations,
          §27-7-12.
        Grounds for refusing,
          §27-7-19.
        Notice of refusal,
          §27-7-21.
        Return for cancellation
          upon refusal,
          §27-7-22.
      Requirement, §27-7-4.
      Revocation, §§27-7-19 to
        27-7-22.
      Solicitors, §27-7-27.

INSURANCE—Cont'd
  Agents—Cont'd
    Property, casualty and surety
      insurance
      representatives—Cont'd
    Licenses—Cont'd
      Stolen licenses.
        Affidavit in lieu of
          return for
          cancellation,
          §27-7-22.
      Suspension or revocation.
        Grounds, §27-7-19.
        Notice, §27-7-21.
        Placing of insurance
          by agent not
          appointed or
          licensed, §27-7-34.
        Proceedings to suspend
          or revoke,
          §27-7-20.
        Return for
          cancellation,
          §27-7-22.
      Temporary license.
        Agent properly
          licensed in another
          state, §27-7-25.
        Applications, §27-7-23.
        Fees, §§27-4-2, 27-7-23.
        Generally, §27-7-23.
        Pending examination
          of agent, §27-7-24.
        When issued, §27-7-23.
    Nonresident agents or
      brokers.
      Commissions, §27-7-28.
      License, §27-7-28.
      Service of process,
        §27-7-29.
    Notice of complaints
      against licensees,
      §27-7-37.
    Orders on complaints
      against licensees,
      §27-7-37.
    Place of business, §27-7-32.
    Placing of insurance by
      agent not appointed or
      licensed, §27-7-34.
    Premiums.
      Accounting for and
        payment of trust
        funds by licensees,
        §27-7-36.
    Privileged information,
      §27-7-38.
    Qualifications for licenses,
      §27-7-5.
    Records, §27-7-33.
    Scope of provisions,
      §27-7-2.
    Service of process.
      Nonresident agents or
        brokers, §27-7-29.
    Solicitors, §27-7-27.
      Licenses, §27-7-27.
    Termination of agent's
      appointment, §27-7-30.
      Rights of agent following
        termination,
        §27-7-31.
    Trust funds.
      Accounting for and
        payment of trust
        funds by licensees,
        §27-7-36.
    Vending machines.
      Applicability of
        provisions, §27-7-3.

INSURANCE—Cont'd
  Agents—Cont'd
    Records.
      Property, casualty and
        surety insurance
        representatives,
        §27-7-33.
    Reports.
      Life and disability
        insurance
        representatives.
        Filing of annual
          statements, §27-8-15.
      Required, §27-3-27.
      Surety insurance
        representatives, §§27-7-1
        to 27-7-38.
    Surplus line insurance.
      Acceptance and placement
        of surplus line
        business for agents,
        §27-10-25.
    Trade practices law,
      §§27-12-1 to 27-12-24.
      See within this heading,
      "Trade practices law."
    Unauthorized insurers.
      Representing, §27-10-1.
    Unfair trade, §§27-12-1 to
      27-12-24. See within this
      heading, "Trade practices
      law."
  Agriculture.
    Department of agriculture
      and industries.
      Insurance for employees at
        shipping points, etc.,
        §2-9-22.
  Air commerce.
    Certificates for common
      carriers and permits for
      contract carriers,
      §37-9-18.
  Alabama health care plan,
    §§27-21-1 to 27-21-6. See
    within this heading,
    "Health insurance."
  Alcoholic beverages.
    Disability insurance.
      Optional policy provision,
      §27-19-26.
  Alcoholism.
    Treatment in group plans,
      §§27-20A-1 to 27-20A-4.
  Alien insurers, §§27-33-1 to
    27-33-16. See within this
    heading, "Insurers."
  Anesthetic coverage.
    Health insurance.
      Certified registered nurse
        anesthetist coverage,
        §§27-46-1 to 27-46-3.
  Annuities.
    Contracts, §§27-15-16 to
      27-15-23.
    Age.
      Misstatement of age,
        §27-15-20.
    Applicability of chapter,
      §27-15-1.
    Dividend provisions,
      §27-15-21.
    Entire contract, §27-15-19.
    Exemption from debt of
      proceeds, §27-14-32.
    Forms.
      Approval, §27-14-8.
      Grounds for
        withdrawal,
        §27-14-9.

INSURANCE—Cont'd
  Annuities—Cont'd
    Contracts—Cont'd
      Forms—Cont'd
        Disapproval, §27-14-8.
        Grounds, §27-14-9.
        Filing, §27-14-8.
      Grace period clause,
        §27-15-17.
      Incontestability clause,
        §27-15-18.
      Misstatement of age or sex,
        §27-15-20.
      Payments.
        Effect of payments,
          §27-14-24.
        Minors.
          Receipt and giving of
            acquittance and
            discharge for
            payment by
            minors, §27-14-25.
      Proceeds.
        Exemption from debt of
          proceeds, §27-14-32.
      Provisions generally,
        §27-15-16.
      Reinstatement, §27-15-22.
      Reversionary annuities.
        Standard provisions in
          contracts, §27-15-23.
      Sex.
        Misstatement of sex,
          §27-15-20.
      Variable contracts,
        §§27-38-2 to 27-38-6.
    Deferred annuities.
      Standard nonforfeiture
      law, §27-15-28.1.
    Defined, §27-5-3.
    Discrimination.
      Exceptions to
        discrimination,
        §27-12-13.
      Unfair discrimination in
        rates, §27-12-11.
    Dividends.
      Contract provisions,
        §27-15-21.
    Exemption from debt of
      proceeds, §27-14-32.
    Inducements.
      Agreements not expressed
        in contract, rebates
        and other
        inducements,
        §27-12-12.
      Exceptions to special
        inducements,
        §27-12-13.
    Insurers.
      Reserve liability for
        variable contracts,
        §27-38-5.
      Variable contracts.
        Licensing of insurers,
        §27-38-3.
    Minors.
      Receipt and giving of
        acquittance and
        discharge for payment
        by minors, §27-14-25.
    Payments.
      Effect of payments,
        §27-14-24.
      Grace period clause,
        §27-15-17.
    Proceeds.
      Exemption from debt of
        proceeds, §27-14-32.

INSURANCE—Cont'd
  Annuities—Cont'd
    Rates.
      Discrimination.
        Exceptions to
          discrimination,
          §27-12-13.
        Unfair discrimination in
          rates, §27-12-11.
      Rebates, §27-12-12.
        Exceptions to rebates,
          §27-12-13.
    Reserves.
      Standard valuation law,
        §27-36-7.
      Variable contracts.
        Reserve liability,
          §27-38-5.
    Rules and regulations.
      Variable contracts,
        §27-38-4.
    Separate accounts.
      Establishment by life
        insurers, §27-38-1.
      Establishment by life
        insurers to provide for
        annuities, §27-38-1.
    Trusts and trustees.
      Investment of trust estate,
        §19-3-125.
    Variable contracts.
      Applicability of title,
        §27-38-6.
      Death benefit provision,
        §27-38-2.
      Determination of benefits.
        Statement of procedures,
        §27-38-2.
      Liability.
        Reserve liability,
        §27-38-5.
      Licensing of insurers,
        §27-38-3.
      Reserve liability for
        variable contracts,
        §27-38-5.
      Rules and regulations,
        §27-38-4.
  Annuity tables.
    See ANNUITY AND
      MORTALITY TABLES.
  Appeals.
    Agents.
      Life and disability
        insurance
        representatives.
        Appeal of order refusing
          to renew or continue
          or suspending or
          revoking license,
          §27-8-16.
    Brokers.
      Life and disability
        insurance
        representatives.
        Appeal of order refusing
          to renew or continue
          or suspending or
          revoking license,
          §27-8-16.
    Commissioner of insurance.
      Appeals from orders of
        commissioner,
        §27-2-32.
      Appeals from orders of
        supervision,
        §27-2-37.
    Holding companies.
      Judicial review of actions
        by commissioner,
        §27-29-13.

INSURANCE—Cont'd
  Appeals—Cont'd
    Insurers.
      Delinquency proceedings,
        §27-32-3.
      Life and disability insurance
        representatives.
        Appeal of order refusing to
          renew or continue or
          suspending or revoking
          license, §27-8-16.
  Applicability of title, §27-1-3.
    Exemptions, §27-1-4.
  Appropriations.
    Appropriations to certain
      universities.
      Determining
        reimbursement for
        patient care activities,
        §27-1-11.1.
  Assessments.
    Insurers.
      Mutual insurers,
        §§27-32-32 to 27-32-35.
      Reciprocal insurers,
        §§27-32-32 to 27-32-36.
    Life and disability insurance
      guaranty association,
      §§27-44-9, 27-44-13,
      27-44-14.
    Reciprocal insurers,
      §§27-32-32 to 27-32-36.
  Assets.
    Insurers, §§27-37-1 to
      27-37-9. See within this
      heading, "Insurers."
  Assigned risks.
    Safety-responsibility act,
      §32-7-35.
  Assignments.
    Policies, §27-14-21.
  Associations.
    Automobile clubs and
      associations, §§27-39-1 to
      27-39-8. See within this
      heading, "Automobile
      clubs and associations."
    Insurance guaranty
      association, §§27-42-1 to
      27-42-20. See within this
      heading, "Insurance
      guaranty association."
    Life and disability insurance
      guaranty association,
      §§27-44-1 to 27-44-21.
      See within this heading,
      "Life and disability
      insurance guaranty
      association."
    Mutual aid associations,
      §§27-30-1 to 27-30-33.
      See within this heading,
      "Mutual aid
      associations."
  Attachment.
    Insurers.
      Delinquency proceedings,
        §27-32-21.
  Attorney general.
    Assistant attorney general.
      Assignment to department
      of insurance, §27-2-11.
    Enforcement of insurance
      code, §27-2-19.
  Attorneys at law.
    Legal expense insurance,
      §§27-43-1 to 27-43-23.
      See within this heading,
      "Legal expense
      insurance."

INSURANCE—Cont'd
  **Automobile clubs and
    associations,** §§27-39-1 to
    27-39-8.
    Agents.
      Control over agents by
        commissioner,
        §27-39-7.
      Licensing, §27-39-7.
    Applicability of chapter,
      §27-39-2.
    Certificates of authority.
      Application, §27-39-6.
      Issuance, §27-39-6.
    Commissioner of insurance.
      Agents and
        representatives.
        Control over by
          commissioner,
          §27-39-7.
      Clubs and associations to
        be under authority,
        etc., of commissioner,
        §27-39-4.
      Powers of commissioner,
        §27-39-5.
    Definitions, §27-39-1.
    Incorporation, §27-39-3.
    Licenses.
      Agents and
        representatives,
        §27-39-7.
      Requirements, §27-39-3.
    Penalties.
      Violations of chapter,
        §27-39-8.
    Representatives.
      Licensing, §27-39-7.
    Violations of chapter.
      Penalty for violation,
        §27-39-8.
  Autopsies.
    Disability insurance.
      Provision in policy as to
        autopsy, §27-19-13.
  Bankruptcy and insolvency.
    Holding companies.
      Delinquency proceedings,
        §27-29-11.
    Insurance guaranty
      association.
      Insolvent insurers.
        Access to assets of
          insolvent insurers,
          §27-42-20.
        Defined, §27-42-5.
        Prevention, §27-42-13.
      Life and disability insurance
        guaranty association,
        §§27-44-14, 27-44-18,
        27-44-21. See within this
        heading, "Life and
        disability insurance
        guaranty association."
  Banks.
    Insurance of deposits.
      See BANKS AND
        FINANCIAL
        INSTITUTIONS.
  Binders, §27-14-18.
  Blanket insurance.
    Disability insurance,
      §§27-20-4 to 27-20-7.
  Bonds, surety.
    Chief receivership division,
      §27-2-51.
    Commissioner of insurance,
      §27-2-3.
  Books.
    Insurance premium finance
      companies, §27-40-6.

INSURANCE—Cont'd
  Boycotts, §27-12-8.
  Brokers.
    Casualty insurance
      representatives.
      Property, casualty and
        surety insurance
        representatives,
        §§27-7-1 to 27-7-38.
        See within this
        heading, "Agents."
    Directory of brokers.
      Annual publication by
        commissioner,
        §27-2-16.
    Examinations.
      Commissioner of insurance,
        §§27-2-20 to 27-2-27.
        See within this
        heading,
        "Commissioner of
        insurance."
    False statements, etc., in
      insurance application,
      §27-12-23.
    Licenses.
      Fees, §27-4-2.
      Property, casualty and
        surety insurance
        representatives,
        §§27-7-4 to 27-7-29.
        See within this
        heading, "Agents."
      Surplus line brokers,
        §27-10-24.
        Revocation or suspension
          of surplus line
          broker's license,
          §27-10-32.
    Life and disability insurance
      representatives, §§27-8-1
      to 27-8-28. See within
      this heading, "Agents."
    Nonresidents.
      Life and disability
        insurance
        representatives,
        §27-8-22.
      Property, casualty and
        surety insurance
        representatives,
        §§27-7-28, 27-7-29.
    Property, casualty and surety
      insurance
      representatives, §§27-7-1
      to 27-7-38. See within
      this heading, "Agents."
    Records.
      Property, casualty and
        surety insurance
        representatives,
        §27-7-33.
      Surplus line brokers,
        §27-10-29.
      Failure to keep records,
        §27-10-32.
    Reports.
      Life and disability
        insurance
        representatives.
        Filing of annual
          statements, §27-8-15.
      Surplus line brokers,
        §27-10-21.
        Annual statement,
          §27-10-30.

INSURANCE—Cont'd
Brokers—Cont'd
Surety insurance representatives.
Property, casualty and surety insurance representatives, §§27-7-1 to 27-7-38. See within this heading, "Agents."
Surplus line insurance.
Generally. See within this heading, "Surplus line insurance."
Licensing of brokers, §27-10-4.
Taxation.
Surplus line brokers.
Annual tax, §27-10-31.
Failure to pay annual tax, §27-10-32.
Buildings.
Casualty insurance generally. See within this heading, "Casualty insurance."
Fire insurance. See within this heading, "Fire insurance."
Insurance in name of less than all owners, §27-22-1.
Burglary insurance.
Casualty insurance generally. See within this heading, "Casualty insurance."
Burial insurance.
Applicability of chapter, §27-17-1.
Applicability of other provisions to chapter, §27-17-15.
Beneficiary, §27-17-10.
Burial reserves.
Valuation of life insurance reserve liabilities, §27-17-16.
Cash benefits.
In lieu of merchandise and services, §27-17-9.
Payment, §27-17-11.
Defined, §27-17-1.
Funeral directors.
Provision in policy for authorized funeral director, §27-17-7.
Investments.
Life, disability and burial insurance companies, §§27-41-1 to 27-41-41. See within this heading, "Investments of life, disability and burial insurance companies."
Merchandise and services.
Cash benefit in lieu of merchandise and services.
Policy provision, §27-17-9.
Policy provision as to furnishing, §27-17-8.
Monument dealers.
Provision in policy for authorized monument dealer, §27-17-7.

INSURANCE—Cont'd
Burial insurance—Cont'd
Policies, §§27-17-1 to 27-17-16.
Authorized funeral director or monument dealer, §27-17-7.
Beneficiary, §27-17-10.
Cash benefits.
In lieu of furnishing of merchandise and services, §27-17-9.
Payments, §27-17-11.
Cash surrender values, §27-17-13.
Conditions.
Waiver, §27-17-12.
Entire contract, §27-17-4.
Grace period provision, §27-17-3.
Incontestability provision, §27-17-5.
Merchandise and services.
Cash benefit in lieu of, §27-17-9.
Provision for furnishing, §27-17-8.
Nonforfeiture benefits, §27-17-13.
Provisions generally, §27-17-2.
Reinstatement provision, §27-17-6.
Representations, §27-17-4.
Terms.
Waiver, §27-17-12.
Title of policy, §27-17-14.
Value.
Cash surrender values, §27-17-13.
Waiver, etc., of policy terms or conditions, §27-17-12.
Premiums.
Grace period provision in policy, §27-17-3.
Valuation of life insurance reserve liabilities, §27-17-16.
Canada.
Insurers.
Trusteed assets.
Canadian insurers, §27-33-16.
Investments of life, disability and burial insurance companies, §§27-41-13, 27-41-15, 27-41-17.
Captions.
Effect of captions, §27-1-7.
Casualty insurance.
Agents and brokers.
Property, casualty and surety insurance representatives, §§27-7-1 to 27-7-38. See within this heading, "Agents."
Creditors.
Rights of judgment creditors, §27-23-2.
Definition, §27-5-6.
Rates and rating organizations, §27-13-60.
Harbors and ports.
Docks department.
Authority of state docks department to carry casualty insurance, §33-1-25.

INSURANCE—Cont'd
Casualty insurance—Cont'd
Inducements.
Unfair inducements, §27-12-14.
Insurers.
Liability.
When absolute, §27-23-1.
Unearned premium reserve, §27-36-3.
Licenses.
Rates and rating organizations, §§27-13-24, 27-13-62.
Medical liability insurance, §§27-26-1 to 27-26-43. See within this heading, "Medical liability insurance."
Motor vehicles.
Automobile clubs and associations, §§27-39-1 to 27-39-8. See within this heading, "Automobile clubs and associations."
General provisions. See MOTOR VEHICLES.
Premiums.
Rebates, §27-12-14.
Unearned premium reserve, §27-36-3.
Rates and rating organizations, §§27-13-1 to 27-13-105. See within this heading, "Rates and rating organizations."
Rebates, §27-12-14.
Representatives, §§27-7-1 to 27-7-38. See within this heading, "Agents."
Reserves.
Unearned premium reserve, §27-36-3.
Unearned premium reserve, §27-36-3.
Certificates of authority.
Insurers, §§27-3-1 to 27-3-29. See within this heading, "Insurers."
Mutual aid associations, §§27-30-8 to 27-30-12. See within this heading, "Mutual aid associations."
Change of place of business, §5-17-23.
Chiropractors.
Insured to have exclusive right to select, §27-1-10.
Payment for health services of chiropractor, §27-1-10.
Civil defense.
Civil defense workers and trainees.
Compensation insurance, §31-9-21.
Claims.
Acts not deemed waiver of provisions or defenses, §27-14-27.
Health insurance.
Limitation period for payment of claims, §27-1-17.
Right of action for recovery of unpaid benefits, §27-1-17.

INSURANCE—Cont'd
Claims—Cont'd
Insurance guaranty
association, §§27-42-5,
27-42-8 to 27-42-12. See
within this heading,
"Insurance guaranty
association."
Coal.
Abandoned mine
reclamation.
Workmen's compensation,
§9-16-134.
Surface mining control and
reclamation.
Permit insurance, §9-16-83.
Coercion, §27-12-8.
Commissioner of insurance,
§§27-2-1 to 27-2-55.
Actions.
Enforcement of insurance
code, §27-2-19.
Agents.
Property, casualty and
surety insurance
representatives.
Filing of agent's
appointment by
insurer with
commissioner,
§27-7-30.
Alien insurers.
Trust agreement.
Approval by
commissioner,
§27-33-5.
Withdrawal of approval,
§27-33-8.
Appeals from orders,
§27-2-32.
Order of supervision,
§27-2-37.
Appointment, §27-2-2.
Attorney general.
Assistant attorney general.
Assignment to
department,
§27-2-11.
Automobile clubs and
associations.
Agents and
representatives.
Control over by
commissioner,
§27-39-7.
Clubs and associations to
be under authority,
etc., of commissioner,
§27-39-4.
Powers of commissioner,
§27-39-5.
Bonds, surety, §27-2-3.
Compensation.
Additional compensation,
§27-2-13.
Conflicts of interest,
§27-2-13.
Contracting for professional
services, §27-2-10.
Defined, §27-1-2.
Delinquency proceedings,
§§27-32-3, 27-32-4,
27-32-15 to 27-32-20. See
within this heading,
"Insurers."
Dental service corporations.
Applicable insurance laws,
§22-21-374.
Generally.
See DENTAL SERVICE
CORPORATIONS.

INSURANCE—Cont'd
Commissioner of insurance
—Cont'd
Destruction.
Records, documents and
files, §27-2-14.
Duties, §27-2-7.
Delegation of duties,
§27-2-8.
Devotion of entire time to
duties, §27-2-4.
Enforcement of insurance
code, §27-2-19.
Evidence.
Examinations, §27-2-26.
Compelling production of
documents, §27-2-27.
Hearings, §27-2-27.
Investigations, §27-2-27.
Records, documents and
files.
Use as evidence,
§27-2-15.
Reports of examinations by
commissioner,
§27-2-24.
Examinations.
Affairs, etc., of insurers,
§27-2-21.
Associations, §27-42-14.
Evaluation of assets,
§27-2-23.
Evidence, §27-2-26.
Compelling production of
documents, §27-2-27.
Examiners.
Appointment, etc.,
§27-2-22.
Expenses, §27-2-25.
How conducted, §27-2-23.
Insurers.
Affairs, etc., of insurers,
§27-2-21.
Power generally, §27-2-20.
Procedure, §27-2-23.
Rates and rating
organizations,
§27-13-74.
Report, §27-2-24.
Witnesses, §27-2-26.
Compelling testimony,
§27-2-27.
Immunity from
prosecution,
§27-2-27.
Expenses.
Examinations by
commissioner,
§27-2-25.
Travel expenses, §27-2-12.
Fees.
Rehabilitation,
reorganization,
conservation and
liquidation of insurers.
Exemption from fees,
§27-32-24.
Finance companies.
Insurance premium finance
companies.
Exclusive jurisdiction of
department of
insurance, §27-40-14.
Licenses.
Information to be
furnished
commissioner,
§27-40-3.
Governor.
Annual report to governor,
§27-2-9.

INSURANCE—Cont'd
Commissioner of insurance
—Cont'd
Governor—Cont'd
Appointment by governor,
§27-2-2.
Health care service plans,
§§10-4-100 to 10-4-115.
See HEALTH CARE
SERVICE PLANS.
Hearings.
Appeals from orders,
§27-2-32.
Conduct.
How conducted, §27-2-30.
Evidence, §27-2-26.
Compelling production of
documents, §27-2-27.
How conducted, §27-2-30.
Notice, §27-2-29.
Order of supervision.
Notice and hearing as to
issuance, §27-2-38.
Order on hearing, §27-2-31.
Power to hold, §27-2-28.
Procedure, §27-2-30.
Property, casualty and
surety insurance
representatives.
Hearing of complaints
against licensees,
§27-7-37.
Rates and rating
organizations.
Fire and inland marine
insurance, §27-13-42.
Witnesses, §27-2-26.
Compelling testimony,
§27-2-27.
Immunity from
prosecution,
§27-2-27.
Holding companies.
Appeal from actions by
commissioner,
§27-29-13.
Effect of chapter on powers
of commissioner,
§27-28-4.
Injunctions against
violations of
commissioner's orders
or rules and
regulations, §27-29-9.
Judicial review of actions
by commissioner,
§27-29-13.
Mandamus.
Petition for mandamus
against
commissioner,
§27-29-13.
Orders by commissioner,
§27-29-8.
Rules and regulations,
§27-29-8.
Inspections.
Records, documents and
files, §27-2-14.
Insurance guaranty
association, §§27-42-9,
27-42-10, 27-42-13.
Insurance premium finance
companies.
Exclusive jurisdiction of
department of
insurance, §27-40-14.

INSURANCE—Cont'd
  Commissioner of insurance
    —Cont'd
    Insurance premium finance
      companies—Cont'd
    Licenses.
      Information to be
        furnished
        commissioner,
        §27-40-3.
    Investigations.
      Evidence, §27-2-26.
      Compelling production of
        documents, §27-2-27.
      Witnesses, §27-2-26.
      Compelling testimony,
        §27-2-27.
      Immunity from
        prosecution,
        §27-2-27.
    Investments of life, disability
      and burial insurance
      companies, §§27-41-1 to
      27-41-41. See within this
      heading, "Investments of
      life, disability and burial
      insurance companies."
    Life and disability insurance
      guaranty association,
      §§27-44-11, 27-44-12,
      27-44-17.
    Liquidation.
      Loans to facilitate,
        §27-32-25.
    Medical liability insurance.
      Joint underwriting
        association.
        Appeal to commissioner,
          §27-26-42.
        Examination of
          association's affairs,
          §27-26-39.
        Judicial review of
          commissioner's
          orders, §27-26-43.
    Mutual aid associations.
      Approval of contracts,
        §27-30-14.
      Examinations by
        commissioner,
        §27-30-24.
      Service of process.
        Commissioner as agent
          for process,
          §27-30-13.
    Notices of commissioner,
      §27-2-18.
      Hearings, §27-2-29.
    Oath, §27-2-3.
    Offices, §27-2-6.
    Order of supervision.
      Appeal, §27-2-37.
      Appointment of supervisor,
        §27-2-34.
      Authority of commissioner,
        §27-2-33.
      Content, §27-2-37.
      Delinquency proceedings.
        Effect on delinquency
          proceedings,
          §27-2-36.
      Duration of order,
        §27-2-35.
      Form, §27-2-37.
      Hearings.
        Notice and hearing as to
          issuance, §27-2-38.
      Liquidation proceedings.
        Effect on liquidation
          proceedings,
          §27-2-36.

INSURANCE—Cont'd
  Commissioner of insurance
    —Cont'd
    Order of supervision—Cont'd
      Notice and hearing as to
        issuance, §27-2-38.
      Prohibited acts during
        term of supervision,
        §27-2-34.
      Reasons for issuance,
        §27-2-33.
      Rehabilitation proceedings.
        Effect on rehabilitation
          proceedings,
          §27-2-36.
      Withdrawal of order,
        §27-2-35.
    Orders, §27-2-18.
      Appeals from orders,
        §27-2-32.
      Hearings, §27-2-31.
      Supervision.
        Order of supervision,
          §§27-2-33 to 27-2-38.
    Pharmaceutical insurance
      coverage.
      Enforcement of provisions,
        §27-45-8.
    Powers, §27-2-7.
      Delegation of powers,
        §27-2-8.
      Examinations, §27-2-20.
      Hearings, §27-2-28.
    Professional services.
      Contracting for
        professional services,
        §27-2-10.
    Publication of materials
      relating to insurance,
      §27-2-16.
    Qualifications, §27-2-2.
    Rates and rating
      organizations.
      Casualty and surety
        insurance.
        Delegation of authority
          by commissioner,
          §27-13-82.
        Examination of business,
          etc., of rating
          organizations and
          insurers making own
          rates, §27-13-74.
        Hearings by
          commissioner,
          §27-13-80.
        Notices by commissioner,
          §27-13-80.
        Orders by commissioner,
          §27-13-80.
          Review of final orders,
            §27-13-81.
        Rating plans.
          Examination and
            approval or
            disapproval,
            §27-13-68.
      Fire and inland marine
        insurance.
        Delegation of authority,
          §27-13-44.
        Examination and
          approval or
          disapproval of rating
          systems, §27-13-30.
        Examination of business,
          etc., of rating
          organizations and
          insurers making own
          rates, §27-13-36.

INSURANCE—Cont'd
  Commissioner of insurance
    —Cont'd
    Rates and rating
      organizations—Cont'd
      Fire and inland marine
        insurance—Cont'd
        Hearings by
          commissioner,
          §27-13-42.
        Notices by commissioner,
          §27-13-42.
        Orders by commissioner,
          §27-13-42.
          Review of final orders,
            §27-13-42.
        Reasonableness of rates.
          Factors to be
            considered in
            determining,
            §27-13-35.
        Review of final orders of
          commissioner,
          §27-13-43.
      Insurance advisory
        organizations.
        Compliance with rules of
          commissioner,
          §27-13-101.
        Filing with
          commissioner,
          §27-13-102.
        Orders by commissioner.
          Casualty and surety
            insurance, §27-13-80.
          Fire and inland marine
            insurance, §27-13-42.
    Receivership division.
      Assumption by receiver of
        certain former powers,
        duties, etc., of
        commissioner,
        §27-2-55.
    Reciprocal insurers.
      Service of process on
        commissioner as agent
        for insurer, §27-31-14.
    Records, documents and files,
      §27-2-14.
      Use as evidence, §27-2-15.
    Rehabilitation.
      Loans to facilitate
        rehabilitation,
        §27-32-25.
    Reports.
      Annual report, §27-2-9.
      Examinations by
        commissioner,
        §27-2-24.
    Rules and regulations,
      §27-2-17.
      Publication, §27-2-16.
    Salary, §27-2-4.
    Seal.
      Official seal, §27-2-5.
    Service of process.
      Appointment of
        commissioner as agent
        for service on insurers,
        §27-3-24.
      Fee for acceptance of
        service on insurers,
        §27-4-2.
    State fire marshal.
      Appointment, etc.,
        §27-2-10.
    Supervision of insurers.
      Order of supervision,
        §§27-2-33 to 27-2-38.

INSURANCE—Cont'd
Commissioner of insurance
—Cont'd
Surplus line insurance.
Production of policies, etc.,
for inspection by
commissioner,
§27-10-36.
Term of office, §27-2-2.
Travel expenses, §27-2-12.
Unauthorized insurers.
Acts constituting
appointment of
commissioner as agent
for service of process,
§27-10-51.
Production of policies, etc.,
for inspection by
commissioner,
§27-10-36.
Witnesses.
Compelling testimony or
production of
documents, §27-2-26.
Immunity from
prosecution, §27-2-27.
Companies.
Corporations provisions.
Applicability, §§10-2A-336,
27-27-61.
Insurers. See within this
heading, "Insurers."
Compliance with title.
Requirement of compliance,
§27-1-5.
Condominiums.
Powers of association,
§35-8-9.
Conflicts of interest.
Commissioner of insurance,
§27-2-13.
Insurers, §27-27-26.
**Construction and
interpretation.**
Effect of captions or
headings, §27-1-7.
Pharmaceutical insurance
coverage.
Pharmaceutical services
not mandated,
§27-45-5.
Policies, §27-14-17.
Prevalence of particular over
general provisions,
§27-1-6.
Consumer finance.
Requirements by creditor,
§5-19-20.
Contracts.
Annuities, §§27-15-16 to
27-15-22. See within this
heading, "Annuities."
Applicability of chapter,
§27-14-2.
Binders, §27-14-18.
Burial insurance policies,
§§27-17-1 to 27-17-16.
See within this heading,
"Burial insurance."
Commissioner of insurance.
Contracting for
professional services,
§27-2-10.
Definitions, §27-14-1.
Disability insurance policies,
§§27-19-1 to 27-19-39.
See within this heading,
"Disability insurance."

INSURANCE—Cont'd
Contracts—Cont'd
Finance companies.
Insurance premium finance
companies.
Cancellation of insurance
contract upon
default, §27-40-11.
Charges for
cancellation,
§27-40-10.
Return of gross
unearned
premiums upon
cancellation,
§27-40-12.
General provisions. See
within this heading,
"Policies."
Industrial life insurance
policies, §§27-16-1 to
27-16-17. See within this
heading, "Industrial life
insurance."
Insurance premium finance
companies.
Cancellation of insurance
contract upon default,
§27-40-11.
Charges, §27-40-10.
Return of gross unearned
premiums upon
cancellation,
§27-40-12.
Insurers.
Exclusive management and
production of business
contracts, §27-27-27.
Life insurance policies,
§§27-15-2 to 27-15-14.
See within this heading,
"Life insurance."
Medicaid.
Denial or reduction of
benefits due to
eligibility for medicaid,
§27-14-11.1.
Minors.
Purchase of insurance by
or for minors, §27-14-5.
Mutual aid associations,
§§27-30-14, 27-30-17.
Policies. See within this
heading, "Policies."
Power to contract, §27-14-5.
Proof of loss.
Forms for proof of loss,
§27-14-26.
Pure endowment contracts,
§§27-15-16 to 27-15-22.
See within this heading,
"Pure endowment
contracts."
Reciprocal insurers.
Execution by attorneys,
§27-31-5.
Nonassessable policies,
§27-31-25.
Right to exchange
contracts, §27-31-18.
Situs of contracts, §27-14-22.
Substitution for standard or
uniform provisions,
§27-14-10.
Unauthorized insurers.
Validity of contracts,
§27-10-1.
Uniform provisions,
§27-14-10.

INSURANCE—Cont'd
Corporations.
Insurance companies.
Applicability of
corporations
provisions,
§§10-2A-336, 27-27-61.
Liability insurance,
§10-2A-21.
Counties.
County commissions.
Powers and duties of
county commissions,
§11-3-11.
Group insurance for officers
and employees, §§11-91-1
to 11-91-8.
See COUNTIES.
Health and accident self-
insurance groups.
Appropriation of funds,
§11-26-2.
Attorneys and employees,
§11-26-4.
Authorized, §11-26-2.
Bylaws.
Filing with insurance
commissioner,
§11-26-5.
Collection of charges,
§11-26-4.
Collection of funds,
§11-26-2.
Establishment, §11-26-2.
Exempt from insurance
premium tax, §11-26-5.
Exempt from regulation by
department of
insurance, §11-26-5.
Governing body of trustees.
Establishment, §11-26-4.
Management and
consultant contracts,
§11-26-4.
Officers.
Liability of officers of
nonprofit
associations,
§§10-11-1 to 10-11-5.
See ASSOCIATIONS.
Powers generally, §11-26-4.
Purpose, §11-26-2.
Schedule of benefits,
§11-26-4.
Filing, §11-26-5.
Schedule of charges,
§11-26-4.
Filing, §11-26-5.
Industry and trade.
Projects for promotion.
Investment in bonds by
insurance
companies,
§11-20-10.
Liability self-insurance
funds, §§11-30-1 to
11-30-7.
See COUNTIES.
Taxation.
Counties not permitted to
tax insurers, §27-4-9.
Credit.
Insurance premium finance
companies, §§27-40-1 to
27-40-18. See within this
heading, "Premiums."
Credit facilities.
Life and disability insurance
representatives.
Use of credit facilities,
§27-8-23.

INSURANCE—Cont'd
Credit insurance.
Casualty insurance
generally, §§27-23-1 to
27-23-28. See within this
heading, "Casualty
insurance."
Credit unions.
Requirements for obtaining
insurance, §5-17-19.
Criminal law and procedure.
Holding companies.
Criminal proceedings
against, §27-29-10.
Default judgments.
Life and disability insurance
guaranty association.
Reopening default
judgments, §27-44-18.
Definitions, §27-1-2.
Adjusters, §27-9-1.
Agents.
Defined, §27-8-1.
Life and disability
insurance
representatives.
§27-8-1.
Property, casualty and
surety insurance
representatives,
§27-7-1.
Annuities, §27-5-3.
Automobile clubs and
associations, §27-39-1.
Burial insurance, §27-17-1.
Casualty insurance, §27-5-6.
Rates and rating
organizations,
§27-13-60.
Certified registered nurse
anesthetist, §27-46-3.
Contracts, §27-14-1.
Dental care services,
§27-19A-2.
Disability insurance, §27-5-4.
Fees and taxes, §27-4-1.
Finance companies.
Insurance premium finance
companies, §27-40-1.
Fire insurance.
Rates and rating
organizations,
§27-13-20.
Fraternal benefit societies,
§27-34-1.
Holding companies, §27-29-1.
Industrial life insurance,
§27-16-1.
Insurable interest, §§27-14-3,
27-14-4.
Insurance guaranty
associations, §27-42-5.
Insurance premium finance
companies, §27-40-1.
Insurers, §§27-1-2, 27-27-1,
27-32-1.
Equity securities,
§27-27-58.
Investments of life, disability
and burial insurance
companies, §27-41-2.
Legal expense insurance,
§27-43-3.
Life and disability insurance
guaranty association,
§27-44-5.
Life insurance, §27-5-2.
Industrial life insurance,
§27-16-1.

INSURANCE—Cont'd
Definitions—Cont'd
Marine insurance, §27-5-8.
Inland marine insurance.
Rates and rating
organizations,
§27-13-20.
Wet marine and
transportation
insurance, §27-5-9.
Medical liability insurance,
§27-26-1.
Medicare supplement policy
minimum standards,
§27-19-52.
Mutual aid associations,
§27-30-1.
Pharmaceutical insurance
coverage, §27-45-2.
Policies, §27-14-1.
Premiums, §27-14-1.
Insurance premium finance
companies, §27-40-1.
Property insurance, §27-5-5.
Rates and rating
organizations.
Advisory organizations,
§27-13-100.
Casualty and surety
insurance, §27-13-60.
Fire and inland marine
insurance, §27-13-20.
Reciprocal insurers, §27-31-1.
Surety insurance, §27-5-7.
Rates and rating
organizations,
§27-13-60.
Title insurance, §27-5-10.
Transportation insurance.
Wet marine and
transportation
insurance, §27-5-9.
Wet marine and
transportation insurance,
§27-5-9.
Dental care services,
§§27-19A-1 to 27-19A-11.
Applicability of chapter,
§27-19A-1.
Commissioner.
Enforcement of chapter,
§27-19A-10.
Nonconforming policies
and plans.
Not to be approved,
§27-19A-9.
Conformity with chapter.
Plans not in conformance
unlawful, §27-19A-8.
Contracts.
Contracting directly with
patients, §27-19A-7.
Definitions, §27-19A-2.
Dental benefits not required,
§27-19A-6.
Enforcement of chapter.
Commissioner, §27-19A-10.
Payment.
Procedure, §27-19A-7.
Penalties.
Violation of chapter,
§27-19A-11.
Policies.
Distribution of information
about, §27-19A-7.
Nonconforming policies.
Denial of approval,
§27-19A-9.
Prohibited provisions,
§27-19A-3.

INSURANCE—Cont'd
Dental care services—Cont'd
Policies—Cont'd
Provisions contrary to
chapter.
Void, §27-19A-5.
Required provisions,
§27-19A-4.
Reimbursement.
Procedures, §27-19A-7.
Scope of chapter, §27-19A-1.
Violation of chapter.
Penalties, §27-19A-11.
Dental hygienists.
"Physicians" under health or
accident insurance
policies, §27-1-11.
Dental service corporations.
Applicable insurance laws,
§22-21-374.
General provisions,
§§22-21-360 to 22-21-391.
See DENTAL SERVICE
CORPORATIONS.
Dentists.
Medical liability insurance,
§§27-26-1 to 27-26-43.
See within this heading,
"Medical liability
insurance."
"Physicians" under health or
accident insurance
policies, §27-1-11.
Department of insurance.
Attorney general.
Assistant attorney general.
Assignment to
department,
§27-2-11.
Commissioner of insurance,
§§27-2-1 to 27-2-55. See
within this heading,
"Commissioner of
insurance."
Defined, §27-1-2.
Establishment, §27-2-1.
Expenditures.
Annual report by
commissioner, §27-2-9.
Expenses, §27-2-1.
Insurance premium finance
companies.
Exclusive jurisdiction of
department of
insurance, §27-40-14.
Receipts.
Annual report by
commissioner, §27-2-9.
Receivership division,
§§27-2-50 to 27-2-55. See
within this heading,
"Receivership division."
Deposits.
Insurers, §§27-6-1 to 27-6-16.
See within this heading,
"Insurers."
Mutual aid associations,
§§27-30-18, 27-30-19.
**Directory of insurers, agents
and brokers.**
Annual publication by
commissioner, §27-2-16.
Disability insurance.
Active life reserve, §27-36-5.
Age.
Misstatement of age,
§27-19-18.
Age limit, §27-19-36.
Agents, §§27-8-1 to 27-8-28.
See within this heading,
"Agents."

INSURANCE—Cont'd
  Disability insurance—Cont'd
    Alcoholic beverages.
      Optional policy provision,
        §27-19-26.
    Applicability of chapter,
      §27-19-1.
    Autopsy provision in policy,
      §27-19-13.
    Beneficiaries.
      Change of beneficiary,
        §27-19-15.
    Benefits, §27-19-21.
      Expense-incurred benefits,
        §27-19-20.
      Hospitalization benefits for
        mental patients in tax-
        supported institutions.
        Exclusion, §27-19-28.
    Blanket disability insurance,
      §§27-20-4 to 27-20-7.
      Benefits.
        Payment of benefits,
          §27-20-7.
      Certificates, §27-20-6.
      Eligible groups, §27-20-4.
      Filing requirement,
        §27-20-5.
      Policies.
        Applications, §27-20-6.
        Certificates, §27-20-6.
        Mandatory provisions,
          §§27-20-5 to 27-20-7.
        Payment of benefits,
          §27-20-7.
      Power to issue, §27-20-5.
    Children.
      Coverage of newly born
        children in health
        insurance policies,
        §27-19-38.
    Claims.
      Forms, §27-19-9.
      Notice of claim provision
        in policy, §27-19-8.
      Payment, §27-19-12.
        Time of payment,
          §27-19-11.
      Proof of loss, §27-19-10.
    Construction of policy
      provisions, §27-19-35.
    Continuance of disability.
      Notice of disability
        continuance provision
        in policy, §27-19-8.
    Coverage.
      Date for termination,
        §27-19-36.
      Newly born children.
        Coverage in health
          insurance policies,
          §27-19-38.
    Defenses.
      Time limit on certain
        defenses, §27-19-5.
    Defined, §27-5-4.
    Discrimination.
      Exceptions to
        discrimination,
        §27-12-13.
      Unfair discrimination in
        rates, §27-12-11.
    Earnings.
      Relation of earnings to
        insurance.
        Optional provision in
          policy, §27-19-22.
    Endorsements.
      Addition of endorsements
        to existing policies,
        §27-19-33.

INSURANCE—Cont'd
  Disability insurance—Cont'd
    Endorsements—Cont'd
      Compliance with chapter
        by endorsement,
        §27-19-34.
    Examination of policies,
      §27-19-32.
    Examinations.
      Provision in policy as to
        physical examination,
        §27-19-13.
    Exemption from debt of
      proceeds, §27-14-31.
    Foreign jurisdictions.
      Provisions of other
        jurisdictions,
        §27-19-30.
    Franchise plan, §27-19-37.
    Fraternal benefit societies.
      Total or permanent
        disability insurance
        contracts, §27-34-32.
    Group disability insurance,
      §§27-20-1 to 27-20-3.
      Direct payment of those
        rendering services,
        §27-20-3.
      Eligible groups, §27-20-1.
      Policies.
        Direct payment of those
          rendering services,
          §27-20-3.
        Mandatory provisions,
          §§27-20-2, 27-20-3.
    Hospitalization benefits.
      Exclusion for mental
        patients in tax-
        supported institutions,
        §27-19-28.
    Inducements, §27-12-12.
      Exceptions to special
        inducements,
        §27-12-13.
    Insurers.
      Active life reserve for
        disability insurance,
        §27-36-5.
    Intoxicants.
      Optional policy provision,
        §27-19-26.
    Investments.
      Life, disability and burial
        insurance companies,
        §§27-41-1 to 27-41-41.
        See within this
          heading, "Investments
          of life, disability and
          burial insurance
          companies."
    Life and disability insurance
      guaranty association,
      §§27-44-1 to 27-44-21.
      See within this heading,
        "Life and disability
        insurance guaranty
        association."
    Life reserve.
      Active life reserve,
        §27-36-5.
    Mental patients.
      Exclusion of hospitalization
        benefits for mental
        patients in tax-
        supported institutions,
        §27-19-28.
    Narcotics.
      Optional policy provision,
        §27-19-26.

INSURANCE—Cont'd
  Disability insurance—Cont'd
    Newly born children.
      Coverage in health
        insurance policies,
        §27-19-38.
    Nonresident agents and
      brokers, §27-8-22.
    Occupations.
      Change of occupation
        provision in policy,
        §27-19-17.
      Illegal occupation,
        §27-19-25.
        Optional provision in
          policy, §27-19-25.
    Ownership of policy in
      person other than
      insured, §27-19-29.
    Physical examination.
      Provision in policy as to
        physical examination,
        §27-19-13.
    Policies, §§27-19-1 to
      27-19-58.
      Actions.
        Provision in policy as to
          legal actions,
          §27-19-14.
      Age.
        Misstatement of age
          provision, §27-19-18.
      Alcoholic beverage
        provision, §27-19-27.
      Autopsy provision,
        §27-19-13.
      Beneficiary.
        Change of beneficiary
          provision, §27-19-15.
      Benefits, §27-19-21.
        Expense-incurred
          benefits, §27-19-20.
      Blanket disability
        insurance, §§27-20-5 to
        27-20-7.
      Changes.
        Provisions as to changes,
          §27-19-4.
      Claims.
        Forms, §27-19-9.
        Notice of claims
          provision, §27-19-8.
        Payment, §27-19-12.
        Time of payment
          provision, §27-19-11.
      Conformity with state
        statutes, §27-19-24.
      Construction of policy
        provisions, §27-19-35.
      Continuance of disability.
        Notice of disability
          continuance
          provision in policy,
          §27-19-8.
      Defenses.
        Time limit on certain
          defenses, §27-19-5.
      Earnings.
        Optional provision as to
          relation of earnings
          to insurance,
          §27-19-22.
      Endorsements.
        Addition of endorsements
          to existing policies,
          §27-19-33.
        Compliance with chapter
          by endorsement,
          §27-19-34.
      Entire contract provision,
        §27-19-4.

INSURANCE—Cont'd
  Disability insurance—Cont'd
    Policies—Cont'd
      Examinations, §27-19-32.
      Format, §27-19-2.
      Grace period provision,
        §27-19-6.
      Group disability insurance,
        §§27-20-2, 27-20-3.
      Insurance with other
        insurers clause,
        §§27-19-20, 27-19-21.
      Intoxicants provision,
        §27-19-26.
      Mandatory provisions,
        §§27-19-3 to 27-19-26.
      Misstatement of age
        provision, §27-19-18.
      Narcotics provision,
        §27-19-26.
      Occupations.
        Change of occupation
          provision, §27-19-17.
      Optional provisions,
        §§27-19-16 to 27-19-26.
      Order of provisions in
        policy, §27-19-27.
      Other insurance in same
        insurer, §27-19-19.
      Ownership of policy.
        Ownership in person
          other than insured,
          §27-19-29.
      Physical examination
        provision, §27-19-13.
      Proof of loss.
        Provision as to proof of
          loss, §27-19-10.
      Provisions generally,
        §27-19-3.
      Reimbursement for visual
        services, §27-19-39.
      Renewability, §27-19-31.
      Return after examination,
        §27-19-32.
      Riders.
        Addition of riders to
          existing policies,
          §27-19-33.
        Compliance with chapter
          by rider, §27-19-34.
      Scope, §27-19-2.
      Statutes.
        Conformity with state
          statutes, §27-19-24.
      Unpaid premiums
        provision, §27-19-23.
    Premiums.
      Agents and brokers.
        Accounting for and
          payment of trust
          funds, §27-8-28.
      Grace period provision in
        policy, §27-19-6.
      Rebates, §27-12-12.
        Exceptions to rebates,
          §27-12-13.
      Reinstatement provision,
        §27-19-7.
      Unpaid premiums.
        Optional provision in
          policy as to unpaid
          premiums,
          §27-19-23.
    Proceeds.
      Exemption from debt of
        proceeds, §27-14-31.
    Proof of loss.
      Provision in policy as to
        proof of loss, §27-19-10.

INSURANCE—Cont'd
  Disability insurance—Cont'd
    Rates.
      Discrimination.
        Exceptions to
          discrimination,
          §27-12-13.
        Unfair discrimination in
          rates, §§27-12-11,
          27-12-13.
      Rebates.
        Exceptions to rebates,
          §§27-12-12, 27-12-13.
      Renewability of policies,
        §27-19-31.
      Reports.
        Filing of annual
          statements by life and
          disability insurance
          representatives,
          §27-8-15.
      Representatives, §§27-8-1 to
        27-8-28. See within this
        heading, "Agents."
      Reserves.
        Active life reserve,
          §27-36-5.
        Standard valuation law,
          §27-36-7.
      Riders.
        Addition of riders to
          existing policies,
          §27-19-33.
        Compliance with chapter
          by rider, §27-19-34.
      Sickle-cell anemia.
        Denial of coverage upon
          diagnosis prohibited,
          §27-5-13.
      Termination of coverage.
        Date for termination,
          §27-19-36.
  Discovery.
    Insurance agreements,
      ARCP, Rule 26 (b).
  Discrimination.
    Insurers.
      Protection of state insurers
        against foreign
        discriminatory or
        onerous requirements,
        §27-3-29.
    Life, annuity and disability
      insurance.
      Exceptions to
        discrimination,
        §27-12-13.
      Unfair discrimination in
        rates, §27-12-11.
  District attorneys.
    Enforcement of insurance
      code, §27-2-19.
  Docks department.
    Authority to carry fire and
      casualty and public
      liability coverage,
      §33-1-25.
  Drugs.
    Disability insurance.
      Optional policy provision
        as to narcotics,
        §27-19-26.
    Pharmaceutical insurance
      coverage, §§27-45-1 to
      27-45-9. See within this
      heading,
      "Pharmaceutical
      insurance coverage."

INSURANCE—Cont'd
  Education.
    City boards of education.
      Insurance on school
        buildings, §16-11-27.
    County boards of education.
      Insurance on school
        buildings, §16-8-42.
    Group insurance.
      Authority of school boards
        to form groups for
        purpose of obtaining,
        §16-22-5.
      Payment of premiums,
        §16-22-5.
      Presumption as to
        payments and
        deductions, §16-22-7.
    Life insurers organized to aid
      nonprofit educational
      and scientific
      institutions.
      Annual license fee, §27-4-8.
    Public education employees
      health insurance,
      §§16-25A-1 to 16-25A-17.
      See EDUCATION.
    Risk management
      cooperatives, §16-8-42.1.
    Salary deductions.
      Group insurance
        premiums, §16-22-6.
    School buses.
      Vehicle liability insurance
        for drivers, §16-27-7.
  Elevator insurance.
    Casualty insurance
      generally, §§27-7-1 to
      27-7-38. See within this
      heading, "Casualty
      insurance."
  Embezzlement.
    Property, casualty and surety
      insurance
      representatives.
      Diversion or appropriation
        of trust funds,
        §27-7-36.
  Endowments, §§27-15-1 to
    27-15-29. See within this
    heading, "Annuities."
  **Enforcement of insurance
    code,** §27-2-19.
  Entertainment insurance.
    Casualty insurance
      generally, §§27-7-1 to
      27-7-38. See within this
      heading, "Casualty
      insurance."
  **Environmental improvement
    authorities.**
    Power to provide, §9-6-8.
  Evidence.
    Commissioner of insurance.
      Examinations, §27-2-26.
      Hearings, §27-2-27.
      Investigations, §27-2-27.
      Records, documents and
        files.
        Use as evidence,
          §27-2-15.
    Policies.
      Application for policy.
        Admissibility into
          evidence, §27-14-6.
    Records, documents and files.
      Use as evidence, §27-2-15.
    Reports.
      Examinations by
        commissioner,
        §27-2-24.

INSURANCE—Cont'd
  Evidence—Cont'd
    Surplus line insurance,
      §27-10-27.
  Examinations.
    Commissioner of insurance,
      §§27-2-20 to 27-2-27. See
      within this heading,
      "Commissioner of
      insurance."
    Disability insurance policy,
      §27-19-32.
    Physical examination,
      §27-19-13.
    Fraternal benefit societies,
      §§27-34-39 to 27-34-41.
      See FRATERNAL
        BENEFIT SOCIETIES.
    Insurance guaranty
      associations, §27-42-13.
  Executions.
    Insurers.
      Delinquency proceedings,
        §27-32-21.
  Exemptions from levy and
    sale under process.
    Rights of beneficiaries and
      assignees under life
      insurance policies,
      §6-10-8.
  Exemptions from title,
    §27-1-4.
  Fees.
    Adjusters.
      Licenses, §§27-4-2, 27-9-2.
    Agents.
      License fee, §27-4-2.
    Brokers.
      Licenses, §27-4-2.
    Commissioner of insurance.
      Rehabilitation,
        reorganization,
        conservation and
        liquidation of insurers.
        Exemption of
          commissioner from
          fees, §27-32-24.
    Definitions, §27-4-1.
    Finance companies.
      Insurance premium finance
        companies, §27-40-3.
    Holding companies.
      Plan for exchange of stock,
        etc., between domestic
        stock insurer and
        holding company.
        Fees, etc., for promotion
          of plan, §27-28-3.
    Insurance premium finance
      companies, §27-40-3.
    Insurers.
      Certificates of authority,
        §27-4-2.
      Exemption from other fees,
        §27-4-10.
      Life insurers organized to
        aid nonprofit
        educational and
        scientific institutions.
        Annual license fee,
          §27-4-8.
      Solicitation permits,
        §§27-4-2, 27-27-5.
    Mail order insurance.
      Service of process on
        unauthorized insurers,
        §27-11-5.
    Mutual aid associations.
      Applicability of fee
        provisions, §27-30-31.

INSURANCE—Cont'd
  Fees—Cont'd
    Rates and rating
      organizations.
      Casualty and surety
        insurance.
        License fee, §27-13-62.
      Fire and inland marine
        insurance.
        License fee, §27-13-24.
    Solicitors.
      Licenses, §27-4-2.
    Surplus line brokers.
      License fees, §27-4-2.
    Vending machines, §27-4-2.
  Filing.
    Existing filings, §27-1-13.
  Finance companies.
    Insurance premium finance
      companies, §§27-40-1 to
      27-40-18. See within this
      heading, "Premiums."
  Financial responsibility.
    Motor vehicle safety-
      responsibility act,
      §§32-7-1 to 32-7-42.
      See MOTOR VEHICLES.
  Fire insurance.
    Casualty insurance
      generally, §§27-7-1 to
      27-7-38. See within this
      heading, "Casualty
      insurance."
    Definitions.
      Insurer, §36-19-40.
    Rates and rating
      organizations,
      §27-13-20.
    Harbors and ports.
      Docks department.
        Authority to carry fire
          insurance, §33-1-25.
    Industrial fire insurance.
      Policies, §27-22-2.
    Licenses.
      Municipal corporations.
        Schedules for fire
          insurance
          companies,
          §11-51-120.
    Policies.
      Industrial fire insurance
        policies, §27-22-2.
    Rates and rating
      organizations, §§27-13-20
      to 27-13-45. See within
      this heading, "Rates and
      rating organizations."
  Foreign insurers. See within
    this heading, "Insurers."
  Forms.
    Existing forms, §27-1-13.
    Health insurance claims.
      Format for claims
        submitted by electronic
        means, §27-1-16.
    Standard health insurance
      claim form, §27-1-16.
  Fraternal benefit societies.
    General provisions, §§27-34-1
      to 27-34-54.
      See FRATERNAL
        BENEFIT SOCIETIES.
  Fraud.
    Policies.
      Application for policy,
        §27-14-7.

INSURANCE—Cont'd
  Funds.
    State insurance fund,
      §§41-15-1 to 41-15-13.
      See within this heading,
      "State insurance fund."
  Funerals.
    Insurers.
      Assets.
        Funeral supplies and
          equipment.
          Valuation, §27-37-8.
  Garnishment.
    Insurers.
      Delinquency proceedings,
        §27-32-21.
  Glass insurance.
    Casualty insurance
      generally, §§27-7-1 to
      27-7-38. See within this
      heading, "Casualty
      insurance."
  Governor.
    Commissioner of insurance.
      Annual report to governor,
        §27-2-9.
      Appointment of
        commissioner, §27-2-2.
  Grain dealers.
    Fire and extended coverage
      insurance required,
      §2-31-6.
    Suspension or revocation of
      license for failure to
      maintain insurance,
      §2-31-7.
  Group insurance.
    Alcoholism treatment in
      group plans, §§27-20A-1
      to 27-20A-4.
      See ALCOHOLISM.
    County officers and
      employees.
      See COUNTIES.
    Disability insurance,
      §§27-20-1 to 27-20-3.
    Life insurance, §§27-18-1 to
      27-18-16. See within this
      heading, "Life
      insurance."
    Municipal officers and
      employees, §§11-91-1 to
      11-91-8.
      See MUNICIPAL
        CORPORATIONS.
  Guaranty associations.
    Insurance guaranty
      associations, §§27-42-1 to
      27-42-20. See within this
      heading, "Insurance
      guaranty associations."
    Life and disability insurance
      guaranty association,
      §§27-44-1 to 27-44-21.
      See within this heading,
      "Life and disability
      insurance guaranty
      association."
  Harbors and ports.
    Docks department.
      Authority to carry fire and
        casualty and public
        liability inusurance,
        §33-1-25.
      Life and health insurance
        for certian salaried
        officers and employees,
        §33-1-5.2.
  Headings.
    Effect of headings, §27-1-7.

INSURANCE—Cont'd
Health care service plans.
Alabama health care plan,
§§27-21-1 to 27-21-6. See
within this heading,
"Health insurance."
Applicability of insurance
laws, §10-4-115.
General provisions,
§§10-4-100 to 10-4-115.
See HEALTH CARE
SERVICE PLANS.
Health insurance.
Alabama health care plan,
§§27-21-1 to 27-21-6.
Administration expenses,
§27-21-3.
Consultants.
Employment, §27-21-5.
Examinations, §27-21-5.
Exemption from premium
tax, §27-21-4.
Expenses.
Administration expenses,
§27-21-3.
Hearings, §27-21-5.
Losses.
Deduction of losses from
premium tax,
§27-21-4.
Offering of insurance,
§27-21-2.
Premiums.
Exemption from
premium tax,
§27-21-4.
Rates, §27-21-3.
Purpose of chapter,
§27-21-1.
Qualifications for plan,
§27-21-5.
Rates, §27-21-3.
Short title of chapter,
§27-21-6.
Taxation.
Exemption from
premium tax,
§27-21-4.
Anesthetic coverage.
Certified registered nurse
anesthetist coverage,
§§27-46-1 to 27-46-3.
Certified registered nurse
anesthetist coverage,
§§27-46-1 to 27-46-3.
Definition of "certified
registered nurse
anesthetist," §27-46-3.
Hospitals not prohibited
from prescribing
policies, rules, etc.,
§27-46-2.
Payment for services,
§27-46-1.
Reimbursement for
services, §27-46-1.
Claims.
Limitation period for
payment, §27-1-17.
Right of action for recovery
of unpaid benefits,
§27-1-17.
Dental care services,
§§27-19A-1 to 27-19A-11.
See within this heading,
"Dental care services."
Dentists and dental
hygienists.
"Physicians" under health
insurance policies,
§27-1-11.

INSURANCE—Cont'd
Health insurance—Cont'd
Forms for claims, §27-1-16.
Fraternal benefit societies.
Health insurance contracts,
§27-34-32.
Health care service plans,
§§10-4-100 to 10-4-115.
See HEALTH CARE
SERVICE PLANS.
Interest.
Limitation period for
payment of claims.
Payment of interest,
§27-1-17.
Mental health services.
Outpatient and inpatient
services, §27-1-18.
Reimbursement for
services, §27-1-18.
Municipal officers and
employees, §§11-91-1 to
11-91-8.
See MUNICIPAL
CORPORATIONS.
Newly born children.
Coverage in health
insurance policies,
§27-19-38.
Pharmaceutical insurance
coverage.
General provisions,
§§27-45-1 to 27-45-9.
See within this
heading,
"Pharmaceutical
insurance coverage."
Podiatrists.
Payment for services,
§27-1-15.
Premiums.
Alabama health care plan.
Exemption from
premium tax,
§27-21-4.
Rates.
Alabama health care plan,
§27-21-3.
Sickle-cell anemia.
Denial of coverage upon
diagnosis of sickle-cell
anemia, §27-5-13.
State employees' health
insurance plan,
§§36-29-1 to 36-29-13.
See PUBLIC OFFICERS
AND EMPLOYEES.
Taxation.
Alabama health care plan.
Exemption from
premium tax,
§27-21-4.
University of Alabama.
Appropriations to
university.
Not considered in patient
care reimbursement,
§27-1-11.1.
**Health maintenance
organizations,** §§27-21A-1
to 27-21A-32.
See HEALTH
MAINTENANCE
ORGANIZATIONS.
Hearings.
Alabama health care plan,
§27-21-5.

INSURANCE—Cont'd
Hearings—Cont'd
Commissioner of insurance,
§§27-2-28 to 27-2-38. See
within this heading,
"Commissioner of
insurance."
Insurers.
Delinquency proceedings.
Claims in delinquency
proceedings,
§27-32-19.
Suspension or revocation of
certificate of authority,
§§27-3-20, 27-3-21.
Property, casualty and surety
insurance
representatives.
Hearings of complaints
against licensees,
§27-7-37.
Rates and rating
organizations.
Casualty and surety
insurance.
Appeals from decisions of
rating organizations,
§27-13-69.
Applications to reduce
rates, §27-13-71.
Hearings by
commissioner,
§27-13-80.
Review of final orders of
commissioner,
§27-13-81.
Fire and inland marine
insurance.
Hearings by
commissioner,
§27-13-42.
Trade practices law,
§27-12-18.
Proceedings on unfair
competition, etc., not
defined under chapter,
§27-12-21.
Service of statements,
notices, orders and
other processes,
§27-12-19.
Highway department.
Self-insurance program for
employees, §23-1-41.
Historic Blakeley authority.
Programs provided for state
employees.
Participation of employees,
§41-10-180.
Holding companies, §§27-29-1
to 27-29-14.
Acquisition of control of
domestic insurers,
§27-29-3.
Affiliates.
Domestic insurers,
§27-29-2.
Records.
Confidential treatment of
information,
§27-29-7.
Examination of records,
§27-29-6.
Standards for transactions
with affiliates,
§27-29-5.
Appeals.
Judicial review of actions
by commissioner,
§27-29-13.

INSURANCE—Cont'd
  Holding companies—Cont'd
    Applicability of Alabama
      business corporation act,
      §27-28-5.
    Authority to engage in
      insurance business.
      Effect of chapter on
        authority, §27-28-4.
      Nonrenewal, §27-29-12.
      Revocation, §27-29-12.
      Suspension, §27-29-12.
    Bankruptcy and insolvency.
      Delinquency proceedings,
      §27-29-11.
    Commissioner of insurance.
      Appeal from actions by
        commissioner,
        §27-29-13.
      Effect of chapter on powers
        of commissioner,
        §27-28-4.
      Injunctions against
        violations of
        commissioner's orders
        or rules and
        regulations, §27-29-9.
      Judicial review of actions
        by commissioner,
        §27-29-13.
      Orders by commissioner,
        §27-29-8.
      Rules and regulations,
        §27-29-8.
    Corporations.
      Applicability of Alabama
        business corporation
        act, §27-28-5.
    Criminal proceedings,
      §27-29-10.
    Definitions, §27-29-1.
    Delinquency proceedings,
      §27-29-11.
    Distributions.
      Dividends and other
        distributions, §27-29-5.
    Dividends, §27-29-5.
    Examination of records, etc.,
      of insurer or affiliates,
      §27-29-6.
      Confidential treatment of
        information examined
        or reported, §27-29-7.
    Exchange of stock, etc.,
      between domestic stock
      insurer and holding
      companies.
      Plan for exchange,
        §§27-28-1 to 27-28-3.
    Fees.
      Plan for exchange of stock,
        etc., between domestic
        stock insurer and
        holding company.
        Fees, etc., for promotion
          of plan, §27-28-3.
    Injunctions, §27-29-9.
    Insolvency.
      Delinquency proceedings,
      §27-29-11.
    Judicial review of actions by
      commissioner, §27-29-13.
    Licenses of insurers.
      Suspension, revocation or
        nonrenewal, §27-29-12.
    Merger with domestic
      insurers, §27-29-3.
    Orders by commissioner,
      §27-29-8.
      Judicial review, §27-29-13.

INSURANCE—Cont'd
  Holding companies—Cont'd
    Records.
      Confidential treatment of
        information, §27-29-7.
      Examination of records,
        etc., of insurer or
        affiliates, §27-29-6.
    Registration of insurers,
      §27-29-4.
    Rehabilitation, §27-29-11.
    Reports.
      Confidential treatment of
        information, §27-29-7.
      Registration of insurers,
        §27-29-4.
    Rules and regulations,
      §§27-29-8, 27-29-9.
      Injunctions for violations,
        §27-29-9.
      Judicial review of actions
        by commissioner,
        §27-29-13.
    Short title of chapter,
      §27-29-14.
    Stock insurers.
      Plan for exchange of stock,
        etc., between domestic
        stock insurer and
        holding company,
        §27-28-3.
      Procedure for exchange,
        §27-28-2.
    Subsidiaries of domestic
      insurers, §27-29-2.
    Surplus.
      Adequacy of surplus,
      §27-29-5.
    Transactions with affiliates.
      Standards for transactions,
      §27-29-5.
    Violations of chapter.
      Criminal proceedings,
        §27-29-10.
      Delinquency proceedings,
        §27-29-11.
      Injunctions, §27-29-9.
      Suspension, revocation or
        nonrenewal of
        insurer's license or
        authority to do
        business, §27-29-12.
    Voting of securities.
      Prohibitions against,
        §27-29-9.
      Sequestration of voting
        securities, §27-29-9.
  Hospitals.
    Medical liability insurance,
      §§27-26-1 to 27-26-43.
    See within this heading,
      "Medical liability
      insurance."
    Payment of claims by
      insurance companies,
      §22-21-7.
  Housing.
    Investments and loans by
      insurance companies,
      §5-5A-23.
  Husband and wife.
    Policy designating wife as
      beneficiary.
      Assignment as security for
        indebtedness.
        Exempted from
          prohibition against
          contracts of
          suretyship by wife,
          §30-4-10.

INSURANCE—Cont'd
  Income tax.
    Corporations.
      Deductions allowed certain
        insurance companies,
        §40-18-35.
    Deductions.
      Accident and health
        insurance.
        Amounts paid for,
          §40-18-15.
      Items not deductible,
        §40-18-17.
    Exemptions.
      Items exempt from income
        tax, §40-18-14.
    Insurers.
      Exemption from income
        tax, §27-4-10.
  Industrial life insurance,
    §§27-16-1 to 27-16-17.
    Age.
      Misstatement of age in
        policy, §27-16-7.
    Applicability of chapter,
      §27-16-2.
    Claims.
      Settlement of claims.
        Provision in policy,
          §27-16-10.
    Conversion to life insurance
      with less frequent
      premium payments,
      §27-16-16.
    Defined, §27-16-1.
    Dividends.
      Policy provisions
        concerning dividends,
        §27-16-8.
    Policies, §§27-16-3 to
      27-16-17.
      Age.
        Misstatement of age,
          §27-16-7.
      Applicability of policy
        provisions to single
        premium policies,
        §27-16-15.
      Beneficiaries, §27-16-12.
      Benefits.
        Nonforfeiture benefits,
          §27-16-13.
      Cash surrender values,
        §27-16-13.
      Conditions.
        Waiver, §27-16-11.
      Conversion to life
        insurance with less
        frequent premium
        payments, §27-16-16.
      Dividend provisions,
        §27-16-8.
      Entire contract, §27-16-5.
      Grace period clause,
        §27-16-4.
      Incontestability clause,
        §27-16-6.
      Nonforfeiture benefits,
        §27-16-13.
      Payment to other than
        designated beneficiary,
        §27-16-12.
      Prohibited provisions,
        §27-16-17.
      Provisions generally,
        §27-16-3.
        Prohibited provisions,
          §27-16-17.
        Reinstatement provision,
          §27-16-9.

INSURANCE—Cont'd
Industrial life insurance
—Cont'd
Policies—Cont'd
Provisions generally
—Cont'd
Settlement of claims
provision, §27-16-10.
Representations, §27-16-5.
Sex.
Misstatement of sex,
§27-16-7.
Terms.
Waiver, §27-16-11.
Title of policy, §27-16-14.
Value.
Cash surrender values,
§27-16-13.
Waiver, etc., of terms or
conditions, §27-16-11.
Premiums.
Applicability of certain
provisions to single
premium policies,
§27-16-15.
Conversion to life
insurance with less
frequent premium
payments, §27-16-16.
Grace period for payment
of premiums, §27-16-4.
Settlement of claims.
Provision in policy,
§27-16-10.
Sex.
Misstatement of sex,
§27-16-7.
Injunctions.
Holding companies, §27-29-9.
Insurers, §27-32-5.
Inland marine insurance.
Licenses.
Municipal corporations.
Schedules for marine
insurance
companies,
§11-51-120.
Rates and rating
organizations, §§27-13-20
to 27-13-45. See within
this heading, "Rates and
rating organizations."
Inspections.
Records.
Commissioner of insurance,
§27-2-14.
Surplus line insurance.
Production of policies, etc.,
for inspection by
commissioner,
§27-10-36.
Unauthorized insurers.
Production of policies, etc.,
for inspection by
commissioner,
§27-10-36.
**Institute for the deaf and
blind.**
Board of trustees.
Insurance of state property,
§21-1-6.
Insurable interest.
Personal insurance, §27-14-3.
Property insurance, §27-14-4.
**Insurance advisory
organizations,**
§§27-13-100 to 27-13-105.
See within this heading,
"Rates and rating
organizations."

INSURANCE—Cont'd
Insurance companies.
Applicability of corporations
provisions, §§10-2A-336,
27-27-61.
Insurers. See within this
heading, "Insurers."
**Insurance guaranty
association,** §§27-42-1 to
27-42-20.
Accounts.
Defined, §27-42-5.
Division into accounts,
§27-42-6.
Applicability of chapter,
§27-42-3.
Assessments.
Credits for assessment
paid, §27-42-16.
Assets.
Access to assets of
insolvent insurer,
§27-42-20.
Disbursement.
Application for court
approval, §27-42-20.
Board of directors, §27-42-7.
Access to records,
§27-42-18.
Expenses, §27-42-7.
Recommendations,
§27-42-13.
Reports, §27-42-13.
Annual financial report,
§27-42-14.
Selections to board,
§27-42-7.
Vacancies, §27-42-7.
Citation, §27-42-1.
Claims.
Covered claim.
Defined, §27-42-5.
Effect of paid claims,
§27-42-11.
Establishment of
procedures for filing
claims, §27-42-9.
Exhaustion of rights,
§27-42-12.
Filing of claims, §27-42-11.
Nonduplication of recovery,
§27-42-12.
Powers and duties of
association, §27-42-8.
Commissioner.
Defined, §27-42-5.
Duties.
Generally, §27-42-10.
Powers.
Generally, §27-42-10.
Reports, §27-42-13.
Submission of plan to
commissioner,
§27-42-9.
Construction of chapter,
§27-42-4.
Creation, §27-42-6.
Creditors.
Preferred creditor status,
§27-42-19.
Credits for assessments paid,
§27-42-16.
Definitions, §27-42-5.
Duties.
Generally, §27-42-8.
Examination of insurers,
§27-42-13.
Commissioner to examine
and regulate
association, §27-42-14.

INSURANCE—Cont'd
**Insurance guaranty
association**—Cont'd
Immunity from liability,
§27-42-17.
Insolvent insurers.
Access to assets of
insolvent insurer,
§27-42-20.
Defined, §27-42-5.
Prevention, §27-42-13.
Life and disability insurance
guaranty association,
§§27-44-1 to 27-44-21.
See within this heading,
"Life and disability
insurance guaranty
association."
Liquidator.
Access to records,
§27-42-18.
Filing of paid claims and
estimates, §27-42-11.
Members, §27-42-6.
Notices.
Disbursement of assets,
§27-42-20.
Plan of operation, §27-42-9.
Failure to submit plan,
§27-42-9.
Powers.
Generally, §27-42-8.
Prevention of insolvency,
§27-42-13.
Purpose of chapter, §27-42-2.
Receiver.
Access to records,
§27-42-18.
Filing of paid claims and
estimates, §27-42-11.
Refunds.
Disposition, §27-42-16.
Reports.
Annual financial report of
directors, §27-42-14.
Duty of commissioner,
§27-42-13.
Short title, §27-42-1.
Stay of proceedings,
§27-42-18.
Taxation.
Exemptions from taxation,
§27-42-15.
Insurers.
Actions.
Time to answer or plead,
§27-3-25.
Agents.
Exceptions to requirement
of agents, §27-3-27.
Execution of contracts,
§27-3-28.
General provisions. See
within this heading,
"Agents."
Insurers to do business
through licensed
agents, §27-3-27.
Alien insurers.
Canadian insurers.
Trusteed assets,
§27-33-16.
Commissioner of insurance.
Trust agreement.
Approval by
commissioner,
§27-33-5.
Withdrawal of
approval, §27-33-8.
Conservation of assets.
Grounds, §27-32-9.

INSURANCE—Cont'd
Insurers—Cont'd
Alien insurers—Cont'd
Conservation of assets
—Cont'd
Property, §27-32-14.
Defined, §27-1-2.
Delinquency proceedings.
Conduct, §27-32-15.
Deposit requirements,
§27-3-14.
Trusteed assets,
§27-3-15.
Examinations.
Trusteed assets,
§27-33-12.
Liquidation.
Grounds, §27-32-7.
Orders, §27-32-13.
Property, §27-32-14.
Records.
Trusteed assets,
§27-33-10.
Trusteed assets, §§27-33-1
to 27-33-16.
Applicability of chapter,
§27-33-1.
Canadian insurers,
§27-33-16.
Compensation of
trustees, §27-33-15.
Defined, §27-33-2.
Deposit of assets in
trust, §27-33-2.
Deposit requirements,
§27-3-15.
Duration of trust,
§27-33-4.
Examination, §27-33-12.
Existing trusts, §27-33-3.
Expenses of trustees,
§27-33-15.
Purpose of trust,
§27-33-4.
Record of trusteed assets,
§27-33-10.
Separation from other
assets, §27-33-10.
Statements.
Trustee statements,
§27-33-11.
Substitution of trustees,
§27-33-14.
Title to trusteed assets,
§27-33-9.
Trust agreement.
Amendment, §27-33-7.
Approval by
commissioner,
§27-33-5.
Authority to make and
execute, §27-33-6.
Requirement, §27-33-5.
Withdrawal of
approval, §27-33-8.
Trustee statements,
§27-33-11.
Withdrawal, §27-33-13.
Unauthorized insurers
process act, §§27-10-50
to 27-10-56. See within
this heading,
"Unauthorized
insurers."
Annuities.
Reserve liability for
variable contracts,
§27-38-5.
Variable contracts.
Licensing of insurers,
§27-38-3.

INSURANCE—Cont'd
Insurers—Cont'd
Appeals.
Delinquency proceedings,
§27-32-3.
Applicability of corporation
statutes to domestic
insurers, §§10-2A-336,
27-27-61.
Assessments.
Mutual insurers.
Collection of assessments
by insurers,
§27-27-33.
Contingent liability of
members.
Levy of assessments,
§27-27-32.
Deficiencies in assets of
mutual insurers.
Curing of deficiency,
§27-27-42.
Nonassessable policies in
mutual insurers,
§§27-27-34, 27-27-35.
Rehabilitation or
liquidation,
§§27-32-32 to
27-32-35.
Reciprocal insurers,
§§27-32-32 to 27-32-36.
See within this
heading, "Reciprocal
insurers."
Rehabilitation or
liquidation.
Order to pay.
Publication and
service, §27-32-35.
Stock insurers.
Collection of assessments
by insurers,
§27-27-33.
Deficiencies in stock
insurer's capital.
Curing of deficiency,
§27-27-42.
Assets.
Alien insurers.
Trusteed assets,
§§27-33-1 to
27-33-16.
Allowable assets, §27-37-1.
Bonds and other evidences
of debts.
Valuation, §27-37-5.
Conservation of assets,
§§27-32-1 to 27-32-41.
Conveyance.
Prohibited during period
of supervision,
§27-2-34.
Deception.
Disallowance of assets
for deception,
§27-37-4.
Deductions from
corresponding
liabilities, §27-37-3.
Disallowance of credits
for deception,
§27-37-4.
Defined, §27-32-1.
§27-37-1.
Deposits by insurers,
§§27-6-1 to 27-6-16.
Disallowance of assets for
deception, §27-37-4.

INSURANCE—Cont'd
Insurers—Cont'd
Assets—Cont'd
Disposal of assets.
Prohibited during period
of supervision,
§27-2-34.
Encumbrance.
Prohibited during period
of supervision,
§27-2-34.
Exclusions, §27-37-2.
Fraternal benefit societies,
§27-34-34.
Funeral supplies and
equipment.
Valuation, §27-37-8.
Generally, §27-37-1.
Maintenance of assets in
state, §27-27-29.
Mortgages and deeds of
trust.
Valuation.
Purchase money
mortgages,
§27-37-9.
Personal property acquired
pursuant to chattel
mortgages.
Valuation, §27-37-7.
Purchase money
mortgages.
Valuation, §27-37-9.
Real property.
Valuation, §27-37-7.
Reciprocal insurers,
§§27-31-27, 27-31-29.
Removal of assets,
§27-27-29.
Securities.
Valuation, §27-37-6.
Valuation, §§27-37-1 to
27-37-9.
Bonds and other
evidences of debts,
§27-37-5.
Chattel mortgages.
Personal property
acquired pursuant
to chattel
mortgages,
§27-37-7.
Debts.
Bonds and other
evidences of debts,
§27-37-5.
Funeral supplies and
equipment, §27-37-8.
Other securities,
§27-37-6.
Personal property
acquired pursuant to
chattel mortgages,
§27-37-7.
Preferred or guaranteed
stocks or shares,
§27-37-6.
Purchase money
mortgages, §27-37-9.
Real property, §27-37-7.
Stocks.
Preferred or
guaranteed stocks
or shares,
§27-37-6.
Attachment.
Delinquency proceedings,
§27-32-21.

INSURANCE—Cont'd
  Insurers—Cont'd
    Authority to transact
      insurance.
    Capital stock and surplus.
      Minimum paid-in capital
        stock and surplus,
        §27-3-7.
    Certificate of authority,
      §§27-3-1 to 27-3-3.
    Eligibility, §27-3-4.
    Holding companies,
      §27-28-4.
      Nonrenewal of authority,
        §27-29-12.
      Revocation of authority,
        §27-29-12.
      Suspension of authority,
        §27-29-12.
    Lloyd's insurers, §27-3-16.
    Mutual insurers,
      §27-27-15.
      Additional kinds of
        insurance, §27-27-20.
    Names.
      Use of name by insurer,
        §27-3-5.
      Restrictions, §27-3-6.
    Surplus.
      Minimum paid-in capital
        stock and surplus,
        §27-3-7.
      Special surplus, §27-3-8.
    Authorized insurers.
      Defined, §27-1-2.
    Bank accounts.
      Withdrawals prohibited
        during period of
        supervision, §27-2-34.
    Beneficiaries.
      Priority of claims,
        §§27-32-37 to 27-32-41.
    Bonds, surety.
      Solicitation permits,
        §27-27-10.
    Bulk reinsurance.
      Mutual insurers,
        §27-27-48.
      Stock insurers, §27-27-47.
    Business transactions.
      Annual report by
        commissioner, §27-2-9.
    Bylaws.
      As part of insurance
        contract, §27-14-13.
      Mutual insurers,
        §27-27-22.
    Canadian insurers.
      Trusteed assets, §27-33-16.
    Casualty insurance.
      Unearned premium
        reserve, §27-36-3.
    Certificate of authority.
      Amendment, §27-3-19.
      Application for certificate.
        Fee, §27-4-2.
        Filing, §27-3-17.
      Continuance, §27-3-19.
        Fees, §27-4-2.
      Exceptions to requirement,
        §§27-3-2, 27-3-3.
      Expiration, §27-3-19.
      Fees, §27-4-2.
      Issuance, §27-3-18.
        Fee, §27-4-2.
      Limitation of certificate,
        §27-3-18.
      Mutual aid associations,
        §§27-30-8 to 27-30-12.
      Ownership of certificate,
        §27-3-18.

INSURANCE—Cont'd
  Insurers—Cont'd
    Certificate of authority
      —Cont'd
      Refusal, §27-3-18.
      Reinstatement.
        Expired certificates,
          §27-3-23.
        Fee, §27-4-2.
        Suspended or revoked
          certificates, §27-3-23.
      Renewal.
        Fee, §27-4-2.
        Required, §27-3-1.
        Exceptions to
          requirement,
          §§27-3-2, 27-3-3.
      Suspension or revocation.
        Duration, §27-3-23.
        Grounds.
          Additional grounds,
            §27-3-21.
          Failure to file annual
            statement,
            §27-3-26.
          Mandatory grounds,
            §27-3-20.
        Hearing, §§27-3-20,
          27-3-21.
        Notice, §§27-3-20 to
          27-3-22.
        Obligations of insurers
          during suspension,
          §27-3-23.
        Reinstatement, §27-3-23.
    Charters.
      As part of contract,
        §27-14-13.
      Charter documents fees,
        §27-4-2.
      Extinguishment, §27-27-50.
      Nullification, §27-27-50.
    Claims against insurers.
      Definitions, §27-32-1.
      Delinquency proceedings,
        §§27-32-17 to 27-32-20.
      Domestic insurers.
        Claims of nonresidents
          against, §27-32-17.
      Foreign insurers.
        Claims of residents
          against, §27-32-18.
      Liquidation.
        Allowance, §27-32-30.
        Priority of claims of
          policyholders and
          beneficiaries,
          §§27-32-37 to
          27-32-41.
      Refusal of insurer to pay or
        settle, §27-12-24.
    Closing business.
      Annual report by
        commissioner of closed
        businesses, §27-2-9.
    Common ownership,
      management and
      directorships, §27-12-16.
    Conflicts of interest,
      §27-27-26.
    Conservation of assets.
      Alien insurers.
        Grounds, §27-32-9.
        Property, §27-32-14.
      Construction of chapter,
        §27-32-2.
      Credits.
        Setoff of credits and
          debts, §27-32-29.

INSURANCE—Cont'd
  Insurers—Cont'd
    Conservation of assets
      —Cont'd
      Debts.
        Setoff of credits and
          debts, §27-32-29.
      Definitions, §27-32-1.
      Delinquency proceedings,
        §§27-32-15 to 27-32-20.
      Deposit of moneys
        collected, §27-32-23.
      Employees.
        Priority of compensation
          owed to employees,
          §27-32-28.
      Foreign insurers.
        Grounds, §27-32-8.
        Property, §27-32-14.
      Grounds.
        Alien insurers, §27-32-9.
        Foreign insurers,
          §27-32-8.
      Liens.
        Voidable liens,
          §27-32-27.
      Loans to facilitate,
        §27-32-25.
      Preference to creditors.
        Voidable transfers and
          liens, §27-32-27.
      Priorities.
        Compensation owing
          employees,
          §27-32-28.
        Property of insurer,
          §27-32-14.
      Purpose of chapter,
        §27-32-2.
      Setoff of credits and debts,
        §27-32-29.
      Transfers.
        Voidable transfers and
          liens, §27-32-27.
    Contracts.
      Exclusive management and
        production of business
        contracts, §27-27-27.
    Corporations statutes.
      Applicability to domestic
        insurers, §§10-2A-336,
        27-27-61.
    Corrupt practices.
      Meeting of stockholders or
        members, §27-27-25.
    Debentures.
      Value of surplus
        debentures, §27-27-40.
    Debts.
      Incurring during period of
        supervision prohibited,
        §27-2-34.
    Definitions, §§27-1-2,
      27-27-1, 27-32-1.
    Equity securities,
      §27-27-58.
    Delinquency proceedings.
      Alien insurers.
        Conduct of proceedings,
          §27-32-15.
      Annual report by
        commissioner, §27-2-9.
      Appeals, §27-32-3.
      Application by
        commissioner.
        Grant or denial,
          §27-32-4.
      Attachment, §27-32-21.
      Claims in delinquency
        proceedings.
        Form, §27-32-19.

INSURANCE—Cont'd
Insurers—Cont'd
Delinquency proceedings
—Cont'd
Claims in delinquency
proceedings—Cont'd
Hearings, §27-32-19.
Nonresidents against
domestic insurers,
§27-32-17.
Notice, §27-32-19.
Orders, §27-32-19.
Priorities, §27-32-20.
Residents against foreign
insurers, §27-32-18.
Rules and regulations,
§27-32-19.
Time for filing,
§27-32-19.
Commencement, §27-32-4.
Commissioner of insurance.
Annual report, §27-2-9.
Exemption from fees,
§27-32-24.
Conduct, §§27-32-15,
27-32-16.
Defined, §27-32-1.
Deposit of moneys
collected, §27-32-23.
Executions, §27-32-21.
Foreign insurers.
Claims of residents
against foreign
insurers, §27-32-18.
Conduct of proceedings,
§27-32-16.
Garnishment, §27-32-21.
Hearings.
Claims in delinquency
proceedings,
§27-32-19.
Injunctions, §27-32-5.
Jurisdiction, §27-32-3.
Liquidation, §§27-32-1 to
27-32-41.
Nonresidents.
Claims against domestic
insurers, §27-32-17.
Notice.
Claims in delinquency
proceedings,
§27-32-19.
Order of supervision by
commissioner.
Effect on delinquency
proceedings,
§27-2-36.
Orders.
Claims in delinquency
proceedings,
§27-32-19.
Priorities.
Claims in delinquency
proceedings,
§27-32-20.
Purpose of chapter,
§27-32-2.
Receivership division,
§§27-2-50 to 27-2-55.
Restraining orders,
§27-32-5.
Setoff of credits and debts,
§27-32-29.
Venue, §27-32-3.
Deposit requirements.
Alien insurers.
Generally, §27-3-14.
Trusteed assets,
§27-3-15.
Generally, §27-3-11.

INSURANCE—Cont'd
Insurers—Cont'd
Deposit requirements
—Cont'd
Special deposit.
Surety insurers,
§27-3-12.
Title insurers, §27-3-13.
Trusteed assets.
Alien insurers, §27-3-15.
Deposits, §§27-6-1 to 27-6-16.
Authorized deposits,
§27-6-1.
Composition, §27-6-3.
Custodian.
State treasurer as
custodian, §27-6-4.
Deficiency in market value
of deposit.
Curing of deficiency,
§27-6-14.
Excess deposits, §27-6-11.
Income from deposits,
§27-6-12.
Inspection by solvent
insurers, §27-6-12.
Purposes for which held,
§27-6-2.
Record of securities and
assets deposited,
§27-6-5.
Release of deposit.
Authorization of release,
§27-6-16.
Filing of statement,
§27-6-16.
Generally, §27-6-15.
Requirements, §§27-3-11 to
27-3-15.
Rights of solvent insurers,
§27-6-12.
Securities and assets
deposited, §27-6-3.
Appraisal, §27-6-6.
Assignment, §27-6-6.
Authority to sell,
§27-6-8.
Deficiency in market
value.
Curing of deficiency,
§27-6-14.
Excess deposits,
§27-6-11.
Income from deposits,
§27-6-12.
Power of attorney to sell,
§27-6-7.
New power, §27-6-10.
Return of power,
§27-6-9.
Safekeeping of power,
§27-6-9.
Reassignment, §27-6-6.
Record, §27-6-5.
Sale.
Authority to sell,
§27-6-8.
Power of attorney to
sell, §§27-6-7,
27-6-9, 27-6-10.
Substitution for
deposited securities
or assets, §27-6-12.
Valuation, §27-6-6.
Curing of deficiency in
market value of
deposit, §27-6-14.
State treasurer as
custodian, §27-6-4.

INSURANCE—Cont'd
Insurers—Cont'd
Deposits—Cont'd
Surety insurers' special
deposit.
Sale to pay outstanding
judgment, §27-6-13.
Directors.
Change of directors.
Notice of change,
§27-27-28.
Common directorships,
§27-12-16.
Conflicts of interest,
§27-27-26.
Election, §27-27-23.
Number, §27-27-23.
Pecuniary interests,
§27-27-26.
Power of domestic insurers
to indemnify directors,
§27-27-3.
Qualifications, §27-27-23.
Removal, §27-27-24.
Vacancies, §27-27-24.
Directory of insurers.
Annual publication by
commissioner,
§27-2-16.
Disability insurance.
Active life reserve for
disability insurance,
§27-36-5.
Disbursements.
Voucher or other document
for disbursements,
§27-27-30.
Discrimination.
Protection of state insurers
against foreign
discriminatory or
onerous requirements,
§27-3-29.
Dishonest practices.
Meeting of stockholders or
members, §27-27-25.
Dissolution.
Loans to facilitate,
§27-32-25.
Dividends.
Holding companies,
§27-29-5.
Illegal dividends.
Liability for illegal
dividends, §27-27-39.
Mutual insurers,
§27-27-38.
Stock insurers, §27-27-37.
Eligibility to transact
insurance, §27-3-1.
Employees.
Conflicts of interest,
§27-27-26.
Indemnification.
Power to indemnify,
§27-27-3.
Rehabilitation,
reorganization,
conservation and
liquidation of insurers.
Priority of compensation
owing employees,
§27-32-28.
Equity securities.
Insider trading of equity
securities, §§27-27-52
to 27-27-60.
Examinations.
Commissioner of insurance.
Affairs, etc., of insurers,
§27-2-21.

INSURANCE—Cont'd
  Insurers—Cont'd
    Examinations—Cont'd
      Commissioner of insurance
        —Cont'd
        Insurers making own
          rates, §27-13-74.
    Executions.
      Contracts, §27-3-28.
      Delinquency proceedings,
        §27-32-21.
    Fair trade.
      Common ownership,
        management and
        directorships,
        §27-12-16.
      Refusal to pay or settle
        claims, §27-12-24.
    Fees.
      Certificates of authority,
        §27-4-2.
      Exemption from other fees,
        §27-4-10.
      Life insurers organized to
        aid nonprofit
        educational and
        scientific institutions.
        Annual license fee,
          §27-4-8.
      Solicitation permits,
        §§27-4-2, 27-27-5.
    Financial condition.
      Annual report by
        commissioner, §27-2-9.
      Annual statement of
        insurers, §27-3-26.
      False statements as to
        financial condition,
        §27-12-7.
      Malicious statements on
        financial condition,
        §27-12-9.
    Foreign insurers.
      Authority to transact
        insurance.
        Eligibility, §27-3-4.
      Conservation of assets.
        Grounds, §27-32-8.
        Property, §27-32-14.
      Defined, §27-1-2.
      Delinquency proceedings.
        Claims of residents
          against foreign
          insurers, §27-32-18.
        Conduct, §27-32-16.
      Deposits.
        Composition, §27-6-3.
      Fraternal benefit societies,
        §§27-34-7, 27-34-8.
      Liquidation.
        Ancillary liquidation.
          Grounds, §27-32-10.
        Property, §27-32-14.
      Property.
        Conservation or
          liquidation,
          §27-32-14.
      Reciprocal insurers.
        Attorneys, §27-31-5.
      Taxation.
        Premium tax, §27-4-4.
      Unauthorized insurers
        process act, §§27-10-50
        to 27-10-56. See within
        this heading,
        "Unauthorized
        insurers."
    War.
      Effect of war on
        contracts of foreign
        insurers, §27-14-23.

INSURANCE—Cont'd
  Insurers—Cont'd
    Fraternal benefit societies,
      §§27-34-1 to 27-34-54.
      See FRATERNAL
        BENEFIT SOCIETIES.
    Garnishment.
      Delinquency proceedings,
        §27-32-21.
    Health care plan.
      Offering of insurance,
        §27-21-2.
    Hearings.
      Delinquency proceedings.
        Claims in delinquency
          proceedings,
          §27-32-19.
      Suspension or revocation of
        certificate of authority,
        §§27-3-20, 27-3-21.
    Holding companies, §§27-29-1
      to 27-29-14. See within
      this heading, "Holding
      companies."
    Housing.
      Investments and loans
        with respect to
        housing, §5-5A-23.
    Impairment.
      Defined, §27-32-1.
      Delinquency proceedings,
        §§27-32-15 to 27-32-20.
      Liquidation, §§27-32-1 to
        27-32-41.
      Order of supervision by
        commissioner,
        §§27-2-33 to 27-2-38.
        See within this
        heading,
        "Commissioner of
        insurance."
      Receivership division,
        §§27-2-50 to 27-2-55.
        See within this
        heading, "Receivership
        division."
      Rehabilitation, §§27-32-1
        to 27-32-41.
    Income tax.
      Exemption from income
        tax, §27-4-10.
    Indemnification of directors.
      Power to indemnify
        directors, §27-27-3.
    Independently procured
      coverages, §27-10-35.
    Injunctions, §27-32-5.
    Insolvency.
      Defined, §27-32-1.
      Delinquency proceedings,
        §§27-32-15 to 27-32-20.
      Liquidation, §§27-32-1 to
        27-32-41.
      Order of supervision by
        commissioner,
        §§27-2-33 to 27-2-38.
        See within this
        heading,
        "Commissioner of
        insurance."
      Receivership division,
        §§27-2-50 to 27-2-55.
        See within this
        heading, "Receivership
        division."
      Rehabilitation, §§27-32-1
        to 27-32-41.

INSURANCE—Cont'd
  Insurers—Cont'd
    Insurance guaranty
      association, §§27-42-1 to
      27-42-20. See within this
      heading, "Insurance
      guaranty association."
    Investments.
      Housing, §5-5A-23.
      Life, disability and burial
        insurance companies,
        §§27-41-1 to 27-41-41.
        See within this
        heading, "Investments
        of life, disability and
        burial insurance
        companies."
      Prohibited during period of
        supervision, §27-2-34.
      Real property, §27-3-3.
      Securities secured by real
        property, §27-3-3.
    Jurisdiction.
      Delinquency proceedings,
        §27-32-3.
    Liabilities.
      Active life reserve for
        disability insurance,
        §27-36-5.
      Casualty insurance.
        When insurer's liability
          absolute, §27-23-1.
      Deductions from
        corresponding assets,
        §27-37-3.
      Fixation of liabilities upon
        liquidation, §27-32-26.
      Generally, §27-36-1.
      Increase of inadequate loss
        reserves, §27-36-6.
      Incurring liability
        prohibited during
        period of supervision,
        §27-2-34.
      Standard valuation law,
        §27-36-7.
      Unearned premium
        reserve, §§27-36-2 to
        27-36-4.
      Valuation of reserves.
        Standard valuation law,
          §27-36-7.
      Variable contracts reserve,
        §27-38-5.
    Licenses.
      Annuities.
        Variable contracts,
          §27-38-3.
      Exemption from other
        licenses, §27-4-10.
      Holding companies.
        Suspension, revocation or
          nonrenewal of
          insurer's license,
          §27-29-12.
      Life insurers organized to
        aid nonprofit
        educational and
        scientific institutions.
        Annual license fee,
          §27-4-8.
      Municipal corporations,
        §§11-51-120 to
        11-51-123.
      Refund of licenses paid by
        mistake, §27-4-11.
      Variable annuities,
        §27-38-3.
    Liens.
      Voidable liens, §27-32-27.

INSURANCE—Cont'd
Insurers—Cont'd
Life insurance.
Investments.
Notes guaranteed under
servicemen's
readjustment act,
§27-1-9.
Notes secured by
mortgages or deeds
of trust, §27-1-8.
New domestic stock life
insurance company.
Minimum capital and
surplus, §27-3-9.
Nonprofit educational and
scientific institutions.
Annual license fee of life
insurers organized to
aid nonprofit
educational and
scientific
institutions, §27-4-8.
Proceeds of policies.
Power of life insurer to
hold, §27-15-26.
Right to proceeds
retained by life
insurer, §27-14-30.
Separate accounts.
Establishment by life
insurers to provide
for annuities and
benefits, §27-38-1.
Standard valuation law,
§27-36-7.
Limits of risk, §27-5-11.
Liquidation.
Alien insurers.
Grounds, §27-32-7.
Orders, §27-32-13.
Property, §27-32-14.
Beneficiaries.
Classification, §27-32-40.
Payment of claims,
§27-32-38.
Priority of claims,
§§27-32-37 to
27-32-41.
Claims.
Allowance, §27-32-30.
Priority of claims of
policyholders and
beneficiaries,
§§27-32-37 to
27-32-41.
Time to file, §27-32-31.
Construction of chapter,
§27-32-2.
Credits.
Setoff of credits and
debts, §27-32-29.
Debts.
Setoff of credits and
debts, §27-32-29.
Definitions, §27-32-1.
Deposit of moneys
collected, §27-32-23.
Employees.
Priority of compensation
owed to employees,
§27-32-28.
Filing.
Time to file, §27-32-31.
Fixation of rights and
liabilities upon
liquidation, §27-32-26.
Foreign insurers.
Ancillary liquidation.
Grounds, §27-32-10.
Property, §27-32-14.

INSURANCE—Cont'd
Insurers—Cont'd
Liquidation—Cont'd
Grounds, §27-32-7.
Alien insurers, §27-32-7.
Foreign insurers.
Ancillary liquidation,
§27-32-10.
Liability.
Receivers, §27-32-41.
Liens.
Voidable liens,
§27-32-27.
Mutual insurers.
Assessments, §§27-32-32
to 27-32-36.
Order of supervision by
commissioner.
Effect on liquidation,
§27-2-36.
Orders, §27-32-12.
Alien insurers,
§27-32-13.
Policyholders.
Classification, §27-32-40.
Payment of claims,
§27-32-38.
Priority of claims,
§§27-32-37 to
27-32-41.
Reinsuring of policies,
§27-32-39.
Preference to creditors.
Voidable transfers and
liens, §27-32-27.
Priorities.
Claims of policyholders
and beneficiaries.
Classification,
§27-32-40.
Established, §27-32-37.
Liability of receiver,
§27-32-41.
Payment of claims,
§27-32-38.
Reinsuring of policies,
§27-32-39.
Compensation owing
employees,
§27-32-28.
Property of insurer,
§27-32-14.
Receivers.
Liability, §27-32-41.
Reciprocal insurers,
§27-31-27.
Assessments, §§27-32-32
to 27-32-36.
Reinsuring of policies,
§27-32-39.
Rights.
Fixation of rights on
liquidation,
§27-32-26.
Setoff of credits and debts,
§27-32-29.
Transfers.
Voidable transfers,
§27-32-27.
Uniform insurers
liquidation act,
§27-32-22.
Voidable transfers and
liens, §27-32-27.
Lloyd's insurers.
Authorization to transact
insurance, §27-3-16.
Loans, §27-27-40.
Housing, §5-5A-23.

INSURANCE—Cont'd
Insurers—Cont'd
Loans—Cont'd
Loans to facilitate
rehabilitation, etc.,
§27-32-25.
Prohibited during period of
supervision, §27-2-34.
Mail order insurance,
§§27-11-1 to 27-11-7. See
within this heading,
"Unauthorized insurers."
Management.
Common management,
§27-12-16.
Marine and transportation
insurance.
Unearned premium
reserve, §27-36-4.
Merger and consolidation.
Holding companies.
Merger with domestic
insurers, §27-29-3.
Mutual insurers,
§27-27-46.
Reciprocal insurers,
§27-31-28.
Stock insurers, §27-27-45.
Monopolies, §27-12-16.
Mortgages and deeds of trust.
Investments by life
insurance companies,
§27-1-8.
Valuation.
Purchase money
mortgages, §27-37-9.
Mutual aid associations,
§§27-30-1 to 27-30-33.
See within this heading,
"Mutual aid
associations."
Mutual insurers, §§27-27-1 to
27-27-61.
Applicability of chapter,
§27-27-2.
Applications for insurance.
Deposit in trust of
premiums or fees on
qualifying
applications,
§27-27-18.
Solicitation of qualifying
applications,
§27-27-17.
Assessments.
Collection, §27-27-33.
Contingent liability of
members.
Levy of assessments,
§27-27-32.
Deficiencies in assets of
mutual insurers.
Curing of deficiency,
§27-27-42.
Nonassessable policies in
mutual insurers,
§27-27-34.
Rehabilitation or
liquidation.
Commissioner's report,
§27-32-32.
Levy, §27-32-33.
Order to pay judgment,
§27-32-34.
Report by
commissioner,
§27-32-32.
Service of order to pay,
§27-32-35.

INSURANCE—Cont'd
  Insurers—Cont'd
    Mutual insurers—Cont'd
     Assets.
      Distribution upon
        liquidation,
        §27-27-49.
     Authorization to transact
      insurance, §27-27-15.
     Additional kinds of
      insurance, §27-27-20.
     Bonds, surety, §27-27-16.
     Bulk reinsurance,
      §27-27-48.
     Bylaws, §27-27-22.
     Certificates of authority,
      §27-27-15.
     Contingent liability of
      members.
      Collection of assessments
        by insurers,
        §27-27-33.
      Generally, §27-27-31.
      Levy of assessments,
        §27-27-32.
      Nonassessable policies in
        mutual insurers,
        §§27-27-34, 27-27-35.
     Conversion into stock
      insurer, §27-27-44.
     Corrupt practices in
      meeting of members,
      §27-27-25.
     Deficiencies in assets.
      Order of supervision by
        commissioner,
        §§27-2-33 to 27-2-38.
        See within this
        heading,
        "Commissioner of
        insurance."
     Defined, §27-27-1.
     Deposit in lieu of bond,
      §27-27-16.
     Dishonest practices in
      meeting of members,
      §27-27-25.
     Dividends, §27-27-38.
     Failure to complete
      organization,
      §27-27-19.
     Fraternal benefit societies.
      Conversion into stock or
        mutual life
        insurance company,
        §§27-35-1 to
        27-35-11.
        See FRATERNAL
          BENEFIT
          SOCIETIES.
     Liability of members.
      Contingent liability,
        §§27-27-31, 27-27-32.
     Liquidation.
      Assessments, §§27-32-32
        to 27-32-36.
      Distribution of assets
        upon liquidation,
        §27-27-49.
     Membership, §27-27-21.
      Contingent liability of
        members,
        §§27-27-31, 27-27-32.
      Corrupt or dishonest
        practices in meeting
        of members,
        §27-27-25.
     Merger and consolidation,
      §27-27-46.
     Mutualization of stock
      insurers, §27-27-43.

INSURANCE—Cont'd
  Insurers—Cont'd
    Mutual insurers—Cont'd
     Nonassessable policies in
      mutual insurers.
      Generally, §27-27-34.
      Revocation of domestic
        insurers authority to
        issue, §27-27-35.
     Organizations.
      Failure to complete
        organization,
        §27-27-19.
     Policies.
      Nonassessable policies,
        §27-27-34.
      Revocation of domestic
        insurers authority
        to issue, §27-27-35.
     Premiums.
      Deposit in trust,
        §27-27-18.
     Rehabilitation.
      Assessments, §§27-32-32
        to 27-32-36.
     Reinsurance.
      Bulk reinsurance,
        §27-27-48.
     Service of process.
      Assessments.
        Service of order to pay
          for rehabilitation
          or liquidation,
          §27-32-35.
     Solicitation of qualifying
      applications for
      insurance, §27-27-17.
     Solicitation permit,
      §§27-27-4 to 27-27-14.
     Stock insurers.
      Conversion of mutual
        insurer into stock
        insurer, §27-27-44.
     Surety insurers.
      Sole surety, §27-24-3.
    Names.
     Use of name by insurer,
      §27-3-5.
    Nonresidents.
     Delinquency proceedings.
      Claims against domestic
        insurers, §27-32-17.
    Notice.
     Delinquency proceedings.
      Claims in delinquency
        proceedings,
        §27-32-19.
     Suspension or revocation of
      certificate of authority,
      §§27-3-20 to 27-3-22.
      Order by commissioner,
        §27-3-22.
    Office.
     Home office, §27-27-29.
    Officers.
     Change of officers.
      Notice of change,
        §27-27-28.
     Conflicts of interest,
      §27-27-26.
     Indemnification.
      Power to indemnify,
        §27-27-3.
     Notice of change,
      §27-27-28.
     Pecuniary interests,
      §27-27-26.

INSURANCE—Cont'd
  Insurers—Cont'd
    Order of supervision by
     commissioner, §§27-2-33
     to 27-2-38. See within
     this heading,
     "Commissioner of
     insurance."
    Ownership.
     Common ownership,
      §27-12-16.
    Payment of claims.
     Refusal to pay claims,
      §27-12-24.
    Penalties.
     Taxation.
      Penalty for violation of
        sections 27-4-3
        through 27-4-6,
        §27-4-7.
    Permits.
     Solicitation permits,
      §§27-27-4 to 27-27-14.
    Policies.
     Issuance.
      Nonparticipating
        policies, §27-27-36.
      Participating policies,
        §27-27-36.
      Prohibited during period
        of supervision,
        §27-2-34.
    Premiums.
     Unearned premium
      reserve, §§27-36-2 to
      27-36-4.
    Principal place of business,
     §27-27-29.
    Priorities.
     Delinquency proceedings.
      Priority of compensation
        owed to employees,
        §27-32-28.
     Liquidation or
      rehabilitation.
      Priority of claims of
        policyholders and
        beneficiaries,
        §§27-32-37 to
        27-32-41.
    Property.
     Foreign or alien insurers.
      Conservation or
        liquidation of
        property, §27-32-14.
     Transfer of property.
      Prohibited during period
        of supervision,
        §27-2-34.
     Valuation, §27-37-7.
    Property insurance.
     Unearned premium
      reserve, §27-36-3.
    Rates and rating
     organizations.
     Filing of data or
      information by
      insurers, §27-13-3.
     General provisions,
      §§27-13-1 to 27-13-105.
      See within this
      heading, "Rates and
      rating organizations."
    Receivership division,
     §§27-2-50 to 27-2-55. See
     within this heading,
     "Receivership division."

INSURANCE—Cont'd
  Insurers—Cont'd
    Reciprocal insurers.
      General provisions,
        §§27-31-1 to 27-31-29.
        See within this
        heading, "Reciprocal
        insurers."
    Records.
      Alien insurers.
        Trusteed assets,
        §27-33-10.
      Deposits.
        Record of securities and
        assets deposited,
        §27-6-5.
      Holding companies.
        Confidential treatment of
        information,
        §27-29-7.
        Examination of records
        of insurer, §27-29-6.
      Removal of records,
        §27-27-29.
    Registration.
      Members of holding
        company systems,
        §27-29-4.
    Rehabilitation.
      Beneficiaries.
        Classification, §27-32-40.
        Payment of claims,
        §27-32-38.
      Claims.
        Priority of claims of
        policyholders and
        beneficiaries,
        §§27-32-37 to
        27-32-41.
      Construction of chapter,
        §27-32-2.
      Credits.
        Setoff of credits and
        debts, §27-32-29.
      Debts.
        Setoff of credits and
        debts, §27-32-29.
      Definitions, §27-32-1.
      Delinquency proceedings,
        §§27-32-15 to 27-32-20.
      Deposit of moneys
        collected, §27-32-23.
      Employees.
        Priority of compensation
        owed to employees,
        §27-32-28.
      Grounds, §27-32-6.
      Liability.
        Receivers, §27-32-41.
      Liens.
        Voidable liens,
        §27-32-27.
      Mutual insurers.
        Assessments, §§27-32-32
        to 27-32-36.
      Order of supervision by
        commissioner.
        Effect on rehabilitation,
        §27-2-36.
      Orders, §27-32-11.
      Policyholders.
        Classification, §27-32-40.
        Payment of claims,
        §27-32-38.
        Priority of claims,
        §§27-32-37 to
        27-32-41.
        Reinsuring of policies,
        §27-32-39.

INSURANCE—Cont'd
  Insurers—Cont'd
    Rehabilitation—Cont'd
      Preference to creditors.
        Voidable transfers and
        liens, §27-32-27.
      Priorities.
        Claims of policyholders
        and beneficiaries.
        Classification of
        policyholders and
        beneficiaries,
        §27-32-40.
        Established, §27-32-37.
        Liability of receiver,
        §27-32-41.
        Payment of claims,
        §27-32-38.
        Reinsuring of policies,
        §27-32-39.
        Compensation owing
        employees,
        §27-32-28.
      Purpose of chapter,
        §27-32-2.
      Receivers.
        Liability, §27-32-41.
      Reciprocal insurers.
        Assessments, §§27-32-32
        to 27-32-36.
      Reinsuring of policies,
        §27-32-39.
      Setoff of credits and debts,
        §27-32-29.
      Transfers.
        Voidable transfers,
        §27-32-27.
      Voidable transfers and
        liens, §27-32-27.
    Reinsurance.
      Bulk reinsurance.
        Mutual insurers,
        §27-27-48.
        Stock insurers,
        §27-27-47.
      Entry into new reinsurance
        contract prohibited
        during period of
        supervision, §27-2-34.
    Reorganization.
      Construction of chapter,
        §27-32-2.
      Credits.
        Setoff of credits and
        debts, §27-32-29.
      Debts.
        Setoff of credits and
        debts, §27-32-29.
      Definitions, §27-32-1.
      Delinquency proceedigns,
        §§27-32-15 to 27-32-20.
      Deposit of moneys
        collected, §27-32-23.
      Employees.
        Priority of compensation
        owed to employees,
        §27-32-28.
      Liens.
        Voidable liens,
        §27-32-27.
      Loans to facilitate,
        §27-32-25.
      Preference to creditors.
        Voidable transfers and
        liens, §27-32-27.
      Priorities.
        Compensation owing
        employees of insurer,
        §27-32-28.
      Purpose of chapter,
        §27-32-2.

INSURANCE—Cont'd
  Insurers—Cont'd
    Reorganization—Cont'd
      Setoff of credits and debts,
        §27-32-29.
      Transfers.
        Voidable transfers,
        §27-32-27.
      Voidable transfers and
        liens, §27-32-27.
    Reports.
      Annual statement of
        insurers, §27-3-26.
      Fee for filing, §27-4-2.
      Furnishing information to
        commissioner,
        §27-3-26.
      Rates and rating
        organizations.
        Annual statistical
        reports of insurers,
        §27-13-66.
      Taxation.
        Annual tax statement,
        §27-4-3.
    Reserves.
      Active life reserve for
        disability insurance,
        §27-36-5.
      Deficiency reserves.
        Standard valuation law,
        §27-36-7.
      Inadequate life loss
        reserves.
        Increase, §27-36-6.
      Increase of inadequate loss
        reserves, §27-36-6.
      Loss reserves.
        Increase of inadequate
        loss reserve,
        §27-36-6.
      Minimum aggregate
        reserves.
        Standard valuation law,
        §27-36-7.
      Standard valuation law,
        §27-36-7.
      Unearned premium
        reserve, §§27-36-2 to
        27-36-4.
      Valuation.
        Standard valuation law,
        §27-36-7.
      Variable contracts,
        §27-38-5.
    Restraining orders, §27-32-5.
    Rules and regulations.
      Insider trading of domestic
        stock insurer equity
        securities, §27-27-60.
      Securities of stock insurers,
        §27-27-51.
    Securities.
      Deposits by insurers,
        §§27-6-3 to 27-6-14.
    Service of process on
      insurers.
      Appointment of
        commissioner as agent,
        §27-3-24.
      Commissioner of insurance.
        Appointment as agent
        for service, §27-3-24.
      Fee for acceptance of
        service by
        commissioner, §27-4-2.
      How served, §27-3-25.

INSURANCE—Cont'd
  Insurers—Cont'd
    Service of process on insurers
        —Cont'd
      Mutual insurers.
        Order to pay assessments
            for rehabilitation or
            liquidation,
            §27-32-35.
        Time to answer or plead,
            §27-3-25.
        Unauthorized insurers,
            §§27-10-50 to 27-10-56.
          See within this
            heading,
            "Unauthorized
            insurers."
    Setoffs.
      Rehabilitation,
          reorganization,
          liquidation or
          conservation of assets.
        Setoff of credits and
            debts, §27-32-29.
    Settlement of claims.
      Refusal to settle claims,
          §27-12-24.
    Solicitation permits.
      Application, §27-27-5.
        Approval, §27-27-6.
        Denial, §27-27-6.
      Bonds, surety, §27-27-10.
      Compliance with terms,
          §27-27-7.
      Contents, §27-27-7.
      Denial of application,
          §27-27-6.
      Deposit in lieu of bond,
          §27-27-10.
      Deposit of permit funds in
          escrow.
        Refund, §27-27-13.
        Requirement, §27-27-12.
        Withdrawal of funds,
            §27-27-13.
      Effect of granting,
          §27-27-8.
      Escrow deposit of funds,
          §§27-27-12, 27-27-13.
      Fees, §§27-4-2, 27-27-5.
      Funds.
        Deposit in escrow,
            §27-27-12.
        Withdrawal, §27-27-13.
      Issuance, §27-27-7.
        Effect of granting,
            §27-27-8.
      Licensing of securities
          salesmen, §27-27-11.
      Modification, §27-27-9.
      Required, §27-27-4.
      Revocation, §27-27-9.
      Subsequent financing,
          §27-27-14.
      Waiver of requirement of
          bond or deposit,
          §27-27-10.
    Standard valuation law,
        §27-36-7.
    State insurers.
      Protection against foreign
          discriminatory or
          onerous requirements,
          §27-3-29.
    Stock insurers, §§27-27-1 to
        27-27-61.
      Applicability of chapter,
          §27-27-2.

INSURANCE—Cont'd
  Insurers—Cont'd
    Stock insurers—Cont'd
      Assessments.
        Collection of assessments
            by insurers,
            §27-27-33.
        Deficiencies in stock
            insurer's capital,
            §27-27-42.
      Bulk reinsurance,
          §27-27-47.
      Capital.
        Collection of
            assessments.
          Curing of deficiency,
              §27-27-33.
        Deficiencies in stock
            insurer's capital,
            §27-27-41.
          Curing of deficiency,
              §27-27-42.
      Capital stock and surplus.
        Minimum paid-in capital
            stock and surplus,
            §27-3-7.
        New domestic life
            insurance
            company, §27-3-9.
      Conversion of mutual
          insurer into stock
          insurer, §27-27-44.
      Corrupt practices in
          meeting of
          stockholders,
          §27-27-25.
      Deficiencies in stock
          insurer's capital,
          §27-27-41.
        Curing of deficiency,
            §27-27-42.
        Collection of
            assessments by
            insurers,
            §27-27-33.
        Order of supervision by
            commission,
            §§27-2-33 to 27-2-38.
      Deficits.
        Application of capital
            surplus to deficit,
            §27-3-10.
      Definition, §27-27-1.
        Equity securities,
            §27-27-58.
      Dishonest practices in
          meeting of
          stockholders,
          §27-27-25.
      Dividends, §27-27-37.
      Exchange of stock.
        Plan for exchange of
            stock, etc., between
            stock insurer and
            holding company,
            §§27-28-1 to 27-28-3.
      Fraternal benefit societies.
        Conversion into stock or
            mutual life
            insurance company,
            §§27-35-1 to
            27-35-11.
          See FRATERNAL
            BENEFIT
            SOCIETIES.

INSURANCE—Cont'd
  Insurers—Cont'd
    Stock insurers—Cont'd
      Holding companies.
        Plan for exchange of
            stock, etc., between
            domestic stock
            insurer and holding
            company, §§27-28-1
            to 27-28-3.
      Insider trading of equity
          securities.
        Applicability of sections
            27-27-53 through
            27-27-55, §§27-27-57,
            27-27-59.
        Definition of equity
            securities, §27-27-58.
        Exemptions from
            sections 27-27-54
            and 27-27-55,
            §27-27-56.
        Ownership statements,
            §27-27-53.
        Profits.
          Recovery of certain
              profits by
              company,
              §27-27-54.
        Recovery of certain
            profits by company,
            §27-27-54.
        Rules and regulations,
            §27-27-60.
        Short title, §27-27-52.
        Unlawful sales,
            §27-27-55.
      Life insurers.
        Minimum capital and
            surplus for new
            domestic stock life
            insurance company,
            §27-3-9.
      Meeting of stockholders.
        Corrupt or dishonest
            practices in meeting,
            §27-27-25.
      Merger and consolidation,
          §27-27-45.
      Minimum paid-in capital
          stock and surplus,
          §27-3-7.
      New domestic stock life
          insurance company,
          §27-3-9.
      Mutual insurers.
        Conversion of mutual
            insurer into stock
            insurer, §27-27-44.
      Mutualization of stock
          insurers, §27-27-43.
      Reinsurance.
        Bulk reinsurance,
            §27-27-47.
      Rules and regulations.
        Insider trading of equity
            securities, §27-27-60.
        Securities of domestic
            stock insurers,
            §27-27-51.
      Solicitation permit,
          §§27-27-4 to 27-27-14.
      Surplus.
        Application of capital
            surplus to reduction
            or elimination of
            deficit, §27-3-10.
      Subsequent financing.
        Solicitation permit for
            subsequent financing,
            §27-27-14.

INSURANCE—Cont'd
Insurers—Cont'd
Supervision.
Order of supervision by
commissioner,
§§27-2-33 to 27-2-38.
Surety insurers.
Deposit requirements.
Special deposit, §27-3-12.
Sale of special deposit
to pay outstanding
judgment,
§27-6-13.
Unearned premium
reserve, §27-36-3.
Surplus.
Minimum paid-in capital
stock and surplus,
§27-3-7.
New domestic stock life
insurance company.
Minimum capital and
surplus, §27-3-9.
Reduction or elimination of
deficit.
Application of capital
surplus to reduction
or elimination,
§27-3-10.
Special surplus, §27-3-8.
Surplus line insurance.
Action or proceeding
against insurer.
Service of process,
§27-10-33.
Eligibility of insurers for
placement, §27-10-26.
Liability of insurer as to
losses and unearned
premiums, §27-10-28.
Service of process in action
or proceeding against
insurer, §27-10-33.
Taxation.
Counties.
Taxation by counties not
allowed, §27-4-9.
Definitions, §27-4-1.
Exemption from other
taxes, §27-4-10.
Foreign insurers.
Premium tax, §27-4-4.
Mistake.
Refund of taxes paid by
mistake, §27-4-11.
Penalty for violation of
sections 27-4-3 through
27-4-6, §27-4-7.
Premium tax, §27-4-5.
Foreign insurers,
§27-4-4.
Penalty for violation of
sections 27-4-3
through 27-4-6,
§27-4-7.
Statement, §27-4-3.
Wet marine and
transportation
insurance, §27-4-6.
Refund of taxes paid by
mistake, §27-4-11.
Wet marine and
transportation
insurance, §27-4-6.
Title insurers.
Deposit requirements.
Special deposit, §27-3-13.
Revocation of charter for
violations, §27-25-1.
Unearned premium
reserve, §27-36-2.

INSURANCE—Cont'd
Insurers—Cont'd
Trade practices law,
§§27-12-1 to 27-12-24.
See within this heading,
"Trade practices law."
Trusteed assets.
Alien insurers, §§27-33-1
to 27-33-16.
Unauthorized insurers,
§§27-10-50 to 27-10-56.
See within this heading,
"Unauthorized insurers."
Unclaimed property.
Uniform disposition of
unclaimed property
act, §§35-12-21,
35-12-23.
Unfair trade, §§27-12-1 to
27-12-24. See within this
heading, "Trade practices
law."
Uniform insurers liquidation
act, §27-32-22.
Variable contracts.
Licensing of insurers,
§27-38-3.
Reserve liability for
variable contracts,
§27-38-5.
Venue.
Delinquency proceedings,
§27-32-3.
Violations.
Rehabilitation, §§27-32-1
to 27-32-41.
Interest.
Health and accident
insurance policies.
Limitation period for
payment of claims.
Payment of interest,
§27-1-17.
Intimidation, §27-12-8.
Investigations.
Commissioner of insurance,
§§27-2-26, 27-2-27.
Investments generally.
Burial insurance companies,
§§27-41-1 to 27-41-41.
See within this heading,
"Investments of life,
disability and burial
insurance companies."
Disability insurance
companies, §§27-41-1 to
27-41-41. See within this
heading, "Investments of
life, disability and burial
insurance companies."
Insurers.
Housing.
Investments with respect
to housing, §5-5A-23.
Prohibited during period of
supervision, §27-2-34.
Real property, §27-3-3.
Securities secured by real
property, §27-3-3.
Life insurance company,
§§27-41-1 to 27-41-41.
See within this heading,
"Investments of life,
disability and burial
insurance companies."
Mortgages and deeds of trust.
Investments of life
insurance companies,
§§27-1-8, 27-41-29.
Mutual aid associations,
§27-30-20.

INSURANCE—Cont'd
Investments generally
—Cont'd
Oil and gas producing
properties and facilities.
Eligible investments of life,
disability and burial
insurance companies,
§27-41-34.1.
Servicemen's readjustment
act.
Investments of life
insurance companies,
§27-1-9.
Water conservation and
irrigation.
Corporations.
Bond issues, §9-10-39.
**Investments of life, disability
and burial insurance
companies.**
Admitted assets.
Defined, §27-41-2.
Effect of failure to dispose
of real estate, personal
property, securities,
etc., within prescribed
period of time,
§27-41-40.
Investments which may be
counted as admitted
assets generally,
§27-41-3.
Only eligible investments
to be counted as
admitted assets,
§27-41-41.
Treatment of investments
partially qualifying as
eligible investments,
§27-41-41.
African development bank
obligations, §27-41-14.
Agricultural property loan
investments, §27-41-32.
American insurance stocks,
§27-41-18.
Applicability of chapter,
§27-41-1.
Authorization of investments.
By board of directors, etc.,
§27-41-5.
Canadian governmental
obligations, §27-41-13.
Certificates, etc., issued by
trustees or receivers,
§27-41-23.
Certified statements as to
ineligible investments.
Filing with commissioner,
§27-41-3.
Chattel mortgages,
§27-41-33.
Collateral loans, §27-41-24.
Common stocks or shares
and capital stocks of
American and Canadian
corporations, §27-41-17.
Corporate obligations
generally, §27-41-15.
Data processing and
accounting systems,
§27-41-31.
Definitions, §27-41-2.
Effect of failure to dispose of
real estate, personal
property, securities, etc.,
within prescribed period
of time, §27-41-40.

INSURANCE—Cont'd
Investments of life, disability and burial insurance companies—Cont'd
Eligible investments.
African development bank obligations, §27-41-14.
Agricultural property loan investments, §27-41-32.
American insurance stocks, §27-41-18.
Assets or funds to which investment limitations based upon amounts of insurer's assets, §27-41-3.
Canadian governmental obligations, §27-41-13.
Certificates, etc., issued by trustees or receivers, §27-41-23.
Chattel mortgages, §27-41-33.
Collateral loans, §27-41-24.
Common stocks or shares and capital stocks of American and Canadian corporations, §27-41-17.
Corporate obligations generally, §27-41-15.
Data processing and accounting systems, §27-41-31.
Defined, §27-41-2.
Federal national mortgage association obligations, §27-41-14.
Filing with commissioner certified statements as to investments or obligations for investments, §27-41-3.
Foreign and alien insurers, §27-41-39.
General requirements, §27-41-4.
Housing authority obligations, §27-41-11.
Insurance stocks, §27-41-18.
International bank for reconstruction and development obligations, §27-41-14.
Investments which may be counted as admitted assets generally, §27-41-3.
Loans, etc., secured by mortgages and leases on real property, §27-41-30.
Loans guaranteed by United States, §27-41-8.
Loans secured by liens on interests in oil, gas or condensate properties, etc., §27-41-22.
Loans secured by pledges of securities or pledges or assignments of life insurance policies, §27-41-24.
Miscellaneous investments, §27-41-35.
Mortgage loans generally, §§27-1-8, 27-41-29.

INSURANCE—Cont'd
Investments of life, disability and burial insurance companies—Cont'd
Eligible investments—Cont'd
Mutual aid associations, §§27-41-37, 27-41-38.
Obligations issued or guaranteed by certain federal agencies, §27-41-12.
Obligations of American and Canadian institutions generally, §27-41-15.
Obligations of religious institutions or societies, §27-41-21.
Obligations secured by lease, etc., relating to machinery and personal property, §27-41-19.
Oil and gas producing properties and facilities, §27-41-34.1.
Oil and gas production loans, §27-41-22.
Particular investments.
General provisions, §§27-41-7 to 27-41-34.
Personal property loans, §27-41-33.
Policy loans, §27-41-25.
Preferred or guaranteed stocks, etc., of American corporations, §27-41-16.
Public improvement obligations, §27-41-10.
Railroad leased line obligations, §27-41-20.
Railroad terminal obligations, §27-41-20.
Real estate, §27-41-34.
Real property lease investments, §27-41-30.
Savings and loan associations shares or savings accounts, §27-41-26.
School district obligations, §27-41-9.
Securities of foreign countries, §27-41-27.
Servicemen's readjustment act.
Loans guaranteed under, §27-1-9.
Ship loans, §27-41-28.
State, county, municipal, etc., obligations, §27-41-9.
Terminal obligations of railroads and other common carriers, §27-41-20.
Transportation equipment trust obligations, §27-41-19.
Treatment of investments partially qualifying as eligible investments, §27-41-41.
Trustees' or receivers' obligations, §27-41-23.
United States government obligations, §27-41-7.

INSURANCE—Cont'd
Investments of life, disability and burial insurance companies—Cont'd
Federal national mortgage association obligations, §27-41-14.
Foreign and alien insurers, §27-41-39.
Foreign securities, §27-41-27.
General requirements as to eligibility, §27-41-4.
Housing authority obligations, §27-41-11.
Insurance stocks, §27-41-18.
International bank for reconstruction and development obligations, §27-41-14.
Limitations upon investments.
Generally, §27-41-6.
Limitations based upon amounts of insurer's assets, §27-41-3.
Loans, etc., secured by mortgages and leases on real property, §§27-1-8, 27-41-30.
Loans guaranteed by United States, §27-41-8.
Loans secured by liens on interests in oil, gas or condensate properties, etc., §27-41-22.
Loans secured by pledges of securities or pledges or assignments of life insurance policies, §27-41-24.
Local public housing authority obligations, §27-41-11.
Miscellaneous investments, §27-41-35.
Mortgage loans generally, §27-41-29.
Mutual aid associations.
Funeral supply inventories and funeral equipment, §27-41-38.
Investments generally, §27-41-37.
Obligations issued or guaranteed by certain federal agencies, §27-41-12.
Obligations of American and Canadian institutions generally, §27-41-15.
Obligations of religious institutions or societies, §27-41-21.
Obligations secured by lease, etc., relating to machinery and personal property, §27-41-19.
Oil and gas producing properties and facilities, §27-41-34.1.
Oil and gas production loans, §27-41-22.
Personal property loans, §27-41-33.
Policy loans, §27-41-25.
Preferred or guaranteed stocks, etc., of American corporations, §27-41-16.
Prohibited investments.
Generally, §27-41-36.

INSURANCE—Cont'd
Investments of life, disability and burial insurance companies—Cont'd
Public improvement obligations, §27-41-10.
Railroad leased line obligations, §27-41-20.
Railroad terminal obligations, §27-41-20.
Real estate, §27-41-34.
Effect of failure to dispose of real estate, etc., §27-41-40.
Real property lease investments, §27-41-30.
Savings and loan associations shares or savings accounts, §27-41-26.
School district obligations, §27-41-9.
Securities of foreign countries, §27-41-27.
Ship loans, §27-41-28.
State, county, municipal, etc., obligations, §27-41-9.
Terminal obligations of railroads and other common carriers, §27-41-20.
Transportation equipment trust obligations, §27-41-19.
Trustees' or receivers' obligations, §27-41-23.
Underwriting, etc., of offerings of securities or property, §27-41-36.
United States government obligations, §27-41-7.
Joinder of claims.
Liability insurance coverage, ARCP, Rule 18 (c).
Joint underwriting association, §§27-26-20 to 27-26-43. See within this heading, "Medical liability insurance."
Judicial building authority, §41-10-273.
Jurisdiction.
Insurers.
Delinquency proceedings, §27-32-3.
Kinds of insurance, §§27-5-1 to 27-5-12.
Definitions not mutually exclusive, §27-5-1.
Exceptions to applicability of chapter, §27-5-1.
Legal expense insurance.
Applicability of chapter, §27-43-4.
Applicability of general insurance laws, §27-43-13.
Authorization.
Requirements generally, §27-43-5.
Bonds, surety.
Requirements, §27-43-9.
Certificate of authority.
Filing of application, §27-43-8.
Contents, §27-43-8.
Issuance, §27-43-8.
Citation of article, §27-43-1.
Construction of chapter, §27-43-23.

INSURANCE—Cont'd
Legal expense insurance —Cont'd
Contracts.
Filing and approval of contracts, §27-43-12.
Definitions, §27-43-3.
Deposits.
Requirements, §27-43-9.
Disposition of moneys received from licenses and fees, §27-43-21.
Eligibility.
Insurers deemed eligible to transact legal expense insurance, §27-43-6.
Fees, §27-43-13.
Disposition of moneys received from licenses and fees, §27-43-21.
Forms, §27-43-10.
Funds belonging to legal service insurers, §27-43-20.
Incorporation.
Procedure generally, §27-43-7.
Penalties.
Imposition, §27-43-19.
Policies.
Forms, §27-43-10.
Issuance, §27-43-10.
Premium rates, §27-43-11.
Prepaid legal expense insurance business.
Authorization required, §27-43-5.
Procedure for incorporation of legal services insurance corporation.
Generally, §27-43-7.
Promulgation of rules and regulations, §27-43-22.
Purpose of chapter, §27-43-2.
Rates.
Premiums, §27-43-11.
Registration requirements.
Administrative penalty in lieu of suspension or revocation of registration, §27-43-19.
Generally, §27-43-14.
Grounds for compulsory refusal, suspension or revocation, §27-43-16.
Grounds for discretionary refusal, suspension or revocation, §27-43-17.
Procedure for refusal, suspension or revocation of registration, §27-43-18.
Sales agent, §27-43-15.
Rules and regulations.
Promulgation, §27-43-22.
Sales agents.
Registration requirements, §27-43-15.
Short title, §27-43-1.
Taxation, §27-43-13.
Trusts and trustees.
Funds belonging to legal service insurers.
Agents to hold in trust, §27-43-20.
Types of legal expense insurance, §27-43-10.

INSURANCE—Cont'd
Liability insurance.
Casualty insurance.
Cancellation of automobile liability insurance, §§27-23-20 to 27-23-28.
See MOTOR VEHICLES.
Corporations, §10-2A-21.
Medical liability insurance, §§27-26-1 to 27-26-43.
See within this heading, "Medical liability insurance."
Licenses.
Adjusters, §§27-9-2 to 27-9-8.
Agents.
Examinations.
Fees, §27-4-2.
Property, casualty and surety insurance representatives, §§27-7-4 to 27-7-26.
Automobile clubs and associations.
Agents and representatives, §27-39-7.
Requirements, §27-39-3.
Brokers.
Fees, §27-4-2.
Life and disability insurance representatives, §§27-8-3 to 27-8-21.
See within this heading, "Brokers."
Property, casualty and surety insurance representatives, §§27-7-4 to 27-7-26.
See within this heading, "Agents."
Surplus line brokers, §27-10-24.
Revocation or suspension of surplus line brokers license, §27-10-32.
Casualty insurance.
Rates and rating organizations, §§27-13-62, 27-13-78, 27-13-79.
Finance companies.
Insurance premium finance companies, §§27-40-3 to 27-40-5.
Fraternal benefit societies, §§27-34-6 to 27-34-8.
Insurance premium finance companies, §§27-40-3 to 27-40-5.
Insurers.
Exemption from other licenses, §27-4-10.
Life insurers organized to aid nonprofit educational and scientific institutions.
Annual license fee, §27-4-8.
Refund of licenses paid by mistake, §27-4-11.
Life and disability insurance representatives, §§27-8-3 to 27-8-21. See within this heading, "Brokers."
Municipal corporations.
Schedules, §§11-51-120 to 11-51-123.

INSURANCE—Cont'd
Licenses—Cont'd
Premiums.
Finance companies,
§§27-40-3 to 27-40-5.
Rating organizations.
Casualty insurance,
§§27-13-62, 27-13-78,
27-13-79.
Fire and inland marine
insurance, §§27-13-24,
27-13-40, 27-13-41.
Securities salesmen,
§27-27-11.
Solicitors.
Property, casualty and
surety insurance
representatives,
§§27-7-4 to 27-7-26.
See within this
heading, "Agents."
Surety insurance.
Rates and rating
organizations,
§§27-13-62, 27-13-78,
27-13-79.
Surplus line insurance.
Brokers, §27-10-24.
Liens.
Insurers.
Voidable liens, §27-32-27.
**Life and disability insurance
guaranty association,**
§§27-44-1 to 27-44-21.
Accounts, §27-44-6.
Defined, §27-44-5.
Appeals.
Actions of board.
Appeal to commissioner,
§27-44-11.
Applicability of chapter,
§27-44-3.
Assessments.
Amounts, §27-44-9.
Board of directors to assess
member insurers,
§27-44-9.
Classes of assessments,
§27-44-9.
Credits for assessments
paid, §27-44-13.
Unpaid assessments.
Liability, §27-44-14.
Association.
Defined, §27-44-5.
Board of directors.
Annual financial report,
§27-44-15.
Expenses.
Reimbursement,
§27-44-7.
Immunity, §27-44-17.
Organizational meetings,
§27-44-7.
Selection of members,
§27-44-7.
Vacancies, §27-44-7.
Citation, §27-44-1.
Commissioner.
Appeals from action of
board or association,
§27-44-11.
Defined, §27-44-5.
Immunity, §27-44-17.
Insolvencies.
Duties of commissioner,
§27-44-12.
Powers and duties,
§27-44-11.
Construction of chapter,
§27-44-4.

INSURANCE—Cont'd
**Life and disability insurance
guaranty association**
—Cont'd
Contractual obligations.
Defined, §27-44-5.
Covered policies.
Defined, §27-44-5.
Creation, §27-44-6.
Creditor of impaired or
insolvent insurer,
§27-44-14.
Credits for assessments paid,
§27-44-13.
Default judgments.
Reopening, §27-44-18.
Definitions, §27-44-5.
Examinations.
Association subject to
examination in
regulation by
commissioner,
§27-44-15.
Immunity under chapter,
§27-44-17.
Impaired insurers.
Defined, §27-44-5.
Insolvent insurers.
Association deemed
creditor, §27-44-14.
Defined, §27-44-5.
Immediate access of
associations to assets,
§27-44-21.
Judicial distribution of
ownership rights of
insolvent insurer,
§27-44-14.
Stay of proceedings,
§27-44-18.
Liberal construction of
chapter, §27-44-4.
Meetings.
Records, §27-44-14.
Member insurers.
Defined, §27-44-5.
Members, §27-44-6.
Plan of operation.
Promulgation of rules in
absence of plan,
§27-44-10.
Submission, §27-44-10.
Powers and duties.
Generally, §27-44-8.
Preferred creditor status,
§27-44-20.
Premiums.
Defined, §27-44-5.
Prevention of insolvencies.
Duties of commissioner,
§27-44-12.
Purpose of chapter, §27-44-2.
Receivers.
Preferred creditor status,
§27-44-20.
Recovery of certain
distributions from
controlling affiliates,
§27-44-14.
Records.
Negotiations and meetings,
§27-44-14.
Scope of chapter, §27-44-3.
Short title, §27-44-1.
Stay of proceedings.
Proceedings in which
insolvent insurer is
party, §27-44-18.
Supervision of commissioner,
§27-44-6.

INSURANCE—Cont'd
**Life and disability insurance
guaranty association**
—Cont'd
Taxation.
Association exempt from
taxation, §27-44-16.
Life insurance.
Accounts.
Separate accounts.
Applicability of title,
§27-38-6.
Establishment by life
insurers to provide
for annuities and
benefits, §27-38-1.
Age.
Misstatement of age in
policies, §27-15-6.
Agents, §§27-8-1 to 27-8-28.
See within this heading,
"Agents."
Annuities.
Establishment of separate
accounts by life
insurers, §27-38-1.
Beneficiaries of policies.
Rights against creditors,
§27-14-29.
Benefits.
Group life insurance.
Adjustment, §27-18-7.
Assignment of benefits
under group policies,
§27-18-16.
Payment of benefits,
§27-18-9.
Separate accounts.
Establishment by life
insurers to provide
for incidental
benefits, §27-38-1.
Cash surrender value,
§27-15-28.
Claims.
Settlement of claims,
§27-15-13.
County officers and
employees, §§11-91-1 to
11-91-7.
See COUNTIES.
Creditors.
Rights of beneficiaries
against creditors,
§27-14-29.
Definitions, §27-5-2.
Industrial life insurance,
§27-16-1.
Discrimination.
Exceptions to
discrimination,
§27-12-13.
Unfair discrimination in
rates, §27-12-11.
Dividends, §27-15-7.
Educational institutions.
Annual license fee of life
insurers organized to
aid nonprofit
educational
institutions, §27-4-8.
Exemptions from levy and
sale under process.
Rights of beneficiaries and
assignees under life
insurance policies,
§6-10-8.

INSURANCE—Cont'd
  Life insurance—Cont'd
    Fraternal benefit societies.
      Conversion into stock or
        mutual life insurance
        company, §§27-35-1 to
        27-35-11.
      See FRATERNAL
        BENEFIT
        SOCIETIES.
    Group life insurance.
      Applicability of chapter,
        §27-18-1.
      Benefits.
        Adjustment, §27-18-7.
        Assignment of benefits
          under group policies,
          §27-18-16.
        Payment of benefits,
          §27-18-9.
      Employee life insurance,
        §27-18-15.
      Policies, §§27-18-2 to
        27-18-13.
        Adjustment of premiums
          and/or benefits,
          §27-18-7.
        Applications, §27-18-5.
        Assignment of rights and
          benefits under group
          policies, §27-18-16.
        Benefits.
          Adjustments, §27-18-7.
          Assignment of
            benefits,
            §27-18-16.
          Payment of benefits,
            §27-18-9.
        Certificates.
          Individual certificates,
            §27-18-10.
        Conversion.
          Death during
            conversion period,
            §27-18-13.
          Notice as to conversion
            rights, §27-18-14.
          Termination of
            eligibility,
            §27-18-11.
          Termination of policy,
            §27-18-12.
        Debtors.
          Furnishing of
            statement to
            debtors, §27-18-8.
        Grace period provision,
          §27-18-3.
        Incontestability
          provision, §27-18-4.
        Individual certificates,
          §27-18-10.
        Insurability provision,
          §27-18-6.
        Provisions generally,
          §27-18-2.
        Representations,
          §27-18-5.
        Statements as evidence,
          §27-18-5.
      Premiums.
        Adjustment of premiums,
          §27-18-7.
        Grace period provision in
          policy, §27-18-3.
      Rights.
        Assignment of rights
          under group policies,
          §27-18-16.
    Homicide.
      Effect of, §43-8-253.

INSURANCE—Cont'd
  Life insurance—Cont'd
    Inducements, §27-12-12.
      Exceptions to special
        inducements,
        §27-12-13.
    Industrial life insurance,
      §§27-16-1 to 27-16-17.
      See within this heading,
        "Industrial life
        insurance."
    Insurers.
      Investments.
        Notes guaranteed under
          servicemen's
          readjustment act,
          §27-1-9.
        Notes secured by
          mortgages or deeds
          of trust, §27-1-8.
      New domestic stock life
        insurance company.
        Minimum capital and
          surplus, §27-3-9.
      Nonprofit educational and
        scientific institutions.
        Annual license fee of life
          insurers organized to
          aid nonprofit
          educational and
          scientific
          institutions, §27-4-8.
      Proceeds of policies.
        Power of life insurer to
          hold proceeds of
          policy, §27-15-26.
        Right to proceeds when
          proceeds retained by
          life insurer,
          §27-14-30.
      Separate accounts.
        Establishment by life
          insurers to provide
          for annuities and
          benefits, §27-38-1.
      Standard valuation law,
        §27-36-7.
    Investments.
      Life, disability and burial
        insurance companies,
        §§27-41-1 to 27-41-41.
        See within this
        heading, "Investments
        of life, disability and
        burial insurance
        companies."
      Life and disability insurance
        guaranty association,
        §§27-44-1 to 27-44-21.
        See within this heading,
        "Life and disability
        insurance guaranty
        association."
    Loans on policy, §27-15-8.
      Maximum rates of interest,
        §27-15-8.1.
    Minors.
      Receipt and giving of
        acquittance and
        discharge for payment
        by minors, §27-14-25.
    Mortgages and deeds of
      trusts.
      Investments.
        Notes secured by
          mortgages or deeds
          of trust, §27-1-8.

INSURANCE—Cont'd
  Life insurance—Cont'd
    Municipal officers and
      employees, §§11-91-1 to
      11-91-7.
      See MUNICIPAL
        CORPORATIONS.
    Natural death act.
      Execution of declaration
        not to effect sale, etc.,
        §22-8A-9.
    Nonforfeiture law.
      Standard nonforfeiture
        law, §27-15-28.
      Individual deferred
        annuities,
        §27-15-28.1.
    Nonprofit educational and
      scientific institutions.
      Annual license fee of life
        insurers organized to
        aid nonprofit
        educational and
        scientific institutions,
        §27-4-8.
    Nonresident agents and
      brokers, §27-8-22.
    Policies.
      Age.
        Misstatement of age,
          §27-15-6.
      Applicability of chapter,
        §27-15-1.
      Beneficiaries.
        Rights of beneficiaries
          against creditors,
          §27-14-29.
      Benefits.
        Paid up nonforfeiture
          benefits, §27-15-28.
        Table of benefits,
          §27-15-9.
      Calculation of values,
        §27-15-28.
      Cash surrender value,
        §27-15-28.
      Dividends, §27-15-7.
      Entire contract, §27-15-5.
      Exclusions in policies,
        §27-15-24.
      Generally, §27-15-2.
      Grace period, §27-15-3.
      Group life insurance,
        §§27-18-2 to 27-18-13.
      Incontestability, §27-15-4.
        Effect of incontestability
          clause, §27-15-15.
      Industrial life insurance,
        §§27-16-1 to 27-16-17.
        See within this
          heading, "Industrial
          life insurance."
      Installments.
        Table of installments,
          §27-15-10.
      Loans on policy, §27-15-8.
      Misstatement of age or sex,
        §27-15-6.
      Nonforfeiture provisions,
        §27-15-28.
      Paid up nonforfeiture
        benefits, §27-15-28.
      Payment of premiums,
        §27-15-10.
        Minors, §27-14-25.
      Proceeds.
        Power of life insurer to
          hold proceeds,
          §27-15-26.

INSURANCE—Cont'd
  Life insurance—Cont'd
    Policies—Cont'd
      Proceeds—Cont'd
        Right to proceeds
          retained by life
          insurer, §27-14-30.
      Prohibited policy plans,
        §27-15-29.
      Reinstatement, §27-15-11.
        Contestability of
          reinstated policies,
          §27-15-25.
      Representations, §27-15-5.
      Restrictions in policies,
        §27-15-24.
      Settlement of claims,
        §27-15-13.
      Sex.
        Misstatement of sex,
          §27-15-6.
      Surrender.
        Cash surrender value,
          §27-15-28.
      Table of installments,
        §27-15-10.
      Table of values and
        benefits, §27-15-9.
      Title to policy, §27-15-14.
      Value.
        Calculation of values,
          §27-15-28.
        Cash surrender value,
          §27-15-28.
        Tables of values,
          §27-15-9.
    Premiums.
      Adjusted premiums,
        §27-15-28.
      Agents and brokers.
        Accounting for and
          payment of trust
          funds, §27-8-28.
      Amount due.
        Deductions in
          determining amount
          due, §27-15-27.
      Deductions in determining
        amount due, §27-15-27.
      Grace period for payment,
        §27-15-3.
      Group life insurance.
        Adjustment of premiums,
          §27-18-7.
        Grace period provision in
          policy, §27-18-3.
      Industrial life insurance,
        §§27-16-4, 27-16-15,
        27-16-16.
      Payment of premiums,
        §27-15-12.
      Table of installments,
        §27-15-10.
      Rebates, §27-12-12.
        Exceptions to rebates,
          §27-12-13.
    Proceeds.
      Right to proceeds retained
        by life insurer,
        §27-14-30.
    Rates.
      Discrimination.
        Exceptions to
          discrimination,
          §27-12-13.
      Unfair discrimination in
        rates, §27-12-11.
      Rebates, §27-12-12.
        Exceptions to rebates,
          §27-12-13.

INSURANCE—Cont'd
  Life insurance—Cont'd
    Reports.
      Filing of annual
        statements by life and
        disability insurance
        representatives,
        §27-8-15.
    Representatives, §§27-8-1 to
      27-8-28. See within this
      heading, "Agents."
    Reserves.
      Standard valuation law,
        §27-36-7.
    Scientific institutions.
      Annual license fee of life
        insurers organized to
        aid scientific
        institutions, §27-4-8.
    Separate accounts.
      Applicability of title,
        §27-38-6.
      Establishment by life
        insurers to provide for
        annuities and benefits,
        §27-38-1.
    Settlement of claims,
      §27-15-13.
    Tables.
      Installments, §27-15-10.
      Values and benefits,
        §27-15-9.
    Trusts and trustees.
      Investment of trust estate,
        §19-3-125.
  Limits of risks.
    Mutual aid associations,
      §§27-5-11, 27-30-15.
  Liquefied petroleum gas.
    Engaging in business of
      selling, distributing, etc.,
      §9-17-105.
  Livestock.
    Markets.
      Commissioner to require
        insurance on livestock
        accepted for sale,
        §2-15-67.
  Lloyd's insurers.
    Authority to transact
      insurance, §27-3-16.
  Loans.
    Insurance premium finance
      companies, §§27-40-1 to
      27-40-18. See within this
      heading, "Premiums."
    Insurers, §27-27-40.
    Life insurance policies.
      Loans on policy, §27-15-8.
      Maximum rates of
        interest, §27-15-8.
  Loss.
    Acts not deemed waiver of
      provisions or defenses,
      §27-14-27.
    Effect of misrepresentations
      in proof of loss,
      §27-14-28.
    Forms for proof of loss,
      §27-14-26.
  Mail order insurance,
    §§27-11-1 to 27-11-7. See
    within this heading,
    "Unauthorized insurers."
  Malpractice.
    Casualty insurance
      generally. See within
      this heading, "Casualty
      insurance."

INSURANCE—Cont'd
  Malpractice—Cont'd
    Medical liability insurance,
      §§27-26-1 to 27-26-43.
      See within this heading,
      "Medical liability
      insurance."
  Mandamus.
    Holding companies.
      Petition for mandamus
        against commissioner
        of insurance,
        §27-29-13.
  Marine and transportation
    insurance.
    Definitions, §27-5-8.
    Inland marine insurance.
      Rates and rating
        organizations,
        §27-13-20.
    Inland marine insurance.
      Rates and rating
        organizations,
        §§27-13-20 to 27-13-45.
        See within this
        heading, "Rates and
        rating organizations."
    Insurers.
      Unearned premium
        reserve, §27-36-4.
    Unearned premium reserve,
      §27-36-4.
    Wet marine and
      transportation insurance.
      Defined, §27-5-9.
      Taxation, §27-4-6.
  Medicaid.
    Denial or reduction of
      benefits due to medicaid
      eligibility, §27-14-11.1.
  Medical insurance generally,
    §§27-21-1 to 27-21-6. See
    within this heading,
    "Health insurance."
  Medical liability insurance,
    §§27-26-1 to 27-26-43.
    Commissioner of insurance.
      Joint underwriting
        association.
        Appeal to commissioner,
          §27-26-42.
        Examination of
          association's affairs,
          §27-26-39.
        Judicial review of
          commissioner's
          orders, §27-26-43.
    Condition of doing business
      in state.
      Sale of medical liability
        insurance, §27-26-3.
    Coverage.
      Joint underwriting
        association.
        Applicability for
          coverage, §27-26-32.
    Definitions, §27-26-1.
    Joint underwriting
      association, §§27-26-1 to
      27-26-43.
      Annual statements,
        §27-26-38.
      Appeal to commissioner,
        §27-26-42.
      Board of directors,
        §27-26-22.
      Commencement of
        operations, §27-26-26.
      Commissioner of insurance.
        Appeal to commissioner,
          §27-26-42.

INSURANCE—Cont'd
Medical liability insurance
—Cont'd
Joint underwriting
association—Cont'd
Commissioner of insurance
—Cont'd
Examination of
association's affairs,
§27-26-39.
Judicial review of
commissioner's
orders, §27-26-43.
Composition, §27-26-21.
Cooperation with board
and policyholders,
§27-26-24.
Coverage.
Application for coverage,
§27-26-32.
Creation, §27-26-21.
Deficit.
Insufficiency of funds,
§27-26-31.
Proration of participation
in losses, §27-26-37.
Recoupment of shares of
deficit, §27-26-29.
Directors.
Board of directors,
§27-26-22.
Duties of association,
§27-26-23.
Examination of
association's affairs,
§27-26-39.
Expenses.
Proration of participation
in expenses,
§27-26-37.
Funds.
Holding in trust,
§27-26-30.
Insufficiency of funds,
§27-26-31.
Investing of funds,
§27-26-30.
Stabilization reserve
fund, §§27-26-27,
27-26-28, 27-26-41.
Insufficiency of funds,
§27-26-31.
Investing of funds,
§27-26-30.
Judicial review of
commissioner's orders,
§27-26-43.
Liability for statements
made during
proceedings under
article, §27-26-40.
Losses.
Proration of participation
in losses, §27-26-37.
Management fees.
Proration of participation
in management fees,
§27-26-37.
Plan of operation,
§27-26-25.
Policies.
Application for coverage,
§27-26-32.
Cancellation, §27-26-35.
Generally, §27-26-33.
Issuance, §27-26-34.
Rating plans, §27-26-36.
Powers of association,
§27-26-23.

INSURANCE—Cont'd
Medical liability insurance
—Cont'd
Joint underwriting
association—Cont'd
Proration of participation
in writings, expenses,
etc., §27-26-37.
Public officers or
employees.
Effect of membership on
board of directors of
stabilization reserve
fund, §27-26-41.
Purpose, §27-26-20.
Rating plans, §27-26-36.
Recoupment of shares of
deficit, §27-26-29.
Reports.
Annual statements,
§27-26-38.
Reserve fund.
Stabilization reserve
fund, §§27-26-27,
27-26-28, 27-26-41.
Servicing allowance.
Proration of participation
in servicing
allowance,
§27-26-37.
Stabilization reserve fund.
Charge, §27-26-28.
Generally, §27-26-27.
Public officers or
employees.
Effect of membership
on board of
directors of fund,
§27-26-41.
Trusts and trustees.
Holding funds in trust,
§27-26-30.
When underwriting
operations commenced,
§27-26-26.
Writings.
Proration of participation
in writings,
§27-26-37.
Policies.
Joint underwriting
association, §§27-26-32
to 27-26-36.
Purpose of chapter, §27-26-2.
Reports.
Annual reports of carriers,
§27-26-4.
Joint underwriting
association.
Annual statements,
§27-26-38.
Judgments and
settlements, §27-26-5.
**Medicare supplement policy
minimum standards,**
§§27-19-50 to 27-19-58.
Applicability of provisions,
§27-19-58.
Benefits.
Minimum standards
generally, §27-19-54.
Citation of article, §27-19-50.
Definitions, §27-19-52.
Disclosure requirements,
§27-19-56.
Loss ratios.
Standards generally,
§27-19-55.

INSURANCE—Cont'd
**Medicare supplement policy
minimum standards**
—Cont'd
Notice of right to return
policy and receive
refunds of premium.
Requirements generally,
§27-19-57.
Purpose of article, §27-19-51.
Short title, §27-19-50.
Standards for policy
provisions.
Generally, §27-19-53.
Provisions as to coverage
of pre-existing
conditions, §27-19-53.
Mental health services.
Exclusion of hospitalization
benefits for mental
patients in tax-supported
institutions, §27-19-28.
Reimbursement for
outpatient and inpatient
services by qualified
psychiatrist or
psychologist, §27-1-18.
Minors.
Annuities.
Receipt and giving of
acquittance and
discharge for payment
by minors, §27-14-25.
Health insurance.
Coverage of newly born
children in health
insurance policies,
§27-19-38.
Life insurance.
Receipt and giving of
acquittance and
discharge for payment
by minors, §27-14-25.
Purchase of insurance by or
for minors, §27-14-5.
Misrepresentations.
Policies.
Application for policy,
§27-14-7.
Proof of loss.
Effect of
misrepresentations in
proof of loss, §27-14-28.
Monopolies.
Insurers.
Common ownership,
management and
directorships,
§27-12-16.
Mortality tables.
See ANNUITY AND
MORTALITY TABLES.
**Mortgages and deeds of
trust.**
Investments.
Life insurance companies
may invest in notes
secured by mortgages
or deeds of trusts,
§§27-1-8, 27-41-29.
Purchase of insurance as
condition precedent to
sale or loan on property,
§27-12-15.
Motor vehicles.
Assigned risks, §32-7-35.
Safety-responsibility act,
§§32-7-1 to 32-7-42.
See MOTOR VEHICLES.

INSURANCE—Cont'd
 Motor vehicles—Cont'd
  Automobile clubs and
   associations, §§27-39-1 to
   27-39-8. See within this
   heading, "Automobile
   clubs and associations."
  Cancellation of automobile
   liability insurance,
   §§27-30-20 to 27-23-28.
   See MOTOR VEHICLES.
  Casualty insurance
   generally. See within
   this heading, "Casualty
   insurance."
  Public officers and
   employees, §36-1-6.
  Safety-responsibility act,
   §§32-7-1 to 32-7-42.
   See MOTOR VEHICLES.
  Uninsured motorists,
   §32-7-23.
   Safety-responsibility act,
   §§32-7-1 to 32-7-42.
   See MOTOR VEHICLES.
 Municipal corporations.
  Group insurance for officers
   and employees, §§11-91-1
   to 11-91-8.
   See MUNICIPAL
    CORPORATIONS.
  Liability insurance.
   Employees.
    Authority to contract for,
    §11-47-24.
  Licensing insurance
   companies.
   Schedules, §§11-51-120 to
   11-51-123.
 Mutual aid associations,
  §§27-30-1 to 27-30-33.
  Accounts, §27-30-21.
   Duty of officers and agents,
   §27-30-23.
  Address.
   Notice of change of
   address, §27-30-13.
  Agents.
   Authorization to act as or
   for associations,
   §27-30-4.
   Duties, §27-30-23.
   Life and disability
   insurance
   representatives.
    Applicability of chapter
    8, §27-30-32.
   Requirements, §27-30-5.
  Annual statement, §27-30-22.
  Applicability of chapter.
   Exceptions, §27-30-3.
   Generally, §27-30-2.
  Applicability of other
   provisions, §27-30-33.
  Authorization to act as or for
   association.
   Generally, §27-30-4.
   Requirements, §27-30-5.
  Capital stock.
   Decrease, §27-30-28.
   Increase, §27-30-28.
   Increase in paid-in capital
   stock, §27-30-6.1.
   Requirements for existing
   associations, §27-30-6.
  Certificates of authority.
   Applications, §27-30-8.
   Denial, §27-30-9.
   Expiration, §27-30-10.
   Issuance, §27-30-9.

INSURANCE—Cont'd
 Mutual aid associations
  —Cont'd
  Certificates of authority
   —Cont'd
   Original certificate,
   §27-30-27.
   Qualification of corporation
   for original certificate,
   §27-30-27.
   Refusal, §27-30-9.
   Renewal, §27-30-10.
   Revocation, §§27-30-11,
   27-30-12.
   Suspension or revocation.
    Grounds, §27-30-21.
    Procedure, §27-30-12.
  Commissioner of insurance.
   Approval of contracts,
   §27-30-14.
   Examinations by
   commissioner,
   §27-30-24.
  Service of process.
   Commissioner as agent
   for process,
   §27-30-13.
  Contracts, §§27-30-14 to
   27-30-17.
   Annual valuation.
    Benefits, aid or services
    other than cash,
    §27-30-17.
    Benefits payable in cash,
    §27-30-16.
   Approval by commissioner,
   §27-30-14.
   Contents, §27-30-14.
   Issuance, §27-30-14.
   Limits of risks, §27-30-15.
   Valuation.
    Annual valuation,
    §§27-30-16, 27-30-17.
  Defined, §27-30-1.
  Deposits.
   Administration, §27-30-19.
   Amounts, §27-30-18.
   Kind, §27-30-18.
   Purpose, §27-30-18.
  Directors, §27-30-30.
  Examinations by
   commissioner, §27-30-24.
  Exceptions to chapter,
   §27-30-3.
  Exemption of resident
   members' interest from
   process, §27-30-25.
  Existing associations.
   Authority to increase paid-
   in capital stock and
   paid-in surplus,
   §27-30-6.1.
   Capital stock for surplus
   requirements,
   §27-30-6.
  Fees.
   Applicability of fee
   provisions, §27-30-31.
  Financing of new
   associations, §27-30-26.
  Funds, §27-30-20.
  Incorporation of new
   associations, §27-30-26.
  Information.
   Furnishing, §27-30-22.
  Investments, §27-30-20.
  Life and disability insurance
   representatives.
   Applicability of chapter 8,
   §27-30-32.
  Limits of risks, §27-30-15.

INSURANCE—Cont'd
 Mutual aid associations
  —Cont'd
  Members, §27-30-29.
   Exemption of resident
   members' interest from
   process, §27-30-25.
   Meetings, §27-30-29.
   Voting rights, §27-30-29.
  Name of association,
   §27-30-7.
  New associations.
   Incorporation and
   financing, §27-30-26.
  Notice.
   Change of address,
   §27-30-13.
  Officers.
   Duties, §27-30-23.
  Policies, §§27-30-14 to
   27-30-17.
  Provision of domestic life and
   disability insurance
   pursuant to chapter 3,
   §27-30-34.
  Records, §27-30-21.
   Duty of officers and agents,
   §27-30-23.
  Reports.
   Annual statement,
   §27-30-22.
   Duty of officers and agents,
   §27-30-23.
  Service of process, §27-30-13.
  Solicitors.
   Authorization to act as or
   for associations,
   §27-30-4.
   Requirements, §27-30-5.
  Stock.
   Capital stock
   requirements.
    Authority to increase
    paid-in capital stock,
    §27-30-6.1.
    Existing associations,
    §27-30-6.
   Decrease of capital stock,
   §27-30-28.
   Increase of capital stock,
   §27-30-28.
  Surplus.
   Authority to increase paid-
   in surplus, §27-30-6.1.
   Requirements for existing
   associations, §27-30-6.
  Taxation.
   Applicability of taxation
   provisions, §27-30-31.
  Trustees, §27-30-30.
 Mutual insurers.
  General provisions, §§27-27-1
   to 27-27-61. See within
   this heading, "Insurers."
 Names.
  Insurers.
   Use of name by insurer,
   §27-3-5.
  Mutual aid associations,
   §27-30-7.
  Reciprocal insurers.
   Business name, §27-31-4.
 Narcotics.
  Disability insurance.
   Optional policy provision,
   §27-19-26.
 Natural death act.
  Life insurance.
   Execution of declaration
   not to effect sale, etc.,
   §22-8A-9.

INSURANCE—Cont'd
  Nonresidents.
    Insurers.
      Delinquency proceedings.
        Claims against domestic
          insurers, §27-32-17.
    Life and disability insurance
      representatives.
      Nonresident agents and
        brokers, §27-8-22.
    Property, casualty and surety
      insurance
      representatives,
      §§27-7-28, 27-7-29.
  Notices.
    Agents.
      Property, casualty and
        surety insurance
        representatives.
        Appointment or removal.
          Notice, §27-7-30.
    Appeals from commissioner,
      §27-2-32.
    Hearings, §27-2-29.
    Notices of commissioner,
      §27-2-18.
    Insurers.
      Delinquency proceedings.
        Claims in delinquency
          proceedings,
          §27-32-19.
      Suspension or revocation of
        certificate of authority,
        §§27-3-20 to 27-3-22.
    Life and disability insurance
      representatives.
      Business address change,
        §27-8-26.
    Mutual aid associations.
      Change of address,
        §27-30-13.
    Order of supervision.
      Notice and hearing as to
        issuance, §27-2-38.
    Property, casualty and surety
      insurance
      representatives.
      Notice of complaints
        against licensees,
        §27-7-37.
    Rates and rating
      organizations.
      Casualty and surety
        insurance.
        Notices by commissioner,
          §27-13-80.
      Fire and inland marine
        insurance.
        Notices by commissioner,
          §27-13-42.
  Nurses.
    Health insurance.
      Certified registered nurse
        anesthetist coverage,
        §§27-46-1 to 27-46-3.
  Penalties.
    Automobile clubs and
      associations.
      Violations of chapter,
        §27-39-8.
    Insurers.
      Taxation.
        Penalty for violation of
          sections 27-4-3
          through 27-4-6,
          §27-4-7.
    Mail order insurance.
      Penalty for violation of
        chapter, §27-11-7.

INSURANCE—Cont'd
  Penalties—Cont'd
    Pharmaceutical insurance
      coverage.
      Violations of provisions,
        §27-45-9.
    Rates and rating
      organizations.
      Casualty and surety
        insurance.
        Penalty for violation of
          article, §27-13-83.
      Fire and inland marine
        insurance.
        Violations of article,
          §27-13-45.
    Surplus line insurance.
      Violations of article,
        §27-10-37.
    Unauthorized insurers.
      Mail order insurance.
        Penalty for violation of
          chapter, §27-11-7.
    Violations of title, §27-1-12.
  Permits.
    Insurers.
      Solicitation permits,
        §§27-27-4 to 27-27-14.
      See within this
        heading, "Insurers."
  Person.
    Defined, §27-1-2.
  Personal insurance.
    Insurable interest, §27-14-3.
  Pest control.
    Subterranean termite
      eradication and control
      work, §2-28-10.
  Pesticides.
    Application.
      Liability insurance,
        §2-27-56.
  **Pharmaceutical insurance
    coverage,** §§27-45-1 to
    27-45-9.
    Applicability of provisions,
      §27-45-1.
    Choice of pharmaceutical
      services, §27-45-3.
    Commissioner of insurance.
      Enforcement of provisions,
        §27-45-8.
    Contracting provider.
      Participation as, §27-45-3.
    Definitions, §27-45-2.
    Employee benefit plans.
      Conformance with
        provisions required,
        §27-45-6.
        Nonconforming plans not
          to be approved for
          sale, §27-45-7.
      Defined, §27-45-2.
      Void plans.
        Plans contrary to
          provisions, §27-45-4.
    Health insurance policies.
      Conformance with
        provisions required,
        §27-45-6.
        Nonconforming policies,
          §27-45-7.
      Defined, §27-45-2.
      Void policies.
        Policies contrary to
          provisions, §27-45-4.
    Penalties.
      Violations of provisions,
        §27-45-9.

INSURANCE—Cont'd
  **Pharmaceutical insurance
    coverage**—Cont'd
    Pharmaceutical services.
      Choice of pharmaceutical
        services, §27-45-3.
      Defined, §27-45-2.
      Provisions of services not
        mandated, §27-45-5.
    Prescriptions.
      Defined, §27-45-2.
    Scope of provisions, §27-45-1.
    Violations of provisions.
      Punishment, §27-45-9.
    Willful violations of
      provisions.
      Punishment, §27-45-9.
  Physicians.
    False statements, etc., in
      insurance application,
      §27-12-23.
    Medical liability insurance,
      §§27-26-1 to 27-26-43.
      See within this heading,
        "Medical liability
        insurance."
  Pleadings.
    Form of complaints on
      insurance policies,
      ARCP, Forms 13 to 15.
  Podiatrists.
    Health insurance.
      Payment for services of
        podiatrists, §27-1-15.
  Police.
    State Capitol police.
      Authority to insure,
        §41-4-185.
      Limits as to amount of
        insurance, §41-4-185.
      Payment for insurance,
        §41-4-185.
  Policies, §§27-14-1 to 27-14-32.
    Applicability of chapter,
      §27-14-2.
    Application for policy.
      Admissibility into
        evidence, §27-14-6.
      Alterations, §27-14-6.
      Evidence.
        Admissibility into
          evidence, §27-14-6.
      Exemptions, §27-14-6.
      Fraud, §27-14-7.
      Misrepresentations,
        §27-14-7.
      Reliance by insurer on
        application, §27-14-6.
      Representations and
        application, §27-14-7.
      Required, §27-14-6.
    Assignment, §27-14-21.
    Binders, §27-14-18.
    Blanket disability insurance,
      §§27-20-5 to 27-20-7.
    Burial insurance, §§27-17-2
      to 27-17-14. See within
      this heading, "Burial
      insurance."
    Cancellation.
      Insurance premium finance
        companies.
        Procedure for
          cancellation of
          insurance contract
          upon default,
          §27-40-11.
    Combination policies,
      §27-14-15.
    Construction, §27-14-17.

INSURANCE—Cont'd
  Policies—Cont'd
    Contents, §27-14-11.
      Additional provisions,
        §27-14-12.
    Definitions, §27-14-1.
    Delivery of policies,
      §27-14-19.
    Disability insurance,
      §§27-19-1 to 27-19-29.
      See within this heading,
        "Disability insurance."
    Endorsement.
      Noncomplying
        endorsements,
        §27-14-16.
    Evidence.
      Application for policy.
        Admissibility into
          evidence, §27-14-6.
    Execution, §27-14-14.
    Extension, §27-14-20.
    Facsimile signatures,
      §27-14-14.
    Finance companies.
      Insurance premium finance
        companies.
        Cancellation of insurance
          contract upon
          default.
          Charges, §27-40-10.
          Return of gross
            unearned
            premiums,
            §27-40-12.
    Fire insurance.
      Industrial fire insurance
        policies, §27-22-2.
    Forms.
      Approval, §27-14-8.
        Grounds for withdrawal
          of previous approval,
          §27-14-9.
      Disapproval, §27-14-8.
        Grounds for disapproval,
          §27-14-9.
      Filing, §27-14-8.
    Fraud.
      Application for policy,
        §27-14-7.
    Group disability insurance,
      §§27-20-2, 27-20-3.
    Group life insurance,
      §§27-18-2 to 27-18-13.
      See within this heading,
        "Life insurance."
    Industrial life insurance,
      §§27-16-3 to 27-16-17.
      See within this heading,
        "Industrial life
        insurance."
    Insurance premium finance
      companies.
      Cancellation of insurance
        contract upon default.
        Charges, §27-40-10.
        Return of gross unearned
          premiums upon
          cancellation,
          §27-40-12.
    Insurers.
      Charter, bylaws, etc., of
        insurer as part of
        contract, §27-14-13.
      Issuance, §§27-2-34,
        27-27-36.
    Issuance.
      Prohibited during period of
        supervision of insurer,
        §27-2-34.

INSURANCE—Cont'd
  Policies—Cont'd
    Issuance—Cont'd
      What constitutes "doing
        business," §6-3-5.
    Legal expense insurance.
      Generally, §§27-43-1 to
        27-43-23. See within
        this heading, "Legal
        expense insurance."
    Life insurance.
      General provisions,
        §§27-15-2 to 27-15-14.
        See within this
        heading, "Life
        insurance."
      Group life insurance,
        §§27-18-2 to 27-18-13.
        See within this
        heading, "Life
        insurance."
      Industrial life insurance,
        §§27-16-3 to 27-16-17.
        See within this
        heading, "Industrial
        life insurance."
    Medical liability insurance.
      Joint underwriting
        association, §§27-26-32
        to 27-26-36.
    Medicare supplement police
      minimum standards,
      §§27-19-50 to 27-19-58.
    Misrepresentations.
      Application for policy,
        §27-14-7.
    Mutual aid associations,
      §§27-30-14 to 27-30-17.
    Noncomplying policies,
      §27-14-16.
    Payments.
      Effect of payments,
        §27-14-24.
      Minors.
        Receipt and giving of
          acquittance and
          discharge for
          payment by minors,
          §27-14-25.
    Provisions.
      Contents of policies,
        §§27-14-11, 27-14-12.
      Standard or uniform
        provisions, §27-14-10.
      Substitution for standard
        or uniform provisions,
        §27-14-10.
      Waiver of standard or
        uniform provisions,
        §27-14-10.
    Reciprocal insurers.
      Execution by attorneys,
        §27-31-5.
      Nonassessable policies,
        §27-31-25.
      Right to exchange
        contracts, §27-31-18.
    Records.
      Property, casualty and
        surety insurance
        representatives,
        §27-7-33.
    Renewal, §27-14-20.
    Riders.
      Noncomplying riders,
        §27-14-16.
    Signatures, §27-14-14.
    Situs of contracts, §27-14-22.

INSURANCE—Cont'd
  Policies—Cont'd
    State insurance fund.
      Director of finance may
        prescribe forms of
        policies, §41-15-9.
    Surplus line insurance.
      Production of policies, etc.,
        for inspection by
        commissioner,
        §27-10-36.
    Trusts consisting of
      insurance policies or
      proceeds, §35-4-260.
    "Twisting," §27-12-6.
    Unauthorized insurers.
      Production of policies, etc.,
        for inspection by
        commissioner,
        §27-10-36.
    Underwriters' policies,
      §27-14-15.
  Premiums.
    Alabama health care plan.
      Exemption from premium
        tax, §27-21-4.
    Casualty insurance.
      Unearned premium
        reserve, §27-36-3.
    Credit.
      Insurance premium finance
        companies, §§27-40-1
        to 27-40-18.
    Definitions, §27-14-1.
      Insurance premium finance
        companies, §27-40-1.
    Disability insurance.
      Rebates, §27-12-12.
        Exceptions to rebates,
          §27-12-13.
    Finance companies, §§27-40-1
      to 27-40-18.
      Agreements.
        Delivery of copy to
          insured, §27-40-18.
        Notification of existence
          of, §27-40-17.
        Purchase of premium
          finance agreement,
          §27-40-16.
      Books, §27-40-6.
      Cancellation upon default.
        Charges for cancellation,
          §27-40-10.
        Duties with respect to
          cancellation,
          §27-40-15.
        Procedure, §27-40-11.
        Return of gross unearned
          premiums,
          §27-40-12.
      Charges.
        Cancellation charges,
          §27-40-10.
        Delinquency charges,
          §27-40-10.
        Service charge, §27-40-9.
      Commissioner of insurance.
        Exclusive jurisdiction of
          department of
          insurance, §27-40-14.
        Licenses.
          Information to be
            furnished,
            §27-40-3.
      Contents of premium
        finance agreement,
        §27-40-8.

The Michie Company solicits your help in making this index as complete, accurate and useful as possible. Please use these postpaid cards to advise us of any errors or omissions you may find, or to recommend any other improvements. You may also contact a member of our Indexing Staff by calling toll-free **1-800-446-3410** to make suggestions or obtain assistance.

Name of Code _____

  (a) I had difficulty/was unable to locate the section pertaining to __

_____

  (b) Section(s) _____ should be identified as _____

_____

and indexed under the heading _____

  (c) The section reference following the index entry _____

_____ on page _____ of Vol. _____ should read § _____

  (d) Other suggestions: _____

_____

Name _____ Phone _____

Firm _____ Address _____

City _____ State _____ Zip _____

Name of Code _____

  (a) I had difficulty/was unable to locate the section pertaining to __

_____

  (b) Section(s) _____ should be identified as _____

_____

and indexed under the heading _____

  (c) The section reference following the index entry _____

_____ on page _____ of Vol. _____ should read § _____

  (d) Other suggestions: _____

_____

Name _____ Phone _____

Firm _____ Address _____

City _____ State _____ Zip _____

BUSINESS REPLY MAIL

FIRST CLASS   PERMIT NO. 6   CHARLOTTESVILLE, VA

POSTAGE WILL BE PAID BY ADDRESSEE

The Michie Company

Post Office Box 7587
Charlottesville, Virginia 22906-9988

NO POSTAGE
NECESSARY
IF MAILED
IN THE
UNITED STATES

BUSINESS REPLY MAIL

FIRST CLASS   PERMIT NO. 6   CHARLOTTESVILLE, VA

POSTAGE WILL BE PAID BY ADDRESSEE

The Michie Company

Post Office Box 7587
Charlottesville, Virginia 22906-9988

INSURANCE—Cont'd
Premiums—Cont'd
Finance companies—Cont'd
Default in payment.
Procedure for
cancellation of
insurance contract,
§27-40-11.
Definitions, §27-40-1.
Delinquency charges,
§27-40-10.
Department of insurance.
Exclusive jurisdiction,
§27-40-14.
Designation of agents,
§27-40-15.
Exemptions from chapter,
§27-40-2.
Fees, §27-40-3.
Filing of premium finance
agreement, §27-40-13.
Form of premium finance
agreement, §27-40-8.
Issuance of drafts, etc.,
§27-40-15.
Jurisdiction.
Exclusive jurisdiction of
department of
insurance, §27-40-14.
Licenses.
Information to be
furnished
commissioner,
§27-40-3.
Investigation of
applicant, §27-40-4.
Issuance, §27-40-4.
Qualifications of
applicant, §27-40-4.
Required, §27-40-3.
Revocation, §27-40-5.
Suspension, §27-40-5.
Premium finance
agreement.
Contents, §27-40-8.
Filing, §27-40-13.
Style, §27-40-8.
Premium to be sent to
insurance company,
§27-40-15.
Prepayment of obligation,
§27-40-9.
Rebates or inducement.
Payment prohibited,
§27-40-16.
Rules and regulations.
Promulgation and
enforcement,
§27-40-7.
Service charge, §27-40-9.
Unearned premiums.
Recovery of, §27-40-15.
Health insurance.
Alabama health care plan.
Exemption from
premium tax,
§27-21-4.
Rates, §27-21-3.
Industrial life insurance,
§§27-16-15, 27-16-16.
Insurance premium finance
companies, §§27-40-1 to
27-40-18.
Insurers.
Unearned premium
reserve, §§27-36-2 to
27-36-4.
Legal expense insurance.
Rates, §27-43-11.

INSURANCE—Cont'd
Premiums—Cont'd
Life and disability insurance
representatives.
Accounting for and
payment of trust funds
by licensees, §27-8-28.
Life insurance.
Generally. See within this
heading, "Life
insurance."
Industrial life insurance,
§§27-16-15, 27-16-16.
Loans.
Insurance premium finance
companies, §§27-40-1
to 27-40-18.
Marine and transportation
insurance.
Unearned premium
reserve, §27-36-4.
Property insurance.
Rebates, §27-12-14.
Unearned premium
reserve, §27-36-3.
Rates and rating
organizations. See within
this heading, "Rates and
rating organizations."
Reciprocal insurers.
Unused premiums.
Distribution, §27-31-26.
Reserves.
Unearned premium
reserve, §§27-36-2 to
27-36-4.
State insurance fund.
Basis upon which
premiums charged,
§41-15-5.
Disgreement between
department of finance
and persons in charge
of state property,
§41-15-8.
Payment, §41-15-6.
Pro rata premiums,
§41-15-7.
Trust fund.
Premiums collected
under chapter to
constitute trust fund,
§41-15-10.
Surety insurance.
Rebates, §27-12-14.
Unearned premium
reserve, §27-36-3.
Surplus line insurance.
Liability of insurer as to
unearned premiums,
§27-10-28.
Records of surplus line
brokers, §27-10-29.
Taxation, §§27-4-3 to 27-4-7.
Title insurance.
Unearned premium
reserve, §27-36-2.
Unearned premium reserve.
Casualty insurance,
§27-36-3.
Marine and transportation
insurance, §27-36-4.
Property insurance,
§27-36-3.
Surety insurance, §27-36-3.
Title insurance, §27-36-2.

INSURANCE—Cont'd
Priorities.
Insurers.
Delinquency proceedings.
Claims in delinquency
proceedings,
§27-32-20.
Priority of compensation
owed to employees,
§27-32-28.
Rehabilitation or
liquidation.
Priority of claims of
policyholders and
beneficiaries,
§§27-32-37 to
27-32-41.
Prior rights, obligations, etc.
Preservation, §27-1-14.
Proof of loss.
Effect of misrepresentations
in proof of loss,
§27-14-28.
Forms for proof of loss,
§27-14-26.
Property.
Insurers.
Foreign or alien insurers.
Conservation or
liquidation of
property, §27-32-14.
Transfer of property.
Prohibited during period
of supervision,
§27-2-34.
Valuation, §27-37-7.
Purchase of insurance as
condition precedent to
sale or loan on property,
§27-12-15.
Property insurance.
Agents, §§27-7-1 to 27-7-38.
See within this heading,
"Agents."
Brokers.
Property, casualty and
surety insurance
representatives,
§§27-7-1 to 27-7-38.
See within this
heading, "Agents."
Casualty insurance. See
within this heading,
"Casualty insurance."
Defined, §27-5-5.
Fire insurance.
Generally. See within this
heading, "Fire
insurance."
Rates and rating
organizations,
§§27-13-20 to 27-13-45.
See within this
heading, "Rates and
rating organizations."
Inducements.
Unfair inducements,
§27-12-14.
Insurable interest, §27-14-4.
Insurers.
Unearned premium
reserve, §27-36-3.
Premiums.
Rebates, §27-12-14.
Unearned premium
reserve, §27-36-3.
Rebates, §27-12-14.
Representatives. See within
this heading, "Agents."

INSURANCE—Cont'd

Property insurance—Cont'd

Reserves.

Unearned premium
reserve, §27-36-3.

Solicitors.

Property, casualty and
surety insurance
representatives,
§§27-7-1 to 27-7-38.
See within this
heading, "Agents."

Title insurance, §27-25-1.

Unearned premium reserve,
§27-36-3.

Public buildings.

Contracts, §§41-16-80 to
41-16-82.
See CONTRACTS.

State insurance fund,
§§41-15-1 to 41-15-13.
See within this heading,
"State insurance fund."

**Public education employees'
health insurance,**
§§16-25A-1 to 16-25A-17.
See EDUCATION.

**Public officers and
employees.**

County officers and
employees, §§11-91-1 to
11-91-8.
See COUNTIES.

Motor vehicles, §36-1-6.

Municipal officers and
employees, §§11-91-1 to
11-91-8.
See MUNICIPAL
CORPORATIONS.

Negligent or wrongful acts of
state employees,
§36-1-6.1.

State employees' health
insurance plan,
§§36-29-1 to 36-29-13.
See PUBLIC OFFICERS
AND EMPLOYEES.

State employees liability
insurance, §36-1-6.1.

Pure endowment contracts,
§§27-15-16 to 27-15-22.

Age.

Misstatement of age,
§27-15-20.

Dividends, §27-15-21.

Entire contract, §27-15-19.

Grace period clause,
§27-15-17.

Incontestability clause,
§27-15-18.

Misstatement of age or sex,
§27-15-20.

Payments.

Grace period clause,
§27-15-17.

Provisions generally,
§27-15-16.

Reinstatement, §27-15-22.

Reserves.

Standard valuation law,
§27-36-7.

Reversionary annuities.

Standard provisions in
contracts, §27-15-23.

Sex.

Misstatement of sex,
§27-15-20.

Railroad authorities.

Powers of authorities as to
insurance, §37-13-7.

INSURANCE—Cont'd

**Rates and rating
organizations.**

Administration of laws
relating to rates and
rating systems, §27-13-2.

Advisory organizations,
§§27-13-100 to 27-13-105.

Alabama health care plan.

Premium rates, §27-21-3.

Casualty and surety
insurance, §§27-13-60 to
27-13-83.

Admission of members or
subscribers, §27-13-64.

Alteration of rating plans,
§27-13-75.

Amendment of rating
plans, §27-13-75.

Appeals from decisions of
rating organizations,
§27-13-69.

Applicability of article,
§27-13-61.

Certificates of authority.

Suspension, §27-13-78.

Commissioner of insurance.

Delegation of authority
by commissioner,
§27-13-82.

Examination of business,
etc., of rating
organizations,
§27-13-74.

Hearings by
commissioner,
§27-13-80.

Notices by commissioner,
§27-13-80.

Orders by commissioner,
§27-13-80.

Review of final orders,
§27-13-81.

Revoking or
suspending
license, §27-13-79.

Plans.

Examination and
approval or
disapproval,
§27-13-68.

Review of final orders of
commissioner,
§27-13-81.

Decisions of rating
organizations.

Appeals from decisions,
§27-13-69.

Decrease in rates.

Application for uniform
percentage decrease
by insurers,
§27-13-72.

Hearings on applications
to reduce rates,
§27-13-71.

Definitions, §27-13-60.

Examination of business,
etc., of rating
organizations,
§27-13-74.

Expulsion of members or
subscribers, §27-13-64.

False information
concerning rates,
§27-13-77.

Fees.

License fee, §27-13-62.

INSURANCE—Cont'd

**Rates and rating
organizations**—Cont'd

Casualty and surety
insurance—Cont'd

Hearings, §27-13-80.

Appeals from decisions of
rating organizations,
§27-13-69.

Applications to reduce
rates, §27-13-71.

Review of final orders of
commissioner,
§27-13-81.

Increase in rates.

Application for uniform
percentage increase
by insurers,
§27-13-72.

Information.

Exchange of information,
§27-13-66.

False information
concerning rates,
§27-13-77.

Furnishing information
as to rates,
§27-13-70.

Misleading information
concerning rates,
§27-13-77.

Licenses.

Applications, §27-13-62.

Fees, §27-13-62.

Renewal, §27-13-62.

Required, §27-13-62.

Revocation.

Order revoking license,
§27-13-79.

Suspension, §27-13-78.

Orders suspending
license, §27-13-78.

Membership.

Admission of members,
§27-13-64.

Expulsion of members,
§27-13-64.

Provisions for insurers to
become members,
§27-13-63.

Readmission of members,
§27-13-64.

Withdrawal of members,
§27-13-64.

Misleading information
concerning rates,
§27-13-77.

Notices by commissioner,
§27-13-80.

Orders by commissioner,
§27-13-80.

Review of final orders,
§27-13-81.

Revoking or suspending
license, §27-13-79.

Penalty for violation of
article, §27-13-83.

Plans.

Alteration of rating
plans, §27-13-75.

Amendment of rating
plans, §27-13-75.

Approval by
commissioner,
§27-13-68.

Disapproval by
commissioner,
§27-13-68.

Examination by
commissioner,
§27-13-68.

INSURANCE—Cont'd
Rates and rating
organizations—Cont'd
Casualty and surety
insurance—Cont'd
Plans—Cont'd
Filing plans with
department by
insurers.
Examination and
approval or
disapproval by
commissioner,
§27-13-68.
Requirements,
§27-13-67.
Making rating plans,
§27-13-65.
Prohibition against
premiums not in
accord with approved
rating systems,
§27-13-76.
Supplementation of
rating plans,
§27-13-75.
Premiums not in accord
with approved rating
system prohibited,
§27-13-76.
Rate-making, §27-13-65.
Readmission of members or
subscribers, §27-13-64.
Reasonableness of rates.
Factors to be considered,
§27-13-73.
Reduction of rates.
Application for uniform
percentage decrease
in rates by insurers,
§27-13-72.
Hearings on applications
to reduce rates,
§27-13-71.
Reports.
Annual statistical
reports of insurers,
§27-13-66.
Review of final orders of
commissioner,
§27-13-81.
Rules and regulations,
§27-13-66.
Subscribers.
Admission, §27-13-64.
Expulsion, §27-13-64.
Provisions for insurers to
become subscribers,
§27-13-63.
Readmission, §27-13-64.
Withdrawal of
subscribers,
§27-13-64.
Supplementation of rating
plans, §27-13-75.
Uniform percentage
increase or decrease in
rates.
Application by insurers,
§27-13-72.
Violations of article.
Penalty for violations,
§27-13-83.
Commissioner of insurance.
Casualty and surety
insurance.
Delegation of authority
by commissioner,
§27-13-82.

INSURANCE—Cont'd
Rates and rating
organizations—Cont'd
Commissioner of insurance
—Cont'd
Casualty and surety
insurance—Cont'd
Examination of business,
etc., of rating
organizations and
insurers making own
rates, §27-13-74.
Hearings by
commissioner,
§27-13-80.
Notices by commissioner,
§27-13-80.
Orders by commissioner,
§27-13-80.
Review of final orders,
§27-13-81.
Rating plans.
Examination and
approval or
disapproval,
§27-13-68.
Fire and inland marine
insurance.
Delegation of authority
by commissioner,
§27-13-44.
Examination and
approval or
disapproval of rating
systems by
commissioner of
insurance, §27-13-30.
Examination of business,
etc., of rating
organizations and
insurers making own
rates, §27-13-36.
Hearings by
commissioner,
§27-13-42.
Notices by commissioner,
§27-13-42.
Orders by commissioner,
§27-13-42.
Review of final orders,
§27-13-43.
Reasonableness of rates.
Factors to be
considered by
commissioner in
determining,
§27-13-35.
Review of final orders of
commissioner,
§27-13-43.
Insurance advisory
organizations.
Compliance with rules of
commissioner,
§27-13-101.
Filing with
commissioner,
§27-13-102.
Orders by commissioner.
Casualty and surety
insurance, §27-13-80.
Fire and inland marine
insurance, §27-13-42.
Construction of chapter,
§27-13-1.
Data.
Filing by insurers,
§27-13-3.
Definitions.
Advisory organizations,
§27-13-100.

INSURANCE—Cont'd
Rates and rating
organizations—Cont'd
Definitions—Cont'd
Casualty and surety
insurance, §27-13-60.
Fire and inland marine
insurance, §27-13-20.
Excessive rates, §27-12-17.
Fees.
Casualty and surety
insurance.
License fee, §27-13-62.
Fire and inland marine
insurance.
License fee, §27-13-24.
Fire and inland marine
insurance, §§27-13-20 to
27-13-45.
Alteration of rating
systems, §27-13-37.
Amendment of rating
systems, §27-13-37.
Applicability of article,
§27-13-21.
Exemptions, §27-13-23.
Inland marine insurance,
§27-13-22.
Approval of rates.
Special types or classes
of risks, §27-13-34.
Certificates of authority.
Suspension, §27-13-40.
Commissioner of insurance.
Delegation of authority
by commissioner,
§27-13-44.
Examination of business
of rating
organizations and
insurers making own
rates, §27-13-36.
Hearings by
commissioner,
§27-13-42.
Notices by commissioner,
§27-13-42.
Orders by commissioner,
§27-13-42.
Review of final orders
of commissioner,
§27-13-43.
Reasonableness of rates.
Factors to be
considered,
§27-13-35.
Review of final orders of
commissioner,
§27-13-43.
Decrease in rates.
Applications for uniform
percentage decrease
by insurers,
§27-13-33.
Hearings on applications
to reduce rates,
§27-13-32.
Definitions, §27-13-20.
Examination of business,
etc., of rating
organizations and
insurers making own
rates, §27-13-36.
Exemptions from article,
§27-13-23.
False information
concerning rates,
§27-13-39.
Fees for licenses,
§27-13-24.

INSURANCE—Cont'd
  Rates and rating
    organizations—Cont'd
  Fire and inland marine
    insurance—Cont'd
  Hearings by commissioner,
    §27-13-42.
  Increase in rates.
    Applications for uniform
      percentage increase
      by insurers,
      §27-13-33.
  Licenses.
    Applications, §27-13-24.
    Fee, §27-13-24.
    Renewal, §27-13-24.
    Required, §27-13-24.
    Revocation, §27-13-40.
      Order revoking
        licenses,
        §27-13-41.
    Suspension, §27-13-40.
      Orders suspending
        licenses,
        §27-13-41.
  Members of organizations.
    Expulsion, §27-13-26.
    Provisions for insurers to
      become members,
      §27-13-25.
    Readmission, §27-13-26.
    Withdrawal, §27-13-26.
  Misleading information
    concerning rates,
    §27-13-39.
  Notices by commissioner,
    §27-13-42.
  Offices, §27-13-24.
  Orders by commissioner,
    §27-13-42.
    Review of final orders,
      §27-13-43.
  Penalties.
    Violations of article,
      §27-13-45.
  Premiums not in accord
    with approved rating
    systems prohibited,
    §27-13-38.
  Rate-making, §27-13-27.
  Reasonableness of rates.
    Factors to be considered,
      §27-13-35.
  Reduction of rates.
    Applications for uniform
      percentage decrease
      of rates by insurers,
      §27-13-33.
    Hearings on applications
      to reduce rates,
      §27-13-32.
  Reports.
    Annual statistical
      reports of insurers,
      §27-13-28.
  Risks.
    Risks rated upon
      schedule.
      Survey of risks,
        §27-13-31.
    Special types or classes
      of risks.
      Approval of rates and
        forms for insuring,
        §27-13-34.
  Special types or classes of
    risks.
    Approval of rates and
      forms for insuring,
      §27-13-34.

INSURANCE—Cont'd
  Rates and rating
    organizations—Cont'd
  Fire and inland marine
    insurance—Cont'd
  Subscribers.
    Expulsion, §27-13-26.
    Provisions for insurers to
      become subscribers,
      §27-13-25.
    Readmission, §27-13-26.
    Withdrawal, §27-13-26.
  Supplementation of rating
    systems, §27-13-37.
  Survey of risks rated upon
    schedule, §27-13-31.
  Systems.
    Alteration of rating
      systems, §27-13-37.
    Amendment of rating
      systems, §27-13-37.
    Approval by
      commissioner,
      §27-13-30.
    Disapproval by
      commissioner,
      §27-13-30.
    Examination by
      commissioner,
      §27-13-30.
    Filing of rating systems
      with department by
      insurers.
      Approval by
        commissioner,
        §27-13-30.
      Examination by
        commissioner,
        §27-13-30.
      Requirements,
        §27-13-29.
    Making rating systems,
      §27-13-27.
    Prohibition against
      premiums not in
      accord with approved
      rating systems,
      §27-13-38.
    Supplementation of
      rating systems,
      §27-13-37.
  Uniform percentage
    increase or decrease of
    rates.
    Applications by insurers,
      §27-13-33.
  Violations of article.
    Penalty, §27-13-45.
  Health insurance.
    Alabama health care plan.
      Premium rates, §27-21-3.
  Hearings.
    Casualty and surety
      insurance.
      Appeals from decisions of
        rating organizations,
        §27-13-69.
      Applications to reduce
        rates, §27-13-71.
      Hearings by
        commissioner,
        §27-13-80.
      Review of final orders of
        commissioner,
        §27-13-81.
    Fire and inland marine
      insurance.
      Hearings by
        commissioner,
        §27-13-42.

INSURANCE—Cont'd
  Rates and rating
    organizations—Cont'd
  Information.
    Filing by insurers,
      §27-13-3.
  Inland marine insurance,
    §§27-13-20 to 27-13-45.
  Insurance advisory
    organizations,
    §§27-13-100 to 27-13-105.
    Administration of article,
      §27-13-104.
    Compliance with article
      and rules, etc., of
      commissioner,
      §27-13-101.
    Construction of article,
      §27-13-105.
    Definitions of advisory
      organization,
      §27-13-100.
    Enforcement of article,
      §27-13-104.
    Examinations, §27-13-103.
    Filing with commissioner,
      §27-13-102.
    Orders by commissioner
      against unfair
      practices, etc., or
      violations, §27-13-102.
    Rules of commissioner.
      Compliance with rules,
        §27-13-101.
    Unfair practices.
      Orders by commissioner
        against, §27-13-102.
    Violations.
      Orders by commissioner
        against violations,
        §27-13-102.
  Insurers.
    Filing of data or
      information by
      insurers, §27-13-3.
  Licenses.
    Casualty and surety
      insurance, §§27-13-62,
      27-13-78, 27-13-79.
    Disposition of licenses
      collected from rating
      organizations,
      §27-13-5.
    Fire and inland marine
      insurance, §§27-13-24,
      27-13-40, 27-13-41.
  Life insurance.
    Discrimination.
      Exception, §27-13-13.
    Unfair discrimination in
      rates, §27-12-11.
  Medical liability insurance.
    Joint underwriting
      association.
      Rating plans, §27-26-36.
  Notices.
    Casualty and surety
      insurance.
      Notices by commissioner,
        §27-13-80.
    Fire and inland marine
      insurance.
      Notices by commissioner,
        §27-13-42.
  Penalties.
    Casualty and surety
      insurance.
      Violation of article,
        §27-13-83.

INSURANCE—Cont'd
  Rates and rating
    organizations—Cont'd
     Penalties—Cont'd
      Fire and inland marine
       insurance.
       Violations of article,
        §27-13-45.
     Purpose of chapter, §27-13-1.
     Rebates.
      Trade practices law,
       §§27-12-12 to 27-12-14.
     Reports.
      Casualty and surety
       insurance.
       Annual statistical
        reports of insurers,
        §27-13-66.
      Fire and inland marine
       insurance.
       Annual statistical
        reports of insurers,
        §27-13-28.
     Rules and regulations,
      §27-13-4.
      Casualty and surety
       insurance, §27-13-66.
      Insurance advisory
       organizations.
       Compliance with rules of
        commissioner,
        §27-13-101.
     Short title of chapter,
      §27-13-6.
     Surety insurance, §§27-13-60
      to 27-13-83.
  Rebates.
   Trade practices law,
    §§27-12-12 to 27-12-14.
  Receivers.
   Insurance guaranty
    association.
    Filing of paid claims with
     receiver, §27-42-11.
   Life and disability insurance
    guaranty association.
    Preferred creditor status,
     §27-44-20.
    Recovery of certain
     distributions from
     controlling affiliates,
     §27-44-14.
  Receivership division,
   §§27-2-50 to 27-2-55.
   Assumption by receiver of
    certain former powers,
    duties, etc., of
    commissioner, §27-2-55.
   Chief of division.
    Appointment, §27-2-50.
    Appointment of chief as
     receiver, §27-2-53.
    Existing receivership,
     §27-2-54.
    Bond of chief, §27-2-51.
    Compensation, §27-2-50.
    Term of office, §27-2-50.
   Commissioner of insurance.
    Assumption by receiver of
     certain former powers,
     duties, etc., of
     commissioner,
     §27-2-55.
   Equipment, §27-2-52.
   Established, §27-2-50.
   Expenses, §27-2-52.
   Offices, §27-2-52.
   Operating expenses,
    §27-2-52.
   Personnel, §27-2-52.

INSURANCE—Cont'd
  Reciprocal insurers,
   §§27-31-1 to 27-31-29.
   Actions.
    By and against insurers,
     §27-31-4.
   Advancement of funds to
    insurers, §27-31-15.
   Annual statement, §27-31-16.
   Applicability of chapter,
    §27-31-2.
   Assessments on subscribers.
    Aggregate liability,
     §27-31-24.
    Levy, §27-31-22.
    Liquidation, §§27-32-32 to
     27-32-36.
    Nonassessable policies,
     §27-31-25.
    Rehabilitation or
     liquidation.
     Commissioner's report,
      §27-32-32.
     Levy of assessment,
      §27-32-33.
     Order to pay, §27-32-34.
     Judgment, §27-32-36.
     Publication, §27-32-35.
     Service, §27-32-35.
     Report by commissioner,
      §27-32-32.
    Time limit, §27-31-23.
   Assets.
    Distribution upon
     liquidation, §27-31-27.
    Insufficient assets.
     Proceedings when assets
      insufficient,
      §27-31-29.
   Attorneys.
    Bond of attorney.
     Action on bond or
      deposit, §27-31-13.
     Deposit in lieu of bond,
      §27-31-12.
     Requirements, §27-31-11.
    Defined, §27-31-5.
    Deposit in lieu of bond,
     §27-31-12.
     Action on deposit,
      §27-31-13.
    Execution of contracts,
     §27-31-5.
    Power of attorney.
     Contents, §27-31-9.
     Generally, §27-31-9.
     Modifications of power,
      §27-31-10.
   Bonds, surety.
    Attorneys, §§27-31-11 to
     27-31-13.
    Action on bond,
     §27-31-13.
   Certificates of authority.
    Applications, §27-31-7.
    Declaration.
     Filing declaration with
      applications,
      §27-31-7.
    Denial, §27-31-8.
    Issuance, §27-31-8.
    Refusal, §27-31-8.
    Revocation, §27-31-8.
    Suspension, §27-31-8.
   Commissioner of insurance.
    Service of process on
     commissioner as agent
     for insurer, §27-31-14.
   Contracts.
    Execution by attorneys,
     §27-31-5.

INSURANCE—Cont'd
  Reciprocal insurers—Cont'd
   Contracts—Cont'd
    Nonassessable policies,
     §27-31-25.
    Right to exchange
     contracts, §27-31-18.
   Conversion, §27-31-28.
   Definitions, §27-31-1.
   Distributions.
    Liquidation.
     Distribution of assets
      upon liquidation,
      §27-31-27.
    Unused premiums,
     §27-31-26.
   Financial condition.
    Determination, §27-31-17.
   Foreign reciprocal insurers.
    Attorneys, §27-31-5.
   Funds.
    Advancement to domestic
     insurers, §27-31-15.
    Surplus funds, §27-31-6.
   Information.
    Supplemental information
     to annual statement,
     §27-31-16.
   Insufficient assets.
    Proceedings when assets
     insufficient, §27-31-29.
   Judgment on process,
    §27-31-14.
   Liability.
    Representatives, §27-31-18.
    Subscribers.
     Judgment, §27-31-21.
   Liquidation.
    Assessments, §§27-32-32 to
     27-32-36.
    Distribution of assets upon
     liquidation, §27-31-27.
   Merger, §27-31-28.
   Name.
    Business name, §27-31-4.
   Power of attorney.
    Generally, §27-31-9.
    Modifications, §27-31-10.
   Powers, §27-31-3.
   Premiums.
    Unused premiums.
     Distribution, §27-31-26.
   Rehabilitation.
    Assessments, §§27-32-32 to
     27-32-36.
   Reports.
    Annual statement,
     §27-31-16.
   Representatives.
    Liability, §27-31-18.
   Service of process, §27-31-14.
    Assessments.
     Rehabilitation or
      liquidation.
      Service of order to pay,
       §27-32-35.
   Subscribers, §27-31-18.
    Advisory committee,
     §27-31-19.
    Agreement.
     Modifications, §27-31-10.
    Assessments.
     Aggregate liability,
      §27-31-24.
     Levy, §27-31-22.
     Nonassessable policies,
      §27-31-25.
     Rehabilitation or
      liquidation,
      §§27-32-32 to
      27-32-36.

INSURANCE—Cont'd
  Reciprocal insurers—Cont'd
    Subscribers—Cont'd
      Assessments—Cont'd
        Time limit, §27-31-23.
      Liability.
        Generally, §27-31-20.
        Judgment, §27-31-21.
        Representatives of
          subscribers,
          §27-31-18.
    Surplus funds, §27-31-6.
  Records.
    Adjusters, §27-9-8.
    Agents.
      Property, casualty and
        surety insurance
        representatives,
        §27-7-33.
    Alien insurers.
      Trusteed assets, §27-33-10.
    Brokers.
      Property, casualty and
        surety insurance
        representatives,
        §27-7-33.
      Surplus line brokers,
        §27-10-29.
      Failure to keep records,
        §27-10-32.
    Commissioner of insurance.
      Custody, §27-2-14.
      Destruction, §27-2-14.
      Evidence.
        Use as evidence,
          §27-2-15.
      Inspection, §27-2-14.
      Reproduction, §27-2-14.
    Destruction, §27-2-14.
    False statements and entries,
      §27-12-7.
    Finance companies.
      Insurance premium finance
        companies, §27-40-6.
    Holding companies.
      Confidential treatment of
        information examined
        or reported, §27-29-7.
      Examination of records,
        etc., of insurer or
        affiliates, §27-29-6.
    Inspection, §27-2-14.
    Insurance premium finance
      companies, §27-40-6.
    Insurers.
      Alien insurers.
        Trusteed assets,
          §27-33-10.
      Deposits.
        Record of securities and
          assets deposited,
          §27-6-5.
      Holding companies.
        Confidential treatment of
          information,
          §27-29-7.
        Examination of records
          of insurer, §27-29-6.
      Removal of records,
        §27-27-29.
    Mutual aid associations.
      Duty of officers and agents,
        §27-30-23.
    Policies.
      Property, casualty and
        surety insurance
        representatives,
        §27-7-33.

INSURANCE—Cont'd
  Records—Cont'd
    Property, casualty and surety
      insurance
      representatives,
      §27-7-33.
    Surplus line insurance.
      Brokers, §27-10-29.
      Failure to keep records,
        §27-10-32.
  Registration.
    Holding companies.
      Registration of insurers,
        §27-29-4.
    Insurers.
      Members of holding
        company systems,
        §27-29-4.
  Reinsurance.
    Acceptance, §27-5-12.
    Cancellation of treaties or
      arrangements, §27-5-12.
    Fraternal benefit societies,
      §27-34-33.
    Insurers.
      Bulk reinsurance.
        Mutual insurers,
          §27-27-48.
        Stock insurers,
          §27-27-47.
    Liquidation of insurers.
      Reinsuring of policies,
        §27-32-39.
    Rehabilitation of insurers.
      Reinsuring of policies,
        §27-32-39.
    State insurance fund,
      §41-15-5.
    Supervision of insurers.
      Entry into new reinsurance
        contract prohibited
        during period of
        supervision, §27-2-34.
    What risks may be
      reinsured, §27-5-12.
  Reports.
    Agents.
      Life and disability
        insurance
        representatives.
        Filing of annual
          statements, §27-8-15.
    Brokers.
      Life and disability
        insurance
        representatives.
        Filing of annual
          statements, §27-8-15.
      Surplus line brokers,
        §27-10-21.
        Annual statement,
          §27-10-30.
    Commissioner of insurance.
      Annual report, §27-2-9.
      Examinations by
        commissioner,
        §27-2-24.
    Disability insurance.
      Filing of annual
        statements by life and
        disability insurance
        representatives,
        §27-8-15.
    Evidence.
      Examinations by
        commissioner,
        §27-2-24.
    Examinations by
      commissioner, §27-2-24.
    False statements and entries,
      §27-12-7.

INSURANCE—Cont'd
  Reports—Cont'd
    Holding companies.
      Confidential treatment of
        information, §27-29-7.
      Registration of insurers,
        §27-29-4.
    Independently procured
      coverages, §27-10-35.
    Insurance guaranty
      association.
      Financial report of
        directors, §27-42-14.
      Report of board of
        directors, §27-42-13.
    Insurers.
      Annual statement of
        insurer.
        Fee for filing, §27-4-2.
      Rates and rating
        organizations.
        Annual statistical
          reports of insurers,
          §27-13-28.
      Taxation.
        Annual tax statement,
          §27-4-3.
    Life insurance.
      Filing of annual
        statements by life and
        disability insurance
        representatives,
        §27-8-15.
    Medical liability insurance.
      Annual reports of carriers,
        §27-26-4.
      Joint underwriting
        association.
        Annual statements,
          §27-26-38.
      Judgments and
        settlements, §27-26-5.
    Mutual aid associations.
      Annual statement,
        §27-30-22.
      Duty of officers and agents,
        §27-30-23.
    Rates and rating
      organizations.
      Casualty and surety
        insurance.
        Annual statistical
          reports of insurers,
          §27-13-66.
      Fire and inland marine
        insurance.
        Annual statistical
          reports of insurers,
          §27-13-28.
    Reciprocal insurers.
      Annual statement,
        §27-31-16.
    Surplus line insurance.
      Brokers, §27-10-21.
      Annual statement,
        §27-10-30.
    Trade practices law.
      False statements and
        entries, §27-12-7.
  Representatives. See within
    this heading, "Agents."
  Risks.
    Assigned risks.
      Safety-responsibility act,
        §32-7-35.
    Fire and inland marine
      insurance.
      Risks rated upon schedule.
        Survey of risks,
          §27-13-31.

INSURANCE—Cont'd
Risks—Cont'd
Fire and inland marine
insurance—Cont'd
Special types or classes of
risks.
Approval of rates and
forms for insuring,
§27-13-34.
Limits of risk, §27-5-11.
Rules and regulations.
Annuities.
Variable contracts,
§27-38-4.
Commissioner of insurance,
§27-2-17.
Hearings, §§27-2-28 to
27-2-38.
Publication, §27-2-16.
Finance companies.
Insurance premium finance
companies.
Promulgation and
enforcement by
commissioner,
§27-40-7.
Hearings.
Commissioner of insurance,
§§27-2-28 to 27-2-32.
See within this
heading,
"Commissioner of
insurance."
Holding companies, §27-29-8.
Injunctions for violations,
§27-29-9.
Judicial review of actions
by commissioner,
§27-29-13.
Insurance premium finance
companies.
Promulgation and
enforcement, §27-40-7.
Insurers.
Insider trading of domestic
stock insurer equity
securities, §27-27-60.
Securities of stock insurers,
§27-27-51.
Rates and rating
organizations, §27-13-4.
Casualty and surety
insurance, §27-13-66.
Insurance advisory
organizations.
Compliance with rules of
commissioner,
§27-13-101.
Rules of civil procedure.
Discovery.
Insurance agreements,
ARCP, Rule 16 (b).
Joinder of claims.
Liability insurance
coverage, ARCP, Rule
18 (c).
Pleadings.
Form of complaints on
insurance policies,
ARCP, Forms 13 to 15.
Safety-responsibility act,
§§32-7-1 to 32-7-42.
See MOTOR VEHICLES.
**St. Stephens historical
commission.**
Participation in programs by
employees of commission,
§41-9-337.
Salaries.
Commissioner of insurance,
§27-2-4.

INSURANCE—Cont'd
Science.
Life insurers organized to aid
nonprofit educational
and scientific
institutions.
Annual license fee, §27-4-8.
**Seals and sealed
instruments.**
Commissioner of insurance.
Official seal, §27-2-5.
Secretary of state.
Mail order insurance.
Service of process on
unauthorized insurers.
Secretary of state as
agent for service,
§27-11-5.
Secured transactions.
Transfer of interest or claim
in policy or annuity
excluded, §7-9-104.
Securities.
Licensing of securities
salesmen, §27-27-11.
**Servicemen's readjustment
act.**
Life insurance companies
may invest in loans
guaranteed under
servicemen's
readjustment act,
§27-1-9.
Service of process.
Commissioner of insurance.
Appointment of
commissioner as agent
for service on insurers,
§27-3-24.
Fee for acceptance of
service on insurers,
§27-4-2.
Fraternal benefit societies,
§27-34-47.
How served, §27-3-25.
Mutual aid associations,
§27-30-13.
Mutual insurers.
Assessments.
Order to pay assessments
for rehabilitation or
liquidation,
§27-32-35.
Property, casualty and surety
insurance
representatives.
Nonresident agents or
brokers, §27-7-29.
Reciprocal insurers,
§27-31-14.
Assessments.
Rehabilitation or
liquidation.
Service of order to pay,
§27-32-35.
Surplus line insurance.
Action or proceeding
against insurer,
§27-10-33.
Time to answer or plead,
§27-3-25.
Trade practices law.
Statements, notices, orders
and other processes,
§27-12-19.
Unauthorized insurers,
§§27-10-50 to 27-10-56.
See within this heading,
"Unauthorized insurers."

INSURANCE—Cont'd
Setoffs.
Insurers.
Reorganization,
rehabilitation,
liquidation or
conservation.
Setoff of credits and
debts, §27-32-29.
Short title, §27-1-1.
Sickle-cell anemia.
Denial of health or disability
insurance upon diagnosis
of sickle cell anemia,
§27-5-13.
Simultaneous death act.
Policies of insurance, §43-7-5.
Small loans.
Security for loans.
Acceptance of insurance as
additional security for
loans, §5-18-17.
**Solicitation permit, §§27-27-4
to 27-27-14. See within
this heading, "Insurers."**
Solicitors.
Casualty insurance
representatives,
§27-7-27.
Licenses, §27-7-27.
False statements, etc., in
insurance application,
§27-12-23.
Fees.
Licenses, §27-4-2.
Licenses.
Examinations.
Fees, §27-4-2.
Fees, §27-4-2.
Property, casualty and
surety insurance
representatives,
§27-7-27.
Mutual aid associations.
Authorization to act as or
for associations,
§27-30-1.
Requirements, §27-30-5.
Permits.
Solicitation permits,
§§27-27-4 to 27-27-14.
See within this
heading, "Insurers."
Property insurance
representatives,
§27-7-27.
Surety insurance
representatives.
Property, casualty and
surety insurance
representatives,
§27-7-27.
**Space science exhibit
finance authority.**
Special funds for payment,
§41-10-326.
Sports.
Agents.
Registration.
Malpractice coverage in
lieu of bond,
§8-26-14.
Standard valuation law,
§27-36-7.
**State employees' health
insurance plan, §§36-29-1
to 36-29-13.**
See PUBLIC OFFICERS
AND EMPLOYEES.

INSURANCE—Cont'd
State insurance fund,
§§41-15-1 to 41-15-13.
Administration of chapter.
Department of finance to
administer, §41-15-2.
Expenses.
Requisition of funds
derived from
operations under
chapter for payment
of administrative
expenses, §41-15-10.
Rules and regulations.
Director of finance may
make rules and
regulations for
administration,
§41-15-9.
Administrator of fund.
Generally, §41-15-2.
Appraisal of property,
§41-15-3.
Appropriations, §§41-15-12,
41-15-13.
County school buildings,
§41-15-4.
Creation, §41-15-1.
Department of finance.
Administration of chapter,
§41-15-2.
Certification to department
of description and
value of buildings and
equipment, §41-15-4.
Disagreements.
Resolution of
disagreements
between department
and person in charge
of state property as
to value of property,
premium rates, etc.,
§41-15-8.
Earnings collected under
chapter to constitute
trust fund, §41-15-10.
Employees.
Subject to merit system,
§41-15-11.
Expenditure of funds.
Limitations upon
expenditure, §41-15-11.
Expenses, §41-15-10.
Fire losses.
Appropriation for payment
of excess fire losses,
§41-15-12.
Appropriation of funds
received in payment
for loss to property by
fire, §41-15-13.
Inspection of property,
§§41-15-3, 41-15-4.
Limitations upon expenditure
of funds, §41-15-11.
Losses.
Appropriation for payment
of excess fire or
tornado losses,
§41-15-12.
Appropriation of funds
received in payment
for loss to property by
fire, etc., §41-15-13.
Requisition of funds
derived from
operations under
chapter for payment of
losses, §41-15-10.

INSURANCE—Cont'd
State insurance fund—Cont'd
Policies.
Director of finance may
prescribe forms of
policies, §41-15-9.
Premiums.
Basis upon which
premiums charged,
§41-15-5.
Disagreements between
department of finance
and persons in charge
of state property as to
premium rates.
Resolution of
disagreements,
§41-15-8.
Payment, §41-15-6.
Pro rata premiums,
§41-15-7.
Trust fund.
Premiums collected
under chapter to
constitute trust fund,
§41-15-10.
Purpose, §41-15-1.
Reinsurance, §41-15-5.
Reports.
Inspections of public
property, §41-15-4.
Rules and regulations.
Director of finance may
prescribe, §41-15-9.
School buildings.
County school buildings,
§41-15-4.
Tornado losses.
Appropriation for payment
of excess tornado
losses, §41-15-12.
Trust fund.
Investment of surplus in
fund, §41-15-10.
Premiums and earnings
collected under chapter
to constitute trust
fund, §41-15-10.
Value for which property to
be insured, §41-15-4.
Resolution of
disagreements between
department of finance
and person in charge
of state property as to
value of property,
§41-15-8.
State treasurer.
Custodian of insurers'
deposits, §27-6-4.
Stay of proceedings.
Life and disability insurance
guaranty association,
§27-44-18.
Stock insurers.
General provisions, §§27-27-1
to 27-27-61. See within
this heading, "Insurers."
Superintendent of insurance.
Assigned risk plans.
Approval of plans by
superintendent of
insurance, §32-7-35.
Surety insurance.
Actions on bonds or
undertakings.
Venue, §27-24-6.

INSURANCE—Cont'd
Surety insurance—Cont'd
Agents.
Property, casualty and
surety insurance
representatives,
§§27-7-1 to 27-7-38.
See within this
heading, "Agents."
Applicability of chapter,
§27-24-1.
Brokers.
Property, casualty and
surety insurance
representatives,
§§27-7-1 to 27-7-38.
See within this
heading, "Agents."
Corporations.
Sole surety, §27-24-2.
Definitions, §27-5-7.
Rates and rating
organizations,
§27-13-60.
Deposit requirements for
insurers.
Sale of surety insurers'
special deposit to pay
outstanding judgment,
§27-6-13.
Special deposit, §27-3-12.
Estoppel to insurer to deny
its power, etc., §27-24-7.
Inducements.
Unfair inducements,
§27-12-14.
Insolvency of surety.
Additional bond upon
insolvency of surety,
§27-24-5.
Insurers.
Deposit requirements.
Special deposit, §27-3-12.
Unearned premium
reserve, §27-36-3.
Licenses.
Rates and rating
organizations,
§§27-13-62, 27-13-78,
27-13-79.
Mutual surety insurers.
Sole surety, §27-24-3.
Premiums.
Rebates, §27-12-14.
Unearned premium
reserve, §27-36-3.
Rates and rating
organizations, §§27-13-60
to 27-13-83. See within
this heading, "Rates and
rating organizations."
Rebates, §27-12-14.
Reciprocal surety insurers.
Sole surety, §27-24-3.
Remedies of insurers,
§27-24-8.
Representatives, §§27-7-1 to
27-7-38. See within this
heading, "Agents."
Reserves.
Unearned premium
reserve, §27-36-3.
Rights of insurers, §27-24-8.
Sole surety.
Corporations, §27-24-2.
Cosureties on bond of state
treasurer, §27-24-4.
Mutual surety insurers,
§27-24-3.
Reciprocal surety insurers,
§27-24-3.

INSURANCE—Cont'd
Surety insurance—Cont'd
Solicitors.
Property, casualty and
surety insurance
representatives,
§§27-7-1 to 27-7-38.
See within this
heading, "Agents."
State treasurer.
Sole surety.
Cosureties on bond of
state treasurer,
§27-24-4.
Unearned premium reserve,
§27-36-3.
Venue of actions on bonds or
undertakings, §27-24-6.
Surplus line insurance,
§§27-10-20 to 27-10-38.
Agents.
Acceptance and placement
of surplus line
business for agents,
§27-10-25.
Brokers.
Acceptance and placement
of surplus line
business for agents or
brokers, §27-10-25.
Annual statement,
§27-10-30.
Endorsement of contract,
§27-10-22.
Licensing, §27-10-24.
Fees, §27-4-2.
Revocation or suspension
of surplus line
broker's license,
§27-10-32.
Office.
Failure to maintain
office in state,
§27-10-32.
Records, §27-10-29.
Failure to keep,
§27-10-32.
Reports, §27-10-21.
Revocation or suspension of
surplus line broker's
license, §27-10-32.
Tax.
Annual tax, §27-10-31.
Failure to pay,
§27-10-32.
Certificate.
Evidence of surplus line
insurance, §27-10-27.
Issuance of false certificate,
§27-10-27.
Changes, §27-10-27.
Commissioner of insurance.
Production of policies, etc.,
for inspection by
commissioner,
§27-10-36.
Eligibility of insurers for
placement, §27-10-26.
Endorsement of contract,
§27-10-22.
Enforceability of contracts,
§27-10-23.
Evidence of surplus line
insurance, §27-10-27.
Exemptions from law,
§27-10-34.
Independently procured
coverages, §27-10-35.

INSURANCE—Cont'd
Surplus line insurance
—Cont'd
Inspections.
Production of policies, etc.,
for inspection by
commissioner,
§27-10-36.
Insurers.
Action or proceeding
against insurer.
Service of process,
§27-10-33.
Eligibility of insurers for
placement, §27-10-26.
Liability of insurer as to
losses and unearned
premiums, §27-10-28.
Service of process in action
or proceeding against
insurer, §27-10-33.
Licenses.
Brokers, §27-10-24.
Losses.
Liability of insurer as to
losses, §27-10-28.
Penalties.
Violations of article,
§27-10-37.
Placement.
Agents or brokers,
§27-10-25.
Eligibility of insurers for
placement, §27-10-26.
Policies.
Production of policies, etc.,
for inspection by
commissioner,
§27-10-36.
Premiums.
Liability of insurer as to
unearned premiums,
§27-10-28.
Records of surplus line
brokers, §27-10-29.
Procuring from unauthorized
insurers, §27-10-20.
Records.
Brokers, §27-10-29.
Failure to keep records,
§27-10-32.
Reports.
Brokers, §27-10-21.
Annual statement,
§27-10-30.
Service of process.
Action or proceeding
against insurer,
§27-10-33.
Short title of article,
§27-10-38.
Taxation.
Annual tax of surplus line
brokers, §27-10-31.
Failure to pay,
§27-10-32.
Unauthorized insurers.
Procuring from
unauthorized insurers,
§27-10-20.
Validity of contracts,
§27-10-23.
Violations of article.
Penalty for violation,
§27-10-37.
Tables.
Annuity tables.
See ANNUITY AND
MORTALITY
TABLES.

INSURANCE—Cont'd
Tables—Cont'd
Life insurance.
Installments, §27-15-10.
Value and benefits,
§27-15-9.
**Tannehill furnace and
foundry commission.**
Programs for employees,
§41-9-330.
Taxation.
Alabama health care plan.
Exemption from premium
tax, §27-21-4.
Brokers.
Surplus line brokers.
Annual tax, §27-10-32.
Counties.
Taxation of insurers by
counties not allowed,
§27-4-9.
Definitions, §27-4-1.
Health insurance.
Alabama health care plan.
Exemption from
premium tax,
§27-21-4.
Independently procured
coverages, §27-10-35.
Insurance companies,
§§27-4-1 to 27-4-11. See
within this heading,
"Insurers."
Insurance guaranty
association.
Exemption from taxation,
§27-42-15.
Mutual aid associations.
Applicability of taxation
provisions, §27-30-31.
Premiums, §§27-4-3 to
27-4-7.
Surplus line insurance.
Annual tax of surplus line
brokers, §27-10-31.
Failure to pay,
§27-10-32.
Wet marine and
transportation insurance,
§27-4-6.
Temporary insurance.
Binders, §27-14-18.
Theft insurance.
Casualty insurance
generally. See within
this heading, "Casualty
insurance."
Threats.
Intimidation, §27-12-8.
Title insurance, §27-25-1.
Defined, §27-5-10.
Deposit requirements for
insurers.
Special deposit, §27-3-13.
Enjoining of certain acts,
§27-25-1.
Insurers.
Deposit requirements.
Special deposit, §27-3-13.
Revocation of charter for
violations, §27-25-1.
Unearned premium
reserve, §27-36-2.
Unearned premium reserve,
§27-36-2.
Trade practices law,
§§27-12-1 to 27-12-24.
Agents.
False statements, etc., in
insurance application,
§27-12-23.

INSURANCE—Cont'd
  Trade practices law—Cont'd
    Boycotts, §27-12-8.
    Brokers.
      False statements, etc., in
        insurance application,
        §27-12-23.
    Cease and desist orders,
      §27-12-18.
      Review of commissioner's
        orders, §27-12-20.
    Charges.
      Collection of charges when
        insurance not
        provided, §27-12-17.
      Excess charges, §27-12-17.
    Claims against insurers.
      Refusal of insurer to pay or
        settle claims,
        §27-12-24.
    Coercion, §27-12-8.
    Common ownership,
      management and
      directorships of insurers,
      §27-12-16.
    Discrimination.
      Life, annuity and disability
        insurance.
        Exceptions to
          discrimination,
          §27-12-13.
        Unfair discrimination in
          rates, etc., §27-12-11.
    False statements and entries,
      §§27-12-7, 27-12-23.
    General prohibition against
      unfair competition,
      §27-12-2.
    Hearings, §27-12-18.
      Proceedings on unfair
        competition, etc., not
        defined under chapter,
        §27-12-21.
      Service of statements,
        notices, orders and
        other processes,
        §27-12-19.
    Inducements.
      Financial inducements to
        purchase insurance,
        §27-12-10.
      Life, annuity and disability
        insurance, §27-12-12.
        Exceptions to special
          inducements,
          §27-12-13.
      Property, casualty or
        surety insurance,
        §27-12-14.
    Insurers.
      Common ownership,
        management and
        directorships,
        §27-12-16.
      Refusal to pay or settle
        claims, §27-12-24.
    Intimidation, §27-12-8.
    Life, annuity and disability
      insurance.
      Exceptions, §27-12-13.
      Inducements, §27-12-12.
      Unfair discrimination in
        rates, etc., §27-12-11.
    Loan on property.
      Purchase of insurance as
        condition precedent to
        loan, §27-12-15.
    Malicious statements on
      financial condition,
      §27-12-9.

INSURANCE—Cont'd
  Trade practices law—Cont'd
    Monopolies.
      Common ownership,
        management and
        directorships of
        insurers, §27-12-16.
    Mortgages and deeds of trust.
      Purchase of insurance as
        condition precedent to
        sale or loan on
        property, §27-12-15.
    Physicians.
      False statements, etc., in
        insurance application,
        §27-12-23.
    Premiums.
      Collection of premiums
        when insurance not
        provided, §27-12-17.
      Excess premiums,
        §27-12-17.
    Proceedings on unfair
      competition, etc., not
      defined under chapter,
      §27-12-21.
      Appeal by intervenor,
        §27-12-22.
    Property.
      Purchase of insurance as
        condition precedent to
        sale or loan on
        property, §27-12-15.
    Property, casualty or surety
      insurance.
      Inducements, §27-12-14.
    Purchase of insurance.
      Financial inducements to
        purchase, §27-12-10.
    Purpose of chapter, §27-12-1.
    Rebates.
      Life, annuity and disability
        insurance, §27-12-12.
      Exceptions to rebates,
        §27-12-13.
      Property, casualty or
        surety insurance,
        §27-12-14.
    Reports.
      False statements and
        entries, §27-12-7.
    Sale of property.
      Purchase of insurance as
        condition precedent to
        sale, §27-12-15.
    Service of process.
      Statements, notices, orders
        and other processes,
        §27-12-19.
    Short title of chapter,
      §27-12-1.
    Solicitors.
      False statements, etc., in
        insurance application,
        §27-12-23.
    Statement of charges,
      §27-12-18.
      Service of statements,
        §27-12-19.
    "Twisting," §27-12-6.
    Unfair competition.
      General prohibition
        against unfair
        competition, §27-12-2.
      Proceedings on unfair
        competition, etc., not
        defined under chapter,
        §27-12-21.
      Appeal by intervenor,
        §27-12-22.

INSURANCE—Cont'd
  Transact.
    Defined, §27-1-2.
  Transportation companies.
    Unclaimed freight.
      Sale.
        Application of proceeds
          for insurance,
          §37-2-30.
  Transportation insurance.
    Wet marine and
      transportation insurance.
      Defined, §27-5-9.
      Taxation, §27-4-6.
  Trusts and trustees.
    Alien insurers.
      Trusteed assets, §§27-33-1
        to 27-33-16. See within
        this heading,
        "Insurers."
    Mutual aid associations.
      Trustees, §27-30-30.
    Policies or proceeds.
      Trusts consisting of
        insurance policies or
        proceeds, §35-4-260.
  Unauthorized insurers,
    §§27-10-50 to 27-10-56.
    Action or proceeding against
      insurer.
      Defense of action,
        §27-10-53.
    Actions by not allowed,
      §27-10-3.
    Adjusters.
      Liability of adjusters,
        §27-10-2.
    Agents.
      Representing unauthorized
        insurer, §27-10-1.
    Aiding unauthorized
      insurers, §27-10-1.
      Liability of persons aiding,
        §27-10-2.
    Commissioner of insurance.
      Production of policies, etc.,
        for inspection by
        commissioner,
        §27-10-36.
    Contracts.
      Validity of contracts,
        §27-10-1.
    Fees.
      Mail order insurance.
        Fees for service on
          unauthorized
          insurers, §27-11-5.
    Independently procured
      coverages, §27-10-35.
    Inspections.
      Production of policies, etc.,
        for inspection by
        commissioner,
        §27-10-36.
    Liability.
      Persons representing or
        aiding unauthorized
        insurers, §27-10-2.
    Mail order insurance,
      §§27-11-1 to 27-11-7.
      Actions against or by
        unauthorized insurers,
        §27-11-6.
      Acts deemed to constitute
        transacting of
        insurance business in
        state, §27-11-3.
      Fees for service on
        insurers, §27-11-5.

INSURANCE—Cont'd
Unauthorized insurers
—Cont'd
Mail order insurance—Cont'd
Jurisdiction.
Attachment of
jurisdiction,
§27-11-5.
Noncomplying insurers.
Actions and proceedings
against, §27-11-4.
Occurrences deemed to
constitute transacting
of insurance business
in state, §27-11-3.
Penalties for violation of
chapter, §27-11-7.
Prohibition against
transaction of
insurance business in
state without license,
§27-11-2.
Purpose of chapter,
§27-11-1.
Service of process on
insurers, §27-11-5.
Secretary of state as
agent for service,
§27-11-5.
Short title of chapter,
§27-11-1.
Validity of acts or
contracts of
unauthorized insurer,
§27-11-6.
Violations of chapter.
Actions and proceedings
against violating
insurers, §27-11-4.
Penalties, §27-11-7.
Penalties.
Mail order insurance,
§27-11-7.
Policies.
Production of policies, etc.,
for inspection by
commissioner,
§27-10-36.
Representing unauthorized
insurer, §27-10-1.
Liability of persons
representing, §27-10-2.
Service of process on
unauthorized insurers,
§27-10-52.
Commissioner of insurance
as agent for service on
foreign or alien
insurer, §27-10-51.
Construction of article,
§27-10-56.
Default judgments,
§27-10-52.
Defense of action or
proceedings by insurer,
§27-10-53.
Exemptions, §27-10-55.
Mail order insurance,
§27-11-5.
Purpose of unauthorized
insurers process act,
§27-10-50.
Short title of article,
§27-10-56.
Transaction of insurance
business not
authorized by article,
§27-10-54.

INSURANCE—Cont'd
Unauthorized insurers
—Cont'd
Surplus line insurance.
Procuring from
unauthorized insurers,
§27-10-20.
Validity of contracts,
§27-10-1.
Unclaimed property.
Uniform disposition of
unclaimed property act,
§§35-12-21, 35-12-23.
**Unemployment
compensation.**
General provisions, §§25-4-1
to 25-4-152.
See UNEMPLOYMENT
COMPENSATION.
Unfair trade.
Trade practices law,
§§27-12-1 to 27-12-24.
See within this heading,
"Trade practices law."
Uninsured motorists.
Safety-responsibility act,
§§32-7-1 to 32-7-42.
See MOTOR VEHICLES.
Universities and colleges.
Appropriations.
Consideration in
determining patient
care reimbursement,
§27-1-11.1.
Life insurers organized to aid
nonprofit educational
and scientific
institutions.
Annual license fee, §27-4-8.
University of Alabama.
Appropriations to university.
Consideration in patient
care reimbursements,
§27-1-11.1.
**USS Alabama battleship
commission.**
Bond issues.
Legal investments for
insurance companies,
§41-9-353.
Employees and property,
§41-9-351.
Vacation time-sharing plans.
Failure to provide liability
insurance, §34-27-58.
Vending machines.
Fees, §27-4-2.
Life and disability insurance
representatives.
Use of vending machines,
§27-8-23.
Property, casualty and surety
insurance agents.
Applicability of provision
on insurance vending
machines, §27-7-3.
Venue.
Insurers.
Delinquency proceedings,
§27-32-3.
Issuance of policies.
Actions against persons,
firms or corporations
issuing, §6-3-5.
Actions against
unincorporated groups
issuing, §6-3-4.
Violations of title.
Enforcement of insurance
code, §27-2-19.

INSURANCE—Cont'd
Violations of title—Cont'd
Penalty for violation,
§27-1-12.
War.
Foreign insurers.
Effect of war on contracts
of foreign insurers,
§27-14-23.
Warehouses, §§8-15-17,
18-15-18.
**Water conservation and
irrigation.**
Corporations.
Bond issues.
Investments, §9-10-39.
**Water system assistance
authority.**
Investments in bonds of
authority.
Insurance companies,
§22-23A-12.
**Wet marine and
transportation
insurance.**
Defined, §27-5-9.
Taxation, §27-4-6.
Witnesses.
Commissioner of insurance.
Examinations,
investigations or
hearings, §27-2-26.
Compelling testimony or
production of
documents, §27-2-27.
Immunity from
prosecution, §27-2-27.
Workmen's compensation,
§§25-5-1 to 25-5-231.
See WORKMEN'S
COMPENSATION.

**INSURRECTION OR
REBELLION.**
**Constitution of the United
States,** Const. U. S., Art. I,
§8.

INTEGRATED BAR ACT.
Attorneys at law.
Board of commissioners,
§§34-3-40 to 34-3-43.

INTEREST.
Annuity tables.
See ANNUITY AND
MORTALITY TABLES.
Appeals.
Judgments, ARAP, Rule 37.
Bad checks.
Charge for bad checks
deemed not finance
charge, §8-8-15.
Change bills.
Unauthorized change bills
not exceeding $1.00,
§8-8-9.
Commercial code.
Commercial paper.
Ambiguous terms and
rules of construction,
§7-3-118.
Interest rates, §7-3-122.
Constitution of Alabama.
Banks and financial
institutions.
Maximum rate, Const.
Ala., art. XIII, §252.
Special, private or local laws
regulating rate of
interest prohibited,
Const. Ala., art. IV,
§104.

INTEREST—Cont'd
Consumer finance.
General provisions, §§5-19-1
to 5-19-31.
See CONSUMER
FINANCE.
Contracts.
Accrual on breach, §8-8-8.
Enforcement of usurious
contracts, §8-8-12.
**Coosa Valley development
authority.**
Bond issues.
Rates of interest,
§33-16-12.
State treasurer to pay
interest, §33-16-14.
Corporations.
Maximum rates of interest.
Credit sales of $2,000 or
more to corporations,
§8-8-5.
Corrections.
Institution finance authority.
Bond issues.
Security, §14-2-21.
Temporary loans in
anticipation of
issuance of bonds,
§14-2-10.
Costs.
Civil cases.
Recovery of full costs by
defendant upon
showing of usurious
interest, §12-19-52.
Counties.
Bond issues.
Exemptions from interest
statutes, §11-14-18.
Interest coupons.
Exemption, §11-81-29.
Maximum rates of
interest.
Exemption, §8-8-7.
Claims and demands against
counties.
Requirements as to
interest coupons,
§11-12-4.
Industrial development
boards.
Exemption of corporation
from interest laws,
§11-20-48.
**County industrial
development authorities.**
Exemption from usury and
interest laws,
§11-92A-17.
Credit unions.
Loans.
Interest rates on loans,
§5-17-18.
**Downtown redevelopment
authorities.**
Bond issues,
§11-54A-10.
Exemption from usury and
interest laws,
§11-54A-16.
Education.
Teachers' retirement system.
Regular interest.
Defined, §16-25-1.
Warrants for special county
and district taxes.
Interest rates, §16-13-95.
Warrants for special license,
privilege or excise taxes.
Interest rates, §16-13-120.

INTEREST—Cont'd
**Electric membership
corporations.**
Bond issues, §37-7-13.
Eminent domain.
Compensation, §18-1A-211.
Deposit of funds.
Allocation of interest,
§18-1A-111.
Interest on award, §18-1A-30.
Estate and inheritance tax.
Delinquent payments,
§40-15-16.
Evidence.
Foreign interest rates.
Secretary of state's
publication rates,
§12-21-92.
**Executors and
administrators.**
Liability of executor or
administrator for
interest, §43-2-509.
Finance.
State funds.
Linked deposits, §5-21-7.
Foreign interest rates.
Evidence.
Secretary of state's
publication rates,
§12-21-92.
Forest products.
Privilege and severance
taxes.
Assessment of taxes due by
department, §9-13-95.
Deficiency in taxes paid,
§§9-13-92, 9-13-96.
Delinquent taxes,
Lien upon property for
payment, §9-13-99.
Hazardous substances.
Fees for disposal of
hazardous waste or
substances.
Time for payment of fees.
Failure to pay within
time required,
§22-30B-5.
Hazardous waste.
Fees for disposal of
hazardous waste or
substances.
Failure to pay within time
required, §22-30B-5.
Health care authorities.
Exemption of authorities
from usury interest
provisions, §22-21-328.
Securities of authority,
§22-21-320.
Highways.
Authority.
Bond issues, §23-1-157.
Federal aid highway finance
authority.
Bonds and notes.
Pledge of funds for
payment, §23-1-311.
Pledge of interest from
investments,
§23-1-315.
**Historical preservation
authorities.**
Exemption from usury or
other interest limiting
laws, §41-10-153.
Hospitals.
Exemption from interest rate
limitation laws, §22-21-6.

INTEREST—Cont'd
Housing.
Maximum rates of interest.
Exemption of debts
incurred pursuant to
national housing act,
§8-8-6.
Income tax.
Bond issues.
Interest received from
obligations of United
States, §40-18-4.
Corporations.
Deductions allowed
corporations generally,
§40-18-35.
Deductions, §40-18-15.
Exemptions.
Interest upon obligations of
the United States,
§40-18-4.
Insurance.
Health and accident
insurance policies.
Limitation period for
payment of claims.
Payment of interest,
§27-1-17.
Judgments.
Appeals, ARAP, Rule 37.
Money judgments and costs,
§8-8-10.
Maximum rates of interest,
§§8-8-1 to 8-8-7.
Aggregation of principal and
interest, §8-8-2.
Associations.
Credit sales to associations,
§8-8-5.
Loans to associations,
§8-8-5.
Constitutional provisions,
Const. Ala., art. XIII,
§252.
Corporations.
Credit sales to
corporations, §8-8-5.
Loans to corporations,
§8-8-5.
Counties.
Exemption of bonds, notes,
etc., §8-8-7.
Credit plans.
Open-end credit plans,
§8-8-14.
Education.
Loans to state board of
education and trustees
of state educational
institutions, §8-8-4.
Generally, §8-8-1.
Housing.
Exemption of debts
incurred pursuant to
national housing act,
§8-8-6.
Indexed to prime rate,
§8-8-14.
Individuals.
Credit sales to individuals,
§8-8-5.
Loans of $2,000 or more to
individuals, §8-8-5.
Installments.
Division into installments,
§8-8-2.
Loans secured by savings
accounts, §8-8-1.2.
Loans under state or federal
law, §8-8-1.1.

INTEREST—Cont'd
Maximum rates of interest
—Cont'd
Municipal corporations.
Exemption of bonds, notes,
etc., §8-8-7.
National housing act.
Exemption of debts
incurred pursuant to,
§8-8-6.
Notes.
Collection on notes
discounted at higher
rate of interest than
eight percent, §8-8-13.
Open-end credit plans,
§8-8-14.
Partnerships.
Credit sales, §8-8-5.
Loans of $2,000 or more,
§8-8-5.
Prime rate.
Indexed to, §8-8-14.
State departments and
agencies.
Exemption of bonds, notes
and instrumentalities,
§8-8-7.
Usurious contracts.
Enforcement, §8-8-12.
Veterans' benefits.
Exemption of debts
incurred pursuant to,
§8-8-6.
Mental health finance
authority.
Bond issues, §41-10-358.
Federal income tax.
Power of authority to
pay and make
agreements for
exemption,
§41-10-371.
Payment of principal and
interest.
Pledge for, §41-10-361.
Sinking fund for,
§41-10-365.
State treasurer,
§41-10-370.
Mortality tables.
See ANNUITY AND
MORTALITY TABLES.
Motor vehicle carriers.
Mileage tax.
Failure to pay on time,
§40-19-7.
Municipal corporations.
Annual appropriations for
interest on indebtedness,
§11-43-57.
Bond issues.
Annual appropriation of
funds for interest on
indebtedness,
§11-43-57.
Interest coupons.
Exempt from taxation,
§11-81-29.
Facsimile signatures,
§11-81-63.
Receivable for payment
of taxes and dues,
§11-81-66.
Maximum rates of interest.
Exemption of municipal
bonds, §8-8-7.
Delinquent property taxes,
§11-51-2.

INTEREST—Cont'd
Municipal corporations
—Cont'd
Maximum rates of interest.
Exemption of bonds, notes,
etc., §8-8-7.
Payment of interest on
warrants not paid for
lack of funds,
§11-43-121.
Water supply and
waterworks.
Customer security deposits.
Payment of interest in
Class 1
municipalities,
§11-50-17.
Nonnegotiable instruments.
Instrument issued to
circulate as money
without authority,
§8-5-1.
Notes.
Collection on notes
discounted at higher rate
of interest than eight
percent, §8-8-13.
Unauthorized notes not
exceeding $1.00,
§8-8-9.
Partial payments.
Application to principal and
interest, §8-8-11.
Partnerships.
Maximum rates of interest.
Credit sales of $2,000 or
more, §8-8-5.
Loans, §8-8-5.
Port authority.
Exemption from usury and
interest laws, §11-94-20.
Power districts.
Bond issues.
Interest on bonds, §37-5-6.
Rates.
Maximum rates of interest,
§§8-8-1 to 8-8-7. See
within this heading,
"Maximum rates of
interest."
Sales tax.
Failure to pay tax.
Penalty plus interest,
§40-23-14.
Overpayments, §40-23-33.
Savings and loan
associations, §5-16-17.
Guaranteed rate of interest.
Agreements to pay
prohibited, §5-16-23.
Securities.
Issuance of interest bearing
securities, §41-1-9.
Provisions deemed
declarative of existing
law, §41-1-10.
Shakespeare festival theatre
finance authority.
Exemption from usury and
interest laws,
§41-10-210.
Small loans, §§5-18-13,
5-18-15.
Solid waste disposal
authorities.
Exemption from usury and
interest laws,
§11-89A-17.

INTEREST—Cont'd
State departments and
agencies.
Maximum rates of interest.
Exemption of bonds, notes,
etc., of state or
instrumentalities,
§8-8-7.
Surcharge on credit sales
and loans, §8-8-14.
Refund upon prepayment,
§8-8-14.
Surcharge on loans, §8-8-14.
Refund upon prepayment,
§8-8-14.
Tables.
Annuity tables.
See ANNUITY AND
MORTALITY
TABLES.
Taxation.
Delinquent taxes, §40-1-44.
Overpayments, §40-1-44.
Sale of land for taxes.
Land sold for taxes not due
at time of sale.
Warrant for interest,
§40-10-105.
Unemployment
compensation.
Compromise or waiver of
interest charges,
§25-4-119.
Payment of interest on
moneys advanced by
federal government,
§25-4-55.
Assessment to discontinue
when all interest paid,
§25-4-57.
Creation of special
payment fund,
§25-4-56.
Disposition of moneys in
fund when assessment
discontinued, §25-4-58.
Money advanced after
previously borrowed
funds repaid, §25-4-57.
Use tax.
Estimate of tax due when no
return made, §40-23-71.
Excess payments, §40-23-79.
Fraud.
Interest on amount
defrauded, §40-23-80.
Taxes not paid when due to
bear interest, §40-23-77.
Usury.
Agricultural development
authority.
Exemption from usury
interest laws,
§2-3A-12.
Commercial code.
Secured transactions.
Validity of security
agreement, §7-9-201.
Costs.
Recovery of full costs by
defendant upon
showing of usurious
interest, §12-19-52.
Counties.
Securities.
Exemption from usury
and interest
statutes, §11-14-18.

INTEREST—Cont'd
Usury—Cont'd
Counties—Cont'd
Warrants in anticipation of
gasoline taxes.
Exemptions from usury
statutes, §11-11-8.
Warrants made in
anticipation of ad
valorem taxes.
Exemption from usury
statutes, §11-11A-4.
Waterworks systems
warrants.
Exemptions from usury
statutes, §11-9-27.
Enforcement of usurious
contracts, §8-8-12.
Gas districts.
Exemption from usury and
interest statutes,
§11-50-415.
Health care authorities.
Exemption from usury
provisions, §22-21-328.
Hospitals.
Public hospital
corporations.
Certain corporations
exempted from usury
laws, §22-21-6.
Maximum rates of interest,
§§8-8-1 to 8-8-7. See
within this heading,
"Maximum rates of
interest."
Municipal corporations.
Boards for operation of
water, sewer, gas and
electric systems.
Exemption from usury
statutes, §11-50-319.
Gas districts.
Exemption from usury
statutes, §11-50-415.
Special health care facility
authorities.
Exemption from usury
statutes, §11-62-19.
Rates.
Maximum rates, §§8-8-1 to
8-8-7. See within this
heading, "Maximum
rates of interest."
Secured transactions.
Validity of security
agreement, §7-9-201.
Shakespeare festival theatre
finance authority.
Exemption from usury and
interest laws,
§41-10-210.
Water, sewer and fire
protection authorities.
Exemption from usury
laws, §11-88-17.
Water system assistance
authority.
Securities issued by
authority.
Exemption from usury
and interest laws,
§22-23A-14.
Witnesses.
Deceased borrower's
representative as
usury witness,
§12-21-164.
Utility services facilities.
Exemption from usury and
interest laws, §11-97-19.

INTEREST—Cont'd
**Water conservation and
irrigation.**
Corporations.
Bond issues, §9-10-36.
**Water management and
drainage.**
Districts.
Bond issues, §§9-9-39,
9-9-40.
**Water pollution control
authority.**
Bond issues.
Usury.
Exemption from usury
laws, §22-34-14.
**Water system assistance
authority.**
Bond issues, §22-23A-7.
Exemption from usury and
interest laws,
§22-23A-14.
Loans in anticipation of bond
issues, §22-23A-9.

INTERIOR DESIGNERS.
Board.
Chairman and secretary,
§34-15A-5.
Creation, §34-15A-5.
Defined, §34-15A-1.
Enforcing provisions of
chapter, §34-15A-6.
Expenses, §34-15A-5.
Membership, §34-15A-5.
Oath, §34-15A-5.
Powers and duties,
§34-15A-6.
Quorum, §34-15A-5.
Terms of office,
§34-15A-5.
Vacancies, §34-15A-5.
Definitions, §34-15A-1.
Enforcement of chapter.
Powers and duties of board,
§34-15A-6.
Examination.
Fees, §34-15A-4.
Requirements for
registration,
§34-15A-3.
Rules and regulations,
§34-15A-4.
Subjects and scope,
§34-15A-4.
When held, §34-15A-4.
Fees.
Examination fees,
§34-15A-4.
Fund, §34-15A-7.
Interior design.
Defined, §34-15A-1.
Qualifications.
Requirements for
registration, §34-15A-3.
Submission of evidence
required, §34-15A-2.
Registration.
Application, §34-15A-2.
Certificates of registration.
Issuance by board,
§34-15A-6.
Required, §34-15A-2.
Requirements, §34-15A-3.

INTERMENT.
General provisions.
See CEMETERIES.

INTERNATIONAL LAW.
Congress.
Power to punish offenses
against, Const. U. S.,
Art. I, §8.

INTERPLEADER, ARCP, Rule
22.
Attorneys' fees, ARCP, Rule
22 (c).
Bills of lading.
Determination of conflicting
claims, §7-7-603.
Commercial code.
Documents of title.
Determination of
conflicting claims,
§7-7-603.
Detinue.
Adverse claimant of property,
§6-6-253.
Form.
General form for interpleader
and declaratory relief,
ARCP, Form 38.
Partition.
Circuit courts, §35-6-21.
Warehouse receipts.
Determination of conflicting
claims, §7-7-603.

INTERPRETATION.
See CONSTRUCTION AND
INTERPRETATION.

INTERPRETERS.
Witnesses.
Appointment, ARCP, Rule 43
(f).
Compensation, §12-21-130;
ARCP, Rule 43 (f).
Generally, §12-21-130;
ARCP, Rule 43 (f).
Handicapped persons,
§§12-21-131 to 12-21-134.

INTERROGATORIES.
Answers.
Failure of party to serve
answers to
interrogatories, ARCP,
Rule 37 (d).
Availability, ARCP, Rule 33
(a).
Business records.
Option to produce business
records, ARCP, Rule 33
(c).
**Failure of party to serve
answers to
interrogatories,** ARCP,
Rule 37 (d).
Forms, ARCP, Rule 33 (d);
ARCP, Forms 47 to 49, 63,
64.
Jury.
Interrogatories to jury,
ARCP, Rule 49.
Motions.
Forms, ARCP, Forms 48, 49,
63, 64.
**Option to produce business
records,** ARCP, Rule 33
(c).
Professional corporations.
Licensing authority.
Procedure upon failure to
answer, §10-4-401.
Propoundment by
authority, §10-4-400.
Scope, ARCP, Rule 33 (b).

INTERROGATORIES—Cont'd

Supplementation of responses, ARCP, Rule 26 (e).

Trial.
Use at trial, ARCP, Rule 33 (b).

Use.
At trial, ARCP, Rule 33 (b).
Procedures for use, ARCP, Rule 33 (a).

INTERSTATE AGREEMENT ON DETAINERS.

Mandatory disposition of detainers, §§15-9-80 to 15-9-88.
See DETAINERS.

INTERSTATE COMMERCE.

Air commerce.
Exemptions from regulation, §37-9-4.
Rates, services, etc.
Powers of commission, §37-9-13.

Alcoholic beverages.
Dry counties.
Transportation of prohibited beverages.
Applicability of article to interstate transportation, §28-4-137.

Aviation.
Aircraft.
Exceptions to regulations, §4-2-80.

Congress, Const. U. S., Art. I, §§8, 9.

Constitution of the United States, Const. U. S., Art. I, §§8, 9.

Corporations.
Application of corporations provisions to interstate commerce, §10-2A-337.

Motor fuels.
Distributors of motor fuels.
Applicability of article, §40-12-205.

Motor vehicle carriers.
Applicability of chapter to interstate commerce, §37-3-3.

Public service commission.
Rates, §§37-1-44, 37-1-47.
Utilities engaged in interstate commerce, §37-1-43.

Public utilities.
Public service commission.
Jurisdiction not regulated under acts of congress, §37-1-43.
Proceedings when interstate rates or rules deemed excessive or discriminatory, §37-1-44.
Sale or lease of utility property.
Sale of property in interstate commerce contrary to federal law not authorized, §37-4-44.

Rates and charges.
Public service commission, §§37-1-80 to 37-1-105.
See PUBLIC SERVICE COMMISSION.

INTERSTATE COMMERCE —Cont'd

Transportation companies.
Concentration and transit privileges and rates, §37-2-20.
General provisions, §§37-2-1 to 37-2-184.
See TRANSPORTATION COMPANIES.

Utilities.
Public service commission.
Jurisdiction over utilities not regulated under acts of congress, §37-1-43.
Proceedings when interstate rates or rules deemed excessive or discriminatory, §37-1-44.
Sale or lease of utility property.
Sale of property in interstate commerce contrary to federal law not authorized, §37-4-44.

INTERSTATE COMPACTS.
See COMPACTS.

INTERSTATE HIGHWAY SYSTEM.

Controlled access facilities, §§23-3-1 to 23-3-8.
See HIGHWAYS.

Designation.
Authority of highway department to classify, designate and mark, §32-5A-30.

Junkyard control, §§23-1-240 to 23-1-251.
See JUNKYARD CONTROL.

Outdoor advertising, §§23-1-270 to 23-1-288.
See ADVERTISING.

Toll bridges, §§23-2-121, 23-2-122.

Toll tunnels, §§23-2-120 to 23-2-122.

INTERSTATE INCOME WITHHOLDING.

Minors.
Custody and support, §§30-3-90 to 30-3-99.
See MINORS.

INTERVAL OWNERSHIP.

Vacation time-sharing plans, §§34-27-50 to 34-27-69.
See VACATION TIME-SHARING PLANS.

INTERVENTION.

Commercial code.
Commercial paper.
Notice to third party of suit, §7-3-803.
Sales.
Notice of claim or litigation to person answerable over, §7-2-607.

Detinue.
Claimant of property, §6-6-252.

Form of motion to intervene, ARCP, Form 32.

Intervention of right, ARCP, Rule 24 (a).

INTERVENTION—Cont'd

Permissive intervention, ARCP, Rule 24 (b).

Procedure, ARCP, Rule 24 (c).

Quieting title.
In rem proceedings, §6-6-568.

INTESTATE SUCCESSION.

Adoption of adults for purposes of inheritance, §§43-4-1 to 43-4-4.
See ADOPTION.

Advancements, §§43-8-50 to 43-8-53.

After-born heirs, §43-8-47.

Aliens.
Status not a disqualification to inheriting, §43-8-56.

Curtesy.
Abolished, §43-8-57.

Debts owing to decedent.
Against whom charged, §43-8-55.

Disclaimer of property interests, §§43-8-290 to 43-8-298.
See DISCLAIMER OF INTERESTS IN PROPERTY.

Distribution of property not disposed of by will, §43-8-40.

Division of estate.
Where representation is involved, §43-8-45.

Escheats, §§43-6-1 to 43-6-9.
See ESCHEATS.

Executors and administrators.
Authorization to sell real property, §43-2-442.
Letters of administration.
Generally, §§43-2-40 to 43-2-48.
See EXECUTORS AND ADMINISTRATORS.

Generic terms.
Construction, §43-8-230.

Heir must survive decedent for five days, §43-8-43.

Heirs other than surviving spouse.
Share, §43-8-42.

Illegitimate child, §43-8-48.

Letters of administration, §§43-2-40 to 43-2-48.
See EXECUTORS AND ADMINISTRATORS.

Parent and child relationship.
Establishment, §43-8-48.

Posthumous heirs, §43-8-47.

Power.
Abolished, §43-8-57.

Pretermitted children, §43-8-91.

Property not disposed by will.
Distributed as prescribed in chapter, §43-8-40.

Relatives of half-blood, §43-8-46.

Representation.
Division of estate where representation is involved, §43-8-45.

INTESTATE SUCCESSION
—Cont'd
Salaries.
Debt for wages owed to
intestate former
employee.
Discharge of debtor from
debt.
Method, §43-8-115.
**Share of persons relating to
decedent through two
lines, §43-8-58.**
Share of surviving spouse,
§43-8-41.
Slayer act, §43-8-253.
Surviving spouse.
Share, §43-8-41.
Wages.
Debt for wages owed to
intestate former
employee.
Discharge of debtor from
debt.
Method, §43-8-115.
When estate passes to state,
§43-8-44.

INTOXICATING LIQUOR,
§§28-1-1 to 28-9-11.
See ALCOHOLIC
BEVERAGES.

**INTOXICATION CHEMICAL
TEST ACT.**
Motor vehicles.
Driving under the influence,
§§32-5-190 to 32-5-194.

INVASION.
**Constitution of the United
States, Const. U. S., Art. I,**
§§8 to 10; Art. IV, §4.

INVENTORIES.
**Banks and financial
institutions.**
Liquidation of insolvent
banks.
Inventory of assets of
bank, §5-8A-41.
Commercial code.
Secured transactions.
Classification of goods,
§7-9-109.
Decedents' estates.
Collection, inventory and
appraisement of personal
property, §§43-2-310 to
43-2-318.
See EXECUTORS AND
ADMINISTRATORS.
Departments.
Nonconsumable personal
property, §41-1-6.
**Executors and
administrators,**
§§43-2-310 to 43-2-318.
See EXECUTORS AND
ADMINISTRATORS.
Farm equipment.
Repurchase of inventory from
retailers, §§8-21-1 to
8-21-14.
See FARM EQUIPMENT.
Guardian and ward.
Uniform guardianship and
protective proceedings
act.
Conservators.
Preparation and filing
complete inventory
of estate.
Duties, §26-2A-146.

INVENTORIES—Cont'd
**Property inventory control
division.**
General provisions, §§36-16-7
to 36-16-11.
See STATE AUDITOR.
Sales.
Going out of business or
distress merchandise
sales.
General provisions,
§§8-21-1 to 8-21-23.
See SALES.
Secured transactions.
Classification of goods,
§7-9-109.
Vacation time-sharing plans.
Failure to furnish buyer with
inventory.
Violations of article,
§34-27-53.

INVESTIGATIONS.
Adoption.
Fees, §26-10-4.1.
Petition for adoption,
§26-10-2.
Attorneys at law.
Disciplinary proceedings.
Rules of disciplinary
enforcement, ARDE,
Rule 8.
Child support programs.
Ability of parents to furnish
child support.
Conducted by department,
§38-10-9.
**Coroners' inquests, §§15-4-1
to 15-4-11.**
See CORONERS.
Corrections.
Inmate community
reintegration under SIR
act.
Investigation of program
by department,
§15-18-114.
Credit unions.
Supervision of bureau.
Generally, §5-2A-100.
Divorce and alimony.
Department of human
resources.
Fees.
Investigation services
fee, §30-3-7.
Elections.
Proceedings to investigate
elections under election
laws, Const. Ala., art.
VIII, §189.
Extradition.
Demand for extradition from
Alabama, §15-9-32.
Felonies.
Presentence investigation,
§13A-5-5.
Fish and game.
Hunting deaths.
Grand jury, §9-11-21.
Habeas corpus.
Inquiry into imprisonment or
detention, §§15-21-17,
15-21-20.
Harbors and ports.
Acquisition of facilities by
state.
Additional investigation by
governor, §33-1-13.

INVESTIGATIONS—Cont'd
Hazardous wastes.
Environmental management
department.
Authority, §22-30-4.
Storage and disposal sites.
Permits, §22-30-12.
Transportation.
Permits, §22-30-12.
Treatment facilities.
Permits, §22-30-12.
Hunting deaths.
Grand jury, §9-11-21.
Income tax.
Unnecessary examination or
investigations, §40-18-56.
Indigent persons.
Defense of indigents.
Investigation of indigency,
§15-12-5.
Marine resources.
Compliance with laws.
Boarding of boats and
entrance into places of
business, §9-12-31.
Military affairs.
Courts of inquiry, §31-2-107.
Municipal corporations.
Class 5 municipalities.
Mayor/commission/city
manager form of
government.
Commission.
Power to investigate
municipal affairs,
§11-44E-44.
Investigations as to
municipal affairs,
§11-44E-181.
Council-manager form of
government.
Right of council, city
manager and designees
to investigate
municipal affairs,
§11-43A-47.
Parole.
Board to investigate
sentenced prisoner's
records, §15-22-25.
Duty of board, §15-22-28.
Penitentiary.
Management and treatment
of convicts, §14-3-54.
Physicians.
General provisions,
§§34-24-360 to 34-24-367.
See PHYSICIANS.
Revocation or suspension of
licenses, §34-24-361.
Presentence investigation.
Persons convicted of felonies,
§13A-5-5.
Prisons and prisoners.
Violations of law, §14-3-9.
Probation.
Board to investigate
sentenced prisoner's
records, §15-22-25.
Probation officer to
investigate defendant,
§15-22-51.
Public defenders.
Approval of expenditures for
investigators, §15-12-45.
Public service commission,
§§37-1-80 to 37-1-105.
See PUBLIC SERVICE
COMMISSION.

INVESTIGATIONS—Cont'd
Sales.
Going out of business or
distress merchandise
sales.
License.
Investigation of
applicant, §8-13-6.
Costs, §8-13-8.
Fee, §8-13-6.
Securities.
Securities commission,
§8-6-15.
Sentencing.
Presentence investigation,
§13A-5-5.
Small loans.
Application for licenses,
§5-18-6.
Supervisor of bureau of
loans, §5-2A-80.
Generally, §5-2A-80.
Soil classifiers.
Board.
Investigation of
complaints, §34-32-13.
Investigation of violations,
§34-32-14.
State toxicologist.
Blood and urine samples
from certain dead bodies.
Authority, §22-19-80.
Exemption from civil and
criminal liability,
§22-19-82.
Motor vehicles.
Safety coordinating
committee.
Member of committee,
§32-3-1.
Safety coordinating
committee.
Member of committee,
§32-3-1.
Vacation time-sharing plans.
Violations of article,
§34-27-68.
Assessment of
investigation costs,
§34-27-64.
Warehouses.
Complaints against
warehouses, §8-15-12.
Welfare.
Application for assistance,
§38-4-2.
Child care facilities.
Licenses.
Issuance, §38-7-4.
Operating without
license, §38-7-10.
Renewal, §38-7-6.
Grand jury.
Recipients of public
assistance, §38-2-6.
Reduction or cancellation of
assistance grants.
Recipients becoming
possessed of income or
resources, §38-4-4.
Youthful offenders.
Inadmissibility of statements,
admission and
confessions, §15-19-5.
Probation officers to assist
court, §15-19-2.

INVESTMENTS.
**Agricultural center
corporation.**
Bond issues.
Legal investments, §2-6-36.
**Banks and financial
institutions.**
General provisions, §§5-1A-1
to 5-21-11.
See BANKS AND
FINANCIAL
INSTITUTIONS.
Housing.
Investments with respect
to housing, §5-5A-23.
Commercial code.
Investment securities,
§§7-8-101 to 7-8-406.
See COMMERCIAL CODE.
Condominiums.
Mortgage investments on
condominium property,
§35-8-19.
Conservators.
Standards for fiduciary
investment and
management,
§19-3-120.2.
Uniform guardianship and
protective proceedings
act.
Powers in administration,
§26-2A-152.
Constitution of Alabama.
Trust funds, Const. Ala.,
amd. 488.
Corrections.
Institution finance authority.
Bond issues.
Proceeds of sale,
§14-2-20.
State funds and trust
funds, §14-2-17.
Counties.
Public building authorities.
Investment of county funds
in warrants, §11-15-15.
Securities issued in
anticipation of grants.
Legal investment status,
§11-11B-6.
Sinking funds.
General provisions.
See COUNTIES.
Surplus funds.
Investment in United
States securities,
§11-8-11.
**County industrial
development authorities.**
Bond issues.
Authorized investments,
§11-92A-16.
County warrants.
Warrants or certificates of
indebtedness for sanitary
sewer systems.
Investment of trust funds,
§11-9-4.
Waterworks systems
warrants.
Investment of trust funds,
§11-9-25.
Credit unions.
Powers of credit unions,
§5-17-4.

INVESTMENTS—Cont'd
Education.
Alabama education
authority.
Bond issues.
Bonds legal investments,
§16-15-9.
Educational building
authorities.
Investments in bonds of
authority, §16-17-17.
Public educational
building authorities,
§16-18-19.
Endowment funds.
Funds held by state board
of education and
trustees of state
institutions, §16-13-2.
Public school and college
authority.
Bond issues.
Investment of fiduciary
funds, §16-16-9.
Tax anticipation warrants in
cities and counties.
Warrants legal
investments for
fiduciaries, §16-13-74.
Warrants for special county
and district taxes.
Investment of unused
proceeds in
government securities,
§16-13-109.
Eminent domain.
Deposit of funds, §18-1A-111.
**Environmental improvement
authorities.**
Powers to invest, §9-6-8.
**Executors and
administrators.**
Authorization of investment
of trust funds by
executors or
administrators in bonds
or stock of private
corporations prohibited,
Const. Ala., art. IV, §74.
Restrictions on investment of
trust funds by executors,
trustees, etc., in private
corporations, Const. Ala.,
amd. 40.
Standards for fiduciary
investment and
management,
§19-3-120.2.
Fiduciaries.
Authorization of investments
of trust funds in bonds or
stock of private
corporations prohibited,
Const. Ala., art. IV, §74.
Restrictions on investments
of trust funds by
fiduciaries in private
corporations, Const. Ala.,
amd. 40.
Standards for fiduciary
investment and
management,
§19-3-120.2.
Fraternal benefit societies,
§27-34-35.
Guardian and ward.
Authorization of investment
of trust funds in bonds or
stock of private
corporations prohibited,
Const. Ala., art. IV, §74.

INVESTMENTS—Cont'd
 Guardian and ward—Cont'd
  Restrictions on investment of
   trust funds by guardians
   in private corporations,
   Const. Ala., amd. 40.
  Standards for fiduciary
   investment and
   management,
   §19-3-120.2.
  Uniform guardianship and
   protective proceedings
   act.
  Conservators.
   Powers in
    administration,
    §26-2A-152.
 Health care authorities.
  Funds of authority,
   §22-21-332.
  Additional powers,
   §22-21-355.
  Legal investments.
   Securities issued under
    article deemed legal
    investments,
    §22-21-326.
  Securities issued under
   article deemed legal
   investments, §22-21-326.
 **Health maintenance
   organization,** §27-21A-11.
 Highways.
  Federal aid highway finance
   authority, §23-1-315.
 Horse racing.
  Commission.
   Funds not needed to
    discharge obligations,
    §11-65-9.
 Hospitals.
  Public hospitals.
   Powers of corporation,
    §11-95-7.
 Industrial parks.
  Warrants.
   Fiduciaries, §11-92-9.
 Insurance.
  General provisions.
   See INSURANCE.
  Investments of life, disability
   and burial insurance,
   §§27-41-1 to 27-41-41.
   See INSURANCE.
 **Mental health finance
   authority.**
  Bond issues.
   Surplus proceeds from sale
    of bonds, §41-10-367.
  Trust funds.
   Investment in bonds,
    §41-10-362.
  Permitted investments.
   Defined, §41-10-351.
 Mobile county.
  Municipal and county funds,
   Const. Ala., amd. 500.
 **Mortgages and deeds of
   trust.**
  Condominium property.
   Mortgage investments on
    condominium property,
    §35-8-19.
 Municipal corporations.
  Securities issued in
   anticipation of grants.
   Legal investment status of
    securities, §11-64-6.
  Sinking funds, §§11-81-19 to
   11-81-21.

INVESTMENTS—Cont'd
 **Peace officers' annuity and
   benefit fund.**
  Investment of moneys,
   §36-21-66.
 Railroad authorities.
  Bonds of authorities.
   County and municipal
    funds, §37-13-17.
   Trust funds.
    Eligibility of bonds as
     investments for,
     §37-13-18.
  Powers of authorities,
   §37-13-7.
 **Savings and loan
   associations.**
  General provisions.
   See SAVINGS AND LOAN
    ASSOCIATIONS.
 Securities.
  Investment securities.
   Generally, §§7-8-101 to
    7-8-406.
   See COMMERCIAL
    CODE.
 Sinking funds.
  Counties, §§11-81-19 to
   11-81-21.
  Municipal corporations,
   §§11-81-19 to 11-81-21.
 **Space science exhibit
   finance authority.**
  Bond issues, §41-10-314.
 State funds.
  Funds which will be in
   treasury 30 days or less,
   §41-14-32.
  Notes and bonds of United
   States or federal
   agencies, §41-14-30.
  Obligations of United States.
   State treasurer authorized
    to invest surplus state
    funds, §36-17-18.
 State treasurer.
  Surplus state funds.
   Investment in obligations
    of United States,
    §36-17-18.
 **Stonewall Jackson memorial
   fund,** §16-32-2.
 Taxation.
  Investment of ad valorem
   taxes, §40-1-47.
 **Trade school and junior
   college authority.**
  Bonds legal investments,
   §16-60-91.
 Transfers to minors.
  Custodians.
   Manner of investment,
    §35-5A-13.
 Trust estates, §§19-3-120 to
   19-3-132.
  See TRUSTS AND
   TRUSTEES.
 Utility services facilities.
  Bond issues.
   Legal investments,
    §11-97-22.
 **Water conservation and
   irrigation.**
  Corporations.
   Bond issues, §9-10-39.
 **Water pollution control
   authority.**
  Bonds issued by authority
   considered legal
   investments, §22-34-12.

INVESTMENTS—Cont'd
 **Water system assistance
   authority.**
  Bond issues, §22-23A-12.
  Water supply assistance
   fund, §22-23A-4.
 Workmen's compensation.
  Second injury trust fund.
   Investment of moneys in
    fund, §25-5-72.

INVITEES.
 **Duty of care owed persons
   on premises for sporting
   or recreational purposes,**
   §§35-15-1 to 35-15-5.
  See PARKS AND
   RECREATION.

**INVOLUNTARY
  COMMITMENT.**
 Mentally ill, §§22-52-1 to
   22-52-17.
  See MENTALLY ILL.

INVOLUNTARY SERVITUDE.
 Constitution of Alabama,
   Const. Ala., art. I, §32.
 **Constitution of the United
   States,** Const. U. S.,
   Amendments XIII, XV.

IRON ORE.
 Licenses for mining.
  Amount of tax, §40-12-128.
  Levy of tax, §40-12-128.
  Limitation of actions,
   §40-12-128.
  Reports.
   Operators, §40-12-129.
   Persons receiving products,
    §40-12-130.
 Mining generally.
  See MINES AND
   MINERALS.

IRRIGATION, §§9-10-1 to
   9-10-47.
  See WATER CONSERVATION
   AND IRRIGATION.

ISLANDS.
 Incorporation, §11-41-1.
 Public lands, §9-2-120.

ISSUE.
 **Posthumous children
   included in "issue,"**
   §35-4-8.
 **Remainders, reversions and
   executory interests.**
  Remainder limited after
   death without heirs or
   issue.
  Construction of words
   "heirs" or "issue,"
   §35-4-213.

ITINERANT VENDORS.
 Licenses, §40-12-139.

                    J

JACKS.
 Liens.
  Owners of stallions, jacks,
   bulls, etc., §§35-11-330,
   35-11-331.

JACKSON COUNTY.
 Economic development.
  Special property tax, Const.
   Ala., amd. 174.

JACKSON COUNTY—Cont'd
Fires and fire prevention.
Fire districts and fire
prevention services,
Const. Ala., amd. 436.
Industrial development.
Special property tax, Const.
Ala., amd. 174.
**Junior college for Jackson
county,** §§16-60-50 to
16-60-67.
See JUNIOR COLLEGES.
Rural development.
Special property tax, Const.
Ala., amd. 174.
School tax.
Additional property tax for
educational purposes,
Const. Ala., amd. 203.
Vocational trade school.
Special property tax for
acquiring, etc., Const.
Ala., amd. 174.
**JACKSON, MUNICIPALITY
OF.**
Port authority, Const. Ala.,
amds. 465, 477.
**JACKSONVILLE,
MUNICIPALITY OF.**
Property tax, Const. Ala.,
amd. 8.
**JACKSONVILLE STATE
UNIVERSITY.**
Administration of university.
Board of trustees.
Powers as to
administration,
§16-52-6.
Agents.
Default, etc., not to work
forfeiture, §16-52-11.
**American Legion
scholarships,** §§16-31-1 to
16-31-4.
Board of trustees, §§16-52-1
to 16-52-10.
Administration of university.
Powers as to
administration,
§16-52-6.
Appointment of members,
§16-52-3.
Body corporate, §16-52-1.
Compensation of members,
§16-52-3.
Composition, §16-52-3.
Courses of instruction.
Powers of board, §16-52-6.
Created, §16-52-3.
Default, etc., not to work
forfeiture, §16-52-11.
Degrees.
Powers of board, §16-52-6.
Endowment funds.
Investment of endowment
funds held by board,
§16-13-2.
Expenses of members,
§16-52-3.
Payment, §16-52-9.
Faculty.
Powers of board, §16-52-6.
Jurisdiction.
Transfer of jurisdiction,
etc., over university to
board of trustees,
§16-52-7.
Legislature.
Reports to legislature,
§16-52-10.

**JACKSONVILLE STATE
UNIVERSITY**—Cont'd
Board of trustees—Cont'd
Meetings, §16-52-4.
Membership, §16-52-3.
Organization of university.
Powers as to organization,
§16-52-6.
Quorum, §16-52-5.
Reports to legislature,
§16-52-10.
Terms of members, §16-52-3.
Transfer of jurisdiction, etc.,
over university to board
of trustees, §16-52-7.
Tuition.
Powers of board, §16-52-6.
Vacancies, §16-52-8.
Body corporate, §16-52-1.
**Commission on higher
education.**
General provisions, §§16-5-1
to 16-5-14.
See UNIVERSITIES AND
COLLEGES.
Student loan program,
§§16-33B-3, 16-33B-4.
Corporation.
Body corporate, §16-52-1.
Rights, privileges, etc., of
corporation, §16-52-2.
Courses of instruction.
Board of trustees.
Powers of board, §16-52-6.
Degrees.
Board of trustees.
Powers of board, §16-52-6.
Faculty.
Appointment, §16-52-6.
Board of trustees.
Powers of board, §16-52-6.
Removal, §16-52-6.
Salaries, §16-52-6.
Gifts.
Not to fail for informality,
§16-52-11.
Grants.
Not to fail for informality,
§16-52-11.
Jurisdiction.
Board of trustees.
Transfer of jurisdiction to
board, §16-52-7.
Legislature.
Board of trustees.
Reports to legislature,
§16-52-10.
**Marine environmental
sciences consortium,**
§§16-45-1 to 16-45-5.
See MARINE
ENVIRONMENTAL
SCIENCES
CONSORTIUM.
Nursing.
School of nursing, §§16-52-13
to 16-52-15.
Officers.
Default, etc., not to work
forfeiture, §16-52-11.
Police officers, §16-52-12.
Organization of university.
Board of trustees.
Powers as to organization,
§16-52-6.
Police, §16-52-12.
General provisions,
§§16-22-1, 16-22-2.
Property.
Certain state property vested
in university, §16-52-16.

**JACKSONVILLE STATE
UNIVERSITY**—Cont'd
Property—Cont'd
Rights, privileges,
responsibilities, etc., of
corporation, §16-52-2.
Reports.
Board of trustees.
Reports to legislature,
§16-52-10.
Salaries.
Faculty, §16-52-6.
Scholarships.
American Legion
scholarships, §§16-31-1
to 16-31-4.
School of nursing, §§16-52-13
to 16-52-15.
School of nursing.
Scholarships, §§16-52-13 to
16-52-15.
Trustees.
Board of trustees, §§16-52-1
to 16-52-16.
Tuition.
Board of trustees.
Powers of board, §16-52-6.

JAILS, §§14-6-1 to 14-6-109.
Alcoholic beverages.
Dry counties.
Sale, delivery, etc., of
liquors to prisoners,
§28-4-165.
Furnishing to prisoners,
§14-6-18.
Allowances.
Feeding of prisoners,
§§14-6-42, 14-6-43,
14-6-48.
Alteration of jails.
Inspection of jails.
Notification of board of
corrections, §14-6-101.
Ordering, §14-6-87.
Penalty for refusal to
obey orders,
§14-6-90.
Removal of prisoners,
§14-6-88.
Refusal to obey orders,
§14-6-90.
Return of prisoners,
§§14-6-89, 14-6-90.
Notice.
Board of corrections,
§14-6-101.
Repairs.
County jails, §11-14-14.
Inspection of jails,
§§14-6-87 to 14-6-90.
Appeals.
Inspection of jails.
When new construction
required, §14-6-82.
Tubercular prisoners.
Persons confined pending
appeal, §14-6-61.
Arrangement.
County jails, §11-14-13.
Arrest.
Copy of arrest writ to be
delivered to jailer,
§15-10-46.
Baths.
Facilities.
Required, §14-6-93.
Prisoners to be compelled to
bathe, §14-6-94.

JAILS—Cont'd
Bedding.
Furnishing of bedding,
§§14-6-19, 14-6-93.
Board of corrections.
Feeding of prisoners,
§§14-6-40 to 14-6-50.
Inspection of jails, §§14-6-80
to 14-6-109.
Circuit courts.
Commitment of prisoners.
Duty of sheriff to report to
clerk, §14-6-15.
Discharge of prisoners.
Duty of sheriff to report to
clerk, §14-6-15.
Lists of confined prisoners.
Furnishing to circuit
courts, §14-6-14.
Clothing.
Furnishing of clothing,
§§14-6-19, 14-6-93.
Commitment of prisoners,
§§14-6-3 to 14-6-16.
Civil process.
Persons committed on civil
process, §14-6-3.
Contempt.
Persons committed for
contempt, §14-6-3.
Federal prisoners, §14-6-3.
Duty to receive and keep,
§14-6-4.
Lists of confined prisoners.
Furnishing to circuit
courts, §14-6-14.
Mentally ill.
Pending transfer to mental
hospital, §14-6-3.
Nearest sufficient jail to
insure safekeeping,
§14-6-6.
Order.
Duty to file process or
order, §14-6-16.
Process.
Duty to file process or
order, §14-6-16.
Refusal to receive prisoners.
Penalties, §14-6-5.
Reports.
Duty of sheriff to report to
clerk of circuit court,
§14-6-15.
Second or subsequent
conviction.
Commencement of
imprisonment,
§14-6-12.
Who may be confined in
county jail, §14-6-3.
Witnesses.
Failure to give security for
their appearance,
§14-6-3.
Condemnation.
Inspection of jails.
Power to condemn jails,
§14-6-83.
Confinement, §§14-6-3 to
14-6-16.
Construction.
County jails, §11-14-13.
Failure to levy tax for
erection when
necessary, §11-14-15.
Levy of tax for erection,
§11-14-14.
Expenses.
Payment, §14-6-104.
Municipal jails, §11-47-7.

JAILS—Cont'd
Construction—Cont'd
Notice.
Board of corrections,
§14-6-101.
Contagious diseases.
Fumigation of jails, §14-6-96.
Tubercular prisoners,
§§14-6-60 to 14-6-62.
Contempt.
Commitment of prisoners.
Nearest sufficient jail,
§14-6-6.
Persons committed for
contempt, §14-6-3.
Coroners.
Special coroners.
Appointment at request of
board of corrections,
§14-6-99.
When coroner to act as
keeper of jail, §11-5-6.
Costs of incarceration.
Misdemeanant required to
pay costs, §14-6-22.
Amount and method of
payment, §14-6-22.
Disposition of costs,
§14-6-22.
Probation or suspension of
sentence.
Payment of costs as
condition of
probation or
suspension, §14-6-22.
Procedure upon default,
§14-6-22.
Remission of costs,
§14-6-22.
County boards of health.
Duties, §22-3-2.
County health officers.
Duties, §22-3-5.
County jails, §§11-14-10 to
11-14-22.
See COUNTIES.
**Custody of jails and
prisoners.**
Sheriffs, §14-6-1.
Death.
Sheriffs.
Delivery of jail to
successor, §14-6-2.
Deductions from sentence,
§§14-9-41 to 14-9-44.
Computation of incentive
time deductions,
§14-9-41.
Good conduct time previously
earned.
Applicability of article,
§14-9-43.
Habitual offender laws.
Effect of article, §14-9-44.
Nonretroactive effect of
article, §14-9-44.
Parole.
Effect of deductions on
parole, §14-9-42.
Depositions.
Form of motion for leave to
take deposition of
prisoner, ARCP, Form
45.
Discharge of prisoners.
Order.
Duty to file process or
order, §14-6-16.
Process.
Duty to file process or
order, §14-6-16.

JAILS—Cont'd
Discharge of prisoners
—Cont'd
Reports.
Duty of sheriff to report to
clerk of circuit court,
§14-6-15.
Diseases.
Notifiable diseases.
Petition for testing and
treatment of inmate,
§22-11A-37.
Sexually transmitted
diseases, §22-11A-17.
District attorneys.
Entitled to free access to
county jail, §12-16-196.
Drugs.
Medicines.
Furnishing to prisoners,
§14-6-19.
Erection of jails, §§11-14-13
to 11-14-16.
Escapes.
General provisions.
See ESCAPE.
Guards.
Summoning to prevent
escape, §14-6-11.
Extradition.
Temporary confinement of
prisoner, §15-9-39.
Federal prisoners.
Commitment of prisoners,
§14-6-3.
Duty to receive and keep,
§14-6-4.
Feeding of prisoners,
§§14-6-40 to 14-6-50.
Account books.
Failure of sheriff to
maintain, §14-6-48.
Allowances.
Account books.
Failure of sheriff to
maintain, §14-6-48.
Amount.
Per capita amount,
§14-6-42.
Per capita amount,
§14-6-42.
Preparation and service of
food.
Amount, §14-6-43.
Two or more jails in
county, §14-6-43.
Cleanliness of food, §14-6-97.
Duty to feed, §14-6-40.
Forms.
Records and statements,
§14-6-47.
Grand juries.
Sheriff to deliver book of
accounts for
examination as to
correctness,
§12-16-193.
Penalties.
Violation of article,
§14-6-50.
Records.
Daily ration sheet or
expense account.
Sheriff not required to
prepare, §14-6-41.
Forms, §14-6-47.
Sanitation requirements,
§14-6-97.
Statements.
Forms, §14-6-47.
Supervision, §14-6-41.

JAILS—Cont'd

Feeding of prisoners—Cont'd
Wholesomeness of food,
§14-6-97.
Fires and fire prevention.
Jail to be fireproof,
§14-6-103.
Removal of prisoners.
Jail building contiguous
thereto on fire,
§14-6-8.
Force.
Use of force by persons with
custodial responsibilities,
§13A-3-24.
Forms.
Feeding of prisoners.
Records and statements,
§14-6-47.
Fumigation.
Infectious diseases, §14-6-96.
Schedule, §14-6-92.
Good conduct.
Deductions from sentence.
Correctional incentive
time, §§14-9-41 to
14-9-44.
Grand jury.
Feeding of prisoners.
Sheriff to deliver book of
accounts with state for
feeding of prisoners to
grand jury for
examination as to
correctness,
§12-16-193.
Free access to county jail,
§12-16-196.
Inspection of jails.
County jail.
Duty as to inspection,
§12-16-191.
Reports.
Furnishing to grand
jury, §14-6-91.
Probate judge to furnish
grand jury report to
board, §14-6-100.
Guards.
Officers and guards.
Escape.
Summoning of guards to
prevent escape,
§14-6-11.
Force.
When use of force
justified, §13A-3-27.
Jailers, §§14-6-1, 14-6-5,
14-6-105.
Removal of prisoners.
Use of guards, §14-6-10.
Habeas corpus.
General provisions, §§15-21-1
to 15-21-34.
See HABEAS CORPUS.
Health.
Authority and jurisdiction of
state board of health,
§22-2-2.
Duties of county boards,
§22-3-2.
Duties of county health
officers, §22-3-5.
Expenses.
Payment, §14-6-104.
Feeding of prisoners,
§§14-6-40 to 14-6-50.
Hospitals.
Removal of prisoners.
Ill health of prisoners,
§14-6-9.

JAILS—Cont'd

Health—Cont'd
Hospitals—Cont'd
Tubercular prisoners,
§§14-6-60 to 14-6-62.
Inspection of jails, §§14-6-80
to 14-6-109.
Sanitation.
Baths, §§14-6-93, 14-6-94.
General provisions. See
within this heading,
"Sanitation."
Inspection of jails,
§§14-6-80 to 14-6-109.
Tubercular prisoners,
§§14-6-60 to 14-6-62.
Heating, §14-6-103.
Hospitals.
Removal of prisoners.
Ill health of prisoners,
§14-6-9.
Tubercular prisoners,
§§14-6-60 to 14-6-62.
**Industries in penal
institutions.**
General provisions, §§14-7-6
to 14-7-20.
See PRISONS AND
PRISONERS.
Insanity.
Mentally ill prisoners,
§§15-16-1 to 15-16-71.
See PRISONS AND
PRISONERS.
Inspection of jails, §§14-6-80
to 14-6-109.
Alterations, repairs, etc.
Notification of board of
corrections, §14-6-101.
Ordering, §14-6-87.
Penalty for refusal to
obey orders,
§14-6-90.
Removal of prisoners,
§14-6-88.
Refusal to obey orders,
§14-6-90.
Return of prisoners,
§§14-6-89, 14-6-90.
Appeals.
When new construction
required, §14-6-82.
Applicability of article.
Municipal corporations,
§14-6-80.
Authority, §14-6-106.
Condemnation.
Powers of board of
corrections, §14-6-83.
Correction of conditions.
Authority of board of
corrections, §14-6-82.
Duties of board of
corrections, §14-6-81.
Frequency of inspections,
§14-6-81.
Grand jury.
Duty of grand juries as to
inspection of county
jail, §12-16-191.
Reports.
Furnishing to grand
jury, §14-6-91.
Judge to furnish report
to board, §14-6-100.
Improvements, §§14-6-87 to
14-6-90, 14-6-101.

JAILS—Cont'd

Inspection of jails—Cont'd
Information.
Furnishing on request,
§14-6-84.
Penalty for failure to
provide, §14-6-85.
Municipal corporations.
Applicability of article,
§14-6-80.
Orders.
Correction of conditions,
§14-6-82.
Effect of orders of board of
corrections, §14-6-107.
Penalties.
Alterations, repairs, etc.
Failure to remove
prisoners, §14-6-90.
Refusal to obey orders,
§14-6-90.
Failure to provide
information, §14-6-85.
Violations of article,
§14-6-109.
Repairs, §§14-6-87 to 14-6-90,
14-6-101.
Reports.
Grand jury.
Probate judge to furnish
grand jury report to
board, §14-6-100.
Publication, §14-6-91.
Schedule of inspections,
§14-6-81.
Sheriffs.
Furnishing information on
request, §14-6-84.
Penalty for failure to
provide, §14-6-85.
Jailers.
Appointment, §14-6-1.
Deputies, watchmen, etc.,
§14-6-105.
Refusal to receive prisoners
into custody, §14-6-5.
Janitors.
Adequate janitor service to
be provided, §14-6-93.
Juvenile proceedings.
When delinquent child may
be detained in jail,
§12-15-61.
Legal custody.
Sheriffs, §14-6-1.
Maintenance.
Expenses.
Payments, §14-6-104.
Municipal corporations,
§11-47-7.
Mattresses and bedding.
Furnishing of bedding,
§§14-6-19, 14-6-93.
Mentally ill.
Commitment of prisoners.
Pending transfer to mental
hospital, §14-6-3.
General provisions, §§15-16-1
to 15-16-71.
See PRISONS AND
PRISONERS.
Security medical facility,
§§22-54-1 to 22-54-5.
Military affairs.
National guard.
Prescribing boundaries
around jails from
which public excluded,
§31-2-123.

JAILS—Cont'd

Minors.
Involuntary commitment of
minors or children.
Authority and procedure,
§12-15-90.
Municipal corporations,
§§11-47-7, 11-47-8.
Inspection of jails.
Applicability of article,
§14-6-80.
General provisions,
§§14-6-80 to 14-6-109.
Notice.
Construction of jails.
Notification of board of
corrections, §14-6-101.
Officers and guards.
Escape.
Summoning of guards to
prevent escape,
§14-6-11.
Force.
When use of force justified,
§13A-3-27.
Jailers, §§14-6-1, 14-6-5,
14-6-105.
Removal of prisoners.
Use of guards, §14-6-10.
Orders of court.
Commitment of prisoners.
Duty to file process or
order, §14-6-16.
Discharge of prisoners.
Duty to file process or
order, §14-6-16.
Painting of jails.
Schedule, §14-6-92.
Parole.
Deductions from sentence.
Effect of deductions on
parole, §14-9-42.
Peace bonds.
Commitment of defendant to
jail, §15-6-25.
Penalties.
Commitment of prisoners.
Failure to receive prisoners
into custody, §14-6-5.
Feeding of prisoners.
Violation of article,
§14-6-50.
Inspection of jails.
Alterations, repairs, etc.
Failure to remove
prisoners, §14-6-88.
Refusal to obey orders,
§14-6-90.
Failure to provide
information, §14-6-85.
Violations of article,
§14-6-109.
Sanitation.
Allowing jail to become
foul or unclean,
§14-6-21.
Penitentiary.
Detention of convicts en
route.
Duty of jailers, §14-3-34.
General provisions, §§14-3-1
to 14-3-60.
See PENITENTIARY.
Temporary confinement of
convict pending removal,
§14-3-30.
Physicians.
Appointment, §14-6-20.
Compensation, §14-6-20.

JAILS—Cont'd

Physicians—Cont'd
Duties.
General provisions,
§14-6-20.
Medical attention.
Furnishing, §14-6-19.
Medicines.
Furnishing necessary
medicines, §14-6-19.
Removal, §14-6-20.
Salaries, §14-6-20.
Terms of office, §14-6-20.
Plumbing.
Adequate sanitary plumbing
connections, §14-6-103.
Preliminary hearings.
Commitment of defendant to
jail, §15-11-3.
When defendant committed
to jail, §15-11-10.
**Prisons and prisoners
generally.**
See PRISONS AND
PRISONERS.
Records.
Feeding of prisoners.
Daily ration sheet or
expense account,
§14-6-41.
Forms, §14-6-47.
Removal of prisoners.
Commitment pending
removal, §14-6-3.
Fires.
Jail building contiguous
thereto on fire,
§14-6-8.
Guards.
Use of guards, §14-6-10.
Hospitals.
Ill health of prisoners,
§14-6-9.
Inspection of jails.
During periods of
alterations, repairs,
etc., §14-6-88.
Municipal corporations,
§11-47-8.
Nearest sufficient jail,
§14-6-7.
Penitentiary.
Temporary confinement
pending removal,
§14-3-30.
Safekeeping of prisoners.
Fires, §14-6-8.
Ill health, §14-6-9.
When made to nearest
sufficient jail, §14-6-7.
Special jails.
During periods of
alterations, repairs,
etc.
Penalty for refusal to
obey orders,
§14-6-90.
Tubercular prisoners,
§§14-6-60 to 14-6-62.
Repairs.
County jails.
Failure to levy tax for
repair when necessary,
§11-14-15.
Levy of tax for repair,
§11-14-14.
Inspection of jails, §§14-6-87
to 14-6-90, 14-6-101.

JAILS—Cont'd

Reports.
Commitment of prisoners.
Duty of sheriff to report to
clerk of circuit court,
§14-6-15.
Discharge of prisoners.
Duty of sheriff to report to
clerk of circuit court,
§14-6-15.
Inspection of jails.
Grand jury.
Furnishing to board,
§14-6-100.
Furnishing to grand
jury, §14-6-91.
Publication of reports,
§14-6-91.
Lists of confined prisoners.
Sheriff to furnish to circuit
courts, §14-6-14.
Monthly report to board of
corrections, §14-6-98.
Return of prisoners.
Inspection of jails.
After periods of alteration,
repairs, etc., §§14-6-89,
14-6-90.
Rules and regulations.
Municipal corporations,
§11-47-7.
Sanitation.
Promulgation, §14-6-86.
Salaries.
Physicians, §14-6-20.
Sanitation.
Allowing jail to become foul
or unclean.
Penalties, §14-6-21.
Baths.
Facilities.
Required, §14-6-93.
Prisoners to be compelled
to bathe, §14-6-94.
Bedding.
Furnishing of bedding,
§§14-6-19, 14-6-93.
Cleaning of jails.
Schedule, §14-6-92.
Cleanliness, §14-6-95.
Clothing.
Furnishing of clothing,
§§14-6-19, 14-6-93.
Expenses.
Payment, §14-6-104.
Fumigation.
Infectious diseases,
§14-6-96.
Schedule, §14-6-92.
Inspection of jails.
Generally, §§14-6-80 to
14-6-109.
Janitor service, §14-6-93.
Painting of jails.
Schedule, §14-6-92.
Plumbing and sewage
connections, §14-6-103.
Rules and regulations.
Promulgation, §14-6-86.
Sentencing.
Commitment of prisoners,
§§14-6-3 to 14-6-16.
Misdemeanant required to
pay costs.
Condition of probation or
suspension of sentence,
§14-6-22.

AILS—Cont'd

Sentencing—Cont'd

Second or subsequent conviction.
Commencement of imprisonment, §14-6-12.

Separation of prisoners.
Men and women, §14-6-13.

Service of process.
How incarcerated person served, ARCP, Rule 4 (c).

Sewers.
Adequate sewage connections, §14-6-103.

Sheriffs.
Allowances.
Feeding of prisoners, §§14-6-40 to 14-6-50.
Circuit courts.
Furnishing lists of confined prisoners, §14-6-14.
Commitment of prisoners.
Duty to report to clerk of circuit court, §14-6-15.
Death.
Delivery of jail, §14-6-2.
Discharge of prisoners.
Duty to report to clerk of circuit court, §14-6-15.
Feeding of prisoners, §§14-6-40 to 14-6-50.
Fees.
Feeding of prisoners, §§14-6-40 to 14-6-50.
Inspection of jails.
Furnishing information on request, §14-6-84.
Penalty for failure to provide, §14-6-85.
Jailer.
Appointment, §14-6-1.
Legal custody in charge of jails and prisoners, §14-6-1.
Officers and guards.
General provisions, §§14-6-10, 14-6-11.
Jailers, §§14-6-1, 14-6-5, 14-6-105.
Removal from office.
Delivery of jail, §14-6-2.
Reports.
Lists of confined prisoners to circuit courts, §14-6-14.
Monthly report to board of corrections, §14-6-98.
Resignation.
Delivery of jail, §14-6-2.
Support of prisoners, §14-6-17.
Terms of office.
Delivery of jail upon expiration of term of office, §14-6-2.

Size.
Requirements, §14-6-103.

State board of health.
Authority and jurisdiction, §22-2-2.

Summons and process.
Commitment of prisoners.
Duty to file process or order, §14-6-16.
Discharge of prisoners.
Duty to file process or order, §14-6-16.

Support of prisoners.
Furnishing of support, §14-6-17.

JAILS—Cont'd

Support of prisoners—Cont'd
When prisoner may furnish his own support, §14-6-17.

Taxation.
County jails.
Levy of tax for erection, etc., §11-14-14.
Failure to levy tax when necessary, §11-14-15.
Special tax for jail, §11-14-16.

Tubercular prisoners.
Appeals.
Persons confined pending appeal, §14-6-61.
Hospitals.
Removal to state hospital, §14-6-60.
Removal of prisoners.
Expenses.
Payment, §14-6-62.
Payment of expenses, §14-6-62.
Persons confined pending appeal, §14-6-61.
State hospital, §14-6-60.

United States.
Federal prisoners.
Commitment of prisoners, §14-6-3.
Duty to receive and keep, §14-6-4.

Violations.
Imprisonment in county jail, §13A-5-7.

Watchman.
When required, §14-6-105.

Witnesses.
Commitment of prisoners.
Witnesses failing to give security for appearances, §14-6-3.

Women.
Separation of men and women, §14-6-13.

JASPER, MUNICIPALITY OF.
Property tax, Const. Ala., amd. 13.
School tax.
Special property tax for educational purposes, Const. Ala., amd. 253.

JEFFERSON COUNTY.
Barbers.
Chapter not applicable to Jefferson county, §34-5-15.
Bingo.
Charitable or nonprofit organizations.
Operation, Const. Ala., amd. 386.
Charities.
Bingo games.
Operation, Const. Ala., amd. 386.
Circuit court holding at Birmingham.
Vacancies in office of judge, Const. Ala., amd. 83.
Circuit court of Jefferson county.
Filling vacancy in office of judge, Const. Ala., amd. 110.
Constables.
Fees.
Exception, §12-19-92.

JEFFERSON COUNTY—Cont'd
Economic and industrial development promotion, Const. Ala., amd. 429.
Fees.
Constables.
Exception, §12-19-92.
Fire protection districts, Const. Ala., amds. 239, 314.
Garbage and trash disposal districts, Const. Ala., amd. 314.
Inferior courts established in lieu of justices of the peace.
Legislation as to jurisdiction, Const. Ala., amds. 258, 283.
Officers.
Fees, Const. Ala., amd. 2.
Probate judgeship.
Additional judgeship for county, Const. Ala., amd. 384.
School tax.
Consolidation school tax amendment, Const. Ala., amd. 82.
Special district tax for furtherance of education, Const. Ala., amds. 175, 260, 298.
Special tax in Mountain Brook school district, Const. Ala., amd. 316.
Sewer bonds, Const. Ala., amd. 73.
Sports hall of fame board.
Display of busts, exhibits, etc., in Jefferson county civic center, §41-9-451.
Weeds.
Prohibition of overgrowth, Const. Ala., amd. 497.
Wills.
Probate code.
Savings provisions for, §43-8-9.

JEWELERS.
Liens.
Declaration of lien, §35-11-150.
Enforcement of lien, §35-11-151.
Sale of articles, §35-11-151.

JOINDER.
Blacksmiths' liens.
Joinder of persons having liens on same property, §35-11-112.
Claims, ARCP, Rule 18 (a).
Form of motion for severance of claims, ARCP, Forms 33, 34.
Liability insurance coverage, ARCP, Rule 18 (c).
Counterclaims and cross-claims.
Joinder of additional parties, ARCP, Rule 13 (h).
Failure to join a party.
Defense of failure to join a party under Rule 19, ARCP, Rule 12 (b), (h).
Forms, ARCP, Forms 32 to 37.

JOINDER—Cont'd
Insurance.
  Joinder of claims.
    Liability insurance
      coverage, ARCP, Rule
      18 (c).
Liability insurance coverage,
  ARCP, Rule 18 (c).
Machinery liens.
  Liens for production,
    manufacture or repair.
    Joinder of persons having
      liens on same property,
      §35-11-112.
Motor vehicle liens.
  Production, manufacture or
    repair.
    Joinder of persons having
      liens on same property,
      §35-11-112.
Nonjoinder.
  Parties.
    Pleading reasons for
      nonjoinder, ARCP,
      Rule 19 (c).
Parties.
  Compulsory joinder, ARCP,
    Rule 19.
  Counterclaim and cross-
    claim, ARCP, Rule 13
    (h).
  Forms, ARCP, Forms 32, 33,
    35 to 37.
  Misjoinder, ARCP, Rule 21.
  Nonjoinder.
    Pleading reasons for
      nonjoinder, ARCP,
      Rule 19 (c).
  Permissive joinder, ARCP,
    Rule 20 (a).
  Persons needed for just
    adjudication, ARCP,
    Rule 19.
  Required joinder, ARCP,
    Rule 19.
Quo warranto.
  Alleged corporation as party
    defendant, §6-6-594.
  Informants, §6-6-595.
Remedies, ARCP, Rule 18 (b).
Rules of criminal procedure,
  ARCrP, Rules 15.3 (a) to
  15.4 (h).
  See RULES OF CRIMINAL
    PROCEDURE.
Trees and timber.
  Damages for destruction,
    injury or removal of
    trees.
    Joinder of actions,
      §35-14-1.
Venue, ARCP, Rule 82 (c).
Woodworkmen's liens.
  Joinder of persons having
    liens on same property,
    §35-11-112.

JOINT APPEALS, ARAP, Rule
  3 (b).

JOINT AUTHORITY.
  Defined, §1-1-2.

**JOINT TENANTS AND
  TENANTS IN COMMON.**
Actions.
  Parties.
    Action against cotenant or
      coparcener, §6-7-40.
Attachment.
  Liens of tenants in common,
    §35-11-351.

**JOINT TENANTS AND
  TENANTS IN COMMON**
  —Cont'd
**Banks and financial
  institutions.**
  Joint deposits.
    See BANKS AND
      FINANCIAL
      INSTITUTIONS.
Condominiums.
  Removal of condominium
    property.
    Property deemed to be
      owned in common,
      §35-8-20.
Credit unions.
  Deposits in names of two
    persons, §5-17-15.
Crops.
  Liens generally, §§35-11-350,
    35-11-351.
  Liens of tenants in common,
    §§35-11-350, 35-11-351.
  Partition, §§35-6-110 to
    35-6-126.
  See PARTITION.
Decedents' estates.
  Survivorship between joint
    tenants, §35-4-7.
**Disclaimer of property
  interests,** §§43-8-290 to
  43-8-298.
  See DISCLAIMER OF
    INTERESTS IN
    PROPERTY.
Dower.
  Ascertainment and payment
    of dower interest,
    §§35-4-190 to 35-4-192.
**Executors and
  administrators.**
  Partition in probate courts.
    Deceased parties, §35-6-65.
Fences.
  Partition fences, §§35-7-1 to
    35-7-7.
  See PARTITION.
Guardian and ward.
  Sale of land for distribution
    among joint owners,
    §§35-6-80 to 35-6-91.
  See PARTITION.
Insane persons.
  Sale of land for distribution
    among joint owners,
    §§35-6-80 to 35-6-91.
  See PARTITION.
Liens of tenants in common.
  Attachment, §35-11-351.
  Declaration of lien,
    §35-11-350.
  Enforcement of lien,
    §35-11-351.
  Liens generally.
    See LIENS.
Life estates.
  Ascertainment and payment
    of life interest,
    §§35-4-190 to 35-4-192.
Mentally ill.
  Sale of land for distribution
    among joint owners,
    §§35-6-80 to 35-6-91.
  See PARTITION.
Minors.
  Sale of land for distribution
    among joint owners,
    §§35-6-80 to 35-6-91.
  See PARTITION.

**JOINT TENANTS AND
  TENANTS IN COMMON**
  —Cont'd
**Mortgages and deeds of
  trust.**
  Joint mortgagees.
    Satisfaction by one of
      several joint
      mortgagees.
      Entry of full payment or
        satisfaction in
        record, §35-10-28.
Municipal corporations.
  Assessments for public
    improvements,
    §§11-48-100 to 11-48-100
  See MUNICIPAL
    CORPORATIONS.
Parties.
  Action against cotenant or
    coparcener, §6-7-40.
Partition.
  General provisions,
    §§35-6-100 to 35-6-104.
Public improvements.
  Assessments for public
    improvements,
    §§11-48-100 to 11-48-100
  See MUNICIPAL
    CORPORATIONS.
**Savings and loan
  associations.**
  Accounts, §5-16-43.
  Deposit in names of two
    persons payable to either
    or survivor, §§5-16-44,
    5-16-45.
Sharecroppers.
  Liens of tenants in common,
    §§35-11-350, 35-11-351.
Simultaneous death act,
  §43-7-4.
**Survivorship between joint
  tenants,** §35-4-7.

JOURNALS.
  Congress, Const. U. S., Art. I,
    §§5, 7.
  Legislature, Const. Ala., art.
    IV, §55.
    Compilation, §29-1-12.
    Compensation, §29-1-13.
    Delivery to secretary of state,
      §29-1-13.
    Filing, §29-1-12.
    Printing.
      Public printing and
        binding, §§41-4-130 to
        41-4-161.
      See PRINTING.

JUDGES.
  Adjudicative responsibilities,
    ACJE, Canon 3A.
  **Administrative
    responsibilities,** ACJE,
    Canon 3B.
  Appointments.
    Canons of judicial ethics.
      See CANONS OF
        JUDICIAL ETHICS.
  Arbitration and award.
    Judge not to act as
      arbitrator, ACJE, Canon
      5E.
  Arts.
    Permitted activities, ACJE,
      Canons 5A, 5G.
  Attorneys at law.
    Canons of judicial ethics,
      ACJE, Canons 3B, 5F.

UDGES—Cont'd
Attorneys at law—Cont'd
  Practice of law by judges
    prohibited, §§34-3-11,
    34-3-14; ACJE, Canon
    5F.
Bail and recognizance.
  Signing of bond for
    appearance or release of
    prisoner.
    Prohibited, §36-10-11.
Benefits.
  Diminishment, §12-1-16.
  Employment benefits,
    §12-1-15.
  Voluntary diminishment of
    benefits, §12-1-16.
Bequests.
  Acceptance prohibited if
    bequest reflects
    expectation of judicial
    favor, ACJE, Canon 5C.
Bias.
  Disqualification for personal
    bias, ACJE, Canon 3C.
Billiard rooms.
  Issuance of license by
    probate judge, §§34-6-31,
    34-6-32.
Bribery, Const. Ala., art. IV,
    §80.
Canons of judicial ethics,
    ACJE, Canons 1 to 7.
  See CANONS OF JUDICIAL
    ETHICS.
Chancery powers.
  Elections.
    Contests.
      Jurisdiction denied,
        §17-15-6.
Charities.
  Permitted activities, ACJE,
    Canon 5B.
**Chief justice of the supreme
    court.**
  See SUPREME COURT.
Circuit court judges.
  General provisions,
    §§12-17-20 to 12-17-40.
  See CIRCUIT COURTS.
Civic activities.
  Permitted activities, ACJE,
    Canon 5B.
Colleges.
  Expenses, §12-5-11.
  Pertaining to administration
    of courts, §12-5-17.
Compensation, Const. Ala.,
    amds. 328, 426.
  Canons of judicial ethics.
    Appointees, ACJE, Canon
      3B.
    Extra-judicial activities.
      Restrictions, ACJE,
        Canon 6.
    Quasi-judicial activities.
      Restrictions, ACJE,
        Canon 6.
  Judicial compensation
    commission, §§12-10-1 to
    12-10-5.
Confidentiality.
  Information acquired in
    judicial capacity not to
    be used for other
    purposes, ACJE, Canon
    5C.
Conflicts of interest.
  Procedure for determining,
    ACJE, Canon 6C.

JUDGES—Cont'd
Conservators.
  Judge to consider himself
    conservator of estates
    under his jurisdiction,
    ACJE, Canon 3B.
Conservators of the peace,
    Const. Ala., art. VI, §157.
Constitution of Alabama.
  See CONSTITUTION OF
    ALABAMA.
**Constitution of the United
    States.**
  Compensation, Const. U. S.,
    Art. III, §1.
  Tenure, Const. U. S., Art. III,
    §1.
Court of civil appeals.
  General provisions, §§12-3-1
    to 12-3-36.
  See COURT OF CIVIL
    APPEALS.
Court of criminal appeals.
  General provisions, §§12-3-1
    to 12-3-36.
  See COURT OF
    CRIMINAL APPEALS.
Court of the judiciary.
  Alternate judges.
    Selection and appointment,
      ARJC, Rule 26.
  Presiding judge, ARJC, Rule
    24.
Decorum.
  Canons of judicial ethics.
    Maintenance at all times,
      ACJE, Canon 2B.
    Proceedings before judge.
      Judge to maintain
        decorum in
        proceedings, ACJE,
        Canon 3A.
Disability, ARCP, Rule 63.
Disqualification, Const. Ala.,
    amd. 328.
  Grounds, §12-1-12.
  Judge acting as such while
    disqualified, AJICR,
    Rule 14.
District attorneys.
  Judicial retirement fund.
    Time of service by judge as
      full-time state
      prosecutor.
      Credit for time,
        §12-18-8.1.
District courts.
  General provisions,
    §§12-17-60 to 12-17-70.
  See DISTRICT COURTS.
Duties.
  Additional duties.
    Establishment by supreme
      court, §12-2-17.
  Canons of judicial ethics,
    ACJE, Canons 3, 5.
Education.
  Expenses, §12-5-11.
Educational activities.
  Judge may accept extra-
    judicial appointment,
    ACJE, Canon 5G.
Elections.
  General provisions.
  See ELECTIONS.
Ethics.
  Canons of judicial ethics,
    ACJE, Canons 1 to 7.
  See CANONS OF
    JUDICIAL ETHICS.

JUDGES—Cont'd
Ethics—Cont'd
  Prohibited activities, Const.
    Ala., amd. 328.
Evidence.
  Canons of judicial ethics.
    Electronic presentation.
      Discretion of trial judge,
        ACJE, Canon 3A.
    Personal knowledge of
      disputed evidentiary
      facts.
      Qualification, ACJE,
        Canon 3C.
    Photographic presentation.
      Discretion of trial judge
        or appellate court,
        ACJE, Canon 3A.
Executions.
  Issuance, §6-9-20.
Expenses.
  Canons of judicial ethics.
    Extra-judicial activities.
      Restrictions on
        reimbursement,
        ACJE, Canon 6B.
    Quasi-judicial activities.
      Restrictions on
        reimbursement,
        ACJE, Canon 6B.
  Judicial compensation
    commission.
    Expenses of members.
      Reimbursement,
        §12-10-3.
Family relationships.
  Canons of judicial ethics.
    Disqualification where
      relative has a financial
      interest, ACJE, Canon
      3C.
    Nepotism.
      Prohibited in
        appointments,
        ACJE, Canon 3B.
    Not to influence conduct or
      judgment, ACJE,
      Canon 2C.
Fiduciaries.
  Canons of judicial ethics.
    Disqualification where
      judge has fiduciary
      interest, ACJE, Canon
      3C.
    Permitted fiduciary
      activities, ACJE,
      Canon 5D.
    Restrictions on fiduciary
      activities, ACJE,
      Canon 5D.
Financial interests.
  Canons of judicial ethics,
    ACJE, Canons 3C, 5C,
    6C.
Funds.
  Judicial retirement fund.
    General provisions,
      §§12-18-1 to 12-18-8.
    Transfer of contributions
      and creditable service,
      §§12-18-110 to
      12-18-114.
Gifts.
  Prohibited if gift reflects
    expectation of judicial
    favor, ACJE, Canon 5C.
Historical activities.
  Judge may accept
    appointment, ACJE,
    Canon 5G.

JUDGES—Cont'd
Impartiality.
Canons of judicial ethics.
Disqualification where
impartiality may be
questioned, ACJE,
Canon 3C.
Judge to perform duties
impartially, ACJE,
Canon 3.
Promoting public
confidence, ACJE,
Canon 2A.
Impeachment.
General provisions, §§36-11-1
to 36-11-25.
See IMPEACHMENT.
Which judges subject to
impeachment, §36-11-1;
Const. Ala., art. VII,
§§174, 175.
Impropriety.
Canons of judicial ethics.
Appearance of impropriety.
Judge to avoid in all his
activities, ACJE,
Canon 2.
Avoidance of impropriety,
ACJE, Canon 2.
Influence.
Canons of judicial ethics.
Prestige of office.
Judge not to lend
prestige to advance
interest of others,
ACJE, Canon 2C.
Special position of
influence.
Judge not to convey or
permit others to
convey, ACJE,
Canon 2C.
**Information acquired in
judicial capacity.**
Not to be used for other
purposes, ACJE, Canon
5C.
Inquiry commission, AJICR,
Rules 1 to 18; Const. Ala.,
amd. 328.
Advisory opinions, AJICR,
Rule 17.
Compensation of members.
Per diem compensation of
members who are not
judges, §12-6-1.
Confidentiality of
proceedings, AJICR,
Rule 5.
Contempt.
Power to punish for
contempt, AJICR, Rule
8.
Court of the judiciary.
Prosecution of charges
before court of the
judiciary, AJICR, Rule
15.
Defamation actions.
Privilege, AJICR, Rule 4.
Disqualification of judge.
Judge acting as such while
disqualified, AJICR,
Rule 14.
Disqualification of member,
AJICR, Rule 2.
Executive committee, AJICR,
Rule 12.

JUDGES—Cont'd
Inquiry commission—Cont'd
Investigations, AJICR, Rule
6.
Institution between
meetings, AJICR, Rule
10.
Matters pending before
judicial commission,
AJICR, Rule 16.
Meetings, AJICR, Rule 9.
Officers, AJICR, Rule 11.
Privilege.
Defamation actions,
AJICR, Rule 4.
Proceedings.
Confidentiality, AJICR,
Rule 5.
Style of proceedings,
AJICR, Rule 3.
Process, AJICR, Rule 7.
Style of process, AJICR,
Rule 3.
Rules of procedure.
Advisory opinions, AJICR,
Rule 17.
Confidentiality of
proceedings, AJICR,
Rule 5.
Contempt, AJICR, Rule 8.
Definitions, AJICR, Rule 1.
Disqualification of member
of commission, AJICR,
Rule 2.
Executive committee,
AJICR, Rule 12.
Investigations, AJICR,
Rule 6.
Institution between
meetings, AJICR,
Rule 10.
Judge acting as such while
disqualified, AJICR,
Rule 14.
Meetings, AJICR, Rule 9.
Officers, AJICR, Rule 11.
Pending matters, AJICR,
Rule 16.
Privilege in defamation
actions, AJICR, Rule
4.
Prosecution of charges
before court of the
judiciary, AJICR, Rule
15.
Publication of rules,
AJICR, Rule 18.
Seal, AJICR, Rule 13.
Style of proceedings and
process, AJICR, Rule
3.
Subpoenas and other
process, AJICR, Rule
7.
Seal, AJICR, Rule 13.
Subpoenas, AJICR, Rule 7.
Integrity of judiciary.
Canons of judicial ethics.
Judge to uphold, ACJE,
Canon 1.
Promoting public
confidence in integrity,
ACJE, Canon 2A.
**Judicial compensation
commission,** §§12-10-1 to
12-10-5.
See JUDICIAL
COMPENSATION
COMMISSION.

JUDGES—Cont'd
Judicial conference, §§12-8-
to 12-8-6.
See JUDICIAL
CONFERENCE.
Judicial inquiry commission
AJICR, Rules 1 to 18.
Judicial retirement fund.
General provisions, §§12-18-
to 12-18-8.
Transfer of contributions an
creditable service,
§§12-18-110 to 12-18-11
**Judicial system study
commission,** §§12-9-1 to
12-9-9.
See JUDICIAL SYSTEM
STUDY COMMISSION.
Jury.
When words "jury" or
"juries" include court or
judge, §12-16-1.
**Justices of the supreme
court.**
See SUPREME COURT.
Juvenile proceedings.
See JUVENILE
PROCEEDINGS.
Lecturing.
Permitted activities, ACJE,
Canons 4A, 5A.
Loans.
Acceptance prohibited if loa
reflects expectation of
judicial favor, ACJE,
Canon 5C.
Magistrates.
Inferior court judges.
Election by inferior court
judges to become
magistrates,
§12-17-253.
Mandamus.
Directed to judge or judges,
ARAP, Rule 21.
Mediators.
Judge not to act as mediato
ACJE, Canon 5E.
Municipal courts.
General provisions,
§§12-14-30 to 12-14-34.
Nepotism.
Prohibited in appointments,
ACJE, Canon 3B.
Oaths, Const. U. S., Art. VI.
Peace bonds.
Authority to require person
to give security, §15-6-2
Offense committed or
threatened in presence
judge, §15-6-3.
Pensions.
Circuit courts, §§12-18-1 to
12-18-41.
See CIRCUIT COURTS.
Court of civil appeals,
§§12-18-1 to 12-18-13.
See COURT OF CIVIL
APPEALS.
Court of criminal appeals,
§§12-18-1 to 12-18-13.
See COURT OF
CRIMINAL APPEAL
District courts, §§12-18-50 t
12-18-61.
See DISTRICT COURTS.
Judicial retirement fund.
General provisions,
§§12-18-1 to 12-18-8.

JUDGES—Cont'd
Pensions—Cont'd
Judicial retirement fund
—Cont'd
Transfer of contributions
and creditable service,
§§12-18-110 to
12-18-114.
Probate courts, §§12-18-80 to
12-18-92.
See PROBATE COURTS.
Supreme court justices,
§§12-18-1 to 12-18-41.
See SUPREME COURT.
Political activity.
Canons of judicial ethics,
ACJE, Canon 7.
Powers, Const. Ala., amd. 328.
**Practice of law by judges
prohibited,** §§34-3-11,
34-3-14.
Canons of judicial ethics,
ACJE, Canon 5F.
Constitutional provisions,
Const. Ala., art. VI,
§162.
Prejudice.
Canons of judicial ethics.
Avoidance of prejudicial
conduct, ACJE, Canon
2B.
Disqualification, ACJE,
Canon 3C.
Probate courts.
General provisions,
§§12-13-30 to 12-13-70.
See PROBATE COURTS.
Prohibited activities, Const.
Ala., amd. 328.
Prohibition, writ of.
Directed to judge or judges,
ARAP, Rule 21.
Qualifications, Const. Ala.,
amd. 328.
Quasi-judicial activities.
Canons of judicial ethics.
Compensation.
Restrictions, ACJE,
Canon 6A.
Expenses.
Restrictions on
reimbursement,
ACJE, Canon 6B.
Permitted activities, ACJE,
Canon 4.
Radio.
When broadcasting in
courtroom permitted,
ACJE, Canon 3A.
Relatives.
Canons of judicial ethics.
Disqualification where
relative has a financial
interest, ACJE, Canon
3C.
Influence.
Family relationships not
to influence conduct
or judgment, ACJE,
Canon 2C.
Nepotism.
Prohibited in
appointments,
ACJE, Canon 3B.
Reports.
Financial interests.
Judge to regularly file
reports of financial
interests, ACJE,
Canon 6C.

JUDGES—Cont'd
Restrictions on conduct.
Canons of judicial ethics,
ACJE, Canons 1 to 7.
See CANONS OF
JUDICIAL ETHICS.
Retirement, §§12-18-1 to
12-18-114; Const. Ala.,
amd. 328.
Benefits.
Failure to apply for
benefits at time of
leaving active state
service, §12-1-15.
Uniformity of treatment as
to benefits, §12-1-15.
Circuit courts, §§12-18-1 to
12-18-41.
See CIRCUIT COURTS.
Confidential secretaries.
Retired justices or judges
performing active
duty, §12-5-21.
Court of civil appeals,
§§12-18-1 to 12-18-41.
See COURT OF CIVIL
APPEALS.
Court of criminal appeals,
§§12-18-1 to 12-18-41.
See COURT OF
CRIMINAL APPEALS.
District courts, §§12-18-50 to
12-58-61.
See DISTRICT COURTS.
Judicial retirement fund,
§§12-18-1 to 12-18-114.
Administration of fund,
§12-18-2.
Appeals from decisions of
board of control,
§12-18-2.
Applicability of article to
future additional state
judicial officers,
§12-18-12.
Appropriations of moneys
by legislature for fund,
§12-18-3.
Composition, §12-18-1.
Construction of article,
§12-18-13.
Contributions by judges
and justices, §12-18-5.
District court judges,
§12-18-52.
Probate judges,
§12-18-82.
Refund of contributions
upon termination of
service prior to
eligibility, §12-18-8.
Contributions made to
employees' retirement
system.
Transfer into judicial
retirement fund,
§12-18-8.
Created, §12-18-1.
Disbursement of funds,
§12-18-2.
District court judges,
§§12-18-50 to 12-18-61.
See DISTRICT COURTS.
State and local governing
bodies authorized to
pick-up contributions,
§12-18-5.

JUDGES—Cont'd
Retirement—Cont'd
Judicial retirement fund
—Cont'd
State contributions.
Payment of state
contributions in
event of failure of
state to appropriate
money, §12-18-3.
Supernumerary justices
and judges.
Election by surviving
spouses to obtain
benefits under
provisions of article
1 of chapter.
Payment to judicial
retirement fund by
surviving spouse
at time of election,
§12-18-33.
Transfer of contributions
and creditable service
to fund.
Adjusted benefits,
§12-18-111.
Article supplemental to
other related laws,
§12-18-114.
District judges.
Adjusted benefit
formulas,
§12-18-112.
Exceptions,
§12-18-111.
Spouse's benefits,
§12-18-112.
Eligibility period.
Requirements,
§§12-18-110,
12-18-111.
Formulas, §12-18-111.
District judges'
adjusted benefits
formulas,
§12-18-112.
Probate judges.
Adjusted benefit
formulas,
§12-18-113.
Exceptions,
§12-18-111.
Spouse's benefits,
§12-18-113.
Procedure, §12-18-110.
Spouse's benefits.
District judges,
§12-18-112.
Supplemental nature of
article, §12-18-114.
Probate judges, §§12-18-80 to
12-18-92.
See PROBATE COURTS.
Supreme court justices,
§§12-18-1 to 12-18-41.
See SUPREME COURT.
Uniformity of treatment as
to benefits, §12-1-15.
Robes.
Suitable black judicial robe,
ARJA, Rule 22.
**Rules of judicial
administration.**
Assignment of judges.
Notification, ARJA, Rule
14.
Temporary assignments,
ARJA, Rule 13.
Presiding judges.
Selection, ARJA, Rule 25.

JUDGES—Cont'd
Rules of judicial administration—Cont'd
Secretarial service, ARJA, Rule 20.
Special judges.
Compensation, ARJA, Rule 12.
Rules of judicial inquiry commission, AJICR, Rules 1 to 8.
Salaries, Const. Ala., amd. 328.
Compensation commission, §§12-10-1 to 12-10-5.
Diminishing.
Voluntary diminution of salaries, §12-1-16.
Searches and seizures.
Searching person charged with felony for weapon or evidence in judge's presence, §15-5-17.
Solicitation of funds.
Judge not to solicit funds for educational, religious, charitable, etc., organizations, ACJE, Canon 5B.
Special sessions of court.
Designation of judge to attend and hold court, §12-2-35.
Forfeiture by judge failing to order or attend special session, §12-2-37.
Notification of chief justice by judge unable to attend, §12-2-35.
Standards of conduct.
Canons of judicial ethics, ACJE, Canons 1 to 7.
See CANONS OF JUDICIAL ETHICS.
Studies, projects, etc., to improve administration of justice, §12-5-18.
Study commission.
Judicial system study commission, §§12-9-1 to 12-9-9.
See JUDICIAL SYSTEM STUDY COMMISSION.
Supernumerary judges.
Benefits.
Failure to apply for supernumerary benefits at time of leaving active state service, §12-1-15.
Uniformity of treatment as to benefits, §12-1-15.
Court of civil appeals.
Continuation of laws concerning duties, benefits, etc., §12-3-7.
Court of criminal appeals.
Continuation of laws concerning duties, benefits, etc., §12-3-7.
Supreme court.
General provisions, §12-2-50.
Supreme court.
Establishment of additional duties for judges, §12-2-17.

JUDGES—Cont'd
Supreme court—Cont'd
Justices.
General provisions, §§12-2-1 to 12-2-50.
See SUPREME COURT.
Television.
When broadcasting in courtroom permitted, ACJE, Canon 3A.
Temperance.
Maintenance at all times, ACJE, Canon 2B.
Terms of office, §36-3-2; Const. Ala., amd. 328.
Incumbents.
Terms of incumbents not abridged, Const. Ala., art. VI, §172.
United States courts, Const. U. S., Art. III, §1.
Vacancies in office, Const. Ala., amd. 328.
Acceptance of another office, §36-9-4.
Witnesses.
Canons of judicial ethics.
Character witness.
Judge not to testify voluntarily, ACJE, Canon 2C.
Disqualification of judge where judge has been material witness, ACJE, Canon 3C.

JUDGMENT BY DEFAULT.
See JUDGMENTS.

JUDGMENTS, §§6-9-1 to 6-9-238.
Actions.
New action after adverse decision, §6-2-39.
Affidavits.
Summary judgment, ARCP, Rule 56; ARCP, Forms 84, 85.
Affirmation of judgment, §§12-22-72 to 12-22-75.
Alteration of judgment.
Motion to alter, ARCP, Rule 59 (e), (g).
Disposition of motion, ARCP, Rule 59.1.
Stay on motion, ARCP, Rule 62 (b).
Amendment of judgment.
Clerical mistakes, ARCP, Rule 60 (a).
Motion to amend, ARCP, Rule 59 (e), (g).
Disposition of motion, ARCP, Rule 59.1.
Stay on motion, ARCP, Rule 62 (b).
Nunc pro tunc, ARCP, Rule 60 (a).
Appeals.
Certificate of judgment.
Issuance.
Date of issuance, ARAP, Rule 41 (a).
Stay of certificate pending petitions for certiorari, ARAP, Rule 41 (b).
Entry of judgment, ARAP, Rule 36.
Interest on judgments, ARAP, Rule 37.
Juvenile courts, §12-15-120.
Assignment, §6-9-196.

JUDGMENTS—Cont'd
Associations.
Actions against.
Satisfaction of judgment, §6-7-81.
Attachments, §§6-6-140 to 6-6-149.
See ATTACHMENTS.
Banks and financial institutions.
Regulation of trust business.
Sale of securities deposited with treasurer for satisfaction of judgment, §5-11A-8.
Reorganization.
Entry of judgment, §5-9A-4.
Boundaries.
Actions to determine boundaries, §35-3-3.
Cemeteries.
Counties.
Appeal from assessment for damages.
Entry of judgment for damages and costs, §11-17-11.
Certificate of judgment.
Appeals, ARAP, Rule 41.
Child custody.
Uniform child custody jurisdiction act, §§30-3-20 to 30-3-44.
See MINORS.
Circuit courts.
Notice of judgments, ARCP, Rule 77 (d).
Record of final judgments in minute book, ARCP, Rule 79 (b).
Commercial code.
Commercial paper.
Confession of judgment, §7-3-112.
Secured transactions.
Transactions excluded from provisions of article, §7-9-104.
Compromise and settlement.
Pro tanto settlements.
Effect of judgments entered pursuant to, §12-21-109.
Confession of judgment.
Agreements to confess judgment or authorize another to confess judgment before commencement of action, §8-9-11.
Defined, §12-22-1.
Misdemeanors.
Collection of docket fees and fines where defendants confess judgment, §12-19-151.
Release of errors, §12-22-1.
Small loans, §5-18-16.
Suretyship.
When surety not to confess judgment, §8-3-12.
When void, §8-9-11.
Constitution of the United States.
Full faith and credit clause, Const. U. S., Art. IV, §1.
Proof, Const. U. S., Art. IV, §1.

JUDGMENTS—Cont'd
Construction and interpretation.
Foreign judgments.
Construction of article, §6-9-238.
Conveyances.
Specific performance.
Judgment for specific performance, §35-4-33.
Corporations.
Prosecution of corporations.
Execution on judgment, §10-7-4.
Corrections.
Board of corrections.
Payment by board of adjustment, §41-9-74.
Costs, ARCP, Rule 54 (d).
Counterclaims, §6-8-80.
Judgment for defendant.
Compulsory counterclaims, §6-8-86.
Permissive counterclaims, §6-8-85.
Separate judgments, ARCP, Rule 13 (i).
Counties.
Bond issues.
Validation, §§6-6-750 to 6-6-757.
See COUNTIES.
Cemeteries.
Appeal from assessment for damages.
Entry of judgment for damages and costs, §11-17-11.
Creditors.
Recordation necessary as to judgment creditors, §§35-4-90 to 35-4-98.
See RECORDATION.
Criminal law and procedure.
Judgment creditors.
Defrauding, §13A-9-47.
Cross-claims.
Separate judgments, ARCP, Rule 13 (i).
Declaratory judgments.
General provisions, §§6-6-220 to 6-6-232.
See DECLARATORY JUDGMENTS.
Default judgments.
Annulment of marriage.
Proof required despite default, ARCP, Rule 55 (e).
Attachments.
Trial proceedings, §6-6-141.
Counterclaimants, ARCP, Rule 55 (d).
Cross-claimants, ARCP, Rule 55 (d).
Divorce.
Proof required despite default, ARCP, Rule 55 (e).
Ejectment.
Effect of default judgment, §6-6-290.
Entry, ARCP, Rule 55 (a), (b).
Forms, ARCP, Forms 79 to 83.
Forms, ARCP, Forms 79 to 83.

JUDGMENTS—Cont'd
Default judgments—Cont'd
Life and disability insurance guaranty association.
Reopening default judgments, §27-44-18.
Mechanics' and materialmen's liens.
Enforcement of liens, §35-11-225.
Motion to set aside.
Form, ARCP, Form 83.
Proof required despite default in certain cases, ARCP, Rule 55 (e).
Setting aside default, ARCP, Rule 55 (c).
Form of motion to set aside, ARCP, Form 83.
Small claims, ASCR, Rule K.
Who entitled to, ARCP, Rule 55 (d).
Definitions, ARCP, Rule 54 (a).
Confession of judgment, §12-22-1.
Foreign judgment, §6-9-231.
Demand for judgment, ARCP, Rule 54 (c).
Detinue.
Assessment of value and damages.
Dismissal of action, §6-6-257.
Failure of defendant to appear and plead, §6-6-258.
Jury to assess, §6-6-256.
Execution upon, §6-6-261.
Dispossession.
Unlawfully taking possession of after dispossession under legal process, §13A-7-60.
Ejectment, §§6-6-280 to 6-6-298.
See EJECTMENT.
Elections.
Contests.
Judgment of court, §17-15-32.
Void elections.
Certification of judgment declaring election void, §36-9-15.
Electricity.
Service territories for electric suppliers.
1984 act.
Judicial determination of legality and validity, §§37-14-13, 37-14-14.
1985 act.
Judicial determination of legality and validity, §37-14-38.
Finality of judgment, §37-14-38.
Eminent domain, §§18-1A-210 to 18-1A-216.
See EMINENT DOMAIN.
Enforcement of judgments.
Executions.
See EXECUTIONS.
Judicial sales.
See JUDICIAL SALES.
Powers of courts, §12-1-7.
Small claims, ASCR, Rule L.

JUDGMENTS—Cont'd
Enforcement of judgments—Cont'd
Stay of proceedings to enforce a judgment.
Automatic stay, ARCP, Rule 62 (a).
Injunction pending appeal, ARCP, Rule 62 (c).
Multiple claims or multiple parties.
Stay of judgment upon, ARCP, Rule 62 (h).
Power of appellate court not limited, ARCP, Rule 62 (g).
State of Alabama or agency of state.
Stay in favor of, ARCP, Rule 62 (e).
Stay on motion for new trial or for judgment, ARCP, Rule 62 (b).
Stay upon appeal, ARCP, Rule 62 (d).
Entry of judgment, ARCP, Rule 58 (c).
Appeals, ARAP, Rule 36 (b).
Sufficiency of minute entry, ARCP, Rule 58 (b).
Evidence, §12-21-100.
Admissibility in evidence, ARCP, Rule 44 (f).
Excessive judgments.
Proceedings when only amount excessive, §12-22-71.
Excusable neglect.
Relief from judgment, ARCP, Rule 60 (b).
Executions.
General provisions.
See EXECUTIONS.
Executors and administrators, §§43-2-134, 43-2-150 to 43-2-155.
See EXECUTORS AND ADMINISTRATORS.
Exemptions from levy and sale under process.
Contest of exemption claim, §6-10-32.
Bonds, surety.
Judgment on bond, §6-10-36.
Fees.
Foreign judgments.
Filing fee, §6-9-235.
Final judgment.
Constitutional provisions, Const. U. S., Art. IV, §1.
Findings by court, ARCP, Rule 52.
Fish and game laws.
Violations.
Appeals.
Judgment on appeal, §9-11-15.
Forcible entry and unlawful detainer.
Form, §6-6-319.
Foreign judgments, §§6-9-230 to 6-9-238.
Citation of article, §6-9-230.
Construction of article, §6-9-238.
Defined, §6-9-231.
Effect, §6-9-232.

JUDGMENTS—Cont'd
  Foreign judgments—Cont'd
    Enforcement, §§6-9-230 to
      6-9-237.
    Actions to enforce.
      Right to bring action
        unimpaired,
        §6-9-236.
    Citation of article,
      §6-9-230.
    Construction and
      interpretation.
      Uniformity of
        construction,
        §6-9-238.
    Execution.
      When execution may
        issue, §6-9-233.
    Fees.
      Filing of foreign
        judgment, §6-9-235.
    Filing, §6-9-232.
      Affidavit, §6-9-233.
      Effect, §6-9-232.
      Fees, §6-9-235.
      Notice, §6-9-233.
      "Foreign judgment"
        defined, §6-9-231.
    Recording of judgment in
      probate office,
      §6-9-237.
    Right to bring action to
      enforce.
      Unimpaired, §6-9-236.
    Short title of article,
      §6-9-230.
    Stay, §6-9-234.
    Fees.
      Filing fee, §6-9-235.
    Filing with clerk of circuit
      court, §6-9-232.
    Fees, §6-9-235.
    Notice of filing, §6-9-233.
    Requirements, §6-9-233.
    Recording in probate office,
      §6-9-237.
    Right to enforce unimpaired,
      §6-9-236.
    Short title of article,
      §6-9-230.
    Stay of enforcement,
      §6-9-234.
  Forms, ARCP, Rule 54 (a).
    Declaratory judgment.
      Form of declarations,
      §6-6-222.
    Default judgments, ARCP,
      Forms 79 to 83.
    Forcible entry and unlawful
      detainer, §6-6-319.
    Offer of judgment, ARCP,
      Forms 86, 87.
    Summary judgment, motion
      for, ARCP, Forms 84, 85.
  Fraternal orders.
    Declaratory actions,
      §10-4-177.
    Repayment and lien for
      unsecured loans from
      parent organization,
      §10-4-178.
  Fraud.
    Agreements to confess
      judgment or authorize
      another to confess
      judgment before
      commencement of action,
      §8-9-11.
    Annulment of illegal
      judgments, §8-9-11.

JUDGMENTS—Cont'd
  Fraud—Cont'd
    Relief from judgment, ARCP,
      Rule 60 (b).
  Full faith and credit clause,
    Const. U. S., Art. IV, §1.
  Garnishment, §§6-6-450 to
    6-6-464.
    See GARNISHMENT.
  Habeas corpus.
    Court not to inquire into
      legal judgment,
      §15-21-23.
  How rendered, ARCP, Rule
    58 (a).
  Illegitimacy.
    Determination of paternity.
      Jurisdiction, §12-15-31.
  Impeachment.
    Judgment of conviction.
      Appeal to supreme court.
        Effect, §36-11-16.
      Effect, §36-11-24.
      Vacancy in office.
        Certification upon final
          judgment, §36-11-23.
  Inadvertence.
    Relief from judgment, ARCP,
      Rule 60 (b).
  Installment payments.
    Malpractice.
      Future damages, §6-5-543.
  Interest.
    Appeals, ARAP, Rule 37.
    Money judgments and costs,
      §8-8-10.
  Judgment by default, ARCP,
    Rule 55; ARCP, Forms 79
    to 83.
  Jury.
    Satisfying or setting aside
      judgments.
      Jury trial on fact issues,
        §6-9-180.
  Juvenile proceedings.
    Modification, ARJP, Rule 27.
  Landlord and tenant.
    Possession wrongfully
      withheld.
      Judgment for landlord,
        §35-9-86.
  Liens.
    Liens for improvements on
      public streets, etc.,
      §35-11-414.
    Registration of judgments.
      Judgment constitutes lien
        on defendant's
        property, §6-9-211.
  Limitation of actions.
    Actions upon.
      Twenty year limitation,
        §6-2-32.
    Arrest or reversal of
      judgment.
      One year limitation from
        arrest or reversal,
        §6-2-38.
    Revival of judgments,
      §6-9-190.
    Savings statute.
      New action after adverse
        decision, §6-2-39.
  Malpractice, §§6-5-540 to
    6-5-552.
    See MALPRACTICE.

JUDGMENTS—Cont'd
  **Mechanics' and
    materialmen's liens,**
    §§35-11-210 to 35-11-234.
    See MECHANICS' AND
      MATERIALMEN'S
      LIENS.
  Mistake.
    Clerical mistakes.
      Relief from judgment,
        ARCP, Rule 60 (a).
    Relief from judgment, ARCP
      Rule 60 (b).
  Motor vehicles.
    Safety-responsibility act,
      §§32-7-1 to 32-7-42.
    See MOTOR VEHICLES.
  **Multiple claims or multiple
    parties,** ARCP, Rule 54
    (b).
    Stay of judgment, ARCP,
      Rule 62 (h).
  Municipal corporations.
    Assessments for public
      improvements,
      §§11-48-100 to 11-48-106
    See MUNICIPAL
      CORPORATIONS.
    Bond issues.
      Validation, §§11-81-220 to
        11-81-227.
    See MUNICIPAL
      CORPORATIONS.
  Newly discovered evidence.
    Relief from judgment, ARCP
      Rule 60 (b).
  Notice, ARCP, Rule 77 (d).
  Nuisances.
    Lewdness, assignation or
      prostitution.
      Action to abate and
        perpetually enjoin,
        §6-5-149.
  Offer of judgment, ARCP,
    Rule 68.
    Forms, ARCP, Forms 86, 87.
  Penitentiary.
    Reversal of judgments.
      Removal of convict,
        §14-3-37.
  Periodic payments.
    Malpractice.
      Future damages, §6-5-543
  Personal property.
    Trial of right of property.
      Execution for amount of
        judgment, §6-6-163.
  Physicians.
    Malpractice judgments,
      §§6-5-480 to 6-5-488,
      34-24-57.
    See MALPRACTICE.
  Pleadings, ARCP, Rule 9 (e).
    Motion for judgment on the
      pleadings, ARCP, Rule
      12 (c).
  Presumptions.
    Satisfaction.
      Judgment presumed
        satisfied 10 years after
        entry or execution,
        §6-9-191.
  **Public officers and
    employees.**
    Vacancies in office.
      Certification of judgment
        declaring office
        vacated, §36-9-15.
  Quieting title, §§6-6-540 to
    6-6-546.
    See QUIETING TITLE.

JUDGMENTS—Cont'd
  Quo warranto, §§6-6-620 to
    6-6-628.
    See QUO WARRANTO.
  Railroads.
    Public service commission.
      Violation of judgment
        regulating railroad's
        business with
        connecting line,
        §37-8-118.
  Real estate brokers.
    Final judgment against
      licensee suspends license,
      §34-27-31.
  Recordation.
    Foreign judgments.
      Recording in probate office,
        §6-9-237.
    Judgment lien on defendant's
      property, §6-9-211.
    Probate judge.
      Registration and indexing.
        Failure to register index,
        §6-9-212.
    Purchasers protected in
      dealing with record
      owner as owner of
      indebtedness, §35-4-64.
    Recordation necessary as to
      judgment creditors,
      §§35-4-90 to 35-4-98.
      See RECORDATION.
    Registration, §§6-9-210 to
      6-9-212.
    Statement of name and
      address of preparer.
      Division not applicable to
        judgments, §35-4-112.
  Records.
    Abolished inferior courts.
      Preserving judgment
        records, §12-20-23.
    Copying of judgments into
      final record not required,
      §12-20-21.
  Registration.
    Judgment lien on defendant's
      property, §6-9-211.
    Probate judge.
      Certificate of clerk or
        register.
        Filing with judge,
        §6-9-210.
      Registration and indexing,
        §6-9-210.
        Failure to register or
          index, §6-9-212.
    Recordation.
      General provisions,
        §§6-9-210 to 6-9-212,
        6-9-237.
      Judgment creditors,
        §§35-4-90 to 35-4-98.
        See RECORDATION.
  Relief from judgment, ARCP,
    Rule 60 (b). ARCP, Rule 60
    (b).
    Clerical mistakes, ARCP,
      Rule 60 (a). ARCP, Rule
      60 (a).
    Excusable neglect, ARCP,
      Rule 60 (b).
    Fraud, ARCP, Rule 60 (b).
    Inadvertence, ARCP, Rule 60
      (b).
    Mistakes, ARCP, Rule 60 (b).
    Newly discovered evidence,
      ARCP, Rule 60 (b).
    Nunc pro tunc, ARCP, Rule
      60 (a).

JUDGMENTS—Cont'd
  Relief from judgment—Cont'd
    Stay on motion for relief,
      ARCP, Rule 62 (b).
  Rendition of judgments,
    ARCP, Rule 58 (a).
  Reversal.
    Procedure upon reversal,
      §12-22-70.
  Revival.
    Executors and
      administrators.
      Issuance of execution
        without revival,
        §6-9-193.
      Revival in favor of
        personal
        representative,
        §6-9-194.
    Judgment of district or
      circuit court on which
      execution did not issue
      within 10 years,
      §6-9-192.
    Limitation, §6-9-190.
    Transferred judgment,
      §6-9-196.
  Rules of civil procedure,
    ARCP, Rules 54 to 63;
    Forms 79 to 83.
    See RULES OF CIVIL
      PROCEDURE.
  Satisfaction of judgment.
    Jury trial on fact issues,
      §6-9-180.
    Presumed satisfied 10 years
      after entry or execution,
      §6-9-191.
    Relief from judgment, ARCP,
      Rule 60 (b).
  Savings statute.
    New action after adverse
      decision, §6-2-39.
  Secured transactions.
    Transactions excluded from
      provisions of article,
      §7-9-104.
  Setting aside.
    Jury trial on fact issues,
      §6-9-180.
  Sewers.
    Liens for improvements on
      public sewers,
      §35-11-414.
  Sheriffs.
    Creditors' actions.
      Complaint for discovery of
        assests.
        Order or judgment,
        §6-6-185.
    Evidence.
      Recitals in sheriff's deed,
        §12-21-99.
  Small claims.
    Default judgments, ASCR,
      Rule K.
    Enforcement of judgments,
      ASCR, Rule L.
  Small loans.
    Confessions of judgment,
      §5-18-16.
  Specific performance.
    Judgment operates as deed to
      convey land without
      conveyance being
      executed, §35-4-33.

JUDGMENTS—Cont'd
  Sports.
    Agents.
      Registration.
        Refusal.
          Effective date of
            orders, §8-26-7.
  State.
    Board of corrections.
      Payment by board of
        adjustment, §41-9-74.
    Judgments against state.
      Generally, §§41-9-60 to
        41-9-74.
      See CLAIMS AGAINST
        STATE.
  **Stay of proceedings to
    enforce a judgment.**
    Affirmation of stayed
      judgment, §§12-22-72 to
      12-22-74.
    Applicability of
      amendatory provisions,
      §12-22-73.1.
    Executions.
      See EXECUTIONS.
    General provisions, ARCP,
      Rule 62.
    Judicial sales.
      See JUDICIAL SALES.
  Streets.
    Liens for improvements on
      public streets,
      §35-11-414.
  Sufficiency of judgment,
    ARCP, Rule 58 (b).
  Summary judgment.
    Affidavits.
      Bad faith affidavits, ARCP,
        Rule 56 (g).
      Form, ARCP, Rule 56 (e).
      When affidavits are
        unavailable, ARCP,
        Rule 56 (f).
    Defense required, ARCP,
      Rule 56 (e).
    For claimant, ARCP, Rule 56
      (a).
    For defending party, ARCP,
      Rule 56 (b).
    Forms.
      Motion for summary
        judgment, ARCP,
        Forms 84, 85.
    Further testimony, ARCP,
      Rule 56 (e).
    Motion for summary
      judgment, ARCP, Rule
      56 (c).
    Case not fully adjudicated
      on motion, ARCP, Rule
      56 (d).
    Forms, ARCP, Forms 84,
      85.
    Sureties entitled to summary
      judgment against
      prinicipal and between
      each other, §8-3-42.
  Suretyship.
    Confession of judgment.
      When surety not to confess
        judgment, §8-3-12.
    Control of judgment by
      endorser upon payment
      of debt, §8-3-10.
    Payment by surety.
      Execution.
        Collection of money from
          principal debtor or
          cosureties, §8-3-41.

JUDGMENTS—Cont'd
  Suretyship—Cont'd
    Payment by surety—Cont'd
      Execution—Cont'd
        Issuance on judgment
          paid by surety,
          §8-3-41.
        Transfer of judgment to
          surety upon, §8-3-40.
      Right of surety paying
        judgment, §6-9-2.
      Rights of surety sued
        separately and paying
        judgment, §8-3-7.
      Summary judgment.
        Sureties entitled to
          summary judgment
          against principal and
          between each other,
          §8-3-42.
  Taxation.
    Actions by state against
      officers.
      Judgment on verdict in
        favor of state,
        §40-1-17.
    Assessments.
      Appeals.
        Judgment of revaluation,
          §40-7-48.
    Sale of land for taxes.
      Rights and remedies of
        purchasers.
        Judgment when party
          claiming adversely
          to tax title has made
          payment or tender,
          §40-10-80.
  Tender.
    Judgment on answer of
      tender, §6-8-100.
  Transfer, §6-9-196.
    Action of revivers, §6-9-196.
    Execution.
      Right of assignee, §6-9-196.
  Trees and timber.
    Condemnation of timber theft
      equipment, §9-13-225.
  Uniform child custody
    jurisdiction act, §§30-3-20
    to 30-3-44.
    See MINORS.
  Uniform enforcement of
    foreign judgment act,
    §§6-9-230 to 6-9-238.
  Vacation of judgment.
    Motion to vacate, ARCP,
      Rule 59 (e), (g).
    Disposition of motion,
      ARCP, Rule 59.1.
    Stay on motion, ARCP,
      Rule 62 (b).
  Venue.
    Action to enjoin judgments,
      §6-3-2.
  Void judgment.
    Relief from judgment, ARCP,
      Rule 60 (b).
  Wills.
    Contesting validity of wills.
      Appeals from probate
        court, §§12-22-20 to
        12-22-27.
      See PROBATE COURTS.
    General provisions,
      §§43-8-190 to 43-8-202.
    See WILLS.
  Workmen's compensation,
    §§25-5-91 to 25-5-93.

JUDICIAL BUILDING
  AUTHORITY, §§41-10-260
  to 41-10-284.
  Acquisition, construction,
    etc., of facilities,
    §41-10-271.
  Board of directors,
    §41-10-265.
    Meetings, §41-10-266.
  Bond issues.
    Authorization, §41-10-268.
    Execution, §41-10-269.
    Fund.
      Creation for payment of
        bond, §41-10-272.
    Investments.
      Lawful investment for
        state, retirement and
        other fiduciary funds,
        §41-10-282.
      Proceeds from sale,
        §41-10-276.
    Issuance, §41-10-268.
    Lawful security for state
      deposits, §41-10-282.
    Negotiable instruments,
      §41-10-280.
    Obligations not debt of state,
      §41-10-281.
    Payment.
      State treasurer to disburse
        funds, §41-10-274.
    Presumption of validity,
      §41-10-278.
    Proceeds.
      Use, §41-10-270.
    Refunding bonds, §41-10-277.
    Revenues pledged to
      payment.
      Collection and application
        of, §41-10-273.
    Rights of holders upon
      default, §41-10-273.
    Sale, §41-10-268.
      Investment of proceeds,
        §41-10-276.
      Use of proceeds,
        §41-10-270.
    Security for bonds,
      §41-10-273.
    Taxation.
      Exemption from taxation,
        §41-10-279.
    Validity.
      Civil action challenging,
        §41-10-278.
      Presumption, §41-10-278.
  Composition, §§41-10-262,
    41-10-265.
  Construction of article.
    Liberal construction,
      §41-10-261.
  Contracts, §41-10-271.
  Definitions, §41-10-260.
  Dissolution, §41-10-284.
    Fees.
      No fees for dissolution,
        §41-10-264.
  Earnings of authority,
    §41-10-283.
  Funds.
    Bond issues.

JUDICIAL COMPENSATION
  COMMISSION, §§12-10-1 to
  12-10-5.
  Chairman, §12-10-1.
  Expenses of members.
    Reimbursement, §12-10-3.

JUDICIAL COMPENSATION
  COMMISSION—Cont'd
  Recommendations to
    legislature.
    Generally, §12-10-4.
    Publication, §12-10-5.
    Recommendations to become
      law upon adjournment of
      legislative, §12-10-5.
    Recordation, §12-10-5.
    When submitted, §12-10-5.
  Subpoenas.
    Powers of members as to
      subpoenas, §12-10-2.
  Witnesses.
    Powers of members as to
      witnesses, §12-10-2.

JUDICIAL CONFERENCE,
  §§12-8-1 to 12-8-6, 41-10-272.
  Chairman, §12-8-5.
  Composition, §12-8-1.
  Creation, §12-8-1.
  Designation of members,
    §12-8-1.
  Duties, §12-8-6.
  Expenses of members.
    Reimbursement, §12-8-4.
  Incorporation, §41-10-262.
    Certificate, §41-10-264.
    Fees.
      No fees for incorporation,
        §41-10-264.
      Procedure, §41-10-263.
  Insurance, §41-10-273.
  Intent of legislature,
    §41-10-261.
  Leases of judicial facilities.
    Conditions, §41-10-275.
    Terms, §§41-10-273,
      41-10-275.
  Legislative oversight
    committee, §41-10-265.
  Maintenance of facilities,
    §41-10-273.
  Meetings, §12-8-5.
  Obligations not debt of state,
    §41-10-281.
  Office.
    Municipal office, §41-10-263.
  Officers, §41-10-265.
  Officers and employees,
    §12-8-5.
  Postage.
    Payment, §12-8-4.
  Powers.
    Generally, §41-10-267.
  Printing expenses.
    Payment, §12-8-4.
  Refunding bonds, §41-10-277.
  Taxation.
    Exemption, §41-10-279.
  Terms of members, §12-8-2.
  Vacancies, §12-8-3.

JUDICIAL INQUIRY
  COMMISSION, AJICR,
    Rules 1 to 18.
  See JUDGES.

JUDICIAL NOTICE.
  Indictments.
    Matters not needing
      statement in indictment,
      §15-8-32.
  Military affairs.
    Courts-martial.
      Signature and handwriting
        of commissioned
        officers of national
        guard, §31-2-98.

JUDICIAL NOTICE—Cont'd
Municipal corporations.
Class I municipalities.
Ordinances.
Judicial notice of,
§11-45-11.
Municipal courts.
Ordinances.
Courts to take judicial
notice of ordinances of
municipality, §12-14-7.

JUDICIAL SALES.
Abstracts of title, §6-8-30.
Affidavits.
Notices.
Publication, §6-8-65.
Bulk transfers.
Transfers excepted from
article, §7-6-103.
Commercial code.
Bulk transfers.
Transfers excepted from
article, §7-6-103.
Constitution of Alabama.
Value of property exempted
from sale under legal
process, Const. Ala., art.
IV, §92.
Costs.
Abstracts of title, §6-8-30.
Notices.
Publication, §§6-8-60 to
6-8-69.
Evidence.
Notices.
Newspapers as evidence of
publication, §6-8-67.
Execution sales, §§6-9-80 to
6-9-150.
See EXECUTIONS.
**Executors and
administrators.**
Notice in probate court,
§6-8-68.
**Exemptions from levy and
sale under process,**
§§6-10-1 to 6-10-43.
See EXEMPTIONS FROM
LEVY AND SALE
UNDER PROCESS.
Fees.
Collection of fees from
proceeds of sales,
§12-19-23.
Fraud.
Report of officer making sale.
Sufficiency as note of
contract, §8-9-4.
Guardian and ward.
Notice to guardians in
probate court, §6-8-68.
Hours of sale, §6-8-41.
Notices, §§6-8-60 to 6-8-69.
Newspapers.
Copies to be furnished to
parties, §6-8-66.
Designation of newspaper,
§6-8-60.
Disregard by officer,
§6-8-60.
Evidence of publication,
§6-8-67.
Subscribing, taking and
filing by probate
judges, §6-8-40.
Suspension or
discontinuance before
publication made or
completed, §6-8-63.

JUDICIAL SALES—Cont'd
Notices—Cont'd
Postponement.
Publication of original
notice, §6-8-69.
Publication.
Costs.
Affidavit, §6-8-65.
Applicability of
provisions, §6-8-64.
Rates, §6-8-64.
Evidence.
Newspapers as evidence
of publication,
§6-8-67.
Executors, administrators
and guardians in
probate court, §6-8-68.
Length, §6-8-61.
Exception, §6-8-61.
Specification of weeks
and days, §6-8-62.
Newspapers, §§6-8-40,
6-8-60 to 6-8-69.
Postponement of sale.
Publication of original
notice, §6-8-69.
Requirements.
Publications required by
law, mortgage or
contract, §6-8-60.
Time for publication prior
to proceeding or act to
be done, §6-8-62.
Postponement, §6-8-69.
**Redemption of real
property,** §§6-5-247 to
6-5-257.
See REAL PROPERTY.
Taxation.
Sale of land for taxes,
§§40-10-1 to 40-10-166.
See TAXATION.

JUDICIAL SYSTEM STUDY
COMMISSION, §§12-9-1 to
12-9-9.
Appointment of members,
§12-9-2.
Chairman, §12-9-4.
Authorized to apply for
grants, §12-9-6.
Composition, §12-9-2.
Consultants, §12-9-7.
Coordination of studies.
Agency for coordination,
§12-9-5.
Creation, §12-9-1.
Duties, §12-9-1.
Executive committee, §12-9-4.
Expenses of members.
Reimbursement, §12-9-3.
Experts.
Employment, §12-9-7.
Funds.
Use of appropriated funds,
§12-9-9.
Grants.
Chairman authorized to
apply for grants, §12-9-6.
Commission to serve as
agency for grants,
§12-9-5.
Use of appropriated grants,
§12-9-9.
Law institute.
Assistance of commission by
institute, §12-9-7.
Legislative reference service.
Assistance of commission by
service, §12-9-7.

JUDICIAL SYSTEM STUDY
COMMISSION—Cont'd
Recommendations, §12-9-8.
Reports, §12-9-8.
Research analyst, §12-9-7.
Secretary, §12-9-4.
Studies.
Agency for conduct and
coordination of studies,
§12-9-5.
Terms of members, §12-9-2.
Vice-chairman, §12-9-4.

JUKE BOXES.
Municipal corporations.
Licenses, §§11-51-98,
11-51-100.
Regulation and control of
vending machines on
which music is played,
§11-51-100.

JUNIOR COLLEGES, §§16-60-1
to 16-60-270.
**Alabama trade school and
junior college authority,**
§§16-60-80 to 16-60-96.
Bond issues.
Trade school and junior
college authority,
§§16-60-90 to 16-60-93.
Buildings.
Approval of plans, §16-60-89.
Expenditures for building,
§16-60-89.
Chancellor.
Appointment, §16-60-111.1.
Chief executive officer of
postsecondary education
department,
§16-60-111.5.
Delegation of decision
making authority to
chancellor, §16-60-111.6.
Powers and duties,
§§16-60-111.1,
16-60-111.5.
Qualifications, §16-60-111.1.
Responsibility for operation
of junior colleges and
trade schools,
§16-60-111.2.
Salary, §16-60-111.3.
Term of office, §16-60-111.1.
**Commission of higher
education.**
General provisions, §§16-5-1
to 16-5-14.
Student loan program,
§§16-33B-3, 16-33B-4.
Contracts.
Competitive bidding,
§16-60-89.
Control, §§16-60-110 to
16-60-114.
Definitions.
Management and control,
§16-60-110.
Trade school and junior
college authority,
§16-60-81.
DeKalb county, §§16-60-50 to
16-60-67.
Equipment.
Expenditures for equipping,
§16-60-89.
Faculty.
Appointment of faculty and
staff, §16-60-111.7.
Qualifications, §16-60-111.7.

JUNIOR COLLEGES—Cont'd
Franklin, Marion and
Winston counties,
§§16-60-20 to 16-60-40.
Accounts of officers,
§16-60-33.
Appropriations, §16-60-26.
Board of trustees.
Appointment of trustees,
§16-60-20.
Compensation of members,
§16-60-21.
Composition, §16-60-20.
Control of college,
§16-60-28.
Establishment, §16-60-20.
Expenses of members,
§16-60-21.
Governor to be ex officio
chairman, §16-60-21.
Meetings, §16-60-21.
Officers.
Governor to be ex officio
chairman, §16-60-21.
Initial officers,
§16-60-20.
Vice-president,
§16-60-21.
Organization, §16-60-20.
Reports, §16-60-37.
Terms of members,
§16-60-21.
Bonds, surety.
Treasurer of college,
§16-60-31.
Certificates, §16-60-36.
Commencement of
operations.
Date of commencement of
operations, §16-60-22.
Control of college, §16-60-28.
Conversion to trade school
and junior college.
Action of state board of
education upon
petition, §16-60-39.
Authority of board of
trustees if petition
granted, §16-60-38.
Conflicting laws,
§16-60-40.
Control of trade school and
junior college,
§16-60-39.
Liberal construction of
sections concerning
conversions, §16-60-40.
Management and control of
trade school and junior
college, §16-60-39.
Petition, §16-60-38.
Sections concerning trade
school supplemental,
§16-60-40.
Courses of instruction.
Programs to be offered,
§16-60-27.
Diplomas, §16-60-36.
Donations, §16-60-24.
Employees.
Exemption from jury duty
and town licenses,
§16-60-35.
Faculty.
Appointment by president,
§16-60-29.
Compensation, §16-60-29.
Exemption from jury duty
and town licenses,
§16-60-35.

JUNIOR COLLEGES—Cont'd
Franklin, Marion and
Winston counties—Cont'd
Fees.
Matriculation, library and
laboratory fees,
§16-60-34.
Funds.
Use of public school funds,
§16-60-26.
Gifts, §16-60-24.
Incorporation of college,
§16-60-23.
Jury duty.
Exemption of officers,
teachers and
employees from jury
duty, §16-60-35.
Laboratory fees, §16-60-34.
Library fees, §16-60-34.
Licenses.
Exemption of officers,
teachers and
employees from town
licenses, §16-60-35.
Location.
Selecting location,
§16-60-22.
Matriculation fees, §16-60-34.
Officers.
Accounts, §16-60-33.
Compensation, §16-60-29.
Exemption from jury duty
and town licenses,
§16-60-35.
President of college,
§§16-60-28, 16-60-29.
Secretary of college,
§16-60-30.
Treasurer of college,
§§16-60-31, 16-60-32.
Petitions.
Conversion to trade school
and junior college,
§16-60-38.
President of college.
Appointment, §16-60-28.
Faculty.
Appointment of faculty,
§16-60-29.
Qualifications, §16-60-28.
Removal, §16-60-28.
Term of office, §16-60-28.
Programs to be offered,
§16-60-27.
Property.
Exemption from taxation,
§16-60-35.
Sale of property, §16-60-24.
Public school funds.
Use of public school funds,
§16-60-26.
Records.
Accounts of officers,
§16-60-33.
Reports, §16-60-37.
Rules and regulations,
§16-60-25.
Secretary of college,
§16-60-30.
Taxation.
Exemption of college
property from taxation,
§16-60-35.
Trade school.
Conversion to trade school
and junior college,
§§16-60-38 to 16-60-40.
Treasurer of college,
§16-60-31.
Removal, §16-60-32.

JUNIOR COLLEGES—Cont'd
Funds.
Authority to borrow in
anticipation of current
revenues, §16-60-113.
Gadsden State Community
College.
Merger of institutions.
Educational institution
resulting from,
§16-60-270.
College designated and
named, §16-60-270.
Gadsden State Junior
College.
Merger of institutions,
§16-60-270.
New college designated
and named,
§16-60-270.
Governor.
Junior college for Franklin,
Marion and Winston
counties.
Board of trustees.
Governor ex officio
chairman, §16-60-21.
Institute for deaf and blind.
Education and training of
handicapped persons,
§21-1-9.
Interpretation of article,
§16-60-112.
Jackson and DeKalb
counties, §§16-60-50 to
16-60-67.
Accounts of officers,
§16-60-63.
Annual reports, §16-60-67.
Appropriations by counties
and municipalities
therein for college,
§16-60-56.
Bequests to college,
§16-60-54.
Board of trustees.
Appointment of trustees,
§16-60-50.
Compensation of members,
§16-60-51.
Composition, §16-60-50.
Establishment, §16-60-50.
Expenses of members,
§16-60-51.
Governor.
Ex officio chairman,
§16-60-51.
Meetings, §16-60-51.
Officers, §16-60-51.
Organization, §16-60-51.
Reports, §16-60-67.
State superintendent of
education.
Member of board,
§16-60-50.
Terms of members,
§16-60-51.
Vice-president, §16-60-51.
Bonds, surety.
Treasurer of college,
§16-60-61.
Certificates, §16-60-66.
Commencement of operations
of college.
Date of commencement,
§16-60-52.
Compensation.
Secretary of college,
§16-60-60.
Treasurer of college,
§16-60-61.

JUNIOR COLLEGES—Cont'd
Jackson and DeKalb counties—Cont'd
Control of college, §16-60-58.
Courses of instruction.
Programs to be offered, §16-60-57.
Devises to college, §16-60-54.
Diplomas, §16-60-66.
Donations to college, §16-60-54.
Employees, §16-60-65.
Faculty.
Appointment, §16-60-59.
Compensation, §16-60-59.
Exemption of teachers from jury duty and town licenses, §16-60-65.
Jury duty.
Exemption from jury duty, §16-60-65.
Licenses.
Exemption of teachers from town licenses, §16-60-65.
Fees.
Matriculation, library and laboratory fees, §16-60-64.
General assembly.
Reports to legislature, §16-60-67.
Gifts to college, §16-60-54.
Incorporation of college, §16-60-53.
Jury duty.
Exemptions, §16-60-65.
Laboratory fees, §16-60-64.
Library fees, §16-60-64.
Licenses.
Exemptions from town licenses, §16-60-65.
Location of college.
Selecting location, §16-60-52.
Matriculation fees, §16-60-64.
Minimum standards, §16-60-57.
Officers.
Accounts of officers, §16-60-63.
Appointment, §16-60-59.
Compensation, §16-60-59.
Exemption from jury duty and town licenses, §16-60-65.
Jury duty.
Exemption from jury duty, §16-60-65.
Licenses.
Exemption from town licenses, §16-60-65.
President of college, §§16-60-58, 16-60-59.
Secretary of college, §§16-60-60, 16-60-63.
Treasurer of college, §§16-60-61 to 16-60-63.
President of college, §§16-60-58, 16-60-59.
Programs to be offered, §16-60-57.
Property.
Exemption of college property from taxation, §16-60-65.
Sale of property, §16-60-54.
Public school funds.
Use of public school funds, §16-60-56.

JUNIOR COLLEGES—Cont'd
Jackson and DeKalb counties—Cont'd
Records.
Accounts of officers, §16-60-63.
Reports.
Generally, §16-60-67.
Rules and regulations, §16-60-55.
Secretary of college, §§16-60-60, 16-60-63.
Taxation.
Exemption of college property from taxation, §16-60-65.
Treasurer of college.
Accounts, §16-60-63.
Bond, §16-60-61.
Compensation, §16-60-61.
Duties, §16-60-61.
Election by board of trustees, §16-60-61.
Removal, §16-60-62.
Term of office, §16-60-61.
Vocational education, §16-60-57.
Loans.
Authority to borrow in anticipation of current revenues, §16-60-113.
Location.
Determination by trade school and junior college authority, §16-60-88.
Management and control.
Borrowing money.
Authority to borrow in anticipation of current revenues, §16-60-113.
Definitions, §16-60-110.
Interpretation of sections 16-60-110 and 16-60-111, §16-60-112.
Teachers' salaries.
Authority to borrow in anticipation of current revenues, §16-60-113.
Marion county, §§16-60-20 to 16-60-40.
Military affairs.
National guard.
Educational assistance, §§31-10-1 to 31-10-4.
National guard.
Educational assistance, §§31-10-1 to 31-10-4.
Police.
General provisions, §§16-22-1, 16-22-2.
Retirement.
Teachers' retirement system.
Purchase of service credit by employees.
Leave of absence time, §16-25-11.3.
Total years of service, §16-25-13.1.
Rules and regulations.
Franklin, Marion and Winston counties, §16-60-25.
Jackson and DeKalb counties, §16-60-55.
Salaries.
Teacher's salaries.
Authority to borrow in anticipation of current revenues, §16-60-113.

JUNIOR COLLEGES—Cont'd
School buses.
Transportation of students on public school buses, §16-27-2.
Sites.
When sites must be donated, §16-60-88.
Snead junior college, §§16-60-150 to 16-60-152.
Southern union college, §§16-60-130 to 16-60-132.
State board of education.
Management and control of colleges,
Generally, §§16-60-110 to 16-60-114.
Superintendent of education.
Exclusive authority, §16-60-111.8.
Teachers.
Salaries.
Authority to borrow in anticipation of current revenues, §16-60-113.
Teachers' retirement system.
Purchase of service credit by employees.
Leave of absence time, §16-25-11.3.
Total years of service, §16-25-13.1.
Trade school and junior college authority, §§16-60-80 to 16-60-96.
Bond issues, §§16-60-90 to 16-60-93.
Authorization to issue, §16-60-90.
Deposit of proceeds, §16-60-93.
Disbursements from proceeds, §16-60-93.
Execution, §16-60-91.
Form, §16-60-91.
Investments.
Bonds legal investments, §16-60-91.
Proceeds.
Deposit, §16-60-93.
Disbursements from, §16-60-93.
Use, §16-60-91.
Refunding bonds, §16-60-92.
Sale, §16-60-91.
Security, §16-60-91.
Terms, §16-60-91.
Use of proceeds, §16-60-91.
Buildings, §16-60-89.
Certificate of incorporation.
Issuance, §16-60-85.
Citation of article, §16-60-80.
Contracts.
Competitive bidding, §16-60-89.
Definitions, §16-60-81.
Disbursement of funds, §16-60-95.
Dissolution, §16-60-96.
Equipment.
Expenditures for equipping trade schools and junior colleges, §16-60-89.
Expenditures.
Building and equipping, §16-60-89.
Findings of fact.
Legislative findings of fact, §16-60-82.

JUNIOR COLLEGES—Cont'd
Trade school and junior college authority—Cont'd
Funds.
  Disbursement of funds, §16-60-95.
  Revenues of authority, §16-60-94.
Incorporation.
  Authorization to form public corporation, §16-60-83.
  Certificate of incorporation. Issuance, §16-60-85.
  Manner of incorporation, §16-60-84.
Investments.
  Bonds legal investments, §16-60-91.
Legislative findings of fact and declaration of intent, §16-60-82.
Location of trade schools and junior colleges, §16-60-88.
Members, §16-60-86.
Officers, §16-60-86.
Powers, §16-60-87.
Proceedings, §16-60-86.
Refunding bonds, §16-60-92.
Revenues of authority, §16-60-94.
  Disbursement of funds, §16-60-95.
Short title of article, §16-60-80.
Sites for trade schools and junior colleges.
  Must be donated, §16-60-86.
Wenonah State Junior College.
  Wenonah state technical junior college designated Wenonah state junior college, §16-60-3.
Wenonah State Technical Junior College.
  Designated Wenonah state junior college, §16-60-3.
Winston county, §§16-60-20 to 16-60-40.

JUNK DEALERS.
Junkyard control, §§23-1-240 to 23-1-251.
  See JUNKYARD CONTROL.
Licenses, §40-12-116.
Milk and milk products.
  Marked containers.
    Possession by junk dealer, §8-12-42.
Salvage generally, §§35-13-1 to 35-13-10.
  See SALVAGE.

JUNKYARD CONTROL, §§23-1-240 to 23-1-250.
Acquisition of land.
  Authority of highway director, §23-1-248.
  Manner of acquisition, §23-1-248.
Citation of division, §23-1-240.
Construction of division, §23-1-251.
Declaration of policy, §23-1-242.
Definitions, §23-1-241.

JUNKYARD CONTROL —Cont'd
Eminent domain.
  Acquisition of land.
    Authority of director, §23-1-248.
Existing junkyards.
  Screening, §23-1-246.
Gifts.
  Acquisition of land.
    Authority of director, §23-1-248.
Licenses.
  Conditions, §23-1-245.
  Fee, §23-1-244.
  Issuance, §23-1-244.
    Conditions, §23-1-245.
  Renewal, §23-1-244.
  Required, §23-1-243.
  Revocation, §23-1-244.
Nuisances.
  Abatement, §23-1-250.
  Nonconforming junkyards, §23-1-242.
Penalties.
  Violations of division, §23-1-250.
Policy.
  Declaration of policy, §23-1-242.
Purchases.
  Acquisition of land.
    Authority of director, §23-1-248.
Rules and regulations.
  Promulgation.
    Director of highways, §23-1-249.
    Screening, §23-1-247.
Screening.
  Existing junkyards, §23-1-246.
  Rules and regulations.
    Promulgation, §23-1-247.
Short title of division, §23-1-240.
United States.
  Agreements with department of transportation.
    Authority to enter into agreements, §23-1-249.

JURISDICTION.
Alabama agricultural and mechanical university.
  Board of trustees.
    Exclusive jurisdiction, §16-49-24.
Alabama State University.
  Board of trustees.
    Exclusive jurisdiction, §16-50-24.
Alcoholic beverages.
  Dry counties.
    Abatement of liquor nuisances.
      Powers of court, §28-4-231.
Ameraport.
  Offshore harbor and terminal commission, §33-10-17.
Attorneys at law.
  Disciplinary proceedings.
    Rules of disciplinary enforcement, ARDE, Rule 1.
Aviation.
  Crimes and torts, §4-2-4.

JURISDICTION—Cont'd
Boats.
  District courts.
    Jurisdiction of offenses, §33-5-32.
Child custody.
  Uniform child custody jurisdiction act, §§30-3-20 to 30-3-44.
  See MINORS.
Circuit courts, §§12-11-30 to 12-11-61.
  See CIRCUIT COURTS.
Claims by and against state.
  Board of adjustment, §41-9-62.
Commercial code.
  Secured transactions.
    Multiple state transactions.
      Perfection of security interest, §7-9-103.
Conservators.
  Appointment by court, §26-2A-130.
  Probate court.
    Appointment of conservator, §26-2A-130.
    Settlements of accounts, §26-5-1.
      Death of conservator, §26-5-50.
    Settlements of accounts of guardians.
      Compulsion of settlement, §26-5-30.
  Uniform guardianship and protective proceedings act.
    General provisions. See within this heading, "Guardian and ward."
Constitution of Alabama.
  See CONSTITUTION OF ALABAMA.
Corporations.
  Liquidation.
    Assets and business of corporation, §10-2A-195.
    Nonprofit corporations, §10-3A-149.
Counties.
  Industrial parks, §11-23-6.
  Navigable streams not within limits of any county, §11-1-3.
Court of civil appeals, Const. Ala., amd. 328.
  Appellate jurisdiction, §12-3-10.
  Original jurisdiction, §12-3-11.
Court of criminal appeals, Const. Ala., amd. 328.
  Appellate jurisdiction, §12-3-9.
  Original jurisdiction, §12-3-11.
Courts-martial.
  Military affairs.
    Militia.
      Courts-martial when militia in active service, §31-2-83.
    National guard, §§31-2-92, 31-2-103.
Criminal jurisdiction.
  All persons liable for offenses committed in Alabama, §15-2-1.

JURISDICTION—Cont'd
Criminal jurisdiction—Cont'd
Vesting, §12-1-3.
Decedents' estates.
Probate courts, §12-13-1.
Defenses.
Lack of jurisdiction, ARCP,
Rule 12 (b), (h).
Litigation on merits after
loss on defense not bar
to raising of same
defense on appeal,
§6-8-101.
Diseases.
Notifiable diseases.
Commitment.
Probate court to retain
jurisdiction over
person committed,
§22-11A-33.
District courts, §§12-12-30 to
12-12-36.
See DISTRICT COURTS.
Domestic relations.
Protection from abuse.
Court jurisdiction, §30-5-3.
Education.
Truancy.
Juvenile court jurisdiction,
§16-28-21.
Elections.
Contests.
Judges or courts exercising
chancery powers.
Jurisdiction denied,
§17-15-6.
Executors and
administrators.
Probate courts, §12-13-1.
Forcible entry and unlawful
detainer.
District courts, §6-6-330.
Foreign causes of action.
Enforcement when
jurisdiction of defendant
can be obtained in this
state, §6-5-430.
Funerals.
Prosecutions under chapter,
§34-13-5.
Guardian and ward.
Probate court, §12-13-1.
Uniform guardianship and
protective proceedings
act.
Conservators.
Submission to by
accepting
appointment,
§26-2A-141.
Incapacitated persons.
Guardians.
Concurrent jurisdiction
where ward
resides,
§26-2A-111.
Submission to court
upon accepting
appointment,
§26-2A-106.
Minors.
Guardians.
Proceedings
subsequent to
appointment,
§26-2A-80.
Submission to court
upon acceptance of
appointment,
§26-2A-77.

JURISDICTION—Cont'd
Guardian and ward—Cont'd
Uniform guardianship and
protective proceedings
act—Cont'd
Probate court.
Subject matter
jurisdiction,
§26-2A-31.
Protective proceedings.
Business affairs of
protected persons,
§26-2A-131.
Subject matter jurisdiction
of court, §26-2A-31.
Habeas corpus.
Ouster of jurisdiction of
nearest judge, §15-21-7.
Harbors and ports.
State docks department,
§33-1-11.
Health.
State board of health,
§22-2-2.
History and archives.
Tannehill furnace and
foundry commission,
§41-9-325.
Hospital liens.
Jurisdiction to determine
matters connected with
lien, §35-11-373.
Insurance.
Insurers.
Delinquency proceedings,
§27-32-3.
Jacksonville State
University.
Board of trustees.
Transfer to board,
§16-52-7.
Justices of the peace, Const.
Ala., art. VI, §168.
Increasing jurisdiction.
Special, private or local
laws prohibited, Const.
Ala., art. IV, §104.
Juvenile proceedings,
§§12-12-34, 12-15-2,
12-15-30 to 12-15-36.
See JUVENILE
PROCEEDINGS.
Lack of jurisdiction.
Defense of lack of
jurisdiction, ARCP, Rule
12 (b), (h).
Liens for improvements on
public streets, etc.,
§35-11-413.
Livingston University.
Transfer to board of trustees,
§16-53-7.
Mechanics' and
materialmen's liens.
Actions for enforcement of
liens, §35-11-220.
Mentally ill.
Involuntary commitment.
Retention of jurisdiction by
probate court,
§22-52-11.
Military affairs.
Militia.
Courts-martial.
When militia in active
service of state,
§31-2-83.
National guard.
Courts-martial, §§31-2-92,
31-2-103.

JURISDICTION—Cont'd
Minors.
Child custody.
Uniform child custody
jurisdiction act,
§§30-3-20 to 30-3-44.
See MINORS.
Motor vehicle carriers.
Examiners, §37-3-9.
Motor vehicles.
Trucks, trailers and semi-
trailers.
Violations of chapter.
Courts having
jurisdiction, §32-9-4.
Municipal corporations.
Annexation.
Cities of twenty-five
thousand inhabitants
or more.
City over annexed
territory, §11-42-72.
Police jurisdiction,
§§11-40-10, 11-47-22.
County industrial parks
not subject to,
§11-23-6.
Reduction of corporate limits,
§11-42-212.
Subdivisions.
Exclusive jurisdiction of
planning commission,
§11-52-36.
Territorial jurisdiction of
planning commissions,
§11-52-30.
Municipal courts, §12-14-1;
Const. Ala., amd. 328.
Criminal jurisdiction.
Vesting, §12-1-3.
Nonresidents.
Suits against state, Const. U.
S., Amendment XI.
Notaries public.
Territorial jurisdiction,
§36-20-30.
Partition.
Circuit courts, §35-6-20.
Probate courts, §12-13-1.
Pilots and pilotage.
State pilotage commission.
Harbor masters.
No jurisdiction, §33-4-10.
Territorial jurisdiction,
§33-4-9.
Preliminary hearings.
District court jurisdiction,
§15-11-2.
Probate courts.
Conservators.
Settlement of accounts,
§26-5-1.
Death of conservators,
§26-5-50.
Settlement of accounts of
guardians.
Compulsion of
settlement, §26-5-30.
Federal service.
Person in federal service,
§12-13-2.
Generally, §12-13-1; Const.
Ala., amd. 328.
Guardian and ward,
§12-13-1.
Uniform guardianship and
protective proceedings
act.
Subject matter
jurisdiction,
§26-2A-31.

JURISDICTION—Cont'd
Probate courts—Cont'd
Water management and
drainage districts.
Jurisdiction to establish,
§9-9-5.
**Public officers and
employees.**
Code of ethics.
Actions for violations of
chapter, §36-25-27.
Public service commission.
Exemptions, §§37-1-33 to
37-1-37.
See PUBLIC SERVICE
COMMISSION.
Rules of civil procedure.
Defense of lack of
jurisdiction, ARCP, Rule
12 (b), (h).
Jurisdiction unaffected,
ARCP, Rule 82 (a).
Secured transactions.
Multiple state transactions.
Perfection of security
interest, §7-9-103.
Sewers.
Liens for improvements on
public sewers,
§35-11-413.
Ships and shipping.
District courts.
Jurisdiction of offenses,
§33-5-32.
State.
Maintenance and defense of
state jurisdiction,
§41-1-2.
Sovereignty and jurisdiction
of state, §41-1-1.
Streets.
Liens for improvements on
public streets,
§35-11-413.
Supreme court.
Certified questions from
federal courts, ARAP,
Rule 18 (b).
Generally, §12-2-7; Const.
Ala., art. VI, §140.
Troy State University.
Board of trustees.
Transfer of jurisdiction,
etc., to board, §16-56-7.
Truancy.
Juvenile court jurisdiction,
§16-28-21.
**Uniform guardianship and
protective proceedings
act.**
General provisions,
§§26-2A-1 to 26-2A-160.
**University of North
Alabama.**
Board of trustees.
Transfer of jurisdiction,
§16-51-7.
**USS Alabama battleship
commission.**
Exclusive control over
battleship, park, etc.,
§41-9-348.
Venue.
General provisions.
See VENUE.

JURY, §§12-16-1 to 12-16-233.
Advisory jury, ARCP, Rule 39
(c).
Motion for trial by advisory
jury.
Form, ARCP, Form 69.
Age.
Challenges of jurors,
§12-16-150.
Qualifications of jurors,
§12-16-60.
Alternate jurors.
Selection, ARCP, Rule 47 (b).
Appeals.
Charge to jury, §12-16-13.
Disqualification of jurors,
§12-16-60.
Attorneys at law.
Relation of juror to attorney,
§12-16-150.
Bribery.
Bribing, §13A-10-125.
Jurors.
Bribing a juror,
§13A-10-125.
Receiving a bribe,
§13A-10-126.
Capital cases.
Challenges.
Grounds for challenge by
state, §12-16-152.
Jury participation in
sentence hearing.
Waiver by defendant,
§13A-5-44.
Selection and separation,
§13A-5-44.
Cemeteries.
County cemeteries.
Appeals from assessment of
damages.
Establishment of
damages, §11-17-10.
Summoning and
impaneling,
§11-17-9.
Challenges.
Capital cases.
Grounds for challenge by
state, §12-16-152.
Challenges for cause.
Grounds, §12-16-150.
Additional grounds for
challenge by,
§12-16-152.
Manner of proof,
§12-16-151.
Charge to jury, §12-16-11;
ARCP, Rule 51.
Appeals, §12-16-13.
Criminal cases.
Appeals.
Presumption that
written charges
asked before jury
retired, §12-22-132.
Filing.
When charge must be
written and filed in
record, §12-16-12.
General charges, §12-16-13.
Lesser included offenses,
§13A-1-9.
Motions by parties,
§12-16-13.
Circuit courts.
Civil cases.
Fees, §12-19-110.
Citizenship.
Qualifications of jurors,
§12-16-60.

JURY—Cont'd
Civil actions.
Fees, §§12-19-110 to
12-19-113.
Selection of juries in civil
actions, §12-16-140.
Striking jurors, §12-16-140.
Commissions.
County jury commissions,
§§12-16-30 to 12-16-51.
Compensation of jurors,
§12-16-8.
Constitution of Alabama.
Discharge of juries from
cases, Const. Ala., art. I,
§9.
Exemption from jury duty.
Special, private or local
laws prohibited, Const.
Ala., art. IV, §104.
**Constitution of the United
States.**
Jury of vicinage, Const. U.
S., Amendment VI.
Continuation of case.
Failure of sheriff to summon
juror or failure of juror
summoned to attend
trial, §12-16-81.
Convicted persons.
Qualifications of jurors,
§12-16-60.
Coroner's inquest, §§15-4-1 to
15-4-11.
See CORONERS.
Counties.
Cemeteries.
Appeals from assessment of
damages.
Establishment of
damages by jury,
§11-17-10.
Summoning and
impaneling of jurors,
§11-17-9.
County jury commissions,
§§12-16-30 to 12-16-51.
Absence of members.
Appointment of persons to
act as members,
§12-16-36.
Appointment of members,
§12-16-32.
Persons to act as members
in event of absence,
§12-16-36.
Successors, §12-16-35.
Clerks of commissions.
Authority for employment,
§12-16-37.
Clerical assistance,
§12-16-37.
Compensation, §12-16-37.
Clerks not to be paid for
Sundays, §12-16-40.
Discharge, §12-16-40.
Clerks to devote such
time as required by
commissions,
§12-16-40.
Oath of office, §12-16-38.
Commissioning of members,
§12-16-33.
Compensation of members,
§12-16-34.
Compilation and
maintenance of master
list, §12-16-145.
Composition, §12-16-31.
Disqualification of members,
§12-16-35.

JURY—Cont'd
County jury commissions
—Cont'd
Dual office holding
prohibited, §12-16-31.
Duties, §12-16-34.
Failure of clerk or member
to perform duty,
§12-16-51.
Establishment, §12-16-30.
Influence.
Attempting to influence
commissioner or other
officer, §12-16-85.
Jury box.
General provisions,
§§12-16-44, 12-16-45,
12-16-58 to 12-16-90.
Jury roll.
General provisions,
§§12-16-44, 12-16-46 to
14-16-48.
Names of persons empaneled
on juries.
Certification to commission
by court clerks,
§12-16-47.
Oath of members, §12-16-33.
President of commission,
§12-16-33.
Qualifications of jurors.
Determination by
commission, §12-16-60.
Qualifications of members,
§12-16-31.
Quorum, §12-16-33.
Records.
Preservation of records
concerning selection
and service of jurors,
§12-16-64.
Sickness of members.
Appointment of persons to
act as members,
§12-16-36.
Supplies.
Probate judge to purchase
supplies for
commission, §12-16-50.
Terms of members,
§12-16-32.
Unqualified persons.
Taxing of cost of
summoning of
unqualified person,
§12-16-49.
Vacancies, §12-16-35.
Witnesses.
Failure of person to attend
or testify before
commission, §12-16-51.
Courts.
When words "jury" or
"juries" include court or
judge, §12-16-1.
Criminal cases.
Capital cases.
Challenges.
Grounds for challenge by
state, §12-16-152.
Jury participation in
sentence hearing.
Waiver by defendant,
§13A-5-44.
Selection and separation,
§13A-5-44.
Drawing, selection and
empaneling of juries.
Generally, §12-16-100.

JURY—Cont'd
Criminal cases—Cont'd
Drawing, selection and
empaneling of juries
—Cont'd
Where two or more persons
tried jointly,
§12-16-101.
Fees, §§12-19-210, 12-19-211.
Joint trial.
Drawing, selection and
empaneling of juries,
§12-16-101.
Verdict.
See VERDICT.
Dams.
Erection of dams for mills,
gins, factories, etc.,
§§18-2-1 to 18-2-21.
See DAMS.
Data processing equipment.
Use for selecting, qualifying,
etc., juries, §12-16-146.
Death penalty.
Capital cases.
Challenges.
Grounds for challenge by
state, §12-16-152.
Jury participation in
sentence hearing.
Waiver by defendant,
§13A-5-44.
Selection and separation,
§13A-5-44.
Defined, §1-1-1.
Demand for trial by jury,
ARCP, Rule 38 (b).
Form, ARCP, Form 68.
Specification of issues,
ARCP, Rule 38 (c).
Discharge, §12-16-233; Const.
Ala., art. I, §9.
After retirement of jury,
§12-16-231.
Consent by parties to
discharge of member of
jury, §12-16-232.
Prior to retirement of jury,
§12-16-230.
Replacements.
Summoning of replacement
prior to retirement of
jury, §12-16-230.
Discrimination.
Prohibited in selection of
jury, §12-16-56.
Diseases.
Qualifications of jurors,
§12-16-60.
Disqualification of jurors.
Alternate plan, §12-16-145.
Appeals, §12-16-60.
Citizens of state, counties,
cities, etc., not
disqualified as interested
in actions in which state,
county, city, etc., a party
or interested, §12-16-3.
County jury commissions.
Certification to commission
by court clerks of
names of persons found
disqualified, §12-16-48.
Probate court jurors,
§12-16-78.
**Drawing of names from jury
box,** §§12-16-59, 12-16-70
to 12-16-90.

JURY—Cont'd
Elections.
Contests, §§17-15-20 to
17-15-35.
See ELECTIONS.
Eminent domain.
Demand for trial by jury,
§18-1A-151.
Highest and best use.
Jury issue, §18-1A-174.
Procedures.
Generally, §18-1A-151.
Waiver, §18-1A-151.
Empaneling jurors,
§12-16-74; ARCP, Rule 47
(b).
Criminal cases, §12-16-100.
Powers of jurors empaneled
under article, §12-16-90.
Probate court jurors.
Certification to jury
commission of names
of persons empaneled,
§12-16-78.
Provisions of article as to
empaneling of jurors
directory, §12-16-90.
Employers and employees.
Compensation to which
employees entitled
during jury service,
§12-16-8.
Discharge of employee on
jury duty forbidden,
§12-16-8.1.
Employee's cause of action
upon discharge.
Damages, §12-16-8.1.
Provision supplemental to
other law, §12-16-8.1.
Excusing of employees for
jury service, §12-16-8.
When employee must return
to work, §12-16-8.1.
Evidence.
Taking of written evidence
by jury on retirement,
§12-16-14.
Examination of jurors,
ARCP, Rule 47 (a).
Excusing from jury service,
§12-16-63.
Hearing of excuses,
§12-16-74.
**Executors and
administrators.**
Insolvent estates.
Trial of issue of insolvency
to be by jury,
§43-2-705.
Removal.
When entitled to jury trial,
§43-2-296.
Exemption from jury duty.
County jury commissions.
Certification to commission
of names of persons,
§12-16-48.
Hearing of claims of
exemptions, §12-16-74.
Junior college for Franklin,
Marion and Winston
counties.
Exemption of officers,
teachers and
employees, §16-60-35.
Junior college for Jackson
and DeKalb counties.
Exemption of officers,
teachers and
employees, §16-60-65.

JURY—Cont'd
Exemption from jury duty
    —Cont'd
  Jury rolls.
    Entry of notation on jury
        roll by clerk,
        §12-16-48.
    No exemptions, §12-16-62.
  Probate court jurors.
    Certification to jury
        commission of names,
        §12-16-78.
  Special, private or local laws
      prohibited, Const. Ala.,
      art. IV, §104.
**Exemptions from levy and
    sale under process.**
  Contest of exemption claim.
    Trial by jury in probate
        court, §6-10-31.
Fees.
  Civil cases.
    Circuit court, §12-19-110.
    Probate court, §§12-19-111
        to 12-19-113.
  Criminal cases, §12-19-210.
    Tales jurors, §12-19-211.
  Payment.
    Establishment and filing of
        special procedures for
        payment, §12-19-7.
  Tales jurors.
    Criminal cases, §12-19-211.
Forms.
  Demand for jury trial, ARCP,
      Form 68.
  Motion for trial by advisory
      jury, ARCP, Form 69.
Fraud.
  Objections to venire,
      §12-16-80.
Grand juries generally.
  See GRAND JURY.
Guardian and ward.
  Uniform guardianship and
      protective proceedings
      act.
    Trial by jury, §26-2A-35.
Guilty pleas.
  When jury impaneled to fix
      punishment, §15-15-24.
Handicapped persons.
  Qualifications of jurors,
      §12-16-60.
Impeachment.
  Drawing where member of
      county commission
      subject to impeachment
      proceedings, §36-11-19.
  Proceedings in circuit court.
    Right to jury trial,
        §36-11-14.
Instructions to jury,
    §§12-16-11 to 12-16-13,
    12-22-132, 13A-1-9.
Insufficiency of jurors.
  Procedure when number of
      qualified jurors in
      attendance at court
      insufficient, §12-16-76.
Interrogatories to jury,
    ARCP, Rule 49 (b) to (d).
Intimidating jurors,
    §13A-10-127.
Irregularity in proceedings.
  Grounds for new trial,
      §15-17-5.
Judges.
  When words "jury" or
      "juries" include court or
      judge, §12-16-1.

JURY—Cont'd
Judgments.
  Satisfying or setting aside
      judgments.
    Jury trial on fact issues,
        §6-9-180.
**Junior college for Franklin,
    Marion and Winston
    counties.**
  Exemption of officers,
      teachers and employees
      from jury duty,
      §16-60-35.
**Junior college for Jackson
    and DeKalb counties.**
  Exemption of officers,
      teachers and employees
      from jury duty,
      §16-60-65.
Juror.
  Defined, §13A-10-120.
Jury box, §§12-16-44,
    12-16-45, 12-16-58 to
    12-16-90.
  Destruction of jury box,
      §12-16-83.
  Drawing names from jury
      box, §§12-16-59, 12-16-70
      to 12-16-90.
  Forwarding names to clerk
      of court, §12-16-70.
  Fraud.
    Objections to venire,
        §12-16-80.
  Influence.
    Attempting to influence
        jury commissioner or
        other officer,
        §12-16-85.
  List of names drawn.
    Preparation, §12-16-70.
  Next session of court.
    Drawing for first week of
        next session,
        §12-16-70.
  Presiding judge.
    When juries for next
        session drawn,
        §12-16-72.
  Performance of act with
      intent to affect fair
      drawing of jury,
      §12-16-86.
  Powers of jurors drawn
      under article,
      §12-16-90.
  Probate court juries,
      §12-16-78.
  Provisions of article as to
      drawing of jurors
      directory, §12-16-90.
  Sealing of names drawn,
      §12-16-70.
  Emptying, §12-16-58.
    Circuit court judge,
        §12-16-45.
  Master jury box.
    Drawings from box,
        §12-16-59.
    Emptying, §12-16-58.
  Number of prospective
      jurors placed in box,
      §12-16-58.
  Placement of names in,
      §12-16-58.
  Refilling, §12-16-58.
  Selection of names to be
      placed in box,
      §12-16-58.

JURY—Cont'd
Jury box—Cont'd
  Preparation, §12-16-58.
    Separate jury boxes for
        courts of territorial
        subdivisions of
        counties, §12-16-44.
  Probate court.
    Drawing of names from
        jury box for juries in
        probate court,
        §12-16-78.
  Refilling, §12-16-58.
    Circuit court judge,
        §12-16-45.
    County jury commission,
        §12-16-46.
    Notification of commission
        as to necessity to refill,
        §12-16-45.
  Separate jury boxes for
      courts of territorial
      subdivisions of counties,
      §12-16-44.
  Trial court jury box.
    Maintenance, §12-16-61.
  Unlawfully placing in or
      withdrawing names from
      jury box, §12-16-83.
Jury of vicinage, Const. U. S.,
    Amendment VI.
Jury roll.
  Certification of new jury roll
      by county jury
      commission, §12-16-46.
  Disqualification of jurors.
    Entry of notation on jury
        roll, §12-16-48.
  Names.
    Entry of juror's name on
        jury roll, §12-16-47.
  New jury roll.
    Certification, §12-16-46.
  Persons empaneled on juries.
    Notation on jury roll,
        §12-16-47.
  Separate jury rolls for courts
      of territorial subdivisions
      of counties, §12-16-44.
Jury tampering, §13A-10-128.
Lesser included offenses.
  Charged to jury, §13A-1-9.
Less than twelve, ARCP, Rule
    48.
Lists of jurors.
  Civil actions.
    Striking jurors, §12-16-140.
  Master list, §12-16-57.
Lodging.
  Jury kept together without
      separation overnight,
      §12-16-10.
Master jury box, §§12-16-58,
    12-16-59.
Master list of jurors,
    §12-16-57.
Meals.
  Jury kept together without
      separation overnight,
      §12-16-10.
Mentally ill.
  Challenges of jurors,
      §12-16-150.
Military affairs.
  Exemptions from state jury
      duty, §31-2-11.
Minors.
  Consent to trial without jury,
      §15-19-1.

JURY—Cont'd

Misconduct.
Grounds for new trial,
§15-17-5.

Misdemeanors.
Demand for jury in
misdemeanor cases in
circuit court, §15-14-30.

Mistrial.
Discharge of jury and entry
of mistrial, §12-16-233.

Motions.
Advisory jury.
Form of motion for trial by
advisory jury, ARCP,
Form 69.

**Multiple claims, parties and
actions.**
Striking jurors, ARCP, Rule
47 (c).

Municipal courts.
Cases to be tried by judge
without jury, §12-14-6.

Names of jurors.
Jury roll.
Entry of juror's name,
§12-16-47.
Persons empaneled on juries.
Certification of names,
§12-16-47.

New trial.
Irregularity or misconduct in
proceedings, §15-17-5.

Number of jurors.
Less than twelve, ARCP,
Rule 48.

Oaths of jurors, §12-16-170.
Defect in administration of
oath.
Reversal of criminal cases,
§12-16-173.
Qualifications of jurors.
Duty of court to ascertain
before administering
oath, §12-16-6.
Swearing jurors, §12-16-74.

Objections.
Instructions to jury, ARCP,
Rule 51.

Partition.
Crops.
Trial by jury, §35-6-122.

**Personal knowledge of juror
as to fact in controversy
during trial.**
Testimony by juror, §12-16-7.

Polling of jurors, §12-16-15.

Preparation, §12-16-59.

Probate court, §12-16-78.
Fees.
Jurors' fees, §§12-19-111 to
12-19-113.

**Public officers and
employees.**
Summary proceedings
involving officials.
Judgment against officer
accepting substitute
for juror or serving
person other than one
to be drawn, §6-6-683.

Qualifications of jurors,
§12-16-60.
Alternative plan, §12-16-145.
Declaration of policy,
§12-16-55.
Determination by jury
commission, §12-16-60.
Duty of court to ascertain
before administering
oath, §12-16-6.

JURY—Cont'd

Qualifications of jurors
—Cont'd
Forms.
Completion by prospective
jurors, §12-16-59.
Contents, §12-16-59.
Misrepresentation of
material facts on
forms, §12-16-59.
Preparation, §12-16-59.
Records.
Preservation of records,
§12-16-64.
Use of data processing
equipment, §12-16-146.

Quieting title.
In personam proceedings.
Trial by jury, §6-6-543.

Quo warranto.
Trial by jury, §6-6-593.

Records.
Preservation of records
concerning selection and
service of jurors,
§12-16-64.

Refilling, §12-16-58.

**Relation of juror to attorney
or parties.**
Grounds for granting
challenge for cause,
§12-16-150.

Replacement of jurors.
Discharge.
Summoning of replacement
prior to retirement of
jury, §12-16-230.

Right to trial by jury, ARCP,
Rule 38 (a).

Roll.
Jury roll, §§12-16-44,
12-16-46 to 12-16-48.

Rules of civil procedure.
General provisions.
See RULES OF CIVIL
PROCEDURE.
Interrogatories to jury,
ARCP, Rule 49 (b) to (d).
Verdict, ARCP, Rules 49, 50.

Selection of jurors, ARCP,
Rule 47 (b).
Alternate plan, §12-16-145.
Disqualification of jurors,
§12-16-145.
Random selection,
§12-16-145.
Civil actions, §12-16-140.
Criminal cases.
Drawing, selection and
empaneling of juries in
criminal cases.
Generally, §12-16-100.
Where two or more
persons tried jointly,
§12-16-101.
Declaration of policy,
§12-16-55.
Discrimination prohibited,
§12-16-56.
Jury box, §§12-16-59,
12-16-70 to 12-16-90.
Master list, §12-16-57.
Records.
Preservation of records,
§12-16-64.
Use of data processing
equipment, §12-16-146.

Sentencing.
Punishment fixed by jury.
See SENTENCING.

Separation of jury, §12-16-9.

JURY—Cont'd

Sequestering jury.
Motion of parties or courts
own initiative, §12-16-9.

Sheriffs.
Summoning jurors,
§§12-16-73, 12-16-81.

Striking jurors, ARCP, Rule
47 (b), (c).
Capital cases.
Challenges.
Grounds for challenge by
state, §12-16-152.
Criminal cases, §12-16-100.

Summoning jurors.
Execution of order to
summon jurors,
§12-16-73.
Failure of juror summoned to
attend trial.
Effect, §12-16-82.
Not grounds for quashing
venire or continuing
case, §12-16-81.
Failure of sheriff to summon
juror drawn.
Not grounds for quashing
venire or continuing
case, §12-16-81.
Favoritism.
Connivance by sheriff of
offense prohibited by
section 12-16-87,
§12-16-88.
Summoning with intent to
produce result
favorable to party,
§12-16-87.
Fraud.
Objections to venire,
§12-16-80.
Influence.
Attempting to influence
jury commissioner or
other officer
summoning jurors,
§12-16-85.
Negligent failure of sheriff or
deputy to summon juror,
§12-16-89.
Powers of jurors summoned
under article, §12-16-90.
Probate juries, §12-16-78.
Provisions of article as to
summoning of jurors
directory, §12-16-90.
Return of order to summon
jurors by sheriff,
§12-16-73.

Swearing jurors, §12-16-74.

Tampering, §13A-10-128.

Threats.
Intimidating jurors,
§13A-10-127.

Trial by consent, ARCP, Rule
39 (c).

Trial by jury, ARCP, Rule 39
(a).
Guardian and ward.
Uniform guardianship and
protective proceedings
act, §26-2A-35.
Right to trial by jury, Const.
Ala., art. I, §11; Const.
U. S., Amendments VI,
VII.
Waiver, ARCP, Rule 38 (d).

University of Montevallo.
Employees exempt from jury
duty, §16-54-12.

JURY—Cont'd

Venire.

Drawing from venire of jurors for session of court, §12-16-74.

Influence.

Attempting to influence jury commissioner or other officer selecting or drawing jurors, §12-16-85.

Issuance of venire to sheriff by clerk, §12-16-70.

Objections to venire, §12-16-80.

Performance of act with intent to affect fair drawing of jury, §12-16-86.

Powers of jurors drawn under article, §12-16-90.

Provisions of article as to drawing of jurors directory, §12-16-90.

Quashing venire.

Failure of sheriff to summon juror drawn or failure of juror summoned to attend trial.

Not grounds for quashing venire, §12-16-81.

Verdict.

General provisions.

See VERDICT.

Polling of jurors, §12-16-15.

Waiver of jury trial, ARCP, Rule 38 (d).

Wills.

Contesting validity of will.

Drawing and summoning of jurors, §43-8-192.

Penalty for default, §43-8-192.

Trial by jury, §§43-8-190, 43-8-202.

Witnesses.

Personal knowledge of juror as to fact in controversy during trial.

Juror to testify as to knowledge, §12-16-7.

Written evidence.

Taking of written evidence by jury on retirement, §12-16-14.

Youthful offenders.

Consent of minor to trial without jury, §15-19-1.

JUSTICES OF THE PEACE.

Abolition of office, Const. Ala., amd. 323.

Appeals from justices, Const. Ala., art. VI, §168.

Constitution of Alabama, Const. Ala., art. VI, §168.

See CONSTITUTION OF ALABAMA.

Election, Const. Ala., art. VI, §168.

Evidence.

Foreign justices.

Copies of proceedings and judgments.

Admissibility in evidence, §12-21-38.

JUSTICES OF THE PEACE —Cont'd

Fees, Const. Ala., art. VI, §168.

Increasing fees.

Special, private or local laws prohibited, Const. Ala., art. IV, §104.

Foreign justices.

Copies of proceedings and judgments.

Admissibility in evidence, §12-21-38.

Impeachment, Const. Ala., art. VII, §175.

Jurisdiction, Const. Ala., art. VI, §168.

Increasing jurisdiction.

Special, private or local laws prohibited, Const. Ala., art. IV, §104.

Terms of office, Const. Ala., art. VI, §168.

JUVENILE PROCEEDINGS, §§12-15-1 to 12-15-120.

Adults.

Procedure and dispositions in cases involving adults, §12-15-76.

Advisory boards, §12-15-4.

Aftercare.

Violation of terms of aftercare.

Proceedings against children violating, §12-15-75.

Appeals, ARJP, Rule 28.

Appointment and compensation of counsel for indigent juveniles, §15-12-22.

District attorneys.

Representation of state by district attorney in cases appealed by juvenile courts, §12-15-5.

From judgments, orders, etc., of juvenile courts, §12-15-120.

Indigent persons.

Appointment and compensation of counsel for indigent juveniles, §15-12-22.

Attorneys at law.

Appearance of counsel, ARJP, Rule 14.

Appointment of counsel, §12-15-63.

Fees.

Issuance of order to parents for payment, §12-15-11.

Liability of counties for attorneys' fees, §12-15-10.

Repeal of provisions, §12-15-10.1.

Involuntary commitment of minors or children, §12-15-90.

Right to counsel, ARJP, Rule 22.

Appointment of counsel, §12-15-63.

Notification of children, parents, guardians, etc., §12-15-63.

JUVENILE PROCEEDINGS —Cont'd

Care of youths under jurisdiction of juvenile court, §§44-3-1 to 44-3-12.

Circuit courts.

Jurisdiction, §§12-12-34, 12-15-2.

Involuntary commitment proceedings, §12-11-10.

Commitment.

Involuntary commitment.

Authority and procedure, §12-15-90.

Transfer of cases to circuit courts, §12-11-10.

Conduct of hearings, §12-15-65; ARJP, Rule 24.

Conduct of parties.

Restraint.

Issuance of orders restraining conduct, §12-15-73.

Confidentiality.

Law enforcement records, ARJP, Rule 19.

Release of information, ARJP, Rule 18.

Contempt.

Punishment for contempt, §12-15-12.

Continuances.

Granting, §12-15-68.

Under terms and conditions agreed to by parties, §12-15-64.

Convictions.

Orders of disposition, etc., not to be deemed convictions, §12-15-72.

Costs, ARJP, Rule 26.

Counties.

Liability for court costs, §12-15-10.

Issuance of order to parents for payment, §12-15-11.

Counties.

Liability for court costs, attorneys' fees and expenses for maintenance and care of children, §12-15-10.

Repeal of attorney fees provisions, §12-15-10.1.

Criminal law and procedure.

Transfer of cases from juvenile court to criminal court, §12-15-34.

Custody of children.

Delivery of children taken into custody, §12-15-58.

Department of pensions and security.

Powers, §12-15-7.

Detention facilities, §§12-15-58 to 12-15-62; ARJP, Rules 9, 10.

Expenses for maintenance and care.

Issuance of order to parents for payment, §12-15-11.

Liability of counties, §12-15-10.

Extension of orders of custody, §12-15-74.

Interference with custody, §12-15-14.

JUVENILE PROCEEDINGS
—Cont'd
Custody of children—Cont'd
Involuntary commitment.
Authority and procedure,
§12-15-90.
Issuance of order for taking
into custody and
bringing before court,
§12-15-57.
Modification of orders,
§12-15-74.
Orders of protective
supervision.
Violation.
Powers of courts with
respect to children
violating, §12-15-12.
Parents.
Order for payment of
support, treatment,
etc., §12-15-9.
Probation officers, §12-15-7.
Regional custody and care of
youths under jurisdiction
of juvenile court.
Definitions, §44-3-1.
Nonprofit public
corporations for
provision of temporary
care and custody.
Amendment of articles of
incorporation,
§44-3-7.
Appropriations to
corporations by
governing bodies,
§44-3-9.
Authorization for
creation, §44-3-2.
Boards of directors,
§44-3-5.
Responsibility for
control and
direction, §44-3-10.
Commencement of
existence, §44-3-12.
Control and direction of
facilities and
programs.
Responsibility of
boards of directors,
§44-3-10.
Effect of formation on
existing facilities,
§44-3-3.
Exemption from
taxation, §44-3-11.
Governing bodies.
Admission into
membership of
corporations,
§44-3-8.
Appropriations to
corporations by,
§44-3-9.
Powers, §44-3-6.
Service areas of
corporations,
§44-3-4.
Release of children taken
into custody, §§12-15-58,
12-15-62.
Revocation of orders of
custody, §12-15-74.
Shelter care facilities,
§§12-15-58 to 12-15-62;
ARJP, Rule 9.
Taking into custody,
§12-15-56.
Decisions, §12-15-65.

JUVENILE PROCEEDINGS
—Cont'd
Decrees.
Consent to supervision,
ARJP, Rule 16.
Entry in separate minute
book, §12-15-2.
Modification, ARJP, Rule 27.
Definitions, §12-15-1.
Regional custody and care of
youths under jurisdiction
of juvenile court, §44-3-1.
Delinquency.
Causing, etc., delinquency,
§12-15-13.
Disposition of delinquent
children, §12-15-71.
Petitions.
Informal adjustment of
delinquency cases prior
to filing of petition,
§12-15-51.
Removal, concealment, etc.,
of delinquent child,
§12-15-15.
Dental care.
Children found in need of
dental care, §12-15-70.
**Department of pensions and
security.**
Custody of children.
Procedure upon taking into
custody of child,
§12-15-7.
Dependency.
Causing, etc., dependency,
§12-15-13.
Disposition of dependent
children, §12-15-71.
Removal, concealment, etc.,
of dependent child,
§12-15-15.
Detention facilities,
§12-15-61.
Continuation of detention.
Authority and criteria for
continuation,
§12-15-59.
Filing of petition and
conduct of hearing as
to necessity, §12-15-60.
Delivery to detention facility
of children taken into
custody, §12-15-58.
Designation, ARJP, Rule 9.
Disruptive behavior in
detention, ARJP, Rule
10.
Powers of probation officers
and department as to
placing children in
detention care, §12-15-7.
Release from detention
facility, §12-15-62.
Disposition.
Adults.
Dispositions in cases
involving adults,
§12-15-76.
Dependent children,
delinquent children or
children in need of
supervision, §12-15-71.
Evidence.
Admissibility of evidence
given in hearings and
disposition of child,
§12-15-72.

JUVENILE PROCEEDINGS
—Cont'd
Disposition—Cont'd
Minors.
Dispositions in cases
involving minors,
§12-15-76.
Orders of disposition not to
be deemed convictions,
impose civil disabilities,
etc., §12-15-72.
Proceedings.
Continuation.
Care or rehabilitation
required.
Exception inapplicable
to criminal
proceedings or
charges, §12-15-65.
Rehabilitation or care
required, §12-15-65.
Generally, §12-15-65.
Violation of terms of
probation, aftercare or
protective supervision.
Disposition of children
violating, §12-15-75.
District attorneys.
Appeals.
Representation of state,
§12-15-5.
Assistance of juvenile court
by district attorney,
§12-15-5.
Exercise of authority by
district attorney,
§12-15-5.
District courts.
Jurisdiction, §§12-12-34,
12-15-2.
Dockets.
Inspection of court dockets,
§12-15-100.
Separate docket, §12-15-2.
Double jeopardy, §12-15-66.
Education.
Truancy.
Jurisdiction of juvenile
court, §16-28-21.
Equity.
Powers, §12-15-2.
Evidence, §12-15-65.
Admissibility.
Sexual offenses.
Minors, §12-15-65.
Evidence given in hearings
and disposition of child.
Admissibility of evidence
against child,
§12-15-72.
Extrajudicial statements,
§12-15-66.
Illegally seized or obtained
evidence, §12-15-66.
Sexual offenses.
Minors, §12-15-65.
Statement by child.
Admissibility, ARJP, Rule
21.
Examinations.
Parents or custodians,
§12-15-69.
Physical and mental
examinations,
§§12-15-69, 12-15-70.
Expungement.
Destruction of records
generally, §12-15-103.

JUVENILE PROCEEDINGS
—Cont'd
Extrajudicial statements of children.
Admissibility in evidence, §12-15-66.
Family court.
Establishment, §12-17-24.1.
Judges.
Appointments of presiding judge, §12-17-24.1.
Findings, ARJP, Rule 25.
Fingerprints.
Taking and disposition of fingerprints, §12-15-102.
Guardian ad litem.
Appointment by courts, §12-15-8.
Guardian and ward.
Appointment of guardians by court, §12-15-8.
Attorneys at law.
Notification of guardians of right to counsel, §12-15-63.
Hearings, §12-15-65; ARJP, Rules 23, 24.
Conduct of hearings, §12-15-65; ARJP, Rule 24.
Hearing to be held within seventy-two hours, §12-15-60.
Involuntary commitment of minors or children, §12-15-90.
Notice, ARJP, Rule 23.
Waiver, ARJP, Rule 23.
Scheduling, ARJP, Rule 23.
Seventy-two hours.
Hearings as to necessity for continuation of detention or shelter care must be held within, §12-15-60.
Illegitimacy.
Determination of paternity.
Jurisdiction of juvenile court, §12-15-31.
Informal adjustment, ARJP, Rule 15.
Initiation of cases, ARJP, Rule 12.
Intake office, ARJP, Rule 8.
Informal adjustment, ARJP, Rule 15.
Initiation of cases, ARJP, Rule 12.
Intake officers.
Initiation of cases by filing of petitions, §12-15-50.
Involuntary commitment of minors or children.
Authority and procedure, §12-15-90.
Jails.
When delinquent child may be detained in jail, §12-15-61.
Judges.
Administrative authority, ARJP, Rule 3.
Appointment, §12-17-24.1.
Assignment, ARJP, Rule 2.
Designation, §12-15-3.
Family court division, §12-17-24.1.
Reports.
Administrative reports, ARJP, Rule 7.

JUVENILE PROCEEDINGS
—Cont'd
Judges—Cont'd
Reports—Cont'd
Requirement of monthly reports by judges as to work of juvenile courts, §12-15-3.
Writs.
Powers as to issuance, §12-15-2.
Judgments.
Modification, ARJP, Rule 27.
Jurisdiction.
Adults or minors, §12-15-31.
Children, §12-15-30.
Illegitimacy.
Determination of paternity, §12-15-31.
Mental illness or retardation.
Proceedings for commitment of minor, §12-15-31.
Minors or adults, §12-15-31.
Original jurisdiction, §§12-15-30, 12-15-31.
Circuit and district courts to exercise original concurrent jurisdiction, §§12-12-34, 12-15-2.
Paternity.
Determination, §12-15-31.
Powers, §12-15-2.
Retention, §12-15-32.
Termination, §12-15-32.
Justices.
Retirement.
State and local governing bodies authorized to pick up member contributions to retirement fund, §12-18-5.
Law enforcement records and files.
Destruction.
Proceedings for destruction, §12-15-103.
Disclosure of information, §12-15-101.
Inspection, §12-15-101.
Maintenance, §12-15-101.
Sealing.
Proceedings for sealing, §12-15-103.
Medical facilities.
Delivery to medical facility of children taken into custody, §12-15-58.
Medical records, §12-15-100.
Medical treatment, §12-15-70.
Mental examinations, §§12-15-69, 12-15-70.
Mental illness or retardation.
Involuntary commitment.
Authority and procedure, §12-15-90.
Jurisdiction of juvenile courts, §12-15-31.
Proceedings as to minors or children believed to be mentally ill or retarded, §12-15-70.
Minors.
Jurisdiction, §12-15-31.
Procedure and dispositions in cases involving minors, §12-15-76.

JUVENILE PROCEEDINGS
—Cont'd
Need of supervision of child.
Causing need of supervision, §12-15-13.
Disposition of children in need of supervision, §12-15-71.
Petitions.
Informal adjustment of need prior to filing of petition, §12-15-51.
Removal, concealment, etc., of child in need of supervision, §12-15-15.
Orders of court, ARJP, Rule 25.
Contempt.
Punishment for disobeying orders, §12-15-12.
Disregarding, etc., of lawful order of court, §12-15-14.
Entry in separate minute book, §12-15-2.
Final dispositional orders.
Authority of court to make in cases where parties served by publication, §12-15-55.
Inspection of orders, §12-15-100.
Interlocutory orders.
Authority of court to make in cases where parties served by publication, §12-15-55.
Modification, ARJP, Rule 27.
Parents.
Attorneys at law.
Fees.
Issuance of order to parents for payment, §12-15-11.
Notification of parents of right to counsel, §12-15-63.
Costs.
Issuance of order to parents for payment of court costs, §12-15-11.
Examination after hearing where ability to care for or supervise child in issue, §12-15-69.
Expenses for support, treatment, etc.
Issuance of order to parents for payment, §12-15-11.
Children in custody of persons other than parents, §12-15-9.
Petitions.
Adjustment of certain cases.
Informal adjustment prior to filing of petition, §12-15-51.
Amendment, ARJP, Rule 17.
Contents, §12-15-52.
Execution, §12-15-52.
Filing.
Cases initiated by filing of petitions by intake officers, §12-15-50.
Informal adjustment of certain cases prior to filing, §12-15-51.
Form, §12-15-52.

JUVENILE PROCEEDINGS
—Cont'd
Petitions—Cont'd
Initiation of cases, ARJP,
Rule 12.
Filing of petitions by
intake officers,
§12-15-50.
Involuntary commitment of
minors or children,
§12-15-90.
Photographs.
Taking and disposition,
§12-15-102.
**Physical and mental
examinations,** §§12-15-69,
12-15-70.
Prisons and prisoners.
When child may be detained
in adult facility,
§12-15-61.
Probation.
Extension of orders of
probation, §12-15-74.
Modification of orders of
probation, §12-15-74.
Revocation of orders of
probation, §12-15-74.
Violation of terms of
probation, §12-15-75.
Youthful offenders.
Court authorized to post
probation, §15-19-6.
Youth services.
See YOUTH SERVICES.
Probation officers, ARJP,
Rule 4.
Appointment, §12-15-7.
Chief probation officer,
ARJP, Rule 5.
Designation, §12-15-7.
Duties, §12-15-7.
Interference with
performance of duties,
§12-15-15.
Interference with
performance of duties by
probation officer,
§12-15-15.
Local merit system or
personnel board.
Applicability of provisions,
§12-15-7.
Powers, §12-15-7.
Terms of office, §12-15-7.
Probation volunteers, ARJP,
Rule 6.
Protective supervision,
§12-15-74.
Psychiatric records.
Filing, §12-15-100.
Inspection, §12-15-100.
Records.
Confidentiality of law
enforcement records,
ARJP, Rule 19.
Disclosure of information
derived from court
records, §12-15-100.
Law enforcement records and
files.
Destruction.
Proceedings for
destruction,
§12-15-103.
Disclosure of information,
§12-15-101.
Inspection, §12-15-101.
Maintenance, §12-15-101.

JUVENILE PROCEEDINGS
—Cont'd
Records—Cont'd
Law enforcement records and
files—Cont'd
Sealing.
Proceedings for sealing,
§12-15-103.
Medical records, §12-15-100.
Proceedings, ARJP, Rule 20.
Psychiatric records,
§12-15-100.
Retention schedule.
Inapplicability to juvenile
records, ARJA, Rule
31.
Social records.
Destruction, §12-15-103.
Filing, §12-15-100.
Inspection, §12-15-100.
Sealing, §12-15-103.
Referees, §12-15-6.
**Regional custody and care
of youths under
jurisdiction of juvenile
court,** §§44-3-1 to 44-3-12.
**Release of children taken
into custody,** §§12-15-58,
12-15-62.
Release of information,
ARJP, Rule 18.
Reports.
Administrative reports,
ARJP, Rule 7.
Continuation of dispositional
hearings to receive
reports, §12-15-65.
Care or rehabilitation
required.
Exception inapplicable to
criminal proceedings
or charges,
§12-15-65.
Predisposition report,
§12-15-69.
Restraint of conduct.
Issuance of orders restraining
conduct of parties to
proceedings, §12-15-73.
Rights of child, ARJP, Rule
11.
Right to counsel, ARJP, Rule
22.
Rules of juvenile procedure,
ARJP, Rules 1 to 30.
Amending petition, ARJP,
Rule 17.
Appeals, ARJP, Rule 28.
Applicability of rules.
Procedure when rules not
applicable, ARJP, Rule
1.
Attorneys at law.
Appearance of counsel,
ARJP, Rule 14.
Right to counsel, ARJP,
Rule 22.
Conduct of hearing, ARJP,
Rule 24.
Confidentiality.
Law enforcement records,
ARJP, Rule 19.
Release of information,
ARJP, Rule 18.
Consent decree, ARJP, Rule
16.
Costs, ARJP, Rule 26.
Decrees.
Consent decree, ARJP,
Rule 16.

JUVENILE PROCEEDINGS
—Cont'd
Rules of juvenile procedure
—Cont'd
Decrees—Cont'd
Modification, ARJP, Rule
27.
Detention facilities.
Designation, ARJP, Rule 9.
Disruptive behavior in
detention, ARJP, Rule
10.
Disruptive behavior in
detention, ARJP, Rule
10.
Effective date of rules, ARJP,
Rule 30.
Evidence.
Admissibility of child's
statement, ARJP, Rule
21.
Findings, ARJP, Rule 25.
Hearings.
Conduct, ARJP, Rule 24.
Notice, ARJP, Rule 23.
Informal adjustment, ARJP,
Rule 15.
Initiation of cases, ARJP,
Rule 12.
Intake office, ARJP, Rule 8.
Informal adjustment,
ARJP, Rule 15.
Initiation of cases, ARJP,
Rule 12.
Judges.
Administrative authority,
ARJP, Rule 3.
Assignment, ARJP, Rule 2.
Reports.
Administrative reports,
ARJP, Rule 7.
Judgments.
Modification, ARJP, Rule
27.
Law enforcement records.
Confidentiality, ARJP,
Rule 19.
Modification of orders,
judgments or decrees,
ARJP, Rule 27.
Notice of hearings, ARJP,
Rule 23.
Orders, ARJP, Rule 25.
Modification, ARJP, Rule
27.
Parent and child.
Termination of parental
rights.
Applicability of rules,
§26-18-4.
Petition.
Amending petition, ARJP,
Rule 17.
Initiation of cases, ARJP,
Rule 12.
Probation officers, ARJP,
Rule 4.
Chief probation officer,
ARJP, Rule 5.
Probation volunteers, ARJP,
Rule 6.
Procedure when rules not
applicable, ARJP, Rule
1.
Promulgation, §12-15-2.
Record of proceedings, ARJP,
Rule 20.
Release of information,
ARJP, Rule 18.

JUVENILE PROCEEDINGS
—Cont'd
Rules of juvenile procedure
—Cont'd
Reports.
Administrative reports,
ARJP, Rule 7.
Rights of child, ARJP, Rule
11.
Right to counsel, ARJP,
Rule 22.
Scheduling hearings, ARJP,
Rule 23.
Service of summons, ARJP,
Rule 13.
Shelter care facilities.
Designation, ARJP, Rule 9.
Statement by child.
Admissibility, ARJP, Rule
21.
Supervision of child.
Continuance under
supervision without
adjudication, ARJP,
Rule 16.
Time.
Limitations, ARJP, Rule 1.
Title of rules, ARJP, Rule 29.
Scheduling hearings, ARJP,
Rule 23.
Searches and seizures.
Illegally seized evidence,
§12-15-66.
Self-incrimination.
Privilege against self-
incrimination, §12-15-66.
Service of process.
Publication.
Authority of court to make
interlocutory or final
dispositional orders in
cases where parties
served by publication,
§12-15-55.
Service of summons,
§12-15-53; ARJP, Rule
13.
Manner of service,
§12-15-54.
Waiver of service,
§12-15-53.
Sexual offenses.
Evidence.
Hearings.
Conduct of hearings,
§12-15-65.
Minors.
Admissibility, §12-15-65.
Shelter care facilities,
§12-15-61.
Continuation of shelter care.
Authority for continuation,
§12-15-59.
Criteria for continuation,
§12-15-59.
Necessity for continuation.
Filing of petition and
conduct of hearing,
§12-15-60.
Hearing to be held
within seventy-two
hours, §12-15-60.
Delivery to shelter care
facility of children taken
into custody, §12-15-58.
Designation, ARJP, Rule 9.

JUVENILE PROCEEDINGS
—Cont'd
Shelter care facilities—Cont'd
Necessity for continuation of
shelter care.
Filing of petition and
conduct of hearing,
§12-15-60.
Hearing to be held
within seventy-two
hours, §12-15-60.
Powers of officers and
department as to placing
children in shelter care,
§12-15-7.
Release from facility,
§12-15-62.
Social records.
Destruction, §12-15-103.
Filing, §12-15-100.
Inspection, §12-15-100.
Sealing, §12-15-103.
Studies.
Predisposition study,
§12-15-69.
Summons and process.
Endorsements upon
summonses, §12-15-53.
Issuance of summonses,
§12-15-53.
Powers of courts as to
issuance, §12-15-2.
Service of summonses,
§12-15-53; ARJP, Rule
13.
Manner of service,
§12-15-54.
Waiver of service,
§12-15-53.
Waiver of service of
summonses, §12-15-53.
Supervision of child.
Consent decree, ARJP, Rule
16.
Continuance under
supervision without
adjudication, ARJP, Rule
16.
Suspension of proceedings.
Under terms and conditions
agreed to by parties,
§12-15-64.
Transcripts.
Inspection of transcripts,
§12-15-100.
Transfer of cases.
Detention facilities.
Transfer of child when case
transferred for
criminal prosecution,
§12-15-61.
Transfer from juvenile court
to criminal court,
§12-15-34.
Transfer of proceedings
between juvenile courts
within state, §12-15-36.
Transfer to juvenile court
from other courts,
§12-15-33.
Truancy.
Evidence.
Attendance register and
rules and regulations
as evidence, §16-28-23.
Jurisdiction of juvenile court,
§16-28-21.
Prosecutions, §16-28-22.
Venue, §12-15-35.

JUVENILE PROCEEDINGS
—Cont'd
Vital statistics.
Release of information,
ARJP, Rule 18.
Welfare.
Department of human
resources.
Advising judges and
officers of juvenile
courts, §38-2-6.
Writs.
Powers of courts as to
issuance, §12-15-2.
Youthful offenders, §§15-19-1
to 15-19-7.
See YOUTHFUL
OFFENDERS.

JUVENILES.
General provisions.
See MINORS.
**Interstate compact on
juveniles,** §§44-2-1 to
44-2-7.
See YOUTH SERVICES.
Juvenile proceedings,
§§12-15-1 to 12-15-120.
See JUVENILE
PROCEEDINGS.
Minors.
See MINORS.
Youthful offenders, §§15-19-1
to 15-19-7.
See YOUTHFUL
OFFENDERS.
Youth services, §§44-1-1 to
44-1-77.
See YOUTH SERVICES.

K

KIDNAPPING.
Abduct.
Defined, §13A-6-40.
Custody.
Interference with custody.
Class C felony, §13A-6-45.
Elements of crime,
§13A-6-45.
Definitions, §13A-6-40.
First degree kidnapping.
Class A felony, §13A-6-43.
Elements of crime,
§13A-6-43.
Releasing victim alive.
Not first degree
kidnapping, §13A-6-43.
Indictments.
Form of indictment,
§15-8-150.
Interference with custody,
§13A-6-45.
Class C felony, §13A-6-45.
Relative.
Defined, §13A-6-40.
Releasing victim alive.
Not first degree kidnapping,
§13A-6-43.
Restrain.
Defined, §13A-6-40.
Second degree kidnapping.
Class B felony, §13A-6-44.
Elements of crime,
§13A-6-44.
Unlawful imprisonment.
First degree, §13A-6-41.
Second degree, §13A-6-42.

KIDNAPPING—Cont'd
Use of force in defense of persons.
When use of deadly physical force justified, §13A-3-23.

KIDNEYS.
Anatomical gifts, §§22-19-40 to 22-19-47, 22-19-60, 22-19-61.
See ANATOMICAL GIFTS.

KINDERGARTENS.
City boards of education, §16-11-16.
County boards of education, §16-8-41.
Pilot programs, §16-2-6.
Teachers, §16-13-52.1.

KINSHIP.
Incestuous marriages, §§30-1-3, 30-1-6.
See MARRIAGE.

KNIGHTS OF PYTHIAS.
Licenses.
Exemptions, §40-9-12.
Taxation.
Exemptions, §40-9-12.

KNIVES.
Weapons.
Licenses.
Dealers in bowie and dirk knives, §40-12-143.

L

LABELS.
Agriculture.
Grading and standards of farm products and fish, §§2-11-50 to 2-11-59.
See AGRICULTURE.
Alcoholic beverages.
Dry counties.
Wine for sacramental or religious purposes, §28-4-119.
Beverage containers.
Defacing, §8-12-21.
Registration, §8-12-20.
Brands and marks.
See BRANDS AND MARKS.
Bread, flour, cornmeal and grits.
Requirements, §20-1-77.
Catfish.
Requirements as to labeling for sale, §2-11-33.
Caustic or corrosive substances.
Approval and registration, §8-17-23.
Commercial feeds, §§2-21-17, 2-21-20.
Drugs.
Identification of drug products, §§20-1-150 to 20-1-154.
See DRUGS.
Eggs and egg products, §2-12-2.
Penalty for failure to affix, §2-12-10.
Feeds, §§2-21-17, 2-21-20.
Fertilizer.
Defined, §2-22-2.
Generally, §2-22-7.

LABELS—Cont'd
Fertilizer—Cont'd
Soil containers and soil amendments.
Labeling requirements for sale, §2-22-8.
Fruits and vegetables.
Grading and standards.
Compulsory labeling in certain areas, §2-11-75.
Labeling requirements, §2-11-73.
Honey, §§2-11-121 to 2-11-123.
Labor unions.
Adoption and use of labels, §25-7-14.
Lime, §§2-23-2, 2-23-4.
Linseed oil.
Labeling of original, unbroken containers, §8-17-42.
Meat and meat products.
General provisions.
See MEAT AND MEAT PRODUCTS.
Misbranding, §§2-17-18 to 2-17-20.
Mellorine.
Requirements as to labeling, §20-1-135.
Milk and milk products.
Marked containers, §§8-12-40 to 8-12-44.
See MILK AND MILK PRODUCTS.
Nuts.
Requirements as to labeling of packages or containers, §20-1-92.
Oleomargarine.
Requirements as to labeling, §20-1-113.
Petroleum products.
Reclaimed or re-refined oil, §8-17-111.
Requirement, §8-17-82.
Poultry.
General provisions.
See POULTRY.
Misbranding, §§2-17-10, 2-17-18 to 2-17-20.
Recorded devices.
Manufacturer's name required on packages, §13A-8-83.
Seeds.
Prohibited acts, §2-26-11.
Registration of symbol of seeds or plant parts, §§2-26-50 to 2-26-52.
Requirements as to labeling of containers in which seeds sold, §2-26-7.
Selling mislabeled commodities.
Deceptive business practices, §13A-9-41.
Trademarks.
See TRADEMARKS.
Turpentine, §§8-17-171, 8-17-172.
Unions.
Adoption and use of labels by unions or associations of workingmen, §25-7-14.

LABOR, §§25-1-1 to 25-10-10.
Accidents.
Rehabilitation and crippled children's service, §§16-38-1 to 16-38-9.
See HANDICAPPED PERSONS.
Accounts of employers.
Access by department of industrial relations to accounts, §25-2-22.
Agriculture.
Laborers.
Liens for wages, §§35-11-91 to 35-11-97.
See AGRICULTURE.
Statistics, §§2-2-50 to 2-2-52.
Appeals.
Board of appeals.
Department of industrial relations, §§25-2-12 to 25-2-25.
Arbitration.
Local boards of arbitration, §§25-7-50 to 25-7-54.
Board of appeals.
Department of industrial relations, §§25-2-12 to 25-2-25.
Bonds, surety.
Commissioner of labor, §25-3-2.
Director of industrial relations, §25-2-6.
Boycotts, §13A-11-122.
Child labor, §§25-8-1 to 25-8-31.
Actors and performers, §25-8-31.
Age certificates.
Employment and age certificates, §§25-8-13 to 25-8-21.
Alcoholic beverages.
Employment of persons under 19 years of age prohibited, §25-8-12.
Certificates.
Employment and age certificates, §§25-8-13 to 25-8-21.
Coal mines.
Persons under 18 not to work in or about mines, §25-9-30.
Correction of insanitary or unhealthy conditions, §25-8-25.
Eighteen years of age.
Prohibited places of employment, §25-8-11.
Employment and age certificates, §§25-8-13 to 25-8-21.
Application for certificates, §25-8-14.
Cancellation of illegally or improperly issued certificate, §25-8-21.
Cancellation upon termination of employment, §25-8-19.
Contents, §25-8-18.
Illegally or improperly issued certificate.
Cancellation, §25-8-21.
Issuance, §25-8-15.
Certain age and special employment certificates, §25-8-16.

LABOR—Cont'd
  Child labor—Cont'd
    Employment and age
        certificates—Cont'd
      Issuance—Cont'd
        Illegal or improper
            issuance.
          Cancellation, §25-8-21.
      Reports.
        Monthly reports to
            department,
            §25-8-20.
      Return upon termination of
          employment, §25-8-19.
      Revocation or suspension
          in event of
          unsatisfactory school
          performance, §25-8-16.
      Schools.
        Special employment
            certificates void
            upon opening of
            public schools,
            §25-8-17.
        Unsatisfactory school
            performance.
          Revocation or
              suspension,
              §25-8-16.
        Special employment
            certificates.
          Issuance, §25-8-16.
          Void upon opening of
              public schools,
              §25-8-17.
      Termination of
          employment.
        Return and cancellation,
            §25-8-19.
      Unsatisfactory school
          performance.
        Revocation or
            suspension, §25-8-16.
      When required, §25-8-13.
    Employment of children
        under 16 years of age,
        §§25-8-1 to 25-8-9.
      Agricultural employment.
        Exceptions to
            prohibition, §25-8-1.
      Children between 14 and
          16 years of age.
        Employment outside
            school hours,
            §25-8-1.
      Children of 14 and 15
          years of age.
        Employment upon
            waiver of school
            attendance, §25-8-5.
      Domestic employment.
        Exceptions to
            prohibition, §25-8-1.
      Evidence of employment,
          §25-8-4.
      Exceptions as to
          agricultural and
          domestic employment,
          §25-8-1.
      Hours of employment,
          §25-8-4.
        Street occupations,
            §25-8-8.
      Occupations.
        Prohibited occupations,
            §25-8-2.
        State board of health
            may declare
            occupation
            dangerous or
            injurious, §25-8-3.

LABOR—Cont'd
  Child labor—Cont'd
    Employment of children
        under 16 years of age
        —Cont'd
      Places of employment.
        Prohibited places,
            §25-8-2.
        State board of health
            may declare place
            dangerous or
            injurious, §25-8-3.
      Posting of notice of law,
          §25-8-6.
      Prohibited generally,
          §25-8-1.
      Prohibited occupations and
          places of employment,
          §25-8-2.
      School hours.
        Employment during
            school hours,
            §25-8-15.
        Employment of children
            between 14 and 16
            years of age outside
            school hours,
            §25-8-1.
      Street occupations.
        Hours persons under 16
            years of age may
            work, §25-8-8.
        Permits for persons
            under 16 years of
            age, §25-8-9.
    Employment of persons
        under 18 years of age.
      Prohibited places of
          employment, §25-8-11.
    Employment of persons
        under 19 years of age.
      Prohibited places of
          employment, §25-8-12.
    Enforcement of chapter,
        §25-8-22.
    Evidence of employment,
        §25-8-4.
    Fourteen years of age.
      Employment of children
          between 14 and 16
          years of age outside
          school hours, §25-8-1.
      Employment of children of
          14 and 15 years of age
          upon waiver of school
          attendance, §25-8-5.
    Illegal employment.
      Removal of children
          illegally employed,
          §25-8-27.
    Insanitary or unhealthful
        conditions.
      Inspection and correction,
          §25-8-25.
    Inspections.
      Correction of insanitary or
          unhealthful conditions,
          §25-8-25.
      Establishments where
          minors employed,
          §25-8-22.
    Nineteen years of age.
      Prohibited places of
          employment, §25-8-12.
    Owners of establishments
        employing minors.
      Duties, §25-8-24.
    Penalties.
      Violations of chapter,
          §25-8-30.

LABOR—Cont'd
  Child labor—Cont'd
    Performers and actors,
        §25-8-31.
    Permits.
      Illegally or improperly
          issued permit.
        Cancellation, §25-8-21.
      Sale of article for resale on
          streets to person under
          16 years of age
          without permits,
          §25-8-28.
      Street occupations.
        Permits for persons
            under 16 years of
            age, §25-8-9.
      Working in public places,
          §§25-8-7 to 25-8-10.
    Places of employment.
      Owners.
        Duties of owners,
            §25-8-24.
      Posting of notice of law,
          §25-8-6.
      Prohibited places.
        Persons under 16 years
            of age, §25-8-2.
        Persons under 18 years
            of age, §25-8-11.
        Persons under 19 years
            of age, §25-8-12.
    Public places.
      Working in public places,
          §§25-8-7 to 25-8-10.
    Removal of children illegally
        employed, §25-8-27.
    Reports.
      Employment and age
          certificates.
        Monthly report to
            department,
            §25-8-20.
      School attendance officers,
          §25-8-23.
    Right of entry.
      School attendance officers,
          §25-8-23.
    School attendance officers.
      Reports to department,
          §25-8-23.
      Right of entry, §25-8-23.
    Sixteen years of age.
      Employment of children
          under 16 years of age,
          §§25-8-1 to 25-8-9.
      Street occupations, §§25-8-7
          to 25-8-10.
    Twelve years of age.
      Persons under 12 years of
          age not to engage in
          certain occupations,
          §25-8-7.
    Violations of chapter.
      Penalty, §25-8-30.
    Working in public places.
      Delinquency.
        Child violating
            provisions as to
            street occupations
            deemed delinquent,
            §25-8-10.
      Hours persons under 16
          years of age may work,
          §25-8-8.
      Permits.
        Persons under 16 years
            of age engaged in
            authorized
            occupations, §25-8-9.

LABOR—Cont'd
Child labor—Cont'd
Working in public places
—Cont'd
Permits—Cont'd
Sale of article for resale
on streets to person
under 16 years of
age without permit,
§25-8-28.
Persons under 12 years of
age not to engage in
certain occupations,
§25-8-7.
Violation of provisions.
Child violating
provisions as to
street occupations
deemed delinquent,
§25-8-10.
Coal.
Child labor.
Persons under 18 not to
work in or about
mines, §25-9-30.
Coal mine safety, §§25-9-1 to
25-9-370.
See COAL.
Solicitation of funds from
employees for purposes of
retaining or procuring
employment, §25-9-28.
Commissioner of labor,
§§25-3-2 to 25-3-5.
Appointment, §25-3-2.
Bond, §25-3-2.
Closing of plants or
industries, §25-3-5.
Duties, §25-3-3.
Full-time position, §25-3-2.
Oath of office, §25-3-2.
Powers, §25-3-3.
Seminars for unemployed or
underemployed
employees, §25-3-5.
State credit union.
Expanding of field of
membership, §25-3-5.
Term of office, §25-3-2.
Vacancies.
Filling, §25-3-2.
Wage claims.
Controversies as to wage
claims.
Investigation and
adjustment, §25-3-4.
Conflicts of interest.
Department of industrial
relations.
Board of appeals, §25-2-12.
Convict labor, §§14-5-1 to
14-5-11.
See PRISONS AND
PRISONERS.
Counties.
Developing, advertising and
promoting labor
resources, §11-3-11.
Dangerous conditions.
Appeals from findings of
board of appeals as to
dangerous condition of
machines, etc., §25-2-13.
Definitions.
Unemployment
compensation, §§25-4-1
to 25-4-17.
See UNEMPLOYMENT
COMPENSATION.
Unions and labor relations,
§25-7-2.

LABOR—Cont'd
**Department of industrial
relations,** §§25-2-1 to
25-2-26.
Accounts of employers.
Access to accounts,
§25-2-22.
Appropriations.
Disposition, §25-2-26.
Expenditure, §25-2-26.
Board of appeals, §§25-2-12
to 25-2-25.
Alternate members,
§25-2-12.
Appeals from findings as to
dangerous condition of
machines, etc.,
§25-2-13.
Appointment of members,
§25-2-12.
Compensation of members,
§25-2-12.
Composition, §25-2-12.
Conflicts of interest,
§25-2-12.
Created, §25-2-12.
Duties, §25-2-13.
Powers, §25-2-13.
Procedure, §25-2-14.
Qualifications of members,
§25-2-12.
Quorum, §25-2-12.
Record of proceedings,
§25-2-14.
Removal of members,
§25-2-12.
Rules and regulations.
Effective date, §25-2-18.
Penalties for violations,
§25-2-25.
Promulgation,
amendment, etc.
Effective date,
§25-2-18.
Hearings, §25-2-17.
Proposals, §25-2-16.
Publication, §25-2-18.
Publication, §25-2-18.
Review of rules or
regulations.
Commencement of
action in circuit
court, §25-2-21.
Petition to board of
appeals, §25-2-20.
Variations from rules or
regulations,
§25-2-19.
Violations.
Penalties for
violations,
§25-2-25.
Sessions, §25-2-15.
Terms of members,
§25-2-12.
Unemployment
compensation,
§§25-4-94 to 25-4-97.
Witnesses.
False statements under
oath, §25-2-25.
Powers of board as to
witnesses, §25-2-23.
Coal mine safety.
Legal representation of
department, §25-9-369.
Conflicts of interest.
Board of appeals, §25-2-12.
Director of industrial
relations, §§25-2-6 to
25-2-11.

LABOR—Cont'd
**Department of industrial
relations**—Cont'd
Divisions of department,
§25-2-3.
Duties, §25-2-2.
Employees, §25-2-4.
Applicability of merit
system, §25-2-5.
Employers to furnish
information to
department, §25-2-22.
Enforcement of laws
administered by
department, §25-2-24.
Established, §25-2-1.
False statements under oath,
§25-2-25.
Federal allotments.
Disposition and
expenditure, §25-2-26.
Information.
Employers to furnish
information to
department, §25-2-22.
Mine safety.
Coal mine safety.
Legal representation of
department,
§25-9-369.
Officers, §25-2-3.
Applicability of merit
system, §25-2-5.
Powers as to witnesses,
§25-2-23.
Penalties for violations of
chapter or rules or
regulations of board of
appeals, §25-2-25.
Records.
Access to records of
employers, §25-2-22.
Rules and regulations.
Board of appeals, §§25-2-12
to 25-2-25.
Director of industrial
relations, §25-2-8.
Seal, §25-2-1.
Small business assistance,
§§25-10-1 to 25-10-10.
See SMALL BUSINESS
ASSISTANCE.
Violations of chapter.
Penalties for violations,
§25-2-25.
Witnesses.
False statements under
oath, §25-2-25.
Powers of officers of
department as to
witnesses, §25-2-23.
Department of labor.
Commissioner of labor,
§§25-3-2 to 25-3-5.
Created, §25-3-1.
**Director of industrial
relations,** §§25-2-6 to
25-2-11.
Agreements with federal
agencies, §25-2-11.
Appointment, §25-2-6.
Bonds, surety, §25-2-6.
Compensation, §25-2-6.
Duties, §25-2-7.
Employment service division.
Designated chief of
division, §25-2-10.
Federal agencies.
Agreements with federal
agencies, §25-2-11.
Oath of office, §25-2-6.

LABOR—Cont'd

Director of industrial relations—Cont'd

Powers, §25-2-7.
  Witnesses.
    Powers as to witnesses, §25-2-23.
Qualifications, §25-2-6.
Right of entry, §25-2-9.
Rules and regulations, §25-2-8.
Salary, §25-2-6.
Term of office, §25-2-6.
Unemployment compensation division.
  Designated chief of division, §25-2-10.
Vacancies.
  Filling, §25-2-6.
Witnesses.
  False statements under oath, §25-2-25.
  Powers of director as to witnesses, §25-2-23.
Workmen's compensation, §§25-5-2, 25-5-3.

District attorneys.
  Enforcement of laws, §25-2-24.

Domestic labor.
  Use for public works, etc., §§39-3-2, 39-3-3.

Elections.
  Fair campaign practices.
    Job discrimination to solicit money, §17-22A-20.

Employment agencies, §§34-10-1 to 34-10-5.
  See EMPLOYMENT AGENCIES.

Evidence.
  Child labor.
    Evidence of employment, §25-8-4.

Income tax.
  Exemption of certain labor organizations, §40-18-32.

Inspections.
  Child labor.
    Establishments where minors employed, §25-8-22.
    Inspection and correction of insanitary or unhealthful conditions, §25-8-25.

Labor unions, §§25-7-1 to 25-7-54.

Liens for wages.
  Agricultural laborers, §§35-11-91 to 35-11-97.
    See AGRICULTURE.
  Lumber employees or laborers, §§35-11-270 to 35-11-273.
  Railroad employees, §§35-11-90 to 35-11-97.
    See RAILROADS.
  Sawmill employees or laborers, §§35-11-270 to 35-11-273.
  Timber employees or laborers, §§35-11-270 to 35-11-273.

Machinery.
  Dangerous condition.
    Appeals from findings, §25-2-13.

LABOR—Cont'd

Minors.
  Child labor, §§25-8-1 to 25-8-31.

Municipal corporations.
  Fire departments.
    Right to join labor organizations, §11-43-143.

Notice.
  Child labor.
    Posting notice of law, §25-8-6.
  Department of industrial relations.
    Board of appeals.
      Hearing on rules and regulations, §25-2-17.

Penalties.
  Child labor.
    Violations of chapter, §25-8-30.
  Unions and labor relations.
    Penalty for violations of article, §25-7-16.

Penitentiary.
  Convict labor, §§14-3-47 to 14-3-49.

Prisons and prisoners.
  Convict labor, §§14-5-1 to 14-5-11.
    See PRISONS AND PRISONERS.
  Industries in penal institutions, §§14-7-6 to 14-7-23.
    See PRISONS AND PRISONERS.
  Work release, §§14-8-30 to 14-8-44.
    See PRISONS AND PRISONERS.

Public works.
  Use of domestic products and resident workmen, §§39-3-1 to 39-3-3.

Records.
  Department of industrial relations.
    Board of appeals.
      Record of proceedings, §25-2-14.
  Employers' records.
    Access of department, §25-2-22.

Reports.
  Employment and age certificates.
    Monthly report to department, §25-8-20.

Resident workmen.
  Use for public works, §§39-3-2, 39-3-3.

Right of entry.
  Child labor.
    Right of entry of school attendance officers, §25-8-23.
  Director of industrial relations, §25-2-9.

Right to work law, §§25-7-30 to 25-7-36.

Rules and regulations.
  Department.
    Board of appeals, §§25-2-16 to 25-2-20.
    Director of industrial relations, §25-2-8.

LABOR—Cont'd

Safety.
  Coal mine safety, §§25-9-1 to 25-9-370.
    See COAL.
  Duties of employers, etc., §25-1-1.

Small business assistance, §§25-10-1 to 25-10-10.
  See SMALL BUSINESS ASSISTANCE.

Strikes.
  Unions and labor relations.
    Fire departments.
      Municipal or state fire fighters or firemen not to strike, etc., §11-43-143.
    Votes.
      Use or threats of use of force, etc., to secure or prevent, §25-7-11.

Threats.
  Unions and labor relations, §§25-7-9, 25-7-11.

Toxic substances in the workplace, §§22-33-1 to 22-33-15.
  See TOXIC SUBSTANCES IN THE WORKPLACE.

Trusts and trustees.
  Trusts for employees or self-employed persons, §35-4-259.

Unemployment compensation, §§25-4-1 to 25-4-152.
  See UNEMPLOYMENT COMPENSATION.

Unions and labor relations, §§25-7-1 to 25-7-54.
  Actions.
    Right to work law.
      Damages for denial of employment, §25-7-35.
  Administrative employees.
    Membership in labor organizations, §25-7-13.
  Antiboycott act, §13A-11-122.
  Arbitration.
    Local boards of arbitration, §§25-7-50 to 25-7-54.
  Boards of arbitration.
    Local boards, §§25-7-50 to 25-7-54.
  Boards of mediation, §25-7-4.
  Boycott.
    Prohibited, §13A-11-122.
  Bylaws.
    Labor organizations to file copies, §25-7-5.
  Constitutions.
    Labor organizations to file copies of constitutions, §25-7-5.
  Construction of article, §25-7-3.
  Declaration of policy, §25-7-1.
  Definitions, §25-7-2.
  Devices.
    Adoption and use of labels or devices, §25-7-14.
  Dues.
    Employer not to require payment as condition of employment, §25-7-34.

LABOR—Cont'd

Unions and labor relations —Cont'd

Engaging in lawful vocation.
  Interference with peaceable
    exercise of lawful
    industry, business,
    etc., §25-7-9.
Executive employees.
  Membership in labor
    organizations,
    §25-7-13.
Fees.
  Collection by labor
    organization of fee as
    work permit or
    condition of work,
    §25-7-12.
Fire departments.
  Rights to join labor
    organizations,
    §11-43-143.
Force and violence.
  Interference with peaceable
    exercise of lawful
    industry, business,
    etc., §25-7-9.
  Strike votes.
    Use or threats of use of
      force, etc., to secure
      or prevent, §25-7-11.
Insurance.
  Membership of executive,
    administrative, etc.,
    employees in labor
    organizations.
    Effect of section on
      existing insurance
      contracts, §25-7-13.
Joining labor organizations.
  Freedom to join or refrain
    from joining, §25-7-6.
  Right to work law,
    §§25-7-30 to 25-7-36.
Labels.
  Adoption and use of labels,
    §25-7-14.
Local boards of arbitration,
    §§25-7-50 to 25-7-54.
  Appointment of members,
    §25-7-50.
  Compensation of members,
    §25-7-52.
  Composition, §25-7-50.
  Consent of members,
    §25-7-51.
  Costs, §25-7-54.
  Decisions of boards,
    §25-7-53.
  Notice of board
    proceedings, §25-7-51.
  Oath of members, §25-7-51.
  Secretary, §25-7-51.
  Witnesses.
    Powers of board as to
      witnesses, §25-7-51.
Penalties.
  Violations of article,
    §25-7-16.
Professional employees.
  Membership in labor
    organizations,
    §25-7-13.
Provisions of article
  cumulative, §25-7-15.
Reports.
  Annual reports, §25-7-5.

LABOR—Cont'd

Unions and labor relations —Cont'd

Right to work law.
  Actions.
    Damages for denial of
      employment,
      §25-7-35.
    Agreement to deny right to
      work prohibited,
      §25-7-31.
    Applicability of article,
      §25-7-36.
    Combination to deny right
      to work prohibited,
      §25-7-31.
    Declaration of policy,
      §25-7-30.
    Dues.
      Employer not to require
        payment as
        condition of
        employment,
        §25-7-34.
    Employers not to require
      abstention from union
      membership, §25-7-33.
    Employers not to require
      membership as
      condition of
      employment, §25-7-32.
    Violations of article.
      Damages for denial of
        employment,
        §25-7-35.
  Strikes.
    Fire departments.
      Municipal or state fire
        fighters or firemen
        not to strike, etc.,
        §11-43-143.
    Votes.
      Use or threats of use of
        force, etc., to secure
        or prevent, §25-7-11.
  Supervisory employees.
    Membership in labor
      organizations,
      §25-7-13.
  Threats.
    Interference with peaceable
      exercise of lawful
      industry, business,
      etc., §25-7-9.
    Strike votes.
      Use or threats of use of
        force, etc., to secure
        or prevent, §25-7-11.
    Violations of article.
      Penalty for violations,
        §25-7-16.
  Witnesses.
    Local boards of arbitration.
      Powers of board as to
        witnesses, §25-7-51.

Wage claims.

Commissioner of labor.
  Investigation and
    adjustment of
    controversies, §25-3-4.

Wages generally.

See WAGES.

Witnesses.

Department of industrial
  relations.
  False statements under
    oath, §25-2-25.
  Powers as to witnesses,
    §25-2-23.

LABOR—Cont'd

Witnesses—Cont'd

Unions and labor relations.
  Local boards of arbitration.
    Powers of board as to
      witnesses, §25-7-51.

Women.

Sitting accommodations.
  Duty of employer to
    provide sitting
    accommodations for
    females, §25-1-2.
Water closets.
  Duty of employer to
    provide separate water
    closets for females,
    §25-1-2.

Workmen's compensation,

  §§25-5-1 to 25-5-231.
See WORKMEN'S
  COMPENSATION.

LABORATORIES.

Agriculture.

Establishment, §2-2-36.
Operation, §2-2-36.
Soil-testing laboratories,
  §§2-24-1 to 2-24-5.
See AGRICULTURE.
Where analysis to be made,
  §2-2-34.

Cancer.

Examination.
  Laboratory examination
    and test of specimens,
    §22-13-11.

Cement.

Testing laboratory,
  §16-47-14.

Diseases.

Notifiable diseases.
  Directors.
    Persons responsible for
      reporting diseases,
      §22-11A-2.
  General provisions,
    §§22-11A-1 to
    22-11A-38.
  See DISEASES.

Junior college for Franklin, Marion and Winston counties.

Laboratory fees, §16-60-34.

Junior college for Jackson and DeKalb counties.

Laboratory fees, §16-60-64.

Medical technicians.

Schools.
  Training schools.
    Certification and
      approval, §34-18-2.
    Laboratory
      requirements,
      §34-18-2.

Pesticides.

State laboratory, §§2-27-30 to
  2-27-32.

Poultry.

Disease diagnostic
  laboratories.
  Establishment, conduct
    and maintenance,
    §2-16-20.

Seeds.

Testing laboratory.
  Establishment, §2-26-4.

Soil testing laboratories,

  §§2-24-1 to 2-24-5.
See AGRICULTURE.

LABORATORIES—Cont'd
Swine diseases.
Diagnostic laboratory,
§2-15-210.
University of Alabama.
Testing laboratories,
§16-47-14.

LACHES.
Affirmative defense, ARCP,
Rule 8 (c).

LAFAYETTE,
MUNICIPALITY OF.
Property tax, Const. Ala.,
amd. 8.

LAGRANGE HISTORICAL
COMMISSION.
Generally, §41-9-270.

LAKES.
Fish and game.
General provisions, §§9-11-80
to 9-11-95.
See FISH AND GAME.
General provisions.
See WATERS AND
WATERCOURSES.

LAMAR COUNTY.
Constable.
Abolition of office, Const.
Ala., amd. 419.
Economic development.
Municipalities in Lamar
county, Const. Ala., amd.
189.
School tax.
Additional tax for school
purposes, Const. Ala.,
amd. 176.

LAND.
Eminent domain, §§18-1A-1
to 18-1A-311.
See EMINENT DOMAIN.
Land-use regulations.
Soil and water conservation.
Districts, §§9-8-26 to
9-8-30.
See SOIL AND WATER
CONSERVATION.
Public lands, §§9-15-1 to
9-15-53.
See PUBLIC LANDS.
Real property.
See REAL PROPERTY.
Soil and water conservation.
General provisions, §§9-8-1 to
9-8-67.
See SOIL AND WATER
CONSERVATION.

LANDFILLS.
Financing collection and
disposal facilities,
§§22-27-20 to 22-27-27.
See GARBAGE AND
TRASH.

LANDLORD AND TENANT,
§§35-9-1 to 35-9-100.
Abandonment.
Crops.
Seizure upon abandonment
of premises, §35-9-12.
Actions.
Use and occupation of land.
When reasonable
satisfaction may be
recovered, §35-9-100.
Advances.
Liens of landlord, §§35-9-30
to 35-9-42.

LANDLORD AND TENANT
—Cont'd
Advances—Cont'd
Maturity of advances,
§35-9-31.
Affidavits.
Liens for advances and rent
of lands, §35-9-35.
Possession wrongfully
withheld.
Arrest of proceedings by
tenant, §35-9-84.
Demand for premises,
§35-9-80.
Trial upon delivery of
counter affidavit,
§35-9-85.
Apartment ownership act,
§§35-8-1 to 35-8-22.
Appeals.
Possession wrongfully
withheld, §35-9-87.
Assignments.
Liens for advances and rent
of lands.
Assignment of claim,
§35-9-33.
Liens for rent of buildings.
Vested in assignee of claim
for rent, §35-9-65.
Attachment.
Liens for advances and rent
of lands, §§35-9-30 to
35-9-42.
Liens for rent of buildings,
§§35-9-60 to 35-9-65.
Attornment.
Prohibited generally, §35-9-1.
Unnecessary upon
conveyance, §35-4-32.
Bonds, surety.
Liens for advances and rent
of lands, §35-9-35.
Breach of lease.
Notice to quit, §35-9-6.
Buildings.
Liens for rent of buildings,
§§35-9-60 to 35-9-65.
Circuit courts.
Possession wrongfully
withheld.
Removal of action to
circuit court, §35-9-83.
Commercial code.
Lien of landlord.
Applicability of secured
transactions provision,
§7-9-104.
Conveyances.
Attornment of tenant
unnecessary, §35-4-32.
Conveyance of greater estate
by tenant for life or
years passes his estate,
§35-4-232.
Payment of rent without
notice of conveyance,
§35-4-32.
Crops.
Advances.
Liens for advances and
rent of lands.
Attachment to crop of
succeeding year,
§35-9-32.
Emblements.
When tenant at will
entitled to
emblements, §35-9-2.
Failure or refusal of tenant
to plant crop, §35-9-38.

LANDLORD AND TENANT
—Cont'd
Crops—Cont'd
Levy upon crop of subtenant,
§35-9-39.
Liens for advances and rent
of lands.
Attachment to crop of
succeeding year,
§35-9-32.
Seizure upon abandonment of
premises, §35-9-12.
Damages.
Reasonable satisfaction for
use and occupation of
land, §35-9-100.
Default of lease.
Notice to quit, §35-9-6.
Demand of possession.
Notice to quit for breach or
default of terms of lease,
§35-9-6.
Service of demand, §35-9-7.
Tenant wrongfully
withholding, §35-9-80.
Unnecessary when tenancy is
for certain period,
§35-9-8.
Duration of tenancy.
Lodgings.
Hiring of lodgings for
indefinite term,
§35-9-3.
When time for termination
not specified, §35-9-3.
Ejectment.
Joinder of landlord as party
defendant, §6-6-287.
Continuation of action
against tenant,
§6-6-287.
Liability.
Tenant in possession,
§6-6-288.
Possession wrongfully
withheld, §§35-9-80 to
35-9-88.
Emblements.
When tenant at will entitled
to emblements, §35-9-2.
Estoppel.
Tenant estopped to deny
landlord's title, §35-9-1.
Executors and
administrators.
Renting of lands for payment
of debts and for division,
§43-2-440.
Fees.
Possession wrongfully
withheld, §35-9-88.
Forms.
Notice to quit for breach or
default of terms of lease,
§35-9-6.
Holding over.
Tenants holding over.
Damages, §35-9-100.
Possession wrongfully
withheld, §§35-9-80 to
35-9-88.
Judgments.
Possession wrongfully
withheld.
Judgment for landlord,
§35-9-86.
Leases.
General provisions.
See LEASES.

LANDLORD AND TENANT
—Cont'd
Liens of landlord, §§35-9-30
to 35-9-65.
Advances and rent of lands,
§§35-9-30 to 35-9-42.
Affidavits.
Attachment, §35-9-35.
Applicability of division to
tenant in chief and
subtenant, §35-9-42.
Assignment of claim for
rent and advances,
§35-9-33.
Attachment.
Affidavit and bond,
§35-9-35.
Bond, §35-9-35.
Crop of succeeding year,
§35-9-32.
Issuance, §35-9-36.
Property leviable,
§35-9-36.
Return, §35-9-36.
Subtenants.
Levy upon crop of
subtenant,
§35-9-39.
Right of subtenant to
require
attachment
against tenant in
chief, §35-9-41.
Trial, §35-9-36.
When lien may be
enforced by
attachment,
§35-9-34.
Bonds, surety.
Attachment, §35-9-35.
Claim for rent and
advances.
Assignment, §35-9-33.
Continuation of lien,
§35-9-32.
Declaration of lien,
§35-9-30.
Enforcement of lien.
Attachment.
When lien may be
enforced by
attachment,
§35-9-34.
Failure of tenant to plant
crop, §35-9-38.
Lien declared, §35-9-30.
Liens of agricultural
superintendents and
laborers.
Prior satisfaction of
claims for rent and
advances, §35-11-96.
Maturity of rent and
advances, §35-9-31.
Refusal of tenant to plant
crop, §35-9-38.
Relation between party
furnishing land and
party furnishing labor,
§35-9-37.
Subtenants.
Applicability of division
to subtenant,
§35-9-42.
Attachment, §35-9-39.
Right of subtenant to
require
attachment
against tenant in
chief, §35-9-41.

LANDLORD AND TENANT
—Cont'd
Liens of landlord—Cont'd
Advances and rent of lands
—Cont'd
Subtenants—Cont'd
Levy upon crop of
subtenant, §35-9-39.
Subrogation of subtenant
to rights, liens and
remedies of landlord,
§35-9-40.
Trial of attachment,
§35-9-36.
Assignees.
Right of landlord to enforce
lien against assignees,
§35-9-11.
Commercial code.
Applicability of secured
transactions provision,
§7-9-104.
Crops.
Liens for advances and
rent of lands.
Attachment to crop of
succeeding year,
§35-9-32.
Enforcement.
Right to enforce against
sublessees or assignees
of tenant, §35-9-11.
Livestock.
Lien of landlord on stock
raised on rented
premises, §35-11-72.
Rent of buildings, §§35-9-60
to 35-9-65.
Affidavits.
Attachment, §35-9-62.
Assignments.
Liens, rights and
remedies vested in
assignee of claim for
rent, §35-9-65.
Attachment.
Affidavit, §35-9-62.
Bond, §35-9-62.
Law governing
proceedings,
§35-9-64.
Property leviable,
§35-9-63.
When lien may be
enforced by
attachment,
§35-9-61.
Bonds, surety.
Attachment, §35-9-62.
Declaration of lien,
§35-9-60.
Enforcement of lien.
Attachment.
When lien may be
enforced by
attachment,
§35-9-61.
Law governing
proceedings, §35-9-64.
Lien declared, §35-9-60.
Priority of lien, §35-9-63.
Secured transactions.
Applicability of secured
transactions provision,
§7-9-104.
Sublessees.
Right of landlord to enforce
lien against sublessees,
§35-9-11.

LANDLORD AND TENANT
—Cont'd
Life estates.
General provisions.
See LIFE ESTATES.
Recovery of rent upon death
of life tenant who has
demised estate, §35-9-13.
Livestock.
Lien of landlord on stock
raised on rented
premises, §35-11-72.
Lodgings.
Hiring of lodgings for
indefinite term, §35-9-4.
**Mechanics' and
materialmen's liens.**
Building or improvement on
leased land, §35-11-212.
Notice.
Breach or default of terms of
lease, §35-9-6.
Eviction notice, §35-9-6.
Service, §35-9-7.
Tenancy for certain period.
Notice unnecessary,
§35-9-8.
Termination of tenancy.
Lodgings, §35-9-4.
Tenancy at will, §35-9-3.
Tenancy for term less than
one year, §35-9-5.
When time for termination
not specified, §35-9-3.
Unnecessary when tenancy is
for certain period,
§35-9-8.
Occupation of land.
When reasonable satisfaction
may be recovered,
§35-9-100.
Option to purchase land.
Limitations on duration of
option, §35-4-76.
Ownership.
Apartment ownership act,
§§35-8-1 to 35-8-22.
Partnerships.
Incidents of tenancy,
§10-8-72.
Personal property.
Conveyances of personal
property brought into
state by tenants for life
or years.
Recordation, §35-4-54.
**Possession wrongfully
withheld,** §§35-9-80 to
35-9-88.
Affidavits.
Arrest of proceedings by
tenant, §35-9-84.
Demand for premises,
§35-9-80.
Trial upon delivery of
counter affidavit,
§35-9-85.
Appeals, §35-9-87.
Arrest of proceedings,
§35-9-85.
Circuit court.
Removal of action to
circuit court, §35-9-83.
Demand of possession.
Notice to quit for breach or
default of terms of
lease, §35-9-6.
Service of demand, §35-9-7.
Tenant wrongfully
withholding, §35-9-80.

LANDLORD AND TENANT
—Cont'd
Possession wrongfully withheld—Cont'd

Demand of possession
—Cont'd
Unnecessary when tenancy is for certain period, §35-9-8.

Fees, §35-9-88.

Judgment for landlord, §35-9-86.

Process.
Issuance of process, §35-9-81.
Service of process, §35-9-82.
Removal of action to circuit court, §35-9-83.
Service of writ or process, §35-9-82.
Trial upon delivery of counter affidavit, §35-9-85.

Writ.
Issuance of writ, §35-9-81.
Service of writ, §35-9-82.

Priorities.
Liens for rent of buildings, §35-9-63.

Remedies.
Landlord's remedies.
Eviction, §35-9-63.
Extended to grantees, etc., §35-9-9.
Liens of landlord, §§35-9-30 to 35-9-65.
Tenant's remedies.
Extended to tenant's grantees, §35-9-10.
Use and occupation of land.
When reasonable satisfaction may be recovered, §35-9-100.

Rent.
Buildings.
Liens for rent of buildings, §§35-9-60 to 35-9-65.
Conveyance of property.
Payment of rent without notice of conveyance, §35-4-32.
Liens for advances and rent of lands, §§35-9-30 to 35-9-42.
Life tenants.
Recovery of rent upon death of life tenant who has demised estate, §35-9-13.
Rent of lands.
Liens for advances and rent of lands, §§35-9-30 to 35-9-42.

Searches and seizures.
Crops.
Seizure upon abandonment of premises, §35-9-12.

Secured transactions.
Lien of landlord.
Applicability of secured transactions provision, §7-9-104.

Self-service storage facilities, §§8-15-30 to 8-15-38.
Applicability of article, §8-15-38.
Citation of article, §8-15-30.

LANDLORD AND TENANT
—Cont'd
Self-service storage facilities —Cont'd

Creditors.
Effect of laws governing rights of creditors, §8-15-37.
Definitions, §8-15-31.
Effect of law governing rights of landlords against tenants, §8-15-37.
Failure to pay charges.
Posting of notice as to effect, §8-15-35.
Landlords.
Effect of laws governing rights of landlords against tenants, §8-15-37.
Liens.
Owner's lien, §8-15-33.
Satisfaction, §8-15-37.
Posting of notice as to effect of failure to pay charges, §8-15-35.
Satisfaction of owner's lien, §8-15-34.
Notice.
Posting of notice as to effect of failure to pay charges, §8-15-35.
Rights provided by article as additional to other rights allowed by law, §8-15-36.
Risk of loss.
Determination, §8-15-32.
Short title, §8-15-30.
Vesting of care in occupant, §8-15-32.

Service of process.
Demand of possession, §35-9-7.
Notice to quit, §35-9-7.
Possession wrongfully withheld, §35-9-82.

Summons and process.
Possession wrongfully withheld.
Issuance of process, §35-9-81.

Tenancy at will.
Duration of tenancy when time for termination not specified, §35-9-3.
Hiring of lodgings for indefinite term, §35-9-4.
Emblements.
When tenant at will entitled to emblements, §35-9-2.
Lodgings.
Hiring of lodgings for indefinite term, §35-9-4.
Notice to terminate, §35-9-3.

Tenants holding over.
Damages, §35-9-100.
Possession wrongfully withheld, §§35-9-80 to 35-9-88.

Termination of tenancy.
Duration of tenancy when time for termination not specified, §35-9-3.
Lodgings, §35-9-4.

LANDLORD AND TENANT
—Cont'd
Termination of tenancy —Cont'd

Less than one year.
Notice to terminate tenancy for term less than one year, §35-9-5.
Lodgings.
Hiring of lodgings for indefinite term, §35-9-4.
Notice, §§35-9-80 to 35-9-88.
Possession wrongfully withheld, §§35-9-80 to 35-9-88.
Tenancy for term less than one year.
Notice to terminate, §35-9-5.

Term of tenancy.
Certain period.
Notice to quit unnecessary when tenancy is for certain period, §35-9-8.

Title.
Tenant estopped to deny landlord's title, §35-9-1.

Trial.
Liens for advances and rent of lands.
Attachment, §35-9-36.
Possession wrongfully withheld.
Trial upon delivery of counter affidavit, §35-9-85.

Use and occupation of land.
When reasonable satisfaction may be recovered, §35-9-100.

Writs.
Possession wrongfully withheld.
Issuance of writ, §35-9-81.
Service of writ, §35-9-82.

Wrongfully withholding possession, §§35-9-80 to 35-9-88.

LAND PATENTS.
Conveyances by governor or state agencies or institutions, §§35-4-380 to 35-4-391.
See CONVEYANCES.

Decedents' estates.
Public lands.
Patents to charge real estate with debts and obligations of decedent, §35-4-386.

Evidence, §12-21-96.

School lands.
When secretary of state issues patent, §16-20-3.

LANDSCAPE ARCHITECTS,
§§34-17-1 to 34-17-27.
Architects.
Exemptions from provisions of chapter, §34-17-27.
Board of examiners, §§34-17-1 to 34-17-3.
Appointment of members, §34-17-2.
Compensation of members, §34-17-2.
Composition of board, §34-17-2.
Creation of board, §34-17-2.
Defined, §34-17-1.

LANDSCAPE ARCHITECTS
—Cont'd
Board of examiners—Cont'd
Enforcement of chapter.
Powers and duties of
board, §34-17-3.
Governor.
Annual report to governor,
§34-17-3.
Appointment of board
members, §34-17-2.
Meetings, §34-17-2.
Oaths.
Administration by board
members, §34-17-3.
Oath of office, §34-17-2.
Officers of board, §34-17-2.
Powers and duties, §34-17-3.
Qualifications of members,
§34-17-2.
Records.
Board to keep record of
proceedings, §34-17-3.
Reports.
Annual report to governor,
§34-17-3.
Rules and regulations.
Examinations.
Board to adopt rules
covering scope of
examinations,
§34-17-22.
Promulgation by board,
§34-17-3.
Seal.
Adoption and use of official
seal, §34-17-3.
Secretary.
Landscape architect's fund.
Duties of secretary,
§34-17-6.
Terms of office, §34-17-2.
Vacancies.
Filling vacancies, §34-17-2.
Corporations.
Certificate of authorization.
Terms and conditions,
§34-17-4.
Licensing or registration of
corporation prohibited,
§34-17-4.
Limitations and conditions
on corporate practice,
§34-17-4.
Definitions, §34-17-1.
Disciplinary actions.
Grounds for disciplinary
actions, §34-17-5.
**Drawings, specifications and
plans.**
Approval.
Seal and signature
required, §34-17-4.
Misrepresentation as to
preparation.
Grounds for disciplinary
actions, §34-17-5.
Signature and seal required,
§34-17-4.
Engineers.
Exemptions from provisions
of chapter, §34-17-27.
Examinations.
Board of examiners,
§§34-17-1 to 34-17-3.
Conduct of examinations,
§34-17-22.
Exemptions from
examination
requirements, §34-17-23.
Fee, §34-17-25.

LANDSCAPE ARCHITECTS
—Cont'd
Examinations—Cont'd
Qualifications of applicants,
§34-17-21.
Rules and regulations.
Board to adopt rules
covering scope of
exam, §34-17-22.
Schedule of examinations,
§34-17-22.
**Exemptions from provisions
of chapter.**
Examination requirements,
§34-17-23.
Generally, §34-17-27.
Fees.
Examination fee, §34-17-25.
License fees, §§34-17-24,
34-17-25.
Foresters.
Exemptions from provisions
of chapter, §34-17-27.
Fraud.
Grounds for disciplinary
actions, §34-17-5.
Funds.
Landscape architect's fund,
§34-17-6.
Governor.
Board of examiners,
§§34-17-2, 34-17-3.
Land surveyors.
Exemptions from provisions
of chapter, §34-17-27.
Licenses.
Fees.
Amount, §34-17-25.
Delinquent fee penalty,
§34-17-24.
Payment, §34-17-24.
Receipt to be issued,
§34-17-24.
Reissuance fee, §34-17-24.
Schedule, §34-17-25.
Nonresidents.
Reciprocity, §34-17-26.
Public policy as to licensing,
§34-17-20.
Qualifications of applicants,
§34-17-21.
Required, §34-17-20.
Nonresidents.
Reciprocity as to licensing,
§34-17-26.
Waiver of examination
requirements, §34-17-23.
Partnerships.
Certificate of authorization.
Terms and conditions,
§34-17-4.
Licensing or registration of
partnerships prohibited,
§34-17-4.
Limitations and conditions
on corporate practice,
§34-17-4.
Penalties.
Violations of chapter,
§34-17-7.
Permits.
Horticulture and floriculture
work, §§2-28-4 to 2-28-7.
Plans, §§34-17-4, 34-17-5.
**Practice of landscape
architecture.**
Corporations.
Licensing and registration
prohibited, §34-17-4.

LANDSCAPE ARCHITECTS
—Cont'd
**Practice of landscape
architecture**—Cont'd
Corporations—Cont'd
Limitations and conditions
on corporate practice,
§34-17-4.
Deemed personal right,
§34-17-4.
Partnerships.
Limitations and conditions
on practice, §34-17-4.
Registration or licensing
prohibited, §34-17-4.
Reciprocity.
Board authorized to permit
reciprocal practice,
§34-17-26.
Records.
Board of examiners.
Record of proceedings,
§34-17-3.
Reports.
Board of examiners.
Annual report to governor,
§34-17-3.
Rules and regulations.
Board of examiners.
Examinations.
Scope of examinations,
§34-17-22.
Promulgation by board,
§34-17-3.
Seals.
Board of examiners.
Adoption and use of official
seal, §34-17-3.
Final drawings, etc., to bear
seal, §34-17-4.
Violations of chapter.
Grounds for disciplinary
actions, §34-17-5.
Penalties, §34-17-7.

LANDSCAPING.
Appeals.
Horticulture and floriculture
work.
Appeals from denial or
revocation of permits,
§2-28-7.
Architects.
Landscape architects,
§§34-17-1 to 34-17-27.
See LANDSCAPE
ARCHITECTS.
Capitol.
Gardener.
Employment of landscape
gardener for Capitol
grounds, §41-4-183.
Definitions.
Horticulture and floriculture
work, §2-28-1.
Fees.
Horticulture and floriculture
work.
Permit fees, §2-28-4.
**Horticulture and floriculture
work,** §§2-28-1 to 2-28-12.
Appeals from denial or
revocation of permits,
§2-28-7.
Applicability of chapter,
§2-28-12.
Commissioner of agriculture
and industries.
Permits.
Appeals from denial or
revocation, §2-28-7.

LANDSCAPING—Cont'd
  **Horticulture and floriculture
    work**—Cont'd
    Commissioner of agriculture
        and industries—Cont'd
      Permits—Cont'd
        Applicants to present
            evidence as to
            qualifications,
            §2-28-5.
        Denial or revocation,
            §2-28-7.
    Definitions, §2-28-1.
    Examinations.
      Applicants for permits,
          §2-28-4.
      Applicability of
          requirement as to
          examination,
          §2-28-6.
      Required, §2-28-2.
    Examining board.
      Generally, §2-28-2.
    Fees.
      Permit fees, §2-28-4.
    Injunctions.
      Restraining performance
          without permit,
          §2-28-11.
    Penalties for violations of
        chapter or rules or
        regulations, §2-28-11.
    Permits.
      Appeals from denial or
          revocation, §2-28-7.
      Commissioner.
        Appeals from denial or
            revocation, §2-28-7.
        Applicants to present
            evidence as to
            qualifications,
            §2-28-5.
        Denial or revocation,
            §2-28-7.
      Denial, §2-28-7.
      Duration, §2-28-4.
      Examination of applicants,
          §2-28-4.
        Applicability of
            requirement as to
            examination,
            §2-28-6.
      Experience of applicants.
        Submission of statements
            as to experience,
            §2-28-4.
      Fees, §2-28-4.
      Injunctive proceedings to
          restrain performance
          of work or services
          without permit,
          §2-28-11.
      Issuance, §§2-28-4, 2-28-5.
      Qualifications of
          applicants.
        Evidence as to
            qualifications,
            §2-28-5.
        Minimum qualifications,
            §2-28-5.
        Submission of statements
            as to training and
            experience, §2-28-4.
      Required for performance
          of professional work,
          §2-28-4.
      Revocation, §2-28-7.
      Testing of applicants,
          §2-28-4.

LANDSCAPING—Cont'd
  **Horticulture and floriculture
    work**—Cont'd
    Permits—Cont'd
      Training.
        Submission of statements
            as to training by
            applicants, §2-28-4.
    Qualifications of persons
        engaged in work.
      Promulgation of rules and
          regulations, §2-28-3.
    Rules and regulations.
      Penalties for violations,
          §2-28-11.
      Promulgation as to
          qualifications and
          practice, §2-28-3.
    Violations of chapter.
      Penalties for violations,
          §2-28-11.
  Injunctions.
    Horticulture and floriculture
        work.
      Performance of professional
          work or services
          without permit,
          §2-28-11.
  Penalties.
    Horticulture and floriculture
        work.
      Commissioner may impose
          penalty, §2-2-18.
      Violations, §2-28-11.
**LAND SURVEYORS, §§34-11-1
    to 34-11-37.**
    See SURVEYS AND
        SURVEYORS.
**LANETT, MUNICIPALITY
    OF.**
    Property tax, Const. Ala.,
        amd. 8.
LARCENY.
  Arrest.
    Goods held for sale.
      Detention and arrest of
          suspect, §15-10-14.
    Livestock.
      Appearance upon arrest,
          §2-2-14.1.
  **Burglary, §§13A-7-1 to
      13A-7-8.**
      See BURGLARY.
  Commercial code.
    Commercial paper.
      Defenses, §7-3-306.
      Stolen instruments,
          §7-3-804.
    Investment securities,
        §7-8-405.
    Sales.
      Power to transfer voidable
          title, §7-2-403.
  False pretenses.
    Bringing into state property
        obtained by false
        pretense elsewhere,
        §13A-8-21.
  **General provisions,
      §§13A-8-1 to 13A-8-144.**
      See THEFT.
  Indictments.
    Form of indictment,
        §15-8-150.
  **Investment securities,
      §7-8-405.**
  Livestock.
    Arrest.
      Appearance upon arrest,
          §2-2-14.1.

LARCENY—Cont'd
  Livestock—Cont'd
    Department to determine
        ownership of stolen
        livestock and furnish
        information to interested
        persons, §2-15-25.
    Forfeiture of vehicles, etc.,
        used in theft, §2-2-14.2.
    Livestock theft investigator,
        §2-2-14.
  Motor vehicles.
    Embezzlement, conversion,
        etc., of vehicles subject to
        larceny, §32-15-7.
    Uniform certificate of title
        and antitheft act,
        §§32-8-1 to 32-8-88.
      See MOTOR VEHICLES.
  Stolen property.
    See STOLEN PROPERTY.
LARGEMOUTH BASS.
  State fresh water fish, §1-2-9.
LAUDERDALE COUNTY.
  Elk river watershed area.
    Development, Const. Ala.,
        amd. 243.
  Officers.
    Compensation of certain
        officers, Const. Ala.,
        amd. 241.
  School tax.
    School district tax, Const.
        Ala., amd. 404.
    Special property tax for
        educational purposes,
        Const. Ala., amd. 177.
  **Special, private or local laws
      relating to Lauderdale
      county and
      municipalities,** Const.
      Ala., amd. 140.
  Tax assessor.
    Combination of offices of tax
        assessor and tax
        collector, Const. Ala.,
        amd. 405.
LAUNDRIES.
  General provisions.
    See CLEANERS, DYERS
        AND PRESSERS.
**LAW ENFORCEMENT
    OFFICERS.**
  Constables.
    See CONSTABLES.
  General provisions.
    See PEACE OFFICERS.
  Police.
    See POLICE.
  Sheriffs.
    See SHERIFFS.
  State police.
    See STATE POLICE.
**LAW ENFORCEMENT
    PLANNING AGENCY,
    §§41-8A-1 to 41-8A-13.**
  Budgets.
    Submission to governor of
        annual budget,
        §41-8A-12.
  Composition, §41-8A-2.
  Conflict of laws.
    Omnibus crime control and
        safe streets act of 1968.
      Effect of chapter in event
          provisions conflict,
          §41-8A-13.
  Construction of chapter,
      §41-8A-13.

**LAW ENFORCEMENT
PLANNING AGENCY**
—Cont'd
Creation, §41-8A-2.
Definitions, §41-8A-1.
**Department of economic and
community affairs.**
Transfer of functions to
department, §41-23-1.
Development.
Office of state planning and
federal programs.
Inapplicability of
provisions, §41-9-214.
Director, §41-8A-2.
Appointment, §41-8A-5.
Duties, §41-8A-4.
Powers, §41-8A-4.
Qualifications, §41-8A-5.
Duties, §41-8A-6.
Establishment, §41-8A-2.
Governor.
Request for funds in
appropriation bill,
§41-8A-12.
Submission of annual budget
and request for funds to
governor, §41-8A-12.
Powers, §41-8A-6.
**Regional advisory boards
and planning units.**
Appointment of members,
§41-8A-8.
Budgeting and other
financial procedures,
§41-8A-10.
Compensation of members,
§41-8A-9.
Composition, §41-8A-8.
Duties, §41-8A-9.
Establishment, §41-8A-8.
Financial procedures,
§41-8A-10.
Officers, §41-8A-8.
Powers, §41-8A-9.
Purpose, §41-8A-8.
Representation of more than
one element or interest
by board member,
§41-8A-11.
Service by same individual
on state supervisory
board and regional
advisory board,
§41-8A-11.
Staff, §41-8A-8.
Request for funds, §41-8A-12.
Staff, §41-8A-3.
State supervisory board.
Appointment of members,
§41-8A-5.
Compensation of members,
§41-8A-5.
Composition, §41-8A-5.
Creation, §41-8A-5.
Duties, §41-8A-6.
Establishment, §41-8A-5.
Executive committee,
§41-8A-5.
Powers and duties,
§41-8A-7.
Officers, §41-8A-5.
Powers, §41-8A-6.
Qualifications of members,
§41-8A-5.
Representation of more than
one element or interest
by board member,
§41-8A-11.

**LAW ENFORCEMENT
PLANNING AGENCY**
—Cont'd
State supervisory board
—Cont'd
Service by same individual
on state supervisory
board and regional
advisory board,
§41-8A-11.
Terms of members, §41-8A-5.
Vacancies, §41-8A-5.
LAW INSTITUTE, §§29-8-1 to
29-8-5.
See ALABAMA LAW
INSTITUTE.
LAWRENCE COUNTY.
Barbers.
Chapter not applicable to
Lawrence county,
§34-5-15.
Bond issues, Const. Ala., amd.
30.
Court costs and charges,
Const. Ala., amd. 321.
**Economic and industrial
development promotion,**
Const. Ala., amd. 429.
Economic development,
Const. Ala., amd. 190.
Health.
Special property tax for
general health purposes,
Const. Ala., amd. 311.
Officers.
Fees, compensation, etc., of
certain officers, Const.
Ala., amd. 321.
School districts.
Authorization of creation of
special school districts,
etc., in Lawrence county,
Const. Ala., amd. 99.
Change in boundaries of
school districts, Const.
Ala., amd. 294.
Special school district in
Lawrence county, Const.
Ala., amd. 79.
School tax.
Special tax in school
districts, Const. Ala.,
amd. 294.
Tax elections in certain
school districts, Const.
Ala., amds. 20, 32.
LAWS.
Code of Alabama.
See CODE OF ALABAMA.
Counties.
See COUNTIES.
International law.
Constitutional provisions.
Power of congress to
punish offenses
against, Const. U. S.,
Art. I, §8.
Local laws.
Counties.
See COUNTIES.
Municipal corporations.
Ordinances.
See MUNICIPAL
CORPORATIONS.
Retroactive laws.
Ex post facto laws.
Prohibited, Const. U. S.,
Art. I, §§9, 10.
Statutes.
See STATUTES.

LAWS—Cont'd
Supreme law of the land.
Constitution of the United
States, Const. U. S., Art.
VI.
LEAD.
Citation of chapter, §22-37-1.
Definitions, §22-37-2.
Materials not lead-free.
Use or sale for drinking
water systems or
plumbing, §22-37-6.
Notice.
Customers of water suppliers.
Notice of potential for lead
contamination,
§22-37-5.
Plumbing codes.
Amendment of city and
county plumbing codes,
§22-37-4.
Rules and regulations.
Promulgation, §22-37-3.
Short title of chapter,
§22-37-1.
**Water supply and
waterworks.**
Notice to customers of
potential for lead
contamination, §22-37-5.
Use or sale of materials not
lead-free, §22-37-6.
LEARNERS' LICENSES.
Drivers' licenses, §§32-6-8,
32-6-21.
LEASES.
Acknowledgments.
Leases for more than 20
years, §35-4-6.
Agricultural center.
Lease of coliseum building
and facilities, §§2-6-50 to
2-6-54.
See AGRICULTURE.
Alcoholic beverages.
Dry counties.
Renting or permitting use
of premises for sale,
manufacture, etc.,
§§28-4-90 to 28-4-93.
Ameraport.
Offshore harbor and terminal
commission, §§33-10-18,
33-10-19.
See AMERAPORT.
Armories.
Duties of armory commission,
§31-4-16.
Breach.
Notice to quit for breach,
§35-9-6.
Coal.
Inspections.
Refusal to permit adjacent
landowner or lessee to
inspect mine,
§25-9-322.
Surface mining control and
reclamation.
Certain lands leased,
§9-16-101.
Condominiums.
Common and limited
common elements.
Lease includes undivided
interest, §35-8-6.
Units, §35-8-8.

LEASES—Cont'd
Convict labor.
Leasing of convicts.
General provisions,
§§14-5-2, 14-5-5.
Penalties, §14-5-4.
State agencies, §14-5-10.
Corrections.
Institution finance authority.
Kilby property, §§14-2-29
to 14-2-32.
Default.
Notice to quit for default,
§35-9-6.
Education.
Lease and sale of school land,
§§16-20-1 to 16-20-9.
See PUBLIC LANDS.
Electric cooperatives.
Lease of property.
Approval of members
required, §37-6-21.
**Electric membership
corporations.**
Power to lease property,
§37-7-11.
Eminent domain.
Rental to former owner or
tenant.
Amount of rent, §18-1A-25.
**Environmental improvement
authorities.**
Power to lease, §9-6-8.
Exemption from taxation,
§11-89-16.
Fees.
Probate judges' fees,
§12-19-90.
Forms.
Notice to quit for breach or
default, §35-9-6.
**Fraudulent leasing or rental
of property, §§13A-8-140
to 13A-8-144.**
Governor.
Conveyances by governor or
state agency or
institution, §§35-4-380,
35-4-383.
Harbors and ports.
Real property, §33-1-17.
Taxation.
Exemption from taxation,
§33-1-19.
Health care authorities.
Agreements with authorizing
subdivisions.
Authorized, §22-21-330.
Options.
Renewal options,
§22-21-330.
Remedies for default in
performance of lease
agreement, §22-21-331.
Security for payment of
rental.
Special pledge as
security, §22-21-330.
Terms, §22-21-330.
Vacant space.
Use, §22-21-330.
Homestead exemptions.
Exemptions from levy and
sale under process.
Effect of leasing
homestead, §6-10-41.
**Landlord and tenant
generally.**
See LANDLORD AND
TENANT.

LEASES—Cont'd
Licenses.
Leasing or renting tangible
personal property,
§§40-12-220 to 40-12-227.
See PERSONAL
PROPERTY.
Marine resources.
Oysters.
Natural oyster reefs,
§§9-12-21 to 9-12-25.
**Mechanics' and
materialmen's liens.**
Building or improvement on
leased land, §35-11-212.
Military affairs.
Taxation.
Exemption of property
leased by units of
armed forces, §31-2-80.
Mines and minerals.
Governor.
Authorization to lease
mineral rights on
public lands,
§35-4-383.
Public lands.
School lands, §9-15-36.
Salt springs.
Conveyance by director of
conservation,
§35-4-380.
Motor vehicles.
Violation where vehicle
leased to another.
Owner not liable,
§32-5-152.1.
Exception upon failure to
maintain vehicle,
§32-5-152.1.
Municipal corporations.
Post office projects.
Leasing of projects.
Authority to lease
facilities to postal
service, §11-55-13.
Powers of municipalities,
§11-55-2.
Requirements as to
leases, §11-55-10.
Public utilities.
Lease of electric, gas, etc.,
plants, §§11-50-140 to
11-50-151.
See MUNICIPAL
CORPORATIONS.
**Oil and gas leases, §§9-17-50
to 9-17-69.**
Mineral documentary tax,
§§40-20-30 to 40-20-37.
See OIL AND GAS.
Option to purchase land.
Limitations on duration,
§35-4-76.
Personal property.
Leasing or renting,
§§40-12-220 to 40-12-227.
See PERSONAL
PROPERTY.
Licenses, §§40-12-220 to
40-12-227.
See PERSONAL
PROPERTY.
Prisons and prisoners.
Convict labor.
Leasing of convicts.
General provisions,
§§14-5-2, 14-5-5.
Penalties, §14-5-4.
State agencies, §14-5-10.

LEASES—Cont'd
Public lands.
Authority to lease, §9-15-18.
Oil and gas leases, §§9-17-50
to 9-17-69.
See OIL AND GAS.
School lands, §9-15-36.
Swamp and overflowed lands
Approval, §9-15-45.
Authority of commissioner,
§9-15-30.
Authorized, §9-15-45.
Public service commission.
Water distribution facilities.
Conveyance without
commission approval,
§37-4-45.
Public utilities.
Lease of property, §§37-4-40
to 37-4-44.
See PUBLIC UTILITIES.
Recordation.
Leases for more than 20
years, §35-4-6.
Memorandum of lease.
Recording in lieu of lease,
§35-4-51.1.
Sales tax.
Personal property.
Leasing or renting,
§§40-12-220 to
40-12-227.
See PERSONAL
PROPERTY.
Salt springs.
Lease by director of
conservation, §35-4-380.
School lands.
General provisions, §§16-20-
to 16-20-9.
See PUBLIC LANDS.
**Southeast interstate low-
level radioactive waste
management compact.**
Bond, surety of leasor,
§22-32-5.
Operation and disposal of
waste, §22-32-4.
**Southern products mart
authority.**
Leasing of buildings,
facilities and structures
§41-10-68.
**Space science exhibit
commission.**
Concessions, §41-9-436.
**State departments and
agencies.**
Conveyances by governor or
state agency or
institution, §§35-4-380,
35-4-383.
Lease-sale agreements.
Authority to enter for
equipment purchasers
§41-4-115.
Taxation.
Personal property.
Leasing or renting,
§§40-12-220 to
40-12-227.
See PERSONAL
PROPERTY.
Term.
Maximum term of leasehold
estate, §35-4-6.

LEASES—Cont'd
Term—Cont'd
More than 20 years.
Acknowledgment or
approval and
recordation of leases
for more than 20
years, §35-4-6.
Theft.
Fraudulent leasing or rental
of property, §§13A-8-140
to 13A-8-144.
See THEFT.
Water conservation and
irrigation.
Corporations.
Property.
Counties, cities, public
departments, etc.,
§9-10-42.
Water supply and
waterworks.
Water distribution facilities.
Conveyance without
commission approval,
§37-4-45.
LEE COUNTY.
Fires and fire prevention.
Fire fighting districts and
fire protection, Const.
Ala., amds. 392, 498.
Juveniles.
Special tax for improving
enforcement of laws
relative to and providing
facilities for, Const. Ala.,
amd. 324.
Officers.
Fees and compensation of
elected officials, Const.
Ala., amd. 362.
School tax.
Special property tax for
educational purposes,
Const. Ala., amd. 147.
Special school district tax,
Const. Ala., amd. 309.
LEGACIES.
Executors and
administrators.
Settlements and
distributions.
Compelling payment of
legacies, §§43-2-580 to
43-2-586.
See EXECUTORS AND
ADMINISTRATORS.
General provisions, §§43-8-1
to 43-8-298.
See WILLS.
LEGAL SERVICES
LIABILITY, §§6-5-570 to
6-5-581.
See ATTORNEYS AT LAW.
LEGISLATIVE
DEPARTMENT.
Constitution of Alabama,
Const. Ala., art. IV, §§44
to 111.
See CONSTITUTION OF
ALABAMA.
General provisions, Const.
Ala., art. IV, §§44 to 111.
See LEGISLATURE.

LEGISLATURE, §§29-1-1 to
29-8-5.
Accounts and accounting.
Legislative committee on
public accounts,
§§41-5-18 to 41-5-20.
Acts of legislature.
Printing, §§41-4-130 to
41-4-161.
See PRINTING.
Public printing and binding,
§§41-4-130 to 41-4-161.
See PRINTING.
Secretary of state, §§36-14-11
to 36-14-13.
Statutes.
See STATUTES.
Administrative procedure
act.
Intent of legislature,
§41-22-2.
Alabama agricultural and
mechanical university.
Reports to legislature,
§16-49-30.
Alabama state university.
Reports to legislature,
§16-50-30.
Amendment of laws by title
only, Const. Ala., art. IV,
§45.
Amendments to constitution.
Basis to representation in
legislature not to be
changed, Const. Ala., art.
XVIII, §284.
Apportionment, Const. Ala.,
art. IV, §50.
Census.
Apportionment of house
based on decennial
census, Const. Ala.,
art. IX, §198.
Duty of legislature to
apportion representatives
among counties, Const.
Ala., art. IX, §199.
Each county entitled to at
least one representative,
Const. Ala., art. IX,
§199.
Enumeration of inhabitants.
State may provide for
enumeration, Const.
Ala., art. IX, §201.
Equality of senatorial
districts, Const. Ala., art.
IX, §200.
Initial apportionment of
house of representatives,
Const. Ala., art. IX,
§202.
Initial apportionment of
senatorial districts,
Const. Ala., art. IX,
§203.
Number of members of house
of representatives.
Maximum number, Const.
Ala., art. IX, §198.
Ratio of senators to
representatives, Const.
Ala., art. IX, §197.
Appropriations.
Allotments of appropriations.
Approval of allotments,
§41-4-91.
Duration of allotments,
§41-4-91.
Modification of allotments,
§41-4-91.

LEGISLATURE—Cont'd
Appropriations—Cont'd
Allotments of appropriations
—Cont'd
Requisition of allotments,
§41-4-91.
Restriction of allotments
by governor, §41-4-90.
Availability, §41-4-90.
Charitable or educational
institutions.
Institutions not under
absolute control of
state, Const. Ala., art.
IV, §73.
Committees.
Legislative interim
committees, §29-1-10.
Effect, §41-4-90.
Emergency appropriations,
§41-4-94.
General appropriation bill.
Restrictions on, Const.
Ala., art. IV, §71.
Lapsing of appropriations,
§41-4-93.
Legislative costs, §29-1-22.
Legislative fiscal office,
§§29-5-1 to 29-5-12.
Paramount duty to make
basic appropriations at
regular sessions, Const.
Ala., amd. 448.
Payment of money out of
state treasury, Const.
Ala., art. IV, §72.
Penalties for violations of
article, §41-4-96.
Restriction of allotments by
governor, §41-4-90.
Restrictions on general
appropriation bill, Const.
Ala., art. IV, §71.
Violations of article.
Penalties, §41-4-96.
Wrongful expenditure,
§41-4-95.
Arrest.
Privilege from arrest,
§29-1-7.
Constitutional provisions,
Const. Ala., art. IV,
§56.
Auburn University.
Board of trustees.
Report made to legislature,
§16-48-11.
Banks and banking.
Authority of legislature
restricted, Const. Ala.,
art. XIII, §247.
Bills.
Amendments.
Procedure for amendment,
Const. Ala., art. IV,
§64.
Restrictions, Const. Ala.,
art. IV, §61.
Revenue bills.
Amendments by senate,
Const. Ala., art. IV,
§70.
Committees of conference.
Adoption of reports of
committees, Const.
Ala., art. IV, §64.
General appropriation bill.
Restrictions on, Const.
Ala., art. IV, §71.
Laws to be passed by bills,
Const. Ala., art. IV, §61.

LEGISLATURE—Cont'd
  Bills—Cont'd
    Passage.
      Majority vote required for
        passage, Const. Ala.,
        art. IV, §63.
      Presentation to governor for
        signature, Const. Ala.,
        art. V, §125.
      Effect of failure to sign,
        Const. Ala., art. V,
        §125.
    Readings.
      Number of readings for
        bills, Const. Ala., art.
        IV, §63.
      Reading of bills at length
        may be dispensed with,
        Const. Ala., art. IV,
        §66.
    Referral to standing
      committees, Const. Ala.,
      art. IV, §62.
    Revenue bills.
      Amendments by senate,
        Const. Ala., art. IV,
        §70.
      House of representatives.
        Revenue bills to
          originate in house,
          Const. Ala., art. IV,
          §70.
      Preparation of general
        revenue bill, Const.
        Ala., art. IV, §70.
      Time limit for passage,
        Const. Ala., art. IV,
        §70.
    Signature by presiding officer
      of each house, Const.
      Ala., art. IV, §66.
    Standing committees.
      Referral to standing
        committees, Const.
        Ala., art. IV, §62.
    Veto.
      Procedure for passage after
        veto, Const. Ala., art.
        V, §125.
    Votes on bills.
      Majority vote required for
        passage, Const. Ala.,
        art. IV, §63.
      Recordation, Const. Ala.,
        art. IV, §63.
  Bribery, Const. Ala., art. IV,
    §§79 to 81.
    Protection of members from
      bribes, Const. Ala., art.
      IV, §53.
  Budgets.
    Contents of annual budget of
      legislature, §29-1-22.
    Legislative budgets.
      Generally, Const. Ala.,
        amd. 448.
    Legislative fiscal office.
      Evaluation of budgetary
        matters, §29-5-10.
    Presentation by legislature of
      annual budget, §29-1-22.
    Transmission of budget to
      legislature, §41-4-82.
  Capitol building.
    Control of space when
      legislature convenes
      outside capitol, §29-1-19.
    Use of space, §29-1-19.

LEGISLATURE—Cont'd
  Census.
    Apportionment of house
      based on decennial
      census, Const. Ala., art.
      IX, §198.
  Chairs or desks.
    Production of restored desks
      to be used in renovated
      state capital building.
      Rate or price established,
        §29-1-23.
    Purchase by members of
      legislature, §29-1-23.
    Revenues generated by desks
      and chairs sold, §29-1-23.
    Unsold desks and chairs
      delivered to department
      of archives and history,
      §29-1-23.
  Civil process.
    Privilege from civil process,
      §29-1-7.
  Coastal areas.
    Legislative findings, §9-7-11.
  Code of ethics, §§36-25-27,
    36-25-28.
  Committees.
    Contract review permanent
      legislative oversight
      committee, §§29-2-40,
      29-2-41.
    Evaluation of prison system
      and board of corrections,
      §§29-2-20 to 29-2-22.
    Joint fiscal committee,
      §§29-5-2, 29-5-8.
    Legislative committee on
      public accounts,
      §§41-5-18 to 41-5-20.
    Legislative council, §§29-6-1
      to 29-6-7.
    Legislative interim
      committees.
      Appropriations, §29-1-10.
      Compensation.
        Employees, §29-1-9.
        Per diem, §29-1-9.
    Permanent joint highway
      committee, §§29-2-1 to
      29-2-8.
    Standing committees.
      Number of members,
        §29-1-18.
    Water assistance legislative
      oversight committee,
      §22-23A-3.
  Committees of conference.
    Reports.
      Adoption of reports, Const.
        Ala., art. IV, §64.
  Compensation, Const. Ala.,
    art. IV, §49; amds. 39, 57.
    Certification, §29-1-11.
    Committees.
      Legislative interim
        committees.
        Employees, §29-1-9.
        Per diem, §29-1-9.
    Journals.
      Compilation, §29-1-13.
    Per diem, §29-1-8.
      Legislative interim
        committees, §29-1-9.
      Permanent joint highway
        committee, §§29-2-5,
        29-2-7.
    Salaries.
      Legislative officers and
        employees, §29-1-21.
    Travel expenses, §29-1-8.

LEGISLATURE—Cont'd
  Compensation—Cont'd
    Treatment of travel expenses
      for state income tax
      purposes, §29-1-8.1.
  Composition of legislature,
    Const. Ala., art. IV, §44.
  Conflicts of interest.
    Disclosure of personal or
      private interest in bills,
      etc., by legislators,
      Const. Ala., art. IV, §82.
  **Conservation and natural
    resources.**
    Commissioner.
      Advisor of the legislature,
        §9-2-5.
    Department.
      Recommendations to
        legislature, §9-2-2.
  Constitution of Alabama.
    Legislative department,
      Const. Ala., art. IV, §§44
      to 111.
    See CONSTITUTION OF
      ALABAMA.
  Contempt.
    Punishment for contempt or
      disorderly behavior,
      Const. Ala., art. IV, §53.
    Not bar to indictment for
      same offense, Const.
      Ala., art. IV, §54.
  **Contract review permanent
    legislative oversight
    committee.**
    Clerical help, §29-2-41.
    Creation, §29-2-40.
    Emergency procedures,
      §29-2-41.1.
    Exclusions from provisions.
      Personal and professional
        service agreements,
        §29-2-41.3.
    Expenses for members,
      §29-2-41.
    Independent contractor
      agreements.
      Inclusion in term personal
        and professional
        services, §29-2-41.2.
    Meetings, §29-2-41.
    Membership, §29-2-40.
    Officers, §29-2-41.
    Organization, §29-2-41.
    Personal and professional
      service agreements.
      Exclusions, §29-2-41.3.
      Independent contractor
        agreements.
        Inclusion in term,
          §29-2-41.2.
    Procedure, §29-2-41.
      Emergency procedure,
        §29-2-41.1.
    Responsibilities, powers, etc.
      §29-2-41.
    Secretary, §29-2-41.
  Convening.
    Governor authorized to
      convene on extraordinary
      occasions, Const. Ala.,
      art. V, §122.
  **Coosa Valley development
    authority.**
    Legislative intent, §33-16-2.
  Corporations.
    Charters.
      Authority of legislature to
        revoke, Const. Ala.,
        art. XII, §238.

LEGISLATURE—Cont'd
Corporations—Cont'd
Nonprofit corporations.
Reservation of power in
legislature,
§10-3A-224.
Corrections.
Board of corrections.
Advisor to the legislature,
§14-1-9.
Evaluation of prison
system and board of
corrections, §§29-2-20
to 29-2-22.
Notice prior to decision on
construction of
permanent facilities,
§14-1-9.
Periodic recommendations,
§14-1-13.
Corruption.
Expulsion for corruption bar
to further service in
legislature, Const. Ala.,
art. IV, §54.
Costs.
Appropriation for legislative
costs, §29-1-22.
Counties.
Local bill introduced in
legislature.
Payment of cost of
advertising, §11-13-6.
Dams.
Dams considered as
authorized by
legislature, §10-4-323.
Death of member.
Notice to governor, §36-9-6.
Disorderly conduct.
Punishment for disorderly
behavior, Const. Ala.,
art. IV, §53.
Not bar to indictment for
same offense, Const.
Ala., art. IV, §54.
Districts.
Enumeration, §29-1-2.3.
Effective date, §29-1-2.4.
Senate, Const. Ala., art. IX,
§§200, 203.
Division of laws, Const. Ala.,
art. IV, §45.
Dual office holding.
Appointment of legislators to
other offices during
terms for which elected,
Const. Ala., art. IV, §59.
Education.
Alabama education study
commission.
Reports to legislature,
§16-6-4.
Duty to establish and
maintain public school
system, Const. Ala., art.
XIV, §256.
Teachers.
Retirement system.
Legislative service as
full-time employee.
Creditable service,
§16-25-11.2.
Elections.
Contests, §§17-15-20 to
17-15-35.
See ELECTIONS.
Generally.
See ELECTIONS.
Emergency appropriations,
§41-4-94.

LEGISLATURE—Cont'd
**Emergency interim
succession,** §§29-3-1 to
29-3-16.
Attack.
Defined, §29-3-3.
Continuity of legislature in
event of enemy attack,
Const. Ala., amd. 159.
Declaration of policy, §29-3-2.
Definitions, §29-3-3.
Expiration of chapter,
§29-3-14.
Extension of provisions,
§29-3-14.
Restoration of provisions,
§29-3-14.
Governor.
Legislative sessions.
Convening of sessions,
§29-3-10.
Place of session, §29-3-9.
Local governments.
Designation of successor,
§29-3-16.
Enabling authority,
§29-3-15.
Oaths.
Successors, §29-3-7.
Policy.
Declaration of policy,
§29-3-2.
Quorum, §29-3-13.
Sessions.
Legislative sessions.
Convening of sessions,
§29-3-10.
Place of legislative session.
Governor may change,
§29-3-9.
Quorum, §29-3-13.
Vote requirements,
§29-3-13.
Short title, §29-3-1.
Successors.
Compensation, §29-3-12.
Designation.
Legislators, §29-3-4.
Officers of political
subdivisions,
§29-3-16.
Records, §29-3-6.
When effective, §29-3-6.
Duties.
Assumes duties of
legislator, §29-3-11.
Current business of
legislature.
Duty of successors to
keep themselves
informed, §29-3-8.
Immunities, §29-3-12.
Oaths, §29-3-7.
Order of succession.
Changes, §29-3-6.
Powers and duties.
Assumes duties of
legislator, §29-3-11.
Privileges and immunities,
§29-3-12.
Qualifications, §29-3-5.
Records.
Public journal, §29-3-6.
Removal.
Records, §29-3-6.
When effective, §29-3-6.
Status, §29-3-5.
Terms, §§29-3-5, 29-3-6.
Title of chapter, §29-3-1.
Unavailable.
Defined, §29-3-3.

LEGISLATURE—Cont'd
Employees, §§29-4-40 to
29-4-50.
Clerk of house of
representatives.
Administrative assistants,
§29-4-44.
Chief clerk, §29-4-43.
Full-time employees,
§§29-4-43, 29-4-44.
Part-time employees,
§29-4-46.
Secretarial employees,
§29-4-44.
Compensation, §29-4-42.
Certification, §29-4-1.
Change, §29-4-2.
Full-time employees,
§29-4-42.
Part-time employees,
§29-4-45.
Salary increases to apply
to legislative
personnel, §29-4-3.
Discrimination in hiring.
Prohibited, §29-4-50.
Doorkeepers.
Employment of retired
state troopers,
§29-4-47.
Full-time employees.
Administrative assistants,
§29-4-44.
Clerks to presiding officers
of legislature,
§29-4-43.
Compensation.
Generally, §29-4-42.
Enumeration, §29-4-42.
Finance and taxation
committee.
Secretarial employees,
§29-4-49.
Secretarial employees,
§§29-4-44, 29-4-49.
Ways and means
committee.
Secretarial employees,
§29-4-49.
Guards.
Employment of retired
state troopers,
§29-4-47.
House of representatives.
Administrative assistance
and secretarial
employees for
presiding officer,
§29-4-44.
Compensation, Const. Ala.,
art. IV, §67.
Marshals.
Employment of retired
state troopers,
§29-4-47.
Number, §29-4-42.
Change of number, §29-4-2.
Pages.
Appointment, §29-4-48.
Part-time employees.
Clerk of house of
representatives.
Secretarial employees,
§29-4-46.
Compensation.
Generally, §29-4-45.
Enumeration, §29-4-45.
Finance and taxation
committee.
Clerks, §29-4-49.

LEGISLATURE—Cont'd
Employees—Cont'd
  Part-time employees—Cont'd
    Secretary of senate.
      Secretarial employees,
        §29-4-46.
    Ways and means
      committee.
      Clerks, §29-4-49.
  Positions authorized,
    §29-4-41.
  Secretary of senate.
    Administrative assistants,
      §29-4-44.
    Chief clerk, §29-4-43.
    Full-time employees,
      §§29-4-43, 29-4-44.
    Part-time employees,
      §29-4-46.
    Secretarial employees,
      §29-4-44.
  Senate, §29-4-44; Const. Ala.,
    art. IV, §67.
  State troopers.
    Employment of retired
      troopers as guards,
      marshals or
      doorkeepers, §29-4-47.
  Supervision.
    Legislative council,
      §29-4-40.
      Delegation of powers and
        duties, §29-4-40.
Enterprise zones.
  Legislative oversight
    committee.
    Appointment of members,
      §41-23-23.
Equipment.
  Purchase of new equipment.
    Trade of old equipment,
      §29-1-20.
**Establishment of legislative
department,** Const. Ala.,
  art. III, §42.
Estimates.
  Amount of money involved
    under provisions of
    certain bills.
    Director of legislative fiscal
      officer to make
      estimate, §29-5-12.
Ethics.
  Code of ethics, §§36-25-27,
    36-25-28.
**Evaluation of prison system
and board of
corrections.**
  Committee.
    Advisors.
      Employment of
        consultants,
        advisors, etc.,
        §29-2-21.
    Chairman, §29-2-20.
    Clerical assistance,
      §29-2-22.
    Compensation of members,
      §29-2-22.
    Consultants.
      Employment of
        consultants,
        advisors, etc.,
        §29-2-21.
    Creation, §29-2-20.
    Duties, §29-2-20.
    Expenses of members,
      §29-2-22.

LEGISLATURE—Cont'd
**Evaluation of prison system
and board of corrections**
—Cont'd
  Committee—Cont'd
    Membership, §29-2-20.
    Compensation and
      expenses of
      members, §29-2-22.
    Purpose, §29-2-20.
    Reports to legislature,
      §29-2-20.
Expulsion of members,
  Const. Ala., art. IV, §53.
  Expulsion for corruption bar
    to further service in
    legislature, Const. Ala.,
    art. IV, §54.
Fiscal office, §§29-5-1 to
  29-5-12.
**Foreign trade and relations
commission.**
  Annual report to legislature,
    §41-9-662.
Forests and forestry.
  State forestry commission.
    Recommendations to
      legislature, §9-3-4.
Former members.
  Lobbying.
    Former members not to be
      extended floor
      privileges for lobbying
      purposes, §36-25-23.
Geological survey.
  State geologist.
    Reports to legislature,
      §9-4-2.
Gerrymandering.
  Senatorial districts, Const.
    Ala., art. IX, §200.
Gift enterprises.
  Prohibited, Const. Ala., art.
    IV, §65.
Governor.
  Convening.
    Extraordinary occasions,
      Const. Ala., art. V,
      §122.
  Emergency interim
    succession, §§29-3-9,
    29-3-10.
  Reports.
    Governor to give certain
      information and
      reports to legislature,
      Const. Ala., art. V,
      §123.
Harbors and ports.
  Port authority.
    Legislative intent,
      §33-13-2.
Health.
  Annual report to legislature
    by state committee of
    public health, §22-2-7.
  Requests for information,
    §22-2-7.
Highways.
  Department.
    Recommendations for
      legislation, §23-1-35.
  Permanent joint highway
    committee, §§29-2-1 to
    29-2-8.

LEGISLATURE—Cont'd
House of representatives,
  Const. Ala., art. IV, §§44
    to 111.
  Adjournment.
    Without consent of senate,
      Const. Ala., art. IV,
      §58.
  Admittance to floor.
    Restrictions on admittance
      Const. Ala., art. IV,
      §57.
  Apportionment of legislators,
    Const. Ala., art. IV, §50.
    General provisions, Const.
      Ala., art. IV, §§197 to
      203.
  Change of place of sitting.
    Without consent of senate,
      Const. Ala., art. IV,
      §58.
  Clerk of house of
    representatives.
    Administrative assistant,
      §29-4-43.1.
    Assistant clerk, §29-4-20.
    Continuing service status,
      §29-4-20.
    Election, §29-4-20.
    Employees, §§29-4-43,
      29-4-44.
    Removal, §29-4-20.
  Compensation of members,
    Const. Ala., amds. 39,
    57.
  Conviction of certain crimes
    bar to eligibility, Const.
    Ala., art. IV, §60.
  Districts.
    Enumeration of districts,
      §29-1-1.2.
    Effective date, §29-1-2.4.
  Doors of each house to be
    open, Const. Ala., art.
    IV, §57.
  Election of representatives,
    Const. Ala., art. IV, §46.
  Each house judge of
    election, returns and
    qualifications of
    members, Const. Ala.,
    art. IV, §51.
  Elections generally.
    See ELECTIONS.
  Special elections to fill
    vacancies, Const. Ala.
    amd. 97.
  Employees.
    Administrative assistants
      and secretarial
      employees for
      presiding officer,
      §29-4-44.
    Clerk of house of
      representatives,
      §§29-4-43, 29-4-44.
    Compensation, Const. Ala.
      art. IV, §67.
    Duties, Const. Ala., art.
      IV, §67.
    Number, Const. Ala., art.
      IV, §67.
  Journal of proceedings,
    Const. Ala., art. IV, §55.
  Number of representatives,
    §29-1-1.2; Const. Ala.,
    art. IV, §50.
    Duty of legislature to fix,
      Const. Ala., art. IX,
      §199.
    Effective date, §29-1-2.4.

LEGISLATURE—Cont'd
House of representatives
—Cont'd
Number of representatives
—Cont'd
Maximum number, Const.
Ala., art. IX, §198.
Officers, Const. Ala., art. IV,
§51.
Clerk of house of
representatives,
§§29-4-20, 29-4-43.1.
Compensation, Const. Ala.,
art. IV, §67.
Duties, Const. Ala., art.
IV, §67.
Number of officers, Const.
Ala., art. IV, §67.
Qualifications of
representatives, Const.
Ala., art. IV, §47.
Conviction of certain
crimes bar to
eligibility, Const. Ala.,
art. IV, §60.
Each house judge of
qualifications of
members, Const. Ala.,
art. IV, §51.
Quorum, Const. Ala., art. IV,
§52.
Ratio of senators to
representatives, Const.
Ala., art. IX, §197.
Revenue bills.
Revenue bills to originate
in house, Const. Ala.,
art. IV, §70.
Rules of proceedings, Const.
Ala., art. IV, §53.
Speaker of house.
Administrative assistant.
Upgraded to confidential
assistant, §29-4-44.
Election, Const. Ala., art.
IV, §51.
Employees.
Confidential assistants
and secretarial
employees, §29-4-44.
Enterprise zones.
Legislative oversight
committee.
Appointment of
members,
§41-23-23.
Signature of bills, Const.
Ala., art. IV, §66.
Synfuels development
authority.
Individuals who may
become public
corporation, §9-6A-3.
Temporary speaker, Const.
Ala., art. IV, §51.
Term of office, Const. Ala.,
art. IV, §51.
Water system assistance
authority.
Appointment of
members, §22-23A-3.
Succession to office.
Emergency interim
succession, §§29-3-1 to
29-3-16.
Terms of representatives,
Const. Ala., art. IV, §46.
Travel allowance of
members, Const. Ala.,
amds. 39, 57.

LEGISLATURE—Cont'd
House of representatives
—Cont'd
Vacancies, Const. Ala., art.
IV, §46.
Special elections to fill,
Const. Ala., amd. 97.
Immunity of legislators,
Const. Ala., art. IV, §56.
Arrest and civil process,
§29-1-7.
**Jacksonville State
University.**
Board of trustees.
Reports to legislature,
§16-52-10.
Joint resolutions.
Printing, §§41-4-130 to
41-4-161.
See PRINTING.
Journals, Const. Ala., art. IV,
§55.
Compilation, §29-1-12.
Compensation, §29-1-13.
Delivery to secretary of state,
§29-1-13.
Filing, §29-1-12.
Printing.
Public printing and
binding, §§41-4-130 to
41-4-161.
See PRINTING.
**Junior college for Jackson
and DeKalb counties.**
Reports to legislature,
§16-60-67.
**Legislative committee on
public accounts,**
§§41-5-18 to 41-5-20.
Legislative council, §§29-6-1
to 29-6-7.
Chairman.
Election, §29-6-3.
Compensation.
Generally, §29-6-4.
Construction of chapter,
§29-6-7.
Created, §29-6-1.
Duties.
Generally, §29-6-6.
Legislative reference service.
Assistance to council,
§29-6-6.
Meetings.
Generally, §29-6-3.
Quorum, §29-6-3.
Members.
Additional members,
§29-6-2.1.
Election, §29-6-2.
Expenses.
Compensation, §29-6-4.
Increase in membership,
§29-6-2.1.
Terms of members, §29-6-2.
Powers.
Generally, §29-6-6.
Quorum, §29-6-3.
Secretary.
Generally, §29-6-5.
Vacancies.
Filling of vacancies,
§29-6-2.
Vice-chairman.
Election, §29-6-3.
Votes.
Generally, §29-6-3.

LEGISLATURE—Cont'd
Legislative fiscal office,
§§29-5-1 to 29-5-12.
Budget.
Evaluation of budgetary
matters, §29-5-10.
Committees.
Assistance to other
legislative committees,
§29-5-8.
Joint fiscal committee.
Created, §29-5-2.
Computers.
Evaluation of budgetary
matters, §29-5-10.
Director.
Appointment, §29-5-3.
Head of office, §29-5-1.
Removal, §29-5-3.
Salary, §29-5-3.
State departments,
institutions and
agencies.
Cooperation, §29-5-5.
State employees'
retirement system.
Participation, §29-5-3.
Duties.
Generally, §29-5-7.
Employees.
Appointment, §29-5-4.
Established, §29-5-1.
Estimate of amount of money
involved under
provisions of certain
bills, §29-5-12.
Functions.
Generally, §29-5-7.
Joint fiscal committee.
Created, §29-5-2.
Legislators.
Assistance to members of
house and senate,
§29-5-9.
Personnel, §29-5-4.
State departments,
institutions and
agencies.
Cooperation.
Director, §29-5-5.
Department of examiners
of public accounts.
Assistance to legislative
fiscal office, §29-5-6.
Legislative reference
service.
Assistance to legislative
fiscal office, §29-5-6.
State employees' retirement
system.
Director of legislative fiscal
office.
Participation, §29-5-3.
Legislative reference service,
§§29-7-1 to 29-7-7.
Compensation.
Director, §29-7-2.
Legislative reference
analysts, §29-7-5.
Construction of chapter,
§29-7-7.
Created, §29-7-1.
Director.
Appointment, §29-7-2.
Compensation, §29-7-2.
Duties.
Generally, §29-7-6.
Employees.
Additional staff members,
§29-7-4.

LEGISLATURE—Cont'd
Legislative reference service
—Cont'd
Employees—Cont'd
Assistant to director,
§29-7-3.
Clerical help, §29-7-4.
Confidential secretary,
§29-7-3.
Legislative reference
analysts.
Compensation, §29-7-5.
Merit system act applies,
§29-7-3.
Exceptions, §§29-7-3,
29-7-4.
Judicial system study
commission.
Assistance of commission
by service, §12-9-7.
Powers.
Generally, §29-7-6.
Length of sessions.
Maximum length, Const.
Ala., art. IV, §48; amds.
39, 57.
Organizational sessions,
§29-1-4.
Regular sessions, §29-1-4;
Const. Ala., amd. 339.
Special sessions, §29-1-5;
Const. Ala., art. IV, §76.
Livingston University.
Board of trustees.
Reports to legislature,
§16-53-10.
Local laws.
Constitution of Alabama,
Const. Ala., art. IV,
§§104 to 107.
Publication by counties,
§§11-13-2 to 11-13-5.
Lotteries.
Authorization by legislature
prohibited, Const. Ala.,
art. IV, §65.
Marine mammal protection.
Findings, §9-11-392.
Meetings.
Time and place of meetings,
Const. Ala., art. IV, §48;
amds. 39, 57, 427.
Members.
Arrest.
Privilege from arrest,
§29-1-7.
Civil process.
Privilege from civil
process, §29-1-7.
Election.
General provisions.
See ELECTIONS.
Number, Const. Ala., art. IV,
§50.
Oath of office, Const. Ala.,
art. XVI, §279.
Administration, §29-1-6.
Military affairs.
Regular military
appropriations,
§31-2-132.
Special appropriations for
national guard in active
military service of state,
§31-2-133.
Motor vehicles.
Safety coordinating
committee.
Recommendations for
enactment of laws,
§32-3-4.

LEGISLATURE—Cont'd
Municipal corporations.
Bills.
Annexation.
Bill to contain accurate
description of
territory and plat or
map, §11-42-6.
Notices.
Vacancies in office to be
filled by legislature.
Notice by governor,
§36-9-16.
Oath of office, Const. Ala.,
art. XVI, §279.
Administration of oath,
§29-1-6.
Officers, Const. Ala., art. IV,
§51.
Clerk of house of
representatives,
§§29-4-20, 29-4-43.1.
Compensation.
Certification, §29-4-1.
Change, §29-4-2.
Generally, §29-4-22.
Salary increases to apply
to legislative officers,
§29-4-3.
Duties.
Generally, §29-4-24.
Election, §29-4-20.
Enumerated, §29-4-20.
Fees.
Sale of copies of bills
introduced in
legislature.
Deposit in state treasury,
§29-4-23.
House of representatives,
Const. Ala., art. IV,
§§51, 67.
Income.
Disclosure of personal
income, §29-4-23.
Number of officers.
Change of number, §29-4-2.
Oaths.
Administration of oaths,
§29-4-21.
Removal, §29-4-20.
Secretary of senate,
§§29-4-20, 29-4-43.1.
Senate, Const. Ala., art. IV,
§§51, 67.
Oversight committees.
Water assistance legislative
oversight committee,
§22-23A-3.
Pardons.
Regulation of pardons, Const.
Ala., amd. 38.
Parole.
Regulation of paroles, Const.
Ala., amd. 38.
**Permanent joint highway
committee,** §§29-2-1 to
29-2-8.
Chairman.
Election, §29-2-3.
Compensation.
Members of committee,
§29-2-5.
Secretary, §29-2-7.
Construction of chapter,
§29-2-1.
Created, §29-2-2.
Duties.
Generally, §29-2-4.
State highway department,
§29-2-6.

LEGISLATURE—Cont'd
**Permanent joint highway
committee**—Cont'd
Elections.
Chairman and vice-
chairman, §29-2-3.
Legislation.
Proposed legislation
referred to committee,
§29-2-8.
Meetings, §29-2-3.
Membership, §29-2-2.
Appointment, §29-2-2.
Compensation, §29-2-5.
Qualifications of members,
§29-2-2.
Terms of members, §29-2-2.
Vacancies.
Filling of vacancies,
§29-2-2.
Powers.
Generally, §29-2-4.
Legislation.
Proposed legislation
referred to
committee, §29-2-8.
Purpose of chapter, §29-2-1.
Quorum, §29-2-3.
Secretary, §29-2-7.
State highway department,
§29-2-6.
Vice-chairman.
Election, §29-2-3.
Place of meetings, Const.
Ala., art. IV, §48.
Printing.
Public printing and binding,
§§41-4-130 to 41-4-161.
See PRINTING.
Private laws.
Constitution of Alabama,
Const. Ala., art. IV,
§§104 to 107.
Privilege from arrest,
§29-1-7; Const. Ala., art.
IV, §56.
Probation.
Regulation of probation,
Const. Ala., amd. 38.
Process.
Enforcement, Const. Ala.,
art. IV, §53.
Promulgation of laws.
Periodic promulgation, Const.
Ala., art. IV, §85.
**Protection of members from
violence, bribes, etc.,**
Const. Ala., art. IV, §53.
Public accounts.
Legislative committee on
public accounts,
§§41-5-18 to 41-5-20.
**Public officers and
employees.**
Code of ethics.
Constitutional rights of
citizens to
communicate with
members.
Chapter not to impair,
§36-25-28.
Disciplinary powers of
legislature.
Chapter not to limit,
§36-25-27.
State employees' retirement
system, §§36-27-1 to
36-27-86.
See PUBLIC OFFICERS
AND EMPLOYEES.

LEGISLATURE—Cont'd
  Quorum in each house,
    Const. Ala., art. IV, §52.
  Railroads.
    Free passes or discount
      tickets to members,
      Const. Ala., art. XII,
      §244.
    Regulation of railroad
      companies, Const. Ala.,
      art. XII, §243.
  Recess.
    Printing of acts when recess
      taken by legislature,
      §41-4-161.
  Records.
    Documents of legislature.
      Deposit with secretary of
        state, §29-1-14.
    Filing, §29-1-16.
    Legislation.
      Engrossed copies of laws.
        Deposit with secretary of
        state, §29-1-15.
    Papers of legislature.
      Deposit with secretary of
        state, §29-1-14.
    Receipt for papers, §29-1-17.
  Reports.
    Budget management act,
      §§41-19-10, 41-19-11.
    Governor to give certain
      reports and information
      to legislature, Const.
      Ala., art. V, §123.
  Resignation of members,
    §36-9-12.
  Resolutions.
    Secretary of state.
      Acts and resolutions of
        legislature, §§36-14-11
        to 36-14-13.
  Revenue bills, Const. Ala.,
    art. IV, §70.
  Revision of laws.
    Periodic revision, Const. Ala.,
      art. IV, §85.
  Revival of laws.
    By title only, Const. Ala.,
      art. IV, §45.
  Rules of proceedings in both
    houses, Const. Ala., art.
    IV, §53.
  Safety coordinating
    committee.
    Recommendations to
      legislature, §32-3-4.
  Salaries, Const. Ala., art. IV,
    §49; amd. 39.
    Compensation generally. See
      within this heading,
      "Compensation."
  Secretary of state.
    Acts and resolutions of
      legislature, §§36-14-11 to
      36-14-13.
    Records.
      Legislation, §29-1-15.
      Papers and documents of
        legislature, §29-1-14.
      Receipt for papers,
        §29-1-17.
  Senate.
    Adjournment.
      Without consent of house,
        Const. Ala., art. IV,
        §58.
    Admittance to floor.
      Restrictions on admittance,
        Const. Ala., art. IV,
        §57.

LEGISLATURE—Cont'd
  Senate—Cont'd
    Apportionment, Const. Ala.,
      art. IX, §§197 to 203.
    Change of place of sitting.
      Without consent of house
        of representatives,
        Const. Ala., art. IV,
        §58.
    Compensation of members,
      Const. Ala., art. IV, §49;
      amds. 39, 57.
    Conviction of certain crimes
      bar to eligibility, Const.
      Ala., art. IV, §60.
    Districts.
      Change in districts.
        Senatorial districts not
          to be changed until
          next apportioning
          session, Const. Ala.,
          art. IX, §200.
      Counties.
        Counties within
          senatorial districts
          to be contiguous,
          Const. Ala., art. IX,
          §200.
        Division of counties
          between senatorial
          districts prohibited,
          Const. Ala., art. IX,
          §200.
      Duty of legislature to
        divide state into
        senatorial districts,
        Const. Ala., art. IX,
        §200.
      Enumeration of districts,
        §29-1-2.3.
      Effective date, §29-1-2.4.
      Equality of senatorial
        districts, Const. Ala.,
        art. IX, §200.
      Initial apportionment,
        Const. Ala., art. IX,
        §203.
    Doors of each house to be
      open, Const. Ala., art.
      IV, §57.
    Election of senators, Const.
      Ala., art. IV, §46.
      Each house judge of
        election, returns and
        qualifications of
        members, Const. Ala.,
        art. IV, §51.
      Elections generally.
        See ELECTIONS.
      Special elections to fill
        vacancies, Const. Ala.,
        amd. 97.
    Employees, §29-4-44; Const.
      Ala., art. IV, §67.
    Journal of proceedings,
      Const. Ala., art. IV, §55.
    Lieutenant governor.
      Ex officio president of
        senate, Const. Ala.,
        art. V, §117.
    Number of senators,
      §29-1-2.3; Const. Ala.,
      art. IV, §50.
      Duty of legislature to fix,
        Const. Ala., art. IX,
        §200.
      Effective date, §29-1-2.4.
    Officers, Const. Ala., art. IV,
      §51.
      Compensation, Const. Ala.,
        art. IV, §67.

LEGISLATURE—Cont'd
  Senate—Cont'd
    Officers—Cont'd
      Duties, Const. Ala., art.
        IV, §67.
      Number of officers, Const.
        Ala., art. IV, §67.
      Secretary of senate,
        §§29-4-20, 29-4-43.1.
      President pro tem.
        Election, Const. Ala., art.
          IV, §51; amds. 39, 57.
        Employees, §29-4-44.
        Signature of bills, Const.
          Ala., art. IV, §66.
        Temporary president,
          Const. Ala., art. IV,
          §51.
        Term of office, Const. Ala.,
          art. IV, §51.
      Qualifications of senators,
        Const. Ala., art. IV, §47.
        Conviction of certain
          crimes bar to
          eligibility, Const. Ala.,
          art. IV, §60.
        Each house judge of
          qualifications of
          members, Const. Ala.,
          art. IV, §51.
      Quorum, Const. Ala., art. IV,
        §52.
      Ratio of senators to
        representatives, Const.
        Ala., art. IX, §197.
      Revenue bills.
        Amendments to revenue
          bills by senate, Const.
          Ala., art. IV, §70.
      Rules of proceedings, Const.
        Ala., art. IV, §53.
      Secretary of senate.
        Administrative assistant,
          §29-4-43.1.
        Assistant secretary.
          Compensation, §29-4-22.
          Election, §29-4-20.
          May be legislative
            employee when
            legislature not in
            session, §29-4-20.
        Continuing service status,
          §29-4-20.
        Election, §29-4-20.
        Employees, §§29-4-20,
          29-4-43.1.
        Removal, §29-4-20.
      Succession to office.
        Emergency interim
          succession, §§29-3-1 to
          29-3-16.
      Terms of senators, Const.
        Ala., art. IV, §46.
      Travel allowance of
        members, Const. Ala.,
        amds. 39, 57.
      Vacancies, Const. Ala., art.
        IV, §46.
  Sessions.
    Annual sessions, §29-1-3;
      Const. Ala., amd. 39.
    Biennial sessions, Const.
      Ala., amds. 39, 57.
    Special sessions, §29-1-5;
      Const. Ala., art. IV,
      §76; amd. 339.
    Length of sessions.
      Maximum length, Const.
        Ala., art. IV, §48;
        amds. 39, 57.

LEGISLATURE—Cont'd
Sessions—Cont'd
Length of sessions—Cont'd
Organizational sessions, §29-1-4.
Regular sessions, §29-1-4; Const. Ala., amd. 339.
Special sessions, §29-1-5; Const. Ala., art. IV, §76.
Maximum length of sessions, Const. Ala., art. IV, §48; amds. 39, 57.
Organizational sessions, Const. Ala., amds. 39, 57.
Special sessions.
Duration, Const. Ala., art. IV, §76.
Restrictions on legislature at special sessions, Const. Ala., art. IV, §76.
Time and place of meetings, §§29-1-3, 29-1-4; Const. Ala., amds. 39, 57.
Small loans.
Legislative findings of fact and declaration of intent, §5-18-2.
Soil and water conservation.
Districts.
Legislative findings, §9-8-21.
Special, private or local laws.
Constitution of Alabama, Const. Ala., art. IV, §§104 to 107.
Special sessions.
Duration, Const. Ala., art. IV, §76.
Restrictions on legislation at special sessions, Const. Ala., art. IV, §76.
Standing committees.
Referral of bills to standing committees, Const. Ala., art. IV, §62.
State departments and agencies.
Sunset law, §§41-20-1 to 41-20-16.
See STATE DEPARTMENTS AND AGENCIES.
Succession to office.
Emergency interim succession, §§29-3-1 to 29-3-16.
Summons and process.
Enforcement of process, Const. Ala., art. IV, §53.
Privilege from arrest and civil process, §29-1-7; Const. Ala., art. IV, §56.
Sunset law, §§41-20-1 to 41-20-16.
See STATE DEPARTMENTS AND AGENCIES.
Taxation.
Travel expenses of legislators.
Treatment for state income tax purposes, §29-1-8.1.
Time of meetings, Const. Ala., art. IV, §48.

LEGISLATURE—Cont'd
Tombigbee-Tennessee waterway development compact.
Legislative approval and ratification, §33-8-1.
Tombigbee Valley development authority.
Legislative intent, §33-17-2.
Travel allowance of members, Const. Ala., amds. 39, 57.
Treatment for state income tax purposes, §29-1-8.1.
Troy State University.
Board of trustees.
Reports to legislature, §16-56-10.
Unemployment compensation.
Reservation of right to repeal or amend chapter, §25-4-144.
Uniform laws.
Commission on uniform state laws.
Reports to legislature, §41-9-373.
University of Alabama.
Board of trustees.
Report to legislature, §§16-47-36, 16-47-53, 16-47-93, 16-47-134, 16-47-175.
Dental college of Alabama.
Report to legislature, §16-47-53.
School of medicine.
Annual report to legislature, §16-47-93.
School of nursing.
Report to legislature, §16-47-134.
School of social work.
Report of board of trustees, §16-47-175.
University of North Alabama.
Board of trustees.
Reports to legislature, §16-51-10.
Vacancies in office, Const. Ala., art. IV, §46.
Death.
Notice to governor, §36-9-6.
Special elections to fill, Const. Ala., amd. 97.
Violence.
Protection of members from violence, Const. Ala., art. IV, §53.
War.
Continuity of legislature in event of enemy attack, Const. Ala., amd. 159.
Waters and watercourses.
Riparian owners.
Repossession of structures by legislature, §33-7-51.
Tolls.
Regulation by legislature, §33-7-52.
Water system assistance authority.
Speaker of house.
Appointments to authority, §22-23A-3.

LEGISLATURE—Cont'd
Water system assistance authority—Cont'd
Water assistance legislative oversight committee.
Monitoring actions of authority, §22-23A-3.
Speaker of house.
Appointments to committee, §22-23A-3.
LEGITIMATION OF CHILDREN, §§26-11-1 to 26-11-3.
LEPROSY.
Notifiable diseases, §§22-11A-1 to 22-11A-38.
See DISEASES.
LESTER, MUNICIPALITY OF.
Economic development, Const. Ala., amd. 244.
LETTERS OF ADMINISTRATION, §§43-2-40 to 43-2-48.
See EXECUTORS AND ADMINISTRATORS.
LETTERS OF CREDIT.
Commercial code, §§7-5-101 to 7-5-117.
See COMMERCIAL CODE.
Corporations.
Authority of public corporations with respect to letters of credit as security for bonds, notes, etc., §11-80-7.
Counties.
Authority of counties with respect to letters of credit as security for bonds, notes, etc., §11-80-7.
Municipal corporations.
Authority of municipalities with respect to letters of credit as security for bonds, notes, etc., §11-80-7.
LETTERS ROGATORY.
Service of process by letter rogatory in foreign country, ARCP, Rule 4.4 (b).
LETTERS TESTAMENTARY, §§43-2-20 to 43-2-29.
See EXECUTORS AND ADMINISTRATORS.
LEVEES.
Municipal corporations.
Assessments for public improvements.
Manner of assessment, §11-48-16.
LEWDNESS.
Actions.
Nuisances, §§6-5-140 to 6-5-154.
See NUISANCES.
Nuisances.
Actions on nuisances, §§6-5-140 to 6-5-154.
See NUISANCES.
Obscenity generally, §§13A-12-130 to 13A-12-200.10.
See OBSCENITY.

LEWDNESS—Cont'd
Public lewdness,
§13A-12-130.

LIBEL AND SLANDER.
Accusation of commission of crime, §6-5-180.
Actions, §§6-5-182 to 6-5-189.
Burden of proof, §6-5-182.
Circumstances.
Evidence, §6-5-183.
Damages.
Actual damages.
When only actual damages recoverable, §6-5-185.
Mitigation, §6-5-183.
Evidence of truth or circumstances, §6-5-183.
Retraction, §6-5-184.
Vindictive or punitive damages.
Prerequisite to recovery, §6-5-186.
Evidence of truth or circumstances, §6-5-183.
Retraction, §6-5-184.
Effect of retraction and tender of money, §6-5-188.
Tender of money.
Effect, §6-5-189.
Retraction and tender of money, §6-5-188.
Truth.
Evidence, §6-5-183.
Mitigation of damages.
Evidence of truth, §6-5-183.
Public persons.
Truth of charges against may be proved, §6-5-187.
Arrest.
Reports of arrests.
Privileged information, §13A-11-161.
Banks and financial institutions.
False, etc., statements affecting financial standing of bank, §5-5A-46.
Breach of peace.
Libel tending to provoke breach, §13A-11-160.
Chastity.
Words falsely imputing woman's chastity actionable, §6-5-181.
Congress.
Privilege of members of congress, Const. U. S., Art. I, §6.
Constitution of Alabama.
Truth as defense in prosecutions for libel, Const. Ala., art. I, §12.
Constitution of the United States.
Congress.
Privilege of members of congress, Const. U. S., Art. I, §6.
Crime.
Accusation of commission, §6-5-180.

LIBEL AND SLANDER
—Cont'd
Criminal or civil proceedings in court.
Pleadings considered privileged, §13A-11-161.
Damages.
Actions, §§6-5-183 to 6-5-186.
Defamation generally,
§13A-11-163.
Evidence.
Truth or circumstances, §6-5-183.
Grand jury.
Reports.
Privileged information, §13A-11-161.
Indictments.
Form of indictment, §15-8-150.
Indictment for libel.
Contents, §13A-11-162.
Reports of return of indictments.
Privileged information, §13A-11-161.
Limitation of actions.
Two year limitation, §6-2-38.
Newspapers.
Refusal to testify by printer, §13A-11-164.
Perjury.
Accusation of false swearing presumptively imports, §6-5-180.
Pleadings.
Privileged information, §13A-11-161.
Printer.
Refusal to testify, §13A-11-164.
Privileged information.
Publication of certain documents considered privileged, §13A-11-161.
Real property.
Slander of title.
Right of action, §6-5-211.
Retraction, §6-5-184.
Effect of retraction and tender of money, §6-5-188.
Tender of money.
Effect, §6-5-189.
Retraction and tender of money, §6-5-188.
Title.
Slander of title.
Right of action, §6-5-211.
Truth.
Actions, §§6-5-183, 6-5-187.
Warrants.
Publication of certain documents considered privileged, §13A-11-161.

LIBRARIES.
Alabama historical commission.
Acquisition, operation, etc., by commission, §41-9-254.
Authorities.
Public library authorities.
Municipal corporations, §§11-57-1 to 11-57-26.
See MUNICIPAL CORPORATIONS.

LIBRARIES—Cont'd
Blind persons.
Operation of library service by department of adult blind and deaf, §21-1-15.
Boards.
Library boards, §§11-90-2, 11-90-3.
Public library service.
Executive board, §§41-8-2 to 41-8-4.
Bond issues.
Public library authorities, §§11-57-1 to 11-57-26.
See MUNICIPAL CORPORATIONS.
Buildings.
Erection.
Powers and duties of library boards, §11-90-3.
City boards of education.
Establishment and maintenance of libraries, §16-11-23.
Compacts.
Interstate library compact, §§41-8-20 to 41-8-25.
Constitution of Alabama.
Special property tax by counties or municipalities for library purposes, Const. Ala., amd. 269.
Counties.
Establishment of free public libraries.
Powers of counties as to establishment, §11-90-1.
Funds, §§11-25-1, 11-25-7, 11-25-9.
Interstate library compact.
Restrictions as to entry into, §41-8-23.
Joint library service.
Establishment and maintenance, §11-90-4.
Law libraries, §§11-25-1 to 11-25-12.
Administration of libraries, §11-25-6.
Advisory committee.
Appointment, §11-25-6.
Applicability of chapter.
Existing libraries, §11-25-2.
Authorized, §11-25-1.
Budgets.
Supplement by counties, §11-25-3.
Code.
Distribution of state code to law libraries, §11-25-10.
County government.
Use at no cost, §11-25-8.
Creation.
Filing of resolutions, §11-25-1.
Custodian.
Appointment, §11-25-5.
Establishment.
Alternative methods, §11-25-2.
Existing libraries.
Applicability of chapter, §11-25-2.
Succession to property and funds, §11-25-2.

LIBRARIES—Cont'd
Counties—Cont'd
Law libraries—Cont'd
Funds, §11-25-1.
Disbursement, §11-25-7.
Establishment, §11-25-7.
Exemption from taxes,
§11-25-7.
Sources of finance,
§11-25-7.
Court cost, §11-25-9.
Gift to libraries, §11-25-8.
Network established,
§11-25-11.
Property.
Transfer between state,
counties and
libraries, §11-25-12.
Public use.
Consideration for
appropriations from
municipal governing
bodies, §11-25-4.
Sites.
Counties to furnish,
§11-25-3.
How to appropriate
space, §11-25-1.
Utilities.
Counties to furnish,
§11-25-3.
Library boards, §§11-9-02,
11-90-3.
Maintenance of free public
libraries.
Powers of counties as to
maintenance, §11-90-1.
Powers of counties as to
establishment and
maintenance of free
public libraries, §11-90-1.
Special property tax for
library purposes, Const.
Ala., amd. 269.
Deaf persons.
Operation of library service
by department of adult
blind and deaf, §21-1-15.
Definitions.
Interstate library compact.
State library agency,
§41-8-20.
Registration records, §41-8-9.
Districts.
Interstate library districts,
§§41-8-21, 41-8-24.
Education.
Scholarships and grants in
the field of library
service, §41-8-6.
School libraries, §§16-21-1 to
16-21-3.
Establishment.
By city boards of education,
§16-11-23.
Executive board.
Library service, §§41-8-2 to
41-8-4.
Expenditures.
Powers and duties of library
boards, §11-90-3.
**Grants in the field of library
service,** §41-8-6.
Handicapped persons.
Operation of library service
by department of adult
blind and deaf, §21-1-15.

LIBRARIES—Cont'd
History and archives.
Alabama historical
commission.
Acquisition, operation, etc.,
of libraries by
commission, §41-9-254.
Interstate library compact,
§§41-8-20 to 41-8-25.
Administrator of compact,
§41-8-22.
Agreements for construction
or maintenance of
libraries by counties,
municipalities, etc.
Restrictions as to entry
into agreements,
§41-8-23.
Contents, §41-8-21.
Counties.
Restrictions as to entry
into, §41-8-23.
Definition of state library
agency, §41-8-20.
Deputy compact
administrators, §41-8-22.
Districts, §41-8-21.
Federal aid.
Application for and
receipt of, §41-8-24.
State aid to interstate
library districts lying
partly within state,
§41-8-24.
Enactment, §41-8-21.
Form, §41-8-21.
Municipal corporations.
Restrictions as to entry
into library
agreements, §41-8-23.
State library agency defined,
§41-8-20.
Withdrawal from compact.
Sending and receipt of
notices required in
event of withdrawal,
§41-8-25.
Joint library service.
Establishment, §11-90-4.
Maintenance, §11-90-4.
**Junior college for Franklin,
Marion and Winston
counties.**
Library fees, §16-60-34.
**Junior college for Jackson
and DeKalb counties.**
Library fees, §16-60-64.
Law libraries.
Counties, §§11-25-1 to
11-25-12.
Librarians.
Election by library boards,
§11-90-3.
Library boards.
Appointment of members,
§11-90-2.
Composition, §11-90-2.
Duties, §11-90-3.
Powers, §11-90-3.
Records, §11-90-3.
Terms of members, §11-90-2.
Vacancies, §11-90-2.
Library service, §§41-8-1 to
41-8-25.
Maintenance.
By city boards of education,
§16-11-23.

LIBRARIES—Cont'd
Municipal corporations.
Authorities.
Public library authorities,
§§11-57-1 to 11-57-26.
See MUNICIPAL
CORPORATIONS.
Boards.
Library boards, §§11-90-2,
11-90-3.
Establishment of free public
libraries.
Powers of municipalities as
to establishment,
§11-90-1.
Interstate library compact.
Restrictions on entry into
library agreements,
§41-8-23.
Joint library service.
Establishment and
maintenance, §11-90-4.
Library boards, §§11-90-2,
11-90-3.
Maintenance of free public
libraries.
Powers of municipalities as
to maintenance,
§11-90-1.
Powers as to establishment
and maintenance of free
public libraries, §11-90-1.
Public library authorities,
§§11-57-1 to 11-57-26.
See MUNICIPAL
CORPORATIONS.
Obscenity.
Anti-obscenity enforcement
act.
Inapplicability of criminal
provisions to,
§13A-12-200.10.
Public library authorities.
Municipal corporations,
§§11-57-1 to 11-57-26.
See MUNICIPAL
CORPORATIONS.
Public library service,
§§41-8-1 to 41-8-25.
Applicability of article,
§41-8-8.
Assistants to director,
§41-8-3.
Chief objective, §41-8-1.
Creation, §41-8-1.
Director, §41-8-3.
Administrator of interstate
library compact,
§41-8-22.
Duties, §41-8-5.
Effect of article, §41-8-8.
Executive board, §§41-8-2 to
41-8-4.
Appointment of members,
§41-8-2.
Compensation of members,
§41-8-2.
Composition, §41-8-2.
Duties, §41-8-2.
Election of officers, §41-8-3.
Expenses of members,
§41-8-2.
Officers.
Election, §41-8-3.
Powers, §41-8-2.
Reports.
Annual report to
governor, §41-8-4.
Terms of members, §41-8-2.
Vacancies, §41-8-2.

LIBRARIES—Cont'd
Public library service
—Cont'd
Grants in the field of library
service, §41-8-6.
Interstate library compact,
§§41-8-20 to 41-8-25.
Powers, §41-8-5.
Reports.
Executive board.
Annual report to
governor, §41-8-4.
Service to obtain reports
from public libraries,
§41-8-7.
Scholarships in the field of
library service, §41-8-6.
**Purchase of books and
equipment.**
Powers and duties of library
boards, §11-90-3.
Records.
Library boards, §11-90-3.
Registration records.
Confidentiality, §41-8-10.
Defined, §41-8-9.
Rights of parents to
inspect, §41-8-10.
Right of citizens to copy.
Exemptions, §36-12-40.
Registration records,
§§41-8-9, 41-8-10.
Reports.
Public library service.
Executive board.
Annual report to
governor, §41-8-4.
Service to obtain reports
from public libraries,
§41-8-7.
**Scholarships in the field of
library service,** §41-8-6.
School libraries.
General provisions, §§16-21-1
to 16-21-3.
Supreme court library,
§§12-2-151 to 12-2-160.
See SUPREME COURT.
Taxation.
Exemptions, §40-9-1.

LIBRARY OF CONGRESS.
**Acts and resolutions of
legislature.**
Secretary of state to furnish
copies, §36-14-12.

LICENSES, §§40-12-1 to
40-12-425.
Abortion.
Parental consent.
Forfeiture of professional
licenses.
Violations, §26-21-6.
Abstract companies,
§40-12-41.
Accountants.
Public accountants,
§40-12-43.
Certified public
accountants, §40-12-71.
**Acetylene gas and carbide
manufacturers,** §40-12-42.
Actions.
Recovery of tax, §40-12-2.
Actuaries, §40-12-43.
Adding machines.
Sales, §40-12-44.
Additional license, §40-12-23.
**Administrative procedure
act,** §41-22-19.
Adoption agencies, §26-10-8.

LICENSES—Cont'd
Advertising, §40-12-45.
Affidavits.
False affidavits, §40-12-8.
Agents.
Brokers and agents of iron,
railway, etc., supplies,
§40-12-67.
Penalty on agents of persons,
firms, etc., who have not
paid tax, §40-12-18.
Agriculture.
Farm products.
Municipalities not to
charge farmers for sale
of farm products,
§11-51-105.
Fees.
Proceeding against persons
delinquent in payment,
§2-9-2.
Marketing of agricultural
products.
Inspectors, §2-11-6.
Air commerce.
Brokers, §37-9-24.
Personal property.
Leasing or renting.
Air carriers.
Exemptions,
§40-12-223.
**Air conditioning plants and
equipment,** §40-12-46.
Airports, §§4-2-72 to 4-2-79.
See AVIATION.
Alcoholic beverages,
§§28-3A-1 to 28-3A-26.
See ALCOHOLIC
BEVERAGES.
Alligator farms.
Cancellation of license upon
violation of chapter,
§9-12-214.
Dealers, §9-12-206.
Endangerment of species.
Effect on license of federal
declaration of
endangerment,
§9-12-213.
Expiration and renewal,
§9-12-203.
Fees, §9-12-202.
Expiration and renewal,
§9-12-203.
Issuance, §9-12-202.
Restaurant licenses,
§9-12-206.
Retailer's license, §9-12-206.
Ambulances, §§22-18-3,
22-18-4, 40-12-247.
Ammunition.
Dealers, §40-12-158.
Amusements.
Amusement parks, §40-12-47.
Municipal corporations.
§§11-51-102, 11-51-104.
Revocation of licenses,
§11-51-103.
Architects, §40-12-48.
Associations.
Exemptions from licenses.
Disabled veterans.
Inapplicability to
associations,
§40-12-348.
Veterans of World War II.
Inapplicability to
associations,
§40-12-375.
Athletics.
Athletic fields, §40-12-147.

LICENSES—Cont'd
Athletics—Cont'd
Municipal corporations.
Licensing of athletic
games, §11-51-104.
Atomic energy.
Exemptions from licenses.
Nuclear fuel assemblies,
§40-9-22.
Radioactive materials.
See ATOMIC ENERGY.
Attorneys at law, §§34-3-4 to
34-3-7, 40-12-49.
See ATTORNEYS AT LAW.
Auctions and auctioneers,
§§34-4-20 to 34-4-32,
40-12-50.
See AUCTIONS AND
AUCTIONEERS.
Audiologists, §§34-28A-20 to
34-28A-27.
See SPEECH
PATHOLOGISTS AND
AUDIOLOGISTS.
Auditors, §40-12-43.
**Automobile clubs and
associations.**
Agents and representatives,
§27-39-7.
Requirements, §27-39-3.
**Automotive dismantlers and
parts recyclers,**
§§40-12-411 to 40-12-418.
See MOTOR VEHICLES.
Bacteriologists, §40-12-126.
**Banks and financial
institutions.**
Industrial development
corporations.
Occupational license taxes,
§10-4-144.
Municipal licenses.
Schedule of tax,
§11-51-130.
Savings and loan
associations.
Municipal license
schedules, §11-51-131.
Barbecue stands, §40-12-153.
Barbers.
Generally, §§34-5-2, 34-5-9,
34-5-10, 40-12-58.
See BARBERS.
Refusal to license, §34-5-8.
Revocation or suspension,
§34-5-8.
Baseball.
Baseball parks, §40-12-59.
Battery shops, §40-12-60.
Beauty parlors, §40-12-61.
Beverages, §§40-12-69,
40-12-70.
Bicycles.
Dealers, §40-12-62.
Tags, §40-12-62.
Billiard rooms, §§34-6-30 to
34-6-35.
See BILLIARD ROOMS.
**Birmingham building trades
towers.**
Exemptions from licenses,
§40-9-12.
**Birmingham Football
Foundation, Inc.**
Exemptions from licenses,
§40-9-12.
Blind persons.
Exemptions from licenses,
§40-12-330.
Blueprint makers, §40-12-63.

LICENSES—Cont'd
  Boats, §§33-5-13, 33-5-15,
      33-5-20.
  Bonds, surety.
    Bond brokers, §40-12-162.
    Bond makers, §40-12-64.
    License inspectors, §40-12-11.
  Bottlers, §40-12-65.
  Bowling alleys, §40-12-66.
    Municipal corporations,
      §11-51-102.
    Revocation of licenses,
      §11-51-103.
  Boxing and wrestling,
      §41-9-96.
  Boy Scouts of America.
    Exemptions from licenses,
      §40-9-12.
  Bridges.
    Special, private or local laws
      prohibited, Const. Ala.,
      art. IV, §104.
  Brokers.
    Brokers and agents of iron,
      railway, etc., supplies,
      §40-12-67.
    Insurance brokers.
      See INSURANCE.
    Merchandise brokers,
      §40-12-81.
    Real estate brokers.
      See REAL ESTATE
        BROKERS.
    Soliciting brokers,
      §40-12-160.
    Stock and bond brokers,
      §40-12-162.
  Brooms.
    Manufacturers, §40-12-68.
  Burial.
    Coffins and caskets.
      Dealers and agents,
        §40-12-79.
      Manufacturers, §40-12-78.
  Cafes, §40-12-151.
  Cafeterias, §40-12-151.
  Calculating machines.
    Sales, §40-12-44.
  Cancer society.
    Exemptions from licenses,
      §40-9-12.
  Cards.
    Playing cards, §40-12-144.
  Carnivals, §40-12-163.
  **Catholic Maritime Club of
      Mobile, Inc.**
    Exemptions from licenses,
      §40-9-12.
  Certificates.
    False certificates, §40-12-8.
  Change of place of business,
      §40-12-1.
  Charities.
    Exemptions from licenses,
      §§40-9-12, 40-9-13.
  Checks.
    Sale of checks, §§8-7-3 to
      8-7-14.
    See CHECKS.
  Chemistry, §40-12-126.
  Child care facilities, §§38-7-3
      to 38-7-10.
    See WELFARE.
  Childhaven, Inc.
    Exemptions from licenses,
      §40-9-12.
  Child-placing agencies,
      §26-10-8.
  Chiropodists, §40-12-155.

LICENSES—Cont'd
  Chiropractors.
    General provisions.
      See CHIROPRACTORS.
    Physicians generally.
      See PHYSICIANS.
  Cigarettes.
    Taxation.
      Gummed cigarette
        papers.
        Effect of tax on other
          licenses, §40-25A-12.
      Required, §40-25A-3.
  Circuses, §40-12-74.
  Civil defense.
    Exemptions of civil defense
      workers from license
      requirements, §31-9-16.
    Shelters.
      Liability of persons,
        §31-9-17.
  Clairvoyants.
    Fee, §40-12-104.
  **Cleaners, dyers and
      pressers.**
    Cleaning and pressing
      establishments,
      §40-12-75.
    Diaper services, §40-12-117.
    Hat-cleaning establishments,
      §40-12-109.
    Laundered towel, apron, etc.,
      rentals, §40-12-117.
    Laundries, §40-12-118.
  Coal and coke dealers,
      §§40-12-76, 40-12-77.
  Coal surface mining,
      §9-16-81.
  Coffins and caskets.
    Agents, §40-12-79.
    Dealers, §40-12-79.
    Manufacturers, §40-12-78.
  Cold storage plants,
      §40-12-137.
  Collection agencies,
      §40-12-80.
  Commercial fishing.
    Hunting, fishing and
      trapping licenses
      generally, §§9-11-30 to
      9-11-66.
      See FISH AND GAME.
    Public impounded waters and
      navigable streams,
      §§9-11-141 to 9-11-146.
      See FISH AND GAME.
  Commissioners, §§40-6-1 to
      40-6-8.
    Supernumerary license
      commissioners.
      Applicability of retirement
        system established for
        elected officials,
        §40-6-6.
      Chapter inapplicable to
        supernumeraries
        appointed prior to
        August 1, 1983,
        §40-6-7.
      Commission as
        supernumeraries.
        When officials
          commissioned,
          §40-6-1.
      Compensation, §40-6-3.
        Deduction from salaries
          of officials charged
          with assessment or
          collection of taxes,
          §40-6-4.

LICENSES—Cont'd
  Commissioners—Cont'd
    Supernumerary license
      commissioners—Cont'd
      Election by officials
        eligible for retirement
        under another plan,
        §40-6-5.
      Fees.
        Deductions from fees of
          officials charged
          with assessment or
          collection of taxes,
          §40-6-4.
      Life tenure, §40-6-3.
      Oath, §40-6-2.
      Retirement.
        Election to participate in
          supernumerary
          retirement program,
          §40-6-8.
      Vacancies.
        Assumption of duties in
          case of vacancy,
          §40-6-2.
  Commission merchants,
      §40-12-81.
  Comptometers.
    Sales, §40-12-44.
  Concerts, §40-12-82.
  Constitution of Alabama.
    Payment of state license tax
      not to excuse payment of
      other privilege and
      license taxes, Const.
      Ala., art. XII, §221.
  Consumer finance, §§5-19-22
      to 5-19-24.
  Contractors.
    General provisions, §§34-8-2
      to 34-8-5.
    State licensing board,
      §§34-8-20 to 34-8-27.
      See CONTRACTORS.
  Contracts.
    Dealers in conditional sales
      contracts, drafts,
      acceptances, etc.,
      §40-12-83.
  Corporations.
    Exemptions from licenses.
      Disabled veterans.
        Inapplicability to
          corporations,
          §40-12-348.
      Veterans of World War II.
        Inapplicability to
          corporations,
          §40-12-315.
  Cosmetologists, §§34-7-2 to
      34-7-21, 40-12-124.
    See COSMETOLOGISTS.
  Cotton, §§40-12-85 to 40-12-88.
  Counties.
    County license tax for school
      purposes, §§40-12-4 to
      40-12-7.
    Generally.
      See COUNTIES.
    Hunting, fishing and
      trapping licenses
      generally, §§9-11-30 to
      9-11-66.
      See FISH AND GAME.
  Credit agencies, §40-12-87.
  Creosoting, §40-12-90.
  **Daughters of the American
      Revolution.**
    Exemptions from licenses,
      §40-9-13.

LICENSES—Cont'd
Defenses.
Affirmative defense, ARCP, Rule 8 (c).
Delicatessens, §40-12-91.
Delinquent license taxes.
Collection, §40-12-10.
Due and delinquent date, §40-12-26.
Dental hygienists, §§34-9-4, 34-9-26.
See DENTISTS.
Dental service corporations, §§22-21-363, 22-21-364, 22-21-367, 22-21-375.
See DENTAL SERVICE CORPORATIONS.
Dentists, §§34-9-1 to 34-9-26, 40-12-92.
See DENTISTS.
Department of finance.
Forms.
Duty to prepare, §40-12-19.
Department of revenue.
Refunds.
Duty of department, §40-12-24.
Detective agencies, §40-12-93.
Detention facilities.
Youth detention facilities, §44-1-27.
Devices for testing skill and strength used for profit, §40-12-95.
Dictaphones.
Sales, §40-12-127.
Dietitians and nutritionists.
Practice act.
Examinations, §34-34A-7.
Waiver, §34-34A-12.
Expiration of license, §34-34A-13.
Qualification for license, §34-34A-7.
Reciprocity, §34-34A-11.
Refusal, revocation or suspension, §34-34A-14.
Reinstatement of license, §34-34A-14.
Renewal of license, §34-34A-13.
Temporary license, §34-34A-9.
Directories.
Selling, §40-12-96.
Disabled veterans.
Exemption from licenses, §§40-12-340 to 40-12-352.
Distress merchandise sales, §§8-13-2 to 8-13-14, 40-12-101.
See SALES.
Dogs.
Shows, §40-12-111.
Trainers, §9-11-52.
Donor eye enucleation licenses, §§34-13-150 to 34-13-152.
Drivers' licenses.
Generally, §§32-6-1 to 32-6-48.
See MOTOR VEHICLES.
Motorcycles, §§32-12-22, 32-12-26.
Motor-driven cycles, §§32-12-22, 32-12-26.
Driver training schools, §§32-14-20 to 32-14-24.
See MOTOR VEHICLES.

LICENSES—Cont'd
Duplicating machines.
Sales, §40-12-127.
Education.
City boards of education.
Allocation of revenue from licenses, §16-11-25.
Teachers.
Exemptions from licenses.
Corporations organized for purpose of aiding retired teachers, §40-9-18.
Unaccredited schools.
Operation of school, §16-46-5.
Review of actions, §16-46-9.
Warrants for special license, privilege or excise taxes, §§16-13-120 to 16-13-122.
Electric companies.
License taxes, §§40-21-53 to 40-21-56.
Elks club.
Exemptions from licenses.
Elks memorial centers, §40-9-12.
Embalmers, §§34-13-90, 34-13-92, 40-12-98.
Employment agencies, §§34-10-1 to 34-10-5.
See EMPLOYMENT AGENCIES.
Engineers, §40-12-99.
Episcopal foundation of Jefferson county.
Exemptions from licenses, §40-9-13.
Examinations.
Conduct, §34-26-44.
Waiver, §34-26-45.
Exemptions from licenses, §§40-9-1 to 40-9-49.
Atomic energy.
Nuclear fuel assemblies, §40-9-22.
Birmingham building trades towers, §40-9-12.
Birmingham Football Foundation, Inc., §40-9-12.
Blind persons, §40-12-330.
Boy Scouts of America, §40-9-12.
Cancer society, §40-9-12.
Catholic Maritime Club of Mobile, Inc., §40-9-12.
Charities, §§40-9-12, 40-9-13.
Childhaven, Inc., §40-9-12.
Corporations.
Disabled veterans, §40-12-348.
Nonprofit corporations, §§40-9-12, 40-9-13.
Corporation organized for purpose of aiding retired teachers, §40-9-18.
Daughters of the American Revolution, §40-9-13.
Disabled veterans, §§40-12-340 to 40-12-352.
Apprentices, §40-12-344.
Associations, §40-12-348.
Certain veterans not included, §§40-12-352.
Corporations, §40-12-348.
County license, §40-12-342.
Eligibility, §40-12-340.
Employees, §40-12-344.

LICENSES—Cont'd
Exemptions from licenses —Cont'd
Disabled veterans—Cont'd
Expiration of license, §40-12-346.
Form of license, §40-12-345.
Fraudulently obtaining license, §40-12-349.
Helpers, §40-12-344.
Issuance of license.
County in which issued, §40-12-350.
Municipal license, §40-12-343.
Partnerships, §40-12-348.
Penalties.
Violations by officials, §40-12-351.
Proof of disability, §40-12-347.
Scope, §40-12-340.
State license, §40-12-341.
Education.
Corporation organized for purpose of aiding retired teachers, §40-9-18.
Elks club.
Elks memorial centers, §40-9-12.
Episcopal foundation of Jefferson county, §40-9-13.
Fire departments.
Volunteer fire departments, §40-9-13.
Freewill Baptist children's home, §40-9-12.
Girl Scouts of America, §40-9-12.
Heart Association, §40-9-13.
Helping Hand Club of Anniston, §40-9-12.
Holy Comforter House, Inc., of Gadsden, §40-9-12.
Knights of Pythias, §40-9-12.
Masonic lodges.
Alabama masonic home, §40-9-12.
Methodist children's home, §40-9-12.
Methodist home for the aging, §40-9-12.
National foundation.
Alabama field offices, §40-9-12.
New hope industries of Dothan, §40-9-12.
Presbyterian Apartments, Inc., §40-9-13.
Presbyterian home for children, §40-9-12.
Salvation Army, Inc., §40-9-12.
Seamen's home of Mobile, §40-9-12.
Shrine clubs.
Annual shrine circus and other events, §40-9-13.
State fair.
Alabama state fair and exhibit association, §40-9-15.
University of Alabama Huntsville foundation, §40-9-12.

LICENSES—Cont'd
Exemptions from licenses
—Cont'd
Veterans.
Disabled veterans,
§§40-12-340 to
40-12-352.
World War II veterans,
§§40-12-370 to
40-12-377.
World War II veterans,
§§40-12-370 to 40-12-377.
Associations, §40-12-375.
Certain veterans not
exempt, §40-12-375.
Corporations, §40-12-375.
County license, §40-12-372.
Eligibility, §40-12-370.
Form of license,
§40-12-374.
Fraudulently obtaining
license, §40-12-376.
Municipal license,
§40-12-373.
Officials.
Duty, §40-12-374.
Violations.
Penalty, §40-12-377.
Partnerships, §40-12-375.
Penalties.
Transfer, §40-12-374.
Violations by officials,
§40-12-377.
Scope, §40-12-370.
State license, §40-12-371.
Transfer of license.
Penalty, §40-12-374.
Young Men's Christian
Association, §40-9-9.
Young Men's Hebrew
Association, §40-9-12.
Young Women's Christian
Association, §40-9-10.
Young Women's Christian
Organization, §40-9-11.
Express companies.
License taxes, §§40-21-60,
40-21-61.
Municipal license schedule,
§11-51-126.
Eyeglasses.
Sales, §40-12-161.
Fairs.
Exemptions from licenses.
Alabama state fair and
exhibit association,
§40-9-15.
Street fairs, §40-12-163.
Farm products.
Municipalities not to charge
farmers for sale etc., of
farm products,
§11-51-105.
Fees.
Alcoholic beverages,
§28-3A-4.
Ferries.
Municipal corporations.
Establishment of ferries on
rivers between two
counties, §§11-49-20 to
11-49-23.
Special, private or local laws
prohibited, Const. Ala.,
art. IV, §104.
Fertilizer.
Factories, §40-12-100.
Licenses for sale of
commercial fertilizer,
§§2-22-5, 2-22-6, 2-22-8.

LICENSES—Cont'd
Finance companies.
Small loans, §§5-18-3 to
5-18-12.
See SMALL LOANS.
Fire departments.
Volunteer fire departments.
Exemptions from licenses,
§40-9-13.
Fireworks.
Dealers, §40-12-102.
Fish and game.
Commercial fishing.
Public impounded waters
and navigable streams,
§§9-11-141 to 9-11-146.
See FISH AND GAME.
Hunting, fishing and
trapping licenses
generally, §§9-11-30 to
9-11-66.
See FISH AND GAME.
Salt water fish, §9-12-114.
Flying jennies, §40-12-103.
Foresters, §§34-12-7 to
34-12-9.
Form, §40-12-2.
Department of finance.
Duty to prepare, §40-12-19.
Transient merchants,
§34-35-5.
Fortunetellers.
Fee, §40-12-104.
Foster care facilities,
§44-1-27.
Fraternal benefit societies,
§§27-34-6 to 27-34-8.
Fraud.
Exemptions from licenses.
Disabled veterans.
Fraudulently obtaining
license, §40-12-349.
Veterans of World War II.
Fraudulently obtaining
license, §40-12-376.
**Freewill Baptist children's
home.**
Exemptions from licenses,
§40-9-12.
Freight.
Transfer of freight,
§40-12-171.
Fruit dealers, §40-12-105.
Funeral services, §§34-13-1 to
34-13-152.
See FUNERALS.
Furs.
Dealers, §40-12-110.
Gambling.
Playing cards, §40-12-144.
Game laws.
Hunting, fishing and
trapping licenses
generally, §§9-11-30 to
9-11-66.
See FISH AND GAME.
Garages.
Automobile garages and
shops, §40-12-54.
Storage garages, §40-12-55.
Garbage and trash.
Collection and disposal.
Private or corporate
agencies, §22-27-5.
Gas districts.
Levy and collection of
privilege license tax by
certain municipalities,
§11-50-413.

LICENSES—Cont'd
Gasoline.
Stations and pumps,
§40-12-106.
Girl Scouts of America.
Exemptions from licenses,
§40-9-12.
Glass.
Selling, §40-12-107.
Going out of business sales,
§§8-13-2 to 8-13-14,
40-12-101.
See SALES.
Golf.
Golf or miniature golf
courses, §40-12-108.
Grain dealers, §§2-31-3 to
2-31-13.
See GRAIN DEALERS.
Hamburger stands,
§40-12-153.
Harbors and ports.
Construction of wharves, etc.,
§33-1-28.
Harbor masters, §33-3-5.
Upland owners.
Revocation or suspension,
§33-1-29.
Health care institutions.
General provisions,
§§22-21-20 to 22-21-33.
See HOSPITALS.
Health care service plan.
License taxes by
municipalities or
counties prohibited,
§10-4-107.
**Health maintenance
organizations.**
Agents, §27-21A-14.
**Hearing aid dealers and
fitters.**
General provisions, §§34-14-1
to 34-14-14.
See HEARING AID
DEALERS AND
FITTERS.
Permits.
Temporary permits,
§§34-14-1, 34-14-7.
Heart Association.
Exemptions from licenses,
§40-9-13.
Heaters.
Dealers, §40-12-97.
**Helping Hand Club of
Anniston.**
Exemptions from licenses,
§40-9-12.
Hide.
Dealers, §40-12-110.
**Historical preservation
authorities.**
Imposition of license tax on
authority, §41-10-147.
**Holy Comforter House, Inc.,
of Gadsden.**
Exemptions from licenses,
§40-9-12.
Horse racing.
Conducting race without
license, §11-65-37.
Misuse, §11-65-42.
Racetracks, §40-12-147.
Operators, §§11-65-18 to
11-65-22.
See HORSE RACING.
Owners, §§11-65-14 to
11-65-17.
Horses.
Dealers, §40-12-112.

LICENSES—Cont'd
Horses—Cont'd
Shows, §40-12-111.
Hospitals, §§22-21-20 to
22-21-33.
See HOSPITALS.
Hotels.
Alcoholic beverage licenses,
§§28-3A-1 to 28-3A-26.
See ALCOHOLIC
BEVERAGES.
Innkeepers and hotels,
§40-12-115.
Hunting licenses.
Hunting, fishing and
trapping licenses
generally, §§9-11-30 to
9-11-66.
See FISH AND GAME.
Ice cream, §40-12-113.
Ice factories, §40-12-114.
**Industrial development
corporations.**
Occupational license taxes,
§10-4-144.
Inspectors.
License inspectors,
§§40-12-10, 40-12-11.
Insurance.
Adjusters, §§27-9-2 to 27-9-8.
See INSURANCE.
Agents.
Examinations.
Fees, §27-4-2.
Property, casualty and
surety insurance
representatives,
§§27-7-4 to 27-7-26.
See INSURANCE.
Automobile clubs and
associations.
Agents and
representatives,
§27-39-7.
Requirements, §27-39-3.
Casualty insurance.
Rates and rating
organizations,
§§27-13-62, 27-13-78,
27-13-79.
Finance companies.
Insurance premium finance
companies, §§27-40-3
to 27-40-5.
Fraternal benefit societies,
§§27-34-6 to 27-34-8.
Insurance premium finance
companies, §§27-40-3 to
27-40-5.
Insurers.
Exemption from other
licenses, §27-4-10.
Life insurers organized to
aid nonprofit
institutions.
Annual license fee,
§27-4-8.
Refund of licenses paid by
mistake, §27-4-11.
Municipal corporations.
Schedules, §§11-51-120 to
11-51-123.
Securities salesmen,
§27-27-11.
Solicitors.
Property, casualty and
surety insurance
representatives,
§§27-7-4 to 27-7-26.
See INSURANCE.

LICENSES—Cont'd
Insurance—Cont'd
Surety insurance.
Rates and rating
organizations,
§§27-13-62, 27-13-78,
27-13-79.
Surplus line insurance.
Brokers, §27-10-24.
Iron ore.
Mining, §§40-12-128 to
40-12-130.
Issuance, §40-12-2.
Itinerant vendors, §40-12-139.
**Junior college for Franklin,
Marion and Winston
counties.**
Exemption of officers,
teachers and employees
from town licenses,
§16-60-35.
**Junior college for Jackson
and DeKalb counties.**
Exemption of officers,
teachers and employees
from town licenses,
§16-60-65.
Junk dealers, §40-12-116.
Junkyards, §§23-1-243 to
23-1-245.
Knights of Pythias.
Exemptions from licenses,
§40-9-12.
Knives.
Dealers in bowie and dirk
knives, §40-12-143.
Landscape architects,
§§34-17-20, 34-17-21,
34-17-24 to 34-17-26.
See LANDSCAPE
ARCHITECTS.
Laundries, §40-12-118.
Leases.
Personal property.
Leasing or renting tangible
personal property,
§§40-12-220 to
40-12-227.
See PERSONAL
PROPERTY.
**Levy of both state and
county license tax.**
Collection and distribution,
§40-12-3.
License inspectors.
Bonds, surety, §40-12-11.
Generally, §40-12-10.
Lightning rods, §40-12-120.
Limitation of actions.
Actions by state or political
subdivision for recovery
of amounts claimed for
licenses.
Five year limitation,
§6-2-35.
Livestock dealers, §§2-15-30,
2-15-132.
Loans.
Small loans, §§5-18-3 to
5-18-12.
See SMALL LOANS.
**Long term quality health
care.**
Facilities.
Responsibility of
department of public
health, §22-6-26.
Machinery.
Repair shops, §40-12-123.

LICENSES—Cont'd
Magic.
Legerdemain and sleight of
hand, §40-12-119.
Marine resources, §§9-12-80
to 9-12-94.
See MARINE RESOURCES.
Marriage.
Blood test for licenses.
Syphilis examination for
marriage license,
§22-11A-15.
Certificates, §§30-1-13,
30-1-14, 30-1-16.
General provisions, §§30-1-9
to 30-1-12.
Syphilis examination for
marriage license,
§22-11A-15.
Masonic lodges.
Exemptions from licenses.
Alabama masonic home,
§40-9-12.
Mentally ill.
Facilities.
License required to
operate, §22-50-17.
Merry-go-rounds, §40-12-103.
Methodist children's home.
Exemptions from licenses,
§40-9-12.
**Methodist home for the
aging.**
Exemptions from licenses,
§40-9-12.
Midwives, §§34-19-3 to
34-19-5, 34-19-9.
Military affairs.
Exemption of certain post
exchanges and canteens
from state and local
licenses, §31-2-81.
Milk and milk products.
Ice cream, §40-12-113.
Operation of testing
apparatus, §2-13-9.
Mimeographs.
Sales, §40-12-127.
Mobile homes.
Fees, §§24-5-6, 24-5-10.
Sale of mobile homes,
§24-5-6.
Monuments.
Selling or erecting,
§40-12-131.
Mops.
Manufacturers, §40-12-68.
Morticians, §34-13-70.
Motion pictures.
Permanent operators,
§40-12-133.
Transient operators,
§40-12-132.
Motorcycles.
Dealers, §40-12-62.
Tags, §40-12-62.
Taxes and registration fees,
§40-12-242.
Additional fee, §40-12-273.
Disposition, §40-12-274.
Motor-driven cycles.
Fees, §32-6-21.
Operator's license.
Age requirement,
§32-12-22.
Issuance, §32-12-22.
Revocation, §32-12-26.
Motor fuels.
Diesel fuel tax, §§40-17-12,
40-17-14.

LICENSES—Cont'd
  Motor fuels—Cont'd
    Distributors of motor fuels,
      §§40-12-190 to 40-12-197.
      See MOTOR FUELS.
  Motor vehicle carriers.
    Brokers, §§37-3-15, 37-3-16.
    General provisions,
      §§37-3-16, 37-3-33.
  Motor vehicles, §§32-6-1 to
      32-6-295.
      See MOTOR VEHICLES.
  Mules.
    Dealers, §40-12-112.
  Multiple businesses.
    Engaging in, §40-12-13.
  **Multiple licenses on same
      business,** §40-12-14.
  Municipal corporations.
    Ferries.
      Establishment on rivers
        between two counties,
        §§11-49-20 to 11-49-23.
    General provisions,
      §§11-51-90 to 11-51-185.
      See MUNICIPAL
        CORPORATIONS.
    Population of municipality as
      determining tax,
      §40-12-17.
  Music.
    Musical entertainments,
      §40-12-82.
    Musical instruments,
      §40-12-141.
  National foundation.
    Exemptions from licenses.
      Alabama field offices,
        §40-9-12.
  Naturopaths, §40-12-155.
  Navigation.
    Aids to navigation.
      State docks department to
        grant licenses for
        construction, §33-1-28.
  **New hope industries of
      Dothan.**
    Exemptions from licenses,
      §40-9-12.
  Newsstands, §40-12-134.
  Nightclubs, §40-12-152.
  Nurses, §§34-21-20 to
      34-21-26.
      See NURSES.
  **Nursing home
      administrators,** §§34-20-1,
      34-20-11 to 34-20-16.
      See NURSING HOMES.
  Nursing homes.
    General provisions,
      §§22-21-20 to 22-21-33.
      See HOSPITALS.
  Oculists, §40-12-135.
  Opticians, §40-12-135.
  Optometrists, §§34-22-20 to
      34-22-24, 40-12-135.
      See OPTOMETRISTS.
  Osteopaths, §40-12-136.
  Packinghouses, §40-12-137.
  Palmists.
    Fee, §40-12-104.
  Parks and recreation.
    Municipal corporations,
      §§11-51-102, 11-51-104.
  Partnerships.
    Exemptions from licenses.
      Disabled veterans,
        §40-12-348.
      Veterans of World War II,
        §40-12-375.
  Part of year, §40-12-25.

LICENSES—Cont'd
  Parts recyclers.
    Motor vehicles, §§40-12-411
      to 40-12-418.
      See MOTOR VEHICLES.
  Pawnbrokers, §40-12-138.
  Payment of license tax.
    When due and payable,
      §40-12-10.
  Peddlers, §40-12-139.
    Transient peddlers,
      §40-12-174.
  Penalties.
    Agents of persons, firms, etc.,
      who have not paid tax,
      §40-12-18.
    Exemptions from licenses.
      Disabled veterans.
        Violations by officials,
          §40-12-351.
      Veterans of World War II.
        Transfer, §40-12-374.
        Violations by officials,
          §40-12-377.
    Failure to take out licenses,
      §40-12-9.
  Personal privilege, §40-12-15.
  Personal property.
    Leasing or renting,
      §§40-12-220 to 40-12-227.
      See PERSONAL
        PROPERTY.
  Pesticides.
    Application of pesticides,
      §§2-27-53 to 2-27-56.
    License to sell, §2-27-10.
  **Pharmacists and
      pharmacies,** §§34-23-30 to
      34-23-53.
      See PHARMACISTS AND
        PHARMACIES.
  Photography.
    Developing and printing
      films, §40-12-94.
    Photographers and
      photograph galleries,
      §40-12-140.
  Physical therapists,
      §§34-24-210 to 34-24-217.
      See PHYSICAL
        THERAPISTS.
  Physicians.
    Certificates of qualification,
      §§34-24-70, 34-24-73,
      34-24-75, 34-24-80.
      See PHYSICIANS.
    Generally, §§34-24-310 to
      34-24-367.
      See PHYSICIANS.
  Pianos.
    Selling or renting,
      §40-12-141.
  Pig iron.
    Storage operators,
      §40-12-142.
  Pilots and pilotage.
    Certification, §§33-4-30,
      33-4-34.
    Examination, §§33-4-30,
      33-4-35, 33-4-36.
    General provisions,
      §§33-4-34, 33-4-37,
      33-4-41 to 33-4-45.
  Pipelines.
    Municipal corporations.
      License schedule for
        pipeline companies,
        §11-51-129.
  Pistols, §§13A-11-73 to
      13A-11-75, 13A-11-81.
      See WEAPONS.

LICENSES—Cont'd
  Place of business.
    Change, §40-12-1.
    License to designate,
      §40-12-12.
  Plates.
    Tags and plates, §§32-6-51 to
      32-6-295.
      See MOTOR VEHICLES.
  Playing cards, §40-12-144.
  Plumbers, §40-12-145.
    Acts, works and conduct
      permitted without
      license, §34-37-15.
    Certification of plumbers and
      gas fitters, §§34-37-6 to
      34-37-15.
      See PLUMBING.
    Restrictions, §34-37-16.
  Podiatrists.
    Examinations, §§34-24-255 to
      34-24-257.
    Generally, §§34-24-270 to
      34-24-276, 40-12-155.
      See PODIATRISTS.
  Polygraph examiners,
      §§34-25-20 to 34-25-36.
      See POLYGRAPH
        EXAMINERS.
  Pool halls, §§34-6-30 to
      34-6-35, 40-12-146.
      See BILLIARD ROOMS.
  **Presbyterian Apartments,
      Inc.**
    Exemptions from licenses,
      §40-9-13.
  **Presbyterian home for
      children.**
    Exemptions from licenses,
      §40-9-12.
  Probate courts, §§40-12-269
      to 40-12-271.
      See PROBATE COURTS.
  Psychologists.
    Examination, §§34-26-43.1 to
      34-26-45.
      See PSYCHOLOGISTS.
    General provisions,
      §§34-26-40 to 34-26-48.
      See PSYCHOLOGISTS.
  Public utilities, §§40-21-50 to
      40-21-64.
      See PUBLIC UTILITIES.
  Public works.
    Improvement authorities.
      Chapter exclusive,
        §39-7-33.
  Quail.
    Commercial quail breeding,
      §§9-11-342, 9-11-349.
      See FISH AND GAME.
  Racetracks, §40-12-147.
  Radios.
    Sales, §40-12-148.
  Radio utilities, §37-4-115.
  Railroads.
    Alcoholic beverages.
      Retail common carrier
        liquor license,
        §28-3A-18.
    Brokers and agents of
      railway supplies,
      §40-12-67.
    Employees, §37-2-85.
      Employment of unlicensed
        persons, §37-2-86.
    License taxes, §40-21-57.
    Municipal corporations.
      Schedules, §11-51-124.

LICENSES—Cont'd
Railroads—Cont'd
Sleeping car companies.
Municipal license schedule,
§11-51-125.
Supply cars, §40-12-164.
Randolph county.
Funding county facilities.
License taxes, Const. Ala.,
amd. 442.
Real estate brokers,
§§34-27-30 to 34-27-38,
40-12-149, 40-12-150.
Records.
Probate judge to keep,
§40-12-21.
Refrigerators.
Dealers, §40-12-97.
Refunds.
Applications, §40-12-23.
Department of revenue.
Duty, §40-12-24.
Rent.
Leasing or renting tangible
personal property,
§§40-12-220 to 40-12-227.
See PERSONAL
PROPERTY.
Requirement.
Who must procure business,
vocational or
occupational licenses,
§40-12-40.
Rescue squads.
Exemption from license fees,
§32-11-2.
Resin.
Resin stills, §40-12-175.
Restaurants, §40-12-151.
Alcoholic beverages.
See ALCOHOLIC
BEVERAGES.
Rifles.
Dealers, §40-12-158.
Roadhouses, §40-12-152.
Road machinery.
Dealers, §40-12-169.
Rodeos, §40-12-111.
Sale of checks, §§8-7-3 to
8-7-14.
See CHECKS.
Sales.
Fire, closing out, etc., sales,
§40-12-101.
Going out of business or
distress merchandise
sales, §§8-13-2 to
8-13-14, 40-12-101.
See SALES.
Salvation army.
Exemptions from licenses,
§40-9-12.
Sandwich shops, §40-12-153.
**Savings and loan
associations.**
Municipal license schedules,
§11-51-131.
Sawmills, §40-12-154.
School bus drivers, §16-27-4.
Scientists, §40-12-155.
Seamen's home of Mobile.
Exemptions from licenses,
§40-9-12.
**Selling throughout state
under one license,**
§40-12-9.
Sentencing.
Article not to deprive court
of authority to suspend
or cancel license,
§13A-5-2.

LICENSES—Cont'd
Sewing machines.
Sales, §40-12-156.
Ships and shipping.
Foreign vessels.
Operation without license,
§33-5-15.
Term of license, §33-5-13.
Shooting galleries,
§40-12-157.
Municipal corporations,
§11-51-102.
Revocation of licenses,
§11-51-103.
Shotguns.
Dealers, §40-12-158.
Shows.
Transient theatrical and
vaudeville shows,
§40-12-173.
Vaudeville and variety
shows, §40-12-166.
Shrine clubs.
Exemptions from licenses.
Annual shrine circus and
other events, §40-9-13.
Skating rinks, §40-12-159.
Small loans, §§5-18-3 to
5-18-12.
See SMALL LOANS.
Social workers, §§34-30-20 to
34-30-28.
See SOCIAL WORKERS.
**Southeast interstate low-
level radioactive waste
management compact.**
Fees, §22-32-5.
Spectacles, §40-12-161.
**Speech pathologists and
audiologists,** §§34-28A-20
to 34-28A-27.
See SPEECH
PATHOLOGISTS AND
AUDIOLOGISTS.
Sports.
Baseball parks, §40-12-59.
Statements.
Sworn statements.
Amount of capital, value of
goods, stock, etc.,
§40-12-16.
Steam fitters, §40-12-145.
Steamships.
Alcoholic beverages.
Generally, §§28-3A-1 to
28-3A-26.
Stills.
Turpentine and resin stills,
§40-12-175.
Stock brokers, §40-12-162.
Stores, §§40-12-310 to
40-12-319.
See STORES.
Stubs.
License and stub must
correspond, §40-12-20.
Sugar.
Factories, §40-12-165.
Surface mining.
Coal surface mining,
§9-16-81.
Syrup.
Factories, §40-12-165.
Tags and plates, §§32-6-51 to
32-6-295.
See MOTOR VEHICLES.
Taxation.
Delinquent taxes.
Collection, §40-12-10.

LICENSES—Cont'd
Taxation—Cont'd
Inspectors, §40-12-10.
Powers and duties,
§40-12-10.
Supernumerary license
commissioners, §§40-6-1
to 40-6-8.
Telegraph companies.
License taxes, §40-21-59.
Municipal license schedule,
§11-51-127.
Telephone companies.
License taxes, §40-21-58.
Municipal license schedule
for telephone companies,
§11-51-128.
Television.
Community antenna
television systems.
Tax, §11-27-3.
Term of license, §40-12-26.
Theaters, §40-12-166.
Municipal corporations,
§11-51-102.
Revocation, §11-51-103.
Ticket scalpers, §40-12-167.
Tobacco.
Cigars, cigarettes, cheroots,
etc.
Retailers, §40-12-72.
Wholesalers, §40-12-73.
Tombstones.
Selling or erecting,
§40-12-131.
Tourist camps, §40-12-168.
Tractors.
Dealers, §40-12-169.
Trading stamps, §40-12-170.
Trailers.
Dealers, §40-12-169.
Transferability, §40-12-15.
Transient dealers, §40-12-172.
Transient merchants,
§§34-35-3 to 34-35-8.
See TRANSIENT
MERCHANTS.
Trees and timber.
Dealers, §40-12-121.
Funds from licenses
pertaining to.
Disposition of proceeds,
§40-12-28.
Lumberyards, §40-12-122.
Mills.
Veneer mills, planing
mills, box factories,
etc., §40-12-177.
Turpentine stills, §40-12-175.
Typewriters.
Sales, §40-12-44.
Undertakers, §34-13-70.
**Unemployment
compensation.**
Revocation or suspension of
required license.
Disqualifications for
benefits, §25-4-78.
University of Alabama.
Huntsville foundation.
Exemptions from licenses,
§40-9-12.
University of Montevallo.
Employees exempt from
license taxes, §16-54-12.
Upholsterers, §40-12-125.
**Vacation time-sharing plans
generally,** §§34-27-50 to
34-27-69.
See VACATION TIME-
SHARING PLANS.

LICENSES—Cont'd
Vending machines,
§40-12-176.
Municipal license tax,
§§11-51-98, 11-51-100.
Vending stands.
Blind persons.
Preference in issuance of
licenses, §21-1-41.
Vendors.
Transient vendors,
§40-12-174.
Veterans.
Exemption from licenses,
§§40-12-340 to 40-12-377.
Veterinarians, §§34-29-71 to
34-29-77.
See VETERINARIANS.
Veterinary surgery,
§40-12-178.
Violations.
Each day's violation
constitutes separate
offense, §40-12-27.
Warehouses, §40-12-179.
Cotton warehouses,
§40-12-88.
Refrigerated warehouses,
§40-12-137.
Waters and watercourses.
Development of docks along
inland waterways.
Occupying state property.
Revocation and
suspension of license
to occupy, §§33-2-3,
33-2-33, 33-2-63,
33-2-93, 33-2-122,
33-2-152.
Upland owners.
Revocation or suspension,
§33-1-29.
Weapons.
False information in
application for licenses,
§13A-11-81.
Pistols, §§13A-11-73 to
13A-11-75, 13A-11-81.
Shotguns, rifles, ammunition,
etc. §40-12-158.
Well drillers, §§22-24-5,
22-24-7.
World War II veterans.
Exemptions from licenses,
§§40-12-370 to 40-12-377.
Wrestling, §41-9-96.
Yards.
Storage yards, §40-12-179.
**Young Men's Christian
Association.**
Exemptions from licenses,
§40-9-9.
**Young Men's Hebrew
Association.**
Exemptions from licenses,
§40-9-12.
**Young Women's Christian
Association.**
Exemption from licenses,
§40-9-10.
**Young Women's Christian
Organization.**
Exemptions from licenses,
§40-9-11.
Youth services.
Detention facilities, §44-1-27.
Foster care facilities,
§44-1-27.

LIE DETECTORS.
Polygraph examiners,
§§34-25-1 to 34-25-36.
See POLYGRAPH
EXAMINERS.

LIENS, §§35-11-1 to 35-11-431.
Abutting landowners.
Liens for improvements on
public streets, etc.,
§§35-11-410 to 35-11-417.
See HIGHWAYS.
Affidavits.
Attachment.
Affidavit required before
issue of attachment,
§35-11-5.
Agisters, §§35-11-70, 35-11-71.
Agriculture.
Cotton gins, §§35-11-290,
35-11-291.
Hay baling machines or
presses, §§35-11-290,
35-11-291.
Peanut machines or pickers,
§§35-11-290, 35-11-291.
Plants for drying or
processing planting
seeds, §§35-11-290,
35-11-291.
Sharecroppers, §§35-11-350,
35-11-351.
Superintendents and
laborers, §§35-11-91 to
35-11-97.
See AGRICULTURE.
Tenants in common,
§§35-11-350, 35-11-351.
Airports.
State airports.
Liens for services rendered,
§4-2-95.
Animals.
Feeding, boarding or
training, §35-11-71.
Livestock.
See LIVESTOCK.
Owners of stallions, jacks,
bulls, etc., §§35-11-330,
35-11-331.
Veterinarians, §§35-11-390,
35-11-391.
**Appliances, machinery and
equipment used for land
clearing or
improvements.**
Declaration of lien,
§35-11-430.
Enforcement of lien,
§35-11-431.
Perfection of lien, §35-11-431.
Attachment.
Affidavit.
Required before issue of
attachment, §35-11-5.
Bond.
Required before issue of
attachment, §35-11-5.
Creation, §6-6-76.
Limitations, §35-11-6.
Trial of cases of attachment,
§35-11-6.
Attorneys at law.
Lien for attorney's fees,
§34-3-61.
Baggage.
Hotel keepers, §§35-11-130,
35-11-131.
Restaurant keepers,
§§35-11-130, 35-11-131.

LIENS—Cont'd
**Banks and financial
institutions.**
Credit unions.
Lien on shares and
deposits of members,
§5-17-14.
Liquidation of insolvent
banks.
Liens against bank in
possession of
superintendent,
§5-8A-28.
Savings and loan
associations.
Accounts, §5-16-26.
**Bear creek development
authority.**
Statutory mortgage lien,
§33-15-10.
Birds.
Feeding, boarding or
training, §35-11-71.
Blacksmiths, §§35-11-110 to
35-11-112.
Blind persons.
Assistance to needy blind
persons.
Hospitalization.
Cost not to constitute
lien on property,
§38-5-5.
Boats.
Declaration of lien on
watercraft, §35-11-60.
Bonds, surety.
Attachment.
Bond required before issue
of attachment,
§35-11-5.
Limitation of actions.
Chapter inapplicable,
§6-2-2.
Booms and bulkheads,
§§35-11-310, 35-11-311.
Buildings.
Landlord and tenant.
Liens for rent of buildings,
§§35-9-60 to 35-9-65.
See LANDLORD AND
TENANT.
Mechanics' and
materialmen's liens,
§§35-11-210 to 35-11-234.
See MECHANICS AND
MATERIALMEN'S
LIENS.
Bulkheads, §§35-11-310,
35-11-311.
Bulls.
Owners of stallions, jacks,
bulls, etc., §§35-11-330,
35-11-331.
Carriers.
Lien of carrier, §7-7-307.
Enforcement, §7-7-308.
Cleaners, §§35-11-170,
35-11-171.
Coal.
Abandoned mine
reclamation.
Property subject to lien,
§9-16-129.
Commercial code.
See COMMERCIAL CODE.
Condominiums.
Against condominium
property.
Generally, §35-8-16.
In favor of association,
§35-8-17.

LIENS—Cont'd
Condominiums—Cont'd
Recordation, §35-8-11.
Termination of condominium, §35-8-20.
Constitution of Alabama.
Laborers' liens and mechanics' liens not barred by homestead exemptions, Const. Ala., art. X, §207.
Special, private or local laws creating, extending or impairing liens prohibited, Const. Ala., art. IV, §104.
Corporations.
Stock.
Lien on shares by corporation, §10-2A-43.
Cotton.
Boll weevil eradication.
Assessment of cotton growers.
Failure to pay assessment, §2-19-135.
Removal from state of cotton subject to purchase money lien, §2-19-13.
Cotton gins, §§35-11-290, 35-11-291.
Creation.
Special, private or local laws prohibited, Const. Ala., art. IV, §104.
Credit unions.
Lien on shares and deposits of members, §5-17-14.
Criminal law and procedure.
Defrauding secured creditors, §13A-9-46.
Crops.
Agricultural superintendents and laborers, §§35-11-91 to 35-11-97.
See AGRICULTURE.
Landlord's liens.
Advances and rent of lands, §§35-9-30 to 35-9-42.
See LANDLORD AND TENANT.
Partition of crops.
Effect on existing liens, §35-6-115.
Rent or advances.
Failure to apply farm produce to payment of lien for rent or advances, §2-1-4.
Tenants in common, §§35-11-350, 35-11-351.
Education.
Private colleges and universities facilities authority.
Bond issues.
Statutory mortgage lien, §16-18A-7.
Educational building authorities.
Bond issues.
Statutory mortgage lien, §16-17-12.
Electric cooperatives.
Mortgages or deeds of trust creating liens, §37-6-23.
Enforcement.
Attachment, §§6-6-76, 35-11-5, 35-11-6.

LIENS—Cont'd
Enforcement—Cont'd
Statutory modes of enforcement not exclusive, §35-11-1.
Environmental improvement authorities.
Bond issues.
Creation of statutory mortgage lien, §9-6-11.
Estrays.
Costs of keeping animal, etc., §3-2-2.
Executions, §§6-9-60, 6-9-61, 6-9-84.
Exemptions from levy and sale under process.
Contest of exemption claim.
Effect of contest on lien on property, §6-10-43.
Homestead exemption.
Liens not affected, §6-10-4.
When no action lies against officer levying, §6-10-42.
Extension.
Special, private or local laws prohibited, Const. Ala., art. IV, §104.
Factors.
Secured transactions, §§7-9-101 to 7-9-507.
See COMMERCIAL CODE.
Forests and forestry.
Fires and fire prevention.
Assessments for forest fire protection.
Failure to pay assessment, §9-13-196.
Lien on property for payment, §9-13-184.
Forest products.
Payment of taxes, interest and penalties, §§9-13-81, 9-13-99.
Fraternal orders.
Effect of article on existing liens, §10-4-179.
Judgment to provide liens for unsecured loans from parent organization, §10-4-178.
Fraud.
Judgment creditors.
Defrauding judgment creditors, §13A-9-47.
Secured creditors.
Defrauding secured creditors, §13A-9-46.
Gasoline.
Gasoline tax.
Delinquents, §40-17-46.
Gins.
Owners of cotton gins, §§35-11-290, 35-11-291.
Hay.
Baling machines or presses, §§35-11-290, 35-11-291.
Hazardous substances.
Fees for disposal of.
Lien upon property of operators, §22-30B-9.
Hazardous waste.
Fees for disposal of.
Liens upon property of operators, §22-30B-9.
Highways.
Improvements on public streets, etc., §§35-11-410 to 35-11-417.
See HIGHWAYS.

LIENS—Cont'd
Homestead exemptions.
Laborers' liens and mechanics' liens not barred by homestead exemptions, Const. Ala., art. X, §207.
Hospitals, §§35-11-370 to 35-11-375.
See HOSPITALS.
Hotel keepers, §§35-11-130, 35-11-131.
Impairment.
Special, private or local laws prohibited, Const. Ala., art. IV, §104.
Improvements on public streets, etc., §§35-11-410 to 35-11-417.
See HIGHWAYS.
Income tax.
Applicability of lien provisions.
Generally, §40-18-51.
Withholding tax.
Property of employer who fails to withhold or pay over, §40-18-74.
Inferior lienors.
Rights of inferior lienors, §35-11-2.
Insurance.
Insurers.
Voidable liens, §27-32-27.
Investment securities.
Issuer's lien, §7-8-103.
Jacks.
Owners of stallions, jacks, bulls, etc., §§35-11-330, 35-11-331.
Jewelers, §§35-11-150, 35-11-151.
Joint tenants and tenants in common.
Liens of tenants in common, §§35-11-350, 35-11-351.
Judgment creditors.
Defrauding, §13A-9-47.
Judgments.
Registration of judgments.
Judgment constitutes lien on defendant's property, §6-9-211.
Land clearing or improvements.
Appliances, machinery and equipment used for land clearing or improvements, §§35-11-430, 35-11-431.
Landlord and tenant, §§35-9-30 to 35-9-65.
See LANDLORD AND TENANT.
Laundries, §§35-11-170, 35-11-171.
Limitation of actions.
Attachment, §35-11-6.
Bonds, surety.
Chapter inapplicable, §6-2-2.
Tax liens.
Chapter inapplicable, §6-2-2.
Lis pendens.
Release of land from lien upon execution of bond, §35-4-137.
Livery stables, §§35-11-190, 35-11-191.

LIENS—Cont'd
Livestock.
Landlord's lien on stock raised on premises, §35-11-72.
Livery stable keepers, §§35-11-190, 35-11-191.
Owners of stallions, jacks, bulls, etc., §§35-11-330, 35-11-331.
Pasturage on training.
Lien on stock, §35-11-70.
Veterinarians, §§35-11-390, 35-11-391.
Machinery.
Appliances, machinery and equipment used for land clearing or improvements, §§35-11-430, 35-11-431.
Production, manufacture or repair, §§35-11-110 to 35-11-112.
Materialmen, §§35-11-210 to 35-11-234.
See MECHANICS' AND MATERIALMEN'S LIENS.
Mechanics' liens, §§35-11-210 to 35-11-234.
See MECHANICS' AND MATERIALMEN'S LIENS.
Mortgages and deeds of trust.
Satisfaction of mortgage liens, §§35-10-20 to 35-10-30.
See MORTGAGES AND DEEDS OF TRUST.
Motor fuels.
Diesel fuel tax.
Delinquents.
Tax lien, §40-17-15.
Motor vehicle carriers.
Mileage tax.
Tax to be lien on property of persons subject to chapter, §40-19-10.
Motor vehicles.
Abandoned vehicles, §§32-13-2 to 32-13-4.
See MOTOR VEHICLES.
Municipal testing stations.
Seizure and impoundment of vehicles.
Expenses of seizure and impounding, §32-18-8.
Production, manufacture or repair, §§35-11-110 to 35-11-112.
See MOTOR VEHICLES.
Uniform certificate of title and antitheft act.
Defined, §32-8-2.
Security interests.
Assignment by lienholder, §32-8-63.
Duty of lienholder to disclose information, §32-8-65.
Excepted liens, §32-8-60.
Municipal corporations.
Assessments for public improvements, §§11-48-32 to 11-48-35, 11-48-49 to 11-48-53.
See MUNICIPAL CORPORATIONS.

LIENS—Cont'd
Municipal corporations —Cont'd
Licenses.
Lien for license taxes, §11-51-96.
Enforcement not to constitute waiver of rights as to respondent's bond, §11-51-159.
Taxation.
Lien for property taxes, §11-51-6.
Optional method for levy and collection, §11-51-44.
Weeds.
Abatement of weeds.
Class 2 municipalities.
Cost of abatement or removal, §11-67-8.
Class 5 municipalities.
Cost of abatement or removal, §11-67-27.
Oil and gas.
Conservation and regulation of production.
Tax for expenses of administration and enforcement.
Payment of tax, interest and penalties, §9-17-30.
Mineral documentary tax, §40-20-32.
Order of resort to different things, §35-11-4.
Partition.
Crops.
Effect of partition on existing liens, §35-6-115.
Effect of partition on liens, §§35-6-51, 35-6-115.
Pasturage.
Lien on stock for pasturage, §35-11-70.
Peanuts.
Machines or pickers, §§35-11-290, 35-11-291.
Personal property.
Trial of right of property.
Claims based on lien, §6-6-164.
Priorities generally.
See PRIORITIES.
Public utilities.
Inspection and supervision fees.
Recovery of delinquent fees, §37-4-24.
Railroad laborers, §§35-11-90 to 35-11-97.
See RAILROADS.
Real property.
Lis pendens.
Release of land from lien upon execution of bond, §35-4-137.
Recordation.
Purchasers protected in dealing with record owner as owner of indebtedness, §35-4-64.
Redemption.
Right to redeem, §35-11-3.
Restaurant keepers, §§35-11-130, 35-11-131.

LIENS—Cont'd
Roads.
Improvements on public streets, etc., §§35-11-410 to 35-11-417.
See HIGHWAYS.
Sales tax.
Tax a lien, §40-23-19.
Tobacco sales tax, §40-25-21.
Savings and loan associations.
Accounts.
Liens on accounts, §5-16-26.
Sawmills.
Employees' or laborers' liens, §§35-11-270 to 35-11-273.
Owners' or operators' liens, §§35-11-250, 35-11-251.
Secured transactions, §§7-9-101 to 7-9-507.
See COMMERCIAL CODE.
Seeds.
Plants for drying or processing planting seeds, §§35-11-290, 35-11-291.
Self-service storage facilities.
Owner's lien, §8-15-33.
Satisfaction, §8-15-34.
Posting of notice as to effect of failure to pay charges, §8-15-35.
Satisfaction of owner's lien, §8-15-34.
Sewers.
Improvements on public streets, etc., §§35-11-410 to 35-11-417.
See HIGHWAYS.
Sharecroppers, §§35-11-350, 35-11-351.
Ships and shipping.
Declaration of lien on watercraft, §35-11-60.
Silversmiths, §§35-11-150, 35-11-151.
Small loans.
Acceptance of liens on real estate as security for loans, §5-18-14.
Stables.
Livery stables, §§35-11-190, 35-11-191.
Stallions.
Owners of stallions, jacks, bulls, etc., §§35-11-330, 35-11-331.
Streets.
Improvements on public streets, etc., §§35-11-410 to 35-11-417.
See HIGHWAYS.
Stumpage.
General provisions, §§35-11-20, 35-11-21.
Subordinate liens.
Order of resort to different things, §35-11-4.
Subrogation.
Inferior lienors.
Rights of inferior lienors, §35-11-2.
Mechanics' and materialmen's liens, §35-11-234.
Redemption.
Subrogation to benefits of lien after redemption, §35-11-3.

LIENS—Cont'd
Tax liens.
  General provisions.
    See TAXATION.
  United States taxes,
    §§35-11-42 to 35-11-48.
    See UNITED STATES.
Tenants in common,
  §§35-11-350, 35-11-351.
Tobacco.
  Sales tax.
    Tax lien, §40-25-21.
  Use tax.
    Tax lien, §40-25-45.
Trainers, §§35-11-70,
  35-11-71.
Transportation companies.
  Inspection and supervision
    fees, §37-2-41.
Trees and timber.
  Booms and bulkheads,
    §§35-11-310, 35-11-311.
  Employees' or laborers' liens,
    §§35-11-270 to 35-11-273.
  Liens for stumpage,
    §§35-11-20, 35-11-21.
Trial.
  Attachment, §35-11-6.
United States.
  Uniform federal lien
    registration act,
    §§35-11-42 to 35-11-48.
    See UNITED STATES.
Use tax.
  Tax a lien, §40-23-81.
  Tobacco use tax, §40-25-45.
Vacation time-sharing plans.
  Statement of liens.
    Required prior to sale,
      lease, encumbrance or
      conveyance, §34-27-51.
Veterinarians, §§35-11-390,
  35-11-391.
Wages.
  Agricultural superintendents
    and laborers, §§35-11-91
    to 35-11-97.
    See AGRICULTURE.
  Lumber employees or
    laborers, §§35-11-270 to
    35-11-273.
  Railroad employees,
    §§35-11-90 to 35-11-97.
    See RAILROADS.
  Sawmill employees or
    laborers, §§35-11-270 to
    35-11-273.
  Timber employees or
    laborers, §§35-11-270 to
    35-11-273.
Warehouseman's lien,
  §7-7-209.
  Enforcement, §7-7-210.
Watchmakers, §§35-11-150,
  35-11-151.
Watercraft.
  Declaration of lien on
    watercraft, §35-11-60.
Water management and
  drainage.
  Districts.
    Taxation.
      Taxes constitute lien,
      §9-9-32.
Woodworkmen, §§35-11-110
  to 35-11-112.
Workmen's compensation.
  Judgment liens.
    Creation, §25-5-91.

LIENS—Cont'd
Workmen's compensation
  —Cont'd
  Judgment liens—Cont'd
    Discharge of lien upon
      judgment payable
      periodically, §25-5-92.

LIEUTENANT GOVERNOR.
Business travel, §29-4-51.
Compensation, Const. Ala.,
  art. V, §118.
Constitution of Alabama.
  Compensation, Const. Ala.,
    art. V, §118.
  Election, Const. Ala., art. V,
    §§114, 115.
  Executive department.
    Member of department,
      Const. Ala., art. V,
      §112.
  Ex officio president of senate,
    Const. Ala., art. V, §117.
  Impeachment, Const. Ala.,
    art. VII, §173.
  Qualifications, Const. Ala.,
    art. V, §117.
    Failure of lieutenant
      governor-elect to
      qualify, Const. Ala.,
      art. V, §127.
  Residency requirements,
    Const. Ala., art. V, §118.
  Succession.
    Ineligible to succeed self,
      Const. Ala., art. V,
      §116.
    One additional term,
      Const. Ala., amd. 282.
  Term of office, Const. Ala.,
    art. V, §116; amd. 282.
Elections, Const. Ala., art. V,
  §§114, 115.
Enterprise zones.
  Legislative oversight
    committee.
    Appointment of members,
      §41-23-23.
Equipment and supplies.
  Authority to purchase and
    lease, §29-4-51.
Executive department.
  Member of department,
    Const. Ala., art. V, §112.
Impeachment, Const. Ala.,
  art. VII, §173.
Oaths, Const. U. S., Art. VI;
  Amendment XIV.
Office separate and distinct
  from legislature, state
  agencies, entity or
  official, §29-4-51.
Personnel.
  Appointment by lieutenant
    governor, §29-4-51.
  Business travel.
    Approval by lieutenant
      governor, §29-4-51.
  Compensation.
    Fixed by lieutenant
      governor, §29-4-51.
  Duties and responsibilities.
    Prescribed by lieutenant
      governor, §29-4-51.
  Service at pleasure of
    lieutenant governor,
    §29-4-51.
Protection.
  General provisions, §§36-33-1
    to 36-33-4.

LIEUTENANT GOVERNOR
  —Cont'd
Qualifications, Const. Ala.,
  art. V, §117.
  Failure of lieutenant
    governor-elect to qualify,
    Const. Ala., art. V, §127.
Residency requirements,
  Const. Ala., art. V, §118.
Senate.
  Ex officio president, Const.
    Ala., art. V, §117.
Succession.
  Ineligible to succeed self,
    Const. Ala., art. V, §116.
Synfuels development
  authority.
  Individuals who may become
    public corporation,
    §9-6A-3.
Term of office, Const. Ala.,
  art. V, §116.
Water system assistance
  authority.
  Appointments to authority,
    §22-23A-3.
  Water assistance legislative
    oversight committee.
    Appointments to
      committee, §22-23A-3.

LIFE AND DISABILITY
  INSURANCE GUARANTY
  ASSOCIATION, §§27-44-1
  to 27-44-21.
See INSURANCE.

LIFE ESTATES.
Acts of life tenants.
  Remainders not defeated by
    acts of life tenants,
    §35-4-170.
Appeals.
  Ascertainment and payment
    of life interests,
    §35-4-192.
Ascertainment and payment
  of life interests.
  Appeals, §35-4-192.
  Application, §35-4-191.
  Costs, §35-4-191.
  Court.
    Duty of court, §35-4-190.
  Guardian ad litem.
    Appointment, §35-4-191.
  Hearing, §35-4-191.
  Mentally ill.
    Appointment of guardian
      ad litem, §35-4-191.
  Minors.
    Appointment of guardian
      ad litem, §35-4-191.
  Notice, §35-4-191.
  Present value.
    Duty of court to ascertain,
      §35-4-190.
  Witnesses, §35-4-191.
Conveyances.
  Conveyance of greater estate
    by tenant for life or
    years passes his estate,
    §35-4-232.
Creditors of life tenants.
  Recordation necessary as to
    creditors, §35-4-91.
Death.
  Rent.
    Recovery of rent upon
      death of life tenant
      who has demised
      estate, §35-9-13.
Dower, §§35-4-190, 35-4-191.

LIFE ESTATES—Cont'd

Estates pur autre vie.
Character, §35-4-231.

Executors and administrators.
Recovery of rent upon death of life tenant who has demised estate, §35-9-13.

Fee simple estates.
Effect of grant of absolute power, §35-4-292.

Guardian ad litem.
Ascertainment and payment of life interests.
Appointment of guardian ad litem, §35-4-191.

Hearings.
Ascertainment and payment of life interests, §35-4-191.

Landlord and tenant.
Recovery of rent upon death of life tenant who has demised estate, §35-9-13.

Mortality tables, §§35-16-1 to 35-16-4.

Notice.
Ascertainment and payment of life interests, §35-4-191.

Payment of life interests, §§35-4-190 to 35-4-192.

Personal property.
Conveyances of personal property brought into state by tenants for life or years.
Recordation, §35-4-54.
Removal of personalty.
Consent of remainderman or reversioner required, §35-4-171.

Powers of disposition.
Effect of grant of absolute power, §35-4-292.

Recordation.
Necessary as to creditors of life tenants, §35-4-91.

Remainders not defeated by acts of life tenants, §35-4-170.

Remainders, reversions and executory interests, §§35-4-210 to 35-4-213.

Rent.
Recovery of rent upon death of life tenant who has demised estate, §35-9-13.

Rule in Shelley's case.
Abolished, §35-4-230.

Value.
Ascertainment and payment of life interests, §§35-4-190 to 35-4-192.

Warranties by tenant for life, §35-4-270.

LIFE EXPECTANCY TABLES.

Annuity tables, §§35-16-1 to 35-16-4.

Mortality tables, §§35-16-1 to 35-16-4.

LIFE-SUPPORT PROCEDURES.

Termination, §§22-8A-1 to 22-8A-10.
See NATURAL DEATH ACT.

LIFE TENANT, §§35-4-54, 35-4-170, 35-4-171.

LIGHTNING RODS.

Licenses, §40-12-120.

LIGNITE, §§40-13-30 to 40-13-36.
See COAL.

LIME, §§2-23-1 to 2-23-11.

Agricultural liming materials.
Defined, §2-23-2.

Analysis.
Commissioner of agriculture and industries, §2-23-6.

Brands.
Defined, §2-23-2.

Burnt lime.
Defined, §2-23-2.

Calcitic limestone.
Defined, §2-23-2.

Calcium carbonate equivalent.
Defined, §2-23-2.

Chalk.
Defined, §2-23-2.

Commissioner of agriculture and industries.
Right of entry upon public or private premises, §2-23-6.

Counties.
Acquisition of lands for lime quarries, §11-14-23.
Conduct of condemnation proceedings, §11-14-24.

Definitions, §2-23-2.

Delivery slips.
False or misleading statements on delivery slips prohibited, §2-23-4.

Distributors.
Deficiencies in agricultural liming materials.
Assessment of penalties against distributors for deficiencies, §2-23-7.

Fees.
Inspection fee, §2-23-5.
Inspection fee, §2-23-5.

Penalties.
Assessment of penalties against distributors for deficiencies in agricultural liming materials, §2-23-7.

Permits, §§2-23-3, 2-23-5.

Records.
Maintenance and examination of sales records, §2-23-5.

Reports.
Monthly reports as to gross sales in tons, §2-23-5.

Dolomitic limestone.
Defined, §2-23-2.

Environmental control.
Materials containing toxic materials in quantities injurious to plants or animals, §2-23-8.

Fees.
Disposition, §2-23-5.
Inspection fee, §2-23-5.
Permits.
Application fees, §2-23-3.
Disposition of permit fees, §2-23-5.

Fineness.
Defined, §2-23-2.

Ground shells.
Defined, §2-23-2.

LIME—Cont'd

Hydrated lime.
Defined, §2-23-2.

Inspections, §2-23-6.
Commissioner of agriculture and industries, §2-23-6.
Fee, §2-23-5.
Right of entry upon public or private premises by commissioner, §2-23-6.

Labels.
Defined, §2-23-2.
False or misleading statements on package labels, §2-23-4.
Requirements as to labeling, §2-23-4.

Limestone.
Defined, §2-23-2.

Manufacturers.
Deficiencies in agricultural liming materials.
Assessment of penalties against manufacturers for deficiencies, §2-23-7.
Fees.
Inspection fee, §2-23-5.
Inspection fee, §2-23-5.
Penalties.
Assessment of penalties for deficiencies in agricultural liming materials, §2-23-7.
Records.
Maintenance and examination of sales records, §2-23-5.
Reports.
Monthly reports as to gross sales in tons, §2-23-5.

Noncompliance with chapter.
Suspension from sale, seizure and condemnation of, §2-23-10.

Noncomplying agricultural liming materials.
Sale or offer for sale, §2-23-8.

Penalties.
Manufacturers.
Assessment of penalties against manufacturers, §2-23-7.

Permits.
Applications for permits, §2-23-3.
Duration of permits, §2-23-3.
Fees.
Application fees, §2-23-3.
Disposition of permit fees, §2-23-5.
Required for manufacture or distribution, §2-23-3.

Poisons and poisoning.
Materials containing toxic materials in quantities injurious to plants or animals, §2-23-8.

Pollution.
Toxic materials.
Materials containing toxic materials in quantities injurious to plants or animals, §2-23-8.

Reports.
Manufacturers and distributors, §2-23-5.

Rules and regulations.
Board of agriculture and industries, §2-23-9.

LIME—Cont'd
Rules and regulations
—Cont'd
Noncomplying agricultural
liming materials.
Sale or offer for sale,
§2-23-8.
Promulgation by board,
§2-23-9.
Violations.
Deemed misdemeanors,
§2-23-11.
Materials not complying
with rules or
regulations, §2-23-8.
Suspension from sale,
seizure and
condemnation of,
§2-23-10.
Sampling.
Commissioner of agriculture
and industries, §2-23-6.
Short title of chapter,
§2-23-1.
Toxic materials.
Materials containing toxic
materials in quantities
injurious to plants or
animals, §2-23-8.
Violations of chapter.
Deemed misdemeanors,
§2-23-11.
Noncomplying agricultural
liming materials.
Sale or offer for sale,
§2-23-8.
Suspension from sale, seizure
and condemnation of,
§2-23-10.

LIMESTONE.
Defined, §2-23-2.
Governor.
Sale of right to quarry
limestone, §35-4-381.

LIMESTONE COUNTY.
Commission.
Authority to dispose of dead
farm animals and
excavate human graves,
Const. Ala., amd. 482.
Elk river watershed area.
Development, Const. Ala.,
amd. 243.
Fires and fire prevention.
Establishment of fire
districts, Const. Ala.,
amd. 371.
Health.
Special property tax for
general health purposes,
Const. Ala., amd. 311.
Malaria control.
Tax for malaria control,
Const. Ala., amd. 34.
Officers.
Fees, salaries, etc., of certain
public officers, Const.
Ala., amd. 64.
Police.
Jurisdiction.
Police jurisdiction of
municipalities, Const.
Ala., amd. 499.
Trade schools, §16-60-193.

LIMITATION OF ACTIONS,
§§6-2-1 to 6-2-40.
Accrual of cause of action.
Fraud, §6-2-3.
Right of entry, §6-2-4.

LIMITATION OF ACTIONS
—Cont'd
Agents.
Commencement of limitation.
Principal against agent,
§6-2-6.
**Agreement or stipulation to
limit time prescribed.**
Void, §6-2-15.
Exception, §6-2-15.
Appeals.
Actions against surety to any
writ of error, appeal,
replevy or forthcoming
bond in courts of the
United States or other
state.
Four year limitation,
§6-2-36.
Arrest or reversal of
judgment on appeal.
Recommencement of
action, §6-2-38.
Applicability of chapter,
§6-2-1.
Exceptions, §6-2-2.
Assault and battery.
Six year limitation, §6-2-34.
Attorneys at law.
Actions for failure to pay
over money or for
neglect or omission of
duty.
Six year limitation,
§6-2-34.
Disbarment.
Three year limitation,
§6-2-37.
Disciplinary proceedings,
ARDE, Rule 23.
Legal services liability
actions, §6-5-574.
Bills of lading.
Limitations in bills of lading
or tariff, §7-7-309.
Bond issues.
Action to test validity of
municipal bond election,
§§6-2-40, 11-81-61.
Contesting validity of
issuance, sale, etc.,
§11-81-14.
Municipal special health care
facility authorities.
Actions determining
validity, §11-62-9.
Bonds, surety.
Actions against surety to any
replevy or forthcoming
bond executed in courts
of the United States or
other state.
Four year limitation,
§6-2-36.
Bulk transfers, §7-6-111.
Carriers.
Actions by or against
carriers for recovery of
charges.
Two year limitation,
§6-2-38.
Cigarettes.
Taxation.
Gummed cigarette papers.
Assessments and actions
to collect tax,
§40-25A-11.

LIMITATION OF ACTIONS
—Cont'd
Claims by and against state.
Award for personal injury or
death.
Limitation on amount of
award, §41-9-70.
Presentation of claims
against state, §41-9-65.
Commencement of actions.
Asbestos.
Actions for injuries
resulting from
exposure to, §6-2-30.
Generally, §6-2-30.
**Commencement of
limitation.**
Demand necessary for action,
§6-2-7.
Principal against deputy or
agent, §6-2-6.
Commercial code.
Bills of lading.
Limitation in bills of
lading or tariff,
§7-7-309.
Bulk transfers, §7-6-111.
Documents of title.
Limitations in bills of
lading or tariff,
§7-7-309.
Duration of financing
statements, §7-7-403.
Sales.
Contracts for sale,
§7-2-725.
Secured transactions.
Duration of financing
statements, §7-9-403.
**Competitive bidding on
public contracts.**
Violations, §41-16-2.
Computation of time.
Absence from state, §6-2-10.
Contracts during war,
§6-2-13.
Injunctions.
Stays by injunction,
§6-2-12.
Letters testamentary or
administration.
Granting, §6-2-14.
Nonmerchant mutual
accounts, §6-2-11.
Statutes.
Stays by statutory
prohibition, §6-2-12.
War.
Contracts during, §6-2-13.
Constables.
Nonfeasance, misfeasance or
malfeasance.
Actions against surety.
Six year limitation,
§6-2-34.
Ten year limitation,
§6-2-33.
Constitution of Alabama.
Special, private or local laws
prohibited, Const. Ala.,
art. IV, §104.
Contracts.
Actions upon sealed
instruments.
Ten year limitation,
§6-2-33.
Actions upon simple
contracts.
Six year limitation,
§6-2-34.

LIMITATION OF ACTIONS
—Cont'd
Contracts—Cont'd
Foreign statutes.
Effect upon actions on
contracts, §6-2-17.
Sales, §7-2-725.
War.
Computation of time as to
contracts during war,
§6-2-13.
Coroners.
Actions for nonfeasance,
misfeasance or
malfeasance.
Actions against surety.
Six year limitation,
§6-2-34.
Ten year limitation,
§6-2-33.
Counterclaims.
Effect of statute of
limitations, §6-8-84.
Counties.
Actions for recovery of
license, franchise or
other taxes.
Five year limitation,
§6-2-35.
Bond issues.
Election contest, §11-81-90.
Validity of issuance, sale,
etc.
Limitation period for
actions to contest
validity, §11-81-14.
Recovery of lands.
No limitation, §6-2-31.
Criminal law and procedure.
Limitations on prosecution,
§§15-3-1 to 15-3-8.
See CRIMINAL LAW AND
PROCEDURE.
Death.
Wrongful death, §§6-2-38,
6-5-410.
Decedents' estates.
Claims to charge real estate
with debts and
obligations of decedent,
§6-2-41.
Suspension of limitation.
Claims against estates,
§6-2-9.
Deceptive trade practices,
§8-19-14.
Decrees.
Actions upon.
Twenty year limitation,
§6-2-32.
Defenses.
Statute of limitations on
affirmative defense,
ARCP, Rule 8 (c).
Descent cast.
Right of entry not tolled,
§6-2-5.
Documents of title.
Limitations in bills of lading
or tariff, §7-7-309.
Elections.
Action to test validity of
municipal election for
bond issues or tax levies.
Six month limitation,
§6-2-40.
**Executors and
administrators.**
Against executor or
administrator, §43-2-131.

LIMITATION OF ACTIONS
—Cont'd
**Executors and
administrators**—Cont'd
Nonfeasance, misfeasance or
malfeasance.
Actions against surety,
§6-2-34.
False imprisonment.
Six year limitation, §6-2-34.
Farm equipment.
Repurchase of inventory from
equipment retailers,
§8-21-14.
Fees.
Actions for recovery of fees.
Two year limitation,
§6-2-38.
**Forcible entry and unlawful
detainer.**
Uninterrupted occupation for
three years bars action,
§6-6-315.
Franchises.
Actions by state or political
subdivision for franchise
taxes.
Five year limitation,
§6-2-35.
Fraud.
Accrual of cause of action,
§6-2-3.
Fruit trees.
Delivery of fruit trees of
different kind, variety,
etc., than sold.
Limitation period for
prosecutions, §2-25-41.
Gasoline tax.
Actions by state, §40-17-41.
Applicability to all other
excise taxes on motor
fuels, §40-17-42.
Guardian ad litem.
Action for improper
appointment, §6-7-103.
Guardian and ward.
Nonfeasance, misfeasance or
malfeasance.
Actions against surety.
Six year limitation,
§6-2-34.
Hazardous substances.
Fees for disposal of.
Time limits for actions
under chapter,
§22-30B-14.
Hazardous waste.
Fees for disposal of.
Time limit for actions
under chapter,
§22-30B-14.
Health care authorities.
Securities.
Limitation of actions to
contest validity,
§22-21-329.
Heirs.
Exceptions to applicability of
chapter, §6-2-2.
Impeachment.
Proceedings not to be barred,
§36-11-24.
Income tax.
Civil actions and proceedings
by taxpayer, §40-18-47.
Involuntary conversion,
§40-18-45.

LIMITATION OF ACTIONS
—Cont'd
Income tax—Cont'd
Period of limitation upon
assessment and
collection, §40-18-45.
Suspension, §40-29-50.
Qualified stock acquisition,
§40-18-45.
Informers.
Actions qui tam.
Two year limitation,
§6-2-38.
Iron ore.
Mining.
Licenses, §40-12-128.
Judgments.
Actions upon.
Twenty year limitation,
§6-2-32.
Arrest or reversal of
judgment.
One year limitation from
arrest or reversal,
§6-2-38.
Revival of judgments,
§6-9-190.
Libel and slander.
Two year limitation, §6-2-38.
Licenses.
Actions by state or political
subdivision for recovery
of amounts claimed for
licenses.
Five year limitation,
§6-2-35.
Liens.
Attachment, §35-11-6.
Bonds, surety.
Chapter inapplicable,
§6-2-2.
Tax liens.
Chapter inapplicable,
§6-2-2.
Loans.
Recovery of money.
Six year limitation,
§6-2-34.
Lost or unclaimed property.
Uniform disposition of
unclaimed property act.
Duties under article not
affected by expiration
of limitation period,
§35-12-37.
Lubricating oils and greases.
Tax.
Actions by state,
§40-17-181.
**Lumber employees' or
laborers' liens,**
§35-11-272.
Malicious prosecution.
Two year limitation, §6-2-38.
Malpractice, §6-5-482.
**Mechanics' and
materialmen's liens,**
§35-11-221.
Mentally ill.
Suspension of limitation for
disabilities, §6-2-8.
Merchants.
Exceptions to applicability of
chapter, §6-2-2.
Military affairs.
Compensation for death of
national guardsmen.
Limitation on time for
presentation of claims,
§31-3-5.

LIMITATION OF ACTIONS
—Cont'd

Money.
Recovery of money due by open or unliquidated account.
Three year limitation, §6-2-37.

Mortgages and deeds of trust.
Actions on equities of redemption where lands have been sold under judgment of circuit court.
Five year limitation, §6-2-35.

Motor fuels taxes, §§40-17-41, 40-17-42.

Motor vehicles.
Manufacturers.
Dealings by manufacturers with dealers, §8-20-12.

Municipal corporations.
Actions for recovery of license, franchise or other taxes, §6-2-35.
Bond issues.
Actions to test validity of issuance, etc., §11-81-14.
Actions to test validity of municipal election for purpose of issuing bonds, §§6-2-40, 11-81-61.
Claims for and against municipalities, §§11-47-23, 11-50-84.
Elections.
Actions to test validity of municipal elections for bond issues or tax levies, §6-2-40.
Recovery of lands.
No limitation, §6-2-31.

Negotiable instruments.
Exceptions to applicability of chapter, §6-2-2.

New promises.
Effect, §6-2-16.

Partial payment.
Effect, §6-2-16.

Penalties.
Actions for recovery of penalties, §6-2-38.

Personal injury.
Two year limitation, §6-2-38.

Post-conviction remedies,
ARCrP, Rule 20.2 (c).

Prisons and prisoners.
Suspension of limitation for disabilities, §6-2-8.

Products liability, §6-5-502.

Prosecution.
Actions for malicious prosecution.
Two year limitation, §6-2-38.
Limitations on prosecution, §§15-3-1 to 15-3-8.
See CRIMINAL LAW AND PROCEDURE.

Public officers and employees.
Actions for nonfeasance, misfeasance or malfeasance.
Ten year limitation, §6-2-33.

LIMITATION OF ACTIONS
—Cont'd

Real property.
Actions for recovery by state, counties and municipal corporations.
No limitation, §6-2-31.
Actions for recovery of lands, tenements or hereditaments.
Ten year limitation, §6-2-33.
Actions for the use and occupation of land.
Six year limitation, §6-2-34.
Claims to charge real estate with debts and obligations of decedent, §6-2-41.

Rent.
Recovery of arrears of rent due upon parol demise.
Six year limitation, §6-2-34.

Replevy.
Actions against surety to any replevy bond executed in courts of the United States or other state.
Four year limitation, §6-2-36.

Right of entry.
Accrual of cause of action, §6-2-4.
Tolling.
Not tolled by a descent cast, §6-2-5.

Rules of criminal procedure.
Post-conviction remedies, ARCrP, Rule 20.2 (c).

Sales.
Contracts, §7-2-725.

Sales tax.
Assessment.
Appeal of assessments, §40-23-18.
Civil suit to collect tax, §40-23-21.
Refunds, §40-23-18.

Savings statute.
New action after adverse decision, §6-2-39.

Sawmill employees' or laborers' liens, §35-11-272.

Seals and sealed instruments.
Actions upon contract or writing under seal.
Ten year limitation, §6-2-33.

Secured transactions.
Duration of financing statements, §7-9-403.

Securities.
Prosecutions for violations of article, §8-6-18.

Seduction.
Two year limitation, §6-2-38.

Sewers.
Liens for improvements on sewers, §35-11-412.

Sheriffs.
Nonfeasance, misfeasance or malfeasance.
Actions against surety.
Six year limitation, §6-2-34.
Ten year limitation, §6-2-33.

LIMITATION OF ACTIONS
—Cont'd

State.
Actions for recovery of license, franchise or other taxes.
Five year limitation, §6-2-35.
Constitution of the United States.
Limitations on powers of the state, Const. U. S., Art. I, §10.
Recovery of certain lands.
No limitation, §6-2-31.

Statutes.
Foreign statutes.
Effect upon actions on contracts, §6-2-17.

Streets.
Liens for improvements on public streets, §35-11-412.

Suretyship.
Actions against surety to any writ of error, appeal, replevy or forthcoming bond executed in United States courts or courts of other states.
Four year limitation, §6-2-36.
Actions for nonfeasance, misfeasance or malfeasance.
Six year limitation on actions against surety, §6-2-34.

Suspension of limitation.
Claims against estates, §6-2-9.
Disabilities, §6-2-8.

Taxation, §§40-29-50 to 40-29-52.

Time.
Computation, §§6-2-10 to 6-2-14.

Trade secrets.
Misappropriation, §8-27-4.

Transportation companies.
Damages for loss, injury or delay in delivery.
Action for damages, §37-2-62.

Trees and timber.
Damages for destruction, injury or removal of trees, §35-14-3.
Timber employees' or laborers' liens, §35-11-272.

Trespass.
Six year limitation.
Trespass to person or liberty, §6-2-34.
Trespass to real or personal property, §6-2-34.

Unclaimed property.
Uniform disposition of unclaimed property act.
Duties under article not affected by expiration of limitation period, §35-12-37.

Unemployment compensation, §25-4-145.

Use tax.
Collection of tax, §40-23-87.

LIMITATION OF ACTIONS
—Cont'd
Wages.
Actions for recovery of
wages.
Two year limitation,
§6-2-38.
War.
Contracts during war.
Computation of time,
§6-2-13.
Welfare.
Civil actions against persons
owning property and
supported at public
charge, §38-1-5.
Wills.
Probate code.
Fraud, §43-8-5.
Workmen's compensation,
§25-5-80.
Occupational diseases.
Limitation period for
claims or actions for
compensation,
§25-5-117.
Pneumoconiosis.
Coal miners, §25-5-178.
Limitation period for
claims or actions for
compensation,
§25-5-147.
Radiation.
Occupational exposure to
radiation.
Limitation period for
claims or actions for
compensation,
§25-5-197.
Wrongful death, §§6-2-38,
6-5-410.

LIMITED PARTNERSHIPS,
§§10-9A-1 to 10-9A-203.
See PARTNERSHIPS.

LINSEED OIL.
Brands and marks.
Mixture or substitute to be
marked as such,
§8-17-43.
Containers.
Labeling of original,
unbroken containers,
§8-17-42.
Enforcement of article,
§8-17-44.
Mixture.
Marking and sale as such,
§8-17-43.
Penalties.
Violation of article, §8-17-45.
Sales.
Mixture or substitute to be
sold as such, §8-17-43.
Suspension from sale of
illegal products,
§8-17-44.
Searches and seizures.
Illegal products, §8-17-44.
Standards.
Boiled linseed oil, §8-17-41.
Raw linseed oil, §8-17-40.
Substitute.
Marking and sale as such,
§8-17-43.
Violations of article.
Penalties, §8-17-45.

LIQUEFIED PETROLEUM
GAS, §§9-17-100 to 9-17-110.
Administrator, §9-17-104.

LIQUEFIED PETROLEUM
GAS—Cont'd
Appeals.
Directive order of
discontinuance,
§9-17-108.
Board, §§9-17-101 to 9-17-104.
Administrator, §9-17-104.
Appointment of members,
§9-17-101.
Assistants.
Employment, §9-17-104.
Bylaws, §9-17-101.
Compensation of members,
§9-17-102.
Composition, §9-17-101.
Consultants.
Employment, §9-17-104.
Created, §9-17-101.
Defined, §9-17-100.
Fund, §9-17-104.
Inspectors.
Employment, §9-17-104.
Invoices.
Percentage of invoice cost
paid to board,
§9-17-106.
Meetings, §9-17-101.
Officers.
Election, §9-17-101.
Qualifications of members,
§9-17-101.
Quorum, §9-17-101.
Reports.
Sale and purchase reports
to board.
Required, §9-17-106.
Rules and regulations.
Promulgation, §9-17-103.
Seal, §9-17-104.
Technical advisors.
Employment, §9-17-104.
Terms of office, §9-17-101.
Vacancies, §9-17-101.
Bonds, surety.
Administrator, §9-17-104.
Engaging in business of
selling, distributing, etc.,
§9-17-105.
Definitions, §9-17-100.
**Directive order of
discontinuance,**
§9-17-108.
Fees.
Assessment, §§9-17-106,
9-17-109, 9-17-110.
Deficiency.
Computation of deficiency,
§9-17-109.
Failure to report and remit.
Penalties, §9-17-109.
Permits, §9-17-106.
Assessment, §§9-17-106,
9-17-109, 9-17-110.
Refund of excess, §9-17-109.
Refunds of certain fees,
§9-17-106.
Fuel tax, §§40-17-160 to
40-17-166.
See LIQUEFIED
PETROLEUM GAS
FUEL TAX.
Funds.
Liquefied petroleum gas
board personal bond
fund, §9-17-105.
Hearings.
Assessment, §9-17-109.
Authority of board,
§9-17-108.
Injunctions, §9-17-108.

LIQUEFIED PETROLEUM
GAS—Cont'd
Inspections.
System, §9-17-103.
Insurance.
Engaging in business of
selling, distributing, etc.,
§9-17-105.
Invoices.
Issuance.
Purchaser or agent,
§8-17-190.
Percentage of invoice cost
paid to board, §9-17-106.
**Liquefied petroleum gas
board.**
Generally, §§9-17-101 to
9-17-104.
Meters.
Invoice.
Issuance, §8-17-190.
Weighing or metering upon
purchase, §8-17-190.
Names.
Permit holder's name.
Change of name,
§9-17-105.
Orders.
Directive order of
discontinuance,
§9-17-108.
Peace officers.
Administrator, §9-17-104.
Penalties.
Failure to report and pay
fees owed, §9-17-109.
Imposition of penalties.
Authority of board,
§9-17-108.
Permits.
Failure to secure and pay
fees by delinquent
date, §9-17-106.
Violations of article, rules,
etc., §9-17-109.
Permits, §9-17-105.
Exemption for permit holders
who are licensed to
install gas piping,
§9-17-106.
Failure to secure.
Penalty, §9-17-106.
Fees, §9-17-106.
Assessment, §§9-17-106,
9-17-109, 9-17-110.
Failure to pay by
delinquent date.
Penalty, §9-17-106.
Refunds of certain fees,
§9-17-106.
When due and delinquent,
§9-17-106.
Name of permit holder.
Change of name,
§9-17-105.
Reinstatement, §9-17-106.
Temporary permit, §9-17-106.
Reports.
Sale and purchase reports to
board, §9-17-106.
Sales.
Invoices, §8-17-190.
Sale and purchase reports to
board.
Required, §9-17-106.
Sales tax.
Exemptions.
Gas sold for agricultural
purposes, §40-23-4.
Storage capacity, §9-17-107.

LIQUEFIED PETROLEUM GAS—Cont'd

System.
Combination, §9-17-103.
Defined, §9-17-100.
Inspection, §9-17-103.
Weights and measures.
Weighing or metering upon purchase, §8-17-190.

LIQUEFIED PETROLEUM GAS FUEL TAX, §§40-17-160 to 40-17-166.

Applicability of provisions.
Exemptions, §40-17-166.
Decals.
Annual decal from liquefied petroleum gas board, §40-17-161.
Failure to timely obtain decal.
Penalty, §40-17-164.
Remittance of cost of decal, §40-17-162.
Exemptions, §40-17-166.
Flat fee, §40-17-160.
Reduced fee for vehicles acquired after September 30, §40-17-161.
Remittance, §40-17-160.
Liquefied petroleum gas board.
Rules and regulations, §40-17-163.
Out-of-state vehicles.
Tax on, §40-17-165.
Penalties.
Failure to timely obtain decal, §40-17-164.
Proceeds.
Disposition, §40-17-162.
Rate of tax.
Flat fee on vehicles using liquefied petroleum gas as fuel, §40-17-160.
Rules and regulations, §40-17-163.

LIQUIDATION.

Banks and financial institutions, §§5-8A-1 to 5-8A-46.
See BANKS AND FINANCIAL INSTITUTIONS.
Contracts.
Specific performance.
Liquidation of damages does not bar specific performance, §8-1-45.
Corporations.
Dissolution, §§10-2A-180 to 10-2A-203.
See CORPORATIONS.
General provisions, §§10-2A-195 to 10-2A-200.
See CORPORATIONS.
Income tax, §40-18-36.
Nonprofit corporations, §§10-3A-149 to 10-3A-156.
See CORPORATIONS.
Credit unions.
Alabama credit union league.
Redemption and purchase of advance dues certificate upon liquidation of member credit union, §5-17-28.
Voluntary dissolution, §5-17-21.

LIQUIDATION—Cont'd

Dental service corporations.
Department supervised, §22-21-388.
Sales.
Going out of business or distress merchandise sales, §§8-13-1 to 8-13-23.
See SALES.
Savings and loan associations.
Involuntary liquidation, §5-6-37.
Voluntary liquidation, §§5-6-32 to 5-6-35.
Small loans.
Receiver to have power to liquidate upon violation of chapter, §5-18-10.
Warehouses.
Liquidation of operations, §8-15-14.

LIQUOR.

Intoxicating liquor, §§28-1-1 to 28-9-11.
See ALCOHOLIC BEVERAGES.

LIS PENDENS, §§35-4-130 to 35-4-139.

Bona fide purchases.
Protected upon failure to record notice, §35-4-135.
Bonds, surety.
Release of land from lien upon execution of bond, §35-4-137.
Constables.
Liability on bonds, §35-4-139.
Fees.
Recording notice, §35-4-138.
Index of notices, §35-4-134.
Indorsements.
Notices in record to be indorsed on original, §35-4-133.
Lessees.
Protected upon failure to record notice, §35-4-135.
Levy on real property.
Notice of levy.
Filing in lis pendens record, §35-4-132.
Liens.
Release of land from lien upon execution of bond, §35-4-137.
Microphotographing, §35-4-136.
Mortgagees.
Protected upon failure to record notice, §35-4-135.
Notice of actions.
Filing in lis pendens record, §35-4-131.
Probate judges.
Keeping lis pendens record, §35-4-130.
Liability on bonds, §35-4-139.
Public officers.
Liability on bonds, §35-4-139.
Record, §35-4-130.
Failure to record notice.
Bona fide purchases, etc., protected upon failure to record notice, §35-4-135.
Fees for recording notice, §35-4-138.
Index of notices, §35-4-134.

LIS PENDENS—Cont'd

Record—Cont'd
Indorsement on original, §35-4-133.
Levy on real property.
Notice of levy, §35-4-132.
Notice of actions.
Filing in record, §35-4-131.
Notices to be recorded in full, §35-4-133.
Release of land from lien upon execution of bond, §35-4-137.
Termination of action, §35-4-136.
Sheriffs.
Liability on bonds, §35-4-139.
Termination of action.
Record of termination, §35-4-136.

LITERARY CLUBS.

Conveyances by literary or social societies, §§35-4-340 to 35-4-344.
See CONVEYANCES.
Deeds.
Conveyances by literary or social socities, §§35-4-340 to 35-4-344.
See CONVEYANCES.
Tax exemption, §40-9-1.

LITIGATION ACCOUNTABILITY.

General provisions, §§12-19-270 to 12-19-276.
See COURTS.

LITTER.

Beautification board.
General provisions, §§41-9-490 to 41-9-498.
See BEAUTIFICATION.
Boats.
Discharge of litter and sewage from watercraft, §§33-6-1 to 33-6-12.
See BOATS.
Caves.
Prohibited acts, §9-19-3.
Criminal littering, §13A-7-29.
Garbage and trash.
See GARBAGE AND TRASH.
Highways.
See HIGHWAYS.
Motor vehicles.
Spilling loads or litter, §32-5-76.
Throwing of litter onto highway, §32-5A-60.
Signs, §23-5-7.
Streets.
See HIGHWAYS.
Watercraft.
Discharge of litter and sewage from watercraft.
See BOATS.

LITTLE MILLER ACT.

Public works, §39-1-1.

LIVERY OF SEISIN.

Unnecessary for conveyance, §35-4-31.

LIVERY STABLES.

Liens of keepers.
Declaration of lien, §35-11-190.
Enforcement of lien, §35-11-191.
Sale of stock, §35-11-191.

LIVESTOCK, §§2-15-1 to
2-15-317.
Abattoirs.
See SLAUGHTERHOUSES.
Agisters.
Lien on stock for pasturage
or training, §35-11-70.
Alligator farms, §§9-12-200 to
9-12-214.
See ALLIGATOR FARMS.
Animals generally.
See ANIMALS.
Appeals.
Running at large.
Appeals from judgment of
district court, §3-5-12.
Arrest.
Sanitary and disease control
laws.
Appearance upon arrest,
§2-2-14.1.
Theft.
Appearance upon arrest,
§2-2-14.1.
Artificial insemination.
Central artificial
insemination unit,
Revenues derived from sale
of semen, bulls, etc.
Disposition of revenues,
§2-30-61.
Supervision of work under
chapter, §2-30-62.
Attachment.
Liens of owners of stallions,
jacks, bulls, etc.,
§35-11-331.
Auctions and auctioneers.
Markets.
Operators not to permit
purchase by owners,
officers, employees,
etc., of market,
§2-15-66.
Audits.
Promotion of cattle industry.
Audit of cattle owner's
associations, §2-8-19.
Promotion of swine industry.
Audit of swine producer's
associations, §2-8-59.
Bang's disease, §§2-15-190 to
2-15-197.
Bills of sale.
Dealers, §2-15-43.
Markets, §2-15-65.
Blacksmiths, §§35-11-110 to
35-11-112.
Bonds, surety.
Dealers, §§2-15-133,
2-15-134.
Market operators, §2-15-63.
Promotion of cattle industry.
Treasurers of cattle
owners' associations,
§2-8-16.
Promotion of swine industry.
Treasurers of swine
producers' associations,
§2-8-56.
Weighing livestock at
markets.
Bond of permittee,
§2-15-93.

LIVESTOCK—Cont'd
Branding of livestock,
§§2-15-20 to 2-15-30.
Actions or criminal
proceedings as to title or
right of possession.
Admissibility of certificate
of registration of
brand, §2-15-22.
Alteration of brand or mark
with intent to defraud,
§3-1-27.
Commissioner of agriculture
and industries.
Positions on which animals
may be branded.
Designation by
commissioner,
§2-15-28.
Rules and regulations.
Promulgation for
implementation of
article, §2-15-28.
Definitions, §2-15-20.
Department of agriculture
and industries.
Forms for registration,
reregistration and
transfer of brands.
Furnishing, etc.,
§2-15-24.
Register of brands.
Maintenance,
publication, etc., by
department,
§2-15-25.
Registration of brands and
issuance of certificates
of registration by
department, §2-15-21.
Evidence.
Admissibility of certificate
of registration as to
title or right of
possession, §2-15-22.
Fees.
Disposition of fees,
§2-15-26.
Registration of brands.
Application fees,
§2-15-21.
Renewal of brands,
§2-15-23.
Transfer of brands,
§2-15-21.
Fraudulently marking or
branding, §3-1-27.
Penalties for violations of
article, §2-15-30.
Disposition of fines,
§2-15-30.
Positions on which animals
may be branded.
Designation by
commissioner,
§2-15-28.
Prohibited acts, §2-15-29.
Register of brands.
Maintenance, publication,
etc., by department,
§2-15-25.
Records required to be
maintained by
operators of livestock
markets, hide dealers,
etc., §2-15-27.
Registration of brands.
Application, §2-15-21.
Approval of applications
for registration,
§2-15-21.

LIVESTOCK—Cont'd
Branding of livestock
—Cont'd
Registration of brands
—Cont'd
Certificates of registration.
Admissibility as to title
or right of
possession, §2-15-22.
Issuance, §2-15-21.
Denial of applications for
registration, §2-15-21.
Department.
Registration and
issuance of
certificates, §2-15-21.
Fees.
Application fees,
§2-15-21.
Disposition of fees,
§2-15-26.
Forms.
Furnishing, etc.,
§2-15-24.
Issuance of certificates,
§2-15-21.
Maintenance of register of
brands, §2-15-25.
Publication of register of
brands, §2-15-25.
Reregistration, §2-15-23.
Furnishing, etc., of
forms, §2-15-24.
Renewal of brands, §2-15-23.
Rules and regulations.
Promulgation by
commissioner,
§2-15-28.
Violations, §2-15-30.
Transfer of brands, §2-15-21.
Furnishing of forms,
§2-15-24.
Violations of article,
§2-15-30.
Revocation of permits or
licenses of livestock
markets or dealers,
§2-15-30.
Breeders.
Protection against bogus or
fraudulent pedigrees,
§§2-15-310 to 2-15-317.
Brucellosis, §§2-15-190 to
2-15-197.
Bulls.
Liens of owners, §§35-11-330,
35-11-331.
Butchers.
Records, §§2-15-3, 2-15-27.
Carcasses.
Inspection, §§2-17-3 to
2-17-5.
Cattle.
Bang's disease, §§2-15-190 to
2-15-197.
Branding, §§2-15-20 to
2-15-30.
Brucellosis or Bang's disease,
§§2-15-190 to 2-15-197.
Appropriations for conduct
of control program.
Expenditure, §2-15-195.
Article cumulative,
§2-15-197.
Commissioner.
Cooperation with federal
agencies, §2-15-194.
Cooperation with federal
agencies, §2-15-194.

LIVESTOCK—Cont'd
 Cattle—Cont'd
  Brucellosis or Bang's disease
   —Cont'd
   Destruction of animals.
    Indemnification of
     owners, §2-15-195.
   Establishment of disease
    control program,
    §2-15-192.
   Federal agencies.
    Cooperation with,
     §2-15-194.
   Indemnification.
    Payment to owners of
     cattle slaughtered
     under program,
     §2-15-2.
   Inspections, §2-15-193.
   Penalty for violations of
    rules and regulations,
    §2-15-196.
   Purpose of article,
    §2-15-190.
   Right of entry of state
    veterinarian, etc.,
    §2-15-193.
   Rules and regulations.
    Penalty for violations,
     §2-15-196.
   Slaughter of cattle.
    Payment of
     indemnification to
     owners, §2-15-2.
   State veterinarian.
    Cooperation with federal
     agencies, §2-15-194.
    Inspection, §2-15-193.
    Interference with
     performance of
     duties, §2-15-193.
    Right of entry,
     §2-15-193.
   Supervision of control
    program, §2-15-193.
   Vaccination of calves.
    Adoption of program,
     §2-15-191.
  Butchers.
   Brucellosis or Bang's
    disease, §§2-15-190 to
    2-15-197.
   Records, §2-15-3.
   Tuberculosis, §§2-15-2,
    3-1-17 to 3-1-19.
  Dipping of cattle.
   Indemnification of owners
    for injuries, etc.,
    §§11-12-1 to 11-12-3.
   Tick eradication,
    §§2-15-290 to 2-15-299.
  Diseases.
   Brucellosis or Bang's
    disease, §§2-15-190 to
    2-15-197.
   Paratuberculosis.
    Payment of
     indemnification to
     owners, §2-15-2.
   Tuberculosis, §§2-15-2,
    3-1-17 to 3-1-19.
  Liens.
   Generally, §§35-11-70,
    35-11-72.
   Livery stable keepers,
    §§35-11-190,
    35-11-191.
   Owners of stallions, jacks,
    bulls, etc., §§35-11-330,
    35-11-331.

LIVESTOCK—Cont'd
 Cattle—Cont'd
  Liens—Cont'd
   Veterinarians, §§35-11-390,
    35-11-391.
  Paratuberculosis.
   Slaughter of cattle.
    Payment of
     indemnification to
     owners, §2-15-2.
  Promotion of cattle industry,
   §§2-8-1 to 2-8-22; Const.
   Ala., amds. 201, 452.
   Assessments.
    Collection, §2-8-12.
    Declared to be in public
     interest, §2-8-3.
    Deductions for expenses,
     §2-8-12.
    Expenditure, §2-8-17.
    Failure to deduct and
     pay over.
     Penalty for failure,
      §2-8-22.
    Penalty for failure to
     deduct and pay over
     assessment, §2-8-22.
   Referendum.
    Application for
     approval to
     conduct, §§2-8-4,
     2-8-5.
    Authority of certified
     association to
     conduct, §2-8-6.
    Canvass of results,
     §2-8-10.
    Conduct, §2-8-8.
    Declared to be in
     public interest,
     §2-8-3.
    Eligibility to vote,
     §2-8-9.
    Majority vote required
     for approval of
     assessment,
     §2-8-10.
    Notice, §2-8-7.
    Payment of expense,
     §2-8-8.
    Question to be voted
     on, §2-8-9.
    Subsequent
     referendums,
     §2-8-11.
   Refund to cattle owner,
    §2-8-15.
   Remittances to treasurer
    of cattle owners'
    association, §2-8-13.
   Audit of cattle owners'
    association.
    Annual audit, §2-8-19.
   Authorized activities.
    Not illegal or in
     restraint of trade,
     §2-8-2.
   Bonds, surety.
    Treasurers of cattle
     owners' associations,
     §2-8-16.
   Certification of cattle
    owners' association.
    Application for.
     Action by board,
      §2-8-5.
     Generally, §2-8-4.
    Revocation of
     certification, §2-8-21.

LIVESTOCK—Cont'd
 Cattle—Cont'd
  Promotion of cattle industry
   —Cont'd
   Commissioner of
    agriculture and
    industries.
    Enforcement duties of
     commissioner,
     §2-8-21.
   Examination of cattle
    owners' associations by
    department of
    examiners of public
    accounts, §2-8-19.
   Joint programs with other
    states, §2-8-18.
   Legislative purpose and
    intent, §2-8-1.
   Rules and regulations,
    §2-8-20.
   Treasurers of cattle
    owners' associations.
    Bond, §2-8-16.
    Remittances to
     treasurers, §2-8-13.
  Quarantine.
   Tuberculous cows, §3-1-18.
  Records.
   Butchers to maintain
    records as to cows
    butchered, §2-15-3.
  Rules and regulations.
   Promotion of cattle
    industry, §2-8-20.
  Rustling.
   Prohibited, §§2-15-40 to
    2-15-48.
  Sale.
   Dealers to obtain bills of
    sale upon purchase,
    §2-15-43.
  Tick eradication, §§2-15-290
   to 2-15-299.
  Tuberculosis.
   Compensation of owners
    for slaughtered cows
    determined not to have
    been affected, §3-1-18.
   Indemnification.
    Payment to owners of
     cattle slaughtered,
     §2-15-2.
   Isolation of tuberculous
    cows, §3-1-18.
   Notification of owners of
    dairies upon discovery
    of cows affected with
    tuberculosis, §3-1-17.
   Penalties for violations,
    §3-1-19.
   Removal from herd of
    tuberculous cows,
    §3-1-18.
   Slaughter of cattle,
    §3-1-18.
    Payment of
     indemnification to
     owners of cattle
     slaughtered, §2-15-2.
   Violations.
    Penalties for violations,
     §3-1-19.
 Cholera.
  Hog cholera, §§2-15-230 to
   2-15-274.
 Commercial alligator
  operations, §§9-12-200 to
  9-12-214.
  See ALLIGATOR FARMS.

LIVESTOCK—Cont'd
Commercial code.
Sale of unborn young.
Definition of goods,
§7-2-105.
Identification of goods,
§7-2-501.
Secured transactions.
Classification of goods,
§7-9-109.
When security interest
attaches, §7-9-204.
**Commissioner of agriculture
and industries.**
Branding of livestock.
Designation of positions on
which animals may be
branded, §2-15-28.
Rules and regulations.
Promulgation, §2-15-28.
Diseases, §§2-15-150 to
2-15-197.
Financial responsibility act,
§§2-15-81 to 2-15-86.
Hog cholera.
Execution and enforcement
of subdivision,
§2-15-235.
Rules and regulations,
§2-15-235.
Markets, §§2-15-64, 2-15-67,
2-15-69.
Pedigrees.
Certificates, §§2-15-312 to
2-15-317.
Common fences.
Allowing stock to run at
large under common
fence, §13A-7-61.
Constitution of Alabama.
Establishing separate stock
districts.
Special, private or local
laws prohibited, Const.
Ala., art. IV, §104.
Promotion of cattle industry,
Const. Ala., amds. 201,
452.
Promotion of production,
research, etc., of swine
and swine products,
Const. Ala., amd. 327.
**Contagious and infectious
diseases.**
Cattle.
Brucellosis or Bang's
disease, §§2-15-190 to
2-15-197.
Paratuberculosis.
Payment of
indemnification for
slaughtered animals,
§2-15-2.
Tuberculosis, §§2-15-2,
3-1-17 to 3-1-19.
Control generally, §§2-15-150
to 2-15-174.
Hog cholera, §§2-15-230 to
2-15-274.
Contracts.
Department of agriculture
and industries.
Inspection or testing
services, §2-15-1.
Counties.
Appropriations to pay
premiums on livestock
exhibited in shows held
in county, §11-3-11.

LIVESTOCK—Cont'd
Counties—Cont'd
Dipping of cattle.
Indemnification of owners
for injuries, etc.,
§§11-12-1 to 11-12-3.
Running at large.
Refunding of counties
where livestock kept
and fed in county
pounds, §3-5-11.
Cruelty to animals,
§§2-15-110 to 2-15-114.
Handling of livestock in
markets and in transit.
Breakdown in transit.
Notice to owner of
livestock, §2-15-111.
Construction of
conveyances used for
transporting,
§2-15-112.
Delay in transit.
Conveyances to proceed
to destination
without delay,
§2-15-111.
Inhumane handling
prohibited, §2-15-110.
Inspection of markets for
enforcement,
§2-15-113.
Liability of managers, etc.,
permitting violations
of article by
employees, etc.,
§2-15-114.
Penalties, §2-15-114.
Rules and regulations.
Penalties for violations,
§2-15-114.
Promulgation by
commissioner,
§2-15-113.
Sticks, whips, chains, etc.
Use in markets,
§2-15-113.
Violations of article.
Handling in violation of
article prohibited,
§2-15-110.
Penalties for violations,
§2-15-114.
Dealers, §§2-15-40 to 2-15-48.
Applicability of article,
§2-15-47.
Bills of sale.
Exhibition, §2-15-43.
Issuance for livestock
hauled or transported,
§2-15-43.
Obtaining bills of sale
upon purchase of
sheep, cattle, etc.,
§2-15-43.
Transporting livestock
without bill of sale,
§2-15-43.
Bonds, surety.
Acceptance of bonds given
under federal packers
and stockyards act,
§2-15-134.
Equivalent.
Bond equivalent,
§2-15-133.
Federal packers and
stockyards act.
Acceptance of bonds
given under,
§2-15-134.

LIVESTOCK—Cont'd
Dealers—Cont'd
Bonds, surety—Cont'd
Generally, §2-15-133.
Books.
Maintenance of books,
§2-15-133.
Commissioner of agriculture
and industries.
Financial responsibility
act.
Promulgation of rules
and regulations,
§2-15-135.
Definitions, §§2-15-40,
2-15-131.
Fees.
License fees, §2-15-132.
Permit fee, §2-15-41.
Financial responsibility act,
§§2-15-130 to 2-15-138.
Applicability of article,
§2-15-137.
Bonds, surety, §§2-15-133,
2-15-134.
Books.
Maintenance of books,
§2-15-133.
Definitions, §2-15-131.
Federal packers and
stockyards act.
Acceptance of bonds,
§2-15-134.
Financial statements.
Furnishing, §2-15-133.
Injunctive proceedings to
restrain operation by
dealer in violation of
article, §2-15-136.
Licenses, §§2-15-30,
2-15-132.
Payment for livestock
purchased.
Requirement as to
payment, §2-15-133.
Penalty for violations of
article, §2-15-136.
Provisions of article
cumulative and
supplemental to article
3 of chapter, §2-15-138
Records.
Maintenance of records,
§2-15-133.
Reporting compliance with
act.
Commissioner.
Authority to inspect
records, §2-15-83.
Promulgation of rules
and regulations,
§2-15-84.
Provision of lists of
licensed livestock
dealers to
markets, §2-15-82.
Construction of division,
§2-15-86.
Definitions, §2-15-81.
Markets.
Authority of
commissioner to
inspect records,
§2-15-83.
Provision of lists of
licensed dealers,
§2-15-82.
Reporting
requirements,
§2-15-82.

LIVESTOCK—Cont'd
Dealers—Cont'd
Financial responsibility act
—Cont'd
Reporting compliance with
act—Cont'd
Penalties.
Willful noncompliance
with reporting
provisions,
§2-15-85.
Permits.
Revocation for willful
noncompliance
with reporting
provisions,
§2-15-85.
Prompt payment for
livestock required,
§2-15-82.
Purpose of division,
§2-15-80.
Rules and regulations.
Promulgation by
commissioner,
§2-15-84.
Willful noncompliance
with reporting
provisions, §2-15-85.
Reports.
Furnishing, §2-15-133.
Rules and regulations.
Promulgation of rules
and regulations,
§2-15-135.
Short title of article,
§2-15-130.
Violations of article.
Penalty for violations,
§2-15-136.
Financial statements.
Furnishing, §2-15-133.
Licenses.
Appeals from denial or
revocation, §2-15-132.
Applications, §2-15-132.
Denial, §2-15-132.
Fees, §2-15-132.
Issuance, §2-15-132.
Required, §2-15-132.
Revocation, §2-15-132.
Violations of provisions
relating to branding
of livestock,
§2-15-30.
Municipal corporations.
Sanitary rules or
regulations.
Article not to prohibit
adoption by
municipalities,
§2-15-48.
Payment for livestock
purchased.
Requirement as to
payment, §2-15-133.
Permits.
Application, §2-15-41.
Cumulative.
Permits required by
article cumulative,
§2-15-48.
Delinquency penalty,
§2-15-41.
Fees, §2-15-41.
Forfeiture, §2-15-42.
Issuance of permit plates,
§2-15-41.
Required, §2-15-41.

LIVESTOCK—Cont'd
Dealers—Cont'd
Permits—Cont'd
Revocation.
Violations of provisions
relating to branding
of livestock,
§2-15-30.
Vehicles used in
transporting livestock.
Dealers to pay permit
fee, §2-15-41.
Records.
Maintenance of records,
§2-15-133.
Reports.
Furnishing reports,
§2-15-133.
Rules and regulations.
Article by municipalities of
sanitary rules or
regulations, §2-15-48.
Financial responsibility
act.
Promulgation of rules
and regulations,
§2-15-135.
Reporting compliance
with act, §2-15-84.
Promulgation, §2-15-45.
Violations of article.
Deemed misdemeanor,
§2-15-46.
Financial responsibility
act.
Penalties for violations,
§2-15-136.
Definitions, §§2-15-60, 3-5-1.
Branding of livestock,
§2-15-20.
Dealers, §2-15-131.
Diseases, §2-15-150.
Hog cholera, §2-15-230.
Markets, §2-15-60.
**Department of agriculture
and industries.**
Branding of livestock,
§§2-15-20 to 2-15-30.
Contracts.
Inspection or testing
services, §2-15-1.
Fees.
Inspection or testing
services, §2-15-1.
Inspections.
Contracts to perform
inspection services,
§2-15-1.
Testing services.
Contracts to perform
testing services,
§2-15-1.
Destruction.
Diseased animals, §§2-15-160
to 2-15-168.
Wanton, malicious, etc.,
destruction of animal of
another, §§3-1-10, 3-1-11.
Dipping of cattle.
Counties.
Indemnification of owners
for injuries, etc.,
§§11-12-1 to 11-12-3.
Tick eradication, §§2-15-290
to 2-15-299.
Diseases, §§2-15-150 to
2-15-174.
Administration of article.
Payment of expenses,
§2-15-173.

LIVESTOCK—Cont'd
Diseases—Cont'd
Appraisal of animals to be
destroyed, §§2-15-161 to
2-15-167.
Board of agriculture and
industries.
Rules and regulations.
Promulgation, §2-15-171.
Brucellosis or Bang's disease,
§§2-15-190 to 2-15-197.
Certificate of health.
Required for livestock
being brought into
state, §2-15-155.
Choking.
Sale or exchange of horse
or mule affected with
choking, §3-1-21.
Cleaning, disinfecting, etc.
Quarantined livestock or
places, §2-15-156.
Vehicles used in
transporting animals,
§2-15-157.
Commissioner of agriculture
and industries.
Authorization to destroy
animals and indemnify
owners, §2-15-160.
Hog cholera, §2-15-235.
Rules and regulations.
Promulgation for control
and eradication,
§2-15-170.
When commissioner to
invite cooperation of
federal government in
arrest or eradication,
§2-15-152.
Definitions, §2-15-150.
Destruction of animals,
§2-15-168.
Appraisal.
Basis for appraisal,
§2-15-164.
Diseased animals to be
appraised prior to
slaughter, §2-15-161.
Exposed animals whose
flesh can be saved
for food, §2-15-163.
Materials to be
destroyed, §2-15-165.
Reporting of appraisal
of materials,
§2-15-167.
Reappraisal of animals,
§2-15-162.
Reporting of appraisals,
§§2-15-166, 2-15-167.
Authority, §2-15-160.
Disposal of carcasses, etc.
Rules and regulations,
§2-15-172.
Disposition of animals and
materials destroyed,
§2-15-168.
Indemnification of owners,
§§2-15-2, 2-15-160.
Reports.
Appraisal, §§2-15-166,
2-15-167.
Salvage value.
Payment of salvage
value to owner,
§2-15-163.
Expenses.
Suppression or eradication
and administration of
article, §2-15-173.

LIVESTOCK—Cont'd
Diseases—Cont'd
Federal government.
When commissioner to
invite cooperation of
federal government in
arrest or eradication,
§2-15-152.
Funds.
Appropriation of funds for
suppression or
eradication by county
commission, §2-15-151.
Glanders.
Sale or exchange of horse
or mule affected with
glanders, §3-1-21.
Hog cholera, §§2-15-230 to
2-15-274.
Inspection of livestock,
§§2-17-1 to 2-17-38.
See MEAT AND MEAT
PRODUCTS.
Inspectors.
Interference with,
§2-15-158.
Right of entry, §2-15-158.
Livestock brought into state.
Certificate of health
required, §2-15-155.
Penalties.
Hog cholera.
Violations of subdivision,
§2-15-236.
Violations of article or
rules and regulations,
§2-15-174.
Brucellosis or Bang's
disease, §2-15-196.
Quarantine.
Cattle.
Tuberculous cows,
§3-1-18.
Cleaning, disinfecting, etc.,
of quarantined
livestock or places,
§2-15-156.
Generally, §2-15-153.
Hog cholera, §2-15-233.
Notice of establishment of
quarantine.
Issuance and service,
§2-15-153.
Rules and regulations.
Promulgation as to
transportation,
disposition, etc., of
quarantined
livestock, §2-15-171.
Running at large.
Permitting in
quarantined district,
§2-15-159.
Tick eradication.
Counties released from
quarantine.
Inspectors to guard
boundary lines,
etc., §2-15-299.
Transportation of livestock
within or from
quarantined districts,
§2-15-154.
Reports.
Appraisal of animals and
materials to be
destroyed, §§2-15-166,
2-15-167.

LIVESTOCK—Cont'd
Diseases—Cont'd
Right of entry.
State veterinarian,
livestock inspectors,
etc., §2-15-158.
Rules and regulations.
Hog cholera.
Promulgation, §2-15-235.
Serum and other
immunizing agents,
§2-15-256.
Control of
manufacture, sale,
etc., §§2-15-270 to
2-15-274.
Manufacture, sale, etc., of
veterinary or biological
products and serums
and disposal of dead
carcasses, etc.,
§2-15-172.
Penalty for violations,
§2-15-174.
Brucellosis or Bang's
disease, §2-15-196.
Quarantined livestock.
Rules and regulations as
to transportation,
disposition, etc.,
§2-15-171.
Rules and regulations for
control and
eradication, §2-15-170.
Running at large.
Quarantined districts.
Permitting, §2-15-159.
Sales of exposed animals,
§2-15-169.
Sanitary and disease control
laws.
Arrest.
Appearance, §2-2-14.1.
Serums.
Rules and regulations as to
manufacture, sale, etc.,
§2-15-172.
State veterinarian.
Certificates of health,
§2-15-155.
Interference with execution
of duties, §2-15-158.
Right of entry, §2-15-158.
Swine diseases, §§2-15-230 to
2-15-274.
Tuberculosis.
Cattle, §§2-15-2, 3-1-17 to
3-1-19.
Veterinary or biological
products.
Rules and regulations as to
manufacture, sale, etc.,
§2-15-172.
Violations of article.
Penalty for violations,
§2-15-174.
Warranty.
No implied warranty that
livestock disease free,
§2-15-4.
When suppression or
eradication to be
commenced within
county, etc., §2-15-151.
Districts.
Establishing separate stock
districts.
Special, private or local
laws prohibited, Const.
Ala., art. IV, §104.

LIVESTOCK—Cont'd
Dogs.
Killing or injuring livestock
Keeping of dog known to
kill, etc., prohibited,
§3-1-1.
Liability of owner, §3-1-1.
Injuries caused by dog
while off premises o
owner, §3-1-6.
Permitting dog known to
kill or injure to run a
large, §3-1-4.
Rabid dogs.
Liability of owner for
injuries caused by,
§3-1-2.
Driving through streets,
§11-47-110.
Estrays, §§3-2-1 to 3-2-23.
See ESTRAYS.
Evidence.
Brands.
Admissibility of certificat
of registration as to
title or right of
possession, §2-15-22.
Executions.
Sustenance.
Levying officer to provide
sustenance for unsold
livestock, §6-9-95.
Fairs.
State aid to livestock shows
§§2-7-50 to 2-7-53.
Federal livestock inspector
Appointment as state
livestock inspectors,
§2-4-3.
Feeds.
Commercial feeds, §§2-21-1
to 2-21-34.
See FEEDS.
Fees.
Branding of livestock,
§§2-15-21, 2-15-23,
2-15-26.
Dealers, §§2-15-41, 2-15-13
Department of agriculture
and industries.
Inspection or testing
srevices, §2-15-1.
Markets, §§2-15-62, 2-15-92
Pedigrees.
Certificate fee, §2-15-313
Running at large, §3-5-5.
Fences.
Common fences.
Allowing stock to run at
large, §13A-7-61.
Construction.
Construction of lawful
fences, §§3-4-1 to 3-4
Lands not enclosed by lawf
fence.
Liability of owner of
animal breaking into
lands, §3-4-6.
Liability of person injuri
or destroying animal
breaking into lands,
§3-4-6.
Rail fences.
Construction of rail fence
for cattle, horses and
mules, §3-4-2.
Railroad fences.
Failure to fence railroads
Liability for injury to
stock, §37-2-89.

LIVESTOCK—Cont'd
Fences—Cont'd
Requirements as to
construction of lawful
fences, §§3-4-1 to 3-4-5.
Stakes, pits, poisons, etc.
Penalty for setting by
person not having
fence as prescribed in
chapter, §3-4-7.
Wire fences.
Seven or more wires.
Requirements as to
construction, §3-4-4.
Standard woven wire
fences.
Requirements as to
construction, §3-4-5.
Three or more wires.
Requirements as to
construction, §3-4-3.
Financial responsibility act.
General provisions,
§§2-15-230 to 2-15-238.
Reporting compliance with
act, §§2-15-80 to 2-15-86.
Fish and game.
Hunting.
Nighttime.
Killing stock, §9-11-258.
Foot and mouth disease. See
within this heading,
"Diseases."
Forfeitures.
Vehicles, etc., used in
livestock theft, §2-2-14.2.
Fraud.
Branding or marking or
altering mark or brand
with intent to defraud,
§3-1-27.
Burning, cauterizing, etc., of
teeth of horse or mule,
§3-1-23.
Pedigrees, §§2-15-310 to
2-15-317.
Garbage.
Swine.
Feeding garbage to swine,
§2-15-211.
Glanders.
Sale or exchange of horse or
mule affected with,
§3-1-21.
Hide dealers.
Records, §2-15-27.
Highways.
Markets.
Purchase of livestock on
public highway within
2,500 feet of public
livestock market,
§2-15-71.
Running at large.
Liability of owner of
livestock for collision
with motor vehicle,
§3-5-3.
Staking, pasturing, etc., of
animals upon highway
rights of way.
Estrays.
Applicability of laws as
to estrays, §3-3-3.
Peace officers empowered
to seize, §3-3-2.
Prohibited, §3-3-1.
Hogs.
Hog cholera, §§2-15-230 to
2-15-274.

LIVESTOCK—Cont'd
Hogs—Cont'd
Promotion of swine industry,
§§2-8-40 to 2-8-62.
Horses.
Glanders.
Sale or exchange of horse
or mule affected with
glanders, etc., §3-1-21.
Stallions.
Lien for services.
Sale of mare subject to
lien, §3-1-22.
Teeth.
Burning, cauterizing, etc.
Effect of possession of
such horse, §3-1-25.
Evidence to be
substantiated by
veterinarian,
§3-1-24.
Prohibited, §3-1-23.
Transportation of horse
into state, §3-1-26.
Tick eradication, §§2-15-296
to 2-15-298.
Immunization.
Hog cholera vaccine,
§§2-15-250 to 2-15-274.
Indictments.
Cattle theft.
Form of indictment,
§15-8-150.
Injunctions.
Markets.
Proceedings to restrain
operation in violation
of provisions of
provisions of division,
§2-15-70.
Injuries.
Counties.
Indemnification of owners
for injuries, etc.,
caused by dipping of
cattle, §§11-21-1 to
11-12-3.
Wanton, malicious, etc.,
injury of animal of
another, §§3-1-10, 3-1-11.
Inspections.
Carcasses, §§2-17-3 to 2-17-5.
Department of agriculture
and industries.
Contracts to perform
inspection or testing
services, §2-15-1.
Handling of livestock in
markets.
Inspection of markets for
enforcement of section,
§2-15-113.
Markets.
Commissioner, state
veterinarian, etc.,
§2-15-69.
Meat and meat products,
§§2-17-1 to 2-17-38.
See MEAT AND MEAT
PRODUCTS.
Inspectors.
State livestock inspectors,
§§2-4-2, 2-4-3.
Tick eradication, §§2-15-293,
2-15-294.
Insurance.
Casualty insurance
generally.
See INSURANCE.

LIVESTOCK—Cont'd
Insurance—Cont'd
Markets.
Commissioner to require
markets to carry,
§2-15-67.
Jacks.
Liens of owners, §§35-11-330,
35-11-331.
Landlord and tenant.
Lien of landlord on stock
raised on rented
premises, §35-11-72.
Larceny.
Arrest.
Appearance upon arrest,
§2-2-14.1.
Department to determine
ownership of stolen
livestock and furnish
information to interested
persons, §2-15-25.
Forfeiture of vehicles, etc.,
used in theft, §2-2-14.2.
Investigators, §2-2-14.
Livestock theft
investigator, §2-2-14.
Licenses.
Dealers, §§2-15-30, 2-15-132.
Liens.
Landlord's lien.
Lien of landlord on stock
raised on rented
premises, §35-11-72.
Livery stable keepers,
§§35-11-190, 35-11-191.
Owners of stallions, jacks,
bulls, etc.
Attachment, §35-11-331.
Declaration of lien,
§35-11-330.
Enforcement of lien,
§35-11-331.
Liens generally.
See LIENS.
Priority of lien, §35-11-330.
Pasturage or training.
Lien on stock for pasturage
or training, §35-11-70.
Veterinarians, §§35-11-390,
35-11-391.
Livery stables.
Liens of keepers,
§§35-11-190, 35-11-191.
Lost livestock.
Department to determine
ownership of lost
livestock and furnish
information to interested
persons, §2-15-25.
Estrays generally, §§3-2-1 to
3-2-23.
See ESTRAYS.
Markets, §§2-15-60 to
2-15-114.
Auctions.
Operators not to permit
purchase by owners,
officers, employees,
etc., of market,
§2-15-66.
Bills of sale.
Disposition by markets,
§2-15-65.
Information to be shown on
bills of sale, §2-15-65.
Issuance by markets,
§2-15-65.
Bonds, surety.
Livestock market
operators, §2-15-63.

LIVESTOCK—Cont'd
　Markets—Cont'd
　　Bonds, surety—Cont'd
　　　Weighing livestock at
　　　　markets.
　　　　Bond of permittee,
　　　　　§2-15-93.
　　Commissioner of agriculture
　　　and industries.
　　　Inspection, §2-15-69.
　　　Insurance.
　　　　Markets to carry
　　　　　insurance on
　　　　　livestock accepted
　　　　　for sale, §2-15-67.
　　　Interference with
　　　　performance of duties,
　　　　§2-15-69.
　　　Right of entry, §2-15-69.
　　　Rules and regulations,
　　　　§2-15-64.
　　　Weighing livestock at
　　　　markets.
　　　　Permit to be obtained,
　　　　　§2-15-92.
　　Cruelty to animals.
　　　Handling of livestock in
　　　　markets and in transit,
　　　　§§2-15-110 to 2-15-114.
　　Dealers, §§2-15-40 to 2-15-48.
　　Definitions, §§2-15-60,
　　　2-15-90.
　　Equipment required,
　　　§2-15-64.
　　Facilities required, §2-15-64.
　　Fees.
　　　Disposition, §2-15-62.
　　　Payment.
　　　　Agricultural marketing
　　　　　cooperatives,
　　　　　§2-15-62.
　　　　Delinquency penalty,
　　　　　§2-15-62.
　　　　Permit fees, §2-15-62.
　　　Weighing livestock at
　　　　markets.
　　　　Permit fee, §2-15-92.
　　Financial responsibility act.
　　　General provisions,
　　　　§§2-15-230 to 2-15-238.
　　　Reporting compliance with
　　　　act, §§2-15-80 to
　　　　2-15-86.
　　Fines.
　　　Disposition of fines,
　　　　§2-15-70.
　　Handling of livestock in
　　　markets and in transit,
　　　§§2-15-110 to 2-15-114.
　　Highways.
　　　Purchase of livestock on
　　　　public highway within
　　　　2,500 feet of public
　　　　market, §2-15-71.
　　Implementation of division.
　　　Rules and regulations,
　　　　§2-15-68.
　　Information received
　　　pertaining to amount or
　　　volume of business
　　　conducted by markets.
　　　Use and disclosure of
　　　　information, §2-15-62.
　　Injunctions.
　　　Restraint of operation in
　　　　violation of division,
　　　　§2-15-70.
　　Inspections.
　　　Commissioner, state
　　　　veterinarian, etc.,
　　　　§2-15-69.

LIVESTOCK—Cont'd
　Markets—Cont'd
　　Insurance.
　　　Markets to carry insurance
　　　　on livestock accepted
　　　　for sale, §2-15-67.
　　Penalties.
　　　Fees.
　　　　Delinquency penalty,
　　　　　§2-15-62.
　　Permits.
　　　Appeals from denial or
　　　　revocation, §2-15-61.
　　　Applications, §2-15-61.
　　　Denial.
　　　　Appeal, §2-15-61.
　　　Fees, §2-15-62.
　　　Issuance, §2-15-61.
　　　Operation of market
　　　　without permit,
　　　　§2-15-70.
　　　Required, §2-15-61.
　　　Revocation, §2-15-61.
　　　Violations of provisions
　　　　relating to branding
　　　　of livestock,
　　　　§2-15-30.
　　　Weighing livestock at
　　　　markets, §§2-15-90 to
　　　　2-15-96.
　　Public road, street or
　　　highway.
　　　Purchase of livestock on
　　　　public road, street or
　　　　highway within 2,500
　　　　feet of public livestock
　　　　market, §2-15-71.
　　Records.
　　　Register of brands.
　　　　Records required to be
　　　　　maintained,
　　　　　§2-15-27.
　　Right of entry by
　　　commissioner, state
　　　veterinarian, etc.,
　　　§2-15-69.
　　Roads.
　　　Purchase of livestock on
　　　　public road within
　　　　2,500 feet of public
　　　　market, §2-15-71.
　　Rules and regulations.
　　　Handling of livestock in
　　　　markets.
　　　　Promulgation, §2-15-113.
　　　Implementation of division,
　　　　§2-15-68.
　　　Promulgation, §2-15-64.
　　State veterinarian.
　　　Interference with
　　　　performance of duties,
　　　　§2-15-69.
　　　Right of entry and
　　　　inspection, §2-15-69.
　　Streets.
　　　Purchase of livestock on
　　　　public street within
　　　　2,500 feet of public
　　　　market, §2-15-71.
　　Violations of division,
　　　§2-15-70.
　　Weighing livestock at
　　　markets.
　　　Bonds, surety.
　　　　Permittee's bond,
　　　　　§2-15-93.
　　　Definition of livestock
　　　　market, §2-15-90.
　　　Exemption of public
　　　　weighmasters from
　　　　division, §2-15-95.

LIVESTOCK—Cont'd
　Markets—Cont'd
　　Weighing livestock at
　　　markets—Cont'd
　　　False weights.
　　　　Giving of false weight,
　　　　　§2-15-96.
　　　Fees.
　　　　Permit fee, §2-15-92.
　　　Livestock not to be sold by
　　　　weight at livestock
　　　　market unless weighed
　　　　by permittee, §2-15-91
　　　Markets employing public
　　　　weighmasters not
　　　　required to employ
　　　　permittees, §2-15-95.
　　　Permits.
　　　　Bond of permittee,
　　　　　§2-15-93.
　　　　Commissioner of
　　　　　agriculture and
　　　　　industries.
　　　　　Permit to be obtained
　　　　　　from
　　　　　　commissioner,
　　　　　　§2-15-92.
　　　　Duration, §2-15-92.
　　　　Fee, §2-15-92.
　　　　Forfeiture of permit by
　　　　　person giving false
　　　　　weight, §2-15-96.
　　　　Operation of scales
　　　　　without permit,
　　　　　§2-15-96.
　　　　Required for operation of
　　　　　scales at livestock
　　　　　market, §2-15-91.
　　　　To be obtained from
　　　　　commissioner,
　　　　　§2-15-92.
　　　Provision of services of
　　　　permittee or public
　　　　weighmaster by
　　　　markets, §2-15-94.
　Meat and meat products,
　　§§2-17-1 to 2-17-38.
　　See MEAT AND MEAT
　　PRODUCTS.
　Misdemeanors.
　　Sanitary and disease control
　　　laws.
　　　Arrest.
　　　　Appearance upon arrest
　　　　　§2-2-14.1.
　　Theft.
　　　Arrest.
　　　　Appearance upon arrest
　　　　　§2-2-14.1.
　Motor vehicle carriers.
　　Vehicles hauling livestock.
　　　Exemptions from chapter,
　　　　§37-3-4.
　Motor vehicles.
　　Running at large on
　　　highways.
　　　Liability of owner of
　　　　livestock for collision,
　　　　§3-5-3.
　　Size and weight of vehicles
　　　transporting.
　　　Exemption from article,
　　　　§32-9-25.
　Mules.
　　Glanders.
　　　Sale or exchange of mule
　　　　affected with glander
　　　　etc., §3-1-21.

LIVESTOCK—Cont'd
 Mules—Cont'd
  Jacks.
   Lien for services.
    Sale of jennet subject to
     lien, §3-1-22.
   Teeth.
    Burning, cauterizing, etc.
    Effect of possession of
     mules, §3-1-25.
    Evidence to be
     substantiated by
     veterinarian,
     §3-1-24.
    Prohibited, §3-1-23.
    Transportation of mule
     into state, §3-1-26.
  Tick eradication, §§2-15-296
   to 2-15-298.
 Municipal corporations.
  Dealers.
   Sanitary rules and
    regulations.
    Adoption by
     municipalities,
     §2-15-48.
  Driving through streets,
   §11-47-110.
  Running at large.
   Authority of
    municipalities, §3-5-14.
   Destruction, §11-47-110.
   Impoundment, §11-47-110.
   Ordinances not repealed,
    §3-5-14.
   Refunding of
    municipalities where
    livestock kept and fed
    in municipal pounds,
    §3-5-11.
 Pasturage.
  Lien on stock for pasturage,
   §35-11-70.
 **Pasturing upon highway
  rights-of-way,** §§3-3-1 to
  3-3-3.
 Pedigrees, §§2-15-310 to
  2-15-317.
  Certificate.
   Display, §2-15-312.
   Disposition of copies of
    certificate, §2-15-312.
   False pretense.
    Obtaining by false
     pretense, §2-15-317.
   Fee for certificate,
    §2-15-313.
   Issuance to owner of sire
    upon receipt of
    statement by
    commissioner,
    §2-15-312.
   Annual report as to
    certificates issued,
    §2-15-316.
   Lien of owner of sire,
    §2-15-314.
    Enforcement of lien,
     §2-15-315.
   Obtaining by false
    pretense, §2-15-317.
   Posting of copy by owner of
    sire, §2-15-312.
  Reports.
   Annual report of
    commissioner as to
    certificates issued,
    etc., §2-15-316.

LIVESTOCK—Cont'd
 Pedigrees—Cont'd
  Commissioner of agriculture
   and industries.
   Annual report of
    commissioner as to
    certificates issued, etc.,
    §2-15-316.
   Issuance of certificate to
    owner of sire upon
    receipt of statement by
    commissioner,
    §2-15-312.
  False pedigree.
   Giving false pedigree of
    animal, §2-15-317.
  Fee for certificate, §2-15-313.
  Liens.
   Lien of owner of sire
    obtaining certificate
    under provisions of
    article, §2-15-314.
    Enforcement of lien,
     §2-15-315.
  Purpose of article, §2-15-310.
  Reports.
   Annual report of
    commissioner as to
    certificates issued, etc.,
    §2-15-316.
  Statement.
   Filing with commissioner
    by owner of sire
    charging service fee,
    §2-15-311.
   Issuance of certificate to
    owner of sire upon
    receipt of statement by
    commissioner,
    §2-15-312.
 Penalties.
  Branding of livestock.
   Violations of article or
    rules and regulations,
    §2-15-30.
  Cattle.
   Promotion of cattle
    industry.
    Failure to deduct and
     pay over assessment,
     §2-8-22.
  Diseases.
   Hog cholera.
    Violations of provisions
     of subdivision,
     §2-15-236.
    Violations of article or
     rules and regulations,
     §§2-15-174, 2-15-196.
   Handling of livestock in
    markets and in transit,
    §2-15-114.
   Hog cholera.
    Violations of provisions of
     subdivision, §2-15-236.
  Markets.
   Fees.
    Delinquency penalty,
     §2-15-62.
   Promotion of cattle industry.
    Failure to deduct and pay
     over assessment,
     §2-8-22.
   Promotion of swine industry.
    Failure to deduct and pay
     over assessment,
     §2-8-62.
 Permits.
  Dealers, §§2-15-41, 2-15-42.
  Markets, §§2-15-61, 2-15-62.

LIVESTOCK—Cont'd
 Poultry.
  General provisions, §§2-16-1
   to 2-16-42.
  See POULTRY.
 Purchase.
  Between sunset and sunrise.
   Prohibited, §3-1-20.
 Quarantine.
  General provisions. See
   within this heading,
   "Diseases."
 Railroads.
  Cattle guards, §37-2-137.
  Connection of tracks and
   interchange of traffic.
   Precedence given livestock,
    §37-2-135.
  Fences.
   Failure to fence railroads.
    Liability for injury to
     stock, §37-2-89.
 Registration.
  Brands, §§2-15-21 to 2-15-26.
 Rules and regulations.
  Branding of livestock.
   Promulgation, §2-15-28.
   Violations, §2-15-30.
  Brucellosis or Bang's disease.
   Penalty for violation,
    §2-15-196.
  Dealers, §§2-15-45, 2-15-48,
   2-15-84, 2-15-135.
  Diseases.
   General provisions,
    §§2-15-170 to 2-15-174.
   Hog cholera, §§2-15-235,
    2-15-256, 2-15-270 to
    2-15-274.
  Handling of livestock in
   markets, §2-15-113.
  Hog cholera, §§2-15-235,
   2-15-256, 2-15-270 to
   2-15-274.
  Markets.
   Handling of livestock in
    markets.
    Promulgation, §2-15-113.
   Implementation of division,
    §2-15-68.
   Promulgation, §2-15-64.
  Promotion of cattle industry,
   §2-8-20.
  Promotion of swine industry,
   §2-8-60.
 Running at large.
  Appeals from judgment of
   district court, §3-5-12.
  Appearance of owner.
   Proceedings where owner
    appears and claims
    livestock, §3-5-8.
  Common fences.
   Allowing stock to run at
    large under common
    fence, §13A-7-61.
  Counties.
   Refunding of counties
    where livestock kept
    and fed in county
    pounds, §3-5-11.
  Damages.
   Determination of amount,
    §3-5-12.
  Discharging livestock.
   Proceedings and entry of
    judgment.
    Discharging livestock
     where not
     unlawfully at large,
     §3-5-9.

LIVESTOCK—Cont'd
  Running at large—Cont'd
    Estrays, §§3-2-1 to 3-2-23.
      See ESTRAYS.
    Fees, §3-5-5.
    General provisions, §§3-2-1 to
        3-2-23.
      See ESTRAYS.
    Judgment lien upon livestock
        causing damage, §3-5-3.
    Liability of owner for
        damages, §3-5-3.
      Running at large on
          highways and collision
          with motor vehicle,
          §3-5-3.
    Municipal corporations.
      Authority to adopt
          ordinances, §3-5-14.
      Impoundment and
          destruction of animals
          running at large,
          §11-47-110.
      Ordinances not repealed,
          §3-5-14.
      Refunding of
          municipalities where
          livestock kept and fed
          in municipal pounds,
          §3-5-11.
    Nonresidents.
      Filing of statement where
          owner not resident of
          county, §3-5-7.
    Notice to owner, §3-5-6.
    Not unlawfully at large.
      Proceedings and entry of
          judgment discharging
          livestock, §3-5-9.
    Permitting livestock to run
        at large, §3-5-2.
    Recovery by owner, §3-5-5.
    Recovery of livestock.
      Proceedings for recovery,
          §3-5-12.
    Sale.
      Disposition of proceeds of
          sale, §3-5-13.
      Procedure for sale when
          animal not reclaimed.
          Reclaimed, §3-5-13.
      Where livestock not
          claimed, §3-5-8.
    Seizure, §3-5-4.
      Determination of validity
          of seizure, §3-5-12.
      Fees and costs, §3-5-12.
      Hearing upon seizure,
          §3-5-8.
      Person seizing entitled to
          possession until
          judgment and costs of
          keeping and caring
          paid, §3-5-10.
      Posting of notice as to
          taking, §3-5-8.
      Validity.
        Determination of validity
            of seizure, §3-5-12.
    Taking up of livestock by
        owner of lands on which
        animals running at
        large, §3-5-6.
    Taking up of livestock
        running at large by
        highway patrol, etc.,
        §3-5-4.

LIVESTOCK—Cont'd
  Running at large—Cont'd
    Unknown owner.
      Filing of statement where
          owner unknown, not
          resident of county, etc.,
          §3-5-7.
  Rustling.
    Livestock theft investigator,
        §2-2-14.
  Sales.
    Between sunset and sunrise.
        Prohibited, §3-1-20.
    Bills of sale.
      Dealers to obtain, §2-15-43.
      Markets, §§2-15-40 to
          2-15-48.
    Dealers for resale, §§2-15-40
        to 2-15-48.
    Running at large, §§3-5-8,
        3-5-13.
  Sales tax.
    Exemptions.
      Gross proceeds of sale of
          livestock, §40-23-4.
  Secured transactions.
    Classification of goods,
        §7-9-109.
    When security interest
        attaches, §7-9-204.
  Shows.
    State aid to livestock
        shows.
      Amount, §2-7-53.
      Declaration of purpose,
          §2-7-50.
      Eligibility for allotments,
          §2-7-52.
      Limitations on allotments,
          §2-7-52.
      Payment of allotment.
        Time of payment,
            §2-7-53.
      Prizes and premiums.
        Expenditures authorized,
            §2-7-51.
      Statement to be filed by
          organization desiring
          allotment, §2-7-53.
      Time of payment, §2-7-53.
  Slaughter.
    Dealers, §§2-15-40 to 2-15-48.
    General provisions, §§2-17-3
        to 2-17-5.
  Slaughterhouses.
    General provisions.
      See SLAUGHTERHOUSES.
  Spotlighting, §32-5-17.
  Stables.
    Livery stables.
      Liens of keepers,
          §§35-11-190,
          35-11-191.
  Staking upon highway rights
      of way, §§3-3-1 to 3-3-3.
  Stallions.
    Liens of owners, §§35-11-330,
        35-11-331.
  State livestock inspectors.
    Appointment, §2-4-2.
    Federal livestock inspectors.
      Appointment as state
          livestock inspectors,
          §2-4-3.
  State veterinarian.
    Brucellosis of Bang's disease,
        §§2-15-193, 2-15-194.
    Diseases, §§2-15-155,
        2-15-158.
    Markets, §2-15-69.

LIVESTOCK—Cont'd
  State veterinarian—Cont'd
    Tick eradication.
      Number of dipping vats,
          inspectors, chemicals,
          etc., required,
          §2-15-293.
  Stolen property.
    Department of agriculture
        and industries to
        determine ownership of
        stolen livestock and
        furnish information to
        interested persons,
        §2-15-25.
  Streets.
    Markets.
      Purchase of livestock on
          public street within
          2,500 feet of public
          livestock market,
          §2-15-71.
  Swine.
    Cholera.
      Hog cholera, §§2-15-230 to
          2-15-274.
    Constitution of Alabama.
      Amendments.
        Promotion of production,
            distribution, etc.,
            Const. Ala., amd.
            400.
    Definitions.
      Hog cholera, §2-15-230.
    Diseases.
      Feeding of garbage to
          swine, §2-15-211.
      Hog cholera, §§2-15-230 to
          2-15-274.
      Laboratory.
        Swine disease diagnostic
            laboratory,
            §2-15-210.
    Garbage.
      Feeding garbage to swine,
          §2-15-211.
    Hog cholera, §§2-15-230 to
        2-15-274.
      Bodies.
        Disposition of bodies of
            hogs dying from hog
            cholera, §2-15-233.
      Burning of hogs dying
          from cholera, etc.,
          §3-1-28.
      Commissioner of
          agriculture and
          industries.
        Execution and
            enforcement of
            subdivision,
            §2-15-235.
        Promulgation of rules
            and regulations,
            §2-15-235.
      Counties.
        Eradication programs,
            §2-15-234.
      Definitions, §2-15-230.
      Disposition of bodies of
          hogs dying from hog
          cholera, §2-15-233.
      Eradication programs.
        Appropriation and
            expenditure of funds
            by counties,
            §2-15-234.

LIVESTOCK—Cont'd
 Swine—Cont'd
  Hog cholera—Cont'd
   Execution and enforcement
    of subdivision.
    Commissioner of
     agriculture and
     industries,
     §2-15-235.
   Inoculation.
    Payment of cost,
     §2-15-251.
   Inspectors, §2-15-234.
   Moving of hogs from
    quarantined premises,
    §2-15-233.
   Penalties for violations of
    subdivision, §2-15-236.
   Possession of hog cholera
    virus prohibited,
    §2-15-231.
   Quarantine, §2-15-233.
    Moving of hogs from
     quarantined
     premises, §2-15-233.
   Rules and regulations.
    Promulgation, §2-15-235.
   Serum and other
    immunizing agents,
    §2-15-256.
    Control of
     manufacture, sale,
     etc., §§2-15-270 to
     2-15-274.
   Sale of hog cholera virus
    prohibited, §2-15-231.
   Sale of swine infected with
    or exposed to hog
    cholera, §2-15-232.
   Serum and other
    immunizing agents,
    §§2-15-250 to 2-15-274.
    Acquisition by
     department,
     §2-15-250.
    Adoption of disease
     control programs,
     §2-15-256.
    Appropriations,
     §2-15-257.
    Control of manufacture,
     sale, etc.
     Rules and regulations,
      §§2-15-270 to
      2-15-274.
    Cost of inoculation.
     Payment, §2-15-251.
    Distribution by
     department,
     §2-15-251.
     To owners of
      commercial
      garbage-fed swine,
      etc., §2-15-253.
    False representations.
     Making false
      representation for
      securing serum or
      other immunizing
      agents, §2-15-254.
    Fund.
     Serum fund, §2-15-255.
    Hog cholera virus.
     Not to be purchased or
      distributed by
      department,
      §2-15-252.
     Possession, sale, etc.,
      prohibited,
      §2-15-251.

LIVESTOCK—Cont'd
 Swine—Cont'd
  Hog cholera—Cont'd
   Serum and other
    immunizing agents
    —Cont'd
    Rules and regulations,
     §2-15-256.
    Control of
     manufacture, sale,
     etc., §§2-15-270 to
     2-15-274.
   Violations of provisions of
    subdivision.
    Penalties, §2-15-236.
  Killing or injuring livestock.
   Permitting hog known to
    kill or injure livestock
    to run at large, §3-1-4.
  Promotion of swine industry,
   §§2-8-40 to 2-8-62; Const.
   Ala., amd. 327.
   Assessments.
    Collection of
     assessments, §2-8-51.
    Declared to be in public
     interest, §2-8-42.
    Deductions for expenses,
     §2-8-51.
    Expenditure of
     assessments, §2-8-57.
    Failure to deduct and
     pay over assessment.
     Penalty for failure,
      §2-8-62.
    Limitations on
     assessments, §2-8-49.
    Penalty for failure to
     deduct and pay over
     assessment, §2-8-62.
   Referendum.
    Application to conduct,
     §§2-8-43, 2-8-44.
    Authority to conduct
     referendum,
     §2-8-45.
    Canvass of results,
     §2-8-49.
    Conduct, §2-8-47.
    Declared to be in
     public interest,
     §2-8-42.
    Eligibility to vote,
     §2-8-48.
    Majority vote required
     for approval of
     assessment,
     §2-8-49.
    Notice, §2-8-46.
    Payment of expense,
     §2-8-47.
    Question to be voted
     on, §2-8-48.
    Subsequent
     referendum,
     §2-8-50.
   Refund to swine
    producer, §2-8-54.
   Remission of collections
    to treasurers of
    associations, §2-8-52.
   Audit of swine producers'
    associations, §2-8-59.
   Authorized activities.
    Not illegal or in
     restraint of trade,
     §2-8-41.
   Bonds, surety.
    Treasurers of swine
     producers'
     associations, §2-8-56.

LIVESTOCK—Cont'd
 Swine—Cont'd
  Promotion of swine industry
   —Cont'd
   Certification of swine
    producers' associations.
    Application for
     certification.
     Action by board on
      application,
      §2-8-44.
     Generally, §2-8-43.
    Revocation of
     certification, §2-8-61.
   Commissioner of
    agriculture and
    industries.
    Enforcement duties of
     commissioner,
     §2-8-61.
   Enforcement duties of
    commissioner, §2-8-61.
   Examination of swine
    producers' associations
    by department of
    examiners of public
    accounts, §2-8-59.
   Exempt sales, §2-8-55.
   Joint programs with other
    states, §2-8-58.
   Legislative purpose and
    intent, §2-8-40.
   Rules and regulations,
    §2-8-60.
   Treasurers of swine
    producers' associations.
    Bonds of treasurers,
     §2-8-56.
    Remission of collections
     to treasurers,
     §2-8-52.
  Quarantine.
   Hog cholera, §2-15-233.
  Rules and regulations.
   Promotion of swine
    industry, §2-8-60.
  Running at large.
   Permitting hog known to
    kill or injure livestock
    to run at large, §3-1-4.
  Vaccination.
   Hog cholera serum,
    vaccine, etc.,
    §§2-15-250 to 2-15-274.
 Theft, §2-2-14.
  Arrest.
   Appearance upon arrest,
    §2-2-14.1.
  Forfeiture of vehicles, etc.,
   used in theft, §2-2-14.2.
  Investigator, §2-2-14.
  Second degree theft of
   property, §13A-8-4.
 Tick eradication, §§2-15-290
  to 2-15-299.
  Appropriations.
   County commissions to
    make appropriations,
    §2-15-290.
  Cattle.
   Dipping of cattle in tick
    infested or
    quarantined ranges,
    farms, etc., §2-15-295.
  Running at large.
   Taking up, dipping, etc.,
    of cattle running at
    large, §2-15-297.
  Transportation into state of
   ticky cattle, §2-15-298.

LIVESTOCK—Cont'd
Tick eradication—Cont'd
Commencement.
Expenditures by county
upon commencement,
§2-15-290.
When to be commenced
within county,
§2-15-290.
Dipping of cattle in tick
infested or quarantined
ranges, farms, etc.,
§2-15-295.
Dipping vats.
Counties to provide and
maintain required
number, §2-15-292.
Number.
Counties to maintain
required number,
§2-15-292.
Required, §2-15-293.
Provision by counties,
§2-15-292.
Expenditures upon
commencement,
§2-15-290.
State aid to counties,
§2-15-291.
Horses.
Dipping of horses kept in
tick infested lots,
§2-15-296.
Running at large.
Taking up, dipping, etc.,
of horses running at
large, §2-15-297.
Transportation into state of
tick infested horses,
§2-15-298.
Inspectors.
Appointment, §2-15-294.
Commissioning, §2-15-294.
Compensation by counties,
§2-15-294.
Counties released from
state or federal
quarantined to provide
for inspectors to guard
boundary lines,
§2-15-299.
State veterinarian to
determine and notify
county commission as
to number required,
§2-15-293.
Supervision, §2-15-294.
Mules.
Dipping of mules kept in
tick infested lots,
ranges, etc., §2-15-296.
Running at large.
Taking up, dipping, etc.,
of mules running at
large, §2-15-297.
Transportation into state of
tick infested mules,
§2-15-298.
Quarantine.
Counties released from
state or federal
quarantine to provide
for inspectors to guard
boundary lines, etc.,
§2-15-299.

LIVESTOCK—Cont'd
Tick eradication—Cont'd
Reinfestation.
Counties becoming
reinfested with ticks to
pay costs of
disinfecting infested
ranges, cattle, etc.,
§2-15-299.
Running at large.
Taking up, dipping, etc., of
cattle, horses, etc.,
running at large or
quarantined on tick
infested ranges, etc.,
§2-15-297.
State aid to counties for
payment of expenses,
§2-15-291.
State veterinarian.
Number of dipping vats,
inspectors, chemicals,
etc., required,
§2-15-293.
Transportation of livestock.
Transportation into state of
tick infested cattle,
horses, mules, etc.,
§2-15-298.
When commenced, §2-15-290.
Title.
Brands.
Admissibility of certificate
as to title or right of
possession, §2-15-22.
Training.
Lien on stock for training,
§35-11-70.
Transportation.
Diseases, §§2-15-110 to
2-15-114.
Handling of livestock in
markets and in transit,
§§2-15-110 to 2-15-114.
Quarantine.
Transportation within or
from quarantined
districts, §2-15-154.
Tick eradiction.
Transportation into state of
tick infested cattle,
houses, mules, etc.,
§2-15-298.
Trespass.
Destruction or injury of
animal of another.
Proof of trespassing by
animal in mitigation
or justification of
offense, §3-1-11.
Fences.
Liability of owner of
animal breaking into
lands not enclosed by
lawful fence, §3-4-6.
Running at large, §§3-5-2 to
3-5-9.
Tuberculosis.
Cattle. See within this
heading, "Cattle."
Use tax.
Exemptions, §40-23-62.
Vaccination.
Hog cholera vaccine,
§§2-15-250 to 2-15-274.
Veterinarians.
General provisions.
See VETERINARIANS.

LIVESTOCK—Cont'd
Veterinarians—Cont'd
State veterinarian.
Brucellosis or Bang's
disease, §§2-15-193,
2-15-194.
Diseases, §§2-15-155,
2-15-158.
Markets, §2-15-69.
Tick eradication.
Number of dipping vats,
inspectors,
chemicals, etc.,
required, §2-15-293.
**Wanton destruction or
injury,** §§3-1-10, 3-1-11.
Warranty.
No implied warranty that
livestock disease free,
§2-15-4.
Weights and measures.
Weighing livestock at
markets, §§2-15-90 to
2-15-96.

LIVING APART ACT.
Husband and wife, §30-2-2.

**LIVINGSTON,
MUNICIPALITY OF.**
Economic development,
Const. Ala., amd. 251.
Property tax, Const. Ala.,
amd. 8.

LIVINGSTON UNIVERSITY,
§§16-53-1 to 16-53-12.
Administration of university.
Board of trustees.
Powers of board, §16-53-6.
Agents.
Default, etc., not to work
forfeiture, §16-53-11.
**American legion
scholarships,** §§16-31-1 to
16-31-4.
Board of trustees, §§16-53-1
to 16-53-11.
Administration of university.
Powers of board, §16-53-6.
Appointment of members,
§16-53-3.
Body corporate, §16-53-1.
Buildings.
Authority of board as to
buildings, §16-53-2.
Capital improvements.
Authority of board as to
buildings and other
capital improvements,
§16-53-2.
Chief executive officer,
§16-53-3.
Compensation of members,
§16-53-3.
Composition, §16-53-3.
Conflicts of interest.
Removal of member
conducting business
with university,
§16-53-3.
Courses of instruction.
Powers of board, §16-53-6.
Created, §16-53-3.
Default, etc., not to work
forfeiture, §16-53-11.
Degrees.
Powers of board, §16-53-6.
Endowment funds.
Investment of endowment
funds held by board,
§16-13-2.

LIVINGSTON UNIVERSITY
—Cont'd
Board of trustees—Cont'd
Executive committee,
§16-53-4.
Expenses of members,
§16-53-3.
Payment, §16-53-9.
Faculty.
Powers of board, §16-53-6.
Funds.
Depository and interest on
funds, §16-53-3.
Powers of board, §16-53-6.
Jurisdiction.
Transfer of jurisdiction to
board of trustees,
§16-53-7.
Legislature.
Reports to legislature,
§16-53-10.
Meetings, §16-53-4.
Membership, §16-53-3.
Officers.
Powers of board, §16-53-6.
Organization of university.
Powers of board, §16-53-6.
Powers as to organization
and administration,
§16-53-6.
Quorum, §16-53-5.
Removal of members.
Members conducting
business with
university, §16-53-3.
Reports to legislature,
§16-53-10.
Terms of members, §16-53-3.
Transfer of jurisdiction to
board of trustees,
§16-53-7.
Tuition.
Powers of board, §16-53-6.
Vacancies, §16-53-8.
Body corporate, §16-53-1.
Buildings.
Board of trustees.
Authority of board as to
buildings, §16-53-2.
Capital improvements.
Board of trustees.
Authority of board as to
buildings and other
capital improvements,
§16-53-2.
Chief executive officer.
Board of trustees, §16-53-3.
Conflicts of interest,
§16-53-3.
**Commission of higher
education.**
General provisions, §§16-5-1
to 16-5-14.
See UNIVERSITIES AND
COLLEGES.
Conflicts of interest.
Board of trustees.
Removal of member
conducting business
with university,
§16-53-3.
Corporation.
Body corporate, §16-53-1.
Rights, privileges,
responsibilities, etc., of
corporation, §16-53-2.
Courses of instruction.
Board of trustees.
Powers of board, §16-53-6.

LIVINGSTON UNIVERSITY
—Cont'd
Degrees.
Board of trustees.
Powers of board, §16-53-6.
Faculty.
Appointment, §16-53-6.
Board of trustees.
Powers of board, §16-53-6.
Eminent scholars trust fund,
§§16-61-1 to 16-61-10.
See UNIVERSITIES AND
COLLEGES.
Removal, §16-53-6.
Salaries, §16-53-6.
Funds.
Board of trustees.
Depository and interest on
funds, §16-53-3.
Powers of board, §16-53-6.
Eminent scholars trust fund,
§§16-61-1 to 16-61-10.
See UNIVERSITIES AND
COLLEGES.
Gifts and grants.
Not to fail for informality,
§16-53-11.
Jurisdiction.
Transfer to board of trustees,
§16-53-7.
Legislature.
Board of trustees.
Reports to legislature,
§16-53-10.
**Marine environmental
sciences consortium,**
§§16-45-1 to 16-45-5.
See MARINE
ENVIRONMENTAL
SCIENCES
CONSORTIUM.
Names, §16-53-1.
Grant or gift not to fail for
misnomer, §16-53-11.
Officers.
Appointment, §16-53-6.
Board of trustees.
Powers of board, §16-53-6.
Default, etc., not to work
forfeiture, §16-53-11.
Police officers, §16-53-12.
Removal, §16-53-6.
Salaries, §16-53-6.
Organization of university.
Board of trustees.
Powers of board, §16-53-6.
Police, §16-53-12.
General provisions,
§§16-22-1, 16-22-2.
Property.
Rights, privileges,
responsibilities, etc., of
corporation, §16-53-2.
Reports.
Board of trustees.
Reports to legislature,
§16-53-10.
Salaries.
Faculty, §16-53-6.
Powers of board of trustees,
§16-53-6.
Scholarships.
American legion
scholarships, §§16-31-1
to 16-31-4.
Trustees.
Board of trustees, §§16-53-1
to 16-53-10.
Tuition.
Board of trustees.
Powers of board, §16-53-6.

LIVING WILL, §§22-8A-1 to
22-8A-10.
See NATURAL DEATH ACT.

LOANS.
**Banks and financial
institutions.**
General provisions.
See BANKS AND
FINANCIAL
INSTITUTIONS.
Bureau of loans, §§5-2A-80 to
5-2A-83.
Burial societies, §10-4-24.
Effect of recital in minutes
on proceedings, §10-4-26.
Canons of judicial ethics.
Acceptance prohibited if loan
reflects expectation of
judicial favor, ACJE,
Canon 5C.
Constitution of Alabama.
Mortgage loans.
Nonresidents making
through licensed
brokers, Const. Ala.,
amd. 154.
Consumer loans, §§5-19-22,
5-19-23.
Contracts.
Small loans, §§5-18-15,
5-18-16.
Corporations.
See CORPORATIONS.
Corrections.
Institution finance authority.
Temporary loans in
anticipation of
issuance of bonds,
§14-2-10.
Counties, §§11-10-1 to 11-10-6.
See COUNTIES.
Credit.
See CREDIT.
Credit unions, §§5-17-17,
5-17-18.
Penalty for concealment of
loans, §5-17-29.
Penalty for receipt of
commission, emolument,
etc., for procuring loans,
§5-17-30.
Debtors and creditors.
See DEBTORS AND
CREDITORS.
**Downtown redevelopment
authorities.**
Loans to authorities by
counties, municipalities,
etc., §11-54A-22.
Education.
Age of majority.
Contracting for educational
loans for college level
education and above,
§26-1-5.
Student loan program,
§§16-33B-1 to 16-33B-8.
See STUDENT LOAN
PROGRAM.
Electric cooperatives.
Power to make loans to
certain persons, §37-6-3.
**Environmental improvement
authorities.**
Power to borrow money,
§9-6-8.
Fraternal benefit societies.
Certificate loans, §27-34-25.

LOANS—Cont'd
Fraternal orders.
From parent organization,
§10-4-178.
Governor.
Temporary loans to meet
deficiencies in treasury.
Negotiation, §36-13-4.
**Industrial development
boards.**
Municipal boards.
Temporary loans,
§11-54-91.
**Industrial development
corporations.**
Members.
Loan limits, §10-4-140.
Loans to corporation by
members, §10-4-140.
When not obligated to
make loans to
corporation, §10-4-135.
Powers of corporations,
§10-4-133.
Institute for deaf and blind.
Negotiation of temporary
loans, §21-1-19.
Insurance companies.
Housing.
Loans with respect to
housing, §5-5A-23.
Insurance premium finance
companies, §§27-40-1 to
27-40-18.
See INSURANCE.
Life insurance policies.
Loans on policy, §27-15-8.
Maximum rates of
interest, §27-15-8.
Loans to facilitate
rehabilitation, etc.,
§27-32-25.
Prohibited during period of
supervision, §27-2-34.
**Insurance premium finance
companies,** §§27-40-1 to
27-40-18.
See INSURANCE.
Interest.
General provisions.
See INTEREST.
Judges.
Acceptance prohibited if loan
reflects expectation of
judicial favor, ACJE,
Canon 5C.
Junior colleges.
Authority to borrow in
anticipation of current
revenues, §16-60-113.
Licenses.
Small loans, §§5-18-4 to
5-18-12.
See SMALL LOANS.
Limitation of actions.
Recovery of money, §6-2-34.
Military affairs.
Veterans.
Minor veterans empowered
to contract liability for
repayment of certain
loans, §31-1-2.
Minors.
Age of majority.
Contracting for educational
loans for college level
education and above,
§26-1-5.

LOANS—Cont'd
**Mowa Choctaw housing
authority.**
Contract with government
for loans, §24-7-6.
Municipal corporations.
General provisions,
§§11-47-1, 11-47-2.
Municipalities not to grant
public money or lend
credit to private persons
or corporations, Const.
Ala., art. IV, §94; amd.
112.
Waterworks and sewer
boards.
Execution, etc., of contracts
as security for
repayment of money
borrowed, §11-50-236.
Nonresidents.
Mortgage loans.
Nonresidents making
mortgage loans
through licensed
mortgage loan brokers,
Const. Ala., amd. 154.
Partnerships.
Loans by partners.
Rights and duties of
partners, §10-8-43.
Personal property.
Effect of loans of personal
property not in writing,
§35-4-95.
Loans in writing.
Creating estates in
personal property,
§35-4-94.
Recordation.
Necessity, §35-4-94.
Pistols.
Loans secured by deposit of
pistol, §13A-11-80.
Pleadings.
Form of complaint for money
lent, ARCP, Form 9.
**Savings and loan
associations.**
General provisions, §§5-16-2,
5-16-23 to 5-16-26.
See SAVINGS AND LOAN
ASSOCIATIONS.
Interest, §5-16-17.
Small loans, §§5-18-1 to
5-18-24.
See SMALL LOANS.
**Space science exhibit
finance authority.**
Temporary loans in
anticipation of issuance
of bonds, §41-10-308.
Student loan program,
§§16-33B-1 to 16-33B-8.
See STUDENT LOAN
PROGRAM.
Universities and colleges.
Age of majority.
Contracting for educational
loans for college level
education and above,
§26-1-5.
**USS Alabama battleship
commission.**
Bond issues, §§41-9-352,
41-9-353.
Borrowing money,
§§41-9-354, 41-9-355.

LOANS—Cont'd
Veterans.
Minor veterans empowered to
contract liability for
repayment of certain
loans, §31-1-2.
**Water management and
drainage.**
Power of board of water
management
commissioners, §9-9-15.
**Water pollution control
authority.**
Accounts and accounting,
§22-34-11.
Default, §22-34-11.
**Watershed conservancy
districts.**
Power to borrow money,
§9-8-61.
**Water system assistance
authority.**
Approval not required,
§22-23A-15.
In anticipation of bond
issues, §22-23A-9.
Weapons.
Pistols.
Loans secured by pistol,
§13A-11-80.

LOBBYISTS.
Constitution of Alabama.
State or county officials.
Lobbying in legislature by
state or county
officials, Const. Ala.,
art. IV, §101.
**Public officers and
employees.**
Code of ethics, §§36-25-18 to
36-25-23.
See PUBLIC OFFICERS
AND EMPLOYEES.
State or county officials.
Lobbying in legislature by
state or county
officials, Const. Ala.,
art. IV, §101.

LOCAL LAWS.
Constitution of Alabama.
See CONSTITUTION OF
ALABAMA.
Publication by counties,
§§11-13-2 to 11-13-5.

LOCAL OPTION.
**Elections as to sale and
distribution of alcoholic
beverages.**
General provisions,
§§28-2A-1 to 28-2A-4.
Special method referendum,
§§28-2-20 to 28-2-25.
See ALCOHOLIC
BEVERAGES.

LOCKJAW.
Notifiable diseases generally,
§§22-11A-1 to 22-11A-38.
See DISEASES.

LODGES.
Vacation time-sharing plans,
§§34-27-50 to 34-27-69.
See VACATION TIME-
SHARING PLANS.

LODGING HOUSES, §§34-15-1
to 34-15-20.
See HOTELS, INNS AND
OTHER TRANSIENT
LODGING PLACES.

LOGS.
See TREES AND TIMBER.

LOITERING.
Begging.
Loitering for purpose of begging, §13A-11-9.
Drugs.
Loitering for purposes of using or possessing, §13A-11-9.
Elections.
Polling places, §17-7-19.
Elements of crime, §13A-11-9.
Gambling.
Loitering for purpose of gambling, §13A-11-9.
Masks.
Being masked in public place, §13A-11-9.
Prostitution.
Loitering for purposes of prostitution, §13A-11-9.
Transportation facilities, §13A-11-9.
Universities and colleges.
Loitering without legitimate reason or permission, §13A-11-9.
Violation, §13A-11-9.

LONG ARM STATUTE.
Foreign countries, ARCP, Rule 4.4.
Out-of-state service, ARCP, Rule 4.2.

LONG TERM QUALITY HEALTH CARE, §§22-6-20 to 22-6-27.
Agency responsible to ensure compliance, §22-6-24.
Appropriations, §22-6-24.
Citation of act.
Short title, §22-6-21.
Construction and interpretation.
References to federal law, §22-6-22.
Definitions.
Facilities, §22-6-23.
Deposits.
Funds received pursuant to act, §22-6-24.
Resident protection trust fund.
Deposit of civil penalties collected, §22-6-27.
Enforcement, §22-6-25.
Facilities.
Defined, §22-6-23.
Licensing.
Responsibility of department of public health, §22-6-26.
Federal law.
References to, §22-6-22.
Funds.
Resident protection trust fund.
Deposit of civil penalties collected, §22-6-27.
Uses, §22-6-27.
Intent of legislature, §22-6-20.
Legislative intent, §22-6-20.
Licenses.
Facilities.
Responsibility of department of public health, §22-6-26.

LONG TERM QUALITY HEALTH CARE—Cont'd
Medicaid.
Designated agency responsible to ensure compliance, §22-6-24.
Enforcement, §22-6-25.
Remedies.
Enforcement of act, §22-6-25.
Resident protection trust fund, §22-6-27.
Uses, §22-6-27.
Rules and regulations.
Enforcement remedies and criteria, §22-6-25.
Short title, §22-6-21.
State health department.
Functions and responsibilities, §22-6-26.
Title of act.
Short title, §22-6-21.

LORD CAMPBELL'S ACT.
Wrongful death, §6-5-410.

LOST OR UNCLAIMED PROPERTY, §§35-12-1 to 35-12-48.
Appliances.
Disposition of unclaimed articles left for service, §35-12-6.
Articles left for service.
Disposition of unclaimed articles left for service, §35-12-6.
Bills of lading.
Lost and missing bills, §7-7-601.
Claims.
Proof of ownership of claimant, §35-12-2.
Cleaners, dyers and pressers.
Disposition of unclaimed articles left for service, §35-12-6.
Commercial code.
Commercial paper.
Lost instruments, §7-3-804.
Documents of title.
Lost and missing documents, §7-7-601.
Investment securities, §7-8-405.
Commissioner of revenue.
Uniform disposition of unclaimed property act.
See within this heading, "Uniform disposition of unclaimed property act."
Conditional sales contract.
When recorded contract received in evidence, §35-4-98.
Contracts.
Substitution of lost papers or records in civil cases, §12-20-30.
Conveyances.
Governor or state agency or institution.
Deeds.
Conveyances in cases of lost deeds, §35-4-391.
Substitution of lost papers or records in civil cases, §12-20-30.
Counties.
Bond issues.
Issuance of duplicates for lost bonds, §11-81-32.

LOST OR UNCLAIMED PROPERTY—Cont'd
Courts.
Substitution of lost or destroyed papers or records in civil cases, §§12-20-26 to 12-20-32.
See COURTS.
Dead bodies.
Distribution of unclaimed bodies for scientific study, §§22-19-20 to 22-19-30.
See DEAD BODIES.
Deeds.
Conveyances by governor or state agency or institution.
Conveyances in cases of lost deeds, §35-4-391.
Substitution of lost papers or records in civil cases, §12-20-30.
Depositaries.
When finder becomes depositary, §35-12-1.
Disposition.
Unclaimed articles left for service, §35-12-6.
Uniform disposition of unclaimed property act, §§35-12-20 to 35-12-48.
Documents of title.
Lost and missing documents, §7-7-601.
Finance.
Warrants.
Issuance of duplicate warrants when originals lost, §41-4-58.
Finders.
Compensation, §35-12-3.
Reward, §35-12-3.
Sale by finder, §35-12-5.
When finder becomes depositary, §35-12-1.
Freight.
Sale of unclaimed freight, §§37-2-28 to 37-2-30.
Indictments.
Lost, mislaid, mutilated or destroyed indictments, §§15-8-110, 15-8-111.
Investment securities, §7-8-405.
Larceny, §§13A-8-6 to 13A-8-9.
Laundries.
Disposition of unclaimed articles left for service, §35-12-6.
Limitation of actions.
Uniform disposition of unclaimed property act.
Duties under article not affected by expiration, §35-12-37.
Livestock.
Department to determine ownership of lost livestock and furnish information to interested persons, §2-15-25.
Estrays generally, §§3-2-1 to 3-2-23.
See ESTRAYS.
Maps and plats.
Town surveys, maps or plats, §35-2-56.

LOST OR UNCLAIMED PROPERTY—Cont'd

Motor vehicles.
Disposition of unclaimed articles left for service, §35-12-6.

Municipal corporations.
Bond issues.
Issuance of duplicates for lost bonds, §11-81-32.
Disposition of proceeds, §11-47-116.
Maps or plats, §35-2-56.
Redemption by owner, §11-47-116.
Sale, §11-47-116.
Storage, §11-47-116.
Uniform disposition of unclaimed property act.
Exemption of incorporated municipalities and municipal boards from act, §11-40-15.

Notice.
Disposition of unclaimed articles left for service, §35-12-6.
Uniform disposition of unclaimed property act, §§35-12-32, 35-12-38.

Partition.
Unclaimed money, §35-6-1.

Payment or delivery of abandoned property.
Uniform disposition of unclaimed property act, §§35-12-33 to 35-12-36.

Penalties.
Uniform disposition of unclaimed property act, §35-12-45.

Presumption of abandonment.
Uniform disposition of unclaimed property act, §§35-12-22 to 35-12-29.

Proof of ownership.
Claimant, §35-12-2.

Radio.
Disposition of unclaimed radios left for service, §35-12-6.

Reciprocity.
Uniform disposition of unclaimed property act.
Property abandoned or escheated under laws of another state, §35-12-30.

Records.
Courts.
Substitution of lost or destroyed papers or records in civil cases, §§12-20-26 to 12-20-32.
See COURTS.
Uniform disposition of unclaimed property act.
Examination by commissioner, §35-12-43.

Reports.
Uniform disposition of unclaimed property act.
Report of abandoned property, §35-12-31.
Penalty for failure to render, §35-12-45.

Rewards.
Finders, §35-12-3.

LOST OR UNCLAIMED PROPERTY—Cont'd

Rules and regulations.
Uniform disposition of unclaimed property act.
Commissioner of revenue, §35-12-46.

Sales.
Disposition of unclaimed articles left for service, §35-12-6.
Finders, §35-12-5.
Uniform disposition of unclaimed property act, §§35-12-38 to 35-12-42.

Salvage.
General provisions, §§35-13-1 to 35-13-10.
See SALVAGE.

Storage.
Placing thing found in storage, §35-12-4.

Television.
Disposition of unclaimed articles left for service, §35-12-6.

Theft of lost property.
General provisions, §§13A-8-6 to 13A-8-9.

Transportation companies.
Sale of unclaimed freight, §§37-2-28 to 37-2-30.

Uniform disposition of unclaimed property act, §§35-12-20 to 35-12-48.
Appeals.
Claims for property or proceeds of sale.
Judicial review of commissioner's decision, §35-12-42.
Attorneys at law.
Special counsel to commissioner, §35-12-46.
Banking organizations.
Defined, §35-12-21.
Intangible property held in course of dissolution, §35-12-26.
Property held by banking organizations.
Presumption of abandonment, §35-12-22.
Bond issues.
Presentation of matured bonds for payment, §35-12-38.
Sale of abandoned securities, §35-12-38.
Business associations.
Defined, §35-12-21.
Dissolution.
Intangible property held in course of dissolution, §35-12-26.
Distributions.
Undistributed distributions, §35-12-25.
Dividends.
Undistributed dividends, §35-12-25.
Intangible property held in course of dissolution, §35-12-26.

LOST OR UNCLAIMED PROPERTY—Cont'd

Uniform disposition of unclaimed property act—Cont'd
Business associations—Cont'd
Property held by business associations.
Presumption of abandonment, §35-12-22.
Undistributed dividends and distributions, §35-12-25.
Claims for property or proceeds of sale.
Determination by commissioner, §35-12-41.
Filing claim, §35-12-40.
Judicial review of commissioner's decision, §35-12-42.
Payment by commissioner, §35-12-41.
Commissioner of revenue.
Claims for property or proceeds of sale.
Determination and payment, §35-12-41.
Judicial review of commissioner's decision, §35-12-42.
Custody of property.
Election to receive custody, §35-12-36.
Election to receive custody of property, §35-12-36.
Employees, §35-12-46.
Notices.
Publishing and mailing by commissioner, §35-12-32.
Payment or delivery to commissioner, §§35-12-33 to 35-12-36.
Records.
Examination of records by commissioner, §35-12-43.
Rules and regulations, §35-12-46.
Construction of article, §35-12-48.
Definitions, §35-12-21.
Delivery of abandoned property, §§35-12-33 to 35-12-36.
Deposit of funds, §35-12-39.
Duties under article.
Not affected by expiration of limitation period, §35-12-37.
Penalties for failure to perform, §35-12-45.
Election by commissioner to receive custody of property, §35-12-36.
Electric cooperatives.
Exemptions from act, §35-12-24.1.
Employees of commissioner, §35-12-46.
Escheats.
Property presumed abandoned or escheated under laws of another state, §35-12-47.

LOST OR UNCLAIMED PROPERTY—Cont'd
Uniform disposition of unclaimed property act —Cont'd
Escheats—Cont'd
Reciprocity for property abandoned or escheated under laws of another state, §35-12-30.
Exemptions.
Electric cooperatives, §35-12-24.1.
Federal courts, officers, authorities or agencies.
Property held by.
Presumption of abandonment, §35-12-28.
Fiduciaries.
Intangible property held by fiduciaries, §35-12-27.
Financial organizations.
Defined, §35-12-21.
Intangible property held in course of dissolution, §35-12-26.
Property held by financial organizations.
Presumption of abandonment, §35-12-22.
Holder.
Defined, §35-12-21.
Liability.
Relief from liability, §35-12-34.
Payment or delivery, §§35-12-33 to 35-12-36.
Reports, §35-12-31.
Insurance corporations.
Defined, §35-12-21.
Unclaimed funds held by insurance corporations.
Definition of unclaimed funds, §35-12-23.
Presumption of abandonment, §35-12-23.
Intangible property.
Business associations and banking or financial organizations.
Intangible property held in course of dissolution, §35-12-26.
Fiduciaries.
Intangible property held by fiduciaries, §35-12-27.
Limitation of actions.
Duties under article not affected by expiration, §35-12-37.
Municipal corporations.
Exemption of incorporated municipalities and municipal boards from act, §11-40-15.
Notice.
Commissioner of revenue.
Publishing and mailing by commissioner of revenue, §35-12-32.
Mailing.
Commissioner of revenue, §35-12-32.

LOST OR UNCLAIMED PROPERTY—Cont'd
Uniform disposition of unclaimed property act —Cont'd
Notice—Cont'd
Publication.
Commissioner of revenue, §35-12-32.
Sale of abandoned property, §35-12-38.
Other states.
Property presumed abandoned or escheated under laws of another state, §35-12-47.
Reciprocity for property abandoned or escheated under laws of another state, §35-12-30.
Owner.
Defined, §35-12-21.
Not entitled to income or other increments accruing after payment or delivery to commissioner, §35-12-35.
Payment or delivery of abandoned property.
Compelling delivery.
Proceedings to compel delivery, §35-12-44.
Election by commissioner to receive custody, §35-12-36.
Generally, §35-12-33.
Liability.
Relief from liability, §35-12-34.
Owner not entitled to income or other increments accruing after payment or delivery, §35-12-35.
Penalties for refusal to deliver, §35-12-45.
Refusal to deliver.
Penalties, §35-12-45.
Proceedings to compel delivery, §35-12-44.
Reimbursement of holder, §35-12-34.
Relief from liability, §35-12-34.
Rights become obligations of state, §35-12-34.
Penalties.
Generally, §35-12-45.
Person.
Defined, §35-12-21.
Presumption of abandonment.
Deposits and refunds held by utilities, §35-12-24.
Federal courts, officers, authorities or agencies.
Property held by, §35-12-28.
Intangible property.
Business associations and banking or financial organizations.
Held in course of dissolution, §35-12-26.

LOST OR UNCLAIMED PROPERTY—Cont'd
Uniform disposition of unclaimed property act —Cont'd
Presumption of abandonment —Cont'd
Intangible property —Cont'd
Fiduciaries.
Held by fiduciaries, §35-12-27.
Miscellaneous personal property not otherwise covered by article, §35-12-29.
Other states.
Property presumed abandoned or escheated under laws of another state, §35-12-47.
Property held by banking or financial organizations or business associations, §35-12-22.
Unclaimed funds held by insurance corporations, §35-12-23.
Undistributed dividends and distributions of business associations, §35-12-25.
United States.
Property held by federal courts, officers, authorities or agencies, §35-12-28.
Reciprocity.
Property abandoned or escheated under laws of another state, §35-12-30.
Records.
Examination by commissioner, §35-12-43.
Report of abandoned property, §35-12-31.
Penalty for failure to render, §35-12-45.
Rules and regulations.
Commissioner of revenue, §35-12-46.
Sale of abandoned property, §35-12-38.
Claims for proceeds.
Determination, §35-12-41.
Filing claim, §35-12-40.
Judicial review of decision, §35-12-42.
Payment by commissioner, §35-12-41.
Deposit of proceeds, §35-12-39.
Proceeds of sale.
Claims for proceeds, §§35-12-40 to 35-12-42.
Deposit of funds, §35-12-39.
Short title of article, §35-12-20.
Statute of limitations.
Duties under article not affected by expiration, §35-12-37.

LOST OR UNCLAIMED PROPERTY—Cont'd
Uniform disposition of unclaimed property act—Cont'd
United States.
Property held by federal courts, officers, authorities or agencies.
Presumption of abandonment, §35-12-28.
Utilities.
Defined, §35-12-21.
Deposits and refunds held by utilities.
Presumption of abandonment, §35-12-24.
Electric cooperatives.
Exemptions from act, §35-12-24.1.
Warehouse receipts.
Lost and missing receipts, §7-7-601.
Warrants.
State warrants.
Issuance of duplicate warrants when originals lost, §41-4-58.

LOTTERIES.
Constitution of Alabama.
Prohibited, Const. Ala., art. IV, §65.
Defenses.
Lottery occurring outside state no defense to prosecution under section 13A-12-22, §13A-12-29.
Defined, §13A-12-20.
Forfeitures.
Transportation of lottery paraphernalia.
Forfeiture of vehicles used to transport, §§13A-12-70 to 13A-12-75.
Gambling generally, §§13A-12-20 to 13A-12-92.
See GAMBLING.
Grand jury.
Witnesses.
Examinations, §12-16-212.
Refusal to testify, §12-16-213.
Indictments.
Form of indictment for carrying on illegal lottery, §15-8-150.
Mortgages and deeds of trust.
Transportation of lottery paraphernalia.
Mortgagees of vehicles used to transport.
Rights of mortgagee, §13A-12-73.
Motor vehicles.
Transportation of paraphernalia, §§13A-12-70 to 13A-12-75.
Numbers game.
Defined, §13A-12-20.
Outside state.
Defenses to prosecution for promoting gambling, §13A-12-29.

LOTTERIES—Cont'd
Paraphernalia.
Transportation.
Articles not commonly used in numbers or policy game, §13A-12-75.
Bailors.
Condition of vendors or mortgagees.
Rights of, §13A-12-73.
By certain persons, §13A-12-70.
Condemnation of vehicles.
Procedure for condemnation, §13A-12-72.
Forfeiture of vehicle.
Disposition of proceeds of sale, §13A-12-74.
Procedure for forfeiture, §13A-12-72.
Sale of forfeited vehicle, §13A-12-73.
Movement of vehicles need not be shown, §13A-12-71.
Sales.
Forfeited vehicles, §13A-12-73.
Disposition of proceeds, §13A-12-74.
Seizure of vehicles used, §13A-12-70.
Pari-mutuel.
Defined, §13A-12-20.
Records.
Possession of gambling records.
General provisions, §§13A-12-24 to 13A-12-26.
See GAMBLING.
Searches and seizures.
Transportation of lottery paraphernalia.
Seizure of vehicles used, §13A-12-70.

LOW-LEVEL RADIOACTIVE WASTE.
Compacts.
Southeast interstate low-level radioactive waste management compact, §§22-32-1 to 22-32-9.
See SOUTHEAST INTERSTATE LOW-LEVEL RADIOACTIVE WASTE MANAGEMENT COMPACT.

LOWNDES COUNTY.
Barbers.
Chapter not applicable to Lowndes county, §34-5-15.
Probate judge.
Compensation, Const. Ala., amd. 483.

LOYAL ORDER OF MOOSE.
Taxation.
Property exempted, §40-9-1.

L.P.N.
Licensed practical nurses.
General provisions, §§34-21-1, 34-21-22.

LSD.
Controlled substances, §§20-2-1 to 20-2-144.
See DRUGS.

LUBRICATING OILS AND GREASES.
Definitions.
Tax, §40-17-170.
Department of revenue.
Tax.
Duty to enforce provisions, §40-17-179.
Education.
Tax.
Church schools.
Exemption, §40-17-171.
City and county boards of education.
Exemption, §40-17-171.
Private schools.
Exemption, §40-17-171.
Excise taxes.
Additional excise tax on gasoline, motor fuel and lubricating oil, §§40-17-220 to 40-17-225.
See TAXATION.
Institute for deaf and blind.
Tax.
Exemption, §40-17-171.
Limitation of actions.
Tax.
Actions by state, §40-17-181.
Penalties.
Tax.
Failure to keep records or make reports, §40-17-178.
Petroleum products generally, §§8-17-80, 8-17-132.
Records.
Tax.
Failure to keep.
Penalty, §40-17-178.
Sales, §40-17-176.
Reports.
Tax, §§40-17-200 to 40-17-203.
Sales tax.
Exemptions, §40-23-4.
Tax, §§40-17-170 to 40-17-186.
Acceptance of money on recovery of balance.
Effect, §40-17-180.
Actions by state.
Limitation, §40-17-181.
Additional excise tax on gasoline, motor fuel and lubricating oil, §§40-17-220 to 40-17-225.
Amount, §40-17-171.
Applicability of tax.
Tax to apply whether withdrawal for use or sale, §40-17-173.
Church schools.
Exemption, §40-17-171.
City and county boards of education.
Exemption, §40-17-171.
Dealers.
Retail dealers.
Defined, §40-17-170.
Report of address, §40-17-177.

LUBRICATING OILS AND GREASES—Cont'd
Tax—Cont'd
Dealers—Cont'd
Wholesale dealers in illuminating, lubricating or fuel oils, §40-17-174.
Definitions, §40-17-170.
Delinquents, §40-17-184.
Department of revenue.
Duty of enforcement, §40-17-179.
Disposition, §40-17-172.
Distributors.
Defined, §40-17-170.
Report of address, §40-17-177.
Education.
Church schools.
Exemption, §40-17-171.
City and county boards of education.
Exemption, §40-17-171.
Private schools.
Exemption, §40-17-171.
Exemptions, §40-17-171.
Certificates of exemption, §40-17-171.
Institute for deaf and blind.
Exemption, §40-17-171.
Levy, §40-17-171.
Limitation of actions, §40-17-181.
Manufacturers.
Report of address, §40-17-177.
Payment.
When tax to be paid, §40-17-186.
Penalties.
Records.
Failure to keep, §40-17-178.
Reports.
Failure to make, §40-17-178.
Private schools.
Exemption, §40-17-171.
Records.
Failure to keep.
Penalty, §40-17-178.
Sales, §40-17-176.
Reports.
Address.
Report by distributor, storer, retail dealer or manufacturer, §40-17-177.
Carriers.
Information not public, §40-17-202.
Penalty for failure to comply, §40-17-203.
When report to be made by carriers, §40-17-200.
Failure to make.
Penalty, §40-17-178.
Forms, §40-17-182.
Warehouses.
Information not public, §40-17-202.
Penalty for failure to comply, §40-17-203.
When reports to be made, §40-17-201.
Returns.
Monthly returns.
Failure to make, §40-17-183.

LUBRICATING OILS AND GREASES—Cont'd
Tax—Cont'd
Statements.
Swearing to, §40-17-175.
When statements to be rendered, §40-17-186.
Storers.
Defined, §40-17-170.
Report of address, §40-17-177.
Violations.
Restraint of violators, §40-17-185.
Youth services.
Department of youth services school districts.
Exemption, §40-17-171.
Youth services.
Tax.
Department of youth services school districts.
Exemption, §40-17-171.

LUMBER.
Attachment.
Sawmill owners' or operators' liens, §35-11-251.
Employees' or laborers' liens.
Attachment, §35-11-273.
Declaration of lien, §35-11-270.
Enforcement of lien, §35-11-273.
Liens generally, §§35-11-270 to 25-22-273.
Limitations, §35-11-272.
Priority of lien, §35-11-271.
Liens.
Employees' or laborers' liens, §§35-11-270 to 35-11-273.
Generally, §§35-11-250 to 35-11-273.
See LIENS.
Sawmills, §§35-11-250 to 35-11-273.
See SAWMILLS.
Motor vehicle carriers.
Vehicles hauling lumber.
Exemptions from chapter, §37-3-4.
Sawmills, §§35-11-250 to 35-11-273.
See SAWMILLS.
Trees and timber.
General provisions.
See TREES AND TIMBER.

LUNATICS.
Defined, §1-1-1.
General provisions, §§22-50-1 to 22-55-4.
See MENTALLY ILL.

LUNG DISEASES.
See TUBERCULOSIS.

LURLEEN B. WALLACE MEMORIAL CANCER HOSPITAL FUND.
Counties.
Appropriations by counties, §11-8-12.

LYE.
Regulation of caustic or corrosive substances, §§8-17-20 to 8-17-24.
See CAUSTIC OR CORROSIVE SUBSTANCES.

LYNN, MUNICIPALITY OF.
Economic development,
Const. Ala., amd. 256.

M

MACHINERY.
Attachment.
Liens for production, manufacture or repair.
Right to enforce lien by attachment, §35-11-111.
Coal mine safety.
Operation and maintenance of machinery.
See COAL.
Land clearing or improvements.
Liens.
Appliances, machinery and equipment used for land clearing or improvements, §§35-11-110 to 35-11-112, 35-11-430, 35-11-431.
Licenses.
Repair shops, §40-12-123.
Liens.
Appliances, machinery and equipment used for land clearing or improvements, §§35-11-110 to 35-11-112, 35-11-430, 35-11-431.
Attachment.
Joinder of persons having liens on same property, §35-11-112.
Right to enforce lien by attachment, §35-11-111.
Declaration of lien, §35-11-110.
Enforcement of lien.
Joinder of persons having liens on same property, §35-11-112.
Right to enforce by attachment, §35-11-111.
Joinder of persons having liens on same property, §35-11-112.
Production, manufacture or repair, §§35-11-110 to 35-11-112.
Manufacture.
Liens for manufacture, §§35-11-110 to 35-11-112.
Production.
Liens for production, §§35-11-110 to 35-11-112.
Repairs.
Licensing repair shops, §40-12-123.
Liens, §§35-11-110 to 35-11-112.

MACON COUNTY.
Abolishing.
Repeal of amendment, Const. Ala., amd. 406.
Area.
Reducing area.
Boundaries.
Altering boundaries.
Repeal of amendment, Const. Ala., amd. 406.

MACON COUNTY—Cont'd
  Area—Cont'd
    Reducing area—Cont'd
      Repeal of amendment,
        Const. Ala., amd. 406.
  **Daniel "Chappie" James
    Aerospace Memorial.**
    Indebtedness for, Const. Ala.,
      amd. 437.
  **Economic and industrial
    development promotion,**
    Const. Ala., amd. 429.
  Taxation.
    School tax.
      Additional tax for
        education purposes,
        Const. Ala., amd. 420.

MADISON COUNTY.
  Bingo.
    Charitable or nonprofit
      organizations.
      Operation of bingo games,
        Const. Ala., amd. 387.
  Charities.
    Bingo.
      Operation of bingo games
        by nonprofit
        organizations in
        Madison county, Const.
        Ala., amd. 387.
  Circuit court.
    Procedure for filling
      vacancies in office of
      judge, Const. Ala., amd.
      334.
  Court costs and charges,
    Const. Ala., amd. 105.
  **Economic and industrial
    development promotion,**
    Const. Ala., amd. 429.
  Economic development.
    Promotion of industrial,
      commercial and
      agricultural
      development, Const.
      Ala., amds. 191, 245.
  Fires and fire prevention.
    Establishment of fire
      districts, Const. Ala.,
      amd. 378.
  Judicial commission, Const.
    Ala., amd. 334.
  Officers.
    Fees, allowances, etc., of
      judge of probate and
      other officers, Const.
      Ala., amd. 135.
  Property tax.
    Delinquent tax notices.
      Local legislation regarding
        delinquent tax notices,
        Const. Ala., amd. 348.
  School bonds.
    Bonds for school buildings,
      Const. Ala., amd. 320.
  School tax.
    Repeal of exemptions, Const.
      Ala., amd. 455.
    Special tax in school district
      no. 1, Const. Ala., amds.
      149, 304.
  Space exhibits.
    Bonds for display of certain
      exhibits, Const. Ala.,
      amd. 224.

MAGIC.
  Licenses.
    Legerdemain and sleight of
      hand, §40-12-119.

MAGISTRATES.
  Administrative agency.
    Divisions.
      District court magistrate
        agency division, ARJA,
        Rule 18.
      Municipal court
        magistrates agency
        division, ARJA, Rule
        18.
    Established, ARJA, Rule 18.
  Appointment, §12-14-51.
    Forms, ARJA, Rule 18.
    Notice, ARJA, Rule 18.
    Qualifications, ARJA, Rule
      18.
    Recommendations, ARJA,
      Rule 18.
  Arrest.
    District court magistrates
      agency division.
      Authority of magistrates
        in, ARJA, Rule 18.
    Municipal court magistrates
      agency division.
      Authority of magistrates
        in, ARJA, Rule 18.
  Bail and recognizance.
    District court magistrates
      agency division.
      Authority of magistrates
        in, ARJA, Rule 18.
    Municipal court magistrates
      agency division.
      Authority of magistrates
        in, ARJA, Rule 18.
  District courts.
    Administrative agency.
      District court magistrates
        agency division, ARJA,
        Rule 18.
        Authority, ARJA, Rule
          18.
        Selection, ARJA, Rule
          18.
    Generally.
      See DISTRICT COURTS.
  **Financial systems for
    receipt, deposit and
    disbursement of funds.**
    Assistance in development,
      ARJA, Rule 28.
  Fines.
    Traffic infractions, ARJA,
      Rule 20.
  Forms.
    Appointment, ARJA, Rule
      18.
    Oath of office, ARJA, Rule
      18.
  Guilty pleas.
    District court magistrates
      agency division.
      Receiving pleas of guilty in
        misdemeanor cases.
        Authority of magistrates
          in, ARJA, Rule 18.
    Municipal court magistrates
      agency division.
      Receiving pleas of guilty in
        municipal ordinance
        cases.
        Authority of magistrates
          in, ARJA, Rule 18.
  Judges.
    Inferior court judges.
      Election by inferior court
        judges, §12-17-253.

MAGISTRATES—Cont'd
  Misdemeanors.
    District court magistrates
      agency division.
      Authority of magistrates
        in, ARJA, Rule 18.
  Motor vehicles.
    Traffic infractions.
      Schedule of fines, ARJA,
        Rule 20.
  Municipal courts.
    Administrative agency.
      Municipal court
        magistrates agency
        division, ARJA, Rule
        18.
    Generally.
      See MUNICIPAL
        COURTS.
  Notice.
    Appointment, ARJA, Rule
      18.
  Oaths.
    Oath of office, ARJA, Rule
      18.
    Form, ARJA, Rule 18.
  Ordinances.
    Municipal court magistrates
      agency division.
      Ordinance violations.
        Authority of magistrates
          in, ARJA, Rule 18.
  Peace bonds.
    See PEACE BONDS.
  Penalties.
    Schedule of fines, ARJA,
      Rule 20.
  Powers, §12-14-51.
  **Qualifications for
    appointment,** ARJA, Rule
    18.
  **Recommendations for
    appointment,** ARJA, Rule
    18.
  **Rules of judicial
    administration,** ARJA,
    Rule 18.
  Supernumerary magistrates.
    Appointment of
      supernumerary
      magistrate to fill
      vacancy, §12-17-263.
    Benefits to surviving spouse,
      §12-17-265.
  Traffic infractions.
    Fines, ARJA, Rule 20.
    Receipt of guilty pleas,
      §12-12-52.

MAIL.
  Air commerce.
    United States mail exempt
      from regulation, §37-9-3.
  Certified mail.
    Notice required to be served
      by registered mail may
      be served by certified
      mail, §1-3-7.
    Service of process by certified
      mail, ARCP, Rule 4.1 (c).
    Foreign countries, ARCP,
      Rule 4.4 (b).
    Out-of-state service, ARCP,
      Rule 4.2 (b).
  Elections.
    Absentee voting generally,
      §§17-10-1 to 17-10-20.
    See ELECTIONS.

MAIL—Cont'd
Elections—Cont'd
Registration of absentee
electors.
Persons entitled to register
by mail, §17-4-134.
Harassing communications,
§13A-11-8.
Motor vehicle carriers.
Certificates of public
convenience and
necessity.
Transportation of
newspapers, baggage
or mail, §37-3-12.
Lighting equipment and
warning devices for
vehicles engaged in mail
service, §32-5-243.
Vehicles used exclusively in
transportation of United
States mail.
Exemptions from chapter,
§37-3-4.
Notice.
Registered mail.
Notice required to be
served by registered
mail may be served by
certified mail, §1-3-7.
Obscenity, §13A-12-131.
Pilots and pilotage.
Delivery of letters by pilot,
§33-4-56.
Quarantine.
Refusal of mail, §22-12-21.
Registered mail.
Notice required to be served
by registered mail may
be served by certified
mail, §1-3-7.
Service of process by mail.
Additional time after service
by mail, ARCP, Rule 6
(e).
Certified mail, ARCP, Rule
4.1 (c).
Foreign countries, ARCP,
Rule 4.4 (b).
Notice required to be
served by registered
mail may be served by
certified mail, §1-3-7.
Out-of-state service by
certified mail, ARCP,
Rule 4.2 (b).
Deposit of money for postage
and registration, §6-4-22.
Taxation.
Exemptions from taxation.
Disabled persons.
Principal residence of
totally disabled
persons.
Verification of
eligibility by mail,
§40-9-21.1.
Homestead exemption.
Verification of eligibility
by mail, §40-9-21.1.
Timely mailing treated as
timely filing and paying,
§40-1-45.
**Unsolicited goods delivered
by mail.**
Disposition, §35-1-3.

MAIL ORDER SCHOOLS.
Unaccredited schools,
§§16-46-1 to 16-46-10.
See EDUCATION.

MAINTENANCE.
Alimony and support,
§§30-2-50 to 30-2-54.
Child custody and support,
§§30-3-1 to 30-3-99.
See MINORS.
Child support programs,
§§38-10-1 to 38-10-33.
See CHILD SUPPORT
PROGRAMS.
Desertion and nonsupport,
§§30-4-50 to 30-4-65.
See DESERTION AND
NONSUPPORT.
General provisions.
See SUPPORT AND
MAINTENANCE.
Indigent persons.
Relief and support by
counties, §§38-8-1 to
38-8-3.
Mentally ill.
Support of persons in state
institutions, §§22-53-1 to
22-53-26.
See MENTALLY ILL.
**Uniform reciprocal
enforcement of support
act,** §§30-4-80 to 34-4-98.
See DESERTION AND
NONSUPPORT.

MAJORITY.
Age of majority, §26-1-1.
Contracting for educational
loans for college level
education and above,
§26-1-5.
Uniform guardianship and
protective proceedings
act.
Termination of
appointment of
guardian upon minor
obtaining, §26-2A-79.
Education.
Age of majority.
Contracting for educational
loans for college level
education and above,
§26-1-5.
**Relief of minor children
from disabilities of
nonage,** §§26-13-1 to
26-13-8; Const. Ala., art.
IV, §104.
See MINORS.

MALARIA.
Notifiable diseases,
§§22-11A-1 to 22-11A-38.
See DISEASES.

MALICIOUS MISCHIEF.
Minors.
Liability of parents for
destruction of property
by minor, §6-5-380.

MALICIOUS PROSECUTION.
Limitation of actions.
Two year limitation, §6-2-38.
Malpractice.
Cause of action, §6-5-550.
Pleadings.
Form of complaint for
malicious prosecution,
ARCP, Form 19.

MALPRACTICE, §§6-5-480 to
6-5-488, 6-5-540 to 6-5-552.
Ad damnum clause.
Elimination, §6-5-483.

MALPRACTICE—Cont'd
Arbitration and award.
Settlement of disputes by
arbitration, §6-5-485.
Attorneys at law.
Legal services liability,
§§6-5-570 to 6-5-581.
See ATTORNEYS AT
LAW.
Burden of proof, §6-5-548.
Civil practice.
Rules of evidence and
procedures in civil
actions preserved,
§6-5-488.
Complaints.
Ad damnum clause.
Elimination, §6-5-483.
Contents, §6-5-551.
Damages.
Future damages.
Defined, §6-5-542.
Not to be reduced to
present value,
§6-5-543.
Periodic payment over a
period of years,
§6-5-543.
Itemization, §6-5-543.
Noneconomic losses.
Recovery, §6-5-544.
Definitions, §§6-5-481,
6-5-542.
Dental practitioner.
Defined, §6-5-481.
Dentist.
Defined, §6-5-481.
Degree of care owed to
patient, §6-5-484.
Discovery.
Information subject to
discovery, §6-5-545.
Evidence.
Admissibility.
Evidence at medical
expenses will be
reimbursed, §6-5-545.
No evidence admitted of
medical liability
insurance, §6-5-548.
Burden of proof, §6-5-548.
Rules of evidence in civil
actions preserved,
§6-5-488.
Scintilla rule of evidence
abolished, §6-5-549.
Substantial evidence.
Defined, §6-5-542.
Standard of proof shall be
proof by substantial
evidence, §6-5-549.
Future damages.
Computation, §6-5-543.
Defined, §6-5-542.
Health care provider.
Defined, §6-5-542.
Hospital.
Defined, §6-5-481.
Insurance.
Casualty insurance
generally.
See INSURANCE.
Medical liability insurance,
§§27-26-1 to 27-26-43.
See INSURANCE.
Judgments and settlements.
Filing reports, §34-24-56.
Grounds for suspension or
revocation of license,
§34-24-57.

MALPRACTICE—Cont'd
Judgments and settlements
　—Cont'd
　Limitations.
　　One million dollar limit on
　　　judgments, §6-5-547.
　　Modification, §6-5-543.
　　Notification of article
　　　requirements, §34-24-57.
　　One million dollar limit on
　　　judgments, §6-5-547.
　　Optional method of payment
　　　of judgments in excess of
　　　$100,000, §6-5-486.
　　Payment, §§6-5-486, 6-5-487.
　　Judgments to specify
　　　payment terms,
　　　§6-5-543.
　　Reports, §34-24-56.
　　　Failure to comply with
　　　　requirements,
　　　　§34-24-57.
　　　Notification of article
　　　　requirements,
　　　　§34-24-57.
　　　Review of reports by board,
　　　　§34-24-57.
　　Security.
　　　Requirement to post
　　　　security or provide
　　　　evidence of insurance,
　　　　§6-5-543.
Legal services liability,
　§§6-5-570 to 6-5-581.
　See ATTORNEYS AT LAW.
Licenses.
　Grounds for suspension or
　　revocation, §34-24-57.
Limitation of actions,
　§6-5-482.
Malicious prosecution.
　Cause of action, §6-5-550.
Medical institution.
　Defined, §6-5-481.
Medical liability act.
　Short title, §6-5-480.
Medical liability act of 1987.
　Applicability of article,
　　§6-5-552.
　Construction of article,
　　§6-5-541.
　Intent of legislature,
　　§6-5-540.
　Legislative intent, §6-5-540.
　Short title, §6-5-541.
　Title of article.
　　Short title, §6-5-541.
Medical liability insurance,
　§§27-26-1 to 27-26-43.
　See INSURANCE.
Medical practitioner.
　Defined, §6-5-481.
Noneconomic losses.
　Recovery, §6-5-544.
Osteopaths.
　Suspension or revocation of
　　license, §34-24-360.
Payment.
　Advance payment.
　　Advance payments in
　　　excess of award not
　　　repayable, §6-5-487.
　　Not to be construed as
　　　admission of liability,
　　　§6-5-487.
　Contempt of court.
　　Continuing pattern of
　　　failure to make
　　　payment, §6-5-543.

MALPRACTICE—Cont'd
Payment—Cont'd
　Judgments in excess of
　　$100,000.
　　Optional method, §6-5-486.
　Judgments in excess of
　　$150,000.
　　Judgments to specify terms
　　　of payment, §6-5-543.
　Periodic payments.
　　Termination, §6-5-543.
Periodic payment.
　Defined, §6-5-542.
　Termination, §6-5-543.
Physician.
　Defined, §6-5-481.
　Degree of care owed to
　　patient, §6-5-484.
　Grounds for suspension or
　　revocation of license,
　　§34-24-57.
Professional corporation.
　Defined, §6-5-481.
　Effect of article on
　　professional liability,
　　§10-4-390.
Reports.
　Judgments and settlements,
　　§§34-24-56, 34-24-57.
Review committees.
　Decisions, opinions, etc.,
　　privileged, §34-24-58.
Settlements. See within this
　heading, "Judgments and
　settlements."
Standard of care, §6-5-484.
　Defined, §6-5-542.
Substantial evidence.
　Defined, §6-5-542.
Title of article.
　Short title, §6-5-480.
Venue, §6-5-546.

MALT BEVERAGES, §§28-3-1,
　28-3-45, 28-3-184 to 28-3-187.
　See ALCOHOLIC
　　BEVERAGES.

MAMMALS.
Marine mammal protection,
　§§9-11-390 to 9-11-398.
　See MARINE MAMMAL
　　PROTECTION.

MANDAMUS.
Appeals.
　Judgments on applications
　　for remedial writs,
　　§12-22-6.
　Review in supreme court of
　　decisions of courts of
　　appeals.
　　Rules of appellate
　　　procedure, ARAP, Rule
　　　21.
Commencement by petition,
　§6-6-640.
　Answer thereto, §6-6-640.
　Relief upon issues presented,
　　§6-6-640.
Counties.
　Special tax for payment of
　　principal and interest on
　　bonds and sinking fund
　　payments.
　　Mandamus proceedings,
　　　§11-81-26.
Court of civil appeals.
　Original jurisdiction of court,
　　§12-3-11.

MANDAMUS—Cont'd
Court of civil appeals
　—Cont'd
　Review in supreme court of
　　decisions of courts of
　　appeals.
　　Rules of appellate
　　　procedure, ARAP, Rule
　　　21.
Court of criminal appeals.
　Original jurisdiction of court,
　　§12-3-11.
　Review in supreme court of
　　decisions of courts of
　　appeals.
　　Rules of appellate
　　　procedure, ARAP, Rule
　　　21.
Directed to judge or judges,
　ARAP, Rule 21.
Forms.
　Petition for writ of
　　mandamus, ARAP, Form
　　19.
Fraud.
　Charitable fraud.
　　Enforcement of provisions
　　　by injunction,
　　　mandamus or other
　　　remedy, §13A-9-76.
Income tax.
　Taxes paid through mistake
　　or error.
　　Failure or refusal of
　　　department of revenue
　　　to refund, §40-18-43.
Insurance.
　Holding companies.
　　Petition for mandamus
　　　against commissioner
　　　of insurance,
　　　§27-29-13.
Judges.
　Directed to judge or judges,
　　ARAP, Rule 21.
Municipal corporations.
　Special tax for payment of
　　principal and interest on
　　bonds and sinking fund
　　payments.
　　Mandamus proceedings,
　　　§11-81-26.
Petition for writ, ARAP, Rule
　21.
　Forms, ARAP, Form 19.
Power districts.
　Bond issues.
　　Rights and remedies of
　　　bondholders, §37-5-8.
Rules of appellate
　procedure, ARAP, Rule
　21.
Service of process.
　Petitions, ARAP, Rule 21.
Supreme court.
　Review in supreme court of
　　decisions of courts of
　　appeals, ARAP, Rule 21.
Use tax.
　Writ of mandamus against
　　collection of tax,
　　§40-23-87.
Water management and
　drainage.
　Districts.
　　Default of bonds, §9-9-40.

MANDATORY DISPOSITION
　OF DETAINERS, §§15-9-80
　to 15-9-88.
　See DETAINERS.

MANICURISTS.
See COSMETOLOGISTS.

MANSLAUGHTER.
Class B felony, §13A-6-3.
Elements, §13A-6-3.
Homicide generally.
See HOMICIDE.
Limitations on prosecution.
First degree manslaughter,
§15-3-5.

MANUFACTURED
BUILDINGS, §§24-4A-1 to
24-4A-7.
Definitions, §24-4A-2.
Enforcement of provisions,
§24-4A-4.
Delegation of authority by
department, §24-4A-4.
Exemptions from provisions,
§24-4A-3.
Pre-engineered metal
buildings, §24-4A-7.
Fees.
Defined, §24-4A-2.
Schedule of fees, §24-4A-3.
Fire marshal, §§24-4A-2 to
24-4A-4.
Definition of "department,"
§24-4A-2.
Enforcement of provisions,
§24-4A-4.
Delegation of authority,
§24-4A-4.
Manufactured housing
commission.
Transfer of functions to
commission, §24-6-4.
Powers, §24-4A-3.
Rules and regulations,
§24-4A-4.
Transfer of functions to
commission, §24-6-4.
Injunctions.
Violations of provisions,
§24-4A-5.
Insignia of approval,
§24-4A-3.
Installation.
Definition of "install,"
§24-4A-2.
Modification of units prior to
or during installation,
§24-4A-3.
Legislative declaration,
§24-4A-1.
Local government.
Authority of local
government agencies,
§24-4A-3.
Defined, §24-4A-2.
Manufactured housing
commission, §§24-6-1 to
24-6-4.
Appointment, §24-6-3.
Compensation, §24-6-3.
Composition, §24-6-3.
Contracts, §24-6-4.
Creation, §§24-6-1, 24-6-2.
Duties.
Generally, §24-6-2.
Employees, §24-6-4.
Expenses, §24-6-3.
Fees, §24-6-4.
Functions, §24-6-2.
Transfer from fire
marshal's division,
§24-6-4.
Fund, §24-6-4.
Intent of chapter, §24-6-1.
Meetings, §24-6-3.

MANUFACTURED
BUILDINGS—Cont'd
Manufactured housing
commission—Cont'd
Officers, §24-6-3.
Powers and duties.
Generally, §24-6-2.
Qualifications of members,
§24-6-3.
Rules and regulations,
§24-6-4.
Vacancies in office, §24-6-3.
Mobile homes.
General provisions, §§24-5-1
to 24-5-34.
See MOBILE HOMES.
Penalties.
Violations of provisions,
§24-4A-6.
Permits.
Special permits for
movement of certain site-
built buildings,
§32-9-29.1.
Pre-engineered metal
buildings.
Exemption, §24-4A-7.
Purpose of provisions,
§24-4A-1.
Rules and regulations,
§24-4A-4.
Violations of provisions.
Injunctions, §24-4A-5.
Penalty, §24-4A-6.

MANUFACTURERS.
Alabama extended
manufacturers' liability
act.
General provisions, §§6-5-500
to 6-5-525.
See PRODUCTS
LIABILITY.
Alcoholic beverages.
See ALCOHOLIC
BEVERAGES.
Canals.
Connections to public ways.
Construction and operation
of connections by
manufacturing
corporations, §10-5-13.
Operation outside state and
making extensions
within state by
manufacturing
companies, §10-5-12.
Connections to public ways.
Construction and operation
by manufacturing
corporations, §10-5-13.
Controlled substances.
Manufacturers and
distributors.
See DRUGS.
Cosmetics.
Adulteration and
misbranding.
Effect of possession by
manufacturer of
adulterated or
misbranded cosmetics,
§20-1-54.
Counties.
Promotion of manufacturing
plants, §11-3-11.
County boards of health.
Duties, §22-3-2.

MANUFACTURERS—Cont'd
Drugs.
Adulterated or misbranded
drugs.
Effect of possession by
manufacturer,
§20-1-31.
Controlled substances.
Manufacturers and
distributors.
See DRUGS.
Definition of manufacturers,
§34-23-1.
Permits, §34-23-32.
Easements.
Condemnation for easements,
§10-5-3.
Eminent domain.
Condemnation for rights of
way or easements by
manufacturing
companies, §10-5-3.
Routes and sites.
Rights of condemning
corporations in
selection of routes and
sites, §10-5-8.
Extended manufacturers'
liability.
General provisions, §§6-5-500
to 6-5-525.
See PRODUCTS
LIABILITY.
Fertilizer.
Chapter not to restrict or
avoid sales or exchanges
between manufacturers,
processors, etc., §2-22-23.
Penalty for manufacture of
commercial fertilizer
short in weight,
§2-22-18.
Food.
Adulteration and
misbranding.
Effect of possession by
manufacturers of
adulterated or
misbranded food,
§20-1-31.
Health.
Authority and jurisdiction of
state board of health,
§22-2-2.
Duties of county boards of
health, §22-3-2.
Helmets.
Duties of manufacturers,
§32-5A-245.
Highways.
Connections to public ways.
Construction and operation
of connections by
manufacturing
corporations, §10-5-13.
Industrial alcohol.
Permits for operation of
distilleries and
denaturing plants.
See INDUSTRIAL
ALCOHOL.
Liability.
Extended manufacturers'
liability generally,
§§6-5-500 to 6-5-525.
See PRODUCTS
LIABILITY.
Lime.
See LIME.
Mobile homes.
See MOBILE HOMES.

MANUFACTURERS—Cont'd
Motorcycle helmets.
Duties of manufacturers,
§32-12-42.
Motor vehicles.
Dealings by manufacturers
with dealers, §§8-20-1 to
8-20-12.
See MOTOR VEHICLES.
**Pharmacists and
pharmacies.**
Defined, §34-23-1.
Permit, §34-23-32.
Public ways.
Connections to public ways.
Construction and operation
by manufacturing
corporations, §10-5-13.
Railroads.
Connections to public ways.
Construction and
operations of
connections by
manufacturing
corporations, §10-5-13.
Operation outside state and
making extensions
within state by
manufacturing
companies, §10-5-12.
Rebates.
Officer, agent, etc., of
manufacturing
corporation taking
rebate, §8-11-4.
Rights of way.
Condemnation for rights of
way by manufacturing
companies, §10-5-3.
Ships and shipping.
Certificates of registration
and numbering.
Description of vessel of
manufacturer or dealer
to be omitted from
certificate, §33-5-14.
Operation of transportation
methods for persons or
property by
manufacturing
companies, §10-5-9.
State board of health.
Authority and jurisdiction,
§22-2-2.
Steamships.
Operation of transportation
methods for persons or
property by
manufacturing
companies, §10-5-9.
Tunnels.
Connections to public ways.
Construction and operation
of connections by
manufacturing
corporations, §10-5-13.
Waters and watercourses.
Connections to public ways.
Construction and operation
of connections to
navigable watercourses
by manufacturing
corporations, §10-5-13.

MAPS AND PLATS.
Aerial photographs or maps.
Recording, §§35-2-80 to
35-2-82.
Assessments for taxation.
Plat books.
See TAXATION.

MAPS AND PLATS—Cont'd
Coal mines.
See COAL.
Conveyances.
Town surveys, plats or maps.
Certification,
acknowledgment and
recordation of plat or
map held to be
conveyance, §35-2-51.
Counties.
See COUNTIES.
Division of land surveys.
Production, reproduction or
sale of maps and plats,
§35-2-35.
Education.
School tax district,
§§16-13-192, 16-13-193,
16-13-198.
Eminent domain.
Map or diagram to
accompany complaint,
§18-1A-72.
Evidence.
Prima facie evidence of facts
of general notoriety and
interest, §12-21-108;
ARCP, Rule 44 (g).
Surveyor general of the
United States.
Admissibility of certified
copies of surveyor
general's books, maps
and field notes,
§12-21-36.
Town surveys, plats or maps.
Certification,
acknowledgment and
recordation of plat or
map.
Copies as evidence,
§35-2-51.
Fees.
Probate judges' fees,
§12-19-90.
Flood-prone areas.
Counties.
Land-use management in
flood-prone areas,
§§11-19-1 to 11-19-24.
See COUNTIES.
Highway department.
Preparation, §23-1-40.
Honeybees and apiaries.
Location of apiaries.
Preparation and
maintenance of county
maps, §2-14-8.
Lost or unclaimed property.
Town surveys, maps or plats,
§35-2-56.
Municipal corporations.
Account surveys.
See MUNICIPAL
CORPORATIONS.
Surveys, plats or maps,
§§35-2-1 to 35-2-82.
See MUNICIPAL
CORPORATIONS.
Public lands.
County maps, §9-15-11.
Preparation, §9-15-11.
Sales.
Division of land surveys,
§35-2-35.
Surveys and surveyors.
See SURVEYS AND
SURVEYORS.

MAPS AND PLATS—Cont'd
Taxation.
Assessments.
Plat books, §§40-7-38 to
40-7-41.
See TAXATION.
School tax district,
§§16-13-192, 16-13-193,
16-13-198.

MARATHON CONTESTS.
Prohibited, §13A-14-3.

MARBLE.
Official rock of state, §1-2-14.

MARENGO COUNTY.
Barbers.
Chapter not applicable to
Marengo county,
§34-5-15.
Courthouse.
Bonds for courthouse, Const.
Ala., amd. 264.
**Economic and industrial
development promotion,**
Const. Ala., amd. 429.
Economic development,
Const. Ala., amd. 308.
Industrial development,
Const. Ala., amd. 468.
Establishment of industrial
development corporation,
Const. Ala., amd. 468.
Officers.
Compensation of certain
officers, Const. Ala.,
amd. 265.

MARGARINE, §§20-1-110 to
20-1-113.
See OLEOMARGARINE.

MARIJUANA.
Controlled substances.
Defined, §20-2-2.
General provisions, §§20-2-1
to 20-2-144.
See DRUGS.
Possession, §§13A-12-213,
13A-12-214.

**MARINE AND
TRANSPORTATION
INSURANCE.**
See INSURANCE.

**MARINE ENVIRONMENTAL
SCIENCES
CONSORTIUM,** §§16-45-1
to 16-45-5.
Board of directors, §16-45-4.
Coastal areas.
Permissible uses, §9-7-13.
Corporation.
Consortium constituted body
corporate, §16-45-3.
Directors, §16-45-4.
Management, §16-45-4.
Member institutions.
Annual expenditures by
governing authorities,
§16-45-5.
Contributions by governing
authorities, §16-45-5.
Governing authorities.
Contributions and annual
expenditures, §16-45-5.
Initial member institutions,
§16-45-1.
Officers, §16-45-4.
Organization, §16-45-1.
Purposes, §16-45-2.

MARINE MAMMAL PROTECTION, §§9-11-390 to 9-11-318.

Applicability of article, §9-11-398.

Citation of article.
Short title, §9-11-390.

Commissioner of conservation and natural resources.
Rules and regulations.
Promulgation, §9-11-395.

Definitions, §9-11-391.

Enforcement of article, §9-11-396.

Funding of programs, §9-11-397.

Law enforcement officers.
Enforcement powers, §9-11-396.

Legislative findings, §9-11-392.

Moratorium.
Defined, §9-11-391.
Exceptions, §9-11-393.
Imposition, §9-11-393.

Penalties.
Disposition of moneys arising from fines and forfeitures, §9-11-396.
Violations of article, §9-11-396.

Policy.
Declaration of policy, §9-11-392.

Possession of marine mammals.
Prohibited, §9-11-394.

Prohibited acts, §9-11-394.

Rules and regulations.
Penalties for violations, §9-11-396.
Promulgation, §9-11-395.

Sale of marine mammals.
Prohibited, §9-11-394.

Scope of article, §9-11-398.

Searches and seizures.
Violations of article.
Custody and disposition of equipment, etc., seized, §9-11-396.

Taking of marine mammals.
Moratorium, §§9-11-391, 9-11-393.
Prohibited, §9-11-394.

Title of article, §9-11-390.

Transportation of marine mammals.
Prohibited, §9-11-394.

Violations of article.
Penalties, §9-11-396.

MARINE PILOTS.

General provisions, §§33-4-1 to 33-4-57.
See PILOTS AND PILOTAGE.

MARINE POLICE.

Division, §§33-5-4 to 33-5-6.
Creation, §33-5-4.
Enforcement of chapter, §33-5-6.

Officers.
Powers of peace officers, §33-5-5.

Peace officers.
Marine police officers to have powers of peace officers, §33-5-5.

Personnel, §33-5-4.

Powers of officers, §33-5-5.

MARINE POLICE—Cont'd

Patrol boats.
See MARINE RESOURCES.

MARINE RESOURCES, §§9-12-1 to 9-12-184.

Affidavits.
Boats.
Licenses.
Tonnage of vessel, §9-12-85.

Appeals.
Violation of chapter.
Bonds, §9-12-7.
Procedure, §9-12-6.

Appropriations.
Gulf states marine fisheries compact.
Commission.
Operating expenses, §9-12-184.

Arrests.
Boats.
Captains of vessels to assist, §9-12-3.
Director of division of marine resources.
Authority to make arrests, §9-2-86.
Inspectors.
Boats.
Captains of vessels to assist inspectors, §9-12-3.

Artificial fishing reefs, §§9-12-140 to 9-12-142.

Bait dealer's license.
Shrimp, §§9-12-54.1 to 9-12-54.7. See within this heading, "Licenses."

Boards and commissions.
Fishing reef ship commission, §9-12-142.
Gulf states marine fisheries commission, §§9-12-181 to 9-12-183.

Boats.
Arrests.
Captains of vessels to assist, §9-12-3.
Boarding of boats.
Investigation of compliance with laws, §9-12-31.
Condemnation.
Violation of chapter. See within this heading, "Violation of chapter."
Fees.
Licenses, §§9-12-80, 9-12-93.
Inspections.
Boarding of boats to investigate compliance with laws, §9-12-31.
Captains of vessels to assist inspectors, §9-12-3.
Refusal to open boat for inspection, §9-12-116.
Licenses.
Affidavits.
Tonnage of vessel, §9-12-85.
Fees.
Nonresidents, §9-12-80.
Shrimp boats, §9-12-93.
Nonresidents.
Fees, §9-12-80.

MARINE RESOURCES —Cont'd

Boats—Cont'd
Licenses—Cont'd
Oysters.
Purchase or sale of oysters taken by unlicensed boats, §9-12-64.
Possession, operation or use of unlicensed boat, §9-12-117.
Purchase of shrimp or oysters taken by unlicensed boats, §9-12-64.
Revocation.
Sales to persons failing to comply with provisions of article, §9-12-65.
Sale of shrimp or oysters taken by unlicensed boats, §9-12-64.
Shrimp.
Purchase or sale of shrimp taken by unlicensed boats, §9-12-64.
Taking or carrying shrimp, §9-12-93.
Tonnage of vessel.
Affidavits of applicants for licenses, §9-12-85.
Use of unlicensed boats, §9-12-63.
Nonresidents.
Licenses.
Fees, §9-12-80.
Patrol boats.
Duties, §9-12-29.
Inspectors.
Manning, §9-12-29.
Manning of boats, §9-12-29.
Oysters.
Private oyster reefs, §9-12-30.
Providing by department of conservation and natural resources, §9-12-29.
Sheriffs.
Summoning into service, §9-12-2.
Shrimp.
Bait dealers.
Furnishing boat numbers, §9-12-54.3.
Notice of substitution of boats, §9-12-54.3.
Licenses.
Taking or carrying shrimp, §9-12-93.
Unlicensed boats.
Used to take oysters or shrimp, §9-12-63.
Summoning into service.
Assisting inspectors in making arrests.
Captains of vessels to assist, §9-12-3.
Sheriffs, §9-12-2.
Violation of chapter.
Condemnation and sale of boat and equipment, §§9-12-5, 9-12-7, 9-12-8.

MARINE RESOURCES
—Cont'd

Bonds, surety.
Division.
Director, §9-2-84.
Oysters.
Mechanical rake dredges, etc.
Use by owners and lessees of private reefs, §9-12-37.
Violation of chapter.
Appeals.
Bonds for stay of sale of condemned boats, §9-12-7.
Burden of proof.
Residency, §9-12-1.
Coastal areas.
Division.
Permissible uses, §9-7-13.
General provisions, §§9-7-10 to 9-7-20.
See COASTAL AREAS.
Commercial seafood fishing agreements, §§9-12-160 to 9-12-162.
Commissioner of conservation and natural resources.
Appointment of director of division, §9-2-82.
Powers and duties.
General provisions, §9-2-7.
Rules and regulations.
Promulgation, §9-2-8.
Compact.
Gulf states marine fisheries compact, §§9-12-180 to 9-12-184. See within this heading, "Gulf states marine fisheries compact."
Condemnation.
Violation of chapter.
Boats and equipment, §§9-12-5, 9-12-7, 9-12-8.
Conservation.
Marine environmental sciences consortium, §§16-45-1 to 16-45-4.
Conspiracy.
Evasion of provisions of article, §9-12-116.
Crab catchers.
Licenses, §9-12-124.
Crabs.
Reciprocal agreements as to commercial seafood fishing, §§9-12-160 to 9-12-162.
Dealers.
Fresh saltwater fish.
Licenses.
Revocation.
False reports, §9-12-115.
Reports.
Wholesale dealers, §9-12-115.
Inspections.
Refusal to open place of business for inspection, §9-12-116.
Reports.
Wholesale dealers, §9-12-115.

MARINE RESOURCES
—Cont'd

Dealers—Cont'd
Shrimp bait dealers.
Licenses, §§9-12-54.1 to 9-12-54.7. See within this heading, "Licenses."
Definitions.
Mussels or mollusks, §9-11-370.
Oysters.
Natural oyster reef, §9-12-21.
Seafoods, §9-2-80.
Department of commerce.
Commissioner of the bureau of fisheries.
Cooperation by department of conservation and natural resources, §9-2-4.
Department of conservation and natural resources.
Powers and duties.
Seafood generally, §9-2-4.
Director. See within this heading, "Division."
District courts.
Violation of chapter.
Jurisdiction, §9-12-4.
Division.
Control.
Director, §9-2-82.
Creation, §9-2-81.
Director.
Appointment, §9-2-82.
Arrest.
Authority to arrest, §9-2-86.
Bonds, surety, §9-2-84.
Firearms.
Authority to carry, §9-2-86.
Full-time position, §9-2-83.
Merit system, §9-2-82.
Oath of office, §9-2-83.
Peace officer.
Director constituted peace officer, §9-2-86.
Powers, §9-2-86.
Salaries, §9-2-83.
Supervision of division, §9-2-82.
Duties.
General provisions, §9-2-81.
Employees, §§9-2-81, 9-2-85.
Expenses.
Payment from seafoods fund, §9-2-89.
Inspections.
Authority to inspect, §9-2-86.
Peace officers.
Director and employees constituted, §9-2-86.
Powers.
General provisions, §9-2-86.
Personnel.
Duties, §9-2-85.
General provisions, §9-2-81.
Seizure of illegal items, §9-2-85.
Powers.
General provisions, §9-2-81.

MARINE RESOURCES
—Cont'd

Division—Cont'd
Supervision.
Director, §9-2-82.
Dredges.
Licenses, §9-12-87.
Private reefs.
Owners and lessees, §9-12-37.
Oysters.
Mechanical devices. See within this heading, "Oysters."
Environmental sciences consortium, §§16-45-1 to 16-45-4.
Fees.
Collection, §9-12-66.
Disposition, §9-12-66.
Licenses. See within this heading, "Licenses."
Violation of chapter.
District attorney, §9-12-6.
Sale of condemned boats and equipment.
County treasurer, §9-12-8.
Fish and game.
General provisions, §§9-11-1 to 9-11-457.
See FISH AND GAME.
Fishing reefs. See within this heading, "Reefs."
Funds.
Seafood fund, §§9-2-87 to 9-2-89.
Garfish.
Killing before returning to waters, §9-12-112.
Gill nets.
Licenses.
Recreational gill net license, §9-12-123.
Gulf states marine fisheries compact, §§9-12-180 to 9-12-184.
Authorized, §9-12-180.
Commission, §§9-12-181 to 9-12-183.
Appropriation.
Annual appropriation for operating expenses, §9-12-184.
Expenses.
Annual appropriation, §9-12-184.
Payment of expenses incident to membership, §9-12-183.
Powers.
Supplemental powers, §9-12-182.
Representatives to commission, §9-12-181.
Contents, §9-12-180.
Form, §9-12-180.
Harbors and ports.
General provisions, §§33-1-1 to 33-3-6.
See HARBORS AND PORTS.
Oysters.
Ports of entry, §9-12-28.
Shrimp.
Ports of entry, §9-12-28.

MARINE RESOURCES
—Cont'd
Health.
Shrimp.
Unfit for human
consumption.
Condemnation,
disposition, etc.,
§9-12-47.
Hearings.
Violation of chapter, §9-12-5.
**Illegal tackle or fishing
devices.**
Possession, operation or use,
§9-12-117.
Inspections.
Boats.
Boarding of boats,
§9-12-31.
Captains of vessels to
assist inspectors,
§9-12-3.
Refusal to open boat for
inspection, §9-12-116.
Compliance with laws.
Boarding of boats and
entrance into places of
business, §9-12-31.
Dealers.
Refusal to open place of
business for inspection,
§9-12-116.
Division.
Authority to inspect,
§9-2-86.
Inspectors.
Boats.
Arrests.
Captains of vessels to
assist inspectors,
§9-12-3.
Patrol boats.
Manning, §9-12-29.
Oyster beds, §9-12-126.
Oysters.
Standard measures,
§9-12-27.
Refusal to allow inspections,
§9-12-116.
Shrimp.
Standard measures,
§9-12-27.
Investigations.
Compliance with laws.
Boarding of boats and
entrance into places of
business, §9-12-31.
Leases.
Oysters.
Natural oyster reefs,
§§9-12-21 to 9-12-25.
Licenses, §§9-12-80 to 9-12-94.
Applications.
False statements, §9-1-1.
Bait dealer's license.
Shrimp bait dealers,
§§9-12-54.1 to
9-12-54.7.
Boats. See within this
heading, "Boats."
Borrowing, §9-1-3.
Use of another's license,
§9-1-3.
Crab catchers, §9-12-124.
Dealers.
Fresh saltwater fish.
Revocation, §9-12-115.
Shrimp bait dealers,
§§9-12-54.1 to
9-12-54.7.

MARINE RESOURCES
—Cont'd
Licenses—Cont'd
Disposition of proceeds,
§9-12-120.
Dredges.
Fees, §9-12-87.
Required, §§9-12-37,
9-12-87.
Term of license, §9-12-87.
Fees.
Collection, §9-12-66.
Crab catcher's license,
§9-12-124.
Disposition of fees,
§§9-12-66, 9-12-120.
Dredges, §9-12-87.
Erroneous or excessive
fees.
Refunds, §9-2-25.
Gill nets.
Recreational gill net
license, §9-12-123.
Issuing authorities,
§9-12-119.
Mussels or mollusks,
§§9-11-372 to 9-11-374.
Nets, §9-12-113.
Nonresidents, §9-12-80.
Reciprocal agreements as
to commercial
seafood fishing,
§9-12-161.
Oysters, §§9-12-37, 9-12-87.
Refunds.
Erroneous or excessive
fees, §9-2-25.
Seafood seller's license,
§9-12-125.
Shrimp.
Boats.
Taking or carrying
shrimp, §9-12-93.
Gill nets.
Recreational gill net
license, §9-12-123.
Issuance.
Crab catcher's license,
§9-12-124.
Disposition of proceeds,
§9-12-120.
Execution, §9-12-118.
False statement to officer
issuing, §9-1-1.
Fees.
Issuing authorities,
§9-12-119.
Gill nets.
Recreational gill net
license, §9-12-123.
Persons authorized,
§9-12-118.
Records, §9-12-118.
Reports, §9-12-119.
Seafood seller's license,
§9-12-125.
Lending, §9-1-3.
Mussels or mollusks.
Taking from fresh waters,
§§9-11-370 to 9-11-374.
Nets.
Duration of license,
§9-12-113.
Fees, §9-12-113.
Required, §9-12-113.
Seines, §9-12-113.
Nonresidents. See within this
heading, "Nonresidents."
Oysters.
Dredges, §§9-12-37,
9-12-87.

MARINE RESOURCES
—Cont'd
Licenses—Cont'd
Oysters—Cont'd
Fees.
Dredges, §§9-12-37,
9-12-87.
Taking for commercial
purposes, §9-12-82.
Disposition of proceeds,
§§9-12-82, 9-12-83.
Possession of licenses,
§9-12-94.
Taking for commercial
purposes, §§9-12-82,
9-12-83.
Penalties.
False statements, §9-1-3.
Lending, borrowing, etc.,
§9-1-3.
Reciprocal agreements as to
commercial seafood
fishing, §§9-12-160 to
9-12-162.
Records, §9-12-118.
Reports.
Issuing authorities,
§9-12-119.
Seafood sellers, §9-12-125.
Shrimp.
Bait dealers, §§9-12-54.1 to
9-12-54.7.
Boats.
Taking or carrying
shrimp, §9-12-93.
Fees.
Boats taking or carrying
shrimp, §9-12-93.
Possession of licenses,
§9-12-94.
Shrimp bait dealers,
§§9-12-54.1 to 9-12-54.7.
Areas open to live bait
shrimping, §9-12-54.6.
Boat numbers.
Furnishing numbers by
dealer, §9-12-54.3.
Catching of shrimp.
Persons other than
licensed dealers,
§9-12-54.5.
Where permitted,
§9-12-54.4.
Closed areas.
Rivers, bayous and
creeks permanently
closed, §9-12-54.6.
Expiration date of license,
§9-12-54.2.
Fees.
Nonresident license fee,
§9-12-54.2.
Issuance of license,
§9-12-54.1.
Limitation on quantities to
be taken, §9-12-54.4.
Manner of taking,
§9-12-54.4.
Nonresidents.
Fee for license,
§9-12-54.2.
Notice.
Substitution of boats,
§9-12-54.3.
Numbers of boats.
Dealers to furnish boat
numbers, §9-12-54.3.
Penalties.
Unlicensed live bait
shrimpers,
§9-12-54.1.

MARINE RESOURCES
—Cont'd
Licenses—Cont'd
Shrimp bait dealers—Cont'd
Penalties—Cont'd
Violation of provisions,
§9-12-54.7.
Quantities to be taken.
Limitation on quantities,
§9-12-54.4.
Revocation of license,
§9-12-54.1.
Rivers, bayous and creeks
permanently closed,
§9-12-54.6.
Substitution of boats.
Notice of substitution,
§9-12-54.3.
**Marine environmental
sciences consortium,**
§§16-45-1 to 16-45-4.
Marine mammal protection,
§§9-11-390 to 9-11-398.
See MARINE MAMMAL
PROTECTION.
Mussels or mollusks,
§§9-11-370 to 9-11-374.
Definitions, §9-11-370.
Taking from fresh waters.
Definitions, §9-11-370.
Licenses.
Buyer's license,
§9-11-373.
Catcher's license,
§9-11-372.
Fees.
Buyer's license,
§9-11-373.
Catcher's license,
§9-11-372.
Disposition of proceeds
of sale, §9-11-374.
Nonresidents.
Burden of proof as to
residence, §9-11-370.
Defined, §9-11-370.
Rules and regulations.
Contents, §9-11-371.
Promulgation, §9-11-371.
Natural oyster reefs,
§§9-12-21 to 9-12-25.
Nets.
Lead lines, §§9-12-110 to
9-12-113.
Length, §9-12-111.
Licenses.
Duration of license,
§9-12-113.
Fees, §9-12-113.
Required, §9-12-113.
Mesh.
Size of mesh, §9-12-110.
Oysters.
Seines.
Dragging over public
reefs or private
oyster grounds,
§9-12-26.
Seines.
Lead lines.
Length, §9-12-111.
Licenses, §9-12-113.
Mesh.
Size of mesh, §9-12-110.
Oysters.
Dragging over public
reefs or private
oyster grounds,
§9-12-26.

MARINE RESOURCES
—Cont'd
Nonresidents.
Burden of proof.
Residency, §9-12-1.
Licenses.
Fees, §9-12-80.
Reciprocal agreements as
to commercial
seafood fishing,
§9-12-161.
Shrimp bait dealers,
§9-12-54.2.
Shrimp bait dealers.
Fee for license,
§9-12-54.2.
Mussels or mollusks.
Taking from fresh waters,
§9-11-370.
Persons considered residents
of state, §9-12-1.
Reciprocal agreements as to
commercial seafood
fishing, §§9-12-160 to
9-12-162.
Notice.
Oysters.
Use of rake dredges,
§9-12-40.
Shrimp.
Bait dealers.
Substitution of boats,
§9-12-54.3.
Oaths.
Division.
Director, §9-2-83.
Oysters.
Accounts.
Audit, §9-2-4.
Ameraport offshore harbor
and terminal
commission.
Compensation of oyster
lessees, §33-10-19.
Boats.
Licenses. See within this
heading, "Boats."
Buoys.
Damaging or removing
buoys marking oyster
reefs, §9-12-62.
Closure of oyster beds,
§9-12-126.
Relay of oysters from
closed areas,
§9-12-126.
Costs.
Replanting of public reefs.
Option to pay replanting
costs, §9-12-42.
Culling of oysters.
Disposition of culled
oysters, §9-12-33.
Required, §9-12-33.
Size limits, §9-12-33.
Definitions.
Natural oyster reef,
§9-12-21.
Gathering of oysters.
Nighttime.
Use of mechanical
devices, §9-12-36.
Owners of land fronting
public waters,
§9-12-22.
Inspection of oyster beds,
§9-12-126.

MARINE RESOURCES
—Cont'd
Oysters—Cont'd
Jurisdiction.
Department of
conservation and
natural resources,
§9-2-4.
Leases.
Ameraport offshore harbor
and terminal
commission.
Compensation of oyster
lessees, §33-10-19.
Licenses.
Boats. See within this
heading, "Boats."
Dredges, §§9-12-37,
9-12-87.
Possession of licenses,
§9-12-94.
Taking for commercial
purposes, §§9-12-82,
9-12-83.
Measures.
Inspections, §9-12-27.
Nonstandard measures.
Use for purchase or sale,
§9-12-27.
Standard measures for
oysters, §9-12-27.
Taking of oysters under
three inches long,
§9-12-61.
Mechanical devices.
Bonds, surety.
Use of devices by owners
and lessees of
private reefs,
§9-12-37.
Licenses.
Dredges, §§9-12-37,
9-12-87.
Nighttime.
Taking of oysters at
night, §9-12-36.
Notice of use of rake
dredges, §9-12-40.
Private reefs.
Use of mechanical rake
dredges, etc.,
§9-12-37.
Rake dredges.
Licenses, §§9-12-37,
9-12-87.
Notice of use, §9-12-40.
Private reefs, §9-12-37.
Supervision of taking of
oysters, §9-12-40.
Natural oyster reefs,
§§9-12-21 to 9-12-25.
Defined, §9-12-21.
Leases.
Ameraport offshore
harbor and terminal
commission.
Compensation of oyster
lessees, §33-10-19.
Application, §9-12-24.
Authority, §9-12-24.
Cancellation, §9-12-24.
Riparian bottoms,
§9-12-23.
Disposition of proceeds,
§9-12-24.
Forfeiture, §9-12-24.
Removal of oysters by
lessee, §9-12-25.
Procedure, §9-12-24.

MARINE RESOURCES
—Cont'd
Oysters—Cont'd
Natural oyster reefs—Cont'd
Leases—Cont'd
Regulations for
protection of rights
of lessees, §9-12-25.
Removal of oysters.
Forfeiture of lease,
§9-12-25.
Riparian bottoms.
Cancellation, §9-12-23.
Riparian bottoms.
Cancellation of leases,
§9-12-23.
Nighttime.
Taking oysters at night,
§9-12-36.
Owners of land fronting
public waters.
Right to plant and gather
oysters, §9-12-22.
Patrol boats, §§9-12-29,
9-12-30.
Penalties.
Harvesting oysters from
closed beds, §9-12-126.
Planting of oysters.
Owners of land fronting
public waters,
§9-12-22.
Replanting on public reefs,
§§9-12-42, 9-12-43.
Ports of entry.
Establishment, §9-12-28.
Use of unauthorized ports,
§9-12-28.
Property.
Owners of land fronting
public waters.
Right to plant and
gather oysters,
§9-12-22.
Purchases.
Oysters taken by
unlicensed tongers,
boats, etc., §9-12-64.
Reciprocal agreements as to
commercial seafood
fishing, §§9-12-160 to
9-12-162.
Reefs.
Buoys.
Damaging or removing,
§9-12-62.
Cultivation of public reefs,
§9-12-35.
Department of
conservation and
natural resources.
Jurisdiction and control,
§9-2-4.
Leases.
Natural oyster reefs,
§§9-12-23 to 9-12-25.
Markers.
Damaging or removing,
§9-12-62.
Natural oyster reefs.
Defined, §9-12-21.
Leases, §§9-12-23 to
9-12-25.
Patrol boats.
Patrolling private oyster
reefs, §9-12-30.
Private reefs.
Marking, §9-12-32.
Permits, §9-12-32.
Replanting on private
reefs, §9-12-43.

MARINE RESOURCES
—Cont'd
Oysters—Cont'd
Reefs—Cont'd
Private reefs—Cont'd
Seed oysters.
Location and
disposition of seed
oysters, §9-12-38.
Seines, §9-12-26.
Surveys, §9-12-32.
Tax on oysters.
Oysters harvested for
commercial
purposes, §9-12-44.
Public reefs.
Cost of replanting,
§9-12-42.
Duty to replant,
§9-12-42.
Replanting of oysters,
§9-12-42.
Taking of oysters for
replanting on
private reefs,
§9-12-43.
Seed oysters.
Cultivation of public
reefs, §9-12-35.
Operators of private
reefs utilizing seed
oysters from public
reefs, §9-12-38.
Purchase of seed
oysters from public
reefs, §9-12-39.
Taking from public
reefs, §9-12-34.
Seines, §9-12-26.
Rules and regulations.
Promulgation and
enforcement, §9-2-4.
Seed oysters.
Designation of seed
oyster areas,
§9-12-34.
Seines.
Dragging over public
reefs or private
oyster grounds,
§9-12-26.
Taking of oysters.
Authority to prohibit,
§9-2-4.
Replanting of oysters.
Private reefs.
Taking of oysters from
public reefs,
§9-12-43.
Public reefs.
Duty to replant,
§9-12-42.
Reports.
Oysters caught or sold,
§9-2-4.
Rules and regulations.
Promulgation and
enforcement, §9-2-4.
Sacking, §9-12-67.
Sales.
Oysters taken by
unlicensed boats,
tongers, etc., §9-12-64.
Oysters under three inches
long, §9-12-61.
Sale to persons failing to
comply with provisions
of article, §9-12-65.
Seed oysters.
Cultivation of public reefs,
§9-12-35.

MARINE RESOURCES
—Cont'd
Oysters—Cont'd
Seed oysters—Cont'd
Designation of seed oyster
areas, beds or reefs,
§9-12-34.
Private reefs.
Location and disposition
of seed oysters,
§9-12-38.
Public reefs.
Cultivation of public
reefs, §9-12-35.
Operators of private
reefs utilizing seed
oysters from public
reefs, §9-12-38.
Purchase of seed oysters
from public reefs,
§9-12-39.
Taking from public reefs,
§9-12-34.
Purchase.
Public reefs, §9-12-39.
Size limitation, §9-12-34.
Taking from public reefs,
§9-12-34.
Transplantation of oysters
and shells, §9-12-35.
Seines.
Dragging over public reefs
or private oyster
grounds, §9-12-26.
Size requirements, §9-12-33.
Harvesting of undersized
oysters, §9-12-41.
Seed oysters, §9-12-34.
Taking of oysters under
three inches long,
§9-12-61.
Undersized oysters.
Harvesting, §9-12-41.
Standard measure, §9-12-27.
Surveys.
Private reefs, §9-12-32.
Tagging, §9-12-67.
Taxation.
Private reefs.
Tax on oysters harvested
from private reefs,
§9-12-44.
Transplantation of oysters
and shells, §9-12-35.
Beyond boundaries of state.
Regulation of
transportation,
§9-12-50.
Boats. See within this
heading, "Boats."
Violations.
Prosecution, §9-12-66.
Patrol boats, §§9-12-29,
9-12-30.
Penalties.
Collection, §9-12-66.
Disposition, §9-12-66.
Imposition of fine, §9-12-5.
Licenses, §9-1-3.
Oysters.
Culling of oysters,
§9-12-33.
Harvesting oysters from
closed beds, §9-12-126.
Replanting oysters.
Public reefs, §9-12-42.
Taking for commercial
purposes.
Violation of provisions,
§9-12-82.

MARINE RESOURCES
—Cont'd
Penalties—Cont'd
Possession or operation of
unlicensed boats or
vessels, §9-12-117.
Possession or use of illegal
tackle or fishing devices,
§9-12-117.
Shrimp.
Bait dealer's license.
Violation of provisions,
§§9-12-54.1,
9-12-54.7.
Trawls.
Commercial shrimp
trawling in waters
closed, §9-12-122.
Violation of article,
§9-12-121.
Permits.
Reefs.
Private reefs, §9-12-32.
Police.
Director and employees of
division constituted as
peace officers, §9-2-86.
General provisions, §§33-5-4
to 33-5-6.
Patrol boats, §§9-12-29,
9-12-30.
Ports of entry, §9-12-28.
Posse comitatus.
Sheriffs.
Summoning into service,
§9-12-2.
**Reciprocal agreements as to
commercial seafood
fishing,** §§9-12-160 to
9-12-162.
Authorized, §9-12-160.
Licenses.
Fees.
Nonresidents, §9-12-161.
Nonresidents.
License fees, §9-12-161.
Rights and privileges.
Exercise in accordance
with Alabama laws,
§9-12-162.
Records.
Licenses.
Issuance, §9-12-118.
Reefs.
Artificial fishing reefs.
Establishment in offshore
waters, §§9-12-140 to
9-12-142.
Fishing reef ship
commission.
Generally, §9-12-142.
Sale or barter of
salvageable parts of
liberty ships.
Approval of
transactions,
§9-12-141.
Authorized, §9-12-140.
Disposition of proceeds,
§9-12-140.
Form of transactions,
§9-12-141.
Informal solicitation of
bids, §9-12-141.
Solicitation of bids,
§9-12-141.
Buoys.
Damaging or removing,
§9-12-62.
Fishing reef ship commission,
§9-12-142.

MARINE RESOURCES
—Cont'd
Reefs—Cont'd
Markers.
Damaging or removing,
§9-12-62.
Natural oyster reefs. See
within this heading,
"Oysters."
Oyster reefs. See within this
heading, "Oysters."
Private reefs.
Marking, §9-12-32.
Permits.
Agents and permittees to
carry permits,
§9-12-32.
Filing lists of agents and
permittees, §9-12-32.
Plats.
Filing, §9-12-32.
Surveys, §9-12-32.
Reports.
Dealers.
Wholesale dealers,
§9-12-115.
Licenses.
Issuing authorities,
§9-12-119.
Oysters caught or sold,
§9-2-4.
Shrimp.
Report of shrimp caught or
sold, §9-2-4.
Residence.
Burden of proof, §9-12-1.
Retail dealers. See within this
heading, "Dealers."
Right of entry.
Investigation of compliance
with laws.
Boarding of boats and
entrance into places of
business, §9-12-31.
Rules and regulations.
Mussels or mollusks.
Taking from fresh waters,
§9-11-371.
Promulgation.
Commissioner, §9-2-8.
Department of
conservation and
natural resources,
§9-2-4.
Publication and distribution,
§9-2-8.
Salaries.
Director of division, §9-2-83.
Sales.
Oysters. See within this
heading, "Oysters."
Shrimp. See within this
heading, "Shrimp."
Violation of chapter.
Condemnation and sale of
boats and equipment,
§§9-12-5, 9-12-7,
9-12-8.
Seafood.
Control of seafood, §9-12-20.
Defined, §9-2-80.
Fund, §§9-2-87 to 9-2-89.
Collections.
Remittance to state
treasurer, §9-2-88.
Composition, §9-2-87.
Creation, §9-2-87.
Credit of seafood fund.
Remittance of collections
to credit of fund,
§9-2-88.

MARINE RESOURCES
—Cont'd
Seafood—Cont'd
Fund—Cont'd
Disbursement, §9-2-89.
Expenditures, §9-2-89.
Use of fund, §9-2-89.
Mussels or mollusks. See
within this heading,
"Mussels or mollusks."
Ownership, §9-12-20.
Oysters. See within this
heading, "Oysters."
Property of state, §9-12-20.
Shrimp. See within this
heading, "Shrimp."
Seafood fund, §§9-2-87 to
9-2-89.
Seafood sellers.
Licenses, §9-12-125.
Searches and seizures.
Division employees.
Seizure of illegal items,
§9-2-85.
Violation of chapter.
Condemnation and sale of
boats and equipment,
§§9-12-5, 9-12-7,
9-12-8.
Seasons.
Authority to establish.
Department of
conservation and
natural resources,
§9-2-4.
Seed oysters. See within this
heading, "Oysters."
Seines. See within this
heading, "Nets."
Sheriffs.
Posse comitatus.
Summoning into service,
§9-12-2.
Shrimp.
Bait dealer's license,
§§9-12-54.1 to 9-12-54.7.
Boats.
Licenses.
Generally. See within
this heading,
"Boats."
Taking or carrying
shrimp, §9-12-93.
Unlicensed boats.
Use for taking shrimp,
§9-12-63.
Canning.
Tax on shrimp canned
within state, §9-12-51.
Condemnation.
Shrimp not fit for human
consumption, §9-12-47.
Importation of shrimp,
§9-12-49.
Licenses.
Bait dealer's license,
§§9-12-54.1 to
9-12-54.7.
Boats.
Generally. See within
this heading,
"Boats."
Taking or carrying
shrimp, §9-12-93.
Possession of licenses,
§9-12-94.
Measures.
Inspections, §9-12-27.

MARINE RESOURCES
—Cont'd
Shrimp—Cont'd
Measures—Cont'd
Nonstandard measures.
Possession and use for
purchase or sale,
§9-12-27.
Standard measures,
§9-12-27.
Packing or processing.
Tax on shrimp processed in
state, §9-12-51.
Ports of entry.
Establishment, §9-12-28.
Use of unauthorized ports,
§9-12-28.
Purchases.
Shrimp taken by
unlicensed tongers,
boats, etc., §9-12-64.
Reciprocal agreements as to
commercial seafood
fishing, §§9-12-160 to
9-12-162.
Reports, §9-2-4.
Rules and regulations.
Promulgation, §9-2-4.
Sales.
Sales to persons failing to
comply with article,
§9-12-65.
Shrimp taken by
unlicensed tongers,
boats, etc., §9-12-64.
Taxation.
Sale for commercial
purposes, §9-12-51.
Unfit for human
consumption, §9-12-47.
Weights and measures.
Minimum weight of
shrimp, §9-12-46.
Taxation.
Canning, drying or
shipping within state,
§9-12-51.
Payment of tax, §9-12-54.
Sale for commercial
purposes, §9-12-51.
Shrimp not to be exported,
§9-12-53.
Transportation to other
states, §9-12-52.
Transportation.
Beyond boundaries of state.
Regulation of
transportation,
§9-12-50.
Licenses.
Boats, §9-12-93.
Taxation.
Shrimp taken for
transportation to
other states,
§9-12-52.
Unfit for human
consumption, §9-12-47.
Trawls.
Commercial shrimp
trawling in waters
closed.
Confiscation and
forfeiture of trawls,
§9-12-122.
Penalty, §9-12-122.
Unfit for human
consumption.
Condemnation, §9-12-47.
Disposition of shrimp,
§9-12-47.

MARINE RESOURCES
—Cont'd
Shrimp—Cont'd
Weights and measures.
Measures.
Standard measures,
§9-12-27.
Minimum weight
requirement, §9-12-46.
Importation of shrimp
into state, §9-12-49.
Nonconforming shrimp.
Possession, sale, etc.,
§9-12-46.
Statutes.
Commissioner.
Publication and
distribution, §9-2-8.
Surveys.
Private reefs.
Surveys and markings,
§9-12-32.
Taxation.
Collection of taxes, §9-12-66.
Disposition of taxes,
§9-12-66.
Oysters.
Private reefs.
Tax on oysters harvested
from private reefs
for commercial
purposes, §9-12-44.
Payment of tax, §9-12-54.
Shrimp.
Canning, drying or
shipping within state,
§9-12-51.
Payment of tax, §9-12-54.
Sales.
Commercial purposes,
§9-12-51.
Tax on shrimp not to be
exported, §9-12-53.
Transportation.
Shrimp taken for
transportation to
other states,
§9-12-52.
Terrapins.
Tax on terrapins caught
for commercial
purposes, §9-12-45.
Terrapins.
Size requirements, §9-12-45.
Taxation.
Terrapins caught for
commercial purposes,
§9-12-45.
Undersized terrapins.
Possession, §9-12-45.
Transportation.
Oysters. See within this
heading, "Oysters."
Shrimp. See within this
heading, "Shrimp."
Turtles, §9-12-45.
Violation of chapter.
Appeals.
Bonds.
Stay of sale of
condemned boat,
§9-12-7.
Procedure, §9-12-6.
Right of appeal, §9-12-6.
Condemnation of boats and
equipment, §9-12-5.
Sale.
Bonds for stay of sale,
§9-12-7.
Disposition of proceeds,
§9-12-8.

MARINE RESOURCES
—Cont'd
Violation of chapter—Cont'd
Condemnation of boats and
equipment—Cont'd
Sale—Cont'd
Fees.
County treasurer,
§9-12-8.
Procedure, §9-12-8.
Conspiracy to evade
provisions, §9-12-116.
Costs.
Affirmation of judgment,
§9-12-6.
Discharge of accused,
§9-12-5.
District attorneys.
Fee, §9-12-6.
District courts.
Jurisdiction, §9-12-4.
Witnesses.
Summoning, §9-12-4.
Fees.
District attorney, §9-12-6.
Sale of condemned boats
and equipment.
County treasurer,
§9-12-8.
Hearings, §9-12-5.
Jurisdiction.
District courts, §9-12-4.
Penalties.
Collection, §9-12-66.
Disposition, §9-12-66.
Imposition of fine, §9-12-5.
Proceedings conducted in
name of state, §9-12-6.
Prosecution, §9-12-66.
Witnesses.
Summoning, §9-12-4.
Weapons.
Authority to carry firearms,
§9-2-86.
Weights and measures.
Oysters, §§9-12-27, 9-12-61.
Shrimp, §9-12-27.
Wholesale dealers. See within
this heading, "Dealers."
Witnesses.
Violation of chapter.
Summoning of witnesses,
§9-12-4.

MARION COUNTY.
Bond issues.
Refunding of certain
securities by certain
municipalities, Const.
Ala., amd. 246.
Economic development.
Municipalities in Marion
county, Const. Ala., amd.
84.
Health facilities.
Bonds, etc., for health
facilities, Const. Ala.,
amd. 75.
Hospitals.
Bonds, etc., for hospital
purposes, Const. Ala.,
amd. 75.
Special tax for hospital
purposes, Const. Ala.,
amd. 69.
**Junior college for Marion
county,** §§16-60-20 to
16-60-40.
See JUNIOR COLLEGES.

MARION COUNTY—Cont'd
Refunding of securities by certain municipalities,
Const. Ala., amd. 246.
School tax.
Special district tax for Hamilton special school district, Const. Ala., amd. 329.
Special property taxes for school purposes, Const. Ala., amd. 205.
Trade schools.
Conversion of junior college for Franklin, Marion and Winston counties to trade school and junior college, §§16-60-38 to 16-60-40.
Water supply and waterworks.
Public water authority. Creation authorized, Const. Ala., amd. 490.

MARKERS.
Monuments and markers.
See MONUMENTS AND MARKERS.

MARKETS.
Agricultural markets.
See AGRICULTURE.
County boards of health.
Duties, §22-3-2.
Farmers' markets.
Authority, §§2-5-1 to 2-5-17.
See AGRICULTURE.
Handicapped persons.
Products produced by handicapped.
Powers of department of adult blind and deaf as to marketing of products, §21-2-1.
Health.
Duties of county boards of health, §22-3-2.
Livestock, §§2-15-60 to 2-15-96.
See LIVESTOCK.
Sundays.
Holding and trading therein on Sunday, §13A-12-2.

MARKET VALUE.
Commercial code, §§7-2-723, 7-2-724.
Evidence.
Testimony as to market value, §12-21-114.

MARRIAGE.
Abatement, revival and survival of actions.
Actions by or against unmarried women not abated upon marriage, §6-5-460.
Adultery, §13A-13-2.
Age.
Minimum age for contracting marriage, §30-1-4.
Alimony, §§30-2-1 to 30-2-55.
See DIVORCE AND ALIMONY.
Annulment of marriage.
Default judgments.
Proof required despite default, ARCP, Rule 55 (e).

MARRIAGE—Cont'd
Annulment of marriage —Cont'd
Wills.
Effect of annulment, §43-8-252.
Revocation of will by annulment, §43-8-137.
Bastards.
See ILLEGITIMACY.
Bigamy, §13A-13-1.
Indictments.
Form, §15-8-150.
Blood tests.
Venereal disease, §22-11A-15.
Certificates.
Corrections, §22-9-6.
Errors.
Correction, §30-1-16.
Evidence.
Certificate deemed presumptive evidence, §30-1-13.
Examination of certificates, §22-9-7.
Forms, §22-9-6.
Furnishing, §22-9-7.
Issuance, §30-1-13.
Failure to issue, §30-1-14.
Records, §§22-9-50, 30-1-13.
Vital statistics.
See VITAL STATISTICS.
Child custody and support, §§30-3-1 to 30-3-99.
See MINORS.
Consanguinity.
Incestuous marriages, §§30-1-3, 30-1-6.
Consent.
Parental consent, §30-1-5.
Contracts.
Breach of contract to marry.
Exemptions from liability, §6-5-330.
Conveyances.
Personal property conveyed in consideration of marriage.
Necessary recordation, §35-4-93.
Recitation of marital status of grantor or vendor required, §35-4-73.
Deeds.
Recitation of marital status of grantor or vendor required, §35-4-73.
Desertion and nonsupport, §§30-4-50 to 30-4-65.
See DESERTION AND NONSUPPORT.
District attorney.
Offenses.
Probate judge to notify district attorney of offenses under chapter, §30-1-18.
Divorce and alimony, §§30-2-1 to 30-2-55.
See DIVORCE AND ALIMONY.
Dower.
See DOWER.
Evidence.
Certificates.
Marriage certificate deemed presumptive evidence of facts, §30-1-13.

MARRIAGE—Cont'd
Evidence—Cont'd
Certified registers of marriages, §12-21-101.
Licenses.
Register of licenses deemed presumptive evidence of facts, §30-1-12.
Fees.
Performance of marriages, §30-1-8.
Probate judges' fees, §12-19-90.
Fraud.
Agreements upon consideration of marriage void unless in writing, §8-9-2.
Guardian and ward.
Uniform guardianship and protective proceedings act.
Minors.
Termination of appointment of guardians, §26-2A-79.
Illegitimacy.
See ILLEGITIMACY.
Incestuous marriages.
Illegitimacy.
Issue not deemed illegitimate, §30-1-3.
Solemnization of marriage of parties within prohibited degrees.
Penalty, §30-1-6.
Kinship.
Incestuous marriages, §§30-1-3, 30-1-6.
Legitimation of children, §§20-11-1 to 20-11-3.
Licenses.
Application.
Errors.
Correction, §30-1-16.
Certificates. See within this heading, "Certificates."
Duration of licenses, §30-1-9.
Errors.
Correction, §30-1-16.
Evidence.
Register of licenses deemed presumptive evidence, §30-1-12.
Expiration of licenses, §30-1-9.
Issuance, §30-1-9.
Minors.
Penalty for issuance of marriage license to minor contrary to provisions of chapter, §30-1-10.
Penalties.
Minors.
Issuance of marriage license to minor contrary to provisions of chapter, §30-1-10.
Solemnization of marriage without license, §§30-1-9, 30-1-11.
Records, §§22-9-50, 30-1-12.
Solemnization of marriage without license, §§30-1-9, 30-1-11.
Syphilis examination for marriage license.
Generally, §22-11A-15.

MARRIAGE—Cont'd
Licenses—Cont'd
Void license.
Solemnization of marriage, §30-1-9.
Minimum age for contracting marriage, §30-1-4.
Minors.
Licenses.
Issuance of marriage license to minor contrary to provisions of chapter.
Penalty, §30-1-10.
Minimum age for contracting marriage, §30-1-4.
Parental consent, §30-1-5.
Solemnization of marriage of parties under age of consent.
Penalty, §30-1-6.
Miscegenation laws, Const. Ala., art. IV, §102.
Nonsupport.
General provisions, §§30-4-50 to 30-4-65.
See DESERTION AND NONSUPPORT.
Offenses.
Certificates.
Failure to issue, §30-1-14.
District attorney.
Probate judge to notify district attorney of offenses under chapter, §30-1-18.
Licenses.
Issuance to minor contrary to provisions of chapter, §30-1-10.
Solemnization of marriages.
Void license, §30-1-9.
Without license, §30-1-9.
Penalty, §30-1-11.
Solemnization of marriages.
Licenses.
Void licenses, §30-1-9.
Without licenses, §30-1-11.
Penalty, §30-1-11.
Parties under age of consent, §30-1-6.
Parties within prohibited degrees, §30-1-6.
Parental consent for marriage of certain minors, §30-1-5.
Parent and child.
Relationship not dependent upon marriage, §26-17-3.
Penalties. See within this heading, "Offenses."
Personal property.
Conveyed in consideration of marriage.
Recordation necessary as to purchasers, mortgagees and judgment creditors, §35-4-93.
Property of wife, §§30-4-1 to 30-4-16.
See HUSBAND AND WIFE.
Recordation.
Personal property conveyed in consideration of marriage.
Necessary recordation, §35-4-93.

MARRIAGE—Cont'd
Recordation—Cont'd
Recitation of marital status of grantor or vendor required, §35-4-73.
Records.
Certificate, §§22-9-50, 30-1-13.
Errors.
Correction, §30-1-17.
Evidence.
Certified registers of marriages, §12-21-101.
Licenses, §§22-9-50, 30-1-12.
Relatives.
Incestuous marriages, §§30-1-3, 30-1-6.
Remarriage.
Termination of alimony, §30-2-55.
Remarriage after divorce.
See DIVORCE AND ALIMONY.
Settlements.
Recordation of conveyance of personal property in consideration of marriage, §35-4-93.
Solemnization.
Incestuous marriages, §30-1-6.
Licenses.
Penalty for solemnization of marriage without license, §30-1-11.
Void licenses, §30-1-9.
Minors, §30-1-6.
Persons authorized to solemnize marriages, §30-1-7.
Support and maintenance.
General provisions.
See SUPPORT AND MAINTENANCE.
Syphilis.
Licenses.
Examination for syphilis as prerequisiste for marriage license, §22-11A-15.
Uniform reciprocal enforcement of support act, §§30-4-80 to 30-4-98.
See DESERTION AND NONSUPPORT.
Venereal diseases.
Licenses.
Syphilis examination for marriage license, §22-11A-15.
Vital statistics.
General provisions, §§22-9-1 to 22-9-79.
See VITAL STATISTICS.
Wills.
Annulment of marriage.
Effect of, §43-8-252.
Revocation of will by annulment, §43-8-137.
Remarriage.
Revival of will, §43-8-137.
Workmen's compensation.
Dependents.
Compensation to cease upon death or marriage of dependent, §25-5-69.

MARRIED WOMEN.
Dower.
See DOWER.

MARRIED WOMEN—Cont'd
Executors and administrators.
Letters testamentary.
Issuance to married women, §43-2-23.
Supplemental letters for married women upon removal of disability, §43-2-24.
Property of wife, §§30-4-1 to 30-4-16.
Savings and loan associations.
Accounts, §5-16-43.
Veterans.
Educational benefits.
See VETERANS.

MARSHALL COUNTY.
Annexation, Const. Ala., amd. 469.
Court costs and charges, Const. Ala., amd. 215.
Fires and fire prevention.
Forest fire protection, Const. Ala., amd. 439.
Motor fuel.
License tax on selling, etc., Const. Ala., amd. 66.
Officers.
Fees, etc., Const. Ala., amd. 215.
School tax.
Special property tax for public school buildings, Const. Ala., amd. 101.

MARSHALS.
Court of civil appeals, §12-3-19.
Court of criminal appeals, §12-3-19.
Forest wardens.
Designation as forest wardens, §9-13-5.
State fire marshals, §§36-19-1 to 36-19-29.

MARTS.
Products marts.
See PRODUCTS MARTS.

MASONIC LODGES.
Licenses.
Exemptions.
Alabama Masonic Home, §40-9-12.
Taxation.
Exemptions from taxation.
Alabama Masonic Home, §40-9-12.

MASTER AND SERVANT.
Agents.
See AGENTS.
General provisions.
See EMPLOYERS AND EMPLOYEES.
Labor.
See LABOR.

MASTERS.
Appointment, ARCP, Rule 53 (a).
Compensation, ARCP, Rule 53 (a).
Meetings, ARCP, Rule 53 (d).
Powers, ARCP, Rule 53 (c).
Proceedings, ARCP, Rule 53 (d).
Reference to master, ARCP, Rule 53 (b).
Reports, ARCP, Rule 53 (e).

MASTERS—Cont'd
Statement of accounts,
ARCP, Rule 53 (d).
**When reference to master
made,** ARCP, Rule 53 (b).
Witnesses, ARCP, Rule 53 (d).

MATERIALMEN'S LIENS,
§§35-11-210 to 35-11-234.
See MECHANICS' AND
MATERIALMEN'S LIENS.

**MATTRESSES AND
BEDDING.**
Destruction.
Nuisances menacing public
health.
Summary destruction
without compensation,
§22-10-3.
Health.
Nuisances menacing public
health, §§22-10-1 to
22-10-3.
Jails.
Furnishing of bedding,
§§14-6-19, 14-6-93.
**Nuisances menacing public
health,** §§22-10-1 to
22-10-3.

**MAYFAIR TOWERS
CORPORATION.**
Taxation.
Exemption from taxation,
§40-9-26.

MAYHEM.
Indictments.
Form of indictment,
§15-8-150.

MAYORS.
See MUNICIPAL
CORPORATIONS.

MEASLES.
Notifiable diseases,
§§22-11A-1 to 22-11A-38.

MEASURES.
General provisions, §§8-16-1
to 8-16-123.
See WEIGHTS AND
MEASURES.

**MEAT AND MEAT
PRODUCTS,** §§2-17-1 to
2-17-38.
Accounts.
False statements or entries,
§2-17-34.
Actions.
Evidence of violations of
chapter or regulations.
Admissibility of evidence of
violations in civil
actions for damages,
§2-17-31.
Adulteration.
Condemnation proceedings,
§2-17-19.
Destruction of adulterated
carcasses, §2-17-4.
Detention of carcasses, meat
food products, etc.,
believed to be
adulterated, §2-17-18.
Inspections.
Refusal or withdrawal of
inspection, §2-17-20.
Marking, stamping, etc.,
prohibited where food
products adulterated,
§2-17-11.

**MEAT AND MEAT
PRODUCTS**—Cont'd
Adulteration—Cont'd
Removal of official marks
from adulterated
products prior to release,
§2-17-18.
Brands and marks.
Misbranding, §§2-17-18 to
2-17-20.
Official marks. See within
this heading, "Marking."
Cans.
Labels, §2-17-10.
**Carcasses of slaughtered
animals.**
Inspections. See within this
heading, "Inspections."
Labels, §2-17-4.
Horses, mules, etc.,
§2-17-15.
Misbranding.
Detention of misbranded
carcasses, §2-17-18.
Certificates.
False statements in
certificates, §2-17-14.
**Commissioner of agriculture
and industries.**
Cooperation with other
governmental branches
and agencies, §2-17-25.
Enforcement of subpoenas
and orders, §2-17-24.
Information obtained by
commissioner.
Disclosure by state officer
or employee without
proper authority,
§2-17-36.
Inspections.
Temporary orders of
commissioner,
§2-17-21.
Jurisdiction of commissioner.
Exclusive as to activities
covered by chapter,
§2-17-25.
Secretary of agriculture.
Designation and powers of
commissioner as state
agency for cooperation
with secretary of
agriculture, §2-17-25.
Subpoenas.
Failure to attend and
testify or produce
evidence, §2-17-33.
Issuance, §2-17-24.
Witnesses.
Failure to attend and
testify, §2-17-33.
Powers of commissioner as
to witnesses, §2-17-24.
Condemnation.
Destruction of condemned
carcasses, §2-17-4.
Generally, §2-17-19.
Construction of chapter,
§2-17-38.
Containers.
Labels, §2-17-10.
Damages.
Evidence of violations of
chapter or regulations.
Admissibility, §2-17-31.
Dead livestock.
Compliance with regulations
of commissioner for
prevention of use for
human food, §2-17-8.

**MEAT AND MEAT
PRODUCTS**—Cont'd
Dead livestock—Cont'd
Inspections. See within this
heading, "Inspections."
Registration of persons,
firms, etc., buying,
selling, transporting,
etc., §2-17-7.
Definitions, §2-17-1.
Destruction.
Adulterated carcasses,
§2-17-4.
Condemned meat food
products, §2-17-9.
Nuisances menacing public
health.
Summary destruction of
property without
compensation,
§22-10-3.
Diseased livestock.
Condemnation, §2-17-19.
Persons, firms, etc., buying,
selling, etc.
Compliance with
regulations of
commissioner for
prevention of use for
human food purposes,
§2-17-8.
Registration, §2-17-7.
Separate slaughter, §2-17-3.
Diseased or unsound meats.
Inspection.
Provision for inspections by
municipal
corporations,
§11-47-136.
Sales.
Prohibition by municipal
corporations,
§11-47-136.
Evidence.
Mutilation, alteration, etc., of
documentary evidence,
§2-17-34.
Violations of chapter or
regulations.
Admissibility, §2-17-31.
Foreign beef.
Purchase with public funds
of beef not raised and
produced within United
States, §2-1-7.
Forgery and counterfeiting.
Official marks, §2-17-14.
Handling.
Rules and regulations.
Promulgation of
regulations as to
handling of carcasses,
meats, etc., §2-17-22.
Injunctions, §2-17-30.
Inspections.
Advisory council, §2-17-26.
Applicability of chapter.
Certain provisions,
§2-17-27.
Carcasses of slaughtered
animals, §§2-17-3,
2-17-4.
Applicability of provisions
as to inspection,
§2-17-5.
Limitation of entry of
carcasses into
establishments
inspected under
chapter, §2-17-5.
Reinspection, §2-17-4.

MEAT AND MEAT PRODUCTS—Cont'd
Inspections—Cont'd
Commissioner of agriculture and industries.
Temporary orders of commissioner, §2-17-21.
Condemnation.
Generally, §2-17-19.
Construction of chapter, §§2-17-2, 2-17-38.
Definitions, §2-17-1.
Exemption of certain activities, §2-17-27.
Federal meat inspection act.
Applicability of chapter to persons, firms, etc., regulated, §2-17-29.
Food products, §2-17-9.
Implementation of chapter.
Regulations for implementation, promulgation, approval, etc., §2-17-21.
Injunctive proceedings under chapter or regulations, §2-17-30.
Inspectors.
Appointment by commissioner, §2-17-16.
Duties, §2-17-16.
Interference with persons performing official duties, §2-17-32.
Legislative findings of fact and declaration of policy, §2-17-2.
Misbranding.
Refusal or withdrawal of inspectors, §2-17-20.
Misrepresentations, §2-17-14.
Municipal corporations, §11-47-136.
Charges for inspection, §11-43-59.
Inspections for other municipalities, §11-47-139.
Penalties for violations of chapter, §2-17-37.
Persons, firms, etc., regulated under federal meat inspection act, §2-17-29.
Prior to slaughter, §2-17-3.
Processing establishments.
See within this heading, "Processing establishments."
Products not intended for human food.
Inspection not to be provided, §2-17-6.
Purpose of chapter, §2-17-2.
Rabbits.
Domestically raised and slaughtered, etc., for human consumption, §§2-17A-1 to 2-17A-5.
Records, §2-17-23.
Rules and regulations, §2-17-16.
Federal regulations.
Regulations promulgated under certain federal acts, §2-17-2.

MEAT AND MEAT PRODUCTS—Cont'd
Inspections—Cont'd
Rules and regulations —Cont'd
Implementation of chapter.
Promulgation, approval, etc., of regulations for implementation, §2-17-21.
Violations, §§2-17-13, 2-17-30, 2-17-31.
Slaughter.
Generally, §§2-17-3 to 2-17-5.
Slaughterhouses, §§2-17-11, 2-17-12.
Refusal or withdrawal of inspection, §2-17-20.
United States department of agriculture.
Exemption of meat, etc., inspected and passed by department, §2-17-28.
Violations of chapter or regulations, §2-17-13.
Admissibility, §2-17-31.
Penalties, §2-17-37.
Intrastate commerce.
Investigations.
Organizations engaged in intrastate commerce, §2-17-24.
Reports.
Requirement of organizations, etc., engaged in intrastate commerce, §2-17-24.
Labels.
Cans, pots, tins, etc., §2-17-10.
Carcasses of slaughtered animals, §2-17-4.
Horses, mules, etc., §2-17-15.
False or misleading labeling, §2-17-10.
Food products, §2-17-9.
Horses, mules, etc.
Labels showing derivations.
Sale, transportation, etc., of carcasses without labels, §2-17-15.
Misbranding. See within this heading, "Misbranding."
Unauthorized casting, printing, etc., of device or label containing official mark, §2-17-14.
Marking.
Adulteration.
Marking, stamping, etc., prohibited where food products adulterated, §2-17-11.
Horses, mules, etc.
Carcasses not marked to show derivation, §2-17-15.
Official marks.
Forgery, §2-17-14.
Refusal to allow markings, stamping, etc., where sanitary conditions adulterate product, §2-17-11.

MEAT AND MEAT PRODUCTS—Cont'd
Marking—Cont'd
Official marks—Cont'd
Removal from detained, adulterated or misbranded carcasses, meat food products, etc., prior to release, §2-17-18.
Unauthorized casting, printing, etc., of device or label containing official mark or simulation, §2-17-14.
Unauthorized use, §2-17-14.
Misbranding, §§2-17-18 to 2-17-20.
Condemnation proceedings, §2-17-19.
Detention of carcasses, meat food products, etc., believed to be misbranded, §2-17-18.
Inspections.
Refusal or withdrawal of inspection, §2-17-20.
Removal of official marks from misbranded products, §2-17-18.
Misrepresentation.
Inspections, §2-17-14.
Municipal corporations.
Diseased or unsound meats.
Sales.
Prohibition of sale, etc., §11-47-136.
Fresh meats.
Regulation of sale, etc., §11-47-138.
Inspections, §11-47-136.
Charges for inspection, §11-43-59.
Inspections for other municipalities, §11-47-139.
Regulation of sales, §§11-47-137, 11-47-138.
Nuisances menacing public health, §§22-10-1 to 22-10-3.
Official marks. See within this heading, "Marking."
Penalties.
Violations of chapter, §2-17-37.
Poultry.
See POULTRY.
Processing establishments.
Days and hours when processing to be done.
Designation, §2-17-12.
Horses, mules, etc., to be prepared in facilities separated from those in which cattle, sheep, swine, etc., are prepared, §2-17-15.
Inspections.
Animals prepared, §2-17-12.
Assignment of inspectors, §2-17-12.
Refusal or withdrawal of inspection, §2-17-20.
Sanitary conditions, §2-17-11.

MEAT AND MEAT PRODUCTS—Cont'd

Processing establishments —Cont'd

Separate facilities.
　Horses, mules, etc., to be prepared in facilities separated from those in which cattle, sheep, swine, etc., are prepared, §2-17-15.

Public officers.

Disclosure of information obtained by commissioner without proper authority, §2-17-36.

Rabbits, §§2-17A-1 to 2-17A-5.

Domestic rabbits.
　Authority of commissioner to contract with federal government, §2-17A-5.

Funds.
　Administration of chapter provisions, §2-17A-5.

Inspections.
　Contract for inspection services by department of agriculture and industries, §2-17A-3.
　Fees for services, §2-17A-3.
　Voluntary unless otherwise provided by congress, §2-17A-4.

Rules and regulations.
　Minimum standards, §2-17A-2.
　Promulgation, §2-17A-2.

Slaughter, etc., for domestic consumption in compliance with chapter, §2-17A-1.

Records.

Classes of persons, firms, etc., required to maintain records, §2-17-23.
Examination, §2-17-23.
Inspections, §2-17-23.

Registration.

Persons, firms, etc., buying, selling, etc., dead, dying, diseased, etc., livestock, §2-17-7.

Reports.

Failure to file annual or special reports, §2-17-35.
False statements or entries, §2-17-34.

Rules and regulations, §2-17-16.

Establishments handling food, §22-20-5.
Federal regulations.
　Adoption and promulgation, §2-17-2.
Handling, §§2-17-22, 22-20-5.
Implementation of chapter, §2-17-21.
Injunctive proceedings under regulations, jurisdiction and prosecution, §2-17-30.
Penalties for violations, §2-17-37.

MEAT AND MEAT PRODUCTS—Cont'd

Rules and regulations —Cont'd

Rabbits.
　Slaughter, processing, inspection, etc., for domestic consumption, §2-17A-2.
Violations, §2-17-13.
　Admissibility of evidence of violations in civil actions for damages, §2-17-31.
　Penalties, §2-17-37.

Sales.

Municipal corporations.
　Regulation by municipal corporations, §§11-47-137, 11-47-138.
Unlawful acts, §§2-17-13, 11-47-136.

Slaughter.

Diseased livestock.
　Separate slaughter, §2-17-3.
Exemption of certain activities from provisions of chapter by commissioner, §2-17-27.
Inspections.
　Carcasses of slaughtered animals, §§2-17-3 to 2-17-5.
　Reinspection, §2-17-4.
　Prior to slaughter, §2-17-3.
Unlawful acts, §2-17-13.

Slaughterhouses.

Days and hours when slaughtering to be done. Designation, §2-17-12.
Horses, mules, etc., to be prepared in facilities separated from those in which cattle, sheep, swine, etc., prepared, §2-17-15.
Inspections.
　Animals slaughtered, §2-17-12.
　Assignment of inspectors, §2-17-12.
　Refusal or withdrawal of inspection, §2-17-20.
　Sanitary conditions, §2-17-11.
Sanitary conditions.
　Inspections, §2-17-11.
Separate facilities.
　Horses, mules, etc., to be prepared in facilities separated from those in which cattle, sheep, swine, etc., are prepared, §2-17-15.

Storage.

Rules and regulations.
　Promulgation of regulations as to storage of carcasses, meats, etc., §2-17-22.

Subpoenas.

Failure to attend and testify or produce documentary evidence in obedience to subpoena, §2-17-33.
Issuance by commissioner, §2-17-24.

Tins.

Labels, §2-17-10.

MEAT AND MEAT PRODUCTS—Cont'd

Transportation of animals, etc.

Unlawful acts, §2-17-13.

United States.

Department of agriculture.
　Exemption of meat inspected and passed by United States department of agriculture, §2-17-28.

Violations of chapter, §2-17-13.

Admissibility of evidence of violations in civil actions for damages, §2-17-31.
Penalties, §2-17-37.

Witnesses.

Commissioner of agriculture and industries.
　Powers of commissioner as to witnesses, §2-17-24.
Failure to attend and testify, §2-17-33.
Generally, §2-17-24.

MECHANICS' AND MATERIALMEN'S LIENS, §§35-11-210 to 35-11-234.

Acknowledgments.

Satisfaction of lien, §35-11-231.

Actions.

Enforcement of liens. See within this heading, "Enforcement of liens."

Assignments, §35-11-233.

Bonds, surety.

Transfer of lien on real property to other security.
　Requirements as to bond, §35-11-233.

Commencement of actions.

Enforcement of liens, §35-11-222.

Contractors.

Original contractor. See within this heading, "Original contractor."
Subcontractors.
　Effect of failure to pay subcontractors, §35-11-219.

Death.

Actions against personal representatives, §35-11-230.
Actions by personal representatives, §35-11-229.

Declaration of lien, §35-11-210.

Default judgments.

Enforcement of liens, §35-11-225.

Definitions.

Owner or proprietor, §35-11-232.

Enforcement of liens, §§35-11-220 to 35-11-230.

Commencement of action, §35-11-222.
Death.
　Actions against personal representatives, §35-11-230.
　Actions by personal representatives, §35-11-229.

**MECHANICS' AND
MATERIALMEN'S LIENS**
—Cont'd
Enforcement of liens—Cont'd
Default judgment,
§35-11-225.
Employees, etc., of
contractor.
Actions by employees, etc.,
§35-11-227.
Defense by contractor,
§35-11-227.
Executors and
administrators.
Actions against personal
representatives,
§35-11-230.
Actions by personal
representatives,
§35-11-229.
Finding or verdict,
§35-11-224.
How action commenced,
§35-11-222.
Issues, §35-11-224.
Judgment, §§35-11-224 to
35-11-226.
Jurisdiction of actions for
enforcement, §35-11-220.
Limitation of actions,
§35-11-221.
Parties, §35-11-223.
Personal representatives.
Actions against personal
representatives,
§35-11-230.
Actions by personal
representatives,
§35-11-229.
Pleadings, §35-11-222.
Practice, §35-11-222.
Proceedings, §35-11-222.
Verdict, §35-11-224.
**Executors and
administrators.**
Actions against personal
representatives,
§35-11-230.
Actions by personal
representatives,
§35-11-229.
Fees.
Verified statement.
Indorsement and
recordation by probate
judge, §35-11-216.
Forfeiture of lien.
Failure to pay materialmen,
laborers, employees and
subcontractors,
§35-11-219.
Forms.
Verified statement,
§35-11-213.
Homestead exemptions.
Not barred by homestead
exemptions, Const. Ala.,
art. X, §207.
Indorsements.
Verified statement.
Indorsement by probate
judge, §35-11-216.
Judgments.
Default judgment,
§35-11-225.
Enforcement of judgments,
§35-11-226.
Generally, §35-11-224.
Jurisdiction.
Actions for enforcement of
liens, §35-11-220.

**MECHANICS' AND
MATERIALMEN'S LIENS**
—Cont'd
Landlord and tenant.
Building or improvement on
leased land, §35-11-212.
Leases.
Building or improvement on
leased land, §35-11-212.
Liens generally.
See LIENS.
Limitation of actions,
§35-11-221.
**List of materialmen, laborers
and employees,**
§35-11-219.
More than one lot.
Selection of land to be
charged, §35-11-217.
**Mortgages and deeds of
trust.**
Priority of mechanics' and
materialmen's liens,
§35-11-211.
Notice.
Lien claimed by persons
other than original
contractor, §35-11-218.
Materialmen's notice to
owner or proprietor,
§35-11-210.
Original contractor.
Actions by employees, etc., to
enforce lien.
Defense by contractor,
§35-11-227.
Forfeiture of lien.
Effect of failure to pay
materialmen, etc.,
§35-11-219.
Lien claimed by persons
other than original
contractor.
Notice, §35-11-218.
List of materialmen, laborers
and employees,
§35-11-219.
Priority of liens arising
under division,
§35-11-228.
Owner.
Defined, §35-11-232.
Parties.
Enforcement of liens,
§35-11-223.
Perfection.
Verified statement,
§35-11-213.
Pleadings.
Enforcement of liens,
§35-11-222.
Priorities, §35-11-211.
Liens arising under division,
§35-11-228.
Proceeds.
Distribution of proceeds,
§35-11-228.
Proprietor.
Defined, §35-11-232.
Real property.
Transfer of lien on real
property to other
security, §35-11-233.
Recordation.
Verified statement,
§35-11-216.
Satisfaction of liens.
Acknowledgment of
satisfaction, §35-11-231.
**Selection of land to be
charged,** §35-11-217.

**MECHANICS' AND
MATERIALMEN'S LIENS**
—Cont'd
Statement.
Verified statement,
§§35-11-213 to 35-11-216.
Streets.
Liens.
Improvements on public
streets, etc.,
§§35-11-410 to
35-11-417.
See HIGHWAYS.
Subcontractors.
Effect of failure to pay
subcontractors,
§35-11-219.
Subdivisions.
Selection of land to be
charged, §35-11-217.
Subrogation, §35-11-234.
**Transfer of lien on real
property to other
security,** §35-11-233.
Verdict.
Enforcement of liens,
§35-11-224.
Verified statement,
§§35-11-213 to 35-11-216.
Contents, §35-11-213.
Duty to file, §35-11-213.
Fee.
Indorsement and
recordation fee,
§35-11-216.
Filing.
Duty to file, §35-11-213.
Time for filing, §35-11-215.
Form, §35-11-213.
Indorsement by probate
judge, §35-11-216.
Oath, §35-11-213.
How oath administered out
of state, §35-11-214.
Probate judge.
Indorsement by probate
judge, §35-11-216.
Recordation, §35-11-216.
Time for filing, §35-11-215.

MEDICAID PROGRAM,
§§22-6-1 to 22-6-9.
See HEALTH.

**MEDICAL ASSOCIATION OF
ALABAMA.**
Constitutes state board of
health, §22-2-1.

MEDICAL CLINIC BOARDS,
§§11-58-1 to 11-58-15.
See MUNICIPAL
CORPORATIONS.

MEDICAL EXAMINER.
Coroners.
See CORONERS.
Diseases.
Notifiable diseases.
General provisions,
§§22-11A-1 to
22-11A-38.
See DISEASES.
State toxicologist.
See STATE
TOXICOLOGIST.

MEDICAL LIABILITY ACT.
Malpractice generally,
§§6-5-480 to 6-5-488,
6-5-540 to 6-5-552.
See MALPRACTICE.

MEDICAL LIABILITY INSURANCE, §§27-26-1 to 27-26-43.
See INSURANCE.

MEDICAL SCHOOLS.
Anatomical gifts.
See ANATOMICAL GIFTS.
Distribution of unclaimed bodies for scientific study.
See DEAD BODIES.
Meharry medical college, §16-3-35.
University of Alabama school of medicine, §§16-47-90 to 16-47-128.
See UNIVERSITY OF ALABAMA.

MEDICAL TECHNICIANS, §§34-18-1 to 34-18-47.
Board of medical technicians examiners.
Annulment or revocation of certificate.
Power of board, §34-18-24.
Appointment of members, §34-18-41.
Compensation of members, §34-18-47.
Composition of board, §34-18-40.
Enforcement of chapter.
Fund for enforcement of chapter, §34-18-47.
Expenses of members, §34-18-47.
Funds.
Secretary-treasurer to receive and disburse, §34-18-45.
Use of fees collected, §34-18-47.
Governor.
Appointment of board members, §34-18-41.
Vacancies.
Filling vacancies, §34-18-42.
Meetings.
Generally, §34-18-46.
Notice of meetings, §34-18-46.
Record of meetings, §34-18-44.
Special meetings, §34-18-46.
Officers of board, §34-18-43.
Qualifications of members, §34-18-40.
Quorum, §34-18-46.
Records.
Meetings, §34-18-44.
Reports.
Annual report to board, §34-18-45.
Rules and regulations.
Promulgation by board, §34-18-43.
Seal, §34-18-43.
Secretary-treasurer.
Annual report to board, §34-18-45.
Bond, §34-18-45.
Receipt and disbursement of funds, §34-18-45.
Salary, §34-18-47.
Terms of office, §34-18-42.
Vacancies.
Filling vacancies, §34-18-42.

MEDICAL TECHNICIANS
—Cont'd
Bonds, surety.
Secretary-treasurer of board, §34-18-45.
Certificates of registration.
See within this heading, "Registration."
Definitions, §34-18-1.
Registered medical technician, §34-18-20.
Examinations, §§34-18-21, 34-18-22.
Fees.
Receipt and disbursement by secretary-treasurer of board, §34-18-45.
Registration without examination, §34-18-22.
Reinstatement of certificate, §34-18-25.
Renewal of certificate, §34-18-25.
Use of funds by board, §34-18-47.
Fraud.
False representation in obtaining certificate, §34-18-3.
Funds.
Receipt and disbursements by secretary-treasurer, §34-18-45.
Use of funds by board, §34-18-47.
Governor.
Appointing board of medical technicians examiners, §34-18-41.
Notice.
Annulment or revocation of certificate.
Notice of charges, §34-18-24.
Board to announce meetings, §34-18-46.
Penalties.
Violations of chapter, §34-18-3.
Registration.
Annulment or revocation of certificate, §34-18-24.
Certificate.
Annulment or revocation of certificate, §34-18-24.
False representation in obtaining, §34-18-3.
Form of certificate, §34-18-23.
Reinstatement of certificate, §34-18-25.
Renewal of certificate, §34-18-25.
Seal of board to be affixed, §34-18-23.
Educational prerequisites, §34-18-21.
Examination, §34-18-21.
Registration without examination, §34-18-22.
Fees.
Registration without examination, §34-18-22.
Reinstatement of certificate, §34-18-25.
Renewal of certificate, §34-18-25.
Qualifications of applicants, §34-18-21.

MEDICAL TECHNICIANS
—Cont'd
Registration—Cont'd
Registered medical technician.
Defined, §34-18-20.
Register of applicants, §34-18-44.
Required, §34-18-20.
Schools.
Educational prerequisites of applicants, §34-18-21.
Waiver of examination requirements, §34-18-22.
Schools.
Educational prerequisites of applicants for registration, §34-18-21.
Training schools, §34-18-2.
Unauthorized practice as medical technician.
Failure to obtain certificate, §34-18-20.
Penalty, §34-18-3.

MEDICINE.
Drugs.
See DRUGS.
Pharmacists and pharmacies, §§34-23-1 to 34-23-118.
See PHARMACISTS AND PHARMACIES.
Physicians.
General provisions, §§34-24- to 34-24-384.
See PHYSICIANS.

MEHARRY MEDICAL COLLEGE.
Contracts for education of Alabama students, §16-3-35.
State board of education.
Contracts for education of Alabama students, §16-3-35.

MELLORINE, §§20-1-130 to 20-1-137.
Adulteration, §20-1-137.
Advertising.
False and misleading advertising, §20-1-136.
Containers.
When container deemed misbranded, §20-1-135.
Definitions, §§20-1-130, 20-1-132.
False advertising, §20-1-136.
Fees.
Permit fee, §20-1-133.
Imitations, §20-1-137.
Labels.
Requirements as to labeling, §20-1-135.
Manufacturers.
Permits, §20-1-133.
Misbranding, §20-1-137.
Sale or offer for sale of misbranded mellorine, §20-1-137.
When package or container deemed misbranded, §20-1-135.
Misleading advertising, §20-1-136.
Packaging.
Permits, §20-1-133.
When package deemed misbranded, §20-1-135.
Permits, §20-1-133.

MELLORINE—Cont'd

Purpose of article, §20-1-131.
Sales.
Adulterated or misbranded mellorine, §20-1-137.
Permits, §20-1-133.
Requirements as to sale, §20-1-134.
Standards, §20-1-132.

MEMORIALS.

Cemeteries.
General provisions, §§11-17-1 to 11-17-16.
See CEMETERIES.
Confederacy, §§9-2-104, 9-2-105.
White house of the confederacy, §§41-12-1 to 41-12-3.
Gorgas memorial board, §41-9-220.
Hobson memorial board, §41-9-222.
State parks.
Monuments and historic sites, §§9-14-1 to 9-14-3.
White House of the Confederacy, §§41-12-1 to 41-12-3.

MENINGITIS.

Notifiable diseases, §§22-11A-1 to 22-11A-38.
See DISEASES.

MEN'S HALL OF FAME,

§§41-9-850 to 41-9-853.
Board.
Appointment.
Governor, §41-9-850.
Chairman, §41-9-850.
Composition, §41-9-850.
Created, §41-9-850.
Governor.
Appointment, §41-9-850.
Meetings, §41-9-850.
Quorum, §41-9-850.
Secretary, §41-9-850.
Terms of office, §41-9-850.
Vacancies in office.
Filling, §41-9-850.
Gifts.
Donations, contributions and gifts.
Exemption from taxation, §41-9-853.
Items pertaining to hall of fame.
Housed at location of hall of fame, §41-9-851.
Location, §41-9-851.
Purposes, §41-9-852.
Selection of persons to be installed, §41-9-852.
Taxation.
Donations, contributions and gifts.
Exemption, §41-9-853.

MENTAL HEALTH CAPITAL OUTLAY OVERSIGHT COMMISSION.

Approval of appropriations, §22-50-25.
Compensation of members, §22-50-25.
Composition, §22-50-25.
Creation, §22-50-25.
Meetings, §22-50-25.
Members, §22-50-25.
Appointment, §22-50-25.
Compensation, §22-50-25.

MENTAL HEALTH CAPITAL OUTLAY OVERSIGHT COMMISSION—Cont'd

Quorum, §22-50-25.
Term, §22-50-25.
Vacancy, §22-50-25.

MENTAL HEALTH FINANCE AUTHORITY, §§41-10-350 to 41-10-371.

Actions.
Power to sue and be sued, §41-10-356.
Attorneys at law.
Power to employ attorneys, §41-10-356.
Auctions and auctioneers.
Bond issues.
Sale of bonds at public auction, §41-10-360.
Bids and bidding.
Bond issues.
Sale of bonds, §41-10-360.
Bond issues.
Amount, §41-10-357.
Auctions.
Sale of bonds at public auction, §41-10-360.
Bids and bidding.
Sale of bonds, §41-10-360.
Community facilities.
Designation of bonds for community facilities, §41-10-359.
Definition of "bonds," §41-10-351.
Delivery of bonds, §41-10-359.
Deposits of state funds.
Bonds as security for, §41-10-362.
Execution of bonds, §41-10-359.
Federal income tax.
Exemption of interest on bonds.
Power of authority to pay and make agreements for exemption, §41-10-371.
Interest, §41-10-358.
Federal income tax.
Exemption.
Power of authority to pay and make agreements for exemption, §41-10-371.
Liability of authority upon bonds, §41-10-361.
Maturity, §41-10-358.
Negotiable instruments, §41-10-361.
Notice.
Sale of bonds, §41-10-360.
Obligations of state.
Bonds do not create, §41-10-366.
Payment of principal and interest.
Pledge for, §41-10-361.
Sinking fund for, §41-10-365.
State treasurer, §41-10-370.
Pledge for payment of principal and interest, §41-10-361.
Power to issue bonds, §§41-10-356, 41-10-357.

MENTAL HEALTH FINANCE AUTHORITY—Cont'd

Bond issues—Cont'd
Proceeds.
Investment of surplus proceeds, §41-10-367.
Mental health facilities building fund, §41-10-364.
Refunding bonds, §41-10-363.
Surplus proceeds.
Investment, §41-10-367.
Use.
Restrictions, §41-10-357.
Recital that bonds issued pursuant to provisions, §41-10-360.
Records.
Payment of principal and interest.
State treasurer, §41-10-370.
Redemption, §41-10-358.
Refunding bonds, §41-10-363.
Sale of bonds, §41-10-360.
Signatures.
Execution of bonds, §41-10-359.
Sinking fund for payment of principal and interest, §41-10-365.
Taxation.
Exemption, §41-10-362.
Terms and conditions of bonds, §41-10-358.
Trust funds.
Investment in bonds, §41-10-362.
Commissioner of mental health and mental retardation.
Definition of "commissioner," §41-10-351.
Community facilities.
Bond issues.
Designation of bonds for community facilities, §41-10-359.
Defined, §41-10-351.
Contracts.
Obligations of state.
Contracts do not create, §41-10-366.
Power to contract, §41-10-356.
Debts.
Bond issues.
Debts of state not created, §41-10-366.
Contracts.
Debts of state not created, §41-10-366.
Definitions, §41-10-351.
Department of mental health and mental retardation.
Definition of "department," §41-10-351.
Directors.
Defined, §41-10-351.
Meetings, §41-10-355.
Members of authority to constitute board of directors, §41-10-355.
Quorum, §41-10-355.
Dissolution of authority, §41-10-369.
Evidence.
Record of proceedings, §41-10-355.

MENTAL HEALTH FINANCE AUTHORITY—Cont'd
Funds.
Mental health facilities building fund, §41-10-364.
Sinking fund for payment of principal and interest on bonds, §41-10-365.
Incorporation of authority.
Application for authority to incorporate, §41-10-353.
Authorized, §41-10-352.
Certificate of incorporation, §41-10-354.
Interest.
Bond issues, §41-10-358.
Investments.
Bond issues.
Surplus proceeds from sale of bonds, §41-10-367.
Trust funds.
Investment in bonds, §41-10-362.
Permitted investments.
Defined, §41-10-351.
Legislative findings, §41-10-350.
Members of authority, §§41-10-352, 41-10-355.
Negotiable instruments.
Bond issues.
Deemed negotiable instruments, §41-10-361.
Nonprofit corporation, §41-10-368.
Notice.
Bond issues.
Sale of bonds, §41-10-360.
Officers, §41-10-355.
Powers, §41-10-356.
Property.
Dissolution of authority.
Disposition of property upon, §41-10-369.
Powers as to property, §41-10-356.
Publication.
Bond issues.
Sale of bonds.
Notice of sale, §41-10-360.
Purpose of provisions, §41-10-350.
Records.
Bond issues.
Payment of principal and interest.
State treasurer, §41-10-370.
Proceedings of authority, §41-10-355.
Seals and sealed instruments.
Power to have and alter corporate seal, §41-10-356.
Secretary of state.
Incorporation of authority.
Application for authority to incorporate.
Presented to secretary of state, §41-10-353.
Certificate of incorporation.
Issuance, §41-10-354.
Signatures.
Bond issues.
Execution of bonds, §41-10-359.

MENTAL HEALTH FINANCE AUTHORITY—Cont'd
State treasurer.
Bond issues.
Payment of principal and interest, §41-10-370.
Records, §41-10-370.
Status.
Nonprofit corporation, §41-10-368.
Taxation.
Exemptions from taxation.
Bonds and income of authority, §41-10-362.
Federal income tax.
Interest on bonds.
Power of authority to pay and make agreements for exemption, §41-10-371.

MENTALLY ILL.
Actions.
Regional mental health programs and facilities.
Officers.
Liability of officers of nonprofit organizations, §§10-11-1 to 10-11-5.
Admission to institutions.
Commitment, §§22-52-1 to 22-52-37, 22-52-70 to 22-52-72. See within this heading, "Commitment."
Mentally retarded.
Generally, §§22-52-51 to 22-52-56. See within this heading, "Mental retardation."
Juvenile proceedings, §§12-15-70, 12-15-90.
Adult protective services, §§38-9-1 to 38-9-11.
See ADULT PROTECTIVE SERVICES.
Appeals.
Commitment.
Involuntary commitment, §22-52-15.
Persons accused of crimes.
Appeals from orders of probate courts as to commitment, §22-52-37.
Department of mental health and mental retardation.
Judicial review of final order or decision of department, §22-50-19.
Involuntary commitment, §22-52-15.
Attorney general, Const. Ala., art. V, §136.
Attorneys at law.
Commitment.
Costs.
Payment of costs, §22-52-14.
Involuntary commitment.
Appointment by probate judge, §22-52-5.
Appointment of attorney for person sought to be committed, §22-52-4.
Employment by petitioners, §22-52-5.
Payment of fees, §22-52-14.

MENTALLY ILL—Cont'd
Attorneys at law—Cont'd
Commitment—Cont'd
Payment of costs, §22-52-14.
Criminal law and procedure.
Release of criminal psychopaths.
Appointed counsel, §15-16-65.
Bail and recognizance.
Execution for acknowledgment of undertaking, §15-13-23.
Bank deposits and collections.
Incompetence of customer.
Authority of payor or collecting bank, §7-4-405.
Bonds, surety.
Support of persons in state mental institutions, §§22-53-5, 22-53-26.
Capital expenditures.
Mental health capital outlay oversight commission, §22-50-25.
Commercial code.
Bank deposits and collections.
Incompetence of customer.
Authority of payor or collecting bank, §7-4-405.
Commercial paper.
Defenses against holder in due course, §7-3-305.
Negotiation effective although subject to rescission, §7-3-207.
Commitment, §§22-52-1 to 22-52-37, 22-52-70 to 22-52-72.
Acquittal on ground of insanity.
Proceedings for commitment of person in custody of department, §22-52-33.
Appeals.
Involuntary commitment, §22-52-15.
Persons accused of crimes.
Appeals from orders of probate courts as to commitment, §22-52-37.
Attorneys at law.
Costs.
Payment of costs, §22-52-14.
Examinations.
Involuntary commitment.
Ordering of examinations of person sought to be committed, §22-52-7.
Federal agencies, §22-52-13.
Habeas corpus.
General provisions, §§15-21-1 to 15-21-34.
See HABEAS CORPUS.
Hearings.
Involuntary commitment, §§22-52-6, 22-52-8, 22-52-9.
Persons accused of crimes, §22-52-35.

MENTALLY ILL—Cont'd
Commitment—Cont'd
Involuntary commitment,
  §§22-52-1 to 22-52-17.
Appeals, §22-52-15.
Applicability of article,
  §22-52-16.
Attorneys at law.
  Appointment by probate
    judge to appear in
    support of petition,
    §22-52-5.
  Appointment for person
    sought to be
    committed, §22-52-4.
  Employment by
    petitioners of
    attorney to appear in
    support of petition,
    §22-52-5.
  Payment of fees,
    §22-52-14.
Confinement when
  treatment for mental
  illness unavailable,
  §22-52-10.
Conveyance of person
  committed to custody
  of department,
  §22-52-12.
Costs.
  Payment of costs,
    §22-52-14.
Examinations.
  Ordering, etc., of
    examinations of
    person sought to be
    committed, §22-52-7.
Expenses of conveyance of
  person committed,
  §22-52-12.
Facilities.
  Notification of probate
    judge of facility to
    which person should
    be sent if committed,
    §22-52-6.
Federal agencies,
  §22-52-13.
Guardian ad litem.
  Appointment for person
    sought to be
    committed, §22-52-4.
Hearings.
  Conduct of hearings,
    §22-52-9.
  Date of final hearing,
    §22-52-6.
  Final hearings, §22-52-8.
    Date, §22-52-6.
  Probable cause hearings,
    §22-52-8.
Jurisdiction.
  Retention by probate
    court over person
    committed,
    §22-52-11.
Limitations upon liberty of
  person sought to be
  committed.
  Imposition of limitations
    pending hearings,
    §22-52-7.
  Restrictions on
    imposition, §22-52-7.

MENTALLY ILL—Cont'd
Commitment—Cont'd
Involuntary commitment
  —Cont'd
Mental evaluations.
  Facilities other than
    department of
    mental health and
    mental retardation
    not required to
    perform, §22-52-17.
Mental retardation. See
  within this heading,
  "Mental retardation."
Minors.
  Juvenile proceedings,
    §§12-11-10, 12-15-90.
Order by probate judge.
  Entry of orders setting
    forth findings,
    granting petition
    and committing
    person to custody of
    department of
    mental health,
    §22-52-10.
Payment of costs,
  §22-52-14.
Petition for involuntary
  commitment, §§22-52-1
  to 22-52-6, 22-52-10.
  Appointment of attorney
    to appear in support
    of petition, §22-52-5.
  Contents, §22-52-1.
  Dismissal, §22-52-2.
  Employment by
    petitioners of
    attorney to appear in
    support of petition,
    §22-52-5.
  Examination of
    petitioner, §22-52-2.
  Filing with probate
    judge, §22-52-1.
  Findings by probate
    judge, §22-52-10.
  Granting or denial,
    §22-52-10.
  Notification of
    department of
    mental health of
    filing, §22-52-6.
  Reading of petition to
    person sought to be
    committed, §22-52-4.
  Review by probate judge,
    §22-52-2.
  Service upon person
    sought to be
    committed, §22-52-3.
Reports as to progress of
  person committed.
  Facilities to report to
    probate judge,
    §22-52-12.
Retention of jurisdiction by
  probate court over
  person committed,
  §22-52-11.
Veterans' administration,
  §22-52-13.
Judges.
  Special probate judges.
    Persons accused of
      crimes, §§22-52-35,
      22-52-36.
Minors, §§12-15-31, 12-15-70,
  12-15-90.

MENTALLY ILL—Cont'd
Commitment—Cont'd
Persons accused of crimes,
  §§15-16-30 to 15-16-43.
Acquittal on grounds of
  insanity.
  Ordering acquitted
    person to state
    hospital, §15-16-43.
  Final hearing,
    §15-16-42.
  Hearing,
    determination of
    necessity for
    hearings,
    §15-16-41.
Proceedings for
  commitment of
  persons in custody of
  department,
  §22-52-33.
Appeals from orders,
  §22-52-37.
Charges nolle prossed or
  dismissed, §22-52-32.
Conduct of proceedings.
  Standards of conduct,
    §22-52-37.
Definitions, §22-52-30.
Dismissal or nolle prossed
  of charges, §22-52-32.
Effect of commitment upon
  statute of limitations,
  §22-52-31.
Hearings.
  Appointment of special
    probate judges for
    hearing, §22-52-35.
  Incapable of standing trial,
    §22-52-31.
  Minimum standards for
    civil commitment,
    §22-52-37.
Not guilty by reason of
  insanity.
  Proceedings for
    commitment,
    §22-52-33.
Orders.
  Appeals from orders,
    §22-52-37.
  Appointment of special
    probate judges for
    entry of orders,
    §22-52-35.
Proceedings for
  commitment,
  §22-52-31.
Proceedings where persons
  found competent to
  stand trial or charges
  nolle prossed or
  dismissed, §22-52-32.
Reevaluation.
  Proceedings for
    reevaluation of
    certain persons in
    custody of
    department,
    §22-52-34.
Special probate judges.
  Appointment for
    consideration,
    hearing and entry of
    orders pertaining to
    commitment,
    §22-52-35.
  Compensation,
    §22-52-36.
  Powers, §22-52-35.
  Qualifications, §22-52-35.

MENTALLY ILL—Cont'd
  Commitment—Cont'd
    Persons accused of crimes
        —Cont'd
      Standards for conduct of
          proceedings, §22-52-37.
      Statute of limitations.
        Effect of commitment
            upon statute,
            §22-52-31.
      Transfer.
        Proceedings for transfer
            of certain persons in
            custody of
            department,
            §22-52-34.
    Petitions.
      Involuntary commitment,
          §§22-52-1 to 22-52-6,
          22-52-10.
    Prisoners.
      Generally, §§22-52-70 to
          22-52-72.
      Investigation of insanity of
          certain confined
          persons, §§15-16-20 to
          15-16-23.
      Procedure for commitment
          to mental health
          facility, §22-52-70.
      Security medical facility,
          §§22-54-1 to 22-54-5.
    Procedures for commitment
        not affected by article,
        §22-50-18.
    Release.
      Procedures for release not
          affected by chapter,
          §22-50-18.
    Security medical facility.
      Applicability of
          commitment statutes
          to patients at facility,
          §22-54-4.
    Veterans' administration,
        §22-52-13.
  Compacts.
    Interstate compact on mental
        health, §§22-55-1 to
        22-55-4.
  Conflict of laws.
    Repeal of conflicting laws,
        §22-50-24.
  Consent for health services.
    General provisions, §§22-8-1
        to 22-8-9.
      See HEALTH.
    Persons deemed incapable of
        consent, §13A-6-70.
  Conservators.
    Incapacitated persons.
      General provisions,
          §§26-2-48 to 26-2-50.
      Removal of person or
          property of minors and
          wards, §§26-8-1 to
          26-8-52.
        See GUARDIAN AND
            WARD.
    Uniform guardianship and
        protective proceedings
        act, §§26-2A-1 to
        26-2A-160.
      See GUARDIAN AND
          WARD.

MENTALLY ILL—Cont'd
  Constitution of Alabama.
    Bond issues.
      Bond issues for acquisition,
          improvement, etc., of
          mental health
          facilities, Const. Ala.,
          amds. 266, 340.
      Building construction and
          improvement purposes
          at Alabama state
          hospitals and Partlow
          state school for mental
          deficients, Const. Ala.,
          amds. 113, 118.
    Governor.
      Procedure when governor
          or acting governor
          appears to be of
          unsound mind, Const.
          Ala., art. V, §128.
    University of Alabama
        medical center.
      Bond issue for mental
          hospital, Const. Ala.,
          amd. 141.
  Contracts.
    Necessaries.
      Liability for, §8-1-170.
    Void contracts, §8-1-170.
      Conveyance of real estate
          not void if made in
          good faith, §8-1-171.
      Exceptions, §8-1-170.
      Mortgage in good faith on
          real estate of insane
          person not void,
          §8-1-172.
  Conveyances.
    Husband and wife.
      Conveyance by spouse of
          insane person,
          §§30-4-12, 30-4-30 to
          30-4-37.
        See HUSBAND AND
            WIFE.
    Void contracts.
      Conveyance of real estate
          not void if made in
          good faith, §8-1-171.
  Corporations.
    Regional mental health
        programs and facilities,
        §§22-51-1 to 22-51-14.
      See within this heading,
          "Regional mental health
          programs and facilities."
  Costs.
    Moving of insane prisoners.
      Recovery of costs by state,
          §15-16-3.
  Counties.
    Regional mental health
        programs and facilities,
        §§22-51-1 to 22-51-14.
      See within this heading,
          "Regional mental health
          programs and facilities."
  Criminal law and procedure.
    Acquittal on grounds of
        insanity.
      Ordering acquitted person
          to state hospital,
          §15-16-43.
      Hearing, §15-16-41.
        Final hearing,
            §15-16-42.
      Proceedings for
          commitment of person
          in custody of
          department, §22-52-33.

MENTALLY ILL—Cont'd
  Criminal law and procedure
      —Cont'd
    Capital cases, §15-16-22.
    Commitment of persons
        accused of crimes,
        §§15-16-30 to 15-16-43.
      See within this heading,
          "Commitment." -52-33.
    Costs of moving prisoners.
      Recovery of costs by state,
          §15-16-3.
      State to pay, §15-16-3.
    Criminal psychopath release
        restriction act,
        §§15-16-60 to 15-16-71.
    Insanity defense, §13A-3-1.
    Investigation into sanity of
        certain confined persons,
        §§15-16-20 to 15-16-23.
      Capital cases, §15-16-22.
      Limitations on
          jurisdiction to
          suspend execution,
          §15-16-23.
      Order upon restoration
          to sanity, §15-16-23.
      Suspending execution of
          death sentence,
          §15-16-23.
      Duty of judge to institute
          investigation,
          §15-16-20.
      Resumption of proceedings
          when sanity restored,
          §15-16-21.
      Suspension of felony trial
          pending inquiry,
          §15-16-21.
    Plea of insanity.
      Special plea required,
          §15-16-1.
    Presumption of responsibility
        for acts, §15-16-2.
    Prisons and prisoners.
      Generally, §§22-52-70 to
          22-52-72.
      Investigation of insanity of
          certain confined
          persons, §§15-16-20 to
          15-16-23.
    Release of criminal
        psychopaths, §§15-16-60
        to 15-16-71.
      Attorneys at law.
        Appointed counsel,
            §15-16-65.
      Conditional releases.
        Appropriate conditions,
            §15-16-68.
        Generally, §15-16-67.
        Hearings.
          Removal of conditions
              §15-16-71.
        Modification, §15-16-70.
        Necessary conditions,
            §15-16-68.
        Notice.
          Hearing on
              modification of
              release, §15-16-70
          Hearing on removal of
              conditions,
              §15-16-71.
        Notice that defendant is
            no longer mentally
            ill, etc., §15-16-63.

MENTALLY ILL—Cont'd
Criminal law and procedure
—Cont'd
Release of criminal
psychopaths—Cont'd
Conditional releases
—Cont'd
Periodic reports
regarding
defendant's
compliance.
Required, §15-16-69.
Removal of conditions,
§15-16-71.
Statement of specific
conditions.
Required, §15-16-69.
Courts.
Defined, §15-16-61.
Defendants.
Defined, §15-16-61.
Definitions, §15-16-61.
Department of mental
health and mental
retardation.
Definition of
"department,"
§15-16-61.
Notice of opinion that
defendant is no
longer mentally ill,
etc., §15-16-63.
Determination as to
condition of defendant,
§15-16-67.
Disposition of defendant,
§15-16-67.
District attorneys.
Defined, §15-16-61.
Hearings, §15-16-64.
Conditional releases.
Modification,
§15-16-70.
Removal of conditions,
§15-16-71.
Failure to hold hearing.
Release of defendant
upon, §15-16-66.
Indigent defendants.
Appointment of counsel,
§15-16-65.
Notice.
Conditional releases.
Hearing on
modification of
release, §15-16-70.
Hearing on removal of
conditions,
§15-16-71.
Plans, §15-16-63.
Hearings, §15-16-64.
Requirement that
department give
notice of opinion
that defendant is no
longer mentally ill,
etc., §15-16-63.
Orders of court.
Requirement of court
order, §15-16-62.
Privileges.
Conditional releases.
Periodic reports not
deemed violative
of doctor-patient
privilege, etc.,
§15-16-69.
Regional or community
mental health
facilities.
Defined, §15-16-61.

MENTALLY ILL—Cont'd
Criminal law and procedure
—Cont'd
Release of criminal
psychopaths—Cont'd
Reports.
Conditional releases.
Periodic reports
regarding
defendant's
compliance,
§15-16-69.
Short title of article,
§15-16-60.
Title of article.
Short title, §15-16-60.
Security medical faiclity,
§§22-54-1 to 22-54-5.
Verdict.
General verdict of not
guilty or verdict of
conviction, §15-16-24.
Special verdict of not
guilty due to insanity,
§15-16-24.
Curators.
General provisions,
§§26-7A-1 to 26-7A-17.
See GUARDIAN AND
WARD.
Dams.
Erection of dams for mills,
gins, factories or electric
generators.
Guardian ad litem.
Appointment, §18-2-4.
Decedents' estates.
Claims and debts.
Time and manner of filing
claims by persons of
unsound mind,
§43-2-351.
Defense of insanity.
Acquittal on grounds of
insanity, §§15-16-41 to
15-16-43, 22-52-33. See
within this heading,
"Criminal law and
procedure."
Definitions, §§13A-6-60,
22-50-1.
Commitment of persons
accused of crimes,
§22-52-30.
Criminal law and procedure.
Release of criminal
psychopaths,
§15-16-61.
Mental retardation,
§22-52-50.
Regional mental health
programs and facilities,
§22-51-1.
**Department of mental health
and mental retardation,**
§§22-50-1 to 22-50-62.
Appeals.
Judicial review of final
order or decision of
department, §22-50-19.
Board of trustees.
Appointment, §22-50-5.
Subsequent
appointments to
board, §22-50-6.
Composition, §22-50-5.
Creation, §22-50-5.
Expenses of trustees,
§22-50-8.
Meetings, §22-50-5.
Terms of office, §22-50-5.

MENTALLY ILL—Cont'd
**Department of mental health
and mental retardation**
—Cont'd
Board of trustees—Cont'd
Vacancies in office,
§22-50-6.
Budget funds.
Request for budget funds,
§22-50-14.
Commissioner, §22-50-16.
Composition, §22-50-2.
Created, §22-50-2.
Criminal law and procedure.
Release of criminal
psychopaths,
§§15-16-61, 15-16-63.
Decisions.
Judicial review of decision
by department,
§22-50-19.
Divisions, §22-50-2.
Fees.
Disposition, §22-50-3.
Forms, §22-50-20.
Funds.
Request for budget funds,
§22-50-14.
Income.
Disposition, §22-50-3.
Legal division, §22-50-12.
Mental health finance
authority, §§41-10-350 to
41-10-371.
See MENTAL HEALTH
FINANCE
AUTHORITY.
Offices, §22-50-2.
Orders.
Judicial review of final
order of department,
§22-50-19.
Powers, §22-50-11.
Generally, §22-50-9.
Public corporation, §22-50-4.
Receipts.
Disposition, §22-50-3.
Reports.
Annual report, §22-50-13.
Youth services board.
Member of board, §44-1-51.
Elections.
Certain persons disqualified
from registering and
voting, Const. Ala., art.
VIII, §182.
Lists of qualified voters.
Purging of registration
lists.
Registrars to receive
information of
incompetency,
§17-4-131.
Eminent domain.
Hearings.
Guardian ad litem.
Appointment,
§18-1A-275.
Examinations.
Involuntary commitment,
§22-52-7.
**Executors and
administrators.**
Claims and debts.
Time and manner of filing
claims, §43-2-351.
Curators.
General provisions,
§§26-7A-1 to 26-7A-17.
See GUARDIAN AND
WARD.

MENTALLY ILL—Cont'd
**Executors and
    administrators**—Cont'd
Grounds for removal,
    §43-2-290.
Insolvent estates.
  Claims against insolvent
    estates.
  Time allowed persons of
    unsound mind for
    filing, §43-2-741.
Real property.
  Sale for payment of debts
    and for division.
    Appointment of guardian
      ad litem, §43-2-445.
    Compensation of
      guardian ad litem,
      §43-2-448.
    Duties of guardian ad
      litem, §43-2-448.
    Order of sale.
      When depositions
        required,
        §43-2-452.
Settlements and
    distributions.
  Appointment of guardian
    ad litem, §43-2-504.
  Arbitration on settlement
    of estates.
    Consent by guardian,
      §43-2-601.
  Special guardians,
    §43-2-517.
Facilities.
Bond issues.
  Acquisition, improvement,
    etc., of mental health
    facilities, Const. Ala.,
    amds. 266, 340.
  Building construction and
    improvement purposes
    at Alabama state
    hospitals and Partlow
    state school for mental
    deficients, Const. Ala.,
    amds. 113, 118.
  Special health care facility
    authorities, §§11-62-1
    to 11-62-21.
    See MUNICIPAL
      CORPORATIONS.
Certificate or license
  required to operate,
  §22-50-17.
Commitment. See within this
  heading, "Commitment."
Criminal psychopaths.
  Release of criminal
    psychopaths,
    §§15-16-60 to 15-16-71.
    See within this
      heading, "Criminal
      law and procedure."
Funds for essential functions,
  §22-50-15.
Health care authorities.
  Generally, §§22-21-310 to
    22-21-356.
    See HEALTH CARE
      AUTHORITIES.
Inspections.
  Board of corrections.
    Authority, §14-6-106.
    Powers and effect of
      orders, §14-6-107.
Licenses.
  Required to operate
    facility, §22-50-17.

MENTALLY ILL—Cont'd
Facilities—Cont'd
Mental health capital outlay
  oversight commission,
  §22-50-25.
Mental retardation.
  Admission. See within this
    heading, "Mental
    retardation."
Municipal corporations.
  Special health care facility
    authorities, §§11-62-1
    to 11-62-70.
    See MUNICIPAL
      CORPORATIONS.
Operation.
  Certificate or license
    required to operate,
    §22-50-17.
Partlow state school and
  hospital.
  Bond issues, Const. Ala.,
    amds. 113, 118.
  Streets, §23-1-42.
Physicians at facilities.
  Exemption from attending
    as witnesses,
    §22-50-22.
Police officers for state
  mental health facilities
  or hospitals, §22-50-21.
Regional mental health
  programs and facilities,
  §§22-51-1 to 22-51-14.
  See within this heading,
    "Regional mental health
    programs and facilities."
Security medical facility,
  §§22-54-1 to 22-54-5.
  Admissions.
    Applications for
      admission, §22-54-3.
    Final decision as to
      admission of patients
      to rest with
      superintendent of
      facility, §22-54-5.
    Sources from which
      patients may be
      admitted to facility,
      §22-54-2.
    When applications not to
      be accepted,
      §22-54-3.
  Commitment of patients.
    Applicability of
      commitment statutes
      to patients, §22-54-4.
  Designation, §22-54-1.
  Discharge of patients,
    §22-54-4.
    Final decision as to
      discharge to rest
      with superintendent,
      §22-54-5.
  Establishment authorized,
    §22-54-1.
  Jurisdiction.
    Facility to be under
      jurisdiction of
      mental health board,
      §22-54-1.
    Institutions, courts, etc.,
      referring patients to
      facility to retain
      constructive
      jurisdiction over
      patients, §22-54-4.

MENTALLY ILL—Cont'd
Facilities—Cont'd
Security medical facility
  —Cont'd
  Release of patients.
    Applicability of release
      statutes to patients,
      §22-54-4.
    Return of patients to
      sources from which
      received, §22-54-4.
    Sources from which
      patients may be
      admitted to facility,
      §22-54-2.
    Return of patients to
      sources from which
      received, §22-54-4.
  Superintendent.
    Final decision as to
      admission or
      discharge of patients
      to rest with
      superintendent,
      §22-54-5.
  Support of patients.
    Applicability of support
      statutes to patients,
      §22-54-4.
Streets.
  Construction and
    maintenance.
    State highway
      department,
      §23-1-42.
Superintendents.
  Exemption from attending
    as witnesses,
    §22-50-22.
Support of persons in state
  mental institutions,
  §§22-53-1 to 22-53-26.
  Bill.
    Monthly bills, §22-53-4.
    Reexamination of
      financial condition
      of inmates and
      relatives,
      §22-53-25.
  Bonds, surety, §22-53-5.
  Reexamination of
    financial condition of
    inmates and
    relatives, §22-53-26.
  Change in amount of
    payment, §22-53-4.
  Failure to make payment,
    §22-53-4.
  Judgments, §22-53-4.
  Liability, §22-53-20.
    Persons liable for
      support and
      maintenance of
      inmates, §22-53-1.
    Proceedings to determine
      liability, §22-53-3.
    Proceedings to
      redetermine,
      §22-53-24.
    Reexamination of
      financial condition of
      inmates and
      relatives, §22-53-20.
  Nonpaying inmates.
    Lists to be furnished to
      probate judges,
      §22-53-23.
    Reexamination required,
      §22-53-21.

MENTALLY ILL—Cont'd
Facilities—Cont'd
Support of persons in state
  mental institutions
  —Cont'd
  Reexamination of financial
    condition of inmates
    and relatives,
    §§22-53-20 to 22-53-26.
  Bond for support,
    §22-53-26.
  Jurisdiction to determine
    liability, §22-53-22.
  Liability for payment for
    care and
    maintenance,
    §22-53-20.
  Jurisdiction to
    determine
    liability,
    §22-53-22.
  Proceedings to
    redetermine
    liability,
    §22-53-24.
  Monthly bill, §22-53-25.
  Nonpaying inmates.
    List furnished to
      probate judges,
      §22-53-23.
  Reexamination
    required,
    §22-53-21.
  Report by county
    department of
    pensions and
    security, §22-53-23.
Security medical facility.
  Applicability of support
    statutes to patients
    at facility, §22-54-4.
University of Alabama
  medical center.
  Bond issue for mental
    hospital, Const. Ala.,
    amd. 141.
Fees.
Department of mental health
  and mental retardation.
  Disposition, §22-50-3.
Probate judges' fees,
  §12-19-90.
Proceedings to pass upon
  soundness of mind of
  person.
Probate court jurors' fees,
  §12-19-113.
Witness fees in probate
  court.
Inquisition proceedings
  regarding mental
  illness, §12-19-135.
Forms, §22-50-20.
Funds.
Essential functions,
  §22-50-15.
Guardian ad litem.
See GUARDIAN AD LITEM.
Guardian and ward.
Curators.
  General provisions,
    §§26-7A-1 to 26-7A-17.
    See GUARDIAN AND
    WARD.
General provisions.
  See GUARDIAN AND
  WARD.

MENTALLY ILL—Cont'd
Guardian and ward—Cont'd
Uniform guardianship and
  protective proceedings
  act, §§26-2A-1 to
  26-2A-160.
  See GUARDIAN AND
  WARD.
Veterans.
  Incompetent veterans and
    dependents.
  Appointment of
    guardian, §§26-9-1 to
    26-9-19.
    See VETERANS.
Habeas corpus.
General provisions, §§15-21-1
  to 15-21-34.
  See HABEAS CORPUS.
Health care authorities,
  §§22-21-310 to 22-21-356.
  See HEALTH CARE
  AUTHORITIES.
Hearings.
Commitment, §§22-52-6,
  22-52-8, 22-52-9.
Criminal law and procedure.
  Release of criminal
    psychopaths,
    §15-16-64.
  Conditional releases.
    Modification,
      §15-16-70.
    Removal of conditions,
      §15-16-71.
  Failure to hold hearing,
    §15-16-66.
Guardian ad litem.
  Appointment.
    Infants or incompetents,
      §18-1A-275.
Hospitals.
Commitment, §§22-52-1 to
  22-52-37. See within this
  heading, "Commitment."
General provisions. See
  within this heading,
  "Facilities."
Mental health capital outlay
  oversight commission,
  §22-50-25.
Regional mental health
  programs and facilities,
  §§22-51-1 to 22-51-14.
  See within this heading,
  "Regional mental health
  programs and facilities."
Security medical facilities,
  §§22-54-1 to 22-54-5.
Support of persons in state
  mental institutions,
  §§22-53-1 to 22-53-26.
  See within this heading,
  "Facilities."
Husband and wife.
Conveyances by spouse of
  insane person, §§30-4-30
  to 30-4-37.
  See HUSBAND AND
  WIFE.
Support of persons in state
  mental institutions,
  §§22-53-1 to 22-53-26.
  See within this heading,
  "Facilities."
Identification.
Nondriver identification
  cards for retarded
  persons, §32-6-4.1.

MENTALLY ILL—Cont'd
Immunity.
Regional mental health
  programs and facilities.
  Officers.
    Liability of officers of
      nonprofit
      organizations,
      §§10-11-1 to 10-11-5.
Indigent persons.
Criminal law and procedure.
  Release of criminal
    psychopaths.
  Appointment of counsel,
    §15-16-65.
Information.
Disclosure of information,
  §22-50-62.
Purpose of article, §22-50-60.
Inspections.
State mental institutions,
  §§14-6-106, 14-6-107.
Institutions. See within this
  heading, "Facilities."
Insurance.
Disability insurance.
  Hospitalization benefits.
    Exclusion, §27-19-28.
**Interstate compact on
  mental health,** §§22-55-1
  to 22-55-4.
Administrator, §§22-55-2,
  22-55-3.
  Designation of compact
    administrator,
    §22-55-2.
  Duties, §22-55-2.
  Powers, §22-55-2.
  Supplementary
    agreements, §22-55-3.
Enactment, §22-55-1.
Financial obligations of state.
  Payment, §22-55-4.
Supplementary agreements
  with officials of other
  states, §§22-55-3,
  22-55-4.
  Payment of financial
    obligations of state
    under supplementary
    agreements, §22-55-4.
  Power of compact
    administrator to enter
    into, §22-55-3.
Terms, §22-55-1.
Investigations.
Certain confined persons,
  §§15-16-20 to 15-16-25.
  See within this heading,
  "Criminal law and
  procedure."
Involuntary commitment,
  §§22-52-1 to 22-52-17. See
  within this heading,
  "Commitment."
Jails.
Commitment of prisoners.
  Pending transfer to mental
    hospital, §14-6-3.
Investigation into sanity of
  certain confined persons,
  §§15-16-20 to 15-16-25.
  See within this heading,
  "Criminal law and
  procedure."
Security medical facility,
  §§22-54-1 to 22-54-5.

MENTALLY ILL—Cont'd
**Joint tenants and tenants in
 common.**
Sale of land of minors and
 insane persons for
 distribution among joint
 owners, §§35-6-80 to
 35-6-90.
 See PARTITION.
Judges.
Special probate judges.
 Commitment hearings.
 Persons accused of
 crimes, §§22-52-35,
 22-52-36.
Jurisdiction.
Involuntary commitment.
 Retention of jurisdiction by
 probate court over
 person committed,
 §22-52-11.
Jury.
Challenges of jurors,
 §12-16-150.
Juvenile proceedings.
Involuntary commitment.
 Authority and procedure,
 §12-15-90.
 Jurisdiction of juvenile
 courts, §12-15-31.
 Proceedings as to minors or
 children believed to be
 mentally ill or retarded,
 §12-15-70.
Licenses.
Facilities.
 Required to operate
 facility, §22-50-17.
Limitation of actions.
Suspension of limitation for
 disabilities, §6-2-8.
Maintenance.
Support of persons in state
 mental institutions,
 §§22-53-1 to 22-53-26.
 See within this heading,
 "Facilities."
**Mandatory disposition of
 detainers.**
Inapplicability of article to
 mentally ill persons,
 §15-9-86.
Mental health board.
Personnel.
 Authority to establish
 personnel policies,
 §22-50-40.
 Salaries.
 Authority to establish
 salary schedules,
 §22-50-40.
 Security medical facility,
 §§23-54-1 to 23-54-5.
 Termination, §22-50-10.
 Transfer of authority to
 department, §22-50-10.
**Mental health capital outlay
 oversight commission,**
 §22-50-25.
Mental retardation.
Admission, §22-52-51.
 Involuntary admission.
 Minors.
 Authority and
 procedure,
 §12-15-90.
 Proceedings for court
 order.
 Expenses, §22-52-56.
 Generally, §22-52-55.

MENTALLY ILL—Cont'd
Mental retardation—Cont'd
Admission—Cont'd
 Involuntary admission
 —Cont'd
 Reception on court order,
 §22-52-54.
 Youth services.
 Commitment of
 retarded youth to
 state hospital,
 §44-1-36.
 Minors.
 Involuntary admissions,
 §12-15-90.
 Youth services.
 Commitment to state
 hospital, §44-1-36.
 Preference in admission,
 §22-52-51.
 Voluntary admission.
 Discharge of individual
 admitted
 voluntarily,
 §§22-52-52, 22-52-53.
Definitions, §22-52-50.
Diagnosis.
 Facilities may receive for
 diagnosis, §22-52-51.
Discharge, §22-52-57.
 Individuals admitted
 voluntarily.
 Generally, §22-52-52.
 Request by parent, etc.,
 §22-52-53.
Education of exceptional
 children, §§16-39-1 to
 16-39-12.
 See EDUCATION.
Identification cards.
 Nondriver identification
 cards for retarded
 persons, §32-6-4.1.
Juvenile proceedings.
 See JUVENILE
 PROCEEDINGS.
Leave from institutions,
 §22-52-57.
Nondriver identification
 cards for retarded
 persons, §32-6-4.1.
Observation.
 Facilities may receive for
 observation, §22-52-51.
Preference in admission,
 §22-52-51.
Transfer of individuals to
 other institutions,
 §22-52-58.
Youth services.
 Commitment of retarded
 youth to state hospital,
 §44-1-36.
**Mortgages and deeds of
 trust.**
Void contracts.
 Mortgage in good faith on
 real estate of insane
 person not void,
 §8-1-172.
Motor vehicles.
Drivers' licenses.
 Persons to whom license
 not to be issued,
 §32-6-7.

MENTALLY ILL—Cont'd
Municipal corporations.
Housing of mentally retarded
 or mentally ill persons.
 Zoning regulations for
 housing in multi-
 family zone,
 §11-52-75.1.
Regional mental health
 programs and facilities,
 §§22-51-1 to 22-51-14.
 See within this heading,
 "Regional mental health
 programs and facilities."
Special health care facility
 authorities, §§11-62-1 to
 11-62-21.
 See MUNICIPAL
 CORPORATIONS.
Negligence.
Regional mental health
 programs and facilities.
 Officers.
 Liability of officers of
 nonprofit
 organizations,
 §§10-11-1 to 10-11-5.
Negotiable instruments. See
 within this heading,
 "Commercial code."
**Nondriver identification
 cards for retarded
 persons,** §32-6-4.1.
Notice.
Criminal law and procedure.
 Release of criminal
 psychopaths.
 Conditional releases,
 §15-16-63.
 Hearing on
 modification of
 release, §15-16-70.
 Hearing on removal of
 conditions,
 §15-16-71.
 Hearings, §15-16-64.
 Requirement that
 department give
 notice of opinion
 that defendant is no
 longer mentally
 ill,etc., §15-16-63.
Optometrists.
Grounds for revocation or
 suspension of license,
 §34-22-23.
Orders of court.
Criminal law and procedure.
 Release of criminal
 psychopaths.
 General provisions,
 §§15-16-60 to
 15-16-71. See within
 this heading,
 "Criminal law and
 procedure."
 Requirement of court
 order, §15-16-62.
Parent and child.
Relief of minor children from
 disabilities of nonage.
 General provisions,
 §§26-13-1 to 26-13-8;
 Const. Ala., art. IV,
 §104.
 See MINORS.
Support of persons in state
 mental institutions,
 §§22-53-1 to 22-53-26.
 See within this heading,
 "Facilities."

MENTALLY ILL—Cont'd
Parties.
Infants and incompetents,
§§6-7-100 to 6-7-103.
See PARTIES.
Partition.
Sale of land of insane
persons for distribution
among joint owners,
§§35-6-80 to 35-6-91.
See PARTITION.
Penalties.
Violations of chapter,
§22-50-23.
Penitentiary.
Removal of convicts,
§14-3-42.
Personal property.
Guardian and ward.
Removal of property of
minors and wards,
§§26-8-1 to 26-8-52.
See GUARDIAN AND
WARD.
Personnel.
Conflicting provisions of
section 22-50-11
repealed, §22-50-43.
Continuation of positions not
under merit system,
§22-50-42.
Mental health board.
Authority to establish
personnel policies,
§22-50-40.
Merit system.
Inclusion or continuation of
positions under merit
system, §22-50-41.
**Persons deemed incapable
of consent, §13A-6-70.**
Petitions.
Involuntary commitment,
§§22-25-1 to 22-25-6. See
within this heading,
"Commitment."
Physicians.
Exemption of physician of
state mental health
facilities from attending
as witnesses, §22-50-22.
Pilots and pilotage.
Branches.
Grounds for depriving pilot
of branch, §33-4-46.
Police.
Officers for state mental
health facilities or
hospitals, §22-50-21.
Presumptions.
Persons over fourteen
presumed responsible for
acts, §15-16-2.
Prisons and prisoners.
General provisions,
§§22-52-70 to 22-52-72.
See PRISONS AND
PRISONERS.
Investigations on sanity of
certain confined persons,
§§15-16-20 to 15-16-23.
Security medical facility,
§§22-54-1 to 22-54-5.

MENTALLY ILL—Cont'd
Privileges.
Criminal law and procedure.
Release of criminal
psychopaths.
Conditional releases.
Periodic reports not
deemed violative
of doctor-patient
privilege, etc.,
§15-16-69.
Probate courts.
Commitment generally. See
within this heading,
"Commitment."
Judges.
Special probate judges for
commitment hearings.
Persons accused of
crimes, §§22-52-35,
22-52-36.
Proceedings to pass upon
soundness of mind of
person.
Jurors' fees, §12-19-113.
Witness fees, §12-19-135.
Programs.
Regional mental health
programs and facilities,
§§22-51-1 to 22-51-14.
See within this heading,
"Regional mental health
programs and facilities."
**Public officers and
employees.**
Judgment of insanity of
officeholder vacates
office, §36-9-3.
Real property.
Conveyances by spouse of
insane person, §§30-4-30
to 30-4-37.
See HUSBAND AND
WIFE.
Executors and
administrators.
Sale for payment of debts
and for division,
§§43-2-445, 43-2-448,
43-2-452.
Records.
Disclosure of information,
§22-50-62.
Purpose of article, §22-50-60.
**Regional mental health
programs and facilities,**
§§22-51-1 to 22-51-14.
Actions.
Officers.
Liability of officers of
nonprofit
organizations,
§§10-11-1 to 10-11-5.
Advisory committee.
Professional advisory
committee, §22-51-10.
Appropriations by local
governing bodies,
§22-51-14.
Board of directors.
Appointment of members,
§22-51-8.
Bylaws, §22-51-9.
Compensation of members,
§22-51-8.
Composition, §22-51-8.
Constitution, §22-51-9.
Executive committee,
§22-51-8.
Meetings, §22-51-9.

MENTALLY ILL—Cont'd
**Regional mental health
programs and facilities**
—Cont'd
Board of directors—Cont'd
Qualifications of members,
§22-51-8.
Quorum, §22-51-9.
Terms of members,
§22-51-8.
Vacancies, §22-51-8.
Bylaws.
Adoption by board of
directors, §22-51-9.
Constitution.
Adoption by board of
directors, §22-51-9.
Control of facilities and
programs, §22-51-12.
Criminal psychopaths.
Release of criminal
psychopaths,
§§15-16-60 to 15-16-71.
See within this
heading, "Criminal
law and procedure."
Definitions, §22-51-1.
Exemption from taxation,
§22-51-13.
Immunity.
Officers.
Liability of officers of
nonprofit
organizations,
See ASSOCIATIONS.
Incorporation of public
corporations.
Application, §§22-51-3,
22-51-4.
Authorized, §22-51-2.
Certificate of incorporation,
§§22-51-5 to 22-51-7.
Mental health capital outlay
oversight commission,
§22-50-25.
Negligence.
Officers.
Liability of officers of
nonprofit
organizations,
§§10-11-1 to 10-11-5.
Powers of corporation,
§22-51-11.
Professional advisory
committee, §22-51-10.
Tax exemption, §22-51-13.
Torts.
Officers.
Liability of officers of
nonprofit
organizations,
§§10-11-1 to 10-11-5.
**Removal of personal
property of minors and
wards, §§26-8-1 to 26-8-52.**
See GUARDIAN AND
WARD.
Reports.
Criminal law and procedure.
Release of criminal
psychopaths.
Conditional releases.
Periodic reports
regarding
defendant's
compliance,
§15-16-69.
Department of mental health
and mental retardation.
Annual report, §22-50-13.

MENTALLY ILL—Cont'd
Research data.
Authority to receive, §22-50-61.
Disclosure of information, §22-50-62.
Purpose of article, §22-50-60.
School children.
Mental examinations, §§26-29-1 to 26-29-6.
See EDUCATION.
Security medical facility, §§22-54-1 to 22-54-5.
Service of process.
How incompetents served, ARCP, Rule 4 (c).
Nonresident insane defendants.
Service in absence of other provisions, §6-4-21.
Settlements and distributions. See within this heading, "Executors and administrators."
Sexual offenses.
Mentally defective and incapacitated, §§13A-6-60, 13A-6-70.
State mental institutions.
Facilities generally. See within this heading, "Facilities."
Support and maintenance.
Persons in state mental institutions, §§22-53-1 to 22-53-26. See within this heading, "Facilities."
Taxation.
Exemptions.
Corporations organized to establish regional mental health programs and facilities, §40-9-23.
Torts.
Regional mental health programs and facilities.
Officers.
Liability of officers of nonprofit organizations, §§10-11-1 to 10-11-5.
Transfer of inmates to other institutions, §22-52-58.
Uniform guardianship and protective proceedings act, §§26-2A-1 to 26-2A-160.
See GUARDIAN AND WARD.
United States.
Condemnation of land or rights of way.
Appointment of guardian ad litem and counsel for infants and persons of unsound mind, §42-2-4.
Veterans.
Commitment.
Veterans' administration, §22-52-13.
Incompetent veterans and dependents, §§26-9-1 to 26-9-19.
See VETERANS.
Violation of chapter.
Penalties, §22-50-23.

MENTALLY ILL—Cont'd
Weapons.
Pistols.
Delivery to persons of unsound mind, §13A-11-76.
Wills.
Contesting validity of will.
Additional time for contest by persons of unsound mind, §43-8-201.
Witnesses.
Fees in probate court.
Inquisition proceedings regarding mental illness, §12-19-135.
Incompetent witnesses, §12-21-165.
Superintendent and physician of state mental health facilities.
Exemption from attending as witnesses, §22-50-22.
Youth services.
Commitment of mentally ill youth to state hospitals, §44-1-36.

MENTAL RETARDATION.
Criminal law and procedure.
Mentally retarded defendants, §§15-24-1 to 15-24-7.
See CRIMINAL LAW AND PROCEDURE.
Education of exceptional children, §§16-39-1 to 16-39-12.
See EDUCATION.
General provisions.
See MENTALLY ILL.
Genetic service, §§22-10A-1 to 22-10A-3.
Guardian and ward.
See GUARDIAN AND WARD.
Minors.
Involuntary commitment, §12-15-90.

MERCHANT MARINE.
Military affairs.
Persons exempted from military service, §31-2-6.

MERCHANTS.
Arrest.
Detention and arrest of person suspected of larceny of goods held for sale, §15-10-14.
Commission merchants.
Sale of farm produce, §§2-29-1 to 2-29-11.
See COMMISSION MERCHANTS.
Executors and administrators.
Stock in trade.
Sale, §43-2-421.
Limitation of actions.
Exceptions to applicability of chapter, §6-2-2.
Retail merchants associations, §10-4-260.
Stores.
See STORES.
Transient merchants, §§34-35-1 to 34-35-9.
See TRANSIENT MERCHANTS.

MERCHANTS—Cont'd
Wholesale merchants associations, §10-4-280.

MERCY KILLING.
Natural death act.
Provisions of chapter not an approval of mercy killing, §22-8A-10.

MERGER.
Banks and trust companies.
Dissenting shareholders' rights, §5-7A-44.
General provisions, §§5-7A-1 to 5-7A-6.
See BANKS AND FINANCIAL INSTITUTIONS.
Resulting banks, §5-7A-45.
Corporations.
Consolidation or merger.
General provisions, §§10-2A-140 to 10-2A-146.
See CORPORATIONS.
Nonprofit corporations, §§10-3A-100 to 10-3A-104.
Credit unions.
Procedures, §5-17-22.
Electric cooperatives.
See ELECTRIC COOPERATIVES.
Fraternal benefit societies, §§27-34-48, 27-34-49.
Savings and loan associations.
See SAVINGS AND LOAN ASSOCIATIONS.

MERIT SYSTEM.
General provisions.
See PUBLIC OFFICERS AND EMPLOYEES.
Municipal corporations.
Civil service merit system for law enforcement officers, §§11-43-180 to 11-43-190.
See MUNICIPAL CORPORATIONS.

MERRY-GO-ROUNDS.
Licenses, §40-12-103.

MESCALINE.
Controlled substances.
General provisions, §§20-2-1 to 20-2-144.
See DRUGS.

METALS.
Molds, dyes or patterns.
Disposal, §§8-28-1 to 8-28-4.
Applicability of provisions, §8-28-4.
Definitions, §8-28-1.
Notice, §8-28-3.
Procedure, §8-28-3.
When molder may dispose of form owned by customer, §8-28-2.

METERS.
Electric meters, §37-8-6.
Gas and electric meters.
Furnishing, §37-8-6.
Inspections.
Open for inspection, §37-8-6.
Public service commission.
Accuracy.
Commission may provide for, §37-1-53.
Public utilities. §37-1-53.

METHODIST CHILDREN'S HOME.
Licenses.
Exemptions, §40-9-12.

METHODIST HOME FOR THE AGING.
Licenses.
Exemptions, §40-9-12.
Taxation.
Exemptions, §40-9-12.

MICROPHOTOGRAPHY.
Banks and financial institutions.
Reproduction of records and books, §5-4A-1.
Educational records, §§16-1-3, 16-1-4.
Evidence.
Records.
Admissibility in evidence, §41-13-40.
Lis pendens, §35-4-136.
Records.
See RECORDS.

MIDWIVES, §§34-19-2 to 34-19-10.
Abnormal childbirth, §34-19-8.
Blind persons.
Infantile blindness.
Prevention, §22-20-2.
Continuation of practice of lay midwifery, §34-19-3.
Death.
Reports.
Failure of midwife to report death, §22-9-78.
Definitions, §34-19-2.
Fees.
Licenses.
Issuance and renewal.
Authority to levy and collect fee, §34-19-5.
Lay midwifery.
Continuation of practice, §34-19-3.
Licenses.
Application, §34-19-4.
Designation of midwife certification.
Professional nursing license, §34-19-9.
Fees.
Issuance, §34-19-5.
Fee, §34-19-5.
Qualifications of applicant, §34-19-4.
Renewal, §34-19-5.
Fee, §34-19-5.
Required, §34-19-3.
Revocation, §34-19-5.
Suspension, §34-19-5.
Practices which may be performed by licensees, §34-19-6.
Attendance in cases of abnormal child birth, §34-19-8.
Restrictions, §34-19-7.
Prevention of infantile blindness, §22-20-2.
Promulgation of procedures and standards, §34-19-10.
Reports.
Death.
Failure of midwife to report death, §22-9-78.
Rules and regulations.
Promulgation, §34-19-10.

MIDWIVES—Cont'd
Vital statistics.
Failure of midwife to report death, §22-9-78.

MIGRATORY BIRDS, §§9-11-263, 9-11-430 to 9-11-435.
See FISH AND GAME.

MILITARY AFFAIRS, §§31-2-1 to 31-2-133.
Accounts and accounting.
Adjutant general, §31-2-68.
Officers, §31-2-68.
Actions.
Arms and equipment.
Proceedings when member of armed forces unable to account for property or money, §31-2-34.
Compensation for death of national guardsmen, §§31-3-1 to 31-3-7. See within this heading, "National guard."
Defense of actions against present or former members of national guard, §31-2-89.
Enlisted men.
Actions against enlisted men for acts performed in line of duty, §31-2-89.
Military courts.
Actions against members of court as to sentences, warrants, etc., §31-2-89.
National guard.
Actions against national guard members for acts or omissions performed in official capacity, §§31-2-89 to 31-2-91.
Appointment of defense counsel, §31-2-90.
Defense of actions against present or former members, §31-2-89.
Security for costs to be given by plantiff, §31-2-91.
Compensation for death of national guardsmen, §§31-3-1 to 31-3-7. See within this heading, "National guard."
Officers.
Actions against officers for acts performed in line of duty, §31-2-89.
Parties.
Persons in federal service and spouses living in state deemed residents for purpose of commencing actions, §6-7-20.
Removal of actions.
Right of national guard members to change of venue, §31-2-118.
Active military or naval service of state.
Enforcement of attendance of officers and enlisted men, §31-2-127.

MILITARY AFFAIRS—Cont'd
Active military or naval service of state—Cont'd
Special appropriations for national guard, §31-2-133.
When officers, enlisted men, etc., deemed to be in active service, §31-2-38.
Adjutant general.
Administration of military affairs, §31-2-69; Const. Ala., amd. 89.
Appointment, §31-2-58.
Standards for appointment, §31-2-69; Const. Ala., amd. 89.
Armory commission.
Member of commission, §31-4-1.
Arms and equipment.
Annual report to governor.
Number and condition of arms and equipment, §31-2-67.
Audit of books, accounts, etc., §31-2-68.
Bonds, surety, §31-2-62.
Clerical assistants, §31-2-63.
Commission, §31-2-58.
Courts of inquiry.
Institution by adjutant general, §31-2-107.
Custodian of state military property, §31-2-25.
Disbanded organizations.
Property.
Officers to return to custody of adjutant general, §31-2-26.
Dropping allowance.
Establishment by adjutant general, §31-2-128.
Duties.
Generally, §31-2-58.
Status and duties upon call into federal service of national guard, §31-2-59.
Federal service of national guard.
Status and duties upon call into, §31-2-59.
Offices, §31-2-63.
Powers.
Generally, §31-2-58.
Property.
Disbanded organizations.
Officers to return to custody of adjutant general, §31-2-26.
Powers and duties of adjutant general as exclusive custodian of state military property, §31-2-25.
Qualifications, §31-2-58.
Rank, §31-2-58.
Removal.
Standards for removal, §31-2-69.
Reports.
Annual report to governor, §31-2-67.
Revolving fund, §31-2-131.
Seal, §31-2-58.
Standards for appointment, removal, etc., §31-2-69.

MILITARY AFFAIRS—Cont'd
Adjutant general—Cont'd
State defense force.
Powers of adjutant general
with respect to state
defense force, §31-2-9.
Terms of office, §31-2-58.
Age.
Militia.
Composition of state
militia, §31-2-2.
Naval militia, §31-2-4.
Unorganized militia, §31-2-5.
Air national guard.
Headquarters and
headquarters
detachment.
Appointment of officers
and enlisted men,
§31-2-55.
National crisis.
Assignment during
national crisis,
§31-2-57.
Leaving state without
permission, §31-2-82.
Officers.
Headquarters and
headquarters
detachment.
Appointment of officers,
§31-2-55.
Alcoholic beverages.
Authority of commanders to
incarcerate and detain
persons interfering with
performance of troops,
§31-2-126.
Invoices and receipts to be
maintained by persons,
firms, etc., selling or
shipping goods to federal
government for military
purposes, §28-3-11.
National guard.
Commanders may order
closing of certain
places and forbid sale
of alcoholic beverages,
§31-2-124.
Compensation for death of
national guardsmen.
When dependents not
entitled to
compensation,
§31-3-2.
Penalties.
Unauthorized sale or
possession of alcoholic
beverages purchased
from military liquor
stores, §28-1-3.1.
Penalty, §28-1-3.1.
Shipment of articles taxed by
chapter to military
reservations within
state, §28-3-8.
**Annual encampments or
cruises,** §31-2-37.
Appeals.
Compensation for death of
national guardsmen.
Decision of awarding
authority to be final,
§31-3-7.
Appropriations.
Armory commission.
Disbursement of regular
military appropriations
for maintenance of
armories, §31-4-19.

MILITARY AFFAIRS—Cont'd
Appropriations—Cont'd
Armory commission—Cont'd
Use of military
appropriations for
payment of commission
expenses or
obligations, §31-4-6.
Counties or municipalities.
Appropriation of funds for
local units, §31-2-129.
National guard.
Appropriations for
operation, support,
etc., §31-2-108.
Special appropriations for
national guard in
active military service
of state, §31-2-133.
Regular military
appropriations,
§31-2-132.
Revolving fund, §31-2-131.
State defense force, §31-2-10.
Unexpended appropriations.
Disposition, §31-2-15.
Armories generally, §§31-4-1
to 31-4-19.
See ARMORIES.
Armory commission, §§31-4-1
to 31-4-9.
Actions.
Commission may sue and
be sued, §31-4-3.
Adjutant general.
Member of commission,
§31-4-1.
Appointment of members by
governor, §31-4-1.
Appropriations.
Disbursement of regular
military appropriations
for maintenance of
armories, §31-4-19.
Use of military
appropriations for
payment of expenses or
obligations of
commission, §31-4-6.
Approval, inspection and
supervision of
construction by state
building commission,
§31-4-13.
Armory boards, §31-4-15.
Arms and equipment.
Bonds for care, §31-4-4.
Attorney general.
Member of commission,
§31-4-1.
Body corporate, §31-4-2.
Bond issues.
Financing or refinancing of
armories, §31-4-5.
Bonds, surety.
Arms, equipment, etc., of
United States reserve
units of state colleges,
§31-4-4.
Buildings.
Acquisition and
construction, §31-4-8.
Counties.
Cooperation of counties
for acquisition of
buildings, §31-4-9.
Compensation of members,
§31-4-3.
Composition, §31-4-1.

MILITARY AFFAIRS—Cont'd
Armory commission—Cont'd
Condemnation.
Exercise of power,
§31-4-10.
Contracts.
Power of commission to
contract, §31-4-3.
Counties.
Buildings.
Cooperation of counties
for acquisition of
buildings, §31-4-9.
Conveyance by counties of
public lands to
commission for use as
armory sites, §31-4-11.
Delegation of powers and
duties to executive
committee, §31-4-3.
Disposition of armories.
Generally, §31-4-14.
Duties.
Delegation to executive
committee, §31-4-3.
Generally, §31-4-3.
Eminent domain.
Exercise of power of
condemnation,
§31-4-10.
Executive committee.
Delegation of powers and
duties to executive
committee, §31-4-3.
Expenses.
Appropriations.
Use of military
appropriations for
payment of expenses,
§31-4-6.
Financing or refinancing of
armories, etc., §31-4-5.
Use of military
appropriations for
payment of expenses
or obligations of
commission, §31-4-6.
Governor.
Appointment of members,
§31-4-1.
Chairman of commission,
§31-4-1.
Grounds.
Acquisition, construction,
etc., of armory
grounds, §31-4-8.
Improvements.
Financing or refinancing,
§31-4-5.
Incorporation.
Certificate of incorporation.
Issuance, §31-4-2.
Procedure, §31-4-2.
Lease of armories.
Duties of commission,
§31-4-16.
Management and care of
armories, §31-4-15.
Meetings, §31-4-3.
Municipal corporations.
Buildings.
Cooperation of
municipalities for
acquisition of
buildings, §31-4-9.
Conveyance of public lands
to commission for use
as armory sites,
§31-4-11.

MILITARY AFFAIRS—Cont'd
Armory commission—Cont'd
Name.
  Succession by corporate
    name, §31-4-2.
National guard.
  Officers.
    Members of commission,
      §31-4-1.
  Provision of armories for
    housing and
    instruction of national
    guard, §31-4-7.
Officers of control, §31-4-15.
Powers.
  Delegation to executive
    committee, §31-4-3.
  Generally, §31-4-3.
Provision of armories for
  housing, instruction of
  national guard and naval
  militia, §31-4-7.
Public buildings.
  Cooperation of counties
    and municipalities for
    acquisition of buildings
    suitable for use as
    public buildings,
    §31-4-9.
Public lands.
  Conveyance by counties or
    municipalities for use
    as armory sites,
    §31-4-11.
Quorum, §31-4-3.
Real property.
  Power to acquire, §31-4-3.
  Taxation.
    Exemption, §31-4-12.
Renting armories.
  Power of armory board of
    officers of control,
    §31-4-15.
Sale of armories.
  Duties of commission,
    §31-4-16.
Sites.
  Conveyance by counties or
    municipalities of
    public lands for use as
    sites, §31-4-11.
Taxation.
  Property used for armory
    and training purposes
    exempt from taxation,
    §31-4-12.
Use of armories.
  Generally, §31-4-14.
Arms and equipment.
Actions.
  Proceedings when member
    of armed forces unable
    to account for property
    or money, §31-2-34.
Adjutant general.
  Annual report to governor.
    Number and condition of
      arms and equipment,
      §31-2-67.
Armories.
  See ARMORIES.
Bearing arms without
  authority of governor.
  Unauthorized military
    organizations,
    §31-2-125.
Bonds, surety.
  Persons required to give
    bond, §§31-2-14,
    31-4-4.

MILITARY AFFAIRS—Cont'd
Arms and equipment—Cont'd
Care.
  Officers and enlisted men
    personally responsible
    for care, §31-2-28.
  Commanders of troops may
    order closing of certain
    places and forbid sale of
    arms, §31-2-124.
Deposit in armories,
  §31-2-23.
Destruction.
  Wilful or malicious
    destruction, §31-2-29.
Disbanded organizations,
  §31-2-26.
Exempt from sale under
  execution, §31-2-78.
Illegally acquired arms or
  equipment.
  Seizure, etc., §31-2-30.
Lost or damaged equipment.
  Liability of officers and
    enlisted men, §31-2-32.
Preservation by officers,
  §31-2-24.
Private use of military
  property, §31-2-27.
Proceedings when member of
  armed forces unable to
  account for property or
  money, §31-2-34.
Property generally. See
  within this heading,
  "Property."
Reports.
  Failure of officers and
    enlisted men to make
    required reports,
    §31-2-33.
Safekeeping, Const. Ala., art.
  XV, §277.
Sale, exchange, etc.,
  §31-2-30.
Unauthorized retention of
  military arms and
  equipment, §31-2-31.
Seizure of unlawfully
  retained property,
  §31-2-31.
Unauthorized use of military
  property for private
  purposes, §31-2-27.
Uniforms. See within this
  heading, "Uniforms."
Arrests.
Exemption of members of
  militia, §31-2-79; Const.
  Ala., art. XV, §275.
Arsenals.
See ARMORIES.
Assault and battery.
National guard.
  Assault on national guard
    members assembled for
    performance of duties,
    §31-2-119.
  Duty to disperse when shot
    fired, etc., at national
    guard, §31-2-121.
  Protection of national
    guard troops from
    assault, §31-2-120.
Attorney general.
Armory commission.
  Member of commission,
    §31-4-1.

MILITARY AFFAIRS—Cont'd
Attorney general—Cont'd
Arms and equipment.
  Proceedings when member
    of armed forces unable
    to account for property
    or money, §31-2-34.
Attorneys at law.
Actions against national
  guard members for acts
  or omissions performed
  in official capacity.
  Appointment of defense
    counsel, §31-2-90.
  Defense of actions against
    present or former
    members, §31-2-89.
Audits.
Adjutant general.
  Audit of books, accounts,
    etc., of adjutant
    general, §31-2-68.
Officers, §31-2-68.
Awards.
Damages caused by national
  guard members acting in
  line of duty.
  Claims filed for damages,
    §31-2-86.
Bond issues.
Armory commission.
  Financing or refinancing of
    armories, §31-4-5.
Bonds, surety.
Actions against national
  guard members for acts
  or omissions performed
  in official capacity.
  Security for costs to be
    given by plaintiff,
    §31-2-91.
Adjutant general, §31-2-62.
Arms and equipment.
  Persons required to give
    bond, §§31-2-14,
    31-4-4.
Military department
  employees, §31-2-62.
Property.
  Persons responsible for
    public or military
    property, §31-2-14.
Boundaries.
Jails, public buildings, etc.
  Commanders of national
    guard troops may
    prescribe boundaries,
    §31-2-123.
Buildings.
Armory commission.
  Acquisition and
    construction of
    buildings, §31-4-8.
  Counties.
    Cooperation of counties
      for acquisition,
      §31-4-9.
  Counties or municipalities.
    Armory commission.
      Cooperation of counties
        for acquisition of
        buildings, §31-4-9.
  Sale of real estate and
    buildings to local
    national guard units,
    §31-2-130.
  Donations.
    Reversion of donations,
      §31-4-18.

MILITARY AFFAIRS—Cont'd
Buildings—Cont'd
Municipal corporations.
Armory commission.
Cooperation of
municipalities for
acquisition of
buildings, §31-4-9.
Sale of real estate and
buildings to local
national guard units,
§31-2-130.
Camps.
Annual encampments,
§31-2-37.
Sanitation laws.
Enforcement in camps,
§31-2-40.
Canteens.
Gasoline taxes.
Exemption, §31-2-81.
Licenses.
Exemptions from state and
local licenses, §31-2-81.
Tobacco taxes.
Exemption, §31-2-81.
Circuit courts.
Ordering out of troops.
Request of judge to
governor, §31-2-111.
Civil defense, §§31-9-1 to
31-9-24.
See CIVIL DEFENSE.
Civil office.
Acceptance of commission in
state armed forces and
United States reserve
components.
Not incompatible with
holding of civil office,
§31-2-36.
Commander-in-chief, §31-2-2;
Const. U. S., Art. II, §2.
Command in the field,
§31-2-51.
Designated, §31-2-51.
Duties.
Generally, §31-2-52.
Flag, §31-2-54.
Personal military staff,
§31-2-53.
Powers.
Generally, §31-2-52.
Constitution of Alabama.
See CONSTITUTION OF
ALABAMA.
Contracts.
Veterans.
Minor veterans empowered
to contract liability for
repayment of certain
loans, §31-1-2.
Counties.
Appropriations.
Counties may appropriate
funds for military
purposes, §31-2-129.
Armories.
Public improvement bonds
generally, §§11-81-140
to 11-81-150.
See COUNTIES.
Armory commission.
Buildings.
Cooperation of counties
for acquisition of
buildings, §31-4-9.
Conveyance by counties of
public lands to
commission for use as
armory sites, §31-4-11.

MILITARY AFFAIRS—Cont'd
Counties—Cont'd
Buildings.
Armory commission.
Cooperation of counties
for acquisition of
buildings, §31-4-9.
Sale of real estate and
buildings to local
national guard units,
§31-2-130.
Donations for aid of local
national guard or naval
militia, §31-4-17.
Real property.
Counties may sell real
estate and buildings to
local national guard
units, §31-2-130.
Reversion of donations,
§31-4-18.
Courts-martial.
Militia, §31-2-83.
National guard. See within
this heading, "National
guard."
Obscenity.
Disruption of proceedings.
Punishment of persons,
§31-2-101.
Officers.
Judicial notice.
Signature and
handwriting of
commissioned
officers, §31-2-98.
Salaries.
Forfeiture of pay and
allowance, §31-2-93.
Sentencing. See within this
heading, "Sentencing."
Sheriffs. See within this
heading, "Sheriffs."
Uniform code of military
justice.
Proceedings to follow code,
§31-2-92.
Witnesses, §§31-2-100,
31-2-102.
Courts. See within this
heading, "Military courts."
**Custom and usage of United
States armed forces.**
Matters governed by,
§31-2-35.
Damages.
Payment for damages caused
by national guard
members acting in line
of duty, §31-2-86.
Death.
Evidence of armed forces
death.
Official notice prima facie
evidence, §12-21-90.
National guardsmen.
Compensation for death of
national guardsmen.
See within this
heading, "National
guard."
Death penalty.
Militia.
Imposition of death penalty
by courts-martial,
§31-2-83.
Defenses.
Actions against present or
former members of
national guard, §31-2-89.
At state expense, §31-2-89.

MILITARY AFFAIRS—Cont'd
Definitions, §31-2-1.
Compensation for death of
national guardsmen,
§31-3-1.
National guard educational
assistance, §31-10-2.
Department of defense.
Regulations of department of
defense. See within this
heading, "Regulations of
department of defense."
Department of military. See
within this heading,
"Military department."
**Department of veterans'
affairs,** §§31-5-1 to
31-5-14.
See VETERANS.
Depositories.
Military property.
See ARMORIES.
Disabilities.
National guard.
Compensation for
disability, §31-2-85.
Disbanded organizations.
Arms and equipment.
Officers to return arms,
equipment, etc., to
custody of adjutant
general, §31-2-26.
Discharges.
Courts-martial.
General courts-martial.
Dishonorable discharge
from service,
§31-2-93.
Dishonorable discharge.
General courts-martial.
Power to order, §31-2-93.
Honorable discharges.
Admissibility as evidence,
§31-1-1.
Recordation, §31-1-1.
Discrimination.
Uniforms.
Discrimination against
person wearing
uniform, §31-2-21.
**Disloyal or insulting
remarks, gestures, etc.,
to or about troops
engaged in performance
of duties,** §31-2-22.
Dispersion of mobs.
Authority to act to disperse
mob, §31-2-117.
Duty to disperse when shot
fired, etc., at national
guard, §31-2-121.
Order to disperse, §31-2-115.
Failure to obey order,
§31-2-116.
Donations.
City and county donations
for aid of local national
guard or naval militia
organizations, §31-4-17.
Reversion of donations,
§31-4-18.
Drills.
Assembly for drill, §31-2-76.
Disloyal or insulting
remarks, gestures, etc.,
to or about troops
engaged in drilling,
§31-2-22.
Time and place for drills,
§31-2-76.

MILITARY AFFAIRS—Cont'd
Drills—Cont'd
Unauthorized military
organizations, §31-2-125.
Dropping allowance.
Adjutant general.
Establishment by adjutant
general, §31-2-128.
Military department.
Dropping allowance as
item of budget,
§31-2-128.
Drunkenness.
Authority of commanders to
incarcerate and detain
persons interfering with
performance of troops,
§31-2-126.
Education.
Military recruiting
representatives.
Access to school facilities,
§16-1-25.
National guard educational
assistance, §§31-10-1 to
31-10-4.
Elections.
Absentee voting.
Application.
Postcard application for
certain military
personnel and wives,
§17-10-3.
Residence of voters.
No loss or acquisition of
residence by military
service, §17-3-11.
Emergency purchases,
§31-2-39.
Eminent domain.
Armory commission.
Exercise of power of
condemnation,
§31-4-10.
Employees.
Military department,
§§31-2-60 to 31-2-62.
Enlisted men.
Actions against enlisted men
for acts performed in line
of duty, §31-2-89.
Active military or naval
service of the state.
When enlisted men deemed
to be in, §31-2-38.
Air national guard.
Appointment, §31-2-55.
Arms and equipment.
Care.
Personal responsibility,
§31-2-28.
Lost or damaged
equipment.
Liability of enlisted men,
§31-2-32.
Personal arms.
Exempt from sale under
execution, §31-2-78.
Reports.
Failure to make required
reports, §31-2-33.
Attendance of enlisted men
called into active
military service of state.
Enforcement of attendance,
§31-2-127.

MILITARY AFFAIRS—Cont'd
Enlisted men—Cont'd
Jury duty.
Exemptions of enlisted
men of national guard,
naval militia and state
guard from state jury
duty, §31-2-11.
National guard. See within
this heading, "National
guard."
Per diem of enlisted men
under military travel
orders, §31-2-16.
Property.
Lost or damaged property.
Liability, §31-2-32.
Personal responsibility for
care, §31-2-28.
Reports.
Failure to make reports,
§31-2-33.
Travel orders.
Per diem of enlisted men
under travel orders,
§31-2-16.
Uniforms.
Personal uniforms.
Exempt from sale under
execution, §31-2-78.
Equipment. See within this
heading, "Arms and
equipment."
Evidence.
Armed forces death.
Official notice.
Prima facie evidence of
death, §12-21-90.
Compensation for death of
national guardsmen.
Rules of evidence for
determination of
claims, §31-3-5.
Courts-martial, §31-2-98.
Missing persons.
Official report of person
missing, §12-21-91.
Executions.
Arms and equipment.
Personally owned arms and
equipment of officers
and enlisted men.
Exempt from sale under
execution, §31-2-78.
Expenses.
Courts-martial.
Payment of expenses,
§31-2-102.
Emergency purchases,
§31-2-39.
Federal service.
Payment of expenses by
state upon call into
federal service,
§31-2-44.
Explosives.
National guard.
Commanders of national
guard troops may
order closing of certain
places and forbid sale
of explosives,
§31-2-124.
Transportation of explosives.
Transportation of military
or naval forces.
Exceptions, §37-8-180.

MILITARY AFFAIRS—Cont'd
Federal service.
Adjutant general.
Status and duties upon call
into federal service of
national guard,
§31-2-59.
Expenses.
Payment of expenses by
state upon call into
federal service,
§31-2-44.
Headquarters and
headquarters detachment
of national guard.
National crisis.
Appointment during
national crisis,
§31-2-57.
Release from active federal
service.
Status of officers and
enlisted men released,
§31-2-43.
Status of officers and enlisted
men released from active
federal service, §31-2-43.
Units.
Designations of units
engaged in federal
service, §31-2-45.
Fiduciaries in war service,
§§19-2-1 to 19-2-5.
Fines.
Courts-martial.
Disposition of fines,
§31-2-105.
Fish and game.
Licenses.
Members of armed forces
during war, §9-11-35.
Flags.
Governor's flag, §31-2-54.
Funds.
Military department billeting
revolving fund, §31-1-3.
Proceedings when member of
armed forces unable to
account for property or
money, §31-2-34.
Reports.
Failure of officers, etc., to
make required reports,
§31-2-33.
Revolving fund.
Authority of adjutant
general, §31-2-131.
Military department
billeting revolving
fund, §31-1-3.
Special appropriations for
national guard in active
military service of state,
§31-2-133.
Garrisons.
Sanitation laws.
Enforcement in garrisons,
§31-2-40.
Gasoline.
Taxation.
Exemption of certain post
exchanges and
canteens from gasoline
taxes, §31-2-81.
General officers of the line,
§31-2-72.
Gifts.
City and county donations
for aid of local national
guard or naval militia
organizations, §31-4-17.

MILITARY AFFAIRS—Cont'd
Gifts—Cont'd
Reversion of donations,
§31-4-18.
Good Samaritan act.
Military assistance to safety
and traffic program.
Medical aidmen rendering
first aid or emergency
care at scene of
accident, etc.
Exemption from liability,
§6-5-332.
Governor.
Annual encampments or
cruises.
Governor may order,
§31-2-37.
Armed forces organizations.
Leaving state without
permission, §31-2-82.
Armory commission. See
within this heading,
"Armory commission."
Commander-in-chief.
General provisions. See
within this heading,
"Commander-in-chief."
Courts-martial.
Execution of sentence.
Approval of governor
prerequisite,
§31-2-103.
General courts-martial for
national guard.
Governor to convene,
§31-2-93.
Review of sentence by
governor, §31-2-103.
Emergency officers.
Appointment in state
militia, §31-2-47.
Flag, §31-2-54.
Military powers of governor,
Const. Ala., art. V, §131.
Ordering out of troops,
§§31-2-109 to 31-2-114.
See within this heading,
"Ordering out of troops."
Personal military staff of
governor, §31-2-53.
Reports.
Adjutant general.
Annual report to
governor, §31-2-67.
Staff, Const. Ala., art. XV,
§276; amd. 89.
State defense force.
Organization of state
defense force by
governor, §31-2-8.
Powers of governor with
respect to state defense
force, §31-2-9.
Unorganized militia.
Ordering out of
unorganized militia,
§31-2-48.
When unorganized militia
may be ordered out for
active service,
§31-2-46.
**Headquarters and
headquarters
detachment.**
Appointment of officers and
enlisted men, §31-2-55.
Assignment during national
crisis, §31-2-57.

MILITARY AFFAIRS—Cont'd
Health.
Abatement of menaces to
health, §31-2-126.
Hearings.
Compensation for death of
national guardsmen.
Hearing by board of
adjustment, §31-3-6.
Highways.
Right of troops to use
highways, §31-2-84.
Income tax.
Deductions.
Amortization of war or
emergency facilities,
§40-18-18.
Exemptions.
Military retirement
benefits, §40-18-20.
Members of armed forces of
United States.
Liability for state income
tax, §40-18-3.
Indictments.
Right of national guard
members under
indictment to change of
venue of trial, §31-2-118.
Injuries.
Compensation for injury,
§31-2-85.
Right of national guard
members under
indictment for injuries to
persons or property to
change of venue,
§31-2-118.
Instruction.
Annual encampments or
cruises, §31-2-37.
Armories.
Provisions of armories for
instruction of national
guard, naval militia,
etc., §31-4-7.
Drills, encampments,
maneuvers, etc.,
§31-2-76.
Other states.
Supervision and command
of national guard
organizations jointly
maintained with other
states for training and
instruction, §31-2-87.
**Insulting remarks and
gestures.**
Making disloyal or insulting
remarks, gestures, etc.,
to or about troops
engaged in performance
of duties, etc., §31-2-22.
**Interfering with
performance of troops.**
Authority of commanders to
incarcerate and detain
persons interfering,
§31-2-126.
Investigations.
Conduct of officers.
Courts of inquiry,
§31-2-107.
Jails.
National guard.
Commanders of national
guard troops may
prescribe boundaries
around jails from
which public excluded,
§31-2-123.

MILITARY AFFAIRS—Cont'd
Judicial notice.
Courts-martial.
Signature and handwriting
of commissioned
officers of national
guard, §31-2-98.
Jurisdiction.
Militia.
Courts-martial.
Jurisdiction of courts-
martial when militia
in active service of
state, §31-2-83.
National guard.
Courts-martial, §§31-2-92,
31-2-103.
Jury.
Exemptions of officers and
enlisted men of national
guard, naval militia and
state guard from state
jury duty, §31-2-11.
Leases.
Taxation.
Exemption from ad
valorem taxes of
property leased by
units of armed forces,
§31-2-80.
Leaves of absence.
Military leave of absence for
public officers and
employees, §31-2-13.
Legislature.
Regular military
appropriations,
§31-2-132.
Special appropriations for
national guard in active
military service of state,
§31-2-133.
Licenses.
Exemption of certain post
exchanges and canteens
from state and local
licenses, §31-2-81.
Fish and game.
Members of armed forces
during war, §9-11-35.
Limitation of actions.
Compensation for death of
national guardsmen.
Limitation on time for
presentation of claims,
§31-3-5.
Loans.
Veterans.
Minor veterans empowered
to contract liability for
repayment of certain
loans, §31-1-2.
Maneuvers.
Time and place for
maneuvers, §31-2-76.
Medals.
National guard and naval
militia medals, §31-2-41.
Uniforms.
Service medals authorized
for wear with national
guard and naval
militia uniforms,
§31-2-77.
Merchant marine.
Persons exempted from
military service, §31-2-6.

MILITARY AFFAIRS—Cont'd
Merit system.
  Military department.
    Applicability to
        department officers
        and employees,
        §31-2-60.
Military courts.
  Actions against members of
      court as to sentences,
      warrants, etc., §31-2-89.
  Courts-martial.
    Militia, §31-2-83.
    National guard. See within
        this heading,
        "National guard."
  Courts of inquiry, §31-2-107.
  Sentences.
    Actions against members
        as to sentences,
        §31-2-89.
  Warrants.
    Actions against members
        as to warrants,
        §31-2-89.
Military department.
  Administration of military
      affairs by department,
      Const. Ala., amd. 89.
  Appointment, §31-2-60.
  Billeting revolving fund,
      §31-1-3.
  Bonds, surety.
    Employees of military
        department, §31-2-62.
  Dropping allowance.
    Item of budget of
        department, §31-2-128.
  Employees.
    Appointment, §31-2-60.
    Assignments, duties and
        authority, §31-2-60.
    Bonds, §31-2-62.
    Merit system.
      Applicability to
          employees, §31-2-60.
    Qualifications, §31-2-60.
    Rank, §31-2-60.
    Salaries, §31-2-61.
  Furniture, §31-2-63.
  Merit system.
    Applicability to officers
        and employees,
        §31-2-60.
  Militia.
    Administration by
        department, §31-2-2.
  Officers.
    Appointment by adjutant
        general, §31-2-60.
    Assignments, duties and
        authority, §31-2-60.
    Merit system.
      Applicability, §31-2-60.
    Qualifications, §31-2-60.
    Salaries, §31-2-61.
  Offices, §31-2-63.
  Organization, §31-2-60.
  Payment for damages caused
      by national guard
      members acting in line
      of duty.
    Appropriations of
        department, §31-2-86.
  Rank, §31-2-60.
  Stationery, §31-2-63.
Military property. See within
    this heading, "Property."

MILITARY AFFAIRS—Cont'd
Militia.
  Adjutant general. See within
      this heading, "Adjutant
      general."
  Administration.
    Generally, §31-2-2.
  Arming, Const. Ala., art. XV,
      §271.
    Safekeeping of arms,
        ammunition, etc.,
        Const. Ala., art. XV,
        §277.
  Arrests.
    Exemptions of members
        from arrest, §31-2-79;
        Const. Ala., art. XV,
        §275.
  Commanders.
    Quarterly allowances,
        §31-2-108.
  Compensation.
    Officers and men not
        entitled when not in
        active service, Const.
        Ala., art. XV, §278.
  Composition, Const. Ala., art.
      XV, §271.
    Generally, §31-2-2.
  Constitution of Alabama.
    See CONSTITUTION OF
        ALABAMA.
  Constitution of the United
      States.
    See CONSTITUTION OF
        THE UNITED
        STATES.
  Courts-martial, §31-2-83.
  Discipline, Const. Ala., art.
      XV, §271.
  Divisions of state militia,
      §31-2-3.
  Emergency officers.
    Appointment by governor,
        §31-2-47.
  Enlisted personnel.
    Compensation.
      Not entitled to
          compensation when
          not in active service,
          Const. Ala., art. XV,
          §278.
  Failure to appear for duty,
      §31-2-50.
  Governor.
    Commander-in-chief of
        militia, §31-2-2.
    Staff, Const. Ala., art. XV,
        §276; amd. 89.
  Laws applicable to militia
      when in active service of
      state, §31-2-83.
  Leaving state without
      permission, §31-2-82.
  Naval militia. See within
      this heading, "Naval
      militia."
  Officers.
    Company and regimental
        officers.
      Election or appointment,
          Const. Ala., art. XV,
          §273.
    Compensation.
      Not entitled to
          compensation when
          not in active service,
          Const. Ala., art. XV,
          §278.
    Emergency officers,
        §31-2-47.

MILITARY AFFAIRS—Cont'd
Militia—Cont'd
  Officers—Cont'd
    General officers.
      Appointment, Const.
          Ala., art. XV, §276;
          amd. 89.
      Terms of office, Const.
          Ala., art. XV, §276.
  Organized militia.
    Composition, §31-2-3.
  Organizing, Const. Ala., art.
      XV, §271.
  Records.
    Safekeeping, Const. Ala.,
        art. XV, §277.
  Retired list.
    Division of state militia,
        §31-2-3.
  Staffs, Const. Ala., art. XV,
      §276.
  State military department.
    Administration of militia
        by department,
        §31-2-2.
  United States army.
    Conformance with
        regulations governing,
        Const. Ala., art. XV,
        §272.
  Unorganized militia. See
      within this heading,
      "Unorganized militia."
  Volunteer organizations,
      Const. Ala., art. XV,
      §274.
Missing in action.
  Official report of person
      missing.
    Prima facie evidence,
        §12-21-91.
Mobs.
  Dispersion of mobs. See
      within this heading,
      "Dispersion of mobs."
  Riots. See within this
      heading, "Riots."
Motor vehicles.
  Drivers' licenses.
    Restricted licenses,
        §32-6-12.
  License taxes and
      registration fees.
    Exemptions, §§31-2-12,
        40-12-244.
  Tags and plates.
    National guard, §§32-6-110
        to 32-6-113.
    Retired military,
        §§32-6-290 to 32-6-295.
    See MOTOR VEHICLES.
Municipal corporations.
  Appropriation of funds for
      local national guard and
      naval militia units,
      §31-2-129.
  Armory commission.
    Buildings.
      Cooperation of
          municipalities for
          acquisition of
          buildings, §31-4-9.
      Conveyance by
          municipalities of
          public lands to
          commission for use as
          armory sites, §31-4-11.
    Donations for aid of local
        national guard or naval
        militia, §31-4-17.

MILITARY AFFAIRS—Cont'd
Municipal corporations
—Cont'd
Real property.
Sale to local national
guard units, §31-2-130.
Reversion of donations,
§31-4-18.
National crisis.
Headquarters and
headquarters
detachments of national
guard.
Appointment during
national crisis,
§31-2-57.
National defense act.
Defined, §31-2-1.
State defense force.
Organization, maintenance
and training under
provisions of act,
§31-2-8.
National guard.
Actions.
Actions against national
guard members for
acts or omissions
performed in official
capacity.
Appointment of defense
counsel, §31-2-90.
Defense of actions
against present or
former members,
§31-2-89.
Security for costs to be
given by plaintiff,
§31-2-91.
Compensation for death of
national guardsmen,
§§31-3-1 to 31-3-7.
Defense of actions against
present or former
members, §31-2-89.
Air national guard. See
within this heading, "Air
national guard."
Alcoholic beverages.
Commanders may forbid
sale, §31-2-124.
Compensation for death of
guardsmen.
When dependents not
entitled to
compensation,
§31-3-2.
Annual encampments,
§31-2-37.
Appropriations.
Operation and support,
§31-2-108.
Special appropriations for
national guard in
active military service
of state, §31-2-133.
Armories.
Officers as members of
armory commission,
§31-4-1.
Provision of armories for
housing and
instruction of national
guard, §31-4-7.
Assaults.
Duty to disperse when shot
fired, etc., at national
guard, §31-2-121.

MILITARY AFFAIRS—Cont'd
National guard—Cont'd
Assaults—Cont'd
National guard members
assembled for
performance of duties,
§31-2-119.
Protection of national
guard troops from
assault, §31-2-120.
Attorneys at law.
Actions against national
guard members for
acts or omissions
performed in official
capacity.
Appointment of defense
counsel, §31-2-90.
Defense of actions
against present or
former members,
§31-2-89.
Buildings.
Counties or municipalities
may sell real estate
and buildings to local
units for military
purposes, §31-2-130.
Commanders.
Boundaries around jails,
public buildings, etc.
Commanders may
prescribe boundaries
from which public
excluded, §31-2-123.
Quarterly allowances,
§31-2-108.
Compensation for death of
national guardsmen,
§31-2-85.
Alcoholic beverages.
When dependents not
entitled to
compensation,
§31-3-2.
Amount of compensation,
§31-3-2.
Appeals.
Decision of awarding
authority to be final,
§31-3-7.
Awarding authority.
Defined, §31-3-1.
Board of adjustment.
Hearing and
determination of
claims, §31-3-6.
Claims.
Hearing on claims by
board of adjustment,
§31-3-6.
Limitation on time for
presentation,
§31-3-5.
Procedure for
determination of
claims, §31-3-5.
Construction of chapter,
§31-3-7.
Decision of awarding
authority to be final,
§31-3-7.
Definitions, §31-3-1.
Dependents.
Apportionment of
compensation among
dependents, §31-3-3.
Defined, §31-3-1.
Residents of United
States, §31-3-4.

MILITARY AFFAIRS—Cont'd
National guard—Cont'd
Compensation for death of
national guardsmen
—Cont'd
Dependents—Cont'd
Right to compensation,
§31-3-2.
Evidence.
Rules of evidence for
determination of
claims, §31-3-5.
Hearing.
Board of adjustment,
§31-3-6.
Limitation on time for
presentation of claims,
§31-3-5.
Payment of compensation.
Apportionment among
dependents, §31-3-3.
Manner, §31-3-3.
Residents.
Dependents must be
residents of United
States, §31-3-4.
Right of dependents to
compensation, §31-3-2.
Composition, §31-2-3.
Counties.
Appropriation of funds for
local national guard,
§31-2-129.
Real property.
Counties may sell to
local national guard
units, §31-2-130.
Courts-martial.
Court reporter.
Employment, §31-2-99.
Disruption of proceedings.
Punishment of persons
disrupting,
§31-2-101.
Evidence, §31-2-98.
Judicial notice, §31-2-98.
Signature and
handwriting of
commissioned
officers, §31-2-98.
Expenses.
Payment of expenses,
§31-2-102.
Findings of courts-martial.
Review by governor,
§31-2-103.
Fines.
Disposition, §31-2-105.
General courts-martial,
§31-2-93.
Governor.
Approval of governor
prerequisite to
execution of
sentence, §31-2-103.
Review of findings and
sentence by
governor, §31-2-103.
Judicial notice.
Signature and
handwriting of
commissioned
officers, §31-2-98.
Jurisdiction, §31-2-92.
Presumption of
jurisdiction,
§31-2-102.
Manual of courts-martial
to govern proceedings,
§31-2-97.
Powers, §§31-2-92, 31-2-96.

MILITARY AFFAIRS—Cont'd
National guard—Cont'd
  Courts-martial—Cont'd
    Presidents.
      Powers, §31-2-96.
      Presumption of jurisdiction
        and legality of
        proceedings, §31-2-103.
      Procedure generally,
        §31-2-92.
      Process.
        Compensation of civil
          officers for execution
          of process, §31-2-106.
        Persons authorized to
          execute, §31-2-104.
    Sentences.
      Delivery of certificate to
        sheriff for execution
        of sentence,
        §31-2-105.
      Persons authorized to
        execute, §31-2-104.
      Review by governor,
        §31-2-103.
    Sheriffs.
      Delivery of certificate to
        sheriff for execution
        of sentence,
        §31-2-105.
      Execution of process and
        sentence, §31-2-104.
      Payment of sheriffs' fees,
        §§31-2-102, 31-2-106.
    Special courts-martial,
      §31-2-94.
    Subpoenas, §31-2-100.
    Summary courts-martial.
      Convening, §31-2-95.
      Officers.
        Power of summary
          court officers,
          §31-2-96.
      Powers of punishment,
        §31-2-95.
    Types, §31-2-92.
    Uniform code of military
      justice.
      Proceedings to follow
        code, §31-2-92.
    Warrants.
      Punishment of persons
        disrupting
        proceedings,
        §31-2-101.
      Summary court officers.
        Power to issue
          warrants,
          §31-2-96.
    Witnesses.
      Payment of witness fees,
        §31-2-102.
      Subpoena, §31-2-100.
  Custom and usage of United
    States armed forces.
    Matters governed by,
      §31-2-35.
  Damages.
    Payment for damages
      caused by members
      acting in line of duty,
      §31-2-86.
  Defenses of actions against
    present or former
    members, §31-2-89.
  Definitions.
    Educational assistance act,
      §31-10-2.
  Disabilities.
    Compensation for
      disability, §31-2-85.

MILITARY AFFAIRS—Cont'd
National guard—Cont'd
  Discharges.
    Enlisted members,
      §31-2-75.
  Donations.
    City and county donations
      for aid of local
      national guard or
      naval militia
      organizations,
      §31-4-17.
  Educational assistance,
    §§31-10-1 to 31-10-4.
    Definitions, §31-10-2.
    Eligibility for tuition
      reimbursement,
      §31-10-3.
    Final authority for
      determining
      applicants, §31-10-4.
    Minimum requirements to
      be eligible, §31-10-4.
    Minimum standards,
      §31-10-3.
    Repayment of benefits if
      service terminated,
      §31-10-4.
    Short title, §31-10-1.
    Tuition reimbursement
      authorized for active
      members of national
      guard, §31-10-3.
  Enforcement of attendance,
    §31-2-127.
  Enlisted men.
    Discharge of enlisted
      members, §31-2-75.
    Headquarters and
      headquarters
      detachment.
      Appointment of enlisted
        men, §31-2-55.
    Jury duty.
      Exemptions from state
        jury duty, §31-2-11.
    Period of enlistments,
      §31-2-74.
    Qualifications, Const. Ala.,
      amd. 89.
    Release from active federal
      service.
      Status of enlisted men
        released, §31-2-43.
    Retirement, §31-2-42.
  Explosives.
    Commanders may forbid
      sale, §31-2-124.
  Federally recognized national
    guard.
    Qualifications, §31-2-69.
  Federal service. See within
    this heading, "Federal
    service."
  Gifts.
    City and county donations
      for aid of local
      national guard,
      §31-4-17.
  Headquarters and
    headquarters
    detachment.
    Appointment of officers
      and enlisted men,
      §31-2-55.
    National crisis.
      Assignment during
        national crisis,
        §31-2-57.

MILITARY AFFAIRS—Cont'd
National guard—Cont'd
  Highways.
    Right to use highways,
      §31-2-84.
  Injuries.
    Compensation for injury,
      §31-2-85.
  Instruction.
    Other states.
      Supervision and
        command, §31-2-87.
  Jails.
    Commanders may
      prescribe boundaries
      around jails from
      which public excluded,
      §31-2-123.
  Jury duty.
    Exemption of officers and
      enlisted men, §31-2-11.
  Leaving state without
    permission, §31-2-82.
  Medals, §31-2-41.
  Motor vehicle tags and
    plates, §§32-6-110 to
    32-6-113.
  Municipal corporations.
    Appropriation of funds for
      local national guard
      units, §31-2-129.
    Real property.
      Municipalities may sell
        real estate and
        buildings to local
        national guard,
        §31-2-130.
  Noncommissioned officers.
    Appointment, §31-2-73.
    Promotion, §31-2-73.
  Officers.
    Armory commission.
      Certain officers members
        of commission,
        §31-4-1.
    Arms and equipment.
      Preservation by officers,
        §31-2-24.
    Headquarters and
      headquarters
      detachment.
      Appointment of officers,
        §31-2-55.
    Jury duty.
      Exemptions from state
        jury duty, §31-2-11.
    Noncommissioned officers,
      §31-2-73.
    Other states.
      Supervision and
        command, §31-2-87.
    Property.
      Preservation by officers,
        §31-2-24.
    Qualifications, Const. Ala.,
      amd. 89.
    Release from active federal
      service.
      Status of officers
        released, §31-2-43.
    Retirement, §31-2-42.
    Same powers and duties as
      officers in armed forces
      of United States,
      §31-2-70.
    Staff officers
      headquartered in other
      states.
      Qualifications and
        appointment,
        §31-2-71.

MILITARY AFFAIRS—Cont'd
National guard—Cont'd
Officers—Cont'd
Uniforms.
Preservation by officers,
§31-2-24.
Ordering out of troops,
§§31-2-109 to 31-2-114.
See within this heading,
"Ordering out of troops."
Other states.
Supervision and command,
§31-2-87.
Pay and subsistence,
§31-2-88.
Peacetime.
Right of state to use
national guard in
peacetime, §31-2-7.
Proceedings.
Presumption of legality,
§31-2-103.
Public buildings.
Commanders of national
guard troops may
prescribe boundaries
around public
buildings from which
public excluded,
§31-2-123.
Qualifications of personnel,
Const. Ala., amd. 89.
Release from active federal
service.
Status of officers and
enlisted men released,
§31-2-43.
Retirement, §31-2-42.
Riots and unlawful
assemblies. See within
this heading, "Riots."
Streets.
Right to use streets,
§31-2-84.
Tags and plates, §§32-6-110
to 32-6-113.
Taxation.
Property exempt, §40-9-1.
Training.
Other states.
Supervision and
command, §31-2-87.
Uniforms.
Medals and decorations.
Authorized for wear with
national guard
uniforms, §31-2-77.
Unauthorized wearing of
uniform while not on
duty, §31-2-20.
Weapons.
Commanders may forbid
sale of weapons,
§31-2-124.
Naval militia.
Active naval service of the
state.
When officers or enlisted
men deemed to be in,
§31-2-38.
Age of members, §31-2-4.
Annual cruises, §31-2-37.
Armories.
Provisions of amories for
housing and
instruction of naval
militia, §31-4-7.
Authorized, Const. Ala., art.
XV, §271.

MILITARY AFFAIRS—Cont'd
Naval militia—Cont'd
Commanders.
Quarterly allowances,
§31-2-108.
Composition, §31-2-4.
Constitution of Alabama.
See CONSTITUTION OF
ALABAMA.
Counties.
Appropriation of funds for
local naval militia
units, §31-2-129.
Custom and usage of United
States armed forces.
Matters governed by,
§31-2-35.
Donations.
City and county donations,
§31-4-17.
Enforcement of attendance,
§31-2-127.
Enlisted men.
Release from active federal
service.
Status of enlisted men
released, §31-2-43.
Federal service. See within
this heading, "Federal
service."
Gifts.
City and county gifts for
aid of local naval
militia, §31-4-17.
Jury duty.
Exemptions of officers and
enlisted men from
state jury duty,
§31-2-11.
Leaving state without
permission, §31-2-82.
Medals, §31-2-41.
Municipal corporations.
Appropriation of funds for
local naval militia
units, §31-2-129.
Officers.
Age, §31-2-4.
Arms and equipment.
Preservation by officers,
§31-2-24.
Property.
Preservation by officers,
§31-2-24.
Release from active federal
service.
Status of officers
released, §31-2-43.
Same powers and duties as
officers in armed forces
of United States,
§31-2-70.
Uniforms.
Preservation by officers,
§31-2-24.
Pay and subsistence,
§31-2-88.
Release from active federal
service.
Status of officers and
enlisted men released,
§31-2-43.
Streets and highways.
Right of troops to use,
§31-2-84.
Uniforms.
Medals and decorations,
§31-2-77.
Unauthorized wearing of
uniform while not on
duty, §31-2-20.

MILITARY AFFAIRS—Cont'd
Noncommissioned officers.
National guard, §31-2-73.
Obscenity.
Courts-martial.
Disruption of proceedings.
Punishment of persons
disrupting,
§31-2-101.
Officers.
Actions against officers for
acts performed in line of
duty, §31-2-89.
Adjutant general. See within
this heading, "Adjutant
general."
Air national guard.
Appointment, §31-2-55.
Appointment, Const. Ala.,
amd. 89.
Air national guard,
§31-2-55.
General officers of the line,
§31-2-72.
National guard. See within
this heading,
"National guard."
Standards for appointment,
§31-2-69.
Arms and equipment.
Care.
Personal responsibility
for care, §31-2-28.
Lost or damaged
equipment.
Liability of officers,
§31-2-32.
Personal arms.
Exempt from sale under
execution, §31-2-78.
Preservation by officers,
§31-2-24.
Reports.
Failure to make required
reports, §31-2-33.
Attendance of officers called
into active military
service of state.
Enforcement of attendance,
§31-2-127.
Audit of accounts, §31-2-68.
Commander-in-chief. See
within this heading,
"Commander-in-chief."
Conduct.
Investigation of conduct.
Courts of inquiry,
§31-2-107.
Courts-martial.
Signature and handwriting
of commissioned
officers.
Judicial notice, §31-2-98.
Courts of inquiry.
Investigation of conduct of
officers, §31-2-107.
Disbanded organizations.
Arms and equipment.
Return to custody of
adjutant general,
§31-2-26.
Discharge, Const. Ala., amd.
89.
Dispersion of mobs.
Order to disperse,
§31-2-115.
Duties.
Officers to have same
duties as officers in
armed forces of United
States, §31-2-70.

MILITARY AFFAIRS—Cont'd
Officers—Cont'd
Emergency officers.
Appointment of emergency
officers in state militia
by governor, §31-2-47.
Emergency purchases,
§31-2-39.
General officers of the line,
§31-2-72.
"In the active military or
naval service of the
state."
When officers deemed to be
in the active military
or naval service of
state, §31-2-38.
Jury duty.
Exemptions of officers,
§31-2-11.
Military department. See
within this heading,
"Military department."
National guard. See within
this heading, "National
guard."
Naval militia. See within
this heading, "Naval
militia."
Other states.
Supervision and command,
§31-2-87.
Pay and subsistence,
§31-2-88.
Per diem, §31-2-16.
Powers.
Officers to have same
powers as officers in
armed forces of United
States, §31-2-70.
Property.
Accountability and
responsibility of
officers for property in
custody, §31-2-25.
Injured or destroyed
property.
Liabilities of officers,
§31-2-25.
Lost or damaged property.
Liability of officers,
§31-2-32.
Personally responsible for
care, etc., of military
property in custody,
§31-2-28.
Reports.
Failure to make required
reports, §31-2-33.
Removal, Const. Ala., amd.
89.
Standards for removal,
§31-2-69.
Reports.
Arms and equipment.
Failure to make required
reports, §31-2-33.
Retirement, Const. Ala.,
amd. 89.
National guard, §31-2-42.
Standards for appointment,
removal, etc., §31-2-69.
Suspension, Const. Ala., amd.
89.
Travel orders.
Per diem of officers under
military travel orders,
§31-2-16.

MILITARY AFFAIRS—Cont'd
Officers—Cont'd
Uniforms.
Personal uniforms.
Execution.
Exempt from sale
under execution,
§31-2-78.
Preservation by officers,
§31-2-24.
Ordering out of troops,
§§31-2-109 to 31-2-114.
Compliance with
instructions, §31-2-113.
Governor.
Authority of governor,
§31-2-109.
Issuance of order,
§31-2-112.
Reports to governor when
troops ordered by civil
authorities, §31-2-114.
Request to governor by
local officials,
§31-2-111.
Local officials.
Authority of local civil
authorities to order out
troops, §31-2-112.
Commanding officers.
Requiring written
instructions from
civil authorities,
§31-2-113.
Reports.
Troops ordered by civil
authorities.
Reports to governor,
§31-2-114.
Request to governor,
§31-2-111.
Purposes, §31-2-109.
Reports.
Troops ordered by civil
authorities.
Reports to governor,
§31-2-114.
Restrictions, §31-2-110.
Unorganized militia,
§31-2-48.
Organized militia.
Composition, §31-2-3.
Other states.
Supervision and command of
national guard
organizations jointly
maintained with other
states for training and
instruction, §31-2-87.
Parties.
Persons in federal service
and spouses living in
state deemed residents
for purpose of
commencing actions,
§6-7-20.
Pay and subsistence.
Courts-martial.
General courts-martial.
Forfeiture of pay and
allowances, §31-2-93.
National guard and naval
militia in active military
or naval service of state,
§31-2-88.
Peacetime.
Maintenance of troops in
time of peace, §31-2-7.

MILITARY AFFAIRS—Cont'd
Peacetime—Cont'd
National guard.
Right of state to use
national guard in
peacetime, §31-2-7.
Penalties.
Courts-martial.
Disposition of fines
collected, §31-2-105.
Imprisonment, §31-2-83.
Death penalty, §31-2-83.
Uniforms.
Unauthorized wearing of
United States armed
forces uniform,
§31-2-17.
Wearing foreign uniforms,
§31-2-19.
Pilots and pilotage.
Persons exempted from
military service.
Pilots employed in sea
service of any citizen
or merchant within
United States, §31-2-6.
Post exchanges.
Licenses.
Exemptions from state and
local licenses, §31-2-81.
Tobacco taxes.
Exemption, §31-2-81.
Presumptions.
Courts-martial.
Presumption of jurisdiction
and legality of
proceedings, §31-2-103.
Probate judges.
Honorable discharges.
Duties of judges as to,
§31-1-1.
Ordering out of troops.
Request to governor by
probate judge,
§31-2-111.
Property.
Actions.
Proceedings when member
of armed forces unable
to account for property
or money, §31-2-34.
Adjutant general.
Powers and duties of
adjutant general as
exclusive custodian of
state military
property, §31-2-25.
Armories.
See ARMORIES.
Arms and equipment. See
within this heading,
"Arms and equipment."
Bonds, surety.
Persons responsible for
public or military
property, §31-2-14.
Care.
Officers and enlisted men
personally responsible
for care, §31-2-28.
Custodian.
Adjutant general as
exclusive custodian of
state military
property, §31-2-25.
Illegally acquired property.
Seizure, etc., §31-2-30.

MILITARY AFFAIRS—Cont'd
Property—Cont'd
Injured or destroyed
property.
Liability of officers and
enlisted men,
§§31-2-25, 31-2-32.
Right of national guard
members under
indictment for injuries
to property to change
of venue, §31-2-118.
Wilful or malicious
destruction, §31-2-29.
Officers.
Accountability and
responsibility of
officers for property in
custody, §31-2-25.
Preservation of property by
officers, §31-2-24.
Pawning military property,
§31-2-31.
Private use of military
property, §31-2-27.
Proceedings when member of
armed forces unable to
account for property or
money, §31-2-34.
Real property. See within
this heading, "Real
property."
Reports.
Failure of officers and
enlisted men to make
required reports,
§31-2-33.
Sale, exchange, etc., of
military property,
§31-2-30.
Taxation.
Exemption from ad
valorem taxes of
property owned or
leased by units of
armed forces, §31-2-80.
Transfer by officers.
Authority of adjutant
general required,
§31-2-25.
Unauthorized retention,
§31-2-31.
Seizure of unlawfully
retained property,
§31-2-31.
Unauthorized use of military
property for private
purposes, §31-2-27.
Uniforms. See within this
heading, "Uniforms."
Wilful or malicious
destruction, §31-2-29.
Public buildings.
Armory commission.
Cooperation of counties
and municipalities for
acquisition of buildings
suitable for use as
public buildings,
§31-4-9.
Commanders of national
guard troops.
Prescribing boundaries
around public
buildings from which
public excluded,
§31-2-123.

MILITARY AFFAIRS—Cont'd
Public lands.
Armory commission.
Conveyance by counties or
municipalities of
public lands for use as
armory sites, §31-4-11.
**Public officers and
employees.**
Acceptance, etc., of
commission, etc., in state
armed forces and United
States reserve
components.
Not incompatible with
holding of civil office,
§31-2-36.
Credit for active federal
service, §31-2-13.
Military leave of absence,
§31-2-13.
Persons exempted from
military service.
State officers, §31-2-6.
Service benefits for
government employees,
§31-2-13.
Service in time of war or
national emergency,
§§36-8-1 to 36-8-6.
See PUBLIC OFFICERS
AND EMPLOYEES.
State employees' retirement
system.
Membership.
Effect of military service,
§36-27-4.
Purchases.
Emergency purchases,
§31-2-39.
Quartering of soldiers, Const.
Ala., art. I, §28; Const. U.
S., Amendment III.
Real property.
Counties or municipalities
may sell real estate and
buildings to local
national guard units,
§31-2-130.
Reversion of donations,
§31-4-18.
Taxation.
Exemption from ad
valorem taxes of
property owned or
leased by units of
armed forces, §31-2-80.
Records.
Discharges.
Honorable discharges,
§31-1-1.
Admissibility as
evidence, §31-1-1.
Safekeeping, Const. Ala., art.
XV, §277.
Recruiting.
Education.
Access to school facilities
by recruiting
representatives,
§16-1-25.
**Regulations of department
of defense.**
Composition of organized
militia and national
guard.
Organization in accordance
with regulations,
§31-2-3.
Defined, §31-2-1.

MILITARY AFFAIRS—Cont'd
**Regulations of department
of defense**—Cont'd
State military forces to
conform with regulations
of department, Const.
Ala., amd. 89.
Religion.
Persons exempted from
military service.
Holding of religious beliefs,
§31-2-6.
**Remainders, reversions and
executory interests.**
Reversion of donations for
national guard or naval
militia, §31-4-18.
Removal of actions.
Right of national guard
members under
indictment for injuries to
persons or property to
change of venue of trial,
§31-2-118.
Reports.
Adjutant general.
Annual report to governor,
§31-2-67.
Emergency purchases,
§31-2-39.
Enlisted men.
Arms and equipment.
Failure of enlisted men
to make required
reports, §31-2-33.
Funds.
Failure of officers, etc., to
make required reports,
§31-2-33.
Officers.
Arms and equipment.
Failure of officers to
make required
reports, §31-2-33.
Ordering out of troops.
Reports to governor when
troops ordered by civil
authorities, §31-2-114.
Property.
Failure of officers, etc., to
make required reports
concerning military
arms, funds, etc.,
§31-2-33.
Residence.
Militia.
Composition of state
militia, §31-2-2.
National guard.
Compensation for death of
national guardsmen.
Dependents must be
residents of United
States, §31-3-4.
Retirement.
Motor vehicles.
Tags and plates for retired
military, §§32-6-290 to
32-6-295.
See MOTOR VEHICLES.
National guard, §31-2-42.
Riots.
Dispersion of mobs. See
within this heading,
"Dispersion of mobs."
Duty to disperse when shot
fired, etc., at national
guard, §31-2-121.

MILITARY AFFAIRS—Cont'd
Riots—Cont'd
National guard.
Compensation for death of
national guardsmen.
Death of national
guardsmen quelling
riot, §31-3-2.
Ordering out of troops. See
within this heading,
"Ordering out of troops."
Regulation of passage and
occupancy on streets
during riot, §31-2-122.
Streets.
Regulation of passage and
occupancy on streets
during riot, §31-2-122.
Rules and regulations.
Regulations of department of
defense. See within this
heading, "Regulations of
department of defense."
Unorganized militia,
§31-2-47.
Safety.
Abatement of menaces to
health or safety of
command, §31-2-126.
Salaries.
Courts-martial.
Forfeiture of pay and
allowance, §31-2-93.
Military department.
Officers and employees,
§31-2-61.
National guard and naval
militia, §31-2-88.
Sales.
Military property.
Sale, exchange, etc.,
§31-2-30.
National guard.
Weapons.
Commanders may forbid
sale, §31-2-124.
Unauthorized retention of
military property,
§31-2-31.
Sanitation.
Enforcement of sanitation
laws in camps or
garrisons, §31-2-40.
Seals.
Adjutant general, §31-2-58.
Searches and seizures.
Illegally acquired military
property.
Seizure, etc., §31-2-30.
Unlawfully retained
property, §31-2-31.
Sentencing.
Courts-martial, §31-2-83.
Governor.
Approval of governor
prerequisite to
execution of
sentence, §31-2-103.
Persons authorized to
execute sentences,
§31-2-104.
Review of sentence by
governor, §31-2-103.
Military courts.
Actions against members
of court as to
sentences, §31-2-89.

MILITARY AFFAIRS—Cont'd
Sheriffs.
Courts-martial.
Compensation for
execution of process,
§31-2-106.
Delivery of certificate to
sheriff for execution of
sentence, §31-2-105.
Execution of processes and
sentences.
Persons authorized to
execute, §31-2-104.
Payment of sheriffs' fees,
§31-2-102.
Ordering out of troops.
Request to governor by
sheriff, §31-2-111.
Unlawfully retained military
property.
Seizure by sheriff,
§31-2-31.
Signatures.
Courts-martial.
Judicial notice of signature
and handwriting of
commissioned officers,
§31-2-98.
Standing army, Const. Ala.,
art. I, §27.
State.
Arms and equipment.
Proceedings by state when
member of armed
forces unable to
account for property or
money, §31-2-34.
Federal service.
Payment of expenses by
state upon call into
federal service,
§31-2-44.
Persons exempted from
military service, §31-2-6.
State defense force, §§31-2-8
to 31-2-10.
Adjutant general.
Powers of adjutant general
with respect to state
defense force, §31-2-9.
Appropriations, §31-2-10.
Disbanding, §31-2-8.
Federal control.
State defense force to be
free from federal
control, §31-2-9.
Governor.
Authority to organize,
equip, train and
maintain, §31-2-8.
Powers of governor with
respect to state defense
force, §31-2-9.
National defense act.
Organization, maintenance
and training under
provisions of act,
§31-2-8.
Organization, §31-2-8.
When organized, §31-2-8.
State guard.
Jury.
Exemptions of officers and
enlisted men from
state jury duty,
§31-2-11.
Leaving state without
permission, §31-2-82.

MILITARY AFFAIRS—Cont'd
State guard—Cont'd
Peacetime.
Right of state to use state
guard in peacetime,
§31-2-7.
State military department.
See within this heading,
"Military department."
State militia.
Generally. See within this
heading, "Militia."
Naval militia. See within
this heading, "Naval
militia."
Streets.
Disloyal or insulting
remarks.
Making disloyal or
insulting remarks,
gestures, etc., to or
about troops at drill on
streets, §31-2-22.
Right of troops to use streets,
§31-2-84.
Riots.
Regulation of passage and
occupancy during riot,
§31-2-122.
Subpoena.
Courts-martial.
Subpoena of witnesses,
§31-2-100.
Taxation.
Exemption from ad valorem
taxes of property owned
or leased by units of
armed forces, §31-2-80.
National guard.
Property exempt, §40-9-1.
Post exchanges and canteens.
Exemption from tobacco
and gasoline taxes,
§31-2-81.
Tobacco.
Taxation.
Exemption of certain post
exchanges and
canteens from tobacco
taxes, §31-2-81.
Training.
Annual encampments or
cruises, §31-2-37.
Armories.
Provisions of armories for
housing, instruction,
etc., of national guard,
naval militia, etc.,
§31-4-7.
Drills, encampments,
maneuvers, etc.,
§31-2-76.
Other states.
Supervision and command,
§31-2-87.
Travel orders.
Per diem of officers or
enlisted men under
orders, §31-2-16.
**Unauthorized military
organizations,** §31-2-125.
**Uniform code of military
justice.**
Courts-martial.
Proceedings to follow code,
§31-2-92.
Defined, §31-2-1.
Uniforms.
Discrimination against
person wearing uniform,
§31-2-21.

MILITARY AFFAIRS—Cont'd
Uniforms—Cont'd
Exempt from sale under
execution, §31-2-78.
Foreign uniforms.
Wearing foreign uniforms.
Penalties, §31-2-19.
Prohibited, §31-2-18.
Exceptions, §31-2-18.
Illegally acquired uniforms.
Seizure, etc., §31-2-30.
Medals and decorations,
§31-2-77.
Personally owned uniforms.
Execution.
Exempt from sale under
execution, §31-2-78.
Preservation by officers,
§31-2-24.
Sale, exchange, etc.,
§31-2-30.
Unauthorized wearing of
uniform of United States
armed forces, §31-2-17.
Unauthorized wearing of
uniform while not on
duty, §31-2-20.
Unit designations.
Defined, §31-2-1.
United States.
Active federal service.
Credit for federal service,
§31-2-13.
Commission in United States
reserve.
Acceptance not
incompatible with
holding of civil office,
§31-2-36.
Compensation for death of
national guardsmen,
§31-3-4.
Custom and usage of United
States armed forces.
Matters governed by,
§31-2-35.
Federally recognized national
guard.
Qualifications, §31-2-69.
Militia.
Conformance with
regulations governing
United States army,
Const. Ala., art. XV,
§272.
Officers to have same powers
and duties as officers in
armed forces of United
States, §31-2-70.
Persons exempted from
military service.
Officers of United States,
§31-2-6.
Release from active federal
service.
Status of officers and
enlisted men of
national guard and
naval militia upon
release, §31-2-43.
Uniforms.
Unauthorized wearing of
uniform of United
States armed forces,
§31-2-17.

MILITARY AFFAIRS—Cont'd
Universities and colleges.
Armory commission.
Bonds, surety.
Arms and equipment.
Care of arms,
equipment, etc.,
§31-4-4.
National guard educational
assistance, §§31-10-1 to
31-10-4.
Unlawful assemblies.
Dispersion of mobs. See
within this heading,
"Dispersion of mobs."
Unorganized militia.
Age requirement, §31-2-5.
Composition, §31-2-5.
Divisions of state militia,
§31-2-3.
Draft of unorganized militia,
§31-2-49.
Manner of ordering out,
§31-2-48.
Officers.
Appointment, §31-2-48.
Organization, §31-2-48.
Rules, regulations, etc.,
governing unorganized
militia in active service,
§31-2-47.
When unorganized militia
may be ordered out for
active service, §31-2-46.
Venue.
Change of venue, §31-2-118.
Veterans.
See VETERANS.
Warrants.
Courts-martial.
Disruption of proceedings.
Punishment of persons
disrupting,
§31-2-101.
Summary court officers.
Power to issue warrants,
§31-2-96.
Military courts.
Actions against members
of courts as to
warrants, §31-2-89.
Weapons.
Arms and equipment. See
within this heading,
"Arms and equipment."
National guard.
Commanders may forbid
sale of weapons,
§31-2-129.
Witnesses.
Courts-martial.
Payment of witness fees,
§31-2-102.
Subpoena of witnesses,
§31-2-100.

MILITIA.
See MILITARY AFFAIRS.

MILK AND MILK
PRODUCTS, §§2-13-1 to
2-13-94.
Adulteration.
Ice cream, §2-13-12.
Advertising.
Substitutes for butter and
cheese.
Use of certain words or
representations in
advertisement,
§2-13-19.

MILK AND MILK PRODUCTS
—Cont'd
Appeals.
Health regulations.
Appeal from order or
action of commissioner,
§2-13-90.
Board of agriculture and
industries.
Powers of board, §2-13-2.
Butter.
Imitation butter, §§2-13-16 to
2-13-20.
Advertisement.
Use of certain words or
representations in
advertisement,
§2-13-19.
Containers.
Required stamping or
marking on
containers, §2-13-17.
Deception of public.
Sale of substitutes
intending to deceive
public, §2-13-20.
Defined, §2-13-16.
Possession of substitutes,
§2-13-19.
Sale.
Deception of public.
Sale of substitutes
intending to
deceive public,
§2-13-20.
Statement required to
accompany sale,
§2-13-18.
Use of certain words or
representations in
sale, §2-13-19.
Transportation through
state, §2-13-18.
Renovated butter, §2-13-21.
Cheese.
Imitation cheese, §§2-13-16
to 2-13-19.
Advertisement.
Use of certain words or
representations in
advertisement,
§2-13-19.
Containers.
Required stamping or
marking on
containers, §2-13-17.
Defined, §2-13-16.
Possession of substitutes,
§2-13-19.
Sale.
Statement required to
accompany sale,
§2-13-18.
Use of certain words or
representations in
sale, §2-13-19.
Transportation through
state, §2-13-18.
Commissioner of agriculture
and industries.
Health regulations. See
within this heading,
"Health regulations."
Permits, §2-13-86.
Containers.
Marked containers, §§8-12-40
to 8-12-44, 8-16-95 to
8-16-97. See within this
heading, "Marked
containers."

MILK AND MILK PRODUCTS
—Cont'd

Cooling stations.
Inspection of milk cooling
stations, §22-20-7.
County boards of health.
Duties, §22-3-2.
County health officers.
Duties, §22-3-5.
Dairies.
Insanitary premises or
utensils, §2-13-7.
Inspection.
Municipal corporations,
§§11-47-137,
11-47-139.
Sanitation of premises and
utensils, §2-13-5.
Definitions.
Ice cream, §2-13-11.
Imitation butter and
imitation cheese,
§2-13-16.
Diseases.
Milk from diseased cows,
§2-13-7.
Distributors.
Permits generally. See
within this heading,
"Permits."
Evidence.
Marked containers.
Possession by secondhand
or junk dealer prima
facie evidence of
violation, §8-12-42.
Farms.
Inspection of dairy farms,
§22-20-7.
Fat.
Adding or blending fat with
milk or cream, §2-13-4.
Fees.
Permits.
Filing fee, §2-13-8.
Fraud.
Imitation butter.
Sale of substitutes
deceiving public,
§2-13-20.
Health regulations.
Appeal from order or action
of commissioner,
§2-13-90.
Boards of health.
Authority and jurisdiction,
§§22-2-2, 22-3-2.
Powers of state and local
boards of health not
restricted, §2-13-91.
Commissioner of agriculture
and industries, §§2-13-90
to 2-13-93.
Appeal from order or
action of commissioner,
§2-13-90.
Examination of records,
§2-13-92.
Investigations and
inspections, §2-13-92.
Resisting or interfering
with commissioner,
§2-13-92.
Right of entry, §2-13-92.
Rules and regulations,
§2-13-93.
Cooperation among state
agencies, §2-13-81.
County boards of health.
Duties, §22-3-2.

MILK AND MILK PRODUCTS
—Cont'd

Health regulations—Cont'd
County boards of health
—Cont'd
Powers not restricted,
§2-13-91.
County health officers.
Duties, §22-3-5.
Insanitary dairy premises
and utensils, §2-13-7.
Inspections. See within this
heading, "Inspections."
Investigations, §2-13-92.
Milk transported into
Alabama, §2-13-84.
Permits. See within this
heading, "Permits."
Purpose of article, §2-13-80.
Records.
Examination of records,
§2-13-92.
Right of entry of
commissioner, §2-13-92.
Rules and regulations of
commissioner, §2-13-93.
Sanitation of dairy premises
and utensils, §2-13-5.
Seizure of milk in transit,
§2-13-89.
State and local boards of
health.
Authority and jurisdiction,
§§22-2-2, 22-3-2.
Powers not restricted,
§2-13-91.
Transportation of milk into
Alabama, §2-13-84.
Violation a misdemeanor,
§2-13-94.
**Ice cream, §§2-13-11 to
2-13-12.**
Adulterated ice cream,
§2-13-12.
Defined, §2-13-11.
Licenses, §40-12-113.
Misbranded ice cream,
§2-13-13.
Standardized, §2-13-11.
**Imitation butter, §§2-13-16 to
2-13-20.**
**Imitation cheese, §§2-13-16 to
2-13-19.**
**Insanitary premises and
utensils, §2-13-7.**
Inspections, §2-13-92.
Applicability of laws relative
to inspection, §2-13-22.
Dairies.
Municipal corporations,
§§11-47-137,
11-47-139.
Dairy farms, milk cooling
stations, etc., §22-20-7.
Labels.
Marked containers, §§8-12-40
to 8-12-44, 8-16-95 to
8-16-97. See within this
heading, "Marked
containers."
Licenses.
Ice cream, §40-12-113.
Operation of testing
apparatus, §2-13-9.
**Marked containers, §§8-12-40
to 8-12-44, 8-16-95 to
8-16-97.**
Capacities, §8-16-95.
Enforcement of article,
§8-12-43.

MILK AND MILK PRODUCTS
—Cont'd

Marked containers—Cont'd
Evidence.
Possession by secondhand
or junk dealer prima
facie evidence of
violation, §8-12-42.
Penalties.
Selling or using
noncomplying
containers, §8-16-96.
Violations of article,
§8-12-44.
Presumption of ownership,
§8-12-41.
Purchase, §8-12-40.
Sale, §8-12-40.
Noncomplying containers,
§8-16-96.
Sealers.
Duties, §8-16-97.
Secondhand or junk dealers.
Possession prima facie
evidence of violation,
§8-12-42.
Violations of article.
Penalty, §8-12-44.
Possession by secondhand
or junk dealer prima
facie evidence of
violation, §8-12-42.
**Mellorine, §§20-1-130 to
20-1-137.**
See MELLORINE.
Misbranding.
Ice cream, §2-13-13.
Motor vehicle carriers.
Vehicles hauling milk.
Exemption from size and
weight requirements,
§32-9-23.
Exemptions from chapter,
§37-3-4.
Municipal corporations.
Codes.
Adoption of technical codes
by reference, §11-45-8.
Dairies.
Inspections, §§11-47-137,
11-47-139.
Regulation, §11-47-137.
Oil.
Adding or blending oil with
milk or cream, §2-13-4.
Penalties.
Marked containers.
Selling or using
noncomplying
containers, §8-16-96.
Violations of article,
§8-12-44.
Permits.
Application, §2-13-8.
Businesses for which permits
required, §2-13-8.
Commissioner.
Issuance on semi-annual
basis, §2-13-86.
Suspension or revocation,
§2-13-86.
Duration, §§2-13-8, 2-13-86.
Fees.
Filing fee, §2-13-8.
Filing fee, §2-13-8.
Issuance, §2-13-87.
Commissioner.
Issuance on semi-annual
basis, §2-13-86.
Required, §2-13-84.

MILK AND MILK PRODUCTS
—Cont'd
Permits—Cont'd
Revocation, §2-13-87.
Permits issued by
commissioner on semi-
annual basis, §2-13-86.
Suspension.
Permits issued by
commissioner on semi-
annual basis, §2-13-86.
Transportation of milk into
Alabama, §2-13-84.
When required, §§2-13-8,
2-13-84.
Presumptions.
Ownership of marked
containers, §8-12-41.
Processors.
Permits generally. See
within this heading,
"Permits."
Producers.
Permits generally. See
within this heading,
"Permits."
**Promotion of production,
distribution, etc., of milk,**
Const. Ala., amd. 388.
Purchasers.
Utensils to be cleaned by
purchasers, §2-13-6.
Purpose of article, §2-13-2.
Records.
Health regulations.
Examination of records,
§2-13-92.
Reports.
Annual reports of creameries,
milk plants, etc.,
§2-13-15.
Rules and regulations.
Health regulations. See
within this heading,
"Health regulations."
Sales.
Imitation butter, §§2-13-18 to
2-13-20.
Imitation cheese, §§2-13-18,
2-13-19.
Marked containers, §8-12-40.
Noncomplying containers,
§8-16-96.
Suspension from sale.
Applicability of laws
relative to suspension
from sale, §2-13-22.
Seizures.
Applicability of laws relative
to seizure, §2-13-22.
Health regulations.
Seizure of milk in transit,
§2-13-89.
State board of health.
Authority and jurisdiction,
§22-2-2.
Powers not restricted,
§2-13-91.
Tests.
License for operation of
testing apparatus,
§2-13-9.
Requirements, §2-13-14.
Use of standard test
required, §2-13-10.
Utensils.
Cleaning.
Utensils to be cleaned by
purchasers, §2-13-6.
Insanitary utensils, §2-13-7.

MILK AND MILK PRODUCTS
—Cont'd
Utensils—Cont'd
Sanitation of utensils,
§2-13-5.
Weights and measures.
Milk and cream bottles and
containers, §§8-16-95 to
8-16-97.

MILLS.
Dams.
Erection of dams for mills,
§§18-2-1 to 18-2-21.
See DAMS.
Sawmills, §§35-11-250,
35-11-251, 35-11-270
to 35-11-273.
See SAWMILLS.

MIMEOGRAPHS.
Licenses.
Sales, §40-12-127.

MINERALS RESOURCE
MANAGEMENT
COMMITTEE, §§9-5-1 to
9-5-3.

MINERAL WATER.
**Names, marks, etc., on
beverage containers.**
§§8-12-20, 8-12-21.

MINES AND MINERALS,
§§9-16-1 to 9-16-134.
Actions.
Surface mining reclamation.
Enforcement of final order
of director, §9-16-11.
Alabama mining academy,
§§16-60-260 to 16-60-264.
Contracts.
Authority of Walker state
technical college
president, §16-60-261.
Duties.
Generally, §16-60-264.
Established, §16-60-260.
Facilities.
Walker state technical
college.
Use of college facilities
authorized,
§16-60-261.
History of Alabama mining.
Walker state technical
college.
Procurement of historical
articles authorized,
§16-60-261.
Location.
Walker state technical
college, §16-60-260.
Personnel.
Walker state technical
college.
Use of college personnel
authorized,
§16-60-261.
Preservation of Alabama
mining history.
Walker state technical
college.
Procurement of historical
articles authorized,
§16-60-261.
Purpose.
Generally, §16-60-260.
Research.
Contracts, §16-60-264.
Generally, §16-60-264.

MINES AND MINERALS
—Cont'd
Alabama mining academy
—Cont'd
Purpose—Cont'd
Technical assistance in
complying with mine
safety laws,
§16-60-263.
Rescue teams.
Maintenance and training,
§16-60-264.
Safety.
Program, §§16-60-262 to
16-60-264.
Generally, §16-60-262.
Purpose, §16-60-262.
Research.
Contracts, §16-60-264.
Generally, §16-60-264.
Technical assistance,
§16-60-263.
Reports.
Preparation and
publication,
§16-60-264.
Research.
Generally, §16-60-264.
Training.
Cooperative educational
and training
agreements authorized,
§16-60-261.
Program.
Generally, §16-60-262.
Walker state technical
college.
Facilities.
Use of college facilities
authorized,
§16-60-261.
Location, §16-60-260.
Personnel.
Use of college personnel
authorized,
§16-60-261.
Preservation of Alabama
mining history.
Procurement of historical
articles authorized,
§16-60-261.
President.
Authority to enter into
safety research
related contracts,
§16-60-261.
Appeals.
Surface mining reclamation.
Violation of article.
Orders of director,
§9-16-10.
Bonds, surety.
Surface mining reclamation.
Permit for surface mining
operations, §§9-16-5,
9-16-8.
Amended applications,
§9-16-6.
Bureau of mines.
University of Alabama.
Cooperation of university
with bureau of mines,
§16-47-13.
Canals.
Connections to public ways.
Construction and operation
of connections by
mining corporations,
§10-5-13.

MINES AND MINERALS
—Cont'd
Canals—Cont'd
Operation outside state and
making extensions
within state by mining
companies, §10-5-12.
Coal.
Abandoned mine
reclamation, §§9-6-120 to
9-6-134.
See COAL.
Mine safety, §§25-9-1 to
25-9-370.
See COAL.
Severance tax, §§40-13-1 to
40-13-10, 40-13-30 to
40-13-36.
See COAL.
Surface mining control and
reclamation, §§9-16-107,
9-16-120 to 9-16-134.
See COAL.
Commercial code.
Sales.
Goods to be severed from
realty, §7-2-107.
Secured transactions.
Description of land,
§7-9-203.
Multiple state transactions.
Perfection of security
interest, §7-9-103.
When security interest
attaches, §7-9-204.
Condemnation.
Rights of way or easements
by mining companies,
§10-5-3.
Connections to public ways.
Construction and operation of
connections by mining
corporations, §10-5-13.
Counties.
Acquisition of lands for
public purposes.
Use of lands for collection
and exhibit of
minerals, §11-18-2.
Developing, advertising and
promoting mineral
resources, §11-3-11.
Exhibit of mineral resources
of county, §§11-3-11,
11-18-2.
Dams.
Surface mining reclamation.
Construction of dams,
§9-16-7.
Definitions.
Surface mining reclamation,
§9-16-2.
Documentary tax, §§40-20-30
to 40-20-37.
See OIL AND GAS.
Easements.
Condemnation for easements
by mining companies,
§10-5-3.
Eminent domain.
Condemnation for rights of
way or easements by
mining companies,
§10-5-3.
Routes and sites.
Rights of condemning
corporations in
selection of routes and
sites, §10-5-8.

MINES AND MINERALS
—Cont'd
Fees.
Surface mining reclamation,
§§9-16-6, 9-16-12.
Funds.
Surface mining reclamation,
§9-16-12.
Geological survey, §§9-4-1 to
9-4-19.
See GEOLOGICAL
SURVEY.
Good Samaritan act.
Mine rescue planning and
recovery operations.
Qualified persons,
§6-5-332.
Hearings.
Management committee.
Conduct of hearing, §9-5-3.
Surface mining reclamation.
Violation of article,
§9-16-10.
Hematite.
Official mineral of state,
§1-2-13.
Highways.
Connections to public ways.
Construction and operation
by mining
corporations, §10-5-13.
Income tax.
Basis for depletion.
Discovery value, §40-18-16.
Corporations.
Deductions allowed
corporations.
Depletion of mines,
§40-18-35.
Deductions.
Depletion allowance,
§§40-18-15, 40-18-35.
Injunctions.
Surface mining reclamation.
Violation of article,
§9-16-11.
Inspections.
Surface mining reclamation,
§§9-16-8, 9-16-9.
Iron ore.
Licenses for mining,
§§40-12-128 to 40-12-130.
Leases.
Governor.
Authorization to lease
mineral rights on
public land, §35-4-383.
Public lands.
School lands, §9-15-36.
Salt springs.
Conveyance by director of
conservation,
§35-4-380.
Licenses.
Iron ore.
License for mining,
§§40-12-128 to
40-12-130.
Management committee,
§§9-5-1 to 9-5-3.
Chairman, §9-5-1.
Compensation of members,
§9-5-2.
Composition, §9-5-1.
Cooperation of state
departments and
agencies, §9-5-3.
Coordination of activities of
state departments and
agencies, §9-5-3.
Creation, §9-5-1.

MINES AND MINERALS
—Cont'd
Management committee
—Cont'd
Duties.
General provisions, §9-5-3.
Expenses of members, §9-5-2.
Hearings.
Conduct of public hearing,
§9-5-3.
Meetings, §9-5-2.
Powers and duties.
General provisions, §9-5-3.
Recommendations to
governor.
Implementation, §9-5-3.
Mineral documentary tax,
§§40-20-30 to 40-20-37.
See OIL AND GAS.
**Minerals resource
management committee,**
§§9-5-1 to 9-5-3.
Mining academy, §§16-60-260
to 16-60-264.
Municipal corporations.
Annexation of mining plants.
Exemption from taxation,
§11-42-59.
Notice.
Surface mining reclamation.
Violation of article,
§9-16-10.
Official mineral, §1-2-13.
Oil and gas, §§9-17-1 to
9-17-110.
See OIL AND GAS.
Penalties.
Surface mining reclamation.
Disposition, §9-16-12.
Engaging in surface
mining without
permit, §9-16-11.
Violation of article,
§9-16-11.
Permits.
Coal.
Surface mining control and
reclamation.
See COAL.
Surface mining operations,
§§9-16-4 to 9-16-6.
Public lands.
Sale of minerals, §9-15-18.
School lands, §§9-15-38,
9-15-39.
Swamp and overflowed
lands, §§9-15-38,
9-15-40.
School lands.
Leases, §9-15-36.
Sale of minerals, §§9-15-38,
9-15-39.
Swamp and overflowed lands.
Sale of minerals, §§9-15-38,
9-15-40.
Public ways.
Connections to public ways.
Construction and operation
by mining
corporations, §10-5-13.
Railroads.
Connections to public ways.
Construction and operation
of connections by
mining corporations,
§10-5-13.
Operation outside state and
making extensions
within state by mining
companies, §10-5-12.

MINES AND MINERALS
　—Cont'd
Rebates.
　Officer, agent, etc., of mining
　　　corporation taking
　　　rebate, §8-11-4.
Reclamation.
　Surface mining reclamation.
　　General provisions,
　　　§§9-16-1 to 9-16-15.
　　　See within this
　　　heading, "Surface
　　　mining reclamation."
Rights of way.
　Condemnation for rights of
　　　way by mining
　　　companies, §10-5-3.
Rules and regulations.
　Surface mining reclamation.
　　Promulgation, §9-16-13.
Safety.
　Alabama mining academy,
　　　§§16-60-260 to 16-60-264.
　Coal mine safety, §§25-9-1 to
　　　25-9-370.
　　See COAL.
Sales.
　Public lands.
　　Minerals from lands,
　　　§9-15-18.
　　School lands, §§19-15-38,
　　　19-15-39.
　　Swamp and overflowed
　　　lands, §§9-15-38 to
　　　9-15-40.
Sales tax.
　Exemptions.
　　Equipment, machinery,
　　　fuel, etc., used in
　　　exploration in offshore
　　　federal waters,
　　　§40-23-4.
　Sales of machines used in
　　　mining.
　　Tax on gross receipts
　　　levied, §40-23-2.
Salt springs.
　Conveyance of lease by
　　　director of conservation,
　　　§35-4-380.
School of mines of Alabama,
　　§16-47-12.
Secured transactions.
　Description of land, §7-9-203.
　Multiple state transactions.
　　Perfection of security
　　　interest, §7-9-103.
　When security interest
　　　attaches, §7-9-204.
Ships and shipping.
　Operation of transportation
　　　methods for persons or
　　　property by mining
　　　companies, §10-5-9.
State mineral, §1-2-13.
Steamships.
　Operation of transportation
　　　methods for persons or
　　　property by mining
　　　companies, §10-5-9.
Strip mining.
　Mine safety.
　　Surface mining operations,
　　　§§25-9-270 to 25-9-284.
　　See COAL.
　Surface mining control and
　　　reclamation.
　　General provisions.
　　　§§9-16-70 to 9-16-107.
　　　See COAL.

MINES AND MINERALS
　—Cont'd
Strip mining—Cont'd
　Surface mining control and
　　　reclamation—Cont'd
　　General provisions,
　　　§§9-16-1 to 9-16-15.
　　　See within this
　　　heading, "Surface
　　　mining reclamation."
Surface mining reclamation,
　　§§9-16-1 to 9-16-15.
　Actions.
　　Enforcement of final order
　　　of director, §9-16-11.
　Administration of article,
　　　§9-16-13.
　Appeals.
　　Orders of director,
　　　§9-16-10.
　Applicability of article,
　　　§9-16-14.
　Article supplemental,
　　　§9-16-15.
　Bonds, surety.
　　Permit for surface mining
　　　operators, §§9-16-5,
　　　9-16-8.
　　Amended applications,
　　　§9-16-6.
　Cash deposits, §9-16-8.
　Citation of article, §9-16-1.
　Dams.
　　Construction of dams,
　　　§9-16-7.
　Definitions, §9-16-2.
　Department.
　　Reclamation and
　　　revegetation of lands
　　　by department,
　　　§9-16-12.
　Enforcement of article.
　　Actions.
　　　Institution, §9-16-11.
　　Appeals from orders of
　　　director, §9-16-10.
　　Hearings, §9-16-10.
　　Notice of violations,
　　　§9-16-10.
　Exemptions from article,
　　　§9-16-14.
　Fees.
　　Disposition, §9-16-12.
　　Permit for surface mining
　　　operations, §9-16-6.
　Funds, §9-16-12.
　Grading.
　　Duties of operators,
　　　§9-16-7.
　Hearings.
　　Violation of article,
　　　§9-16-10.
　Injunctions.
　　Violation of article,
　　　§9-16-11.
　Inspections, §9-16-8.
　　Completed operations,
　　　§9-16-8.
　　Right of entry upon lands,
　　　§9-16-9.
　Notices.
　　Violations, §9-16-10.
　Operators.
　　Bonds, surety.
　　　General provisions,
　　　§9-16-8.
　　Permits, §§9-16-4 to
　　　9-16-6.
　　Cash deposits, §9-16-8.
　　Duties generally, §9-16-7.

MINES AND MINERALS
　—Cont'd
Surface mining reclamation
　　—Cont'd
　Operators—Cont'd
　　Grading operations,
　　　§9-16-7.
　　Securities deposits, §9-16-8.
　Penalties.
　　Disposition, §9-16-12.
　　Engaging in operation
　　　without permit,
　　　§9-16-11.
　　Violation of article,
　　　§9-16-11.
　Permit for surface mining
　　　operations.
　　Application.
　　　Amendments, §9-16-6.
　　　Contents, §9-16-5.
　　　Filing, §9-16-5.
　　Bonds, surety, §§9-16-5,
　　　9-16-8.
　　　Amended application,
　　　§9-16-6.
　　Duration, §9-16-5.
　　Fees, §9-16-6.
　　Issuance, §9-16-5.
　　　Amended permit,
　　　§9-16-6.
　　Required, §9-16-4.
　　　Operating without valid
　　　permit, §9-16-11.
　　Separate permit for each
　　　operation, §9-16-4.
　　Term, §9-16-5.
　Purposes of article, §9-16-3.
　Repeal of conflicting laws,
　　　§9-16-15.
　Revegetation.
　　Duties of operators,
　　　§9-16-7.
　　Work performed by
　　　department, §9-16-12.
　Right of entry upon lands.
　　Inspections as to
　　　compliance with
　　　article, §9-16-9.
　Roads.
　　Fire lanes or access roads,
　　　§9-16-7.
　Rules and regulations.
　　Promulgation, §9-16-13.
　Securities deposits, §9-16-8.
　Seeding.
　　Duties of operators,
　　　§9-16-7.
　Supplemental provisions,
　　　§9-16-15.
　Title of article, §9-16-1.
　Violation of article.
　　Appeals.
　　　Orders of director,
　　　§9-16-10.
　　Hearings, §9-16-10.
　　Injunctions, §9-16-11.
　　Notices, §9-16-10.
　　Orders.
　　　Appeals, §9-16-10.
　　　Entry by director,
　　　§9-16-10.
　　Penalties, §9-16-11.
Surveys.
　Geological survey, §§9-4-1 to
　　　9-4-19.
　　See GEOLOGICAL
　　　SURVEY.
Taxation.
　Coal severance tax, §§40-13-1
　　　to 40-13-36.
　　See COAL.

MINES AND MINERALS
—Cont'd

Taxation—Cont'd

Mineral documentary tax, §§40-20-30 to 40-20-37. See OIL AND GAS.

Tunnels.

Connections to public ways. Construction and operation of connections by mining corporations, §10-5-13.

University of Alabama.

Bureau of mines. Cooperation of university with bureau of mines, §16-47-13.

Department of mining engineering. Declared to be school of mines, §16-47-12.

School of mines of Alabama, §16-47-12.

Use tax.

Exemptions. Exploration in offshore federal waters. Equipment, machinery, fuel, etc., used in, §40-23-62.

Tax on machines used in mining, §40-23-61.

Waters and watercourses.

Connections to public ways. Construction and operation of connections to navigable watercourses by mining corporations, §10-5-13.

MINISTERS.
See CLERGY.

MINORS.

Abandonment of child, §13A-13-5.

Abortion.

Parental consent to performing abortions upon minors, §§26-21-1 to 26-21-8. See ABORTION.

Abuse.

Child abuse act, §§26-15-1 to 26-15-4.

Child abuse and neglect generally. See within this heading, "Child abuse and neglect."

Child abuse and neglect prevention act, §§26-16-1 to 26-16-13. See within this heading, "Child abuse and neglect."

Domestic violence facilities, §§30-6-1 to 30-6-13. See DOMESTIC VIOLENCE FACILITIES.

Protection from abuse, §§30-5-1 to 30-5-11. See DOMESTIC RELATIONS.

Reporting child abuse or neglect, §§26-14-1 to 26-14-13. See within this heading, "Child abuse and neglect."

MINORS—Cont'd

Actions.

Destruction of property by minor. Liability of parents, §6-5-380.

Injury to minor child. Right of action of parents, §6-5-390.

Wrongful death of minor, §6-5-391.

Adoption, §§26-10-1 to 26-10-30. See ADOPTION.

Adult.

Defined, §35-5A-2.

Age.

Majority, §26-1-1. Contracting for educational loans for college level education and above, §26-1-5.

Relief from disabilities of nonage, §§26-13-1 to 26-13-8. See within this heading, "Relief from disabilities of nonage."

Aid to dependent children.

Eligibility, §38-4-1.

Public assistance generally. See WELFARE.

Alcoholic beverages.

See ALCOHOLIC BEVERAGES.

Alcoholism.

Consent for health services. Consent of any minor as to alcohol toxicity, §22-8-6.

Anatomical gifts.

See ANATOMICAL GIFTS.

Appeals.

Juvenile proceedings. See JUVENILE PROCEEDINGS.

Bail and recognizance.

Execution for acknowledgment of undertaking, §15-13-23.

Banks and financial institutions.

Deposits. Disposition of deposits of deceased persons, §5-5A-38.

Time for payment, §5-5A-39.

Rights of minors, §5-5A-37.

Savings and loan associations. Accounts, §5-16-43.

Bastards.

See ILLEGITIMACY.

Benefit plan.

Defined, §35-5A-2.

Bicycles.

Violations. Parents or guardians of child not to authorize violations, §32-5A-266.

Billiard rooms, §§34-6-9 to 34-6-11.

Blind persons.

Infantile blindness. Notifiable diseases generally, §§22-11A-1 to 22-11A-38. See DISEASES.

Prevention, §22-20-2.

Blood donations.

Persons 17 or older, §26-1-3.

MINORS—Cont'd

Bond issues.

Ownership of securities by minors, §§8-6-90 to 8-6-95. See SECURITIES.

Bonds, surety.

Custody and support. Guaranteeing payment of overdue support or compliance with visitation order, §30-3-6.

Bone marrow donation.

Consent of minors and parents, §22-8-9.

Bowie knives.

Sale to minor prohibited, §13A-11-57.

Broker.

Defined, §35-5A-2.

Child abuse act, §§26-15-1 to 26-15-4.

Child abuse and neglect.

Child abuse act, §§26-15-1 to 26-15-4.

Effect of chapter upon existing rights or liabilities, pending prosecutions, etc., §26-15-4.

Penalty. Torture, willful abuse, etc., of child under 18 by responsible person, §26-15-3.

Responsible person. Defined, §26-15-2.

Short title, §26-15-1.

Torture, willful abuse, etc., of child under 18 by responsible person, §26-15-3.

Child abuse and neglect prevention act, §§26-16-1 to 26-16-33.

Board. Appointment, §26-16-4.

Committees, §26-16-4.

Compensation, §26-16-4.

Composition, §26-16-4.

Creation, §26-16-3.

Criteria for making grants to local councils, §26-16-10.

Disbursements. Generally, §26-16-9.

Duties. Generally, §26-16-6.

Executive director, §26-16-3.

Federal funds, §26-16-8.

Functions. Generally, §26-16-6.

Grants to local councils. Criteria, §26-16-10.

Meetings, §26-16-5.

Officers, §26-16-4.

Recommendations to governor. Changes in state program, §26-16-7.

Records, §26-16-5.

Review of board conducted every five years, §26-16-12.

Rules. Promulgation, §26-16-11.

Staff, §26-16-3.

Terms of office, §26-16-4.

MINORS—Cont'd
Child abuse and neglect
—Cont'd
Child abuse and neglect
prevention act—Cont'd
Definitions, §26-16-2.
Investigations.
State agencies to share
information
concerning,
§26-16-13.
Protection from abuse,
§§30-5-1 to 30-5-11.
See DOMESTIC
RELATIONS.
Short title, §26-16-1.
State agencies to share
information, §26-16-13.
Department of human
resources.
Multi-disciplinary child
protection teams,
§§26-15-50 to 26-15-53.
Reporting child abuse or
neglect, §§26-14-1 to
26-14-13.
Domestic violence facilities.
General provisions,
§§30-6-1 to 30-6-13.
See DOMESTIC
VIOLENCE
FACILITIES.
Prevention act, §§26-16-1 to
26-16-23.
Protection from abuse.
General provisions,
§§30-5-1 to 30-5-11.
See DOMESTIC
RELATIONS.
Reporting child abuse or
neglect, §§26-14-1 to
26-14-13.
Abuse.
Defined, §26-14-1.
Attorneys.
Appointment of attorney
to represent child,
§26-14-11.
Authority.
Defined, §26-14-1.
Child.
Defined, §26-14-1.
Citizen reports.
Confidentiality, §26-14-8.
Immunity from liability,
§26-14-9.
Permissive reporting,
§26-14-4.
Communications.
Privileged
communications.
Not grounds for
exclusion of
evidence,
§26-14-10.
Contents of reports,
§26-14-5.
Custody.
Temporary protective
custody of child,
§26-14-6.
Day care workers.
Mandatory reporting,
§26-14-3.
Definitions, §26-14-1.
Department of human
resources.
Central registry of
records.
Establishment,
§26-14-8.

MINORS—Cont'd
Child abuse and neglect
—Cont'd
Reporting child abuse or
neglect—Cont'd
Department of human
resources—Cont'd
Duties, §§26-14-7,
26-14-8.
Investigations, §26-14-7.
Records.
Central registry,
§26-14-8.
Reports to be made to
department,
§26-14-3.
Rules and regulations,
§26-14-12.
Records and reports,
§26-14-8.
Duly constituted authority.
Defined, §26-14-1.
Evidence.
Privileged
communications.
Not grounds for
exclusion of
evidence,
§26-14-10.
Hospitals and clinics.
Mandatory reporting,
§26-14-3.
Immunity.
Actions under chapter
immune from
liability, §26-14-9.
Law enforcement officials.
Mandatory reporting,
§26-14-3.
Liability.
Immunity from liability
for actions under
chapter, §26-14-9.
Mandatory reports,
§26-14-3.
Confidentiality, §26-14-8.
Failure to make required
report.
Penalty, §26-14-13.
Immunity from liability,
§26-14-9.
Mental health
professionals.
Mandatory reporting,
§26-14-3.
Neglect.
Defined, §26-14-1.
Penalties.
Failure to make required
report, §26-14-13.
Permissive reports,
§26-14-4.
Confidentiality, §26-14-8.
Immunity from liability,
§26-14-9.
Pharmacists.
Mandatory reporting,
§26-14-3.
Physicians and surgeons.
Mandatory reporting,
§26-14-3.
Privileged communications.
Not grounds for
exclusion of
evidence, §26-14-10.
Protective custody.
Temporary protective
custody of child,
§26-14-6.
Purpose of chapter,
§26-14-2.

MINORS—Cont'd
Child abuse and neglect
—Cont'd
Reporting child abuse or
neglect—Cont'd
Records.
Central registry.
Establishment,
§26-14-8.
Confidentiality, §26-14-8.
Rules and regulations.
Department of human
resources, §26-14-12.
Records and reports,
§26-14-8.
Social workers.
Mandatory reporting,
§26-14-3.
Teachers and school
officials.
Mandatory reporting,
§26-14-3.
Temporary protective
custody of child,
§26-14-6.
Victim counselors.
Confidentiality.
Victim counselors not
relieved of duty to
report child abuse
or neglect,
§15-23-45.
Sexual abuse victim
protection, §§15-26-1 to
15-26-10.
Citation of chapter,
§15-25-30.
"Crime involving child
abuse" defined,
§15-26-10.
Victim counselors.
Confidentiality.
Victim counselors not
relieved of duty to
report child abuse or
neglect, §15-23-45.
**Child abuse and neglect
prevention act.**
Generally, §§26-16-1 to
26-16-33. See within this
heading, "Child abuse
and neglect."
Child care and treatment.
Providing criminal conviction
information on
applicants for
employment, §26-1-4.
Welfare.
See WELFARE.
**Child care facilities, §§38-7-1
to 38-7-18.**
See WELFARE.
**Child custody and support,
§§30-3-1 to 30-3-99. See
within this heading,
"Custody and support."**
**Child labor, §§25-8-1 to
25-8-31.**
See LABOR.
Child placement.
Interstate compact on the
placement of children,
§§44-2-20 to 44-2-26. See
within this heading,
"Interstate compact on
child placement."

MINORS—Cont'd
Child pornography.
Obscene materials containing visual reproduction of children, §§13A-12-190 to 13A-12-198.
See OBSCENITY.
Children's trust fund,
§§26-16-30 to 26-16-33.
Construction of article, §26-16-33.
Creation, §26-16-30.
Disposition, §26-16-30.
Disposition of contributions, §26-16-32.
Income tax.
Refund designation, §26-16-31.
Investment, §26-16-30.
Purpose, §26-16-30.
Repeal of conflicting acts, §26-16-33.
Child support.
Child support programs, §§38-10-1 to 38-10-33.
See CHILD SUPPORT PROGRAMS.
Garnishment, §30-3-67.
General provisions, §§30-3-1 to 30-3-99. See within this heading, "Custody and support."
Cigarettes.
Selling cigarettes to minors, §13A-12-3.
Circuit courts.
Juvenile proceedings.
See JUVENILE PROCEEDINGS.
Coal.
Persons under 18 not to work in or about mines, §25-9-30.
Commercial code.
Commercial paper.
Defenses against holder in due course, §7-3-305.
Negotiation effective although subject to rescission, §7-3-207.
Commitment.
Involuntary commitment, §§12-11-10, 12-15-90.
Compacts.
Interstate compact on juveniles, §§44-2-1 to 44-2-8.
Interstate compact on the placement of children, §§44-2-20 to 44-2-26.
Consent for health services,
§§22-8-1 to 22-8-9.
See HEALTH.
Conservators.
Appointment of conservators.
General conservators for county, §26-2-26.
Defined, §35-5A-2.
Removal of person or property of minors and wards, §§26-8-1 to 26-8-52.
See GUARDIAN AND WARD.
Uniform guardianship and protective proceedings act, §§26-2A-1 to 26-2A-160.
See GUARDIAN AND WARD.

MINORS—Cont'd
Constitution of Alabama.
Relieving minors of disabilities of nonage.
Special, private or local laws prohibited, Const. Ala., art. IV, §104.
Contracts.
Age of majority.
Contracting for educational loans for college level education and above, §26-1-5.
Contributing to delinquency,
§12-15-13.
Conveyances.
Powers of disposition.
Disposition to or among children, §35-4-300.
Corporations.
Stock and stockholders.
See CORPORATIONS.
Courts.
Defined, §35-5A-2.
Juvenile proceedings.
General provisions, §§12-15-1 to 12-15-120.
See JUVENILE PROCEEDINGS.
Credit unions.
Deposits, §5-17-15.
Criminal law and procedure.
Abandonment of child, §13A-13-5.
Dependent or neglected children.
Causing, etc., of delinquency, dependency or need of supervision of children, §12-15-13.
Defined, §12-15-1.
Endangering welfare of child, §13A-13-6.
Force.
Use of force by persons with parental, custodial or special responsibilities, §13A-3-24.
Hazards.
Creating hazards, §13A-11-220.
Immaturity as defense to criminal liability, §13A-3-3.
Juvenile proceedings.
Transfer of cases, §12-15-34.
Crippled and disabled children, §§21-3-1 to 21-3-8.
See HANDICAPPED PERSONS.
Custodial property.
Defined, §35-5A-2.
Custodian.
Defined, §35-5A-2.
Custody and support,
§§30-3-1 to 30-3-99.
Abandonment by wife of husband, §30-3-1.
Award of visitation rights to grandparents, §30-3-4.
Basic child support obligations, ARJA, Rule 32.
Bonds, surety.
Securing payment of overdue support, §30-3-6.

MINORS—Cont'd
Custody and support—Cont'd
Child support programs.
See CHILD SUPPORT PROGRAMS.
Definitions.
Child support guidelines, ARJA, Rule 32.
Uniform child custody jurisdiction act, §30-3-22.
Withholding orders for child support, §30-3-60.
Divorce, §30-3-1.
Dockets.
Expedited process for child support.
Initial case settings, ARJA, Rule 35.
Expedited process for child support.
Dockets.
Initial case settings, ARJA, Rule 35.
Hearings.
Before referees, ARJA, Rule 35.
Initial case settings, ARJA, Rule 35.
Rehearings before courts, ARJA, Rule 35.
Monitors.
Appointment of expedited process monitors, ARJA, Rule 35.
Referees.
Appointment, ARJA, Rule 35.
Hearings before, ARJA, Rule 35.
Rehearings before courts, ARJA, Rule 35.
Scope, ARJA, Rule 35.
Forms.
Standardized child support guideline form and income statement form, ARJA, Rule 32.
Garnishment.
Withholding orders for child support.
Priority over garnishments, §30-3-67.
Guidelines.
Child support guidelines.
Basic child support obligations, ARJA, Rule 32.
Computation of child support, ARJA, Rule 32.
Definitions, ARJA, Rule 32.
Effective date, ARJA, Rule 32.
Established, ARJA, Rule 32.
Forms.
Standardized child support guideline form and income statement form, ARJA, Rule 32.
Income statements, ARJA, Rule 32.
Forms, ARJA, Rule 32.
Payment of support to court, ARJA, Rule 32.

MINORS—Cont'd
Custody and support—Cont'd
Hearings.
Expedited process for child
support, ARJA, Rule
35.
Withholding orders for
child support.
Obligor to be served
notice and given
opportunity for
hearing, §30-3-62.
Income statements, ARJA,
Rule 32.
Interference with custody,
§13A-6-45.
Interstate income
withholding, §§30-3-90 to
30-3-99.
Additional remedies,
§30-3-92.
Adoption of other state's
support order,
§30-3-95.
Amendment of withholding
order.
Amendment of support
order, §30-3-96.
Choice of laws, §30-3-94.
Citation of article,
§30-3-90.
Costs.
Court costs, §30-3-97.
Defenses, §30-3-94.
Definitions, §30-3-91.
Docket fees, §30-3-97.
Documents filed with clerk,
§30-3-93.
Entry of income
withholding order,
§30-3-95.
Evidence, §30-3-94.
Request by another state
for evidence from
person in this state,
§30-3-99.
Hearings, §30-3-93.
Prima facie case,
§30-3-94.
Obligor obtaining
employment or other
income in another
state.
Notification of agency
requesting
withholding,
§30-3-96.
Petition for adoption of
support order in
another jurisdiction.
Purpose of obtaining
withholding,
§30-3-99.
Petition for enforcement of
order, §30-3-93.
Purpose of article,
§30-3-90.
Remedies additional to
those now existing,
§30-3-92.
Service on obligor,
§30-3-93.
Short title of article,
§30-3-90.
Voluntary income
withholding, §30-3-98.
Withholding by court of
this state, §30-3-93.

MINORS—Cont'd
Custody and support—Cont'd
Monitors.
Expedited process for child
support.
Appointment of
expedited process
monitor, ARJA, Rule
35.
Notice.
Obligor and employer to
give notice of change
of employer, §30-3-66.
Withholding orders for
child support.
Obligee to give notice of
change of address,
§30-3-65.
Payment of support to court,
ARJA, Rule 32.
Reciprocal state enforcement
of duty to support.
General provisions,
§§30-4-80 to 30-4-98.
See DESERTION AND
NONSUPPORT.
Referees.
Expedited process for child
support.
Appointment of referees,
ARJA, Rule 35.
Hearings before, ARJA,
Rule 35.
Right of department to
support owed by parents
to child, §§38-10-30 to
38-10-33.
Action to assure that
parents provide
support, §38-10-32.
Assignment to department
of right of support
owed to child,
§38-10-31.
Child in custody of
department or
receiving maintenance
payments, §§38-10-31
to 38-10-33.
Action to assure that
parents provide
support, §38-10-32.
Assignment of right to
support, §38-10-31.
Collection and payment
to department,
§38-10-33.
Collection and payment to
department, §38-10-33.
Definitions, §38-10-30.
Service of process.
Withholding orders for
child support.
New employer to be
served with order,
§30-3-66.
Obligor to be served
notice and given
opportunity for
hearing, §30-3-62.
When order served on
employer, §30-3-61.
Uniform child custody
jurisdiction act,
§§30-3-20 to 30-3-44.
Applicability of chapter,
§30-3-43.
Assistance to courts of
foreign states,
§30-3-40.

MINORS—Cont'd
Custody and support—Cont'
Uniform child custody
jurisdiction act—Cont'd
Calendar.
Priority, §30-3-44.
Citation, §30-3-20.
Conduct.
Cause for abscission from
exercise of
jurisdiction,
§30-3-28.
Construction and
interpretation,
§30-3-21.
Costs.
Appearance of parties
and child, §30-3-31.
Inconvenient forum.
Payment of expenses,
§30-3-27.
Custody decrees.
Certified copies.
Furnished to other
states, §30-3-37.
Res judicata effect,
§30-3-32.
Definitions, §30-3-22.
Depositions.
Taking testimony in
another state,
§30-3-38.
Documents.
Preservation for use in
foreign states,
§30-3-41.
Evidence.
Continuing duty to
inform court,
§30-3-29.
Information under oath
submitted to court,
§30-3-29.
Taking testimony in
another state,
§30-3-38.
Foreign custody decrees.
Filing and enforcement,
§30-3-35.
Modification, §30-3-34.
Recognization and
enforcement.
Generally, §30-3-33.
Registry and
proceedings,
§30-3-36.
Request for foreign court
records, §30-3-42.
Forum non conveniens,
§30-3-27.
Hearings.
Foreign state hearings.
Orders to appear,
§30-3-39.
Notice, §30-3-24.
Inconvenient forum,
§30-3-27.
International application,
§30-3-43.
Judgments and decrees.
Custody decree.
Res judicata effect,
§30-3-32.
Preservation of
documents for use
foreign states,
§30-3-41.
Jurisdiction.
Declined by reason of
conduct, §30-3-28.

MINORS—Cont'd
Custody and support—Cont'd
Uniform child custody
jurisdiction act—Cont'd
Jurisdiction—Cont'd
Determination of child
custody.
Effect of physical
presence of child,
§30-3-23.
Submission to
jurisdiction,
§30-3-25.
Notice.
Appearance of parties
and child, §30-3-31.
Hearings, §30-3-24.
Persons outside state,
§30-3-25.
Opportunity to be heard,
§30-3-24.
Orders and decrees.
Preservation of
documents for use in
foreign states,
§30-3-41.
Parties.
Additional parties,
§30-3-30.
Appearance of parties
and child, §30-3-31.
Pleadings.
Preservation for use in
foreign states,
§30-3-41.
Priority on calendar,
§30-3-44.
Records.
Foreign custody decrees.
Request for court
records, §30-3-42.
Res judicata.
Effect of custody decree,
§30-3-32.
Short title, §30-3-20.
Simultaneous proceedings
in other states,
§30-3-26.
Studies in foreign states,
§30-3-39.
Venue.
Modification of child
custody, visitation
rights or child support,
§30-3-5.
Visitation.
Bonds, security or other
guarantee to secure
compliance with order,
§30-3-6.
Voluntary separation of
husband and wife,
§30-3-2.
Withholding orders for child
support, §§30-3-60 to
30-3-71.
Answer of employer,
§30-3-64.
Liability for failure to
answer, §30-3-69.
Change of address.
Obligee to give notice of
change, §30-3-65.
Termination of order
when unable to
deliver payments,
§30-3-65.

MINORS—Cont'd
Custody and support—Cont'd
Withholding orders for child
support—Cont'd
Compliance with orders.
Employers who comply
not liable for
wrongful
withholding,
§30-3-68.
Contents of order, §30-3-62.
Costs.
Filing fees and costs,
§30-3-63.
Service, §30-3-62.
Deducting fee for expenses.
Employer authorized to
deduct, §30-3-71.
Definitions, §30-3-60.
Discharging person due to
withholding order.
Employers not to
discharge, §30-3-70.
Employer to withhold
support from income
due and pay to
designee, §30-3-61.
Existing support orders,
§30-3-62.
Expenses of employer.
Authority to deduct fee
for expenses,
§30-3-71.
Failure or refusal to
withhold.
Liability of employers,
§30-3-69.
Fees.
Employer authorized to
deduct fee, §30-3-71.
Filing fees and costs,
§30-3-63.
Garnishments.
Withholding orders to
have priority over
garnishments,
§30-3-67.
Hiring persons due to
withholding order.
Employers not to
discharge or refuse
to hire, §30-3-70.
Issuance, §30-3-62.
Liability of employers who
fail or refuse to
withhold, §30-3-69.
Maximum amounts
prescribed, §30-3-67.
Modification by court,
§30-3-64.
New employer.
Obligor and employer to
give notice of change
of employer,
§30-3-66.
Service of order on new
employer, §30-3-66.
Notice of change of
address.
Obligee to give notice,
§30-3-65.
Termination of order
when unable to
deliver payments,
§30-3-65.
Notice of change of
employer.
Obligor and employer to
give notice, §30-3-66.

MINORS—Cont'd
Custody and support—Cont'd
Withholding orders for child
support—Cont'd
Obligor to be served notice
and given opportunity
for hearing, §30-3-62.
Order binding on employer,
§30-3-64.
Priority over
garnishments,
§30-3-67.
Refusal to withhold.
Liability of employers
who fail or refuse to
withhold, §30-3-69.
Required, §30-3-61.
Termination of
withholding, §30-3-62.
When orders served on
employer, §30-3-61.
When order takes effect,
§30-3-62.
Who may petition for
order, §30-3-62.
Wrongful withholding.
Employers who comply
not liable, §30-3-68.
Dams.
Erection of dams for mills,
gins, factories or electric
generators.
Guardian ad litem.
Appointment, §18-2-4.
Day care centers.
Child care facilities, §§38-7-1
to 38-7-18.
See WELFARE.
Debts.
Exemptions from
administration and
payment of debts.
See EXEMPTIONS FROM
ADMINISTRATION
AND PAYMENT OF
DEBTS.
Decedents' estates.
Claims and debts.
Time and manner of filing
claims, §43-2-351.
Definitions.
Child abuse.
"Responsible person"
defined, §26-15-2.
Child abuse and neglect
prevention act, §26-16-2.
Custody and support.
Child support guidelines,
ARJA, Rule 32.
Right of department to
support owed by
parents to child,
§38-10-30.
Interstate compact on child
placement, §44-2-20.
Uniform child custody
jurisdiction act, §30-3-22.
Withholding orders for child
support, §30-3-60.
Delinquency.
Causing, etc., §12-15-13.
Institutional care.
Interstate compact on child
placement, §44-2-20.
Juvenile proceedings.
See JUVENILE
PROCEEDINGS.
Youthful offenders, §§15-19-1
to 15-19-7.
See YOUTHFUL
OFFENDERS.

MINORS—Cont'd
Delinquency—Cont'd
Youth services.
General provisions,
§§44-1-1 to 44-1-77.
See YOUTH SERVICES.
Department of human resources.
Multi-disciplinary child protection teams, §§26-15-50 to 26-15-53.
Reporting child abuse or neglect, §§26-14-1 to 26-14-13. See within this heading, "Child abuse or neglect."
Department of youth services.
General provisions, §§44-1-1 to 44-1-77.
See YOUTH SERVICES.
Disability.
Crippled and disabled children, §§21-3-1 to 21-3-8.
See HANDICAPPED PERSONS.
Relief from disabilities of nonage, §§26-13-1 to 26-13-8. See within this heading, "Relief from disabilities of nonage."
Diseases.
Notifiable diseases.
Consent for health services.
Consent of any minor as to reportable diseases, §22-8-6.
Sexually transmitted diseases.
Consent may be given by minor for medical treatment, §22-11A-19.
Informing parent or guardian.
Authority of medical care provider, §22-11A-19.
District courts.
Juvenile jurisdiction, §§12-12-34, 12-15-2.
Divorce and alimony.
Child custody and support, §30-3-1.
Venue of proceedings seeking modification of child custody, visitation rights or child support, §30-3-5.
Visitation rights of grandparents, §30-3-4.
Drugs.
Consent for health services.
Consent of any minor as to drug dependency, §22-8-6.
Controlled substances.
Immunity of persons reporting suspected use by, §20-2-3.
Sale, furnishing, etc., of controlled substances by persons over age eighteen to persons under age eighteen.
Penalties, §13A-2-215.
Education.
General provisions.
See EDUCATION.

MINORS—Cont'd
Emancipation of minors,
§§26-13-1 to 26-13-8; Const. Ala., art. IV, §104.
See within this heading, "Relief from disabilities of nonage."
Eminent domain.
Hearings.
Guardian ad litem.
Appointment, §18-1A-275.
Endangering welfare of child, §13A-13-6.
Executors and administrators.
Claims and debts.
Time and manner of filing, §43-2-351.
Conveyances by executors and administrators.
Application to compel conveyance.
Notice to guardians of minor heirs, §35-4-323.
Insolvent estates.
Claims against insolvent estates.
Time allowed certain minors for filing, §43-2-741.
Letters testamentary.
Supplemental letters for minors upon removal of disability, §43-2-24.
Real property.
Sale for payment of debts and for division.
Appointment of guardian ad litem, §43-2-445.
Duties and compensation of guardian ad litem, §43-2-448.
Order of sale.
When depositions required, §43-2-452.
Settlements and distributions.
Appointment of guardian ad litem, §43-2-504.
Arbitration on settlement of estates.
Consent by guardian, §43-2-601.
Expenses.
Credit for expenses of minor distributees, §43-2-510.
Special guardians, §43-2-517.
Financial institution.
Defined, §35-5A-2.
Fingerprints.
Juvenile proceedings, §12-15-102.
Fish and game.
Licenses.
Fishing licenses.
Persons under sixteen years of age, §9-11-53.
Hunting license.
Persons under sixteen years of age, §9-11-50.
Fraternal benefit societies.
Benefits.
Lives of children, §27-34-24.

MINORS—Cont'd
Garnishment.
Child support, §30-3-67.
Gifts to minors.
Uniform transfers to minor act, §§35-5A-1 to 35-5A-24.
See TRANSFERS TO MINORS.
Grandparents.
Visitation.
Award of visitation rights, §30-3-4.
Guardian ad litem.
See GUARDIAN AD LITEM.
Guardian and ward.
See GUARDIAN AND WARD.
Handicapped persons.
Crippled and disabled children, §§21-3-1 to 21-3-8.
See HANDICAPPED PERSONS.
Rehabilitation and crippled children's service, §§16-38-1 to 16-38-9.
See HANDICAPPED PERSONS.
Health.
Consent for health services, §§22-8-1 to 22-8-9.
See HEALTH.
Prevention of infantile blindness, §22-20-2.
Hearings.
Custody and support.
Expedited process for child support, ARJA, Rule 35.
Withholding orders for child support.
Obligor to be served notice and given opportunity for hearing, §30-3-62.
Husband and wife.
See HUSBAND AND WIFE.
Hypothyroidism.
Testing of infants, §22-20-3.
Illegitimacy.
See ILLEGITIMACY.
Income tax.
Children's trust fund.
State income tax refund designation, §26-16-31.
Deductions.
Contributions or gifts made to institutions for the prevention of cruelty to children, §40-18-15.
Corporations, §40-18-35.
Injury to minor child.
Right of action of parents, §6-5-390.
Insurance.
Annuities.
Receipt and giving of acquittance and discharge for payment by minors, §27-14-25.
Health insurance.
Coverage of newly born children in health insurance policies, §27-19-38.
Life insurance.
Receipt and giving of acquittance and discharge for payment by minors, §27-14-25.

MINORS—Cont'd
  Insurance—Cont'd
    Purchase of insurance by or
      for minors, §27-14-5.
    Transfers to minors,
      §§33-5A-1 to 33-5A-24.
      See TRANSFERS TO
        MINORS.
  **Interstate compact on child
    placement,** §§44-2-20 to
    44-2-26.
    Administrator, §44-2-20.
      Commissioner of
        department of human
        resources, §44-2-26.
    Agreements.
      Authority to make,
        §44-2-24.
    Applicability of compact,
      §44-2-20.
    Child.
      Defined, §44-2-20.
    Commissioner.
      Department of human
        resources.
        Administrator of
          compact, §44-2-26.
        Approval of financial
          commitments,
          §44-2-24.
        Rules and regulations.
          Promulgation,
            §44-2-26.
    Conditions for placement,
      §44-2-20.
    Construction and
      interpretation, §44-2-20.
    Definitions, §44-2-20.
    Delinquent children.
      Institutional care,
        §44-2-20.
    Enactment, §44-2-20.
    Executive head.
      Governor deemed executive
        head, §44-2-25.
    Exemption from compact,
      §44-2-20.
    Financial obligations of state,
      §44-2-21.
      Approval.
        Commissioner of
          department of
          human resources,
          §44-2-24.
    Governor.
      Activities as executive
        head, §44-2-25.
    Illegal placement.
      Penalties, §44-2-20.
    Limitations on scope,
      §44-2-20.
    Penalties.
      Illegal placement, §44-2-20.
    Placement.
      Commissioner.
        Department of human
          resources.
          Deemed appropriate
            authority in
            receiving state,
            §44-2-23.
      Conditions of placement,
        §44-2-20.
      Defined, §44-2-20.
      Department of human
        resources.
        To act as appropriate
          public authority,
          §44-2-22.
      Illegal placement.
        Penalties, §44-2-20.

MINORS—Cont'd
  **Interstate compact on child
    placement**—Cont'd
    Purpose, §44-2-20.
    Receiving state.
      Defined, §44-2-20.
    Rules and regulations.
      Commissioner to
        promulgate, §44-2-26.
    Sending agency.
      Defined, §44-2-20.
      Jurisdiction.
        Retention of jurisdiction,
          §44-2-20.
    Severability of provisions,
      §44-2-20.
    Withdrawal, §44-2-20.
  **Interstate income
    withholding.**
    Custody and support,
      §§30-3-90 to 30-3-99. See
      within this heading,
      "Custody and support."
  Involuntary commitment.
    Juvenile proceedings, §12-15-90.
  Jails.
    Involuntary commitment.
      Juvenile proceedings,
        §§12-15-61, 12-15-90.
  **Joint tenants and tenants in
    common.**
    Sale of land of minors and
      insane persons for
      distribution among joint
      owners, §§35-6-80 to
      35-6-90.
      See PARTITION.
  Juvenile proceedings.
    General provisions, §§12-15-1
      to 12-15-120.
      See JUVENILE
        PROCEEDINGS.
  Kidnapping.
    General provisions,
      §§13A-6-40 to 13A-6-45.
      See KIDNAPPING.
  Labor.
    Child labor, §§25-8-1 to
      25-8-31.
      See LABOR.
  Legitimation of children,
    §§26-11-1 to 26-11-3.
  Loans.
    Age of majority.
      Contracting for educational
        loans for college level
        education and above,
        §26-1-5.
  Majority.
    Age of majority, §26-1-1.
      Contracting for educational
        loans for college level
        education and above,
        §26-1-5.
    Relief of minor children from
      disabilities of nonage,
      §§26-13-1 to 26-13-8.
  Malicious mischief.
    Liability of parents for
      destruction of property
      by minor, §6-5-380.
  Marriage.
    See MARRIAGE.
  Mentally ill.
    Involuntary commitment,
      §12-15-90.
  Missing persons, §§26-19-1 to
    26-19-10.
    See MISSING PERSONS.

MINORS—Cont'd
  Motor vehicles.
    Driver training schools.
      Persons under sixteen
        years of age operating
        motor vehicles,
        §32-5-64.
    Permitting persons under
      sixteen years of age to
      operate motor vehicles,
      §32-5-65.
    Sexual offenses.
      Enticing child to enter
        vehicle for immoral
        purposes, §13A-6-69.
  **Multi-disciplinary child
    protection teams,**
    §§20-16-50 to 20-16-53.
    Advisory committee,
      §26-16-52.
    Composition, §26-16-50.
    Creation, §26-16-50.
    Criteria, §26-16-51.
    Existing child abuse
      prevention teams.
      Exemption from article,
        §26-16-53.
    Preservation, §26-16-53.
    Functions.
      Generally, §26-16-51.
    Guidelines, §26-16-51.
  Neglect. See within this
    heading, "Child abuse and
    neglect."
  Nonage.
    Relief from disabilities of
      nonage, §§26-13-1 to
      26-13-8; Const. Ala., art.
      IV, §104. See within this
      heading, "Relief from
      disabilities of nonage."
  Notice.
    Withholding orders for child
      support.
      Obligee to give notice of
        change of address,
        §30-3-65.
      Obligor and employer to
        give notice of change
        of employer, §30-3-66.
  Obscenity.
    Obscene materials containing
      visual reproduction of
      children, §§13A-12-190
      to 13A-12-198.
      See OBSCENITY.
  Orders.
    Withholding orders for child
      support, §§30-3-60 to
      30-3-71. See within this
      heading, "Custody and
      support."
  Out-of-court statement,
    §§15-26-2 to 15-26-9.
    Admissibility, §15-25-31.
    Cooperative evidence
      prerequisite,
      §15-25-34.
    Requirements,
      §15-25-32.
    Court to inform jury as
      to statement,
      §15-25-36.
    Notice of intent to
      introduce, §15-25-35.
    Recorded findings of
      court, §15-25-38.

MINORS—Cont'd
Out-of-court statement
—Cont'd
Recorded findings of
court—Cont'd
Short title of chapter,
§15-25-30.
Trustworthiness of
statement.
Factors in considering,
§15-26-8.
Unavailability of child to
testify.
Expert testimony as to,
§15-25-33.
Parent and child.
General provisions.
See PARENT AND
CHILD.
Parties.
Infants and incompetents,
§§6-7-100 to 6-7-103.
Partition.
Probate courts.
Interests of minors
considered, §35-6-45.
Sale of land of minors for
distribution among joint
owners, §§35-6-80 to
35-6-91.
See PARTITION.
Personal property.
Conveyances of personalty to
minors, §35-4-96.
Guardian and ward.
Removal of property of
minors and wards,
§§26-8-1 to 26-8-52.
See GUARDIAN AND
WARD.
Phenylketonuria.
Testing infants for
phenylketonuria,
§22-20-3.
Photographs.
Juvenile proceedings,
§12-15-102.
Pistols.
Delivery to minors,
§13A-11-76.
Selling to minors,
§13A-11-57.
Pool halls, §§34-6-9 to 34-6-11.
See BILLIARD ROOMS.
Pornography.
Obscenity.
Obscene materials
containing visual
reproduction of
children, §§13A-12-190
to 13A-12-198.
See OBSCENITY.
Posthumous children.
Included in "heirs," "issue"
or "children," §35-4-8.
Pregnancy.
Consent for health services.
Consent of any minor as to
pregnancy, §22-8-6.
Presumptions.
Responsibility for criminal
acts, §15-16-2.
**Prevention of infantile
blindness,** §22-20-2.
Prisons and prisoners.
Department of youth
services.
Confinement of youth in
adult penal
institutions, §44-1-8.

MINORS—Cont'd
Probation.
General provisions.
See JUVENILE
PROCEEDINGS.
Youth services.
See YOUTH SERVICES.
Property.
Conveyances of personalty to
minors, §35-4-96.
Conveyances of realty.
Powers of disposition.
Disposition to or among
children, §35-4-300.
Destruction of property by
minor.
Liability of parents,
§6-5-380.
Public assistance.
Child care facilities, §§38-7-1
to 38-7-18.
See WELFARE.
Real property.
Conveyances.
Powers of disposition.
Disposition to or among
children, §35-4-300.
Executors and
administrators.
Sale for payment of debts
and for division. See
within this heading,
"Executors and
administrators."
Records.
Juvenile proceedings.
See JUVENILE
PROCEEDINGS.
Relief from disabilities of
nonage.
Foreign judgments,
§26-13-8.
Judgment of court.
Records to be kept by
judge of probate,
§26-13-7.
Referees.
Custody and support.
Expedited process for child
support.
Appointment of referees,
ARJA, Rule 35.
Hearings before referees,
ARJA, Rule 35.
**Relief from disabilities of
nonage,** §§26-13-1 to
26-13-8.
Authorization.
Generally, §26-13-1.
Hearings, §§26-13-4 to
26-13-7.
Contesting of petition,
§26-13-4.
Judgment of court.
Effect, §26-13-5.
Records, §26-13-7.
Restriction of rights of
minor, §26-13-6.
Judgment of court, §§26-13-5
to 26-13-8.
Effect, §26-13-5.
Foreign judgments,
§26-13-8.
Record of judgment.
Probate court, §26-13-7.
Restriction of rights of
minor, §26-13-6.
Jurisdiction, §26-13-1.
Notices.
Filing of petitions,
§26-13-3.

MINORS—Cont'd
**Relief from disabilities of
nonage**—Cont'd
Petition, §§26-13-2 to
26-13-4.
Contesting of petition,
§26-13-4.
Filing, §26-13-2.
Notice, §26-13-3.
Probate court.
Records.
Foreign judgments,
§26-13-8.
Judgment of juvenile
court, §26-13-7.
Records.
Foreign judgments,
§26-13-8.
Judgment of court.
Records to be kept by
judge of probate,
§26-13-7.
Special, private or local laws
prohibited, Const. Ala.,
art. IV, §104.
When authorized, §26-13-1.
Religion.
Remedial treatment by
spiritual means.
Not crime of endangering
welfare of child,
§13A-13-6.
**Removal of personal
property,** §§26-8-1 to
26-8-52.
See GUARDIAN AND
WARD.
Reports.
Child abuse and neglect,
§§26-14-1 to 26-14-13.
See within this heading,
"Child abuse and
neglect."
**Savings and loan
associations.**
Accounts, §5-16-43.
Securities.
Ownership by minors,
§§8-6-90 to 8-6-95.
See SECURITIES.
Transfers to minors,
§§35-5A-1 to 35-5A-24.
See TRANSFERS TO
MINORS.
Service of process.
How infants served, ARCP,
Rule 4 (c).
Nonresident minors, §6-4-21
Withholding orders for child
support.
New employer to be served
with order, §30-3-66.
Obligor to be served notice
and given opportunity
for hearing, §30-3-62.
When order served on
employer, §30-3-61.
**Settlements and
distributions.** See within
this heading, "Executors
and administrators."
**Sex crime records of certain
employees,** §§26-20-1 to
26-20-5.
Certain employers to check,
§26-20-1.
Confidentiality of
information, §26-20-6.
Disposition of statement,
§26-20-2.

MINORS—Cont'd
Sex crime records of certain employees—Cont'd
"Sex crime" defined, §26-20-5.
Statements of employees, §§26-20-2 to 26-20-4.
Disclosure of sex crimes, §26-20-2.
Exempt employees required to submit statement, §26-20-4.
Penalty for false statements, §26-20-3.
Verification, §26-20-2.
Sexual offenses.
Child abuse and neglect. See within this heading, "Child abuse and neglect."
Child victim.
Interviewing child victim of sexual crime.
Limitations authorized, §15-1-2.
Prosecutions involving, §§15-25-1 to 15-25-6.
Sexual abuse victim protection, §§15-25-30 to 15-25-40. See within this heading, "Child abuse and neglect."
Child witness.
Prosecutions involving, §§15-25-1 to 15-25-6.
Enticing child to enter vehicle, house, etc., for immoral purposes, §13A-6-69.
Obscenity.
Obscene materials containing visual reproduction of children, §§13A-12-190 to 13A-12-198.
See OBSCENITY.
Sheriffs.
Guardian and ward.
Appointment of sheriff as guardian, §26-2-27.
Sickle cell anemia.
Testing of infants, §22-20-3.
Sickle cell trait.
Testing of infants, §22-20-3.
Stock and stockholders.
Corporations.
See CORPORATIONS.
Ownership of securities by minors, §§8-6-90 to 8-6-95.
See SECURITIES.
Transfers to minors, §§35-5A-1 to 35-5A-24.
See TRANSFERS TO MINORS.
Support and maintenance.
Child support programs, §§38-10-1 to 38-10-33.
See CHILD SUPPORT PROGRAMS.
Custody and support, §§30-3-1 to 30-3-99. See within this heading, " Custody and support."
Divorce, §30-3-1.
Trusts and trustees.
See TRUSTS AND TRUSTEES.

MINORS—Cont'd
Support and maintenance —Cont'd
Uniform child custody jurisdiction act, §§30-3-20 to 30-3-44. See within this heading, "Custody and support."
Voluntary separation of husband and wife, §30-3-2.
Torts.
Torts to property.
Liability for, §6-5-380.
Transfers to minors, §§35-5A-1 to 35-5A-24.
See TRANSFERS TO MINORS.
Trusts and trustees.
General provisions.
See TRUSTS AND TRUSTEES.
Uniform child custody jurisdiction act, §§30-3-20 to 30-3-44. See within this heading, "Custody and support."
Uniform guardianship and protective proceedings act, §§26-2A-1 to 26-2A-160.
See GUARDIAN AND WARD.
Uniform reciprocal enforcement of support act.
Reciprocal state enforcement of duty to support, §§30-4-80 to 30-4-98.
See DESERTION AND NONSUPPORT.
Uniform transfers to minors act, §§35-5A-1 to 35-5A-24.
See TRANSFERS TO MINORS.
United States.
Condemnation of land or rights-of-way.
Appointment of guardian ad litem and counsel for infants and persons of unsound mind, §42-2-4.
Universities and colleges.
Age of majority.
Contracting for educational loans for college level education and above, §26-1-5.
Vandalism.
Liability of parents for destruction of property by minor, §6-5-380.
Venereal diseases.
Consent by minor to diagnosis or treatment.
Consent of any minor as to venereal disease, §22-8-6.
Venue.
Child custody, visitation rights or child support.
Proceedings seeking modification of child custody, etc., §30-3-5.
Unlawful detaining of child, §15-2-8.
Veterans.
Educational benefits, §§31-6-1 to 31-6-17.
See VETERANS.

MINORS—Cont'd
Veterans—Cont'd
Loans.
Minor veterans empowered to contract liability for repayment of certain loans, §31-1-2.
Visitation.
Orders.
Bond, security or other guarantee to secure compliance, §30-3-6.
Weapons.
Bowie knives.
Selling to minors, §13A-11-57.
Pistols.
Delivery to minors, §13A-11-78.
Selling to minors, §13A-11-57.
Welfare.
Aid to dependent children.
See WELFARE.
Child care facilities, §§38-7-1 to 38-7-18.
See WELFARE.
Wills.
Contesting validity of wills.
Additional time for contest by infants, §43-8-201.
Notice of probate, §43-8-165.
Pretermitted children, §43-8-91.
Who may make will, §43-8-130.
Withholding orders for child support, §§30-3-60 to 30-3-71. See within this heading, "Custody and support."
Witnesses.
Incompetent witnesses, §12-21-165.
Workmen's compensation.
Double compensation when minor illegally employed, §25-5-34.
Payment of awards to minors.
Effect, §25-5-55.
Wrongful death.
Action for wrongful death of minor, §6-5-391.
Youthful offenders, §§15-19-1 to 15-19-7.
See YOUTHFUL OFFENDERS.
Youth services,
General provisions, §§44-1-1 to 44-1-77.
See YOUTH SERVICES.

MISBRANDING.
Agriculture, §§2-2-31 to 2-2-37.
See AGRICULTURE.
Brake fluid, §§8-17-4, 8-17-5.
Caustic or corrosive substances, §§8-17-20, 8-17-21.
Cosmetics.
Adulteration and misbranding.
See COSMETICS.
Drugs.
Adulteration and misbranding.
See DRUGS.

MISBRANDING—Cont'd
Food.
Adulteration and
misbranding.
See FOOD.
Indictment, §15-8-150.
Meat and meat products,
§§2-17-18 to 2-17-20.
Mellorine, §§20-1-135,
20-1-137.
Poultry, §§2-17-10, 2-17-18 to
2-17-20.
See POULTRY.

MISCEGENATION LAWS.
Constitution of Alabama,
Const. Ala., art. IV, §102.

MISDEMEANORS.
Abortion.
Parental consent to
performing abortion
upon minors.
Disclosure of records or
information, §26-21-8.
Penalty for violation of
chapter, §26-21-6.
Appeals.
Bonds, §12-22-171.
Bail and recognizance.
Discharge of defendant by
sheriff after indictment,
§15-13-5.
Discretionary bail schedule,
ARJA, Rule 2.
When new bail allowed,
§15-13-64.
Caves, §§9-19-3 to 9-19-5.
Cemeteries.
Defacing or injuring tomb,
gravestone, flowers, etc.,
§13A-7-23.1.
Class A misdemeanor.
Arson.
Third degree arson,
§13A-7-43.
Bail jumping, §13A-10-40.
Bait advertising, §13A-9-43.
Banks and financial
institutions.
Receiving deposits in
failing financial
institutions,
§13A-9-50.
Bribery.
Commercial bribery,
§13A-11-120.
Receiving a commercial
bribe, §13A-11-121.
Sports bribery,
§13A-11-141.
Caves.
Violations of provisions.
Subsequent offenses,
§9-19-5.
Cemeteries.
Desecration of venerated
objects, §13A-11-12.
Coal.
Sale and delivery.
Mixed with other
substances or with
different quality,
§13A-9-52.
Compounding, §13A-10-7.
Conflicts of interest.
Failure of public servant to
disclose, §13A-10-62.
Corpses.
Abuse, §13A-11-13.
Criminal coercion, §13A-6-25.

MISDEMEANORS—Cont'd
Class A misdemeanor
—Cont'd
Criminally negligent
homicide, §13A-6-4.
Criminal mischief.
Second degree criminal
mischief, §13A-7-22.
Criminal simulation,
§13A-9-10.
Dead bodies.
Abuse of corpse,
§13A-11-13.
Defrauding secured creditors,
§13A-9-46.
Desecration of venerated
objects, §13A-11-12.
Drugs.
Marihuana.
Unlawful possession of
marihuana in the
second degree,
§13A-12-214.
Eavesdropping, §13A-11-31.
Possession of devices,
§13A-11-34.
Escape.
Hindering apprehension of
escapee, §13A-10-45.
Second degree escape.
Permitting or
facilitating,
§13A-10-35.
Evidence.
Tampering with physical
evidence, §13A-10-129.
False alarms, §13A-10-8.
Falsely reporting incidents,
§13A-11-11.
Fines.
Limitations on amount,
§13A-5-12.
Flags.
Desecration of venerated
objects, §13A-11-12.
Food stamps.
Illegal possession of food
stamps.
Third degree illegal
possession of food
stamps, §13A-9-91.
Forgery.
Possession of forged
instruments.
Third degree possession,
§13A-9-7.
Third degree forgery,
§13A-9-4.
Fraud.
Charitable fraud.
Third degree charitable
fraud, §13A-9-75.
Gambling.
Conspiracy to promote
gambling, §13A-12-23.
Possession of gambling
devices, §13A-12-27.
Possession of gambling
records, §§13A-12-24,
13A-12-25.
Promoting gambling,
§13A-12-22.
Hindering prosecution.
Second degree hindering,
§13A-10-44.
Inciting a riot, §13A-11-4.
Indecent exposure,
§13A-6-68.
Minors.
Abandonment, §13A-13-5.

MISDEMEANORS—Cont'd
Class A misdemeanor
—Cont'd
Misapplication of property,
§13A-9-51.
Motor vehicles.
Unauthorized use of
vehicle, §13A-8-11.
Nonsupport, §13A-13-4.
Noxious substances.
Criminal possession of,
§13A-7-28.
Criminal use of, §13A-7-27.
Nurses.
Violations of provisions,
§34-21-7.
Obstructing governmental
operations, §13A-10-2.
Offering false instruments
for recording, §13A-9-12.
Peace officers.
Reports.
False reporting to law
enforcement
authorities,
§13A-10-9.
Perjury.
Second degree perjury,
§13A-10-102.
Prostitution.
Promoting prostitution in
the third degree,
§13A-12-113.
Receiving stolen property.
Third degree receiving
stolen property,
§13A-8-19.
Reckless endangerment,
§13A-6-24.
Records.
Tampering with
governmental records,
§13A-10-12.
Religion.
Desecration of venerated
objects, §13A-11-12.
Reports.
Falsely reporting incidents,
§13A-11-11.
False reporting to law
enforcement
authorities, §13A-10-9.
Rioting, §13A-11-3.
Inciting a riot, §13A-11-4.
Sentence of imprisonment,
§13A-5-7.
Sexual abuse.
Second degree sexual
abuse, §13A-6-67.
Sexual misconduct,
§13A-6-65.
Signatures.
Obtaining by deception,
§13A-9-11.
Sports.
Tampering with sports
contest, §13A-11-143.
Theft.
Lost property.
Third degree theft of lost
property, §13A-8-9.
Services.
Third degree theft of
services,
§13A-8-10.3.
Third degree theft,
§13A-8-5.
Third degree assault,
§13A-6-22.
Trading in public office,
§13A-10-63.

MISDEMEANORS—Cont'd
Class A misdemeanor
—Cont'd
Trespass.
First degree criminal
trespass, §13A-7-2.
Unauthorized use of vehicle,
§13A-8-11.
Unlawful imprisonment.
First degree unlawful
imprisonment,
§13A-6-41.
Class B misdemeanor.
Adultery, §13A-13-2.
Arrest.
Resisting arrest,
§13A-10-41.
Caves.
Violations of provisions.
Second offense, §9-19-5.
Contraband.
Promoting prison
contraband in the
third degree,
§13A-10-38.
Courts.
Interference with judicial
proceedings,
§13A-10-130.
Criminal mischief.
Third degree criminal
mischief, §13A-7-23.
Criminal tampering.
Second degree tampering,
§13A-7-26.
Cruelty to animals,
§13A-11-14.
Deceptive business practices,
§13A-9-41.
Eavesdropping.
Divulging illegally
obtained information,
§13A-11-35.
Failure of disorderly persons
to disperse, §13A-11-6.
False advertising, §13A-9-42.
Financial statements.
Issuing false statements,
§13A-9-49.
Fines.
Limitation on amount,
§13A-5-12.
Fire protection sprinkler
systems.
Violations of provisions,
§34-33-12.
Hazards.
Creating hazards,
§13A-11-220.
Hindering transportation of
commodities,
§13A-11-221.
Impersonation.
Criminal impersonation,
§13A-9-18.
Insolvency.
Fraud in insolvency,
§13A-9-48.
Judgment creditors.
Defrauding, §13A-9-47.
Judicial proceedings.
Interference with,
§13A-10-130.
Jury.
Tampering with jury,
§13A-10-128.
Menacing, §13A-6-23.
Party lines.
Falsely requesting use for
emergency,
§13A-11-223.

MISDEMEANORS—Cont'd
Class B misdemeanor
—Cont'd
Perjury.
Third degree perjury,
§13A-10-103.
Public officers and
employees.
Misuse of confidential
information,
§13A-10-82.
Resisting arrest, §13A-10-41.
Sentence of imprisonment,
§13A-5-7.
Service of process.
Simulating legal process,
§13A-10-131.
Slugs.
Unlawful use, §13A-9-17.
Summons and process.
Simulating legal process,
§13A-10-131.
Witnesses.
Tampering, §13A-10-124.
Class C misdemeanor.
Caves.
Violations of provisions.
First offense, §9-19-5.
Cotton.
Boll weevil eradication.
Violations of provisions,
§2-19-129.
Disorderly conduct,
§13A-11-7.
Fines.
Limitation on amount,
§13A-5-12.
Fire control.
Refusing to assist,
§13A-10-6.
Gambling.
Simple gambling,
§13A-12-21.
Harassment, §13A-11-8.
Impersonating public
servants, §13A-10-10.
Inspections.
Refusal to permit public
officers to inspect,
§13A-10-3.
Lewdness.
Public lewdness,
§13A-12-130.
Littering, §13A-7-29.
Marine resources.
Crab catcher licenses.
Violations of provisions,
§9-12-124.
Seafood seller's license.
Violations of provisions,
§9-12-125.
Obscenity.
Public display of obscene
sticker, sign, etc.,
§13A-12-131.
Peace officers.
Impersonating a public
servant, §13A-10-10.
Refusing to aid, §13A-10-5.
Public officers and
employees.
Impersonating public
servants, §13A-10-10.
Sentence of imprisonment,
§13A-5-7.
Trespass.
Second degree criminal
trespass, §13A-7-3.

MISDEMEANORS—Cont'd
Class C misdemeanor
—Cont'd
Unlawful imprisonment.
Second degree unlawful
imprisonment,
§13A-6-42.
Unsworn falsification to
authorities, §13A-10-109.
Classification, §13A-5-3.
**Confession of judgment for
fees and fines.**
Collection of docket fees and
fines, §12-19-151.
Corporations.
Officers and directors,
§10-2A-284.
Costs of incarceration.
Requirement that
misdemeanant pay costs,
§14-6-22.
Criminal simulation,
§13A-9-10.
Deceptive trade practices.
Violations.
Willful violation a
misdemeanor,
§8-19-12.
Designation of offenses,
§13A-5-4.
District courts.
Criminal jurisdiction,
§12-12-32.
Drugs.
Controlled substances.
Manufacturers and
distributors, §§20-2-71,
20-2-72.
Elections.
Fair campaign practices,
§17-22A-22.
Precincts.
Task force.
Failure to cooperate with
task force, §17-5A-9.
Fines.
Authorized, §13A-5-2.
Collection of docket fees and
fines, §12-19-151.
Distribution of fines
collected, §12-19-152.
Limitations on amount,
§13A-5-12.
Firearms.
Possession of firearms by
persons at
demonstrations in public
places, §13A-11-59.
Fires and fire prevention.
Sprinkler systems.
Class B misdemeanor.
Violations of provisions,
§34-33-12.
Food stamps.
Class A misdemeanor.
Illegal possession of food
stamps.
Third degree illegal
possession of food
stamps, §13A-9-91.
Fraud.
Charitable fraud.
Class A misdemeanor,
§13A-9-75.
Class C misdemeanor,
§13A-9-71.
Gambling.
Class A misdemeanor. See
within this heading,
"Class A misdemeanor."

MISDEMEANORS—Cont'd
Ginseng.
Violations of provisions,
§9-13-250.
Grand jury.
Not required in misdemeanor
cases, Const. Ala., art. I,
§8; amd. 37.
**Hazardous substances or
waste.**
Fees for disposal of
hazardous waste or
substances.
Assistants or agents of
department of revenue.
Refusal to perform
duties, §22-30B-15.
Confidentiality of fee
reports.
Violation of section,
§22-30B-15.
Records of hazardous
substances received for
disposal.
Violations of section,
§22-30B-11.
Homicide.
Criminally negligent
homicide.
Class A misdemeanor,
§13A-6-4.
Imprisonment.
Limitations on term of
imprisonment, §13A-5-7.
Place of imprisonment,
§13A-5-8.
Term of imprisonment for
misdemeanors, §13A-5-7.
Indictments.
Finding of indictments for
misdemeanors,
§12-16-203.
Offenses which are
indictable, §15-8-2.
Jury.
Demand for jury in
misdemeanor cases in
circuit court, §15-14-30.
Limitations on prosecution,
§15-3-2.
Livestock.
Sanitary and disease control
laws.
Arrest.
Appearance upon arrest,
§2-2-14.1.
Theft.
Arrest.
Appearance upon arrest,
§2-2-14.1.
Magistrates.
District court magistrates
agency division.
Authority of magistrates
in, ARJA, Rule 18.
Menacing.
Class B misdemeanor,
§13A-6-23.
Motor vehicles.
See MOTOR VEHICLES.
Municipal corporations.
Class 5 municipalities.
Mayor/commission/city
manager form of
government.
Acceptance of gifts,
§11-44E-183.
Elections.
Bribery, §11-44E-164.

MISDEMEANORS—Cont'd
Municipal corporations
—Cont'd
Class 5 municipalities
—Cont'd
Mayor/commission/city
manager form of
government—Cont'd
Investigations as to
municipal affairs.
Failure to obey
subpoenas,
§11-44E-181.
Officers or employees.
Interest in contracts
with city or public
utilities,
§11-44E-183.
Penalties for violations
of chapter,
§11-44E-167.
Negotiable instruments.
Negotiating worthless
negotiable instrument,
§13A-9-13.1.
Nurses.
Violations of provisions,
§34-21-7.
Offenses.
Designation, §13A-5-4.
Penalties.
General provisions.
See PENALTIES.
Pleas in abatement.
Abatement of prosecution in
circuit court when case
pending in district or
municipal court,
§15-15-43.
Plumbing.
Violations of provisions,
§34-37-17.
Police.
Fleeing officer, §32-5A-193.
Probate judges.
Failure to perform duties,
§17-1-5.
Probation.
Authorized, §13A-5-2.
Property.
Damage to property.
See PROPERTY.
Reckless endangerment.
Class A misdemeanor,
§13A-6-24.
Recordation.
Recitation of marital status
of grantor or vendor.
False recitation a
misdemeanor,
§35-4-73.
Sentencing.
Imprisonment.
Place of imprisonment,
§13A-5-8.
Term of imprisonment,
§13A-5-7.
Weapons.
Firearms.
Possession of firearms by
persons at
demonstrations in
public places,
§13A-11-59.
Youthful offenders.
Disposition of case upon
adjudication, §15-19-6.

MISREPRESENTATION.
Commercial code.
Commercial paper.
Defenses against holder in
due course, §7-3-305.
Sales.
Remedies, §7-2-721.
Solvency of buyer.
Seller's remedies on
discovery of buyer's
insolvency, §7-2-702.
Fraud.
General provisions.
See FRAUD.
Right of action.
Misrepresentation of
material facts,
§6-5-101.
**Hotels, inns and other
transient lodging places.**
Obtaining accommodations
by misrepresentation,
§§34-15-19, 34-15-20.
Insurance.
Policies, §27-14-7.
Proof of loss, §27-14-28.
Meat and meat products.
Inspections, §2-17-14.
Partnerships.
Rights where contract
rescinded for
misrepresentation,
§10-8-44.
Podiatrists.
Revocation or suspension of
license, §34-24-276.
Vacation time-sharing plans
Violations of article,
§§34-27-56, 34-27-60.
Veterans.
Pensions for widows of
Confederate veterans.
Proceedings as to pensions
secured by
misrepresentation,
§31-8-17.

MISSING PERSONS, §§26-19-1
to 26-19-10.
Agents.
Presumption of signer's
authority, §12-21-91.
Boards of education.
List of missing school
children.
Compilation and
distribution, §26-19-9.
Definitions, §26-19-1.
Evidence.
Official report of person
missing, etc., §12-21-91.
Location.
Duties of law enforcement
agencies upon locating,
§26-19-8.
Missing school children.
School to notify
department of
education and bureau,
§26-19-10.
Missing children's bureau,
§§26-19-2 to 26-19-4.
Creation, §26-19-2.
Director required to
establish, §26-19-3.
Functions.
Specific functions,
§26-19-4.
Personnel.
Authority to transfer, hire
etc., §26-19-3.

MISSING PERSONS—Cont'd
Missing school children.
Boards of education.
Compilation and
distribution of list,
§26-19-9.
Location.
School to notify
department of
education and bureau,
§26-19-10.
Reports, §§26-19-5 to 26-19-7.
Contents, §26-19-5.
Duties of law enforcement
agencies upon receiving,
§26-19-7.
Forwarding to other law
enforcement agencies,
§26-19-6.
Law enforcement agencies to
report to bureau,
§26-19-5.

**MISSISSIPPI-ALABAMA SEA
GRANT CONSORTIUM.**
Coastal areas.
Permissible uses, §9-7-13.

MISTAKE.
Commercial code.
Letters of credit.
Error in statement of
terms, §7-5-107.
Negotiation effective
although subject to
rescission, §7-3-207.
Contracts.
Specific performance.
Cases in which specific
performance not
enforced, §8-1-40.
Written contract not
expressing parties' intent
may be revised, §8-1-2.
Conveyances.
Reformation, §35-4-153.
Counties.
Money erroneously paid into
county treasury, etc.
Transfer to state treasury,
§11-1-6.
Criminal law and procedure.
Culpability generally,
§§13A-2-1 to 13A-2-7.
See CRIMINAL LAW AND
PROCEDURE.
Effect upon criminal liability,
§13A-2-6.
Deeds.
Reformation, §35-4-153.
Forms.
Form of complaint for money
paid by mistake, ARCP,
Form 10.
Income tax.
Tax paid through mistake or
error, §40-18-43.
Judgments.
Clerical mistakes.
Relief from judgment,
ARCP, Rule 60 (a).
Relief from judgment, ARCP,
Rule 60 (b).
**Mortgages and deeds of
trust.**
Reformation, §35-4-153.
Orders of court.
Clerical mistakes.
Relief from order, ARCP,
Rule 60 (a).
Relief from order, ARCP,
Rule 60 (b).

MISTAKE—Cont'd
Pleadings, ARCP, Rule 9 (b).
Form of complaint for money
paid by mistake, ARCP,
Form 10.
**Relief from judgment or
order,** ARCP, Rule 60 (b).
Clerical mistakes, ARCP,
Rule 60 (a).
Taxation.
Refunds.
Taxes paid by mistake,
§§40-10-160 to
40-10-165.
See TAXATION.
Sale of land for taxes.
Land sold for taxes not due
at time of sale,
§§40-10-100 to
40-10-105.
See TAXATION.

MISTRIAL.
Entry of mistrial, §12-16-233.
Jury.
Discharge of jury and entry
of mistrial, §12-16-233.

MOBILE BAY.
Harbors and ports.
General provisions, §§33-1-1
to 33-3-6.
See HARBORS AND
PORTS.
Marine resources.
General provisions, §§9-12-1
to 9-12-184.
See MARINE
RESOURCES.

MOBILE COLLEGE.
**Marine environmental
sciences consortium,**
§§16-45-1 to 16-45-5.

MOBILE COUNTY.
Bingo.
Operation of bingo games in,
Const. Ala., amd. 440.
Bond issues, Const. Ala.,
amds. 29, 463.
Debt limit, Const. Ala., amd.
60.
Extension of debt limit,
Const. Ala., amd. 100.
Change in purposes of levy
and distribution of
special tax, Const.
Ala., amd. 301.
General obligation bonds,
Const. Ala., amds. 447,
463.
Capital improvements.
Bond issue for capital
improvements, Const.
Ala., amd. 301.
Debt limit, Const. Ala., amd.
60.
Extension of debt limit,
Const. Ala., amd. 301.
**Economic and industrial
development promotion,**
Const. Ala., amd. 429.
Education.
Constitution of Alabama.
Applicability of education
article, Const. Ala.,
art. XIV, §270.
Amendment to section
270, Const. Ala.,
amd. 111.

MOBILE COUNTY—Cont'd
Health.
Special property tax, Const.
Ala., amd. 351.
Amount, Const. Ala., amd.
393.
Hospitals.
Bond issues, Const. Ala.,
amd. 151.
Change in purposes of levy
and distribution of
special tax, Const.
Ala., amd. 301.
Budget of Mobile county
public hospital board,
Const. Ala., amd. 194.
Special property tax for
public hospital purposes,
Const. Ala., amd. 275.
Special tax for public
hospital purposes, Const.
Ala., amd. 301.
Investments.
Municipal and county funds,
Const. Ala., amd. 500.
Judges.
Procedure for filling
vacancies in office,
Const. Ala., amd. 408.
Mosquitoes.
Special property tax for
control, Const. Ala.,
amds. 351, 361.
Officers.
Costs, fees, salaries etc., of
certain officers, Const.
Ala., amd. 28.
Pensions of former officers,
Const. Ala., amd. 192.
**Pension or retirement
system,** Const. Ala., amd.
150.
Comprehensive health
insurance plan for
retired employees, Const.
Ala., amd. 441.
Privilege license taxes.
Levy of certain privilege
license taxes by
municipalities, Const.
Ala., amd. 219.
Public buildings.
Bonds for certain public
buildings, Const. Ala.,
amd. 300.
Roads.
Bond issues, Const. Ala.,
amds. 18, 152.
Change in purposes of levy
and distribution of
special tax, Const.
Ala., amd. 301.
Districts to build and
maintain roads, Const.
Ala., amd. 15.
Rodents.
Special property tax for
control, Const. Ala., amd.
351.
School bonds.
Bonds for public school
buildings, Const. Ala.,
amds. 122, 151.
Change in purposes of levy
and distribution of
special tax, Const. Ala.,
amd. 301.
School lands.
Title to sixteenth section of
school lands, Const. Ala.,
amd. 289.

MOBILE COUNTY—Cont'd
School tax, Const. Ala., amd.
  16.
    Special property tax for
      school capital outlay
      purposes, Const. Ala.,
      amd. 179.
Seawalls.
    Districts to build and
      maintain seawalls,
      Const. Ala., amd. 15.
Sheriff.
    Fees, commissions, salaries,
      etc., Const. Ala., amd.
      47.
Welfare.
    Special property tax, Const.
      Ala., amd. 351.
Wills.
    Probate code.
      Savings provisions for,
        §43-8-9.

MOBILE HARBOR.
Constitution of Alabama.
    Bonds for Theodore ship
      channel project, Const.
      Ala., amd. 286.
    Development, improvement,
      etc., of state docks
      facilities, Const. Ala.,
      amd. 338.
Development of docks and
  other facilities along
  inland waterways,
  §§33-2-1 to 33-2-213.
    See WATERS AND
      WATERCOURSES.
General provisions, §§33-3-1
  to 33-3-6.
    See HARBORS AND PORTS.

MOBILE HOMES, §§24-5-1 to
  24-5-34.
Administration of article,
  §24-5-12.
Anchoring, §§24-5-30 to
  24-5-34.
    Conflict of laws.
      Certain local laws,
        municipal ordinances,
        etc., not repealed,
        §24-5-34.
    Definitions, §24-5-31.
    License tags.
      Suspension of license tags
        for violations of article,
        §24-5-33.
    Local laws.
      Certain local laws not
        repealed, §24-5-34.
    Ordinances.
      Certain municipal
        ordinances not
        repealed, §24-5-34.
    Penalties for violations of
      article, §24-5-33.
    Requirements.
      Anchorage requirements,
        §24-5-32.
    Short title of article,
      §24-5-30.
    Violations of article.
      Additional relief from
        violations, §24-5-33.
      Penalties, §24-5-33.
      Suspension of license tags,
        §24-5-33.
Certificates of title, §§32-8-30,
  32-8-31.
Certification of
  manufacturer, §24-5-4.

MOBILE HOMES—Cont'd
Conflict of laws.
    Anchoring.
      Certain local laws,
        municipal ordinances,
        etc., not repealed,
        §24-5-34.
Definitions, §24-5-31.
Enforcement of article,
  §24-5-13.
Fees.
    Licenses and seals, §§24-5-6,
      24-5-10.
Fire marshal.
    State fire marshal. See
      within this heading,
      "State fire marshal."
Homestead exemption.
    Levy and sale under process,
      exemptions from,
      §6-10-2.
Inspections.
    Label of approval required,
      §24-5-4.
    Local ordinances providing
      for inspection of mobile
      homes, §24-5-13.
    Manufacturing, sales, etc.,
      establishments, §24-5-9.
Label of approval.
    Manufacture of mobile homes
      not bearing label and
      certification, §24-5-5.
    Required prior to sale or
      offer for sale of new
      mobile homes, §24-5-4.
    Sale of new mobile homes
      without label, §24-5-7.
Licenses, §§40-12-255 to
  40-12-257.
    Anchoring.
      Suspension of license tags
        for violations of article,
        §24-5-33.
    Fees, §§24-5-6, 24-5-10.
    Sale of mobile homes,
      §24-5-6.
    Temporary tags and
      certificates.
      Issuance, §32-6-212.
Manufactured buildings
  generally, §§24-4A-1 to
  24-4A-7.
    See MANUFACTURED
      BUILDINGS.
Manufactured housing
  commission, §§24-6-1 to
  24-6-4.
Manufacturers.
    Certification of
      manufacturer.
      Manufacture of mobile
        homes not bearing
        label and certification,
        §24-5-5.
      Required, §24-5-4.
    Inspection of manufacturing
      establishments, §24-5-9.
    Records and statistics as to
      manufacture, §24-5-11.
Movement of oversized
  vehicles.
    Permits, §32-9-29.
Ordinances.
    Anchoring.
      Certain local laws,
        municipal ordinances,
        etc., not repealed,
        §24-5-34.

MOBILE HOMES—Cont'd
Ordinances—Cont'd
    Local ordinances providing
      for inspection of mobile
      homes, §24-5-13.
Penalties.
    Anchoring.
      Penalties for violations of
        article, §24-5-33.
    State fire marshal.
      Violations of article,
        §24-5-14.
    Violations of article,
      §24-5-14.
    Disposition of fines,
      §24-5-14.
Permits.
    Movement of oversized
      vehicles or loads.
      General provisions,
        §32-9-29.
    Special permits.
      Movement of certain site-
        built buildings,
        §32-9-29.1.
Records.
    Statistics as to manufacture,
      sale, etc., of mobile
      homes, §24-5-11.
    Test records, §24-5-9.
Sales.
    Inspection of sales
      establishments, §24-5-9.
    Licenses for sale, §24-5-6.
    New mobile homes without
      label, §24-5-7.
    Records and statistics as to
      manufacture, sale, etc.,
      of mobile homes,
      §24-5-11.
Sales tax, §40-23-101.
Short title of article, §24-5-1.
Standards.
    Establishment of uniform
      standards, §24-5-3.
    State fire marshal.
      Enforcement of uniform
        standards, §24-5-13.1.
State fire marshal.
    Funds.
      State fire marshal's fund,
        §24-5-10.
    Violations of article.
      Disposition of fine,
        §24-5-14.
    Penalties.
      Violations of article,
        §24-5-14.
    Standards.
      Enforcement of uniform
        standards, §24-5-13.1.
    Transfer of functions to
      manufacture housing
      commission, §24-6-4.
Statistics.
    Records and statistics as to
      manufacture, sale, etc.,
      of mobile homes,
      §24-5-11.
Taxation.
    Ad valorem tax, §§40-12-256,
      40-12-257.
    Decals, §40-7-1.
    Gas or electric service.
      Report of connection,
        §40-7-1.
    Owner of real estate.
      Report of name and
        address of owner of
        mobile home, §40-7-1.

MOBILE HOMES—Cont'd
Testing of products, etc.,
§24-5-9.
**Uniform certificate of title
and antitheft act.**
Travel trailers.
Certificate of title.
Exemption of certain
travel trailers,
§32-8-31.
Uniform standards code,
§§24-5-1 to 24-5-14.
Use tax.
Excise tax on storage or use,
§40-23-102.
Violations of article.
Penalties, §24-5-14.

**MOLDS, DYES OR
PATTERNS.**
Disposal, §§8-28-1 to 8-28-4.
Applicability of provisions,
§8-28-4.
Definitions, §8-28-1.
Notice, §8-28-3.
Procedure, §8-28-3.
When molder may dispose of
form owned by customer,
§8-28-2.

MOLLUSKS.
Mussels or mollusks,
§§9-11-370 to 9-11-374.

MONARCH BUTTERFLY.
State insect, §1-2-25.

MONEY.
**Banks and financial
institutions.**
Machines, §5-5A-30.
Commercial code.
Defined, §7-1-201.
Corporations.
Change bills.
See CORPORATIONS.

MONOPOLIES.
Actions.
By whom and against whom
action may be
commenced, §6-5-60.
Venue, §6-5-60.
Agriculture.
Incorporated marketing
associations.
Association not a
monopoly, §2-10-71.
Catfish.
Promotion of industry.
Activities to promote
industry not illegal or
in restraint of trade,
§2-8-271.
Commodities.
Monopolizing commodities or
business, §8-10-3.
Constitution of Alabama.
Regulation of monopolies,
Const. Ala., art. IV,
§103.
**Contracts restraining
business void,** §8-1-1.
Exceptions, §8-1-1.
Insurers.
Common ownership,
management and
directorship, §27-12-16.
Trade and commerce.
Restraint of trade or
production, §§8-10-1 to
8-10-3.

MONROE COUNTY.
Fires and fire prevention.
Fire protection districts.
Property tax.
Additional property tax,
Const. Ala., amd.
501.
Property tax.
Fire protection and rescue
squads.
Additional property tax for,
Const. Ala., amd. 501.
School tax.
Special school tax, Const.
Ala., amd. 86.

**MONROEVILLE,
MUNICIPALITY OF.**
Property tax, Const. Ala.,
amd. 8.

MONTEVALLO.
University of Montevallo,
§§16-54-1 to 16-54-15.
See UNIVERSITY OF
MONTEVALLO.

MONTGOMERY, CITY OF.
Capitol grounds.
City council authorized to
adopt ordinances to
protect, §41-4-186.
Court of civil appeals.
Judges to reside in
Montgomery during
terms of court, §12-3-5.
Court of criminal appeals.
Judges to reside in
Montgomery during
terms of court, §12-3-5.
**Public officers and
employees.**
Residence requirement,
§36-2-4.
Failure to comply deemed
ground for
impeachment or
removal, §36-2-5.
Public service commission.
Residence of commissioners,
§37-1-9.

MONTGOMERY COUNTY.
Bingo.
Operation of games by
nonprofit organizations,
Const. Ala., amd. 413.
Court costs and charges,
Const. Ala., amd. 139.
Fires and fire prevention.
Establishment of fire
districts, Const. Ala.,
amd. 379.
Hospitals.
Special tax for hospital and
public health purposes,
Const. Ala., amd. 63.
Officers.
Salaries, Const. Ala., amd. 4.
Public health.
Special tax for hospital and
public health purposes,
Const. Ala., amd. 63.

MONTH.
Defined, §1-1-1.

**MONUMENTS AND
MARKERS.**
**Actions to determine
boundaries.**
Landmarks, §35-3-3.

**MONUMENTS AND
MARKERS—Cont'd**
Alabama coordinate system.
Descriptions of monuments,
markers, etc., §35-2-6.
Cemeteries, §§11-17-1 to
11-17-16.
See CEMETERIES.
Confederacy, §§9-2-104,
9-2-105.
Criminal law and procedure.
Desecration of venerated
objects, §13A-11-12.
**Desecration of venerated
objects,** §13A-11-12.
Geological survey, §§9-4-1 to
9-4-19.
See GEOLOGICAL
SURVEY.
Licenses.
Selling or erecting,
§40-12-131.
Public societies, §§10-4-20 to
10-4-26.
See CORPORATIONS.
State parks, §§9-14-1 to
9-14-29.
See STATE PARKS.
Surveys and surveyors.
General provisions, §§34-11-1
to 34-11-37.
See SURVEYS AND
SURVEYORS.

MOOSE, LOYAL ORDER OF.
Taxation.
Property exempted, §40-9-1.

MOPS.
Licenses.
Manufacturers, §40-12-68.

MORGAN COUNTY.
Consolidation of offices,
Const. Ala., amd. 330.
**Economic and industrial
development promotion,**
Const. Ala., amd. 429.
Economic development.
Promotion of industrial,
commercial and
agricultural
development, Const.
Ala., amd. 303.
Health.
Special property tax for
general health purposes,
Const. Ala., amd. 311.
Hospitals.
Special tax for hospital
purposes, Const. Ala.,
amd. 52.
Jail.
Bonds for erection, etc., of
jail, Const. Ala., amd.
36.
Libraries.
Special property tax for
library service, Const.
Ala., amd. 318.
Officers.
Regulation of salaries, etc., of
officers, Const. Ala.,
amd. 44.
Offices.
Consolidation, Const. Ala.,
amd. 330.
School tax.
Additional taxes for public
school purposes, Const.
Ala., amd. 106.

MORGAN COUNTY—Cont'd
  Sheriff's posse.
    Grant of money to.
      Authorized, Const. Ala.,
        amd. 502.
  Sheriff's reserve.
    County commission
      authorized to grant
      money to, Const. Ala.,
      amd. 457.
  Taxation.
    Additional ad valorem tax,
      Const. Ala., amd. 484.

MORGUES.
  Coroners.
    See CORONERS.
  Dead bodies.
    See DEAD BODIES.
  Municipal corporations,
    §11-47-7.

MORPHINE.
  Controlled substances.
    General provisions, §§20-2-1
      to 20-2-144.
    See DRUGS.

MORTALITY TABLES.
  **Annuity and mortality
    tables,** §§35-16-1 to
    35-16-4.

**MORTGAGES AND DEEDS
  OF TRUST,** §§35-10-1 to
  35-10-51.
  Abstract of mortgages.
    Failure to keep, §12-13-54.
  Acknowledgments.
    Conveyances generally.
      See CONVEYANCES.
  Actions.
    Reformation of deeds,
      mortgages and
      conveyances, §§35-4-150
      to 35-4-153.
  Affidavits.
    Conveyances generally,
      §§35-4-69 to 35-4-71.
  Agriculture.
    Marketing associations.
      Authority to execute
        mortgages, §2-10-27.
  **Banks and financial
    institutions.**
    Investments and loans,
      §5-5A-23.
    Powers, §5-5A-18.
  **Bear creek development
    authority.**
    Exemption from taxation,
      §33-15-12.
    Statutory mortgage lien,
      §33-15-10.
  Blanket mortgages.
    Condominium property,
      §35-8-18.
  Brokers.
    Mortgage brokerage
      business.
      Savings and loan
        associations prohibited
        from engaging in
        mortgage brokerage
        business, §5-16-48.
  Burial societies.
    Securing loans by mortgage
      or deed of trust,
      §10-4-24.
    Effect of recital in minutes
      on proceedings,
      §10-4-26.

**MORTGAGES AND DEEDS
  OF TRUST**—Cont'd
  Chattel mortgages.
    Fraud, §8-9-1.
    Secured transactions,
      §§7-9-101 to 7-9-507.
    See COMMERCIAL CODE.
    Trial of right of property.
      Claims based on mortgage,
      §6-6-164.
  Commercial code.
    Secured transactions,
      §§7-9-101 to 7-9-507.
    See COMMERCIAL CODE.
  Condominiums.
    Blanket mortgage on
      condominium property,
      §35-8-18.
    Common and limited
      common elements.
      Mortgage includes
        undivided interest in
        common and limited
        common elements,
        §35-8-6.
    Investments.
      Mortgage investments on
        condominium property,
        §35-8-19.
    Recordation, §35-8-11.
    Units, §35-8-8.
  Constitution of Alabama.
    Nonresidents.
      Making mortgage loans
        through licensed
        mortgage loan brokers,
        Const. Ala., amd. 154.
  Conveyances.
    Corporations, §10-4-25.
    Foreclosure. See within this
      heading, "Foreclosure."
    Generally, §§35-4-1 to
      35-4-412.
    See CONVEYANCES.
  Corporations.
    Churches.
      Securing loans by
        mortgage or deed of
        trust, §10-4-24.
    Foreign corporations.
      Mortgage loans by
        nonresident
        corporation not
        constituting doing
        business in state,
        Const. Ala., amd. 154.
    Graveyard owners.
      Securing loans by
        mortgage or deed of
        trust, §10-4-24.
      Effect of recital in
        minutes on
        proceedings,
        §10-4-26.
    Powers of corporations,
      §10-2A-20.
    Proof of conveyances
      executed in name of
      corporation, §35-4-67.
    Public societies.
      Securing loans by
        mortgage or deed of
        trust, §10-4-26.
    Sale and conveyance of
      property, §10-4-25.

**MORTGAGES AND DEEDS
  OF TRUST**—Cont'd
  Counties.
    Bond issues.
      Execution of mortgages or
        deeds of trust upon
        property acquired with
        proceeds of bond
        issues, §11-81-2.
  Deeds.
    Foreclosure deeds.
      Deeds in lieu of
        foreclosure, §§35-10-50,
        35-10-51.
      Generally. See within this
        heading, "Foreclosure."
  Definitions.
    Foreclosure.
      Deeds in lieu of
        foreclosure, §35-10-50.
    Power of sale, §35-10-11.
  Description of land.
    Erroneous description.
      Reformation, §§35-4-151,
      35-4-152.
  Detinue.
    Actions by mortgagee or
      against mortgagor,
      §6-6-259.
  Education.
    Private colleges and
      universities.
      Facilities authority.
        Bond issues.
          Statutory mortgage
            lien, §16-18A-7.
  **Educational building
    authorities.**
    Bond issues.
      Statutory mortgage lien,
      §16-17-12.
  Ejectment.
    Actions by mortgagee against
      mortgagor, §6-6-282.
  Electric cooperatives.
    Board of trustees.
      Powers as to, §37-6-21.
    Encumbrance of property.
      Approval of members
        required, §37-6-21.
    Liens.
      Instruments creating liens,
      §37-6-23.
  **Electric membership
    corporations.**
    Encumbering property,
      §37-7-11.
  **Environmental improvement
    authorities.**
    Bond issues.
      Creation of statutory
        mortgage lien, §9-6-11.
  Erroneous descriptions.
    Reformation, §§35-4-151,
      35-4-152.
  Executions.
    Void or irregular sale under
      foreclosure.
      Purchaser succeeds to
        interest of mortgagee,
        §6-9-146.
  **Executors and
    administrators.**
    Assignment or transfer,
      §43-2-420.
    Releases.
      Executors and
        administrators
        authorized to execute,
        §35-10-25.

MORTGAGES AND DEEDS OF TRUST—Cont'd

Fees.
Probate judges' fees, §12-19-90.

Foreclosure.
Contrary to article.
Applicability of section 35-10-9, §35-10-10.
Sales contrary to article null and void, §35-10-9.
Counties.
Sale to be held in county where property situated, §35-10-7.
Applicability of section 35-10-7, §35-10-10.
Two or more counties.
Sale of lands situated in two or more counties, §35-10-4.
Deeds.
Convey legal title, §35-10-5.
Index of foreclosure deeds, §35-10-1.
Deeds in lieu of foreclosure, §§35-10-50, 35-10-51.
Effect of conveyance, §35-10-1.
Hours of sale, §6-8-41.
Index of foreclosure deeds, §35-10-1.
Lands situated in two or more counties, §35-10-4.
Notice of sale.
Applicability of section 35-10-8, §35-10-10.
How notice given, §35-10-8.
Partial sale.
Additional satisfaction permitted under continuing power of sale, §35-10-6.
Place of sale.
Lands situated in two or more counties, §35-10-4.
Sale to be held in county where property situated, §35-10-7.
Applicability of section 35-10-7, §35-10-10.
Sale under power where instrument silent as to place of sale, §35-10-2.
Redemption, §§6-5-247 to 6-5-257.
See REAL PROPERTY.
Situs of property.
Sale of lands situated in two or more counties, §35-10-4.
Sale to be held in county where property situated, §35-10-10.
Terms of sale.
Sale under power where instrument silent as to place or terms of sale, §35-10-2.
Title.
Foreclosure deed conveys legal title, §35-10-5.
Void sales.
Applicability of section 35-10-9, §35-10-10.
Sales contrary to article null and void, §35-10-9.

MORTGAGES AND DEEDS OF TRUST—Cont'd

Foreclosure—Cont'd
When instrument contains no power of sale, §35-10-3.

Fraternal orders.
Effect of article on existing mortgages, §10-4-179.

Fraud.
Mortgage of personalty, §8-9-1.
Reformation, §35-4-153.

Health care authorities.
Powers of authority, §22-21-318. §23-1-207.

Housing authorities.
County housing authorities.
See HOUSING AUTHORITIES.
Industry and trade.
Projects for promotion, §§11-20-1 to 11-20-13.
See COUNTIES.
Municipal housing authorities.
See HOUSING AUTHORITIES.
Power of sale.
Situs of property.
Sale of lands situated in two or more counties, §35-10-4.
Sale to be held in county where land situated, §35-10-7.
Public property.
Mortgage for payment of debts, §11-81-27.

Industrial development boards.
Liability of municipalities upon obligations of boards, §11-54-92.
Security for payment of principal and interest of bonds, §11-54-90.

Industrial development corporations.
Powers of corporations, §10-4-133.
Taking of security by mortgage, §10-4-142.

Insurance.
Investments.
Life insurance companies may invest in notes secured by mortgages or deeds of trust, §27-1-8.
Purchase of insurance as condition precedent to sale or loan on property, §27-12-15.

Interest generally.
See INTEREST.

Investments.
Condominium property.
Mortgage investments on condominium property, §35-8-19.

Joint mortgagees.
Satisfaction by one of several joint mortgagees.
Entry of full payment or satisfaction in record, §35-10-28.

Judicial sales generally.
See JUDICIAL SALES.

MORTGAGES AND DEEDS OF TRUST—Cont'd

Liens.
Satisfaction of mortgage liens, §§35-10-20 to 35-10-30. See within this heading, "Satisfaction of mortgage liens."

Limitation of actions.
Actions on equities of redemption where lands have been sold under judgment of circuit court, §6-2-35.

Lis pendens.
Mortgagees protected upon failure to record notice, §35-4-135.

Literary or social societies.
Conveyances by literary or social societies.
Societies not prevented from taking mortgage, §35-4-343.

Lotteries.
Transportation of lottery paraphernalia.
Mortgagees of vehicles used to transport.
Rights of mortgagee, §13A-12-73.

Mechanics' and materialmen's liens.
Priority of mechanics' and materialmen's liens, §35-11-211.

Mentally ill.
Void contracts.
Mortgage in good faith on real estate of insane person not void, §8-1-172.

Mistake.
Reformation, §35-4-153.

Mortality tables.
Annuity and mortality tables, §§35-16-1 to 35-16-4.

Municipal corporations.
Boards for operation of water, sewer, gas and electric systems.
Bond issues.
Mortgaging of systems for payment of bonds, §11-50-317.
Provisions in mortgages or deeds of trust executed by corporation as to rights of parties, §11-50-314.
Bond issues, §11-81-2.
Electric lighting or power plants.
Execution as security for debts, etc., incurred in construction, acquisition, etc., §§11-50-8 to 11-50-11.
Gas districts.
Bond issues.
Properties, persons, etc., subject to mortgages, §11-50-408.
Provisions as to rights of parties in mortgages and deeds of trust executed as security for bonds, §11-50-407.

MORTGAGES AND DEEDS OF TRUST—Cont'd
Municipal corporations —Cont'd
Gas districts—Cont'd
Bond issues—Cont'd
When mortgages effective, §11-50-408.
Housing authorities.
Municipal housing authorities.
See HOUSING AUTHORITIES.
Industrial development boards.
Liability of municipalities upon obligations of boards, §11-54-92.
Security for payment of principal and interest of bonds, §11-54-90.
Post-office projects.
Notice to, approval or consent of governmental body not to be required for execution of mortgages, §11-55-7.
Security for payment of principal and interest of bonds, §11-55-4.
Public property.
Mortgage for payment of debts, §11-81-27.
Water supply and waterworks.
Execution as security for debts, etc., incurred in construction, acquisition, etc., §§11-50-8 to 11-50-11.
Waterworks and sewer boards.
Acquisition, operation, etc., of gas plants and systems.
Execution of mortgages as security for indebtedness, §11-50-262.
Provisions in mortgages and deeds of trust.
Executed by corporation as to rights of parties, §11-50-235.
Nonresidents.
Mortgage loans through licensed mortgage loan brokers, Const. Ala., amd. 154.
Notice.
Foreclosure sale.
Applicability of section 35-10-8, §35-10-10.
How notice of sale given, §35-10-8.
Origination of mortgages.
Savings and loan associations, §5-16-48.
Partial payments, §§35-10-22 to 35-10-24.
Parties.
Reformation.
Grantors, etc., may be made parties defendant, §35-4-152.
Payment, §§35-10-20 to 35-10-30. See within this heading, "Satisfaction of mortgage liens."

MORTGAGES AND DEEDS OF TRUST—Cont'd
Penalties.
Failure to enter satisfaction or payment in record, §35-10-30.
Personal property.
Commercial code.
Secured transactions, §§7-9-101 to 7-9-507.
See COMMERCIAL CODE.
Fraud, §8-9-1.
Trial of right of property.
Claims based on mortgage, §6-6-164.
Post-office projects.
Notice to, approval or consent of governmental body not to be required for execution of mortgages, §11-55-7.
Security for payment of principal and interest of bonds, §11-55-4.
Power districts.
Power to make and enter, §37-5-3.
Power of sale.
Additional satisfaction permitted under continuing power of sale, §35-10-6.
Contrary to article.
Applicability of section 35-10-9, §35-10-10.
Sales contrary to article null and void, §35-10-9.
Definitions, §35-10-11.
Execution of foreclosure, §§35-10-12 to 35-10-16.
Applicability of provisions, §35-10-16.
Effect, §35-10-12.
Indexing of deeds, §35-10-12.
Notice of sale, §35-10-13.
Place for conducting foreclosure, §35-10-14.
Successive sale, §35-10-15.
Time for conducting foreclosure, §35-10-14.
Foreclosure when instrument contains no power of sale, §35-10-3.
Instrument silent as to place or terms of sale.
Sale under power where instrument silent, §35-10-2.
Notice of sale.
Minimum standards, §35-10-13.
Security.
Constitutes part of security, §35-10-1.
Situs of property.
Sale of lands situated in two or more counties, §35-10-4.
Sale to be held in county where property situated, §35-10-7.
Applicability of section 35-10-7, §35-10-10.
Successive sales, §35-10-15.
Void sales.
Applicability of section 35-10-9, §35-10-10.
Who may execute, §35-10-1.

MORTGAGES AND DEEDS OF TRUST—Cont'd
Presumptions.
Satisfaction of mortgage liens.
When indebtedness presumed to have been paid, §35-10-20.
Purchase of mortgages.
Savings and loan associations, §5-16-48.
Real property.
Redemption, §§6-5-247 to 6-5-257.
See REAL PROPERTY.
Recordation.
See RECORDATION.
Recordation tax, §§40-22-1 to 40-22-12.
See RECORDATION.
Redemption of real property, §§6-5-247 to 6-5-257.
See REAL PROPERTY.
Reformation, §§35-4-150 to 35-4-153.
Releases.
Executors and administrators authorized to execute, §35-10-25.
Sale of property, §19-3-171.
Contrary to article.
Applicability of section 35-10-9, §35-10-10.
Sales contrary to article null and void, §35-10-9.
Counties.
Sale to be held in county where property situated, §35-10-10.
Two or more counties.
Sale of lands situated in two or more counties, §35-10-4.
Foreclosure. See within this heading, "Foreclosure."
Hours of sale for public sales, §6-8-41.
Lands situated in two or more counties, §35-10-4.
Notice.
Applicability of section 35-10-8, §35-10-10.
How notice of sale given, §35-10-8.
Partial sale.
Additional satisfaction permitted under continuing power of sale, §35-10-6.
Place of sale.
Lands situated in two or more counties, §35-10-4.
Sale to be held in county where property situated, §35-10-7.
Applicability of section 35-10-7, §35-10-10.
Sale under power where instrument silent as to place or terms of sale, §35-10-2.
Power of sale. See within this heading, "Power of sale."
Savings and loan associations, §5-16-48.

MORTGAGES AND DEEDS OF TRUST—Cont'd
Sale of property—Cont'd
Void sales.
Applicability of section 35-10-9, §35-10-10.
Purchaser succeeds to interest of mortgagee, §6-9-146.
Sales contrary to article null and void, §35-10-9.
Satisfaction of mortgage liens, §§35-10-20 to 35-10-30.
Execution of releases.
Executors and administrators authorized to execute, §35-10-25.
Executors and administrators.
Authorized to execute releases, etc., §35-10-25.
Full payment or satisfaction.
Entry in record, §§35-10-21, 35-10-27 to 35-10-29.
Partial payments.
Entry by execution and delivery of separate instrument, §35-10-24.
Notices or demands to enter, §35-10-23.
When entered on margin of record, §35-10-22.
Penalties.
Failure to enter payment or satisfaction in record, §35-10-30.
Presumptions.
When indebtedness presumed to have been paid, §35-10-20.
Recordation, §§35-10-22 to 35-10-30.
Entry of full payment or satisfaction in record.
Generally, §35-10-27.
Penalty for violation, §35-10-30.
Satisfaction by one of several joint mortgagees, §35-10-28.
Vendor's or other lien reserved in conveyance, §35-10-29.
Executors and administrators authorized to enter satisfaction, §35-10-25.
Partial payments, §§35-10-22 to 35-10-24.
Penalties.
Failure to enter full payment or satisfaction in record, §35-10-30.
When payment required to be entered in record, §35-10-21.
Releases.
Executors and administrators authorized to execute, §35-10-25.

MORTGAGES AND DEEDS OF TRUST—Cont'd
Satisfaction of mortgage liens—Cont'd
Title.
Revested upon payment of debt, §35-10-26.
When indebtedness presumed to have been paid, §35-10-20.
Savings and loan associations.
Generally, §5-16-48.
Secured transactions, §§7-9-101 to 7-9-507.
See COMMERCIAL CODE.
Taxation.
Recordation tax, §§12-13-53, 40-22-1 to 40-22-12.
See RECORDATION.
Title.
Foreclosure deed conveys legal title, §35-10-5.
Revested upon payment of debt, §35-10-26.
Trees and timber.
Transfers of standing timber, trees and cutting rights.
Void and inoperative as against purchasers, mortgagees and judgment creditors without notice or prior recordation, §35-4-92.
Witnesses.
Form of proof of conveyances, §35-4-68.

MORTICIANS.
General provisions, §§34-13-1 to 34-13-152.
See FUNERALS.

MOSQUITOES.
Cisterns.
Construction, regulation, etc., of public cisterns, §11-47-140.
Municipal corporations.
Construction, regulation, etc., of public wells, cisterns, etc., §11-47-140.
Wells.
Construction, regulation, etc., of public wells, §11-47-140.

MOTELS, §§34-15-1 to 34-15-20, 40-26-1 to 40-26-21.
See HOTELS, INNS AND OTHER TRANSIENT LODGING PLACES.

MOTHERS AND BABIES INDIGENT CARE TRUST FUND.
Perinatal health, §§22-12B-1 to 22-12B-4.

MOTION PICTURES.
Definitions.
Fair competition, §8-18-2.
Depiction of criminal activities.
Profits from crime, §§41-9-80 to 41-9-84.
Fair competition, §§8-18-1 to 8-18-6.
Actions.
Award of damages and attorney's fees in civil actions, §8-18-6.

MOTION PICTURES—Cont'd
Fair competition—Cont'd
Attorney's fees.
Award in civil actions, §8-18-6.
Bids and bidding.
Blind bidding prohibited, §8-18-4.
Definitions, §8-18-2.
Procedures, §8-18-5.
Damages.
Award in civil actions, §8-18-6.
Definitions, §8-18-2.
Distributors.
Defined, §8-18-2.
Enforcement of chapter, §8-18-6.
Exhibitors.
Defined, §8-18-2.
Injunctions, §8-18-6.
Legislative intent, §8-18-3.
License agreements.
Defined, §8-18-2.
Notice.
Trade screening.
Notice required, §8-18-4.
Run.
Defined, §8-18-2.
Short title of act, §8-18-1.
Theaters.
Defined, §8-18-2.
Trade screening.
Defined, §8-18-2.
Notice of trade screening required, §8-18-4.
Licenses, §§40-12-132, 40-12-133.
Obscenity generally.
See OBSCENITY.

MOTIONS.
Alteration of judgment, ARCP, Rule 59 (e), (g).
Disposition of motion, ARCP, Rule 59.1.
Stay on motion, ARCP, Rule 62 (b).
Amendment of judgment, ARCP, Rule 59 (e), (g).
Disposition of motion, ARCP, Rule 59.1.
Stay on motion, ARCP, Rule 62 (b).
Appeals.
Rules of appellate procedure.
See APPEALS.
Stay pending appeal, ARAP, Rule 8 (b).
Attorneys at law.
Signing of motions, ARCP, Rule 11.
Circuit courts.
Motion day, ARCP, Rule 78.
Consolidation.
Form of motion to consolidate, ARCP, Form 72.
Default judgments.
Form of motion to set aside, ARCP, Form 83.
Defenses.
Consolidation of defenses in motion, ARCP, Rule 12 (g).
Defenses that may be made by motion, ARCP, Rule 12 (b).
Forms, ARCP, Form 26.

MOTIONS—Cont'd
Depositions.
Forms of motions, ARCP,
Forms 42 to 46, 62, 67.
Termination or limitation of
oral examination, ARCP,
Rule 30 (d).
Form of motion to limit,
ARCP, Form 44.
Directed verdict, ARCP, Rule
50; ARCP, Form 77.
Stay on motion, ARCP, Rule
62 (b).
Discovery.
Order compelling discovery,
ARCP, Rule 37 (a).
Forms of motions, ARCP,
Forms 62 to 67.
Dropping defendant.
Form of motion, ARCP, Form
33.
Eminent domain.
Withdrawal of deposited
funds before judgment,
§18-1A-110.
Evidence on motions, ARCP,
Rule 43 (e).
Findings by court.
Motion for amendment,
ARCP, Rule 52 (b).
Interrogatories.
Forms, ARCP, Forms 48, 49,
63, 64.
Intervention.
Form of motion to intervene,
ARCP, Form 32.
Joinder of parties.
Forms of motions, ARCP,
Forms 35 to 37.
**Judgment notwithstanding
verdict,** ARCP, Rule 50;
ARCP, Form 78.
Judgment on the pleadings,
ARCP, Rule 12 (c).
Jury.
Advisory jury.
Form of motion for trial by
advisory jury, ARCP,
Form 69.
More definite statement,
ARCP, Rule 12 (e).
New trial, ARCP, Rule 50 (b).
Affidavits.
Time for serving, ARCP,
Rule 59 (c).
Disposition of new trial
motion, ARCP, Rule
59.1.
Form, ARCP, Form 78.
Granting, §§12-22-241,
12-22-242.
Appeal, §12-22-10.
Presentation of motions not
required, ARCP, Rule 59
(g).
Stay on motion for new trial,
ARCP, Rule 62 (b).
Time for motion, ARCP, Rule
59 (b).
**Physical examination of
persons.**
Form of motion for physical
examination, ARCP,
Form 53.
**Production of documents
and things.**
Order compelling production.
Form of motion for order,
ARCP, Form 52.
Records.
Final record, §12-20-22.

MOTIONS—Cont'd
Requests for admission.
Form of motions, ARCP,
Forms 58, 59, 61, 61A.
**Rules of appellate
procedure.**
See APPEALS.
Rules of civil procedure.
See RULES OF CIVIL
PROCEDURE.
Rules of criminal procedure.
See RULES OF CRIMINAL
PROCEDURE.
Severance of claims.
Forms of motions, ARCP,
Forms 33, 34.
Signing of motions, ARCP,
Rule 11.
Stay pending appeal, ARAP,
Rule 8 (d).
Striking pleadings.
Motion to strike, ARCP, Rule
12 (f).
Summary judgment, ARCP,
Rule 56.
Forms, ARCP, Forms 84, 85.
Third-party defendants.
Motions to bring in.
Form, ARCP, Form 28.
Vacation of judgment, ARCP,
Rule 59 (e), (g).
Disposition of motion, ARCP,
Rule 59.1.
Stay on motion, ARCP, Rule
62 (b).
Verdict.
See VERDICT.

MOTORBOATS.
Carburetors, §33-5-22.
General provisions, §§33-5-1
to 33-5-36.
See BOATS.
Muffling devices, §§33-5-23.

MOTOR CARRIERS, §§37-3-1
to 37-3-34, 40-17-140 to
40-17-155, 40-19-1 to
40-19-17.
See MOTOR VEHICLE
CARRIERS.

MOTORCYCLES.
**Attachment to other
vehicles.**
Prohibited, §32-5A-243.
Brakes.
Number of brakes required,
§§32-5-212, 32-12-24.
Clinging to other vehicles.
Prohibited, §32-5A-243.
Clubs.
Shrine motorcycle clubs,
§§32-6-190, 32-6-191.
Dealers.
Licenses, §40-12-62.
Definitions, §§32-1-1.1,
40-12-240.
Motor-driven cycles,
§32-1-1.1.
Footrests.
Required equipment,
§32-5A-244.
Guardian and ward.
Authorizing or permitting
violations, §32-12-20.
Handlebars.
Type and form of handlebars,
§32-5A-244.
Head lamps.
Required, §32-5-240.

MOTORCYCLES—Cont'd
Helmets.
Manufacturers.
Duties, §32-12-42.
Operators to wear helmets,
§32-5A-245.
Passengers to wear helmets,
§32-5A-245.
Sale.
Helmets failing to comply
with specifications,
§32-5A-245.
Specifications, §32-12-41.
Violations.
Penalty for violation,
§32-12-44.
Licenses.
Dealers, §40-12-62.
Tags, §40-12-62.
Motor-driven cycles,
§§32-12-21, 32-12-22,
32-12-26.
Shrine motorcycle clubs,
§§32-6-190, 32-6-191.
Taxes and registration fees,
§40-12-242.
Additional fees,
§40-12-273.
Disposition, §40-12-274.
"Motorcycles" defined,
§40-12-240.
Motor-driven cycles,
§§32-12-20 to 32-12-27.
Age.
Licenses, §32-12-22.
Brakes, §32-12-24.
Defined, §32-12-20.
Guardian.
Authorizing or permitting
violations, §32-12-20.
Licenses.
Fees, §32-6-21.
Operator's license,
§§32-12-22, 32-12-26.
Lighting equipment on
motor-driven cycles,
§32-5-242.
Limited-access roads.
Restrictions on use,
§32-5A-92.
Manner of riding,
§32-5A-242.
Night.
Speed limit at night,
§32-5A-175.
Operator's license.
Age requirement,
§32-12-22.
Issuance, §32-12-22.
Revocation, §32-12-26.
Overtaking.
Manner of overtaking,
§32-5A-242.
Parents.
Authorizing or permitting
violations, §32-12-20.
Penalties.
Violations, §32-12-27.
Registration.
Required, §32-12-22.
Speed limits.
Nighttime speed limit,
§32-5A-175.
Traffic regulations.
Persons riding or operating
cycles.
Subject to traffic
regulations,
§32-5A-240.

MOTORCYCLES—Cont'd
  Motor-driven cycles—Cont'd
    Violations.
      Operator's license.
        Revocation for violation,
          §32-12-26.
      Parent or guardian not to
        authorize or permit
        violations, §32-12-20.
      Penalties, §32-12-27.
  Motor vehicles generally,
    §§32-1-1 to 32-18-8.
    See MOTOR VEHICLES.
  Parent and child.
    Authorizing or permitting
      violations by child,
      §32-12-20.
  Passengers, §32-5A-241.
  Penalties.
    Violations, §32-12-44.
  Riding on motorcycles,
    §32-5A-241.
  Seats, §32-5A-241.
  Shrine motorcycle clubs.
    Distinctive license plates,
      §32-6-191.
      Authorized, §32-6-190.
      Color, §32-6-190.
      Design, §32-6-190.
      Issuance, §32-6-191.
        Fees, §32-6-191.
      One per person, §32-6-190.
      Preparation, §32-6-191.
  Violations, §32-5A-241.

MOTOR-DRIVEN CYCLES,
  §§32-12-20 to 32-12-27.
  See MOTORCYCLES.

MOTOR FUELS.
  Agriculture.
    Sales tax.
      Diesel fuel used for off-
        highway agricultural
        purposes.
        Exemption of gross
          proceeds from sale,
          §40-23-4.
    Use tax.
      Diesel fuel used for off-
        highway agricultural
        purposes.
        Exemption, §40-23-62.
  Appeals.
    Distributors of motor fuels.
      Decisions of department of
        revenue.
        Appeals to courts,
          §40-12-203.
  Bonds, surety.
    Diesel fuel tax.
      Application for license for
        sale, withdrawal or
        use, §40-17-14.
    Distributors of motor fuels.
      Licenses, §40-12-194.
  Contracts.
    Marketing.
      Violation of chapter.
        Void and unenforceable,
          §8-22-14.
  Counties.
    Taxation.
      Public roads, bridges and
        ferries.
        Expenditure of funds
          derived from taxes
          levied on fuels,
          §23-1-84.

MOTOR FUELS—Cont'd
  Damages.
    Marketing.
      Violation of chapter,
        §8-22-17.
  Definitions.
    Diesel fuel tax.
      Motor fuel, §40-17-1.
    Distributors of motor fuels.
      Licenses, §40-12-190.
    Marketing, §8-22-4.
  Diesel fuel tax, §§40-17-1 to
    40-17-21.
    Amount, §40-17-2.
    Application, §40-17-3.
    Bonds, surety.
      Application for license for
        sale, withdrawal or
        use, §40-17-14.
    Books.
      Keeping for three years,
        §40-17-7.
    Delinquents, §§40-17-15 to
      40-17-17.
      Bonding company.
        Demand on, §40-17-16.
        Claim against, §40-17-17.
      Execution, §40-17-15.
      Levy on property,
        §40-17-16.
      Liens, §40-17-15.
      Notice to show cause,
        §40-17-15.
    Enforcement.
      Cost, §40-17-8.
    Gasoline tax.
      Effect on provisions of
        gasoline tax,
        §40-17-19.
    Levy, §40-17-2.
    Licenses.
      Bulk purchaser's license,
        §40-17-12.
      Sale, withdrawal or use.
        Application, §40-17-14.
        Bond, §40-17-14.
    Motor carrier fuel tax.
      Credit of payment of motor
        fuel tax, §40-17-142.
    "Motor fuel" defined,
      §40-17-1.
    Motor fuel upon which tax
      not paid or assumed.
      Use unlawful, §40-17-4.
    Payment.
      Monthly payment,
        §40-17-5.
        Failure to make,
          §40-17-10.
    Proceeds.
      Disposition, §40-17-13.
    Records.
      Failure to keep, §40-17-9.
    Reports.
      Failure to make, §40-17-9.
      Forms, §40-17-8.
    Returns.
      Monthly returns.
        Failure to make,
          §40-17-10.
    Rules and regulations,
      §40-17-18.
    Sales.
      Books showing.
        Keeping for three years,
          §40-17-7.
      Sales without liability for
        tax on part of
        distributor or storer,
        §40-17-11.

MOTOR FUELS—Cont'd
  Diesel fuel tax—Cont'd
    Same pump sale of diesel
      fuel for highway and off-
      highway purposes.
      Records.
        Separate maintenance
          required, §40-17-21.
    Statement.
      Forms, §40-17-8.
      Monthly statement,
        §40-17-5.
      Sworn, §40-17-6.
    Violations of article.
      Restraint of violators,
        §40-17-20.
  Distributors of motor fuels,
    §§40-12-190 to 40-12-206.
    Appeals.
      Decisions of department of
        revenue.
        Appeals to courts,
          §40-12-203.
    Applicability of article.
      Interstate and foreign
        commerce, §40-12-205.
    Definitions.
      Licenses, §40-12-190.
    Delivery of gasoline.
      Illegal delivery.
        Forfeiture of vehicles
          and boats,
          §40-12-201.
      Tank trucks.
        Delivery from tank truck
          to motor vehicle
          tank prohibited,
          §40-12-200.
    Department of revenue.
      Appeals to courts from
        decisions, §40-12-203.
    Enforcement of article.
      Rewards, §40-12-202.
    Foreign commerce.
      Applicability of article,
        §40-12-205.
    Information.
      Exchange with other
        states, §40-12-206.
    Injunctions.
      Restraining and enjoining
        violations of article,
        §40-12-204.
    Interstate commerce.
      Applicability of article,
        §40-12-205.
    Licenses, §§40-12-190 to
      40-12-197.
      Application, §40-12-191.
        Filing fee, §40-12-193.
      Bonds, surety.
        Required, §40-12-194.
      Definitions, §40-12-190.
      Discontinuance of business.
        Reports and payments,
          §40-12-197.
      Engaging in business
        without license,
        §40-12-196.
      Fees.
        Filing fee, §40-12-193.
        Issuance, §40-12-195.
        Not granted to certain
          persons, §40-12-192.
        Required, §40-12-191.
        Revocation, §40-12-195.
      Transfer.
        Nontransferability,
          §40-12-195.
        Reports and payments,
          §40-12-197.

MOTOR FUELS—Cont'd
Distributors of motor fuels
—Cont'd
Transportation of gasoline.
Highways.
Public highways,
§40-12-198.
Illegal transportation.
Forfeiture of vehicles
and boats,
§40-12-201.
Waters of the state.
Transportation by boats
over navigable
waters of the state,
§40-12-199.
Violations of article.
Fines.
Disposition of proceeds,
§40-12-202.
Restraining and enjoining,
§40-12-204.
Excise taxes.
Additional excise tax on
gasoline, motor fuel and
lubricating oil,
§§40-17-220 to 40-17-225.
See TAXATION.
Executions.
Diesel fuel tax.
Delinquents, §40-17-15.
Fees.
Distributors of motor fuels.
Filing fee for license
application,
§40-12-193.
Highway department.
Purchases, §23-1-51.
Injunctions.
Distributors of motor fuels.
Restraining and enjoining
violations of article,
§40-12-204.
Marketing.
Violation of chapter,
§8-22-17.
Interstate commerce.
Distributors of motor fuels.
Applicability of article,
§40-12-205.
Licenses.
Diesel fuel tax, §§40-17-12,
40-17-14.
Distributors of motor fuels,
§§40-12-190 to 40-12-197.
See within this heading,
"Distributors of motor
fuels."
Liens.
Diesel fuel tax, §40-17-15.
Limitation of actions.
Taxation, §§40-17-41,
40-17-42.
Marketing, §§8-22-1 to
8-22-18.
Applicability of chapter,
§8-22-12.
Below cost combined selling
price of motor fuel and
promotional gifts,
§8-22-10.
Below cost fuel sales.
Certain sales prohibited,
§8-22-6.
Below cost fuel transfers.
Certain transfers
prohibited, §8-22-7.
Citation of chapter, §8-22-1.
Competitive sales, §8-22-13.

MOTOR FUELS—Cont'd
Marketing—Cont'd
Contracts.
Violation of chapter.
Void and unenforceable,
§8-22-14.
Cost to wholesaler and
retailer.
Determination, §8-22-15.
Damages.
Violation of chapter,
§8-22-17.
Declaration of legislature,
§8-22-3.
Definitions, §8-22-4.
Differentials between sales
and transfer price,
§8-22-8.
Disclosure of oil transfer
price, §8-22-5.
Exemptions from chapter,
§8-22-12.
Injunctions.
Violation of chapter,
§8-22-17.
Intent of legislature, §8-22-3.
Legislative declaration and
intent, §8-22-3.
Legislative findings, §8-22-2.
Oil transfer price.
Disclosure, §8-22-5.
Penalties.
Violation of chapter,
§8-22-16.
Prima facie showing of
violation of chapter,
§8-22-18.
Purpose of chapter, §8-22-3.
Sales and transfer price
differentials, §8-22-8.
Sales between wholesalers,
§8-22-11.
Short title of act, §8-22-1.
Unlawful acts generally,
§8-22-9.
Violation of chapter,
§§8-22-16 to 8-22-18.
Motor carrier fuel tax,
§§40-17-140 to 40-17-155.
See MOTOR VEHICLE
CARRIERS.
Notice.
Diesel fuel tax.
Delinquents.
Notice to show cause,
§40-17-15.
**Petroleum products
generally.**
See OIL AND GAS.
Pumps.
Diesel fuel for highway and
off-highway purposes.
Same pump sales.
Separate maintenance of
records required,
§40-17-21.
Records.
Same pump sale of diesel
fuel for highway and off-
highway purposes.
Separate maintenance of
records, §40-17-21.
Reports.
Diesel fuel tax, §§40-17-8,
40-17-9.
Taxation generally,
§§40-17-200 to 40-17-203.
Rules and regulations.
Diesel fuel tax, §40-17-18.

MOTOR FUELS—Cont'd
Sales tax.
Diesel fuel tax, §§40-17-7,
40-17-11.
Diesel fuel used for off-
highway agricultural
purposes.
Exemption of gross
proceeds from sale,
§40-23-4.
Taxation.
Additional excise tax on
gasoline, motor fuel and
lubricating oil,
§§40-17-220 to 40-17-225.
See TAXATION.
Diesel fuel tax, §§40-17-1 to
40-17-21. See within this
heading, "Diesel fuel
tax."
Expenditure of taxes, Const.
Ala., amd. 93.
Gasoline tax, §§40-17-30 to
40-17-133.
See GASOLINE.
Limitation of actions,
§§40-17-41, 40-17-42.
Motor carrier fuel tax,
§§40-17-140 to 40-17-155.
See MOTOR VEHICLE
CARRIERS.
Reports, §§40-17-200 to
40-17-203.
Carriers.
Information not public,
§40-17-202.
Penalty for failure to
comply, §40-17-203.
When report to be made
by carriers,
§40-17-200.
Warehouses.
Information not public,
§40-17-202.
Penalty for failure to
comply, §40-17-203.
When reports to be made
by warehousemen
and transfer
companies,
§40-17-201.
Sales tax.
Exemption, §40-23-4.
Diesel fuel used for off-
highway agricultural
purposes, §40-23-4.
Use tax.
Diesel fuel used for off-
highway agricultural
purposes.
Exemption, §40-23-62.
Use tax.
Diesel fuel used for off-
highway agricultural
purposes.
Exemptions, §40-23-62.
Exemptions, §40-23-62.

**MOTOR SPORTS HALL OF
FAME COMMISSION,**
§§41-9-470 to 41-9-478.
Accounts and accounting.
Books of account, §41-9-477.
Appointment of members,
§41-9-471.
Audits, §41-9-477.
Bond issues, §§41-9-473 to
41-9-476.
Counties.
Bonds not obligation of
counties, §41-9-475.

MOTOR SPORTS HALL OF FAME COMMISSION —Cont'd

Bond issues—Cont'd
Execution, §41-9-473.
Exemptions from taxation, §41-9-474.
Form, §41-9-473.
Maturity, §41-9-473.
Municipal corporations.
Bonds not obligation of municipalities, §41-9-475.
Payment.
Pledge of revenues for payment, §41-9-476.
Sale, §41-9-473.
State.
Bonds not obligation of state, §41-9-475.
Books, §41-9-477.
Chairman, §41-9-471.
Compensation of members, §41-9-471.
Composition, §41-9-471.
Construction of article.
Liberal construction, §41-9-478.
Counties.
Bonds not obligation of counties, §41-9-475.
Created, §41-9-470.
Duties, §41-9-472.
Executive committee, §41-9-471.
Exemptions from taxation, §41-9-474.
Exhibition facility.
Location, §41-9-470.
Meetings, §41-9-471.
Municipal corporations.
Bonds not obligation of municipalities, §41-9-475.
Powers, §41-9-472.
Additional powers, §41-9-478.
Purpose, §41-9-470.
Qualifications of members, §41-9-471.
Quorum, §41-9-471.
Records, §41-9-477.
Removal of members, §41-9-471.
Rules and regulations.
Adoption, §41-9-471.
State.
Bonds not obligation of state, §41-9-475.
Taxation.
Exemptions from taxation, §41-9-474.
Terms of members, §41-9-471.
Vacancies, §41-9-471.

MOTOR VEHICLE CARRIERS, §§37-3-1 to 37-3-34.

Accounts and accounting.
Public service commission.
Authority of commission as to, §§37-3-7, 37-3-22.
Actions.
Mileage tax.
Tax constitutes debt collectable by civil action, §40-19-3.
Other rights of action not extinguished, §37-3-19.

MOTOR VEHICLE CARRIERS—Cont'd

Administration of chapter.
Employment of personnel to aid public service commission, §37-3-27.
Public service commission to administer, §37-3-7.
Agriculture.
Vehicles hauling agricultural commodities.
Exemptions from chapter, §37-3-4.
Ambulances.
Exemptions from chapter, §37-3-4.
Appeals.
Final action or order of commission, §37-3-29.
Mileage tax.
Appeals by tax payers of assessments, §40-19-9.
Applicability of chapter.
Exemptions, §37-3-4.
Interstate commerce, §37-3-3.
Appropriations, §37-3-31.
Baggage.
Certificates of public convenience and necessity.
Transportation of newspapers, baggage or mail, §37-3-12.
Public service commission.
Regulations as to, §37-3-7.
Bills of lading.
Commercial code.
See COMMERCIAL CODE.
Contents, §37-3-23.
Documents of title, §§7-7-101 to 7-7-603.
See COMMERCIAL CODE.
Forms.
Commission to prescribe, §37-3-23.
Issuance to shipper, §37-3-23.
Liability, §37-3-23.
Bonds, surety.
Brokers.
Bond required for issuance of license, §37-3-15.
Certificates of public convenience and necessity.
Bond required, §37-3-18.
Contract carrier permit.
Bond required, §37-3-18.
Fuel tax.
Motor carriers to give bond, §40-17-143.
Mileage tax.
Bond or other security for collection of tax, §40-19-16.
Brokers.
Bonds, surety.
Required for license, §37-3-15.
Defined, §37-3-2.
Licenses.
Bond required, §37-3-15.
Effective date, §37-3-16.
Issuance, §37-3-15.
Qualifications of brokers, §37-3-15.
Required, §37-3-15.
Suspension, change or revocation, §37-3-16.

MOTOR VEHICLE CARRIERS—Cont'd

Brokers—Cont'd
Public service commission.
Pecuniary interest in brokers by commission members, §37-3-8.
Regulation of brokers by commission, §37-3-7.
Qualifications of brokers.
Licenses, §37-3-15.
Records.
Authority of public service commission, §37-3-15.
Regulation of brokers, §37-3-15.
Certificates of public convenience and necessity.
Abandonment or discontinuance of service, §37-3-12.
Amendment of certificate.
Fee, §37-3-32.
Application, §37-3-10.
Baggage.
Transportation of newspapers, baggage or mail, §37-3-12.
Bonds, surety.
Required, §37-3-18.
Charter parties, §37-3-12.
Defined, §37-3-2.
Determination by commission, §37-3-10.
Deviations, §37-3-12.
Dual operations.
Holding certificate and permit as contract carrier at same time, §37-3-14.
Effective date, §37-3-16.
Factors considered before granting, §37-3-11.
Fee, §37-3-32.
Highways.
Rights in highway use not conferred, §37-3-11.
Issuance.
Factors considered before granting, §37-3-11.
When issued, §37-3-11.
Mail.
Transportation of newspapers, baggage or mail, §37-3-12.
Mileage tax.
Suspension or revocation upon delinquency, §40-19-12.
Newspapers.
Transportation of newspapers, baggage or mail, §37-3-12.
Prior operations.
Continuance, §37-3-10.
Public service commission.
Determination by commission, §37-3-10.
Rights in highway use not conferred, §37-3-11.
Routes.
Certificate to specify routes, §37-3-12.
Scope of authority granted, §37-3-12.
Service.
Certificate to specify service rendered, §§37-3-11, 37-3-12.

MOTOR VEHICLE
   CARRIERS—Cont'd
Certificates of public
   convenience and
   necessity—Cont'd
Suspension, change or
   revocation, §§37-3-16,
   40-19-12.
Transfer, §37-3-17.
When required, §37-3-10.
Charities.
Discounts.
   Exemptions for charities,
     §37-8-28.
Free passage.
   Exemptions for charities,
     §37-8-28.
Rebates.
   Exemptions for charities,
     §37-8-28.
Charters.
Certificates of public
   convenience and
   necessity, §37-3-12.
Intrastate charter rights.
   Grant to certain common
     carriers, §37-3-12.1.
Circuit courts.
Appeals from final action or
   orders of commission to
   circuit court, §37-3-29.
Citation, §37-3-1.
Claims.
Soliciting claims from
   shippers or consignees
   against carriers,
   §37-8-280.
Coal.
Vehicles hauling coal.
   Exemptions from chapter,
     §37-3-4.
Commissioner of revenue.
Fuel tax.
   Authority to adopt rules
   and regulations,
   §40-17-152.
Compacts.
Mileage tax.
   Reciprocal agreements
   with other states,
   §40-19-11.
Complaints.
Public service commission.
   Rates and charges,
   §37-3-19.
Conflicts of interest.
Commission members not to
   have pecuniary interest,
   etc., in carriers or
   brokers, §37-3-8.
Continuance of prior
   operations.
Certificates of convenience
   and necessity, §37-3-10.
Contract carriers.
Charges.
   Generally, §37-3-21.
Defined, §37-3-2.
Permits.
   Applications, §37-3-13.
   Bonds, surety.
     Required, §37-3-18.
   Business covered under
     permit.
     Commission to specify,
      §37-3-13.
   Dual operations, §37-3-14.
   Effective date, §37-3-16.
   Fees, §37-3-32.
   Generally, §37-3-13.
   Issuance, §37-3-13.

MOTOR VEHICLE
   CARRIERS—Cont'd
Contract carriers—Cont'd
Permits—Cont'd
   Notice of application,
     §37-3-13.
   Required, §37-3-13.
   Suspension, change or
     revocation, §§37-3-16,
     40-19-12.
   Transfer, §37-3-17.
Public service commission.
   Regulation of contract
   carriers, §37-3-7.
Rules and regulations,
   §37-3-21.
Schedules.
   Filing with commission,
     §37-3-21.
   Publication, §37-3-21.
   Public inspection, §37-3-21.
Contracts.
True copies of contracts.
   Commission may require
   carriers to file,
   §37-3-22.
Cooperative associations.
Vehicles controlled and
   operated by cooperative
   associations.
   Exemptions from chapter,
     §37-3-4.
Cotton.
Vehicles hauling cotton.
   Exemptions from chapter,
     §37-3-4.
Counties.
Vehicles owned and operated
   by counties.
   Exemptions from chapter,
     §37-3-4.
Debts.
Mileage tax.
   Tax constitutes debt
   collectable by civil
   action, §40-19-3.
Definitions, §§37-3-2, 40-19-1.
Fuel tax, §40-17-140.
Delivery.
Property delivered to
   consignee other than
   shipper or consignor.
   Liability of carrier,
   §37-3-26.
Discounts.
Exemptions, §37-8-28.
Penalties for violations,
   §37-8-27.
Discrimination.
Charging or collecting higher
   than lawful rate,
   §37-8-23.
Violation of statutes relating
   to unjust
   discriminations,
   §37-8-20.
Dual operations.
Holding certificates and
   permits at same time,
   §37-3-14.
Effective date of certificates,
   permits or licenses,
   §37-3-16.
Employees.
Discounts.
   Exemptions for employees,
     §37-8-28.
Free passage.
   Exemptions for employees,
     §37-8-28.
Rebates, §37-8-28.

MOTOR VEHICLE
   CARRIERS—Cont'd
Employees—Cont'd
Wages.
   Biweekly payment,
     §37-8-270.
Enforcement of chapter.
Employment of personnel to
   aid public service
   commission, §37-3-27.
Public service commission to
   enforce, §37-3-7.
Equipment.
Duty of common carrier to
   provide, §37-3-19.
Examiners.
Books and papers.
   Power to compel
     production, §37-3-28.
Certifying official acts.
   Power to certify, §37-3-28.
Designation, §37-3-28.
Jurisdiction, §37-3-9.
Oaths.
   Power to administer,
     §37-3-28.
Orders, §37-3-9.
Reference of matters to
   examiners by
   commission, §37-3-9.
Subpoenas.
   Power to issue, §37-3-28.
Witnesses.
   Power to compel
     attendance, §37-3-28.
Executions.
Mileage tax.
   Execution against property
     of delinquent taxpayer,
     §40-19-10.
Exemptions, §37-3-4.
Expenses.
Appropriations to meet
   expenses, §37-3-31.
Public service commission.
   Appropriations to meet
     expenses, §37-3-31.
Explosives.
Transportation of explosives,
   §§37-8-180 to 37-8-184.
Facilities.
Duty of common carrier to
   provide, §37-3-19.
Fares.
Transportation of passengers,
   §§37-3-19, 37-3-20.
Fees.
Certificates of public
   convenience and
   necessity, §37-3-32.
Contract carrier permits,
   §37-3-32.
Municipal privilege license
   fee, §37-3-33.
Payment to commission,
   §37-3-32.
Registration fees, §37-3-32.
Fertilizer.
Vehicles hauling fertilizer.
   Exemptions from chapter,
     §37-3-4.
Fraud.
Mileage tax.
   Making false or erroneous
     statements, reports or
     representations,
     §40-19-14.
Free passage, §37-3-20.
Exemptions, §37-8-28.
Penalties for violations,
   §37-8-27.

MOTOR VEHICLE
 CARRIERS—Cont'd
Free passage—Cont'd
 Public service commission.
  Exemptions for commission
   members, §§37-3-20,
   37-8-28.
Freight.
 Claims.
  Soliciting claims from
   shippers or consignees
   against carriers,
   §37-8-280.
Fuel tax, §§40-17-140 to
  40-17-155.
 Amount, §40-17-141.
 Appropriations.
  Administration and
   enforcement costs,
   §40-17-146.
 Bonds, surety.
  Motor carriers to give,
   §40-17-143.
 Books and records,
   §40-17-149.
 Commissioner of revenue.
  Rules and regulations.
   Authority to adopt,
    §40-17-152.
 Cumulative effect of article,
   §40-17-154.
 Definitions, §40-17-140.
 Exemptions, §40-17-153.
 Expenditure, Const. Ala.,
   amd. 93.
 False statements.
  Penalty, §40-17-144.
 Gasoline tax.
  Credit of payment,
   §40-17-142.
 Identification markers for
   motor vehicles,
   §40-17-150.
 Levy, §40-17-141.
 Motor fuel tax.
  Credit of payment,
   §40-17-142.
 Motor fuel used in state.
  How amount ascertained,
   §40-17-147.
 Payment, §40-17-145.
 Penalties, §40-17-155.
  False statements,
   §40-17-144.
 Proceeds.
  Disposition, §40-17-146.
 Reports of motor carrier,
   §40-17-148.
  Information not public,
   §40-17-202.
  Penalty for failure to
   comply, §40-17-203.
  When report to be made by
   carriers, §40-17-200.
 Reports of warehouses.
  Information not public,
   §40-17-202.
  Penalty for failure to
   comply, §40-17-203.
  When reports to be made
   by warehousemen and
   transfer companies,
   §40-17-201.
 Rules and regulations.
  Authority of commissioner
   to adopt, §40-17-152.
 Sales without liability for tax
   on part of distributor,
   §40-17-151.

MOTOR VEHICLE
 CARRIERS—Cont'd
Garnishment.
 Mileage tax.
  Execution against property
   of delinquent taxpayer,
   §40-19-10.
Hearings.
 Examiners generally. See
  within this heading,
  "Examiners."
 Public service commission.
  See within this heading,
  "Public service
  commission."
Highways.
 Certificates of public
  convenience and
  necessity.
  Rights in highway use not
   conferred, §37-3-11.
 Defined, §37-3-2.
 Proprietary or property
  rights in use of highways
  not conferred by chapter,
  §37-3-6.
Hotels, inns and other
 transient lodging places.
 Exemptions from chapter,
  §37-3-4.
Interest.
 Mileage tax.
  Failure to pay tax on time,
   §40-19-7.
Interstate commerce.
 Applicability of chapter to
  interstate commerce,
  §37-3-3.
Jurisdiction.
 Examiners, §37-3-9.
Licenses, §40-12-246.
 Brokers, §§37-3-15, 37-3-16.
 Effective date, §37-3-16.
 Local authorities.
  Power to charge license,
   §32-5-1.
 Municipal privilege license
  tax, §37-3-33.
 Suspension, change or
  revocation, §37-3-16.
Liens.
 Mileage tax.
  Tax to be lien on property
   of persons subject to
   chapter, §40-19-10.
Livestock.
 Vehicles hauling livestock.
  Exemptions from chapter,
   §37-3-4.
Local authorities.
 Licenses or taxes.
  Power to charge, §32-5-1.
Lumber.
 Vehicles hauling lumber.
  Exemptions from chapter,
   §37-3-4.
Mail.
 Certificates of public
  convenience and
  necessity.
 Transportation of
  newspapers, baggage
  or mail, §37-3-12.
 Vehicles used exclusively in
  transportation of United
  States mail.
  Exemptions from chapter,
   §37-3-4.

MOTOR VEHICLE
 CARRIERS—Cont'd
Mileage tax, §§40-19-1 to
  40-19-17.
 Actions.
  Tax constitutes debt
   collectable by civil
   action, §40-19-3.
 Assessment, §40-19-9.
 Axle.
  Defined, §40-19-1.
 Bonds, surety.
  Security for collection of
   tax, §40-19-16.
 Certificates of public
  convenience and
  necessity.
  Suspension or revocation
   upon delinquency,
   §40-19-12.
 Collection.
  Bond or other security for
   collection of tax,
   §40-19-16.
  Department of revenue and
   power to collect,
   §40-19-13.
  Employment of personnel
   for collection,
   §40-19-15.
  Tax constitutes debt
   collectable by civil
   action, §40-19-3.
 Compacts.
  Reciprocal agreements
   with other states,
   §40-19-11.
 Deficiencies, §40-19-8.
 Definitions, §40-19-1.
 Delinquency.
  Executions against
   property of delinquent
   taxpayer, §40-19-10.
 Department of revenue.
  Appearance before,
   §40-19-9.
  Employment of personnel
   for collection of tax,
   §40-19-15.
  Rules and regulations,
   §40-19-13.
 Employment of personnel for
   collection of tax,
   §40-19-15.
 Executions.
  Failure to pay tax.
   Executions against
    property of
    delinquent taxpayer,
    §40-19-10.
 Expenditure, Const. Ala.,
   amd. 93.
 Fraud.
  Making false or erroneous
   statements, reports or
   representations,
   §40-19-14.
 Funds.
  Motor carrier fund,
   §40-19-17.
 Imposition of tax, §40-19-3.
 Interest.
  Failure to pay tax on time,
   §40-19-7.
 Liens.
  Tax to be lien on property
   of persons subject to
   tax, §40-19-10.

MOTOR VEHICLE
CARRIERS—Cont'd
Mileage tax—Cont'd
Mileage traveled in this
state.
Statement to be filed with
department of revenue,
§40-19-13.
Motor carrier fund.
Use of fund, §40-19-17.
Notice.
Appearance before
department of revenue,
§40-19-9.
Assessments, §40-19-9.
Returns.
Written notice of failure
to make returns,
§40-19-6.
Other states.
Reciprocal agreements
with other states,
§40-19-11.
Payments.
Correct payments,
§40-19-8.
Delinquency, §40-19-12.
Failure to pay tax on time.
Penalty for failure,
§40-19-7.
Installment payments,
§40-19-4.
Refunds or deficiencies,
§40-19-8.
Suspension or revocation of
certificate or permit
upon delinquency,
§40-19-12.
When tax is payable,
§40-19-4.
Penalties.
Payment.
Failure to pay tax on
time, §40-19-7.
Returns.
Failure to make returns,
§40-19-6.
Violations, §40-19-14.
Permits.
Suspension or revocation
upon delinquency,
§40-19-12.
Personal property.
Execution against property
of delinquent taxpayer,
§40-19-10.
Purpose of tax, §40-19-2.
Real property.
Execution against property
of delinquent taxpayer,
§40-19-10.
Reciprocal agreements with
other states, §40-19-11.
Records.
Duty of motor carriers to
keep records, §40-19-5.
Failure to keep records,
§40-19-5.
Refunds, §40-19-8.
Regular passenger carrying
seats.
Defined, §40-19-1.
Reports.
Failure to make report,
§40-19-5.
Making false or erroneous
reports, §40-19-14.
Monthly reports.
Information required,
§40-19-4.

MOTOR VEHICLE
CARRIERS—Cont'd
Mileage tax—Cont'd
Returns.
Contents, §40-19-4.
Examination of returns,
§40-19-8.
Extension of time for
filing, §40-19-4.
Failure to make returns.
Penalty, §40-19-6.
Notice.
Written notice of failure
to make returns,
§40-19-6.
Rules and regulations.
Department of revenue to
prescribe, §40-19-13.
Seating capacity.
Defined, §40-19-1.
Sheriffs.
Execution against property
of delinquent taxpayer.
Duties of sheriff
generally, §40-19-10.
Statements of taxpayer.
Mileage traveled in this
state.
Making false or
erroneous
statements,
§40-19-14.
Statement to be filed,
§40-19-13.
To whom paid, §40-19-2.
Violations.
Penalty, §40-19-14.
Milk and milk products.
Vehicles hauling milk.
Exemptions from chapter,
§37-3-4.
Motor carrier fuel tax,
§§40-17-140 to 40-17-155.
See within this heading,
"Fuel tax."
Motor carrier fund.
Mileage tax.
Taxes collected to be paid
into fund, §40-19-17.
Motor vehicles.
General provisions, §§32-1-1
to 32-18-8.
See MOTOR VEHICLES.
Local authorities.
Traffic regulations.
Power to tax, §32-5-1.
Municipal corporations.
Taxation.
Municipal privilege license
tax, §37-3-33.
Vehicles owned and operated
by municipalities.
Exemptions from chapter,
§37-3-4.
Newspapers.
Certificates of public
convenience and
necessity.
Transportation of
newspapers, baggage
or mail, §37-3-12.
Oaths.
Examiners.
Power to administer oaths,
§37-3-28.
Reports.
Annual, periodical or
special reports.
Under oath, §37-3-22.

MOTOR VEHICLE
CARRIERS—Cont'd
Officers.
Free transportation,
§37-3-20.
Rebates, §37-3-25.
Operation.
Accordance with provisions of
chapter, §37-3-5.
Passengers.
Transportation of passengers.
See within this heading,
"Transportation of
passengers."
Peanuts.
Vehicles hauling peanuts.
Exemptions from chapter,
§37-3-4.
Penalties.
Free passes, rebates or
discounts, §37-8-27.
Fuel tax, §§40-17-144,
40-17-155.
Mileage tax. See within this
heading, "Mileage tax."
Violations, §37-3-25.
Permits.
Contract carrier permits. See
within this heading,
"Contract carriers."
Prior operations.
Continuance.
Certificates of public
convenience and
necessity, §37-3-10.
Property.
Highways.
Proprietary or property
rights in use of
highways not conferred
by chapter, §37-3-6.
Public service commission.
Abandonment or
discontinuance of service.
Order of commission
required, §37-3-12.
Accounts and accounting.
Authority of commission as
to, §§37-3-7, 37-3-22.
Administration and
enforcement of chapter,
§37-3-7.
Appeals.
Final action or order of
commission, §37-3-29.
Baggage.
Regulations as to, §37-3-7.
Brokers.
Pecuniary interest in
brokers by commission
members, §37-3-8.
Regulation of brokers by
commission, §37-3-7.
Carriers subject to regulation
of commission, §37-3-5.
Certificates of public
convenience and
necessity. See within this
heading, "Certificates of
public convenience and
necessity."
Compensation of members,
§37-3-30.
Complaints.
Rates and charges,
§37-3-19.
Conflicts of interest.
Commission members not
to have pecuniary
interest in carriers or
brokers, §37-3-8.

**MOTOR VEHICLE
CARRIERS**—Cont'd
Public service commission
—Cont'd
Contract carriers.
Permits generally. See
within this heading,
"Contract carriers."
Regulation by commission,
§37-3-7.
Definition of "commission,"
§37-3-2.
Divulging facts or
information during
course of examination of
accounts or records,
§37-3-25.
Duties.
Generally, §37-3-7. See
Enforcement of chapter,
§37-3-7.
Employment of personnel
to aid public service
commission, §37-3-27.
Equipment.
Duties of commission as to
equipment of common
carriers, §37-3-7.
Examiners, §§37-3-9, 37-3-28.
Expenses.
Appropriations to meet
expenses, §37-3-31.
Facilities.
Duties of commission as to
facilities of common
carriers, §37-3-7.
Fees.
Payment to commission,
§37-3-32.
Free transportation,
§§37-3-20, 37-8-28.
General provisions.
See PUBLIC SERVICE
COMMISSION.
Hearings.
Disposition of matters
requiring hearing,
§37-3-9.
Examiners generally. See
within this heading,
"Examiners."
Generally, §37-3-7.
New rates and charges,
§37-3-19.
Rehearing, §37-3-7.
Where held, §37-3-9.
Orders.
Appeals from orders of
commission, §37-3-29.
Effective date, §37-3-24.
Exceptions to orders,
§37-3-9.
Generally, §37-3-7.
Service upon parties in
interest, §37-3-9.
Written orders, §37-3-9.
Pecuniary interest of
commission members in
carriers or brokers,
§37-3-8.
Powers.
Generally, §37-3-7.
Rates and charges.
Complaints regarding,
§37-3-19.
Records.
Duties of commission as to
records, §37-3-7.
Reports.
Commission authorized to
require, §37-3-22.

**MOTOR VEHICLE
CARRIERS**—Cont'd
Public service commission
—Cont'd
Rules and regulations.
Commission to prescribe,
§37-3-7.
Power and authority to
make general rules
and regulations,
§37-3-34.
Substantial compliance by
commission, §37-3-34.
Securities of carriers.
Commission members not
to own, §37-3-8.
Service.
Regulation of carriers as to
adequate service,
§37-3-7.
Transfer of certificates or
permits, §37-3-17.
Transportation of passengers.
Duties of commission as to,
§37-3-7.
Public utilities generally.
See PUBLIC UTILITIES.
Rates and charges.
Changes in rates and
charges, §37-3-20.
Collection, §37-3-26.
Collecting higher than
lawful rate, §37-8-23.
Collecting lower than
lawful rate, §37-8-22.
Complaints regarding rates
and charges, §37-3-19.
Contract carriers. See within
this heading, "Contract
carriers."
Delivery of property
transported to consignee
other than shipper or
consignor.
Liability of carrier,
§37-3-26.
Demanding or receiving
greater or lesser
compensation than
enumerated in tariffs,
§37-3-20.
Filing, §37-3-20.
Generally, §37-3-19.
Joint rates.
Duty of common carriers to
establish, §37-3-19.
New rates and charges.
Hearings on lawfulness,
§37-3-19.
Public service commission,
Complaints regarding,
§37-3-19.
Tariffs. See within this
heading, "Tariffs of
common carriers."
Violation of statutes relating
to reasonable rates,
§37-8-20.
Rebates.
Exemptions, §37-8-28.
Penalties for violations,
§37-8-27.
Rebates in violation of
chapter, §37-3-25.
Records.
Brokers.
Authority of public service
commission, §37-3-15.
Mileage tax, §40-19-5.

**MOTOR VEHICLE
CARRIERS**—Cont'd
Records—Cont'd
Public service commission.
Duties of commission as to
records, §37-3-7.
Registration.
Fees, §37-3-32.
Number, §37-3-32.
Remedies.
Other remedies not
extinguished, §37-3-19.
Rented and hired vehicles.
Exemptions from chapter,
§37-3-4.
Reports.
Annual, periodical or special
reports.
Commission authorized to
require, §37-3-22.
Mileage tax, §§40-19-5,
40-19-14.
Motor carrier fuel tax. See
within this heading,
"Fuel tax."
Oaths.
Reports to be under oath,
§37-3-22.
Routes.
Certificates of public
convenience and
necessity.
Certificate to specify,
§37-3-12.
Duty of common carriers to
establish reasonable
routes, §37-3-19.
Rules and regulations.
Fuel tax.
Authority of commissioner
to adopt, §40-17-152.
Mileage tax.
Department of revenue to
prescribe, §40-19-13.
Public service commission.
Commission to prescribe,
§37-3-7.
Power and authority to
make, §37-3-34.
Schedules.
Contract carriers, §37-3-21.
Tariffs of common carriers.
See within this heading,
"Tariffs of common
carriers."
School buses.
Exemption from chapter,
§37-3-4.
Securities.
Public service commission.
Members not to own any
securities of carriers or
brokers, §37-3-8.
Service.
Abandonment or
discontinuance of service,
§37-3-12.
Certificates of public
convenience and
necessity.
Abandonment or
discontinuance of
service, §37-3-12.
Certificate to specify
service to be rendered,
§37-3-12.
Defined, §37-3-2.
Duty of common carrier to
provide, §37-3-19.

MOTOR VEHICLE
  CARRIERS—Cont'd
Service—Cont'd
  Public service commission.
    Regulation of carriers as to
      adequate service,
      §37-3-7.
    Violation of statutes relating
      to adequate service,
      §37-8-20.
Sheriffs.
  Execution against property of
    delinquent taxpayer.
    Duties of sheriff generally,
      §40-19-10.
Short title of chapter,
  §37-3-1.
Solicitation.
  Claims.
    Soliciting claims from
      shippers or consignees
      against carriers,
      §37-8-280.
State.
  Vehicles owned and operated
    by state.
    Exemptions from chapter,
      §37-3-4.
Stations.
  Taxation.
    Municipal privilege license
      tax, §37-3-33.
Subpoenas.
  Examiners.
    Power to issue subpoenas,
      §37-3-28.
Supreme court.
  Appeals, §37-3-29.
Tariffs of common carriers.
  Charging or accepting rate
    lower than published
    tariff, §37-8-22.
  Charging or collecting higher
    than lawful rate,
    §37-8-23.
  Demanding or collecting
    greater or less
    compensation than
    enumerated in tariff,
    §37-3-20.
  Filing with commission,
    §37-3-20.
  Public inspection, §37-3-20.
  Rates and charges. See
    within this heading,
    "Rates and charges."
  Rejection of certain tariffs,
    §37-3-20.
Taxation.
  Fuel tax, §§40-17-140 to
    40-17-155. See within
    this heading, "Fuel tax."
  Local authorities.
    Power to tax, §32-5-1.
  Mileage tax, §§40-19-1 to
    40-19-17. See within this
    heading, "Mileage tax."
  Municipal privilege license
    tax, §37-3-33.
Terminals.
  Taxation.
    Municipal privilege license
      tax, §37-3-33.
Tires, §32-5-210.

MOTOR VEHICLE
  CARRIERS—Cont'd
Transportation of
  passengers.
  Alcoholic beverages.
    Public drinking of
      prohibited liquors and
      beverages on railway
      passenger cars or in
      waiting rooms,
      §37-8-160.
  Charter parties.
    Certificates of public
      convenience and
      necessity, §37-3-12.
  Defined, §37-3-2.
  Duty of common carrier to
    provide service and
    facilities, §37-3-19.
  Fares.
    Free passage, §37-3-20.
    Joint fares.
      Duty of common carriers
        to establish,
        §37-3-19.
  Free passage, §37-3-20.
  Municipal privilege license
    fees or taxes, §37-3-33.
  Public service commission.
    Duties of commission as to,
      §37-3-7.
Trees and timber.
  Vehicles hauling trees or
    timber.
    Exemptions from chapter,
      §37-3-4.
United States.
  Vehicles owned and operated
    by the United States.
    Exemptions from chapter,
      §37-3-4.
Venue.
  Violations committed on
    trains or buses, §37-8-94.
Violations.
  Free passes, rebates or
    discounts.
    Penalties for violations,
      §37-8-27.
  Penalties for violations,
    §37-3-25.
  Venue for violations
    committed on trains or
    buses, §37-8-94.
Wages.
  Biweekly payment of wages,
    §37-8-270.
Witnesses.
  Examiners.
    Power to compel
      attendance, §37-3-28.

MOTOR VEHICLES, §§32-1-1
  to 32-18-8.
Abandoned motor vehicles,
  §§32-13-1 to 32-13-8.
  Appeals.
    Hearing to determine
      whether vehicle
      abandoned, §32-13-4.
  Auctions.
    Authority to sell, §32-13-3.
  Chapter cumulative,
    §32-13-8.
  Defined, §32-13-1.
  Failure to redeliver hired
    vehicle, §32-15-6.
  Garages.
    Disposition of unclaimed
      vehicles left for
      service, §35-12-6.

MOTOR VEHICLES—Cont'd
Abandoned motor vehicles
  —Cont'd
  Garages—Cont'd
    Reports of operator to
      department, §32-8-84.
    Hearing to determine
      whether vehicle
      abandoned, §32-13-4.
    Appeals, §32-13-4.
  Liens.
    Clear bill of sale, §32-13-3.
    Notice of sale, §§32-13-3,
      32-13-4.
    Removal.
      Lien on vehicles
        removed, §32-13-2.
  Municipal corporations.
    Power of municipality not
      restricted, §32-13-8.
  Notice.
    Posted notice, §32-13-1.
    Sale, §§32-13-3, 32-13-4.
  Operators of garages, repair
    shops and parking lots.
    Reports of unclaimed
      vehicles, §32-8-84.
  Police.
    Responsibility, §32-13-2.
  Removal.
    Lien on vehicles removed,
      §32-13-2.
    Notice of removal,
      §32-13-2.
    Property owners, §32-13-2.
    Wrecked or damaged
      vehicles from highway,
      §32-5A-60.
  Sale, §§32-13-3 to 32-13-7.
    Authority to sell, §32-13-3.
    Clear bill of sale.
      Issuance, §32-13-3.
    Hearing to determine
      whether vehicle
      abandoned, §32-13-4.
      Appeals, §32-13-4.
    Notice of sale, §§32-13-3,
      32-13-4.
    Proceeds.
      Deductions from
        proceeds, §32-13-6.
      Disposition, §32-13-7.
    Rejection of bids, §32-13-5.
    Report of sale, §32-13-6.
      Fee of circuit court for
        filing, §12-19-76.
      Filing, §32-13-6.
Accidents, §§32-10-1 to
  32-10-12.
  Aid.
    Duty to render aid,
      §32-10-2.
  Bullet damage.
    Garages to report bullet
      damage, §32-10-10.
  Coroners.
    Reports.
      Immediate report of
        accident, §32-10-5.
      Written report to
        director, §32-10-9.
  Death.
    Accidents involving death,
      §32-10-1.
    Duty to give information
      and render aid in
      accidents resulting in
      death, §32-10-2.
  Guests.
    Liability for death of
      guest, §32-1-2.

MOTOR VEHICLES—Cont'd
Accidents—Cont'd
Death—Cont'd
Reports required following
accident involving
death, §32-7-5.
Duty to give information and
render aid, §32-10-2.
Failure to stop and render
aid.
Revocation of driver's
license.
Grounds for revocation,
§32-5A-195.
Fixtures.
Highway fixtures.
Duty upon striking,
§32-10-4.
Garages.
Bullet damage, §32-10-10.
Reports, §32-10-10.
Glass.
Removing glass, etc.,
remaining from
accident, §32-5A-60.
Good Samaritan act.
Rendering first aid or
emergency care at
scence of accident.
Exemption from liability,
§6-5-332.
High or potentially high
accident locations.
Surveillance of traffic for
detection and
correction, §32-10-12.
Highway fixtures.
Duty upon striking,
§32-10-4.
Hit and run driving,
§§32-10-1 to 32-10-3.
Penalty, §32-10-6.
Information.
Duty to give information,
§32-10-2.
Injuries.
Reports required following
accident involving
personal injury,
§32-7-5.
Leaving scene of accident,
§§32-10-1 to 32-10-3.
Penalty, §32-10-6.
Nonresidents.
Safety-responsibility act.
See within this
heading, "Safety-
responsibility act."
Penalties.
Violations, §32-10-6.
Personal injuries.
Accidents involving
injuries, §32-10-1.
Police.
Written reports of
accidents, §32-10-7.
Reports.
Confidentiality, §32-10-11.
Contents, §32-10-8.
Coroners, §32-10-9.
Director of public safety.
Filing accident reports,
§32-6-14.
Tabulation and analysis
of accident reports,
§32-10-12.
Evidence.
Use of reports as
evidence, §32-10-11.

MOTOR VEHICLES—Cont'd
Accidents—Cont'd
Reports—Cont'd
Failure to make report.
Penalty for violation,
§§32-7-37, 32-10-6.
Forms, §32-10-8.
Garages, §32-10-10.
Highway patrol.
Report to highway
patrol, §32-10-5.
Immediate reports of
accident.
Required, §32-10-5.
Safety-responsibility act.
Reports required
following accidents,
§32-7-5.
Written reports of
accidents, §32-10-7.
Rescue squads, §§32-11-1 to
32-11-4.
See RESCUE SQUADS.
Safety-responsibility act,
§§32-7-1 to 32-7-42. See
within this heading,
"Safety-responsibility
act."
Unattended vehicles.
Duty upon striking,
§32-10-3.
Violations, §32-10-6.
Witnesses.
Police to interview
witnesses, §32-10-7.
Actions.
Safety-responsibility act.
Chapter not to prevent
other process, §32-7-41.
Matters not to be evidence
in civil actions,
§32-7-12.
Used car sales.
Right of action dependent
upon compliance with
provisions of chapter,
§32-16-3.
Ad valorem taxes.
Certificate of title.
Prerequisite to
assessments, §32-8-83.
Advertising.
Signs, signals or markers
bearing commercial
advertising prohibited,
§32-5A-36.
Age.
Drivers' licenses.
Temporary instruction and
learners' permits. See
within this heading,
"Drivers' licenses."
Driver training schools.
Persons under sixteen
years of age operating
motor vehicles,
§32-5-64.
Persons under sixteen years
of age operating motor
vehicles.
Permitting, §32-5-65.
Prohibited, §32-5-64.
Agents.
Uniform certificate of title
and antitheft act.
Designated agents. See
within this heading,
"Uniform certificate of
title and antitheft act."

MOTOR VEHICLES—Cont'd
Agriculture.
Tractors. See within this
heading, "Tractors."
Air pollution.
Emissions, §22-28-12.
Airports.
Trespass and operation of
vehicles on airports,
landing fields, etc.,
§4-2-7.
**Alabama driver license
compact,** §§32-6-30 to
32-6-36. See within this
heading, "Drivers'
licenses."
Alcoholic beverages.
Chemical tests for
intoxication, §§32-5-190
to 32-5-194, 32-5A-194.
See within this heading,
"Driving under the
influence."
Contraband.
See ALCOHOLIC
BEVERAGES.
Drivers' licenses.
Grounds for revocation,
§32-5A-195.
Persons to whom license
not to be issued,
§32-6-7.
Driving under the influence,
§32-5A-194.
Chemical tests for
intoxication,
§§32-5-190 to 32-5-194,
32-5A-194. See within
this heading, "Driving
under the influence."
Dry counties.
Storage, possession, etc., of
beverages in passenger
area of vehicles or in
view of passengers,
§28-4-200.
Pedestrians under influence,
§32-5A-221.
Renting to intoxicated
person, §32-15-2.
Alleys.
Defined, §32-1-1.1.
Stopping before emerging
from alley, §§32-5A-153,
32-5A-218.
Amateur radio operators.
Tags and plates, §§32-6-70 to
32-6-73, 32-6-90 to
32-6-93. See within this
heading, "Tags and
plates."
Ambulances.
Counties, §§11-87-1 to
11-87-5.
Emergency vehicles
generally. See within
this heading,
"Emergency vehicles."
General provisions, §§22-18-1
to 22-18-7.
See AMBULANCES.
Municipal corporations,
§§11-87-1 to 11-87-5.
**Ameraport offshore harbor
and terminal
commission.**
Purchase of vehicles,
§§33-10-22.

MOTOR VEHICLES—Cont'd

Anatomical gifts by holders of drivers' licenses or nondriver identification cards, §§22-19-60, 22-19-61.

Specific gift to be noted on license or card, §22-19-60.

Animals.

Certificate of title.
Animal-drawn vehicles.
Exemption, §32-8-31.
Horse-drawn wagons.
Reflectors or similar warning devices, §32-5-245.

Lamps.
Animal-drawn vehicles, §32-5-240.
Persons riding animals or driving animal-drawn vehicles, §32-5A-5.
Reflective devices on ridden animals, §32-5-249.

Antique vehicles, §§40-12-290 to 40-12-296.

Department of revenue.
List of registrants.
Department to furnish, §40-12-295.
License taxes and registration fees.
Disposition of funds, §40-12-296.
Exemption, §40-12-293.
Registration, §40-12-290.
Funds.
Disposition, §40-12-296.
List of registrants.
Department of revenue to furnish, §40-12-295.
Tags and plates.
Design, §40-12-291.
Renewal, §40-12-291.
Replacement.
Defaced, lost or destroyed tags or plates, §40-12-292.
Rules and regulations as to issuance, §40-12-294.
Taxation.
Ad valorem taxes.
Exemption, §40-12-293.

Antitheft act.

Uniform certificate of title and antitheft act, §§32-8-1 to 32-8-88. See within this heading, "Uniform certificate of title and antitheft act."

Appeals.

Abandoned vehicles.
Hearing to determine whether vehicle abandoned, §32-13-4.
Automotive dismantlers and parts recyclers.
License.
Refusal, cancellation or revocation, §40-12-417.
Cancellation, suspension or revocation of drivers' licenses, §32-5A-195.
Suspension by medical advisory board, §32-6-47.

MOTOR VEHICLES—Cont'd

Appeals—Cont'd

Safety-responsibility act, §32-7-3.
Assigned risk plans, §32-7-35.
Uniform certificate of title and antitheft act.
Actions of department, §§32-8-4, 32-8-5.

Arrest.

Speed.
Measuring devices.
Officer operating.
Violation communicated to other officer, §32-5A-177.

Arrests.

Appearance upon arrest for misdemeanor, §32-1-4.
Bonds, §§32-1-4 to 32-1-6.
Driving under the influence.
Arrest without warrant, §32-5-171.
Highway patrol.
Disposition of arrest fees, §32-2-25.
Misdemeanors.
Procedure upon arrest for misdemeanor, §32-1-4.
Municipal officers.
Disposition of fines and forfeitures, §32-5A-10.
Police.
Duty to make arrests for violations, §32-5-310.
Procedure upon arrest for misdemeanor, §32-1-4.
Procedure upon arrest for violations, §32-5-310.
Trucks, trailers and semi-trailers.
Violations of chapter, §32-9-3.
Without warrant.
Driving under the influence, §32-5-171.
Taking accused before nearest court, §32-5-310.
Trucks, trailers and semi-trailers.
Violations of chapter, §32-9-3.

Arterial streets.

Defined, §32-1-1.1.

Assigned risks.

Safety-responsibility act, §32-7-35.

Assignments.

Uniform certificate of title and antitheft act.
Security interests.
Assignment by lienholder, §32-8-63.

Attachment.

Liens for production, manufacture or repair.
Right to enforce liens by attachment, §35-11-111.

Attorney general.

Safety coordinating committee.
Member of committee, §32-3-1.

Auctions.

Abandoned motor vehicles, §32-13-3.

MOTOR VEHICLES—Cont'd

Automobile clubs and associations, §§27-9-1 to 27-9-8.

See INSURANCE.

Automotive dismantlers and parts recyclers, §§40-12-410 to 40-12-425.

Certificates of title.
Transfer of title, §40-12-420.
Definitions, §40-12-410.
Fees.
Licenses, §40-12-413.
Hearings.
License.
Refusal, cancellation or revocation, §40-12-416.
Injunctions.
Violations of article, §40-12-425.
Licenses, §§40-12-412 to 40-12-418.
Application, §40-12-412.
Fee, §40-12-413.
Financial responsibility.
Proof, §40-12-414.
Other licenses not required, §40-12-418.
Proof of financial responsibility, §40-12-414.
Refusal, cancellation or revocation.
Appeal to circuit court, §40-12-417.
Authority of commissioner of revenue, §40-12-416.
Grounds, §40-12-416.
Hearing, §40-12-417.
Renewal, §40-12-415.
Required, §40-12-411.
Term, §40-12-415.
Penalties.
Violations of article, §40-12-424.
Plates.
License plates to be forwarded to department of revenue, §40-12-423.
Records.
Inspection, §40-12-419.
Maintenance, §40-12-419.
Salvage pool or salvage disposal sale.
Buyers' identification cards.
Revocation, §40-12-421.
Defined, §40-12-410.
Identification cards.
Buyers' identification cards, §40-12-421.
Out-of-state salvage dealers, §40-12-422.
Restrictions on sales, §40-12-421.
Transfer of vehicle certificate of title, §40-12-420.
Violations.
Injunctions, §40-12-425.
Penalties, §40-12-424.

Backing vehicles.

Limitations on backing, §§32-5-72, 32-5A-51.

Bail and recognizance. See within this heading, "Bonds, surety."

MOTOR VEHICLES—Cont'd
Beaches.
Operation of vehicles on
beaches of Gulf of
Mexico.
Prohibited, §32-1-7.
Bicycles.
See BICYCLES.
Bills of lading.
Transportation companies.
See TRANSPORTATION
COMPANIES.
Blind persons.
Guide dogs, §§21-7-6, 21-7-7.
Pedestrians, §32-5A-220.
Right to use of public
conveyances and
transportation facilities,
§21-7-3.
White cane law, §§21-7-6,
21-7-7.
Blood tests.
Chemical tests for
intoxication, §§32-5-190
to 32-5-194, 32-5A-194.
See within this heading,
"Driving under the
influence."
Boards and commissions.
Drivers' licenses.
Medical advisory board,
§§32-6-40 to 32-6-48.
See within this
heading, "Drivers'
licenses."
Bombs.
Throwing fire bombs into
occupied vehicle,
§32-5-11.
Bonds, surety.
Arrests, §§32-1-4 to 32-1-6.
Depositing driver's license
in lieu of bail in
certain cases, §32-1-5.
Procedure, §32-1-5.
Violation of traffic
ordinance of
incorporated
municipality,
§32-1-6.
Giving bond upon arrest
for misdemeanor,
§32-1-4.
Option of depositing
driver's license in
lieu of bail, §§32-1-5,
32-1-6.
Revocation of license
for forfeiture of
bail, §32-5A-195.
Refusal to give bond,
§32-1-4.
Violating written bond to
appear, §32-1-4.
Bail bond, §32-5-310.
Discretionary bail
schedule, ARJA, Rule
2.
Driver's license.
Forfeiture of bail.
Grounds for
revocation,
§32-5A-195.
Discretionary bail schedule,
ARJA, Rule 2.
Drivers' licenses.
Depositing driver's license
in lieu of bail,
§§32-1-5, 32-1-6.

MOTOR VEHICLES—Cont'd
Bonds, surety—Cont'd
Drivers' licenses—Cont'd
Forfeiture of bail.
Grounds for revocation,
§32-5A-195.
Driver training schools.
Bond required, §32-14-21.
Forfeiture of bonds.
Grounds for revocation of
driver's license,
§32-5A-195.
Highway patrol, §§32-2-23,
32-2-24.
Safety-responsibility act.
Security. See within this
heading, "Safety-
responsibility act."
Trucks, trailers and semi-
trailers.
Bond for arrest for
violation of chapter,
§32-9-3.
Uniform certificate of title
and antitheft act.
Certificate of title.
Application for
certificate with bond,
§32-8-36.
Used car sales.
Nonresident dealers,
§32-16-2.
Brakes.
Brake fluid, §§8-17-1 to
8-17-9.
See BRAKE FLUID.
Number of brakes required,
§32-5-212.
Required, §32-5-212.
Unattended vehicles.
Setting brake before
leaving vehicle,
§32-5A-50.
Bricks.
Spilling loads, §32-5-76.
Bridges.
Overtaking and passing.
Limitations on passing,
§32-5A-85.
Pedestrians.
Entry restricted by signals,
gates or barriers,
§32-5A-222.
Size and weight of vehicles.
Rules and regulations.
Promulgation by
highway
department,
§23-1-59.
Speed limitations on bridges,
§§32-5-92, 32-5A-176.
Trucks, trailers and semi-
trailers.
Weight on bridges,
§32-9-20.
Buses.
Church buses, §32-5A-154.
Definitions, §§32-1-1.1,
32-9-21, 40-12-240.
Flares.
Required, §32-5-220.
Jitney bus.
Defined, §40-12-240.
License taxes and
registration fees,
§40-12-246.
License taxes and
registration fees.
Jitney buses, §40-12-245.
Motor buses, §40-12-246.

MOTOR VEHICLES—Cont'd
Buses—Cont'd
Motor bus.
Defined, §32-9-21.
License taxes and
registration fees,
§40-12-246.
School buses.
Defined, §32-1-1.1.
General provisions,
§§16-27-1 to 16-27-7.
See EDUCATION.
Signal lights, §32-5A-155.
Business districts.
Alley or driveway.
Stopping before emerging
from alley or driveway,
§§32-5A-153,
32-5A-218.
Defined, §32-1-1.1.
Pedestrians.
Crossing roadways in
business districts,
§32-5A-210.
Carriages.
Reflectors or similar warning
devices on horse-drawn
wagons, §32-5-245.
Carriers.
Motor vehicle carriers,
§§37-3-1 to 37-3-34.
See MOTOR VEHICLE
CARRIERS.
Certificate of title.
Uniform certificate of title
and antitheft act,
§§32-8-1 to 32-8-88. See
within this heading,
"Uniform certificate of
title and antitheft act."
Certification permits.
Effect of certification permits
issued by state board of
health, §32-5A-194.1.
Chains.
Tire chains, §32-5-210.
Change of ownership.
Recording, §40-12-260.
Fee, §40-12-261.
Rules and regulations for
enforcement, §40-12-272.
**Chemical tests for
intoxication**, §§32-5-190 to
32-5-194, 32-5A-194. See
within this heading,
"Driving under the
influence."
Child passenger restraints.
Contributory negligence.
Failure to wear restraint
system not considered
contributory
negligence, §32-5-222.
Required for children under
six, §32-5-222.
Church buses, §32-5A-154.
Citizens' band radios.
Amateur radio operators.
Tags and plates, §§32-6-70
to 32-6-73, 32-6-90 to
32-6-93. See within
this heading, "Tags
and plates."
Civil air patrol.
License taxes and
registration fees.
Exemption, §40-12-244.
Clerks of court.
Uniform traffic infractions.
Fines and court costs paid
to, ARJA, Rule 19.

MOTOR VEHICLES—Cont'd
Clubs.
Automobile clubs and
associations, §§27-39-1 to
27-39-8.
See INSURANCE.
Coastal areas.
Operation of vehicles on
beaches and sand dunes
of Gulf of Mexico.
Prohibited, §32-1-7.
Coasting prohibited,
§32-5A-57.
Commercial code.
Secured transactions.
Applicability of filing
provisions, §7-9-302.
Commercial driver licenses,
§§32-6-310 to 32-6-331.
Applicability of provisions.
Offenses committed after
certain date,
§32-6-49.20.
Applications, §32-6-49.9.
False information,
§32-6-49.9.
Change of name, address, or
residence.
Application for duplicate
license, §32-6-49.9.
Class D driver's license.
When holder may driver
commercial vehicle,
§32-6-49.8.
Classifications, §32-6-49.10.
Construction and
interpretation.
Cumulative nature of
sanctions and
penalties, §32-6-330.
Liberal construction of
provisions, §32-6-49.2.
Contents, §32-6-49.10.
Convictions.
Applicability of provisions
to certain offenses,
§32-6-49.20.
Defined, §32-6-49.3.
Disqualification from
driving commercial
vehicle, §32-6-49.11.
Information regarding
driving record.
Furnishing by
department,
§32-6-49.15.
Notification required of
driver, §32-6-49.5.
Reports, §32-6-49.14.
Definitions, §32-6-49.3.
Department of public safety.
Agreements.
Authority to enter into,
§32-6-49.17.
Definition of "department,"
§32-6-49.3.
Information regarding
driving record.
Furnishing, §32-6-49.15.
Rules and regulations,
§32-6-49.16.
Disqualification from driving
commercial vehicle,
§32-6-49.11.
Use of alcohol while
driving, §32-6-49.12.

MOTOR VEHICLES—Cont'd
Commercial driver licenses
—Cont'd
Driving under the influence,
§§32-6-320 to 32-6-322.
Disqualification from
driving commercial
vehicle, §32-6-49.11.
Use of alcohol while
driving, §32-6-49.12.
Tests of blood or breath,
§32-6-49.13.
Use of alcohol while
driving, §32-6-49.12.
Duration, §32-6-49.19.
Employer.
Defined, §32-6-49.3.
Notifications by driver to
employer.
Requirements,
§32-6-49.5.
Prohibited acts, §32-6-49.6.
Responsibilities,
§32-6-49.6.
Exceptions to requirement,
§32-6-49.7.
Expiration, §32-6-49.10.
Fees, §32-6-49.19.
Application fee, §32-6-49.9.
Information regarding
driving record.
Furnishing by
department,
§32-6-49.15.
Violations of provisions,
§32-6-49.22.
Information on license,
§32-6-49.10.
Information regarding
driving record.
Furnishing by department,
§32-6-49.15.
Misdemeanors.
Violations of provisions,
§32-6-49.22.
Number of licenses.
Limitation, §32-6-49.4.
One license per driver,
§32-6-49.4.
Other jurisdictions.
Licenses issued by,
§32-6-49.9.
Penalties.
Cumulative nature,
§32-6-330.
Purpose of provisions,
§32-6-49.2.
Qualifications, §32-6-49.8.
Reciprocity, §32-6-49.18.
Renewal, §32-6-49.10.
Reports.
Convictions, §32-6-49.14.
Required, §32-6-49.7.
Exceptions, §32-6-49.7.
Revocation or suspension.
Disqualification from
driving commercial
vehicle.
Generally, §§32-6-49.12,
32-6-320.
False information in
application, §32-6-49.9.
Notification required of
driver, §32-6-49.5.
Records to be updated,
§32-6-49.11.
Rules and regulations,
§32-6-49.16.
Sanctions.
Cumulative nature,
§32-6-330.

MOTOR VEHICLES—Cont'd
Commercial driver licenses
—Cont'd
Short title of act, §32-6-49.1.
Term, §32-6-49.19.
Tests, §32-6-49.8.
Waiver of tests, §32-6-49.8.
Commissioner of revenue.
Reciprocal agreements for
registration on an
apportionment or
allocation basis.
Powers of commissioner,
§32-6-56.
Tags and plates.
Rules and regulations of
commissioner,
§32-6-53.
Compact.
Alabama driver license
compact, §§32-6-30 to
32-6-36. See within this
heading, "Drivers'
licenses."
Condemnation.
Nighttime hunting of deer,
§9-11-252.1.
Consent.
Chemical tests for
intoxication.
Driving under the
influence.
Implied consent,
§32-5-192.
Constitution of Alabama.
Conecuh county.
Taxation.
Annual license taxes and
registration on
trucks, trailers, etc.,
Const. Ala., amd.
435.
Fees or taxes relating to use
of vehicles and to fuels
used for vehicles.
Expenditure, Const. Ala.,
amd. 93.
**Construction and
interpretation.**
Commercial driver licenses.
Cumulative nature of
sanctions and
penalties, §32-6-49.21.
Liberal construction of
provisions, §32-6-49.2.
Safety-responsibility act.
Uniformity of
interpretation,
§32-7-42.
Tags and plates.
Retired military.
Provisions cumulative,
§32-6-295.
Uniform vehicle code.
Rules of the road act.
Uniformity of
interpretation,
§32-5A-11.
Consuls.
License taxes and
registration fees.
Exemption of private
passenger vehicles,
§40-12-243.
Special plates,
§40-12-243.
Contracts.
Drivers' licenses.
Contracts for lease or
purchase of equipment
§32-6-20.

MOTOR VEHICLES—Cont'd
Controlled-access highways.
Defined, §32-1-1.1.
Controlled substances.
Driving under the influence
of narcotic drugs. See
within this heading,
"Driving under the
influence."
Forfeiture of motor vehicle.
Controlled substance
violations, §20-2-93.
Conversion.
Antitheft laws, §§32-8-1 to
32-8-88. See within this
heading, "Uniform
certificate of title and
antitheft act."
Renting and hiring.
Conversion of vehicle
subject to larceny,
§32-15-7.
Coroners.
Accidents.
Reports, §§32-10-5, 32-10-9.
Costs.
Uniform traffic infractions.
Costs paid to clerk of court,
ARJA, Rule 19.
Cotton.
Cotton wagons.
Towing cotton wagons,
§32-9-2.
Loads which must be
fastened by cables or
chains, §32-5-75.
Module-movers used to haul
cotton from field,
§32-9-2.
Counties.
Arrest made by county
officers.
Disposition of fines and
forfeitures, §32-5A-10.
Fees.
Public roads, bridges and
ferries.
Expenditure of funds
derived from fees
levied on vehicles,
§23-1-84.
Highway and traffic safety
coordination act.
Powers of counties, §32-4-7.
Highway patrol.
Fees and costs.
When not to be paid by
county, §32-2-25.
Powers generally, §32-5-1.
Tags.
County vehicles,
§40-12-250.
Courts.
Prohibiting operation of
motor vehicles by
persons convicted of
violations, §32-5-316.
Trucks, trailers and semi-
trailers.
Violations of chapter.
Jurisdiction of courts,
§32-9-4.
Crest of grades.
Turning on crest,
§32-5A-131.
Criminal law and procedure.
Arrests. See within this
heading, "Arrests."

MOTOR VEHICLES—Cont'd
Criminal law and procedure
—Cont'd
Disorderly conduct.
Obstructing vehicular or
pedestrian traffic,
§13A-11-7.
Driving under the influence.
See within this heading,
"Driving under the
influence."
Hindering transportation of
commodities,
§13A-11-221.
Obscuring identity of vehicle,
§13A-8-22.
Traffic offenses.
District courts, §§12-12-50
to 12-12-56.
Violations generally. See
within this heading,
"Violations."
Uniform certificate of title
and antitheft act,
§§32-8-1 to 32-8-88. See
within this heading,
"Uniform certificate of
title and antitheft act."
Crossings.
Grade crossings. See within
this heading,
"Railroads."
Crosswalks. See within this
heading, "Pedestrians."
Curves.
Overtaking and passing.
Limitations on passing,
§32-5A-85.
Speed limitations,
§32-5A-170.
Turning on curves
prohibited, §32-5A-131.
Damages.
Highways.
Liability for damage to
highway, §32-5-9.
Safety-responsibility act.
Matters not to be evidence
in civil actions for
damages, §32-7-12.
Dealers.
Dealings by manufacturers
with dealers, §§8-20-1 to
8-20-12. See within this
heading,
"Manufacturers."
Defined, §32-1-1.1.
Licenses, §40-12-51.
Accessory dealers,
§40-12-53.
Dealers, reconditioners,
rebuilders and
wholesalers,
§§40-12-390 to
40-12-400. See within
this heading,
"Licenses."
Motor vehicle franchise act.
Dealings by manufacturers
with dealers, §§8-20-1
to 8-20-12. See within
this heading,
"Manufacturers."
Tags, §40-12-264.
Uniform certificate of title
and antitheft act,
§§32-8-1 to 32-8-88. See
within this heading,
"Uniform certificate of
title and antitheft act."

MOTOR VEHICLES—Cont'd
Dealers—Cont'd
Used car sales, §§32-16-1 to
32-16-4.
Warranty work on motor
vehicles, §§32-17-1,
32-17-2.
Death.
Accidents involving death.
See within this heading,
"Accidents."
Homicide by vehicle,
§32-5A-192.
Definitions, §32-1-1.1.
Abandoned vehicles,
§32-13-1.
Alabama driver license
compact, §32-6-31.
Automobile clubs and
associations, §27-39-1.
Automotive dismantlers and
parts recyclers,
§40-12-410.
Commercial driver licenses,
§32-6-49.3.
Dealers', reconditioners',
rebuilders' and
wholesalers' licenses,
§40-12-390.
Drivers' licenses.
Alabama driver license
compact, §32-6-31.
Commercial driver
licenses, §32-6-49.3.
Medical advisory board,
§32-6-40.
Driver training schools,
§32-14-2.
Fire fighters, §32-6-270.
Handicapped persons,
§32-6-230.
Insurance.
Cancellation of automobile
liability insurance,
§27-23-20.
License taxes and
registration fees,
§40-12-240.
Manufacturers.
Dealings by manufacturers
with dealers, §8-20-3.
Moving violations, §32-5-313.
Municipal corporations.
Stopping, standing and
parking, §11-61-1.
Municipal testing stations,
§32-18-1.
Nonoriginal equipment
manufacturer
aftermarket crash parts,
§32-17A-1.
Retired military, §32-6-290.
Safety-responsibility act,
§32-7-2.
Sales tax, §40-23-100.
Temporary tags and
certificates, §32-6-210.
Traffic infractions.
Defined, §32-5-313.
Uniform certificate of title
and antitheft act,
§32-8-2.
Used car sales, §32-16-1.
Use tax, §40-23-100.
Department of public safety,
§§32-2-1 to 32-2-44.
Anatomical gifts.
Gifts made by affidavit.
Filing with department,
§22-19-60.

MOTOR VEHICLES—Cont'd
Department of public safety
—Cont'd
Anatomical gifts—Cont'd
Immunity from civil
liability of officers and
employees, §22-19-61.
Assistant director, §32-2-2.
Appointment, §32-2-2.
Duties, §32-2-2.
Salary, §32-2-2.
Commercial driver licenses.
Agreements.
Authority to enter into,
§32-6-49.17.
Definition of "department,"
§32-6-49.3.
Information regarding
driving record.
Furnishing, §32-6-49.15.
Rules and regulations,
§32-6-49.16.
Compensation and expenses
of officers, employees,
etc.
Method of payment
generally, §32-2-6.
Creation, §32-2-1.
Criminal history records
search.
Fee, §32-2-8.1.
Defined, §32-1-1.1.
Director.
Accident reports.
Director to file all
accident reports,
§32-6-14.
Appointment, §32-2-1.
Assistant director, §32-2-2.
Convictions.
Director to file, §32-6-14.
Divisions of department.
Creation by director,
§32-2-3.
Drivers' licenses.
Examinations.
Rules and regulations
for examinations,
§32-6-3.
Reciprocal agreements,
§32-6-10.
Records to be kept by
director, §32-6-14.
Restrictions on licenses.
Imposition by director,
§32-6-12.
Rules and regulations,
§32-6-13.
Enforcement of laws.
What laws director to
enforce, §32-2-5.
Head of department,
§32-2-1.
Lights, lamps and
reflective devices.
Issuance and
enforcement of
regulations,
§32-5-252.
Minimum speed limits,
§32-5A-174.
Powers, §32-2-5.
Records and reports.
Fees for copies.
Collection of fees by
director, §32-2-8.
Rules and regulations.
Promulgation by
director, §32-2-9.

MOTOR VEHICLES—Cont'd
Department of public safety
—Cont'd
Director—Cont'd
Safety coordinating
committee.
Director member of
committee, §32-3-1.
Safety-responsibility act.
General provisions. See
within this heading,
"Safety-
responsibility act."
Speed zones.
Establishment,
§32-5A-172.
Term of office, §32-2-1.
Divisions.
Chiefs, §32-2-4.
Holding positions subject
to merit system,
§32-2-4.
Creations, §32-2-3.
Employees.
Appointment by director,
§32-2-4.
Positions subject to merit
system, §32-2-4.
Enumeration, §32-2-3.
Employees.
Controlling civil
disturbances, §32-2-7.
Insurance for employees,
§32-2-10.
Rescue or protective duties,
§32-2-7.
Expenses.
Controlling civil
disturbances, §32-2-7.
Method of payment
generally, §32-2-6.
Warrants.
Method of payment
generally, §32-2-6.
Head of department.
Director to be head,
§32-2-1.
Identification cards for
nondrivers, §32-6-1.
Insurance.
Employees, §32-2-10.
Officers.
Controlling civil
disturbances, §32-2-7.
Rescue or protective duties,
§32-2-7.
Records.
Copies.
Fees for copies, §32-2-8.
Reports.
Copies.
Fees for copies, §32-2-8.
Rules and regulations.
Promulgation by director,
§32-2-9.
Salaries.
Assistant director, §32-2-2.
Method of payment
generally, §32-2-6.
Derelict vehicles.
Abandoned motor vehicles,
§§32-13-1 to 32-13-8. See
within this heading,
"Abandoned motor
vehicles."
Destruction.
Nuisances menacing public
health.
Summary destruction
without compensation,
§22-10-3.

MOTOR VEHICLES—Cont'd
Director.
Defined, §32-1-1.1.
Disabled vehicles.
Stopping on highways,
§32-5A-136.
Towing or hauling, §32-5-51.
Dismantlers, §§40-12-410 to
40-12-425. See within this
heading, "Automotive
dismantlers and parts
recyclers."
Disorderly conduct.
Obstructing vehicular or
pedestrian traffic,
§13A-11-7.
**Distress flag for
handicapped or
paraplegic drivers,**
§§32-5-12 to 32-5-14.
District courts.
Traffic infractions.
General provisions,
§§12-12-50 to 12-12-56.
See DISTRICT COURTS.
Schedule of fines, ARJA,
Rule 20.
Divided highways.
Driving on, §32-5A-90.
Doors of vehicles.
Opening and closing.
Restricted, §32-5A-54.
Down grades.
Coasting prohibited,
§32-5A-57.
**Driveaway-towaway
operations.**
Defined, §32-1-1.1.
Driver education, §§16-40-5.1
to 16-40-5.4.
Authorized, §16-40-5.1.
Driver training schools,
§§32-14-1 to 32-14-24.
See within this heading,
"Driver training
schools."
Fees.
Boards of education may
establish reasonable
fees, §16-40-5.4.
General provisions,
§§16-40-5.1 to 16-40-5.4.
Notification, §16-40-5.2.
Performance based
instructional program,
§16-40-5.3.
Reassigned teachers.
Salaries, §16-40-5.2.
Rules and regulations,
§16-40-5.4.
Teachers.
Salary of reassigned
teachers, §16-40-5.2.
Drivers.
Defined, §32-1-1.1.
Drivers' licenses, §§32-6-1 to
32-6-48.
Alabama driver license
compact, §§32-6-30 to
32-6-36.
Applicability of other laws,
§32-6-31.
Application for new
licenses, §32-6-31.
Citation, §32-6-30.
Compact administrator,
§32-6-31.
Compensation, §32-6-33.
Expenses, §32-6-33.
Construction and
severability, §32-6-31.

MOTOR VEHICLES—Cont'd
Drivers' licenses—Cont'd
Alabama driver license
    compact—Cont'd
Declaration of policy,
    §32-6-31.
Definitions, §32-6-31.
Director of public safety.
    Duties under compact,
    §32-6-32.
Effect of conviction,
    §32-6-31.
    Application to offenses
        enumerated in,
        §32-5A-195.
Entry into force, §32-6-31.
Executive head.
    Defined, §32-6-34.
Findings, §32-6-31.
Information.
    Interchange of
        information,
        §32-6-31.
Licensing authority,
    §32-6-32.
Reports.
    Convictions, §32-6-31.
    Courts to report
        suspension of
        licenses, §32-6-35.
Revocation and suspension.
    Courts to report,
        §32-6-35.
Short title, §32-6-30.
Terms of compact,
    §32-6-31.
Title, §32-6-30.
Withdraw, §32-6-31.
Anatomical gifts by holders
    of drivers' licenses or
    nondriver identification
    cards, §§22-19-60,
    22-19-61.
Applications.
    Certificate of examination
        results.
        Attachment to
            application, §32-6-3.
    Oath before judge of
        probate, §32-6-4.
    Record of applications.
        Director of public safety
            to keep records,
            §32-6-14.
Arrests.
    Depositing driver's license
        in lieu of bail in
        certain cases.
        Procedure, §32-1-5.
    Violation of traffic
        ordinance of
        incorporated
        municipality,
        §32-1-6.
Cancellation, suspension or
    revocation.
    Alabama driver license
        compact.
        Courts to report
            suspension, etc., of
            licenses to director of
            public safety,
            §32-6-35.
    Appeals, §32-5A-195.
        Suspension by medical
            advisory board,
            §32-6-47.

MOTOR VEHICLES—Cont'd
Drivers' licenses—Cont'd
Cancellation, suspension or
    revocation—Cont'd
    Bail.
        Forfeiture of bail.
            Grounds for
                revocation,
                §32-5A-195.
    Chemical tests for
        intoxication.
        Suspension of license for
            refusal to submit to
            test, §32-5-192.
    Definitions, §32-1-1.1.
    Driving under the
        influence, §32-5A-191.
        Grounds for revocation,
            §32-5A-195.
    Drugs.
        Grounds for revocation,
            §32-5A-195.
    Failure or refusal to take
        examination or test.
        Grounds for suspension
            or revocation,
            §32-6-3.
    Failure to stop and render
        aid.
        Grounds for revocation,
            §32-5A-195.
    Felonies.
        Use of motor vehicle in
            commission of
            felony, §32-5A-195.
    Generally, §32-5A-195.
    Grounds, §32-5A-195.
    Habitually, reckless or
        negligent drivers.
        Grounds for suspension,
            §32-5A-195.
    Hearings.
        Rights to file petitions,
            §32-5A-195.
    Medical advisory board.
        Appeal, §32-6-47.
        No driving while appeal
            pending, §32-6-47.
    Reinstatement.
        Application, §32-6-17.
        Duplicate license,
            §32-6-17.
        Fees, §32-6-17.
    Reports, §32-6-35.
    Safety-responsibility act.
        See within this
            heading, "Safety-
            responsibility act."
    Suspension of license
        without hearing,
        §32-5A-195.
    Temporary instruction and
        learner's licenses,
        §32-6-8.
    Violation by person whose
        license has been
        cancelled, suspended or
        revoked, §32-6-19.
Certificate of title.
    Use of duplicate copy of
        application for
        certificate as permit to
        operate motor vehicle,
        §32-8-38.
Chemical tests for
    intoxication.
    Refusal to submit to tests.
        Suspension of license,
            §32-5-192.

MOTOR VEHICLES—Cont'd
Drivers' licenses—Cont'd
Commercial driver licenses,
    §§32-6-49.1 to 32-6-49.22.
    See within this heading,
        "Commercial driver
        licenses."
Compact, §§32-6-30 to
    32-6-36.
Contents of licenses, §32-6-6.
Definitions.
    Commercial driver
        licenses, §32-6-49.3.
    Medical advisory board,
        §32-6-40.
Destroyed licenses, §32-6-15.
Display, §32-6-9.
Drugs.
    Grounds for revocation,
        §32-5A-195.
    Persons to whom license
        not to be issued,
        §32-6-7.
Duplicate license, §32-6-15.
    Making false affidavit to
        obtain, §32-6-15.
    Reinstatement of cancelled,
        suspended or revoked
        license, §32-6-17.
Duration, §32-6-4.
Enforcement of article,
    §32-6-13.
Equipment to implement
    article.
    Contracts for lease or
        purchase of equipment,
        §32-6-20.
    Standards and
        requirements for
        equipment, §32-6-20.
Examinations.
    Certificate of results,
        §32-6-3.
        Attaching to application,
            §32-6-3.
    Counties.
        Examination in county
            other than county of
            residence, §32-6-3.
    Examination prior to
        application, §32-6-3.
    Failing examination,
        §32-6-3.
    Kind of examination given,
        §32-6-3.
    Method and manner of
        giving examination,
        §32-6-3.
    Refusal to take
        examinations.
        Grounds for suspension
            or revocation of
            license, §32-6-3.
    Renewal of license, §32-6-3.
    Results.
        Certificate of results,
            §32-6-3.
        Reporting results,
            §32-6-3.
    Rules and regulations.
        Director of public safety
            to promulgate,
            §32-6-3.
    Temporary instruction and
        learner's licenses.
        Examination required,
            §32-6-8.
Exemptions.
    Persons exempt from
        securing license,
        §32-6-2.

MOTOR VEHICLES—Cont'd
Drivers' licenses—Cont'd
Expiration date, §32-6-1.
Fees, §32-6-4.
  Disposition of fees
    collected, §32-6-5.
  Duplicate of lost or
    destroyed license,
    §32-6-15.
  Examination conducted in
    county of applicant's
    residence, §32-6-21.
  Photo license or card,
    §32-6-6.
  Reinstatement of cancelled,
    suspended or revoked
    license, §32-6-17.
  Temporary instruction and
    learner's licenses,
    §32-6-8.
Handicapped persons.
  Persons to whom license
    not to be issued,
    §32-6-7.
Hearings.
  Cancellation, suspension or
    revocation.
    Right to file petitions,
      §32-5A-195.
Identification cards.
  Nondriver identification
    cards.
    Department of public
      safety to make
      available, §32-6-1.
Ineligible persons, §32-6-7.
Issuance.
  Manner of issuance,
    §32-6-4.
  Persons to whom license
    not to be issued,
    §32-6-7.
Learner's licenses, §32-6-8.
Local authorities.
  Additional licenses or
    permits.
    No power to require,
      §32-5-1.
Lost licenses, §32-6-15.
Medical advisory board,
  §§32-6-40 to 32-6-48.
  Appointment, §32-6-41.
  Creation, §32-6-41.
  Definitions, §32-6-40.
  Duties, §32-6-42.
  Immunity from civil
    liability, §32-6-45.
  Meetings, §32-6-41.
    Closed meetings of
      board, §32-6-46.
  Promulgation of vision
    standards.
    Division not to prohibit
      director from
      utilizing other
      agencies, §32-6-48.
  Purposes of board,
    §32-6-41.
  Qualification of members,
    §32-6-41.
  Quorum, §32-6-41.
  Recommendations.
    Consideration by
      director, §32-6-44.
  Records.
    Confidentiality, §32-6-43.
    Consideration of opinion
      by director, §32-6-44.

MOTOR VEHICLES—Cont'd
Drivers' licenses—Cont'd
Medical advisory board
  —Cont'd
  Refusal of examination.
    Driver considered
      unqualified to drive,
      §32-6-44.
  Reports.
    Confidentiality, §32-6-43.
    Consideration of opinion
      by director, §32-6-44.
  Responsibilities, §32-6-42.
  Suspension or revocation of
    license.
    Appeals, §32-6-47.
    No driving while appeal
      pending, §32-6-47.
  Terms of office, §32-6-41.
Mentally ill.
  Persons to whom license
    not to be issued,
    §32-6-7.
Motor-driven cycles,
  §§32-12-22, 32-12-26.
New residents, §32-6-1.
Nondriver identification
  cards.
  Department of public
    safety to make
    available, §32-6-1.
Nonresidents.
  Persons exempt from
    securing license,
    §32-6-2.
Number assigned to licensee,
  §32-6-6.
Oaths.
  Application under oath,
    §32-6-4.
Penalties, §32-6-18.
Persons exempt from
  securing license, §32-6-2.
Persons to whom license not
  to be issued, §32-6-7.
Photographs, §32-6-4.
  Specifications, §32-6-6.
Possession, §32-6-9.
Probate judge.
  Application for license
    under oath to judge,
    §32-6-4.
  Collection of fee, §32-6-4.
  Compensation, §32-6-5.
  Reports, §32-6-5.
  Temporary instruction and
    learner's licenses,
    Duties of judge as to,
      §32-6-8.
Reciprocal agreements.
  Alabama driver license
    compact, §§32-6-30 to
    32-6-36.
  Annulment of agreement,
    §32-6-10.
  Commercial driver
    licenses, §32-6-49.18.
  Director of public safety
    empowered to enter
    into, §32-6-10.
  Federal military
    installations.
    Authorities in charge of,
      §32-6-11.
  Other states, §32-6-10.
Records.
  Director of public safety to
    keep records, §32-6-14.
Renewal, §32-6-1.
  Examinations, §32-6-3.

MOTOR VEHICLES—Cont'd
Drivers' licenses—Cont'd
Renewal—Cont'd
  Failure to make
    application for
    renewal, §32-6-1.
Reports.
  Medical advisory board.
    Confidentiality, §32-6-4
  Probate judge reports,
    §32-6-5.
Required, §32-6-1.
Restricted licenses, §32-6-1
Rules and regulations.
  Promulgation by director
    public safety, §32-6-1
School bus drivers, §16-27-4
Signature of licensee,
  §32-6-6.
Speeding.
  Notation of conviction on
    driver's license,
    §32-5-97.
Standards.
  Director of public safety t
    prescribe standards,
    §32-6-20.
Temporary instruction and
  learner's licenses.
  Age of person who may
    obtain, §32-6-8.
  Applications.
    Who may apply, §32-6-
  Examination.
    Required, §32-6-8.
  Fee, §§32-6-8, 32-6-21.
  Form, §32-6-8.
  Issuance, §32-6-8.
  Licensed drivers to
    accompany, §32-6-8.
  Probate judge.
    Duties of judge as to,
      §32-6-8.
  Renewal, §32-6-8.
  Revocation or suspension
    §32-6-8.
United States.
  Persons in service of
    federal government.
    Persons exempt from
      securing license,
      §32-6-2.
  Reciprocal agreements.
    Authorities in charge o
      federal military
      installations,
      §32-6-11.
Driver training schools,
  §§32-14-1 to 32-14-24.
Citation, §32-14-1.
Definitions, §32-14-2.
Driver education and
  training fund.
  Allocation of funds by
    safety coordinating
    committee, §32-3-7.
  Penalties collected credit
    to fund, §32-5-313.
Exemptions, §32-14-5.
Expenditure of taxes and
  fees, Const. Ala., amd.
  354.
Instructors.
  Qualifications, §32-14-22
Insurance.
  Required, §32-14-21.
Licenses, §§32-14-20 to
  32-14-24.
  Cancellation, suspension
    revocation, §32-14-2
  Expiration, §32-14-23.

MOTOR VEHICLES—Cont'd
Driver training schools
—Cont'd
Licenses—Cont'd
Issuance, §32-14-23.
Qualifications.
Instructor for driving
school, §32-14-22.
Insurance, §32-14-21.
Operation of driving
school, §32-14-21.
Surety bond, §32-14-21.
Renewal, §32-14-23.
Refusal to renew,
§32-14-24.
Required, §32-14-20.
Minors.
Persons under sixteen
years of age operating
motor vehicles,
§32-5-64.
Money.
Disposition of moneys
received, §32-14-4.
Penalties.
Violations, §32-14-6.
Rules and regulations.
Superintendent authorized
to prescribe, §32-14-3.
Safety coordinating
committee.
Allocation of funds for
prelicensing driver
education and training
program, §32-3-7.
Short title, §32-14-1.
Superintendent.
Defined, §32-14-2.
Licenses.
Cancellation, suspension
or revocation by
superintendent,
§32-14-24.
Superintendent to issue,
§§32-14-20, 32-14-23.
Rules and regulations,
§32-14-3.
Surety bond.
Required, §32-14-21.
Title.
Short title, §32-14-1.
Truck driver education and
training program.
Appropriation for
instituting and
conducting, §32-5-313.
Violations.
Penalty for violations,
§32-14-6.
Driveways.
Rights of way.
Exceptions to right-of-way
rule, §32-5A-114.
Stopping before emerging
from alley or driveway,
§§32-5A-153, 32-5A-218.
Stopping, standing and
parking.
Prohibited in specified
places, §32-5A-137.
Driving under the influence,
§32-5A-191.
Arrests.
Warrantless arrest,
§32-5-171.
Chemical tests for
intoxication, §§32-5-190
to 32-5-194, 32-5A-194,
32-6-322.
By whom test made,
§32-5A-194.

MOTOR VEHICLES—Cont'd
Driving under the influence
—Cont'd
Chemical tests for
intoxication—Cont'd
Citation, §32-5-190.
Commercial driver
licenses, §32-6-49.13.
Consent.
Implied consent,
§32-5-192.
Drivers' licenses.
Failure to submit to
tests.
Suspension of license,
§32-5-192.
Driving privilege.
Defined, §32-5-191.
Evidence.
Admissibility of results
of test in evidence,
§32-5A-194.
Refusal to submit to test,
§32-5A-194.
Failure to submit to
chemical tests.
Suspension of privilege
to operate motor
vehicle, §32-5-192.
Highway patrol.
Which officers may be
authorized to make
tests, §32-5-194.
How test made,
§32-5A-194.
Immunity from liability,
§32-5A-194.
Implied consent, §32-5-192.
Nonresidents, §32-5-192.
Physicians.
By whom test made,
§32-5A-194.
Liability, §32-5A-194.
Police.
Which law enforcement
officers authorized to
make tests,
§32-5-194.
Presumptions, §32-5A-194.
Privilege.
Defined, §32-5-191.
Refusal to submit to test.
Admissibility of evidence
of refusal,
§32-5A-194.
Results of test.
Admissibility in
evidence,
§32-5A-194.
Availability of test
results, §32-5A-194.
Short title, §32-5-190.
When tests administered,
§32-5-192.
Commercial driver licenses,
§§32-6-320 to 32-6-322.
Disqualification from
driving commercial
vehicle, §32-6-49.11.
Use of alcohol while
driving, §32-6-49.12.
Tests of blood or breath,
§32-6-49.13.
Use of alcohol while
driving, §32-6-49.12.
Consent.
Chemical tests for
intoxication.
Implied consent,
§32-5-192.

MOTOR VEHICLES—Cont'd
Driving under the influence
—Cont'd
Drivers' licenses.
Grounds for revocation,
§32-5A-195.
Evidence.
Chemical tests for
intoxication,
§32-5A-194.
Implied consent.
Chemical tests for
intoxication, §32-5-192.
Penalties, §32-5A-191.
Prohibited, §32-5A-191.
Renting to intoxicated
person, §32-15-2.
Drugs.
Drivers' licenses.
Grounds for revocation,
§32-5A-195.
Persons to whom license
not to be issued,
§32-6-7.
Driving under the influence
of narcotic drugs,
§§32-5-190 to 32-5-194,
32-5A-191, 32-5A-194.
See within this heading,
"Driving under the
influence."
Forfeiture of vehicle.
Controlled substance
violations, §20-2-93.
Pedestrians under influence,
§32-5A-221.
Renting to intoxicated
person, §32-15-2.
Drunkenness.
Driving under the influence,
§§32-5-190 to 32-5-194,
32-5A-191, 32-5A-194.
See within this heading,
"Driving under the
influence."
Education.
Driver education, §§16-40-5.1
to 16-40-5.4.
See EDUCATION.
Driver training schools,
§§32-14-1 to 32-14-24.
See within this heading,
"Driver training
schools."
Eye protective devices for
pupils and teachers
participating in certain
courses, §16-1-7.
School buses, §§16-27-1 to
16-27-7.
See EDUCATION.
Eggs and egg products.
Inspection of vehicles,
§2-12-10.
Embezzlement.
Renting and hiring.
Embezzlement of vehicle
subject to larceny,
§32-15-7.
Emergency vehicles.
Ambulances, §§22-18-1 to
22-18-7.
See AMBULANCES.
Approaching.
Duty of driver on
approach, §32-5-113.
Defined, §32-1-1.1.
Drivers of emergency
vehicles.
Duty to drive safely,
§32-5A-115.

MOTOR VEHICLES—Cont'd
  Emergency vehicles—Cont'd
    Duty of driver on approach,
      §32-5-113.
    Following authorized
      emergency vehicles,
      §32-5-113.
    Following prohibited,
      §32-5A-58.
    Lights, lamps and reflective
      devices, §32-5A-115.
    Pedestrians.
      Pedestrians to yield right
        of way, §32-5A-219.
    Sirens, §32-5-213.
    Warning devices, §32-5-213.
  Employers and employees.
    Safety-responsibility act.
      Employment of necessary
        employees by director
        of public safety,
        §32-7-38.
      Proof of financial
        responsibility.
        Owner may give proof
          for employees,
          §32-7-28.
  Enforcement of chapter,
    §32-5-310.
  Engines.
    Fumes or smoke.
      Preventing of fumes or
        smoke, §32-5-216.
    Mufflers, §32-5-216.
    Noise.
      Prevention of noise,
        §32-5-216.
    Removal.
      Salvage.
        Motor vehicle declared
          salvage upon
          removal of engine,
          §32-8-87.
    Unattended vehicles.
      Stopping engine,
        §32-5A-50.
    Vehicle identification
      number.
      Removed, falsified or
        unauthorized
        identification number,
        §32-8-86.
  Equipment.
    Brakes, §32-5-212.
      Unattended vehicles.
        Setting brakes,
          §32-5A-50.
    Definitions, §32-17A-1.
    Disclosure, §32-17A-2.
      Document, §32-17A-3.
    Flares, §§32-5-220,
      32-5-221.
    Headlights, §§32-5-240 to
      32-5-253. See within this
      heading, "Lights, lamps
      and reflective devices."
    Horns, §32-5-213.
    Inspections.
      Municipal testing stations,
        §§32-18-1 to 32-18-8.
        See within this
        heading, "Municipal
        testing stations."
    Lights, lamps and reflective
      devices, §§32-5-240 to
      32-5-253. See within this
      heading, "Lights, lamps
      and reflective devices."
    Mirrors, §32-5-214.
    Mufflers, §32-5-216.

MOTOR VEHICLES—Cont'd
  Equipment—Cont'd
    Municipal testing stations,
      §§32-18-1 to 32-18-8. See
      within this heading,
      "Municipal testing
      stations."
    Nonoriginal equipment
      manufacturer
      aftermarket crash parts.
      Disclosure, §§32-17A-1 to
        32-17A-3.
    Reflective devices, §§32-5-240
      to 32-5-253. See within
      this heading, "Lights,
      lamps and reflective
      devices."
    Safety glazing material,
      §32-5-218.
    Seat belts. See within this
      heading, "Seat belts."
    Tail lamps. See within this
      heading, "Lights, lamps
      and reflective devices."
    Testing stations.
      Municipal testing stations,
        §§32-18-1 to 32-18-8.
        See within this
        heading, "Municipal
        testing stations."
    Tires. See within this
      heading, "Tires."
    Warning devices. See within
      this heading, "Warning
      devices."
    Windshields, §32-5-215.
  Essential parts.
    Defined, §32-1-1.1.
  **Established place of
    business.**
    Defined, §32-1-1.1.
  Evidence.
    Accident report, §32-10-11.
    Certificate of title.
      Prima facie evidence of
        facts appearing on it,
        §32-8-39.
    Chemical tests for
      intoxication, §32-5A-194.
    Safety responsibility act.
      Matters not to be evidence
        in civil actions,
        §32-7-12.
      Proof of financial
        responsibility. See
        within this heading,
        "Safety-responsibility
        act."
    Size and weight of vehicles.
      Scales.
        Certificate of approval
          prima facie evidence
          of accuracy,
          §32-9-32.
  Examinations.
    Drivers' licenses, §§32-6-3,
      32-6-8.
  Explosives.
    Decal, plate or placard.
      Vehicles transporting.
        Prominent display
          required,
          §32-5A-171.
    Defined, §32-1-1.1.
    Equipment required of
      vehicles transporting,
      §32-5-74.
    Flammable liquid.
      Defined, §32-1-1.1.

MOTOR VEHICLES—Cont'd
  Explosives—Cont'd
    Flammable liquid—Cont'd
      Vehicles transporting.
        Decal, plate or placard.
          Prominent display
            required,
            §32-5A-171.
        Maximum speed,
          §32-5A-171.
    Flares.
      Vehicles carrying
        explosives.
        Flares required,
          §32-5-220.
    Marking of vehicles
      transporting, §32-5-74.
    Speed.
      Vehicles transporting.
        Maximum speed,
          §32-5A-171.
    Transportation of explosives
      General provisions,
        §§37-8-180 to 37-8-184.
      Vehicles transporting,
        §32-5-74.
        Decal, plate or placard.
          Prominent display
            required,
            §32-5A-171.
        Maximum speed,
          §32-5A-171.
  Farm tractors. See within the
    heading, "Tractors."
  Fees.
    Automotive dismantlers and
      parts recyclers.
      Licenses, §40-12-413.
    Circuit courts.
      Abandoned vehicles.
        Fee for filing a report of
          sale, §12-19-76.
    Commercial driver licenses,
      §32-6-49.19.
      Application fee, §32-6-49.5.
      Information regarding
        driving record.
        Furnishing by
          department,
          §32-6-49.15.
    Department of public safety
      Criminal history records
        search, §32-2-8.1.
      Records and reports.
        Fees for copies, §32-2-8.
    Drivers' licenses. See within
      this heading, "Drivers'
      licenses."
    Highway patrol, §§32-2-21,
      32-2-25.
    License taxes and
      registration fees,
      §§40-12-240 to 40-12-27
      See within this heading
      "License taxes and
      registration fees."
    Municipal testing stations,
      §32-18-3.
    National guard.
      Exemptions from motor
        vehicle license tax an
        registration fee,
        §31-2-12.
    Recording change of
      ownership of motor
      vehicle, §40-12-261.
    Registration fees,
      §§40-12-240 to 40-12-27
      See within this heading
      "License taxes and
      registration fees."

MOTOR VEHICLES—Cont'd

Fees—Cont'd
Safety-responsibility act.
Operating records.
Furnishing of abstracts
by director, §32-7-4.
Temporary tags and
certificates, §32-6-215.
Uniform certificate of title
and antitheft act,
§§32-8-6, 32-8-7.
Felonies.
Embezzlement, conversion,
etc., of vehicles subject to
larceny, §32-15-7.
Failure to redeliver hired
vehicle, §32-15-6.
Hiring with intent to
defraud, §32-15-5.
Homicide.
Criminally negligent
homicide.
Drivers of motor vehicles
driving under
influence.
Class C felony,
§13A-6-4.
Obtaining possession by
trick, false
representation, etc.,
§32-15-4.
Penalties for felonies
generally, §32-5A-9.
Uniform certificate of title
and antitheft act,
§§32-8-12, 32-8-14.
Financial responsibility.
Safety-responsibility act,
§§32-7-1 to 32-7-42. See
within this heading,
"Safety-responsibility
act."
Fines and forfeitures. See
within this heading,
"Penalties."
Firearms.
Weapons generally. See
within this heading,
"Weapons."
Fire bombs.
Throwing fire bombs into
occupied vehicle,
§32-5-11.
Fires and fire prevention.
Drivers of fire vehicles.
Duty to drive safely,
§32-5A-115.
Duty on approach of
emergency vehicle,
§32-5-113.
Fire hoses.
Crossing fire hoses,
§32-5A-59.
Following emergency
vehicles prohibited,
§32-5A-58.
Lights, lamps and reflective
devices on fire vehicles,
§32-5A-115.
Obedience to firemen
required, §32-5A-4.
Rights of way.
Pedestrians required to
yield, §32-5A-219.
Sirens and warning devices,
§32-5-213.
Speed limits.
When speed limit not
applicable, §32-5A-7.

MOTOR VEHICLES—Cont'd

Fires and fire prevention
—Cont'd
Stopping, standing and
parking.
Certain privileges
available, §32-5A-7.
Prohibited in specified
places, §32-5A-137.
Stop signals and stop signs.
Authorized to proceed
through signals or
signs, §32-5A-7.
Tags and plates.
Special tags and plates for
firefighters, §§32-6-270
to 32-6-274. See within
this heading, "Tags
and plates."
Flags.
Distress flag for handicapped
or paraplegic drivers,
§§32-5-12 to 32-5-14.
Loads.
Flag or light at end of
load, §32-5-211.
Flammable liquids.
Defined, §32-1-1.1.
Flares.
Vehicles transporting
inflammable liquids.
Flares required to be
carried, §32-5-220.
Flares.
Carrying required by certain
vehicles, §32-5-220.
Display, §32-5-221.
Specifications, §32-5-220.
Flashing signals, §32-5A-34.
Fog lamps, §32-5-241.
Following too closely,
§32-5A-89.
Foreign vehicles.
Defined, §32-1-1.1.
Forfeitures. See within this
heading, "Penalties."
Forms.
Uniform certificate of title
and antitheft act.
Department to provide,
§32-8-9.
Uniform traffic infractions,
ARJA, Rule 19.
Frames.
Removal of frame.
Motor vehicle declared
salvage upon removal,
§32-8-87.
Franchises.
Dealers.
Motor vehicle franchise
act.
Dealings by
manufacturers with
dealers, §§8-20-1 to
8-20-12. See within
this heading,
"Manufacturers."
Fraud.
Certificate of title.
Refusal to issue certificate,
§32-8-42.
Suspension or revocation of
certificate.
Grounds for suspension
or revocation,
§32-8-49.
Renting and hiring. See
within this heading,
"Renting and hiring."

MOTOR VEHICLES—Cont'd

Fuel.
Gasoline tax, §§40-17-30 to
40-17-133.
See GASOLINE.
Motor fuels.
See MOTOR FUELS.
Motor vehicle carriers,
§§37-3-1 to 37-3-34.
See MOTOR VEHICLE
CARRIERS.
Fumes.
Preventing escape of
excessive fumes or
smoke, §32-5-216.
Funds.
Driver education and
training fund.
Penalties.
Moneys collected credited
to fund, §32-5-313.
Gambling.
Forfeiture of vehicle used in
violation of article,
§13A-12-30.
Transportation of lottery
paraphernalia,
§§13A-12-70 to
13A-12-75.
See LOTTERIES.
Garages.
Accidents.
Bullet damage.
Garages to report bullet
damage, §32-10-10.
Reports, §32-10-10.
Licenses, §40-12-54.
Storage garages, §40-12-55.
Unclaimed vehicles.
Disposition of unclaimed
vehicles left for
service, §35-12-6.
Reports of operator to
department, §32-8-84.
Garbage and trash.
Spilling loads or litter,
§32-5-76.
Throwing of litter onto
highway, §32-5A-60.
Glass.
Depositing glass on
highways, §32-5A-60.
Removing glass remaining
from accidents,
§32-5A-60.
Safety glazing material,
§32-5-218.
Tinting.
Restrictions, §32-5-215.
Windshields, §32-5-215.
Good Samaritan act.
Exemption from liability,
§6-5-332.
Governor.
Highway and traffic safety
coordination act.
Authority of governor,
§32-4-2.
Cooperation with and
participation in
programs of federal
and other agencies,
§32-4-6.
Highway patrol.
Establishment and
maintenance, §32-2-20.
Safety coordinating
committee.
Chairman of committee,
§32-3-1.

MOTOR VEHICLES—Cont'd
Governor—Cont'd
Speed limits.
Maximum speeds.
Governor authorized to prescribe, §32-5A-171.
Speed zones.
Establishment of state speed zones, §32-5A-172.
Grade crossings. See within this heading, "Railroads."
Gravel.
Spilling loads, §32-5-76.
Gross weight.
Defined, §32-1-1.1.
Guest statute.
Liability for injury or death of guest, §32-1-2.
Guide dogs, §§21-7-6, 21-7-7.
Gulf of Mexico.
Operation of vehicles on beaches and sand dunes of Gulf of Mexico.
Prohibited, §32-1-7.
Ham radio operators.
Amateur radio operators.
Tags and plates, §§32-6-70 to 32-6-73, 32-6-90 to 32-6-93. See within this heading, "Tags and plates."
Handicapped persons.
Blind persons. See within this heading, "Blind persons."
Definitions, §32-6-230.
Disabled veterans.
Tags and plates, §§32-6-130 to 32-6-133.
Distress flag for handicapped or paraplegic drivers, §§32-5-12 to 32-5-14.
Authorized, §32-5-12.
Card authorizing use, §32-5-13.
Design, §32-5-12.
Fee for issuance, §32-5-13.
Illegal use.
Penalty for illegal use, §32-5-14.
Issuance.
Fee, §32-5-13.
Penalty for illegal use, §32-5-14.
Replacement flags, §32-5-13.
Drivers' licenses.
Persons to whom license not to be issued, §32-6-7.
License plates, §§40-12-300 to 40-12-302.
Misuse of privileges, §32-6-233.
Parking.
Agreements with other states as to parking privileges, §32-6-234.
Unauthorized use of handicapped parking place, §32-6-233.1.
Unlimited parking periods, §32-6-232.
Pedestrians, §32-5A-220.
Reciprocity.
Agreements concerning parking privileges, §32-6-234.

MOTOR VEHICLES—Cont'd
Handicapped persons
—Cont'd
Right to use public conveyances and transportation facilities, §21-7-3.
Veterans.
Disabled veterans.
Tags and plates, §§32-6-130 to 32-6-133.
Hay.
Loads which must be fastened by cables or chains, §32-5-75.
Headlamps, §§32-5-240 to 32-5-253. See within this heading, "Lights, lamps and reflective devices."
Health.
Nuisances menacing public health, §§22-10-1 to 22-10-3.
Hearings.
Abandoned vehicles.
Hearing to determine whether vehicle abandoned, §32-13-4.
Automotive dismantlers and parts recyclers.
License.
Refusal, cancellation or revocation, §40-12-417.
Drivers' licenses.
Cancellation, suspension or revocation.
Right to file petitions, §32-5A-195.
Uniform certificate of title and antitheft act.
Protesting actions of department, §32-8-4.
Hearses.
License taxes and registration fees, §40-12-247.
Heavy motor vehicles.
Registration.
Applicants to furnish evidence of paying federal taxes, §32-6-58.
Helmets.
Motorcycles.
See MOTORCYCLES.
Highway and traffic safety coordination act, §§32-4-1 to 32-4-7.
Citation, §32-4-1.
Coordinator of highway and traffic safety.
Appointment by governor, §32-4-3.
Duties.
Generally, §32-4-3.
Office created, §32-4-3.
Quarters, §32-4-4.
Staff.
Authority to employ and secure staff, §32-4-4.
Supplies, §32-4-4.
Term of office, §32-4-3.
Counties.
Powers of local governing bodies, §32-4-7.
Declaration of policy, §32-4-2.
Governor.
Authority, §32-4-2.
Chief administrator, §32-4-2.

MOTOR VEHICLES—Cont'd
Highway and traffic safety coordination act—Cont'd
Governor—Cont'd
Cooperation with participation in programs of federal and other agencies, §32-4-6.
Local governing bodies.
Powers.
Generally, §32-4-7.
Municipal corporations.
Powers of local governing bodies, §32-4-7.
National highway safety act of 1966.
Participation in benefits of act, §32-4-5.
Policy.
Declaration of policy, §32-4-2.
Safety coordinating committee, §§32-3-1 to 32-3-7. See within this heading, "Safety coordinating committee."
Short title, §32-4-1.
Highway patrol.
Accidents.
Reports.
Immediate report to highway patrol, §32-10-5.
Arrests.
Fees.
Disposition, §32-2-25.
Badges.
Officers to receive as part of retirement benefits, §32-2-26.
Bonds, surety.
Execution of bonds, §32-2-23.
Liabilities under bonds, §32-2-24.
Chemical tests for intoxication.
Which law enforcement officers may be authorized to make tests, §32-5-194.
Closing highways, §32-5-16.
Costs.
Disposition of costs, §32-2-21.
When costs not to be paid by county, §32-2-25.
Counties.
Fees and costs.
When not to be paid by county, §32-2-25.
Court attendance.
Troopers entitled to costs, fees or mileage for attending court, §32-2-21.
Equipment.
Officers to receive as part of retirement benefits, §32-2-26.
Establishment.
Governor authorized to establish, §32-2-20.
Fees.
Arrest fee.
Disposition, §32-2-25.
Disposition, §32-2-21.
When fees not to be paid by county, §32-2-25.

MOTOR VEHICLES—Cont'd
Highway patrol—Cont'd
Governor.
Establishment and
maintenance by
governor, §32-2-20.
Mileage.
Disposition, §32-2-21.
Powers.
Officers have powers of
peace officers,
§32-2-22.
Retirement benefits.
Officers to receive badge,
pistol, etc., as part of
benefits, §32-2-26.
Highways.
Closing highways.
State trooper may close
highways, §32-5-16.
Construction and
maintenance.
Working signs.
Speed limit between
working signs,
§32-5-93.
Yielding right of way to
construction vehicles,
§32-5A-116.
Damage to highway.
Liability for damage,
§32-5-9.
Dangerous conditions.
State trooper may close
highways, §32-5-16.
Defined, §32-1-1.1.
Department.
Director.
Speed zones.
Establishment of state
speed zones,
§32-5A-172.
Licenses.
Exemptions, §23-1-52.
Divided highways.
Driving on, §32-5A-90.
Fixtures.
Accidents.
Duty upon striking
highway fixtures,
§32-10-4.
General provisions.
See HIGHWAYS.
Glass, nails, etc.
Depositing on highways,
§32-5A-60.
Interstate highway system.
Controlled access facilities.
Restrictions on use by
various classes of
vehicles.
Authority of highway
director, §23-3-3.
Laned roadways, §32-5A-88.
Limited-access highways. See
within this heading,
"Limited-access
highways."
Littering.
Vehicles loaded with
gravel, rock, sawdust,
wood, etc.
Restrictions on and
penalty for spilling
loads, §32-5-76.
Mountain highways.
Driving on mountain
highways, §32-5A-56.

MOTOR VEHICLES—Cont'd
Highways—Cont'd
National highway safety act
of 1966. See within this
heading, "Highway and
traffic safety
coordination act."
No passing zones.
Designation by highway
department,
§32-5A-86.
Obstructions.
Removal by highway
director, §32-5-5.
One-way roadways.
Designation by highway
department,
§32-5A-87.
Overtaking and passing.
No passing zones,
§32-5A-86.
Parking on highways,
§32-5A-138.
Racing on highways.
Prohibited, §32-5A-178.
Restrictions on right to use,
§32-1-3.
Rights of way.
Vehicles entering
interstate or limited-
access highways,
§§32-5A-110 to
32-5A-112.
Signs.
Restrictions on highway
use.
Erection and
maintenance of signs
by local authorities,
§32-1-3.
Size and weight of vehicles.
Rules and regulations.
Promulgation by
highway
department,
§23-1-59.
Spilling loads on highways,
§32-5-76.
Stopping on highways,
§32-5A-136.
Through highways.
Stopping at certain
through highways,
§32-5A-113.
Trucks, trailers and semi-
trailers.
Restrictions on operation
on highways, §32-1-3.
Weight restrictions.
Promulgation of rules and
regulations by
highway department,
§23-1-59.
Workers.
Persons working on
highway excepted from
rules of the road act,
§32-5A-6.
**Hindering transportation of
commodities,**
§13A-11-221.
Hiring vehicles.
General provisions, §§32-15-1
to 32-15-8. See within
this heading, "Renting
and hiring."
Hit and run driving,
§§32-10-1 to 32-10-3.
Penalty, §32-10-6.

MOTOR VEHICLES—Cont'd
Hitchhiking.
Prohibition against
hitchhiking, §32-5A-216.
Homicide, §32-5A-192.
Criminally negligent
homicide.
Drivers of motor vehicles
driving under
influence.
Class C felony, §13A-6-4.
Horns.
Distance horn to be heard,
§32-5-213.
Pedestrians.
Warning pedestrians,
§32-5A-213.
Required, §32-5-213.
Horse-drawn wagons.
Reflectors or similar warning
devices, §32-5-245.
Husband and wife.
Safety-responsibility act.
Proof of financial
responsibility.
Owner may give proof
for member of
immediate family,
§32-7-28.
Identification cards.
Issuance of identification
cards for nondrivers,
§32-6-1.
Identification numbers.
Uniform certificate of title
and antitheft act.
Vehicle identification
numbers. See within
this heading, "Uniform
certificate of title and
antitheft act."
Ignition.
Unattended vehicles.
Locking ignition,
§32-5A-50.
Implements of husbandry,
§32-1-1.1.
Implied consent.
Chemical tests for
intoxication, §32-5-192.
Infractions.
Uniform traffic infractions.
Clerks of court.
Fines and costs paid to,
ARJA, Rule 19.
Complaint and summons,
ARJA, Rule 19.
Costs.
Paid to clerks of court,
ARJA, Rule 19.
Defendant's appearance.
Plea and waiver of trial,
ARJA, Rule 19.
Fines.
Paid to clerks of court,
ARJA, Rule 19.
Forms, ARJA, Rule 19.
Law enforcement officers.
Issuance of ticket to,
ARJA, Rule 19.
Municipal parking
offenses, ARJA, Rule
19.
Notice.
Failure of defendant to
appear.
Issuance of additional
notice, ARJA,
Rule 19.

MOTOR VEHICLES—Cont'd
Infractions—Cont'd
Uniform traffic infractions
—Cont'd
Parking.
Municipal parking
offenses, ARJA, Rule
19.
Pleas.
Defendant's appearance,
ARJA, Rule 19.
Procedures.
Generally, ARJA, Rule
19.
Trial.
Defendant's appearance.
Waiver, ARJA, Rule
19.
Uniform traffic ticket and
complaint, ARJA, Rule
19.
Warrants.
Defendant's failure to
appear.
Issuance of
supplemental
summons or
warrant, ARJA,
Rule 19.
Violations generally. See
within this heading,
"Violations."
Injunctions.
Automotive dismantlers and
parts recyclers.
Violations of article,
§40-12-425.
Inspections.
Municipal testing stations,
§§32-18-1 to 32-18-8. See
within this heading,
"Municipal testing
stations."
Uniform certificate of title
and antitheft act,
§32-8-8.
Instructors.
Driver training schools,
§32-14-22.
Insurance.
Assigned risk plans.
Safety-responsibility act,
§32-7-35.
Automobile clubs and
associations, §§27-39-1 to
27-39-8.
See INSURANCE.
Cancellation of automobile
liability insurance,
§§27-23-20 to 27-23-27.
Assigned risk plan.
Notification of
availability,
§27-23-24.
Definitions, §27-23-20.
Liability of insurers for
statements, etc.,
§27-23-27.
Nonrenewal.
Applicability of article to
nonrenewal,
§27-23-28.
Notice of cancellation.
Availability of assigned
risk plan
notification,
§27-23-24.
Proof of notice,
§27-23-25.
Reasons, §27-23-23.

MOTOR VEHICLES—Cont'd
Insurance—Cont'd
Cancellation of automobile
liability insurance
—Cont'd
Notice of cancellation
—Cont'd
Time of notice,
§27-23-23.
Reasons for cancellation,
§27-23-21.
Notice, §27-23-23.
Specification upon
insured's request,
§27-23-26.
Renewal.
Effect of renewal,
§27-23-22.
Casualty insurance
generally.
See INSURANCE.
Definitions.
Cancellation of automobile
liability insurance,
§27-23-20.
Department of public safety.
Employees.
Insurance for employees,
§32-2-10.
Driver training schools.
Required, §32-14-21.
Liability insurance.
Cancellation, §§27-23-20 to
27-23-27.
Proof of financial
responsibility. See within
this heading, "Safety-
responsibility act."
Public officers and
employees.
State employees operating
motor vehicles in
performance of duties,
§36-1-6.
Renewal.
Effect of renewal on
cancellation,
§27-23-22.
Safety-responsibility act,
§§32-7-1 to 32-7-42. See
within this heading,
"Safety-responsibility
act."
Self-insurers.
Safety-responsibility act,
§32-7-34.
Uninsured motorists.
Safety responsibility act,
§32-7-23.
**International registration
plan,** §40-12-262.
Intersections.
Crossing intersections.
Keep to the right in
crossing, §32-5-54.
Defined, §32-1-1.1.
Obstruction of traffic.
Entry into obstructed
intersections,
§32-5A-61.
Pedestrians.
Subject to traffic control
signals, §32-5A-210.
Rights of way.
Approaching or entering
intersections,
§§32-5A-110 to
32-5A-112.
Speed limits upon
approaching, §32-5A-170.

MOTOR VEHICLES—Cont'd
Intersections—Cont'd
Stopping, standing and
parking.
Prohibited in specified
places, §32-5A-137.
Turning at intersections,
§32-5A-130.
Interstate highways.
Speed limits, §32-5A-171.
Intoxicating liquor.
Driving under the influence,
§§32-5-190 to 32-5-194,
32-5A-191, 32-5A-194.
See within this heading,
"Driving under the
influence."
Judges.
Probate judges. See within
this heading, "Probate
judges."
Judgments.
Safety-responsibility act. See
within this heading,
"Safety-responsibility
act."
Junked vehicles.
Abandoned motor vehicles,
§§32-13-1 to 32-13-8. See
within this heading,
"Abandoned motor
vehicles."
Junkyard control, §§23-1-240
to 23-1-251.
See JUNKYARD
CONTROL.
Removal of manufacturer's
identification number
plates, serial plates and
license plates.
Required, §32-8-87.
Jurisdiction.
Trucks, trailers and semi-
trailers.
Violations of chapter.
Courts having
jurisdiction, §32-9-4.
Keys.
Unattended vehicles.
Removing key, §32-5A-50.
Lamps, §§32-5-240 to 32-5-253.
See within this heading,
"Lights, lamps and
reflective devices."
Laned roadways.
Defined, §32-1-1.1.
Driving on roadways laned
for traffic, §32-5A-88.
Left side of highway.
Driving in extreme left
side restricted,
§32-5-77.
Signs.
Slow-moving traffic,
§32-5A-88.
Larceny.
Embezzlement, conversion,
etc., of vehicles subject to
larceny, §32-15-7.
Suspension of registration of
stolen vehicles, §32-8-84.
Uniform certificate of title
and antitheft act,
§§32-8-1 to 32-8-88. See
within this heading,
"Uniform certificate of
title and antitheft act."
Learners' licenses, §32-6-8.

MOTOR VEHICLES—Cont'd
  Leases.
    Violation where vehicle
      leased to another.
      Owner not liable,
      §32-5-152.1.
  Left side of highway.
    Driving in extreme left side
      restricted, §32-5-77.
  Legislature.
    Safety coordinating
      committee.
      Recommendations to
        legislature for
        enactment of laws,
        §32-3-4.
  Length of vehicles, §§32-9-20
    to 32-9-32. See within this
    heading, "Size and weight
    of vehicles."
  License plates.
    Forwarding to department of
      revenue, §40-12-423.
  Licenses.
    Antique vehicles.
      Exemption from other
        licensing
        requirements,
        §40-12-293.
    Automotive dismantlers and
      parts recyclers,
      §§40-12-412 to 40-12-418.
    Commercial driver licenses,
      §§32-6-49.1 to 32-6-49.22.
      See within this heading,
      "Commercial driver
      licenses."
    Dealers, §40-12-51.
      Accessory dealers,
        §40-12-53.
    Dealers, reconditioners,
      rebuilders and
      wholesalers, §§40-12-390
      to 40-12-400.
      Additional places of
        business, §40-12-395.
      Appeal to circuit court
        from denial,
        cancellation,
        suspension or
        revocation, §40-12-397.
      Application, §40-12-392.
      Bonds, surety.
        Prerequisite to issuance,
          §40-12-398.
      Cancellation.
        Appeal to circuit court,
          §40-12-397.
      Definitions, §40-12-390.
      Denial.
        Appeal to circuit court,
          §40-12-397.
      Fee, §40-12-392.
        Disposition of fees
          collected, §40-12-393.
      Issuance of certificate,
        §40-12-394.
        Bond or net worth
          statement
          prerequisite to
          issuance, §40-12-398.
      Net worth statement.
        Prerequisite to issuance,
          §40-12-398.
      One licensed dealer only
        permitted at same
        place of business,
        §40-12-395.
      Penalty for violations,
        §40-12-400.

MOTOR VEHICLES—Cont'd
  Licenses—Cont'd
    Dealers, reconditioners,
      rebuilders and
      wholesalers—Cont'd
      Records to be kept by
        licensees, §40-12-399.
      Required, §40-12-391.
      Restrictions on sales by
        wholesalers,
        reconditioners and
        rebuilders, §40-12-392.
      Revocation, §40-12-396.
        Appeal to circuit court
          from revocation,
          §40-12-397.
        Notice and hearing on
          revocation,
          §40-12-396.
      Sales tax.
        State sales tax number,
          §40-12-391.
      Same place of business.
        One licensed dealer only,
          §40-12-395.
      Supplemental license for
        each additional place
        of business,
        §40-12-395.
      Suspension, §40-12-396.
        Appeal to circuit court
          from suspension,
          §40-12-397.
      Term, §40-12-394.
      Violations.
        Penalty, §40-12-400.
      Wholesalers, reconditioners
        or rebuilders who are
        also dealers,
        §40-12-392.
    Drivers' licenses, §§32-6-1 to
      32-6-48. See within this
      heading, "Drivers'
      licenses."
    Driver training schools,
      §§32-14-20 to 32-14-24.
    Exemptions.
      Civil air patrol,
        §40-12-244.
      National guard,
        §40-12-244.
      Rescue squads, §40-12-244.
      Reserves, §40-12-244.
      Veterans.
        Disabled veterans,
          §40-12-244.
    Garages, §40-12-54.
      Storage garages, §40-12-55.
    Highway department.
      Exemptions, §23-1-52.
    Learners' licenses, §32-6-8.
    Plates, §§32-6-50 to 32-6-295.
      See within this heading,
      "Tags and plates."
    Salesmen, §40-12-52.
    Shops, §40-12-54.
      Tire retreading shops,
        §40-12-57.
    Staggered licensing,
      registration and
      taxation, §§32-6-60 to
      32-6-67.
    Storage.
      Storage garages, §40-12-55.
      Storage other than in
        garages, §40-12-56.
    Tags and plates, §§32-6-50 to
      32-6-295. See within this
      heading, "Tags and
      plates."

MOTOR VEHICLES—Cont'd
  Licenses—Cont'd
    Taxes, §§40-12-240 to
      40-12-274. See within
      this heading, "License
      taxes and registration
      fees."
  **License taxes and
    registration fees,**
    §§40-12-240 to 40-12-274.
    Ambulances, §40-12-247.
    Buses.
      Jitney buses, §40-12-245.
      Motor buses, §40-12-246.
    County license commissioner.
      Fee for issuing license,
        §40-12-271.
    Date due and delinquent,
      §40-12-267.
    Definitions, §40-12-240.
      Self-propelled campers or
        house cars, §40-12-240.
    Disbursement of proceeds,
      §40-12-270.
    Exemptions.
      Foreign consuls.
        Private passenger
          vehicles, §40-12-243.
        Special plates,
          §40-12-243.
      Veterans.
        Disabled veterans.
          Motor vehicles issued
            to disabled
            veterans,
            §40-12-254.
    Expenditure of taxes and
      fees, Const. Ala., amd.
      93.
    Fee for issuance, §40-12-271.
    Foreign consuls.
      Exemption of private
        passenger vehicles,
        §40-12-243.
      Special plates,
        §40-12-243.
    Hearses, §40-12-247.
    Highway department.
      Exemptions, §23-1-52.
    Jeeps.
      Private passenger
        automobiles,
        §40-12-241.
    Jitney buses, §40-12-245.
      Defined, §40-12-240.
    Lists of motor vehicles.
      Certification by probate
        judge, §40-12-269.
    Motor buses, §40-12-246.
    Motorcycles, §40-12-240.
    Motor tractors, §40-12-251.
    Nonresidents.
      Effect of provisions relative
        to registration,
        §40-12-262.
    Other taxes precluded,
      §40-12-268.
    Part of year, §40-12-258.
    Payment.
      Quarterly declining basis,
        §40-12-259.
    Private passenger
      automobiles, §40-12-242.
      Additional fees,
        §40-12-273.
      Disposition, §40-12-274.
      Defined, §40-12-240.
      Station wagons, jeeps, etc.,
        included, §40-12-241.

MOTOR VEHICLES—Cont'd
License taxes and
    registration fees—Cont'd
Probate judge.
  Fee for issuing license,
    §40-12-271.
Proceeds.
  Disbursement, §40-12-270.
Remittance of money,
  §40-12-269.
Station wagons.
  Private passenger
    automobiles,
    §40-12-241.
Trailers and semitrailers.
  Basis of tax, §40-12-252.
  Defined, §40-12-240.
Travel trailers.
  Defined, §40-12-240.
  Noncompliance.
    Citations, §40-12-257.
    Penalties, §40-12-255.
  Registration fee,
    §40-12-255.
  Fees for collection,
    §40-12-255.
Trucks or truck tractors,
  §40-12-248.
  Additional fees,
    §40-12-273.
    Disposition, §40-12-274.
  Change in gross vehicle
    weight allowance or
    use of vehicle,
    §40-12-249.
  Defined, §40-12-240.
Truck trailers, tractor
  trailers and semitrailers.
  Bases of tax, §40-12-242.
Vehicles transporting
  passengers for hire,
  §40-12-246.
Veterans.
  Exemption of vehicles
    issued to disabled
    veterans, §40-12-254.
Liens.
Abandoned motor vehicles,
  §§32-13-3, 32-13-4.
Municipal testing stations.
  Seizure and impoundment
    of vehicles.
    Expenses of seizure and
      impounding to be
      lien, §32-18-8.
Production, manufacture or
  repair, §§35-11-110 to
  35-11-112.
  Attachment.
    Joinder of persons
      having liens on same
      property, §35-11-112.
    Right to enforce lien by
      attachment,
      §35-11-111.
  Declaration of lien,
    §35-11-110.
  Enforcement of lien.
    Joinder of persons
      having liens on same
      property, §35-11-112.
    Right to enforce by
      attachment,
      §35-11-111.
  Joinder of persons having
    liens on same property,
    §35-11-112.

MOTOR VEHICLES—Cont'd
Liens—Cont'd
Uniform certificate of title
  and antitheft act.
  Security interest. See
    within this heading,
    "Uniform certificate of
    title and antitheft act."
Lights, lamps and reflective
  devices, §§32-5-240 to
  32-5-253.
Additional equipment
  required on certain
  vehicles, §32-5-240.
Approval of lighting devices,
  §32-5-252.
Casting light on real
  property at night,
  §32-5-17.
Clearance lamps, §32-5-242.
Director of public safety.
  Duties as to, §32-5-252.
Driving lamps.
  Auxiliary driving lamps,
    §32-5-241.
Enforcement of provisions,
  §32-5-253.
Flag or light at end of load,
  §32-5-211.
Fog lamps, §32-5-241.
Head lamps.
  Height of lamps, §32-5-242.
  Multiple-beam road-
    lighting equipment,
    §32-5-242.
  Parked vehicles.
    Dimming headlights on
      parked vehicles,
      §32-5-244.
  Required, §32-5-240.
  Single-beam road-lighting
    equipment, §32-5-242.
  Visibility distance,
    §32-5-241.
Loads.
  Flag or light at end of
    load, §32-5-211.
Mail.
  Vehicles engaged in mail
    service.
    Lighting equipment and
      warning devices,
      §32-5-243.
Marker lamps.
  Visibility, §32-5-242.
Misdemeanors.
  Casting light on real
    property at night,
    §32-5-17.
Mounting reflectors,
  clearance lamps and side
  marker lamps, §32-5-242.
Multiple-beam road-lighting
  equipment, §32-5-242.
Nuisance.
  Casting light on real
    property at night,
    §32-5-17.
Number required, §32-5-240.
Parked vehicles.
  Lights on parked vehicles,
    §32-5-244.
Passing lamps.
  Auxiliary passing lamps,
    §32-5-241.
Police vehicles, §32-5A-115.
Prohibited lamps and
  devices, §32-5-252.

MOTOR VEHICLES—Cont'd
Lights, lamps and reflective
  devices—Cont'd
Real property.
  Casting light from motor
    vehicle on real
    property at night,
    §32-5-17.
Regulations.
  Issuance and enforcement
    by director of public
    safety, §32-5-252.
Required lighting equipment
  and illuminating devices
  of vehicles, §32-5-240.
Sales.
  Approval required,
    §32-5-252.
  Noncompliance with
    requirements of
    division, §32-5-253.
Side marker lamps and
  reflectors.
  Color, §32-5-242.
  Mounting, §32-5-242.
Signal lamps and signal
  devices, §32-5-241.
Signals for starting, stopping
  and turning,
    §§32-5A-133, 32-5A-134.
Single-beam road-lighting
  equipment, §32-5-242.
Slow-moving vehicles.
  Reflective devices for slow-
    moving vehicles,
    §§32-5-246 to 32-5-250.
Special restrictions on lamps,
  §32-5-241.
Spot lamps, §32-5-241.
Standards and specifications.
  Establishment by director
    of public safety,
    §32-5-252.
Tail lamps, §32-5-240.
Turn signals, §§32-5A-133,
  32-5A-134.
Visibility, §32-5-242.
When lighted lamps
  required, §32-5-240.
Limited-access highways.
Backing on shoulders,
  §32-5-72.
Driving onto or off,
  §32-5A-91.
Interstate highway system.
  Restrictions on use by
    various classes of
    vehicles.
    Authority of highway
      director, §23-3-3.
Restrictions on use,
  §32-5A-92.
Rights of way upon entering,
  §§32-5A-110 to
  32-5A-112.
Litter.
Spilling loads or litter,
  §32-5-76.
Throwing of litter onto
  highway, §32-5A-60.
Livestock.
Running at large on
  highways.
  Liability of owner of
    livestock for collision
    with motor vehicle,
    §3-5-3.
Size and weight of vehicles
  transporting livestock.
  Exemptions from
    restrictions, §32-9-25.

MOTOR VEHICLES—Cont'd
Loading.
  Cables or chains.
    Loads which must be
      fastened by cables or
      chains, §32-5-75.
  Extension of load beyond
    rear of vehicle.
  Flag or light at end of
    load, §32-5-211.
  Flag or light at end of load,
    §32-5-211.
  Logs and lumber.
    Unloading logs, lumber,
      etc., on or near
      highways, §32-5-4.
  Obstructions to driver's view
    or driving mechanism,
    §32-5A-53.
  Ramps, platforms or other
    devices, §32-5-3.
  Removal of ramps, platforms
    and obstructions,
    §32-5-5.
  Size and weight of vehicles.
    General provisions,
      §§32-9-20 to 32-9-32.
    See within this
      heading, " Size and
      weight of vehicles."
  Spilling loads, §32-5-76.
Local authorities.
  Defined, §32-1-1.1.
  Highways.
    When rights to use
      highways may be
      restricted, §32-1-3.
  Licenses.
    No power to require
      additional license or
      permit, §32-5-1.
  Parking.
    Angle parking on roadway,
      §32-5A-138.
  Powers.
    Generally, §32-5-1.
  Regulation of traffic.
    Power to provide for by
      ordinance, §32-5-1.
  Speed.
    Power to pass, enforce or
      maintain speed
      ordinances, §32-5-1.
  Traffic-control devices.
    Highways under local
      jurisdiction, §32-5-31.
Lost or unclaimed property.
  Disposition of unclaimed
    articles left for service,
    §35-12-6.
Lotteries.
  Lottery paraphernalia.
    Transportation,
      §§13A-12-70 to
      13A-12-75.
Lumber.
  Loads which must be
    fastened by cables or
    chains, §32-5-75.
  Unloading on or near
    highways, §32-5-4.
Magistrates.
  Traffic infractions.
    Schedule of fines, ARJA,
      Rule 20.
Mail.
  Defined, §32-1-1.1.
  Lighting equipment and
    warning devices for
    vehicles engaged in mail
    service, §32-5-243.

MOTOR VEHICLES—Cont'd
Manufacturers.
  Dealings by manufacturers
    with dealers, §§8-20-1 to
    8-20-12.
  Citation of chapter,
    §8-20-1.
  Damages.
    Transportation damages,
      §8-20-9.
  Deceptive trade practices,
    §8-20-4.
  Declaration of purpose,
    §8-20-2.
  Definitions, §8-20-3.
  Franchise relationships.
    Limitations on
      cancellation,
      modification,
      terminations and
      nonrenewals,
      §8-20-5.
  Free association.
    Dealer's right of free
      association with
      other dealers,
      §8-20-10.
  Legislative purpose,
    §8-20-2.
  Limitation of actions,
    §8-20-12.
  Predelivery obligations,
    §8-20-6.
  Remedies, §8-20-11.
  Short title, §8-20-1.
  Time of accrual of cause of
    action, §8-20-12.
  Transportation damages,
    §8-20-9.
  Unfair and deceptive trade
    practices, §8-20-4.
  Warranty obligations of
    manufacturers and
    dealers to consumers,
    §8-20-8.
  Warranty obligations to
    dealers, §8-20-7.
  Definitions.
    Dealings by manufacturers
      with dealers, §8-20-3.
  Uniform certificate of title
    and antitheft act. See
    within this heading,
    "Uniform certificate of
    title and antitheft act."
  Warranty work on motor
    vehicles, §§32-17-1,
    32-17-2.
Markings.
  Signs, signals and markings,
    §§32-5A-30 to 32-5A-37.
    See within this heading,
    "Signs, signals and
    markings."
Mechanics.
  Liens.
    Production, manufacture or
      repair, §§35-11-110 to
      35-11-112.
Medal of honor recipients.
  Tags and plates, §§32-6-250
    to 32-6-255. See within
    this heading, "Tags and
    plates."
Medical advisory board.
  Drivers' license medical
    advisory board, §§32-6-40
    to 32-6-48. See within
    this heading, "Drivers'
    licenses."

MOTOR VEHICLES—Cont'd
Meeting of vehicles,
  §32-5A-81.
Mentally ill.
  Drivers' licenses.
    Persons to whom license
      not to be issued,
      §32-6-7.
Metal tires.
  Defined, §32-1-1.1.
Mileage.
  Renting and hiring.
    Fraudulent determination,
      §32-15-1.
    Tampering with mileage
      device, §32-15-3.
Military affairs.
  Drivers' licenses.
    Restricted licenses,
      §32-6-12.
  License tax.
    Exemptions, §31-2-12.
    Members of national
      guard or reserves,
      §40-12-244.
  Tags and plates for national
    guard, §§32-6-110 to
    32-6-114.
  Tags and plates for retired
    military, §§32-6-290 to
    32-6-295. See within this
    heading, "Tags and
    plates."
Milk and milk products.
  Size and weight of vehicles.
    Trucks or semi-trailers
      used for transportating
      milk.
      Exemption from size and
        weight
        requirements,
        §32-9-23.
Minors.
  Driver training schools.
    Persons under sixteen
      years of age operating
      motor vehicles,
      §32-5-64.
  Permitting persons under
    sixteen years of age to
    operate motor vehicles,
    §32-5-65.
  Persons under sixteen years
    of age operating motor
    vehicles.
    Prohibited, §32-5-64.
  Sexual offenses.
    Enticing child to enter
      vehicle for immoral
      purposes, §13A-6-69.
Mirrors.
  Distance reflected in mirror,
    §32-5-214.
  Required, §32-5-214.
  Towed vehicles.
    Mirror required, §32-5-214.
Misdemeanors.
  Appearance upon arrest for
    misdemeanor, §32-1-4.
  Disobedience of traffic laws,
    §32-5A-3.
  Fleeing or attempting to
    elude a police officer,
    §32-5A-193.
  Lights, lamps and reflective
    devices.
    Casting light on real
      property at night,
      §32-5-17.

MOTOR VEHICLES—Cont'd
Misdemeanors—Cont'd
Nonresidents.
International registration
plan.
Violations of provisions,
§40-12-262.
Penalties for misdemeanors
generally, §32-5A-8.
Police.
Fleeing or attempting to
elude, §32-5A-193.
Registration.
International registration
plan.
Violations of provisions,
§40-12-262.
Spilling loads or litter,
§32-5-76.
Tags and plates.
International registration
plan.
Violations of provisions,
§40-12-262.
Uniform certificate of title
and antitheft act,
§§32-8-13, 32-8-14.
Missiles.
Throwing or shooting deadly
or dangerous missile into
occupied vehicle,
§32-5-11.
Mobile homes.
Uniform certificate of title
and antitheft act.
Certificate of title,
§§32-8-30, 32-8-31.
Motorcycles.
See MOTORCYCLES.
Motor-driven cycles,
§§32-12-20 to 32-12-27.
See MOTORCYCLES.
Motor vehicle carriers,
§§37-3-1 to 37-3-34.
See MOTOR VEHICLE
CARRIERS.
Mountain highways.
Crest of grades.
Turning on, §32-5A-131.
Driving on, §32-5A-56.
Moving violations, §32-5-313.
Mufflers, §32-5-216.
Municipal corporations.
Abandoned motor vehicles.
Power of municipality not
restricted, §32-13-8.
Arrest made by municipal
officers.
Disposition of fines and
forfeitures, §32-5A-10.
Bridges.
Maximum speed on
bridges.
Signs stating maximum
speed, §32-5-92.
Codes of traffic regulations.
Adoption of technical codes
by reference, §11-45-8.
Elections.
Provision of automobiles,
etc., to bring voters to
polls, §11-44-52.
Highway and traffic safety
coordination act.
Powers of municipalities,
§32-4-7.

MOTOR VEHICLES—Cont'd
Municipal corporations
—Cont'd
Inspection.
Municipal testing stations,
§§32-18-1 to 32-18-8.
See within this
heading, "Municipal
testing stations."
Parking.
Power to regulate or
prohibit, §32-5-1.
Violation of municipal
ordinance, §32-5-152.
Powers generally, §32-5-1.
Regulation of running of
automobiles within
corporate limits,
§11-47-114.
Speed limits.
Bridges, §32-5-92.
Establishment within
corporate limits,
§11-49-4.
Posting of sign boards as to
municipal speed limits,
§11-49-5.
Tags.
Municipal vehicles,
§40-12-250.
Trucks, trailers and semi-
trailers.
Size and weight of
vehicles.
Exemption from article,
§32-9-22.
Violation of traffic ordinance
of incorporated
municipality.
Depositing driver's license
in lieu of bail, §32-1-5.
Municipal courts.
Traffic infractions.
Schedule of fines, ARJA,
Rule 20.
Municipal testing stations,
§§32-18-1 to 32-18-8.
Applicability.
Residents or persons who
maintain place of
business in city,
§32-18-7.
Compliance with ordinance.
Use of streets dependent
upon compliance,
§32-18-4.
Control of tests, §32-18-5.
Definitions, §32-18-1.
Expenses.
City may pay for testing
stations from earnings
or out of general fund,
§32-18-6.
Fees.
Power of city to fix amount
of fees, §32-18-3.
General fund.
City may pay for testing
stations from general
fund, §32-18-6.
Impoundment, §32-18-8.
Inspections.
Fee for inspection,
§32-18-3.
Inspections by owner
between inspection
period fixed by city,
§32-18-3.
Seizure and impoundment
of vehicles not
inspected, §32-18-8.

MOTOR VEHICLES—Cont'd
Municipal testing stations
—Cont'd
Inspections—Cont'd
Stickers.
Issuance, §32-18-4.
Liens.
Expenses incurred in
seizure and
impounding of
vehicles, §32-18-8.
Penalties.
Violations, §32-18-8.
Power of city to set up or
designate, §32-18-2.
Privately operated status.
Designation by city,
§32-18-2.
Residents or persons who
maintain place of
business in city.
Applicability, §32-18-7.
Rules and regulations.
Power of city to make,
§32-18-2.
Seizure of motor vehicle,
§32-18-8.
Stickers.
Approval by director of
public safety, §32-18-5.
Issuance, §32-18-5.
Placing on windshield,
§32-18-5.
Streets.
Use of streets dependent
upon compliance with
ordinance, §32-18-4.
Violations.
Penalties, §32-18-8.
Seizure of motor vehicle,
§32-18-8.
Narcotics.
Driving under the influence.
See within this heading,
"Driving under the
influence."
National guard.
Tags and plates, §§32-6-110
to 32-6-114.
Negligence.
Child passenger restraints.
Failure to wear restraint
system not considered
contributory
negligence, §32-5-222.
Safety-responsibility act.
Matters not to be evidence
in civil actions,
§32-7-12.
Noise.
Mufflers.
Required, §32-5-216.
**Nondriver identification
cards,** §32-6-1.
Nonresidents, §32-1-1.1.
Chemical tests for
intoxication, §32-5-192.
Drivers' licenses.
Persons exempt from
securing license,
§32-6-2.
International registration
plan, §40-12-262.
Misdemeanors.
International registration
plan.
Violations of provisions,
§40-12-262.

MOTOR VEHICLES—Cont'd
Nonresidents—Cont'd
Registration, §§40-12-262 to
40-12-264.
International registration
plan, §40-12-262.
Safety-responsibility act. See
within this heading,
"Safety-responsibility
act."
Tags and plates.
Effect of provisions relative
to display of tags,
§40-12-262.
International registration
plan, §40-12-262.
Misdemeanors.
Violations of
provisions,
§40-12-262.
Requirements,
§40-12-262.
Temporary trip permits,
§40-12-262.
Uniform certificate of title
and antitheft act,
§§32-8-2, 32-8-31.
Used car sales.
Registration of vehicles
brought into state by
nonresident dealers,
§32-16-2.
Notice.
Abandoned vehicles.
Posted notice, §32-13-1.
Removal.
Notice of removal,
§32-13-2.
Uniform certificate of title
and antitheft act.
Security interest,
§§32-8-66, 32-8-67.
Uniform traffic infractions.
Failure of defendant to
appear.
Issuance of additional
notice, ARJA, Rule
19.
Nuisances.
Lights, lamps and reflective
devices.
Casting light from motor
vehicle on real
property at night,
§32-5-17.
Numbers.
Vehicle identification
numbers.
Uniform certificate of title
and antitheft act. See
within this heading,
"Uniform certificate of
title and antitheft act."
Oaths.
Drivers' licenses.
Application under oath,
§32-6-4.
Obscenity.
Bumper stickers, etc.
Public display of obscene
sticker, §13A-12-131.
**Obscuring identity of
vehicle,** §13A-8-22.
Odometers.
Renting and hiring.
Tampering with odometer,
§32-15-3.
**Official traffic-control
devices,** §32-1-1.1.
One-way roadways,
§32-5A-87.

MOTOR VEHICLES—Cont'd
Operators' licenses, §§32-6-1
to 32-6-48. See within this
heading, "Drivers'
licenses."
Organ donors.
Anatomical gifts by holders
of drivers' licenses or
nondriver identification
cards, §§22-19-60,
22-19-61.
Specific gift to be noted on
license or card,
§22-19-60.
Oversized vehicles, §§32-9-20
to 32-9-32. See within this
heading, "Size and weight
of vehicles."
Overtaking and passing,
§§32-5A-81 to 32-5A-86.
Audible warning, §32-5A-82.
Bridges.
Limitations on passing,
§32-5A-85.
Curves.
Limitations on passing,
§32-5A-84.
Following too closely,
§32-5A-89.
Generally, §32-5A-82.
Giving way to overtaking
vehicle, §32-5A-82.
Horns.
Audible warning of
passing, §32-5A-82.
Lamps.
Auxiliary passing lamps,
§32-5-241.
Limitations on privilege,
§32-5A-84.
Meeting of vehicles,
§32-5A-81.
No passing zones, §32-5A-86.
Signs indicating,
§32-5A-86.
Overtaking on the right.
When permitted,
§32-5A-83.
Railroad grade crossings.
Limitations on passing,
§32-5A-85.
Tunnels.
Overtaking and passing,
§32-5A-85.
Vehicles proceeding in
opposite direction,
§32-5A-81.
Vehicles proceeding in same
direction, §32-5A-82.
Owners.
Defined, §32-1-1.1.
Real property.
Regulation of use of real
property by owner,
§32-5-2.
Traffic-control devices,
§32-5-2.
Transfer of ownership.
Uniform certificate of title
and antitheft act,
§§32-8-44 to 32-8-47.
Paraplegic drivers.
Distress flags, §§32-5-12 to
32-5-14.

MOTOR VEHICLES—Cont'd
Parent and child.
Safety-responsibility act.
Proof of financial
responsibility.
Owner may give proof
for member of
immediate family,
§32-7-28.
Parking.
Defined, §32-1-1.1.
General provisions. See
within this heading,
"Stopping, standing and
parking."
Parts.
Nonoriginal equipment
manufacturer
aftermarket crash parts,
§§32-17A-1 to 32-17A-3.
Definitions, §32-17A-1.
Disclosure, §32-17A-2.
Document, §32-17A-3.
Parts recyclers, §§40-12-410
to 40-12-425. See within
this heading, "Automotive
dismantlers and parts
recyclers."
Passenger cars.
Defined, §32-1-1.1.
Passengers.
Guest statute.
Liability for death or
injury of guest,
§32-1-2.
Interfering with driver's
control, §32-5A-53.
Number of passengers.
Obstructions to driver's
view or driving
mechanism, §32-5A-53.
Passing, §§32-5A-81 to
32-5A-86. See within this
heading, "Overtaking and
passing."
Pedestrians.
Alcoholic beverages.
Under influence of alcohol
or drugs, §32-5A-221.
Blind persons, §32-5A-220.
Guide dogs, §§21-7-6,
21-7-7.
White cane law, §§21-7-6,
21-7-7.
Business districts.
Prohibiting pedestrians
from crossing
roadways in business
districts, §32-5A-210.
Crosswalks.
Business districts.
Prohibiting pedestrians
from crossing
roadways in business
districts except by
crosswalks,
§32-5A-210.
Crossing at other than
crosswalks,
§32-5A-212.
Defined, §32-1-1.1.
Overhead pedestrian
crossings, §32-5A-212.
Pedestrians to use right
half of crosswalks,
§32-5A-214.
Right of way, §32-5A-211.
Stopping, standing and
parking.
Prohibited in specified
places, §32-5A-137.

MOTOR VEHICLES—Cont'd
Pedestrians—Cont'd
Crosswalks—Cont'd
Using right half of
crosswalks,
§32-5A-214.
Defined, §32-1-1.1.
Drivers to exercise due care
to avoid pedestrians,
§32-5A-213.
Drugs.
Under influence of alcohol
or drugs, §32-5A-221.
Emergency vehicles.
Pedestrians to yield right
of way, §32-5A-219.
Hitchhiking.
Prohibited, §32-5A-216.
Horns.
Warning pedestrians,
§32-5A-213.
Incapacitated persons,
§32-5A-220.
Intersections.
Pedestrians subject to
traffic control signals
at intersections,
§32-5A-210.
Limited-access highways.
Restrictions on use by
pedestrians, §32-5A-92.
Overhead pedestrian
crossings, §32-5A-212.
Police.
Right of way.
Pedestrians required to
yield, §32-5A-219.
Railroads.
Entry restricted by signals,
gates or barriers,
§32-5A-222.
Rights of way.
Crosswalks, §32-5A-211.
Yielding to pedestrian,
§32-5A-218.
Roadways.
Pedestrians on roadways
prohibited, §32-5A-215.
Signs, signals and markings.
Pedestrians subject to
signals at
intersections,
§32-5A-210.
Walk and wait signals,
§32-5A-33.
Traffic regulations.
Pedestrians subject to,
§32-5A-210.
Tunnels, §32-5A-212.
Warning by driver,
§32-5A-213.
Penalties.
Accident reports.
Failure to file, §§32-7-37,
32-10-6.
Automotive dismantlers and
parts recyclers.
Violations of article,
§40-12-424.
Commercial driver licenses.
Cumulative nature of
sanctions and
penalties, §32-6-49.21.
Disposition of penalties
collected, §32-5-313.
Driver education and
training fund.
Amounts collected credited
to fund, §32-5-313.

MOTOR VEHICLES—Cont'd
Penalties—Cont'd
Drivers' licenses.
Disposition of funds
collected, §32-6-18.
Violations generally,
§32-6-18.
Driver training schools.
Violations of chapter,
§32-14-6.
Driving under the influence,
§32-5A-191.
Embezzlement, conversion,
etc., of vehicles subject to
larceny, §32-15-7.
Failure to redeliver hired
vehicle, §32-15-6.
Felonies.
Penalties for felonies
generally, §32-5A-9.
Fines and forfeitures.
Controlled substance
violation, §20-2-93.
Disposition.
Generally, §32-5A-10.
Schedule, ARJA, Rule 20.
Traffic infractions.
Uniform traffic
infractions.
Payment of fines and
costs paid to clerk
of court, ARJA,
Rule 19.
Handicapped persons.
Distress flag for
handicapped or
paraplegic drivers.
Penalty for illegal use,
§32-5-14.
Hiring with intent to
defraud, §32-15-5.
Hit and run driving,
§32-10-6.
Misdemeanors.
Penalties for misdemeanors
generally, §32-5A-8.
Moving violations.
Additional penalty,
§32-5-313.
Municipal testing stations,
§32-18-8.
Obtaining possession by
trick, false
representation, etc.,
§32-15-4.
Personalized tags or plates.
Operation of motor vehicle
bearing tag or plate
not issued therefor or
transferred thereto,
§32-6-155.
Reckless driving, §32-5A-190.
Safety-responsibility act,
§32-7-37.
Sales and use tax.
Failure to pay, §40-23-110.
Schedule of fines for traffic
offenses, ARJA, Rule 20.
Signs, signals and markings.
Injuring signs, §32-5A-37.
Slow-moving vehicles.
Reflective devices on slow-
moving vehicles,
§32-5-251.
Temporary tags and
certificates, §32-6-219.
Traffic infractions.
Additional penalty,
§32-5-313.

MOTOR VEHICLES—Cont'd
Penalties—Cont'd
Traffic infractions—Cont'd
Uniform traffic infractions.
Fines and costs paid to
clerks of court,
ARJA, Rule 19.
Travel trailers.
Noncompliance with
provisions as to
registration fee and
identification tag,
§40-12-255.
Trucks, trailers and semi-
trailers.
Disposition of fines and
forfeitures, §32-9-6.
Violations of chapter,
§32-9-5.
Uniform certificate of title
and antitheft act,
§32-8-14.
Uniform traffic infractions.
Fines and costs paid to
clerks of court, ARJA,
Rule 19.
Used car sales.
Violations by vendors or
dealers, §32-16-4.
Violations of certain sections,
§32-5-312.
Warranty work on motor
vehicles.
Violations by
manufacturers or
dealers, §32-17-2.
Permits.
Certification permits issued
by state board of health.
Effect, §32-5A-194.1.
Oversized vehicles.
Permits for movement of
oversized vehicles,
§32-9-29.
Personal injuries.
Accidents, §32-10-1.
Plates, §§32-6-50 to 32-6-295.
See within this heading,
"Tags and plates."
Pleas.
Uniform traffic infractions.
Defendant's appearance.
Plea and waiver of trial,
ARJA, Rule 19.
Pneumatic tires.
Defined, §32-1-1.1.
Required, §32-5-210.
Tires generally. See within
this heading, "Tires."
Pole trailers.
Defined, §32-1-1.1.
Police.
Abandoned vehicles.
Responsibility of police,
§32-13-2.
Accidents.
Written reports of
accidents, §32-10-7.
Arrests. See within this
heading, "Arrests."
Chemical tests for
intoxication, §32-5-194.
Defined, §32-1-1.1.
Drivers of police vehicles.
Duty to drive safely,
§32-5A-115.
Fleeing or attempting to
elude a police officer,
§32-5A-193.

MOTOR VEHICLES—Cont'd
Police—Cont'd
Highway patrol. See within
this heading, "Highway
patrol."
Highways.
Closing of highways by
state trooper, §32-5-16.
Horns and warning devices,
§32-5-213.
Lights, lamps and reflective
devices, §32-5A-115.
Measuring and weighing
vehicles, §32-9-31.
Obedience to officers
required, §32-5A-4.
Pedestrians.
Right of way.
Pedestrians required to
yield, §32-5A-219.
Sirens, §32-5-213.
Speed limitations.
When speed limit not
applicable, §32-5A-7.
Stopping, standing and
parking.
Authority of police to move
vehicles stopped on
highways, §32-5A-139.
Certain privileges
available, §32-5A-7.
Stop signals and stop signs.
Authority to proceed
through signals or
signs, §32-5A-7.
Trucks, trailers and semi-
trailers.
Enforcement of chapter,
§32-9-3.
Uniform traffic infractions.
Uniform traffic ticket and
complaint.
Issuance of tickets to,
ARJA, Rule 19.
Accountability, ARJA,
Rule 19.
Pools.
State-owned vehicles,
§§4-17-3 to 4-17-7.
Presumptions.
Chemical test for
intoxication, §32-5A-194.
Stopping, standing and
parking.
Parking in violation of
municipal ordinances.
Presumption as to person
committing
violation, §32-5-152.
Prisoners of war.
Tags and plates.
Medal of honor recipients
and prisoners of war,
§§32-6-250 to 32-6-255.
See within this
heading, "Tags and
plates."
Private road or driveway.
Defined, §32-1-1.1.
Probate judges.
Drivers' licenses.
Duties as to. See within
this heading, "Drivers'
licenses."
License taxes and
registration fees.
Fee for issuing license,
§40-12-271.
Temporary tags and
certificates.
Issuance, §32-6-213.

MOTOR VEHICLES—Cont'd
Probate judges—Cont'd
Uniform certificate of title
and antitheft act,
§32-8-34.
Production.
Liens.
Production, manufacture
and repair,
§§35-11-110 to
35-11-112.
Proof of insurance.
Safety-responsibility act. See
within this heading,
"Safety-responsibility
act."
**Public officers and
employees.**
Insurance of state employees
operating motor vehicles
in performance of duties,
§36-1-6.
Public safety.
Department of public safety,
§§32-2-1 to 32-2-44. See
within this heading,
"Department of public
safety."
Pulpwood.
Loads which must be
fastened by cables or
chains, §32-5-75.
Racing.
Motor sports hall of fame
commission, §§41-9-470
to 41-9-478.
See MOTOR SPORTS
HALL OF FAME
COMMISSION.
Radio.
Amateur radio operators.
Tags and plates for,
§§32-6-70 to 32-6-73,
32-6-90 to 32-6-93. See
within this heading,
"Tags and plates."
Railroads.
Defined, §32-1-1.1.
Grade crossings.
Dangerous grade crossings.
Warning signs,
§32-5A-150.
Keep to the right in
crossing railroads,
§32-5-54.
Moving heavy equipment
at crossings,
§32-5A-152.
Overtaking and passing at
crossings, §32-5A-85.
Speed limits, §32-5A-170.
Warning signals,
§32-5A-151.
Moving heavy equipment at
grade crossings,
§32-5A-152.
Operation of transportation
methods for persons or
property by railroad
companies, §10-5-9.
Pedestrians.
Entry restricted by signals,
gates or barriers,
§32-5A-222.
Railroad sign or signal.
Defined, §32-1-1.1.
Railroad train.
Defined, §32-1-1.1.
Signals at grade crossings,
§32-5A-150.

MOTOR VEHICLES—Cont'd
Railroads—Cont'd
Stopping, standing and
parking.
Prohibited in specified
places, §32-5A-137.
Real property.
Lights, lamps and reflective
devices.
Casting light from motor
vehicle on real
property at night,
§32-5-17.
Regulation and use of real
property by owner.
Erection and maintenance
of traffic-control
devices, §32-5-2.
Rebuilders.
Dealers, reconditioners,
rebuilders and
wholesalers.
Licenses, §§40-12-390 to
40-12-400. See within
this heading,
"Licenses."
Reciprocal agreements.
Commercial driver licenses,
§32-6-49.18.
Drivers' licenses. See within
this heading, "Drivers'
licenses."
Registration of vehicles on
an apportionment or
allocation basis.
Powers of commissioner of
revenue as to
reciprocal agreements,
§32-6-56.
Reckless driving.
Generally, §32-5A-190.
Penalty, §32-5A-190.
Reconditioners.
Dealers, reconditioners,
rebuilders and
wholesalers.
Licenses, §§40-12-390 to
40-12-400. See within
this heading,
"Licenses."
Reconstructed vehicles.
Defined, §32-1-1.1.
Recordation.
Transfer of vehicle,
§40-12-260.
Fee for recording change of
ownership, §40-12-261.
Records.
Automotive dismantlers and
parts recyclers,
§40-12-419.
Change in ownership,
§40-12-260.
Convictions.
Director of public safety to
file, §32-6-14.
License taxes and
registration fees,
§§40-12-240 to 40-12-274.
See within this heading,
"License taxes and
registration fees."
Temporary tags and
certificates, §32-6-217.
Uniform certificate of title
and antitheft act. See
within this heading,
"Uniform certificate of
title and antitheft act."

MOTOR VEHICLES—Cont'd
  Reflective devices, §§32-5-240
    to 32-5-253. See within
    this heading, "Lights,
    lamps and reflective
    devices."
  Registration.
    Antique vehicles. See within
      this heading, "Antique
      vehicles."
    Apportionment or allocation
      basis.
      Reciprocal agreements
        with other states for
        registration.
        Powers of commissioner
          of revenue, §32-6-56.
    Defined, §32-1-1.1.
    Heavy motor vehicles.
      Applicants to furnish
        evidence of paying
        federal taxes, §32-6-58.
    International registration
      plan, §40-12-262.
    Misdemeanors.
      International registration
        plan.
        Violations of provisions,
          §40-12-262.
    National guard.
      Exemptions from
        registration fee,
        §31-2-12.
    Nonresidents.
      Effect of provisions relative
        to registration,
        §40-12-264.
      International registration
        plan, §40-12-262.
      Registration of certain
        commercial vehicles
        owned by nonresidents
        prohibited, §40-12-263.
      Used car sales.
        Registration of motor
          vehicles brought into
          state by nonresident
          dealers, §32-16-4.
    Plates, §§32-6-50 to 32-6-295.
      See within this heading,
      "Tags and plates."
    Reciprocal agreements for
      registration on an
      apportionment or
      allocation basis.
      Powers of commissioner of
        revenue, §32-6-56.
    Safety-responsibility act. See
      within this heading,
      "Safety-responsibility
      act."
    Staggered licensing,
      registration and
      taxation, §§32-6-60 to
      32-6-67.
    Stolen or converted vehicles.
      Suspension of registration,
        §32-8-84.
    Tags and plates, §§32-6-50 to
      32-6-295. See within this
      heading, "Tags and
      plates."
    Temporary license tags and
      registration certificates,
      §§32-6-210 to 32-6-218.
    Used car sales.
      Nonresident dealers.
        Registration of vehicles
          brought into state,
          §32-16-4.

MOTOR VEHICLES—Cont'd
  Renting and hiring, §§32-15-1
    to 32-15-8.
    Alcoholic beverages.
      Renting to intoxicated
        person, §32-15-2.
    Conversion of vehicle subject
      to larceny, §32-15-7.
    Delivery of hired vehicle.
      Failure to deliver,
        §32-15-6.
        Service of written
          demand, §32-15-6.
    Drugs.
      Renting to intoxicated
        person, §32-15-2.
    Embezzlement of vehicle
      subject to larceny,
      §32-15-7.
    Failure to redeliver hired
      vehicle, §32-15-6.
      Service of written demand,
        §32-15-6.
    Fraud.
      Hiring with intent to
        defraud, §32-15-5.
      Mileage, §32-15-1.
      Obtaining possession by
        trick, false
        representation, etc.,
        §32-15-4.
      Tampering with mileage
        device, §32-15-3.
    Intoxicated persons, §32-15-2.
    Licenses to lease or rent
      tangible personal
      property, §§40-12-220 to
      40-12-227.
      See PERSONAL
        PROPERTY.
    Mileage.
      Fraudulent determination
        of mileage, §32-15-1.
      Person hiring tampering
        with mileage device,
        §32-15-3.
      Obtaining possession by
        trick, false
        representation, etc.,
        §32-15-4.
    Odometer.
      Tampering with mileage
        device, §32-15-3.
    Permitting another to drive
      hired car, §32-15-8.
    Proof of financial
      responsibility, §32-7-36.
    Safety-responsibility act.
      Exceptions to act, §32-7-36.
  Repairs.
    Liens.
      Production, manufacture
        and repair,
        §§35-11-110 to
        35-11-112. See within
        this heading, "Liens."
    State-owned vehicles,
      §41-17-8.
    Warranty work on motor
      vehicles, §§32-17-1,
      32-17-2.
  Reports.
    Accident reports. See within
      this heading,
      "Accidents."
    Change in ownership,
      §40-12-260.
    Commercial driver licenses.
      Convictions, §32-6-49.14.

MOTOR VEHICLES—Cont'd
  Reports—Cont'd
    Drivers' licenses.
      Alabama driver license
        compact, §§32-6-31,
        32-6-35.
      Medical advisory board.
        Confidentiality, §32-6-43.
      Report of probate judge,
        §32-6-5.
      Safety-responsibility act. See
        within this heading,
        "Safety-responsibility
        act."
  Rescue squads.
    Distinctive license tags or
      plates for members'
      vehicles, §§32-6-170 to
      32-6-174.
    General provisions, §§32-11-1
      to 32-11-4.
  Residence district.
    Alley or driveway.
      Stopping before emerging
        from, §32-5A-153.
    Defined, §32-1-1.1.
  **Revocation of drivers'
    license.** See within this
    heading, "Drivers'
    licenses."
  Right side of highway.
    Driving on right side,
      §32-5A-80.
    Mountain highways.
      Driving on mountain
        highways, §32-5A-56.
    Rotary traffic islands.
      Passing in rotary traffic
        islands, §32-5A-87.
    Slow-moving vehicles,
      §32-5A-80.
  Rights of way.
    Defined, §32-1-1.1.
    Driveways.
      Exceptions to right-of-way
        rule, §32-5A-114.
    Emergency vehicles.
      Yielding right of way to
        emergency vehicles,
        §32-5A-219.
    Exceptions to right-of-way
      rule, §32-5A-114.
    Fire department vehicles.
      §32-5A-219.
    Highway construction and
      maintenance.
      Duty of driver on
        approach, §32-5A-116.
    Intersections.
      Approaching or entering
        intersections,
        §§32-5A-110 to
        32-5A-112.
    Limited-access highways,
      §§32-5A-110 to
      32-5A-112.
    Pedestrians.
      Yielding right of way to
        pedestrians,
        §32-5A-153.
      Yielding to rights of way,
        §32-5A-218.
    Police.
      Yielding right of way to
        police, §32-5A-219.
    Signs.
      Interstate or limited-access
        highways, §§32-5A-110
        to 32-5A-112.
  Road tractors.
    Defined, §32-1-1.1.

MOTOR VEHICLES—Cont'd
Rocks.
Spilling loads, §32-5-76.
Throwing rocks into occupied
vehicle, §32-5-11.
Rotary traffic islands.
Designation by highway
department, §32-5A-87.
Rules and regulations.
Commercial driver licenses,
§32-6-49.16.
Expired tags.
Operating vehicle with,
§32-6-219.
False statements on
application, §32-6-219.
Operating with expired tags,
§32-6-219.
Penalties, §32-6-219.
Speed.
Construction zones.
Rural and urban
construction zones,
§32-5A-176.1.
State board's of health
regulations.
Effect, §32-5A-194.1.
Temporary tags and
certificates, §32-6-218.
Rules of the road act,
§§32-5A-1 to 32-5A-266.
Applicability of chapter,
§32-5A-2.
Persons working on
highways excepted,
§32-5A-6.
Chapter deemed not
retroactive, §32-5A-12.
Citation, §32-5A-1.
Laws not repealed,
§32-5A-13.
Provisions deemed
cumulative, §32-5A-13.
Short title, §32-5A-1.
Safety.
Committee.
Safety coordinating
committee, §§32-3-1 to
32-3-7. See within this
heading, "Safety
coordinating
committee."
Department of public safety,
§§32-2-1 to 32-2-44. See
within this heading,
"Department of public
safety."
Highway and traffic safety
coordination act,
§§32-4-1 to 32-4-7. See
within this heading,
"Highway and traffic
safety coordination act."
Inspections.
Municipal testing stations,
§§32-18-1 to 32-18-8.
See within this
heading, "Municipal
testing stations."
Lights, lamps and reflective
devices, §§32-5-240 to
32-5-253. See within this
heading, "Lights, lamps
and reflective devices."
Loads.
Spilling loads, §32-5-76.
Municipal testing stations,
§§32-18-1 to 32-18-8. See
within this heading,
"Municipal testing
stations."

MOTOR VEHICLES—Cont'd
Safety—Cont'd
Reflective devices, §§32-5-240
to 32-5-253. See within
this heading, "Lights,
lamps and reflective
devices."
Safety-responsibility act,
§§32-7-1 to 32-7-42. See
within this heading,
"Safety-responsibility
act."
Seat belts. See within this
heading, "Seat belts."
Spilling loads or litter,
§32-5-76.
State safety coordinating
committee, §§32-3-1 to
32-3-7. See within this
heading, "Safety
coordinating committee."
Zones.
Defined, §32-1-1.1.
Driving through safety
zone prohibited,
§32-5A-217.
Safety belts. See within this
heading, "Seat belts."
**Safety coordinating
committee,** §§32-3-1 to
32-3-7.
Administrative expenses,
§32-3-5.
Chairman.
Governor to be chairman,
§32-3-1.
Composition, §32-3-1.
Driver education and
training program.
Allocation of funds by
committee to
department of
education or
educational
institutions, §32-3-7.
Establishment, §32-3-1.
Expenses.
Administrative expenses,
§32-3-5.
Funds.
Allocation of funds.
Generally, §§32-3-6,
32-3-7.
Governor.
Chairman, §32-3-1.
Highway and traffic safety
coordination act,
§§32-4-1 to 32-4-7. See
within this heading,
"Highway and traffic
safety coordination act."
Highway and traffic safety
programs.
Allocation of funds by
committee, §32-3-6.
Legislature.
Recommendations to
legislature for
enactment of laws,
§32-3-4.
Meetings.
Time of meetings, §32-3-2.
Members.
Ex officio members,
§32-3-1.
Terms of members, §32-3-1.
Problems to be specifically
studied, §32-3-3.
Purpose of meetings, §32-3-2.
Recommendations of
committee, §32-3-4.

MOTOR VEHICLES—Cont'd
**Safety coordinating
committee**—Cont'd
Terms of members, §32-3-1.
Safety glazing material.
Approved types of material,
§32-5-218.
Defined, §32-5-218.
Required, §32-5-218.
Vehicles needing safety
glazing material,
§32-5-218.
Safety-responsibility act,
§§32-7-1 to 32-7-42.
Accidents.
Death.
Reports required
following accidents
involving death,
§32-7-5.
Reports required following
accidents, §32-7-5.
Actions.
Chapter not to prevent
other actions,
§32-7-41.
Evidence.
Matters not to be
evidence in civil
actions, §32-7-12.
Administration of chapter.
Director of public safety to
administer, §32-7-3.
Expenses of administering
chapter, §32-7-39.
Appeals.
Assigned risk plans.
Persons denied insurance
under such plans,
§32-7-35.
Stays, §32-7-3.
When appeal may be
taken, §32-7-3.
Who may appeal, §32-7-3.
Written notice of appeal,
§32-7-3.
Assigned risk plans.
Appeals from denial,
§32-7-35.
Applicants, §32-7-35.
Apportionment among
insurance companies,
§32-7-35.
Approval by
superintendent of
insurance, §32-7-35.
Bonds, surety.
Security, §§32-7-6 to
32-7-11.
Certificate of insurance.
Cancellation of certificate.
Substitution of proof,
§32-7-29.
Defaults of insurance
carriers, §32-7-21.
Nonresidents.
Certificate furnished by
nonresident as proof,
§32-7-21.
Notice of cancellation or
termination of certified
policy, §32-7-24.
Proof of financial
responsibility.
Certificate as proof,
§32-7-20.
Self-insurers, §32-7-34.
Chapter not to affect other
policies, §32-7-25.
Chapter not to prevent other
process, §32-7-41.

MOTOR VEHICLES—Cont'd
Safety-responsibility act
   —Cont'd
   Chapter supplemental to
      other laws, §32-7-40.
   Citation, §32-7-1.
   Construction and
      interpretation.
      Uniformity of
         interpretation,
         §32-7-42.
   Courts.
      Nonpayment of judgments.
         Courts to report,
            §32-7-13.
   Damages.
      Matters not to be evidence
         in civil actions for
         damages, §32-7-12.
   Defaults by insurance
      carriers, §32-7-21.
   Definitions, §32-7-2.
   Director.
      Administration of chapter,
         §32-7-3.
      Defined, §32-7-2.
      Operating records.
         Director to furnish,
            §32-7-4.
      Suspension of licenses.
         When director to
            suspend, §32-7-6.
   Employers and employees.
      Employment of necessary
         employees to discharge
         duties imposed by
         chapter, §32-7-38.
      Proof of financial
         responsibility.
         Owner may give proof
            for employees,
            §32-7-28.
   Enforcement of chapter.
      Director of public safety to
         enforce, §32-7-3.
   Evidence.
      Civil actions.
         Matters not to be
            evidence in civil
            actions, §32-7-12.
   Exceptions, §32-7-36.
   Expenses.
      Administration of chapter,
         §32-7-39.
   Fees.
      Operating records.
         Furnishing of abstracts
            by director, §32-7-4.
   Husband and wife.
      Proof of financial
         responsibility.
         Owner may give proof
            for member of
            immediate family,
            §32-7-28.
   Judgments.
      Courts to report
         nonpayment of
         judgment, §32-7-13.
      Defined, §32-7-2.
      Failure to satisfy
         judgment.
         Bond as proof of
            financial
            responsibility.
            Actions against
               persons executing
               bonds, §32-7-26.
      Installment payment of
         judgments, §32-7-17.

MOTOR VEHICLES—Cont'd
Safety-responsibility act
   —Cont'd
   Judgments—Cont'd
      Nonpayment of judgments.
         Courts to report,
            §32-7-13.
         Suspension of license,
            registration or
            operating privilege,
            §32-7-14.
         Nonresidents,
            §32-7-14.
         Suspension to continue
            until judgments
            paid and proof
            given, §32-7-15.
      Nonresidents.
         Failure to satisfy
            judgments,
            §§32-7-13, 32-7-14.
      Payments sufficient to
         satisfy judgments,
         §32-7-16.
      Security.
         Payment of judgment
            with security
            deposits, §32-7-11.
      Self-insurers, §32-7-34.
   Negligence.
      Matters not to be evidence
         in civil actions,
         §32-7-12.
   Nonresidents.
      Application to
         nonresidents, §32-7-9.
      Certificate of insurance.
         Furnishing certificate as
            proof, §32-7-21.
      Defined, §32-7-2.
      Judgments.
         Failure to satisfy
            judgments,
            §§32-7-13, 32-7-14.
      Proof of financial
         responsibility.
         Certificate of insurance
            furnished as proof,
            §32-7-21.
   Operating records.
      Abstracts.
         Director to furnish,
            §32-7-4.
   Operators.
      Defined, §32-7-2.
   Owners.
      Defined, §32-7-2.
      Proof of financial
         responsibility.
         Owner may give proof
            for others, §32-7-28.
   Parent and child.
      Proof of financial
         responsibility.
         Owner may give proof
            for member of
            immediate family,
            §32-7-28.
   Penalties.
      Violations, §32-7-37.
   Policies.
      Cancellation or
         termination of certified
         policy, §32-7-24.
      Chapter not to affect other
         policies, §32-7-25.
      Coverage, §32-7-22.
      Motor vehicle liability
         policy.
         Defined, §32-7-22.

MOTOR VEHICLES—Cont'd
Safety-responsibility act
   —Cont'd
   Proof of financial
      responsibility.
      Additional proof may be
         required, §32-7-30.
      Alternate methods of
         giving proof, §32-7-19.
      Bond as proof, §32-7-26.
         Actions against persons
            executing bond for
            failure to satisfy
            judgment, §32-7-26.
      Certificate of insurance as
         proof, §32-7-20.
      Defined, §32-7-2.
      Duration of proof, §32-7-31.
      Employees.
         Owner may give proof
            for employees,
            §32-7-28.
      Failure to furnish proof.
         Surrender of license and
            registration,
            §32-7-33.
      Husband and wife.
         Owner may give proof
            for member of
            immediate family,
            §32-7-28.
      Money or securities as
         proof, §32-7-27.
         Return of money,
            §32-7-31.
      Owner may give proof for
         others, §32-7-28.
      Parent and child.
         Owner may give proof
            for member of
            immediate family,
            §32-7-28.
      Payment of judgments.
         Licenses or registration
            not to be suspended,
            §32-7-17.
      Registration of vehicles of
         person required to give
         proof, §32-7-19.
      Renting and hiring,
         §32-7-36.
      Required upon certain
         convictions, §32-7-18.
      Return or cancellation of
         proof.
         When proof may be
            cancelled or
            returned, §32-7-31.
      Securities as proof,
         §32-7-27.
         Return of securities,
            §32-7-31.
      Substitution of proof,
         §32-7-29.
      Suspension of license or
         registration.
         License or registration
            not to be suspended.
            When proof of
               financial
               responsibility is
               given, §32-7-18.
      Waiver of requirement of
         filing proof, §32-7-31.
      When proof may be
         cancelled or returned,
         §32-7-31.
   Registration.
      Defined, §32-7-2.

MOTOR VEHICLES—Cont'd
Safety-responsibility act
—Cont'd
Registration—Cont'd
Proof of financial
responsibility.
Registration of motor
vehicle of person
required to give
proof, §32-7-19.
Surrender of registration,
§32-7-33.
Suspension of registration.
Nonpayment of
judgments, §32-7-14.
Nonresidents,
§32-7-14.
Suspension to continue
until judgments
paid and proof
given, §32-7-15.
Persons operating
vehicles after
suspension.
Penalty, §32-7-37.
Proof of financial
responsibility.
Registration not to be
suspended upon
proof, §32-7-18.
Surrender upon
suspension, §32-7-33.
Transfer to defeat
purpose of chapter,
§32-7-32.
Transfer of registration to
defeat purpose of
chapter.
Prohibited, §32-7-32.
Unregistered motor
vehicles, §32-7-9.
Renting and hiring.
Exceptions to act, §32-7-36.
Repeal.
Chapter supplemental to
other laws, §32-7-40.
Reports.
Accidents.
Reports required
following accidents,
§32-7-5.
Matters not to be evidence
in civil actions,
§32-7-12.
Nonpayment of judgments.
Courts to report,
§32-7-13.
Rules and regulations.
Director of public safety to
make rules and
regulations for
administration,
§32-7-3.
Satisfaction of judgments.
Payment sufficient to
satisfy requirements,
§32-7-16.
Security.
Amount of security,
§32-7-10.
Custody, §32-7-11.
Deposits, §32-7-10.
Disposition, §32-7-11.
Exceptions, §32-7-6.
Further exceptions to
requirement of
security, §32-7-7.
Form of security, §32-7-10.
Person on whose behalf
deposit is made,
§32-7-10.

MOTOR VEHICLES—Cont'd
Safety-responsibility act
—Cont'd
Security—Cont'd
Reducing amount of
security.
Director may reduce,
§32-7-10.
Required, §32-7-6.
Return, §32-7-11.
Suspension of licenses.
Deposit of security upon
suspension, §32-7-8.
When security determined,
§32-7-6.
Self-insurers.
Certificate of insurance,
§32-7-34.
Who may qualify as self-
insurer, §32-7-34.
Suspension of licenses.
Duration of suspension,
§32-7-8.
Nonpayment of judgments,
§32-7-14.
Licenses not to be
suspended.
When judgment debtor
gives proof of
financial
responsibility,
§32-7-18.
Nonresidents, §32-7-14.
Suspension to continue
until judgments paid
and proof given,
§32-7-15.
Nonresidents, §32-7-9.
Persons operating vehicles
after suspension of
license.
Penalty, §32-7-37.
Proof of financial
responsibility.
License not to be
suspended when
proof given,
§32-7-18.
Security.
Deposit of security upon
suspension, §32-7-8.
Surrender of license upon
suspension, §32-7-33.
When director to suspend,
§32-7-6.
Uninsured motorists,
§32-7-23.
Defined, §32-7-23.
Limitations on recovery,
§32-7-23.
United States.
Vehicles owned by United
States.
Exceptions to chapter,
§32-7-36.
Violations, §32-7-37.
Penalties, §32-7-37.
Waiver.
Proof of financial
responsibility,
§32-7-31.
Sales.
Abandoned motor vehicles,
§§32-13-3 to 32-13-7.
Fee for recording change of
ownership, §40-12-261.
Lighting devices.
Approval required,
§32-5-252.

MOTOR VEHICLES—Cont'd
Sales—Cont'd
Lighting devices—Cont'd
Noncompliance with
requirements of
division, §32-5-253.
Record of transfer,
§40-12-260.
Restrictions on sales by
wholesalers,
reconditioners and
rebuilders, §40-12-392.
Seat belts.
Prohibited sales, §32-5-217.
Tires.
Unsafe tires, §32-5-210.
Used car sales. See within
this heading, "Used car
sales."
Salesmen.
Licenses, §40-12-52.
Sales tax, §40-23-2.
Applicability of general sales
tax provisions,
§40-23-105.
Automotive parts, §40-23-2.
Automotive vehicles, truck
trailers, etc., §40-23-101.
Collection before registration
or licensing, §40-23-104.
Definitions, §40-23-100.
Disposition of taxes collected,
§40-23-108.
Failure to pay.
Penalty, §40-23-110.
Fees for collection,
§40-23-107.
License commissioners.
Duties, §40-23-109.
Payment.
Proof of payment,
§40-23-104.
Proof of purchase price,
§40-23-104.
Reciprocity, §40-23-106.
Registration or licensing.
Prerequisite, §40-23-104.
Tax levied on gross receipts,
§40-23-2.
Trade-ins.
Sales tax levied on sales
price less credit for
trade-in, §40-23-103.
Trailers, §40-23-2.
Salvage.
Antitheft act, §32-8-87.
Scales. See within this
heading, "Size and weight
of vehicles."
School buses.
Defined, §32-1-1.1.
General provisions, §§16-27-1
to 16-27-7.
See EDUCATION.
Signal lights, §32-5A-155.
Schools.
Driver training schools,
§§32-14-1 to 32-14-24.
See within this heading,
"Driver training
schools."
**Scrapping, dismantling or
destroying vehicle.**
Automotive dismantlers,
§§40-12-410 to 40-12-425.
See within this heading,
"Automotive dismantlers
and parts recyclers."
Certificate of title, §32-8-49.

MOTOR VEHICLES—Cont'd
Searches and seizures.
Municipal testing stations.
Inspections.
Seizure and
impoundment of
uninspected vehicles,
§32-18-8.
Uniform certificate of title
and antitheft act.
Identifiable component
part, §32-8-86.
Seat belts.
Child passenger restraints.
Contributory negligence,
§32-5-222.
Penalty for violation,
§32-5-222.
Required for children
under six, §32-5-222.
Sales.
Prohibited sales, §32-5-217.
School buses, §16-27-6.
Specifications, §32-5-217.
Secondhand vehicles.
Used car sales, §§32-16-1 to
32-16-4.
Secured transactions.
Applicability of filing
provisions, §7-9-302.
Security agreements.
Uniform certificate of title
and antitheft act,
§§32-8-2 to 32-8-65.
Semi-trailers.
Defined, §32-1-1.1.
General provisions, §§32-9-1
to 32-9-32. See within
this heading, "Trucks,
trailers and semi-
trailers."
Motor vehicle carriers,
§§37-3-1 to 37-3-34.
See MOTOR VEHICLE
CARRIERS.
Serial number.
Obscuring serial number,
§13A-8-22.
Sexual offenses.
Minors.
Enticing child to enter
vehicle for immoral
purposes, §13A-6-69.
Sheriffs.
Tags and plates.
Amateur radio operators.
Lists to be furnished to
sheriff, §§32-6-72,
32-6-92.
Uniform certificate of title
and antitheft act,
§32-8-8.
**Shooting into occupied
vehicle,** §32-5-11.
Shops.
Licenses, §40-12-54.
Tire retreading shops,
§40-12-57.
Sidewalks.
Defined, §32-1-1.1.
Driving upon sidewalks
restricted, §32-5A-52.
Pedestrians.
When pedestrians allowed
on roadways,
§32-5A-215.
Stopping before driving onto
sidewalk, §§32-5A-153,
32-5A-218.

MOTOR VEHICLES—Cont'd
Sidewalks—Cont'd
Stopping, standing and
parking.
Prohibited in specified
places, §32-5A-137.
Signs, signals and markings,
§§32-5A-30 to 32-5A-37.
Approval, §32-5A-36.
Bridges.
Entry by pedestrians
restricted, §32-5A-222.
Municipal corporations.
Signs stating maximum
speed on bridges,
§32-5-92.
Commercial advertising.
Signs or signals bearing
commercial advertising
prohibited, §32-5A-36.
Defacing, §32-5A-37.
Emergency vehicles.
Authorized to proceed
through stop signals or
signs, §32-5A-7.
Fire vehicles.
Authorized to proceed
through stop signals or
signs, §32-5A-7.
Flashing signals, §32-5A-34.
Grade crossings.
Warning signals to be
obeyed, §32-5A-150.
Hand signals.
Method of giving,
§32-5A-135.
Starting, stopping and
turning, §§32-5A-133,
32-5A-134.
Highway construction or
repairs.
Working signs.
Speed limit, §32-5-93.
Highway department may
place signs prohibiting or
restricting, §32-5A-138.
Injuring signs, §32-5A-37.
Lane-direction-control
signals, §32-5A-35.
Laned roadways, §32-5A-88.
Left side of highway.
Driving in extreme left
side restricted.
Notice to director to
erect marker,
§32-5-77.
Local authorities.
Power to provide for
regulation of traffic by
local ordinance,
§32-5-1.
Minimum speed regulations,
§32-5A-174.
Necessity for signs,
§32-5A-31.
Obedience generally,
§32-5A-31.
Overtaking and passing.
No passing zones,
§32-5A-86.
Parking prohibitions.
Highway department may
erect signs,
§32-5A-138.
Pedestrians.
Subject to traffic control
signals at
intersections,
§32-5A-210.
Walk and wait signals,
§32-5A-33.

MOTOR VEHICLES—Cont'd
Signs, signals and markings
—Cont'd
Police.
Authorized to proceed
through stop signals or
signs, §32-5A-7.
Railroad sign or signal.
Defined, §32-1-1.1.
Entry by pedestrians
restricted, §32-5A-222.
Warning signals at
crossings, §§32-5A-150,
32-5A-151.
Real property.
Owner to erect and
maintain, §32-5-2.
Restrictions on highway use.
Erection and maintenance
of signs, §32-1-3.
Rights of way.
Interstate or limited-access
highways, §§32-5A-110
to 32-5A-112.
Sale of signs, signals or other
devices not conforming to
provisions of section,
§32-5A-36.
Signal lamps and signal
devices, §32-5-241.
Speed limitations.
Construction zones.
Urban and rural
construction zones,
§32-5A-176.1.
Minimum speed
regulations,
§32-5A-174.
Municipalities, §11-49-5.
Starting, stopping and
turning, §§32-5A-133,
32-5A-134.
Stopping, standing and
parking.
Prohibited in specified
places, §32-5A-137.
Stop signs.
Through highways,
§32-5A-113.
Submission to highway
director for approval,
§32-5A-36.
Tests, §32-5A-36.
Through highways.
Stopping at certain
through highways,
§32-5A-113.
Traffic-control devices.
Colors used, §32-5-31.
Defined, §32-1-1.1.
Legend.
Colors used, §32-5A-32.
Local authorities, §32-5-31.
Jurisdiction, §32-5-31.
Obedience, §32-5A-31.
Traffic-control signal.
Defined, §32-1-1.1.
Turn signals, §§32-5A-133,
32-5A-134.
Unauthorized signs, markers,
etc.
Use, §32-5A-36.
Visibility.
Signs must be sufficiently
legible, §32-5A-31.
Walk and wait signals,
§32-5A-33.
Working signs.
Speed limit between signs,
§32-5-93.

MOTOR VEHICLES—Cont'd
Sirens.
Emergency vehicles,
§32-5-213.
Prohibited, §32-5-213.
Size and weight of vehicles,
§§32-9-20 to 32-9-32.
Axle spacing requirements,
§32-9-20.
Bridges.
Rules and regulations.
Promulgation by
highway
department,
§23-1-59.
Weight on bridges,
§32-9-20.
Evidence.
Scales.
Certificate of approval as
prima facie evidence,
§32-9-32.
Exemptions, §§32-9-22 to
32-9-25.
Cotton.
Trucks, trailers or semi-
trailers carrying
cotton, §32-9-22.
Farm tractors, §32-9-24.
Generally, §32-9-22.
Implements of husbandry,
§32-9-22.
Livestock.
Vehicles transporting,
§32-9-25.
Milk transporters,
§32-9-23.
Municipal corporations.
Trucks, trailers or semi-
trailers licensed by
municipal
corporations,
§32-9-22.
Steel.
Vehicles transporting
steel, §32-9-25.
Trees and timber.
Vehicles transporting,
§32-9-25.
Two to eight wheel, one to
four-axle trailers,
§32-9-26.
Farm tractors.
Exemptions, §32-9-24.
Gross weight.
Defined, §32-1-1.1.
Height, §32-9-20.
Implements of husbandry.
Exemption from article,
§32-9-22.
Length, §32-9-20.
Livestock.
Vehicles transporting
livestock.
Exemptions from
restrictions of
article, §32-9-25.
Load and weight limits.
Unloading vehicles to
decrease gross weight,
§32-9-31.
When highway department
may prescribe load and
weight limits, §32-1-3.
Measuring and weighing
vehicles, §32-9-31.
Refusal of operator to have
truck or trailer
measured or weighed,
§32-9-31.

MOTOR VEHICLES—Cont'd
Size and weight of vehicles
—Cont'd
Milk trucks.
Exemption from size and
weight requirements,
§32-9-23.
Motor bus.
Defined, §32-9-21.
Maximum permissible
length and width,
§32-9-21.
Municipal corporations.
Trucks, trailers or semi-
trailers licensed by
municipal
corporations.
Exemption from article,
§32-9-22.
Oversized vehicles.
Permits for movement.
Bonds, surety.
Condition for issuance,
§32-9-29.
Cost, §32-9-29.
Designation of routes.
Director of highway
department may
designate,
§32-9-29.
Issuance, §32-9-29.
Renewal, §32-9-29.
Police.
Measuring and weighing
vehicles, §32-9-31.
Restrictions.
Schedule of restrictions,
§32-9-20.
When local authorities
may impose
restrictions, §32-1-3.
Rules and regulations.
Promulgation by highway
department, §23-1-59.
Scales.
Certificate of approval,
§32-9-32.
Prima facie evidence,
§32-9-32.
Director of highway
department to furnish,
§32-9-32.
Expensive weighing
vehicles, §32-9-32.
Portable scales, §32-9-20.
Schedule of restrictions,
§32-9-20.
Steel.
Vehicles transporting steel.
Exemptions from
restrictions of
article, §32-9-25.
Trees and timber.
Vehicles transporting.
Exemption from
restrictions of
article, §32-9-25.
Two to eight wheel, one to
four-axle trailers,
§§32-9-26 to 32-9-28.
Equipment, §32-9-27.
Size of trailer, §32-9-27.
Transporting agricultural
commodities.
Exemptions from
restrictions of
article, §32-9-26.
Violations.
Misdemeanor, §32-9-28.
Weight of trailer and load,
§32-9-26.

MOTOR VEHICLES—Cont'd
Size and weight of vehicles
—Cont'd
Two to eight wheel, one to
four-axle trailers—Cont'd
Width, §32-9-27.
United States.
Trucks, trailers or semi-
trailers owned by
United States.
Exempt from article,
§32-9-22.
Weight, §32-9-20.
Gross weight table,
§32-9-20.
Width, §32-9-20.
Slag.
Spilling loads, §32-5-76.
Slow-moving vehicles.
Laned highways.
Signs indicating laned or
slow-moving traffic,
§32-5A-88.
Reflective devices for slow-
moving vehicles,
§§32-5-246 to 32-5-250.
Animals.
Exceptions as to ridden
animals, §32-5-249.
Bicycles.
Exceptions as to bicycles,
§32-5-249.
Design, §32-5-246.
Height above ground,
§32-5-247.
Mounting, §32-5-247.
Other provisions not
repealed, §32-5-250.
Penalties for violations,
§32-5-251.
Repeal.
Other provisions not
repealed, §32-5-250.
Required, §32-5-246.
Restrictions on use,
§32-5-248.
Violations.
Penalty for violations,
§32-5-251.
Right side of highways,
§32-5A-80.
Smoke.
Preventing escape of
excessive fumes or
smoke, §32-5-216.
Snowmobiles.
Operation limited, §32-5A-62.
Sodomy.
Minors.
Enticing child to enter
vehicle for immoral
purposes, §13A-6-69.
Solicitation.
Soliciting rides, §32-5A-216.
**Specially constructed
vehicles.**
Defined, §32-1-1.1.
Special mobile equipment.
Defined, §32-1-1.1.
Speed.
Alteration of maximum
limits, §32-5A-173.
Ambulances.
When speed limit not
applicable, §32-5A-7.

MOTOR VEHICLES—Cont'd
Speed—Cont'd
Arrest.
Measuring devices.
Officer operating.
Violation
communicated to
other officer,
§32-5A-177.
Bridges.
Special speed limitations
on bridges, §§32-5-92,
32-5A-176.
Business districts,
§32-5A-170.
Construction zones.
Urban and rural
construction zones,
§32-5A-176.1.
Curves.
Restrictions as to speed,
§32-5A-170.
Driver's license.
Notation of conviction on
license, §32-5-97.
Emergency vehicles.
When speed limit not
applicable, §32-5A-7.
Exemptions, §32-5A-7.
Explosives or flammable
liquids.
Passenger vehicles, motor
trucks or passenger
buses carrying or
transporting.
Maximum speed,
§32-5A-171.
Fire vehicles.
When speed limit not
applicable, §32-5A-7.
Governor.
Maximum speeds.
Governor authorized to
prescribe,
§32-5A-171.
Intersections.
Approaching intersections,
§32-5A-170.
Interstate highways.
Speed limits, §32-5A-171.
Local authorities.
Power of local authorities
to pass, enforce or
maintain regulations
of speed, §32-5-1.
Maximum speed limits,
§32-5A-171.
Measuring devices.
Officer operating.
Violation communicated
to other officer.
Arrest for, §32-5A-177.
Testimony derived from
use, §32-5A-177.
Minimum speed regulations.
Establishment, §32-5A-174.
Municipal corporations.
Bridges, §32-5-92.
Establishment of speed
limits within corporate
limits, §11-49-4.
Posting of signboards as to
municipal speed limits,
§11-49-5.
Police.
When speed limit not
applicable, §32-5A-7.
Railroad grade crossings.
Restrictions as to speed on
approach, §32-5A-170.

MOTOR VEHICLES—Cont'd
Speed—Cont'd
Residence districts,
§32-5A-171.
Restrictions as to speed in
certain locations,
§32-5A-170.
Rules and regulations.
Construction zones.
Rural and urban
construction zones,
§32-5A-176.1.
Schools.
Speed limits upon passing
schools, §32-5A-170.
Signs.
Construction zones.
Urban and rural
construction zones,
§32-5A-176.1.
Minimum speed,
§32-5A-174.
Posting of signboards as to
municipal speed limits,
§11-49-5.
State troopers.
When speed limit not
applicable, §32-5A-7.
Trucks.
Maximum speeds,
§32-5A-171.
Urban districts.
Speed limitations,
§32-5A-171.
Violations.
Generally, §32-5A-177.
Measuring devices.
Officer operating.
Arrest for violation
communicated to
other officer,
§32-5A-177.
Notation of conviction on
driver's license,
§32-5-97.
Penalties for violations,
§32-5A-177.
Summons to specify speed,
§32-5A-177.
When speed limit not
applicable, §32-5A-7.
Working signs.
Speed limit between
working signs,
§32-5-93.
Zones.
Establishment of state
speed zones,
§32-5A-172.
Spilling loads or litter,
§32-5-76.
Spotlighting, §32-5-17.
**Staggered licensing,
registration and
taxation,** §§32-6-60 to
32-6-67.
Centralized registration
prohibited, §32-6-65.
Change of county of
residence, §32-6-63.
Construction of subdivision,
§32-6-66.
Determination of month.
Individual's last name
determines, §32-6-61.
Trucks and commercial
vehicles, §32-6-61.
Duration of validity of plates,
§32-6-62.
Effective date, §32-6-60.

MOTOR VEHICLES—Cont'd
Staggered licensing,
registration and taxation
—Cont'd
Fees.
Proration during
implementation period,
§32-6-60.
Forms.
Uniform registration
renewal form,
§32-6-65.
Implementation period,
§32-6-60.
Individual's last name
determines month,
§32-6-61.
Legislative oversight
committee, §32-6-67.
Penalties.
Registration penalty,
§32-6-65.
Plates, §§32-6-62 to 32-6-64.
Characters designate
county of issuance,
§32-6-64.
Design.
Regulations of revenue
commissioner,
§32-6-64.
Duration of validity,
§32-6-62.
Handicapped persons.
Special plates, §32-6-64.
Handling and distribution,
§32-6-64.
Tabs and stamps in lieu of
plates, §32-6-63.
Proration, §32-6-61.
Purchased vehicles.
Reregistration, §32-6-61.
Registration.
Centralized registration
prohibited, §32-6-65.
Late registration penalty,
§32-6-65.
Uniform registration
renewal form,
§32-6-65.
Residence.
Changing county of
residence, §32-6-63.
Tabs and stamps.
Use in lieu of license
plates, §32-6-63.
Trucks and commercial
vehicles.
Determination of month,
§32-6-61.
Uniform registration renewal
form, §32-6-65.
Standing. See within this
heading, "Stopping,
standing and parking."
**Starting, stopping and
turning.**
Safety requirements for
starting parked vehicle,
§32-5A-132.
Signals required,
§§32-5A-133, 32-5A-134.
Stopping, standing and
parking. See within this
heading, "Stopping,
standing and parking."
State.
Defined, §32-1-1.1.

MOTOR VEHICLES—Cont'd
State coordinating committee.
Chairman.
Governor to be chairman, §32-3-1.
State-owned vehicles, §§41-17-1 to 41-17-9.
Alteration, etc., of license plate affixed to state vehicle, §41-17-9.
Area transportation pools.
Establishment, operation, etc., §41-17-6.
Fees and charges.
Disposition of fees collected for use of pool cars, §41-17-5.
Establishment of mileage fees and charges for use of pool cars, §41-17-3.
Funds.
Establishment of transportation revolving fund, §41-17-5.
License plates, §40-12-250.
Alteration, etc., §41-17-9.
Maintenance, §41-17-8.
Passenger automobiles.
Purchase for or assignment to state officers or employees, §41-17-2.
Pool, §§41-17-3 to 41-17-7.
Area transportation pools.
Establishment, operation, etc., §41-17-6.
Fees and charges.
Disposition of fees collected for use of pool cars, §41-17-5.
Establishment of mileage fees and charges for use of pool cars, §41-17-3.
Maintenance of transportation pool in city of Montgomery by department of finance, §41-17-3.
Number of automobiles to be kept in pool, §41-17-4.
Operation of pool, §41-17-3.
Rules and regulations.
Promulgation for provision of parking and storage for pool, etc., by director of finance, §41-17-7.
Self-supporting.
Transportation pool to be self-supporting, §41-17-5.
Repair, §41-17-8.
Rules and regulations.
Promulgation for provision of parking and storage for pool, etc., by director of finance, §41-17-7.
Standards, §41-17-1.
Tags, §40-12-250.
Alteration, etc., §41-17-9.
Unauthorized use, etc., §41-17-9.

MOTOR VEHICLES—Cont'd
State police.
Highway patrol. See within this heading, "Highway patrol."
State safety coordinating committee, §§32-3-1 to 32-3-7. See within this heading, "Safety coordinating committee."
State toxicologist.
Safety coordinating committee.
Member of committee, §32-3-1.
State treasurer.
Surety insurance.
Sole surety.
Cosureties on bond of state treasurer, §27-24-4.
State troopers. See within this heading, "Highway patrol."
Steel.
Size and weight of vehicles transporting structural steel.
Exemptions from restrictions, §32-9-25.
Stickers.
Inspection stickers. See within this heading, "Municipal testing stations."
Stopping, standing and parking.
Alleys.
Stopping before emerging from alley, §§32-5A-153, 32-5A-218.
Angle parking, §32-5A-138.
Church buses.
Approaching church bus, §32-5A-154.
Defined, §32-1-1.1.
Disabled vehicles, §32-5A-136.
Driveways.
Prohibited in specified places, §32-5A-137.
Stopping before emerging from alley or private driveway, §32-5A-153.
Emergency vehicles.
Certain privileges available, §32-5A-7.
Fires and fire prevention.
Certain privileges available, §32-5A-7.
Fire stations.
Prohibited in specified places, §32-5A-137.
Grade crossings.
Failure to bring vehicle to complete stop before traversing grade crossing, §32-5A-150.
Handicapped persons.
Agreements with other states as to parking privileges, §32-6-234.
Unauthorized use of handicapped parking place, §32-6-233.1.
Unlimited parking periods, §32-6-232.
Highways.
Parking on highways, §32-5A-136.

MOTOR VEHICLES—Cont'd
Stopping, standing and parking—Cont'd
Intersections.
Prohibited in specified places, §32-5A-137.
Lights on parked vehicles, §32-5-244.
Municipal corporations.
Applicability of provisions, §11-61-3.
Authority of towns and cities with respect to parking facilities, §11-61-2.
Definitions, §11-61-1.
Off-street parking facilities, §§11-47-240 to 11-47-243.
Parking in violation of municipal ordinances, §32-5-152.
Presumption as to person committing violation, §32-5-152.
Uniform traffic infractions.
Municipal parking offenses, ARJA, Rule 19.
Power to regulate or prohibit parking of vehicles, §32-5-1.
Uniform traffic infractions.
Municipal parking offenses, ARJA, Rule 19.
Parallel parking, §32-5A-138.
Police.
Certain privileges available, §32-5A-7.
Vehicles standing upon highways.
Authority to move, §32-5A-139.
Prohibited in specified places, §32-5A-137.
Railroad grade crossings.
Failure to come to a stop, §§32-5A-150, 32-5A-151.
Prohibited in specified places, §32-5A-137.
School buses.
Approaching school bus or vehicle, §32-5A-154.
Sidewalks.
Prohibited in specified places, §32-5A-137.
Stopping before emerging onto sidewalk, §32-5A-153.
Signals of starting, stopping and turning, §32-5A-133.
Signs, signals and markings.
Prohibited in specified places, §32-5A-137.
Starting parked vehicle.
Safe movement required, §32-5A-132.
Through highways.
Stopping at through highways required, §32-5A-113.
Unattended vehicles, §32-5A-50.
Unclaimed vehicles.
Operators of parking lots.
Reports of unclaimed vehicles, §32-8-84.

MOTOR VEHICLES—Cont'd
Stopping, standing and parking—Cont'd
Uniform traffic infractions.
Municipal parking offenses, ARJA, Rule 19.
Stop signs, §32-5A-113.
Storage.
Licenses.
Storage garages, §40-12-55.
Storage other than in garages, §40-12-56.
Streets.
Defined, §32-1-1.1.
Summons and process.
Speed limitations.
Violations of speed limitations.
Summons to specify speed, §32-5A-177.
Uniform traffic infractions.
Complaint and summons, ARJA, Rule 19.
Suspension of drivers' license. See within this heading, "Drivers' licenses."
Tags and plates, §§32-6-50 to 32-6-295.
Alteration of tags, §40-12-265.
Amateur radio operators, §§32-6-70 to 32-6-73, 32-6-90 to 32-6-93.
Amateur radio operators licensed by civil air patrol, §§32-6-90 to 32-6-93.
Department of revenue.
Rules and regulations, §32-6-91.
Issuance of special tags, §32-6-90.
Lists to be furnished to sheriff, §32-6-92.
Provisions supplemental, §32-6-93.
Rules and regulations, §32-6-91.
Sheriff.
Lists to be furnished to sheriff, §32-6-92.
Fee, §32-6-70.
Additional fee, §32-6-70.
Issuance of special tags, §32-6-70.
Lists to be furnished to sheriff, §32-6-72.
Licensed by civil air patrol, §32-6-92.
Provisions supplemental, §32-6-73.
Rules and regulations.
Department of revenue to make rules and regulations, §32-6-71.
Sheriff.
Lists to be furnished to sheriff, §32-6-72.
Antique vehicles, §§40-12-290 to 40-12-296.
See within this heading, "Antique vehicles."
Antitheft laws.
Removed, falsified or unauthorized identification number, registration or license date, §32-8-86.

MOTOR VEHICLES—Cont'd
Tags and plates—Cont'd
Attachments.
Manufacturing specifications for license tags or plates, §32-6-57.
Automotive dismantlers and parts recyclers.
Plates from dismantled vehicles to be forwarded to department of revenue, §40-12-423.
Certificate of title.
Certificate prerequisite to issuance of license plates, §32-8-32.
Refusal to issue certificate.
Return of tags upon refusal to issue, §32-8-38.
Citizens' band radio, §§32-6-70 to 32-6-73, 32-6-90 to 32-6-93.
Commissioner of revenue.
Rules and regulations.
Power of commissioner to make rules and regulations, §32-6-53.
Construction and interpretation.
Provisions cumulative, §32-6-295.
County vehicles, §40-12-250.
Dealers' tags, §40-12-264.
Design.
Specifications for design, §32-6-133.
Tag to show heart and words "Heart of Dixie," §32-6-54.
Destruction or wreckage of vehicle, §40-12-266.
Disabled veterans, §§32-6-130 to 32-6-133.
Design of special plates, §32-6-130.
Fee, §32-6-130.
Issuance of special plates, §32-6-130.
Provisions supplementary, §32-6-132.
Rules and regulations.
Commissioner of revenue to make, §32-6-131.
Specifications for design, §32-6-133.
Transferability, §32-6-130.
Use.
Wrongful use, §32-6-131.
Wrongful acquisition or use, §32-6-131.
Enforcement of certain sections, §40-12-272.
Federal performance standards.
Minimum standards to be met, §32-6-57.
Fire fighters, §§32-6-270 to 32-6-274.
Authorized, §32-6-271.
Definitions, §32-6-270.
Distinctive plate or tag authorized, §32-6-271.
Fees.
Additional fee, §32-6-272.
Form, §32-6-271.
Issuance, §32-6-272.

MOTOR VEHICLES—Cont'd
Tags and plates—Cont'd
Fire fighters—Cont'd
Lists of eligible fire fighters, §32-6-272.
Newly acquired vehicles.
Transfer of plates, §32-6-273.
Nontransferability, §32-6-273.
Plates furnished for licensing year commencing January 1, 1984 and thereafter, §32-6-274.
Preparation, §32-6-272.
Use of plates or tags, §32-6-272.
Foreign consuls.
Special plates for private passenger vehicles, §40-12-243.
Handicapped persons.
Distinctive license plate decals, §§32-6-230 to 32-6-234.
Agreements with other states as to parking privileges, §32-6-234.
Authorized, §32-6-231.
Definition, §32-6-230.
False representations to obtain, §32-6-233.
Misuse of privileges, §32-6-233.
Parking.
Unlimited parking periods, §32-6-232.
Prerequisite, §32-6-231.
Temporary identification placard, §32-6-231.
Distinctive license plates, §§40-12-300 to 40-12-302.
Applications, §40-12-300.
Design, §40-12-302.
Display.
No requirement to display, §40-12-300.
Fees, §40-12-300.
Issuance, §40-12-300.
Standard license plates, §40-12-301.
Transfer, §40-12-301.
"Heart of Dixie" to be shown on tag, §32-6-54.
Improper classification.
Using license tag of improper classification, §32-6-52.
Improper tags.
Use, §40-12-265.
International registration plan, §40-12-262.
Issuance.
Limitations, §32-6-292.
Licensing year, §32-6-294.
Manufacturing specifications, §32-6-57.
Medal of honor recipients and prisoners of war, §§32-6-250 to 32-6-255.
Construction and interpretation, §32-6-253.
Distinctive plate authorized, §§32-6-250, 32-6-251.

MOTOR VEHICLES—Cont'd
Tags and plates—Cont'd
Medal of honor recipients
and prisoners of war
—Cont'd
Fees.
No fee required,
§32-6-250.
Fraud in obtaining,
§32-6-253.
National guard and air
national guard plates.
Applicability of
provisions
concerning,
§32-6-254.
Rules and regulations,
§32-6-255.
Surviving spouse.
Use by, §32-6-254.
Transfer of plates,
§32-6-252.
Use and transferability,
§32-6-254.
Use by surviving spouse,
§32-6-254.
Violations of provisions,
§32-6-253.
Misdemeanors.
International registration
plan.
Violations of provisions,
§40-12-262.
Municipal vehicles,
§40-12-250.
Mutilation of tags,
§40-12-265.
National guard, §§32-6-110
to 32-6-114.
Applicants for distinctive
plates, §32-6-111.
Authority for distinctive
plates or tags,
§32-6-110.
Color, §32-6-110.
Design, §32-6-110.
Distinctive national guard
license tags, §31-2-12.
Issuance, §32-6-111.
Licensing year, §32-6-113.
Number of plates required.
Adjutant general to
estimate number of
plates, §32-6-113.
Permanence of plates,
§32-6-254.
Preparation, §32-6-111.
Probate judge.
Issuance, §32-6-111.
Proof of membership.
Submission of proof by
applicant, §32-6-111.
Provisions supplementary,
§32-6-114.
Transferability, §32-6-112.
Use, §32-6-111.
Nonresidents.
Effect of provisions relative
to display of tags,
§40-12-262.
International registration
plan, §40-12-262.
Misdemeanors.
Violations of
provisions,
§40-12-262.
Requirements,
§40-12-262.
Temporary trip permits,
§40-12-262.

MOTOR VEHICLES—Cont'd
Tags and plates—Cont'd
Personalized tags or plates.
Application, §32-6-150.
Department of revenue.
Promulgation of rules
and regulations,
§32-6-151.
Fees, §32-6-150.
Disposition, §32-6-156.
Issuance.
Generally, §32-6-150.
Issuance of identical tags
or plates, §32-6-153.
Operation of motor vehicle
bearing tag or plate
not issued therefor or
transferred thereto,
§32-6-155.
Rules and regulations.
Promulgation by
department of
revenue, §32-6-151.
Transfer.
Generally, §32-6-154.
Troy State University
commemorative tags,
§32-6-150.
Violation.
Operation of motor
vehicles bearing tag
or plate not issued
therefor or
transferred thereto,
§32-6-155.
Placement of license tags,
§40-12-258.
Prisoners of war, §§32-6-250
to 32-6-255.
Provisions cumulative,
§32-6-295.
Rear tags.
Required, §32-6-51.
Replacement tags,
§40-12-265.
Rescue squad members,
§§32-6-170 to 32-6-174.
Authorized, §32-6-171.
Distinctive lettering,
§32-6-171.
Issuance, §32-6-172.
Licensing year, §32-6-174.
Preparation, §32-6-172.
Proof to be submitted by
applicant, §32-6-172.
Transferability, §32-6-173.
Use, §32-6-172.
"Volunteer rescue squad"
defined, §32-6-170.
Rescue squad vehicles.
Special tags, §32-11-4.
Retired military, §§32-6-290
to 32-6-292.
Authorization of distinctive
plates, §32-6-291.
Defined, §32-6-290.
Distinctive plates.
Authorized, §32-6-291.
Fees, §32-6-292.
Issuance.
Procedure, §32-6-292.
Rules and regulations.
Commissioner of revenue
to make, §32-6-53.
Enforcement of certain
sections, §40-12-272.
Medal of honor recipients
and prisoners of war,
§32-6-255.

MOTOR VEHICLES—Cont'd
Tags and plates—Cont'd
Sale or transfer of vehicle.
Tags remain with vehicle,
§40-12-260.
Specifications for design,
§32-6-133.
Staggered licensing,
registration and
taxation, §§32-6-60 to
32-6-67.
State vehicles, §40-12-250.
Alteration, etc., §41-17-9.
Temporary tags, §§32-6-210
to 32-6-218. See within
this heading,
"Temporary tags and
certificates."
Time limit for purchase of
tags, §40-12-264.
Transferability.
Plates not transferable,
§32-6-293.
Exception, §32-6-293.
When tags may be
transferred,
§40-12-260.
Transfer of ownership.
Delivery of plates,
§32-8-47.
Travel trailers.
Identification tag.
Display, §40-12-255.
Issuance.
Fee, §40-12-255.
Noncompliance.
Citations, §40-12-257.
Penalties, §40-12-255.
USS Alabama battleship
commission.
Special tag number for
chairman, §32-6-55.
Veterans.
Disabled veterans,
§§32-6-130 to 32-6-133.
Year.
Licensing year, §32-6-294.
Tailgating.
Following too closely,
§32-5A-89.
Staggered licensing,
registration and
taxation, §§32-6-60 to
32-6-67.
Tail lamps, §32-5-240.
Tar wood.
Loads which must be
fastened by cables or
chains, §32-5-75.
Taxation.
Ad valorem taxes,
§40-12-253.
Antique vehicles.
Exemption, §40-12-293.
Certificate of title
prerequisite to
assessment, §32-8-33.
Motor vehicles issued to
disabled veterans
exempt, §40-12-254.
Travel trailers, §40-12-256.
Citations for
noncompliance,
§40-12-257.
Certificate of title.
Ad valorem taxes.
Certificate prerequisite
to assessment,
§32-8-33.

MOTOR VEHICLES—Cont'd
Taxation—Cont'd
Department of revenue.
Uniform certificate of title
and antitheft act. See
within this heading,
"Uniform certificate of
title and antitheft act."
Heavy motor vehicles.
Applicants for registration
to furnish proof of
paying federal taxes,
§32-6-58.
License taxes and
registration fees,
§§40-12-240 to 40-12-274.
See within this heading,
"License taxes and
registration fees."
Motor carrier mileage tax,
§§40-19-1 to 40-19-17.
See MOTOR VEHICLE
CARRIERS.
Registration of heavy motor
vehicles.
Applicant to furnish proof
of paying federal taxes,
§32-6-58.
Sales tax. See within this
heading, "Sales tax."
Use tax. See within this
heading, "Use tax."
Television.
Location of television viewers
in vehicle, §32-5-219.
**Temporary instruction and
learners' licenses,**
§32-6-8.
**Temporary tags and
certificates,** §§32-6-210 to
32-6-218.
Contents, §32-6-216.
Copies of certificate,
§32-6-216.
County officials.
Issuance, §32-6-213.
Definitions, §32-6-210.
Department.
Design and supply,
§32-6-218.
Investigations, §32-6-218.
Rules and regulations.
Promulgation, §32-6-218.
Design.
Department to design,
§32-6-218.
Designated agents.
Issuance, §32-6-211.
Duration, §32-6-214.
Fees, §32-6-215.
Issuance.
Authority.
Designated agents,
§32-6-211.
Probate judge, §32-6-213.
County officials, §32-6-213.
Fees, §32-6-215.
Mobile homes and travel
trailers.
Manufacturers, dealers,
etc., §32-6-212.
Revocation of authority,
§32-6-218.
Mobile homes and travel
trailers.
Issuance.
Manufacturers, dealers,
etc., §32-6-212.
Probate judge.
Issuance, §32-6-213.

MOTOR VEHICLES—Cont'd
**Temporary tags and
certificates**—Cont'd
Records.
Inspection, §32-6-217.
Maintenance, §32-6-217.
Renewal, §32-6-214.
Revocation of issuing
authority, §32-6-218.
Rules and regulations.
Promulgation, §32-6-218.
Successive tags, §32-6-214.
Term of validity, §32-6-214.
Tests.
Chemical tests for
intoxication, §§32-5-190
to 32-5-194, 32-5A-194.
See within this heading,
"Driving under the
influence."
Drivers' licenses.
Examination for licenses,
§32-6-3.
Municipal testing stations,
§§32-18-1 to 32-18-8. See
within this heading,
"Municipal testing
stations."
Signs, signals and markings.
Submission to highway
director for tests,
§32-5A-36.
Theft.
First degree theft of
property, §13A-8-3.
Unauthorized use of vehicle,
§13A-8-11.
Uniform certificate of title
and antitheft act,
§§32-8-1 to 32-8-88. See
within this heading,
"Uniform certificate of
title and antitheft act."
Unlawful breaking and
entering of vehicle,
§13A-8-11.
Through highway.
Defined, §32-1-1.1.
**Throwing or shooting deadly
or dangerous missile
into occupied vehicle,**
§32-5-11.
Tickets.
Uniform traffic infractions.
Uniform traffic ticket and
complaint, ARJA, Rule
19.
Tires.
Chains, §32-5-210.
Leaving unattended vehicles.
Turning front wheels to
curb side of highway,
§32-5A-50.
Metal tires.
Defined, §32-1-1.1.
Movable tracks.
Permits authorizing
operation, §32-5-210.
Pneumatic tires.
Defined, §32-1-1.1.
Required, §32-5-210.
Restrictions as to tire
equipment, §32-5-210.
Retreading shops.
Licenses, §40-12-57.
Sales.
Unsafe tires, §32-5-210.
Solid rubber tires, §32-5-210.
Solid tires.
Defined, §32-1-1.1.

MOTOR VEHICLES—Cont'd
Tires—Cont'd
Studs.
Prohibited, §32-5-210.
Traction, §32-5-210.
Tread, §32-5-210.
Title.
Uniform certificate of title
and antitheft act,
§§32-8-1 to 32-8-88. See
within this heading,
"Uniform certificate of
title and antitheft act."
Towing.
Abandoned motor vehicles
generally. See within
this heading,
"Abandoned motor
vehicles."
Disabled vehicles, §32-5-51.
Display of red flag or signal
cloth at rear of vehicle,
§32-5-51.
Drawbars.
Specifications, §32-5-51.
Mirrors.
Required, §32-5-214.
Trucks, trailers and semi-
trailers generally. See
within this heading,
"Trucks, trailers and
semi-trailers."
Trackless trolley coach.
Defined, §32-1-1.1.
Tractors.
Farm tractors.
Defined, §32-1-1.1.
Drivers' licenses.
Persons exempt from
securing license,
§32-6-2.
Size and weight of
vehicles.
Exemptions from
restrictions,
§32-9-24.
License or privilege tax.
Motor tractors, §40-12-251.
Railroad grade crossings.
Moving heavy equipment
at grade crossings,
§32-5A-152.
Road tractor.
Defined, §32-1-1.1.
Trucks, trailers and semi-
trailers, §§32-9-1 to
32-9-32. See within this
heading, "Trucks,
trailers and semi-
trailers."
Trade and commerce.
Motor vehicle franchise act.
Dealings by manufacturers
with dealers, §§8-20-1
to 8-20-12. See within
this heading,
"Manufacturers."
Traffic.
Defined, §32-1-1.1.
Traffic-control signals.
Defined, §32-1-1.1.
General provisions.
Signs, signals and
markings, §§32-5A-30
to 32-5A-37. See
within this heading,
"Signs, signals and
markings."
Traffic offenses.
District courts.
See DISTRICT COURTS.

MOTOR VEHICLES—Cont'd
  Traffic offenses—Cont'd
    General provisions. See
      within this heading,
      "Violations."
    Penalties. See within this
      heading, "Penalties."
  Trailers.
    Mobile homes, §§24-5-1 to
      24-5-34.
      See MOBILE HOMES.
    Trucks, trailers and semi-
      trailers, §§32-9-1 to
      32-9-32. See within this
      heading, "Trucks,
      trailers and semi-
      trailers."
  Training schools.
    Driving training schools,
      §§32-14-1 to 32-14-24.
      See within this heading,
      "Driver training
      schools."
  Transfer of ownership.
    Fee for recording change of
      ownership, §40-12-261.
    Record of transfer,
      §40-12-260.
    Rules and regulations for
      enforcement, §40-12-272.
    Uniform certificate of title
      and antitheft act,
      §§32-8-44 to 32-8-47.
  Transportation companies.
    Bills of lading or receipts.
      See TRANSPORTATION
      COMPANIES.
  Transporters.
    Defined, §32-1-1.1.
  Travel homes.
    General provisions, §§24-5-1
      to 24-5-34.
      See MOBILE HOMES.
    License taxes and
      registration fees.
      Travel trailers. See within
        this heading, "License
        taxes and registration
        fees."
    Permits for movement of
      oversized vehicles,
      §32-9-29.
    Tags and plates.
      Travel trailers,
        §§40-12-255,
        40-12-257.
    Temporary tags and
      certificates.
      Issuance, §32-6-212.
  Travel trailers.
    Ad valorem taxation,
      §40-12-256.
    Citations for
      noncompliance,
      §40-12-257.
    General provisions.
      See MOBILE HOMES.
    License taxes and
      registration fees. See
      within this heading,
      "License taxes and
      registration fees."
    Permits for movement of
      oversized vehicles,
      §32-9-29.
    Riding in moving trailers
      prohibited, §32-5A-55.
    Tags and plates, §§40-12-255,
      40-12-257.

MOTOR VEHICLES—Cont'd
  Trees and timber.
    Loads which must be
      fastened by cables or
      chains, §32-5-75.
    Size and weight of vehicles
      transporting.
      Exemption from article,
        §32-9-25.
    Unloading logs, lumber, etc.,
      on or near highways,
      §32-5-4.
  Trial.
    Uniform traffic infractions.
      Defendant's appearance.
        Plea and waiver of trial,
          ARJA, Rule 19.
  **Trucks, trailers and semi-
    trailers,** §§32-9-1 to
    32-9-32.
    Arrests.
      Bond, §32-9-3.
      Violations of chapter,
        §32-9-3.
    Cotton wagons.
      Towing cotton wagons,
        §32-9-2.
    Dealers in trailers.
      Licenses, §40-12-169.
    Defined, §§32-1-1.1,
      40-12-240.
    Disabled trucks upon
      highways.
      Flares required, §32-5-221.
    Enforcement of chapter,
      §32-9-3.
    Flares.
      Disabled trucks upon
        highways, §32-5-221.
      Required, §32-5-220.
    Four wheel, two-axle trailers.
      Size and weight of
        vehicles. See within
        this heading, "Size and
        weight of vehicles."
    Highways.
      Restrictions on rights to
        use highways, §32-1-3.
    Jurisdiction.
      Courts having jurisdiction
        over violations,
        §32-9-4.
    License taxes and
      registration fees,
      §§40-12-240 to 40-12-274.
      See within this heading,
      "License taxes and
      registration fees."
    Lighting equipment,
      §32-5-240.
    Milk transporters.
      Size and weight of
        vehicles.
        Exemptions from article,
          §32-9-23.
    Module-movers.
      Hauling cotton from field
        to gin, §32-9-2.
    Motor vehicle carriers,
      §§37-3-1 to 37-3-34.
      See MOTOR VEHICLE
      CARRIERS.
    Municipal corporations.
      Size and weight of
        vehicles.
        Vehicles owned by
          municipal
          corporations exempt,
          §32-9-22.

MOTOR VEHICLES—Cont'd
  **Trucks, trailers and semi-
    trailers**—Cont'd
    Penalties.
      Disposition of fines and
        forfeitures, §32-9-6.
      Violations of chapter,
        §32-9-5.
    Pole trailers.
      Defined, §32-1-1.1.
    Police.
      Enforcement of chapter,
        §32-9-3.
    Registration fees,
      §§40-12-240 to 40-12-274.
      See within this heading,
      "License taxes and
      registration fees."
    Sales tax.
      Tax levied on gross
        receipts, §40-23-2.
    Semi-trailers.
      Defined, §32-1-1.1.
    Size and weight of vehicles,
      §§32-9-20 to 32-9-32. See
      within this heading,
      "Size and weight of
      vehicles."
    Speed limits.
      Maximum speeds,
        §32-5A-171.
    Tires.
      Requirements, §32-5-210.
    Trailers.
      Operation, §32-9-1.
      Passengers.
        Hauling of passengers,
          §32-9-1.
      Permits.
        Movement of trailers,
          §32-9-1.
      Regulation of movement.
        Special permits, §32-9-1.
      Uses for which allowed,
        §32-9-1.
    United States.
      Vehicles owned by United
        States exempt from
        article, §32-9-22.
    Use tax, §40-23-61.
    Violations.
      Arrest for violation,
        §32-9-3.
      Courts having jurisdiction,
        §32-9-4.
      Disposition of fines and
        forfeitures, §32-9-6.
      Penalties, §32-9-5.
    Weight of vehicles, §§32-9-20
      to 32-9-32. See within
      this heading, "Size and
      weight of vehicles."
  Tunnels.
    Overtaking and passing.
      Limitations on passing,
        §32-5A-85.
  Turning at intersections,
    §32-5A-130.
    Turns on red traffic signals,
      §32-5A-32.
  Turn signals, §32-5A-133.
  U-haul-it vehicles, §§32-15-1
    to 32-15-8. See within this
    heading, "Renting and
    hiring."
  Unattended vehicles.
    Abandoned motor vehicles
      generally, §§32-13-1 to
      32-13-8. See within this
      heading, "Abandoned
      motor vehicles."

MOTOR VEHICLES—Cont'd
Unattended vehicles—Cont'd
Accidents.
Duty upon striking
unattended vehicle,
§32-10-3.
Procedure before leaving
vehicle unattended,
§32-5A-50.
Unauthorized use of vehicle,
§13A-8-11.
State vehicles, §41-17-9.
Uniform certificate of title
and antitheft act,
§32-8-81.
Unclaimed property,
§§32-13-1 to 32-13-8. See
within this heading, "
Abandoned motor
vehicles."
**Uniform certificate of title
and antitheft act,**
§§32-8-1 to 32-8-88.
Aiding, abetting, etc., in
violations, §32-8-11.
Animal-drawn vehicles,
§§32-8-80 to 32-8-88.
Antitheft laws.
Exceptions from
provisions of article,
§32-8-80.
Certificate of title.
Exemption, §32-8-31.
Antitheft laws.
Animal-drawn vehicles.
Exceptions from
provisions of article,
§32-8-80.
Damaging or tampering
with vehicles.
Unauthorized damaging
or tampering,
§32-8-83.
Exceptions from provisions
of article, §32-8-80.
Garages.
Unclaimed vehicles.
Reports of operators,
§32-8-84.
Identity of vehicle.
Dismantling, destroying
or changing identity,
§32-8-87.
Implements of husbandry.
Exceptions from
provisions of article,
§32-8-80.
License date.
Removed, falsified or
unauthorized license
date, §32-8-86.
Receiving or disposing of
vehicles.
Unauthorized receiving
or disposing,
§32-8-82.
Records.
Stolen, converted,
recovered and
unclaimed vehicles,
§32-8-84.
Registration.
Removed, falsified or
unauthorized
registration,
§32-8-86.
Suspension of
registration of stolen
or converted
vehicles, §32-8-84.

MOTOR VEHICLES—Cont'd
**Uniform certificate of title
and antitheft act**—Cont'd
Antitheft laws—Cont'd
Reports.
False report of theft or
conversion, §32-8-85.
Stolen, converted,
recovered and
unclaimed vehicles,
§32-8-84.
Salvage.
Motor vehicle declared
salvage, §32-8-87.
Special mobile equipment.
Exceptions from
provisions of article,
§32-8-80.
Theft facilities.
Definitions, §32-8-88.
Prohibited, §32-8-88.
Seizure and forfeiture of
property, §32-8-88.
Total loss.
Defined, §32-8-87.
Unauthorized use of
vehicles, §32-8-81.
Unclaimed vehicles.
Operators of garages,
repair shops and
parking lots.
Reports of unclaimed
vehicles, §32-8-84.
Vehicle identification
number.
Removed, falsified or
unauthorized
identification
number, §32-8-86.
Wheelchairs.
Self-propelled
wheelchairs.
Exceptions from
provisions of
article, §32-8-80.
Appeals.
Actions of department,
§§32-8-4, 32-8-5.
Assignments.
Security interests.
Assignment by
lienholder, §32-8-63.
Automotive dismantlers and
parts recyclers.
Transfer of certificate of
title, §40-12-420.
Certificate of title.
Animal-drawn vehicles.
Exemption, §32-8-31.
Application.
Bond or cash to
accompany, §32-8-36.
Certificate of designated
agent to accompany,
§32-8-35.
Check of vehicle
identification
number.
Upon receipt of
application,
§32-8-37.
Department may require
proof of no security
interest, §32-8-36.
Examination of
application by
department,
§32-8-37.
First certificate,
§32-8-35.
Lienholders, §32-8-35.

MOTOR VEHICLES—Cont'd
**Uniform certificate of title
and antitheft act**—Cont'd
Certificate of title.
Application—Cont'd
Manufacturer's
statement of origin,
§32-8-35.
New vehicles, §32-8-35.
Use of duplicate copy of
application as permit
to operate motor
vehicle, §32-8-38.
Vehicles previously
registered in another
state or country,
§32-8-35.
Who required to apply,
§32-8-30.
Bonds, surety.
Application for
certificate with bond
or cash, §32-8-36.
Contents, §32-8-39.
Dealers.
Compliance with
chapter, §32-8-30.
Vehicles owned by
dealers.
Exemption, §32-8-31.
Delivery, §32-8-41.
Distinctive certificates for
certain vehicles,
§32-8-40.
Drivers' licenses.
Use of duplicate copy of
application for
certificate as permit
to operate motor
vehicle, §32-8-38.
Effect, §32-8-39.
Evidence.
Certificate issued by
department prima
facie evidence of
facts appearing on it,
§32-8-39.
Exemption, §32-8-31.
Failure to furnish
information or
documents.
Refusal to issue
certificate, §32-8-42.
False or fraudulent
statements.
Refusal to issue
certificate, §32-8-42.
Fees.
Unpaid fees, §32-8-42.
Form, §32-8-37.
Implement of husbandry.
Exemption, §32-8-31.
Issuance, §32-8-37.
Conditions of issuance,
§32-8-36.
Refusal to issue
certificate, §32-8-42.
Return of duplicate and
tags upon refusal to
issue certificate,
§32-8-38.
Lost, stolen or mutilated
certificates, §32-8-43.
Manufacturers.
Vehicles owned by
manufacturers.
Exemption, §32-8-31.
Mobile homes, §32-8-30.
Exemption of certain
mobile homes,
§32-8-31.

MOTOR VEHICLES—Cont'd
**Uniform certificate of title
and antitheft act**—Cont'd
Certificate of title—Cont'd
New vehicles.
Manufacturer's
statement of origin,
§32-8-35.
Nonresidents.
Exemption, §32-8-31.
Pole trailers.
Exemption, §32-8-31.
Records, §32-8-37.
Refusing certificate,
§32-8-42.
Replacement of lost, stolen
or mutilated
certificates, §32-8-43.
Required, §32-8-30.
Scrapping, dismantling or
destroying vehicle.
Suspension or revocation
of certificate,
§32-8-49.
Security interests.
Distinctive certificates
for certain vehicles,
§32-8-40.
Perfection by delivery of
certificate, §32-8-61.
Special mobile equipment.
Exemption, §32-8-31.
Tags and plates.
Return of tags upon
refusal to issue
certificate, §32-8-38.
Travel trailers.
When required, §32-8-30.
Undisclosed security
interest.
Department may
withhold issuance of
certificate until proof
of no undisclosed
interest, §32-8-36.
United States.
Vehicles owned by
United States.
Exemption, §32-8-31.
Use of duplicate copy of
application as permit
to operate motor
vehicle, §32-8-38.
Vehicles engaged in
interstate
transportation of
persons or property.
Exemption, §32-8-31.
Vehicles registered in
other state or country.
Application for first
certificate, §32-8-35.
Citation, §32-8-1.
Creditors.
Perfection of security
interests, §32-8-61.
Dealers.
Compliance with chapter
required, §32-8-30.
Defined, §32-8-2.
Designated agents of
department, §32-8-34.
Inspections.
Right of inspection for
violations, §32-8-8.
Revocation of authority.
Department authorized
to revoke, §32-8-3.

MOTOR VEHICLES—Cont'd
**Uniform certificate of title
and antitheft act**—Cont'd
Dealers—Cont'd
Security interests.
Excepted liens and
security interests,
§32-8-60.
Transfer of ownership.
Records of dealers,
§32-8-45.
Vehicles owned by dealers.
Certificates of title not
necessary, §32-8-31.
Definitions, §32-8-2.
Department.
Actions of department.
Court review of
department actions,
§32-8-5.
Protest of actions,
§32-8-4.
Appeals, §§32-8-4, 32-8-5.
Dealers.
Revocation of authority,
§32-8-3.
Defined, §32-8-2.
Designated agents.
Form.
Department to provide,
§32-8-9.
Duties.
Generally, §32-8-3.
Enforcement of chapter,
§32-8-10.
Hearings.
Protesting actions of
department, §32-8-4.
Information concerning
status of title, §32-8-3.
Inspections.
Right of inspection for
violations, §32-8-8.
Investigations, §32-8-3.
Powers.
Generally, §32-8-3.
Protest of actions of
department, §32-8-4.
Court review of
department actions,
§32-8-5.
Rules and regulations,
§32-8-3.
Vehicle identification
number.
Assignment of new
number, §32-8-3.
Designated agents.
Application for first
certificate of title.
Certificate of designated
agent to accompany,
§32-8-35.
Appointment by
department, §32-8-34.
Defined, §32-8-2.
Enumerated, §32-8-34.
Transfer of ownership,
§32-8-46.
Drivers' licenses.
Certificate of title.
Use of duplicate copy of
application as permit
to operate motor
vehicle, §32-8-38.
Evidence.
Certificate of title.
Prima facie evidence of
facts appearing on it,
§32-8-39.

MOTOR VEHICLES—Cont'd
**Uniform certificate of title
and antitheft act**—Cont'd
Fees.
Additional commission
fees, §32-8-7.
Schedule of fees, §32-8-6.
Felonies.
Offenses constituting
felonies, §32-8-12.
Penalties, §32-8-14.
Forms.
Department to provide,
§32-8-9.
Fraud.
Certificate of title.
Refusal to issue.
Grounds for refusal,
§32-8-42.
Suspension or revocation,
§32-8-49.
Hearings.
Protesting actions of
department, §32-8-4.
Identifiable component part.
Disposition of forfeited
property, §32-8-86.
Seizure of vehicle, part,
etc., §32-8-86.
When number altered, etc.,
§32-8-86.
Identity of vehicle.
Dismantling, destroying or
changing identity of
vehicle, §32-8-87.
Implement of husbandry.
Antitheft laws.
Exceptions from
provisions of article,
§32-8-80.
Certificate of title.
Exemption, §32-8-31.
Defined, §32-8-2.
Inspections, §32-8-8.
Investigations.
Department to make
investigations, §32-8-3.
License plates.
Certificate prerequisite to
issuance of plates,
§32-8-32.
Liens.
Defined, §32-8-2.
Manufacturers.
Application for first
certificate.
Manufacturer's
statement of origin,
§32-8-35.
Defined, §32-8-2.
Security interests.
Excepted liens and
security interests,
§32-8-60.
Vehicles owned by
manufacturers.
Certificate of title.
Not required, §32-8-31.
Misdemeanors.
Offenses constituting
misdemeanors,
§32-8-13.
Penalties, §32-8-14.
Mobile homes.
Cancellation of title.
Certain mobile homes
affixed to realty,
§32-8-30.

MOTOR VEHICLES—Cont'd
Uniform certificate of title
and antitheft act—Cont'd
Mobile homes—Cont'd
Certificates of title.
Exemption of certain
mobile homes,
§32-8-31.
Reapplication when
mobile home
detached, §32-8-30.
When required, §32-8-30.
Defined, §32-8-2.
Nonresidents.
Certificate of title.
Exemption, §32-8-31.
Defined, §32-8-2.
Notice.
Security interests,
§§32-8-66, 32-8-67.
Penalties, §32-8-14.
Pole trailers.
Certificate of title.
Exemption, §32-8-31.
Defined, §32-8-2.
Police.
Right of inspection for
violations, §32-8-8.
Probate judges.
Designated agents of
department of revenue,
§32-8-34.
Records.
Certificate of title.
Records of certificates
issued, §32-8-37.
Security interests.
Examinations of records,
§32-8-67.
Recording notices of
security interest,
§32-8-67.
Transfer of ownership.
Dealers, §32-8-45.
Registration.
Antitheft laws.
Suspension of
registration of stolen
or converted
vehicles, §32-8-84.
Rules and regulations.
Department to adopt and
enforce, §32-8-3.
Department to promulgate,
§32-8-9.
Salvage.
Motor vehicle declared
salvage, §32-8-87.
Scrap metal processors.
Defined, §32-8-2.
Scrapping, dismantling or
destroying vehicle.
Certificate of title.
Suspension or revocation
of certificate,
§32-8-49.
Scrap vehicle.
Defined, §32-8-2.
Security agreements.
Defined, §32-8-2.
Disclosure of information
by lienholders,
§32-8-65.
Security interests.
Application of first
certificate of title.
Department may require
proof of no
undisclosed security
interest, §32-8-36.

MOTOR VEHICLES—Cont'd
Uniform certificate of title
and antitheft act—Cont'd
Security interests—Cont'd
Assignment by lienholder,
§32-8-63.
Certificate of title.
Distinctive certificates
for certain vehicles,
§32-8-40.
Exclusiveness of
procedure, §32-8-66.
Execution of release on
certificate, §32-8-64.
Perfection of security
interest by delivery
of certificate of title,
§32-8-61.
Creation by owner,
§32-8-62.
Creditors.
Perfection of security
interests, §32-8-61.
Dealers.
Excepted liens and
security interests,
§32-8-60.
Defined, §32-8-2.
Exceptions, §32-8-60.
Liens.
Assignment by
lienholder, §32-8-63.
Duty of lienholder to
disclose information,
§32-8-65.
Excepted liens, §32-8-60.
Manufacturers.
Excepted liens and
security interests,
§32-8-60.
Notice.
Exclusiveness of
procedure of giving
notice, §32-8-66.
Filing and recording
notices, §32-8-67.
Perfection, §32-8-61.
Exclusiveness of
procedure, §32-8-66.
Procedure when owner
creates security
interest, §32-8-62.
Records.
Examination of records,
§32-8-67.
Recording notices of
security interest,
§32-8-67.
Release, §32-8-64.
Satisfaction.
Release of interest,
§32-8-64.
Sheriff.
Inspections.
Right of inspection for
violations, §32-8-8.
Short title, §32-8-1.
Special mobile equipment.
Antitheft laws.
Exceptions from
provisions of article,
§32-8-80.
Certificate of title.
Exemption, §32-8-31.
Defined, §32-8-2.
Stolen vehicles.
Vehicle identification
number.
Check of number against
list of stolen
vehicles, §32-8-37.

MOTOR VEHICLES—Cont'd
Uniform certificate of title
and antitheft act—Cont'd
Tags and plates.
Certificate of title.
Prerequisite to issuance
of license plates,
§32-8-32.
Return of tags upon
refusal to issue
certificate, §32-8-38.
Transfer of ownership.
Delivery of plates,
§32-8-47.
Title, §32-8-1.
Total loss.
Defined, §32-8-87.
Transfer of ownership,
§§32-8-44 to 32-8-47.
Automotive dismantlers
and parts recyclers,
§40-12-420.
Certificate of title,
§32-8-44.
Lienholders in
possession, §32-8-44.
Transfer of ownership to
or from dealer,
§32-8-45.
When department to
issue new certificate
§32-8-47.
Dealers.
Automotive dismantlers
and parts recyclers,
§40-12-420.
To or from dealer,
§32-8-45.
Designated agent.
Transfer by operation of
law, §32-8-46.
Execution of application for
new certificate,
§32-8-44.
Execution of assignment,
§32-8-44.
Generally, §32-8-44.
Operation of law, §32-8-46.
Records.
Dealers, §32-8-45.
Security interests.
Creation at time of
transfer, §32-8-44.
Tags and plates.
Delivery, §32-8-47.
Warranty of title, §32-8-44.
Travel trailers.
Certificates of title.
When required, §32-8-30.
Defined, §32-8-2.
Unauthorized use, §32-8-81.
United States.
Vehicles owned by United
States.
Certificate of title.
Exemption from
requirement,
§32-8-31.
Used vehicles.
Defined, §32-8-2.
Vehicle identification
numbers.
Assignment of new
numbers.
Department to assign,
§32-8-3.
Check of number against
list of stolen vehicles,
§32-8-37.
Defined, §32-8-2.

MOTOR VEHICLES—Cont'd
**Uniform certificate of title
and antitheft act**—Cont'd
Vehicle identification
numbers—Cont'd
Inspection of numbers,
§32-8-8.
Removed, falsified or
unauthorized
identification number,
§32-8-86.
Vehicles engaged in
interstate transportation
of persons or property.
Certificate of title.
Exemption, §32-8-31.
Vehicles registered in
another state or country.
Application for first
certificate of title,
§32-8-35.
Violations.
Aiding and abetting in
violations, §32-8-11.
Felonies.
Offenses constituting
felonies, §32-8-12.
Inspection for violations,
§32-8-8.
Misdemeanors.
Offenses constituting
misdemeanors,
§32-8-13.
Penalties, §32-8-14.
Uninsured motorists.
Safety-responsibility act,
§32-7-23.
United States.
Certificate of title.
Exemption, §32-8-31.
Drivers' licenses.
Persons in service of
federal government
while driving official
motor vehicles.
Exemptions from
securing license,
§32-6-2.
Reciprocal agreements.
Authorities in charge of
federal military
installations,
§32-6-11.
Safety-responsibility act.
Exceptions to act, §32-7-36.
Trucks, trailers and semi-
trailers.
Size and weight of
vehicles.
Exemption from article,
§32-9-22.
**Unlawful breaking and
entering of vehicle,**
§13A-8-11.
Urban districts.
Defined, §32-1-1.1.
Speed limitations,
§32-5A-171.
Used car sales, §§32-16-1 to
32-16-4.
Actions.
Right of action dependent
upon compliance with
chapter, §32-16-3.
Bonds, surety.
Dealers, §32-16-2.
Compliance with chapter.
Right of action dependent
upon compliance,
§32-16-3.

MOTOR VEHICLES—Cont'd
Used car sales—Cont'd
Dealers.
Bonds, §32-16-2.
Dealers with no permanent
place of business.
Registration and bond
required, §32-16-2.
Defined, §32-16-1.
Nonresident dealers.
Registration of vehicles
brought into state,
§32-16-2.
Violations.
Penalty, §32-16-4.
Definitions, §32-16-1.
Nonresident dealers.
Registration, §32-16-2.
Penalties.
Violations, §32-16-4.
Registration.
Nonresident dealers,
§32-16-2.
Vendor.
Defined, §32-16-1.
Violations.
Penalty for violations,
§32-16-4.
Use tax, §40-23-61.
Collection before registration
or licensing, §40-23-104.
Definitions, §40-23-100.
Disposition of taxes collected,
§40-23-108.
Excise tax on storage or use
of automotive vehicles,
truck trailers, etc.,
§40-23-102.
Failure to pay.
Penalty, §40-23-110.
Fees for collection,
§40-23-107.
License commissioners.
Duties, §40-23-109.
Payment.
Proof of payment,
§40-23-104.
Proof of purchase price,
§40-23-104.
Reciprocity, §40-23-106.
Registration or licensing.
Prerequisites, §40-23-104.
**USS Alabama battleship
commission.**
Tags and plates.
Special tag number for
chairman of
commission, §32-6-55.
Vehicles.
Defined, §32-1-1.1.
Veterans.
Disabled veterans.
Ad valorem taxes.
Exemption.
Motor vehicles issued
to disabled
veterans,
§40-12-254.
License taxes and
registration fees.
Exemption, §40-12-244.
Motor vehicles issued
to disabled
veterans,
§40-12-254.
Tags and plates,
§§32-6-130 to 32-6-133.
Violations.
Arrests. See within this
heading, "Arrests."

MOTOR VEHICLES—Cont'd
Violations—Cont'd
District courts.
Traffic offenses.
See DISTRICT COURTS.
Drivers' licenses.
Cancellation, suspension or
revocation.
Violation by person
whose license has
been cancelled,
suspended or
revoked, §32-6-19.
Penalties, §32-6-18.
Enforcement of chapter,
§32-5-310.
Fines.
Schedule of fines, ARJA,
Rule 20.
Magistrates.
Receipt of guilty pleas,
§12-12-52.
Misdemeanors.
Procedure upon arrest for
misdemeanor, §32-1-4.
Moving violations.
Additional penalty,
§32-5-313.
Defined, §32-5-313.
Municipal courts.
Procedure, §12-14-8.
Penalties. See within this
heading, "Penalties."
Prohibiting operation of
motor vehicles by
persons convicted of
violations, §32-5-316.
Records of convictions.
Director of public safety to
file, §32-6-14.
Traffic infractions.
Additional penalty,
§32-5-313.
Defined, §32-5-313.
Uniform traffic infractions,
ARJA, Rule 19.
Violations deemed
misdemeanor,
§32-5A-3.
Uniform traffic infractions,
ARJA, Rule 19.
Accountability for tickets,
ARJA, Rule 19.
Clerks of court.
Fines and costs paid to,
ARJA, Rule 19.
Complaint and summons,
ARJA, Rule 19.
Costs.
Paid to clerks of court,
ARJA, Rule 19.
Defendant's appearance.
Plea and waiver of trial,
ARJA, Rule 19.
Fines.
Paid to clerks of court,
ARJA, Rule 19.
Forms, ARJA, Rule 19.
Law enforcement officers.
Issuance of tickets to,
ARJA, Rule 19.
Municipal parking
offenses, ARJA, Rule
19.
Notice.
Failure of defendant to
appear.
Issuance of further
notice, ARJA,
Rule 19.

MOTOR VEHICLES—Cont'd
Violations—Cont'd
Uniform traffic infractions
—Cont'd
Parking offenses.
Municipal parking
offenses, ARJA, Rule
19.
Pleas.
Defendant's appearance,
ARJA, Rule 19.
Procedures generally,
ARJA, Rule 19.
Summons.
Complaint and summons,
ARJA, Rule 19.
Trial.
Defendant's appearance.
Waiver, ARJA, Rule
19.
Uniform traffic ticket and
complaint.
Accountability for
tickets, ARJA, Rule
19.
Declaration of approval,
ARJA, Rule 19.
Form of complaint and
summons, ARJA,
Rule 19.
Issuance to law
enforcement officers,
ARJA, Rule 19.
Use, ARJA, Rule 19.
Warrants.
Failure of defendant to
appear.
Issuance of
supplemental
summons or
warrants, ARJA,
Rule 19.
Waiver.
Safety-responsibility act.
Proof of financial
responsibility.
Waiving requirement of
filing proof,
§32-7-31.
Warning devices.
Emergency vehicles,
§32-5-213.
Flares, §§32-5-220, 32-5-221.
Horns, §32-5-213.
Horse-drawn wagons,
§32-5-245.
Mail service.
Warning devices for
vehicles engaged in
mail service,
§32-5-243.
Pedestrians.
Warning pedestrians,
§32-5A-213.
Warrants.
Department of public safety.
Compensation and
expenses of officers,
employees, etc.
Method of payment
generally, §32-2-6.
Uniform traffic infractions.
Failure of defendant to
appear.
Issuance of supplemental
summons or
warrant, ARJA,
Rule 19.

MOTOR VEHICLES—Cont'd
**Warranty work on motor
vehicles.**
Compensation by
manufacturer, etc., for
work performed by
dealer or representative,
§32-17-1.
Dealers.
Compensation by
manufacturer for work
performed by dealer,
§32-17-1.
Violations.
Penalty, §32-17-2.
Manufacturers.
Compensation by
manufacturer for work
performed by dealer or
representative,
§32-17-1.
Violations.
Penalty, §32-17-2.
Obligations of manufacturers
and dealers to
consumers, §8-20-8.
Obligations to dealers,
§8-20-7.
Penalties.
Violations by
manufacturers or
dealers, §32-17-2.
Weapons.
Bullets.
Motor vehicle accidents.
Garages to report bullet
damage, §32-10-10.
Discharging firearm into
automobile or truck,
§13A-11-61.
Highway patrol.
Officers to receive pistols
as part of retirement
benefits, §32-2-26.
Pistols.
License to carry pistol in
vehicle.
See WEAPONS.
Shooting into occupied
vehicle, §32-5-11.
Weight of vehicles, §§32-9-20
to 32-9-32. See within this
heading, "Size and weight
of vehicles."
White cane law, §§21-7-6,
21-7-7.
Wholesalers.
Dealings by manufacturers
with dealers, §§8-20-1 to
8-20-12. See within this
heading,
"Manufacturers."
Licenses.
Dealers, reconditioners,
rebuilders and
wholesalers,
§§40-12-390 to
40-12-400. See within
this heading,
"Licenses."
Windshields.
Defrosters, §32-5-215.
Obstructions.
Prohibited, §32-5-215.
Safety glazing material,
§32-5-218.
Tinting.
Restrictions, §32-5-215.
Wipers.
Required, §32-5-215.

MOTOR VEHICLES—Cont'd
Witnesses.
Accidents.
Police to interview
witnesses, §32-10-7.
Working signs.
Speed limit between signs,
§32-5-93.

**MOUNTAIN BROOK,
MUNICIPALITY OF.**
Property tax.
Additional tax, Const. Ala.,
amds. 209, 336.

MOVIES.
See MOTION PICTURES.

**MOWA CHOCTAW HOUSING
AUTHORITY,** §§24-7-1 to
24-7-6.
**Applicability of municipal
housing authority law,**
§24-7-3.
Area of operation, §24-7-4.
Contracts.
With government for loans
and contributions,
§24-7-6.
**Cooperation with
municipalities and
regional housing
authorities,** §24-7-5.
Creation, §24-7-2.
Definitions, §24-7-1.
Duties.
Generally, §24-7-3.
Loans.
Contract with government,
§24-7-6.
Meetings.
Location, §24-7-2.
Membership, §24-7-2.
Municipalities.
Cooperation with, §24-7-5.
Officers, §24-7-2.
Powers and duties.
Generally, §24-7-3.
Proxies, §24-7-2.
**Regional housing
authorities.**
Cooperation with, §24-7-5.
Removal of members,
§24-7-2.
Quorum, §24-7-2.
Services.
State to provide, §24-7-6.
Terms of office, §24-7-2.

MULES.
Estrays.
See ESTRAYS.
General provisions.
See LIVESTOCK.
Licenses.
Dealers, §40-12-112.

MULTIPLE ACTIONS.
Elections between actions,
§6-5-440.

MUMPS.
Notifiable diseases,
§§22-11A-1 to 22-11A-38.
See DISEASES.

**MUNICIPAL
CORPORATIONS.**
Abandoned property.
Uniform disposition of
unclaimed property act.
Exemption of
municipalities,
§11-40-15.

MUNICIPAL CORPORATIONS—Cont'd

Abandonment.
Cemeteries, §§11-47-60 to 11-47-74. See within this heading, "Cemeteries."
Class 5 municipalities.
Mayor/commission/city manager form of government, §§11-44E-200 to 11-44E-202.
Commission form of government.
Class 7 municipalities, §§11-44A-1 to 11-44A-32. See within heading, "Class 7 municipalities."
General provisions, §§11-40-150 to 11-40-162. See within this heading, "Commission form of government."

Abattoirs.
Establishment, §11-47-138.
Regulation, §§11-47-137, 11-47-138.

Absorbed municipalities.
Duties of expanded municipalities as to properties and obligations of absorbed municipalities, §§11-42-180 to 11-42-187. See within this heading, "Expanded municipalities."

Abutting landowners.
Assessments for public improvements, §11-48-14.
Maps or plats.
Vacation of streets or alleys by abutting landowners, §35-2-54.
Validation, §35-2-55.

Accountants.
Finance.
Duties as to, §11-43-85.

Accounts and accounting.
Class 5 municipalities.
Mayor/commission/city manager form of government, §11-44E-54.
Clerk, §11-43-102.
Commission form of government, §11-44-50.
Council-manager form of government, §§11-43A-27, 11-43A-29, 11-43A-31.
Finance generally. See within this heading, "Finance."
Mayor/commission/city manager form of government, §11-44E-54.
Weeds.
Abatement of weeds.
Class 2 municipalities.
Cost of abatement of nuisance, §11-67-7.
Class 5 municipalities.
Cost of abatement of nuisance, §11-67-26.

MUNICIPAL CORPORATIONS—Cont'd

Acknowledgments.
Surveys, plats or maps, §35-2-51.

Actions.
Attorney general may be required to defend against, Const. Ala., amd. 111.
Class 5 municipalities.
Mayor/commission/city manager form of government.
Succession of government.
Continuance of pending actions, §11-44E-146.
Council-manager form of government.
Pending litigation.
Effect of chapter upon, §11-43A-40.
Historic preservation commissions.
Prevention of violations and recovery of damages, §11-68-12.
Mayor/commission/city manager form of government.
Succession of government.
Continuance of pending actions, §11-44E-146.
Nuisances.
Actions to enjoin and abate, §§6-5-122, 11-47-118.
Rights of action.
Preserved and enforced.
Notwithstanding change of name or organization, §11-40-4.

Advertising.
Authorized, §11-47-9.
Costs, §11-47-10.
Municipal resources, §11-47-11.
Streets.
Municipal connecting link roads, §23-1-113.

Aged persons.
Recreational, social and cultural facilities.
Planning, establishment, etc., §11-80-5.
Special health care facility authorities, §§11-62-1 to 11-62-21. See within this heading, "Special health care facility authorities."

Agents.
Bonds, surety.
Recordation, §36-5-3.
Negligence.
Liability for negligence of agents, etc., §§11-47-190 to 11-47-192.
Waterworks and sewer boards.
Management of systems as agents of municipalities, §§11-50-290 to 11-50-291.

MUNICIPAL CORPORATIONS—Cont'd

Agriculture.
Farmers' market authority.
Local appropriations authorized, §2-5-17.
Sale of farm products.
Municipalities not to charge farmers for sale, §11-51-105.
Regulation of sale by farmers or other producers, §2-29-10.

Air pollution.
Local air pollution control programs, §22-28-23.

Airports, §§4-4-1 to 4-4-16.
Abatement of hazards, §4-4-10.
Acquisition, construction, etc.
Authority to acquire, §4-4-2.
Bond issues.
Authority to issue, §§4-1-1, 4-4-11.
Financial and technical assistance, §4-2-38.
Methods of acquisition, §§4-4-5, 4-4-6.
Air rights.
Acquisition, §4-4-10.
Authorities.
Assistance and cooperation by municipalities, §4-3-13.
Alternate procedure for incorporation, §4-3-49.
Bond issues.
Investment in funds, §4-3-57.
Borrowing of money to assist authority, §4-3-80.
Investment of municipal funds in bonds of authority, §4-3-20.
Bond issues, §4-4-11.
Authority to issue bonds for acquisition, etc., §§4-1-1, 4-4-11.
Public improvement bonds.
Revenue-producing undertakings, §§11-81-140 to 11-81-150.
See COUNTIES.
Codes.
Adoption of technical codes by reference, §11-45-8.
Concessions.
Grant of concessions, §4-4-8.
Condemnation.
Acquisition of lands by condemnation, §§4-4-5, 4-4-6.
Control.
Municipal governing bodies, §4-4-7.
Cumulative provisions.
Provisions of chapter cumulative, §4-4-16.
Definitions, §4-4-1.
Establishment.
Authority to establish, §4-4-2.

MUNICIPAL
CORPORATIONS—Cont'd
Airports—Cont'd
Furnishing goods, services,
    etc., §4-4-8.
Municipal liens for
    supplies, services, etc.,
    §4-4-9.
Governing bodies.
    Control by municipal
        governing bodies,
        §4-4-7.
    Delegation of powers to
        other bodies or officers,
        §4-4-7.
Hazards.
    Abatement of hazards,
        §4-4-10.
Joint airports, §4-4-12.
Liability for negligence.
    Municipal immunity from
        liability, §4-4-4.
Liens.
    Concessionaires, §4-4-9.
    Municipal liens for
        supplies, services, etc.,
        §4-4-9.
Lights on hazards, §4-4-10.
Negligence.
    Municipal immunity from
        liability for negligence,
        §4-4-4.
Operation.
    Authority to operate,
        §4-4-2.
Parks.
    Use of parks for airports,
        etc., §4-4-3.
Police powers as to airports,
    §4-4-15.
Powers.
    Police powers as to
        airports, §4-4-15.
Priority of liens, §4-4-9.
Private airports, §4-4-14.
Provision of goods and
    services, §4-4-8.
Municipal liens for
    supplies, services, etc.,
    §4-4-9.
Provisions of chapter
    cumulative, §4-4-16.
Removal of hazards, §4-4-10.
Rules and regulations,
    §4-4-14.
    Authority to regulate,
        §4-4-2.
Sale.
    Disposition of proceeds of
        sale, §4-4-13.
    Procedure for sale, §4-4-13.
Zoning, §§4-6-1 to 4-6-15.
See AVIATION.
Alabama privatization act.
Utility services facilities,
    §§11-97-1 to 11-97-27.
See UTILITY SERVICES
    FACILITIES.
Alcoholic beverages.
Elections.
    Drunkenness at polling
        place during election,
        §§11-46-68, 11-46-139.
    Officers of election.
        Drinking while election
            being held,
            §11-46-132.

MUNICIPAL
CORPORATIONS—Cont'd
Alcoholic beverages—Cont'd
Elections—Cont'd
    Watchers.
        Drinking of intoxicating
            liquors by watcher,
            §§11-46-65,
            11-46-136.
Emergencies.
    Temporary closings,
        §28-3-47.
General provisions.
    See ALCOHOLIC
        BEVERAGES.
Licenses.
    Retail liquor license
        applications.
        Approval by governing
            authority,
            §28-3A-23.
Local option, §§28-2A-1 to
    28-2A-4.
Privilege or license tax,
    §28-3A-21.
Sales tax.
    Exemption of alcoholic
        beverage control board,
        §11-51-200.
Suppression of intemperance,
    §11-47-112.
Taxation.
    Audit and collection of
        taxes on beer or table
        wine for benefit of
        local governing bodies
        generally, §§28-7A-1 to
        28-7A-6.
    See ALCOHOLIC
        BEVERAGES.
Temperance.
    Promotion of temperance,
        §11-47-112.
Traffic in certain beverages
    in violation of law.
    Suppression, §11-47-112.
Alleys.
Closing and vacating streets,
    alleys and highways,
    §§23-4-1 to 23-4-20.
    See HIGHWAYS.
General provisions. See
    within this heading,
    "Streets."
**Alteration of corporate
limits.**
Annexation, §§11-42-1 to
    11-42-88. See within this
    heading, "Annexation."
Consolidation, §§11-42-100 to
    11-42-167. See within
    this heading,
    "Consolidation."
Reduction of corporate limits,
    §§11-42-200 to 11-42-213.
    See within this heading,
    "Reduction of corporate
    limits."
**Ambulance service, §§11-87-1
to 11-87-5.**
Appropriations, §11-87-2.
Chapter cumulative,
    §11-87-5.
Contracts for services,
    §11-87-3.
Counties.
    Joint operation with
        counties, §11-87-1.
Creation.
    Authorized, §11-87-1.

MUNICIPAL
CORPORATIONS—Cont'd
Ambulance service—Cont'd
Establishment.
    Authorized, §11-87-1.
Fees, §11-87-4.
Joint operation with
    counties, §11-87-1.
Maintenance.
    Authorized, §11-87-1.
Operation.
    Authorized, §11-87-1.
Powers of municipalities,
    §22-18-7.
Rules and regulations.
    Promulgation, §11-87-1.
Amusements.
Houses of amusement.
    Closing, §11-51-102.
Licenses, §§11-51-102,
    11-51-104.
Revocation, §11-51-103.
Provision of music and other
    exhibitions, §11-47-19.
Animals.
Livestock.
    Dealers.
        Sanitary rules and
            regulations,
            §2-15-48.
    Driving through streets,
        §11-47-160.
    Running at large.
        Authority to adopt
            ordinances, §3-5-14.
        Destruction, §11-47-110.
        Impoundment, etc.,
            §11-47-110.
        Reimbursement where
            livestock kept in
            municipal pounds,
            §3-5-11.
    Violations of ordinances.
        Summons and complaint
            in lieu of arrest,
            §11-40-10.1.
**Annexation, §§11-42-1 to
11-42-88.**
Aldermen.
    Election, §11-42-73.
Applicability of article,
    §11-42-1.
Billiard rooms.
    Territory exempt from
        taxation.
        Licensing of billiard
            rooms, §11-42-81.
Bills.
    Accurate description of
        territory, plat or map
        required, §11-42-6.
Boundaries.
    Cities of twenty-five
        thousand or more,
        §§11-42-45, 11-42-74,
        11-42-75.
Cities of twenty-five
    thousand or more,
    §§11-42-40 to 11-42-88.
Applicability of article,
    §11-42-40.
Boundaries.
    Designation for voting,
        §11-42-45.
    Rearrangement of voting
        precincts, §11-42-74.
    Rearrangement of wards,
        §11-42-75.
Compensation of probate
    judge, §11-42-87.

MUNICIPAL CORPORATIONS—Cont'd
Annexation—Cont'd
Cities of twenty-five
thousand or more
—Cont'd
Contracts.
Territory exempt from
taxation.
Article as contract
between city and
exempt territory,
§11-42-88.
Costs of election,
§11-42-53.
Education.
Territory exempt from
taxation.
Attendance at city
schools, §11-42-85.
Election, §§11-42-43 to
11-42-53, 11-42-56.
Aldermen or
representatives,
§11-42-73.
Applicability of general
election laws,
§11-42-48.
Ascertainment of results,
§11-42-50.
Ballots, §11-42-49.
Canvassing of returns,
§11-42-51.
Certification of results,
§11-42-50.
Contests of election,
§11-42-52.
Costs of election,
§11-42-53.
Delivery of results,
§11-42-50.
General election laws.
Applicability,
§11-42-48.
Inspectors.
Appointment,
§11-42-46.
Notice of election,
§11-42-44.
Ordering of election,
§11-42-43.
Qualifications for voting,
§11-42-47.
Representatives,
§11-42-73.
Results, §11-42-50.
Returning officers.
Appointment,
§11-42-46.
Returns.
Canvassing of returns,
§11-42-51.
Subsequent elections.
When held, §11-42-56.
Voting places.
Designation,
§11-42-45.
Electors to vote at
designated voting
places, §11-42-47.
Enforcement of article.
Territory exempt from
taxation, §11-42-88.
Exclusiveness of article.
Provisions of article not
exclusive, §11-42-40.
Fees of probate judge,
§11-42-87.
Hearings.
Taxation.
Contests, §11-42-65.

MUNICIPAL CORPORATIONS—Cont'd
Annexation—Cont'd
Cities of twenty-five
thousand or more
—Cont'd
Hearings—Cont'd
Taxation—Cont'd
Show cause, §11-42-61.
Industrial plants.
Exemption from
taxation, §11-42-59.
Inspectors.
Duty, §11-42-46.
Jurisdiction.
City governing body over
annexed territory,
§11-42-72.
Laws.
Annexed territory
subject to laws of
city, §11-42-72.
License tax.
Territory exempt from
taxation.
Assessment and
collection of
license tax,
§§11-42-83,
11-42-84.
Levy and collection of
license tax,
§11-42-82.
Manufacturing plants.
Exemption from
taxation, §11-42-59.
Maps and plats.
Certification by probate
judge, §11-42-42.
Filing with probate
judge, §11-42-42.
Recordation, §11-42-51.
Taxation.
Endorsements on map,
§§11-42-69,
11-42-70.
Filing of map of
annexed territory
subject to taxation,
§11-42-60.
Recordation of map,
§11-42-71.
Withdrawal of map
from files of
probate judge for
use in circuit
court, §11-42-68.
Mining plants.
Exemption from
taxation, §11-42-59.
Notice.
Requirement as to
notices under article,
§11-42-55.
Single notice for
separately owned
lands, §11-42-62.
Taxation.
Appeals, §11-42-67.
Orders.
Entry of orders,
§11-42-51.
Recordation, §11-42-51.
Requirement as to orders
under article,
§11-42-55.
Taxation.
Recordation, §11-42-71.

MUNICIPAL CORPORATIONS—Cont'd
Annexation—Cont'd
Cities of twenty-five
thousand or more
—Cont'd
Ordinances.
Annexed territory
subject to ordinances
of city, §11-42-72.
Powers.
Territory exempt from
taxation.
City's powers as to,
§11-42-88.
Precincts.
Division of wards into
voting precincts,
§11-42-74.
Rearrangement of
boundaries,
§11-42-74.
Voting in precincts of
residence, §11-42-74.
Privilege tax.
Territory exempt from
taxation.
Assessment and
collection of
privilege tax,
§§11-42-83,
11-42-84.
Levy and collection of
privilege tax,
§11-42-82.
Recordation.
Orders, maps, etc.,
§11-42-51.
Taxation.
Resolution, map,
orders, etc.,
§11-42-71.
Resolutions.
Certification, §11-42-42.
Filing, §11-42-42.
Passage of resolutions to
annex territory,
§11-42-41.
Requirements, §11-42-55.
Taxation.
Certification of
resolution,
§11-42-60.
Filing resolution with
probate judge,
§11-42-60.
Notice of passage,
§11-42-61.
Passage of resolution
declaring annexed
territory subject to
taxation,
§11-42-60.
Recordation, §11-42-71.
Single resolution for
separately owned
lands, §11-42-62.
Withdrawal of certified
resolution from
files of probate
judge for use in
circuit court,
§11-42-68.
Schools.
Territory exempt from
taxation.
Right of children to
attend public
schools, §11-42-85.

**MUNICIPAL
  CORPORATIONS**—Cont'd
Annexation—Cont'd
Cities of twenty-five
    thousand or more
    —Cont'd
Sewers.
  Territory exempt from
      taxation.
    Enforcement of
        sanitary
        connections and
        assessment of
        costs, §11-42-78.
Sidewalks.
  Territory exempt from
      taxation.
    Construction of
        sidewalks and
        assessment of
        costs, §11-42-79.
Subsequent extensions of
    corporate limits,
    §11-42-54.
Taxation.
  Appeals from judgment
      of circuit court,
      §11-42-69.
  Appeals from judgment
      of probate judge.
    Endorsement on map,
        §11-42-69.
    Filing, §11-42-66.
    Issuance of notice of
        appeal, §11-42-67.
    Notice of appeal,
        §11-42-67.
    Right to jury trial,
        §11-42-66.
    Security for costs,
        §11-42-66.
    Service of notice of
        appeal, §11-42-67.
    Transmittal of papers
        to clerk of circuit
        court, §11-42-68.
    Trial and entry of
        judgment by
        circuit court,
        §11-42-69.
    Withdrawal of map
        and certified
        resolution from
        files of probate
        judge, §11-42-68.
  Contests.
    City to file separate
        causes against
        contesting
        property owners,
        §11-42-63.
    Filing of contest as to
        right of city to tax
        lands or property,
        §11-42-63.
    Hearings, §11-42-65.
  Decree adjudging
      property subject to
      taxation, §11-42-65.
    Rendition as to
        noncontesting
        property owners,
        §11-42-64.
  Entry of judgment by
      circuit court,
      §11-42-69.

**MUNICIPAL
  CORPORATIONS**—Cont'd
Annexation—Cont'd
Cities of twenty-five
    thousand or more
    —Cont'd
Taxation—Cont'd
  Exemption from
      taxation, §11-42-57.
    Article as contract
        between city and
        exempt territory,
        §11-42-88.
    Attendance at city
        schools, §11-42-85.
    Common carriers,
        street railroads,
        etc., §11-42-84.
    Construction of
        improvements in
        territory,
        §11-42-77.
    Dance halls, §11-42-81.
    Entitlement to benefits
        derived from city
        taxes, §11-42-76.
    Industrial plants in
        annexed territory,
        §11-42-59.
    Landowners to file
        petition requesting
        betterments,
        §11-42-79.
    Manufacturing plants
        in annexed
        territory,
        §11-42-59.
    Mining plants in
        annexed territory,
        §11-42-59.
    Pool rooms, §11-42-81.
    Privilege or license
        tax, §§11-42-82 to
        11-42-84.
    Rights of resident
        citizens for persons
        residing in
        territory,
        §11-42-86.
    Sewers, §11-42-78.
    Sidewalks, §11-42-79.
    Street tax, §11-42-80.
  Hearings.
    Show cause, §11-42-61.
  Imposition on annexed
      territory and
      property after five
      years, §11-42-58.
  Judgment by circuit
      court.
    Appeals from
        judgment,
        §11-42-69.
    Certification to probate
        judge, §11-42-70.
    Entry of judgment,
        §11-42-69.
  Maps.
    Endorsements on
        maps, §§11-42-69,
        11-42-70.
    Filing with probate
        judge, §11-42-60.
    Recordation,
        §11-42-71.
    Withdrawal of map
        from files of
        probate judge,
        §11-42-68.

**MUNICIPAL
  CORPORATIONS**—Cont'd
Annexation—Cont'd
Cities of twenty-five
    thousand or more
    —Cont'd
Taxation—Cont'd
  Noncontesting property
      owners.
    Decree imposing tax,
        §11-42-64.
  Notice.
    Appeals, §11-42-67.
    Single notice for
        separately owned
        lands, §11-42-62.
  Orders.
    Recordation, §11-42-71
  Payment of taxes,
      §11-42-71.
  Resolutions.
    Certification,
        §11-42-60.
    Filing with probate
        judge, §11-42-60.
    Imposition of tax,
        §11-42-60.
    Notice of passage,
        §11-42-61.
    Recordation, §11-42-71
    Single resolution or
        notice for
        separately owned
        lands, §11-42-62.
    Withdrawal from files
        of probate judge,
        §11-42-68.
  Single resolution or
      notice for separately
      owned lands,
      §11-42-62.
  Trial by circuit court,
      §11-42-69.
  Wards.
    Boundaries, §11-42-75.
    Creation, etc., §11-42-73.
    Division into voting
        precincts, §11-42-74.
    Election of aldermen or
        representatives,
        §11-42-73.
Class 5 municipalities.
  Mayor/commission/city
      manager form of
      government.
    Inclusion of annexed
        territory into
        district,
        §11-44E-187.
Common carriers.
  Territory exempt from
      taxation.
    Assessment and
        collection of
        privilege or license
        tax, §11-42-84.
Consent.
  Proceedings where parties
      consent, §11-42-2.
Consolidation of contiguous
    municipalities.
  Alternate mode,
      §§11-42-120 to
      11-42-134.
  General provisions,
      §§11-42-100 to
      11-42-106.
Dance halls.
  Generally, §11-42-2.
  Subsequent elections.
    When held, §11-42-4.

MUNICIPAL
  CORPORATIONS—Cont'd
 Annexation—Cont'd
  Dance halls—Cont'd
   Territory exempt from
    taxation.
    Licensing of dance halls,
     §11-42-81.
  Elections.
   Cities of twenty-five
    thousand inhabitants
    or more, §§11-42-43 to
    11-42-53, 11-42-56.
  Exclusiveness of article.
   Provisions not exclusive,
    §11-42-1.
  Expanded municipalities.
   Duties as to absorbed
    municipalities,
    §§11-42-180 to
    11-42-187. See within
    this heading,
    "Expanded
    municipalities."
  Fees.
   Cities of twenty-five
    thousand or more.
    Fees of probate judges,
     §11-42-87.
  Incorporated municipalities,
   §§11-42-20 to 11-42-24.
   Construction of article,
    §11-42-24.
   Definition of owners,
    §11-42-20.
   Ordinances, §11-42-21.
   Owners defined, §11-42-20.
   Petition for annexation,
    §11-42-21.
   Proceedings, §11-42-21.
   Provisions of article not
    exclusive, §11-42-23.
   Subsequent extensions of
    corporate limits,
    §11-42-22.
  Industrial parks.
   County industrial parks.
    Exemption from
     annexation,
     §11-23-6.
  Jurisdiction.
   Cities of twenty-five
    thousand inhabitants
    or more.
    Jurisdiction of city over
     annexed territory,
     §11-42-72.
  Maps and plats.
   Cities of twenty-five
    thousand or more,
    §§11-42-42, 11-42-51.
   Copies of map to be
    furnished to judge of
    probate, §11-42-6.
   Taxation, §§11-42-68 to
    11-42-71.
  Mayor/commission/city
   manager form of
   government.
   Inclusion of annexed
    territory into district,
    §11-44E-187.
  Notice.
   Cities of twenty-five
    thousand or more.
    Requirements, §11-42-55.
    Taxation.
     Appeals, §11-42-67.
     Single notice for
      separately owned
      lands, §11-42-62.

MUNICIPAL
  CORPORATIONS—Cont'd
 Annexation—Cont'd
  Notice—Cont'd
   Notice of intention to apply
    for local law annexing
    territory required,
    §11-42-6.
   Requirements,
    §11-42-3.
  Orders.
   Cities of twenty-five
    thousand or more,
    §§11-42-51, 11-42-55,
    11-42-71.
   Requirements, §11-42-3.
  Ordinances.
   Cities of twenty-five
    thousand or more,
    §11-42-72.
   Contiguous municipalities.
    Mode of consolidation.
     When municipality to
      annex city or
      town,
      §11-42-100.1.
   Incorporated
    municipalities,
    §11-42-21.
  Petitions.
   Contiguous municipalities.
    Mode of consolidation.
     When municipality to
      annex city or
      town,
      §11-42-100.1.
   Incorporated
    municipalities,
    §11-42-21.
  Pool rooms.
   Territory exempt from
    taxation.
    Licensing of pool rooms,
     §11-42-81.
  Precincts.
   Cities of twenty-five
    thousand or more,
    §11-42-74.
  Proceedings.
   Generally, §11-42-2.
   Incorporated
    municipalities,
    §11-42-21.
   Where parties consent to
    annexation, §11-42-2.
  Recordation.
   Cities of twenty-five
    thousand or more.
    Recordation of orders,
     maps, etc.,
     §§11-42-51, 11-42-71.
  Resolutions.
   Cities of twenty-five
    thousand or more,
    §§11-42-41, 11-42-42,
    11-42-60 to 11-42-62.
   Requirements, §11-42-3.
  Street railroads.
   Territory exempt from
    taxation.
    Assessment and
     collection of
     privilege or license
     tax, §11-42-84.
  Streets.
   Territory exempt from
    taxation.
    Street tax, §11-42-80.

MUNICIPAL
  CORPORATIONS—Cont'd
 Annexation—Cont'd
  Subsequent elections.
   Cities of twenty-five
    thousand or more.
    When held, §11-42-56.
  Subsequent extensions of
   corporate limits,
   §11-42-54.
   Incorporated
    municipalities,
    §11-42-22.
  Telephone and telegraph
   lines.
   Territory exempt from
    taxation.
    Assessment and
     collection of
     privilege or license
     tax from operators,
     §11-42-84.
  Validation of certain prior
   annexations, §11-42-5.
  Wards.
   Change of boundaries upon
    annexation, §11-40-8.
   Cities of twenty-five
    thousand or more,
    §§11-42-73 to 11-42-75.
  Waterworks.
   Territory exempt from
    taxation.
    Privilege or license tax,
     §11-42-84.
 Appeals.
  Annexation.
   Cities of twenty-five
    thousand or more.
    Taxation, §§11-42-66 to
     11-42-69.
  Assessments for public
   improvements,
   §§11-48-36 to 11-48-47.
   See within this heading,
    "Assessments for public
    improvements."
  Bond issues.
   Validation.
    Judgment of circuit
     court, §§6-6-754,
     11-81-223.
  Charter.
   Forfeiture of charter.
    Appeal from decree of
     forfeiture, §11-41-26.
  Class 5 municipalities.
   Mayor/commission/city
    manager form of
    government.
    Removal of officers and
     employees,
     §11-44E-180.
  Demolition of unsafe
   structures, §11-40-32.
  Dissolution.
   Appeal from decree of
    dissolution, §11-41-26.
  Eminent domain.
   Procedure, §11-47-172.
   Right of entry pending
    appeal, §11-47-173.
  Forfeiture of charter.
   Appeal from decree of
    forfeiture and
    dissolution, §11-41-26.

MUNICIPAL
  CORPORATIONS—Cont'd
Appeals—Cont'd
Historic preservation
    commissions.
  Changes in historic
      properties or districts.
    Certificate of
        appropriateness.
      Denial, §11-68-10.
Mayor/commission/city
    manager form of
    government.
  Removal of officers and
      employees,
      §11-44E-180.
Zoning, §§11-52-80, 11-52-81.
Appearance bonds.
Designation of persons to
    approve, §11-43-5.
Appropriations.
Ambulance service, §11-87-2.
Bands, §11-80-4.
Capital improvement,
    §11-66-5.
Farmers' markets.
  Local appropriations
      authorized, §2-5-17.
Fire fighters' personnel
    standards and education.
  Appropriations authorized,
      §36-32-10.
Forests and forestry.
  Research and educational
      programs, §2-30-23.
Health.
  Public health work,
      §22-3-11.
Industry.
  Promotion of industry,
      §11-47-11.
Interest on indebtedness,
    §11-43-57.
Peace officers' standards and
    training commission,
    §36-21-48.
State parks.
  Improvement, operation,
      etc., of state park
      system, §9-14-6.
Tannehill furnace and
    foundry commission,
    §41-9-328.
Welfare, §38-2-9.
Architectural review boards.
Bridges.
  Applicability of provisions,
      §11-68-15.
Composition, §11-68-13.
Establishment, §§11-68-2,
    11-68-13.
Expenses of members.
  Reimbursement, §11-68-13.
Federal provisions.
  Applicability, §11-68-15.
Highways.
  Applicability of provisions,
      §11-68-15.
Meetings, §11-68-13.
Multiple boards, §11-68-13.
Nomination of members,
    §11-68-13.
Number of members,
    §11-68-13.
Officers, §11-68-13.
Personnel, §11-68-13.
Preexisting boards.
  Effect of provisions on,
      §11-68-14.
Purpose of provisions,
    §11-68-1.

MUNICIPAL
  CORPORATIONS—Cont'd
Architectural review boards
  —Cont'd
Qualifications of members,
    §11-68-13.
Removal of members,
    §11-68-13.
Rules of procedure,
    §11-68-13.
Streets.
  Applicability of provisions,
      §11-68-15.
Terms of members,
    §11-68-13.
Vacancies, §11-68-13.
Armories.
Conveyance of public lands
    for use as armory sites,
    §31-4-11.
Cooperation to acquire
    buildings for use as
    armories, §31-4-9.
General provisions.
  See MILITARY AFFAIRS.
Public improvement bonds.
  Certain revenue-producing
      undertakings,
      §11-81-140.
Real property.
  Sale to local national
      guard unit, §31-2-130.
Arrest.
Gambling, §11-47-111.
Motor vehicle arrest by
    municipal officers.
  Disposition of fines and
      forfeitures, §32-5A-10.
Police.
  Summons and complaint in
      lieu of arrest,
      §11-40-10.1.
Art galleries.
Powers as to, §11-47-16.
Assessments.
Abatement of nuisances,
    §11-47-117.
Demolition of unsafe
    structures.
  Costs, §§11-40-34,
      11-40-35.
Property taxes, §§11-51-1,
    11-51-4, 11-51-22.
Sales and use taxes,
    §§11-51-90, 11-51-204,
    11-51-205.
**Assessments for public
  improvements,** §§11-48-1
    to 11-48-106.
Abatement, §11-48-29.
  Erroneous assessments,
      §11-48-31.
  Excessive assessments,
      §11-48-31.
  Government or charitable
      property, §11-48-30.
Abutting property, §11-48-14.
Acceptance of work.
  Council to accept for
      municipality,
      §11-48-13.
Amount of assessments.
  Fixing by council,
      §11-48-29.
  Reduction, §11-48-29.
    Erroneous assessments,
        §11-48-31.
    Excessive assessments,
        §11-48-31.

MUNICIPAL
  CORPORATIONS—Cont'd
**Assessments for public
  improvements**—Cont'd
Amount of assessments
    —Cont'd
  Reduction—Cont'd
    Government or
        charitable property,
        §11-48-30.
    Reconveyance of
        property acquired
        through
        foreclosure of
        assessment,
        §11-48-30.
    Tenants in common.
      Property owned by
          tenants in
          common,
          §§11-48-105,
          11-48-106.
Appeals from judgment of
    circuit court, §§11-48-43
    to 11-48-47.
  By municipality.
    Authorized, §11-48-46.
    Bond not required,
        §11-48-46.
    Execution.
      Issuance, §11-48-47.
  By property owner.
    Authorized, §11-48-43.
    Bonds, §11-48-43.
    Conduct of appeal,
        §11-48-44.
  Judgment from
      municipality.
    Interest and damages
        upon affirmance,
        §11-48-45.
  Order of sale.
    Issuance of execution
        and order of sale
        upon entry of final
        judgment in favor of
        municipality,
        §11-48-47.
Appeals to circuit court from
    assessments, §§11-48-36
    to 11-48-42.
  Authorized, §11-48-36.
  Bond, §11-48-37.
  Conduct, §11-48-41.
  Costs.
    Assessment of costs,
        §11-48-41.
  Defective assessment.
    Judgment for amounts
        properly chargeable,
        §11-48-42.
  Docket.
    Entry on trial docket,
        §11-48-38.
  Entry on trial docket,
      §11-48-38.
  Evidence.
    Transcript for appeal.
      Prima facie evidence,
          §11-48-40.
  Judgment.
    Appeals from judgment
        of circuit court,
        §§11-48-43 to
        11-48-47.

MUNICIPAL
CORPORATIONS—Cont'd
Assessments for public
improvements—Cont'd
Appeals to circuit court from
assessments—Cont'd
Judgment—Cont'd
Entry of judgment,
§11-48-41.
For amounts properly
chargeable where
assessment
defective,
§11-48-42.
Jury trial.
Right of jury trial,
§11-48-41.
Transcript for appeal.
Contents, §11-48-39.
Prima facie evidence,
§11-48-40.
Applicability of article,
§11-48-3.
Assessment book.
Delivery to city or town
clerk, §11-48-22.
Publication of notice as
to delivery,
§11-48-22.
Inspection.
Publication of notice as
to inspection of book,
§11-48-22.
List of property owners to
be assessed.
Entry of list in
assessment book,
§11-48-21.
Benefited property,
§11-48-14.
Street and sewer
improvements outside
certain cities,
§11-48-81.
Bond issues.
Applicability of provisions
of law, §11-48-63.
Issuance after completion
of work, §11-48-62.
Public improvement bonds,
§§11-81-114,
11-81-115, 11-18-117,
11-81-118.
Bonds, surety.
Appeals from judgment of
circuit court.
By property owner,
§11-48-43.
Appeals to circuit court
from assessments,
§11-48-37.
Book.
Assessment book,
§§11-48-21, 11-48-22.
Charitable organizations.
Property owned by
charitable
organizations.
Reconveyance of property
acquired through
foreclosure,
§11-48-30.
Reduction or abatement
of assessments,
§11-48-30.
Circuit court.
Appeals from judgment of
circuit court,
§§11-48-43 to 11-48-47.

MUNICIPAL
CORPORATIONS—Cont'd
Assessments for public
improvements—Cont'd
Circuit court—Cont'd
Appeals to circuit court
from assessments,
§§11-48-36 to 11-48-42.
Enforcement of assessment
liens in circuit court,
§11-48-33.
Class 5 municipalities.
Mayor/commission/city
manager form of
government.
Commission.
Imposition of
assessments,
§11-44E-44.
Collection of property taxes.
Special taxes.
Separation of general
and special taxes,
§11-51-28.
Completion of work.
Issuance of bonds after
completion, §11-48-62.
Contracts for improvements.
Acceptance of work.
Council to accept for
municipality,
§11-48-13.
Advertisement, §11-48-11.
Letting of contract,
§11-48-11.
Notice, §11-48-11.
Rejection of work.
Council to reject for
municipality,
§11-48-13.
Supervision of work by city
or town engineer,
§11-48-12.
Definitions, §11-48-2.
Street and sewer
improvements outside
certain cities,
§11-48-81.
Delinquent property taxes.
Optional method for levy
and collection of
property taxes,
§§11-51-40 to 11-51-74.
Dikes.
Manner of assessment,
§11-48-16.
Disbursement of property
taxes.
Special taxes.
Separation of general
and special taxes,
§11-51-28.
Division of assessment.
Joint tenants and tenants
in common,
§§11-48-101 to
11-48-104.
Drawings of proposed
improvements.
Filing in office of engineer
for public inspection,
§11-48-6.
Ordering preparation,
§11-48-5.
Effect of assessments,
§11-48-29.
Engineer.
City or town engineer to
supervise work,
§11-48-12.

MUNICIPAL
CORPORATIONS—Cont'd
Assessments for public
improvements—Cont'd
Erroneous assessments.
Abatement, §11-48-31.
Appeals to circuit court,
§§11-48-36 to 11-48-42.
Reduction, §11-48-31.
Estimates for proposed
improvements.
Filing in office of engineer
for public inspection,
§11-48-6.
Ordering preparation of
estimates, §11-48-5.
Excessive assessments.
Abatement, §11-48-31.
Reduction, §11-48-31.
Failure to pay assessment.
Sale of land upon failure of
owner to pay,
§§11-48-49 to 11-48-53.
Foreclosure of assessments.
Enforcement of assessment
liens, §§11-48-33,
11-48-35.
Government or charitable
property.
Reconveyance of property
acquired through,
§11-48-30.
Sale of land upon failure of
owner to pay,
§§11-48-49 to 11-48-53.
Government organizations.
Property owned by,
Reduction or abatement
of assessment,
§11-48-30.
Grade of street, alley, etc., to
be improved.
When council to establish
grade, §11-48-10.
Hearings.
Establishment of date for
hearing, §11-48-6.
Objections as to
improvements,
§11-48-8.
Objections to assessments.
Conduct, §11-48-27.
Notice of hearing,
§11-48-23.
Powers of council as to
subpoena of
witnesses, etc.,
§11-48-28.
Interest.
Sale of land upon failure of
owner to pay,
§§11-48-49 to 11-48-60.
Intersections of streets,
alleys, etc.
Manner of assessment,
§§11-48-16, 11-48-17.
Joint tenants, §§11-48-100 to
11-48-106.
Lands purchased by state at
sale for nonpayment of
taxes.
Assessment of costs of
street improvements
and sewers authorized,
§11-48-15.
Levees.
Manner of assessment,
§11-48-16.

MUNICIPAL CORPORATIONS—Cont'd
Assessments for public improvements—Cont'd
Levy of property taxes.
Optional method, §§11-51-40 to 11-51-174.
Special taxes.
Separation of general and special taxes, §11-51-28.
Liens.
Assessment against property owned by tenants in common, §§11-48-100, 11-48-102.
Assessments to constitute liens, §11-48-29.
Assignment, §11-48-32.
Duration of assessment lien, §11-48-34.
Effect of sales of property for taxes upon assessment liens, §11-51-21.
Enforcement of assessment liens, §11-48-33.
Effect of sales of property for other assessment liens upon same property, §11-48-35.
Sale of land upon failure of owner to pay, §§11-48-49 to 11-48-53.
Sale of land upon failure of owner to pay, §§11-48-49 to 11-48-53.
Tax liens.
Effect of enforcement of tax liens upon assessment liens, §11-48-34.
Transfer of assessment liens, §§11-48-29, 11-48-32.
Limitation, Const. Ala., art. XII, §223.
Lists of property owners to be assessed.
Entry of list in assessment book, §11-48-21.
Preparation, §11-48-20.
Manner of assessment, §§11-48-16 to 11-48-18.
Dikes, §11-48-16.
Intersections of streets, alleys, etc., §11-48-17.
Levees, §11-48-16.
Seawalls, §11-48-16.
Sewers, §11-48-16.
Sidewalk improvements, §11-48-18.
Swamp drainage, §11-48-16.
Mayor/commission/city manager form of government.
Commission.
Imposition of assessments, §11-44E-44.
Notice.
Contents of notice, §11-48-24.
Defects or errors in notice.
Effect and correction, §11-48-25.

MUNICIPAL CORPORATIONS—Cont'd
Assessments for public improvements—Cont'd
Notice—Cont'd
Delivery and inspection of assessment book, §11-48-22.
Objections to assessments.
Notice of hearing upon objections, §11-48-23.
Property owned by tenants in common.
Notice of division of assessment, §11-48-103.
Objections as to improvements.
Hearing date, §11-48-6.
Objections to assessments.
Filing of written objections, §11-48-26.
Hearing.
Conduct, §11-48-27.
Notice of hearing, §11-48-23.
Subpoena of witnesses, etc., §11-48-28.
Notice of hearing, §11-48-23.
Written objections.
Filing, §11-48-26.
Optional method for levy and collection of property taxes, §§11-51-40 to 11-51-74.
Collection of taxes.
County tax collectors to collect, §11-51-43.
County tax assessor.
Ordinance or resolution levying taxes.
Certification and delivery to county tax assessor, §11-51-42.
County tax collectors.
Duty to collect taxes, §11-51-43.
Delinquent taxes.
When tax is delinquent, §11-51-41.
Levy of taxes, §11-51-42.
Ordinance or resolution levying taxes, §11-51-42.
Operation under provisions of article by certain cities, §11-51-40.
Ordinance levying taxes.
Certification and delivery to county tax assessor, §11-51-42.
Ordinance providing for payment upon basis of state and county assessments for preceding tax year, §11-51-40.
Resolution levying taxes, §11-51-42.
When tax is due, §11-51-41.
Ordinances and resolutions.
Amendment, §11-48-8.
Description of proposed improvement, §11-48-5.
Modification, §11-48-8.

MUNICIPAL CORPORATIONS—Cont'd
Assessments for public improvements—Cont'd
Ordinances and resolutions —Cont'd
Notice to certain property owners, §11-48-7.
Publication, §11-48-7.
Rescission, §11-48-8.
Payment of assessments.
Generally, §11-48-48.
Reduction of assessments, §§11-48-29 to 11-48-31.
Sale of land upon failure of owner to pay, §§11-48-49 to 11-48-53.
Payment of proportional costs of improvements by council, §11-48-9.
Plans of proposed improvements.
Filing in office of engineer for public inspection, §11-48-6.
Ordering preparation, §11-48-5.
Powers of municipalities.
General powers as to public improvements, §11-48-4.
Property benefited, §11-48-14.
Street and sewer improvements outside certain cities, §11-48-81.
Property owned by tenants in common, §§11-48-100 to 11-48-105.
Apportionment of assessment, §11-48-100.
Petition for division of assessment, §11-48-101.
Description of ownership of property.
Correction, §11-48-105.
Division of assessment, §11-48-102.
Acceptance of payment, §11-48-102.
Appeals from division, §11-48-104.
Discharge of lien upon proportionate shares of assessment, §11-48-102.
Notice to property owners, §11-48-103.
Petition of assessment, §11-48-101.
Liens.
Discharge of apportionment assessment lien, §§11-48-100, 11-48-102.
Division of assessments.
Discharge of lien upon proportionate shares, §11-48-102.
Reduction of assessment.
Effect upon assessment lien, §11-48-106.
Notice of division of assessment, §11-48-103.

MUNICIPAL CORPORATIONS—Cont'd
Assessments for public improvements—Cont'd

Property owned by tenants in common—Cont'd
Ownership of property.
Correction of description of ownership, §11-48-105.
Payment.
Acceptance of payment, §11-48-102.
Petition for division of assessment among joint owners, §11-48-101.
Reduction of assessment, §11-48-105.
Effect upon assessment lien, §11-48-106.
Railroads.
Assessment of costs against railroads, §11-48-19.
Redemption of property after sale, §§11-48-54 to 11-48-60.
Reduction of assessments, §11-48-29.
Assessments in excess of benefits derived, etc., §11-48-31.
Erroneous assessments, §11-48-31.
Excessive assessments, §11-48-31.
Government or charitable property.
Authority, §11-48-30.
Reconveyance of property acquired through foreclosure, §11-48-30.
Property owned by tenants in common, §§11-48-105, 11-48-106.
Rejection of work.
Council to reject for municipality, §11-48-13.
Sale of land upon failure of owner to pay assessment, §§11-48-49 to 11-48-59.
Costs of notice and sale charged against land, §11-48-51.
Deed.
Certificate of warning to redeem.
Recordation, §§11-48-56, 11-48-57.
Execution, etc., of deed to purchaser at sale, §11-48-52.
Mailing copies of deed to persons last assessed, §11-48-57.
Defect in sale, §11-48-53.
Error in sale.
Effect of error, §11-48-53.
Execution of deed to purchaser at sale, §11-48-52.
Notice of proceedings, §11-48-49.
Costs of notice charged against land, §11-48-51.

MUNICIPAL CORPORATIONS—Cont'd
Assessments for public improvements—Cont'd

Sale of land upon failure of owner to pay assessment —Cont'd
Notice of proceedings —Cont'd
Effect of error or defect in notice, §11-48-53.
Payment prior to sale, §11-48-50.
Purchase of property by municipality, §11-48-52.
Redemption of property after sale, §11-48-54.
Applicability of provisions of sections 11-48-54 through 11-48-58, §11-48-60.
Certificate of warning to redeem, §11-48-56.
Contents, §11-48-56.
Mailing of copies of certificate to persons last assessed, §11-48-57.
Recordation, §11-48-57.
Extension of redemption period, §11-48-55.
Redemption of property during extended redemption period, §11-48-58.
Liability of probate judge, §11-48-59.
Redemption during extended redemption period, §11-48-58.
Surplus from sale.
Disposition, §11-48-52.
Sales of property for taxes.
Certification to circuit court of unpaid assessments, §11-51-21.
Collection of assessments from proceeds of sale, §11-51-21.
Seawalls.
Manner of assessment, §11-48-16.
Sewers.
Acquisition, operation, etc., §§11-50-50 to 11-50-54.
Waterworks and sewer boards.
Management of systems as agents of municipalities, §§11-50-290, 11-50-291.
Assessment against lands purchased by state at sale for nonpayment of taxes, §11-48-15.
Manner of assessment, §11-48-16.
Authorized, §11-81-161.
Boards for operation of water, sewer, gas and electric systems, §§11-50-310 to 11-50-324. See within this heading, "Public utilities."

MUNICIPAL CORPORATIONS—Cont'd
Assessments for public improvements—Cont'd

Sewers—Cont'd
Manner of assessment —Cont'd
Eminent domain, §11-50-51.
Expenses.
Payment of expenses of operation out of general fund, §11-81-182.
Notice, §11-50-56.
Operation by public water corporations, §§11-50-370 to 11-50-372.
Rules and regulations.
Adoption, §11-50-108.
State board of health.
Supervision of operation, §11-81-185.
Purchase, §§11-50-70 to 11-50-108.
Revenue bonds, §§11-51-161, 11-51-162.
Short title of article, §11-48-1.
Sidewalk improvements.
Manner of assessment, §11-48-18.
Municipality may compel owners to repair sidewalks, etc., §11-48-65.
Specification of cost, §11-48-9.
Specifications of proposed improvements.
Filing in office of engineer for public inspection, §11-48-6.
Ordering preparation of specifications, §11-48-5.
Street and sewer improvements outside certain cities.
Bond issues.
General obligation bonds.
Issuance to pay cost of improvements, §11-48-82.
Payable from proceeds of assessments, §11-48-83.
Street improvements.
Assessment against lands purchased by state at sale for nonpayment of taxes, §11-48-15.
Grade of street, alley, etc., to be improved.
When council to establish grade, §11-48-10.
Intersections.
Manner of assessment, §§11-48-16, 11-48-17.
Surveys of proposed improvements.
Filing in office of engineer for public inspection, §11-48-6.

**MUNICIPAL
CORPORATIONS**—Cont'd
**Assessments for public
improvements**—Cont'd
Surveys of proposed
improvements—Cont'd
Ordering preparation,
§11-48-5.
Swamp drainage.
Manner of assessment,
§11-48-16.
Tenants in common,
§§11-48-100 to 11-48-105.
Who may be assessed,
§§11-48-14, 11-48-15.
Railroads, §11-48-19.
Street and sewer
improvements outside
certain cities,
§11-48-81.
Athletics.
Licensing of athletic games,
§11-51-104.
Public athletic boards,
§§11-59-1 to 11-59-17.
See within this heading,
"Parks and recreation."
Atomic energy.
Radiation.
Effect of chapter on local
ordinances, §22-14-15.
Attachment.
Licenses.
Collection of license taxes.
Equitable attachment,
§11-51-160.
Taxation.
Collection of taxes in
anticipation of
nonpayment,
§11-51-26.
Attorney general.
Allegations, municipal
ordinance or franchise
unconstitutional.
Entitled to be heard,
§6-6-227.
Service upon attorney
general, §6-6-227.
Defense of actions against
political subdivisions,
Const. Ala., amd. 111.
Duty to give opinions to local
officers, §36-15-18.
Certificate of officer
requesting, §36-15-20.
Moot or private questions
not to be submitted for
opinion, §36-15-20.
Resolution of municipality
required, §36-15-20.
Written opinion protects
officer, governing body,
etc., §36-15-19.
Ordinances.
Constitutionality
questioned.
Notice to attorney
general, §6-6-227.
Auctions and auctioneers.
General provisions, §§34-4-1
to 34-4-54.
See AUCTIONS AND
AUCTIONEERS.
Licensing of auction sales,
§11-51-97.
Limitation on authority of
municipalities to tax,
§34-4-6.

**MUNICIPAL
CORPORATIONS**—Cont'd
Auditors.
Clerks.
Devolution of duties upon
auditors, §11-43-103.
Duties, §11-43-3.
Devolution of clerk duties
upon auditor,
§11-43-103.
Election, §11-43-3.
Terms of office, §11-43-3.
Audits.
Boards of water and sewer
commissioners,
§11-50-355.
Bond issues, §11-81-68.
Claims against municipality.
Auditing by clerks,
§11-43-101.
Commission form of
government.
Optional form A,
§11-44-95.
Optional form B,
§11-44-139.
Transportation service in
class 3 municipalities,
§11-49A-18.
Authorities.
Airports. See within this
heading, "Airports."
Buildings.
Hospitals.
Building authorities,
§§22-21-130 to
22-21-156.
See HOSPITALS.
Public building authorities,
§§11-56-1 to 11-56-22.
See within this
heading, "Public
building authorities."
Counties.
Establishment, aid, etc., of
hospitals in counties,
§11-47-134.
Electricity.
Municipal electric
authority, §§11-50A-1
to 11-50A-33. See
within this heading,
"Electricity."
Establishment, §§11-47-7,
11-47-134, 22-21-1.
Hospitals.
Building authorities,
§§22-21-130 to
22-21-156.
See HOSPITALS.
Housing authorities,
§§24-1-20 to 24-1-45.
See HOUSING
AUTHORITIES.
Improvement authorities,
§§39-7-1 to 39-7-34.
See PUBLIC WORKS.
Indigent persons.
Appropriation of funds for
care, §11-47-133.
Maintenance, §11-47-7.
Medical clinic boards,
§§11-58-1 to 11-58-15.
See within this heading,
"Medical clinic boards."
Police jurisdiction over
hospitals, §11-47-22.

**MUNICIPAL
CORPORATIONS**—Cont'd
Authorities—Cont'd
Public building authorities,
§§11-56-1 to 11-56-22.
See within this heading,
"Public building
authorities."
Public hospital associations.
Appropriations, §22-21-56.
Public library authorities,
§§11-57-1 to 11-57-26.
See within this heading,
"Libraries."
Regulation, §11-47-7.
Transfer of hospitals and
funds by municipalities,
§22-21-81.
Transportation service in
class 3 municipalities.
Defined, §11-49A-2.
Dissolution of authority,
§11-49A-19.
Incorporation of additional
authorities in same
county.
Prohibited, §11-49A-20.
Organization, §11-49A-7.
Powers, §11-49A-8.
Authority of municipalities.
Acquisition of authority
granted, §11-40-3.
Generally, §11-40-1.
Bands.
Appropriations for municipal
bands, §11-80-4.
**Banks and financial
institutions.**
Deposits.
Pledge of assets as security
for deposits by
municipalities,
§5-5A-28.
Industrial development
corporations.
Occupational license taxes,
§10-4-144.
Licenses.
Schedule of license tax,
§11-51-130.
Savings and loan
associations.
Schedule of license tax,
§11-51-131.
**Bear creek development
authority.**
Monetary contributions by
certain municipalities,
§33-15-13.
Beverages.
Impure, adulterated, etc.,
drink.
Prohibition of sale, etc.,
§11-47-136.
Provision for inspections,
§11-47-136.
Billiard rooms.
Annexation.
Territory exempt from
taxation.
Licensing of billiard
rooms, §11-42-81.
Authority of municipalities,
§34-6-3.
Closing, §11-51-102.
General provisions, §§34-6-1
to 34-6-35.
See BILLIARD ROOMS.
Keeping tables outside cities
or towns, §§34-6-8,
34-6-8.1.

MUNICIPAL
CORPORATIONS—Cont'd
Billiard rooms—Cont'd
Licenses, §11-51-102.
Annexation.
Territory exempt from
taxation, §11-42-81.
Application to city clerk,
§34-6-34.
Ordinance may prohibit
issuance, §34-6-35.
Revocation, §11-51-103.
Blind persons.
Elections.
Assistance to disabled
voters, §§11-46-40,
11-46-111, 11-46-122,
11-46-138.
Deception of disabled
voters by marker, etc.,
§§11-46-64, 11-46-135.
False declaration
requesting assistance,
§11-46-138.
Mayor-council form.
Assistance of disabled
electors, §11-46-40.
Voting machines,
§11-46-51.
Employment by
municipalities, §21-7-8.
Board of adjustment,
§§11-52-80, 11-52-81.
Board of commissioners. See
within this heading,
"Commission form of
government."
Boards of education,
§§16-11-1 to 16-11-27.
See EDUCATION.
Boards of water and sewer
commissioners,
§§11-50-340 to 11-50-358.
Appointment of members,
§11-50-342.
Audits.
Annual audits, §11-50-355.
Bond issues, §§11-50-345 to
11-50-350, 11-50-353 to
11-50-356.
Authorization of issuance,
§11-50-345.
Denominations,
§11-50-345.
Disposition of proceeds
from sale, §11-50-345.
Execution, §11-50-345.
Exemption from taxation,
§11-50-354.
Form, §11-50-345.
Interim receipts.
Issuance, §11-50-345.
Issuance, §11-50-356.
Authorization,
§11-50-345.
Liability upon revenue
bonds, §11-50-348.
Payment, §11-50-348.
Trust agreement as
security, §11-50-346.
Proceeds from sale.
Disposition, §11-50-345.
Refunding bonds,
§§11-50-350,
11-50-356.
Remedies of bondholders
and trustees,
§11-50-349.
Resolutions, §11-50-347.
Issuance of bonds,
§11-50-346.

MUNICIPAL
CORPORATIONS—Cont'd
Boards of water and sewer
commissioners—Cont'd
Bond issues—Cont'd
Resolutions—Cont'd
Trustees, §11-50-353.
Sale, §11-50-345.
Disposition of proceeds,
§11-50-345.
Taxation.
Exemption from
taxation, §11-50-354.
Temporary bonds,
§11-50-345.
Terms, §11-50-345.
Trust agreements,
§11-50-347.
Execution as security for
payment,
§11-50-346.
Bonds, surety.
Members of boards,
§11-50-342.
Compensation of members,
§11-50-342.
Conflicting laws, §11-50-358.
Conflicts of interest.
Members, agents or
employees of board,
§11-50-355.
Connection of buildings to
sewers.
Rules and regulations,
§11-50-352.
Construction of article.
Liberal construction,
§11-50-357.
Conveyances.
Powers of board as to,
§11-50-344.
Creation, §11-50-341.
Cumulative provisions,
§11-50-356.
Definitions, §11-50-340.
Dissolution of board.
Upon payment of bonds in
full, §11-50-355.
Exemption from taxation,
§11-50-354.
Expenses.
Payment, §11-50-348.
Money received under article.
Deemed trust funds,
§11-50-353.
Oaths of members,
§11-50-342.
Officers.
Election, §11-50-342.
Ordinance creating,
§11-50-341.
Powers, §11-50-343.
Conveyance, etc., of title to
systems, §11-50-344.
Qualifications of members,
§11-50-342.
Quorum, §11-50-342.
Rates and charges,
§11-50-351.
Removal of members,
§11-50-342.
Reports.
Annual reports,
§11-50-355.
Resolutions of board.
Authentication,
§11-50-343.
Bond issues, §§11-50-346,
11-50-347.
Trustees, §11-50-353.
Publication, §11-50-343.

MUNICIPAL
CORPORATIONS—Cont'd
Boards of water and sewer
commissioners—Cont'd
Resolutions of board—Cont'd
Recordation, §11-50-343.
Sewer connections.
Rules and regulations,
§11-50-352.
Taxation.
Exemption from taxation,
§11-50-354.
Terms of members,
§11-50-342.
Title to systems.
Conveyances, §11-50-344.
Vesting in city upon
payment of bonds,
§11-50-355.
Transfer of existing system
to board, §11-50-344.
Trust agreements.
Bond issues, §11-50-347.
Provisions for issuance of
bonds, §11-50-346.
Security for payment of
revenue bonds,
§11-50-346.
Provisions in trust
agreements as to
trustee, §11-50-353.
Remedies of trustees,
§11-50-349.
Vacancies, §11-50-342.
Boats.
Local regulation, §33-5-31.
Municipal boats.
Exemption from
numbering provisions,
§33-5-19.
Bodies politic and corporate.
Declared bodies politic and
corporate, §11-40-1.
Bond issues, Const. Ala., art.
XII, §222.
Absorbed municipalities.
Duties of expanded
municipalities as to,
§§11-42-180,
11-42-186.
Airports, §4-4-11.
Authority to issue bonds
for acquisition,
improvement, etc.,
§4-1-1.
Anticipation notes,
§11-81-28.
Appeals.
Validation, §§6-6-754,
11-81-223.
Audits, §11-81-68.
Authorization of issuance.
After reorganization,
§11-47-4.
Boards for operation of
water, sewer, gas and
electric systems,
§§11-50-315 to 11-50-318.
Boards of water and sewer
commissioners,
§§11-50-345 to 11-50-350,
11-50-353 to 11-50-356.
See within this heading,
"Boards of water and
sewer commissioners."
Buildings.
Authorized for
construction,
extension, etc.,
§11-47-3.

MUNICIPAL CORPORATIONS—Cont'd
Bond issues—Cont'd
Buildings—Cont'd
Public building authorities, §§11-56-10 to 11-56-18. See within this heading, "Public building authorities."
Civic organizations.
Acquisition of projects to provide of buildings, etc., for certain national organizations, §§11-54-54 to 11-54-61. See within this heading, "Civic organizations."
Class 5 municipalities.
Mayor/commission/city manager form of government.
Commission.
Power to authorize issuance, §11-44E-44.
Commercial development authorities, §§11-54-179 to 11-54-183.
Commercial paper, §11-81-30.
Debt limit, Const. Ala., art. XII, §225; amd. 268.
See CONSTITUTION OF ALABAMA.
Definitions.
"Municipality," §11-81-50.
Validation prior to issuance, §§6-6-750, 11-81-220.
Delivery, §11-81-63.
Validity of delivery.
Limitation of actions, §11-81-14.
Presumption, §11-81-14.
Department of finance.
Consent of department not required for issuance, §41-4-16.
Destroyed bonds.
Issuance of duplicates, §11-81-32.
Disposition of proceeds, §11-81-13.
District electric corporations.
See within this heading, "Electricity."
Duplicate bonds.
Issuance for lost, mutilated or destroyed bonds, §11-81-32.
Elections, §§11-81-52 to 11-81-61, 11-81-67.
Applicability of provisions of general election laws, §11-81-67.
Ballots, §11-81-54.
Board of canvassers, §11-81-57.
Canvassers.
Board of canvassers, §11-81-57.
Clerks.
Appointment, §11-81-55.
Compensation, §11-81-56.
Conduct of election, §11-81-55.
Contest.
Authorized, §11-81-59.
Bond required, §11-81-59.

MUNICIPAL CORPORATIONS—Cont'd
Bond issues—Cont'd
Elections—Cont'd
Contest—Cont'd
Hearing, §11-81-60.
Limitation of action, §§6-2-40, 11-81-61.
Notice, §11-81-60.
Directory provisions of article, §11-81-67.
Expenses, §11-81-56.
Facsimile signatures, §11-81-33.
General election laws.
Applicability, §11-81-67.
Hearings.
Contest, §11-81-60.
Irregular elections.
Ratification, §11-81-31.
Limitation of actions.
Contest, §§6-2-40, 11-81-61.
Managers.
Appointment, §11-81-55.
Compensation, §11-81-56.
Mandatory provisions of article, §11-81-67.
Notice of election, §11-81-53.
Ratification of certain irregular elections for issuance of bonds, §11-81-31.
Recordation of results, §11-81-58.
Results.
Recordation, §11-81-58.
Returning officers.
Appointment, §11-81-55.
Compensation, §11-81-56.
Electricity.
Alternate borrowing for electric systems, §§11-81-200 to 11-81-206. See within this heading, "Electricity."
Authorized, §11-47-3.
District electric corporations, §§11-50-526 to 11-50-529.
Revenue bonds, §§11-81-160 to 11-81-190. See within this heading, "Public utilities."
Security for bonds issued to purchase, etc. light and power plants, §11-81-1.
Engraved signature.
Execution of bonds with engraved or otherwise reproduced facsimile of signature, seal, etc., §11-81-33.
Exchange, §11-81-11.
Refunding bonds, §§11-81-11, 11-81-64.
Execution, §11-81-63.
Facsimile signature, §11-81-33.
Interest coupons, §11-81-63.
Validity of execution.
Limitation period for actions to contest validity, §11-81-14.

MUNICIPAL CORPORATIONS—Cont'd
Bond issues—Cont'd
Execution—Cont'd
Validity of execution —Cont'd
Presumption as to validity, §11-81-14.
Exemption from taxation, §§40-9-1, 11-81-29.
Facsimile signature, §11-81-33.
Interest coupons, §11-81-63.
Fire protection districts.
Construction of sewerage facilities in resort areas, §§11-88-91 to 11-88-111.
Generally, §§11-88-8 to 11-88-11, 11-88-16, 11-88-21.
Form, §11-81-9.
Gas.
Gas districts, §§11-50-405 to 11-50-410, 11-50-412.
Revenue bonds, §§11-81-160 to 11-81-190. See within this heading, "Public utilities."
Security for bonds issued in purchase, etc., in gas plants, §11-81-1.
Health care facility authorities, §§11-62-8 to 11-62-12.
Hotels.
Projects to promote hotel services, §§11-54-143, 11-54-144.
Improvement for which bonds issued.
Estimate as to period of usefulness, §11-81-8.
Industrial development boards, §§11-54-89 to 11-54-92.
Interest.
Appropriation for interest, §11-43-57.
Maximum rates of interest.
Exemption of municipal bonds, §8-8-7.
Interest coupons.
Exempt from taxation, §11-81-29.
Facsimile signatures, §11-81-63.
Receivable for payment of taxes and dues, §11-81-66.
Irregularities in proceedings for issuance, etc., not to affect validity, §11-81-30.
Issuance, §11-81-62.
Authority for issuance after reorganization, §11-47-4.
Duplicates, §11-81-32.
Elections for issuance, §§11-81-52 to 11-81-61, 11-81-67.
Generally, §11-81-62.
Irregularities in proceedings for issuance not to affect validity, §11-81-30.

MUNICIPAL
  CORPORATIONS—Cont'd
Bond issues—Cont'd
  Issuance—Cont'd
    Powers of counties
      authorizing issuance,
      §11-81-3.
    Purposes for which bonds
      may be issued,
      §11-81-51.
    Refunding bonds.
      Authority for issuance,
        §11-81-64.
    Revenue bonds and other
      revenue securities,
      Const. Ala., amd. 107.
    Validation of bonds prior
      to issuance, §§6-6-750
      to 6-6-757, 11-81-220
      to 11-81-227.
  Judgment as to validity,
    §§6-6-753 to 6-6-755,
    11-81-223, 11-81-224.
  Letters of credit.
    Security for bonds,
      §11-80-7.
  Libraries.
    Public library authorities,
      §§11-57-11 to 11-57-21.
      See within this
      heading, "Libraries."
  Licenses.
    Pledge of revenue to pay,
      §§11-81-16, 11-81-18.
  Limitation of actions.
    Testing validity of
      issuance, etc.,
      §11-81-14.
    Testing validity of
      municipal election for
      purpose of issuing
      bonds, §§6-2-40,
      11-81-61.
  Lost bond.
    Issuance of duplicates,
      §11-81-32.
  Maturity, §11-81-6.
    Bonds issued and sold in
      series, §11-81-7.
  Mayor/commission/city
    manager form of
    government.
    Commission.
      Power to authorize
        issuance,
        §11-44E-44.
  Medical clinic boards,
    §§11-58-7 to 11-58-10.
  Mortgages and deeds of trust.
    Execution upon property
      acquired with
      proceeds, §11-81-2.
    Recordation, §11-81-2.
  Mutilated bonds.
    Issuance of duplicates,
      §11-81-32.
  Notes.
    Anticipation notes.
      Issuance, sale, etc., of
        negotiable notes in
        anticipation of sale
        of bonds, §11-81-28.
  Notice of election, §11-81-53.
  Outstanding bonds.
    Funding of bonds
      outstanding,
      §§11-81-64, 11-81-65.
  Payment, §11-81-6.
    Bonds issued and sold in
      series, §11-81-7.

MUNICIPAL
  CORPORATIONS—Cont'd
Bond issues—Cont'd
  Payment—Cont'd
    Places of payment,
      §11-81-5.
    Pledge of revenues from
      certain taxes, utilities,
      etc., for payment,
      §§11-50-240, 11-81-16
      to 11-81-18.
    Tax for payment.
      Collection of special tax,
        §11-81-15.
      Disposition of special
        tax, §11-81-15.
      Levy of special tax,
        §11-81-15.
      Mandamus proceedings,
        §11-81-26.
    Pledge of revenues from
      certain taxes for
      payment, §§11-81-16,
      11-81-18.
    Waterworks system.
      Pledge of revenues from
        waterworks system,
        §§11-81-16, 11-81-17.
  Period of usefulness of
    improvement or property
    for which bonds issued.
    Estimate, §11-81-8.
  Pledge of revenues from
    certain taxes, utilities,
    etc., for payment,
    §§11-50-240, 11-81-16 to
    11-81-18.
  Post office projects, §§11-55-3
    to 11-55-8, 11-55-11. See
    within this heading,
    "Post office projects."
  Powers of municipalities
    authorizing issuance,
    §11-81-3.
  Price.
    Sale price, §11-81-10.
  Proceeds from sale.
    Disposition, §11-81-13.
    Execution of mortgages or
      deeds of trust upon
      property acquired with
      proceeds, §11-81-2.
  Promotion of industry, trade
    and pollution control,
    §§11-54-24 to 11-54-29.
  Property for which bonds
    issued.
    Estimate as to period of
      usefulness of property,
      §11-81-8.
  Public athletic boards,
    §§11-59-9 to 11-59-11,
    11-59-16. See within this
    heading, "Parks and
    recreation."
  Public building authorities,
    §§11-56-10 to 11-56-18.
    See within this heading,
    "Public building
    authorities."
  Public corporations, Const.
    Ala., amd. 108.
    Assistance to related public
      corporations, §§11-63-1
      to 11-63-4.
  Public improvement bonds,
    §§11-81-110 to 11-81-123.
    Adjustment of bonds,
      §11-81-119.

MUNICIPAL
  CORPORATIONS—Cont'd
Bond issues—Cont'd
  Public improvement bonds
    —Cont'd
    Assessments.
      Bonds, surety of
        collector, §11-81-115.
      Disposition, §11-81-114.
      Liability for diversion of
        funds, §11-81-115.
      Pledge of proceeds,
        §11-81-110.
      Refunding of excess
        assessments,
        §§11-81-117,
        11-81-118.
    Consolidation of
      municipalities.
      Liability upon bonds,
        §11-81-123.
    Delivery.
      In payment for work,
        §11-81-111.
    Disposition of proceeds
      from sale, §11-81-112.
    Enforcement of
      maintenance of
      accounts.
      Payment of bonds, etc.,
        §11-81-114.
    Grouping of improvements
      for issuance of bonds,
      §11-81-113.
    Issuance, §11-81-110.
      Grouping of
        improvements,
        §11-81-113.
      Refunding bonds,
        §§11-81-119 to
        11-81-121.
    Maintenance of accounts.
      Enforcement, §11-81-114.
    Maturity, §11-81-111.
    Payment, §11-81-114.
      Liability for diversion of
        funds, §11-81-115.
      Pledge of proceeds of
        assessments as
        security for
        payment,
        §11-81-110.
    Pledge of proceeds,
      §11-81-110.
    Proceeds from sale.
      Disposition, §11-81-112.
    Redemption of bonds,
      §11-81-116.
    Refunding of bonds,
      §11-81-119.
      Consolidation of issues,
        §11-81-121.
      Issuance of refunding
        bonds, §§11-81-119
        to 11-81-121.
      Sale or issuance to
        custodian of special
        fund, etc., of
        refunding bonds,
        §11-81-120.
    Sinking funds,
      §11-81-122.
    Refunding of excess
      assessments.
      Authority, §11-81-117.
      Disposition of amounts
        not refunded,
        §11-81-118.
      Limitation period for
        claims, §11-81-118.
      Procedure, §11-81-117.

MUNICIPAL
  CORPORATIONS—Cont'd
Bond issues—Cont'd
Public improvement bonds
  —Cont'd
Sale.
  Disposition of proceeds
    from sale,
    §11-81-112.
  In payment for work,
    §11-81-111.
  Refunding bonds,
    §§11-81-119,
    11-81-120.
Security.
  Disposition of
    assessments securing
    bonds in certain
    cities, §11-81-114.
  Pledge of proceeds of
    assessments,
    §11-81-110.
Settlement of bonds,
    §11-81-119.
Sinking fund accounts.
  Disposition, §11-81-114.
  Maintenance,
    §11-81-114.
  Refunding bond issues,
    §11-81-122.
Public improvement bonds
  for certain revenue-
  producing undertakings,
  §§11-81-140 to 11-81-150.
  See COUNTIES.
Public library authorities,
  §§11-57-11 to 11-57-21.
  See within this heading,
  "Libraries."
Public utilities.
  Boards for operation of
    water, sewer, gas and
    electric system,
    §§11-50-315 to
    11-50-318.
  Electric systems.
    Alternate borrowing for
      electric systems,
      §§11-81-200 to
      11-81-206. See
      within this heading,
      "Electricity."
  Exemption from taxation,
    §11-50-322.
  Public improvement bonds,
    §§11-81-110 to
    11-81-123.
  Revenue bonds for
    waterworks, gas, sewer
    or electric systems,
    §§11-81-160 to
    11-81-190. See within
    this heading, "Public
    utilities."
  Waterworks and sewer
    boards, §§11-50-237,
    11-50-239, 11-50-240.
Redemption of securities,
  §§11-82-1 to 11-82-7. See
  within this heading,
  "Redemption of
  securities."
Refunding bonds.
  Exchange, §§11-81-11,
    11-81-64.
  Holders.
    Rights of holders,
      §11-81-64.
  Issuance, §11-81-4.
    Authority for issuance,
      §11-81-64.

MUNICIPAL
  CORPORATIONS—Cont'd
Bond issues—Cont'd
Refunding bonds—Cont'd
Payment.
  Pledge of tax, revenues
    for payment,
    §11-81-4.
  Powers of municipalities as
    to, §11-81-3.
  Rights of holders,
    §11-81-64.
  Sale, §§11-81-11, 11-81-64.
  Security, §11-81-65.
  Sinking funds, §§11-81-22
    to 11-81-25.
Registration, §11-81-9.
Reorganization of
  municipalities.
  Authority for issuance
    after reorganization,
    §11-47-4.
Revenue bonds for
  waterworks, gas, sewer
  or electric systems,
  §§11-81-160 to 11-81-190.
  See within this heading,
  "Public utilities."
Sale, §§11-81-11 to 11-81-14.
  Bids, §11-81-11.
    Determination of highest
      bidder, §11-81-12.
  Disposition of proceeds,
    §11-81-13.
  Price, §11-81-10.
  Proceeds from sale.
    Disposition, §11-81-13.
    Execution of mortgages
      or deeds of trust
      upon property
      acquired with
      proceeds of bond
      issues, §11-81-2.
  Refunding bonds,
    §§11-81-11, 11-81-64.
  Validity of sale.
    Limitation of actions,
      §11-81-14.
    Presumption, §11-81-14.
School buildings.
  Security for bonds to
    purchase, etc.,
    §11-81-1.
Securities issued in
  anticipation of grants,
  §§11-64-1 to 11-64-7. See
  within this heading,
  "Securities issued in
  anticipation of grants."
Series.
  Maturity of bonds issued
    and sold in series,
    §11-81-7.
  Payment of bonds issued
    and sold in series,
    §11-81-7.
Sewers.
  Boards for operation of
    water, sewer, gas and
    electric systems,
    §§11-50-315 to
    11-50-318.
  Boards of water and sewer
    commissioners,
    §§11-50-345 to
    11-50-350, 11-50-353 to
    11-50-356. See within
    this heading, "Boards
    of water and sewer
    commissioners."

MUNICIPAL
  CORPORATIONS—Cont'd
Bond issues—Cont'd
Sewers—Cont'd
  Public improvement bonds,
    §§11-81-110 to
    11-81-123.
  Purchase of sewers,
    §§11-50-96 to
    11-50-102, 11-50-105.
    See within this
    heading, "Sewers."
  Revenue bonds,
    §§11-81-160 to
    11-81-190. See within
    this heading, "Public
    utilities."
  Waterworks and sewer
    boards, §§11-50-237,
    11-50-239, 11-50-240.
Sidewalks.
  Public improvement bonds,
    §§11-81-110 to
    11-81-123.
Signatures, §§11-81-14,
  11-81-33, 11-81-63.
Sinking fund.
  General provisions,
    §§11-81-22 to 11-81-25.
  Public improvement bonds,
    §§11-81-114,
    11-81-122.
Special, private or local laws
  prohibited, Const. Ala.,
  art. IV, §104.
Streets.
  Public improvement bonds,
    §§11-81-110 to
    11-81-123.
Taxation.
  Bonds and coupons
    receivable for
    payment, §11-81-66.
  Exemption from taxation,
    §§11-50-354, 11-81-29,
    40-9-1.
  Pledge of revenues,
    §§11-81-16, 11-81-18.
  Special tax for payment of
    principal and interest.
    Levy, collection and
      disposition,
      §11-81-15.
    Mandamus proceedings,
      §11-81-26.
    Pledge of revenues,
      §§11-81-16, 11-81-18.
Transfer.
  Provision for transfer,
    §11-81-9.
Transportation service in
  class 3 municipalities,
  §§11-49A-10, 11-49A-11,
  11-49A-13, 11-49A-15.
Validation, §§6-6-750 to
  6-6-757, 11-81-30,
  11-81-220 to 11-81-227.
  Appeals from judgment of
    circuit court,
    §§6-6-754, 11-81-223.
  Applicability of article,
    §11-81-227.
  Complaint for
    determination as to
    legality of proposed
    issuance.
    Contents, §§6-6-752,
      11-81-222.
    Filing, §§6-6-751,
      11-81-221.

MUNICIPAL CORPORATIONS—Cont'd
Bond issues—Cont'd
Validation—Cont'd
Costs of proceedings, §§6-6-757, 11-81-226.
Definitions, §§6-6-750, 11-81-220.
District attorney.
Defined, §6-6-750.
Service on, §6-6-752.
Entry of judgment on validity, §11-81-223.
Hearing to show cause why obligations not valid, §§6-6-753, 11-81-223.
Notice, §§6-6-752, 11-81-222.
Order, §§6-6-752, 11-81-222.
Irregularities in proceedings for issuance, etc., not to affect validity, §11-81-30.
Judgment on validity.
Appeals from judgment of circuit court, §§6-6-754, 11-81-223.
Conclusiveness, §§6-6-755, 11-81-224.
Contents, §6-6-753.
Entry of judgment, §11-81-223.
Legend to appear on validated obligations, §§6-6-756, 11-81-225.
Limitation period for actions, §§6-2-40, 11-60-10, 11-81-14.
Marking of validated obligations, §§6-6-756, 11-81-225.
Notice of hearing, §§6-6-752, 11-81-222.
Order to show cause, §§6-6-752, 11-81-222.
Petition.
Contents, §§6-6-752, 11-81-222.
Right to file, §§6-6-751, 11-81-221.
Service on district attorney, §6-6-752.
Presumption as to validity, §11-81-14.
Validated obligations.
Legend to appear on, §§6-6-756, 11-81-225.
Water supply and waterworks.
Authorized for construction, extension, etc., §11-47-3.
Boards for operation of water, sewer, gas and electric systems, §§11-50-315 to 11-50-318.
Boards of water and sewer commissioners, §§11-50-345 to 11-50-350, 11-50-353 to 11-50-356. See within this heading, "Boards of water and sewer commissioners."
Issuance, §11-50-6.

MUNICIPAL CORPORATIONS—Cont'd
Bond issues—Cont'd
Water supply and waterworks—Cont'd
Public improvement bonds, §§11-81-110 to 11-81-123.
Revenue bonds, §§11-81-160 to 11-81-190. See within this heading, "Public utilities."
Security, §§11-50-6, 11-81-1.
Waterworks and sewer boards, §§11-50-237, 11-50-239, 11-50-240.
Bonds, surety.
Agents.
Recordation, §36-5-3.
Appearance bonds.
Designation of persons to approve, §11-43-5.
Assessments for public improvements.
Appeals from judgment of circuit court.
By property owner, §11-48-43.
Appeals to circuit court from assessments, §11-48-37.
Boards of water and sewer commissioners, §11-50-342.
Class 5 municipalities.
Mayor/commission/city manager form of government.
Commissioners, §11-44E-43.
Employees, §11-44E-184.
Manager, §11-44E-95.
Mayor, §11-44E-73.
Clerks, §11-43-104.
Commissioners, §§11-44-9, 11-44-79, 11-44-128.
Mayor/commission/city manager form of government, §11-44E-43.
Council-manager form of government.
City manager and other officers and employees, §11-43A-49.
Electric utility boards.
Depositories, §11-50-505.
Employees, §11-50-499.
Officers, §11-50-499.
Employees, §11-43-13.
Mayor/commission/city manager form of government.
Bond of employees, §11-44E-184.
Gas utility boards.
Depositories, §11-50-475.
Official bonds of certain officers and employees, §11-50-468.
Licenses.
Collection of license taxes.
Injunction against delinquent payment.
Bond to dissolve temporary injunctive relief, §§11-51-154 to 11-51-156.

MUNICIPAL CORPORATIONS—Cont'd
Bonds, surety—Cont'd
Manager, §11-43-21.
Mayor/commission/city manager form of government.
Commissioners, §11-44E-43.
Employees, §11-44E-184.
Manager, §11-44E-95.
Mayor, §11-44E-73.
Mayors.
Execution of bonds, §11-43-83.
Officers, §11-43-13.
Municipalities may provide for bond of officers, §11-46-1.
Recordation, §36-5-3.
Taxation.
Optional method for levy and collection of property taxes.
Official bonds, §11-51-73.
Treasurers, §11-43-120.
Waterworks utility boards.
Depositories, §11-50-445.
Official bonds of certain officers and employees, §11-50-438.
Borrowing money. See within this heading, "Loans."
Boundaries.
Annexation, §§11-42-1 to 11-42-88. See within this heading, "Annexation."
Class 8 municipalities.
Mayor-council form of government, §11-44F-2.
Commission form of government.
Continuation of territorial limits, §11-44-25.
Consolidation, §§11-42-100 to 11-42-167. See within this heading, "Consolidation."
Corporate limits.
Not altered or affected by adoption of code, §11-40-5.
Expanded municipalities, §§11-42-180 to 11-42-187. See within this heading, "Expanded municipalities."
Reduction of corporate limits, §§11-42-200 to 11-42-213. See within this heading, "Reduction of corporate limits."
Zoning districts, §§11-52-70, 11-52-76, 11-52-78, 11-52-84.
Bowling alleys.
Closing, §11-51-102.
Licenses, §11-51-102.
Revocation, §11-51-103.
Bribery.
Class 5 municipalities.
Mayor/commission/city manager form of government.
Elections, §11-44E-161.
Misdemeanor, §11-44E-164.

MUNICIPAL
CORPORATIONS—Cont'd
Bribery—Cont'd
Class 5 municipalities
—Cont'd
Mayor/commission/city
manager form of
government—Cont'd
Persons appointed by
city manager or
seeking
appointment,
§11-44E-94.
Elections.
Commission form,
§§11-46-138,
11-46-139.
Mayor/commission/city
manager form of
government,
§11-44E-161.
Misdemeanor,
§11-44E-164.
Mayor-council form,
§§11-46-67, 11-46-68.
Offering or accepting
bribes for votes,
§11-44-53.
Bridges.
Access roads or bridges to
certain facilities.
Aid for development by
municipalities,
§23-1-91.
Aid by benefited
municipalities, §23-1-90.
Architectural review boards.
Applicability of provisions
to bridges, §11-68-15.
Bond issues.
Public improvement bonds.
Revenue-producing
undertakings,
§§11-81-140 to
11-81-150.
See COUNTIES.
Construction and
maintenance.
Railroads.
When required to
construct and
maintain, §§11-49-40
to 11-49-45.
Counties.
Operation, etc., of bridges
over navigable
streams.
Bridges in municipal
corporations,
§11-3-17.
Establishment within
municipalities, §23-1-86.
Historic preservation
commissions.
Applicability of provisions
to bridges, §11-68-15.
Maintenance.
Authority of highway
department, §23-1-47.
Public roads, bridges and
ferries generally.
See COUNTIES.
Speed limit on bridges.
Signs stating maximum
speed, §32-5-92.
Taxation.
Apportionment of road and
bridge taxes between
counties and
municipalities,
§§11-83-1 to 11-83-3.

MUNICIPAL
CORPORATIONS—Cont'd
Budgets.
Civic organizations.
Acquisition to projects to
provide buildings, etc.,
for certain national
organizations,
§§11-54-50 to 11-54-62.
See within this
heading, "Civic
organizations."
Class 5 municipalities.
Mayor/commission/city
manager form of
government.
Commission, §11-44E-44.
Fiscal year, §11-44E-110.
Five year plan,
§11-44E-112.
Preparation of budgets,
§11-44E-92.
Submission of budgets,
§11-44E-111.
Transportation service in
class 3 municipalities.
Annual budget,
§11-49A-18.
Buildings.
Bond issues.
Authorized for
construction,
extension, etc.,
§11-47-3.
Capital improvement
generally, §§11-66-1 to
11-66-7. See within this
heading, "Capital
improvement."
Class 1 municipalities.
Demolition of unsafe
structures, §§11-40-30
to 11-40-36.
Codes.
Adoption, §§11-43-59,
11-45-8.
Minimum building
standards code.
Adoption, §41-9-166.
Condemnation, §11-43-59.
Construction.
Approval process,
§§11-52-11, 11-85-7.
Contracts authorized,
§11-47-3.
Indebtedness authorized,
§11-47-3.
Contracts.
Authorized for
construction, etc.,
§11-47-3.
Contracts between counties
and municipalities as
to use and occupancy
of public buildings
located in
municipalities,
§11-80-3.
Demolition.
Class 1 municipalities,
§§11-40-30 to 11-40-36.
Regulation of unsafe
buildings, §§11-53-1 to
11-53-4.
Eminent domain.
Condemnation of lands for
public building sites,
§11-80-1.
Extension.
Contracts authorized,
§11-47-3.

MUNICIPAL
CORPORATIONS—Cont'd
Buildings—Cont'd
Extension—Cont'd
Indebtedness authorized,
§11-47-3.
Hospitals.
Building authorities,
§§22-21-130 to
22-21-156.
See HOSPITALS.
Indebtedness.
Construction, extension,
etc.
Indebtedness authorized
§11-47-3.
Laws.
Adoption, §11-43-59.
Minimum building standard
code.
Adoption by municipalitie
§41-9-166.
Nuisances.
Minimum housing
standards and
regulation of unsafe
buildings.
Power to enjoin or abate
public nuisances no
impaired by chapter
§11-53-3.
Ordinances.
Adoption, §11-43-59.
Planning.
Approval process,
§§11-52-11, 11-85-7.
Public building authorities,
§§11-56-1 to 11-56-22.
See within this heading
"Public building
authorities."
Public improvement bonds.
Revenue-producing
undertakings,
§§11-81-140 to
11-81-150.
See COUNTIES.
Regulation of unsafe
buildings, §§11-53-1 to
11-53-4.
Repairs.
Contracts authorized,
§11-47-3.
Indebtedness authorized,
§11-47-3.
Streets.
Reservation of lands for
future acquisition for
streets.
No compensation for
buildings erected
during reservation
period, §11-52-54.
Vacation of streets for
erection of public
buildings, §§11-49-100
to 11-49-106. See
within this heading,
"Streets."
Subdivisions.
Access streets, §11-52-35.
When permits may be
issued, §11-52-35.
Unsafe buildings.
Wharves.
Construction, maintenanc
etc., on or near
wharves, §11-47-15.

MUNICIPAL CORPORATIONS—Cont'd

Buildings—Cont'd
Zoning, §§11-52-70, 11-52-73, 11-52-82, 11-52-83. See within this heading, "Zoning."

Burial grounds. See within this heading, "Cemeteries."

Bylaws.
Commission form of government. See within this heading, "Commission form of government."
Evidence, §12-21-95.

Canals.
Construction and maintenance.
Authorized, §11-50-50.

Capital improvement, §§11-66-1 to 11-66-7.
Appropriations, §11-66-5.
Citation of chapter, §11-66-1.
Class 2 municipalities, §§11-44C-60, 11-44C-61, 11-44C-80.
Definitions, §11-66-3.
Fiscal year.
Defined, §11-66-3.
Funds.
Appropriations, §11-66-5.
Creation, §11-66-4.
Definition of fund, §11-66-3.
Distribution of fund capital, §11-66-6.
Fund capital.
Defined, §11-66-3.
Distribution, §11-66-6.
Payment of allocations by state comptroller, §11-66-7.
Trust fund.
Defined, §11-66-3.
Legislative findings, §11-66-2.
Payment of allocation, §11-66-7.
Purpose declared, §11-66-2.
Short title of chapter, §11-66-1.
State.
Defined, §11-66-3.
Trust fund.
Defined, §11-66-3.
Trust income.
Defined, §11-66-3.

Carriages.
Licensing, §11-51-101.

Carts.
Licensing, §11-51-101.

Cemeteries, §§11-47-40 to 11-47-74.
Abandonment, §§11-47-60 to 11-47-74.
Board of health.
Notice of removal of remains, §11-47-64.
Removal of remains.
Notice to board, §11-47-64.
Rules and regulations of board, §11-47-64.
Declaration for abandonment and removal of human remains, §§11-47-60 to 11-47-62.
Adoption, §11-47-60.

MUNICIPAL CORPORATIONS—Cont'd

Cemeteries—Cont'd
Abandonment—Cont'd
Declaration for abandonment and removal of human remains—Cont'd
Notice of declaration.
Publication, posting and mailing, §11-47-62.
Posting of notice of declaration, §11-47-62.
Publication of notice of declaration, §11-47-62.
Time.
Specification as to removal of remains, §11-47-61.
Expenses.
Payment, §11-47-73.
Funds remaining after abandonment.
Disposition, §11-47-73.
Lands in abandoned cemeteries.
Confirmation of sales by probate court, §11-47-71.
Sale, etc., by corporations, etc., §11-47-71.
Reinterment of remains, §§11-47-63 to 11-47-74.
Care, etc., of lands, etc., in which remains reinterred, §11-47-69.
Expenses.
Payment, §11-47-73.
Generally, §11-47-67.
Maps, §11-47-68.
Markers, §11-47-68.
Mausoleums.
Reservation of lands in abandoned cemeteries for erection of memorial mausoleum, etc., §11-47-66.
Notices, §11-47-63.
Plans, §11-47-68.
Procedure, §11-47-67.
Purchase of lands, etc., for reinterment, §11-47-66.
Sale of lands, etc., for reinterment, §11-47-66.
Removal of remains.
Affidavit of person removing, §11-47-65.
All remains.
Filing of declaration as to, §11-47-72.
Board of health.
Notice to board, §11-47-64.
Rules and regulations of board, §11-47-64.
Churches.
Cemeteries owned by churches, §11-47-74.

MUNICIPAL CORPORATIONS—Cont'd

Cemeteries—Cont'd
Abandonment—Cont'd
Removal of remains —Cont'd
Completion of removal.
Filing, etc., of declaration as to removal of all remains, §11-47-72.
Declaration as to removal of all remains.
Filing, etc., §11-47-72.
Declaration for abandonment and removal of remains, §§11-47-60 to 11-47-62.
Expenses.
Payment, §11-47-73.
Friends.
Voluntary removal by friend of person interred, §11-47-65.
Generally, §11-47-63.
Headstones.
Removal, etc., from graves, §11-47-70.
Markers.
Removal, etc., from graves, §11-47-70.
Monuments.
Removal, etc., from graves, §11-47-70.
Notices, §§11-47-63, 11-47-64.
Owners of plot or lot.
Voluntary removal, §11-47-65.
Relatives.
Voluntary removal, §11-47-65.
Religious denominations.
Removal of remains from cemeteries owned by churches, etc., §11-47-74.
Voluntary removal by relative or friend, §11-47-65.
Care and maintenance.
Contracts for municipal care and maintenance.
Authorized, §11-47-41.
Manner of contracting, §11-47-42.
Reinterment of remains from abandoned cemeteries, §11-47-69.
Churches.
Removal of remains from cemeteries owned by churches, etc., §11-47-74.
Contracts.
Municipal care and maintenance, §§11-47-41, 11-47-42.
Ownership of municipal cemeteries, §11-47-40.
Police jurisdiction over cemeteries, §11-47-22.
Private cemeteries.
Regulation, etc., of establishment or use, §11-47-40.

MUNICIPAL CORPORATIONS—Cont'd

Cemeteries—Cont'd

Regulation of municipal cemeteries, §11-47-40.

Census, §§11-47-90 to 11-47-95.

Arrangement of enumeration, §11-47-91.

Authorization for conduct by municipality, §11-47-90.

Certification of results to secretary of state, §11-47-91.

Effect of taking, §11-47-94.

Enumerators, §11-47-90.

False enumeration, §11-43-15.

Federal bureau of census.

Authorization for conduct by federal bureau, §11-47-92.

Limitation, §11-47-92.

Use, §11-47-93.

Incorporation.

Census enumeration of inhabitants, §11-41-4.

Limitation upon taking, §11-47-95.

Federally conducted census, §11-47-92.

Reports.

Effect of filing report of census, §11-47-94.

Return of enumeration, §11-47-91.

School census.

Effect as to conduct of school census, §11-47-91.

General provisions.

See EDUCATION.

Certificates of indebtedness.

Redemption of securities, §§11-82-1 to 11-82-7. See within this heading, "Redemption of securities."

Charities.

Assessments for public improvements.

Reduction or abatement of assessment on charitable property, §11-48-30.

Charter.

Forfeiture of charter, §§11-41-24 to 11-41-26, 11-41-28.

Appeals.

From decree of forfeiture, §11-41-26.

Decree of forfeiture.

Appeal from decree, §11-41-26.

Hearing upon petition for decree, §11-41-25.

Notice of petition for decree, §11-41-25.

Petition to probate judge for decree, §11-41-25.

Rendition of decree, §11-41-26.

Fee of probate judge, §11-41-28.

Grounds for forfeiture, §11-41-24.

Petition to probate judge for decree of forfeiture, §11-41-25.

MUNICIPAL CORPORATIONS—Cont'd

Charter—Cont'd

Special, private or local laws prohibited, Const. Ala., art. IV, §104.

Churches.

Cemeteries.

Removal of remains, etc., from church cemeteries, §11-47-74.

Cigarettes.

License tax on vending machines, §11-51-98.

Circuit courts.

Appeals from judgments of circuit courts, §12-14-71.

Assessments for public improvements.

Appeals from judgment of circuit court, §§11-48-43 to 11-48-47.

Appeals to circuit court from assessments, §§11-48-36 to 11-48-42.

See within this heading, "Assessments for public improvements."

Costs.

Docket fees, fines, etc., collected in municipal ordinance cases.

Distribution, §12-19-154.

Inapplicability of provisions, §12-19-155.

Prosecution assistance by municipality, ARJA, Rule 16.

Vacation and annulment of map or plats, §§35-2-58 to 35-2-62.

Cisterns.

Construction, regulation, etc., of public cisterns, etc., §11-47-140.

City clerks. See within this heading, "Clerks."

City manager, §§11-43-20 to 11-43-22.

Civic organizations.

Acquisition of projects to provide buildings for certain national organizations, §§11-54-50 to 11-54-62.

Bond issues, §§11-54-54 to 11-54-59, 11-54-61.

Approval of governmental body not required for issuance or sale, §11-54-58.

Delivery, §11-54-54.

Denominations, §11-54-54.

Disposition of proceeds, §11-54-56.

Execution, §11-54-54.

Exemption from taxation, §11-54-61.

Form of bonds, §11-54-54.

Insurance companies.

Investment in bonds, §11-54-59.

Interest, §11-54-54.

Security, §11-54-55.

Investment in bonds, §11-54-59.

MUNICIPAL CORPORATIONS—Cont'd

Civic organizations—Cont'd

Acquisition of projects to provide buildings for certain national organizations—Cont'd

Bond issues—Cont'd

Maturity, §11-54-54.

Notice to governmental body not required for issuance or sale, §11-54-58.

Payment.

Security, §11-54-55.

Proceeds from sale.

Disposition, §11-54-56.

Redemption, §11-54-54.

Refunding bonds, §11-54-57.

Sale, §11-54-54.

Approval, etc., of governmental body not required, §11-54-58.

Disposition of proceeds, §11-54-56.

Savings banks.

Investment in bonds, §11-54-59.

Security for payment, §11-54-55.

Terms, §11-54-54.

Construction of article, §11-54-62.

Contributions.

Municipalities not to contribute to costs, §11-54-60.

Definitions, §11-54-50.

Exemptions from taxation, §11-54-61.

Insurance companies.

Investment in bonds, §11-54-59.

Leasing of projects.

Powers of municipalities, §11-54-52.

Requirements, §11-54-53.

Legislative intent, §11-54-51.

Mortgages and deeds of trust.

Approval, etc., of governmental body not to be required, §11-54-58.

Security for payment, §11-54-55.

Municipal lands.

Not to be used for projects, §11-54-60.

Powers of municipalities, §11-54-52.

Savings banks.

Investment in bonds, §11-54-59.

Civil defense.

Employees.

Powers and duties of employees rendering outside aid, §31-9-11.

Officers.

Military service in time of war or national emergency.

See PUBLIC OFFICERS AND EMPLOYEES.

Powers with respect to civil defense, §31-9-10.

MUNICIPAL
CORPORATIONS—Cont'd
Civil defense—Cont'd
State grants to political
subdivisions, §31-9-24.
Torts.
Immunity from liability for
torts resulting from
civil defense activities,
§31-9-16.
Civil service merit systems
for law enforcement
officers, §§11-43-183 to
11-43-190.
Applicability of article,
§11-43-190.
Authorized, §11-43-183.
Chief of police.
Exemption of chief of
police and deputy
chief, §11-43-187.
Classification of law
enforcement officers,
§11-43-185.
Classification of law
enforcement officers.
Agreement with state
personnel department.
Rules and regulations,
§11-43-185.
Determination of salaries
to be paid
classifications,
§11-43-186.
Establishment of merit
systems, §11-43-182.
Exemptions from merit
systems.
Chief of police and deputy
chief, §11-43-187.
"Law enforcement officer"
defined, §11-43-181.
Personnel boards.
Appointment of member,
§11-43-189.
Probationary employment.
Provision for probationary
periods of employment,
§11-43-188.
Purpose of article,
§11-43-180.
Reimbursement of state for
costs, §11-43-184.
Disposition of funds,
§11-43-184.
Rules and regulations.
Agreement with state
personnel department
for services and
facilities.
Applicability of state
merit system rules
and regulations,
§11-43-185.
Salaries.
Determination of salaries
to be paid
classifications,
§11-43-186.
Civil service system.
Municipality of less than
5,000.
Abolition or creation,
§11-43-5.1.
Claims for and against
municipalities.
Abandonment of commission
form.
Civil actions, etc., not
affected, §11-44-160.

MUNICIPAL
CORPORATIONS—Cont'd
Claims for and against
municipalities—Cont'd
Ante litem notice,
§11-47-192.
Auditing of claims against
municipality, §11-43-101.
Employees.
Dealing in claims,
§11-43-14.
Limitation periods for
presentation, §§11-47-23,
11-50-84.
Negligence of agents, etc.,
§§11-47-190 to 11-47-192.
Notice.
Ante litem notice,
§11-47-192.
Officers.
Dealing in claims,
§11-43-14.
Presentation.
Hearings.
Objections, etc., to
assessments,
§11-50-84.
Limitation periods for
presentation,
§§11-47-23, 11-50-84.
Hearing upon objections,
etc., §11-50-84.
Recordation of claims against
municipality, §11-43-101.
Torts.
Definitions, §11-93-1.
Liability for negligence of
agents, etc.,
§§11-47-190 to
11-47-192.
Liability of municipalities
not extended, §11-93-3.
Maximum amount of
damages, §11-93-2.
Settlement or compromises,
§11-93-2.
Treasurers.
Money due municipalities
to be paid to treasurer,
§11-43-123.
Warrants.
Issuance of warrants for
claims against
municipality,
§11-43-101.
Class 1 municipalities.
Buildings.
Demolition of unsafe
structures, §§11-40-30
to 11-40-36.
Commercial development
authorities, §§11-54-170
to 11-54-192. See within
this heading,
"Commercial
development
authorities."
Council.
Members.
Expense allowances,
§11-43-7.1.
Districts.
Division of municipality
into single-member
districts.
Exception, §11-43-63.
Employee benefits,
§§11-40-17, 11-40-18.
Enterprise zones, §11-40-16.

MUNICIPAL
CORPORATIONS—Cont'd
Class 1 municipalities
—Cont'd
Firemen's pensions and relief
plans.
Minimum monthly
benefits, §11-40-18.
Government.
Expenses.
Allowance for members
of governing body,
§§11-40-14,
11-43-7.1.
Reimbursement for
expenses incurred
beyond corporate
limits, §§11-40-14,
11-43-7.1.
Harbors and ports.
Construction of port
facilities, §11-47-14.1.
Horse racing, §§11-65-1 to
11-65-47.
See HORSE RACING.
Hotels and related facilities.
Operation by class 1
municipalities,
§11-40-19.
Hotel management
contracts, §11-40-20.
Interest.
Water supply and
waterworks.
Customer security
deposits.
Payment of interest,
§11-50-17.
Judicial notice of ordinances
of class 1 municipalities,
§11-45-11.
Mayors.
Attendance at certain
meetings, §11-43-86.
Chief administrative
assistants.
Authority of mayors to
appoint, §11-43-81.1.
Compensation, §11-43-86.
Powers.
Appointment and
removal.
Chief administrative
assistants,
§11-43-81.1.
Motor fuel taxes.
Exemption from certain
fuel taxes, §40-17-240.
Ordinances and resolutions.
Judicial notice of
ordinances of class 1
municipalities,
§11-45-11.
Pension and retirement
plans.
Minimum monthly
benefits, §11-40-17.
Policemen's and
firemen's pension
and relief plans,
§11-40-18.
Planning.
Municipal planning
commission.
Composition, §11-52-3.
Policemen's pensions and
relief plans.
Minimum monthly
benefits, §11-40-18.

MUNICIPAL
　　CORPORATIONS—Cont'd
Class 1 municipalities
　　—Cont'd
Retirement.
　Minimum monthly
　　retirement and
　　survivor's benefits,
　　§11-40-17.
　Policemen's and
　　firemen's pension
　　and relief plans,
　　§11-40-18.
Class 2 municipalities,
　§§11-44C-1 to 11-44C-93.
Abatement of weeds,
　§§11-67-1 to 11-67-9.
Accounting year, §11-44C-41.
Actions.
　Pending legal actions and
　　proceedings,
　　§11-44C-81.
Applicability of chapter,
　§11-44C-1.
Appropriations.
　Additional appropriations,
　　§11-44C-57.
　Capital improvement
　　program.
　Lapse, §11-44C-61.
　Emergency appropriations,
　　§11-44C-58.
　Expenditures not to exceed,
　　§11-44C-67.
　Payments and obligations
　　must be in accord
　　with, §11-44C-62.
　Reserve fund for
　　permanent public
　　improvements,
　　§11-44C-61.
　Transfer of unencumbered
　　balance from one
　　department to another,
　　§11-44C-56.
Attorneys at law.
　City attorney.
　　Appointment,
　　　§11-44C-38.
　　Outside counsel,
　　　§11-44C-38.
Audits.
　Annual examination of
　　books and accounts,
　　§11-44C-31.
Budget, §§11-44C-41 to
　11-44C-54, 11-44C-60,
　11-44C-61.
　Budget message.
　　Contents, §11-44C-46.
　　Printing and
　　　distribution,
　　　§11-44C-47.
　Budget year, §11-44C-41.
　Capital budget,
　　§11-44C-61.
　Certification, §11-44C-53.
　Compilation of budget
　　information by director
　　of finance, §11-44C-43.
　Copies.
　　Printing and
　　　distribution,
　　　§11-44C-47.
　Disapproval of expenditure
　　line item, §11-44C-52.
　Effective upon final
　　adoption, §11-44C-53.

MUNICIPAL
　　CORPORATIONS—Cont'd
Class 2 municipalities
　　—Cont'd
Budget—Cont'd
　Estimates of revenue and
　　expenditures,
　　§11-44C-43.
　Review and revision,
　　§11-44C-43.
　Existing budget continued
　　in force, §11-44C-63.
　General fund budget,
　　§11-44C-44.
　　Adoption, §11-44C-51.
　　Failure to adopt,
　　　§11-44C-51.
　Hearings.
　　Public hearing,
　　　§11-44C-47.
　　Requirement,
　　　§11-44C-48.
　　Revision after hearing,
　　　§11-44C-49.
　Increase in expenditures
　　over mayor's
　　recommendation,
　　§11-44C-49.
　Printing and distribution,
　　§11-44C-53.
　Public hearing on budget
　　required, §11-44C-48.
　Public utility budgets,
　　§11-44C-45.
　　Estimates for public
　　　utilities, §11-44C-54.
　　Presentation to council,
　　　§11-44C-54.
　Receipts estimated to
　　exceed expenditures,
　　§11-44C-45.
　Recommended
　　expenditures not to
　　exceed estimated
　　receipts, §11-44C-45.
　Revision, §11-44C-49.
　Submission to council,
　　§11-44C-42.
　Summary, §11-44C-50.
Capital improvement
　　program.
　Amendment. §11-44C-60.
　Capital budget,
　　§11-44C-61.
　Lapse of appropriation,
　　§11-44C-61.
　Public improvements for
　　which legislative step
　　taken, §11-44C-80.
　Submission, §11-44C-60.
City attorney.
　Appointment, §11-44C-38.
City clerk, §11-44C-24.
Commission form of
　　government.
　Generally, §11-44C-92.
Conflicts of interest.
　Contracts, §11-44C-88.
Continuation as municipal
　　corporation, §11-44C-10.
Contracts, §§11-44C-70 to
　11-44C-72, 11-44C-80,
　11-44C-88.
　Certification of balance
　　sufficient to pay for,
　　§11-44C-72.
　City improvements costing
　　more than $2,000,
　　§11-44C-71.
　Bidding on contracts,
　　§11-44C-71.

MUNICIPAL
　　CORPORATIONS—Cont'd
Class 2 municipalities
　　—Cont'd
Contracts—Cont'd
　Competitive bidding,
　　§11-44C-70.
　Conflicts of interest,
　　§11-44C-88.
　Existing contracts.
　　Continuation in force,
　　　§11-44C-80.
　　Written requisition,
　　　§11-44C-72.
Council.
　Compensation, §11-44C-18.
　　Additional stipend for
　　　president of council,
　　　§11-44C-18.
　Composition, §11-44C-13.
　Districts.
　　Composition, §11-44C-13.
　　Reapportionment,
　　　§11-44C-90.
　Elections, §11-44C-6.
　　Filing as candidate,
　　　§11-44C-14.
　　Filing of pauper's oath or
　　　petition, §11-44C-15.
　　No primary election,
　　　§11-44C-15.
　　Qualifying fee,
　　　§11-44C-14.
　Holding other offices,
　　§11-44C-17.
　Journal of proceedings,
　　§11-44C-27.
　Judging of election and
　　qualifications of
　　members, §11-44C-26.
　Majority vote requirement,
　　§11-44C-28.
　Meetings, §§11-44C-25,
　　11-44C-28.
　Participation,
　　§11-44C-86.
　Oath of office, §11-44C-16.
　Offices, departments or
　　agencies.
　　Assigning additional
　　　functions to,
　　　§11-44C-23.
　　Creating, changing or
　　　abolishing,
　　　§11-44C-23.
　Order of business,
　　§11-44C-27.
　Ordinances.
　　Procedures, §11-44C-28.
　　Publication, §11-44C-28.
　Powers.
　　Generally, §11-44C-21.
　President, §11-44C-19.
　Procedures.
　　Generally, §11-44C-28.
　Qualifications of members,
　　§11-44C-17.
　Quorum, §11-44C-28.
　Retirement.
　　Pensions for certain
　　　elected public
　　　officials, §11-43-19.
　Rules, §11-44C-27.
　Succession in office,
　　§11-44C-7.
　Term of office, §11-44C-7.
　Vacancies in office,
　　§11-44C-22.
　Vice-president, §11-44C-20.
　When elected councilmen
　　take office, §11-44C-7.

MUNICIPAL
CORPORATIONS—Cont'd
Class 2 municipalities
—Cont'd
Department of finance.
Creation, §11-44C-64.
Director of finance.
Appointment,
§11-44C-64.
Bond, surety,
§11-44C-65.
Duties.
Generally, §11-44C-66.
Powers.
Generally, §11-44C-66.
Qualifications,
§11-44C-65.
Purchases, §§11-44C-69,
11-44C-70, 11-44C-72.
Departments.
Allotments for each
department.
Monthly or quarterly
allotments,
§11-44C-55.
Revision, §11-44C-55.
Inquiry into conduct of,
§11-44C-87.
Transfer of unencumbered
balance from one
department to another,
§11-44C-56.
Districts.
Division of municipality
into single-member
districts, §11-43-63.
Divisions of city government.
Distribution of work
among departmental
divisions, §11-44C-39.
Enumeration, §11-44C-38.
Executive directors,
§11-44C-38.
Elections, §§11-44C-2 to
11-44C-9.
Adoption of commission or
mayor-council
government.
Special election,
§11-44C-2.
Ballots, §11-44C-3.
Conduct, §11-44C-4.
Council, §11-44C-6.
Filing as candidate,
§11-44C-14.
Filing of pauper's oath or
petition, §11-44C-15.
No primary elections,
§11-44C-15.
Qualification of
candidates,
§11-44C-7.
Qualifying fee,
§11-44C-14.
Expenses, §11-44C-4.
Majority vote
requirements,
§11-44C-7.
Mayor, §11-44C-8.
Mayor, §11-44C-6.
Filing as candidate,
§11-44C-32.
Filing of pauper's oath or
petition, §11-44C-33.
No primary election,
§11-44C-33.
Qualifying fee,
§11-44C-32.
Special election to fill
vacancy, §11-44C-36.

MUNICIPAL
CORPORATIONS—Cont'd
Class 2 municipalities
—Cont'd
Elections—Cont'd
Run-off elections,
§11-44C-7.
Mayor, §11-44C-8.
Schedule, §11-44C-7.
Mayor, §11-44C-9.
Succession in office.
Mayor, §11-44C-9.
Votes cast by each voter,
§11-44C-7.
Voting machines.
Use, §11-44C-3.
Emergency notes,
§11-44C-74.
Expenses.
Monthly statement,
§11-44C-31.
Fees.
Received by officers and
employees.
Disposition, §11-44C-68.
Fiscal year, §11-44C-41.
Form of government.
Commission form.
Generally, §11-44C-92.
Elections, §§11-44C-2 to
11-44C-9.
Mayor-council form.
Change from prohibited
for two years,
§11-44C-91.
Procedure for changing,
§11-44C-91.
Provisions applicable
regardless of form
chosen, §11-44C-93.
Franchises.
Grant by ordinance or
resolution, §11-44C-29.
Hearings.
Budgets, §11-44C-48.
Lapse of unexpended and
unencumbered
appropriation,
§11-44C-59.
Leases.
Grant by ordinance or
resolution, §11-44C-29.
Right to use of streets.
Granting by ordinance or
resolution,
§11-44C-29.
Mayor.
Acting mayor, §11-44C-36.
Compensation, §11-44C-35.
Duties.
Generally, §11-44C-37.
Election, §11-44C-6.
Filing as candidate,
§11-44C-32.
Filing of pauper's oath or
petition, §11-44C-33.
Majority vote
requirements,
§11-44C-8.
No primary election,
§11-44C-33.
Qualifying fee,
§11-44C-32.
Run-off election,
§11-44C-8.
Schedule, §11-44C-9.
Special election to fill
vacancy, §11-44C-36.
Succession in office,
§11-44C-9.
Oath, §11-44C-9.

MUNICIPAL
CORPORATIONS—Cont'd
Class 2 municipalities
—Cont'd
Mayor—Cont'd
Participation in council
meetings, §11-44C-86.
Powers and duties.
Generally, §11-44C-37.
Qualifications, §11-44C-34.
Term of office, §11-44C-36.
Vacancies in office,
§11-44C-36.
Mayor-council form of
government.
Government known as,
§11-44C-11.
Provisions applicable to,
§11-44C-5.
Notes.
Emergency notes,
§11-44C-74.
Not payable on demand,
§11-44C-75.
Private sale, §11-44C-75.
Redemption prior to
maturity, §11-44C-75.
Revenue notes, §11-44C-73.
Nuisances.
Weed abatement, §§11-67-1
to 11-67-9.
Oath of office.
City officers, §11-44C-89.
Council, §11-44C-16.
Officers and employees.
Acceptance of gifts, etc.,
§11-44C-88.
Conflicts of interest,
§11-44C-88.
Continuation in office.
Personnel holding
administrative office,
§11-44C-77.
Existing laws not
inconsistent with
personnel provisions of
chapter, §11-44C-76.
Existing rights and
privileges, §11-44C-76.
Inquiry into conduct of,
§11-44C-87.
Merit system officers and
employees.
Removal, §11-44C-85.
Oath of office, §11-44C-89.
Transfer of powers and
duties of office
abolished, §11-44C-77.
Offices.
Abolition by chapter.
Transfer of powers and
duties, §11-44C-77.
Continuation of offices,
§11-44C-79.
Inquiry into conduct of,
§11-44C-87.
Transfer of records,
property and
equipment,
§11-44C-78.
Ordinances.
Codification, §11-44C-30.
Continuation in effect,
§11-44C-84.
Procedure, §11-44C-28.
Publication, §11-44C-28.
Revision, §11-44C-30.
Parks, fairgrounds or
exhibitions.
Laws continued,
§11-44C-83.

MUNICIPAL
 CORPORATIONS—Cont'd
Class 2 municipalities
   —Cont'd
Pension and retirement
   plans.
   Elected public officials,
      §11-43-19.
   Laws relating to continued
      in force, §11-44C-82.
Personnel.
   Mayor authorized to
      employ additional
      personnel, §11-44C-40.
Powers of city generally,
   §11-44C-12.
Purchases.
   Certification of balance
      sufficient to pay for,
      §11-44C-72.
   Competitive bidding,
      §11-44C-70.
   Division of department of
      finance, §11-44C-69.
   Written requisition,
      §11-44C-72.
Receipts.
   Monthly statement,
      §11-44C-31.
Retirement or relief funds.
   Laws relating to continued
      in force, §11-44C-82.
Revenue notes, §11-44C-73.
Weed abatement, §§11-67-1
   to 11-67-9.
   Account of cost, §11-67-7.
   Applicability of provisions,
      §11-67-1.
   Authorization, §11-67-2.
   Construction and
      interpretation,
      §11-67-1.
   Cost.
      Collection with taxes,
         §11-67-8.
      Hearing on, §11-67-8.
      Lien of cost, §11-67-8.
      Report of cost, §11-67-7.
   Decision of council of city
      of Mobile, §11-67-5.
   Hearings.
      Cost of abatement,
         §11-67-8.
      Public hearing.
         Notice, §11-67-4.
         Procedure generally,
            §11-67-5.
   Jurisdiction to remove
      weeds, §11-67-5.
   Liens.
      Cost of abatement,
         §11-67-8.
   Notice.
      Public hearing, §11-67-4.
   Order of abatement,
      §11-67-3.
      City of Mobile.
         Decision of council,
            §11-67-5.
   Owner's right to have
      weeds removed at own
      expense, §11-67-6.
   Private contractors,
      §11-67-6.
   Public nuisance.
      Authority to declare,
         §11-67-2.
      Resolution declaring,
         §11-67-3.

MUNICIPAL
 CORPORATIONS—Cont'd
Class 2 municipalities
   —Cont'd
Weed abatement—Cont'd
   Reports.
      Cost of abating nuisance.
         Report to tax collector,
            §11-67-8.
      Cost of removing
         nuisance, §11-67-7.
      Effect of account reports
         confirmed before
         enactment of article,
         §11-67-9.
   Resolutions.
      Effect of resolutions
         enacted before
         article, §11-67-9.
      Public nuisance.
         Declaration of weeds
            as, §11-67-3.
   Right of entry, §11-67-6.
Zoning.
   Comprehensive zone map,
      §11-44C-30.
Class 3 municipalities.
Districts.
   Division of municipality
      into single-member
      districts, §11-43-63.
Elections.
   Date of election, §11-46-5.
Planning.
   Municipal planning
      commissions.
      Alternate structure,
         §11-52-12.
Public transportation service,
   §§11-49A-1 to 11-49A-20.
   See within this heading,
   "Transportation service
   in class 3
   municipalities."
Class 4 municipalities.
Commission form of
   government.
   Abandonment, §§11-44B-1
      to 11-44B-22.
   Administrative offices
      continued,
      §§11-44B-11,
      11-44B-13.
   Adoption of mayor-
      council form.
      Ordinance, §11-44B-1.
   Civil service officers
      continued,
      §11-44B-14.
   Claims against cities,
      §11-44B-11.
   Compliance with voting
      rights act,
      §11-44B-2.
   Contracts continued,
      §11-44B-16.
   Effect of chapter on
      employees,
      §§11-44B-11,
      11-44B-12.
   Election.
      Conduct, §11-44B-5.
   Existing rights and
      privileges of officers
      and employees,
      §11-44B-12.
   Initial territorial limits,
      §11-44B-10.
   Judicial proceedings
      unaffected,
      §11-44B-17.

MUNICIPAL
 CORPORATIONS—Cont'd
Class 4 municipalities
   —Cont'd
Commission form of
   government—Cont'd
   Abandonment—Cont'd
   Laws relating to certain
      boards continued,
      §11-44B-19.
   Mayor and council,
      §§11-44B-2 to
      11-44B-8.
      Assumption of office,
         §11-44B-3.
      Election, §11-44B-2.
      Election date,
         §11-44B-4.
      Majority vote
         requirement,
         §11-44B-6.
      Meetings, §11-44B-6.
      Ordinances and
         resolutions,
         §11-44B-6.
      Powers and duties of
         mayor, §11-44B-7.
      President pro tempore
         of council,
         §11-44B-8.
      Qualifications,
         §11-44B-5.
      Quorum, §11-44B-6.
      Record of proceedings,
         §11-44B-6.
      Salaries, §11-44B-2.
      Terms of office,
         §11-44B-4.
   Office space, supplies
      and other support,
      §11-44B-11.
   Ordinances, §11-44B-1.
      Establishing
         boundaries of
         seven-council
         districts,
         §11-44B-2.
      Salaries of mayor and
         council members,
         §11-44B-2.
   Ordinances and
      resolutions
      continued,
      §11-44B-21.
   Inconsistent or
      conflicting laws,
      §11-44B-22.
   Pension, retirement and
      relief fund laws
      continued,
      §11-44B-18.
   Public works completion
      required,
      §11-44B-16.
   Reapportionment of
      council districts,
      §11-44B-10.
   Reassignment of powers
      and duties of
      abolished agencies,
      §11-44B-13.
   Streets and highways.
      Franchise, lease or
         right to use,
         §11-44B-9.
   Termination of duties,
      etc., of
      commissioners,
      §11-44B-3.

MUNICIPAL CORPORATIONS—Cont'd
Class 4 municipalities —Cont'd
Commission form of government—Cont'd
Abandonment—Cont'd
Transfer of records, equipment, etc., §11-44B-15.
Vesting of existing rights, powers and properties, §11-44B-20.
Mayor-council form of government.
Actions.
Pending actions, §11-43B-25.
Adoption.
Authority, §11-43B-1.
Ordinance, §11-43B-1.
When deemed adopted, §11-43B-2.
Applicability of laws relating to existing offices, §11-43B-21.
Appointment or removal of employees.
Council not to direct, §11-43B-7.
Appropriations, §11-43B-10.
Audits, §11-43B-9.
Boards and commissions.
Creation, §11-43B-17.
Laws continued, §11-43B-27.
Boundaries.
District boundaries, §11-43B-15.
Redistricting after census, §11-43B-16.
Initial territorial limits, §11-43B-14.
Budgets, §11-43B-10.
Civil service employees.
Appointment, §11-43B-7.
Chapter not to supersede existing system, §11-43B-22.
Continuance in office, §11-43B-22.
Continuation of administrative offices, §11-43B-20.
Contracts.
Continuance of contracts in effect, §11-43B-24.
Limit on duration, §11-43B-18.
Validity, §11-43B-18.
Departments.
Creation by ordinance, §11-43B-17.
Discontinuance of functions assigned by law, §11-43B-17.
Elections.
Qualifying fee, §11-43B-4.
Statement of campaign expenses and contributions, §11-43B-4.
Expenditures, §11-43B-10.
Franchises.
Grant, §11-43B-13.
Initial territorial limits, §11-43B-14.

MUNICIPAL CORPORATIONS—Cont'd
Class 4 municipalities —Cont'd
Mayor-council form of government—Cont'd
Laws relating to city continued in effect, §11-43B-31.
Lease of right to use streets or public property, §11-43B-13.
Mayor and council.
Elections.
Conduct, §11-43B-4.
Date, §11-43B-2.
Exercise of powers, §11-43B-8.
Expenses, §11-43B-5.
Holding of compensated appointive office by former council member or mayor, §11-43B-6.
Holding other public office during term, §11-43B-6.
Insurance.
Participation in programs, §11-43B-5.
Meetings.
Agenda, §11-43B-8.
Number of council members, §11-43B-15.
President of council, §11-43B-11.
Vacancies in office, §11-43B-12.
President pro tempore, §11-43B-11.
Quorum, §11-43B-8.
Residency requirements, §11-43B-4.
Salaries, §11-43B-5.
Terms of office, §11-43B-3.
Vacancies in office, §11-43B-12.
Officers and employees.
Effect of chapter on, §11-43B-19.
Purchase of labor, etc., from, §11-43B-30.
Offices, etc., abolished by chapter.
Exercise of powers and duties of, §11-43B-20.
Ordinances.
Continued in effect, §11-43B-29.
References to city commission, etc., deemed to refer to city council, §11-43B-29.
Pension, retirement and relief fund laws.
Continuation in effect, §11-43B-26.
Powers.
Generally, §11-43B-28.
Inconsistent laws as to exercise of powers, §11-43B-31.
Vested in council, §11-43B-8.
Receipts and expenses.
Statement of, §11-43B-9.

MUNICIPAL CORPORATIONS—Cont'd
Class 4 municipalities —Cont'd
Mayor-council form of government—Cont'd
Supervision of employees.
Limits on supervision by council, §11-43B-7.
Title of government, §11-43B-8.
Transfer of powers and duties, §11-43B-21.
Transfer of records, equipment, etc., §11-43B-23.
Violation of chapter, §11-43B-32.
Class 5 municipalities.
Alternate structure of planning commission, §11-52-13.
City manager, mayor commission form of government, §11-52-14.
Commission form of government.
Mayor/commission/city manager form of government, §§11-44E-40 to 11-44E-54.
Salaries and expenses of mayor and associate commissioners, §11-44-18.1.
Council.
Vacancies, §11-43-18.
Disbursements, §11-44-18.1.
Dogs.
Canine leash ordinances.
Procedure for adoption or repeal, §11-45-10.
Elections.
Date of election, §11-46-6.
Mayor-council for of government, §§11-43C-2 to 11-43C-6, 11-43C-13.
Electricity.
Hydroelectric generating facilities.
Referendum on issuing obligations to construct, §11-50-6.1.
Mayor/commission/city manager form of government, §§11-44E-40 to 11-44E-54.
Government.
Vacancies.
Governing bodies, §11-43-18.
Managers.
Mayor/commission/city manager form of government, §§11-44E-44, 11-44E-90 to 11-44E-100.
Mayor/commission/city manager form of government, §§11-44E-1 to 11-44E-221.
Abandonment of form of government, §§11-44E-200 to 11-44E-202.
Authority, §11-44E-200.

MUNICIPAL
  CORPORATIONS—Cont'd
Class 5 municipalities
  —Cont'd
Mayor/commission/city
  manager form of
  government—Cont'd
Abandonment of form of
  government—Cont'd
Commission.
  Termination of term of
    office,
    §11-44E-201.
  Elections, §11-44E-201.
  New officers and
    governing body,
    §11-44E-201.
  No election on change
    within two years,
    §11-44E-202.
Mayor.
  Termination of term of
    office,
    §11-44E-201.
  Petition for change,
    §11-44E-201.
Accounts.
  Examination of books
    and accounts,
    §11-44E-54.
Acquisition of property.
  Powers, §11-44E-22.
Actions.
  Continuance of pending
    actions, §11-44E-146.
Administrative
  departments.
  Power of commission to
    establish,
    §11-44E-44.
  Powers, §11-44E-92.
  Powers of city managers,
    §11-44E-92.
Administrative head of
  city, §11-44E-92.
Administrative service.
  Dealings with,
    §11-44E-93.
Adoption of form of
  government.
  Authority, §11-44E-2.
  Cities to which chapter
    applies, §11-44E-1.
  Continuation as
    municipal
    corporation,
    §11-44E-20.
  Government to be known
    as, §11-44E-21.
Airport boards.
  Continuation of laws,
    §11-44E-186.
Annexation.
  Inclusion of annexed
    territory into
    districts,
    §11-44E-187.
Appeals.
  Removal of officers and
    employees,
    §11-44E-180.
Applicability of chapter,
  §11-44E-1.
  Effect on existing laws,
    §11-44E-220.
Appointment, §11-44E-91.
Assessments.
  Imposition of
    assessments,
    §11-44E-44.

MUNICIPAL
  CORPORATIONS—Cont'd
Class 5 municipalities
  —Cont'd
Mayor/commission/city
  manager form of
  government—Cont'd
Authority to adopt form of
  government,
  §11-44E-2.
Authority to change form
  of government,
  §11-44E-200.
Boards and commissions.
  Continuation of laws,
    §11-44E-186.
  Power of commission to
    appoint members,
    §11-44E-44.
Bond issues.
  Power to authorize,
    §11-44E-44.
Bonds, surety.
  Commissioners,
    §11-44E-43.
  Employees, §11-44E-184.
  Managers, §11-44E-95.
  Mayor, §11-44E-73.
Boundaries.
  Continuation,
    §11-44E-120.
Bribery.
  City manager,
    §11-44E-94.
  Elections, §§11-44E-161,
    11-44E-164.
Budgets.
  Fiscal year, §11-44E-110.
  Five year plan,
    §11-44E-112.
  Power of commission to
    adopt, §11-44E-44.
  Preparation, §11-44E-92.
  Preparation by city
    manager,
    §11-44E-92.
  Submission of budgets by
    city manager,
    §11-44E-111.
Bylaws.
  Enactment, §11-44E-51.
  Revision and
    codification,
    §11-44E-53.
Candidates for public
  office.
  Ineligiblity to continue
    employment,
    §11-44E-94.
Change of form of
  government.
  Authority, §11-44E-200.
  Elections.
    No election on change
      within two years,
      §11-44E-202.
Chief executive officer.
  Mayor, §11-44E-75.
Citation of chapter.
  Short title, §11-44E-221.
Cities to which chapter
  applies, §11-44E-1.
City.
  Defined, §11-44E-20.
Clerks.
  Civil service or merit
    system, §11-44E-47.
  Duties, §11-44E-47.
  Signing of warrants for
    payment of money,
    §11-44E-76.

MUNICIPAL
  CORPORATIONS—Cont'd
Class 5 municipalities
  —Cont'd
Mayor/commission/city
  manager form of
  government—Cont'd
Code of conduct,
  §§11-44E-160 to
  11-44E-168.
Bribery.
  Elections,
    §§11-44E-161,
    11-44E-164.
Conflicts of interest,
  §11-44E-163.
Elections, §§11-44E-160
  to 11-44E-168.
  Bribery, §§11-44E-161,
    11-44E-164.
  Disqualification of
    candidates,
    §11-44E-167.
  Employee involvement
    in elections,
    §11-44E-165.
  False statements as to
    qualifications to
    vote, §11-44E-164.
  Hiring of persons to
    solicit votes,
    §11-44E-166.
  Misdemeanors,
    §11-44E-164.
  Party caucuses or
    primaries
    prohibited,
    §11-44E-160.
  Recall of elected
    officials,
    §11-44E-168.
  Statement of campaign
    contributions,
    §11-44E-162.
  Transportation of
    voters to polls,
    §11-44E-161.
  Voting or offering to
    vote by person not
    qualified,
    §11-44E-164.
Misdemeanors.
  Elections, §11-44E-164.
  Violations of chapter,
    §11-44E-167.
Public service utilities.
  Financial interest in
    prohibited,
    §11-44E-163.
Violations of chapter.
  Misdemeanors,
    §11-44E-167.
Codes.
  Resolutions, bylaws and
    ordinances,
    §11-44E-53.
Commencement of form of
  government,
  §11-44E-4.
Commission, §§11-44E-40
  to 11-44E-54.
Accounts.
  Examination of,
    §11-44E-54.
Administrative
  departments.
  Power to establish,
    §11-44E-44.
Administrative service.
  Dealings with,
    §11-44E-45.

MUNICIPAL
  CORPORATIONS—Cont'd
Class 5 municipalities
  —Cont'd
Mayor/commission/city
    manager form of
    government—Cont'd
Commission—Cont'd
  Appointment of officers
    and employees.
    Interference in
      prohibited,
      §11-44E-45.
  Assessments,
    §11-44E-44.
  Audits, §11-44E-54.
  Boards and commissions.
    Power to appoint
      members,
      §11-44E-44.
  Bond issues.
    Power to authorize
      issuance,
      §11-44E-44.
  Bonds, surety,
    §11-44E-43.
  Budgets.
    Power to adopt,
      §11-44E-44.
  Bylaws.
    Enactment,
      §11-44E-51.
    Revision and
      codification,
      §11-44E-53.
  City manager.
    Power to employ and
      discharge,
      §11-44E-44.
  Codes.
    Resolutions, bylaws
      and ordinances,
      §11-44E-53.
  Committees.
    Appointment of
      members,
      §11-44E-181.
  Conduct of offices,
    departments or
    agencies.
    Power to inquire into,
      §11-44E-44.
  Conflicts of interest.
    Acceptance of gifts,
      §11-44E-183.
    Dealings with
      administrative
      service,
      §11-44E-45.
    Financial interest in
      public service
      utilities,
      §11-44E-163.
    Inteference in
      appointment or
      removal of officers
      and employees,
      §11-44E-45.
    Interest in contracts
      with city or public
      utilities,
      §11-44E-183.
  Contracts.
    Conflicts of interest,
      §11-44E-183.
    Employment contract
      with city manager,
      §11-44E-44.

MUNICIPAL
  CORPORATIONS—Cont'd
Class 5 municipalities
  —Cont'd
Mayor/commission/city
    manager form of
    government—Cont'd
Commission—Cont'd
  Districts.
    Division into four
      single-member
      districts,
      §11-44E-120.
    Inclusion of annexed
      territory into
      district,
      §11-44E-187.
    Reapportionment,
      §11-44E-121.
  Duties, §11-44E-4.
  Elections, §11-44E-40.
    Canvassing votes,
      §11-44E-49.
    Caucus or primaries
      prohibited,
      §11-44E-160.
    First commission,
      §11-44E-3.
    Judge of elections,
      §11-44E-49.
    Majority vote
      requirements,
      §§11-44E-3,
      11-44E-40.
    Ordinances for
      election,
      §11-44E-2.
    Run-off elections,
      §§11-44E-3,
      11-44E-40.
    Statement of
      candidacy,
      §11-44E-41.
    Terms of office,
      §11-44E-3.
  Electric plants and
    systems.
    Conveyance to board
      or public
      corporation,
      §11-44E-52.
  Examinations.
    Books and accounts,
      §11-44E-54.
  Financial plans.
    Powers to adopt,
      §11-44E-44.
  Franchises.
    Granting, §11-44E-52.
  Gas plants and systems.
    Conveyance to board
      or public
      corporation,
      §11-44E-52.
  Gifts.
    Acceptance of gifts
      prohibited,
      §11-44E-183.
  Hearings.
    Powers to hold public
      hearing,
      §11-44E-44.
  Improvements.
    Assessments,
      §11-44E-44.
  Investigations.
    Powers as to,
      §11-44E-44.
    Subpoenas,
      §11-44E-181.

MUNICIPAL
  CORPORATIONS—Cont'd
Class 5 municipalities
  —Cont'd
Mayor/commission/city
    manager form of
    government—Cont'd
Commission—Cont'd
  Journal.
    Commission to keep,
      §11-44E-50.
  License taxes.
    Powers to impose and
      collect,
      §11-44E-44.
  Maps.
    Comprehensive zoning
      maps, §11-44E-53.
  Mayor.
    Presiding officer,
      §11-44E-75.
  Mayor and commission
    known as
    commission,
    §11-44E-4.
  Meetings, §§11-44E-48,
    11-44E-51.
    Enactment of
      resolutions, bylaws
      or ordinances,
      §11-44E-51.
    First meeting,
      §11-44E-48.
    Mayor to preside,
      §11-44E-51.
    Quorum, §11-44E-51.
    Records, §11-44E-51.
  Oath of office,
    §11-44E-40.
  Officers and employees.
    Interference with
      appointment or
      removal
      prohibited,
      §11-44E-45.
  Operation of city.
    Power to adopt
      policies,
      §11-44E-44.
  Ordinances.
    Election of
      commissioners,
      §11-44E-2.
    Enactment,
      §11-44E-51.
    Granting of franchises,
      §11-44E-52.
    Powers to enact,
      §11-44E-44.
    Revision and
      codification,
      §11-44E-53.
  Petitions.
    Election for or against
      proposed grants
      for franchises,
      §11-44E-52.
  Policies for operation of
    city.
    Power to adopt,
      §11-44E-44.
  Powers, §11-44E-4.
    Generally, §11-44E-44.
    Transfer of powers,
      §11-44E-44.
    Vested in commission,
      §11-44E-21.
  Property taxes.
    Power to levy,
      §11-44E-44.

MUNICIPAL CORPORATIONS—Cont'd
Class 5 municipalities —Cont'd
Mayor/commission/city manager form of government—Cont'd
Commission—Cont'd
Publication.
Resolution or ordinance granting franchises, §11-44E-52.
Public property.
Granting of franchises' right to use, §11-44E-52.
Public service utilities.
Conflicts of interest, §§11-44E-163, 11-44E-183.
Qualifications and taking of office, §§11-44E-4, 11-44E-40.
Vacancy upon disqualification, §11-44E-42.
Quorum, §11-44E-51.
Records.
Examination of books and accounts, §11-44E-54.
Meetings, §11-44E-51.
Removal of officers or employees.
Determination, §11-44E-45.
Resolutions.
Enactment, §11-44E-51.
Granting of franchises, §11-44E-52.
Powers to enact, §11-44E-44.
Revision and codification, §11-44E-53.
Rules of procedure.
Adoption, §11-44E-44.
Determination, §11-44E-50.
Salaries, §11-44E-43.
Power to set, §11-44E-44.
Sewer plants and systems.
Conveyance to board of public corporation, §11-44E-52.
Streets and highways.
Granting franchise to use, §11-44E-52.
Subpoenas.
Investigations as to municipal affairs, §11-44E-181.
Taxation.
Powers, §11-44E-44.
Terms of office, §§11-44E-3, 11-44E-40.
Vacancies, §11-44E-46.
Commissioner ceases to possess qualifications, §11-44E-42.
Filling, §11-44E-46.

MUNICIPAL CORPORATIONS—Cont'd
Class 5 municipalities —Cont'd
Mayor/commission/city manager form of government—Cont'd
Commission—Cont'd
Warrants for the payment of money.
Power to authorize issuance, §11-44E-44.
Waterworks plants and systems.
Conveyance to board or public corporation, §11-44E-52.
Zoning.
Comprehensive zoning map, §11-44E-53.
Compensation.
Commissioner, §11-44E-43.
Manager, §11-44E-96.
Mayor, §11-44E-73.
Acting mayor, §11-44E-74.
Power of commission to set, §11-44E-44.
Conflicts of interest.
Acceptance of gifts by officials or employees, §11-44E-183.
City manager.
Improper influences on prohibited, §11-44E-94.
Commission, §11-44E-45.
Financial interest in public service utilities, §11-44E-163.
Interest of officials or employees in contracts with city or public utilities, §11-44E-183.
Continuation of laws, §11-44E-186.
Contracts.
Conflicts of interest, §11-44E-183.
Employment of city manager, §11-44E-44.
Existing contracts.
Continued in force, §11-44E-145.
Extending beyond one year, §11-44E-182.
Manager.
Contract between city manager and cities, §11-44E-98.
Criminal law and procedure.
Continuance of criminal proceedings, §11-44E-146.
Dealings with administrative service, §11-44E-93.
Districts.
Commission.
Division into four single-member districts, §11-44E-120.

MUNICIPAL CORPORATIONS—Cont'd
Class 5 municipalities —Cont'd
Mayor/commission/city manager form of government—Cont'd
Districts—Cont'd
Commission—Cont'd
Inclusion of annexed territory into district, §11-44E-187.
Reapportionment, §11-44E-121.
Duties.
Adoption of form of government.
Enjoyment, §11-44E-20.
Generally, §11-44E-92.
Effect of chapter on existing laws, §11-44E-220.
Elected officials.
Candidates for office not to continue employment, §11-44E-94.
Noneligibility, §11-44E-91.
Elections.
Abandonment of form of government, §11-44E-201.
Election of new officers and governing body, §11-44E-201.
When held, §11-44E-202.
Bribery, §§11-44E-161, 11-44E-164.
Campaign contributions.
Statement of, §11-44E-162.
Candidates.
Qualifications and eligibility, §§11-44E-3, 11-44E-42, 11-44E-72.
Statement of candidacy, §§11-44E-41, 11-44E-71.
Canvassing votes.
Commission, §11-44E-49.
Caucuses prohibited, §11-44E-160.
Change of form of government, §11-44E-201.
Election of new officers and governing body, §11-44E-201.
When held, §11-44E-202.
Commission, §11-44E-40.
Caucus or primaries prohibited, §11-44E-160.
Eligibility of candidate, §11-44E-42.
Judge of elections, §11-44E-49.
Majority vote requirement, §11-44E-40.

MUNICIPAL
CORPORATIONS—Cont'd
Class 5 municipalities
—Cont'd
Mayor/commission/city
manager form of
government—Cont'd
Elections—Cont'd
Commission—Cont'd
Qualifications and
eligibility,
§11-44E-42.
Run-off elections,
§11-44E-40.
Statement of
candidacy,
§11-44E-41.
Commission districts.
Division into four
single-member
districts,
§11-44E-120.
Reapportionment,
§11-44E-121.
Commissioners.
First commission,
§11-44E-3.
Contributions.
Statement of campaign
contributions,
§11-44E-162.
Disqualification of
candidates,
§11-44E-167.
Duties of municipal
officials, §11-44E-3.
Eligibility of candidates,
§§11-44E-3,
11-44E-42,
11-44E-72.
Employee involvement
in, §11-44E-165.
Expenses, §11-44E-3.
Forms.
Statement of campaign
contributions,
§11-44E-162.
Statement of
candidacy,
§§11-44E-41,
11-44E-71.
Granting of franchises,
§11-44E-52.
Hiring of persons to
solicit votes,
§11-44E-166.
Judge of election.
Commission,
§11-44E-49.
Majority vote
requirements,
§§11-44E-3,
11-44E-40,
11-44E-70.
Mayor, §11-44E-70.
Caucus or primary
prohibited,
§11-44E-160.
Eligibility of
candidates,
§11-44E-72.
First mayor,
§11-44E-3.
Majority vote
requirements,
§11-44E-70.
Run-off elections,
§11-44E-70.
Statement of
candidacy,
§11-44E-71.

MUNICIPAL
CORPORATIONS—Cont'd
Class 5 municipalities
—Cont'd
Mayor/commission/city
manager form of
government—Cont'd
Elections—Cont'd
Mayor—Cont'd
Vacancy in office of
mayor,
§11-44E-74.
Misdemeanors,
§11-44E-164.
Municipal officials.
Duties, §11-44E-3.
Notice, §11-44E-3.
Vacancy in office of
mayor,
§11-44E-74.
Ordinances.
Election of
commissioners,
§11-44E-2.
Primaries prohibited,
§11-44E-160.
Publication.
Notice, §11-44E-3.
Qualifications of
candidates,
§11-44E-3.
Qualifications to vote,
§11-44E-164.
Reapportionment of
commission districts,
§11-44E-121.
Recall of elected officials,
§11-44E-168.
Run-off elections,
§§11-44E-3,
11-44E-70.
Commission,
§11-44E-40.
Soliciting votes at polls
on election day.
Hiring of persons,
§11-44E-166.
Special elections.
Vacancy in office of
mayor,
§11-44E-74.
Statement of campaign
contributions,
§11-44E-162.
Statement of candidacy,
§§11-44E-41,
11-44E-71.
Terms of office,
§11-44E-3.
Transportation of voters
to polls,
§11-44E-161.
Vacancy in office of
mayor, §11-44E-74.
Voters.
False statements as to
qualifications,
§11-44E-164.
Transportation to
polls, §11-44E-161.
Employees.
Appointment and
removal, §11-44E-92.
Elections.
Involvement in,
§11-44E-165.
Ethics.
Code of conduct,
§§11-44E-160 to
11-44E-168.

MUNICIPAL
CORPORATIONS—Cont'd
Class 5 municipalities
—Cont'd
Mayor/commission/city
manager form of
government—Cont'd
Financial plans.
Power of commission to
adopt, §11-44E-44.
Fiscal year, §11-44E-110.
Forms.
Recall of elected officials,
§11-44E-168.
Franchises.
Adoption of form of
government.
Enjoyment,
§11-44E-20.
Granting, §11-44E-52.
Full time duties,
§11-44E-92.
Gifts.
Acceptance by officials or
employees,
§11-44E-183.
Government's title,
§11-44E-21.
Hearings.
Power of commission to
hold public hearings,
§11-44E-44.
Hospitals.
Board.
Continuation of laws,
§11-44E-186.
Housing authority.
Continuation of laws,
§11-44E-186.
Immunities.
Adoption of form of
government.
Enjoyment,
§11-44E-20.
Improvements.
Assessments,
§11-44E-44.
Continuance of public
improvements,
§11-44E-145.
Insurance.
City manager.
Eligibility for group
insurance,
§11-44E-97.
Investigations, §11-44E-92.
Power of commission as
to, §11-44E-44.
Journal.
Commission to keep,
§11-44E-50.
Laws.
Continuation of laws,
§11-44E-186.
Effect of chapter on
existing laws,
§11-44E-220.
Library boards.
Continuation of laws,
§11-44E-186.
License taxes.
Imposition, §11-44E-44.
Manager, §§11-44E-90 to
11-44E-100.
Absence or disability,
§11-44E-100.
Acting city manager.
Vacancies in office,
§11-44E-99.
Bonds, surety,
§11-44E-95.

MUNICIPAL
CORPORATIONS—Cont'd
Class 5 municipalities
—Cont'd
Mayor/commission/city
manager form of
government—Cont'd
Manager—Cont'd
Budgets.
Five year plan,
§11-44E-112.
Submission,
§11-44E-111.
Compensation,
§11-44E-96.
Contract of employment.
Contract between city
manager and
cities, §11-44E-98.
Power of commission
to enter into,
§11-44E-44.
Creation of office,
§11-44E-90.
Discharge.
Power of commission
to discharge,
§11-44E-44.
Duties.
Noninterference by
commission or
mayor with,
§11-44E-93.
Employment.
Power of commission
to employ,
§11-44E-44.
Insurance.
Eligibility for group
insurance,
§11-44E-97.
Noneligibility of elected
official, §11-44E-91.
Power of commission to
employ, §11-44E-44.
Retirement system.
Eligibility for,
§11-44E-97.
Salaries, §11-44E-96.
Vacancies, §11-44E-99.
Temporary absence or
disability,
§11-44E-100.
Maps.
Comprehensive zoning
maps, §11-44E-53.
Mayor, §§11-44E-70 to
11-44E-76.
Abandonment of form of
government.
Termination of term of
office,
§11-44E-201.
Absence of mayor.
Designation of mayor
protem,
§11-44E-75.
Acting mayor.
Appointment,
§11-44E-74.
Compensation,
§11-44E-74.
Appointment of
committees,
§11-44E-181.
Bonds, surety,
§11-44E-73.
Ceremonial functions.
Representing city in,
§11-44E-75.

MUNICIPAL
CORPORATIONS—Cont'd
Class 5 municipalities
—Cont'd
Mayor/commission/city
manager form of
government—Cont'd
Mayor—Cont'd
Chief executive officer,
§11-44E-75.
Commissioners and
mayor known as
commission,
§11-44E-4.
Compensation,
§11-44E-73.
Acting mayor,
§11-44E-74.
Increasing or
decreasing during
term of office,
§11-44E-73.
Conflicts of interest.
Acceptance of gifts,
§11-44E-183.
Financial interest in
public service
utilities,
§11-44E-163.
Interest in contracts
with city or public
utility,
§11-44E-183.
Contracts.
Conflicts of interest,
§11-44E-183.
Duties, §11-44E-75.
Successor when
vacancy in office of
mayor,
§11-44E-74.
Elections, §11-44E-70.
Caucus or primary
prohibited,
§11-44E-160.
Eligibility of
candidates,
§11-44E-72.
First mayor,
§11-44E-3.
Majority vote
requirements,
§§11-44E-3,
11-44E-70.
Run-off elections,
§§11-44E-3,
11-44E-70.
Special election upon
vacancy in office,
§11-44E-74.
Statement of
candidacy,
§11-44E-71.
Terms of office,
§11-44E-3.
Vacancy, §11-44E-74.
Gifts.
Acceptance of gifts
prohibited,
§11-44E-183.
Meetings of commission.
Presiding officer,
§11-44E-51.
Notice.
Special election to fill
vacancy,
§11-44E-74.
Oath of office,
§11-44E-70.

MUNICIPAL
CORPORATIONS—Cont'd
Class 5 municipalities
—Cont'd
Mayor/commission/city
manager form of
government—Cont'd
Mayor—Cont'd
Payment of funds.
Countersigned by
mayor,
§11-44E-76.
Powers.
Generally, §11-44E-75.
Successor when
vacancy in office of
mayor,
§11-44E-74.
Presiding officer of
commission,
§11-44E-75.
Protem.
Designation by mayor
protem,
§11-44E-75.
Public service utilities.
Financial interest in
prohibited,
§11-44E-163.
Interest in contracts
with prohibited,
§11-44E-183.
Qualification and taking
of office, §11-44E-70.
Successor when
vacancy in office of
mayor,
§11-44E-74.
Salaries, §11-44E-73.
Acting mayor,
§11-44E-74.
Successor mayor.
Vacancy in office of
mayor,
§11-44E-74.
Term of office,
§§11-44E-3,
11-44E-70.
Successor when
vacancy in office of
mayor,
§11-44E-74.
Vacancy in office of
mayor, §11-44E-74.
Meetings.
Commission,
§§11-44E-48,
11-44E-51.
Attendance required,
§11-44E-92.
Mayor to preside,
§11-44E-51.
Misdemeanors.
Acceptance of gifts,
§11-44E-183.
Conflicts of interest,
§11-44E-183.
Elections, §11-44E-164.
Investigations as to
municipal affairs.
Failure to obey
subpoenas,
§11-44E-181.
Violations of chapter,
§11-44E-167.
Notice.
Elections, §11-44E-3.
Special election when
vacancy in office of
mayor, §11-44E-74.

MUNICIPAL
CORPORATIONS—Cont'd
Class 5 municipalities
  —Cont'd
Mayor/commission/city
  manager form of
  government—Cont'd
Oaths.
  Commission, §11-44E-40.
  Mayor, §11-44E-70.
  Officers, §11-44E-185.
Officers and employees.
  Appeals.
    Removal, §11-44E-180.
  Bonds, surety,
    §11-44E-184.
  City manager.
    Powers as to
      employees,
      §11-44E-92.
  Commission.
    Interference in
      appointment or
      removal,
      §11-44E-45.
  Conflicts of interest,
    §11-44E-183.
  Continuance of those in
    classified service,
    §§11-44E-141,
    11-44E-142.
  Contracts.
    Conflicts of interest,
      §11-44E-183.
  Gifts.
    Acceptance of gifts
      prohibited,
      §11-44E-183.
  Oath of office,
    §11-44E-185.
  Public utilities.
    Interest in contracts
      with prohibited,
      §11-44E-183.
  Removal, §11-44E-180.
  Rights preserved,
    §11-44E-140.
Ordinances.
  Adoption of form of
    government,
    §11-44E-2.
  Annexation,
    §11-44E-187.
  Continued in effect,
    §11-44E-149.
  Election of
    commissioners,
    §11-44E-2.
  Enactment, §11-44E-51.
  Power of commission to
    enact, §11-44E-44.
  Revision and
    codification,
    §11-44E-53.
Parks and recreation.
  Continuation of laws,
    §§11-44E-148,
    11-44E-186.
Payment of funds,
  §11-44E-76.
Pensions and retirement
  plans.
  Laws continued,
    §11-44E-147.
Personal property.
  Powers concerning,
    §11-44E-22.

MUNICIPAL
CORPORATIONS—Cont'd
Class 5 municipalities
  —Cont'd
Mayor/commission/city
  manager form of
  government—Cont'd
Petitions.
  Abandonment of form of
    government.
    Termination of term of
      office,
      §11-44E-201.
  Changing form of
    government,
    §11-44E-201.
  Franchises.
    Elections for or against
      granting,
      §11-44E-52.
  Recall of elected officials,
    §11-44E-168.
Planning board.
  Continuation of laws,
    §11-44E-186.
Plumbers or electricians
  board.
  Continuation of laws,
    §11-44E-186.
Political opinions or
  affiliations.
  Appointing, etc.,
    manager based on,
    §11-44E-94.
Powers.
  Adoption of form of
    government.
    Enjoyment,
      §11-44E-20.
  Enumeration of powers
    not exclusive,
    §11-44E-22.
  Exercise of power,
    §11-44E-21.
  Generally, §§11-44E-22,
    11-44E-92.
  Vested in commission,
    §11-44E-21.
Property.
  Powers concerning,
    §11-44E-22.
  Transfer of property,
    §11-44E-143.
Property taxes.
  Power of commission to
    levy, §11-44E-44.
Publication.
  Elections.
    Notice, §11-44E-3.
  Granting of franchises,
    §11-44E-52.
  Notice.
    Elections, §11-44E-3.
    Special election when
      vacancy in office of
      mayor,
      §11-44E-74.
  Resolutions, bylaws or
    ordinances,
    §11-44E-51.
Public service utilities.
  Conflicts of interest,
    §11-44E-183.
  Continuation of laws,
    §11-44E-186.
  Contracts.
    Conflicts of interest,
      §11-44E-183.
    Financial interest in.
    Prohibited,
      §11-44E-163.

MUNICIPAL
CORPORATIONS—Cont'd
Class 5 municipalities
  —Cont'd
Mayor/commission/city
  manager form of
  government—Cont'd
Purchasing agent,
  §11-44E-92.
Qualifications, §11-44E-91.
Real property.
  Powers concerning,
    §11-44E-22.
Reapportionment of
  commission districts,
  §11-44E-121.
Recall of elected officials,
  §11-44E-168.
Records.
  Examination of books
    and accounts,
    §11-44E-54.
  Meetings, §11-44E-51.
  Transfer of agency
    records,
    §11-44E-143.
Reports, §11-44E-92.
Residency requirements,
  §11-44E-91.
Resolutions.
  Continued in effect,
    §11-44E-149.
  Enactment, §11-44E-51.
  Power to enact,
    §11-44E-44.
  Revision and
    codification,
    §11-44E-53.
Retirement.
  City manager.
    Eligibility, §11-44E-97.
Rights.
  Adoption of form of
    government.
    Enjoyment,
      §11-44E-20.
Salaries.
  Commissioner,
    §11-44E-43.
  Manager, §11-44E-96.
  Mayor, §11-44E-73.
    Acting mayor,
      §11-44E-74.
  Power of commission to
    set compensation,
    §11-44E-44.
School boards.
  Continuation of laws,
    §11-44E-186.
Short title, §11-44E-221.
Subpoenas.
  Investigations as to
    municipal affairs,
    §11-44E-181.
Succession of government.
  Abolished agencies.
    Exercise of powers by
      agencies
      designated by
      commission,
      §11-44E-141.
  Continuance of offices,
    etc., §11-44E-144.
  Contracts.
    Existing contracts
      continued in force,
      §11-44E-145.

MUNICIPAL
   CORPORATIONS—Cont'd
Class 5 municipalities
   —Cont'd
Mayor/commission/city
   manager form of
   government—Cont'd
Succession of government
   —Cont'd
Officers and employees.
   Continuance of those
     in classified
     service,
     §§11-44E-141,
     11-44E-142.
   Rights preserved,
     §11-44E-140.
Offices, departments,
   boards or agencies.
   Name or powers and
     duties same or
     substantially
     same,
     §11-44E-144.
Ordinances and
   resolutions
   continued in effect,
   §11-44E-149.
Parks and recreation.
   Laws continued,
     §11-44E-148.
Pending legal actions
   and proceedings,
   §11-44E-146.
Pension or retirement
   and relief funds.
   Laws continued,
     §11-44E-147.
Property.
   Transfers,
     §11-44E-143.
Public improvements.
   Continuance,
     §11-44E-145.
Records.
   Transfers,
     §11-44E-143.
Transfer of records and
   property,
   §11-44E-143.
Taxation.
   Power of commissions,
     §11-44E-44.
Title of chapter.
   Short title, §11-44E-221.
Vacancies.
   Commission.
     Filling, §11-44E-46.
   Manager, §11-44E-99.
   Temporary absence or
     disability,
     §11-44E-100.
Violations of chapter,
   §11-44E-167.
Warrants for the payment
   of money.
   Payment of all funds by,
     §11-44E-76.
   Power of commission to
     authorize issuance,
     §11-44E-44.
Zoning.
   Comprehensive zoning
     maps, §11-44E-53.
   Continuation of laws,
     §11-44E-186.

MUNICIPAL
   CORPORATIONS—Cont'd
Class 5 municipalities
   —Cont'd
Mayor-council form of
   government, §§11-43C-1
   to 11-43C-92.
Accountant.
   Appointment,
     §11-43D-17.
   Duties, §11-43D-17.
Accounting year,
   §11-43C-41.
Actions.
   Pending actions,
     §§11-43C-81,
     11-43D-11.
Administrative assistants,
   §11-43D-16.
Administrative service.
   Council not to
     interfere with,
     §11-43D-15.
Adoption.
   Actions.
     Pending legal actions
       and proceedings,
       §11-43D-11.
   Applicability of
     provisions,
     §11-43D-1.
   Authorities.
     Continuance,
       §11-43D-13.
   Boards.
     Continuance,
       §11-43D-13.
   Commissions.
     Continuance,
       §11-43D-13.
   Continuation of city as
     municipal
     corporation,
     §11-43C-10.
   Contracts.
     Existing contracts
       continued in force,
       §11-43D-10.
   Improvements.
     Completion of public
       improvements,
       §11-43D-10.
   Officers and employees.
     Continuance in office,
       §§11-43D-7,
       11-43D-8.
     Rights preserved,
       §11-43D-6.
   Ordinance.
     Continuance of
       ordinances and
       resolutions,
       §11-43D-22.
     Establishment of
       boundaries,
       §11-43D-2.
     Form, §11-43D-1.
   Pending actions,
     §11-43D-11.
   Pensions, retirement,
     and relief funds.
     Continuation in force
       of laws,
       §11-43D-12.
   Transfer of certain
     records and property,
     §11-43D-9.
Agencies.
   Continuation,
     §11-43C-79.

MUNICIPAL
   CORPORATIONS—Cont'd
Class 5 municipalities
   —Cont'd
Mayor-council form of
   government—Cont'd
Allocations.
   Agencies serving poor
     and needy,
     §11-43C-92.
Amusement facilities.
   Continuation in force of
     laws relating to,
     §11-43C-83.
Appeals.
   Officers and employees.
     Removal, §11-43C-85.
Applicability of chapter,
   §11-43C-1.
   Election to determine,
     §11-43C-5.
Appropriations.
   Additional, §11-43C-57.
   Allotment, §11-43C-55.
   Emergency, §11-43C-58.
   Emergency notes,
     §11-43C-74.
   Lapse of appropriations
     for capital
     improvement
     projects, §11-43C-61.
   Unexpended and
     unencumbered
     appropriation.
     Lapse of, §11-43C-59.
     Transfer, §11-43C-56.
Bids and bidding,
   §11-43C-71.
Bonds, surety.
   Division of finance.
     Head of division,
       §11-43C-65.
   Expenditures financed by
     bond, §11-43C-67.
Budgets.
   Capital budget,
     §§11-43C-42,
     11-43C-61.
   Certification of adopted
     budget required,
     §11-43C-53.
   Compilation of budget
     information,
     §11-43C-43.
   Continuation of existing
     budget, §11-43C-63.
   Contracts for period
     exceeding budget
     year, §11-43C-67.
   Effective upon final
     adoption,
     §11-43C-53.
   Estimates for public
     utilities, §11-43C-54.
   General fund budget,
     §11-43C-42.
     Adoption of budget and
       any necessary
       revenue measure,
       §11-43C-51.
     Failure to adopt,
       §11-43C-51.
     Public utility
       appropriations,
       §11-43C-44.
   Leases for period
     exceeding budget
     year, §11-43C-67.
   Mayor to submit budget,
     §11-43C-42.

MUNICIPAL
CORPORATIONS—Cont'd
Class 5 municipalities
—Cont'd
Mayor-council form of
government—Cont'd
Budgets—Cont'd
Message of mayor,
§11-43C-42.
Contents, §11-43C-46.
Printing and distribution
of budgets,
§§11-43C-47,
11-43C-53.
Public hearing on
budget, §11-43C-48.
Revision of budget
after hearing,
§11-43C-49.
Public utility budgets,
§§11-43C-42,
11-43C-45.
Presentation of budget
to council,
§11-43C-54.
Revenues and
expenditures.
Estimates, §11-43C-43.
Revision of budget after
hearing, §11-43C-49.
Summary of budget,
§11-43C-50.
When effective,
§11-43C-53.
Budget year, §11-43C-41.
Capital improvement
program.
Basis, §11-43C-92.
Generally, §11-43C-60.
Changing form of
government.
Procedure, §11-43C-91.
Prohibited for four years,
§11-43C-91.
City clerk, §11-43C-24.
City government divisions.
Appointment of
executive directors of
divisions,
§11-43C-38.
Distribution of work
among departments,
§11-43C-39.
Temporary divisions,
§11-43C-39.
Conflicts of interest,
§11-43C-88.
Contracts.
Conflicts of interest,
§11-43C-88.
Contracts for period
exceeding budget
year, §11-43C-67.
Existing contracts
continued in force,
§§11-43C-80,
11-43D-10.
Public improvements,
§11-43C-71.
Socially and
economically
disadvantaged.
Participation in
contracts by,
§11-43C-92.
Cultural development.
Continuation in force of
laws relating to,
§11-43C-83.

MUNICIPAL
CORPORATIONS—Cont'd
Class 5 municipalities
—Cont'd
Mayor-council form of
government—Cont'd
Departments.
Continuation,
§11-43C-79.
Discontinuation of mayor-
council form of
government.
Change prohibited for
four years,
§11-43C-91.
Procedure, §11-43C-91.
Districts.
Changing boundaries
where population
varies by over five
percent, §11-43C-13.
Division of municipality
into districts,
§11-43C-13.
Reapportionment.
Change of population,
§§11-43C-90,
11-43D-5.
Elections, §§11-43C-2 to
11-43C-6, 11-43C-13.
Ballots, §11-43C-3.
Conduct of election,
§11-43C-4.
Division of municipality
into districts,
§11-43C-13.
Expenses, §11-43C-4.
Mayor and council
members,
§§11-43C-6,
11-43D-2.
Procedure, §11-43D-4.
Provisions applicable if
mayor-council form
of government
chosen, §11-43C-5.
Special election as to
adoption of mayor-
council form of
government,
§11-43C-2.
Adoption of proposal,
§11-43C-2.
Ballots, §11-43C-3.
Conduct of election,
§11-43C-4.
Expenses of election,
§11-43C-4.
Voting machines,
§11-43C-3.
Voting machines.
Use, §11-43C-3.
Equipment.
Transfer of equipment
where powers and
duties reassigned,
§11-43C-78.
Exhibitions.
Continuation in force of
laws relating to,
§11-43C-83.
Expenditures.
Classification,
§11-43C-67.
Excessive expenditures,
§11-43C-67.
Receipts in surplus not
to be exceeded
unless additional
revenue measures
adopted, §11-43C-49.

MUNICIPAL
CORPORATIONS—Cont'd
Class 5 municipalities
—Cont'd
Mayor-council form of
government—Cont'd
Fairgrounds.
Continuation in force of
laws relating to,
§11-43C-83.
Fees.
Officers and employees.
Disposition of,
§11-43C-68.
Finance.
Division of finance,
§11-43C-64.
Bond required for head
of division,
§11-43C-65.
Head of division,
§11-43C-64.
Powers and duties of
division head,
§11-43C-66.
Purchasing
responsibilities,
§§11-43C-70 to
11-43C-72.
Qualifications of head
of division,
§11-43C-65.
Firefighters.
Through transportation
of firefighters in
discharge of duties,
§11-43C-88.
Fiscal year, §11-43C-41.
Improvements.
Adoption of form of
government.
Completion of public
improvements,
§11-43D-10.
Investigations, §11-43C-87.
Leases for period exceeding
budget year,
§11-43C-67.
Legal actions.
Pending actions,
§11-43C-81.
Mayor and council.
Absence or disability of
mayor, §11-43D-21.
Accounts.
Annual examination,
§11-43C-31.
Actions.
Pending actions,
§11-43C-81.
Administrative
assistants,
§11-43D-16.
Administrative offices.
Continuation,
§11-43C-79.
Administrative service.
Noninterference of
council with,
§11-43D-15.
Agencies.
Continuation,
§11-43C-79.
Allocations.
Agencies serving poor
and needy,
§11-43C-92.
Amusement facilities.
Continuation in force
of laws relating to,
§11-43C-83.

MUNICIPAL CORPORATIONS—Cont'd
Class 5 municipalities
—Cont'd
Mayor-council form of
government—Cont'd
Mayor and council—Cont'd
Appeals.
Removal of merit
system officers and
employees,
§11-43C-85.
Appropriations.
Additional,
§11-43C-57.
Allotments,
§11-43C-55.
Certification,
§11-43C-62.
Emergency,
§11-43C-58.
Emergency notes,
§11-43C-74.
Lapse, §§11-43C-59,
11-43C-61.
Payments in accord
with
appropriations,
§11-43C-62.
Transfer of
unencumbered
balance from one
department to
another,
§11-43C-56.
Assumption of office,
§11-43D-2.
Bond issues.
Expenditures financed
by bond,
§11-43C-67.
Books and accounts.
Annual examination
of, §11-43C-31.
Budgets.
Adoption, §11-43C-51.
Capital budget,
§§11-43C-42,
11-43C-61.
Certification,
§11-43C-53.
Compilation of budget
information by
director of finance,
§11-43C-43.
Contents of budget
message,
§11-43C-46.
Contracts for period
exceeding budget
year, §11-43C-67.
Effectiveness upon
final adoption,
§11-43C-53.
Existing budget
continued in force,
§11-43C-63.
Failure to adopt,
§11-43C-51.
General fund budget,
§11-43C-44.
Hearing, §§11-43C-48,
11-43C-49.
Leases for period
exceeding budget
year, §11-43C-67.
Mayor to submit
budget to council,
§11-43C-42.

MUNICIPAL CORPORATIONS—Cont'd
Class 5 municipalities
—Cont'd
Mayor-council form of
government—Cont'd
Mayor and council—Cont'd
Budgets—Cont'd
Printing and
distribution,
§§11-43C-47,
11-43C-53.
Public utility budgets,
§§11-43C-42,
11-43C-54.
Review and revision of
estimates,
§11-43C-43.
Revision of budget
after hearing,
§11-43C-49.
Summary of budget,
§11-43C-50.
When effective,
§11-43C-53.
Bylaws.
Revision and
codification,
§11-43C-30.
Candidates, §11-43C-32.
Capital improvement
program.
Generally, §11-43C-60.
Capital improvements.
Basis, §11-43C-92.
Changing form of
government.
Procedure, §11-43C-91.
Prohibited for four
years, §11-43C-91.
City attorney.
Mayor to appoint,
§11-43C-38.
Compensation of council,
§§11-43C-18,
11-43D-18.
Compensation of mayor,
§§11-43C-18,
11-43D-18.
Composition of council,
§11-43C-13.
Contracts.
Contracts for period
exceeding budget
year, §11-43C-67.
Participation by the
socially and
economically
disadvantaged,
§11-43C-92.
Conviction.
Effect, §11-43C-17.
Councilman may succeed
himself, §11-43C-7.
Creating, changing,
abolishing or
assigning additional
functions to offices,
departments or
agencies,
§11-43C-23.
Cultural development.
Continuation in force
of laws relating to,
§11-43C-83.
Departments.
Continuation,
§11-43C-79.

MUNICIPAL CORPORATIONS—Cont'd
Class 5 municipalities
—Cont'd
Mayor-council form of
government—Cont'd
Mayor and council—Cont'd
Discontinuation of
mayor-council form
of government.
Change prohibited for
four years,
§11-43C-91.
Procedure, §11-43C-91.
District council
members.
Composition,
§11-43C-13.
Fees required,
§11-43C-14.
Filing as candidate,
§11-43C-14.
Districts.
Reapportionment,
§§11-43C-90,
11-43D-5.
Division of city
government.
Mayor to appoint
executive directors
of divisions,
§11-43C-38.
Division of finance.
Bond required for head
of division,
§11-43C-65.
Head of division,
§11-43C-64.
Qualifications of head
of division,
§11-43C-65.
Duties of mayor,
§§11-43C-37,
11-43D-14.
Elections, §11-43D-2.
Council to judge
election,
§11-43C-26.
Filing of pauper's oath
or petition to
become candidate,
§11-43C-15.
Majority vote
requirements,
§§11-43C-7,
11-43C-8.
Primary elections
prohibited,
§§11-43C-15,
11-43C-33.
Quadrennially held,
§§11-43C-7,
11-43C-9.
Qualifications of
candidates,
§§11-43C-7,
11-43C-17.
Qualifications of
mayor,
§11-43C-34.
Run-off election,
§§11-43C-7,
11-43C-8.
Votes cast by each
voter, §11-43C-7.
When elected
councilmen to take
office, §11-43C-7.
When held,
§§11-43C-7,
11-43C-9.

**MUNICIPAL
CORPORATIONS**—Cont'd
Class 5 municipalities
—Cont'd
Mayor-council form of
government—Cont'd
Mayor and council—Cont'd
Employees.
Amount available for
salaries,
§11-43C-40.
Mayor authorized to
employ additional
personnel,
§11-43C-40.
Merit system
inapplicable,
§11-43C-40.
Equipment.
Transfer, §11-43C-78.
Exhibitions.
Continuation of laws,
§11-43C-83.
Expenditures,
§11-43C-67.
Expenses.
Monthly statement of
receipts and
expenses,
§11-43C-31.
Filing as candidate for
mayor, §11-43C-32.
Filing of pauper's oath,
§11-43C-33.
Finance.
Division of finance,
§11-43C-64.
Powers and duties of
head of division,
§11-43C-66.
Firemen.
Free transportation
during discharge
of duties,
§11-43C-88.
Holding other public
office during term,
§11-43C-17.
Investigations.
Municipal affairs,
§11-43C-87.
Leases for period
exceeding budget
year, §11-43C-67.
Legal actions.
Pending actions,
§11-43C-81.
Majority vote
requirements,
§§11-43C-7,
11-43C-8.
Mayoral candidate
qualifications,
§11-43C-34.
Mayor may succeed
himself, §11-43C-9.
Meetings, §11-43C-28.
First meeting,
§11-43C-25.
Journal of proceedings,
§11-43C-27.
Mayor's rights in
council meetings,
§11-43D-20.
Notice, §11-43D-20.
Open, §11-43C-25.
Order of business of
council,
§11-43C-27.

**MUNICIPAL
CORPORATIONS**—Cont'd
Class 5 municipalities
—Cont'd
Mayor-council form of
government—Cont'd
Mayor and council—Cont'd
Meetings—Cont'd
Participation in
meetings of
council by mayor,
department heads,
etc., §11-43C-86.
Regular, §11-43C-25.
Rules and order of
business of
council,
§11-43C-27.
Merit system.
Appeal of decision for
removal of officers
and employees,
§11-43C-85.
Employees not subject
to, §11-43C-40.
Notes.
Emergency notes,
§11-43C-74.
Notes not payable on
demand,
§11-43C-75.
Private sale,
§11-43C-75.
Redemption prior to
maturity,
§11-43C-75.
Revenue notes,
§11-43C-73.
Oaths.
City officers required
to take,
§11-43C-89.
Elected officials
required to take,
§11-43C-16.
Mayor, §11-43C-9.
Oath of office,
§11-43C-16.
Officers and employees.
Acceptance of gifts,
§11-43C-88.
Administrative
services
employees,
§11-43C-21.
Appointments to
reflect make-up of
community,
§11-43C-92.
Conflicts of interest,
§11-43C-88.
Continuation in office
of personnel
holding
administrative
offices,
§11-43C-77.
Disposition of fees
received by,
§11-43C-68.
Exercise of powers and
duties as to,
§11-43C-21.
Existing laws not
inconsistent with
personnel or
provisions of
chapter,
§11-43C-76.

**MUNICIPAL
CORPORATIONS**—Cont'd
Class 5 municipalities
—Cont'd
Mayor-council form of
government—Cont'd
Mayor and council—Cont'd
Officers and employees
—Cont'd
Existing rights and
privileges of,
§11-43C-76.
Free transportation in
discharge of
duties, §11-43C-88.
Oath, §11-43C-89.
Participation in
contracts by the
socially and
economically
disadvantaged,
§11-43C-92.
Removal of merit
system officers and
employees,
§11-43C-85.
Transfer of powers and
duties of office
abolished by
chapter,
§11-43C-77.
Ordinances.
Changing functions of
offices, etc.,
§11-43C-23.
Continued in effect,
§11-43C-84.
Grant of franchises to
use streets, etc.,
§11-43C-29.
Revision and
codification,
§11-43C-30.
Outside counsel.
Authority to obtain,
§11-43C-38.
Parks.
Continuation of laws,
§11-43C-83.
Payments and
obligations,
§11-43C-62.
Pensions.
Continuation of laws,
§11-43C-82.
Personnel.
Amount available for
salaries,
§11-43C-40.
Mayor authorized to
employ additional
personnel,
§11-43C-40.
Merit system
inapplicable,
§11-43C-40.
Petition to become
candidate,
§11-43C-33.
Policemen.
Free transportation of
policemen in
discharge of
duties, §11-43C-88.
Powers.
Changing functions of
offices, etc.,
§11-43C-23.
Council, §11-43C-21.

MUNICIPAL CORPORATIONS—Cont'd
Class 5 municipalities
—Cont'd
Mayor-council form of
government—Cont'd
Mayor and council—Cont'd
Powers—Cont'd
Manner in which
powers exercised,
§11-43C-11.
Mayor, §§11-43C-37,
11-43D-14.
President of council,
§11-43D-19.
Additional
compensation,
§11-43C-18.
Duties, §11-43C-19.
Election, §11-43C-19.
President pro tem,
§11-43D-19.
Term, §11-43C-19.
Vacancies, §11-43C-19.
Primary elections
prohibited,
§11-43C-33.
Procedure for changing
form of government,
§11-43C-91.
Procurement,
§11-43C-72.
Property.
Transfer, §11-43C-78.
Public hearings.
Budget, §11-43C-48.
Public improvements.
Alteration, §11-43C-71.
Bidding on contract,
§11-43C-71.
Capital improvement
program,
§11-43C-60.
Compilation after
change in form of
government,
§11-43C-80.
Contracts for,
§11-43C-71.
Lapse of
appropriations,
Reserve fund for
permanent public
improvements,
§11-43C-61.
Public utilities,
§11-43C-54.
Purchasing.
Certification of balance
sufficient to pay,
§11-43C-72.
Competitive bidding,
§11-43C-70.
Division of finance
responsible for,
§11-43C-68.
Written requisition,
§11-43C-72.
Qualifications.
Council to judge
qualifications,
§11-43C-26.
Effect of loss,
§11-43C-17.
Mayoral qualifications,
§11-43C-34.
Reapportionment,
§§11-43C-90,
11-43D-5.

MUNICIPAL CORPORATIONS—Cont'd
Class 5 municipalities
—Cont'd
Mayor-council form of
government—Cont'd
Mayor and council—Cont'd
Records.
Transfer of records
where powers and
duties reassigned,
§11-43C-78.
Recreation.
Continuation of laws,
§11-43C-83.
Relief funds.
Continuation of laws,
§11-43C-82.
Resolutions.
Continued in effect,
§11-43C-84.
Grant of franchises to
use streets, etc.,
§11-43C-29.
Revision and
codification of
resolutions,
§11-43C-30.
Retirement.
Continuation of laws,
§11-43C-82.
Revenues and
expenditures.
Adherence by council
to expenditure,
§11-43C-52.
Disapproval by mayor
of expenditure line
item, §11-43C-52.
Estimates for each
department,
§11-43C-43.
Excessive
expenditures,
§§11-43C-49,
11-43C-57.
Expenditures financed
by bond,
§11-43C-67.
Increase in
expenditures over
mayor's
recommendation,
§11-43C-49.
Recommendations
where receipts
estimated to
exceed
expenditures,
§11-43C-45.
Revenue notes,
§11-43C-73.
Transfer of
expenditures,
§11-43C-56.
Socially and
economically
disadvantaged.
Participation in
contracts by,
§11-43C-92.
Subpoena power,
§11-43C-87.
Term of office,
§§11-43C-7,
11-43D-3.
Transfer of records, etc.,
upon reassignment,
§11-43C-78.

MUNICIPAL CORPORATIONS—Cont'd
Class 5 municipalities
—Cont'd
Mayor-council form of
government—Cont'd
Mayor and council—Cont'd
Transportation.
Free transportation of
officials, policemen
and firemen in
discharge of
duties, §11-43C-88.
Vacancies, §11-43C-22.
Filling vacancies,
§11-43D-21.
Mayor's office,
§11-43C-36.
Vice-president of council,
§11-43C-20.
Voting, §11-43C-7.
Zoning.
Comprehensive zone
map, §11-43C-30.
Merit system.
Officers and employees.
Removal, §11-43C-85.
Notes, §§11-43C-73 to
11-43C-75.
Emergency notes,
§11-43C-74.
Not payable on demand,
§11-43C-75.
Private sale, §11-43C-75.
Redemption prior to
maturity,
§11-43C-75.
Revenue notes,
§11-43C-73.
Oaths.
City officers required to
take, §11-43C-89.
Officers and employees.
Acceptance of gifts,
§11-43C-88.
Adoption of form of
government.
Continuance in office,
§§11-43D-7,
11-43D-8.
Rights of officers and
employees
preserved,
§11-43D-6.
Appointments to reflect
make-up of
community,
§11-43C-92.
Conflicts of interest,
§11-43C-88.
Continuation in office of
personnel holding
administrative office,
§11-43C-77.
Continuation of office,
§11-43C-79.
Existing laws not
inconsistent with
personnel and
provisions of
chapter, §11-43C-76.
Existing rights and
privileges of,
§11-43C-76.
Fees.
Disposition of,
§11-43C-68.

MUNICIPAL
CORPORATIONS—Cont'd
Class 5 municipalities
—Cont'd
Mayor-council form of
government—Cont'd
Officers and employees
—Cont'd
Mayor and council.
Dealings with those in
administrative
services,
§11-43C-21.
Merit system.
Removal, §11-43C-85.
Removal.
Appeal of decision,
§11-43C-85.
Transfer of powers and
duties of office
abolished by chapter,
§11-43C-77.
Offices.
Records and property.
Transfer on adoption of
form of
government,
§11-43D-9.
Ordinances.
Adoption of form of
government.
Continuance of
ordinances and
resolutions,
§11-43D-22.
Form of ordinance,
§11-43D-1.
Continued in effect,
§11-43C-84.
Districts.
Establishment of
boundaries,
§11-43D-2.
Parks.
Continuation in force of
laws relating to,
§11-43C-83.
Payments and obligations.
Certification of
accordance with
appropriations,
§11-43C-62.
Penalty.
Violations, §11-43C-62.
Void, §11-43C-62.
Penalties.
Payments and
obligations.
Knowing violation,
§11-43C-62.
Pensions.
Continuation of laws,
§11-43C-82.
Adoption of form of
government,
§11-43D-12.
Policemen.
Free transportation of
policemen in
discharge of duties,
§11-43C-88.
Powers, §11-43C-11.
Manner in which powers
exercised,
§11-43C-11.
Powers of city,
§11-43C-12.
Vested in council,
§11-43C-11.

MUNICIPAL
CORPORATIONS—Cont'd
Class 5 municipalities
—Cont'd
Mayor-council form of
government—Cont'd
Procedure for changing
form of government,
§11-43C-91.
Property.
Transfer of property
where powers and
duties reassigned,
§11-43C-78.
Public hearing.
Budgets, §11-43C-48.
Public improvements.
Appropriations.
Lapse, §11-43C-61.
Capital improvement
program,
§11-43C-60.
Completion after change
in form of
government,
§11-43C-80.
Contracts for,
§11-43C-71.
Reserve fund for
permanent public
improvements,
§11-43C-61.
Public officers and
employees.
Oaths, §11-43C-89.
Public utilities.
Budgets.
Budget estimates,
§11-43C-54.
Generally,
§11-43C-45.
Presentation,
§11-43C-54.
Officers and employees.
Conflicts of interest,
§11-43C-88.
Purchasing division.
Bids and bidding,
§§11-43C-70,
11-43C-71.
Certification of balance
sufficient to pay,
§11-43C-72.
Competitive bidding,
§§11-43C-70,
11-43C-71.
Generally, §11-43C-69.
Powers and duties of
division head,
§11-43C-69.
Written requisition,
§11-43C-72.
Qualifications of officials,
§11-43C-17.
Reapportionment.
Districts.
Population change,
§11-43C-90.
Records.
Transfer of records
where powers and
duties reassigned,
§11-43C-78.
Recreation.
Continuation of laws,
§11-43C-83.
Resolutions.
Continued in effect,
§11-43C-84.

MUNICIPAL
CORPORATIONS—Cont'd
Class 5 municipalities
—Cont'd
Mayor-council form of
government—Cont'd
Retirement.
Continuation of laws,
§11-43C-82.
Adoption of form of
government,
§11-43D-12.
Revenues and
expenditures.
Adherence by council to
expenditure,
§11-43C-52.
Disapproval by mayor of
expenditure line
item, §11-43C-52.
Estimates for each
department,
§11-43C-43.
Recommendations
where receipts
estimated to
exceed
expenditures,
§11-43C-45.
Excessive expenditures,
§11-43C-67.
Expenditures financed by
bonds, §11-43C-67.
Increase in expenditures
over mayor's
recommendation,
§11-43C-49.
Recommended
expenditures not to
exceed estimated
receipts unless
additional revenue
measures adopted,
§11-43C-45.
Revenue notes,
§11-43C-73.
Transfer of expenditures,
§11-43C-56.
Scope of chapter,
§11-43C-1.
Socially and economically
disadvantaged.
Contracts.
Participation in,
§11-43C-92.
Subpoena power.
Mayor and council,
§11-43C-87.
Title of government,
§11-43C-11.
Transfer of records, etc.,
upon reassignment,
§11-43C-78.
Transportation.
Free transportation of
officials, policemen
and firemen in
discharge of duties,
§11-43C-88.
Nuisances.
Weed abatement,
§§11-67-20 to 11-67-28.
Oaths.
Mayor/commission/city
manager form of
government.
Commission, §11-44E-40.
Oath of office,
§11-44E-185.

MUNICIPAL
CORPORATIONS—Cont'd
Class 5 municipalities
—Cont'd
Payment of funds out of
treasury by warrant,
§11-44-18.1.
Weed abatement, §§11-67-20
to 11-67-28.
Account of cost, §11-67-26.
Applicability of article,
§11-67-20.
Authorization, §11-67-21.
Construction and
interpretation,
§11-67-20.
Cost.
Collection with taxes,
§11-67-27.
Lien of costs, §11-67-27.
Report of cost.
Hearing on, §11-67-27.
Decision of city council,
§11-67-24.
Hearings.
Cost of abatement,
§11-67-27.
Notice, §11-67-23.
Procedure, §11-67-24.
Liens.
Cost as lien, §11-67-27.
Notice.
Public hearing,
§11-67-23.
Order of abatement,
§11-67-22.
Decision of city council,
§11-67-24.
Owner's right to have
weeds removed at own
expense, §11-67-25.
Private contractors,
§11-67-25.
Public nuisance.
Authority to declare
weeds as, §11-67-21.
Resolution declaring
weeds as, §11-67-22.
Reports.
Cost of abating or
removing nuisance,
§§11-67-26, 11-67-27.
Effect of account reports
confirmed before
enactment of article,
§11-67-28.
Resolutions.
Effect of resolutions
enacted before
article, §11-67-28.
Public nuisance.
Declaration of weeds
as, §11-67-22.
Right of entry, §11-67-25.
Class 6 municipalities,
§§11-44D-1 to 11-44D-21.
Commission form of
government.
Abandonment.
Elections.
Conduct, §§11-44D-3,
11-44D-7.
Effect of results,
§11-44D-3.
Expenses, §11-44D-3.
Form of ballot,
§11-44D-2.
Use of voting
machines,
§11-44D-2.

MUNICIPAL
CORPORATIONS—Cont'd
Class 6 municipalities
—Cont'd
Commission form of
government—Cont'd
Abandonment—Cont'd
Manager-council form of
government,
§11-44D-5.
Mayor-council form of
government,
§11-44D-4.
Ordinances, §11-44D-1.
Adoption of mayor-
council or
manager-council
form, §11-44D-1.
Provisions applicable to
both mayor-council
and manager-council
forms of government,
§11-44D-6.
Reapportionment of council
districts, §11-44D-8.
Administrative offices
continued,
§11-44D-13.
Civil service officers
continued,
§11-44D-14.
Contracts continued,
§11-44D-16.
Effect of chapter on
employees,
§§11-44D-12,
11-44D-13.
Existing rights, etc.,
continued,
§11-44D-10.
Initial territorial limits,
§11-44D-11.
Judicial proceedings
unaffected,
§11-44D-17.
Laws relating to certain
boards continued,
§11-44D-19.
Ordinances and
resolutions
continued,
§11-44D-20.
Inconsistent or
conflicting laws,
§11-44D-21.
Pension, retirement and
relief fund laws
continued,
§11-44D-18.
Powers of cities,
§11-44D-9.
Public improvements
completion required,
§11-44D-16.
Reassignment of powers
and duties of
abolished agencies,
§11-44D-13.
Transfer of records,
equipment, etc.,
§11-44D-15.
Council-manager form of
government.
Election, §11-43A-3.1.
Provision to supersede
other laws,
§11-43A-3.2.

MUNICIPAL
CORPORATIONS—Cont'd
Class 7 municipalities,
§§11-44A-1 to 11-44A-32.
Commission form of
government.
Abandonment.
Administrative offices
continued,
§11-44A-8.
Applicability of chapter,
§11-44A-15.
Civil service officers
continued,
§11-44A-9.
Contracts continued,
§11-44A-11.
Duties of commission
terminated,
§11-44A-3.
Effect of chapter on
employees,
§11-44A-7.
Election.
Calling, §11-44A-1.
Conduct, §11-44A-5.
Proposition submitted
to voters,
§11-44A-1.
Establishment of council
districts, §11-44A-2.
Judicial proceedings
unaffected,
§11-44A-12.
Laws relating to certain
boards continued,
§11-44A-14.
Mayor-council to assume
office, §11-44A-3.
Ordinances and
resolutions
continued,
§11-44A-16.
Pension and retirement
plans continued,
§11-44A-13.
Powers and duties of
mayor-council,
§11-44A-2.
Public works completion
required,
§11-44A-11.
Reapportionment of
council districts,
§11-44A-6.
Reassignment of powers
and duties of
abolished agencies,
§11-44A-8.
Referenda, §11-44A-1.
Conduct, §11-44A-5.
Salaries of mayor and
council members,
§11-44A-2.
Terms of mayor and
council members,
§11-44A-4.
Transfer of records,
equipment, etc.,
§11-44A-10.
Mayor.
Designation by
ordinance, §11-44-58.
Mayor-council form of
government.
Adoption where
commission form
violates federal
voting rights act,
§§11-44A-30 to
11-44A-32.

**MUNICIPAL
CORPORATIONS**—Cont'd
Class 7 municipalities
—Cont'd
Commission form of
government—Cont'd
Public safety
commissioner.
Designation by
ordinance, §11-44-58.
Public works
commissioner.
Designation by
ordinance, §11-44-58.
Conflicts of interest,
§11-43-12.1.
Federal voting rights act.
Mayor-council form of
government.
Adoption where
commission form
violates act,
§§11-44A-30 to
11-44A-32.
Mayor-council form of
government.
Adoption where
commission form
violates federal voting
rights act, §11-44A-30.
Boundaries of districts,
§11-44A-31.
Candidates for election.
Residency
requirements,
§11-44A-30.
Elections, §11-44A-30.
Governing bodies,
§11-44A-32.
Ordinance, §11-44A-30.
Powers and duties of
municipalities,
§11-44A-32.
Residency requirements.
Candidates and
electors,
§11-44A-30.
Single-member districts.
Boundaries,
§11-44A-31.
Division into,
§11-44A-30.
Class 8 municipalities.
Conflicts of interest,
§11-43-12.1.
Mayor-council form of
government, §§11-44F-1
to 11-44F-3.
Adoption where
commission form
violates federal voting
rights act, §11-44F-1.
Boundaries of districts,
§11-44F-2.
Candidates.
Residence
requirements,
§11-44F-1.
Elections, §11-44F-1.
Electors.
Residence
requirements,
§11-44F-1.
Governing body of
municipalities,
§11-44F-3.
Ordinance, §11-44F-1.
Powers and duties of
municipalities,
§11-44F-3.

**MUNICIPAL
CORPORATIONS**—Cont'd
Class 8 municipalities
—Cont'd
Mayor-council form of
government—Cont'd
Adoption where
commission form
violates federal voting
rights act—Cont'd
Residence requirements
for candidates and
electors, §11-44F-1.
Single-member districts.
Boundaries, §11-44F-2.
Municipality divided
into 5 single-
member districts,
§11-44F-1.
Classification.
Classification by legislature,
Const. Ala., amd. 375.
Eight classes of
municipalities,
§11-45-9.1.
Municipal corporations
classified as cities or
towns, §11-40-6.
Clerks.
Auditors.
Devolution of duties upon
auditors, §11-43-103.
Bonds, surety, §11-43-104.
Books and accounts.
Maintenance, §11-43-102.
Claims for and against
municipality.
Auditing, recordation, etc.,
§11-43-101.
Warrants for claims,
§11-43-101.
Class 5 municipalities.
Mayor/commission/city
manager form of
government,
§11-44E-47.
Council, §11-43-100.
Duties, §11-43-3.
Additional duties,
§11-43-104.
Class 5 municipalities.
Mayor/commission/city
manager form of
government,
§11-44E-47.
Devolution of duties upon
auditor, §11-43-103.
Election of clerks.
Cities having less than
6,000 inhabitants,
§11-43-4.
Cities having more than
6,000 inhabitants,
§11-43-3.
Offenses, §§11-46-60,
11-46-131.
Voting machines.
Duties, §§11-46-33,
11-46-104, 17-9-17.
Fees.
Disposition of fees of clerk,
§11-43-7.
Finance.
Maintenance, etc., of books
and accounts,
§11-43-102.
Licenses.
Issuance, §11-43-103.

**MUNICIPAL
CORPORATIONS**—Cont'd
Clerks—Cont'd
Mayor/commission/city
manager form of
government.
Civil service or merit
system.
Appointment where not
subject to,
§11-44E-47.
Continuation in office
where subject to,
§11-44E-47.
Duties, §11-44E-47.
Officers generally. See within
this heading, "Officers."
Ordinances and resolutions.
Custody of ordinances,
§11-43-100.
Publication by clerk,
§11-45-3.
Penalties.
Election offenses,
§§11-46-60, 11-46-131.
Salary, §§11-43-3, 11-43-4.
Term of office, §11-43-4.
Clinics.
Medical clinic boards,
§§11-58-1 to 11-58-15.
See within this heading,
"Medical clinic boards."
Coal.
Severance tax.
State preemption, §40-13-9.
Code of Alabama.
Corporate limits not altered
or affected by adoption,
§11-40-5.
Code of conduct.
Class 5 municipalities.
Mayor/commission/city
manager form of
government,
§§11-44E-160 to
11-44E-168. See within
this heading, "Class 5
municipalities."
**Commercial development
authorities,** §§11-54-170 to
11-54-192.
Applicants.
Defined, §11-54-171.
Applications.
Approval or denial by
governing body,
§11-54-175.
Contents, §11-54-173.
Filing, §§11-54-173,
11-54-175.
Recordation, §11-54-175.
Authorizing municipality.
Defined, §11-54-171.
Liability, §11-54-184.
Authorizing resolution.
Defined, §11-54-171.
Autonomy of authority,
§11-54-187.
Board, §§11-54-171,
11-54-176.
Composition, §11-54-176.
Defined, §11-54-171.
Election of members,
§11-54-176.
Expenses, §11-54-176.
Qualifications, §11-54-176.
Removal of members,
§11-54-176.
Terms of office, §11-54-176.
Vacancies, §11-54-176.

MUNICIPAL
CORPORATIONS—Cont'd
Commercial development
authorities—Cont'd
Bond issues, §§11-54-179 to
11-54-183.
Eligibility for investment,
§11-54-179.
Execution, §11-54-179.
Exemption from certain
taxes and fees,
§11-54-183.
Form, §11-54-179.
Interest rate, §11-54-179.
Limitation on proceedings
questioning or taxing
bonds, §11-54-182.
Negotiability, §11-54-179.
Notice of bond resolution,
§11-54-182.
Payment, §11-54-179.
Pledge of revenues,
§11-54-179.
Proceeds from sale,
§11-54-180.
Refunding bonds,
§11-54-181.
Sale, §11-54-179.
Competitive bid laws.
Exemption, §11-54-186.
Continued existence of
authority, §11-54-191.
Cumulative provisions,
§11-54-192.
Definitions, §11-54-171.
Construction of definitions,
§11-54-172.
Director.
Defined, §11-54-171.
Dissolution, §11-54-189.
Earnings of authority,
§11-54-188.
Election of officers,
§11-54-177.
Governing body.
Defined, §11-54-171.
Incorporation.
Authorization or denial,
§11-54-173.
Certificate of incorporation.
Amendments,
§11-54-175.
Contents, §11-54-174.
Execution of certificate,
§11-54-174.
Existence of authority to
prevent incorporation
of another by same
municipality,
§11-54-190.
Procedure to incorporate,
§11-54-174.
Incorporators.
Defined, §11-54-171.
Interest.
Exemption from interest
laws, §11-54-185.
Legislative intent,
§11-54-170.
Liability.
Authorizing municipality,
§11-54-184.
Liberal construction of
article, §11-54-170.
Meaning of phrases,
§11-54-172.
Meetings.
Public meetings,
§11-54-178.
Nonprofit corporation,
§11-54-188.

MUNICIPAL
CORPORATIONS—Cont'd
Commercial development
authorities—Cont'd
Notice.
Bond resolution,
§11-54-182.
Officers, §11-54-177.
Pollution.
Defined, §11-54-171.
Pollution control facility.
Defined, §11-54-171.
Powers.
Generally, §11-54-178.
Preventing corporation of
another by same
municipality, §11-54-190.
Principal office.
Defined, §11-54-171.
Projects.
Defined, §11-54-171.
Location of projects,
§11-54-178.
Provisions of article
cumulative, §11-54-192.
State supervision.
Freedom of authority from
state supervision,
§11-54-187.
Taxation.
Exemption of bond issues,
§11-54-183.
Usury.
Exemption from usury
laws, §11-54-185.
Commercial projects.
Bonds for enlargement, etc.,
of municipally-owned
projects, Const. Ala.,
amd. 228.
Commission form of
government, §§11-44-1 to
11-44-162.
Abandonment, §§11-44-150 to
11-44-162.
Abolition of office of
commissioner,
§11-44-161.
Actions for or against
municipality.
Actions not affected,
§11-44-160.
Adoption of provisions as
to mayor-council form
of government,
§11-44-155.
Aldermen, §11-44-157.
Duties, §11-44-162.
Election, §11-44-156.
Powers, §11-44-162.
Bylaws.
Continuation,
§11-44-158.
Class 4 municipalities. See
within this heading,
"Class 4
municipalities."
Class 6 municipalities. See
within this heading,
"Class 6
municipalities."
Class 7 municipalities. See
within this heading,
"Class 7
municipalities."
Commissioners.
Abolishment of office,
§11-44-161.

MUNICIPAL
CORPORATIONS—Cont'd
Commission form of
government—Cont'd
Abandonment—Cont'd
Corporate existence of
municipality.
Continuation,
§11-44-158.
Election.
Ballots, §11-44-154.
Calling of election,
§11-44-152.
Canvassing of vote,
§11-44-155.
Certification of
provisions as to
mayor-council form
of government,
§11-44-155.
Conduct of election,
§11-44-155.
Petition to probate judge
for election,
§11-44-150.
Examination and
certification of
petition,
§11-44-151.
Proposition submitted to
voters, §11-44-154.
Results.
Declaration of result,
§11-44-155.
Subsequent elections.
When held,
§11-44-153.
Employees.
Continuation in office,
§11-44-161.
Laws.
Continuation,
§11-44-158.
Liabilities of municipality.
Not affected, §11-44-160.
Management, etc., of
municipalities
abandoning
commission form,
§11-44-162.
Mayor.
Duties, §§11-44-157,
11-44-162.
Election, §11-44-156.
Powers, §11-44-162.
Officers.
Continuation in office,
§11-44-161.
Ordinances.
Continuation,
§11-44-158.
Powers of municipality.
Vesting of powers,
§11-44-159.
Resolutions.
Continuation,
§11-44-158.
Rights of municipalities.
Not affected, §11-44-160.
Vesting of rights,
§11-44-159.
Territorial limits.
Continuation,
§11-44-159.
Wards.
Creation, §11-44-159.
Abolition of certain boards,
etc., §11-44-23.
Accounts and accounting,
§11-44-50.

MUNICIPAL
CORPORATIONS—Cont'd
Commission form of
government—Cont'd
Administrative powers and
duties.
Distribution among
departments,
§11-44-29.
Adoption of provisions of
article, §11-44-6.
Applicability of article,
§11-44-1.
Audits.
Optional form A,
§11-44-95.
Optional form B,
§11-44-139.
Bonds, surety.
Commissioners, §§11-44-9,
11-44-79, 11-44-128.
Optional form A,
§11-44-79.
Optional form B,
§11-44-128.
Bribery.
Offering or accepting
bribes for votes,
§11-44-53.
Bylaws.
Abandonment of
commission form.
Continuation in force,
§11-44-158.
Continuation, §§11-44-24,
11-44-158.
Form, §11-44-32.
Granting franchises, etc.,
for use of streets, etc.
Effective date, §11-44-33.
Elections, §11-44-34.
Determination of
result, §11-44-35.
Objections, §11-44-34.
Optional form A,
§11-44-88.
Publication, §11-44-33.
Manner of enactment,
§11-44-31.
Optional form A,
§§11-44-87, 11-44-88.
Voting, §11-44-32.
Certification of provisions of
article, §11-44-6.
Class 2 municipalities,
§11-44C-92.
Class 4 municipalities,
§§11-44B-1 to 11-44B-22.
See within this heading,
"Class 4 municipalities."
Class 6 municipalities,
§§11-44D-1 to 11-44D-21.
See within this heading,
"Class 6 municipalities."
Class 7 municipalities,
§§11-44A-1 to 11-44A-32.
See wiithin this heading,
"Class 7 municipalities."
Commissioners.
Abandonment of
commission form.
Abolition of office of
commissioners,
§11-44-161.
Assignment of powers,
§11-44-30.
Authority upon
organization,
§11-44-23.
Bond, §§11-44-9, 11-44-79,
11-44-128.

MUNICIPAL
CORPORATIONS—Cont'd
Commission form of
government—Cont'd
Commissioners—Cont'd
Compensation, §§11-44-18,
11-44-80, 11-44-104,
11-44-129.
Death.
Filling of vacancies
caused by death,
§§11-44-12, 11-44-77.
Delegation of duties,
§11-44-30.
Departments.
Determination and
exercise of powers
and duties of
departments,
§11-44-29.
Designation, §§11-44-8,
11-44-81, 11-44-121.
Duties.
Assignment or
delegation,
§§11-44-30, 11-44-86.
Election, §11-44-7.
At large, §11-44-25.
Ballots, §11-44-39.
Specification in ballot
as to term,
§11-44-40.
Candidacy.
Statement of
candidacy,
§11-44-37.
Commissioners at large,
§11-44-25.
Expenses.
Statement of campaign
expenses,
§11-44-44.
Filing candidacy,
§11-44-37.
Majority of votes
required, §11-44-41.
Optional form A,
§§11-44-73 to
11-44-75, 11-44-90 to
11-44-92, 11-44-97 to
11-44-100.
Procedure for adoption,
§11-44-72.
Optional form B,
§§11-44-121,
11-44-123 to
11-44-125,
11-44-134.
Procedure for election,
§11-44-7.
Qualifications of
candidates,
§11-44-38.
Qualified voters only to
vote, §11-44-43.
Run-off election,
§11-44-42.
Statement of campaign
expenses, §11-44-44.
Statement of candidacy,
§11-44-37.
Specification in
statement as to
term, §11-44-40.
Term of office.
Specification in
statement of
candidacy and
ballot as to term,
§11-44-40.

MUNICIPAL
CORPORATIONS—Cont'd
Commission form of
government—Cont'd
Commissioners—Cont'd
Election—Cont'd
Vacancies.
Filling of two
simultaneous
vacancies,
§11-44-13.
Voting.
Majority of votes
required,
§11-44-41.
Manner of voting,
§11-44-41.
Qualified voters only
to vote, §11-44-43.
Eligibility for office,
§11-44-38.
Filling of vacancies
caused by
ineligibility,
§§11-44-11, 11-44-76.
Entry into office,
§11-44-10.
Ineligibility.
Filling of vacancies
caused by,
§§11-44-11, 11-44-76.
Mayor/commission/city
manager form of
government.
Commission generally,
§§11-44E-40 to
11-44E-54. See
within this heading,
"Class 5
municipalities."
Mayor to be president of
board of
commissioners,
§§11-44-15, 11-44-83.
Meetings.
Optional form A,
§11-44-82.
Optional form B,
§§11-44-126,
11-44-127.
Presiding officer,
§11-44-20.
Quorum, §11-44-20.
Record of proceedings,
§11-44-22.
Time, etc., §11-44-19.
When open to public,
§11-44-21.
Oath, §§11-44-9, 11-44-79,
11-44-123.
Optional form A,
§§11-44-73 to
11-44-105.
Optional form B,
§§11-44-120 to
11-44-140.
Powers.
Assignment or
delegation,
§§11-44-30, 11-44-96.
Optional form A,
§§11-44-84, 11-44-86.
Optional form B,
§11-44-121.
Upon organization,
§11-44-23.
President of board of
commissioners,
§§11-44-14 to 11-44-18,
11-44-83, 11-50-16.
Public meetings, §11-44-21.

MUNICIPAL
CORPORATIONS—Cont'd
Commission form of
government—Cont'd
Commissioners—Cont'd
Qualification for office,
§§11-44-8, 11-44-38,
11-44-76, 11-44-81,
11-44-123, 11-44-124.
Quorum, §§11-44-20,
11-44-82, 11-44-126.
Record of proceedings,
§§11-44-22, 11-44-126.
Removal.
Filling of vacancies
caused by,
§§11-44-12, 11-44-77,
11-44-130 to
11-44-134.
Resignation.
Filling of vacancies
caused by,
§§11-44-12, 11-44-77.
Terms of office, §§11-44-7,
11-44-73, 11-44-74,
11-44-123.
Vacancies, §11-44-125.
Filling of two
simultaneous
vacancies,
§§11-44-13, 11-44-78.
Filling of vacancies
caused by death,
resignation or
removal, §§11-44-12,
11-44-77, 11-44-130
to 11-44-134.
Filling of vacancies
caused by
ineligibility,
§§11-44-11, 11-44-76.
Conflicts of interest.
Officers and employees,
§§11-44-46 to 11-44-48,
11-44-94, 11-44-138.
Optional form A,
§11-44-94.
Optional form B,
§11-44-138.
Corporate existence of
municipality.
Continuation, §11-44-23.
Corporate limits.
Continuation, §11-44-25.
Definitions.
Optional form B,
§11-44-120.
Departments.
Determination and exercise
of powers and duties,
§11-44-29.
Election as to commission
form, §§11-46-90 to
11-46-144. See within
this heading, "Elections."
Electricity.
Municipal officers or
employees.
Conflicts of interest,
§§11-44-46 to
11-44-48.
President of board of
commissioners.
Employment as
superintendent of
light system,
§11-50-16.
Validation of prior
employment,
§11-50-16.

MUNICIPAL
CORPORATIONS—Cont'd
Commission form of
government—Cont'd
Employees.
Compensation, §§11-44-28,
11-44-85, 11-44-104.
Conflicts of interest,
§§11-44-46 to 11-44-48,
11-44-94, 11-44-138.
Continuation in office,
§§11-44-27, 11-44-122,
11-44-161.
Gifts.
Acceptance from
railways, gas works,
etc., §11-44-48.
Optional form A,
§§11-44-70 to
11-44-105.
Option form B,
§§11-44-122,
11-44-138.
Removal, §11-44-28.
Selection, §§11-44-28,
11-44-45, 11-44-85,
11-44-93.
Solicitation of votes by
municipal employees,
§§11-44-54, 11-44-98.
Examinations.
Books and accounts,
§§11-44-50, 11-44-95,
11-44-139.
Executive powers and duties.
Distribution among
departments,
§11-44-29.
Expenses.
Optional form A.
Publication of statement,
§11-44-95.
Optional form B.
Publication of statement,
§11-44-139.
Publication of statement,
§11-44-49.
Federal voting rights act.
Mayor-council form of
government.
Adoption where
commission form
violates act.
Class 7 municipalities,
§§11-44A-30 to
11-44A-32.
Class 8 municipalities,
§§11-44F-1 to
11-44F-3.
Finance.
Examinations of books and
accounts, §§11-44-50,
11-44-95, 11-44-139.
Optional form A.
Examination of books
and accounts,
§11-44-95.
Publication of statement
of receipt and
expenses, §11-44-95.
Optional form B.
Audit of books and
accounts, §11-44-139.
Publication of statement
of receipt and
expenses,
§11-44-139.
Publication of statement of
expenses, §11-44-49.

MUNICIPAL
CORPORATIONS—Cont'd
Commission form of
government—Cont'd
Franchises.
Use of streets, etc.
Procedure for granting,
§11-44-36.
Resolutions, etc.,
granting franchises.
Effective date,
§11-44-33.
Elections, §§11-44-34,
11-44-35.
Objections, §11-44-34.
Optional form A,
§11-44-88.
Optional form B,
§11-44-137.
Publication, §11-44-33.
Gas.
Municipal officers or
employees.
Conflicts of interest,
§§11-44-46 to
11-44-48.
President of board of
commissioners.
Employment as
superintendent of
gas systems,
§11-50-16.
Validation of prior
employment,
§11-50-16.
Initiative and referendum.
Optional form A.
Adoption of ordinances
by, §11-44-105.
Laws.
Abandonment of
commission form.
Continuation of laws,
§11-44-158.
Continuation, §§11-44-24,
11-44-122, 11-44-158.
Liability.
Continuation, §11-44-26.
Limits.
Continuation of territorial
limits, §11-44-25.
Mayor/commission/city
manager form of
government, §§11-44E-1
to 11-44 E-222. See
within this heading,
"Class 5 municipalities."
Mayor-council form of
government.
Class 7 municipalities.
Adoption where
commission form
violates federal
voting rights act,
§§11-44A-30 to
11-44A-32.
Class 8 municipalities.
Adoption where
commission form
violates federal
voting rights act,
§§11-44F-1 to
11-44F-3.
Nepotism.
Optional form A,
§§11-44-102,
11-44-103.
Optional form B,
§11-44-138.

MUNICIPAL CORPORATIONS—Cont'd
Commission form of government—Cont'd
Officers.
Compensation, §§11-44-28, 11-44-85, 11-44-104.
Conflicts of interest, §§11-44-46 to 11-44-48, 11-44-94, 11-44-138.
Continuation in office, §§11-44-27, 11-44-121, 11-44-122.
Employment by public service utilities prohibited, §11-44-47.
Gifts.
Acceptance from railways, gas works, etc., §11-44-48.
Removal, §11-44-28.
Selection, §§11-44-28, 11-44-85.
Optional form A, §§11-44-70 to 11-44-105.
Abolition of certain boards, etc., §11-44-84.
Administrative powers and duties.
Distribution among departments, §11-44-85.
Adoption.
Election, §11-44-72.
Procedure for adoption, §11-44-71.
Applicability of article, §11-44-70.
Audit of books and accounts, §11-44-95.
Boards.
Abolition of certain boards, §11-44-84.
Bonds, surety.
Commissioners, §11-44-79.
Bylaws.
Enactment, §11-44-87.
Granting franchises, etc., for use of streets, etc.
Procedure for adoption, §11-44-88.
Commissioners.
Authority, §11-44-84.
Bond, §11-44-79.
Compensation, §§11-44-80, 11-44-104.
Death.
Filling vacancies caused by death, §11-44-77.
Designation, §11-44-81.
Positions, §11-44-75.
Duties.
Assignment or delegation, §11-44-86.
Election, §11-44-73.
Applicability of general state laws, §11-44-100.
Ballots, §11-44-91.
Commissioners elected after September 1, 1945, §11-44-74.
Election to designated position, §11-44-75.

MUNICIPAL CORPORATIONS—Cont'd
Commission form of government—Cont'd
Optional form A—Cont'd
Commissioners—Cont'd
Election—Cont'd
Solicitation of votes, §11-44-98, 11-44-99.
Statement of campaign expenses, §11-44-92.
Statement of candidacy, §11-44-90.
Use of influence or contributions by municipal officers or employees, §11-44-97.
Voting, §11-44-91.
Ineligibility.
Filling vacancies caused by, §11-44-76.
Meetings, §11-44-82.
Not to receive profits, wages, etc., from municipality, §11-44-102.
Oath, §11-44-79.
Powers, §11-44-84.
Assignment or delegation, §11-44-86.
President of board of commissioners.
Mayor, §11-44-83.
Qualifications, §§11-44-76, 11-44-81.
Quorum, §11-44-82.
Removal.
Filling vacancies caused by removal, §11-44-77.
Resignation.
Filling vacancies caused by, §11-44-77.
Taking of office, §11-44-81.
Terms of office, §11-44-73.
Commissioners elected after September 1, 1945, §11-44-74.
Vacancies.
Filling of two or more simultaneous vacancies, §11-44-78.
Filling vacancies caused by death, resignation or removal, §11-44-77.
Filling vacancies caused by ineligibility, §11-44-76.
Commissions.
Abolition of certain commissions, §11-44-84.
Conflicts of interest.
Municipal officers and employees, §11-44-94.
Corporate existence.
Continuation, §11-44-84.

MUNICIPAL CORPORATIONS—Cont'd
Commission form of government—Cont'd
Optional form A—Cont'd
Departments.
Distribution of executive and administrative powers and duties among departments, §11-44-85.
Election.
Commissioners, §§11-44-73 to 11-44-75, 11-44-90 to 11-44-92, 11-44-97 to 11-44-100.
Procedure for adoption, §11-44-72.
Employees.
Appointment, §§11-44-85, 11-44-93.
Certain persons not to become employees, §11-44-103.
Conflicts of interest, §11-44-94.
Elections for commissioners.
Solicitation of votes by employees, §11-44-98.
Use of influence or contribution of money by employees, §11-44-97.
Not to receive profits, wages, etc., from municipality, §11-44-102.
Salaries, §11-44-85.
To receive regular compensation only, §11-44-104.
Executive powers and duties.
Distribution among departments, §11-44-85.
Expenses.
Publication of statement, §11-44-95.
Franchises.
Streets.
Use of streets, §11-44-88.
Initiative.
Adoption of ordinances, §11-44-105.
Nepotism, §§11-44-102, 11-44-103.
Officers.
Abolition of certain officers, §11-44-84.
Appointment, §11-44-85.
Certain persons not to become officers, §11-44-103.
Compensation.
To receive regular compensation only, §11-44-104.
Conflicts of interest, §11-44-94.
Elections for commissioners.
Use of influence or contribution of money by officers, §11-44-97.

MUNICIPAL
  CORPORATIONS—Cont'd
Commission form of
  government—Cont'd
Optional form A—Cont'd
  Officers—Cont'd
    Not to receive profits,
      wages, etc., from
      municipality,
      §11-44-102.
    Salaries, §11-44-85.
  Ordinances.
    Adoption by initiative
      and referendum,
      §11-44-105.
    Enactment generally,
      §11-44-87.
    Franchises for use of
      streets.
      Procedure for adoption,
        §11-44-88.
  Petitions.
    Requirements,
      §11-44-101.
  Probate judges.
    Fee for examination of
      petitions for
      elections, §11-44-96.
    Maintenance of record
      books and
      compensation,
      §11-44-96.
  Procedure for adoption.
    Election, §11-44-72.
    Generally, §11-44-71.
  Receipts.
    Publication of statement,
      §11-44-95.
  Records.
    Maintenance of record
      books, §11-44-96.
  Referendum.
    Adoption of ordinances
      by initiative and
      referendum,
      §11-44-105.
  Resolutions.
    Enactment generally,
      §11-44-87.
    Franchises for use of
      streets.
      Procedure for adoption,
        §11-44-88.
  Streets.
    Contracts for
      construction.
      Procedure for letting,
        §11-44-89.
    Franchises for use,
      §11-44-88.
    Territorial limits of
      municipality.
      Continuation, §11-44-84.
Optional form B, §§11-44-120
  to 11-44-140.
  Accounts.
    Audit, §11-44-139.
  Adoption by ordinance,
    §11-44-121.
  Alteration of form,
    §11-44-140.
  Audit of books and
    accounts, §11-44-139.
  Bonds, surety.
    Commissioners,
      §11-44-128.
  Books and accounts.
    Audit, §11-44-139.

MUNICIPAL
  CORPORATIONS—Cont'd
Commission form of
  government—Cont'd
Optional form B—Cont'd
  Commissioners.
    Authority as head of
      departments,
      §11-44-135.
    Bonds, surety,
      §11-44-128.
    Compensation,
      §11-44-129.
    Conflicts of interest,
      §11-44-138.
    Designation, §11-44-121.
    Designation of positions,
      §11-44-123.
    Disqualification from
      certain offices,
      §11-44-128.
    Dual office holding,
      §11-44-128.
    Election, §§11-44-121,
      11-44-123.
      Filling vacancies,
        §11-44-125.
      Qualification of
        candidates,
        §11-44-124.
      Recall election,
        §11-44-134.
      Special election for
        selection of
        successor after
        removal,
        §11-44-134.
    Meetings.
      Open to public,
        §11-44-127.
      Place, §11-44-127.
      Presiding officer,
        §11-44-126.
      Quorum, §11-44-126.
      Record of proceedings,
        §11-44-126.
      Time, §11-44-126.
    Oath.
      Qualification for
        taking oath,
        §11-44-123.
    Powers, §11-44-121.
    President of board.
      Additional duties,
        §11-44-135.
      Qualification for office,
        §11-44-123.
    Qualification of
      candidates,
      §11-44-124.
    Quorum, §11-44-126.
    Recall election,
      §11-44-134.
    Record of proceedings,
      §11-44-126.
    Removal.
      Certification of lists of
        electors to probate
        judge where
        municipality
        situated in two or
        more counties,
        §11-44-131.
      Delivery of petition
        and certificate to
        board, §11-44-134.
      Examination of
        petition
        requesting,
        §11-44-130.

MUNICIPAL
  CORPORATIONS—Cont'd
Commission form of
  government—Cont'd
Optional form B—Cont'd
  Commissioners—Cont'd
    Removal—Cont'd
      Fee of probate judge,
        §11-44-133.
      Filing petition
        requesting
        resignation,
        §11-44-130.
      Issuance of certificate,
        etc., by probate
        judge, §11-44-130.
      Payment of security
        upon presentation
        of petition,
        §11-44-133.
      Recall election,
        §11-44-134.
      Special election for
        selection of
        successor,
        §11-44-134.
      Unauthorized signing
        of petition,
        §11-44-132.
    Terms of office,
      §11-44-123.
    Vacancies, §11-44-125.
  Conflicts of interest.
    Commissioners, officers
      or employees,
      §11-44-138.
  Definitions, §11-44-120.
  Departments.
    Authority of
      commissioners as
      heads of
      departments,
      §11-44-135.
    Distribution of municipal
      powers and duties
      among departments,
      §11-44-135.
  Elections.
    Commissioners,
      §§11-44-121,
      11-44-123 to
      11-44-125,
      11-44-134.
  Employees.
    Conflicts of interest,
      §11-44-138.
    Continuation in force of
      appointment,
      §11-44-122.
  Expenses.
    Publication of
      semiannual
      statement of
      expenses,
      §11-44-139.
  Franchises.
    Ordinances granting
      franchises for use of
      public highways or
      property, §11-44-137.
  Funds.
    Disbursement from
      municipal treasury,
      §11-44-129.
  Governing body.
    Continuation in office,
      §11-44-121.
  Laws.
    Continuation,
      §11-44-122.
  Nepotism, §11-44-138.

MUNICIPAL
   CORPORATIONS—Cont'd
Commission form of
   government—Cont'd
Optional form B—Cont'd
Officers.
   Conflicts of interest,
      §11-44-138.
   Continuation in office,
      §§11-44-121,
      11-44-122.
   Immunities, §11-44-138.
   Privileges, §11-44-138.
Ordinances.
   Adoption of form by
      ordinance,
      §11-44-121.
   Continuation in force,
      §11-44-122.
   Enactment, §11-44-136.
   Granting franchise for
      use of property,
      §11-44-137.
   Publication, §11-44-136.
Property.
   Ordinances granting
      franchises for use of
      property, §11-44-137.
Receipts.
   Publication of statement
      of receipts,
      §11-44-139.
Records.
   Commissioners.
      Record of proceedings,
         §11-44-126.
Resolutions.
   Continuation,
      §11-44-122.
   Enactment, §11-44-136.
   Publication, §11-44-136.
Streets.
   Ordinances granting
      franchises for use of
      highways,
      §11-44-137.
Treasury.
   Disbursement of funds
      from municipal
      treasury, §11-44-129.
Ordinances.
   Abandonment of
      commission form.
   Continuation in force of
      ordinances,
      §11-44-158.
   Continuation, §§11-44-24,
      11-44-122, 11-44-158.
   Enactment, §§11-44-31,
      11-44-87, 11-44-136.
   Form, §11-44-32.
   Granting franchises, etc.,
      for use of streets, etc.
      Effective date, §11-44-33.
      Elections, §11-44-34.
      Proceedings upon
         determination of
         election result,
         §11-44-35.
      Objections, §11-44-34.
      Optional form A,
         §11-44-88.
      Optional form B,
         §11-44-137.
   Publication, §11-44-33.
   Optional form A,
      §§11-44-87, 11-44-88,
      11-44-105.

MUNICIPAL
   CORPORATIONS—Cont'd
Commission form of
   government—Cont'd
Ordinances—Cont'd
   Optional form B,
      §§11-44-121,
      11-44-122, 11-44-136,
      11-44-137.
   Voting, §11-44-32.
Organization under
   commission form of
   government.
   Powers and authority of
      commissioners,
      §11-44-23.
Penalties.
   Violations of article,
      §11-44-57.
Petitions.
   Election.
      Petition for election as to
         organization under
         commission form,
         §11-44-2.
   Optional form A.
      Requirements as to
         petitions,
         §11-44-101.
Political support.
   Promising employment to
      obtain, §11-44-52.
Powers.
   Continuation, §11-44-26.
President of board of
   commissioners,
      §§11-44-14 to 11-44-18,
      11-44-83, 11-50-16.
   Compensation, §11-44-18.
   Designation as mayor,
      §§11-44-15, 11-44-83.
   Duties, §§11-44-14,
      11-44-135.
   Election, §11-44-14.
   Electric light systems.
      Employment of president
         as superintendent,
         §11-50-16.
      Validation of prior
         employment,
         §11-50-16.
   Gas systems.
      Employment of president
         as superintendent,
         §11-50-16.
   Mayor.
      Designation as mayor,
         §§11-44-15, 11-44-83.
      Duties as president of
         board of
         commissioners and
         as mayor, §11-44-17.
      Performance of duties,
         §11-44-16.
      Powers, §11-44-14.
   Sewer systems.
      Employment of president
         as superintendent,
         §11-50-16.
   Water systems.
      Employment of president
         as superintendent.
      Validation of prior
         employment,
         §11-50-16.
Probate judges.
   Compensation, §11-44-51.
   Maintenance of record
      books by probate
      judges, §11-44-51.

MUNICIPAL
   CORPORATIONS—Cont'd
Commission form of
   government—Cont'd
Probate judges—Cont'd
   Optional form A.
      Compensation,
         §11-44-96.
      Fee for examination of
         petitions for
         elections, §11-44-96.
      Maintenance of record
         books, §11-44-96.
Property.
   Optional form B.
      Ordinances granting
         franchises for use of
         property, §11-44-137.
Public utilities.
   Municipal officers or
      employees.
      Conflicts of interest,
         §§11-44-46 to
         11-44-48.
Railroads.
   Municipal officers or
      employees.
      Conflicts of interest,
         §11-44-46.
Receipts.
   Optional form A.
      Publication of statement,
         §11-44-95.
   Optional form B.
      Publication of statement,
         §11-44-139.
   Publication of statement,
      §11-44-49.
Records.
   Commissioners.
      Record of proceedings,
         §§11-44-22,
         11-44-126.
   Maintenance of record
      books by probate
      judges, §11-44-51.
   Optional form A.
      Maintenance of record
         books by probate
         judges, §11-44-96.
   Optional form B.
      Commissioners.
         Record of proceedings,
            §11-44-126.
Resolutions.
   Abandonment of
      commission form.
   Continuation in force of
      resolutions,
      §11-44-158.
   Continuation, §§11-44-24,
      11-44-122, 11-44-158.
   Form, §11-44-32.
   Granting franchises, etc.,
      for use of streets, etc.
      Effective date, §11-44-33.
      Elections, §11-44-34.
      Proceedings upon
         determination of
         result, §11-44-35.
      Objections, §11-44-34.
      Optional form A,
         §11-44-88.
      Publication, §11-44-33.
   Manner of enactment,
      §§11-44-31, 11-44-87,
      11-44-136.
   Optional form A,
      §§11-44-87, 11-44-88.

MUNICIPAL
  CORPORATIONS—Cont'd
**Commission form of
  government**—Cont'd
Resolutions—Cont'd
  Optional form B,
    §§11-44-122,
    11-44-136.
  Voting, §11-44-32.
Rights.
  Continuation, §11-44-26.
Sewers.
  President of board of
    commissioners.
    Employment as
      superintendent of
      sewer systems,
      §11-50-16.
    Validation of prior
      employment,
      §11-50-16.
Streets.
  Contracts for construction,
    improvement, etc.
    Procedure for letting.
      Optional form A,
        §11-44-89.
  Franchises for use of
    streets.
    Objections, §11-44-34.
    Optional form A,
      §11-44-88.
    Optional form B,
      §11-44-137.
    Procedure for granting,
      §11-44-36.
  Resolutions, etc.,
    granting.
    Effective date,
      §11-44-33.
    Elections, §11-44-34.
    Proceedings upon
      determination of
      election result,
      §11-44-35.
    Publication, §11-44-33.
  Optional form A.
    Contracts for
      construction,
      §11-44-89.
    Franchises for use of
      streets, §11-44-88.
  Optional form B.
    Ordinances granting
      franchises for use of
      highways,
      §11-44-137.
Telephones.
  Municipal officers or
    employees.
    Conflicts of interest,
      §11-44-46.
Violations of article.
  Penalties, §11-44-57.
Wards.
  Creation upon
    abandonment of
    commission form,
    §11-44-159.
  Discontinuance, §11-44-25.
Water supply and
  waterworks.
  Municipal officers or
    employees.
    Conflicts of interest,
      §§11-44-46 to
      11-44-48.

MUNICIPAL
  CORPORATIONS—Cont'd
**Commission form of
  government**—Cont'd
Water supply and
  waterworks—Cont'd
  President of board of
    commissioners.
    Employment as
      superintendent of
      water systems,
      §11-50-16.
    Validation of prior
      employment,
      §11-50-16.
Common carriers.
  Annexation.
    Territory exempt from
      taxation.
    Assessment and
      collection of
      privilege or license
      tax from operators,
      §11-42-84.
Community action agencies.
  Appropriations to agencies,
    §11-80-4.1.
  Contributions to agencies,
    §11-80-4.1.
Concert halls.
  Establishment, acquisition,
    administration, etc.,
    §11-47-16.
Condemnation. See within
  this heading, "Eminent
  domain."
Conflict of laws.
  Boards of water and sewer
    commissioners,
    §11-50-358.
  Health laws.
    Between municipal and
      general health laws,
      §22-1-2.
  Municipalities not to pass
    laws in conflict with
    general laws of state,
    Const. Ala., art. IV, §89.
  Zoning, §11-52-82.
Conflicts of interest.
  Boards of water and sewer
    commissioners,
    §11-50-355.
  Class 5 municipalities.
    Mayor/commission/city
      manager form of
      government.
      Acceptance of gifts from
        public utilities,
        §11-44E-183.
      Commission.
        Dealings with
          administrative
          service,
          §11-44E-45.
        Interference and
          appointment or
          removal of officers
          and employees,
          §11-44E-45.
      Interest of officials or
        employees in
        contracts with city
        or public utilities,
        §11-44E-183.
      Manager.
        Improper influences on
          prohibited,
          §11-44E-94.

MUNICIPAL
  CORPORATIONS—Cont'd
Conflicts of interest—Cont'd
Class 5 municipalities
  —Cont'd
  Mayor/commission/city
    manager form of
    government—Cont'd
    Public service utilities.
      Financial interest in,
        §11-44E-163.
  Mayor-council form of
    government,
    §11-43C-88.
Commission form of
  government.
  Officers or employees,
    §§11-44-46 to 11-44-48,
    11-44-94, 11-44-138.
  Optional form A,
    §11-44-94.
  Optional form B,
    §11-44-138.
Council-manager form of
  government.
  Mayor and council
    prohibited from
    involvement in
    administrative service,
    §11-43A-18.
Councilmen, §11-43-53.
  Aldermen not to vote on
    certain matters,
    §11-43-54.
  Generally, §11-43-12.
Employees.
  Commission form of
    government,
    §§11-44-46 to 11-44-48,
    11-44-94, 11-44-138.
  Generally, §11-43-12.
  Mayor/commission/city
    manager form of
    government.
    Acceptance of gifts,
      §11-44E-183.
    Interest in contracts with
      city or public
      utilities,
      §11-44E-183.
Mayor/commission/city
  manager form of
  government.
  Acceptance of gifts from
    public utilities,
    §11-44E-183.
  Commission.
    Dealings with
      administrative
      service, §11-44E-45.
    Interference in
      appointment or
      removal of officers
      and employees,
      §11-44E-45.
  Interest of officials or
    employees in contracts
    with city or public
    utilities, §11-44E-183.
  Manager.
    Political or other
      improper influences
      on prohibited,
      §11-44E-94.
  Public service utilities.
    Financial interest in,
      §11-44E-163.

MUNICIPAL
CORPORATIONS—Cont'd
Conflicts of interest—Cont'd
Nepotism.
Commission form of
government.
Optional form A,
§§11-44-102,
11-44-103.
Optional form B,
§§11-44-102,
11-44-103.
Officers.
Commission form of
government,
§§11-44-46 to 11-44-48,
11-44-94, 11-44-138.
Employment by
corporations holding
franchises as to use of
streets, §11-43-11.
Generally, §11-43-12.
Grounds for impeachment,
§11-43-161.
Mayor/commission/city
manager form of
government.
Acceptance of gifts,
§11-44E-183.
Penalties, §§11-43-12,
11-43-53.
Personal property.
Purchase from elected
officials, etc.,
§11-43-12.1.
Services.
Purchase from elected
officials, etc.,
§11-43-12.1.
Consolidation.
Bond issues.
Public improvement bonds.
Liability upon bonds
when municipalities
consolidated,
§11-81-123.
Contiguous municipalities,
§§11-42-100 to 11-42-134.
Actions.
Continuation,
§11-42-106.
Alternate mode,
§§11-42-120 to
11-42-134.
Actions.
Continuation,
§11-42-131.
Agreement as to terms of
annexation and
merger.
Approval, §11-42-122.
Confirmation,
§11-42-122.
Execution, §11-42-122.
Filing, §11-42-127.
Recordation,
§11-42-127.
Taxation in
municipality
annexed,
§11-42-132.
Aldermen.
Election, §11-42-133.
Annexation and merger.
Agreement as to
terms,
§§11-42-122,
11-42-127.
Costs, §11-42-129.

MUNICIPAL
CORPORATIONS—Cont'd
Consolidation—Cont'd
Contiguous municipalities
—Cont'd
Alternate mode—Cont'd
Annexation and merger
—Cont'd
Declaration of
annexation,
§11-42-126.
Expenses, §11-42-129.
Ownership of property
of municipality
annexed,
§11-42-130.
When deemed
perfected,
§11-42-128.
Commissioners.
Appointment,
§11-42-121.
Costs of annexation,
§11-42-129.
Election.
Aldermen, §11-42-133.
Ballots, §11-42-125.
Inspectors, §11-42-124.
Ordering by
proclamation,
§11-42-123.
Results, §§11-42-125,
11-42-126.
Expenses of annexation,
§11-42-129.
Generally, §11-42-120.
Ownership of property of
municipality
annexed, §11-42-130.
Perfection of annexation.
When deemed
perfected,
§11-42-128.
Precincts.
Division of wards into
voting precincts,
§11-42-133.
Rearrangement of
boundaries,
§11-42-133.
Property.
Ownership of property
of municipality
annexed,
§11-42-130.
Provisions of division not
exclusive,
§11-42-134.
Recordation.
Copy of agreement and
merger,
§11-42-127.
Taxation.
Provisions in
annexation
agreement as to,
§11-42-132.
Wards.
Creation, etc.,
§11-42-133.
Division into voting
precincts,
§11-42-133.
Rearrangement of
boundaries,
§11-42-133.
Commissioners,
§11-42-103.
Compensation,
§11-42-104.

MUNICIPAL
CORPORATIONS—Cont'd
Consolidation—Cont'd
Contiguous municipalities
—Cont'd
Commissioners—Cont'd
Division of consolidated
municipality into
wards, §11-42-103.
Failure to act,
§11-42-104.
Oath, §11-42-104.
Corporate organization.
Continuation,
§11-42-105.
Duties of consolidated
municipalities,
§11-42-106.
Elections, §11-42-100.1.
Alternate mode,
§§11-42-123 to
11-42-126.
Mayor and other officers,
§11-42-103.
Industrial plants.
Exemption from
taxation, §11-42-102.
Manufacturing plants.
Exemption from
taxation, §11-42-102.
Mayor.
Election, §11-42-103.
Mode of consolidation.
Alternate mode,
§§11-42-120 to
11-42-134.
When municipalities to
form new corporate
organization,
§11-42-101.
When municipality to
annex city or town,
§11-42-100.1.
Officers.
Continuation of officers
of municipalities,
§11-42-105.
Election, §11-42-103.
Qualification and
assumption of duties
of officers elected for
consolidated
municipalities,
§11-42-105.
Rights and powers of
consolidated
municipalities,
§11-42-106.
Wards.
Division of consolidated
municipality into
wards, §11-42-103.
When municipality to
annex city or town,
§11-42-100.1.
Elections.
Contiguous municipalities,
§11-42-100.1.
Alternate mode,
§§11-42-123 to
11-42-126,
11-42-133.
Noncontiguous
municipalities,
§§11-42-151 to
11-42-154, 11-42-157,
11-42-159.

MUNICIPAL
   CORPORATIONS—Cont'd
Consolidation—Cont'd
Expanded municipalities.
   Duties as to absorbed
      municipalities,
      §§11-42-180 to
      11-42-187. See within
      this heading,
      "Expanded
      municipalities."
New corporate organization.
   When municipalities to
      form, §11-42-101.
Noncontiguous
   municipalities,
   §§11-42-150 to 11-42-167.
Actions.
   Continuation,
      §11-42-161.
   Continuation of rights of
      action, §§11-42-160,
      11-42-162.
Agreement of annexation.
   Deemed contract
      between
      municipalities,
      §11-42-164.
   Enforcement, §11-42-164.
   Ordinances and
      resolutions.
      Enactment to carry out
         agreement,
         §11-42-165.
Aldermen.
   Continuation in office,
      §11-42-156.
   Powers and duties,
      §11-42-156.
Applicability of article,
   §11-42-150.
Boards of education.
   Continuation in office,
      §11-42-159.
   Election, §11-42-159.
Boundaries of territory to
   be incorporated.
   Councils to define upon
      receipt of petition
      requesting election,
      §11-42-151.
Bylaws.
   Applicability,
      §11-42-166.
Contracts.
   Annexation agreement
      as, §11-42-164.
   Assumption by
      consolidated
      municipality,
      §11-42-155.
   Disposition of property,
      etc., §11-42-155.
   Dissolution of annexed
      municipality,
      §11-42-166.
   Rights, powers, duties,
      etc., of annexing
      municipality,
      §11-42-167.
Election.
   Ballots.
      Form and marking,
         §11-42-153.
   Boards of education,
      §11-42-159.
   Calling of election,
      §11-42-152.
   Canvassing of returns,
      §11-42-154.
   Conduct, §11-42-152.

MUNICIPAL
   CORPORATIONS—Cont'd
Consolidation—Cont'd
Noncontiguous municipalities
   —Cont'd
   Election—Cont'd
      Notice of election,
         §11-42-152.
      Officers, §11-42-157.
      Results.
         Ascertainment and
            publication,
            §11-42-154.
      Returns.
         Canvassing of returns,
            §11-42-154.
      Statement of vote.
         Forwarding to probate
            judge, §11-42-154.
   Indebtedness of
      municipality annexed.
      Payment or assumption,
         §11-42-163.
   Liabilities.
      Payment or assumption,
         §11-42-163.
   Mayors.
      Continuation in office,
         §11-42-156.
      Powers and duties,
         §11-42-156.
   Name of consolidated
      municipality,
      §11-42-155.
   Officers.
      Election, §11-42-157.
   Ordinances.
      Applicability,
         §11-42-166.
      Enactment and passage
         of ordinances to
         carry out annexation
         agreement,
         §11-42-165.
   Property.
      Ownership of property of
         municipalities
         consolidated,
         §11-42-155.
   Resolutions.
      Applicability,
         §11-42-166.
      Enactment to carry out
         agreement,
         §11-42-165.
   Rights, powers and duties
      of consolidated
      municipality,
      §11-42-155.
   Taxation.
      Collection of taxes,
         §11-42-158.
      Disbursement of taxes,
         §11-42-158.
   Wards.
      Division of consolidated
         municipality into
         wards, §11-42-157.
Constitution of Alabama.
   See CONSTITUTION OF
      ALABAMA.
Construction and
   interpretation.
Annexation.
   Incorporated
      municipalities.
      Construction of article,
         §11-42-24.

MUNICIPAL
   CORPORATIONS—Cont'd
Construction and
   interpretation—Cont'd
Demolition of unsafe
   structures.
   Cumulative nature of
      provisions, §11-40-36.
Weeds.
   Abatement of weeds.
      Class 2 municipalities,
         §11-67-1.
      Class 5 municipalities,
         §11-67-20.
Contiguous municipalities.
Consolidation, §§11-42-100 to
   11-42-134. See within
   this heading,
   "Consolidation."
Contracts.
Advertisement of
   municipalities, §11-47-9.
Ambulance service.
   Contracts for services,
      §11-87-3.
Bids.
   Award to lowest
      responsible bidder,
      §11-47-6.
   Manner of awarding
      contracts on bids,
      §11-45-2.
   Resolutions.
      Required to award
         contracts on bids,
         §11-45-2.
Boards for operation of
   water, sewer, gas and
   electric systems.
   Conveyance of system in
      other municipality,
      §11-50-320.
   Execution, etc., as security
      for repayment of
      money borrowed,
      §11-50-315.
Buildings.
   Authorized for
      construction,
      extension, etc.,
      §11-47-3.
   Between counties and
      municipalities as to
      use of buildings
      located in
      municipalities,
      §11-80-3.
Cemeteries.
   Municipal care and
      maintenance,
      §§11-47-41, 11-47-42.
Class 5 municipalities.
   Mayor/commission/city
      manager form of
      government.
      Conflicts of interest,
         §11-44E-183.
      Contract between city
         manager and cities,
         §11-44E-98.
      Contracts extending
         beyond one year,
         §11-44E-182.
      Succession of
         government.
         Existing contracts
            continued in force,
            §11-44E-145.

**MUNICIPAL
CORPORATIONS**—Cont'd
Contracts—Cont'd
Conflicts of interest,
§11-43-12.
Mayor/commission/city
manager form of
government.
Contracts, §11-44E-183.
Consolidation of
municipalities,
§§11-42-155, 11-42-164.
Council-manager form of
government.
Continuation of contracts,
§11-43A-39.
Limit on contracts
involving money
payments, §11-43A-48.
Requirements for validity,
§11-43A-48.
Electricity, §§11-47-3,
11-50-1.
Execution, §11-47-5.
Mayors, §11-43-83.
Fire departments.
Operation beyond corporate
limits and police
jurisdiction.
Contracts with
municipalities,
counties and
manufacturing or
industrial concerns,
§11-43-142.
Gas.
Bond issues by gas
districts.
Execution, etc., of
contracts as security
for repayment of
moneys borrowed,
§11-50-407.
Furnishing of gas,
§11-50-1.
Mayor/commission/city
manager form of
government.
Conflicts of interest,
§11-44E-183.
Contract between city
manager and cities,
§11-44E-98.
Contracts extending
beyond one year,
§11-44E-182.
Succession of government.
Existing contracts
continued in force,
§11-44E-145.
Mayors.
Execution of contracts,
§11-43-83.
Officers.
Execution of contracts,
§11-47-5.
Public contracts.
Competitive bidding.
See CONTRACTS.
Public improvements,
§§11-48-11 to 11-48-13.
Public utilities.
Mayor/commission/city
manager form of
government.
Conflicts of interest,
§11-44E-183.
Rates and service
regulations established
by contract, §37-4-22.

**MUNICIPAL
CORPORATIONS**—Cont'd
Contracts—Cont'd
Public utilities—Cont'd
Waiver by utility of terms
or conditions, §37-1-48.
Resolutions.
Manner of awarding
contracts on bids,
§11-45-2.
Sewers.
Public water corporations
and public sewer
corporations.
Contracts for operation
and management of
sanitary sewer
systems, §11-50-371.
Purchase of sewers,
§§11-50-74, 11-50-77.
Streets.
Paving of city streets.
Highway department,
§23-1-40.
Utilities.
Rates and service
regulations established
by contract, §37-4-22.
Water supply and
waterworks.
Authorized for
construction, etc.,
§11-47-3.
Furnishing of water,
§11-50-1.
Public water corporations.
Contracts between public
water corporations
and public sewer
corporations for
operation of sewer
systems, §11-50-371.
Conveyances.
Town surveys, plats or maps.
Certification,
acknowledgment and
recordation of plat or
map held to be
conveyance, §35-2-51.
**Coosa valley development
authority.**
Cooperation with
municipalities, §33-16-2.
Corporate limits.
Annexation, §§11-42-1 to
11-42-88. See within this
heading, "Annexation."
Commission form of
government.
Continuation of territorial
limits, §11-44-25.
Consolidation, §§11-42-100 to
11-42-167. See within
this heading,
"Consolidation."
Expanded municipalities,
§§11-42-180 to 11-42-187.
See within this heading,
"Expanded
municipalities."
Not altered by adoption of
code, §11-40-5.
Reduction of corporate limits,
§§11-42-200 to 11-42-213.
See within this heading,
"Reduction of corporate
limits."

**MUNICIPAL
CORPORATIONS**—Cont'd
Corporations.
District electric corporations,
§§11-50-520 to 11-50-533.
See within this heading,
"Electricity."
Municipalities not to grant
money to private
corporations, Const. Ala.,
art. IV, §94; amd. 112.
Obligations of corporations
held by municipalities,
Const. Ala., art. IV,
§100.
Public corporations,
§§11-63-1 to 11-63-4.
Public water corporations,
§§11-50-370 to 11-50-372.
Special health care facility
authorities, §§11-62-1 to
11-62-21. See within this
heading, "Special health
care facility authorities."
Corrections.
Institution finance authority.
Leasing of facilities,
§14-2-30.
Costs.
Bond issues.
Validation proceedings,
§§6-6-757, 11-81-226.
Demolition of unsafe
structures, §§11-40-33 to
11-40-35.
Council.
Annexation.
Election of aldermen or
representatives,
§11-42-73.
Attendance of members.
Compulsion of attendance,
§11-43-51.
Clerks.
Attendance at council
meetings, §11-43-100.
Custody of seal and rules,
ordinances, etc., of
council, §11-43-100.
Preparation of record of
council meetings,
§11-43-100.
Composition, §11-43-40.
Conflicts of interest,
§§11-43-12, 11-43-53.
Aldermen not to vote on
certain matters,
§11-43-54.
Consolidation of contiguous
municipalities.
Election of aldermen,
§11-42-133.
Consolidation of
noncontiguous
municipalities.
Continuation in office and
powers and duties of
aldermen, §11-42-156.
Departments.
Appropriation for
expenditures of
departments,
§11-43-57.
Dual office holding.
Aldermen not to hold other
municipal offices,
§11-43-53.

**MUNICIPAL
　　CORPORATIONS**—Cont'd
Council—Cont'd
Duties of councilmen,
　　§11-43-43.
Abandonment of
　　commission form of
　　government,
　　§§11-44-157,
　　11-44-162.
Election of councilmen,
　　§11-44-156.
After incorporation,
　　§§11-41-5, 11-41-6.
Annexed territory,
　　§11-42-73.
Consolidation of contiguous
　　municipalities.
　　Alternate mode,
　　§11-42-133.
Elections.
　　General provisions. See
　　　　within this heading,
　　　　"Elections."
　　Judging of election by
　　　　council, §§11-43-40,
　　　　11-43-58.
Executive sessions.
　　Prohibited, §13A-14-2.
Exercise of legislative
　　functions, §11-43-2.
Expenses.
　　When reimbursed,
　　　　§11-43-7.1.
Finances of municipality.
　　Management and control,
　　　　§11-43-56.
Functions.
　　Exercise of legislative
　　　　functions, §11-43-2.
Journal, §11-43-52.
Mayors.
　　Absence or disability.
　　　　Exercise of functions of
　　　　　　mayor, §11-43-42.
Meetings.
　　Clerks.
　　　　Attendance at and
　　　　　　preparation of
　　　　　　record, §11-43-100.
　　Compulsion of attendance
　　　　of members, §11-43-51.
　　Holding of regular
　　　　meetings, §11-43-50.
　　Organizational meeting,
　　　　§11-43-44.
　　Place, §11-43-49.
　　Record.
　　　　Preparation by clerk,
　　　　　　§11-43-100.
　　Regular meetings,
　　　　§11-43-50.
　　Rules of procedure,
　　　　§11-43-52.
　　Special meetings.
　　　　Calling, §11-43-50.
　　Time of meetings,
　　　　§11-43-49.
Officers. See within this
　　heading, "Officers."
Ordinances and resolutions.
　　General provisions. See
　　　　within this heading,
　　　　"Ordinances and
　　　　resolutions."
Organizational meeting,
　　§11-43-44.
Police. See within this
　　heading, "Police."

**MUNICIPAL
　　CORPORATIONS**—Cont'd
Council—Cont'd
Powers, §11-43-43.
Abandonment of
　　commission form of
　　government,
　　§§11-44-157,
　　11-44-162.
President of council.
　　Qualifications.
　　　　Judging of qualifications
　　　　　　by council,
　　　　　　§11-43-58.
　　Right to vote, §11-43-40.
　　Term of office, §11-43-40.
　　Vacancies in office.
　　　　Filling, §11-43-42.
President pro tempore.
　　Election, §11-43-49.
　　Vacancies.
　　　　Filling, §11-43-42.
Property of municipality.
　　Management and control,
　　　　§11-43-56.
Qualifications of councilmen,
　　§11-43-1.
Quorum, §11-43-48.
Records.
　　Clerks.
　　　　Preparation of records of
　　　　　　council meetings,
　　　　　　§11-43-100.
Removal of councilmen,
　　§11-43-54.
Residence of councilmen,
　　§11-43-1.
Resolutions.
　　General provisions. See
　　　　within this heading,
　　　　"Ordinances and
　　　　resolutions."
Retirement.
　　Pensions for certain elected
　　　　public officials of class
　　　　2 municipalities,
　　　　§11-43-19.
Rules of procedure,
　　§11-43-52.
Salary of councilmen,
　　§11-43-2.
　　Ratification of certain
　　　　salaries, §11-43-17.
Seal.
　　Custody of seal,
　　　　§11-43-100.
Secret sessions.
　　Prohibited, §13A-14-2.
Temporary chairman.
　　Appointment, §11-43-49.
Terms of councilmen,
　　§11-43-40.
Treasurers.
　　Reports and statements to
　　　　council, §11-43-120.
Vacancies, §11-43-4.
　　Filling, §11-43-41.
　　Governing bodies of class 5
　　　　municipalities,
　　　　§11-43-18.
Voting.
　　Aldermen not to vote on
　　　　certain matters,
　　　　§11-43-54.
　　President, §11-43-40.
**Council-manager form of
　　government,** §§11-43A-1
　　to 11-43A-52.
Abolished offices.
　　Transfer of powers and
　　　　duties, §11-43A-35.

**MUNICIPAL
　　CORPORATIONS**—Cont'd
**Council-manager form of
　　government**—Cont'd
Accounts and accounting,
　　§11-43A-27.
Budget and accounting
　　year, §11-43A-29.
Fiscal year, §11-43A-29.
Monthly statement and
　　summary, §11-43A-27.
Municipal funds.
　　Payment and deposit,
　　　　§11-43A-31.
Publication of results,
　　§11-43A-27.
Actions.
　　Pending litigation.
　　　　Effect of chapter upon,
　　　　　　§11-43A-40.
Adoption.
　　Authorized, §11-43A-1.
　　Petition.
　　　　Examination of petition
　　　　　　and certification to
　　　　　　mayor, §11-43A-2.
　　Provisions of chapter,
　　　　§11-43A-6.
　　Revision and codification,
　　　　§11-43A-26.
　　Time for change in form of
　　　　government,
　　　　§11-43A-7.
Agencies.
　　Continuation of laws
　　　　relating to agencies,
　　　　§11-43A-42.
Applicability of chapter,
　　§11-43A-1.
　　Effect of chapter upon
　　　　existing laws,
　　　　§11-43A-52.
　　Existing officers and
　　　　employees, §11-43A-3.
　　Laws relating to pensions,
　　　　retirement and relief
　　　　funds for employees,
　　　　§11-43A-41.
　　Pending litigation,
　　　　§11-43A-40.
　　When chapter applicable,
　　　　§11-43A-43.
Appointments.
　　City manager, §11-43A-14.
　　Designation of
　　　　administrative
　　　　officer to perform
　　　　duties of manager,
　　　　§11-43A-28.
　　Continuation in office of
　　　　persons holding
　　　　administrative office,
　　　　§11-43A-35.
Authorities.
　　Continuation of laws,
　　　　§11-43A-42.
Authorized, §11-43A-1.
Ballots.
　　Form, §11-43A-5.
　　Marking of ballots,
　　　　§11-43A-5.
Boards.
　　Continuation of laws
　　　　relating to boards,
　　　　§11-43A-42.
Bonds, surety.
　　City manager and other
　　　　officers and employees,
　　　　§11-43A-49.
Budget.
　　Adoption, §11-43A-29.

MUNICIPAL CORPORATIONS—Cont'd
Council-manager form of government—Cont'd
Budget—Cont'd
Changes in budget,
§11-43A-29.
Submission, §11-43A-29.
Budget and accounting year,
§11-43A-29.
Candidates.
Determination of
qualifications by
council members,
§11-43A-22.
Filing of statement of
candidacy, §11-43A-13.
Qualifications and
eligibility, §§11-43A-9,
11-43A-13.
Change from council-
manager form of
government, §11-43A-51.
Change in form of
government.
Time, §11-43A-7.
City clerk.
Duties.
Assignment of duties as
clerk-treasurer,
§11-43A-30.
City manager.
Appointment, §11-43A-18.
Bonds, surety, §11-43A-49.
Duties, §11-43A-28.
Eligibility, §11-43A-18.
Investigations.
Right to investigate
affairs, §11-43A-47.
Meetings.
Right to attend council
meetings,
§11-43A-46.
Special or adjourned
meetings.
Notification,
§11-43A-46.
Oath or affirmation,
§11-43A-50.
Qualifications, §11-43A-28.
Removal from office,
§11-43A-18.
Temporary absence or
disability.
Appointment of
replacement,
§11-43A-28.
Temporary acting city
manager, §11-43A-18.
Term, §11-43A-18.
Class 6 municipalities.
Election.
Time, procedure, etc.,
§11-43A-3.1.
Provisions to supersede
other laws in 1983,
§11-43A-3.2.
Clerk of municipality.
Designation, §11-43A-20.
Duties, §11-43A-20.
When subject to civil
service or merit
system, §11-43A-20.
Compensation of mayors and
councilmen, §11-43A-15.
Composition of council,
§11-43A-8.

MUNICIPAL CORPORATIONS—Cont'd
Council-manager form of government—Cont'd
Conflicts of interest.
Mayor and council
prohibited from
involvement in
administrative service,
§11-43A-18.
Continuation of corporation,
§11-43A-10.
Contracts.
Continuation of contracts,
§11-43A-39.
Limit on contracts
involving money
payments, §11-43A-48.
Requirements for validity,
§11-43A-48.
Councilman-at-large.
Establishment of posts,
§11-43A-32.
Departments.
Continuation of offices and
departments,
§11-43A-38.
Meetings.
Right of department
heads to attend,
§11-43A-46.
Discrimination.
Prohibited, §11-43A-45.
Districts.
Division of municipality
into districts,
§11-43A-9.
Establishment of council
districts, §11-43A-32.
Reapportionment,
§11-43A-33.
Filing of recommended
plan with council,
§11-43A-33.
Redistricting ordinance,
§11-43A-33.
Duties.
Abolished offices.
Transfer of powers and
duties, §11-43A-35.
Generally, §11-43A-12.
Effect of chapter on existing
laws, §11-43A-52.
Elections.
Adoption and certification
of provisions of
chapter, §11-43A-6.
Ballots.
Form, §11-43A-5.
Marking, §11-43A-5.
Printing and separation,
§11-43A-14.
Candidates.
Determination of
qualifications by
council, §11-43A-22.
Eligibility, §11-43A-9.
Filing of statement of
candidacy,
§11-43A-13.
Qualifications,
§11-43A-9.
Canvassing of vote,
§11-43A-6.
Change from council-
manager form of
government,
§11-43A-51.
When election
authorized,
§11-43A-51.

MUNICIPAL CORPORATIONS—Cont'd
Council-manager form of government—Cont'd
Elections—Cont'd
Class 6 municipalities,
§11-43A-3.1.
Conduct, §§11-43A-6,
11-43A-14.
Declaration of results,
§11-43A-6.
Investigation, §11-43A-22.
Next council, §11-43A-8.
Officers, §11-43A-9.
Order of probate judge,
§11-43A-3.
Proclamation of mayor,
§11-43A-3.
Provisions to supersede
other laws in 1983,
§11-43A-3.2.
Reapportionment.
Effect, §11-43A-33.
Runoff election, §11-43A-9.
Submission of question for
election, §11-43A-3.
Subsequent elections.
When held, §11-43A-4.
Treasurer, §11-43A-30.
When allowed, §11-43A-4.
Employees.
Bonds, surety, §11-43A-49.
Continuation in office of
persons holding
administrative office,
§11-43A-35.
Continuation in office of
persons in civil service
or merit system,
§11-43A-36.
Effect of chapter upon
existing employees,
§11-43A-34.
Oath or affirmation,
§11-43A-50.
Existing laws.
Effect of chapter upon,
§11-43A-52.
Fiscal year, §11-43A-29.
Franchises.
Ordinances granting
franchise.
Effective date,
§11-43A-25.
Funds.
Deposit of municipal funds,
§11-43A-31.
Payment of municipal
funds, §11-43A-31.
Improvements.
Completion of public
improvements,
§11-43A-39.
Investigations, §11-43A-47.
Mayors.
Assistants.
Councilman-at-large as
assistant mayor,
§11-43A-16.
At-large posts, §11-43A-32.
Compensation, §11-43A-15.
Conflicts of interest,
§11-43A-18.
Duties, §11-43A-16.
Mayor pro tem,
§11-43A-16.
Oath or affirmation,
§11-43A-50.
Vacancies in office.
Filling by councilman-at-
large, §11-43A-16.

MUNICIPAL
CORPORATIONS—Cont'd
Council-manager form of
government—Cont'd
Meetings.
Adjournment, §11-43A-24.
City manager.
Right to attend council
meetings,
§11-43A-46.
Department heads.
Right to attend council
meetings,
§11-43A-46.
Journal, §11-43A-24.
Open to public,
§11-43A-21.
Quorum, §11-43A-24.
Record of proceedings,
§11-43A-24.
Regular public meetings of
council, §11-43A-24.
Rules of council,
§11-43A-23.
Special or adjourned
meetings.
City manager to be
notified, §11-43A-46.
Special or other meetings,
§11-43A-24.
Times for meetings of
council, §11-43A-21.
Unanimous consent for
passage of certain
ordinances,
§11-43A-24.
Name.
Governing body,
§11-43A-8.
Title of government,
§11-43A-11.
Notice.
Special or adjourned
meetings.
City manager to be
notified, §11-43A-46.
Oaths.
Councilmen, officers and
employees, §11-43A-50.
Officers.
Bonds, surety, §11-43A-49.
Continuation in office of
persons holding
administrative office,
§11-43A-35.
Continuation in office of
persons in civil service
or merit system,
§11-43A-36.
Effect of chapter upon
existing officers,
§11-43A-34.
Election, §11-43A-9.
Oath or affirmation,
§11-43A-50.
Terms of office, §11-43A-9.
Offices.
Abolished offices,
§11-43A-35.
Continuation, §11-43A-38.
Power of council to create,
change and abolish,
§11-43A-19.
Reassignment of duties.
Transfer of records,
property and
equipment,
§11-43A-37.
Ordinances.
Continuation, §11-43A-44.

MUNICIPAL
CORPORATIONS—Cont'd
Council-manager form of
government—Cont'd
Ordinances—Cont'd
Publication.
Expense of grantee,
§11-43A-25.
Redistricting ordinance,
§11-43A-33.
Revision and codification,
§11-43A-26.
Thirty day delay in effect
of ordinance granting
franchises, §11-43A-25.
Pending litigation.
Effect of chapter upon,
§11-43A-40.
Pensions.
Effect of chapter on laws
relating to pensions,
§11-43A-41.
Petitions.
Examination of petition
and certification to
mayor, §11-43A-2.
Powers.
Abolished offices.
Transfer of powers and
duties, §11-43A-35.
Creation, change and
abolishing of offices,
§11-43A-19.
Generally, §§11-43A-12,
11-43A-17.
Vesting of powers in
council, §11-43A-11.
Procedural rules of council,
§11-43A-23.
Records.
Transfer of records,
property, etc., when
reassigned,
§11-43A-37.
Relief funds.
Effect of chapter on laws
relating to,
§11-43A-41.
Resolutions.
Continuation, §11-43A-44.
Revision and codification,
§11-43A-26.
Retirement.
Effect of chapter on laws
relating to retirement,
§11-43A-41.
Rules of council, §11-43A-23.
Runoff elections, §11-43A-9.
Seating of initial council,
§11-43A-8.
Short title, §11-43A-1.
Temporary acting city
manager, §11-43A-18.
Terms of office, §11-43A-9.
Time for change in form of
government, §11-43A-7.
Treasurer.
Duties.
Assignment, §11-43A-30.
Elections, §11-43A-30.
Establishment of office,
§11-43A-30.
Vacancies.
Filling, §11-43A-16.
Counties.
Ambulance service.
Joint operation with
counties, §11-87-1.

MUNICIPAL
CORPORATIONS—Cont'd
Counties—Cont'd
Buildings.
Contracts between counties
and municipalities as
to use of buildings
located in
municipalities,
§11-80-3.
Payment for improvement
to sidewalks and
streets around county
buildings.
Appropriations, §11-14-7.
Authorized, §11-14-6.
Ratification of and
discharge from
liability for prior
payments, §11-14-8.
Water supply and
waterworks, §§11-14-3,
11-21-2, 11-21-3.
Courthouses located in
municipalities.
Costs of improvements
which benefit property
of county, §11-14-5.
Fire departments.
Contracts with counties,
§11-43-142.
General provisions.
See COUNTIES.
Hospitals, poorhouses, etc.
Establishment in counties,
§11-47-134.
Public roads, bridges and
ferries.
Access roads or bridges to
certain facilities.
Aid for development by
municipalities,
§23-1-91.
Establishment within
municipalities.
Authority of county
commissions,
§23-1-86.
Extension of aid by
benefited
municipalities,
§23-1-90.
Operation, etc., of bridges
over navigable
streams.
Bridges in municipal
corporations,
§11-3-17.
Streets.
Assumption of authority
over streets controlled
by counties,
§§11-49-80, 11-49-81.
Construction,
improvement, etc., by
counties.
Payment of costs by
municipal
corporations,
§§11-49-60 to
11-49-63.
Subdivisions, §§11-52-30 to
11-52-54. See within this
heading, "Subdivisions."
Waterworks plants and
distribution systems.
Conveyance to municipal
corporations, §11-14-3.

MUNICIPAL
 CORPORATIONS—Cont'd
Court of civil appeals.
 Offices and other physical
  facilities for courts.
  Contracting with
   municipalities,
   §12-1-20.
Court of criminal appeals.
 Offices and other physical
  facilities.
  Contracting with
   municipalities for,
   §12-1-20.
Courts.
 Municipal courts, §§12-14-1
  to 12-14-71.
  See MUNICIPAL
   COURTS.
Criminal law.
 Election offenses, §§11-46-61
  to 11-46-68, 11-46-71,
  11-46-73. See within this
  heading, "Elections."
Criminal law and procedure.
 General provisions.
  See CRIMINAL LAW AND
   PROCEDURE.
Cultural facilities.
 Establishment, acquisition,
  administration, etc.,
  §11-47-16.
Dairies.
 Inspection, §11-47-139.
Death.
 Commissioners.
  Filling of vacancies caused
   by death, §§11-44-12,
   11-44-77.
 Fire fighters.
  Compensation for death
   from occupational
   disease, §11-43-144.
 Police, §§36-30-20 to
  36-30-23.
Debts.
 Absorbed municipalities.
  Duties of expanded
   municipalities as to
   property and
   obligations,
   §§11-42-180 to
   11-42-187. See within
   this heading,
   "Expanded
   municipalities."
 Claims for and against
  municipalities. See
  within this heading,
  "Claims for and against
  municipalities."
 Limitation.
  See CONSTITUTION OF
   ALABAMA.
Declaratory judgments.
 Construction and validity of
  ordinances, §6-6-223.
Decrees.
 Dissolution, §§11-41-23,
  11-41-26.
 Forfeiture of charter. See
  within this heading,
  "Charter."
Deeds.
 Mayors.
  Execution, etc., §11-43-83.
Definitions.
 Airports, §4-4-1.

MUNICIPAL
 CORPORATIONS—Cont'd
Definitions—Cont'd
 Assessments for public
  improvements.
  Street and sewer
   improvements outside
   corporate limits of
   certain cities,
   §11-48-81.
 Boards of water and sewer
  commissioners,
  §11-50-340.
 Bond issues.
  Validation, §§6-6-750,
   11-81-220.
 Capital improvement,
  §11-66-3.
 Commission form of
  government.
  Optional form B,
   §11-44-120.
 Demolition of unsafe
  structures.
  Appropriate city official,
   §11-40-31.
 Electric corporations.
  District electric
   corporations,
   §11-50-520.
 Gas.
  Districts, §11-50-390.
  Transfer of gas system
   without elections,
   §11-50-210.
 Industrial development
  boards, §11-54-80.
 Industrial parks, §11-54-1.
 Medical clinic boards,
  §11-58-1.
 Motor vehicles.
  Parking.
   Authority of towns and
    cities, §11-61-1.
 Off-street parking facilities,
  §11-47-240.
 Parking.
  Authority of towns and
   cities, §11-61-1.
 Parks, playgrounds and other
  recreational and athletic
  areas and facilities.
  Authorities, §11-47-210.
 Planning, §11-52-1.
 Police.
  Compensation for death or
   disability from
   occupational diseases,
   §36-30-20.
 Public athletic boards,
  §11-59-1.
 Public corporations.
  Financial assistance,
   §11-63-1.
 Public improvements.
  Street and sewer
   improvements outside
   certain cities,
   §11-48-80.
 Public park and recreation
  boards, §11-60-1.
 Securities issued in
  anticipation of grants,
  §11-64-1.
 Sewers.
  Boards of water and sewer
   commissioners,
   §11-50-340.

MUNICIPAL
 CORPORATIONS—Cont'd
Definitions—Cont'd
 Sewers—Cont'd
  Operation of systems by
   public water
   corporations,
   §11-50-370.
  Transfer of water and
   sewer systems by
   municipalities without
   elections, §11-50-190.
 Special health care facility
  authorities, §11-62-1.
 Water supply and
  waterworks.
  Boards of water and sewer
   commissioners,
   §11-50-340.
  Operation of sewer systems
   by public water
   corporations,
   §11-50-370.
  Transfer of water and
   sewer systems by
   municipalities without
   elections, §11-50-190.
**Demolition of unsafe
 structures.**
 Appeals, §11-40-32.
 Authorized, §11-40-30.
 Costs.
  Assessment, §11-40-34.
  Payment, §11-40-35.
  Report, §11-40-33.
  Resolution fixing,
   §11-40-33.
   Objections to findings,
    §11-40-33.
 Cumulative nature of
  provisions, §11-40-36.
 Definitions.
  Appropriate city official,
   §11-40-31.
 Hearings, §11-40-32.
 Notice.
  Costs.
   Meeting at which cost
    fixed, §11-40-33.
  Unsafe or dangerous
   condition of structure,
   §11-40-31.
 Power of class 1 cities,
  §11-40-30.
Departments.
 Commission form of
  government.
  Determination and exercise
   of powers and duties of
   departments by
   commissioners,
   §11-44-29.
  Executive and
   administrative powers
   and duties.
   Distribution among
    departments,
    §11-44-29.
 Council.
  Appropriation for
   expenditures of
   departments,
   §11-43-57.
 Expenditures.
  Appropriation for,
   §11-43-57.
 Fire departments,
  §§11-43-140 to 11-43-144.
 Police. See within this
  heading, "Police."

MUNICIPAL
CORPORATIONS—Cont'd
Depositories.
Electric utility boards,
§§11-50-503 to 11-50-505.
Treasurers.
Deposit of public money in
depositories,
§11-43-122.
Destruction of public
records, §12-20-50.
Development.
Industrial development
boards, §§11-54-80 to
11-54-123. See within
this heading, "Industrial
development boards."
Redevelopment projects,
§§24-2-1 to 24-2-10.
See REDEVELOPMENT
PROJECTS.
Regional planning and
development, §§11-85-1
to 11-85-73.
See PLANNING.
Subdivisions, §§11-52-30 to
11-52-54. See within this
heading, "Subdivisions."
Urban renewal projects,
§§24-3-1 to 24-3-9.
See URBAN RENEWAL
PROJECTS.
Dikes.
Assessments for public
improvements.
Manner of assessment,
§11-48-16.
Discrimination.
Council-manager form of
government.
Prohibited, §11-43A-45.
Housing.
Zoning regulations.
Housing discrimination
prohibited,
§11-52-75.
Diseases.
Contagious diseases.
Removal and detention of
persons with,
§11-47-134.
Fire fighters.
Compensation for death or
disability from
occupational diseases,
§11-43-144.
Vaccination.
Compulsory vaccination,
§11-47-132.
Dissolution, §§11-41-20 to
11-41-28.
Appeals.
From decree of forfeiture
and dissolution,
§11-41-26.
Authority, §11-41-20.
Charter, §§11-41-24 to
11-41-26, 11-41-28.
Forfeiture of charter.
Appeal from decree,
§11-41-26.
Fee of probate judge,
§11-41-28.
Grounds, §11-41-24.
Hearing upon petition,
§11-41-25.
Notice of petition,
§11-41-25.
Petition to probate judge
for decree, §11-41-25.

MUNICIPAL
CORPORATIONS—Cont'd
Dissolution—Cont'd
Charter—Cont'd
Forfeiture of charter
—Cont'd
Rendition of decree,
§11-41-26.
Consolidation of
noncontiguous
municipalities,
§§11-42-166, 11-42-167.
Decree of dissolution.
Appeal from decree,
§11-41-26.
Issuance, §11-41-23.
Rendition, §11-41-26.
Disposition of property after
dissolution, §11-41-27.
Fee of probate judge,
§11-41-28.
Forfeiture of charter.
Appeal from decree,
§11-41-26.
Fee of probate judge,
§11-41-28.
Grounds for forfeiture,
§11-41-24.
Hearing upon petition,
§11-41-25.
Notice of petition,
§11-41-25.
Petition to probate judge
for decree, §11-41-25.
Rendition of decree,
§11-41-26.
Hearings.
Petition to probate judge
for dissolution.
Hearing upon petition,
§11-41-22.
Notice.
Petition to probate judge
for dissolution,
§11-41-22.
Petition to probate judge for
dissolution, §11-41-21.
Hearing, §11-41-22.
Notice of hearing,
§11-41-22.
Property.
Disposition after
dissolution, §11-41-27.
District attorneys.
Bond issues.
Validation, §§6-6-750,
6-6-752.
District courts.
Costs.
Docket fees, fines, etc.,
collected in municipal
ordinance cases.
Distribution, §12-19-154.
Inapplicability of
provisions,
§12-19-155.
Courtrooms and judicial and
clerical facilities.
Provision by
municipalities,
§12-19-4.
Districts.
Class 5 municipalities.
Mayor/commission/city
manager form of
government.
Annexed territory.
Inclusion into districts,
§11-44E-187.

MUNICIPAL
CORPORATIONS—Cont'd
Districts—Cont'd
Class 5 municipalities
—Cont'd
Mayor/commission/city
manager form of
government—Cont'd
Division into four single-
member districts,
§11-44E-120.
Reapportionment,
§11-44E-121.
Council-manager form of
government.
Division of municipality
into districts,
§11-43A-9.
Establishment of council
districts, §11-43A-32.
Reapportionment,
§11-43A-33.
Filing of recommended
plan with council,
§11-43A-33.
Redistricting ordinance,
§11-43A-33.
Division of municipality into
single-member districts,
§11-43-63.
Class 1 municipalities.
Exception, §11-43-63.
Class 2 municipalities.
Exception, §11-43-63.
Class 3 municipalities.
Exception, §11-43-63.
Class 5 municipalities.
Mayor/commission/city
manager form of
government,
§11-44E-120.
Class 7 municipalities.
Mayor-council form of
government,
§§11-44A-30,
11-44A-31.
Class 8 municipalities.
Mayor-council form of
government,
§§11-44F-1,
11-44F-2.
Mayor/commission/city
manager form of
government,
§11-44E-120.
Electricity.
District electric
corporations,
§§11-50-520 to
11-50-533.
Gas districts, §§11-50-390 to
11-50-417. See within
this heading, "Gas."
Mayor/commission/city
manager form of
government.
Commission districts.
Annexed territory.
Inclusion into district,
§11-44E-187.
Division into four single-
member districts,
§11-44E-120.
Reapportionment,
§11-44E-121.
Power districts, §§37-5-1 to
37-5-9.
See POWER DISTRICTS.

MUNICIPAL
CORPORATIONS—Cont'd
Districts—Cont'd
Reapportionment.
Class 5 municipalities.
Mayor/commission/city
manager form of
government,
§11-44E-121.
Water, sewer and fire
protection districts,
§§11-89-1 to 11-89-19.
See WATER, SEWER AND
FIRE PROTECTION
DISTRICTS.
Zoning. See within this
heading, "Zoning."
Dogs.
Canine leash ordinances.
Procedure for adoption or
repeal, §11-45-10.
Running at large.
Destruction, §11-47-110.
Impoundment, §11-47-110.
Permitting dogs to run at
large, §3-1-5.
Downtown redevelopment
authorities, §§11-54A-1 to
11-54A-24.
See DOWNTOWN
REDEVELOPMENT
AUTHORITIES.
Drains.
Connections.
Regulation, installation,
etc., §§11-50-53,
11-50-54.
Construction and
maintenance of drains,
§11-50-50.
Regulation, installation, etc.,
§11-50-54.
Drunkenness.
Elections.
Drunkenness at polling
place during election,
§§11-46-68, 11-46-139.
Duties.
Generally, §11-40-1.
Easements.
Acquisition by condemnation,
§§11-47-170 to 11-47-173.
Sewers.
Acquisition by
condemnation,
§11-50-51.
Education.
Annexation.
Territory exempt from
taxation.
Attendance at city
schools, §11-42-85.
Boards of education.
City boards, §§16-11-1 to
16-11-27.
See EDUCATION.
Bond issues.
Security for bonds for
purchase, etc., of
school buildings,
§11-81-1.
Consolidation of
noncontiguous
municipalities.
Boards of education.
Continuation in office,
§11-42-159.
Election, §11-42-159.

MUNICIPAL
CORPORATIONS—Cont'd
Education—Cont'd
County boards of education.
Municipality may remain
under county board,
§16-13-199.
Erection of school buildings,
§11-47-13.
General provisions.
See EDUCATION.
Independent cities.
Apportionment of state and
county funds to
independent cities,
§16-13-34.
Levy of tax for school
buildings, §11-47-13.
Local aid to state educational
institutions, §§16-19-1 to
16-19-8.
See UNIVERSITIES AND
COLLEGES.
Purchase of school property,
§11-47-13.
Superintendents of schools.
City superintendents,
§§16-12-1 to 16-12-21.
See EDUCATION.
Textbooks.
Local textbook selection
committees, §§16-36-4
to 16-36-6.
Elections.
Absentee voting.
Designation of clerk or
register in election
held at different time
from general election,
§17-10-15.
Alcoholic beverages,
§§11-46-68, 11-46-139.
Amendments to constitution
of Alabama.
Claims against
municipalities for
expenses, §17-17-6.
Annexation.
Cities of twenty-five
thousand or more,
§§11-42-43 to 11-42-53.
See within this
heading, "Cities of
twenty-five thousand
or more."
Generally, §11-42-12.
Subsequent elections.
When held, §11-42-4.
Applicability of general state
laws as to municipal
elections, §§11-44-56,
17-1-1.
Auditors, §11-43-3.
Ballots.
Cities to pay for ballots,
§17-8-23.
Commission form of
government,
§§11-46-110 to
11-46-114 to 11-46-118.
Duties of mayor, §17-8-26.
Incorporation elections,
§11-41-3.
Mayor-council form of
government,
§§11-46-39, 11-46-43 to
11-46-47, 11-46-52.
Blind electors.
Assistance, §§11-46-40,
11-46-111, 11-46-122,
11-46-138.

MUNICIPAL
CORPORATIONS—Cont'd
Elections—Cont'd
Blind electors—Cont'd
Deception of disabled
voters by official,
§§11-46-64, 11-46-135.
Mayor-council form,
§§11-46-40, 11-46-51.
Bond issues, §§11-81-52 to
11-81-61, 11-81-67. See
within this heading,
"Bond issues."
Bribery.
Commission form,
§§11-46-138,
11-46-139.
Mayor/commission/city
manager form of
government,
§11-44E-161.
Misdemeanors,
§11-44E-164.
Mayor-council form,
§§11-46-67, 11-46-68.
Offering or accepting
bribes for votes,
§11-44-53.
Campaign contributions.
Mayor/commission/city
manager form of
government.
Statement of campaign
contributions,
§11-44E-162.
Candidates.
Fees.
Qualification fee,
§11-46-2.
Caucuses.
Mayor/commission/city
manager form of
government.
Party caucus for
nomination of
candidates
prohibited,
§11-44E-160.
Change in government.
Holding of election after
change in government,
§11-40-6.
City clerks.
Election of clerks,
§§11-43-3, 11-43-4.
Offenses, §§11-46-60,
11-46-131.
Voting machines.
Duties of clerks,
§§11-46-33,
11-46-104, 17-9-17.
Class 2 municipalities,
§§11-44C-2 to 11-44C-9.
See within this heading,
"Class 2 municipalities."
Class 5 municipalities.
Mayor/commission/city
manager form of
government. See
within this heading,
"Class 5
municipalities."
Mayor-council form of
government,
§§11-43C-2 to
11-43C-6, 11-43C-13.
See within this
heading, "Class 5
municipalities."

MUNICIPAL
  CORPORATIONS—Cont'd
Elections—Cont'd
  Class 7 municipalities.
  Mayor-council form of
      government.
    Adoption where
      commission form
      violates federal
      voting rights act,
      §11-44A-30.
  Class 8 municipalities.
  Mayor-council form of
      government.
    Adoption where
      commission form
      violates federal
      voting rights act,
      §11-44F-1.
  Commission form of
      government, §§11-46-90
      to 11-46-144.
    Abandonment of form,
      §§11-44-151 to
      11-44-155.
    Absentee ballots,
      §§11-46-127 to
      11-46-129, 11-46-138,
      11-46-139.
      Applicability of other
        laws relating to
        absentee voting,
        §11-46-128.
      Casting and handling of
        ballots generally,
        §11-46-128.
      Deletion of voters by
        absentee ballot from
        list of qualified
        electors, §11-46-99.
      Duties of registers,
        clerks, etc.,
        generally,
        §11-46-128.
      Eligibility, §11-46-127.
      Failure or refusal to
        perform or discharge
        duties relating to,
        §11-46-139.
      False oath, §11-46-138.
      Lists of applicants for
        absentee ballots.
        Marking, posting, etc.,
          §11-46-129.
        Marking, posting, etc., of
          lists of applicants,
          §11-46-129.
    Adoption of provisions of
      article, §11-44-6.
    Alcoholic beverages.
      Drunkenness in polling
        place during
        election, §11-46-139.
      Officers of election.
        Drinking during
          election,
          §11-46-132.
      Watchers.
        Drinking, §11-46-136.
    Altering votes, §11-46-139.
    Annulment of election,
      §11-46-142.
    Applicability of article,
      §11-46-90.
    Assistance to voters.
      Disabled voters,
        §11-46-111.
      False declaration
        requesting
        assistance,
        §11-46-138.

MUNICIPAL
  CORPORATIONS—Cont'd
Elections—Cont'd
  Commission form of
      government—Cont'd
    Assistance to voters
        —Cont'd
      Voting machines,
        §§11-46-121,
        11-46-122.
    Assumption of duties by
        officers elected,
        §11-46-92.
    Ballot boxes.
      Delivery, §11-46-116.
      Destruction, §11-46-117.
      Opening.
        When ballot boxes may
          be opened,
          §11-46-117.
      Retention, §11-46-117.
      Sealing, §11-46-116.
    Ballots, §11-46-96.
      Cities to pay for ballots,
        §17-8-23.
      Comparing number on
        ballot with poll lists,
        §11-46-139.
      Copying or disclosing
        number on ballot,
        §11-46-139.
      Counting, §11-46-115.
      Delivery of ballot boxes,
        §11-46-116.
      Destruction of ballot
        boxes, §11-46-117.
      Examination of ballots,
        §11-46-118.
      Forging names of
        inspectors on ballots,
        §11-46-139.
      Form and marking,
        §11-44-5.
      Opening of ballot boxes,
        §11-46-117.
      Packaging of ballots,
        §11-46-116.
      Procedure where paper
        ballots used,
        §11-46-110.
      Removal by electors,
        §11-46-138.
      Retention of ballot boxes,
        §11-46-117.
      Right of secret ballot,
        §11-46-114.
      Sealing ballot boxes,
        §11-46-116.
    Secret ballot.
      Right of secret ballot,
        §11-46-114.
    Supplies.
      Election supplies,
        §11-46-103.
      Voting machines.
        Certification as to
          ballots,
          §11-46-118.
        Disposition of ballots,
          §11-46-123.
        Examination of ballots,
          §11-46-118.
        Voting procedure where
          paper ballots used,
          §11-46-110.
    Blind voters.
      Assistance, §§11-46-121,
        11-46-122.
      Deception by marker,
        etc., §11-46-135.

MUNICIPAL
  CORPORATIONS—Cont'd
Elections—Cont'd
  Commission form of
      government—Cont'd
    Blind voters—Cont'd
      False declaration
        requesting
        assistance,
        §11-46-138.
    Booths.
      Destruction, defacing,
        etc., §11-46-139.
      Voting booths,
        §11-46-105.
        Time limit, etc., for
          occupation of
          booth, §11-46-113.
    Bribery, §§11-46-138,
      11-46-139.
      Offering or accepting
        bribes for votes,
        §11-44-53.
    Candidacy.
      Statements of candidacy,
        §11-46-96.
      Unopposed, §11-46-97.
      Withdrawal, §11-46-96.
    Canvassing of returns,
      §§11-44-6, 11-46-126.
      Preparation of returns of
        canvass, §11-46-123.
    Certificate of election.
      Issuance by board of
        commissioners,
        §11-46-126.
    Certification of provisions
      of article, §11-44-6.
    Challengers.
      Duties, §11-46-99.
      Selection, §11-46-99.
    Challenges.
      Disposition of affidavits,
        §11-46-115.
      Generally, §11-46-109.
      Identification of voters
        challenged,
        §11-46-110.
      Oath of voters
        challenged,
        §11-46-110.
        Forms of oath,
          §11-46-112.
        Penalty for false oath,
          §11-46-112.
        Refusal to take oath,
          §11-46-112.
      Offenses, §11-46-138.
      Penalty for false oaths,
        §11-46-112.
      Refusal to take oath,
        §11-46-112.
      Voting machines,
        §11-46-121.
    Changing votes,
      §11-46-139.
    Class 7 municipalities.
      Mayor-council form of
        government.
        Adoption where
          commission form
          violates federal
          voting rights act,
          §11-44A-30.

MUNICIPAL CORPORATIONS—Cont'd
Elections—Cont'd
Commission form of government—Cont'd
Class 8 municipalities.
Mayor-council form of government.
Adoption where commission form violates federal voting rights act, §11-44F-1.
Clerks.
Offenses, §11-46-131.
Voting machines.
Duties as to voting machines, §11-46-104.
Closing days.
Effect of closing days, §11-46-91.
Conduct of elections, §11-44-6.
Contests.
Commencement of action, §11-46-140.
Entry of judgment, §11-46-141.
Grounds, §11-46-140.
Opening of ballot boxes, §11-46-117.
Trial, §11-46-141.
Voting machines.
Locking during period for filing of contest, §11-46-124.
Costs of elections, §11-46-90.
Counting votes.
Canvassing returns, §11-46-126.
Preparation of returns of canvass, §11-46-123.
Opening of ballot boxes, §11-46-117.
Statement of votes, §11-46-116.
Votes not to be counted until polls closed, §11-46-115.
Voting machines.
Certification as to counters, §11-46-118.
Certification as to number of votes on counters, §11-46-123.
Examination of counters, §11-46-118.
Cumulative provisions.
Offenses, §11-46-144.
Date of election, §11-46-145.
Declaration of votes.
Voting machines, §11-46-123.
Definition of municipal governing body, §11-46-91.
Disabled voters.
Assistance, §§11-46-111, 11-46-122.
Deception by marker, etc., §11-46-135.

MUNICIPAL CORPORATIONS—Cont'd
Elections—Cont'd
Commission form of government—Cont'd
Disabled voters—Cont'd
False declaration requesting assistance, §11-46-138.
Drunkenness.
At polling place during election, §11-46-139.
Electioneering, §11-46-139.
Executive officers.
Offenses, §11-46-130.
False impersonations, §11-46-138.
Fraudulently altering or changing votes, §11-46-139.
Fraudulent voting, §11-46-138.
Governing body.
Municipal governing body defined, §11-46-91.
Handicapped voters.
Assistance, §§11-46-111, 11-46-122.
Deception by marker, etc., §11-46-135.
False declaration requesting assistance, §11-46-138.
Holidays.
Effect of legal holidays, §11-46-91.
Identification of voters.
Where voting machines used, §11-46-121.
Influencing voters.
Undue influence, §11-46-139.
Instruction of voters.
Removing, defacing, etc., instructions, §11-46-139.
Interference with voters, §11-46-139.
Lists of qualified electors.
Certification, §§11-46-107, 11-46-108.
Deletion of voters by absentee ballot from lists, §11-46-99.
Disqualification of mayor or chief executive officer.
Preparation, etc., of lists upon, §11-46-108.
Filing, §§11-46-107, 11-46-108.
Mayor or chief executive officer.
Lists of qualified voters upon disqualification, §11-46-108.
Preparation, §§11-46-107, 11-46-108.
Publication, §§11-46-107, 11-46-108.
Mayor-council form of government, §§11-46-20 to 11-46-73.

MUNICIPAL CORPORATIONS—Cont'd
Elections—Cont'd
Commission form of government—Cont'd
Mayors.
Calling of elections, §11-44-3.
Lists of qualified voters upon disqualification of mayor, §11-46-108.
Offenses, §11-46-130.
Municipal employees, §11-44-54.
Notice of elections, §11-46-93.
Offenses.
Annulment of elections, §11-46-142.
Challenges, §11-46-138.
Clerks, §11-46-131.
Cumulative provisions, §11-46-144.
Electors, §11-46-138.
Executive officers, §11-46-130.
Inspectors, §11-46-133.
Markers.
Deception of disabled voters, §11-46-135.
Mayors, §11-46-130.
Miscellaneous offenses, §11-46-139.
Returning officers.
Failure to deliver statement of votes and poll list, §11-46-134.
Voters, §11-46-138.
Watchers.
Drinking, §11-46-136.
Officers elected.
Assumption of duties by officers elected, §11-46-92.
Officers of election.
Alcoholic beverages.
Drinking by watchers, §11-46-136.
Drinking during election, §11-46-132.
Appointment, §11-46-98.
Upon failure of others to attend polls, §11-46-100.
Assistance to voters, §11-46-111.
Attendance at polls, §11-46-99.
Appointment of officers upon failure of others to attend, §11-46-100.
Certification, §11-46-101.
Challengers.
Selection and duties, §11-46-99.
Compensation, §11-46-98.
Disabled voters.
Assistance, §11-46-111.
Duties.
Neglect, failure or refusal to perform, §11-46-132.
Inspectors.
Offenses, §11-46-133.
List of officers appointed, §11-46-98.

MUNICIPAL CORPORATIONS—Cont'd

Elections—Cont'd

Commission form of government—Cont'd

Officers of election—Cont'd

Notice of appointment, §11-46-98.

Oath, §11-46-99.

Offenses, §11-46-132.

Opening of polls, §11-46-99.

Qualifications, §11-46-101.

Returning officers.

Failure to deliver statement of votes and poll list, §11-46-134.

Schools for instruction in use of voting machines, §11-46-101.

Vacancies, §§11-46-98, 11-46-100.

Voting machines.

Election officers for voting machines, §11-46-120.

Schools for instruction in use of voting machines, §11-46-101.

Watchers, §11-46-106.

Drinking, §11-46-136.

Optional form A, §§11-44-70 to 11-44-105. See within this heading, "Commission form of government."

Optional form B, §§11-44-120 to 11-44-140. See within this heading, "Commission form of government."

Order.

Preservation of order, §11-46-99.

Payment of persons to solicit votes, §11-44-55.

Petitions to probate judges, §11-44-2.

Place of voting.

Designation of voting places, §11-46-95.

Polling places.

Attendance at polls by election officers, §11-46-99.

Appointment of election officers upon failure of others to attend polls, §11-46-100.

Closing of polls.

Votes not to be counted until polls closed, §11-46-115.

Voting machines, §11-46-123.

Designation of voting places, §11-46-95.

Division into groups and assignment to voting places of voters in certain wards or voting places, §11-46-95.

MUNICIPAL CORPORATIONS—Cont'd

Elections—Cont'd

Commission form of government—Cont'd

Polling places—Cont'd

Drunkenness at polling place during election, §11-46-139.

Hours during which polls open, §11-46-99.

Number of electors allowed, §11-46-113.

Opening of polls, §11-46-118.

Election officers, §11-46-99.

Voting machines.

Opening of polls, §11-46-118.

Poll lists.

Certification, §11-46-116.

Comparing number on ballot with poll list, §11-46-139.

Copying, §11-46-139.

Delivery, §11-46-116.

Disposition, §11-46-115.

Failure of returning officer to deliver, §11-46-134.

Sealing, §11-46-116.

Preservation of order, §11-46-99.

President of board of commissioners, §11-44-14.

Proposition submitted to voters, §11-44-5.

Qualifications for voting, §11-46-109.

Registration.

Voting without registering, §11-46-138.

Removing, destroying, etc., instructions, §11-46-139.

Residence.

Electors to vote in ward or precinct of residence, §11-46-109.

Result.

Declaration of election result, §§11-44-6, 11-46-123, 11-46-126.

Voting machines.

Declaration of election results, §11-46-123.

Returns.

Delivery to governing body, §11-46-117.

Preparation, etc., §11-46-123.

Run-off elections, §11-46-126.

Time of holding, §11-46-92.

Secret ballot.

Right of secret ballot, §11-46-114.

Selling votes, §11-46-138.

Solicitation of votes.

Accepting pay to solicit votes, §11-44-55.

Special elections.

Time of holding, §11-46-92.

MUNICIPAL CORPORATIONS—Cont'd

Elections—Cont'd

Commission form of government—Cont'd

State laws.

Applicability to municipal elections, §11-44-56.

Statement of votes.

Certification, §11-46-116.

Delivery, §11-46-116.

Failure of returning officer to deliver, §11-46-134.

Preparation, §11-46-116.

Sealing, §11-46-116.

Statements of candidacy, §11-46-96.

Unopposed candidates, §11-46-97.

Subsequent elections.

When not to be held, §11-44-4.

Supplies.

Election supplies, §§11-46-103, 11-46-119.

Time.

Election dates, §11-46-145.

Electors remaining longer than time allowed, §11-46-138.

Limit for occupation of booth, §11-46-113.

Official time applicable, §11-46-91.

Procedure where election not held on day appointed, §11-46-143.

Regular election, §11-46-92.

Run-off elections, §11-46-92.

Special elections, §11-46-92.

Unopposed candidates, §11-46-97.

Proceedings, §11-46-97.

Voters, §§11-46-107 to 11-46-113.

Assistance to voters, §11-46-111.

Voting machines, §§11-46-121, 11-46-122.

Booths, §11-46-105.

Time limit, etc., for occupation of booth, §11-46-113.

Challenge of voters.

Forms of oaths to be taken by challenged voter, §11-46-112.

Generally, §11-46-109.

Oath of challenged voter, §11-46-112.

Penalty for false oath, §11-46-112.

Refusal to take oath, §11-46-112.

Division into groups and assignment to voting places of voters in certain wards or voting districts, §11-46-95.

MUNICIPAL CORPORATIONS—Cont'd
Elections—Cont'd
Commission form of
government—Cont'd
Wards—Cont'd
Electors to vote in ward
or precinct of
residence,
§11-46-109.
Voting centers.
General provisions,
§11-46-95.
Watchers, §11-46-106.
Drinking, §11-46-136.
When elections held,
§11-46-92.
Procedure where election
not held on day
appointed,
§11-46-143.
Write-in voting.
Prohibited, §11-46-114.
Consolidation.
Contiguous municipalities,
§11-42-100.1.
Alternate mode,
§§11-42-120 to
11-42-134. See
within this heading,
"Consolidation."
Noncontiguous
municipalities,
§§11-42-151,
11-42-154, 11-42-157.
Contests.
Commission form,
§§11-46-117,
11-46-124, 11-46-140,
11-46-141.
Mayor-council form,
§§11-46-46, 11-46-53,
11-46-69, 11-46-70.
Council, §11-43-2.
Election after
incorporation,
§§11-41-5, 11-41-6.
General provisions,
§§11-46-20 to 11-46-73.
Incorporation, §§11-41-1 to
11-41-6.
Mayor-council form,
§§11-46-20 to 11-46-73.
Council-manager form of
government. See within
this heading, "Council-
manager form of
government."
Councilmen.
Abandonment of
commission form of
government,
§11-44-156.
Annexed territory,
§11-42-73.
Consolidation of contiguous
municipalities.
Alternate mode,
§11-42-133.
Definition of municipal
governing body,
§11-46-91.
Judging of elections by
council, §§11-43-40,
11-43-58.
Date of elections.
Certain class 3
municipalities,
§11-46-5.

MUNICIPAL CORPORATIONS—Cont'd
Elections—Cont'd
Date of elections—Cont'd
Certain class 5
municipalities,
§11-46-6.
Districts.
Division of municipality
into single member
districts or wards,
§11-43-63.
Mayor/commission/city
manager form of
government,
§11-44E-120.
Mayor/commission/city
manager form of
government.
Division into four single-
member districts,
§11-44E-120.
Reapportionment,
§11-44E-121.
Federal voting rights act.
Class 7 municipalities.
Mayor-council form of
government.
Adoption where
commission form
violates act,
§11-44A-30.
Class 8 municipalities.
Mayor-council form of
government.
Adoption where
commission form
violates act,
§11-44F-1.
Fees.
Qualification fee for
candidates.
Establishment, §11-46-2.
Franchises.
Mayor/commission/city
manager form of
government.
Elections for or against
proposed grant,
§11-44E-52.
General provisions.
See ELECTIONS.
Handicapped voters.
Commission form of
government,
§§11-46-111,
11-46-122, 11-46-135,
11-46-138.
Mayor-council form of
government,
§§11-46-40, 11-46-51,
11-46-64.
Holidays.
Effect of legal holidays,
§§11-46-20, 11-46-91.
Illegal voting at municipal
elections, §17-23-2.
Impersonating another,
§§11-46-67, 11-46-138,
17-23-2.
Incorporation.
Ballots, §11-41-3.
Conduct of election,
§11-41-3.
Costs of elections, §11-41-6.
Mayor and councilmen.
Conduct of election,
§11-41-5.
Costs of elections,
§11-41-6.

MUNICIPAL CORPORATIONS—Cont'd
Elections—Cont'd
Incorporation—Cont'd
Mayor and councilmen
—Cont'd
Notice of election,
§11-41-5.
Ordering of election,
§11-41-5.
Qualifications for voting,
§11-41-5.
Record of elections,
§11-41-6.
Result of election.
Approval, §11-41-6.
Report to probate
judge, §11-41-6.
Setting aside, etc., of
elections, §11-41-6.
Notice of election, §11-41-2.
Ordering election,
§11-41-2.
Qualifications for voting,
§11-41-3.
Record of elections,
§11-41-6.
Required for incorporation,
§11-41-1.
Results.
Certification, §11-41-4.
Instruction cards.
Cities to pay for, §17-8-23.
Removing, destroying, etc.,
instructions,
§§11-46-68, 11-46-139.
Mayor/commission/city
manager form of
government.
Abandonment of form of
government,
§11-44E-201.
New officers in
governing bodies,
§11-44E-201.
No election within two
years, §11-44E-202.
Bribery, §11-44E-161.
Misdemeanor,
§11-44E-164.
Campaign contributions.
Statement of,
§11-44E-162.
Candidates.
Disqualification of
candidates,
§11-44E-167.
Qualifications and
eligibility,
§§11-44E-3,
11-44E-42,
11-44E-72.
Statement of candidacy,
§§11-44E-41,
11-44E-71.
Canvassing votes.
Commission, §11-44E-49.
Caucuses.
Prohibited, §11-44E-160.
Commission, §11-44E-40.
Candidates.
Qualifications and
eligibility,
§11-44E-42.
Caucuses prohibited,
§11-44E-160.
Eligibility of candidate,
§11-44E-42.
First commission,
§11-44E-3.

MUNICIPAL CORPORATIONS—Cont'd
Elections—Cont'd
Mayor/commission/city
manager form of
government—Cont'd
Commission—Cont'd
Judge of election,
§11-44E-49.
Majority vote
requirements,
§11-44E-40.
Ordinances.
Election of
commissioners,
§11-44E-2.
Primaries prohibited,
§11-44E-160.
Run-off elections,
§11-44E-40.
Statement of candidacy,
§11-44E-41.
Contributions.
Statement of campaign
contributions,
§11-44E-162.
Disqualification of
candidates.
Penalties for violations
of chapter,
§11-44E-167.
Districts.
Division in four single-
member districts,
§11-44E-120.
Reapportionment,
§11-44E-121.
Duties of municipal
officials, §11-44E-3.
Eligibility of candidates,
§§11-44E-3, 11-44E-42,
11-44E-72.
Employee involvement in
elections, §11-44E-165.
Expenses, §11-44E-3.
Forms.
Recall of elected officials,
§11-44E-168.
Statement of candidacy,
§11-44E-71.
Franchises.
Elections for or against
proposed grant,
§11-44E-52.
Judge of election.
Commission, §11-44E-49.
Majority vote
requirements,
§§11-44E-3, 11-44E-40,
11-44E-70.
Mayor, §11-44E-70.
Caucuses prohibited,
§11-44E-160.
Eligibility of candidate,
§11-44E-72.
First mayor, §11-44E-3.
Majority vote
requirements,
§11-44E-70.
Primaries prohibited,
§11-44E-160.
Run-off elections,
§11-44E-70.
Special elections.
Vacancy in office of
mayor,
§11-44E-74.
Statement of candidacy,
§11-44E-71.

MUNICIPAL CORPORATIONS—Cont'd
Elections—Cont'd
Mayor/commission/city
manager form of
government—Cont'd
Mayor—Cont'd
Vacancy in office of
mayor.
Special elections,
§11-44E-74.
Misdemeanors,
§11-44E-164.
Municipal officials.
Duties, §11-44E-3.
Notice, §11-44E-3.
Vacancy in office of
mayor.
Special elections,
§11-44E-74.
Ordinances.
Election of
commissioners,
§11-44E-2.
Petitions.
Recall of elected officials,
§11-44E-168.
Primaries.
Prohibited, §11-44E-160.
Publication.
Vacancy in office of
mayor.
Special elections,
§11-44E-74.
Qualifications of
candidates,
§§11-44E-3, 11-44E-42,
11-44E-72.
Qualifications to vote.
False statements as to,
§11-44E-164.
Voting or offering to vote
by person not
qualified,
§11-44E-164.
Recall of elected officials,
§11-44E-168.
Run-off elections,
§§11-44E-3, 11-44E-40,
11-44E-70.
Soliciting votes at polls at
election day.
Hiring of persons,
§11-44E-166.
Special elections.
Vacancy in office of
mayor, §11-44E-74.
Statement of campaign
contributions,
§11-44E-162.
Statement of candidacy,
§11-44E-41.
Transportation of voters to
polls.
Prohibited, §11-44E-161.
Vacancy in office of mayor.
Special elections,
§11-44E-74.
Violations of chapter.
Disqualification of
candidates,
§11-44E-167.
Voting.
False statements as to
qualifications,
§11-44E-164.
Voting or offering to vote
by person not
qualified,
§11-44E-164.

MUNICIPAL CORPORATIONS—Cont'd
Elections—Cont'd
Mayor-council form of
government, §§11-46-20
to 11-46-73.
Absentee ballots,
§11-46-25.
Applicability of other
laws relating to,
§11-46-57.
Casting and handling,
§11-46-57.
Deletion of voters by
absentee ballot from
lists of qualified
electors, §11-46-28.
Duties of registers,
clerks, etc.,
generally, §11-46-57.
Eligibility, §11-46-56.
Lists of applicants for
absentee ballots.
Marking, posting, etc.,
§11-46-58.
Miscellaneous offenses,
§11-46-68.
Offenses of electors,
§11-46-67.
Alcoholic beverages.
Drinking by watcher,
§11-46-65.
Drunkenness at polling
place during
election, §11-46-68.
Altering votes, §11-46-68.
Annulment of elections,
§11-46-71.
Applicability of article,
§11-46-20.
Assistance to voters.
Voting machines,
§11-46-51.
Assumption of duties by
officers elected,
§11-46-21.
Ballot boxes.
Delivery, §11-46-45.
Destruction, §11-46-46.
Opening.
When opened,
§11-46-46.
Retention, §11-46-46.
Sealing, §11-46-45.
Ballots.
Certification as to
ballots, §11-46-47.
Cities to pay for ballots,
§17-8-23.
Counting, §11-46-44.
Delivery, §11-46-45.
Destruction, §11-46-46.
Disposition, §11-46-52.
Election supplies,
§11-46-32.
Examination of ballots,
§11-46-47.
Generally, §11-46-25.
Miscellaneous offenses,
§11-46-68.
Offenses by electors,
§11-46-67.
Opening ballot boxes,
§11-46-46.
Packaging, §11-46-45.
Paper ballots.
Procedure, §11-46-39.
Retention of ballot boxes,
§11-46-46.
Sealing of ballot boxes,
§11-46-45.

MUNICIPAL
    CORPORATIONS—Cont'd
Elections—Cont'd
  Mayor-council form of
    government—Cont'd
    Ballots—Cont'd
      Secret ballot, §11-46-43.
      Write-in voting
        prohibited,
        §11-46-43.
    Blind voters.
      Deception by marker,
        etc., §11-46-64.
      Voting machines,
        §11-46-51.
    Booths.
      Time limit, etc., for
        occupation of voting
        booth, §11-46-42.
      Voting booths, §11-46-34.
    Bribery.
      Buying votes, §11-46-68.
      Selling votes, §11-46-67.
    Buying votes, §11-46-68.
    Candidates.
      Statements of candidacy,
        §11-46-25.
      Unopposed, §11-46-26.
      Withdrawal of candidacy,
        §11-46-25.
    Canvass of returns,
      §11-46-55.
      Preparation, etc., of
        returns of canvass,
        §11-46-52.
    Certificate of election.
      Issuance by governing
        body, §11-46-55.
    Challengers.
      Duties, §11-46-28.
      Selection, §11-46-28.
    Challenges.
      Disposition of affidavits,
        §11-46-52.
      Generally, §11-46-38.
      Identification of voters
        challenged,
        §11-46-39.
      Oath of challenged
        voters, §11-46-39.
      Forms of oaths,
        §11-46-41.
      Penalty for false oath,
        §11-46-41.
      Refusal to take oath,
        §11-46-41.
    Offenses of electors,
      §11-46-67.
    Voting machines.
      Challenges to voters,
        §11-46-50.
    Changing votes, §11-46-68.
    Class 5 municipalities,
      §§11-43C-2 to
      11-43C-6, 11-43C-13.
      See within this
      heading, "Class 5
      municipalities."
    Class 7 municipalities.
      Adoption where
        commission form
        violates federal
        voting rights act,
        §11-44A-30.
    Class 8 municipalities.
      Adoption where
        commission form
        violates federal
        voting rights act,
        §11-44F-1.

MUNICIPAL
    CORPORATIONS—Cont'd
Elections—Cont'd
  Mayor-council form of
    government—Cont'd
    Clerks.
      Duties of clerk as to
        voting machines,
        §11-46-33.
      Offenses, §11-46-60.
    Closing days.
      Effect of closing days,
        §11-46-20.
    Contests.
      Commencement of
        action, §11-46-69.
      Entry of judgment,
        §11-46-70.
      Grounds, §11-46-69.
      Opening ballot boxes,
        §11-46-46.
      Trial, §11-46-70.
      Voting machines.
        Locking during period
        for filing of
        contests,
        §11-46-53.
    Cost of elections,
      §11-46-20.
    Counting votes.
      Certification of voting
        machine counters,
        §11-46-47.
      Determination of
        majority vote,
        §11-46-55.
      Not to be counted until
        polls closed,
        §11-46-44.
      Number of votes on
        voting machine
        counters, §11-46-52.
    Date of election, §11-46-74.
    Procedure when election
      not held on day
      appointed, §11-46-72.
    Declaration of votes,
      §11-46-52.
    Diagrams.
      Posting and placement of
        diagrams, §11-46-48.
    Disabled voters.
      Assistance, §11-46-40.
      Deception by marker,
        etc., §11-46-64.
      Voting machines,
        §11-46-51.
    Drunkenness.
      At polling place during
        election, §11-46-68.
    Duties of officers elected.
      Assumption of duties,
        §11-46-21.
    Electioneering, §11-46-68.
    Executive officers.
      Offenses, §11-46-59.
    False impersonations.
      Offenses of electors,
        §11-46-67.
    Federal voting rights act.
      Class 7 municipalities.
        Adoption where
          commission form
          violates act,
          §11-44A-30.
      Class 8 municipalities.
        Adoption where
          commission form
          violates act,
          §11-44F-1.

MUNICIPAL
    CORPORATIONS—Cont'd
Elections—Cont'd
  Mayor-council form of
    government—Cont'd
    Forgery.
      Writing name of
        inspectors on ballot,
        §11-46-68.
    Handicapped voters.
      Assistance, §11-46-40.
      Deception by marker,
        etc., §11-46-64.
      Voting machines,
        §11-46-51.
    Holidays.
      Effect of legal holidays,
        §11-46-20.
    Hours during which polls
      open, §11-46-28.
    Identification of voters.
      Where voting machines
        used, §11-46-50.
    Incorporation, §§11-41-5,
      11-41-6.
    Instructions to voters.
      Willfully tearing down,
        destroying, etc.,
        §11-46-68.
    Lighting facilities.
      Preparation, §11-46-48.
    Lists of qualified electors.
      Certification, §11-46-36.
      Upon disqualification
        of mayor, etc.,
        §11-46-37.
      Deletion of voters by
        absentee ballot from,
        §11-46-28.
      Disposition, §11-46-44.
      Disqualification of
        mayor, etc.
        Preparation, etc., of
          lists, §11-46-37.
      Filing, §11-46-36.
      Upon disqualification
        of mayor, etc.,
        §11-46-37.
      Preparation, §11-46-36.
      Upon disqualification
        of mayor, etc.,
        §11-46-37.
      Publication, §11-46-36.
      Upon disqualification
        of mayor, etc.,
        §11-46-37.
    Majority vote.
      Determination of
        majority vote,
        §11-46-55.
    Mayor.
      Offenses, §11-46-59.
    Models.
      Posting and placement,
        §11-46-48.
    Nominations.
      Proceedings where only
        one nominee for
        office, §11-46-26.
    Notice of elections,
      §11-46-22.
    Offenses.
      Alcoholic beverages.
        Drinking by watcher,
        §11-46-65.
      Annulment of election,
        §11-46-71.
      Clerks, §11-46-60.
      Cumulative provisions,
        §11-46-73.

MUNICIPAL CORPORATIONS—Cont'd
Elections—Cont'd
Mayor-council form of government—Cont'd
Offenses—Cont'd
Disabled voters.
Deception by marker, etc., §11-46-64.
Election officers, §§11-46-61 to 11-46-68.
Electors, §11-46-67.
Executive officers, §11-46-59.
Inspectors, §11-46-62.
Markers.
Deception of disabled voters by marker, etc., §11-46-64.
Mayor, §11-46-59.
Miscellaneous offenses, §11-46-68.
Returning officers.
Failure to deliver statement of votes and poll lists, §11-46-63.
Voters, §11-46-67.
Watchers.
Drinking, §11-46-65.
Officers of election.
Appointment, §11-46-27.
Upon failure of others to attend polls, §11-46-29.
Attendance at polls, §11-46-28.
Appointment upon failure of others to attend polls, §11-46-29.
Certification, §11-46-30.
Challengers, §11-46-28.
Compensation, §11-46-27.
Custodians of voting machines and keys.
Designation, etc., §11-46-54.
Disabled voters.
Deception by marker, etc., §11-46-64.
Inspectors.
Offenses, §11-46-62.
Markers.
Deception of disabled voters by marker, etc., §11-46-64.
Notice of appointment, §11-46-27.
Oath of officers, §§11-46-28.
Offenses, §§11-46-61 to 11-46-68.
Miscellaneous offenses, §11-46-68.
Opening of polls, §11-46-28.
Publication of list, §11-46-27.
Qualifications, §11-46-30.
Returning officers.
Failure to deliver statement of votes and poll lists, §11-46-63.
Vacancies, §11-46-27.

MUNICIPAL CORPORATIONS—Cont'd
Elections—Cont'd
Mayor-council form of government—Cont'd
Officers of election—Cont'd
Voting machines, §11-46-49.
Instruction of election officials in use of voting machines, §11-46-30.
Watchers, §11-46-35.
Drinking, §11-46-65.
Official time applicable, §11-46-20.
Places of voting.
Designation, §11-46-24.
Electors to vote in ward or precinct of residence, §11-46-38.
Polling places.
Attendance at polls by election officers, §11-46-28.
Appointment of election officers upon failure of others to attend polls, §11-46-29.
Closing of polls, §11-46-52.
Votes not to be counted until polls closed, §11-46-44.
Designation, §11-46-24.
Hours during which polls open, §11-46-28.
Number of electors allowed, §11-46-42.
Opening of polls, §11-46-47.
By election officers, §11-46-28.
Hours during which polls open, §11-46-28.
Talking in polling place, §11-46-42.
Poll lists.
Comparing number on ballot with poll list, §11-46-68.
Copying poll lists, §11-46-68.
Delivery, §11-46-45.
Disposition, §11-46-44.
Failure of returning officer to deliver, §11-46-63.
Sealing, §11-46-45.
Preservation of order, §11-46-28.
Preventing voters from freely casting ballots, §11-46-68.
Qualifications for voting, §11-46-38.
Registration.
Voting without registering, §11-46-67.
Residence.
Electors to vote in ward or precinct of residence, etc., §11-46-38.
Results.
Declaration of election result, §§11-46-52, 11-46-55.

MUNICIPAL CORPORATIONS—Cont'd
Elections—Cont'd
Mayor-council form of government—Cont'd
Returns.
Canvassing of returns, §11-46-55.
Delivery to governing body, §11-46-46.
Run-off elections, §11-46-55.
Time of holding, §11-46-21.
Secret ballot, §11-46-43.
Selling votes, §11-46-67.
Special elections.
Time of holding, §11-46-21.
Statements of candidacy, §11-46-25.
Statements of vote.
Certification, §11-46-45.
Delivery, §11-46-45.
Failure of returning officer to deliver, §11-46-63.
Preparation, §11-46-45.
Sealing, §11-46-45.
Supplies.
Election supplies, §11-46-32.
Provision of supplies, §11-46-48.
Time.
Central standard time, §11-46-20.
Election dates, §11-46-74.
Official time applicable, §11-46-20.
Procedure when election not held on day appointed, §11-46-72.
Regular elections, §11-46-21.
Run-off elections, §11-46-21.
Special elections, §11-46-21.
Unopposed candidates, §11-46-26.
Voters.
Assignment to voting places of voters in certain wards or voting districts, §11-46-24.
Bribery, §11-46-68.
Disclosing how electors voted, §11-46-68.
Disturbing voters, §11-46-68.
Division into groups in certain wards or voting districts, §11-46-24.
Identification where voting machines used, §11-46-50.
Interference with, §11-46-68.
Lists of qualified electors.
Certification, §11-46-36.
Deletion of voters by absentee ballot from lists of qualified electors, §11-46-28.

MUNICIPAL
CORPORATIONS—Cont'd
Elections—Cont'd
Mayor-council form of
  government—Cont'd
Voters—Cont'd
Lists of qualified electors
  —Cont'd
  Disposition, §11-46-44.
  Filing, §11-46-36.
  Preparation,
    §§11-46-36,
    11-46-37.
  Publication, §11-46-36.
Number of electors
  allowed in polling
  place, §11-46-42.
Offenses, §11-46-67.
Selling votes, §11-46-67.
Unduly influencing,
  §11-46-68.
Voting booths, §11-46-34.
Time limit, etc., for
  occupation of booth,
  §11-46-42.
Voting centers.
  Designation, §11-46-24.
  Procedure for conduct of
    elections, §11-46-24.
  Rights generally,
    §11-46-24.
Voting machines.
  Assistance of voters,
    §§11-46-50, 11-46-51.
  Blind persons, §11-46-51.
  Challenges to voters,
    §11-46-50.
  Contests.
    Locking during period
      for filing of
      contests,
      §11-46-53.
  Counters.
    Certification as to
      counters,
      §11-46-47.
    Examination of
      counters,
      §11-46-47.
    Number of votes on
      counters,
      §11-46-52.
  Custodians, §11-46-54.
  Declaration of votes,
    §11-46-52.
  Delivery of keys,
    §11-46-47.
  Disabled voters,
    §11-46-51.
  Disposition of keys,
    §11-46-52.
  Duties of clerk as to,
    §11-46-33.
  Election supplies,
    §11-46-32.
  Examination of keys,
    §11-46-47.
  Identification of keys,
    §11-46-47.
  Identification of voters,
    §11-46-50.
  Instruction of officials in
    use of machines,
    §11-46-30.
  Instruction of voters in
    use of machines,
    §11-46-51.
  Keys.
    Certification as to
      keys, §11-46-47.

MUNICIPAL
CORPORATIONS—Cont'd
Elections—Cont'd
Mayor-council form of
  government—Cont'd
Voting machines—Cont'd
Keys—Cont'd
  Delivery, examination
    and identification,
    §11-46-47.
  Designation of
    custodians,
    §11-46-54.
  Disposition, §11-46-52.
Locking machines,
  §11-46-52.
Number of votes on
  counters, §11-46-52.
Officers of election,
  §11-46-49.
  Instruction in use of
    machines,
    §11-46-30.
Opening of machines,
  §11-46-47.
Posting, etc., of diagrams
  furnished with
  voting machines,
  §11-46-31.
Procedure for voting,
  §11-46-50.
Protection, §11-46-54.
Provision of election
  materials and
  supplies, §11-46-48.
Public exhibition for
  instruction and
  information of
  voters, §11-46-31.
Records.
  Disposition of records
    taken from
    machines,
    §11-46-53.
Seals.
  When seals may be
    broken, §11-46-53.
Storage, §11-46-54.
Transportation,
  §11-46-54.
Voting centers,
  §11-46-24.
Wards.
  Boundaries.
    Adjustment, §11-46-23.
  Designation of voting
    places, §11-46-24.
  Division into voting
    districts, §11-46-23.
Watchers, §11-46-35.
  Drinking, §11-46-65.
Write-in voting.
  Prohibited, §11-46-43.
Mayors, §11-43-2.
  Abandonment of
    commission form of
    government,
    §11-44-156.
  Consolidation of contiguous
    municipalities,
    §11-42-103.
  Duties of mayor, §17-8-26.
  Election after
    incorporation,
    §§11-41-5, 11-41-6.
  Failure to elect.
    Grounds for forfeiture of
      charter, §11-41-24.
  Judging of election by
    council, §11-43-58.

MUNICIPAL
CORPORATIONS—Cont'd
Elections—Cont'd
Mayors—Cont'd
  Mayor/commission/city
    manager form of
    government,
    §11-44E-70.
  Mayor-council form
    generally, §§11-46-20
    to 11-46-73.
  Offenses, §§11-46-59,
    11-46-130.
Motor vehicles.
  Provision of automobiles,
    etc., to bring voters to
    polls, §11-44-52.
Notice.
  Mayor/commission/city
    manager form of
    government,
    §11-44E-3.
Offenses.
  Mayor-council form of
    government.
    Election officers,
      §§11-46-61 to
      11-46-68.
Officers of election,
  §§11-43-3, 11-43-4,
  11-43-45.
  Commission form,
    §§11-46-98 to
    11-46-101.
  Mayor-council form,
    §§11-46-27 to 11-46-30.
  Officer or employee of city
    acting as election
    officer, §17-6-15.
Participation by public
  employees.
  Improper use of position to
    influence vote or
    political action,
    §17-1-7.
Partisan election.
  Abolished in certain
    municipalities,
    §11-46-3.
Political parties.
  Primary elections by
    political parties
    abolished in certain
    municipalities,
    §11-46-3.
Precincts.
  Inapplicability of general
    election laws to
    municipal elections,
    §17-5A-10.
Primary elections.
  Mayor/commission/city
    manager form of
    government.
    Primaries for nomination
      of candidates
      prohibited,
      §11-44E-160.
  Where abolished, §11-46-3.
Provisions for elections.
  Municipalities may provide
    for election of officers,
    §11-46-1.
Publication.
  Mayor/commission/city
    manager form of
    government.
    Notice of election,
      §11-44E-3.

MUNICIPAL
    CORPORATIONS—Cont'd
  Elections—Cont'd
    Public utilities.
      Sale, lease, etc., of electirc,
        gas or waterworks
        plants by
        municipalities,
        §§11-50-143 to
        11-50-149. See within
        this heading, "Public
        utilities."
    Recall of elected officials.
      Mayor/commission/city
        manager form of
        government,
        §11-44E-168.
    Reduction of corporate limits,
      §§11-42-201, 11-42-204 to
      11-42-207, 11-42-209. See
      within this heading,
      "Reduction of corporate
      limits."
    Register.
      Designation of register
        when election held at
        different time from
        primary or general
        election, §17-10-15.
    Solicitation of votes.
      Acceptance of pay to solicit
        votes, §11-44-55.
    Time.
      Commission form of
        government.
        Hours during which polls
          open, §11-46-99.
      Date of elections in certain
        class 3 municipalities,
        §11-46-5.
      Date of elections in certain
        class 5 municipalities,
        §11-46-6.
      Mayor-council form of
        government.
        Hours during which polls
          open, §11-46-28.
    Treasurer, §11-43-3.
    Unauthorized voting,
      §11-44-53.
    Voters.
      Identification of electors
        eligible to vote.
        Contract with counties,
          §11-46-4.
        Official poll list,
          §11-46-4.
      List of electors eligible to
        vote.
        Official poll list,
          §11-46-4.
      Mayor/commission/city
        manager form of
        government.
        False statement as to
          qualifications to
          vote, §11-44E-164.
        Transportation of voters
          to polls prohibited,
          §11-44E-161.
        Voting or offering to vote
          by person not
          qualified,
          §11-44E-164.
      Provision of automobiles,
        etc., to bring voters to
        polls, §11-44-52.

MUNICIPAL
    CORPORATIONS—Cont'd
  Elections—Cont'd
    Voting machines.
      Applicability of laws to use
        of voting machines in
        municipalities,
        §17-9-39.
      Compensation of election
        officials, §17-9-20.
      Use, §17-9-6.
    Wards.
      Commission form of
        government,
        §§11-46-94, 11-46-95,
        11-46-109.
      Division of municipality
        into single member
        districts, §11-43-63.
      Mayor-council form,
        §§11-46-23, 11-46-24.
  Electric authority.
    Municipal electric authority,
      §§11-50A-1 to 11-50A-33.
      See within this heading,
      "Electricity."
  Electricity.
    Acquisition of systems.
      Authorized, §§11-81-161,
        11-81-200.
      Borrowing money,
        §11-81-202.
      Debts incurred in
        construction,
        acquisition, etc.,
        §§11-50-8 to 11-50-11.
      Purchase of electric plants,
        §11-50-1.
      Purchase of public utilities
        generally, §§37-4-60 to
        37-4-65.
      See PUBLIC UTILITIES.
    Security for bonds and
      indebtedness, §11-81-1.
    Alternate borrowing for
      electric systems,
      §§11-81-200 to 11-81-206.
      Acquisition of systems.
        Authorized, §11-81-200.
        Borrowing money for,
          §11-81-202.
      Charges for electric energy
        and service.
        Limitation, §11-81-204.
      Construction of article,
        §11-81-206.
      Contracts for security of
        lender, §11-81-204.
      Election as to proposed
        undertaking,
        §11-81-201.
      Extension of systems.
        Authorized, §11-81-200.
        Borrowing money for
          extension,
          §11-81-202.
      Form of instrument
        evidencing loan,
        §11-81-205.
      Limitations on borrowing,
        §11-81-202.
      Maturity of instrument
        evidencing loan,
        §11-81-205.
      Operation of systems.
        Authorized, §11-81-200.
        Borrowing money for,
          §11-81-202.
      Pledges of plants as
        security for repayment,
        §11-81-203.

MUNICIPAL
    CORPORATIONS—Cont'd
  Electricity—Cont'd
    Alternate borrowing for
      electric systems—Cont'd
      Repayment of money
        borrowed.
        Contracts for security,
          §11-81-204.
        Pledges of plants as
          security, §11-81-203.
      Rights of way.
        Acquisition, §11-81-200.
      Security for repayment of
        money borrowed.
        Contracts, §11-81-204.
        Pledges of plants,
          §11-81-203.
      Terms of instrument
        evidencing loan,
        §11-81-205.
    Authority, §§11-50A-1 to
      11-50A-33.
    Boards.
      Boards for operation of
        water, sewer, gas and
        electric systems,
        §§11-50-310 to
        11-50-324. See within
        this heading, "Public
        utilities."
      Electric utility boards,
        §§11-50-490 to
        11-50-506.
    Bond issues.
      Alternate borrowing for
        electric systems,
        §§11-81-200 to
        11-81-206.
      Authorized, §11-47-3.
      District electric
        corporations,
        §§11-50-526 to
        11-50-529.
      Public improvement bonds.
        Revenue-producing
          undertakings,
          §§11-81-140 to
          11-81-150.
        See COUNTIES.
      Referendum.
        Issuing obligations to
          construct
          hydroelectric
          generating facilities
          in class 5
          municipality,
          §11-50-6.1.
      Revenue bonds,
        §§11-81-160 to
        11-81-190. See within
        this heading, "Public
        utilities."
      Security for bonds for
        construction, etc., of
        light and power plants,
        §11-81-1.
    Bonds, surety.
      Electric utility boards,
        §§11-50-499,
        11-50-505.
    Calendar basis, §11-81-187.
    Codes.
      Adoption of technical codes
        by reference, §11-45-8.
    Combination of electric light
      and power plants with
      waterworks plants,
      §11-50-12.

MUNICIPAL
CORPORATIONS—Cont'd
Electricity—Cont'd
Commission form of
government.
Municipal officers or
employees.
Conflicts of interest,
§§11-44-46 to
11-44-48.
President of board of
commissioners as
superintendent of
lighting systems,
§11-50-16.
Consolidation of systems.
Authorized, §§11-47-3,
11-81-161.
Construction of systems.
Contracts and indebtedness
authorized, §11-47-3.
Debts incurred in,
§§11-50-8 to 11-50-11.
Security for bonds and
indebtedness, §11-81-1.
Contracts.
Construction, extension,
etc., of electric light
and power plants,
§11-47-3.
Furnishing of electricity,
§11-50-1.
Conveyance of plants to
boards organized to own
plants, §§11-50-13,
11-50-14.
Corporations.
District electric
corporations,
§§11-50-520 to
11-50-533.
Debts incurred in
construction, acquisition,
etc., §§11-50-8 to
11-50-11.
Authorized, §11-47-3.
Mortgages and deeds of
trust.
Conditions, §11-50-9.
Covenants, §11-50-9.
Execution as security,
§11-50-8.
Franchise right, etc., of
purchaser at
foreclosure sale,
§11-50-10.
Rates and charges,
§11-50-11.
Revenues from plants.
Disposition, §11-50-11.
Terms, §11-50-9.
Warranties, §11-50-9.
Security generally,
§11-81-1.
Definitions.
District electric
corporations,
§11-50-520.
District electric corporations,
§§11-50-520 to 11-50-533.
Aid from municipalities,
§11-50-533.
Board of directors,
§11-50-525.
Bond issues, §§11-50-526 to
11-50-529, 11-50-531,
11-50-532.
Consent of department of
finance, §11-50-527.
Denominations,
§11-50-526.

MUNICIPAL
CORPORATIONS—Cont'd
Electricity—Cont'd
District electric corporations
—Cont'd
Bond issues—Cont'd
Department of finance.
Consent of department
required,
§11-50-527.
Execution, §11-50-526.
Exemption from
taxation, §11-50-531.
Interest, §11-50-526.
Interim receipts,
§11-50-526.
Issuance, §11-50-526.
Consent of department
of finance,
§11-50-527.
Nature of obligations,
§11-50-528.
Payment.
Dissolution of
corporation upon
payment in full,
§11-50-532.
Refunding bonds,
§11-50-526.
Remedies of bondholders,
§11-50-529.
Rights of bondholders,
§11-50-529.
Sale, §11-50-526.
Temporary bonds,
§11-50-526.
Certificate of incorporation,
§11-50-522.
Amendment, §11-50-523.
Charges for services
rendered, §11-50-530.
Definitions, §11-50-520.
Directors.
Board of directors,
§11-50-525.
Dissolution, §11-50-532.
Exemption from taxation,
§11-50-531.
Income.
Exemption from
taxation, §11-50-531.
Incorporation.
Authority to incorporate,
§11-50-521.
Certificate of
incorporation,
§11-50-522.
Amendment,
§11-50-523.
Procedure, §11-50-522.
Municipal aid, §11-50-533.
Powers.
Corporate powers,
§11-50-524.
Property.
Exemption from
taxation, §11-50-531.
Rates for services rendered,
§11-50-530.
Taxation.
Exemption, §11-50-531.
Electric utility boards,
§§11-50-490 to 11-50-506.
Accountant.
Appointment,
§11-50-500.
Bonds, surety.
Depositories, §11-50-505.
Employees, §11-50-499.
Officers, §11-50-499.

MUNICIPAL
CORPORATIONS—Cont'd
Electricity—Cont'd
Electric utility boards
—Cont'd
Books and accounts.
Examination,
§11-50-500.
Chairman.
Election, §11-50-494.
Vacancies, §11-50-494.
Compensation of members,
§11-50-495.
Composition, §11-50-490.
Construction.
Expenditures for new
construction,
§11-50-502.
Creation, §11-50-490.
Depositories.
Bonds, surety,
§11-50-505.
Deposit of money
received from use of
electric system,
§11-50-504.
Securities, §11-50-505.
Segregation of funds,
§11-50-503.
Withdrawal of funds,
§11-50-503.
Distribution of money
received from use of
electric system,
§11-50-504.
Duties, §11-50-497.
Effect of chapter on
existing laws, etc.,
§11-50-506.
Election of members,
§11-50-492.
Employees.
Bonds, surety,
§11-50-499.
Funds.
Segregation of funds,
§11-50-503.
Withdrawal of funds,
§11-50-503.
Impeachment of members,
§11-50-498.
Meetings, §11-50-496.
Money received from use of
electric system.
Deposit and distribution,
§11-50-504.
Oaths of members,
§11-50-493.
Officers.
Bonds, surety,
§11-50-499.
Election, §11-50-494.
Vacancies, §11-50-494.
Powers, §11-50-497.
Qualifications of members,
§11-50-491.
Record of proceedings,
§11-50-496.
Removal of members,
§11-50-498.
Reports.
Annual report,
§11-50-501.
Examination of books
and accounts,
§11-50-500.
Secretary.
Election, §11-50-494.
Vacancies in office,
§11-50-494.

MUNICIPAL CORPORATIONS—Cont'd
Electricity—Cont'd
Electric utility boards —Cont'd
Segregation of funds, §11-50-503.
Terms of members, §11-50-492.
Vacancies.
Filling, §11-50-492.
Withdrawal of funds, §11-50-503.
Establishment of electric plants.
Generally, §11-50-1.
Expanded municipalities.
Duty to operate electric light systems of absorbed municipalities, §11-42-185.
Extension of systems.
Authorized, §§11-81-161, 11-81-200.
Borrowing money, §11-81-202.
Contracts and indebtedness authorized, §11-47-3.
Financial condition of system.
Accounting, §11-81-188.
Fiscal year basis, §11-81-187.
Inspections.
Charges for electric wiring inspection, §11-43-59.
License schedule, §11-51-129.
Maintenance of electric plants.
Debts incurred in construction, §§11-50-8 to 11-50-11.
Expenses.
Payment out of general funds, §11-81-182.
Generally, §11-50-1.
Mayors.
Employment as superintendent of municipal light systems, §§11-43-80, 11-50-16.
Mortgages and deeds of trust.
Security for debts, etc., §§11-50-8 to 11-50-11.
Municipal electric authority, §§11-50A-1 to 11-50A-33.
Actions.
Jurisdiction, §11-50A-24.
Annual audit, §11-50A-6.
Authority.
Defined, §11-50A-1.
Board, §11-50A-6.
Compensation, §11-50A-6.
Composition, §11-50A-6.
Defined, §11-50A-1.
Election committee.
Additional members, §11-50A-6.
Designation of elector, §11-50A-6.
Distribution of vote, §11-50A-6.
Duties, §11-50A-6.
Quorum, §11-50A-6.
Election of officers, §11-50A-6.
Majority required for action, §11-50A-6.

MUNICIPAL CORPORATIONS—Cont'd
Electricity—Cont'd
Municipal electric authority —Cont'd
Board—Cont'd
Meetings, §11-50A-6.
Special meetings, §11-50A-6.
Terms, §11-50A-6.
Vacancies, §11-50A-6.
Bond anticipation notes.
Defined, §11-50A-1.
Bond issues, §§11-50A-8 to 11-50A-15, 11-50A-25, 11-50A-26.
Authority to issue, §11-50A-8.
Cancellation, §11-50A-12.
Contracts.
Validation, §11-50A-11.
Covenants in resolutions to issue, §11-50A-9.
Credit not pledged, §11-50A-13.
Default.
Duties of receiver, §11-50A-14.
Holder right to receivership upon default, §11-50A-14.
Jurisdiction of court, §11-50A-14.
Termination of receivership, §11-50A-14.
Defined, §11-50A-1.
Destroyed bonds, §11-50A-12.
Execution, §11-50A-9.
Immunity from liability, §11-50A-13.
Interest, §11-50A-12.
Legal investments, §11-50A-16.
Negotiability, §11-50A-15.
Paying agent, §11-50A-12.
Prerequisite to issuance, §11-50A-9.
Procedure for authorization, §11-50A-9.
Proceeds of bonds, §11-50A-21.
Provisions of resolution deemed irrevocable contract, §11-50A-26.
Public service commission.
Review and regulation, §11-50A-25.
Records, §11-50A-12.
Trust agreements, §11-50A-20.
Validation, §11-50A-10.
Competitive bid laws.
Exemption, §11-50A-29.
Construction of act, §§11-50A-1, 11-50A-30.
Contracts.
Enforcement, §11-50A-17.
Indemnity, §11-50A-17.
Payment of charges, §11-50A-17.

MUNICIPAL CORPORATIONS—Cont'd
Electricity—Cont'd
Municipal electric authority —Cont'd
Contracts—Cont'd
Public service commission.
Review and regulation of authority contracts, §11-50A-25.
Purchase of electric power, §11-50A-17.
Use of projects, §11-50A-17.
Validation, §11-50A-11.
Corporation.
Application.
Contents, §11-50A-4.
Certificate of incorporation, §11-50A-5.
Costs.
Defined, §11-50A-1.
Definitions, §11-50A-1.
Dissolution of authority.
Procedure, §11-50A-27.
Effectiveness of pledges and security interests, §11-50A-31.
Exemptions.
Competitive bid laws, §11-50A-29.
Sunset law, §11-50A-28.
Taxation, §11-50A-27.
Incorporation.
Application.
Procedure, §11-50A-4.
Certificate of incorporation.
Fees not required, §11-50A-5.
Intent of legislature, §11-50A-2.
Jurisdiction of actions, §11-50A-24.
Municipality.
Defined, §11-50A-1.
Notes.
Bond anticipation notes.
Contractual nature of resolution, §11-50A-26.
Issuance, §11-50A-22.
Defined, §11-50A-1.
Issuance, §11-50A-22.
Officers and employees.
Bonds, surety.
Required, §11-50A-8.
Person.
Defined, §11-50A-1.
Pledge of revenues, §11-50A-19.
Pledges and security interests.
Effectiveness, §11-50A-31.
Powers.
Acquisition of property, §11-50A-8.
Agreements for electric power, §11-50A-8.
Bond issues, §11-50A-8.
Contracts, §11-50A-8.
Delegation of powers, §11-50A-8.
Eminent domain, §11-50A-8.
Generally, §11-50A-8.
Investment, §11-50A-8.

MUNICIPAL
 CORPORATIONS—Cont'd
Electricity—Cont'd
Municipal electric authority
 —Cont'd
 Powers—Cont'd
  Litigation, §11-50A-8.
  Promulgation of bylaws,
   rules and
   regulations,
   §11-50A-8.
  Transfers of property,
   §11-50A-8.
 Project.
  Contract fees for projects,
   §11-50A-17.
  Defined, §11-50A-1.
 Public service commission.
  Duties generally,
   §11-50A-25.
  Review and regulation of
   authority,
   §11-50A-25.
 Purpose of authority,
  §11-50A-3.
 Records, §11-50A-6.
 Revenues.
  Assignment of trustee,
   §11-50A-18.
  Defined, §11-50A-1.
  Pledge, §11-50A-19.
  Rates, §11-50A-18.
  Use of revenues,
   §11-50A-18.
 Seal, §11-50A-8.
 Severability of provisions,
  §11-50A-33.
 Sunset law.
  Exemptions, §11-50A-28.
 Supplementary nature of
  provisions, §11-50A-32.
 Taxation.
  Exemptions, §11-50A-7.
  Fee in lieu of taxes,
   §11-50A-7.
 Trust agreement,
  §11-50A-20.
 Trust funds, §11-50A-23.
Operation of systems.
 Authorized, §11-81-200.
 Boards for operation of
  water, sewer, gas and
  electric systems,
  §§11-50-310 to
  11-50-324. See within
  this heading, "Public
  utilities."
 Borrowing money for
  operation, §11-81-202.
 Debts incurred, §§11-50-8
  to 11-50-11.
 Expenses.
  Payment of expenses out
   of general funds,
   §11-81-182.
 Generally, §11-50-1.
Other municipalities.
 Sale of power to other
  municipalities,
  §11-50-3.
Payment by municipalities
 for services furnished by
 system, §11-81-186.
Power districts, §§37-5-1 to
 37-5-9.
 See POWER DISTRICTS.
Power lines.
 Acquisition of power lines
  and rights of way,
  §11-50-2.

MUNICIPAL
 CORPORATIONS—Cont'd
Electricity—Cont'd
President of board of
 commissioners,
 §11-50-16.
Superintendent of light
 systems.
 Employment as
  superintendent,
  §11-50-16.
 Validation of prior
  employment,
  §11-50-16.
Properties of system.
 Accounting, §11-81-188.
Purchase of electric plants.
 Debts incurred in
  purchase, §§11-50-8 to
  11-50-11.
 Generally, §11-50-1.
 Security for bonds and
  indebtedness, §11-81-1.
Purchase of public utilities
 generally, §§37-4-60 to
 37-4-65.
 See PUBLIC UTILITIES.
Quality.
 Regulation of quality,
  §11-50-1.
Rates.
 District electric
  corporations,
  §11-50-530.
 Establishment, §11-81-184.
 Limitation, §11-81-204.
 Mortgages and deeds of
  trust.
  Provision as to rates,
   §11-50-11.
 Regulation of rates,
   §11-50-1.
 State supervision or
  regulation.
  Not subject to,
   §11-81-185.
Repair of systems.
 Authorized, §11-81-161.
 Contracts and indebtedness
  authorized, §11-47-3.
Revenue bonds, §§11-81-160
 to 11-81-190. See within
 this heading, "Public
 utilities."
Revenues.
 Depository.
  Designation, §11-81-183.
 Disposition, §§11-50-12,
  11-81-181.
 Gross revenue account.
  Disposition and
   disbursement,
   §11-81-183.
 Mortgages or deeds of
  trust.
  Provision as to
   disposition of
   revenues, §11-50-11.
 Pledge of revenues,
  §§11-81-16, 11-81-181.
Rights of way.
 Acquisition, §11-50-2.
Sale, lease, etc., of plants by
 municipalities,
 §§11-50-140 to 11-50-151.
 See within this heading,
 "Public utilities."
Sale of power to other
 municipalities, §11-50-3.

MUNICIPAL
 CORPORATIONS—Cont'd
Electricity—Cont'd
Streets.
 Regulation of use of streets
  for electric lines,
  §11-43-62.
Superintendent of light
 systems.
 Employment of mayor or
  president of board of
  commissioners as,
  §11-50-16.
Transfer of plants to boards
 organized and
 incorporated to own and
 operate plants,
 §§11-50-13, 11-50-14.
Trees.
 Attachment of wires to
  trees, §9-13-15.
Use of electric light and
 power plants, §11-50-12.
Utility boards.
 Electric utility boards,
  §§11-50-490 to
  11-50-506.
Waterworks plants.
 Combination of electric
  light and power plants
  with waterworks
  plants, §11-50-12.
Elk river development
 agency.
Contributions to work of
 agency, §33-12-6.
Emergencies.
Ambulance service, §§11-87-1
 to 11-87-5.
Fire departments.
 Operation beyond corporate
  limits and police
  jurisdiction,
  §11-43-141.
Military service by municipal
 officers in time of
 national emergency,
 §§36-8-1 to 36-8-5.
Eminent domain, Const. Ala.,
 art. XII, §235.
Airports, §4-4-6.
Appeals.
 Procedure for appeal,
  §11-47-172.
 Right of entry of
  municipality pending
  appeal, §11-47-173.
Authorized.
 By municipal governing
  body, §11-47-171.
 Generally, §11-47-170.
Buildings.
 Condemnation for sites,
  §11-80-1.
Gas districts, §11-50-397.
Medical clinic boards.
 Powers, §11-58-5.1.
Procedure.
 Appeals, §11-47-172.
 Generally, §11-47-172.
Public improvements.
 Acquisition of lands,
  easements, etc., for
  public improvements,
  §11-48-64.
Public library authorities,
 §11-57-9.
Relocation assistance,
 §11-80-2.

MUNICIPAL
CORPORATIONS—Cont'd
Eminent domain—Cont'd
Right of entry of
municipality pending
appeal, §11-47-173.
Sewers.
Acquisition of easements,
§11-50-51.
Streets.
Condemnation of lands for
streets and
construction materials,
§11-80-1.
Employees.
Abandonment of commission
form.
Continuation in office,
§11-44-161.
Accident insurance.
Group insurance for
officers and employees,
§§11-91-1 to 11-91-8.
See within this
heading, "Insurance."
Bonds, surety, §11-43-13.
Mayor/commission/city
manager form of
government.
Bonds of employees,
§11-44E-184.
Civil defense.
Powers and duties of
employees rendering
outside aid, §31-9-11.
Claims for or against town.
Dealing in claims,
§11-43-14.
Class 5 municipalities.
Mayor/commission/city
manager form of
government.
Bonds, surety,
§11-44E-184.
Conflicts of interest.
Acceptance of gifts,
§11-44E-183.
Contracts,
§11-44E-183.
Continuation of those in
classified service,
§11-44E-142.
Contracts.
Conflicts of interest,
§11-44E-183.
Elections.
Involvement in
prohibited,
§11-44E-165.
Gifts.
Acceptance of,
§11-44E-183.
Managers.
Powers, §11-44E-92.
Misdemeanors.
Acceptance of gifts,
§11-44E-183.
Conflicts of interest,
§11-44E-183.
Public utilities.
Interest in contracts
with, §11-44E-183.
Removal of officers and
employees,
§11-44E-180.
Succession of
government.
Rights of officers and
employees
preserved,
§11-44E-140.

MUNICIPAL
CORPORATIONS—Cont'd
Employees—Cont'd
Code of conduct.
Class 5 municipalities.
Mayor/commission/city
manager form of
government,
§§11-44E-160 to
11-44E-168. See
within this heading,
"Class 5
municipalities."
General provisions,
§§36-25-1 to 36-25-30.
See PUBLIC OFFICERS
AND EMPLOYEES.
Commission form of
government.
Compensation, §§11-44-28,
11-44-85, 11-44-104.
Conflicts of interest,
§§11-44-46 to 11-44-48,
11-44-94, 11-44-138.
Continuation in office,
§§11-44-27, 11-44-122,
11-44-161.
Gifts.
Acceptance from
railways, gas works,
etc., §11-44-48.
Optional form A. See
within this heading,
"Commission form of
government."
Optional form B,
§§11-44-122,
11-44-138.
Removal, §11-44-28.
Selection, §§11-44-28,
11-44-45, 11-44-85,
11-44-93.
Solicitation of votes by
municipal employees,
§§11-44-54, 11-44-98.
Conflicts of interest,
§11-43-12.
Commission form of
government,
§§11-44-46 to 11-44-48.
Optional form A,
§11-44-94.
Optional form B,
§11-44-138.
Mayor/commission/city
manager form of
government.
Acceptance of gifts,
§11-44E-183.
Contracts, §11-44E-183.
Damages.
Employees' suit for
damages arising out of
official duties.
Indemnification,
§11-47-24.
Municipality to provide
counsel, §11-47-24.
Elections.
Class 5 municipalities.
Mayor/commission/city
manager form of
government.
Involvement in
elections
prohibited,
§11-44E-165.
Improper use of position to
influence votes or
political action,
§17-1-7.

MUNICIPAL
CORPORATIONS—Cont'd
Employees—Cont'd
Elections—Cont'd
Mayor/commission/city
manager form of
government.
Involvement in elections
prohibited,
§11-44E-165.
Right of city and county
employees to
participate in political
activities, §17-1-7.
Solicitation, etc., of votes
by municipal
employees, §11-44-54.
Ethics.
Code of ethics, §§36-25-1 to
36-25-30.
See PUBLIC OFFICERS
AND EMPLOYEES.
Fees.
Establishment, §11-43-7.
Indemnification.
Damages arising out of
performance of official
duties, §11-47-24.
Insurance.
Group insurance for
officers and employees,
§§11-91-1 to 11-91-8.
See within this
heading, "Insurance."
Liability insurance,
§11-47-24.
Liability of municipality for
negligence of agents,
§§11-47-190 to 11-47-192.
Mayor/commission/city
manager form of
government.
Acceptance of gifts,
§11-44E-183.
Bonds, surety,
§11-44E-184.
Conflicts of interest.
Contracts, §11-44E-183.
Contracts.
Conflicts of interest,
§11-44E-183.
Elections.
Involvement in elections
prohibited,
§11-44E-165.
Gifts.
Acceptance of gifts,
§11-44E-183.
Managers.
Powers, §11-44E-92.
Misdemeanors.
Acceptance of gifts,
§11-44E-183.
Conflicts of interest,
§11-44E-183.
Public utilities.
Interest in contracts
with, §11-44E-183.
Removal of officers and
employees,
§11-44E-180.
Rights of officers and
employees preserved,
§11-44E-140.
Succession of government.
Continuance of those in
classified service,
§11-44E-142.

MUNICIPAL
CORPORATIONS—Cont'd
Employees—Cont'd
Negligence.
Liability for negligence of
agents, etc.,
§§11-47-190 to
11-47-192.
Pension and retirement
plans. See within this
heading, "Pension and
retirement plans."
Political activities.
Improper use of position to
influence votes or
political action,
§17-1-7.
Right of employees to
participate, §17-1-7.
Retirement plans. See within
this heading, "Pension
and retirement plans."
Salaries.
Commission form of
government, §11-44-28.
Optional form A,
§11-44-85.
Optional form B,
§11-44-104.
Establishment, §11-43-7.
Ordinances and resolutions
fixing salaries.
Veto, §11-45-5.
Social security, §§36-28-1 to
36-28-10.
See SOCIAL SECURITY.
State employees' retirement
system.
Participation of city
employees, §36-27-6.
Torts.
Liability of municipality
for negligence of
agents, etc.,
§§11-47-190 to
11-47-192.
Warrants.
Dealing in warrants,
§11-43-14.
Engineer.
Appointment, §11-48-12.
Public improvements.
City or town engineer to
supervise work,
§11-48-12.
Supervision of projects by
professional engineers,
§34-11-10.
Enterprise zones.
Creation within class 1
cities, §11-40-16.
General provisions,
§§41-23-20 to 41-23-32.
See ENTERPRISE ZONES.
Environmental improvement
authorities.
Aid and cooperation of
municipal corporations,
§9-6-13.
Ethics.
Class 5 municipalities.
Mayor/commission/city
manager form of
government.
Code of conduct,
§§11-44E-160 to
11-44E-168. See
within this heading,
"Class 5
municipalities."

MUNICIPAL
CORPORATIONS—Cont'd
Ethics—Cont'd
Code of ethics, §§36-25-1 to
36-25-30.
See PUBLIC OFFICERS
AND EMPLOYEES.
Evidence.
Ordinances, bylaws and
resolutions, §12-21-95.
Proof of certain official
documents, §12-21-73.
Reduction of corporate limits.
Map or plat.
Evidence of municipal
boundaries,
§11-42-211.
Examinations.
Commission form of
government.
Books and accounts,
§§11-44-50, 11-44-95,
11-44-139.
Finance.
Accounting, §11-43-85.
Exemptions from levy and
sale under process.
Municipal property, §6-10-10.
Exhibitions.
Provision of music and other
exhibitions, §11-47-19.
Expanded municipalities.
Duties as to absorbed
municipalities,
§§11-42-180 to 11-42-187.
Actions of absorbed
municipalities.
Pending actions,
§11-42-183.
Bonds of absorbed
municipalities.
Partial annexation.
Payment of
proportionate
share by expanded
municipality,
§11-42-186.
Payment, execution, etc.,
§11-42-180.
Books of absorbed
municipalities.
Disposition, §11-42-184.
Contracts for local
improvements of
absorbed
municipalities.
Payment, execution, etc.,
§11-42-180.
Debts of absorbed
municipalities.
Payment, execution, etc.,
§11-42-180.
Documents of absorbed
municipalities.
Disposition, §11-42-184.
Electric light systems.
Operation, etc.,
§11-42-185.
Fines.
Collection, §11-42-183.
Gas systems.
Operation, etc.,
§11-42-185.
Judgments.
Collection, §11-42-183.
Papers of absorbed
municipalities.
Disposition, §11-42-184.

MUNICIPAL
CORPORATIONS—Cont'd
Expanded municipalities
—Cont'd
Duties as to absorbed
municipalities—Cont'd
Partial annexation.
Bonds for improvements.
Payment of
proportionate
share by expanded
municipality,
§11-42-186.
School property.
Payment of value by
expanded
municipality,
§11-42-187.
Property of absorbed
municipalities.
Disposition, §11-42-181.
Partial annexation.
Payment of value by
expanded
municipality,
§11-42-187.
School property.
Partial annexation.
Payment of value by
expanded
municipality,
§11-42-187.
Special assessments of
absorbed
municipalities.
Collection, §11-42-182.
Taxes of absorbed
municipalities.
Collection, §11-42-182.
Waterworks.
Operation, etc.,
§11-42-185.
Explosives.
Storage.
Provision of building for
storage of gunpowder,
etc., §11-47-12.
Regulation, §11-43-60.
Express companies.
License schedules,
§11-51-126.
Fair trial tax.
Disposition when collected in
municipal court,
§12-19-251.1.
Farmers' markets.
Local appropriations
authorized, §2-5-17.
Farm products.
Licenses.
Municipalities not to
charge farmers to sell,
§11-51-105.
Regulation of sale, §2-29-10.
Federal voting rights act.
Class 7 municipalities.
Mayor-council form of
government.
Adoption where
commission form
violates act,
§§11-44A-30 to
11-44A-32.
Class 8 municipalities.
Mayor-council form of
government.
Adoption where
commission form
violates act,
§§11-44F-1 to
11-44F-3.

MUNICIPAL CORPORATIONS—Cont'd
Fees.
Ambulance service, §11-87-4.
Annexation.
Cities of twenty-five thousand inhabitants or more.
Fees of probate judges, §11-42-87.
Clerks.
Disposition of fees of clerk, §11-43-7.
Dissolution.
Fee of probate judge, §11-41-28.
Elections.
Qualification fee for candidates, §11-46-2.
Employees, §11-43-7.
Enterprise zones.
Creation within class 1 cities.
Reduction in municipal fees, §11-40-16.
Forfeiture of charter.
Fee of probate judge, §11-41-28.
Garbage and trash, §11-47-135.
Incorporation.
Filing order of incorporation, §11-41-4.
Officers.
Disposition of fees collected, §11-43-6.
Payment into local treasury, §1-3-6.
Unchanged during term of office, §11-43-9.
Probate judges.
Annexation.
Cities of twenty-five thousand or more.
Fees and compensation of probate judges, §11-42-87.
Commission form of government.
Optional form A, §11-44-96.
Dissolution, §11-41-28.
Forfeiture of charter, §11-41-28.
Reduction of corporate limits, §11-42-213.
Public utilities.
Boards for operation of water, sewer, gas and electric systems.
Directors' fees, §11-50-15.
Inspection and supervision fees.
Assessment by municipality prohibited, §37-4-23.
Reduction of corporate limits.
Probate judge and other officers, §11-42-213.
Ferries.
Licenses.
Establishment on rivers between two counties, §§11-49-20 to 11-49-23.
See FERRIES.
Public roads, bridges and ferries, §§23-1-86, 23-1-90, 23-1-91.
See COUNTIES.

MUNICIPAL CORPORATIONS—Cont'd
Ferries—Cont'd
Railroads.
When required to construct within cities, §§11-49-40 to 11-49-45.
See within this heading, "Railroads."
Finance.
Accountants.
Appointment, §11-43-85.
Accounts and accounting.
Commission form of government.
Examinations of books and accounts, §11-44-50.
Maintenance, etc., of municipal books and accounts, §11-43-102.
Clerks.
Maintenance of books and accounts, §11-43-102.
Commission form of government.
Examinations of books and accounts, §§11-44-50, 11-44-95, 11-44-139.
Optional form A.
Examination of books and accounts, §11-44-95.
Publication of statement of receipts and expenses, §11-44-95.
Optional form B.
Audit of books and accounts, §11-44-139.
Publication of statement of receipts and expenses, §11-44-139.
Publication of quarterly statement, §11-44-49.
Control of finances by council, §11-43-56.
Examinations, §11-43-85.
Commission form of government, §§11-44-50, 11-44-95, 11-44-139.
Management by council, §11-43-56.
Mayors.
Statement to council of financial condition, §11-43-84.
Fines.
Schedule of fines for nontraffic violations.
Authorized to establish by ordinance, ARJA, Rule 20.
Fire departments, §§11-43-5, 11-43-140 to 11-43-144.
Authorized, §11-43-140.
Chiefs, §11-43-5.
Commissioners.
Council may delegate power to control and manage, §11-43-140.
Contracts.
Operation beyond corporate limits and police jurisdiction, §11-43-142.
Control, §11-43-140.

MUNICIPAL CORPORATIONS—Cont'd
Fire departments—Cont'd
Diseases.
Occupational diseases.
Compensation for death or disability, §11-43-144.
Emergencies.
Operation beyond corporate limits and police jurisdiction, §11-43-141.
Labor organizations.
Rights to join, §11-43-143.
Liabilities.
Operation beyond corporate limits and police jurisdiction, §§11-43-141, 11-43-142.
Management, §11-43-140.
Occupational diseases.
Compensation for death or disability of fire fighters, §11-43-144.
Operation beyond corporate limits and police jurisdiction.
Contracts, §11-43-142.
Emergencies, §11-43-141.
Exemptions, §11-43-141.
Immunities, §11-43-141.
Liabilities, §§11-43-141, 11-43-142.
Strikes.
Municipal or state fire fighters or firemen not to strike, etc., §11-43-143.
Unions.
Rights to join, §11-43-143.
Volunteer fire departments.
Donation of money, property, etc.
Authority of municipality, §9-3-18.
Fire limits.
Adoption, §11-43-59.
Fires and fire prevention.
Class 1 municipalities.
Firemen's pensions and relief plans.
Minimum monthly benefits, §11-40-18.
Codes.
Adoption of technical codes by reference, §11-45-8.
Fire departments, §§11-43-5, 11-43-140 to 11-43-144.
See within this heading, "Fire departments."
Fire fighters' personnel standards and education.
Appropriations and grants authorized, §36-32-10.
Powers and duties of municipal governments, §36-32-12.
Fire limits.
Adoption, §11-43-59.
Sprinkler systems.
Regulation of work of contractors, §34-33-9.

MUNICIPAL
  CORPORATIONS—Cont'd
Fires and fire prevention
  —Cont'd
  Water, sewer and fire
    protection authorities,
    §§11-88-1 to 11-88-111.
    See WATER, SEWER AND
    FIRE PROTECTION
    AUTHORITIES.
  Water, sewer and fire
    protection districts,
    §§11-89-1 to 11-89-19.
    See WATER, SEWER AND
    FIRE PROTECTION
    DISTRICTS.
Floods.
  Assessments for public
    improvements.
  Manner of assessment of
    costs of seawalls,
    levees, etc., §11-48-16.
Food.
  Impure, adulterated, etc.,
    food.
    Inspections, §11-47-136.
    Prohibition of sale, etc.,
      §11-47-136.
  Inspection, §11-47-136.
    Charges for inspection,
      §11-43-59.
  Markets and marketing of
    food products.
    Regulation, etc.,
      §11-47-137.
  Regulation of sales,
    §11-47-137.
Foreign municipal
  corporations.
  Acquisition of water supply
    by, §§11-50-30 to
    11-50-36. See within this
    heading, "Water supply
    and waterworks."
Forests and forestry.
  Acquisition and
    administration of forest
    lands.
    Authorized, §11-84-1.
    Seedlings.
      Provision, §11-84-2.
    Technical assistance.
      Provision, §11-84-2.
    Transplants.
      Provision, §11-84-2.
  Forest products.
    Privilege and severance
      taxes.
      Payments by
        municipalities
        purchasing,
        §9-13-106.
  Research and educational
    programs.
    Appropriation, §2-30-23.
    Receipt of donations from
      municipalities,
      §2-30-23.
Forfeiture of charter,
  §§11-41-24 to 11-41-26,
  11-41-28.
Forms.
  Class 5 municipalities.
    Mayor/commission/city
      manager form of
      government.
      Elections.
        Statement of
          candidacy,
          §§11-44E-41,
          11-44E-71.

MUNICIPAL
  CORPORATIONS—Cont'd
Forms—Cont'd
  Class 5 municipalities
    —Cont'd
    Mayor/commission/city
      manager form of
      government—Cont'd
      Recall of elected officials,
        §11-44E-168.
  Mayor/commission/city
    manager form of
    government.
    Elections.
      Statement of candidacy,
        §§11-44E-41,
        11-44E-71.
    Recall of elected officials,
      §11-44E-168.
  Recall of elected officials.
    Mayor/commission/city
      manager form of
      government,
      §11-44E-168.
Franchises.
  Class 5 municipalities.
    Mayor/commission/city
      manager form of
      government.
      Granting, §11-44E-52.
  Commission form of
    government.
    Use of streets, etc.
      Procedure to grant
        franchises,
        §11-44-36.
      Resolutions, bylaws or
        ordinances granting
        franchises.
        Effective date,
          §11-44-33.
        Elections, §§11-44-34,
          11-44-35.
        Objections, §11-44-34.
        Optional form A,
          §11-44-88.
        Optional form B,
          §11-44-137.
        Publication, §11-44-33.
  Council-manager form of
    government.
    Ordinances granting
      franchise.
      Thirty day delay in
        effect, §11-43A-25.
  Disposition of money from
    sale or lease, §11-43-62.
  Elections.
    Class 5 municipalities.
      Mayor/commission/city
        manager form of
        government.
        Voting for or against
          proposed grant,
          §11-44E-52.
  Lease, §11-43-62.
  Mayor/commission/city
    manager form of
    government.
    Granting, §11-44E-52.
  Property.
    Commission form of
      government.
      Ordinances granting
        franchises for use of
        property.
        Optional form B,
          §11-44-137.
  Sale, §11-43-62.

MUNICIPAL
  CORPORATIONS—Cont'd
Franchises—Cont'd
  Streets.
    Class 5 municipalities.
      Mayor/commission/city
        manager form of
        government.
        Granting of franchise
          to use streets,
          §11-44E-52.
    Commission form of
      government.
      Procedure for granting
        franchise to use
        streets, §11-44-36.
      Resolutions, bylaws or
        ordinances granting
        franchises to use
        streets.
        Effective date,
          §11-44-33.
        Elections, §11-44-34.
        Objections, §11-44-34.
        Optional form A,
          §11-44-88.
        Optional form B,
          §11-44-137.
        Proceedings upon
          determination of
          election result,
          §11-44-35.
        Publication, §11-44-33.
    Mayor/commission/city
      manager form of
      government.
      Granting right to use
        streets, etc.,
        §11-44E-52.
    Term.
      Maximum term in cities or
        towns of six thousand
        or more, Const. Ala.,
        art. XII, §228.
Fruits and vegetables.
  Decayed fruits and
    vegetables.
    Sales.
      Prohibition, §11-47-136.
  Inspections.
    Provision for inspections,
      §11-47-136.
  Regulation of sales,
    §11-47-137.
Fugitives from justice.
  Rewards when high crime or
    misdemeanor committed
    in municipality, §15-9-2.
Funds.
  Capital improvement,
    §§11-66-3 to 11-66-7.
    Appropriations to,
      §11-66-5.
    Creation, §11-66-4.
    Definition of fund,
      §11-66-3.
    Fund capital.
      Defined, §11-66-3.
      Distribution, §11-66-6.
    Payment of allocations by
      state comptroller,
      §11-66-7.
    Trust fund.
      Defined, §11-66-3.
  Investment.
    Sinking funds, §§11-81-19
      to 11-81-21.
  Sinking funds, §§11-81-15,
    11-81-19 to 11-81-26. See
    within this heading,
    "Sinking funds."

MUNICIPAL CORPORATIONS—Cont'd

Gambling.

Prohibition of gaming and gambling houses, etc., §11-47-111.

Garbage and trash, §11-47-135.

Incinerators.
Establishment, §11-47-135.

Solid waste management plan.
General provisions, §§22-27-40 to 22-27-49.
See SOLID WASTE.

Garnishment.

Taxation.
Collection of taxes, §§11-51-8, 11-51-26.

Gas.

Acquisition, operation, etc., of gas plants and systems.
Authorization, §11-81-161.

Boards for operation of water, sewer, gas and electric systems, §§11-50-310 to 11-50-324. See within this heading, "Public utilities."

Conveyance of gas plants to boards organized to own plants, §§11-50-13, 11-50-14.

Expenses.
Payment out of general fund, §11-81-182.

Gas utility boards, §§11-50-460 to 11-50-475.

Generally, §11-50-1.

Purchase of public utilities generally, §§37-4-60 to 37-4-65.
See PUBLIC UTILITIES.

Revenue bonds, §§11-81-161, 11-81-612.

Security for bonds, §11-81-1.

Waterworks and sewer boards, §§11-50-260 to 11-50-273. See within this heading, "Waterworks and sewer boards."

Appliances.
Gas districts.
Rules and regulations, §§11-50-401, 11-50-402.

Assessments for public improvements, §§11-48-1 to 11-48-106. See within this heading, "Assessments for public improvements."

Boards.
Boards for operation of water, gas, sewer and electric systems, §§11-50-310 to 11-50-324. See within this heading, "Public utilities."

Conveyance of gas plants to boards organized to own plants, §§11-50-13, 11-50-14.

MUNICIPAL CORPORATIONS—Cont'd

Gas—Cont'd

Boards—Cont'd
Districts.
Board of directors, §§11-50-393 to 11-50-395.
Gas utility boards, §§11-50-460 to 11-50-475.
Waterworks and sewer boards.
Acquisition, operation, etc., of plants and systems, §§11-50-260 to 11-50-273. See within this heading, "Waterworks and sewer boards."

Bond issues.
Gas districts, §§11-50-405 to 11-50-410, 11-50-412.
Revenue bonds, §§11-81-160 to 11-81-190. See within this heading, "Public utilities."
Security for bonds, §11-81-1.

Bonds, surety.
Gas utility boards, §§11-50-468, 11-50-475.

Calendar basis, §11-81-187.

Code.
Adoption of technical codes by reference, §11-45-8.

Commission form of government.
Municipal officers or employees.
Conflicts of interest, §§11-44-46 to 11-44-48.
President of board of commissioners as superintendent of gas systems, §11-50-16.

Consolidation of systems.
Authorized, §11-81-161.

Construction of gas plants, §§11-50-260 to 11-50-273.

Contracts.
Furnishing of gas, §11-50-1.
Gas districts.
Bond issues.
Security for repayment, §11-50-407.

Conveyance of gas plants to boards organized to own plants, §§11-50-13, 11-50-14.

Definitions.
Districts, §11-50-390.
Transfer of gas system without elections, §11-50-210.

Districts, §§11-50-390 to 11-50-417.
Acquisition.
Competing gas systems, §11-50-399.
Distribution systems outside territory of municipalities, §11-50-398.

MUNICIPAL CORPORATIONS—Cont'd

Gas—Cont'd

Districts—Cont'd
Appliances.
Rules and regulations, §11-50-401.
Procedure, §11-50-402.
Board of directors, §§11-50-393 to 11-50-395.
Compensation, §11-50-393.
Election, §11-50-393.
Officers, §11-50-394.
Organization, §11-50-394.
Powers, §11-50-395.
Qualifications, §11-50-393.
Removal of members, §11-50-393.
Resolutions, §11-50-395.
Terms of office, §11-50-393.
Vacancies, §11-50-393.
Bond issues, §§11-50-392, 11-50-405 to 11-50-410, 11-50-412.
Authorization, §11-50-405.
Contracts.
Security for repayment, §11-50-407.
Delivery, §11-50-405.
Denominations, §11-50-405.
Disposition of proceeds from sale, §11-50-406.
Exchange, §11-50-405.
Execution, §11-50-405.
Exemption from taxation, §11-50-412.
Form of bond, §11-50-405.
Interim receipts, §11-50-405.
Liability upon bonds, §11-50-409.
Liens.
Properties, persons, etc., subject to liens, §11-50-408.
When liens effective, §11-50-408.
Mortgages and deeds of trust.
Properties, persons, etc., subject to mortgages, §11-50-408.
Security for bonds as to rights of parties, §11-50-407.
When effective, §11-50-408.
Payment, §11-50-409.
Dissolution of district and disposition of systems upon payment of indebtedness, §11-50-392.
Security for repayment, §11-50-407.

**MUNICIPAL
CORPORATIONS**—Cont'd
Gas—Cont'd
  Districts—Cont'd
    Bond issues—Cont'd
      Pledges of property or
        revenues.
        Properties, persons,
          etc., subject to
          pledges,
          §11-50-408.
        When effective,
          §11-50-408.
      Proceeds from sale.
        Disposition,
          §11-50-406.
      Refunding bonds,
        §11-50-405.
      Remedies of bondholders
        and trustees,
        §11-50-410.
      Rights of bondholders
        and trustees,
        §11-50-410.
      Sale, §11-50-405.
        Disposition of proceeds,
        §11-50-406.
      Temporary bonds,
        §11-50-405.
      Terms, §11-50-405.
    Certificate of incorporation,
      §11-50-392.
    Competing gas systems.
      Acquisition, §11-50-399.
    Construction.
      Distribution systems
        outside territory of
        municipalities,
        §11-50-398.
    Contracts.
      Bond issues.
        Security for
          repayment,
          §11-50-407.
    Creation, §11-50-391.
    Definitions, §11-50-390.
    Directors, §§11-50-393 to
      11-50-395.
    Dissolution.
      Payment of indebtedness
        of district,
        §11-50-392.
    Distribution systems
      outside of
      municipalities,
      §11-50-398.
    Eminent domain,
      §11-50-397.
    Exclusiveness of article,
      §11-50-417.
    Exemption from taxation,
      §11-50-412.
    Fixtures.
      Rules and regulations,
        §11-50-401.
        Procedure, §11-50-402.
    Highways.
      Use of public highway
        rights-of-way,
        §11-50-400.
    Income.
      Exemption from
        taxation, §11-50-412.
    Incorporation.
      Certificate of
        incorporation,
        §11-50-392.

**MUNICIPAL
CORPORATIONS**—Cont'd
Gas—Cont'd
  Districts—Cont'd
    Incorporation—Cont'd
      Proceedings, notices, etc.,
        required by article
        for incorporation
        exclusive,
        §11-50-416.
      Validation of proceedings
        to incorporate,
        §11-50-414.
    Interest statutes.
      Exemption, §11-50-415.
    License tax.
      Levy and collection,
        §11-50-413.
    Liens.
      Bond issues.
        Properties, persons,
          etc., subject to
          liens, §11-50-408.
        When liens effective,
          §11-50-408.
    Mortgages and deeds of
      trust.
      Bond issues.
        Security for bonds as
          to rights of
          parties,
          §11-50-407.
        When effective,
          §11-50-408.
    Notices.
      Required notices
        exclusive,
        §11-50-416.
    Operation.
      Distribution systems
        outside of
        municipalities,
        §11-50-398.
    Pipes.
      Rules and regulations,
        §11-50-401.
        Procedure, §11-50-402.
    Powers of districts,
      §11-50-396.
      Eminent domain,
        §11-50-397.
    Profits.
      Disposition of net profits,
        §11-50-411.
      Exemption from
        taxation, §11-50-412.
      "Net income" defined,
        §11-50-411.
    Property.
      Exemption from
        taxation, §11-50-412.
    Provisions of article
      exclusive, §11-50-417.
    Public service commission.
      Exemption of districts
        from jurisdiction of
        commission,
        §11-50-416.
    Purpose of article,
      §11-50-416.
    Rights-of-way.
      Use of public highway
        rights-of-way,
        §11-50-400.
    Rules and regulations.
      Conflict with municipal
        rules and
        regulations,
        §11-50-403.

**MUNICIPAL
CORPORATIONS**—Cont'd
Gas—Cont'd
  Districts—Cont'd
    Rules and regulations
      —Cont'd
      Installation,
        maintenance, etc., of
        gas fixtures, pipes,
        etc., §§11-50-401,
        11-50-402.
    Taxation.
      Exemption of property,
        etc., §11-50-412.
      Privilege license tax.
        Levy and collection,
        §11-50-413.
    Transfer of systems to
      district by
      municipalities,
      §11-50-404.
    Usury statutes.
      Exemption, §11-50-415.
  Elections.
    Transfer of gas system
      without election,
      §§11-50-210 to
      11-50-213.
  Eminent domain.
    Districts, §11-50-397.
  Expanded municipalities.
    Operation, etc., of gas
      systems of absorbed
      municipalities,
      §11-42-185.
  Extension of gas systems.
    Authorized, §11-81-161.
  Financial condition of
    system.
    Accounting, §11-81-188.
  Fiscal year basis, §11-81-18⁰
  Fixtures.
    Gas districts.
      Rules and regulations,
        §§11-50-401,
        11-50-402.
  Gas utility boards,
      §§11-50-460 to 11-50-47
    Accounting, §11-50-470.
    Bonds, surety.
      Depositories.
        Fixing of bonds
          required from
          depositories,
          §11-50-475.
      Official bonds of certain
        officers and
        employees,
        §11-50-468.
    Books and accounts.
      Accounting, §11-50-470
      Report to municipal
        governing body,
        §11-50-471.
    Compensation of member
      §11-50-465.
    Composition, §11-50-460.
    Construction.
      Expenditures for new
        construction to gas
        distribution system
        §11-50-472.
    Creation, §11-50-460.
    Depositories.
      Fixing of bonds require
        from depositories,
        §11-50-475.
    Disbursement of funds,
      §11-50-473.

MUNICIPAL
CORPORATIONS—Cont'd
Gas—Cont'd
Gas utility boards—Cont'd
Disposition of money
received from
operation of gas
distribution system,
§11-50-474.
Duties, §11-50-469.
Election of members,
§11-50-462.
Employees.
Bonds, surety,
§11-50-468.
Examination of books and
accounts, §11-50-470.
Expenditures.
New construction,
additions, etc., to gas
distribution systems,
§11-50-472.
Funds.
Disbursement,
§11-50-473.
Maintenance,
§11-50-473.
Impeachment of members,
§11-50-464.
Maintenance of funds,
§11-50-473.
Meetings, §11-50-467.
Oaths of members,
§11-50-463.
Officers.
Bonds, surety,
§11-50-468.
Election, §11-50-466.
Vacancies, §11-50-466.
Operation of gas
distribution system.
Disposition of money
received, §11-50-474.
Powers, §11-50-469.
Qualifications of members,
§11-50-461.
Record of proceedings,
§11-50-467.
Removal of members,
§11-50-464.
Reports.
Accounting, §11-50-470.
Annual report to
municipal governing
body, §11-50-471.
Terms of members,
§11-50-462.
Vacancies, §11-50-462.
Licenses.
Gas districts.
Levy and collection of
privilege license tax,
§11-50-413.
Schedules for gas
companies, §11-51-129.
Liens.
Gas districts.
Bond issues.
Properties, persons,
etc., subject to
liens, §11-50-408.
When liens effective,
§11-50-408.
Maintenance of systems.
Boards for operation of
water, sewer, gas and
electric systems,
§§11-50-310 to
11-50-324. See within
this heading, "Public
utilities."

MUNICIPAL
CORPORATIONS—Cont'd
Gas—Cont'd
Maintenance of systems
—Cont'd
Waterworks and sewer
boards, §§11-50-230 to
11-50-291. See within
this heading,
"Waterworks and
sewer boards."
Mayors.
Employment, salary, etc.,
as superintendent of
gas systems,
§§11-43-80, 11-50-16.
Mortgages and deeds of trust.
Gas districts.
Bond issues.
Properties, persons,
etc., subject to
mortgages,
§11-50-408.
Security for bonds as
to rights of
parties,
§11-50-407.
When mortgages
effective,
§11-50-408.
Operation of gas plants and
systems, §§11-50-260 to
11-50-273.
Ordinances.
Transfer of gas system
without elections,
§11-50-211.
Payment by municipalities
for services furnished by
system, §11-81-186.
Pipes.
Gas districts.
Rules and regulations,
§§11-50-401,
11-50-402.
Plants.
Acquisition, operation, etc.,
of gas plants and
systems.
General provisions,
§§11-50-260 to
11-50-273.
Sale, lease, etc., by
municipalities,
§§11-50-140 to
11-50-151. See within
this heading, "Public
utilities."
Pledge and collateral
security.
Gas districts.
Bond issues.
Properties, persons,
etc., subject to
pledges,
§11-50-408.
Security for bonds,
§11-50-407.
When pledges
effective,
§11-50-408.
Power districts, §§37-5-1 to
37-5-9.
See POWER DISTRICTS.

MUNICIPAL
CORPORATIONS—Cont'd
Gas—Cont'd
President of board of
commissioners.
Superintendent of gas
systems.
Employment as
superintendent,
§11-50-16.
Validation of prior
employment,
§11-50-16.
Properties of system.
Accounting, §11-81-188.
Public improvements
generally. See within
this heading, "Public
improvements."
Purchase of gas plants,
§§11-50-260 to 11-50-273.
Purchase of public utilities
generally, §§37-4-60 to
37-4-65.
See PUBLIC UTILITIES.
Quality.
Regulation, §11-50-1.
Rates.
Establishment, §11-81-184.
Regulation, §11-50-1.
State supervision or
regulation.
Not subject to,
§11-81-185.
Repair of systems.
Authorized, §11-81-161.
Resolutions.
Transfer of gas system
without elections,
§11-50-211.
Revenue bonds, §§11-81-160
to 11-81-190. See within
this heading, "Public
utilities."
Revenues.
Depository.
Designation, §11-81-183.
Disposition of gross
revenue account and
special funds,
§11-81-183.
Disposition of gross
revenues, §§11-81-181,
11-81-183.
Pledge of revenues,
§11-81-181.
Rules and regulations.
Gas districts, §§11-50-401
to 11-50-403.
Sale, lease, etc., of gas plants
by municipalities,
§§11-50-140 to 11-50-151.
See within this heading,
"Public utilities."
Superintendent of gas
systems.
Employment of mayor or
president of board of
commissioners as
superintendent,
§§11-43-80, 11-50-16.
Transfer of gas system
without elections,
§§11-50-210 to 11-50-213.
Article supplemental,
§11-50-213.
Authorization of
conveyance,
§11-50-211.
Conditions, §11-50-211.

MUNICIPAL
   CORPORATIONS—Cont'd
Gas—Cont'd
   Transfer of gas system
      without elections
      —Cont'd
      Conveyance authorized,
         §11-50-211.
      Definitions, §11-50-210.
      Implementation of article,
         §11-50-212.
      Ordinances, §11-50-211.
      Resolutions, §11-50-211.
      Terms, §11-50-211.
   Transfer of plants to boards
      organized to own plants,
      §§11-50-13, 11-50-14.
   Utility boards.
      Gas utility boards,
         §§11-50-460 to
         11-50-475.
   Waterworks and sewer
      boards.
      Acquisition, operation, etc.,
         of gas plants and
         systems, §§11-50-260
         to 11-50-273. See
         within this heading,
         "Waters and sewer
         boards."
Gifts.
   Class 5 municipalities.
      Mayor/commission/city
         manager form of
         government.
         Officers and employees.
            Acceptance of gifts
               from public
               utilities
               prohibited,
               §11-44E-183.
Golf courses.
   Public athletic boards,
      §§11-59-1 to 11-59-17.
      See within this heading,
      "Parks and recreation."
   Public improvement bonds.
      Certain revenue-producing
         undertakings,
         §§11-81-140 to
         11-81-150.
      See COUNTIES.
Government.
   Change in government.
      Extension of term of
         commissioner,
         §11-40-11.
      Holding of election after
         change in government,
         §11-40-6.
      When change in form of
         government takes
         effect, §11-40-11.
   Commission form of
      government, §§11-44-1 to
      11-44-162. See within
      this heading,
      "Commission form of
      government."
   Council. See within this
      heading, "Council."
   Expenses.
      Allowances for members of
         governing body,
         §11-40-14.
   Mayors. See within this
      heading, "Mayors."
   Vacancies.
      Governing bodies of class 5
         municipalities,
         §11-43-18.

MUNICIPAL
   CORPORATIONS—Cont'd
Governor.
   Municipal police.
      Employment within state
         by governor during
         riots, etc., §§36-21-20
         to 36-21-24.
      Order of governor.
         Refusal of municipal
            official to comply,
            §15-6-4.
Granaries.
   Public improvement bonds.
      Certain revenue-producing
         undertakings,
         §§11-81-140 to
         11-81-150.
      See COUNTIES.
Grants.
   Securities issued in
      anticipation of grants,
      §§11-64-1 to 11-64-7. See
      within this heading,
      "Securities issued in
      anticipation of grants.'"
   Special health care facility
      authorities, §11-62-16.
Graveyards, §§11-47-40 to
   11-47-74. See within this
   heading, "Cemeteries."
Group insurance for officers
   and employees.
   Retired employees.
      Health or medical
         insurance for retired
         employees, §11-91-8.
Gunpowder.
   Provision of building for
      storage, §11-47-12.
   Storing in city or town,
      §13A-11-224.
Gutters.
   Proper setting of gutters,
      etc., §11-47-140.
Handguns.
   Ordinances and resolutions.
      Subject matter of handguns
         reserved to state
         legislature, §11-45-1.1.
Handicapped persons.
   Bond issues.
      Public improvement bonds
         for certain revenue-
         producing
         undertakings,
         §§11-81-140 to
         11-81-150.
      See COUNTIES.
   Elections.
      Assistance to disabled
         electors, §§11-46-40,
         11-46-51, 11-46-111,
         11-46-122.
      Deception of disabled
         voters by marker, etc.,
         §§11-46-64, 11-46-135.
      False declaration
         requesting assistance,
         §11-46-138.
      Mayor-council form,
         §11-46-51.
      Assistance of disabled
         electors, §11-46-40.
      Voting machines,
         §11-46-51.
   Employment, §21-7-8.
   False declaration requesting
      assistance, §11-46-138.

MUNICIPAL
   CORPORATIONS—Cont'd
Handicapped persons
   —Cont'd
   Special health care facility
      authorities, §§11-62-1 to
      11-62-21. See within this
      heading, "Special health
      care facility authorities."
Harbors and ports.
   Alteration of channel of
      watercourse, §11-47-15.
   Bond issues.
      Construction of port
         facilities by class 1
         municipalities,
         §11-47-14.1.
   Channel of watercourse.
      Alteration of channel,
         §11-47-15.
   Construction, maintenance,
      etc., of wharves and
      buildings, §11-47-15.
   Construction of port facilities
      by class 1 municipalities,
      §11-47-14.1.
   Improvement of waterfronts,
      §11-47-14.
   Provision of wharves and
      landings, §11-47-14.
Hazards.
   Markers or lights on hazards
      §4-4-10.
Health.
   Appropriations by
      municipalities for public
      health work, §22-3-11.
   Cemeteries, §§11-47-40 to
      11-47-74. See within this
      heading, "Cemeteries."
   Certain county and local
      laws unaffected by title,
      §22-1-9.
   Codes.
      Adoption of technical codes
         by reference, §11-45-8.
   Conflicts between municipal
      and general health laws,
      §22-1-2.
   Maintenance of health,
      §11-47-130.
   Medical clinic boards,
      §§11-58-1 to 11-58-15.
      See within this heading,
      "Medical clinic boards."
   Morgues, §11-47-7.
   Powers as to health,
      §11-47-131.
   Sanitary regulations.
      Territorial operation of
         ordinances for
         enforcement,
         §11-40-10.
   State health department.
      Payment of health
         department claims out
         of municipal budgets,
         §22-3-12.
Health care authorities,
   §§22-21-310 to 22-21-356.
   See HEALTH CARE
   AUTHORITIES.
Health care service plan.
   License, privilege or other
      taxes by municipalities
      prohibited, §10-4-107.

MUNICIPAL
CORPORATIONS—Cont'd
Hearings.
Assessments for public
improvements.
Objections, §11-48-8.
Date for hearing,
§11-48-6.
Objections to assessments.
Conduct, §11-48-27.
Notice of hearing,
§11-48-23.
Subpoena of witnesses,
etc., §11-48-28.
Bond issues.
Validation, §6-6-753.
Class 5 municipalities.
Mayor/commission/city
manager form of
government.
Commission.
Power to hold public
hearing,
§11-44E-44.
Demolition of unsafe
structures, §11-40-32.
Dissolution.
Hearing on petition to
probate judge,
§11-41-22.
Historic preservation
commissions.
Changes in historic
properties or districts.
Certificate of
appropriateness,
§11-68-9.
Designation of historic
properties and
districts.
Proposed
recommendations,
§11-68-7.
Mayor/commission/city
manager form of
government.
Commission.
Power to hold public
hearing, §11-44E-44.
Reduction of corporate limits.
Show cause hearing why
proposed boundary
should not be
established,
§11-42-202.
Weeds.
Abatement of weeds.
Class 2 municipalities.
Cost of abatement,
§11-67-8.
Notice of public
hearing, §11-67-4.
Procedure generally,
§11-67-5.
Class 5 municipalities.
Cost of abatement,
§11-67-27.
Notice of public
hearing,
§11-67-23.
Procedure generally,
§11-67-24.
Highway department.
General provisions.
See HIGHWAYS.
Highways.
Architectural review boards.
Applicability of provisions
to highways,
§11-68-15.

MUNICIPAL
CORPORATIONS—Cont'd
Highways—Cont'd
Closing and vacating streets,
alleys and highways,
§§23-4-1 to 23-4-20.
See HIGHWAYS.
General provisions. See
within this heading,
"Streets."
Historic preservation
commission.
Applicability of provisions
to highways,
§11-68-15.
Interstate highway system.
Controlled access facilities,
§§23-3-1 to 23-3-8.
See HIGHWAYS.
Municipal connecting link
roads, §§23-1-110 to
23-1-113.
Resolutions, bylaws or
ordinances granting
franchises for use of
streets, etc., §§11-44-33
to 11-44-35, 11-44-88.
See within this heading,
"Commission form of
government."
Rights of way.
Acquisition.
When deemed necessary
by director of
highways, §23-1-45.
Streets.
Designation as part of
state highways,
§23-1-40.
General provisions. See
within this heading,
"Streets."
Historical preservation
authorities.
Loans, sales, etc., of money,
property, etc., by
municipal corporations,
§41-10-146.
Historical research.
Authorization to undertake,
§16-42-1.
Contracts with historical
corporations, etc.,
authorized, §16-42-3.
Funds.
Use of municipal funds,
§16-42-2.
Historic Blakeley authority.
Appropriation, §41-10-178.
Construction and
maintenance of roads
and other public
facilities.
Authorized, §41-10-178.
Historic preservation
commissions.
Actions.
Injunctions and damages,
§11-68-12.
Appeals.
Changes in historic
properties or districts.
Certificate of
appropriateness,
§11-68-10.
Bridges.
Applicability of provisions
to, §11-68-15.
Bylaws, §11-68-3.

MUNICIPAL
CORPORATIONS—Cont'd
Historic preservation
commissions—Cont'd
Changes in historic
properties or districts.
Certificate of
appropriateness.
Applications, §11-68-9.
Denial, §11-68-11.
Appeal, §11-68-10.
Reconsideration,
§11-68-11.
Expedited procedure,
§11-68-9.
Issuance, §11-68-11.
Required, §11-68-9.
Composition, §11-68-3.
Designation of historic
properties and districts.
Notice, §11-68-8.
Recommendations.
Criteria, §11-68-6.
Hearing, §11-68-7.
Duties, §11-68-5.
Establishment, §11-68-2.
Expenses of members.
Reimbursement, §11-68-3.
Federal provisions.
Applicability, §11-68-15.
Hearings.
Changes in historic
properties or districts.
Certificate of
appropriateness,
§11-68-9.
Designation of historic
properties and
districts.
Proposed
recommendations,
§11-68-7.
Highways.
Applicability of provisions
to highways,
§11-68-15.
Historic properties and
districts.
Changes.
Certificate of
appropriateness,
§§11-68-9 to
11-68-11.
Designation, §§11-68-6 to
11-68-8.
Meetings, §11-68-3.
Nomination of members,
§11-68-3.
Nonprofit agency, §11-68-4.
Notice.
Designation of historic
properties and
districts, §11-68-8.
Number of members,
§11-68-3.
Officers, §11-68-3.
Ordinances.
Establishment of
commission, §11-68-2.
Violations of ordinances.
Actions for injunctions
and damages,
§11-68-12.
Personnel, §11-68-3.
Powers, §11-68-5.
Preexisting commissions.
Effect of provisions on,
§11-68-14.
Purpose of provisions,
§11-68-1.

MUNICIPAL
   CORPORATIONS—Cont'd
Historic preservation
   commissions—Cont'd
Qualifications of members,
   §11-68-3.
Recommendations.
   Designation of historic
      properties and
      districts, §11-68-6.
   Hearings, §11-68-7.
Removal of members,
   §11-68-3.
Reports, §11-68-3.
Rules of procedure, §11-68-3.
Status.
   Nonprofit agency, §11-68-4.
Streets.
   Applicability of provisions
      to streets, §11-68-15.
Taxation.
   Exemption from taxation,
      §11-68-4.
Terms of members, §11-68-3.
Vacancies, §11-68-3.
Holidays.
Elections.
   Commission form.
      Effect of legal holidays,
         §11-46-91.
   Mayor-council form.
      Effect of legal holidays,
         §11-46-20.
Horse racing.
Class 1 municipalities,
   §§11-65-1 to 11-65-47.
See HORSE RACING.
Hospitals.
General provisions.
   See HOSPITALS.
Public hospitals, §§11-95-1 to
   11-95-21.
See HOSPITALS.
Hotels, inns and other
   transient lodging places.
Acquisition of projects,
   §§11-54-140 to 11-54-153.
Additional powers of
   municipalities,
   §11-54-142.
Bond issues.
   Execution, §11-54-143.
   Exemption from
      taxation, §11-54-150.
   Financing project,
      §11-54-143.
   Legal investments,
      §11-54-149.
   Notice not required,
      §11-54-152.
   Not indebtedness of
      municipality,
      §11-54-143.
   Payment, §11-54-143.
   Sale, §11-54-143.
   Security for bonds,
      §11-54-144.
   Use of proceeds,
      §11-54-147.
Competitive bidding.
   Exemption, §11-54-153.
Construction of article,
   §11-54-151.
Contributions by
   municipalities.
   No payment out of
      general funds,
      §11-54-148.
Costs of acquiring project,
   §11-54-147.
Definitions, §11-54-140.

MUNICIPAL
   CORPORATIONS—Cont'd
Hotels, inns and other
   transient lodging places
   —Cont'd
Acquisition of projects
   —Cont'd
   Investments.
      Bonds made legal
         investments,
         §11-54-149.
   Leases, §11-54-145.
   Legislative intent,
      §11-54-141.
   Liberal construction of
      article, §11-54-141.
   Mortgages.
      Notice not required,
         §11-54-152.
   Notice.
      Sale or issuance of bond,
         §11-54-152.
   Refunding bonds.
      Authorized, §11-54-146.
      Legal investments,
         §11-54-149.
      Use of proceeds from
         sale, §11-54-147.
   Security for bonds,
      §11-54-144.
   Taxation.
      Bonds exempt from
         taxation, §11-54-150.
Industrial development
   boards.
   Ad valorem taxes.
      Hotels and motor inns
         built under act not
         exempt from,
         §11-54-96.1.
Operation of hotels and
   related facilities.
   Class 1 municipalities and
      certain public
      corporations,
      §11-40-19.
   Hotel management
      contracts, §11-40-20.
Housing.
Alienation of certain public
   improvements by
   political subdivisions,
   §§35-4-410 to 35-4-412.
See HOUSING.
Authorities, §§24-1-20 to
   24-1-45.
See HOUSING
   AUTHORITIES.
Codes.
   Adoption of technical codes
      by reference, §11-45-8.
Discrimination by zoning
   regulation.
   Prohibited, §11-52-75.
Minimum housing standards
   and regulation of unsafe
   buildings, §§11-53-1 to
   11-53-4.
Abatement of nuisances.
   Power not impaired,
      §11-53-3.
Construction of chapter,
   §11-53-4.
Injunctions.
   Availability, §11-53-3.
Legislative declarations,
   §11-53-1.
Nuisances.
   Power to abate not
      impaired, §11-53-3.

MUNICIPAL
   CORPORATIONS—Cont'd
Housing—Cont'd
Minimum housing standards
   and regulation of unsafe
   buildings—Cont'd
   Ordinances regulating use,
      repair, maintenance,
      etc., of domiciles,
      §11-53-2.
Redevelopment projects,
   §§24-2-1 to 24-2-10.
See REDEVELOPMENT
   PROJECTS.
Urban renewal projects,
   §§24-3-1 to 24-3-9.
See URBAN RENEWAL
   PROJECTS.
Zoning.
   Discrimination prohibited,
      §11-52-75.
   Mentally retarded or
      mentally ill persons.
      Regulation as to housing
         in multi-family
         zones, §11-52-75.1.
   Regulation as to housing of
      different classes of
      inhabitants in
      residential districts,
      §11-52-75.
Housing authorities,
   §§24-1-20 to 24-1-45.
See HOUSING
   AUTHORITIES.
Immunity.
Airports.
   Municipal immunity from
      liability for negligence,
      §4-4-4.
Civil defense activities.
   Municipal immunity from
      liability for negligence,
      §31-9-16.
Claims for and against
   municipalities. See
   within this heading,
   "Claims for and against
   municipalities."
Fire departments.
   Operation beyond corporate
      limits and police
      jurisdiction,
      §11-43-141.
Negligence of agents,
   §§11-47-190 to 11-47-192.
Impeachment.
Municipal officers,
   §§11-43-161 to 11-43-163;
   Const. Ala., art. VII,
   §175. See within this
   heading, "Officers."
Improvement authorities.
General provisions, §§39-7-1
   to 39-7-34.
See PUBLIC WORKS.
Improvements.
Assessments for public
   improvements, §§11-48-1
   to 11-48-106. See within
   this heading,
   "Assessments for public
   improvements."
Capital improvement,
   §§11-66-1 to 11-66-7. See
   within this heading,
   "Capital improvement."

MUNICIPAL
CORPORATIONS—Cont'd
Improvements—Cont'd
Class 5 municipalities.
Mayor/commission/city
manager form of
government.
Commission.
Power to impose
improvement
assessments,
§11-44E-44.
Succession of
government.
Continuance of public
improvements,
§11-44E-145.
Council-manager form of
government.
Completion of public
improvements,
§11-43A-39.
Public improvements
generally. See within
this heading, "Public
improvements."
Incorporation, §§11-41-1 to
11-41-8.
Attempted incorporations.
Validation, §11-41-8.
Authority, §11-41-1.
Census enumeration of
inhabitants, §11-41-4.
Certificate of incorporation,
§§11-60-4 to 11-60-6.
Acknowledgment, §11-60-4.
Amendment, §11-60-6.
Approval, §11-60-5.
Contents, §11-60-4.
Examination, §11-60-5.
Execution, §11-60-4.
Filing, §11-60-5.
Recordation, §11-60-5.
Costs, §11-41-6.
Councilmen, §§11-41-5 to
11-41-7.
Dormant municipalities.
Reinstatement of corporate
organization, §11-41-7.
Elections, §§11-41-2 to
11-41-6.
Ballots.
Provision and form of
ballot, §11-41-3.
Conduct of election,
§§11-41-3, 11-41-5.
Costs of elections, §11-41-6.
Mayor and councilmen.
Conduct of election,
§11-41-5.
Notice of election,
§11-41-5.
Ordering election,
§11-41-5.
Qualifications for voting,
§11-41-5.
Record of elections,
§11-41-6.
Result of election,
§11-41-6.
Setting aside, etc., of
elections, §11-41-6.
Notice of election, §11-41-2.
Ordering election,
§11-41-2.
Qualifications for voting,
§11-41-3.
Record of elections,
§11-41-6.
Required for incorporation,
§11-41-1.

MUNICIPAL
CORPORATIONS—Cont'd
Incorporation—Cont'd
Elections—Cont'd
Results.
Certification of result to
probate judge,
§11-41-4.
Fee for filing order, §11-41-4.
Islands, §11-41-1.
Mayor and councilmen,
§§11-41-5 to 11-41-7.
Appointment.
Reinstatement of
corporate
organization of
dormant
municipalities,
§11-41-7.
Election.
Conduct of election,
§11-41-5.
Costs of elections,
§11-41-6.
Issuance and recordation
of order approving
report and election
result, §11-41-6.
Notice of election,
§11-41-5.
Ordering of election,
§11-41-5.
Qualifications for voting,
§11-41-5.
Record of elections,
§11-41-6.
Report of result,
§11-41-6.
Result.
Report to probate
judge, §11-41-6.
Setting aside, etc., of
elections, §11-41-6.
Reinstatement of corporate
organization of
dormant
municipalities.
Appointment of mayor
and councilmen,
§11-41-7.
Vacancies, §11-41-6.
Order of incorporation.
Fee for filing, §11-41-4.
Filing, §11-41-4.
Issuance, §11-41-4.
Petition to probate judge
for order, §11-41-1.
Recordation, §11-41-4.
Petition to probate judge for
order of incorporation,
§11-41-1.
Procedural irregularities.
Validation of prior
attempted
incorporations,
§11-41-8.
Record of proceedings,
§11-41-6.
Reinstatement of corporate
organization of dormant
municipalities, §11-41-7.
Reports.
Election of mayor and
councilmen.
Results, §11-41-6.
Special, private or local laws
prohibited, Const. Ala.,
art. IV, §104.

MUNICIPAL
CORPORATIONS—Cont'd
Incorporation—Cont'd
Validation.
Prior attempted
incorporations,
§11-41-8.
Indemnification.
Employees, §11-47-24.
Indigent persons.
Counties.
Establishment, aid, etc., of
poorhouses, etc., in
counties, §11-47-134.
Hospitals.
Appropriation for care of
sick, etc., §11-47-133.
Industrial development
boards, §§11-54-80 to
11-54-123.
Agreements.
Liability of municipalities
upon agreements,
§11-54-92.
Ancillary facilities,
§§11-54-120 to 11-54-123.
Construction and
interpretation,
§11-54-121.
Definitions, §11-54-120.
Legislative intent,
§11-54-121.
Powers, §11-54-122.
Cumulative, §11-54-123.
Board of directors, §11-54-86.
Meetings, §11-54-87.
Bond issues, §§11-54-89 to
11-54-92.
Default.
Remedies, §11-54-90.
Delivery, §11-54-89.
Denominations, §11-54-89.
Execution, §11-54-89.
Exemption from taxation,
§11-54-96.
Form, §11-54-89.
Interest, §11-54-89.
Security for payment,
§11-54-90.
Liability of municipalities
upon bonds, §11-54-92.
Maturity, §11-54-89.
Mortgages and deeds of
trust.
Security for payment,
§11-54-90.
Payment.
Security, §11-54-90.
Preissuance procedures,
§§8-6-110 to 8-6-122.
See INDUSTRIAL
REVENUE BONDS.
Redemption, §11-54-89.
Refunding of bonds,
§11-54-89.
Remedies upon default,
§11-54-90.
Sale, §11-54-89.
Security for payment,
§11-54-90.
Temporary revenue bonds,
§11-54-91.
Terms, §11-54-89.
Borrowing money for
temporary use,
§11-54-91.
Certificates of incorporation,
§§11-54-82 to 11-54-85,
11-54-95.
Chapter cumulative,
§11-54-101.

MUNICIPAL CORPORATIONS—Cont'd

Industrial development boards—Cont'd

Competitive bid laws.
Exemption, §11-54-98.
Construction of article, §§11-54-81, 11-54-100.
Definitions, §11-54-80.
Directors, §11-54-86.
Meetings, §11-54-87.
Dissolution.
Authority, §11-54-94.
Procedure, §11-54-94.
Vesting of title to funds and properties in municipalities, §11-54-94.
Earnings.
Disposition of net earnings, §11-54-93.
Exemption from taxation, §11-54-96.
Exemption from taxation, §11-54-96.
Hotels and motor inns not exempt, §11-54-96.1.
Funds.
Dissolution.
Vesting of title to funds in municipalities upon dissolution, §11-54-94.
Hotels, inns and other transient lodging places.
Ad valorem taxes required of, §11-54-96.1.
Incorporation.
Application for authority to incorporate, §11-54-82.
Attempted incorporation.
Validation, §11-54-99.
Certificate of incorporation, §§11-54-82 to 11-54-85, 11-54-95.
Acknowledgment, §§11-54-82, 11-54-83.
Amendment, §11-54-85.
Approval, §11-54-84.
Contents, §11-54-83.
Examination, §11-54-84.
Execution, §§11-54-82, 11-54-83.
Filing, §§11-54-82, 11-54-84.
Recordation, §11-54-84.
Exemption from fees or taxes, §11-54-95.
Resolution, §11-54-82.
Validation of attempted incorporation, §11-54-99.
Interest laws.
Exemption, §11-54-97.
Legislative intent, §11-54-81.
Location of projects, §11-54-87.
Mortgages and deeds of trust.
Bond issues.
Security for payment, §11-54-90.
Liability of municipalities upon obligations of boards, §11-54-92.
Obligations.
Liability of municipalities, §11-54-92.
Operation of projects, §11-54-87.
Pollution control facilities.
Powers of board, §11-54-88.

MUNICIPAL CORPORATIONS—Cont'd

Industrial development boards—Cont'd

Powers of boards, §§11-54-87, 11-54-88.
Projects.
Location, §11-54-87.
Operation, §11-54-87.
Property.
Dissolution.
Vesting of title to properties, §11-54-94.
Exemption from taxation, §11-54-96.
Recordation of documents.
Without payment of taxes or certain fees, §11-54-95.
Resolutions.
Authorizing incorporation, §11-54-82.
Temporary loans, §11-54-91.
Usury.
Exemption from usury laws, §11-54-97.

Industrial development corporations.

Occupational license taxes, §10-4-144.

Industrial parks.

Acquisition and development of lands, §§11-54-1 to 11-54-4.
Authorized, §11-54-2.
Definitions, §11-54-1.
Sale of lands comprising industrial parks.
Authorization and procedure, §11-54-3.
Binding option agreements, §11-54-4.
County industrial parks.
Contracts with municipalities for services, §11-23-6.
Not subject to annexation or police jurisdiction of municipalities, §11-23-6.
Sale of lands comprising industrial parks.
Authorization and procedure, §11-54-3.
Binding option agreements, §11-54-4.

Industrial projects.

Bonds for enlargement, etc., of muncipally-owned projects, Const. Ala., amd. 228.

Industry.

Annexation.
Exemption of industrial plants from taxation, §11-42-59.
Promotion.
Appropriations, §11-47-11.
Generally, §§11-54-20 to 11-54-32. See within this heading, "Promotion of industry, trade and pollution control."

MUNICIPAL CORPORATIONS—Cont'd

Initiative and referendum.

Commission form of government.
Optional form A.
Ordinances by initiative and referendum, §11-44-105.

Injunctions.

Enjoining or restraining enforcement of ordinance, §6-6-502.
Nuisances.
Public nuisances.
Right of action to enjoin, §§6-5-122, 11-47-118.

Injuries.

Liability for negligence of agents, etc., §§11-47-190 to 11-47-192.

Insects.

Control of conditions favorable to harboring insects, §11-47-140.

Inspections.

Charges for inspections, §11-43-59.
Dairies, §11-47-139.
Electric wiring.
Charges for inspection, §11-43-59.
Food.
Charges for inspection, §11-43-59.
Impure, adulterated, etc., food, etc., §11-47-136.
Jails, §§11-47-7, 11-47-8.
General provisions, §§14-6-80 to 14-6-109.
See JAILS.
Meat.
Charges for inspection, §11-43-59.
Inspections for other municipalities, §11-47-139.
Motor vehicles.
Municipal testing stations, §§32-18-1 to 32-18-8.
See MOTOR VEHICLES.
Vegetables.
Charges for inspection, §11-43-59.
Weights and measures, §11-43-59.

Insurance.

Accident insurance.
Group insurance for officers and employees, §§11-91-1 to 11-91-8.
Class 5 municipalities.
Mayor/commission/city manager form of government.
City managers.
Eligibility for group insurance, §11-44E-97.
Companies.
License schedules, §§11-51-120 to 11-51-131. See within this heading, "Licenses."
Employees.
Group insurance for employees, §§11-91-1 to 11-91-8.

**MUNICIPAL
 CORPORATIONS**—Cont'd
Insurance—Cont'd
Group insurance for officers
 and employees, §§11-91-1
 to 11-91-8.
Amount of insurance.
 Determination, §11-91-3.
 Requirements, §11-91-2.
Appropriation of funds.
 Implementation of
 provisions of
 chapter, §11-91-6.
Authorization of provision
 by governing bodies,
 §11-91-1.
Class 5 municipalities.
 Mayor/commission/city
 manager form of
 government.
 Eligibility and
 participation of
 city manager in
 group insurance
 plan, §11-44E-97.
Contracting for policies,
 §11-91-2.
Coverage of policies.
 Requirements as to
 coverage, §11-91-2.
Eligibility for insurance.
 Determination, §11-91-3.
Implementation of
 provisions of chapter.
 Appropriation of funds
 for implementation,
 §11-91-6.
Kind of insurance.
 Determination, §11-91-3.
Health or medical
 insurance for retired
 employees, §11-91-8.
Mayor/commission/city
 manager form of
 government.
 Eligibility of city
 manager for group
 insurance,
 §11-44E-97.
Nature of insurance.
 Determination, §11-91-3.
Payment of premiums,
 §11-91-4.
Manner of paying,
 §11-91-3.
Validation of premiums,
 §11-91-7.
Persons to be insured.
 Determination, §11-91-3.
Policies.
 Amounts of insurance.
 Determination,
 §11-91-3.
 Requirements,
 §11-91-2.
 Contracting for policies,
 §11-91-2.
 Coverage of policies.
 Requirements as to
 coverage, §11-91-2.
 Purchase of policies,
 §11-91-2.
 Validation of policies
 issued prior to
 August 16, 1947,
 §11-91-7.
Premiums.
 Manner of payment,
 §11-91-3.

**MUNICIPAL
 CORPORATIONS**—Cont'd
Insurance—Cont'd
Group insurance for officers
 and employees—Cont'd
Premiums—Cont'd
 Payment, §11-91-4.
 Manner of payment,
 §11-91-3.
 Validation, §11-91-7.
 Return of premiums,
 §11-91-5.
 Validation of premiums
 paid, §11-91-7.
Provision by governing
 bodies authorized,
 §11-91-1.
Purchase of policies,
 §11-91-2.
Return of premiums,
 §11-91-5.
Validation of policies
 issued prior to August
 16, 1947, §11-91-7.
Health insurance.
 Group insurance for
 officers and employees,
 §§11-91-1 to 11-91-8.
Liability insurance.
 Employees.
 Authority to contract for,
 §11-47-24.
License schedules,
 §§11-51-120 to 11-51-131.
 See within this heading,
 "Licenses."
Life insurance.
 Group insurance for
 officers and employees,
 §§11-91-1 to 11-91-8.
Managers.
 Mayor/commission/city
 manager form of
 government.
 Eligibility for group
 insurance,
 §11-44E-97.
Mayor/commission/city
 manager form of
 government.
 City manager.
 Eligibility for group
 insurance,
 §11-44E-97.
Officers.
 Group insurance for
 officers and employees,
 §§11-91-1 to 11-91-8.
Interest.
Annual appropriations for
 interest on indebtedness,
 §11-43-57.
Delinquent property taxes,
 §11-51-2.
Maximum rates of interest.
 Exemption of bonds, notes,
 etc., of municipalities,
 §8-8-7.
Payment of interest on
 warrants not paid for
 lack of funds, §11-43-121.
Water supply and
 waterworks.
 Customer security deposits.
 Payment of interest in
 class 1
 municipalities,
 §11-50-17.
Interstate commerce.
Licensing of persons engaged
 in, §11-51-90.

**MUNICIPAL
 CORPORATIONS**—Cont'd
Investigations.
Class 5 municipalities.
 Mayor/commission/city
 manager form of
 government.
 Commission, §11-44E-44.
 Investigations as to
 municipal affairs,
 §11-44E-181.
Council-manager form of
 government, §11-43A-47.
Investments.
Securities issued in
 anticipation of grants.
 Legal investment,
 §11-64-6.
Sinking funds, §§11-81-15,
 11-81-19 to 11-81-26. See
 within this heading,
 "Sinking funds."
Islands.
Incorporation, §11-41-1.
Jails.
Erection, §11-47-7.
Establishment, §11-47-7.
General provisions.
 See JAILS.
Inspection, §14-6-80.
 General provisions,
 §§14-6-80 to 14-6-109.
 See JAILS.
Maintenance, §11-47-7.
Regulations, §11-47-7.
Removal of prisoners to
 another jail, §11-47-8.
**Joint tenants and tenants in
 common.**
Assessments for public
 improvements,
 §§11-48-100 to 11-48-106.
 See within this heading,
 "Assessments for public
 improvements."
Judgments.
Assessments for public
 improvements,
 §§11-48-100 to 11-48-106.
 See within this heading,
 "Assessments for public
 improvements."
Bond issues.
 Validation, §§6-6-753 to
 6-6-755, 11-81-223,
 11-81-224.
Judicial notice.
Class I municipalities.
 Ordinances, §11-45-11.
Jukeboxes.
Licenses, §§11-51-98,
 11-51-100.
Regulation and control,
 §11-51-100.
Jurisdiction.
Annexation.
 Cities of twenty-five
 thousand or more.
 Jurisdiction of city
 governing body over
 annexed territory,
 §11-42-72.
Police jurisdiction,
 §§11-40-10, 11-47-22.
County industrial parks
 not subject to,
 §11-23-6.
Reduction of corporate limits,
 §11-42-212.

MUNICIPAL
  CORPORATIONS—Cont'd
Jurisdiction—Cont'd
Subdivisions.
  Exclusive jurisdiction of
    planning commission
    as to subdivision plats,
    §11-52-36.
  Territorial jurisdiction of
    planning commissions,
    §11-52-30.
Labor.
  Fire departments.
    Right to join labor
      organizations,
      §11-43-143.
Landings.
  Provision of landings,
    §11-47-14.
Leases.
  Electric, gas or waterworks
    plants by municipalities,
    §§11-50-140 to 11-50-151.
    See within this heading,
    "Public utilities."
  Post-office projects,
    §§11-55-2, 11-55-10,
    11-55-13.
Legislative reference service,
  §§29-7-1 to 29-7-7.
  See LEGISLATURE.
Legislature.
  Bills.
    Annexation.
      Bill to contain accurate
        description of
        territory and plat or
        map, §11-42-6.
    General laws applying to
      single municipality.
      Notice of intention to
        enact.
        Required, §11-40-13.
Letters of credit.
  Security for bonds, notes,
    etc., §11-80-7.
Levees.
  Assessments for public
    improvements,
    §11-48-16.
Liability.
  Airports.
    Municipal immunity,
      §4-4-4.
  Civil defense activities.
    Municipal immunity,
      §31-9-16.
  Claims for and against
    municipalities. See
    within this heading,
    "Claims for and against
    municipalities."
  Commission form of
    government.
    Continuation of liabilities,
      §11-44-26.
  Fire departments.
    Operation beyond corporate
      limits and police
      jurisdiction,
      §§11-43-141,
      11-43-142.
  Negligence of agents, etc.,
    §§11-47-190 to 11-47-912.
Libraries.
  Authorities.
    Public library authorities,
      §§11-57-1 to 11-57-26.
  Boards.
    Library boards.
      See LIBRARIES.

MUNICIPAL
  CORPORATIONS—Cont'd
Libraries—Cont'd
Bond issues.
  Public library authorities,
    §§11-57-11 to 11-57-21.
Establishment of free public
  libraries.
  Powers of municipalities,
    §11-90-1.
Interstate library compact.
  Restrictions as to entry
    into agreements by
    municipalities,
    §41-8-23.
Joint library service.
  Establishment and
    maintenance, §11-90-4.
Library boards, §§11-90-2,
  11-90-3.
  See LIBRARIES.
Maintenance of free public
  libraries.
  Powers of municipalities,
    §11-90-1.
Public library authorities,
  §§11-57-1 to 11-57-26.
  Board of directors,
    §11-57-6.
  Bond issues, §§11-57-11 to
    11-57-21.
    Authority for issuance,
      §11-57-11.
      Notice of resolution
        authorizing,
        §11-57-12.
      Recital as to authority
        for issuance,
        §11-57-12.
    Default.
      Remedies, §11-57-20.
    Delivery, §11-57-13.
    Denominations,
      §11-57-11.
    Disposition of proceeds
      from sale, §11-57-16.
    Execution, §11-57-13.
    Exemption from
      taxation, §11-57-25.
    Form, §11-57-11.
    Interest.
      Security for payment,
        §§11-57-11,
        11-57-15.
    Investment in bonds.
      Executors and
        administrators,
        §11-57-19.
      Fiduciaries, §11-57-19.
      Guardians, §11-57-19.
      Insurance companies,
        §11-57-19.
      Municipalities,
        §11-57-18.
      Savings banks,
        §11-57-19.
      Trustees, §11-57-19.
    Liability of state or
      municipalities on
      bonds, §11-57-21.
    Limitation of actions,
      §11-57-12.
    Maturity, §11-57-11.
    Negotiability, §11-57-14.
    Payment.
      Remedies upon default,
        §11-57-20.

MUNICIPAL
  CORPORATIONS—Cont'd
Libraries—Cont'd
Public library authorities
  —Cont'd
  Bond issues—Cont'd
    Payment—Cont'd
      Security for payment
        of principal and
        interest,
        §§11-57-11,
        11-57-15.
    Proceeds from sale.
      Disposition, §11-57-16.
    Redemption, §11-57-11.
    Refunding bonds,
      §11-57-17.
    Remedies upon default,
      §11-57-20.
    Sale, §11-57-11.
      Disposition of proceeds,
        §11-57-16.
    Security for payment,
      §§11-57-11, 11-57-15.
    State.
      Liability of state on
        bonds, §11-57-21.
    Terms, §11-57-11.
    Validity of proceedings
      for issuance.
      Limitation of actions,
        §11-57-12.
  Construction of chapter,
    §§11-57-2, 11-57-26.
  Definitions, §11-57-1.
  Directors.
    Board of directors,
      §11-57-6.
  Dissolution of authorities,
    §11-57-24.
  Eminent domain, §11-57-9.
  Executors and
    administrators.
    Bond issues.
      Investment in bonds,
        §11-57-19.
  Exemption from taxation of
    properties bonds, etc.,
    §11-57-25.
  Fiduciaries.
    Investment in bonds,
      §11-57-19.
  Funds.
    Investment of funds of
      authorities,
      §11-57-22.
  Guardians.
    Investment in bonds,
      §11-57-19.
  Incorporation.
    Application for authority
      to form, §11-57-3.
    Certificate of
      incorporation.
      Acknowledgment,
        §11-57-4.
      Approval by governing
        body, §11-57-4.
      Contents, §11-57-4.
      Execution, §11-57-4.
      Filing, §11-57-5.
      Recordation, §11-57-5.
    Procedure, §11-57-3.
    Resolution, §11-57-3.
    Subsequent formation of
      other authorities by
      same municipalities
      not precluded,
      §11-57-24.

MUNICIPAL
CORPORATIONS—Cont'd
Libraries—Cont'd
Public library authorities
—Cont'd
Insurance companies.
Investment in bonds,
§11-57-19.
Investment of funds of
authorities, §11-57-22.
Lease agreements.
Exemption from
taxation, §11-57-25.
Projects, §11-57-10.
Remedies upon default,
§11-57-20.
Legislative intent,
§11-57-2.
Obligations.
Liability of state or
municipalities,
§11-57-21.
Officers, §11-57-7.
Powers, §11-57-8.
Property.
Conveyances to
authorities by
municipalities,
§11-57-23.
Exemption from
taxation, §11-57-25.
Vesting of title to assets
or properties in
municipalities upon
dissolution,
§11-57-24.
Records.
Proceedings of board of
directors, §11-57-6.
Resolutions.
Authorizing
incorporation,
§11-57-3.
Bond issues.
Notice of resolution
authorizing,
§11-57-12.
Savings banks.
Investment in bonds,
§11-57-19.
State.
Liability of state on
bonds and
obligations of
authorities,
§11-57-21.
Trustees.
Investment in bonds,
§11-57-19.
Special property tax for
library purposes, Const.
Ala., amd. 269.
Licenses, §§11-51-90 to
11-51-207.
Amount of license tax.
Licenses taken out after
July 1, §11-51-92.
Proration for licenses
taken out after July
1, §11-51-92.
Amusements, §§11-51-102,
11-51-104.
Revocation of licenses,
§11-51-103.
Athletic games, §11-51-104.
Attachment.
Collection of license taxes.
Equitable attachment,
§11-51-160.
Auction sales, §11-51-97.

MUNICIPAL
CORPORATIONS—Cont'd
Licenses—Cont'd
Authorization of licensing,
§11-51-90.
Banks.
Schedule, §11-51-130.
Billiard tables, §11-51-102.
Annexation.
Territory exempt from
taxation, §11-42-81.
Issuance prohibited where
billiard room
prohibited by
ordinance, §34-6-35.
Revocation, §11-51-103.
Bond issues.
Pledge of revenues,
§§11-81-16, 11-81-18.
Bonds, surety.
Injunction against
delinquent business.
Temporary injunctions,
§§11-51-154 to
11-51-156.
Bowling alleys, §11-51-102.
Revocation, §11-51-103.
Carriages, §11-51-101.
Carts, §11-51-101.
Classification in certain
cities, §11-51-94.
Clerks.
Issuance of licenses,
§11-43-103.
Collection of license taxes,
§§11-51-150 to 11-51-185.
Accounting as to tax due,
§11-51-152.
Attachment.
Equitable attachment,
§11-51-160.
Cumulative provisions,
§11-51-161.
Duties of department,
§11-51-185.
Equitable attachment,
§11-51-160.
Injunction against
delinquent business.
Appeals, §§11-51-153,
11-51-157.
Bond to dissolve
temporary injunctive
relief.
Amount, §11-51-154.
Effect as security for
judgment and
costs upon final
hearing,
§§11-51-154,
11-51-155.
Execution, §11-51-154.
Forfeiture, §11-51-156.
Issuance of execution,
§11-51-156.
Dissolution of injunction
upon appeal,
§11-51-153.
Bond to dissolve,
§§11-51-154 to
11-51-156.
Entry of judgment,
§11-51-152.
Filing petition for
injunction,
§11-51-150.
Granting, §11-51-151.
Hearings, §11-51-151.
Notice of filing of
petition for,
§11-51-151.

MUNICIPAL
CORPORATIONS—Cont'd
Licenses—Cont'd
Collection of license taxes
—Cont'd
Injunction against
delinquent business
—Cont'd
Reinstatement of
injunction when
judgment reversed,
§11-51-153.
Temporary injunctive
relief.
Bond to dissolve,
§§11-51-154 to
11-51-156.
Liens, §11-51-96.
Enforcement not to
constitute waiver of
rights as to
respondent's bond,
§11-51-159.
Limitation of actions,
§6-2-35.
Outside corporate limits,
§11-51-91.
Pending actions.
Effect upon institution of
subsequent action
becoming due after
institution of prior
action, §11-51-158.
Provisions of division
cumulative,
§11-51-161.
State department of
revenue, §§11-51-180
to 11-51-185.
Attorneys at law.
Employment of special
counsel,
§11-51-184.
Authority of department,
§11-51-182.
Certification of taxes
collected, §11-51-183.
Charge for collection,
§11-51-183.
Disposition of taxes
collected, §11-51-183.
Duties of department,
§11-51-182.
Inspection of reports by
municipal governing
body, §11-51-181.
Ordinance levying tax to
be collected.
When amendment
effective,
§11-51-185.
Prerequisites for
collection,
§11-51-180.
Reports.
Distribution,
§11-51-182.
Inspection by
governing body,
§11-51-181.
Preparation,
§11-51-182.
Special counsel.
Employment,
§11-51-184.
Time of collection,
§11-51-181.
Companies.
Schedule, §§11-51-120 to
11-51-131.

MUNICIPAL
    CORPORATIONS—Cont'd
Licenses—Cont'd
  Delinquent taxes.
    Collection, §§11-51-150 to
      11-51-185.
  Electric companies.
    Schedule, §11-51-129.
  Exemptions from licenses.
    Disabled veterans,
      §40-12-343.
    Veterans of World War II,
      §40-12-373.
  Express companies.
    Schedule, §11-51-126.
  Failure to obtain.
    Engaging in business
      without license
      unlawful, §11-51-93.
  Farmers.
    Municipalities not to
      charge farmers for sale
      etc., of farm products,
      §11-51-105.
  Ferries.
    See FERRIES.
  Firearms.
    Revocation of licenses of
      places of sale,
      §11-51-103.
  Gas companies.
    Schedules, §11-51-129.
  Gas districts.
    Levy and collection of
      privilege license tax by
      certain municipalities,
      §11-50-413.
  Health care service plans.
    License taxes by
      municipalities
      prohibited, §10-4-107.
  Industrial development
    corporations, §10-4-144.
  Insurance companies.
    Agents.
      Exemption from further
        privilege or
        occupational taxes,
        §11-51-123.
    Gross premiums.
      Provision of statement of
        gross premiums,
        §11-51-122.
    Payment of license tax,
      §11-51-122.
    Engaging in business
      upon payment of tax,
      §11-51-123.
    Schedules, §§11-51-120 to
      11-51-123.
  Interstate commerce.
    Licensing persons engaged
      in interstate
      commerce, §11-51-90.
  Jukeboxes, §§11-51-98,
    11-51-100.
  Lien for license taxes,
    §11-51-96.
    Enforcement not waiver of
      rights as to
      respondent's bond,
      §11-51-159.
  Limitation of actions.
    Actions to recover license
      taxes, §6-2-35.
  More than one business.
    License required for each,
      §11-51-95.

MUNICIPAL
    CORPORATIONS—Cont'd
Licenses—Cont'd
  Ordinances.
    Penalty for violation of
      ordinances requiring
      licenses, §11-51-93.
  Outside corporate limits.
    Business conducted
      outside, §11-51-91.
  Parks, §§11-51-102,
    11-51-104.
    Exemption of public park
      and recreation boards,
      §11-60-17.
  Penalties, §11-51-93.
  Pipeline companies.
    Schedule, §11-51-129.
  Place of business.
    Change of place, §11-51-94.
    Conduct only at place
      designated in license,
      §11-51-94.
  Pledge of revenues from
    licenses for payment of
    bonds, §§11-81-16,
    11-81-18.
  Pool tables, §11-51-102.
  Revocation, §11-51-103.
  Powers.
    Purposes for which
      licensing power may
      be exercised,
      §11-51-90.
  Public park and recreation
    boards.
    Exemption from license
      taxes, §11-60-17.
  Public sales, §11-51-97.
  Railroads.
    Schedules, §11-51-124.
  Revenues.
    Pledge of revenues from
      licenses for payment of
      bonds, §§11-81-16,
      11-81-18.
  Sales.
    Auction sales, public sales
      and street sales,
      §11-51-97.
    Farm products.
      Municipalities not to
        charge farmers for
        sale, etc.,
        §11-51-105.
  Sales and use taxes.
    Levy and assessment in
      lieu of license tax,
      §11-51-205.
  Savings and loan
    associations.
    Schedule, §11-51-131.
  Schedules, §§11-51-120 to
    11-51-131.
    Banks, §11-51-130.
    Electric companies,
      §11-51-129.
    Express companies,
      §11-51-126.
    Gas companies, §11-51-129.
    Insurance companies.
      Fire insurance
        companies,
        §11-51-120.
      Marine insurance
        companies,
        §11-51-120.
      Other than fire and
        marine insurance
        companies,
        §11-51-121.

MUNICIPAL
    CORPORATIONS—Cont'd
Licenses—Cont'd
  Schedules—Cont'd
    Pipeline companies,
      §11-51-129.
    Railroads, §11-51-124.
    Savings and loan
      associations,
      §11-51-131.
    Street railroads,
      §11-51-129.
    Telegraph companies,
      §11-51-127.
    Telephone companies,
      §11-51-128.
    Waterworks companies,
      §11-51-129.
  Shooting galleries,
    §11-51-102.
    Revocation, §11-51-103.
  State department of revenue.
    Collection of certain
      municipal license
      taxes, §§11-51-180 to
      11-51-185.
  State license tax.
    Payment of state license
      tax not to excuse
      payment of other
      license taxes, Const.
      Ala., art. XII, §221.
    Population of municipality
      as determining tax,
      §40-12-17.
  Street railroads.
    Schedule, §11-51-129.
  Street sales, §11-51-97.
  Telegraph companies.
    Schedule, §11-51-127.
  Telephones.
    Coin telephones.
      License tax, §11-51-98.
    Schedule for telephone
      companies, §11-51-128.
  Theaters, §11-51-102.
    Revocation, §11-51-103.
  Transfer of licenses,
    §11-51-92.
  Two or more businesses.
    License required for each,
      §11-51-95.
  Uniformity of license tax,
    §11-51-94.
  Vending machines.
    Authorized, §11-51-98.
    Music machines,
      §§11-51-98, 11-51-100.
  Veterans.
    Disabled veterans.
      Exemptions from
        licenses, §40-12-343.
    World War II veterans.
      Exemptions from
        licenses, §40-12-373.
  Violations of provisions.
    Penalties, §11-51-93.
  Wagons, §11-51-101.
  Waterworks companies.
    Schedule, §11-51-129.
  Weapons.
    Revocation of licenses of
      places of sale,
      §11-51-103.
  Weighing machines.
    Authorized, §11-51-98.

MUNICIPAL
CORPORATIONS—Cont'd
Liens.
Assessments for public
improvements. See
within this heading,
"Assessments for public
improvements."
Gas districts.
Bond issues.
Properties, persons, etc.,
subject to liens,
§11-50-408.
Provisions in pledge
agreements executed
as security for bonds
as to rights of
parties, §11-50-407.
When liens effective,
§11-50-408.
Licenses.
Lien for license taxes,
§11-51-96.
Enforcement not waiver
of rights as to
respondent's bond,
§11-51-159.
Public utilities.
Revenue bonds for
waterworks, etc.
Statutory mortgage lien
for bondholders,
§§11-81-178,
11-81-179.
Taxation.
Lien for property taxes,
§11-51-6.
Optional method for levy
and collection,
§11-51-44.
Sale of land for payment
of taxes, §11-51-21.
Weeds.
Abatement of weeds.
Class 2 municipalities.
Cost of abatement as
weed liens,
§11-67-8.
Class 5 municipalities.
Cost of abatement as
weed liens,
§11-67-27.
Limitation of actions.
Bond issues.
Testing validity of
issuance, etc.,
§11-81-14.
Testing validity of
municipal election,
§§6-2-40, 11-81-61.
Claims for and against
municipalities,
§§11-47-23, 11-50-84.
Licenses.
Recovery of license taxes,
§6-2-35.
Recovery of lands.
No limitation, §6-2-31.
Taxation.
Recovery of license,
franchise or other
taxes, §6-2-35.
Testing validity of
municipal elections for
tax levies, §6-2-40.
Livestock.
Dealers.
Sanitary rules and
regulations, §2-15-48.
Driving through streets,
§11-47-110.

MUNICIPAL
CORPORATIONS—Cont'd
Livestock—Cont'd
Running at large.
Ordinances, §3-5-14.
Reimbursement where
livestock kept in
municipal pounds,
§3-5-11.
Loans.
Interest.
Appropriation for interest,
§11-43-57.
Municipalities not to grant
public money or lend
credit to private persons
or corporations, Const.
Ala., art. IV, §94; amd.
112.
Public improvements.
Temporary loans.
Progress payments,
§11-48-61.
Special health care facility
authorities.
Making of loans to
authority by other
governmental entities,
§11-62-16.
Thirty year loans.
Agreement to levy special
tax as security,
§11-47-2.
Authorized, §11-47-2.
Twelve month renewable
loans.
Authorized, §11-47-1.
Pledge of certain taxes or
revenues as security,
§11-47-1.
Waterworks and sewer
boards.
Security for repayment,
§11-50-236.
Lost or unclaimed property.
Bond issues.
Issuance of duplicates,
§11-81-32.
Disposition of proceeds,
§11-47-116.
Maps or plats, §35-2-56.
Redemption by owner,
§11-47-116.
Sale, §11-47-116.
Storage, §11-47-116.
Uniform disposition of
unclaimed property act.
Exemption of
municipalities,
§11-40-15.
Managers, §11-43-21.
Affirmative action necessary
to exercise powers, etc.,
conferred by article,
§11-43-22.
Authority to employ,
§11-43-20.
Bonds, surety, §11-43-21.
Class 5 municipalities.
Mayor/commission/city
manager form of
government,
§§11-44E-1 to 11-44
E-221. See within this
heading, "Class 5
municipalities."
Compensation, §11-43-21.

MUNICIPAL
CORPORATIONS—Cont'd
Managers—Cont'd
Council-manager form of
government, §§11-43A-1
to 11-43A-52. See within
this heading, "Council-
manager form of
government."
Duties, §11-43-21.
Employment, §11-43-20.
Mayor/commission/city
manager form of
government, §§11-44E-1
to 11-44 E-221. See
within this heading,
"Class 5 municipalities."
Municipal planning
commissions.
Alternate structure of
planning commission
in certain cities,
§11-52-14.
Powers, §11-43-21.
Procedure for employment,
§11-43-20.
Provisions of article
cumulative, §11-43-22.
Qualifications, §11-43-21.
Removal, §11-43-21.
Term of office, §11-43-21.
Mandamus.
Special tax for payment of
principal and interest on
bonds and sinking fund
payments.
Mandamus proceedings,
§11-81-26.
Manufacturing projects.
Bonds for enlargement, etc.,
of municipally-owned
projects, Const. Ala.,
amd. 228.
Maps.
Surveys, plats or maps,
§§35-2-50 to 35-2-62. See
within this heading,
"Surveys, plats or maps."
Markers on hazards, §4-4-10.
Markets.
Bond issues.
Public improvement bonds.
Certain revenue-
producing
undertakings,
§§11-81-140 to
11-81-150.
See COUNTIES.
Regulation, etc., for markets
and marketing of food
products, etc.,
§11-47-137.
Mayor/commission/city
manager form of
government.
Class 5 municipalities,
§§11-44E-1 to
11-44E-221. See within
this heading, "Class 5
municipalities."
Elections. See within this
heading, "Elections."
Managers generally,
§§11-43-20 to 11-43-22.
Mayors generally, §§11-43-80
to 11-43-85. See within
this heading, "Mayors."

MUNICIPAL
CORPORATIONS—Cont'd
Mayor-council form of government.
Class 2 municipalities, §§11-44C-1 to 11-44C-93. See wiithin this heading, "Class 2 municipalities."
Class 4 municipalities, §§11-43B-1 to 11-43B-32. See within this heading, "Class 4 municipalities."
Class 5 municipalities, §§11-43C-1 to 11-43C-92. See wiithin this heading, "Class 5 municipalities."
Class 7 municipalities.
Adoption where commission form violates federal voting rights act, §11-44A-30.
Boundaries of districts, §11-44A-31.
Governing bodies, §11-44A-32.
Powers and duties of municipalities, §11-44A-32.
Single-member districts. Boundaries, §11-44A-31.
Class 8 municipalities.
Adoption where commission form violates federal voting rights act, §§11-44F-1 to 11-44F-3.
Council. See within this heading, "Council."
Elections, §§11-46-20 to 11-46-73. See within this heading, "Elections."
Mayor. See within this heading, "Mayors."
Mayors.
Absence.
Exercise of functions during absence, §11-43-42.
Bonds, surety.
Execution of bonds, §11-43-83.
Chief administrative assistants.
Authority of mayors to appoint, §11-43-81.1.
Chief executive officer.
Designated, §11-43-81.
Class 5 municipalities.
Mayor/commission/city manager form of government.
Generally, §§11-44E-1 to 11-44E-221. See within this heading, "Class 5 municipalities."
Consolidation.
Contiguous municipalities.
Election of mayor, §11-42-103.
Noncontiguous municipalities.
Continuation in office, §11-42-156.
Contracts.
Execution, §11-43-83.
Council.
Absence or disability.
Exercise of functions of mayor, §11-43-42.

MUNICIPAL
CORPORATIONS—Cont'd
Mayors—Cont'd
Council-manager form of government.
Assistants.
Councilman-at-large as assistant mayor, §11-43A-16.
At-large posts, §11-43A-32.
Compensation, §11-43A-15.
Conflicts of interest, §11-43A-18.
Duties, §11-43A-16.
Elections. See within this heading, "Elections."
Mayor pro tem, §11-43A-16.
Oath or affirmation, §11-43A-50.
Vacancies in office.
Filling by councilman-at large, §11-43A-16.
Deeds.
Execution, etc., §11-43-83.
Designated chief executive officer, §11-43-81.
Disability.
Exercise of functions during disability, §11-43-42.
Duties, §11-43-80.
Abandonment of commission form of government, §§11-44-157, 11-44-162.
Election, §11-44-156.
After incorporation, §§11-41-5, 11-41-6.
Consolidation of contiguous municipalities.
Election of mayor, §11-42-103.
Failure to elect.
Grounds for forfeiture of charter, §11-41-24.
Judging of election by council, §11-43-58.
Mayor-council form generally, §§11-46-20 to 11-46-73. See within this heading, "Elections."
Offenses, §§11-46-59, 11-46-130.
Electricity.
Employment as superintendent of municipal light systems, §§11-43-80, 11-50-16.
Finance.
Accounting, §11-43-85.
Statement to council of financial condition of municipality, §11-43-84.
Functions.
Exercise during absence or disability, §11-43-42.
Gas.
Employment as superintendent of gas systems, §§11-43-80, 11-50-16.

MUNICIPAL
CORPORATIONS—Cont'd
Mayors—Cont'd
Mayor/commission/city manager form of government.
Generally, §§11-44E-1 to 11-44E-221. See within this heading, "Class 5 municipalities."
Meetings.
Authorized to attend certain meetings.
Class 1 municipality, §11-43-86.
Office, §11-43-80.
Officers.
Generally. See within this heading, "Officers."
Powers of appointment and removal, §11-43-81.
Requiring of reports by municipal officers, §11-43-84.
Ordinances and resolutions.
Approval, §11-45-3.
Recall from mayor, §11-45-3.
Transmittal to mayor for consideration, §11-45-3.
Veto, §11-45-4.
Penalties.
Election offenses, §11-46-59.
Powers, §11-43-80.
Abandonment of commission form of government, §§11-44-157, 11-44-162.
Appointment and removal, §11-43-81.
Chief administrative assistants, §11-43-81.1.
President of board of commissioners.
Designation as mayor, §§11-44-15, 11-44-83.
Duties as president of board of commissioners and as mayor, §11-44-17.
Performance of duties and responsibilities of mayor in certain municipalities, §11-44-16.
Qualifications, §11-43-1.
Judging of qualifications by council, §11-43-58.
Reports.
Financial condition.
Statement to council of financial condition of municipality, §11-43-84.
Requiring of reports by municipal officers, §11-43-84.
Residence, §11-43-1.
Salary, §11-43-80.
Class 1 municipality, §11-43-86.
Ratification of certain salaries of mayors, §11-43-80.

MUNICIPAL
    CORPORATIONS—Cont'd
Mayors—Cont'd
Sewers.
  Employment as
    superintendent of
    sewage systems,
    §§11-43-80, 11-50-16.
Vacancies.
  Filling, §11-43-42.
Water supply and
  waterworks.
  Employment as
    superintendent of
    water systems,
    §§11-43-80, 11-50-16.
Meat and meat products.
Diseased or unsound meats.
  Sales.
    Prohibition of sale, etc.,
      §11-47-136.
Fresh meats.
  Regulation of sale, etc.,
    §11-47-138.
Inspections.
  Charges for inspection,
    §11-43-59.
  Inspections for other
    municipalities,
    §11-47-139.
  Regulation of sales,
    §§11-47-137, 11-47-138.
Mechanical codes.
Adoption by reference,
  §11-45-8.
Medical clinic boards,
  §§11-58-1 to 11-58-15.
Board of directors, §11-58-4.
Bond issues, §§11-58-7 to
  11-58-11, 11-58-14.
  Default.
    Remedies, §11-58-8.
  Delivery, §11-58-7.
  Denominations, §11-58-7.
  Disposition of proceeds
    from sale, §11-58-9.
  Execution, §11-58-7.
  Exemption from taxation,
    §11-58-14.
  Form, §11-58-7.
  Insurance companies.
    Investment in bonds,
      §11-58-11.
  Investment in bonds by
    savings banks and
    insurance companies,
    §11-58-11.
  Payment.
    Dissolution of
      corporation upon,
      §11-58-7.
    Remedies upon default,
      §11-58-8.
    Security, §11-58-8.
  Preissuance procedure,
    §§8-6-110 to 8-6-122.
    See INDUSTRIAL
      REVENUE BONDS.
  Proceeds from sale.
    Disposition, §11-58-9.
  Refunding bonds,
    §11-58-10.
  Remedies upon default,
    §11-58-8.
  Sale, §11-58-7.
    Disposition of proceeds,
      §11-58-9.
  Savings banks.
    Investment in bonds,
      §11-58-11.

MUNICIPAL
    CORPORATIONS—Cont'd
Medical clinic boards
    —Cont'd
Bond issues—Cont'd
  Security for payment,
    §11-58-8.
  Terms, §11-58-7.
Definitions, §11-58-1.
Directors.
  Board of directors,
    §11-58-4.
Dissolution of corporation,
  §11-58-7.
  Authority for dissolution,
    §11-58-13.
  Effect of dissolution,
    §11-58-13.
  Procedure, §11-58-13.
Eminent domain, §11-58-5.1.
Exemptions of corporations.
  Exemption from taxation,
    §11-58-14.
  Exemption from usury and
    interest laws,
    §11-58-15.
Funds.
  Dissolution of corporation.
    Vesting of title to funds,
      §11-58-13.
Incorporation, §§11-58-2,
  11-58-3.
  Application for authority,
    §11-58-2.
  Certificate of incorporation.
    Acknowledgment,
      §11-58-3.
    Contents, §11-58-3.
    Execution, §11-58-2.
    Filing, §§11-58-2,
      11-58-3.
    Recordation, §11-58-3.
  Effect of granting of
    authority for
    incorporation,
    §11-58-2.
  Resolution authorizing,
    §11-58-2.
Interest laws.
  Exemption, §11-58-15.
Leasing of medical clinics or
  clinical facilities.
  Exemption of lease
    agreements from
    taxation, §11-58-14.
  Requirements as to
    leasing, §11-58-6.
Operation of clinic.
  Disposition of revenue,
    §11-58-6.
Powers, §§11-58-5, 11-58-5.1.
Property.
  Conveyances of properties
    to corporations by
    municipalities,
    §11-58-12.
  Dissolution of corporation.
    Vesting of title to
      properties in
      municipalities upon
      dissolution,
      §11-58-13.
  Exemption from taxation,
    §11-58-14.
Purpose of chapter, §11-58-2.
Resolutions.
  Incorporation.
    Authorizing, §11-58-2.

MUNICIPAL
    CORPORATIONS—Cont'd
Medical clinic boards
    —Cont'd
Revenue from operation of
  clinic.
  Disposition of revenue,
    §11-58-6.
Usury.
  Exemption from usury
    laws, §11-58-15.
Mentally ill.
Housing of mentally retarded
  or mentally ill persons.
  Zoning regulations for
    housing in multi-
    family zone,
    §11-52-75.1.
Regional mental health
  programs and facilities,
  §§22-51-1 to 22-51-14.
  See MENTALLY ILL.
Merit systems.
Civil service merit systems
  for law enforcement
  officers, §§11-43-180 to
  11-43-190. See within
  this heading, "Civil
  service merit systems for
  law enforcement
  officers."
Military affairs.
Appropriation for local
  national guard and naval
  militia units, §31-2-129.
Armory commission.
  Buildings.
    Cooperation of
      municipalities for
      acquisition of
      buildings, §31-4-9.
    Conveyance by
      municipalities of
      public lands to
      commission for use as
      armory sites, §31-4-11.
  Donations for aid of local
    national guard or naval
    militia, §31-4-17.
  Reversion of donations,
    §31-4-18.
Milk and milk products.
Codes.
  Adoption by reference,
    §11-45-8.
Dairies.
  Inspections, §11-47-139.
  Regulation, §11-47-137.
Mining plants.
Annexation.
  Exemption from taxation,
    §11-42-59.
Misdemeanors.
Class 5 municipalities.
  Mayor/commission/city
    manager form of
    government.
    Acceptance of gifts,
      §11-44E-183.
    Elections.
      Bribery, §11-44E-164.
    Investigations.
      Failure to obey
        subpoenas,
        §11-44E-181.
    Officers or employees.
      Conflicts of interest,
        §11-44E-183.
    Penalties for violations
      of chapter,
      §11-44E-167.

MUNICIPAL CORPORATIONS—Cont'd

Morgues.
Establishment, §11-47-7.
Maintenance, §11-47-7.
Regulation, §11-47-7.

Mortgages and deeds of trust.
Boards for operation of water, sewer, gas and electric systems.
Bond issues.
Mortgaging of systems for payment, §11-50-317.
Rights of parties, §11-50-314.
Bond issues.
Execution upon property acquired with proceeds, §11-81-2.
Electric lighting or power plants.
Security for debts, etc., incurred in construction, acquisition, etc., §§11-50-8 to 11-50-11.
Gas districts.
Bond issues.
Properties, persons, etc., subject to mortgages, §11-50-408.
Security for bonds, §11-50-407.
When mortgages effective, §11-50-408.
Industrial development boards.
Liability of municipalities upon obligations of boards, §11-54-92.
Security for payment, §11-54-90.
Post-office projects.
Consent, etc., of governmental body not to be required for execution, §11-55-7.
Security for payment of bonds, §11-55-4.
Public property.
Mortgage for payment of debts, §11-81-27.
Public utilities.
Revenue bonds for waterworks, gas, sewer or electric systems.
Statutory mortgage lien of bondholders, §§11-81-178, 11-81-179.
Water supply and waterworks.
Security for debts, etc., incurred in construction, acquisition, etc., §§11-50-8 to 11-50-11.
Waterworks and sewer boards.
Acquisition, operation, etc., of gas plants and systems.
Security for indebtedness, §11-50-262.
Provisions in mortgages and deeds of trust.
Rights of parties, §11-50-235.

MUNICIPAL CORPORATIONS—Cont'd

Mosquitoes.
Construction, regulation, etc., of public wells, cisterns, etc., §11-47-140.

Motor fuels.
Additional excise tax on gasoline, motor fuel and lubricating oil.
Exemptions, §40-17-220.

Motor sports hall of fame commission.
Bonds not obligation of municipalities, §41-9-475.

Motor vehicle carriers.
Taxation.
Municipal privilege license tax, §37-3-33.

Motor vehicles.
Abandoned vehicles.
Power of municipality not restricted, §32-13-8.
Arrest made by municipal officers.
Disposition of fines and forfeitures, §32-5A-10.
Bridges.
Maximum speed.
Signs stating, §32-5-92.
Codes of traffic regulations,
Adoption by reference, §11-45-8.
Elections.
Provision of automobiles, etc., to bring voters to polls, §11-44-52.
Highway and traffic safety coordination act.
Powers of municipalities, §32-4-7.
Inspection.
Municipal testing stations, §§32-18-1 to 32-18-8.
See MOTOR VEHICLES.
Municipal testing stations, §§32-18-1 to 32-18-8.
See MOTOR VEHICLES.
Parking.
Applicability of provisions, §11-61-3.
Authority of towns and cities with respect to facilities, §11-61-2.
Definitions, §11-61-1.
Parking in violation of municipal ordinances, §32-5-152.
Presumption as to person committing violation, §32-5-152.
Power to regulate or prohibit, §32-5-1.
Uniform traffic infractions.
Municipal parking offenses, ARJA, Rule 19.
Violation of municipal ordinance, §32-5-152.
Uniform traffic infractions, ARJA, Rule 19.
Powers generally, §32-5-1.
Regulation within corporate limits, §11-47-114.
Speed limits.
Bridges, §32-5-92.
Establishment within corporate limits, §11-49-4.

MUNICIPAL CORPORATIONS—Cont'd

Motor vehicles—Cont'd
Speed limits—Cont'd
Posting of sign boards as to, §11-49-5.
Tags.
Municipal vehicles, §40-12-250.
Testing stations.
Municipal testing stations, §§32-18-1 to 32-18-8.
See MOTOR VEHICLES.
Trucks, trailers and semi-trailers.
Size and weight of vehicles.
Exemption from article, §32-9-22.
Violation of traffic ordinance of incorporated municipality.
Depositing driver's license in lieu of bail, §32-1-5.

Municipal connecting link roads, §§23-1-110 to 23-1-113.

Municipal courts, §§12-14-1 to 12-14-71.
See MUNICIPAL COURTS.

Municipal electric authority, §§11-50A-1 to 11-50A-33.
See within this heading, "Electricity."

Municipal government capital improvement, §§11-66-1 to 11-66-7. See within this heading, "'Capital improvement."

Municipal planning commissions, §§11-52-2 to 11-52-14. See within this heading, "Planning."

Museums.
Establishment, acquisition, administration, etc., §11-47-16.

Music.
Bands.
Appropriations for municipal bands, §11-80-4.
Establishment, etc., of concert halls, §11-47-16.
Juke boxes.
Regulation and control, §11-51-100.
Provision of music and other exhibitions, §11-47-19.

Names, §11-40-1.
Change of name, §11-40-7.
Property rights preserved, §11-40-4.
Council-manager form of government.
Governing body, §11-43A-8.
Government to be known as "council-manager form of government," §11-43A-11.

MUNICIPAL
CORPORATIONS—Cont'd
National organizations.
Civic organizations.
Acquisition, etc., of projects
for promotion of
buildings and other
facilities for certain
national organizations,
§§11-54-50 to 11-54-62.
See within this
heading, "Civic
organizations."
Natural gas. See within this
heading, "Gas."
Negligence.
Airports.
Municipal immunity from
liability, §4-4-4.
Liability for negligence of
agents, §§11-47-190 to
11-47-192.
Nepotism.
Commission form of
government.
Optional form A,
§§11-44-102,
11-44-103.
Optional form B,
§11-44-138.
Noncontiguous
municipalities.
Consolidation, §§11-42-150 to
11-42-167. See within
this heading,
"Consolidation."
Notes.
Anticipation of sale of bonds.
Issuance, sale, etc., of
negotiable notes in
anticipation,
§11-81-28.
Elections.
Ordering of election for
determination as to
issuance, §11-81-52.
Execution.
Anticipation notes,
§11-81-28.
Facsimile signature,
§11-81-33.
Issuance.
Anticipation notes,
§11-81-28.
Election.
Ordering to determine
issuance, §11-81-52.
Maturity.
Anticipation notes,
§11-81-28.
Purposes for which issued,
§11-81-51.
Redemption of securities.
Generally. See within this
heading, "Redemption
of securities."
Refunding notes.
Issuance, §11-81-4.
Payment.
Pledge of tax, revenues
for payment,
§11-81-4.
Sale.
Anticipation notes,
§11-81-28.

MUNICIPAL
CORPORATIONS—Cont'd
Notice.
Annexation.
Cities of twenty-five
thousand or more,
§11-42-55.
Taxation.
Appeals, §11-42-67.
Single notice for
separately owned
lands, §11-42-62.
Notice of intention to apply
for local law annexing
territory required,
§11-42-6.
Requirement, §11-42-3.
Ante litem notice,
§11-47-192.
Assessments for public
improvements,
§§11-48-22 to 11-48-25,
11-48-103. See within
this heading,
"Assessments for public
improvements."
Bond issues.
Hearing on validation.
Publication of notice,
§§6-6-752, 11-81-222.
Notice of election,
§11-81-53.
Class 5 municipalities.
Mayor/commission/city
manager form of
government.
Elections, §11-44E-3.
Special election when
vacancy in office of
mayor,
§11-44E-74.
Demolition of unsafe
structures.
Costs.
Meeting at which cost
fixed, §11-40-33.
Unsafe or dangerous
condition of structure,
§11-40-31.
Dissolution.
Petition to probate judge,
§11-41-22.
Elections.
Mayor/commission/city
manager form of
government,
§11-44E-3.
Special election when
vacancy in office of
mayor, §11-44E-74.
Historic preservation
commissions.
Designation of historic
properties and
districts, §11-68-8.
Mayor/commission/city
manager form of
government.
Elections, §11-44E-3.
Special election when
vacancy in office of
mayor, §11-44E-74.
Reduction of corporate limits,
§§11-42-202, 11-42-205.
Sewers.
Assessments for cost of
purchase, §§11-50-81,
11-50-82.
Giving of notice under
provisions of division,
§11-50-56.

MUNICIPAL
CORPORATIONS—Cont'd
Notice—Cont'd
Weeds.
Abatement of weeds.
Class 2 municipalities.
Public hearing,
§11-67-4.
Class 5 municipalities.
Public hearing,
§11-67-23.
Nuisances.
Abatement, §11-47-117.
Actions to enjoin and
abate, §§6-5-122,
11-47-118.
Weeds.
Class 2 municipalities,
§§11-67-1 to 11-67-9.
See within this
heading, "Class 2
municipalities."
Class 5 municipalities,
§§11-67-20 to
11-67-28. See within
this heading, "Class
5 municipalities."
Actions to enjoin and abate,
§§6-5-122, 11-47-118.
Assessment of costs of
abatement, §11-47-117.
Buildings.
Minimum housing
standards and
regulation of unsafe
buildings.
Abating nuisances not
impaired by chapter,
§11-53-3.
Factories.
When nuisance after
operating for one year.
Effect of section on
municipal
ordinances, §6-5-127.
Housing.
Minimum housing
standards and
regulation of unsafe
buildings.
Abating nuisances not
impaired by chapter,
§11-53-3.
Injunctions.
Actions to enjoin,
§11-47-118.
Public nuisances,
§6-5-122.
Weeds.
Abatement of weeds.
Class 2 municipalities,
§§11-67-1 to 11-67-9.
See within this
heading, "Class 2
municipalities."
Class 5 municipalities,
§§11-67-20 to
11-67-28. See within
this heading, "Class
5 municipalities."
Oaths.
Class 5 municipalities.
Mayor/commission/city
manager form of
government.
Commission, §11-44E-40.
Mayor, §11-44E-70.
Officers, §11-44E-185.
Commissioners, §§11-44-9,
11-44-79, 11-44-123.

**MUNICIPAL
CORPORATIONS**—Cont'd
Oaths—Cont'd
Council-manager form of
government.
Councilmen, officers and
employees, §11-43A-50.
Designation of persons to
administer, §11-43-5.
Mayor/commission/city
manager form of
government.
Commission, §11-44E-40.
Mayor, §11-44E-70.
Officers, §11-44E-185.
Officers, §36-4-6.
Officers.
Abandonment of commission
form.
Continuation in office,
§11-44-161.
Accident insurance.
Group insurance for
officers and employees,
§§11-91-1 to 11-91-8.
See within this
heading, "Insurance."
Appointment, §11-43-45.
Class 5 municipalities.
Mayor/commission/city
manager form of
government.
Interference in
appointment or
removal by
commission,
§11-44E-45.
Municipalities may provide
for appointment of
officers, §11-46-1.
Bonds, surety, §11-43-13.
Municipalities may provide
for bond of officers,
§11-46-1.
Recordation, §36-5-3.
Bribery. See within this
heading, "Bribery."
Cities of less than 6,000.
Election, etc., §11-43-4.
Cities of more than 6,000.
Election, etc., §11-43-3.
Claims for or against town.
Dealing in claims,
§11-43-14.
Class 5 municipalities.
Mayor/commission/city
manager form of
government.
Commission.
Interference in
appointment or
removal of officers
and employees,
§11-44E-45.
Conflicts of interest.
Acceptance of gifts,
§11-44E-183.
Contracts,
§11-44E-183.
Contracts.
Conflicts of interest,
§11-44E-183.
Gifts.
Acceptance,
§11-44E-183.
Misdemeanors.
Acceptance of gifts,
§11-44E-183.
Conflicts of interest,
§11-44E-183.

**MUNICIPAL
CORPORATIONS**—Cont'd
Officers—Cont'd
Class 5 municipalities
—Cont'd
Mayor/commission/city
manager form of
government—Cont'd
Public utilities.
Conflicts of interest,
§11-44E-183.
Removal of officers and
employees,
§11-44E-180.
Succession of
government.
Continuance of present
officers,
§11-44E-141.
Continuance of those
in classified
service,
§11-44E-142.
Rights of officers and
employees
preserved,
§11-44E-140.
Mayor-council form of
government. See
within this heading,
"Class 5
municipalities."
Clerks, §§11-43-100 to
11-43-104.
Generally. See within this
heading, "Clerks."
Code of ethics, §§36-25-1 to
36-25-30.
See PUBLIC OFFICERS
AND EMPLOYEES.
Commission form of
government.
Compensation, §§11-44-28,
11-44-85, 11-44-104.
Conflicts of interest,
§§11-44-46 to 11-44-48,
11-44-94, 11-44-138.
Continuation in office,
§§11-44-27, 11-44-121,
11-44-122.
Gifts.
Acceptance from
railways, gas works,
etc., §11-44-48.
Optional form A,
§§11-44-84, 11-44-85,
11-44-102 to 11-44-104.
Optional form B,
§§11-44-121,
11-44-122, 11-44-138.
Removal, §11-44-28.
Selection, §§11-44-28,
11-44-85.
Conflicts of interest,
§11-43-12.
Commission form of
government,
§§11-44-46 to 11-44-48.
Optional form A,
§11-44-94.
Optional form B,
§11-44-138.
Employment of municipal
officers by corporations
holding franchises as
to use of streets,
§11-43-11.
Grounds for impeachment,
§11-43-161.

**MUNICIPAL
CORPORATIONS**—Cont'd
Officers—Cont'd
Conflicts of interest—Cont'd
Mayor/commission/city
manager form of
government.
Acceptance of gifts,
§11-44E-183.
Interest in contracts with
city or public
utilities,
§11-44E-183.
Penalty, §11-43-12.
Contracts.
Execution, §11-47-5.
Mayor/commission/city
manager form of
government.
Conflicts of interest,
§11-44E-183.
Corporations.
Employment of municipal
officers by corporations
holding franchises as
to use of streets,
§11-43-11.
Councilmen. See within this
heading, "Council."
Duties, §11-43-47.
Assumption of duties by
officers elected,
§11-46-92.
Municipalities may provide
for duties of officers,
§11-46-1.
Election.
Cities of less than 6,000,
§11-43-4.
Cities of more than 6,000,
§11-43-3.
General provisions. See
within this heading,
"Elections."
Judging of election by
council, §11-43-58.
Municipalities may provide
for election, §11-46-1.
Engineer. See within this
heading, "Engineer."
Expenses.
Traveling expenses,
§§36-7-1 to 36-7-5.
Fees.
Disposition, §11-43-6.
Paid into local treasury,
§1-3-6.
Unchanged during term of
office, §11-43-9.
Financial dealings with
municipality, etc.
Grounds for impeachment,
§11-43-161.
Impeachment, §§11-43-161 to
11-43-163; Const. Ala.,
art. VII, §175.
Committee of council.
Secretary of committee,
§11-43-163.
Conflicts of interest.
Grounds for
impeachment,
§11-43-161.
Financial dealings with
municipality.
Grounds for
impeachment,
§11-43-161.
Grounds for impeachment,
§§11-43-161,
11-43-162.

MUNICIPAL
CORPORATIONS—Cont'd
Officers—Cont'd
Impeachment—Cont'd
Misapplication of funds
from special tax.
Grounds for
impeachment,
§11-43-162.
Public service corporations.
Acceptance of
employment from
public service
corporation.
Grounds for
impeachment,
§11-43-161.
Witnesses.
Powers of council or
committee as to,
§11-43-163.
Insurance.
Group insurance for
officers and employees,
§§11-91-1 to 11-91-8.
See within this
heading, "Insurance."
Liabilities.
Liability of municipality
for negligence of
agents, etc.,
§§11-47-190 to
11-47-192.
Municipalities may
prescribe officers'
liability, §11-46-1.
Managers, §§11-43-20 to
11-43-22.
Class 5 municipalities.
Mayor/commission/city
manager form of
government,
§§11-44E-1 to 11-44
E-222. See within
this heading, "Class
5 municipalities."
Council-manager form of
government,
§§11-43A-1 to
11-43A-52. See within
this heading, "Council-
manager form of
government."
Municipal planning
commission.
Alternate structure in
certain cities,
§11-52-14.
Mayor/commission/city
manager form of
government.
Commission.
Interference in
appointment or
removal of officers
and employees,
§11-44E-45.
Conflicts of interest.
Acceptance of gifts,
§11-44E-183.
Contracts, §11-44E-183.
Contracts.
Conflicts of interest,
§11-44E-183.
Gifts.
Acceptance, §11-44E-183.
Misdemeanors.
Acceptance of gifts,
§11-44E-183.
Conflicts of interest,
§11-44E-183.

MUNICIPAL
CORPORATIONS—Cont'd
Officers—Cont'd
Mayor/commission/city
manager form of
government—Cont'd
Public utilities.
Interest in contracts
with, §11-44E-183.
Removal of officers and
employees,
§11-44E-180.
Succession of government.
Continuance of those in
classified service,
§§11-44E-141,
11-44E-142.
Rights of officers and
employees preserved,
§11-44E-140.
Mayors.
General provisions. See
within this heading,
"Mayors."
Powers of appointment and
removal, §11-43-81.
Requiring of reports by
municipal officers,
§11-43-84.
Military service by officers in
time of national
emergency, §§36-8-1 to
36-8-6.
See PUBLIC OFFICERS
AND EMPLOYEES.
Misapplication of funds from
special tax.
Grounds for impeachment,
§11-43-162.
Neglect.
Liability of municipality
for negligence of
agents, etc.,
§§11-47-190 to
11-47-192.
Oaths, §36-4-6.
Offenses, §11-46-59.
Penalties.
Election offenses,
§11-46-59.
Pension and retirement
plans. See within this
heading, "Pension and
retirement plans."
Powers, §11-43-47.
Municipalities may provide
for, §11-46-1.
Public money received.
Daily balances required,
§11-43-10.
Officers to pay over,
§11-43-10.
Public service corporations.
Acceptance of employment
from public service
corporation.
Grounds for
impeachment,
§11-43-161.
Qualifications, §11-43-1.
Judging of qualifications
by council, §11-43-58.

MUNICIPAL
CORPORATIONS—Cont'd
Officers—Cont'd
Removal, §11-43-160.
Class 5 municipalities.
Mayor/commission/city
manager form of
government,
§11-44E-180.
Commission
interference in
appointment or
removal of officers,
§11-44E-45.
Reports.
Requiring of reports by
municipal officers,
§11-43-84.
Residence, §11-43-1.
Salaries.
Commission form of
government, §11-44-28.
Optional form A,
§11-44-85.
Optional form B,
§11-44-104.
Establishment, §11-43-8.
Municipalities may provide
for, §§11-43-6, 11-46-1.
Ordinances and resolutions
fixing salaries.
Veto, §11-45-5.
Suspension of restriction
on diminishing public
salaries, Const. Ala.,
amd. 26A.
Unchanged during term of
office, §11-43-9.
Suspension of restriction
on diminishing
public salaries,
Const. Ala., amd.
26A.
Streets.
Corporations holding
franchises as to use of
streets.
Employment of
municipal officers,
§11-43-11.
Terms of office, §11-43-46.
Municipalities may provide
for terms, §11-46-1.
Torts.
Liability for negligence of
agents, etc.,
§§11-47-190 to
11-47-192.
Traveling expenses.
Advancement, §36-7-3.
Statement of expenses.
Approval, §36-7-4.
Effect of failure to
present and secure
approval, §36-7-4.
Presentation, §36-7-4.
Drawing or approval of
warrant in violation of
article, §36-7-5.
Reimbursement.
Statement of expenses.
Approval, §§36-7-1,
36-7-2.
Disallowance, §36-7-2.
Presentation, §§36-7-1,
36-7-2.
Treasurers, §§11-43-120 to
11-43-123.
Warrants.
Dealing in warrants by
officers, §11-43-14.

MUNICIPAL CORPORATIONS—Cont'd

Off-street parking facilities.
Applicability of article,
§11-47-242.
Construction of article,
§11-47-243.
Definitions, §11-47-240.
Powers of cities as to,
§11-47-241.

Oil and gas.
Privilege tax on production.
Allocation and distribution,
§40-20-8.
Exemption from ad
valorem taxes,
§40-20-12.
Levy of tax by
municipalities,
§40-20-2.

Orders of court.
Annexation.
Cities of twenty-five
thousand or more.
Entry of orders,
§11-42-51.
Recordation, §11-42-51.
Requirement as to orders
under article,
§11-42-55.
Recordation, §11-42-71.

Ordinances and resolutions.
Adoption, §11-45-7.
Authorized, §11-45-1.
Procedure for adoption,
§11-45-2.
Amendment, §11-45-6.
Annexation. See within this
heading, "Annexation."
Approval.
By mayor, §11-45-3.
Assessments for public
improvments, §§11-48-5,
11-48-7, 11-48-8.
Attorney general.
Constitutionality of
ordinance questioned.
Notice to attorney
general, §6-6-227.
Boards of water and sewer
commissioners,
§§11-50-341, 11-50-343,
11-50-346, 11-50-347. See
within this heading,
"Boards of water and
sewer commissioners."
Bridges, tunnels, etc.
Requirements of
construction and
maintenance by
railroads within limits
of certain cities,
§§11-49-42 to 11-49-45.
Buildings.
Adoption, §11-43-59.
Class 1 municipalities.
Judicial notice of
ordinances, §11-45-11.
Class 5 municipalities.
Mayor/commission/city
manager form of
government.
Commission.
Power to enact,
§11-44E-44.
Enactment, §11-44E-51.
Revision and
codification,
§11-44E-53.

MUNICIPAL CORPORATIONS—Cont'd

Ordinances and resolutions —Cont'd
Class 5 municipalities
—Cont'd
Mayor/commission/city
manager form of
government—Cont'd
Succession of
government.
Ordinances and
resolutions
continued in effect,
§11-44E-149.
Mayor-council form of
government. See
within this heading,
"Class 5
municipalities."
Class 7 municipalities.
Mayor-council form of
government.
Adoption where
commission form
violates federal
voting rights act,
§11-44A-30.
Class 8 municipalities.
Mayor-council form of
government.
Adoption where
commission form
violates federal
voting rights act,
§11-44F-1.
Clerks.
Custody of ordinances,
§11-43-100.
Publication by clerk,
§11-45-3.
Codification of ordinances,
§11-45-7.
Class 5 municipalities.
Mayor/commission/city
manager form of
government,
§11-44E-53.
Commission form of
government. See within
this heading,
"Commission form of
government."
Consideration.
Transmittal to mayor for
consideration,
§11-45-3.
Consolidation of
noncontiguous
municipalities.
Applicability of annexing
municipality's
resolutions,
§11-42-166.
Contracts.
Awarding contracts on
bids, §11-45-2.
Declaratory judgments.
Questions of construction
or validity, §6-6-223.
Dogs.
Leash ordinances,
§11-45-10.
Effective date, §11-45-8.
Enforcement, §11-45-1.
Evidence, §12-21-73.

MUNICIPAL CORPORATIONS—Cont'd

Ordinances and resolutions —Cont'd
Fines.
Schedule of fines for
nontraffic violations.
Establishment by
ordinance, ARJA,
Rule 20.
Gas systems.
Transfer without election,
§11-50-211.
Handguns.
Subject matter of handguns
reserved to state
legislature, §11-45-1.1.
Historic preservation
commissions.
Establishment of
commission, §11-68-2.
Violations of ordinances.
Actions for injunctions
and damages,
§11-68-12.
Housing.
Minimum housing
standards and
regulation of unsafe
buildings, §11-53-2.
Industrial development
boards.
Resolution authorizing
incorporation,
§11-54-82.
Injunctions or restraint on
enforcement, §6-6-502.
Judicial notice.
Class 1 municipalities,
§11-45-11.
Mayor/commission/city
manager form of
government.
Commission.
Power to enact,
§11-44E-44.
Enactment, §11-44E-51.
Revision and codification,
§11-44E-53.
Succession of government.
Ordinances and
resolutions
continued in effect,
§11-44E-149.
Mayor-council form of
government.
Class 7 municipalities.
Adoption where
commission form
violates federal
voting rights act,
§11-44A-30.
Class 8 municipalities.
Adoption where
commission form
violates federal
voting rights act,
§11-44F-1.
Mayors.
Approval by mayor,
§11-45-3.
Recall from mayor,
§11-45-3.
Transmittal to mayor for
consideration,
§11-45-3.
Veto, §11-45-4.

MUNICIPAL CORPORATIONS—Cont'd
Ordinances and resolutions
—Cont'd
Parties.
Validity of municipal ordinance or franchise, §6-6-227.
Allegations of unconstitutionality, §6-6-227.
Persons to be made parties, §6-6-227.
Rights of persons not parties, §6-6-227.
Service upon attorney general, §6-6-227.
Penalties for violation, §11-45-9.
Police regulations.
Territorial operation of ordinances for enforcement of police regulations, §11-40-10.
Public athletic boards.
Resolution authorizing incorporation, §11-59-3.
Publication, §§11-45-3, 11-45-8.
Class 5 municipalities.
Mayor/commission/city manager form of government, §11-44E-51.
Public building authorities.
Bond issues.
Notice of resolution authorizing issuance, §11-56-11.
Resolution authorizing incorporation, §11-56-3.
Public improvements.
Amendment, §11-48-8.
Assessments for public improvements, §§11-48-5, 11-48-7, 11-48-8.
Modification, §11-48-8.
Notice to certain property owners, §11-48-7.
Ordinance or resolution describing proposed improvement, §11-48-5.
Publication, §11-48-7.
Rescission, §11-48-8.
Public library authorities.
Bond issues.
Notice of resolution authorizing issuance of bonds, §11-57-12.
Resolution authorizing incorporation, §11-57-3.
Public park and recreation boards.
Bond issues.
Notice of resolution authorizing issuance, §11-60-10.
Incorporation.
Resolution authorizing incorporation, §11-60-3.
Public utilities.
Revenue bonds, §§11-81-163, 11-81-176.

MUNICIPAL CORPORATIONS—Cont'd
Ordinances and resolutions
—Cont'd
Public utilities—Cont'd
Waiver by utility of terms of municipal ordinance, §37-1-48.
Recall from mayor, §11-45-3.
Recordation, §11-45-8.
Reduction of corporate limits, §§11-42-200 to 11-42-202.
Sanitary regulations.
Territorial operation of ordinances, §11-40-10.
Sewers, §§11-50-75 to 11-50-77.
Streets.
Franchises right to use of streets, §§11-44-33 to 11-44-35, 11-44-388, 11-44-137.
Technical codes.
Adoption by reference, §11-45-8.
Unconstitutionality.
Validity of municipal ordinances or franchises, §6-6-227.
Allegations of unconstitutionality, §6-6-227.
Persons to be made parties, §6-6-227.
Rights of persons not parties, §6-6-227.
Service upon attorney general, §6-6-227.
Vacation of streets for erection of public buildings, §§11-49-100 to 11-49-103.
Vetoes, §11-45-4.
Ordinances and resolutions fixing salaries of officers and employees, §11-45-5.
Passage over veto, §11-45-4.
Violations.
Penalties which may be imposed, §11-45-9.
Summons and complaint in lieu of arrest, §11-40-10.1.
Weeds.
Abatement of weeds.
Class 2 municipalities, §§11-67-3, 11-67-9.
Class 5 municipalities, §§11-67-22, 11-67-28.
Zoning, §§11-52-76 to 11-52-78, 11-52-82 to 11-52-84. See within this heading, "Zoning."
Organization.
Commission form of government.
Powers and authority of commissioners upon organization, §11-44-23.
Continuation of present organization, §11-40-9.
Council, §§11-43-40 to 11-43-62. See within this heading, "Council."
Property rights preserved notwithstanding change of organization, §11-40-4.

MUNICIPAL CORPORATIONS—Cont'd
Parking.
Motor vehicles, §§11-61-1 to 11-61-3, 32-5-1, 32-5-152; ARJA, Rule 19. See within this heading, "Motor vehicles."
Off-street parking facilities, §§11-47-240 to 11-47-243.
Parks and recreation.
Airports.
Use of parks for airports, §4-4-3.
Alienation of certain public improvements, §§35-4-410 to 35-4-412.
Appropriations.
State parks, §9-14-6.
Athletic boards, §§11-59-1 to 11-59-17.
Authorities, §§11-47-210 to 11-47-220.
Authorization, §11-47-214.
Board of directors.
Generally, §11-47-217.
Construction of article, §11-47-220.
Cooperating municipalities, §11-47-213.
Definitions, §11-47-210.
Dissolution.
Authority, §11-47-219.
Procedure, §11-47-219.
Vesting of title, etc., to properties in municipalities upon, §11-47-219.
Eminent domain.
Exercise of power, §11-47-218.
Incorporation, §§11-47-214 to 11-47-216.
Application of authority to form corporation, §11-47-214.
Certificate, §§11-47-214 to 11-47-216.
Acknowledgment, §11-47-216.
Contents, §11-47-215.
Execution, §11-47-216.
Filing with probate judge, §11-47-216.
Recordation by probate judge, §11-47-216.
Procedure generally, §11-47-214.
Resolutions authorizing incorporation, §11-47-214.
Powers.
Eminent domain, §11-47-218.
Generally, §11-47-218.
Powers as to acquisition of lands for parks, etc.
Cooperating municipalities, §11-47-213.
Generally, §11-47-211.
Outside corporate limits, §11-47-212.
Boards.
Athletic boards, §§11-59-1 to 11-59-17.
Public park and recreation boards, §§11-60-1 to 11-60-20.

MUNICIPAL
  CORPORATIONS—Cont'd
Parks and recreation—Cont'd
Bond issues.
  Public athletic boards,
    §§11-59-1 to 11-59-17.
  Public improvement bonds.
  Certain revenue-
    producing
    undertakings,
    §§11-81-140 to
    11-81-150.
  See COUNTIES.
  Public park and recreation
    boards, §§11-60-1 to
    11-60-20.
Class 5 municipalities.
  Mayor/commission/city
    manager form of
    government.
    Succession of
    government.
    Laws continued,
    §11-44E-148.
Codes.
  Adoption by reference,
    §11-45-8.
Definitions, §11-47-210.
Eminent domain.
  Authority, §11-47-218.
Establishment of public
  parks, etc., §11-47-19.
  Authorities, §§11-47-210 to
    11-47-220.
Improving public parks, etc.,
  §11-47-19.
Industrial parks, §§11-54-1 to
  11-54-4.
Licensing of parks,
  §§11-51-102, 11-51-104.
  Exemption of public park
    and recreation boards
    from license taxes,
    §11-60-17.
Mayor/commission/city
  manager form of
  government.
  Succession of government.
    Laws continued,
    §11-44E-148.
Police jurisdiction over parks,
  §11-47-22.
Powers as to acquisition, etc.,
  of lands, etc., for parks,
  §§11-47-211 to 11-47-213.
  Cooperation by
    municipalities,
    §11-47-213.
  Generally, §11-47-211.
  Outside corporate limits,
    §11-47-212.
Public athletic boards,
  §§11-59-1 to 11-59-17.
  Agreements.
    Liability of
      municipalities upon,
      §11-59-11.
  Board of directors,
    §11-59-7.
  Bond issues.
    Default.
      Remedies, §11-59-10.
    Delivery, §11-59-9.
    Denominations, §11-59-9.
    Execution, §11-59-9.
    Exemption from
      taxation, §11-59-16.
    Form, §11-59-9.
    Liability of
      municipalities,
      §11-59-11.

MUNICIPAL
  CORPORATIONS—Cont'd
Parks and recreation—Cont'd
Public athletic boards
  —Cont'd
Bond issues—Cont'd
  Payment, §11-59-10.
    Security for payment,
    §11-59-10.
  Redemption, §11-59-9.
  Refunding of bonds,
    §11-59-9.
  Remedies upon default,
    §11-59-10.
  Sale, §11-59-9.
  Security for payment of
    principal and
    interest, §11-59-10.
  Terms, §11-59-9.
Construction of chapter,
  §§11-59-2, 11-59-17.
Definitions, §11-59-1.
Directors.
  Board of directors,
    §11-59-7.
Dissolution of corporations,
  §11-59-14.
Documents of corporations.
  Filing for record without
    payment of taxes or
    fees, §11-59-15.
Exemption from taxation,
  §11-59-16.
Facilities.
Incorporation.
  Application for authority
    to incorporate,
    §11-59-3.
  Certificate of
    incorporation.
    Acknowledgment,
      §§11-59-3, 11-59-4.
    Amendment, §11-59-6.
    Approval, §11-59-5.
    Contents, §11-59-4.
    Examination, §11-59-5.
    Execution, §§11-59-3,
      11-59-4.
    Filing, §§11-59-3,
      11-59-5.
    Filing for record
      without payment
      of taxes or certain
      fees, §11-59-15.
    Recordation, §§11-59-5,
      11-59-15.
    Resolution authorizing,
      §11-59-3.
Legislative intent,
  §11-59-2.
Liability of municipalities
  upon bonds, etc., of
  corporations,
  §11-59-11.
Powers of corporations,
  §11-59-8.
  Conveyances of title to
    facilities, §11-59-13.
Probate judges.
  Certificate of
    incorporation,
    §11-59-5.
Property.
  Conveyance to
    corporations by
    municipalities,
    §11-59-12.

MUNICIPAL
  CORPORATIONS—Cont'd
Parks and recreation—Cont'd
Public athletic boards
  —Cont'd
Property—Cont'd
  Dissolution of
    corporations.
    Vesting of title to
      facilities,
      §11-59-14.
  Powers of corporations as
    to conveyances of
    title to facilities,
    §11-59-13.
Public park and recreation
  boards, §§11-60-1 to
  11-60-20.
  Agreements.
    Liability of
      municipalities upon,
      §11-60-13.
  Board of directors,
    §11-60-7.
  Bond issues, §§11-60-9 to
    11-60-13, 11-60-17,
    11-60-20.
    Authorization of
      issuance, §11-60-9.
    Limitation of actions,
      §11-60-10.
    Notice of resolution
      authorizing,
      §11-60-10.
    Delivery, §11-60-9.
    Denominations, §11-60-9.
    Execution, §11-60-9.
    Exemption from
      taxation, §11-60-17.
    Form, §11-60-9.
    Further proceedings as
      to issuance not
      required, §11-60-20.
    Liability of
      municipalities upon,
      §11-60-13.
    Limitation period for
      actions as to validity
      of proceedings for
      issuance, §11-60-10.
    Payment, §11-60-9.
      Remedies upon default,
      §11-60-11.
      Security for payment,
      §11-60-11.
    Redemption, §11-60-9.
    Refunding of bonds,
      §11-60-9.
    Remedies upon default,
      §11-60-11.
    Sale, §11-60-9.
    Security for payment of
      principal or interest,
      §11-60-11.
    Temporary bonds,
      §11-60-12.
    Terms, §11-60-9.
    Validity of proceedings
      for issuance.
      Limitation of actions,
      §11-60-10.
  Borrowing money.
    Temporary use,
      §11-60-12.
  Construction of chapter,
    §11-60-2.
  Contracts.
    Exemption of
      corporations from
      competitive bid laws,
      §11-60-19.

MUNICIPAL
CORPORATIONS—Cont'd
Parks and recreation—Cont'd
Public park and recreation
boards—Cont'd
Definitions, §11-60-1.
Dissolution of corporations,
§11-60-15.
Documents of corporations.
Filing for record without
payment of taxes or
certain fees,
§11-60-16.
Earnings of corporations.
Disposition of net
earnings, §11-60-14.
Exemption from
taxation, §11-60-17.
Exemptions of
corporations,
§§11-60-17 to 11-60-19.
Competitive bid laws,
§11-60-19.
Interest laws, §11-60-18.
Taxation, §11-60-17.
Usury laws, §11-60-18.
Funds of corporations.
Dissolution of
corporations.
Vesting of title to
funds in
municipalities
upon dissolution,
§11-60-15.
Governmental
subdivisions.
Police powers not
impaired, §11-60-20.
Incorporation, §§11-60-3,
11-60-16, 11-60-20.
Application for authority
to form corporation,
§11-60-3.
Certificate of
incorporation.
Acknowledgment,
§11-60-3.
Execution, §11-60-3.
Filing, §11-60-3.
Filing for record
without payment
of taxes or certain
fees, §11-60-16.
Recordation, §11-60-16.
Effect of granting of
authority for
incorporation,
§11-60-3.
Further proceedings as
to incorporation not
required, §11-60-20.
Resolution authorizing,
§11-60-3.
Interest laws.
Exemption of
corporations,
§11-60-18.
Legislative intent,
§11-60-2.
Liability of municipalities
upon bonds, etc., of
corporations,
§11-60-13.
Licenses.
Exemption from license
tax, §11-60-17.
Obligations of corporations.
Liability of
municipalities upon,
§11-60-13.

MUNICIPAL
CORPORATIONS—Cont'd
Parks and recreation—Cont'd
Public park and recreation
boards—Cont'd
Powers of corporations,
§11-60-8.
Cumulative, §11-60-20.
Projects.
Location of projects,
§11-60-8.
Property.
Dissolution of
corporations.
Vesting of title to
properties in
municipalities,
§11-60-15.
Exemption from
taxation, §11-60-17.
Recreation boards,
§§11-86-1 to 11-86-6.
See PARKS AND
RECREATION.
Resolutions.
Bond issues.
Notice of resolution
authorizing,
§11-60-10.
Incorporation.
Resolution authorizing,
§11-60-3.
State.
Police powers of state
not impaired,
§11-60-20.
Taxation.
Exemption of
corporations from
taxation, §11-60-17.
Temporary loans,
§11-60-12.
Usury laws.
Exemption of
corporations,
§11-60-18.
Recreation boards, §§11-86-1
to 11-86-6.
See PARKS AND
RECREATION.
State parks.
Appropriations for
improvement,
operation, etc., §9-14-6.
Parties, §6-6-227.
Allegations.
Statute, ordinance or
franchise
unconstitutional,
§6-6-227.
Persons to be made parties,
§6-6-227.
Rights of persons not parties,
§6-6-227.
Service upon attorney
general, §6-6-227.
Peace bonds.
Refusal of municipal official
to comply with order of
governor, §15-6-4.
Peace officers' standards
and training
commission.
Appropriations and grants by
municipalities,
§36-21-48.
Municipal police chiefs.
Continuing education,
§36-21-51.

MUNICIPAL
CORPORATIONS—Cont'd
Penalties.
Census.
False enumeration,
§11-43-15.
Clerks.
Election offenses,
§§11-46-60, 11-46-131.
Commission form of
government.
Violations of article,
§11-44-57.
Conflicts of interest,
§§11-43-12, 11-43-53.
Election offenses. See within
this heading, "Elections."
Failure of municipal official
to comply with order of
governor, §15-6-4.
Fines.
Schedule of fines for
nontraffic violations,
ARJA, Rule 20.
Licenses.
Violations of provisions of
division or ordinances
requiring licenses,
§11-51-93.
Maximum fine, §11-45-9.
Mayors.
Election offenses,
§11-46-59.
Officers.
Election offenses,
§11-46-59.
Ordinances.
Violations of ordinances,
§11-45-9.
Permissible penalties,
§11-45-9.
Summons and complaint in
lieu of arrest.
Additional penalty for
failure to appear,
§11-40-10.1.
Violations of ordinances,
§11-45-9.
Pension and retirement
plans.
Administration of funds,
§§36-31-1 to 36-31-3.
Applicability of chapter,
§36-31-3.
Trustees.
Compensation, §36-31-2.
Designation, §36-31-1.
Powers and duties.
Prescription, §36-31-1.
Class 1 municipalities.
Firemen's pension and
relief plan.
Minimum monthly
benefits, §11-40-18.
Policemen's pension and
relief plan.
Minimum monthly
benefits, §11-40-18.
Class 5 municipalities.
Mayor/commission/city
manager form of
government.
City manager.
Eligibility for city
retirement system,
§11-44E-97.
Succession of
government.
Laws continued,
§11-44E-147.

**MUNICIPAL
CORPORATIONS**—Cont'd
**Pension and retirement
plans**—Cont'd
Class 5 municipalities
—Cont'd
Mayor-council form of
government.
Continuation of laws
relating to pensions
or retirement and
relief funds,
§11-43C-82.
Continuation of laws
relating to pensions,
etc. §11-43D-12.
Council-manager form of
government.
Effect of chapter on laws
relating to pensions,
etc., §11-43A-41.
Elected public officials of
class 2 municipalities,
§11-43-19.
Managers.
Eligibility for city
retirement system,
§11-44E-97.
Mayor/commission/city
manager form of
government.
City manager.
Eligibility for city
retirement system,
§11-44E-97.
Succession in government.
Laws continued,
§11-44E-147.
State employees' retirement
system.
Credit to municipal officer
or employee for prior
service with another
municipality,
§36-27-51.
Participation of city
employees, §36-27-6.
Personal injuries.
Liability for negligence of
agents, etc., §§11-47-190
to 11-47-192.
Personal property. See
within this heading,
"Property."
Petitions.
Annexation.
Contiguous municipalities.
Mode of consolidation.
When municipality to
annex city or
town,
§11-42-100.1.
Incorporated
municipalities,
§11-42-21.
Charter.
Forfeiture of charter,
§11-41-25.
Class 5 municipalities.
Mayor/commission/city
manager form of
government.
Abandonment of form of
government.
Petition for change,
§11-44E-201.
Granting of franchises.
Elections for or against
proposed grant,
§11-44E-52.

**MUNICIPAL
CORPORATIONS**—Cont'd
Petitions—Cont'd
Class 5 municipalities
—Cont'd
Mayor/commission/city
manager form of
government—Cont'd
Recall of elected officials,
§11-44E-168.
Commission form of
government.
Election.
Petition for election as to
organization,
§11-44-2.
Optional form A,
§11-44-101.
Council-manager form of
government.
Examination of petition
and certification to
mayor, §11-43A-2.
Dissolution, §§11-41-21,
11-41-22.
Forfeiture of charter,
§11-41-25.
Franchises.
Mayor/commission/city
manager form of
government.
Elections for or against
proposed grant,
§11-44E-52.
Incorporation.
Petition to probate judge
for order of
incorporation,
§11-41-1.
Mayor/commission/city
manager form of
government.
Abandonment of form of
government,
§11-44E-201.
Granting of franchises.
Elections for or against,
§11-44E-52.
Recall of elected officials,
§11-44E-168.
Recall of elected officials.
Mayor/commission/city
manager form of
government,
§11-44E-168.
Physically disabled.
Special health care facility
authorities, §§11-62-1 to
11-62-21. See within this
heading, "Special health
care facility authorities."
Pipelines.
License schedules,
§11-51-129.
Planning, §§11-52-1 to
11-52-14.
Adoption of municipal plan,
§11-52-2.
Amendment of municipal
plan, §11-52-2.
Commissions.
Municipal planning
commission, §§11-52-2
to 11-52-14.
Regional planning
commissions, §§11-85-1
to 11-85-7, 11-85-40.
See PLANNING.
Definitions, §11-52-1.
Execution of municipal plan,
§11-52-2.

**MUNICIPAL
CORPORATIONS**—Cont'd
Planning—Cont'd
Extension of municipal plan,
§11-52-2.
Master plan for physical
development, §§11-52-8
to 11-52-10.
Authorization for adoption,
§11-52-8.
Contents of plan, §11-52-8.
Procedure for adoption,
§§11-52-8, 11-52-10.
Purpose of plan, §11-52-9.
Studies.
Conduct of studies,
§11-52-9.
Surveys.
Conduct of surveys,
§11-52-9.
Municipal planning
commissions, §§11-52-2
to 11-52-14.
Alternate structures,
§§11-52-12 to 11-52-14.
Appointment of members,
§11-52-3.
Chairman, §11-52-4.
Compensation of members,
§11-52-3.
Composition, §11-51-3.
Alternate structures,
§§11-52-12 to
11-52-14.
Comprehensive advisory
planning and research.
Powers of local planning
commissions,
§11-85-40.
Consultants, §11-52-5.
Creation authorized,
§11-52-2.
Designations of planning
commissions, §11-52-2.
Duties, §11-52-6.
Employees, §11-52-5.
Expenditure of funds,
§11-52-5.
Master plan for physical
development,
Adoption, §§11-52-8 to
11-52-10.
Meetings, §11-52-4.
Officers, §11-52-4.
Overruling of commission,
§11-52-11.
Powers, §11-52-6.
Zoning powers, §11-52-7.
Proposed construction of
streets, public
buildings, utilities,
etc., to be submitted
for approval after
adoption, §11-52-11.
Qualifications of members,
§11-52-3.
Records.
Maintenance of record of
resolutions,
transactions, etc.,
§11-52-4.
Regional planning.
Adoption of master plan,
§11-85-6.
Removal of members,
§11-52-3.
Rules of procedure,
§11-52-4.

**MUNICIPAL
CORPORATIONS**—Cont'd
Planning—Cont'd
Municipal planning
commissions—Cont'd
Subdivisions, §§11-52-30 to
11-52-36. See within
this heading,
"Subdivisions."
Terms of members,
§11-52-3.
Vacancies, §11-52-3.
Zoning powers, §11-52-7.
Records.
Municipal planning
commission, §11-52-4.
Regional planning and
development, §§11-85-1
to 11-85-73.
See PLANNING.
Subdivisions, §§11-52-30 to
11-52-54. See within this
heading, "Subdivisions."
Zoning, §§11-52-70 to
11-52-84. See within this
heading, "Zoning."
Plats.
Town surveys, plats or maps,
§§35-2-50 to 35-2-62. See
within this heading,
"Surveys, plats or maps."
**Pledge and collateral
security.**
Boards for operation of
water, sewer, gas and
electric systems.
Pledge of revenues from
systems for payment of
bonds, §11-50-317.
Rights of parties,
§11-50-314.
Gas districts.
Bond issues, §11-50-408.
Security for bonds,
§11-50-407.
When pledges effective,
§11-50-408.
Waterworks and sewer
boards.
Acquisition, operation, etc.,
of gas plants and
systems.
Security for
indebtedness,
§11-50-262.
Rights of parties,
§11-50-235.
Plumbing.
Codes.
Adoption by reference,
§11-45-8.
Permits for installation
within police jurisdiction
of municipalities,
§22-26-4.
Regulation, installation, etc.,
§11-50-54.
Police.
Arrest.
Summons and complaint in
lieu of arrest,
§11-40-10.1.
Chief of police.
Continuing education,
§36-21-51.
Provision for chief of
police, §11-43-5.

**MUNICIPAL
CORPORATIONS**—Cont'd
Police—Cont'd
Civil service merit systems
for law enforcement
officers, §§11-43-180 to
11-43-190. See within
this heading, "Civil
service merit systems for
law enforcement
officers."
Class 1 municipalities.
Policemen's pensions and
relief plans.
Minimum monthly
benefits, §11-40-18.
Compensation for death or
disability from
occupational diseases,
§§36-30-20 to 36-30-23.
Authorized, §36-30-21.
Definitions, §36-30-20.
Eligibility for benefits.
Generally, §36-30-22.
Where physical
examination not
required at time of
entry into service,
§36-30-23.
Physical examination.
Eligibility for benefits
where examination
not required at time
of entry into service,
§36-30-23.
Continuing education.
Chief of police, §36-21-51.
County deputy sheriffs.
Employment as police,
§11-43-16.
Death.
Compensation for death
from occupational
diseases, §§36-30-20 to
36-30-23.
Disability.
Compensation for disability
from occupational
diseases, §§36-30-20 to
36-30-23.
Diseases.
Compensation for death or
disability from
occupational diseases,
§§36-30-20 to 36-30-23.
Enforcement of police
regulations.
Territorial operation of
ordinances for
enforcement,
§11-40-10.
Establishment of police force,
§11-43-55.
Jurisdiction, §§11-40-10,
11-47-22.
County industrial parks
not subject to,
§11-23-6.
Occupational diseases.
Compensation for death or
disability, §§36-30-20
to 36-30-23.
Organization of police force,
§11-43-55.

**MUNICIPAL
CORPORATIONS**—Cont'd
Police—Cont'd
Riots.
Employment of municipal
police within state by
governor during riots,
§§36-21-20 to 36-21-24.
Additional men.
Employment and
compensation,
§36-21-23.
Authorization, §36-21-20.
Command of police,
§36-21-24.
Compensation of police,
§36-21-22.
Additional men,
§36-21-23.
Duties of police,
§36-21-21.
Municipal authorities.
Duty when called upon
to furnish police,
§36-21-21.
Powers of police,
§36-21-21.
Privileges of police,
§36-21-21.
Station houses.
Provision of station houses,
§11-43-55.
Summons and complaint in
lieu of arrest,
§11-40-10.1.
Pollution.
Industrial development
boards.
Powers as to pollution
control facilities,
§11-54-88.
Promotion of pollution
control, §§11-54-1 to
11-54-211. See within
this heading, "Promotion
of industry, trade and
pollution control."
Pool tables. See within this
heading, "Billiard rooms."
Poorhouses.
Establishment, aid, etc., of
poorhouses in counties,
§11-47-134.
Police jurisdiction over
poorhouses, §11-47-22.
Population based acts.
Classification of
municipalities.
Eight classes, §11-45-9.1.
Post-office projects, §§11-55-1
to 11-55-13.
Acquisition of projects,
§§11-55-2, 11-55-13.
Bond issues, §§11-55-1 to
11-55-13.
Approval not required for
sale or issuance,
§11-55-7.
Delivery, §11-55-3.
Denominations, §11-55-3.
Disposition of proceeds
from sale, §11-55-5.
Execution, §11-55-3.
Exemption from taxation,
§11-55-11.
Form, §11-55-3.
Insurance companies.
Investment in bonds,
§11-55-8.

MUNICIPAL
   CORPORATIONS—Cont'd
Post-office projects—Cont'd
Bond issues—Cont'd
  Interest, §11-55-3.
    Security for payment,
      §11-55-4.
  Investment in bonds by
    savings banks and
    insurance companies,
    §11-55-8.
  Issuance of bonds.
    Consent, etc., of
      government not
      required, §11-55-7.
    Powers of municipalities,
      §11-55-2.
  Mortgages and deeds of
    trust.
    Security for payment,
      §11-55-4.
  Negotiability, §11-55-3.
  Notice to government not
    required, §11-55-7.
  Payment.
    Security for payment of
      principal and
      interest, §11-55-4.
  Powers of municipalities as
    to issuance, §11-55-2.
  Proceeds from sale.
    Disposition, §11-55-5.
  Redemption, §11-55-3.
  Refunding bonds, §11-55-6.
  Sale, §11-55-3.
    Consent, etc., of
      government not
      required, §11-55-7.
    Disposition of proceeds,
      §11-55-5.
  Savings banks.
    Investment in bonds,
      §11-55-8.
  Security for payment of
    principal and interest,
    §11-55-4.
  Terms, §11-55-3.
Construction of chapter,
  §11-55-12.
Contribution by
  municipalities to costs of
  acquisition of projects,
  §11-55-9.
Definitions, §11-55-1.
Donations.
  Acceptance of donations of
    property or money,
    §11-55-9.
  Use of municipal lands for
    acquisition of projects,
    §11-55-9.
Exemption from taxation,
  §11-55-11.
Insurance companies.
  Investment in bonds,
    §11-55-8.
Investments.
  Bond issues.
    Investment by savings
      banks and insurance
      companies, §11-55-8.
Leasing of projects.
  Authority to lease facilities
    to United States postal
    service, §11-55-13.
  Powers of municipalities,
    §11-55-2.
  Requirements as to leases,
    §11-55-10.

MUNICIPAL
   CORPORATIONS—Cont'd
Post-office projects—Cont'd
Mortgages and deeds of trust.
  Bond issues.
    Security for payment,
      §11-55-4.
  Consent, etc., of
    govermment not
    required for execution,
    §11-55-7.
  Security for payment,
    §11-55-4.
Municipal land.
  Use for costs of acquisition
    of projects, §11-55-9.
Powers of municipalities,
  §11-55-2.
Property.
  Acceptance of donations for
    projects, §11-55-9.
  Acquisition for use of
    United States postal
    service, §11-55-13.
  Lease to United States
    postal service,
    §11-55-13.
Savings banks.
  Investment in bonds,
    §11-55-8.
Power districts, §§37-5-1 to
  37-5-9.
See POWER DISTRICTS.
Powers of municipalities.
Acquisition of powers
  granted, §11-40-3.
Generally, §11-40-1.
Precincts.
Annexed territory.
  Cities of twenty-five
    thousand or more,
    §11-42-74.
Consolidation of contiguous
  municipalities.
  Alternate mode,
    §11-42-133.
Prisons and prisoners.
Jails, §§11-47-7, 11-47-8.
General provisions.
  See JAILS.
Inspection, §14-6-80.
Police jurisdiction over
  workhouses and houses
  of correction, §11-47-22.
Privies.
Regulation, installation, etc.,
  §11-50-55.
Probate judges.
Annexation.
  Compensation of probate
    judge, §11-42-87.
Attempted incorporations.
  Validation, §11-41-8.
Charters.
  Forfeiture of charter,
    §§11-41-24 to 11-41-26,
    11-41-28. See within
    this heading,
    "Charter."
Commission form of
  government, §§11-44-51,
  11-44-96.
Compensation.
  Annexation by cities of
    twenty-five thousand
    or more.
  Compensation of probate
    judges, §11-42-87.

MUNICIPAL
   CORPORATIONS—Cont'd
Probate judges—Cont'd
Compensation—Cont'd
  Commission form of
    government, §11-44-51.
  Optional form A,
    §11-44-96.
  Reduction of corporate
    limits, §11-42-213.
Dissolution, §§11-41-20 to
  11-41-28. See within this
  heading, "Dissolution."
Fees.
  Annexation.
    Cities of twenty-five
      thousand or more.
    Fees and compensation
      of probate judges,
      §11-42-87.
  Commission form of
    government.
    Optional form A,
      §11-44-96.
  Dissolution, §11-41-28.
  Forfeiture of charter,
    §11-41-28.
  Reduction of corporate
    limits, §11-42-213.
Forfeiture of charter,
  §§11-41-24 to 11-41-26,
  11-41-28. See within this
  heading, "Charter."
Incorporation.
  Petition to probate judge
    for order, §11-41-1.
Procedural irregularities.
  Validation, §11-41-8.
Validation.
  Prior attempted
    incorporations,
    §11-41-8.
Promotion of industry, trade
  and pollution control.
Acquisition of projects for
  promotion, §§11-54-20 to
  11-54-32.
Bond issues.
  Approval of government
    not required,
    §11-54-28.
  Default in payment.
    Remedies upon default,
      §11-54-25.
  Delivery, §11-54-24.
  Denominations,
    §11-54-24.
  Disposition of proceeds
    from sale, §11-54-26.
  Execution, §11-54-24.
  Exemption from
    taxation, §11-54-31.
  Form, §11-54-24.
  Interest, §11-54-24.
  Investment in bonds,
    §11-54-29.
  Notice to government not
    required, §11-54-28.
  Payment.
    Remedies upon default,
      §11-54-25.
    Security for payment,
      §11-54-25.
  Preissuance procedure,
    §§8-6-110 to 8-6-122.
  See INDUSTRIAL
    REVENUE
    BONDS.
  Proceeds from sale.
    Disposition, §11-54-26.
  Redemption, §11-54-24.

MUNICIPAL CORPORATIONS—Cont'd

Promotion of industry, trade and pollution control—Cont'd

Acquisition of projects for promotion—Cont'd

Bond issues—Cont'd

Refunding bonds, §11-54-27.

Remedies upon default, §11-54-25.

Sale, §11-54-24.

Consent, etc., of government not required, §11-54-28.

Disposition of proceeds, §11-54-26.

Security for payment, §11-54-25.

Terms, §11-54-24.

Construction of article, §§11-54-21, 11-54-32.

Contributions to cost of acquisition.

Municipalities not to contribute, §11-54-30.

Definitions, §11-54-20.

Exemption from taxation of projects, bonds, etc., §11-54-31.

Insurance companies.

Investment in bonds, §11-54-29.

Investments, §11-54-29.

Leasing of projects.

Powers of municipalities as to leasing, §11-54-22.

Requirements as to leasing, §11-54-23.

Legislative intent, §11-54-21.

Mortgages and deeds of trust.

Consent, etc., of government not required for execution, §11-54-28.

Municipal lands.

Not to be used for projects, §11-54-30.

Powers of municipalities as to, §11-54-22.

Requirements as to leasing of projects, §11-54-23.

Savings banks.

Investment in bonds, §11-54-29.

Taxation.

Exemption from taxation of projects, bonds, etc., §11-54-31.

Appropriations for promotion of industry, §11-47-11.

Generally, §§11-54-1 to 11-54-211.

Property.

Absorbed municipalities.

Duties of expanded municipalities, §§11-42-180 to 11-42-187. See within this heading, "Expanded municipalities."

Acquisition by condemnation, §§11-47-170 to 11-47-173.

MUNICIPAL CORPORATIONS—Cont'd

Property—Cont'd

Actions for recovery.

No limitation of time, §6-2-31.

Class 5 municipalities.

Mayor/commission/city manager form of government.

Powers of city, §11-44E-22.

Succession of government.

Transfer of property, §11-44E-143.

Commission form of government.

Optional form B.

Ordinances granting franchises for use of property, §11-44-137.

Condemnation, §§11-47-170 to 11-47-173.

Control by council, §11-43-56.

Disposition of unneeded real estate.

Generally, §11-47-20.

Leasing thereof, §11-47-21.

Dissolution.

Disposition of property after dissolution, §11-41-27.

Eminent domain, §§11-47-170 to 11-47-173.

Generally. See within this heading, "Eminent domain."

Franchises.

Commission form of government.

Ordinances granting franchises for use of property.

Optional form B, §11-44-137.

Industrial development boards.

Dissolution of boards.

Vesting of title to properties in municipalities upon, §11-54-94.

Exemption from taxation, §11-54-96.

Libraries.

Public library authorities, §§11-57-23 to 11-57-25.

Management, §11-43-56.

Mayor/commission/city manager form of government.

Powers of city, §11-44E-22.

Succession of government.

Transfer of property, §11-44E-143.

Medical clinic boards, §§11-58-12 to 11-58-14.

Mortgage for payment of debts, §11-81-27.

Post-office projects.

Use of municipal land for costs of acquisition, §11-55-9.

Promotion of industry, trade or pollution control.

Municipal lands not to be used for projects, §11-54-30.

Public athletic boards, §§11-59-12 to 11-59-14.

MUNICIPAL CORPORATIONS—Cont'd

Property—Cont'd

Public building authorities, §§11-56-19, 11-56-20.

Public library authorities, §§11-57-23 to 11-57-25.

Public park and recreation boards, §§11-60-15, 11-60-17.

Reservation of lands for future acquisition, §§11-52-50 to 11-52-54.

Rights.

Preserved and enforced.

Notwithstanding change of name or organization, §11-40-4.

Surveys, plats or maps, §§35-2-50 to 35-2-62. See within this heading, "Surveys, plats or maps."

Taxation, §§11-51-1 to 11-51-74. See within this heading, "Taxation."

Unneeded real estate.

Disposition, §11-47-20.

Leasing, §11-47-21.

Use of public property for public utility or private enterprise purposes.

Consent of municipal corporation prerequisite, Const. Ala., art. XII, §220.

Public athletic boards, §§11-59-1 to 11-59-17. See within this heading, "Parks and recreation."

Publication.

Class 5 municipalities.

Mayor/commission/city manager form of government.

Elections.

Notice, §11-44E-3.

Special election when vacancy in office of mayor, §11-44E-74.

Granting of franchises, §11-44E-52.

Ordinances, §11-44E-51.

Elections.

Mayor/commission/city manager form of government.

Notice, §§11-44E-3, 11-44E-74.

Public building authorities, §§11-56-1 to 11-56-22.

Board of directors, §11-56-6.

Record of proceedings, §11-56-6.

Bond issues, §§11-56-10 to 11-56-18, 11-56-21.

Authority for issuance, §11-56-10.

Notice of resolution authorizing, §11-56-11.

Default.

Remedies, §11-56-13.

Delivery, §11-56-12.

Denominations, §11-56-10.

Disposition of proceeds from sale, §11-56-14.

Execution, §11-56-12.

Exemption from taxation, §11-56-21.

MUNICIPAL
   CORPORATIONS—Cont'd
Public building authorities
   —Cont'd
Bond issues—Cont'd
   Form, §11-56-10.
   Interest.
      Security for payment,
         §§11-56-10, 11-56-13.
   Investment in bonds.
      Executors and
         administrators,
         §11-56-18.
      Fiduciaries, §11-56-18.
      Municipalities,
         §11-56-17.
      Savings banks,
         §11-56-18.
      Trustees, §11-56-18.
   Limitation of actions,
      §11-56-11.
   Maturity, §11-56-10.
   Payment.
      Remedies upon default,
         §§11-56-13, 11-56-15.
      Security for payment,
         §§11-56-10, 11-56-13.
   Proceeds from sale.
      Disposition, §11-56-14.
   Redemption, §11-56-10.
   Refunding bonds,
      §11-56-16.
   Remedies upon default,
      §§11-56-13, 11-56-15.
   Resolutions.
      Notice of resolution
         authorizing issuance
         of bonds, §11-56-11.
   Sale, §11-56-10.
      Disposition of proceeds,
         §11-56-14.
      Security for payment,
         §§11-56-10, 11-56-13.
   Terms, §11-56-10.
   Validity of proceedings for
      issuance.
      Limitation of actions,
         §11-56-11.
Certificate of incorporation,
   §§11-56-3 to 11-56-5,
   11-56-20.
Construction of chapter,
   §§11-56-2, 11-56-22.
Definitions, §11-56-1.
Directors.
   Board of directors,
      §11-56-6.
Dissolution.
   Generally, §11-56-20.
Executors and
   administrators.
   Investment in bonds,
      §11-56-18.
Exemption from taxation of
   projects, bonds, etc.,
   §11-56-21.
Fiduciaries.
   Investment in bonds,
      §11-56-18.
Incorporation, §§11-56-3 to
   11-56-5, 11-56-20.
   Application for authority to
      form corporation,
      §11-56-3.
   Certificate of incorporation,
      §§11-56-3 to 11-56-5.
      Acknowledgment,
         §11-56-5.
      Approval, §11-56-4.
      Contents, §11-56-4.
      Execution, §11-56-5.

MUNICIPAL
   CORPORATIONS—Cont'd
Public building authorities
   —Cont'd
Incorporation—Cont'd
   Certificate of incorporation
      —Cont'd
      Filing, §11-56-5.
      Recordation, §11-56-5.
   Procedure, §11-56-3.
   Resolution authorizing,
      §11-56-3.
   Subsequent formation of
      other corporations
      permitted, §11-56-20.
Insurance companies.
   Investment in bonds,
      §11-56-18.
Leasing of projects, §11-56-9.
Legislative intent, §11-56-2.
Officers, §11-56-7.
Powers, §11-56-8.
Projects.
   Exemption from taxation,
      §11-56-21.
Property.
   Conveyance to corporations
      by municipalities,
      §11-56-19.
   Vesting of title in
      municipalities upon
      dissolution, §11-56-20.
Records.
   Board of directors.
      Record of proceedings,
         §11-56-6.
Resolutions.
   Authorizing incorporation,
      §11-56-3.
   Bond issues.
      Notice of resolution
         authorizing issuance
         of bonds, §11-56-11.
Savings banks.
   Investment in bonds,
      §11-56-18.
Trustees.
   Investment in bonds,
      §11-56-18.
Public contracts.
General provisions, §§41-16-1
   to 41-16-125.
See CONTRACTS.
Public corporations.
   §§11-63-1 to 11-63-4.
Definitions.
   Financial assistance,
      §11-63-1.
Financial assistance.
   Bonds and securities of
      corporations,
      §§11-63-3, 11-63-4.
   Payments.
      Power to make,
         §11-63-2.
   Code.
      Defined, §11-63-1.
   Corporation securities.
      Defined, §11-63-1.
   Funds.
      Creation of irrevocable
         trust funds.
         Payment of corporate
            securities,
            §11-63-2.
   Grants to corporations.
      Power to make, §11-63-2.
   Loans to corporations.
      Power to make, §11-63-2.
   Municipality.
      Defined, §11-63-1.

MUNICIPAL
   CORPORATIONS—Cont'd
Public corporations—Cont'd
Financial assistance—Cont'd
   Municipal revenues.
      Defined, §11-63-1.
   Municipal securities.
      Defined, §11-63-1.
   Related public corporation.
      Defined, §11-63-1.
   Securities.
      Defined, §11-63-1.
Public improvements,
   §§11-48-1 to 11-48-106.
Acceptance of work.
   Council to accept for
      municipality,
      §11-48-13.
Acquisition of lands,
   easements, etc.,
   §11-48-64.
Assessments for public
   improvements, §§11-48-1
   to 11-48-106. See within
   this heading,
   "Assessments for public
   improvements."
Authorities.
   Improvement authorities.
      General provisions,
         §§39-7-1 to 39-7-34.
      See PUBLIC WORKS.
Bond issues.
   Public improvement bonds.
      Revenue producing
         undertakings,
         §§11-81-140 to
         11-81-150.
      See COUNTIES.
Completion of work.
   Issuance of bonds after
      completion, §11-48-62.
Contracts for improvements,
   §§11-48-11 to 11-48-13.
Costs of proposed
   improvements.
   Assessments, §§11-48-1 to
      11-48-106. See within
      this heading,
      "Assessments for
      public improvements."
   Payment of portion by
      council, §11-48-9.
   Specified, §11-48-9.
Definitions.
   Street and sewer
      improvements outside
      certain cities,
      §11-48-80.
Drawings of proposed
   improvements.
   Filing in office of engineer
      for public inspection,
      §11-48-6.
   Ordering preparation,
      §11-48-5.
Eminent domain, §11-48-64.
Engineer.
   City or town engineer to
      supervise work,
      §11-48-12.
Estimates of proposed
   improvements.
   Filing in office of engineer
      for public inspection,
      §11-48-6.
   Ordering preparation,
      §11-48-5.

MUNICIPAL CORPORATIONS—Cont'd
Public improvements—Cont'd
Grade of street, alley, etc., to be improved.
When council to establish grade, §11-48-10.
Hearings.
Objections as to improvements, §11-48-8.
Date for hearing, §11-48-6.
Housing projects.
Alienation of certain public improvements by political subdivisions, §§35-4-410 to 35-4-412.
Improvement authorities, §§39-7-1 to 39-7-34.
See PUBLIC WORKS.
Joint tenants.
Assessments against property owned by tenants in common, §§11-48-100 to 11-48-106. See within this heading, "Assessments for public improvements."
Loans.
Temporary loans.
Progress payments, §11-48-61.
ments."
Objections as to improvements.
Hearings, §11-48-8.
Date for hearing, §11-48-6.
Ordinances and resolutions.
Description of proposed investment, §11-48-5.
Generally, §§11-48-7, 11-48-8.
Parks and recreation.
Alienation of certain public improvements by political subdivisions, §§35-4-410 to 35-4-412.
Plans of proposed improvements.
Filing in office of engineer for public inspection, §11-48-6.
Ordering preparation of plans, §11-48-5.
Powers of municipalities, §11-48-4.
Rejection of work.
Council to reject for municipality, §11-48-13.
Sewers.
Outside certain cities, §§11-48-80 to 11-48-83.
Sidewalks.
Compelling owners to repair, §11-48-65.
Specifications of proposed improvements.
Filing in office of engineer for public inspection, §11-48-6.
Ordering preparation, §11-48-5.

MUNICIPAL CORPORATIONS—Cont'd
Public improvements—Cont'd
Street and sewer improvements outside certain cities, §§11-48-80 to 11-48-83.
Assessment of costs against property benefited, §11-48-81.
Bond issues.
Source of payments, §11-48-83.
Consent of property owners, §11-48-81.
Benefited property, §11-48-81.
Bond issues.
General obligation bonds.
Issuance to pay cost of improvements, §11-48-82.
Source of payments, §11-48-83.
Consent of property owners.
Requirement, §11-48-81.
Construction.
Powers of cities, §11-48-81.
Definitions, §11-48-80.
Powers of cities as to construction, §11-48-81.
Who may be assessed, §11-48-81.
Surveys of proposed improvements.
Filing in office of engineer for public inspection, §11-48-6.
Ordering preparation of surveys, §11-48-5.
Tenants in common.
Assessments against property owned by tenants in common, §§11-48-100 to 11-48-106. See within this heading, "Assessments for public improvements."
Waterworks and sewer boards.
Acquisition, operation, etc., of gas plants and systems, §§11-50-268 to 11-50-270, 11-50-273. See within this heading, "Waterworks and sewer boards."
Public library authorities, §§11-57-23 to 11-57-25.
Public service commission.
Exercise of certain municipal powers.
Title not intended to limit, §37-1-35.
Gas districts.
Exemption from jurisdiction of commission, §11-50-416.
Municipal utilities.
Jurisdictional exemptions, §37-1-34.

MUNICIPAL CORPORATIONS—Cont'd
Public service commission —Cont'd
Utilities.
Waiver in municipal ordinances or contracts, §37-1-48.
Public transportation service in class 3 municipalities, §§11-49A-1 to 11-49A-20.
See within this heading, "Transportation service in class 3 municipalities."
Public utilities.
Assessments for public improvements, §§11-48-1 to 11-48-106. See within this heading, "Assessments for public improvements."
Boards.
Boards for operation of water, sewer, gas and electric systems, §§11-50-310 to 11-50-324.
Boards of water and sewer commissioners, §§11-50-340 to 11-50-358. See within this heading, "Boards of water and sewer commissioners."
Electric utility boards, §§11-50-490 to 11-50-506. See within this heading, "Electricity."
Gas utility boards, §11-50-230.
Waterworks and sewer boards, §§11-50-230 to 11-50-291. See within this heading, "Waterworks and sewer boards."
Waterworks utility boards, §§11-50-430 to 11-50-445. See within this heading, "Water supply and waterworks."
Boards for operation of water, sewer, gas and electric systems, §§11-50-310 to 11-50-324.
Agreements of governing bodies with boards, §11-50-14.
Applicability of provisions pertaining to other boards, §11-50-324.
Board of health.
Jurisdiction, etc., §11-50-323.
Bond issues, §§11-50-315 to 11-50-318.
Contracts.
Security for repayment, §11-50-315.
Denominations, §11-50-316.
Execution, §11-50-316.
Interest, §11-50-316.
Mortgaging of systems for payment, §11-50-317.

MUNICIPAL
    CORPORATIONS—Cont'd
Public utilities—Cont'd
Boards for operation of
  water, sewer, gas and
  electric systems—Cont'd
Bond issues—Cont'd
  Payment.
    Mortgaging of systems,
      §11-50-317.
    Pledge of revenues,
      §11-50-317.
    Source, §11-50-316.
    Vesting of title to
      systems in
      municipality upon
      payment in full,
      §11-50-316.
  Pledge of revenues for
    payment,
    §11-50-317.
  Proceeds from sale.
    Disposition,
    §11-50-318.
  Refunding bonds,
    §11-50-316.
  Sale, §11-50-316.
    Disposition of proceeds,
    §11-50-318.
  Terms, §11-50-316.
Certificate of incorporation,
  §11-50-312.
Consolidation of systems,
  §11-50-321.
Construction of article,
  §11-50-323.
Contracts.
  Conveyance of system in
    other municipality.
    Execution upon
      payment,
      §11-50-320.
  Security for repayment,
    §11-50-315.
Conveyance of plants and
  systems to boards,
  §11-50-13.
Conditions as to control
  and operation of
  plants by boards,
  §11-50-14.
Definitions, §11-50-310.
Directors, §11-50-313.
  Fees, §11-50-15.
Dissolution of corporation,
  §11-50-316.
Exemption from usury and
  interest statutes,
  §11-50-319.
Fees, §11-50-313.
  Directors, §11-50-15.
Governing bodies'
  agreements with
  boards, §11-50-14.
Incorporation.
  Application for
    authority,
    §11-50-311.
  Certificate of
    incorporation,
    §11-50-312.
  Resolution authorizing,
    §11-50-311.
Interest statutes.
  Exemption, §11-50-319.
Jurisdiction, etc., of state
  board of health and
  public service
  commission,
  §11-50-323.

MUNICIPAL
    CORPORATIONS—Cont'd
Public utilities—Cont'd
Boards for operation of
  water, sewer, gas and
  electric systems—Cont'd
Mortgages and deeds of
  trust.
  Bond issues.
    Mortgaging of systems
      for payment,
      §11-50-317.
  Rights of parties,
    §11-50-314.
Operation by public water
  coprorations,
  §§11-50-370 to
  11-50-372.
Other municipalities.
  Acquisition, operation,
    etc., of systems
    located in other
    municipality,
    §11-50-320.
Pledge agreements.
  Bond issues.
    Pledge of revenues for
      payment,
      §11-50-317.
  Rights of parties,
    §11-50-314.
Powers of corporation,
  §11-50-314.
Public service commission.
  Jurisdiction, etc.,
    §11-50-323.
Resolution authorizing
  incorporation,
  §11-50-311.
Title to plants and
  systems.
  Powers of boards as to
    conveyance, etc., of
    title, §11-50-14.
  Vesting in municipality
    upon payment of
    bonds, §11-50-316.
Transfer of plants and
  systems to boards,
  §11-50-13.
  Conditions, etc., in
    instruments of
    transfer as to control
    and operation,
    §11-50-14.
Usury statutes.
  Exemption, §11-50-319.
Bond issues.
  Boards for operation of
    water, sewer, gas and
    electric systems,
    §§11-50-315 to
    11-50-318.
  Electric systems.
    Alternate borrowing for
      electric systems,
      §§11-81-200 to
      11-81-206. See
      within this heading,
      "Electricity."
  Exemption from taxation,
    §11-50-322.
  Public improvement bonds.
    Revenue-producing
      undertakings,
      §§11-81-140 to
      11-81-150.
    See COUNTIES.

MUNICIPAL
    CORPORATIONS—Cont'd
Public utilities—Cont'd
Bond issues—Cont'd
  Revenue bonds for
    waterworks, gas, sewer
    or electric systems,
    §§11-81-160 to
    11-81-190.
  Waterworks and sewer
    boards, §§11-50-237,
    11-50-239, 11-50-240.
Class 5 municipalities.
  Mayor/commission/city
    manager form of
    government.
    Conflicts of interest.
    Contracts,
      §11-44E-183.
Commission form of
  government.
  Municipal officers or
    employees.
    Conflicts of interest,
      §§11-44-46 to
      11-44-48.
Conflicts of interest.
  Mayor/commission/city
    manager form of
    government.
    Contracts, §11-44E-183.
Construction.
  Proposed construction to be
    submitted for approval
    of regional planning
    commission, §11-85-7.
  Proposed construction to be
    submitted for approval
    of municipal planning
    commission, §11-52-11.
Contracts.
  Mayor/commission/city
    manager form of
    government.
    Conflicts of interest,
      §11-44E-183.
  Rates and service
    regulations established
    by contract, §37-4-22.
  Waiver by utility of terms
    or conditions, §37-1-48.
Corporations.
  Compulsion of efficient
    service, §11-43-60.
  District electric
    corporations,
    §§11-50-520 to
    11-50-533. See within
    this heading,
    "Electricity."
  Public water corporations,
    §§11-50-370 to
    11-50-372.
Damages to abutting
  property owners.
  Liability, Const. Ala., art.
    XII, §227.
Definitions.
  Boards for operation of
    water, sewer, gas and
    electric systems,
    §11-50-310.
  Revenue bonds for
    waterworks, gas, sewer
    or electric systems,
    §11-81-160.

**MUNICIPAL
CORPORATIONS**—Cont'd
Public utilities—Cont'd
Districts.
Electric corporations,
§§11-50-520 to
11-50-533. See within
this heading,
"Electricity."
Gas districts, §§11-50-390
to 11-50-417. See
within this heading,
"Gas."
Efficient service.
Compulsion of efficient
service, §11-43-60.
Elections.
Boards for operation of
water, sewer, gas and
electric systems,
§§11-50-310 to
11-50-324.
Bond issues.
Boards for operation of
water, sewer, gas
and electric systems,
§§11-50-315 to
11-50-318.
Revenue bonds,
§§11-81-160 to
11-81-190. See within
this heading, "Revenue
bonds for waterworks,
gas, sewer or electric
systems."
Sale, lease, etc., of electric,
gas or waterworks
plants by
municipalities,
§§11-50-140 to
11-50-151.
Sale, lease, etc., of electric
plants by
municipalities,
§§11-50-140 to
11-50-151.
Electricity.
Alternate borrowing for
electric systems,
§§11-81-200 to
11-81-206. See within
this heading,
"Electricity."
District electric
corporations,
§§11-50-520 to
11-50-533. See within
this heading,
"Electricity."
Electric utility boards,
§§11-50-490 to
11-50-506. See within
this heading,
"Electricity."
General provisions. See
within this heading,
"Electricity."
Improvement authorities.
General provisions,
§§39-7-1 to 39-7-34.
See PUBLIC WORKS.
Public improvement bonds.
Revenue-producing
undertakings,
§§11-81-140 to
11-81-150.
See COUNTIES.
Exemption from taxation,
§11-50-322.

**MUNICIPAL
CORPORATIONS**—Cont'd
Public utilities—Cont'd
Fees.
Boards for operation of
water, sewer, gas and
electric systems.
Directors' fees,
§11-50-15.
Inspection and supervision
fees.
Assessment by
municipality
prohibited, §37-4-23.
Franchises.
Maximum term in cities
and towns of six
thousand or more,
Const. Ala., art. XII,
§228.
Taxation, §§40-21-26 to
40-21-28.
Gas.
Assessments for public
improvements,
§§11-48-1 to 11-48-106.
See within this
heading, "Assessments
for public
improvements."
Boards for operation of
water, sewer, gas and
electric systems,
§§11-50-310 to
11-50-324.
Districts, §§11-50-390 to
11-50-417. See within
this heading, "Gas."
Gas utility boards,
§§11-50-460 to
11-50-475. See within
this heading, "Gas."
General provisions. See
within this heading,
"Gas."
Improvement authorities.
General provisions,
§§39-7-1 to 39-7-34.
See PUBLIC WORKS.
Revenue bonds,
§§11-81-160 to
11-81-190.
Sale, lease, etc., of gas
plants by
municipalities,
§§11-50-140 to
11-50-151.
Transfer of gas system
without elections,
§§11-50-210 to
11-50-213.
Waterworks and sewer
boards.
Acquisition, operation of
gas plants and
systems, §§11-50-260
to 11-50-273. See
within this heading,
"Waterworks and
sewer boards."
Improvement authorities.
General provisions,
§§39-7-1 to 39-7-34.
See PUBLIC WORKS.
Leases.
Sale, lease, etc., of electric,
gas or waterworks
plants, §§11-50-140 to
11-50-151.

**MUNICIPAL
CORPORATIONS**—Cont'd
Public utilities—Cont'd
Mayor/commission/city
manager form of
government.
Conflicts of interest.
Contracts, §11-44E-183.
Officers.
Acceptance of employment
from public service
corporation.
Grounds for
impeachment,
§11-43-161.
Ordinances.
Revenue bonds,
§§11-81-163,
11-81-176.
Waiver by utility of terms
or conditions in
ordinances, §37-1-48.
Planning.
Proposed construction to be
submitted for approval
of commission,
§§11-52-11, 11-85-7.
Regional planning
commissions.
Eminent domain or
rights under
franchises not
impaired, §11-85-24.
Proposed construction to
be submitted for
approval, §11-85-7.
Property.
Exemption from taxation,
§11-50-322.
Public improvements,
§§11-48-1 to 11-48-106.
See within this heading,
"Public improvements."
Public roads and places.
Contracting with local
authorities for use,
§10-5-14.
Purchase by municipality or
governmental agency.
Electric systems, §§11-47-3,
11-50-8 to 11-50-11.
See within this
heading, "Electricity."
ontracts with
Gas systems. See within
this heading, "Gas."
Generally, §§37-4-60 to
37-4-65.
See PUBLIC UTILITIES.
Sewers, §§11-50-70 to
11-50-108. See within
this heading, "Sewers."
ntracts with
Waterworks, §§11-50-1,
11-50-5 to 11-50-11.
See within this
heading, "Water
supply and
waterworks."
Rates.
Boards of water and sewer
commissioners.
Establishment,
§11-50-351.
Electricity. See within this
heading, "Electricity."
Establishment by contract,
§37-4-22.
Gas, §§11-50-1, 11-50-184,
11-50-185.

**MUNICIPAL
CORPORATIONS**—Cont'd
Public utilities—Cont'd
Rates—Cont'd
Sewers, §§11-50-120 to
11-50-122.
Water supply and
waterworks. See
within this heading,
"Water supply and
waterworks."
Revenue bonds for
waterworks, gas, sewer
or electric systems,
§§11-81-160 to 11-81-190.
Acquisition of systems.
Authorized, §11-81-161.
Estimate of costs,
§11-81-162.
Additional bonds.
Issuance, §11-81-173.
Payment, §11-81-173.
Alternate borrowing for
electric systems,
§§11-81-200 to
11-81-206. See within
this heading,
"Electricity."
Anticipatory borrowing
authorized, §11-81-165.
Applicability of limitations
in other provisions of
chapter, §11-81-175.
Consolidation of systems.
Authorized, §11-81-161.
Estimate of costs,
§11-81-162.
Construction of article,
§11-81-190.
Contracts.
Impairment of valid
contracts,
§11-81-189.
Default in payment of
bonds.
Receivers, §11-81-180.
Definitions, §11-81-160.
Delivery of bonds,
§§11-81-166,
11-81-167.
Denominations of bonds,
§11-81-166.
Disposition of proceeds
from sale, §§11-81-169,
11-81-170.
Elections.
Not required, §11-81-176.
Execution of bonds,
§§11-81-166,
11-81-167.
Executors and
administrators.
Investment in bonds,
§11-81-177.
Exemption from taxation,
§11-81-172.
Extension of systems.
Authorized, §11-81-161.
Estimate of costs,
§11-81-162.
Fiduciaries.
Investment in bonds,
§11-81-177.
Form of bonds, §11-81-166.
Insurance companies.
Investment in bonds,
§11-81-177.
Investment of bonds,
§11-81-177.

**MUNICIPAL
CORPORATIONS**—Cont'd
Public utilities—Cont'd
Revenue bonds for
waterworks, gas, sewer
or electric systems
—Cont'd
Issuance of bonds.
Additional bonds,
§11-81-173.
Authorization
proceedings,
§11-81-166.
Limitation of actions
to set aside,
§11-81-164.
Notice of adoption,
§11-81-164.
Borrowing in
anticipation of
issuance authorized,
§11-81-165.
Elections.
Not required,
§11-81-176.
Ordinances or
resolutions.
Adoption, amendment,
recordation, etc.,
§11-81-163.
Publication of
ordinances,
resolutions, etc., not
required, §11-81-176.
Refunding bonds,
§11-81-174.
Restraining issuance.
Limitation of actions,
§11-81-164.
Liens.
Impairment not
authorized,
§11-81-189.
Statutory mortgage lien
of bondholders,
§§11-81-178,
11-81-179.
Limitation of actions.
Issuance of bonds,
§11-81-164.
Limitations in other
provisions of chapter,
§11-81-175.
Maintenance of systems.
Payment of expenses,
§11-81-182.
Maturity, §11-81-166.
Negotiability of bonds,
§11-81-168.
Operation of systems.
Payment of expenses out
of general funds,
§11-81-182.
Ordinances.
Issuance of bonds,
§11-81-163.
Publication not required,
§11-81-176.
Payment of bonds,
§11-81-166.
Additional bonds,
§11-81-173.
Default in payment.
Receivers, §11-81-180.
Pledge of revenues,
§11-81-181.
Proceeds from sale.
Disposition, §§11-81-169,
11-81-170.

**MUNICIPAL
CORPORATIONS**—Cont'd
Public utilities—Cont'd
Revenue bonds for
waterworks, gas, sewer
or electric systems
—Cont'd
Receivers.
Appointment upon
default, §11-81-180.
Powers, §11-81-180.
Redemption, §11-81-171.
Refunding bonds,
§11-81-174.
Repair of systems.
Authorized, §11-81-161.
Estimate of costs,
§11-81-162.
Resolutions.
Issuance of bonds,
§11-81-163.
Publication not required,
§11-81-176.
Revenues from systems.
Disposition, §11-81-181.
Pledge of revenues,
§11-81-181.
Sale of bonds, §11-81-166.
Borrowing in
anticipation,
§11-81-165.
Disposition of proceeds,
§11-81-169.
Excess proceeds,
§11-81-170.
Purposes, §11-81-170.
Elections.
Not required,
§11-81-176.
Publication of
ordinances,
resolutions, etc., not
required, §11-81-176.
Savings banks.
Investment in bonds,
§11-81-177.
Segregation of revenues,
§11-81-163.
Statutory mortgage lien of
bondholders.
Creation, §11-81-178.
Duration, §11-81-179.
Enforcement, §11-81-179.
Filing, §11-81-178.
Notice, §11-81-178.
Recordation, §11-81-178.
Taxation.
Exemption from
taxation, §11-81-172.
Terms of bonds,
§11-81-166.
Trustees.
Investment in bonds,
§11-81-177.
Trust indentures,
§11-81-166.
Sale, lease, etc., of electric,
gas or waterworks plants
by municipalities,
§§11-50-140 to 11-50-151.
Approval by governing
body, §37-4-42.
Assumption of payment of
existing bonded
indebtedness,
§11-50-151.
Authorized, §11-50-141.
Ordering of special
election, §11-50-143.
Definitions, §11-50-140.

**MUNICIPAL
CORPORATIONS**—Cont'd
Public utilities—Cont'd
Sale, lease, etc., of electric,
gas or waterworks plants
by municipalities
—Cont'd
Elections, §§11-50-143 to
11-50-149.
Appointment of clerks,
returning officers,
etc., §11-50-146.
Ballots, §§11-50-147 to
11-50-149.
Disposition,
§11-50-149.
Form, §11-50-148.
Marking, §11-50-148.
Provision of ballots,
§11-50-147.
Calling of election,
§11-50-144.
Canvassing of returns,
§11-50-149.
Clerks.
Appointment,
§11-50-146.
Conduct of election,
§11-50-147.
Managers.
Appointment,
§11-50-146.
Notice of election,
§11-50-145.
Ordering of special
election for
authorization,
§11-50-143.
Qualifications for voting,
§11-50-147.
Results.
Declaration,
§11-50-149.
Returning officers.
Appointment,
§11-50-146.
Transfer of gas system
without, §§11-50-210
to 11-50-213.
Transfer of water and
sewer systems
without, §§11-50-190
to 11-50-192.
Transfer of water
systems without
elections,
§§11-50-170 to
11-50-174.
Voting places.
Designation,
§11-50-146.
Execution, §11-50-150.
Existing bonded
indebtedness.
Assumption, §11-50-151.
Notice of election,
§11-50-145.
Purchaser to assume
bonded indebtedness,
§11-50-151.
Resolution, §11-50-142.
Terms of sale, lease, etc.,
§11-50-150.
Service.
Compulsion of efficient
service, §11-43-60.
Sewers.
Authorities.
Improvement authorities,
§§39-7-1 to 39-7-34.
See PUBLIC WORKS.

**MUNICIPAL
CORPORATIONS**—Cont'd
Public utilities—Cont'd
Sewers—Cont'd
Boards of water and sewer
commissioners,
§§11-50-340 to
11-50-358. See within
this heading, "Boards
of water and sewer
commissioners."
General provisions. See
within this heading,
"Sewers."
Improvement authorities.
General provisions,
§§39-7-1 to 39-7-34.
See PUBLIC WORKS.
Public improvement bonds.
General provisions,
§§11-81-110 to
11-81-123. See
within this heading,
"Bond issues."
Revenue-producing
undertakings,
§§11-81-140 to
11-81-150.
See COUNTIES.
Waterworks and sewer
boards, §§11-50-230 to
11-50-291. See within
this heading,
"Waterworks and
sewer boards."
Streets.
Consent of municipality as
to use of streets for
construction, §11-49-1.
Contracting with local
authorities on use of
streets, §10-5-14.
Taxation.
Franchises and intangibles,
§40-21-26.
Local taxes on.
Apportionment,
§40-21-27.
Entry and collection,
§40-21-28.
Telephones.
General provisions. See
within this heading,
"Telephones."
Improvement authorities.
General provisions,
§§39-7-1 to 39-7-34.
See PUBLIC WORKS.
Water supply and
waterworks.
Boards for operation of
water, sewer, gas and
electric systems,
§§11-50-310 to
11-50-324.
Boards of water and sewer
commissioners,
§§11-50-340 to
11-50-358. See within
this heading, "Boards
of water and sewer
commissioners."
General provisions. See
within this heading,
"Water supply and
waterworks."
Improvement authorities,
§§39-7-15, 39-7-19 to
39-7-21.
See PUBLIC WORKS.

**MUNICIPAL
CORPORATIONS**—Cont'd
Public utilities—Cont'd
Water supply and
waterworks—Cont'd
Public improvement bonds.
General provisions,
§§11-81-110 to
11-81-123. See
within this heading,
"Bond issues."
Revenue-producing
undertakings.
§§11-81-140 to
11-81-150.
See COUNTIES.
Public water corporations,
§§11-50-370 to
11-50-372.
Sale, lease, etc., of electric,
gas or waterworks
plants by
municipalities,
§§11-50-140 to
11-50-151.
Transfer of water systems
without elections,
§§11-50-170 to
11-50-174.
Waterworks and sewer
boards, §§11-50-230 to
11-50-291. See within
this heading,
"Waterworks and
sewer boards."
Waterworks utility boards,
§§11-50-430 to
11-50-445. See within
this heading, "Water
supply and
waterworks."
Public water corporations,
§§11-50-370 to 11-50-372.
Public works.
General provisions.
See PUBLIC WORKS.
Improvement authorities.
General provisions,
§§39-7-1 to 39-7-34.
See PUBLIC WORKS.
Public improvements,
§§11-48-1 to 11-48-106.
See within this heading,
"Public improvements."
Radioactive fallout
protection.
Requirement in new public
buildings, §39-6-2.
Quarantine.
Enforcement, §22-12-13.
Expense, §22-12-16.
Proclamation, §22-12-12.
Report of local quarantine to
state, §22-12-17.
Rabies.
Effect of chapter on
municipalities, §3-7-13.
Radiation.
Effect of chapter on local
ordinances, §22-14-15.
Radio utilities.
Inspection and supervision
fees.
Prohibited, §37-4-116.
Railroad authorities.
Cooperation of cities,
§37-13-9.
Railroads.
Assessment of costs of
improvements against
railroads, §11-48-19.

MUNICIPAL CORPORATIONS—Cont'd
Railroads—Cont'd
Bridges, tunnels, etc.,
§§11-49-40 to 11-49-45.
When construction
required within cities,
§§11-49-40 to 11-49-45.
Appeal from ordinances
requiring, §11-49-45.
Apportionment of costs
between railroads,
§11-49-42.
Authorized, §11-49-40.
Cost.
Apportionment,
§11-49-42.
Enforcement of
ordinance by action
in circuit court,
§11-49-44.
Failure to comply with
ordinance.
Appeal from orders
imposing
penalties,
§11-49-45.
Penalties, §11-49-43.
Ordinances, §§11-49-42
to 11-49-45.
Action to enforce,
§11-49-44.
Appeal from
ordinances,
§11-49-45.
Penalties for failure to
comply, §11-49-43.
Vacation of street,
§11-49-41.
Commission form of
government.
Municipal officers or
employees.
Conflicts of interest,
§11-44-46.
Connection of tracks and
interchange of traffic.
Railroads running to or
through same town or
city, §37-2-132.
License schedules,
§11-51-124.
Rights-of-way.
Abandoned rights-of-way.
Transfer to
municipalities,
§10-5-2.1.
Running, etc., of trains
within corporate limits.
Regulation, §11-47-114.
Sleeping car companies.
License schedules,
§11-51-125.
Street railroads. See within
this heading, "Street
railroads."
Streets, etc.
Regulation of running,
switching, etc., on
crossings, etc.,
§11-43-61.
Subways.
Construction, §18-1A-274.
Viaducts.
Construction, §18-1A-274.
Real property. See within this
heading, "Property."

MUNICIPAL CORPORATIONS—Cont'd
Recall of elected officials.
Class 5 municipalities.
Mayor/commission/city
manager form of
government,
§11-44E-168.
Recordation.
Annexation.
Cities of twenty-five
thousand or more.
Orders, maps, etc.,
§§11-42-51, 11-42-71.
Claims against municipality,
§11-43-101.
Incorporation.
Order of incorporation,
§11-41-4.
Ordinances, §11-45-8.
Reduction of corporate limits.
Recordation of map or plat,
§11-42-203.
Town surveys, plats or maps,
§§35-2-51, 35-2-57.
Records.
Class 5 municipalities.
Mayor/commission/city
manager form of
government.
Examination,
§11-44E-54.
Succession of
government.
Transfer of agency
records,
§11-44E-143.
Commission form of
government.
Commissioners.
Record of proceedings,
§§11-44-22,
11-44-126.
Maintenance of record
books, §11-44-51.
Optional form A.
Maintenance of record
books, §11-44-96.
Optional form B.
Commissioners.
Record of proceedings,
§11-44-126.
Council.
Clerks.
Preparation of records of
council meetings,
§11-43-100.
Council-manager form of
government.
Meetings, §11-43A-24.
Transfer of records upon
reassignment,
§11-43A-37.
Destruction of public records.
Establishment of
restoration, §12-20-50.
Electric utility boards.
Meetings.
Record of proceedings,
§11-50-496.
Gas utility boards.
Meetings.
Record of proceedings,
§11-50-467.
Incorporation proceedings,
§11-41-6.
Local government records
commission, §§41-13-22
to 41-13-25.

MUNICIPAL CORPORATIONS—Cont'd
Records—Cont'd
Lost records.
Establishment or
restoration, §12-20-50.
Mayor/commission/city
manager form of
government.
Examination, §11-44E-54.
Succession of government.
Transfer of agency
records,
§11-44E-143.
Municipal planning
commissions, §11-52-4.
Photographing or
microphotographing.
Appropriation, §41-13-43.
Public building authorities.
Board of directors,
§11-56-6.
Streets.
Municipal connecting link
roads.
Designation of roads,
§23-1-111.
Waterworks utility boards.
Record of proceedings,
§11-50-437.
Recreation. See within this
heading, "Parks and
recreation."
Redemption of securities,
§§11-82-1 to 11-82-7.
Definitions, §11-82-1.
Option to redeem.
Applicability of provisions,
§11-82-6.
Limitation on prices,
§11-82-4.
Prices.
Limitation, §11-82-4.
Retention, §11-82-2.
Securities maturing
more than 10 years
after date, §11-82-3.
To be provided in
proceedings for
issuance of securities,
§11-82-5.
Validation of certain
proceedings, §11-82-7.
Redevelopment projects,
§§24-2-1 to 24-2-10.
See REDEVELOPMENT
PROJECTS.
**Reduction of corporate
limits,** §§11-42-200 to
11-42-213.
Adoption of proposed limits.
Entry of order, §11-42-207.
Boundaries.
Establishment of proposed
boundary.
Hearing.
Notice, §11-42-202.
Evidence, §11-42-211.
Costs of proceedings,
§11-42-210.
Dismissal of proposal for
adoption of proposed
limits.
Entry of order, §11-42-208.
Election.
Ballots, §11-42-207.
Clerks, §11-42-207.
Conduct of election,
§11-42-207.
Contests, §11-42-209.
Inspectors, §11-42-207.

MUNICIPAL CORPORATIONS—Cont'd
Reduction of corporate limits—Cont'd
Election—Cont'd
List of qualified electors.
Certification and filing, §11-42-201.
Notice, §11-42-205.
Order directing election, §11-42-204.
Places of voting, §11-42-206.
Qualified electors, §11-42-206.
Certification and filing of list, §11-42-201.
Question submitted, §11-42-204.
Results, §11-42-207.
Returning officers, §11-42-207.
Evidence.
Map or plat, etc., evidence of municipal boundaries, §11-42-211.
Expenses of proceedings, §11-42-210.
Fees, §11-42-213.
Hearings.
Notice, §11-42-202.
Jurisdiction of territory within corporate limits established pursuant to article, §11-42-212.
Maps and plats.
Certification, §11-42-201.
Evidence of municipal boundaries, §11-42-211.
Filing, §§11-42-201, 11-42-202.
Hearings, §11-42-202.
Recordation, §11-42-203.
Notice.
Election, §§11-42-202, 11-42-205.
Orders.
Adoption of proposed limits, §11-42-207.
Dismissing adoption of proposed limits, §11-42-208.
Election on corporate limit, §11-42-204.
Establishing corporate limits as defined in resolution and map or plat when no protest filed, §11-42-203.
Recordation.
Maps and plats, §11-42-203.
Resolution.
Certification, §11-42-201.
Defining proposed reduced corporate limits, §11-42-200.
Filing, §§11-42-201, 11-42-202.
Regional planning and development, §§11-85-1 to 11-85-73.
See PLANNING.
Registration.
Bond issues, §11-81-9.

MUNICIPAL CORPORATIONS—Cont'd
Relief funds.
Council-manager form of government.
Effect of chapter on laws relating to, §11-43A-41.
Relocation assistance, §11-80-2.
Reports.
Boards of water and sewer commissioners, §11-50-355.
Census.
Effect of filing report of census, §11-47-94.
Class 5 municipalities.
Mayor/commission/city manager form of government.
Semiannual reports of city manager, §11-44E-92.
Electric utility boards.
Annual report, §11-50-501.
Examination of books and accounts, §11-50-500.
Finance.
Accounting, §11-43-85.
Gas utility boards, §11-50-471.
Accounting, §11-50-470.
Incorporation.
Election of mayor and councilmen.
Results, §11-41-6.
Mayor/commission/city manager form of government.
City manager, §11-44E-92.
Mayors.
Financial condition.
Statement to council, §11-43-84.
Requiring of reports by municipal officers, §11-43-84.
Officers.
Requiring of reports by, §11-43-84.
Quarantine.
Report of local quarantine to state, §22-12-17.
Sinking funds.
Investment or deposit, §11-81-19.
Treasurers.
Reports to council, §11-43-120.
Waterworks utility boards, §11-50-441.
Accounting, §11-50-440.
Weeds.
Abatement of weeds.
Class 2 municipalities, §§11-67-7 to 11-67-9.
Cost of abating, §11-67-8.
Cost of removing, §11-67-7.
Effect of account reports confirmed before enactment of article, §11-67-9.
Class 5 municipalities, §§11-67-26 to 11-67-28.
Cost of abating, §11-67-27.

MUNICIPAL CORPORATIONS—Cont'd
Reports—Cont'd
Weeds—Cont'd
Abatement of weeds —Cont'd
Class 5 municipalities —Cont'd
Cost of removing, §11-67-26.
Effect of account reports confirmed before enactment of article, §11-67-28.
Reservation of land sfor future acquisition, §§11-52-50 to 11-52-54.
Resolutions. See within this heading, "Ordinances and resolutions."
Resources.
Promotion of municipal resources.
Appropriations, etc., §11-47-11.
Restitution to victims of crimes.
Restitution centers.
Cooperation of municipalities, §15-18-76.
Powers of municipalities, §15-18-77.
Retirement plans. See within this heading, "Pension and retirement plans."
Rewards.
High crime or misdemeanor committed in municipality, §15-9-2.
Right of entry.
Eminent domain, §11-47-173.
Rights of municipalities.
Acquisition of rights granted, §11-40-3.
Commission form of government.
Continuation, §11-44-26.
Property rights.
Preserved and enforced.
Notwithstanding change of name or organization, §11-40-4.
Rights of way.
Gas districts.
Use of public highway rights of way, §11-50-400.
Police jurisdiction over, §11-47-22.
Railroads.
Abandoned rights-of-way.
Transfer to municipalities, §10-5-2.1.
Transportation service in class 3 municipalities.
Use of rights of way, §11-49A-17.
Riots.
Alcoholic beverages.
Temporary closings of licensed places, §28-3-47.
Police.
Employment of municipal police within state during, §§36-21-20 to 36-21-24.

MUNICIPAL CORPORATIONS—Cont'd

Riots—Cont'd

Proclamation closing shops and forbidding sale of arms, ammunition, etc., §11-43-82.

Roads. See within this heading, "Streets."

Rules and regulations.

Airports, §4-4-14.
Authority to regulate, §4-4-2.
Ambulance service, §11-87-1.
Gas districts, §§11-50-401 to 11-50-403.
Sales and use taxes, §11-51-204.
Subdivisions, §§11-52-50 to 11-52-54.
Zoning, §§11-52-70 to 11-52-84. See within this heading, "Zoning."

Safe buildings.

Codes.
Adoption by reference, §11-45-8.

St. Stephens historical commission.

Appropriation.
Authorized, §41-9-336.
Public facilities and improvements on commission land.
Powers as to, §41-9-336.

Salaries.

Class 5 municipalities.
Mayor/commission/city manager form of government.
Commission, §11-44E-43.
Power to set, §11-44E-44.
Manager, §11-44E-96.
Mayor, §11-44E-73.
Acting mayor, §11-44E-74.
Clerks, §§11-43-3, 11-43-4.
Commissioners, §§11-44-18, 11-44-80, 11-44-104, 11-44-129.
Mayor/commission/city manager form of government, §11-44E-43.
Councilmen, §11-43-2.
Ratification of certain salaries of councilmen, §11-43-17.
Employees.
Commission form of government, §11-44-28.
Optional form A, §11-44-85.
Optional form B, §11-44-104.
Establishment, §11-43-7.
Ordinances and resolutions fixing salaries.
Veto, §11-45-5.
Mayor/commission/city manager form of government.
Commission, §11-44E-43.
Power to set, §11-44E-44.
Manager.
Compensation, §11-44E-96.
Mayor, §11-44E-73.
Acting mayor, §11-44E-74.

MUNICIPAL CORPORATIONS—Cont'd

Salaries—Cont'd

Mayors, §11-43-80.
Class 1 municipality, §11-43-86.
Ratification of certain salaries of mayors, §11-43-17.
Officers.
Commission form of government, §11-44-28.
Optional form A, §11-44-85.
Optional form B, §11-44-104.
Establishment, §11-43-8.
Municipalities may provide for compensation, §§11-43-6, 11-46-1.
Ordinances and resolutions fixing salaries.
Veto, §11-45-5.
Unchanged during term of office, §11-43-9.
Ordinances and resolutions fixing salaries.
Veto, §11-45-5.
Treasurer, §11-43-3.

Sales.

Airports, §4-4-13.
Bond issues, §§11-81-11 to 11-81-14. See within this heading, "Bond issues."
Electric, gas or waterworks plants by municipalities, §§11-50-140 to 11-50-151. See within this heading, "Public utilities."
Licenses.
Auction sales, public sales and street sales, §11-51-97.
Farm products.
Municipalities not to charge farmers, §11-51-105.
Special health care facility authorities.
Sales of property to authority by other governmental entities, §11-62-16.
Taxation.
Sales of property to pay taxes, §§11-51-7, 11-51-16 to 11-51-25. See within this heading, "Taxation."

Sales and use taxes, §§11-51-200 to 11-51-207.

Administration by state department of revenue, §11-51-207.
Alcoholic beverage control board.
Exemption from sales tax, §11-51-200.
Applicability of provisions.
State excise or use tax law, §11-51-203.
State sales tax law, §11-51-201.
Ascertainment of taxes.
Rules and regulations, §11-51-204.
Assessment.
In lieu of license tax under section 11-51-90, §11-51-205.

MUNICIPAL CORPORATIONS—Cont'd

Sales and use taxes—Cont'd

Assessment—Cont'd
Pledge of proceeds of license tax.
Effect, §11-51-205.
Rules and regulations, §11-51-204.
Chilton county rescue squad.
Exemption, §40-23-5.
Collection of sales or use tax on same sale.
Only one tax collectible, §40-23-2.1.
Collection of taxes by state department of revenue, §11-51-207.
Diabetes Trust Fund, Inc.
Exemption from tax, §40-23-5.
Exemption from sales tax, §§11-51-200, 40-23-5.
Eye Foundation, Inc.
Exemption, §40-23-5.
King Ranch, Inc.
Exemption, §40-23-5.
Levy.
Excise or use tax levy authorized, §11-51-202.
In lieu of license tax under section 11-51-90, §11-51-205.
Outside corporate limits, §11-51-206.
Pledge of proceeds of license tax.
Effect, §11-51-205.
Rules and regulations, §11-51-204.
Sales tax levy authorized, §11-51-200.
License tax under section 11-51-90.
Levy and assessment of taxes in lieu of license tax, §11-51-205.
Pledge of proceeds of license tax.
Effect, §11-51-205.
Outside corporate limits.
Levy of tax outside limits, §11-51-206.
Rate.
Establishment, §11-51-205.
Rules and regulations, §11-51-204.
State department of revenue.
Administration and collection of taxes, §11-51-207.
State excise or use tax law.
Applicability, §11-51-203.
Exemptions, §40-23-62.
State sales tax law.
Applicability, §11-51-201.
Exclusion of certain municipal privilege license taxes, §40-23-3.
Exemptions, §40-23-4.

Sanitation.

Codes.
Adoption by reference, §11-45-8.
Inspections, §§11-43-59, 11-47-136, 11-47-139.

MUNICIPAL
CORPORATIONS—Cont'd
Sanitation—Cont'd
Jurisdiction.
Territorial operation of
ordinances for
enforcement of
sanitary regulations,
§11-40-10.
Maintenance of cleanliness,
§11-47-130.
Powers as to sanitation,
§11-47-131.
Savings and loan
associations.
Licenses.
Schedule of license tax,
§11-51-131.
Schools.
Annexation.
Territory exempt from
taxation.
Attendance at city
schools, §11-42-85.
City superintendents of
schools, §§16-12-1 to
16-12-21.
See EDUCATION.
General provisions.
See EDUCATION.
Police jurisdiction over
schoolhouses, §11-47-22.
Taxes.
See EDUCATION.
Seals and sealed
instruments, §11-40-1.
Council.
Custody of seal,
§11-43-100.
Description of seal, §11-40-2.
Searches and seizures.
Gambling implements,
§11-47-111.
Seawalls.
Assessments for public
improvements.
Manner of assessment,
§11-48-16.
Securities.
Bond issues. See within this
heading, "Bond issues."
Notes. See within this
heading, "Notes."
Redemption, §§11-82-1 to
11-82-7. See within this
heading, "Redemption of
securities."
Warrants. See within this
heading, "Warrants."
Securities issued in
anticipation of grants,
§§11-64-1 to 11-64-7.
Amount, §11-64-4.
Authority, §11-81A-3.
Construction and
interpretation, §11-64-7.
Definitions, §11-64-1.
Denominations, §11-64-4.
Execution, §11-64-4.
Grantee.
Defined, §11-64-1.
Powers, §11-64-2.
Interest.
Coupons, §11-64-4.
Investments.
Legal investments,
§11-64-6.
Maturity, §11-64-4.
Municipalities.
Defined, §11-64-1.

MUNICIPAL
CORPORATIONS—Cont'd
Securities issued in
anticipation of grants
—Cont'd
Municipalities—Cont'd
Powers, §§11-64-3,
11-81A-3.
Powers, §§11-64-3, 11-81A-3.
Public corporations.
Defined, §11-64-1.
Powers, §11-64-3.
Taxation.
Exemption from taxation,
§11-64-5.
Senior citizens.
Recreational, social and
cultural facilities.
Planning, establishment,
etc., §11-80-5.
Septic tanks.
Regulation, installation, etc.,
§11-50-55.
Service of process.
How city served, ARCP, Rule
4 (c).
Sewers.
Acquisition, operation, etc.,
§§11-50-50 to 11-50-54.
Authorized, §11-81-161.
Boards for operation of
water, sewer, gas and
electric systems,
§§11-50-310 to
11-50-324. See within
this heading, "Public
utilities."
Eminent domain, §11-50-1.
Expenses.
Payment, §11-81-182.
Notice, §11-50-56.
Public water corporations.
operation by,
§§11-50-370 to
11-50-372.
Purchase, §§11-50-70 to
11-50-108.
Revenue bonds,
§§11-51-161,
11-51-162. See within
this heading, "Public
utilities."
Rules and regulations,
§11-50-108.
State board of health.
Supervision of operation
by state board of
health, §11-81-185.
Waterworks and sewer
boards.
Management of systems
as agents of
municipalities,
§§11-50-290,
11-50-291.
Alteration of system,
§11-50-52.
Annexation.
Territory exempt from
taxation.
Construction of sanitary
sewers.
Connection required,
§11-42-78.
Assessments.
Acquisition, operation, etc.,
of sewers, §§11-50-50
to 11-50-54.
Lands purchased by state
at sale for taxes,
§11-48-15.

MUNICIPAL
CORPORATIONS—Cont'd
Sewers—Cont'd
Assessments—Cont'd
Manner of assessments,
§11-48-16.
Public improvements
generally, §§11-48-1 to
11-48-106. See within
this heading,
"Assessments for
public improvements."
Purchase, §§11-50-70 to
11-50-108.
Authorities.
Improvement authorities.
General provisions,
§§39-7-1 to 39-7-34.
See PUBLIC WORKS.
Boards.
Boards for operation of
water, sewer, gas and
electric systems,
§§11-50-310 to
11-50-324. See within
this heading, "Public
utilities."
Boards of water and sewer
commissioners,
§§11-50-340 to
11-50-358. See within
this heading, "Boards
of water and sewer
commissioners."
Waterworks and sewer
boards, §§11-50-230 to
11-50-291. See within
this heading,
"Waterworks and
sewer boards."
Bond issues.
Boards for operation of
water, sewer, gas and
electric systems,
§§11-50-315 to
11-50-318.
Boards of water and sewer
commissioners,
§§11-50-345 to
11-50-350, 11-50-353 to
11-50-356. See within
this heading, "Boards
of water and sewer
commissioners."
Public improvement bonds,
§§11-81-110 to
11-81-123. See within
this heading, "Bond
issues."
Purchase of sewers,
§§11-50-96 to
11-50-102, 11-50-105.
Waterworks and sewer
boards, §§11-50-237,
11-50-239, 11-50-240.
Calendar basis, §11-81-187.
Codes.
Adoption by reference,
§11-45-8.
Commissioners.
Boards of water and sewer
commissioners,
§§11-50-340 to
11-50-358. See within
this heading, "Boards
of water and sewer
commissioners."

**MUNICIPAL
CORPORATIONS**—Cont'd

Sewers—Cont'd

Commission form of
government.
President of board as
superintendent of
sewer systems,
§11-50-16.
Condemnation of easements,
etc., §11-50-51.
Connections.
Boards of water and sewer
commissioners.
Rules and regulations,
§11-50-352.
Failure to make
connection, §11-50-54.
Installation, §§11-50-53,
11-50-54.
Penalty for failure to make
connection, §11-50-54.
Regulation, §11-50-53.
Consolidation of systems.
Authorized, §11-81-161.
Construction.
Authorized, §11-50-50.
Contracts.
Public water corporations
and public sewer
corporations.
Operation and
management of
systems, §11-50-371.
Purchase of sewers,
§11-50-74.
Amendment, etc., of
contract, §11-50-77.
Conveyance to boards
organized to own sewer
plants, §§11-50-13,
11-50-14.
Corporations.
Operation of systems by
public water
corporations,
§§11-50-370 to
11-50-372.
Definitions.
Operation of systems by
public water
corporations,
§11-50-370.
Transfer of water and
sewer systems by
municipalities without
elections, §11-50-190.
Drains.
Construction and
maintenance,
§11-50-55.
Easements.
Condemnation, §11-50-51.
Eminent domain, §11-50-51.
Extension of system,
§11-50-52.
Authorized, §11-81-161.
Financial condition of
system.
Accounting, §11-81-188.
Fiscal year basis, §11-81-187.
Improvement authorities.
General provisions,
§§39-7-1 to 39-7-34.
See PUBLIC WORKS.
Maintenance of systems.
Authorized, §11-50-50.
Expenses.
Payment, §11-81-182.
Rules and regulations,
§11-50-108.

**MUNICIPAL
CORPORATIONS**—Cont'd

Sewers—Cont'd

Maps.
Purchase of sewers.
Filing of maps in office
of engineer for
public inspection,
§11-50-73.
Ordering preparation,
§11-50-72.
Mayors.
Employment as
superintendent of
systems, §§11-43-80,
11-50-16.
Notice, §11-50-56.
Assessments for costs of
purchase, §§11-50-81,
11-50-82.
Operation of systems,
§§11-50-50 to 11-50-54.
Ordinances.
Purchase of sewers,
§§11-50-75 to 11-50-77.
Transfer of systems by
municipalities without
elections, §11-50-191.
Outside certain cities,
§§11-48-80 to 11-48-83.
Payment by municipalities
for services furnished by
system, §11-81-186.
Penalties.
Connections.
Failure to make,
§11-50-54.
Plumbing.
Regulation, installation,
etc., §11-50-54.
Police jurisdiction over
sewers, §11-47-22.
President of board of
commissioners.
Superintendent of sewer
systems, §11-50-16.
Privies.
Regulation, installation,
etc., §11-50-55.
Properties of system.
Accounting, §11-81-188.
Public improvements.
Bond issues, §§11-81-110 to
11-81-123. See within
this heading, "Bond
issues."
General provisions. See
within this heading,
"Public
improvements."
Improvement authorities.
General provisions,
§§39-7-1 to 39-7-34.
See PUBLIC WORKS.
Public water corporations.
Operation of systems,
§§11-50-370 to
11-50-372.
Purchase, §§11-50-70 to
11-50-108.
Assessments, §11-50-75.
Account, §11-50-103.
Amount.
Fixing amount,
§11-50-85.
Appeals, §11-50-90.
Assessment book,
§§11-50-80 to
11-50-82.
Authorized, §11-50-79.

**MUNICIPAL
CORPORATIONS**—Cont'd

Sewers—Cont'd

Purchase—Cont'd
Assessments—Cont'd
Deposit of proceeds in
bank, §11-50-104.
Disbursement of
proceeds, §11-50-103.
Excess assessments.
Refunds, §§11-50-106,
11-50-107.
Lien for assessments,
§11-50-85.
Assignment, §11-50-86.
Effect of enforcement
of tax liens upon,
§11-50-88.
Effect of sale of
property for
enforcement of
other assessment
liens, §11-50-89.
Enforcement,
§§11-50-87,
11-50-89, 11-50-92,
11-50-94.
Sale of property for
enforcement,
§11-50-89.
Transfer, §11-50-86.
List of property owners
to be assessed.
Entry in assessment
book, §11-50-80.
Preparation of list,
§11-50-80.
Notice, §11-50-82.
Effect and correction of
defects or errors in
notice, §11-50-82.
Objections to
assessments.
Filing, §§11-50-83,
11-50-84.
Hearing, §§11-50-81,
11-50-84.
Payment, §11-50-91.
Prior to sale of land
upon failure to
pay, §11-50-92.
Proceeds from
assessments,
§§11-50-103 to
11-50-105.
Accounting,
§11-50-103.
Deposit in bank,
§11-50-104.
Disposition of excess,
§11-50-105.
Use, §11-50-105.
Withdrawal from
bank, §11-50-104.
Redemption of property
after sale, §11-50-95.
Refunding of excess
assessments.
Authority, §11-50-106.
Disposition of amounts
not refunded,
§11-50-107.
Limitation period for
presentation of
claims, §11-50-107.
Procedure, §11-50-106.

MUNICIPAL
CORPORATIONS—Cont'd
Sewers—Cont'd
Purchase—Cont'd
Assessments—Cont'd
Sale of land upon failure to pay, §§11-50-89, 11-50-92 to 11-50-95.
Cost of notice and sale charged against land, §11-50-92.
Defect in notice or sale, §11-50-94.
Disposition of surplus, §11-50-93.
Effect of sale upon other assessment liens upon same property, §11-50-89.
Error in notice or sale, §11-50-94.
Execution of deed, §11-50-93.
Notice, §11-50-92.
Payment prior to sale, §11-50-92.
Purchase by municipality, §11-50-93.
Redemption of property after sale, §11-50-95.
Withdrawal of proceeds, §11-50-104.
Authorized, §11-50-71.
Bond issues, §§11-50-96 to 11-50-105.
Authorized, §11-50-96.
Denominations, §11-50-98.
Disposition of proceeds from sale, §11-50-99.
Diversion of funds for payment of bonds.
Liability, §11-50-102.
Execution of bonds, §11-50-98.
Form of bonds, §11-50-98.
Interest, §11-50-98.
Liability for diversion of funds for payment, §11-50-102.
Municipalities of less than six thousand.
Issuance, etc., §11-50-101.
Payment of bonds, §11-50-100.
Liability for diversion of funds for payment, §11-50-102.
Redemption of bonds, §11-50-100.
Use of proceeds from assessments, §11-50-105.
Sale of bonds, §11-50-98.
Disposition of proceeds, §11-50-99.
Terms, §11-50-98.
Contracts.
Amendment, §11-50-77.
Contents, §11-50-74.
Execution, §11-50-74.
Modification, §11-50-77.
Rescission, §11-50-77.
Terms, §11-50-74.

MUNICIPAL
CORPORATIONS—Cont'd
Sewers—Cont'd
Purchase—Cont'd
Costs.
Payment of portion of costs by council, §11-50-78.
Specification of costs, §11-50-78.
Council defined, §11-50-70.
Loans.
Making of loans to pay for sewers, §11-50-97.
Maps.
Filing of maps in office of engineer for public inspection, §11-50-73.
Ordering preparation, §11-50-72.
Notice.
Assessments, §§11-50-81, 11-50-82.
Objections to purchase.
Hearing, §11-50-77.
Date, §11-50-75.
Ordinance or resolution describing system, §11-50-72.
Ordinance or resolution providing for purchase, §§11-50-75 to 11-50-77.
Amendment, §11-50-77.
Modification, §11-50-77.
Passage, §11-50-75.
Publication, §11-50-76.
Rescission, §11-50-77.
Payment of portion of costs by council, §11-50-78.
Profiles.
Filing of profiles in office of engineer for public inspection, §11-50-73.
Ordering preparation, §11-50-72.
Purchase of public utilities generally, §§37-4-60 to 37-4-65.
See PUBLIC UTILITIES.
Rates, fees and charges, §11-50-128.
Boards of water and sewer commissioners, §11-50-351.
Definitions, §11-50-120.
Enforcement, §11-50-122.
Establishment, §§11-50-121, 11-50-351, 11-81-184.
Revenues, §§11-81-16, 11-81-181, 11-81-183.
Schedule.
Single schedule for combined sewer and water systems, §11-50-121.
State supervision or regulation.
Not subject to, §11-81-185.
Repair.
Authorized, §11-81-161.
Resolutions.
Purchase of sewers, §§11-50-75 to 11-50-77.
Transfer of water and sewer systems without elections, §11-50-191.

MUNICIPAL
CORPORATIONS—Cont'd
Sewers—Cont'd
Resort areas.
Construction of sewerage facilities in resort areas, §§11-88-40 to 11-88-111.
Revenue bonds, §§11-81-160 to 11-81-190. See within this heading, "Public utilities."
Revenues.
Depository.
Designation, §11-81-183.
Disposition of gross revenue account and special funds, §11-81-183.
Disposition of gross revenues, §§11-81-181, 11-81-183.
Gross revenue account.
Disposition, §§11-81-181, 11-81-183.
Pledge of revenues, §§11-81-16, 11-81-181.
Rules and regulations, §11-50-108.
Septic tanks.
Regulation, installation, etc., §11-50-55.
State board of health.
Supervision of operation of sewer systems, §11-81-185.
Superintendent of sewer systems.
Employment of mayor or president of board of commissioners as, §§11-43-80, 11-50-16.
Transfer of plants to boards organized to own and operate, §§11-50-13, 11-50-14.
Transfer of water and sewer systems without elections, §§11-50-190 to 11-50-192.
Agreements, §11-50-192.
Authorization of conveyance, §11-50-191.
Conveyance authorized, §11-50-191.
Definitions, §11-50-190.
Ordinance, §11-50-191.
Resolution, §11-50-191.
Terms, §11-50-191.
Trusts and trustees.
Boards of water and sewer commissioners, §§11-50-346, 11-50-347, 11-50-349, 11-50-353. See within this heading, "Boards of water and sewer commissioners."
Water closets.
Regulation, installation, etc., §11-50-55.
Water, sewer and fire protection authorities, §§11-88-1 to 11-88-111.
See WATER, SEWER AND FIRE PROTECTION AUTHORITIES.

**MUNICIPAL
CORPORATIONS**—Cont'd
Sewers—Cont'd
Water, sewer and fire
protection districts,
§§11-89-1 to 11-89-19.
See WATER, SEWER AND
FIRE PROTECTION
DISTRICTS.
Water supply and
waterworks.
Combination of sewer
system and water
distribution system,
§11-50-121.
Waterworks and sewer
boards, §§11-50-230 to
11-50-291. See within
this heading,
"Waterworks and sewer
boards."
Sheriffs.
County deputy sheriffs.
Employment as police,
§11-43-16.
General provisions.
See SHERIFFS.
Ships and shipping.
Local regulation, §33-5-31.
Municipal boats.
Exemption from
numbering provisions,
§33-5-19.
Shooting galleries.
Closing, §11-51-102.
Licenses, §11-51-102.
Revocation, §11-51-103.
Sidewalks.
Annexation.
Territory exempt from
taxation.
Construction of
sidewalks and
curbing and
assessment of costs,
§11-42-79.
Assessments for public
improvements.
Compelling repair of
sidewalks, §11-48-65.
Manner of assessments,
§11-48-18.
Awnings.
Regulation of awnings
overhanging
sidewalks, §11-49-2.
Bond issues.
Public improvement bonds,
§§11-81-110 to
11-81-123. See within
this heading, "Bond
issues."
Cellar openings.
Regulation of cellar
openings on sidewalks,
§11-49-2.
Public improvements,
§§11-48-1 to 11-48-106.
See within this heading,
"Public improvements."
Repairs.
Public improvements.
Compelling repair,
§11-48-65.
Regulation, construction,
etc., §11-49-2.
Signs.
Municipal connecting link
roads, §23-1-113.

**MUNICIPAL
CORPORATIONS**—Cont'd
Signs—Cont'd
Regulation of signs
overhanging streets or
sidewalks, §11-49-2.
Speed limits, §11-49-5.
Sinking funds, §§11-81-15,
11-81-19 to 11-81-26.
Bond issues, §§11-81-22 to
11-81-25.
Designation, §11-81-23.
Disposition, §11-81-23.
Duties of trustee of sinking
fund, §11-81-24.
Execution, §11-81-22.
Interest, §11-81-23.
Issuance, §11-81-22.
Maturity, §11-81-23.
Powers of trustee of
sinking fund,
§11-81-25.
Creation, §11-81-24.
Deposit.
Reports as to deposit,
§11-81-19.
Establishment, §11-81-24.
Investment, §§11-81-19 to
11-81-21.
Generally, §11-81-19.
Investment of funds
received to credit of
sinking fund,
§11-81-20.
Municipal funds,
§11-81-21.
Reports as to investment,
§11-81-19.
Payments.
Special tax.
Mandamus proceedings,
§11-81-26.
Public improvement bonds,
§§11-81-110 to 11-81-123.
See within this heading,
"Bond issues."
Reports.
Investment or deposit,
§11-81-19.
Savings certificates.
Contracts for purchases,
§11-81-19.
Taxation.
Special tax for payments,
§11-81-15.
Mandamus proceedings,
§11-81-26.
Trustee of sinking fund.
Duties, §11-81-24.
Employment, §11-81-24.
Powers, §11-81-25.
Slaughterhouses.
Establishment, §11-47-138.
Regulation, §§11-47-137,
11-47-138.
Social security.
Public employees, §§36-28-1
to 36-28-10.
See SOCIAL SECURITY.
Solid waste.
Management plan.
General provisions,
§§22-27-40 to 22-47-49.
See SOLID WASTE.
**Southeast interstate low-
level radioactive waste
management compact.**
Cooperation with
commission, §22-32-7.

**MUNICIPAL
CORPORATIONS**—Cont'd
**Special health care facility
authorities,** §§11-62-1 to
11-62-21.
Acquisitions by authority,
§11-62-16.
Assets.
Acquisition by authority,
§11-62-16.
Dissolution of authority.
Vesting of title to assets
and properties,
§11-62-17.
Authority to form.
Applications, §11-62-3.
Effect, §11-62-3.
Authorized purpose
obligation.
Defined, §11-62-1.
Board.
Defined, §11-62-1.
Board of directors, §11-62-5.
Bond issues, §§11-62-8 to
11-62-12.
Counties.
Investment, §11-62-11.
Debt servicing.
Special debt service
reserve funds,
§11-62-12.
Default.
Remedies, §11-62-8.
Delivery, §11-62-8.
Denominations, §11-62-8.
Execution, §11-62-8.
Form, §11-62-8.
Municipalities.
Investment, §11-62-11.
Notice.
Resolution authorizing
issuance, §11-62-9.
Redemption, §11-62-8.
Refunding bonds and notes,
§11-62-10.
Remedies.
Default, §11-62-8.
Resolution.
Authorizing, §11-62-8.
Notice, §11-62-9.
Sale, §11-62-8.
Security for payment,
§11-62-8.
Series, §11-62-8.
State.
Investment by state,
§11-62-11.
State obligations.
Debt not created by
bonds, §11-62-8.
Terms, §11-62-8.
Validity.
Actions concerning.
Limitations, §11-62-9.
Certificates of incorporation,
§§11-62-3, 11-62-4.
Acknowledgment, §11-62-3.
Amendment, §11-62-4.
Contents, §11-62-3.
Execution, §11-62-3.
Filing, §11-62-3.
Recordation, §11-62-3.
Competitive bid laws.
Exemptions, §11-62-20.
Construction of chapter,
§11-62-21.
County.
Defined, §11-62-1.
Definitions, §11-62-1.
Determining municipality.
Defined, §11-62-1.

MUNICIPAL CORPORATIONS—Cont'd
Special health care facility authorities—Cont'd
Director.
Defined, §11-62-1.
Dissolution of authority.
Authority to dissolve, §11-62-17.
Procedure, §11-62-17.
Earnings of authority.
Disposition of net earnings, §11-62-15.
Eligible investment.
Defined, §11-62-1.
Facilities.
Defined, §11-62-1.
Operation by authority, §11-62-7.
Administration or management by third parties, §11-62-13.
Limitations, §11-62-13.
Religious activities.
Use of facilities to promote or inhibit, §11-62-14.
Formation of corporations, §11-62-3.
Grants.
Receipt by authority, §11-62-16.
Herein.
Defined, §11-62-1.
Incorporators.
Defined, §11-62-1.
Legislative intent, §11-62-2.
Loans.
Making of loans to authority, §11-62-16.
Municipalities.
Defined, §11-62-1.
Officers, §11-62-6.
Powers of authority, §11-62-7.
Purpose of chapter, §11-62-2.
Sales of property to authority, §11-62-16.
State.
Defined, §11-62-1.
Taxation.
Exemptions, §11-62-18.
Users.
Defined, §11-62-1.
Usury and interest laws.
Exemptions, §11-62-19.
Speed limits.
Bridges, §32-5-92.
Establishment within corporate limits, §11-49-4.
Posting of signs, §11-49-5.
Stadiums.
Public athletic boards, §§11-59-1 to 11-59-17.
See within this heading, "Parks and recreation."
Public improvement bonds.
Revenue-producing undertakings, §§11-81-140 to 11-81-150.
See COUNTIES.
State.
Legislation applying to single municipality.
Notice of intention to enact, §11-40-13.

MUNICIPAL CORPORATIONS—Cont'd
State—Cont'd
Streets.
Construction, improvement, etc., by state.
Payment of costs by municipal corporations, §§11-49-60 to 11-49-62.
State parks.
Appropriations.
Improvement, operation, etc., of state park system, §9-14-6.
Grants of land to state park system, §9-14-6.
Stolen property.
Disposition of proceeds, §11-47-116.
Redemption by owner, §11-47-116.
Sale, §11-47-116.
Storage, §11-47-116.
Taking up stolen property, §11-47-116.
Street railroads.
Annexation.
Territory exempt from taxation.
Privilege or license tax, §11-42-84.
Licenses.
Schedule, §11-51-129.
Operation over tracks of another company.
Regulation, §11-47-115.
Repairs.
Railroads and public utilities using streets to be required to keep streets in repair, etc., §11-49-3.
Streets.
Advertising.
Municipal connecting link roads, §23-1-113.
Animals.
Running at large, §11-47-110.
Architectural review boards.
Applicability of provisions to streets, §11-68-15.
Assessments for public improvements, §§11-48-10, 11-48-15 to 11-48-17. See within this heading, "Assessments for public improvements."
Assumption of authority over streets controlled by counties, §§11-49-80, 11-49-81.
Resolutions.
Adoption, §11-49-80.
Contents, §11-49-81.
When effective, §11-49-81.
Bond issues.
Public improvement bonds, §§11-81-110 to 11-81-123. See within this heading, "Bond issues."

MUNICIPAL CORPORATIONS—Cont'd
Streets—Cont'd
Buildings.
Vacation of streets for erection of public buildings, §§11-49-100 to 11-49-106.
Capital improvement generally, §§11-66-1 to 11-66-7. See within this heading, "Capital improvement."
Cleaning.
Provision for cleaning, §11-47-18.
Closing and vacating streets.
General provisions, §§23-4-1 to 23-4-20.
See HIGHWAYS.
Commission form of government.
Contracts for construction, improvement, etc.
Procedure for letting.
Optional form A, §11-44-89.
Franchises for use of streets.
Objections, §11-44-34.
Procedure for granting, §11-44-36.
Resolutions, bylaws or ordinances granting.
Effective date, §11-44-33.
Elections, §11-44-34.
Optional form A, §11-44-88.
Optional form B, §11-44-137.
Proceedings upon determination of election result, §11-44-35.
Publication, §11-44-33.
Optional form A.
Contracts for construction, improvement, etc., §11-44-89.
Franchises, etc., for use of streets, §11-44-88.
Optional form B.
Ordinances granting franchises for use of streets, §11-44-137.
Connecting link roads, §§23-1-110 to 23-1-113.
Constructed, improved, etc., by county, state or federal government.
Payment of cost, §§11-49-60 to 11-49-63.
Assessment of proportionate share, §11-49-60.
Enforcement of lien, §11-49-61.
Bond issues.
Payment of proportionate share of cost, §11-49-62.
Conduct of proceedings under article, §11-49-63.

MUNICIPAL
CORPORATIONS—Cont'd
Streets—Cont'd
Constructed, improved, etc.,
   by county, state or
   federal government
   —Cont'd
  Payment of cost—Cont'd
   Contract by municipality
    for payment of
    proportionate share
    of cost.
    Authorized, §11-49-60.
   Lien on property
    assessed.
    Enforcement,
     §11-49-61.
    Establishment,
     §11-49-61.
   Proportionate share of
    cost, §§11-49-60 to
    11-49-62.
   Assessment against
    property benefited,
    §11-49-60.
   Bond issues to pay,
    §11-49-62.
   Contract by
    municipality
    authorized,
    §11-49-60.
   Enforcement of lien,
    §11-49-61.
Construction.
  Proposed construction
   submitted for approval
   of municipal planning
   commission, §11-52-11.
  Proposed construction
   submitted for approval
   of regional planning
   commission, §11-85-7.
  Use of proceeds of gasoline
   tax, §40-17-79.
Contracts.
  Paving of city streets.
   Highway department,
    §23-1-40.
Counties.
  Assumption of authority
   over streets controlled
   by counties,
   §§11-49-80, 11-49-81.
  Payment of costs of streets
   constructed, improved,
   etc., §§11-49-60 to
   11-49-63.
Electric lines.
  Regulation of use of streets
   for electric lines,
   §11-43-62.
Eminent domain, §11-80-1.
Failure to maintain.
  Grounds for forfeiture of
   charter, §11-41-24.
Franchises.
  Commission form of
   government.
   Procedure to grant,
    §11-44-36.
   Resolutions, bylaws or
    ordinances granting
    franchise for use of
    streets, §§11-44-33 to
    11-44-35, 11-44-88,
    11-44-137.
   Effective date,
    §11-44-33.
   Elections, §11-44-34.
   Objections, §11-44-34.

MUNICIPAL
CORPORATIONS—Cont'd
Streets—Cont'd
Franchises—Cont'd
  Commission form of
   government—Cont'd
   Resolutions, bylaws or
    ordinances granting
    franchise for use of
    streets—Cont'd
    Optional form A,
     §11-44-88.
    Optional form B,
     §11-44-137.
    Proceedings upon
     determination of
     election result,
     §11-44-35.
    Publication, §11-44-33.
Gasoline tax.
  Use of proceeds for
   construction and
   maintenance of streets,
   §40-17-79.
General provisions.
  See HIGHWAYS.
Highways.
  Designation as state
   highways.
   Highway department,
    §23-1-40.
Historic preservation
  commissions.
  Applicability of provisions
   to streets, §11-68-15.
Intersections.
  Assessments for
   improvements,
   §11-48-17.
Interstate highways.
  Municipal connecting link
   roads, §§23-1-110 to
   23-1-113.
Lighting.
  Municipal connecting link
   roads, §23-1-113.
  Provision for lighting,
   §11-47-18.
Livestock.
  Driving through streets,
   §11-47-110.
  Running at large,
   §11-47-110.
Maintenance.
  Authority of highway
   department, §23-1-47.
  Counties.
   Maintenance declared
    county matter,
    §11-83-1.
  Use of proceeds of gasoline
   tax, §40-17-79.
Maps or plats.
  Approval of municipal
   authorities, §35-2-52.
  Vacation of streets by
   abutting landowners,
   §35-2-54.
  Validation, §35-2-55.
Municipal connecting link
  roads, §§23-1-110 to
  23-1-113.
  Advertising signs,
   §23-1-113.
  Designation, §23-1-111.
  Drainage, §23-1-113.
  Intent of article, §23-1-110.
  Lighting, §23-1-113.
  Maintenance and repair.
   Conditions, §23-1-113.

MUNICIPAL
CORPORATIONS—Cont'd
Streets—Cont'd
Municipal connecting link
  roads—Cont'd
  Maintenance and repair
   —Cont'd
   Responsibility,
    §23-1-112.
   Scope of highway
    department
    responsibility,
    §23-1-113.
   Stipulations,
    §23-1-113.
  Marking of roads,
   §23-1-113.
  Purpose of article,
   §23-1-110.
  Records.
   Designation of roads,
    §23-1-111.
  Traffic control, §23-1-113.
Officers.
  Corporations holding
   franchises as to use of
   streets.
   Employment of
    municipal officers,
    §11-43-11.
Paving.
  Contracts by highway
   department, §23-1-40.
Planning.
  Proposed construction
   submitted for approval
   of commission,
   §11-52-11.
Plats or maps.
  Approval of municipal
   authorities required,
   §35-2-52.
  Vacation of streets or
   alleys by abutting
   landowners, §§35-2-54,
   35-2-55.
Private enterprises.
  Consent of municipality as
   to use of streets, etc.,
   for private enterprises
   required, §11-49-1.
Public improvements.
  Assessments for public
   improvements,
   §§11-48-10, 11-48-15 to
   11-48-17. See within
   this heading,
   "Assessments for
   public improvements."
  Bond issues, §§11-81-110 to
   11-81-123. See within
   this heading, "Bond
   issues."
  General provisions,
   §§11-48-1 to 11-48-106.
   See within this
   heading, "Public
   improvements."
Public roads generally.
  See COUNTIES.
Public utilities.
  Consent of municipality as
   to use of streets,
   §11-49-1.
  Contracting with local
   authorities on use of
   streets, §10-5-14.

MUNICIPAL
CORPORATIONS—Cont'd
Streets—Cont'd
Public utilities—Cont'd
Repairs.
Railroads and public
utilities using
streets to keep in
repair, §11-49-3.
Railroads.
Regulation of running, etc.,
trains on streets,
crossings, etc.,
§11-43-61.
Repairs.
Keeping streets in
repair, §11-49-3.
Street railroads. See within
this heading, "Street
railroads."
Reservation of lands for
future acquisition,
§§11-52-50 to 11-52-54.
Resolutions, bylaws or
ordinances granting
franchises for use of
streets, §§11-44-33 to
11-44-36, 11-44-88,
11-44-137.
Sales.
Licensing of street sales,
§11-51-97.
Sidewalks, §11-49-2.
Signs.
Municipal connecting link
roads, §23-1-113.
Regulation of signs
overhanging streets,
§11-49-2.
Sprinkling.
Provision for sprinkling,
§11-47-18.
State.
Payment of costs of streets,
etc., constructed by
county, state or federal
government,
§§11-49-60 to 11-49-63.
Subdivisions, §§11-52-30 to
11-52-54. See within this
heading, "Subdivisions."
Taxation.
Apportionment of road and
bridge taxes between
counties and
municipalities,
§§11-83-1 to 11-83-3.
Maintenance of
municipal streets
declared county
matter, §11-83-1.
One half of road tax
collected in county to
be paid to
municipalities
therein, §11-83-2.
Use of taxes paid over to
municipalities,
§11-83-3.
Telephone and telegraph
lines.
Regulation of use of streets
for, §11-43-62.
Trees.
Public utilities.
Attachment of wires to
trees, §9-13-15.
Vacation by abutting
landowners, §35-2-55.

MUNICIPAL
CORPORATIONS—Cont'd
Streets—Cont'd
Vacation for erection of
public buildings,
§§11-49-100 to 11-49-106.
Damages, §11-49-106.
General provisions.
See HIGHWAYS.
Ordinance, §11-49-100.
Notice as to introduction
of ordinance,
§§11-49-101,
11-49-102.
Time for consideration,
§11-49-100.
Two-thirds vote of
council required,
§11-49-103.
Portion of street to remain
open, §11-49-104.
Property rights in vacated
portion of street,
§11-49-105.
Strikes.
Fire departments.
Municipal or state fire
fighters or firemen not
to strike, §11-43-143.
Style of ordinances, §11-45-2.
Subdivisions, §§11-52-30 to
11-52-54.
Buildings.
Access streets, §11-52-35.
Erection.
When permitted,
§11-52-35.
Reservation of lands for
future acquisition for
streets.
Compensation for taking
of buildings erected
on reserved lands
prohibited,
§11-52-54.
When building permits
may be issued,
§11-52-35.
Jurisdiction.
Plats.
Jurisdiction of planning
commission,
§11-52-36.
Territorial jurisdiction of
planning commissions,
§11-52-30.
Penalties.
Transfer, sale, etc., of
lands prior to approval
of plat, §11-52-33.
Planning commissions.
Territorial jurisdiction,
§11-52-30.
Plats.
Approval, §§11-52-30,
11-52-31.
Legal effect, §11-52-32.
Procedure for approval or
disapproval,
§11-52-32.
Remedies and penalty for
transfer, sale, etc., of
lands prior to,
§11-52-33.
Jurisdiction of planning
commission as to
subdivision plats,
§11-52-36.
Statutes.
Status of other platting
statutes, §11-52-36.

MUNICIPAL
CORPORATIONS—Cont'd
Subdivisions—Cont'd
Plats—Cont'd
Streets.
Reservation of lands for
future acquisition.
Adoption and approval
of plats, §11-52-50.
Regulations, §11-52-31.
Remedies for transfer or sale
of lands prior to approval
of plat, §11-52-33.
Reservation of lands.
Future acquisition for
public streets,
§§11-52-50 to 11-52-54.
Sale of lands prior to
approval of plat.
Remedies and penalty,
§11-52-33.
Statutes.
Status of other subdivision
statutes, §11-52-36.
Streets, §§11-52-30 to
11-52-54.
Access streets, §11-52-35.
Arrangement.
Provisions in regulations
as to arrangement,
§11-52-31.
Buildings.
Access streets, §11-52-35.
Completion.
Provisions as to
completion,
§11-52-31.
Grading, §11-52-34.
Improvement, §11-52-34.
Provisions in subdivision
regulations as to
arrangement, etc.,
§11-52-31.
Reservation of lands for
future acquisition,
§§11-53-50 to 11-52-54.
Abandonment of
reservations,
§11-52-50.
Liability to property
owners for
expenses upon
abandonment,
§11-52-51.
Appeals from
compensation
awards, §11-52-53.
Authorized, §11-52-50.
Board of appraisers.
Appointment,
§11-52-51.
Hearings upon claims
for compensation,
§11-52-51.
Meetings, §11-52-51.
Objections to
reservations,
§11-52-52.
Reports, §11-52-51.
Buildings.
Compensation for
taking of buildings
erected during
reservation period
prohibited,
§11-52-54.

MUNICIPAL
    CORPORATIONS—Cont'd
Subdivisions—Cont'd
Streets—Cont'd
Reservation of lands for
    future acquisition
    —Cont'd
Claims for damages or
    compensation for
    reservations.
Agreements as to
    releases,
    §11-52-51.
Hearings, §11-52-51.
Compensation,
    §§11-52-50 to
    11-52-54.
Agreements as to
    releases,
    §11-52-50.
Appeals from awards,
    §11-52-53.
Establishment of
    amount, §11-52-51.
Hearings upon claims,
    §11-52-51.
Payment to property
    owners, §11-52-52.
When prohibited,
    §11-52-54.
Damages.
Agreements as to
    releases of claims
    for damages,
    §11-52-50.
Objections, §11-52-52.
Plats.
Adoption, §11-52-50.
Approval, §11-52-50.
Releases of claims for
    damages or
    compensation for
    reservations.
Agreements between
    planning
    commission and
    landowners,
    §11-52-50.
Reports.
Board of appraisers,
    §11-52-52.
Use of reserved lands by
    owner.
Reservation not to
    impair, §11-52-54.
Transfer of lands prior to
    approval of plat.
Remedies and penalty,
    §11-52-33.
Zoning.
Powers of planning
    commission, §11-52-32.
Subpoenas.
Class 5 municipalities.
Mayor/commission/city
    manager form of
    government.
Investigations,
    §11-44E-181.
Subways.
Construction, §18-1A-274.
Summons and process.
Violations of certain
    ordinances.
Summons and complaint in
    lieu of arrest,
    §11-40-10.1.

MUNICIPAL
    CORPORATIONS—Cont'd
Sunshine law.
Council.
Executive or secret
    sessions prohibited,
    §13A-14-2.
Superintendents of schools.
City superintendents of
    schools, §§16-12-1 to
    16-12-21.
See EDUCATION.
Surveys, plats or maps,
    §§35-2-50 to 35-2-62.
Abutting landowners.
Vacation of streets or
    alleys, §35-2-54.
Validation, §35-2-55.
Acknowledgment of plat or
    map, §35-2-51.
Conveyance.
Acknowledgment and
    recording of plat as,
    §35-2-51.
Annexation. See within this
    heading, "Annexation."
Certification, §35-2-51.
Class 5 municipalities.
Mayor/commission/city
    manager form of
    government.
Zoning.
Comprehensive zoning
    maps, §11-44E-53.
Evidence.
Certification,
    acknowledgment and
    recordation, §35-2-51.
Lost maps or plats, §35-2-56.
Master plan for physical
    development of
    municipality.
Conduct of surveys,
    §11-52-9.
Mislaid maps or plats,
    §35-2-56.
Mutilated maps or plats,
    §35-2-56.
Public improvements,
    §§11-48-5, 11-48-6.
Recordation of plat or map,
    §35-2-51.
Conveyance.
Acknowledgment and
    recording of plat as,
    §35-2-51.
Vacated map or plat.
Duty of probate judge
    upon recording,
    §35-2-57.
Reduction of corporate limits,
    §§11-42-201, 11-42-202,
    11-42-211.
Remedies not exclusive,
    §35-2-62.
Required survey, §35-2-50.
Sewers, §§11-50-72, 11-50-73.
Streets, alleys and public
    ways.
Lands platted or mapped
    as.
Approval of municipal
    authorities required,
    §35-2-52.
Vacation by abutting
    landowners, §35-2-54.
Validation, §35-2-55.
Subdivisions, §§11-52-30 to
    11-52-33, 11-52-36,
    11-52-50. See within this
    heading, "Subdivisions."

MUNICIPAL
    CORPORATIONS—Cont'd
Surveys, plats or maps
    —Cont'd
Vacation and annulment by
    circuit court, §§35-2-58
    to 35-2-62.
Appeals, §35-2-59.
Conduct of proceedings,
    §35-2-59.
Entry of judgment,
    §35-2-59.
Fee for recordation and
    registration, §35-2-61.
Jurisdiction, §35-2-58.
Parties, §35-2-58.
Recordation of judgment,
    §35-2-60.
Remedies not exclusive,
    §35-2-62.
Vacation of plat or map by
    owner of lands, §35-2-53.
Duty of probate judge upon
    recording vacated map
    or plat, §35-2-57.
Remedies not exclusive,
    §35-2-62.
What plat or map must
    show, §35-2-50.
Swamps.
Assessments for public
    improvements.
Manner of assessment for
    drainage, §11-48-16.
Swimming pools.
Codes.
Adoption by reference,
    §11-45-8.
Public athletic boards,
    §§11-59-1 to 11-59-17.
See within this heading,
    "Parks and recreation."
Public improvement bonds.
Revenue-producing
    undertakings,
    §§11-81-140 to
    11-81-150.
See COUNTIES.
**Tannehill furnace and
    foundry commission.**
Appropriations, §41-9-328.
Taxation, §§11-51-1 to
    11-51-207.
Annexation.
Cities of twenty-five
    thousand or more,
    §§11-42-62 to 11-42-71,
    11-42-79 to 11-42-88.
See within this
    heading, "Annexation."
Assessment of property taxes,
    §11-51-1.
Assessment rolls.
Acceptance by county
    commission,
    §11-51-4.
Adoption by county
    commission,
    §11-51-4.
Submission to county
    commission,
    §11-51-4.
Assessors.
Provision for tax
    assessors, §11-43-5.
Effect of assessments,
    §11-51-7.
Enforcement by levy of
    execution upon and
    sale of property,
    §11-51-7.

MUNICIPAL
CORPORATIONS—Cont'd
Taxation—Cont'd
Assessment of property taxes
—Cont'd
Entry of civil actions for
assessments on trial
docket, §11-51-12.
Escaped taxes.
Assessments against
property for,
§11-51-22.
Informality in assessment.
Reassessment, §11-51-22.
Irregularity in assessment.
Reassessment, §11-51-22.
Objections to assessments.
Hearing upon objections,
§11-51-1.
Optional method for levy and
collection of property
taxes, §§11-51-45 to
11-51-49, 11-51-55.
Reassessment, §11-51-22.
Assessments for public
improvements,
§§11-51-28, 11-51-40 to
11-51-43. See within this
heading, "Assessments
for public
improvements."
Assessors.
Provision for tax assessor,
§11-43-5.
Attachments.
Anticipation of
nonpayment,
§11-51-26.
Boards of water and sewer
commissioners.
Exemption from taxation,
§11-50-354.
Bond issues. See within this
heading, "Bond issues."
Charges payable from state
treasury.
Municipal corporations
exempt from payment,
Const. Ala., art. XI,
§218.
Class 5 municipalities.
Mayor/commission/city
manager form of
government.
Commission.
Powers, §11-44E-44.
Collection of property taxes.
Anticipation of
nonpayment.
Attachment or
garnishment,
§11-51-26.
Attachment for collection,
§11-51-26.
Failure to collect.
Grounds for forfeiture of
charter, §11-41-24.
Garnishment for collection,
§11-51-8.
Anticipation of
nonpayment,
§11-51-26.
Limitation of actions,
§6-2-35.
Optional method for levy
and collection of
property taxes,
§§11-51-40 to 11-51-74.
Tax collectors.
Provision for, §11-43-5.

MUNICIPAL
CORPORATIONS—Cont'd
Taxation—Cont'd
Collection of property taxes
—Cont'd
Unknown owners.
Collection of taxes due
upon property
assessed to unknown
owner, §11-51-9.
Consolidation of contiguous
municipalities.
Alternate mode.
Provisions as to taxation
in municipality
annexed, §11-42-132.
Exemption of industrial or
manufacturing plants,
§11-42-102.
Consolidation of
noncontiguous
municipalities.
Collection and
disbursement of taxes,
§11-42-158.
Constitution of Alabama,
Const. Ala., art. XI,
§§216, 218; amd. 56.
Delinquent property taxes,
§§11-51-2, 11-51-3,
11-51-11 to 11-51-15.
Appeal from judgment of
circuit court,
§11-51-15.
Entry of civil actions for
assessments on trial
docket, §11-51-12.
Entry of judgment by
circuit court,
§11-51-14.
Interest rate on delinquent
taxes, §11-51-2.
Judgment.
Appeal from judgment of
circuit court,
§11-51-15.
Entry of judgment by
circuit court,
§11-51-14.
List of delinquent taxes,
§§11-51-11 to 11-51-13.
Filing in circuit court,
§11-51-12.
Preparation of certified
list, §11-51-11.
Publication of notice of
filing of tax list as to
owners unknown or
not found, §11-51-13.
Notice required from
certain tax collectors
as to delinquent taxes,
§11-51-3.
Sale for taxes, §§11-51-7,
11-51-14, 11-51-16 to
11-51-25.
Summons notifying owners
of institution of
proceedings against
property.
Issuance, execution and
return, §11-51-12.
Unknown owners.
Publication of notice of
filing of tax list, etc.,
as to, §11-51-13.
When taxes delinquent,
§11-51-2.
Demand for payment of
property taxes,
§11-51-10.

MUNICIPAL
CORPORATIONS—Cont'd
Taxation—Cont'd
Due date, §11-51-2.
Education.
General provisions.
See EDUCATION.
Elimination of small
payments, §40-1-31.2.
Enterprise zones.
Creation within class 1
cities.
Reduction in municipal
tax and license
rates, §11-40-16.
Error.
Refund of taxes paid by,
§§40-10-164 to
40-10-166.
Escaped taxes.
Assessments against
property for escaped
taxes, §11-51-22.
Excess proceeds from special
taxes.
Disposition, §11-51-28.
Exemptions from taxation.
Annexed territory,
§§11-42-57, 11-42-59,
11-42-79 to 11-42-86.
See within this
heading, "Annexation."
Boards for operation of
water, sewer, gas and
electric systems,
§11-50-322.
Boards of water and sewer
commissioners,
§11-50-354.
Bond issues, §11-81-29.
Consolidation of contiguous
municipalities.
Exemption from taxation
of industrial or
manufacturing
plants, §11-42-102.
District electric
corporations,
§11-50-531.
Factories, industries and
plants.
Application, §40-9-41.
Cessation of exemption,
§40-9-42.
Consolidation of
contiguous
municipalities,
§11-42-102.
Generally, §40-9-40.
Inapplicability to taxes
to which factories,
plants, etc., already
subject, §40-9-46.
New or extended
factories, industries
and plants, §40-9-47.
Sections as to local
and state taxation
cumulative,
§40-9-49.
Gas districts, §11-50-412.
Health care service plans,
§10-4-107.
Property used for public
purposes, §40-9-14.
Waterworks and sewer
boards, §11-50-235.
Garnishment.
Collection of taxes,
§§11-51-8, 11-51-26.

MUNICIPAL
    CORPORATIONS—Cont'd
  Taxation—Cont'd
    Gas districts.
      Exemption from taxation,
        §11-50-412.
      Privilege license tax,
        §11-50-413.
    Gasoline tax, §§40-17-50,
      40-17-51.
    General taxes.
      Separation of general and
        special taxes,
        §11-51-28.
    Health care service plans.
      Municipal taxes prohibited,
        §10-4-107.
    Historic preservation
      commissions.
      Exemption from taxation,
        §11-68-4.
    Interest.
      Delinquent property taxes,
        §11-51-2.
    Levy of property taxes,
      §11-51-1.
      Optional method for levy,
        §§11-51-40 to 11-51-74.
    License taxes, §§11-51-90 to
      11-51-185. See within
      this heading, "Licenses."
    Lien for taxes, §11-51-6.
      Optional method for levy
        and collection,
        §11-51-44.
      Sale of property for
        payment of taxes.
        Effect of sale on liens,
          §11-51-21.
    Limitation of actions.
      Recovery of taxes, §6-2-35.
      Testing validity of
        municipal elections for
        tax levies, §6-2-40.
    Mayor/commission/city
      manager form of
      government.
      Commission.
        Powers, §11-44E-44.
    Mistake.
      Refund of taxes paid by,
        §§40-10-164 to
        40-10-166.
    Motor fuels.
      Additional excise tax on
        gasoline, motor fuel
        and lubricating oil.
        Exemptions, §40-17-220.
      Exemption of class 1
        municipalities from
        certain fuel taxes,
        §40-17-240.
    Optional method for levy and
      collection of property
      taxes, §§11-51-40 to
      11-51-74.
      Assessments.
        Assessment book,
          §11-51-47.
        Computation and entry
          of amount,
          §11-51-48.
        Certificate of assessment,
          §11-51-49.
        Crediting of tax collector
          with taxes on
          assessment lists,
          §11-51-55.
        Forms.
          Preparation, §11-51-46.

MUNICIPAL
    CORPORATIONS—Cont'd
  Taxation—Cont'd
    Optional method for levy and
      collection of property
      taxes—Cont'd
      Assessments—Cont'd
        Indication on list of
          property located in
          municipalities and
          ascertainment of
          value of property,
          §11-51-45.
        Preparation of
          assessment forms,
          §11-51-46.
      Bonds, surety.
        Probate judge, county
          tax assessor and
          county tax collector,
          §11-51-73.
      Collection of taxes.
        Insolvent taxes,
          §11-51-58.
        Payment to municipal
          treasurers,
          §11-51-52.
        Procedure, §11-51-50.
        Receipt of municipal
          treasurers,
          §11-51-52.
        Receipt of tax collector,
          §11-51-51.
      Commission of tax
        assessors and tax
        collectors, §11-51-74.
      Computation of amount
        owed, §11-51-48.
      County tax assessor.
        Ascertainment of value
          of property,
          §11-51-45.
        Assessment book,
          §11-51-47.
        Bonds, surety, §11-51-73.
        Commission, §11-51-74.
        Forms.
          Preparation of forms
          for use by tax
          assessor,
          §11-51-46.
        Indication on assessment
          list of property
          located in
          municipalities,
          §11-51-45.
      County tax collector.
        Annual settlement,
          §11-51-53.
        Bonds, surety, §11-51-73.
        Charging insolvent taxes
          and taxes in
          litigation against tax
          collector, §11-51-56.
        Commission, §11-51-74.
        Crediting for uncollected
          balances of insolvent
          taxes and taxes in
          litigation, §11-51-59.
        Crediting with municipal
          taxes on assessment
          list and with taxes
          in litigation,
          §11-51-55.
        Entry in docket book of
          taxes due, §11-51-60.
        Payment of balance of
          taxes collected,
          §11-51-53.
        Procedure for collection,
          §11-51-50.

MUNICIPAL
    CORPORATIONS—Cont'd
  Taxation—Cont'd
    Optional method for levy and
      collection of property
      taxes—Cont'd
      County tax collector
        —Cont'd
        Receipt of tax collector,
          §11-51-51.
        Report, §11-51-52.
        Final report as to
          uncollected
          balances of
          insolvent taxes
          and taxes in
          litigation,
          §11-51-59.
      Docket book.
        Entry by tax collector in
          docket book of taxes
          due, §11-51-60.
      Erroneous payment.
        Procedure for recovery,
          §11-51-72.
      Insolvent taxes, §§11-51-56
        to 11-51-59.
        Charging against tax
          collector, §11-51-56.
        Collection, §11-51-58.
        Crediting tax collector
          for uncollected
          balances, §11-51-59.
        Lists of insolvents.
          Preparation, §11-51-57.
        Monthly reports,
          §11-51-58.
        Payment, §11-51-58.
        Settlement, §11-51-58.
        Uncollected balances.
          Report, §11-51-59.
      Lien for taxes, §11-51-44.
      Payment of taxes.
        Insolvent taxes,
          §11-51-58.
        Recovery of taxes
          erroneously paid,
          §11-51-72.
        Sale of land for payment,
          §§11-51-61 to
          11-51-69.
      Probate judge.
        Official bonds, §11-51-73.
      Receipt of municipal
        treasurers, §11-51-52.
      Receipt of tax collector.
        Preparation, contents
          and effect, §11-51-51.
      Report of tax collector,
        §11-51-52.
        Uncollected balances of
          insolvent taxes and
          taxes in litigation,
          §11-51-59.
      Sale for taxes, §§11-51-61
        to 11-51-71.
        Amount for which
          property to be sold,
          §11-51-67.
        Amount of taxes due on
          property.
          Entry in books,
          §11-51-67.
        Appeal by state from
          decree of sale,
          §11-51-62.
        Cancellation of sale.
          Proceedings upon,
          §11-51-70.
        Certificate of purchase,
          §11-51-63.

MUNICIPAL
 CORPORATIONS—Cont'd
Taxation—Cont'd
 Optional method for levy and
  collection of property
  taxes—Cont'd
 Sale for taxes—Cont'd
  Decree of sale, §11-51-61.
   Appeal by state,
    §11-51-62.
  Deed.
   Execution, §11-51-64.
  Duties of tax assessor as
   to descriptive list,
   §11-51-66.
  Execution of deed,
   §11-51-64.
  Invalid sale.
   Repayment of state,
    §11-51-69.
   Rights of purchaser,
    §11-51-65.
  Redemption.
   Disposition of
    redemption money,
    §11-51-71.
  Rights of purchaser
   where sale invalid,
   §11-51-65.
  State.
   Payment of
    municipality
    where lands bid in
    by state sold by
    state, §11-51-68.
   Repayment of state
    when sale invalid,
    §11-51-69.
 Special taxes.
  Separation of general
   and special taxes,
   §11-51-54.
 Taxes in litigation.
  Charging against tax
   collector, §11-51-56.
  Crediting tax collector
   with taxes in
   litigation,
   §§11-51-55, 11-51-59.
  Report as to uncollected
   balances, §11-51-59.
 Treasurers.
  Payment of taxes
   collected to,
   §11-51-52.
  Receipt of municipal
   treasurers,
   §11-51-52.
 Valuation of property.
  Ascertainment by county
   tax assessor,
   §11-51-45.
 Payment of property taxes.
  Anticipation of
   nonpayment.
   Attachment or
    garnishment,
    §11-51-26.
  Demand for payment,
   §11-51-10.
  Optional method,
   §§11-51-40 to 11-51-74.
  Penalties for nonpayment.
   Releases, §11-51-27.
 Pledge of revenues from
  certain taxes for
  payment on bonds,
  §11-81-16.

MUNICIPAL
 CORPORATIONS—Cont'd
Taxation—Cont'd
 Property used for public
  purposes.
  Exemption from state ad
   valorem taxation,
   §40-9-14.
 Public improvements.
  Assessments. See within
   this heading,
   "Assessments for
   public improvements."
 Public utilities, §§40-21-26 to
  40-21-28.
 Rates of taxation, §11-51-1.
  Limitation on property tax
   rates, Const. Ala., art.
   XI, §216.
 Redemption of property
  sold for taxes,
  §§11-51-7, 11-51-23 to
  11-51-25.
 Refund of taxes paid by
  mistake or error,
  §§40-10-164 to 40-10-166.
 Releases from property taxes,
  §11-51-27.
 Settlement of claims and
  releases from
  penalties, §11-51-27.
 Revenues.
  Pledge of revenues from
   certain taxes for
   payment on bonds,
   §§11-81-16, 11-81-18.
 Road and bridge taxes.
  Apportionment between
   counties and
   municipalities,
   §§11-83-1 to 11-83-3.
 Sales and use taxes,
  §§11-51-200 to 11-51-207.
  See within this heading,
  "Sales and use taxes."
 Sales for taxes, §§11-51-7,
  11-51-14, 11-51-16 to
  11-51-25.
  Assessments for public
   improvements.
   Certification to court of
    unpaid assessments,
    §11-51-21.
   Collection from proceeds
    of sale, §11-51-21.
  Disposition of proceeds,
   §11-51-16.
  Enforcement of
   assessments by levy of
   execution upon and
   sale of property,
   §11-51-7.
  Invalidity of sale.
   Grounds, §11-51-20.
   Liabilities of purchaser,
    §11-51-18.
  Liens.
   Effect of sales upon tax
    and assessment
    liens, §11-51-21.
  Optional method for levy
   and collection of
   property taxes,
   §§11-51-61 to 11-51-71.
  Proceeds.
   Disposition, §11-51-16.
  Purchase of property by
   municipalities,
   §11-51-17.
  Redemption.
   Authorization, §11-51-23.

MUNICIPAL
 CORPORATIONS—Cont'd
Taxation—Cont'd
 Sales for taxes—Cont'd
  Redemption—Cont'd
   By municipality,
    §11-51-25.
   Conveyance of property,
    etc., to redeemer,
    §11-51-24.
   From municipality,
    §11-51-25.
   Procedure, §11-51-23.
   Right of redemption of
    owner, §11-51-7.
  Rights of purchaser,
   §11-51-18.
  Title acquired by
   purchaser, §11-51-19.
  Invalid sale, §11-51-20.
 School taxes.
  See EDUCATION.
 Securities issued in
  anticipation of grants.
  Exemption from taxation,
  §11-64-5.
 Settlement of claims and
  releases from penalties,
  §11-51-27.
 Sinking funds.
  Special tax for payments,
   §§11-81-15, 11-81-26.
 Special taxes.
  Disposition of excess
   proceeds, §11-51-28.
  Optional method for levy
   and collection of
   property taxes.
   Separation of general
    and special taxes,
    §11-51-54.
  Separation of general and
   special taxes,
   §11-51-28.
  Sinking fund payments,
   §§11-81-15, 11-81-26.
 State department of revenue.
  Collection of certain
   municipal license taxes
   by state department,
   §§11-51-180 to
   11-51-185. See within
   this heading,
   "Licenses."
 Streets.
  Apportionment of road and
   bridge taxes between
   counties and
   municipalities,
   §§11-83-1 to 11-83-3.
 Unknown property owners.
  Collection of taxes due
   upon property
   assessed, §11-51-9.
  Publication of notice of
   filing of tax list, etc.,
   as to, §11-51-13.
 Use taxes, §§11-51-200 to
  11-51-207. See within
  this heading, "Sales and
  use taxes."
 Valuation of property.
  Contesting valuation.
   Right of property owners
    to contest, §11-51-5.
   Notice to property owners
    where valuation by
    city higher than
    county valuation,
    §11-51-5.

MUNICIPAL
CORPORATIONS—Cont'd
Taxation—Cont'd
Valuation of property
—Cont'd
Optional method for levy
and collection of
property taxes.
Ascertainment of value,
§11-51-45.
Right to contest, §11-51-5.
Waterworks and sewer
boards.
Exemption from taxation of
property and income of
corporation,
§11-50-235.
When property taxes due,
§11-51-2.
Tax increment districts,
§§11-99-1 to 11-99-10;
Const. Ala., amd. 475.
See TAX INCREMENT
DISTRICTS.
Telegraph companies.
License schedule, §11-51-127.
Streets.
Regulation of use of streets
for telegraph lines,
§11-43-62.
Telephones.
Annexation.
Territory exempt from
taxation.
Privilege or license tax
from operators,
§11-42-84.
Commission form of
government.
Municipal officers or
employees.
Conflicts of interest,
§§11-44-46 to
11-44-48.
Improvement authorities.
General provisions,
§§39-7-1 to 39-7-34.
See PUBLIC WORKS.
License tax on coin
telephones, §11-51-98.
Licensing of telephone
companies.
Schedule, §11-51-128.
Streets.
Regulation of use of streets
for telephone lines,
§11-43-62.
Trees.
Attachment of wires to
trees, §9-13-15.
Temperance.
Promotion of temperance,
§11-47-112.
Tenants in common.
Assessments for public
improvements,
§§11-48-100 to 11-48-106.
See within this heading,
"Assessments for public
improvements."
Tennis courts.
Public athletic boards,
§§11-59-1 to 11-59-17.
See within this heading,
"Parks and recreation."
Public improvement bonds.
Revenue-producing
undertakings,
§§11-81-140 to
11-81-150.
See COUNTIES.

MUNICIPAL
CORPORATIONS—Cont'd
Theaters.
Closing, §11-51-102.
Licenses, §11-51-102.
Revocation, §11-51-103.
Time.
Elections, §§11-46-5, 11-46-6,
11-46-28, 11-46-99. See
within this heading,
"Elections."
Tobacco.
Sales tax, §40-25-29.
Tombigbee Valley
development authority.
Contracts with
municipalities, §33-17-8.
Torts.
Claims for and against
municipalities, §§11-93-1
to 11-93-3.
Liability for negligence of
agents, etc., §§11-47-190
to 11-47-192.
Actions, §11-47-191.
Airports.
Municipal immunity,
§4-4-4.
Ante litem notice,
§11-47-192.
Civil defense activities.
Municipal immunity,
§31-9-16.
Damages.
Filing of statement as to
damages claimed,
§11-47-192.
Death.
Filing of statement as to
manner of injury,
§11-47-192.
Injury.
Filing of statement as to
manner of injury,
§11-47-192.
Joint liability of other
persons or
corporations,
§11-47-190.
Actions, §11-47-191.
Judgments.
Entry and execution,
§11-47-191.
Manner of injury.
Filing of statement as to,
§11-47-192.
Statement.
Filing of statement as to
manner of injury,
damages claimed,
etc., §11-47-192.
When municipality liable,
§11-47-190.
Limitation on claims against
municipalities, §§11-93-1
to 11-93-3.
Definitions, §11-93-1.
Liability of governmental
units not extended,
§11-93-3.
Maximum amount of
damages recoverable,
§11-93-2.
Notice.
Ante litem notice,
§11-47-192.
Town surveys, plats or
maps, §§35-2-50 to
35-2-62. See within this
heading, "Surveys, plats or
maps."

MUNICIPAL
CORPORATIONS—Cont'd
Trade and commerce.
Promoting, §§11-54-20 to
11-54-32. See within this
heading, "Promotion of
industry, trade and
pollution control."
Transportation companies,
§§37-2-2, 37-2-6, 37-2-40.
Transportation service in
class 3 municipalities,
§§11-49A-1 to 11-49A-20.
Agencies.
Powers of localities,
agencies, etc.,
§11-49A-14.
Applicants.
Defined, §11-49A-2.
Applications, §11-49A-4.
Audits, §11-49A-18.
Authorities.
Defined, §11-49A-2.
Dissolution, §11-49A-19.
Incorporation of additional
authorities in same
county.
Prohibited, §11-49A-20.
Organization, §11-49A-7.
Powers, §11-49A-8.
Authorizing municipality.
Defined, §11-49A-2.
Authorizing resolution.
Defined, §11-49A-2.
Board of directors, §11-49A-7.
Defined, §11-49A-2.
Bond issues, §§11-49A-2,
11-49A-10, 11-49A-11,
11-49A-13.
Contracts as security,
§11-49A-11.
Defined, §11-49A-2.
Exemption from taxation,
§11-49A-15.
Form, §11-49A-10.
Payment.
Contracts as security,
§11-49A-11.
Source, §11-49A-10.
Sale, §11-49A-10.
Seal, §11-49A-10.
Signatures, §11-49A-10.
Terms, §11-49A-10.
Trust indentures,
mortgages, etc.,
§11-49A-10.
Use of proceeds,
§11-49A-13.
Budget, §11-49A-18.
Chief executive officer.
Defined, §11-49A-2.
Definitions, §11-49A-2.
Construction of definitions,
§11-49A-3.
Dissolution of authority,
§11-49A-19.
Exemption from additional
proceedings, regulation,
etc., §11-49A-16.
Exemption from taxes, fees
and costs, §11-49A-15.
Fees, §11-49A-9.
Exemption, §11-49A-15.
Herein.
Defined, §11-49A-3.
Incorporation, §§11-49A-4 to
11-49A-6, 11-49A-20.
Additional authorities in
same county.
Prohibited, §11-49A-20.

MUNICIPAL
CORPORATIONS—Cont'd
Transportation service in
class 3 municipalities
—Cont'd
Incorporation—Cont'd
Additional documents,
§11-49A-5.
Application, §11-49A-4.
Certificate of incorporation.
Amendments, §11-49A-6.
Contents, §11-49A-5.
Denial or approval of
governing body,
§11-49A-6.
Filing, §§11-49A-5,
11-49A-6.
Signing and
acknowledging,
§11-49A-5.
Notice to secretary of state,
§11-49A-5.
Resolution of denial or
approval, §11-49A-4.
Legislative findings,
§11-49A-1.
Liens.
Statutory mortgage lien,
§11-49A-12.
Localities.
Powers of localities,
agencies, etc.,
§11-49A-14.
Mortgages.
Statutory mortgage lien,
§11-49A-12.
Notice.
Statutory mortgage liens,
§11-49A-12.
Organization of authority,
§11-49A-7.
Public transportation service.
Defined, §11-49A-2.
Purpose, §11-49A-1.
Rates, §11-49A-9.
Rights of way.
Use, §11-49A-17.
Transit system.
Defined, §11-49A-2.
Treasurers.
Bonds, surety, §11-43-120.
Claims for and against
municipalities.
Money due municipalities
to be paid to treasurer,
§11-43-123.
Council.
Reports and statements to
council, §11-43-120.
Depositories.
Deposit of public money in
depositories,
§11-43-122.
Duties, §§11-43-3, 11-43-120.
Additional duties,
§11-43-121.
Election, §11-43-3.
Liabilities.
Losses arising from deposit
of public money in
depositories,
§11-43-122.
Money due municipalities.
Payment to treasurer,
§11-43-123.
Officers generally. See within
this heading, "Officers."
Public moneys.
Deposit in depositories,
§11-43-122.

MUNICIPAL
CORPORATIONS—Cont'd
Treasurers—Cont'd
Reports to council,
§11-43-120.
Salary, §11-43-3.
Statements to council,
§11-43-120.
Taxation.
Optional method for levy
and collection of
property taxes.
Payment of taxes
collected to
municipal
treasurers,
§11-51-52.
Warrants.
Payment of interest upon
warrants not paid for
lack of funds,
§11-43-121.
Payment of warrants,
§11-43-120.
Trees and timber.
Forests and forestry.
§§2-30-23, 9-13-106,
11-84-1, 11-84-2. See
within this heading,
"Forests and forestry."
Public utilities.
Attachment of wires to
trees in towns or
cities, §9-13-15.
Trusts and trustees.
Sinking funds.
Trustee of sinking fund,
§§11-81-24, 11-81-25.
Tunnels.
Bond issues.
Public improvement bonds.
Revenue-producing
undertakings,
§§11-81-140 to
11-81-150.
See COUNTIES.
Construction and
maintenance.
When construction
required within cities,
§§11-49-40 to 11-49-45.
Unemployment
compensation.
Coverage.
Election of coverage under
chapter, §25-4-131.
Unions.
Fire fighters.
Right to join unions,
§11-43-143.
United States.
Donation of property to U. S.
for defense purposes.
Authority, §11-54-211.
Legislative declarations
and findings,
§11-54-210.
Universities and colleges.
Local aid to state educational
institutions, §§16-19-1 to
16-19-8.
See UNIVERSITIES AND
COLLEGES.
Urban renewal projects,
§§24-3-1 to 24-3-9.
See URBAN RENEWAL
PROJECTS.
Use taxes, §§11-51-200 to
11-51-207. See within this
heading, "Sales and use
taxes."

MUNICIPAL
CORPORATIONS—Cont'd
USS Alabama battleship
commission.
Appropriations by
municipalities,
§41-9-356.
Usury.
Boards for operation of
water, sewer, gas and
electric systems.
Exemption, §11-50-319.
Gas districts.
Exemption, §11-50-415.
Utilities, §§11-50-1 to
11-50-533. See within this
heading, "Public utilities."
Utility services facilities,
§§11-97-1 to 11-97-27.
See UTILITY SERVICES
FACILITIES.
Vaccination.
Provision for system of
compulsory vaccination,
etc., §11-47-132.
Validation of obligations,
§§6-6-750 to 6-6-757,
11-81-30, 11-220 to
11-81-227. See within this
heading, "Bond issues."
Vegetables.
Inspections.
Charges for inspection,
§11-43-59.
Vending machines.
License tax.
Authorized, §11-51-98.
Juke boxes, §§11-51-98,
11-51-100.
Music.
Regulation and control of
juke boxes, §11-51-100.
Venue.
Damages for personal injury,
death or property
damage, §6-3-11.
Veterans.
Licenses.
Exemptions from licenses,
§§40-12-343,
40-12-373.
Wagons.
Licensing, §11-51-101.
Wards.
Abandonment of commission
form.
Creation of wards,
§11-44-159.
Annexation, §§11-40-8,
11-42-73 to 11-42-75. See
within this heading,
"Annexation."
Change of ward lines,
§11-40-8.
Class 5 municipalities.
Mayor-council form of
government.
Division of municipality
into electoral
districts, §11-43C-13.
Commission form of
government.
Creation upon
abandonment of
commission form,
§11-44-159.
Discontinuance, §11-44-25.
Consolidation of
municipalities.
Alternate mode,
§11-42-133.

MUNICIPAL CORPORATIONS—Cont'd

Wards—Cont'd

Consolidation of municipalities—Cont'd

Division of consolidated municipalities into wards, §§11-42-103, 11-42-157.

Creation of new wards, §§11-40-8, 11-44-159.

Division of municipalities into wards, §11-40-8.

Elections.

Commission for of government, §§11-46-94, 11-46-95, 11-46-109.

Division of municipality into single member districts, §11-43-63.

Mayor-council form of government, §§11-46-23, 11-46-24.

Warehouses.

Public improvement bonds.

Revenue-producing undertakings, §§11-81-140 to 11-81-150.

See COUNTIES.

Warrants.

Claims for and against municipality.

Issuance of warrants, §11-43-101.

Class 5 municipalities.

Mayor/commission/city manager form of government.

Commission.

Power to authorize issuance, §11-44E-44.

Payment of funds by, §11-44E-76.

Education.

General provisions.

See EDUCATION.

Local aid to state educational institutions, §§16-19-3 to 16-19-5, 16-19-7.

See UNIVERSITIES AND COLLEGES.

Employees.

Dealing in warrants, §11-43-14.

Industrial parks.

Acquisition and development of lands for industrial parks, §§11-54-1 to 11-54-4.

Generally, §§11-92-6 to 11-92-10.

Interest.

Appropriation, §11-43-57.

Payment of interest upon warrants not paid for lack of funds, §11-43-121.

Issuance.

Designation of persons to issue, §11-43-5.

Officers.

Dealing in warrants by officers, §11-43-14.

Payment of warrants.

Treasurers, §11-43-120.

MUNICIPAL CORPORATIONS—Cont'd

Warrants—Cont'd

Redemption of securities generally, §§11-82-1 to 11-82-7. See within this heading, "Redemption of securities."

Refunding warrants.

Issuance, §11-81-4.

Payment.

Pledge of tax revenues, §11-81-4.

Treasurers.

Payment of interest upon warrants not paid for lack of funds, §11-43-121.

Payment of warrants, §11-43-120.

Universities and colleges.

Local aid to state educational institutions, §§16-19-3 to 16-19-5, 16-19-7.

See UNIVERSITIES AND COLLEGES.

Water closets.

Regulation, installation, etc., §11-50-55.

Water conservation and irrigation.

Agency.

Contributing money for work of agency, §9-10-9.

Taxation.

Collection of taxes for work of agency, §9-10-9.

Corporations.

Property.

Lease or conveyance of real property, §9-10-42.

Waterfronts.

Improvement, §11-47-14.

Waters and watercourses.

Alteration of channel of watercourses, §11-47-15.

Water, sewer and fire protection authorities, §§11-88-1 to 11-88-111.

See WATER, SEWER AND FIRE PROTECTION AUTHORITIES.

Water, sewer and fire protection districts, §§11-89-1 to 11-89-19.

See WATER, SEWER AND FIRE PROTECTION DISTRICTS.

Water supply and waterworks.

Acquisition.

Consent of governing board of corporation or association operating, §11-50-1.1.

Annexation.

Territory exempt from taxation.

Privilege or license tax from operators, §11-42-84.

Assessments for public improvements, §§11-48-1 to 11-48-106. See within this heading, "Assessments for public improvements."

MUNICIPAL CORPORATIONS—Cont'd

Water supply and waterworks—Cont'd

Authorities.

Boards for operation of water, sewer, gas and electric systems, §§11-50-310 to 11-50-324. See within this heading, "Public utilities."

Boards of water and sewer commissioners, §§11-50-340 to 11-50-358. See within this heading, "Boards of water and sewer commissioners."

Improvement authorities.

General provisions, §§39-7-1 to 39-7-34. See PUBLIC WORKS.

Waterworks and sewer boards, §§11-50-230 to 11-50-291. See within this heading, "Waterworks and sewer boards."

Waterworks utility boards, §§11-50-430 to 11-50-445.

Bond issues.

Authorized for construction, extension, etc., §11-47-3.

Boards for operation of water, sewer, gas and electric systems, §§11-50-315 to 11-50-318.

Boards of water and sewer commissioners, §§11-50-345 to 11-50-350, 11-50-353 to 11-50-356. See within this heading, "Boards of water and sewer commissioners."

Payment for plants, etc., purchased, §11-50-6.

Security for bonds, §§11-50-6, 11-81-1.

Public improvement bonds, §§11-81-110 to 11-81-123. See within this heading, "Bond issues."

Referendum.

Construction of hydroelectric generating facilities in class 5 municipality, §11-50-6.1.

Revenue bonds, §§11-81-160 to 11-81-190. See within this heading, "Public utilities."

Waterworks and sewer boards, §§11-50-237, 11-50-239, 11-50-240.

Bonds, surety.

Waterworks utility boards, §§11-50-438, 11-50-445.

Calendar basis, §11-81-187.

MUNICIPAL
CORPORATIONS—Cont'd
Water supply and
waterworks—Cont'd
Cisterns.
  Construction, regulation,
    etc., of public cisterns,
    §11-47-140.
Codes.
  Adoption by reference,
    §11-45-8.
Commissioners.
  Boards of water and sewer
    commissioners,
    §§11-50-340 to
    11-50-358. See within
    this heading, "Boards
    of water and sewer
    commissioners."
Commission form of
  government.
  Municipal officers or
    employees.
    Conflicts of interest,
      §§11-44-46 to
      11-44-48.
  President of board of
    commissioners as
    superintendent of
    water systems,
    §11-50-16.
Consolidation of systems,
  §11-47-3.
  Authorized, §11-81-161.
Construction of waterworks.
  Contracts and indebtedness
    authorized, §11-47-3.
  Expenditure of municipal
    funds, §11-50-5.
Contracts.
  Authorized for
    construction,
    extension, etc.,
    §11-47-3.
  Furnishing of water,
    §11-50-1.
  Public water corporations.
    Contracts between public
      water corporations
      and public sewer
      corporations for
      operation of sanitary
      sewer systems,
      §11-50-371.
Conveyance of waterworks to
  boards organized to own,
    §§11-50-13, 11-50-14.
Corporations.
  Public water corporations,
    §§11-50-370 to
    11-50-372.
Counties.
  Conveyance of waterworks
    to municipal
    corporations, §11-14-3.
  Sale of waterworks plants
    or distribution systems
    to counties.
    Power to sell, §11-21-2.
    Publication of notice,
      §11-21-3.
Customer security deposits.
  Payment of interest in
    class 1 municipalities,
    §11-50-17.

MUNICIPAL
CORPORATIONS—Cont'd
Water supply and
waterworks—Cont'd
Debts incurred in
  construction, acquisition,
  etc.
  Mortgages and deeds of
    trust, §§11-50-8 to
    11-50-11.
    Conditions, §11-50-9.
    Covenants, §11-50-9.
    Franchise right, etc., of
      purchaser at
      foreclosure sale,
      §11-50-10.
    Rates and charges,
      §11-50-11.
    Revenues from plants,
      §11-50-11.
    Security for debts,
      §11-50-8.
    Terms, §11-50-9.
    Warranties, §11-50-9.
Definitions.
  Boards of water and sewer
    commissioners,
    §11-50-340.
  Operation of sanitary
    sewer systems by
    public water
    corporations,
    §11-50-370.
  Transfer of water and
    sewer systems by
    municipalities without
    elections, §11-50-190.
Eminent domain.
  Sources of water so as to
    secure supply,
    §11-50-4.
Establishment of
  waterworks.
  Expenditure of municipal
    funds, §11-50-5.
  Generally, §11-50-1.
Expanded municipalities.
  Operation, etc., of
    waterworks of
    absorbed
    municipalities,
    §11-42-185.
Extension of waterworks
  systems.
  Authorized, §11-81-161.
  Contracts and indebtedness
    authorized, §11-47-3.
Financial condition of
  system.
  Accounting, §11-81-188.
  Fiscal year basis, §11-81-187.
Foreign municipal
  corporations.
  Acquisition of water supply
    by, §§11-50-30 to
    11-50-36.
    Attachments.
      Exemptions from
        attachment, etc.,
        §11-50-35.
    Authorized, §11-50-30.
    Consent of counties and
      municipalities
      required, §11-50-33.
    Contracts, §11-50-32.
    Counties.
      Consent required,
        §11-50-33.
    Executions.
      Exemption from levy,
        etc., §11-50-35.

MUNICIPAL
CORPORATIONS—Cont'd
Water supply and
waterworks—Cont'd
Foreign municipal
  corporations—Cont'd
  Acquisition of water supply
    by—Cont'd
    Exemption from levy,
      etc., §11-50-35.
    Jurisdiction over
      territory acquired,
      §11-50-34.
    Powers, §§11-50-31,
      11-50-32.
    Property necessary to
      afford adequate
      water supply.
      Acquisition authorized,
        §11-50-30.
    Taxation, §11-50-36.
  Franchises.
    Purchase of waterworks.
    Right of purchaser at
      foreclosure sale,
      §11-50-7.
  Improvement authorities.
    General provisions,
      §§39-7-1 to 39-7-34.
    See PUBLIC WORKS.
  Interest.
    Customer security deposits.
      Payment of interest in
        class 1
        municipalities,
        §11-50-17.
  Licenses.
    Schedule for waterworks
      companies, §11-51-129.
  Maintenance of systems.
    Debts incurred, §§11-50-8
      to 11-50-11.
    Expenditure of municipal
      funds, §11-50-5.
    Expenses.
      Payment, §11-81-182.
    Foreign municipal
      corporations,
      §§11-50-30 to 11-50-36.
    Generally, §11-50-1.
  Mayors.
    Employment as
      superintendent of
      water systems,
      §§11-43-80, 11-50-16.
  Mortgages and deeds of trust.
    Security for debts incurred
      in construction,
      acquisition, etc.,
      §§11-50-8 to 11-50-11.
  Operation of systems.
    Boards for operation of
      water, sewer, gas and
      electric systems,
      §§11-50-310 to
      11-50-324. See within
      this heading, "Public
      utilities."
    Debts incurred, §§11-50-8
      to 11-50-11.
    Expenditure of municipal
      funds, §11-50-5.
    Expenses.
      Payment out of general
        funds, §11-81-182.
    Generally, §11-50-1.
  Ordinances.
    Transfer of water and
      sewer systems by
      municipalities without
      elections, §11-50-191.

**MUNICIPAL
CORPORATIONS**—Cont'd
**Water supply and
waterworks**—Cont'd
Other municipalities.
Sale of water to other
municipalities,
§11-50-3.
Payment by municipalities
for services furnished by
system, §11-81-186.
Plants.
Sale, lease, etc., by
municipalities,
§§11-50-140 to
11-50-151. See within
this heading, "Public
utilities."
President of board of
commissioners.
Superintendent of water
systems.
Employment as
superintendent,
§11-50-16.
Validation of prior
employment,
§11-50-16.
Properties of system.
Accounting, §11-81-188.
Public improvements.
Bond issues, §§11-81-110 to
11-81-123. See within
this heading, "Bond
issues."
General provisions,
§§11-48-1 to 11-48-65.
See within this
heading, "Public
improvements."
Improvement authorities,
§§39-7-15, 39-7-19 to
39-7-21.
Generally, §§39-7-1 to
39-7-34.
See PUBLIC WORKS.
Public utilities generally,
§§11-50-1 to 11-50-533.
See within this heading,
"Public utilities."
Public water corporations,
§§11-50-370 to 11-50-372.
Board of health.
Rights and powers not
impaired by article,
§11-50-372.
Contracts.
Between public water
corporations and
public sewer
corporations,
§11-50-371.
Definitions, §11-50-370.
Powers of public water
corporations.
Not impaired by article,
§11-50-372.
Rights not impaired by
article, §11-50-372.
Purchase of public utilities
generally, §§37-4-60 to
37-4-65.
See PUBLIC UTILITIES.
Purchase of waterworks.
Authorized, §11-81-161.
Bond issues, §11-50-6.
Security, §11-50-6.
Debts incurred, §§11-50-8
to 11-50-11.
Expenditure of municipal
funds, §11-50-5.

**MUNICIPAL
CORPORATIONS**—Cont'd
**Water supply and
waterworks**—Cont'd
Purchase of waterworks
—Cont'd
Foreign municipal
corporations,
§§11-50-30 to 11-50-36.
Franchise right of
purchaser at
foreclosure sale,
§11-50-7.
Generally, §11-50-1.
Revenue bonds,
§§11-81-160 to
11-81-190. See within
this heading, "Public
utilities."
Revenues from plants.
Disposition, §11-50-6.
Quality.
Regulation of water
quality, §11-50-1.
Rates.
Boards of water and sewer
commissioners,
§11-50-351.
Combination of sewer and
water distribution
system.
Single schedule of
charges, §11-50-121.
Establishment, §11-81-184.
Mortgages or deeds of trust
as security for debts
incurred, §11-50-11.
Regulation of water rates,
§11-50-1.
State supervision or
regulation.
Not subject to,
§11-81-185.
Repair of systems.
Authorized, §11-81-161.
Contracts and indebtedness
authorized, §11-47-3.
Resolutions.
Transfer of water and
sewer systems by
municipalities without
elections, §§11-50-170,
11-50-171, 11-50-191.
Revenue bonds, §§11-81-160
to 11-81-190. See within
this heading, "Public
utilities."
Revenues.
Depository.
Designation, §11-81-183.
Disposition of gross
revenue account and
special funds by
depository,
§11-81-183.
Disposition, §11-81-181.
Gross revenue account.
Disposition, §11-81-183.
Pledge of revenues for
payment of bonds,
§§11-81-16, 11-81-17.
Provision in purchase
agreement as to
disposition, §11-50-6.
Revenue bonds.
Pledge of revenues for
payment of bonds,
§11-81-181.

**MUNICIPAL
CORPORATIONS**—Cont'd
**Water supply and
waterworks**—Cont'd
Sale, lease, etc., of
waterworks plants by
municipalities,
§§11-50-140 to 11-50-151.
See within this heading,
"Public utilities."
Sale of water.
To other municipalities,
§11-50-3.
Securing water supply.
Condemnation of sources of
water, §11-50-4.
Superintendent of water
systems.
Employment of mayor or
president of board of
commissioners as,
§§11-43-80, 11-50-16.
Transfer of water and sewer
systems by
municipalities without
elections, §§11-50-170 to
11-50-174, 11-50-190 to
11-50-192.
Agreements, §11-50-192.
Execution, §11-50-173.
Authorization of
conveyance,
§§11-50-170,
11-50-191.
Bond issues.
Security, §11-50-172.
Construction of article,
§11-50-174.
Conveyance authorized,
§§11-50-170,
11-50-191.
Definitions, §11-50-190.
Execution of necessary
agreements,
§11-50-173.
Indentures.
Security, §11-50-172.
Instruments.
Execution, §11-50-173.
Limitation of actions to
restrain, §11-50-171.
Mortgages.
Security, §11-50-172.
Ordinance, §11-50-191.
Public service commission.
Exemption from
jurisdiction,
§11-50-174.
Regulatory bodies.
Exemption from
jurisdiction,
§11-50-174.
Resolutions.
Authorizing transfer,
§11-50-170.
Publication of notice of
adoption, §11-50-171.
Restraint of transfer.
Limitation of actions,
§11-50-171.
Terms, §11-50-170.
Transfer of waterworks to
boards organized and
incorporated to own and
operate waterworks,
§§11-50-13, 11-50-14.
Utility boards.
Waterworks utility boards,
§§11-50-430 to
11-50-445.

**MUNICIPAL
  CORPORATIONS**—Cont'd
**Water supply and
  waterworks**—Cont'd
Water, sewer and fire
  protection authorities,
  §§11-88-1 to 11-88-111.
  See WATER, SEWER AND
    FIRE PROTECTION
    AUTHORITIES.
Water, sewer and fire
  protection districts,
  §§11-89-1 to 11-89-19.
  See WATER, SEWER AND
    FIRE PROTECTION
    DISTRICTS.
Waterworks and sewer
  boards, §§11-50-230 to
  11-50-291. See within
  this heading,
  "Waterworks and sewer
  boards."
Waterworks utility boards,
  §§11-50-430 to 11-50-445.
Accountant.
  Duties, §11-50-440.
Additions.
  Expenditures for
    additions to
    waterworks plant,
    §11-50-442.
Bonds, surety, §§11-50-430
  to 11-50-445.
Depositories.
  Fixing of bonds
    required from,
    §11-50-445.
  Official bonds of certain
    officers and
    employees,
    §11-50-438.
Compensation of members,
  §11-50-435.
Composition, §11-50-430.
Construction.
  Expenditures for new
    construction,
    §11-50-442.
Creation, §11-50-430.
Depositories.
  Bonds, surety.
    Fixing of bonds
      required from,
      §11-50-445.
Duties, §11-50-439.
Election of members,
  §11-50-432.
Employees.
  Bonds, surety,
    §11-50-438.
Expenditures.
  New construction,
    additions, etc., to
    waterworks plant,
    §11-50-442.
Funds.
  Disbursement,
    §11-50-443.
  Fixing of bonds required
    from depositories,
    §11-50-445.
  Maintenance,
    §11-50-443.
Impeachment of members,
  §11-50-434.
Meetings, §11-50-437.
Oath of members,
  §11-50-433.
Officers, §11-50-436.
  Bonds, surety, §11-50-438.

**MUNICIPAL
  CORPORATIONS**—Cont'd
**Water supply and
  waterworks**—Cont'd
Waterworks utility boards
  —Cont'd
Operation of waterworks
  plant and system.
  Disposition of money
    received, §11-50-444.
Powers, §11-50-439.
Qualifications of members,
  §11-50-431.
Record of proceedings,
  §11-50-437.
Removal of members,
  §11-50-434.
Reports, §11-50-441.
  Accountant's report,
    §11-50-440.
Terms of members,
  §11-50-432.
Vacancies, §11-50-432.
Wells.
  Construction regulation,
    etc., of public wells,
    §11-47-140.
**Water system assistance
  authority.**
Investments in bonds of
  authority, §22-23A-12.
**Waterworks and sewer
  boards,** §§11-50-230 to
  11-50-291.
Acquisition, operation, etc.,
  of gas plants and
  systems, §§11-50-260 to
  11-50-273.
Appeal from order of public
  service commission,
  §11-50-269.
Completion of sale
  pursuant to final
  determination,
  §11-50-270.
Authorization, §11-50-260.
Bond issues, §§11-50-262 to
  11-50-264.
Contracts.
  Security for
    repayment,
    §11-50-263.
Denominations,
  §11-50-264.
Exemption from
  taxation, §11-50-264.
Interest, §11-50-264.
Issuance, §§11-50-262,
  11-50-264.
Payment, §11-50-264.
Pledge of revenues for
  payment,
  §11-50-264.
Refunding bonds,
  §11-50-264.
Sale, §11-50-264.
Terms, §11-50-264.
Vesting of title to system
  in municipality upon
  payment,
  §11-50-264.
Borrowing money,
  §11-50-262.
Contracts as security for
  repayment,
  §11-50-263.

**MUNICIPAL
  CORPORATIONS**—Cont'd
**Waterworks and sewer
  boards**—Cont'd
Acquisition, operation, etc.,
  of gas plants and
  systems—Cont'd
Completion of sale.
  Pursuant to final
    determination of
    commission or court,
    §11-50-270.
Conditions of acquisition.
  Issuance of order by
    commission as to,
    §11-50-268.
Consolidation of gas and
  waterworks plants and
  systems, §11-50-271.
Construction of division,
  §11-50-273.
Contracts.
  Security for repayment,
    §11-50-263.
Deeds.
  Failure of seller to
    tender or board to
    accept, §11-50-270.
Existing plant or system.
  Notice of owner of
    intention of
    waterworks board to
    operate, §11-50-266.
Voluntary sale to board
  by owner,
  §11-50-267.
Hearing on acquisition,
  §11-50-268.
Appeal from order of
  commission,
  §11-50-269.
Intention to operate gas
  plant or system.
  Notice to owner of
    existing gas plant or
    system, §11-50-266.
Mortgages and deeds of
  trust.
  Provisions as to rights of
    parties, §11-50-262.
  Security for
    indebtedness,
    §11-50-262.
Name of board.
  Change upon acquisition
    of gas plant or
    system, §11-50-272.
Notice to owner of existing
  gas plant or system in
  territory of intention
  to operate, §11-50-266.
Pledges.
  Security for
    indebtedness,
    §11-50-262.
Powers of boards as to gas
  plants and systems.
  Additional powers,
    §11-50-261.
Public service commission.
  Appeal from order of
    commission,
    §11-50-269.
  Application to
    commission for
    determination as to
    terms of acquisition,
    §11-50-268.

MUNICIPAL CORPORATIONS—Cont'd
Waterworks and sewer boards—Cont'd
Acquisition, operation, etc., of gas plants and systems—Cont'd
Public service commission—Cont'd
Completion of sale pursuant to final determination of commission or court, §11-50-270.
Exemption from jurisdiction, §11-50-273.
Issuance of order as to terms, conditions, etc., of acquisition, §11-50-268.
Purchase price.
Failure of board to pay, §11-50-270.
Sale of gas to municipalities.
Authorized, §11-50-262.
Sale of plant or system by board to utility regulated by commission, §11-50-265.
Terms of acquisition.
Issuance of order by commission as to terms, §11-50-268.
Public service commission determination, §11-50-268.
Transfer of gas plant or system by board to utility regulated by state public service commission, §11-50-265.
Transfer of gas plant or system to waterworks board, §11-50-265.
Acquisition, operation, etc., of waterworks system located in another municipality, §11-50-239.
Board of directors.
Generally, §11-50-234.
Board of health.
Jurisdiction, etc., §11-50-241.
Bond issues.
Acquisition, operation, etc., of gas plants and systems, §§11-50-262 to 11-50-264.
Application of revenues, §11-50-237.
Denominations, §11-50-237.
Execution, §11-50-237.
Gas plants.
Acquisition, operation, etc., of gas plants and systems, §§11-50-262 to 11-50-264.
Improvement and extension of waterworks plants, §11-50-240.
Interest, §11-50-237.

MUNICIPAL CORPORATIONS—Cont'd
Waterworks and sewer boards—Cont'd
Bond issues—Cont'd
Payment.
Conveyance of system in other municipality upon payment of indebtedness, §11-50-239.
Pledge of revenues, §§11-50-237, 11-50-240.
Vesting of title to systems in municipality upon payment of bonds in full, §11-50-237.
Refunding bonds, §11-50-237.
Sale, §11-50-237.
Terms, §11-50-237.
Borrowing money.
Contracts as security for repayment, §11-50-236.
Certificate of incorporation, §§11-50-232, 11-50-233.
Consolidation of gas and waterworks plants and systems, §11-50-271.
Construction of division, §11-50-241.
Contracts.
Acquisition, operation, etc., of gas plants and systems.
Security for repayment, §11-50-263.
Conveyance of system in other municipality upon payment of indebtedness, §11-50-239.
Management and operation of sanitary sewer systems as agents of municipalities, §11-50-290.
Security for repayment of moneys borrowed, §11-50-236.
Definitions, §11-50-230.
Directors.
Generally, §11-50-234.
Dissolution of corporation.
Upon payment of bonds in full, §11-50-237.
Electric light and power plants.
Combination with waterworks, §11-50-12.
Expenses.
Meeting expense allowance, §11-50-234.1.
Gas plants.
Acquisition, operation, etc., §§11-50-260 to 11-50-273.
Powers of boards.
Additional powers, §11-50-261.
Revenues from gas systems.
Pledge for payment of bonds, §11-50-240.
Income.
Exemption from taxation of income of corporation, §11-50-235.

MUNICIPAL CORPORATIONS—Cont'd
Waterworks and sewer boards—Cont'd
Incorporation.
Application for authority, §11-50-231.
Certificate of incorporation.
Acknowledgment, §11-50-233.
Amendment, §11-50-232.
Contents, §11-50-232.
Filing, §11-50-233.
Recordation, §11-50-233.
Resolution.
Authorizing incorporation, §11-50-231.
Loans.
Contracts as security for repayment, §11-50-236.
Management of sewer systems as agents of municipalities, §§11-50-290, 11-50-291.
Board of health.
Rights and powers not impaired by division, §11-50-291.
Contracts.
Between municipalities and waterworks board, §11-50-290.
Powers of municipalities and state board of health.
Not impaired by division, §11-50-291.
Rights of municipalities and state board of health.
Not impaired by division, §11-50-291.
Meetings.
Expense allowance, §11-50-234.1.
Mortgages and deeds of trust.
Acquisition, operation, etc., of gas plants and systems.
Security for indebtedness, §11-50-262.
Rights of parties, §11-50-235.
Name of board.
Change upon acquisition of gas plant or system, §11-50-272.
Pledges.
Acquisition, operation, etc., of gas plants and systems.
Security for indebtedness, §11-50-262.
Rights of parties, §11-50-235.
Powers of corporation.
As to conveyance of title to systems, §11-50-238.
Gas plants and systems, §11-50-261.
Generally, §11-50-235.
Property.
Exemption from taxation of property of corporation, §11-50-235.

MUNICIPAL CORPORATIONS—Cont'd
Waterworks and sewer boards—Cont'd
Public service commission.
Acquisition, operation, etc., of gas plants and systems, §§11-50-168 to 11-50-273.
Jurisdiction, etc., §11-50-241.
Resolution.
Incorporation, §11-50-231.
Taxation.
Exemption from taxation, §11-50-235.
Title to systems.
Conveyance, §11-50-238.
Vesting in municipality upon payment of bonds in full, §11-50-237.
Transfer of systems to corporation, §11-50-238.

Weapons.
Closing places for sale of firearms, §11-51-102.
Ordinances and resolutions.
Subject matter of handguns reserved to state legislature, §11-45-1.1.
Revocation of licenses of places where firearms kept for sale, §11-51-103.
Riots.
Proclamation forbidding sale of arms, etc., during, §11-43-82.

Weeds.
Abatement of weeds.
Class 2 municipalities, §§11-67-1 to 11-67-9.
See within this heading, "Class 2 municipalities."
Class 5 municipalities, §§11-67-20 to 11-67-28.
See within this heading, "Class 5 municipalities."
Requirement of cutting, §11-47-140.

Weights and measures.
Inspections, §11-47-17.
Charges for inspection, §11-43-59.
Local sealers, §§8-16-7, 8-16-11, 8-16-30 to 8-16-32.
See WEIGHTS AND MEASURES.
Provision of public scales, §11-47-17.
Weighing machines.
License tax, §11-51-98.

Wells.
Construction, regulation, etc., of public wells, §11-47-140.

Wharves.
Bond issues.
Public improvement bonds.
Revenue producing undertakings, §§11-81-140 to 11-81-150.
See COUNTIES.
Construction, §11-47-15.
Leasing, §11-47-15.
Maintenance, §11-47-15.
Provision of wharves, §11-47-14.

MUNICIPAL CORPORATIONS—Cont'd
Workmen's compensation.
Applicability of chapter to municipalities, §25-5-13.

Zoning, §§11-52-70 to 11-52-84.
Airports, §§4-6-1 to 4-6-15.
See AVIATION.
Appeals.
Appeals to circuit court from final decisions of board of adjustment, §11-52-81.
Board of adjustment.
Appeals to board from decisions of administrative officials, §11-52-80.
Board of adjustment, §§11-52-80, 11-52-81.
Appeals to board, §11-52-80.
Appeals to circuit court from final decision of board, §11-52-81.
Appointment of members, §11-52-80.
Composition, §11-52-80.
Creation, §11-52-80.
Decisions of board.
Appeals from final decision, §11-52-81.
Meetings, §11-52-80.
Qualifications of members, §11-52-80.
Record of proceedings, §11-52-80.
Removal of members, §11-52-80.
Rules of procedure.
Adoption, §11-52-80.
Terms of members, §11-52-80.
Vacancies, §11-52-80.
Boundaries.
District boundaries, §11-52-70.
Amendment, §11-52-78.
Municipal legislative body to provide procedure, §11-52-76.
Existing boundaries.
Article not to repeal, modify, etc., §11-52-84.
Repeal, §11-52-78.
Buildings.
Height regulations, §11-52-73.
Conflict of laws, §11-52-82.
Provision as to type, use, etc., authorized, §11-52-70.
Remedies for construction, etc., of buildings in violation of article, §11-52-83.
Size of buildings.
Regulation and restriction, §11-52-73.
Business districts.
Establishment, etc., authorized, §11-52-70.

MUNICIPAL CORPORATIONS—Cont'd
Zoning—Cont'd
Class 5 municipalities.
Mayor/commission/city manager form of government.
Comprehensive zoning maps, §11-44E-53.
Mayor-council form of government, §11-43C-30.
Commission.
Generally, §11-52-79.
Conflict of laws, §11-52-82.
Density of population.
Regulation and restriction, §11-52-73.
Discrimination.
Prohibited in housing, §11-52-75.
Districts.
Area, §11-52-71.
Authorization of establishment, etc., §11-52-70.
Boundaries, §11-52-70.
Amendment, §11-52-78.
Procedure, §11-52-76.
Existing boundaries.
Article not to repeal, modify, etc., §11-52-84.
Repeal, §11-52-78.
Division of territory into districts, §11-52-70.
Establishment, §11-52-70.
Number, §11-52-71.
Shape, §11-52-71.
Housing.
Mentally retarded or mentally ill persons.
Regulation as to housing in multi-family zones, §11-52-75.1.
Regulation as to housing of different classes of inhabitants in residential districts, §11-52-75.
Industrial districts.
Establishment, etc., authorized, §11-52-70.
Lot sizes.
Conflict of laws, §11-52-82.
Regulation and restriction, §11-52-73.
Mayor/commission/city manager form of government.
Comprehensive zoning maps, §11-44E-53.
Municipal planning commission.
Powers as to zoning, §11-52-7.
Ordinances.
Adoption of ordinances for implementation of article, §11-52-76.
Amendment, §11-52-78.
Article not to repeal, modify, etc., existing ordinances, §11-52-84.
Conflict of laws, §11-52-82.
Existing ordinances.
Article not to repeal, modify, etc., §11-52-84.

MUNICIPAL
CORPORATIONS—Cont'd
Zoning—Cont'd
Ordinances—Cont'd
Procedure for adoption of
ordinances authorized
by article, §11-52-77.
Repeal, §11-52-78.
Violations.
Remedies, §11-52-83.
Population.
Regulation of density,
§11-52-73.
Records.
Board of adjustment.
Record of proceedings,
§11-52-80.
Regulations.
Amendment, §11-52-78.
Procedure, §11-52-76.
Conflict of laws, §11-52-82.
Considerations in
establishment,
§11-52-72.
Density of population,
§11-52-73.
Enforcement, §11-52-76.
Establishment.
Considerations in
establishment,
§11-52-72.
Procedure, §11-52-76.
Existing regulations.
Article not to repeal,
modify, etc.,
§11-52-84.
Height of buildings,
§11-52-73.
Conflict between
regulations,
§11-52-82.
Housing.
Regulation as to housing
of different classes of
inhabitants in
residential districts,
§11-52-75.
Lot sizes, §11-52-73.
Purposes, §11-52-72.
Remedies for violation,
§11-52-83.
Repeal, §11-52-78.
Uniformity, §11-52-71.
Violations.
Remedies, §11-52-83.
Yard regulations,
§11-52-73.
Conflict of laws,
§11-52-82.
Residential districts.
Establishment, etc.,
authorized, §11-52-70.
Regulation as to housing of
different classes of
inhabitants in
residential districts,
§11-52-75.
Subdivisions.
Powers of planning
commission, §11-52-32.
Uniformity of regulations,
§11-52-71.
Violations.
Remedies, §11-52-83.
Yard regulations, §11-52-73.
Conflict of laws, §11-52-82.

MUNICIPAL COURTS,
§§12-14-1 to 12-14-71.
Abolition, Const. Ala., amd.
328.
Effect, §12-14-17.
Procedure, §12-14-17.
Reestablishment.
Procedure and effect,
§12-14-19.
Remittance of costs, fines
and forfeitures
previously collected,
§12-14-18.
Administrative agency,
§§12-14-50 to 12-14-52.
Authorized, §12-14-50.
Duties, §12-14-50.
Magistrates.
Deemed chief officers of
agency, §12-14-51.
Officials of agency.
Judicial powers, §12-14-50.
Magistrates deemed chief
officers, §12-14-51.
Persons deemed officials,
§12-14-50.
Powers, §12-14-50.
Rules.
Supreme court to provide
rules of administration
for agency, §12-14-52.
Administrative personnel.
Coordination of functions and
duties, §12-5-13.
Appeals.
Appeals to circuit court,
§§12-14-70, 12-14-71,
12-19-150, 12-19-153.
Costs, §12-19-150.
Collection, §12-19-153.
Bonds, surety, §12-14-31.
From judgments of circuit
courts, §12-14-71.
Appearances.
Bonds, surety, §12-14-31.
Arrest warrants.
Execution, §12-14-4.
Issuance, §12-14-32.
Bail and recognizance.
Admission to bail of persons
charged with violations
of municipal ordinances,
§12-14-5.
Waiver of appearance
bond, §12-14-5.
Bonds, surety.
Appeal bonds, §12-14-31.
Appearance bonds, §12-14-31.
Inability to pay fines and
costs.
Defendant's bond,
§12-14-11.
Circuit courts.
Superintendence of muncipal
courts, §12-11-30.
Clerks of court.
Clerks generally.
See CLERKS OF COURT.
Fees.
Monthly reports as to fees
collected, §12-1-19.
Fines.
Monthly reports as to fines
collected, §12-1-19.
Commutation of sentences.
Power of mayor to commute,
§12-14-15.
Constitution of Alabama,
Const. Ala., amd. 328.

MUNICIPAL COURTS—Cont'd
Costs, §12-14-14.
Abolition of municipal court.
Remittance of costs
previously collected
upon abolition of court,
§12-14-18.
Additional fees.
Charge and collection,
§12-19-250.1.
Distribution to fair trial
tax fund, §12-19-250.1.
Imposition, §12-19-250.1.
Criminal cases.
Imposition of court costs,
§12-19-153.
Fair trial tax.
Additional fee.
Distribution to fair trial
tax fund,
§12-19-250.1.
Retention and disposition
of tax, §12-19-251.1.
Inability to pay.
Defendant's bond,
§12-14-11.
Mayor.
Power to remit, §12-14-15.
Working out amount of
judgment, §12-14-12.
Courts generally.
See COURTS.
Criminal jurisdiction.
Vesting, §12-1-3.
Disposition of cases.
Powers of courts, §12-14-10.
Establishment, §12-14-1.
Reestablishment.
Procedure and effect,
§12-14-19.
Facilities.
Provision by municipality,
§12-14-2.
Fair trial tax.
Additional fee.
Distribution to fair trial
tax fund, §12-19-250.1.
Retention and disposition of
tax when collected in
municipal court,
§12-19-251.1.
Fines.
Abolition of municipal court.
Remittance of fines
previously collected,
§12-14-18.
Clerks of court.
Monthly reports as to fines
collected, §12-1-19.
Inability to pay.
Defendant's bond,
§12-14-11.
Mayor.
Power to remit fines,
§12-14-15.
Traffic infractions.
Schedule, ARJA, Rule 20.
Working out amount of
judgment, §12-14-12.
Forfeitures.
Abolition of municipal court.
Remittance of forfeitures
previously collected,
§12-14-18.
Indigent persons.
Defense of indigents.
General provisions,
§§15-12-1 to 15-12-46.
See INDIGENT
PERSONS.

MUNICIPAL COURTS—Cont'd
Indigent persons—Cont'd
Defense of indigents—Cont'd
Provision of indigent
defense services,
§12-14-9.
Judges, §§12-1-18, 12-14-30 to
12-14-34.
Absence.
Acting municipal judges,
§12-14-34.
Acting municipal judges,
§12-14-34.
Appointment, Const. Ala.,
amd. 328.
Conferences, seminars, etc.
Failure to attend when
ordered, §12-1-18.
Reimbursement of travel
expenses, §12-1-18.
Death.
Acting municipal judges,
§12-14-34.
Disability.
Acting municipal judges,
§12-14-34.
Disqualification.
Acting municipal judges,
§12-14-34.
Grounds, §12-14-30.
Expenses.
Reimbursement of travel
expenses for attending
conferences, etc.,
§12-1-18.
General provisions.
See JUDGES.
Number of judges.
Municipal governing body
to provide for,
§12-14-3.
Powers, §12-14-31.
Practice of law.
Prohibited by full-time
judges, §12-14-30.
Presiding judge.
Designation, §12-14-30.
Qualifications, §12-14-30;
Const. Ala., amd. 328.
Retirement, §12-14-33.
Election of rights,
§12-18-51.
Robes.
Judges encouraged to wear
suitable black judicial
robe, ARJA, Rule 22.
Salary, §12-14-33.
Terms of office, §12-14-30.
Travel expenses.
Reimbursement of judges
attending conferences,
etc., §12-1-18.
Unauthorized remuneration
for judicial services by
full-time judges
prohibited, §12-14-30.
Vacancies.
Acting municipal judges,
§12-14-34.
Filling, §12-14-30; Const.
Ala., amd. 328.
Warrants.
Issuance of arrest and
search warrants,
§12-14-32.
Judicial notice.
Ordinances, §12-14-7.
Jurisdiction, §12-14-1; Const.
Ala., amd. 328.
Criminal jurisdiction.
Vesting, §12-1-3.

MUNICIPAL COURTS—Cont'd
Jury.
Cases to be tried by judge
without jury, §12-14-6.
Locations.
Municipal governing body to
provide for, §12-14-3.
Magistrates.
Administrative agency.
Municipal court
magistrates agency
division, ARJA, Rule
18.
Authority, ARJA, Rule
18.
Selection, ARJA, Rule
18.
Appointment, §12-14-51.
Deemed chief officers of
administrative agency of
court, §12-14-51.
Powers, §12-14-51.
Mayor.
Commutation of sentences,
§12-14-15.
Fines and costs.
Power to remit, §12-14-15.
Motor vehicles.
Traffic infractions.
Procedure, §12-14-8.
Schedule of fines, ARJA,
Rule 20.
Officers and employees.
Conferences, seminars, etc.,
§12-1-18.
Ordinances.
Judicial notice, §12-14-7.
Personnel.
Provision by municipality,
§12-14-2.
Places for holding court,
§12-14-3.
Police.
Execution of warrants and
processes, §12-14-4.
Powers.
Trial and disposition of cases,
§12-14-10.
Probation, §12-14-13.
Process.
Execution by sheriffs and
municipal law
enforcement officers,
§12-14-4.
Prosecutorial services.
Provision by municipality,
§12-14-2.
Reestablishment.
Procedure and effect,
§12-14-19.
Reports.
Actions.
Report to municipal
governing body,
§12-14-15.
Clerks of court, §12-1-19.
Proceedings of courts,
§12-14-16.
Retirement.
Judges, §12-14-33.
Election by judges entitled
to receive commissions
as district judges,
§12-18-51.
Salaries.
Judges, §12-14-33.
Search warrants.
Issuance, §12-14-32.
Sentences.
Commutation.
Power of mayor, §12-14-15.

MUNICIPAL COURTS—Cont'd
Sentences—Cont'd
Mayor.
Power to commute,
§12-14-15.
Sheriffs.
Execution of warrants and
processes, §12-14-4.
Supreme court.
Administrative agency for
municipal court.
Supreme court to provide
rules of administration
for agency, §12-14-52.
Times for holding court.
Municipal governing body to
provide for, §12-14-3.
**Traffic infractions or
defenses.**
Fines, ARJA, Rule 20.
Procedure, §12-14-8.
Trial.
Cases to be tried by judge
without jury, §12-14-6.
Powers of courts as to trial,
§12-14-10.
Warrants.
Execution by sheriffs and
municipal law
enforcement officers,
§12-14-4.
Issuance, §12-14-32.

**MUNICIPAL ELECTRIC
AUTHORITY,** §§11-50A-1 to
11-50A-33.
See MUNICIPAL
CORPORATIONS.

**MUSCLE SHOALS,
MUNICIPALITY OF.**
School tax.
Special property tax for
educational purposes,
Const. Ala., amd. 172.

MUSEUMS.
**Alabama Agricultural and
Mechanical University.**
State Black Archives,
Research Center And
Museum, §§16-49-50 to
16-49-55.
See HISTORY AND
ARCHIVES.
**Alabama historical
commission.**
Acquisition, operation, etc.,
§41-9-254.
**Black Heritage Museum of
West Alabama,** §§16-62-1
to 16-62-6.
See BLACK HERITAGE
MUSEUM OF WEST
ALABAMA.
Counties.
Acquisition of lands,
§11-18-2.
Establishment, acquisition,
administration, etc.,
§11-47-16.
History and archives.
Alabama historical
commission.
Acquisition, operation, etc.,
of museums by
commission, §41-9-254.
Municipal corporations.
Establishment, acquisition,
administration, etc.,
§11-47-16.

MUSEUMS—Cont'd
State Black Archives,
  Research Center And
  Museum, §§16-49-50 to
  16-49-55.
See HISTORY AND
  ARCHIVES.
University of Alabama
  museum, §§16-47-190 to
  16-47-204.
See UNIVERSITY OF
  ALABAMA.

MUSIC.
Bands.
  Appropriations for bands,
    §11-80-4.
Counties.
  Bands.
    Appropriations for bands,
      §11-80-4.
  Establishment, etc., of
    concert halls, §11-47-16.
Hall of fame board,
  §§41-9-680 to 41-9-684.
  Appointment of members,
    §41-9-680.
  Appropriations, §41-9-684.
  Bond issues, Const. Ala.,
    amd. 489.
  Compensation of members,
    §41-9-680.
  Composition, §41-9-680.
  Creation, §41-9-680.
  Domicile of board, §41-9-681.
  Executive secretary or
    director, §41-9-681.
  Expenditures, §41-9-684.
  Functions, §41-9-682.
  Gifts.
    Solicitation and
      acceptance, §41-9-683.
    Taxation.
      Exemption from
        taxation, §41-9-683.
  Location, §41-9-681.
  Meetings, §41-9-680.
  Membership, §41-9-680.
  Officers, §41-9-680.
  Powers and duties, §41-9-682.
  Qualifications of members,
    §41-9-680.
  Quorum, §41-9-680.
  Staff, §41-9-681.
  Taxation.
    Gifts.
      Exemptions, §41-9-683.
  Terms of office, §41-9-680.
Licenses.
  Musical entertainments,
    §40-12-82.
  Musical instruments,
    §40-12-141.
Municipal corporations.
  Bands.
    Appropriations for
      municipal bands,
      §11-80-4.
    Establishment, etc., of
      concert halls, §11-47-16.
    Provision of music and other
      exhibitions, §11-47-19.
    Vending machines.
      Regulation and control of
        vending machines on
        which music is played,
        §11-51-100.
Official state reunion theme
  song, §1-2-24.
State song of Alabama.
  Adoption, §1-2-16.

MUSSELS, §§9-11-370 to
9-11-374.

MUTUAL INSURANCE.
See INSURANCE.

N

NAMES.
Adoption.
  Change of name of child,
    §26-10-1.
Agriculture.
  Cooperatives.
    Use of word "cooperative"
      in name, §2-10-1.
Alabama Agricultural and
  Mechanical University.
  Board of trustees, §16-49-21.
  Grants or gifts not to fail
    because of misnomer,
    etc., §16-49-3.
Alabama coordinate system.
  Limitation on use of name of
    system, §35-2-7.
Alabama State University.
  Board of trustees, §16-50-21.
  Grants or gifts not to fail
    because of misnomer,
    etc., §16-50-3.
Banks and financial
  institutions.
  Savings and loan
    associations, §5-16-9.
  Use of word "trust" in
    corporate or partnership
    name, §§5-11A-1,
    5-11A-4.
Beverage containers,
  §§8-12-20, 8-12-21.
Bishop of diocese.
  Corporate name, §10-4-4.
Brands and marks.
  See BRANDS AND MARKS.
Change of name.
  Adoption.
    Change of name of child,
      §26-10-1.
  Fees.
    Probate judges' fees,
      §12-19-90.
  Jurisdiction of probate
    courts, §12-13-1.
  Special, private or local laws
    prohibited, Const. Ala.,
    art. IV, §104.
Constitution of Alabama.
  Change of name.
    Special, private or local
      laws prohibited, Const.
      Ala., art. IV, §104.
Corporations.
  See CORPORATIONS.
Counties, §11-1-1.
Credit unions.
  Use of words "credit union"
    in name or title, §5-17-3.
Dentists.
  Improper use of name in
    practice of dentistry,
    §34-9-17.
Divorce.
  Wife may be enjoined from
    using husband's name,
    §30-2-11.
Drugs.
  Controlled substances.
    Nomenclature of controlled
      substances in
      schedules, §20-2-21.
Elections, §§17-7-15, 17-8-2.

NAMES—Cont'd
Electric cooperatives.
  Use of words electric, power
    or cooperative in
    cooperative's name,
    §37-6-4.
Fees.
  Change of name.
    Probate judges' fees,
      §12-19-90.
Health care authorities.
  Powers of authority,
    §22-21-318.
Health care service plan.
  Change of corporate name,
    §10-4-105.
Highways, §§23-1-8, 23-1-8.1.
Indictments, §§15-8-28,
  15-28-90.
Insurance.
  Insurers.
    Use of name by insurer,
      §27-3-5.
  Mutual aid associations,
    §27-30-7.
  Reciprocal insurers.
    Business name, §27-31-4.
Labels.
  See LABELS.
Liquefied petroleum gas.
  Permit holder's name.
    Change of name,
      §9-17-105.
Livingston University,
  §16-53-1.
  Grant or gift not to fail for
    misnomer, §16-53-11.
Municipal corporations,
  §11-40-1.
  Change of name, §11-40-7.
  Property rights.
    Rights of action, etc.,
      preserved and
      enforced.
      Notwithstanding
        change of name,
        §11-40-4.
  Council-manager form of
    government.
    Governing body,
      §§11-43A-8, 11-43A-11.
Parties.
  Pleadings, ARCP, Rule 10
    (a).
Partnerships.
  Limited partnerships,
    §10-9A-2.
  Foreign limited
    partnerships,
    §10-9A-163.
Probate courts.
  Change of name.
    Jurisdiction of probate
      courts, §12-13-1.
Professional corporations.
  Corporate name, §10-4-387.
Savings and loan
  associations.
  Corporate name, §5-16-9.
Trademarks.
  See TRADEMARKS.
Troy state university.
  Grant or gift not to fail for
    misnomer, §16-56-11.
Unincorporated professional
  associations, §10-10-5.
University of Montevallo,
  §16-54-1.

NAMES—Cont'd
Welfare.
Recipients of public
assistance.
Filing names with probate
judge.
County boards of
pensions and
security, §38-1-4.

NARCOTICS.
Driving under the influence,
§32-5A-191.
Arrest, §32-5-171.
Chemical test, §§32-5-190 to
32-5-194, 32-5A-194.
Education.
Drug abuse education,
§§16-41-1 to 16-41-10.
See EDUCATION.
General provisions.
See DRUGS.
Motor vehicles.
Driving under the influence,
§32-5A-191.
Arrest, §32-5-171.
Chemical test, §§32-5-190
to 32-5-194, 32-5A-194.

NATIONAL BANKS.
Applicability of provisions,
§5-1A-5.
Banks generally, §§5-1A-1 to
5-13A-10.
See BANKS AND
FINANCIAL
INSTITUTIONS.
Defined, §5-1A-2.
**State banks to have powers
of national banks,**
§5-5A-18.1.

**NATIONAL CONFERENCE
OF STATE
LEGISLATURES.**
Sales and use taxes.
Exemption from tax,
§40-23-5.

NATIONAL FORESTS.
Acquisition of lands.
Consent to acquisition,
§42-1-2.
Administration.
Consent to acquisition of
lands needed for
administration, §42-1-2.
Consolidation.
Consent to acquisition of
lands needed for
consolidation, §42-1-2.
Receipts.
Distribution and expenditure,
§9-13-2.
**Shooting preserves, game
refuges, etc.**
Establishment, §9-11-4.
United States.
Consent to acquisition of
lands needed for
consolidation and
administration of
national forests, §42-1-2.

NATIONAL FOUNDATION.
Licenses.
Exemptions.
Alabama field offices,
§40-9-12.
Taxation.
Exemptions.
Alabama field offices,
§40-9-12.

NATIONAL GUARD.
See MILITARY AFFAIRS.

**NATIONAL YOUTH
ADMINISTRATION.**
**Public officers and
employees.**
State employees' retirement
system.
Granting of credit for
service, §36-27-15.1.

NATIVE FARM WINE.
**Regulation of production,
sale, etc.,** §§28-6-1 to
28-6-6.
See ALCOHOLIC
BEVERAGES.

NATURAL DEATH ACT,
§§22-8A-1 to 22-8A-10.
Chapter cumulative,
§22-8A-9.
**Condition for receipt of
health care services.**
Declaration not to be
condition for receipt,
§22-8A-9.
**Declaration for withdrawal
of life-support
procedures.**
Competency of declarant,
§22-8A-7.
Condition for receipt of
health care services.
Declaration not to be
condition for receipt,
§22-8A-9.
Form, §22-8A-4.
Life insurance.
Execution of declaration
not to affect sale, etc.,
§22-8A-9.
Notice to physician,
§22-8A-4.
Penalties for willful
concealment, etc.,
§22-8A-8.
Refusal of attending
physician to comply with
declaration, §22-8A-8.
Requirements, §22-8A-4.
Revocation of declaration,
§22-8A-5.
Penalties for concealment,
§22-8A-8.
Who may execute, §22-8A-4.
Witnesses, §22-8A-4.
Writing required, §22-8A-4.
Definitions, §22-8A-3.
Euthanasia.
Provisions of chapter not an
approval of mercy
killing, §22-8A-10.
Forgery.
Penalties for forging
declaration, §22-8A-8.
Forms.
Declaration for withdrawal of
life-support, §22-8A-4.
Hospitals.
Liability of participating
facility, §22-8A-7.
Legislative intent, §22-8A-2.
Mercy killing.
Provisions of chapter not an
approval, §22-8A-10.
Physicians.
Certification and
confirmation of terminal
condition, §22-8A-6.
Definition of attending
physician, §22-8A-3.

**NATURAL DEATH ACT
—Cont'd**
Physicians—Cont'd
Liability of participating
physician, §22-8A-7.
Notice of declaration,
§22-8A-4.
Refusal of attending
physician to comply with
declaration, §22-8A-8.
Short title, §22-8A-1.
Suicide.
Withholding or withdrawal
not suicide, §22-8A-9.
Terminal condition.
Certification and
confirmation of,
§22-8A-6.
Defined, §22-8A-3.

NATURAL GAS.
**Conservation and regulation
of production.**
See OIL AND GAS.
Gas pipeline systems.
See PIPELINES.
General provisions.
See GAS.
Municipal corporations.
See MUNICIPAL
CORPORATIONS.
Production.
Conservation and regulation.
See OIL AND GAS.

NATURALIZATION.
Constitutional provisions,
Const. U. S., Art. I, §§8, 9.

NATURAL RESOURCES.
See CONSERVATION AND
NATURAL RESOURCES.

NATURE STUDY SOCIETIES.
Corporations.
Public societies, §§10-4-20 to
10-4-26.
See CORPORATIONS.

NATUROPATHS.
Licenses, §40-12-155.

NAVAL MILITIA.
See MILITARY AFFAIRS.

NAVIGATION.
Aids to navigation.
Licenses.
State docks department to
grant, §33-1-28.
**Coosa Valley development
authority.**
Authority of authority,
§33-16-11.
Counties.
Opening and cleaning
navigable streams.
County commission
authorized to make
contracts, §33-7-2.
Damages.
Diverting streams.
Damages for diversion,
§33-7-4.
Harbor masters, §§33-3-2 to
33-3-6, 33-4-10.
Licenses.
Aids to navigation.
State docks department to
grant licenses for
construction, §33-1-28.
Marine police, §§33-5-4 to
33-5-6.

NAVIGATION—Cont'd

Mobile harbor.
Obstructions to navigation.
Depositing substance that
will form obstruction,
§33-1-35.

Obstructing navigation.
Dams on navigable rivers.
See DAMS.
Diverting streams.
Damages, §33-7-4.
Mobile harbor.
Depositing substance that
will form obstruction,
§33-1-35.
Opening and cleaning
navigable streams.
County commission
authorized to make
contracts, §33-7-2.
Penalty, §33-7-3.
Public thoroughfares.
Navigable waters as public
thoroughfares, §33-7-1.
Riparian owners.
Structures built or
maintained by owners.
Obstructing navigation
prohibited, §33-7-51.
Trees and timber.
Floating logs, timber or
lumber upon
watercourse without
sufficient force to
prevent obstruction,
§33-7-6.
Obstructing streams used
for floating timber to
market, §33-7-5.
Opening or cutting loose of
boom without
authority, §§33-7-7,
33-7-8.

Penalties.
Obstructing navigable
watercourse, §33-7-3.

Pilots and pilotage.
See PILOTS AND
PILOTAGE.

Police.
Marine police.
See MARINE POLICE.

Ports.
General provisions.
See HARBORS AND
PORTS.

Public thoroughfares.
Navigable waters in state
are public thoroughfares,
§33-7-1.

State docks department.
Aids to navigation.
Licenses.
Department to grant,
§33-1-28.

Trees and timber.
Floating logs, timber or
lumber upon watercourse
without sufficient force
to prevent obstruction,
§33-7-6.
Obstructing streams used for
floating timber to
market, §33-7-5.
Opening or cutting loose of
boom without authority,
§§33-7-7, 33-7-8.

Waters and watercourses.
General provisions.
See WATERS AND
WATERCOURSES.

NEEDY PERSONS.

See INDIGENT PERSONS.

NEGLIGENCE.

Agents.
Employer's liability for
certain injuries.
See EMPLOYERS AND
EMPLOYEES.
Principal responsible for
negligence of agent in
transacting agency,
§8-2-7.

Airport authorities.
Immunity of authority and
directors from liability
for negligence, §4-3-7.
Alternate procedure for
incorporation, §4-3-50.

Airports.
Municipal airports.
Municipal immunity from
liability for negligence,
§4-4-4.

Associations.
Officers.
Liability of officers of
nonprofit associations,
§§10-11-1 to 10-11-5.

Authorities.
Officers.
Liability of officers of
nonprofit
organizations,
§§10-11-1 to 10-11-5.

Boards and commissions.
Officers.
Liability of officers of
nonprofit
organizations,
§§10-11-1 to 10-11-5.

Boats.
Operation in reckless or
negligent manner,
§33-5-24.

Carriers.
Contractual limitation of
liability.
Bill of lading, §7-7-309.
Duty of carrier.
Carrier issuing bill of
lading, §7-7-309.
Railroads.
Railway policemen.
Liability of corporation
for acts of policemen,
§37-2-155.

Commercial code.
Commercial paper.
Negligence contributing to
alteration or
unauthorized
signature, §7-3-406.

Contributory negligence.
Affirmative defense, ARCP,
Rule 8 (c).
Motor vehicles.
Child passenger restraints.
Failure to wear restraint
system not
considered
contributory
negligence,
§32-5-222.

Corporations.
Nonprofit corporations.
Officers.
Liability, §§10-11-1 to
10-11-5.

**Criminally negligent
homicide, §13A-6-4.**

NEGLIGENCE—Cont'd

Employers and employees.
Employer's liability for
certain injuries, §§25-6-1
to 25-6-4.

Hazards.
Creating hazards,
§13A-11-220.

Homicide.
Criminally negligent
homicide, §13A-6-4.

Malpractice.
General provisions.
See MALPRACTICE.

Mentally ill.
Regional mental health
programs and facilities.
Officers.
Liability of officers of
nonprofit
organizations,
§§10-11-1 to 10-11-5.

Motor vehicles.
Child passenger restraints.
Failure to wear restraint
system not considered
contributory
negligence, §32-5-222.
Safety-responsibility act.
Matters not to be evidence
in civil actions,
§32-7-12.

Municipal corporations.
Airports.
Municipal immunity from
liability, §4-4-4.
Liability for negligence of
agents, etc., §§11-47-190
to 11-47-192.
Airports.
Immunity, §4-4-4.
Civil defense.
Immunity, §31-9-10.
Limitation on claims,
§§11-93-1 to 11-93-3.

Nonprofit organizations.
Officers.
Liability of officers.
Gross negligence as
exception to
immunity from suit,
§10-11-3.

Pilots and pilotage.
Branches.
Grounds for depriving pilot
of branch, §33-4-46.

Pleadings.
Form of complaint for
negligence or
wantonness, ARCP,
Form 16.

Podiatrists.
Revocation or suspension of
license, §34-24-276.

Railroads.
Railway policemen.
Liability of corporation for
acts of policemen,
§37-2-155.

Real property.
Recreational or sporting
premises liability,
§§35-15-1 to 35-15-28.
See REAL PROPERTY.

Recreation.
Recreational or sporting
premises liability,
§§35-15-1 to 35-15-28.
See REAL PROPERTY.

NEGLIGENCE—Cont'd
Signatures.
Commercial paper.
Negligence contributing to alteration or unauthorized signature, §7-3-406.
Torts generally.
See TORTS.

NEGOTIABLE
INSTRUMENTS.
Actions.
Defenses.
Actions on promissory notes, bonds or other contracts for payment of money, §6-5-286.
Holder of worthless check, draft or order.
Right of action, §6-5-285.
Instrument lost or destroyed by theft, etc., §6-5-284.
Execution bond, §6-5-284.
Bad checks.
Charge for bad checks.
Deemed not to be a finance charge, §8-8-15.
Imposition authorized, §8-8-15.
Negotiating worthless instruments. See within this heading, "Criminal law and procedure."
Penalty and service charge, §8-8-15.
Service charge, §8-8-15.
Banks and financial institutions.
Commercial code.
See COMMERCIAL CODE.
Discounting notes illegally, §5-6A-20.
Transactions involving shipment of goods.
Acceptance of drafts or bills of exchange.
Authority, §5-5A-25.
Limitations, §5-5A-26.
Bills of exchange, §§8-4-1 to 8-4-4.
Bonds, surety.
Actions.
Instrument lost or destroyed by theft, etc.
Execution bond, §6-5-284.
Checks.
Bad checks.
Charge for bad checks.
Deemed not to be finance charge, §8-8-15.
Imposition authorized, §8-8-15.
Penalty and service charge, §8-8-15.
Service charge, §8-8-15.
Commercial code.
See COMMERCIAL CODE.
General provisions.
See CHECKS.
Negotiating worthless instruments. See within this heading, "Criminal law and procedure."
Commercial code.
See COMMERCIAL CODE.
Commercial paper, §§7-3-101 to 7-3-805.
See COMMERCIAL CODE.

NEGOTIABLE
INSTRUMENTS—Cont'd
Corrections.
Institution finance authority.
Bond issues.
Deemed negotiable instruments, §14-2-23.
Counterclaims.
Exemptions.
Negotiated commercial paper, §6-8-83.
Criminal law and procedure.
Negotiating worthless instruments.
Conduct constituting, §13A-9-13.1.
Evidence.
Prima facie evidence.
Identity, §13A-9-13.3.
Identity.
Prima facie evidence of identity, §13A-9-13.3.
Notice of refusal of payment upon instrument, §13A-9-13.2.
Prima facie evidence, §13A-9-13.1.
Identity, §13A-9-13.3.
Worthless check unit of special services division of district attorney, §12-17-224.
District attorneys.
Special services division.
Worthless check unit, §12-17-224.
Drafts.
Commercial code.
See COMMERCIAL CODE.
Education.
Public school and college authority.
Bonds as negotiable instruments, §16-16-9.
Environmental control.
Environmental improvement authorities.
Bond issues, §9-6-9.
Evidence.
Certificate of notary, etc., as to presentment for acceptance, etc., of instrument governed by commercial law, §12-21-105.
Instrument lost or destroyed by theft, etc.
Evidence of loss, destruction and contents, §6-5-284.
Fiduciaries.
Uniform fiduciaries act.
Transfer of negotiable instrument by fiduciary, §19-1-4.
Forms.
Complaint on a promissory note, ARCP, Form 2.
Health care authorities.
Securities and coupons as negotiable instruments, §22-21-327.
Limitation of actions.
Exceptions to applicability of chapter, §6-2-2.

NEGOTIABLE
INSTRUMENTS—Cont'd
Mental health finance authority.
Bond issues.
Deemed negotiable instruments, §41-10-361.
Misdemeanors.
Negotiating worthless negotiable instruments, §13A-9-13.1.
Negotiating worthless instruments. See within this heading, "Criminal law and procedure."
Notice.
Negotiating worthless instrument.
Notice of refusal of payment upon instruments, §13A-9-13.2.
Space science exhibit finance authority.
Bond issues.
Bonds and coupons deemed, §41-10-320.
Uniform commercial code.
See COMMERCIAL CODE.
Water conservation and irrigation.
Corporations.
Bond issues, §9-10-36.
Water management and drainage.
Districts.
Bond issues, §9-9-37.
Water system assistance authority.
Bonds and coupons deemed, §22-23A-16.

NEPOTISM.
Canons of judicial ethics.
Prohibited in appointments, ACJE, Canon 3B.
Judges.
Prohibited in appointments, ACJE, Canon 3B.
Municipal corporations.
Commission form of government.
Optional form A, §§11-44-102, 11-44-103.
Optional form B, §11-44-138.
State service.
Prohibited in employment, §41-1-5.

NETS.
Fish and game, §§9-11-88, 9-11-91, 9-11-245, 9-11-246.
See FISH AND GAME.
Marine resources, §§9-12-110 to 9-12-113.

NEW HOPE INDUSTRIES OF DOTHAN.
Licenses.
Exemptions, §40-9-12.
Taxation.
Exemptions, §40-9-12.

NEWSPAPERS.
Banks and financial institutions.
Publication of semi-annual reports, §5-3A-14.

NEWSPAPERS—Cont'd
Evidence.
Proof of publication of notice, §12-21-68.
Freedom of press and speech, Const. Ala., art. I, §4; Const. U. S., Amendment I.
Gambling.
Evidence.
Published reports of occurrence of sporting events, §13A-12-28.
Judicial sales.
Notices.
See JUDICIAL SALES.
Libel and slander.
Refusal to testify by printer, §13A-11-164.
Licenses for newsstands, §40-12-134.
Motor vehicle carriers.
Certificates of public convenience and necessity.
Transportation of newspapers, baggage or mail, §37-3-12.
Reporters.
Exemption of news-gathering persons from disclosing sources, §12-21-142.

NEW TRIAL.
Abuse of discretion.
Grounds for granting, §15-17-5.
Accident.
Grounds for granting new trial, §15-17-5.
Affidavits.
Time for serving, ARCP, Rule 59 (c).
Appeals.
Automatic appeals.
Granting of new trial, §12-22-241.
Grant or refusal of motion for new trial, §12-22-10.
Costs, §15-17-5.
Disability of judge, ARCP, Rule 63.
Error of law.
Grounds for new trial, §15-17-5.
Evidence.
Newly discovered evidence.
Grounds for new trial, §15-17-5.
Forms.
Motion for new trial, ARCP, Form 78.
Granting, §§12-22-241, 12-22-242.
Appeal, §12-22-10.
Grounds for granting, §15-17-5; ARCP, Rule 59 (a).
Grounds for granting, §15-17-5; ARCP, Rule 59 (a).
Initiative of court, ARCP, Rule 59 (d).
Irregularity in proceedings.
Grounds for granting, §15-17-5.
Jury.
Misconduct.
Grounds for granting, §15-17-5.

NEW TRIAL—Cont'd
Limit of two new trials, §6-8-104.
Motion for new trial, ARCP, Rule 50 (b).
Affidavits.
Time for serving, ARCP, Rule 59 (c).
Disposition, ARCP, Rule 59.1.
Form, ARCP, Form 78.
Granting, §§12-22-241, 12-22-242, 15-17-5.
Appeal, §12-22-10.
Grounds, ARCP, Rule 59 (a).
Presentation of motions not required, ARCP, Rule 59 (g).
Refusal of motion.
Appeal, §12-22-10.
Stay on motion, ARCP, Rule 62 (b).
Time for motion, ARCP, Rule 59 (b).
When filed and served, §15-17-5; ARCP, Rule 59 (b).
Newly discovered evidence.
Grounds for new trial, §15-17-5.
Probate courts, §12-13-11.
Prosecution.
Misconduct.
Grounds for granting new trial, §15-17-5.
Remittitur, ARCP, Rule 59 (f).
State.
Misconduct.
Grounds for granting new trial, §15-17-5.
Stay on motion for new trial, ARCP, Rule 62 (b).
Verdict.
Not sustained beyond reasonable doubt or contrary to law.
Grounds for granting new trial, §15-17-5.

NEXT FRIEND.
Appeals.
Probate courts.
Appeals by next friends of minors or persons of unsound mind from probate courts, §12-22-26.
Fiduciaries generally.
See FIDUCIARIES.
Guardian and ward generally.
See GUARDIAN AND WARD.
Parties.
Infants and incompetents.
Substitution of guardian for next friend pending action, §6-7-100.
Suit by next friend, ARCP, Rule 17 (c).
Uniform fiduciaries act.
See FIDUCIARIES.

NIGHTCLUBS.
Licenses, §40-12-152.

NITRATE OF SILVER.
Prevention of infantile blindness, §22-20-2.

NITROGEN.
Fertilizer, §§2-22-12 to 2-22-16.

NOISE.
Criminal law and procedure.
Making unreasonable noise.
Disorderly conduct, §13A-11-7.
Motor vehicles.
Mufflers.
Required, §32-5-216.

NONAGE.
Relief from disabilities of nonage, §§26-13-1 to 26-13-8; Const. Ala., art. IV, §104.
See MINORS.

NONCLAIM ACT.
Executors and administrators.
Claims and debts, §§43-2-350 to 43-2-354.

NON COMPOS MENTIS.
Defined, §1-1-1.
Mentally ill.
See MENTALLY ILL.

NONNEGOTIABLE INSTRUMENTS.
Corporations.
Change bills, etc.
Issuance prohibited, §8-5-2.
Endorsements generally.
See ENDORSEMENTS.
Interest.
Instrument issued to circulate as money without authority, §8-5-1.

NONPROFIT CORPORATIONS, §§10-3A-1 to 10-3A-225.
See CORPORATIONS.

NONRESIDENTS.
Accountants.
Registration of foreign accounts, §34-1-5.
Temporary annual permits, §34-1-7.
Adoption.
Conditions precedent to bringing child into state, §38-7-15.
Subsidized adoptions.
Effect of nonresidence of adopting parents, §26-10-27.
Affidavits.
Taking of affidavits outside state, §12-21-4.
Attachment.
Issuance when defendant resides out of state, §6-6-42.
One nonresident against another, §6-6-48.
Security for costs, §6-6-50.
Attorneys at law.
Disciplinary proceedings.
Reciprocal discipline, ARDE, Rule 17.
Auctioneers.
Licensing of nonresidents, §34-4-25.
Commissioners.
Appointment of commissioners in other states or territories, §36-1-1.

NONRESIDENTS—Cont'd
Constitution of the United States.
Jurisdiction of suits against state, Const. U. S., Amendment XI.
Contractors.
Public works.
Out-of-state contractors.
Preference to resident contractors in letting of certain contracts, §39-3-5.
Corporations.
Foreign corporations.
See CORPORATIONS.
Cosmetologists.
Licenses or registration, §34-7-12.
Criminal law and procedure.
Liability for offenses committed in Alabama, §15-2-1.
Dentists and dental hygienists.
Licensed in other states, §34-9-10.
District attorneys.
Vacation of office for nonresidency, §12-17-183.
Estate and inheritance tax.
Nonresident decedents, §40-15-7.
Executors and administrators, §§43-2-190 to 43-2-200.
See EXECUTORS AND ADMINISTRATORS.
Fish and game.
General provisions.
See FISH AND GAME.
Fishing licenses, §§9-11-55 to 9-11-56.1.
Foresters.
Reciprocity, §34-12-11.
Garbage and trash.
Out-of-state transporters.
Permits.
Issuance, §22-27-5.
Handicapped persons.
Institute for deaf and blind.
Education and training, §21-1-14.
Hearing aid dealers and fitters.
License reciprocity requirements, §34-14-3.
Hunting licenses, §§9-11-46 to 9-11-49.2.
See FISH AND GAME.
Income tax.
Computation of tax, §40-18-5.
Exemptions.
Personal exemptions allowed, §40-18-19.
Persons and subjects taxable, §40-18-2.
Insurance.
Insurers.
Delinquency proceedings.
Claims against domestic insurers, §27-32-17.
Life and disability insurance representatives.
Nonresident agents and brokers, §27-8-22.
Property, casualty and surety insurance representatives, §§27-7-28, 27-7-29.

NONRESIDENTS—Cont'd
Jurisdiction.
Suits against state, Const. U. S., Amendment XI.
Landscape architects.
Reciprocity to licensing, §34-17-26.
Waiver of examination, §34-17-23.
Loans.
Mortgage loans.
Nonresidents making mortgage loans through licensed mortgage loan brokers, Const. Ala., amd. 154.
Marine resources.
See MARINE RESOURCES.
Mortgages and deeds of trust.
Nonresidents making mortgage loans through licensed mortgage loan brokers, Const. Ala., amd. 154.
Motor vehicles.
See MOTOR VEHICLES.
Optometrists.
Licenses, §34-22-21.
Partition.
Crops, §35-6-113.
Probate courts.
Nonresidents as parties, §35-6-43.
Sale instead of partition.
Nonresidents as parties, §35-6-60.
Pesticides.
Application.
Licenses, §2-27-55.
Physicians.
See PHYSICIANS.
Podiatrists.
Licenses, §§34-24-271, 34-24-272.
Polygraph examiners.
Licenses.
Nonresident applicants, §34-25-23.
Probate courts.
Costs.
Security for costs in suits by or for nonresidents, §12-19-48.
Psychologists.
Waiver of license examination, §34-26-45.
Public works.
Contracts.
Out-of-state contractors.
Preference to resident contractors in letting of certain contracts, §39-3-5.
Real estate brokers.
See REAL ESTATE BROKERS.
Receivers.
Service of process on foreign receivers, §6-6-627.
Seafood fishing.
Reciprocal agreements, §§9-12-160 to 9-12-162.
Service of process.
See SERVICE OF PROCESS.
Speech pathologists and audiologists.
Exemption of temporary in state practice from provisions of chapter, §34-28A-3.

NONRESIDENTS—Cont'd
Use tax.
Exemptions.
Tangible personal property brought into state by nonresident, §40-23-62.
Venue, §6-3-2.
Weapons.
Firearms.
Sale of firearms or ammunition, §13A-11-58.
Welfare.
Child care facilities.
Conditions precedent to bringing child into state for placement, §38-7-15.
Wills.
Notice of probate, §43-8-166.
Probate of foreign will, §43-8-175.

NONSUPPORT.
General provisions.
See DESERTION AND NONSUPPORT.

NORTHEAST CRENSHAW WATER AND FIRE PROTECTION AUTHORITY.
Exemption from gross receipt tax, §40-21-82.1.

NOTARIES PUBLIC.
Appointment, Const. Ala., art. VI, §168.
Notaries public for state at large, §36-20-30.
Bonds, surety, §36-20-3.
Notaries public for state at large, §36-20-31.
Commissioning, §36-20-1.
Fee of probate judge for issuance of commission, §36-20-1.
Notaries public for state at large, §36-20-30.
Performance or assumption of authority to perform notarial act without commission, §36-20-11.
Probate judges.
Fee for issuance of commissions, §§12-19-90, 36-20-1, 36-20-30.
Report to secretary of state by probate judge, §36-20-1.
Duties.
Notaries public for state at large, §36-20-30.
Evidence.
Certificate of notary as to presentment for acceptance, etc., of instrument governed by commercial law, §12-21-105.
Fees, §36-20-6.
Notaries public for state at large.
Fee of probate judge for issuance of notary commission, §36-20-30.
Probate judge.
Fee for issuance of commission, §§12-19-90, 36-20-1, 36-20-30.

NOTARIES PUBLIC—Cont'd
Impeachment, Const. Ala.,
   art. VII, §175.
   General provisions.
   See IMPEACHMENT.
   Subject to impeachment,
      §36-11-1.
Jurisdiction.
   Territorial jurisdiction of
      notaries public for state
      at large, §36-20-30.
Powers, §36-20-5.
   Notaries public for state at
      large, §36-20-30.
Probate judges.
   Fee for issuance of notary
      commissions, §§12-19-90,
      36-20-1, 36-20-30.
   Register of official acts. See
      within this heading,
      "Register of official acts."
   Report to secretary of state,
      §36-20-1.
Public officers generally.
   See PUBLIC OFFICERS
      AND EMPLOYEES.
Register of official acts.
   Copies.
      Provision of certified copies
         from register, §36-20-7.
      Duty of probate judge in
         possession,
         §36-20-10.
   Maintenance, §36-20-7.
   Probate judges.
      Delivery of register to
         probate judge upon
         death, resignation,
         etc., of notary,
         §36-20-8.
      Judge may deliver
         register to another
         notary, §36-20-10.
      Penalty for failure to
         deliver register to
         judge on demand,
         §36-20-9.
Seal, §36-20-4.
   Notaries public for state at
      large, §36-20-32.
State at large.
   Appointment, §36-20-30.
   Bond, §36-20-31.
   Commissioning, §36-20-30.
   Duties, §36-20-30.
   Jurisdiction.
      Territorial jurisdiction,
         §36-20-30.
   Powers, §36-20-30.
   Seal, §36-20-32.
   Term of office, §36-20-30.
Term of office, §36-20-1;
   Const. Ala., art. VI, §168.
   Notaries public for state at
      large, §36-20-30.
Vacancies in office.
   Removal from county,
      §36-20-2.
Veterans.
   State service commissioner.
      Appointment and powers
         as notaries public,
         §31-5-12.

NOTES.
Commercial paper generally,
   §§7-3-101 to 7-3-805.
   See COMMERCIAL CODE.
Corrections.
   Institution finance authority.
      See CORRECTIONS.

NOTES—Cont'd
Counties, §§11-81-28,
   11-81-33.
Facsimile signatures.
   Execution of notes with
      facsimile signatures,
      §1-3-3.
Interest.
   Collection on notes
      discounted at higher rate
      of interest than eight
      percent, §8-8-13.
   Unauthorized notes not
      exceeding $1.00, §8-8-9.
Municipal corporations.
   See MUNICIPAL
      CORPORATIONS.
**Negotiable instruments
   generally.**
   See NEGOTIABLE
      INSTRUMENTS.
Seals.
   Execution of notes with
      facsimile seals, §1-3-3.
Signatures.
   Execution of notes with
      facsimile signatures,
      §1-3-3.
Uniform commercial code.
   Commercial paper generally,
      §§7-3-101 to 7-3-805.
      See COMMERCIAL CODE.

NOTICE.
Abortion.
   Parental consent to
      performing abortions
      upon minors.
      Pregnancy by minor's
         natural father,
         adoptive father or
         stepfather or legal
         guardian.
         Written notice to minor's
            mother, §26-21-3.
      Waiver of written consent
         requirement.
         Notice by court to
            minor's parents or
            legal guardian not
            required or
            permitted, §26-21-4.
Accountants.
   Hearings before board of
      public accountancy,
      §34-1-14.
Actions.
   Filing notice of actions in lis
      pendens record,
      §35-4-131.
Agents.
   Both principal and agent
      have notice of whatever
      either has notice of,
      §8-2-8.
   Claim against agent before
      notice of agency.
      Set-off against principal's
         claim by person
         having, §8-2-9.
Agriculture.
   Evidence of notices, §2-2-17.
   Rules and regulations,
      §2-2-16.

NOTICE—Cont'd
Alcoholic beverages.
   Beer.
      Business relations between
         wholesalers and
         suppliers.
         Amendment or
            cancellation of
            agreement.
            Written notice to
               wholesaler,
               §28-9-6.
         Arbitration procedures,
            §28-9-8.
         Transfer of wholesaler's
            business.
            Written notice to
               supplier, §28-9-5.
Ante litem notice.
   Municipal corporations.
      Liability for negligence of
         agents, etc.
         Filing of statement as to
            manner of injury,
            damages claimed,
            etc.
            Required, §11-47-192.
Assignments.
   Payments, set-offs and
      discounts prior to notice
      of assignment.
      Contracts, writings and
         paper circulating as
         money subject to,
         §8-5-25.
Attachment.
   Levy.
      Nonresident defendant,
         §6-6-81.
      Resident defendant,
         §6-6-82.
   Sale of property levied on.
      Order for receipt of sale
         proceeds by plaintiff
         pending action.
         Notice of motion,
            §6-6-78.
Attorney general.
   Constitutional validity of
      statutes, ordinances, etc.,
      questioned.
      Attorney general to be
         notified, §6-6-227;
         ARAP, Rule 44.
**Banks and financial
   institutions.**
   See BANKS AND
      FINANCIAL
      INSTITUTIONS.
Boats.
   Change of address or transfer
      of interest, §33-5-16.
Catfish.
   Promotion of industry.
      Referendum of
         assessments, §2-8-276.
Certified mail.
   Notice required to be served
      by registered mail may
      be served by certified
      mail, §1-3-7.
Child labor.
   Employment of children
      under 16 years of age.
      Posting of notice of law,
         §25-8-6.
Chiropractors.
   Refusal, revocation or
      suspension of licenses.
      Notice of hearing,
         §34-24-167.

NOTICE—Cont'd
Circuit courts.
Fees.
Administrative fee for
periodic payments.
Notice of fee, §12-19-26.
Orders or judgments, ARCP,
Rule 77 (d).
Coal.
Surface mining control and
reclamation.
Suspension or revocation of
permits.
Public hearing, §9-16-93.
Commercial code.
See COMMERCIAL CODE.
Conservators.
Incapacitated persons.
Revocation of
conservatorship.
Application by person
ascertained to be
incapacitated.
Notice to conservator,
§26-2-52.
Petitions for appointment,
§26-2A-134.
Settlements of accounts of
guardians.
Filing of annual, partial or
final settlement,
§26-5-15.
Day for settlement,
§§26-5-3, 26-5-9.
Conveyances.
Acknowledgments.
Disqualification of
corporate officers or
shareholders from
acknowledging
conveyances, §35-4-25.
Purchasers, mortgagees or
judgment creditors.
Notice of conveyances,
§35-4-90.
Corporations.
See CORPORATIONS.
Corrections.
Inmate community
reintegration under SIR
act.
Investigation by
department regarding
inmate suitability,
§15-18-114.
Institution finance authority.
Bond issues.
Authorizing resolutions,
§14-2-15.
Sale, §14-2-16.
Kilby property.
Sale or lease, §14-2-26.
Cotton.
Promotion of cotton products.
Assessments.
Referendum to levy
assessment,
§2-8-196.
**County industrial
development authorities.**
Boards of directors.
Meetings, §11-92A-9.
Credit unions.
Board.
Meetings, §5-17-56.
Crime victims compensation.
Action to recover damages,
§15-23-14.

NOTICE—Cont'd
Dams.
Erection of dams for mills,
gins, factories or electric
generators.
Application to erect.
Owner of land on
opposite side of
stream, §18-2-4.
Hearing to show cause
against grant of
application, §18-2-10.
Dental service corporations.
Sales representatives.
Termination of contracting
sales representatives,
§22-21-377.
Depositions.
See DEPOSITIONS.
Desertion and nonsupport.
Payment of overdue support.
Bond, security, or other
guarantee to secure.
Petition or original
pleading to clearly
notify obligor,
§30-3-6.
Diseases.
Notifiable diseases.
General provisions.
See DISEASES.
Persons responsible for
reporting disease,
§22-11A-2.
District courts.
Administrative fee for
periodic payments.
Notice of fee, §12-19-26.
Dogs.
Wildlife management areas.
Impoundment of dogs,
§9-11-306.
Dower interests.
Ascertainment and payment,
§35-4-191.
Education.
County boards of education.
Meetings, §§16-8-3, 16-8-4.
Nonteacher, nonclassified,
etc., employees.
Termination, §§36-26-101,
36-26-104.
One-mill county school tax.
Election, §16-13-161.
Textbooks.
Public meetings to consider
adoption, §16-36-9.
Eggs and egg products.
Promotion of industry.
Assessments.
Referendum, §2-8-156.
Elections.
See ELECTIONS.
Electric cooperatives.
Waiver of provisions
requiring notice,
§37-6-24.
Electricity.
Service territories for electric
suppliers.
1984 act.
Judicial determination of
legality and validity
of provisions.
Hearing, §37-14-12.
1985 act.
Judicial determination of
legality and validity
of provisions.
Hearing, §37-14-38.

NOTICE—Cont'd
Eminent domain.
Appeals.
Notice of appeal,
§18-1A-283.
Commissioners.
Appointment.
Service of notice,
§18-1A-280.
Dismissal of action,
§18-1A-75.
Termination of occupancy,
§18-1A-24.
Enterprise zones.
Agreement by appropriate
governing authorities,
§41-23-28.
**Environmental improvement
authorities.**
Governor.
Formation of authority,
§9-6-5.
Environmental management.
Commission.
Hearings and procedures
before commission,
§22-22A-7.
Rules and regulations.
Adoption, §22-22A-8.
Escheats.
Notice by representative,
§43-6-2.
Contents, §43-6-3.
Estrays.
Publication and posting of
notice as to estrayed
animal where owner not
located, §3-2-4.
Seizure.
Notice to department of
agriculture, §3-2-2.
Evidence.
Posting of notice.
Proof of posting, §12-21-69.
Publication of notice.
Proof of publication,
§12-21-68.
Executions.
Execution sales, §6-9-87.
Notice of plaintiff of money
made, §6-9-92.
Levy.
Notice where levy on real
estate, §6-9-82.
**Executors and
administrators.**
See EXECUTORS AND
ADMINISTRATORS.
**Exemptions from
administration and
payment of debts.**
See EXEMPTIONS FROM
ADMINISTRATION
AND PAYMENT OF
DEBTS.
**Exemptions from levy and
sale under process.**
Declaration of claimed
exemptions.
Effect as notice, §6-10-23.
Fish and game.
Exhibitions.
Possession of wildlife for
public exhibitions.
Notice of violations,
§9-11-325.
Spearfishing.
Competitive events,
§9-11-170.

NOTICE—Cont'd
Fish and game—Cont'd
Wildlife management areas.
Dogs.
Impoundment, §9-11-306.
Forcible entry and unlawful detainer, §6-6-317.
Process, §6-6-332.
Foreclosure.
Notice requirements, §6-8-69.
Forests and forestry.
See FORESTS AND FORESTRY.
Fraternal benefit societies.
Conversion into stock or mutual life insurance company.
Notice to subordinate lodges or branches, §27-35-3.
Garnishment.
Answer of garnishee, §6-6-450.
Notice to defendant, §6-6-394.
Gasoline tax.
Delinquents.
Notice to show cause, §40-17-46.
Grain.
Promotion of grain industry.
Assessments.
Referendum to levy assessment, §2-8-236.
Grain dealers.
Refusal, suspension or revocation of license, §2-31-11.
Guardian and ward.
See GUARDIAN AND WARD.
Habeas corpus.
Bail without notice, §15-21-13.
District attorney, prosecutor or arrestor, §15-21-13.
Other interested parties, §15-21-12.
Harbors and ports.
Docks.
State docks facilities contingency trust fund.
Director of department to give notice of expected deficiency, §33-2-211.
Hazardous waste or substances.
Cleanup fund.
Orders to implement cleanup plans.
Notice to liable parties, §22-30A-5.
Fees for disposal of hazardous waste or substances.
Monthly reports.
Notice of failure to make, §22-30B-8.
Permits.
Applications, §22-30-12.
Health care authorities.
Board meetings.
Waiver, §22-21-316.
Securities.
Issuance, §22-21-329.
Health studio services.
Assignment of contract, §8-23-7.

NOTICE—Cont'd
Hearing aid dealers and fitters.
Business address of licensee, §34-14-8.
Heating and air conditioning contractors.
Examinations, §34-31-29.
Highways.
Closing and vacating streets, alleys and highways, §23-4-2.
Historical preservation authority.
Incorporation in multiple county area.
Governor to notify respective county governing bodies, §41-10-138.
Hotels, inns and other transient lodging places.
See HOTELS, INNS AND OTHER TRANSIENT LODGING PLACES.
Income tax.
Assessment.
Mailing of tax blank to be only notice required, §40-18-40.
Setoff debt collection, §§40-18-103, 40-18-105.
Industrial alcohol.
Permittees to notify governor of changes in officers, directors, etc., §28-5-11.
Industrial revenue bonds.
Action by director upon receipt of notification, §8-6-116.
Certificate of notification, §8-6-120.
Intent to issue bonds.
Notifications of intent, §8-6-115.
Insurance.
See INSURANCE.
Jails.
Construction of jails.
Notification of board of corrections, §14-6-101.
Judgments, ARCP, Rule 77 (d).
Judicial sales, §§6-8-60 to 6-8-67.
See JUDICIAL SALES.
Labor.
Child labor.
Employment of children under 16 years of age.
Posting of notice of law, §25-8-6.
Department of industrial relations.
Board of appeals.
Promulgation of rules and regulations, §25-2-17.
Landlord and tenant, §§35-9-3 to 35-9-8.
See LANDLORD AND TENANT.
Lead.
Customers of water suppliers.
Notice of potential for lead contamination, §22-37-5.
Legislature.
Vacancies to be filled by legislature, §36-9-16.

NOTICE—Cont'd
Life interests.
Ascertainment and payment, §35-4-191.
Lis pendens, §§35-4-130 to 35-4-139.
See LIS PENDENS.
Lost or unclaimed property.
Disposition of unclaimed articles left for service, §35-12-6.
Uniform disposition of unclaimed property act, §§35-12-32, 35-12-38.
Magistrates.
Appointment, ARJA, Rule 18.
Mail.
Registered mail.
Notice required to be served by registered mail may be served by certified mail, §1-3-7.
Mandatory disposition of detainers.
Notice to prisoners, §§15-9-82, 15-9-87.
Marine resources.
Oysters.
Use of rake dredges, §9-12-40.
Shrimp.
Bait dealers.
Substitution of boats, §9-12-54.3.
Mechanics' and materialmen's liens.
Lien claimed by person other than original contracts, §35-11-218.
Materialman's notice to owner or proprietor, §35-11-210.
Medical technicians.
Annulment or revocation of certificate.
Notice of charges, §34-18-24.
Board to announce meetings, §34-18-46.
Mental health finance authority.
Bond issues.
Sale of bonds, §41-10-360.
Mentally ill.
Criminal law and procedure.
Release of criminal psychopaths.
See MENTALLY ILL.
Mines and minerals.
Surface mining reclamation.
Notice of violations, §9-16-10.
Minors.
Withholding orders for child support.
Obligee to give notice of change of address, §30-3-65.
Obligor and employer to give notice of change of employer, §30-3-66.
Molds, dyes or patterns.
Disposal, §8-28-1.
Mortgages and deeds of trust.
Foreclosure sale, §§35-10-8, 35-10-10.

NOTICE—Cont'd
Motion picture fair competition.
Trade screening.
Notice of trade screening required, §8-18-4.
Motor fuels.
Diesel fuel tax.
Delinquents.
Notice to show cause, §40-17-15.
Motor vehicles.
See MOTOR VEHICLES.
Municipal corporations.
See MUNICIPAL CORPORATIONS.
Negotiable instruments.
Negotiating worthless instrument.
Notice of refusal of payment upon instrument, §13A-9-13.2.
Nuts, bulbs, fruits and vegetables.
Promotion of industry.
Assessments.
Notice of referendum, §2-8-126.
Orders of court, ARCP, Rule 77 (d).
Supreme court, ARAP, Rule 17 (a).
Oysters.
Mechanical devices.
Notice of use of rake dredges, §9-12-40.
Parole.
Board of pardons and paroles.
Meetings, §15-22-23.
Required notice prior to action, §15-22-36.
Partition.
See PARTITION.
Partnerships.
Construction of "notice" of fact, §10-8-3.
Effect of notice to one partner, §10-8-51.
Pawnbrokers.
Sale of pledges by pawnbroker, §8-1-81.
Pharmacists and pharmacies.
Bankruptcy sales, auction sales, etc., of drugs and medicines, §34-23-6.
Pilots.
Revocation or suspension of license for cause.
Notice of specific charges, §33-4-41.
Plumbing.
Certification of plumbers and gas fitters.
Change of place of business or name under which business carried on, §34-37-14.
Revocation of certificate, §34-37-12.
Post-conviction remedies.
Appeal of petitioner's conviction pending.
Notification of appellate court, ARCrP, Rule 20.6 (c).
Probate judges.
Death, §36-9-10.

NOTICE—Cont'd
Probate of will.
Notice to surviving spouse and next of kin, §§43-8-164 to 43-8-166.
Publication of legal notice.
Copies of paper with advertisement to be furnished to parties, §6-8-66.
Cost of publication, §6-8-64.
Affidavits, §6-8-65.
Evidentiary effect of newspaper containing advertisement, §6-8-67.
Length of publication, §6-8-61.
Newspaper designation, §6-8-60.
Postponement of sale, §6-8-69.
Probate court proceedings, §6-8-68.
Requirements for publication, §6-8-60.
Suspension or discontinuance of paper before publication made or completed, §6-8-63.
Time requirements, §6-8-62.
Public lands, §§9-15-10, 9-15-12.
Public officers and employees.
See PUBLIC OFFICERS AND EMPLOYEES.
Public works.
See PUBLIC WORKS.
Quieting title.
In rem proceedings.
Publication of notice, §6-6-564.
Railroad authorities.
Bond resolution, §37-13-19.
Railroads.
See RAILROADS.
Real estate brokers.
Licensee to notify commission of citations and suits, §34-27-31.
Recordation.
See RECORDATION.
Registered mail.
Notice required to be served by registered mail may be served by certified mail, §1-3-7.
Rules of criminal procedure.
Post-conviction remedies.
Appeal of petitioner's conviction pending.
Notification of appellate court, ARCrP, Rule 20.6 (c).
Sales tax.
Assessments, §40-23-17.
Returns.
Failure to make return.
Notice to taxpayer, §40-23-15.
Salvage, §35-13-3.
Securities.
Minors.
Ownership by minors.
Notice of minority.
Minor may not disaffirm security transaction unless prior written notice given, §8-6-93.

NOTICE—Cont'd
Self-service storage facilities.
Charges.
Failure to pay charges.
Posting of notice as to effect, §8-15-35.
Sheriffs.
Discovery of assets.
Notice to debtor to file statement of assets, §6-6-200.
Ships and shipping.
See SHIPS AND SHIPPING.
Small claims.
Forms.
Notice to defendant and complainant, ASCR, Forms 1 to 3, 5.
Social workers.
Board of social work examiners.
Meetings, §34-30-56.
Disciplinary proceedings, §34-30-5.
Soil and water conservation.
See SOIL AND WATER CONSERVATION.
Sports.
Agents.
Registration.
Refusal, §8-26-7.
Support and maintenance.
Payment of overdue support.
Bond, security, or other guarantee to secure.
Petition or original pleading to clearly notify obligor, §30-3-6.
Supreme court.
Appeals.
Form of notice of appeal, ARAP, Form 1.
Orders, ARAP, Rule 17 (a).
Taxation.
General provisions.
See TAXATION.
Hotels, inns and other transient lodging places.
Transient occupancy tax.
Assessment, §40-26-13.
Income tax.
Assessment.
Mailing of tax to be only notice required, §40-18-40.
Setoff debt collection, §§40-18-103, 40-18-105.
Motor vehicle carriers.
Mileage tax.
See MOTOR VEHICLE CARRIERS.
Public utilities.
Valuation notice, §40-21-23.
Sales tax.
See SALES TAX.
Securities tax, §40-24-7.
Use tax.
Additional amounts due.
When notice to be mailed, §40-23-76.
Tax increment districts.
Assessed and equalized value of property and tax increment base, §11-99-5.
Time.
Publication of legal notice, §6-8-62.

NOTICE—Cont'd
Toxic substances in the workplace.
Fire departments, emergency medical service providers and law enforcement agencies, §22-33-10.
Transportation companies.
See TRANSPORTATION COMPANIES.
Trees and timber.
Transfers of standing timber, trees and cutting rights.
Void and inoperative as against purchasers, mortgagees and judgment creditors without notice or prior recordation, §35-4-92.
Trial.
Notice that case has been placed on trial docket, ARCP, Rule 40 (b).
Trusts and trustees.
See TRUSTS AND TRUSTEES.
Unclaimed property.
Uniform disposition of unclaimed property act, §§35-12-32, 35-12-38.
Underground storage tanks.
Owners of tanks.
Notice of provisions of chapter, §22-35-11.
Uniform child custody jurisdiction act.
Hearings, §§30-3-24, 30-3-25.
Uniform commercial code.
See COMMERCIAL CODE.
Use tax.
Additional amounts due.
When notice to be mailed, §40-23-76.
Utility services facilities.
Bond issues.
Notice of bond resolution, §11-97-25.
Venue.
Change or transfer, §6-3-22.
Visitation.
Compliance with visitation order.
Bond, security, or other guarantee to secure.
Petition or other original pleading to clearly notify obligor, §30-3-6.
Warehouses.
Permits.
Grant or denial, §8-15-6.
Water management and drainage.
See WATER MANAGEMENT AND DRAINAGE.
Water pollution control act.
Department of environmental management.
Hearings.
Establishment of standards, §22-22-9.
Water pollution control authority.
Corporation of authority.
No notice required, §22-34-15.

NOTICE—Cont'd
Water system assistance authority.
Bond issues.
Notice of public sale, §22-23A-8.
Welfare.
Appeals, §38-4-5.
Application for assistance.
Notice of action taken, §38-4-2.
Wills.
Probate.
Notice to surviving spouse and next of kin, §§43-8-164 to 43-8-166.

NOTIFIABLE DISEASES,
§§22-11A-1 to 22-11A-38.
See DISEASES.

NUCLEAR ENERGY.
General provisions, §§22-14-1 to 22-14-35.
See ATOMIC ENERGY.
Radioactive waste.
Southeast interstate low-level radioactive waste management compact, §§22-32-1 to 22-32-9.

NUDITY.
Indecent exposure, §§13A-6-68, 13A-6-69, 13A-12-130.

NUISANCES.
Abatement.
Junkyard control, §23-1-250.
Lewdness, assignation or prostitution. See within this heading, "Lewdness, assignation or prostitution."
Municipal corporations, §§6-5-122, 11-47-117, 11-47-118.
Actions.
Lewdness, assignation or prostitution.
Generally. See within this heading, "Lewdness, assignation or prostitution."
Public nuisances.
Generally. See within this heading, "Public nuisances."
Right of action.
Generally, §6-5-121.
Alcoholic beverages.
Dry counties.
Abatement of liquor nuisances, §§28-4-220 to 28-4-232.
See ALCOHOLIC BEVERAGES.
Alienees.
Rights and responsibilities for continuance, §6-5-126.
Assignation.
Generally. See within this heading, "Lewdness, assignation or prostitution."

NUISANCES—Cont'd
Bonds, surety.
Lewdness, assignation or prostitution.
Bond for preliminary injunction or temporary restraining order prior to hearing, §6-5-144.
Closing place pending final decision.
Release of property on bond, §6-5-148.
Contempt.
Lewdness, assignation or prostitution, §§6-5-145, 6-5-154.
Costs.
Lewdness, assignation or prostitution.
Action to abate and perpetually enjoin, §6-5-149.
Damages.
Special damage to individual by public nuisance.
Right of action, §6-5-123.
Dams.
Erection of dams for mills, gins, factories or electric generators.
Building or raising dam without authority, §18-2-18.
Definitions, §6-5-120.
Lewdness, assignation or prostitution, §6-5-140.
Evidence.
Lewdness, assignation or prostitution.
Action to abate and perpetually enjoin, §6-5-149.
Factories.
When not deemed nuisances after operating one year, §6-5-127.
Effect of section on municipal ordinances, §6-5-127.
Fish and game.
Prohibited devices used in hunting, fishing or trapping, §9-11-16.
Health.
Nuisances menacing public health.
See HEALTH.
Injunctions.
Injunction before completion, §6-5-125.
Lewdness, assignation or prostitution. See within this heading, "Lewdness, assignation or prostitution."
Public nuisances.
Municipal corporations, §§6-5-122, 11-47-118.
Judgments.
Lewdness, assignation or prostitution.
Action to abate and perpetually enjoin, §6-5-149.
Junkyard control.
Abatement, §23-1-250.
Nonconforming junkyards, §23-1-242.

NUISANCES—Cont'd

Lewdness, assignation or prostitution.

Abatement.

Order of abatement, §6-5-151.

Action to abate and perpetually enjoin.

Closing place pending final decision.

Order, §6-5-147.

Release of property on bond, §6-5-148.

Commencement.

By whom commenced, §6-5-142.

Complaint.

Filing, §6-5-143.

Continuance, §6-5-149.

Costs, §6-5-149.

Dismissal, §6-5-149.

Evidence, §6-5-149.

Judgment, §6-5-149.

Venue, §6-5-143.

Bonds, surety.

Bond for preliminary injunction or temporary restraining order prior to hearing, §6-5-144.

Closing place pending final decision.

Release of property on bond, §6-5-148.

Closing place pending final decision.

Order, §6-5-147.

Release of property on bond, §6-5-148.

Complaint.

Service and answer, §6-5-146.

Contempt.

Proceedings on, §6-5-154.

Temporary restraining order.

Violation, §6-5-145.

Violations constituting, §6-5-145.

Criminal proceedings.

Effect of establishment of nuisance in criminal proceedings, §6-5-153.

Definitions, §6-5-140.

Injunctions.

By whom action to perpetually enjoin commenced, §6-5-142.

Permanent injunction.

Grant and effect, §6-5-150.

Preliminary injunction.

Application, §6-5-143.

Bond, §6-5-144.

Granting, §6-5-146.

Maintaining nuisance.

Who deemed guilty, §6-5-141.

Sale of property.

Fees of officers selling property, §6-5-152.

Generally, §6-5-151.

Temporary restraining order.

Bond, §6-5-144.

Inventory.

Return, §6-5-145.

Issuance, §6-5-145.

Return, §6-5-145.

Violation.

Contempt of court, §6-5-145.

NUISANCES—Cont'd

Motor vehicles.

Lights, lamps and reflective devices.

Casting light from motor vehicle on real property at night, §32-5-17.

Municipal corporations.

Abatement, §11-47-117.

Maintenance of civil actions to enjoin and abate, §§6-5-122, 11-47-118.

Weeds.

Class 2 municipalities, §§11-67-1 to 11-67-9.

See MUNICIPAL CORPORATIONS.

Class 5 municipalities, §§11-67-20 to 11-67-28.

See MUNICIPAL CORPORATIONS.

Actions.

Maintenance of civil actions to enjoin and abate, §§6-5-122, 11-47-118.

Assessment of costs of abatement, §11-47-117.

Factories.

When not deemed nuisances after operating one year.

Effect of section on municipal ordinances,

Housing.

Minimum housing standards and regulation of unsafe buildings.

Power to enjoin or abate public nuisances not impaired by chapter, §11-53-3.

Injunctions.

Maintenance of civil actions to enjoin and abate, §11-47-118.

Public nuisances, §6-5-122.

Weeds.

Abatement of weeds.

Class 2 municipalities, §§11-67-1 to 11-67-9.

See MUNICIPAL CORPORATIONS.

Class 5 municipalities, §§11-67-20 to 11-67-28.

See MUNICIPAL CORPORATIONS.

Nurses.

Practice by unlicensed persons declared nuisance, §34-21-26.

Private nuisances.

Actions.

Right of action, §6-5-124.

Distinguished from public nuisances, §6-5-121.

Prostitution.

Generally. See within this heading, "Lewdness, assignation or prostitution."

NUISANCES—Cont'd

Public nuisances.

Abatement.

Municipalities.

Right of action, §6-5-122.

Distinguished from private nuisances, §6-5-121.

Injunctions, §6-5-122.

Municipal corporations.

Abatement or enjoining.

Right of action by municipalities, §6-5-122.

Special damage to individual.

Right of action, §6-5-123.

Red light abatement act, §§6-5-140 to 6-5-154.

Temorary restraining order.

Lewdness, assignation or prostitution, §§6-5-144, 6-5-145.

Venue.

Lewdness, assignation or prostitution.

Action to abate and perpetually enjoin, §6-5-143.

Water supply and waterworks.

Safe drinking water act.

Violations deemed public nuisances, §22-23-53.

NUMBER.

Singular includes plural and vice versa, §1-1-2.

NUMBERS GAMES.

Lotteries.

See LOTTERIES.

NUNC PRO TUNC.

Amendment of judgments, ARCP, Rule 60 (a).

NURSERIES.

Agents.

Registration, §2-25-7.

Appeals.

Insect and disease control.

Appeals to state board from actions of commissioner, §2-25-18.

Board of agriculture and industries.

Insect and disease control.

See within this heading, "Insect and disease control."

Commissioner of agriculture and industries.

Insect and disease control.

See within this heading, "Insect and disease control."

Dealers in nursery stock.

Registration, §2-25-7.

Disease control. See within this heading, "Insect and disease control."

Evidence.

Insect and disease control.

Rules and regulations.

Admissibility in evidence, §2-25-20.

Fees.

Insect and disease control.

Inspection certificates, §2-25-6.

Registration of agents or salesmen, §2-25-7.

NURSERIES—Cont'd
Forgery and counterfeiting.
Insect and disease control.
Forgery of inspection
certificates, §2-25-22.
Fraud.
Delivery of fruit trees of
different kind, variety,
etc., than sold, §2-25-40.
Limitation period for
prosecutions, §2-25-41.
Sale, etc., of falsely named
trees, plants, etc.,
§2-25-42.
Fruit trees.
Delivery of fruit trees of
different kind, variety,
etc., than sold, §2-25-40.
Limitation period for
prosecutions, §2-25-41.
Insect and disease control,
§§2-25-1 to 2-25-22.
Agents.
Registration, §2-25-7.
Appeals to state board from
actions of commissioner,
§2-25-18.
Board of agriculture and
industries.
Appeals to state board
from actions of
commissioner,
§2-25-18.
Powers of board as to
protection of
agricultural and
horticultural interests,
§2-25-4.
Rules and regulations,
§2-25-20.
Review by board,
§2-25-21.
Commissioner of agriculture
and industries.
Appeals to state board
from actions of
commissioner,
§2-25-18.
Powers of commissioner as
to protection of
agricultural and
horticultural interests,
§2-25-3.
Quarantine powers.
Exercise of quarantine
powers of board by
commissioner,
§2-25-5.
Rules and regulations,
§2-25-20.
Treatment of infested or
diseased trees or
plants, §2-25-17.
Proceedings to compel
execution of
treatment prescribed
by commissioner,
§2-25-19.
Compliance with article.
Sale, carriage, shipment,
etc., of nursery stock,
§2-25-14.
Cuttings, prunings, etc.
Destruction of diseased or
infested cuttings,
§2-25-16.
Throwing into public roads,
fields, etc., §2-25-16.
Dealers in nursery stock.
Registration, §2-25-7.
Definitions, §2-25-1.

NURSERIES—Cont'd
Insect and disease control
—Cont'd
Evidence.
Rules and regulations.
Admissibility in
evidence, §2-25-20.
Fees.
Inspection certificates,
§2-25-6.
Forgery of inspection
certificates, §2-25-22.
Fruits, nuts, etc.
Importation, sale,
possession, etc., of
fruits, nuts, etc.,
infested or infected
with insects or
diseases, §2-25-15.
Inspections.
Certificates.
Application for
certificates, §2-25-6.
Bonds, surety.
Actions upon bonds for
damages caused by
shipment of plants
infested with plant
pests or diseases,
§2-25-8.
When commissioner
may require
person reapplying
for certificate to
post surety bond,
§2-25-8.
Destruction, §2-25-22.
Fees, §2-25-6.
Forgery, §2-25-22.
Obtaining certificates,
§2-25-6.
Reciprocity with other
states, §2-25-6.
Refusal or recall,
§2-25-8.
Wrongful or improper
use, §2-25-22.
Forgery of certificates,
§2-25-22.
Reciprocity with other
states, §2-25-6.
Introduction into state of live
insects or specimens of
diseases injurious to
plants, §2-25-10.
Powers of board of
agriculture and
industries.
Exercise of powers by
commissioner, §2-25-5.
Purposes of article, §2-25-2.
Quarantine.
Exercise of quarantine
powers of board by
commissioner, §2-25-5.
Movement into state or
within state of plants,
plant products, etc.,
during quarantines,
§2-25-13.
Powers of board of
agriculture and
industries, §2-25-4.
Reciprocity.
Inspections, §2-25-6.
Registration.
Agents or salesmen,
§2-25-7.
Rules and regulations.
Admissibility in evidence,
§2-25-20.

NURSERIES—Cont'd
Insect and disease control
—Cont'd
Rules and regulations
—Cont'd
Promulgation, §2-25-20.
Review by board, §2-25-21.
Violations, §2-25-22.
Salesmen.
Registration, §2-25-7.
Specimens of diseases.
Introduction into state of
specimens injurious to
plants, §2-25-10.
Tags.
Affixation of official tags to
boxes, packages, etc.,
§2-25-9.
Common carriers.
Not to accept for
shipment or deliver
nursery stock
without official tags,
§2-25-11.
Not to be liable for
damages for refusal
to receive, deliver,
etc., boxes or
packages without
official tags,
§2-25-12.
Confiscation of boxes,
packages, etc., shipped
into state without
official tags, §2-25-9.
Furnishing of official tags,
§2-25-9.
Treatment of trees or plants
found to be infested or
diseased by
commissioner, §2-25-17.
Proceedings to compel
execution of treatment,
§2-25-19.
Violations of article,
§2-25-22.
Inspections.
Insect and disease control.
See within this heading,
"Insect and disease
control."
Quarantine.
Insect and disease control,
§§2-25-4, 2-25-5, 2-25-13.
Reciprocity.
Insect and disease control.
Inspection certificates,
§2-25-6.
Registration.
Insect and disease control.
Registration of agents or
salesmen, §2-25-7.
Rules and regulations.
Insect and disease control,
§§2-25-20 to 2-25-22.
Salesmen.
Registration, §2-25-7.
Sales tax.
Exemptions, §40-23-4.

NURSES.
Accidents.
Rendering aid at scene of
accidents.
Exemptions from liability,
§6-5-332.
Advisory councils.
Appointment, §34-21-3.
Compensation of members,
§34-21-3.
Defined, §34-21-1.

NURSES—Cont'd
  Advisory councils—Cont'd
    Expenses of members,
      §34-21-3.
  Aides.
    Exemptions from provisions
      of chapter, §34-21-6.
  Appeals.
    Denial, suspension or
      revocation of license,
      §34-21-25.
  Applicability of chapter.
    Exemptions from provisions
      of chapter, §34-21-6.
  Associations.
    Professional corporations,
      §§10-4-380 to 10-4-406.
    See PROFESSIONAL
      CORPORATIONS.
    Unincorporated professional
      associations, §§10-10-1 to
      10-10-16.
    See UNINCORPORATED
      PROFESSIONAL
      ASSOCIATIONS.
  Blind persons.
    Infantile blindness.
      Prevention, §22-20-2.
  **Blood and urine samples
    from certain dead
    bodies, §§22-19-81,
    22-19-82.**
  Board of nursing.
    Appointment of members,
      §34-21-2.
    Authority, §34-21-2.
      Transfer from board of
        nurses' examiners and
        registration, §34-21-4.
    Board of nurses' examiners
      and registration.
      Transfer of powers and
        duties to board of
        nursing, §34-21-4.
    Bonds, surety.
      Executive officer, §34-21-2.
    Compensation of members,
      §34-21-2.
    Composition, §34-21-2.
    Created, §34-21-2.
    Defined, §34-21-1.
    Denial, suspension or
      revocation of license.
      Procedure, §34-21-25.
    Educational programs.
      Supervision by board,
        §34-21-5.
    Executive officer.
      Bond, §34-21-2.
      Employment and
        qualifications,
        §34-21-2.
    Expenses of members,
      §34-21-2.
    Funds, §34-21-4.
    Governor.
      Annual report to governor,
        §34-21-2.
      Appointment and removal
        of members, §34-21-2.
    Hearings.
      Denial, suspension or
        revocation of license,
        §34-21-25.
    Immunity from individual
      civil liability, §34-21-2.
    Injunctions.
      Unauthorized practice of
        nursing, §34-21-26.

NURSES—Cont'd
  Board of nursing—Cont'd
    Licensed practical nurse
      members.
      Service and advisory
        capacities, §34-21-2.
    Meetings, §34-21-2.
    Powers and duties, §34-21-2.
    Qualifications of members,
      §34-21-2.
    Records.
      Public record of
        proceedings, §34-21-2.
    Terms of office, §34-21-2.
    Vacancies.
      Filling vacancies, §34-21-2.
  **Child abuse or neglect
    reporting, §§26-14-1 to
    26-14-13.**
    See MINORS.
  **Continuing education,
    §§34-21-40 to 34-21-43.**
  Corporations.
    Professional corporations,
      §§10-4-380 to 10-4-406.
    See PROFESSIONAL
      CORPORATIONS.
  Dead bodies.
    Blood and urine samples
      from certain dead bodies.
      Exemption from civil and
        criminal liability,
        §22-19-82.
      May be directed to
        withdraw samples,
        §22-19-81.
  Definitions, §34-21-1.
  Diplomas.
    Fraudulently obtaining or
      furnishing diploma.
      Penalty, §34-21-7.
  Education.
    Continuing education,
      §34-21-23.
  **Educational programs,
    §34-21-5.**
    Approval of board required.
      Penalty for conducting
        without approval,
        §34-21-7.
    Continuing education,
      §§34-21-23, 34-21-40.
    Contracts with individuals,
      institutions and
      agencies, §34-21-41.
    Duty of board of nursing to
      provide programs,
      seminars and
      workshops, §34-21-40.
    Funds.
      Source of funds,
        §34-21-43.
    Grants with individuals,
      institutions and
      agencies, §34-21-41.
    Plans, programs and
      criteria.
      Development, §34-21-42.
    Scholarships. See within this
      heading, "Scholarships."
  Emergencies.
    Exemptions from licensing
      provisions, §34-21-6.
  Examinations.
    Board of nurses' examiners
      and registration.
      Transfer of powers and
        duties to board of
        nursing, §34-21-4.
    License examinations,
      §§34-21-21, 34-21-22.

NURSES—Cont'd
  Examinations—Cont'd
    Practical nurse, §34-21-22.
    Professional nurse,
      §34-21-21.
  **Exemptions from chapter,
    §34-21-6.**
  Fees, §34-21-24.
    Licenses, §34-21-24.
    Witnesses at license
      hearings, §34-21-25.
  Fraud.
    Denial, revocation or
      suspension of license,
      §34-21-25.
    Obtaining or furnishing
      license or diploma,
      §34-21-7.
  Funds.
    Board of nursing, §34-21-4.
    Educational programs.
      Continuing education.
        Source of funds,
        §34-21-43.
  Good Samaritan Act.
    Nurses rendering first aid or
      emergency care at scene
      of accident, etc.
      Exemption from liability,
        §6-5-332.
  Health care authorities.
    Generally, §§22-21-310 to
      22-21-356.
    See HEALTH CARE
      AUTHORITIES.
  Hearings.
    Denial, revocation or
      suspension of licenses,
      §34-21-5.
  Immunity.
    Board of nursing.
      Members immune from
        individual civil
        liability, §34-21-2.
    Persons reporting violations
      of provisions, §34-21-25.
  Injunctions.
    Practicing nursing without
      license, §34-21-26.
  Insurance.
    Health insurance.
      Certified registered nurse
        anesthetist coverage,
        §§27-46-1 to 27-46-3.
  **Jacksonville State
    University.**
    School of nursing, §§16-52-13
      to 16-52-15.
  Liability.
    Exemptions.
      Good Samaritan Act,
        §6-5-332.
  Licenses.
    Appeals.
      Denial, suspension or
        revocation of license,
        §34-21-25.
    Applications.
      Practical nurse, §34-21-22.
      Professional nurse,
        §34-21-21.
      Renewal of license,
        §34-21-23.
    Continuing education
      requirements, §34-21-23.
    Denial.
      Appeal from decision of
        board, §34-21-25.
      Grounds, §34-21-25.
      Procedure, §34-21-25.

NURSES—Cont'd
Licenses—Cont'd
Discipline of licensees,
§34-21-25.
Education.
Continuing education
requirements,
§34-21-23.
Examinations.
Practical nurse, §34-21-22.
Professional nurse,
§34-21-21.
Fees, §34-21-24.
Fines.
Administrative fines.
Disciplining licensees,
§34-21-25.
Fraud.
Denial, suspension or
revocation of license,
§34-21-25.
Fraudulently obtaining or
furnishing license.
Penalty, §34-21-7.
Lapsed license, §34-21-23.
Penalties, §34-21-7.
Practical nurse.
Application for license,
§34-21-22.
Licensed practical nurse
defined, §34-21-1.
Temporary permit,
§34-21-22.
Use of title licensed
practical nurse,
§34-21-22.
Practice without license.
Declared public nuisance,
§34-21-26.
Injunctive relief, §34-21-26.
Penalties, §34-21-7.
Professional nurse.
Application for license,
§34-21-21.
Licensed professional nurse
defined, §34-21-1.
Manner of obtaining
license, §34-21-21.
Temporary permit,
§34-21-21.
Use of title registered
nurse, §34-21-21.
Register of licensees to be
kept, §34-21-2.
Renewal of license,
§34-21-23.
Required.
Generally, §34-21-20.
Suspension or revocation.
Appeal from decision of
board, §34-21-25.
Grounds, §34-21-25.
Procedure, §34-21-25.
Midwives.
See MIDWIVES.
Misdemeanors.
Violations of provisions,
§34-21-7.
Nuisances.
Practice by unlicensed
persons declared
nuisance, §34-21-26.
Penalties.
Administrative fines.
Disciplining licensees,
§34-21-25.
Injunctions.
Practice of nursing without
license, §34-21-26.
Violations of chapter,
§34-21-7.

NURSES—Cont'd
Practical nurses.
Defined, §34-21-1.
Injunctions.
Unauthorized practice,
§34-21-26.
Licenses, §§34-21-1, 34-21-22.
Nuisances.
Practice by unlicensed
persons declared
nuisance, §34-21-26.
Penalty for practice without
license, §34-21-7.
Professional corporations.
See PROFESSIONAL
CORPORATIONS.
Professional nurses.
Defined, §34-21-1.
Health insurance coverage.
Certified registered nurse
anesthetist coverage,
§§27-46-1 to 27-46-3.
Injunctions.
Unauthorized practice,
§34-21-26.
Licenses. See within this
heading, "Licenses."
Nuisances.
Practice by unlicensed
persons declared
nuisance, §34-21-26.
Penalty for practice without
license, §34-21-7.
Registered nurse.
Use of title registered
nurse, §34-21-21.
Records.
Board of nursing.
Public record of
proceedings, §34-21-2.
Registered nurse.
General provisions. See
within this heading,
"Professional nurses."
Use of title, §34-21-21.
Religion.
Applicability of chapter.
Certain religious healing
and care exempt,
§34-21-6.
Reports.
Child abuse or neglect,
§§26-14-1 to 26-14-13.
See MINORS.
Scholarships.
Jacksonville State
University, §§16-52-13 to
16-52-15.
Post-baccalaureate
scholarships.
Amount of scholarship,
§34-21-62.
Applications, §34-21-61.
Appropriations.
Annual appropriation,
§34-21-63.
Criteria for selection of
recipients, §34-21-62.
Established, §34-21-60.
Failure to complete course
or serve as nurse,
§34-21-62.
Number, §34-21-60.
Qualifications of recipients,
§34-21-61.
Renewal, §34-21-62.
Repayment.
When liable for
repayment,
§34-21-62.

NURSES—Cont'd
Scholarships—Cont'd
Sylacauga Nurses' Training
School, §§16-58-1 to
16-58-3.
Troy State University,
§§16-56-13 to 16-56-15.
Tuskegee Institute, §§16-57-2
to 16-57-4.
University of Alabama,
§§16-47-135 to 16-47-137,
16-47-150 to 16-47-152.
University of North
Alabama, §§16-55-13 to
16-55-15.
University of South
Alabama, §§16-55-7 to
16-55-9.
**Sylacauga Nurses' Training
School, §§16-58-1 to
16-58-3.**
Troy State University.
School of nursing, §§16-56-13
to 16-56-15.
Tuskegee Institute.
School of nursing, §§16-57-2
to 16-57-4.
**Unincorporated professional
associations, §§10-10-1 to
10-10-16.**
See UNINCORPORATED
PROFESSIONAL
ASSOCIATIONS.
University of Alabama.
School of nursing,
§§16-47-135 to 16-47-137,
16-47-150 to 16-47-152.
**University of Alabama,
Huntsville, §§16-47-150 to
16-47-152.**
**University of North
Alabama.**
School of nursing.
Scholarships, §§16-51-13 to
16-51-15.
**University of South
Alabama.**
School of nursing, §§16-55-7
to 16-55-9.
Violations of chapter.
Penalty, §34-21-7.

NURSING HOMES.
Accreditation.
Confidentiality, §22-21-8.
**Administrators, §§34-20-1 to
34-20-16.**
Advisory council, §34-20-8.
Appeals.
Decisions of board of
examiners, §34-20-6.
Board of examiners.
Advisory council, §34-20-8.
Appeals from decisions of
board, §34-20-6.
Appointment of members,
§34-20-4.
Chairman, §34-20-4.
Compensation of members,
§34-20-4.
Composition of board,
§34-20-4.
Defined, §34-20-1.
Duties, §34-20-5.
Enforcement of chapter,
§34-20-14.
Functions, §34-20-5.
Funds.
Annual audit, §34-20-7.

NURSING HOMES—Cont'd
Administrators—Cont'd
Board of examiners—Cont'd
Funds—Cont'd
Authorization to receive
and expend funds,
§34-20-7.
Meetings, §34-20-4.
Officers, §34-20-4.
Powers, §34-20-5.
Qualifications of members,
§34-20-4.
Removal of members,
§34-20-4.
Restoration of license,
§34-20-15.
Revocation or suspension of
licenses, §34-20-14.
Rules and regulations.
Promulgation by board,
§34-20-5.
Secretary, §34-20-4.
Terms of office, §34-20-4.
Vacancies.
Filling vacancies,
§34-20-4.
Continuing education
requirements, §34-20-13.
Death.
Replacement of
administrator,
§34-20-2.
Definitions, §34-20-1.
Disciplinary proceedings,
§34-20-14.
Diseases.
Notifiable diseases.
Persons responsible for
reporting disease,
§22-11A-2.
Education.
Continuing education
requirements,
§34-20-13.
Enforcement of chapter,
§34-20-14.
Examinations.
Contents, §34-20-10.
Fee, §34-20-9.
Prerequisite to issuance of
license, §34-20-11.
Qualifications for
admission, §34-20-9.
Schedule, §34-20-10.
Fees.
Examination fee, §34-20-9.
Reciprocal licenses,
§34-20-12.
Renewal of license,
§34-20-13.
Fines.
Administrative fines.
Disciplining of licensees,
§34-20-14.
Licenses.
Continuing education
requirements,
§34-20-13.
Expiration and
reactivation,
§34-20-13.
File of applications and
licensees, §34-20-13.
Fines.
Administrative fines.
Disciplining of
licensees,
§34-20-14.
Inactive status, §34-20-13.
Issuance of license,
§34-20-11.

NURSING HOMES—Cont'd
Administrators—Cont'd
Licenses—Cont'd
List of persons holding
license, §34-20-13.
Provisional license.
Defined, §34-20-1.
Qualifications of
applicants, §34-20-9.
Reciprocity, §34-20-12.
Register of applicants,
§34-20-13.
Renewal, §34-20-13.
Replacement of
administrator upon
death or unexpected
resignation, §34-20-2.
Required, §34-20-2.
Restoration of license,
§34-20-15.
Revocation or suspension.
Grounds, §34-20-14.
Procedure, §34-20-14.
Penalties.
Administrative fines,
§34-20-14.
Revocation or suspension of
license, §34-20-14.
Violations of chapter,
§34-20-16.
Practice of nursing home
administration.
Defined, §34-20-1.
License required, §34-20-2.
Prohibited acts, §34-20-16.
Provisional nursing home
administrator.
Defined, §34-20-1.
Resignation.
Replacement of
administrator,
§34-20-2.
Appeals.
Board of examiners of
nursing home
administrators.
Decisions of board,
§34-20-6.
**Board of examiners of
nursing home
administrators.** See
within this heading,
"Administrators."
Definitions.
Administrators, §34-20-1.
Diseases.
Notifiable diseases.
Administrators.
Persons responsible for
reporting diseases,
§22-11A-2.
Education.
Administrators.
Continuing education,
§34-20-13.
Fees.
Administrators. See within
this heading,
"Administrators."
Funds.
Board of examiners of
nursing home
administrators.
Annual audit, §34-20-7.
Authority to receive and
expend funds,
§34-20-7.
Health care authorities,
§§22-21-310 to 22-21-356.
See HEALTH CARE
AUTHORITIES.

NURSING HOMES—Cont'd
Hospitals generally.
See HOSPITALS.
Licenses.
General provisions.
See HOSPITALS.
Nursing home
administrators. See
within this heading,
"Administrators."
**Long-term residential health
care recipient
ombudsmen,** §§22-5A-1 to
22-5A-7.
Advisory committee on
program, §22-5A-4.
Area plan to describe
program, §22-5A-4.
Certification, §22-5A-4.
Citation of chapter, §22-5A-1.
Commission.
Duties, §22-5A-3.
Notification as to
prospective
ombudsmen, §22-5A-4.
Community ombudsmen.
Selection, §22-5A-4.
Complaints.
Receiving.
Procedures for receiving,
§22-5A-5.
Resolution of complaints.
Procedures for resolution
of complaints,
§22-5A-6.
Definitions, §22-5A-2.
Duties, §22-5A-4.
Immunity.
Limited immunity of
person or agency
making reports,
§22-5A-7.
Informing recipients of
ombudsmen program,
§22-5A-5.
Selection, §22-5A-4.
Short title of chapter,
§22-5A-1.
State ombudsmen.
Duties, §22-5A-3.
Training, §22-5A-4.
Penalties.
Nursing home
administrators. See
within this heading,
"Administrators."
**Quality assurance
credentials.**
Confidentiality, §22-21-8.
Reciprocity.
Administrators.
Licenses, §34-20-12.
**Statement of services
rendered.**
Itemized to be furnished
patient upon request,
§22-21-7.

NUTRITIONISTS.
General provisions, §§34-34-1
to 34-34-4.
See DIETITIANS AND
NUTRITIONISTS.
Practice act, §§34-34A-1 to
34-34A-15.
See DIETITIANS AND
NUTRITIONISTS.

NUTS.
"Blow-outs."
Sale or offer for sale,
§20-1-91.

NUTS—Cont'd
Containers.
Requirements as to labeling, §20-1-92.
"Culls."
Sale or offer for sale, §20-1-91.
Decayed nuts.
Sale or offer for sale, §20-1-90.
Diseased nuts.
Importation, §2-25-15.
Infested nuts.
Importation, §2-25-15.
Sale or offer for sale, §20-1-90.
Labels.
Requirements as to labeling of packages or containers, §20-1-92.
Mouldy nuts.
Sale or offer for sale, §20-1-90.
Packages.
Requirements as to labeling, §20-1-92.
Peanuts.
See PEANUTS.
Pecans.
Taxation.
Pecans stored in licensed warehouse, §40-9-3.
"Pops."
Sale or offer for sale, §20-1-91.
Promotion of industry.
Assessments.
Collection, §2-8-133.
Disposition, §2-8-133.
Maximum assessment, §2-8-126.
Referendum.
Affirmative vote, §2-8-130.
Subsequent referendum after affirmative vote, §2-8-135.
Application for approval to conduct, §§2-8-123, 2-8-124.
Authority of certified organization to conduct, §2-8-125.
Ballots, §2-8-132.
Canvass of results, §2-8-132.
Conduct, §2-8-127.
Declared to be in public interest, §2-8-122.
Eligibility to vote, §2-8-128.
Hours, §2-8-131.
Negative vote, §2-8-129.
Subsequent referendum after negative vote, §2-8-134.
Notice, §2-8-126.
Payment of expense, §2-8-127.
Poll holders, §2-8-132.
Question to be voted on, §2-8-128.
Rules and regulations, §2-8-131.
Voting places, §2-8-131.
Refund, §2-8-136.
Authorized activities.
Not illegal or in restraint of trade, §2-8-121.

NUTS—Cont'd
Promotion of industry —Cont'd
Bonds, surety.
Treasurer of growers' organization, §2-8-137.
Certification of growers' association.
Application for certification.
Action by board on application, §2-8-124.
Generally, §2-8-123.
Declaration of policy, §2-8-120.
Notice.
Assessments.
Notice of referendum, §2-8-126.
Reports.
Annual statements by treasurer of growers' organization, §2-8-137.
Treasurer of growers' organization, §2-8-137.
Rejected nuts.
Sale or offer for sale, §20-1-91.
Sales.
"Blow-outs," §20-1-91.
"Culls."
Sale or offer for sale, §20-1-91.
Infested, mouldy, decayed, etc., nuts.
Sale or offer for sale, §20-1-90.
"Pops," §20-1-91.
Rejected nuts, §20-1-91.
Standards.
Adoption, §20-1-93.
State nut.
Pecan designated as state nut, §1-2-19.

O

OATHS.
Accounts and accounting.
Department of examiners of public accounts.
Authority to administer oaths, §41-5-15.
Chief examiners.
Oath of office, §41-5-5.
Arbitration and award.
Arbitrators, §§6-6-6, 6-6-7.
Attachment.
Oath of plaintiff, §6-6-44.
Attorneys at law.
Admission oath, §34-3-15.
Banks and financial institutions.
Directors, §5-6A-2.
Examination of banks.
Bank examiners, §5-2A-17.
Superintendent of banks, §5-2A-4.
Child custody.
Uniform child custody jurisdiction act.
Information under oath to be submitted to court, §30-3-29.
Chiropractors.
Board of chiropractic examiners.
Oath of members, §34-24-141.

OATHS—Cont'd
Civil defense.
Loyalty oath, §31-9-20.
Comptroller.
Oath of office, §41-4-6.
Congress.
Oath of office, Const. U. S., Art. VI.
Conservation and natural resources.
Commissioner.
Oath of office, §9-2-5.
Constitution of Alabama.
Oaths of office, Const. Ala., art. XVI, §279.
Constitution of the United States.
Congress, Const. U. S., Art. VI.
Governor, Const. U. S., Art. VI.
Lieutenant governor, Const. U. S., Amendment XIV.
House of representatives.
United States, Const. U. S., Art. VI.
Public officers, Const. U. S., Art. VI.
Senate.
United States, Const. U. S., Art. VI.
Contractors.
State licensing board.
Oath of board, §34-8-21.
Coroner's inquest.
Oath of jurors, §15-4-1.
Right of coroner to administer, §15-4-6.
Corrections.
Board of corrections.
Oath of chiefs of divisions, §14-1-7.
Commissioner of corrections, §14-1-1.4.
Courts.
Powers of courts, §12-1-7.
Credit unions.
Bureau of credit unions.
Supervisor, §5-2A-100.
Credit union administration.
Administrator, §5-17-42.
Examiners, §5-17-52.
Defined, §1-1-1.
Education.
State board of education.
Authority to administer oaths, §16-3-24.
Oath of members, §16-3-26.
State superintendent of education.
Oath of office, §16-4-2.
Elections.
See ELECTIONS.
Exemptions from administration and payment of debts.
Commissioners, §6-10-103.
Fences.
Partition fences.
Fence viewers, §35-7-6.
Finance.
Department of finance.
Oaths of office.
Officers and chiefs of divisions, §41-4-6.
Chief of legal division, §41-4-202.
Fish and game.
Director of game and fish division, §9-2-62.

OATHS—Cont'd

Fish and game—Cont'd
Wardens, §9-2-64.
Forests and forestry.
State forester, §9-3-5.
Governor.
Oath of office, §36-13-1.
Grand jury.
See GRAND JURY.
**Hazardous waste or
substances.**
Fees for disposal of
hazardous waste or
substances.
Monthly reports to be
sworn, §22-30B-10.
Highway department.
Power to administer oaths,
§23-1-39.
Income tax.
Corporations.
Statement furnished to
department of revenue,
§40-18-55.
**Industrial development
advisory board.**
Members' oath, §41-9-185.
Judges, Const. U. S., Art. VI.
Jurors.
See JURY.
Landscape architects.
Board of examiners,
§§34-17-2, 34-17-3.
Legislature.
Oath of office, Const. Ala.,
art. XVI, §279.
Administration of oath,
§29-1-6.
Lieutenant governor, Const.
U. S., Art. VI; Amendment
XIV.
Loyalty oath, §31-9-20.
Magistrates.
Oath of office, ARJA, Rule
18.
Marine resources.
Director.
Division, §9-2-83.
Motor vehicles.
Drivers' licenses.
Application under oath,
§32-6-4.
Municipal corporations.
See MUNICIPAL
CORPORATIONS.
Oil and gas board.
Administration of oaths,
§9-17-5.
Partition fences.
Fence viewers, §35-7-6.
Perjury, §§13A-10-100 to
13A-10-109.
See PERJURY.
Pharmacists.
Oath of office, §34-23-90.
Pilots and pilotage.
Oath of pilot, §33-4-37.
State pilotage commission.
Chairman of commission.
Administration of oaths
by chairman,
§33-4-5.
Podiatrists.
Board of podiatry,
§§34-24-250, 34-24-252.
Prisons and prisoners.
Officers and guards.
Oath of office, §14-3-13.
Superintendent of public
works, §14-4-14.

OATHS—Cont'd

Probate judges.
Filing, §36-4-3.
Public officers.
General provisions, §§36-4-1
to 36-4-9.
See PUBLIC OFFICERS
AND EMPLOYEES.
Public service commission.
See PUBLIC SERVICE
COMMISSION.
Railroads.
Railway policemen,
§37-2-151.
Sales tax.
Reports under oath,
§40-23-10.
Searches and seizures.
Warrants.
Supported by oath or
affirmation, Const.
Ala., art. I, §5; Const.
U. S., Amendment IV.
Small loans.
Bureau of loans.
Supervisor, §5-2A-80.
Sports.
Agents.
Athlete agent regulatory
commission.
Members to take oath,
§8-26-3.
State parks.
Division of parks.
Director, §9-2-101.
Supreme court.
Justices.
Administration of oaths,
§12-2-3.
Taxation.
See TAXATION.
Telephones.
Securities of telephone
companies.
Applications to issue
securities or assume
obligations, §37-2-172.
**Unsworn falsification to
authorities,** §13A-10-109.
Veterans.
County service
commissioners, §31-5-11.
State service commissioner.
Oath of office, §31-5-11.
**Vice-president of the United
States,** Const. U. S., Art.
VI; Amendment XIV.
**Water management and
drainage.**
Board of water management
commissioners.
Oath of office, §9-9-14.
Weights and measures.
Weighmasters, §8-16-50.
Welfare.
Witnesses, §38-4-6.
Witnesses.
See WITNESSES.

OATS.
See GRAIN.

OBSCENITY.

Actions.
Violations of anti-obscenity
enforcement act.
Injunctive relief,
§13A-12-200.7.
Affect on other laws.
Anti-obscenity enforcement
act, §13A-12-200.9.

OBSCENITY—Cont'd

Attorney general.
Anti-obscenity enforcement
act.
Injunctive relief for
violations,
§13A-12-200.7.
Forfeiture actions.
Initiating, §13A-12-200.8.
Bumper stickers.
Public display of obscene
sticker, sign, etc.,
§13A-12-131.
Child pornography.
Obscene materials containing
visual reproduction of
children, §§13A-12-190
to 13A-12-198.
**Construction and
interpretation.**
Anti-obscenity enforcement
act.
Affect on other laws,
§13A-12-200.9.
Criminal procedure.
Minors.
Sale, exhibition, etc., of
obscene materials to
minors.
Prosecution. See within
this heading,
"Minors."
Defenses.
Displaying materials harmful
to minors.
Affirmative defenses,
§13A-12-200.5.
Disseminating obscene
materials.
Affirmative defenses,
§13A-12-200.4.
Distributing obscene
materials.
Affirmative defenses,
§13A-12-200.4.
Producing obscene materials.
Affirmative defenses,
§13A-12-200.4.
Definitions, §13A-12-200.1.
Obscene materials containing
visual reproduction of
children, §13A-12-190.
Disorderly conduct.
Using abusive or obscene
language or making
obscene gestures,
§13A-11-7.
Display.
Public display of obscene
sticker, sign, etc.,
§13A-12-131.
Class C misdemeanor,
§13A-12-131.
**Displaying materials
harmful to minors,**
§13A-12-200.5.
Affirmative defenses,
§13A-12-200.5.
**Disseminating obscene
materials,** §13A-12-200.3.
Affirmative defenses,
§13A-12-200.4.
**Distributing obscene
materials.**
Affirmative defenses,
§13A-12-200.4.
Minors.
Distributing to,
§13A-12-200.5.
Prohibited, §13A-12-200.2.

OBSCENITY—Cont'd
Education.
Libraries.
Public school or college or
university libraries.
Anti-obscenity
enforcement act.
Inapplicability of
criminal
provisions to,
§13A-12-200.10.
Evidence.
Exclusion of audience where
evidence vulgar, obscene,
etc., §§12-21-9,
12-21-202.
Obscene materials containing
visual reproduction of
children. See within this
heading, "Minors."
Extradition.
Anti-obscenity enforcement
act.
Persons in violation of,
§13A-12-200.6.
Felonies.
Producing obscene materials.
Class C felony,
§13A-12-200.2.
Forfeitures.
Property subject to
forfeitures,
§13A-12-200.8.
Forfeiture of equipment,
materials, etc.,
§13A-12-198.
Obscene materials
containing visual
reproduction of
children,
Governor.
Extradition of persons in
violation of anti-
obscenity enforcement
act, §13A-12-200.6.
Guardian and ward.
Obscene materials containing
visual reproduction of
children.
Parents or guardians
permitting children to
engage in production
of, §13A-12-196.
Hearings.
Anti-obscenity enforcement
act.
Preliminary injunctions for
violations,
§13A-12-200.7.
Forfeitures of property,
§13A-12-200.8.
**Importation, display, sale,
etc.**
Public display of obscene
sticker, sign, etc.,
§13A-12-131.
Class C misdemeanor,
§13A-12-131.
Indecent exposure,
§13A-12-130.
Injunctions.
Anti-obscenity enforcement
act.
Attorney general may
initiate,
§13A-12-200.7.

OBSCENITY—Cont'd
Libraries.
Anti-obscenity enforcement
act.
Inapplicability of criminal
provisions to,
§13A-12-200.10.
Mail.
Importation. See within this
heading, "Importation,
display, sale, etc."
Military affairs.
Courts-martial.
Disruption of proceedings.
Punishment of persons
disrupting,
§31-2-101.
Minors.
Displaying materials harmful
to minors,
§13A-12-200.5.
Distributing obscene
materials to,
§13A-12-200.5.
Obscene materials containing
visual reproduction of
children.
Commercial exploitation.
Indicative of prurient
interest,
§13A-12-195.
Definitions, §13A-12-190.
Dissemination or public
display, §13A-12-191.
Forfeiture of equipment,
etc., §13A-12-198.
Possession with intent,
§13A-12-192.
Evidence.
Identity of person
engaged in obscene
act not required,
§13A-12-194.
Indication of commercial
exploitation may be
probative in
determining whether
matter appeals to
prurient interest,
§13A-12-195.
Inferences as to age
permitted to jury or
court, §13A-12-193.
Possession with intent to
disseminate, prima
facie evidence of,
§13A-12-192.
Proof of age of person
depicted,
§13A-12-193.
Forfeiture of equipment,
materials, etc.,
§13A-12-198.
Identity of person engaged
in obscene act not
required, §13A-12-194.
Parents or guardians
permitting children to
engage in production
of, §13A-12-196.
Possession with intent to
disseminate,
§13A-12-192.
Production of obscene
matter, §13A-12-197.
Forfeiture of equipment,
materials, etc.,
§13A-12-198.
Proof of age of person
depicted, §13A-12-193.

OBSCENITY—Cont'd
Misdemeanors.
Displaying materials harmful
to minors,
§13A-12-200.5.
Disseminating obscene
materials,
§13A-12-200.3.
Distributing obscene
materials,
§13A-12-200.2.
Public display of obscene
sticker, sign, etc.,
§13A-12-131.
Wholesalers.
Distributing obscene
materials,
§13A-12-200.2.
Motor vehicles.
Bumper stickers, etc.
Public display of obscene
sticker, §13A-12-131.
Parent and child.
Obscene materials containing
visual reproduction of
children.
Parents or guardians
permitting children to
engage in production
of, §13A-12-196.
**Producing obscene
materials,** §13A-12-200.2.
Affirmative defenses,
§13A-12-200.4.
Public lewdness,
§13A-12-130.
Sale.
Minors.
Sale, exhibition, etc., of
obscene materials to
minors. See within this
heading, "Minors."
Searches and seizures.
Seizure of property,
§13A-12-200.8.
Signs.
Public display of obscene
sticker, sign, etc.,
§13A-12-131.
Universities and colleges.
Libraries.
Anti-obscenity enforcement
act.
Inapplicability of
criminal provisions
to, §13A-12-200.10.
Wholesalers.
Distributing obscene
materials,
§13A-12-200.2.
Affirmative defenses,
§13A-12-200.4.

OBSTRUCTION OF TRAFFIC.
**Drivers prohibited from
proceeding towards
obstruction,** §32-5A-61.

OCCUPATIONS.
See PROFESSIONS AND
OCCUPATIONS.

OCEANOGRAPHY.
**Marine environmental
sciences consortium,**
§§16-45-1 to 16-45-5.

OCULISTS.
Licenses, §40-12-135.

ODOMETERS, §32-15-3.

OFFER OF JUDGMENT,
ARCP, Rule 68; Forms 86, 87.

OFFICE OF PROSECUTION SERVICES, §§12-17-230 to 12-17-233.1.
Assistance to prosecuting attorneys, §12-17-230.
Audits.
Annual audit, §12-17-233.
Budgets.
Transfer of budget excesses, §12-17-233.1.
Established, §12-17-230.
Executive director, §12-17-232.
Merit system.
Not subject to merit system, §12-17-231.
Retirement benefits.
Eligibility for state retirement benefits, §12-17-231.
Tenure, §12-17-232.
Funding, §12-17-233.
Powers of office.
Restriction on powers of office, §12-17-234.
Purpose, §12-17-230.
Transfer of budget excesses, §12-17-233.1.

OFFICERS.
See PUBLIC OFFICERS AND EMPLOYEES.

OFFICIAL BONDS, §§36-5-1 to 36-5-68.
See PUBLIC OFFICERS AND EMPLOYEES.

OIL AND GAS.
Actions.
Conservation and regulation of production. See within this heading, "Conservation and regulation of production."
Adulteration.
Petroleum products, §§8-17-83, 8-17-134.
Advertisements.
Leases by state.
Parties requesting advertisement of lands for lease purposes to pay for necessary legal advertisements, §9-17-66.
Petroleum products.
Reclaimed or re-refined oil, §8-17-112.
Appeals.
Conservation and regulation of production.
Injunctions, §9-17-18.
Board. See within this heading, "Conservation and regulation of production."
Commercial code.
Sales.
Goods to be severed from realty, §7-2-107.
Secured transactions.
Applicability of filing provisions, §7-9-302.
Description of land, §7-9-203.
When security interest attaches, §7-9-204.

OIL AND GAS—Cont'd
Conservation and regulation of production, §§9-17-1 to 9-17-33.
Actions.
Fines.
Payment not to abridge private cause of action, §9-17-32.
Oil and gas board.
Representation in litigation, §9-17-5.
Violations of article, rules, etc.
Civil actions for damages, §9-17-19.
Appeals.
Injunctions, §9-17-18.
Definitions, §9-17-1.
Disposition of proceeds derived from sales, §9-17-33.
Drilling units.
Establishment, §9-17-12.
Locations for drilling of wells within, §9-17-12.
Separately owned tracts of land.
Allowable production shares of unintegrated tracts, §9-17-13.
Integration and development as drilling units, §9-17-13.
Applicability of antitrust laws, §9-17-13.
Orders requiring integration, etc., §9-17-13.
Fees.
Petitions.
Filing fee, §9-17-24.
Wells.
Drilling, §9-17-24.
Status determination, §9-17-24.
Illegal oil, gas or product.
Acquisition, §9-17-21.
Condemnation, §9-17-22.
Defined, §9-17-1.
Handling, §9-17-21.
Penalty for each prohibited transaction, §§9-17-32.
Processing, §9-17-21.
Sale, §9-17-21.
Property forfeited to state, §9-17-22.
Seizure, §9-17-22.
Transportation, §9-17-21.
Injunctions.
Appeals, §9-17-18.
Board.
Issuance against, §9-17-16.
Violations of article, rules, etc.
Actions by private parties to enjoin, §9-17-19.
Issuance against violators, §9-17-17.
Oaths.
Administration by oil and gas board, §9-17-5.
Oil.
Defined, §9-17-1.

OIL AND GAS—Cont'd
Conservation and regulation of production—Cont'd
Oil and gas board.
Actions.
Representation in litigation, §9-17-5.
Appointment of members, §9-17-3.
Compensation of members, §9-17-3.
Composition, §9-17-3.
Created, §9-17-3.
Duties.
Generally, §9-17-6.
Expenses of members, §9-17-3.
Funds.
Special fund, §9-17-24.
Geological survey.
Retention of faculty members and students for research, §§9-4-14 to 9-4-19.
See GEOLOGICAL SURVEY.
Hearings, §9-17-3.
Rules of procedure, §9-17-7.
Injunctions against, §9-17-16.
Meetings, §9-17-3.
Unit operations.
Meeting to consider need, §9-17-81.
Oaths.
Administration, §9-17-5.
Orders.
Judicial review, §9-17-15.
Limits on production allowable within state or from separate pools.
Limitations upon orders establishing, §9-17-14.
Pools.
Limitations as to orders limiting or prorating production, §9-17-12.
Promulgation, §9-17-7.
Emergency orders, §9-17-7.
Unit operations. See within this heading, "Unit operations."
Votes required for promulgation, §9-17-4.
Powers.
Generally, §9-17-6.
Qualifications of members, §9-17-3.
Quorum, §9-17-4.
Rules and regulations.
Judicial review, §9-17-15.
Limits on production allowable within state or from separate pools.
Limitations upon rules or regulations establishing, §9-17-14.

OIL AND GAS—Cont'd
Conservation and regulation of production—Cont'd
Oil and gas board—Cont'd
Rules and regulations —Cont'd
Pools.
Limitations as to rules and regulations limiting or prorating production, §9-17-12.
Promulgation, §9-17-7.
Votes required for promulgation, §9-17-4.
Subpoenas.
Enforcement of subpoenas issued by board, §9-17-8.
Terms of office, §9-17-3.
Vacancies in office, §9-17-3.
Wells.
Control, §9-17-23.
Witnesses.
Powers as to, §9-17-8.
Subpoenas.
Enforcement, §9-17-8.
Oil and gas supervisor, §9-17-9.
Personnel.
Employment, §9-17-10.
Wells.
Notification of supervisor prior to drilling, §9-17-24.
Penalties.
Illegal oil, gas or product.
Each prohibited transaction, §9-17-32.
Violations of article, §9-17-32.
Policy.
Declaration of public policy, §9-17-2.
Pools.
Cycling of gas, §9-17-13.
Defined, §9-17-1.
Production.
Determination of producers' shares, §9-17-12.
Exceeding established allowable production prohibited, §9-17-14.
Unauthorized manner of production.
Prohibited, §9-17-14.
Reservoir energy.
Determination of producers' shares, §9-17-12.
Rules, regulations or orders limiting or prorating production.
Limitations, §9-17-12.
Proceeds.
Disposition of proceeds derived from sales, §9-17-33.
Purpose of article, §9-17-2.
Reservoirs.
Introduction of gas into, §9-17-13.
Sales.
Disposition of proceeds, §9-17-33.

OIL AND GAS—Cont'd
Conservation and regulation of production—Cont'd
Tax for expenses of administration and enforcement, §§9-17-25 to 9-17-31.
Collection.
Recovery of tax improperly collected, §9-17-27.
Disposition and expenditures, §9-17-31.
Levy, §9-17-25.
Liens.
Payment of tax, interest and penalties, §9-17-30.
Payment, §9-17-25.
Failure to pay.
Penalty and interest, §§9-17-28, 9-17-29.
Penalties.
Failure to make return, §9-17-29.
Failure to pay tax, §§9-17-28, 9-17-29.
Records, §9-17-26.
Returns, §9-17-26.
Failure to make.
Penalty and interest, §9-17-29.
Notice to make, §9-17-29.
Violations of article.
Aiding and abetting.
Penalties, §9-17-32.
Civil actions for damages, §9-17-19.
Injunctions, §9-17-17.
Actions by private parties to enjoin, §9-17-19.
Penalties, §9-17-32.
Waste.
Defined, §9-17-1.
Prohibited, §9-17-11.
Wells.
Control.
Duty of owners, §9-17-23.
Oil and gas board.
Power to secure payment by owners of costs and expenses of controlling, §9-17-23.
Rights upon failure of owners to control, §9-17-23.
Drilling.
Fee, §9-17-24.
Disposition, §9-17-24.
Payment, §9-17-24.
Notification of oil and gas supervisor, §9-17-24.
Status determination.
Fee, §9-17-24.
Witnesses.
Oil and gas board.
Powers, §9-17-8.
Contracts.
Oil and gas board.
Geological survey.
Retention of faculty members and students for research, §§9-4-15, 9-4-16.

OIL AND GAS—Cont'd
Counties.
Funds.
Severance tax trust funds, §40-20-50.
Privilege tax on production.
Allocation and distribution of net taxes collected to counties, §40-20-8.
Exemption from ad valorem taxes levied by counties, §40-20-12.
Funds.
Severance tax trust funds, §40-20-50.
Levy of taxes by counties, §40-20-2.
Severance tax trust funds, §40-20-50.
Definitions.
Conservation and regulation of production, §9-17-1.
Mineral documentary tax, §40-20-30.
Petroleum products, §8-17-80.
Posting price and tax.
"Motor vehicle" defined, §8-17-150.
Reclaimed or re-refined oil, §8-17-110.
Privilege tax on production, §40-20-1.
Unit operations.
"Secondary recovery methods" defined, §9-17-80.
Disposition of proceeds from sale.
Conservation and regulation of production, §9-17-33.
Drilling units, §§9-17-12, 9-17-13.
Exploration in offshore federal waters.
Equipment, machinery, fuel, etc., used in, §40-23-4.
Fees.
Drilling, §9-17-24.
Petition filing fee, §9-17-24.
Petroleum products. See within this heading, "Petroleum products."
Status determination, §9-17-24.
Fraud and deceit in sale of petroleum products, §§8-17-130 to 8-17-139.
Funds.
Counties.
Severance tax trust funds, §40-20-50.
Oil and gas board.
Special fund, §9-17-24.
Gasoline.
Petroleum products generally. See within this heading, "Petroleum products."
Tax, §§40-17-30 to 40-17-124.
See GASOLINE.
Geological survey.
General provisions, §§9-4-1 to 9-4-19.
See GEOLOGICAL SURVEY.
Illegal oil, gas or product.
See within this heading, "Conservation and regulation of production."

OIL AND GAS—Cont'd
Income tax.
Basis for depletion.
Discovery value, §40-18-16.
Corporations.
Deductions allowed
corporations.
Allowance for depletion,
§40-18-35.
Deductions.
Depletion allowance,
§40-18-15.
Injunctions.
Conservation and regulation
of production, §§9-17-16
to 9-17-19.
Petroleum products, §8-17-92.
Violations of article,
§40-20-11.
Inspections.
Petroleum products,
§§8-17-87, 8-17-91.
Leases, §§9-17-50 to 9-17-69.
Cancellation on records.
Failure or refusal.
Liability of lessees,
§9-17-50.
Lapsed optional leases,
§9-17-50.
Leases by state, §§9-17-60 to
9-17-69.
Advertisements.
Parties requesting
advertisement to
pay, §9-17-66.
Authorization.
Lands of department of
conservation and
natural resources,
§9-17-60.
Lands of state
department,
institutions or
agencies, §9-17-61.
Lands under navigable
streams, waters, etc.,
§9-17-62.
Bids, §9-17-65.
Charts.
Charges for oil and gas
lease tract charts,
§9-17-67.
Governor.
Authorization to lease oil
and gas rights,
§35-4-383.
Pooling or unitization.
Agreements to authorize,
§9-17-64.
Amendments to leases to
authorize, §9-17-64.
Lease may authorize,
§9-17-63.
Revenues from leases.
Disposition, §9-17-68.
Expenditure, §9-17-69.
School lands, §9-15-36.
Mineral documentary tax
generally. See within
this heading, "Mineral
documentary tax."
Public lands.
School lands, §9-15-36.
Salt springs.
Lease of salt springs by
director of
conservation,
§35-4-380.

OIL AND GAS—Cont'd
Liens.
Conservation and regulation
of production.
Tax for expenses of
administration and
enforcement.
Payment of tax, interest
and penalties,
§9-17-30.
Mineral documentary tax,
§40-20-32.
Linseed oil, §§8-17-40 to
8-17-45.
See LINSEED OIL.
Liquefied petroleum gas,
§§9-17-100 to 9-17-110.
See LIQUEFIED
PETROLEUM GAS.
Lubricating oils and greases.
Petroleum products
generally. See within
this heading, "Petroleum
products."
Tax, §§40-17-170 to
40-17-186.
See LUBRICATING OILS
AND GREASES.
Mineral documentary tax,
§§40-20-30 to 40-20-37.
Ad valorem taxes.
Nonproducing leaseholds.
Exemption from ad
valorem taxes,
§40-20-35.
How exemption
obtained upon
existing interests,
§40-20-36.
Tax to be in lieu of,
§40-20-35.
Amount, §40-20-32.
Applicability of tax,
§40-20-31.
By whom payable, §40-20-33.
Collection.
Probate judge to collect
tax, §40-20-33.
Definitions, §40-20-30.
Entries on instrument and
record, §40-20-34.
Exemptions.
How exemption obtained
upon existing
interests, §40-20-36.
Nonproducing leaseholds.
Exemption from ad
valorem taxes,
§40-20-35.
Fees.
Probate judge, §40-20-37.
Levied, §40-20-31.
Liens.
Tax to be lien, §40-20-32.
Mineral acre.
Defined, §40-20-30.
Nonproducing leaseholds.
Exemption from ad
valorem taxes,
§40-20-35.
How exemption obtained
upon existing
interests, §40-20-36.
Payment, §§40-20-33,
40-20-34.
Primary term.
Defined, §40-20-30.
Probate judges.
Collection of tax,
§40-20-33.
Fees, §40-20-37.

OIL AND GAS—Cont'd
Mineral documentary tax
—Cont'd
Probate judges—Cont'd
Where tax to be paid,
§40-20-34.
Remainder of tax.
Disposition, §40-20-37.
Royalty acre.
Defined, §40-20-30.
When payable, §40-20-33.
Municipal corporations.
Privilege tax on production.
Allocation and distribution
of net taxes collected
to certain
municipalities,
§40-20-8.
Exemption from ad
valorem taxes levied
by municipalities,
§40-20-12.
Levy of tax by
municipalities,
§40-20-2.
Oil and gas board. See within
this heading,
"Conservation and
regulation of production."
Penalties.
Petroleum products. See
within this heading,
"Petroleum products."
Permits.
Petroleum products. See
within this heading,
"Petroleum products."
Petroleum products,
§§8-17-80 to 8-17-155.
Adulteration.
Fraud and deceit in sale,
§8-17-134.
Prohibited, §8-17-83.
Advertising.
Reclaimed or re-refined oil,
§8-17-112.
Applicability of provisions.
Reclaimed or re-refined oil.
Nonapplicability of
division to certain
sales, §8-17-115.
Standards and inspections.
Inapplicability to certain
shipments, §8-17-94.
Containers.
Changing contents,
§8-17-136.
Definitions, §8-17-80.
Posting price and tax.
"Motor vehicle" defined,
§8-17-150.
Reclaimed or re-refined oil,
§8-17-110.
Diesel fuel.
Defined, §8-17-80.
Examinations, §8-17-85.
Fees.
Disposition, §8-17-91.
Inspection fee, §8-17-87.
Disposition, §8-17-91.
Overpayments.
Refund, §8-17-91.
Permit fee, §8-17-85.
Disposition, §8-17-91.
Fraud and deceit in sale,
§§8-17-130 to 8-17-139.
Adulteration, §8-17-134.
Containers.
Changing contents,
§8-17-136.

OIL AND GAS—Cont'd
  Petroleum products—Cont'd
    Fraud and deceit in sale
      —Cont'd
      Enforcement of division,
        §8-17-138.
      Generally, §8-17-130.
      Imitation of markings with
        intent to deceive,
        §8-17-137.
      Marking of pumps.
        Liquid motor fuels,
          §8-17-131.
        Lubricating oils,
          §8-17-132.
        Motor greases, §8-17-132.
        Removing markings,
          §8-17-133.
      Misnomer.
        Selling product other
          than that indicated,
          §8-17-135.
        Selling under other
          name, §8-17-134.
      Penalties.
        Violations of division,
          §8-17-139.
    Gasoline.
      Defined, §8-17-80.
      Tax.
        See GASOLINE.
    Importation.
      Notification, §8-17-89.
    Injunctions, §8-17-92.
    Inspections.
      Fee, §8-17-87.
        Disposition, §8-17-91.
        Overpayments.
          Refund, §8-17-91.
    Invoices.
      Driver of delivery vehicle
        to deliver, §8-17-90.
    Kerosene.
      Defined, §8-17-80.
    Labels.
      Reclaimed or re-refined oil,
        §8-17-111.
      Requirement, §8-17-82.
    Liquid motor fuels.
      Marking of pumps.
        Fraud and deceit in sale,
          §8-17-131.
    Lubricating oil.
      Defined, §8-17-80.
      Marking of pumps.
        Fraud and deceit in sale,
          §8-17-132.
    Motor greases.
      Marking of pumps.
        Fraud and deceit in sale,
          §8-17-132.
    Nonstandard products,
      §8-17-88.
    Penalties.
      Disposition, §8-17-91.
      Fraud and deceit in sale.
        Violation of division,
          §8-17-139.
      Overpayments.
        Refund, §8-17-91.
      Posting price and tax.
        Violation of division,
          §8-17-155.
      Reclaimed or re-refined oil.
        Violation of division,
          §8-17-116.
      Standards and inspections.
        Violation of division,
          §8-17-93.
    Permits.
      Application, §8-17-85.

OIL AND GAS—Cont'd
  Petroleum products—Cont'd
    Permits—Cont'd
      Expiration date, §8-17-85.
      Fee, §8-17-85.
        Disposition, §8-17-91.
        Overpayments.
          Refund, §8-17-91.
      Nonapplicability of section
        to certain persons,
        §8-17-85.
      Required, §8-17-85.
      Revocation, §8-17-93.
    Posting of price and tax,
      §§8-17-150 to 8-17-155.
      Construction of division,
        §8-17-151.
      Courts.
        Jurisdiction in
          enforcement of
          division, §8-17-153.
      Enforcement of division,
        §8-17-154.
        Jurisdiction, §8-17-153.
      Jurisdiction.
        Enforcement of division,
          §8-17-153.
      "Motor vehicle" defined,
        §8-17-150.
      Penalties.
        Violation of division,
          §8-17-155.
      Purpose of division,
        §8-17-151.
      Required, §8-17-152.
      Violation of division.
        Penalties, §8-17-155.
    Reclaimed or re-refined oil,
      §§8-17-110 to 8-17-116.
      Advertising, §8-17-112.
      Condemnation.
        Illegal oil, §8-17-114.
      Definitions, §8-17-110.
      Enforcement of division,
        §8-17-113.
      Labels.
        Requirements, §8-17-111.
      Penalties.
        Violation of division,
          §8-17-116.
      Sale.
        Illegal oil.
          Suspension from sale,
          §8-17-114.
        Nonapplicability of
          division to certain
          sales, §8-17-115.
      Seizure.
        Illegal oil, §8-17-114.
      Violation of division.
        Penalties, §8-17-116.
    Records.
      Inspection, §8-17-84.
      Preservation, §8-17-84.
      Regulations as to keeping,
        §8-17-84.
      Requirement, §8-17-84.
    Rules and regulations.
      Promulgation, §8-17-81.
      Records.
        Keeping, §8-17-84.
    Sale.
      Nonstandard products.
        Sale prohibited, §8-17-88.
        Suspension from sale,
          §8-17-88.
      Permit.
        Required, §8-17-85.
    Samples.
      Duty to test, §8-17-86.

OIL AND GAS—Cont'd
  Petroleum products—Cont'd
    Searches and seizures.
      Illegal products, §9-17-22.
      Reclaimed or re-refined oil.
        Seizure of illegal oil,
          §8-17-114.
    Standards.
      Determination and
        adoption, §8-17-81.
      Lowering.
        Prohibited, §8-17-83.
      Prior standards.
        Effect, §8-17-81.
    Storage.
      Nonstandard products.
        Storage prohibited,
          §8-17-88.
      Permit.
        Required, §8-17-85.
    Tests, §8-17-85.
      Certificate of tests,
        §8-17-86.
      Methods.
        Determination and
          adoption, §8-17-81.
      Samples.
        Duty to test, §8-17-86.
  Pools. See within this heading,
    "Conservation and
    regulation of production."
  Price.
    Posting of price and tax,
      §§8-17-150 to 8-17-155.
  Privilege tax on production,
    §§40-20-1 to 40-20-13.
    Additional taxes.
      Collection and
        disbursement,
        §40-20-13.
    Ad valorem taxes.
      Exemption from, §40-20-12.
    Allocation and distribution of
      taxes collected, §40-20-8.
    Amount of tax, §40-20-2.
    Assessment of taxes,
      §40-20-6.
    By whom tax paid, §40-20-3.
    Collection of tax, §40-20-4.
      Additional taxes,
        §40-20-13.
      Allocation and distribution
        of net taxes collected,
        §40-20-8.
    Counties.
      Allocation and distribution
        of net taxes collected,
        §40-20-8.
      Exemption from ad
        valorem taxes levied
        by counties, §40-20-12.
      Imposition of tax by
        counties, §40-20-2.
    Definitions, §40-20-1.
    Department of revenue.
      Deduction of appropriation
        for expenses of
        department, §40-20-7.
      Injunctions against
        violations, §40-20-11.
      Reports.
        Department to furnish
          blanks, §40-20-9.
    Development wells.
      Defined, §40-20-1.
    Discovery wells.
      Defined, §40-20-1.
    Enforcement of article,
      §40-20-4.
    Enhanced recovery projects.
      Defined, §40-20-1.

OIL AND GAS—Cont'd
Privilege tax on production
—Cont'd
Enhanced recovery projects
—Cont'd
Qualified enhanced
recovery projects.
Defined, §40-20-1.
Supplemental enhanced
recovery projects.
Defined, §40-20-1.
Exemption from ad valorem
taxes, §40-20-12.
Failure to deduct and
withhold tax, §40-20-3.
Incremental oil or gas
production.
Defined, §40-20-1.
Injunctions.
Enjoining violation of
article, §40-20-11.
Leases in production.
Exemption from ad
valorem taxes,
§40-20-12.
Levy of tax, §40-20-2.
Mineral rights in producing
properties.
Exemption from ad
valorem taxes,
§40-20-12.
Municipal corporations.
Allocation and distribution
of net taxes collected
to certain
municipalities,
§40-20-8.
Exemption from ad
valorem taxes levied
by municipalities,
§40-20-12.
Imposition of tax by
municipal
corporations, §40-20-2.
Oaths.
Reports to department of
revenue.
Certificate required,
§40-20-9.
Offshore drilling or
production facilities.
Defined, §40-20-1.
Offshore production.
Defined, §40-20-1.
Onshore wells.
Defined, §40-20-1.
Ownership.
Tax levied on producers in
proportion to
ownership at time of
severance, §40-20-3.
Payment.
By whom tax paid,
§40-20-3.
Penalties.
Reports.
Penalty for failure to
file, §40-20-5.
Producers.
Defined, §40-20-1.
Statements, §40-20-4.
Tax levied and
proportioned to
ownership at time of
severance, §40-20-3.
Records.
Inspection of records,
§40-20-4.
Required, §40-20-4.
Replacement wells.
Defined, §40-20-1.

OIL AND GAS—Cont'd
Privilege tax on production
—Cont'd
Reports.
Certificate, §40-20-9.
Failure to file.
Penalty, §40-20-5.
Monthly reports required,
§40-20-5.
Payments to accompany
reports, §40-20-5.
Penalties.
Failure to file report,
§40-20-5.
Verification, §40-20-9.
Royalty interest.
Tax levied on basis of
entire production in
state including royalty
interest, §40-20-2.
Severed.
Defined, §40-20-1.
Statements of producers,
§40-20-4.
Submerged lands.
Defined, §40-20-1.
Violations.
Enjoining violation of
article, §40-20-11.
When tax to accrue,
§40-20-2.
Probate judges.
Mineral documentary tax.
See within this heading,
"Mineral documentary
tax."
Production.
Conservation and regulation.
See within this heading,
"Conservation and
regulation of
production."
Privilege tax on production,
§§40-20-1 to 40-20-13.
See withinthis heading,
"Privilege tax on
production."
Products, §§8-17-80 to
8-17-155. See within this
heading, "Petroleum
products."
Public lands.
Leases by state, §§8-17-60 to
8-17-69. See within this
heading, "Leases."
Reclaimed or re-refined oil,
§§8-17-110 to 8-17-116. See
within this heading,
"Petroleum products."
Reports.
Privilege tax on production,
§§40-20-5, 40-20-9.
Sales.
Conservation and regulation
of production.
Disposition of proceeds,
§9-17-33.
Petroleum products,
§§8-17-85, 8-17-88.
Sales tax.
Exemptions.
Equipment, machinery,
fuel, etc., used in
exploration in offshore
federal waters,
§40-23-4.
Gross proceeds of sales of
lubricating oil and
gasoline, §40-23-4.

OIL AND GAS—Cont'd
Searches and seizures.
Illegal oil, gas or product,
§§8-17-114, 9-17-22.
Secured transactions.
Applicability of filing
provisions, §7-9-302.
Description of land, §7-9-203.
When security interest
attaches, §7-9-204.
Severance taxes.
County severance tax trust
funds, §40-20-50.
State.
Leases by state, §§8-17-60 to
8-17-69. See within this
heading, "Leases."
Taxation.
Gasoline tax, §§40-17-30 to
40-17-124.
See GASOLINE.
Lubricating oils and greases,
§§40-17-170 to 40-17-186.
See LUBRICATING OILS
AND GREASES.
Mineral documentary tax,
§§40-20-30 to 40-20-37.
See within this heading,
"Mineral documentary
tax."
Privilege tax on production,
§§40-20-1 to 40-20-13.
See within this heading,
"Privilege tax on
production."
Use tax, §40-23-62.
Unit operations, §§9-17-80 to
9-17-88.
Applicability of article,
§9-17-88.
Definitions.
"Secondary recovery
methods," §9-17-80.
Oil and gas board.
Meeting to consider need
for unit operations,
§9-17-81.
Order requiring.
Amending orders, §9-17-85.
Contents, §9-17-83.
Issuance, §9-17-82.
New orders, §9-17-85.
Revocation.
When automatically
revoked, §9-17-84.
When effective, §9-17-84.
Production and operations,
§9-17-87.
Separately owned tracts.
Alteration of contribution,
§9-17-86.
Use tax.
Exemptions, §40-23-62.
Weights and measures.
Sale of oil at retail regulated,
§8-16-105.
Wells.
Privilege tax on production.
See within this heading,
"Privilege tax on
production."

OLD AGE.
See AGED PERSONS.

OLEOMARGARINE.
**Board of agriculture and
industries.**
Changes of specifications as
to addition of vitamins,
§20-1-112.

OLEOMARGARINE—Cont'd
Labels.
Requirements as to labeling, §20-1-113.
Requirements.
Labeling, §20-1-113.
Minimum requirements as to units of vitamin A, §20-1-111.
Short title of article, §20-1-110.
Vitamins.
Changes of specification as to addition of vitamins by state board of agriculture and industries, §20-1-112.

ONEONTA, MUNICIPALITY OF.
School tax.
Special school tax, Const. Ala., amd. 299.

OPELIKA, MUNICIPALITY OF.
Property tax, Const. Ala., amd. 8.
School tax.
Special property tax for educational purposes, Const. Ala., amd. 147.

OPERAS.
Sales tax.
Exemptions.
Gross proceeds of sales of admissions, §40-23-4.

OPHTHALMIA NEONATORUM.
Notifiable diseases, §§22-11A-1 to 22-11A-38.
See DISEASES.
Prevention of infantile blindness, §22-20-2.

OPIUM.
Controlled substances generally, §§20-2-1 to 20-2-144.
See DRUGS.

OPOSSUMS.
Hunting at night, §§9-11-235, 9-11-235.1.

OPP, MUNICIPALITY OF.
Property tax, Const. Ala., amd. 17.

OPTICIANS.
Licenses, §40-12-135.

OPTIONS.
Commercial code.
Acceleration at will, §7-1-208.
Contracts for sale, §7-2-311.
Municipal corporations.
Industrial parks.
Sale of lands comprising industrial parks.
Binding option agreements, §11-54-4.
Real property.
Limitations on duration of option to purchase land, §35-4-76.

OPTOMETRISTS, §§34-22-1 to 34-22-65.
Advertising.
Licenses.
Unauthorized advertising as grounds for revocation or suspension, §34-22-23.
Alcoholic beverages.
Licenses.
Habitual drunkenness as grounds for revocation or suspension, §34-22-23.
Appeals.
Disciplinary actions against licensees, §34-22-8.
Applicability of chapter.
Intent of chapter, §34-22-3.
Limitation on application, §34-22-4.
Objects and purposes of chapter, §34-22-2.
Associations.
Professional corporations, §§10-4-380 to 10-4-406.
See PROFESSIONAL CORPORATIONS.
Unincorporated professional associations, §§10-10-1 to 10-10-16.
See UNINCORPORATED PROFESSIONAL ASSOCIATIONS.
Blind persons.
Assistance to needy blind persons.
Freedom of choice in selection of specialists to make examinations, §38-1-2.
General provisions.
See BLIND PERSONS.
Board of optometric scholarship awards.
Appropriations.
Conditional appropriations for scholarship awards, §34-22-61.
Composition, §34-22-60.
Contractual agreement of recipients.
Penalties for breach, §34-22-64.
Created, §34-22-60.
Loans.
Repayment, §34-22-63.
Localities in need of optometrists.
Applications to board, §34-22-65.
Penalties.
Breach of contract, §34-22-64.
Powers and duties generally, §34-22-61.
Recipients of scholarships, §34-22-64.
Repayment of loans.
Interest, §34-22-63.
Service contracts, §34-22-63.
Terms of office, §34-22-60.
Types of scholarships.
Establishment by board, §34-22-62.
Board of optometry.
Annual meeting, §34-22-40.
Appointment of members, §34-22-40.
Bonds, surety, §34-22-41.

OPTOMETRISTS—Cont'd
Board of optometry—Cont'd
Compensation of members, §34-22-41.
Composition, §34-22-40.
Creation, §34-22-40.
Defined, §34-22-1.
Disciplinary action against licensees, §34-22-8.
Duties.
Generally, §34-22-42.
Education.
Establishment of standards by board, §34-22-42.
Election of candidates, §34-22-40.
Evidence.
Assisting prosecution of violations of chapter, §34-22-6.
Examinations.
Authority to conduct, §34-22-42.
Generally, §34-22-20.
Funds.
Deposit and expenditure of funds, §34-22-41.
Use and disposition of funds, §34-22-24.
Governor.
Annual report to governor, §34-22-41.
Appointment of members, §34-22-40.
Injunctions.
Board may enjoin violations of chapter, §34-22-7.
Licenses.
Authority to grant and deny licenses, §34-22-42.
Meetings.
Annual meeting, §34-22-40.
Generally, §34-22-41.
Office of board, §34-22-43.
Officers, §34-22-41.
Powers.
Generally, §34-22-42.
Qualifications of members, §34-22-40.
Quorum, §34-22-41.
Records, §34-22-43.
Registry, §§34-22-42, 34-22-43.
Removal of members, §34-22-40.
Reports.
Annual report, §34-22-41.
Rules and regulations.
Promulgation by board, §34-22-42.
Secretary.
Registry of licensees, §34-22-43.
Staff.
Authority to employ staff, §34-22-42.
Subpoenas.
Authority of board, §34-22-42.
Disciplinary proceedings, §34-22-8.
Terms of office, §34-22-40.
Vacancies.
Filling vacancies, §34-22-40.
Violations of chapter.
Board may enjoin violations, §34-22-7.

OPTOMETRISTS—Cont'd
Board of optometry—Cont'd
Violations of chapter—Cont'd
Board to assist in
prosecutions, §34-22-6.
Witnesses.
Authority of board,
§34-22-42.
Disciplinary proceedings,
§34-22-8.
Bonds, surety.
Board of optometry.
Bond of members,
§34-22-41.
Corporations.
Professional corporations,
§§10-4-380 to 10-4-406.
See PROFESSIONAL
CORPORATIONS.
Definitions, §34-22-1.
Diplomas.
Unlawful use or sale of
diploma, §34-22-6.
Disciplinary action, §34-22-8.
Education.
Board of optometry.
Authority to establish
standards, §34-22-42.
Continuing education
requirements, §34-22-22.
Limited teaching licenses,
§34-22-5.
Qualifications of applicants,
§34-22-20.
Evidence.
Board of optometry.
Admissibility of copies of
board records,
§34-22-43.
Examinations.
Board of optometry.
Authority to conduct,
§34-22-42.
Continuing education
requirements, §34-22-22.
Licenses. See within this
heading, "Licenses."
Limited teaching licenses,
§34-22-5.
Subjects examined,
§34-22-20.
**Exemptions from provisions
of chapter,** §34-22-4.
Fees.
Board of optometry.
Disposition of fees,
§34-22-24.
Disposition of fees, §34-22-24.
Licenses. See within this
heading, "Licenses."
Limited teaching licenses,
§34-22-5.
Fraud.
Grounds for revocation or
suspension of license,
§34-22-23.
Penalty for fraudulently
obtaining license,
§34-22-6.
Governor.
Board of optometry.
Annual report to governor,
§34-22-41.
Appointment of board
members, §34-22-40.
Hearings.
Disciplinary action, §34-22-8.
Injunctions.
Board may enjoin violations
of chapter, §34-22-7.
Intent of chapter, §34-22-3.

OPTOMETRISTS—Cont'd
Licenses, §40-12-135.
Application for examination,
§34-22-20.
Board of optometry.
Authority to grant and
deny, §34-22-42.
Continuing education
requirements, §34-22-22.
Disciplinary action against
licensees, §34-22-8.
Education.
Continuing education
requirements,
§34-22-22.
Educational qualifications,
§34-22-20.
Examinations, §34-22-20.
Fees.
Application fee, §34-22-20.
Disposition of license fees,
§34-22-24.
Renewal, §34-22-22.
Revocation or suspension of
license for fee
splitting, §34-22-23.
Fraud in obtaining license,
§34-22-6.
Issuance, §34-22-20.
Limited teaching licenses,
§34-22-5.
Nonresidents.
Reciprocity requirements,
§34-22-21.
Qualifications of applicants,
§34-22-20.
Reciprocity, §34-22-21.
Reinstatement or restoration
of license, §34-22-22.
Renewal, §34-22-22.
Revocation or suspension.
Failure to renew license,
§34-22-22.
Grounds, §34-22-23.
Teaching licenses.
Limited teaching licenses,
§34-22-5.
Temporary license,
§34-22-20.
Mentally ill.
Grounds for revocation or
suspension of license,
§34-22-23.
Nonresidents.
Licenses, §34-22-21.
Objects of chapter, §34-22-2.
Penalties.
Fee for failure to renew
licenses, §34-22-22.
Violations of chapter,
§34-22-6.
Practice of optometry.
Defined, §34-22-1.
Objects and purposes of
chapter, §34-22-2.
Unlawful practice, §34-22-6.
Professional corporations,
§§10-4-380 to 10-4-406.
See PROFESSIONAL
CORPORATIONS.
Purposes of chapter,
§34-22-2.
Reciprocity.
Licenses, §34-22-21.
Rules and regulations.
Board of optometry.
Authority to promulgate,
§34-22-42.
Limited teaching licenses,
§34-22-5.

OPTOMETRISTS—Cont'd
Scholarships.
Board of optometric
scholarship awards,
§§34-22-60 to 34-22-65.
Subpoenas.
Disciplinary proceedings,
§34-22-8.
Power of board, §34-22-42.
Time.
Disciplinary hearings,
§34-22-8.
**Unincorporated professional
associations,** §§10-10-1 to
10-10-16.
See UNINCORPORATED
PROFESSIONAL
ASSOCIATIONS.
Violations of chapter.
Assistance in prosecutions,
§34-22-6.
Disciplinary action, §34-22-8.
Injunctions.
Board may enjoin
violations of chapter,
§34-22-7.
Penalties, §34-22-6.
Witnesses.
Authority of board to compel
attendance and
administer oaths,
§34-22-42.
Disciplinary proceedings
before board, §34-22-8.

ORCHESTRAS.
Sales tax.
Exemptions.
Gross proceeds from sales
of admissions to
orchestral concerts,
§40-23-4.

ORDERS OF COURT.
Adoption.
Orders of adoption.
See ADOPTION.
Appeals.
Notice of orders, ARAP, Rule
17 (a).
Bankruptcy and insolvency.
See BANKRUPTCY AND
INSOLVENCY.
Child support.
Withholding orders for child
support, §§30-3-60 to
30-3-71.
See MINORS.
Chiropractors.
Final orders.
Form and content,
§34-24-174.
Licenses.
Refusal, revocation or
suspension.
Form and content of
final order,
§34-24-174.
Discovery.
Protective orders, ARCP,
Rule 26 (c).
Domestic relations.
Protection from abuse,
§§30-5-6 to 30-5-8,
30-5-10.
Eminent domain.
Entry, §§18-1A-51,
18-1A-276.
Modification, §18-1A-53.
Entry of order.
Sufficiency of minute entry,
ARCP, Rule 58 (b).

ORDERS OF COURT—Cont'd
Excusable neglect.
Relief from order, ARCP,
Rule 60 (b).
Fences.
Partition fences, §35-7-4.
Fraud.
Relief from order, ARCP,
Rule 60 (b).
Guardian and ward.
Removal of person or
property of minors and
wards.
Removal to another county,
§26-8-22.
Removal to another state.
Application, §26-8-41.
Entry of order, §26-8-42.
Uniform guardianship and
protective proceedings
act.
Appointment of
conservators or other
protective orders.
Permissible court orders,
§26-2A-136.
Petitions for orders
subsequent to
appointment of
conservators,
§26-2A-144.
Procedure concerning
order on original
petition, §26-2A-135.
Termination of
conservatorship.
Evidence and
recordation,
§26-2A-149.
Incapacitated persons.
Court appointment of
guardian.
Order of appointment,
§26-2A-105.
Termination of
incapacity.
Request for order,
§26-2A-110.
Protective orders.
See GUARDIAN AND
WARD.
How rendered, ARCP, Rule
58 (a).
Inadvertence.
Relief from order, ARCP,
Rule 60 (b).
Jails.
Commitment or discharge of
prisoner.
Duty to file process or
order, §14-6-16.
Juvenile proceedings.
See JUVENILE
PROCEEDINGS.
Liquefied petroleum gas.
Directive order of
discontinuance,
§9-17-108.
Mentally ill.
Criminal law and procedure.
Release of criminal
psychopaths.
Requirement of court
order, §15-16-62.
Minors.
Custody and support.
Withholding orders for
child support,
§§30-3-60 to 30-3-71.
See MINORS.

ORDERS OF COURT—Cont'd
Mistake.
Clerical mistakes.
Relief from order, ARCP,
Rule 60 (a).
Relief from order, ARCP,
Rule 60 (b).
Motions.
New trial.
Time for motion, ARCP,
Rule 59 (b).
Newly discovered evidence.
Relief from order, ARCP,
Rule 60 (b).
Notice, ARCP, Rule 77 (d).
Supreme court orders, ARAP,
Rule 17 (a).
Partition.
See PARTITION.
Partnerships.
Dissolution, §10-8-92.
Probate courts, §§12-13-1,
12-13-3.
Protective orders, ARCP,
Rule 26 (c).
Recordation.
Statement of name and
address of preparer.
Division not applicable to
orders of court,
§35-4-112.
Records.
Copying of orders into final
record not required,
§12-20-21.
Relief from order.
Clerical mistakes, ARCP,
Rule 60 (a).
Excusable neglect, ARCP,
Rule 60 (b).
Fraud, ARCP, Rule 60 (b).
Inadvertence, ARCP, Rule 60
(b).
Mistakes, ARCP, Rule 60 (b).
Newly discovered evidence,
ARCP, Rule 60 (b).
Stay on motion for relief,
ARCP, Rule 62 (b).
Rendition of orders, ARCP,
Rule 58 (a).
**Restitution to victims of
crimes.**
Effect of restitution order,
§15-18-78.
Employment income
withholding order,
§§15-18-140 to 15-18-151.
See RESTITUTION TO
VICTIMS OF
CRIMES.
Enforceability where
defendant imprisoned,
§15-18-71.
Objections to order,
§15-18-69.
Restitution order, §15-18-67.
Rights of victims, §15-18-78.
Section cumulative and in
para materia with other
statutes, §15-18-78.
Withholding.
Employment income
withholding order,
§§15-18-140 to
15-18-151.
See RESTITUTION TO
VICTIMS OF
CRIMES.
Rules of civil procedure,
ARCP, Rules 58, 60.

ORDERS OF COURT—Cont'd
**Southeast interstate low-
level radioactive waste
management compact.**
Issuance of order prohibiting
use of source of ionizing
radiation, §22-32-8.
Sufficiency of order, ARCP,
Rule 58 (b).
Supreme court.
Notice of orders, ARAP, Rule
17 (a).
Visitation.
Bond, security, or other
guarantee to secure
compliance with
visitation order, §30-3-6.
**Withholding orders for child
support.**
Custody and support,
§§30-3-60 to 30-3-71.
See MINORS.

**ORDERS OF THE EASTERN
STAR.**
**Grand chapter of all orders
of the Eastern Star.**
Exemptions from sales and
use taxes, §40-23-5.

ORDINANCES.
Atomic energy.
Radiation.
Effect of chapter on local
ordinances, §22-14-15.
Attorney general.
Constitutionality questioned.
Notice to attorney general,
§6-6-227; ARAP, Rule
44.
Condominiums.
Building or zoning
ordinances.
Construction and
application, §35-8-21.
Evidence.
Municipal ordinances,
§12-21-95.
Injunctions.
Enjoining or restraining
enforcement, §6-6-502.
Magistrates.
Municipal court magistrates
agency division.
Ordinance violations.
Authority of magistrates
in, ARJA, Rule 18.
Mobile homes.
Anchoring.
Certain local laws,
municipal ordinances,
etc., not repealed,
§24-5-34.
Local ordinances providing
for inspection of mobile
homes, §24-5-13.
Municipal corporations.
See MUNICIPAL
CORPORATIONS.
Municipal courts.
Judicial notice.
Courts to take judicial
notice of ordinances of
municipality, §12-14-7.
Pleadings, ARCP, Rule 9 (d).
Soil and water conservation.
Districts.
Land-use regulations,
§9-8-26.

ORDINANCES—Cont'd
Validity of municipal
ordinances or
franchises.
Persons to be made parties,
§6-6-227.
Zoning.
Municipal corporations.
See MUNICIPAL
CORPORATIONS.

ORGAN DONORS.
General provisions,
§§22-19-40 to 22-19-61,
22-19-120 to 22-19-144.
See ANATOMICAL GIFTS.

ORPHANS AND
ORPHANAGES.
Child care facilities, §§38-7-1
to 38-7-18.
See WELFARE.
Churches.
Conventions or associations
of churches.
Establishment of
orphanages, §10-4-61.
Municipal corporations.
Special health care facility
authorities, §§11-62-1 to
11-62-21.
See MUNICIPAL
CORPORATIONS.
Relief of minors from
disabilities of nonage,
§§26-13-1 to 26-13-8.
See MINORS.

OSTEOPATHS.
See PHYSICIANS.

OUTDOOR ADVERTISING,
§§23-1-270 to 23-1-288.
See ADVERTISING.

OWELTY.
Partition in circuit courts,
§35-6-24.

OXFORD, MUNICIPALITY
OF.
Property tax, Const. Ala.,
amd. 13.

OZARK, MUNICIPALITY OF.
School tax.
Special property tax for
educational purposes,
Const. Ala., amds. 295,
462.

P

PACKAGES.
Containers generally.
See CONTAINERS.

PACKINGHOUSES.
Licenses, §40-12-137.

PAGERS.
Education.
When pupils prohibited from
carrying, §16-1-27.

PAINT.
Jails.
Painting of jails.
Schedule, §14-6-92.

PALMISTS.
Licenses.
Fee, §40-12-104.

PANDERING.
Promoting prostitution,
§§13A-12-111 to
13A-12-113.

PAPER.
Forest products generally,
§§9-13-60 to 9-13-107.
See FORESTS AND
FORESTRY.

PARAPHERNALIA.
Drugs.
Controlled substances.
Contraband, §13A-12-260.
Definition, §13A-12-260.
Delivery or sale,
§13A-12-260.
Possession of
paraphernalia,
§13A-12-260.

PARDONS.
Authority of board to grant,
§15-22-36.
Board of pardons and
paroles.
See PAROLE.
Civil disabilities.
Pardon not relieved from
civil disability unless
specifically provided,
Const. Ala., amd. 38.
Constitution of Alabama,
Const. Ala., art. V, §124.
Legislature to regulate,
Const. Ala., amd. 38.
Constitution of the United
States, Const. U. S., Art.
II, §2.
Death penalty.
Pardon of person having
death sentence
commuted to life
imprisonment, §15-22-27.
Postponing execution of
sentence pending
pardons, §15-18-100.
Elections.
Disqualification from
registration and voting.
Convicted persons.
Restoration of right to
vote by pardon,
§17-3-10.
Governor, Const. Ala., art. V,
§124.
Legislature.
Regulation of pardons, Const.
Ala., amd. 38.
Political disabilities.
Pardon not relieved from
civil and political
disabilities unless
specifically provided,
Const. Ala., amd. 38.
President, Const. U. S., Art.
II, §2.
Violations of article.
Pardons granted in violation
null and void, §15-22-40.

PARENT AND CHILD.
Abandonment of minors.
Child support programs,
§§38-10-1 to 38-10-33.
See CHILD SUPPORT
PROGRAMS.
Relief of minor children from
disabilities of nonage,
§§26-13-1 to 26-13-8.
See MINORS.

PARENT AND CHILD—Cont'd
Abandonment of minors
—Cont'd
Termination of parental
rights.
Presumption arising from
abandonment,
§26-18-7.
Abortion.
Inducing or attempting to
induce abortion,
§13A-13-7.
Parental consent to
perform abortions
upon minors, §§26-21-1
to 26-21-8.
See ABORTION.
Actions.
Alcoholic beverages.
Illegal sales to minors.
Right of action of parent,
§6-5-70.
Destruction of property by
minor.
Liability of parents,
§6-5-380.
Determination of paternity.
See within this heading,
"Determination of
paternity."
Injury to minor child.
Right of action of parents,
§6-5-390.
Prosecution or defense of
actions in name of father
by mother, §6-7-1.
Wrongful death of minor,
§6-5-391.
Action to determine mother
and child relationship.
Applicability of father and
child provisions,
§26-17-18.
Who may bring, §26-17-18.
Adoption.
Consent of parents, §26-10-3.
General provisions, §§26-10-1
to 26-10-30.
See ADOPTION.
Termination of parental
rights.
Authority of one in custody
to place for adoption,
§26-18-10.
Review of efforts to achieve
adoption, §26-18-9.
Alcoholic beverages.
Illegal sales to minors.
Right of action of parent,
§6-5-70.
Appeals.
Determination of paternity,
§26-17-20.
Termination of parental
rights.
Precedence of appeals,
§26-18-2.
Artificial insemination.
Relationship of father and
child, §26-17-21.
Bastards.
Determination of paternity,
§§26-17-1 to 26-17-21.
See within this heading,
"Determination of
paternity."
General provisions.
See ILLEGITIMACY.

PARENT AND CHILD—Cont'd
Bicycles.
Violations of regulations.
Parent not to permit or
authorize violations,
§32-5A-266.
Blind persons.
Educational benefits for
dependents of blind
parents, §§16-33-1 to
16-33-12.
See UNIVERSITIES AND
COLLEGES.
Bone marrow donation.
Consent by parents, §22-8-9.
Child protection.
Termination of parental
rights. See within this
heading, "Termination of
parental rights."
Child support.
General provisions.
See CHILD SUPPORT.
Child support programs,
§§38-10-1 to 38-10-33.
See CHILD SUPPORT
PROGRAMS.
Consent for health services,
§§22-8-1 to 22-8-9.
See HEALTH.
Criminal law and procedure.
Immaturity as bar to
criminal liability,
§13-3-3.
Interference with custody,
§13A-6-45.
Justification and excuse.
Use of force by persons
with parental
responsibilities,
§13A-3-24.
**Crippled and disabled
children.**
Physical examination of
children having
malformations or
disabilities.
Information to be given
parents, §21-3-7.
Custody.
Interference with custody,
§13A-6-45.
Termination of parental
rights.
Transfer of custody,
§26-18-8.
Death of parent.
Visitation rights of
grandparents, §30-3-4.
Definitions.
Parent and child
relationship, §26-17-2.
Termination of parental
rights, §26-18-3.
**Destruction of property by
minor.**
Liability of parents, §6-5-380.
Determination of paternity,
§§26-17-1 to 26-17-21.
Actions to determine.
Evidence, §26-17-9.
Confidentiality,
§26-17-19.
Intercourse with other
men, §26-17-13.
Presumptions, §26-17-5.
Types of evidence,
§26-17-13.
Hearing, §26-17-10.
Joinder, §26-17-9.

PARENT AND CHILD—Cont'd
Determination of paternity
—Cont'd
Actions to determine—Cont'd
Jurisdiction, §26-17-10.
Concurrent jurisdiction
among juvenile,
district and circuit
courts, §38-10-7.
Jury, §26-17-10.
Nature of actions, §26-17-9.
Process, §26-17-10.
Prosecution of proceedings,
§26-17-7.
Rules of procedure,
§26-17-9.
Style of proceedings,
§26-17-7.
Venue, §26-17-10.
Who may bring action,
§26-17-6.
Witnesses, §26-17-9.
Immunity, §26-17-13.
Refusal to testify,
§26-17-13.
Adopted children, §26-17-6.
Appeals, §26-17-20.
Attorneys at law.
Representation of minors,
§26-17-17.
Right to counsel,
§26-17-17.
Birth certificates, §26-17-19.
Blood tests, §26-17-12.
Order of court, §26-17-14.
Enforcement, §26-17-15.
Parties, §§26-17-11, 26-17-12.
Presumption of paternity,
§26-17-5.
Rights of inheritance and
succession, §26-17-8.
Stay until birth, §26-17-6.
Stipulations barring
paternity actions.
Unenforceable, §26-17-16.
Support.
Amount, §26-17-14.
Enforcement under
criminal code,
§26-17-9.
Liability.
Limitation on liability
for education and
support, §26-17-8.
Limitation of actions,
§26-17-8.
Orders of court, §26-17-14.
Enforcement, §26-17-15.
Promise to render support,
§26-17-16.
When action may be brought,
§26-17-6.
Diseases.
Notifiable diseases.
Sexually transmitted
diseases.
Treatment of minor.
Notification of parent
allowed,
§22-11A-19.
Domestic violence facilities.
General provisions, §§30-6-1
to 30-6-13.
See DOMESTIC
VIOLENCE
FACILITIES.

PARENT AND CHILD—Cont'd
Evidence.
Determination of paternity.
Actions to determine. See
within this heading,
"Determination of
paternity."
**Exemptions from
administration and
payment of debts.**
See EXEMPTIONS FROM
ADMINISTRATION
AND PAYMENT OF
DEBTS.
**Exemptions from levy and
sale under process.**
Homestead exemption.
Interposition of claim or
defense of contest by
minor children,
§6-10-39.
**Father and child
relationship.**
Determination. See within
this heading,
"Determination of
paternity."
Genetic service, §§22-10A-1 to
22-10A-3.
Health services.
Consent for health services,
§§22-8-1 to 22-8-9.
See HEALTH.
Illegitimacy.
Determination of paternity,
§§26-17-1 to 26-17-21.
See within this heading,
"Determination of
paternity."
General provisions.
See ILLEGITIMACY.
Incest.
See INCEST.
Injury to minor child.
Right of action of parents,
§6-5-390.
Juvenile proceedings.
See JUVENILE
PROCEEDINGS.
Kidnapping.
Interference with custody,
§13A-6-45.
Legitimation of children,
§§26-11-1 to 26-11-3.
Liability.
Destruction of property by
minor.
Liability of parent,
§6-5-380.
Marriage.
Consent for marriage of
certain minors, §30-1-5.
Relationship between parent
and child.
Not dependent upon
marriage, §26-17-3.
Mentally ill.
Relief of minor children from
disabilities of nonage,
§§26-13-1 to 26-13-8.
See MINORS.
Support of persons in state
mental institutions,
§§22-53-1 to 22-53-26.
See MENTALLY ILL.
Motor-driven cycles.
Authorizing or permitting
violations, §32-12-20.

PARENT AND CHILD—Cont'd
Motor vehicles.
Safety-responsibility act.
Proof of financial
responsibility
Owner may give proof
for member of
immediate family,
§32-7-28.
Obscenity.
Obscene materials containing
visual reproduction of
children.
Parents or guardians
permitting children to
engage in production
of, §13A-12-196.
Parties.
Prosecution or defense of
actions in name of father
by mother, §6-7-1.
Personal property.
Conveyances of personalty to
minors.
Recordation necessary as to
purchasers,
mortgagees and
judgment creditors,
§35-4-96.
Presumptions.
Paternity, §26-17-5.
Termination of parental
rights.
Presumption arising from
abandonment,
§26-18-7.
Protection from abuse.
General provisions, §§30-5-1
to 30-5-11.
See DOMESTIC
RELATIONS.
Relationship.
Artificial insemination,
§26-17-21.
Defined, §26-17-2.
Establishment.
How established, §26-17-4.
Father and child
relationship.
Determination, §§26-17-1
to 26-17-21. See within
this heading,
"Determination of
paternity."
Marriage.
Not dependent upon
marriage, §26-17-3.
Paternity.
Determination of paternity,
§§26-17-1 to 26-17-21.
See within this
heading,
"Determination of
paternity."
Scholarships.
Educational benefits for
dependents of blind
parents, §§16-33-1 to
16-33-12.
See UNIVERSITIES AND
COLLEGES.
Seduction.
Action by father or mother
for seduction of
daughter, §6-5-351.
Service of process.
Termination of parental
rights, §26-18-6.
State parent locator,
§38-2-6.1.

PARENT AND CHILD—Cont'd
Taxation.
Assessments.
By whom property should
be listed, §40-7-17.
Returns.
Separate returns in
individual and
fiduciary capacity,
§40-7-20.
**Termination of parental
rights,** §§26-18-1 to
26-18-21.
Abandonment.
Presumption arising from,
§26-18-7.
Ability to assume custody of
child.
Allegation and proof
required, §26-18-4.
Adoption.
Authority of one in custody
to place for adoption,
§26-18-10.
Review of efforts to achieve
adoption, §26-18-9.
Appeals.
Precedence of appeals,
§26-18-2.
Citation of chapter, §26-18-1.
Custody.
Transfer of custody,
§26-18-8.
Definitions, §26-18-3.
Factors considered, §26-18-7.
Grounds, §26-18-7.
Petition.
Who may file, §26-18-5.
Purpose of chapter, §26-18-2.
Rules of juvenile procedure.
Applicability, §26-18-4.
Service of process, §26-18-6.
Short title of chapter,
§26-18-1.
Torts.
Liability.
Destruction of property by
minor, §6-5-380.
Uniform parentage act.
Parent and child
relationship. See within
this heading,
"Relationship."
Short title of chapter,
§26-17-1.
Welfare.
Child support programs,
§§38-10-1 to 38-10-33.
See CHILD SUPPORT
PROGRAMS.
Wrongful death of minor,
§6-5-391.

PARI-MUTUEL BETTING.
See HORSE RACING.

PARKING.
General provisions.
See MOTOR VEHICLES.

PARKING LOTS.
Shopping carts.
Abandonment on parking
lots, §13A-8-62.
State highway department.
Construction and
maintenance, §23-1-42.

PARKS AND RECREATION.
**Africatown, U.S.A. state
park,** §§41-10-230 to
41-10-240.
See AFRICATOWN, U.S.A.
STATE PARK.
Airports.
Municipal corporations.
Use of parks for airports,
§4-4-3.
**Alienation of certain public
improvements by
political subdivisions.**
Authorization to alienate
public recreational
facilities, §35-4-410.
Ordinance describing
proposed conveyance,
§35-4-411.
Referendum.
Authorization to alienate
public recreational
facilities, §35-4-410.
Election, §35-4-412.
Resolution describing
proposed conveyance,
§35-4-411.
Authorities.
Municipal corporations.
Parks, playgrounds and
other recreational and
athletic areas and
facilities, §§11-47-210
to 11-47-220.
See MUNICIPAL
CORPORATIONS.
Beautification board.
General provisions,
§§41-9-490 to 41-9-498.
See BEAUTIFICATION.
Boards of recreation,
§§11-86-1 to 11-86-6. See
within this heading,
"Recreation boards."
**Capital development
assistance fund,** §§9-7A-1
to 9-7A-17.
Allocation of fund.
Disposition of money
received, §9-7A-16.
Priority, §9-7A-17.
Commissioner.
Consultation with state
departments, §9-7A-15.
Cooperation and
collaboration with
other agencies,
§9-7A-14.
Duties.
Generally, §9-7A-13.
Functions.
Generally, §9-7A-13.
Powers.
Generally, §9-7A-13.
Composition, §9-7A-1.
Conversion of property.
Approval of commissioner
required, §9-7A-10.
Cooperation and
collaboration with other
agencies.
Commissioner authorized,
§9-7A-14.
Creation, §9-7A-1.
Definitions, §9-7A-2.
Disbursement of funds,
§9-7A-7.
Disposition of money received
under chapter, §9-7A-16.

PARKS AND RECREATION
—Cont'd

Capital development assistance fund—Cont'd

Grants.
Applications, §9-7A-3.
Applicants required to assume post completion cost of maintenance, §9-7A-4.
Composition of applicant's share, §9-7A-5.
Conformity of projects with state comprehensive outdoor recreation plan, §9-7A-6.
Conformity of requests with guidelines promulgated by commissioner, §9-7A-12.
Contribution of matching amount to applicant, §9-7A-5.
Description of project, §9-7A-3.
Disbursement, §9-7A-7.
Maximum amount, §9-7A-5.
Procedures for applications, §9-7A-3.
Projects receiving financial assistance must conform to state plan, §9-7A-6.
Records.
Examination of records by commissioner, §9-7A-11.
Required, §9-7A-9.
Requests must conform to guidelines promulgated by commissioner, §9-7A-12.
Legislative declaration, §9-7A-1.
Purpose, §9-7A-1.
Real property.
Conversion of property acquired under chapter requires commissioner's approval, §9-7A-10.
Records.
Applicants for grants required to maintain records, §9-7A-9.
Examination of records by commissioner, §9-7A-11.
Reports, §9-7A-8.

Constitution of Alabama.
Alienation of public parks, playgrounds, recreational facilities and housing projects by political subdivisions and public bodies, Const. Ala., amd. 112.
Bond issue to acquire, develop, etc., state parks and facilities, Const. Ala., amd. 267.

Conveyances.
Alienation of certain public improvements by political subdivisions, §§35-4-410 to 35-4-412.

PARKS AND RECREATION
—Cont'd

Counties.
Alienation of certain public improvements by political subdivisions, §§35-4-410 to 35-4-412.
General provisions.
See COUNTIES.
Recreation boards. See within this heading, "Recreation boards."

Definitions.
Capital development assistance fund, §9-7A-2.
Rivers.
Limitation of liability for non-commercial public recreational use of land, §35-15-21.

Division of parks.
See STATE PARKS.

Duty of care owed to persons on premises for sporting or recreational purposes, §§35-15-1 to 35-15-5.
Existing liability.
Otherwise existing liability not limited, §35-15-3.
General duty of care.
Not created, §35-15-4.
Liability.
General duty of care or ground of liability not created, §35-15-4.
Limitation of liability.
Otherwise existing liability not limited, §35-15-3.
No duty owed except as provided in section 35-15-3, §35-15-1.
Permission to use premises.
Effect of permission, §35-15-2.
Right to go on lands of another without permission not created, §35-15-5.

Funds.
Capital development assistance fund, §§9-7A-1 to 9-7A-17. See within this heading, "Capital development assistance fund."

Liability.
Duty of care owed to persons on premises, §§35-15-1 to 35-15-15.
Limitation, §§35-15-20 to 35-15-28. See within this heading, "Limitation of liability for non-commercial public recreational use of land."

Licenses.
Municipal corporations, §§11-51-102, 11-51-104.

Limitation of liability for non-commercial public recreational use of land, §§35-15-20 to 35-15-28.
Commercial recreational enterprises.
Provisions not applicable, §35-15-26.
Definitions, §35-15-21.

PARKS AND RECREATION
—Cont'd

Limitation of liability for non-commercial public recreational use of land —Cont'd
Establishment of non-commercial public recreational use.
Acts creating rebuttable presumption, §35-15-28.
Exceptions, §35-15-24.
Commercial recreational enterprises, §35-15-26.
Generally, §35-15-23.
Governmental immunity unaffected, §35-15-27.
Inspection not required, §35-15-22.
Legislative declaration.
Purpose of provisions, §35-15-20.
Outdoor recreational land.
Defined, §35-15-21.
Duty of care by persons using, §35-15-25.
Presumptions.
Acts by owner creating rebuttable presumption of non-commercial public recreational use, §35-15-28.
Purpose of provisions, §35-15-20.
Warning not required, §35-15-22.

Municipal corporations.
Alienation of certain public improvements by political subdivisions, §§35-4-410 to 35-4-412.
General provisions.
See MUNICIPAL CORPORATIONS.
Public athletic boards, §§11-59-1 to 11-59-17.
See MUNICIPAL CORPORATIONS.
Public park and recreation boards, §§11-60-1 to 11-60-20.
See MUNICIPAL CORPORATIONS.
Recreation boards. See within this heading, "Recreation boards."

Negligence.
Duty of care owed persons on premises for sporting or recreational purposes, §§35-15-1 to 35-15-5.

Parkways, §9-14-2.

Presumptions.
Limitation of liability for non-commercial public recreational use of land.
Acts by owner creating rebuttable presumption of non-commercial public recreational use, §35-15-28.

Public improvements.
Alienation of certain public improvements by political subdivisions, §§35-4-410 to 35-4-412.

PARKS AND RECREATION —Cont'd

Records.
Capital development assistance fund.
Applicants required to maintain records, §9-7A-9.
Examination of records by commissioner, §9-7A-11.

Recreation boards, §§11-86-1 to 11-86-6.
Appointment of members, §11-86-2.
Appropriations, §11-86-5.
Buildings.
Designation, acquisition, improvement, etc., of buildings for recreational purposes, §11-86-5.
Compensation of members, §11-86-2.
Composition, §11-86-2.
Construction of chapter, §11-86-6.
Counties.
Joint actions by counties and municipalities, §11-86-5.
Creation, §11-86-1.
Director of recreation.
Employment, §11-86-4.
Duties, §11-86-3.
Joint actions by counties and municipalities, §11-86-5.
Lands.
Designation, acquisition, improvement, etc., of lands for recreational purposes, §11-86-5.
Municipalities.
Joint actions by counties and municipalities, §11-86-5.
Public park and recreation boards, §§11-60-1 to 11-60-20.
See MUNICIPAL CORPORATIONS.
Officers, §11-86-2.
Powers, §11-86-3.
Qualifications of members, §11-86-2.
Rules and regulations.
Adoption, §11-86-2.
Staff, §11-86-4.
Terms of members, §11-86-2.

Referendum.
Alienation of certain public improvements by political subdivisions, §§35-4-410, 35-4-412.

Reports.
Capital development assistance fund.
Requirements, §9-7A-8.

Societies for establishing parks and places of public recreation.
Public societies, §§10-4-20 to 10-4-26.
See CORPORATIONS.

State parks, §§9-2-100 to 9-2-108, 9-14-1 to 9-14-29.
See STATE PARKS.

PARKS AND RECREATION —Cont'd

Torts.
Duty of care owed persons on premises for sporting or recreational purposes, §§35-15-1 to 35-15-5.
Limitation of liability, §§35-15-20 to 35-15-28.
See within this heading, "Limitation of liability for non-commercial public recreational use of land."

Wildlife parks.
Possession of wildlife for public exhibition purposes, §§9-11-320 to 9-11-328.
See FISH AND GAME.

PARKWAYS.
State parks, §9-14-2.

PAROLE.

Arrest.
Parole officers.
Powers and duties, §15-22-73.
Retaking of parolee without warrant, §15-22-31.
Violations, §15-22-76.

Authority of board to grant, §15-22-36.

Board of corrections.
Cooperation with board of pardons and paroles, §15-22-28.
Furnishing records, §15-22-34.

Board of pardons and paroles.
Appointment of members, §15-22-20.
Appointment of secretary and other assistants, §15-22-21.
Authority to grant pardons and paroles, §15-22-36.
Chairman, §15-22-20.
Compensation, §15-22-20.
Constitution of Alabama, Const. Ala., art. V, §124.
Cooperation with board of corrections, §15-22-28.
Creation, §15-22-20.
Due notice.
Defined, §15-22-23.
Duties.
Generally, §15-22-24.
Mandatory nature of board duties, §15-22-38.
Penalty for neglecting or failing to perform, §15-22-39.
Holding other offices prohibited, §15-22-20.
Incentive awards, §15-22-24.
Investigations, §§15-22-25, 15-22-28.
Limitation on powers of board, §15-22-37.
Meetings, §15-22-23.
Neglecting or failing to perform duty.
Penalty, §15-22-39.
Notice.
Action after notice, §15-22-23.
Meetings, §15-22-23.
Required prior to action, §15-22-36.

PAROLE—Cont'd

Board of pardons and paroles—Cont'd
Oath, §15-22-20.
Offices.
Furnishing of offices, §15-22-22.
Orders of board.
Conditions for ordering pardons, paroles, etc., §15-22-23.
Policy and procedural guidelines, §15-22-24.
Powers.
Generally, §15-22-24.
Qualifications of members, §15-22-20.
Quorum, §15-22-20.
Remission of fines or forfeitures.
Prerequisite conditions, §15-22-23.
Removal of members, §15-22-20.
Reports.
Annual report, §15-22-24.
Sentenced prisoner's social and criminal records, §15-22-25.
Representation of applicants before board.
No state official to appear or represent applicant, §15-22-24.
Restitution to victims of crimes.
Restitution centers.
Powers of board, §15-18-77.
Supervision of parolee's restitution, §15-18-74.
Restoration of civil and political rights.
Prerequisite conditions, §15-22-23.
Retirement.
Badge and pistol part of retirement benefits, §15-22-24.
Rules and regulations.
Adoption, §15-22-37.
Secretary.
Appointment, §15-22-21.
State employees' retirement system.
Members, §36-27-5.
Strict construction of board powers, §15-22-38.
Supplies.
Furnishing of supplies, §15-22-22.
Terms of office, §15-22-20.
Transfer of prisoners to federal government or other jurisdiction, §15-22-24.
Vacancies.
Filling vacancies, §15-22-20.

Community residential facility.
Fees and charges to parolees, §15-22-30.

Compacts.
Interstate compacts, §15-22-1.

Conditions of parole.
Rules and regulations, §15-22-29.

PAROLE—Cont'd

Constitution of Alabama.
Authority of governor, Const. Ala., art. V, §124.
Board of pardons and parole, Const. Ala., art. V, §124.
Legislature to regulate, Const. Ala., amd. 38.

Costs.
Community residential facilities.
Charging parolees room and board, §15-22-30.
Contributions by parolees toward costs of supervision and rehabilitation.
Generally, §15-22-2.
Retaking of parolee.
Fees for execution of warrant, §15-22-31.

County jails.
Deductions from sentence.
Effect of deductions on parole, §14-9-42.

Death sentence commuted to life imprisonment, §15-22-27.

Definitions.
Board of pardons and paroles.
Due notice, §15-22-23.

Delinquency.
Criminal justice information center.
Supplying information on delinquent parolees, §41-9-635.
Declaration of parole violator as delinquent, §15-22-32.

Discharge from parole, §15-22-33.

Educational release.
Escape, §15-22-74.
Violations, §15-22-74.

Eligibility.
Minimum sentence to be served prior to eligibility, §15-22-28.
Standards for release, §15-22-26.

Executions.
Retaking of parolee.
Execution of warrant, §15-22-31.

Felonies.
Certain repeat offenders, §15-22-27.1.
Persons sentenced to life imprisonment upon second conviction of class A felonies, §15-22-27.2.

Hearing.
Parole court to be held upon return of prisoner, §15-22-32.

Investigations.
Board to investigate sentenced prisoner's social and criminal records, §15-22-25.
Duty of board, §15-22-28.

Jails.
Deductions from sentence.
Effect of deductions on parole, §14-9-42.

Legislature.
Regulation of paroles, Const. Ala., amd. 38.

PAROLE—Cont'd

Life sentence without parole.
Appointment of experienced counsel for indigent defendants, §13A-5-54.

Minimum sentence to be served prior to eligibility, §15-22-28.

Municipal parole boards.
Appointment of members, §15-22-70.
Approval of board.
Number required, §15-22-71.
Authority, §15-22-72.
Construction and interpretation of article, §15-22-77.
Duties, §15-22-72.
Meetings, §15-22-71.
Number of members, §15-22-70.
Parole officers.
Appointment, §15-22-73.
Powers, §15-22-72.
Quorum, §15-22-70.
Terms of office, §15-22-70.

Notice.
Board of pardons and paroles.
Meetings, §15-22-23.
Due notice, §15-22-23.
Required notice prior to action, §15-22-36.

Parole officers.
Appointment, §15-22-73.
Cooperation with courts, §15-22-35.
Disclosure.
Public inspection of reports, records and data, §15-22-73.
Powers and duties, §15-22-73.
Reports.
Municipal parole boards may require, §15-22-73.

Penalties.
Board of pardons and paroles.
Liability of members for neglecting or failing to perform duty, §15-22-39.

Penitentiary.
Deductions from sentence.
Effect of deductions on parole, §14-9-42.

Permission to leave state or county, §15-22-33.

Prisons and prisoners.
Deductions from sentence.
Effect, §14-9-42.

Records.
Board to report on prisoner's social and criminal records, §15-22-25.
Furnishing by board of corrections, §15-22-34.

Remission of fines and forfeitures.
Authority of board, §15-22-36.

Repeat offenders.
Certain felonies, §§15-22-27.1, 15-22-27.2.

Reports.
Board of pardons and paroles, §15-22-24.

PAROLE—Cont'd

Reports—Cont'd
Board to report on sentenced prisoner's social and criminal records, §15-22-25.
Parole officers.
Municipal parole boards may require, §15-22-73.
Relief from reports, §15-22-33.

Restitution to victims of crimes.
Default by parolee.
Effect, §15-18-72.
Payment of restitution.
Condition of parole, §15-18-71.
Restitution centers.
Powers of board of pardons and paroles, §15-18-77.
Supervision of parolee's restitution, §15-18-74.

Retaking parolee.
Arrest without warrant, §15-22-31.
Parole court to be held upon return of prisoner, §15-22-32.
Warrant, §15-22-31.

Rules and regulations.
Adoption by board of pardons and paroles, §§15-22-29, 15-22-37.

Standards for release of prisoners on parole, §15-22-26.

Temporary leave, §15-22-28.

Travel.
Permission to leave state or county, §15-22-33.

Violations.
Arrest, §15-22-76.
Declaration of parole violator as delinquent, §15-22-32.
Educational release, §15-22-74.
Paroles granted in violation null and void, §15-22-40.
Retaking parolee, §15-22-31.
Work release, §15-22-74.

Void parole.
Parole granted contrary to provisions of article, §15-22-40.

Warrants.
Retaking of parolee, §15-22-31.

Weapons.
Pistol of probation and parole officer included in retirement benefits, §15-22-24.

Work release.
Revocation, §15-22-74.
Violations, §15-22-74.
Wages.
Deduction and disbursement by city, §15-22-75.

PAROL EVIDENCE.

Commercial code.
Sales contracts.
Parol or extrinsic evidence, §7-2-202.

Foreign countries.
Production of books, etc.
Parol in lieu of, §12-21-3.

PAROL EVIDENCE—Cont'd
Foreign countries—Cont'd
Proof of laws of foreign
countries, §12-21-64.
Receipt of money, §12-21-110.
Void writing.
Admissibility of parol
evidence to show,
§12-21-33.
General provisions.
See EVIDENCE.
Sales.
Contracts.
Parol or extrinsic evidence,
§7-2-202.

PARTIES.
Appeals.
Substitution of parties,
ARAP, Rule 43.
Associations.
Actions against, §6-7-81.
Right to commence actions,
§6-7-80.
Bankruptcy and insolvency.
Proceedings when defendant
involved in bankruptcy,
§6-7-30.
Capacity, ARCP, Rule 17 (b).
Pleading, ARCP, Rule 9 (a).
Child custody proceedings.
Uniform child custody
jurisdiction act.
Joinder and appearance of
parties, §§30-3-30,
30-3-31.
Class actions, ARCP, Rule 23.
Commercial code.
See COMMERCIAL CODE.
Conveyances.
Reformation.
Grantors, etc., may be
made parties
defendant, §35-4-152.
Criminal law and procedure,
§§13A-2-20 to 13A-2-26.
See CRIMINAL LAW AND
PROCEDURE.
Death.
Abatement, revival and
survival of actions,
§§6-5-460 to 6-5-466;
Const. Ala., art. IV, §95.
See ABATEMENT,
REVIVAL AND
SURVIVAL OF
ACTIONS.
Substitution of parties,
ARCP, Rule 25 (a), (d).
Declaratory judgments.
Persons to be made parties,
§6-6-227.
Deeds.
Reformation of deeds.
Grantors, etc., may be
made parties
defendant, §35-4-152.
Defendants.
Multiple defendants.
Service of process, ARCP,
Rule 4 (f).
Fictitious parties, ARCP,
Rule 9 (h).
Guardian and ward.
Curators.
Appeals, §26-7A-16.
Infants and incompetents.
Actions against guardians
of persons of unsound
mind, §6-7-102.

PARTIES—Cont'd
Guardian and ward—Cont'd
Infants and incompetents
—Cont'd
Substitution of guardian
for next friend pending
action, §6-7-100.
Husband and wife.
Prosecution or defense of
actions in name of
husband by wife, §6-7-1.
Infants and incompetents,
ARCP, Rule 17 (c).
Guardian ad litem.
Action for improper
appointment, §6-7-103.
Guardians.
Actions against guardians
of persons of unsound
minds, §6-7-102.
Substitution for next friend
pending action,
§6-7-100.
Next friend.
Substitution of guardian
for next friend pending
action, §6-7-100.
Substitution pending action,
ARCP, Rule 25 (b).
Death of ward, §6-7-101.
Guardian for next friend,
§6-7-100.
Interpleader, ARCP, Rule 22.
Interrogatories to parties,
ARCP, Rule 33; Forms 47
to 49, 63, 64.
Intervention.
Form of motion to intervene,
ARCP, Form 32.
Intervention of right, ARCP,
Rule 24 (a).
Permissive intervention,
ARCP, Rule 24 (b).
Procedure, ARCP, Rule 24
(c).
Joinder.
See JOINDER.
**Joint tenants and tenants in
common.**
Action against cotenant or
coparcener, §6-7-40.
**Mechanics' and
materialmen's liens.**
Enforcement of liens,
§35-11-223.
Mentally ill.
Infants and incompetents.
See within this heading,
"Infants and
incompetents."
Substitution of parties,
ARCP, Rule 25 (b).
Military affairs.
Persons in federal service
and spouses living in
state deemed residents
for purpose of
commencing actions,
§6-7-20.
Minors.
Infants and incompetents.
See within this heading,
"Infants and
incompetents."
**Mortgages and deeds of
trust.**
Reformation.
Grantors, etc., may be
made parties
defendant, §35-4-152.

PARTIES—Cont'd
Multiple parties.
Defendants.
Service of process, ARCP,
Rule 4 (f).
Judgments involving
multiple parties, ARCP,
Rule 54 (b).
Service of process.
Multiple defendants,
ARCP, Rule 4 (f).
Striking jurors, ARCP, Rule
47 (c).
Municipal corporations.
Allegations.
Statute, ordinance or
franchise
unconstitutional,
§6-6-227.
Persons to be made parties,
§6-6-227.
Service upon attorney
general, §6-6-227.
Names of parties.
Pleadings, ARCP, Rule 10
(a).
Next friend.
Infants and incompetents.
Substitution of guardian
for next friend pending
action, §6-7-100.
Nonconsenting plaintiff.
Right to recovery, §6-7-50.
Use of name by another
plaintiff, §6-7-50.
Nonjoinder, ARCP, Rule 21.
Parent and child.
Prosecution or defense of
actions in name of father
by mother, §6-7-1.
Partition.
Action against cotenant or
coparcener, §6-7-40.
Probate courts.
See PARTITION.
Partnerships.
Commencing action against
partnership in common
name or against any
associates thereof,
§6-7-70.
Persons to be made parties,
§6-6-227.
Plaintiffs.
Nonconsenting plaintiff,
§6-7-50.
Political parties.
General provisions.
See ELECTIONS.
Public officers.
Death or separation from
office.
Substitution of parties,
ARCP, Rule 25 (d).
Public service commission.
Proceedings before
commission, §37-1-87.
Right of party to be heard in
person or by attorney,
§37-1-88.
Real party in interest, ARCP,
Rule 17 (a).
**Rights of persons not
parties,** §6-6-227.
Rules of civil procedure.
See RULES OF CIVIL
PROCEDURE.
Service of process.
Multiple defendants, ARCP,
Rule 4 (f).

PARTIES—Cont'd
  Substitution of parties.
    Death, ARCP, Rule 25 (a).
      Public officers, ARCP, Rule
        25 (d).
    Forms, ARCP, Forms 39, 40.
    Incompetency, ARCP, Rule
      25 (b).
    Public officers.
      Death or separation from
        office, ARCP, Rule 25
        (d).
    Transfer of interest, ARCP,
      Rule 25 (c).
  Third-party practice.
    See THIRD-PARTY
      PRACTICE.
  Transfer of interest.
    Substitution of parties,
      ARCP, Rule 25 (c).
  Uniform commercial code.
    See COMMERCIAL CODE.
  United States.
    Actions to which United
      States a party, Const. U.
      S., Art. III.
    Persons in federal service
      and spouses living in
      state deemed residents
      for purpose of
      commencing actions,
      §6-7-20.
  Wills.
    Contesting validity of wills,
      §43-8-200.

PARTITION, §§35-6-1 to
  35-6-126.
  Actions.
    Fences.
      Action to recover costs and
        expenses, §35-7-7.
    Trial of title or adverse claim
      issues, §6-8-1.
  Adverse claim or title.
    Probate courts.
      Partition not made when
        adverse claim or title
        asserted, §35-6-55.
  Annulment.
    Circuit courts, §35-6-50.
  Appeals.
    Crops, §35-6-124.
  Application for partition.
    Crops. See within this
      heading, "Crops."
    Probate courts. See within
      this heading, "Probate
      courts."
  Assignments.
    Crops.
      Article applicable to
        assignees, §35-6-126.
  Attorneys at law.
    Fees.
      Attorney's fees paid as part
        of costs, §34-3-60.
  Bonds, surety.
    Crops.
      Forthcoming bond,
        §35-6-114.
  Circuit courts, §§35-16-20 to
    35-16-25.
    Adjustment of equities,
      §35-6-23.
    Annulment of partition,
      §35-6-50.
    Commissioner.
      Partition without
        commissioners,
        §35-6-24.

PARTITION—Cont'd
  Circuit courts—Cont'd
    Defendants.
      Judgment not affected by
        death of defendant,
        §35-6-25.
      Service of process on
        certain parties
        defendant, §35-6-25.
    Equity.
      Adjustment of equities,
        §35-6-23.
    Guardian ad litem.
      Appointment, §35-6-25.
    Interpleader, §35-6-21.
    Jurisdiction to divide or sell
      for partition, §35-6-20.
    Owelty, §35-6-24.
    Questions of title.
      Determination, §35-6-23.
    Rights of parties.
      Duty of court to declare
        rights of parties,
        §35-6-22.
    Service of process on certain
      parties defendant,
      §35-6-25.
    Title.
      Questions of title.
        Determination, §35-6-23.
  Commissioners.
    Circuit courts.
      Partition without
        commissioners,
        §35-6-24.
    Crops. See within this
      heading, "Crops."
    Fees, §35-6-53.
    Probate courts. See within
      this heading, "Probate
      courts."
    Sale instead of partition,
      §§35-6-62, 35-6-64.
  Contingent interest.
    Partition of freehold devised
      with contingent interest,
      §19-3-170.
  Conveyances.
    Sale of land of minors and
      insane persons for
      distribution among joint
      owners, §§35-6-87,
      35-6-88.
  Costs.
    Crops, §35-6-123.
    Fences.
      Action to recover costs and
        expenses, §35-7-7.
    Probate courts, §35-6-54.
  Counties.
    Probate courts.
      Partition of land lying
        partly in different
        counties, §35-6-41.
    Unclaimed money.
      Deposit in county treasury,
        §35-6-1.
  Crops, §§35-6-110 to 35-6-126.
    Appeals, §35-6-124.
    Applicability of article.
      Article applicable to
        assignees, §35-6-126.
    Application for partition.
      By whom application
        made, §35-6-110.
      Contents of application,
        §35-6-111.
      Notice, §35-6-113.
    Assignments.
      Article applicable to
        assignees, §35-6-126.

PARTITION—Cont'd
  Crops—Cont'd
    Bonds, surety.
      Forthcoming bond,
        §35-6-114.
    Commissioners.
      Appointment, §35-6-117.
      Duties, §35-6-117.
      Oath of commissioners,
        §35-6-117.
      Replacement of
        commissioners upon
        failure to act,
        §35-6-119.
      Reports, §35-6-117.
      Confirming or setting
        aside report,
        §35-6-120.
      Impracticability of
        partition, §35-6-118.
      Objections to
        commissioners'
        report, §35-6-120.
      Return, §35-6-117.
    Costs, §35-6-123.
    Decrees.
      Partition or sale,
        §35-6-115.
    Delivery of shares, §35-6-121.
    Fees, §35-6-123.
    Forthcoming bond, §35-6-114.
    Guardian ad litem.
      Appointment, §35-6-112.
    Hearing.
      Notice of hearing,
        §35-6-113.
      Time for hearing,
        §35-6-112.
    Impracticability of partition.
      Sale when partition
        impracticable,
        §35-6-118.
    Jury trial, §35-6-122.
    Liens.
      Effect of partition on
        existing liens,
        §35-6-115.
    Nonresidents, §35-6-113.
    Notice.
      Application and hearing,
        §35-6-113.
    Objections to commissioners'
      report, §35-6-120.
    Probate courts.
      Partition in probate courts.
        Article not applicable to
        partition of crops,
        §35-6-66.
    Probate judge.
      Distribution of proceeds of
        sale by probate judge,
        §35-6-116.
    Recordation of papers,
      §35-6-125.
    Remedies not exclusive,
      §35-6-126.
    Reports.
      Commissioners, §35-6-117.
      Confirming or setting
        aside report,
        §35-6-120.
      Impracticability of
        partition, §35-6-118.
      Objections to
        commissioners'
        report, §35-6-120.
    Return of division by
      commissioners,
      §35-6-117.
    Sale.
      Decree of sale, §35-6-115.

PARTITION—Cont'd
Crops—Cont'd
Sale—Cont'd
Distribution of proceeds by
probate judge,
§35-6-116.
Sheriff, §35-6-116.
When partition
impracticable,
§35-6-118.
Seizure of crops to be divided
by sheriff, §35-6-117.
Shares.
Delivery of shares,
§35-6-121.
Sheriff.
Sale by sheriff, §35-6-116.
Seizure of crops to be
divided by sheriff,
§35-6-117.
When sheriff ordered to
take possession of
crops, §35-6-114.
Trial by jury, §35-6-122.
What crops subject to
partition, §35-6-110.
Custodians.
Sale of land of minors and
insane persons for
distribution among joint
owners.
Contest by custodian,
§35-6-84.
Death.
Circuit courts.
Judgment not affected by
death of defendant,
§35-6-25.
Executors or administrators
of deceased parties.
Partition in probate courts.
Applicability of article,
§35-6-65.
Probate courts.
Completion of partition by
substitute
commissioner,
§35-6-52.
Sale instead of partition.
Completion of sale by
substitute
commissioner,
§35-6-64.
Decrees.
Crops.
Decree of partition or sale,
§35-6-115.
Probate courts.
Decree for partition,
§35-6-45.
Sale instead of partition,
§35-6-62.
Recordation of decrees,
§35-6-58.
Definitions.
Partition fence, §35-7-1.
Equity.
Circuit courts.
Adjustment of equities,
§35-6-23.
Evidence.
Probate courts.
Record of application as
evidence, §35-6-49.
Sale instead of partition,
§35-6-61.

PARTITION—Cont'd
**Executors and
administrators.**
Partition in probate courts.
Article applicable to
executors or
administrators of
deceased parties,
§35-6-65.
Expenses.
Probate courts, §35-6-54.
Family.
Sale of land of minors and
insane persons for
distribution among joint
owners.
Contest by next of kin,
§35-6-84.
Fees.
Attorney's fees paid as part
of costs, §34-3-60.
Commissioners, §35-6-53.
Crops, §35-6-123.
Fences.
Orders of court, §35-7-5.
Fences.
Action to recover costs and
expenses, §35-7-7.
Costs.
Action to recover costs and
expenses, §35-7-7.
Defined, §35-7-1.
Expenses.
Action to recover expenses,
§35-7-7.
Expenses to be borne
proportionately by
adjoining owners,
§35-7-3.
Failure of parties to agree.
Ascertainment of amount
to be paid upon
failure, §35-7-4.
Fees.
Orders of court, §35-7-5.
Orders of court.
Amount to be paid upon
failure of parties to
agree, §35-7-4.
Fees, §35-7-5.
Repairs.
Action to recover costs and
expenses, §35-7-7.
Expenses to be borne
proportionately by
adjoining owners,
§35-7-3.
Joint owners authorized to
make repairs, §35-7-2.
Viewers.
Generally, §35-7-6.
Oath of viewers, §35-7-6.
**Forthcoming and delivery
bonds.**
Crops.
Forthcoming bond,
§35-6-114.
Guardian ad litem.
Circuit courts.
Appointment of guardian
ad litem, §35-6-25.
Crops.
Appointment of guardian
ad litem for partition
of crops, §35-6-112.
Probate courts.
Appointment of guardian
ad litem, §35-6-43.
Sale instead of partition,
§35-6-60.

PARTITION—Cont'd
Guardian ad litem—Cont'd
Sale instead of partition,
§35-6-60.
Sale of land of minors and
insane persons for
distribution among joint
owners.
Appointment of guardian
ad litem, §35-6-83.
Guardian and ward.
Sale of land of minors and
insane persons for
distribution among joint
owners, §§35-6-80 to
35-6-91. See within this
heading, "Sale of land of
minors and insane
persons for distribution
among joint owners."
Hearings.
Crops.
Notice, §35-6-113.
Time, §35-6-112.
Probate courts, §35-6-43.
Sale instead of partition,
§§35-6-59, 35-6-60.
Sale of land of minors and
insane persons for
distribution among joint
owners, §§35-6-82,
35-6-85.
Insane persons.
Sale of land of insane
persons for distribution
among joint owners,
§§35-6-80 to 35-6-91. See
within this heading,
"Sale of land of minors
and insane persons for
distribution among joint
owners."
Interpleader.
Circuit courts, §35-6-21.
Jurisdiction.
Circuit courts, §35-6-20.
Probate courts, §12-13-1.
Jury.
Crops.
Trial by jury, §35-6-122.
Liens.
Crops.
Effect of partition on
existing liens, §35-6-115.
Effect of partition on liens,
§35-6-51.
Mentally ill.
Sale of land of insane
persons for distribution
among joint owners,
§§35-6-80 to 35-6-91. See
within this heading,
"Sale of land of minors
and insane persons for
distribution among joint
owners."
Minors.
Probate courts.
Interests of minors
considered, §35-6-45.
Sale of land of minors for
distribution among joint
owners, §§35-6-80 to
35-6-91. See within this
heading, "Sale of land of
minors and insane
persons for distribution
among joint owners."
Nonresidents.
Crops, §35-6-113.

PARTITION—Cont'd
  Nonresidents—Cont'd
    Probate courts.
      Nonresidents as parties,
        §35-6-43.
    Sale instead of partition.
      Nonresidents as parties,
        §35-6-60.
  Notice.
    Crops.
      Notice of application and
        hearing for partition of
        crops, §35-6-113.
    Probate courts.
      Notice of partition,
        §§35-6-43, 35-6-47.
    Sale instead of partition.
      Notice of hearing, §35-6-60.
    Sale of land of minors and
      insane persons for
      distribution among joint
      owners.
      Notice of hearing, §35-6-82.
  Orders of court.
    Fences.
      Amount to be paid upon
        failure of parties to
        agree, §35-7-4.
      Fees for orders, §35-7-5.
    Sale instead of partition,
      §35-6-62.
    Sale of land of minors and
      insane persons for
      distribution among joint
      owners, §§35-6-85,
      35-6-87.
    Unclaimed money.
      Payment upon order of
        court, §35-6-1.
  Owelty.
    Partition in circuit courts,
      §35-6-24.
  Parties.
    Action against cotenant or
      coparcener, §6-7-40.
    Probate courts. See within
      this heading, "Probate
      courts."
    Sale instead of partition.
      Nonresidents as parties,
        §35-6-60.
  Probate courts, §§35-6-40 to
    35-6-66.
    Adverse claim or title.
      Partition not made when
        adverse claim or title
        asserted, §35-6-55.
    Annulment of partition by
      circuit court, §35-6-50.
    Applicability of article.
      Crops.
        Article not applicable to
          partition of crops,
          §35-6-66.
      Executors or
        administrators of
        deceased parties,
        §35-6-65.
    Application for partition.
      By whom application
        made, §35-6-40.
      Contents, §35-6-42.
      Filing of application,
        §35-6-49.
      Recordation, §35-6-49.
    Commissioners.
      Appointment, §35-6-45.

PARTITION—Cont'd
  Probate courts—Cont'd
    Commissioners—Cont'd
      Death.
        Completion of partition
          by substitute
          commissioner,
          §35-6-52.
      Determination and
        statement by
        commissioners,
        §35-6-48.
      Duties, §35-6-46.
      Fees, §35-6-53.
      Neglect.
        Completion of partition
          by substitute
          commissioner,
          §35-6-52.
      Notice of partition,
        §35-6-47.
      Oath of commissioners,
        §35-6-46.
      Resignation.
        Completion of partition
          by substitute
          commissioner,
          §35-6-52.
      Statement by
        commissioners,
        §35-6-48.
      Substitute commissioners.
        Completion of partition
          by substitute
          commissioner,
          §35-6-52.
    Costs, §35-6-54.
    Crops.
      Article not applicable to
        partition of crops,
        §35-6-66.
      Distribution of proceeds of
        sale by probate judge,
        §35-6-116.
    Death of commissioner.
      Completion of partition by
        substitute
        commissioner,
        §35-6-52.
    Death of party.
      Executors or
        administrators of
        deceased parties.
        Applicability of article,
          §35-6-65.
    Decrees, §35-6-45.
      Sale instead of partition,
        §§35-6-58, 35-6-62.
    Defendants.
      Proceedings against
        unknown persons and
        certain other parties
        defendant, §35-6-44.
    Different counties.
      Partition of land lying
        partly in different
        counties, §35-6-41.
    Evidence.
      Record of application as
        evidence, §35-6-49.
    Executors or administrators
      of deceased parties.
      Applicability of article,
        §35-6-65.
    Expenses, §35-6-54.
    Fees of commissioners,
      §35-6-53.
    Guardian ad litem.
      Appointment, §35-6-43.
      Sale instead of partition,
        §35-6-60.

PARTITION—Cont'd
  Probate courts—Cont'd
    Hearing, §35-6-43.
      Sale instead of partition,
        §§35-6-59, 35-6-60.
      Time of hearing, §35-6-43.
    Jurisdiction, §12-13-1.
    Liens.
      Effect of partition on liens,
        §35-6-51.
    Minors.
      Interests of minors
        considered, §35-6-45.
    Nonresidents as parties,
      §35-6-43.
    Notice of hearing, §35-6-43.
    Notice of partition, §35-6-47.
    Orders of court.
      Sale instead of partition,
        §35-6-62.
    Parties.
      Executors or
        administrators of
        deceased parties.
        Applicability of article,
          §35-6-65.
      Nonresidents as parties,
        §35-6-43.
      Proceedings against
        unknown persons and
        certain other parties
        defendant, §35-6-44.
    Property subject to partition,
      §35-6-40.
    Recordation of application for
      partition, §35-6-49.
    Remedy not exclusive,
      §35-6-56.
    Sale instead of partition. See
      within this heading,
      "Sale instead of
      partition."
    Title.
      Adverse claim or title.
        Partition not made when
          adverse claim or
          title asserted,
          §35-6-55.
      Partition vests title,
        §35-6-50.
    Unknown persons.
      Proceedings against
        unknown persons,
        §35-6-44.
  Purchase of interest of joint
    owner filing for
    partition.
    Appraisal.
      Costs, §35-6-104.
    Court appointment of
      appraisers or
      commissioners,
      §35-6-101.
    Effect of failure to pay
      purchase price,
      §35-6-103.
    Notice by prospective
      purchasers.
      Required, §35-6-100.
    Payment, §35-6-102.
    Provision by court for
      purchase of filing joint
      owners' interests,
      §35-6-100.
    Transfer of title to property,
      §35-6-102.
  Questions of title.
    Circuit courts.
      Determination of questions
        of title, §35-6-23.

PARTITION—Cont'd
Recordation.
Crops.
Recordation of papers,
§35-6-125.
Decree of sale, §35-6-58.
Probate courts.
Recordation of application
for partition, §35-6-49.
Relatives.
Sale of land of minors and
insane persons for
distribution among joint
owners.
Contest by next of kin,
§35-6-84.
**Remainders, reversions and
executory interests.**
Freehold devised with
contingent interest,
§19-3-170.
Remedies.
Crops.
Remedies not exclusive,
§35-6-126.
Reports.
Crops. See within this
heading, "Crops."
Sale of land of minors and
insane persons for
distribution among joint
owners, §§35-6-81,
35-6-87.
Sale instead of partition,
§§35-6-57 to 35-6-64.
Application for sale.
By whom made, §35-6-58.
Commissioners.
Appointment of
commissioner,
§35-6-62.
Death.
Completion of sale by
substitute
commissioner,
§35-6-64.
Neglect.
Completion of sale by
substitute
commissioner,
§35-6-64.
Resignation.
Completion of sale by
substitute
commissioner,
§35-6-64.
Substitute commissioner.
Completion of sale by
substitute
commissioner,
§35-6-64.
Conduct of sale, §35-6-62.
Crops. See within this
heading, "Crops."
Decree, §35-6-62.
Recordation, §35-6-58.
Distribution of purchase
money, §35-6-63.
Evidence, §35-6-61.
Guardian ad litem.
Appointment, §35-6-60.
Hearing.
Notice of hearing, §35-6-60.
Time for hearing, §35-6-59.
Nonresidents as parties,
§35-6-60.
Notice of hearing, §35-6-60.
Orders of court, §35-6-62.
Parties.
Nonresidents as parties,
§35-6-60.

PARTITION—Cont'd
Sale instead of partition
—Cont'd
Payment of purchase money,
§35-6-63.
Place of sale, §35-6-58.
Property subject to sale,
§35-6-58.
Purchase money.
Payment and distribution,
§35-6-63.
Recordation of decrees,
§35-6-58.
When sale ordered, §35-6-57.
Where sale held, §35-6-58.
**Sale of land of minors and
insane persons for
distribution among joint
owners, §§35-6-80 to
35-6-91.**
Confirmation of sale.
Certificate of conveyance
by judge, §35-6-88.
Order confirming sale,
§35-6-85.
Sale void unless to
advantage of ward and
confirmed by court,
§35-6-89.
Contest by custodian and
next of kin, §35-6-84.
Conveyances.
Certificate by judge,
§35-6-88.
Order for conveyance,
§35-6-87.
Presenting to court.
Required, §35-6-88.
Custodian.
Contest by custodian,
§35-6-84.
Disadvantageous sales.
Sale void unless to
advantage of ward,
§35-6-89.
Guardian ad litem.
Appointment, §35-6-83.
Guardians.
Authority of guardian,
§35-6-90.
Successor guardian,
§35-6-90.
Contest by custodian and
next of kin, §35-6-84.
Eligibility to make sale,
§35-6-80.
Limitation on guardian's
authority, §35-6-90.
Report of sale to court,
§35-6-81.
Hearing.
Conduct generally,
§35-6-85.
Notice of hearing, §35-6-82.
Time of hearing, §35-6-82.
Multiple sales, §35-6-86.
Next of kin.
Contest by next of kin,
§35-6-84.
Notice of hearing, §35-6-82.
Orders of court.
Confirmation of sale,
§35-6-85.
Order for conveyance,
§35-6-87.
Payment.
Report of payment,
§35-6-87.
Provisions of article not
exclusive, §35-6-91.

PARTITION—Cont'd
**Sale of land of minors and
insane persons for
distribution among joint
owners**—Cont'd
Reports.
Guardian to report sale to
court, §35-6-81.
Payment, §35-6-87.
Time of sale, §35-6-80.
Void sale.
Sale void unless to
advantage of ward and
confirmed by court,
§35-6-89.
When sale made, §35-6-80.
Who may make sale,
§35-6-80.
Searches and seizures.
Crops.
Seizure of crops to be
divided by sheriff,
§35-6-117.
Service of process.
Circuit courts.
Service on certain parties
defendant, §35-6-25.
Sheriffs.
Crops. See within this
heading, "Crops."
Title.
Circuit courts.
Determination of questions
of title, §35-6-23.
Probate courts.
Adverse claim or title.
Partition not made when
adverse claim or
title asserted,
§35-6-55.
Partition vests title,
§35-6-50.
Trial.
Crops.
Trial by jury, §35-6-122.
Unclaimed money.
Deposit in county treasury,
§35-6-1.
Unknown persons.
Probate courts.
Proceedings against
unknown persons,
§35-6-44.

**PARTLOW STATE SCHOOL
AND HOSPITAL.**
Bond issues.
Building construction and
improvement purposes,
Const. Ala., amds. 113,
118.
State school and hospital.
Streets.
Construction and
maintenance.
State highway
department,
§23-1-42.

PARTNERSHIPS, §§10-8-1 to
10-9A-200.
Accountants.
See ACCOUNTANTS.
Accounts and accounting.
Dissolution.
Partner's right to account
of interest in
partnership, §10-8-98.

PARTNERSHIPS—Cont'd
Accounts and accounting
  —Cont'd
  Limited partnerships formed
    since January 1, 1972.
    Dissolution.
      Settling of accounts,
        §10-9A-144.
  Partner accountable as
    fiduciary, §10-8-48.
  Right of partner to formal
    accounting, §10-8-47.
Actions.
  Derivative actions.
    Limited partnerships,
      §§10-9A-180 to
      10-9A-183.
  Parties.
    Commencing action
      against partnership in
      common name or
      against any associates
      thereof, §6-7-70.
Admission of partner.
  Evidence against
    partnership, §10-8-50.
Agents.
  Dissolution.
    Binding of partnership by
      partner after
      dissolution, §10-8-95.
    Effect on authority of
      partners, §10-8-94.
  Liability of partner by
    estoppel, §10-8-55.
  Limited partnerships.
    Maintenance, §10-9A-3.
  Partners as agents of
    partnership, §10-8-49.
Agriculture.
  Acts or omissions of officers
    or agents, §2-1-2.
Applicability of chapter.
  Certain associations not
    affected by chapter,
    §10-8-5.
  Certain statutes not affected
    by chapter, §10-8-7.
  Limited partnerships.
    Applicability of chapter to
      limited partnerships,
      §10-8-5.
Architects.
  Certificates of authorization,
    §34-2-35.
  Renewal.
    Fee, §34-2-35.
Assets.
  Dissolution.
    Distribution of assets,
      §10-8-99.
Assignments, §§10-8-72,
  10-8-102.
  Limited partnerships.
    Assignment of partnership
      interest, §10-9A-121.
    Right of assignee to
      become limited
      partner, §10-9A-123.
  Partner's interest, §§10-8-41,
    10-8-72.
  Rights of assignees, §10-8-41.
Attachment.
  Exemption of partner's
    interest, §10-8-72.
Auctions and auctioneers.
  Effect of license issued to
    partnership, §34-4-28.

PARTNERSHIPS—Cont'd
Authority of partners.
  Dissolution.
    Binding of partnership by
      partner after
      dissolution, §10-8-95.
    Effect on authority,
      §10-8-94.
Bankruptcy and insolvency.
  Dissolution, §10-8-91.
Books.
  Inspection of partnership
    books, §10-8-45.
  Keeping of partnership
    books, §10-8-45.
Breach of trust.
  Liability of partnership for
    breach of trust, §10-8-54.
**Cases not provided for by
  chapter.**
  Rules, §10-8-4.
Citation of chapter, §10-8-1.
**Conduct of partnership
  business.**
  Rights and duties of
    partners, §10-8-43.
Constitution of Alabama.
  Regulation of partnerships,
    Const. Ala., art. IV,
    §103.
**Construction and
  interpretation.**
  Construction of chapter,
    §10-8-6.
  "Knowledge" or "notice" of a
    fact, §10-8-3.
  Limited partnerships.
    Construction of article,
      §10-9A-200.
Contracts.
  Dissolution.
    Covenants not to compete,
      §8-1-1.
  Fraud.
    Rights where contracts
      rescinded for fraud,
      §10-8-44.
  Misrepresentation.
    Rights where contract
      rescinded for
      misrepresentation,
      §10-8-44.
Contributions by partners.
  Dissolution, §10-8-99.
    Right to contribution from
      copartners, §10-8-100.
  Limited partnerships. See
    within this heading,
    "Limited partnerships."
Conveyances.
  Real property, §10-8-73.
Corporations.
  Participation in partnerships,
    §10-2A-23.
Curtesy.
  Property not subject to
    curtesy, §10-8-72.
Death.
  Disposition of partnership
    property, §10-8-72.
  Dissolution.
    Death of partner, §10-8-91.
    Liability of deceased
      partners, §10-8-101.
  Duty of partners to render
    information to legal
    representative of
    deceased partner,
    §10-8-46.

PARTNERSHIPS—Cont'd
Death—Cont'd
  Limited partnerships.
    Death of general partner,
      §10-9A-61.
    Powers of successors in
      interest, §10-9A-124.
    Rights of estate of deceased
      partners, §10-8-103.
Debtors and creditors.
  Charging interest of debtor
    partner on application by
    judgment creditor,
    §10-8-42.
  Limited partnerships.
    Rights of judgment
      creditors of partners,
      §10-9A-122.
Decedents' estates.
  Disposition of partner's
    interest, §10-8-72.
  Rights of estate of deceased
    partner, §10-8-103.
Definitions, §§10-8-2, 10-8-3.
  Dissolution, §10-8-90.
  Limited partnerships,
    §10-9A-1.
Different partners.
  Continuing business with
    different partners,
    §10-8-102.
Disability.
  Duty of partners to render
    information to legal
    representative of partner
    under legal disability,
    §10-8-46.
Dissolution, §§10-8-90 to
  10-8-103.
  Accounts and accounting.
    Partner's right to account
      of interest in
      partnership, §10-8-98.
  Assets.
    Distribution of assets,
      §10-8-99.
  Authority of partners.
    Binding of partnership by
      partner after
      dissolution, §10-8-95.
    Effect on authority,
      §10-8-94.
  Causes, §10-8-91.
  Continuing business with
    new or different
    partners, §10-8-102.
  Contracts.
    Covenants not to compete,
      §8-1-1.
  Contributions by partners,
    §10-8-99.
    Right to contribution from
      copartners, §10-8-100.
    Exceptions, §10-8-100.
  Court ordered dissolution,
    §10-8-92.
  Deceased partners.
    Rights of estate of deceased
      partners, §10-8-103.
  Defined, §10-8-90.
  Different partners.
    Continuing business with
      different partners,
      §10-8-102.
  Effect on authority of
    partners, §10-8-94.
  Grounds, §10-8-91.
    Court-ordered dissolution,
      §10-8-92.

PARTNERSHIPS—Cont'd
Dissolution—Cont'd
Liability.
Binding of partnership by
partner after
dissolution, §10-8-95.
Deceased partners,
§10-8-101.
Discharge, §10-8-101.
Distribution of liabilities,
§10-8-99.
Effect of partner's existing
liability, §10-8-101.
New and retiring partners,
§10-8-102.
Right of contribution from
copartners, §10-8-100.
Limited partnerships. See
within this heading,
"Limited partnerships."
New partners, §10-8-102.
Order of court, §10-8-92.
Partnership not terminated,
§10-8-93.
Property.
Rights of partners
regarding partnership
property, §10-8-97.
Retiring partners.
Liability of retiring
partners, §10-8-102.
Rights of retiring partners,
§10-8-103.
Right to wind up affairs,
§10-8-96.
Termination.
Partnership not
terminated, §10-8-93.
Dower.
Property not subject to
dower, §10-8-72.
Duties of partners, §10-8-43.
Employment agencies.
Effect of admission of
partners on license,
§34-10-4.
Engineers.
Certificate of authorization,
§34-11-9.
Practice of engineering,
§34-11-9.
Disciplinary action,
§34-11-11.
Estoppel.
Liability of partner by
estoppel, §10-8-55.
Evidence.
Admission or representation
of partner as evidence
against partnership,
§10-8-50.
**Exemptions from levy and
sale under process.**
Partnership property,
§§6-10-9, 10-8-72.
Existence.
Continuation after
termination of term or
undertaking, §10-8-21.
Determination of whether
partnership exists,
§10-8-20.
Dissolution.
Partnership not
terminated, §10-8-93.
Term existence.
Continuation after
termination of term,
§10-8-21.

PARTNERSHIPS—Cont'd
Fiduciaries.
Definition of fiduciary,
§19-3-150.
Liability of fiduciary, estate
and beneficial owners,
§19-3-151.
Power of fiduciary to limit
liability of estate or
himself, §19-3-152.
Liability of partnership for
breach of trust, §10-8-54.
Partner accountable as
fiduciary, §10-8-48.
Right to participate in
partnership, §19-3-151.
**Foreign limited
partnerships,** §§10-9A-160
to 10-9A-167.
Foresters.
Partnerships not to be
licensed under chapter,
§34-12-10.
Fraud.
Rights where contract
rescinded for fraud,
§10-8-44.
Funeral establishments.
See FUNERALS.
**Hearing aid dealers and
fitters.**
Licenses.
Compliance with licensing
provisions, §34-14-2.
Homestead rights.
Property not subject to,
§10-8-72.
Income tax.
Generally, §40-18-24.
Returns, §40-18-28.
Indemnification of partners.
Rights and duties of
partners, §10-8-43.
Information.
Duty of partners to render
information, §10-8-46.
Injunctions.
Limited partnerships.
Foreign limited
partnerships.
Transaction of business
in violation of
provisions,
§10-9A-167.
Inspections.
Partnership books, §10-8-45.
Interest.
Maximum rates of interest.
Credit sales of $2,000 or
more to partnerships,
§8-8-5.
Loans of $2,000 or more to
partnerships, §8-8-5.
Interest of partners. See
within this heading,
"Partner's interest."
**Joint and several liability of
partners,** §10-8-52.
Knowledge.
Construction of "knowledge"
of a fact, §10-8-3.
Knowledge of one partner
operates as knowledge of
partnership, §10-8-51.
Landlord and tenant.
Incidents of tenancy,
§10-8-72.
Landscape architects,
§34-17-4.
Land surveyors, §34-11-9.

PARTNERSHIPS—Cont'd
Liability.
Breach of trust.
Liability of partnership for
breach of trust,
§10-8-54.
Deceased partners.
Liability upon dissolution,
§10-8-101.
Dissolution.
Binding of partnership by
partner after
dissolution, §10-8-95.
Deceased partners,
§10-8-101.
Discharge, §10-8-101.
Distribution of liabilities,
§10-8-99.
Effect of partner's existing
liability, §10-8-101.
New and retiring partners,
§10-8-102.
Right of contribution from
copartners, §10-8-100.
Estoppel.
Liability of partner by
estoppel, §10-8-55.
Joint and several liability of
partners, §10-8-52.
Limited partnerships. See
within this heading,
"Limited partnerships."
New partners, §10-8-102.
Obligations arising before
admission to partnership.
Liability of partner,
§10-8-56.
Partners' wrongful acts or
omissions.
Liability of partnership for
partners' wrongful acts
or omissions, §10-8-53.
Retiring partners, §10-8-102.
Licenses.
Applicability of chapter on
partnerships to limited
partnerships, §10-8-5.
Exemptions from licenses.
Disabled veterans,
§40-12-348.
Veterans of World War II,
§40-12-375.
Limited partnerships,
§§10-9A-1 to 10-9A-200.
Additional limited partners.
Admission, §10-9A-40.
Agents.
Maintenance, §10-9A-3.
Alabama partnership act.
Applicability, §10-9A-203.
Assignment of partnership
interest, §10-9A-121.
Right of assignee to
become limited
partner, §10-9A-123.
Businesses which may be
carried on, §10-9A-5.
Certificate of limited
partnership.
Amendment, §10-9A-21.
Judicial act, §10-9A-24.
Cancellation, §10-9A-22.
Judicial act, §10-9A-24.
Contents, §10-9A-20.
Defined, §10-9A-1.
Execution, §§10-9A-20,
10-9A-23.

PARTNERSHIPS—Cont'd
Limited partnerships—Cont'd
Certificate of limited
partnership—Cont'd
False statements and
certificates.
Liability of false
statements,
§10-9A-26.
Filing with probate judge,
§§10-9A-20, 10-9A-25.
Constructive notice that
partnership is
limited partnership,
§10-9A-27.
Liability for false
statements in
certificate, §10-9A-26.
Citation of chapter,
§10-9A-201.
Construction of article,
§10-9A-200.
Contributions.
Defined, §10-9A-1.
Form of contributions,
§10-9A-80.
General partners,
§10-9A-63.
Liability to partnership,
§10-9A-81.
Return.
Liability upon return,
§10-9A-107.
Creditors.
Rights of judgment
creditors of partners,
§10-9A-122.
Death of limited partner.
Powers of successors in
interest, §10-9A-124.
Definitions, §10-9A-1.
Derivative actions.
Costs, §10-9A-183.
Expenses, §10-9A-183.
Pleading, §10-9A-182.
Proper plaintiff,
§10-9A-181.
Right of action,
§10-9A-180.
Dissolution.
Judicial dissolution,
§10-9A-141.
Nonjudicial dissolution,
§10-9A-140.
Settling of accounts,
§10-9A-144.
Winding up, §10-9A-142.
Distribution.
In kind distribution,
§10-9A-104.
Interim distribution,
§10-9A-100.
Limitations, §10-9A-106.
Right to distribution,
§10-9A-105.
Sharing, §10-9A-83.
Winding up of partnership.
Distribution of assets,
§10-9A-143.
Withdrawal of partner,
§10-9A-103.
Foreign limited partnerships,
§§10-9A-160 to
10-9A-167.
Defined, §10-9A-1.
Law governing,
§10-9A-160.
Name, §10-9A-163.

PARTNERSHIPS—Cont'd
Limited partnerships—Cont'd
Foreign limited partnerships
—Cont'd
Registration.
Application, §10-9A-161.
Changes and
amendments,
§10-9A-164.
Cancellation,
§10-9A-165.
Certificate of
registration.
Issuance, §10-9A-162.
Failure to register,
§§10-9A-166,
10-9A-167.
Fees, §10-9A-161.
Filing requirements,
§10-9A-161.
Injunctions.
Transaction of
business in
violation of
provisions,
§10-9A-167.
General partners.
Admission of additional
general partners,
§10-9A-60.
Contributions, §10-9A-63.
Death, §10-9A-61.
Defined, §10-9A-1.
Liability, §10-9A-62.
Powers, §10-9A-62.
Voting, §10-9A-64.
Withdrawal, §§10-9A-61,
10-9A-101.
Inspection.
Records, §10-9A-4.
Judgment creditors.
Rights of judgment
creditors of partners,
§10-9A-122.
Judicial dissolution,
§10-9A-141.
Liability.
General partners,
§10-9A-62.
Limited partners,
§10-9A-42.
Partners to partnership,
§10-9A-81.
Return of contribution,
§10-9A-107.
Limited partners, §§10-9A-40
to 10-9A-43.
Withdrawal, §10-9A-102.
Limited partnerships formed
since January 1, 1972.
Accounts and accounting.
Dissolution.
Settling of accounts,
§10-9A-144.
Dissolution.
Settling of accounts,
§10-9A-144.
Loans by partners, §10-9A-6.
Losses.
Sharing, §10-9A-82.
Names, §10-9A-2.
Foreign limited
partnerships,
§10-9A-163.
Nature of business, §10-9A-5.
Nonjudicial dissolution,
§10-9A-140.
Obligations.
Liability of limited
partners to third
parties, §10-9A-42.

PARTNERSHIPS—Cont'd
Limited partnerships—Cont'd
Offices.
Maintenance, §10-9A-3.
Partner's interest.
Assignment of partnership
interest, §10-9A-121.
Right of assignee to
become limited
partner, §10-9A-123.
Limited partners interest
is personal property,
§10-9A-120.
Permitted businesses,
§10-9A-5.
Powers of partners.
General partners,
§10-9A-62.
Profits.
Sharing, §10-9A-82.
Property.
Partnership interest is
personal property,
§10-9A-120.
Records, §10-9A-4.
Repeal of prior provisions.
Effect, §10-9A-202.
Reports.
Initial report to secretary
of state, §10-9A-3.
Restriction of partners.
General partners,
§10-9A-62.
Rights of partners.
Financial records,
§10-9A-44.
General partners,
§10-9A-62.
Inspect and copy records,
§10-9A-44.
Rules for cases not provided
for in chapter,
§10-9A-203.
Short title of chapter,
§10-9A-201.
Status of person erroneously
believing himself limited
partner, §10-9A-43.
Third parties.
Liability of limited
partners to, §10-9A-42.
Time of formation,
§10-9A-20.
Transactions of partner with
partnership, §10-9A-6.
Voting.
General partners,
§10-9A-64.
Limited partners,
§10-9A-41.
Winding up, §10-9A-142.
Distribution of assets,
§10-9A-143.
Loans by partners.
Rights and duties of
partners, §10-8-43.
Management of partnership.
Rights and duties of
partners, §10-8-43.
Misrepresentation.
Rights where contract
rescinded for
misrepresentation,
§10-8-44.
Names.
Limited partnerships,
§10-9A-2.
Foreign limited
partnerships,
§10-9A-163.

PARTNERSHIPS—Cont'd
Names—Cont'd
  Use of word "trust" in
    corporate or partnership
    name, §§5-11A-1,
    5-11A-4.
New partners, §10-8-102.
Notice.
  Construction of "notice" of a
    fact, §10-8-3.
  Notice to one partner
    operates as notice to
    partnership, §10-8-51.
Omissions.
  Liability of partnership for
    partners' omissions,
    §10-8-53.
Orders of court.
  Dissolution, §10-8-92.
Parties.
  Commencing action against
    partnership in common
    name or against any
    associates thereof,
    §6-7-70.
Partner's interest.
  Assignment, §10-8-41.
  Debtor partner.
    Charging interest of debtor
      partner on application
      by judgment creditor,
      §10-8-42.
  Limited partnerships.
    Assignment of partnership
      interest, §10-9A-121.
    Right of assignee to
      become limited
      partner, §10-9A-123.
    Partnership interest is
      personal property,
      §10-9A-120.
  Nature of partner's interest,
    §10-8-40.
  Rights of assignees, §10-8-41.
Powers of partners.
  Limited partnerships.
    General partners,
      §10-9A-62.
Presumptions.
  Property.
    Presumptions as to
      partnership property,
      §10-8-70.
Promissory estoppel.
  Liability of partner by
    estoppel, §10-8-55.
Property.
  Conveyance of real property,
    §10-8-73.
  Co-ownership of specific
    partnership property,
    §10-8-72.
  Dissolution.
    Rights of partners
      regarding partnership
      property, §10-8-97.
  Dower, curtesy and
    homestead rights.
    Property not subject to,
      §10-8-72.
  Incidents of tenancy,
    §10-8-72.
  Limited partnerships.
    Partnership interest is
      personal property,
      §10-9A-120.
  Presumptions as to
    partnership property,
    §10-8-70.

PARTNERSHIPS—Cont'd
Property—Cont'd
  Rights of partners, §10-8-71.
  Dissolution.
    Rights of partners
      regarding
      partnership
      property, §10-8-97.
  Sale of real property,
    §10-8-73.
  What property considered
    partnership property,
    §10-8-70.
Real estate brokers,
  §34-27-32.
Real property. See within this
  heading, "Property."
Receivers.
  See RECEIVERS.
Records.
  Limited partnerships,
    §10-9A-4.
  Maintenance, §10-9A-4.
Reports.
  Limited partnerships.
    Initial report to secretary
      of state, §10-9A-3.
Representation of partner.
  Evidence against
    partnership, §10-8-50.
**Restitution to victims of
  crimes.**
  Default by partnership.
    Forfeiture of right to do
      business, §15-18-73.
    Requirements, §15-18-73.
Restriction of partners.
  Limited partnerships.
    General partners,
      §10-9A-62.
Retiring partners.
  Liability, §10-8-102.
  Rights of retiring partners,
    §10-8-103.
Rights of partners, §10-8-43.
  Dissolution.
    Rights of partners
      regarding partnership
      property, §10-8-97.
  Estate of deceased partners,
    §10-8-103.
  Limited partnerships.
    Access to records and
      financial statements,
      §10-9A-44.
    Property rights, §10-8-71.
    Dissolution, §10-8-97.
  Retiring partners, §10-8-103.
Service of process.
  How partnership served,
    ARCP, Rule 4 (c).
Short title of chapter,
  §10-8-1.
Social workers.
  Practice of social work in
    partnerships, §34-30-30.
Soil classifiers.
  Practice by partnerships not
    prohibited, §34-32-4.
Surveyors, §34-11-9.
Taxation.
  Assessments.
    By whom property should
      be listed, §40-7-17.
  Returns.
    Separate returns in
      individual and
      fiduciary capacity,
      §40-7-20.

PARTNERSHIPS—Cont'd
**Unincorporated professional
  associations.**
  Certain statutes not affected
    by chapter, §10-8-7.
Veterinarians.
  All partners to be licensed,
    §34-29-87.
Winding up affairs, §§10-8-90
  to 10-8-103. See within
  this heading, "Dissolution."
  A-44.
Wrongful acts.
  Liability of partnership for
    partners' wrongful acts,
    §10-8-53.

PARTS RECYCLERS.
**Automotive dismantlers and
  parts recyclers,**
  §§40-12-410 to 40-12-425.
  See MOTOR VEHICLES.

PASSENGERS.
Motor vehicle carriers.
  Transportation of passengers.
    See MOTOR VEHICLE
      CARRIERS.
Motor vehicles, §§32-1-2,
  32-5A-53.
Railroads.
  See RAILROADS.
Transportation companies,
  §§37-2-35 to 37-2-39.

PASTORS.
  See CLERGY.

PASTURAGE.
Lien on stock for pasturage,
  §35-11-70.

PATENTS.
Commercial code.
  Sales.
    Buyer's obligation against
      infringement, §7-2-312.
    Notice of claim or
      litigation to person
      answerable over,
      §7-2-607.
    Warranty against
      infringement, §7-2-312.
Congress, Const. U. S., Art. I,
  §8.
**Conveyances by governor or
  state agencies or
  institutions.**
  Public land patents,
    §§35-4-386 to 35-4-389.
Decedents' estates.
  Public land patents.
    Patent to decedent vests
      title in his successors,
      §35-4-386.
Evidence.
  Land patents, §12-21-96.
Inventions.
  Constitutional provisions,
    Const. U. S., Art. I, §8.
Public lands.
  Conveyances by governor or
    state agencies,
    §§35-4-386 to 35-4-389.
  Evidence, §12-21-96.
  School lands.
    Exchanges of school lands,
      §9-15-44.
    Issuance of patents,
      §§9-15-42, 16-20-3.
  Sales.
    Issuance of patents to
      purchasers, §9-15-42.

PATENTS—Cont'd
  Public lands—Cont'd
    Swamp and overflowed lands.
      Claims of title.
        Issuance upon
          settlement, §9-15-48.
      Sale of lands.
        Issuance of patents to
          purchasers, §9-15-46.
  Recordation, §35-4-56.
    Public land patents,
      §35-4-387.
  School lands. See within this
    heading, "Public lands."
  Titles.
    Swamp and overflowed lands.
      Claims of title, §9-15-48.

PATERNITY.
  Determination of paternity,
    §§26-17-1 to 26-17-21.
    See PARENT AND CHILD.
  Indigent persons.
    Representation of defendants
      prior to arraignment.
    Matters to be ascertained
      by trial judges,
      §15-12-20.
  Legitimation of children,
    §§26-11-1 to 26-11-3.

PATHOLOGISTS.
  Plant pathologists, §§2-28-1
    to 2-28-12.
    See PLANTS.
  Speech pathologists and
    audiologists, §§34-28A-1
    to 34-28A-44.
    See SPEECH
      PATHOLOGISTS AND
      AUDIOLOGISTS.

PATRIOTIC SOCIETIES.
  Public societies, §§10-4-20 to
    10-4-26.
    See CORPORATIONS.

PATROLMEN.
  Police.
    See POLICE.

PAUPERS.
  General provisions.
    See INDIGENT PERSONS.

PAWNBROKERS, §§8-1-80 to
  8-1-84.
  Auctions.
    Sale of pledges at public
      auction, §8-1-81.
  Books.
    Description of security.
      Entry in book, §8-1-80.
    Examination, §8-1-80.
  Consumer finance.
    Nonapplicability of chapter,
      §5-19-31.
  Description of security.
    Entry in book, §8-1-80.
  Licenses, §40-12-138.
  Notice.
    Sale of pledges, §8-1-81.
  Payment of debt.
    Borrower may pay prior to
      sale, §8-1-83.
  Penalties.
    Violation of article, §8-1-84.
  Receipts.
    Pawnbroker to give to
      borrower, §8-1-80.
  Sale of pledges.
    Auction.
      Public auction, §8-1-81.
    Notice, §8-1-81.

PAWNBROKERS—Cont'd
  Sale of pledges—Cont'd
    Payment of debt prior to
      sale, §8-1-83.
    Time.
      Not to be sold until 60
        days after delivery to
        pawnbroker, §8-1-82.
  Violations of article.
    Penalty, §8-1-84.

PEACE BONDS, §§15-6-1 to
  15-6-61.
  Affidavits.
    Form, §15-6-20.
  Appeals.
    Costs, §15-6-42.
    Failure to sustain appeal.
      Effect, §15-6-43.
    Form of undertaking on
      appeals, §15-6-40.
    Return on appeal, §15-6-41.
      Liability of judge.
        Examination anew on
          appeals, §15-6-42.
    Undertaking on appeal.
      Form, §15-6-40.
  Appearance.
    Not required unless offense
      committed, §15-6-24.
  Arrest.
    Discharge of defendant,
      §§15-6-22, 15-6-25.
    Issuance of warrant,
      §15-6-21.
  Commitment warrant.
    Contents, §15-6-25.
  Complainant.
    Examination by judge,
      §15-6-20.
    When costs to be paid by
      complainant, §15-6-23.
  Costs.
    Appeals, §15-6-42.
    Execution for collection,
      §15-6-26.
    Prosecution costs, §15-6-26.
    When paid by complainant,
      §15-6-23.
  Discharge of defendant,
    §15-6-25.
  Executions.
    Collection of costs, §15-6-26.
  Fees.
    When paid by complainant,
      §15-6-23.
  Form of bond, §15-6-24.
  Hearing, §15-6-22.
  Jails.
    Commitment of defendant to
      jail, §15-6-25.
  Judges.
    Authority to require persons
      to give security, §15-6-2.
    Offense committed or
      threatened in presence of
      judge, §15-6-3.
  Municipal corporations.
    Refusal of municipal official
      to comply with order of
      governor, §15-6-4.
  Requiring security by
    defendant, §15-6-24.
  Undertakings.
    Appeals.
      Form, §15-6-40.
    Forfeiture, §15-6-61.
    Remittance of amount
      specified, §15-6-61.
    Upon conviction, §15-6-60.

PEACE BONDS—Cont'd
  Warrants.
    Commitment warrant.
      Contents, §15-6-25.
    Issuance of arrest warrant,
      §15-6-21.
  Witnesses.
    Examination of witnesses,
      §15-6-20.

PEACE OFFICERS.
  Actions.
    Defense.
      Payment of fees and costs
        in certain cases,
        §36-21-1.
  Advertisements.
    State or federal peace officer
      magazines.
      Solicitation of
        advertisements,
        §13A-14-5.
  Age.
    Minimum standards,
      §36-21-46.
  Aiding.
    Refusal to aid, §13A-10-5.
  Annuity and benefit fund,
    §§36-21-60 to 36-21-78.
    Annuities.
      Adjustment of amount,
        §36-21-76.
      Adjustments by board
        pursuant to report of
        actuary, §36-21-73.
        Liability for deficiencies
          in payments
          pursuant to,
          §36-21-73.
      Attachment, garnishment,
        assignment, etc.
        Annuities not subject,
          §36-21-77.
      Cumulative, §36-21-78.
      No vested rights,
        §36-21-76.
      Payment directly to
        member or beneficiary,
        §36-21-77.
      Reinstatement of benefits
        of certain members,
        §36-21-76.
      Retirement annuity,
        §36-21-70.
      Subject to change by
        legislature, §36-21-76.
      When determination of
        years of qualified
        service conclusive,
        §36-21-76.
    Audits.
      Annual audit of acts and
        affairs of board,
        §36-21-75.
    Benefits.
      Adjustment of amount of
        benefits, §36-21-76.
      Adjustments by board
        pursuant to report of
        actuary, §36-21-73.
        Liability for deficiencies
          in payment pursuant
          to, §36-21-73.
      Attachment, garnishment,
        assignment, etc.
        Benefits not subject,
          §36-21-77.
      Cumulative, §36-21-78.
      Death benefits, §36-21-72.
      Disability benefits,
        §36-21-71.

PEACE OFFICERS—Cont'd
Annuity and benefit fund
—Cont'd
Benefits—Cont'd
No vested rights,
§36-21-76.
Payment directly to
member or beneficiary,
§36-21-77.
Reinstatement of benefits
of certain members,
§36-21-76.
Retirement annuity,
§36-21-70.
Subject to change by
legislature, §36-21-76.
Board of commissioners,
§36-21-75.
Agents, §36-21-63.
Appointment of members,
§36-21-61.
Audit.
Annual audits of acts
and affairs of board,
§36-21-75.
Bonds, surety.
Members and employees
handling funds,
§36-21-63.
Compensation of members,
§36-21-62.
Composition, §36-21-61.
Creation, §36-21-61.
Duties.
Generally, §36-21-64.
Employees, §36-21-63.
Executive director,
§36-21-63.
Remittance of proceeds of
certain additional
court costs to
director, §36-21-67.
Officers.
Generally, §36-21-63.
Powers.
Generally, §36-21-64.
Qualifications of members,
§36-21-61.
Quorum, §36-21-63.
Records.
Maintenance, §36-21-65.
Terms of office, §36-21-61.
Vacancies, §36-21-61.
Composition, §36-21-66.
Created, §36-21-66.
Death benefits, §36-21-72.
Definitions, §36-21-60.
Disability benefits,
§36-21-71.
Expenditure of moneys,
§36-21-66.
Fees.
Monthly membership fee,
§36-21-68.
Exemption from
payment, §36-21-68.
Refund, §36-21-74.
Garnishment.
Benefits, annuities, etc.,
not subject, §36-21-77.
Imposition of additional court
costs in certain
proceedings, §36-21-67.
Remittance of proceeds to
executive director,
§36-21-67.
Investment of moneys,
§36-21-66.
Membership.
Application, §36-21-68.
Eligibility, §36-21-68.

PEACE OFFICERS—Cont'd
Annuity and benefit fund
—Cont'd
Membership—Cont'd
Fee.
Exemption from monthly
fee, §36-21-68.
Monthly fee, §36-21-68.
Refund, §36-21-74.
Military service.
Receipt of service credit,
§36-21-69.
Official designation,
§36-21-66.
Participation in other plans,
systems, etc.
Not to bar participation in
fund, §36-21-78.
Purpose, §36-21-66.
Receipts and income.
Actuarial valuation,
§36-21-73.
Retirement annuity.
Schedule of benefits,
§36-21-70.
Appropriations.
Hall of fame.
Expenditures of
appropriations and
donated funds,
§41-9-873.
Survivor's education
assistance act.
Annual appropriation from
state general fund,
§36-21-105.
Arrest.
Force.
Resisting arrest.
Use of force in resisting
arrest prohibited,
§13A-3-28.
Use of force in making
arrest, §13A-3-27.
General provisions.
See ARREST.
Refusing to aid peace officer,
§13A-10-5.
Resisting arrest, §13A-10-41.
Assembly.
Killing dogs used by peace
officers.
Persons violating
provisions in course of
orderly
demonstrations.
Inapplicability of section,
§13A-11-15.
Badges.
Death in line of duty.
Providing badge for
survivors of officer
killed in line of duty,
§36-21-8.1.
Disablement in line of duty.
Providing badge for
survivor of officer
killed or disabled in
line of duty,
§36-21-8.1.
Benefits.
Annuity and benefit fund,
§§36-21-60 to 36-21-78.
See within this heading,
"Annuity and benefit
fund."
Compensation for death,
§§36-30-1 to 36-30-7. See
within this heading,
"Death."

PEACE OFFICERS—Cont'd
Bonds, surety.
Annuity and benefit fund.
Board of commissioners.
Members and employees
handling funds,
§36-21-63.
Character.
Minimum standards,
§36-21-46.
Compensation.
Compensation for death,
§§36-30-1 to 36-30-7. See
within this heading,
"Death."
Counties.
Minimum starting salary,
§36-21-10.
Lump-sum payment,
§36-21-3.
Overtime.
County non-elected law
enforcement officers,
§36-21-4.1.
Generally, §36-21-4.
Method of compensation.
Statement of election,
§36-21-5.
Pay or compensation leave
for non-elected law
enforcement officer in
service of county,
§36-21-4.1.
"State law enforcement
officer" defined,
§36-21-6.
Subsistence allowance,
§36-21-2.
**Conservation and natural
resources.**
Commissioner of
conservation and natural
resources.
Constituted peace officer,
§9-11-5.
Constables.
See CONSTABLES.
Death.
Annuity and benefit fund
generally, §§36-21-60 to
36-21-78. See within this
heading, "Annuity and
benefit fund."
Badges.
Providing badge for
survivor of officer
killed or disabled in
line of duty,
§36-21-8.1.
Compensation for death,
§§36-30-1 to 36-30-7.
Amount, §36-30-2.
Awarding authority.
Decision final, §36-30-7.
Defined, §36-30-1.
Entry of judgment and
order for payment,
§36-30-6.
Hearing and
determination of
claims, §36-30-6.
Claims.
Determination.
Forms, §36-30-5.
Hearing, §36-30-6.
Rules of evidence and
procedures,
§36-30-5.
Presentation.
Form and manners,
§36-30-5.

PEACE OFFICERS—Cont'd
Death—Cont'd
Compensation for death
—Cont'd
Claims—Cont'd
Presentation—Cont'd
Limitation period,
§36-30-5.
Proof of facts, §36-30-5.
Construction of article,
§36-30-7.
Deaths deemed
compensable, §36-30-2.
Definitions, §36-30-1.
Dependents.
Persons deemed
dependents or
partial dependent,
§36-30-1.
Evidence.
Determination of claims.
Adoption of rules of
evidence, §36-30-5.
Payment, §36-30-3.
Order, §36-30-6.
United States residents
only, §36-30-4.
Education.
Survivor's education
assistance act,
§§36-21-100 to
36-21-105. See within
this heading,
"Survivor's education
assistance act."
Definitions.
Annuity and benefit fund,
§36-21-60.
Death.
Compensation for death,
§36-30-1.
Overtime compensation.
"State law enforcement
officer," §36-21-6.
Standards and training
commission, §36-21-40.
Survivor's education
assistance act,
§36-21-101.
Disability.
Annuity and benefit fund,
§36-21-71.
Badges.
Providing badge for
survivor of officer
killed or disabled in
line of duty,
§36-21-8.1.
Diseases.
Unknown cure.
Preference given to police
officers and fire
fighters suffering from
diseases without
known cure in
admission to research
programs, §36-21-11.
Dogs.
Killing dogs used by peace
officers, §13A-11-15.
Education.
Continuing education
courses.
Municipal chiefs of police
to complete annually,
§36-21-51.

PEACE OFFICERS—Cont'd
Education—Cont'd
Death.
Survivor's education
assistance act,
§§36-21-100 to
36-21-105. See within
this heading,
"Survivor's education
assistance act."
Minimum standards,
§36-21-46.
Municipal chiefs of police to
complete annual
continuing education
courses, §36-21-51.
Entrapment.
When entrapment defense to
criminal liability,
§13A-3-31.
Escape.
Force.
Use of force to prevent
escape, §13A-3-27.
Fires and fire prevention.
Refusing to assist in fire
control, §13A-10-6.
Fish and game.
Wardens, §§9-2-64, 9-2-65,
9-11-5, 9-11-17.
Force.
Deadly physical force.
When use justified,
§13A-3-27.
Funds.
Annuity and benefit fund,
§§36-21-60 to 36-21-78.
See within this heading,
"Annuity and benefit
fund."
Peace officers' standards and
training fund, §36-21-47.
Court costs.
Remittance to fund,
§36-21-47.1.
Gambling.
Gambling places.
Duty of officer to break
into and enter house,
§13A-12-55.
Gifts.
Hall of fame.
Donations, contributions
and gifts.
Exemption from
taxation, §41-9-872.
Guards.
Prisons.
Officers and guards.
General provisions.
See PRISONS AND
PRISONERS.
Jails.
See JAILS.
Penitentiary.
See PENITENTIARY.
Hall of fame.
Appropriations.
Expenditures, §41-9-873.
Board, §§41-9-870, 41-9-871.
Bylaws.
Adoption by board,
§41-9-871.
Contributions.
Exemption from taxation,
§41-9-872.
Funds.
Expenditures, §41-9-873.
Donations.
Exemption from taxation,
§41-9-872.

PEACE OFFICERS—Cont'd
Hall of fame—Cont'd
Donations—Cont'd
Funds.
Expenditures, §41-9-873.
Gifts.
Exemption from taxation,
§41-9-872.
Rules and regulations.
Adoption by board,
§41-9-871.
Taxation.
Donations, contributions
and gifts.
Exemption from
taxation, §41-9-872.
Highway patrol.
General provisions, §§32-2-20
to 32-2-44.
See MOTOR VEHICLES.
Impersonation, §13A-10-11.
Public servants, §13A-10-10.
**Killing dogs used by peace
officers,** §13A-11-15.
Liquefied petroleum gas.
Administrator, §9-17-104.
Magazines.
Solicitation of advertisements
for state or federal peace
officer magazines or
journals, §13A-14-5.
Marine police, §§33-5-4 to
33-5-6.
Order to disperse.
Failure to comply disorderly
conduct, §13A-11-7.
Overtime compensation. See
within this heading,
"Compensation."
Penalties.
Peace officers' standards and
training commission.
Violation of article or
standards, rules, etc.,
promulgated
thereunder, §36-21-50.
Pensions.
Annuity and benefit fund,
§§36-21-60 to 36-21-78.
See within this heading,
"Annuity and benefit
fund."
Physical qualifications.
Minimum standards,
§36-21-46.
Police.
See POLICE.
Prisons and prisoners.
Officers and guards.
General provisions.
See PRISONS AND
PRISONERS.
Jails.
See JAILS.
Penitentiary.
See PENITENTIARY.
Public service commission.
Enforcement division.
Members to have powers of
peace officers,
§37-1-66.
Records.
Annuity and benefit fund.
Board of commissioners,
§36-21-65.
Reports.
Child abuse or neglect.
See MINORS.
False reporting to law
enforcement authorities,
§13A-10-9.

PEACE OFFICERS—Cont'd
Retirement.
Annuity and benefit fund, §§36-21-60 to 36-21-78.
See within this heading, "Annuity and benefit fund."
Riots.
Failure of disorderly person to disperse, §13A-11-6.
Rules and regulations.
Hall of fame.
Adoption by board, §41-9-871.
Sheriffs.
See SHERIFFS.
Solicitation.
State or federal peace officer magazines or journals.
Solicitation of advertisements, §13A-14-5.
Standards and training commission, §§36-21-40 to 36-21-51.
Appropriations by municipalities and counties, §36-21-48.
Disposition, §36-21-48.
Bylaws.
Adoption, §36-21-41.
Compensation of members, §36-21-44.
Composition, §36-21-41.
Created, §36-21-41.
Definitions, §36-21-40.
Designation of members, §36-21-41.
Duties.
Generally, §36-21-45.
Expenses of members.
Reimbursement, §36-21-44.
Functions.
Generally, §36-21-45.
Fund, §36-21-47.
Court costs.
Remittance to fund, §36-21-47.1.
Grants by federal and state governments, §36-21-47.1.
Grants by municipalities and counties, §§36-21-47.1, 36-21-48.
Disposition, §36-21-48.
Law enforcement agencies.
Agreements and cooperation, §36-21-49.
Meetings, §36-21-43.
Minimum standards for applicants and appointees for peace officers, §36-21-46.
Municipal chiefs of police to complete annual continuing education courses, §36-21-51.
Officers and employees, §36-21-42.
Penalties.
Violations of article, §36-21-50.
Qualifications of members, §36-21-41.
Seal.
Official seal, §36-21-43.
Terms of office, §36-21-41.
State police.
General provisions.
See STATE POLICE.

PEACE OFFICERS—Cont'd
State police—Cont'd
Highway patrol, §§32-2-20 to 32-2-44.
See MOTOR VEHICLES.
Subsistence allowance, §36-21-2.
Survivor's education assistance act, §§36-21-100 to 36-21-105.
Applications.
State department of education to provide application for implementation, §36-21-103.
Appropriations.
Annual appropriation from state general fund, §36-21-105.
Assistance authorized, §36-21-102.
Board, §36-21-104.
Creation, §36-21-104.
Defined, §36-21-101.
Citation of act, §36-21-100.
Definitions, §36-21-101.
Eligibility for benefits, §36-21-102.
Eligible programs.
Defined, §36-21-101.
Forms.
State department of education to supply, §36-21-103.
Short title, §36-21-100.
Tuition.
Defined, §36-21-101.
Taxation.
Department of revenue.
Agents and employees constituted peace officers, §40-2-10.
Hall of fame.
Donations, contributions and gifts.
Exemption from taxation, §41-9-872.
Training.
Expenses.
Reimbursement by new employer, §36-21-7.
Minimum standards, §36-21-46.
Standards and training commission, §§36-21-40 to 36-21-51. See within this heading, "Standards and training commission."
Tuition.
Death.
Survivor's education assistance act, §§36-21-100 to 36-21-105.
Weapons.
Handguns.
Eligibility of honorably retired law enforcement officers to carry handguns, §36-21-9.

PEANUTS.
Attachment.
Liens of owners of peanut machines or pickers, §35-11-291.

PEANUTS—Cont'd
Farmers.
Indemnification program, Const. Ala., amd. 383.
Garnishment.
Liens of owners of peanut machines or pickers.
Enforcement of lien, §35-11-291.
Indemnification program for peanut farmers, Const. Ala., amd. 383.
Liens.
Owners of peanut machines or pickers.
Attachment, §35-11-291.
Declaration of lien, §35-11-290.
Enforcement of lien, §35-11-291.
Garnishment, §35-11-291.
Priority of lien, §35-11-290.
Sale of peanuts, §35-11-291.
Machines.
Liens of owners of peanut machines. See within this heading, "Liens."
Motor vehicle carriers.
Vehicles hauling peanuts.
Exemptions from chapter, §37-3-4.
Nuts generally.
See NUTS.
Pickers.
Liens of owners of peanut pickers. See within this heading, "Liens."
Sales.
Liens of owners of peanut machines or pickers.
Enforcement of lien, §35-11-291.
Taxation.
Exemptions.
Peanuts stored in licensed warehouses, §40-9-3.

PECANS.
Nuts generally.
See NUTS.
State nut.
Designation as state nut, §1-2-19.
Taxation.
Exemptions.
Pecans stored in licensed warehouses, §40-9-3.

PEDDLERS.
Bonds, surety.
Sales tax.
Itinerant vendors to file bond, §40-23-24.
Licenses, §40-12-139.
Transient peddlers, §40-12-174.
Sales tax.
Bonds, surety.
Itinerant vendors to file bond, §40-23-24.

PEDESTRIANS.
See MOTOR VEHICLES.

PEDIGREES.
Livestock, §§2-15-310 to 2-15-317.
See LIVESTOCK.

PELLAGRA.
Notifiable diseases, §§22-11A-1 to 22-11A-38.
See DISEASES.

PELL CITY, MUNICIPALITY OF.
Property tax, Const. Ala., amd. 8.

PENAL INSTITUTIONS.
Jails.
See JAILS.
Penitentiary, §§14-3-30 to 14-3-60.
See PENITENTIARY.
Prisons and prisoners.
See PRISONS AND PRISONERS.

PENALTIES.
Abortion.
Parental consent to performing abortion upon minors, §26-21-6.
Accountants.
Unlawful practice, §34-1-19.
Actions for statutory penalties.
Commencement.
Who may commence, §6-5-50.
Adoption, §26-10-9.
Adult protective services.
Abuse, neglect and exploitation, §38-9-7.
Failure to make report, §38-9-10.
Advertising.
Outdoor advertising.
Violations of division and rules and regulations, §23-1-288.
Aged persons.
Medical assistance to elderly persons.
False representations, §38-6-8.
Agriculture.
Violations of title, §2-1-9.
Air commerce, §37-9-31.
Air conditioning contractors, §§34-31-25, 34-31-32.
Air pollution, §22-28-22.
Alcoholic beverages.
See ALCOHOLIC BEVERAGES.
Alligator farms, §9-12-211.
Ambulances.
Violations of chapter or rules and regulations, §22-18-6.
Appeals.
Disposition of appeals.
Affirmation of stayed judgment generally, §12-22-72.
Frivolous appeal.
Damages for frivolous appeal, ARAP, Rule 38.
Architects, §§34-2-35, 34-2-36.
Asbestos.
Contractors accreditation.
Certification of removal projects.
Violations, §22-39-5.
Atomic energy.
Radiation.
Penalty for violation of chapter or rules, regulations or orders, §22-14-14.
Civil penalties, §22-14-14.
Attorneys at law.
See ATTORNEYS AT LAW.

PENALTIES—Cont'd
Auctions and auctioneers.
Violation of article, §§8-14-24, 34-4-7.
Audiologists.
Violations of provisions, §34-28A-4.
Aviation, §4-2-12.
Banks and financial institutions.
See BANKS AND FINANCIAL INSTITUTIONS.
Barbers.
Violations of chapter, §34-5-16.
Billiard rooms.
See BILLIARD ROOMS.
Blind persons.
Sale, etc., of blind-made products or services.
Penalties for violation of article, §21-1-62.
Boats.
See BOATS.
Boxing and wrestling.
Athletic commission, §41-9-90.1.
Brake fluid.
Violations of article, §8-17-9.
Budgets.
Violations of article, §41-4-96.
Capital punishment.
See CAPITAL PUNISHMENT.
Catfish.
Marketing of catfish.
Violations of article, §§2-11-39, 2-11-40.
Promotion of industry.
Failure to deduct and pay over assessments, §2-8-291.
Cattle.
Promotion of cattle industry.
Failure to deduct and pay over assessment, §2-8-22.
Caustic or corrosive substances.
Violation of article, §8-17-24.
Checks.
Sale of checks.
Violations of chapter, §8-7-15.
Child abuse or neglect.
Failure to make required report, §26-14-13.
Child labor.
Violations of chapter, §25-8-30.
Child support programs.
Violations.
Falsification of financial reports, §38-10-9.
Chiropractors.
Licenses.
Refusal, revocation or suspension.
Fines, §34-24-170.
Violations of article, §34-24-123.
Cigarettes.
Taxation.
Gummed cigarette papers, §§40-25A-6 to 40-25A-9.
Civil defense.
Violations, §31-9-22.

PENALTIES—Cont'd
Coal.
Severance tax of 1977.
See COAL.
Surface mining control and reclamation.
Permits.
Violations of provisions, §9-16-94.
Concurrent sentences.
Service of state sentence concurrently with federal sentence in federal penal system, §15-18-4.
Conservation and natural resources, §§9-1-4, 9-2-15.1.
Conservators.
Settlements of accounts of conservators.
Compulsion of settlement by probate court.
Appearance by conservator or representative.
Failure to appear, §26-5-35.
Constitution of Alabama.
Cruel or unusual punishment, Const. Ala., art. I, §15.
Excessive fines.
Prohibited, Const. Ala., art. I, §15.
Special, private or local laws fixing punishment prohibited, Const. Ala., art. IV, §104.
Consumer finance, §5-19-30.
Contractors, §§34-8-6, 34-8-10.
Controlled substances.
See DRUGS.
Corporations.
See CORPORATIONS.
Corrections.
Inmate community reintegration under SIR act.
Failure to remain within limits of confinement, etc., §15-18-121.
Cosmetics.
Violations of provisions, §20-1-5.
Cosmetologists.
Violations of chapter, §34-7-25.
Cotton.
Promotion of cotton products
Violations of provisions, §2-8-211.
Counties.
See COUNTIES.
Courts.
Punishment fixed by court.
Offense punishable by imprisonment in county jail, §15-18-21.
Credit.
Escape.
Time between recapture and return to penal system, §15-18-6.
Applicability to prisoner presently incarcerated, §15-18-7.

PENALTIES—Cont'd
Credit—Cont'd
Time spent incarcerated
pending trial, §15-18-5.
Applicability to prisoners
presently incarcerated,
§15-18-7.
Credit cards.
Cease and desist orders.
Violation by credit card
banks, §5-20-7.
Credit unions.
Concealment of discounts or
loans, §5-17-29.
False or omitted entries,
§5-17-32.
Overdraws, §5-17-30.
Receipt of commission,
emolument, etc., for
procuring loans,
§5-17-30.
Receipt of property other
than in payment for just
demand, §5-17-31.
Crime victims compensation.
Alteration of commission
records, §15-23-20.
Assessment of additional
costs and penalties,
§15-23-17.
Failure of commission
members to disclose
conflict of interest,
§15-23-19.
Failure to omit or disclose
material fact, etc.,
§15-23-21.
Furnishing false information,
§15-23-21.
Influence peddling,
§15-23-18.
Money or securities of
commission.
Unauthorized control,
§15-23-22.
Dead bodies.
Distribution for scientific
study.
Violations of provisions,
§22-19-30.
Death penalty.
General provisions.
See CAPITAL
PUNISHMENT.
Deceptive trade practices.
Violations, §8-19-11.
Willful violation a
misdemeanor,
§8-19-12.
Dental service corporations.
Sales representatives.
Administrative penalty in
lieu of discretionary
suspension, revocation,
etc., §22-21-382.
Diversion or appropriation
of funds, §22-21-378.
Violations of article,
§22-21-390.
Dentists.
See DENTISTS.
Dietitians and nutritionists.
False representation,
§34-34-3.
Practice act.
Violations, §34-34A-15.
Diseases.
Notifiable diseases.
Reports.
Failure to make report,
§22-11A-6.

PENALTIES—Cont'd
Diseases—Cont'd
Notifiable diseases—Cont'd
Reports—Cont'd
Physicians' failure to
make report,
§22-11A-6.
Dogs.
Fighting of dogs, §3-1-29.
Training without license,
§9-11-52.
Drugs.
General provisions.
See DRUGS.
Education.
Diversion of funds by
officials, §16-13-4.
Exceeding budget,
§16-13-144.
Unaccredited schools.
Violation of provisions of
chapters, §16-46-10.
Eggs and egg products.
Delinquency in payment of
permit fee, §2-12-4.
Failure to pay inspection fee
or affix labels, §2-12-10.
Promotion of industry.
Failure to deduct and pay
over assessments,
§2-8-171.
Elections.
Ballots.
Removing or breaking
seals, §17-8-37.
Fair campaign practices,
§17-22A-22.
Electrocution.
Capital punishment,
§§15-18-1, 15-18-82.
Engineers.
Violations of chapter,
§34-11-15.
**Enumeration of legal
punishments,** §15-18-1.
**Environmental management
department.**
Civil penalty for violations of
chapter, §22-22-9.
Criminal penalty for
violation of chapter,
§22-22-14.
**Executors and
administrators.**
Notice of appointment.
Failure to give, §43-2-62.
Extradition.
Failure to inform arrestee of
rights, §15-9-38.
Habeas corpus.
Failure to allow prisoner to
apply, §15-9-38.
Felonies.
Habitual felony offenders.
Additional penalties,
§13A-5-9.
Deductions from sentences
of correctional
incentive time.
Effect on habitual
offender laws,
§14-9-44.
Restriction on imposition of
penalty, §13A-5-10.
Persons previously convicted
of felonies, §15-18-9.
Fertilizer.
Manufacture of commercial
fertilizer short in weight,
§2-22-18.

PENALTIES—Cont'd
Finance companies.
Small loans.
Violations of provisions,
§§5-18-4, 5-18-24.
Fines.
Assessment, §12-19-22.
Constitution of Alabama.
Excessive fines, Const.
Ala., art. I, §15.
Constitution of the United
States.
Excessive fines, Const. U.
S., Amendment VIII.
Criminal cases.
Collection of docket fees
and fines where
defendants convicted of
misdemeanors confess
judgment for fees and
fines, §12-19-151.
Distribution of fines
collected, §12-19-152.
Criminal procedure, rules of.
Restitution and fines.
Generally, ARCrP, Rule
10.
Disposition of appeals.
Affirmation of stayed
judgment.
Generally, §12-22-72.
Distribution, §12-19-22.
Felonies.
Limitations on fines,
§13A-5-11.
Fish and game.
Commercial fee fishing
ponds.
Violations of provisions,
§9-11-457.
Misdemeanors.
Limitations on amount,
§13A-5-12.
Transfer to circuit clerks of
fines collected and in
possession on January
15, 1977 of clerks of
courts abolished,
§12-19-22.
Fires and fire prevention.
Fire marshal.
See FIRES AND FIRE
PREVENTION.
Firemen.
Personnel standards and
education.
Appointing or paying fire
fighter failing to
meet standards,
§36-32-8.
Sprinkler systems.
Violations of provisions,
§34-33-12.
Fireworks.
Violations of provisions,
§8-17-224.
Fish and game.
See FISH AND GAME.
Food.
Violations of provisions,
§20-1-5.
Forests and forestry.
See FORESTS AND
FORESTRY.
Fraternal benefit societies.
Failure to file annual
statements, §27-34-38.
Misrepresentations,
§27-34-45.

PENALTIES—Cont'd
  Fruits and vegetables.
    Grading and standards.
      Penalty for violation of
        article or rules and
        regulations, §2-11-78.
  Funeral services.
    See FUNERALS.
  Garbage and trash.
    Violation of article, §22-27-7.
  Gasoline tax, §40-17-37.
  Grain.
    Promotion of grain industry.
      Violation of provisions,
        §2-8-252.
  Grain dealers.
    Violations of provisions,
      §2-31-17.
  Habeas corpus.
    Refusal or neglect to deliver
      true copy of detention
      order, §15-21-28.
    Transferring custody so as to
      elude service or effect of
      writ, §15-21-31.
    Unlawful detention or arrest
      after discharge,
      §15-21-27.
  Handicapped persons.
    Rights of blind or other
      physically disabled
      persons.
      Penalty for denial of or
        interference with
        enumerated rights,
        §21-7-5.
  Harbors and ports.
    Violation of rules and
      regulations of
      department, §33-1-31.
  Hard labor.
    Imposition of additional hard
      labor to pay costs,
      §15-18-63.
    Permissible legal
      punishments, §15-18-1.
  **Hazardous waste or
    substances.**
    Cleanup fund.
      Orders to implement
        cleanup plans.
        Failure to comply,
          §22-30A-5.
      Violations of chapter.
        Civil penalties,
          §22-30A-11.
      Fees for disposal of
        hazardous waste or
        substances.
        Failure to submit monthly
          reports, §22-30B-6.
        Waiver of penalties for
          good cause,
          §22-30B-8.
        False or fraudulent reports,
          §22-30B-7.
        Time for payment of fees.
          Failure to pay within
            time required,
            §22-30B-5.
  Health.
    Violation of health or
      quarantine law, §22-1-8.
    Violation of state board of
      health rules or
      regulations, §22-2-14.
  **Health maintenance
    organizations.**
    Violations of chapter.
      Administrative penalty,
        §27-21A-22.

PENALTIES—Cont'd
  **Hearing aid dealers and
    fitters.**
    Administrative fines.
      Disciplining of licensees,
        §34-14-9.
    Violations of chapter,
      §34-14-14.
  **Heating and air conditioning
    contractors.**
    Use of penalties collected,
      §34-31-25.
    Violations of chapter,
      §34-31-32.
  Highways.
    Contracts.
      Qualification of bidders.
        False representations,
          §23-1-56.
    Department.
      Rules and regulations.
        Violations, §23-5-13.
    Detours.
      Signs.
        Driving around,
          destruction, etc.,
          §23-5-2.
  Historic Blakeley authority.
    Charging, receiving or
      obtaining of fees,
      §41-10-173.
    Rules and regulations.
      Violations, §41-10-181.
  Honey.
    Labeling.
      Violations of provisions,
        §2-11-123.
  Honeybees and apiaries.
    Violations of article or rules
      and regulations,
      §2-14-15.
  Hospitals.
    Violation of licensing article,
      §22-21-33.
  **Hotels, inns and other
    transient lodging places.**
    See HOTELS, INNS AND
      OTHER TRANSIENT
      LODGING PLACES.
  Impeachment, Const. Ala.,
    art. VII, §176.
  Income tax.
    See INCOME TAX.
  Industrial alcohol.
    Violations of chapter,
      §28-5-14.
  Industrial revenue bonds.
    Criminal penalties, §8-6-121.
  Insurance.
    See INSURANCE.
  Jails.
    Commitment of prisoners.
      Failure to receive prisoners
        into custody, §14-6-5.
    Feeding of prisoners.
      Violations of article,
        §14-6-50.
    Inspection of jails.
      Alterations, repairs, etc.
        Failure to remove
          prisoners, §§14-6-88,
          14-6-90.
        Refusal to obey orders,
          §14-6-90.
      Failure to provide
        information, §14-6-85.
    Violations of article,
      §14-6-109.

PENALTIES—Cont'd
  Jails—Cont'd
    Sanitation.
      Allowing jail to become
        foul or unclean,
        §14-6-21.
  Junkyard control.
    Violations of division,
      §23-1-250.
  Labor.
    Child labor.
      Violations,
        §25-8-30.
    Unions and labor relations.
      Violations, §25-7-16.
  Landscape architects.
    Violations of provisions,
      §34-17-7.
  Landscaping.
    Horticulture and floriculture
      work.
      Commissioner of
        agriculture may
        impose penalty,
        §2-2-18.
      Penalties for violations of
        chapter or rules or
        regulations, §2-28-11.
  Licenses.
    See LICENSES.
  Lime.
    Assessment of penalties
      against manufacturers,
      distributors, etc., for
      deficiencies in
      agricultural liming
      materials, §2-23-7.
  Limitation of actions.
    Actions for recovery of
      penalties, §6-2-38.
  Linseed oil.
    Violation of article, §8-17-45.
  Liquefied petroleum gas,
    §§9-17-106, 9-17-109.
    Imposition of penalties.
      Authority of board,
        §9-17-108.
  **Liquefied petroleum gas fuel
    tax.**
    Failure to timely obtain
      decal, §40-17-164.
  Livestock.
    See LIVESTOCK.
  Lubrication oils and greases.
    Tax.
      Failure to keep records or
        make reports,
        §40-17-178.
  Magistrates.
    Schedule of fines, ARJA,
      Rule 20.
  Manufactured buildings.
    Violations of provisions,
      §24-4A-6.
  Marine mammal protection.
    Violations of article,
      §9-11-396.
  Marine resources.
    See MARINE RESOURCES.
  Meat and meat products.
    Violations of chapter,
      §2-17-37.
  Medical technicians.
    Violations of chapter,
      §34-18-3.
  Mentally ill.
    Violations of chapter,
      §22-50-23.
  Military affairs.
    See MILITARY AFFAIRS.

PENALTIES—Cont'd
Milk and milk products.
Marked containers.
Selling or using
noncomplying
containers, §8-16-96.
Violations of article,
§8-12-44.
Mines and minerals,
§§9-16-11, 9-16-12.
Mobile homes.
Anchoring.
Penalties for violations of
article, §24-5-33.
Violations of article,
§24-5-14.
**Mortgages and deeds of
trust.**
Failure to enter satisfaction
or payment in record,
§35-10-30.
Motorcycles.
Violations of provisions,
§32-12-44.
Motor-driven cycles.
Violations of provisions,
§32-12-27.
Motor vehicle carriers.
See MOTOR VEHICLE
CARRIERS.
Motor vehicles.
See MOTOR VEHICLES.
Municipal corporations.
See MUNICIPAL
CORPORATIONS.
Navigation.
Obstructing navigable
waterways, §33-7-3.
Nurses.
Administrative fines.
Disciplining licensees,
§34-21-25.
Violations of provisions,
§34-21-7.
**Nursing home
administrators.**
Administrative fines.
Disciplining of licensees,
§34-20-14.
Violations of provisions,
§34-20-16.
Optometrists.
Violations of provisions,
§34-22-6.
Parole.
Board of pardons and
paroles.
Liability of members for
neglecting or failing to
perform duty,
§15-22-39.
Pawnbrokers.
Violation of article, §8-1-84.
Peace officers.
Peace officers' standards and
training commission.
Violation of article or
standards, rules, etc.,
promulgated
thereunder, §36-21-50.
Penitentiary.
Violation of chapter,
§14-3-16.
Warden.
Wrongful discharge of
convicts, §14-10-3.
**Permissible legal
punishments,** §15-18-1.

PENALTIES—Cont'd
Pest control.
Commissioner of agriculture
and industries may
impose, §2-2-18.
Violations of chapter or rules
or regulations, §2-28-11.
Pesticides.
Application.
Penalty for violations of
article, §2-27-62.
Commissioner of agriculture
and industries may
impose, §2-2-18.
Violations of article,
§2-27-16.
Petroleum products,
§8-17-139.
**Pharmacists and
pharmacies.**
See PHARMACISTS AND
PHARMACIES.
Physical therapists.
Administrative fines.
Disciplining of licensees,
§34-24-193.
Violations of article,
§34-24-196.
Physicians.
See PHYSICIANS.
Pilots and pilotage.
Licenses.
Acting without license,
§33-4-47.
State pilotage commission.
Civil actions to recover
forfeitures, §33-4-12.
Pipelines.
Gas pipeline systems,
§37-4-87.
Plant pathologists.
Commissioner of agriculture
may impose penalties,
§2-2-18.
Violations of chapter or rules
or regulations, §2-28-11.
Plumbing.
Installation of facilities.
Violations of chapter,
§22-26-6.
Podiatrists.
Practicing without licenses,
§34-24-270.
Violations of provisions,
§34-24-234.
Polygraph examiners.
Violations of chapter,
§34-25-8.
Poultry.
Violations of chapter,
§2-17-37.
Prisons and prisoners.
Convict labor.
Coal mines.
Working convicts in coal
mines, §14-5-4.
Hard labor sentence.
Failure to report by
probate judge,
§14-4-4.
Hiring or leasing of
convicts, §14-5-4.
County convicts.
Convict labor, §14-5-4.
Hard labor sentence.
Failure to report by
probate judge,
§14-4-4.

PENALTIES—Cont'd
Prisons and prisoners
—Cont'd
Discharging convicts.
Wrongful discharge by
public official,
§14-10-3.
Joint act of prisoners.
Three or more prisoners,
§14-11-11.
Officers and guards.
Violation of law, §14-11-4.
Overworking, maltreatment
or inflicting of
unauthorized
punishment, §14-11-1.
Property.
State property.
Injury to or destruction
of, §14-11-10.
Public buildings.
Injury to or destruction of,
§14-11-10.
Solitary confinement.
Noncompliance by officers
and guards, §14-11-5.
State property.
Injury to or destruction of,
§14-11-10.
Trespassing about prisons,
§14-11-9.
Violation of chapter,
§14-3-16.
Witnesses.
Management and
treatment of convicts.
Failure to appear or
testify, §14-11-3.
Work release.
Violations of chapter,
§14-8-10.
Probation.
See PROBATION.
Professional corporations.
False statements, answers,
etc., §10-4-401.
Psychologists.
Unlicensed practice,
§34-26-42.
Public lands.
Surplus lands.
Transfer to volunteer fire
departments,
§41-4-33.1.
**Public officers and
employees.**
Bonds, surety.
Failure to endorse date of
filing on bond,
§36-5-10.
Failure to file, §36-5-17.
Performance of official act
by public officer,
§36-5-22.
Code of ethics.
Violations, §36-25-27.
Commissions.
Exercise of duties of office
without first obtaining,
§36-2-9.
Entering into public office of
person disqualified by
law, §36-2-2.
Merit system.
Violations, §36-26-47.
Public service commission.
See PUBLIC SERVICE
COMMISSION.

PENALTIES—Cont'd
Public works.
Resident workmen.
Employment required.
Violations of section,
§39-3-3.
Punishment fixed by court.
Offense punishable by
imprisonment in county
jail, §15-18-21.
Quarantine.
Violation of quarantine law,
§22-1-8.
Rabies.
Tags.
Penalty when animal
found without tag,
§3-7-6.
Violations of chapter,
§3-7-11.
Radiation, §22-14-14.
Railroads.
Free passes, rebates or
discounts, §37-8-27.
Noncompliance with certain
commission orders,
§37-8-110.
Real estate brokers.
See REAL ESTATE
BROKERS.
Recorded devices, §13A-8-86.
**Remission of fines and
forfeitures,** §15-22-36.
Repeat offenders, §15-18-9.
**Restitution to victims of
crimes.**
Employment income
withholding order.
Generally, §15-18-143.
Noncompliance with order,
§15-18-148.
Sales.
Going-out-of-business or
distress merchandise
sales, §8-13-22.
Sales tax.
See SALES TAX.
**Savings and loan
associations.**
Members, §5-16-13.
Searches and seizures.
Search warrants, §15-5-19.
Sewers, §22-26-6.
Ships and shipping.
Disposition of fines, §33-5-32.
Violations of provisions,
§33-5-35.
Shopping carts, §13A-8-64.
Small loans, §§5-18-4, 5-18-24.
Soil classifiers, §34-32-18.
**Southeast interstate low-
level radioactive waste
management compact.**
Violation of chapter,
§22-32-8.
Soybeans.
Promotion of soybean
industry.
Failure to deduct and pay
over assessment,
§2-8-103.
**Special, private or local laws
fixing punishment
prohibited,** Const. Ala.,
art. IV, §104.
**Speech pathologists and
audiologists.**
Administrative fines.
Disciplining of licensees,
§34-28A-42.

PENALTIES—Cont'd
**Speech pathologists and
audiologists**—Cont'd
Violations of provisions,
§34-28A-4.
Sports.
Violations of chapter,
§8-26-41.
State parks.
Rules and regulations.
Violations, §9-2-9.
Stores.
Licenses.
Failure to take out license,
§40-12-319.
Student grant program.
False statements and
representations,
§16-33A-10.
Surveys and surveyors.
Alteration or destruction of
survey corners and
accessories, §34-2-31.
Violations of provisions,
§34-11-15.
Swine.
Promotion of swine industry.
Failure to deduct and pay
over assessment,
§2-8-62.
Taxation.
Alcoholic beverages.
Malt or brewed beverages.
Excise tax, §§28-3-186,
28-3-187.
Cigarettes.
Gummed cigarette papers.
See CIGARETTES.
Gasoline tax, §40-17-37.
General provisions.
See TAXATION.
Income tax.
See INCOME TAX.
Insurance companies,
§27-4-7.
Liquefied petroleum gas fuel
tax, §40-17-164.
Lubricating oils and greases,
§40-17-178.
Motor vehicle carriers.
Fuel tax, §§40-17-144,
40-17-155.
Mileage tax.
See MOTOR VEHICLE
CARRIERS.
Public utilities, §§40-21-17,
40-21-31.
Sales tax.
See SALES TAX.
Tobacco.
Sales tax.
See TOBACCO.
Use tax, §§40-23-69,
40-23-80.
Tobacco.
Sales tax.
See TOBACCO.
Transportation companies.
See TRANSPORTATION
COMPANIES.
Tree surgery.
Commissioner of agriculture
may impose penalty,
§2-2-18.
Violations of chapter or rules
or regulations, §2-28-11.
Turpentine.
Violations of article,
§8-17-174.

PENALTIES—Cont'd
Unclaimed property.
Uniform disposition of
unclaimed property act,
§35-12-45.
**Unemployment
compensation.**
Compromise or waiver of
civil penalties, §25-4-119.
Delinquent contribution
payments and reports,
§25-4-133.
Generally, §25-4-145.
Trust fund.
Disposition of penalties,
§25-4-31.
Unions, §25-7-16.
Use tax.
Failure to pay, §40-23-69.
Fraud, §40-23-80.
Vacation time-sharing plans.
Violations of article,
§34-27-61.
Veterans.
Pensions for widows of
Confederate veterans.
Violation of laws, §31-8-33.
Veterinarians.
Unauthorized practice,
§34-29-82.
Vital statistics.
Death.
Violation of article or state
board of health
regulations, §22-9-79.
Warehouses.
Operating without permit,
§8-15-10.
**Water and wastewater
systems and treatment
plants.**
Violations of chapter,
§22-25-15.
**Water conservation and
irrigation.**
Agency.
Conflicts of interest,
§9-10-12.
Corporations.
Conflicts of interest,
§9-10-45.
**Water management and
drainage.**
Districts.
Taxation.
Delinquent taxes,
§9-9-32.
Tax collector failing to
make prompt
payment to
treasurer, §9-9-34.
Waters and watercourses.
Fish.
Preventing passage of fish
up streams, §9-11-92.
Obstructing navigable
watercourse, §33-7-3.
**Water supply and
waterworks.**
Wells.
Violations of chapter,
§22-24-11.
Weights and measures.
Violations of chapter,
§8-16-18.
Welfare.
Child care facilities.
Violations of chapter,
§38-7-16.

PENALTIES—Cont'd
Welfare—Cont'd
Recipients of public
assistance.
Disclosure of names,
§38-1-4.
Witnesses.
Failure of subpoenaed
witness to attend and
remain, §12-21-182.
Failure or refusal to testify,
§12-21-143.
Workmen's compensation.
Overdue compensation
payments, §25-5-59.
Youth services.
Violations of chapter,
§44-1-10.

PENITENTIARY, §§14-3-30 to
14-3-60.
Alcoholic beverages.
Introducing into
penitentiary, §14-3-60.
Baggage.
Search of convicts' baggage,
§14-3-35.
Bail and recognizance.
Commission of offense during
incarceration, §14-3-56.
Bibles.
Board of corrections to
supply, §14-3-46.
Bond issues.
Improvement of penal and
correctional facilities,
Const. Ala., amd. 374.
Books.
Reading material.
Board of corrections to
supply, §14-3-46.
Cells.
Unhealthy or unfit cells.
Confinement in, §14-3-50.
Chains.
When authorized on convicts,
§14-3-52.
Clothing of convicts.
Requirements, §14-3-44.
Commission of offense
during incarceration.
Bail, §14-3-56.
Confinement of convict,
§14-3-56.
Evidence.
Fact of confinement in
penitentiary, §14-3-57.
Contagious diseases.
Removal of convicts,
§14-3-43.
Tuberculosis, §14-3-41.
Convict labor, §§14-3-47 to
14-3-49.
Corporal punishment,
§14-3-52.
Correctional incentive time
act, §§14-9-40 to 14-9-44.
County convicts.
Costs.
Sentencing of convicts,
§14-4-10.
Cruel or excessive
punishment, §14-3-52.
Death of convicts.
Disposition of effects,
§14-3-36.
Deductions from sentence.
Computation of incentive
time deductions,
§14-9-41.

PENITENTIARY—Cont'd
Deductions from sentence
—Cont'd
Good conduct time previously
earned.
Applicability of article,
§14-9-43.
Habitual offender laws.
Effect of article, §14-9-44.
Nonretroactive effect of
article, §14-9-44.
Parole.
Effect of deductions on
parole, §14-9-42.
Delivery of prisoners.
Detention of convicts en
route.
Duty of jailers, §14-3-34.
Sheriff, §14-3-33.
Depositions.
Convict in penitentiary.
Taking testimony of
convict on
interrogatories by
defendant, §12-21-263.
Diet, §14-3-45.
Discharging convicts.
General provisions.
See PRISONS AND
PRISONERS.
Diseases.
Contagious diseases.
Removal of prisoners,
§14-3-43.
Notifiable diseases.
Petition for testing and
treatment of inmate of
correctional facility,
§22-11A-37.
Sexually transmitted
diseases.
Prisoner testing
generally,
§22-11A-17.
Tuberculosis, §14-3-41.
Effects of convicts.
Disposition upon death,
§14-3-36.
Taking charge of, §14-3-36.
Eminent domain.
Acquisition of land, etc.,
§18-1A-271.
Escape.
See ESCAPE.
Evidence.
Commission of offense during
incarceration.
Fact of confinement in
penitentiary, §14-3-57.
Federal prisoners.
Board of corrections to
receive, §14-3-32.
Feeding of prisoners.
Diet, §14-3-45.
Female convicts.
Officers and guards,
§14-3-39.
Separation of convicts by sex,
§14-3-40.
Good conduct.
Deductions from sentence.
Correctional incentive
time, §§14-9-41 to
14-9-44.
Two or more convictions.
Effect of conduct thereon,
§14-3-38.
Guards. See within this
heading, "Officers and
guards."

PENITENTIARY—Cont'd
Hearings.
Management and treatment
of convicts, §14-3-54.
Hospitals.
Removal of convicts.
Contagious diseases,
§14-3-43.
Mentally ill, §14-3-42.
Separation of convicts.
Tubercular prisoners,
§14-3-41.
Housing.
Unhealthy or unfit cells.
Confinement in, §14-3-50.
Industries in penal
institutions.
See PRISONS AND
PRISONERS.
Inspection of penitentiary.
Board of corrections.
Authority, §14-6-106.
Effect of orders of board,
§14-6-107.
Investigations.
Management and treatment
of convicts, §14-3-54.
Jails.
Generally.
See JAILS.
Judgments.
Reversal of judgments.
Removal of convict,
§14-3-37.
Labor.
Convict labor, §§14-3-47 to
14-3-49.
Management of convicts.
Comments on and in
presence of convicts,
§14-3-55.
Inquiry, §14-3-54.
Mentally ill.
Removal of convicts,
§14-3-42.
Officers and guards.
Female convicts, §14-3-39.
General provisions.
See PRISONS AND
PRISONERS.
Management of convicts.
Comments on and in
presence of convicts,
§14-3-55.
Investigation, §14-3-54.
Parole.
Deductions from sentence.
Effect of deductions on
parole, §14-9-42.
Penalties.
Violation of chapter,
§14-3-16.
Warden.
Discharging convicts.
Wrongful discharge,
§14-10-3.
Prisons and prisoners
generally.
See PRISONS AND
PRISONERS.
Property.
Convict's property.
Disposition upon death,
§14-3-36.
Taking charge of, §14-3-36.
Punishment. See within this
heading, "Sentencing."
Reading material.
Board of corrections to
supply, §14-3-46.

PENITENTIARY—Cont'd
Records.
Punishment, §14-3-52.
Statistics.
Information regarding new
convicts, §14-3-35.
Removal of convicts.
Contagious diseases,
§14-3-43.
Insanity, §14-3-42.
Judgment reversed, §14-3-37.
Mentally ill, §14-3-42.
Temporary confinement of
convict in jail pending
removal, §14-3-30.
Urgent necessity, §14-3-43.
Rules and regulations.
Convict labor, §14-3-47.
Posting, §14-3-59.
Searches.
Baggage of convicts,
§14-3-35.
Person of convicts.
New arrival, §14-3-35.
Sentencing.
Commuted sentence.
Imprisonment on, §14-3-31.
Good conduct.
Deductions from sentence.
Correctional incentive
time, §§14-9-41 to
14-9-44.
Two or more convictions.
Effect of conduct on,
§14-3-38.
Punishment.
Corporal punishment,
§14-3-52.
Cruel or excessive
punishment, §14-3-52.
Records, §14-3-52.
Restrictions, §14-3-51.
Two or more convictions.
Effect of convict's conduct
thereon, §14-3-38.
How sentences to be
served, §14-3-38.
Separation of convicts.
Male and female, §14-3-40.
Sex.
Separation of convicts,
§14-3-40.
Shackles.
When authorized on convicts,
§14-3-53.
Sheriffs.
Delivery of convicts by
sheriff, §14-3-33.
Statistics.
Information regarding
convicts.
Entering on records,
§14-3-35.
Tuberculosis.
Convicts suffering from,
§14-3-41.
Violation of chapter.
Commission of offense during
incarceration, §§14-3-56,
14-3-57.
Warden.
Discharging convicts.
Penalty for wrongful
discharge, §14-10-3.
Women.
Officers and guards,
§14-3-39.
Separation of convicts by sex,
§14-3-40.

PENITENTIARY—Cont'd
Work, §§14-3-47 to 14-3-49.
Convict labor. See within
this heading, "Convict
labor."

PENNY TRUST FUND.
Deposits, §41-15A-1.
Division of proceeds,
§41-15A-2.
**Gifts, donations and
bequests.**
Authorization to accept,
§41-15A-1.
Income tax.
Return, §41-15A-4.
State and local public funds.
Not to be deposited into fund,
§41-15A-5.
Taxation.
Deduction, §41-15A-3.

PENSIONS.
Annuity tables, §§35-16-1,
35-16-2.
Circuit court judges.
Retirement.
See CIRCUIT COURTS.
Confederate veterans.
Widows of Confederate
veterans, §§31-8-1 to
31-8-33.
See VETERANS.
Counties.
See COUNTIES.
District court judges.
Retirement.
See DISTRICT COURTS.
Governor.
Widows or widowers of
governors, §36-13-12.
Income tax.
Corporations.
Deductions allowed
corporations.
Contributions paid by
employer to pension
plans, §40-18-35.
Deductions.
Contributions paid by
employer to pension
plans, §40-18-15.
Exemptions, §40-18-19.
Judges.
Retirement generally.
Circuit courts.
See CIRCUIT COURTS.
Court of civil appeals.
See COURT OF CIVIL
APPEALS.
Court of criminal appeals.
See COURT OF
CRIMINAL
APPEALS.
District courts.
See DISTRICT COURTS.
Judicial retirement fund.
See JUDGES.
Probate courts.
See PROBATE COURTS.
Supreme court justices.
See SUPREME COURT.
Mortality tables, §§35-16-3,
35-16-4.
Municipal corporations.
See MUNICIPAL
CORPORATIONS.
Peace officers.
Annuity and benefit fund,
§§36-21-60 to 36-21-78.
See PEACE OFFICERS.

PENSIONS—Cont'd
Probate judges.
Retirement.
See PROBATE COURTS.
Sheriffs.
Retirement system,
§§36-22-40 to 36-22-45.
See SHERIFFS.
Social security.
General provisions.
See SOCIAL SECURITY.
**State employees' retirement
system,** §§36-27-1 to
36-27-86.
See PUBLIC OFFICERS
AND EMPLOYEES.
Supreme court justices.
Retirement.
See SUPREME COURT.
Teachers' retirement system,
§§16-25-1 to 16-25-47.
See EDUCATION.
Trusts and trustees.
Trusts for employees or self-
employed persons,
§35-4-259.
Veterans.
Widows of Confederate
veterans, §§31-8-1 to
31-8-33.
See VETERANS.

PERDIDO RIVER.
State boundary, §§41-2-3,
41-2-4.

PERINATAL HEALTH.
**Mothers and babies indigent
care trust fund,**
§§22-12B-1 to 22-12B-4.
Perinatal health act.
General provisions,
§§22-12A-1 to 22-12A-6.
See HEALTH.

PERJURY.
**Banks and financial
institutions.**
False reports by bank
examiners, §5-3A-10.
False swearing, etc., before
bank examiner or
superintendent, §5-3A-7.
Child support programs.
Falsification of financial
reports, §38-10-9.
Corroboration.
Required for conviction,
§13A-10-105.
Defenses.
Irregularities no defense,
§13A-10-108.
**Denial of guilt in previous
trials.**
Not to be prosecuted as
perjury, §13A-10-106.
First degree perjury.
Class C felony, §13A-10-101.
Elements, §13A-10-101.
Fraternal benefit societies,
§27-34-53.
**Hazardous waste or
substances.**
Fees for disposal of
hazardous waste or
substances.
Monthly reports to be
sworn.
Perjury in making
reports, §22-30B-10.

PERJURY—Cont'd
Income tax.
Affidavits.
Making false affidavits,
§40-18-52.
Returns, §40-18-27.
Inconsistent statements.
Degree of perjury for which
defendant may be
convicted, §13A-10-104.
Indictments.
Form of indictment,
§15-8-150.
Inconsistent statements.
Single count indictment,
§13A-10-104.
**Irregularities no defense to
prosecution,** §13A-10-108.
Libel and slander.
Accusation of false swearing,
§6-5-180.
Oaths.
Administration of oath in
irregular manner.
No defense to prosecution,
§13A-10-108.
Previous trials.
Denial of guilt in previous
trial not to be prosecuted
as perjury, §13A-10-106.
Public service commission.
Hearings on rate and other
regulations.
Perjury prosecution not
barred, §37-1-91.
**Retraction of false
statements.**
When bar to perjury
prosecution,
§13A-10-107.
Sales tax.
Reports.
False statements,
§40-23-10.
Second degree perjury,
§13A-10-102.
**Statements made in separate
hearings at separate
stages of same trial,**
§13A-10-107.
Third degree perjury,
§13A-10-103.
Unsworn falsification.
Elements of crime,
§13A-10-109.
Witnesses.
Corroboration required,
§13A-10-105.

PERMITS.
Accountants.
See ACCOUNTANTS.
Advertising.
Outdoor advertising.
Erection and maintenance
of signs.
See ADVERTISING.
Agriculture.
See AGRICULTURE.
Air commerce.
Certificates and permits,
§§37-9-16 to 37-9-23,
37-9-25.
See AIR COMMERCE.
Air pollution, §22-28-16.
Airports.
Zoning permits, §4-6-8.
**Banks and financial
institutions,** §§5-5A-1,
5-5A-10, 5-5A-11.

PERMITS—Cont'd
Boxing and wrestling,
§41-9-96.
Brake fluid.
Sale or distribution, §8-17-2.
Burial permits.
See BURIAL.
Child labor.
See LABOR.
Coastal areas, §9-7-20.
Commission merchants.
Sale of farm produce.
See COMMISSION
MERCHANTS.
Contract carrier permits.
Motor vehicle carriers.
See MOTOR VEHICLE
CARRIERS.
Corporations, §§40-14-20 to
40-14-23.
Cotton gins, §§2-19-61,
2-19-63, 2-19-64.
Counties.
Land-use management in
flood-prone areas.
Construction and
development permits,
§11-19-7.
Dead bodies.
Burial permits.
See BURIAL.
Removal permits.
See DEAD BODIES.
Dentists.
Anesthesia.
Use of general anesthesia.
See DENTISTS.
Teaching permits, §34-9-8.
Education.
Unaccredited schools.
See EDUCATION.
Eggs and egg products,
§§2-8-170, 2-12-4.
**Environmental management
department,** §22-22-9.
Fertilizer dealers, §2-22-4.
**Fire protection sprinkler
systems,** §§34-33-4 to
34-33-8.
Fireworks, §§8-17-210 to
8-17-216.
See FIREWORKS.
Fish and game.
Collection of wild animals
and birds for scientific
purposes, §9-11-231.
Commercial fee fishing
ponds, §§9-11-450,
9-11-453, 9-11-454.
Exhibitions, §§9-11-324 to
9-11-327.
Propagation.
Private purposes,
§9-11-261.
Raccoons.
Coon on the log contests,
§§9-11-248, 9-11-249.
Garbage and trash, §22-27-3.
Out-of-state transporters,
§22-27-5.
Ginseng.
Exportation of ginseng,
§9-13-245.
Refusal or recall of permits.
Powers of commissioner,
§9-13-249.
Hazardous waste, §22-30-12.
**Hearing aid dealers and
fitters,** §§34-14-1, 34-14-7.

PERMITS—Cont'd
Highways.
Movement of oversized
vehicles or loads.
General provisions,
§32-9-29.
Special permits for
movement of certain site-
built buildings,
§32-9-29.1.
Utilities.
Digging up roads, §23-1-4.
Honeybees and apiaries.
Used beekeeping equipment.
Shipment, movement, etc.,
without permit,
§2-14-6.
Horse racing, §§11-65-23 to
11-65-26, 11-65-42.
Industrial alcohol.
See INDUSTRIAL
ALCOHOL.
Insurers.
Solicitation permits.
See INSURANCE.
Landscaping.
Horticulture and floriculture
work, §§2-28-4 to 2-28-7,
2-28-11.
Lime.
Manufacture or distribution
of agricultural liming
materials, §§2-23-3,
2-23-5.
Liquefied petroleum gas.
See LIQUEFIED
PETROLEUM GAS.
Livestock.
Dealers.
See LIVESTOCK.
Markets.
See LIVESTOCK.
Manufactured buildings.
Special permits for
movement of certain site-
built buildings,
§32-9-29.1.
Marine resources.
Reefs.
Permits to use private
reefs, §9-12-32.
Mellorine, §20-1-133.
Milk and milk products.
See MILK AND MILK
PRODUCTS.
Mines and minerals.
Coal surface mining.
See COAL.
Surface mining.
See MINES AND
MINERALS.
Mobile homes, §§32-9-29,
32-9-29.1.
Motor vehicle carriers.
Contract carrier permits.
See MOTOR VEHICLE
CARRIERS.
Motor vehicles.
See MOTOR VEHICLES.
Outdoor advertising.
Erection and maintenance of
signs.
See ADVERTISING.
Pest control, §§2-28-4 to
2-28-7.
Pesticides.
Use permits, §2-27-11.
Petroleum products.
See OIL AND GAS.

PERMITS—Cont'd
Pharmacists and pharmacies, §§34-23-30 to 34-23-34.
See PHARMACISTS AND PHARMACIES.
Plant pathology, §§2-28-4 to 2-28-7.
Plumbing.
Installation of facilities, §§22-26-4, 22-26-5.
Poultry.
Hatcheries and chick dealers, §2-16-3.
Public works.
Improvement authorities.
Chapter exclusive, §39-7-33.
Railroads.
Conductors, §37-2-86.1.
Engineers, §37-2-86.1.
Sales tax.
Manufacturers.
Purchasing tangible personal property without payment of sales tax, §40-23-31.
Savings and loan associations, §5-2A-62.
Schools.
Unaccredited schools, §16-46-6.
Seeds, §§2-26-5, 2-26-6.
Sentencing.
Article not to deprive court of authority to suspend or cancel permit, §13A-5-2.
Solid waste.
Management plan.
Moratorium on issuance of permits, §22-27-49.
Soybeans.
Buyers, §2-8-102.
Surface mining.
Coal surface mining.
See COAL.
General provisions.
See MINES AND MINERALS.
Tobacco.
Sales tax.
Permit for wholesalers or jobbers, §40-25-16.
Transportation companies, §§37-2-5 to 37-2-7.
Tree surgery.
See TREES AND TIMBER.
Utilities.
Digging up of roads, §23-1-4.
Veterinarians.
Premise permits, §§34-29-88, 34-29-89.
Warehouses, §§8-15-3 to 8-15-10, 8-15-14.
See WAREHOUSES.
Water conservation and irrigation.
Agency.
Construction permits, §9-10-6.
Corporations, §9-10-35.
Water supply and waterworks.
Safe drinking water act.
Permit to construct or modify water system, §§22-23-40 to 22-23-43.

PERMITS—Cont'd
Welfare.
Child care facilities.
Temporary permits, §38-7-5.
Wrestling, §41-9-96.

PERPETUITIES.
Rule against perpetuities, §§35-4-4, 35-4-5.

PERRY COUNTY.
Probate judge.
Compensation, Const. Ala., amd. 485.

PERSONAL INJURY.
Claims against state.
Limitation on amount of award, §41-9-70.
Damages generally.
See DAMAGES.
Dogs injuring persons, §§3-6-1 to 3-6-4.
Employer's liability for certain injuries.
See EMPLOYERS AND EMPLOYEES.
Felonious injury.
Civil action without criminal prosecution, §6-5-370.
Limitation of actions.
Two year limitation, §6-2-38.
Motor vehicles.
Accidents involving injuries, §32-10-1.
Municipal corporations.
Liability for negligence of agents, etc.
Filing of statement as to manner of injury, §11-47-192.
Pleadings.
Form of complaint for personal injuries, ARCP, Form 31.
Torts generally.
See TORTS.
Workmen's compensation.
Injuries.
See WORKMEN'S COMPENSATION.

PERSONAL PROPERTY.
Actions.
Detinue, §§6-6-250 to 6-6-264.
See DETINUE.
Possession.
Deprivation of owner of possession, §6-5-260.
Interference with mere possession, §6-5-261.
Remainderman or reversioner.
Rights of action, §6-5-264.
Replevin, §§6-6-100 to 6-6-102.
Trespass.
Bailments, §6-5-263.
Generally, §6-5-262.
Trial of right of property, §§6-6-160 to 6-6-167. See within this heading, "Trial of right of property."
Affidavits.
Trial of right of property, §§6-6-160, 6-6-161.
Agriculture.
Sale of farm products, §43-2-419.

PERSONAL PROPERTY —Cont'd
Air commerce.
Leasing or renting.
Licenses.
Air carriers.
Exemptions, §40-12-223.
Aliens.
Right of aliens to take, hold and transmit property, §35-1-1.
Attachments.
See ATTACHMENTS.
Bailments.
See BAILMENTS.
Bequests.
Wills, §§43-8-140, 43-8-224.
Bonds, surety.
Trial of right of property. See within this heading, "Trial of right of property."
Brands and marks.
Defacing identifying mark on encumbered personal property, §8-12-3.
Bulk transfers, §§7-6-101 to 7-6-111.
See COMMERCIAL CODE.
Chattel mortgages.
Fraud, §8-9-1.
Secured transactions, §§7-9-101 to 7-9-507.
See COMMERCIAL CODE.
Trial of right of property.
Claims based on mortgage, §6-6-164.
Commercial code.
Secured transactions, §§7-9-101 to 7-9-507.
See COMMERCIAL CODE.
Conditional sales.
Evidence.
When conditional sales contract received in evidence, §35-4-98.
Secured transactions, §§7-9-101 to 7-9-507.
See COMMERCIAL CODE.
Contracts.
Specific performance.
Breach of agreement to transfer.
Pecuniary compensation presumed adequate, §8-1-47.
Conveyances.
General provisions.
See CONVEYANCES.
Minors.
Conveyances of personalty to minors, §35-4-96.
Corporations.
Property generally.
See CORPORATIONS.
Counties.
Property generally.
See COUNTIES.
Decedents' estates.
Executors and administrators.
General provisions.
See EXECUTORS AND ADMINISTRATORS.
Sale of personal property, §§43-2-410 to 43-2-422.
See EXECUTORS AND ADMINISTRATORS.

PERSONAL PROPERTY
—Cont'd

Definitions, §1-1-1.
Leasing or renting.
Licenses, §40-12-220.
Departments.
Inventory of nonconsumable personal property, §41-1-6.
Detinue, §§6-6-250 to 6-6-264.
See DETINUE.
Equity of redemption.
Executions, §6-9-40.
Escheats.
Action by state to recover personal property distributed without authority, §43-6-8.
Disposition of personalty when no heir appears, §43-6-4.
Executions.
See EXECUTIONS.
Executors and administrators.
General provisions.
See EXECUTORS AND ADMINISTRATORS.
Sale of personal property, §§43-2-410 to 43-2-422.
See EXECUTORS AND ADMINISTRATORS.
Exemptions from administration and payment of debts, §§6-10-67 to 6-10-107.
See EXEMPTIONS FROM ADMINISTRATION AND PAYMENT OF DEBTS.
Exemptions from levy and sale under process, §§6-10-1 to 6-10-43.
See EXEMPTIONS FROM LEVY AND SALE UNDER PROCESS.
Farm products.
Sale, §43-2-419.
Fraud.
Mortgage of personalty, §8-9-1.
Fraudulent leasing or rental of property, §§13A-8-140 to 13A-8-144.
Garnishment.
Proceedings when garnishee liable for delivery, §6-6-455.
Gifts generally.
See GIFTS.
Husband and wife.
Property generally.
See HUSBAND AND WIFE.
Income tax.
Dealers in personal property.
Installment method, §40-18-44.
Installment method.
Dealers in personal property, §40-18-44.
Gain or loss upon disposition of installment obligations, §40-18-44.
Judgments.
Trial of right of property.
Execution for amount of judgment, §6-6-163.

PERSONAL PROPERTY
—Cont'd

Landlord and tenant.
Conveyances of personal property brought into state by tenants for life or years.
Recordation, §35-4-54.
Larceny.
See LARCENY.
Leasing or renting.
Licenses.
Amount of tax, §40-12-222.
Collection of tax, §40-12-224.
Definitions, §40-12-220.
Exemption, §40-12-223.
Interest on overpayment, §40-12-225.
Levy of tax, §40-12-222.
Payment of tax.
Overpayment.
Interest, §40-12-225.
Proceeds of tax.
Deposit in state treasury, §40-12-226.
Disposition, §40-12-227.
Required, §40-12-221.
Liens.
Trial of right of property.
Claims based on lien, §6-6-164.
Life estates.
Conveyances of personal property brought into state by tenants for life or years.
Recordation, §35-4-54.
Removal of personalty.
Consent of remainderman or reversioner required, §35-4-171.
Loans.
Effect of loans of personal property not in writing, §35-4-95.
Loans in writing, §35-4-94.
Lost or unclaimed property, §§35-12-1 to 35-12-48.
See LOST OR UNCLAIMED PROPERTY.
Marriage.
Conveyed in consideration of marriage.
Recordation necessary as to purchasers, mortgagees and judgment creditors, §35-4-93.
Minors.
Conveyances of personalty to minors, §35-4-96.
Mortgages and deeds of trust.
Fraud, §8-9-1.
Secured transactions, §§7-9-101 to 7-9-507.
See COMMERCIAL CODE.
Trial of right of property.
Claims based on mortgage, §6-6-164.
Municipal corporations.
Property generally.
See MUNICIPAL CORPORATIONS.

PERSONAL PROPERTY
—Cont'd

Parent and child.
Conveyances of personalty to minors.
Recordation necessary as to purchasers, mortgagees and judgment creditors, §35-4-96.
Partition.
General provisions, §§35-6-1 to 35-6-126.
See PARTITION.
Partnerships.
Property generally.
See PARTNERSHIPS.
Probate courts.
Trial of right of property.
Return where execution issued from probate court, §6-6-165.
Property generally.
See PROPERTY.
Recordation.
Choses in action not personal property within meaning used in division, §35-4-55.
Conveyances in consideration of marriage.
Necessary recordation, §35-4-93.
Conveyances of personal property brought into state by tenants for life or years, §35-4-54.
Remainders, reversions and executory interests.
Actions.
Rights of remainderman or reversioner, §6-5-264.
Recordation, §35-4-94.
Removal of personalty by life tenant.
Consent of remainderman or reversioner required, §35-4-171.
Renting, §§40-12-220 to 40-12-227. See within this heading, "Leasing or renting."
Replevin, §§6-6-100 to 6-6-102.
Rule against perpetuities, §§35-4-4, 35-4-5.
Sales tax.
Exemptions, §40-23-4.
Salvage, §§35-13-1 to 35-13-10.
See SALVAGE.
Secured transactions, §§7-9-101 to 7-9-507.
See COMMERCIAL CODE.
Space science exhibit commission, §41-9-436.
State departments and agencies.
Inventory of nonconsumable personal property, §41-1-6.
Surplus personal property, §§41-16-120 to 41-16-125.
See SURPLUS PERSONAL PROPERTY.
Taxation.
Exemptions, §40-9-1.
Holding by warehousemen for distribution, §40-9-7.
Storage for shipment outside state, §40-9-6.

PERSONAL PROPERTY
—Cont'd
Taxation—Cont'd
Subjects of taxation,
§40-11-1.
Tax collectors.
Levy and sale of personal
property.
See TAXATION.
Theft.
Fraudulent leasing or rental
of property, §§13A-8-140
to 13A-8-144.
Transfers.
Bulk transfers, §§7-6-101 to
7-6-111.
See COMMERCIAL CODE.
Trespass, §§6-2-34, 6-5-262,
6-5-263.
Trial of right of property,
§§6-6-160 to 6-6-167.
Affidavit, §6-6-160.
Return, §6-6-161.
Assessment.
Damages for delay,
§6-6-162.
Property value, §6-6-162.
Bonds, surety, §6-6-160.
Forfeited bonds, §§6-6-165,
6-6-166.
Forfeiture of claimant's
bond, §6-6-163.
Return, §6-6-161.
Burden of proof, §6-6-161.
Claims based on mortgage or
lien, §6-6-164.
Costs.
Execution for amount,
§6-6-163.
Damages.
Execution for amount,
§6-6-163.
Delivery of property to
claimant, §6-6-160.
Execution.
Judgment, damages and
costs, §6-6-163.
Judgments.
Execution for amount,
§6-6-163.
Levy.
Other property.
Levy by plaintiff not
precluded, §6-6-167.
Liens.
Claims based on liens,
§6-6-164.
Mortgages.
Claims based on
mortgages, §6-6-164.
Persons not party to writ of
execution or attachment.
Claim to personal property
levied on, §6-6-160.
Probate courts.
Return where execution
issued from probate
court, §6-6-165.
Return.
Affidavit, §6-6-161.
Bond, §6-6-161.
Execution issued from
probate court,
§6-6-165.
Levy made in different
county than where
judgment entered or
original attachment
issued, §6-6-166.
Writ, §6-6-161.

PERSONAL PROPERTY
—Cont'd
Trial of right of property
—Cont'd
Sheriffs.
Release from damages for
seizure, §6-6-168.
Writ.
Return, §6-6-161.
Trusts and trustees.
General provisions.
See TRUSTS AND
TRUSTEES.
Unclaimed property,
§§35-12-1 to 35-12-48.
See LOST OR UNCLAIMED
PROPERTY.
**Unincorporated professional
associations.**
Conveyances, §10-10-9.
Wills.
General provisions.
See WILLS.

**PERSONAL
REPRESENTATIVES.**
**Abatement, revival and
survival.**
Claims by and against in
proceedings not of an
equitable nature,
§6-5-462.
Substitution where no action
filed, §6-5-465.
Attorneys at law.
See ATTORNEYS AT LAW.
**Executors and
administrators,** §§43-2-1
to 43-2-813.
See EXECUTORS AND
ADMINISTRATORS.
Fiduciaries generally.
See FIDUCIARIES.
Guardian and ward.
See GUARDIAN AND
WARD.
Trusts and trustees.
See TRUSTS AND
TRUSTEES.

PERSONNEL SYSTEM.
**Fire fighters' personnel
standards and education
commission,** §§36-32-1 to
36-32-12.
See FIRES AND FIRE
PREVENTION.
Merit system, §§36-26-1 to
36-26-108.
See PUBLIC OFFICERS
AND EMPLOYEES.

PEST CONTROL, §§2-28-1 to
2-28-12.
Appeals.
Denial or revocation of
permits, §2-28-7.
Applicability of chapter,
§2-28-12.
Bonds, surety.
Subterranean termite
eradication and control
work, §2-28-10.
Branch offices.
Operation and supervision,
§2-28-8.
Conduct of business, §2-28-8.
County health officers.
Duties, §22-3-5.
Definitions, §2-28-1.

PEST CONTROL—Cont'd
Examinations.
Applicants for permits,
§2-28-4.
Applicability of
requirement as to
examination, §2-28-6.
Persons engaged in
entomological work to be
examined, §2-28-2.
Examining board, §2-28-2.
Fees.
Permit fees, §2-28-4.
Garbage and trash, §22-27-4.
Injunctions.
Proceedings to restrain
performance of
professional work or
services without permit,
§2-28-11.
Insurance.
Subterranean termite
eradication and control
work, §2-28-10.
Nurseries.
Insect and disease control,
§§2-25-1 to 2-25-22.
See NURSERIES.
Offices.
Operation and supervision of
main offices, etc.,
§2-28-8.
Penalties.
Commissioner of agriculture
and industries may
impose, §2-2-18.
Violations of chapter or rules
or regulations, §2-28-11.
**Performance of structural
pest control work.**
Regulation, §2-28-8.
Permits.
Appeal from denial or
revocation, §2-28-7.
Applicants.
Evidence as to
qualifications.
Applicants to present to
commissioner,
§2-28-5.
Minimum qualifications,
§2-28-5.
Submission of statements
as to training and
experience by
applicants, §2-28-4.
Testing and examination,
§2-28-4.
Applicability of
requirement as to
examination,
§2-28-6.
Commissioner of agriculture
and industries.
Appeals from denial or
revocation of permits,
§2-28-7.
Applicants to present
evidence as to
qualifications to
commissioner, §2-28-5.
Denial or revocation of
permits, §2-28-7.
Denial, §2-28-7.
Duration, §2-28-4.
Examination of applicants,
§§2-28-4, 2-28-6.
Fees, §2-28-4.

PEST CONTROL—Cont'd
Permits—Cont'd
Injunctive proceedings to restrain performance of professional work or services without permit, §2-28-11.
Issuance, §§2-28-4, 2-28-5.
Required for performance of professional work or services governed by chapter, §2-28-4.
Revocation, §2-28-7.
Pesticides.
See PESTICIDES.
Qualifications.
Applicants for permits, §2-28-5.
Promulgation of rules and regulations as to qualifications, §2-28-3.
Rules and regulations.
Penalties for violations, §2-28-11.
Performance of structural pest control work, §2-28-8.
Performance of subterranean termite eradication and control work, §2-28-9.
Qualifications and practice of persons engaged in work governed by chapter.
Promulgation of rules and regulations, §2-28-3.
Violations.
Penalties, §2-28-11.
Subterranean termite eradication and control work.
Bond, surety, §2-28-10.
Insurance, §2-28-10.
Regulation of performance, §2-28-9.
Training.
Submission of statements as to training by applicants for permits, §2-28-4.
Violations of chapter.
Penalties for violations, §2-28-11.

PESTICIDES, §§2-27-1 to 2-27-63.
Administration of article, §2-27-4.
Advertising.
False advertising prohibited, §2-27-14.
Advisory committee.
Generally, §2-27-6.
Agreements.
Intergovernmental agreements, §2-27-7.
Analysis, §2-27-12.
Deficiencies in analysis, §2-27-13.
State laboratory generally.
See within this heading, "State laboratory."
Appeals.
Application of pesticides.
Licenses.
Appeals from suspension, revocation or modification of licenses, §2-27-54.
Applicability of article.
Exceptions to applicability, §2-27-5.

PESTICIDES—Cont'd
Application of pesticides, §§2-27-50 to 2-27-62.
Appeals from suspension, revocation or modification of licenses, §2-27-54.
Applicability of article.
Exceptions to applicability, §2-27-52.
Article deemed cumulative, §2-27-63.
Bonds, surety, §2-27-56.
Commissioner of agriculture and industries.
Rules and regulations, §2-27-57.
Suspension, revocation or modification of licenses.
Appeals from actions of commissioner, §2-27-54.
Definitions, §2-27-50.
Disposal of pesticides.
Rules and regulations, §2-27-59.
Enforcement of article, §2-27-61.
Exceptions to applicability of article, §2-27-52.
Fee.
License fee, §2-27-53.
Handling of pesticides.
Rules and regulations, §2-27-59.
Injunctions.
Violations of article, §2-27-62.
Inspections, §2-27-61.
Insurance.
Liability insurance, §2-27-56.
Liability insurance, §2-27-56.
Licenses.
Appeals from actions of commissioner, §2-27-54.
Applications, §2-27-53.
Bonds, surety, §2-27-56.
Duration, §2-27-53.
Examination of applicants, §2-27-53.
Expiration date, §2-27-53.
Fee, §2-27-53.
Liability insurance, §2-27-56.
Modification, §2-27-54.
Nonresidents, §2-27-55.
Renewal, §2-27-53.
Required, §2-27-53.
Revocation, §2-27-54.
Suspension, §2-27-54.
Method of application.
Rules and regulations, §2-27-58.
Nonresidents.
Licenses, §2-27-55.
Penalties.
Violations of article, §2-27-62.
Purpose of article, §2-27-51.
Records, §2-27-60.
Reports, §2-27-60.
Rules and regulations.
Disposal of pesticides, §2-27-59.
Generally, §2-27-57.
Handling of pesticides, §2-27-59.

PESTICIDES—Cont'd
Application of pesticides —Cont'd
Rules and regulations —Cont'd
Method of application, §2-27-58.
Time of application, §2-27-58.
Type of application, §2-27-58.
Violations of article.
Injunctions, §2-27-62.
Penalty for violations, §2-27-62.
Bonds, surety.
Application of pesticides, §2-27-56.
Condemnation.
Noncomplying articles, §2-27-15.
Cooperation.
Intergovernmental cooperation, §2-27-7.
Definitions, §2-27-2.
Application of pesticides, §2-27-50.
Disposal.
Rules and regulations, §2-27-59.
Enforcement of article, §2-27-4.
Exceptions to applicability of article, §2-27-5.
Exports.
Exception to applicability of article, §2-27-5.
Fees.
Application of pesticides.
License fee, §2-27-53.
Handling.
Rules and regulations, §2-27-59.
Injunctions.
Application of pesticides, §2-27-62.
Violations of article, §2-27-16.
Inspections, §2-27-12.
Application of pesticides, §2-27-61.
Insurance.
Application of pesticides.
Liability insurance, §2-27-56.
Intergovernmental cooperation and agreements, §2-27-7.
Labels.
Altering, defacing, etc., prohibited, §2-27-14.
Laboratories.
State laboratory, §§2-27-30 to 2-27-33.
Licenses.
Required to sell, §2-27-10.
Nonresidents.
Application of pesticides.
Licenses, §2-27-55.
Penalties.
Application of pesticides.
Penalty for violations of article, §2-27-62.
Commissioner of agriculture and industries may impose, §2-2-18.
Violations of article, §2-27-16.
Permits.
Use permits, §2-27-11.

PESTICIDES—Cont'd
Pesticide residue laboratory,
§§2-27-30 to 2-27-33.
Prohibited acts, §2-27-14.
Purpose of article, §2-27-3.
Records.
Application of pesticides,
§2-27-60.
Registration.
Generally, §2-27-9.
Reports.
Application of pesticides,
§2-27-60.
Rules and regulations,
§2-27-8.
Application of pesticides,
§§2-27-50 to 2-27-62. See
within this heading,
"Application of
pesticides."
Sales.
Prohibited acts, §2-27-14.
Sales tax.
Exemptions.
Gross proceeds of sales of
insecticides and
fungicides, §40-23-4.
Sampling, §2-27-12.
Deficiencies in analysis,
§2-27-13.
Seizure.
Noncomplying articles,
§2-27-15.
Short title of article, §2-27-1.
State laboratory.
Additional powers and
authority, §2-27-33.
Director, §2-27-32.
Establishment, §2-27-30.
Executive committee,
§2-27-30.
Location, §2-27-31.
Operation, §2-27-30.
Policy committee, §2-27-30.
Suspension from sale.
Noncomplying articles,
§2-27-15.
Use tax.
Exemptions, §40-23-62.
Violations of article.
Injunctions to restrain,
§2-27-16.
Penalties, §2-27-16.
Suspension from sale, seizure
and condemnation of
noncomplying articles,
§2-27-15.

PESTS.
Control, §§2-28-1 to 2-28-12.
See PEST CONTROL.
Insects.
See INSECTS.
**Nuisances menacing public
health,** §§22-10-1 to
22-10-3.
Pesticides, §§2-27-1 to 2-27-63.
See PESTICIDES.

PETITIONS.
Abortion.
Parental consent to
performing abortion
upon minors.
Waiver of written consent
requirement, §26-21-4.
Adoption, §§26-10-1, 26-10-2.
Bankruptcy and insolvency.
Recordation, §35-4-52.

PETITIONS—Cont'd
Coal.
Surface mining control and
reclamation.
Designation of areas
unsuitable for surface
coal mining, §9-16-96.
Conservators.
Appointment, §§26-2A-133,
26-2A-134, 26-2A-135.
**Constitution of the United
States.**
Right of, Const. U. S.,
Amendment I.
Counties.
Cemeteries.
Petition for appointment of
commission, §11-17-1.
Relocation of county seats,
§§11-16-1, 11-16-32.
Diseases.
Notifiable diseases.
Commitment of afflicted
persons.
Attorney to be appointed,
§22-11A-29.
Confinement when no
treatment available,
§22-11A-32.
Content of petition,
§22-11A-25.
Findings, §22-11A-32.
Generally, §22-11A-25.
Guardian ad litem to be
appointed,
§22-11A-29.
Hearings.
Rules to apply,
§22-11A-31.
Notice of petition to be
served, §22-11A-27.
Order for person to
appear for hearing
and to be examined
by a physician,
§22-11A-30.
Petitions without merit
to be dismissed,
§22-11A-26.
Placing limitations upon
liberty of person
afflicted, §22-11A-28.
Probate judge may take
sworn testimony of
petitioners,
§22-11A-26.
Rehearing, §22-11A-32.
Rules to apply at
hearings,
§22-11A-31.
Prisoner testing.
Petition for testing and
treatment of inmate
of correctional
facility, §22-11A-37.
Elections.
Presidential and vice-
presidential elections.
Nominating petitions,
§17-19-2.
Electric cooperatives.
Initiative by members,
§37-6-17.
Extraordinary writs, ARAP,
Rule 21.
Forests and forestry.
Taxation.
Special county taxes for
forest protection.
Request for assessment,
§9-13-163.

PETITIONS—Cont'd
Guardian and ward.
Curators.
Appointment, §26-7A-2.
Uniform guardianship and
protective proceedings
act.
Appointment of
conservators or other
protective orders.
Petitions for orders
subsequent to
appointment of
conservators,
§26-2A-144.
Procedure concerning
hearing and order on
original petition,
§26-2A-135.
Resignation or removal
of conservators,
§26-2A-143.
Termination of
conservatorships,
§26-2A-158.
Court appointment of
guardians for minors,
§26-2A-75.
Incapacitated persons.
Guardians.
Court appointment,
§26-2A-102.
Removal or petition to
resign,
§26-2A-110.
Temporary guardians,
§26-2A-107.
Minors.
Guardians.
Removal or for
permission to
resign, §26-2A-81.
Protective proceedings.
Appointment of
conservators or other
protective orders,
§26-2A-130.
Original petition,
§26-2A-133.
Habeas corpus, §§15-21-4 to
15-21-7.
Highways.
Closing and vacating streets,
alleys and highways,
§23-4-2.
Improvement authorities,
§§39-7-3 to 39-7-6.
**Junior college for Franklin,
Marion and Winston
counties.**
Petition for conversion to
trade school and junior
college, §16-60-38.
Juvenile proceedings.
General provisions.
See JUVENILE
PROCEEDINGS.
Mandamus.
Rules of appellate procedure,
ARAP, Rule 21.
Municipal corporations.
General provisions.
See MUNICIPAL
CORPORATIONS.
Post-conviction remedies.
Appeals.
Release of petitioners,
ARCrP, Rule 20.10 (b).
Commencement of
proceedings, ARCrP,
Rule 20.6 (a), (b).

PETITIONS—Cont'd
Post-conviction remedies
—Cont'd
Filing, ARCrP, Rule 20.6 (a).
Notification of appellate
courts, ARCrP, Rule 20.6
(c).
Release of petitioners.
Appeals, ARCrP, Rule
20.10 (b).
Service, ARCrP, Rule 20.6
(a).
Specificity, ARCrP, Rule 20.6
(b).
Successive petitions.
Preclusion of remedy,
ARCrP, Rule 20.2 (b).
Prohibition, writ of.
Rules of appellate procedure,
ARAP, Rule 21.
Public works.
Improvement authorities,
§§39-7-3 to 39-7-6.
**Right to petition for a
redress of grievances,**
Const. U. S., Amendment
I.
Rules of criminal procedure.
Commencement of
proceedings, ARCrP,
Rule 20.6.
Post-conviction remedies.
Successive petitions.
Preclusion of remedy,
ARCrP, Rule 20.2
(b).
Soil and water conservation.
Districts.
Incorporation of districts,
§§9-8-23.
Watershed conservancy
districts.
Petition for formation,
§§9-8-53 to 9-8-55.
Transfers to minors.
Accounting.
Petition for accounting by
custodian, §35-5A-20.
**Water management and
drainage.**
Water management districts.
See WATER
MANAGEMENT AND
DRAINAGE.

PETIT JURIES.
See JURY.

PETIT LARCENY.
General provisions.
See LARCENY.

PETROLEUM PRODUCTS,
§§8-17-80 to 8-17-155.
See OIL AND GAS.

PEYOTE.
Controlled substances.
See DRUGS.

**PHARMACISTS AND
PHARMACIES,** §§34-23-1
to 34-23-118.
Adulterated drugs.
Sale prohibited, §34-23-9.
Alcohol.
Sale, purchase, and
prescription, §§28-4-150
to 28-4-166.
See ALCOHOLIC
BEVERAGES.
Applicability of chapter.
Objects and purposes of
chapter, §34-23-2.

PHARMACISTS AND
PHARMACIES—Cont'd
Applicability of chapter
—Cont'd
Physicians, dentists, etc.,
exempt from chapter,
§34-23-11.
Assistant's certificate.
Requirements, §34-23-50.
Association.
Defined, §34-23-1.
Attorney general.
Board of pharmacy.
Attorney general counsel
to board, §34-23-93.
Auctions and auctioneers.
Notice of auction sales of
drugs and medicines,
§34-23-6.
Bankruptcy and insolvency.
Notice of sale of drugs and
medicines, §34-23-6.
Board of pharmacy,
§§34-23-90 to 34-23-94.
Annual report to governor,
§34-23-92.
Appeals.
Judicial review of board
orders, §34-23-94.
Appointment of members,
§34-23-90.
Compensation.
Members of board,
§34-23-91.
Secretary, §34-23-91.
Composition, §34-23-90.
Defined, §34-23-1.
Election of officers,
§34-23-90.
Enforcement of chapter.
Assisting prosecuting
officers, §34-23-93.
Injunctions against
violations of chapter.
Authority of board,
§34-23-12.
Evidence.
Books and records of board,
§34-23-92.
Furnishing evidence to
prosecuting officers,
§34-23-93.
Governor.
Annual report to governor,
§34-23-92.
Appointment of members,
§34-23-90.
Injunctions against violations
of chapter, §34-23-12.
Inspectors, §34-23-3.
Judicial review of orders,
§34-23-94.
Legal counsel, §34-23-93.
Meetings, §34-23-91.
Public notice, §34-23-91.
Notification by pharmacists
of change of employment,
§34-23-10.
Oath of office, §34-23-90.
Officers.
Duties, §34-23-91.
Election, §34-23-90.
Orders.
Judicial review of orders,
§34-23-94.
Powers and duties.
Generally, §34-23-92.
Officers, §34-23-91.
Qualifications of members,
§34-23-90.
Quorum, §34-23-91.

PHARMACISTS AND
PHARMACIES—Cont'd
Board of pharmacy—Cont'd
Removal of members,
§34-23-90.
Rules and regulations.
Pharmacies in hospitals
and related
institutions.
Promulgation of rules
and regulations,
§34-23-74.
Promulgation by board,
§34-23-92.
Schools and colleges of
pharmacy.
Recognition, §34-23-4.
Secretary, §34-23-91.
Election by board,
§34-23-90.
Staff and assistants.
Employment by board,
§34-23-92.
Subpoena power of board,
§34-23-92.
Terms of office, §34-23-90.
Treasurer, §34-23-91.
Vacancies, §34-23-90.
Violations of chapter.
Authority of board to
investigate, §34-23-92.
Injunctions, §34-23-12.
Witnesses.
Compelling attendance at
board proceedings,
§34-23-92.
Bonds, surety.
Board of pharmacy.
Secretary and treasurer to
furnish bond,
§34-23-91.
State drug inspectors,
§34-23-3.
Change of employment.
Notification of board of
pharmacy, §34-23-10.
Chemical.
Defined, §34-23-1.
Child abuse or neglect.
Reports, §26-14-3.
Controlled substances.
General provisions.
See DRUGS.
Maintenance of records and
inventories by registered
pharmacies, §20-2-58.
Corporations.
Professional corporations,
§§10-4-380 to 10-4-406.
See PROFESSIONAL
CORPORATIONS.
Unincorporated professional
associations, §§10-1-1 to
10-1-16.
See UNINCORPORATED
PROFESSIONAL
ASSOCIATIONS.
Definitions, §34-23-1.
Impaired professionals,
§34-38-1.
Robbery, §13A-8-51.
Degrees.
Professional degree.
Defined, §34-23-1.
Dentists.
Exemptions from provisions
of chapter, §34-23-11.
Drugs.
Bankruptcy sales, auction
sales, etc., of drugs,
§34-23-6.

**PHARMACISTS AND
    PHARMACIES**—Cont'd
Drugs—Cont'd
  Brands.
    Substitution of brands,
      §34-23-8.
  Defined, §34-23-1.
  General provisions.
    See DRUGS.
  Illegal possession of
    prescription drugs,
    §34-23-7.
  Legend drug.
    Defined, §34-23-1.
  Prescriptions. See within this
    heading, "Prescriptions."
  Sale of adulterated drugs,
    §34-23-9.
  State drug inspectors,
    §34-23-3.
  Substitution of drugs or
    brands, §34-23-8.
Education.
  Internship training,
    §§34-23-50, 34-23-72.
  Preceptor, §§34-23-1,
    34-23-73.
  Schools and colleges of
    pharmacy, §§34-23-4,
    34-23-50.
  Training program for
    candidates for licensure,
    §34-23-53.
Enforcement of chapter.
  Board of pharmacy.
    Assisting prosecuting
      officers, §34-23-93.
    Injunctions against
      violations of chapter.
      Authority of board,
        §34-23-12.
  Duties of state drug
    inspectors, §34-23-3.
  Duty of district attorney,
    §34-23-93.
Evidence.
  Board of pharmacy.
    Furnishing evidence to
      prosecuting officers,
      §34-23-93.
    Records and books as
      evidence, §34-23-91.
Examinations.
  Licenses, §34-23-51.
Exemptions from chapter.
  Pharmacy internship,
    §34-23-50.
  Physicians, dentists, etc.,
    exempt, §34-23-11.
Fees.
  Assistant's certificate,
    §34-23-50.
  Drug manufacturer's permit,
    §34-23-32.
  Examination and registration
    fee, §34-23-51.
  Lapsed licenses, §34-23-52.
  Pharmacy permits,
    §34-23-30.
  Reciprocal licensure,
    §34-23-51.
  Renewal of license,
    §34-23-52.
Fraud.
  Grounds for revocation or
    suspension of licenses or
    permits, §34-23-33.
Generic drugs, §34-23-8.

**PHARMACISTS AND
    PHARMACIES**—Cont'd
Governor.
  Board of pharmacy.
    Annual report to governor,
      §34-23-92.
    Appointment and removal
      of members, §34-23-90.
Health care service plans.
  Prescriptions.
    Third party prescription
      program.
      Provisions inapplicable
        to corporations
        organized for
        establishment and
        operation of plans,
        §34-23-116.
Hospital, §34-23-74.
  Defined, §34-23-1.
  Permits, §§34-23-30 to
    34-23-34.
**Illegal possession of
    prescription drugs,**
    §34-23-7.
Impaired professionals,
    §§34-38-1 to 34-38-8.
  Definitions, §34-38-1.
  Illness, inebriation, etc.
    Confidentiality of
      information, records
      and proceedings,
      §34-38-6.
    Disclosure and joint review
      of information,
      §34-38-4.
    Evaluation of professionals
      believed impaired,
      §34-38-8.
    Impaired professionals
      committee, §34-38-2.
      Authority of board to
        contract to
        undertake certain
        functions, §34-38-3.
      Nonliability of personnel,
        §34-38-5.
    Reports.
      Annual report,
        §34-38-7.
    Promotion of early
      treatment, etc.,
      §34-38-2.
    Reports.
      Procedures for reporting
        impaired
        professional program
        activity, §34-38-4.
Injunctions.
  Board may enjoin violations
    of chapter, §34-23-12.
Inspectors, §34-23-3.
Insurance.
  Pharmaceutical insurance
    coverage, §§27-45-1 to
    27-45-9.
    See INSURANCE.
Internship training.
  Qualification and
    requirements of
    pharmacies, §34-23-72.
  Requirements, §34-23-50.
Legislative intent.
  Objects and purposes of
    chapter, §34-23-2.
Licenses, §§34-23-30 to
    34-23-53.
  Application, §34-23-51.
  Change of employment.
    Notification of board,
    §34-23-10.

**PHARMACISTS AND
    PHARMACIES**—Cont'd
Licenses—Cont'd
  Defined, §34-23-1.
  Examinations, §34-23-51.
  Expiration, §34-23-52.
  Fees.
    Examination and
      registration fee,
      §34-23-51.
    Lapsed licenses.
      Penalty fee, §34-23-52.
    Reciprocal licensure,
      §34-23-51.
    Renewal fee, §34-23-52.
  Internship exemption,
    §34-23-50.
  Lapsed licenses.
    Penalty fee, §34-23-52.
  Practice without license.
    Penalty, §34-23-13.
  Qualifications of applicants,
    §34-23-51.
  Reciprocity.
    Licensure without
      examination,
      §34-23-51.
  Renewal, §34-23-52.
  Required, §34-23-50.
  Revocation or suspension.
    Grounds, §34-23-33.
    Notice of hearing,
      §34-23-34.
    Statement of charges,
      §34-23-34.
  Training program for
    candidates, §34-23-53.
Mail-order houses.
  Permits, §34-23-31.
Manufacturers.
  Defined, §34-23-1.
  Permit for drug
    manufacturers,
    §34-23-32.
Medical practitioner.
  Defined, §34-23-1.
Medicine.
  Bankruptcy sales, auction
    sales, etc., of medicine,
    §34-23-6.
  Defined, §34-23-1.
Notices.
  Bankruptcy sales, auction
    sales, etc., of drugs and
    medicines, §34-23-6.
Objects of chapter, §34-23-2.
Penalties.
  Brands.
    Substitution of drug
      brands, §34-23-8.
  Drug manufacturers.
    Violation of permit
      provisions, §34-23-32.
  General penalty, §34-23-13.
  Illegal possession of
    prescription drugs,
    §34-23-7.
  Lapsed licenses.
    Penalty fee, §34-23-52.
  Licenses.
    Grounds for revocation or
      suspension, §34-23-33.
    Lapsed licenses, §34-23-52.
    Practicing pharmacy
      without a license,
      §34-23-13.
  Prescriptions.
    Permitting compounding or
      dispensing by
      unauthorized persons,
      §34-23-13.

PHARMACISTS AND PHARMACIES—Cont'd

Penalties—Cont'd

Revocation or suspension of licenses or permits.
Grounds, §34-23-33.
Robbery.
Violation of article, §13A-8-52.
Rules and regulations.
Penalty for violations, §34-23-13.
Sale of adulterated drugs, §34-23-9.
Substitution of drugs, §34-23-8.
Violations of chapter.
General penalty, §34-23-13.
Violations of pharmacy and prescription requirements, §34-23-70.

Permits.
Defined, §34-23-1.
Drug manufacturers, §34-23-32.
Mail-order houses, §34-23-31.
Pharmacy permits.
Generally, §34-23-30.
Revocation or suspension, §§34-23-33, 34-23-34.

Person.
Defined, §34-23-1.

Pharmacy.
Defined, §34-23-1.
Display of certificate, §34-23-70.
General requirements, §34-23-70.
Internship training.
Qualification and requirements, §34-23-72.
Location in hospital, nursing home or related institution.
Requirements, §34-23-74.
Management, §34-23-70.
Permits, §§34-23-30, 34-23-33, 34-23-34.
Prescription rooms.
Requirements, §34-23-71.
Supervision by pharmacists, §34-23-70.

Physicians.
Exemptions from provisions of chapter, §34-23-11.
Physicians not restricted by chapter, §34-23-70.

Poison.
Defined, §34-23-1.
Restriction on sale in pharmacy, §34-23-70.

Preceptor.
Defined, §34-23-1.
General qualifications, §34-23-73.
Reports, §34-23-73.

Prescriptions.
Compounding or dispensing by unauthorized persons.
Penalty, §34-23-13.
Controlled substances, §20-2-91.
Defined, §34-23-1.
Files, §34-23-70.
General requirements, §34-23-70.
Requirements for prescription rooms, §34-23-71.

PHARMACISTS AND PHARMACIES—Cont'd

Prescriptions—Cont'd

Third party prescription program, §§34-23-110 to 34-23-118.
Applicability of provisions.
Exception as to medicaid services, §34-23-116.
Cancellation of program, §34-23-113.
Citation of act.
Short title, §34-23-110.
Compliance with provisions.
Required, §34-23-118.
Contracts.
Required contractual provisions, §34-23-112.
Defined, §34-23-111.
Denial of payment, §34-23-114.
Health care service plans.
Provisions inapplicable to corporations organized for establishment and operation of plans, §34-23-116.
Identification cards.
Use after cancellation of program, §34-23-113.
Medicaid.
Provisions not applicable to medicaid services, §34-23-116.
Notice.
Required before institution of program, §34-23-117.
Reimbursement.
Denial of payment, §34-23-114.
Rates, §34-23-115.
Title of act.
Short title, §34-23-110.

Professional corporations, §§10-4-380 to 10-4-406.
See PROFESSIONAL CORPORATIONS.

Purposes of chapter, §34-23-2.

Reciprocity.
Licensure without examination, §34-23-51.

Robbery.
Citation of act, §13A-8-50.
Definitions, §13A-8-51.
Penalties.
Violation of article, §13A-8-52.
Second or subsequent conviction.
Penalty, §13A-8-52.
Short title of act, §13A-8-50.
Violation of article.
Penalty for violation, §13A-8-52.

Rules and regulations.
Board of pharmacy.
Promulgation, §34-23-92.
Penalty for violations, §34-23-13.
Pharmacies in hospitals and related institutions.
Promulgation of rules and regulations, §34-23-74.

Sale.
Adulterated drugs, §34-23-9.

PHARMACISTS AND PHARMACIES—Cont'd

Sale—Cont'd

Bankruptcy sales, auction sales, etc., of drugs and medicines, §34-23-6.
Defined, §34-23-1.
Notice of bulk sale of drugs, §34-23-6.

Schools and colleges of pharmacy.
Board of pharmacy.
Recognition of schools and colleges, §34-23-4.
Licenses.
Exemption of student interns, §34-23-50.
Recognition, §34-23-4.

State drug inspectors, §34-23-3.

Subpoenas.
Board of pharmacy.
Subpoena power of board, §34-23-92.

Third party prescription program, §§34-23-110 to 34-23-118. See within this heading, "Prescriptions."

Unincorporated professional associations, §§10-1-1 to 10-1-16.
See UNINCORPORATED PROFESSIONAL ASSOCIATIONS.

Violations of chapter.
Board of pharmacy.
Assisting prosecuting officers, §34-23-93.
Injunctions against violations, §34-23-12.
General penalty, §34-23-13.

Wholesalers.
Defined, §34-23-1.

Witnesses.
Board of pharmacy.
Compelling attendance at board proceedings, §34-23-92.

PHENYLKETONURIA.
Testing infants, §22-20-3.
Treatment.
Rules and regulations for treatment, §22-20-3.

PHOENIX, MUNICIPALITY OF.
Property tax, Const. Ala., amd. 8.

PHONOGRAPH RECORDS.
Copying and sale of recorded devices, §§13A-8-80 to 13A-8-86.
See RECORDED DEVICES.

PHOSPHORUS.
Fertilizer, §§2-22-12 to 2-22-16.

PHOTOGRAPHY.
Aerial photographs.
Recording, §§35-2-80, 35-2-81.
Banks and financial institutions.
Reproduction of records and books, §5-4A-1.
Canons of judicial ethics.
When taking of photographs in courtroom permitted, ACJE, Canon 3A.
Educational records, §§16-1-3, 16-1-4.

PHOTOGRAPHY—Cont'd
Elections.
Voting machines.
Photographing name of candidates or question together with total vote cast, §17-9-34.
Evidence.
Records.
Photographed records, §41-13-40.
Juvenile proceedings.
Taking and disposition of photographs of children, §12-15-102.
Licenses.
Developing and printing films, §40-12-94.
Photographers and photograph galleries, §40-12-140.
Microphotographing.
Records, §§41-13-40 to 41-13-44.
Recordation.
Aerial photographs or maps, §§35-2-80, 35-2-81.
Records.
Educational records, §§16-1-3, 16-1-4.
Photographing and microphotographing, §§41-13-40 to 41-13-44.
Secretary of state.
Photographic reproduction, §36-14-15.

PHYSICAL FITNESS COMMISSION, §§22-5-1 to 22-5-9.
See HEALTH.

PHYSICAL THERAPISTS, §§34-24-190 to 34-24-217.
Advertising.
Revocation or suspension of licenses.
Unethical advertising, §34-24-217.
Appeals.
Refusal, revocation or suspension of licenses.
Judicial review of board decision, §34-24-194.
Board of physical therapy, §§34-24-191 to 34-24-195.
Appointment of members, §34-24-192.
Compensation of members, §34-24-192.
Complaints charging violation of article.
Filing with board, §34-24-194.
Composition, §34-24-192.
Defined, §34-24-191.
Fees.
Certification fee, §34-24-193.
Governor.
Appointment of members, §34-24-192.
Officers, §34-24-192.
Physical therapist fund.
Authority of board, §34-24-195.
Powers and duties.
Generally, §34-24-193.
Qualifications of members, §34-24-192.

PHYSICAL THERAPISTS —Cont'd
Board of physical therapy —Cont'd
Rules and regulations.
Authority of board, §34-24-193.
Subpoenas.
Power to issue, §34-24-194.
Terms of members, §34-24-192.
Vacancies, §34-24-192.
Continuing education, §34-24-216.
Definitions, §34-24-191.
Education.
Continuing education, §34-24-216.
Examinations.
Registration and licenses, §§34-24-211 to 34-24-213.
Fees.
Board of physical therapy.
Certification fee, §34-24-193.
Registration and licenses, §§34-34-211, 34-24-216.
Felonies.
Revocation or suspension of licenses.
Conviction as grounds, §34-24-217.
Fraud.
False statement in registration application.
Penalty, §34-24-196.
Revocation or suspension of licenses.
Fraud as grounds, §34-24-217.
Funds.
Physical therapist fund, §34-24-195.
Licenses, §§34-24-210 to 34-24-217. See within this heading, "Registration and licenses."
Penalties.
Administrative fines.
Disciplining of licensees, §34-24-193.
Violations of article, §34-24-196.
Physical therapist technician.
Defined, §34-24-191.
Physical therapy assistant.
Defined, §34-24-191.
Physiotherapist.
Defined, §34-24-191.
Registration and licenses, §§34-24-210 to 34-24-217.
Applicability of article.
Other healing arts not affected, §34-24-210.
Application, §34-24-211.
Continuing education requirements, §34-24-216.
Examinations, §34-24-212.
License issued to applicants passing exam, §34-24-213.
License issued without exam, §34-24-214.
Fees.
Application fee, §34-24-211.
Renewal of licenses, §34-24-216.

PHYSICAL THERAPISTS —Cont'd
Registration and licenses —Cont'd
Issuance of license.
Applicants passing exam, §34-24-213.
Without examination, §34-24-214.
Refusal, suspension or revocation of license.
Grounds, §34-24-217.
Judicial review of board decision, §34-24-194.
Renewal of licenses, §34-24-216.
Required, §34-24-210.
Temporary licenses, §34-24-215.
Short title of article, §34-24-190.
State licensing board.
General provisions.
See PHYSICIANS.
Title.
Short title of article, §34-24-190.
Violations of article.
Complaint charging violation, §34-24-194.
Hearing, §34-24-194.
Applicability of evidentiary rules, §34-24-194.
Penalties, §34-24-196.

PHYSICIANS.
Abortion.
Inducing or attempting to induce abortion, §13A-13-7.
Parental consent to performing abortion upon minors, §§26-21-1 to 26-21-8.
See ABORTION.
Accidents.
Rendering aid at scene of accidents.
Exemptions from liability, §6-5-332.
Adult protective services.
Reports.
Abuse, neglect and exploitation, §§38-9-7 to 38-9-10.
Aged persons.
Medical assistance to elderly persons, §38-6-2.
Alcoholic beverages.
Acquisition, dispensing, etc., for medicinal, scientific, etc., purposes, §28-3-15.
Dry counties.
Sale, purchase and prescription, §§28-4-150 to 28-4-166.
See ALCOHOLIC BEVERAGES.
Anatomical gifts.
General provisions.
See ANATOMICAL GIFTS.
Appeals.
Foreign medical school graduates.
Off-shore medical schools.
Reviewing court bound by determination of board, §34-24-82.

PHYSICIANS—Cont'd
  Applicability of chapter.
    Practicing medicine or
        osteopathy without
        license.
      Certain activity exempt
          from licensing
          requirements,
          §34-24-51.
  Assistants to physicians,
      §§34-24-290 to 34-24-294.
    Approved program.
      Defined, §34-24-290.
    Authority of trainees and
        assistants, §34-24-292.
    Board of medical examiners.
      Generally. See within this
          heading, "State board
          of medical examiners."
      Powers and duties,
          §34-24-293.
    Certificates of approval.
      Issuance by board,
          §34-24-293.
    Definitions, §34-24-290.
    Injunctions.
      Enjoining violations of
          article, §34-24-294.
    Legislative intent and
        declaration, §34-24-291.
    Penalties.
      Injunctive proceedings,
          §34-24-294.
      Violation of rules and
          regulations,
          §34-24-293.
    Purpose of article,
        §34-24-291.
    Qualifications.
      Formulation of guidelines
          by board, §34-24-293.
    Rules and regulations.
      Penalty for violations,
          §34-24-293.
      Promulgation by board,
          §34-24-293.
    Services performed by
        trainees and assistants,
        §34-24-292.
    Standards.
      Adoption and publication
          by board, §34-24-293.
    Trainees.
      Defined, §34-24-290.
      Services performed by
          trainees, §34-24-292.
  Associations.
    Professional corporations,
        §§10-4-380 to 10-4-406.
      See PROFESSIONAL
          CORPORATIONS.
    Unincorporated professional
        associations, §§10-1-1 to
        10-1-16.
      See UNINCORPORATED
          PROFESSIONAL
          ASSOCIATIONS.
  Blind persons.
    Assistance to needy blind
        persons.
      Freedom of choice in
          selection of specialists
          to make examinations,
          §38-1-2.
    Infantile blindness.
      Prevention, §22-20-2.
  **Blood and urine samples
      from certain dead
      bodies,** §§22-19-81,
      22-19-82.

PHYSICIANS—Cont'd
  Boards.
    Board of chiropractic
        examiners, §§34-24-140
        to 34-24-144.
    Medical association board of
        censors.
      Constituted as board of
          examiners, §34-24-53.
    State board of medical
        examiners. See within
        this heading, "State
        board of medical
        examiners."
  Burden of proof.
    Foreign medical school
        graduates.
      Off-shore medical schools.
        Certificate of
            qualification.
          Proof required for,
              §34-24-83.
        Substantial equivalence
            of program to
            accredited schools.
          Burden of
              demonstrating,
              §34-24-80.
  Cancer.
    Reports, §22-13-10.
  Certificates of qualification.
    Application.
      Submitting of false or
          fraudulent application,
          §13A-9-21.
    Examinations, §§34-24-70 to
        34-24-72, 34-24-75.
    Foreign medical school
        graduates.
      Off-shore medical schools.
        Denial of certificate,
            §34-24-80.
    Issuance.
      Certain certificates issued
          without examination,
          §34-24-75.
    Licenses.
      Generally. See within this
          heading, "Licenses."
    Qualifications of applicants,
        §34-24-70.
    Reciprocity, §34-24-73.
  Certificates of registration,
      §§34-24-337 to 34-24-340.
    Applications, §34-24-337.
    Change of address,
        §34-24-338.
    Contents, §34-24-338.
    Duration, §34-24-337.
    Failure to register.
      Revocation of license,
          §34-24-337.
    Fees.
      Application fee,
          §34-24-337.
      Collection by state board of
          medical examiners,
          §34-24-340.
    Issuance, §34-24-338.
    Retired persons.
      Exception to requirement,
          §34-24-339.
    Suspension or revocation,
        §§34-24-360 to 34-24-367.
      See within this heading,
          "Licenses."
  Child abuse or neglect.
    Reports, §26-14-3.

PHYSICIANS—Cont'd
  Chiropractors.
    General provisions,
        §§34-24-120 to 34-24-176.
    See CHIROPRACTORS.
  Committees.
    Decisions, opinions, etc., of
        medical committees
        privileged, §34-24-58.
  Consent for health services,
      §§22-8-1 to 22-8-9.
    See HEALTH.
  **Construction and
      interpretation.**
    Licenses, §34-24-342.
  Consultants.
    Nonresident consultants.
      Practice, §34-24-74.
  Coroner's inquest, §§15-4-1 to
      15-4-11.
    See CORONERS.
  Corporations.
    Professional corporations,
        §§10-4-380 to 10-4-406.
    See PROFESSIONAL
        CORPORATIONS.
  Cosmetologists.
    Certificate of health, §34-7-7.
  Crime victims compensation.
    Waiver of physician-patient
        privilege.
      Filing claim under chapter
          constitutes waiver,
          §15-23-11.
  Criminal law and procedure.
    Force.
      Use of force for certain
          treatment, §13A-3-24.
  Dead bodies.
    Blood and urine samples
        from certain dead bodies.
      Exemption from civil and
          criminal liability,
          §22-19-82.
    May be directed to
        withdraw samples,
        §22-19-81.
  Definitions, §§6-5-481, 25-5-1.
    Assistants to physicians,
        §34-24-290.
    Practice of medicine or
        osteopathy, §34-24-50.
  Dentists.
    General provisions.
      See DENTISTS.
  Depositions.
    Revocation or suspension of
        licenses, §34-24-365.
  Disciplinary actions.
    Administrative fines,
        §34-24-381.
    Chief administrative officer
        of hospitals.
      Reporting to board of
          medical examiners,
          §34-24-59.
  Diseases.
    Notifiable diseases,
        §§22-11A-1 to 22-11A-38.
    See DISEASES.
  Domestic remedies.
    Exemption from provisions of
        chapter, §34-24-55.

PHYSICIANS—Cont'd
Education.
Foreign medical school
graduates.
Off-shore medical schools,
§§34-24-79 to 34-24-84.
See within this
heading, "Foreign
medical school
graduates."
Public education employees'
health insurance.
Payment to physicians,
§16-25A-10.
Elections.
Absentee voting.
Physician's certificate.
When required, §17-10-4.
Emergencies.
Doctors rendering first aid or
emergency care at scene
of accident, etc.
Exemption from liability,
§6-5-332.
Emergency services.
Exemption from provisions of
chapter, §34-24-55.
Enforcement of chapter.
Malpractice.
Investigation of judgments
and settlements by
board, §34-24-57.
Examinations, §§34-24-70 to
34-24-78.
Board of chiropractic
examiners, §§34-24-140
to 34-24-144.
Certificates of qualification.
Additional examinations
allowed on failure,
§34-24-72.
Application for
examination,
§34-24-71.
Failure of examination.
Additional examinations
allowed, §34-24-72.
Issuance without
examination in certain
cases, §34-24-75.
Scope of examination,
§34-24-70.
Waiver of examination,
§34-24-75.
Fees, §34-24-77.
Foreign medical school
graduates.
Oral examinations.
Legislative intent,
§34-24-70.1.
Montgomery.
Examinations held at
Montgomery,
§34-24-76.
Place of examinations,
§34-24-76.
Records.
Board to keep complete
records of
examinations,
§34-24-78.
State board of medical
examiners. See within
this heading, "State
board of medical
examiners."
Time.
Board of examiners to fix
time, §34-24-76.

PHYSICIANS—Cont'd
**Exemptions from provisions
of chapter.**
Domestic remedies,
§34-24-55.
Emergency services,
§34-24-55.
Practicing medicine or
osteopathy without
license.
Certain activity exempt
from requirements,
§34-24-51.
Family remedies.
Exemption from provisions of
chapter, §34-24-55.
Fees.
Certificate of registration.
Application fee,
§34-24-337.
Collection by state board of
medical examiners,
§34-24-340.
Examinations, §34-24-77.
Licenses, §34-24-334.
Collection by state board of
examiners, §34-24-340.
Reciprocity.
Application for
reciprocity.
Certification,
§34-24-331.
Postmortem examinations,
§12-19-193.
Fines.
Administrative fines,
§§34-24-381 to
34-24-384.
Alabama physicians
education fund,
§34-24-382.
**Foreign medical school
graduates,** §§34-24-79 to
34-24-84.
Off-shore medical schools.
Appeals.
Reviewing court bound
by determination of
board, §34-24-82.
Burden of proof.
Certificate of
qualification.
Proof required for,
§34-24-83.
Substantial equivalence
of program to
accredited schools,
§34-24-80.
Certificate of qualification.
Denial to licensee,
§34-24-80.
Proof required for,
§34-24-83.
Exception for,
§34-24-83.
Findings of legislature,
§34-24-79.
Judicial review.
Reviewing court bound
by determination of
board, §34-24-82.
Legislative finding,
§34-24-79.
Liability.
State board of medical
examiners.
Immunity of board and
staff, §34-24-84.
Rules and regulations,
§34-24-81.

PHYSICIANS—Cont'd
**Foreign medical school
graduates**—Cont'd
Off-shore medical schools
—Cont'd
State board of medical
examiners.
Denial of certificate of
qualification for
licensee, §34-24-80.
Immunity from liability,
§34-24-84.
Reviewing court bound
by determination of
board, §34-24-82.
Rules and regulations,
§34-24-81.
Substantial equivalence of
program to accredited
schools.
Burden of
demonstrating,
§34-24-80.
Oral examinations.
Legislative intent,
§34-24-70.1.
Fraud.
State employees
investigating and
bringing charges against
doctors relating to fraud.
Exemption from liability,
§6-5-334.
Funds.
State board of medical
examiners.
Defraying litigation costs,
§34-24-53.
Deposit and expenditure of
funds received,
§34-24-54.
Good Samaritan Act.
Rendering aid at scene of
accidents.
Exemptions from liability,
§6-5-332.
Health care authorities.
Generally, §§22-21-310 to
22-21-356.
See HEALTH CARE
AUTHORITIES.
Health care service plans,
§§10-4-100 to 10-4-116.
See HEALTH CARE
SERVICE PLANS.
**Hearing aid dealers and
fitters,** §§34-14-1 to
34-14-33.
See HEARING AID
DEALERS AND
FITTERS.
Hearings.
Licenses.
Suspension or revocation,
§§34-24-361,
34-24-363.
Impaired physicians,
§§34-24-400 to 34-24-406.
Illness, inebriation, etc.
Duty to promote early
treatment, etc.,
§34-24-400.
Evaluation of physician
believed impaired,
§34-24-406.
Report of findings,
§34-24-406.
Impaired physician's
committee, §34-24-400.
Annual report,
§34-24-405.

PHYSICIANS—Cont'd
Impaired physicians—Cont'd
Illness, inebriation, etc
—Cont'd
Impaired physician's
committee—Cont'd
Confidentiality of
information,
§34-24-404.
Contracts.
Authority of board of
medical examiners
to contract for,
§34-24-401.
Disclosure and joint
review of
information,
§34-24-402.
Liability of members,
§34-24-403.
Reports, §34-24-405.
Procedures for
reporting impaired
physician program
activity,
§34-24-402.
Indictments.
Practice of medicine without
license.
Form of indictment,
§15-8-150.
Injunctions.
Assistants to physicians.
Enjoining violations of
article, §34-24-294.
Practice of medicine or
osteopathy.
Proceedings to restrain
unlawful practice,
§34-24-52.
Unlicensed practice,
§34-24-341.
Insurance.
False statements, etc., in
insurance application,
§27-12-23.
Medical liability insurance,
§§27-26-1 to 27-26-43.
See INSURANCE.
Jails, §§14-6-19, 14-6-20.
Judgments.
Malpractice judgments and
settlements, §§6-5-486,
6-5-487, 6-5-543.
Liability.
Consent for health services.
Liability of physicians for
reliance and good
faith, §22-8-7.
Exemptions.
Good Samaritan Act,
§6-5-332.
State employees
investigating fraud or
abuse of medicaid
program, §6-5-334.
Foreign medical school
graduates.
Off-shore medical schools.
State board of medical
examiners.
Immunity of board and
staff, §34-24-84.
Medical liability insurance,
§§27-26-1 to 27-26-43.
See INSURANCE.
Licenses, §40-12-126.
Administrative fines.
Payment prerequisite to
renewal, §34-24-383.

PHYSICIANS—Cont'd
Licenses—Cont'd
Application for license.
Denial, §34-24-335.
Submitting of false or
fraudulent application,
§13A-9-21.
Certificates of qualification.
Appeal from action of
board, §34-24-330.
Generally. See within this
heading, "Certificates
of qualification."
Issuance, §§34-24-330,
34-24-333.
New certificate where
license lost or name
changed, §34-24-332.
Construction and
interpretation,
§34-24-342.
Continuing medical
education, §34-24-336.
County probate judges.
Filing of licenses with,
§34-24-342.
Denial of application,
§34-24-335.
Design, §34-24-334.
Fees, §34-24-334.
Collection by state board of
examiners, §34-24-340.
Reciprocity.
Application for
reciprocity.
Certification,
§34-24-331.
Issuance, §34-24-334.
Medical licensure
commission.
Appointment of members,
§34-24-310.
Composition, §34-24-310.
Creation, §34-24-310.
Discretion in issuance of
licenses, §34-24-333.
Exclusive power over
licenses, §34-24-342.
Number of members,
§34-24-310.
Personnel.
Employment, §34-24-313.
State board of medical
examiners to
furnish, §34-24-312.
Powers, §34-24-311.
Prosecuting attorneys.
Assistance by,
§34-24-313.
Qualifications of members,
§34-24-310.
State board of medical
examiners.
Furnishing of personnel,
facilities and funds,
§34-24-312.
Terms of members,
§34-24-310.
Unlicensed practice.
Commencement of
action, §34-24-341.
Numbering, §34-24-334.
Osteopaths, §40-12-136.
Practice without license,
§34-24-51.
Suspension or revocation,
§34-24-360.
Penalties.
Practicing medicine or
osteopathy without
license, §34-24-51.

PHYSICIANS—Cont'd
Licenses—Cont'd
Penalties—Cont'd
Violations of provisions,
§34-24-343.
Practicing medicine or
osteopathy without
license, §34-24-51.
Reciprocity.
Application for reciprocity.
Certification, §34-24-313.
Fee, §34-24-331.
Certificates of
qualification.
Appeal from action of
board, §34-24-330.
Issuance, §34-24-333.
Collection of fees,
§34-24-340.
Suspension or revocation.
Appeals, §34-24-367.
Depositions, §34-24-365.
Effect of commission order,
§34-24-367.
Failure to register,
§34-24-337.
Grounds, §§34-24-57,
34-24-360.
Authority to implement
provisions,
§34-24-360.1.
Hearings, §34-24-361.
Notice, §34-24-361.
Subpoenas, §34-24-363.
Witnesses, §34-24-363.
Immunities, §34-24-361.
Investigations, §34-24-361.
Malpractice as grounds,
§§34-24-57, 34-24-360.
Authority to implement
provisions,
§34-24-360.1.
Order by commission.
Effect, §34-24-367.
Vacation by court,
§34-24-367.
Vote necessary,
§34-24-366.
Power of medical licensure
commission,
§34-24-360.
Practice of medicine when
license suspended or
revoked, §34-24-362.
Procedure, §34-24-361.
Reissue of license,
§34-24-362.
Reporting of offenses.
Duty to report,
§34-24-361.
Temporary suspension,
§34-24-361.
Venue, §34-24-367.
Vote of commission
necessary, §34-24-366.
Witnesses, §34-24-363.
Depositions, §34-24-365.
Per diem and travel
expenses,
§34-24-364.
Subpoenas, §34-24-363.
Unlicensed practice.
Aiding or abetting by
physician.
Grounds for suspension
or revocation of
license, §34-24-360.
Injunction, §34-24-341.
Jurisdiction, §34-24-341.

PHYSICIANS—Cont'd
Licenses—Cont'd
Unlicensed practice—Cont'd
Medical licensure
commission.
Commencement of
action, §34-24-341.
Venue.
Judicial review of
administrative
decisions of
commission,
§34-24-367.
Violations of provisions.
Penalties, §34-24-343.
Witnesses.
Revocation or suspension of
licenses, §§34-24-363
to 34-24-365.
Malpractice.
Administrative fines,
§34-24-381.
General provisions.
See MALPRACTICE.
Medical liability insurance,
§§27-26-1 to 27-26-43.
See INSURANCE.
Suspension or revocation of
license.
Grounds, §§34-24-57,
34-24-360.
Authority to implement
provisions,
§34-24-360.1.
Medicaid program.
State employees
investigating fraud or
abuse of program.
Exemption from liability,
§6-5-334.
Medical association.
Board of censors.
Constituted as board of
medical examiners,
§34-24-53.
Constitutes state board of
health, §22-2-1.
Medical examiners.
General provisions.
See MEDICAL
EXAMINER.
State board of medical
examiners. See within
this heading, "State
board of medical
examiners."
Medical liability insurance,
§§27-26-1 to 27-26-43.
See INSURANCE.
**Medical licensure
commission.** See within
this heading, "Licenses."
Medical technicians,
§§34-18-1 to 34-18-47.
See MEDICAL
TECHNICIANS.
Mentally ill.
Exemption of physician of
state mental health
facilities from attending
as witnesses, §22-50-22.
Midwives, §§34-19-2 to
34-19-10.
See MIDWIVES.
Natural death act, §§22-8A-1
to 22-8A-10.
See NATURAL DEATH
ACT.
Nonresidents.
Consultants.
Practice, §34-24-74.

PHYSICIANS—Cont'd
Nonresidents—Cont'd
Physicians accompanying
patient being transported
into state for treatment,
§34-24-74.
Reciprocity, §§34-24-73,
34-24-77.
Notifiable diseases,
§§22-11A-1 to 22-11A-38.
See DISEASES.
Nurses, §§34-21-1 to 34-21-43.
See NURSES.
Off-shore medical schools,
§§34-24-79 to 34-24-84. See
within this heading,
"Foreign medical school
graduates."
Optometrists, §§34-22-1 to
34-22-65.
See OPTOMETRISTS.
Osteopaths.
Licenses, §40-12-136.
Practicing without license,
§34-24-51.
Suspension or revocation,
§34-24-360.
Malpractice.
Suspension or revocation of
license, §34-24-360.
Practice defined, §34-24-50.
Peer review committees.
Exemption from liability of
physicians constituting,
§6-5-333.
Penalties.
Administrative fines,
§§34-24-381 to
34-24-384.
Licenses and registration.
Practicing medicine or
osteopathy without
license, §34-24-51.
Revocation or suspension of
licenses, §§34-24-360
to 34-24-367. See
within this heading,
"Licenses."
Violations of provisions,
§34-24-343.
Malpractice.
Report of judgments and
settlements.
Failure to comply with
requirements,
§34-24-57.
**Pharmacists and
pharmacies.**
General provisions, §§34-23-1
to 34-23-94.
See PHARMACISTS AND
PHARMACIES.
Postmortem examinations.
Fees, §12-19-193.
**Practice of medicine or
osteopathy.**
Defined, §34-24-50.
Licenses.
Practicing without license,
§34-24-51.
Revocation or suspension.
Generally, §§34-24-360
to 34-24-367. See
within this heading,
"Licenses."
Pregnant women.
Inducing or attempting to
induce abortion,
miscarriage or
premature delivery of
women, §13A-13-7.

PHYSICIANS—Cont'd
**Prevention of infantile
blindness,** §22-20-2.
Privileged communications.
Crime victims compensation.
Filing claim under chapter
constitutes waiver of
physician-patient
privilege, §15-23-11.
Criminal psychopath
conditional releases.
Periodic reports not
deemed violative of
privilege, §15-16-69.
Decisions, opinions, etc., of
committees privileged,
§34-24-58.
Psychiatrist-patient
privilege, §34-26-2.
Professional corporations,
§§10-4-380 to 10-4-406.
See PROFESSIONAL
CORPORATIONS.
**Professional standards
review committees.**
Exemption of physician
members from liability,
§6-5-333.
Psychiatrists.
Psychiatrist-patient
privilege, §34-26-2.
Reciprocity.
Certificates of qualification.
Generally, §34-24-73.
Fees, §34-24-77.
Licenses. See within this
heading, "Licenses."
Records.
Examinations.
Board to keep complete
records of
examinations,
§34-24-78.
Registration.
Certificates of registration,
§§34-24-337 to 34-24-340.
Religion.
Exemptions from chapter,
§34-24-55.
Reports.
Adult protective services.
Abuse, neglect and
exploitation, §§38-9-8
to 38-9-10.
See ADULT
PROTECTIVE
SERVICES.
Cancer, §22-13-10.
Child abuse or neglect,
§26-14-3.
Diseases.
Notifiable diseases,
§22-11A-2.
Malpractice judgments and
settlements, §34-24-57.
Rules of civil procedure.
Physical and mental
examination of
persons.
Report of examining
physician, ARCP,
Rule 35 (b).
**Restraining unlawful
practice.**
Unlawful practice of
medicine or osteopathy,
§34-24-52.

PHYSICIANS—Cont'd
Rules and regulations.
Foreign medical school
graduates.
Off-shore medical schools.
State board of medical
examiners,
§34-24-81.
State board of medical
examiners.
Authority to promulgate,
§34-24-53.
Rules of civil procedure.
Physical and mental
examination of persons.
Report of examining
physician, ARCP, Rule
35 (b).
State board of medical
examiners.
Malpractice judgments and
settlements, §34-24-56.
Settlements.
Malpractice judgments and
settlements.
See MALPRACTICE.
**Speech pathologists and
audiologists.**
Exemptions from provisions
of chapter, §34-28A-3.
**State board of chiropractic
examiners, §§34-24-140 to
34-24-144.**
**State board of medical
examiners.**
Assistants to physicians.
Powers and duties of
board, §34-24-293.
Board of censors of medical
association.
Constituted as board of
medical examiners,
§34-24-53.
Examinations.
Board to fix time of
examination,
§34-24-76.
Board to keep records of
examinations,
§34-24-78.
Expenses, §34-24-54.
Foreign medical school
graduates.
Off-shore medical schools.
Denial of certificate of
qualification for
licensee, §34-24-80.
Determinations of board.
Reviewing court bound
by, §34-24-82.
Immunity of board and
staff from liability,
§34-24-84.
Rules and regulations,
§34-24-81.
Funds.
Defraying litigation costs,
§34-24-53.
Deposit and expenditure of
funds received,
§34-24-54.
Hearings.
Revocation or suspension of
licenses, §§34-24-361,
34-24-363.
Malpractice judgments and
settlements.
Filing report with board,
§34-24-56.
Review of reports,
§34-24-57.

PHYSICIANS—Cont'd
**State board of medical
examiners**—Cont'd
Medical association board of
censors.
Constituted as board of
medical examiners,
§34-24-53.
Powers and duties.
Authority to carry out
powers and duties,
§34-24-53.
Proceedings.
Board to keep record of
minutes, §34-24-78.
Quorum, §34-24-53.
Records.
Board to keep certain
records, §34-24-78.
Reports.
Malpractice judgments and
settlements, §34-24-56.
Rules and regulations.
Authority to promulgate,
§34-24-53.
**Unincorporated professional
associations, §§10-1-1 to
10-1-16.**
See UNINCORPORATED
PROFESSIONAL
ASSOCIATIONS.
**University of Alabama
school of medicine.**
See UNIVERSITY OF
ALABAMA.
**Utilization review and
quality control
committees.**
Decisions, opinions, etc.,
privileged, §34-24-58.
Exemption of members from
liability, §6-5-333.
Venue.
Medical licensure
commission.
Judicial review of
decisions, §34-24-367.
**Veterinarians, §§34-29-60 to
34-29-94.**
See VETERINARIANS.
Violations of chapter.
Restraining unlawful
practice.
Unlawful practice of
medicine or
osteopathy, §34-24-52.
Witnesses.
Revocation or suspension of
licenses, §§34-24-363 to
34-24-365.
Workmen's compensation.
Defined, §25-5-1.

PIANOS.
Licenses.
Selling or renting,
§40-12-141.

PICKENS COUNTY.
Economic development.
Municipalities in Pickens
county, Const. Ala., amd.
302.

PICKEREL.
See FISH AND GAME.

PIEDMONT, MUNICIPALITY
OF.
Property tax, Const. Ala.,
amd. 17.

PIERS.
Booms and bulkheads.
See BOOMS AND
BULKHEADS.
Eminent domain.
Power of eminent domain in
internal improvement
corporations, §10-5-1.
Harbors and ports.
See HARBORS AND PORTS.
Inland waterways.
Development of docks and
other facilities along
inland waterways.
See WATERS AND
WATERCOURSES.

PIG IRON.
Licenses.
Storage operators,
§40-12-142.

PIGS.
General provisions.
See LIVESTOCK.
Running at large.
See ESTRAYS.

PIKE COUNTY.
Fishing lake.
Fishing in county public lake
without paying
admission fee, §9-11-66.
**Modernization of county
government,** Const. Ala.,
amd. 503.
Probate judge.
Compensation, Const. Ala.,
amd. 421.
Disposition of charges
collected by judge, Const.
Ala., amd. 421.
Truck tax, Const. Ala., amd.
458.

PILOTS AND PILOTAGE,
§§33-4-1 to 33-4-57.
Absences without leave.
Branches.
Grounds for depriving pilot
of branch, §33-4-46.
Actions.
Bond of pilot.
Actions on bonds, §33-4-40.
State pilotage commission.
Civil actions to recover
forfeitures, §33-4-12.
Affidavits.
Licenses.
Application for license.
Affidavit to accompany,
§33-4-34.
Age.
Apprentices.
Age limitations for
apprentices, §33-4-31.
Compulsory retirement of bar
pilots, §33-4-53.
Requirements, §33-4-31.
Alcoholic beverages.
Branches.
Grounds for depriving pilot
of branch, §33-4-46.
Appeals.
Apprentices.
Discharge, §33-4-33.
Apprentices.
Age.
Limitations on age,
§33-4-31.
Approval.
State pilotage commission
to approve, §33-4-32.

PILOTS AND PILOTAGE
—Cont'd
  Apprentices—Cont'd
    Certificate of apprenticeship.
      Application for license.
        Certificate to accompany,
          §33-4-34.
      Discharge.
        Appeal of discharge,
          §33-4-33.
      Examination.
        Second examination.
          Apprentice pilots not
            required to take
            second examination,
            §33-4-36.
      Selection, §33-4-32.
      Seniority.
        Branching or licensing
          according to seniority,
          §33-4-34.
  Attorneys at law.
    Revocation or suspension of
      licenses.
      Representation of pilot at
        hearing, §33-4-45.
  Ballast.
    Unlawful discharge of
      ballast.
      Reports, §33-4-57.
  **Board of pilotage
    commissioners.** See
    within this heading, "State
    pilotage commission."
  Bonds, surety.
    Actions on bonds, §33-4-40.
    Approval by state pilotage
      commissioners, §33-4-39.
    New bonds, §33-4-40.
    Preserving bonds, §33-4-40.
    Required, §33-4-39.
    Secretary of commission,
      §33-4-6.
    State pilotage commission,
      §33-4-4.
  Branches.
    Examination and
      certification required
      prior to branching,
      §33-4-35.
    Grounds for depriving pilot
      of branch, §33-4-46.
    Seniority.
      Branching according to
        seniority, §33-4-34.
  Certification.
    Applications for licenses.
      Certificate to accompany
        application, §33-4-34.
    Required for license,
      §33-4-30.
  Citizenship.
    Qualifications of pilots,
      §33-4-31.
  Commission. See within this
    heading, "State pilotage
    commission."
  Detaining pilots on vessels.
    Fees of pilots detained,
      §33-4-50.
  Discharges.
    Unlawful discharge of
      ballast, sweepings,
      rubbish, etc., in bay.
      Reports, §33-4-57.
  Discrimination.
    Pay of pilots.
      No discrimination in pilot's
        fees, §33-4-51.

PILOTS AND PILOTAGE
—Cont'd
  Evidence.
    Physical and mental fitness
      of pilots.
      State pilotage commission.
        Authority to require
          evidence, §33-4-11.
  Examination.
    Commission to prepare
      examination, §33-4-35.
    Committee to examine
      answers of applicants,
      §33-4-35.
    Required for license,
      §33-4-30.
    Second examination.
      Apprentice pilots not
        required to take,
        §33-4-36.
  Expenses.
    State pilotage commission.
      Traveling expenses of
        commissioners,
        §33-4-3.
  Fees.
    Exemptions from payment of
      pilot's fees, §33-4-52.
    License tax.
      Levy, payment and
        disposition, §33-4-38.
    Pay of pilots, §§33-4-48 to
      33-4-53. See within this
      heading, "Pay of pilots."
    State pilotage commission.
      Fees enumerated, §33-4-13.
    Witness fees, §33-4-43.
  Forfeitures.
    State pilotage commission.
      Civil actions to recover,
        §33-4-12.
  Garbage and trash.
    Unlawful discharge.
      Report by pilot, §33-4-57.
  Harbor masters, §§33-3-1 to
    33-3-6.
    See HARBORS AND PORTS.
  Harbors and ports.
    Generally.
      See HARBORS AND
        PORTS.
  Hearings.
    Revocation or suspension of
      licenses, §33-4-45.
      Representation of pilot at
        hearing, §33-4-45.
  Jurisdiction.
    State pilotage commission,
      §§33-4-9, 33-4-10.
  Letters.
    Delivery of letters by pilot,
      §33-4-56.
  Licenses.
    Acting without license.
      Penalty, §33-4-47.
    Application, §33-4-34.
    Certification, §§33-4-30,
      33-4-34.
    Examination. See within this
      heading, "Examination."
    Exhibition, §33-4-37.
    Federal pilot license for
      Mobile bay.
      Harbor masters.
        License required,
          §33-3-5.
    Harbor masters.
      Federal pilot license for
        Mobile bay required,
        §33-3-5.

PILOTS AND PILOTAGE
—Cont'd
  Licenses—Cont'd
    Harbor masters—Cont'd
      State pilot license required,
        §33-3-5.
    Issuance.
      State pilotage commission
        to issue, §33-4-37.
    Possession, §33-4-37.
    Revocation or suspension for
      cause, §§33-4-41 to
      33-4-45.
      Decision of commission,
        §33-4-45.
      Fees.
        Witness fees, §33-4-43.
      Generally, §33-4-41.
      Hearings.
        Generally, §33-4-45.
      Mileage.
        Witnesses' mileage,
          §33-4-43.
      Subpoenas.
        Failure of witness to
          answer, §33-4-42.
        Issuance in behalf of
          pilot, §33-4-44.
      Witnesses.
        Failure of witness to
          answer subpoena,
          §33-4-42.
        Fees and mileage,
          §33-4-43.
    Seniority.
      Branching or licensing
        according to seniority,
        §33-4-34.
    Surrender.
      Compulsory retirement of
        bar pilots, §33-4-53.
    Tax.
      Levy, payment and
        disposition of license
        tax, §33-4-38.
    Violations.
      Revocation or suspension
        for violation, §33-4-41.
  Mail.
    Delivery of letters by pilot,
      §33-4-56.
  Mentally ill.
    Branches.
      Grounds for depriving pilot
        of branch, §33-4-46.
  Military affairs.
    Persons exempted from
      military service.
      Pilots employed in sea
        service, §31-2-6.
  Navigation.
    Generally.
      See NAVIGATION.
  Negligence.
    Branches.
      Grounds for depriving pilot
        of branch, §33-4-46.
  Notice.
    Revocation or suspension of
      license for cause.
      Notice of specific charges,
        §33-4-41.
  Number of pilots, §33-4-30.
  Oaths.
    Oath of pilot, §33-4-37.
    State pilotage commission.
      Chairman of commission.
        Administration of oaths
          by chairman,
          §33-4-5.

PILOTS AND PILOTAGE
—Cont'd
Offering services to vessels nearest bar, §33-4-55.
Order of boats piloted.
Pilot boats must offer services to vessels nearest bar, §33-4-55.
Orders.
Delivery of orders by pilot, §33-4-56.
Pay of pilots, §§33-4-48 to 33-4-52.
Discrimination.
No discrimination of pilot's fees, §33-4-51.
Exemptions from payment, §33-4-52.
Failure to pay.
Refusal by pilot to carry vessel out, §33-4-49.
Generally, §33-4-48.
Master of ship or vessel must pay, §33-4-48.
Pilots detained on vessels.
Fees, §33-4-50.
Rates, §33-4-48.
Rebating.
No rebating of pilot's fees, §33-4-51.
Refusal to carry vessel out.
Failure to pay, §33-4-49.
Time of payment, §33-4-49.
Wind and weather.
Pilots detained on vessels.
Fees, §33-4-50.
Penalties.
Licenses.
Acting without license, §33-4-47.
State pilotage commission.
Civil actions to recover forfeitures, §33-4-12.
Physical and mental fitness of pilots.
Branches.
Grounds for depriving pilot of branch, §33-4-46.
State pilotage commission.
Authority to require evidence of physical and mental fitness, §33-4-11.
Qualifications.
Generally, §33-4-31.
Physical and mental fitness of pilots.
State pilotage commission.
Authority to require evidence of, §33-4-11.
Rates, §§33-4-48 to 33-4-52.
Rebates.
Prohibited, §33-4-51.
Records.
State pilotage commission, §33-4-14.
Reports.
Unlawful discharge of ballast, sweepings, rubbish, etc., in bay, §33-4-57.
Retirement.
Compulsory retirement of bar pilots, §33-4-53.
Rules and regulations.
State pilotage commission.
Authority to make and enforce, §33-4-11.
Records, §33-4-14.
Salaries, §§33-4-48 to 33-4-52.

PILOTS AND PILOTAGE
—Cont'd
Seniority.
Branching or licensing according to seniority, §33-4-34.
State pilotage commission.
Accounts.
Secretary to keep accounts, §33-4-6.
Actions.
Civil actions to recover forfeitures, §33-4-12.
Appeals.
Discharges of apprentices.
Appeals to commission, §33-4-33.
Appointment by governor, §33-4-3.
Apprentices.
Appeals of discharge, §33-4-33.
Approval by commission, §33-4-32.
Discharge, §33-4-33.
Bond, §33-4-4.
Chairman, §33-4-5.
Citizenship, §33-4-2.
Compensation, §33-4-3.
Composition, §33-4-1.
Duties.
Generally, §33-4-1.
Examinations.
Preparation by commission, §33-4-35.
Expenses.
Traveling expenses, §33-4-3.
Fees.
Enumerated, §33-4-13.
Forfeitures.
Civil actions to recover, §33-4-12.
Jurisdiction.
Harbor masters.
No jurisdiction over harbor masters, §33-4-10.
Territorial jurisdiction, §33-4-9.
Licenses.
Revocation or suspension of license for cause, §§33-4-41, 33-4-45.
Meetings.
Chairman, §33-4-5.
Place of meetings, §33-4-7.
Records.
Secretary to keep records, §33-4-6.
When meetings held, §33-4-7.
Number of members, §33-4-1.
Number of pilots.
Discretion of commission, §33-4-30.
Oaths.
Administration by chairman, §33-4-5.
Physical and mental fitness of active bar pilots.
Authority to require evidence of, §33-4-11.
Powers.
Generally, §33-4-1.
Qualifications, §33-4-2.
Records.
Access to records, §33-4-14.
Rules and regulations, §33-4-14.

PILOTS AND PILOTAGE
—Cont'd
State pilotage commission
—Cont'd
Revocation or suspension of licenses, §33-4-41.
Decision of commission, §33-4-45.
Rules and regulations.
Authority to make and enforce, §33-4-11.
Records, §33-4-14.
Secretary, §33-4-6.
Subpoenas.
Power of commission to subpoena witnesses, §33-4-41.
Terms, §33-4-3.
Vacancies.
Appointment of successors by governor, §33-4-8.
Witnesses.
Power of commission to subpoena witnesses, §33-4-41.
Subpoenas.
Failure of witness to answer, §33-4-42.
Issuance of subpoenas in behalf of pilot, §33-4-44.
Power of commission to subpoena witnesses, §33-4-41.
Service by sheriff, §33-4-41.
Taxation.
License tax.
Levy, payment and disposition, §33-4-38.
Vessels in distress, §33-4-55.
Vessels required to take pilots, §33-4-54.
Fees.
Exemptions from payment of pilot's fees, §33-4-52.
Violations.
Branches.
Grounds for depriving pilot of branch, §33-4-46.
Revocation or suspension of license for violation, §33-4-41.
Wages, §§33-4-48 to 33-4-52.
Witnesses, §§33-4-41 to 33-4-44.

PINE HILL, MUNICIPALITY OF.
Property tax, Const. Ala., amd. 8.

PINE TAR.
Forest products generally.
See FORESTS AND FORESTRY.

PIPELINES.
Bonds, surety.
Highways.
Digging up of roads, §23-1-4.
Circuit courts.
Gas pipeline systems.
Jurisdiction of circuit court, §37-4-86.
Commercial code.
Secured transactions.
Applicability of filing provisions, §7-9-302.
Companies.
Transportation companies.
See TRANSPORTATION COMPANIES.

PIPELINES—Cont'd
Construction.
Condemnation of ways and
rights of way, §10-5-4.
Corporations.
Foreign corporations.
Extension of pipelines into
state, §10-2A-225.
Definitions.
Gas pipeline systems,
§37-4-80.
Hazardous liquid pipeline
facilities, §37-4-90.
Dwellings.
Construction through
curtilage of house
without consent, §10-5-5.
Eminent domain.
Companies constructing,
operating or maintaining
internal improvement.
Condemnation of ways and
rights of way, §10-5-4.
Power of eminent domain in
internal improvement
corporations, §10-5-1.
Routes and sites.
Rights of condemning
corporations in
selection of routes and
sites, §10-5-8.
Fees.
Safety inspection fees,
§37-4-88.
Gas pipeline systems,
§§37-4-80 to 37-4-88.
Circuit court.
Jurisdiction, §37-4-86.
Commission.
Defined, §37-4-80.
Inspections, §37-4-83.
Inspectors.
Employment of
inspectors, §37-4-84.
Right of access and
entry, §37-4-83.
Limitation on powers,
§37-4-85.
Penalties.
Civil penalties may be
compromised by
commission,
§37-4-87.
Personnel.
Employment, §37-4-84.
Powers.
Generally, §37-4-82.
Limitation on powers,
§37-4-85.
Records.
Right to require pipeline
systems to make
records, §37-4-83.
Right of entry, §37-4-83.
Rules and regulations.
Promulgation, §37-4-83.
Definitions, §37-4-80.
Federal safety standards.
Compliance with minimum
standards, §37-4-81.
Defined, §37-4-80.
Injunctions.
Jurisdiction of circuit court
to restrain violations,
§37-4-86.
Inspection.
Fees, §37-4-88.

PIPELINES—Cont'd
Gas pipeline systems—Cont'd
Penalties.
Civil penalties.
Compromise by
commission,
§37-4-87.
Violations, §37-4-87.
Public utility.
Defined, §37-4-80.
Safety standards.
Circuit court.
Jurisdiction to enforce
compliance,
§37-4-86.
Compliance with federal
minimum safety
standards, §37-4-81.
Enforcement by public
service commission,
§37-4-82.
Inspection.
Fees, §37-4-88.
Transportation companies.
See TRANSPORTATION
COMPANIES.
Transportation of gas.
Defined, §37-4-80.
United States.
Federal minimum safety
standards.
Compliance with,
§37-4-81.
Violations.
Circuit court.
Jurisdiction, §37-4-86.
Penalties, §37-4-87.
Hazardous liquid pipeline
facilities.
Commission.
Duties, §37-4-92.
Inspectors and other
qualified employees.
Authorization to employ,
§37-4-95.
Powers and duties,
§37-4-92.
Limitation on powers,
§37-4-97.
Promulgation of rules
and regulations,
§37-4-93.
Definitions, §37-4-90.
Federal standards.
Compliance with, §37-4-91.
Injunctions.
Violation of article,
§37-4-94.
Inspectors.
Authority to employ,
§37-4-95.
Operation and maintenance.
Compliance with federal
standards, §37-4-91.
Penalties.
Violation of article,
§37-4-96.
Rules and regulations.
Promulgation, §37-4-93.
Violation of article.
Injunctions, §37-4-94.
Penalties, §37-4-96.
Highways.
Digging up of roads, §23-1-4.
Housing.
Construction through
curtilage of house
without consent, §10-5-5.

PIPELINES—Cont'd
Injunctions.
Gas pipeline systems.
Jurisdiction of circuit cour
to restrain violations,
§37-4-86.
Inspections.
Safety inspection fees,
§37-4-88.
Licenses.
Municipal corporations.
License schedule for
pipeline companies,
§11-51-129.
Municipal corporations.
License schedules,
§11-51-129.
Operation.
Condemnation of ways and
rights of way by
companies operating
internal improvement,
§10-5-4.
Penalties.
Gas pipeline systems,
§37-4-87.
Public service commission.
Gas pipeline systems. See
within this heading,
"Gas pipeline systems."
Public utilities.
Gas pipeline systems,
§§37-4-80 to 37-4-88. See
within this heading,
"Gas pipeline systems."
Secured transactions.
Applicability of filing
provisions, §7-9-302.
Taxation.
General provisions.
See PUBLIC UTILITIES.
United States.
Gas pipeline systems.
Federal minimum safety
standards.
Compliance with,
§37-4-81.

PIRACY.
Copying and sale of
recorded devices,
§§13A-8-80 to 13A-8-86.
See RECORDED DEVICES.
Powers of congress, Const.
U. S., Art. I, §8.

PISTACHIOS.
Manufacture and sale.
See NUTS.

PISTOLS.
See WEAPONS.

PLAGUE.
Notifiable diseases,
§§22-11A-1 to 22-11A-38.
See DISEASES.

PLANNING.
Commissions.
County planning
commissions.
See COUNTIES.
Municipal planning
commissions, §§11-52-1
to 11-52-14.
See MUNICIPAL
CORPORATIONS.
Regional planning and
development commissio
§§11-85-1 to 11-85-73.
Comprehensive advisory
planning.
Defined, §11-85-40.

PLANNING—Cont'd
Comprehensive advisory planning—Cont'd
Powers of Alabama development office and local, regional and joint planning commissions as to comprehensive advisory planning and research, §11-85-40.
Regional planning commissions for comprehensive advisory planning and research, §§11-85-20 to 11-85-24.
Counties.
County planning commissions.
See COUNTIES.
Flood-prone areas.
Comprehensive land use management in flood-prone areas, §§11-19-1 to 11-19-24.
See COUNTIES.
Regional planning and development, §§11-85-1 to 11-85-73.
Definitions.
Comprehensive advisory planning, §11-85-40.
Regional planning commissions for comprehensive advisory planning and research, §11-85-20.
Regional planning and development commissions, §11-85-50.
Flood-prone areas.
Counties.
Comprehensive land use management in flood-prone areas, §§11-19-1 to 11-19-24.
See COUNTIES.
Health.
State health planning and development, §§22-4-1 to 22-4-17.
See HEALTH.
Housing authorities.
County housing authorities.
Authority projects subject to local planning laws, §24-1-69.
Municipal housing authorities.
Authority projects subject to local planning laws, §24-1-30.
Joint planning commissions.
Powers as to comprehensive advisory planning and research, §11-85-40.
Municipal corporations.
General provisions.
See MUNICIPAL CORPORATIONS.
Municipal planning commission, §§11-52-1 to 11-52-14.
See MUNICIPAL CORPORATIONS.
Regional planning and development, §§11-85-1 to 11-85-73.

PLANNING—Cont'd
Office of state planning and federal programs.
Environmental management, §§22-22A-1 to 22-22A-15.
See ENVIRONMENTAL MANAGEMENT.
General provisions.
See DEVELOPMENT.
Regional planning and development, §§11-85-1 to 11-85-73.
Commissions.
Flood-prone areas, §§11-19-1 to 11-19-24.
See COUNTIES.
Regional planning and development commissions, §§11-85-1 to 11-85-73.
Regional planning commissions for comprehensive advisory planning and research, §§11-85-20 to 11-85-24.
Contracts.
Regional planning and development commissions.
Authority to enter into contracts with other agencies, §11-85-73.
Definitions.
Regional planning and development commissions, §11-85-50.
Regional planning commissions for comprehensive advisory planning and research, §11-85-20.
Establishment of regions, §11-85-1.
Regional planning and development commissions, §§11-85-1 to 11-85-73.
Additional governmental units becoming members of commission.
Procedure, §§11-85-53, 11-85-71.
Adjoining counties, municipalities, etc.
Joint planning agreements with.
Authorized, §11-85-57.
Advisory committees.
Appointment, §11-85-54.
Agreements.
Joint planning agreements.
Authorized with adjoining counties, municipalities, etc., §11-85-57.
Bistate commissions, §11-85-52.
Boundaries of districts.
Changes to include adjacent counties, §11-85-57.
Composition, §11-85-53.
Confirmation of existing commissions, §11-85-70.

PLANNING—Cont'd
Regional planning and development—Cont'd
Regional planning and development commissions—Cont'd
Contracts.
Authority to enter into contracts with other agencies, §11-85-73.
Definitions, §11-85-50.
Dissolution, §11-85-53.
Districts.
Boundaries.
Changes to include adjacent counties, §11-85-57.
Designation of state planning and development districts by governor, §11-85-51.
Effect of population changes upon establishment and operation, §11-85-59.
Single county state planning and development districts.
Designation, §11-85-51.
State planning and development districts.
Designation by governor, §11-85-51.
Use for other purposes and programs, §11-85-58.
Duties, §§11-85-56, 11-85-72.
Establishment.
Effect of population changes upon establishment of commissions, §11-85-59.
Financing, §11-85-53.
Receipt of state financial support, §11-85-55.
Formation.
Effect of population changes upon formation, §§11-85-52, 11-85-59.
Governor.
Designation of state planning and development districts, §11-85-51.
Joint planning agreements.
Authorized with adjoining counties, municipalities, etc., §11-85-57.
Multistate commissions, §11-85-52.
Officers, §11-85-54.
Operation of commissions.
Effect of population changes upon operation, §11-85-59.
Powers, §§11-85-56, 11-85-72.
Ratification of existing commissions, §11-85-70.

PLANNING—Cont'd
**Regional planning and
development**—Cont'd
Regional planning and
development
commissions—Cont'd
Replacement of
representatives,
§11-85-53.
Selection of representatives,
§11-85-53.
Single county commissions,
§§11-85-52.
Single county state
planning and
development districts.
Designation, §11-85-51.
State financial support.
Receipt, §11-85-55.
State planning and
development districts.
Designation by governor,
§11-85-51.
Effect of population
changes, §11-85-59.
Use for other purposes
and programs,
§11-85-58.
Terms of representatives,
§11-85-53.
Withdrawal of
governmental units.
Procedure, §11-85-53.
Regional planning commissions,
§§11-85-1 to 11-85-7.
Appointment of members,
§11-85-2.
Appropriation of funds,
§11-85-3.
Buildings.
Proposed construction of
public buildings to
be submitted for
approval, §11-85-7.
Compensation of members,
§11-85-2.
Composition, §11-85-2.
Comprehensive advisory
planning and research.
Powers, §11-85-40.
Counties.
Certification of master
plan to counties,
§11-85-5.
Creation, §11-85-1.
Establishment of regions,
§11-85-1.
Expenditure of funds,
§11-85-3.
Funds.
Appropriation of funds,
§11-85-3.
Expenditure of funds,
§11-85-3.
Governor.
Certification of master
plan to governor,
§11-85-5.
Master plan for physical
development of region.
Adoption, §11-85-4.
Amendments.
Certification of proposed
amendments to
regional planning
commission for
approval, §11-85-6.
Certification of plan to
governor,
municipalities,
counties, etc.,
§11-85-5.

PLANNING—Cont'd
**Regional planning and
development**—Cont'd
Regional planning
commissions—Cont'd
Master plan for physical
development of region
—Cont'd
Contents, §11-85-4.
Municipal planning
commission.
Adoption of plan,
§11-85-6.
Purpose, §11-85-4.
Municipalities.
Adoption of master plan,
§11-85-6.
Certification of master
plan, §11-85-5.
Organization, §11-85-3.
Overruling of commission,
§11-85-7.
Procedure, §11-85-3.
Qualifications of members,
§11-85-2.
Removal of members,
§11-85-2.
Staff, §11-85-3.
Streets.
Proposed construction to
be submitted for
approval, §11-85-7.
Terms of members,
§11-85-2.
Utilities.
Proposed construction to
be submitted for
approval, §11-85-7.
Vacancies, §11-85-2.
Regional planning
commissions for
comprehensive advisory
planning and research,
§§11-85-20 to 11-85-24.
Appointment of members,
§11-85-22.
Composition, §11-85-22.
Creation, §11-85-21.
Definitions, §11-85-20.
Duties, §11-85-23.
Eminent domain.
Article not to impair
right of eminent
domain of utilities,
§11-85-24.
Establishment of region for
advisory planning,
§11-85-21.
Franchises.
Article not to impair
rights under
franchises of
utilities, §11-85-24.
Powers, §§11-85-23,
11-85-40.
Qualifications of members, ·
§11-85-22.
Utilities.
Article not to impair
right of eminent
domain or rights
under franchises,
leases, etc., of
utilities, §11-85-24.
Vacancies, §11-85-22.

PLANNING—Cont'd
Solid waste.
Management plan,
§§22-27-40 to
22-27-49.
See SOLID WASTE.
**Southern growth policies
agreement,** §§41-18-1 to
41-18-3.
State planning.
Office of state planning and
federal programs,
§§41-9-208 to
41-9-214.
See DEVELOPMENT.
Subdivisions.
County regulation of
subdivisions, §§11-24-1
to 11-24-7.
See COUNTIES.
Generally.
See SUBDIVISIONS.
United States.
Office of state planning and
federal programs,
§§41-9-208 to
41-9-214.
See DEVELOPMENT.

PLANTATIONS.
Superintendents.
Liens, §§35-11-91 to
35-11-97.
See AGRICULTURE.

PLANTS.
Agriculture.
General provisions.
See AGRICULTURE.
Diseases.
Insect and disease
control, §§2-25-1 to
2-25-22.
See NURSERIES.
Pathologists, §§2-28-1 to
2-28-12.
Floriculture.
See LANDSCAPING.
Horticulture.
See LANDSCAPING.
**Insect and disease
control.**
Nurseries, §§2-25-1 to
2-25-22.
See NURSERIES.
Pest control generally.
See PEST CONTROL.
Pesticides.
See PESTICIDES.
Landscaping.
See LANDSCAPING.
Nurseries.
See NURSERIES.
Pathologists, §§2-28-1 to
2-28-12.
Appeals.
Denial or revocation of
permits, §2-28-7.
Applicability of chapter,
§2-28-12.
Commissioner of
agriculture
and industries.
Appeals from denial or
revocation of permits,
§2-28-7.
Denial or revocation of
permits, §2-28-7.
Penalties.
Authority to impose,
§2-2-18.

PLANTS—Cont'd
  Pathologists—Cont'd
    Commissioner of agriculture
      and industries—Cont'd
      Permits.
        Applicants to present
          evidence as to
          qualification,
          §2-28-5.
      Definitions, §2-28-1.
      Examinations.
        Applicants for permits,
          §2-28-4.
        Applicability of
          requirement as to
          examination,
          §2-28-6.
        Persons engaged in
          pathological work,
          §2-28-2.
      Examining board,
        §2-28-2.
      Fees.
        Permit fees, §2-28-4.
      Injunctions.
        Restraining performance of
          professional work or
          services without
          permit, §2-28-11.
      Penalties.
        Commission of agriculture
          may impose, §2-2-18.
        Violations of chapter or
          rules or regulations,
          §2-28-11.
      Permits, §§2-28-4 to
        2-28-11.
        Appeals from denial or
          revocation of permits,
          §2-28-7.
        Applicants.
          Evidence as to
            qualifications,
            §2-28-5.
          Examination, §§2-28-4,
            2-28-6.
          Qualifications, §2-28-5.
          Submission of statements
            as to training and
            experience, §2-28-4.
        Commissioner of
          agriculture and
          industries.
          Appeal from denial or
            revocation of
            permits, §2-28-7.
          Applicants to present
            evidence as to
            qualifications to
            commissioner,
            §2-28-5.
          Denial or revocation of
            permits, §2-28-7.
        Denial, §2-28-7.
        Duration, §2-28-4.
        Examination of applicants,
          §§2-28-4, 2-28-6.
        Experience by applicants.
          Submission of statements
            as to experience,
            §2-28-4.
        Fees, §2-28-4.
        Injunctive proceedings to
          restrain performance
          of work or services
          without permit,
          §2-28-11.
        Issuance, §2-28-5.

PLANTS—Cont'd
  Pathologists—Cont'd
    Permits—Cont'd
      Qualifications of
        applicants.
        Evidence.
          Applicants to present
            to commissioner,
            §2-28-5.
        Minimum qualifications,
          §2-28-5.
        Submission of statements
          as to training and
          experience, §2-28-4.
      Required for performance
        of professional work or
        services governed by
        chapter, §2-28-4.
      Revocation, §2-28-7.
      Testing of applicants,
        §2-28-4.
      Training of applicants.
        Submission of statements
          as to training, §2-28-4.
    Rules and regulations.
      Penalties for violations,
        §2-28-11.
      Promulgation as to
        qualifications and
        practice of persons
        engaged in work or
        services governed by
        chapter, §2-28-3.
    Violations of chapter.
      Penalties for violations,
        §2-28-11.
  Quarantine.
    Insect and disease control.
      See NURSERIES.
  Sales.
    Fraud.
      See NURSERIES.
  Seeds.
    See SEEDS.
  Symbol of plant parts.
    Registration, §§2-26-50 to
      2-26-52.

PLASTICS.
  Molds, dyes or patterns.
    Disposal.
      Applicability of provisions,
        §8-28-4.
      Definitions, §8-28-1.
      Notice, §8-28-3.
      Procedure, §8-28-3.
      When molder may dispose
        of form owned by
        customer, §8-28-2.

PLATS.
  General provisions.
    See MAPS AND PLATS.
  Taxation.
    Assessments.
      Plat books, §§40-7-37 to
        40-7-41.

PLAYGROUNDS.
  Education.
    General provisions.
      See EDUCATION.

PLEADINGS.
  Abatement.
    Pleas in abatement.
      Criminal pleading,
        §§15-15-40 to 15-15-44.

PLEADINGS—Cont'd
  Abortion.
    Parental consent to
      performing abortion
      upon minors.
    Waiver of written consent
      requirements.
      Pleadings to identify
        minors by initials
        only, §26-21-4.
  **Adoption of statements by
    reference,** ARCP, Rule 10
    (c).
  Affirmative defenses, ARCP,
    Rule 8 (c).
  Allowed pleadings, ARCP,
    Rule 7 (a).
  **Alternative claims or
    defenses,** ARCP, Rule 8
    (e).
  Ambiguity.
    Motion for more definite
      statement, ARCP, Rule
      12 (e).
  Amendments, ARCP, Rule 15
    (a).
    Amendments to conform to
      evidence, ARCP, Rule 15
      (b).
    Counterclaims, ARCP, Rule
      13 (f).
    Relation back of
      amendments, ARCP,
      Rule 15 (c).
  Attorneys at law.
    Signing of pleadings, ARCP,
      Rule 11.
  Capacity, ARCP, Rule 9 (a).
  Capital offenses.
    Guilty pleas, §13A-5-42.
  Caption, ARCP, Rule 10 (a).
  Claims for relief.
    Contents, ARCP, Rule 8 (a).
  Class actions.
    Form of complaint, ARCP,
      Form 24.
  Commercial code.
    Interpleader and
      intervention.
      Commercial paper.
        Notice to third party of
          suit, §7-3-803.
      Sales.
        Notice of claim or
          litigation to person
          answerable over,
          §7-2-607.
  Conciseness, ARCP, Rule 8 (e).
  Condition of the mind,
    ARCP, Rule 9 (b).
  Conditions precedent, ARCP,
    Rule 9 (c).
  Consistency, ARCP, Rule 8
    (e).
  **Construction and
    interpretation,** ARCP,
    Rule 8 (f).
  Contents of claims for relief,
    ARCP, Rule 8 (a).
  Copies.
    Filing of copies in place of
      missing pleadings,
      §6-8-102.
  Counterclaims.
    See COUNTERCLAIMS.
  Criminal pleading.
    Capital offenses.
      Guilty pleas, §13A-5-42.
    Demurrers.
      Forms, §15-15-4.

PLEADINGS—Cont'd
Criminal pleading—Cont'd
Forms of pleas, §15-15-4.
Guilty pleas.
Appeals.
No right of appeal,
§15-15-26.
Capital offenses,
§13A-5-42.
Determination of degree of
offense and fixing of
punishment, §15-15-24.
Entry of judgment,
§15-15-23.
Felony cases, §15-15-20.
Fixing of date to formally
make and enter plea,
§15-15-22.
Hearing of testimony,
§15-15-23.
Information preferred and
filed against
defendant, §15-15-21.
Magistrates.
District court
magistrates agency
division.
Receiving pleas of
guilty in
misdemeanor
cases, ARJA, Rule
18.
Municipal court
magistrates agency
division.
Receiving pleas of
guilty in
municipal
ordinance cases,
ARJA, Rule 18.
No right of appeal,
§15-15-26.
Receiving of plea,
§15-15-23.
Sentencing of defendant,
§15-15-23.
When plea not accepted,
§15-15-25.
How plea determined,
§15-15-3.
Insanity defense.
Special plea required,
§15-16-1.
Jurisdiction.
Judgment may be pleaded
without averring
jurisdictional facts,
§15-15-2.
Not guilty plea.
Entry for defendant upon
refusal to plead,
§15-15-1.
Pleas in abatement,
§§15-15-40 to 15-15-44.
Case pending in district or
municipal court.
Abatement of
prosecution of
misdemeanor in
circuit court,
§15-15-43.
Grand jury.
Objection to formation,
§15-15-40.
Plea on grounds of
improperly drawn
jury, §15-15-44.
Indictment.
Objection to indictment,
§15-15-40.
Verification, §15-15-42.

PLEADINGS—Cont'd
Criminal pleading—Cont'd
Pleas in abatement—Cont'd
When filed, §15-15-41.
Plea on grounds grand
jurors improperly
drawn, §15-15-44.
Refusal to plead.
Entry of not guilty plea for
defendant, §15-15-1.
Rejoinders.
Forms, §15-15-4.
Replications.
Forms, §15-15-4.
Cross-claims.
See CROSS-CLAIMS.
Damages.
Special damage, ARCP, Rule
9 (g).
Defenses, ARCP, Rule 8 (b).
Affirmative defenses, ARCP,
Rule 8 (c).
Alternative defenses, ARCP,
Rule 8 (e).
Answer presenting defenses
under Rule 12 (b),
ARCP, Form 27.
Assertion in pleadings,
ARCP, Rule 12 (b).
Effect of failure to deny,
ARCP, Rule 8 (d).
Forms, ARCP, Forms 26, 27.
Denials, ARCP, Rule 8 (b).
Denials.
Effect of failure to deny,
ARCP, Rule 8 (d).
Form of denials, ARCP, Rule
8 (b).
Dilatory pleadings, ARCP,
Rule 11.
Court of the judiciary, ARJC,
Rule 7.
Directness, ARCP, Rule 8 (e).
Exhibits, ARCP, Rule 10 (c).
Failure to deny.
Effect of failure, ARCP, Rule
8 (d).
Failure to state a claim.
Defense of failure to state a
claim, ARCP, Rule 12
(b), (h).
False imprisonment.
Form of complaint, ARCP,
Form 18.
Felonies. See within this
heading, "Criminal
pleading."
Fictitious parties, ARCP,
Rule 9 (h).
Filing, ARCP, Rule 5 (d).
Definition of filing with the
court, ARCP, Rule 5 (e).
Forms, ARCP, Rule 10; ARCP,
Forms 2 to 29.
Criminal pleading, §15-15-4.
Fraud, ARCP, Rule 9 (b).
Form of complaint for fraud,
ARCP, Form 20.
Frivolous pleadings, ARCP,
Rule 11.
Court of the judiciary, ARJC,
Rule 7.
General rules of pleading,
ARCP, Rule 8.
Guilty pleas. See within this
heading, "Criminal
pleading."
Insufficiency of pleading.
Exceptions for insufficiency.
Abolished, ARCP, Rule 7
(c).

PLEADINGS—Cont'd
Judgments, ARCP, Rule 9 (e).
Motion for judgment on the
pleadings, ARCP, Rule
12 (c).
Libel and slander.
Privileged information,
§13A-11-161.
Lost or destroyed papers.
Substitution of lost or
destroyed papers or
records in civil cases,
§§12-20-1, 12-20-26 to
12-20-32.
See COURTS.
Malicious prosecution.
Form of complaint, ARCP,
Form 19.
**Mechanics' and
materialmen's liens.**
Enforcement of liens,
§35-11-222.
Mistake, ARCP, Rule 9 (b).
Form of complaint for money
paid by mistake, ARCP,
Form 10.
More definite statement.
Motion for more definite
statement, ARCP, Rule
12 (e).
Names of parties, ARCP,
Rule 10 (a).
Negligence.
Form of complaint, ARCP,
Form 16.
Nonjoinder.
Pleading reasons for
nonjoinder, ARCP, Rule
19 (c).
Official document or act,
ARCP, Rule 9 (d).
Ordinances, ARCP, Rule 9 (d)
Paragraphs, ARCP, Rule 10
(b).
Permitted pleadings, ARCP,
Rule 7 (a).
Place, ARCP, Rule 9 (f).
Pleas in abatement.
Criminal pleading,
§§15-15-40 to 15-15-44.
Post-conviction remedies,
ARCrP, Rule 20.7.
Probate courts.
Applicability of provisions
pertaining to pleading in
circuit courts, §12-13-12.
**Public officers and
employees.**
Official document or act,
ARCP, Rule 9 (d).
Record.
Original or copies of
pleadings final record in
civil actions, §12-20-22.
Rules of criminal procedure.
See RULES OF CRIMINAL
PROCEDURE.
Separate statement, ARCP,
Rule 10 (b).
Service, ARCrP, Rule 5.
Signing of pleadings, ARCP,
Rule 11.
Statutes.
Special statute, ARCP, Rule
9 (d).
**Stockholder's derivative
action.**
Form of complaint, ARCP,
Form 25.

PLEADINGS—Cont'd
Striking pleading.
Motion to strike, ARCP, Rule 12 (f).
Supplemental pleadings,
ARCP, Rule 15 (d).
Counterclaims, ARCP, Rule 13 (e).
Third-party practice, ARCP, Rule 14.
Form of third-party complaint, ARCP, Form 29.
Time, ARCP, Rule 9 (f).
Vagueness.
Motion for more definite statement, ARCP, Rule 12 (e).
Warranty.
Form of complaint on a warranty, ARCP, Form 21.
Wrongful death.
Form of complaint, ARCP, Form 31.

PLEAS.
Abolished, ARCP, Rule 7 (c).
Motor vehicles.
Uniform traffic infractions.
Defendant's appearance.
Plea and waiver of trial, ARJA, Rule 19.

PLEAS IN ABATEMENT,
§§15-15-40 to 15-15-44.

PLEDGE AND COLLATERAL SECURITY.
Acknowledgment.
Receipt or acknowledgment for collateral required, §8-1-3.
Appeals.
Costs on appeal.
See APPEALS.
Banks.
See BANKS AND FINANCIAL INSTITUTIONS.
Commercial code.
Secured transactions.
See COMMERCIAL CODE.
Counties.
Depositories, §11-4-42.
Education.
Tax anticipation warrants in cities and counties.
Public school funds and minimum school program fund moneys not to be pledged, §16-13-76.
Mortgages and deeds of trust.
See MORTGAGES AND DEEDS OF TRUST.
Motor vehicles.
Uniform certificate of title and antitheft act, §§32-8-1 to 32-8-88.
See MOTOR VEHICLES.
Municipal corporations.
Boards for operation of water, sewer, gas and electric systems.
Pledge of revenues from systems for payment of bonds, §11-50-317.

PLEDGE AND COLLATERAL SECURITY—Cont'd
Municipal corporations —Cont'd
Boards for operation of water, sewer, gas and electric systems—Cont'd
Provisions in pledge agreements executed by corporation as to rights of parties, §11-50-314.
Gas districts.
Bond issues.
Properties, persons, etc., subject to pledges, §11-50-408.
Provisions in pledge agreements executed as security for bonds as to rights of parties, §11-50-407.
When pledges effective, §11-50-408.
Waterworks and sewer boards.
Acquisition, operation, etc., of gas plants and systems.
Execution of pledges, etc., as security for indebtedness, §11-50-262.
Provisions in pledge agreements executed by corporation as to rights of parties, §11-50-235.
Peace bonds.
See PEACE BONDS.
Receipt.
Receipt or acknowledgment for collateral required, §8-1-3.
Savings and loan associations.
See SAVINGS AND LOAN ASSOCIATIONS.
Secured transactions,
§§7-9-101 to 7-9-507.
See COMMERCIAL CODE.
Small loans.
See SMALL LOANS.
Tennessee Valley Authority.
Exhibit commission.
Bond issues.
Payment of principal or interest.
Pledge of amounts necessary from revenues retained by state, §41-9-783.
Uniform commercial code.
See COMMERCIAL CODE.

PLUMBING, §§34-37-1 to 34-37-18.
Apprentice gas fitter or plumber.
Defined, §34-37-1.
Registration of applicants for registration certificates, §34-37-6.
Boards of health.
Authority to require installation of plumbing facilities, §22-26-2.

PLUMBING—Cont'd
Bonds, surety.
Certification of plumbers and gas fitters.
Revocation of certificates.
Issuance of license to licensee, §34-37-12.
Master plumbers and gas fitters, §34-37-13.
Plumbers and gas fitters examining board.
Executive director, §34-37-5.
Certification of plumbers and gas fitters, §§34-37-1 to 34-37-15.
Acts, works and conduct permitted without certificate, §34-37-15.
Defined, §34-37-1.
Examinations, §34-37-6.
Failure to pass.
Reexamination, §34-37-7.
Waiver of examination, §34-37-6.
Reciprocal agreements, §34-37-11.
Expiration of certificates, §34-37-9.
Fees.
Board to set, §34-37-9.
Grandfather clause, §34-37-6.
Inactive status.
Affidavit, §34-37-14.
Issuance of certificate, §§34-37-6, 34-37-9.
Renewal, §34-37-8.
Temporary certificate, §34-37-10.
Name under which business carried on.
Change.
Notice, §34-37-14.
Place of business.
Change.
Notice, §34-37-14.
Reciprocal agreements, §34-37-11.
Renewal, §34-37-8.
Required, §34-37-6.
Exceptions, §34-37-15.
Revocation of certificates, §34-37-12.
Temporary certificate, §34-37-10.
Wrongful use of certificate, §34-37-14.
Codes.
Lead.
Amendment of city and county codes to include provisions of chapter, §22-37-4.
Conflict of laws.
Other laws repealed, §34-37-18.
Construction and interpretation.
Conflicting laws repealed, §34-37-18.
Definitions, §34-37-1.
Examinations.
Certification of plumbers and gas fitters, §§34-37-6, 34-37-7.
Fees.
Certification of plumbers and gas fitters.
Board to set fees, §34-37-9.

PLUMBING—Cont'd
Gas fitters.
Apprentice gas fitters.
Defined, §34-37-1.
Registration of applicants
for registration
certificates, §34-37-6.
Journeyman gas fitters.
Defined, §34-37-1.
Master gas fitters.
Bonds, surety, §34-37-13.
Defined, §34-37-1.
Hearings.
Certification of plumbers and
gas fitters.
Revocation of certificate,
§34-37-12.
Installation of facilities.
Authority of state and county
boards of health to
require, §22-26-2.
Permits.
Outside jurisdiction of
municipal
corporations, §22-26-5.
Within police jurisdiction
of municipal
corporations, §22-26-4.
Plans or specifications.
Approval, §22-26-3.
Violations of chapter.
Penalty, §22-26-6.
Jails.
Adequate sanitary plumbing
connections, §14-6-103.
Journeyman gas fitters.
Defined, §34-37-1.
Journeyman plumbers.
Defined, §34-37-1.
Lead.
General provisions, §§22-37-1
to 22-37-6.
See LEAD.
Licensing of plumbers,
§40-12-145.
Acts, works and conduct
permitted without
license, §34-37-15.
Certification of plumbers and
gas fitters. See within
this heading, "
Certification of plumbers
and gas fitters."
Restrictions, §34-37-16.
Master gas fitters.
Bonds, surety, §34-37-13.
Defined, §34-37-1.
Master plumbers.
Bonds, surety, §34-37-13.
Defined, §34-37-1.
Misdemeanors.
Violations of provisions,
§34-37-17.
Municipal corporations.
Codes.
Adoption of technical codes
by reference, §11-45-8.
Permits for installation
within police jurisdiction
of municipalities,
§22-26-4.
Regulation, installation, etc.,
§11-50-54.
Notice.
Certification of plumbers and
gas fitters.
Change of place of business
or name under which
business carried on,
§34-37-14.

PLUMBING—Cont'd
Notice—Cont'd
Certification of plumbers and
gas fitters—Cont'd
Revocation of certificate,
§34-37-12.
Conducting business.
Notice of address of place
of business, §34-37-14.
Penalties.
Installation of facilities.
Violations of chapter,
§22-26-6.
Permits.
Installation of facilities.
Outside jurisdiction of
municipal
corporations, §22-26-5.
Permits for installation
within police
jurisdiction of
municipal
corporations, §22-26-4.
**Plumbers and gas fitters
examining board.**
Appointment of members,
§34-37-3.
Bonds, surety.
Executive director,
§34-37-5.
Compensation of members,
§34-37-4.
Composition, §34-37-3.
Definition of "board,"
§34-37-1.
Duties, §§34-37-6, 34-37-9.
Executive director.
Bonds, surety, §34-37-5.
Expenses of members,
§34-37-4.
Fund, §34-37-5.
Meetings, §34-37-4.
Name.
Renamed, §34-37-2.
Powers.
Expansion of authority,
§34-37-2.
Quorum, §34-37-4.
Terms of members, §34-37-3.
Reciprocity.
Certification of plumbers and
gas fitters, §34-37-11.
Registration.
Apprentice plumbers or gas
fitters.
Applicants for registration
certificate, §34-37-6.
Subpoenas.
Certification of plumbers and
gas fitters.
Revocation of certificates.
Compelling attendance of
witnesses, §34-37-12.
Witnesses.
Certification of plumbers and
gas fitters.
Revocation of certificate,
§34-37-12.

PNEUMOCONIOSIS.
Workmen's compensation,
§§25-5-140 to 25-5-180.
See WORKMEN'S
COMPENSATION.

PNEUMONIA.
Notifiable diseases,
§§22-11A-1 to 22-11A-38.
See DISEASES.

PODIATRISTS, §§34-24-230 to
34-24-276.
Advertising.
False or misleading
advertising, §34-24-231.
Revocation or suspension of
license, §34-24-276.
Applicability of article.
Exemption of other healing
arts, §34-24-233.
Board of podiatry,
§§34-24-250 to 34-24-257.
Appointment of members,
§34-24-250.
Compensation of members,
§34-24-253.
Composition, §34-24-250.
Examinations generally. See
within this heading,
"Examinations."
Fees.
Disposition of funds
realized from fees,
§34-24-253.
Funds.
Disposition of funds
realized from fees,
§34-24-253.
Governor.
Annual report to governor,
§34-24-252.
Appointment and removal
of members,
§34-24-250.
Meetings.
Generally, §34-24-251.
Oaths.
Authority to administer
oaths, §34-24-252.
Oath of office, §34-24-250.
Powers and duties.
Generally, §34-24-252.
Qualifications of members,
§34-24-250.
Quorum, §34-24-251.
Removal of members,
§34-24-250.
Secretary-treasurer.
Bond, §34-24-254.
Salary, §34-24-254.
Terms of office, §34-24-250.
Vacancies.
Filling vacancies,
§34-24-250.
Bonds, surety.
Board of podiatry.
Bond of secretary-
treasurer, §34-24-254.
Deceit.
Revocation or suspension of
license, §34-24-276.
Definitions, §34-24-230.
Unprofessional conduct,
§34-24-276.
Diagnosis.
Defined, §34-24-230.
Disciplinary action.
Revocation or suspension of
license, §34-24-276.
Electrical treatment.
Defined, §34-24-230.
Examinations, §§34-24-255 to
34-24-257.
Application, §34-24-255.
Conduct of examination,
§34-24-256.
Contents of examination,
§34-24-255.
Fees, §§34-24-255, 34-24-257.

PODIATRISTS—Cont'd
  Examinations—Cont'd
    Passing examination.
      Issuance of license,
        §34-24-255.
    Qualifications of applicants,
      §34-24-255.
    Required, §34-24-255.
    Scope of examination,
      §34-24-255.
    Second or subsequent
      examination, §34-24-257.
  Exemptions from provisions
    of article, §34-24-233.
  Fees.
    Disposition of funds realized
      from fees, §34-24-253.
    Examinations, §34-24-255.
      Second or subsequent
        examination,
        §34-24-257.
    Licenses.
      Podiatrists coming into
        state, §34-24-271.
      Renewal registration fee,
        §34-24-275.
      Special certificate for
        nonresidents,
        §34-24-272.
    Prior practice of podiatry,
      §34-24-232.
  Fraud.
    Revocation or suspension of
      license, §34-24-276.
  Funds.
    Board of podiatry.
      Disposition of funds
        realized from fees,
        §34-24-253.
  Governor.
    Board of podiatry,
      §§34-24-250, 34-24-252.
  Grandfather clause,
    §34-24-232.
  Human foot.
    Defined, §34-24-230.
  Insurance.
    Health insurance.
      Payment for services of
        podiatrists, §27-1-15.
  Liability.
    Licenses.
      Revocation or suspension.
        Members of board
          immune from suit,
          §34-24-276.
  Licenses.
    Chiropodists, §40-12-155.
    Contents of license,
      §34-24-273.
    Display by holder,
      §34-24-273.
    Examinations, §§34-24-255 to
      34-24-257.
    Fees.
      Podiatrists coming into
        state, §34-24-271.
      Renewal registration fee,
        §34-24-275.
      Special certificate for
        nonresidents,
        §34-24-272.
    Issuance, §§34-24-255,
      34-24-273.
    Nonresidents.
      Podiatrists coming into
        state, §34-24-271.
      Special certificate,
        §34-24-272.

PODIATRISTS—Cont'd
  Licenses—Cont'd
    Penalties.
      Practicing podiatry without
        license, §34-24-270.
      Podiatrists coming into state,
        §34-24-271.
      Practicing podiatry without
        license, §34-24-270.
      Registration of licensees in
        record books, §34-24-273.
      Renewal, §34-24-275.
      Revocation or suspension.
        Grounds, §34-24-276.
  Manipulative treatment.
    Defined, §34-24-230.
  Mechanical treatment.
    Defined, §34-24-230.
  Medical treatment.
    Defined, §34-24-230.
  Misrepresentation.
    Revocation or suspension of
      license, §34-24-276.
  Negligence.
    Revocation or suspension of
      license, §34-24-276.
  Nonresidents.
    Licenses, §§34-24-271,
      34-24-272.
  Oaths.
    Board of podiatry,
      §§34-24-250, 34-24-252.
  Penalties.
    Practicing podiatry without
      license, §34-24-270.
    Violations of article,
      §34-24-234.
  Practice of podiatry.
    Defined, §34-24-230.
    Examinations, §§34-24-255 to
      34-24-257.
    Exemptions from provisions
      of article, §34-24-233.
    Licenses.
      Practice without license,
        §34-24-270.
    Prior to October 1, 1967.
      Grandfather clause,
        §34-24-232.
  Records.
    Licenses.
      Registration of licensees in
        record book,
        §34-24-273.
  State board of medical
    examiners.
    See PHYSICIANS.
  Surgical treatment.
    Defined, §34-24-230.
  Unprofessional conduct.
    Defined, §34-24-276.
    Revocation or suspension of
      license, §34-24-276.
  Violations of article.
    Penalties, §34-24-234.
    Practicing podiatry without
      license, §34-24-270.

POET LAUREATE, §1-2-15.

POISONS AND POISONING.
  Caustic or corrosive
    substances, §§8-17-20 to
    8-17-24.
  Defined, §34-23-1.
  Fishing.
    Catching or killing of fish,
      §9-11-93.
    Private ponds, lakes, pools or
      reservoirs, §9-11-91.

POISONS AND POISONING
  —Cont'd
  Hunting.
    Taking of protected birds or
      animals by use of
      poisons, §9-11-245.
    Penalties, §9-11-246.
  Lime.
    Sale or offer for sale of
      agricultural liming
      materials containing
      toxic materials in
      quantities injurious to
      plants or animals,
      §2-23-8.
  Notifiable diseases,
    §§22-11A-1 to 22-11A-38.
    See DISEASES.
  Pharmacists and
    pharmacies.
    See PHARMACISTS AND
      PHARMACIES.
  Radiation.
    See ATOMIC ENERGY.
  Sales.
    Restrictions on retail sales of
      certain poisons,
      §22-20-11.
    Restrictions on sale in
      pharmacies, §34-23-70.
  State toxicologist.
    See STATE
      TOXICOLOGIST.

POLICE.
  Accidents.
    Rendering aid at scene of
      accidents.
      Exemptions from liability,
        §6-5-332.
  Advertisements.
    State or federal peace officer
      magazines.
      Solicitation of
        advertisements,
        §13A-14-5.
  Aiding.
    Refusing to aid, §13A-10-5.
  Alabama Agricultural and
    Mechanical University.
    University police officers.
      General provisions,
        §§16-22-1, 16-22-2.
      Powers and duties,
        §16-49-4.
  Alabama Institute for deaf
    and blind, §§16-22-1,
    16-22-2.
  Alabama State University.
    General provisions,
      §§16-22-1, 16-22-2.
    Powers and duties, §16-50-4.
    University police officers,
      §16-50-4.
  Arrest.
    General provisions.
      See ARREST.
    Refusing to aid police in
      making arrest,
      §13A-10-5.
    Resisting arrest, §13A-10-41.
  Assault upon peace officer.
    See ASSAULT AND
      BATTERY.
  Auburn University,
    §16-48-12.
    Generally, §§16-27-1,
      16-27-2.
  Capitol.
    Color of uniforms, §41-4-184.

POLICE—Cont'd
 Capitol—Cont'd
  Employment by director of
    finance, §41-4-182.
  Equipment.
    Necessary equipment to be
      furnished, §41-4-185.
  Insurance,
    Authority to insure,
      §41-4-185.
  Powers, §41-4-184.
 Child abuse and neglect.
  See MINORS.
 Civil service merit systems.
  Municipal law enforcement
    officers, §§11-43-180 to
    11-43-190.
  See MUNICIPAL
    CORPORATIONS.
 Constables.
  General provisions.
    See CONSTABLES.
 Criminal law and procedure.
  Attempting to elude officer.
    Bail jumping, §§13A-10-39,
      13A-10-40.
    Escape generally,
      §§13A-10-31 to
      13A-10-35.
    Hindering prosecution or
      apprehension,
      §§13A-10-42 to
      13A-10-45.
    Resisting arrest,
      §13A-10-41.
  Fleeing officer.
    Bail jumping, §§13A-10-39,
      13A-10-40.
    Escape generally,
      §§13A-10-31 to
      13A-10-35.
    Hindering prosecution or
      apprehension,
      §§13A-10-42 to
      13A-10-45.
    Motor vehicle cases,
      §32-5A-193.
    Resisting arrest,
      §13A-10-41.
 Criminal procedure.
  Attempting to elude officer.
    Motor vehicle cases,
      §32-5A-193.
 Death.
  Municipal police.
    Compensation from death
      or disability from
      occupational diseases,
      §§36-30-20 to 36-30-23.
  Peace officers generally.
    See PEACE OFFICERS.
  State police.
    Occupational diseases.
      Compensation for death
        or disability,
        §§36-30-20 to
        36-30-23.
 Diseases.
  Unknown cure.
    Preference given to police
      officers in admission to
      research programs,
      §36-21-11.
 Disorderly conduct.
  Orders to disperse.
    Failure to comply with
      lawful order,
      §13A-11-7.

POLICE—Cont'd
 Eluding officer.
  Attempting to elude officer.
    Motor vehicle cases,
      §32-5A-193.
  Bail jumping, §§13A-10-39,
    13A-10-40.
  Escape generally,
    §§13A-10-31 to
    13A-10-35.
  Hindering prosecution or
    apprehension,
    §§13A-10-42 to
    13A-10-45.
  Resisting arrest, §13A-10-41.
 Entrapment.
  When entrapment defense,
    §13A-3-31.
 Escape.
  Use of force in preventing
    escape, §13A-3-27.
 Fires and fire prevention.
  Refusing to assist in fire
    control, §13A-10-6.
 Flight.
  Bail jumping, §§13A-10-39,
    13A-10-40.
  Escape generally,
    §§13A-10-31 to
    13A-10-35.
  Fleeing officer.
    Motor vehicle cases,
      §32-5A-193.
  Hindering prosecution or
    apprehension,
    §§13A-10-42 to
    13A-10-45.
  Resisting arrest, §13A-10-41.
 Force.
  Use of force in making arrest
    or preventing escape,
    §13A-3-27.
 Fraternal order of police.
  Taxation.
    Property exempt, §40-9-1.
 Gambling.
  Gambling places.
    Duty of officer to break
      into and enter house,
      §13A-12-55.
 Good Samaritan act.
  Policemen rendering first aid
    or emergency care at
    scene of accident, etc.
    Exemption from liability,
    §6-5-332.
 Harbors and ports.
  Marine police, §§33-5-4 to
    33-5-6.
  State docks department.
    Police duties of state docks
      department, §33-3-1.
 Highway patrol.
  General provisions.
    See MOTOR VEHICLES.
 Historic Blakeley authority.
  Deputy police officers.
    Designation, §41-10-181.
 Impersonation.
  Peace officers, §13A-10-11.
  Public servants, §13A-10-10.
 Insurance.
  State Capitol police,
    §41-4-185.
    Authority to insure,
      §41-4-185.
 **Jacksonville State
    University,** §16-52-12.
  Universities and colleges
    generally, §§16-22-1,
    16-22-2.

POLICE—Cont'd
 Junior colleges, §§16-22-1,
    16-22-2.
 Jurisdiction.
  Universities and colleges.
    Extension of jurisdiction,
      §16-22-2.
 Limestone county.
  Jurisdiction.
    Police jurisdiction of
      municipalities located
      within, Const. Ala.,
      amd. 499.
 Livingston University,
    §§16-22-1, 16-22-2,
    16-53-12.
 Magazines.
  Solicitation of advertisements
    for state or federal peace
    officer magazines or
    journals, §13A-14-5.
 Marine police, §§33-5-4 to
    33-5-6.
 Mentally ill.
  Officers for state mental
    health facilities or
    hospitals, §22-50-21.
 Misdemeanors.
  Eluding officer.
    Attempting to elude,
      §32-5A-193.
  Fleeing officer, §32-5A-193.
 Motor vehicles.
  See MOTOR VEHICLES.
 Municipal corporations.
  See MUNICIPAL
    CORPORATIONS.
 Municipal courts.
  Execution of warrants and
    processes, §12-14-4.
 Order to disperse.
  Failure to comply disorderly
    conduct, §13A-11-7.
 Peace officers generally.
  See PEACE OFFICERS.
 Prisons and prisoners.
  Guards.
    See PRISONS AND
      PRISONERS.
 Public buildings.
  Color of uniforms, §41-4-184.
  Employment by director of
    finance, §41-4-182.
  Equipment.
    Necessary equipment to be
      furnished, §41-4-185.
  Insurance, §41-4-185.
    Authority to insure,
      §41-4-185.
  Powers, §41-4-184.
 Railway policemen.
  See RAILROADS.
 Reports.
  Child abuse or neglect.
    See MINORS.
  False reporting to law
    enforcement authorities,
    §13A-10-9.
 Riots.
  Employment of municipal
    police within state by
    governor during riots,
    etc., §§36-21-20 to
    36-21-24.
  Failure of disorderly persons
    to disperse, §13A-11-6.
 Sheriffs.
  See SHERIFFS.

POLICE—Cont'd
Solicitation.
State or federal peace officer magazines or journals. Solicitation of advertisements, §13A-14-5.
State capitol police, §§41-4-182, 41-4-184, 41-4-185.
State parks.
Deputy police officers, §9-2-9.
State police.
See STATE POLICE.
Stopping on highways.
Authority of police to move vehicles stopped on highways, §32-5A-139.
Sylacauga Nurses' Training School, §§16-22-1, 16-22-2.
Taxation.
Fraternal order of police. Property exempt, §40-9-1.
Tickets.
Unauthorized disposition of traffic ticket, §12-12-56.
Troy State University.
Generally, §16-56-12.
Universities and colleges generally, §§16-22-1, 16-22-2.
Tuskegee Institute, §§16-22-1, 16-22-2.
Unemployment compensation.
Certain employees of department of industrial relations constituted peace officers to enforce certain provisions, §25-4-146.
Universities and colleges.
Alabama state university, §16-50-4.
Auburn university, §16-48-12.
Duties, §16-22-1.
Employment, §16-22-1.
Jurisdiction.
Extension of jurisdiction, §16-22-2.
Powers, §16-22-1.
University of Alabama, §§16-47-10, 16-47-11, 16-47-199.
University of Alabama.
Appointment, §16-47-10.
Duties, §16-47-10.
Extended jurisdiction, §16-47-11.
Museum.
Powers of police officers appointed by university president, §16-47-199.
Powers, §16-47-10.
Universities and colleges generally, §§16-22-1, 16-22-2.
University of Montevallo, §§16-22-1, 16-22-2.
University of North Alabama.
Generally, §16-51-12.
Universities and colleges generally, §§16-22-1, 16-22-2.
University of South Alabama. See within this heading, "Universities and colleges."

POLICY GAMES.
Lotteries.
See LOTTERIES.

POLIO.
Notifiable diseases, §§22-11A-1 to 22-11A-38.
See DISEASES.

POLITICAL PARTIES.
Elections.
See ELECTIONS.
Income tax.
Voluntary check off designations on returns. Designated contribution by taxpayer filing state income tax return, §40-18-146.

POLITICAL SUBDIVISIONS.
Counties.
See COUNTIES.
Municipal corporations.
See MUNICIPAL CORPORATIONS.

POLLARD, MUNICIPALITY OF.
Property tax, Const. Ala., amd. 8.

POLLING PLACES.
See ELECTIONS.

POLL TAX.
Constitution of Alabama.
See CONSTITUTION OF ALABAMA.
Constitution of the United States.
Payment not required in federal elections, Const. U. S., Amendment XXIV.
General provisions.
See ELECTIONS.

POLLUTION.
Agricultural nonpoint source pollution, §§22-38-1 to 22-38-8.
See WATER POLLUTION.
Air pollution, §§22-28-1 to 22-28-23.
See AIR POLLUTION.
Authorities.
Environmental improvement authorities, §§9-6-1 to 9-6-17.
See ENVIRONMENTAL IMPROVEMENT AUTHORITIES.
Pollution control finance authority, §§22-29-1 to 22-29-23.
See WATER POLLUTION.
Caves.
Underground water resources.
Risk of pollution. Misdemeanor, §9-19-4.
Environmental improvement authorities, §§9-6-1 to 9-6-17.
See ENVIRONMENTAL IMPROVEMENT AUTHORITIES.
Environmental management.
Generally, §§22-22A-1 to 22-22A-16.
See ENVIRONMENTAL MANAGEMENT.

POLLUTION—Cont'd
Funds.
Pollution control grant fund, §22-22A-16.
Hazardous waste, §§22-30-1 to 22-30-24.
See HAZARDOUS WASTE.
Industrial development boards.
Powers as to pollution control facilities, §11-54-88.
Lime.
Toxic materials.
Sale or offer for sale of agricultural liming materials containing toxic materials in quantities injurious to plants or animals, §2-23-8.
Municipal corporations.
Industrial development boards.
Powers as to pollution control facilities, §11-54-88.
Promotion of pollution control, §§11-54-20 to 11-54-31.
See MUNICIPAL CORPORATIONS.
Pesticides.
General provisions, §§2-27-1 to 2-27-63.
See PESTICIDES.
Taxation.
Pollution control equipment exempt, §40-9-1.
Water pollution.
General provisions.
See WATER POLLUTION.
Pollution control finance authority, §§22-29-1 to 22-29-23.
See WATER POLLUTION.
Safe drinking water act.
Polluting public water supply prohibited, §22-23-47.
Water pollution control act, §§22-22-1 to 22-22-14.
See WATER POLLUTION CONTROL ACT.

POLL WATCHERS.
See ELECTIONS.

POLYGRAPH EXAMINERS, §§34-25-1 to 34-25-36.
Actions.
License required to maintain actions, §34-25-30.
Administration of chapter.
Board to issue regulations, §34-25-5.
Appeals.
Refusal, suspension or revocation of licenses. Judicial review of board decisions, §34-25-35.
Applications for licenses, §§34-25-22 to 34-25-24.
Board of polygraph examiners.
Administration of chapter. Issuance of regulations, §34-25-5.
Advisory consultants, §34-25-4.
Chairman.
Defined, §34-25-2.

POLYGRAPH EXAMINERS
—Cont'd
**Board of polygraph
examiners**—Cont'd
Chairman—Cont'd
Election, §34-25-4.
Composition, §34-25-4.
Definitions, §34-25-2.
Employees, §34-25-4.
Enforcement of chapter.
Injunctions, §34-25-7.
Issuance of regulations,
§34-25-5.
Established, §34-25-4.
Expenses of members,
§§34-25-4, 34-25-5.
Fees.
Disbursement of collected
funds, §34-25-5.
Hearings.
Refusal, suspension or
revocation of licenses,
§34-25-34.
Per diem of members,
§34-25-5.
Refusal, suspension or
revocation of licenses,
§§34-25-32 to 34-25-36.
Rules and regulations.
Promulgation of
administration and
enforcement
regulations, §34-25-5.
Terms of office, §34-25-4.
Travel expenses of members,
§34-25-5.
Voting.
Majority vote required,
§34-25-4.
Bonds, surety.
Licensees required to furnish,
§34-25-21.
Change of business address.
Notification of secretary of
board, §34-25-28.
Definitions, §34-25-2.
Enforcement of chapter.
Polygraph examiners board.
Injunctions, §34-25-7.
Regulations, §34-25-5.
Evidence.
Applicability of chapter.
Chapter not to affect
admissibility.
Rules, §34-25-6.
Polygraph examiners board.
Board seal and signatures.
Prima facie proof,
§34-25-5.
Refusal, suspension or
revocation of licenses.
Board to base decision on
evidence, §34-25-34.
Examinations.
Fees.
Examination and license
fees, §34-25-26.
Fees.
Disbursement of collected
funds, §34-25-5.
Examination and license
fees, §34-25-26.
License fees, §§34-25-22 to
34-25-26.
Felonies.
Refusal, suspension or
revocation of licenses.
Conviction as grounds,
§34-25-32.

POLYGRAPH EXAMINERS
—Cont'd
Fraud.
Grounds for refusal,
suspension or revocation
of license, §34-25-32.
Hearings.
Refusal, suspension or
revocation of licenses,
§34-25-34.
Instrumentation.
Minimum requirements,
§34-25-3.
Use of instruments not
meeting minimum
requirements
prohibited, §34-25-3.
Requirements, §34-25-3.
Internship.
Defined, §34-25-2.
Licenses, §§34-25-20 to
34-25-36.
Actions.
License required to
maintain actions,
§34-25-30.
Applications.
Applicants, §§34-25-23,
34-25-24.
Original license, §34-25-22.
Bond required of licensees,
§34-25-21.
Change of business address.
Notification of secretary,
§34-25-28.
Display, §34-25-27.
Fees.
Examination and license
fees, §34-25-26.
Internship license,
§34-25-25.
Nonresident applicants,
§34-25-23.
Original license, §34-25-22.
Out-of-state license,
§34-25-24.
Schedule, §34-25-26.
Governmental agency
employees.
Exemption for fee
requirements,
§34-25-26.
Hearing.
Refusal, suspension or
revocation, §34-25-34.
Illegal use of license.
Grounds for revocation or
suspension, §34-25-32.
Nonresidents, §34-25-23.
Out-of-state license,
§34-25-24.
Practice without license
unlawful, §34-25-20.
Qualifications of licensees,
§34-25-21.
Refusal, suspension or
revocation.
Appeals.
Judicial review of board
decisions, §34-25-35.
Grounds, §34-25-32.
Hearing, §34-25-34.
Notification of charges,
§34-25-34.
Reissuance of license,
§34-25-36.
Subpoena of witnesses and
documents, §34-25-34.
Surrender of license,
§34-25-36.

POLYGRAPH EXAMINERS
—Cont'd
Licenses—Cont'd
Refusal, suspension or
revocation—Cont'd
Violation by one examiner
or trainee not to affect
employer, §34-25-33.
Renewal, §34-25-29.
Required, §34-25-20.
Signature required on
license, §34-25-27.
Termination, §34-25-29.
Nonresidents.
Licenses.
Nonresident applicants,
§34-25-23.
Penalties.
Violations of chapter,
§34-25-8.
Probationary grounds,
§34-25-32.
**Refusal, suspension or
revocation of licenses,**
§§34-25-32 to 34-25-36.
Registration.
Licenses, §§34-25-20 to
34-25-36.
Reprimands.
Grounds, §34-25-32.
Short title of chapter,
§34-25-1.
Subpoenas.
Refusal, suspension or
revocation of licenses.
Board authorized to issue
subpoenas, §34-25-34.
Title of chapter.
Short title of chapter,
§34-25-1.
Violations of chapter.
Injunctions, §34-25-7.
Penalties, §34-25-8.
Refusal, suspension or
revocation of licenses,
§§34-25-32 to 34-25-36.
Violation by one examiner or
trainee not to affect
employer, §34-25-33.

PONDS.
Fish and game.
See FISH AND GAME.

POOLHALLS, §§34-6-1 to
34-6-35.
See BILLIARD ROOMS.

POORHOUSES.
Municipal corporations.
Establishment, aid, etc., of
poorhouses in counties,
§11-47-134.
Police jurisdiction over
poorhouses, §11-47-22.

POOR PEOPLE.
See INDIGENT PERSONS.

POPULAR NAMES.
Abortion act, §13A-13-4.
Administrative procedure
act, §§41-22-1 to 41-22-27.
Adoption act, §§26-10-1 to
26-10-30.
Adult protective services
act, §§38-9-1 to 38-9-11.
Alcoholic beverage control
act, §§28-3-1 to 28-3-286.
Alimony act, §§30-2-50 to
30-2-55.
Anatomical gift act,
§§22-19-40 to 22-19-61.

POPULAR NAMES—Cont'd
Antiadvertising liquor law,
§28-3-16.
Antiblacklist act,
§13A-11-123.
Antiboycott act, §13A-11-122.
Anti cattle rustling act,
§§2-15-40 to 2-15-48.
Anti-lapse act, §43-8-224.
Anti-obscenity enforcement
act, §§13A-12-200.1 to
13A-12-200.10.
Apartment ownership act,
§§35-8-1 to 35-8-22.
Automatic appeal act,
§12-22-150.
Automobile guest law,
§32-1-2.
Bad check law, §§13A-9-13.1
to 13A-9-20.
Bastardy law, §§26-11-1 to
26-11-8.
Beef promotion act, §§2-8-1
to 2-8-22.
Beverage control act,
§§28-3-1 to 28-3-286.
Blacklisting act, §13A-11-123.
Blood test act, §§22-16-5,
22-16-6.
Blue law, §§13A-12-1,
13A-12-2.
Blue sky law, §§8-6-1 to
8-6-60.
Bone dry law, §§28-4-1 to
28-4-326.
Boycotting and picketing
act, §13A-11-122.
Brain death act, §§22-31-1 to
22-31-4.
Business records act,
§§12-21-42 to 12-21-44.
Chain store tax act,
§§40-12-310 to 40-12-319.
Child abuse act, §§26-14-1 to
26-14-13.
Child abuse and neglect
prevention act, §§26-16-1
to 26-16-53.
Child care act, §§38-7-1 to
38-7-17.
Child custody jurisdiction
act, §§30-3-20 to 30-3-44.
Child labor law, §§25-8-1 to
25-8-31.
Child placement compact
act, §§44-2-1 to 44-2-26.
Child protection act,
§§26-18-1 to 26-18-10.
Child support act, §§30-4-50
to 30-4-98.
Child support act of 1979,
§§38-10-1 to 38-10-33.
Civil libel act, §§6-5-180 to
6-5-189.
Coal mine safety law,
§§25-9-1 to 25-9-370.
Code of ethics, §§36-25-1 to
36-25-30.
Cogeneration act, §§37-12-1
to 37-12-5.
Common law reception act,
§1-3-1.
Comprehensive
kindergarten act,
§§16-13-52, 16-13-52.1.
Compulsory attendance law,
§§16-28-1 to 16-28-24.
Compulsory unitization act,
§§9-17-80 to 9-17-88.
Computer crime act,
§§13A-8-100 to 13A-8-103.

POPULAR NAMES—Cont'd
Correctional good time act,
§§14-9-40 to 14-9-44.
Correctional incentive time
act, §§14-9-40 to 14-9-44.
Crime victims compensation
act, §§15-23-1 to 15-23-46.
Crime victims' court
attendance act,
§§15-14-50 to 15-14-57.
Criminal libel act,
§§13A-11-160 to
13A-11-164.
Criminal mischief act,
§§13A-7-20 to 13A-7-29.
Criminal trespass act,
§§13A-7-2 to 13A-7-4.
Curve act, §37-2-81.
Cy Pres act, §35-4-251.
Dead man's act, §12-21-163.
Death sentence appeal act,
§12-22-150.
Death with dignity act,
§§22-8A-1 to 22-8A-10.
Deceptive trade practices
act, §§8-19-1 to 8-19-15.
Declaratory judgment act,
§§6-6-220 to 6-6-232.
Defamation act, §§6-5-180 to
6-5-189.
Defamation and libel act,
§§13A-11-160 to
13A-11-164.
Desertion and non-support
act, §§30-4-50 to 30-4-65.
Divorce act, §§30-2-1 to
30-2-31.
Doing business act,
§§10-2A-235 to 10-2A-237.
Dram shop act, §§6-5-70,
6-5-71.
Drug Baron's enforcement
act, §§13A-12-231,
13A-12-232.
Elective compensation law,
§§25-5-50 to 25-5-93.
Equality of citizenship act,
§§17-1-7, 36-26-38.
Exceptional child education
act, §§16-39-1 to 16-39-12.
Felon registration act,
§§13A-11-180 to
13A-11-186.
Five-gallon act, §28-4-115.
Forced share act, §43-8-70.
Free textbook act, §§16-36-1
to 16-36-39.
Fresh pursuit act, §15-10-74.
Fugitive spouse's law,
§§30-4-80 to 30-4-98.
Good Samaritan act,
§6-5-332.
Good time law, §§14-9-40 to
14-9-44.
Guest law, §32-1-2.
Heart balm law, §§6-5-330,
6-5-331.
Hit and run act, §§32-10-1 to
32-10-12.
Hospital lien act, §§35-11-370
to 35-11-375.
Illegitimacy inheritance act,
§43-8-48.
Indecent liberty act,
§§13A-6-66 to 13A-6-70.
Inmate community
reintegration under sir
act, §§15-18-110 to
15-18-123.
Integrated bar act, §§34-3-40
to 34-3-43.

POPULAR NAMES—Cont'd
Intoxication chemical test
act, §§32-5-190 to
32-5-194.
Lie detector act, §§34-25-1 to
34-25-36.
Lis pendens act, §§35-4-130 to
35-4-139.
Little Miller act, §39-1-1.
Living apart act, §30-2-2.
Living wills act, §§22-8A-1 to
22-8A-10.
Lord Campbell's act,
§6-5-410.
Majority age act, §26-1-1.
Marriage act, §§30-1-3 to
30-1-18.
Married women's property
act, §§30-4-1 to 30-4-16.
Mechanics' lien act,
§§35-11-110 to 35-11-112.
Medical liability act,
§§6-5-480 to 6-5-488.
Medical practice act,
§§34-24-50 to 34-24-367.
Mini-code, §§5-19-1 to 5-19-31.
Minor homicide act, §6-5-391.
Motor vehicle guest act,
§32-1-2.
Motor vehicle safety-
responsibility act,
§§32-7-1 to 32-7-42.
Natural death act, §§22-8A-1
to 22-8A-10.
Newsman's privilege act,
§12-21-142.
Nonclaim act, §§43-2-350 to
43-2-354.
Nonsupport and desertion
act, §§30-4-50 to 30-4-98.
Paternity act, §§26-11-1 to
26-11-3.
Perpetuities act, §35-4-4.
Pharmacy robbery act,
§§13A-8-50 to 13A-8-53.
Polygraph examiners act,
§§34-25-1 to 34-25-36.
Pour-over act, §43-8-140.
Prenatal health act,
§§22-12A-1 to 22-12A-6.
Pretermitted child act,
§43-8-91.
Prison-made goods act,
§§14-7-6 to 14-7-23.
Prohibition law, §§28-4-1 to
28-4-326.
Protection from abuse act,
§§30-5-1 to 30-5-11.
Quiet title act, §§6-6-540 to
6-6-573.
Rabies law, §§3-7-1 to 3-7-13.
Red light abatement act,
§§6-5-140 to 6-5-154.
Residential health care
recipient ombudsman
act, §§22-5A-1 to 22-5A-7.
Restitution withholding act,
§§15-18-140 to 15-18-151.
Retarded defendant act,
§§15-24-1 to 15-24-7.
Revised reciprocal
enforcement of support
act, §§30-4-80 to 30-4-97.
Right to die law, §§22-8A-1 to
22-8A-10.
Right to work act, §§25-7-30
to 25-7-36.
Riot act, §§13A-11-3,
13A-11-4.
Rule against perpetuities,
§35-4-4.

POPULAR NAMES—Cont'd
Rules of the road act, §§32-5A-1 to 32-5A-266.
Runaway parent's law, §§30-4-80 to 30-4-98.
Safe drinking water act, §§22-23-30 to 22-23-54.
School bus safety act, §§16-27-1 to 16-27-7.
Search and seizure act, §§15-5-1 to 15-5-31.
Seduction act, §13A-6-65.
Separation from bed and board, §30-2-2.
Simultaneous death act, §§43-7-1 to 43-7-8.
Skippers act, §§30-4-80 to 30-4-97.
Slayer act, §43-8-253.
Small business assistance act, §§25-10-1 to 25-10-10.
Small estates act, §§43-2-690 to 43-2-696.
Sobriety test act, §§32-5-190 to 32-5-194.
Son of Sam law, §§15-18-140 to 15-18-151.
Speed limit act, §32-5A-171.
Spotlighting, §32-5-17.
Statute of frauds, §§8-9-1 to 8-9-12.
Statute of limitations--civil actions, §§6-2-30 to 6-2-41.
Statute of limitations-- criminal actions, §§15-3-1 to 15-3-8.
Statute of limitations-- paternity, §26-12-7.
Statute of uses, §35-4-250.
Stink bomb act, §§13A-7-27, 13A-7-28.
Stop and frisk act, §§15-5-30, 15-5-31.
Sunday closing law, §§13A-12-1, 13A-12-2.
Sunset law, §§41-20-1 to 41-20-16.
Taxpayer convenience act, §40-7-9.1.
Tax refund act, §§40-1-11, 40-1-12.
Tractor gas act, §§40-17-100 to 40-17-108.
Twenty hook law, §§9-11-140 to 9-11-156.
Uniform reciprocal enforcement of support act, §§30-4-80 to 30-4-97.
Uninsured motorist act, §32-7-23.
Unlawful assembly act, §13A-11-5.
Voter registration act, §§17-4-20 to 17-4-215.
Voting machine law, §§17-9-1 to 17-9-41.
Wallace-Cater act, §§11-54-80 to 11-54-123.
Wallace-Folsom prepaid college tuition act, §16-33C-2.
Witness disqualification act, §12-21-162.
Work release act, §§14-8-30 to 14-8-44.
Wrongful death act, §§6-5-410, 6-5-411.
Wrongful death act--minor child, §6-5-391.
Wrongful life act, §§22-8A-1 to 22-8A-10.

POPULAR NAMES—Cont'd
Youthful offenders act, §§15-19-1 to 15-19-7.

POPULATION ACTS.
Classification of laws, Const. Ala., amd. 375.
Municipal corporations.
Classification of municipalities.
Eight classes, §11-45-9.1.
Not repealed, §1-1-10.
Validation, Const. Ala., amd. 389.

PORNOGRAPHY.
Child pornography.
Minors.
Obscene materials containing visual reproduction of children, §§13A-12-190 to 13A-12-198.
See OBSCENITY.
Obscenity.
General provisions, §§13A-12-130 to 13A-12-200.10.
See OBSCENITY.

PORPOISES.
Marine mammal protection.
General provisions, §§9-11-390 to 9-11-398.
See MARINE MAMMAL PROTECTION.

PORT AUTHORITY, §§11-94-1 to 11-94-23, 33-13-1 to 33-13-13.
See HARBORS AND PORTS.

PORTS.
See HARBORS AND PORTS.

POSSE COMITATUS.
Marine resources.
Sheriffs.
Summoning into service, §9-12-2.

POST-CONVICTION REMEDIES.
Appeals.
Court to which appeal taken, ARCrP, Rule 20.10 (a).
Release of petitioners, ARCrP, Rule 20.10 (b).
Who may appeal, ARCrP, Rule 20.10 (a).
Assignment of judge, ARCrP, Rule 20.6 (d).
Attorneys at law.
Appointment of counsel, ARCrP, Rule 20.7 (c).
Burden of proof, ARCrP, Rule 20.3.
Court of criminal appeals.
Court to which appeal taken, ARCrP, Rule 20.10 (a).
Hearings, ARCrP, Rule 20.9 (a).
Decision, ARCrP, Rule 20.9 (c).
Findings of fact, ARCrP, Rule 20.9 (d).
Testimony of petitioners, ARCrP, Rule 20.9 (b).
Limitation of actions, ARCrP, Rule 20.2 (c).
Nature of proceeding, ARCrP, Rule 20.4.

POST-CONVICTION REMEDIES—Cont'd
Notice.
Appeal of petitioner's conviction pending.
Notification of appellate court, ARCrP, Rule 20.6 (c).
Petitions.
Appeals.
Release of petitioners, ARCrP, Rule 20.10 (b).
Commencement of proceedings, ARCrP, Rule 20.6.
Filing, ARCrP, Rule 20.6 (a).
Notification of appellate courts, ARCrP, Rule 20.6 (c).
Release of petitioners.
Appeals, ARCrP, Rule 20.10 (b).
Service, ARCrP, Rule 20.6 (a).
Specificity, ARCrP, Rule 20.6 (b).
Successive petitions.
Preclusion of remedy, ARCrP, Rule 20.2 (b).
Pleadings.
Amendment of pleadings, ARCrP, Rule 20.7 (b).
Prosecutor's response, ARCrP, Rule 20.7 (a).
Preclusion of remedy.
Grounds, ARCrP, Rule 20.2 (a).
Statute of limitations, ARCrP, Rule 20.2 (c).
Successive petitions, ARCrP, Rule 20.2 (b).
Prehearing conference, ARCrP, Rule 20.8.
Prosecutor's response, ARCrP, Rule 20.7 (a).
Relation to other remedies, ARCrP, Rule 20.4.
Release of petitioners.
Appeals, ARCrP, Rule 20.10 (b).
Scope of remedy, ARCrP, Rule 20.1.
Summary disposition, ARCrP, Rule 20.7 (d).
Venue, ARCrP, Rule 20.5.

POSTHUMOUS CHILDREN.
Included in "heirs," "issue" or "children," §35-4-8.

POSTMORTEM EXAMINATIONS.
Coroners.
Fees, §12-19-193.
Physicians.
Fees, §12-19-193.
State toxicologist.
See STATE TOXICOLOGIST.

POST OFFICES.
Constitutional provisions, Const. U. S., Art. I, §8.
Municipal corporations.
Post-office projects, §§11-55-1 to 11-55-13.
See MUNICIPAL CORPORATIONS.

POTASH.
Regulation of caustic or corrosive substances, §§8-17-20 to 8-17-24.

POTASSIUM.
  Fertilizer, §§2-22-12 to
    2-22-16.

POTATOES.
  Artificial coloring.
    Sale, offer for sale, etc.,
      §20-1-30.
  **Fruits and vegetables
    generally.**
    See FRUITS AND
      VEGETABLES.

POULTRY.
  Accounts.
    False statements or entries,
      §2-17-34.
  Actions.
    Evidence of violations of
      chapter or regulations.
      Admissibility in civil
        actions for damages,
        §2-17-31.
  Adulteration.
    Condemnation proceedings,
      §2-17-19.
    Destruction of adulterated
      carcasses, §2-17-4.
    Detention of poultry food
      products believed to be
      adulterated, §2-17-18.
    Inspections.
      Refusal or withdrawal,
        §2-17-20.
      Official marks.
        Removal from adulterated
          products, §2-17-18.
  Avian influenza, §2-16-23.
  Brands and marks.
    Misbranding, §§2-17-10,
      2-17-18 to 2-17-20.
    Official marks, §§2-17-14,
      2-17-18.
  **Carcasses of slaughtered
    animals.**
    Destruction of adulterated
      carcasses, §2-17-4.
    Inspections. See within this
      heading, "Inspections."
  Certificates.
    False statements in
      certificates, §2-17-14.
  Chick dealers, §§2-16-1 to
    2-16-9.
  **Commissioner of agriculture
    and industries.**
    Cooperation with other
      governmental branches
      and agencies, §2-17-25.
    Enforcement of subpoenas
      and orders, §2-17-24.
    Information obtained by
      commissioner.
      Disclosure by state officer
        or employee without
        proper authority,
        §2-17-36.
    Jurisdiction of commissioner
      exclusive as to activities
      covered by chapter,
      §2-17-25.
    Secretary of agriculture.
      Designation and powers of
        commissioner as state
        agency for cooperating
        with secretary of
        agriculture, §2-17-25.

POULTRY—Cont'd
  **Commissioner of agriculture
    and industries**—Cont'd
    Subpoenas.
      Failure to attend and
        testify or produce
        documentary evidence
        in obedience to
        subpoena, §2-17-33.
      Issuance, §2-17-24.
      Temporary orders, §2-17-21.
    Witnesses.
      Failure to attend and
        testify, §2-17-33.
      Powers of commissioner as
        to witnesses, §2-17-24.
  Condemnation.
    Destruction of condemned
      carcasses, §2-17-4.
    Generally, §2-17-19.
    Poultry food products,
      §2-17-9.
  Constitution of Alabama.
    Promotion of poultry and
      poultry products, Const.
      Ala., amds. 214, 428.
  Construction of chapter,
    §2-17-38.
  **Contagious and infectious
    diseases.**
    General provisions,
      §§2-15-150 to 2-15-174.
    See LIVESTOCK.
  Containers.
    Labeling of cans, pots, tins,
      etc., §2-17-10.
  Damages.
    Evidence of violations of
      chapter or regulations.
      Admissibility of evidence
        in civil actions for
        damages, §2-17-31.
  Dead poultry, §§2-16-40 to
    2-16-42.
    Carcasses of slaughtered
      animals.
      Destruction of adulterated
        carcasses, §2-17-4.
      Inspections. See within this
        heading, "Inspections."
  Definitions.
    Chick dealers, §2-16-1.
    Inspections, §2-17-1.
    Public hatchery, §2-16-1.
  Destruction.
    Adulterated carcasses,
      §2-17-4.
    Condemned poultry food
      products, §2-17-9.
    Poultry waste, dead poultry
      and unhatched or unused
      eggs, §2-16-41.
  Diseases, §§2-17-19 to 2-17-23.
    Avian influenza.
      Legislative declaration as
        to serious nature of
        disease, §2-16-23.
      Penalties for violation of
        laws, §2-16-23.
    Condemnation proceedings.
      Generally, §2-17-19.
    Cooperation by department
      with other state and
      federal agencies,
      §2-16-21.
    Department of agriculture
      and industries.
      Cooperation by department
        with other state and
        federal agencies,
        §2-16-21.

POULTRY—Cont'd
  Diseases—Cont'd
    Expenditure of funds
      appropriated for purpose
      of carrying out
      provisions of division,
      §2-16-22.
    Laboratories.
      Establishment, conduct
        and maintenance of
        poultry disease
        diagnostic laboratories,
        §2-16-20.
    Livestock generally.
      See LIVESTOCK.
    Persons, firms, etc., buying,
      selling, etc., diseased
      poultry.
      Compliance with
        regulations of
        commissioner for
        prevention of use for
        food purposes, §2-17-8.
      Registration, §2-17-7.
    Poultry waste, dead poultry
      and unhatched or unused
      eggs, §§2-16-40 to
      2-16-42.
    Program for prevention,
      eradication and control.
      Adoption, conduct, etc.,
        §2-16-21.
    Registration of persons,
      firms, etc., buying,
      selling, etc., diseased
      poultry, §2-17-7.
    Rules and regulations,
      §2-16-2.
    Slaughter of diseased
      poultry.
      Separate slaughter,
        §2-17-3.
  Eggs.
    General provisions.
      See EGGS AND EGG
        PRODUCTS.
    Hatcheries, §§2-16-1 to
      2-16-9. See within this
      heading, "Hatcheries and
      chick dealers."
    Unhatched or unused eggs,
      §§2-16-40 to 2-16-42.
  Evidence.
    Mutilation, alteration, etc., of
      documentary evidence,
      §2-17-34.
    Violations of chapter or
      regulations.
      Admissibility of evidence of
        violations in civil
        actions for damages,
        §2-17-31.
  Facilities.
    Examination, §2-17-23.
  Feeds.
    Commercial feeds.
      See FEEDS.
  Fees.
    Grading.
      Collection and disposition
        of fees by department,
        §2-18-3.
    Hatcheries and chick dealers,
      §§2-16-3, 2-16-8.
  Forgery and counterfeiting.
    Official marks, §2-17-14.

POULTRY—Cont'd

Grading, §§2-18-1 to 2-18-3.
Board of agriculture and industries.
Promulgation of rules and regulations for grading, §2-18-1.
Contracts.
Department may enter into contracts to perform grading, §2-18-3.
Department of agriculture and industries.
Contracts to perform grading, §2-18-3.
Fees.
Collection and disposition of fees by department, §2-18-3.
Inspection at poultry slaughtering, dressing and processing establishments, §2-18-2.
Rules and regulations.
Slaughtering, dressing or processing plants or establishments, §2-18-1.

Handling.
Rules and regulations.
Promulgation of regulations as to handling of carcasses, meats, etc., §2-17-22.

Hatcheries and chick dealers, §§2-16-1 to 2-16-9.
Appeals from denial or revocation of permits, §2-16-3.
Definitions, §2-16-1.
Fees.
Permit fee, §2-16-3.
Fines.
Disposition of fines, §2-16-9.
National poultry improvement plan.
Department to conduct program in accordance with, §2-16-8.
Permits, §2-16-3.
Records.
Maintenance of records by public hatcheries and chick dealers or jobbers, §2-16-6.
Rules and regulations, §2-16-2.
Violations deemed misdemeanors, §2-16-9.
Sales.
Requirements for baby chicks, turkey poults and hatching eggs sold or offered for sale, §2-16-4.
Shipment into state.
Requirements for baby chicks, turkey poults and hatching eggs shipped or brought into state, §2-16-5.
Unhatched or unused eggs, §§2-16-40 to 2-16-42.
Violations of article or rules or regulations deemed a misdemeanor, §2-16-9.

Health regulations for establishments handling food, §22-20-5.

POULTRY—Cont'd

Injunctions.
Jurisdiction and prosecution of injunctive proceedings under chapter or regulations, §2-17-30.
Inspections, §§2-17-1 to 2-17-42.
Advisory council, §2-17-26.
Applicability of certain provisions of chapter, §2-17-27.
Applicability of chapter to persons, firms, etc., regulated under federal poultry products inspection act, §2-17-29.
Carcasses of slaughtered animals, §§2-17-3, 2-17-4.
Applicability of provisions as to inspection, §2-17-5.
Limitation of entry of carcasses into establishments inspected under chapter, §2-17-5.
Reinspection, §2-17-4.
Commissioner of agriculture and industries.
Temporary orders, issuance, etc., §2-17-21.
Condemnation, §2-17-19.
Construction of chapter, §§2-17-2, 2-17-38.
Definitions, §2-17-1.
Exemption of certain activities from provisions of chapter by commissioner, §2-17-27.
Federal poultry products inspection act.
Applicability of chapter to persons, firms, etc., regulated under federal act, §2-17-29.
Food products, §2-17-9.
Implementation of chapter.
Regulations for implementation, §2-17-21.
Injunctive proceedings.
Jurisdiction and prosecution of injunctive proceedings under chapter or regulations, §2-17-30.
Inspectors.
Appointment, §2-17-16.
Duties, §2-17-16.
Interference with person engaged in performance of official duties under chapter, §2-17-32.
Legislative findings of fact and declaration of policy, §2-17-2.
Misrepresentations, §2-17-14.
Penalties for violations of chapter, §2-17-37.
Poultry waste, dead poultry and unhatched or unused eggs, §2-16-42.
Prior to slaughter, §2-17-3.
Processing establishments.
See within this heading, "Processing establishments."

POULTRY—Cont'd

Inspections—Cont'd
Products not to be used for human food.
Inspection not to be provided, §2-17-6.
Purpose of chapter, §2-17-2.
Records, §2-17-23.
Refusal, §2-17-20.
Rules and regulations, §2-17-16.
Federal regulations.
Adoption and promulgation of regulations promulgated under certain federal acts, §2-17-2.
Implementation of chapter.
Promulgation, approval, etc., of regulations for implementation, §2-17-21.
Slaughterhouses. See within this heading, "Slaughterhouses."
United States department of agriculture.
Exemption of poultry inspected and passed by United States department of agriculture, §2-17-28.
Violations of chapter or regulations.
Admissibility of evidence of violations in civil actions for damages, §§2-17-13, 2-17-31.
Penalties, §2-17-37.
Withdrawal, §2-17-20.

Intrastate commerce.
Investigations.
Conduct of investigations as to organizations, etc., engaged in intrastate commerce, §2-17-24.
Reports.
Requirement as to organizations, etc., engaged in intrastate commerce, §2-17-24.

Inventories.
Examination, §2-17-23.

Labels.
Carcasses of slaughtered animals, §2-17-4.
False or misleading labeling, §2-17-10.
Food products, §2-17-9.
Misbranding, §§2-17-10, 2-17-18 to 2-17-20.
Unauthorized casting, printing, etc., of device or label containing official mark or simulation, §2-17-14.

Laboratories.
Disease diagnostic laboratories.
Establishment, conduct and maintenance, §2-16-20.

POULTRY—Cont'd
Marking.
Adulteration.
Commissioner to refuse to
allow markings,
stamping, etc., in
establishments where
sanitary conditions
adulterate, §2-17-11.
Official mark.
Commissioner to refuse to
allow markings,
stamping, etc., of
poultry food products
in establishments
where sanitary
conditions adulterate
products, §2-17-14.
Forgery, §2-17-14.
Removal from adulterated
or misbranded poultry
food products,
§2-17-18.
Unauthorized use,
§2-17-14.
Misbranding, §§2-17-10,
2-17-18 to 2-17-20.
Condemnation proceedings,
§2-17-19.
Detention of poultry food
products believed to be
misbranded, §2-17-18.
False or misleading labeling,
§2-17-10.
Inspections.
Refusal or withdrawal,
§2-17-20.
Official marks.
Removal from misbranded
products, §2-17-18.
**National poultry
improvement plan.**
Department to conduct
program in accordance
with plan, §2-16-8.
Fees.
Acceptance and disposition
of fees by department,
§2-16-8.
Official marks, §§2-17-14,
2-17-18.
Penalties.
Violations of chapter,
§2-17-37.
Permits.
Hatcheries and chick dealers,
§2-16-3.
**Poultry waste, dead poultry
and unhatched or
unused eggs,** §§2-16-40 to
2-16-42.
Administration of division,
§2-16-42.
Destruction, §2-16-41.
Disposal, §§2-16-41, 2-16-42.
Enforcement of division,
§2-16-42.
Handling, §2-16-41.
Inspections.
State veterinarian,
§2-16-42.
Purpose of division, §2-16-40.
Right of entry and inspection
of state veterinarian,
etc., §2-16-42.
Rules and regulations.
Handling.
Destruction and disposal,
§2-16-41.

POULTRY—Cont'd
**Poultry waste, dead poultry
and unhatched or
unused eggs**—Cont'd
State veterinarian.
Right of entry and
inspection, §2-16-42.
Processing establishments.
Days and hours when
processing to be done.
Designation, §2-17-12.
Department of agriculture
and industries.
Contracts to perform
grading, §2-18-3.
Grading. See within this
heading, "Grading."
Inspections, §2-18-2.
Animals prepared,
§2-17-12.
Assignment of inspectors,
§2-17-12.
Refusal or withdrawal of
inspection by
commissioner,
§2-17-20.
Sanitary conditions,
§2-17-11.
Rules and regulations.
Grading.
Promulgation of rules
and regulations for
grading by state
board, §2-18-1.
**Promotion of poultry and
poultry products,** Const.
Ala., amd. 214.
**Public officers and
employees.**
Disclosure by state officer or
employee of information
obtained by
commissioner without
proper authority,
§2-17-36.
Quarantine.
Poultry waste, dead poultry
and unhatched or unused
eggs. §2-16-42.
Records.
Classes of persons, firms,
etc., required to
maintain records,
§2-17-23.
Examination, §2-17-23.
Grading.
Slaughtering, dressing or
processing plants or
establishments.
Promulgation of rules
and regulations for
grading, §2-18-1.
Handling.
Promulgation of
regulations as to
handling of carcasses,
meats, etc., §2-17-22.
Hatcheries and chick dealers.
Maintenance of records,
§2-16-6.
Registration.
Persons, firms, etc., buying,
selling, etc., dead, dying,
diseased, poultry,
§2-17-7.
Reports.
Failure to file annual or
special reports, §2-17-35.
False statements or entries,
§2-17-34.

POULTRY—Cont'd
Rules and regulations.
Injunctive proceedings under
regulations, jurisdiction
and prosecution,
§2-17-30.
Violations of regulations.
Admissibility of evidence of
violations in civil
actions for damages,
§§2-17-13, 2-17-31.
Sales.
Illegal acts, §2-17-13.
Sales tax.
Exemptions.
Feed for poultry, §40-23-4.
Gross proceeds of sale of
baby chicks and poults,
§40-23-4.
Slaughter.
Exemption of certain
activities from provisions
of chapter by
commissioner, §2-17-27.
Illegal acts, §2-17-13.
Slaughterhouses.
Days and hours when
slaughtering to be done.
Designation, §2-17-12.
Department of agriculture
and industries.
Contracts to perform
grading, §2-18-3.
Grading, §§2-18-1 to 2-18-3.
Inspections, §2-18-2.
Animals slaughtered,
§2-17-12.
Assignment of inspectors,
§2-17-12.
Refusal or withdrawal of
inspection by
commissioner,
§2-17-20.
Sanitary conditions,
§2-17-11.
Rules and regulations.
Grading.
Promulgation of rules
and regulations for
grading by state
board, §2-18-1.
Sanitary conditions.
Inspection, §2-17-11.
Storage.
Rules and regulations.
Promulgation of
regulations as to
storage of carcasses,
meats, etc., §2-17-22.
Subpoenas.
Failure to attend and testify
or produce documentary
evidence in obedience to
subpoena, §2-17-33.
Issuance by commissioner,
§2-17-24.
Taxation.
Sales tax.
Exemptions.
Gross proceeds of sale of
baby chicks and
poults, §40-23-4.
**Transportation of animals,
etc.**
Illegal acts, §2-17-13.
Unhatched or unused eggs,
§§2-16-40 to 2-16-42.

POULTRY—Cont'd

United States.
Department of agriculture.
Exemption of poultry
inspected and passed
by, §2-17-28.
Use tax.
Exemptions, §40-23-62.
Violations of chapter.
Admissibility of evidence of
violations in civil actions
for damages, §2-17-31.
Penalties, §2-17-37.
Waste, §§2-16-40 to 2-16-42.
Witnesses.
Commissioner of agriculture
and industries.
Powers of commissioner as
to witnesses, §2-17-24.
Failure to attend and testify,
§2-17-33.
Generally, §2-17-24.

POUR-OVER TRUSTS,
§43-8-140.

POWER DISTRICTS, §§37-5-1
to 37-5-9.
Actions.
Bond issues.
Rights and remedies of
bondholders, §37-5-8.
Power to sue and be sued,
§37-5-3.
Assets.
Disposition upon dissolution,
§37-5-2.
Board of directors.
Appointment, §37-5-4.
Compensation, §37-5-4.
Consolidation.
Determination of board of
each district, §37-5-2.
Defined, §37-5-1.
Dissolution.
Board to have powers of
receivers, §37-5-2.
Expenses, §37-5-4.
Oath, §37-5-4.
Powers.
Generally, §37-5-5.
Rules and regulations,
§37-5-5.
Terms, §37-5-4.
Vacancies, §37-5-4.
Body corporate, §37-5-2.
Bond issues, §§37-5-5 to
37-5-8.
Authority to issue, §37-5-6.
Department of finance.
Consent required, §37-5-7.
Form, §37-5-6.
Injunctions.
Rights and remedies of
bondholders, §37-5-8.
Interest, §37-5-6.
Mandamus.
Rights of bondholders,
§37-5-8.
Manner of issuance, §37-5-6.
Maturity, §37-5-6.
Power to issue, §37-5-3.
Purpose for which bond may
be issued, §37-5-6.
Receipts.
Interim receipts, §37-5-6.
Repurchase, §37-5-6.
Rights and remedies of
bondholders, §37-5-8.
Consolidation, §37-5-2.
Approval of commission,
§37-5-2.

POWER DISTRICTS—Cont'd

Consolidation—Cont'd
Effect on preexisting rights
and liabilities, §37-5-2.
Contracts.
Power to make and enter
into, §37-5-3.
Conveyances.
Power to make and enter
into, §37-5-3.
Creation, §37-5-2.
Public service commission.
Approval or disapproval of
creation, §37-5-2.
Definitions, §37-5-1.
Dissolution.
Disposition of assets, §37-5-2.
Finding of commission,
§37-5-2.
Winding up of affairs,
§37-5-2.
Eminent domain.
District to have power,
§37-5-3.
Expenses.
Municipal aid, §37-5-9.
Governing body.
Creation of district, §37-5-2.
Defined, §37-5-1.
Highways.
Right to use and occupy
highways, §37-5-3.
Injunctions.
Bond issues.
Rights and remedies of
bondholders, §37-5-8.
Interest.
Bond issues.
Interest on bonds, §37-5-6.
Limits of district, §37-5-2.
Mandamus.
Bond issues.
Rights and remedies of
bondholders, §37-5-8.
**Mortgages and deeds of
trust.**
Power to make and enter,
§37-5-3.
Municipal corporations.
Districts to be created and
constitute municipal
corporation, §37-5-2.
Municipal aid, §37-5-9.
Powers.
Exercise of powers, §37-5-2.
Generally, §37-5-3.
Public service commission.
Approval of creation, §37-5-2.
Consolidation.
Approval of commission,
§37-5-2.
Dissolution of district,
§37-5-2.
Orders, §37-5-2.
Purchase of public utilities,
§§37-4-60 to 37-4-65.
See PUBLIC UTILITIES.
Purpose, §37-5-3.
Rates and charges.
Power to fix, maintain and
collect, §37-5-3.
Real property.
Acquisition, §37-5-3.
Receivers.
Bond issues.
Rights and remedies of
bondholders, §37-5-8.
Dissolution.
Board of directors to have
powers of receivers,
§37-5-2.

POWER DISTRICTS—Cont'd

**Seals and sealed
instruments.**
District to have seal, §37-5-3.
Winding up of affairs.
Dissolution, §37-5-2.

POWERS OF ATTORNEY.

Acknowledgments, §35-4-28.
Conveyances generally.
See CONVEYANCES.
Durable power of attorney.
Appointment by court of
guardian, §26-1-2.
Creation, §26-1-2.
Death of principal.
Effect, §26-1-2.
Effect of acts performed
pursuant to, §26-1-2.
Guardian and ward.
Uniform guardianship and
protective proceedings
act.
Delegation of powers.
Parents or guardians,
§26-2A-7.
**Uniform guardianship and
protective proceedings
act.**
Delegation of powers.
Parents or guardians,
§26-2A-7.
Veterans.
Department of veterans'
affairs.
Execution of power of
attorney, §31-5-4.

POWERS OF DISPOSITION.

General provisions.
See CONVEYANCES.

PRACTICAL NURSES.
See NURSES.

PRAYERS.
Education.
School prayer, §16-1-20.2.

PREACHERS.
See CLERGY.

PRECINCTS.
Elections.
Counties.
See COUNTIES.
General provisions.
See ELECTIONS.
Municipal corporations.
See MUNICIPAL
CORPORATIONS.

PREFABRICATED HOUSING,
§§24-4A-1 to 24-4A-7.
See MANUFACTURED
BUILDINGS.

PREGNANCY.
Abortion.
Inducing or attempting to
induce, §13A-13-7.
Consent for health services.
Consent of any minor as to
pregnancy, §22-8-6.
Death penalty.
Procedure when condemned
female believed
pregnant, §15-18-86.
Midwives, §§34-19-2 to
34-19-10.
See MIDWIVES.
Minors.
Consent for health services.
Consent of any minor as to
pregnancy, §22-8-6.

PRELIMINARY HEARINGS,
§§15-11-1 to 15-11-15.
Adjournment, §15-11-3.
Appearance.
Failure of defendant to
appear at hearing,
§15-11-1.
Attorneys at law.
Appearance by counsel for
defendant, §15-11-7.
Bail and recognizance.
Amount to be endorsed on
commitment, §15-11-11.
Commitment of defendant to
bail, §15-11-3.
Default.
Certification to circuit
court, §15-11-4.
District court certificate as
presumptive evidence,
§15-11-4.
Issuance of alias warrant
upon default, §15-11-5.
Discharge of defendant,
§15-11-11.
When defendant committed
to bail, §15-11-10.
**Commitment of defendant to
jail or bail,** §15-11-3.
Form of commitment,
§15-11-10.
Reports, §15-11-15.
When defendant to be
committed, §15-11-10.
Conduct of hearing, §15-11-7.
Discharge.
Giving of sufficient bail,
§15-11-11.
When defendant to be
discharged, §15-11-9.
**Examination of complainant
and witnesses,** §15-11-6.
**Failure of defendant to
appear at hearing,**
§15-11-1.
Felonies.
Right of person arrested for
felony to hearing,
§15-11-1.
Gambling.
Gambling places.
Court to hear evidence and
bind parties over for
trial, §13A-12-57.
Jails.
Commitment of defendant to
jail, §15-11-3.
When defendant committed
to jail, §15-11-10.
Jurisdiction.
District court jurisdiction,
§15-11-2.
Probable cause.
Prosecution not barred by
finding of no probable
cause, §15-11-2.
Reports.
Court to report when person
held on indictment,
§15-11-15.
When no committal,
§15-11-15.
**Right of person arrested for
felony to hearing,**
§15-11-1.
**When defendant to be
discharged,** §15-11-9.
Witnesses.
Duty of court to examine,
§15-11-8.

**PRELIMINARY HEARINGS
—Cont'd**
Witnesses—Cont'd
Examination of witnesses,
§15-11-6.
Separation of witnesses,
§15-11-7.
Undertaking.
Discharge of witness upon
entering of
undertaking,
§15-11-14.
Form of undertaking,
§15-11-12.
Married women and
minors, §15-11-13.
Refusal or failure of
witness to enter,
§15-11-14.
Requiring witness to enter
undertaking,
§15-11-12.

**PRERETIREMENT DEATH
BENEFIT PROGRAM,**
§§36-27B-1 to 36-27B-5.

**PRESBYTERIAN
APARTMENTS, INC.**
Licenses.
Exemptions, §40-9-13.
Taxation.
Exemptions, §40-9-13.

**PRESBYTERIAN
APARTMENTS OF
BIRMINGHAM, INC.**
Taxation.
Exemption from taxation,
§40-9-26.

**PRESBYTERIAN HOME FOR
CHILDREN.**
Licenses.
Exemptions, §40-9-12.
Taxation.
Exemptions, §40-9-12.

**PRESBYTERIAN HOMES OF
DECATUR, INC.**
Taxation.
Exemption from taxation,
§40-9-26.

PRESCRIPTIONS.
Alcohol.
Dry counties, §§28-4-151 to
28-4-164.
See ALCOHOLIC
BEVERAGES.
Controlled substances.
See DRUGS.
**Identification of drug
products,** §§20-1-150 to
20-1-154.
**Pharmacists and
pharmacies.**
General provisions.
See PHARMACISTS AND
PHARMACIES.
**Third party prescription
program,** §§34-23-110 to
34-23-118.
See PHARMACISTS AND
PHARMACIES.
Victim counselors.
Confidentiality provisions not
to authorize prescribing
of drugs, §15-23-46.

**PRESIDENT OF THE
UNITED STATES.**
Age, Const. U. S., Art. II, §1.

**PRESIDENT OF THE
UNITED STATES—Cont'd**
Aliens.
Ineligible for presidency,
Const. U. S., Art. II, §1.
Ambassadors and consuls,
Const. U. S., Art. II, §§2, 3.
Appointment of officers, etc.,
Const. U. S., Art. II, §2.
Approval of laws, Const. U.
S., Art. I, §7.
**Approval of order,
resolution or vote of
congress,** Const. U. S.,
Art. I, §7.
Bribery, Const. U. S., Art. II,
§4.
Commander-in-chief, Const.
U. S., Art. II, §2.
Compensation, Const. U. S.,
Art. II, §1.
Congress.
Adjourning congress, Const.
U. S., Art. II, §3.
Convening congress, Const.
U. S., Art. II, §3.
Declaration of president's
disability.
Determination of issue,
Const. U. S.,
Amendment XXV, §4.
Messages to congress, Const.
U. S., Art. II, §3.
Special sessions of congress,
Const. U. S., Art. II, §3.
Death.
Duty of congress, Const. U.
S., Art. II, §1.
President elect.
Provision in case of, Const.
U. S., Amendment XX.
Succession upon death,
Const. U. S., Amendment
XXV, §1.
Disability, Const. U. S., Art.
II, §1.
Declaration by president.
Inability to perform duties,
Const. U. S.,
Amendment XXV, §3.
Declaration by vice-president
and other officers, Const.
U. S., Amendment XXV,
§4.
Duties, Const. U. S., Art. II,
§3.
Declaration by president of
inability to perform
duties, Const. U. S.,
Amendment XXV, §3.
Elections.
General provisions.
See ELECTIONS.
Eligibility, Const. U. S., Art.
II, §1.
Execution of laws, Const. U.
S., Art. II, §3.
Executive power, Const. U.
S., Art. II, §1.
Failure to qualify, Const. U.
S., Amendment XX.
Impeachment, Const. U. S.,
Art. II, §4.
Inability, Const. U. S., Art. II,
§1.
Limitation on terms, Const.
U. S., Amendment XXII.
Message to congress, Const.
U. S., Art. II, §3.

PRESIDENT OF THE UNITED STATES—Cont'd

Ministers.
Receiving, Const. U. S., Art. II, §3.
Pardons, Const. U. S., Art. II, §2.
Powers of president, Const. U. S., Art. II, §§2, 3.
Public officers.
Commissions, Const. U. S., Art. II, §3.
Qualifications, Const. U. S., Art. II, §1.
Removal, Const. U. S., Art. II, §§1, 4.
Succession upon removal, Const. U. S., Amendment XXV, §1.
Resignation, Const. U. S., Art. II, §1.
Succession upon resignation, Const. U. S., Amendment XXV, §1.
Signing bills, Const. U. S., Art. I, §7.
Statutes.
Approval of laws by president, Const. U. S., Art. I, §7.
Veto, Const. U. S., Art. I, §7.
Succession to office, Const. U. S., Art. II, §1; Amendment XX.
Upon death, resignation or removal of president, Const. U. S., Amendment XXV, §1.
Supreme court.
Appointment of justices, Const. U. S., Art. II, §2.
Terms of office, Const. U. S., Art. II, §1; Amendments XX, XXI.
Limitation on terms, Const. U. S., Amendment XXII.
Time of taking office, Const. U. S., Amendment XX.
Treason, Const. U. S., Art. II, §4.
Treaties, Const. U. S., Art. II, §2.
Vacancies during senate recess, Const. U. S., Art. II, §2.
Veto, Const. U. S., Art. I, §7.

PRESS.

Constitution of Alabama.
Freedom of press, Const. Ala., art. I, §4.
Constitution of the United States.
Freedom of press, Const. U. S., Amendment I.
Newspapers generally.
See NEWSPAPERS.

PRESUMPTIONS.

Abandonment.
Contracts.
When recorded contract presumed abandoned, §35-4-75.
Uniform disposition of unclaimed property act, §§35-12-22 to 35-12-29.
See LOST OR UNCLAIMED PROPERTY.

PRESUMPTIONS—Cont'd

Alcoholic beverages.
Stamps, crowns or lids.
Sale of alcoholic beverages without proper stamps.
Presumption as to sale, §28-3-224.
Brands and marks.
Personal property.
Defacing identifying marks on encumbered personal property, §8-12-3.
Commercial code.
Commercial paper.
Date presumed correct, §7-3-114.
Genuineness or authorization of signatures, §7-3-307.
General provisions.
See COMMERCIAL CODE.
Sales.
Burden of establishing breach after acceptance, §7-2-607.
Conservators.
Settlements of accounts of guardians.
Partial settlement.
Correctness, §26-5-6.
Contracts.
Abandonment.
When recorded contract presumed abandoned, §35-4-75.
Specific performance.
Presumptions as to availability as remedies, §8-1-47.
Conveyances.
Powers of disposition.
Presumption that power not personal, §35-4-303.
Criminal law and procedure.
Persons over 14 presumed responsible for acts, §15-16-2.
Death.
Executors and administrators.
Persons presumed dead, §§43-2-230 to 43-2-238.
See EXECUTORS AND ADMINISTRATORS.
Presumption of death generally, §43-8-6.
Decedents' estates.
Administration of estates.
Executors and administrators.
Persons presumed dead, §§43-2-230 to 43-2-238.
See EXECUTORS AND ADMINISTRATORS.
Settlement after twenty years, §§43-2-660 to 43-2-664.
Elections.
Primary elections.
Presumption of acceptance of chapter, §17-16-5.

PRESUMPTIONS—Cont'd

Executors and administrators.
Persons presumed dead.
Administration of estates, §§43-2-230 to 43-2-238.
See EXECUTORS AND ADMINISTRATORS.
Settlement of estate after twenty years, §§43-2-660 to 43-2-664.
Fish and game.
Fur dealers.
Presumptions as to dealership, §9-11-62.
Highways.
Littering.
Driver presumed offender, §23-5-6.
Income tax.
Nonresidents, §40-18-5.
Presumption of residents for income tax liability, §40-18-2.
Indictments.
Legal presumption need not be stated, §15-8-32.
Investment securities.
Action on securities, §7-8-105.
Judgments.
Satisfaction.
Judgment presumed satisfied 10 years after entry or execution, §6-9-191.
Mentally ill.
Persons over 14 presumed responsible for acts, §15-16-2.
Military affairs.
Courts-martial.
Presumption of jurisdiction and legality of proceedings, §31-2-103.
Milk and milk products.
Marked containers.
Presumption of ownership, §8-12-41.
Minors.
Responsibility for criminal acts, §15-16-2.
Mortgages and deeds of trust.
Satisfaction of mortgage liens.
When indebtedness presumed to have been paid, §35-10-20.
Motor vehicles.
Chemical test for intoxication, §32-5A-194.
Stopping, standing and parking.
Parking in violation of municipal ordinances, §32-5-152.
Parent and child.
Paternity, §26-17-5.
Termination of parental rights.
Presumption arising from abandonment, §26-18-7.
Parks and recreation.
Limitation of liability for non-commercial public recreational use of land.
Acts by owner creating rebuttal presumption, §35-15-28.

PRESUMPTIONS—Cont'd
Partnerships.
  Property.
    Presumptions as to
      partnership property,
      §10-8-70.
Powers of disposition.
  Presumption that power not
    personal, §35-4-303.
Probate courts.
  Judgments, orders, etc.
    Presumptions to be
      accorded to, §12-13-1.
Public utilities.
  Gross receipts tax.
    Exemptions.
      Presumptions as to
        exemptions,
        §40-21-81.
Railroads.
  Advertising signs resembling
    railroad signs.
    Name of person on
      advertising.
      Presumed guilty party,
        §37-8-200.
Search warrants.
  Issuance for containers
    unlawfully used or held,
    §8-12-23.
Securities.
  Fiduciary security transfers.
    Presumption that
      registered owner
      continues to be
      fiduciary, §8-6-74.
Specific performance.
  Contracts.
    Availability as remedy,
      §8-1-47.
  Minors.
    Ownership by minors.
      Presumption that holder
        not minor, §8-6-92.
Tobacco.
  Sales tax.
    Possession of unstamped
      tobacco products,
      §40-25-25.
Unclaimed property.
  Uniform disposition of
    unclaimed property act.
  See LOST OR
    UNCLAIMED
    PROPERTY.
Uniform commercial code.
  See COMMERCIAL CODE.
Weights and measures.
  Existence in place of sale,
    etc., presumptive proof of
    use and ownership,
    §8-16-13.
Wills.
  Death.
    Presumption of death,
      §43-8-6.
Workmen's compensation.
  See WORKMEN'S
    COMPENSATION.

RETERMITTED CHILDREN,
  §43-8-91.

RIESTS.
See CLERGY.

RIMARY ELECTIONS.
General provisions, §§17-16-1
  to 17-16-89.
  See ELECTIONS.

PRINCIPAL AND AGENT.
General provisions.
  See AGENTS.

**PRINCIPAL AND INCOME
  ACT.**
See TRUSTS AND TRUSTEES.

PRINTING.
Actions.
  Public printing and binding.
    Venue of actions on
      contracts, §41-4-138.
Bonds, surety.
  Public printing and binding,
    §§41-4-133, 41-4-136.
  Printer of acts and
    journals, §41-4-160.
Contracts.
  Public printing and binding,
    §§41-4-130 to 41-4-138.
  See within this heading,
    "Public printing and
    binding."
Department of finance.
  Publications.
    Certain departments and
      agencies exempt from
      provisions, §41-4-243.
Governor.
  Public printing and binding.
    Approval of contract and
      bond, §41-4-136.
Legislature.
  Acts and joint resolutions,
    §§41-4-143 to 41-4-161.
    See within this heading,
      "Public printing and
      binding."
  Journals. See within this
    heading, "Public printing
    and binding."
Libel and slander.
  Refusal to testify by printer,
    §13A-11-164.
**Manager of printing and
  publications,** §§41-4-240
  to 41-4-242.
  Creation of office, §41-4-240.
  Duties, §41-4-241.
  Functions, §41-4-241.
  Powers, §41-4-241.
Public printing and binding,
  §§41-4-130 to 41-4-161.
  Actions on contracts.
    Venue, §41-4-138.
  Acts and joint resolutions,
    §§41-4-143 to 41-4-161.
  Bond of printer, §41-4-160.
  Certification, §41-4-146.
  Delivery by printer.
    When acts must be
      delivered by printer,
      §41-4-150.
  Delivery of material to
    printer, §§41-4-143,
    41-4-146.
    Penalty for not
      delivering copies to
      printer, §41-4-147.
  Index, §41-4-148.
  Pamphlet form.
    Certain officers to keep
      pamphlets in books
      until acts published
      in permanent form,
      §41-4-156.
    Delivery in 10 days,
      §41-4-159.

PRINTING—Cont'd
Public printing and binding
  —Cont'd
  Acts and joint resolutions
    —Cont'd
    Pamphlet form—Cont'd
      Distribution to certain
        officers,
        departments, etc.,
        §41-4-156.
      New contract upon
        failure of printer to
        deliver, §41-4-159.
      Order of printing acts,
        §41-4-158.
      Page size, §41-4-157.
      Paper, §41-4-157.
      Required heading,
        §41-4-158.
      Size of pamphlets,
        §41-4-158.
      Type size, §41-4-157.
    Payment for printing,
      §§41-4-151, 41-4-152.
    Penalty for not delivering
      copies of acts to
      printer, §41-4-147.
    Preparation for printing,
      §41-4-142.
    Quality of paper,
      §41-4-148.
    Recess by legislature.
      Printing of acts when
        recess taken by
        legislature,
        §41-4-161.
    Revenue laws.
      Separate printing,
        §41-4-149.
    Style of printing,
      §41-4-148.
    Volumes of acts.
      Certification, §41-4-144.
      Number, size and
        contents of volumes,
        §41-4-143.
    When acts must be printed
      and delivered by
      printer, §41-4-150.
  Bids, §§41-4-132 to 41-4-134.
  Blanks.
    Paper and parchment for
      blanks, §41-4-140.
  Bonds, surety, §§41-4-133,
    41-4-136.
    Approval by governor,
      auditor and treasurer,
      §41-4-136.
    Filing, §41-4-136.
  Printer of acts and
    journals, §41-4-160.
  Classification, §41-4-131.
  Contracts, §§41-4-130 to
    41-4-138.
    Actions on contracts.
      Venue of actions,
        §41-4-138.
    Approval by governor,
      auditor and treasurer,
      §41-4-136.
  Auditor.
    Approval by auditor,
      §41-4-136.
  Bids.
    Acceptance, §41-4-134.
    Advertisements for bids.
      Biennial
        advertisement,
        §41-4-132.
      Readvertisement of
        bids, §41-4-134.

PRINTING—Cont'd
Public printing and binding
—Cont'd
Contracts—Cont'd
Bids—Cont'd
Opening of bids,
§41-4-134.
Proposals to be in
writing, §41-4-133.
Rejection, §41-4-134.
Bonds, surety, §41-4-133.
Approval by governor,
auditor and
treasurer, §41-4-136.
Filing of bonds,
§41-4-136.
Deductions from contract
price for failure to
perform within time,
§41-4-160.
Entering into contract,
§41-4-135.
Failure to perform within
time.
Deductions from contract
price for failure,
§41-4-160.
Forfeiture of contract for
cause, §41-4-137.
Governor.
Approval by governor,
§41-4-136.
New contract after
forfeiture for cause,
§41-4-137.
Required, §41-4-130.
Treasurer.
Approval by treasurer,
§41-4-136.
Venue of actions on
contracts, §41-4-138.
Forfeiture of contract for
cause, §41-4-137.
Governor.
Approval of contract and
bond, §41-4-136.
Journals.
Bond of printer of journals,
§41-4-160.
Payment for printing,
§41-4-152.
Preparation, §41-4-145.
Quality of paper,
§41-4-148.
Style of printing,
§41-4-148.
When journals must be
printed and delivered
by printer, §41-4-150.
Manager of printing and
publications, §§41-4-240
to 41-4-242.
Pamphlet form.
Size of pamphlets,
§41-4-158.
Paper and parchment for
blanks, §41-4-140.
Payment for printing.
Charge for matters ordered
to be printed by both
houses, §41-4-155.
Deductions from contract
price for failure to
perform within time,
§41-4-160.
Generally, §41-4-151.
Laws and journals,
§41-4-152.
Revenue laws, §41-4-153.
Source of funds, §41-4-154.

PRINTING—Cont'd
Public printing and binding
—Cont'd
Reports by departments,
officers, boards, etc.,
§41-4-141.
Revenue laws.
Separate printing,
§41-4-149.
Venue of actions on
contracts, §41-4-138.
Where printing to be done,
§41-4-139.
State auditor.
Public printing and binding.
Approval of contract and
bond, §41-4-136.
State treasurer.
Public printing and binding.
Approval of contract and
bond, §41-4-136.
Taxation.
Subjects of taxation,
§40-11-1.
Venue.
Public printing and binding.
Venue of actions on
contracts, §41-4-138.

PRIORITIES.
Buildings.
Liens for rent, §35-9-63.
Bulls.
Liens of owners, §35-11-330.
Cotton gins.
Liens of owners, §35-11-290.
Counties.
Claims and demands against
counties.
Preferred claims and order
of their priority,
§11-12-15.
Enterprise zones.
Manufacturers, suppliers,
contractors and laborers,
§41-23-30.
Guardian and ward.
Uniform guardianship and
protective proceedings
act.
Conservators.
Appointment,
§26-2A-138.
**Hay baling machines or
presses.**
Liens of owners, §35-11-290.
Insurance.
Insurers.
Delinquency proceedings.
Claims in delinquency
proceedings,
§27-32-20.
Priority of compensation
owed to employees,
§27-32-28.
Rehabilitation or
liquidation.
Priority of claims of
policyholders and
beneficiaries,
§§27-32-37 to
27-32-41.
Jacks.
Liens of owners, §35-11-330.
Landlord and tenant.
Liens for rent of buildings,
§35-9-63.
Liens generally.
See LIENS.

PRIORITIES—Cont'd
Livestock.
Liens of owners of stallions,
jacks, bulls, etc.,
§35-11-330.
**Lumber employees' or
laborers' liens,**
§35-11-271.
**Mechanics' and
materialmen's liens,**
§35-11-211.
Liens arising under division,
§35-11-228.
Peanut machines or pickers.
Liens of owners, §35-11-290.
Rent.
Liens for rent of buildings,
§35-9-63.
**Sawmill employees' or
laborers' liens,**
§35-11-271.
Secured transactions.
See COMMERCIAL CODE.
Seeds.
Liens of owners of plants for
drying or processing
planting seeds,
§35-11-290.
Sewers.
Liens for improvements on
sewers, §35-11-411.
Stallions.
Liens of owners, §35-11-330.
Streets.
Liens for improvements on
public streets,
§35-11-411.
**Timber employees' or
laborers' liens,**
§35-11-271.

PRISONERS OF WAR.
**Bonus for Southeast Asian
War prisoners,** §§31-7-1
to 31-7-5.
Educational benefits,
§§31-6-4, 31-6-5.

PRISONS AND PRISONERS.
Agents.
Work release.
Inmate not deemed agent
of board of corrections,
§14-8-5.
Alcoholic beverages.
Dry counties.
Sale, delivery, etc., of
liquors to prisoners,
§28-4-165.
Appropriations.
Convict labor.
State lands.
Purchase of land,
§14-3-2.
Arrest.
Officers and guards.
Escaped convicts, §14-3-15.
Powers of arrest, §14-3-14.
Blood.
Donation of blood.
Deductions from sentences,
§14-9-3.
Board of corrections.
Correspondence.
Official correspondence,
§14-3-6.
County convicts.
Applicability of laws and
rules pertaining to
state convicts, §14-4-1.

PRISONS AND PRISONERS
—Cont'd
Board of corrections—Cont'd
Duties.
General provisions,
§14-3-1.
General provisions.
See CORRECTIONS.
Prison-made goods. See
within this heading,
"Prison-made goods."
Records.
Convicts, §14-3-7.
Official correspondence,
§14-3-6.
Reports.
Annual report to governor,
§14-1-13.
Transmission to
legislature, §14-3-11.
Supervision and employment
of provisions, §14-1-8.
Bond issues.
Improvement of penal and
correctional facilities,
Const. Ala., amd. 374.
Bonds, surety.
Superintendent of public
works, §14-4-12.
Bridges.
Convict labor.
Use on public roads and
bridges, §23-1-37.
Chaplains, §14-3-12.
Clothing.
Discharging convicts.
Furnishing to discharged
convicts, §14-10-1.
Coal.
Mines.
Convict labor.
Working convicts in coal
mines, §§14-5-3,
14-5-5.
Penalties, §14-5-4.
Confessions.
Threatening of prisoners for
purposes of extorting.
Prohibited, §36-10-16.
Contraband.
Defined, §§13A-10-30,
13A-10-36.
First degree promoting
prison contraband.
Class C felony, §13A-10-36.
Elements, §13A-10-36.
Second degree promoting
prison contraband.
Class C felony, §13A-10-37.
Elements, §13A-10-37.
Third degree promoting
prison contraband.
Class B misdemeanor,
§13A-10-38.
Elements, §13A-10-38.
Contracts.
Highways.
Convict labor.
Use on public roads and
bridges, §23-1-37.
Controlled substances.
Providing drugs to prisoners,
§§13A-10-36 to
13A-10-38.
Convict labor.
Board of corrections.
Supervision of employment
of prisoners, §14-1-8.
Bridges.
Use on public roads and
bridges, §23-1-37.

PRISONS AND PRISONERS
—Cont'd
Convict labor—Cont'd
Coal mines.
Working convicts in coal
mines, §§14-5-3,
14-5-5.
County convicts.
General provisions,
§§14-5-1 to 14-5-8. See
within this heading,
"County convicts."
District attorneys, judges,
sheriffs, etc.
Hiring of convicts
prohibited, §14-5-11.
Drainage.
Work on drains or
drainage districts,
§14-5-7.
Agreement to use of
convict labor,
§14-5-9.
Hard labor for the county,
§§14-4-2 to 14-4-4.
Highways.
Use on public roads and
bridges, §23-1-37.
Hiring of convicts.
County convicts, §§14-4-2
to 14-4-4.
District attorneys, judges,
sheriffs, etc.
Employment prohibited,
§14-5-11.
General provisions,
§14-5-2.
Penalties, §14-5-4.
State agencies, §14-5-10.
Income.
Use of net income, §14-3-5.
Industries in penal
institutions.
General provisions,
§§14-7-6 to 14-7-20.
See within this
heading, "Prison-made
goods."
Institution finance authority.
Construction of facilities,
§14-2-28.
Leasing of convicts.
County convicts, §§14-5-2,
14-5-4, 14-5-5.
General provisions,
§14-5-2.
Penalties, §14-5-4.
State agencies, §14-5-10.
Overworking, §14-11-1.
Penitentiary, §§14-3-47 to
14-3-49.
Proceeds.
Use of net income, §14-3-5.
State convicts.
Drainage.
Work on drains or
drainage districts,
§14-5-7.
Agreement to use of
convict labor,
§14-5-9.
Superintendent of public
works, §§14-4-11 to
14-4-14.
Termination of sentence.
Working convict after
termination, §14-11-2.
Work release, §§14-8-1 to
14-8-44. See within this
heading, "Work release."

PRISONS AND PRISONERS
—Cont'd
**Correctional incentive time
act,** §§14-9-40 to 14-9-44.
Corrections generally.
See CORRECTIONS.
Costs.
County convicts.
Sentencing of convicts.
Cost of conviction,
§14-4-10.
Insane prisoners.
Moving costs, §15-16-3.
County boards of health.
Duties, §22-3-2.
County convicts.
Applicability of laws and
rules pertaining to state
convicts, §14-4-1.
Board of corrections.
State convicts.
Applicability of laws and
rules pertaining to,
§14-4-1.
Convict labor, §§14-5-1 to
14-5-8.
Authority to work, §14-5-5.
Coal mines.
Working convicts in coal
mines, §§14-5-3,
14-5-5.
Drainage.
Districts.
Working on drains,
§14-5-6.
Work on drains, §14-5-6.
Agreement to use of
convict labor,
§14-5-8.
Feeding of prisoners.
Work on public roads,
§14-4-8.
Hard labor for the county.
Control of convicts,
§14-4-2.
Defined, §14-5-1.
Hiring of guards,
§14-4-2.
Report of sentence,
§14-4-4.
Reports by probate judge,
§14-4-3.
Superintendence of
convicts, §14-4-2.
Hiring of convicts, §14-5-2.
Penalties, §14-5-4.
Leasing of convicts,
§14-5-2.
General provisions,
§14-5-5.
Penalties, §14-5-4.
Officers and guards.
Employment, §14-4-2.
Public buildings.
Working in and around,
§14-5-5.
Public roads.
Work on public roads.
Female convicts,
§14-4-7.
Noon meals, §14-4-8.
Rules and regulations,
§14-4-6.
Tobacco allowance,
§14-4-8.
Public works.
Working in and around,
§14-5-5.
Rules and regulations.
Public roads, §14-4-6.

PRISONS AND PRISONERS
—Cont'd
County convicts—Cont'd
Convict labor—Cont'd
Work on public roads.
Female convicts, §14-4-7.
Noon meals, §14-4-8.
Rules and regulations, §14-4-6.
Tobacco allowance, §14-4-8.
Definitions.
Hard labor for the county, §14-5-1.
Feeding of prisoners.
Work on public roads, §14-4-8.
Hard labor for the ocunty.
Generally, §§14-4-2 to 14-4-4.
Hiring of convicts, §14-5-2.
Penalties, §14-5-4.
Leasing of convicts, §14-5-2.
General provisions, §14-5-5.
Penalties, §14-5-4.
Oaths, §14-4-14.
Officers and guards.
Oath of office, §14-4-14.
Records.
Maintaining of records, §14-4-3.
Probate judge, §14-4-5.
Reports.
Probate judge, §14-4-3.
Sentencing of convicts.
Cost of conviction, §14-4-10.
Good conduct, §14-4-9.
Two or more convictions, §14-4-9.
State convicts.
Applicability of laws and rules pertaining to, §14-4-1.
Streets.
Work on public roads, §§14-4-6 to 14-4-8.
Superintendent of public works, §§14-4-11 to 14-4-14.
Deductions from sentence.
Blood.
Donation of blood, §14-9-3.
Computation of incentive time deductions, §14-9-41.
Correctional incentive time act.
Short title of act, §14-9-40.
Good conduct time previously earned.
Applicability of article, §14-9-43.
Parole.
Effect of deductions on parole, §14-9-42.
Work release programs, §14-8-7.
Definitions, §13A-10-30.
County convicts.
Hard labor for the county, §14-5-1.
Release for educational purposes and seeking employment and residence, §14-8-60.
Work release, §14-8-1.
County inmates and state inmates in county custody, §14-8-30.

PRISONS AND PRISONERS
—Cont'd
Depositions.
Form of motion for leave to take deposition of prisoner, ARCP, Form 45.
Detainers.
Mandatory disposition of detainers, §§15-9-80 to 15-9-88.
See DETAINERS.
Detention.
Illegal detention after termination of sentence, §14-11-2.
Discharging convicts.
Cash payments.
Additional payments upon release, §14-10-2.
Clothing.
Furnishing to discharged prisoners, §14-10-1.
County convicts.
Convict labor.
Working on drains, §14-5-6.
Delivery of person charged with other criminal offense, §14-10-1.
Felon registration act, §§13A-11-180 to 13A-11-186.
See FELONIES.
Money.
Additional cash payments upon release, §14-10-2.
Penalties.
Wrongful discharge by public official, §14-10-3.
Transportation.
Furnishing to discharged convicts, §14-10-1.
Wrongful discharge.
Penalties, §14-10-3.
Diseases.
Notifiable diseases.
Petition for testing and treatment of inmate of correctional facility, §22-11A-37.
Sexually transmitted diseases, §22-11A-17.
Tubercular prisoners.
Generally. See within this heading, "Tubercular prisoners."
Jails.
See JAILS.
Drainage.
County convicts.
Convict labor.
Agreement to use of convict labor, §§14-5-6, 14-5-8.
State convicts.
Convict labor.
Work on drains or drainage districts, §14-5-9.
Drugs.
Providing drugs to prisoners, §§13A-10-36 to 13A-10-38.

PRISONS AND PRISONERS
—Cont'd
Education.
Release for educational purposes and seeking employment and residence, §§14-8-60 to 14-8-67. See within this heading, "Release."
Schools at correctional units, §§14-12-1 to 14-12-4.
State board of education.
Supervision of educational work of special institutions, §16-3-20.
Eminent domain.
Acquisition of land, etc., §18-1A-271.
Escape.
General provisions.
See ESCAPE.
Tools for escape.
Providing prisoners with tools, §§13A-10-36 to 13A-10-38.
Evaluation of prison system.
Legislative committee for evaluation, etc., of prison system and board of corrections, §§29-2-20 to 29-2-22.
Extradition.
General provisions.
See EXTRADITION.
Federal prisoners.
Jails, §§14-6-3, 14-6-4.
Penitentiary.
Board of corrections to receive, §14-3-32.
Feeding of prisoners.
County convicts.
Work on public roads, §14-4-8.
Jails.
See JAILS.
Penitentiary.
Diet, §14-3-45.
Records.
Daily ration sheet or expense account.
Form, §14-6-47.
Sheriff not required to prepare, §14-6-41.
Female convicts.
Convict labor.
Work on public roads, §14-4-7.
Force.
Use of force by persons with custodial responsibilities, §13A-3-24.
Good conduct.
County convicts.
Two or more convictions.
Effect of convict's conduct thereon, §14-4-9.
Deductions from sentence.
Correctional incentive time, §§14-9-40 to 14-9-43.
Two or more convictions.
Effect of conduct thereon, §14-3-38.
Work release.
Eligibility for good time, §14-8-7.
Guards. See within this heading, "Officers and guards."

PRISONS AND PRISONERS
—Cont'd

Habeas corpus.
General provisions.
See HABEAS CORPUS.
Hard labor for the county,
§§14-4-2 to 14-4-4.
Health.
Duties of county boards of
health, §22-3-2.
Highways.
Convict labor.
County convicts, §§14-4-6
to 14-4-8.
Use on public roads and
bridges, §23-1-37.
Holding incommunicado.
Prohibited, §36-10-16.
Hospitals.
Prisoners needing long-time
hospitalization.
Treatment, care and
segregation, §14-1-12.
Tubercular prisoners.
Treatment, care and
segregation, §14-1-12.
**Industries in penal
institutions.**
General provisions, §§14-7-6
to 14-7-20. See within
this heading, "Prison-
made goods."
**Inmate community
reintegration under SIR
act,** §§15-18-110 to
15-18-123.
See CORRECTIONS.
Insanity. See within this
heading, "Mentally ill
prisoners."
Inspections.
Authority of board of
corrections, §14-6-106.
Effect of orders of board of
corrections, §14-6-107.
Jails.
See JAILS.
Penitentiary, §§14-6-106,
14-6-107.
Investigations.
Violations of law, §14-3-9.
Jails, §§14-6-80 to 14-6-109.
See JAILS.
Joint acts of prisoners.
Three or more prisoners.
Penalties, §14-11-11.
Juvenile proceedings.
When delinquent child may
be detained in adult
detention facility,
§12-15-61.
Labor.
County convicts, §§14-4-1 to
14-4-14, 14-5-1 to 14-5-8.
See within this heading,
"County convicts."
General provisions. See
within this heading,
"Convict labor."
Industries in penal
institutions.
General provisions,
§§14-7-6 to 14-7-20.
See within this
heading, "Prison-made
goods."
Superintendent of public
works, §§14-4-11 to
14-4-14.

PRISONS AND PRISONERS
—Cont'd

Labor—Cont'd
Work release, §§14-8-1 to
14-8-44. See within this
heading, "Work release."
Leases.
Convict labor.
Generally. See within this
heading, "Convict
labor."
Limitation of actions.
Suspension of limitation for
disabilities, §6-2-8.
Management of convicts.
Witnesses.
Failure to appear or
testify, §14-11-3.
**Mandatory disposition of
detainers,** §§15-9-80 to
15-9-88.
See DETAINERS.
**Manufactured and produced
goods.**
Industries in penal
institutions.
General provisions,
§§14-7-6 to 14-7-20.
See within this
heading, "Prison-made
goods."
Mentally ill prisoners.
Capital cases.
Inquiry into sanity,
§15-16-22.
Removal of insane
defendant to state
hospital, §15-16-22.
Commitment.
Procedure for commitment
to mental health
facility, §22-52-70.
Conveyance to mental health
facility.
Prerequisites to
conveyance, §22-52-71.
Costs of moving insane
prisoners, §15-16-3.
Investigation on sanity of
certain confined persons.
Capital cases, §§15-16-22,
15-16-23.
Duty of judge to institute,
§15-16-20.
Proceedings where person
found insane,
§15-16-20.
Suspension of felony trial
pending inquiry,
§15-16-21.
Transfer to state hospital
upon finding of
insanity, §15-16-21.
Recovery.
Report of recovery,
§22-52-72.
Reports.
Recovery of prisoners,
§22-52-72.
Security medical facility,
§§22-54-1 to 22-54-5.
Mines.
Convict labor.
Working convicts in coal
mines, §§14-5-3,
14-5-5.

PRISONS AND PRISONERS
—Cont'd

Minors.
Department of youth
services.
Confinement of youth in
adult penal
institutions, §44-1-8.
Detaining in adult facility,
§12-15-61.
Involuntary commitment.
Juvenile proceedings,
§12-15-90.
Municipal corporations.
Police jurisdiction over
workhouses and houses
of correction, §11-47-22.
Oaths.
Officers and guards.
Oath of office, §14-3-13.
Superintendent of public
works, §14-4-14.
Officers and guards.
Arrest.
Escaped convicts, §14-3-15.
Powers of arrest, §14-3-14.
Board of corrections.
Duties generally, §14-3-1.
Control.
Board of corrections,
§14-3-1.
County convicts.
Convict labor.
Employment of guards,
§14-4-2.
Oath of office, §14-4-14.
Discharging convicts.
Penalty for wrongful
discharge, §14-10-3.
Duties.
Failure of duty, §14-11-4.
Escaped convicts.
Pursuit and arrest,
§14-3-15.
Female convicts, §14-3-39.
Force.
When use of force justified,
§13A-3-27.
Maltreatment of convicts,
§14-11-1.
Oath of office, §§14-3-13,
14-4-14.
Penitentiary, §§14-3-54,
14-3-55.
Powers.
Policemen, §14-3-14.
Violation of law.
Penalties, §14-11-4.
Pardons.
See PARDONS.
Parole.
Deductions from sentence.
Effect of deductions on
parole, §14-9-42.
General provisions.
See PAROLE.
Penalties.
Convict labor.
Hiring or leasing of
convicts, §14-5-4.
County convicts.
Hard labor sentence.
Failure to report by
probate judge,
§14-4-4.
Discharging convicts.
Wrongful discharge by
public official,
§14-10-3.
Hiring of convicts, §14-5-4.

PRISONS AND PRISONERS
—Cont'd
Penalties—Cont'd
Joint acts of prisoners.
Three or more prisoners
joined to do unlawful
act, §14-11-11.
Leasing of convicts, §14-5-4.
Officers and guards.
Violation of law, §14-11-4.
Property.
State property.
Injury to or destruction
of, §14-11-10.
Punishment.
Inflicting of unauthorized
punishment, §14-11-1.
Sentences.
General provisions. See
within this heading,
"Sentences."
Solitary confinement.
Noncompliance by officers
and guards, §14-11-5.
Trespassing about prisons,
§14-11-9.
Violations of chapter,
§14-3-16.
Witnesses.
Management and
treatment of convicts.
Failure to appear or
testify, §14-11-3.
Work release.
Violations of chapter,
§14-8-10.
Penitentiary.
General provisions.
See PENITENTIARY.
**Permissible legal
punishments.**
Imprisonment in hard labor,
§15-18-1.
**Prison-made goods, §§14-7-6
to 14-7-23.**
Administration of chapter.
Preparation and
promulgation of
policies, §14-7-18.
Audits.
Reports of annual audit by
state auditor, §14-7-17.
Board of corrections.
Administration of chapter.
Preparation and
promulgation of
policies, §14-7-18.
Hearing on decision to
obligate funds.
Notice, §14-7-9.
Price.
Determination, §14-7-11.
Catalogues, §14-7-12.
Citation of chapter.
Short title, §14-7-6.
Construction of chapter,
§14-7-23.
Equipment and supplies.
Purchase, §14-7-8.
Industrial revolving fund.
Authorization, §14-7-19.
Excess funds.
Transfer to state general
fund, §14-7-20.
Expenditures, §14-7-19.
Price, §14-7-11.
Purchases.
Equipment, etc., §14-7-8.
Political subdivisions,
§14-7-13.

PRISONS AND PRISONERS
—Cont'd
Prison-made goods—Cont'd
Purchases—Cont'd
State offices, etc., §14-7-13.
Exceptions to
requirement,
§14-7-14.
Reports, §14-7-15.
Purpose of chapter, §14-7-7.
Priorities, §14-7-16.
Reports.
Audits.
Annual audits by state
auditor, §14-7-17.
Purchases by state offices,
etc., §14-7-15.
Requests for manufacture or
production of articles,
§14-7-12.
Sale of goods, §14-7-22.
Authority of board of
corrections, §14-1-8.
Disposition of proceeds,
§14-7-20.
Price, §14-7-11.
Surplus agricultural
products and personal
property, §14-7-21.
Specifications of goods,
§14-7-10.
Supervisory personnel.
Employment, §14-7-8.
Title of chapter, §14-7-6.
Probate judges.
County convicts.
Hard labor sentence.
Reports, §14-4-4.
Records, §14-4-5.
Reports by probate judge,
§14-4-3.
**Profits from crime, §§41-9-80
to 41-9-84.**
See PROFITS FROM
CRIME.
**Promoting prison
contraband, §§13A-10-36
to 13A-10-38.**
Property.
State property.
Injury to or destruction of.
Penalties, §14-11-10.
Public buildings.
Injury to or destruction of.
Penalties, §14-11-10.
**Public lands, §§14-3-2 to
14-3-4.**
**Public officers and
employees.**
Felonies.
Conviction of felony
vacates office, §36-9-2.
Public works.
Convict labor generally. See
within this heading,
"Convict labor."
Superintendent of public
works, §§14-4-11 to
14-4-14.
Punishment.
Inflicting of unauthorized
punishment, §14-11-1.
Purchases.
Industries in penal
institutions.
General provisions,
§§14-7-6 to 14-7-20.
See within this
heading, "Prison-made
goods."

PRISONS AND PRISONERS
—Cont'd
Purchases—Cont'd
State lands.
Appropriations for
purchases, §14-3-2.
Records.
Contents of records of
convicts, §14-3-7.
County convicts.
Maintenance by board of
corrections, §14-4-3.
Probate judge, §14-4-5.
Feeding of prisoners.
Daily ration sheet or
expense account.
Sheriff not required to
prepare, §14-6-41.
Forms, §14-6-47.
Penitentiary.
Information regarding new
convicts, §14-3-35.
Punishment, §14-3-52.
**Reintegration of inmate into
society.**
Inmate community
reintegration under SIR
act, §§15-18-110 to
15-18-123.
See CORRECTIONS.
Release.
Discharging convict,
§§14-10-1 to 14-10-3.
Educational purposes and
seeking employment and
residence, §§14-8-60 to
14-8-67.
Board of corrections.
Inmates not deemed
agents of board
while going to and
from employment,
§14-8-65.
Investigations and
recommendations by
employees of board
as to requests for
visits or job
opportunities,
§14-8-64.
Definitions, §14-8-60.
Public understanding.
Promotion, §14-8-66.
Reports.
Annual report, §14-8-66.
Rules and regulations,
§§14-8-61 to 14-8-63.
State agencies.
Encouragement of
cooperation,
§14-8-66.
Violations.
Willful failure of inmate
to remain within
extended limits of
confinement or
return to place of
confinement,
§14-8-67.
Work release, §§14-8-1 to
14-8-44. See within this
heading, "Work release."
Removal of prisoners.
Jails.
See JAILS.
Reports.
Board of corrections,
§§14-1-13, 14-3-11.
County convicts.
Hard labor sentence.
Probate judge, §14-4-4.

PRISONS AND PRISONERS
—Cont'd
Reports—Cont'd
County convicts—Cont'd
Probate judge, §§14-4-3,
14-4-4.
Mentally ill prisoners.
Recovery of prisoners,
§22-52-72.
Prison-made goods,
§§14-7-15, 14-7-17.
Violations of law, §14-3-9.
Work release.
Annual report, §14-8-9.
Restitution to victims of
crimes.
Enforceability of restitution
order for prisoner,
§15-18-71.
Suspension of sentence.
Default by defendant with
suspended sentence.
Effect, §15-18-72.
Payment of restitution as
condition to
suspension, §15-18-70.
Roads.
Work on public roads.
County convicts, §§14-4-6
to 14-4-8.
Rules and regulations.
Board of corrections.
Promulgation, §14-1-8.
County convicts.
Convict labor.
Public roads, §14-4-6.
Release for educational
purposes and seeking
employment and
residence, §§14-8-61 to
14-8-63.
Work release.
Adoption, §14-8-2.
County inmates and state
inmates in county
custody, §§14-8-31,
14-8-33.
Earnings.
Disposition, §14-8-6.
Salaries.
Superintendent of public
works, §14-4-11.
Work release, §§14-8-4,
14-8-6.
Sales.
Prison-made goods. See
within this heading,
"Prison-made goods."
State lands, §14-3-2.
Schools at correctional
units, §§14-12-1 to 14-12-4.
Sentences.
Cards.
Contents, §14-3-8.
County convicts, §§14-4-9,
14-4-10.
Deductions from sentences.
See within this heading,
"Deductions from
sentence."
Determination of sentence.
Illegal detention, §14-11-2.
Working after termination
of sentence, §14-11-2.
Furnishing sentence card to
each convict, §14-3-8.
Good conduct. See within
this heading, "Good
conduct."

PRISONS AND PRISONERS
—Cont'd
Sentences—Cont'd
Restitution to victims of
crimes.
Payment of restitution as
condition to
suspension, §15-18-70.
Solitary confinement.
Noncompliance by officers
and guards.
Penalties, §14-11-5.
Suspended sentence.
Restitution to victims of
crimes.
Effect of default,
§15-18-72.
Payment as condition to
suspension,
§15-18-70.
Service of process.
How incarcerated person
served, ARCP, Rule 4 (c).
Solitary confinement.
Noncompliance with
sentence.
Officers and guards.
Penalties, §14-11-5.
State lands.
Improvements, §14-3-3.
Renting out of surplus land,
§14-3-4.
Sale and purchase.
Appropriations for
purchase, §14-3-2.
Streets.
Convict labor.
County convicts.
Work on public roads,
§§14-4-6 to 14-4-8.
Use on public roads and
bridges, §23-1-37.
Superintendent of public
works.
Bonds, surety, §14-4-12.
Compensation, §14-4-11.
Duties.
General provisions,
§14-4-13.
Oath of office, §14-4-14.
Terms of office, §14-4-11.
Supervised intensive
restitution program.
Inmate community
reintegration under SIR
act, §§15-18-110 to
15-18-123.
See CORRECTIONS.
Tobacco.
County convicts.
Work on public roads.
Tobacco allowance,
§14-4-8.
Tools.
Contraband, §§13A-10-36 to
13A-10-38.
Trade schools.
Frank Lee youth center,
§§16-60-170 to 16-60-173.
Transportation.
Discharging convicts.
Furnishing to discharged
convicts, §14-10-1.
Treatment of convicts.
Witnesses.
Failure to appear or
testify, §14-11-3.
Trespassing.
Penalties, §14-11-9.

PRISONS AND PRISONERS
—Cont'd
Tubercular prisoners.
Jails.
See JAILS.
Penitentiary, §14-3-41.
Segregation, §14-1-12.
Separation, §14-3-41.
Treatment, §14-1-12.
Uniform mandatory
disposition of detainers,
§§15-9-80 to 15-9-88.
See DETAINERS.
United States.
Jails, §§14-6-3, 14-6-4.
Venue.
Actions where prison system
involved, §6-3-9.
Violations of law.
Where violations tried,
§14-3-9.
Violations of law.
Penalties, §14-3-16.
Reporting by board of
corrections, §14-3-9.
Venue of trial, §14-3-9.
Weapons.
Contraband.
Promotion of prison
contraband.
§§13A-10-36 to
13A-10-38.
Welfare.
See WELFARE.
Witnesses.
Management and treatment
of convicts.
Failure to appear or
testify, §14-11-3.
Women.
Working female convicts on
public roads, §14-4-7.
Work.
County convicts, §§14-4-1 to
14-4-14, 14-5-1 to 14-5-8.
See within this heading,
"County convicts."
General provisions. See
within this heading,
"Convict labor."
Industries in penal
institutions, §§14-7-6 to
14-7-23. See within this
heading, "Prison-made
goods."
Release.
Educational purposes and
seeking employment
and residence,
§§14-8-60 to 14-8-67.
See within this
heading, "Release."
Work release, §§14-8-1 to
14-8-44. See within
this heading, "Work
release."
Superintendent of public
works, §§14-4-11 to
14-4-14.
Work release, §§14-8-1 to
14-8-44. See within this
heading, "Work release."
Work release, §§14-8-1 to
14-8-44.
Agent of board of corrections.
Inmate not deemed agent,
§14-8-5.

PRISONS AND PRISONERS
—Cont'd
Work release—Cont'd
County inmates and state
inmates in county
custody.
Authorization for
programs, §14-8-31.
Board of corrections.
Contracts with counties
as to costs, §14-8-31.
Designation of officers
and employees,
§14-8-41.
Investigations and
recommendations by
employees of board,
§14-8-34.
Conditions of employment,
§14-8-35.
Construction of article,
§14-8-44.
Counties.
Designation of
employees, §14-8-41.
Employment of inmates,
§14-8-36.
Inmates not deemed
agents of counties
while going to and
from employment,
§14-8-40.
Definitions, §14-8-30.
Earnings of inmates.
Disposition, §14-8-37.
Effect of article upon
existing programs,
§14-8-44.
Establishment of programs,
§14-8-31.
Good time credit.
Eligibility of inmates,
§14-8-38.
Leaves.
Granting to inmates,
§14-8-39.
Passes.
Granting to inmates,
§14-8-39.
Penalty for violations,
§14-8-43.
Protests as to participation
by inmate, §14-8-33.
Rules and regulations.
Promulgation, §§14-8-31,
14-8-33.
State.
Employment of inmates,
§14-8-36.
Wages, §14-8-36.
Inmates not deemed
agents of state while
going to and from
employment,
§14-8-40.
Violations.
Penalty, §14-8-43.
Willful failure of inmate
to remain within
extended limits of
confinement or
return to place of
confinement,
§14-8-42.
Work release camps.
Establishment, §14-8-32.
Definitions, §14-8-1.
Earnings, §§14-8-4, 14-8-6.
Good time credit.
Eligibility, §14-8-7.

PRISONS AND PRISONERS
—Cont'd
Work release—Cont'd
Investigations.
Employees of the board,
§14-8-3.
Limitations on securing
employment, §14-8-4.
Penalties.
Violations of chapter,
§14-8-10.
Policies.
Adoption, §14-8-2.
Public understanding.
Commissioner to provide,
§14-8-9.
Recommendations.
Employees of the board,
§14-8-3.
Reports.
Annual report, §14-8-9.
Rules and regulations.
Adoption, §14-8-2.
County inmates and state
inmates in county
custody, §§14-8-31,
14-8-33.
Earnings.
Disposition of earnings,
§14-8-6.
Types of employment.
Limitations, §14-8-4.
Wages.
Disposition of earnings,
§14-8-6.
Requirements as to
amount, §14-8-4.

PRIVACY.
Invasions of privacy.
Eavesdropping, §§13A-11-30
to 13A-11-37.
See EAVESDROPPING.

PRIVATE ACTIVITY BONDS.
State ceiling, §§41-10-35 to
41-10-43.
See BOND ISSUES.

PRIVATE SCHOOLS.
See EDUCATION.

PRIVIES.
Municipal corporations.
Regulation, installation, etc.,
§11-50-55.
**Nuisances menacing public
health,** §§22-10-1 to
22-10-3.

PRIVILEGES.
Attorneys at law.
Attorney-client privilege.
Testimony of attorney for
or against client,
§12-21-161.
**Communications with
clergymen.**
Refusal to disclose in legal or
quasi-legal proceedings.
Protected by privilege,
§12-21-166.
Constitution of Alabama.
Irrevocable or exclusive
grants of special
privileges, Const. Ala.,
art. I, §22.
Counselors.
Generally, §34-8A-21.
Victim counselors.
Confidentiality generally,
§§15-23-40 to 15-23-46.
See VICTIM
COUNSELORS.

PRIVILEGES—Cont'd
Diseases.
Notifiable diseases.
Confidentiality of
information.
Notification of third
parties of diseases,
§22-11A-38.
**Hazardous waste or
substances.**
Fees for disposal of
hazardous waste or
substances.
Confidentiality of fee
reports, §22-30B-15.
Libel and slander.
Publication of certain
documents considered
privileged, §13A-11-161.
Mentally ill.
Criminal law and procedure.
Release of criminal
psychopaths.
Conditional releases.
Periodic reports not
deemed violative
of doctor-patient
privilege, etc.,
§15-16-69.
News-gathering persons.
Exemption from disclosing
sources, §12-21-142.
Physician-patient privilege.
Crime victims compensation.
Filing claim under chapter
constitutes waiver of
privilege, §15-23-11.
Criminal psychopath
conditional releases.
Periodic reports not
deemed violative of
privilege, §15-16-69.
Professional corporations.
Privileged communications.
Effect of article on
privileged
communications,
§10-4-391.
Psychiatrist-patient, §34-26-2.
Criminal psychopath
conditional releases.
Periodic reports not
deemed violative of
privilege, §15-16-69.
**Psychologist-patient
privilege,** §34-26-2.
Criminal psychopath
conditional releases.
Periodic reports not
deemed violative of
privilege, §15-16-69.
Victim counselors.
Confidentiality, §§15-23-40 to
15-23-46.
See VICTIM
COUNSELORS.

PROBATE.
Conveyances.
See CONVEYANCES.
General provisions.
See WILLS.

PROBATE CODE.
Descent and distribution.
Intestate succession,
§§43-8-40 to 43-8-58.
See WILLS.

PROBATE CODE—Cont'd
Disclaimer of interests in property, §§43-8-290 to 43-8-298.
See DISCLAIMER OF INTERESTS IN PROPERTY.
Elective share of surviving spouse, §§43-8-70 to 43-8-76.
See WILLS.
Exempt property and allowances, §§43-8-110 to 43-8-115.
See WILLS.
General provisions, §§43-8-1 to 43-8-298.
See WILLS.
Intestate succession, §§43-8-40 to 43-8-58.
See WILLS.
Uniform disclaimer of property interests, §§43-8-290 to 43-8-298.
See DISCLAIMER OF INTERESTS IN PROPERTY.
Wills.
Construction, §§43-8-220 to 43-8-231.
See WILLS.
Contesting validity, §§43-8-190 to 43-8-202.
See WILLS.
Execution, §§43-8-130 to 43-8-141.
See WILLS.
Generally, §§43-8-130 to 43-8-202.
See WILLS.

PROBATE COURTS.
Adoption.
Reports to department of pensions and security.
Required, §12-13-44.
Ad quod damnum proceedings.
Witness fees, §12-19-136.
Agriculture.
Rules and regulations.
Copies furnished to probate judges, §2-2-17.
Appeals from probate court.
Bond on appeal.
Appeal of order removing executor or administrator, §12-22-24.
Circuit court judgment on appeal.
Appeal from circuit court judgment on appeal, §12-22-22.
Contest of will removed to probate court of another county, §12-22-23.
Costs on appeal.
Execution for unpaid costs, §12-22-76.
Reimbursement of costs from estate of testator, etc., §12-22-27.
Security for costs, §12-22-25.
Final judgments, orders or decrees, §§12-22-2, 12-22-20.

PROBATE COURTS—Cont'd
Appeals from probate court —Cont'd
Guardian and ward.
Appeals by guardians of minors or persons of unsound mind, §12-22-26.
Uniform guardianship and protective proceedings act.
Procedure governing, §26-2A-36.
Next friend.
Appeals by next friends of minors or persons of unsound mind, §12-22-26.
Other orders, judgments or decrees, §12-22-21.
Record on appeal.
Delayed or defective record.
Liability of probate judge, §12-22-60.
Removal of executor or administrator.
Bond on appeal of order removing, §12-22-24.
Attachment.
Issuance by judge, §6-6-43.
Attorneys at law.
Surety bond of judges.
Attorneys not deemed sufficient sureties on official bonds, §36-5-13.
Bonds, surety.
Attorneys at law.
Not deemed sufficient sureties on certain official bonds, §36-5-13.
Chief clerk, §12-13-13.
Judges. See within this heading, "Judges."
Chiropractors.
License to be recorded with judge of probate, §34-24-164.
Circuit courts.
Administration of estates.
Removal of administration from probate court, §12-11-41.
Correction of errors in probate court.
Irregular sales of lands under decrees of court of probate may be confirmed, §12-11-61.
Settlements of estates.
Correction of errors in probate court, §12-11-60.
Superintendence of probate courts, §12-11-30.
Clerks of court.
Chief clerk.
Authority performance of official acts of chief clerk, §12-13-14.
Bonds, surety, §12-13-13.
Oath, §12-13-13.
Powers, §12-13-14.
Probate judges.
Vacancies in office of probate judge, §12-13-15.

PROBATE COURTS—Cont'd
Clerks of court—Cont'd
Failure to deliver books, papers, money, etc., to successor of probate judge, §12-13-18.
Guardian and ward.
Uniform guardianship and protective proceedings act.
Records and certified copies.
Duties, §26-2A-34.
Conservators.
Bonds, surety.
Additional bond.
Authority to require, §26-3-7.
Neglect in taking.
Liability of probate judge, §26-3-13.
New or additional bond.
Authority to require, §26-3-7.
Omission in taking.
Liability of probate judge, §26-3-13.
Recordation, §26-3-12.
Jurisdiction.
Accounts of conservators.
Settlements, §26-5-1.
Settlements of accounts of conservators.
Compulsion of settlement, §26-5-30.
Removal of conservatorship to circuit courts, §26-2-2.
Settlements of accounts of conservators.
Compulsion of settlement by probate court, §§26-5-30 to 26-5-39.
See CONSERVATORS.
Death of conservators.
Jurisdiction, §26-5-50.
Final settlement.
Account and vouchers.
Examination, §26-5-10.
Guardian ad litem appointed, §26-5-8.
Settlements of accounts of guardians.
Finality of orders or decrees, §26-5-15.
Final settlement.
Account and vouchers.
Filing by conservators, §26-5-8.
Day for settlement, §26-5-9.
Decree, §26-5-11.
Recordation.
Decree, §26-5-11.
Partial settlement.
Day for settlement, §26-5-3.
Examination of vouchers, §26-5-4.
Recordation.
Decree as to vouchers and accounts, §26-5-5.
Constitution of Alabama.
See CONSTITUTION OF ALABAMA.
Contempt.
Powers of courts as to punishment for contempt, §12-13-9.

PROBATE COURTS—Cont'd
Contesting validity of wills,
§§43-8-190 to 43-8-202.
See WILLS.
Costs.
Appeals.
Execution for unpaid costs,
§12-22-76.
Reimbursement of costs on
appeal from estate of
testator, etc.,
§12-22-27.
Security for costs of appeal,
§12-22-25.
Excessive costs.
Proceedings for retaxation
of excessive costs in
probate courts,
§12-19-54.
Nonresidents.
Security for costs in suits
by or for nonresidents,
§12-19-48.
Probate judges' fees. See
within this heading,
"Judges."
Retaxation of excessive costs,
§12-19-54.
Counties.
General provisions.
See COUNTIES.
Courts generally.
See COURTS.
Curators.
Mentally or physically
incapacitated persons.
Appointment of curator,
§26-7A-1.
Damnum.
Ad quod damnum
proceedings.
Jurors' fees, §12-19-112.
Decrees.
Irregular sales of lands
under decrees of court of
probate may be
confirmed by circuit
court, §12-11-61.
**Developmentally disabled
persons.**
Appointment of guardian,
§12-13-21.
District courts.
Adoption.
Transfer of proceedings to
district court from
probate court,
§12-12-35.
Dower.
Jurisdiction of probate
courts, §12-13-1.
Electric cooperatives.
Transmitting copies of article
to judge, §37-6-19.
Eminent domain.
§§18-1A-270, 18-1A-294.
Errors.
Correction of errors in
probate court.
Irregular sales of lands
under decrees of court
of probate may be
confirmed by circuit
court, §12-11-61.
Settlements of estates,
§12-11-60.
Escheats.
Probate judges, §§43-6-6,
43-6-7, 43-6-9.

PROBATE COURTS—Cont'd
Establishment.
Legislature may establish in
each county, Const. Ala.,
art. VI, §149.
Evidence.
Applicability of provisions
pertaining to evidence in
circuit courts, §12-13-12.
**Executors and
administrators.**
General provisions.
See EXECUTORS AND
ADMINISTRATORS.
**Exemptions from levy and
sale under process.**
Contest of exemption claim.
Trial by jury in probate
court, §6-10-31.
Expenses.
Judges.
Attending state or national
conferences, schools,
etc., §12-13-19.
Fees.
Judges. See within this
heading, "Judges."
Jurors' fees, §§12-19-111 to
12-19-113.
Schedule of fees, §12-19-90.
Witnesses, §§12-19-135,
12-19-136.
**Fiduciary funds in hands of
officials,** §§19-3-80 to
19-3-87.
See FIDUCIARIES.
Garnishment.
Applicability of provisions
pertaining to
garnishments in circuit
courts, §12-13-8.
Enforcement, §12-13-7.
Issuance, §12-13-7.
Grand juries.
Examination of fee book of
probate judge,
§12-16-194.
Guardian ad litem.
Appeals by guardians of
minors or persons of
unsound mind,
§12-22-26.
Curator of mentally or
physically incapacitated
persons, §§26-7A-1 to
26-7A-17.
See GUARDIAN AND
WARD.
Developmentally disabled
persons.
Appointment of guardian
for, §12-13-21.
Guardian and ward.
Developmentally disabled
persons.
Appointment of guardian,
§12-13-21.
General provisions.
See GUARDIAN AND
WARD.
Uniform guardianship and
protective proceedings
act.
Clerks of court.
Records and certified
copies.
Duties, §26-2A-34.
Jurisdiction.
Subject matter
jurisdiction,
§26-2A-31.

PROBATE COURTS—Cont'd
Hours.
When courts deemed open,
§12-13-3.
Judges.
Absence.
Appointment of special
judge when probate
judge absent,
§12-13-37.
Abstract of mortgages, etc.
Failure to keep, §12-13-54.
Acts and resolutions of
legislature.
Secretary of state to
furnish copies for
certain officers,
§36-14-13.
Adoption.
Fees, §12-19-90.
Reports to department of
pensions and security.
Required, §12-13-44.
Attachments.
Issuance, §6-6-43.
Attorneys at law.
Attorneys not deemed
sufficient sureties on
official bonds of
probate judges,
§36-5-13.
Billiard rooms.
Issuance of license by
probate judge,
§§34-6-31, 34-6-32.
Bonds, surety, §12-13-33.
Amount of bond, §12-13-33.
Attorneys not deemed
sufficient sureties on
official bonds of
probate judges,
§36-5-13.
Lis pendens.
Liability of judges on
bonds, §35-4-139.
Persons who may institute
civil actions on bonds
of judges, §12-13-34.
Books.
Examination of fee book by
district attorney and
grand jury, §12-16-194
Rebinding or recopying.
Authorization by county
commission,
§12-13-46.
Compensation of probate
judge, §12-13-46.
Execution of contract by
probate judge,
§12-13-47.
Manner, §12-13-46.
Surrender of custody of
books for rebinding,
§12-13-47.
Canons of judicial ethics.
See CANONS OF
JUDICIAL ETHICS.
Compensation.
Expenses incurred in
attending state or
national conferences,
schools, etc., §12-13-19
Funds to come from
county's general fund,
§12-13-20.
Maximum compensation.
Income on fee basis,
§12-19-90.1.
Minimum compensation,
§12-13-20.

PROBATE COURTS—Cont'd
Judges—Cont'd
Compensation—Cont'd
Special judges, ARJA, Rule 14.
Conferences.
Payment of expenses, §12-13-19.
Conservators of peace.
Probate judges deemed conservators, §12-13-39.
Costs on appeal.
Execution for unpaid costs, §12-22-76.
Counties.
See COUNTIES.
Death.
Notice to governor, §36-9-10.
Duties.
Generally, §12-13-41.
Election of probate judge, Const. Ala., art. VI, §152.
Elections generally.
See ELECTIONS.
Electric cooperatives.
Articles.
Transmission of copies of articles to probate judge, §37-6-19.
Elmore county.
Duties, §12-13-41.
Escheats, §§43-6-6, 43-6-7, 43-6-9.
Fee book.
Examination of fee book by district attorney and grand jury, §12-16-194.
Fees, §12-19-90.
Copies of fees.
Furnishing, §12-19-40.
Due date, §12-19-43.
Examination of fee book by district attorney and grand jury, §12-16-194.
General provisions.
See COSTS.
Licenses.
Fee for issuing, §40-12-271.
Lists of fees.
Posting, §12-19-40.
Preparation of bills for fees or costs, §12-19-42.
Records.
Maintenance of record book of fees, §12-19-45.
Schedule of fees, §12-19-90.
Unauthorized fees.
Liability for receiving, §12-19-47.
When fees allowed for services in proceedings before probate judges due, §12-19-43.
Fiduciary funds in hands of officials, §§19-3-80 to 19-3-87.
See FIDUCIARIES.
Fish and game.
Licenses.
See FISH AND GAME.
Funds.
Fiduciary funds in hands of officials, §§19-3-80 to 19-3-87.
See FIDUCIARIES.

PROBATE COURTS—Cont'd
Judges—Cont'd
Hours.
Office hours, §12-13-36.
Impeachment.
General provisions.
See IMPEACHMENT.
Subject to impeachment, §36-11-1; Const. Ala., art. VII, §174.
Incompetence.
Appointment of special judge when probate judge incompetent, §12-13-37.
Judges generally.
See JUDGES.
Judicial sales.
Notices.
Subscribing, taking and filing of weekly newspapers, §6-8-40.
Licenses. See within this heading, "Licenses."
Lis pendens, §§35-4-130, 35-4-139.
Military affairs.
Honorable discharges.
Duties of judges as to, §31-1-1.
Ordering out troops.
Request to governor by probate judge, §31-2-111.
Mineral documentary tax, §§40-20-33, 40-20-34, 40-20-37.
Motor vehicles.
Drivers' licenses, §§32-6-4, 32-6-5, 32-6-8.
License taxes and registration fees.
Fee for issuance, §40-12-271.
Temporary tags and certificates.
Issuance, §32-6-213.
Municipal corporations.
General provisions.
See MUNICIPAL CORPORATIONS.
Notaries public.
Commissioning.
Fee of probate judge for issuance of commission, §§12-19-90, 36-20-1, 36-20-30.
Reports to secretary of state, §§36-20-1, 36-20-30.
Notaries public for state at large.
Fee of probate judge for issuance of commissions, §36-20-30.
Report to secretary of state of commissioning, §36-20-30.
Register of official acts.
Deliver to judge upon death, resignation, etc., of notary, §36-20-8.
Judge may deliver register to another notary, §36-20-10.

PROBATE COURTS—Cont'd
Judges—Cont'd
Notaries public—Cont'd
Register of official acts —Cont'd
Liability of person failing to deliver register to judge on demand, §36-20-8.
Penalty for failure to deliver register to judge on demand, §36-20-9.
Provision of certified copies from register, §36-20-10.
Oaths.
Filing, §36-4-3.
Officers' fees generally.
See COSTS.
Offices, §12-13-36.
Papers, documents, etc.
Preparation by probate judge of papers, documents, etc., to be heard by judge, §12-13-16.
Pending actions.
Taking file in pending action from office of judge, §12-20-25.
Pensions, §§12-18-80 to 12-18-92.
Powers, §12-13-40.
Prisons and prisoners, §§14-4-3 to 14-4-5.
Qualifications, §12-13-31.
Recordation.
General provisions.
See RECORDATION.
Records.
Examination of records, §12-13-50.
Fees.
Maintenance of record book of fees received by probate judges, §12-19-45.
Proceeds of crime.
Confiscation of profits, §41-9-81.
Taking file in pending action from office of judge, §12-20-25.
Registration of judgments.
See JUDGMENTS.
Required duties.
Generally, §12-13-41.
Retirement, §§12-18-80 to 12-18-92.
Applicability of provisions of article 1 of chapter to probate judges elected or appointed to office after October 1, 1976, §12-18-81.
Benefits, §12-18-87.
Cost of living increase for 1984, §12-18-92.
Entitlement to receipt of pension, §12-18-80.
Contributions to retirement fund by judges, §12-18-82.
Cost of living increase.
1984 increase, §12-18-92.
Declaration as to intention to retire, §12-18-85.

PROBATE COURTS—Cont'd
Judges—Cont'd
Retirement—Cont'd
Election by probate judges
holding office on
December 27, 1973 to
come under provisions
of article 1 of chapter,
§12-18-81.
Eligibility for retirement.
Generally, §12-18-84.
Entitlement to retirement
and receipt of pension,
§12-18-80.
Intention to retire.
Declaration as to
intention, §12-18-85.
Judicial retirement fund.
General provisions.
See JUDGES.
1984 cost of living
increase, §12-18-92.
Retirement order,
§12-18-80.
State and local governing
bodies authorized to
pick up member
contributions to
retirement fund,
§12-18-81.
Supernumerary probate
judges, §12-18-90.
Termination of service
prior to eligibility for
retirement benefits,
§12-18-83.
Transfer of contributions
and creditable service
to judicial retirement
fund, §§12-18-110 to
12-18-114.
Vacancy in office,
§12-18-86.
Robes.
Judges encouraged to wear
suitable black judicial
robe, ARJA, Rule 22.
Schools.
Attendance.
Payment of expenses,
§12-13-19.
Seal of office, §12-13-35.
Settlements by executors,
administrators and
guardians.
Payment to probate judge
of money due on
decree upon
settlement, §12-13-48.
Payment of probate
judge for receipt of
money under section
12-13-48, §12-13-49.
Sickness.
Appointment of special
judge when probate
judge sick, §12-13-37.
Special judges.
Appointment, §§12-13-27,
12-13-38.
Compensation, ARJA, Rule
14.
Duties, §12-13-37.
Judgments, orders and
decrees.
Force, effect, etc.,
§12-13-37.
Oath of office, §12-1-14.
Powers, §12-1-14.
Qualifications, §12-1-14.

PROBATE COURTS—Cont'd
Judges—Cont'd
Special judges—Cont'd
Refusal to act, death, etc.
Appointment of special
judge in event of
refusal, death, etc.,
of original special
judge, §12-13-38.
Successors.
Failure of clerk, etc., to
deliver books, papers,
money, etc., to
successor of probate
judge, §12-13-18.
Summary proceedings
involving officials,
§§6-6-720, 6-6-721,
6-6-723.
Supernumerary judges.
Continuation of laws
concerning duties,
benefits, etc.,
§12-13-70.
Retirement, §12-18-90.
Tax.
Recordation or registration
tax.
Failure to collect,
§12-13-53.
Terms of office, §12-13-30;
Const. Ala., art. VI,
§155.
Incumbents.
Terms of incumbents not
abridged, Const.
Ala., art. VI, §172.
Trusts and trustees.
Fiduciary funds in hands
of officials, §§19-3-80
to 19-3-87.
See FIDUCIARIES.
Vacancies, §12-18-86.
Acts which may be
performed by chief
clerk during vacancy
in office of probate
judge, §12-13-15.
Death.
Notice, §36-9-10.
Filling, §12-13-32.
Judgments.
Presumptions, §12-13-1.
Registration of judgments.
Probate judge, §§6-9-210,
6-9-212.
Validity, §12-13-1.
Jurisdiction.
Conservators.
Accounts of conservators.
Settlements, §26-5-1.
Settlements of accounts of
conservators.
Compulsion of
settlement.
Partial settlement,
§26-5-30.
Death of conservator,
§26-5-50.
Curators of mentally or
physically incapacitated
persons.
Appointment, §26-7A-1.
Federal service.
Person in federal service,
§12-13-2.
Generally, §12-13-1.

PROBATE COURTS—Cont'd
Jurisdiction—Cont'd
Guardian and ward.
Uniform guardianship and
protective proceedings
act.
Subject matter
jurisdiction,
§26-2A-31.
Water management and
drainage.
Districts.
Jurisdiction to establish,
§9-9-5.
Jury.
Disqualified, exempt and
empaneled jurors.
Certification to jury
commission, §12-16-78.
Drawing of jurors by probate
judge, §12-16-78.
Drawing of names from jury
box for juries in probate
court, §12-16-78.
Fees.
Jurors' fees, §§12-19-111 to
12-19-113.
Summoning jurors,
§12-16-78.
Letters of administration,
§§43-2-40 to 43-2-48.
See EXECUTORS AND
ADMINISTRATORS.
Letters testamentary,
§§43-2-20 to 43-2-29.
See EXECUTORS AND
ADMINISTRATORS.
Licenses.
Issuance of license.
Fee of probate judge,
§40-12-271.
Probate judge.
Disposition of moneys by
judge, §40-12-22.
Fee for issuing license,
§40-12-271.
Lists of motor vehicles.
Certification, §40-12-269.
Records to be kept by
judge, §40-12-21.
Remittance of moneys,
§40-12-269.
Proceeds.
Disbursement, §40-12-270.
Lis pendens, §§35-4-130,
35-4-139.
Location.
Where cases may be heard in
counties where terms
held in places other than
county seat, §12-13-4.
Mentally ill.
Commitment, §§22-52-35,
22-52-36.
Curator.
Appointment, §26-7A-1.
Proceedings to pass upon
soundness of mind of
person.
Jurors' fees, §12-19-113.
Witness fees, §12-19-135.
Motor vehicles.
General provisions.
See MOTOR VEHICLES.
Names.
Change of name.
Jurisdiction of probate
courts, §12-13-1.
New trials, §12-13-11.

PROBATE COURTS—Cont'd
Next friend.
Appeals by next friends of
minors or persons of
unsound mind,
§12-22-26.
Nonresidents.
Costs.
Security for costs in suits
by or for nonresidents,
§12-19-48.
Notaries public.
Commissioning.
Notaries public for state at
large, §36-20-30.
Report to secretary of
state, §36-20-1.
Orders.
Amendment.
Limitation period,
§12-13-3.
Presumptions, §12-13-1.
Setting aside limitation
period, §12-13-3.
Validity, §12-13-1.
When courts deemed open for
making, §12-13-3.
Partition, §§35-6-40 to 35-6-66.
See PARTITION.
Pensions.
Retirement of judges,
§§12-18-80 to 12-18-92.
See within this heading,
"Judges."
Personal property.
Trial of right of property.
Return where execution
issued from probate
court, §6-6-165.
Pleading.
Applicability of provisions
pertaining to pleading in
circuit courts, §12-13-12.
Powers, Const. Ala., art. VI,
§149.
Practice.
Applicability of provisions
pertaining to practice in
circuit courts, §12-13-12.
Presumptions.
Judgments, orders, etc.
Presumptions to be
accorded to, §12-13-1.
Probate of wills.
General provisions.
See WILLS.
Process.
When process of courts may
be made returnable,
§12-13-6.
Public welfare, §§38-1-3,
38-1-4.
Real estate brokers.
List of licensees.
Commission to provide
upon request of judge,
§34-27-5.
Recordation.
General provisions.
See RECORDATION.
Registration of judgments.
Probate judge, §§6-9-210,
6-9-212.
Reopening of cases.
Limitation period, §12-13-3.
Retirement.
Judges, §§12-18-80 to
12-18-92. See within this
heading, "Judges."
Sale of land for taxes.
See TAXATION.

PROBATE COURTS—Cont'd
Sales.
Going out of business or
distress merchandise
sales.
When probate judge to
issue license, §8-13-9.
Settlements of estates.
Correction of errors in
probate court, §12-11-60.
Sheriffs.
Liability for failure to take
money on or return
execution issued by
probate court, §12-13-17.
Special judges. See within
this heading, "Judges."
Supernumerary judges,
§§12-13-70, 12-18-90.
Taxation.
See TAXATION.
United States.
Condemnation of land or
rights-of-way.
Jurisdiction of probate
court, §42-2-1.
Validity.
Judgments, orders, etc.,
§12-13-1.
Venue.
Change of venue, §12-13-10.
**Water management and
drainage.**
Districts.
See WATER
MANAGEMENT AND
DRAINAGE.
Welfare, §§38-1-3, 38-1-4.
**Where cases may be heard
in counties where terms
held in places other than
county seat,** §12-13-4.
Wills.
General provisions.
See WILLS.
Witnesses.
Fees, §§12-19-135, 12-19-136.

PROBATION.
**Administrative procedure
act.**
Applicability, §15-18-8.1.
Arrest.
Violations of probation
terms, §15-22-54.
**Authority of circuit and
district courts,** §15-22-50.
Compacts.
Interstate compacts,
§15-22-1.
Conditions of probation,
§15-22-52.
Effect of fullfillment,
§15-18-8.
Modification, §15-18-8.
Constitution of Alabama.
Legislature to regulate,
Const. Ala., amd. 38.
Costs.
Assessment and payment of
termination costs,
§15-22-55.
Contributions by
probationers toward costs
of supervision and
rehabilitation, §15-22-2.

PROBATION—Cont'd
Costs—Cont'd
Misdemeanant required to
pay costs of
incarceration.
Payment of costs as
condition of probation,
§14-6-22.
Desertion and nonsupport.
Criminal proceedings.
See DESERTION AND
NONSUPPORT.
Fees.
Intensive supervision
program, §15-22-56.
Felonies.
Authorized, §13A-5-2.
**Intensive supervision
program,** §15-22-56.
Investigations.
Board to investigate
sentenced prisoner's
social and criminal
records, §15-22-25.
Probation officer to
investigate defendant,
§15-22-51.
Juvenile probation.
General provisions,
§§12-15-74, 12-15-75.
Youth services, §§44-1-24,
44-1-26.
Legislature.
Regulation of probation,
Const. Ala., amd. 38.
Misdemeanors.
Authorized, §13A-5-2.
Municipal courts, §12-14-13.
Period of probation,
§15-22-54.
**Placement of convicted
persons on probation.**
Generally, §15-18-8.
Probation officers.
Child labor.
See LABOR.
Investigations, §15-22-51.
Juvenile proceedings,
§§12-15-7, 12-15-15.
Powers and duties, §15-22-53.
Records.
Confidentiality, §15-22-53.
Records.
Board to report on sentenced
prisoner's social and
criminal records,
§15-22-25.
Confidentiality of probation
officers' records,
§15-22-53.
Reports.
Board to report on sentenced
prisoner's social and
criminal records,
§15-22-25.
Defendant to report to
probation authorities
during term of probation,
§15-18-8.
**Restitution to victims of
crimes.**
Default by probationer.
Effect, §15-18-72.
Payment of restitution as
condition to probation,
§15-18-70.
Revocation of probation,
§15-18-8.

PROBATION—Cont'd
Rules and regulations.
Administration procedure
act.
Applicability, §15-18-8.1.
Supervision.
Intensive supervision
program, §15-22-56.
Termination, §15-22-54.
Assessment and payment of
costs of termination,
§15-22-55.
Violations.
Arrest and disposition of
person, §15-22-54.
Persons convicted of
violations may be placed
on probation, §13A-5-2.
Youthful offenders.
Court authorized to post
probation, §15-19-6.
Juvenile probation generally,
§§12-15-74, 12-15-75.

PROCESS.
Service of process.
See SERVICE OF PROCESS.
Simulating legal process,
§13A-10-131.
Summons and process.
See SUMMONS AND
PROCESS.

PRODUCTS LIABILITY.
Applicability of division,
§6-5-503.
Collateral source rule.
Modified, §6-5-520.
Damages.
Collateral source rule.
Modification, §6-5-520.
Mitigation of recoverable
damages.
Evidence of medical
expense
reimbursement,
§6-5-522.
Legislative findings and
intent, §6-5-520.
Reimbursement of medical
expenses.
Cost of obtaining
reimbursement
recoverable, §6-5-522.
Definitions, §6-5-501.
Product liability actions,
§6-5-521.
Evidence.
Discovery.
Reimbursement of medical
expenses discoverable,
§6-5-523.
Mitigation of damages.
Reimbursement for medical
expenses admissible,
§6-5-522.
Reimbursement for medical
or hospital expenses.
Inadmissible if recipient
must pay, §6-5-524.
Legislative findings and
intent, §6-5-500.
Limitation of actions,
§6-5-502.
Prior rights of parties not
affected, §6-5-525.
Retroactive, §6-5-503.
Severability of provisions.
Sections and clauses of
division inseparable and
nonseverable, §6-5-504.

PRODUCTS MARTS.
Bond issues.
Southern products mart
authority, §§41-10-55 to
41-10-69.
State products mart and
coliseum authority,
§§41-10-93 to 41-10-108.
See within this heading,
"State products mart and
coliseum authority."
Definitions.
Southern products mart
authority, §41-10-51.
State products mart and
coliseum authority,
§41-10-81.
Southern products mart
authority, §§41-10-55 to
41-10-69.
Accounts and accounting.
Audit of books and
accounts of authority,
§41-10-66.
Agreements.
Liability upon agreements
of authority, §41-10-62.
Audits.
Annual audit of books and
accounts of authority,
§41-10-66.
Bond issues, §§41-10-55 to
41-10-69.
Authorization of issuance
and sale, §§41-10-55,
41-10-56.
Consent of department of
finance, etc., not a
prerequisite to
issuance, §41-10-58.
Delivery, §41-10-57.
Denominations, §41-10-55.
Disposition of proceeds
from sale, §41-10-60.
Execution, §41-10-57.
Exemption from taxation,
§41-10-61.
Form, §41-10-55.
Hearings.
Public hearing not a
prerequisite to
issuance, §41-10-58.
Investment of trust funds
in bonds, §41-10-61.
Issuance.
Authorized, §§41-10-55,
41-10-56.
Public hearing not a
prerequisite to,
§41-10-58.
Liability upon bonds,
§41-10-62.
Negotiable instruments,
§41-10-55.
Payment, §§41-10-55,
41-10-65.
Conveyance of lands,
buildings, properties,
etc., of authority to
state upon payment
in full of bonds,
§41-10-69.
Default in payment.
Remedies, §41-10-63.

PRODUCTS MARTS—Cont'd
Southern products mart
authority—Cont'd
Bond issues—Cont'd
Payment—Cont'd
Pledge of revenues of
authority and
creation of statutory
lien upon facilities
and properties of
authority for
payment.
Authority in
procedure,
§41-10-63.
Records pertaining to
payment.
Maintenance by state
treasurer,
§41-10-65.
Remedies upon default in
payment, §41-10-63.
Trust fund for payment.
Special and continuing
trust fund,
§41-10-64.
Redemption, §41-10-55.
Refunding bonds,
§41-10-59.
Disposition of proceeds
from sale, §41-10-60.
Resolution authorizing
issuance to contain
recital as to authority
for issuance, §41-10-56.
Sale, §41-10-58.
Authorized, §41-10-55.
Disposition of proceeds
from sale, §41-10-60.
State funds.
Use of bonds as security
for deposits of state
funds, §41-10-61.
Taxation.
Exemption from
taxation, §41-10-61.
Terms, §41-10-55.
Trust funds.
Investment in bonds,
§41-10-61.
Validity.
Limitation period and
venue for actions to
contest validity of
resolutions, bonds,
etc., §41-10-56.
Buildings.
Construction.
Generally, §41-10-67.
Conveyance to state upon
payment in full of
bonds, §41-10-69.
Leasing, §41-10-68.
Construction of article,
§41-10-52.
Construction of facilities,
buildings and structures,
§41-10-67.
Contracts.
Construction of facilities,
buildings and
structures, §41-10-67.
Liability upon agreements
of authority, §41-10-62.
Debts.
Liability upon debts of
authority, §41-10-62.
Definitions, §41-10-51.
Directors of authority,
§41-10-53.
Dissolution, §41-10-69.

PRODUCTS MARTS—Cont'd
Southern products mart authority—Cont'd
Eminent domain.
  Acquisition by eminent domain of real property or rights owned by railroads or utilities not authorized, §41-10-54.
Exemption from taxation, §41-10-61.
Facilities.
  Construction.
    Awarding of contracts for construction, §41-10-67.
    Supervision of construction, §41-10-67.
  Leasing, §41-10-68.
  Maintenance.
    Special and continuing trust fund for maintenance, §41-10-64.
  Trust fund.
    Special and continuing trust fund for maintenance of facilities, §41-10-64.
Funds.
  Special and continuing trust fund for payment of bonds and maintenance of facilities of authority, §41-10-64.
Income.
  Exemption from taxation, §41-10-61.
Incorporation, §41-10-53.
Lands of authority.
  Conveyance to state upon payment in full of bonds, §41-10-69.
Leases.
  Buildings, facilities and structures, §41-10-68.
Maintenance of facilities of authority.
  Special and continuing trust fund for maintenance, §41-10-64.
Members of authority, §41-10-53.
Officers of authority, §41-10-53.
Powers of authority, §41-10-54.
Property.
  Conveyance to state upon payment in full of bonds, §41-10-69.
  Exemption from taxation, §41-10-61.
Purpose of article, §41-10-52.
Railroads.
  Acquisition by eminent domain of rights owned by railroads not authorized, §41-10-54.
Real property.
  Acquisition by eminent domain not authorized, §41-10-54.
Records.
  Payment of bond issues, §41-10-65.

PRODUCTS MARTS—Cont'd
Southern products mart authority—Cont'd
Reports.
  Disposition of reports of annual audit, §41-10-66.
Short title, §41-10-50.
Structures.
  Construction, §41-10-67.
  Leasing, §41-10-68.
Taxation.
  Exemption from taxation, §41-10-61.
Utilities.
  Acquisition by eminent domain of rights owned by utilities not authorized, §41-10-54.
State products mart and coliseum authority, §§41-10-80 to 41-10-108.
Appropriations.
  Authorized by municipalities or counties, §41-10-106.
Attorneys at law.
  Bond issues.
    Attorneys' fees.
      Maximum amount payable to attorneys for services rendered, §41-10-98.
Board of directors, §§41-10-87 to 41-10-89.
  Additional members.
    Appointment, §41-10-89.
    Terms of office, §41-10-89.
  Compensation of members, §41-10-87.
  Composition, §41-10-87.
  Election of members, §41-10-88.
  Reelection, §41-10-87.
  Evidence.
    Recordation and admissibility in evidence of proceedings of board, §41-10-87.
  Expenses of members, §41-10-87.
  Qualifications, §41-10-87.
  Quorum, §41-10-87.
  Reelection of members, §41-10-87.
  Terms of members, §§41-10-88, 41-10-89.
  Vacancies, §41-10-87.
Bond issues, §§41-10-93 to 41-10-108.
  Attorneys' fees.
    Maximum amount payable to attorneys for services rendered, §41-10-98.
  Authority for issuance, §41-10-93.
    Bonds to contain recital as to authority, §41-10-93.
    Notice of resolution authorizing issuance, §41-10-94.
  Payment of expenses in connection with authorization, §41-10-93.

PRODUCTS MARTS—Cont'd
State products mart and coliseum authority—Cont'd
Bond issues—Cont'd
  County funds.
    Investment of surplus county funds in bonds, §41-10-100.
  Default in payment.
    Remedies upon default, §41-10-102.
  Delivery, §41-10-95.
  Denominations, §41-10-93.
  Disposition of proceeds from sale, §41-10-97.
  Execution, §41-10-95.
    Proceeds of bonds not to be used for payment of fees, commissions, etc., for services in execution, §41-10-98.
  Exemption from taxation, §41-10-107.
  Expenses.
    Payment of expenses in connection with authorization, sale and issuance, §41-10-93.
  Fiduciaries.
    Investment in bonds, §41-10-101.
  Form, §41-10-93.
  Insurance companies.
    Investment in bonds, §41-10-101.
  Investments.
    County funds.
      Investment of surplus county funds in bonds, §41-10-100.
    Fiduciaries.
      Investment in bonds, §41-10-101.
    Insurance companies.
      Investment in bonds, §41-10-101.
    Savings and investment in bonds, §41-10-101.
  Issuance.
    Authority for issuance, §§41-10-93, 41-10-94.
    Expenses.
      Payment of expenses in connection with authorization and issuance, §41-10-93.
    Proceeds of bonds not to be used for payment of fees, commissions, etc., for services in issuance, §41-10-98.
  Liability upon bonds, §41-10-93.
  Limitation period for actions contesting validity, §41-10-94.
  Negotiable instruments, §41-10-93.
  Payment.
    Default in payment.
      Remedies upon default, §41-10-102.
    Security for payment, §41-10-96.
  Vesting of title to projects upon payment in full, §41-10-108.

PRODUCTS MARTS—Cont'd
State products mart and coliseum authority
—Cont'd
Bond issues—Cont'd
Proceeds from sale.
Disposition, §41-10-97.
Not to be used for payment of fees, commissions, etc., for services in sale, issuance, execution, etc., of bonds, §41-10-98.
Redemption, §41-10-93.
Refunding bonds, §41-10-99.
Remedies upon default, §41-10-102.
Sale, §41-10-93.
Disposition of proceeds from sale, §41-10-97.
Expenses.
Payment of expenses in connection with sale, §41-10-93.
Proceeds from sale.
Disposition, §41-10-97.
Not to be used for payment of fees, commissions, etc., for services in sale, issuance, etc., of bonds, §41-10-98.
Savings banks.
Investment in bonds, §41-10-101.
Security for payment, §41-10-96.
Taxation.
Exemption from taxation, §41-10-107.
Terms, §41-10-93.
Trustees.
Investment in bonds, §41-10-101.
Validity.
Limitation period for actions contesting validity, §41-10-94.
Construction of article, §§41-10-82, 41-10-109.
Counties.
Appropriations to corporation by county authorized, §41-10-106.
Bond issues.
Investment of surplus county funds in bonds of corporation, §41-10-100.
Conveyances of property to corporation by county authorized, §41-10-105.
Subsequent formations, §41-10-108.
Definitions, §41-10-81.
Dissolution of corporation, §41-10-108.
Eminent domain.
Powers of corporation, §41-10-92.
Evidence.
Proceedings of board of directors.
Admissibility in evidence, §41-10-87.
Exemptions from taxation, §41-10-107.

PRODUCTS MARTS—Cont'd
State products mart and coliseum authority
—Cont'd
Exhibits.
Conduct in projects, §41-10-104.
Income.
Exemption from taxation, §41-10-107.
Incorporation.
Application for, §41-10-83.
Authorization.
Adoption by governing body of resolution, §41-10-83.
Certificate of incorporation.
Amendment, §41-10-86.
Contents, §41-10-84.
Execution, §41-10-85.
Filing, §41-10-85.
Recordation, §41-10-85.
Resolution by governing body approving form and contents of certificate, §41-10-84.
Subsequent formation.
Formation of corporation not to prevent subsequent formation of other corporations by same county, §41-10-108.
Leasing of projects, §41-10-103.
Municipal corporations.
Appropriations to corporation by municipality authorized, §41-10-106.
Conveyances of property to corporation by municipality authorized, §41-10-105.
Officers of corporation, §41-10-90.
Powers of corporation.
Eminent domain, §41-10-92.
Generally, §41-10-91.
Projects.
Conduct of sporting events, exhibits, etc., in projects, §41-10-104.
Exemption from taxation, §41-10-107.
Leasing, §41-10-103.
Vesting of title to projects upon payment of bonds, §41-10-108.
Property.
Conveyances to corporation by municipality, county or state authorized, §41-10-105.
Exemption from taxation, §41-10-107.
Vesting of title to properties of corporation upon dissolution, §41-10-108.
Purpose of article, §41-10-82.
Recordation.
Certificate of incorporation, §41-10-85.
Proceedings of board of directors, §41-10-87.
Short title of article, §41-10-80.

PRODUCTS MARTS—Cont'd
State products mart and coliseum authority
—Cont'd
Sporting events.
Conduct in projects, §41-10-104.
State.
Conveyances of property to corporation by state authorized, §41-10-105.
Taxation.
Exemption from taxation, §41-10-107.

PROFANITY.
See OBSCENITY.

PROFESSIONAL ASSOCIATIONS.
Unincorporated professional associations, §§10-1-1 to 10-1-16.
See UNINCORPORATED PROFESSIONAL ASSOCIATIONS.

PROFESSIONAL CORPORATIONS, §§10-4-380 to 10-4-406.
Accountants.
See ACCOUNTANTS.
Applicability of article.
Existing corporations, §10-4-403.
Generally, §10-4-384.
Professional associations, §10-4-406.
Articles of incorporation.
Amendments, §10-4-394.
Penalties for false statements, §10-4-401.
Profession limited by, §10-4-385.
Business corporation act.
Applicability, §10-4-381.
Charter, §10-1-1.
Consolidation, §10-4-395.
Death.
Stock and stockholders.
Transfer of shares upon death of shareholder, §10-4-389.
Definitions, §§6-5-481, 10-4-382.
Directors, §10-4-393.
Dissolution.
Involuntary dissolution.
Request of licensing authority, §10-4-396.
Domestic professional corporation.
Defined, §10-4-382.
Existing corporations.
Applicability of article, §10-4-403.
Foreign professional corporations.
Admission, §10-4-397.
Certificate of authority.
Qualification, §10-4-397.
Required, §10-4-397.
Revocation, §10-4-398.
Defined, §10-4-382.
Reports.
Annual report, §10-4-394.
Interrogatories.
Licensing authority.
Penalties for false statements, §10-4-401.
Procedure upon failure to answer, §10-4-401.

PROFESSIONAL CORPORATIONS—Cont'd
Interrogatories—Cont'd
Licensing authority—Cont'd
Propounding to any
professional
corporation, §10-4-400.
Investments, §10-4-385.
Liability.
Effect of article on
professional liability,
§10-4-390.
Licensing authority.
Article does not restrict
regulation by, §10-4-402.
Defined, §10-4-382.
Interrogatories.
Penalties for false
statements, §10-4-401.
Procedure upon failure to
answer, §10-4-401.
Propounding to any
professional
corporation, §10-4-400.
Involuntary dissolution.
Request of authority,
§10-4-396.
Malpractice.
Definition of professional
corporation, §6-5-481.
Effect of article on
professional liability,
§10-4-390.
Merger, §10-4-395.
Names.
Corporate name, §10-4-387.
Nonprofit corporation act.
Applicability, §10-4-381.
Officers, §10-4-393.
Penalties.
False statements, answers,
etc., §10-4-401.
Powers generally, §10-4-385.
Privileged communications.
Effect of article on privileged
communications,
§10-4-391.
Professional associations.
Applicability of article to
unincorporated
professional associations,
§10-4-406.
Professional relationships.
Effect of article on
professional
relationships, §10-4-391.
Professional services.
Defined, §10-4-382.
Rendition, §10-4-386.
Purposes, §10-4-383.
Qualified person.
Defined, §10-4-382.
Real estate brokers.
Death, disability or
retirement of licensed
broker, §34-27-32.
Fee, §34-27-35.
Licensed broker required as
designated officer,
§34-27-32.
Relationships.
Effect of article on
professional
relationships, §10-4-391.
**Rendition of professional
services,** §10-4-386.
Repeal of prior acts.
Effect, §10-4-405.

PROFESSIONAL CORPORATIONS—Cont'd
Reports.
Annual report, §10-4-399.
Penalties for false
statements, §10-4-401.
**Reservation of power of
legislature,** §10-4-404.
Short title of article,
§10-4-380.
Stock and stockholders.
Death of shareholder.
Transfer of shares upon
death, §10-4-389.
Disqualification of
shareholders.
Transfer of shares upon
disqualification,
§10-4-389.
Issuance of shares, §10-4-388.
**Unincorporated professional
associations,** §§10-1-1 to
10-1-16.
See UNINCORPORATED
PROFESSIONAL
ASSOCIATIONS.
Voting trusts.
All trustees and beneficiaries
to be qualified persons,
§10-4-392.

**PROFESSIONS AND
OCCUPATIONS,** §§34-1-1
to 34-38-8.
Accountants, §§34-1-1 to
34-1-32.
See ACCOUNTANTS.
Air conditioning contractors.
General provisions, §§34-31-1
to 34-31-34.
See HEATING AND AIR
CONDITIONING
CONTRACTORS.
Architects.
General provisions, §§34-2-1
to 34-2-42.
See ARCHITECTS.
Landscape architects,
§§34-17-1 to 34-17-27.
See LANDSCAPE
ARCHITECTS.
Associations.
Unincorporated professional
associations.
General provisions,
§§10-10-1 to 10-10-16.
See UNINCORPORATED
PROFESSIONAL
ASSOCIATIONS.
Attorneys at law, §§34-3-1 to
34-3-108.
See ATTORNEYS AT LAW.
Auctioneers.
General provisions, §§34-4-1
to 34-4-54.
See AUCTIONS AND
AUCTIONEERS.
Audiologists.
General provisions,
§§34-28A-1 to
34-28A-44.
See SPEECH
PATHOLOGISTS AND
AUDIOLOGISTS.
Barbers, §§34-5-1 to 34-5-16.
See BARBERS.
Beauticians.
General provisions, §§34-7-1
to 34-7-47.
See COSMETOLOGISTS.

**PROFESSIONS AND
OCCUPATIONS**—Cont'd
Chiropractors.
General provisions,
§§34-24-120 to 34-24-176.
See CHIROPRACTORS.
Contractors.
Electrical contractors,
§§34-36-1 to 34-36-17.
See ELECTRICAL
CONTRACTORS.
General provisions, §§34-8-1
to 34-8-27.
See CONTRACTORS.
Heating and air conditioning
contractors, §§34-31-1 to
34-31-34.
See HEATING AND AIR
CONDITIONING
CONTRACTORS.
Corporations.
Professional corporations.
General provisions,
§§10-4-380 to 10-4-406.
See PROFESSIONAL
CORPORATIONS.
Cosmetologists, §§34-7-1 to
34-7-47.
See COSMETOLOGISTS.
Counselors, §§34-8A-1 to
34-8A-23.
See COUNSELORS.
Dental hygienists.
See DENTISTS.
Dentists.
General provisions, §§34-9-1
to 34-9-65.
See DENTISTS.
Impaired professionals,
§§34-38-1 to 34-38-8.
See DENTISTS.
Designers.
Interior designers,
§§34-15A-1 to 34-15A-7.
See INTERIOR
DESIGNERS.
Landscape architects,
§§34-17-1 to 34-17-27.
See LANDSCAPE
ARCHITECTS.
Dietitians.
General provisions, §§34-34-1
to 34-34-4.
Practice act, §§34-34A-1 to
34-34A-15.
See DIETITIANS AND
NUTRITIONISTS.
Electrical contractors,
§§34-36-1 to 34-36-17.
See ELECTRICAL
CONTRACTORS.
Embalmers.
General provisions,
§§34-13-90 to 34-13-94.
Employment agencies,
§§34-10-1 to 34-10-5.
Engineers.
General provisions, §§34-11-1
to 34-11-37.
See ENGINEERS.
Foresters, §§34-12-1 to
34-12-37.
See FORESTS AND
FORESTRY.
Funeral directors.
General provisions,
§§34-13-70 to 34-13-74.

PROFESSIONS AND OCCUPATIONS—Cont'd
Gas fitters.
Plumbers and gas fitters generally, §§34-37-1 to 34-37-18.
See PLUMBING.
Hearing aid dealers and fitters, §§34-14-1 to 34-14-33.
See HEARING AID DEALERS AND FITTERS.
Heating contractors.
General provisions, §§34-31-1 to 34-31-34.
See HEATING AND AIR CONDITIONING CONTRACTORS.
Injunctions.
Enjoining unauthorized or unlawful practice, §6-6-503.
Interior designers, §§34-15A-1 to 34-15A-7.
See INTERIOR DESIGNERS.
Junk dealers.
Junkyard control, §§23-1-240 to 23-1-251.
See JUNKYARD CONTROL.
Licenses, §40-12-116.
Milk and milk products.
Marked containers.
Possession by junk dealer prima facie evidence of violation, §8-12-42.
Salvage generally, §§35-13-1 to 35-13-10.
See SALVAGE.
Landscape architects, §§34-17-1 to 34-17-27.
See LANDSCAPE ARCHITECTS.
Lie detectors, §§34-25-1 to 34-25-36.
See POLYGRAPH EXAMINERS.
Medical technicians, §§34-18-1 to 34-18-47.
See MEDICAL TECHNICIANS.
Midwives, §§34-19-2 to 34-19-10.
See MIDWIVES.
Nurses, §§34-21-1 to 34-21-63.
See NURSES.
Nursing home administrators, §§34-20-1 to 34-20-16.
See NURSING HOMES.
Nutritionists.
General provisions, §§34-34-1 to 34-34-4.
Practice act, §§34-34A-1 to 34-34A-15.
See DIETITIANS AND NUTRITIONISTS.
Optometrists, §§34-22-1 to 34-22-65.
See OPTOMETRISTS.
Osteopaths.
Physicians generally, §§34-24-50 to 34-24-78, 34-24-310 to 34-24-406.
See PHYSICIANS.

PROFESSIONS AND OCCUPATIONS—Cont'd
Pharmacists.
General provisions, §§34-23-1 to 34-23-118.
See PHARMACISTS AND PHARMACIES.
Impaired professionals, §§34-38-1 to 34-38-8.
See PHARMACISTS AND PHARMACIES.
Physical therapists, §§34-24-190 to 34-24-217.
See PHYSICAL THERAPISTS.
Physicians.
General provisions, §§34-24-50 to 34-24-78, 34-24-310 to 34-24-406.
See PHYSICIANS.
Plumbing, §§34-37-1 to 34-37-18.
See PLUMBING.
Podiatrists, §§34-24-230 to 34-24-276.
See PODIATRISTS.
Polygraph examiners, §§34-25-1 to 34-25-36.
See POLYGRAPH EXAMINERS.
Psychologists, §§34-26-1 to 34-26-48.
See PSYCHOLOGISTS.
Quo warranto.
Judgments.
Prohibiting practice of profession, §6-6-600.
Usurpation of profession.
Right of action and venue, §6-6-591.
Real estate brokers, §§34-27-1 to 34-27-69.
See REAL ESTATE BROKERS.
Social workers, §§34-30-1 to 34-30-58.
See SOCIAL WORKERS.
Soil classifiers, §§34-32-1 to 34-32-19.
See SOIL CLASSIFIERS.
Speech pathologists.
General provisions, §§34-28A-1 to 34-28A-44.
See SPEECH PATHOLOGISTS AND AUDIOLOGISTS.
Surveyors.
General provisions, §§34-11-1 to 34-11-37.
See SURVEYS AND SURVEYORS.
Transient merchants, §§34-35-1 to 34-35-9.
See TRANSIENT MERCHANTS.
Veterinarians, §§34-29-60 to 34-29-94.
See VETERINARIANS.

PROFITS FROM CRIME, §§41-9-80 to 31-9-84.
Applicability of article, §41-9-84.
Escrow accounts.
Restitution to victims, §41-9-80.
Reversion to state after five years, §41-9-82.
Limitations.
Escrow account, §41-9-83.

PROFITS FROM CRIME —Cont'd
Payment to board of adjustment, §41-9-80.
Records.
Criminal for whom money held in escrow.
Public access to records, §41-9-81.
Son of Sam law, §§15-18-140 to 15-18-151.
See RESTITUTION TO VICTIMS OF CRIMES.
Victims.
Escrow account, §41-9-80.

PROHIBITION LAW.
Alcoholic beverages.
Dry counties, §§28-4-1 to 28-4-326.
See ALCOHOLIC BEVERAGES.

PROHIBITION, WRIT OF.
Appeals.
Judgments on applications for remedial writs, §12-22-6.
Review in supreme court of decisions of courts of appeals.
Rules of appellate procedure, ARAP, Rule 21.
Commencement by petition, §6-6-640.
Court of civil appeals.
Review in supreme court of decisions of.
Rules of appellate procedure, ARAP, Rule 21.
Court of criminal appeals.
Review in supreme court of decisions of.
Rules of appellate procedure, ARAP, Rule 21.
Directed to judge or judges, ARAP, Rule 21.
Judges.
Directed to judge or judges, ARAP, Rule 21.
Petitions.
Rules of appellate procedure, ARAP, Rule 21.
Rules of appellate procedure, ARAP, Rule 21.
Supreme court.
Review in supreme court of decisions of courts of appeals.
Rules of appellate procedure, ARAP, Rule 21.

PROMISSORY ESTOPPEL.
Affirmative defense, ARCP, Rule 8 (c).
Partnerships.
Liability of partner by estoppel, §10-8-55.

PROMISSORY NOTES.
Commercial code.
See COMMERCIAL CODE.
General provisions.
See NEGOTIABLE INSTRUMENTS.

PROMPT PAYMENT LAW.
Public contracts, §41-16-3.

PROOF OF FINANCIAL RESPONSIBILITY.
Safety-responsibility act, §§32-7-1 to 32-7-42.
See MOTOR VEHICLES.

PROPAGANDA.
Instruction in history, doctrines, etc., of communism, §16-40-3.

PROPAGATION.
Fish and game.
See FISH AND GAME.

PROPERTY.
Affidavits.
Seizure of property.
Procedure, ARCP, Rule 64 (b).
Aliens.
Right of aliens to take, hold and transmit property, §35-1-1.
Attachments.
See ATTACHMENTS.
Banks and financial institutions.
See BANKS AND FINANCIAL INSTITUTIONS.
Bishop of diocese.
Power of corporation, §10-4-4.
Blind persons.
Assistance to needy blind persons.
Hospitalization.
Cost not to constitute lien, §38-5-5.
Retention of certain property by applicant, §38-5-4.
Bridges.
See BRIDGES.
Cemeteries.
Sale and conveyance, §10-4-25.
Effect of recital in minutes on proceedings, §10-4-26.
Constitution of Alabama.
Sale of property of any individual or estate.
Special, private or local laws providing for sale prohibited, Const. Ala., art. IV, §104.
Counties.
See COUNTIES.
County industrial development authorities.
Dissolution of authority.
Vesting of title to property, §11-92A-22.
Credit unions.
See CREDIT UNIONS.
Criminal damage to property.
Criminal tampering.
Definitions, §13A-7-24.
First degree criminal tampering, §13A-7-25.
Second degree criminal tampering, §13A-7-26.
Definitions, §13A-7-20.
First degree criminal mischief, §13A-7-21.
Second degree criminal mischief, §13A-7-22.
Third degree criminal mischief, §13A-7-23.

PROPERTY—Cont'd
Dams.
Erection of dams for mills, gins, factories or electric generators.
Assessment of lands.
See DAMS.
Defined, §1-1-1.
Disclaimer of property interests, §§43-8-290 to 43-8-298.
See DISCLAIMER OF INTERESTS IN PROPERTY.
District courts.
Seizure of property.
Rules of civil procedure.
Procedure for seizure of property.
Applicability of rules to district courts, ARCP, Rule 64 (b).
Education.
See EDUCATION.
Electric cooperatives, §§37-6-18, 37-6-21, 37-6-23.
Electric membership corporations, §§37-7-10, 37-7-11.
Eminent domain.
General provisions.
See EMINENT DOMAIN.
Executions.
See EXECUTIONS.
Exemptions from property.
HUD 202 property, §40-9-1.
Fiduciaries.
Management.
Standards for fiduciary investment and management, §19-3-120.2.
Fish and game.
State game lands, §§9-11-2, 9-11-3.
Forests and forestry.
See FORESTS AND FORESTRY.
Fraternal orders.
Right of majority group of local organization in fraternal property, §10-4-171.
Use of fraternal property free from trust clause, §10-4-172.
Governor.
Control of state property, §36-13-10.
Guardian and ward.
Removal of person or property of minors and wards, §§26-8-1 to 26-8-52.
See GUARDIAN AND WARD.
Hearings.
Seizure of property.
Rules of civil procedure.
Procedure, ARCP, Rule 64 (b).
Hospitals.
Public hospitals.
See HOSPITALS.
Husband and wife.
See HUSBAND AND WIFE.
Indictments.
Alleging ownership of property, §15-8-33.

PROPERTY—Cont'd
Industrial development authority.
Dissolution of authority.
Title to property of authority to vest in state upon dissolution, §41-10-32.
Industrial development corporations.
Powers, §10-4-133.
Industrial parks.
Acquisition and development.
Powers of counties and municipalities, §11-92-3.
Insurance.
See INSURANCE.
Jacksonville state university.
Certain state property vested in university, §16-52-16.
Rights, privileges, responsibilities, etc., of corporation, §16-52-2.
Junior college for Franklin, Marion and Winston counties.
Exemption from taxation, §16-60-35.
Sale of property, §16-60-24.
Junior college for Jackson and DeKalb counties.
Exemption of college property from taxation, §16-60-65.
Sale of property of college, §16-60-54.
Littering.
Criminal littering, §13A-7-29.
Livingston university.
Rights, privileges, responsibilities, etc., of corporation, §16-53-2.
Lost or unclaimed property, §§35-12-21 to 35-12-48.
See LOST OR UNCLAIMED PROPERTY.
Mental health finance authority.
Dissolution of authority.
Disposition of property upon, §41-10-369.
Powers as to property, §41-10-356.
Military property.
General provisions.
See MILITARY AFFAIRS.
Minors.
Conveyances of personalty to minors, §35-4-96.
Conveyances of realty to minors.
Powers of disposition.
Disposition to or among children, §35-4-300.
Destruction of property by minor.
Liability of parents, §6-5-380.
Transfers to minors, §§35-5A-1 to 35-5A-24.
See TRANSFERS TO MINORS.
Municipal corporations.
See MUNICIPAL CORPORATIONS.
Partnerships.
See PARTNERSHIPS.

PROPERTY—Cont'd

Personal property.
See PERSONAL PROPERTY.

Public lands.
See PUBLIC LANDS.

Public officers and employees.
Public property, papers, etc.
See PUBLIC OFFICERS AND EMPLOYEES.

Public utilities.
See PUBLIC UTILITIES.

Public welfare.
See WELFARE.

Railroad authorities.
Dissolution of authority.
Effect, §37-13-21.
Powers as to, §37-13-7.
Taxation.
Exemption from taxation, §37-13-16.

Railroads.
See RAILROADS.

Real property.
See REAL PROPERTY.

Removal of person or property of minors and wards, §§26-8-1 to 26-8-52.
See GUARDIAN AND WARD.

Salvage.
See SALVAGE.

Savings and loan associations.
See SAVINGS AND LOAN ASSOCIATIONS.

Searches and seizures.
See SEARCHES AND SEIZURES.

Sentencing.
Forfeiture of property.
Article not to deprive court of authority, §13A-5-2.

Snead junior college.
Governor authorized to accept property, §16-60-150.

Southern union college.
Acceptance of facilities by governor, §16-60-130.

State property.
Buildings.
Rent charged for use, §41-4-17.
Contracts for sale of certain state property.
See CONTRACTS.
Governor.
Control of state property, §36-13-10.
Property inventory control division, §§36-16-8 to 36-16-11.
Public buildings.
See PUBLIC BUILDINGS.
Public lands.
See PUBLIC LANDS.

Stolen property.
See STOLEN PROPERTY.

Tennessee Valley Authority.
Exhibit commission.
Powers as to, §41-9-782.

Troy State University.
Rights, privileges, responsibilities, etc., of corporation, §16-56-2.

Trusts and trustees.
See TRUSTS AND TRUSTEES.

PROPERTY—Cont'd

Unclaimed property,
§§35-12-21 to 35-12-48.
See LOST OR UNCLAIMED PROPERTY.

Unincorporated professional associations.
Conveyances, §10-10-9.

University of Alabama.
See UNIVERSITY OF ALABAMA.

University of Montevallo.
See UNIVERSITY OF MONTEVALLO.

University of North Alabama.
Rights, privileges, responsibilities, etc., of corporation, §16-51-2.

USS Alabama battleship commission.
Insurance, §41-9-351.

Utilities.
See PUBLIC UTILITIES.

Water conservation and irrigation.
See WATER CONSERVATION AND IRRIGATION.

Welfare.
See WELFARE.

Women.
Rights of females, Const. Ala., art. X, §209.

PROSECUTION SERVICES.

Office of prosecution services, §§12-17-230 to 12-17-234.

PROSECUTORS.

District attorneys.
See DISTRICT ATTORNEYS.

PROSTITUTION.

Actions for nuisance,
§§6-5-140 to 6-5-154.
See NUISANCES.

Advance prostitution.
Defined, §13A-12-110.

Definitions, §13A-12-110.

Houses of prostitution.
Prohibition by municipal corporations, §11-47-113.

Loitering.
Loitering for purposes of prostitution, §13A-11-9.

Nuisances.
Actions for nuisances, §§6-5-140 to 6-5-154.
See NUISANCES.

Pandering, §§13A-12-111 to 13A-12-113.

Profit from prostitution.
Defined, §13A-12-110.
Second degree promoting prostitution.
Felony, §13A-12-112.

Promoting prostitution.
First degree promotion, §13A-12-111.
Second degree promotion, §13A-12-112.
Third degree promotion, §13A-12-113.

PROTECTIVE SERVICES.

Adult protective services,
§§38-9-1 to 38-9-11.
See ADULT PROTECTIVE SERVICES.

PSILOCYBIN.

Controlled substances.
See DRUGS.

PSYCHIATRISTS.

Consent for health services,
§§22-8-1 to 22-8-9.
See HEALTH.

Privileged communications.
Psychiatrist-patient privilege, §34-26-2.

Professional corporations,
§§10-4-380 to 10-4-406.
See PROFESSIONAL CORPORATIONS.

PSYCHOLOGISTS, §§34-26-1 to 34-26-48.

American Psychological Association.
Adoption of association code of ethics, §34-26-3.

Appeals.
Refusal, suspension or revocation of licenses.
Review of action of board, §34-26-48.

Associations.
Professional corporations, §§10-4-380 to 10-4-406.
See PROFESSIONAL CORPORATIONS.
Unincorporated professional associations, §§10-1-1 to 10-1-16.
See UNINCORPORATED PROFESSIONAL ASSOCIATIONS.

Board of examiners.
Appointment of members.
Governor to appoint, §§34-26-20, 34-26-21.
Assistants.
Authority of board to employ, §34-26-21.
Authority of board.
Generally, §34-26-22.
Certification of psychologists.
Authority of board, §34-26-22.
Chairman.
Elections, §34-26-21.
Code of ethics.
Adoption by board, §34-26-3.
Creation, §34-26-20.
Examinations, §§34-26-43.1 to 34-26-45.
Expenses of members, §34-26-21.
Payment, §34-26-43.
Fees.
Disbursement of collected fees, §34-26-43.
Governor.
Appointment of members, §§34-26-20, 34-26-21.
Removal of members, §34-26-21.
Liability of members, §34-26-21.
List of registered psychologists.
Board to keep and make available, §34-26-22.
Meetings, §34-26-21.
Powers and duties.
Generally, §34-26-22.
Qualifications of members, §34-26-21.
Quorum, §34-26-21.

PSYCHOLOGISTS—Cont'd
  Board of examiners—Cont'd
    Removal of members,
      §34-26-21.
    Rules and regulations.
      Adoption by board,
        §34-26-21.
      Promulgation, §34-26-22.
    Subpoenas.
      Power to issue for
        revocation hearings,
        §34-26-47.
    Suspension or revocation of
      licenses, §§34-26-46 to
      34-26-48.
    Terms of office, §34-26-21.
  Certificates, §§34-26-46 to
    34-26-48.
    Refusal to issue.
      Appeal of decision of board,
        §34-26-48.
      Grounds, §34-26-46.
      Hearing, §34-26-47.
      Subpoena of witnesses and
        documents, §34-26-47.
  Client.
    Protection of confidentiality
      of communications,
      §34-26-2.
  Code of ethics.
    Adoption by board, §34-26-3.
    Violation as grounds for
      revocation of license,
      §34-26-46.
  Confidential
    communications.
    Protection of client
      relationships, §34-26-2.
  Consent for health services,
    §§22-8-1 to 22-8-9.
    See HEALTH.
  Construction of chapter.
    Practice as "psychologist"
      defined, §34-26-1.
  Continuing education.
    Requirements, §34-26-22.
  Corporations.
    Professional corporations,
      §§10-4-380 to 10-4-406.
    See PROFESSIONAL
      CORPORATIONS.
  Definitions.
    Practice as "psychologist,"
      §34-26-1.
  Education.
    Continuing education.
      Requirements, §34-26-22.
  Ethics.
    Code of ethics, §§34-26-3,
      34-26-46.
  Examinations.
    Conduct of examinations,
      §34-26-44.
    Licensure fee, §34-26-43.1.
    Persons licensed in other
      states, §34-26-45.
    Waiver, §34-26-45.
  Examiners. See within this
    heading, "Board of
    examiners."
  Fees.
    Disbursement of funds
      collected, §34-26-43.
    Permanent license fee,
      §34-26-43.
    Registration fee, §34-26-22.
  Fraud.
    Refusal, suspension or
      revocation of licenses.
      Fraud as grounds,
        §34-26-46.

PSYCHOLOGISTS—Cont'd
  Governor.
    Board of examiners,
      §§34-26-20, 34-26-21.
  Licenses.
    Application, §34-26-41.
    Examinations, §§34-26-43.1
      to 34-26-45.
    Exemptions from
      requirements, §34-26-40.
    Fees.
      Permanent license fee,
        §34-26-43.
    Nonresidents.
      Waiver of examination,
        §34-26-45.
    Persons licensed in other
      states, §34-26-45.
    Psychological interns,
      §34-26-40.
    Psychological trainees,
      §34-26-40.
    Qualifications of applicants,
      §34-26-41.
    Reciprocity, §34-26-41.
    Required, §34-26-40.
    Revocation or suspension.
      Appeals of decision of
        board, §34-26-48.
      Grounds, §34-26-46.
      Hearing, §34-26-47.
      Notice of charges,
        §34-26-47.
      Reinstatement of license,
        §34-26-46.
      Subpoena of witnesses and
        documents, §34-26-47.
    Unlicensed practice.
      Penalty, §34-26-42.
  Nonresidents.
    Waiver of license
      examination, §34-26-45.
  Penalties.
    Unlicensed practice as
      psychologist, §34-26-42.
  Practice as "psychologist."
    Defined, §34-26-1.
    Penalty for unlicensed
      practice, §34-26-42.
  Privileged communications.
    Criminal psychopath
      conditional releases.
      Periodic reports not
        deemed violative of
        privilege, §15-16-69.
  Professional corporations,
    §§10-4-380 to 10-4-406.
    See PROFESSIONAL
      CORPORATIONS.
  Reciprocity.
    Licenses, §34-26-41.
  Registration, §34-26-22.
  Revocation or suspension of
    licenses, §§34-26-46 to
    34-26-48.
  Rules and regulations.
    Adoption by board,
      §34-26-21.
  Unincorporated professional
    associations, §§10-1-1 to
    10-1-16.
    See UNINCORPORATED
      PROFESSIONAL
      ASSOCIATIONS.

PSYCHOPATHS.
  Criminal law and procedure.
    Mentally ill.
      General provisions.
        See MENTALLY ILL.

PSYCHOPATHS—Cont'd
  Criminal law and procedure
    —Cont'd
    Mentally ill—Cont'd
      Prisoners.
        See PRISONS AND
          PRISONERS.
      Release of criminal
        psychopaths, §§15-16-60
        to 15-16-71.
      See MENTALLY ILL.
    Sexual psychopaths.
      See SEXUAL OFFENSES.
  Mentally ill.
    See MENTALLY ILL.

PUBLIC
  ACCOMMODATIONS.
  Blind persons.
    Right to use of places of
      public accommodations,
      §21-7-3.
  Handicapped persons.
    Right to use of places of
      public accommodations,
      §21-7-3.
  Hotels, inns and other
    transient lodging places.
    See HOTELS, INNS AND
      OTHER TRANSIENT
      LODGING PLACES.
  Restaurants.
    See RESTAURANTS.

PUBLIC ACCOUNTANTS.
  See ACCOUNTANTS.

PUBLIC ACCOUNTS.
  Accounts and accounting.
    See ACCOUNTS AND
      ACCOUNTING.
  Department of examiners of
    public accounts.
    See ACCOUNTS AND
      ACCOUNTING.
  Division of control and
    accounts, §§41-4-50,
    41-4-54.
  Finance.
    See FINANCE.
  Legislative committee on
    public accounts,
    §§41-5-18 to 41-5-20.
  State auditor.
    See STATE AUDITOR.

PUBLIC ASSISTANCE.
  See WELFARE.

PUBLICATION.
  Counties.
    Laws, §§11-13-1 to 11-13-6.
    See COUNTIES.
    Semi-annual publication of
      county receipts and
      expenditures, §§11-3-21
      to 11-3-23.
  Heating and air conditioning
    contractors.
    List of certified contractors,
      §34-31-31.
  Judicial sales.
    Notice, §§6-8-60 to 6-8-69.
    See JUDICIAL SALES.
  Mental health finance
    authority.
    Bond issues.
      Sale of bonds.
        Notice of sale,
          §41-10-360.

PUBLICATION—Cont'd
Municipal corporations.
Class 5 municipalities.
Mayor/commission/city
manager form of
government.
Elections.
Notice, §11-44E-3.
Special election when
vacancy in office of
mayor,
§11-44E-74.
Granting of franchises,
§11-44E-52.
Ordinances, §11-44E-51.
Elections.
Mayor/commission/city
manager form of
government.
Notice, §11-44E-3.
Printing.
See PRINTING.
Sports.
Agents.
Publication of false,
fraudulent or
misleading information
prohibited, §8-26-33.
Time.
Publication of legal notice.
Time for publication,
§6-8-62.
**Water system assistance
authority.**
Bond issues.
Notice of public sale,
§22-23A-8.

PUBLIC BID LAW.
Public contracts, §§41-16-1 to
41-16-125.
See CONTRACTS.

PUBLIC BUILDINGS.
**Alabama building
corporation,** §41-10-3.
Armories, §§31-4-1 to 31-4-19.
See ARMORIES.
Authorities.
Counties.
See COUNTIES.
Municipal corporations.
See MUNICIPAL
CORPORATIONS.
Beautification board.
General provisions,
§§41-9-490 to 41-9-498.
See BEAUTIFICATION.
Blind persons.
Accessibility to and use of
public buildings and
facilities by physcially
handicapped persons,
§§21-4-1 to 21-4-7.
Operation of vending stands
by blind persons in
public buildings,
§21-1-41.
Right to full use of public
buildings and facilities,
§21-7-2.
Confederacy.
White house of the
confederacy, §§41-12-1 to
41-12-3.
Contracts.
Public contracts.
See CONTRACTS.
Corporation.
Alabama building
corporation, §41-10-3.

PUBLIC BUILDINGS—Cont'd
Counties.
See COUNTIES.
County boards of health.
Duties, §22-3-2.
County health officers.
Duties, §22-3-5.
Executive mansion,
§§41-9-530 to 41-9-532.
Fallout shelters.
Construction of public
buildings with
radioactive fallout
protection, §§39-6-1,
39-6-2.
Governor's mansion,
§§41-9-530 to 41-9-532.
Handicapped persons.
Accessibility to and use of
public buildings and
facilities, §§21-4-1 to
21-4-7.
Architectural plans and
specifications.
Additional rules and
regulations.
Review, §21-4-6.
Definitions, §21-4-2.
Enforcement of chapter,
§21-4-7.
Fire marshal.
Authority to inspect
buildings, §21-4-7.
Promulgation of
standards and
specifications for
public buildings and
facilities, §21-4-3.
Inspection of buildings.
Authority of fire marshal
to inspect buildings,
§21-4-7.
Legislative intent, §21-4-1.
Standards and
specifications for
public buildings and
facilities.
Applicability, §21-4-4.
Construction and
interpretation,
§21-4-5.
Orders to conform with
standards and
specifications,
§21-4-7.
Promulgation, §21-4-3.
Waivers, §21-4-5.
Right to full use of public
buildings and facilities,
§21-7-2.
Health.
Authority and jurisdiction of
state board of health,
§22-2-2.
Duties of county boards of
health, §22-3-2.
Duties of county health
officers, §22-3-5.
Insurance.
State insurance fund.
See INSURANCE.
Jails.
See JAILS.
Military affairs.
Armory commission.
Cooperation of counties
and municipalities for
acquisition of buildings
suitable for use as
public buildings,
§31-4-9.

PUBLIC BUILDINGS—Cont'd
Military affairs—Cont'd
Commanders of national
guard troops.
Prescribing boundaries
around public
buildings from which
public excluded,
§31-2-123.
Municipal corporations.
See MUNICIPAL
CORPORATIONS.
Office of space management,
§§41-4-260 to 41-4-263.
Penitentiary.
See PENITENTIARY.
Police.
Color of uniforms, §41-4-184.
Director of finance.
Employment by director at
Capitol and other state
buildings, §41-4-182.
Equipment.
Necessary equipment to be
furnished, §41-4-185.
Insurance.
Authority to insure,
§41-4-185.
Limits as to amount of
insurance, §41-4-185.
Payment for insurance,
§41-4-185.
Powers, §41-4-184.
Prisons.
General provisions.
See PRISONS AND
PRISONERS.
Penitentiary.
See PENITENTIARY.
Public works.
See PUBLIC WORKS.
Signs.
Expenditure of state funds.
Erection and maintenance
of signs.
Signs designating
building in honor or
memory of
individual, §23-1-8.1.
Space management.
Office of space management,
§§41-4-260 to 41-4-263.
State board of health.
Authority and jurisdiction,
§22-2-2.
**White House of the
Confederacy,** §§41-12-1 to
41-12-3.

PUBLIC CONTRACTS.
See CONTRACTS.

PUBLIC DEFENDERS,
§§15-12-40 to 15-12-46.
Appointed counsel systems.
Division not to exclude
establishment of parallel
systems, §15-12-46.
Attorney-client privilege.
Confidentiality of
communications,
§15-12-44.
Compensation, §15-12-43.
**Confidentiality of attorney-
client communications,**
§15-12-44.
Conflicts of interest.
Division not to exclude
alternative appointment
in cases of conflict,
§15-12-46.
Defined, §15-12-1.

PUBLIC DEFENDERS—Cont'd
Expenses, §15-12-43.
  Approval of expenditures,
    §15-12-45.
Fair trial tax.
  Payment of share of costs of
    maintaining public
    defender offices,
    §12-19-252.
Full-time service required,
  §15-12-41.
Investigations.
  Approval of expenditures for
    investigators, §15-12-45.
Powers and duties.
  Generally, §15-12-42.
Records.
  Maintenance of certain
    records, §15-12-44.
Removal from office,
  §15-12-41.
Reports, §15-12-44.
**Rules of judicial
  administration,** ARJA,
  Rule 8.
Selection, §15-12-40.
Term of office, §15-12-41.

**PUBLIC EDUCATION
  EMPLOYEES' HEALTH
  INSURANCE,** §§16-25A-1 to
  16-25A-17.
  See EDUCATION.

**PUBLIC EMPLOYEES
  INDIVIDUAL
  RETIREMENT ACCOUNT
  FUND,** §§36-27A-1 to
  36-27A-7.
  See PUBLIC OFFICERS AND
    EMPLOYEES.

PUBLIC FUNDS.
  See FINANCE.

PUBLIC HEALTH.
  See HEALTH.

PUBLIC IMPROVEMENTS.
Counties.
  See COUNTIES.
Housing projects.
  Alienation of certain public
    improvements by
    political subdivisions,
    §§35-4-410 to 35-4-412.
Municipal corporations.
  See MUNICIPAL
    CORPORATIONS.
Parks and recreation.
  Alienation of certain public
    improvements by
    political subdivisions,
    §§35-4-410 to 35-4-412.
Public works.
  See PUBLIC WORKS.

PUBLICITY.
**Bureau of tourism and
  travel.**
  Appropriations.
    Use of appropriations,
      §41-7-4.
  Composition, §41-7-1.
  Created, §41-7-1.
  Division heads, §41-7-2.
  Duties, §41-7-1.
  Employees, §41-7-2.
  Powers, §41-7-1.
  Unit heads, §41-7-2.
**Director of the bureau of
  tourism and travel.**
  Advisory board, §41-7-3.
  Appointment, §41-7-2.

PUBLICITY—Cont'd
**Director of the bureau of
  tourism and travel**
  —Cont'd
  Compensation, §41-7-2.
  Head of bureau, §41-7-2.
  Southern travel directors
    council.
    Director may contract with
      and spend funds in
      support of, §41-7-5.
  Term of office, §41-7-2.
**Industrial development
  advisory board.**
  Bureau of publicity and
    information.
    Cooperation of director of
      bureau with board,
      §41-9-188.
**Southern travel directors
  council.**
  Director may contract with
    and spend funds in
    support of, §41-7-5.
Welcome centers.
  Workers.
    Retention of employment
      positions, §41-7-2.

PUBLIC LANDS.
Acquisition.
  Lands to which state
    entitled, §9-15-13.
  Notice, §9-15-10.
    County tax assessors,
      §9-15-12.
Actions.
  School lands.
    Clearing of title, §9-15-37.
Adverse possession.
  Conveyances by governor or
    state agency or
    institution.
    Conveyances in cases of
      adverse possession,
      §35-4-391.
Agent, §9-2-130.
**Ameraport offshore harbor
  and terminal
  commission.**
  Lease of state lands,
    §33-10-19.
Armories.
  Counties or municipalities.
    Conveyance of public lands
      for use as armory
      sites, §31-4-11.
Blind persons.
  Operation of vending stands
    by blind persons on
    properties of state,
    §21-1-41.
Clay.
  Sale of right to quarry clay,
    §35-4-381.
Coastal areas, §§9-7-10 to
  9-7-20.
  See COASTAL AREAS.
Constitution of Alabama.
  Restrictions on donation or
    sale of state lands to
    private corporations or
    individuals, Const. Ala.,
    art. IV, §99.
  Special, private or local laws
    donating lands owned or
    under control by state to
    any person or
    corporation prohibited,
    Const. Ala., art. IV,
    §104.

PUBLIC LANDS—Cont'd
Contracts.
  Sand or gravel.
    Sale or leasing, §§9-15-52,
      9-15-53.
**Conveyances by governor or
  state agencies or
  institutions,** §§35-4-380 to
  35-4-391.
  See CONVEYANCES.
Counties.
  Effect of article.
    Local laws governing
      ownership of land,
      §9-15-19.
  Maps.
    Ownership and location of
      public lands.
      Preparation of county
        maps, §9-15-11.
  Tax assessors.
    Lists of used and unused
      lands.
      Preparation for county
        assessor, §9-15-12.
    Notice of acquisition or
      disposition of lands,
      §9-15-12.
**Data and information on all
  state owned lands.**
  Land resources information
    center.
    Center to compile,
      §9-2-121.
Decedents' estates.
  Patent to decedent vests title
    in his successors,
    §35-4-386.
Deeds.
  Conveyances by governor or
    state agency or
    institution, §§35-4-380 to
    35-4-391.
  See CONVEYANCES.
Definitions.
  Unused public lands, §9-15-1.
**Department of conservation
  and natural resources.**
  Powers and duties.
    General provisions, §9-2-2.
Director of finance.
  Sale of certain surplus lands,
    §41-4-33.
Director of lands division.
  Land resources information
    center.
    Supervision of, §9-2-121.
Disposition.
  Authority to dispose of,
    §9-15-18.
  Notice, §9-15-10.
    County tax assessors,
      §9-15-12.
  Swamp and overflowed lands.
    Authority of commissioner,
      §9-15-30.
Division of lands, §§9-2-120,
  9-2-121.
  Development of certain state-
    owned islands, §9-2-120.
  Islands.
    Certain state-owned
      islands.
      Supervision and
        development,
        §9-2-120.
  Land resources information
    center.
    Agencies to file legal
      instruments, §9-2-121.

PUBLIC LANDS—Cont'd
  Division of lands—Cont'd
    Land resources information
        center—Cont'd
      Compiling data and
          information on all
          state owned lands,
          §9-2-121.
      Created, §9-2-121.
      Director of lands division.
        Center under supervision
            of, §9-2-121.
      Purpose.
        Compiling data and
            information on all
            state owned lands,
            §9-2-121.
      Supervision of center.
        Director of lands
            division, §9-2-121.
      Supervision of certain state-
          owned islands, §9-2-120.
  Eminent domain.
    See EMINENT DOMAIN.
  Evidence.
    Sale or transfer of state
        lands.
      Pre-1879 documents or
          certified copies
          executed by governor
          as evidence of sale or
          transfer of state lands,
          §12-21-97.
  Fires and fire prevention.
    Enforcement of state fire
        laws.
      School lands, §9-15-34.
      Swamp and overflowed lands.
        Enforcement of state fire
            laws, §9-15-34.
  Forests and forestry.
    Practice of forestry.
      School lands, §9-15-34.
      Swamp and overflowed
          lands, §§9-15-30,
          9-15-35.
    Unused public lands.
      Use as state forests,
          §9-15-3.
  Funds.
    Unused public lands.
      Management of unused
          lands, §9-15-17.
  Governor.
    Conveyances by governor,
        §§35-4-380 to 35-4-391.
      See CONVEYANCES.
  Gravel.
    Sale or leasing, §§9-15-52,
        9-15-53.
  Improvements.
    Lists of improvements.
      Disposition, §9-15-8.
      Filing, §9-15-8.
    Sale by person making,
        §8-1-103.
  Islands.
    Division of lands.
      Supervision and
          development of certain
          state-owned islands,
          §9-2-120.
  Land agent, §9-2-130.
  Land clerk.
    Appointment, §9-15-32.
    Examination of lands,
        §9-15-33.
    Expenses, §9-15-33.
    Qualifications, §9-15-32.
  Leases.
    Authority to lease, §9-15-18.

PUBLIC LANDS—Cont'd
  Leases—Cont'd
    Oil and gas leases, §§9-17-60
        to 9-17-69.
      See OIL AND GAS.
    School lands, §9-15-36.
    Swamp and overflowed lands,
        §§9-15-30, 9-15-45.
  Limestone.
    Sale of right to quarry
        limestone, §35-4-381.
  **Lists of used and unused
      lands.**
    County tax assessors.
      Preparation for assessors,
          §9-15-12.
    Disposition of lists, §9-15-8.
    Filing.
      State departments and
          institutions, §9-15-8.
    Preparation.
      Use by county tax
          assessors, §9-15-12.
  Locations.
    Ascertainment, §9-15-6.
  Maps.
    County maps.
      Ownership and location of
          public lands.
        Preparation, §9-15-11.
  Military affairs.
    Armory commission.
      Conveyance by counties or
          municipalities of
          public lands for use as
          armory sites, §31-4-11.
  Mines and minerals.
    Sale of minerals from lands,
        §9-15-18.
    School lands, §§9-15-38,
        9-15-39.
    Swamp and overflowed
        lands, §§9-15-38,
        9-15-40.
    School lands.
      Leases, §9-15-36.
      Sale of minerals, §§9-15-38,
          9-15-39.
    Swamp and overflowed lands.
      Sale of minerals, §§9-15-38,
          9-15-40.
  Notice.
    Acquisition.
      County tax assessors,
          §9-15-12.
    Acquisition of land, §9-15-10.
    Change in status, §9-15-10.
    Counties.
      Tax assessors.
        Acquisition or disposition
            of lands, §9-15-12.
    Disposition of land, §9-15-10.
    County tax assessors,
        §9-15-12.
  Office of land agent,
      §9-2-130.
  Oil and gas.
    Leases by state, §§9-17-60 to
        9-17-69.
      See OIL AND GAS.
  Overflowed lands. See within
      this heading, "Swamp and
      overflowed lands."
  Ownership.
    Records. See within this
        heading, "Records."

PUBLIC LANDS—Cont'd
  Patents.
    Conveyances by governor or
        state agencies or
        institutions, §§35-4-380
        to 35-4-391.
      See CONVEYANCES.
    Evidence, §12-21-96.
    School lands.
      Exchanges of school lands,
          §9-15-44.
      Issuance of patents,
          §§9-15-42, 16-20-3.
      Sales.
        Issuance of patents to
            purchasers, §9-15-42.
    Swamp and overflowed lands.
      Claims of title.
        Issuance upon
            settlement, §9-15-48.
      Sale of lands.
        Issuance of patents to
            purchasers, §9-15-46.
  Penalties.
    Surplus lands.
      Transfer to volunteer fire
          departments,
          §41-4-33.1.
  Prison system, §§14-3-2 to
      14-3-4.
  **Private corporations or
      individuals.**
    Restrictions on donation or
        sale of state lands to,
        Const. Ala., art. IV, §99.
  Quarries.
    Sale of right to quarry
        limestone and clay,
        §35-4-381.
  Recordation.
    Land patents, §35-4-387.
  Records.
    Disposition, §§9-15-7, 9-15-9.
    Land resources information
        center.
      Compiling data and
          information on all
          state owned lands,
          §9-2-121.
    Ownership records.
      Addition of lands as
          acquired, §9-15-13.
      Contents, §9-15-9.
      Disposition, §§9-15-7,
          9-15-9.
      Preparation, §§9-15-6,
          9-15-9.
    Preparation of records of
        ownership, §§9-15-6,
        9-15-9.
    School lands, §§9-15-49 to
        9-15-51.
    Swamp and overflowed lands
      Correction of records,
          §§9-15-49 to 9-15-51.
  Sales.
    Bids under agreements to
        transfer.
      Prohibited, §8-1-101.
        Contracts in violation
            void, §8-1-102.
    Disposition. See within this
        heading, "Disposition."
    Evidence.
      Pre-1879 documents or
          certified copies
          executed by governor
          as evidence of sale or
          transfer of state lands,
          §12-21-97.

PUBLIC LANDS—Cont'd
  Sales—Cont'd
    Improvements.
      Sale by person making,
        §8-1-103.
    Sand or gravel, §§9-15-52,
      9-15-53.
    School lands. See within this
      heading, "School lands."
    Swamp and overflowed lands.
      See within this heading,
      "Swamp and overflowed
      lands."
  Salt springs.
    Lease of salt springs, etc.,
      §35-4-380.
  Salt springs lands
    reservation.
    Examination.
      Land clerk, §9-15-33.
    Management and
      supervision, §9-15-31.
  Sand or gravel.
    Sale or leasing.
      Public water bottoms and
        certain state lands.
        Consummation of
          contracts or leases,
          §9-15-52.
        Contracts, §9-15-52.
        Disposition of revenues,
          §9-15-53.
        Expenditure of revenues,
          §9-15-53.
  School lands.
    Actions.
      Clearing of title, §9-15-37.
    Adverse possession.
      When title acquired by
        adverse possession,
        §16-20-6.
    Defined, §16-20-1.
    Examination.
      Land clerk, §9-15-33.
    Exchanges, §9-15-44.
    Fires and fire prevention.
      Enforcement of state fire
        laws, §9-15-34.
    Forests and forestry.
      Practice of forestry,
        §9-15-34.
    Interest.
      State pledged to pay
        interest on school land
        funds, §16-20-5.
    Lease.
      Adverse possession.
        When title acquired by
          adverse possession,
          §16-20-6.
      Approval, §9-15-36.
      Authority of commissioner
        of conservation and
        natural resources,
        §9-15-36.
      Definition of school lands,
        §16-20-1.
      Interest.
        State pledged to pay
          interest on school
          land funds, §16-20-5.
      Notes.
        Placed with attorney
          general for
          collection, §16-20-4.
      Oil and gas, §9-15-36.
      Patent.
        When secretary of state
          issues patent,
          §16-20-3.
      Purposes, §9-15-36.

PUBLIC LANDS—Cont'd
  School lands—Cont'd
    Lease—Cont'd
      Timber on reserved lots
        not to be injured,
        §16-20-2.
      Township lines abolished,
        §16-20-7.
    Management, §9-15-31.
    Mines and minerals.
      Leases, §9-15-36.
      Sale of minerals.
        Authorized, §9-15-38.
        Bids, §9-15-38.
        Disposition of revenues,
          §9-15-39.
        Notice, §9-15-38.
    Oil and gas.
      Leases, §9-15-36.
    Patents.
      Exchanges of school lands,
        §9-15-44.
      Lease of school lands.
        When secretary of state
          issues, §16-20-3.
      Sale of school lands.
        Issuance of patents to
          purchasers,
          §§9-15-42, 16-20-3.
    Records.
      Correction of errors.
        Certification of corrected
          records, §9-15-51.
        File of proof, §9-15-50.
        Proof.
          File of proof submitted,
            §9-15-50.
          Required, §9-15-49.
          When required, §9-15-49.
    Sales.
      Adverse possession.
        When title acquired by
          adverse possession,
          §16-20-6.
      Approval, §9-15-41.
      Authorized, §9-15-41.
      Sale of lands deeded to
        state for school
        purposes, §16-20-8.
    Deeds.
      Sale of lands deeded to
        state for school
        purposes, §16-20-8.
    Definition of school lands,
      §16-20-1.
    Disposition of revenues,
      §16-20-9.
    Interest.
      State pledged to pay
        interest on school
        land funds, §16-20-5.
    Minerals, §§9-15-38,
      9-15-39.
    Notes.
      Placed with attorney
        general for
        collection, §16-20-4.
    Patents.
      Issuance to purchasers,
        §§9-15-42, 16-20-3.
    Principal to be preserved,
      Const. Ala., art. XIV,
      §257.
    Timber, §§9-15-38, 9-15-39.
    Township lines abolished,
      §16-20-7.
    Supervision, §9-15-31.
    Survey.
      Authority of commissioner,
        §9-15-37.

PUBLIC LANDS—Cont'd
  School lands—Cont'd
    Title.
      Actions to clear, §9-15-37.
      Clearing of title, §9-15-37.
      Exchanges of school lands,
        §9-15-44.
    Township lines abolished,
      §16-20-7.
    Trees and timber.
      Cruising of timber,
        §9-15-37.
      Lease of state lands.
        Timber on reserved lots
          not to be injured,
          §16-20-2.
      Sale of timber,
        Disposition of revenues,
          §9-15-39.
    Trespass.
      Enforcement of state
        trespass laws,
        §9-15-34.
  Soil and water conservation.
    General provisions.
      See SOIL AND WATER
        CONSERVATION.
  State parks.
    See STATE PARKS.
  Status.
    Change in status.
      Notice, §9-15-10.
  Surplus lands, §§41-4-33 to
    41-4-33.2.
    Ambulance services.
      Transfer of surplus
        property to volunteer
        nonprofit ambulance
        services, §41-4-33.2.
    Rescue squads.
      Transfer of surplus
        property to volunteer
        nonprofit rescue squad,
        §41-4-33.2.
    Sale of certain surplus lands
      by director of finance,
      §41-4-33.
    Volunteer fire departments.
      Transfer of surplus
        property to volunteer
        fire departments,
        §41-4-33.1.
  Surveys and surveyors.
    Land resources information
      center.
      Survey to determine data
        and information on
        state owned lands,
        §9-2-121.
    School lands.
      Surveying of lands,
        §9-15-37.
  Swamp and overflowed
    lands.
    Correction of records.
      Required, §9-15-49.
    Disposition.
      Authority of commissioner,
        §9-15-30.
    Examination.
      Land clerk, §9-15-33.
    Exchanges.
      Approval, §9-15-45.
      Authorized, §9-15-45.
    Fires and fire prevention.
      Enforcement of state fire
        laws, §9-15-34.

PUBLIC LANDS—Cont'd
Swamp and overflowed lands—Cont'd
Forests and forestry.
 Practice of forestry, §9-15-35.
  Authority of commissioner, §9-15-30.
Indemnity lands.
 Title.
  Vested in division of lands, §9-15-30.
Leases.
 Approval, §9-15-45.
 Authority of commissioner, §9-15-30.
 Authorized, §9-15-45.
Management, §9-15-31.
Mines and minerals.
 Sale of minerals, §9-15-38.
 Disposition of revenues, §9-15-40.
Patents, §35-4-389.
 Sale of lands.
  Issuance of patents to purchasers, §9-15-46.
 Settlement of claims of title.
  Issuance of patents, §9-15-48.
Records.
 Correction of records.
  Certification of corrected records, §9-15-51.
  File of proof, §9-15-50.
 Proof.
  File of proof submitted, §9-15-50.
  When required, §9-15-49.
Sales.
 Approval, §9-15-45.
 Authorized, §9-15-45.
 Disposition of revenue, §§9-15-43, 9-15-47.
 Minerals, §§9-15-38, 9-15-40.
 Patents.
  Issuance, §9-15-46.
 Timber, §§9-15-38, 9-15-40.
Supervision, §9-15-31.
Title.
 Claims of title, §9-15-48.
 Vested in division of lands, §9-15-30.
Trees and timber.
 Sale of timber.
  Authorized, §9-15-38.
  Bids, §9-15-38.
  Disposition of revenues, §9-15-40.
  Notice, §9-15-38.
Trespass.
 Enforcement of state trespass laws, §9-15-35.
Uses.
 Authority of commissioner of conservation and natural resources, §9-15-30.
Taxation.
County tax assessors, §9-15-12.
Title.
School lands.
 Clearing of title, §9-15-37.
 Exchanges of school lands, §9-15-44.

PUBLIC LANDS—Cont'd
Title—Cont'd
Swamp and overflowed lands.
 Indemnity lands.
  Vested in division of lands, §9-15-30.
  Vested in division of lands, §9-15-30.
Trees and timber.
Sale of timber from lands, §9-15-18.
School lands.
 Cruising of timber, §9-15-37.
 Sale of timber, §§9-15-38, 9-15-39.
Swamp and overflowed lands.
 Sale of timber, §§9-15-38, 9-15-40.
Trespass.
School lands.
 Enforcement of state trespass laws, §9-15-34.
Swamp and overflowed lands.
 Enforcement of state trespass laws, §9-15-35.
Trusts and trustees.
Unused public lands.
 Rights of trust beneficiaries.
  Duties of department to be performed without prejudice, §9-15-5.
University of South Alabama Foundation.
Settlement of dispute as to certain property.
 Conveyed to foundation, §35-4-393.
Unused lands, §§9-15-1 to 9-15-19.
Acquisition.
 Notice, §9-15-10.
  County tax assessors, §9-15-12.
Change in status.
 Notice, §9-15-10.
Concentration of ownership.
 Scattered state-owned lands, §9-15-4.
Control, §9-15-2.
Cost of administering, etc.
 Amount.
  Maximum amount, §9-15-16.
 Charge against income, §9-15-15.
 Fund for management of unused lands, §9-15-17.
 Maximum amount for charges, §9-15-16.
Counties.
 Effect of article.
  Local laws governing ownership, management, etc., §9-15-19.
Definitions, §9-15-1.
Department of conservation and natural resources.
 Duties to be performed without prejudice.
  Rights of trust beneficiaries or state institutions, §9-15-5.
 Technical advisor, §9-15-5.

PUBLIC LANDS—Cont'd
Unused lands—Cont'd
Determination of best use, §9-15-14.
Disposition.
 Notice, §9-15-10.
  County tax assessors, §9-15-12.
Effect of article.
 Local laws governing ownership, management, etc., §9-15-19.
Forests and forestry.
 Determination of lands suitable for devotion to forest culture, §9-15-3.
 Listing of unused lands suitable for devotion to forest culture, §9-15-3.
 State forests.
  Use as state forests, §9-15-3.
  Use as state forests, §9-15-3.
Funds.
 Management of unused lands, §9-15-17.
Improvements.
 List of improvements, §9-15-8.
Jurisdiction.
 Department of conservation and natural resources, §9-15-2.
Lists of unused lands.
 County tax assessors.
  Preparation of lists for assessors, §9-15-12.
 Disposition, §9-15-8.
 Filing, §9-15-8.
Notice.
 Acquisition, §9-15-10.
  County tax assessors, §9-15-12.
 Change in status, §9-15-10.
 Disposition, §9-15-12.
Ownership records. See within this heading, "Records."
Policies.
 Recommendations, §9-15-2.
Records of ownership. See within this heading, "Records."
Revenues.
 Cost of administering, etc.
  Charge against revenue, §9-15-15.
 Disposition of revenues from unused lands, §9-15-15.
Scattered state-owned lands.
 Concentration of ownership, §9-15-4.
State parks.
 Use as state parks, §9-15-3.
Trusts and trustees.
 Rights of trust beneficiaries.
  Duties of department to be performed without prejudice, §9-15-5.
Use.
 Determination of best use, §9-15-14.
 Purposes for which best suited, §9-15-14.

PUBLIC LANDS—Cont'd
Waters and watercourses.
Sand or gravel.
Public water bottoms,
§§9-15-32, 9-15-33.

PUBLIC MONEY.
State funds.
See FINANCE.

**PUBLIC OFFICERS AND
EMPLOYEES.**
Abuse of public office.
Bribery.
General provisions.
See BRIBERY.
Confidential information.
Misuse, §13A-10-82.
Conflicts of interest.
General provisions.
See CONFLICTS OF
INTEREST.
Definitions, §13A-10-80.
Harm.
Defined, §13A-10-80.
Misuse of confidential
information, §13A-10-82.
Accounts and accounting.
Department of examiners of
public accounts, §§41-5-1
to 41-5-24.
See ACCOUNTS AND
ACCOUNTING.
Uniform accounts.
Officers to keep uniform
accounts, §41-5-23.
Actions.
Attorney general may be
required to defend suits
against officers, Const.
Ala., amd. 111.
Bonds, surety.
Actions on official bonds,
§§6-5-30, 6-5-31.
Affidavits.
Public property, papers, etc.
Recovery of papers,
property, etc., by
successors to office,
§§36-12-22 to 36-12-24.
Alcoholic beverages.
Impeachment.
Intemperance in use as
grounds, §36-11-1.
Allowances.
Special, private or local laws
creating, increasing or
decreasing prohibited,
Const. Ala., art. IV,
§104.
Uniformity of laws
regulating, Const. Ala.,
art. IV, §96.
Appeals.
Substitution of parties,
ARAP, Rule 43 (b).
Appointment.
Void appointments.
Certification of judgment
declaring appointment
void, §36-9-15.
Appropriations.
Insurance.
State employees' health
insurance plan,
§36-29-13.
Attachments.
State employees' retirement
system.
Exemption of pension,
annuity, etc.,
§36-27-28.

**PUBLIC OFFICERS AND
EMPLOYEES**—Cont'd
Attorney general.
See ATTORNEY GENERAL.
Attorneys at law.
Bonds, surety.
Attorneys not deemed
sufficient sureties on
official bonds of
probate judges, clerks,
sheriffs, constables,
etc., §36-5-13.
Practice of law by certain
officials.
See ATTORNEYS AT
LAW.
Awards.
Employee suggestion award
program, §36-1-7.
Bail and recognizance.
Judicial and ministerial
officers prohibited from
signing bonds, etc.,
§15-13-24.
Bailiffs.
See BAILIFFS.
Bank examiners.
See BANKS AND
FINANCIAL
INSTITUTIONS.
**Banks and financial
institutions.**
Federal laws.
Officers not to incur
liability or penalties
for compliance with
federal laws,
§5-10A-17.
Savings and loan
associations.
Acknowledgment, etc., of
instruments, §5-16-41.
Superintendent of banks.
Officers not to incur
liability or penalties
for compliance with
orders of
superintendent,
§5-10A-17.
Boards and commissions.
General provisions.
See BOARDS AND
COMMISSIONS.
Bonds, surety.
Actions on official bonds.
Assignment of breaches on
penal bonds or other
writings, §6-5-31.
Right of aggrieved person
to commence actions,
§6-5-30.
Additional bond.
Conditions, §36-5-4.
Procedure, §36-5-41.
Requirement, §36-5-4.
When required, §36-5-40.
Applicability of provisions,
§36-5-25.
Approval.
Filing.
Not to be filed unless
properly approved,
§36-5-8.
Generally, §36-5-6.
Improper approval.
Effect of bonds
improperly approved,
§36-5-20.
Liability, §36-5-7.

**PUBLIC OFFICERS AND
EMPLOYEES**—Cont'd
Bonds, surety—Cont'd
Approval—Cont'd
Irregularities.
Effect on validity,
§36-5-19.
New bond upon discharge
of surety, §36-5-63.
Performance of official acts
prior to approval,
§36-5-22.
Attorneys at law.
Attorneys not deemed
sufficient sureties on
official bonds of
probate judges, clerks,
sheriffs, constables,
etc., §36-5-13.
Cancellation.
Termination, consolidation,
etc., of positions,
§36-5-45.
Conditions, §36-5-19.
Additional bonds, §36-5-4.
Generally, §36-5-5.
Liability of sureties on
bonds conditionally
executed, §36-5-14.
Consolidation of positions.
Cancellation of bonds,
§36-5-45.
Contents.
Irregularities.
Effect on validity,
§36-5-19.
Counties.
See COUNTIES.
Discharge.
Bonds not discharged by
single recovery,
§36-5-23.
Discharge of sureties.
Application.
Officer to whom
addressed to require
principal to give new
bond, §36-5-62.
Sworn, §36-5-61.
To whom addressed,
§36-5-61.
When surety may apply,
§36-5-60.
Effect, §36-5-66.
New bond.
Approval, §36-5-63.
Effect, §36-5-64.
Failure to execute within
prescribed time.
Proceedings upon
failure, §36-5-68.
Filing, §36-5-63.
Requisition, §36-5-62.
When effective, §36-5-64.
When surety discharged,
§36-5-65.
Endorsement.
Date of filing, §36-5-9.
Failure to endorse,
§36-5-10.
Evidence.
Copies of required official
bonds, §12-21-104.
Execution.
Improper execution.
Effect, §36-5-20.
Filing.
Approval.
Not to be filed unless
properly approved,
§36-5-8.

PUBLIC OFFICERS AND EMPLOYEES—Cont'd
Bonds, surety—Cont'd
Filing—Cont'd
Date.
Endorsement on bonds, §36-5-9.
Failure to endorse, §36-5-10.
Failure to file.
Certification of failure to appointing power, §36-5-15.
Notification of district attorney, §36-5-16.
Failure to give notice, §36-5-17.
Vacation of office, §36-5-15.
Generally, §36-5-1.
Improper filing.
Effect of bonds improperly filed, §36-5-20.
New bond upon discharge of surety, §36-5-63.
Performance of official acts prior to filing, §36-5-22.
Time of filing, §36-5-2.
Form.
Irregularities.
Effect on validity, §36-5-19.
Legal effect, §36-5-18.
Bonds improperly executed, approved or filed, §36-5-20.
New bond upon discharge of surety, §36-5-64.
Liability.
Officer improperly approving bond, §36-5-7.
Officials collecting and paying out money under law declared unconstitutional, void, etc., §36-5-24.
Sureties.
Bonds conditionally executed, §36-5-14.
Municipal corporations.
See MUNICIPAL CORPORATIONS.
Official bonds.
Actions for breach.
Venue, §6-3-8.
Attorneys at law.
Not deemed sufficient sureties on certain official bonds, §36-5-13.
Counties.
See COUNTIES.
Lis pendens.
Liability of officers on bonds, §35-4-139.
Payment.
To whom payable, §36-5-5.
Penalties.
Failure to endorse date of filing on bond, §36-5-10.
Failure to give notice of omission of public officer to file official bonds, §36-5-17.

PUBLIC OFFICERS AND EMPLOYEES—Cont'd
Bonds, surety—Cont'd
Penalties—Cont'd
Performance of official act by public officer prior to approval and filing of bond, §36-5-22.
Premiums, §36-5-43.
Payment, §36-5-44.
Proof, §36-5-21.
Recordation.
Generally, §36-5-1.
Secretary of state, §36-5-1.
State treasurer.
Deposit with and payments to treasurer, §36-17-19.
Sureties, §36-5-5.
Bonds to be made by surety or guaranty companies, §36-5-42.
Discharge, §§36-5-60 to 36-5-68.
Liability.
Bonds conditionally executed, §36-5-14.
Qualifications, §36-5-11.
Rights and remedies of sureties among themselves, §36-5-67.
Sufficiency, §§36-5-11 to 36-5-13.
Termination of positions.
Cancellation of bonds, §36-5-45.
Bribery.
See BRIBERY.
Budget officers, §§41-4-6, 41-4-81.
Charities.
Payroll deductions, §§36-1-4, 36-1-4.1.
Circuit registers.
See CIRCUIT COURTS.
Civil defense.
Military service in time of war or national emergency, §§36-8-1 to 36-8-6. See within this heading, "Military affairs."
Classified service. See within this heading, "Merit system."
Clerks of court.
General provisions.
See CLERKS OF COURT.
Code of ethics, §§36-25-1 to 36-25-30.
Agricultural development authority.
Applicability of code, §2-3A-13.
Appropriations, §36-25-29.
Candidates for state office.
Notice of candidacy, §36-25-15.
Statements of economic interests, §36-25-15.
Complaints.
False accusations, §36-25-25.
Filing by citizens, §36-25-24.
Confidential information.
Use or disclosure for private financial gain, §36-25-8.
Conflicting laws.
Repeal, §36-25-30.

PUBLIC OFFICERS AND EMPLOYEES—Cont'd
Code of ethics—Cont'd
Construction of chapter, §36-25-30.
Contracts.
Former officials or employees.
Requirement as to notice, §36-25-13.
Persons related to state officials or employees.
Reports when contracting with state, §36-25-16.
State agencies.
Entering into contracts with, §36-25-11.
Criminal laws.
Chapter not to repeal, §36-25-27.
Definitions, §36-25-2.
Disclosure statement, §36-25-7.
False statements.
Making for purpose of influencing legislation, §36-25-26.
Favors.
Offering, receiving, etc., §36-25-6.
Fees.
Receipt for services provided by state, §36-25-7.
Disclosure statement, §36-25-7.
Gifts.
Offering, receiving, etc., §36-25-6.
Jurisdiction.
Actions for violations of chapter, §36-25-27.
Legislative findings and declarations, §36-25-2.
Legislature.
Constitutional rights of citizens to communicate with members.
Chapter not to impair, §36-25-28.
Disciplinary powers.
Chapter not to limit, §36-25-27.
Lobbying.
Former members of legislature not to be extended floor privileges for lobbying purposes, §36-25-23.
Former officials or employees.
Requirements as to notice, §36-25-13.
Provisions not to be construed as affecting certain professional services, §36-25-22.
Registration of lobbyist.
Required, §36-25-18.
Supplemental registration.
Filing, §36-25-18.
Reports.
Monthly reports by lobbyists, §36-25-19.
Public inspection, §36-25-21.
Public records, §36-25-21.

**PUBLIC OFFICERS AND
EMPLOYEES**—Cont'd
Code of ethics—Cont'd
Lobbying—Cont'd
Termination of activities.
Notice.
Effect as to
requirement for
filing of reports,
§36-25-20.
Filings, §36-25-20.
Money.
Solicitation or receipt for
advice or assistance,
§36-25-7.
Notice.
Candidates for state office.
Notice of candidacy,
§36-25-15.
Lobbyists.
Requirements as to
notice, §36-25-13.
Termination of lobbying
activities, §36-25-20.
Penalties.
Violations of chapter,
§36-25-27.
Personal gain.
Use of official position or
office, §36-25-5.
Use or disclosure of
confidential
information, §36-25-8.
Purpose of chapter, §36-25-2.
Regulatory boards and
commissions.
Promises of future
employment, favors,
etc., for members,
§36-25-12.
Representation of client or
constituent before,
§36-25-10.
Service on boards and
commissions
regulating business
with which person
associated, §36-25-9.
Relatives.
Reports when representing
persons before state
agencies or contracting
with state, §36-25-16.
Reports.
Lobbyists.
Monthly reports,
§36-25-19.
Public inspection,
§36-25-21.
Public records,
§36-25-21.
Violations of chapter,
§36-25-17.
State agencies.
Contracts with, §36-25-11.
Disciplinary powers.
Chapter not to limit,
§36-25-27.
Persons related to state
officials or employees.
Reports when
representing persons
before state
agencies, §36-25-16.
Representation of client or
constituent before,
§36-25-10.
Violations of chapter.
Cooperation of agency
heads, §36-25-17.

**PUBLIC OFFICERS AND
EMPLOYEES**—Cont'd
Code of ethics—Cont'd
State ethics commission,
§§26-5-3, 26-5-4.
Applicability of chapter to
members, employees,
etc., §36-25-3.
Appointment of members,
§36-25-3.
Composition, §36-25-3.
Creation, §36-25-3.
Duties, §36-25-4.
Powers, §36-25-4.
Reports.
Annual reports, §36-25-3.
Rules and regulations.
Waiver, §36-25-3.
Statements of economic
interests.
Candidates for state office,
§36-25-15.
Filing, §36-25-14.
Information required,
§36-25-14.
Venue.
Actions for violations of
chapter, §36-25-27.
Violations.
Penalties, §36-25-27.
Reports, §36-25-17.
Review and appeal.
Procedures, §36-25-17.
Commissioner of revenue.
See TAXATION.
Commissioners.
Appointment in other states
or territories to take and
certify depositions,
receive acknowledgment
and take proof of
conveyances of property,
etc., within state,
§36-1-1.
Commissions.
Boards and commissions.
General provisions.
See BOARDS AND
COMMISSIONS.
County officers.
Commencement of duties
and functions of
offices, §36-2-10.
Execution, §36-2-7; Const.
Ala., art. V, §135.
Exercise of duties of office
without first obtaining,
§36-2-9.
Issuance.
Generally, §36-2-7; Const.
Ala., art. V, §135.
When issued, §36-2-8.
Requirement.
Officers required to obtain,
§36-2-6.
Uniformity of laws
regulating, Const. Ala.,
art. IV, §96.
Compensation. See within
this heading, "Salaries."
Comptroller.
See COMPTROLLER.
Confidential information.
Misuse by public servants,
§13A-10-82.
Conservation officers.
See FISH AND GAME.
Constables.
See CONSTABLES.

**PUBLIC OFFICERS AND
EMPLOYEES**—Cont'd
Constitution of Alabama.
General provisions.
See CONSTITUTION OF
ALABAMA.
Contracts.
Code of ethics.
Entering into contracts
with state agencies,
§36-25-11.
Former officials or
employees.
Notice required,
§36-25-13.
Reports by persons related
to state officials or
employees who
contract with state,
§36-25-16.
**Conviction of certain crimes
bar to eligibility for
office,** Const. Ala., art. IV,
§60.
Corrections.
Board of corrections, §§14-1-4
to 14-1-18.
See CORRECTIONS.
Commissioner of corrections,
§§14-1-1.3, 14-1-1.4.
Corruption.
Impeachment.
Grounds for impeachment,
§36-11-1.
Offenses by officers. See
within this heading,
"Offenses by officers."
Counties.
See COUNTIES.
County administrators,
§§43-2-170 to 43-2-175.
See EXECUTORS AND
ADMINISTRATORS.
Courts.
See COURTS.
Criminal law and procedure.
Abuse of public office. See
within this heading,
"Abuse of public office."
Code of ethics.
Chapter not to repeal any
provisions of criminal
law, §36-25-27.
Impersonating public
servants, §13A-10-10.
Inspections.
Refusal to permit
inspections, §13A-10-3.
Obstructing governmental
operations.
Definitions, §13A-10-1.
Reports.
Failing to file required
reports, §13A-10-4.
Sentencing.
Article not to deprive court
of authority to remove
person from office,
§13A-5-2.
Trading in public office,
§13A-10-63.
Death.
Notice, §36-9-6.
Payment of salary of
deceased officer after
date of death, Const.
Ala., art. IV, §97.
Preretirement death benefit
program, §§36-27B-1 to
36-27B-5.

PUBLIC OFFICERS AND EMPLOYEES—Cont'd

Death—Cont'd

Public property, papers, etc.
Recovery of papers, property, etc., by successor to office upon death of incumbent, §36-12-26.

Vacation of office, §36-9-1.

De facto officials.
Liability, §36-1-2.
Validity of official act, §36-1-2.

Definitions.
Code of ethics, §36-25-1.
Insurance.
State employees' health insurance plan, §36-29-1.
Merit system, §36-26-2.
Classified service, §36-26-10.
County and district health departments, §36-26-80.
Exempt service, §36-26-10.
State institutions, §36-26-60.
Unclassified service, §36-26-10.
"Military service of the United States," §36-8-1.
Protection of certain state officers and visitors, §36-33-1.
Social security, §36-28-1.
State employees' retirement system, §36-27-1.
Reopening of system for certain employees, §36-27-40.

Department of finance, §§41-4-1 to 41-4-263.
See FINANCE.

Director of finance, §§41-4-30 to 41-4-37.
See FINANCE.

Director of irrigation, §9-2-16.

Director of personnel.
Appointment, §36-26-7.
Duties, §36-26-8.
Investigations and hearings.
Generally. See within this heading, "Merit system."
Powers, §36-26-8.
Qualifications, §36-26-7.
Reports, §36-26-40.
Rules and regulations.
Promulgation, §36-25-9.
Salary, §36-26-7.
State personnel department.
Executive head, §§36-26-4, 36-26-8.
Studies, §36-26-40.

District attorneys.
See DISTRICT ATTORNEYS.

District courts.
See DISTRICT COURTS.

Dual office-holding, §36-2-1; Const. Ala., art. XVII, §280.
Congress, Const. U. S., Art. I, §6.
Salary of officer or employee filling more than one position or office, §36-6-3.

PUBLIC OFFICERS AND EMPLOYEES—Cont'd

Duties.
Neglect of duty.
Deductions from salaries or compensation, Const. Ala., art. IV, §87.

Education.
Diversion of funds by officials.
Penalty, §16-13-4.
State superintendent of education.
See EDUCATION.

Elections.
See ELECTIONS.

Eligibility for office.
Conviction of certain crimes bar to eligibility, Const. Ala., art. IV, §60.
Persons not eligible, §36-2-1.
Entering into public office of person disqualified by law, §36-2-2.

Emergencies.
Military service in time of national emergency, §§36-8-1 to 36-8-6. See within this heading, "Military affairs."

Employees' retirement system.
Military service.
Purchase of credit for active military service.
Option must be exercised and paid before October 1, 1986, §36-27-49.1.

Ethics.
Code of ethics, §§36-25-1 to 36-25-30. See within this heading, "Code of ethics."

Evidence.
Bonds, surety.
Proof of bonds or recognizances, §36-5-21.
Copies of required official bonds, etc., and transcripts, §12-21-104.
Exemplifications or copies of records, etc., kept in public office.
Proof, §12-21-67.
State employees' retirement system.
Photo-reproduced copies of records or documents.
Admissibility, §36-27-29.
Summary proceedings involving officials.
Sheriffs, coroners, etc.
Copy of execution and certification of clerk as evidence, §6-6-682.

Executions.
Summary proceedings involving officials.
Judgment against clerk, register or their sureties, §6-6-700.
Judgment against sheriff or coroner, §§6-6-681, 6-6-682.

Expenses.
Moving expenses, §§36-7-40 to 36-7-42.

PUBLIC OFFICERS AND EMPLOYEES—Cont'd

Expenses—Cont'd

Statement of expenses of state officers and employees to be filed with comptroller before warrant issued, §41-4-57.
Traveling expenses, §§36-7-20 to 36-7-23.

Fees.
Code of ethics.
Receipt of fees for services provided by state, §36-25-7.
Court costs generally.
See COSTS.
Creating, increasing or decreasing.
Special, private or local laws prohibited, Const. Ala., art. IV, §104.
Restrictions on receipt of fees, Const. Ala., art. V, §137; amd. 111.
Uniformity of laws regulating, Const. Ala., art. IV, §96.

Felonies.
Conviction of felony vacates office, §36-9-2.

Fiduciary funds in hands of officials, §§19-3-80 to 19-3-87.
See FIDUCIARIES.

Finance.
Statement of expenses of state officers and employees to be filed with comptroller before warrant issued, §41-4-57.

Fire fighters.
See FIRES AND FIRE PREVENTION.

Fire marshal.
See FIRES AND FIRE PREVENTION.

Foreign office or title, Const. U. S., Art. I, §9.

Foresters.
State forester, §§9-3-5, 9-3-6.

Forest fire wardens, §§9-13-6 to 9-13-9.

Fraud.
State employees' retirement system.
False statements for purpose of defrauding system, §36-27-27.

Game and fish wardens.
See FISH AND GAME.

Garnishment.
See GARNISHMENT.

General administrators, §§43-2-170 to 43-2-175.
See EXECUTORS AND ADMINISTRATORS.

Geologists.
State geologist, §§9-4-1 to 9-4-10.
See GEOLOGICAL SURVEY.

Governor.
See GOVERNOR.

Grand jury.
Bonds of county officers.
Examination, §12-16-192.

PUBLIC OFFICERS AND EMPLOYEES—Cont'd

Handicapped persons.
Merit system.
Certification for employment, §36-26-16.

Harbor masters, §§33-3-1 to 33-3-6.
See HARBORS AND PORTS.

Health.
State health officer, §22-2-8.

Health care authorities.
Code of ethics.
Applicability of ethics act, §22-21-334.

Health insurance plan.
State employees' health insurance plan, §§36-29-1 to 36-29-13.
See within this heading, "Insurance."

Hearings.
Merit system.
Investigations and hearings, §§36-26-40, 36-26-41, 36-26-43.
Public property, papers, etc.
Recovery by successors to office, §36-12-22.
Summary proceedings involving officials, §6-6-663.

Highways.
Director, §§23-1-21 to 23-1-21.3.

Holidays.
Compensatory leave.
When holiday worked, §1-3-8.

Impeachment.
See IMPEACHMENT.

Impersonating public servants, §13A-10-10.

Incompetency.
Impeachment.
See IMPEACHMENT.

Individual retirement account fund, §§36-27A-1 to 36-27A-7.
Administration, §36-27A-2.
Administrative cost, §36-27A-7.
Board of control, §§36-27A-2, 36-27A-3.
Contributions, §36-27A-6.
Creation, §36-27A-2.
Deduction of contributions, §36-27A-6.
Eligibility, §36-27A-5.
Investments, §36-27A-4.
Legislative intent, §36-27A-1.
Rules and regulations.
Authority of board to promulgate, §36-27A-3.
Voluntary participation, §36-27A-5.

Insanity.
Judgment of insanity of officeholder vacates office, §36-9-3.

Inspections.
Refusal to permit inspections, §13A-10-3.

Insurance.
County officers and employees, §§11-91-1 to 11-91-7.
See COUNTIES.

PUBLIC OFFICERS AND EMPLOYEES—Cont'd

Insurance—Cont'd

Motor vehicles.
Insurance of state employees operating motor vehicles in performance of duties, §36-1-6.
Municipal officers and employees, §§11-91-1 to 11-91-7.
See MUNICIPAL CORPORATIONS.
Negligent or wrongful acts of state employees, §36-1-6.1.
State employees' health insurance plan, §§36-29-1 to 36-29-13.
Appropriations, §36-29-13.
Benefits.
Payment, §36-29-11.
Board, §36-29-2.
Appropriations.
Subsequent appropriations to board, §36-29-13.
Defined, §36-29-1.
Design of plan.
Factors to be considered, §36-29-3.
Certificates.
Issuance to covered employees, §36-29-6.
Contracts with health insurance agencies or corporations, §36-29-6.
Coverage.
Persons covered generally, §36-29-8.
Coverage.
Dependents, §36-29-7.
Option, §36-29-8.
Persons covered under contract, §36-29-8.
Temporary legislative employees, §36-27-50.
Definitions, §36-29-1.
Dependents.
Inclusion in coverage.
Option, §36-29-8.
Retiring employees.
Contracts to provide for health insurance for spouses and dependents, §36-29-9.
Establishment, §36-29-4.
Provisions.
Generally, §36-29-4.
Retired employees.
Election to continue coverage, §36-29-10.
Retiring employees.
Contracts to provide for health insurance, §36-29-9.
Election as to participation in plan, §36-29-9.
Rules and regulations.
Adoption, §36-29-4.
Promulgation, §36-29-12.

PUBLIC OFFICERS AND EMPLOYEES—Cont'd

Insurance—Cont'd

State employees liability insurance.
Insurance coverage for negligent, wrongful acts of state employees, §36-1-6.1.

Irrigation.
Director of irrigation, §9-2-16.

Judges.
See JUDGES.

Jurisdiction.
Code of ethics.
Actions for violations of chapter, §36-25-27.

Jury.
Summary proceedings involving officials.
Judgment against officer accepting substitute for juror or serving person other than one to be drawn, §6-6-683.

Land agents, §9-2-130.

Legislature.
See LEGISLATURE.

Limitation of actions.
Actions for nonfeasance, misfeasance or malfeasance.
Ten year limitation, §6-2-33.

Lis pendens.
Liability of officers on bonds, §35-4-139.

Livestock inspectors, §§2-4-2, 2-4-3.

Lobbyists.
Code of ethics.
Former members of legislature not to be extended floor privileges for lobbying purposes, §36-25-23.
Notice required, §36-25-13.
Provisions not to be construed as affecting certain professional services, §36-25-22.
Registration of lobbyists.
Required, §36-25-18.
Reports.
Monthly reports to be filed by lobbyists, §36-25-19.
Public inspection, §36-25-21.
Public records, §36-25-21.
Termination of lobbying activities.
Notice.
Effect as to requirement for filing of reports, §36-25-20.
Filing, §36-25-20.
State or county officials.
Lobbying in legislature by state or county officials, Const. Ala., art. IV, §101.

Marine resources.
Division, §§9-2-81 to 9-2-89.
See MARINE RESOURCES.

PUBLIC OFFICERS AND EMPLOYEES—Cont'd

Meat and meat products.
Disclosure of information obtained by commissioner without proper authority, §2-17-36.

Mental health.
Judgment of insanity of officeholder vacates office, §36-9-3.

Mental health board.
Personnel policies and salary schedules, §22-50-40.

Merit system, §§36-26-1 to 36-26-108.
Appointments, Const. Ala., amd. 88.
Classified service, §36-26-17.
Extraordinary appointments, §36-26-18.
Offenses as to appointment for positions in classified service, §36-26-39.
Public health service personnel, §36-26-81.
Classification of positions, §36-26-11.
Classified service.
Applicability of rules and regulations of employment, §36-26-10.
Appointments, §36-26-17.
Capitol security police officers in department of finance, §36-26-66.
Defined, §36-26-10.
Disability determination division of state of education.
Certain employees of division, §36-26-65.
Employment registers.
Tests for establishment, §36-26-15.
Military service.
Effect of entry into active service, §36-26-30.
Offenses.
Testing, certification, appointment, etc., §36-26-39.
Restoration to merit or civil service classification after acceptance of non-merit appointment, §36-26-32.1.
Vacancies.
Filling, §36-26-17.
Compensation.
Annuities.
Tax-deferred annuity programs, §36-26-14.
Deferred compensation programs, §36-26-14.
Improper payments.
Actions to restrain, recover moneys, etc., §36-26-13.

PUBLIC OFFICERS AND EMPLOYEES—Cont'd

Merit system—Cont'd
Compensation—Cont'd
Pay plan.
Cooperation of board with federal government in establishing, §36-26-15.
Preparation, §36-26-12.
Payrolls.
Certification, §36-26-13.
Corrections.
Board of corrections.
Officers and employees, §14-1-4.
County and district health departments.
Definitions, §36-26-80.
Employees covered by system, §36-26-82.
Exceptions, §36-26-83.
Public health service personnel.
Appointment, §36-26-81.
Definitions, §36-26-2.
Classified service, §36-26-10.
County and district health departments, §36-26-80.
Exempt service, §36-26-10.
State institutions, §36-26-60.
Unclassified service, §36-26-10.
Demotions, §36-26-25.
Director of personnel, §§36-26-7, 36-26-8.
Disability determination division of state of education.
Certain employees of division, §36-26-65.
Discipline, §36-26-27.
Limitation period for charges, §36-26-29.
Dismissals, §36-26-29.
Domestic positions.
Adoption of procedures for filling, §36-26-19.
Educational or public television network.
Employees, §36-26-67.
Exempt service.
Defined, §36-26-10.
Extension of provisions to additional positions, §36-26-10.
Geological survey.
Retention of faculty members and students for research.
Persons retained not subject to merit system, §9-4-18.
Hale Memorial hospital.
Employees subject to merit system, §36-26-64.
Handicapped persons.
Certification for employment, §36-26-15.
Hearings, §§36-26-41 to 36-26-43.
Highways.
Department.
Chief engineer, §23-1-22.

PUBLIC OFFICERS AND EMPLOYEES—Cont'd

Merit system—Cont'd
Highways—Cont'd
Department—Cont'd
Legal division.
Assistant counsel, §23-1-26.
Chief counsel, §23-1-25.
Personnel, §23-1-33.
Investigations and hearings.
Buildings.
Use of state, county, etc., buildings, §36-26-43.
Generally, §36-26-40.
Witnesses.
Failure to appear and testify, §36-26-41.
False testimony.
Giving under oath, §36-26-41.
Fees, §36-26-41.
Layoffs, §36-26-26.
Leave.
Annual leave, §36-26-35.
Compensatory leave when holiday worked, §1-3-8.
Military service.
Granting of leave of absence, §36-26-31.
Sick leave.
Conversion of unused leave into membership service for retirement purposes, §36-26-36.1.
Partial payment for accrued sick leave at time of retirement, §36-26-36.
Longevity service recognition pins.
Design, purchase and awarding, §36-26-37.
Marine resources.
Director of division, §9-2-80.
Military affairs.
Effect of entry into active service upon status of classified employees, §36-26-30.
Granting of leave of absence for service in armed forces, §36-26-31.
Restoration of employee to former position after service in armed forces, §36-26-32.
Rights and privileges upon entry into military service.
Employees not in classified service, §36-26-33.
Penalties.
Violations, §36-26-47.
Political activities.
Generally, §36-26-38.
Promotions, §36-26-23; Const. Ala., amd. 88.
Purposes, §36-26-3.
Religion.
Granting of time off to comply with religious obligations, §36-26-34.

PUBLIC OFFICERS AND EMPLOYEES—Cont'd
Merit system—Cont'd
Restoration to merit or civil service classification after acceptance of non-merit appointment, §36-26-32.1.
Retirement.
Sick leave.
Conversion of unused leave into membership service for retirement purposes, §36-26-36.1.
Partial payment for accrued sick leave at retirement, §36-26-36.
Rules and regulations.
Promulgation by director, §36-26-9.
Semiskilled positions.
Adoption of procedures for filling, §36-26-19.
Service ratings, §36-26-22.
Short title, §36-26-1.
Standards of performance and output.
Establishment, §36-26-22.
State capitol guides.
Classified as "capitol hostesses," §36-26-46.
State institutions.
Applicability of merit system, §§36-26-61, 36-26-62.
Repeal of conflicting provisions, §36-26-63.
Defined, §36-26-60.
Employees subject to merit system, §36-26-61.
State personnel board.
General provisions, §§36-26-5, 36-26-6.
State personnel department, §36-26-4.
State treasurer.
Officers and employees subject to system, §36-17-5.
Suspensions, §36-26-28.
Test period.
Generally, §36-26-21.
Removal at expiration.
Restoration to eligibility list, §36-26-21.
Removal during, §36-26-21.
Tests.
Establishment of employment registers for positions in classified service, §36-26-15.
Offenses as to testing for positions in classified service, §36-26-39.
Training.
Programs, §36-26-20.
Transfers, §36-26-24.
Unclassified service.
Applicability of rules and regulations of employment, §36-26-10.
Defined, §36-26-10.
Unskilled positions.
Adoption of procedures for filling, §36-26-19.

PUBLIC OFFICERS AND EMPLOYEES—Cont'd
Merit system—Cont'd
Violations.
Penalties, §36-26-47.
Welfare.
County departments of pensions and security.
Personnel covered by provisions of state merit system, §38-2-8.
Military affairs.
Acceptance, etc., of commission, etc., in state armed forces and United States reserve components.
Not incompatible with holding of civil office, §31-2-36.
Credit for active federal service, §31-2-13.
Military leave of absence, §31-2-13.
Persons exempted from military service.
State officers, §31-2-6.
Service benefits for government employees, §31-2-13.
Service in time of war or national emergency, §§36-8-1 to 36-8-6.
Applicability of chapter, §36-8-6.
Compensation.
Effect of military service upon compensation of regular officials, §36-8-5.
Temporary acting officials, §36-8-3.
"Military service of the United States" defined, §36-8-1.
Powers.
Effect of military service upon powers of regular officials, §36-8-5.
Temporary acting officials, §36-8-3.
Temporary acting officials.
Appointment, §36-8-3.
Powers, §36-8-3.
Tenure, §36-8-4.
Tenure.
Effect of military service upon tenure of regular officials, §36-8-5.
Temporary acting officials, §36-8-4.
Vacancies in office.
Entry into military service not deemed vacation of office, §36-8-2.
State employees' retirement system.
Membership.
Military service, §36-27-4.
Misconduct.
Impeachment.
See IMPEACHMENT.

PUBLIC OFFICERS AND EMPLOYEES—Cont'd
Montgomery.
Residence requirement, §36-2-4.
Failure to comply deemed ground for impeachment or removal, §36-2-5.
Motor vehicles.
Insurance of state employees operating motor vehicles in performance of duties, §36-1-6.
Moving expenses, §§36-7-40 to 36-7-42.
Damages resulting from moving of household goods.
State not liable, §36-7-42.
Reimbursement.
Entitlement, §36-7-40.
Maximum amount, §36-7-40.
Procedure, §36-7-41.
Rules and regulations.
Eligibility and amount, §36-7-41.
Source of funds, §36-7-41.
Multiple office-holding, §36-2-1; Const. Ala., art. XVII, §280.
Congress, Const. U. S., Art. I, §6.
Salary of officer or employee filling more than one office, position, etc., §36-6-3.
Municipal corporations.
See MUNICIPAL CORPORATIONS.
Narcotics.
Impeachment.
Intemperance in use as grounds, §36-11-1.
Neglect of duty.
Deductions from salaries or compensation, Const. Ala., art. IV, §87.
Grounds for impeachment, §36-11-1.
Nepotism.
Prohibited in state service, §41-1-5.
Notaries public.
See NOTARIES PUBLIC.
Notice.
Code of ethics.
Lobbyists, §36-25-13.
Termination of lobbying activities, §36-25-20.
Notice of candidacy for state office, §36-25-15.
Removal of officer from county, etc., for which elected or appointed, §36-9-14.
Vacancies in office.
Death of officers, §36-9-6.
Notice to legislature of vacancies to be filled, §36-9-16.
Oaths, §§36-4-1 to 36-4-9.
Administration, §36-4-1.
Oaths of deputies, §36-4-5.
Applicability of chapter, §36-4-9.
Auditor.
Oaths required to be filed with auditor, §36-4-2.

PUBLIC OFFICERS AND EMPLOYEES—Cont'd

Oaths—Cont'd

Corrections.

Board of corrections.

Chiefs of divisions.

Constitutional oath of office, §14-1-7.

Deputies.

Administration, §36-4-5.

Filing, §36-4-5.

Endorsement.

Date of filing, §36-4-7.

Filing.

Endorsement with date of filing, §36-4-7.

Oaths of deputies, §36-4-5.

Oaths to be filed with secretary of state and auditor, §36-4-2.

Secretary of state.

Oaths required to be filed with secretary, §36-4-2.

Obstructing governmental operations.

Class A misdemeanor, §13A-10-2.

Definitions, §13A-10-1.

Elements of crime, §13A-10-2.

Offenses by officers.

Bribery.

See BRIBERY.

Code of ethics, §§36-25-1 to 36-25-30. See within this heading, "Code of ethics."

Conflicts of interest generally.

See CONFLICTS OF INTEREST.

Elections.

See ELECTIONS.

Prisoners.

Keeping incommunicado, §36-10-16.

Threatening for purpose of extorting confession, §36-10-16.

Offices.

Location, §36-2-3.

Rental of offices, §§36-24-1 to 36-24-4.

Official bonds. See within this heading, "Bonds, surety."

Papers.

Public property, papers, etc., §§36-12-1 to 36-12-64. See within this heading, "Public property, papers, etc."

Parties.

Death or separation from office.

Substitution of parties, ARCP, Rule 25 (d).

Payroll deductions.

Charitable organizations, §36-1-4.1.

Community chests, etc., §36-1-4.

Dues and contributions for employee organizations, §36-1-4.4.

Dues, contributions and premiums.

Statewide policy, §36-1-4.3.

Termination of deductions, §36-1-4.3.

PUBLIC OFFICERS AND EMPLOYEES—Cont'd

Payroll deductions—Cont'd

Firefighters, §36-1-4.2.

National health agencies, §36-1-4.1.

State comptroller.

Policy for deductions for dues, contributions and premiums, §36-1-4.3.

Peace officers.

General provisions.

See PEACE OFFICERS.

Penalties.

Bonds, surety.

Failure to endorse date of filing on bond, §36-5-10.

Failure to file.

Failure to give notice of omission of public officer to file official bonds, §36-5-17.

Performance of official act by public officer prior to approval and filing of bond, §36-5-22.

Code of ethics.

Violations, §36-25-27.

Commissions.

Exercise of duties of office without first obtaining, §36-2-9.

Entering into public office of person disqualified by law, §36-2-2.

Merit system.

Violations, §36-26-47.

Pensions.

State employees' retirement system, §§36-27-1 to 36-27-86. See within this heading, "State employees' retirement system."

Personnel board.

General provisions, §§36-26-5, 36-26-6.

Personnel department.

General provisions, §36-26-4.

Personnel system.

Fire fighters' personnel standards and education commission, §§36-32-1 to 36-32-6.

See FIRES AND FIRE PREVENTION.

Merit system, §§36-26-1 to 36-26-108. See within this heading, "Merit system."

Pleadings.

Official document or act, ARCP, Rule 9 (d).

Police.

See POLICE.

Politics.

Improper use of position to influence vote or political action, §17-1-7.

Participation in political activities, §17-1-7.

Right of city and county employees to participate in political activities, §17-1-7.

Use of state-owned property for political purposes, §§36-12-60 to 36-12-64.

PUBLIC OFFICERS AND EMPLOYEES—Cont'd

Poultry.

Disclosure by state officer or employee of information obtained by commissioner without proper authority, §2-17-36.

Preretirement death benefit program, §§36-27B-1 to 36-27B-5.

Amount of benefits, §36-27B-3.

Contributions.

Certification of decrease in rate of employer contributions, §36-27B-5.

Creation, §36-27B-1.

Effective date of program, §36-27B-1.

Funds.

Established, §36-27B-2.

Transfer of funds, §36-27B-2.

Group life insurance.

Authorized as death benefit, §36-27B-4.

Payment of benefits, §36-27B-3.

Presents from foreign states, Const. U. S., Art. I, §9.

Property.

Acquiring pecuniary interest in property.

Misuse of confidential information, §13A-10-82.

Public property, papers, etc., §§36-12-1 to 36-12-64. See within this heading, "Public property, papers, etc."

Protection of certain state officers and visitors, §§36-33-1 to 36-33-4.

Authorized, §36-33-2.

Definitions, §36-33-1.

Obstruction of protective functions, §36-33-3.

Threatening certain state officers, §36-33-4.

Public employees individual retirement account fund, §§36-27A-1 to 36-27A-7.

Administrative cost, §36-27A-7.

Board of control, §36-27A-2.

Rules and regulations.

Promulgation, §36-27A-3.

Contributions, §36-27A-6.

Costs.

Administrative costs, §36-27A-7.

Creation, §36-27A-2.

Administration by board of control, §36-27A-2.

Eligibility, §36-27A-5.

Investments, §36-27A-4.

Legislative intent, §36-27A-1.

Rules and regulations.

Authority of board to promulgate, §36-27A-3.

Public property, papers, etc., §§36-12-1 to 36-12-64.

Definitions.

Public officer or servant, §36-12-1.

PUBLIC OFFICERS AND EMPLOYEES—Cont'd

Public property, papers, etc. —Cont'd
Disposition when no longer current, §36-12-5.
Inspection and copying of records.
See RECORDS.
Maintenance, §36-12-2.
Permanence.
Required, §36-12-3.
Preservation, §36-12-2.
Recovery of papers, property, etc., by successors to office, §§36-12-21 to 36-12-26.
Affidavit, §§36-12-22 to 36-12-24.
Complaint.
Filing, §36-12-21.
Death of incumbent, §36-12-26.
Hearing, §36-12-22.
Orders.
Issuance, §36-12-21.
Seizure.
Delivery to complainant, §36-12-25.
Examination upon, §36-12-25.
Issuance of warrant, §36-12-24.
Termination of proceedings upon making of affidavit, §36-12-22.
Selection of materials.
Factors, §36-12-3.
Successors in office.
Delivery to, §§36-12-4, 36-12-20.
Recovery of papers, property, etc., by successors to office, §§36-12-21 to 36-12-26.
Uniformity in size, style, etc.
Required, §36-12-3.
Use for political purposes, §§36-12-60 to 36-12-64.
Campaign literature.
Transportation in state-owned vehicles, §36-12-62.
Candidates.
Promotion or advancement of interests, §36-12-61.
Department heads.
Duty to discharge violators of article, §36-12-63.
Liability for violations, §36-12-64.
Purpose of article, §36-12-60.
Violations of article.
Duty of department heads to discharge violators, §36-12-63.
Liability, §36-12-64.
Public service commission.
See PUBLIC SERVICE COMMISSION.
Public works.
Superintendent of public works.
General provisions, §§14-4-11 to 14-4-14.
Quo warranto.
See QUO WARRANTO.

PUBLIC OFFICERS AND EMPLOYEES—Cont'd

Records.
Certificate of public officer on nonexistence of record.
Admissibility and proof of artifact, §12-21-34.
Public property, papers, etc., §§36-12-1 to 36-12-64.
See within this heading, "Public property, papers, etc."
State employees' retirement system, §§36-27-27, 36-27-29.
State personnel department, §36-26-44.
Registers.
Circuit registers.
See CIRCUIT COURTS.
Religious tests.
Prohibited, Const. U. S., Art. VI.
Removal.
Failure to reside in Montgomery, §36-2-5.
Rental of offices, §§36-24-1 to 36-24-4.
Authorized, §36-24-1.
Contract.
Termination, §36-24-3.
Payment, §36-24-2.
Purposes, §36-24-4.
Termination of contracts, §36-24-3.
Reporter of decisions of supreme court and courts of appeals.
See REPORTER OF DECISIONS OF SUPREME COURT AND COURTS OF APPEALS.
Reports.
Code of ethics.
Lobbyists.
Monthly reports, §36-25-19.
Public inspection, §36-25-21.
Public records, §36-25-21.
State ethics commission.
Annual reports, §36-25-3.
Violations, §36-25-17.
Copies.
Reduction of number of printed copies, §36-1-3.
Director of personnel, §36-26-40.
Failure to file required reports, §13A-10-4.
Printing, §41-4-141.
Time for making, §41-4-141.
Representatives.
Congress.
See CONGRESS.
General assembly.
See LEGISLATURE.
Residence, §36-2-3.
Montgomery, §36-2-4.
Failure to comply deemed ground for impeachment or removal, §36-2-5.
Resignation.
Vacation of office, §36-9-1.

PUBLIC OFFICERS AND EMPLOYEES—Cont'd

Retirement.
Payments or grants to retiring officers, Const. Ala., art. IV, §98.
State employees' retirement system, §§36-27-1 to 36-27-86. See within this heading, "State employees' retirement system."
Rules and regulations.
Code of ethics.
State ethics commission.
Waiver of rules and regulations, §36-25-3.
Director of personnel.
Promulgation, §36-26-9.
Insurance.
Expenses not included, §36-29-5.
State employees' health insurance plan, §36-29-4.
Treatment not included, §36-29-5.
Merit system.
Applicability to employees in classified and unclassified service, §36-26-10.
Moving expenses.
Reimbursement.
Eligibility and amount, §36-7-41.
Salaries.
Death.
Payment of salary of deceased officer after date of death, Const. Ala., art. IV, §97.
Deductions from salaries for neglect of duty, Const. Ala., art. IV, §87.
Extra compensation not to be granted after service rendered, Const. Ala., art. IV, §68.
Garnishment.
See GARNISHMENT.
General provisions.
See SALARIES.
Increase or decrease in salary, Const. Ala., amd. 92.
Increase or decrease of compensation during term of office, Const. Ala., art. IV, §68; art. XVII, §281.
Suspension of restriction on diminishing public salaries, Const. Ala., amd. 26A.
Suspension of restriction on diminishing public salaries, Const. Ala., amd. 26A.
Salary deductions.
Charitable organizations, §§36-1-4, 36-1-4.1.
Dues, contributions and premiums, §36-1-4.3.
Employee organization dues and contributions, §36-1-4.4.
Firefighters.
Political subdivisions may provide for, §36-1-4.2.

PUBLIC OFFICERS AND EMPLOYEES—Cont'd

Salary deductions—Cont'd

State employees.

Charitable organizations, §§36-1-4, 36-1-4.1.

Dues, contributions and premiums, §36-1-4.3.

Savings and loan associations.

Acknowledgment, etc., of instruments by public officers employed by associations validated, §5-16-41.

Secretary of state.

See SECRETARY OF STATE.

Senators.

General assembly.

See LEGISLATURE.

Sentencing.

Article not to deprive court of authority to remove person from office, §13A-5-2.

Sheriffs.

See SHERIFFS.

Social security, §§36-28-1 to 36-28-10.

See SOCIAL SECURITY.

Southeast interstate low-level radioactive waste management compact.

Cooperation with commission, §22-32-7.

Speculation through misuse of confidential information, §13A-10-82.

State auditor.

See STATE AUDITOR.

State employees' retirement system, §§36-27-1 to 36-27-86.

Actuary, §36-27-23.

Designation, §36-27-23.

Duties, §36-27-23.

Allowances.

Cancellation of survivor allowances, §36-27-16.1.

Retirement allowances, §§36-27-16 to 36-27-22.

Survivor allowances.

Cancellation, §36-27-16.1.

Nomination of recipient of surviving spouse benefits prior to date of retirement, §36-27-16.2.

Annuities.

Exemption from taxation, attachment, etc., §36-27-28.

Appropriations.

Funds, §36-27-24.

Reopening of system for certain employees, §36-27-47.

Attachments.

Exemption of pension, annuity, etc., §36-27-28.

Auburn University.

Employees of cooperative extension service under federal appointment.

Participation in systems, §36-27-7.

PUBLIC OFFICERS AND EMPLOYEES—Cont'd

State employees' retirement system—Cont'd

Benefits.

Cost-of-living increase.

Amount, §§36-27-80, 36-27-81.

Board of control's and employer's duties and responsibilities §36-27-84.

Employers may elect to come under provisions, §36-27-84.

Medicaid benefits.

Effect, §36-27-85.

Provisions supplemental to other laws regulating payment, §36-27-86.

Survivor allowance adjustments, §36-27-83.

Right to decline portion of benefits, §36-1-5.

Disposition of amounts declined, §36-1-5.

Board of control, §36-27-23.

Attorney general.

Legal adviser to board, §36-27-23.

Composition, §36-27-23.

Elected members, §36-27-23.

Expenses of members, §36-27-23.

Oath of office of members, §36-27-23.

Record of proceedings, §36-27-23.

Reports.

Publication of annual report, §36-27-23.

Secretary-treasurer, §36-27-23.

Vacancies in office, §36-27-23.

Cities.

Participation of employees, §36-27-6.

Contributions.

County engineers.

Payment of member's and employer's contributions by state highway department, §36-27-9.

Department heads.

Credit for service as department head.

Payment of employee's contributions, §36-27-15.

Disposition upon death, §36-27-16.

Elected officials.

Credit for service as elected official of state.

Payment of employee's contributions, §36-27-15.

Legislature.

Credit for years served as member.

Payment of employee's contribution, §36-27-13.

PUBLIC OFFICERS AND EMPLOYEES—Cont'd

State employees' retirement system—Cont'd

Contributions—Cont'd

Legislature—Cont'd

Credit for years served as officer or subordinate officer.

Payment of employee's contributions, §36-27-14.

Makeup contributions.

Payment by certain persons, §36-27-11.

Reopening of system for certain employees.

Interest on contributions, §36-27-44.

Payment of contributions, §36-27-41.

Counties.

County engineers.

Administration of provisions, §36-27-10.

Future service.

Procedure as to, §36-27-10.

Payment of member's and employer's contributions by state highway department, §36-27-9.

Prior service and membership service in county.

Procedure for receipt of full credits, §36-27-10.

Participation of employees, §36-27-6.

Creation, §36-27-2.

Creditable service.

Claiming and purchasing credit for active military service, §36-27-49.2.

Option to be exercised and paid before October 1, 1988, §36-27-49.2.

Claiming and purchasing credit for retirement system service, §36-27-49.2.

Option to be exercised and paid before October 1, 1988, §36-27-49.2.

Computation at retirement, §36-27-11.

Department heads, §36-27-15.

Determination of prior creditable service, §36-27-11.

Elected officials, §36-27-15.

Legislative employment.

Purchase of credit, §36-27-53.

Legislature, §§36-27-13, 36-27-14.

Municipal officers or employees.

Credit for prior service with another municipality, §36-27-51.

PUBLIC OFFICERS AND EMPLOYEES—Cont'd
State employees' retirement system—Cont'd
Creditable service—Cont'd
National youth administration, §36-27-15.1.
Public employment out of state, §36-27-15.2.
Purchase by member prohibited from participating because of age, §36-27-4.1.
Purchase of credit for active military service, §36-27-49.
Option to be exercised and paid before October 1, 1986, §36-27-49.1.
Purchase of prior service credits by certain active members, §36-27-48.
Temporary legislative employees, §36-27-50.
Reopening of system for certain employees.
Credit for prior service, §§36-27-42, 36-27-43.
Restoration to certain persons.
Procedure, §36-27-11.
Retirement with not less than 30 years' creditable service, §36-27-18.
Teachers' retirement system of Alabama.
Transfer of service credits from, §36-27-12.
Withdrawal from service.
Effect, §36-27-16.
Death benefits.
Preretirement death benefit program, §§36-27B-1 to 36-27B-5.
Definitions, §36-27-1.
Reopening of system for certain employees, §36-27-40.
Departments.
Credit for service as department head, §36-27-15.
Employee who becomes director or employee of department.
Continuation of participation in system, §36-27-8.
Matching contributions, §36-27-8.
Designation, §36-27-2.
Documents.
Photo-reproduced copies.
Admissibility in evidence, §36-27-29.
Elected officials.
Credit for service as elected official of state.
Applicability of provisions, §36-27-15.
Granting, §36-27-15.
Maximum credit, §36-27-15.

PUBLIC OFFICERS AND EMPLOYEES—Cont'd
State employees' retirement system—Cont'd
Elected officials—Cont'd
Credit for service as elected official of state —Cont'd
Payment of employee's contributions, §36-27-15.
Fraud.
False statements for purpose of defrauding, §36-27-27.
Funds.
Appropriations, §36-27-24.
Composition, §36-27-24.
Contributions to, §36-27-24.
Creation, §36-27-24.
Disbursements, §36-27-24.
Management, §36-27-25.
Health insurance.
Withholding of amounts from retirement pay to pay premium on state group hospitalization or health insurance plan, §36-27-22.
Highway department.
Payment of member's and employer's contributions for county engineers, §36-27-9.
Hospitalization.
Withholding of amounts from retirement pay to pay premium on state group hospitalization or health insurance plan, §36-27-22.
Legislation affecting system.
Proposed legislation to be accompanied by actuarial estimate of cost, §36-27-26.
Legislative employees.
Contributions of part time employees.
Additional payment and credit, §36-27-103.
Amount, §36-27-101.
Definitions, §36-27-100.
Eligibility, §36-27-101.
Restrictions on purchase of additional retirement time, §36-27-102.
Time for payment, §36-27-102.
Creditable service.
Purchase of credit, §36-27-53.
Legislature.
Credit for years served as member, §36-27-13.
Credit for years served as officer or subordinate officer.
Applicability of provisions, §36-27-14.
Granting, §36-27-14.
Maximum credit, §36-27-14.
Payment of employee's contributions, §36-27-14.

PUBLIC OFFICERS AND EMPLOYEES—Cont'd
State employees' retirement system—Cont'd
Legislature—Cont'd
Temporary legislative employees.
Coverage by retirement system, §36-27-50.
Management, §36-27-2.
Medical board, §36-27-23.
Membership.
Absence from service, §36-27-4.
Age limitation.
Purchase of service credit by member prohibited from participating, §36-27-4.1.
Applicability of other provisions pertaining to pensions or retirement benefits for state employees to members, §36-27-30.
Board of pardons and paroles.
Members, §36-27-5.
Denial, §36-27-4.
Generally, §36-27-4.
Military service, §36-27-4.
Physical fitness department.
Director, §36-27-5.
Temporary legislative employees, §36-27-50.
Military service.
Claiming and purchasing credit for active military service, §§36-27-49, 36-27-49.2.
Option to be exercised and paid before October 1, 1988, §36-27-49.2.
Municipal officers or employees.
Creditable service.
Credit for prior service with another municipality, §36-27-51.
National youth administration.
Granting of credit for service, §36-27-15.1.
Optional retirement for previously retired state employees, §36-27-8.1.
Payments.
Correction of errors, §36-27-27.
Powers, §36-27-2.
Corporate powers, §36-27-3.
Privileges, §36-27-2.
Public or quasi-public organizations.
Participation of employees, §36-27-6.
Purchase of prior service credits by certain active members, §36-27-48.
Purpose, §36-27-2.
Records.
Correction of errors, §36-27-27.
Photo-reproduced copies.
Admissibility in evidence, §36-27-29.

PUBLIC OFFICERS AND EMPLOYEES—Cont'd
State employees' retirement system—Cont'd
Reopening of system for certain employees, §§36-27-40 to 36-27-47.
Allowance payments due on or after October 1, 1975.
Redetermination, §36-27-45.
Appropriations, §36-27-47.
Contributions.
Interest, §36-27-44.
Payment, §36-27-41.
Credit for prior service.
Generally, §36-27-42.
School bus driver, mechanic or maintenance worker, §36-27-43.
Definitions, §36-27-40.
Employees for whom system reopened, §36-27-41.
Employer cost continuing liability, §36-27-46.
Retirement.
Allowances, §36-26-16.
Additional cost of benefits, §36-27-16.3.
Cancellation of survivor allowance, §36-27-16.1.
Cost-of-living increase for persons whose date of retirement is prior to October 1, 1984.
Amount, §36-27-21.5.
Appropriations,
Eligibility where medicaid eligibility would be impaired, §36-27-21.4.
Funding, §§36-27-21.4, 36-27-21.5.
Cost-of-living increase for persons whose date of retirement is prior to October 1, 1987, §16-25-42.
Additional adjustments, §16-25-43.
Appropriations, §16-25-45.
Impairment of eligibility under medicaid, §16-25-46.
Provisions of article supplemental, §16-25-47.
Disability retirement allowance, §36-27-16.
Disposition upon death, §36-27-16.
Effective date of benefits, §36-27-16.3.
Exemption from taxation, attachment, etc., §36-27-28.

PUBLIC OFFICERS AND EMPLOYEES—Cont'd
State employees' retirement system—Cont'd
Retirement—Cont'd
Allowances—Cont'd
Increase in maximum retirement allowance.
Cost-of-living increase for persons whose date of retirement is prior to October 1, 1984, §36-27-21.4.
1969 ten percent increase, §36-27-19.
1971 five percent increase, §36-27-20.
1975 fifteen percent increase, §36-27-21.
1978 cost-of-living increase, §36-27-21.1.
1980 cost-of-living increase, §36-27-21.2.
1982 cost-of-living increase, §36-27-21.3.
Nomination of recipient of surviving spouse benefits prior to date of retirement, §36-27-16.2.
Optional allowances, §36-27-16.
Redetermination of allowances, §36-27-16.
Allowances due on or after October 1, 1975, §36-27-17.
Reopening of system for certain employees.
Redetermination of allowance payments due on or after October 1, 1975, §36-27-45.
Survivor allowance.
Cancellation, §36-27-16.1.
Nomination of recipient of surviving spouse benefits prior to date of retirement, §36-27-16.2.
Withholding to pay premium on state group hospitalization or health insurance plan, §36-27-22.
Disabled employees, §36-27-16.
Generally, §36-27-16.
Not less than 30 years' creditable service, §36-27-18.
Public hospitals or related facilities.
Cost-of-living increase for retirees, §36-27-21.6.
Service retirement allowance.
Amount, §36-27-16.

PUBLIC OFFICERS AND EMPLOYEES—Cont'd
State employees' retirement system—Cont'd
Sick leave.
Conversion of unused leave into membership service, §36-26-36.1.
Taxation.
Exemption of pension, annuity, etc., §36-27-28.
Teachers' retirement system of Alabama.
Creditable service for public employment out of state, §36-27-15.2.
Nomination of recipient of surviving spouse benefits prior to date of retirement, §36-27-16.2.
Transfer of service credits, §36-27-12.
Towns.
Participation of employees, §36-27-6.
Withdrawal from service, §36-27-16.
State ethics commission, §§36-25-3, 36-25-4.
State forester, §§9-3-5, 9-3-6.
State geologist, §§9-4-1 to 9-4-10.
See GEOLOGICAL SURVEY.
State personnel board, §§36-26-5, 36-26-6.
Appointment of members, §36-26-5.
Classified employee member.
Procedure for electing, §36-26-5.
Compensation of members, §36-26-5.
Composition, §36-26-5.
Duties, §36-26-6.
Federal government.
Cooperation with board in establishing and administering standards of personnel qualifications, pay plans, etc., §36-26-15.
Meetings, §36-26-6.
Powers, §36-26-6.
Qualifications of members, §36-26-5.
Removal of members, §36-26-5.
Terms of office, §36-26-5.
State personnel department.
Composition, §36-26-4.
Created, §36-26-4.
Executive head, §36-26-4.
Expenses.
Payment, §36-26-45.
Judicial proceedings.
Representation of department, §36-26-42.
Municipal corporations.
Civil service merit systems for law enforcement officers, §§11-43-180 to 11-43-190.
See MUNICIPAL CORPORATIONS.
Offices, §36-26-4.
Records.
Inspection, §36-26-44.

PUBLIC OFFICERS AND EMPLOYEES—Cont'd
State personnel department
—Cont'd
Rules and regulations.
Exemptions.
Board of corrections, §14-1-4.
State police.
See STATE POLICE.
State service commissioner.
See VETERANS.
State toxicologist.
See STATE TOXICOLOGIST.
State treasurer.
See STATE TREASURER.
Succession to office.
Actions by the state.
Right of successor of public officer to commence, §6-5-3.
Recovery of papers, property, etc., by successors to office, §§36-12-21 to 36-12-26. See within this heading, "Public property, papers, etc."
Suggestions.
Employee suggestion award program, §36-1-7.
Board, §36-1-7.
Maximum cash award, §36-1-7.
Ratification of suggestion, §36-1-7.
Implementation of suggestion by department, §36-1-7.
Summary proceedings involving officials.
Attorneys at law.
Judgment for failure to pay over money collected or deliver personal property recovered in capacity as attorney, §6-6-740.
Clerks and registers.
Entry of judgment against, §6-6-700.
Failure to pay over moneys collected or received for county, §6-6-723.
County treasurers, §6-6-720.
Failure to pay allowed claim, §6-6-722.
Hearing and determination, §6-6-663.
Notice of motion for judgment, §6-6-660.
Parties, §6-6-662.
Probate judges, §6-6-720.
Failure to pay over moneys collected or received for county, §6-6-723.
Forfeiture of half of compensation for failure to discharge duties, §6-6-721.
Sheriffs, coroners, etc.
Executions.
Copy of execution and certification of clerk as evidence, §6-6-682.
Judgment in favor of clerk of supreme court, §6-6-682.

PUBLIC OFFICERS AND EMPLOYEES—Cont'd
Summary proceedings involving officials
—Cont'd
Sheriffs, coroners, etc
—Cont'd
Executions—Cont'd
Judgment in favor of defendant in execution, §6-6-681.
Failure to pay over moneys collected or received for county, §6-6-723.
Juries.
Judgment against officer accepting substitute for juror or serving person other than one to be drawn, §6-6-683.
Summary judgment in favor of sheriff or coroner, §6-6-684.
Writs.
Judgment against sheriff, etc., receiving or executing, §6-6-680.
Tax assessors, §6-6-720.
Forfeiture of half of compensation for failure to discharge duties, §6-6-721.
Tax collectors, §6-6-720.
Failure to pay over moneys collected or received for county, §6-6-723.
Forfeiture of half of compensation for failure to discharge duties, §6-6-721.
Venue, §6-6-661.
Superintendent of banks.
See BANKS AND FINANCIAL INSTITUTIONS.
Superintendent of education.
See EDUCATION.
Tax assessors.
See TAXATION.
Taxation.
General provisions.
See TAXATION.
State employees' retirement system.
Exemption of pension, annuity, etc., §36-27-28.
Tax collectors.
See TAXATION.
Terms of office.
Abridgement.
Vacation of office, §36-9-1.
Threats.
Protection of certain state officers and visitors, §§36-33-1 to 36-33-4.
Trading in public office, §13A-10-63.
Transcripts.
Evidence.
Copies of transcripts, §12-21-104.
Traveling expenses, §§36-7-20 to 36-7-23.
Applicability of article, §36-7-23.
Conflicting laws.
Repeal, §36-7-23.
In-state travel, §36-7-20.

PUBLIC OFFICERS AND EMPLOYEES—Cont'd
Traveling expenses—Cont'd
Mileage allowance.
Persons traveling on official business in privately owned vehicles, §36-7-22.
Out-of-state travel, §36-7-21.
Privately owned vehicles.
Mileage allowance for persons traveling on official business in, §36-7-22.
Treasurer.
State treasurer.
See STATE TREASURER.
United States.
Appointment, Const. U. S., Art. II, §2.
Bribery, Const. U. S., Art. II, §4.
Commissions, Const. U. S., Art. II, §3.
Emoluments, Const. U. S., Art. I, §9.
Holding more than one office, Const. U. S., Art. I, §6.
Impeachment, Const. U. S., Art. II, §4.
Ineligibility of members of congress, Const. U. S., Art. I, §6.
Presents from foreign states, Const. U. S., Art. I, §9.
Presidential electors.
Eligibility, Const. U. S., Art. II, §1.
Religious tests, Const. U. S., Art. VI.
Removal, Const. U. S., Art. II, §4.
Treason, Const. U. S., Art. II, §4.
Vacancies, Const. U. S., Art. II, §2.
Vacancies in office.
Bonds, surety.
Failure to give bond within prescribed time vacates office, §36-5-15.
Death, §36-9-1.
Notice, §36-9-6.
Failure to elect successor.
Offices vacated by failure, §36-9-5.
Felonies.
Conviction of felony vacates office, §36-9-2.
Filling.
Generally, §36-9-17.
How offices vacated.
Generally, §36-9-1.
Insanity.
Judgment vacates office, §36-9-3.
Judgments.
Certification of judgment declaring office vacated, §36-9-15.
Military service during war and national emergencies.
Entry into military service not to be deemed vacation of office, §36-8-2.

PUBLIC OFFICERS AND EMPLOYEES—Cont'd

Vacancies in office—Cont'd

Notice to legislature of vacancies to be filled, §36-9-16.

President.
Appointments during senate recess, Const. U. S., Art. II, §2.

Public property, papers, etc.
Delivery to successor upon vacation of office, §36-12-20.

Residence requirements.
Incumbents ceasing to be resident, §36-9-1.

Resignation, §36-9-1.

State ethics commission.
Filling, §36-25-3.

Void election, §36-9-1.
Declaration vacates office, §36-9-1.
Judgment declaring election or appointment void or office vacated.
Certification, §36-9-15.

Validation.
De facto officials.
Official act, §36-1-2.

Venue.
Bonds, surety.
Breach of official bond, §6-3-8.
Code of ethics.
Actions for violations of chapter, §36-25-27.

Veterans.
State service commissioner.
See VETERANS.

Veterinarians.
State veterinarian, §§2-4-1 to 2-4-4.
See VETERINARIANS.

Visitors.
Protection of certain state officers and visitors, §§36-33-1 to 36-33-4.

War.
Military service in time of war, §§36-8-1 to 36-8-6.
See within this heading, "Military affairs."

Water conservation and irrigation.
Director of irrigation, §9-2-16.

Weighmasters, §§8-16-50 to 8-16-59.
See WEIGHTS AND MEASURES.

Witnesses.
Merit system.
Investigations and hearings, §§36-26-40, 36-26-41, 36-26-43.

Writs.
Summary proceedings involving officials.
Judgment against sheriff, etc., receiving or executing writ, §6-6-680.

PUBLIC RECORDS.

Appeals.
Record on appeal.
See APPEALS.

PUBLIC RECORDS—Cont'd

Cahaba trace commission.
Revenues and expenditures, §41-9-809.

Circuit courts.
Clerks of court.
Records.
See CIRCUIT COURTS.
Registers.
See CIRCUIT COURTS.

Constitution of the United States.
Full faith and credit clause, Const. U. S., Art. IV, §1.
Proof, Const. U. S., Art. IV, §1.

Copies, §§36-12-40, 36-12-41.

Counties.
Local government records commission, §§41-13-22 to 41-13-25.
Records generally.
See COUNTIES.

Courts generally.
See COURTS.

Criminal law and procedure.
Crime victims' compensation.
Alteration of commission records.
Penalties, §15-23-20.
Criminal justice information center, §§41-9-590 to 41-9-648.
See CRIMINAL LAW AND PROCEDURE.
Indictments.
Records.
See INDICTMENTS.
Tampering with government records, §13A-10-12.

Defined, §41-13-1.

Department of archives and history.
Photography or microphotography centralized in department, §41-13-41.
Preservation, filing, etc., of public records.
Assistance of public officials by department, §41-13-4.

Destruction.
Courts.
Records.
Substitution of lost or destroyed papers or records in civil cases.
See COURTS.

District courts.
Records.
See DISTRICT COURTS.

Education.
Records.
See EDUCATION.

Environmental management commission.
Proceedings, §§22-22A-6, 22-22A-7.

Fees.
Copies, §36-12-41.
Court records, ARJA, Rule 30.
Court records.
Copies and certification, ARJA, Rule 30.
Substitution of lost or destroyed records, §12-20-1.

PUBLIC RECORDS—Cont'd

Finance.
Counties.
Record of financial status, §§11-8-7, 11-8-8.
General provisions.
See FINANCE.

Forests and forestry.
Records generally.
See FORESTS AND FORESTRY.

Full faith and credit, Const. U. S., Art. IV, §1.

Funerals, §22-9-7.
Board of funeral services, §§34-13-4, 34-13-25.

Health.
County health officers, §22-3-5.

Health care authorities.
Board.
Meetings, §22-21-316.

Hospitals.
Publicly owned medical institutions.
Annual audit, §22-21-4.

Impeachment.
Final record of impeachment proceedings.
Preparation, §36-11-22.

Income tax records, §§40-18-48, 40-18-107.

Indian affairs commission.
Fiscal records, §41-9-717.

Indictments.
Records.
See INDICTMENTS.

Inspection or examination.
Right of citizens, §36-12-40.

Judgments, §§12-20-21, 12-20-23.

Jury.
Selection and service, §12-16-64.

Juvenile offenders, §15-19-7.

Juvenile proceedings.
Records generally.
See JUVENILE PROCEEDINGS.

Legislature.
Records, §§29-1-14 to 29-1-17.

Libraries.
Right of citizens to copy.
Exemption, §36-12-40.

Library boards, §11-90-3.

Lis pendens records, §§35-4-130 to 35-4-138.
See LIS PENDENS.

Local government records commission, §§41-13-22 to 41-13-25.

Lost records.
Courts.
Establishment of lost record of state, county or municipality, §12-20-50.
Substitution of lost or destroyed paper or records in civil cases.
See COURTS.

Marriage.
Records.
See MARRIAGE.

Mental illness, §§22-50-60, 22-50-62.

Microphotographing.
Photographing or microphotographing.
See RECORDS.

PUBLIC RECORDS—Cont'd
Military affairs.
Honorable discharge, §31-1-1.
Safekeeping, Const. Ala., art.
XV, §277.
**Motor sports hall of fame
commission,** §41-9-470.
Motor vehicles.
Records generally.
See MOTOR VEHICLES.
Municipal corporations.
Local government records
commission, §§41-13-22
to 41-13-25.
Municipal records generally.
See MUNICIPAL
CORPORATIONS.
Nonexistence.
Certificate of public officer
on nonexistence of
record.
Evidentiary admissibility
of artifact, §12-21-34.
Orders of court, §12-20-21.
Parole, §§15-22-25, 15-22-34.
**Peace officers annuity and
benefit fund.**
Board of commissioners,
§36-21-65.
**Photographing or
microphotographing.**
See RECORDS.
Preservation.
Assistance of department of
archives and history,
§41-13-4.
Local government records
commission, §41-13-23.
State records commission,
§41-13-21.
Prisons and prisoners.
Records.
See PRISONS AND
PRISONERS.
Probate judges.
Records.
See PROBATE COURTS.
Probation, §§15-22-25,
15-22-53.
Public defenders, §15-22-44.
Public lands.
Records generally.
See PUBLIC LANDS.
**Public officers and
employees.**
Records generally.
See PUBLIC OFFICERS
AND EMPLOYEES.
Public service commission.
Records.
See PUBLIC SERVICE
COMMISSION.
Records generally.
See RECORDS.
**Reporter of decisions of
supreme court and court
of appeals.**
Records, §12-4-4.
Restoration.
Lost, etc., records of state,
county or municipalities,
§12-20-50.
**Rules of judicial
administration.**
Transfer of cases, ARJA,
Rule 26.
School records.
Educational records
generally.
See EDUCATION.

PUBLIC RECORDS—Cont'd
Sheriffs.
Records generally.
See SHERIFFS.
**Soil and water conservation
committee of state,**
§9-8-22.
Soil classifiers board.
Proceedings, §34-32-8.
**Southern products mart
authority.**
Bond payments, §41-10-65.
**Space science exhibit
commission,** §41-9-437.
State records commission,
§§41-13-20, 41-13-21,
41-13-24, 41-13-25.
Surveys and surveyors.
Records generally.
See SURVEYS AND
SURVEYORS.
**Synfuels development
authority.**
Proceedings of board of
directors, §9-6A-6.
**Tampering with
governmental records,**
§13A-10-12.
Tax records.
Generally, §40-1-5.
Income tax, §§40-18-48,
40-18-107.
Water management and
drainage districts,
§§9-9-31, 9-9-32, 9-9-35.
Tennessee Valley Authority.
Exhibit commission,
§41-9-785.
**Toxic substances and
marketplace,** §22-33-11.
**Unemployment
compensation,** §25-4-116.
**USS Alabama battleship
commission,** §41-9-350.
Vital statistics.
See VITAL STATISTICS.
**Water conservation and
irrigation.**
Agency.
Board of directors.
Proceedings of board,
§9-10-4.
Corporations.
Board of directors.
Proceedings of board,
§9-10-33.
**Water management and
drainage.**
Districts.
Recordbooks, §9-9-6.
Tax records, §§9-9-31, 9-9-32,
9-9-35.
Waters and watercourses.
Development of docks
along inland
waterways.
Separate records as to each
unit of development,
§§33-2-41, 33-2-73,
33-2-103, 33-2-132,
33-2-162.
Weights and measures.
Local sealers, §8-16-32.
Welfare records.
See WELFARE.
Youthful offenders, §15-9-7.

PUBLIC RECORDS—Cont'd
Youth services.
Department of youth
services.
Records of examinations,
etc., §§44-1-38,
44-1-39.
Youth services board.
Records of proceedings,
§44-1-51.

PUBLIC ROADS.
See COUNTIES.

PUBLIC SCHOOLS.
See EDUCATION.

**PUBLIC SERVICE
COMMISSION,** §§37-1-1 to
37-1-157.
Accounts and accounting.
Accountants.
Employment, §37-1-12.1.
Public inspection, §37-1-62.
Railroads.
Separation of intrastate
railroad operations for
accounting purposes,
§37-1-55.
Supervisor of accounts.
Bond, surety, §37-1-14.
Uniform systems of accounts
for utilities.
Commission to establish,
§37-1-54.
Actions.
Attorney general.
Representation of
commission in legal
proceedings, §37-1-64.
Representation of
consumers and state in
legal proceedings,
§37-1-16.
Enforcement of penalties or
forfeitures, §37-1-65.
Injunctions or restraining
orders.
Injunction bond.
Action on bond,
§37-1-155.
Jurisdiction in actions
against commission,
§37-1-10.
Special counsel.
Employment, §37-1-64.
Suspension of rates or orders.
Action on bond for
damages resulting
from, §37-1-135.
Venue for violations of
commission rules or
orders or statutes
relating to commission,
§37-8-2.
Air commerce.
See AIR COMMERCE.
Appeals.
Bonds, surety, §37-1-122.
Action on bond for
damages resulting
from suspension of
rates or orders,
§37-1-135.
Appeal by commission or
state without bond,
§37-1-133.
Appeal by utility,
§37-1-134.
Rate cases, §37-1-140.
Supersedeas bond,
§37-1-141.

PUBLIC SERVICE
COMMISSION—Cont'd
Appeals—Cont'd
Bonds, surety—Cont'd
Rate suspension to affect
only utilities giving
bond, §37-1-131.
Supersedeas bond,
§§37-1-125 to 37-1-130.
Certification of record or
transcript, §37-1-123.
Circuit court.
Right of appeal to circuit
court of Montgomery
county, §37-1-120.
Commission or state may
appeal, §37-1-133.
Evidence.
New or additional
evidence.
Introduction, §37-1-124.
Grounds for setting aside
order, §37-1-124.
Injunctions or restraining
orders, §§37-1-150 to
37-1-157. See within this
heading, "Injunctions or
restraining orders
against rates or orders of
commission."
Intervenors or interested
parties, §37-1-121.
Notice of appeal, §37-1-122.
Perfection.
How appeal perfected,
§37-1-122.
Proceedings on appeal,
§37-1-124.
Rate cases.
Accountants.
Employment of special
accountants,
§37-1-143.
Bonds, surety.
Supersedeas bonds,
§37-1-141.
When required,
§37-1-140.
Collection of denied rate
increases prior to final
disposition of case,
§37-1-141.
Conflicting laws.
Repealed, §37-1-144.
Consultants.
Employment of
consultants by chief
justice, §37-1-143.
Manner of taking,
§37-1-141.
Masters.
Employment of special
masters, §37-1-143.
Notice of appeal, §37-1-140.
Preferred setting of
appeals, §37-1-140.
Record or transcript of
proceedings before
commission,
§§37-1-142, 37-1-143.
Remand of case to
commission for
additional proceedings,
§37-1-143.
Repeal of conflicting laws,
§37-1-144.
Subdivision cumulative,
§37-1-144.
Supersedeas.
Application for,
§37-1-141.

PUBLIC SERVICE
COMMISSION—Cont'd
Appeals—Cont'd
Rate cases—Cont'd
Supersedeas—Cont'd
Bonds, §37-1-141.
Supreme court.
Direct appeal to supreme
court as matter of
right, §37-1-140.
Employment of special
masters,
accountants,
consultants, etc.,
§37-1-143.
Record or transcript of
proceedings before
commission.
Certification to
supreme court,
§37-1-142.
Time for taking, §37-1-140.
Who may appeal,
§37-1-141.
Rate suspensions.
Only utilities giving bond
affected, §37-1-131.
Record of proceedings before
commission, §37-1-123.
Remanding case to
commission, §37-1-124.
State may appeal, §37-1-133.
Stays.
Supersedeas order,
§§37-1-125 to 37-1-130.
Supersedeas.
Rate cases, §37-1-141.
Superseding orders.
Bond.
Additional bond,
§37-1-129.
Amount of bond,
§37-1-128.
Order stayed and
superseded upon
giving bond,
§37-1-130.
Right to supersede order
by giving bond,
§37-1-125.
Order of stay or
supersedeas, §37-1-126.
Termination, §37-1-130.
Order stayed and
superseded upon
giving bond, §37-1-130.
Right to supersede order
by giving bond,
§37-1-125.
Statement of approximate
effect on revenues,
§37-1-127.
Termination of stay or
supersedeas, §37-1-130.
Supreme court.
Rate cases, §§37-1-140 to
37-1-144.
Right of appeal to supreme
court, §37-1-132.
Time for appeal, §37-1-122.
Transcript of proceedings
before commission,
§37-1-123.
Utilities.
Security for costs,
§37-1-134.
Appointment of
commissioners, §37-1-3.

PUBLIC SERVICE
COMMISSION—Cont'd
Attorney general.
Appointment of assistant
attorney general as legal
advisor, §36-15-7.
Appointment of assistant
attorney general as
representative of
consumers and state,
§37-1-16.
Consumers.
Representing consumers in
proceedings before
commission, §37-1-16.
Representing commission in
legal proceedings,
§37-1-64.
Special counsel.
Employment, §37-1-64.
Attorneys at law.
Right of party to be heard in
person or by attorney,
§37-1-88.
Special counsel, §§37-1-12,
37-1-64.
Boards for operation of
water, sewer, gas and
electric systems.
Jurisdiction, etc., of
commission, §11-50-323.
Bonds, surety.
Action on bond for damages
resulting from
suspension of rates or
orders, §37-1-135.
Appeal bonds. See within
this heading, "Appeals."
Injunctions or restraining
orders. See within this
heading, "Injunctions or
restraining orders
against rates or orders of
commission."
Supersedeas bonds,
§§37-1-125 to 37-1-130.
Supervisor of accounts,
§37-1-14.
Capital.
Domicile of commission,
§37-1-10.
Residence of commissioners,
§37-1-9.
Circuit courts.
Appeals.
Right of appeal to circuit
court of Montgomery
county, §37-1-120.
Orders of commission.
Power of circuit court to
compel compliance,
§37-1-104.
Clerk of commission.
Rendering professional
service to utilities,
§37-1-5.
Commissions of other states.
Sitting or conferring with,
§37-1-45.
Common carriers.
General provisions.
See CARRIERS.
Persons passing free of
charge on common
carriers, §37-1-15.
Complaints.
Unfair rates or inadequate
service, §§37-1-83,
37-1-84.

**PUBLIC SERVICE
COMMISSION**—Cont'd
Conflict of laws.
Appeal of rate cases.
Repeal of conflicting laws,
§37-1-144.
Consumers.
Attorney general.
Assistant attorney general
representing
consumers before
commission, §37-1-16.
Utility rate hearing fund,
§37-1-18.
Contempt.
Compliance with commission
orders.
Power of circuit court,
§37-1-104.
**Deaf and hearing-impaired
persons.**
Telephones.
Dual-party relay system.
Administration,
§37-1-80.2.
Definitions.
Utility, §37-1-30.
Department of revenue.
Furnishing information to
department, §37-1-42.
Depositions.
Hearings on rate and other
regulations.
Depositions of witnesses,
§37-1-92.
**Devotion of full time to
official business of
commission, §37-1-9.**
**Domicile of commission,
§37-1-10.**
Duties.
Exclusive, §37-1-31.
**Economic and financial
studies and surveys of
public utility services,**
§37-1-17.
Economists.
Employment, §37-1-12.1.
Elections.
Candidates for public service
commission.
Public utility corporations.
Giving aid or
contributions to
candidates,
§§10-2A-70.1,
10-2A-70.2.
Commissioners, §37-1-3.
General elections.
Offices for which general
election held, §17-2-2.
Time, §17-2-3.
State officers elected by the
people, §17-2-1.
Electric cooperatives.
Exemption from jurisdiction
of commission, §37-6-27.
Electricity.
Distribution, generation or
transmission.
Jurisdictional exemptions
or limitations,
§37-1-33.
General provisions, §§37-1-1
to 37-1-157.
See ELECTRICITY.
Eligibility for membership.
Certain persons ineligible to
be commissioners,
§37-1-6.

**PUBLIC SERVICE
COMMISSION**—Cont'd
Employees.
Accountant, §37-1-12.1.
Appointment, §37-1-12.
Divulging certain
information.
Penalty, §37-1-13.
Economist, §37-1-12.1.
Salaries, §37-1-12.
Special counsel, §37-1-12.
Special investigators.
Employment, §37-1-12.2.
Stenographer and other
clerical assistants.
Employment, §37-1-12.2.
Utility rates analyst,
§37-1-12.1.
Energy.
Cogeneration facilities.
Implementation of chapter,
§37-12-4.
Enforcement division.
Powers of members, §37-1-66.
Established, §37-1-1.
Evidence.
Appeals.
Introduction of new or
additional evidence,
§37-1-124.
Hearings on rates, §§37-1-89,
37-1-99.
Injunctions or restraining
orders.
Bonds.
Receipt in evidence,
§37-1-156.
Rates and orders of
commission.
Deemed prima facie
reasonable and valid,
§37-1-99.
Examiners, §37-1-63.
Executive sessions.
Prohibited, §13A-14-2.
Exemptions.
Electric cooperatives.
Exemption from
jurisdiction of
commission, §37-6-27.
Electricity, §37-1-33.
Gas, §37-1-33.
Municipal utilities,
§§37-1-34, 37-1-35.
Nonutility business,
§37-1-36.
Railroads.
Logging or private
railroads, §37-1-37.
Steam, §37-1-33.
Explosives.
Transportation of explosives.
See EXPLOSIVES AND
EXPLOSIONS.
**Federal commissions or
agencies.**
Sitting or conferring with,
§37-1-46.
**Federal communications
commission.**
Intervention in federal
proceedings involving
interstate rates, etc., in
Alabama, §37-1-47.
Federal power commission.
Intervention in federal
proceedings involving
interstate rates, etc., in
Alabama, §37-1-47.

**PUBLIC SERVICE
COMMISSION**—Cont'd
**Federal proceedings
involving interstate
rates.**
Intervention, §37-1-47.
Fees.
Rate hearings.
Witnesses, §37-1-93.
**Financial and economic
data, §37-1-17.**
**Free passage on common
carriers.**
Exemptions for commission
members, §37-8-28.
Funds.
Consumer's utility rate
hearing fund, §37-1-18.
Gas.
Distribution or furnishing.
Jurisdictional exemptions
or limitations,
§37-1-33.
General provisions.
See GAS.
Gas districts.
Exemption of districts from
jurisdiction and
regulation of
commission, §11-50-416.
Governor.
Reports to governor,
§37-1-41.
Vacancies.
Filling, §37-1-3.
Grand jury.
Witnesses.
Requiring witnesses to
testify, §37-8-4.
Hearings.
Abandonment of service by
utilities.
Application for certificate
of abandonment,
§37-1-50.
Attorney general.
Assistant attorney general
representing
consumers and state,
§37-1-16.
Consumer's utility rate
hearing fund, §37-1-18.
Injunctions or restraining
orders, §37-1-151.
Rate and other regulations.
See within this heading,
"Rate and other
regulations."
Rules and regulations.
Adoption, §37-1-38.
**Impeachment of
commissioners, §37-1-7.**
**Injunctions or restraining
orders against rates or
orders of commission.**
Appeals.
Bond required upon appeal
by utility, §37-1-154.
Costs, §37-1-157.
Right of appeal to supreme
court, §37-1-153.
Bonds.
Action on bond, §37-1-155.
Condition precedent to
issuance, §37-1-150.
Condition to pay damages,
§37-1-152.
Delivery of bond upon
dissolution of
injunction, §37-1-156.

**PUBLIC SERVICE
COMMISSION**—Cont'd
**Injunctions or restraining
orders against rates or
orders of commission**
—Cont'd
Bonds—Cont'd
Failure to give injunction
bond, §37-1-150.
Filing, §§37-1-150,
37-1-152.
Receipt in evidence,
§37-1-156.
Required upon appeal by
utility, §37-1-154.
Costs.
Appeals, §37-1-157.
Damages.
Condition to pay damages,
§37-1-152.
Dissolution of injunction.
Delivery of bond upon
dissolution, §37-1-156.
Evidence.
Bonds.
Receipt in evidence,
§37-1-156.
Hearings, §37-1-151.
Issuance.
Bond as condition
precedent, §37-1-150.
Notice to commission,
§37-1-151.
Supreme court.
Appeals to supreme court,
§37-1-153.
Inspections.
Books and records of
utilities, §37-1-82.
Employees.
Divulging information
respecting inspections,
§37-1-13.
Meters and measuring
devices, §37-1-53.
Interstate commerce.
Interstate rates, §§37-1-44,
37-1-47.
Jurisdiction not regulated
under acts of congress,
§37-1-43.
**Interstate commerce
commission.**
Intervention in federal
proceedings involving
interstate rates, etc., in
Alabama, §37-1-47.
Investigations.
Rate and other regulations,
§37-1-83.
Right of party to be heard in
person or by attorney,
§37-1-88.
Rules and regulations.
Adoption, §37-1-38.
Unfair rates or inadequate
service, §37-1-83.
Jurisdiction.
Actions or proceedings
against commission,
§37-1-10.
Electric cooperatives.
Exemption from
jurisdiction, §37-6-27.
Electricity.
Distribution or furnishing.
Jurisdictional
exemptions or
limitations, §37-1-33.
Exclusive, §37-1-31.

**PUBLIC SERVICE
COMMISSION**—Cont'd
Jurisdiction—Cont'd
Exemptions. See within this
heading, "Exemptions."
Gas.
Distribution or furnishing.
Jurisdictional
exemptions or
limitations, §37-1-33.
Limited as to nonutilities,
§37-4-2.
Municipal utilities,
§§37-1-34, 37-1-35.
Nonutility business.
Jurisdictional exemptions
or limitations,
§37-1-33.
Power.
Distribution or furnishing.
Jurisdictional
exemptions or
limitations, §37-1-33.
Railroads.
Logging or private
railroads.
Jurisdictional
exemptions or
limitations, §37-1-37.
Steam.
Distribution or furnishing.
Jurisdictional
exemptions or
limitations, §37-1-33.
Leases.
Water distribution facilities.
Conveyance without
commission approval,
§37-4-45.
Legal counsel.
Appointment of assistant
attorney general,
§36-15-7.
Meetings, §37-1-8.
Membership, §37-1-1.
**Meters and measuring
devices.**
Accuracy.
Commission may provide
for accuracy, §37-1-53.
Motor vehicle carriers.
See MOTOR VEHICLE
CARRIERS.
Municipal corporations.
See MUNICIPAL
CORPORATIONS.
Oaths.
Commissioners to take oath
of office, §37-1-4.
Powers of commissioners and
examiners to administer
oaths, §37-1-63.
Required reports.
Originals to be subscribed
and sworn to, §37-1-61.
Office, §37-1-8.
Opinions.
Publication, §37-1-39.
Orders.
Action on bond for damages
resulting from
suspension of rates or
orders, §37-1-135.
Appeals. See within this
heading, "Appeals."
Circuit court.
Power to compel
compliance with
commission orders,
§37-1-104.

**PUBLIC SERVICE
COMMISSION**—Cont'd
Orders—Cont'd
Injunctions or restraining
orders against rates or
orders of commission.
See within this heading,
"Injunctions or
restraining orders
against rates or orders of
commission."
Publication, §37-1-39.
Railroads.
Regulations for
convenience of
passengers.
See RAILROADS.
Rate and other regulations.
See within this heading,
"Rate and other
regulations."
Superseding order. See
within this heading,
"Appeals."
Suspension of orders.
Action on bond for
damages resulting
from, §37-1-135.
Transportation companies.
Repairs, improvements or
changes in property or
devices, §37-2-9.
Utilities.
Duty to comply with
orders, §37-1-40.
Venue for violations of
commission orders,
§37-8-2.
Violation of commission
orders.
Generally, §37-8-1.
Parties.
Proceedings before
commission, §37-1-87.
Right of party to be heard in
person or by attorney,
§37-1-88.
Peace officers.
Enforcement division.
Members to have powers of
peace officers,
§37-1-66.
Penalties.
Actions to enforce penalties,
§37-1-65.
Employees.
Divulging certain
information, §37-1-13.
Orders of commission.
Violation of orders,
§37-8-1.
Perjury.
Hearings on rate and other
regulations.
Perjury prosecution not
barred, §37-1-91.
Pipelines.
Gas pipeline systems,
§§37-4-80 to 37-4-87.
See PIPELINES.
Power.
Distribution or furnishing.
Jurisdictional exemptions
or limitations,
§37-1-33.
Power districts, §37-5-2.
Powers of commission.
Exclusive, §37-1-31.
Utilities generally. See
within this heading,
"Utilities."

PUBLIC SERVICE COMMISSION—Cont'd
President.
Salary, §37-1-11.
Publication.
Orders and opinions, §37-1-39.
Public utilities. See within this heading, "Utilities."
Radio utilities.
General provisions.
See RADIO.
Railroad authorities.
Exemption from jurisdiction of public service commission, §37-13-20.
Railroads.
General provisions.
See RAILROADS.
Transportation companies generally, §§37-2-1 to 37-2-184.
See TRANSPORTATION COMPANIES.
Rate and other regulations.
Action on bond for damages resulting from suspension of rates or orders, §37-1-135.
Appeals, §§37-1-140 to 37-1-144.
Changing existing rates or service regulations, §37-1-81.
Complaints.
Commencement of action by complaint, §37-1-84.
Contents, §37-1-84.
Filing, §§37-1-83, 37-1-84.
Who may file complaints, §37-1-83.
Consumer's utility rate hearing fund, §37-1-18.
Denial of rate increases.
Collection of denied increases prior to final disposition of case, §37-1-141.
Excessive or discriminatory rates.
Proceedings when interstate rates or rules deemed excessive or discriminatory, §37-1-44.
Hearings.
Attorney general.
Assistant attorney general representing consumers and state before commission, §37-1-16.
Attorneys at law.
Right of party to be heard in person or by attorney, §37-1-88.
Consumer's utility rate hearing fund, §37-1-18.
Copies of orders.
Certified copies, §37-1-98.
Decision.
Time allowed commission for making decision, §37-1-94.
Depositions of witnesses, §37-1-92.
Effective date of orders, §37-1-100.

PUBLIC SERVICE COMMISSION—Cont'd
Rate and other regulations —Cont'd
Hearings—Cont'd
Evidence.
Orders deemed prima facie reasonable and valid, §37-1-99.
Special examiners, §37-1-89.
Fees.
Witnesses, §37-1-93.
Further investigations, §37-1-89.
Intervention in proceedings before commission, §37-1-87.
Laws governing conduct of hearing, §37-1-89.
Modification of orders, §37-1-101.
Necessity for hearing prior to order affecting rate or service, §37-1-96.
Notice to utility, §37-1-86.
Parties.
Intervention in proceedings before commission, §37-1-87.
Perjury.
Perjury prosecution not barred, §37-1-91.
Place of hearing, §37-1-85.
Reasonable rate.
Order fixing reasonable rate, §37-1-97.
Record of proceedings.
Stenographer to take down testimony, §37-1-102.
Rehearing, §37-1-105.
Right of party to be heard in person or by attorney, §37-1-88.
Separate hearings on several matters, §37-1-90.
Service of process, §37-1-86.
Special examiners, §37-1-89.
Stenographers.
Record of proceedings, §37-1-102.
Subpoenas.
Not excused from obedience to subpoena for reasons of incrimination or forfeiture, §37-1-91.
Taking of testimony, §37-1-89.
Testimony.
Stenographer to take down testimony, §37-1-102.
Time allowed commission for making decision, §37-1-94.
Time of hearing, §37-1-85.
Transcript.
Conveyance to secretary of commission, §37-1-89.
Unfair rates.
Order fixing reasonable rate, §37-1-97.

PUBLIC SERVICE COMMISSION—Cont'd
Rate and other regulations —Cont'd
Hearings—Cont'd
Violations.
Order requiring discontinuance or rectification of violation, §37-1-95.
Witnesses.
Compelling witnesses to testify.
Power of circuit court to compel, §37-1-104.
Depositions, §37-1-92.
Fees, §37-1-93.
Forfeiture.
Witnesses not excused for reasons of forfeiture, §37-1-91.
Laws governing conduct of hearing, §37-1-89.
Mileage, §37-1-93.
Not excused for reasons of incrimination or forfeiture, §37-1-91.
Inadequate service.
Investigation, §37-1-83.
Injunction against rates or orders, §§37-1-150 to 37-1-157. See within this heading, "Injunctions or retraining orders against rates or orders of commission."
Interstate rates.
Excessive or discriminatory rates.
Proceedings when interstate rates or rules deemed excessive or discriminatory, §37-1-44.
Federal proceedings.
Intervention in proceedings involving interstate rates, etc., in Alabama, §37-1-47.
Investigation, §37-1-83.
Jurisdiction.
Limited as to nonutilities, §37-4-2.
Municipal utilities.
Title not intended to limit certain municipal powers, §37-1-35.
Orders.
Amending orders, §37-1-101.
Appeals generally. See within this heading, "Appeals."
Circuit court.
Power to compel compliance with commission orders, §37-1-104.
Hearing necessary prior to order affecting rate or service, §37-1-96.
Inadequate service.
Order fixing reasonable rate, §37-1-97.

PUBLIC SERVICE
COMMISSION—Cont'd
Rate and other regulations
—Cont'd
Orders—Cont'd
Injunctions or restraining
orders against rates or
orders of commission,
§§37-1-150 to 37-1-157.
See within this
heading, "Injunctions
or restraining orders
against rates or ordes
of commission."
Public utilities generally.
See PUBLIC UTILITIES.
Rates to be just and
reasonable, §37-1-80.
Right of utility to earn fair
net return, §37-1-80.
Schedules of rates or service
regulations.
Changing existing rates.
Utility to file new
schedule with
commission,
§37-1-81.
Form for schedules.
Prescribing changes in
form, §37-1-56.
Special examiners, §37-1-89.
Subpoenas, §37-1-91.
Substantial compliance by
commission with
requirements of title
sufficient, §37-1-103.
Suspending operation of
new schedules,
§37-1-81.
Suspension of rates.
Action on bond for
damages resulting
from suspension of
rates or orders,
§37-1-135.
Telephone companies.
Connecting companies.
Review and adjustment
when South Central
Bell receives
increase in net
return, §37-1-80.1.
Deaf and hearing-impaired
customers.
Telephone surcharge for
service, §37-1-80.2.
Unfair rates.
Investigation, §37-1-83.
Utility rates analyst.
Employment, §37-1-12.1.
Records, §37-1-8.
Production and inspection of
books or records of
utilities, §37-1-82.
Public inspection, §37-1-62.
Rate hearings.
Record of proceedings,
§37-1-102.
Removal of commissioners,
§37-1-7.
Reports.
Annual report to governor,
§37-1-41.
Public inspection, §37-1-62.
Requiring reports and
information from
utilities, §37-4-15.
Additional reports of
earnings and operating
expenses, §37-1-59.

PUBLIC SERVICE
COMMISSION—Cont'd
Reports—Cont'd
Requiring reports and
information from
utilities—Cont'd
Annual return of business,
§37-1-58.
Failure to make return.
Penalty, §37-1-58.
Form of reports and
records, §37-1-60.
Generally, §37-1-57.
Oaths.
Originals to be
subscribed and
sworn to, §37-1-61.
Originals, §37-1-61.
Residence of commissioners,
§37-1-9.
Restraining orders,
§§37-1-150 to 37-1-157. See
within this heading,
"Injunctions or restraining
orders against rates or
orders of commission."
Rules and regulations,
§37-1-38.
Meters and measuring
devices, §37-1-53.
Rate and other regulations.
See within this heading,
"Rate and other
regulations."
Salaries of commissioners,
§37-1-11.
Seal, §37-1-2.
Secret sessions.
Prohibited, §13A-14-2.
Security and exchange
commission.
Intervention in federal
proceedings involving
interstate rates, etc., in
Alabama, §37-1-47.
Self-incrimination.
Compelling testimony of
employees who violate
code, §37-8-3.
Hearings on rate and other
regulations.
Witnesses not excused for
reasons of self-
incrimination,
§37-1-91.
Service of process.
Rate and other regulations.
Hearings on unfair rates or
inadequate service,
§37-1-86.
Special counsel, §37-1-12.
Compensation, §37-1-64.
Employment by attorney
general, §37-1-64.
Special examiners.
Rate hearings, §37-1-89.
State.
Appeals.
State may appeal,
§37-1-133.
Stays.
Appeals, §§37-1-125 to
37-1-130.
Steam.
Distribution or furnishing.
Jurisdictional exemptions
or limitations,
§37-1-33.

PUBLIC SERVICE
COMMISSION—Cont'd
Subpoenas.
Compliance with subpoenas.
Power of circuit court,
§37-1-104.
Hearings on rate and other
regulations, §37-1-91.
Powers of commissioners and
examiners to issue
subpoenas, §37-1-63.
Sunshine law.
Executive or secret sessions
prohibited, §13A-14-2.
Supervisor of accounts.
Bond, surety, §37-1-14.
Supreme court.
Appeals.
Rate cases, §§37-1-140 to
37-1-144.
Right of appeal to supreme
court, §37-1-132.
Injunctions or
restraining orders,
§37-1-153.
Telephone companies.
Deaf and hearing-impaired
persons.
Dual-party relay system.
Administration,
§37-1-80.2.
Rural telephone service,
§§37-6-47, 37-6-48.
Securities of telephone
companies, §§37-2-171 to
37-2-174.
Terms of office, §37-1-3.
Transcripts.
Appeals.
Record or transcript of
proceedings before
commission, §37-1-123.
Rate hearings.
Furnishing parties with
copies, §37-1-102.
Transcript to be conveyed
and filed with
secretary of
commission, §37-1-89.
Transportation companies.
Abandonment of service.
Grant or refusal of permit
to abandon, §37-2-7.
Permits.
When permit to abandon
required, §37-2-5.
Actions.
Rights of action not
waived, §37-2-44.
Duty of commission to
supervise, regulate and
control companies,
§37-2-3.
Enforcement of regulations,
§37-2-3.
Inspection fee, §37-2-41.
Joint rates.
Establishment, §37-2-11.
Rates.
Special rates, §37-2-15.
Temporary rates, §37-2-14.
Repairs and improvements in
property or devices.
Order of commission,
§37-2-9.
Reparation.
Order of reparation,
§37-2-19.

PUBLIC SERVICE
COMMISSION—Cont'd
Transportation companies
—Cont'd
Tickets, passes and mileage
books.
Lists to be filed with
commission, §37-2-8.
United States.
Federal commissions or
agencies.
Sitting or conferring with,
§37-1-46.
Intervention in federal
proceedings involving
interstate rates, etc., in
Alabama, §37-1-47.
Utilities.
Abandonment of service.
Certificate for
abandonment.
Application to
commission for
issuance, §37-1-50.
Accounts.
Establishing uniform
systems of accounts,
§37-1-54.
Adequate service.
Duty to render adequate
service to the public,
§37-1-49.
Annual return of business.
Required reports, §37-1-58.
Books and records of
utilities.
Production and inspection,
§37-1-82.
Charges.
Nonpayment of charges.
Abandonment of service
for nonpayment,
§37-1-50.
Classification of utility
services, §37-1-51.
Contracts.
Submission to commission
for approval, §37-4-22.
Corporations.
Elections.
Political candidates.
Giving aid or
contributions to,
§§10-2A-70.1,
10-2A-70.2.
Defined, §37-1-30.
Facilities.
Duty to maintain in good
working condition,
§37-1-49.
Fees.
Inspection and supervision
fees, §§37-4-23,
37-4-24.
General supervision of
utilities, §37-1-32.
Impairment of capital.
Order directing utility to
cease paying
dividends, §37-4-6.
Information from utilities.
Requiring reports and
information from
utilities. See within
this heading,
"Reports."
Meters and measuring
devices.
Providing for accuracy,
§37-1-53.

PUBLIC SERVICE
COMMISSION—Cont'd
Utilities—Cont'd
Municipal ordinances or
contracts.
Waiver by utility of terms
or conditions, §37-1-48.
Municipal utilities.
Exercise of certain
municipal powers,
§37-1-35.
Jurisdictional exemption or
limitation, §37-1-34.
Nonutility business.
Jurisdictional exemptions
or limitations,
§§37-1-33, 37-4-2.
Orders of commission.
Duty of utilities to comply,
§37-1-40.
Violation of utility orders,
§37-8-1.
Penalties.
Utilities subject to penalty.
Actions to recover
penalty, §37-1-65.
Persons owning stock in
utilities.
Ineligible to be
commissioners,
§37-1-6.
Property.
Valuation of utility
property, §§37-4-17 to
37-4-21, 37-4-25.
Public utilities generally,
§§37-4-1 to 37-4-131.
See PUBLIC UTILITIES.
Rate and other regulations.
See within this heading,
"Rate and other
regulations."
Regulations for testing of
service, §37-1-52.
Rendering professional
service to utilities.
Commissioners and clerks
not to render, §37-1-5.
Reports.
Reports to governor,
§37-1-41.
Requiring reports and
information from
utilities. See within
this heading,
"Reports."
Securities.
Application to issue
securities or assume
obligations, §§37-4-7 to
37-4-11.
Standards of service.
Prescribing, §37-1-52.
Supervision, §37-1-32.
Utilities engaged in
interstate commerce.
Jurisdiction not regulated
under acts of congress,
§37-1-43.
Waiver of terms or conditions
in municipal ordinances
or contracts, §37-1-48.
Vacancies.
Filling, §37-1-3.
Venue.
Violations of commission
rules or orders or
statutes relating to
commission, §37-8-2.

PUBLIC SERVICE
COMMISSION—Cont'd
Violations.
Compelling testimony of
employees who violate
code, §37-8-3.
Orders of commission,
§37-8-1.
Venue for violations of
commission rules or
orders or statutes
relating to commission,
§37-8-2.
Witnesses.
Compelling testimony of
employees who violate
code, §37-8-3.
Requiring witnesses to
testify before grand
jury, §37-8-4.
**Water, sewer and fire
protection authorities.**
Exemption from jurisdiction
and regulation of public
service commission,
§11-88-21.
**Water, sewer and fire
protection districts.**
Jurisdiction over and
regulation of districts by
public service
commission, §11-89-19.
**Water supply and
waterworks.**
Conveyance of water
distribution facilities
without commission
approval, §37-4-45.
**Waterworks and sewer
boards.**
Acquisition, operation, etc.,
of gas plants and
systems, §§11-88-7,
11-88-12.
Jurisdiction, etc., of public
service commission,
§11-50-241.
Witnesses.
Compelling testimony of
employees who violate
code, §37-8-3.
Fees.
Rate hearings, §37-1-93.
Grand jury.
Requiring witnesses to
testify, §37-8-4.
Hearings on rate and other
regulations. See within
this heading, "Rate and
other regulations."
Power to compel attendance
of witnesses, §37-1-63.
Rate and other regulations.
See within this heading,
"Rate and other
regulations."

PUBLIC UTILITIES.
Abandonment of service.
Certificate for abandonment,
§37-1-50.
Abutting landowners.
Damages to abutting owners.
Liability of public utilities
in municipal
corporations, Const.
Ala., art. XII, §227.
Accounts and accounting.
Uniform systems of accounts.
Public service commission
to establish, §37-1-54.

PUBLIC UTILITIES—Cont'd
Actions.
Utility services actions,
§§6-5-600 to 6-5-605.
See UTILITY SERVICES
ACTIONS.
Alabama privatization act.
Utility services facilities,
§§11-97-1 to 11-97-27.
See UTILITY SERVICES
FACILITIES.
**Ameraport offshore harbor
and terminal
commission.**
Contracts for public utilities,
§33-10-21.
Appeals.
Purchase of property by
municipality or
governmental agency.
Forced sales.
Appeals to circuit court,
§37-4-63.
Taxation.
Protest of incorrect
valuation, §40-21-24.
Valuation of utility property,
§37-4-21.
Appeals of commission
order, §37-4-19.
Assessment.
Taxation. See within this
heading, "Taxation."
Assignment.
Taxation.
Duties of assignees,
§40-21-33.
Authorities.
Water, sewer and fire
protection authorities,
§§11-88-1 to 11-88-111.
See WATER, SEWER AND
FIRE PROTECTION
AUTHORITIES.
**Bear creek development
authority.**
Eminent domain.
Acquisition of certain
property controlled by
utilities, §33-15-5.
Bond issues.
Counties.
See COUNTIES.
Municipal corporations.
See MUNICIPAL
CORPORATIONS.
Provisions of article not
applicable to certain
notes, §37-4-13.
Bridges.
Rights of way.
Rules and regulations.
Promulgation by
highway
department,
§23-1-59.
**Certificate of convenience
and necessity.**
Application, §37-4-28.
Issuance, §37-4-28.
Motor vehicle carriers,
§§37-3-1 to 37-3-34.
See MOTOR VEHICLE
CARRIERS.
Time for exercising authority
conferred, §37-4-29.
Transportation companies,
§§37-2-1 to 37-2-184.
See TRANSPORTATION
COMPANIES.
When required, §37-4-28.

PUBLIC UTILITIES—Cont'd
Charges.
Nonpayment of charges.
Abandonment of service.
Certificate for
abandonment,
§37-1-50.
Circuit courts.
Appeals.
Purchase or property by
municipality or
governmental agency.
Forced sales.
Appeals to circuit
court, §37-4-63.
Jurisdiction to sell property
and franchises of public
utility corporations,
§12-11-32.
Commission.
Public service commission,
§§37-1-1 to 37-1-157.
See PUBLIC SERVICE
COMMISSION.
Concessions.
Accepting rebates,
concessions or
discrimination, §37-8-25.
Granting unlawful
concessions, §37-8-24.
Constitution of Alabama.
Damages to abutting
property owners.
Liability of public utilities
in municipal
corporations, Const.
Ala., art. XII, §227.
Contracts.
Ameraport offshore harbor
and terminal
commission.
Contracts for public
utilities, §33-10-21.
Bridges.
Rights of way.
Entering into contracts
with highway
department,
§23-1-59.
Highways.
Rights of way.
Entering into contracts
with highway
department,
§23-1-59.
Municipal corporations.
Rates and service
regulations established
by contract, §37-4-22.
Submission to commission,
§37-4-22.
Corporations.
Application of corporations
provisions, §10-2A-336.
Elections.
Political parties or
candidates.
Giving aid or
contributions to,
§§10-2A-70.1,
10-2A-70.2.
Eminent domain.
Power of eminent domain
in internal
improvement or public
utility corporations,
§10-5-1.
Counties.
See COUNTIES.

PUBLIC UTILITIES—Cont'd
Courts.
Receiver's certificate or
debentures.
Power to issue, §37-4-14.
Debentures.
Receiver's certificate or
debentures.
Power of court to issue,
§37-4-14.
Deeds.
Purchase of property by
municipality or
governmental agency.
Forced sales.
Tender of deed, §37-4-64.
Definitions.
Gross receipts tax, §40-21-80.
Rate and other regulations,
§37-4-1.
Deposits.
Unclaimed deposits.
Uniform disposition of
unclaimed property
act, §§35-12-1 to
35-12-48.
See LOST OR
UNCLAIMED
PROPERTY.
Directors.
Duties.
Delegation of duties,
§37-4-4.
Discharge of duties,
§37-4-3.
Fiduciaries.
Officers and directors
occupy fiduciary
relationship, §37-4-3.
Discrimination.
Accepting rebates,
concessions or
discrimination, §37-8-25.
Motor vehicle carriers,
§§37-3-1 to 37-3-34.
See MOTOR VEHICLE
CARRIERS.
Railroads.
See RAILROADS.
Transportation companies,
§§37-2-1 to 37-2-184.
See TRANSPORTATION
COMPANIES.
Districts.
Water, sewer and fire
protection districts,
§§11-89-1 to 11-89-19.
See WATER, SEWER AND
FIRE PROTECTION
DISTRICTS.
Dividends.
Impairment of capital.
Order directing utility to
cease paying
dividends, §37-4-6.
Payment, §37-4-6.
Electric cooperatives,
§§37-6-1 to 37-6-49.
See ELECTRIC
COOPERATIVES.
Electricity.
Condemnation by electric
utilities, §§10-5-4,
37-4-130, 37-4-131.
Counties.
See COUNTIES.

PUBLIC UTILITIES—Cont'd
Electricity—Cont'd
Electric membership
corporations, §§37-7-1 to
37-7-21.
See ELECTRIC
MEMBERSHIP
CORPORATIONS.
General provisions.
See ELECTRICITY.
Municipal corporations.
See MUNICIPAL
CORPORATIONS.
Rates.
Generally. See within this
heading, "Rate and
other regulations."
Taxation.
Generally. See within this
heading, "Taxation."
License taxes. See within
this heading, "License
taxes."
Eminent domain.
Companies constructing,
operating or maintaining
public utility, §10-5-4.
Power of eminent domain in
public utility
corporations, §10-5-1.
Radio utility systems.
Construction and
maintenance of
antennas and towers,
§37-4-113.
Employees.
Free service, §37-4-27.
Securities.
Sale or purchase of
securities by utility
employees, §37-4-5.
Special or reduced rates,
§37-4-27.
Equipment.
Duty to maintain in good
operating condition,
§37-1-49.
Examiners.
Valuation of utility property,
§37-4-17.
Facilities.
Duty to maintain facilities,
§37-1-49.
Fees.
Inspection and supervision
fees, §§37-4-23, 37-4-24.
Delinquent fees.
Recovery, §37-4-24.
Generally, §37-4-23.
Liens.
Delinquent fees,
§37-4-24.
Measure of fees, §37-4-23.
Municipal corporations.
Levy of fees by
municipal
corporations
prohibited, §37-4-23.
Payment over of total fees
due for preceding year,
§37-4-24.
Payment to commission,
§37-4-23.
Failure to pay.
Recovery of delinquent
fees, §37-4-24.
Recovery of delinquent
fees, §37-4-24.

PUBLIC UTILITIES—Cont'd
Fiduciaries.
Officers and directors occupy
fiduciary relationship,
§37-4-3.
Forests and forestry.
Municipal corporations.
Attachment of wires to
trees in cities or
towns, §9-13-15.
Franchises.
Circuit courts.
Jurisdiction to sell
franchises of public
utility corporations,
§12-11-32.
Sale or lease generally. See
within this heading,
"Property."
Taxation. See within this
heading, "Taxation."
Term.
Maximum term in cities
and towns having
population of six
thousand or more,
Const. Ala., art. XII,
§228.
**Freight lines and equipment
companies.**
License tax, §40-21-52.
Gas.
Counties.
See COUNTIES.
General provisions.
See GAS.
Municipal corporations.
See MUNICIPAL
CORPORATIONS.
Rates.
Generally. See within this
heading, "Rate and
other regulations."
Taxation. See within this
heading, "Taxation."
Gas pipeline systems.
See PIPELINES.
Governmental agencies.
Purchase by governmental
agencies, §§37-4-60 to
37-4-65.
Gross receipts tax, §§40-21-80
to 40-21-86.
Additional charge, §40-21-86.
Administration of article,
§40-21-85.
Application of tax.
Legislative intent,
§40-21-81.
Collection of tax, §40-21-85.
Definitions, §40-21-80.
Determination of amount of
tax, §40-21-82.
Disposition of proceeds,
§40-21-87.
Exclusions, §40-21-83.
Exemptions.
Northeast Crenshaw water
and fire protection
authority, §40-21-82.1.
Presumptions as to tax
exemptions, §40-21-81.
Smith's water authority in
Lee county,
§40-21-82.1.
Legislative intent, §40-21-81.
Levy of tax, §40-21-82.

PUBLIC UTILITIES—Cont'd
Gross receipts tax—Cont'd
Licenses.
Payment of tax
prerequisite to
issuance of utility
license, §40-21-84.
Northeast Crenshaw water
and fire protection
authority.
Exemption from tax,
§40-21-82.1.
Responsibility of utilities,
§40-21-81.
Smith's water authority in
Lee county.
Exemption from tax,
§40-21-82.1.
Highways.
See HIGHWAYS.
Holding companies.
Agreements with holding
companies.
Utilities to file statement
with public service
commission, §37-4-26.
Defined, §37-4-1.
Impairment of capital.
Commission may order
utility to cease paying
dividends, §37-4-6.
Inspections.
Fees, §§37-4-23, 37-4-24.
Intercorporate relations.
Agreements with holding
companies or affiliated
interests, §37-4-26.
Holding companies.
Agreements with holding
companies or affiliated
interests, §37-4-26.
Defined, §37-4-1.
Treatment of utility as part
of general system,
§37-4-25.
Interstate commerce.
Public service commission.
Jurisdiction not regulated
under acts of congress,
§37-1-43.
Proceedings when
interstate rates or
rules deemed excessive
or discriminatory,
§37-1-44.
Sale or lease of utility
property.
Sale of property in
interstate commerce
contrary to federal law
not authorized,
§37-4-44.
Leases.
Sale or lease of property,
§§37-4-140 to 37-4-144.
License taxes, §§40-21-50 to
40-21-64.
Computation, §40-21-50.
Counties.
Electric, hydroelectric or
gas utilities.
License tax not to
constitute part of
gross receipts for
purposes of
computation of
county tax,
§40-21-54.
Privilege or license tax by
counties prohibited,
§40-21-64.

PUBLIC UTILITIES—Cont'd
License taxes—Cont'd
Distribution of revenues,
§40-21-51.
Electric, hydroelectric or gas
utilities, §40-21-53.
Aged persons.
Credit on electric bills
for certain persons,
§40-21-53.
County tax.
License tax not to
constitute part of
gross receipts for
purposes of
computation of
county tax,
§40-21-54.
Credit on electric bills for
certain persons,
§40-21-53.
Distribution of revenues
collected, §40-21-55.
Manufacturers and sellers
of hydroelectric power,
§40-21-56.
Municipal tax.
License tax not to
constitute part of
gross receipts for
purposes of
computation of
municipal tax,
§40-21-54.
Not to constitute part of
gross receipts for
purposes of
computation of state,
county or municipal
tax, §40-21-54.
Records.
Inspection of records by
department of
revenue, §40-21-53.
Statement of officers.
Failure to make
statement,
§40-21-53.
Payment to be
accompanied by
statement,
§40-21-53.
State tax.
License tax not to
constitute part of
gross receipts for
purposes of
computation of state
tax, §40-21-54.
Express companies.
Alternative tax, §40-21-61.
Computation, §40-21-60.
Levy, §40-21-60.
Payment, §40-21-60.
Freight lines and equipment
companies, §40-21-52.
Inspections.
Books of utilities open for
inspection, §40-21-50.
Levied, §40-21-50.
Municipal corporations.
Electric, hydroelectric or
gas utilities.
License tax not to
constitute part of
gross receipts for
purposes of
computation of
municipal tax,
§40-21-54.

PUBLIC UTILITIES—Cont'd
License taxes—Cont'd
New public utilities.
Payment of tax, §40-21-50.
Payment of tax prerequisite
to issuance of license,
§40-21-84.
Railroads.
Computation, §40-21-57.
Levy, §40-21-57.
Payment, §40-21-57.
Receipts from department of
revenue, §40-21-63.
Records.
Inspection of records,
§40-21-50.
Reports.
Gross receipts, §40-21-62.
State.
Electric, hydroelectric or
gas utilities.
License tax not to
constitute part of
gross receipts for
purposes of
computation of state
tax, §40-21-54.
Statements to accompany
payment, §40-21-50.
Telegraph business.
Determination of gross
intrastate earnings,
§40-21-59.
Levy, §40-21-59.
Payment of tax, §40-21-59.
Telephone business.
Computation, §40-21-58.
Levy of tax, §40-21-58.
Payment, §40-21-58.
Liens.
Inspection and supervision
fees.
Recovery of delinquent
fees, §37-4-24.
**Meters and measuring
devices.**
Accuracy.
Public service commission
to provide for,
§37-1-53.
Inspections.
Public service commission
to inspect for accuracy,
§37-1-53.
Motor vehicle carriers,
§§37-3-1 to 37-3-34.
See MOTOR VEHICLE
CARRIERS.
Municipal corporations.
See MUNICIPAL
CORPORATIONS.
New public utilities.
License tax, §40-21-50.
Nonutility.
Defined, §37-4-1.
Public service commission.
Jurisdiction of commission
limited as to
nonutilities, §37-4-2.
**Northeast Crenshaw water
and fire protection
authority.**
Exemption from gross
receipts tax, §40-21-82.1.
Notes.
Applicability of article.
Provisions not applicable to
certain notes, §37-4-13.

PUBLIC UTILITIES—Cont'd
Officers.
Duties.
Discharge of duties,
§37-4-3.
Fiduciaries.
Officers and directors
occupy fiduciary
relationship, §37-4-3.
Free transportation,
§37-4-27.
Securities.
Application to issue
securities or assume
obligations.
Filing by officer, §37-4-8.
Special or reduced rates,
§37-4-27.
Penalties.
Securities issued without
authorization.
Penalty for violation,
§37-4-16.
Permits.
Certificate of convenience
and necessity. See within
this heading, "Certificate
of convenience and
necessity."
Personal property. See
within this heading,
"Property."
Pipelines.
Gas pipeline systems,
§§37-4-80 to 37-4-87.
See PIPELINES.
Taxation, §§40-21-10,
40-21-21.
License taxes generally.
See within this
heading, "License
taxes."
Transportation companies,
§§37-2-4, 37-2-4.1,
37-2-6, 37-2-7.
Power districts.
Purchase of power utilities,
§§37-4-60 to 37-4-65.
See POWER DISTRICTS.
Presumptions.
Gross receipts tax.
Exemptions.
Presumptions as to
exemptions,
§40-21-81.
Property.
Deeds.
Purchase of property by
municipality or
governmental agency.
Forced sales.
Tender of deed,
§37-4-64.
Jurisdiction to sell property
of public utility
corporation, §12-11-32.
Purchase by municipality or
governmental agency,
§§37-4-60 to 37-4-65.
Exemptions.
Certain systems or
projects exempted,
§37-4-65.
Forced sales.
Acceptance or rejection,
§37-4-64.
Appeals.
Right of appeal to
circuit court,
§37-4-63.

PUBLIC UTILITIES—Cont'd
Property—Cont'd
  Purchase by municipality or
    governmental agency
    —Cont'd
    Forced sales—Cont'd
      Application to
        commission,
        §37-4-62.
      Deeds.
        Tender of deed,
          §37-4-64.
        Hearing, §37-4-62.
        Notice, §37-4-62.
        Order, §37-4-62.
        Time for compliance,
          §37-4-64.
    Notice of intention to
      engage in business,
      §37-4-60.
    Voluntary sales, §37-4-61.
  Sale or lease.
    Approval by commission,
      §§37-4-41, 37-4-42.
    Interstate commerce.
      Sale of property in
        interstate commerce
        contrary to federal
        law not authorized,
        §37-4-44.
    Legal sales.
      Otherwise legal sales,
        etc., not affected,
        §37-4-43.
    Property located within
      single municipality.
      Approval by commission,
        §37-4-42.
    Restrictions on right to
      sell.
      Otherwise legal sales not
        affected, §37-4-43.
    Right to sell or lease
      property, §37-4-40.
  Valuation of utility property.
    Access of commission to
      property, accounts and
      records of utility,
      §37-4-17.
    Appeals, §§37-4-19,
      37-4-21.
    Assistants.
      Employment by
        commission,
        §37-4-17.
    Corrections, §37-4-19.
    Examiners, §37-4-17.
    Factors considered,
      §37-4-17.
    Finality, §37-4-18.
    Final order of commission,
      §37-4-19.
    Franchises, §40-21-25.
    Hearings.
      Protest, §37-4-19.
    Notice, §37-4-18.
    Protest.
      Filing of protest,
        §37-4-18.
      Hearing on protest,
        §37-4-19.
    Revaluation, §37-4-20.
    Supreme court.
      Appeals to supreme
        court, §37-4-21.
    When made, §37-4-17.
Public service commission.
  Fees.
    Inspection and supervision
      fees, §§37-4-23,
      37-4-24.

PUBLIC UTILITIES—Cont'd
Public service commission
  —Cont'd
    General provisions, §§37-1-1
      to 37-1-157.
      See PUBLIC SERVICE
        COMMISSION.
    Securities.
      Application to issue
        securities or assume
        obligations generally.
        See within this
        heading, "Securities."
    Valuation of utility property
      generally. See within
      this heading, "Property."
Purchase by municipality or
  government agency,
  §§37-4-60 to 37-4-65.
Radio utilities.
  See RADIO.
Railroads.
  General provisions.
    See RAILROADS.
  Taxation.
    Generally. See within this
      heading, "Taxation."
    License taxes. See within
      this heading, "License
      taxes."
  Transportation companies,
    §§37-2-1 to 37-2-184.
    See TRANSPORTATION
      COMPANIES.
Rate and other regulations.
  Charging rate in violation of
    tariff.
    Generally, §37-8-21.
  Contract rates.
    Contracts between
      municipality and
      utility, §37-4-22.
  Definitions, §37-4-1.
  Granting unlawful
    concessions or rebates,
    §37-8-24.
  Interstate rates.
    Regulation by public
      service commission,
      §§37-1-44, 37-1-47.
  Motor vehicle carriers.
    See MOTOR VEHICLE
      CARRIERS.
  Public service commission.
    General provisions,
      §§37-1-1 to 37-1-157.
      See PUBLIC SERVICE
        COMMISSION.
  Reduced rates, §37-4-27.
  Special rates, §37-4-27.
  Transportation companies.
    See TRANSPORTATION
      COMPANIES.
Real property. See within this
  heading, "Property."
Rebates.
  Accepting rebates,
    concessions or
    discrimination, §37-8-25.
  Granting unlawful
    concessions or rebates,
    §37-8-24.
  Motor vehicle carriers.
    Rebates in violation of
      chapter, §37-3-25.
  Railroads.
    See RAILROADS.
  Transportation companies,
    §§37-2-16, 37-8-27,
    37-8-28.

PUBLIC UTILITIES—Cont'd
Receivers.
  Certificate or debentures.
    Power of court to issue,
      §37-4-14.
  Taxation.
    Duties of receivers
      generally, §40-21-33.
Records.
  Public service commission.
    See PUBLIC SERVICE
      COMMISSION.
  Valuation of utility property.
    Access of commission to
      utility records,
      §37-4-17.
Redevelopment projects,
  §§24-2-1 to 24-2-10.
  See REDEVELOPMENT
    PROJECTS.
Refunds.
  Unclaimed refunds.
    Uniform disposition of
      unclaimed property
      act, §§35-12-1 to
      35-12-48.
    See LOST OR
      UNCLAIMED
      PROPERTY.
Regulations.
  Public service commission,
    §§37-1-1 to 37-1-157.
    See PUBLIC SERVICE
      COMMISSION.
Relocation of facilities.
  Construction of highways.
    Payment of cost, §23-1-5.
Reports.
  Public service commission.
    See PUBLIC SERVICE
      COMMISSION.
  Required by public service
    commission, §37-4-15.
Rights of way.
  Counties.
    Public roads, bridges and
      ferries.
      See COUNTIES.
Rules and regulations.
  Highways.
    Rights of way.
      Promulgation by
        highway
        department,
        §23-1-59.
Rural telephone service,
  §§37-6-47, 37-6-48.
Sale of property, §§37-4-140
  to 37-4-144.
Sales tax.
  Exemptions, §40-23-4.
Securities.
  Application to issue
    securities or assume
    obligations.
    Contents, §37-4-8.
    Continuance of application,
      §37-4-9.
    Disposition by commission.
      Time for disposition of
        applications, §37-4-9.
    Filing.
      By whom filed, §37-4-8.
    Form, §37-4-8.
    Grant or denial, §37-4-10.
    Modifications, §37-4-10.
    Oath.
      Application to be made
        under oath, §37-4-8.
    Order of commission,
      §37-4-7.

PUBLIC UTILITIES—Cont'd
  Securities—Cont'd
    Application to issue
      securities or assume
      obligations—Cont'd
      Placing at head of
        commission docket,
        §37-4-9.
      Public service commission.
        Notice to commission of
          sale, pledge or other
          dispositions,
          §37-4-11.
        Orders, §37-4-7.
          Supplemental orders,
            §37-4-10.
        Time for disposition,
          §37-4-9.
        Signatures, §37-4-8.
        Supplemental orders of
          commission, §37-4-10.
        Time for disposition,
          §37-4-9.
        When required, §37-4-7.
    Defined, §37-4-1.
    Disposition.
      Notice to commission,
        §37-4-11.
    Employees.
      Sale or purchase of
        securities by
        employees, §37-4-5.
    Guarantee or obligation on
      part of state not to be
      implied, §37-4-12.
    Issuance.
      Securities issued without
        authorization,
        §37-4-16.
    Notice.
      Sale, pledge or other
        disposition.
        Notice to commission,
          §37-4-11.
    Pledge.
      Notification of commission,
        §37-4-11.
    Reports.
      Required reports.
        Disposition of securities,
          §37-4-15.
    Sale.
      Employees, §37-4-5.
      Notification of commission,
        §37-4-11.
    Telephone companies,
      §§37-2-171 to 37-2-174.
    Validity.
      Securities issued without
        authorization,
        §37-4-16.
  Service.
    Abandonment of service.
      Certificate for
        abandonment,
        §37-1-50.
    Classification of utility
      services by public service
      commission, §37-1-51.
    Duty to render adequate
      service, §37-1-49.
    Form for service regulations.
      Prescribing changes in
        form, §37-1-56.
    Free service, §37-4-27.
    Regulations for testing of
      service.
      Public service commission
        may prescribe,
        §37-1-52.

PUBLIC UTILITIES—Cont'd
  Service—Cont'd
    Standards of service.
      Public service commission
        may prescribe,
        §37-1-52.
  Service use tax, §§40-21-100
    to 40-21-107.
    Collection.
      Procedure for collecting
        tax, §40-21-106.
      Seller to collect tax,
        §40-21-105.
    Computation of tax,
      §40-21-102.
    Contracts.
      Utilities to furnish
        information as to
        contracts, §40-21-104.
    Definitions, §40-21-100.
    Exclusions, §40-21-103.
    Legislative intent,
      §40-21-101.
    Levy of tax, §40-21-102.
      Legislative intent,
        §40-21-101.
    Proceeds.
      Disposition, §40-21-107.
    Receipts.
      Tax required to be
        collected by seller from
        purchaser to be
        displayed separately,
        §40-21-105.
    Registration.
      Utilities to register,
        §40-21-104.
  Sewers.
    Counties.
      See COUNTIES.
    General provisions, §§11-88-1
      to 11-88-111.
      See SEWERS.
    Municipal corporations.
      See MUNICIPAL
        CORPORATIONS.
  **Smith's water authority in
    Lee county.**
    Exemption from gross
      receipts tax, §40-21-82.1.
  **Southern products mart
    authority.**
    Eminent domain.
      Acquisition by eminent
        domain of real
        property or rights
        owned by utilities not
        authorized, §41-10-54.
  State.
    Securities.
      Guarantee or obligation on
        part of state not to be
        implied, §37-4-12.
  Statement of utilities.
    Pipeline companies,
      §40-21-10.
    Water companies.
      Contents of statements,
        §40-21-10.
  Stock and stockholders.
    Taxation.
      Ad valorem taxes,
        §40-21-29.
  Supervision fees, §§37-4-23,
    37-4-24.
  Supreme court.
    Valuation of utility property.
      Appeals to supreme court,
        §37-4-21.

PUBLIC UTILITIES—Cont'd
  Tariffs.
    Charging rate in violation of
      tariff.
      Generally, §37-8-21.
  Taxation, §§40-21-1 to
    40-21-107.
    Appeals.
      Protest of incorrect
        valuation, §40-21-24.
    Applicability of chapter,
      §40-21-1.
    Assessment.
      Appeals, §40-21-24.
      Apportionment of assessed
        value, §40-21-17.
      Department of revenue to
        assess all property,
        §40-21-1.
      Determining tax value of
        franchises and
        intangibles, §40-21-25.
      Entries by assessors,
        §40-21-34.
      Franchises.
        Description, §40-21-30.
      Individuals or
        unincorporated
        associations, §40-21-5.
      Intangible property.
        Description, §40-21-30.
      Penalizing delinquent
        taxpayer, §40-21-17.
      Procuring information from
        other sources when
        taxpayer fails to
        comply, §40-21-32.
      Report to tax assessor.
        Report to contain
          description of
          property, §40-21-17.
      Right of assessment,
        §40-21-17.
      What considered in
        arriving at taxable
        value of property,
        §40-21-20.
    Assignment.
      Duties of assignees,
        §40-21-33.
    Bankruptcy.
      Trustees in bankruptcy.
        Duties, §40-21-33.
    Basis.
      Proportion of value or
        receipts within state to
        total value or receipts
        forms basis, §40-21-22.
    Counties.
      Local taxes on franchises
        and other intangible
        property, §40-21-26.
      Apportionment of local
        taxes, §40-21-27.
      Entry and collection,
        §40-21-28.
    Department of revenue.
      Additional information,
        §40-21-16.
      Assessment of all property
        by department,
        §40-21-1.
      Attendance of officers and
        individuals at
        hearings, §40-21-19.
      Evidence and witnesses
        before department,
        §40-21-18.
      Notice of valuation,
        §40-21-23.

PUBLIC UTILITIES—Cont'd
Taxation—Cont'd
Department of revenue
—Cont'd
Receipt of statements.
Endorsement by
department,
§40-21-16.
Report to tax assessor of
each county, §40-21-34.
Returns.
Examination of returns,
§40-21-17.
Subpoenas, §40-21-18.
Value of property.
Determination by
department,
§40-21-17.
Witnesses, §40-21-18.
Electric power companies.
Intangible property subject
to taxation, §40-21-21.
License taxes. See within
this heading, "License
taxes."
Real property.
Description of real
property, fixtures
and other tangible
property within
state, §40-21-12.
Returns.
Contents, §40-21-9.
Evidence.
Default in furnishing
evidence.
Penalty, §40-21-31.
Department of revenue.
Evidence and witnesses
before department,
§40-21-18.
Express companies.
Intangible property subject
to taxation, §40-21-21.
License taxes, §§40-21-60,
40-21-61.
Generally. See within
this heading,
"License taxes."
Statements, §40-21-15.
Failure to pay.
Penalizing delinquent
taxpayer, §40-21-17.
Franchises.
Description of franchises,
§40-21-30.
Local taxes on franchises,
§40-21-26.
Apportionment of local
taxes, §40-21-27.
Entry and collection,
§40-21-28.
Subject to taxation,
§40-21-21.
Tax value.
Determination,
§40-21-25.
Gas companies.
Intangible property subject
to taxation, §40-21-21.
License taxes. See within
this heading, "License
taxes."
Real property.
Description of real
property, fixtures
and other tangible
property within
state, §40-21-12.
Statements.
Contents, §40-21-10.

PUBLIC UTILITIES—Cont'd
Taxation—Cont'd
Gross receipts tax,
§§40-21-80 to 40-21-86.
Hearings.
Incorrect valuations,
§40-21-24.
Intangible property.
Description, §40-21-30.
Local taxes, §§40-21-26 to
40-21-88.
Stockholders not required
to list shares or pay ad
valorem taxes,
§40-21-29.
Subject to taxation,
§40-21-21.
Tax value.
Determination,
§40-21-25.
License taxes, §§40-21-50 to
40-21-64. See within this
heading, "License taxes."
Local taxes.
Franchises and intangibles,
§40-21-26.
Municipal corporations.
Local taxes on franchises
and intangible
property, §§40-21-26 to
40-21-28.
Notice.
Valuation.
Department of revenue
to send notice of
valuation, §40-21-23.
Officers.
Compelling attendance of
officers at department
hearings, §40-21-19.
Penalties.
Default in making returns,
§40-21-31.
Delinquent taxpayers,
§40-21-17.
Pipeline companies.
Intangible property subject
to taxation, §40-21-21.
License taxes generally.
See within this
heading, "License
taxes."
Statements.
Contents, §40-21-10.
Railroads.
Intangible property subject
to taxation, §40-21-21.
License taxes. See within
this heading, "License
taxes."
Number of cars in system.
Reports of railroad
companies, §40-21-7.
Real property.
Description of real
property, §40-21-12.
Reports, §40-21-7.
Sleeping, parlor, dining
and chair car
companies.
Statements required,
§40-21-11.
Subjects of taxation,
§40-11-1.
Total length of railroad
lines, §40-21-13.
Reports of railroad
companies, §40-21-7.

PUBLIC UTILITIES—Cont'd
Taxation—Cont'd
Real property.
Description of real
property, fixtures and
other tangible property
within state,
§40-21-12.
Statement of property held
outside state,
§40-21-14.
Receipts.
Basis of tax value.
Proportion of value or
receipts within state
to total value or
receipts forms basis
of tax value,
§40-21-22.
Receivers.
Duties.
Generally, §40-21-33.
Records.
Compelling production of
records, documents,
etc., §40-21-19.
Reports.
Contents, §40-21-4.
Department of revenue
report to assessors,
§40-21-34.
Individuals or associations
not incorporated,
§40-21-5.
Railroad companies,
§40-21-7.
Required, §40-21-3.
Tax assessors.
Reports to assessors,
§40-21-17.
Unincorporated
associations, §40-21-5.
Returns.
Default in making returns,
§40-21-31.
Examination by
department, §40-21-17.
Procuring information from
other sources when
taxpayer fails to
comply, §40-21-32.
Securities.
Ad valorem taxes.
Stockholders not
required to list
shares or pay ad
valorem taxes
thereon, §40-21-29.
Service use tax, §§40-21-100
to 40-21-107. See within
this heading, "Service
use tax."
Statement of utilities.
Additional information,
§40-21-16.
Default in making
statement or
furnishing evidence or
information.
Penalty, §40-21-31.
Express companies,
§40-21-15.
Gas companies.
Details of statements,
§40-21-10.
Procuring information from
other sources when
taxpayer fails to
comply, §40-21-32.

PUBLIC UTILITIES—Cont'd
Taxation—Cont'd
Statement of utilities
—Cont'd
Receipt of statements by
department of revenue,
§40-21-16.
Verified statements to be
filed, §40-21-2.
Stock and stockholders.
Ad valorem taxes.
Stockholders not
required to list
shares or pay ad
valorem taxes
thereon, §40-21-29.
Subjects of taxation,
§40-11-1.
Subpoenas.
Department of revenue
power to subpoena,
§40-21-18.
Tax assessors.
Entries by assessors in
assessment book,
§40-21-34.
Local taxes.
Entry and collection,
§40-21-28.
Reports to tax assessor,
§§40-21-17, 40-21-34.
What considered in
arriving at taxable
value of property,
§40-21-20.
Telegraph and telephone
companies.
Dual-party relay system
for deaf and hearing-
impaired customers.
Surcharge collected for
service.
Exemption from
taxation,
§37-1-80.2.
Intangible property subject
to taxation, §40-21-21.
License taxes, §§40-21-58,
40-21-59.
Generally. See within
this heading,
"License taxes."
Real property.
Description of real
property, fixtures
and other tangible
property within
state, §40-21-12.
Returns to department of
revenue describing
property belonging
to company,
§40-21-8.
Returns, §40-21-8.
Contents, §40-21-9.
Trustees in bankruptcy.
Duties, §40-21-33.
Unincorporated associations.
Reports, §40-21-5.
Use tax.
Exemptions, §40-23-62.
Utility service use tax,
§§40-20-100 to 40-20-107.
See within this heading,
"Service use tax."

PUBLIC UTILITIES—Cont'd
Taxation—Cont'd
Value of property.
Basis of tax value.
Proportion of value or
receipts within state
to total value or
receipts forms basis
of tax value,
§40-21-22.
Determination by
department, §40-21-17.
Factors to be considered in
determining true value
of entire property,
§40-21-6.
Hearings before
department of revenue,
§40-21-18.
Intangible property.
Determining tax value,
§40-21-25.
Notice of valuation sent by
department, §40-21-23.
Procuring information from
other sources when
taxpayer fails to
comply, §40-21-32.
Protest of incorrect
valuation, §40-21-24.
What considered in
arriving at taxable
value of property,
§40-21-20.
Water companies.
Intangible property subject
to taxation, §40-21-21.
License taxes. See within
this heading, "License
taxes."
Real property.
Description of real
property, fixtures
and other tangible
property within
state, §40-21-12.
Statements.
Contents, §40-21-10.
Witnesses.
Hearings before
department of revenue,
§40-21-18.
Telephones.
General provisions.
See TELEPHONES.
Rural telephone service,
§§37-6-47, 37-6-48.
Securities of telephone
companies, §§37-2-171 to
37-2-174.
Taxation.
Generally. See within this
heading, "Taxation."
License taxes, §40-21-58.
Generally. See within
this heading,
"License taxes."
Transportation companies,
§§37-2-1 to 37-2-184.
See TRANSPORTATION
COMPANIES.
Trees and timber.
Municipal corporations.
Attachment of wires to
trees in towns or
cities, §9-13-15.

PUBLIC UTILITIES—Cont'd
Unclaimed property.
Uniform disposition of
unclaimed property act,
§§35-12-1 to 35-12-48.
See LOST OR
UNCLAIMED
PROPERTY.
United States.
Sale or lease of utility
property.
Sale of property in
interstate commerce
contrary to federal law
not authorized,
§37-4-44.
Use tax.
Exemptions, §40-23-62.
Service use tax, §§40-21-100
to 40-21-107. See within
this heading, "Service
use tax."
Utility gross receipts tax,
§§40-21-80 to 40-21-86. See
within this heading, "Gross
receipts tax."
Utility services actions,
§§6-5-600 to 6-5-605.
See UTILITY SERVICES
ACTIONS.
Utility services facilities,
§§11-97-1 to 11-97-27.
See UTILITY SERVICES
FACILITIES.
Valuation of utility property.
See within this heading,
"Property."
Violations.
Rebates or concessions.
Accepting rebates,
concessions or
discrimination,
§37-8-25.
Granting unlawful
concessions or rebates,
§37-8-24.
Waiver.
Municipal corporations.
Waiver by utility of terms
or conditions in
municipal ordinances
or contracts, §37-1-48.
**Water and wastewater
systems and treatment
plants.**
See WATER AND
WASTEWATER
SYSTEMS AND
TREATMENT PLANTS.
Water distribution facilities.
Conveyance to public
authority or corporation
without necessity of
commission approval,
§37-4-45.
**Water supply and
waterworks.**
Counties.
See COUNTIES.
General provisions.
See WATER SUPPLY
AND WATERWORKS.
Municipal corporations.
See MUNICIPAL
CORPORATIONS.
Taxation. See within this
heading, "Taxation."

PUBLIC WELFARE.
See WELFARE.

PUBLIC WORKS.
Accounts and accounting.
Improvement authorities,
§39-7-28.
Actions.
Contracts. See within this
heading, "Contracts."
Improvement authorities.
Bond issues.
Rights and remedies of
bondholders,
§39-7-25.
Power to sue and be sued,
§39-7-22.
**American-made products
and labor.**
Contracts to provide for use
if available, §39-3-1.
Asphalt plants.
Inspection prerequisite to
eligibility to bid on sale
of mix, §39-1-2.
Atomic energy.
Radioactive fallout
protection, §§39-6-1,
39-6-2.
Audits.
Improvement authorities.
Accounts and books.
Special audit, §39-7-28.
Authorities.
Improvement authorities,
§§39-7-1 to 39-7-34. See
within this heading,
"Improvement
authorities."
Water, sewer and fire
protection authorities,
§§11-88-1 to 11-88-111.
See WATER, SEWER AND
FIRE PROTECTION
AUTHORITIES.
Bids.
Contracts. See within this
heading, "Contracts."
Bond issues.
Improvement authorities,
§§39-7-22 to 39-7-26.
Bonds, surety.
Actions upon.
Commencement by
contractor's suppliers,
§39-1-1.
Applicability of section,
§39-1-1.
Contracts.
Bids.
Guaranties by bidders.
See within this
heading,
"Contracts."
Out-of-state contractors,
§39-2-14.
Performance bonds by
bidders awarded
contracts, §39-2-8.
Approval of bonds,
§39-2-9.
Proceedings upon failure
to furnish, §39-2-11.
Final settlement, §39-1-1.
Notice of completion of
project, §39-1-1.
Requirement, §39-1-1.
Contracts, §§39-2-1 to 39-2-14.
Actions.
Contract to let in violation
of law.
Actions to enjoin letting
or execution of such
contracts, §39-5-4.

PUBLIC WORKS—Cont'd
Contracts—Cont'd
Actions—Cont'd
Contract to let in violation
of law—Cont'd
Actions to recover funds
received under such
contracts, §39-5-3.
Application of chapter,
§39-5-6.
Construction of chapter,
§39-5-6.
No civil action to be
brought on contract,
§39-5-1.
Notice of chapter
presumed, §39-5-5.
Provisions of chapter
mandatory, §39-5-6.
Award, §39-2-6.
Applicability and
construction of
provisions, §39-2-6.
Awarding authorities.
Bonds.
Approval, §39-2-9.
Defined, §39-2-1.
Execution of contracts.
Completion, §39-2-9.
Effect of failure to
complete, §39-2-11.
Fees for proposals, plans
and specifications,
§39-2-3.
Payment of contractors,
§39-2-12.
Proceed orders.
Issuance, §39-2-10.
Effect of failure to
issue, §39-2-11.
Rules and regulations,
§39-2-13.
Bids.
Advertisement for sealed
bids, §39-2-2.
Errors and discrepancies of
prices in bids.
Effect, §39-2-7.
Guaranties.
Disposition when award
not made within 30
days of opening of
proposals, §39-2-5.
Filing by bidders,
§39-2-4.
Return to bidders,
§39-2-5.
Opening, §39-2-2.
Effect of contracts
entered into in
violation, §39-2-2.
Proceedings when all bids
found unreasonable,
§39-2-6.
Applicability and
construction of
provisions, §39-2-6.
Proceedings when no bids
received at time stated
in advertisement,
§39-2-6.
Bonds, surety.
Out-of-state contractors,
§39-2-14.
Performance bonds.
Filing by bidders
awarded contracts,
§39-2-8.
Approval of bonds,
§39-2-9.

PUBLIC WORKS—Cont'd
Contracts—Cont'd
Bonds, surety—Cont'd
Performance bonds—Cont'd
Filing by bidders
awarded contracts
—Cont'd
Proceedings upon
failure to furnish,
§39-2-11.
Certificate of compliance,
§39-5-1.
Issuance of false or
fraudulent certificate,
§39-5-2.
Definitions, §39-2-1.
Payment of contractors,
§39-2-12.
Domestic products.
Provision for use if
available, §39-3-1.
Liquidated damages for
breach, §39-3-1.
Enforceability.
Contracts let in violation
of law unenforceable,
§39-5-1.
Execution, §39-2-8.
Completion by awarding
authorities, §39-2-9.
Effect of failure to
complete, §39-2-11.
Failure of bidders awarded
contracts to execute.
Proceedings upon,
§39-2-11.
Improvement authorities.
Municipal corporations.
Obligations of municipal
contracts not to be
impaired, §39-7-21.
Power to contract,
§39-7-22.
Injunctions.
Contract to let in violation
of law.
Actions to enjoin,
§39-5-4.
Out-of-state contractors.
Bonds, surety, §39-2-14.
Deposits, §39-2-14.
Preference to resident
contractors in letting
of certain contracts,
§39-3-5.
Registration, §39-2-14.
Performance bonds.
Furnishing by bidders
awarded contracts,
§39-2-8.
Plans and specifications.
Fees to awarding
authorities, §39-2-3.
Furnishing to building
exchanges, §39-2-3.
Proceed orders.
Issuance by awarding
authorities, §39-2-10.
Effect of failure to issue,
§39-2-11.
Resident contractors.
Preference in letting of
certain public
contracts, §39-3-5.
Rules and regulations.
Promulgation, §39-2-13.
Counties.
Convict labor.
See PRISONS AND
PRISONERS.

PUBLIC WORKS—Cont'd
Counties—Cont'd
Radioactive fallout
protection.
Requirement in new public
buildings or structures
and additions, §39-6-2.
Definitions.
Contracts, §39-2-1.
Payment of contractors,
§39-2-12.
Improvement authorities,
§39-7-1.
Radioactive fallout
protection, §39-6-1.
Districts.
Water, sewer and fire
protection districts,
§§11-89-1 to 11-89-19.
See WATER, SEWER AND
FIRE PROTECTION
DISTRICTS.
Domestic products.
Contracts to provide for use
if available, §39-3-1.
Liquidated damages for
breach, §39-3-1.
Elections.
Improvement authorities.
Incorporation. See within
this heading,
"Improvement
authorities."
Eminent domain.
Improvement authorities.
Powers, §39-7-22.
Engineers.
General provisions.
See ENGINEERS.
Preparation of plans and
supervision of
construction by
engineers, §34-11-10.
Fees.
Contracts.
Fees to be paid awarding
authorities for
proposals, plans and
specifications, §39-2-3.
Franchises.
Improvement authorities.
Chapter exclusive,
§39-7-33.
Fraud.
Contracts.
Certificates of compliance.
Issuance of fraudulent
certificate, §39-5-2.
Improvement authorities,
§§39-7-1 to 39-7-34.
Accounts and books.
Audit.
Special audit, §39-7-28.
Examination, §39-7-28.
Copy to board of
trustees, §39-7-28.
Special examination,
§39-7-28.
Actions.
Bondholders.
Rights and remedies,
§39-7-25.
Power to sue and be sued,
§39-7-22.
Application of chapter.
Matters as to which
chapter exclusive,
§§39-7-33, 39-7-34.
Audits.
Accounts and books.
Special audit, §39-7-28.

PUBLIC WORKS—Cont'd
Improvement authorities
—Cont'd
Boards of trustees.
Appointment of members,
§39-7-14.
Composition, §39-7-14.
Examinations of accounts
and books.
Copy of examination to
be furnished to
board, §39-7-28.
Officers.
Selection, §39-7-16.
Organization meeting,
§39-7-16.
Powers, §39-7-17.
Public offices under
municipality.
Members not to hold,
§39-7-15.
Terms of office, §39-7-14.
Vacancies in office,
§39-7-14.
Bond issues, §§39-7-22 to
39-7-26.
Bondholders.
Rights and remedies,
§39-7-25.
Pledge as to alteration,
impairment, etc.,
by state, §39-7-26.
Denominations of bonds,
§39-7-23.
Interim receipts,
certificates, etc.
Issuance, §39-7-23.
Issuance, §§39-7-22,
39-7-23.
Interim receipts,
certificates, etc.,
§39-7-23.
Liability, §39-7-24.
Redemption of bonds,
§39-7-23.
Sale, §39-7-23.
Terms of bonds, §39-7-23.
Contracts.
Power to contract,
§39-7-22.
Definitions, §39-7-1.
Eminent domain.
Powers, §39-7-22.
Financial standing.
Statement and analysis to
be published, §39-7-28.
Franchises.
Chapter exclusive,
§39-7-33.
Incorporation.
Authorization, §39-7-2.
Declaration, §§39-7-10,
39-7-11.
Election.
Ballot, §39-7-9.
General election.
Submission of question
proposed by
petition, §39-7-7.
Petition for election,
§§39-7-3 to 39-7-6.
Question to be submitted
to voters, §§39-7-6 to
39-7-8.
Special election.
Conduct, §39-7-8.
Holding for submission
of question to
voters, §39-7-8.

PUBLIC WORKS—Cont'd
Improvement authorities
—Cont'd
Incorporation—Cont'd
Election—Cont'd
Special election—Cont'd
Limitation as to
number of special
elections, §39-7-31.
Payment of expenses,
§39-7-8.
Notice.
Filing of petition and
question to be
submitted at
election, §39-7-6.
Petition for election.
Filing, §39-7-3.
Publication of notice,
§39-7-6.
Form, §39-7-4.
Sufficiency.
Summary proceedings
for review,
§39-7-5.
Verification, §39-7-4.
Resolution.
Adoption, §39-7-10.
Copy.
Transmission of
certified copy to
secretary of state,
§39-7-11.
When authority deemed
incorporated,
§39-7-11.
Secretary of state.
Copy of resolution.
Transmission of
certified copy to
secretary,
§39-7-11.
Statement of names of
authorities
incorporated.
Effect, §39-7-11.
Furnishing to
department of
finance, §39-7-11.
Publication, §39-7-11.
Licenses.
Chapter exclusive,
§39-7-33.
Moneys.
Disposition, §39-7-27.
Municipal corporations.
Bonds.
Payment of obligations
issued by
municipality,
§39-7-21.
Contracts.
Obligations not to be
impaired, §39-7-21.
Notes.
Payment of obligations
issued by
municipality,
§39-7-21.
Officers and employees.
Powers and duties.
Continuation in effect
of provisions as to
powers and duties,
§39-7-19.
Transfer to authority,
§39-7-20.
Offices.
Trustees not to hold,
§39-7-15.

PUBLIC WORKS—Cont'd
Improvement authorities
—Cont'd
Municipal corporations
—Cont'd
Plant or system.
Assumption of municipal
contracts as to,
§39-7-21.
Transfer of supervision,
possession, control,
etc., to authority,
§39-7-19.
Permits.
Chapter exclusive,
§39-7-33.
Powers, §39-7-13.
Boards of trustees,
§39-7-18.
Delegation of powers to
employees, §39-7-17.
Exercise, §39-7-12.
Generally, §§39-7-13,
39-7-21.
Pledge as to alteration,
impairment, etc., by
state, §39-7-26.
Public corporations, §3-7-12.
Purpose of chapter, §39-7-33.
Seals and sealed
instruments.
Power to have and alter
seal, §39-7-22.
Services.
Diminishing.
Authorization and
procedure, §39-7-30.
Limitation as to number
of special elections
on question,
§39-7-31.
Enlarging.
Authorization and
procedure, §39-7-29.
Limitation as to number
of special elections
on question,
§39-7-31.
Furnishing outside
municipal boundaries,
§39-7-32.
Water system.
Sale, transfer and
conveyance to public
corporation, §39-7-13.
Injunctions.
Contract to let in violation of
law.
Actions to enjoin, §39-5-4.
Inspections.
Asphalt plants.
Prerequisite to eligibility
to bid on asphalt plant
mix, §39-1-2.
Labor.
Resident workmen, §§39-2-2,
39-2-3.
Licenses.
Improvement authorities.
Chapter exclusive,
§39-7-33.
Little Miller act, §39-1-1.
Municipal corporations.
Assessments for public
improvements.
See MUNICIPAL
CORPORATIONS.
Improvement authorities. See
within this heading,
"Improvement
authorities."

PUBLIC WORKS—Cont'd
Municipal corporations
—Cont'd
Radioactive fallout
protection.
Requirement in new public
buildings or structures
or additions, §39-6-2.
Nonresidents.
Contracts.
Out-of-state contractors.
Preference to resident
contractors in letting
of certain contracts,
§39-3-5.
Notice.
Completion of project.
Notice by contractor,
§39-1-1.
Contracts.
Actions on contracts let in
violation of law.
Notice of chapter
presumed, §39-5-5.
Improvement authorities.
Incorporation.
Filing of petition and
question to be
submitted at
election, §39-7-6.
Penalties.
Resident workmen.
Employment required.
Violations of section,
§39-3-3.
Permits.
Improvement authorities.
Chapter exclusive,
§39-7-33.
Petitions.
Improvement authorities.
Incorporation.
Petition for election. See
within this heading,
"Improvement
authorities."
Prisons and prisoners.
See PRISONS AND
PRISONERS.
Products.
Domestic products, §39-3-1.
**Radioactive fallout
protection.**
Municipal and county public
buildings.
Requirement, §39-6-2.
State funded public
buildings.
Certification of planning or
construction.
Powers and duties of
state building
commission, §39-6-1.
Incorporation in certain
buildings, §39-6-1.
Resident workmen.
Certificates of sheriffs as to
residence.
Reliance by employers,
§39-3-3.
Employment required,
§39-3-2.
Penalties for violations of
section, §39-3-3.
Rules and regulations.
Contracts.
Promulgation by awarding
authorities, §39-2-13.

PUBLIC WORKS—Cont'd
**Seals and sealed
instruments.**
Improvement authorities.
Power to have and alter
seal, §39-7-22.
Secretary of state.
Improvement authorities.
Incorporation, §39-7-11.
Sheriffs.
Resident workmen.
Certificates of sheriffs as to
residence.
Reliance by employers,
§39-3-3.
State.
Domestic products, §39-3-1.
Resident workmen, §§39-3-2,
39-3-3.
Steel purchases.
Produced in United States.
Contractors for state
projects to use, §39-3-4.

PUGILISM.
Boxing and wrestling.
See BOXING AND
WRESTLING.

PUNISHMENT.
General provisions.
See PENALTIES.
Sentencing.
See SENTENCING.

PUNITIVE DAMAGES.
General provisions, §§6-11-20
to 6-11-30.
See DAMAGES.
Structured damages.
General provisions, §§6-11-1
to 6-11-7.
See DAMAGES.

PUPILS.
Education.
See EDUCATION.

PURCHASES AND STORES.
Affidavits.
Vendor's affidavit.
When not necessary before
payment of invoices for
state purchases,
§41-4-112.
Agent.
Purchasing agent. See within
this heading,
"Purchasing agent."
Conflicts of interest.
Stationery, printing, fuel,
etc., Const. Ala., art. IV,
§69.
Constitution of Alabama.
Stationery, printing, fuel, etc.
Furnishing by lowest
responsible bidder,
Const. Ala., art. IV,
§69.
Counties.
Joint purchasing agreements,
§41-16-21.1.
Courts.
Local purchasing procedures,
§12-19-10.
Division of purchasing.
Contracts for stationery,
printing, paper and fuel,
§41-4-110.
Duties, §41-4-110.
Established, §41-4-110.
Functions, §41-4-110.
Head of division, §41-4-111.

PURCHASES AND STORES
—Cont'd

Division of purchasing
—Cont'd
Printing.
Public printing and
binding.
See PRINTING.
Purchasing agent. See within
this heading,
"Purchasing agent."
Fuel.
Contract for fuel by division,
§41-4-110.
Hospitals.
County and municipal
hospital authorities.
Applicability of state
competitive bid law,
§22-21-190.
Invoices for state purchases.
Vendor's affidavit.
When not necessary before
payment of invoices,
§41-4-112.
Lease-sale contracts.
State departments and
agencies authorized to
enter into, §41-4-115.
**Obtaining supplies or
materials for
departments or
institutions.**
Procedure for obtaining,
§41-4-113.
Paper.
Contracts for paper by
division, §41-4-110.
Printing.
Contracts for printing by
division, §41-4-110.
General provisions.
See PRINTING.
Prisons and prisoners.
Industries in penal
institutions.
See PRISONS AND
PRISONERS.
Purchasing agent.
Appointment, §41-4-111.
Bond, surety, §41-4-7.
Full time service, §41-4-6.
Head of division, §41-4-111.
Oath of office, §41-4-6.
Subject to merit system,
§41-4-6.
Railroad authorities.
Exemption from certain
purchasing laws,
§37-13-20.
Rental-purchase agreements,
§§8-25-1 to 8-25-6.
See RENTAL-PURCHASE
AGREEMENTS.
Small business assistance.
Percentage of state purchases
awarded to, §25-10-9.
Stationery.
Contracts for stationery by
division, §41-4-110.
United States.
Purchase of property from
United States or its
agencies, §41-4-114.

PYROTECHNICS.
Fireworks.
See FIREWORKS.

Q

QUAIL.
Commercial quail breeding,
§§9-11-340 to 9-11-351.
See FISH AND GAME.
Hunting.
Commercial fowl hunting
preserves, §§9-11-410 to
9-11-419.
See FISH AND GAME.

QUARANTINE, §§22-12-1 to
22-12-29.
Affidavits.
Persons desiring to enter or
remain in certain places,
§22-12-29.
Afflicted persons, §22-11A-3.
Amendment of regulations,
§22-12-5.
Arrest.
Without warrants, §22-12-26.
**Attempted escapes from
detention, §22-12-20.**
**Authority of state
paramount, §22-12-2.**
Aviation.
Refusal of freight, §22-12-21.
Supervision of public
conveyances affected by
quarantine, §22-12-21.
Transportation of person or
thing in violation of
quarantine, §22-12-22.
Buses.
Free rides on public
transports for quarantine
officers, §22-12-23.
Supervision of public
conveyances affected by
quarantine, §22-12-21.
Transportation of person or
thing in violation of
quarantine, §22-12-22.
Cattle.
Tuberculous cows, §3-1-18.
Changes of territory,
§22-12-5.
Cotton.
Boll weevil eradication,
§2-19-125.
Counties.
County commissions.
Powers and duties of
county commissions,
§11-3-11.
Enforcement.
Expense of enforcing local
quarantine, §22-12-16.
Local quarantine,
§22-12-13.
Expense of enforcing,
§22-12-16.
Quarantine of infected
portions of county,
§22-12-15.
Infected portions of county.
Enforcement, §22-12-15.
Establishment of
quarantine, §22-12-14.
Proclamation in counties,
§22-12-12.
Report of local quarantine to
state, §22-12-17.
County quarantine officers,
§22-3-8.
Detention.
Escape, §22-12-20.
Attempted escapes,
§22-12-20.

QUARANTINE—Cont'd
Detention—Cont'd
Place of detention.
Establishment, §22-12-19.
Enforcement, §22-12-1.
Local quarantine, §22-12-13.
Expense of enforcing,
§22-12-16.
Infected portions of county,
§22-12-15.
Escape.
Escapes from detention,
§22-12-20.
Governor.
Proclamation of quarantine
by governor, §22-12-4.
Honeybees and apiaries.
Diseased apiary or colony,
§2-14-10.
Investigations, §22-12-6.
Refusal of investigation by
authorities outside state,
§22-12-7.
Lines.
Affidavits by persons
desiring to enter or
remain in certain places,
§22-12-29.
Passing of quarantine lines
by state quarantine
officers and guards,
§22-12-24.
Livestock.
Diseases generally.
See LIVESTOCK.
Mail.
Refusal of mail, §22-12-21.
Municipal corporations.
Enforcement, §22-12-13.
Expense of enforcing,
§22-12-16.
Powers as to quarantine,
§11-47-131.
Proclamation in cities or
towns, §22-12-12.
Report of local quarantine to
state, §22-12-17.
Notifiable diseases.
Quarantine of afflicted
persons, §22-11A-3.
Sexually transmitted
diseases.
Isolation of person.
Compulsory treatment
and quarantine,
§22-11A-18.
Tuberculosis.
Probate court may order,
§22-11A-10.
Nurseries.
Insect and disease control.
Exercise of quarantine
powers of board by
commissioner, §2-25-2.
Movement into state or
within state during
quarantine, §2-25-13.
Powers of board of
agriculture and
industries, §2-25-4.
Officers.
County quarantine officers,
§27-3-8.
State quarantine officers,
§§22-12-23, 22-12-24.
Penalties.
Violation of quarantine law,
§22-1-8.
**Person coming from infected
place, §22-12-18.**

QUARANTINE—Cont'd
**Persons afflicted with
notifiable diseases,**
§22-11A-3.
Plants.
Insect and disease control.
Exercise of quarantine
powers of board by
commissioner, §2-25-5.
Movement into state or
within state during
quarantines, §2-25-13.
Powers of board of
agriculture and
industries, §2-25-4.
Poultry.
Poultry waste, dead poultry
and unhatched or unused
eggs.
Premises not equipped
with prescribed
disposal facilities,
§2-16-42.
Proclamation.
Governor, §22-12-4.
In county, city or town,
§22-12-12.
Public health committees.
Exercise of rights and duties,
§22-12-3.
Rabies.
Exotic and wildlife pets,
§3-7-2.
Generally, §3-7-12.
Railroads.
Free rides on public
transports for quarantine
officers, §22-12-23.
Refusal of freight, §22-12-21.
Supervision of public
conveyances affected by
quarantine, §22-12-21.
Transportation of person or
thing in violation of
quarantine, §22-12-22.
Reports.
Local quarantine.
Report of local quarantine
to state, §22-12-17.
Rules and regulations.
Amendment of regulations,
§22-12-5.
Arriving vessels.
Violation of regulations as
to arriving vessels,
§22-12-11.
State board of health,
§22-2-2.
Ships and shipping.
Duties of vessel master
ordered to perform
quarantine, §22-12-9.
Free rides on public
transports for quarantine
officers, §22-12-23.
Refusal of freight, §22-12-21.
Supervision of public
conveyances affected by
quarantine, §22-12-21.
Transportation of person or
thing in violation of
quarantine, §22-12-22.
Unauthorized removal of
vessel from quarantine,
§22-12-10.
Violation of regulations as to
arriving vessels,
§22-12-11.
State authority paramount,
§22-12-2.

QUARANTINE—Cont'd
State board of health.
Rules and regulations,
§22-2-2.
State quarantine officers.
Exercise of rights and duties,
§22-12-3.
Free rides on public
transports, §22-12-23.
Passing of quarantine lines
by officers and guards,
§22-12-24.
Travelers.
Quarantine of persons
coming from infected
place, §22-12-18.
Tuberculosis.
Probate court may order
quarantine, §22-11A-10.
Tuberculous cows, §3-1-18.
Violation of quarantine law.
Penalty, §22-1-8.
Transportation of person or
thing in violation of
quarantine, §22-12-22.
Warrants.
Arrests without warrants,
§22-12-26.

QUARRIES.
Canals.
Connections to public ways.
Construction and operation
of connections,
§10-5-13.
Operation outside state and
making extensions
within state, §10-5-12.
Condemnation.
Rights of way or easements,
§10-5-3.
Connections to public ways.
Construction and operation,
§10-5-13.
Counties.
Lime and stone quarries.
Acquisition of lands for
lime and stone
quarries, §11-14-23.
Conduct of condemnation
proceedings,
§11-14-24.
Easements.
Condemnation for easements,
§10-5-3.
Eminent domain.
Condemnation for rights of
way or easements,
§10-5-3.
Sites.
Rights of condemning
corporations in
selection of sites,
§10-5-8.
Governor.
Sale of right to quarry
limestone or clay,
§35-4-381.
Highways.
Connections to public ways.
Construction and operation
of connections,
§10-5-13.
Sand, gravel, etc.
Use in construction and
maintenance of
highways and bridges.
Acquisition of land,
§23-1-3.

QUARRIES—Cont'd
Public ways.
Connections to public ways.
Construction and
operation, §10-5-13.
Quarrying companies,
§§10-5-3, 10-5-9, 10-5-12,
10-5-13.
Railroads.
Connections to public ways.
Construction and operation
of connections,
§10-5-13.
Operation outside state and
making extensions
within state, §10-5-12.
Rights of way.
Condemnation for rights of
way by quarrying
companies, §10-5-3.
Ships and shipping.
Operation of transportation
methods for persons or
property, §10-5-9.
Steamships.
Operation of transportation
methods for persons or
property, §10-5-9.
Tunnels.
Connections to public ways.
Construction and operation
of connections,
§10-5-13.
Waters and watercourses.
Connections to public ways.
Construction and operation
of connections to
navigable
watercourses, §10-5-13.

QUAYS.
Docks.
Development of docks
along inland
waterways,
§§33-2-1 to 33-2-213.
See WATERS AND
WATERCOURSES.
General provisions, §§33-1-1
to 33-1-36.
See HARBORS AND
PORTS.
Wharves.
See WHARVES.

QUIETING TITLE, §§6-6-540 to
6-6-573.
Costs.
In personam proceedings,
§6-6-545.
In rem proceedings, §6-6-571.
Evidence.
In rem proceedings,
§§6-6-566, 6-6-567.
Guardian ad litem.
In rem proceedings.
Appointment, §6-6-562.
In personam proceedings.
Answer.
Contents, §6-6-542.
Complaint.
Contents, §6-6-541.
Costs, §6-6-545.
Judgment.
Effect, §6-6-543.
Entry, §6-6-543.
Filing, §6-6-544.
Jury trial, §6-6-543.
Right of action.
Person in peaceable
possession, §6-6-540.

QUIETING TITLE—Cont'd
In personam proceedings
—Cont'd
State.
Commencement of action
by state, §6-6-546.
In rem proceedings.
Answer.
Time to answer, §6-6-565.
Complaint.
Contents, §6-6-561.
Who may file, §6-6-560.
Costs.
Assessment, §6-6-571.
Default judgments, §6-6-565.
Evidence.
Interest or title.
Proof by legal evidence,
§6-6-567.
Prima facie and conclusive
evidence of title,
§6-6-566.
Guardian ad litem.
Appointment, §6-6-562.
Intervention, §6-6-568.
Judgments.
Contents, §6-6-569.
Default judgments,
§6-6-565.
Recordation, §6-6-570.
Lis pendens.
Filing notice of action,
§35-4-131.
Notice.
Filing notice, §35-4-131.
Publication, §6-6-564.
Remedy and procedure
cumulative, §6-6-573.
Service of process, §6-6-563.
Title or interest.
Evidence, §§6-6-566,
6-6-567.
To whom inures, §6-6-572.
Intervention.
In rem proceedings, §6-6-568.
Judgments.
In personam proceedings,
§§6-6-543, 6-6-544.
In rem proceedings,
§§6-6-565, 6-6-569,
6-6-570.
Jury.
In personam proceedings.
Trial by jury, §6-6-543.
Notice.
In rem proceedings.
Publication of notice,
§6-6-564.
Service of process.
In rem proceedings, §6-6-563.
State.
In personam proceedings.
Maintenance of action by
state, §6-6-546.

QUO WARRANTO, §§6-6-590 to
6-6-604.
Appeals.
Generally, §6-6-603.
Judgments on applications
for remedial writs,
§12-22-6.
Stay of execution on
judgment, §6-6-604.
Complaint.
Clearness and conciseness,
§6-6-592.
Constitution of Alabama.
Power of supreme court to
issue writs, Const. Ala.,
art. VI, §140.

QUO WARRANTO—Cont'd
Corporations.
Annulling existence.
Right of action and venue,
§6-6-590.
Charter.
Vacating.
Right of action and
venue, §6-6-590.
Joinder.
Alleged corporation as
party defendant,
§6-6-594.
Judgments.
Dissolving corporation,
§6-6-599.
Officers.
Usurpation of office.
Right of action and
venue, §6-6-591.
Venue.
Usurpation of corporate
office, §6-6-591.
Vacating charter or
annulling existence,
§6-6-590.
Costs.
Assessment, §6-6-601.
Informants.
Liability of informant's
sureties, §6-6-602.
Court of civil appeals.
Original jurisdiction of court,
§12-3-11.
Court of criminal appeals.
Original jurisdiction of court,
§12-3-11.
Courts.
Trial by court, §6-6-593.
Elections.
Validity of election not
triable, §6-6-598.
Franchises.
Judgments.
Excluding defendant from
franchise, §6-6-600.
Usurpation.
Excluding defendant from
franchise, §6-6-600.
Right of action and venue,
§6-6-591.
Fraternal benefit societies.
Actions in quo warranto,
§27-34-50.
Harbors and ports.
See HARBORS AND PORTS.
Informants.
Death.
Effect, §6-6-596.
Joinder.
Alleged corporation as party
defendant, §6-6-594.
Informants, §6-6-595.
Judgments.
Appeals.
Stay of execution on
judgment, §6-6-604.
Corporations.
Dissolving corporation and
excluding same from
corporate rights, etc.,
§6-6-599.
Franchises.
Excluding defendant from
franchise, §6-6-600.
Professions and occupations.
Prohibiting practice of
profession, §6-6-600.

QUO WARRANTO—Cont'd
Judgments—Cont'd
Public officers and
employees.
Excluding defendant from
office, §6-6-600.
Usurpation of office.
Addition of person rightly
entitled to office.
Entry of judgment on
such right, §6-6-597.
Jury.
Trial by jury, §6-6-593.
**Professions and
occupations.**
Usurpation of profession.
Right of action and venue,
§6-6-591.
**Public officers and
employees.**
Usurpation of office.
Person rightly entitled to
office.
Addition, §6-6-597.
Delivery of books, papers
and property,
§6-6-597.
Entry of judgment on
such rights,
§6-6-597.
Right of action and venue,
§6-6-591.
Summons.
Return, §6-6-593.
Supreme court.
Power to issue writs, Const.
Ala., art. VI, §140.
Trial.
Court or jury, §6-6-593.
Setting of case for trial,
§6-6-593.
Venue.
Corporations.
Usurpation of corporate
office, §6-6-591.
Vacating charter or
annulling existence,
§6-6-590.
Franchise.
Usurpation, §6-6-591.
Professions.
Usurpation, §6-6-591.
Public officers and
employees.
Usurpation of office,
§6-6-591.
Wharves.
See WHARVES.

R

RABBIS.
See CLERGY.

RABBIT FEVER.
Notifiable diseases,
§§22-11A-1 to 22-11A-38.
See DISEASES.

RABIES, §§3-7-1 to 3-7-13.
Biting animals.
Confinement of animals
which have bitten
humans, §3-7-9.
**Confinement of animals
which have bitten
humans,** §3-7-9.
Definitions, §3-7-1.

RABIES—Cont'd
Destruction of animals.
When biting animals may be destroyed and head submitted for examination, §3-7-9.
Examination of head of animal, §3-7-9.
Exotic pets.
Quarantine and inoculation, §3-7-2.
Fees.
Inoculation fee, §3-7-3.
Guard dogs, §3-7-9.
Impounding of animals running at large in violation of chapter.
Authorized, §3-7-7.
Disposition of unclaimed animal, §3-7-8.
Facilities for impoundment, §3-7-7.
Notice to owner, §3-7-7.
Redemption of impounded animals, §3-7-8.
Unclaimed animals.
Disposition, §3-7-8.
Inoculation.
Exotic pets, §3-7-2.
Fee, §3-7-3.
Requirements as to inoculation, §3-7-2.
Wildlife pets, §3-7-2.
Inspectors.
Appointment, §3-7-10.
Compensation, §3-7-10.
Deputies, §3-7-10.
Generally, §3-7-10.
Powers, §3-7-10.
Removal from office, §3-7-10.
Vaccine.
Sale, etc., of anti-rabies vaccine to persons other than rabies inspectors or licensed veterinarians, §3-7-2.
Law enforcement work.
Procedure as to sentry or guard dogs used in law enforcement work, §3-7-9.
Liability of owner for injuries caused by rabid dog, §3-1-2.
Municipal corporations.
Effect of chapter on municipalities, §3-7-13.
Notifiable diseases, §§22-11A-1 to 22-11A-38.
See DISEASES.
Penalties.
Tags.
Penalty when animal found without tag, §3-7-6.
Violations of chapter, §3-7-11.
Quarantine.
Exotic and wildlife pets, §3-7-2.
Generally, §3-7-12.
Reports.
Bites.
Failure of person having knowledge of person having been bitten to report, §3-7-9.
Sentry dogs, §3-7-9.
Tags.
Contents, §3-7-4.
Display, §3-7-4.

RABIES—Cont'd
Tags—Cont'd
Issuance, §3-7-4.
Lost tags.
Replacement, §3-7-5.
Penalty when animal found without tag, §3-7-6.
Replacement of lost tags, §3-7-5.
Wearing requirement, §3-7-4.
Vaccination, §§3-7-2, 3-7-3.
Vaccine.
Sale, etc., of anti-rabies vaccine to persons other than rabies inspectors or licensed veterinarians, §3-7-2.
Veterinarians.
Sale, etc., of anti-rabies vaccine to persons other than rabies inspectors or licensed veterinarians, §3-7-2.
Violations of chapter.
Impounding of animals running at large in violation of chapter, §§3-7-7, 3-7-8.
Penalties, §3-7-11.
Wildlife pets.
Quarantine and inoculation, §3-7-2.

RACCOONS.
Coon on the log contests, §§9-11-247 to 9-11-249.
Hunting.
Coon on the log contests, §§9-11-247 to 9-11-249.
Nighttime, §§9-11-235, 9-11-235.1.

RACETRACKS.
Licenses, §40-12-147.
Public athletic boards, §§11-59-1 to 11-59-17.
See MUNICIPAL CORPORATIONS.

RACIAL MINORITIES.
Constitution of Alabama.
Miscegenation laws, Const. Ala., art. IV, §102.
Constitution of the United States, Const. U. S., Amendments XIV, XV.
Indian affairs commission, §§41-9-708 to 41-9-717.
See INDIANS.
Miscegenation laws, Const. Ala., art. IV, §102.

RACING.
Boats.
Safety regulations, §33-5-27.
Horse racing, §§11-65-1 to 11-65-47.
See HORSE RACING.
Motor sports hall of fame commission, §§41-9-470 to 41-9-478.
See MOTOR SPORTS HALL OF FAME COMMISSION.

RACKING HORSE.
State horse, §1-2-10.

RADIATION.
Compensation for occupational exposure to radiation, §§25-5-190 to 25-5-203.
See WORKMEN'S COMPENSATION.
General provisions, §§22-14-1 to 22-14-16.
See ATOMIC ENERGY.
Occupational exposure to radiation, §§25-5-190 to 25-5-203.
See WORKMEN'S COMPENSATION.
Public buildings.
Construction with radioactive fallout protection, §§39-6-1, 39-6-2.
Radioactive waste.
Southeast interstate low-level radioactive waste management compact, §§22-32-1 to 22-32-9.
Southeast interstate low-level radioactive waste management compact, §§22-32-1 to 22-32-9.
Workmen's compensation.
Compensation for occupational exposure to radiation, §§25-5-190 to 25-5-203.
See WORKMEN'S COMPENSATION.

RADIO, §§37-4-100 to 37-4-117.
Amateur radio operators.
Motor vehicle tags and plates, §§32-6-70 to 32-6-93.
See MOTOR VEHICLES.
Antennas.
Construction and maintenance of antennas and towers.
Right of eminent domain, §37-4-113.
Appeals.
Radio utilities.
Final actions or orders of public service commission, §37-4-114.
Supreme court.
Appeals to supreme court, §37-4-114.
Assignments.
Radio utilities.
Certificate of public convenience and necessity.
Approval of public service commission required, §37-4-105.
Bait advertising.
Limitation on criminal liability, §13A-9-44.
Canons of judicial ethics.
When broadcasting in courtroom permitted, ACJE, Canon 3A.
Certificate of public convenience and necessity. See within this heading, "Utilities."
Citizen's band radios.
Motor vehicle tags and plates, §§32-6-70 to 32-6-93.
See MOTOR VEHICLES.

RADIO—Cont'd
Construction.
Antennas and towers.
Right of eminent domain,
§37-4-113.
Counties.
Radio utilities.
Inspection and supervision
fees.
Prohibited, §37-4-116.
Courts.
When broadcasting in
courtroom permitted,
ACJE, Canon 3A.
Dispatchers.
Radio utilities.
General provisions,
§§37-4-100 to 37-4-117.
See within this
heading, "Utilities."
Eminent domain.
Radio utilities.
Right of eminent domain,
§37-4-113.
False advertising.
Limitation on criminal
liability, §13A-9-44.
Fees.
Radio utilities.
Inspection and supervision
fees.
Payment to commission,
§37-4-116.
Horse racing.
Transmission of racing
events, §11-65-32.
Injunctions.
Radio utilities.
Certificate of public
convenience and
necessity.
Persons operating
without certificate,
§37-4-115.
Judges.
When broadcasting in
courtroom permitted,
ACJE, Canon 3A.
Licenses.
Sales, §40-12-148.
Utilities.
Operating without license.
Injunction against
operation, §37-4-115.
When required, §37-4-115.
Lost or unclaimed property.
Disposition of unclaimed
radios left for service,
§35-12-6.
Motor vehicles.
Tags and plates, §§3-6-70 to
3-6-93.
See MOTOR VEHICLES.
Municipal corporations.
Radio utilities.
Inspection and supervision
fees.
Prohibited, §37-4-116.
Paging services.
General provisions,
§§37-4-100 to 37-4-117.
See within this heading,
"Utilities."
Penalties.
Radio utilities.
Penalty for violations,
§37-4-115.

RADIO—Cont'd
Public service commission.
Radio utilities.
General provisions,
§§37-4-100 to 37-4-117.
See within this
heading, "Utilities."
Radio utilities, §§37-4-100 to
37-4-117. See within this
heading, "Utilities."
Sales.
Licenses, §40-12-148.
Supreme court.
Radio utilities.
Appeals to supreme court,
§37-4-114.
Telegraphs.
Construction and
maintenance of antennas
and towers.
Right of eminent domain,
§37-4-113.
Radio utility systems.
Interconnecting radio
utility systems with
existing telephone or
telegraph companies,
§37-4-112.
Certificate of public
convenience and
necessity required,
§37-4-103.
Telephones.
Construction and
maintenance of antennas
and towers.
Right of eminent domain,
§37-4-113.
Radio utilities.
Interconnecting systems
with existing
telephone or telegraph
companies, §37-4-103.
Mobile radio telephone
service.
Article not applicable to,
§37-4-111.
Towers.
Construction and
maintenance of antennas
and towers.
Right of eminent domain,
§37-4-113.
Unclaimed property.
Disposition of unclaimed
radios left for service,
§35-12-6.
Utilities, §§37-4-100 to
37-4-117.
Actions.
Public service commission.
Intervening as party,
§37-4-108.
Antennas.
Construction and
maintenance,
§37-4-113.
Appeals.
Final action or orders of
commission, §37-4-114.
Applicability of article.
Mobile radio telephone
service.
Article inapplicable,
§37-4-111.
Certificate of public
convenience and
necessity.
Application.
Form, §37-4-102.

RADIO—Cont'd
Utilities—Cont'd
Certificate of public
convenience and
necessity—Cont'd
Application—Cont'd
Hearing on application,
§37-4-103.
Assignment of certificate,
§37-4-105.
Construction or operation
of radio utility system.
Certificate required,
§37-4-102.
Encumbrance of certificate,
§37-4-105.
Established service area.
Entry or extension into.
Commission shall not
grant certificate,
§37-4-110.
Factors considered in
determining whether
to issue, §37-4-103.
Hearing.
Commission to fix time
and place for
hearing, §37-4-103.
Injunctions.
Persons operating
without certificate,
§37-4-115.
Issuance, §37-4-103.
Factors considered in
determining whether
to issue, §37-4-103.
Rules governing,
§37-4-102.
Operating without
certificate.
Injunctions against
operation, §37-4-115.
Revocation, suspension or
alteration of
certificate, §37-4-107.
Telephone or telegraph
companies.
Interconnecting radio
utility system with
existing telephone or
telegraph company.
Certificate required,
§37-4-103.
Transfer of certificate,
§37-4-105.
When required, §37-4-102.
Construction.
Antennas and towers.
Right of eminent
domain, §37-4-113.
Continuation of facilities
existing prior to
September 28, 1971,
§37-4-104.
Continuation of facilities
existing prior to
September 28, 1971,
§37-4-104.
Counties.
Inspection and supervision
fees.
Assessment prohibited,
§37-4-116.
Definitions, §37-4-101.
Eminent domain, §37-4-113.
Enforcement of article.
Powers of public service
commission, §37-4-108.

RADIO—Cont'd
Utilities—Cont'd
Fees.
Inspection and supervision
fees.
Payment to commission,
§37-4-116.
General system.
Treatment of utility as
part of general system,
§37-4-117.
Injunctions.
Certificate of public
convenience and
necessity.
Persons operating
without certificate,
§37-4-115.
Inspections.
Fees.
Payment to commission,
§37-4-116.
Public service commission.
Power to inspect,
§37-4-108.
Interconnection with other
communications,
§37-4-112.
Certificate of public
convenience and
necessity required,
§37-4-103.
Continuation of facilities
existing prior to
September 28, 1971,
§37-4-104.
Licenses.
Operating without license.
Injunction against
operation, §37-4-115.
When required, §37-4-115.
Merger or consolidation.
Approval of public service
commission required,
§37-4-106.
Mobile radio telephone
service.
Article not applicable,
§37-4-111.
Municipal corporations.
Inspection and supervision
fees.
Prohibited, §37-4-116.
Penalties.
Violations, §37-4-115.
Public service commission.
Actions.
Intervening as a party in
actions, §37-4-108.
Appeals.
Final action or order of
commission,
§37-4-114.
Certificate of public
convenience and
necessity.
Issuance of certificate.
Rules and regulations
governing
issuance,
§37-4-102.
Transfer, assignment or
encumbrance of
certificate.
Approval of
commission
required,
§37-4-105.
Duties.
Generally, §37-4-108.

RADIO—Cont'd
Utilities—Cont'd
Public service commission
—Cont'd
Enforcement of article.
Powers of commission,
§37-4-108.
Fees.
Inspection and
supervision fees,
§37-4-116.
General system.
Treatment of utility as
part of general
system, §37-4-117.
Inspection of books,
accounts, etc.
Fees, §37-4-116.
Power of commission,
§37-4-108.
Intervening as a party in
actions, §37-4-108.
Investigations.
Power to institute
investigations,
§37-4-108.
Merger or consolidation.
Approval of commission
required, §37-4-106.
Orders.
Appeals, §37-4-114.
Power to issue,
§37-4-108.
Powers.
Generally, §37-4-108.
Rates and charges for
services.
Commission to prescribe,
§37-4-109.
Records.
Authority to examine,
§37-4-108.
Fees paid, §37-4-116.
Regulation of radio
utilities.
Power to regulate,
§37-4-108.
Repair or improvement of
radio systems.
Commission may order,
§37-4-108.
Revocation, suspension or
alteration of
certificate, §37-4-107.
Supervision of radio
utilities, §37-4-108.
Radio utility systems.
Construction.
Certificate of public
convenience and
necessity required,
§37-4-102.
Continuation of facilities
existing prior to
September 28, 1971,
§37-4-104.
Defined, §37-4-101.
Operation.
Certificate of public
convenience and
necessity required,
§37-4-102.
Continuation of facilities
existing prior to
September 28, 1971,
§37-4-104.

RADIO—Cont'd
Utilities—Cont'd
Radio utility systems—Cont'd
Telephone or telegraph
companies.
Interconnecting radio
utility system with
existing telephone or
telegraph company,
§37-4-112.
Certificate of public
convenience and
necessity required,
§37-4-103.
Rates and charges.
Commission to prescribe
just and reasonable
rates and charges,
§37-4-109.
Tariffs.
Filing, §37-4-109.
Service areas.
Entry or extension into
established areas,
§37-4-110.
Services.
Rates, charges and
classifications for
services.
Commission to prescribe,
§37-4-109.
Short title of article,
§37-4-100.
Supreme court.
Appeals to supreme court,
§37-4-114.
Tariffs.
Filing of rate tariffs,
§37-4-109.
Telephone or telegraph
companies.
Interconnecting radio
utility system with
existing telephone or
telegraph company,
§37-4-112.
Certificate of public
convenience and
necessity required,
§37-4-103.
Mobile radio telephone
service.
Article not applicable,
§37-4-111.
Title of article.
Short title, §37-4-100.
Towers.
Construction and
maintenance,
§37-4-113.
Violations.
Penalty for violations,
§37-4-115.

RADIOACTIVE WASTE.
Compacts.
Southeast interstate low-
level radioactive waste
management compact,
§§22-32-1 to 22-32-9.

RAILROAD AUTHORITIES,
§§37-13-1 to 37-13-21.
Actions.
Power to sue and be sued,
§37-13-7.
Suits against manager or
director of authority,
§37-13-10.
Boards of directors.
Definition of "board,"
§37-13-1.

RAILROAD AUTHORITIES
—Cont'd

Boards of directors—Cont'd
Expenses of directors.
Reimbursement, §37-13-5.
Number of directors.
Certificate of incorporation
to state, §37-13-3.
Officers.
Election, §37-13-6.
Quorum, §37-13-5.
Record of proceedings,
§37-13-5.
Removal of directors,
§37-13-5.
Residence requirement,
§37-13-5.
Vacancies.
Filling, §37-13-5.
Bond issues, §§37-13-11 to
37-13-19.
Coupons, §37-13-11.
Defined, §37-13-1.
Signatures, §37-13-12.
Definition of "bond,"
§37-13-1.
Execution of bonds,
§37-13-12.
Indentures.
Defined, §37-13-1.
Security for bonds,
§37-13-13.
Investment in bonds of
authority.
County and municipal
funds, §37-13-17.
Trust funds.
Eligibility of bonds as
investments,
§37-13-18.
Issuance of bonds, §37-13-11.
Notice.
Bond resolution, §37-13-19.
Power to issue bonds,
§§37-13-7, 37-13-11.
Proceeds of sale.
Disposition, §37-13-14.
Refunding bonds,
§37-13-15.
Refunding bonds, §37-13-15.
Sale of bonds.
Disposition of proceeds,
§37-13-14.
Refunding bonds,
§37-13-15.
Security for bonds, §37-13-13.
Taxation.
Exemption from taxation,
§37-13-16.
Terms and conditions,
§37-13-11.
Contracts.
Construction and purchasing
contracts.
Exemption from certain
provisions, §37-13-20.
Power to execute contracts,
§37-13-7.
Counties.
Cooperation by counties,
§37-13-9.
Definitions, §37-13-1.
Dissolution, §37-13-21.
Eminent domain, §37-13-7.
Grants.
Power to receive and accept,
§§37-13-7, 37-13-8.
Incorporation.
Authority to incorporate,
§37-13-2.

RAILROAD AUTHORITIES
—Cont'd

Incorporation—Cont'd
Certificate of incorporation.
Application to incorporate.
Proposed form of
certificate to be
attached, §37-13-2.
Contents, §37-13-3.
Execution, §37-13-4.
Recordation, §37-13-4.
Effect, §37-13-4.
Procedure, §37-13-2.
Insurance.
Powers of authorities,
§37-13-7.
Investments.
Bonds of authorities.
County and municipal
funds, §37-13-17.
Trust funds.
Eligibility of bonds as
investments,
§37-13-18.
Powers of authorities,
§37-13-7.
Municipal corporations.
Cooperation of cities,
§37-13-9.
Notice.
Bond resolution, §37-13-19.
Officers, §37-13-6.
Election, §37-13-6.
Terms of office, §37-13-6.
Powers, §37-13-7.
Property.
Dissolution of authority.
Effect, §37-13-21.
Powers, §37-13-7.
Taxation.
Exemption, §37-13-16.
Public service commission.
Exemption from jurisdiction,
§37-13-20.
Purchases and stores.
Exemption from certain
purchasing laws,
§37-13-20.
**Seals and sealed
instruments.**
Power to adopt and use
corporate seal, §37-13-7.
Taxation.
Exemption, §37-13-16.
Trusts and trustees.
Bonds of authorities.
Eligibility as investments
for trust funds,
§37-13-18.

RAILROADS.
Abandonment.
Rights-of-way.
Authorized to transfer,
§10-5-2.1.
Accidents.
Precautions.
Failure to use to prevent
accidents, §37-8-114.
Reports, §37-2-91.
Accounts and accounting.
Separation of intrastate
railroad operations for
accounting purposes,
§37-1-55.

RAILROADS—Cont'd
Actions.
Accommodations for
passengers.
Orders of public service
commission.
Failure to comply with
orders, §37-2-113.
Action for damages not
barred, §37-2-116.
Advertising.
Failure of trains to stop at
advertised stations,
§37-2-114.
Grand jury.
Sheriff to report facts to
grand jury, §37-8-200.
Name appearing on sign.
Presumption of guilt,
§37-8-200.
Penalties.
Violations, §37-8-200.
Private property.
Signs on private property,
§37-8-200.
Sheriffs.
Report to grand jury,
§37-8-200.
Signs resembling railroad
signs.
Erection or maintenance,
§37-8-200.
Violations.
Penalty, §37-8-200.
**Aiding another corporation
in construction,** §10-5-11.
Alcoholic beverages.
Licenses.
Retail common carrier
liquor license,
§28-3A-18.
Arrest.
Railway policemen.
Powers of arrest,
§37-2-153.
Assignments.
Property injury claims
against railroads
assignable, §8-5-23.
Attachment.
Liens of railroad laborers
and employees,
§§35-11-90 to 3-11-97.
See within this heading,
"Liens."
Attorney general.
Noncompliance with
commission order to
erect depot or provide
conveniences for
travelers.
Failure of commission to
notify attorney
general, §37-8-111.
Passengers.
Failure of railroad
companies to comply
with orders of
commission in regards
to passenger
accommodations.
Civil action by attorney
general, §37-2-113.
Authorities, §§37-13-1 to
37-13-21.
See RAILROAD
AUTHORITIES.

RAILROADS—Cont'd
Aviation.
Operation of transportation
methods for persons or
property by railroad
companies, §10-5-9.
Baggage.
Personal baggage of
passengers, §§37-2-35 to
37-2-39.
**Bear creek development
authority.**
Eminent domain.
Acquisition of property
controlled by railroads,
§33-15-5.
Bills of lading.
Commercial code.
Defined, §7-1-201.
Overseas shipment.
Form of bill, §7-2-323.
Third-party documents.
Prima facie evidence,
§7-1-202.
Documents of title, §§7-7-101
to 7-7-603.
See COMMERCIAL CODE.
Blind persons.
Right to use of public
conveyances and
transportation facilities,
§21-7-3.
Bonds, surety.
Highways.
Digging up of roads,
§23-1-4.
Railway policemen,
§37-2-151.
Bridges.
Drawbridges.
Steamboats passing
through railroad
drawbridges, §37-2-88.
Grade crossings. See within
this heading,
"Crossings."
Municipal corporations.
Requirement of
construction and
maintenance by
railroads of bridges,
tunnels, etc., within
limits of certain cities,
§§11-49-40 to 11-49-45.
See MUNICIPAL
CORPORATIONS.
Burden of proof.
Compliance with
requirements of sections
37-2-80 through 37-2-82.
Burden of proof on
company, §37-2-83.
Canals.
Operation of canals outside
state and making
extensions within state
by railroad companies,
§10-5-12.
Cars.
Procuring railroad cars
without bona fide
intention for use,
§37-8-148.
Cattle guards.
Required, §37-2-137.
Charges.
Charging or accepting rate
lower than published
tariff, §37-8-22.
Higher than lawful rate,
§37-8-23.

RAILROADS—Cont'd
Charges—Cont'd
Violation of statutes relating
to reasonable rates,
§37-8-20.
Charities.
Free passes, rebates or
discounts.
Exemptions for charities,
§37-8-28.
Circuit courts.
Judgment confirming
commission award
regulating railroad's
business with connecting
line.
Violation of circuit court
judgment, §37-8-118.
Claims.
Soliciting claims from
shippers or consignees
against carriers,
§37-8-280.
Coal mine safety.
Hoisting and haulage,
§§25-9-210 to 25-9-216.
See COAL.
Commercial code.
Secured transactions.
Applicability of filing
provisions, §7-9-302.
Determination of validity
and perfection of
security interest in
rolling stock, §7-9-103.
Transactions excluded from
provisions of article,
§7-9-104.
Common carriers, Const.
Ala., art. XII, §242.
Companies, Const. Ala., art.
XII, §242.
Regulation.
Legislature, Const. Ala.,
art. XII, §243.
Rights.
Generally, Const. Ala., art.
XII, §242.
Transportation companies,
§§37-2-1 to 37-2-184.
See TRANSPORTATION
COMPANIES.
Condemnation.
Condemnation for ways and
rights of way, §§10-5-2,
10-5-4.
Depots, yards and tracks.
Condemnation of lands for
depots, yards and
tracks, §10-5-7.
General provisions. See
within this heading,
"Eminent domain."
Conductors.
Alcoholic beverages.
Conductors may exercise
powers of police
officers, §37-8-160.
Intoxication of persons
employed upon
railways, §37-8-161.
Employees generally. See
within this heading,
"Employees."
Examinations, §37-2-85.
Instruction of conductors,
§37-2-87.
Licenses, §37-2-85.
Employment of unlicensed
persons, §37-2-86.
Permits, §37-2-86.1.

RAILROADS—Cont'd
Conductors—Cont'd
Warning devices.
Failure of railroad
superintendent to
instruct conductors
regarding blowing
horn, whistle, etc.,
§37-8-113.
**Connection of tracks and
interchange of traffic,**
§§37-2-131 to 37-2-135.
Costs.
Each connecting line to be
liable for proportionate
share, §37-2-134.
Delay.
Duty to deliver freight or
cars without
unreasonable delay,
§37-2-135.
Discrimination.
Duty to deliver freight or
cars without
unreasonable delay or
discrimination,
§37-2-135.
Duty to provide equal and
reasonable facilities,
§37-2-134.
Equal and reasonable
facilities.
Duty to provide, §37-2-134.
Railroads to afford
reasonable and proper
facilities, §37-2-132.
Gauge of track.
Railroads not required to
receive or transport
cars of other railroads
unless such cars adapt
to gauge of track,
§37-2-131.
Generally, §37-2-131.
Livestock.
Precedence given livestock,
§37-2-135.
Perishable freight.
Precedence given,
§37-2-135.
Public service commission.
Violation of judgment
confirming commission
award regulating
railroad's business
with connecting line,
§37-8-118.
Railroads running to or
through same town or
city, §37-2-132.
Switch connections,
§37-2-133.
Transferring cars.
Duty to provide equal and
reasonable facilities,
§37-2-134.
From one company to
another, §37-2-132.
Two or more railroads
running to or through
same town or city,
§37-2-132.
Constitution of Alabama.
Acceptance of article
prerequisite to benefits
of future legislation,
Const. Ala., art. XII,
§246.
Bonuses in nature of rebates.
Prohibited, Const. Ala.,
art. XII, §245.

RAILROADS—Cont'd
Constitution of Alabama
—Cont'd
Free passes or discount
tickets.
Giving to members of
legislature or judicial
officers, Const. Ala.,
art. XII, §244.
Grant of easements to
railroad companies,
Const. Ala., art. IV, §99.
Public highways.
When deemed, Const. Ala.,
art. XII, §242.
Railroad companies, Const.
Ala., art. XII, §242.
Regulation.
Legislature, Const. Ala.,
art. XII, §243.
Rights.
Generally, Const. Ala.,
art. XII, §242.
Rates.
Deceiving or misleading
public, Const. Ala., art.
XII, §245.
Rebates.
Prohibited, Const. Ala.,
art. XII, §245.
Construction.
Aiding of another corporation
in railroad construction,
§10-5-11.
Condemnation of ways and
rights of way by
companies constructing
internal improvement,
§10-5-4.
Drainage.
Duty to drain areas in
construction works,
§22-20-10.
Dwelling houses.
Construction through
curtilage of house
without consent,
§10-5-5.
Corporations.
Application of corporations
provisions, §10-2A-336.
Foreign corporations.
Extension of tracks into
state, §10-2A-225.
County boards of health.
Duties, §22-3-2.
Criminal law and procedure.
Force.
Use of force by persons
responsible for
maintenance of order
in contract carriers,
§13A-3-24.
Crossings.
Abandonment, §37-2-84.
Cattle guards at crossings,
§37-2-137.
Easements.
Eminent domain.
Acquisition of easement,
§18-1A-273.
Crossing line of another
railroad, §18-1A-72.
Elimination, §23-1-9.
Eminent domain.
Easements.
Acquisition of easements,
§18-1A-273.
Crossing line of another
railroad, §18-1A-72.

RAILROADS—Cont'd
Crossings—Cont'd
Motor vehicles.
Keeping to the right,
§32-5-54.
Obstruction of crossings.
Crew members acting on
instructions not
responsible, §37-8-115.
Drivers to remain clear of
obstructed crossings,
§32-5A-61.
Right of way at crossings,
§37-2-82.
Stopping trains at crossings,
§37-2-82.
Liability for failure to
comply, §37-2-83.
Warning devices.
Duty of engineer to ring
bell or blow horn at
crossing, §37-2-81.
Liability of railroad for
failure to comply,
§37-2-83.
Curve act, §§37-2-81, 37-2-83.
Definitions.
Authorities, §37-13-1.
Preservation, §37-10-2.
Depots.
Condemnation of lands for
depots, §10-5-7.
Duty of railroad to provide
accommodations
generally, §37-2-110.
Duty to maintain depots,
§37-2-130.
Noncompliance with
commission order to
erect depot.
Attorney general.
Failure of commission to
notify, §37-8-111.
District attorneys.
Failure of commission to
notify, §37-8-111.
Failure of commission to
notify district attorney
or attorney general,
§37-8-111.
Penalty for noncompliance,
§37-8-110.
Stations generally. See
within this heading,
"Stations."
Tariffs.
Failure of railroad to post
freight tariffs at
depots, §37-8-31.
Discounts.
Exemptions, §37-8-28.
General assembly.
Discounts to members,
Const. Ala., art. XII,
§244.
Penalties for violations,
§37-8-27.
Discrimination.
Charging or collecting higher
than lawful rate,
§37-8-23.
Public utilities generally.
See PUBLIC UTILITIES.
Violation of statutes relating
to unjust discrimination,
§37-8-20.

RAILROADS—Cont'd
District attorneys.
Noncompliance with
commission order to
erect depot or provide
conveniences for
travelers.
Failure of commission to
notify district attorney,
§37-8-111.
Passengers.
Failure of companies to
comply with orders in
regard to passenger
accommodations.
District attorney to bring
civil action,
§37-2-113.
Drawbridges.
Steamboats passing
drawbridges, §37-2-88.
Drinking cups.
Use of common drinking cups
prohibited, §22-20-1.
Drunkenness.
Public drinking on railway
passenger cars or in
waiting rooms,
§37-8-160.
Dwellings.
Construction through
curtilage of house
without consent, §10-5-5.
Easements.
Crossings.
Eminent domain.
Acquisition of easements,
§18-1A-273.
Crossing line of another
railroad, §18-1A-72.
Grant of easements to
railroad, Const. Ala., art.
IV, §99.
Electricity.
Overhead conductors.
Operations in proximity to
high voltage overhead
conductors.
Exemption from
provision of sections,
§37-8-54.
Eminent domain.
Condemnation for ways and
rights of way, §§10-5-2,
10-5-4.
Crossings.
Easements.
Acquisition, §18-1A-273.
Crossing line of another
railroad, §18-1A-72.
Depots, yards and tracks.
Condemnation of lands for
depots, yards and
tracks, §10-5-7.
Easements.
Crossings.
Acquisition of easements,
§18-1A-273.
Line of another railroad,
§18-1A-72.
Power of eminent domain in
internal improvement
corporations, §10-5-1.
Routes and sites.
Rights of condemning
corporations in
selection of routes and
sites, §10-5-8.

RAILROADS—Cont'd
  Eminent domain—Cont'd
    Subways.
      Municipal corporations.
        Acquisition of land,
          §18-1A-274.
    Viaducts.
      Municipal corporations.
        Acquisition of land,
          §18-1A-274.
  Employees.
    Alcoholic beverages.
      Intoxication of persons
        employed upon
        railways, §37-8-161.
    Conductors. See within this
      heading, "Conductors."
    Discounts.
      Exemptions, §37-8-28.
    Engineers. See within this
      heading, "Engineers."
    Examinations, §37-2-85.
    Free passage, §37-1-15.
      Exemption from
        prohibition, §37-8-28.
    Intoxication, §37-8-161.
    Liability.
      Obstructing streets,
        crossings, etc.
        Crew members acting on
          instructions not
          responsible,
          §37-8-115.
    Licenses, §37-2-85.
      Employment of unlicensed
        persons, §37-2-86.
    Liens, §§35-11-90 to
      35-11-97. See within this
      heading, "Liens."
    Obstructing streets, etc.
      Crew members acting on
        instructions not
        responsible, §37-8-115.
    Passengers.
      Failure of employees to
        comply with
        provisions.
        Action for damages not
          barred, §37-2-116.
    Rebates, §8-11-4.
      Exemption from
        prohibition, §37-8-28.
    Wages.
      Biweekly payment,
        §37-8-270.
  Engineers.
    Duty to ring bell or blow
      horn, §37-2-81.
    Liability of railroad for
      failure to comply,
      §37-2-83.
    Employees generally. See
      within this heading,
      "Employees."
    Examinations, §37-2-85.
    Failure to ring bell, blow
      horn or whistle on
      trains, §37-8-112.
    Instruction of engineers,
      §37-2-87.
    Intoxication, §37-8-161.
    Licenses, §37-2-85.
      Employment of unlicensed
        persons, §37-2-86.
    Permits, §37-2-86.1.
    Precautions.
      Failure to use to prevent
        accidents, §37-8-114.

RAILROADS—Cont'd
  Engineers—Cont'd
    Warning devices.
      Failure of railroad
        superintendent to
        instruct engineers
        regarding blowing of
        horn, whistle, etc.,
        §37-8-113.
  Examinations.
    Employees, §37-2-85.
  **Execution and text of
    compact, §37-11-1.**
  Explosives.
    Transportation of explosives,
      §§37-8-180 to 37-8-184.
  Fences.
    Cattle guards, §37-2-137.
    Failure after notice to fence
      railroads.
      Liability for injury to
        stock, §37-2-89.
    Notification of person or
      corporation operating
      railroad, §37-2-89.
  Fires and fire prevention.
    Locomotives.
      Equipping with appliances
        to prevent escape of
        fire, §9-13-14.
  Fish and game.
    Hunting or discharge of
      firearm from, upon or
      across railroads,
      §9-11-257.
  Forests and forestry.
    Fires and fire prevention.
      Locomotives.
        Equipping with
          appliances to
          prevent escape of
          fire, §9-13-14.
  Franchises.
    Conveyance to another
      railroad corporation,
      §10-5-10.
  Free passage.
    Employees, §§37-1-15,
      37-8-28.
    Exemptions, §37-8-28.
    General assembly.
      Free passes to members,
        Const. Ala., art. XII,
        §244.
    Penalties for violations,
      §37-8-27.
  Freight.
    Charging or collecting higher
      than lawful rate for
      transportation of freight,
      §37-8-23.
    Claims.
      Soliciting claims from
        shippers or consignees
        against carriers,
        §37-8-280.
    Connection of tracks and
      interchange of traffic.
      Duty to deliver freight
        without unreasonable
        delay or
        discrimination,
        §37-2-135.
    Perishable freight.
      Precedence given
        perishable freight,
        §37-2-135.

RAILROADS—Cont'd
  Freight—Cont'd
    Perishable freight.
      Connection of tracks and
        interchange of traffic.
        Precedence given
          perishable freight,
          §37-2-135.
      Pooling of freights.
        Unlawful pooling, §37-8-30.
      Procuring railroad cars
        without bona fide
        intention for use in
        transportation of freight,
        §37-8-148.
    Tariffs.
      Failure to post tariffs at
        depots, §37-8-31.
  Garnishment.
    Laborers' and employees'
      liens.
      Property or proceeds
        subject to
        garnishment,
        §35-11-95.
  **General provisions, §§37-2-1
    to 37-2-184.**
    See TRANSPORTATION
      COMPANIES.
  Governor.
    Railway policemen.
      Appointment, §37-2-150.
      Removal, §37-2-157.
  Grade crossings. See within
    this heading, "Crossings."
  Grand jury.
    Signs resembling railroad
      signs.
      Erection or maintenance of
        advertising signs
        resembling railroad
        signs.
        Sheriff to report
          violations to grand
          jury, §37-8-200.
  Handicapped persons.
    Right to use of public
      conveyances and
      transportation facilities,
      §21-7-3.
  Harbors and ports.
    Acquisition of property and
      rights-of-way necessary
      by purchase or eminent
      domain, §33-1-22.
    Terminal railroads.
      State may acquire, operate,
        etc., §33-1-16.
  Headlights.
    Exceptions, §37-2-90.
    Failure to provide power
      headlights on engines,
      §37-8-117.
    Required, §37-2-90.
  Health.
    Authority and jurisdiction of
      state board of health,
      §22-2-2.
    Duties of county boards of
      health, §22-3-2.
  Highways.
    Grade crossings, §23-1-9.
    Obstruction of streets, etc.,
      §37-8-115.
    Signs.
      Erection, §§37-2-80,
        37-2-83, 37-2-200.
  Horns.
    Failure to blow horn,
      §37-8-112.

RAILROADS—Cont'd
Horns—Cont'd
Precautions.
Failure to use to prevent
accidents, §37-8-114.
Superintendents.
Failure to instruct
engineers and
conductors regarding
blowing horn,
§37-8-113.
Housing.
Construction through
curtilage of house
without consent, §10-5-5.
Hunting.
Hunting or discharge of
firearm from, upon or
across railroads,
§9-11-257.
Indigent persons.
Free tickets, §37-1-15.
Interchange of traffic,
§§37-2-131 to 37-2-135.
**Iron, brass or other metal
articles manufactured
exclusively for railroad
purposes.**
Unlawful purchase or receipt,
§37-8-149.
Judgments.
Public service commission.
Violation of judgment
confirming commission
award regulating
railroad's business
with connecting line,
§37-8-118.
Jumping on or off trains,
§37-8-91.
Laborers.
Liens, §§35-11-90 to
35-11-97. See within this
heading, "Liens."
Legislature.
Free passes or discount
tickets to members,
Const. Ala., art. XII,
§244.
Regulation of railroad
companies, Const. Ala.,
art. XII, §243.
Liability.
Failure to comply with
sections 37-2-80 through
37-2-82, §37-2-83.
Railway policemen.
Liability of corporation for
acts of policemen,
§37-2-155.
Licenses.
Alcoholic beverages.
Retail common carrier
liquor license,
§28-3A-18.
Brokers and agents of
railway supplies,
§40-12-67.
Employees, §37-2-85.
Employment of unlicensed
persons, §37-2-86.
Municipal corporations.
Schedules, §11-51-124.
Sleeping car companies.
Municipal license schedule,
§11-51-125.
Supply cars, §40-12-164.
Tax, §40-21-57.

RAILROADS—Cont'd
Liens.
Laborers and employees.
Attachment.
Right to enforce liens by
attachment,
§35-11-92.
Declaration of lien,
§35-11-90.
Enforcement of liens.
Right to enforce by
attachment,
§35-11-92.
Garnishment.
Property or proceeds
subject to
garnishment,
§35-11-95.
Liens generally, §§35-11-1
to 35-11-431.
See LIENS.
Prior liens.
Satisfaction of prior
liens, §35-11-97.
Line arrangements.
Entering into line
arrangements by
railroad corporations,
§10-5-11.
Livestock.
Cattle guards, §37-2-137.
Connection of tracks and
interchange of traffic.
Precedence given livestock,
§37-2-135.
Fences.
Failure to fence railroads.
Liability for injury to
stock, §37-2-89.
Logging railroads.
Public service commission.
Jurisdictional exemptions
or limitations,
§37-1-37.
Manufacturers.
Connections to public ways.
Construction and operation
of connections,
§10-5-13.
Operation outside state and
making extensions
within state, §10-5-12.
Mines and minerals.
Connections to public ways.
Construction and operation
of connections,
§10-5-13.
Operation outside state and
making extensions
within state, §10-5-12.
Motor fuels.
Additional excise tax on
gasoline, motor fuel and
lubricating oil.
Exemptions, §40-17-220.
Motor vehicles.
Grade crossings.
Keeping to the right,
§32-5-54.
Operation of transportation
methods for persons or
property by railroad
companies, §10-5-9.
Municipal corporations.
Assessment of costs of
improvements against
railroads, §11-48-19.

RAILROADS—Cont'd
Municipal corporations
—Cont'd
Bridges, tunnels, etc.
Requirement of
construction and
maintenance by
railroads within limits
of certain cities,
§§11-49-40 to 11-49-45.
See MUNICIPAL
CORPORATIONS.
Commission form of
government.
Municipal officers or
employees.
Conflicts of interest,
§11-44-46.
Connection of tracks and
interchange of traffic.
Railroads running to or
through same town or
city, §37-2-132.
License schedules,
§11-51-124.
Running, etc., of trains
within corporate limits.
Regulation, §11-47-114.
Sleeping car companies.
License schedules,
§11-51-125.
Street railroads.
See MUNICIPAL
CORPORATIONS.
Streets, etc.
Regulation of running,
switching, etc., of cars,
trains and locomotives
on streets, crossings,
highways, etc.,
§11-43-61.
Subways and viaducts.
Construction, §18-1A-274.
Eminent domain.
Acquisition of land,
§18-1A-274.
Negligence.
Railway policemen.
Liability of corporation for
acts of policemen,
§37-2-155.
Notice.
Fences.
Notification by public
service commission,
§37-2-89.
Railway policemen,
§§37-2-156, 37-2-157.
Oaths.
Railway policemen,
§37-2-151.
Operation.
Condemnation of ways and
rights of way by
companies operating
internal improvement,
§10-5-4.
Outside state.
Operation outside state,
§10-5-12.
Passengers.
Accommodations.
Duty of railroad to provide,
§37-2-110.
Actions.
Action for damages not
barred, §37-2-116.
Advertised stations.
Failure of trains to stop,
§37-2-114.

RAILROADS—Cont'd
Passengers—Cont'd
Alcoholic beverages.
Public drinking on railway
passenger cars or in
waiting rooms,
§37-8-160.
Charging or collecting higher
than lawful rate for
transportation of
passengers, §37-8-23.
Connection of tracks and
interchange of traffic.
Railroads to afford
reasonable and proper
facilities for
forwarding and
delivering passengers,
§37-2-135.
Failure of trains to stop at
advertised stations,
§37-2-114.
Noncompliance with
commission order to
provide conveniences for
travelers.
Attorney general.
Failure of commission to
notify, §37-8-111.
District attorneys.
Failure of commission to
notify, §37-8-111.
Failure of commission to
notify district attorney
or attorney general,
§37-8-111.
Penalty for noncompliance,
§37-8-110.
Personal baggage of
passengers, §§37-2-35 to
37-2-39.
Public service commission.
Orders of commission.
Notice, §37-2-112.
Remedy for
noncompliance,
§37-2-113.
Time for compliance,
§37-2-112.
Sitting or waiting rooms,
§37-2-110.
Failure of railroad
companies to erect,
§37-2-113.
Public drinking in waiting
rooms, §37-8-160.
Penalties.
Free passes, rebates or
discounts, §37-8-27.
Noncompliance with
commission order to
erect depot or to provide
conveniences for
travelers, §37-8-110.
Permits.
Conductors, §37-2-86.1.
Engineers, §37-2-86.1.
Police.
Railway policemen,
§§37-2-150 to 37-2-157.
See within this heading,
"Railway policemen."
Pooling of freights.
Unlawful pooling, §37-8-30.
Precautions.
Failure to use to prevent
accidents, §37-8-114.
Preservation, §§37-10-1 to
37-10-7.
Appropriations, §37-10-7.

RAILROADS—Cont'd
Preservation—Cont'd
Data and information.
Confidential information,
§37-10-5.
Reimbursement of
railroads for expenses,
§37-10-5.
Requests for by
department, §37-10-5.
Definitions, §37-10-2.
Federal aid.
Expenditure, §37-10-4.
Local or regional
transportation
authorities.
Cooperation with, §37-10-4.
Rules and regulations.
Promulgation, §37-10-6.
Short title of chapter,
§37-10-1.
State highway department.
Cooperation with local or
regional transportation
authorities, §37-10-4.
Expenditure of federal
funds, §37-10-4.
Powers, §37-10-3.
Requests for data and
information, §37-10-5.
Rules and regulations.
Promulgation, §37-10-6.
Title of chapter, §37-10-1.
Presumptions.
Advertising signs resembling
railroad signs.
Name of person on
advertising.
Presumed guilty party,
§37-8-200.
Private railroads.
Public service commission.
Jurisdictional exemptions
or limitations,
§37-1-37.
Property.
Conveyance to another
railroad corporation,
§10-5-10.
Rights-of-way.
Authorized to transfer
abandoned rights-of-
way, §10-5-2.1.
Transfers.
Rights-of-way.
Authorized to transfer
abandoned rights-of-
way, §10-5-2.1.
Unlawful purchase or receipt
of railroad property,
§37-8-149.
Public service commission.
Accounts.
Separation of intrastate
railroad operations for
accounting purposes,
§37-1-55.
Fences.
Notification of corporations
or persons operating
railroads, §37-2-89.
Free tickets.
Persons passing free of
charge, §37-1-15.
Judgment confirming
commission award
regulating railroad's
business with connecting
line.
Violation of judgment,
§37-8-118.

RAILROADS—Cont'd
Public service commission
—Cont'd
Logging or private railroads.
Jurisdictional exemptions
or limitations,
§37-1-37.
Noncompliance with
commission order to
erect depot or to provide
conveniences for
travelers, §37-8-110.
Failure of commission to
notify district attorney
or attorney general,
§37-8-111.
Penalty for noncompliance,
§37-8-110.
Passengers, §§37-2-112,
37-2-113.
Rate and other regulations,
§§37-1-80 to 37-1-105.
See PUBLIC SERVICE
COMMISSION.
Regulations for convenience
of passengers, §§37-2-110
to 37-2-116. See within
this heading,
"Passengers."
Quarantine.
Free rides on public
transports for quarantine
officers, §22-12-23.
Refusal of freight, §22-12-21.
Supervision of public
conveyances affected by
quarantine, §22-12-21.
Transportation of person or
thing in violation of
quarantine, §22-12-22.
Quarries.
Connections to public ways.
Construction and operation
of connections by
quarrying
corporations, §10-5-13.
Operation outside state and
making extensions
within state by
quarrying companies,
§10-5-12.
Railway policemen,
§§37-2-150 to 37-2-157.
Appointment, §37-2-150.
Arrest.
Powers of arrest,
§37-2-153.
Authority.
When authority ceases,
§37-2-153.
Badge, §37-2-152.
Bond, §37-2-151.
Compensation, §37-2-154.
Firearms.
Right to bear firearms,
§37-2-153.
Governor.
Appointment, §37-2-150.
Removal, §37-2-157.
Liability of corporation for
acts of policemen,
§37-2-155.
Misconduct.
Liability of corporation for
acts of policemen,
§37-2-155.
Negligence.
Liability of corporation for
acts of policemen,
§37-2-155.

RAILROADS—Cont'd

Railway policemen—Cont'd

Notice.

Removal, §37-2-157.

Services no longer required.

Filing of notice, §37-2-156.

Oath, §37-2-151.

Powers, §37-2-153.

When powers cease, §37-2-153.

Removal by governor, §37-2-157.

Torts.

Liability of corporation for acts of policemen, §37-2-155.

Rapid rail transit compact.

Execution and text of compact, §37-11-1.

Rates.

Charging or collecting higher than lawful rate for freight transportation, §37-8-23.

Deceiving or misleading public, Const. Ala., art. XII, §245.

Public service commission.

See PUBLIC SERVICE COMMISSION.

Transportation companies generally, §§37-2-1 to 37-2-46.

See TRANSPORTATION COMPANIES.

Rebates.

Exemptions, §37-8-28.

Officer, agent, etc., of railroad corporation taking rebate, §8-11-4.

Penalties for violations, §37-8-27.

Prohibited, Const. Ala., art. XII, §245.

Public utilities generally.

See PUBLIC UTILITIES.

Records.

Separation of intrastate railroad operations for accounting purposes, §37-1-55.

Reports.

Accident reports, §37-2-91.

Restraint of trade.

Unlawful pooling of freights, §37-8-30.

Rights.

Conveyance to another railroad corporation, §10-5-10.

Rights-of-way.

Authorized to transfer abandoned rights-of-way, §10-5-2.1.

Condemnation for right of way, §10-5-2.

Crossings, §37-2-82.

Roadbed.

Conveyance to another transportation company, §10-5-10.

Rolling stock.

Secured transactions.

Determination of validity and perfection of security interest in rolling stock, §7-9-103.

RAILROADS—Cont'd

Rules and regulations.

Preservation.

Promulgation by department, §37-10-6.

Safety.

Crossings, §§37-8-81 to 37-8-83.

Signs.

Erection by companies, §37-2-80.

Liability for failure to comply, §37-2-83.

Salaries.

Railway policemen, §37-2-154.

Sales.

Conveyance of franchises, rights, roadbed and property to another railroad corporation, §10-5-10.

Sales tax.

Exemptions.

Gross proceeds of sale of railroad cars, §40-23-4.

Secured transactions.

Applicability of filing provisions, §7-9-302.

Determination of validity and perfection of security interest in rolling stock, §7-9-103.

Transactions excluded from provisions of article, §7-9-104.

Sharing lines, §10-5-11.

Sheriffs.

Signs resembling railroad signs.

Erection or maintenance of advertising signs resembling railroad signs.

Sheriff to report violations to grand jury, §37-8-200.

Ships and shipping.

Drawbridges.

Steamboats passing through railroad drawbridges, §37-2-88.

Operation of transportation methods for persons or property by railroad companies, §10-5-9.

Signs.

Erection by railroad company, §37-2-80.

Liability for failure to comply, §37-2-83.

Signs resembling railroad signs.

Erection or maintenance, §37-8-200.

Sleeping car companies.

Licenses.

Municipal license schedule, §11-51-125.

Solicitation.

Soliciting claims from shippers or consignees against carriers, §37-8-280.

Southern products mart authority.

Eminent domain.

Acquisition by eminent domain of rights owned by railroads not authorized, §41-10-54.

RAILROADS—Cont'd

Spur tracks.

Construction required, §37-2-136.

State board of health.

Authority and jurisdiction, §22-2-2.

Stations.

Alcoholic beverages.

Public drinking in waiting rooms, §37-8-160.

Depots generally. See within this heading, "Depots."

Failure of trains to stop at advertised stations, §37-2-114.

Sitting or waiting rooms, §37-2-110.

Failure of railroad companies to erect, §37-2-113.

Public drinking in waiting rooms, §37-8-160.

Union stations, §37-2-111.

Steamships.

Operation of transportation methods for persons or property by railroad companies, §10-5-9.

Streets.

Crew members acting on instructions not responsible for obstruction, §37-2-84.

Subways.

Municipal corporations.

Construction, §18-1A-274.

Eminent domain.

Acquisition of land, §18-1A-274.

Superintendents.

Warning devices.

Failure of superintendent to instruct engineers and conductors regarding blowing horn, whistle, etc., §37-8-113.

Switches and sidetracks.

Connection of tracks and interchange of traffic.

Switch connections, §37-2-133.

Construction required, §37-2-136.

Duty to maintain, §37-2-130.

Repairs, improvements or changes in property or devices, §37-2-9.

Taxation.

General provisions.

See PUBLIC UTILITIES.

License taxes, §§40-21-51, 40-21-57.

Motor fuels.

Additional excise tax on gasoline, motor fuel and lubricating oil.

Exemptions, §40-17-220.

Terminals.

Repairs, improvements or changes in property or devices.

Order by public service commission, §37-2-9.

Torts.

Railway policemen.

Liability of corporation for acts of policemen, §37-2-155.

RAILROADS—Cont'd
Towels.
Use of common towels
prohibited, §22-20-1.
Tracks.
Condemnation of lands for
tracks, §10-5-7.
Connection of tracks and
interchange of traffic,
§§37-2-131 to 37-2-135.
Gauge.
Connection of tracks and
interchange of traffic.
Cars transported or
received to be
adapted to gauge of
track, §37-2-131.
Spur tracks.
Construction required,
§37-2-136.
Switches and sidetracks,
§§37-2-9, 37-2-130 to
37-2-136. See within this
heading, "Switches and
sidetracks."
Traffic.
Interchange of traffic.
Connection of tracks and
interchange of traffic,
§§37-2-131 to 37-2-135.
Transfers.
Rights-of-way.
Authorized to transfers
abandoned rights-of-
way, §10-5-2.1.
Transportation companies,
§§37-2-1 to 37-2-184.
See TRANSPORTATION
COMPANIES.
Transportation methods.
Operation of transportation
methods for persons or
property by railroad
companies, §10-5-9.
Tunnels.
Grade crossings. See within
this heading,
"Crossings."
Municipal corporations.
Requirement of
construction and
maintenance by
railroads of bridges,
tunnels, etc., within
limits of certain cities,
§§11-49-40 to 11-49-45.
See MUNICIPAL
CORPORATIONS.
Union stations, §37-2-111.
Use tax.
Exemptions.
Storage, use or
consumption of
railroad cars, vessels
and barges, §40-23-62.
Venue.
Violations committed on
trains, §37-8-94.
Viaducts.
Municipal corporations.
Construction, §18-1A-274.
Eminent domain.
Acquisition of land,
§18-1A-274.
Violations.
Charging or collecting higher
than lawful rate for
transportation of
passengers or freight,
§37-8-23.

RAILROADS—Cont'd
Violations—Cont'd
Free passes, rebates or
discounts.
Penalties for violations,
§37-8-27.
Venue for violations
committed on trains,
§37-8-94.
Wages.
Biweekly payment of wages,
§37-8-270.
Warning devices.
Duty of locomotive engineer
to ring bell or blow horn,
§37-2-81.
Liability of railroad for
failure to comply,
§37-2-83.
Failure to ring bell or blow
horn or whistle on
trains, §37-8-112.
Precautions.
Failure to use to prevent
accidents, §37-8-114.
Superintendents.
Failure of superintendent
to instruct engineers
and conductors
regarding blowing
horn, whistle, etc.,
§37-8-113.
**Water management and
drainage.**
Districts,
Construction of
improvements crossing
railroad right-of-way,
§9-9-47.
Improvements.
Procedure as to proposed
improvements
crossing right-of-
way, §9-9-24.
Waters and watercourses.
Development of docks
along inland
waterways,
§§33-2-1 to 33-2-213.
See WATERS AND
WATERCOURSES.
Weapons.
Discharging firearm into
railroad locomotive or
car, §13A-11-61.
Whistles.
Failure to blow whistle,
§37-8-112.
Precautions.
Failure to use to prevent
accidents, §37-8-114.
Superintendents.
Failure of superintendent
to instruct engineers
and conductors
regarding blowing
horn, whistle, etc.,
§37-8-113.
Workers.
Employees generally. See
within this heading,
"Employees."
Liens of laborers and
employees, §§35-11-90 to
35-11-97. See within this
heading, "Liens."
Yards.
Condemnation of lands for
yards, §10-5-7.

RANDOLPH COUNTY.
Bond issues.
Funding county facilities.
County facilities building
fund, Const. Ala., amd.
444.
Securities, Const. Ala.,
amd. 442.
Counties generally.
See COUNTIES.
Funding county facilities.
County facilities building
fund, Const. Ala., amd.
444.
Privilege, license, etc., taxes
and securities, Const.
Ala., amd. 442.
Judge of probate, Const.
Ala., amd. 459.
Licenses.
Funding county facilities.
License taxes, Const. Ala.,
amd. 442.
School tax.
Special property tax for
educational purposes in
school district No. 2,
Const. Ala., amd. 180.

RAPE.
Evidence.
Exclusion of audience where
evidence vulgar, etc.,
§§12-21-9, 12-21-202.
Past sexual behavior of
complaining witness.
Admissibility of evidence,
§12-21-203.
Rape shield law, §12-21-203.
**Exclusion of persons from
courtroom in cases of
rape,** Const. Ala., art. VI,
§169.
First degree rape.
Class A felony, §13A-6-61.
Elements of crime,
§13A-6-61.
Indictments.
Form of indictment,
§15-8-150.
Rape shield law, §12-21-203.
Second degree rape.
Class B felony, §13A-6-62.
Elements of crime,
§13A-6-62.
Sexual offenses.
General provisions.
See SEXUAL OFFENSES.
Trial.
Exclusion of persons from
courtroom in cases of
rape, Const. Ala., art.
VI, §169.
**Use of force in defense of
persons.**
When deadly physical force
justified, §13A-3-23.

RAPE SHIELD LAW.
General provisions,
§12-21-203.

RATE OF TAXATION, §§40-8-1
to 40-8-4; Const. Ala., art.
IX, §§214, 217.
See TAXATION.

RAZORS.
Weapons.
See WEAPONS.

REAL ESTATE BROKERS,
§§34-27-1 to 34-27-69.
Actions.
Notice to commission of
actions against licensees,
§34-27-31.
Advertising.
Disciplinary actions.
Unlawful advertising as
grounds, §34-27-36.
Appeals.
Disciplinary actions.
Appeal from decision of
commission, §34-27-38.
Applicability of chapter.
Exemptions from provisions,
§34-27-2.
Provisions cumulative,
§34-27-10.
Associate broker.
Defined, §34-27-2.
Bonds, surety.
Disciplinary actions.
Appeal bond, §34-27-38.
Broker.
Defined, §34-27-2.
Business address.
Required on license,
§34-27-35.
Citation of chapter, §34-27-1.
Commission.
General provisions, §§34-27-4
to 34-27-8.
Licenses, §§34-27-30 to
34-27-38. See within this
heading, "Licenses."
Refusal, suspension or
revocation, §§34-27-36 to
34-27-38.
Companies.
Death, disability or
retirement of licensed
broker, §34-27-32.
Licensed broker required as
designated officer,
§34-27-32.
Licenses.
Fees, §34-27-35.
Conflict of laws.
Provisions of chapter
cumulative, §34-27-10.
Contracts.
Agency disclosure clause,
§34-27-8.
Commission authorized to
contract for educational
services, §34-27-6.
Death.
License broker.
Effect on company,
§34-27-32.
Definitions, §34-27-2.
Disciplinary actions.
Appeals from decision of
commission, §34-27-38.
Complaints, §34-27-37.
Evidence.
Authority of commission to
compel production,
§34-27-37.
Grounds, §34-27-36.
Hearings, §34-27-37.
Notice of charges, §34-27-37.
Procedures, §34-27-37.
Subpoenas.
Authority of commission,
§34-27-37.
Education.
Authority of commission to
conduct courses,
§34-27-6.

REAL ESTATE BROKERS
—Cont'd
Engaged.
Defined, §34-27-2.
Evidence.
Disciplinary actions.
Authority of commission to
compel production,
§34-27-37.
Examinations.
Fees, §§34-27-33, 34-27-35.
**Exemptions from provisions
of chapters,** §34-27-2.
Fees.
Examinations, §§34-27-33,
34-27-35.
Licenses.
Broker's license, §34-27-35.
Companies, §34-27-35.
Renewal fees, §34-27-35.
Salesman's license,
§34-27-35.
Payment into real estate
commission fund,
§34-27-4.
Salesman changing broker,
§34-27-34.
Fraud.
Disciplinary actions.
Fraud as grounds,
§34-27-36.
Funds.
Real estate commission fund,
§34-27-4.
Procedure for
disbursement,
§34-27-4.
Recovery fund, §34-27-31.
Hearings.
Disciplinary actions,
§34-27-37.
Rehearings, §34-27-37.
Judgments.
Final judgment against
licensee suspends license,
§34-27-31.
Licenses, §§34-27-30 to
34-27-38.
Applications for license,
§34-27-32.
Contents, §34-27-35.
Corporations.
Applications for license,
§34-27-32.
Educational requirements for
license, §34-27-32.
Examinations, §34-27-33.
Fees, §§34-27-33 to 34-27-35.
Form, §34-27-35.
Inactive status, §34-27-35.
Defined, §34-27-2.
Reactivation, §34-27-35.
Issuance, §34-27-33.
List of licensees, §34-27-5.
Partnerships.
Applications for license,
§34-27-32.
Period.
Defined, §34-27-2.
Place of business.
Maintenance, §34-27-32.
Public display, §34-27-35.
Qualifications of applicants,
§34-27-32.
Reactivation, §34-27-35.
Realty situated within state,
§40-12-149.
Realty situated without
state, §40-12-150.

REAL ESTATE BROKERS
—Cont'd
Licenses—Cont'd
Refusal, suspension or
revocation.
Appeals from decision of
commission, §34-27-38.
Authority of commission,
§34-27-36.
Charges.
Filing of charges,
§34-27-37.
Complaints, §34-27-37.
Evidence.
Authority of commission
to compel
production,
§34-27-37.
Final judgment against
licensee suspends
license, §34-27-31.
Grounds, §34-27-36.
Hearings, §34-27-37.
Rehearings, §34-27-37.
Notice of charges,
§34-27-37.
Procedures, §34-27-37.
Reprimand or fine in lieu
of or in addition to,
§34-27-31.
Subpoenas.
Authority of commission,
§34-27-37.
Witnesses.
Authority of commission
to compel
attendance,
§34-27-37.
Renewal, §34-27-35.
Required, §34-27-30.
Responsibilities of qualifying
broker, §34-27-31.
Suspension or revocation.
General provisions,
§§34-27-36 to 34-27-38.
Term, §34-27-35.
Nonresidents.
Co-brokerage agreements.
Written agreement to be
filed, §34-27-3.
Cooperation with licensed
broker of state.
Required, §34-27-3.
Notices.
Licensee to notify
commission of citations
and suits, §34-27-31.
Partnerships.
Death, disability or
retirement of licensed
broker, §34-27-32.
Licensed broker required as
designated officer,
§34-27-32.
Penalties.
Refusal, suspension or
revocation of licenses,
§34-27-31.
Reprimand or fine in lieu
of or in addition to,
§34-27-31.
Violations of chapter,
§34-27-11.
Person.
Defined, §34-27-2.
Place of business.
Defined, §34-27-2.
Licensing requirements,
§34-27-32.
Maintenance, §34-27-32.

REAL ESTATE BROKERS
—Cont'd
Probate courts.
List of licensees.
Commission to provide
upon request of judge,
§34-27-5.
Qualifying broker.
Change of qualifying broker,
§34-27-34.
Defined, §34-27-2.
Direction and supervision of
branch offices, §34-27-32.
Responsibilities, §34-27-34.
Securing following passing of
examination, §34-27-33.
Termination of relationship,
§34-27-34.
Who may serve as qualifying
broker, §34-27-34.
Real estate commission,
§§34-27-4 to 34-27-8.
Action by majority of
members, §34-27-8.
Appeals from decision of
commission, §34-27-38.
Appointment of members,
§34-27-7.
Assistant executive director.
Employment, §34-27-7.
Compensation of members,
§34-27-7.
Composition, §34-27-7.
Contracts.
Authority to contract for
educational services,
§34-27-6.
Created, §34-27-7.
Education.
Authority to conduct
courses, §34-27-6.
Executive director.
Employment, §34-27-7.
Fund, §34-27-4.
Procedure for
disbursement,
§34-27-4.
Governor.
Appointment of
commission, §34-27-7.
Liability of commissioner for
official acts, §34-27-7.
Licenses, §§34-27-30 to
34-27-38. See within this
heading, "Licenses."
List of licensees.
Commission to provide
upon request of
probate judge,
§34-27-5.
Organization, §34-27-7.
Qualifications of members,
§34-27-7.
Records, §34-27-7.
Refusal, suspension or
revocation of licenses,
§§34-27-36 to 34-27-38.
Rules and regulations.
Authority of commission to
promulgate, §34-27-8.
Seal of commission, §34-27-7.
Terms of office, §34-27-7.
Real estate salesmen.
Defined, §34-27-2.
Licenses, §§34-27-30 to
34-27-38. See within this
heading, "Licenses."
Procedure for broker
terminating employment
of salesman, §34-27-34.

REAL ESTATE BROKERS
—Cont'd
Real estate salesmen—Cont'd
Procedure for salesman
changing broker,
§34-27-34.
Rebates.
Unlawful rebates as grounds
for disciplinary action,
§34-27-36.
Records.
Brokers to keep records of
sales, etc., §34-27-36.
Recovery fund, §34-27-31.
**Refusal, suspension or
revocation of licenses,**
§§34-27-36 to 34-27-38.
Rules and regulations.
Authority of commission to
promulgate, §34-27-8.
Salesmen.
Defined, §34-27-2.
Licenses, §§34-27-30 to
34-27-38. See within this
heading, "Licenses."
Procedure for broker
terminating employment
of salesman, §34-27-34.
Procedure for salesman
changing broker,
§34-27-34.
Short title of chapter,
§34-27-1.
Signs.
Disciplinary actions.
Unlawful placement of
signs as grounds,
§34-27-36.
Subpoenas.
Disciplinary actions.
Authority of commission,
§34-27-37.
Time-sharing.
Vacation time-sharing plans,
§§34-27-50 to 34-27-69.
See VACATION TIME-
SHARING PLANS.
Title.
Short title of chapter,
§34-27-1.
Vacation time-sharing plans,
§§34-27-50 to 34-27-69.
See VACATION TIME-
SHARING PLANS.
Violations of chapter.
Penalties, §34-27-11.
Witnesses.
Disciplinary actions.
Authority of commission to
compel attendance,
§34-27-37.

REAL PROPERTY, §§35-1-1 to
35-16-4.
**Abatement, revival and
survival.**
Survival of real property
claims.
Type of action filed,
§6-5-463.
Acknowledgments.
Conveyances, §§35-4-23 to
35-4-28.
See CONVEYANCES.
Actions, §§6-5-210 to 6-5-214.
Adverse possession.
See ADVERSE
POSSESSION.
Attachment.
See ATTACHMENTS.
Bare possession, §6-5-213.

REAL PROPERTY—Cont'd
Actions—Cont'd
Bare right of possession,
§6-5-212.
Bare title.
Action for trespass by
person having,
§6-5-214.
Ejectment.
Action of ejectment.
Election to proceed by
action of ejectment
or action in nature
of ejectment,
§6-6-280.
Proceedings upon,
§6-6-280.
Forcible entry and unlawful
detainer.
See FORCIBLE ENTRY
AND UNLAWFUL
DETAINER.
Lis pendens, §§35-4-130 to
35-4-139.
See LIS PENDENS.
Notice.
Filing notice in lis pendens
record, §35-4-131.
Partition.
See PARTITION.
Rights above and below
surface.
Unlawful interference,
§6-5-210.
Slander of title, §6-5-211.
Survival of actions, §6-5-463.
Trespass.
Action by person having
bare title, §6-5-214.
Adverse possession.
See ADVERSE
POSSESSION.
**Alabama coordinate
systems,** §§35-2-1 to
35-2-9.
See SURVEYS AND
SURVEYORS.
Alienation.
General provisions.
See CONVEYANCES.
Aliens.
Right of aliens, §35-1-1.
Attachments, §§6-6-30 to
6-6-149.
See ATTACHMENTS.
**Bear Creek development
authority.**
Eminent domain.
Acquisition by eminent
domain of certain
property or rights not
authorized, §33-15-5.
Land acquisition, §33-15-6.
Taxation.
Exemption, §33-15-12.
Boundaries.
General provisions.
See BOUNDARIES.
Brokers.
Real estate brokers,
§§34-27-1 to 34-27-69.
See REAL ESTATE
BROKERS.
Churches.
Conveyance by church
corporations, §10-4-25.
Independence of church
corporations, §10-4-22.
Sale by church corporations,
§10-4-25.

REAL PROPERTY—Cont'd

Civil defense.
Shelters.
Tort liability of persons, §31-9-17.

Claims to land.
Determination, §§6-6-540 to 6-6-573.
See QUIETING TITLE.

Commercial code.
Sales.
Goods to be severed from realty, §7-2-107.
Price payable in realty, §7-2-304.
Secured transactions, §§7-9-101 to 7-9-507.
See COMMERCIAL CODE.

Condemnation.
General provisions.
See EMINENT DOMAIN.

Condominiums.
Units to constitute real property, §35-8-4.

Confidence.
Effect of confidence for mere benefit of third persons, §35-4-250.

Construction and interpretation.
Estate taken as fee simple unless expressly limited, §35-4-2.
Fee tail converted into fee simple, §35-4-3.

Contracts.
Death of person contracting to sell real property.
Conveyances by executors and administrators, §§35-4-320 to 35-4-323.
Sale of real property.
See CONVEYANCES.
Specific performance.
Breach of agreement to transfer.
Pecuniary compensation presumed inadequate, §8-1-47.
Judgments for specific performance, §35-4-33.
Obligation on real estate.
Specific enforcement against person subsequently claiming title, §8-1-46.

Conveyances.
General provisions.
See CONVEYANCES.

Coordinate systems.
Alabama coordinate system, §§35-2-1 to 35-2-9.
See SURVEYS AND SURVEYORS.

Coosa Valley development authority.
Dissolution of authority.
Disposition of real property upon dissolution, §33-16-15.

Counties.
See COUNTIES.

Criminal law and procedure.
Trespass.
See TRESPASS.

REAL PROPERTY—Cont'd

Dams.
Erection of dams for mills, gins, factories or electric generators.
Assessment of lands, §§18-2-7, 18-2-13, 18-2-19.

Death.
Person contracting to sell real property.
Conveyances by executors and administrators, §§35-4-320 to 35-4-323.

Decedents' estates.
Sale of real estate.
See EXECUTORS AND ADMINISTRATORS.

Deeds generally.
See DEEDS.

Deeds of trust.
Foreclosure deeds.
Deeds in lieu of foreclosure, §§35-10-50, 35-10-51.
Generally.
See MORTGAGES AND DEEDS OF TRUST.

Definitions, §1-1-1.
Redemption, §6-5-247.

Devises.
Wills, §§43-8-224 to 43-8-228.

Disclaimer of interests in property.
Eminent domain, §§18-1A-90, 18-1A-92.
General provisions, §§43-8-290 to 43-8-298.
See DISCLAIMER OF INTERESTS IN PROPERTY.

Dispossession.
Unlawfully taking possession of or going back into possession of real estate after dispossession under legal process, §13A-7-60.

Disputed possession.
Party with legal title deemed in possession, §6-5-215.

Dower.
See DOWER.

Easements.
See EASEMENTS.

Education.
Federal grants.
Principal to be preserved, Const. Ala., art. XIV, §257.
School lands.
General provisions.
See PUBLIC LANDS.

Ejectment.
See EJECTMENT.

Eminent domain.
General provisions.
See EMINENT DOMAIN.

Equity of redemption.
Executions, §6-9-40.

Escheats.
Disposition of real estate, §43-6-5.

Evidence.
Title to lands.
Admissibility of evidence, §12-21-41.

Executions.
Levy.
Notice where levy on real estate, §6-9-82.

REAL PROPERTY—Cont'd

Executions—Cont'd
Property subject to execution §6-9-40.
Equity of redemption, §6-9-40.
Redemption, §§6-5-247 to 6-5-257. See within this heading, "Redemption."

Executors and administrators.
Sale of real estate.
See EXECUTORS AND ADMINISTRATORS.

Fee simple estates.
Estate taken as fee simple unless expressly limited, §35-4-2.
Fee tail converted into fee simple, §35-4-3.

Fee tail estates.
Converted into fee simple, §35-4-3.

Fish and game.
Recreational or sporting premises liability, §§35-15-1 to 35-15-28.
See within this heading, "Recreational or sporting premises liability."

Forcible entry and unlawful detainer, §§6-6-310 to 6-6-353.
See FORCIBLE ENTRY AND UNLAWFUL DETAINER.

Fraud.
Contracts for sale of lands void unless in writing, §8-9-2.
Realty conveyance wherein grantee agrees to support grantor during life voidable, §8-9-12.
Exceptions, §8-9-12.

Fraudulent transfers.
See FRAUDULENT TRANSFERS.

Future interests.
Remainders, reversions and executory interests.
See REMAINDERS, REVERSIONS AND EXECUTORY INTERESTS.
Rule against perpetuities.
Avoidance of rule, §35-4-5.
Generally, §35-4-4.

Harbors and ports.
Appraisal of real estate, §33-1-14.
Eminent domain.
Acquisition by eminent domain, §33-1-22.
Insurance.
Authority of department to carry insurance, §33-1-25.
Leases.
Exemptions from taxation, §33-1-19.
Generally, §33-1-17.
Sales.
Generally, §33-1-17.
Lands submerged, lying under or abutting tidal waters, §33-1-18.
Title to property acquired under chapter vests in state, §33-1-17.

REAL PROPERTY—Cont'd
Health care authorities.
Powers of authority,
§22-21-318.
Husband and wife.
Conveyances by spouse of
insane person, §§30-4-30
to 30-4-37.
See HUSBAND AND
WIFE.
Dower.
See DOWER.
General provisions, §§6-10-3,
30-4-12.
Mentally ill.
Conveyance by spouse of
insane person,
§§30-4-30 to 30-4-37.
See HUSBAND AND
WIFE.
Property generally.
See HUSBAND AND
WIFE.
Improvements.
Damages,
Rule of prescription,
§6-5-218.
Redemption of real estate.
Value of permanent
improvements.
How ascertained,
§6-5-254.
Payment, §6-5-254.
Income tax.
Amortization of ad valorem
tax, §40-18-41.
Basis of property.
Gain or loss, §§40-18-6 to
40-18-9.
Capital gain or loss,
§§40-18-6 to 40-18-9.
Deductions.
Gifts of real property for
public purposes,
§40-18-15.
Interval ownership.
Vacation time-sharing plans,
§§34-27-50 to 34-27-69.
See VACATION TIME-
SHARING PLANS.
Invitees.
Recreational or sporting
premises liability,
§§35-15-1 to 35-15-28.
See within this heading,
"Recreational or sporting
premises liability."
Landlord and tenant.
See LANDLORD AND
TENANT.
Levy on real property.
Notice of levy.
Filing with probate judge,
§35-4-132.
Liability.
Recreational or sporting
premises, §§35-15-1 to
35-15-28. See within this
heading, "Recreational or
sporting premises
liability."
Liens.
Lis pendens.
Release of land from lien
upon execution of
bond, §35-4-137.
Mortgages and deeds of trust,
§§35-10-20 to 35-10-30.
See MORTGAGES AND
DEEDS OF TRUST.

REAL PROPERTY—Cont'd
Limitation of actions,
§§6-2-31 to 6-2-34.
Lis pendens, §§35-4-130 to
35-4-139.
See LIS PENDENS.
**Mechanics' and
materialmen's liens.**
Transfer of lien on real
property to other
security, §35-11-233.
Mentally ill.
Conveyances by spouse of
insane person, §§30-4-30
to 30-4-37.
See HUSBAND AND
WIFE.
Military affairs.
Counties or municipalities
may sell real estate and
buildings to local
national guard units,
§31-2-130.
Leases.
Taxation.
Exemption from ad
valorem taxes,
§31-2-80.
Taxation.
Exemption from ad
valorem taxes,
§31-2-80.
Minors.
Powers of disposition.
Disposition to or among
children, §35-4-300.
**Mortgages and deeds of
trust.**
Redemption, §§6-5-247 to
6-5-257. See within this
heading, "Redemption."
Motor vehicles.
Lights, lamps and reflective
devices.
Casting light from motor
vehicle on real
property at night,
§32-5-17.
Regulation of use of real
property by owner,
§32-5-2.
Erection and maintenance
of traffic-control
devices, §32-5-2.
Municipal corporations.
See MUNICIPAL
CORPORATIONS.
Options to purchase.
Limitations on duration of
option to purchase land,
§35-4-76.
Partition.
See PARTITION.
Partnerships, §§10-8-70 to
10-8-73.
Permissive liability theories.
Recreational or sporting
premises, §§35-15-1 to
35-15-28. See within this
heading, "Recreational or
sporting premises
liability."
Permittees.
Recreational or sporting
premises liability,
§§35-15-1 to 35-15-28.
See within this heading,
"Recreational or sporting
premises liability."
Power districts.
Acquisition, §37-5-3.

REAL PROPERTY—Cont'd
Powers of disposition,
§§35-4-290 to 35-4-306.
See CONVEYANCES.
Property generally.
See PROPERTY.
Public lands.
See PUBLIC LANDS.
Public utilities.
See PUBLIC UTILITIES.
Quieting title, §§6-6-540 to
6-6-573.
See QUIETING TITLE.
Real estate brokers,
§§34-27-1 to 34-27-69.
See REAL ESTATE
BROKERS.
**Recreational or sporting
premises liability,**
§§35-15-1 to 35-15-28.
Duty of care owed persons on
premises.
Existing liability.
No limitations on
otherwise existing
liability, §35-15-3.
Extent of duty owed,
§35-15-1.
General duty of care.
Not created, §35-15-4.
Grounds for liability.
General grounds not
created, §35-15-4.
Permission to use
premises.
Right of entry without
permission not
created, §35-15-5.
Right of entry without
permission.
Not created, §35-15-5.
Limitation of liability.
No limitation on otherwise
existing liability,
§35-15-3.
Noncommercial public
recreational use of land,
§§35-15-20 to 35-15-28.
Limitations of liability,
§35-15-23.
Definitions, §35-15-21.
Duty of persons using,
§35-15-25.
Establishment of public
use, §35-15-28.
Governmental immunity
not required by
chapter, §35-15-27.
Inapplicability of
provisions to
commercial
recreational
enterprises,
§35-15-26.
Inspection by owner not
required, §35-15-22.
Legal liability of owner
limited, §35-15-23.
Legislative declaration of
purpose, §35-15-20.
Otherwise existing
liability not limited,
§35-15-24.
Presumptions of public
use.
Acts of owner giving
use to
presumption,
§35-15-28.

REAL PROPERTY—Cont'd
Recreational or sporting premises liability—Cont'd
Noncommercial public recreational use of land —Cont'd
Limitations of liability —Cont'd
Public use.
Establishment, §35-15-28.
Warnings by owner not required, §35-15-22.
Permission to use premises.
Effect, §35-15-2.
Redemption, §§6-5-247 to 6-5-257.
Applicability of article, §6-5-257.
Charges.
Payment or tender of purchase money and other lawful charges with interest, §6-5-253.
Statement of debt and lawful charges.
Demand by person entitled to redeem, §6-5-252.
Circuit courts.
Settlement and adjustment of rights and equities, §6-5-256.
Definitions, §6-5-247.
Delivery of possession to purchaser, §6-5-251.
Executors and administrators.
Redemption by and against, §6-5-249.
Improvements.
Value of permanent improvements.
How ascertained, §6-5-254.
Payment, §6-5-254.
Personal privilege not property or property right, §6-5-250.
Priorities, §6-5-248.
Purchase money.
Payment or tender with interest, §6-5-253.
Right to redeem.
Personal privilege and not property or property right, §6-5-250.
Who may redeem, §6-5-248.
Statement of debt and lawful charges.
Demand by person entitled to redeem, §6-5-252.
Time for delivery of possession, §6-5-251.
Title.
Failure or refusal of purchaser to reconvey, §6-5-255.
Who may redeem, §6-5-248.
Rights above and below surface.
Right of action for unlawful interference, §6-5-210.
Rights-of-way.
See RIGHTS-OF-WAY.
Rule against perpetuities.
Conveyance to avoid perpetuities, §35-4-5.
Generally, §35-4-4.

REAL PROPERTY—Cont'd
Sales.
Conveyances.
See CONVEYANCES.
Execution sales.
Endorsements on execution writs, §§6-9-98 to 6-9-101.
General provisions, §§6-9-140 to 6-9-150.
See EXECUTIONS.
Redemption, §§6-5-247 to 6-5-257. See within this heading, "Redemption."
Judicial sales.
See JUDICIAL SALES.
Tax sales, §§40-10-1 to 40-10-166.
See TAXATION.
Savings and loan associations, §§5-16-2, 5-16-24.
School lands.
See PUBLIC LANDS.
Schools.
See EDUCATION.
Secured transactions, §§7-9-101 to 7-9-507.
See COMMERCIAL CODE.
Sheriffs.
Levy on real property.
Notice of levy.
Filing with probate judge, §35-4-132.
Slander of title.
Right of action, §6-5-211.
Southern products mart authority.
Eminent domain.
Acquisition of real property not authorized, §41-10-54.
Sporting purposes.
Recreational or sporting premises liability, §§35-15-1 to 35-15-28.
See within this heading, "Recreational or sporting premises liability."
Spotlighting, §32-5-17.
State parks.
See STATE PARKS.
Subdivision of land.
Counties.
See COUNTIES.
Surveys and surveyors.
General provisions.
See SURVEYS AND SURVEYORS.
Survival of action, §6-5-463.
Taxation.
Capital gain or loss, §§40-18-6 to 40-18-9.
Recordation tax, §§40-22-1 to 40-22-12.
See RECORDATION.
Subjects of taxation, §40-11-1.
Time-sharing.
Vacation time-sharing plans, §§34-27-50 to 34-27-69.
See VACATION TIME-SHARING PLANS.
Title.
General provisions.
See TITLE.
Quieting title.
See QUIETING TITLE.

REAL PROPERTY—Cont'd
Tombigbee Valley development authority.
Dissolution.
Disposition upon dissolution, §33-17-15.
Power to receive, take and hold, §33-17-8.
Trees and timber.
See TREES AND TIMBER.
Trespass.
General provisions.
See TRESPASS.
Trusts and trustees.
General provisions.
See TRUSTS AND TRUSTEES.
Unincorporated professional associations.
Conveyances, §10-10-9.
Use.
Effect of use for mere benefit of third persons, §35-4-250.
Vacation time-sharing plans, §§34-27-50 to 34-27-69.
See VACATION TIME-SHARING PLANS.
Venue.
Actions against individuals for recovery or possession, §6-3-2.
Equitable proceedings where real estate is subject matter, §6-3-2.
Waste.
See WASTE.
Wills.
Who may convey lands by will, §35-4-1.

REBATES.
Attorneys at law, §8-11-5.
Auctioneers, §8-11-5.
Brokers, §8-11-5.
Commission merchants, §8-11-5.
Constitution of Alabama.
Railroad companies.
Prohibited, Const. Ala., art. XII, §245.
Consumer finance.
Inducement for aiding sale or lease.
Prohibited, §5-19-14.
Corporations.
Officer, agent, etc., of railroad, manufacturing or mining corporation taking rebate, §8-11-4.
Factors, §8-11-5.
Fraternal benefit societies, §27-34-46.
Insurance.
Trade practices law, §§27-12-1 to 27-12-24.
See INSURANCE.
Manufacturers.
Officer, agent, etc., of manufacturing corporation taking rebate, §8-11-4.
Mines and minerals.
Officer, agent, etc., of mining corporation taking rebate, §8-11-4.
Motor vehicle carriers.
Exemptions, §37-8-28.
Penalites for violations, §37-8-27.

REBATES—Cont'd
Motor vehicle carriers
—Cont'd
Rebates in violation of
chapter, §37-3-25.
Pilots.
Rebates prohibited, §33-4-51.
Railroads.
Exemptions, §37-8-28.
Officer, agent, etc., of
railroad corporation
taking rebate, §8-11-4.
Penalties for violations,
§37-8-27.
Prohibited, Const. Ala., art.
XII, §245.
Public utilities generally.
See PUBLIC UTILITIES.
Real estate brokers.
Unlawful rebates as grounds
for disciplinary actions,
§34-27-36.

REBELLION.
**Anarchy and subversive
activities.**
Civil defense.
Employment of subversives
by civil defense
organizations,
§31-9-20.
Treason, §13A-11-2; Const.
Ala., art. I, §§18, 19.
Treason.
Constitution of the United
States.
See TREASON.
General provisions,
§13A-11-2; Const. Ala.,
art. I, §§18, 19.

**RECEIVERS, §§6-6-220 to
6-6-224.**
Actions.
Commencement of actions
against receivers,
§6-6-626.
Creditor's actions.
Appointment of receiver,
§6-6-185.
Appeals.
Appointment by clerk or
register of circuit court,
§6-6-621.
Order appointing or refusing
to appoint receiver,
§12-22-9.
Appointment.
Appeal of order appointing or
refusing to appoint
receiver, §12-22-9.
Bonds, surety.
Posting by applicant,
§6-6-622.
Recovery, §6-6-622.
Circuit courts.
Appeal when appointed by
clerk or register,
§6-6-621.
Power of judge, register or
clerk, §6-6-620.
Corporations.
Dissolution of attachments
and levies of
executions against
corporations, §6-6-624.
Partnerships, §6-6-623.
Dissolution of attachments
and levies of
executions against
partnerships, §6-6-624.

RECEIVERS—Cont'd
Appointment—Cont'd
Partnerships—Cont'd
Modification or vacation of
appointment, §6-6-623.
Orders relative to business,
etc.
Modification or vacation
of orders, §6-6-623.
Power of court to make,
§6-6-623.
**Banks and financial
institutions.**
General provisions.
See BANKS AND
FINANCIAL
INSTITUTIONS.
Insolvent banks.
Liquidation.
See BANKS AND
FINANCIAL
INSTITUTIONS.
Bonds, surety.
Appointment, §6-6-622.
Circuit courts.
Appointment, §§6-6-620,
6-6-621.
Commercial code.
Secured transactions.
Priority over unperfected
security interests,
§7-9-301.
Corporations.
Appointment.
Dissolution of attachments
and levies of
executions against
corporations, §6-6-624.
Liquidation, §§10-2A-196,
10-2A-197.
Salaries, commissions and
wages.
Payment before general
liabilities of
corporations paid,
§6-6-625.
Voting of shares, §10-2A-53.
Creditors' actions.
Complaint for discovery of
assets.
Appointment of receiver,
§6-6-185.
Criminal law and procedure.
Fraud in insolvency,
§13A-9-48.
Fraternal benefit societies.
Receivership, §27-34-50.
Fraud.
Fraud in insolvency,
§13A-9-48.
Insurance.
Insurance guaranty
association.
Filing of paid claims with
receiver, §27-42-11.
Life and disability insurance
guaranty association,
§§27-44-14, 27-44-20.
Receivership division of
department of insurance,
§§27-2-50 to 27-2-55.
See INSURANCE.
**Life and disability insurance
guaranty association,**
§§27-44-14, 27-44-20.
Nonresidents.
Service of process on foreign
receivers, §6-6-627.
Partnerships.
Appointment, §§6-6-623,
6-6-624.

RECEIVERS—Cont'd
Partnerships—Cont'd
Salaries, commissions and
wages.
Payment before general
liabilities of
partnership paid,
§6-6-625.
Power districts.
Bond issues.
Rights and remedies of
bondholders, §37-5-8.
Dissolution.
Board of directors to have
powers of receivers,
§37-5-2.
Public utilities.
Receiver's certificate or
debentures.
Power of court to issue,
§37-4-14.
Taxation.
Duties of receivers
generally, §40-21-33.
Removal, §6-6-628.
Rules of civil procedure,
ARCP, Rule 66.
Secured transactions.
Priority over unperfected
security interests,
§7-9-301.
Securities.
Injunctions.
Appointment of receivers
or conservators for
defendants or
defendants' assets,
§8-6-16.
Service of process.
Foreign or domestic
receivers, §6-6-627.
Small loans.
Appointment upon violation
of chapter, §5-18-10.
Taxation.
Assessments.
By whom property should
be listed, §40-7-17.
Liability, §40-1-8.
Returns.
Separate returns in
individual and
fiduciary capacity,
§40-7-20.
Tax assessors.
Notification of appointment
of fiduciaries, §40-7-30.
Vacancies.
Filling, §6-6-628.
**Water management and
drainage.**
Districts.
Bond issues.
Remedies upon default,
§9-9-40.

**RECEIVING STOLEN
PROPERTY.**
**Conviction, apprehension or
identification of thief.**
No defense to charge of
receiving stolen property,
§13A-8-16.
Definition, §13A-8-16.
Elements generally,
§13A-8-16.
**First degree receiving stolen
property.**
Class B felony, §13A-8-17.
Elements of crime,
§13A-8-17.

RECEIVING STOLEN PROPERTY—Cont'd
First degree receiving stolen property—Cont'd
Value of stolen property, §13A-8-17.
Indictments.
Form of indictment, §15-8-150.
Second degree receiving stolen property.
Class C felony, §13A-8-18.
Elements of crime, §13A-8-18.
Value of stolen property, §13A-8-18.
Stolen property generally.
See STOLEN PROPERTY.
Third degree receiving stolen property.
Class A misdemeanor, §13A-8-19.
Elements of crime, §13A-8-19.
Value of stolen property, §13A-8-19.
Value of stolen property.
First degree receiving stolen property, §13A-8-17.
Second degree receiving stolen property, §13A-8-18.
Third degree receiving stolen property, §13A-8-19.

RECIPROCAL ENFORCEMENT OF SUPPORT ACT, §§30-4-80 to 30-4-98.
See DESERTION AND NONSUPPORT.

RECIPROCITY.
Accountants.
See ACCOUNTANTS.
Attorneys at law.
Disciplinary proceedings, ARDE, Rule 17.
Banks and financial institutions.
Regional reciprocal banking, §§5-13A-1 to 5-13A-10.
See BANKS AND FINANCIAL INSTITUTIONS.
Dietitians and nutritionists.
Practice act, §34-34A-11.
Estate and inheritance tax, §40-15-9.
Unconstitutionality of provision.
Effect, §40-15-9.
Fires and fire prevention.
Sprinkler systems.
State fire marshal's permit, §34-33-4.
Fish and game.
Licenses.
Fishing licenses.
Reciprocal agreement with Florida, §9-11-53.
Fishing.
Commercial seafood fishing, §§9-12-160 to 9-12-162.
Reciprocal agreements as to freshwater fishing, §§9-11-210 to 9-11-213.
Gas fitters.
Certification of plumbers and gas fitters, §34-37-11.

RECIPROCITY—Cont'd
Hearing aid dealers and fitters.
Licenses, §34-14-3.
Hunting.
Reciprocal agreements as to waterfowl hunting, §§9-11-280 to 9-11-283.
Landscape architects.
Board authorized to permit reciprocal practice, §34-17-26.
Lost or unclaimed property.
Uniform disposition of unclaimed property act.
Property abandoned or escheated under laws of another state, §35-12-30.
Motor vehicles.
Commercial driver licenses, §32-6-49.18.
Drivers' licenses, §§32-6-10, 32-6-11.
Registration of vehicles on an apportionment or allocation basis.
Powers of commissioner of revenue as to reciprocal agreements, §32-6-56.
Nurseries.
Insect and disease control.
Inspection certificates, §2-25-6.
Nursing homes.
Administrators.
Licenses, §34-20-12.
Optometrists.
Licenses, §34-22-21.
Pharmacists and pharmacies.
Licensure without examination, §34-23-51.
Physicians.
General provisions, §§34-24-73, 34-24-77.
Licenses, §§34-24-313, 34-24-331.
Plumbing.
Certification of plumbers and gas fitters, §34-37-11.
Psychologists.
Licenses, §34-26-41.
Seafood fishing.
Reciprocal agreements as to commercial seafood fishing, §§9-12-160 to 9-12-162.
Social workers.
Licenses, §34-30-24.
Support and maintenance.
Reciprocal state enforcement of duties to support, §§30-4-80 to 30-4-98.
See DESERTION AND NONSUPPORT.
Unclaimed property.
Uniform disposition of unclaimed property act.
Reciprocity for property abandoned or escheated under laws of another state, §35-12-30.
Unemployment compensation.
Reciprocal arrangements with state and federal agencies, §25-4-120.

RECIPROCITY—Cont'd
Veterans.
State service commissioner.
Reciprocal agreements with other states, §31-5-6.
Waterfowl hunting.
Reciprocal agreements, §§9-11-280 to 9-11-283.

RECKLESS DRIVING.
Generally, §32-5A-190.
Penalties, §32-5A-190.

RECKLESS ENDANGERMENT, §§13A-6-20 to 13A-6-25.
See ASSAULT AND BATTERY.

RECOGNIZANCE, §§15-13-1 to 15-13-82.
See BAIL AND RECOGNIZANCE.

RECORDATION.
Abstract of mortages.
Failure to keep, §12-13-54.
Acknowledgments.
Form of acknowledgment of conveyances, §35-4-68.
Improperly acknowledged instruments as evidence, §35-4-72.
Actions.
Lis pendens, §§35-4-131 to 35-4-139.
See LIS PENDENS.
Aerial photographs or maps.
Article cumulative, §35-2-82.
County engineer.
Approval, §35-2-81.
Fees.
Recordation by probate judge without fee, §35-2-81.
Manner of recordation and maintenance, §35-2-80.
Probate judges.
Duty to record, §35-2-80.
Recordation without fee, §35-2-81.
Use after recordation, §35-2-81.
Affidavits.
Record as notice of facts recited, §35-4-69.
Recordation by probate judge, §35-4-71.
Agriculture.
Taxation.
Farm loans.
Exemption from tax, §40-22-5.
Production credit corporations and associations.
Exemption, §40-22-4.
Alabama coordinate system.
Limitation on recordation of coordinates defining position of point on land boundary, §35-2-6.
Assignment for benefit of creditors.
Deeds of assignment, §35-4-57.
Bankruptcy and insolvency.
Petitions, decrees or orders of bankruptcy, §35-4-52.

RECORDATION—Cont'd
Banks and financial institutions.
Certificate of incorporation, §5-5A-7.
Credit unions.
Seal.
Administrator to record, §5-17-43.
Permit to transact business, §5-5A-11.
Superintendent of banks.
Executed papers, §5-2A-5.
Bonds, surety.
Bonds for title, §35-4-53.
Official bonds.
See PUBLIC OFFICERS AND EMPLOYEES.
Books, §35-4-58.
Access to books, §35-4-60.
Transcripts from books, §35-4-60.
Business trusts.
Declaration of trust, §19-3-64.
Choses in action.
Choses in action not personal property within meaning used in division, §35-4-55.
Commercial code.
Sales.
Goods to be severed from realty, §7-2-107.
Secured transactions, §§7-9-101 to 7-9-507.
See COMMERCIAL CODE.
Conditional sales contracts.
When received in evidence, §35-4-98.
Condominiums.
Bylaws, §35-8-8.
Declaration, §35-8-7.
Documents and instruments, §35-8-11.
Conservators.
Bonds, surety, §26-3-12.
Settlements of accounts of conservators.
Final settlement.
Accounts and vouchers, §26-5-11.
Decree of probate court, §26-5-11.
Partial settlement.
Decree as to vouchers and accounts, §26-5-5.
Uniform guardianship and protective proceedings act.
Letters of conservatorship, §26-2A-149.
Orders terminating conservatorships, §26-2A-149.
Contracts.
Abandonment.
When recorded contract presumed abandoned, §35-4-75.
Conditional sales contract.
When conditional sales contract received in evidence, §35-4-98.
Written contract for sale of land, §35-4-53.
Copies.
Certified copies of instruments, §35-4-66.

RECORDATION—Cont'd
Corporations.
Filing and recording by probate judge or secretary of state.
Generally, §10-2A-93.
Organization, reorganization or dissolution.
Statement of name and address of preparer of certain instruments, §§35-4-110 to 35-4-113.
Corrections.
Institution finance authority.
Incorporation, §14-2-4.
Counties.
Cemeteries.
Damages from taking of property, etc.
Recordation of proceedings upon payment of costs, §11-17-5.
Conveyances recorded in county where property situated, §35-4-62.
Official bonds, §11-2-3.
Publication of legislative laws of local nature.
Recordation of copies, §11-13-5.
Public building authorities.
Certificate of incorporation, §11-15-5.
Relocation of county seats.
Recordation of certified copy of election result, §11-16-25.
Treasurers.
Annual account.
Recordation and posting of copy, §11-4-28.
County industrial development authorities.
Articles, §11-92A-8.
Boards of directors.
Proceedings, §11-92A-9.
Credit unions.
Seal.
Administrator to record, §5-17-43.
Criminal law and procedure.
Offering a false instrument for recording, §13A-9-12.
Decrees.
Statement of name and address of preparer, §§35-4-110 to 35-4-113.
Division not applicable to decrees, §35-4-112.
Deeds.
Recordation tax. See within this heading, "Taxation."
Delivery to probate judge.
Conveyance operative as record from date of delivery, §35-4-59.
Destroyed record books.
Replacement, §11-3-24.
Eminent domain.
Arbitration agreement, §18-1A-257.
Notice of pending action, §18-1A-75.
Evidence.
Improperly recorded instruments as evidence, §35-4-72.
Proof of documents recorded under recording act, ARCP, Rule 44 (e).

RECORDATION—Cont'd
Evidence—Cont'd
When conveyance receivable in evidence, §35-4-65.
Executors and administrators.
Bonds, surety, §43-2-1.
Letters, §43-2-1.
Resignation, §43-2-270.
False instruments.
Offering for recording, §13A-9-12.
Fees, §35-4-58.
Probate court.
Recording fees, §12-19-90.
Recordation tax, §§40-22-1 to 40-22-12. See within this heading, "Taxation."
Filing for registration.
Notice of contents, §35-4-51.
Forms.
Statement of name and address of preparer of certain instruments, §35-4-113.
Fraud.
Offering a false instrument for recording, §13A-9-12.
Guardian and ward.
Conservators.
Bonds, surety, §26-3-12.
Settlement of accounts of conservators, §§26-5-5, 26-5-11.
Uniform guardianship and protective proceedings act, §26-2A-149.
Health care authorities.
Certificate of authority.
Amended certificate, §22-21-315.
Certificate of incorporation, §22-21-314.
Highways.
Closing and vacating streets, alleys and highways.
Report by commissioner, §23-4-4.
Historical preservation authorities.
Certificate of incorporation, §41-10-139.
Hospitals.
Liens of hospitals, §35-11-371.
Improperly recorded instruments.
Use as evidence, §35-4-72.
Indexes.
General direct and reverse indexes.
Maintenance by probate judge for instruments filed for record, §12-13-43.
Industrial development authority.
Application for incorporation, §41-10-23.
Certificate of incorporation, §41-10-24.
Judgment creditors.
Recordation necessary as to purchasers, mortgagees and judgment creditors, §§35-4-90 to 35-4-97. See within this heading, "Necessary as to purchasers, mortgagees and judgment creditors."

RECORDATION—Cont'd
Judgments.
Foreign judgments.
Recording in probate office, §6-9-237.
Purchasers protected in dealing with record owner as owner of indebtedness, §35-4-64.
Statement of name and address of preparer.
Division not applicable to judgments, §35-4-112.
Land patents.
Public land patents, §35-4-387.
Leases.
Leases for more than 20 years, §35-4-6.
Memorandum of lease.
Recording in lieu of lease, §35-4-51.1.
Liens.
Purchasers protected in dealing with record owner as owner of indebtedness, §35-4-64.
Life estates.
Creditors of life tenants.
Recordation necessary as to creditors of life tenants, §35-4-91.
Lis pendens, §§35-4-130 to 35-4-139.
See LIS PENDENS.
Maps.
Aerial photographs or maps, §§35-2-80 to 35-2-82.
Town surveys, plats or maps, §§35-2-51, 35-2-57.
Marginal entries.
Date, §35-4-58.
Marriage.
Personal property conveyed in consideration of marriage.
Necessary recordation, §35-4-93.
Recitation of marital status of grantor or vendor required, §35-4-73.
Mechanics' and materialmen's liens.
Verified statement, §35-11-216.
Misdemeanors.
Recitation of marital status of grantor or vendor.
False recitation a misdemeanor, §35-4-73.
Mode of recording.
Generally, §35-4-58.
Mortgages and deeds of trust.
Purchasers protected in dealing with record owner as owner of indebtedness, §35-4-64.
Recordation necessary as to mortgagees, §§35-4-90 to 35-4-97. See within this heading, "Necessary as to purchasers, mortgagees and judgment creditors."
Recordation tax, §§40-22-1 to 40-22-12. See within this heading, "Taxation."

RECORDATION—Cont'd
Mortgages and deeds of trust—Cont'd
Satisfaction of mortgage liens, §§35-10-21 to 35-10-30.
Motor vehicles.
Transfer of vehicle, §40-12-260.
Fee for recording change of ownership, §40-12-261.
Municipal corporations.
Annexation.
Cities of twenty-five thousand inhabitants or more.
Recordation of orders, maps, etc., §§11-42-51, 11-42-71.
Claims against municipality, §11-43-101.
Incorporation.
Order of incorporation, §11-41-4.
Ordinances, §11-45-8.
Reduction of corporate limits.
Recordation of map or plat, §11-42-203.
Surveys, plats or maps, §§35-2-51, 35-2-57.
Name and address of preparer of certain instruments, §§35-4-110 to 35-4-113.
Necessary as to purchasers, mortgagees and judgment creditors, §§35-4-90 to 35-4-97.
Conveyances of real property generally, §35-4-90.
General provisions, §35-4-90.
Gifts.
Effect of parol gifts of personal property, §35-4-97.
Loans.
In writing, §35-4-94.
Not in writing.
Effect of loans of personal property, §35-4-95.
Marriage settlements, §35-4-93.
Minors.
Conveyances of personalty to minors, §35-4-96.
Personal property.
Conveyances to minors, §35-4-96.
Effect of loans of personal property not in writing, §35-4-95.
Parol gifts of personal property.
Effect, §35-4-97.
Wills or conveyances creating estates in personal property on condition, etc., §35-4-94.
Real property.
Generally.
Conveyances, §35-4-90.
Remainders, reversions and executory interests.
Instruments creating estates in remainder, etc., §35-4-91.

RECORDATION—Cont'd
Necessary as to purchasers, mortgagees and judgment creditors—Cont'd
Trees and timber.
Transfers of standing timber, trees and cutting rights, §35-4-92.
Wills.
Creating estates in personal property on condition, etc., §35-4-94.
Instruments creating estates in remainder, etc., §35-4-91.
Notice.
Filing for registration to constitute notice of contents, §35-4-51.
Recordation necessary as to purchasers, mortgagees and judgment creditors, §§35-4-90 to 35-4-97. See within this heading, "Necessary as to purchasers, mortgagees and judgment creditors."
Recording effective as notice of contents of conveyance, §35-4-63.
Offering a false instrument for recording, §13A-9-12.
Orders of court.
Statement of name and address of preparer.
Division not applicable to orders of court, §35-4-112.
Partition.
Application for partition, §35-6-49.
Crops.
Recordation of papers, §35-6-125.
Decree of sale, §35-6-58.
Patents, §35-4-56.
Public land patents, §35-4-387.
Personal property.
Choses in action not personal property within meaning used in division, §35-4-55.
Conveyances of personal property brought into state by tenants for life or years, §35-4-54.
Marriage settlements.
Recordation necessary as to purchasers, mortgagees and judgment creditors, §35-4-93.
Photographs.
Aerial photographs or maps, §§35-2-80 to 35-2-82.
Place of recordation.
Conveyances recorded in county where property situated, §35-4-62.
Plats.
Necessity for including plat or description of plat book, etc., §35-4-74.

RECORDATION—Cont'd
Preparer of instruments and conveying property.
Statement of name and address of preparer, §§35-4-110 to 35-4-113.
Probate judges.
Affidavits, §35-4-71.
Conveyances required to be recorded in office of probate judge, §35-4-50.
Liability.
Failure to perform duties, §35-4-61.
Marital status of grantor or vendor.
Probate judge not liable for good faith error in recitation of marital status, §35-4-73.
Plats.
Judge not liable for good faith error in requirement to include plat or description of plat book, etc., §35-4-74.
Statement of name and address of preparer of certain instruments.
Probate judge not liable for good faith errors, §35-4-111.
Marital status of grantor or vendor.
Good faith error in recitation requirement.
Probate judge not liable, §35-4-73.
Mode of recording, §35-4-58.
Taxation, §§40-22-1, 40-22-2.
Public lands.
Land patents, §35-4-387.
Purchase money notes, §35-4-53.
Purchasers.
Protected in dealing with record owner as owner of indebtedness, §35-4-64.
Recordation necessary as to purchasers, mortgagees and judgment creditors, §§35-4-90 to 35-4-97. See within this heading, "Necessary as to purchasers, mortgagees and judgment creditors."
Receipt, §35-4-59.
Refusal, §35-4-58.
Remainders, reversions and executory interests.
Creditors of life tenants.
Recordation necessary as to creditors of life tenants, §35-4-91.
Satisfaction of mortgage liens, §§35-10-21 to 35-10-30.
Small loans.
Fees, §5-18-13.
Soil and water conservation.
Watershed conservancy districts.
Referendum upon creation. Recordation of results, §9-8-58.
Stamps.
Time stamp, §35-4-58.

RECORDATION—Cont'd
Statement of name and address of preparer of certain instruments, §§35-4-110 to 35-4-113.
Applicability of division.
When division not applicable, §35-4-112.
Decrees.
Division not applicable to recording of decrees, §35-4-112.
Errors.
Probate judge not liable for good faith errors, §35-4-111.
Form, §35-4-113.
Judgments.
Division not applicable to recordation of judgment, §35-4-112.
Orders of court.
Division not applicable to recordation of court order, §35-4-112.
Probate judge.
Not liable for good faith errors, §35-4-111.
Required for recordation, §35-4-110.
Wills.
Division not applicable to recording of wills, §35-4-112.
State products mart and coliseum authority.
Certificate of incorporation, §41-10-85.
Proceedings of board of directors, §41-10-87.
Synfuels development authority.
Application for authority to incorporate.
Secretary of state to record, §9-6A-4.
Dissolution of authority.
Application for dissolution recorded by secretary of state, §9-6A-10.
Taxation, §§40-22-1 to 40-22-12.
Additional security for previously filed instruments, §40-22-2.
Agriculture.
Farm loans.
Exemption, §40-22-5.
Production credit corporations and associations.
Exemptions with respect to instruments executed to secure loan, §40-22-4.
Amount of tax due.
Probate judges.
Determination of amount by judge, §40-22-1.
Banks.
Tax on mortgages not applicable to any bank unless applicable to all, §40-22-3.
Deeds.
Farm loans.
Exemption, §40-22-5.
Instruments requiring payment of tax, §40-22-1.

RECORDATION—Cont'd
Taxation—Cont'd
Deeds—Cont'd
Unpaid purchase money.
Treatment and collection as mortgage, §40-22-2.
Exempt institutions, §§40-22-5.1 to 40-22-12.
Ad valorem taxes.
Debt secured by instrument.
Exemption from ad valorem taxes, §40-22-9.
Certification of payment, §40-22-7.
Construction of sections 40-22-6 through 40-22-11, §40-22-12.
Liberal construction of sections 40-22-6 through 40-22-11, §40-22-12.
Payment.
Certification of payment, §40-22-7.
Previously paid taxes.
Exemption of debt secured by instrument, §40-22-10.
Waiver of exemption from payment, §40-22-11.
Probate judge.
Certification of payment, §40-22-7.
Religious organizations, §40-22-5.1.
Transfers not subject to tax imposed by section 40-22-1, §40-22-8.
Waiver of exemption, §40-22-11.
Exemptions.
Instruments exempted from payment of tax, §40-22-1.
Production credit corporations and associations, §40-22-4.
Failure to collect upon mortgages and deeds of trust, §12-13-53.
Instruments requiring payment of tax, §40-22-1.
Value of instruments, §40-22-1.
Mortgages and deeds of trust.
Deeds reciting part of purchase money unpaid.
Treatment and collection as mortgage, §40-22-2.
Failure to collect, §12-13-53.
Farm loans.
Exemption, §40-22-5.
General provisions, §40-22-2.
Tax on mortgages not applicable to any bank unless applicable to all, §40-22-3.
Previously filed instruments.
Additional or substantial security, §40-22-2.

RECORDATION—Cont'd
Taxation—Cont'd
Probate judges.
Commission for collecting tax, §40-22-1.
Determination of amount of tax due, §40-22-1.
Failure to collect, §12-13-53.
Filing instruments without collection, §40-22-2.
Production credit corporations and associations.
Exemption, §40-22-4.
Property located outside of state, §40-22-2.
Property situated in two or more counties.
Taxation of instruments conveying, §40-22-1.
Religion.
Exemption of certain conveyances by religious organizations, §40-22-5.1.
Security agreements.
Instruments evidencing secured indebtedness, §40-22-2.
Tenants in common.
Taxation of deeds executed by tenants in common, §40-22-1.
Time.
Conveyance operative as record from date of delivery, §35-4-59.
Recordation necessary as to purchasers, mortgagees and judgment creditors, §§35-4-90 to 35-4-97. See within this heading, "Necessary as to purchasers, mortgagees and judgment creditors."
Time stamp, §35-4-58.
Title.
Bonds for title, §35-4-53.
Town surveys, plats or maps, §§35-2-51, 35-2-57.
Trademarks and service marks.
New certificate, recordation of, §8-12-11.
Effect of failure to record, §8-12-11.
Transcripts, §35-4-60.
Trees and timber.
Transfers of standing timber, trees and cutting rights.
Void and inoperative as against purchasers, mortgagees and judgment creditors without notice or prior recordation, §35-4-92.
Trusts and trustees.
Business trusts.
Declaration of trust, §19-3-64.
Notice of trust, §35-4-257.
Uniform commercial code, §§7-1-101 to 7-11-108.
See COMMERCIAL CODE.
Validation.
Improperly recorded instruments as evidence, §35-4-72.

RECORDATION—Cont'd
Vendor's liens.
Purchasers protected in dealing with record owner as owner of indebtedness, §35-4-64.
Water system assistance authority.
Application to become corporation, §22-23A-5.
What instruments admitted to record, §35-4-51.
Witnesses.
Form of proof of conveyances, §35-4-68.

RECORDED DEVICES.
Actions.
Civil actions.
Damages, §13A-8-85.
Confiscation.
Nonconforming recordings, equipment and components, §13A-8-84.
Containers.
Manufacturer's name required on packages, §13A-8-83.
Damages.
Civil actions, §13A-8-85.
Definitions.
Owners, §13A-8-80.
Forfeitures.
Nonconforming recordings, equipment and components.
Confiscation, §13A-8-84.
Persons convicted of offenses under article.
Disposition of infringing recordings and equipment and components, §13A-8-86.
Labels.
Manufacturer's name required on packages, §13A-8-83.
Manufacturer's name required on packages, §13A-8-83.
Motion pictures.
See MOTION PICTURES.
Owner.
Defined, §13A-8-80.
Packages.
Manufacturer's name required on package, §13A-8-83.
Penalties.
Sales, rental, possession, etc., in contravention of article, §13A-8-86.
Photography.
See PHOTOGRAPHY.
Possession, sale, rental, etc.
Recorded devices produced, manufactured, distributed, etc., in violation of provisions of article.
Prohibited, §13A-8-82.
Produced, manufactured, distributed, etc., in violation of article.
Possession, sale, rental, etc.
Prohibited, §13A-8-82.
Sentencing.
Sales, rental, etc., in contravention of article.
Penalties, §13A-8-86.

RECORDED DEVICES—Cont'd
Transfer of certain sounds prohibited, §13A-8-81.
Exception, §13A-8-81.
Manufacturing, distributing of certain articles, §13A-8-81.
Unauthorized recordings.
Confiscation, §13A-8-84.

RECORDS.
Abortion.
Confidentiality of records and information involving court proceedings, §26-21-8.
Persons disclosing records or information guilty of misdemeanor, §26-21-8.
Transcript of proceedings to be recorded, §26-21-4.
Accountants.
Board of public accountancy, §34-1-3.
Disciplinary investigations.
Confidentiality, §34-1-3.
Hearings, §34-1-14.
Actions.
Orders, judgments and decrees.
Copying into final record not required, §12-20-21.
Pleadings, motions or other papers.
Original or copies final record in civil actions, §12-20-22.
Adoption.
General provisions, §§26-10-4, 26-10-5.
Affidavits.
Final record, §12-20-22.
Agriculture.
Agricultural center corporation.
Record of proceedings, §2-6-24.
Air pollution, §§22-28-9, 22-28-10, 22-28-20.
Airports.
Zoning, §4-6-10.
Alabama school of trades.
Records to be preserved, §16-60-220.
Alcoholic beverages.
See ALCOHOLIC BEVERAGES.
Alligator farms.
Bill of sale.
Availability for inspection, §9-12-207.
Ameraport.
Offshore harbor and terminal commission.
Executive director.
Duties as to records, §33-10-8.
Open to inspection, §33-10-13.
Appeals.
Record on appeal.
See APPEALS.
Arrests.
Criminal justice information center, §§41-9-590 to 41-9-648.
See CRIMINAL LAW AND PROCEDURE.

RECORDS—Cont'd

Atomic energy.
Radiation, §22-14-8.
Attorneys at law.
Disciplinary proceedings, §34-3-85.
Auctions and auctioneers.
Board of auctioneers, §§34-4-50, 34-4-54.
Sale of personal property at auction, §8-14-1.
Aviation.
Airports.
Zoning, §4-6-10.
Banks and financial institutions.
See BANKS AND FINANCIAL INSTITUTIONS.
Barbers.
Board of barber examiners, §34-5-13.
Beautification board.
Proceedings of board.
Maintenance and examination of record of proceedings, §41-9-494.
Bishop of diocese.
Prima facie evidence, §10-4-9.
Boats.
Keeping of records, §33-5-7.
Business records.
Falsifying business records, §13A-9-45.
Butchers, §§2-15-3, 2-15-27.
Cattle.
Butchers to maintain records as to cows butchered, §2-15-3.
Inspections, §2-15-3.
Cahaba trace commission.
Revenues and expenditures, §41-9-809.
Child abuse or neglect, §26-14-8.
Chiropractors.
Board of chiropractic examiners.
Secretary-treasurer or executive secretary to keep, §34-24-143.
Circuit courts.
Clerks of court, ARCP, Rule 79.
General provisions, §§12-17-94, 12-20-25.
Registers, §§12-17-117 to 12-17-119.
Substitution of lost or destroyed papers or records in civil cases, §§12-20-26 to 12-20-32.
See COURTS.
Classification of records.
Local government records commission, §41-13-23.
Issuance by commission of regulations for classifying public records, §41-13-24.
State records commission, §41-13-24.
Coal.
Severance tax of 1977.
Inspection of records, §40-13-34.

RECORDS—Cont'd

Coal—Cont'd
Surface mining control and reclamation.
Confidentiality of records, §9-16-100.
Division of surface mining control and reclamation.
Transfer of records, §9-16-80.
Permits.
Maintenance of records, etc., by permitee, §9-16-92.
Commission merchants.
Sale of farm produce.
Maintenance of records, §2-29-7.
Commissions.
Local government records commission, §§41-13-22 to 41-13-25.
Condominiums.
Accounting records, §35-8-10.
Constitution of the United States.
Full faith and credit clause, Const. U. S., Art. IV, §1.
Proof, Const. U. S., Art. IV, §1.
Contractors.
State licensing board, §34-8-25.
Convictions.
Criminal justice information center, §§41-9-590 to 41-9-648.
See CRIMINAL LAW AND PROCEDURE.
Copies.
Admissibility in evidence, §36-12-41.
Certified copies.
Public officers to provide upon payment of fees, §36-12-41.
Fees.
Public officers to provide certified copies upon payment, §36-12-41.
Right of citizens to copy, §36-12-40.
Corporations, §§10-2A-73, 10-2A-79.
Corrections.
Board of corrections.
Convicts, §14-3-7.
Correspondence.
Preservation of official correspondence, §14-3-6.
Cosmetics.
Investigation, §20-1-3.
Cosmetologists.
Board of cosmetology, §34-7-44.
Counties.
General provisions.
See COUNTIES.
Local government records commission, §§41-13-22 to 41-13-25.
Semiannual publication of county receipts and expenditures, §§11-3-21 to 11-3-23.
Courts.
General provisions, ARJA, Rules 30, 31.

RECORDS—Cont'd

Courts—Cont'd
Substitution of lost or destroyed papers or records in civil cases, §§12-20-26 to 12-20-32.
See COURTS.
Courts of the unified judicial system.
Disposal of records according to procedures of surpeme court, §41-13-21.
Credit unions.
See CREDIT UNIONS.
Crime victims compensation.
Alteration of commission records.
Penalties, §15-23-20.
Criminal justice information center, §§41-9-590 to 41-9-648.
See CRIMINAL LAW AND PROCEDURE.
Criminal law and procedure.
Criminal justice information center, §§41-9-590 to 41-9-648.
See CRIMINAL LAW AND PROCEDURE.
Indictments generally. See within this heading, "Indictments."
Tampering with governmental records, §13A-10-12.
Unsworn falsification to authorities, §13A-10-109.
Dairy commission.
Health regulations.
Examination of records, §2-13-92.
Dead bodies.
Unclaimed bodies.
Distribution for scientific study.
Records of board for distribution and delivery, §22-19-21.
Decrees.
Copying of decrees into final record not required, §12-20-21.
Definitions.
Public records, §41-13-1.
Dentists.
Board of dental examiners, §34-9-44.
Department of archives and history.
Photographing or microphotographing centralized in department, §41-13-41.
Preservation, filing, etc., of public records.
Assistance of public officials by department of archives and history, §41-13-4.
Depositions, ARCP, Rules 30 (c), 31 (b).
Destruction of public records.
Courts.
Substitution of lost or destroyed papers or records in civil cases, §§12-20-26 to 12-20-32.
See COURTS.

RECORDS—Cont'd
Destruction of public records—Cont'd
Insurance.
Commissioner of insurance, §27-2-14.
Local government records commission.
Commission to make determination as to local government records to be preserved or destroyed, §41-13-23.
Microfilmed copies.
State and county officials not to destroy public records until microfilmed copies processed and checked for accuracy, §41-13-44.
Records having no significance, importance or value, §41-13-5.
Restoration of destroyed records of state, county or municipality, §12-20-50.
State records commission.
Approval required, §41-13-21.
Commission to make determination as to state records to be preserved or destroyed, §41-13-21.
Diseases.
Notifiable diseases.
Sexually transmitted diseases.
Medical records, §22-11A-22.
District courts.
General provisions, §§12-2-2, 12-2-54.
Substitution of lost or destroyed papers or records in civil cases, §§12-20-26 to 12-20-32.
See COURTS.
Drugs.
Investigation, §20-1-3.
Education.
See EDUCATION.
Eggs and egg products.
Inspection of records, §2-12-10.
Environmental management.
Commission.
Hearings and procedures before commission, §22-22A-7.
Proceedings of commission, §22-22A-6.
Evidence.
See EVIDENCE.
Examination.
Inspection.
Right of citizens, §36-12-40.
Executors and administrators.
General administrators, §43-2-175.
Fees.
Copies.
Public officers to provide certified copies upon payment of fee, §36-12-41.

RECORDS—Cont'd
Fees—Cont'd
Court records.
Copies and certification, ARJA, Rule 30.
Substitution of lost or destroyed records or papers, §12-20-1.
Filing of public records.
Assistance of public officials by department of archives and history, §41-13-4.
Finance.
Counties.
General provisions.
See COUNTIES.
Records of financial status, §§11-8-7, 11-8-8.
General provisions, §§41-4-14, 41-4-36.
Fireworks.
Keeping of records by permit holders, §8-17-213.
Fish and game.
See FISH AND GAME.
Food.
Investigation of records, §20-1-3.
Forests and forestry.
See FORESTS AND FORESTRY.
Fraternal benefit societies.
Conversion into stock or mutual life insurance company.
Separate record of premiums, §27-35-11.
Minutes of governing body, §27-34-19.
Full faith and credit clause,
Const. U. S., Art. IV, §1.
Funerals, §22-9-77.
Gambling.
Forfeiture of gambling records, §13A-12-30.
Possession of gambling records, §§13A-12-24 to 13A-12-26.
Ginseng.
Collectors, dealers and growers, §9-13-244.
Guardian and ward.
Removal of person or property of minors and wards to another country.
Record of proceedings.
Certification, §26-8-23.
Filed in county in which removal to be made, §26-8-23.
Uniform guardianship and protective proceedings act.
Clerks of court.
Duties, §26-2A-34.
Conservators, §26-2A-146.
Harbors and ports.
Advisory committee, §33-1-9.
Harbor masters, §33-3-5.
Hazardous substances.
Fees.
Location of records, §22-30B-16.
Records of hazardous substances received for disposal, §22-30B-11.

RECORDS—Cont'd
Hazardous waste.
Fees.
Records of hazardous waste or substances received for disposal, §22-30B-11.
Generators, §22-30-18.
Health.
County health officers, §22-3-5.
Health care authorities.
Board.
Meetings, §22-21-316.
Health maintenance organizations.
Examination, §27-21A-16.
Highways.
General provisions, §§23-1-33, 23-1-34.
Hospitals, §§12-21-4 to 12-21-6.
Hotels, inns and other transient lodging places.
Transient occupancy tax, §§40-26-6 to 40-26-9.
Impeachment.
Final record of impeachment proceedings.
Preparation, §36-11-22.
Income tax.
Custody of records, §40-18-48.
Setoff debt collection.
Confidentiality of taxpayer's records, §40-18-107.
Indexes.
General direct and reverse indexes.
Maintenance by probate judge for instruments filed for record, §12-13-43.
Indians.
Indian affairs commission.
Fiscal record, §41-9-717.
Indictments.
Arrest of judgment.
Preferring of new indictments, §15-8-131.
Clerk to record returned indictments, §15-8-72.
Lost, mislaid, mutilated or destroyed indictments, §15-8-110.
Utilization of record copy, §15-8-111.
Photographing or photostating indictments, §15-8-72.
Quashing indictment.
Preferring of new indictments, §15-8-131.
Industrial development authority.
Payment of bonds, §41-10-31.
Industrial development corporations.
First meeting, §10-4-132.
Inspection.
Right of citizens, §36-12-40.
Insurance.
See INSURANCE.
Jails.
Feeding of prisoners.
Daily ration sheet or expense account.
Sheriff not required to prepare, §14-6-41.
Forms, §14-6-47.

RECORDS—Cont'd

Judgments.
Abolished inferior courts.
Preserving judgment
records, §12-20-23.
Copying of judgments into
final record not required,
§12-20-21.
Judicial system.
Courts of unified judicial
system.
Disposal of records
according to
procedures prescribed
by supreme court,
§41-13-21.
**Junior college for Jackson
and DeKalb counties.**
Accounts of officers,
§16-60-63.
Jury.
Preservation of records
concerning selection and
service of jurors,
§12-16-64.
Juvenile offenders.
Confidentiality, §15-19-7.
Inspection of record,
§15-19-7.
Juvenile proceedings.
General provisions,
§§12-15-100 to 12-15-103.
Labor, §§25-2-14, 25-2-22.
Landscape architects.
Board of examiners.
Record of proceedings,
§34-17-3.
Larceny.
Public records.
See LARCENY.
Legislature, §§29-1-14 to
29-1-17.
Libraries.
Right of citizens to copy.
Exemption, §36-12-40.
Library boards, §11-90-3.
Licenses.
Probate judge to keep,
§40-12-21.
Lime, §2-23-5.
Lis pendens, §§35-4-130 to
35-4-138.
See LIS PENDENS.
**Local government records
commission,** §§41-13-22 to
41-13-25.
Attorney general.
Member of commission,
§41-13-22.
Classification of records,
§41-13-23.
Issuance by commission of
regulations classifying
public records,
§41-13-24.
Compensation of members,
§41-13-22.
Created, §41-13-22.
Department of archives and
history.
Director.
Chairman of commission,
§41-13-22.
Department of examiners of
public accounts.
Chief examiner.
Member of commission,
§41-13-22.

RECORDS—Cont'd

**Local government records
commission**—Cont'd
Destruction of public records.
Commission to make
determination as to
local government
records to be preserved
or destroyed,
§41-13-23.
Expenses of members.
Payment of expenses of
certain members,
§41-13-25.
Meetings, §41-13-22.
Preservation of public
records.
Commission to make
determination as to
local government
records to be preserved
or destroyed,
§41-13-23.
Removal of members.
Certain members subject to
removal, §41-13-22.
Secretary of state.
Member of commission,
§41-13-22.
Surveys.
Conduct authorized,
§41-13-24.
Lost records.
Courts.
Substitution of lost or
destroyed papers or
records in civil cases,
§§12-20-26 to 12-20-32.
See COURTS.
Establishment of lost records
of state, county or
municipality, §12-20-50.
Marine resources.
Licenses.
Issuance, §9-12-118.
Marriage.
Certificate, §§22-9-50,
30-1-13.
Errors.
Correction, §30-1-17.
Evidence.
Certified registers of
marriages, §12-21-101.
Licenses, §§22-9-50, 30-1-12.
Meat and meat products,
§2-17-23.
Medical records.
Diseases.
Notifiable diseases.
Sexually transmitted
diseases, §22-11A-22.
**Mental health finance
authority.**
Bond issues.
Payment of principal and
interest.
State treasurer,
§41-10-370.
Proceedings of authority,
§41-10-355.
Mentally ill, §§22-50-60,
22-50-62.
Microphotographing.
Educational records, §§16-1-3
to 16-1-5.
Photographing or
microphotographing.
General provisions,
§§41-13-40 to 41-13-44.
Military affairs, §31-1-1;
Const. Ala., art. XV, §277.

RECORDS—Cont'd

Milk and milk products.
Health regulations.
Examination of records,
§2-13-92.
Minors.
Juvenile proceedings.
General provisions,
§§12-15-100 to
12-15-103.
Mobile homes.
Statistics as to manufacture,
sale, etc., §24-5-11.
Test records, §24-5-9.
Motions.
Final record, §12-20-22.
Motor fuels.
Same pump sale of diesel
fuel for highway and off-
highway purposes.
Separate maintenance of
records, §40-17-21.
**Motor sports hall of fame
commission,** §41-9-477.
Motor vehicles.
General provisions.
See MOTOR VEHICLES.
Temporary tags and
certificates, §32-6-217.
Municipal corporations.
General provisions.
See MUNICIPAL
CORPORATIONS.
Local government records
commission, §§41-13-22
to 41-13-25.
Nonexistence.
Certificate of public officer
on nonexistence of
record.
Admissibility in evidence
of certificate,
§12-21-34.
Orders of courts.
Copying of orders into final
record not required,
§12-20-21.
Parks and recreation.
Capital development
assistance fund.
Applicants required to
maintain records,
§9-7A-9.
Examination of records by
commissioner,
§9-7A-11.
Parole.
Board to report on prisoner's
social and criminal
records, §15-22-25.
Furnishing by board of
corrections, §15-22-34.
Partnerships.
Limited partnerships.
Maintenance, §10-9A-4.
Right of inspection,
§10-9A-4.
Peace officers.
Annuity and benefit fund.
Board of commissioners,
§36-21-65.
Penitentiary.
Information regarding new
convicts, §14-3-35.
Punishment, §14-3-52.
Pesticides.
Application, §2-27-60.

RECORDS—Cont'd
Phonograph records.
Copying and sale of recorded devices, §§13A-8-80 to 13A-8-86.
See RECORDED DEVICES.
Photographing or microphotographing, §41-13-40.
Charges for photographing or microphotographing by department of archives and history, §41-13-41.
Counties.
Appropriation of funds, §41-13-43.
Department of archives and history.
Photographing or microphotographing centralized in department, §41-13-41.
Destruction of public records.
State and county officials not to destroy public records until microfilmed copies processed and checked for accuracy, §41-13-44.
Educational records.
Authorized, §16-1-3.
Destruction, §16-1-4.
Effect, §16-1-3.
Force and effect, §16-1-3.
Intent of provision, §16-1-5.
Retention, §16-1-4.
Equipment and supplies.
Purchase or lease by department of archives and history, §41-13-42.
Evidence.
Admissibility in evidence of photographs, microfilms, etc., §41-13-40.
Indictments.
Recording returned indictments, §15-8-72.
Insurance.
Commissioner of insurance, §27-2-14.
Lis pendens record, §35-4-136.
Municipalities.
Appropriation of funds, §41-13-43.
Secretary of state, §36-14-15.
Welfare.
Commissioner of human resources.
See WELFARE.
Physicians.
Examinations.
Board to keep complete records of examinations, §34-24-78.
Pilots and pilotage.
State pilotage commission, §33-4-14.
Podiatrists, §34-24-273.
Preservation of public records.
Assistance of public officials by department of archives and history, §41-13-4.

RECORDS—Cont'd
Preservation of public records—Cont'd
Local government records commission.
Commission to make determination as to local government records to be preserved or destroyed, §41-13-23.
State records commission.
Commission to make determination as to state records to be preserved or destroyed, §41-13-21.
Prisons and prisoners.
General provisions.
See PRISONS AND PRISONERS.
Probate judges.
See PROBATE COURTS.
Probation.
Board to report on sentenced prisoner's social and criminal records, §15-22-25.
Confidentiality of probation officers' records, §15-22-53.
Public defenders.
Maintenance of certain records, §15-12-44.
Public lands.
General provisions, §§9-15-6 to 9-15-9.
School lands, §§9-15-49 to 9-15-51.
Public officers and employees.
Assistance of official in preserving, filing, etc., by department of archives and history, §41-13-4.
Certificate of public officer on nonexistence of record.
Admissibility and proof of certificate in evidence, §12-21-34.
Public property, papers, etc., §§36-12-1 to 36-12-40.
See PUBLIC OFFICERS AND EMPLOYEES.
State employees' retirement system, §§36-27-27, 36-27-29.
State personnel department, §36-26-44.
Public service commission.
See PUBLIC SERVICE COMMISSION.
Public welfare.
General provisions, §§38-2-11, 38-2-12.
Radiation, §22-14-8.
Real estate brokers.
Brokers to keep records of sales, etc., §34-27-36.
Registers, §§12-17-117 to 12-17-119.
Reporter of decisions of supreme court and courts of appeals.
Receipt and disposition of records, etc., in cases by reporter, §12-4-4.

RECORDS—Cont'd
Restoration.
Lost, etc., records of state, county or municipality, §12-20-50.
Rules of judicial administration.
Transfer of cases, ARJA, Rule 26.
Savings and loan associations, §§5-16-15, 5-16-17.
School records.
See EDUCATION.
Secretary of state.
Local government records commission.
Member of commission, §41-13-22.
Securities.
Securities commission, §8-6-53.
Access to, §8-6-53.
Seeds, §2-26-10.
Sex offenses.
Availability to law enforcement officers, etc., §15-20-5.
Courts to forward records of convictions to director of public safety, §15-20-3.
Report of information to be recorded and indexed by department of public safety, §15-20-5.
Sexual abuse.
Confidentiality of records of victims under eighteen years of age, §15-1-2.
Sheriffs, §§36-22-8 to 36-22-13.
See SHERIFFS.
Small loans, §§5-18-9 to 5-18-11.
Soil and water conservation.
State soil and water conservation committee, §9-8-22.
Soil classifiers.
Board.
Record of proceedings, §34-32-8.
Southern products mart authority.
Maintenance of records pertaining to payment of bonds, §41-10-65.
Space science exhibit commission.
Maintenance and audit, §41-9-437.
Speech pathologists and audiologists.
Board of examiners.
Admissibility of board records as evidence, §34-28A-44.
Sports.
Agents.
Athlete agent regulatory commission, §8-26-3.
Inspection of books and records, §8-26-27.
Records to be kept by agent, §8-26-26.

RECORDS—Cont'd
State records commission.
Classification of records,
§41-13-21.
Issuance by commission of
regulations classifying
public records,
§41-13-24.
Compensation of members,
§41-13-20.
Composition, §41-13-20.
Created, §41-13-20.
Destruction of public records.
Commission to make
determination as to
state records to be
preserved or destroyed,
§41-13-21.
Expenses of members.
Payment of expenses of
certain members,
§41-13-25.
Meetings, §41-13-20.
Preservation of public
records.
Commission to make
determination as to
state records to be
preserved or destroyed,
§41-13-21.
Removal of members.
Certain members subject to
removal, §41-13-20.
Surveys.
Conduct authorized,
§41-13-24.
Unified judicial system.
Disposal of records in
accordance with
procedures, §41-13-21.
Surveys and surveyors.
Division of land surveys.
General provisions,
§§35-2-33, 35-2-35.
**Synfuels development
authority.**
Board of directors.
Proceedings to be reduced
to writing and
recorded, §9-6A-6.
**Tampering with
governmental records,**
§13A-10-12.
Taxation.
Cigarettes.
Gummed cigarette papers.
See CIGARETTES.
Education.
Warrants for special
county and district
taxes, §16-13-106.
General provisions.
See TAXATION.
Hotels, inns and other
transient lodging places.
Transient occupancy tax.
See HOTELS, INNS
AND OTHER
TRANSIENT
LODGING PLACES.
Income tax, §§40-18-48,
40-18-107.
Custody, §40-18-48.
Setoff debt collection.
Confidentiality,
§40-18-107.
Inspection, §40-1-5.
Lubricating oils and greases,
§§40-17-176, 40-17-178.
Maintenance, §40-1-5.

RECORDS—Cont'd
Taxation—Cont'd
Motor fuels.
Diesel fuel tax.
Failure to keep records,
§40-17-9.
Gasoline tax, §§40-17-35,
40-17-37.
Motor vehicle carriers.
Fuel tax, §40-17-149.
Mileage tax, §40-19-5.
Public utilities.
Compelling production of
records, §40-21-19.
Tobacco sales tax,
§§40-25-13, 40-25-26.
Teachers' retirement system.
Admissibility in evidence of
photo-reproduced copies
of records or documents
maintained by system,
§16-25-27.
Tennessee Valley authority.
Exhibit commission,
§41-9-785.
Tickets.
Traffic tickets, §12-12-54.
Tobacco.
Sales tax, §§40-25-13,
40-25-26.
Use tax, §40-25-46.
**Toxic substances in the
workplace.**
Maintenance by employer,
§22-33-11.
**Trademarks and service
marks.**
Registration.
Maintenance of records for
public examination,
§8-12-12.
Transcribed records.
Evidence, §12-21-103.
Transfer of cases, ARJA,
Rule 26.
Transfers to minors,
§§35-5A-1 to 35-5A-24.
See TRANSFERS TO
MINORS.
Duty of custodian to keep
records of transactions,
§35-5A-13.
Trees and timber.
Condemnation of timber theft
equipment.
State forester, §9-13-225.
**Unemployment
compensation,** §25-4-116.
Unified judicial system.
State records commission.
Disposal of records in
accordance with
procedures, §41-13-21.
University of Montevallo.
Transactions, §16-54-10.
**USS Alabama battleship
commission.**
Maintenance and audits,
§41-9-350.
Vacation time-sharing plans.
Failure to keep certian items
among business records.
Violations of article,
§34-27-52.
Failure to provide certain
documents at
registration.
Violations of article,
§34-27-51.

RECORDS—Cont'd
Vital statistics.
Births.
Records of births in
institutions, §22-9-11.
Warehouses.
Character of records.
Promulgation by state
board of agriculture
and industries,
§8-15-2.
**Water conservation and
irrigation.**
Agency.
Board of directors.
Proceedings of board,
§9-10-4.
Corporations.
Board of directors.
Proceedings of board,
§9-10-33.
**Water management and
drainage.**
Districts.
Record book, §9-9-6.
Tax records, §9-9-31.
District treasurer,
§9-9-35.
Preparation of tax
records, §9-9-32.
Waters and watercourses.
Development of docks and
other facilities along
inland waterways.
Units of government,
§§33-2-41, 33-2-73,
33-2-103, 33-2-132,
33-2-162.
**Water system assistance
authority.**
Board of directors.
Record of proceedings,
§22-23A-5.
Weights and measures.
Local sealers, §8-16-32.
Welfare, §§38-2-11, 38-2-12.
Workmen's compensation.
Injuries for which
compensation claimed,
§25-5-4.
Youthful offenders.
Confidentiality, §15-19-7.
Inspection of record,
§15-19-7.
Youth services.
Department of youth
services.
Records of examinations,
etc., §44-1-38.
Restrictions on release or
use of records,
§44-1-39.
Youth services board.
Record of proceedings,
§44-1-51.

RECREATION.
See PARKS AND
RECREATION.

**REDEMPTION OF
PROPERTY.**
Real property.
General provisions, §§6-5-247
to 6-5-257.
See REAL PROPERTY.

REDEVELOPMENT
PROJECTS, §§24-2-1 to
24-2-10.
Acquisition of property.
Powers of housing authorities
or municipalities,
§24-2-2.
Advisory board, §24-2-5.
**Assistance of projects by
cities, counties, etc.,**
§24-2-4.
Bond issues.
Investment by public bodies,
etc., in bonds, etc., issued
by housing authorities,
etc., §24-2-9.
Issuance, §24-2-3.
Clearing of property.
Powers of housing authorities
or municipalities,
§24-2-2.
Conflict of laws, §24-2-10.
Contracts.
Powers of housing authorities
or municipalities,
§24-2-3.
Counties.
Approval of redevelopment
plan by governing bodies
of counties in which
projects situated, §24-2-4.
Assistance of redevelopment
projects by counties,
§24-2-4.
Disposal of property.
Powers of housing authorities
or municipalities,
§24-2-2.
Eminent domain.
Powers of housing authorities
or municipalities,
§24-2-3.
Federal financial aid,
§24-2-8.
Financial aid.
Assistance of redevelopment
projects by cities,
counties, etc., §24-2-4.
Federal financial aid,
§24-2-8.
Housing authorities.
Powers, §§24-2-2, 24-2-3.
**Investment by public bodies,
etc., in bonds, etc.,
issued by housing
authorities,** §24-2-9.
**Legislative findings and
declaration of necessity,**
§24-2-1.
Municipal corporations.
Approval of redevelopment
plan by governing bodies
of cities in which projects
situated, §24-2-4.
Assistance of redevelopment
projects by cities,
§24-2-4.
Powers, §§24-2-2, 24-2-3.
Plan.
Approval of redevelopment
plan by governing bodies
of cities, counties, etc., in
which project situated,
§24-2-4.
Land in project may be made
available for use by
private enterprise or
public agencies in
accordance with
redevelopment plan,
§24-2-6.

REDEVELOPMENT
PROJECTS—Cont'd
Private enterprise.
Land in project may be made
available for use by
private enterprise,
§24-2-6.
Tax status of land sold or
leased to private
individuals or
corporations for
redevelopment, §24-2-7.
**Provisions of chapter
cumulative,** §24-2-10.
Public agencies.
Land in project may be made
available for use by
public agencies, §24-2-6.
Taxation.
Tax status of land sold or
leased to private
individuals or
corporations for
redevelopment, §24-2-7.
United States.
Federal financial aid,
§24-2-8.
Urban renewal projects,
§§24-3-1 to 24-3-9.
See URBAN RENEWAL
PROJECTS.
Utilities.
Installation of utilities.
Powers of housing
authorities or
municipalities, §24-2-2.

RED LIGHT ABATEMENT
ACT.
Nuisances.
Lewdness, assignation or
prostitution, §§6-5-140 to
6-5-154.
See NUISANCES.

REEFS.
Marine resources.
Artificial fishing reefs,
§§9-12-140 to 9-12-142.
Buoys.
Damaging or removing,
§9-12-62.
Fishing reef ship commission,
§9-12-142.
Markers.
Damaging or removing,
§9-12-62.
Natural oyster reefs,
§§9-12-23 to 9-12-25.
Oyster reefs, §§9-12-20 to
9-12-44.
See MARINE
RESOURCES.
Private reefs, §9-12-32.

REFEREES.
Circuit courts.
See CIRCUIT COURTS.
District courts.
See DISTRICT COURTS.
Masters, ARCP, Rule 53 (a) to
(e).
Minors.
Custody and support.
Expedited process for child
support.
Appointment of referees,
ARJA, Rule 35.
Hearings before referees,
ARJA, Rule 35.

REFERENDUM.
Alcoholic beverages.
Elections as to sale and
distribution.
See ALCOHOLIC
BEVERAGES.
Catfish.
Promotion of industry.
Assessments.
Referendum on
imposition of
assessment,
§§2-8-272 to 2-8-280
Cotton.
Promotion of cotton products
Referendum to levy
assessment, §§2-8-193
to 2-8-200.
See COTTON.
Elections generally.
See ELECTIONS.
Forests and forestry.
Fires and fire prevention.
Assessments for forest fire
protection.
State assessment,
§§9-13-193 to
9-13-195.
Housing projects.
Alienation of certain public
improvements by
political subdivisions of
state, §§35-4-410 to
35-4-412.
Municipal corporations.
Commission form of
government.
Optional form A.
Adoption of ordinances
by initiative and
referendum,
§11-44-105.
Parks and recreation.
Alienation of certain public
improvements by
political subdivisions of
state, §§35-4-410 to
35-4-412.
Voting machines.
Referendum on adoption,
§17-9-3.

REFORMATION OF DEEDS,
MORTGAGES AND
CONVEYANCES,
§§35-4-150 to 35-4-153.
See CONVEYANCES.

REFORMATORIES.
Education.
Supervision of educational
work, §16-3-20.

REFORM, MUNICIPALITY
OF.
Property tax, Const. Ala.,
amd. 8.

REFRIGERATORS.
Creating hazards,
§13A-11-220.
Licenses.
Dealers, §40-12-97.

REFUSE, §§22-27-1 to 22-27-27
See GARBAGE AND TRASH.

REGIONAL RECIPROCAL
SAVINGS INSTITUTIONS
§§5-14A-1 to 5-14A-8.
See SAVINGS AND LOAN
ASSOCIATIONS.

REGISTERED MAIL.
Service of process.
Deposit of money for postage
and registration, §6-4-22.
Notice, etc., required to be
served by registered mail
may be served by
certified mail, §1-3-7.

REGISTERED NURSES.
See NURSES.

REGISTERS.
Circuit court registers,
§§12-17-110 to 12-17-147.
See CIRCUIT COURTS.
Fiduciary funds in hands of
officials, §§19-3-80 to
19-3-85.
See FIDUCIARIES.
Financial systems for
receipt, deposit and
disbursement of funds.
Assistance in development,
ARJA, Rule 28.
General provisions,
§§12-17-110 to 12-17-147.
See CIRCUIT COURTS.
Summary proceedings
involving officials.
General provisions,
§§6-6-700, 6-6-723.
Trusts and trustees.
Fiduciary funds in hands of
officials, §§19-3-80 to
19-3-87.
See FIDUCIARIES.

REGISTRARS.
Elections, §§17-4-120 to
17-4-160.
See ELECTIONS.

REGISTRATION.
Accountants, §§34-1-5 to
34-1-15.
See ACCOUNTANTS.
Architects, §§34-2-32 to
34-2-35.
Beauty shops.
Certificates of registration,
§§34-7-3 to 34-7-21.
See COSMETOLOGISTS.
General provisions, §§34-7-5
to 34-7-12.
See COSMETOLOGISTS.
Births.
Districts.
Registration districts,
§22-9-4.
State board of health,
§22-9-2.
Boats.
Numbering, §§33-5-9 to
33-5-19.
See BOATS.
Registration of vessels,
§§33-5-11 to 33-5-17.
See BOATS.
Brake fluid.
Sale or distribution, §8-17-2.
Prohibited if unregistered,
§8-17-5.
Brands.
Livestock brands, §§2-15-20
to 2-15-30.
See LIVESTOCK.
Chiropractors.
See PHYSICIANS.
Commercial feeds.
See FEEDS.

REGISTRATION—Cont'd
Commercial weighing and
measuring technicians,
§§8-16-120 to 8-16-123.
Constitution of the United
States.
Full faith and credit clause,
Const. U. S., Art. IV, §1.
Cosmetologists.
Certificates of registration,
§§34-7-3 to 34-7-21.
See COSMETOLOGISTS.
General provisions, §§34-7-5
to 34-7-12.
See COSMETOLOGISTS.
Cosmetology.
Schools of cosmetology.
General provisions.
See COSMETOLOGISTS.
Instructors, §§34-7-1,
34-7-4, 34-7-11.
Cotton buyers, §§2-19-100 to
2-19-106.
See COTTON.
Counties.
Bond issues, §11-81-9.
Claims and demands against
counties, §§11-12-4,
11-12-5, 11-12-9.
Death.
State board of health,
§22-9-2.
Dentists, §§34-9-13 to 34-9-16,
34-9-22.
Drugs.
Controlled substances.
Manufacturers and
distributors, §§20-2-50
to 20-2-58.
See DRUGS.
Education.
Private schools, §16-1-11.
Elections, §§17-4-120 to
17-4-215.
See ELECTIONS.
Engineers.
Board of registration,
§§34-11-30 to 34-11-37.
See ENGINEERS.
Examinations, §§34-11-4,
34-11-6.
General provisions, §§34-11-1
to 34-11-15.
See ENGINEERS.
Evidence.
Copies.
When certified copy good
secondary evidence,
§12-21-107.
Official entry on paper as
evidence of registry,
§12-21-106.
Feeds.
See FEEDS.
Felons, §§13A-11-180 to
13A-11-186.
See FELONIES.
Foresters.
Board of registration,
§§34-12-30 to 34-12-37.
See FORESTS AND
FORESTRY.
Full faith and credit clause,
Const. U. S., Art. IV, §1.
Funeral directors.
See FUNERALS.
Ginseng.
Dealers, growers and
collectors, §9-13-243.

REGISTRATION—Cont'd
Healing arts.
Certificates of registration.
General provisions,
§§34-24-337 to
34-24-340.
Revocation, §§34-24-360 to
34-24-367.
See PHYSICIANS.
Suspension, §§34-24-360 to
34-24-367.
See PHYSICIANS.
Health studio services.
Salespersons, §8-23-3.
Honeybees and apiaries,
§2-14-3.
See HONEYBEES AND
APIARIES.
Insurance, §27-29-4.
See INSURANCE.
Interior designers,
§§34-15A-2, 34-15A-3,
34-15A-6.
Investment securities,
§§7-8-101 to 7-8-406.
See COMMERCIAL CODE.
Judgments, §§6-9-210 to
6-9-212.
Recordation.
General provisions.
See JUDGMENTS.
Land surveyors.
Board of registration,
§§34-11-30 to 34-11-37.
See SURVEYS AND
SURVEYORS.
Examinations, §§34-11-4,
34-11-6.
General provisions, §§34-11-1
to 34-11-15.
See SURVEYS AND
SURVEYORS.
Libraries.
Registration records,
§§41-8-9, 41-8-10.
Livestock.
Brands, §§2-15-20 to 2-15-30.
See LIVESTOCK.
Meat and meat products.
Persons, firms, etc., buying,
selling, etc., dead, dying,
diseased, etc., livestock,
§2-17-7.
Medical technicians,
§§34-18-20 to 34-18-25.
See MEDICAL
TECHNICIANS.
Morticians.
See FUNERALS.
Motor vehicle carriers,
§37-3-32.
Motor vehicles.
See MOTOR VEHICLES.
Municipal corporations.
Bond issues, §11-81-9.
Nurseries.
Insect and disease control.
Registration of agents or
salesmen, §2-25-7.
Partnerships.
Foreign limited partnerships.
See PARTNERSHIPS.
Pesticides.
Generally, §2-27-9.
Physical therapists,
§§34-24-210 to 34-24-217.
See PHYSICAL
THERAPISTS.

REGISTRATION—Cont'd
Physicians.
　Certificates of registration.
　　General provisions,
　　　§§34-24-337 to
　　　34-24-340.
　　Revocation, §§34-24-360 to
　　　34-24-367.
　　See PHYSICIANS.
　　Suspension, §§34-24-360 to
　　　34-24-367.
　　See PHYSICIANS.
Plumbing.
　Apprentice plumbers or gas
　　fitters.
　　Applicants for registration
　　　certificate, §34-37-6.
Polygraph examiners,
　§§34-25-20 to 34-25-36.
　See POLYGRAPH
　　EXAMINERS.
Poultry.
　Persons, firms, etc., buying,
　　selling, etc., dead, dying,
　　diseased, etc., poultry,
　　§2-17-7.
Real property.
　See RECORDATION.
Recordation.
　See RECORDATION.
Sanitarians.
　See SANITARIANS.
Securities.
　General provisions.
　　See SECURITIES.
　Investment securities.
　　Commercial code,
　　　§§7-8-401 to 7-8-406.
　　See COMMERCIAL
　　　CODE.
Seeds.
　Symbol of seeds or plant
　　parts, §§2-26-50 to
　　2-26-52.
Sexual offenders,
　§§13A-11-200 to
　13A-11-203.
Ships and shipping.
　Registration of vessels,
　　§§33-5-10 to 33-5-16.
　See SHIPS AND
　　SHIPPING.
Soil classifiers, §§34-32-9 to
　34-32-12, 34-32-17.
Surveyors.
　Board of registration,
　　§§34-11-30 to 34-11-37.
　See SURVEYS AND
　　SURVEYORS.
　Examinations, §§34-11-4,
　　34-11-6.
　General provisions, §§34-11-1
　　to 34-11-15.
　See SURVEYS AND
　　SURVEYORS.
Vacation time-sharing plans,
　§§34-27-62 to 34-27-68.
　See VACATION TIME-
　　SHARING PLANS.
Vital statistics.
　See VITAL STATISTICS.
Weights and measures.
　Commercial weighing and
　　measuring technicians,
　　§§8-16-120 to 8-16-123.

REHABILITATION.
Handicapped persons.
　See HANDICAPPED
　　PERSONS.

REHABILITATION—Cont'd
Physical therapists.
　See PHYSICAL
　　THERAPISTS.
**Rehabilitation and crippled
　children's service,**
　§§16-38-1 to 16-38-9.
　See HANDICAPPED
　　PERSONS.

RELATIVES.
Adoption.
　Procedure for adoption by
　　relatives, §26-10-7.
Intestate succession.
　General provisions, §§43-8-40
　　to 43-8-58.
　See WILLS.
　Letters of administration,
　　§§43-2-40 to 43-2-48.
　See EXECUTORS AND
　　ADMINISTRATORS.
Marriage.
　Incestuous marriages.
　　Illegitimacy.
　　　Issue not deemed
　　　　illegitimate, §30-1-3.
　　Solemnization of marriage.
　　　Parties within prohibited
　　　　degrees.
　　　　Penalty, §30-1-6.
Parent and child.
　See PARENT AND CHILD.
Partition.
　Sale of land of minors and
　　insane persons for
　　distribution among joint
　　owners.
　　Contest by next of kin,
　　　§35-6-84.
Trusts and trustees.
　Support and maintenance of
　　relatives.
　　Express trust for support
　　　and maintenance,
　　　§19-3-1.

RELEASES.
Compromise and settlement.
　Pro tanto settlements.
　　Effect of releases entered,
　　　§12-21-109.
Consideration.
　Required, §8-1-23.
Contracts.
　Consideration.
　　Required, §8-1-23.
　Written release.
　　No consideration required,
　　　§8-1-23.
Evidence, §12-21-109.
Pro tanto settlements.
　Effect of release entered,
　　§12-21-109.
Written release.
　No consideration required,
　　§8-1-23.
　Pro tanto release.
　　Effect of release entered,
　　　§12-21-109.

RELIEF.
Counties.
　Relief and support of poor
　　persons.
　　See INDIGENT PERSONS.
General provisions, §§38-1-1
　to 38-8-3.
　See WELFARE.

RELIGION.
Alcoholic beverages.
　Dry counties.
　　Wine for sacramental or
　　　religious purposes,
　　　§§28-4-180 to 28-4-184.
　Wet counties.
　　Acquisition, etc., of wine
　　　for sacramental or
　　　religious purposes by
　　　ministers, pastors, etc.,
　　　§28-3-15.
Bishop of diocese, §§10-4-1 to
　10-4-9.
　See BISHOP OF DIOCESE.
Child care facilities.
　Exceptions to provisions,
　　§38-7-3.
Church buses.
　Approaching church bus or
　　vehicle, §32-5A-154.
　Signal lights, §32-5A-155.
　Stopping when approaching
　　church bus, §32-5A-154.
Corporations.
　Bishop of diocese, §§10-4-1 to
　　10-4-9.
　See BISHOP OF
　　DIOCESE.
　Nonprofit corporations.
　　See CORPORATIONS.
　Religious societies.
　　See CORPORATIONS.
Criminal law and procedure.
　Desecration of venerated
　　objects, §13A-11-12.
　Endangering welfare of child
　　Remedial treatment by
　　　spiritual means,
　　　§13A-13-6.
**Desecration of venerated
　objects,** §13A-11-12.
Drug abuse education.
　Religious objection.
　　Exemption of child by
　　　parents, §16-41-6.
Education.
　Church-related schools.
　　See CHURCHES.
　Drug abuse education.
　　Religious objection.
　　　Exemption of child by
　　　　parents, §16-41-6.
　Parochial schools.
　　See CHURCHES.
Freedom of religion, Const.
　Ala., art. I, §3.
Income tax.
　Corporations.
　　Deductions allowed
　　　corporations.
　　　Contributions or gifts
　　　　made to religious
　　　　institutions,
　　　　§40-18-35.
　Deductions.
　　Contributions or gifts made
　　　to religious
　　　institutions, §40-18-15.
Military affairs.
　Persons exempted from
　　military service.
　　Holding of religious beliefs,
　　　§31-2-6.
Minors.
　Remedial treatment by
　　spiritual means.
　　Not crime of endangering
　　　welfare of child,
　　　§13A-13-6.

RELIGION—Cont'd
Nonprofit corporations.
See CORPORATIONS.
Nurses.
Applicability of chapter.
Certain religious healing
and care exempt,
§34-21-6.
Parochial schools.
See CHURCHES.
Physicians.
Domestic remedies exempt
from provisions of
chapter, §34-24-55.
**Public officers and
employees.**
Merit system.
Granting of time off to
comply with religious
obligations, §36-26-34.
Recordation.
Taxation.
Exempt transactions,
§40-22-5.1.
Religious tests.
Constitution of the United
States, Const. U. S., Art.
VI.
Sacramental wine.
Dry counties, §§28-4-180 to
28-4-184.
Schools.
Parochial schools.
See CHURCHES.
Taxation.
Property of religious
organizations exempt,
§40-9-1.
Use tax.
Exemptions.
Religious magazines and
publications,
§40-23-62.
Use tax.
Exemptions.
Storage, use or
consumption of
religious magazines
and publications,
§40-23-62.
Wine.
Dry counties.
Wine for sacramental or
religious purposes,
§§28-4-180 to 28-4-184.
Wet counties.
Acquisition, etc., of wine
for sacramental or
religious purposes,
§28-3-15.

RELOCATION ASSISTANCE.
**Conservation and natural
resources.**
Department.
Compliance with uniform
relocation assistance
and land acquisition
policies act, §9-2-27.
Highways, §§23-1-210 to
23-1-212.
Municipal corporations,
§11-80-2.

**REMAINDERS, REVERSIONS
AND EXECUTORY
INTERESTS,** §§35-4-210 to
35-4-213.
Actions.
Rights of remainderman or
reversioner of personalty,
§6-5-264.

**REMAINDERS, REVERSIONS
AND EXECUTORY
INTERESTS**—Cont'd
Acts of life tenants.
Remainders not defeated by
acts of life tenants,
§35-4-170.
Contingent remainders.
Defined, §35-4-211.
Generally, §35-4-211.
In lands.
Contingent remainder in
lands equivalent to
executory devise,
§35-4-212.
Creditors of life tenants.
Recordation necessary as to
creditors, §35-4-91.
Death without heirs or issue.
Remainder limited after
death without heirs or
issue.
Construction of words
"heirs" or "issue,"
§35-4-213.
Definitions, §§35-4-210,
35-4-211.
Heirs.
Limited to heirs, issue or
heirs of the body of
person to whom life
estate in same property
is given.
Entitlement to take as
purchasers upon
termination of life
estate, §35-4-230.
Remainder limited after
death without heirs or
issue.
Construction of words
"heirs" or "issue,"
§35-4-213.
Issue.
Limited to heirs, issue or
heirs of the body of
person to whom life
estate in same property
is given.
Entitlement to take as
purchasers upon
termination of life
estate, §35-4-230.
Remainder limited after
death without heirs or
issue.
Construction of words
"heirs" or "issue,"
§35-4-213.
Life tenants.
Recordation necessary,
§35-4-91.
Remainders not defeated by
acts of life tenants,
§35-4-170.
**Limited to heirs, issue or
heirs of the body of
person to whom life
estate in same property
is given.**
Entitled to take as
purchasers upon
termination of life
estates, §35-4-230.
Military affairs.
Reversion of donations for
national guard or naval
militia, §31-4-18.

**REMAINDERS, REVERSIONS
AND EXECUTORY
INTERESTS**—Cont'd
Partition.
Freehold devised with
contingent interest,
§19-3-170.
Personal property.
Actions.
Rights of remainderman or
reversioner, §6-5-264.
Loans in writing, wills or
conveyances creating
estates in personal
property on condition,
etc.
Recordation necessary as to
purchasers,
mortgagees and
judgment creditors,
§35-4-94.
Removal of personalty by life
tenant.
Consent of remainderman
or reversioner
required, §35-4-171.
Principal and income,
§§19-3-270 to 19-3-282.
See TRUSTS AND
TRUSTEES.
Recordation.
Creditors of life tenants.
Recordation necessary,
§35-4-91.
Rights of reversioner.
Defined, §35-4-210.
Rule against perpetuities,
§§35-4-4, 35-4-5.
Rule in Shelley's case.
Abolished, §35-4-230.
Trees and timber.
Conveyances of standing
timber.
Reversion of title to uncut
timber, §35-4-362.
Vested remainders.
Defined, §35-4-211.
Generally, §35-4-211.
**Warranties by tenant for
life,** §35-4-270.

REMEDIES, §§6-6-1 to 6-6-757.
Actions.
See ACTIONS.
Arbitration and award,
§§6-6-1 to 6-6-16.
See ARBITRATION AND
AWARD.
Attachment, §§6-6-30 to
6-6-149.
See ATTACHMENTS.
Barred rights or remedies.
Revival, Const. Ala., art. IV,
§95.
Bond issues.
County obligations.
Validation, §§6-6-750 to
6-6-757.
See COUNTIES.
Municipal corporations.
Validation of city
obligations, §§6-6-750
to 6-6-757, 11-81-220
to 11-81-227.
See MUNICIPAL
CORPORATIONS.
Claim and delivery.
Trial of right of property,
§§6-6-160 to 6-6-168.
See PERSONAL
PROPERTY.

REMEDIES—Cont'd
Code of Alabama.
Existing remedies preserved,
§1-1-9.
Commercial code.
Defined, §7-1-201.
Liberal administration of
remedies, §7-1-106.
Performance or acceptance
under reservation of
rights, §7-1-207.
Sales, §§7-2-701 to 7-2-725.
See COMMERCIAL CODE.
Constitution of Alabama.
Remedies for all injuries,
Const. Ala., art. I, §13.
Contracts.
Commercial code.
See COMMERCIAL CODE.
General provisions.
See CONTRACTS.
Corporations.
Dissolution.
Survival of remedy after
dissolution,
§10-2A-203.
Counties.
Validation of county
obligations, §§6-6-750 to
6-6-757.
See COUNTIES.
Creditor's actions, §§6-6-180
to 6-6-204.
See DEBTORS AND
CREDITORS.
Debtors and creditors.
Creditor's actions, §§6-6-180
to 6-6-204.
See DEBTORS AND
CREDITORS.
Declaratory judgments,
§§6-6-220 to 6-6-232.
See DECLARATORY
JUDGMENTS.
Detinue, §§6-6-250 to 6-6-264.
See DETINUE.
Ejectment, §§6-6-280 to
6-6-298.
See EJECTMENT.
Farm equipment.
Repurchase of inventory from
farm equipment
retailers, §8-21-13.
Forcible entry and unlawful
detainer, §§6-6-310 to
6-6-353.
See FORCIBLE ENTRY
AND UNLAWFUL
DETAINER.
Fraud.
Charitable fraud.
Enforcement of provisions
by injunction,
mandamus, etc.,
§13A-9-76.
Fraudulent transfers.
Creditors' remedies, §8-9A-7.
Garnishment, §§6-6-370 to
6-6-484.
See GARNISHMENT.
Health care authorities.
Lease agreements.
Default, §22-21-331.
Injunctions, §§6-6-500 to
6-6-503.
Landlord and tenant.
General provisions, §§35-9-9,
35-9-10, 35-9-100.

REMEDIES—Cont'd
Landlord and tenant—Cont'd
Liens of landlord, §§35-9-30
to 35-9-65.
See LANDLORD AND
TENANT.
Long term quality health
care.
Enforcement of act, §22-6-25.
Municipal corporations.
Validation of city obligations,
§§6-6-750 to 6-6-757,
11-81-220 to 11-81-227.
See MUNICIPAL
CORPORATIONS.
Partition.
Crops.
Remedies not exclusive,
§35-6-126.
Personal property.
Trial of right of property,
§§6-6-160 to 6-6-168.
See PERSONAL
PROPERTY.
Public officers and
employees.
Summary proceedings
involving officials,
§§6-6-660 to 6-6-740.
See PUBLIC OFFICERS
AND EMPLOYEES.
Quieting title.
General provisions, §§6-6-540
to 6-6-573.
See QUIETING TITLE.
In personam proceedings,
§§6-6-540 to 6-6-546.
See QUIETING TITLE.
In rem proceedings,
§§6-6-560 to 6-6-573.
See QUIETING TITLE.
Quo warranto, §§6-6-590 to
6-6-604.
See QUO WARRANTO.
Receivers, §§6-6-620 to
6-6-628.
See RECEIVERS.
Reformation.
Deeds, mortgages and
conveyances, §§35-4-150
to 35-4-153.
Replevin, §§6-6-100 to 6-6-102.
Revival of barred rights or
remedies, Const. Ala., art.
IV, §95.
Sales.
Commercial code, §§7-2-701
to 7-2-725.
See COMMERCIAL CODE.
Salvage.
Owner.
Remedy of owner when
taker refuses to deliver
property, §35-13-8.
Specific performance.
General provisions.
See CONTRACTS.
Summary proceedings
involving officials,
§§6-6-660 to 6-6-740.
See PUBLIC OFFICERS
AND EMPLOYEES.
Taxation.
Sale of land for taxes,
§§40-10-1 to 40-10-166.
See TAXATION.
Title.
Quieting title.
General provisions,
§§6-6-540 to 6-6-573.
See QUIETING TITLE.

REMEDIES—Cont'd
Title—Cont'd
Quieting title—Cont'd
In personam proceedings,
§§6-6-540 to 6-6-546.
See QUIETING TITLE.
In rem proceedings,
§§6-6-560 to 6-6-573.
See QUIETING TITLE.
Trademarks and service
marks.
Registration of, §8-12-18.
Trade secrets.
Misappropriation.
Actual or threatened
misappropriation of
trade secrets, §8-27-4.
Trial of right of property,
§§6-6-160 to 6-6-168.
See PERSONAL
PROPERTY.
Uniform commercial code.
Defined, §7-1-201.
Liberal administration of
remedies, §7-1-106.
Performance or acceptance
under reservation of
rights, §7-1-207.
Sales, §§7-2-701 to 7-2-725.
See COMMERCIAL CODE.
Unlawful detainer, §§6-6-310
to 6-6-353.
See FORCIBLE ENTRY
AND UNLAWFUL
DETAINER.
Waste.
Intemperates and inebriates,
§§6-6-520 to 6-6-527.
See WASTE.
Water management and
drainage.
Exclusive remedies, §9-9-58.
Writs.
Remedial writs, §§6-6-640 to
6-6-642.

REMITTITUR.
Rules of civil procedure,
ARCP, Rule 59 (f).

REMOVAL OF ACTIONS.
Change of venue.
Civil actions, §§6-3-20 to
6-3-22.
Constitution of Alabama,
Const. Ala., art. I, §6;
art. IV, §75.
Criminal law and procedure,
§§15-2-20 to 15-2-27.
See VENUE.
Probate courts, §12-13-10.
Special, private or local laws
prohibited, Const. Ala.,
art. IV, §104.
Probate courts.
Removal of estate
administration from
probate court, §12-11-41.

REMOVAL OF CRIME
VICTIMS.
Trial.
Removal or exclusion of
crime victims, §15-14-54.

RENAISSANCE FAIRE.
State renaissance faire.
Designation, §1-2-21.

RENT.
Alcoholic beverages.
Dry counties.
Renting or permitting use
of premises for sale,
manufacture, etc.,
§§28-4-90 to 28-4-93.
**Appliances, machinery and
equipment used for land
clearing or
improvements.**
Liens, §§35-11-430,
35-11-431.
Contracts.
Hirings, §§8-1-60 to 8-1-63.
Convicts.
Renting out convicts.
County convicts, §§14-5-2,
14-5-4, 14-5-5.
General provisions,
§14-5-2.
Penalties, §14-5-4.
State agencies, §14-5-10.
**Fraudulent leasing or rental
of property,** §§13A-8-140
to 13A-8-144.
Hirings.
Contracts, §§8-1-60 to 8-1-63.
Landlord and tenant.
Buildings.
Liens for rent of buildings,
§§35-9-60 to 35-9-65.
See LANDLORD AND
TENANT.
Conveyance of property.
Payment of rent without
notice of conveyance,
§35-4-32.
Liens for advances and rent
of lands, §§35-9-30 to
35-9-42.
See LANDLORD AND
TENANT.
Life tenants.
Death of life tenant.
Recovery of rent.
Demised estate,
§35-9-13.
Rent of lands.
Liens for advances and
rent of lands,
§§35-9-30 to 35-9-42.
See LANDLORD AND
TENANT.
Leases.
General provisions.
See LEASES.
Personal property.
Leasing or renting,
§§40-12-220 to
40-12-227.
See PERSONAL
PROPERTY.
Licenses.
Leasing or renting tangible
personal property,
§§40-12-220 to 40-12-227.
See PERSONAL
PROPERTY.
Limitation of actions.
Recovery of arrears of rent
due upon parol demise,
§6-2-34.
Motor vehicles.
Renting and hiring.
General provisions,
§§32-7-36, 32-15-1 to
32-15-8.
See MOTOR VEHICLES.

RENT—Cont'd
Motor vehicles—Cont'd
Renting and hiring—Cont'd
Licenses to lease or rent
tangible personal
property, §§40-12-220
to 40-12-227.
See PERSONAL
PROPERTY.
Personal property.
Leasing or renting,
§§40-12-220 to 40-12-227.
See PERSONAL
PROPERTY.
Licenses, §§40-12-220 to
40-12-227.
See PERSONAL
PROPERTY.
Prisons and prisoners.
Renting out convicts.
County convicts, §§14-5-2,
14-5-4, 14-5-5.
General provisions,
§14-5-2.
Penalties, §14-5-4.
State agencies, §14-5-10.
**Public officers and
employees.**
Rental of offices for state
officers, §§36-24-1 to
36-24-4.
Sales tax.
Personal property.
Leasing or renting,
§§40-12-220 to
40-12-227.
See PERSONAL
PROPERTY.
State officers.
Rental of offices, §§36-24-1 to
36-24-4.
Taxation.
Personal property.
Leasing or renting,
§§40-12-220 to
40-12-227.
See PERSONAL
PROPERTY.
Theft.
Fraudulent leasing or rental
of property, §§13A-8-140
to 13A-8-144.

**RENTAL-PURCHASE
AGREEMENTS.**
Advertisements.
Required provisions, §8-25-5.
Definitions, §8-25-1.
**Disclosures by merchant to
consumer,** §8-25-2.
Form, §8-25-2.
Inaccuracy due to acts, etc.,
after delivery, §8-25-2.
**Inaccuracy due to acts, etc.,
after delivery,** §8-25-2.
Prohibited provisions,
§8-25-3.
Reinstatement.
After failure to make time
payment, §8-25-4.
Time payments.
Failure to make.
Reinstatement of
agreement, §8-25-4.
Violations of chapter.
Damages and fees
recoverable, §8-25-6.
Merchant discovers error,
gives notice and makes
adjustments.
Nonliability, §8-25-6.

RENTAL VEHICLES,
§§32-7-36, 32-15-1 to 32-15-8.
See MOTOR VEHICLES.

REPLEVIN.
Alcoholic beverages.
Dry counties.
Contraband.
Beverages seized not to
be recovered by writ
of replevin during
pendency of
proceedings under
article, §28-4-265.
Bonds, surety.
Collateral security.
Seizure of property if not
given, §8-3-30.
Disposition of seized
perishable property,
§8-3-30.
When surety on replevy
bond may demand
collateral security,
§8-3-30.
Execution of bond, §§6-6-100,
6-6-101.
Forfeiture, §6-6-101.
Commercial code.
Sales.
Buyer's right to replevin,
§7-2-716.
Defendant in attachment.
Right to replevy property,
§6-6-100.
Limitation of actions.
Actions against surety to any
replevy bond executed in
courts of the United
States or other state.
Four year limitation,
§6-2-36.
Tender of value.
Property dead or destroyed,
§6-6-102.
Who may replevy property,
§6-6-100.

**REPORTER OF DECISIONS
OF SUPREME COURT
AND COURTS OF
APPEALS.**
Creation of office, §12-4-1.
Election, §12-4-1.
Records, §12-4-4.
Removal, §12-4-1.
Salary, §12-4-2.
Stenographer for reporter,
§12-4-3.

REPORTERS.
Newspapers generally.
See NEWSPAPERS.
Witnesses.
Exemption from disclosing
sources, §12-21-142.

REPORTS.
Abandoned property.
Uniform disposition of
unclaimed property act.
Report of abandoned
property, §35-12-31.
Penalty for failure to
render, §35-12-45.
Abortion.
Reports to bureau of vital
statistics.
Information required to be
furnished, §26-21-8.
Accountants, §34-1-21.

REPORTS—Cont'd
Accounts and accounting.
Department of examiners of
public accounts.
Audits, §41-5-21.
Adoption.
Probate judges, §12-13-44.
Violations of chapter,
§26-10-9.
Aged persons.
Commission on the aging.
Duty to give to legislature,
§38-3-2.
Agriculture.
See AGRICULTURE.
Air pollution.
Availability of reports,
§22-28-20.
**Alabama Agricultural and
Mechanical University.**
Reports to legislature,
§16-49-30.
Alabama Law Institute.
Distribution, §29-8-5.
Alabama State University.
Board of trustees.
Reports to legislature,
§16-50-30.
Alcoholic beverages.
See ALCOHOLIC
BEVERAGES.
Art commission.
Annual report to governor,
§41-9-23.
Atomic energy.
Radiation, §22-14-8.
Auburn University.
Board of trustees.
Reports to legislature,
§16-48-11.
Aviation.
Aeronautics commission.
Annual report to governor,
§4-2-31.
Hearings, §4-2-49.
**Banks and financial
institutions.**
General provisions.
See BANKS AND
FINANCIAL
INSTITUTIONS.
Superintendent of banks,
§§5-2A-12 to 5-2A-14.
**Bear Creek development
authority.**
Annual reports of directors,
§33-15-15.
Beautification board,
§41-9-497.
Boards and commissions.
Printing, §41-4-141.
Time for making, §41-4-141.
Boats.
Accident reports, §33-5-25.
Bureaus.
Printing, §41-4-141.
Time for making, §41-4-141.
Cancer.
Physicians, §22-13-10.
Canons of judicial ethics.
Financial interests.
Judge to regularly file
reports of financial
interests, ACJE,
Canon 6C.
Child abuse or neglect,
§§26-14-1 to 26-14-13.
See MINORS.
Child labor, §§25-8-20,
25-8-23.

REPORTS—Cont'd
Child support programs.
Parents to report financial
status.
Violations, §38-10-9.
Circuit courts.
Clerks of court.
Monthly reports as to
fines, fees, etc.,
collected, §12-1-19.
Coal.
Blasting and explosives.
Premature explosions,
§25-9-137.
Mine safety.
See COAL.
Severance tax of 1971,
§§40-13-3 to 40-13-7.
Surface mining control and
reclamation.
Sales of coal, §9-16-102.
**Commission on uniform
state laws.**
Reports to legislature,
§41-9-373.
**Conservation and natural
resources.**
Department.
Annual report to governor,
§9-2-2.
Constitution of Alabama.
Banks and financial
institutions.
Semiannual reports, Const.
Ala., art. XIII, §254.
Failure to file.
Impeachable offense,
Const. Ala., art. V,
§121.
Governor.
Governor may require from
officers of executive
department and
officers and managers
of state institutions,
Const. Ala., art. V,
§121.
Reports and information to
be given legislature,
Const. Ala., art. V,
§123.
**Continuing women's
commission.**
Reports to legislature and
governor, §41-9-414.
Contractors.
State licensing board.
Annual report, §34-8-26.
Copies.
Reduction of number of
printed copies, §36-1-3.
Copyright.
Duty of governor, §36-13-5.
Corporations.
Franchise tax.
See CORPORATIONS.
General provisions.
See CORPORATIONS.
Corrections.
Board of corrections.
Annual report to governor,
§14-1-13.
Transmission of reports to
legislature, §14-3-11.
Inmate community
reintegration under SIR
act.
Annual report required,
§15-18-119.

REPORTS—Cont'd
Cotton.
Boll weevil eradication.
Reports of cotton growers
required, §2-19-124.
Counties.
Cemeteries, §§11-17-3,
11-17-4.
Depositories, §11-4-45.
Semiannual publication of
county receipts and
expenditures, §§11-3-21
to 11-3-23.
Treasurers, §11-4-23.
Proceedings upon
resignation, removal,
death, etc., of
treasurer, §11-4-29.
Credit cards.
False reporting of lost, stolen
or mislaid credit cards,
§13A-9-15.
Credit unions, §§5-17-8,
5-17-48.
Crime victims compensation.
Annual report of commission
required, §15-23-6.
Criminal law and procedure.
Criminal justice advisory
commission, §41-9-573.
Failing to file required
reports, §13A-10-4.
Falsely reporting incidents,
§13A-11-11.
False reporting to law
enforcement authorities,
§13A-10-9.
Unsworn falsification to
authorities, §13A-10-109.
**Crippled and disabled
children.**
Disposition of reports,
§21-3-8.
Forms for reporting
malformations and
disabilities, §21-3-8.
Physical examination of
children having
malformations or
disabilities.
Report of findings, §21-3-6.
Crops.
Partition, §§35-6-117 to
35-6-120.
Dental service corporations.
Annual report to
commissioner,
§22-21-373.
**Department of examiners of
public accounts.**
Legislative committee on
public accounts,
§41-5-20.
Diagnostic evaluation.
Disclosure of report, ARCrP,
Rule 5.
Pronouncement of judgment
or sentence, ARCrP,
Rule 4.
Diseases.
Notifiable diseases,
§§22-11A-1 to 22-11A-38.
See DISEASES.
District courts.
Clerks of court.
Monthly reports as to
fines, fees, etc.,
§12-1-19.
Domestic violence facilities.
District attorneys.
Reports to office, §30-6-5.

REPORTS—Cont'd
Domestic violence facilities
—Cont'd
Office of prosecution services.
Reports to legislature,
§30-6-5.
Drugs.
Therapeutic research.
Annual reports to governor
and legislature,
§20-2-118.
Education.
See EDUCATION.
Elections.
Fair campaign practices.
Candidates, committees
and officials to report
contributions and
expenditures,
§§17-22A-8 to
17-22A-10.
**Elk river development
agency.**
Annual reports by directors
to governor, §33-12-7.
Eminent domain.
Commissioners.
Assessments, §18-1A-282.
Enterprise zones.
Department of economic and
community affairs.
Annual report, §41-23-27.
**Environmental improvement
authorities,** §9-6-16.
Estate and inheritance tax.
Appraisement upon failure to
make reports, §40-15-10.
**Executors and
administrators.**
See EXECUTORS AND
ADMINISTRATORS.
**Exemptions from
administration and
payment of debts.**
Appraisers, §§6-10-80 to
6-10-93.
See EXEMPTIONS FROM
ADMINISTRATION
AND PAYMENT OF
DEBTS.
Felonies.
Presentence investigation.
Written reports of
investigation required
by court, §13A-5-5.
Fertilizer, §§2-22-9, 2-22-10.
Finance.
State funds.
Linked deposits.
Annual report by
treasurer, §5-21-10.
Finance companies.
Small loans.
Annual report, §5-18-11.
Public access to reports,
§5-18-23.
Fire marshal, §§36-19-24,
36-19-26, 36-19-43.
Fish and game.
See FISH AND GAME.
**Foreign trade and relations
commission.**
Annual report to governor or
legislature, §41-9-662.
Forests and forestry.
See FORESTS AND
FORESTRY.
Fraternal benefit societies.
Annual statements,
§27-34-36.
Failure to file, §27-34-38.

REPORTS—Cont'd
Fraternal benefit societies
—Cont'd
Publication of report of
examinations, §27-34-41.
Requirements, §27-34-36.
Reserves, §27-34-37.
Valuation of certificates,
§27-34-37.
Fruits and vegetables.
Promotion of industry.
Annual statement by
treasurer of growers'
organization, §2-8-137.
Funerals, §22-9-77.
Board of funeral service.
Annual report of
apprentices,
§34-13-132.
Annual report to governor
and legislature,
§34-13-28.
Gas.
See GAS.
Gasoline tax, §§40-17-200 to
40-17-203.
Geological survey.
State geologist.
Procedure for publication,
§9-4-10.
Reports to legislature,
§9-4-2.
Special reports, §9-4-2.
Governor.
Copyright, §36-13-5.
Governor may require from
officers of executive
department and
managers of state
institutions, Const. Ala.,
art. V, §121.
Handicapped persons.
Rehabilitation and crippled
children service.
Annual report, §16-38-9.
Legislature.
Governor to give certain
information and
reports to legislature,
Const. Ala., art. V,
§123.
Grain dealers, §2-31-10.
Grand jury.
Impeachment.
Investigations of alleged
misconduct or
incompetency.
Disposition of grand jury
reports, §36-11-3.
Jails.
Inspection of jails.
Furnishing to grand
jury, §14-6-91.
Probate judge to furnish
grand jury report to
board, §14-6-100.
Guardian and ward.
Curators.
Accounts and accounting.
Filing in office of probate
judge, §26-7A-13.
Handicapped persons.
Crippled and disabled
children.
Disposition of reports,
§21-3-8.
Forms for reporting
malformations and
disabilities, §21-3-8.

REPORTS—Cont'd
Handicapped persons
—Cont'd
Crippled and disabled
children—Cont'd
Physical examination of
children having
malformations or
disabilities.
Report of findings,
§21-3-6.
Rehabilitation and crippled
children service.
Annual report to governor
on rehabilitation,
§16-38-9.
Hazardous substances.
Cleanup fund.
Annual reports, §22-30A-7.
Fees for disposal of
hazardous waste or
substances.
Confidentiality,
§22-30B-15.
Failure to make monthly
reports.
Notice of faillure,
§22-30B-8.
False or fraudulent reports.
Penalties, §22-30B-7.
Location of reports,
§22-30B-16.
Oaths, §22-30B-10.
Penalty for failure to
submit monthly
reports, §22-30B-6.
Hazardous waste.
Fees for disposal of
hazardous waste or
substances.
Confidentiality of fee
reports, §22-30B-15.
Failure to make monthly
reports.
Notice, §22-30B-8.
False or fraudulent reports.
Penalties, §22-30B-7.
Location of reports,
§22-30B-16.
Monthly reports to be
sworn, §22-30B-10.
Perjury in making false
or fraudulent
statements,
§22-30B-10.
Penalty for failure to
submit monthly
reports, §22-30B-6.
Generators.
Trade secrets.
When reports deemed
trade secrets,
§22-30-18.
Wastes generated,
§22-30-18.
Trade secrets, §22-30-18.
Transporters, §22-30-18.
Health.
See HEALTH.
**Health maintenance
organizations.**
Annual report, §27-21A-8.
Complaint system,
§27-21A-10.
Public documents,
§27-21A-24.
Highways.
Closing and vacating streets,
alleys and highways.
Commissioners.
Filing, §23-4-3.

REPORTS—Cont'd
Highways—Cont'd
Closing and vacating streets, alleys and highways —Cont'd
Commissioners—Cont'd
Recordation, §23-4-4.
Department.
Annual report to governor, §23-1-35.
Historical preservation authorities.
Reports by authority to governor, §41-10-148.
Hospitals.
Child abuse and neglect, §§26-14-1 to 26-14-13.
See MINORS.
Hotels, inns and other transient lodging places.
Transient occupancy tax.
Failure to make, §40-26-8.
Monthly reports, §40-26-3.
Verification, §40-26-7.
Willful refusal to make, §40-26-9.
Housing authorities.
County housing authorities.
Annual report, §24-1-82.
Municipal housing authorities.
Annual report, §24-1-43.
Impeachment.
Grand juries.
Disposition of reports, §36-11-3.
Income tax.
Information from source of income.
Report to department of revenue, §40-18-26.
Report from source.
Defined, §40-18-1.
Indian affairs commission.
Annual report, §41-9-716.
Industrial alcohol.
Requirements, §28-5-9.
Industrial development corporations.
Annual report, §10-4-147.
Institute for deaf and blind.
Treasurers' reports, §21-1-7.
Insurance.
See INSURANCE.
Iron ore.
Licenses for mining, §§40-12-129, 40-12-130.
Jacksonville State University.
Board of trustees.
Reports to legislature, §16-52-10.
Jails.
See JAILS.
Judges.
Financial interests.
Judge to regularly file reports of financial interests, ACJE, Canon 6C.
Judicial system study commission, §12-9-8.
Junior college for Jackson and DeKalb counties.
Generally, §16-60-67.
Juvenile proceedings, §§12-15-65, 12-15-69; ARJP, Rule 7.

REPORTS—Cont'd
Labor.
Employment in age certificates.
Monthly report to department of industrial relations, §25-8-20.
Labor unions.
Annual report, §25-7-5.
Landscape architects.
Board of examiners.
Annual report to governor, §34-17-3.
Legislative committee on public accounts, §41-5-20.
Legislature.
Governor to give certain reports and information to legislature, Const. Ala., art. V, §123.
Libraries.
Public library service.
Executive board.
Annual report to governor, §41-8-4.
Service to obtain reports from public libraries, §41-8-7.
Lime.
Manufacturers and distributors, §2-23-5.
Liquefied petroleum gas.
Sale and purchase reports to board, §9-17-106.
Livingston University.
Board of trustees.
Reports to legislature, §16-53-10.
Lost or unclaimed property.
Uniform disposition of unclaimed property act.
Report of abandoned property, §35-12-31.
Penalty for failure to render, §35-12-45.
Lubricating oils and greases.
Taxation, §§40-17-200 to 40-17-203.
Malpractice, §§34-24-56, 34-24-57.
Marine resources, §§9-2-4, 9-12-115, 9-12-119.
Masters, ARCP, Rule 53 (e).
Meat and meat products, §§2-17-34, 2-17-35.
Mental health examination.
Disclosure of report, ARCrP, Rule 5.
Pronouncement of judgment or sentence, ARCrP, Rule 4.
Mentally ill, §§15-16-69, 22-50-13.
Midwives.
Death.
Failure of midwife to report death, §22-9-78.
Military affairs, §§31-2-33, 31-2-39, 31-2-67, 31-2-114.
See MILITARY AFFAIRS.
Milk and milk products.
Annual reports of creameries, milk plants, etc., §2-13-15.
Minors.
Child abuse or neglect, §§26-14-1 to 26-14-13.
See MINORS.
Missing persons.
Contents, §26-19-5.

REPORTS—Cont'd
Missing persons—Cont'd
Duties of law enforcement agencies upon receiving, §26-19-7.
Forwarding to other law enforcement agencies, §26-19-6.
Law enforcement agencies to report to bureau, §26-19-5.
Motor fuels.
Diesel fuel tax, §§40-17-8, 40-17-9.
Taxation generally, §§40-17-200 to 40-27-203.
Motor vehicle carriers.
General provisions, §37-3-22.
Mileage tax, §§40-19-4, 40-19-5, 40-19-14.
Motor carrier fuel tax, §§40-17-200 to 40-17-203.
Motor vehicles.
Accident reports, §§32-10-7 to 32-10-12.
See MOTOR VEHICLES.
General provisions.
See MOTOR VEHICLES.
Safety-responsibility act, §§32-7-5, 32-7-12, 32-7-13.
Municipal corporations.
See MUNICIPAL CORPORATIONS.
Municipal courts, §§12-1-19, 12-14-15, 12-14-16.
Neglect.
Child abuse or neglect, §§26-14-1 to 26-14-13.
See MINORS.
Notaries public.
Probate judges.
Commissioning, §36-20-30.
Report to secretary of state, §36-20-1.
Nurses.
Child abuse or neglect, §§26-14-1 to 26-14-13.
See MINORS.
Nuts, bulbs, fruits and vegetables.
Promotion of industry.
Annual statements by treasurer of organization, §2-8-137.
Parks and recreation.
Capital development assistance fund.
Requirements, §9-7A-8.
Parole.
Board of pardons and paroles.
Annual report, §15-22-24.
Board to report on sentenced prisoner's social and criminal records, §15-22-25.
Relief of parolee from reports, §15-22-33.
Partition of crops, §§35-6-117 to 35-6-120.
Partnerships.
Limited partnerships.
Initial report to secretary of state, §10-9A-3.
Peace officers.
Child abuse or neglect, §§26-14-1 to 26-14-13.
See MINORS.

REPORTS—Cont'd
  Peace officers—Cont'd
    False reporting to law
        enforcement authorities,
        §13A-10-9.
  Pesticides.
    Application, §2-27-60.
  Physicians.
    Adult protective services.
      Abuse, neglect and
          exploitation, §§38-9-8
          to 38-9-10.
    Child abuse or neglect,
        §§26-14-1 to 26-14-13.
      See MINORS.
    Malpractice judgments and
        settlements, §§34-24-56,
        34-24-57.
    Rules of civil procedure.
      Physical and mental
          examination of
          persons.
        Report of examining
            physician, ARCP,
            Rule 35 (b).
    Venereal diseases.
      Notifiable diseases,
          §§22-11A-1 to
          22-11A-38.
        See DISEASES.
  Pilots and pilotage, §33-4-57.
  Police.
    Child abuse or neglect,
        §§26-14-1 to 26-14-13.
      See MINORS.
    False reporting to law
        enforcement authorities,
        §13A-10-9.
  Presentence report.
    Disclosure of, ARCrP, Rule 5.
    Generally, ARCrP, Rule 3.
  Printing, §41-4-141.
  Prisons and prisoners.
    Board of corrections,
        §§14-1-13, 14-3-11.
    County convicts.
      Hard labor sentence.
        Probate judge, §14-4-4.
      Probate judge, §§14-4-3,
          14-4-4.
    Mentally ill prisoners.
      Recovery of prisoners,
          §22-52-72.
    Prison-made goods,
        §§14-7-15, 14-7-17.
    Violations of law, §14-3-9.
    Work release.
      Annual report, §14-8-9.
  Probate courts.
    Notaries public.
      Commissioning.
        Report to secretary of
            state, §36-20-1.
  Probation.
    Board to report on sentenced
        prisoner's social and
        criminal records,
        §15-22-25.
    Defendant to report to
        probation authorities
        during term of probation,
        §15-18-8.
  Professional corporations.
    Annual report, §10-4-399.
    Penalties for false
        statements, §10-4-401.
  Public defenders, §15-12-44.

REPORTS—Cont'd
  **Public officers and
      employees.**
    Code of ethics.
      Lobbyists.
        Monthly reports,
            §36-25-19.
        Public records,
            §36-25-21.
        Violations, §36-25-17.
    Copies.
      Reduction of number of
          printed copies, §36-1-3.
    Director of personnel,
        §36-26-40.
    Failure to file required
        reports, §13A-10-4.
    Printing, §41-4-141.
    Time for making, §41-4-141.
  Public service commission,
      §§37-1-57 to 37-1-62,
      37-4-15.
    See PUBLIC SERVICE
        COMMISSION.
  Public utilities.
    General provisions.
      See PUBLIC UTILITIES.
  Public welfare.
    See WELFARE.
  Quarantine.
    Local quarantine.
      Report of local quarantine
          to state, §22-12-17.
  Rabies.
    Bites.
      Failure of person having
          knowledge of person
          having been bitten to
          report, §3-7-9.
  Radiation, §22-14-8.
  Railroads.
    Accident reports, §37-2-91.
  **Rehabilitation and crippled
      children service.**
    Annual report to governor on
        rehabilitation, §16-38-9.
  Sales.
    Generally.
      See SALES.
  Sales tax, §§40-23-7 to
      40-23-12, 40-23-15,
      40-23-29.
    See SALES TAX.
  **Savings and loan
      associations,** §5-16-36.
  Schools.
    Child abuse or neglect,
        §§26-14-1 to 26-14-13.
      See MINORS.
    General provisions.
      See EDUCATION.
    Teachers and officials.
  Securities.
    Securities commission,
        §8-6-53.
  Sex offenses.
    Failure to report arrest or
        conviction, §15-20-4.
    Officers to report arrests to
        department of public
        safety, §15-20-2.
  Sextons, §22-9-76.
  Sheriffs.
    Child abuse or neglect,
        §§26-14-1 to 26-14-13.
      See MINORS.
    Preparation of reports as to
        alleged violations of law,
        §36-22-5.

REPORTS—Cont'd
  Small business assistance.
    Department of industrial
        relations, §25-10-7.
  **Small business office of
      advocacy.**
    Annual report, §41-9-767.
  Small loans.
    Annual report, §5-18-11.
    Public access to reports,
        §5-18-23.
  Social workers.
    Child abuse or neglect,
        §§26-14-1 to 26-14-13.
      See MINORS.
  **Southern products mart
      authority.**
    Disposition of reports of
        authority, §41-10-66.
  **Speech pathologists and
      audiologists.**
    Board of examiners.
      Monthly report,
          §34-28A-44.
  **State departments and
      agencies.**
    Printing, §41-4-141.
    Time for making, §41-4-141.
  State toxicologist.
    Investigations.
      See STATE
          TOXICOLOGIST.
  Taxation.
    Cigarettes.
      Gummed cigarette papers.
        Penalty for failure to
            report, §40-25A-6.
    Estate and inheritance taxes.
      Failure to make.
        Appraisement, §40-15-10.
    General provisions.
      See TAXATION.
    Income tax.
      Information from source of
          income.
        Definition of "report
            from source,"
            §40-18-1.
        Report to revenue
            department,
            §40-18-26.
    Lubricating oils and greases.
      See LUBRICATING OILS
          AND GREASES.
    Motor fuels.
      Diesel fuel tax, §§40-17-8,
          40-17-9.
      Gasoline tax.
        See GASOLINE.
      General provisions.
        See MOTOR FUELS.
    Motor vehicle carriers.
      Fuel tax.
        See MOTOR VEHICLE
            CARRIERS.
      Mileage tax.
        See MOTOR VEHICLE
            CARRIERS.
    Public utilities.
      See PUBLIC UTILITIES.
    Sales tax.
      See SALES TAX.
    Tax collectors, §§40-5-23,
        40-5-35 to 40-5-37.
    Tobacco sales tax, §40-25-14.
  Teachers.
    Assaults on teachers.
      Report of assault, §16-1-24.
    Child abuse or neglect,
        §§26-14-1 to 26-14-13.
      See MINORS.

REPORTS—Cont'd
Tickets.
Traffic tickets, §12-12-54.
Tobacco.
Sales tax.
Wholesalers, §40-25-14.
Toxic substances in the workplace.
Annual report of director, §22-33-12.
Troy State University.
Board of trustees.
Reports to legislature, §16-56-10.
Tuberculosis.
See TUBERCULOSIS.
Unclaimed property.
Uniform disposition of unclaimed property act.
Report of abandoned property, §35-12-31.
Penalty for failure to render, §35-12-45.
Unemployment compensation.
Employing units, §25-4-116.
Penalties for delinquent reports, §25-4-133.
Uniform laws.
Commission on uniform state laws.
Reports to legislature, §41-9-373.
Unincorporated professional associations.
Furnishing of statements to secretary of state, §10-10-10.
United States.
Condemnation of land or rights-of-way.
Commissioners for assessment of damages and compensation, §42-2-8.
University of Alabama.
See UNIVERSITY OF ALABAMA.
University of North Alabama.
Board of trustees.
Reports to legislature, §16-51-10.
Venereal diseases.
General provisions.
See VENEREAL DISEASES.
Notifiable diseases, §§22-11A-1 to 22-11A-38.
See DISEASES.
Veterans.
State veterans' homes, §31-5A-9.
Administration of homes.
Department representative, §31-5A-5.
Veterinarians.
State veterinarian.
Annual report, §2-4-4.
Victim counselors.
Confidentiality.
Victim counselors not relieved to report certain crimes, §15-23-45.
Vital statistics.
See VITAL STATISTICS.
Warehouses.
See WAREHOUSES.

REPORTS—Cont'd
Water conservation and irrigation.
Agency.
Annual reports, §9-10-10.
Water management and drainage.
Board of water management commissioners.
Annual reports, §9-9-18.
Districts.
Board of viewers.
See WATER MANAGEMENT AND DRAINAGE.
Water pollution control authority.
Water pollution control revolving loan fund, §22-34-3.
Water supply and waterworks.
Safe drinking water act.
Applicants or suppliers required to report condition of water supply, plant, etc., §22-23-46.
Water system assistance authority.
Governor to deliver annual report, §22-23A-6.
Weights and measures.
Local sealers, §8-16-32.
Welfare.
See WELFARE.
Workmen's compensation, §§25-5-4, 25-5-5.
Youth services.
Youth services board.
Annual report to governor, §44-1-55.

REPRESENTATIVES.
Congress.
See CONGRESS.
General assembly.
See LEGISLATURE.

REPRIEVES.
Capital punishment.
Authority of governor to grant reprieves to persons under sentence of death, Const. Ala., amd. 38.
Governor.
Authority to grant, Const. Ala., art. V, §124; amd. 38.

REPUBLICAN FORM OF GOVERNMENT.
Guaranteed, Const. U. S., Art. IV, §4.

REQUESTS FOR ADMISSIONS.
Discovery, ARCP, Rule 36.
Failure to admit.
Expenses on failure, ARCP, Rule 37 (c).
Forms, ARCP, Forms 54 to 61A.

RESCUE SQUADS, §§32-11-1 to 32-11-4.
Chilton county rescue squad.
Exemption from sales and use taxes, §40-23-5.
Definitions, §32-11-1.
Volunteer rescue squads, §32-6-170.

RESCUE SQUADS—Cont'd
Fees.
Exemption from license and registration fees, §32-11-2.
Good Samaritan act.
Rescue squad members rendering first aid or emergency care at scene of accident, etc.
Exemption from liability, §6-5-332.
Liability.
Entering and attempting to preserve and protect burning buildings, etc.
Exemption from liability, §6-5-335.
Licenses.
Exemption from license fees, §32-11-2.
Members' private vehicles.
Distinctive license plates, §§32-6-170 to 32-6-174.
Members' private vehicles.
Distinctive license plates or tags.
Authorized, §32-6-171.
Distinctive lettering, §32-6-171.
Issuance, §32-6-172.
Licensing year, §32-6-174.
Preparation, §32-6-172.
Proof to be submitted by applicant, §32-6-172.
Transferability, §32-6-173.
Use, §32-6-172.
"Volunteer rescue squad" defined, §32-6-170.
Surplus property.
Voluntary nonprofit rescue squads.
Transfer of state owned surplus property to, §41-4-33.2.
Taxation.
Exemption from ad valorem taxes, §32-11-2.
Vehicles.
Ad valorem taxes.
Exemptions, §32-11-2.
Color, §32-11-3.
Lettering, §32-11-3.
License and registration fees.
Exemptions, §32-11-2.
Members' private vehicles.
Distinctive license plates, §§32-6-170 to 32-6-174.
Tags.
Special tags, §32-11-4.

RESEARCH.
Black archives, research center and museum, §§16-49-50 to 16-49-55.
See HISTORY AND ARCHIVES.
Controlled substances therapeutic research.
Annual reports to governor and legislature, §20-2-118.
Diseases.
Unknown cure.
Preference given to police officers and fire fighters in admission to research programs, §36-21-11.

RESEARCH—Cont'd
Forest research and educational programs, §§2-30-20 to 2-30-24.
Geological survey.
Research and experiments.
Retention of faculty members and students, §§9-4-14 to 9-4-19.
See GEOLOGICAL SURVEY.
Historical research, §§16-42-1 to 16-42-3.
Housing authorities.
Housing research and studies, §24-1-2.
Mental health, §§22-50-60 to 22-50-62.
Scientific research societies.
Corporations.
Public societies, §§10-4-20 to 10-4-28.
See CORPORATIONS.
Water resources research institute, §§9-8-1 to 9-8-4.

RESERVOIRS.
Fishing.
Catching fish, §9-11-91.
Water supply and waterworks, §§22-23-1 to 22-23-54.
See WATER SUPPLY AND WATERWORKS.

RESIDENCE.
Banks and financial institutions.
Directors, §5-6A-1.
Constitution of Alabama.
Not forfeited by temporary absence from state, Const. Ala., art. I, §31.
District attorneys.
Residence requirements, §12-17-183.
District courts.
Requirements for judges, §12-17-64.
Elections.
See ELECTIONS.
Military affairs.
Militia.
Composition of state militia, §31-2-2.
National guard.
Compensation for death of national guardsmen.
Dependents must be residents of United States, §31-3-4.
Public officers and employees.
General provisions.
See PUBLIC OFFICERS AND EMPLOYEES.
Veterans.
Pensions for widows of Confederate veterans.
Persons becoming resident citizens of other states to be dropped from pension roll, §31-8-13.
Voters.
Qualifications, §§17-3-11 to 17-3-13; Const. Ala., art. VIII, §178; amd. 96.

RESIN.
Forest products generally, §§9-13-60 to 9-13-107.
See FORESTS AND FORESTRY.

RESIN—Cont'd
Licenses.
Resin stills, §40-12-175.

RESISTING ARREST.
Bail and recognizance, §15-5-4.

RES JUDICATA.
Affirmative defense, ARCP, Rule 8 (c).
Commercial code.
Effect of notice to person answerable over, §§7-2-607, 7-3-803.

RESOLUTIONS.
Corrections.
Alabama corrections institution finance authority.
Bond issues.
Authorizing resolutions.
Recital, notice and contest, §14-2-15.
Resolutions of board of directors, §14-2-7.
Evidence.
Municipal resolutions, §12-21-95.
Highways.
Closing and vacating streets, alleys and highways, §23-4-2.
Municipal corporations.
Ordinances and resolutions.
See MUNICIPAL CORPORATIONS.
Water system assistance authority.
Authorizing resolutions.
Defined, §22-23A-1.

RESORTS.
Blind persons.
Right to use of public resorts, §21-7-3.
Handicapped persons.
Right to use of public resorts, §21-7-3.
Water, sewer and fire protection authorities.
Construction of sewerage facilities in resort areas, §§11-88-40 to 11-88-111.
See WATER, SEWER AND FIRE PROTECTION AUTHORITIES.

RESPONDEAT SUPERIOR.
Employer's liability for certain injuries, §§25-6-1 to 25-6-4.
Principal and agent.
Employer's liability for certain injuries, §§25-6-1 to 25-6-4.
General provisions, §§8-2-6, 8-2-7.
Telephones.
Securities of telephone companies.
Acts of employees or officers deemed acts of company, §37-2-181.

RESTAURANTS.
Alcoholic beverages.
General provisions, §§28-3-1, 28-3A-13.
Licenses, §§28-3A-13, 28-3A-21.
Alligator farms.
Licenses, §9-12-206.

RESTAURANTS—Cont'd
County health officers.
Duties, §22-3-5.
Criminal law and procedure.
Theft of services, §13A-8-10.
Drinking cups.
Common drinking cups.
Use prohibited, §22-20-1.
Fraud.
Obtaining food by fraud or misrepresentation.
Posting of law, §34-15-20.
Prima facie evidence of offense, §34-15-19.
Goods of customers.
Liens of restaurant keepers, §§35-11-130, 35-11-131.
Health.
Duties of county health officers, §22-3-5.
Regulations, §22-20-5.
Keepers.
Liens, §§35-11-130, 35-11-131.
Licenses, §40-12-151.
Alcoholic beverages, §§28-3A-13, 28-3A-21.
Liens of restaurant keepers.
Declaration of lien, §35-11-130.
Enforcement of lien, §35-11-131.
Seizure and sale of goods and baggage, §35-11-131.
Searches and seizures.
Liens of restaurant keepers.
Seizure and sale of goods and baggage of customers, §35-11-131.
Theft.
Theft of restaurant services, §13A-8-10.
Towels.
Use of common towels prohibited, §22-20-1.

RESTITUTION TO VICTIMS OF CRIMES, §§15-18-65 to 15-18-78.
Actions.
Civil action by victim of crime.
Credit for restitution paid against judgment in favor of victim, §15-18-75.
Associations.
Default by association.
Forfeiture of right to do business, §15-18-73.
Requirements, §15-18-73.
Attachments.
Employment income withholding order.
Authority to attach, etc., assets, etc., of defendant, §15-18-144.
Priority of orders, §15-18-150.
Centers.
Restitution centers, §§15-18-76, 15-18-77.
Civil action by victim.
Credit for restitution paid against judgment in favor of victim, §15-18-75.
Profits from crime, §§41-9-80 to 41-9-84.
Construction and interpretation, §15-18-65.

RESTITUTION TO VICTIMS OF CRIMES—Cont'd
Contempt.
Employment income
withholding order.
Violations of provisions,
§15-18-143.
Conversion.
Employment income
withholding order.
Person complying protected
from actions for
wrongful conversion,
§15-18-149.
Corporations.
Default by corporation.
Forfeiture of right to do
business, §15-18-73.
Requirements, §15-18-73.
Counties.
Restitution centers.
Cooperation of counties
and municipalities,
§15-18-76.
Powers of counties,
§15-18-77.
Crime victims compensation,
§§15-23-1 to 15-23-23.
See CRIME VICTIMS
COMPENSATION.
Criteria for determining
restitution, §15-18-68.
Default.
Defendant with suspended
sentence.
Effect of default, §15-18-72.
Parolee.
Effect of default, §15-18-72.
Probationer.
Effect of default, §15-18-72.
Definitions, §15-18-66.
Withholding act, §15-18-142.
District attorneys.
Special services division.
Worthless check unit,
§12-17-224.
Employment income
withholding order,
§§15-18-143 to 15-18-151.
Factors considered in
determining restitution,
§15-18-68.
Hearings.
Findings.
Statement of findings,
§15-18-69.
Objections to order,
§15-18-69.
Persons entitled to be heard,
§15-18-67.
Restitution hearing,
§15-18-67.
Standing to be heard,
§15-18-67.
Statement of findings,
§15-18-69.
Inmate community
reintegration under SIR
act, §§15-18-110 to
15-18-123.
See CORRECTIONS.
Legislative findings,
§15-18-65.
Municipal corporations.
Restitution centers.
Cooperation of counties
and municipalities,
§15-18-76.
Powers of municipalities,
§15-18-77.

RESTITUTION TO VICTIMS OF CRIMES—Cont'd
Orders of court.
Effect of restitution order,
§15-18-78.
Enforceability where
defendant imprisoned,
§15-18-71.
Objections to order,
§15-18-69.
Restitution order, §§15-18-67,
15-18-78.
Rights of victims, §15-18-78.
Section cumulative and in
para materia with other
statutes, §15-18-78.
Parole.
Default by parolee.
Effect, §15-18-72.
Payment of restitution.
Condition of parole,
§15-18-71.
Restitution centers.
Powers of board of pardons
and paroles, §15-18-77.
Supervision of parolee's
restitution, §15-18-74.
Partnerships.
Default by partnership.
Forfeiture of right to do
business, §15-18-73.
Requirements, §15-18-73.
Payment of restitution.
Condition of sentence
suspension or probation,
§15-18-70.
Default.
Effect, §15-18-72.
Method, §15-18-70.
Parole.
Condition of parole,
§15-18-71.
Parolees.
Supervision of parolee's
restitution, §15-18-74.
Probation.
Payment as condition to
probation, §15-18-70.
Suspension of sentence.
Payment as condition to
suspension, §15-18-70.
Penalties.
Employment income
withholding order.
Generally, §15-18-143.
Noncompliance with order,
§15-18-148.
Prisons and prisoners.
Enforceability of restitution
order for prisoner,
§15-18-71.
Suspended sentence.
Default by defendant with
suspended sentence.
Effect, §15-18-72.
Payment of restitution as
condition to
suspension, §15-18-70.
Probation.
Default by probationer.
Effect, §15-18-72.
Payment of restitution as
condition to probation,
§15-18-70.
Profits from crime, §§41-9-80
to 41-9-84.
Purpose of article, §15-18-65.
Restitution centers.
Board of pardons and
paroles.
Powers, §15-18-77.

RESTITUTION TO VICTIMS OF CRIMES—Cont'd
Restitution centers—Cont'd
Counties.
Cooperation of counties
and municipalities,
§15-18-76.
Powers, §15-18-77.
Establishment, §15-18-76.
Municipal corporations.
Cooperation of counties
and municipalities,
§15-18-76.
Powers, §15-18-77.
Operation, §15-18-76.
Powers of counties,
municipalities and board
of pardons and paroles,
§15-18-77.
Services to be provided,
§15-18-77.
Rights of victims, §15-18-78.
Son of Sam law, §§15-18-140
to 15-18-151. See within
this heading,
"Withholding."
Supervised intensive
restitution program.
Inmate community
reintegration under SIR
act, §§15-18-110 to
15-18-123.
See CORRECTIONS.
Withholding.
Citation of act, §15-18-140.
Declarations of legislature,
§15-18-141.
Definitions, §15-18-142.
Determinations of
legislature, §15-18-141.
Employment income
withholding order,
§§15-18-143 to 15-18-151.
Alteration of order,
§15-18-151.
Attachment, etc., of assets,
etc., of defendant
authorized, §15-18-144.
Change in employment,
§15-18-143.
Compliance with order.
Person complying
protected from
actions for wrongful
conversion, etc.,
§15-18-149.
Contents, §15-18-143.
Continuing order,
§15-18-145.
Disposition of income, etc.,
§15-18-147.
Generally, §15-18-143.
Modification of order,
§15-18-151.
Nature of order,
§15-18-145.
Noncompliance.
Penalty for
noncompliance,
§15-18-148.
Penalty for noncompliance,
§15-18-148.
Persons complying
protected from actions,
§15-18-149.
Priority, §15-18-150.
Receipt and disposition of
income, etc.,
§15-18-147.
Rescinding order,
§15-18-151.

RESTITUTION TO VICTIMS OF CRIMES—Cont'd
Withholding—Cont'd
Employment income withholding order —Cont'd
Service of copy of order, §15-18-146.
Support of dependent children of defendant.
Priority of order, §15-18-150.
Wrongful conversion.
Person complying protected from actions, §15-18-149.
Legislative findings, §15-18-141.
Title of article, §15-18-140.

RESTRAINING ORDERS.
See INJUNCTIONS.

RESTRAINT OF TRADE.
General provisions, §§8-10-1 to 8-10-3.
Monopolies.
See MONOPOLIES.
Motion picture fair competition, §§8-18-1 to 8-18-6.
See MOTION PICTURES.

RETAIL INSTALLMENT SALES.
Commercial code.
Secured transactions.
Validity of security agreement, §7-9-201.

RETAIL MERCHANTS ASSOCIATIONS.
Incorporation.
Authority to form corporation, §10-4-260.

RETIREMENT.
Circuit courts.
Judges.
General provisions, §§12-18-1 to 12-18-13.
See CIRCUIT COURTS.
Judicial retirement fund, §§12-18-1 to 12-18-13.
See JUDGES.
Constitution of Alabama.
State retirement systems.
Use of assets, Const. Ala., amd. 472.
Counties.
General provisions.
See COUNTIES.
Court of civil appeals.
Judges, §§12-18-1 to 12-18-13.
See COURT OF CIVIL APPEALS.
Court of criminal appeals.
Judges, §§12-18-1 to 12-18-13.
See COURT OF CRIMINAL APPEALS.
District attorneys.
Election by former district attorneys serving as circuit judges on January 16, 1977 to come under provisions of article 1 of chapter, §12-18-55.
District courts.
Judges, §§12-18-50 to 12-18-61.
See DISTRICT COURTS.

RETIREMENT—Cont'd
Governor.
Allowance for former governors, §36-13-11.
Harbors and ports.
Docks department.
Retirement plans for employees of state docks department, §33-1-5.1.
Highway patrol.
Badges, pistols, etc.
Officers to receive badge, pistol, etc., as part of retirement benefits, §32-2-26.
Income tax.
Exemptions.
Military retirement benefits, §40-18-20.
Retirement allowances, §40-18-19.
Judges.
Circuit court judges, §§12-18-1 to 12-18-13.
See CIRCUIT COURTS.
Court of civil appeals, §§12-18-1 to 12-18-13.
See COURT OF CIVIL APPEALS.
Court of criminal appeals, §§12-18-1 to 12-18-13.
See COURT OF CRIMINAL APPEALS.
District courts, §§12-18-50 to 12-18-61.
See DISTRICT COURTS.
Judicial retirement fund, §§12-18-1 to 12-18-13.
See JUDGES.
Probate judges, §§12-18-80 to 12-18-92.
See PROBATE COURTS.
Supreme court justices, §§12-18-30 to 12-18-34.
Municipal corporations.
See MUNICIPAL CORPORATIONS.
Peace officers.
Annuity and benefit fund.
See PEACE OFFICERS.
Pilots and pilotage.
Compulsory retirement of bar pilots, §33-4-53.
Probate judges, §§12-18-80 to 12-18-92.
See PROBATE COURTS.
Sheriffs.
See SHERIFFS.
State employees' retirement system.
See PUBLIC OFFICERS AND EMPLOYEES.
State police.
Completion of 25 years service.
State trooper may retire upon completion of 25 years service, §36-21-12.
Supreme court justices, §§12-18-30 to 12-18-34.
Taxation.
Supernumerary tax officials.
Election to participate in supernumerary retirement program, §40-6-8.

RETIREMENT—Cont'd
Teachers' retirement system.
General provisions, §§16-25-1 to 16-25-47.
See EDUCATION.
Transfer of contributions and creditable service to judicial retirement fund, §§12-18-110 to 12-18-114.
Trusts and trustees.
Trusts for employees or self-employed persons, §35-4-259.

RETIREMENT HOMES.
General provisions.
Health care authorities, §§22-21-310 to 22-21-356.
See HEALTH CARE AUTHORITIES.

RETURN BOTTLES.
Names, marks, etc., on beverage containers, §§8-12-20, 8-12-21.

REVENUE AND TAXATION.
General provisions, §§40-1-1 to 40-29-120.
See TAXATION.
State funds, §§41-14-1 to 41-14-38.
See FINANCE.

REVERSIONS.
See REMAINDERS, REVERSIONS AND EXECUTORY INTERESTS.

REVIVAL OF ACTIONS.
See ABATEMENT, REVIVAL AND SURVIVAL OF ACTIONS.

REVIVAL OF JUDGMENTS, §§6-9-190 to 6-9-196.
See JUDGMENTS.

REVOLVERS, §§13A-11-70 to 13A-11-84.
See WEAPONS.

REWARDS.
Alcoholic beverages, §§28-4-25, 28-4-54, 28-4-311.
Banks and financial institutions.
Directors, officers and employees.
Receipt of rewards to procure loans, purchases, discounts, etc., §5-6A-22.
Capital crimes.
Information leading to arrest and conviction for capital crimes, §15-9-1.
Fugitives from justice.
Information leading to arrest and conviction, §§15-9-1 to 15-9-4.
Governor.
Apprehension or rearrest of felons, §15-9-3.
Lost or unclaimed property.
Finders, §35-12-3.
Municipal corporations.
High crime or misdemeanor committed in municipality, §15-9-2.
Penitentiary.
Escape of convict, §14-3-58.

RIFLES, §§13A-11-62 to
13A-11-66.
See WEAPONS.

RIGHT OF ENTRY.
Air pollution.
Inspections, §22-28-19.
Airports.
Surveys and examinations,
§4-2-93.
Child labor.
School attendance officers,
§25-8-23.
Coal.
Abandoned mine
reclamation, §9-16-126.
Cosmetics.
Commissioner of agriculture
and industries, §20-1-3.
Counties.
Land-use management in
flood-prone areas.
Preparation of
examinations and
surveys, §11-19-10.
Surveyors.
Execution of surveys
requested by interested
persons, §11-7-11.
For execution of court
ordered survey,
§11-7-5.
**Director of industrial
relations,** §25-2-9.
Drugs.
Commissioner of agriculture
and industries, §20-1-3.
Eminent domain,
§§18-1A-284, 18-1A-289.
Ginseng.
Commission of agriculture
and industries, §9-13-248.
Hazardous substances.
Cleanup fund.
Department of
environmental
management.
Right of entry to perform
actions necessary to
carry out provisions
of chapter,
§22-30A-10.
Hotels.
Police power of hotel
inspectors, §34-15-6.
Labor.
Child labor.
School attendance officers,
§25-8-23.
Director of industrial
relations, §25-2-9.
Limitation of actions, §§6-2-4,
6-2-5.
Marine resources.
Investigation of compliance
with laws.
Boarding of boats and
entrance into places of
business, §9-12-31.
Municipal corporations.
Eminent domain.
Right of entry of
municipality pending
appeal, §11-47-173.

RIGHT OF ENTRY—Cont'd
Rules of civil procedure.
Entry upon land for
inspection and other
purposes, ARCP, Rule
34.
Failure of party to respond
to request for
inspection, ARCP,
Rule 37 (d).
Surveys and surveyors.
Counties, §§11-7-5, 11-7-11,
11-19-10.
General provisions,
§§23-1-44, 35-2-32.
**Water supply and
waterworks.**
Safe drinking water act,
§22-23-45.

RIGHTS.
Bill of rights, Const. U. S.,
Amendments I to X.
See CONSTITUTION OF
THE UNITED STATES.
Declaration of rights, Const.
Ala., art. I, §§1 to 36.
See CONSTITUTION OF
ALABAMA.

RIGHTS OF WAY.
Abandoned rights of way.
Railroads.
Authorized to transfer,
§10-5-2.1.
**Bear creek development
authority.**
Authority to use rights of
way of all public roads in
the state, §33-15-16.
Bridges, §23-1-59.
Cemeteries.
Eminent domain.
Private parties, §§18-3-20
to 18-3-22.
Condemnation.
Electric utilities, §§37-4-130,
37-4-131.
Highways.
Authority, §23-1-45.
United States, §§42-2-1 to
42-2-12.
See UNITED STATES.
Counties.
Public roads, bridges and
ferries.
Public utilities.
Construction of facilities,
§23-1-85.
Eminent domain.
Private parties, §§18-3-1 to
18-3-22.
See EMINENT DOMAIN.
Graveyards.
Eminent domain.
Private parties, §§18-3-20
to 18-3-22.
Harbors and ports.
Acquisition by purchase or
eminent domain
proceedings, §33-1-22.
Highways.
Eminent domain.
Private parties, §§18-3-1 to
18-3-3.
General provisions.
See HIGHWAYS.
Industrial companies.
Condemnation for rights of
way, §10-5-3.

RIGHTS OF WAY—Cont'd
**Interference with rights of
way.**
Unlawful interference,
§6-5-216.
Littering, §§13A-7-29, 23-5-6
to 23-5-9.
Manufacturers.
Condemnation for rights of
way by manufacturing
companies, §10-5-3.
Mines and minerals.
Condemnation for rights of
way by mining
companies, §10-5-3.
Motor vehicles, §§32-5A-110
to 32-5A-116, 32-5A-218,
32-5A-219.
See MOTOR VEHICLES.
Municipal corporations,
§§11-47-170 to 11-47-173.
**Public roads, bridges and
ferries.**
Counties.
Public utilities.
Construction of facilities,
§23-1-85.
Quarries.
Condemnation for rights of
way by quarrying
companies, §10-5-3.
Railroads.
Abandoned rights of way.
Authorized to transfer,
§10-5-2.1.
Transfers.
Authorized to transfer
abandoned rights of
way, §10-5-2.1.
Roads.
Eminent domain.
Private parties, §§18-3-1 to
18-3-3.
Telegraph companies.
Rules and regulations of
company promulgated by
highway department,
§23-1-59.
Telephone companies.
Eminent domain.
Condemnation of ways and
rights of way by
companies
constructing, operating
or maintaining public
utility, §10-5-4.
Foreign telephone
companies.
Acquisition of easements
for connecting lines,
§18-1A-272.
Grant of easements to
telephone and
telegraph companies,
Const. Ala., art. IV,
§99.
Power in public utility
corporations, §10-5-1.
Routes and sites.
Rights of condemning
corporations in
selection of routes
and sites, §10-5-8.
Transfers.
Railroads.
Abandoned rights of way.
Authorized to transfer,
§10-5-2.1.

RIGHTS OF WAY—Cont'd
Trees and timber.
Conveyances of standing
timber.
Right of way over
timberlands,
§35-4-361.
Trespass.
Unlawful interference with
right of way, §6-5-216.
United States.
Condemnation of rights of
way, §§42-2-1 to 42-2-12.
See UNITED STATES.
Vacation.
Fee, §11-49-6.
Venue.
Actions for breach of right of
way contracts, §6-3-3.
Waters and watercourses.
Development of docks and
other facilities along
inland waterways.
1957 provisions, §33-2-6.
1959 provisions, §33-2-35.
1961 provisions, §33-2-65.
1963 provisions, §33-2-95.
1967 provisions, §33-2-124.
1969 provisions, §33-2-154.
Navigable waters as public
thoroughfares, §33-7-1.

RIGHT TO DIE.
Natural death act, §§22-8A-1
to 22-8A-10.
See NATURAL DEATH
ACT.

RIGHT TO VOTE.
See ELECTIONS.

RIGHT TO WORK LAW,
§§25-7-30 to 25-7-36.
See LABOR.

RIOTS.
Alcoholic beverages.
Temporary closings of
licensed places in
municipalities during
emergencies, §28-3-47.
Civil defense, §§31-9-1 to
31-9-24.
See CIVIL DEFENSE.
Class A misdemeanor,
§13A-11-3.
Department of public safety.
Officers who are employees
of department.
Controlling civil
disturbances.
Expenses, §32-2-7.
Disorderly conduct.
See DISORDERLY
CONDUCT.
Elections.
Sheriffs.
Duty to preserve order at
elections, §17-1-2.
Elements of crime, §13A-11-3.
**Failure of disorderly
persons to disperse,**
§13A-11-6.
Governor.
Municipal police.
Employment within state
by governor during
riots, etc., §§36-21-20
to 36-21-24.
Ordering out of troops,
§§31-2-109 to 31-2-114.
See MILITARY AFFAIRS.

RIOTS—Cont'd
Inciting to riot, §13A-11-4.
Class A misdemeanor,
§13A-11-4.
Military affairs.
Ordering out of troops,
§§31-2-109 to 31-2-114.
See MILITARY AFFAIRS.
Municipal corporations.
Alcoholic beverages.
Temporary closings of
licensed places in
municipalities during
emergencies, §28-3-47.
Proclamation closing shops
and forbidding sale of
arms, ammunition, etc.
Issuance by mayor,
§11-43-82.
Municipal police.
Employment within state by
governor during riots,
etc., §§36-21-20 to
36-21-24.
National guard.
Death of national guardsmen
quelling riot.
Compensation for death of
national guardsmen,
§31-3-2.
Ordering out of troops,
§§31-2-109 to 31-2-114.
See MILITARY AFFAIRS.
Police.
Employment of municipal
police within state by
governor during riots,
etc., §§36-21-20 to
36-21-24.
Failure of disorderly persons
to disperse, §13A-11-6.
Streets.
National guard.
Regulation of passage and
occupancy during riot,
§31-2-122.
Unlawful assembly,
§§13A-11-5, 13A-11-6.

RIPARIAN OWNERS.
**Liens of owners of booms
and bulkheads,**
§§35-11-310, 35-11-311.
Rights of riparian owners,
§§33-7-50 to 33-7-54.
**Water supply and
waterworks.**
Condemnation of riparian
rights by waterworks
corporation, §10-5-6.

RISKS.
Insurance generally.
See INSURANCE.
Safety-responsibility act.
Assigned risk plans,
§32-7-35.

RIVERS.
Waters and watercourses.
Dams on navigable rivers,
§§33-7-30 to 33-7-32.
Development of docks and
other facilities along
inland waterways,
§§33-2-1 to 33-2-213.
See WATERS AND
WATERCOURSES.

ROADHOUSES.
Licenses, §40-12-152.

ROADS.
Agriculture.
Experiment station system.
Construction and
maintenance.
State highway
department,
§23-1-43.
Bicycles, §§32-5A-260 to
32-5A-266.
See BICYCLES.
Bond issues, Const. Ala.,
amds. 11, 21, 87.
Constitution of Alabama.
Bond issues for
construction of roads,
Const. Ala., amd. 11.
United States.
Bond issue for acquiring
public roads in
conjunction with
United States, Const.
Ala., amd. 87.
Constitution of Alabama.
Bond issues, Const. Ala.,
amds. 11, 21, 87.
Bond issue for acquiring in
conjunction with
United States, Const.
Ala., amd. 87.
Bonds for construction,
Const. Ala., amd. 11.
Construction, maintenance,
etc., of public roads,
Const. Ala., amds. 12,
58.
Districts to build and
maintain public roads,
Const. Ala., amd. 15.
State not to engage in
internal improvements
or lend money or credit
for same.
Exception as to public
roads, Const. Ala.,
amd. 1.
Counties.
Closing and vacating streets,
alleys and highways,
§§23-4-1 to 23-4-20.
See HIGHWAYS.
Funds.
Public roads, bridges and
ferries, §§23-1-83,
23-1-84, 23-1-102,
23-1-106.
See COUNTIES.
Oil and gas.
Petroleum products.
Use of fees, §18-17-91.
Private roads, §§23-1-130,
23-1-131.
Public roads, bridges and
ferries, §§23-1-80 to
23-1-95.
See COUNTIES.
Secondary road committee
generally, §8-17-91.
Warrants for construction of
public buildings, bridges
and roads, §§11-28-1 to
11-28-7.
See COUNTIES.
Damages.
Private roads.
Damages caused by road,
§23-1-131.
Detours.
Signs.
Driving around, §23-5-2.

ROADS—Cont'd
Detours—Cont'd
Signs—Cont'd
Injuring, destroying, etc.,
§23-5-2.
Eminent domain.
Rights of way.
Private parties, §§18-3-1 to
18-3-3.
Highways, §§23-1-1 to 23-6-12.
See HIGHWAYS.
**Improvements on public
streets.**
Liens, §§35-11-410 to
35-11-417.
See HIGHWAYS.
Interstate highway system.
Controlled access facilities,
§§23-3-1 to 23-3-8.
See HIGHWAYS.
Designation.
Authority of highway
department to classify,
designate and mark,
§32-5A-30.
Junkyard control, §§23-1-240
to 23-1-251.
See JUNKYARD
CONTROL.
Outdoor advertising,
§§23-1-270 to 23-1-288.
See ADVERTISING.
Toll bridges, §§23-2-140 to
23-2-161.
See TOLL ROAD, BRIDGE
AND TUNNEL
AUTHORITY.
Toll tunnels, §§23-2-120 to
23-2-122.
Utilities.
Relocation necessitated by
construction of
highways.
Payment of cost, §23-1-5.
Licenses.
Road machinery.
Dealers, §40-12-169.
Liens.
Improvements on public
streets, etc., §§35-11-410
to 35-11-417.
See HIGHWAYS.
**Littering, §§13A-7-29, 23-5-6
to 23-5-9.**
Motor vehicles.
Rules of the road, §§32-5A-1
to 32-5A-266.
See MOTOR VEHICLES.
**Municipal connecting link
roads, §§23-1-110 to
23-1-113.**
**Municipal corporations,
§§11-49-1 to 11-49-106.**
See MUNICIPAL
CORPORATIONS.
Prisons and prisoners.
Work on public roads,
§§14-4-6 to 14-4-8.
Private roads.
Damages.
Caused by private road,
§23-1-131.
Establishment.
Application, §23-1-130.
Authority of county
commissions,
§23-1-130.
Proceedings, §23-1-131.
Location.
Limitations, §23-1-130.
Maintenance, §23-1-130.

ROADS—Cont'd
Private roads—Cont'd
Width, §23-1-130.
**Public roads, bridges and
ferries.**
General provisions, §§23-1-80
to 23-1-95.
See COUNTIES.
Rights of way.
Eminent domain.
Private parties, §§18-3-1 to
18-3-3.
Vacation.
Fee, §11-49-6.
**Secondary road committee,
§40-12-270.**
Signs.
Detours, §23-5-2.
Littering.
Erection of signs, §23-5-7.
United States.
Bond issue for acquiring
public roads in
conjunction with United
States, Const. Ala., amd.
87.
Washington county.
Indebtedness to improve
roads and bridges, Const.
Ala., amd. 410.

**ROANOKE, MUNICIPALITY
OF.**
Property tax, Const. Ala.,
amd. 17.

**ROBBERY, §§13A-8-40 to
13A-8-44.**
**Claims of right not defenses
in robbery prosecution,
§13A-8-44.**
Deadly weapons.
Use of deadly weapons or
dangerous instruments.
First degree robbery,
§13A-8-41.
Defenses.
Claims of right not defense,
§13A-8-44.
Definitions, §13A-8-40.
First degree robbery.
Class A felony, §13A-8-41.
Elements of crime,
§13A-8-41.
Force.
Use of force to overcome
physical resistance.
Third degree robbery,
§13A-8-43.
Indictments.
Form of indictment,
§15-8-150.
**Pharmacists and
pharmacies.**
Citation of act, §13A-8-50.
Definitions, §13A-8-51.
Penalties.
Violation of article,
§13A-8-52.
Second or subsequent
conviction.
Penalty, §13A-8-52.
Short title of act, §13A-8-50.
Violation of article.
Penalty for violation,
§13A-8-52.
Second degree robbery.
Class B felony, §13A-8-42.
Elements of crime,
§13A-8-42.
Third degree robbery.
Class C felony, §13A-8-43.

ROBBERY—Cont'd
Third degree robbery
—Cont'd
Elements of crime,
§13A-8-43.
Threats of imminent force.
Third degree robbery,
§13A-8-43.
**Use of force in defense of
person.**
When deadly physical force
justified, §13A-3-23.
Weapons.
Use of deadly weapons or
dangerous instrument.
First degree robbery,
§13A-8-41.

ROCKS.
Motor vehicles.
Spilling loads, §32-5-76.
Throwing rocks into occupied
vehicle, §32-5-11.
Official rock of state, §1-2-14.

**ROCKY MOUNTAIN
SPOTTED FEVER.**
Notifiable diseases,
§§22-11A-1 to 22-11A-38.
See DISEASES.

RODENTS.
Exterminators, §§2-28-1 to
2-28-12.
See PEST CONTROL.
Pest control, §§2-28-1 to
2-28-12.
See PEST CONTROL.
Pesticides, §§2-27-1 to 2-27-63.
See PESTICIDES.

RODEOS.
Licenses, §40-12-111.

ROOMING HOUSES, §§34-15-1
to 34-15-20.
See HOTELS, INNS AND
OTHER TRANSIENT
LODGING PLACES.

RUBBING ALCOHOL, §§28-5-1
to 28-5-14.
See INDUSTRIAL ALCOHOL.

RUBBISH.
See GARBAGE AND TRASH.

**RULE AGAINST
PERPETUITIES.**
**Conveyance to avoid
perpetuities,** §35-4-5.
Generally, §35-4-4.

RULE IN SHELLEY'S CASE.
Abolished, §35-4-230.

RULES AND REGULATIONS.
Academy of honor.
Adoption, §41-11-5.
Accountants, §§34-1-3, 34-1-7.
**Administrative procedure
act,** §§41-22-1 to 41-22-27.
See ADMINISTRATIVE
PROCEDURE ACT.
Adoption.
Subsidized adoption.
Department of pensions
and security to
promulgate, §26-10-30.
Advertising.
Outdoor advertising.
Penalties.
Violations, §23-1-288.
Promulgation, §23-1-286.

RULES AND REGULATIONS
—Cont'd

Aged persons.
Medical assistance to elderly persons.
Determination of eligibility for assistance, §38-6-4.

Agriculture.
Agricultural center board, §2-6-1.
Board of agriculture and industries.
State aid to agricultural fairs, §2-7-32.
Copies furnished to probate judges, §2-2-17.
Evidence of rules and regulations, §2-2-17.
Farmer's market authority.
Conduct of market, §2-5-7.
Ejection of persons from markets for violations, §2-5-11.
Enforcement of chapters, §2-5-10.
Grading and standards of farm products and fish.
Commissioner authorized to make, §2-11-51.
Marketing of agricultural products, §2-11-8.
Markets, §2-3-23.
Conduct of market, §2-5-7.
Notice, §2-2-16.
Promulgation, §2-2-16.

Air commerce.
Public service commission, §37-9-8.

Air pollution, §§22-28-13 to 22-28-15.

Alcoholic beverages.
General provisions, §§28-3-49 to 28-3-51.

Ambulances, §§22-18-1 to 22-18-7.
See AMBULANCES.

Ameraport.
Offshore harbor and terminal commission, §33-10-11.

Appeals.
Briefs.
References in briefs to parties, ARAP, Rule 28 (d).
Rules of appellate procedure.
See APPEALS.

Architects.
Board of registration.
Promulgation, §34-2-39.

Art commission, §41-9-22.

Atomic energy.
Radiation, §22-14-8.

Auctions and auctioneers.
Board of auctioneers.
Promulgation by board, §34-4-50.

Aviation.
Aeronautics commission, §4-2-37.
Airports.
Zoning, §§4-6-4 to 4-6-12.
See AVIATION.

Banks, §§5-2A-7 to 5-2A-9, 5-10A-2, 5-10A-3.
See BANKS AND FINANCIAL INSTITUTIONS.

Barbers.
Board of barber examiners, §34-5-13.

RULES AND REGULATIONS
—Cont'd

Billiard rooms.
Compliance with health department regulations, §34-6-5.

Boats.
Discharge of litter and sewage from watercraft, §§33-6-4, 33-6-5, 33-6-10, 33-6-12.
General provisions, §§33-5-28 to 33-5-30.
See BOATS.

Bond issues.
Securities regulation.
See SECURITIES.

Boxing and wrestling.
Athletic commission, §41-9-90.1.

Brake fluid.
Promulgation, §8-17-6.

Bread, flour, cornmeal and grits.
Publication and effective date, §20-1-78.

Bridges.
Federal assistance.
Promulgation, §23-1-1.
Promulgation, §§23-1-1, 23-1-59.

Building commission.
Adoption, §41-9-141.

Cahaba trace commission.
Adoption, §41-9-803.

Catfish.
Marketing of catfish, §2-11-35.
Proceedings for enforcement, §2-11-38.
Promotion of industry, §2-8-289.

Cattle.
Promotion of cattle industry, §2-8-20.

Child abuse or neglect.
Reporting child abuse or neglect.
Department of pensions and security, §26-14-12.
Records and reports, §26-14-8.

Chiropractors.
Board of chiropractic examiners.
Authority of board, §34-24-144.
Licenses, §34-24-165.
Licenses.
Refusal, revocation or suspension, §34-24-168.
Preceptorship and extern program.
Establishment and implementation of program, §34-24-145.

Coal.
Surface mining control and reclamation.
Commission.
Revision of rules.
Oversight committee to be consulted, §9-16-73.
Emergency rules, §9-16-75.
Procedure for rule making, §9-16-75.
Underground coal mining operations, §9-16-91.

RULES AND REGULATIONS
—Cont'd

Commercial code.
Secured transactions.
Central filing system.
Implementation, §7-9-410.

Condominiums.
Building or zoning regulations.
Construction and application, §35-8-21.

Conservation and natural resources.
See CONSERVATION AND NATURAL RESOURCES.

Consumer finance.
Administrator authorized to make, §5-19-21.

Contractors.
Promulgation by state licensing board, §34-8-22.

Cornmeal.
Publication and effective date, §20-1-78.

Corporations.
Powers of corporations, §10-2A-20.

Corrections.
Board of corrections, §§14-1-4, 14-1-8, 14-1-11.
Inmate community reintegration under SIR act.
Extension of limits of confinement authorized, §15-18-112.

Cosmetology.
Promulgation by board of cosmetology, §34-7-40.

Cotton.
Boll weevil eradication.
Authority to promulgate appropriate regulations, §2-19-128.
Promotion of cotton products, §2-8-208.

Counties.
Public roads, bridges and ferries.
County commissions.
Promulgation, §23-1-80.
Penalties.
Violations, §23-5-14.
Promulgation.
County commissions, §23-1-80.
Violations, §23-1-95.
Penalties, §23-5-14.

Credit cards.
Superintendent of banks.
Promulgation, §5-20-7.

Credit unions.
Procedure for adopting, amending or repealing, §5-17-47.
Reliance on regulations and interpretations, §5-17-46.

Dental service corporations.
Commissioner to promulgate, §22-21-391.

Dentists.
Board of dental examiners.
Penalty for violation, §34-9-5.
Promulgation, §34-9-43.

Department of examiners of public accounts.
Publication, §41-5-17.

RULES AND REGULATIONS
—Cont'd
Depositions.
Criminal cases.
Rules governing use,
§12-21-262.
Domestic violence facilities,
§30-6-10.
Drugs.
Adoption, §20-1-2.
Controlled substances.
Promulgation, §20-2-54.1.
Identification of drug
products.
State board of health.
Promulgation, §20-1-152.
Penalties for violations,
§20-1-5.
Therapeutic research.
Promulgation, §20-2-113.
**Economic and community
affairs.**
Director.
Promulgation, §41-23-6.
Education.
General provisions.
See EDUCATION.
State board of education,
§§16-3-12 to 16-3-14.
Eggs and egg products,
§2-12-8.
Promotion of industry,
§2-8-167.
Energy.
Cogeneration facilities.
Federal rules and
regulations.
Incorporation by
reference, §37-12-3.
**Energy management and
conservation.**
Authority of department of
energy, §41-6A-6.
Scope of rules, §41-6A-6.
Enterprise zones.
Authority to formulate,
§41-23-31.
Exemption from local
regulations.
Nontax incentives,
§41-23-25.
Tax credits or incentives.
Rules to implement,
§41-23-24.
Environmental management.
Procedure for adoption,
§22-22A-8.
Ferries.
Federal assistance.
Promulgation, §23-1-1.
Fertilizer,
See FERTILIZER.
Finance, §41-4-35.
See FINANCE.
Fires and fire prevention.
Firemen.
Personnel standards and
education commission,
§§36-32-1 to 36-32-12.
See FIRES AND FIRE
PREVENTION.
Promulgation by fire
marshal, §36-19-9.
Fish and game.
Exhibitions.
Possession of wildlife for
public exhibition
purposes, §§9-11-320 to
9-11-328.
See FISH AND GAME.

RULES AND REGULATIONS
—Cont'd
Fish and game—Cont'd
Violations of fish and game
laws, §§9-11-6 to 9-11-15.
See FISH AND GAME.
Flour.
Publication and effective
date, §20-1-28.
Food.
Adoption, §20-1-2.
Violations.
Penalty for violations,
§20-1-5.
Forests and forestry.
Fires and fire prevention.
Assessments for forest fire
protection.
State assessment,
§9-13-190.
State forestry commission.
Promulgation and
enforcement, §9-3-4.
Fruits and vegetables.
Grading and standards,
§2-11-77.
Penalty for violation,
§2-11-78.
Funerals.
Board of funeral service.
Certified copies, §34-13-8.
Challenging unreasonable
rules and regulations,
§34-13-6.
Distribution by board,
§34-13-4.
Procedural rules and
regulations of board,
§34-13-23.
Promulgation by board,
§34-13-26.
Scope of rules and
regulations, §34-13-27.
Garbage and trash, §22-27-7.
Ginseng, §9-13-246.
Grain.
Promotion of grain industry,
§2-8-249.
Grain dealers.
Commissioner of agriculture,
§2-31-16.
Grits.
Publication and effective
date, §20-1-28.
Harbors and ports.
State dock department,
§§33-1-24, 33-1-31,
33-3-4.
Hazardous substances.
Fees for disposal of
hazardous waste or
substances.
Adoption, §22-30B-17.
Hazardous waste.
Environmental management
department.
Duties of department as to,
§22-30-9.
Generally, §22-30-11.
Fees for disposal of
hazardous waste or
substances.
Adoption, §22-30B-17.
Generators.
Powers and duties of
environmental
management
department, §22-30-14.

RULES AND REGULATIONS
—Cont'd
Hazardous waste—Cont'd
Permit program.
Duties of environmental
management
department, §22-30-12.
Storage and disposal site
operators.
Authority of environmental
management
department, §22-30-16.
Transporters.
Authority of department,
§22-30-15.
Penalty for violation of
safety and hazardous
materials regulations,
§22-30-15.1.
Treatment facility operators.
Powers and duties of
department, §22-30-16.
Health.
See HEALTH.
Health care authorities.
Powers of authority,
§22-21-318.
**Health maintenance
organizations.**
Promulgation, §27-21A-19.
Highways, §§23-1-1, 23-1-59,
23-1-156.
Historic Blakeley authority.
Promulgation and alteration,
§41-10-181.
Violation.
Penalty, §41-10-181.
Honeybees and apiaries.
Implementation of chapter.
Promulgation, §2-14-13.
Penalties for violations,
§2-14-15.
Hospitals.
Licenses, §22-21-28.
Service program for
indigents, §22-21-212.
**Hotels, inns and other
transient lodging places,**
§§34-15-2 to 34-15-4,
34-15-9, 34-15-10.
See HOTELS, INNS AND
OTHER TRANSIENT
LODGING PLACES.
Income tax.
Department of revenue to
promulgate, §40-18-57.
Indigent persons.
Indigent defense systems,
§15-12-1.
Industrial alcohol.
Promulgation of regulations,
§28-5-9.
**Industrial development
advisory board,**
§41-9-185.
Industrial relations.
Department of industrial
relations.
Board of appeals, §§25-2-16
to 25-2-21, 25-2-25.
See LABOR.
Director of industrial
relations, §25-2-8.
Insurance.
See INSURANCE.
**Interstate compact on child
placement.**
Promulgation by
commissioner of
department of pensions
and security, §44-2-26.

RULES AND REGULATIONS
—Cont'd

Jails.
Sanitation.
Promulgation, §14-6-86.
See JUDGES.

Junior colleges.
Franklin, Marion and
Winston counties,
§16-60-25.
Jackson and DeKalb
counties, §16-60-55.

Junkyard control.
Promulgation, §23-1-249.
Screening, §23-1-247.

Labor.
Department of industrial
relations.
Board of appeals, §§25-2-16
to 25-2-21, 25-2-25.
See LABOR.
Director of public relations,
§25-2-8.

Landscape architects.
Board of examiners.
Examinations.
Rules covering scope of
examinations,
§34-17-22.
Promulgation by board,
§34-17-3.

Landscaping.
Horticulture and floriculture
work.
Penalties for violations,
§2-28-11.
Promulgation as to
qualifications and
practice of persons
engaged in work or
services governed by
chapter, §2-28-3.

Lead.
Promulgation, §22-37-3.

Lime, §§2-23-8 to 2-23-11.

Liquefied petroleum gas.
Promulgation by board,
§9-17-103.

**Liquefied petroleum gas fuel
tax,** §40-17-163.

Livestock.
Branding of livestock.
Promulgation by
commissioner,
§2-15-28.
Violations, §2-15-30.
Brucellosis or Bang's disease.
Penalty for violation,
§2-15-196.
Dealers, §§2-15-45, 2-15-48,
2-15-84, 2-15-135.
See LIVESTOCK.
Diseases, §§2-15-170 to
2-15-174.
Handling of livestock in
markets, §2-15-113.
Markets.
Handling of livestock in
markets.
Treatment in markets.
Promulgation,
§2-15-113.
Implementation of division,
§2-15-68.
Promulgation, §2-15-64.
Promotion of cattle industry,
§2-8-20.
Promotion of swine industry,
§2-8-60.

RULES AND REGULATIONS
—Cont'd

Livestock—Cont'd
Swine.
Hog cholera, §§2-15-235,
2-15-256, 2-15-270 to
2-15-274.
See LIVESTOCK.

**Long term quality health
care.**
Enforcement remedies and
criteria, §22-6-25.

Lost or unclaimed property.
Uniform disposition of
unclaimed property act.
Commissioner of revenue,
§35-12-46.

Manufactured buildings,
§24-4A-4.

Marine mammal protection.
Penalties for violations,
§9-11-396.
Promulgation, §9-11-395.

Marine resources, §§9-2-4,
9-2-8, 9-11-371.

Meat and meat products.
See MEAT AND MEAT
PRODUCTS.

Midwives.
Promulgation, §34-19-10.

Military affairs, §§3-2-1, 3-2-3;
Const. Ala., amd. 89.

Milk and milk products.
Health regulations, §2-13-93.

Mines and minerals.
Surface mining reclamation.
Promulgation, §9-16-13.

Motor fuels.
Diesel fuel tax, §40-17-18.

**Motor sports hall of fame
commission.**
Adoption, §41-9-471.

Motor vehicle carriers.
Fuel tax.
Authority of commissioner
to adopt, §40-17-152.
Mileage tax.
Department of revenue to
prescribe, §40-19-13.
Public service commission.
Commission to prescribe,
§37-3-7.
Power and authority to
make, §37-3-34.

Motor vehicles.
General provisions,
§§32-6-218, 32-6-219.
Rules of the road, §§32-5A-1
to 32-5A-266.
See MOTOR VEHICLES.
State board's of health
regulations.
Effect, §32-5A-194.1.

Municipal corporations.
Airports, §4-4-14.
Authority to regulate,
§4-4-2.
Ambulance service, §11-87-1.
Gas districts, §§11-50-401 to
11-50-403.
Sales and use taxes,
§11-51-204.
Subdivisions, §11-52-31.
Zoning, §§11-52-70 to
11-52-84.
See MUNICIPAL
CORPORATIONS.

Nurseries.
Insect disease and control,
§§2-25-20 to 2-25-22.

RULES AND REGULATIONS
—Cont'd

**Nuts, bulbs, fruits and
vegetables.**
Promotion of industry.
Assessments.
Referendum, §2-8-131.

Oil and gas.
Conservation and regulation
of production.
Oil and gas board,
§§9-17-12, 9-17-14,
9-17-15.

Optometrists.
Board of optometry.
Promulgation, §34-22-42.
Limited teaching licenses,
§34-22-5.

Parole.
Adoption by board of pardons
and paroles, §15-22-37.
Adoption of rules concerning
conditions of parole,
§15-22-29.

Peace officers.
Hall of fame.
Adoption by board,
§41-9-871.

Penitentiary.
Convict labor, §14-3-47.
Posting, §14-3-59.

Pest control, §§2-28-3, 2-28-8,
2-28-9, 2-28-11.
See PEST CONTROL.

Pesticides, §2-27-8.
Application of pesticides,
§§2-27-57 to 2-27-59.

Petroleum products,
§§8-17-81, 8-17-84.

**Pharmacists and
pharmacies,** §§34-23-13,
34-23-74, 34-23-92.

Physical therapists.
Board of physical therapy.
Authority of board,
§34-24-193.

Physicians.
Foreign medical school
graduates.
Off-shore medical schools.
State board of medical
examiners,
§34-24-81.

Plant pathologists, §§2-28-3,
2-28-11.

Polygraph examiners.
Board of polygraph
examiners.
Promulgation, §34-25-5.

Poultry, §§2-17-13, 2-17-30,
2-17-31.

Prisons and prisoners.
Work release.
Adoption, §14-8-2.
Earnings.
Disposition, §14-8-6.

Probation.
Administration procedure
act.
Applicability, §15-18-8.1.

Psychologists.
Adoption by board,
§34-26-21.

**Public officers and
employees.**
Code of ethics.
State ethics commission.
Waiver of rules and
regulations,
§36-25-3.

RULES AND REGULATIONS
—Cont'd

Public officers and employees—Cont'd

Director of personnel.
Promulgation, §36-26-9.

Insurance.
State employees' health insurance plan, §§36-29-4, 36-29-12.

Merit system.
Applicability to employees in classified and unclassified service, §36-26-10.

Moving expenses.
Reimbursement.
Eligibility and amount, §36-7-41.

Public service commission, §§37-1-80 to 37-1-105.
See PUBLIC SERVICE COMMISSION.

Public utilities.
Highways.
Rights of way.
Promulgation by highway department, §23-1-59.

Public works.
Contracts.
Promulgation by awarding authorities, §39-2-13.

Railroads.
Preservation.
Promulgation by department, §37-10-6.

Real estate brokers.
Real estate commission.
Authority of commission to promulgate, §34-27-8.

Securities.
Liability for acts or omissions in good faith under rules, §8-6-24.
Securities commission.
Making, amending and rescinding, §8-6-23.

Seeds, §§2-26-3, 2-26-11, 2-26-13.

Small business assistance.
Adoption of administrative rules, regulations, etc., §25-10-8.

Small loans.
Copies.
Certified copies of official documents, §5-18-12.
Promulgation by supervisor, §5-18-12.
Rates, terms or conditions for loans, §5-18-13.

Social security.
Public employees.
Promulgation, §36-28-10.

Soil and water conservation.
State soil and water conservation committee.
Promulgation, §9-8-22.

Soil classifiers.
Board.
Powers generally, §34-32-8.

Soybeans.
Promotion of soybean industry, §2-8-100.

Speech pathologists and audiologists.
Authority of board to promulgate, §34-28A-42.

RULES AND REGULATIONS
—Cont'd

Sports.
Athlete agents regulatory commission, §§8-26-3, 8-26-28.

Sports hall of fame board.
Adoption, §41-9-452.

State parks, §§9-2-3, 9-2-9.

Stock and stockholders.
Securities regulation, §§8-6-23, 8-6-24.

Surface mining control and reclamation.
Oversight committee.
Consulted on all proposed revisions of commission's rules and regulations, §9-16-73.

Swine.
Promotion of swine industry, §2-8-60.

Taxation.
Cigarettes.
Gummed cigarette papers, §40-25A-16.
Hotels, inns and other transient lodging places.
Transient occupancy tax, §40-26-19.
Income tax, §40-18-57.
Motor fuels.
Diesel fuel tax, §40-17-18.
Motor vehicle carriers fuel tax, §40-17-152.
Motor vehicle carriers.
Fuel tax, §40-17-152.
Mileage tax, §40-19-13.
Tobacco sales tax, §40-25-10.

Tennessee Valley Authority.
Exhibit commission.
Power to adopt, §41-9-782.

Tobacco.
Sales tax.
Interstate common carriers, §40-25-10.

Transient occupancy tax, §40-26-19.

Tunnels.
Federal assistance.
Promulgation, §23-1-1.

Underground storage tanks.
Adoption, §22-35-10.
Tank and wellhead protection, §22-36-3.
Adoption, §22-36-10.
Establish and protect wellhead areas, §22-36-7.
Trust fund.
No disbursements from fund until adoption of rules and regulations, §22-35-13.

Unemployment compensation, §§25-4-111, 25-4-112.

Vacation time-sharing plans.
Promulgation, §34-27-62.

Veterans.
State veterans' homes.
Admissions and discharges, §31-5A-8.
Applicable regulations, §31-5A-11.

Warehouses.
Promulgation by board of agriculture and industries, §8-15-2.

RULES AND REGULATIONS
—Cont'd

Water and wastewater systems and treatment plants, §22-25-13.

Water conservation and irrigation.
Corporations.
Promulgation, §9-10-34.

Water supply and waterworks.
Wells.
Promulgation, §22-24-3.

Weights and measures, §§8-16-15, 8-16-72, 8-16-121.

Welfare.
Department of human resources, §38-2-6.
Adoption, §38-2-3.

Workmen's compensation.
Violations.
Grounds for denial of compensation, §25-5-51.

RULES FOR MANDATORY CONTINUING LEGAL EDUCATION, ARMCLE,
Rules 1 to 8.
See ATTORNEYS AT LAW.

RULES OF APPELLATE PROCEDURE, ARAP,
Rules 1 to 51.
See APPEALS.

RULES OF CIVIL PROCEDURE, ARCP,
Rules 1 to 86.

Accord and satisfaction.
Affirmative defense, ARCP, Rule 8 (c).

Accounts and accounting.
Complaints.
Forms of complaints.
On account stated, ARCP, Form 6.
On open accounts, ARCP, Form 5.
Forms.
Complaint on account stated, ARCP, Form 6.
Complaint on open account, ARCP, Form 5.

Admissions.
Requests for admission, ARCP, Rules 36, 37; Forms 54 to 61A.

Affidavits.
New trial.
Time for serving affidavits, ARCP, Rule 59 (c).
Seizure of person or property.
Procedure for seizure of property, ARCP, Rule 64 (b).
Summary judgment, ARCP, Rule 56 (e) to (g).
Time for motions supported by affidavits, ARCP, Rule 6 (d).

Agreements.
Complaints.
Form of complaint on covenant or agreement, ARCP, Form 3.

RULES OF CIVIL PROCEDURE—Cont'd

Annulment of marriage.
Default judgments.
Proof required despite default, ARCP, Rule 55 (e).

Appeals.
Counterclaims and cross-claims, ARCP, Rule 13 (j).
Discovery pending appeal, ARCP, Rule 27 (b).
Rules of appellate procedure. See APPEALS.
Stay upon appeal, ARCP, Rule 62 (d).

Applicability of rules, ARCP, Rule 81.

Arbitration and award.
Defenses.
Affirmative defense, ARCP, Rule 8 (c).

Art.
Evidence.
Books of art prima facie evidence of facts of general notoriety and interest, ARCP, Rule 44 (g).

Assault and battery.
Pleadings.
Form of complaint for assault and battery, ARCP, Form 17.

Associations.
Unincorporated associations.
Actions relating to unincorporated associations, ARCP, Rule 23.2.

Assumption of risk.
Affirmative defense, ARCP, Rule 8 (c).

Attachments.
Seizure of person or property.
Procedure for seizure of property, ARCP, Rule 64 (b).

Attorneys at law.
Fees.
Interpleader, ARCP, Rule 22 (c).
Interpleader.
Attorneys' fees, ARCP, Rule 22 (c).
Interrogatories to jury.
Court to provide attorneys with questions or interrogatories, ARCP, Rule 49 (d).
Motions.
Signing, ARCP, Rule 11.
Pleadings.
Signing, ARCP, Rule 11.
Signing of pleadings, motions or other papers, ARCP, Rule 11.
Verdict.
Court to provide attorneys with questions or interrogatories for jury, ARCP, Rule 49 (d).

Audita querela.
Writ abolished, ARCP, Rule 60 (b).

Bankruptcy and insolvency.
Discharge in bankruptcy.
Affirmative defense, ARCP, Rule 8 (c).

RULES OF CIVIL PROCEDURE—Cont'd

Bills of review.
Abolished, ARCP, Rule 60 (b).

Bonds, surety.
Proceedings against sureties, ARCP, Rule 65.1.

Capacity.
Determination, ARCP, Rule 17 (b).
Pleadings, ARCP, Rule 9 (a).

Circuit courts, ARCP, Rules 77 to 80.
Always open, ARCP, Rule 77 (a).
Calendars, ARCP, Rule 79 (c).
Chambers.
Orders in chambers, ARCP, Rule 77 (b).
Clerks of court, ARCP, Rules 77 to 80.
Books and records, ARCP, Rule 79.
Calendars, ARCP, Rule 79 (c).
Dockets.
Civil docket, ARCP, Rule 79 (a).
Files of cases, ARCP, Rule 79.
Hours office open, ARCP, Rule 77 (c).
Indexes, ARCP, Rule 79 (c).
Microfilm, ARCP, Rule 79 (b).
Minute book, ARCP, Rule 79 (b).
Notice of orders or judgments, ARCP, Rule 77 (d).
Office, ARCP, Rule 77 (c).
Orders by clerk, ARCP, Rule 77 (c).
Records, ARCP, Rule 79.
Other books and records, ARCP, Rule 79 (d).
Removing files in cases, ARCP, Rule 79 (e).
Transfer of files, ARCP, Rule 79 (f).
Deemed always open, ARCP, Rule 77 (a).
Dockets.
Civil docket, ARCP, Rule 79 (a).
Hearings.
Conduct in open court, ARCP, Rule 77 (b).
Hours open, ARCP, Rule 77 (a).
Judgments.
Notice of judgments, ARCP, Rule 77 (d).
Record of final judgments in minute book, ARCP, Rule 79 (b).
Motion day, ARCP, Rule 78.
Notice.
Orders or judgments, ARCP, Rule 77 (d).
Orders of court.
Notice of orders, ARCP, Rule 77 (d).
Record of appealable orders in minute book, ARCP, Rule 79 (b).

RULES OF CIVIL PROCEDURE—Cont'd

Circuit courts—Cont'd
Records.
Clerks of court, ARCP, Rule 79.
Other books and records, ARCP, Rule 79 (d).
Removing files in cases, ARCP, Rule 79 (e).
Transfer of files, ARCP, Rule 79 (f).
Registers.
Preservation of office of register, ARCP, Rule 81 (d).
Trial.
Conduct in open court, ARCP, Rule 77 (b).

Class actions, ARCP, Rule 23.
Form of complaint, ARCP, Form 24.
Maintainable class actions, ARCP, Rule 23 (b).
Orders, ARCP, Rule 23 (d).
Prerequisites, ARCP, Rule 23 (a).

Clerical mistakes.
Amendment of judgment, ARCP, Rule 60 (a).

Clerks of court, ARCP, Rules 77 to 80.

Commencement of action, ARCP, Rule 3.

Complaints.
Accounts and accounting.
Forms of complaints.
On account stated, ARCP, Form 6.
On open accounts, ARCP, Form 5.
Agreements.
Form of complaint on covenant or agreement, ARCP, Form 3.
Convenants.
Form of complaint on covenant or agreement, ARCP, Form 3.
Conversion.
Form of complaint for conversion, ARCP, Form 22.
Forms, ARCP, Forms 2 to 25.
Recovery of chattels in specie.
Form of complaint, ARCP, Form 23.

Compromise and settlement.
Class actions, ARCP, Rule 23 (e).

Condition of the mind.
Pleadings, ARCP, Rule 9 (b).

Conditions precedent.
Pleadings, ARCP, Rule 9 (c).

Construction of rules, ARCP, Rule 1 (c).

Contempt.
Forms.
Motion for order to show cause.
Why defendant should not be held in contempt, ARCP, Form 66.
Subpoenas.
Failure to obey subpoena, ARCP, Rule 45 (f).

RULES OF CIVIL PROCEDURE—Cont'd

Contracts.
　Failure of consideration.
　　Affirmative defense, ARCP, Rule 8 (c).
　Illegality.
　　Affirmative defense, ARCP, Rule 8 (c).
Conversion.
　Complaints.
　　Form of complaint for conversion, ARCP, Form 22.
　Forms.
　　Complaint for conversion, ARCP, Form 22.
Coram nobis.
　Writ abolished, ARCP, Rule 60 (b).
Coram vobis.
　Writ abolished, ARCP, Rule 60 (b).
Corporations.
　Actions.
　　Derivative actions by shareholders, ARCP, Rule 23.1.
　　Form of complaint, ARCP, Form 25.
Costs.
　Generally, ARCP, Rule 54 (d).
　Judgments, ARCP, Rule 54 (d).
　Previously dismissed action, ARCP, Rule 41 (d).
　Taxation of costs, ARCP, Rule 54 (d).
Counterclaims.
　Appealed actions, ARCP, Rule 13 (j).
　Compulsory counterclaims, ARCP, Rule 13 (a).
　Default judgments, ARCP, Rule 55 (d).
　Dismissal, ARCP, Rule 41 (c).
　Exceeding opposing claim, ARCP, Rule 13 (c).
　Judgments.
　　Separate judgments, ARCP, Rule 13 (i).
　Omitted counterclaim, ARCP, Rule 13 (f).
　Permissive counterclaims, ARCP, Rule 13 (b).
　State.
　　Counterclaim against the state of Alabama, ARCP, Rule 13 (d).
　Supplemental pleadings, ARCP, Rule 13 (e).
　Trial.
　　Separate trials, ARCP, Rule 13 (i).
Courts.
　Deposit in court, ARCP, Rule 67.
　Findings by court.
　　Stay on motion for amendment to or addition to findings, ARCP, Rule 62 (b).
Covenants.
　Complaints.
　　Form of complaint on covenant or agreements, ARCP, Form 3.

RULES OF CIVIL PROCEDURE—Cont'd

Cross-claims.
　Against co-party, ARCP, Rule 13 (g).
　Appealed actions, ARCP, Rule 13 (j).
　Default judgments, ARCP, Rule 55 (d).
　Dismissal, ARCP, Rule 41 (c).
　Joinder of additional parties, ARCP, Rule 13 (h).
　Judgments.
　　Separate judgments, ARCP, Rule 13 (i).
　Separate trials, ARCP, Rule 13 (i).
Damages.
　Pleadings.
　　Special damage, ARCP, Rule 9 (g).
Death.
　Parties.
　　Substitution of parties, ARCP, Rule 25 (a), (d).
Declaratory judgments, ARCP, Rule 57.
Default judgments, ARCP, Rule 55; Forms 79 to 83.
Defenses, ARCP, Rule 12.
　Affirmative defenses, ARCP, Rule 8 (c).
　Alternative defenses, ARCP, Rule 8 (e).
　Consolidation in motion, ARCP, Rule 12 (g).
　Denials.
　　Effect of failure to deny, ARCP, Rule 8 (d).
　　Form of denials, ARCP, Rule 8 (b).
　Failure to join a party under Rule 19, ARCP, Rule 12 (b), (h).
　Failure to state a claim, ARCP, Rule 12 (b), (h).
　Form of denials, ARCP, Rule 8 (b).
　Forms, ARCP, Forms 26, 27.
　How presented, ARCP, Rule 12 (b).
　Improper venue, ARCP, Rule 12 (b), (h).
　Insufficiency of process, ARCP, Rule 12 (b), (h).
　Lack of jurisdiction, ARCP, Rule 12 (b), (h).
　Motions.
　　Consolidation of defenses in motion, ARCP, Rule 12 (g).
　　Defenses which may be made by motion, ARCP, Rule 12 (b).
　　Forms, ARCP, Form 26.
　Pleadings, ARCP, Rule 8.
　Preservation of certain defenses, ARCP, Rule 12 (h).
　Waiver of certain defenses, ARCP, Rule 12 (h).
　When presented, ARCP, Rule 12 (a).
Definitions.
　Judgments, ARCP, Rule 54 (a).
Demurrers.
　Abolished, ARCP, Rule 7 (c).
Deposit in court, ARCP, Rule 67.

RULES OF CIVIL PROCEDURE—Cont'd

Depositions, ARCP, Rules 26 to 37.
　Attendance.
　　Failure of party to attend at own deposition, ARCP, Rule 37 (d).
　Cross-examination.
　　Depositions upon oral examination, ARCP, Rule 30 (c).
　Effect of taking, ARCP, Rule 32 (c).
　Errors.
　　Effect, ARCP, Rule 32 (d).
　Evidence.
　　Objections to admissibility, ARCP, Rule 32 (b).
　Failure of party to attend at own deposition, ARCP, Rule 37 (d).
　Forms, ARCP, Forms 41 to 46, 62, 67.
　Irregularities.
　　Effect, ARCP, Rule 32 (d).
　Motions.
　　Depositions upon oral examination.
　　　Motion to terminate or limit examination, ARCP, Rule 30 (d).
　　　Form, ARCP, Form 44.
　Forms, ARCP, Forms 42 to 46, 62, 67.
　Notice.
　　Effect of errors and irregularities in notice, ARCP, Rule 32 (d).
　Objections.
　　Admissibility.
　　　Objections to admissibility in evidence, ARCP, Rule 32 (b).
　　Depositions upon oral examination, ARCP, Rule 30 (c).
　　Oral examination, ARCP, Rule 30 (c).
　Certification by officer, ARCP, Rule 30 (f).
　Changes, ARCP, Rule 30 (e).
　Copies, ARCP, Rule 30 (f).
　Cross-examination, ARCP, Rule 30 (c).
　Exhibits, ARCP, Rule 30 (f).
　Failure to attend or to serve subpoena, ARCP, Rule 30 (g).
　Filing by officer, ARCP, Rule 30 (f).
　Limitation of examination.
　　Motion to limit, ARCP, Form 44.
　Motions.
　　Termination or limitation of examination, ARCP, Rule 30 (d).
　Notice of examination, ARCP, Rule 30 (b).
　　Forms, ARCP, Forms 41, 42.
　Notice of filing, ARCP, Rule 30 (f).
　Oath, ARCP, Rule 30 (c).
　Objections, ARCP, Rule 30 (c).

RULES OF CIVIL
PROCEDURE—Cont'd
Depositions—Cont'd
Oral examination—Cont'd
Procurement of documents
and things, ARCP,
Rule 30 (b).
Record of examination,
ARCP, Rule 30 (c).
Signing, ARCP, Rule 30
(e).
Submission to witness,
ARCP, Rule 30 (e).
Termination of
examination, ARCP,
Rule 30 (d).
When depositions may be
taken, ARCP, Rule 30
(a).
Perpetuation of testimony,
ARCP, Rule 27.
Persons before whom
depositions taken.
Depositions to be used in
state.
Taken in foreign
countries, ARCP,
Rule 28 (b).
Taken within United
States, ARCP, Rule
28 (a).
Depositions to be used
outside state.
Taken within state,
ARCP, Rule 28 (c).
Disqualification for
interest, ARCP, Rule
28 (d).
Objections to deposition
because of
disqualification,
ARCP, Rule 32 (d).
District courts.
Applicability of rule to,
ARCP, Rule 28 (dc).
Stipulations as to persons,
ARCP, Rule 29.
Place of examination, ARCP,
Rule 45 (d).
Prisoners.
Form of motion for leave to
take deposition of
prisoner, ARCP, Form
45.
Records.
Depositions upon oral
examination.
Record of examination,
ARCP, Rule 30 (c).
Depositions upon written
questions.
Officer to take responses
and prepare record,
ARCP, Rule 31 (b).
Stays.
Form of motion to stay
taking of deposition,
ARCP, Form 43.
Subpoena for taking
depositions, ARCP, Rule
45 (d).
Form, ARCP, Form 75.
Supplementation of
responses, ARCP, Rule
26 (e).
Use in court, ARCP, Rule 32
(a).
Effect of using depositions,
ARCP, Rule 32 (c).

RULES OF CIVIL
PROCEDURE—Cont'd
Depositions—Cont'd
Written questions.
Filing.
Notice of filing, ARCP,
Rule 31 (c).
Forms.
Notice of taking
deposition upon
written questions,
ARCP, Form 46.
Notice, ARCP, Rule 31 (a).
Form of notice, ARCP,
Form 46.
Officer to take responses
and prepare record,
ARCP, Rule 31 (b).
Record.
Officer to take responses
and prepare record,
ARCP, Rule 31 (b).
Service of questions,
ARCP, Rule 31 (a).
Detinue.
Seizure of personal property,
ARCP, Rule 64 (b).
Discovery, ARCP, Rules 26 to
37.
Appeals.
Discovery pending appeal,
ARCP, Rule 27 (b).
Before action, ARCP, Rule 27
(a).
Compelling discovery.
Failure to comply with
order compelling
answers.
Form of motion for order
to show cause why
defendant should not
be held in contempt,
ARCP, Form 66.
Form of motion to
dismiss action,
ARCP, Form 65.
Form of motion to hold
in contempt, ARCP,
Form 64.
Motion for order
compelling discovery,
ARCP, Rule 37 (a).
Forms, ARCP, Forms 62
to 67.
Order compelling
discovery.
Failure to comply with
order, ARCP, Rule
37 (b).
Motion for order, ARCP,
Rule 37 (a).
Forms, ARCP, Forms
62 to 67.
Depositions, ARCP, Rules 26
to 37. See within this
heading, "Depositions."
Entry upon land for
inspection and other
purposes, ARCP, Rule
34.
Failure of party to respond
to request for
inspection, ARCP,
Rule 37 (d).
Failure to make discovery,
ARCP, Rule 37.

RULES OF CIVIL
PROCEDURE—Cont'd
Discovery—Cont'd
Inspections.
Entry upon land for
inspection and other
purposes, ARCP, Rule
34.
Failure of party to
respond to request
for inspection,
ARCP, Rule 37 (d).
Insurance agreements,
ARCP, Rule 26 (b).
Interrogatories, ARCP, Rules
38, 37; Forms 47 to 49,
63, 64.
Methods, ARCP, Rule 26 (a).
Motions.
Order compelling
discovery, ARCP, Rule
37 (a).
Forms of motions, ARCP,
Forms 62 to 67.
Pending appeal, ARCP, Rule
27 (b).
Perpetuation of testimony by
action, ARCP, Rule 27
(c).
Physical and mental
examination of persons.
Form of motion for
physical examination,
ARCP, Form 53.
Order for examination,
ARCP, Rule 35 (a).
Report of examining
physician, ARCP, Rule
35 (b).
Production of documents and
things.
Depositions upon oral
examination.
Request for documents
and things
accompanying notice
of examination,
ARCP, Rule 30 (b).
Forms, ARCP, Forms 50 to
52.
Procedure, ARCP, Rule 34
(b).
Scope, ARCP, Rule 34 (a).
Protective orders, ARCP,
Rule 26 (c).
Requests for admission,
ARCP, Rule 36.
Effect of admission, ARCP,
Rule 36 (b).
Failure to admit.
Expenses on failure,
ARCP, Rule 37 (c).
Forms, ARCP, Forms 54 to
61A.
Procedure, ARCP, Rule 36
(a).
Sanctions.
Failure to make discovery,
ARCP, Rule 37.
Scope of discovery, ARCP,
Rule 26 (b).
Sequence, ARCP, Rule 26 (d).
Stipulations regarding
discovery procedure,
ARCP, Rule 29.
Supplementation of
responses, ARCP, Rule
26 (e).
Timing, ARCP, Rule 26 (d).

RULES OF CIVIL PROCEDURE—Cont'd

Dismissal of actions.
Class actions, ARCP, Rule 23 (e).
Costs.
Previously dismissed action, ARCP, Rule 41 (d).
Counterclaims, ARCP, Rule 41 (c).
Cross-claims, ARCP, Rule 41 (c).
Forms, ARCP, Forms 70, 71.
Involuntary dismissal, ARCP, Rule 41 (b).
Notice of dismissal, ARCP, Rule 41 (a).
Form of notice, ARCP, Form 70.
Stipulation for dismissal, ARCP, Rule 41 (a).
Form of stipulation, ARCP, Form 71.
Third-party claim, ARCP, Rule 41 (c).
Voluntary dismissal, ARCP, Rule 41 (a).

District courts.
Applicability of Alabama rules of civil procedure, §12-12-11.
Depositions.
Persons before whom depositions taken.
Applicability of rule to district courts, ARCP, Rule 28 (dc).
Local court rules and administrative orders.
Applicability to district courts, ARCP, Rule 83 (dc).
Seizure of person or property.
Procedure for seizure of property.
Applicability of rules to district courts, ARCP, Rule 64 (b).

Divorce and alimony.
Default judgments.
Proof required despite default, ARCP, Rule 55 (e).

Dockets.
Circuit courts.
Civil docket, ARCP, Rule 79 (a).

Domestic relations.
Divorce and annulment.
Default judgments.
Proof required despite default, ARCP, Rule 55 (e).
Service by publication.
Alternative to publication in certain domestic proceedings, ARCP, Rule 4.3 (e).

Duress.
Affirmative defense, ARCP, Rule 8 (c).

Effective date of rules, ARCP, Rule 86.

Effect of rules, ARCP, Rule 1 (b).

Eminent domain.
Governing procedure for condemnation of property, §18-1A-70.

RULES OF CIVIL PROCEDURE—Cont'd

Employers and employees.
Injury by fellow servant.
Affirmative defense, ARCP, Rule 8 (c).

Entry upon land for inspection and other purposes, ARCP, Rule 34.
Failure of party to respond to request for inspection, ARCP, Rule 37 (d).

Error.
Harmless error, ARCP, Rule 61.

Estoppel.
Affirmative defense, ARCP, Rule 8 (c).

Evidence, ARCP, Rules 43, 44.
Admissibility, ARCP, Rule 43 (a).
Art.
Books of art prima facie evidence of facts of general notoriety and interest, ARCP, Rule 44 (g).
Authentication of documents, ARCP, Rule 44 (a).
Foreign documents, ARCP, Rule 44 (a).
Lack of record, ARCP, Rule 44 (b).
Original documents, ARCP, Rule 44 (d).
Recordation.
Documents recorded under recording act, ARCP, Rule 44 (e).
Business records, ARCP, Rule 44 (h).
Depositions.
Objections to admissibility, ARCP, Rule 32 (b).
Documents.
Proof of documents, ARCP, Rule 44.
Excluded evidence.
Record of excluded evidence, ARCP, Rule 43 (c).
Foreign law.
Determination of foreign law, ARCP, Rule 44.1.
Form, ARCP, Rule 43 (a).
Historical works.
Prima facie evidence of facts of general notoriety and interest, ARCP, Rule 44 (g).
Judgments.
Admissibility, ARCP, Rule 44 (f).
Maps and plats.
Prima facie evidence of facts of general notoriety and interest, ARCP, Rule 44 (g).
Motions.
Evidence on motions, ARCP, Rule 43 (e).
Newly discovered evidence.
Relief from judgment or order, ARCP, Rule 60 (b).
Private documents.
Proof of private documents, ARCP, Rule 44 (i).

RULES OF CIVIL PROCEDURE—Cont'd

Evidence—Cont'd
Recordation.
Proof of documents recorded under recording act, ARCP, Rule 44 (e).
Records.
Alternative proof of records, ARCP, Rule 44 (c).
Excluded evidence, ARCP, Rule 43 (c).
Lack of record, ARCP, Rule 44 (b).
Science.
Books of science prima facie evidence of facts of general notoriety and interest, ARCP, Rule 44 (g).
Stenographic reports.
Admissibility of stenographically reported testimony, ARCP, Rule 80.
Subpoenas, ARCP, Rule 45.
Transcripts.
Admissibility, ARCP, Rule 80.
Writing.
Handwriting.
Proof of handwriting, ARCP, Rule 44 (j).

Examinations.
Physical and mental examination of persons, ARCP, Rule 35.
Form of motion for physical examination, ARCP, Form 53.

Exceptions.
Unnecessary, ARCP, Rule 46.

Executions, ARCP, Rule 69.
Forms.
Notice of right to claim exemption from execution, ARCP, Form 92.

Exhibits.
Pleadings, ARCP, Rule 10 (c).

False imprisonment.
Pleadings.
Form of complaint for false imprisonment, ARCP, Form 18.

Fictitious defendants.
Dismissal, ARCP, Rule 4 (f).

Filing.
Pleadings and other papers, ARCP, Rule 5 (d), (e).

Findings by court, ARCP, Rule 52.
Amendment, ARCP, Rule 52 (b).
Effect, ARCP, Rule 52 (a).
Stay on motion for amendment to findings or for addition to findings, ARCP, Rule 62 (b).

Foreign countries.
Service of process in a foreign country, ARCP, Rule 4.4.

Foreign law.
Determination of foreign law, ARCP, Rule 44.1.

RULES OF CIVIL PROCEDURE—Cont'd

Forms, ARCP, Rule 84; Forms 1A to 51A.

Accounts and accounting.
  Complaint on account stated, ARCP, Form 6.
  Complaint on open account, ARCP, Form 5.

Agreements.
  Complaint on covenant or agreement, ARCP, Form 3.

Chattels.
  Complaint for recovery of chattels in specie, ARCP, Form 23.

Civil subpoena for production of documents, ARCP, Form 51A.

Class actions.
  Form of complaint, ARCP, Form 24.

Complaints, ARCP, Forms 2 to 25.

Consolidation.
  Motion to consolidate, ARCP, Form 72.

Contempt.
  Motion for order to show cause.
    Why defendant should not be held in contempt, ARCP, Form 66.

Conversion.
  Complaint for conversion, ARCP, Form 22.

Covenants.
  Complaint on covenant or agreement, ARCP, Form 3.

Default judgments, ARCP, Forms 79 to 83.

Defenses raised by motion, ARCP, Form 26.

Depositions, ARCP, Forms 41 to 46, 62, 67.

Dismissal of actions, ARCP, Forms 70, 71.

Execution.
  Notice of right to claim exemption from execution, ARCP, Form 92.

Goods sold and delivered.
  Complaints for, ARCP, Form 7.

Interpleader, ARCP, Form 38.

Interrogatories, ARCP, Forms 47 to 49, 63, 64.

Joinder of parties, ARCP, Forms 32, 33, 35 to 37.

Judgments, ARCP, Rule 54 (a).
  Sufficiency of judgment, ARCP, Rule 58 (b).
  Words required, ARCP, Rule 58 (b).

Jury.
  Demand for trial by jury, ARCP, Form 68.
  Motion for trial by advisory jury, ARCP, Form 69.

Money had and received.
  Complaint for, ARCP, Form 7.

RULES OF CIVIL PROCEDURE—Cont'd

Forms—Cont'd

Money lent.
  Complaint for, ARCP, Form 9.

Money paid by mistake.
  Complaint for, ARCP, Form 10.

Money paid by plaintiff for defendant.
  Complaint for, ARCP, Form 12.

Motions and other papers, ARCP, Rule 7 (b).

Negotiable instruments.
  Complaint on a promissory note, ARCP, Form 2.

New trial.
  Motion for new trial, ARCP, Form 78.

Notice of intent to serve subpoena on nonparty, ARCP, Form 51.

Offer of judgment, ARCP, Forms 86, 87.

Physical examination of persons.
  Form of motion for physical examination, ARCP, Form 53.

Pleadings, ARCP, Forms 2 to 25.

Pre-trial order, ARCP, Form 30.

Production of documents and things, ARCP, Forms 50 to 52.
  Civil subpoena for production of documents, ARCP, Form 51A.
  Notice of intent to serve subpoena on nonparty, ARCP, Form 51.

Recovery of chattels in specie.
  Complaint for recovery, ARCP, Form 23.

Requests for admission, ARCP, Forms 54 to 61A.
  Facts and automobile accidents, ARCP, Form 55.
  Genuineness of document, ARCP, Form 57.
  Statement in response, ARCP, Form 60.

Seizure of person or property, ARCP, Forms 88 to 91.
  Motion for dissolution of writ and request for hearing, ARCP, Form 90.
  Motion for writ of seizure, ARCP, Form 88.
  Order for writ of seizure, ARCP, Form 89.

Severance of claims, ARCP, Forms 33, 34.

Stockholder's derivative action.
  Complaint for stockholder's derivative action, ARCP, Form 25.

Subpoenas, ARCP, Rule 45 (a).

Substitution of parties, ARCP, Forms 39, 40.

RULES OF CIVIL PROCEDURE—Cont'd

Forms—Cont'd

Summary judgment.
  Motion for summary judgment, ARCP, Forms 84, 85.

Summons, ARCP, Rule 4 (a); ARCP, Forms 1A, 1B.

Third-party practice, ARCP, Forms 28, 29.

Verdict.
  Majority verdict.
    Stipulation for majority verdict, ARCP, Form 76.
  Motion for directed verdict, ARCP, Form 77.
  Motion for judgment notwithstanding verdict, ARCP, Form 78.

Work and labor done.
  Complaint for, ARCP, Form 8.

Fraud.

Defenses.
  Affirmative defense, ARCP, Rule 8 (c).

Judgments.
  Relief from judgment, ARCP, Rule 60 (b).

Orders of court.
  Relief from order, ARCP, Rule 60 (b).

Pleadings, ARCP, Rule 9 (b).
  Form of complaint for fraud, ARCP, Form 20.

Relief from judgment or order, ARCP, Rule 60 (b).

Fraudulent conveyances.

Joinder of remedies, ARCP, Rule 18 (b).

Guardian ad litem.

Appointment, ARCP, Rule 17 (c).

Compensation, ARCP, Rule 17 (d).

How chosen, ARCP, Rule 17 (d).

Guardian and ward.

Uniform guardianship and protective proceedings act.
  Rules govern proceedings under chapter, §26-2A-33.

Harmless error, ARCP, Rule 61.

Hearings.

Seizure of person or property.
  Procedure for seizure of property, ARCP, Rule 64 (b).

History and archives.

Evidence.
  Historical works prima facie evidence of facts of general notoriety and interest, ARCP, Rule 44 (g).

Injunctions.

Appeals.
  Injunction pending appeal, ARCP, Rule 62 (c).

Bonds, surety, ARCP, Rule 65 (c).

Form, ARCP, Rule 65 (d).

Preliminary injunctions, ARCP, Rule 65 (a).

RULES OF CIVIL PROCEDURE—Cont'd

Injunctions—Cont'd
Scope, ARCP, Rule 65 (d).
Security, ARCP, Rule 65 (c).
Temporary restraining orders, ARCP, Rule 65 (b).
Duration, ARCP, Rule 65 (b).
Form, ARCP, Rule 65 (d).
Hearing, ARCP, Rule 65 (b).
Notice, ARCP, Rule 65 (b).
Scope, ARCP, Rule 65 (d).

Inspections.
Entry upon land for inspection and other purposes, ARCP, Rule 34.
Failure of party to respond to request for inspection, ARCP, Rule 37 (d).

Insurance.
Discovery.
Insurance agreements, ARCP, Rule 26 (b).
Joinder of claims.
Liability insurance coverage, ARCP, Rule 18 (c).
Pleadings.
Form of complaints on insurance policies, ARCP, Forms 13 to 15.

Interpleader, ARCP, Rule 22.
Attorneys' fees, ARCP, Rule 22 (c).
General form for interpleader and declaratory relief, ARCP, Form 38.
Plaintiffs or defendants, ARCP, Rule 22 (a).
Release from liability, ARCP, Rule 22 (b).

Interpreters, ARCP, Rule 43 (f).

Interrogatories.
Answers.
Failure of party to serve answers to interrogatories, ARCP, Rule 37 (d).
Availability, ARCP, Rule 33 (a).
Business records.
Option to produce business records, ARCP, Rule 33 (c).
Failure of party to serve answers to interrogatories, ARCP, Rule 37 (d).
Forms, ARCP, Rule 33 (d); ARCP, Forms 47 to 49, 63, 64.
Jury.
Interrogatories to jury, ARCP, Rule 49.
Motions.
Forms, ARCP, Forms 48, 49, 63, 64.
Option to produce business records, ARCP, Rule 33 (c).
Scope, ARCP, Rule 33 (b).
Supplementation of responses, ARCP, Rule 26 (e).

RULES OF CIVIL PROCEDURE—Cont'd

Interrogatories—Cont'd
Trial.
Use at trial, ARCP, Rule 33 (b).
Use.
At trial, ARCP, Rule 33 (b).
Procedures for use, ARCP, Rule 33 (a).

Intervention.
Form of motion to intervene, ARCP, Form 32.
Intervention of right, ARCP, Rule 24 (a).
Permissive intervention, ARCP, Rule 24 (b).
Procedure, ARCP, Rule 24 (c).

Jails.
Depositions.
Form of motion for leave to take deposition of prisoner, ARCP, Form 45.

Joinder.
Claims, ARCP, Rule 18 (a).
Form of motion for severance of claims, ARCP, Forms 33, 34.
Counterclaims and cross-claims, ARCP, Rule 13 (h).
Default judgments.
Forms.
Default judgment entered by court, ARCP, Form 82.
Default judgment entered on application to clerk, ARCP, Form 80.
Docket of entry of default, ARCP, Form 81.
Motion to set aside entry of default, ARCP, Form 83.
Failure to join a party.
Defense of failure to join a party under Rule 19, ARCP, Rule 12 (b), (h).
Forms, ARCP, Forms 32 to 37.
Liability insurance coverage, ARCP, Rule 18 (c).
Parties.
Compulsory joinder, ARCP, Rule 19.
Counterclaim and cross-claim, ARCP, Rule 13 (h).
Forms, ARCP, Forms 32, 33, 35 to 37.
Misjoinder, ARCP, Rule 21.
Nonjoinder.
Pleading reasons for nonjoinder, ARCP, Rule 19 (c).
Permissive joinder, ARCP, Rule 20 (a).
Persons joined if feasible, ARCP, Rule 19 (a).
Persons needed for just adjudication, ARCP, Rule 19.
Required joinder, ARCP, Rule 19.
Remedies, ARCP, Rule 18 (b).

RULES OF CIVIL PROCEDURE—Cont'd

Joinder—Cont'd
Venue, ARCP, Rule 82 (c).

Judges.
Disability, ARCP, Rule 63.

Judgments, ARCP, Rules 54 to 63.
Alteration of judgment.
Motion to alter, ARCP, Rule 59 (e), (g).
Disposition of motion, ARCP, Rule 59.1.
Stay on motion, ARCP, Rule 62 (b).
Amendment of judgment.
Clerical mistakes, ARCP, Rule 60 (a).
Motion to amend, ARCP, Rule 59 (e), (g).
Disposition of motion, ARCP, Rule 59.1.
Stay on motion, ARCP, Rule 62 (b).
Nunc pro tunc, ARCP, Rule 60 (a).
Costs, ARCP, Rule 54 (d).
Counterclaims and cross-claims.
Separate judgments, ARCP, Rule 13 (i).
Default judgments.
Annulment of marriage.
Proof required despite default, ARCP, Rule 55 (e).
Counterclaimants, ARCP, Rule 55 (d).
Cross-claimants, ARCP, Rule 55 (d).
Divorce.
Proof required despite default, ARCP, Rule 55 (e).
Entry, ARCP, Rule 55 (a), (b).
Forms, ARCP, Forms 79 to 83.
Forms, ARCP, Forms 79 to 83.
Motion to set aside.
Form, ARCP, Form 83.
Proof required despite default in certain cases, ARCP, Rule 55 (e).
Setting aside default, ARCP, Rule 55 (c).
Form of motion to set aside, ARCP, Form 83.
Who entitled to, ARCP, Rule 55 (d).
Defined, ARCP, Rule 54 (a).
Demand for judgment, ARCP, Rule 54 (c).
Enforcement of judgment.
Executions, ARCP, Rule 69.
Stay of proceedings to enforce a judgment.
Automatic stay, ARCP, Rule 62 (a).
Injunction pending appeal, ARCP, Rule 62 (c).
Multiple claims or multiple parties.
Stay of judgment upon ARCP, Rule 62 (h).

RULES OF CIVIL PROCEDURE—Cont'd

Judgments—Cont'd

Enforcement of judgment —Cont'd

Stay of proceedings to enforce a judgment —Cont'd

Power of appellate court not limited, ARCP, Rule 62 (g).

State of Alabama or agency of state.

Stay in favor of, ARCP, Rule 62 (e).

Stay on motion for new trial or for judgment, ARCP, Rule 62 (b).

Stay upon appeal, ARCP, Rule 62.

Entry of judgment, ARCP, Rule 58 (c).

Sufficiency of minute entry, ARCP, Rule 58 (b).

Evidence.

Admissibility in evidence, ARCP, Rule 44 (f).

Excusable neglect.

Relief from judgment, ARCP, Rule 60 (b).

Findings by court, ARCP, Rule 52.

Forms, ARCP, Rule 54 (a).

Sufficiency of judgment, ARCP, Rule 58 (b).

Words required, ARCP, Rule 58 (b).

Fraud.

Relief from judgment, ARCP, Rule 60 (b).

How rendered, ARCP, Rule 58 (a).

Inadvertence.

Relief from judgment, ARCP, Rule 60 (b).

Language.

Wordage and phraseology, ARCP, Rule 58 (b).

Mistake.

Clerical mistakes.

Relief from judgment, ARCP, Rule 60 (a).

Relief from judgment, ARCP, Rule 60 (b).

Multiple claims or multiple parties, ARCP, Rule 54 (b).

Stay of judgment upon multiple claims or as to multiple parties, ARCP, Rule 62 (h).

Newly discovered evidence.

Relief from judgment, ARCP, Rule 60 (b).

Notice, ARCP, Rule 77 (d).

Offer of judgment, ARCP, Rule 68.

Forms, ARCP, Forms 86, 87.

Pleadings, ARCP, Rule 9 (e).

Relief from judgment, ARCP, Rule 60 (b).

Clerical mistakes, ARCP, Rule 60 (a).

Excusable neglect, ARCP, Rule 60 (b).

Fraud, ARCP, Rule 60 (b).

Inadvertence, ARCP, Rule 60 (b).

RULES OF CIVIL PROCEDURE—Cont'd

Judgments—Cont'd

Relief from judgment—Cont'd

Mistakes, ARCP, Rule 60 (b).

Newly discovered evidence, ARCP, Rule 60 (b).

Stay on motion for relief, ARCP, Rule 62 (b).

Rendition of judgments, ARCP, Rule 58 (a).

Satisfaction of judgment.

Relief from judgment, ARCP, Rule 60 (b).

Sufficiency of judgment, ARCP, Rule 58 (b).

Summary judgment.

Affidavits.

Bad faith affidavits, ARCP, Rule 56 (g).

Form, ARCP, Rule 56 (e).

When affidavits are unavailable, ARCP, Rule 56 (f).

Defense required, ARCP, Rule 56 (e).

For claimant, ARCP, Rule 56 (a).

For defending party, ARCP, Rule 56 (b).

Forms.

Motion for summary judgment, ARCP, Forms 84, 85.

Further testimony, ARCP, Rule 56 (e).

Motion for summary judgment, ARCP, Rule 56 (c).

Case not fully adjudicated on motion, ARCP, Rule 56 (d).

Forms, ARCP, Forms 84, 85.

Vacation of judgment.

Motion to vacate, ARCP, Rule 59 (e), (g).

Disposition of motion, ARCP, Rule 59.1.

Stay on motion, ARCP, Rule 62 (b).

Void judgment.

Relief from judgment, ARCP, Rule 60 (b).

Words required, ARCP, Rule 58 (b).

Jurisdiction.

Jurisdiction unaffected, ARCP, Rule 82 (a).

Lack of jurisdiction.

Defense of lack of jurisdiction, ARCP, Rule 12 (b), (h).

Jury.

Advisory jury, ARCP, Rule 39 (c).

Motion for trial by advisory jury.

Form, ARCP, Form 69.

Alternate jurors.

Selection, ARCP, Rule 47 (b).

Charge to jury, ARCP, Rule 51.

Demand for trial by jury, ARCP, Rule 38 (b).

Form, ARCP, Form 68.

RULES OF CIVIL PROCEDURE—Cont'd

Jury—Cont'd

Demand for trial by jury —Cont'd

Specification of issues, ARCP, Rule 38 (c).

Examination of jurors, ARCP, Rule 47 (a).

Forms.

Demand for jury trial, ARCP, Form 68.

Motion for trial by advisory jury, ARCP, Form 69.

Impaneling jurors, ARCP, Rule 47 (b).

Instructions to jury, ARCP, Rule 51.

Interrogatories to jury, ARCP, Rule 49.

Less than twelve, ARCP, Rule 48.

Motions.

Advisory jury.

Form of motion for trial by advisory jury, ARCP, Form 69.

Multiple claims, parties and actions.

Striking jurors, ARCP, Rule 47 (c).

Objections.

Instructions to jury, ARCP, Rule 51.

Right to trial by jury, ARCP, Rule 38 (a).

Selection of jurors, ARCP, Rule 47 (b).

Striking jurors, ARCP, Rule 47 (b), (c).

Trial by consent, ARCP, Rule 39 (c).

Trial by jury, ARCP, Rules 39 (a), 49.

Waiver of jury trial, ARCP, Rule 38 (d).

Laches.

Affirmative defense, ARCP, Rule 8 (c).

Letters rogatory.

Service of process by letter rogatory in foreign country, ARCP, Rule 4.4 (b).

Licenses.

Defenses.

Affirmative defense, ARCP, Rule 8 (c).

Limitation of actions.

Defenses.

Statute of limitations as affirmative defense, ARCP, Rule 8 (c).

Loans.

Pleadings.

Form of complaint for money lent, ARCP, Form 9.

Local court rules, ARCP, Rule 83.

Long arm statute.

Foreign countries, ARCP, Rule 4.4.

Out-of-state service, ARCP, Rule 4.2.

Malicious prosecution.

Pleadings.

Form of complaint for malicious prosecution, ARCP, Form 19.

RULES OF CIVIL PROCEDURE—Cont'd

Maps and plats.
Evidence.
Prima facie evidence of facts of general notoriety and interest, ARCP, Rule 44 (g).

Masters.
Appointment, ARCP, Rule 53 (a).
Compensation, ARCP, Rule 53 (a).
Meetings, ARCP, Rule 53 (d).
Powers, ARCP, Rule 53 (c).
Proceedings, ARCP, Rule 53 (d).
Reference to master, ARCP, Rule 53 (b).
Reports, ARCP, Rule 53 (e).
Statement of accounts, ARCP, Rule 53 (d).
When reference to master made, ARCP, Rule 53 (b).
Witnesses, ARCP, Rule 53 (d).

Mentally ill.
Parties, ARCP, Rule 17 (c).
Substitution of parties, ARCP, Rule 25 (b).

Minors.
Parties, ARCP, Rule 17 (c).

Mistake.
Judgments.
Clerical mistakes.
Relief from judgment, ARCP, Rule 60 (a).
Relief from judgment, ARCP, Rule 60 (b).
Orders of court.
Clerical mistakes.
Relief from order, ARCP, Rule 60 (a).
Relief from order, ARCP, Rule 60 (b).
Pleadings, ARCP, Rule 9 (b).
Form of complaint for money paid by mistake, ARCP, Form 10.
Relief from judgment or order, ARCP, Rule 60 (b).
Clerical mistakes, ARCP, Rule 60 (a).

Modernization of terminology, ARCP, Rule 81 (e).

Money.
Forms.
Complaint for money had and received, ARCP, Form 11.
Complaint for money lent, ARCP, Form 9.
Complaint for money paid by mistake, ARCP, Form 10.
Complaint for money paid by plaintiff for defendant, ARCP, Form 12.

Motion day, ARCP, Rule 78.

Motions, ARCP, Rules 7 to 16.
Affidavits.
Time for motions supported by affidavits, ARCP, Rule 6 (d).

RULES OF CIVIL PROCEDURE—Cont'd

Motions—Cont'd
Alteration of judgment, ARCP, Rule 59 (e), (g).
Disposition of motion, ARCP, Rule 59.1.
Stay on motion, ARCP, Rule 62 (b).
Amendment of judgment, ARCP, Rule 59 (e), (g).
Disposition of motion, ARCP, Rule 59.1.
Stay on motion, ARCP, Rule 62 (b).
Attorneys at law.
Signing of motions, ARCP, Rule 11.
Consolidation.
Form of motion to consolidate, ARCP, Form 72.
Default judgments.
Form of motion to set aside, ARCP, Form 83.
Defenses.
Consolidation of defenses in motion, ARCP, Rule 12 (g).
Defenses that may be made by motion, ARCP, Rule 12 (b).
Forms, ARCP, Form 26.
Depositions.
Forms of motions, ARCP, Forms 42 to 46, 62, 67.
Termination or limitation of oral examination, ARCP, Rule 30 (d).
Form of motion to limit, ARCP, Form 44.
Directed verdict, ARCP, Rule 50; ARCP, Form 77.
Stay on motion, ARCP, Rule 62 (b).
Discovery.
Order compelling discovery, ARCP, Rule 37 (a).
Forms of motions, ARCP, Forms 62 to 67.
Dropping defendant.
Form of motion, ARCP, Form 33.
Evidence on motions, ARCP, Rule 43 (e).
Findings by court.
Motion for amendment, ARCP, Rule 52 (b).
Form, ARCP, Rule 7 (b).
Interrogatories.
Forms, ARCP, Forms 48, 49, 63, 64.
Intervention.
Form of motion to intervene, ARCP, Form 32.
Joinder of parties.
Forms of motions, ARCP, Forms 35 to 37.
Judgment notwithstanding verdict, ARCP, Rule 50; ARCP, Form 78.
Judgment on the pleadings, ARCP, Rule 12 (c).
Jury.
Advisory jury.
Form of motion for trial by advisory jury, ARCP, Form 69.

RULES OF CIVIL PROCEDURE—Cont'd

Motions—Cont'd
More definite statement, ARCP, Rule 12 (e).
New trial, ARCP, Rule 50 (b).
Affidavits.
Time for serving, ARCP, Rule 59 (c).
Disposition of new trial motion, ARCP, Rule 59.1.
Form, ARCP, Form 78.
Grounds, ARCP, Rule 59 (a).
Presentation of motions not required, ARCP, Rule 59 (g).
Stay on motion for new trial, ARCP, Rule 62 (b).
Time for motion, ARCP, Rule 59 (b).
Physical examination of persons.
Form of motion for physical examination, ARCP, Form 53.
Production of documents and things.
Order compelling production.
Form of motion for order, ARCP, Form 52.
Requests for admission.
Form of motions, ARCP, Forms 58, 59, 61, 61A.
Severance of claims.
Forms of motions, ARCP, Forms 33, 34.
Signing of motions, ARCP, Rule 11.
Striking pleadings.
Motion to strike, ARCP, Rule 12 (f).
Summary judgment, ARCP, Rule 56.
Forms, ARCP, Forms 84, 85.
Third-party defendants.
Motions to bring in.
Form, ARCP, Form 28.
Time for motions, ARCP, Rule 6 (d).
Vacation of judgment, ARCP, Rule 59 (e), (g).
Disposition of motion, ARCP, Rule 59.1.
Stay on motion, ARCP, Rule 62 (b).
Verdict.
Directed verdict, ARCP, Form 77.
Judgment notwithstanding verdict, ARCP, Form 78.

Negligence.
Contributory negligence.
Affirmative defense, ARCP, Rule 8 (c).
Pleadings.
Form of complaint for negligence or wantonness, ARCP, Form 16.

Negotiable instruments.
Forms.
Complaint on a promissory note, ARCP, Form 2.

RULES OF CIVIL PROCEDURE—Cont'd

New trial.
Affidavits.
Time for serving, ARCP, Rule 59 (c).
Disability of judge, ARCP, Rule 63.
Forms.
Motion for new trial, ARCP, Form 78.
Initiative of court, ARCP, Rule 59 (d).
Motion for new trial, ARCP, Rule 50 (b).
Affidavits.
Time for serving, ARCP, Rule 59 (c).
Disposition, ARCP, Rule 59.1.
Form, ARCP, Form 78.
Grounds, ARCP, Rule 59 (a).
Presentation of motions not required, ARCP, Rule 59 (g).
Stay on motion, ARCP, Rule 62 (b).
Time for motion, ARCP, Rule 59 (b).
Remittitur, ARCP, Rule 59 (f).
Stay on motion for new trial, ARCP, Rule 62 (b).

Next friend.
Suit by next friend, ARCP, Rule 17 (c).

Notice.
Judgments, ARCP, Rule 77 (d).
Orders of court, ARCP, Rule 77 (d).

Nunc pro tunc.
Amendment of judgment, ARCP, Rule 60 (a).

Objections.
Exceptions unnecessary, ARCP, Rule 46.
Instructions to jury, ARCP, Rule 51.

Offer of judgment, ARCP, Rule 68.

One form of action, ARCP, Rule 2.

Orders of court.
Class actions, ARCP, Rule 23 (d).
Entry of order, ARCP, Rule 58 (c).
Sufficiency of minute entry, ARCP, Rule 58 (b).
Excusable neglect.
Relief from order, ARCP, Rule 60 (b).
Fraud.
Relief from order, ARCP, Rule 60 (b).
How rendered, ARCP, Rule 58 (a).
Inadvertence.
Relief from order, ARCP, Rule 60 (b).
Mistake.
Clerical mistakes.
Relief from order, ARCP, Rule 60 (a).
Relief from order, ARCP, Rule 60 (b).

RULES OF CIVIL PROCEDURE—Cont'd

Orders of court—Cont'd
Newly discovered evidence.
Relief from order, ARCP, Rule 60 (b).
Notice, ARCP, Rule 77 (d).
Relief from order.
Clerical mistakes, ARCP, Rule 60 (a).
Excusable neglect, ARCP, Rule 60 (b).
Fraud, ARCP, Rule 60 (b).
Inadvertence, ARCP, Rule 60 (b).
Mistakes, ARCP, Rule 60 (b).
Clerical mistakes, ARCP, Rule 60 (a).
Newly discovered evidence, ARCP, Rule 60 (b).
Stay on motion for relief, ARCP, Rule 62 (b).
Rendition of orders, ARCP, Rule 58 (a).
Sufficiency of order, ARCP, Rule 58 (b).

Ordinances.
Pleadings, ARCP, Rule 9 (d).

Papers.
Signing, ARCP, Rule 11.

Parties.
Capacity, ARCP, Rule 17 (b).
Pleading, ARCP, Rule 9 (a).
Class actions, ARCP, Rule 23.
Death.
Substitution of parties, ARCP, Rule 25 (a), (d).
Fictitious parties, ARCP, Rule 9 (h).
Defendants.
Dismissal, ARCP, Rule 4 (f).
Incompetence.
Substitution of parties, ARCP, Rule 25 (b).
Infants or incompetent persons, ARCP, Rule 17 (c).
Interpleader, ARCP, Rule 22.
Interrogatories to parties, ARCP, Rule 37.
Intervention.
Form of motion to intervene, ARCP, Form 32.
Intervention of right, ARCP, Rule 24 (a).
Permissive intervention, ARCP, Rule 24 (b).
Procedure, ARCP, Rule 24 (c).
Joinder, ARCP, Rules 19, 20.
Mentally ill, ARCP, Rule 17 (c).
Substitution of parties, ARCP, Rule 25 (b).
Minors, ARCP, Rule 17 (c).
Multiple parties.
Judgments involving multiple parties, ARCP, Rule 54 (b).
Striking jurors, ARCP, Rule 47 (c).
Names of parties.
Pleadings, ARCP, Rule 10 (a).
Nonjoinder, ARCP, Rule 21.

RULES OF CIVIL PROCEDURE—Cont'd

Parties—Cont'd
Public officers.
Death or separation from office.
Substitution of parties, ARCP, Rule 25 (d).
Real party in interest, ARCP, Rule 17 (a).
Substitution of parties.
Death, ARCP, Rule 25 (a).
Public officers, ARCP, Rule 25 (d).
Forms, ARCP, Forms 39, 40.
Incompetency, ARCP, Rule 25 (b).
Public officers.
Death or separation from office, ARCP, Rule 25 (d).
Transfer of interest, ARCP, Rule 25 (c).
Third-party practice, ARCP, Rules 14, 41; Forms 28, 29.
Transfer of interest.
Substitution of parties, ARCP, Rule 25 (c).

Personal injury.
Pleadings.
Form of complaint for personal injuries, ARCP, Form 31.

Physicians.
Physical and mental examination of persons.
Report of examining physician, ARCP, Rule 35 (b).

Place.
Pleadings, ARCP, Rule 9 (f).

Pleadings, ARCP, Rules 7 to 16.
Adoption of statements by reference, ARCP, Rule 10 (c).
Affirmative defenses, ARCP, Rule 8 (c).
Allowed pleadings, ARCP, Rule 7 (a).
Alternative claims or defenses, ARCP, Rule 8 (e).
Ambiguity.
Motion for more definite statement, ARCP, Rule 12 (e).
Amendments, ARCP, Rule 15 (a).
Amendments to conform to evidence, ARCP, Rule 15 (b).
Counterclaims, ARCP, Rule 13 (f).
Relation back of amendments, ARCP, Rule 15 (c).
Assault and battery.
Form of complaint for assault and battery, ARCP, Form 17.
Attorneys at law.
Signing of pleadings, ARCP, Rule 11.
Capacity, ARCP, Rule 9 (a).
Caption, ARCP, Rule 10 (a).
Claims for relief.
Contents, ARCP, Rule 8 (a).

RULES OF CIVIL PROCEDURE—Cont'd
Pleadings—Cont'd
Class actions.
Form of complaint, ARCP, Form 24.
Conciseness, ARCP, Rule 8 (e).
Condition of the mind, ARCP, Rule 9 (b).
Conditions precedent, ARCP, Rule 9 (c).
Consistency, ARCP, Rule 8 (e).
Construction of pleadings, ARCP, Rule 8 (f).
Contents of claims for relief, ARCP, Rule 8 (a).
Damages.
Special damage, ARCP, Rule 9 (g).
Defenses, ARCP, Rule 8 (b).
Affirmative defenses, ARCP, Rule 8 (c).
Alternative defenses, ARCP, Rule 8 (e).
Answer presenting defenses under Rule 12 (b), ARCP, Form 27.
Assertion in pleadings, ARCP, Rule 12 (b).
Effect of failure to deny, ARCP, Rule 8 (d).
Form of denials, ARCP, Rule 8 (b).
Denials.
Effect of failure to deny, ARCP, Rule 8 (d).
Form of denials, ARCP, Rule 8 (b).
Directness, ARCP, Rule 8 (e).
Exhibits, ARCP, Rule 10 (c).
Failure to deny.
Effect of failure, ARCP, Rule 8 (d).
Failure to state a claim.
Defense of failure to state a claim, ARCP, Rule 12 (b), (h).
Fictitious parties, ARCP, Rule 9 (h).
Filing, ARCP, Rule 5 (d).
Definition of filing with the court, ARCP, Rule 5 (e).
Forms, ARCP, Rule 10; ARCP, Forms 2 to 29.
Fraud, ARCP, Rule 9 (b).
Form of complaint for fraud, ARCP, Form 20.
General rules of pleading, ARCP, Rule 8.
Insufficiency of pleading.
Exceptions for insufficiency.
Abolished, ARCP, Rule 7 (c).
Judgments, ARCP, Rule 9 (e).
Motion for judgment on the pleadings, ARCP, Rule 12 (c).
Malicious prosecution.
Form of complaint for malicious prosecution, ARCP, Form 19.
Mistake, ARCP, Rule 9 (b).
Form of complaint for money paid by mistake, ARCP, Form 10.

RULES OF CIVIL PROCEDURE—Cont'd
Pleadings—Cont'd
More definite statement.
Motion for more definite statement, ARCP, Rule 12 (e).
Names of parties, ARCP, Rule 10 (a).
Negligence.
Form of complaint for negligence or wantonness, ARCP, Form 16.
Nonjoinder.
Pleading reasons for nonjoinder, ARCP, Rule 19 (c).
Official document or act, ARCP, Rule 9 (d).
Ordinances, ARCP, Rule 9 (d).
Paragraphs, ARCP, Rule 10 (b).
Permitted pleadings, ARCP, Rule 7 (a).
Personal injury.
Form of complaint for personal injuries, ARCP, Form 31.
Place, ARCP, Rule 9 (f).
Public officers and employees.
Official document or act, ARCP, Rule 9 (d).
Separate statement, ARCP, Rule 10 (b).
Service.
How made, ARCP, Rule 5 (b).
Numerous defendants, ARCP, Rule 5 (c).
When required, ARCP, Rule 5 (a).
Signing of pleadings, ARCP, Rule 11.
Statutes.
Special statute, ARCP, Rule 9 (d).
Stockholder's derivative action.
Form of complaint, ARCP, Form 25.
Striking pleading.
Motion to strike, ARCP, Rule 12 (f).
Supplemental pleadings, ARCP, Rule 15 (d).
Counterclaims, ARCP, Rule 13 (e).
Third-party practice, ARCP, Rule 14.
Form of third-party complaint, ARCP, Form 29.
Time, ARCP, Rule 9 (f).
Vagueness.
Motion for more definite statement, ARCP, Rule 12 (e).
Warranties.
Form of complaint on a warranty, ARCP, Form 21.
Wrongful death.
Form of complaint for wrongful death, ARCP, Form 31.
Pleas.
Abolished, ARCP, Rule 7 (c).

RULES OF CIVIL PROCEDURE—Cont'd
Preliminary hearings, ARCP, Rule 12 (d).
Pre-trial procedure, ARCP, Rule 16.
Pre-trial procedure, ARCP, Rule 16.
Form of pre-trial order, ARCP, Form 30.
Prisons and prisoners.
Depositions.
Form of motion for leave to take deposition of prisoner, ARCP, Form 45.
Process. See within this heading, "Summons and process."
Production of documents and things, ARCP, Rule 34.
Depositions upon oral examination.
Request for production of documents and things accompanying notice of oral examination, ARCP, Rule 30 (b).
Forms, ARCP, Forms 50 to 52.
Civil subpoena for production of documents, ARCP, Form 51A.
Notice of intent to serve subpoena on nonparty, ARCP, Form 51.
Promissory estoppel.
Affirmative defense, ARCP, Rule 8 (c).
Publication.
Service by publication, ARCP, Rule 4.3.
Public officers and employees.
Parties.
Death or separation from office.
Substitution of parties, ARCP, Rule 25 (d).
Pleadings.
Official document or act, ARCP, Rule 9 (d).
Receivers, ARCP, Rule 66.
Registers.
Office of register preserved, ARCP, Rule 81 (d).
Remittitur, ARCP, Rule 59 (f).
Reports.
Masters, ARCP, Rule 53 (e).
Requests for admission, ARCP, Rule 36.
Effect of admission, ARCP, Rule 36 (b).
Failure to admit.
Expenses on failure to admit, ARCP, Rule 37 (c).
Forms, ARCP, Forms 54 to 61A.
Facts and automobile accidents, ARCP, Form 55.
Genuineness of document, ARCP, Form 57.
Statement in response, ARCP, Form 60.
Procedure, ARCP, Rule 36 (a).

RULES OF CIVIL PROCEDURE—Cont'd

Res judicata.
Affirmative defense, ARCP, Rule 8 (c).
Right of entry.
Entry upon land for inspection and other purposes, ARCP, Rule 34.
Failure of party to respond to request for inspection, ARCP, Rule 37 (d).
Scintilla evidence rule.
Directed verdict or judgment not withstanding verdict.
When court may grant motion, ARCP, Rule 50 (e).
Scire facias.
Abolished, ARCP, Rule 81 (c).
Scope of rules, ARCP, Rule 1 (a).
Security.
Proceedings against sureties, ARCP, Rule 65.1.
Seizure of person or property, ARCP, Rule 64.
Affidavits.
Procedure for seizure of property, ARCP, Rule 64 (b).
District courts.
Applicability of rules to district courts, ARCP, Rule 64 (b).
Forms, ARCP, Forms 88 to 91.
Motion for dissolution of writ and request for hearing, ARCP, Form 10.
Motion for writ of seizure, ARCP, Form 88.
Order for hearing on application for writ of seizure, ARCP, Form 91.
Order for writ of seizure, ARCP, Form 89.
Generally, ARCP, Rule 64 (a).
Preliminary examinations.
Procedure for seizure of property, ARCP, Rule 64 (b).
Procedure for seizure of property.
Affidavit, ARCP, Rule 64 (b).
Attachment.
Dissolution.
Hearing, ARCP, Rule 64 (b).
Hearing on dissolution of writ, ARCP, Rule 64 (b).
Hearing on issuance of writ, ARCP, Rule 64 (b).
Issuance of writ without hearing.
Preliminary finding for plaintiff, ARCP, Rule 64 (b).

RULES OF CIVIL PROCEDURE—Cont'd

Seizure of person or property—Cont'd
Procedure for seizure of property—Cont'd
Hearings.
Dissolution of writ of seizure or attachment.
Pre-judgment hearing, ARCP, Rule 64 (b).
Failure to make preliminary finding for plaintiff, ARCP Rule 64 (b).
Writ of seizure or attachment, ARCP, Rule 64 (b).
Preliminary examinations, ARCP, Rule 64 (b).
Failure to make finding for plaintiff, ARCP, Rule 64 (b).
Finding for plaintiff, ARCP, Rule 64 (b).
Writ of seizure.
Dissolution.
Hearing on, ARCP, Rule 64 (b).
Hearing on dissolution of writ, ARCP, Rule 64 (b).
Hearings on writ, ARCP, Rule 64 (b).
Issued without hearing.
Preliminary finding for plaintiff, ARCP, Rule 64 (b).
Service of process, ARCP, Rules 4 to 4.4.
Acceptance of service, ARCP, Rule 4 (h).
Alternative modes of service.
Effect of availability, ARCP, Rule 4 (g).
Amendment of proof of service, ARCP, Rule 4 (d).
Avoidance of service.
Service by publication, ARCP, Rule 4.3 (c).
Certified mail.
Additional time after service by mail, ARCP, Rule 6 (e).
Foreign countries, ARCP, Rule 4.4 (b).
Out-of-state service by certified mail, ARCP, Rule 4.2 (b).
Service by certified mail, ARCP, Rule 4.1 (c).
Class actions, ARCP, Rule 23 (c).
Delivery by process server, ARCP, Rule 4.1 (b).
Foreign countries, ARCP, Rule 4.4 (b).
Out-of-state service, ARCP, Rule 4.2 (b).
Domestic relations.
Service by publication.
Alternative to publication in certain domestic proceedings, ARCP, Rule 4.3 (e).
Dual modes of service.
Effect of availability, ARCP, Rule 4 (g).

RULES OF CIVIL PROCEDURE—Cont'd

Service of process—Cont'd
Foreign countries, ARCP, Rule 4.4.
How served, ARCP, Rules 4 (c), 4.1 (a), 4.2 (b).
Incomplete service, ARCP, Rule 4 (f).
Insufficiency of service.
Defense of insufficiency of service, ARCP, Rule 12 (b), (h).
Letters rogatory.
Service by letter rogatory in foreign country, ARCP, Rule 4.4 (b).
Limits of effective service, ARCP, Rule 4 (b).
Long arm statute.
Foreign countries, ARCP, Rule 4.4.
Out-of-state service, ARCP, Rule 4.2.
Mail.
Additional time after service by mail, ARCP, Rule 6 (e).
Foreign countries, ARCP, Rule 4.4 (b).
Out-of-state service by certified mail, ARCP, Rule 4.2 (b).
Service by certified mail, ARCP, Rule 4.1 (c).
Methods of service.
Foreign countries, ARCP, Rule 4.4 (b).
In-state service, ARCP, Rule 4.1 (a).
Out-of-state service, ARCP, Rule 4.2 (b).
Publication, ARCP, Rule 4.3.
Multiple defendants, ARCP, Rule 4 (f).
Dismissal of fictitious defendants, ARCP, Rule 4 (f).
Out-of-state service.
Basis for out-of-state service, ARCP, Rule 4.2 (a).
Methods of out-of-state service, ARCP, Rule 4.2 (b).
Pleadings and other papers, ARCP, Rule 5.
Publication.
Service by publication, ARCP, Rule 4.3.
Refusal of service, ARCP, Rule 4 (e).
Subpoenas, ARCP, Rule 45 (c).
Third-party practice, ARCP, Rule 14 (a).
Waiver of service, ARCP, Rule 4 (h).
Signatures.
Pleadings, motions and other papers, ARCP, Rule 11.
Small claims rules.
Applicability of small claims cases, ASCR, Rule N.
General provisions.
See SMALL CLAIMS.
Specific performance.
Judgment for specific acts, ARCP, Rule 70.

RULES OF CIVIL PROCEDURE—Cont'd
Specific performance—Cont'd
Pleadings.
Form of complaint for specific performance, ARCP, Form 4.
State.
Counterclaim against state of Alabama, ARCP, Rule 13 (d).
Statute of frauds.
Defenses.
Affirmative defense, ARCP, Rule 8 (c).
Statute of limitations.
Affirmative defense, ARCP, Rule 8 (c).
Statutes.
Pleadings.
Special statute, ARCP, Rule 9 (d).
Stays.
Depositions.
Form of motion to stay taking of deposition, ARCP, Form 43.
Enforcement of judgment.
Stay of proceedings to enforce a judgment, ARCP, Rule 62.
Stipulations.
Discovery.
Stipulations regarding discovery procedure, ARCP, Rule 29.
Dismissal of actions, ARCP, Rule 41 (a).
Form of stipulation, ARCP, Form 71.
Subpoenas.
Contempt.
Failure to obey subpoena, ARCP, Rule 45 (f).
Depositions.
Form of subpoenas, ARCP, Form 75.
Subpoena for taking depositions, ARCP, Rule 45 (d).
Documentary evidence, ARCP, Rule 45 (b).
Production of documentary evidence.
Form, ARCP, Form 75.
Failure to obey.
Contempt, ARCP, Rule 45 (f).
Forms, ARCP, Rule 45 (a); ARCP, Forms 73 to 75.
Hearings, ARCP, Rule 45 (e).
Issuance, ARCP, Rule 45 (a).
Production of documentary evidence, ARCP, Rule 45 (b).
Form, ARCP, Form 75.
Service, ARCP, Rule 45 (c).
Subpoena duces tecum, ARCP, Form 74.
Trial.
Subpoena for trial, ARCP, Rule 45 (e).
Witnesses generally, ARCP, Rule 45 (a).
Substitution of parties, ARCP, Rule 25.
Forms, ARCP, Forms 39, 40.
Summary judgment, ARCP, Rule 56; Forms 84, 85.

RULES OF CIVIL PROCEDURE—Cont'd
Summons and process.
Amendment, ARCP, Rule 4 (d).
Copy of complaint or other document to be attached, ARCP, Rule 4 (a).
Definition of plaintiff and defendant, ARCP, Rule 4 (a).
Forms, ARCP, Rule 4 (a); ARCP, Forms 1A, 1B.
Instructions, ARCP, Rule 4 (a).
Insufficiency of process.
Defense of insufficiency of process, ARCP, Rule 12 (b), (h).
Issuance, ARCP, Rule 4 (a).
Persons not parties.
Process in behalf of and against persons not parties, ARCP, Rule 71.
Service of process, ARCP, Rules 4 to 4.4.
Supersedeas.
Writ abolished, ARCP, Rule 60 (b).
Suretyship.
Proceedings against sureties, ARCP, Rule 65.1.
Temporary restraining orders, ARCP, Rule 65.
Terminology.
Modernization of terminology, ARCP, Rule 81 (e).
Third-party practice.
Defendant.
When defendant may bring in third-party, ARCP, Rule 14 (a).
Dismissal of third-party claim, ARCP, Rule 41 (c).
Forms, ARCP, Forms 28, 29.
Plaintiff.
When plaintiff may bring in third-party, ARCP, Rule 14 (b).
Pleadings, ARCP, Rule 14.
Forms, ARCP, Form 29.
Service of process, ARCP, Rule 14 (a).
When third-party may be brought in, ARCP, Rule 14.
Time.
Computation, ARCP, Rule 6 (a).
Enlargement, ARCP, Rule 6 (b).
Motions, ARCP, Rule 6 (d).
Pleadings, ARCP, Rule 9 (f).
Title.
Vesting title, ARCP, Rule 70.
Title of rules, ARCP, Rule 85.
Trial.
Assignment of cases for trial, ARCP, Rule 40.
Calendar.
Setting of cases, ARCP, Rule 40 (a).
Consolidation, ARCP, Rule 42 (a).
Form of motion to consolidate, ARCP, Form 72.

RULES OF CIVIL PROCEDURE—Cont'd
Trial—Cont'd
Counterclaims and cross-claims.
Separate trials, ARCP, Rule 13 (i).
Court.
Trial by court, ARCP, Rule 39 (b).
Findings by court, ARCP, Rule 52.
Stay on motion for amendment to finding or for additional findings, ARCP, Rule 62 (b).
Interrogatories.
Use at trial, ARCP, Rule 33 (b).
Jury.
Advisory jury, ARCP, Rule 39 (c).
Trial by consent, ARCP, Rule 39 (c).
Trial by jury, ARCP, Rule 39 (a).
Notice.
Notice that case has been placed on trial docket, ARCP, Rule 40 (b).
Preparation for trial.
Discovery of trial preparation, ARCP, Rule 26 (b).
Separate trials, ARCP, Rules 20 (b), 42 (b).
Setting of cases, ARCP, Rule 40 (a).
Subpoena for trial, ARCP, Rule 45 (e).
Tribunals other than courts.
Applicability to, ARCP, Rule 81 (b).
Venue, ARCP, Rule 82.
Improper venue, ARCP, Rule 82 (d).
Defense of improper venue, ARCP, Rule 12 (b), (h).
Joinder, ARCP, Rule 82 (c).
Resolution of inconsistencies, ARCP, Rule 82 (b).
Verdict.
Attorneys at law.
Court to provide attorneys with questions or interrogatories, ARCP, Rule 49 (d).
Directed verdict.
Motion for directed verdict.
Effect, ARCP, Rule 50 (a).
Form, ARCP, Form 77.
Stay on motion, ARCP, Rule 62 (b).
When court may grant, ARCP, Rule 50 (e).
When made, ARCP, Rule 50 (a).
Forms.
Majority verdict.
Stipulation for majority verdict, ARCP, Form 76.
Motion for directed verdict, ARCP, Form 77.
Motion for judgment notwithstanding verdict, ARCP, Form 78.

ULES OF CIVIL
PROCEDURE—Cont'd
Verdict—Cont'd
General verdicts, ARCP,
Rule 49 (a).
Accompanied by answer to
interrogatories, ARCP,
Rule 49 (c).
Interrogatories to jury,
ARCP, Rule 49 (d).
Court to provide attorneys
with questions or
interrogatories, ARCP,
Rule 49 (d).
General verdict
accompanied by
answer to
interrogatories, ARCP,
Rule 49 (c).
Judgment notwithstanding
verdict.
Motion for judgment
notwithstanding
verdict, ARCP, Rule 50
(b).
Conditional rulings on
grant of motion,
ARCP, Rule 50 (c).
Denial of motion, ARCP,
Rule 50 (d).
Form, ARCP, Form 78.
When court may grant,
ARCP, Rule 50 (e).
Majority verdict, ARCP, Rule
48.
Form of stipulation for
majority verdict,
ARCP, Form 76.
Motions.
Directed verdict, ARCP,
Rule 50 (a), (e).
Form, ARCP, Form 77.
Stay on motion, ARCP,
Rule 62 (b).
Judgment notwithstanding
verdict, ARCP, Rule 50
(b).
Conditional rulings on
grant of motion,
ARCP, Rule 50 (c).
Denial of motion, ARCP,
Rule 50 (d).
Form, ARCP, Form 78.
When court may grant,
ARCP, Rule 50 (e).
Questions to jury, ARCP,
Rule 49.
Special verdicts, ARCP, Rule
49 (b).
Written findings.
Special verdicts, ARCP,
Rule 49 (b).
Waiver.
Affirmative defense, ARCP,
Rule 8 (c).
Warranties.
Pleadings.
Form of complaint on a
warranty, ARCP, Form
21.
Witnesses.
Affirmation.
In lieu of oath, ARCP,
Rule 43 (d).
Applicability of provisions
regulating admissibility
or proof of facts,
§12-21-145.
Cross-examination.
Scope of cross-examination,
ARCP, Rule 43 (b).

RULES OF CIVIL
PROCEDURE—Cont'd
Witnesses—Cont'd
Expert witnesses.
Discovery of trial
preparation, ARCP,
Rule 26 (b).
Impeachment, ARCP, Rule
43 (b).
Interpreters.
Appointment, ARCP, Rule
43 (f).
Compensation, ARCP, Rule
43 (f).
Leading questions, ARCP,
Rule 43 (b).
Masters, ARCP, Rule 53 (d).
Oaths.
Affirmation in lieu of oath,
ARCP, Rule 43 (d).
Scope of examination, ARCP,
Rule 43 (b).
Stenographic reports of
testimony.
Admissibility in evidence,
ARCP, Rule 80.
Subpoenas, ARCP, Rule 45.
Transcripts of testimony.
Admissibility in evidence,
ARCP, Rule 80.
Writs.
Seizure of person or property.
Procedure for seizure of
property.
Writs of seizure or
attachment, ARCP,
Rule 64 (b).
Wrongful death.
Pleadings.
Form of complaint for
wrongful death, ARCP,
Form 31.

RULES OF CONSTRUCTION.
See CONSTRUCTION AND
INTERPRETATION.

RULES OF COURT.
Appeals.
Rules of appellate procedure,
ARAP, Rules 1 to 51.
See APPEALS.
Juvenile procedure, ARJP,
Rules 1 to 30.
See JUVENILE
PROCEEDINGS.
Rules of civil procedure,
ARCP, Rules 1 to 86.
See RULES OF CIVIL
PROCEDURE.
Small claims rules, ASCR,
Rules A to N.
See SMALL CLAIMS.

RULES OF CRIMINAL
PROCEDURE, ARCrP,
Rules 1 to 20.
Abatement.
Pleas in abatement.
Abolished, ARCrP, Rule
16.1 (b).
Acquittal.
Time of pronouncing, ARCrP,
Rule 2.
Amendments.
Indictments, informations
and complaints, ARCrP,
Rule 15.5 (a).
Appeals.
Post-conviction remedies,
ARCrP, Rule 20.10.

RULES OF CRIMINAL
PROCEDURE—Cont'd
Appeals—Cont'd
State from pre-trial rulings.
Briefs and arguments on
appeal, ARCrP, Rule
17 (e).
Certiorari, ARCrP, Rule 17
(g).
Effect of ruling in pre-trial
appeal, ARCrP, Rule
17 (h).
Effect on trial court
proceedings, ARCrP,
Rule 17 (d).
Generally, ARCrP, Rule 17
(a).
Notice of appeal, ARCrP,
Rule 17 (b).
Preference, ARCrP, Rule
17 (c).
Record on appeal, ARCrP,
Rule 17 (f).
Rehearings, ARCrP, Rule
17 (g).
Time for taking appeal,
ARCrP, Rule 17 (b).
Arraignment.
Necessity for arraignment,
ARCrP, Rule 19.
Attorneys at law.
Post-conviction remedies.
Appointment of counsel,
ARCrP, Rule 20.7 (c).
Burden of proof.
Post-conviction remedies,
ARCrP, Rule 20.3.
Capital punishment.
Minute entries.
Old-style minute entries
for appeals and cases
in which death
sentence imposed,
ARCrP, Rule 22.
Case action summary sheets,
ARCrP, Rule 22.
Admissibility into evidence,
ARCrP, Rule 22.
Case files.
Copy filed with, ARCrP,
Rule 22.
Contents, ARCrP, Rule 22.
Filing, ARCrP, Rule 22.
Form of entries, ARCrP,
Rule 22.
Retroactive effect of rule,
ARCrP, Rule 22.
Sufficiency as record, ARCrP,
Rule 22.
Complaints.
Amendment of charges,
ARCrP, Rule 15.5 (a).
Consolidation.
Of defendants, ARCrP,
Rule 15.4 (b).
Additional jurors,
ARCrP, Rule 15.4
(h).
Trial, ARCrP, Rule 15.4
(c).
Of offenses, ARCrP, Rule
15.3 (b).
Trial and sentencing,
ARCrP, Rule 15.3
(c).
Defects in charges, ARCrP,
Rule 15.5 (b).
Effect of defect in charge,
ARCrP, Rule 15.5 (c).
Defined, ARCrP, Rule 15.1
(c).

RULES OF CRIMINAL PROCEDURE—Cont'd
Complaints—Cont'd
Failure of charge to state an offense.
Objection which may be raised at any time, ARCrP, Rule 16.2 (d).
Joinder.
Of defendants, ARCrP, Rule 15.4 (a).
Additional jurors, ARCrP, Rule 15.4 (h).
Trial, ARCrP, Rule 15.4 (c).
Of offenses, ARCrP, Rule 15.3 (a).
Trial and sentencing, ARCrP, Rule 15.3 (c).
Judgment and sentence.
Joinder and consolidation of offenses, ARCrP, Rule 15.3 (c).
Severance.
Of defendants.
Grounds for severance, ARCrP, Rule 15.4 (d).
Inspection of statements, ARCrP, Rule 15.4 (e).
Jeopardy, ARCrP, Rule 15.4 (g).
Severance during trial, ARCrP, Rule 15.4 (g).
Timing of severance motion, ARCrP, Rule 15.4 (f).
Of offenses.
Grounds for severance, ARCrP, Rule 15.3 (d).
Jeopardy, ARCrP, Rule 15.3 (f).
Severance during trial, ARCrP, Rule 15.3 (f).
Timing of severance motion, ARCrP, Rule 15.3 (e).
Trial.
Joinder and consolidation of defendants, ARCrP, Rule 15.4 (c).
Joinder and consolidation of offenses, ARCrP, Rule 15.3 (c).
Concurrent sentences, ARCrP, Rule 11.
Consecutive sentences, ARCrP, Rule 11.
Consolidation.
Complaints.
Of defendants, ARCrP, Rule 15.4 (b).
Additional jurors, ARCrP, Rule 15.4 (h).
Trial, ARCrP, Rule 15.4 (c).
Of offenses, ARCrP, Rule 15.3 (b).
Trial and sentencing, ARCrP, Rule 15.3 (c).

RULES OF CRIMINAL PROCEDURE—Cont'd
Consolidation—Cont'd
Indictments and informations.
Of defendants, ARCrP, Rule 15.4 (b).
Additional jurors, ARCrP, Rule 15.4 (h).
Trial, ARCrP, Rule 15.4 (c).
Of offenses, ARCrP, Rule 15.3 (b).
Trial and sentencing, ARCrP, Rule 15.3 (c).
Conviction.
Post-conviction remedies, ARCrP, Rule 20.
Time of pronouncing, ARCrP, Rule 2.
Court reporters.
Duties, ARCrP, Rule 21.
Death sentence cases.
Minute entries.
Old-style minute entries for, ARCrP, Rule 22.
Defects in charges, ARCrP, Rule 15.5 (b).
Effect of defect in charge, ARCrP, Rule 15.5 (c).
Defenses.
Waiver, ARCrP, Rule 16.2 (c).
Which must be raised by motion.
Effect of motion on plea, ARCrP, Rule 16.2 (e).
Objections which may be raised at any time, ARCrP, Rule 16.2 (d).
Pre-trial motion, ARCrP, Rule 16.2 (a).
All objections and defenses included, ARCrP, Rule 16.2 (b).
Waiver for failure to present, ARCrP, Rule 16.2 (c).
Definitions.
Complaints, ARCrP, Rule 15.1 (c).
Determination of guilt, ARCrP, Rule 1.
Indictments and informations, ARCrP, Rule 15.1.
Judgment, ARCrP, Rule 1.
Scope, ARCrP, Rule 1.
Sentence, ARCrP, Rule 1.
Demurrers.
Abolished, ARCrP, Rule 16.1 (b).
Diagnostic evaluation.
Disclosure of report, ARCrP, Rule 5.
When required, ARCrP, Rule 4.
Discovery, ARCrP, Rule 18.
Continuing duty to disclose, ARCrP, Rule 18.3.
Defendant.
Discovery under other provisions of law, ARCrP, Rule 18.1 (f).
Documents and tangible objects, ARCrP, Rule 18.1 (c).

RULES OF CRIMINAL PROCEDURE—Cont'd
Discovery—Cont'd
Defendant—Cont'd
Information not discoverable, ARCrP, Rule 18.1 (e).
Reports of examinations and tests, ARCrP, Rule 18.1 (d).
Statement of co-defendant or accomplice, ARCrP, Rule 18.1 (b).
Statements of defendant, ARCrP, Rule 18.1 (a).
Noncompliance.
Relief for noncompliance, ARCrP, Rule 18.5 (a).
Protective orders and conditions of discovery.
Effect of protective orders, ARCrP, Rule 18.4 (b).
General and special conditions of discovery, ARCrP, Rule 18.4 (c).
Showing, ARCrP, Rule 18.4 (a).
Reciprocal discovery, ARCrP, Rule 18.5 (b).
State.
Documents and tangible objects, ARCrP, Rule 18.2 (a).
Information not discoverable, ARCrP, Rule 18.2 (d).
Personal physical evidence, ARCrP, Rule 18.2 (b).
Reports of examinations and tests, ARCrP, Rule 18.2 (c).
Double jeopardy.
Severance of defendants.
Subsequent trial not barred, ARCrP, Rule 15.4 (g).
Severance of offenses.
Subsequent trial not barred, ARCrP, Rule 15.3 (f).
Evidence.
Case action summary sheets.
Admissibility into evidence, ARCrP, Rule 22.
Motions.
Pre-trial determination of admissibility of evidence, ARCrP, Rule 16.6.
Admissibility of evidence, ARCrP, Rule 16.6 (b).
Effect of granting motion, ARCrP, Rule 16.6 (d).
Hearing on motion, ARCrP, Rule 16.6 (c).
Orders in limine, ARCrP, Rule 16.6 (e).
Unlawful search, ARCrP, Rule 16.6 (a).
Fines and restitution.
Action upon failure to pay, ARCrP, Rule 10.
Collection of costs, ARCrP, Rule 10.

RULES OF CRIMINAL PROCEDURE—Cont'd

Fines and restitution—Cont'd

Deferred and installment payments, ARCrP, Rule 10.

Execution of fine and costs, ARCrP, Rule 10.

Imposition of, ARCrP, Rule 10.

Incarceration for nonpayment, ARCrP, Rule 10.

Inquiry into defendant's ability to pay, ARCrP, Rule 10.

Remedies for nonpayment, ARCrP, Rule 10.

To whom payment is made, ARCrP, Rule 10.

Forms.

Post-conviction remedies. Petitions, ARCrP, Rule 20.

Hearing.

Post-conviction remedies, ARCrP, Rule 20.9.

Sentence hearing, ARCrP, Rule 6.

Presence of defendant, ARCrP, Rule 7.

Indictments and informations, ARCrP, Rule 15.

Amendment of charges, ARCrP, Rule 15.5 (a).

Charging the offense, ARCrP, Rule 15.2 (b).

Consolidation.

Of defendants, ARCrP, Rule 15.4 (b).

Additional jurors, ARCrP, Rule 15.4 (h).

Trial, ARCrP, Rule 15.4 (c).

Of offenses, ARCrP, Rule 15.3 (b).

Trial and sentencing, ARCrP, Rule 15.3 (c).

Defects in charges, ARCrP, Rule 15.5 (b).

Effect of defects in charge, ARCrP, Rule 15.5 (c).

Definitions, ARCrP, Rule 15.1.

Failure to state an offense.

Objection which may be raised at any time, ARCrP, Rule 16.2 (d).

Generally, ARCrP, Rule 15.2 (a).

Joinder.

Of defendants, ARCrP, Rule 15.4 (a).

Additional jurors, ARCrP, Rule 15.4 (h).

Trial, ARCrP, Rule 15.4 (c).

Of offenses, ARCrP, Rule 15.3 (a).

Trial and sentencing, ARCrP, Rule 15.3 (c).

Judgment and sentence.

Joinder and consolidation of offenses, ARCrP, Rule 15.3 (c).

RULES OF CRIMINAL PROCEDURE—Cont'd

Indictments and informations—Cont'd

Motions.

More definite statement, ARCrP, Rule 15.2 (e).

Nature and contents.

Charging the offense, ARCrP, Rule 15.2 (b).

Generally, ARCrP, Rule 15.2 (a).

Motion for more definite statement, ARCrP, Rule 15.2 (e).

Notice of necessarily included offenses, ARCrP, Rule 15.2 (c).

Unnecessary allegations, ARCrP, Rule 15.2 (d).

Necessarily included offenses.

Notice of, ARCrP, Rule 15.2 (c).

Notice.

Necessarily included offenses, ARCrP, Rule 15.2 (c).

Place where offense committed.

Unnecessary to allege, ARCrP, Rule 15.2 (d).

Presentments.

Indictment includes presentment, ARCrP, Rule 15.1 (a).

Severance.

Of defendants.

Grounds for severance, ARCrP, Rule 15.4 (d).

Inspection of statements, ARCrP, Rule 15.4 (e).

Jeopardy, ARCrP, Rule 15.4 (g).

Severance during trial, ARCrP, Rule 15.4 (g).

Timing of severance motion, ARCrP, Rule 15.4 (f).

Of offenses.

Grounds for severance, ARCrP, Rule 15.3 (d).

Jeopardy, ARCrP, Rule 15.3 (f).

Severance during trial, ARCrP, Rule 15.3 (f).

Timing of severance motion, ARCrP, Rule 15.3 (e).

Time.

Statements of time or place unnecessary, ARCrP, Rule 15.2 (d).

Trial.

Joinder and consolidation of defendants, ARCrP, Rule 15.4 (c).

Joinder and consolidation of offenses, ARCrP, Rule 15.3 (c).

Unnecessary allegations, ARCrP, Rule 15.2 (d).

Instructions to the jury, ARCrP, Rule 14.

RULES OF CRIMINAL PROCEDURE—Cont'd

Joinder and consolidation of offenses, ARCrP, Rule 15.3 (c).

Complaints.

Of defendants, ARCrP, Rule 15.4 (a).

Additional jurors, ARCrP, Rule 15.4 (h).

Trial, ARCrP, Rule 15.4 (c).

Of offenses, ARCrP, Rule 15.3 (a).

Trial and sentencing, ARCrP, Rule 15.3 (c).

Indictments and informations.

Of defendants, ARCrP, Rule 15.4 (a).

Additional jurors, ARCrP, Rule 15.4 (h).

Trial, ARCrP, Rule 15.4 (c).

Of offenses, ARCrP, Rule 15.3 (a).

Trial and sentencing, ARCrP, Rule 15.3 (c).

Judges.

Motions.

Pre-trial motions.

Determination of issues of fact raised, ARCrP, Rule 16.4 (c).

Judgment and sentence.

Acquittal.

Time of pronouncing, ARCrP, Rule 2.

Complaints.

Joinder and consolidation of offenses, ARCrP, Rule 15.3 (c).

Concurrent sentences, ARCrP, Rule 11.

Consecutive sentences, ARCrP, Rule 11.

Conviction.

Time of pronouncing, ARCrP, Rule 2.

Diagnostic evaluation prior to sentencing, ARCrP, Rule 4.

Disclosure of report, ARCrP, Rule 5.

Hearing, ARCrP, Rule 6.

Presence of defendant, ARCrP, Rule 7.

Imposition of sentence, ARCrP, Rule 6.

Indictments and informations.

Joinder and consolidation of offenses, ARCrP, Rule 15.3 (c).

Mental health examination prior to sentencing, ARCrP, Rule 4.

Disclosure of report, ARCrP, Rule 5.

Motion for judgment of acquittal.

After verdict or judgment of conviction.

Denial by operation of law, ARCrP, Rule 12.3 (f).

RULES OF CRIMINAL PROCEDURE—Cont'd

Judgment and sentence —Cont'd

Motion for judgment of acquittal—Cont'd

After verdict or judgment of conviction—Cont'd

Finding of not guilty by reason of insanity, ARCrP, Rule 12.3 (d).

Generally, ARCrP, Rule 12.3 (a).

Joinder with other motions, ARCrP, Rule 12.3 (c).

Presentation to judge not required, ARCrP, Rule 12.3 (e).

Time for making motion, ARCrP, Rule 12.3 (b).

Tolling of period for appeal from district or municipal courts, ARCrP, Rule 12.3 (g).

Decision on motion, ARCrP, Rule 12.2 (b).

Effect of motion, ARCrP, Rule 12.2 (c).

Form of motion, ARCrP, Rule 12.1 (b).

Nature of motion, ARCrP, Rule 12.1 (a).

Time for making motion, ARCrP, Rule 12.2 (a).

After verdict of judgment of conviction, ARCrP, Rule 12.3 (b).

Presence of defendant when required, ARCrP, Rule 7.

Principles of sentencing, ARCrP, Rule 6.

Pronouncement of judgment, ARCrP, Rule 8.

Duty of court after pronouncement, ARCrP, Rule 9.

Pronouncement of sentence, ARCrP, Rule 8.

Duty of court after prouncement, ARCrP, Rule 9.

Time of pronouncing, ARCrP, Rule 2.

Duty of court after pronouncement, ARCrP, Rule 9.

Jurisdiction.

Lack of subject matter jurisdiction.

Objection which may be raised at any time, ARCrP, Rule 16.2 (d).

Jury.

Joinder and consolidation of defendants.

Additional jurors, ARCrP, Rule 15.4 (h).

Trial by jury.

Pre-trial motion issues of fact, ARCrP, Rule 16.4 (b).

Jury instructions, ARCrP, Rule 14.

RULES OF CRIMINAL PROCEDURE—Cont'd

Limitation of actions.

Motions.

Defects in commencement of proceedings or in charge.

Statutes of limitations tolled, ARCrP, Rule 16.5 (c).

Post-conviction remedies, ARCrP, Rule 20.2 (c).

Mental health.

Pleadings by defendant.

Not guilty and not guilty by reason of mental disease or defect, ARCrP, Rule 16.1 (b).

Mental health examination.

Disclosure of report, ARCrP, Rule 5.

When required, ARCrP, Rule 4.

Minute entries.

Case action sheets, ARCrP, Rule 22.

Admissibility into evidence, ARCrP, Rule 22.

Case files.

Copy filed in case files, ARCrP, Rule 22.

Filing of entries, ARCrP, Rule 22.

Form and contents of entries, ARCrP, Rule 22.

Retroactive effect of rule, ARCrP, Rule 22.

Sufficiency as record, ARCrP, Rule 22.

Death sentence cases.

Old-style minute entries for, ARCrP, Rule 22.

Motions, ARCrP, Rules 13, 16.

Effect of motion on plea, ARCrP, Rule 16.2 (e).

Evidence.

Pre-trial determination of admissibility of evidence, ARCrP, Rule 16.6.

Admissibility of evidence, ARCrP, Rule 16.6 (b).

Effect of granting motion, ARCrP, Rule 16.6 (d).

Hearing on motion, ARCrP, Rule 16.6 (c).

Orders in limine, ARCrP, Rule 16.6 (e).

Unlawful search, ARCrP, Rule 16.6 (a).

Indictments and informations.

More definite statement, ARCrP, Rule 15.2 (e).

Judges.

Pre-trial motions.

Determination of issues of fact raised, ARCrP, Rule 16.4 (c).

RULES OF CRIMINAL PROCEDURE—Cont'd

Motions—Cont'd

Limitation of actions.

Defects in commencement of proceedings or in charge.

Statutes of limitations tolled, ARCrP, Rule 16.5 (c).

Motions to quash.

Abolished, ARCrP, Rule 16.1 (b).

Objections which may be raised at any time, ARCrP, Rule 16.2 (d).

Pleadings.

General provisions. See PLEADINGS.

Post trial motions.

Arrest of judgment, ARCrP, Rule 13 (b).

Denial by operation of law, ARCrP, Rule 13 (d).

District and municipal courts, ARCrP, Rule 13 (e).

New trial, ARCrP, Rule 13 (a).

Presentation to judge not required, ARCrP, Rule 13 (c).

Pre-trial motions, ARCrP, Rule 16.

All objections and defenses included, ARCrP, Rule 16.2 (b).

Court trial, ARCrP, Rule 16.4 (c).

Determination of admissibility of evidence, ARCrP, Rule 16.6.

Admissibility of evidence, ARCrP, Rule 16.6 (b).

Effect of granting motion, ARCrP, Rule 16.6 (d).

Hearing on motion, ARCrP, Rule 16.6 (c).

Orders in limine, ARCrP, Rule 16.6 (e).

Unlawful search, ARCrP, Rule 16.6 (a).

Determination of motions, ARCrP, Rule 16.4 (a).

Effect of determination of motion.

Adverse determination, ARCrP, Rule 16.5 (b).

Granting motion based on defect in commencement of proceedings or in charge, ARCrP, Rule 16.5 (a).

Statutes of limitations tolled, ARCrP, Rule 16.5 (c).

Failure to present objections or defense.

Waiver of objection or defense, ARCrP, Rule 16.2 (c).

Issues of fact raised.

Court trial, ARCrP, Rule 16.4 (c).

RULES OF CRIMINAL PROCEDURE—Cont'd

Motions—Cont'd

Pre-trial motions—Cont'd

Issues of fact raised —Cont'd

Jury trial, ARCrP, Rule 16.4 (b).

Jury trial, ARCrP, Rule 16.4 (b).

Objections and defenses which must be raised, ARCrP, Rule 16.2 (a).

Hearing on motion, ARCrP, Rule 16.4.

Court trial, ARCrP, Rule 16.4 (c).

Determination of motions, ARCrP, Rule 16.4 (a).

Jury trial, ARCrP, Rule 16.4 (b).

Objections which may be raised at any time, ARCrP, Rule 16.2 (d).

Time of making motion, ARCrP, Rule 16.3 (a).

Extension or limitation of time, ARCrP, Rule 16.3 (b).

Searches and seizures.

Pre-trial determination of admissibility of evidence.

Unlawful search, ARCrP, Rule 16.6 (a).

Severance.

Timing of severance motion.

Severance of defendants, ARCrP, Rule 15.4 (f).

Severance of offenses, ARCrP, Rule 15.3 (e).

Motions for judgment of acquittal, ARCrP, Rule 12.

Notice.

Indictments and informations.

Necessarily included offenses, ARCrP, Rule 15.2 (c).

Post-conviction remedies.

Appeal of petitioner's conviction pending.

Notification of appellate court, ARCrP, Rule 20.6 (c).

Objections.

Instructions to the jury, ARCrP, Rule 14.

Which must be raised by motion.

Effect of determination of motion.

Adverse determination, ARCrP, Rule 16.5 (b).

Effect of granting motion based upon defect in commencement of proceedings or in charge, ARCrP, Rule 16.5 (a).

Limitation of actions.

Statutes of limitations tolled, ARCrP, Rule 16.5 (c).

RULES OF CRIMINAL PROCEDURE—Cont'd

Objections—Cont'd

Which must be raised by motion—Cont'd

Effect of determination of motion—Cont'd

Statutes of limitations tolled, ARCrP, Rule 16.5 (c).

Effect of motion on plea, ARCrP, Rule 16.2 (e).

Objections which may be raised at any time, ARCrP, Rule 16.2 (d).

Pre-trial motions, ARCrP, Rule 16.2 (a).

All objections and defenses included, ARCrP, Rule 16.2 (b).

Waiver for failure to present, ARCrP, Rule 16.2 (c).

Orders in limine, ARCrP, Rule 16.6 (e).

Parties.

Joinder, consolidation and severance of defendants, ARCrP, Rule 15.4.

Pleadings by the defendant, ARCrP, Rule 16.1 (b).

Petitions.

Commencement of proceedings, ARCrP, Rule 20.6.

Post-conviction remedies.

Successive petitions.

Preclusion of remedy, ARCrP, Rule 20.2 (b).

Pleadings.

Abolishment of pleas generally, ARCrP, Rule 16.1 (b).

Defendants.

Guilty, ARCrP, Rule 16.1 (b).

Not guilty, ARCrP, Rule 16.1 (b).

Not guilty by reason of mental disease or defect, ARCrP, Rule 16.1 (b).

Demurrers.

Abolished, ARCrP, Rule 16.1 (b).

Motions.

General provisions.

See MOTIONS.

Motions to quash.

Abolished, ARCrP, Rule 16.1 (b).

Pleas in abatement.

Abolished, ARCrP, Rule 16.1 (b).

Post-conviction remedies.

Amendment, ARCrP, Rule 20.7 (b).

Prosecutor's response, ARCrP, Rule 20.7 (a).

Successive petitions.

Preclusion of remedy, ARCrP, Rule 20.2 (b).

State of Alabama.

Formal charges by indictment, information or complaint, ARCrP, Rule 16.1 (a).

RULES OF CRIMINAL PROCEDURE—Cont'd

Pleas.

Abolishment of certain pleas, ARCrP, Rule 16.1 (b).

Pleadings.

General provisions.

See PLEADINGS.

Post-conviction remedies, ARCrP, Rule 20.

Amendment of pleadings, ARCrP, Rule 20.7 (b).

Appeals, ARCrP, Rule 20.10.

Court to which appeal taken, ARCrP, Rule 20.10 (a).

Release of petitioner, ARCrP, Rule 20.10 (b).

Who may appeal, ARCrP, Rule 20.10 (a).

Assignment of judges, ARCrP, Rule 20.6 (d).

Attorneys at law.

Appointment of counsel, ARCrP, Rule 20.7 (c).

Burden of proof, ARCrP, Rule 20.3.

Commencement of proceedings, ARCrP, Rule 20.6.

Forms.

Petitions, ARCrP, Rule 20.

Grounds.

Preclusion of remedy, ARCrP, Rule 20.2 (a).

Hearing, ARCrP, Rule 20.9. (a).

Decision, ARCrP, Rule 20.9 (c).

Findings of fact, ARCrP, Rule 20.9 (d).

Testimony of petitioner, ARCrP, Rule 20.9 (b).

Limitation of actions, ARCrP, Rule 20.2 (c).

Nature of proceeding, ARCrP, Rule 20.4.

Petitions.

Appeals.

Release of petitioner, ARCrP, Rule 20.10 (b).

Filing, ARCrP, Rule 20.6 (a).

Forms, ARCrP, Rule 20.

Notification of appellate courts, ARCrP, Rule 20.6 (c).

Release of petitioner.

Appeals, ARCrP, Rule 20.10 (b).

Service, ARCrP, Rule 20.6 (a).

Specificity, ARCrP, Rule 20.6 (b).

Successive petitions.

Preclusion of remedy, ARCrP, Rule 20.2 (b).

Testimony of petitioner, ARCrP, Rule 20.9 (b).

Pleadings generally.

Amendment, ARCrP, Rule 20.7 (b).

Prosecutor's response, ARCrP, Rule 20.7 (a).

Preclusion of remedy, ARCrP, Rule 20.2.

Prehearing conference, ARCrP, Rule 20.8.

RULES OF CRIMINAL PROCEDURE—Cont'd

Post-conviction remedies —Cont'd

Prosecutor's response, ARCrP, Rule 20.7 (a).

Relation to other remedies, ARCrP, Rule 20.4.

Scope of remedy, ARCrP, Rule 20.1.

Statute of limitations, ARCrP, Rule 20.2 (c).

Summary disposition, ARCrP, Rule 20.7 (d).

Venue, ARCrP, Rule 20.5.

Prehearing conferences.

Post-conviction remedies, ARCrP, Rule 20.8.

Presentence report.

Availability of, ARCrP, Rule 3.

Content, ARCrP, Rule 3.

Disclosure of, ARCrP, Rule 5.

When required, ARCrP, Rule 3.

Presentments.

Indictment includes presentment, ARCrP, Rule 15.1 (a).

Report.

Presentence report, ARCrP, Rule 3.

Disclosure of, ARCrP, Rule 5.

Reporters.

Duties, ARCrP, Rule 21.

Restitution, ARCrP, Rule 10.

Searches and seizures.

Motions.

Pre-trial determination of admissibility of evidence.

Unlawful search, ARCrP, Rule 16.6 (a).

Sentencing.

Post-conviction remedies, ARCrP, Rule 20.

Severance, ARCrP, Rule 15.

Complaints.

Of defendants.

Grounds for severance, ARCrP, Rule 15.4 (d).

Inspection of statements, ARCrP, Rule 15.4 (e).

Jeopardy, ARCrP, Rule 15.4 (g).

Severance during trial, ARCrP, Rule 15.4 (g).

Timing of severance motion, ARCrP, Rule 15.4 (f).

Of offenses.

Grounds for severance, ARCrP, Rule 15.3 (d).

Jeopardy, ARCrP, Rule 15.3 (f).

Severance during trial, ARCrP, Rule 15.3 (f).

Timing of severance motion, ARCrP, Rule 15.3 (e).

RULES OF CRIMINAL PROCEDURE—Cont'd

Severance—Cont'd

Indictments and informations.

Of defendants.

Grounds for severance, ARCrP, Rule 15.4 (d).

Inspection of statements, ARCrP, Rule 15.4 (e).

Jeopardy, ARCrP, Rule 15.4 (g).

Severance during trial, ARCrP, Rule 15.4 (g).

Timing of severance motion, ARCrP, Rule 15.4 (f).

Of offenses.

Grounds for severance, ARCrP, Rule 15.3 (d).

Jeopardy, ARCrP, Rule 15.3 (f).

Severance during trial, ARCrP, Rule 15.3 (f).

Timing of severance motion, ARCrP, Rule 15.3 (e).

Motions.

Timing of severance motion.

Severance of defendants, ARCrP, Rule 15.4 (f).

Severance of offenses, ARCrP, Rule 15.3 (e).

State of Alabama.

Pleadings.

Formal charges by indictment, information or complaint, ARCrP, Rule 16.1 (a).

Temporary rules, ARCrP, Rules 1 to 22.

Time.

Indictments and informations.

Statements of time or place unnecessary, ARCrP, Rule 15.2 (d).

Pre-trial motions, ARCrP, Rule 16.3 (a).

Circuit courts.

Time of making motions, ARCrP, Rule 16.3 (a).

District courts.

Time of making motions, ARCrP, Rule 16.3 (a).

Extension or limitation of time, ARCrP, Rule 16.3 (b).

Municipal courts.

Time of making motions, ARCrP, Rule 16.3 (a).

Trial.

Complaints.

Joinder and consolidation of defendants, ARCrP, Rule 15.4 (c).

Joinder and consolidation of offenses, ARCrP, Rule 15.3 (c).

RULES OF CRIMINAL PROCEDURE—Cont'd

Trial—Cont'd

Indictments and informations.

Joinder and consolidation of defendants, ARCrP, Rule 15.4 (c).

Joinder and consolidation of offenses, ARCrP, Rule 15.3 (c).

Motions.

Pretiral motions, ARCrP, Rule 16.

Venue.

Post-conviction remedies, ARCrP, Rule 20.5.

Waiver.

Objections and defenses.

For failure to present as required, ARCrP, Rule 16.2 (c).

RULES OF DISCIPLINARY ENFORCEMENT, ARDE, Rules 1 to 24.

See ATTORNEYS AT LAW.

RULES OF JUDICIAL ADMINISTRATION, ARJA, Rules 1 to 35.

See COURTS.

RULES OF JUVENILE PROCEDURE, ARJP, Rules 1 to 30.

See JUVENILE PROCEEDINGS.

RULES OF THE ROAD, §§32-5A-1 to 32-5A-266.

See MOTOR VEHICLES.

RUMORS.

Criminal law and procedure.

Falsely reporting incidents, §13A-11-11.

RUNAWAY PARENT'S LAW.

Reciprocal state enforcement of duty to support, §§30-4-80 to 30-4-98.

See DESERTION AND NONSUPPORT.

RUNNING AT LARGE.

Dogs.

General provisions, §§3-1-4 to 3-1-6.

Impound of dogs running at large.

Rabies, §§3-7-7, 3-7-8.

Municipal corporations, §§3-1-5, 11-45-10, 11-47-110.

Estrays, §§3-2-1 to 3-2-23.

See ESTRAYS.

RURAL ELECTRIC COOPERATIVES.

Terminating or declining services.

Applicants or customers indebtedness to cooperative for services at present or former locations, §37-6-30.

Applicability of section, §37-6-30.

Definition of rural electric cooperatives, §37-6-30.

Indebtedness for services previously rendered in dispute, §37-6-30.

RURAL TELEPHONE SERVICE, §§37-6-40 to 37-6-49.
See TELEPHONES.

RUSSELL COUNTY.
Barbers.
Chapter not applicable to Russell county, §34-5-15.
Counties generally.
See COUNTIES.
Fires and fire protection.
Fire fighting districts, Const. Ala., amd. 381.
Officers and employees.
Compensation, Const. Ala., amd. 380.
Probate court.
Costs and charges, Const. Ala., amd. 380.
School tax.
Special school tax, Const. Ala., amd. 124.
Tax anticipation bonds, Const. Ala., amd. 124.

RUSSELLVILLE, MUNICIPALITY OF.
Property tax, Const. Ala., amd. 8.

RYE.
General provisions.
See GRAIN.
Grading and standards, §§2-11-90 to 2-11-103.
See GRAIN.
Promotion of grain industry, §§2-8-230 to 2-8-252.
See GRAIN.

S

SABOTAGE.
Civil defense, §§31-9-1 to 31-9-24.
See CIVIL DEFENSE.
Legislature.
Emergency interim succession, §§29-3-1 to 29-3-16.
See LEGISLATURE.

SAFETY.
Boats, §§33-5-21, 33-5-22.
Civil defense, §§31-9-1 to 31-9-24.
See CIVIL DEFENSE.
Coal mine safety, §§25-9-1 to 25-9-370.
See COAL.
Department of public safety.
General provisions, §§32-2-1 to 32-2-44.
See MOTOR VEHICLES.
Electricity.
Operations in proximity to high voltage overhead conductors, §§37-8-52 to 37-8-55.
Harbors and ports.
State docks department. Powers, §§33-3-1, 33-3-2.
Highway and traffic safety coordination act, §§32-4-1 to 32-4-7.
See MOTOR VEHICLES.
Labor.
Coal mine safety, §§25-9-1 to 25-9-370.
See COAL.

SAFETY—Cont'd
Labor—Cont'd
Duties of employers, etc., §25-1-1.
Military affairs.
Abatement of menaces to safety of command, §31-2-126.
Motor vehicles.
Spilling loads or litter, §32-5-76.
Zones.
Defined, §32-1-1.1.
Driving through safety zone prohibited, §32-5A-217.
Railroads.
Crossings, §§37-2-81 to 37-2-83.
Signs.
Erection by companies, §37-2-80.
Liability for failure to comply, §37-2-83.
School buses.
Inspections, §16-27-3.
Monthly safety inspections, §16-27-5.
Seat belts, §16-27-6.
Ships and shipping.
Declaration of policy, §33-5-1.
State safety coordinating committee, §§32-3-1 to 32-3-7.
See MOTOR VEHICLES.
White cane safety day.
Annual proclamation, §21-7-10.

SAFETY-RESPONSIBILITY ACT, §§32-7-1 to 32-7-42.
See MOTOR VEHICLES.

SAILBOARDS.
Defined, §33-5-22.1.
Hull.
Deemed flotation device, §33-5-22.1.

ST. CLAIR COUNTY.
Annexation, Const. Ala., amd. 460.
Courts.
Costs.
Repeal of amendment, Const. Ala., amd. 422.
Economic development, Const. Ala., amd. 197.
Officers.
Compensation.
Repeal of amendment, Const. Ala., amd. 422.
School tax.
Special school tax, Const. Ala., amd. 77.

ST. STEPHENS HISTORICAL COMMISSION, §§41-9-335 to 41-9-337.
Appointment of members, §41-9-335.
Appropriations.
Counties and municipalities. Authorization, §41-9-336.
Benefits.
Status of employees of commission, §41-9-337.
Bonds, surety.
Treasurer, §41-9-335.
Composition, §41-9-335.

ST. STEPHENS HISTORICAL COMMISSION—Cont'd
Counties.
Appropriations.
Authorized, §41-9-336.
Public facilities and improvements on commission land. Powers as to, §41-9-336.
Creation, §41-9-335.
Employees.
Part-time employees. Employment, §41-9-337.
Status for purpose of insurance and benefit programs, §41-9-337.
Expenses of members, §41-9-335.
Insurance.
Participation in programs by employees, §41-9-337.
Meetings, §41-9-335.
Municipal corporations.
Appropriations.
Authorized, §41-9-336.
Public facilities and improvements on commission land. Powers as to, §41-9-336.
Number of members, §41-9-335.
Officers, §41-9-335.
Powers, §41-9-335.
Quorum, §41-9-335.
Terms of members, §41-9-335.

SALARIES.
Accounts and accounting.
Department of examiners of public accounts, §41-5-9.
Aged persons.
Commission on the aging, §38-3-4.
Agriculture.
Commissioner of agriculture and industries, §2-2-5.
Alabama Agricultural and Mechanical University.
Faculty and president, §16-49-23.
Alabama State University.
Faculty and president, §16-50-23.
Attorney general, §36-15-3.
Auburn University.
Powers of board of trustees, §16-48-4.
Circuit courts.
Clerks of court, §§12-17-80, 12-17-81.
Judges, §§12-17-30, 12-18-10; Const. Ala., art. VI, §150.
Officers and employees.
Establishment of rates, §12-17-2.
Registers, §§12-17-80, 12-17-81; Const. Ala., art. VI, §163.
Reporters, §§12-17-274, 12-17-292, 12-17-293.
Coal.
Legislative surface mining oversight committee, §9-16-73.
Surface mining commission, §9-16-73.

SALARIES—Cont'd
  Commercial code.
    Secured transactions.
      Transactions excluded from
        provisions, §7-9-104.
  **Conservation and natural
    resources.**
    Proration among divisions of
      department, §9-2-19.
  Corporations.
    See CORPORATIONS.
  Corrections.
    Board of corrections.
      Chiefs of divisions, §14-1-7.
    Commissioner of corrections,
      §14-1-1.3.
    Deputy commissioners,
      §14-1-1.5.
    Institution finance authority.
      Board of directors, §14-2-6.
  Counties.
    See COUNTIES.
  Court of civil appeals.
    See COURT OF CIVIL
      APPEALS.
  Court of criminal appeals.
    See COURT OF CRIMINAL
      APPEALS.
  Courts, §12-1-21.
  Debts.
    Intestate former employee
      owed wages.
      Discharge of debtor from
        debt, §43-8-115.
  Dentists.
    Public health dentists,
      §22-1-5.
  **Department of examiners of
    public accounts.**
    Chief examiner and assistant
      chief examiner, §41-5-9.
  District attorneys, §12-17-182.
  District courts.
    Court personnel, §12-17-2.
    Judges, §12-17-68; Const.
      Ala., art. VI, §150.
    Retired judges on active
      duty, §12-18-61.
  Education.
    See EDUCATION.
  Elections.
    Election officers, §17-6-13.
    Registrars, §17-4-153.
  **Environmental improvement
    authorities.**
    Board of directors, §9-6-6.
  Escambia county.
    Officers, Const. Ala., amd.
      391.
  Forests and forestry.
    State forester, §9-3-5.
    Assistant state forester,
      §9-3-6.
    State forestry commission,
      §9-3-2.
  Garnishment.
    See GARNISHMENT.
  Geological survey.
    Research and experiments.
      Retention of faculty
        members and students,
        §9-4-19.
  Governor.
    Councillor, §36-13-13.
  Health.
    Dentists.
      Public health dentists,
        §22-1-5.
    How salaries to be paid,
      §22-2-12.

SALARIES—Cont'd
  Health—Cont'd
    State health department
      personnel, §22-2-11.
  Highways.
    Closing and vacating streets,
      alleys and highways.
      Commissioners, §23-4-3.
    Department.
      Chief engineer, §23-1-22.
      Legal division.
        Charging of salary,
          §23-1-29.
        Chief counsel and
          assistant counsel,
          §23-1-27.
      Personnel, §23-1-33.
    Finance corporation,
      §23-1-174.
    Highway authority,
      §23-1-154.
  Income tax.
    Withholding tax.
      Declaration of estimated
        tax, §§40-18-80 to
        40-18-85.
        See INCOME TAX.
      General provisions,
        §§40-18-70 to 40-18-80.
        See INCOME TAX.
  Insurance.
    Commissioner of insurance,
      §27-2-4.
  **Jacksonville State
    University.**
    Faculty, §16-52-6.
  Jails.
    Physicians, §14-6-20.
  Judges, Const. Ala., amd. 328.
    Compensation commission,
      §§12-10-1 to 12-10-5.
    Diminishing.
      Voluntary diminution of
        salaries, §12-1-16.
  Junior colleges.
    Teachers' salaries.
      Authority to borrow in
        anticipation of current
        revenues if funds not
        sufficient to pay,
        §16-60-113.
  Legislature, Const. Ala., art.
    IV, §49.
  Livingston University.
    Faculty, §16-53-6.
  Marine resources.
    Director of division of marine
      resources, §9-2-83.
  Mentally ill.
    Mental health board.
      Authority to establish
        salary schedules,
        §22-50-40.
  Military department,
    §31-2-61.
  Municipal corporations.
    See MUNICIPAL
      CORPORATIONS.
  Municipal courts.
    Judges, §12-14-33.
  National guard, §31-2-88.
  Naval militia, §31-2-88.
  Prisons and prisoners.
    County convicts.
      Superintendent of public
        works, §14-4-11.

SALARIES—Cont'd
  **Public officers and
    employees.**
    Additional salary.
      Receipt from funds of
        United States or
        philanthropic source,
        §36-6-4.
    Appointing authorities.
      Certain salaries to be fixed
        by, §36-6-6.
    Constitutional officers,
      §36-6-8.
    Diminution.
      Voluntary diminution,
        §36-6-10.
    Entitlement.
      Succeeding officer entitled
        to salary for day upon
        which inducted into
        office, §36-6-2.
    Garnishment, §§6-6-480 to
      6-6-484.
    Governor.
      Certain salaries to be fixed
        by, §36-6-6.
      Salaries of persons whose
        salary not set by
        governor, §36-6-8.
    Longevity pay, §36-6-11.
    Merit system.
      Salaries of persons not
        covered by system,
        §36-6-8.
      State personnel board to
        provide for salaries of
        employees in pay plan
        of system, §36-6-7.
    Officer or employee filling
      more than one office,
      position, etc., §36-6-3.
    Payment.
      Time, §36-6-1.
    State personnel board.
      Providing for salaries of
        employees, §36-6-5.
    Time of payment, §36-6-1.
    Voluntary diminution,
      §36-6-10.
  Public service commission,
    §37-1-11.
  Railroads.
    Railway policemen,
      §37-2-154.
  **Savings and loan
    associations.**
    Officers and employees.
      Power of directors to fix,
        §5-16-24.
  Secured transactions.
    Transactions excluded from
      provisions of article,
      §7-9-104.
  Sheriffs, §36-22-16.
  Small loans.
    Bureau of loans.
      Payment of salaries,
        §5-2A-83.
  State health officer, §22-2-8.
  Supreme court justices,
    §12-2-4; Const. Ala., art.
    VI, §150.
    Retired justices on active
      duty status, §12-18-10.
  Surviving spouse.
    Debt for wage owed to
      intestate former
      employee.
      Discharge by payment to
        surviving spouse,
        §43-8-115.

SALARIES—Cont'd
Taxation.
Department of revenue.
Division chiefs, §40-2-24.
Trade schools.
Teachers' salaries.
Authority to borrow in
anticipation of current
revenues if funds not
sufficient to pay,
§16-60-113.
Troy State University.
Faculty and officers,
§16-56-6.
University of Montevallo,
§§16-54-5 to 16-54-8.
**University of North
Alabama.**
Faculty and president,
§16-51-6.
**University of South
Alabama.**
Faculty, officers and
employees, §16-55-4.
**Water conservation and
irrigation.**
Director of irrigation,
§9-2-16.
Welfare.
Board of human resources,
§38-2-2.
County boards of human
resources, §38-2-7.
Widows.
Debt for wages owed to
intestate former
employee.
Discharge by payment to
surviving spouse,
§43-8-115.
Withholding tax, §§40-18-70
to 40-18-80.
See INCOME TAX.
Youth services.
Responsibilities of
department of pensions
and security, §44-1-26.

SALES.
Abandoned property.
Uniform disposition of
unclaimed property act,
§§35-12-20 to 35-12-48.
See LOST OR
UNCLAIMED
PROPERTY.
Abandoned vehicles.
General provisions, §§32-13-1
to 32-13-8.
See MOTOR VEHICLES.
Solid waste disposal act,
§§22-27-1 to 22-27-7.
See GARBAGE AND
TRASH.
Advertising.
Going out of business or
distress merchandise
sales, §8-13-16.
License.
Display of license
number and date of
issuance, §8-13-2.
Agriculture, §§2-1-3, 2-2-30.
Alcohol.
Industrial alcohol, §§28-5-5
to 28-5-7.
Alcoholic beverages, §§28-8-1
to 28-8-8.
See ALCOHOLIC
BEVERAGES.

SALES—Cont'd
Alligator farms.
Restrictions on buyers,
§9-12-204.
Animals.
Domestic animals or fowl.
Sale between sunset and
sunrise, §3-1-20.
Veterinarians' liens.
Sale of animal to enforce
lien, §35-11-391.
Armories.
Duties of armory commission,
§31-4-16.
Attachment, §§6-6-77 to
6-6-79.
Auctions and auctioneers,
§§34-4-1 to 34-4-54.
See AUCTIONS AND
AUCTIONEERS.
Audits.
Going out of business or
distress merchandise
sales.
License applications.
Cost of independent
audit, §8-13-6.
Bankruptcy sales.
Going out of business or
distress merchandise
sales, §§8-13-1 to
8-13-23. See within this
heading, "Going out of
business or distress
merchandise sales."
Blind persons.
Division of rehabilitation and
crippled children service.
Business enterprise
program.
Blind vendors associated
with.
Exemption from sales
or use tax,
§40-23-5.
Sale, etc., of blind-made
products or services,
§§21-1-60 to 21-1-62.
Bonds, surety.
Going out of business or
distress merchandise
sales.
License.
Requirement, §8-13-4.
Brake fluid, §§8-17-2, 8-17-5,
8-17-7.
**Bread, flour, cornmeal and
grits.**
General provisions.
See BREAD, FLOUR,
CORNMEAL AND
GRITS.
Bulk sales.
Commercial code, §§7-6-101
to 7-6-111.
See COMMERCIAL CODE.
Caskets.
Notice and certificates to be
enclosed in sold casket,
§22-9-77.
Record and report of casket
sales, §22-9-77.
Catfish.
Marketing of catfish,
§§2-11-30 to 2-11-40.
See CATFISH.
Promotion of industry.
Occasional sales between
producers.
Exemption, §2-8-284.

SALES—Cont'd
**Caustic or corrosive
substances.**
Misbranded containers,
§8-17-21.
Checks.
Sale of checks, §§8-7-1 to
8-7-15.
See CHECKS.
Cigarettes.
Minors.
Sale to, §13A-12-3.
Coal.
Coal mixed with other
substances or with
different quality of coal,
§13A-9-52.
Code of Alabama.
Publisher, §41-21-4.
Commercial code, §§7-2-101
to 7-2-725.
See COMMERCIAL CODE.
Commission contracts.
Sales representative's
commission contracts,
§§8-24-1 to 8-24-5.
Commission merchants,
§§2-29-1 to 2-29-11.
See COMMISSION
MERCHANTS.
Conditional sales.
Secured transactions,
§§7-9-101 to 7-9-507.
See COMMERCIAL CODE.
Contracts.
Commercial code.
See COMMERCIAL CODE.
Cornmeal.
Manufacture and sale.
See BREAD, FLOUR,
CORNMEAL AND
GRITS.
Corrections.
Institution finance authority.
Bond issues, §§14-2-12 to
14-2-24.
See CORRECTIONS.
Kilby property, §§14-2-25
to 14-2-27.
Cotton.
Generally, §§2-19-1 to
2-19-106.
See COTTON.
Decedents' estates.
Personal property, §§43-2-410
to 43-2-422.
See EXECUTORS AND
ADMINISTRATORS.
Real property, §§43-2-440 to
43-2-482.
See EXECUTORS AND
ADMINISTRATORS.
Deceptive sales practices,
§§8-19-1 to 8-19-15.
See DECEPTIVE TRADE
PRACTICES.
Definitions.
Commercial code, §§7-2-103
to 7-2-106.
Going out of business or
distress merchandise
sales, §8-13-1.
Detinue.
Conditional sales contracts.
Actions by vendor or
against vendee,
§6-6-259.

SALES—Cont'd

Distress merchandise sales,
§§8-13-1 to 8-13-23. See
within this heading,
"Going out of business or
distress merchandise
sales."

Drugs.
General provisions,
§§13A-2-215, 20-1-4.
Pharmacists and pharmacies,
§§34-23-1, 34-23-6,
34-23-9.

Education.
Lease and sale of school land.
General provisions.
See EDUCATION.

Eggs and egg products.
General provisions, §§2-12-2
to 2-12-9.
See EGGS AND EGG
PRODUCTS.
Permits, §2-12-4.
See EGGS AND EGG
PRODUCTS.

Estrays, §3-2-4.
Highways.
Animals running at large
on, §3-2-22.

Evidence.
Contracts.
Parol or extrinsic evidence,
§7-2-202.

Execution sales.
Endorsements on execution
writs, §§6-9-98 to
6-9-101.
General provisions, §§6-9-140
to 6-9-150.
See EXECUTIONS.
Redemption, §§6-5-247 to
6-5-257.
See REAL PROPERTY.

**Executors and
administrators.**
Claims and debts.
Sale, compromise and
settlement, §§43-3-390
to 43-3-394.
Sale of real property for
payment of debts and
for division, §§43-2-440
to 43-2-468.
See EXECUTORS AND
ADMINISTRATORS.
Going out of business or
distress merchandise
sales, §§8-13-1 to
8-13-23. See within this
heading, "Going out of
business or distress
merchandise sales."
Personal property, §§43-2-410
to 43-2-422.
See EXECUTORS AND
ADMINISTRATORS.
Real property.
Sale for payment of debts
and for division,
§§43-2-440 to 43-2-468.
See EXECUTORS AND
ADMINISTRATORS.
Sale of land for payment of
legacies, §§43-2-480 to
43-2-482.

**Exemptions from levy and
sale under process,**
§§6-10-1 to 6-10-126.
See EXEMPTIONS FROM
LEVY AND SALE
UNDER PROCESS.

SALES—Cont'd

Fair trade.
General provisions.
See TRADE AND
COMMERCE.
Motion picture fair
competition, §§8-18-1 to
8-18-6.
See MOTION PICTURES.
Restraint of trade or
production, §§8-1-1,
8-10-1 to 8-10-3.
See TRADE AND
COMMERCE.

Fire sales.
Going out of business or
distress merchandise
sales, §§8-13-1 to
8-13-23. See within this
heading, "Going out of
business or distress
merchandise sales."

Fireworks, §§8-17-210,
8-17-211, 8-17-220 to
8-17-222.
See FIREWORKS.

Fish and game.
See FISH AND GAME.

Flour.
Manufacture and sale.
See BREAD, FLOUR,
CORNMEAL AND
GRITS.

Food.
See FOOD.

Foreclosure.
Deeds in lieu of foreclosure,
§§35-10-50, 35-10-51.
General provisions, §§35-10-1
to 35-10-10.
See MORTGAGES AND
DEEDS OF TRUST.
Power of sale, §§35-10-1 to
35-10-10.
See MORTGAGES AND
DEEDS OF TRUST.
Redemption, §§6-5-247 to
6-5-257.
See REAL PROPERTY.

**Going out of business or
distress merchandise
sales,** §§8-13-1 to 8-13-23.
Advertising, §8-13-16.
License.
Display of number and
date of issuance,
§8-13-2.
Applicability of chapter.
Exceptions, §8-13-23.
Attendance at sale.
Licensee, §8-13-21.
Audits.
License applications.
Costs, §8-13-6.
Bidding.
False bidders.
Prohibited, §8-13-20.
Bonds, surety.
License.
Requirement, §8-13-4.
Business licenses.
Surrender on issuance of
license for sale,
§8-13-11.
Definitions, §8-13-1.
Exemptions, §8-13-23.
Fees.
Licenses, §§8-13-2 to
8-13-14.

SALES—Cont'd

**Going out of business or
distress merchandise
sales**—Cont'd
Hearings.
License.
Applications, §8-13-5.
Costs, §8-13-8.
Hours.
Regular store hours,
§8-13-15.
Exceptions, §8-13-15.
Inventory, §8-13-7.
Additions, §8-13-17.
Defined, §8-13-1.
Sale limited to inventoried
stock, §8-13-17.
Investigations.
License, §8-13-6.
Costs, §8-13-8.
Fee, §8-13-6.
Licenses, §40-12-101.
Advertising.
Display of license
number and date of
issuance, §8-13-2.
Application, §8-13-3.
Audit.
Costs, §8-13-6.
Bond required of applicant,
§8-13-4.
Costs.
Applicant's refusal to
pay, §8-13-6.
Display.
Advertising.
License number and
date of issuance,
§8-13-2.
Premises of sale, §8-13-2.
Duration, §8-13-12.
Extension, §8-13-12.
Fees.
Generally, §8-13-8.
Investigation fee,
§8-13-6.
Applicant's refusal to
pay, §8-13-6.
Issuing fee, §8-13-8.
Renewal fee, §8-13-8.
Hearing.
Applications, §8-13-5.
Costs, §8-13-8.
Investigation, §8-13-6.
Costs, §8-13-8.
Applicant's refusal to
pay, §8-13-6.
Fee, §8-13-6.
Issuance.
Fee, §8-13-8.
Restrictions, §8-13-10.
Use of trade, business or
firm name of
licensee after,
§8-13-14.
When probate judge to
issue, §8-13-9.
Merchants.
Issuance only to bona
fide merchant,
§8-13-7.
Probate judge.
Issuance, §8-13-9.
Renewal.
Fee, §8-13-8.
Required, §8-13-2.
Revocation, §8-13-13.
Failure to report as
ground, §8-13-18.

SALES—Cont'd
Going out of business or distress merchandise sales—Cont'd
Licenses—Cont'd
Sale prohibited between November 15 and December 31, §8-13-12.
Surrender of business licenses, §8-13-11.
Suspension, §8-13-13.
Penalties.
Violations of chapter, §8-13-22.
Probate judge.
License.
Issuance, §8-13-9.
Report.
Daily report of merchandise received, §8-13-18.
Failure to report ground for license revocation, §8-13-18.
Trade, business or firm name of licensee.
Use after issuance of license, §8-13-14.
Violations of chapter.
Each sale constitutes separate offense, §8-13-22.
Penalties, §8-13-22.
Responsibility of licensee, §8-13-21.
Grits.
Manufacture and sale.
See BREAD, FLOUR, CORNMEAL AND GRITS.
Guardian and ward.
Removal of person or property of minors and wards.
Sale of property.
Removal to another state, §§26-8-48 to 26-8-51.
Uniform guardianship and protective proceedings act.
Conservators.
Conflicts of interest, §26-2A-150.
Harbors and ports.
Real property, §33-1-17.
Submerged lands and lands lying under or abutting tidal waters, §33-1-18.
Hay.
Liens of owners of baling machines or presses.
Sale to enforce lien, §35-11-291.
Hearings.
Going out of business or distress merchandise sales.
License.
Applications, §8-13-5.
Costs, §8-13-8.
Highways.
Finance corporation.
Bond issues, §23-1-177.
Highway authority.
Bond issues, §23-1-157.
Hours of sale.
Alcoholic beverages, §28-3A-25.
Public sales, §6-8-41.

SALES—Cont'd
Income tax.
Payment of tax on basis of percentage of sales.
Option of taxpayer, §40-18-23.
Industrial alcohol, §§28-5-5 to 28-5-7.
Industrial parks.
Property, §11-92-5.
Inspections.
Commercial code, §§7-2-512 to 7-2-515.
Investigations.
Going out of business or distress merchandise sales.
License.
Investigation of applicant, §8-13-8.
Fee, §8-13-6.
Judicial sales generally.
See JUDICIAL SALES.
Licenses.
Fire, closing out, etc., sales, §40-12-101.
Going out of business or distress merchandise sales, §§8-13-2 to 8-13-14. See within this heading, "Going out of business or distress merchandise sales."
Limitation of actions.
Contracts, §7-2-725.
Linseed oil, §§8-17-43, 8-17-44.
Liquefied petroleum gas.
Invoices, §8-17-190.
Liquidation sales, §§8-13-1 to 8-13-23. See within this heading, "Going out of business or distress merchandise sales."
Livestock.
Between sunset and sunrise.
Prohibited, §3-1-20.
Bills of sale.
Dealers to obtain, §2-15-43.
Markets, §2-15-65.
Running at large, §§3-5-8, 3-5-13.
Lost or unclaimed property.
Disposition of unclaimed articles left for service, §35-12-6.
Finders, §35-12-5.
Maps and plats.
Division of land surveys, §35-2-35.
Marine resources generally.
See MARINE RESOURCES.
Meat and meat products, §§11-47-136 to 11-47-138.
Mellorine.
Adulterated or misbranded mellorine, §20-1-137.
Permits, §20-1-133.
Requirements, §20-1-134.
Military affairs.
Military property.
Unauthorized retention, §31-2-31.
National guard.
Weapons.
Commanders may forbid sale, §31-2-124.
Milk and milk products.
General provisions.
See MILK AND MILK PRODUCTS.

SALES—Cont'd
Milk and milk products—Cont'd
Imitation butter, §§2-13-16 to 2-13-21.
See MILK AND MILK PRODUCTS.
Imitation cheese, §§2-13-16 to 2-13-21.
See MILK AND MILK PRODUCTS.
Mines and minerals.
Public lands, §9-15-18.
School lands, §§9-15-36, 9-15-38, 9-15-39.
Swamp or overflowed lands, §§9-15-38, 9-15-40.
Mobile homes, §§24-5-6 to 24-5-11.
See MOBILE HOMES.
Mortgages and deeds of trust, §§35-10-1 to 35-10-10.
See MORTGAGES AND DEEDS OF TRUST.
Motor vehicles generally.
See MOTOR VEHICLES.
Municipal corporations.
See MUNICIPAL CORPORATIONS.
Nuts, §20-1-91.
Oil and gas.
Conservation and regulation of production.
Disposition of proceeds, §9-17-33.
Oleomargarine.
Manufacture and sale, §§20-1-110 to 20-1-113.
Oysters, §§9-12-61, 9-12-64, 9-12-65.
Partition.
General provisions.
See PARTITION.
Sale instead of partition, §§35-6-57 to 35-6-64.
See PARTITION.
Pawnbrokers, §§8-1-80 to 8-1-84.
Peanuts, §§35-11-290, 35-11-291.
Penalties.
Going out of business or distress merchandise sales.
Violations, §8-13-22.
Petroleum products.
Fraud and deceit in sale, §§8-17-130 to 8-17-139.
See OIL AND GAS.
General provisions, §§8-17-85, 8-17-88.
Reclaimed or re-refined oil, §§8-17-110 to 8-17-116.
See OIL AND GAS.
Pharmacists and pharmacies generally.
See PHARMACISTS AND PHARMACIES.
Poisons.
Restrictions on retail sales, §22-20-11.
Restrictions on sale in pharmacies, §34-23-70.
Prisons and prisoners.
Convict labor, §§14-5-1 to 14-5-11.
See PRISONS AND PRISONERS.

SALES—Cont'd
Prisons and prisoners
—Cont'd
Industries in penal
institutions, §§14-7-6 to
14-7-23.
See PRISONS AND
PRISONERS.
Probate courts.
Going out of business or
distress merchandise
sales.
When probate judge to
issue license, §8-13-9.
**Public lands, §§9-15-1 to
9-15-53.**
See PUBLIC LANDS.
Public sales.
Bidding.
Consideration for bidding
or not bidding.
Prohibited, §8-1-100.
Contracts in violation
void, §8-1-102.
Hours of sale, §6-8-41.
**Public utilities, §§37-4-40 to
37-4-45.**
See PUBLIC UTILITIES.
Railroads.
Conveyance of franchises,
rights, roadbed and
property to another
railroad corporation,
§10-5-10.
Remedies.
Commercial code, §§7-2-700
to 7-2-725.
See COMMERCIAL CODE.
Reports.
Going out of business or
distress merchandise
sales.
Daily report of
merchandise received,
§8-13-18.
Failure to report ground
for license revocation,
§8-13-18.
Resales.
Fair trade.
See TRADE AND
COMMERCE.
**Savings and loan
associations.**
Accounts, §5-16-40.
Assets, §5-16-28.
**School lands, §§16-20-1 to
16-20-9.**
See PUBLIC LANDS.
**Secured transactions,
§§7-9-101 to 7-9-507.**
See COMMERCIAL CODE.
Securities, §§8-6-17, 8-6-19.
Seeds.
See SEEDS.
Shrimp, §§9-12-64, 9-12-65.
State parks.
Trees and timber.
Disposition and
expenditure of
revenues, §9-2-108.
Surveys and surveyors.
Division of land surveys.
Maps, plats, etc., §35-2-35.
**Swamp and overflowed
lands, §§9-15-45 to
9-15-47.**
Taxation.
Sale of land for taxes,
§§40-10-1 to 40-10-166.
See TAXATION.

SALES—Cont'd
Taxation—Cont'd
Sales tax, §§40-23-1 to
40-23-50.
See SALES TAX.
Use tax, §§40-23-60 to
40-23-88.
See USE TAX.
Tires.
Unsafe tires, §32-5-210.
**Transient merchants,
§§34-35-1 to 34-35-9.**
See TRANSIENT
MERCHANTS.
Transportation companies.
Sale of unclaimed freight,
§§37-2-28 to 37-2-30.
Unauthorized sale or transfer
of property, §37-2-25.
Trees and timber.
Condemnation of timber theft
equipment.
Sale of equipment seized,
§§9-13-225, 9-13-226.
State parks.
Disposition and
expenditure of
revenues, §9-2-108.
Unclaimed property.
Uniform disposition of
unclaimed property act,
§§35-12-20 to 35-12-48.
See LOST OR
UNCLAIMED
PROPERTY.
**Uniform commercial code,
§§7-2-101 to 7-2-725.**
See COMMERCIAL CODE.
**Used car sales, §§32-16-1 to
32-16-4.**
**Vacation time-sharing plans,
§§34-27-50 to 34-27-69.**
See VACATION TIME-
SHARING PLANS.
**Water conservation and
irrigation.**
Corporations.
Bond issues, §9-10-36.
**Water management and
drainage.**
Districts.
Bond issues, §9-9-38.
Delinquent tax lands,
§9-9-40.
**Water pollution control
authority.**
Bond issues, §22-34-8.
**Water system assistance
authority.**
Bond issues.
Procedure, §22-23A-8.
Weapons.
Pistols, §13A-11-77.
See WEAPONS.

**SALES REPRESENTATIVE'S
COMMISSION
CONTRACTS, §§8-24-1 to
8-24-5.**
Commission.
Defined, §8-24-1.
When due and payable.
Unwritten contract,
§8-24-4.
Definitions, §8-24-1.
Principal.
Defined, §8-24-1.
Written contract.
Liability for failure to
comply, §8-24-5.
Required, §8-24-2.

**SALES REPRESENTATIVE'S
COMMISSION
CONTRACTS**—Cont'd
Sales representatives.
Defined, §8-24-1.
Unwritten contracts.
Commission.
When due and payable,
§8-24-4.
Written contract.
Contents.
Required content, §8-24-2.
Copy of contract.
Receipt by sales
representative,
§8-24-3.
Liability of principal for
failure to comply,
§8-24-5.
Required, §8-24-2.

**SALES TAX, §§40-23-1 to
40-23-50.**
Actions.
Street and highway
contractors.
Collection of tax by civil
action, §40-23-50.
Tax collectible by civil suit,
§40-23-21.
Taxes recovered by action,
§40-23-32.
Additional tax, §40-23-28.
**Administration of division,
§40-23-30.**
Aged persons.
Exemptions.
Medicines prescribed by
physicians, §40-23-4.
Agents and employees.
Appointment, §40-23-30.
Agriculture.
Diesel fuel used for off-
highway agricultural
purposes.
Exemption, §40-23-4.
Machinery and equipment.
Application of
administrative
provisions, §40-23-38.
Enforcement, §40-23-38.
Imposition of tax,
§40-23-37.
Rate of tax, §40-23-37.
Seeds for planting purposes.
Exemption, §40-23-4.
Air commerce.
Air carriers.
Exemptions, §40-23-4.
Air pollution control.
Exemptions, §40-23-4.
Alcoholic beverages.
Exemption of alcoholic
beverage control board
from municipal sales tax,
§11-51-200.
Tax levied on gross receipts,
§40-23-2.
American Legion.
Exemptions, §40-23-5.
Amusements.
Tax levied on gross receipts,
§40-23-2.
Appeals.
Assessments, §40-23-18.
Assessment.
Appeals, §40-23-18.
Failure to make returns.
Assessment of tax upon
failure, §40-23-15.

SALES TAX—Cont'd
  Assessment—Cont'd
    Finality of assessment,
      §40-23-18.
    Hearings, §40-23-17.
    Limitation of actions.
      Appeals of assessment,
        §40-23-18.
    Municipal sales tax,
      §§11-51-204, 11-51-205.
    Notice, §40-23-17.
    Rules and regulations,
      §40-23-31.
  Athletics.
    Tax levied on gross receipts,
      §40-23-2.
  Attorney general.
    Violations.
      Injunctions against
        violators, §40-23-27.
  Auburn university.
    Tax levied on gross receipts,
      §40-23-2.
  Ballets and operas.
    Exemptions.
      Gross proceeds from sales
        of admissions,
        §40-23-4.
  Billiard rooms.
    Tax levied on gross receipts,
      §40-23-2.
  Boats, §40-23-2.
  Bonds, surety.
    Agents of department.
      Bond required, §40-23-30.
    Itinerant vendors, §40-23-24.
  Books and papers.
    Examination by department
      of revenue, §40-23-22.
    Failure to produce,
      §40-23-22.
  Boxing and wrestling.
    Tax levied on gross receipts,
      §40-23-2.
  Cash and credit sales.
    Report of sales, §40-23-8.
  Chilton county rescue
    squad.
    Exemptions, §40-23-5.
  Coin-operated machines.
    Tax levied on gross receipts,
      §40-23-2.
  Collection of tax on same
    sale.
    Only one municipal or
      county sales tax collected
      on same sale, §40-23-2.1.
  Comptroller.
    Refunds.
      Issuance of warrant,
        §40-23-32.
  Contractors.
    Tax on street and highway
      contractors, §40-23-50.
  Council of state
    governments.
    Exemptions, §40-23-5.
  Counties.
    Collection of tax on same
      sale.
      Only one county sales or
        use tax collectible,
        §40-23-2.1.
    County tax for school
      purposes.
      Authority to levy, §40-12-4.
    Exemptions.
      Sales of tangible personal
        property, §40-23-4.
  Credit collections.
    Reports, §40-23-8.

SALES TAX—Cont'd
  Cystic Fibrosis Research
    Foundation.
    Exemption, §40-23-4.
  Debts.
    Tax levied to constitute debt,
      §40-23-21.
  Definitions, §40-23-1.
    Gross receipts, §§40-23-1,
      40-23-50.
  Department of revenue.
    Deduction of revenues from
      amounts appropriated for
      operation by department,
      §40-23-35.
    Examination of taxpayer and
      books, §40-23-22.
    Failure to appear before
      department, §40-23-22.
    Rules and regulations.
      Promulgation, §40-23-31.
    Witnesses.
      Failure to appear before
        department, §40-23-22.
  Diabetes Trust Fund, Inc.
    Exemption, §40-23-5.
  Disabled American veterans.
    Exemption, §40-23-5.
  Discounts.
    Governor may authorize
      allowance of discount,
      §40-23-36.
  Disposition of revenues from
    tax, §40-23-35.
  Dog racing.
    Admissions to track or
      handle.
      Exemption, §40-11-5.
  Drugs.
    Exemptions, §§40-23-4,
      40-23-4.1.
  Eastern Star.
    Grand chapter of all orders of
      Eastern Star.
      Exemption, §40-23-5.
  Education.
    Exemptions.
      School boards.
        Sale of tangible personal
          property, §40-23-4.
    Tax levied on gross receipts
      of educational
      institutions, §40-23-2.
    Use of county sales tax funds
      for educational purposes,
      §16-13-37.
  Electricity.
    Exemptions.
      Sale of electric power or
        energy, §40-23-4.
  Estimated payments,
    §40-23-7.
  Executions.
    Failure to pay tax, §40-23-20.
  Exemptions, §40-23-4.
    Aged persons.
      Medicines prescribed by
        physicians for,
        §40-23-4.
    Agriculture.
      Diesel fuel used for off-
        highway agricultural
        purposes, §40-23-4.
      Seeds for planting
        purposes,
    Air carriers, §40-23-4.
    Air pollution control
      equipment, §40-23-4.
    Alabama Special Olympics,
      Inc., §40-9-25.
    American Legion, §40-23-5.

SALES TAX—Cont'd
  Exemptions—Cont'd
    Ballets and operas.
      Sales of admissions,
        §40-23-4.
    Blind persons.
      Division of rehabilitation
        and crippled children
        service.
      Business enterprise
        program.
        Blind vendors
          associated with,
          §40-23-5.
    Chilton county rescue squad,
      §40-23-5.
    Christian Service Mission,
      Inc., §40-23-5.
    Constitution of Alabama.
      Businesses which the state
        is prohibited from
        taxing, §40-23-4.
    Council of state governments,
      §40-23-5.
    Counties.
      Sales of tangible personal
        property to, §40-23-4.
    County public hospital
      associations, §40-23-5.
    Cystic fibrosis research
      foundation, §40-23-4.
    Diabetes Trust Fund, Inc.,
      §40-23-5.
    Disabled American veterans,
      §40-23-5.
    Drugs, §§40-23-4, 40-23-4.1.
    Eastern Star.
      Grand chapter of all orders
        of Eastern Star,
        §40-23-5.
    Education.
      Sale of tangible personal
        property to county, city
        and independent school
        boards, §40-23-4.
    Electricity.
      Sale of electric power or
        energy, §40-23-4.
    Fertilizer, §40-23-4.
    Fish and game.
      Fish feeds, §40-23-4.
    Food stamps, §40-23-4.2.
    George Lindsey Celebrity
      Benefit, Inc., §40-9-25.
    Goodwill industries, §40-23-5.
    Herbicides, §40-23-4.
    Hospitals.
      Sales by hospital canteens,
        §40-23-4.
    King Ranch, Inc., §40-23-5.
    Liquefied petroleum gas.
      Gas used for agricultural
        purposes, §40-23-4.
    Livestock sales, §40-23-4.
    Manufacturers.
      Purchase of tangible
        personal property
        without payment of
        sales tax, §40-23-31.
    Mines and minerals.
      Exploration and offshore
        federal waters.
        Equipment, machinery,
          fuel, etc., used in,
          §40-23-4.
    Municipal corporations.
      Sales of tangible personal
        property to
        municipalities,
        §40-23-4.

SALES TAX—Cont'd
Exemptions—Cont'd
Municipal sales tax,
§11-51-200.
National conference of state
legislatures, §40-23-5.
Nurseries, §40-23-4.
Oil and gas.
Lubricating oil and
gasoline, §40-23-4.
Orchestral concerts.
Sales of admissions,
§40-23-4.
Orders of the Eastern Star,
§40-23-5.
Poultry.
Feed for poultry, §40-23-4.
Sale of baby chicks and
poults, §40-23-4.
Public utilities, §40-23-4.
Railroads.
Sale of railroad cars,
§40-23-4.
Seeds for planting,
Ships and shipping, §40-23-4.
Sight conservation
association, §40-23-5.
South Alabama State Fair
Association Southeastern
Livestock Exposition,
§40-23-5.
Sports.
Sales of admissions,
§40-23-4.
State.
Sales of tangible personal
property to the state,
§40-23-4.
Tomatoes.
Certain items used in the
production and
marketing, §40-23-4.
Tuberculosis.
Jefferson tuberculosis
sanatorium, §40-23-4.
Tunnels.
Fabricated steel tube
sections, §40-23-4.
United States constitution.
Businesses which the state
is prohibited from
taxing, §40-23-4.
Veterans, §40-23-5.
Violation of tax exempt
privilege.
Collection or recovery of
taxes due on illegal
purchases, §40-23-121.
Liability of retailer,
§40-23-120.
Vitamins.
Prescriptions for vitamins
and supplements,
§40-9-27.
Water pollution control
equipment, §40-23-4.
Women's clubs, §40-23-5.
Fertilizer.
Exemptions, §40-23-4.
Fish and game.
Exemptions.
Fish feeds, §40-23-4.
Food.
Sale through coin-operated
dispensing machines.
Tax levied on gross
receipts, §40-23-2.
Food stamps.
Exemptions, §40-23-4.2.
Fraud.
Reports, §40-23-10.

SALES TAX—Cont'd
Fraud—Cont'd
Returns, §40-23-88.
Gasoline.
Exemptions, §40-23-4.
Goodwill industries.
Exemption, §40-23-5.
Governor.
Allowance by governor,
§40-23-36.
Gross proceeds of sale.
Defined, §40-23-1.
Gross receipts.
Defined, §§40-23-1, 40-23-50.
Records.
Disclosing contents,
§40-23-29.
Required, §40-23-9.
Reports, §40-23-7.
Tax levied on gross receipts,
§40-23-2.
Hearings.
Assessment hearings,
§40-23-17.
Herbicides.
Exemption, §40-23-4.
Highways.
Contractors, §40-23-50.
Horse racing.
Tax levied on gross receipts
§40-23-2.
Hospitals.
Exemptions.
Sales by hospital canteens,
§40-23-4.
Incorrect payments,
§40-23-16.
Information.
Disclosure of contents of
returns, §40-23-29.
Release of information.
Rules and regulations,
§40-23-29.
Unlawful use of information
obtained in returns,
reports, etc., §40-23-29.
Injunctions.
Violations.
Restraining violators from
continuing in business,
§40-23-27.
Inspections.
Department of revenue.
Authority to inspect books
and records of
taxpayer, §40-23-22.
Interest.
Failure to pay tax.
Penalty plus interest,
§40-23-14.
Overpayments, §40-23-33.
Itinerant vendors.
Bonds, surety.
Required, §40-23-24.
King Ranch, Inc.
Exemption, §40-23-5.
Leases.
Personal property.
Leasing or renting,
§§40-12-220 to
40-12-227.
See PERSONAL
PROPERTY.
Levied, §40-23-2.
Municipal sales tax,
§§11-51-200 to 11-51-207.
See MUNICIPAL
CORPORATIONS.
Licenses.
License required to engage in
business, §40-23-6.

SALES TAX—Cont'd
Liens.
Tax a lien on property,
§40-23-19.
Limitation of actions.
Assessment.
Appeal, §40-23-18.
Civil suit to collect tax,
§40-23-21.
Refunds, §40-23-18.
Liquefied petroleum gas.
Exemptions.
Sale of gas used for
agricultural purposes,
§40-23-4.
Livestock.
Exemptions, §40-23-4.
Lubricating oils and greases.
Exemptions, §40-23-4.
Mines and minerals.
Exemptions.
Equipment, machinery,
fuel, etc., used in
exploration in offshore
federal waters,
§40-23-4.
Sales of machines used in
mining.
Tax on gross receipts
levied, §40-23-2.
Motion pictures.
Tax levied on gross receipts,
§40-23-2.
Motor fuels.
Diesel fuel used for off-
highway agricultural
purposes.
Exemption, §40-23-4.
Motor vehicles, §40-23-2.
Automotive parts, §40-23-2.
Tax levied on gross receipts,
§40-23-2.
Trailers, §40-23-2.
Municipal corporations.
Exclusion of certain
municipal privilege
license taxes, §40-23-3.
Exemptions.
Sales of tangible personal
property to
municipalities,
§40-23-4.
Sales or use tax collected on
same sale.
Only one municipal sales
or use tax collectible,
§40-23-2.1.
Municipal sales tax,
§§11-51-200 to 11-51-207.
See MUNICIPAL
CORPORATIONS.
**National conference of state
legislatures.**
Exemptions, §40-23-5.
Notice.
Assessments.
Notification by
department, §40-23-17.
Returns.
Failure to make return.
Notice to taxpayer,
§40-23-15.
Nurseries.
Exemptions, §40-23-4.
Oaths.
Reports under oath,
§40-23-10.

SALES TAX—Cont'd
  Oil and gas.
    Exemption.
      Equipment, machinery,
        fuel, etc., used in
        exploration in offshore
        federal waters,
        §40-23-4.
      Sales of lubricating oil and
        gasoline, §40-23-4.
  Operas.
    Exemption, §40-23-4.
  Orchestras.
    Exemptions.
      Sales of admissions to
        orchestral concerts,
        §40-23-4.
  Orders of the Eastern Star.
    Grand chapter of all orders.
      Exemption, §40-23-5.
  Other states.
    Credit for sales tax paid to
      another state, §40-23-65.
  Payment.
    Deficiencies, §40-23-13.
    Estimated payments,
      §40-23-7.
    Failure to pay tax.
      Execution, §40-23-20.
      Penalty, §40-23-14.
    Immediate payment,
      §40-23-23.
    Incorrect payments.
      Procedures governing,
        §40-23-16.
    Installments, §40-23-7.
    Refunds, §40-23-13.
      Overpayments, §40-23-32.
    When tax becomes
      immediately due,
      §40-23-23.
    When taxes due, §40-23-7.
  Peddlers.
    Bonds, surety.
      Itinerant vendors to file
        bond, §40-23-24.
  Penalties.
    Failure to pay tax, §40-23-14.
    Records.
      Examinations.
        Willful refusal to permit,
          §40-23-12.
      Failure to keep records,
        §40-23-11.
    Reports.
      Failure to make report,
        §40-23-11.
      Willful refusal to make
        report, §40-23-12.
    Returns.
      Failure to furnish return,
        §40-23-88.
      False or fraudulent return,
        §40-23-88.
  Perjury.
    Reports.
      False statements,
        §40-23-10.
  Permits.
    Manufacturers.
      Purchasing tangible
        personal property
        without payment of
        sales tax, §40-23-31.
  Personal property.
    Exemptions.
      State.
        Sales of tangible
          personal property to
          the state, §40-23-4.

SALES TAX—Cont'd
  Personal property—Cont'd
    Leasing or renting,
      §§40-12-220 to 40-12-227.
      See PERSONAL
        PROPERTY.
    State.
      Sales of tangible personal
        property to the state,
        §40-23-4.
  Pesticides.
    Exemptions, §40-23-4.
  Poultry.
    Exemptions.
      Feed for poultry, §40-23-4.
      Gross proceeds of sale of
        baby chicks and poults,
        §40-23-4.
  Proceeds.
    Deposit in treasury,
      §40-23-34.
    Disposition of revenues from
      tax, §40-23-35.
  Public utilities.
    Exemptions, §40-23-4.
  Purchase price.
    Failure to add tax to
      purchase price,
      §40-23-26.
    Refunds of tax paid on
      purchase price unlawful,
      §40-23-26.
    Tax a direct tax on retail
      consumer, §40-23-26.
    Tax to be added, §40-23-26.
  Railroads.
    Exemptions.
      Sale of railroad cars,
        §40-23-4.
  Rate, §40-23-2.
    Municipal sales tax,
      §11-51-205.
  Records.
    Duty to preserve, §40-23-9.
    Examination by department
      of revenue, §40-23-22.
      Willful refusal to permit,
        §40-23-12.
    Failure to keep records.
      Penalty, §40-23-11.
    Required, §40-23-9.
  Refunds, §§40-23-13, 40-23-32.
    Claims.
      Extension of time allowed
        for filing, §40-23-18.
    Interest, §40-23-33.
  Rent.
    Personal property.
      Leasing or renting,
        §§40-12-220 to
        40-12-227.
        See PERSONAL
          PROPERTY.
  Reports.
    Access of tax collecting
      authority to information
      contained in reports,
      §40-23-29.
    Cash and credit sales,
      §40-23-8.
    Contents, §40-23-7.
    Failure to make report.
      Notice to taxpayer and
        assessment of tax,
        §40-23-15.
      Penalty, §40-23-11.
    Filing, §40-23-7.
      Extensions of time,
        §40-23-7.

SALES TAX—Cont'd
  Reports—Cont'd
    Oaths.
      Reports to be made under
        oath, §40-23-10.
      Willful refusal to make
        report.
        Penalty, §40-23-12.
  Retail sales.
    Defined, §40-23-1.
    Purchase price.
      Failure to add tax to
        purchase price,
        §40-23-26.
      Refunds of tax added to
        purchase price
        unlawful, §40-23-26.
      Tax to be added to
        purchase price,
        §40-23-26.
    Tax a direct tax on retail
      consumer, §40-23-26.
  Returns.
    Access of tax collecting
      authority to information
      contained in returns,
      §40-23-29.
    Disclosure of contents,
      §40-23-29.
    Examination, §40-23-13.
    Extensions of time for
      making return, §40-23-7.
    Failure to make returns.
      Notice to taxpayer and
        assessment of tax,
        §40-23-15.
      Penalty, §40-23-88.
    Persons selling out or
      quitting business to file
      return, §40-23-25.
  Rules and regulations.
    Department of revenue.
      Promulgation, §40-23-31.
    Municipal sales tax,
      §11-51-204.
  Seeds.
    Exemptions.
      Sale of seeds for planting,
        §40-23-4.
  **Selling out or quitting
    business.**
    Part of purchase money to be
      withheld, §40-23-25.
    Return required, §40-23-25.
  Sheriffs.
    Failure to pay tax.
      Execution directed to
        sheriff, §40-23-20.
    Levy and sale of property,
      §40-23-20.
  Ships and shipping.
    Exemptions, §40-23-4.
  **Sight conservation
    association.**
    Exemption, §40-23-5.
  **South Alabama State Fair
    Association
    Southeastern Livestock
    Exposition.**
    Exemption, §40-23-5.
  Sports.
    Sales of admissions.
      Exemptions, §40-23-4.
  State.
    Exemptions.
      Sales of tangible personal
        property to state,
        §40-23-4.

SALES TAX—Cont'd
Street and highway contractors.
Actions.
Collection of tax, §40-23-50.
Collection, §40-23-50.
Enforcement, §40-23-50.
Levied, §40-23-50.
Tax enforcement and compliance act, §§40-29-1 to 40-29-120.
See TAXATION.
Tobacco, §§40-25-1 to 40-25-29.
See TOBACCO.
Tomatoes.
Exemptions.
Certain items necessary to market tomatoes, §40-23-4.
Tuberculosis.
Exemptions.
Jefferson tuberculosis sanatorium, §40-23-4.
Tunnels.
Exemptions.
Fabricated steel tube sections, §40-23-4.
United States constitution.
Exemptions.
Businesses which the state is prohibited from taxing, §40-23-4.
University of Alabama.
Tax levied on gross receipts, §40-23-2.
Use tax, §§40-23-60 to 40-23-88.
See USE TAX.
Veterans.
Exemptions, §40-23-5.
Violations.
Attorney general.
Injunctions against violators, §40-23-27.
Collection or recovery of taxes due on illegal purchases, §40-23-121.
Liability of retailer, §40-23-120.
Restraining violators from continuing in business, §40-23-27.
Vitamins.
Prescriptions for vitamins and supplements.
Exemption, §40-9-27.
Warrants.
Refunds, §40-23-32.
Water pollution control equipment.
Exemptions, §40-23-4.
Wholesale sales.
Defined, §40-23-1.
Purchase price.
Failure to add tax, §40-23-26.
Refunds of tax added to purchase price unlawful, §40-23-26.
Tax to be added, §40-23-26.
Witnesses.
Department of revenue.
Failure to appear before department, §40-23-22.

SALT SPRINGS.
Examination of land reservation.
Land clerk, §9-15-33.

SALT SPRINGS—Cont'd
Lease of Salt Springs, etc., §35-4-380.
Management and supervision of reservation, §9-15-31.

SALT WATER FISHING.
See MARINE RESOURCES.

SALVAGE, §§35-13-1 to 35-13-10.
Applicability of chapter.
Taker's personal representative, §35-13-10.
Appraisement of property, §35-13-2.
Fees of appraisers, §35-13-6.
Commercial code.
Sales.
Buyer's options as to salvage of rightfully rejected goods, §7-2-604.
Seller's right to salvage unfinished goods, §7-2-704.
Concealment of property.
Liability, §35-13-9.
Death.
Applicability of chapter to taker's personal representative, §35-13-10.
Delivery of property.
Remedy of owner when taker refuses to deliver, §35-13-8.
Restoration of property upon proof by owner, §35-13-4.
Description of property, §35-13-2.
Destruction of property.
Liability, §35-13-9.
District courts.
Exhibition of property to district court, §35-13-2.
Executors and administrators.
Taker of property.
Applicability of chapter to taker's personal representative, §35-13-10.
Exhibition of property to district court, §35-13-2.
Fees.
Appraisers, §35-13-6.
Finder of property, §§35-13-7 to 35-13-10.
History and archives.
Contracts for recovery or salvage of archaeological treasure, etc., §41-9-249.1.
Liability.
Concealment or destruction, etc., of property, §35-13-9.
Limitations on proof by owner, §35-13-7.
Motor vehicles.
Antitheft act, §32-8-87.
Notice, §35-13-3.
Owner of property.
Limitations on proof by owner, §35-13-7.
Proof by owner.
Limitations, §35-13-7.
Restoration of property upon, §35-13-4.

SALVAGE—Cont'd
Owner of property—Cont'd
Remedy when taker refuses to deliver property, §35-13-8.
Remedies.
Owner.
Remedy of owner when taker refuses to deliver property, §35-13-8.
Restoration of property.
Upon proof by owner, §35-13-4.
Right to take up and secure property adrift, §35-13-1.
Taker of property.
Compensation, §35-13-5.
Death.
Applicability of chapter to taker's personal representative, §35-13-10.
Liability for concealment, destruction, etc., §35-13-9.
Personal representative of taker.
Applicability of chapter to personal representative, §35-13-10.
Refusal to deliver property to owner.
Remedy, §35-13-8.
Right to take up and secure property adrift, §35-13-1.
When right to property vested in taker, §35-13-7.

SALVATION ARMY.
Licenses.
Exemptions, §40-9-12.
Taxation.
Exemptions, §40-9-12.

SAMFORD UNIVERSITY.
Marine environmental sciences consortium, §§16-45-1 to 16-45-5.

SAND PITS.
Counties.
Acquisition of lands for sand pits, §11-14-23.
Conduct of condemnation proceedings, §11-14-24.
Sale or leasing of sand or gravel.
Public water bottoms, §§9-15-52, 9-15-53.

SANITARIANS.
Professional corporations, §§10-4-380 to 10-4-406.
See PROFESSIONAL CORPORATIONS.
Unincorporated professional associations, §§10-10-1 to 10-10-16.
See UNINCORPORATED PROFESSIONAL ASSOCIATIONS.

SANITARY LANDFILLS.
Financing solid waste collection and disposal facilities, §§22-27-20 to 22-27-26.
See GARBAGE AND TRASH.

SANITATION.
  Beautification board.
    General provisions,
      §§41-9-490 to 41-9-498.
    See BEAUTIFICATION.
  County health officers.
    Duties, §22-3-5.
  Garbage and trash, §§22-27-1
    to 22-27-27.
    See GARBAGE AND
      TRASH.
  Health generally.
    See HEALTH.
  Jails.
    Baths, §§14-6-93, 14-6-94.
    General provisions, §§14-6-92
      to 14-6-96.
    Inspection of jails, §§14-6-80
      to 14-6-109.
    See JAILS.
  Military affairs.
    Enforcement of sanitation
      laws in camps or
      garrisons, §31-2-40.
  Municipal corporations.
    General provisions,
      §§11-47-130, 11-47-131.
    Inspections, §11-43-59.
  **Nuisances menacing public
    health,** §§22-10-1 to
    22-10-3.
  Sewers generally.
    See SEWERS.

SANITORIUMS.
  Health care authorities,
    §§22-21-310 to 22-21-356.
    See HEALTH CARE
      AUTHORITIES.
  Tuberculosis.
    District tuberculosis
      sanatoria.
    Bonds, Const. Ala., amd.
      74.

**SATISFACTION OF
  JUDGMENT.**
  See JUDGMENTS.

SATURDAYS.
  Holiday falls on Saturday,
    §1-3-8.

**SAVINGS AND LOAN
  ASSOCIATIONS,** §§5-16-1
  to 5-16-53.
  Accounts.
    Account books, §5-16-16.
    Bonuses, §5-16-27.
    Certificate evidencing
      ownership of account.
      Form, §5-16-16.
    Certificate of account.
      Issuance in lieu of account
        book, §5-16-16.
    Date of investment, §5-16-19.
    Death, §§5-16-44 to 5-16-47.
    Deposit in names of two
      persons payable to
      either or survivor.
      How payable, §5-16-44.
      Title to deposit upon
        death of either,
        §5-16-45.
      When construed as
        belonging to
        survivor, §5-16-44.
    Disposition of account of
      deceased person,
      §5-16-46.

**SAVINGS AND LOAN
  ASSOCIATIONS**—Cont'd
  Accounts—Cont'd
    Death—Cont'd
      Trusts and trustees.
        Disposition of deposit in
          trust for another
          upon death of
          trustee, §5-16-47.
    Decedents' estates.
      Disposition of account of
        deceased person,
        §5-16-46.
    Dissolution.
      Voluntary liquidation.
        Unclaimed share
          accounts, §§5-16-33
          to 5-16-35.
    Executors and
      administrators, §5-16-43.
    Federal savings and loan
      insurance corporation.
      Insuring accounts with,
        §5-16-24.
    Fiduciaries, §5-16-43.
    Generally, §5-16-16.
    Guardians, §5-16-43.
    Insuring accounts.
      Power to enter into
        contracts, §5-16-51.
      Power to insure with
        federal savings and
        loan insurance
        corporation, §5-16-24.
    Interest due and accrued
      account, §5-16-17.
    Investments.
      Legal investments for
        fiduciaries, §5-16-43.
    Joint accounts, §5-16-43.
      Deposit in names of two
        persons payable to
        either or survivor.
      How payable, §5-16-44.
      Title to deposit upon
        death of either,
        §5-16-45.
      When construed as
        belonging to
        survivor, §5-16-44.
    Liens on accounts, §5-16-26.
    Liquidation.
      Voluntary liquidation.
        Unclaimed share
          accounts, §§5-16-33
          to 5-16-35.
    Loans.
      Pledges of accounts as
        security, §5-16-26.
    Married women, §5-16-43.
    Minors, §5-16-43.
    Payments on accounts.
      Power of directors to limit
        amounts, §5-16-24.
    Pledges of accounts as
      security for loans,
      §5-16-26.
    Powers of associations,
      §5-16-24.
    Preference between accounts
      prohibited, §5-16-16.
    Redemption of accounts,
      §5-16-21.
      Joint accounts, §5-16-43.
      Powers of associations,
        §5-16-24.
    Repurchase of accounts,
      §5-16-20.
      Joint accounts, §5-16-43.
      Powers of associations,
        §5-16-24.

**SAVINGS AND LOAN
  ASSOCIATIONS**—Cont'd
  Accounts—Cont'd
    Required books, §5-16-15.
    Reserve accounts, §5-16-17.
      Bonus reserve account,
        §5-16-27.
    Sales of accounts, §5-16-40.
    Tenants in common.
      Prohibited, §5-16-43.
    Transferability of accounts,
      §5-16-16.
    Trustees, §5-16-43.
    Unclaimed share accounts.
      Voluntary liquidation,
        §§5-16-33 to 5-16-35.
    Undivided profits account,
      §5-16-18.
    Voluntary liquidation.
      Unclaimed share accounts,
        §§5-16-33 to 5-16-35.
    Women.
      Married women, §5-16-43.
  Acknowledgments.
    Public officers employed by
      or members of
      associations.
      Validation of
        acknowledgment of
        instruments, §5-16-41.
  Actions.
    Powers of associations,
      §5-16-24.
  Activities not restricted,
    §5-1A-7.
  **Alabama savings
    institutions.**
    Regional reciprocal savings
      institutions act.
      Definition, §5-14A-2.
  Appeals.
    Orders of commissioner or
      board, §5-2A-63.
  Applicability of chapter,
    §5-16-3.
  Appraisals.
    Real estate appraisals to be
      made in time of
      acquisition, §5-16-15.
    Reports, §5-16-15.
  Assessments.
    Fees, §5-16-38.1.
  Assets.
    Exchange of assets, §5-16-28.
    Sale of assets, §5-16-28.
    Transfer of assets, §5-16-28.
      Reorganization.
        Transfer to new
          association, §5-16-31.
      Voluntary liquidation,
        §5-16-32.
  Audits, §5-16-36.
  Board.
    Savings and loan board,
      §5-2A-63.
  Bonds, surety.
    Commissioner of savings and
      loan.
      Guarantee of amount
        subscribed by
        incorporators, §5-16-4.
  Bonus plans.
    Abolishing, §5-16-27.
    Adoption, §5-16-27.
    Bonus reserve account,
      §5-16-27.
    Generally, §5-16-27.
    Long-term bonus plans,
      §5-16-27.
    Payment of cash bonuses on
      accounts, §5-16-27.

SAVINGS AND LOAN ASSOCIATIONS—Cont'd

Bonus plans—Cont'd
Power to pay bonus to members, §5-16-24.
Required bonus reserve, §5-16-17.
Short-term bonus plans, §5-16-27.

Borrowing members.
Certificate evidencing membership of borrower. Form, §5-16-16.
Power of directors to extend leniency and indulgence to, §5-16-24.
Real estate loans, §5-16-25.

Borrowing money.
Power of association to borrow money, §5-16-24.

Branch offices.
Establishment, §5-16-11.
Regional reciprocal savings institutions act.
Definition, §5-14A-2.
Power to establish or acquire branch offices, §5-14A-8.

Bureau of savings and loan.
Administration, §5-2A-61.
Commissioner of savings and loan, §§5-2A-61 to 5-2A-63.
Composition, §5-2A-60.
Created, §5-2A-61.
Establishment, §5-2A-61.
Expenses, §5-2A-61.
Liability for acts, §5-2A-61.
Savings and loan board, §5-2A-63.

Bylaws.
Adoption, §5-16-24.
Amendment, §§5-16-7, 5-16-24.
Approval by commissioner.
Form of approval, §5-16-49.
Form, §5-16-49.
Generally, §5-16-7.
Proposed bylaws, §5-16-4.
Required provisions, §5-16-7.

Capital.
Accumulation, §5-16-16.
Composition, §5-16-16.
Defined, §5-16-2.
Generally, §5-16-16.
Impairment of capital.
Defined, §5-16-2.
Minimum capital, §5-16-4.
Not limited, §5-16-16.
Subscription by incorporators, §5-16-4.
Thirty percent capital lending power, §5-16-24.

Certificate of incorporation, §§5-16-4 to 5-16-6.

Certificates of indebtedness.
Issuance, etc., prohibited, §5-16-23.

Circuit courts.
Appeals from orders of savings and loan board, §5-2A-63.

Collection agents.
Bonds, surety, §5-16-14.

Combination home and business structure.
Defined, §5-16-2.

Commencement of business.
Forfeiture of corporate existence for nonuse, §5-16-12.

SAVINGS AND LOAN ASSOCIATIONS—Cont'd

Commencement of business —Cont'd
Period for commencement, §5-16-12.

Commercial code.
Secured transactions.
Transfer of accounts excluded from provisions, §7-9-104.

Commissioner of savings and loan, §§5-2A-61 to 5-2A-63.
Appeals from order of commissioner, §5-2A-63.
Appointment of examiners, §5-2A-61.
Approval by commissioner.
Bylaws.
Form for approval of bylaws, §5-16-49.
Certificate of incorporation.
Form for approval, §5-16-49.
Change of location of home office, §5-16-10.
Form for approval of change, §5-16-49.
Conversions, §5-16-30.
Corporate name and offices, §5-16-9.
Forms, §5-2A-62.
Incorporation, §5-16-5.
Mergers, §5-16-29.
Operating or management contracts, §5-16-42.
Reorganizations, §5-16-31.
Sales, transfers or exchanges of assets, §5-16-28.
Voluntary liquidation, §5-16-32.
Conflicts of interest, §5-2A-61.
Defined, §5-16-2.
Deputy commissioner.
Deputy superintendent of banks, §5-2A-61.
Salary, §5-2A-61.
Secretary of savings and loan board, §5-2A-61.
Disclosure of information, §5-2A-61.
Examiners.
Appointment, §5-2A-61.
Generally, §5-2A-62.
Liability, §5-2A-61.
Orders.
Appeals from, §5-2A-63.
Powers.
Supervisory powers, §5-2A-62.
Recommendations upon petition for incorporation, §5-16-4.
Regional reciprocal savings institutions act.
Cooperation with other savings institutions regulatory agencies, §5-14A-6.
Definition of commissioner, §5-14A-2.
Enforcement of chapter, §5-14A-4.
Salary, §5-2A-61.
Savings and loan board.
Chairman of board, §5-2A-63.
Seal of office, §5-2A-61.

SAVINGS AND LOAN ASSOCIATIONS—Cont'd

Commissioner of savings and loan—Cont'd
Superintendent of banks to be commissioner of savings and loan, §5-2A-61.
Supervisory power, §5-2A-62.

Compromise and settlement.
Power of directors, §5-16-24.

Conflicts of interest.
Commissioner of savings and loan, §5-2A-61.

Conservatorship.
Generally, §5-16-37.

Constitution of Alabama.
Exemption of federal associations from franchise taxes, Const. Ala., amd. 27.

Contracts.
Operating on management contracts, §5-16-42.
Power to contract, §5-16-51.
State associations may make contracts available to federal associations, §5-16-52.

Conversions.
Generally, §5-16-30.
Mutual association into capital stock form of organization, §5-16-31.

Corporate existence.
Forfeiture for nonuse, §5-16-12.

Corporations.
Application of corporations provisions, §10-2A-336.

Death, §§5-16-44 to 5-16-47.
Accounts.
Disposition of account of deceased person, §5-16-46.
Deposit in names of two persons payable to either or survivor.
How payable, §5-16-44.
Title to deposit upon death of either, §5-16-45.
When construed as belonging to survivor, §5-16-44.
Trusts and trustees.
Disposition of deposit in trust for another upon death of trustee, §5-16-47.

Decedents' estates.
Accounts.
Disposition of account of deceased person, §5-16-46.

Definitions, §5-16-2.
Regional reciprocal savings institutions, §5-14A-2.

Deposits.
Receipt of public deposits prohibited, §5-16-23.
Regional reciprocal savings institutions act.
Definition, §5-14A-2.

Directors.
Bonds, surety, §5-16-14.
Committees.
Power to appoint committees, §5-16-24.
Compensation.
Power to fix compensation of directors, §5-16-24.

SAVINGS AND LOAN ASSOCIATIONS—Cont'd

Directors—Cont'd
Election, §5-16-14.
Meetings.
Organizational meeting, §5-16-8.
Number, §5-16-14.
Organizational meeting, §5-16-8.
Powers and duties, §§5-16-14, 5-16-24.
Qualifications, §5-16-14.
Reorganization, §5-16-31.
Terms of office, §5-16-14.
Vacancies, §5-16-14.
Voluntary liquidation, §5-16-32.

Dissolution.
Certificate of dissolution, §5-16-32.
Involuntary liquidation, §5-16-37.
Powers of dissolved association, §5-16-32.
Power to dissolve, §5-16-24.
Voluntary liquidation, §§5-16-32 to 6-16-35.

Dividends.
Cash dividends, §5-16-19.
Date of investment, §5-16-19.
Declaring, §5-16-19.
Dissolution.
Unclaimed dividends, §§5-16-33 to 5-16-35.
Equal participation, §5-16-19.
Fixed amounts.
Agreement to pay prohibited, §5-16-23.
Generally, §5-16-19.
Joint accounts, §5-16-43.
Liquidation.
Unclaimed dividends, §§5-16-33 to 5-16-35.
Redemption of accounts, §5-16-21.
Repurchase of accounts, §5-16-20.
Unclaimed dividends.
Voluntary liquidation, §§5-16-33 to 5-16-35.
Voluntary liquidation.
Unclaimed dividends, §§5-16-33 to 5-16-35.
When credited, §5-16-19.

Earnings.
Net earnings.
Defined, §5-16-2.
Net earnings available for dividends.
Defined, §5-16-2.

Examinations.
Generally, §5-16-36.

Examiners.
Disclosure of information, §5-2A-61.

Exchange of assets, §5-16-28.

Executors and administrators.
Accounts, §5-16-43.

Expenses.
Operating expenses.
Defined, §5-16-2.
Real estate expenses.
Defined, §5-16-2.

Federal home loan bank.
Power of association to act as fiscal agent of United States, §5-16-24.
Power to qualify as member of, §5-16-24.

SAVINGS AND LOAN ASSOCIATIONS—Cont'd

Federal savings and loan associations.
Contracts.
State associations may make contracts available to, §5-16-52.
Conversions into federal associations, §5-16-30.
Conversions into state chartered associations, §5-16-30.
Privileges, etc., §5-16-39.

Federal savings and loan insurance corporation.
Contracts.
Insurance of accounts, etc., §5-16-51.
Power to insure accounts with, §5-16-24.
Reports to corporation, §5-16-36.
Termination of status as insured corporation, §5-16-53.

Federal savings institutions.
Regional reciprocal savings institutions act.
Definition, §5-14A-2.

Fees.
Assessment fees, §5-16-38.1.

Fiduciaries.
Accounts, §5-16-43.
Investments.
Accounts legal investments, §5-16-43.

Financial statement.
Annual financial statement, §5-16-13.

Fines.
Members.
Assessment against members, §5-16-13.

Foreign corporations.
Not to transact business in state, §5-16-39.

Forms.
Generally, §5-16-49.

Guardian and ward.
Accounts, §5-16-43.

Holding companies.
Regional reciprocal savings institutions act.
Alabama savings and loan holding company.
Acquisition by regional holding or institution, §5-14A-3.
Defined, §5-14A-2.
Application fee, §5-14A-7.
Definition of savings and loan holding company, §5-14A-2.
Southern region savings and loan holding companies.
Applicable law, §5-14A-5.
Defined, §5-14A-2.

Home.
Defined, §5-16-2.

Housing.
Investment and loans with respect to, §5-5A-23.

Income.
Gross income.
Defined, §5-16-2.
Operating income.
Defined, §5-16-2.

SAVINGS AND LOAN ASSOCIATIONS—Cont'd

Income—Cont'd
Real estate income.
Defined, §5-16-2.

Income tax.
Exemptions of certain organizations, §40-18-32.

Incorporation, §§5-16-4 to 5-16-6.
Certificate of approval.
Filing, §5-16-4.
Form of certificate, §5-16-49.
Issuance, §5-16-4.
Certificate of incorporation.
Execution, §5-16-4.
Filing, §5-16-4.
Form, §5-16-6.
Petition for certificate, §5-16-49.
Issuance, §5-16-6.
Petition for certificate, §5-16-4.
Approval, §5-16-5.
Form, §5-16-49.
Expense fund.
Contributions, §5-16-4.
Creation, §5-16-4.
Reorganization, §5-16-31.
Subscription by incorporators, §5-16-4.
Minimum subscription, §5-16-4.

Insurance of accounts.
Power to enter into contracts, §5-16-51.
Power to insure with federal savings and loan insurance corporation, §5-16-24.

Insured associations.
Defined, §5-16-2.
Federal savings and loan insurance corporation.
See within this heading, "Federal savings and loan insurance corporation."
Reports, §5-16-36.
Termination of status as insured corporation, §5-16-53.

Interest.
Account.
Interest due and accrued account, §5-16-17.
Accrued monthly, §5-16-17.
Due and accrued account, §5-16-17.
Guaranteed rate of interest.
Agreements to pay prohibited, §5-16-23.

Investments.
Accounts legal investments for fiduciaries, §5-16-43.
Date of investment, §5-16-19.
Federal savings and loan associations.
State associations may make investments available to, §5-16-52.
Housing.
Investments with respect to, §5-5A-23.
Powers of associations, §5-16-24.

Involuntary liquidation, §5-16-37.

**SAVINGS AND LOAN
   ASSOCIATIONS**—Cont'd
**Joint tenants and tenants in
   common.**
Accounts, §5-16-43.
Deposit in names of two
   persons payable to either
   or survivor, §§5-16-44,
   5-16-45.
Licenses.
Municipal license schedules,
   §11-51-131.
Liens.
Accounts.
   Liens on, §5-16-26.
Liquidation.
Involuntary liquidation,
   §5-16-37.
Voluntary liquidation,
   §§5-16-32 to 5-16-35.
Loans.
Accounts.
   Pledges of accounts as
      security, §5-16-26.
Direct reduction loans.
   Defined, §5-16-2.
   Power to make, §5-16-24.
Federal savings and loan
   associations.
   State associations may
      make loans available
      to, §5-16-52.
Home loans, §5-5A-23.
   Defined, §5-16-2.
   Direct reduction home
      loans.
      Powers of associations,
         §5-16-24.
   Thirty percent capital
      lending power,
      §5-16-24.
Interest, §§5-16-17, 5-16-23.
Other real estate loan.
   Defined, §5-16-2.
Powers of associations,
   §5-16-24.
Purchase of loans, §5-16-48.
Real estate loans.
   Amortization, §5-16-25.
   Defined, §5-16-2.
   Expenses.
      Borrowing members to
         pay, §5-16-25.
   General provisions,
      §5-16-25.
   Required security,
      §5-16-25.
   Thirty percent capital
      lending power,
      §5-16-24.
   Transfer of real estate
      security by borrowing
      member, §5-16-13.
Losses.
Liability for losses, §5-16-16.
Management contracts,
   §5-16-42.
Married women.
Accounts, §5-16-43.
Meetings.
Directors, §5-16-8.
Members, §5-16-13.
Organizational meeting,
   §5-16-8.
Members.
Annual meeting, §5-16-13.
Certificates evidencing
   membership.
   Account holders, §5-16-16.
   Borrowers, §5-16-16.

**SAVINGS AND LOAN
   ASSOCIATIONS**—Cont'd
Members—Cont'd
Certificates evidencing
   membership—Cont'd
   Issuance of duplicate
      certificates, §5-16-22.
Defined, §5-16-2.
Duplicate membership
   certificates.
   Issuance, §5-16-22.
Eligibility for membership,
   §5-16-13.
Meetings.
   Annual meeting, §5-16-13.
   Powers and duties, §5-16-13.
Records.
   Membership records,
      §5-16-15.
Rejection of application for
   membership.
   Power of directors,
      §5-16-24.
Rights, privileges and
   liabilities, §5-16-13.
Transfer of real estate
   security by borrowing
   member, §5-16-13.
Voting, §5-16-13.
Merger.
Form of merger agreement,
   §5-16-49.
Generally, §5-16-29.
Power to merge, §5-16-24.
Minors.
Accounts, §5-16-43.
**Mortgages and deeds of
   trust.**
Brokerage business.
   Engaging in, §5-16-48.
Origination, §5-16-48.
Purchase, §5-16-48.
Required security for real
   estate loans, §5-16-25.
Sale of mortgages, §5-16-48.
Municipal corporations.
Licenses.
   Schedule of license tax,
      §11-51-131.
Names.
Corporate name, §5-16-9.
Officers and employees.
Bonds, surety, §5-16-14.
Election of officers, §5-16-8.
Powers and duties, §5-16-14.
Power to appoint, §5-16-24.
Salaries.
   Power of directors to fix,
      §5-16-24.
Offices.
Approval by commissioner,
   §5-16-9.
Branch offices.
   Establishment, §5-16-11.
Change of location of home
   office, §§5-16-9, 5-16-10.
   Form of approval, §5-16-49.
Location, §5-16-9.
Operating contracts,
   §5-16-42.
Organizational meeting,
   §5-16-8.
Participating value.
Defined, §5-16-2.
Penalties.
Members.
   Assessment against
      members, §5-16-13.
Permits.
Required permits, §5-2A-62.

**SAVINGS AND LOAN
   ASSOCIATIONS**—Cont'd
**Pledge and collateral
   security.**
Accounts.
   Pledges of accounts as
      security for loans,
      §5-16-26.
   Power to make loans on
      sole security of
      accounts, §5-16-24.
Powers, §5-16-24.
Profits.
Undivided profits.
   Account, §5-16-18.
Property.
Home property.
   Defined, §5-16-2.
Improved real estate.
   Defined, §5-16-2.
Investments.
   Powers of associations,
      §5-16-24.
Powers of associations,
   §5-16-24.
Purchase of property,
   §5-16-48.
**Public officers and
   employees.**
Acknowledgment, etc., of
   instruments by public
   officers employed by
   associations validated,
   §5-16-41.
Real property. See within this
   heading, "Property."
Records.
Accrued liabilities.
   Records to reflect, §5-16-17.
Membership records,
   §5-16-15.
Required records, §5-16-15.
Redemption of accounts,
   §5-16-21.
Joint accounts, §5-16-43.
Powers of associations,
   §5-16-24.
**Regional reciprocal savings
   institutions act.**
Acquire.
   Defined, §5-14A-2.
Alabama savings
   institutions.
   Acquisition by regional
      holding or institution,
      §5-14A-3.
   Definition, §5-14A-2.
Applicable law, §5-14A-5.
Branch offices.
   Definition, §5-14A-2.
   Power to establish or
      acquire, §5-14A-8.
Citation of provisions,
   §5-14A-1.
Commissioner of savings and
   loan.
   Cooperation with other
      regulatory agencies,
      §5-14A-6.
   Definition, §5-14A-2.
   Enforcement of chapter,
      §5-14A-4.
Companies.
   Defined, §5-14A-2.
Control.
   Defined, §5-14A-2.
Definitions, §5-14A-2.
Deposits.
   Definition, §5-14A-2.
Enforcement of chapter.
   Commissioner, §5-14A-4.

SAVINGS AND LOAN ASSOCIATIONS—Cont'd

Regional reciprocal savings institutions act—Cont'd
Federal savings institutions.
Definition, §5-14A-2.
Fees.
Application for acquisition, §5-14A-7.
Holding companies.
Alabama savings and loan holding companies.
Acquisition by regional holding or institution, §5-14A-3.
Defined, §5-14A-2.
Application fee, §5-14A-7.
Definition of savings and loan holding company, §5-14A-2.
Southern region savings and loan holding companies.
Applicable law, §5-14A-5.
Defined, §5-14A-2.
Principal place of business.
Defined, §5-14A-2.
Regulatory supervision in cooperation with other regulatory agencies.
Commissioner authorized to enter into cooperative agreements, §5-14A-6.
Savings institutions.
Defined, §5-14A-2.
Service corporations.
Definition, §5-14A-2.
Short title of provisions, §5-14A-1.
Southern region savings institutions.
Applicable law, §5-14A-5.
Definition, §5-14A-2.
Southern region states.
Defined, §5-14A-2.
States.
Defined, §5-14A-2.
State savings institutions.
Defined, §5-14A-2.
Subsidiaries.
Definition, §5-14A-2.
Power to establish or acquire, §5-14A-8.
Title of provisions.
Short title, §5-14A-1.
Regular lending area.
Defined, §5-16-2.
Reorganization.
Conservatorship, §5-16-37.
Generally, §5-16-31.
Power to reorganize, §5-16-24.
Reports.
Annual report, §5-16-36.
Federal savings and loan insurance corporation.
Reports to, §5-16-36.
Required reports, §5-16-36.
Repurchase of accounts, §5-16-20.
Joint accounts, §5-16-43.
Powers of associations, §5-16-24.
Reserves.
Bonus reserve account, §5-16-27.
Charging off assets to reserves, §5-16-15.

SAVINGS AND LOAN ASSOCIATIONS—Cont'd

Reserves—Cont'd
Participating reserve, §5-16-31.
Reorganizations.
Participating reserves, §5-16-31.
Required reserves, §5-16-17.
Reserve accounts, §5-16-17.
Salaries.
Officers and employees.
Power of directors to fix, §5-16-24.
Sales.
Accounts, §5-16-40.
Assets, §5-16-28.
Savings and loan board, §5-2A-63.
Appeals from orders, §5-2A-63.
Appointment of members, §5-2A-63.
Chairman, §5-2A-63.
Compensation, §5-2A-63.
Composition, §5-2A-63.
Defined, §5-16-2.
Governor.
Appointment of members, §5-2A-63.
Hearings.
Appeals from orders of commissioner, §5-2A-63.
Offices, §5-2A-63.
Orders.
Appeals from orders, §5-2A-63.
Personnel, §5-2A-63.
Powers, §5-2A-63.
Qualifications of members, §5-2A-63.
Records, §5-2A-63.
Terms of members, §5-2A-63.
Vacancies, §5-2A-63.
Seals and sealed instruments.
Commissioner of savings and loan.
Seal of office, §5-2A-61.
Corporate seal, §5-16-24.
Secured transactions.
Transfer of accounts excluded from provisions of article, §7-9-104.
Securities.
Deposits with state treasurer, etc., of securities issued by associations, §5-16-50.
Investments.
Powers of associations, §5-16-24.
Issued by associations.
Deposits with state treasurer, §5-16-50.
Service corporations.
Regional reciprocal savings institutions act.
Definition, §5-14A-2.
Short title of chapter, §5-16-1.
Southern region savings institutions.
Regional reciprocal savings institutions act.
Applicable law, §5-14A-5.
Definition, §5-14A-2.

SAVINGS AND LOAN ASSOCIATIONS—Cont'd

State treasurer.
Securities issued by associations.
Deposits with state treasurer, §5-16-50.
Voluntary liquidation.
Unclaimed dividends and share accounts.
Certification and transmittal to state treasurer, §5-16-34.
Payment of creditors or investors by state treasurer, §5-16-35.
Subsidiaries.
Regional reciprocal savings institutions act.
Definition of subsidiary, §5-14A-2.
Power to establish or acquire subsidiaries, §5-14A-8.
Taxation.
Exemption from income tax, §40-18-32.
Transfer of assets, §5-16-28.
Reorganization.
Transfer to new association, §5-16-31.
Trusts and trustees.
Accounts, §5-16-43.
Death.
Disposition of deposit in trust for another upon death, §5-16-47.
United States.
Federal savings and loan associations. See within this heading, "Federal savings and loan associations."
Federal savings and loan insurance corporation. See within this heading, "Federal savings and loan insurance corporation."
Power to act as fiscal agent of United States, §5-16-24.
Violations.
Conservatorship, §5-16-37.
Involuntary liquidation, §5-16-37.
Reorganization, §5-16-37.
Voluntary liquidation, §§5-16-32 to 5-16-35.
Approval, §5-16-32.
Certificate of dissolution, §5-16-32.
Creditors.
Distribution of assets, §5-16-32.
Unclaimed dividends and share accounts.
Payment of creditors by commissioner, §5-16-33.
Payment of creditors by state treasurer, §5-16-35.
Distribution of assets, §5-16-32.
Unclaimed dividends and share accounts, §§5-16-33 to 5-16-35.
Investors.
Distribution of assets, §5-16-32.

SAVINGS AND LOAN ASSOCIATIONS—Cont'd
Voluntary liquidation —Cont'd
Investors—Cont'd
Unclaimed dividends and share accounts.
Payment of investors by commissioner, §5-16-33.
Payment of investors by state treasurer, §5-16-35.
Powers of dissolved association, §5-16-32.
Procedure, §5-16-32.
Unclaimed dividends and share accounts, §§5-16-33 to 5-16-35.
Certification and transmittal to state treasurer, §5-16-34.
Payment of creditors and investors by commissioner, §5-16-33.
Payment of creditors or investors by state treasurer, §5-16-35.
Remittance by receiver, §5-16-33.
Winding up business, §5-16-32.
Women.
Married women.
Accounts, §5-16-43.

SAWMILLS.
Attachment.
Employees' or laborers' liens, §35-11-273.
Owners' or operators' liens, §35-11-251.
Employees' or laborers' liens.
Attachment, §35-11-273.
Declaration, §35-11-270.
Enforcement, §35-11-273.
Liens generally.
See LIENS.
Limitations, §35-11-272.
Priority of lien, §35-11-271.
Floating logs on watercourses, §§33-7-5 to 33-7-8.
Licenses, §40-12-154.
Liens.
Employees' or laborers' liens, §§35-11-270 to 35-11-273.
Owners or operators, §§35-11-250, 35-11-251.
Owners' or operators' liens.
Attachment, §35-11-251.
Declaration, §35-11-250.
Enforcement, §35-11-251.
Liens generally.
See LIENS.
Sale of lumber, §35-11-251.
Waters and watercourses.
Floating logs on watercourses, §§33-7-5 to 33-7-8.

SCALES.
Coal mines, §§25-9-340 to 25-9-345.
See COAL.
General provisions, §§8-16-1 to 8-16-123.
See WEIGHTS AND MEASURES.

SCALES—Cont'd
Motor vehicles.
Size and weight of vehicles, §32-9-32.

SCARLET FEVER.
Notifiable diseases, §§22-11A-1 to 22-11A-38.
See DISEASES.

SCENIC ENHANCEMENT.
Highways, §§23-1-220 to 23-1-223.

SCHOLARSHIPS.
American Legion scholarships, §§16-31-1 to 16-31-4.
Blind persons.
Educational benefits for dependents of blind parents, §§16-33-1 to 16-33-12.
See UNIVERSITIES AND COLLEGES.
Dental college of Alabama, §§16-47-50 to 16-47-81.
See UNIVERSITY OF ALABAMA.
Emergency secondary education scholarship fund, §16-23-18.
Administration, §16-23-20.
Amount of grant, §16-23-18.
Commission on higher education.
Authority, §16-23-23.
Contracts of commitment.
Duration, §16-23-21.
Execution, §16-23-21.
Duration of state funding, §16-23-22.
Establishment, §16-23-18.
Number of scholarships, §16-23-18.
Exceptional children.
Special teachers, §16-39-12.
Handicapped persons.
Special teachers, §16-39-12.
Hospitals.
Professional and technical personnel at public hospitals, §22-21-3.
Jacksonville state university, §§16-52-13 to 16-52-15.
Libraries.
Field of library service, §41-8-6.
Library science and library education, §§41-8-1 to 41-8-25.
See LIBRARIES.
Nurses.
Jacksonville state university, §§16-52-13 to 16-52-15.
Post baccalaureate scholarships, §§34-21-60 to 34-21-63.
Sylacauga nurses' training school, §§16-58-1 to 16-58-3.
Troy state university, §§16-56-13 to 16-56-15.
Tuskegee institute, §§16-57-2 to 16-57-4.
University of Alabama, §§16-47-135 to 16-47-137.
University of North Alabama, §§16-55-7 to 16-55-9.

SCHOLARSHIPS—Cont'd
Nurses—Cont'd
University of South Alabama, §§16-55-7 to 16-55-9.
Optometrists.
Board of optometric scholarship awards, §§34-22-60 to 34-22-65.
See OPTOMETRISTS.
Parent and child.
Educational benefits for dependents of blind parents, §§16-33-1 to 16-33-12.
See UNIVERSITIES AND COLLEGES.
Sylacauga nurses' training school, §§16-58-1 to 16-58-3.
Teachers.
Elementary teachers' scholarship fund, §16-23-17.
Exceptional children.
Special teachers, §16-39-12.
Troy state university.
School of nursing, §§16-56-13 to 16-56-15.
Tuskegee institute.
School of nursing, §§16-57-2 to 16-57-4.
University of Alabama.
Dental college of Alabama, §§16-47-76 to 16-47-81.
See UNIVERSITY OF ALABAMA.
School of medicine, §§16-47-121 to 16-47-129.
See UNIVERSITY OF ALABAMA.
School of nursing, §§16-47-135 to 16-47-137.
University of Alabama, Huntsville, §§16-47-150 to 16-47-152.
University of North Alabama, §§16-51-13 to 16-51-15.
University of South Alabama.
School of nursing, §§16-55-7 to 16-55-9.

SCHOOL BUSES.
General provisions, §§16-27-1 to 16-27-7.
See EDUCATION.

SCHOOL LANDS.
General provisions, §§9-15-30 to 9-15-53.
See PUBLIC LANDS.

SCHOOLS.
Air schools, §§4-2-72, 4-2-77, 4-2-79.
Alabama school of trades, §§16-60-210 to 16-60-221.
Alcoholic beverages, §16-1-10.
Barber colleges, §§34-5-6, 34-5-7.
Boards of school trustees, §§16-10-1 to 16-10-11.
See EDUCATION.
Buildings.
General provisions.
See EDUCATION.
Church schools.
See CHURCHES.
Consolidation of schools, §§16-8-13 to 16-8-17.

SCHOOLS—Cont'd
  Corporations.
    Educational institutions,
      §§10-4-80 to 10-4-82.
  Corrections.
    Schools at correctional units,
      §§14-12-1 to 14-12-4.
  Cosmetology.
    General provisions, §§34-7-1
      to 34-7-16.
    See COSMETOLOGISTS.
    Instructors, §§34-7-4, 34-7-11.
  Districts.
    Independent school districts.
      Boards of education.
        Association of school
          board members,
          §16-1-6.
        Review of local actions
          by state
          superintendent,
          §16-3-27.
  Driver training schools,
    §§32-14-1 to 32-14-24.
    See MOTOR VEHICLES.
  Education generally.
    See EDUCATION.
  **Elementary schools
    generally.**
    See EDUCATION.
  General provisions.
    See EDUCATION.
  High schools, §§16-26-1 to
    16-26-4.
  Holidays.
    Enumerated, §1-3-8.
  Independent school districts.
    Boards of education.
      Association of school board
        members, §16-1-6.
      Review of local action by
        state superintendent,
        §16-3-27.
  **Jacksonsville state
    university,** §§16-52-1 to
    16-52-16.
    See JACKSONVILLE
      STATE UNIVERSITY.
  Land.
    General provisions, §§9-15-30
      to 9-15-53.
    See PUBLIC LANDS.
  Libraries, §§16-21-1 to
    16-21-3.
  Motor vehicles.
    Driver training schools,
      §§32-14-1 to 32-14-24.
    See MOTOR VEHICLES.
  **Partlow state school and
    hospital,** §23-1-42; Const.
    Ala., amds. 113, 118.
  Prisons and prisoners.
    Schools at correctional units,
      §§14-12-1 to 14-12-4.
  Real property.
    General provisions.
      See EDUCATION.
    School lands, §§9-15-30 to
      9-15-53.
    See PUBLIC LANDS.
  School lands, §§9-15-30 to
    9-15-53.
    See PUBLIC LANDS.
  **Sylacauga nurses' training
    school,** §§16-58-1 to
    16-58-3.
  Teachers generally.
    See EDUCATION.
  Textbooks, §§16-36-1 to
    16-36-39.
    See EDUCATION.

SCHOOLS—Cont'd
  Trade schools generally.
    See TRADE SCHOOLS.
  Troy state university,
    §§16-56-1 to 16-56-15.
    See TROY STATE
      UNIVERSITY.
  Trustees.
    Boards of school trustees,
      §§16-10-1 to 16-10-11.
    See EDUCATION.
  Tuskegee institute, §§16-57-1
    to 16-57-4.
  Unaccredited schools,
    §§16-46-1 to 16-46-10.
    See EDUCATION.
  **Universities and colleges
    generally.**
    See UNIVERSITIES AND
      COLLEGES.
  University of Alabama,
    §§16-47-1 to 16-47-204.
    See UNIVERSITY OF
      ALABAMA.
  **University of North
    Alabama,** §§16-51-1 to
    16-51-15.
    See UNIVERSITY OF
      NORTH ALABAMA.
  **University of South
    Alabama,** §§16-55-1 to
    16-55-9.
    See UNIVERSITY OF
      SOUTH ALABAMA.
  Youth services, §§44-1-1 to
    44-3-12.
    See YOUTH SERVICES.

SCIENCE.
  Dead bodies.
    Distribution of unclaimed
      bodies for scientific
      study, §§22-19-20 to
      22-19-30.
    See DEAD BODIES.
  Evidence.
    Books of science as evidence
      of facts of general
      notoriety and interest,
      §12-21-108; ARCP, Rule
      44 (g).
  Exhibition.
    Space science exhibit
      commission, §§41-9-430
      to 41-9-439.
    See SPACE SCIENCE
      EXHIBIT
      COMMISSION.
    Space science exhibit finance
      authority, §§41-10-300 to
      41-10-332.
  Fish and game.
    Collection of animals and
      birds for scientific
      purposes.
      Permits, §9-11-231.
  Insurance.
    Life insurers organized to aid
      nonprofit educational
      and scientific
      institutions.
      Annual license fee, §27-4-8.
  Library science.
    Scholarships and grants,
      §41-8-6.
    See LIBRARIES.
  Licenses.
    Scientists, §40-12-155.

SCIENCE—Cont'd
  **Space science exhibit
    commission,** §§41-9-430 to
    41-9-439.
    See SPACE SCIENCE
      EXHIBIT
      COMMISSION.

**SCIENTIFIC RESEARCH
  SOCIETIES.**
  Corporations.
    Public societies, §§10-4-20 to
      10-4-28.
    See CORPORATIONS.

SCINTILLA RULE.
  Abolished, §12-21-12.
  Rules of civil procedure.
    Directed verdict or judgment
      not withstanding verdict.
      Motions.
        When court may grant,
          ARCP, Rule 50 (e).

SCIRE FACIAS.
  Abolished, ARCP, Rule 81 (c).

S CORPORATIONS,
  §§40-18-160 to 40-18-176.
  See CORPORATIONS.

**SCOTTSBORO,
  MUNICIPALITY OF.**
  Property tax, Const. Ala.,
    amd. 8.

SCRAP DEALERS.
  Junk dealers.
    Junkyard control, §§23-1-240
      to 23-1-251.
    See JUNKYARD
      CONTROL.
    Licenses, §40-12-116.
    Milk and milk products.
      Marked containers.
        Possession by junk
          dealer prima facie
          evidence of violation,
          §8-12-42.
    Salvage generally, §§35-13-1
      to 35-13-10.
    See SALVAGE.

SCRIP.
  **Banks and financial
    institutions,** §§5-10A-12,
    5-10A-13.

SCURVY.
  Notifiable diseases,
    §§22-11A-1 to 22-11A-38.
    See DISEASES.

SEAFOOD.
  General provisions.
    See MARINE RESOURCES.

**SEALS AND SEALED
  INSTRUMENTS.**
  Acknowledgments.
    Proof of official seal,
      §35-4-27.
  Actions.
    Consideration of sealed
      instruments.
      Impeachment of or inquiry
        into, §6-5-287.
  Alabama school of trade.
    Corporate seal, §16-60-212.
  Architects, §§34-2-35, 34-2-39.
  Auctions and auctioneers.
    Board of auctioneers,
      §34-4-50.
  Ballots, §§17-8-35 to 17-8-38.
  **Bear Creek development
    authority,** §33-15-15.
  Bishop of diocese, §10-4-4.

SEALS AND SEALED INSTRUMENTS—Cont'd

Bond issues.
Execution with facsimile seals, §1-3-3.
Chiropractors.
Board of chiropractic examiners, §34-24-144.
Circuit courts, ARJA, Rule 24.
Commercial code.
Commercial paper.
Negotiability not affected, §7-3-113.
Contracts for sale.
Seal inoperative, §7-2-203.
Conservation and natural resources.
Department, §9-2-1.
Construction and interpretation.
Effect of writings importing to be under seal, §35-4-22.
Contractors.
State licensing board, §34-8-23.
Contracts.
Commercial code.
Sales contracts.
Seals inoperative, §7-2-203.
Conveyances.
Seal unnecessary, §35-4-21.
Corporations.
Corporate seal, §10-2A-20.
Corrections.
Alabama corrections institution finance authority, §14-2-8.
Institution finance authority.
Execution of bonds and notes, §14-2-11.
Cosmetology.
Board of cosmetology, §34-7-43.
Credit unions.
Credit union administration.
Administrator, §5-17-43.
Deeds.
Seals unnecessary, §35-4-21.
Dentists.
Board of dental examiners, §34-9-41.
District courts, ARJA, Rule 24.
Effect of writings importing to be under seal, §35-4-22.
Elections.
Ballots, §§17-8-35 to 17-8-38.
Electric cooperatives.
Adoption of corporate seal, §37-6-3.
Electric membership corporations.
Power to have and alter seal, §37-7-10.
Engineers.
Board of registration, §34-11-35.
Registered professional engineer, §34-11-7.
Environmental improvement authorities, §9-6-8.
Facsimile seals.
Execution of bonds, warrants, notes, etc., with, §1-3-3.
Fire fighters' personnel standards and education commission, §36-32-4.

SEALS AND SEALED INSTRUMENTS—Cont'd

Funerals.
Board of funeral service, §34-13-27.
Great seal of state, §1-2-4; Const. Ala., art. V, §133.
Health care authorities.
Powers of authority, §22-21-318.
Highways.
Authority, §23-1-155.
Bond issues, §23-1-157.
Department, §23-1-39.
Finance corporation, §23-1-175.
Historic Blakely authority, §41-10-174.
Industrial development advisory board, §41-9-185.
Industrial relations department, §25-2-1.
Insurance.
Commissioner of insurance, §27-2-5.
Judicial inquiry commission, AJICR, Rule 13.
Landscape architects.
Board of examiners, §34-17-3.
Final drawings, etc., to bear seal, §34-17-4.
Land surveyors.
Professional land surveyor, §34-11-7.
Limitation of actions.
Actions upon contract or writing under seal.
Ten year limitation, §6-2-33.
Medical technicians.
Board of medical technicians examiners, §34-18-43.
Mental health finance authority, §41-10-356.
Military affairs.
Adjutant general, §31-2-58.
Mobile homes.
State fire marshal seal.
See MOBILE HOMES.
Municipal corporations, §§11-40-1, 11-40-2.
Council.
Custody of seal, §11-43-100.
Notaries public.
Notaries public for state at large, §36-20-32.
Seal of office, §36-20-4.
Notes.
Execution of notes with facsimile seals, §1-3-3.
Peace officers' standards and training commission, §36-21-43.
Power districts, §37-5-3.
Probate judges, §12-13-35.
Public service commission, §37-1-2.
Public works.
Improvement authorities.
Power to have and alter seal, §39-7-22.
Railroad authorities, §37-13-7.
Real estate commission, §34-27-7.

SEALS AND SEALED INSTRUMENTS—Cont'd

Savings and loan associations.
Commissioner of savings and loan.
Seal of office, §5-2A-61.
Corporate seal, §5-16-24.
Securities.
Facsimiles of corporate seals.
Issuance of securities with, §41-1-8.
Soil and water conservation.
Districts, §9-8-25.
State.
Great seal of state, §1-2-4; Const. Ala., art. V, §133.
Surveys and surveyors.
Board of registration.
Official seal of board, §34-11-35.
Professional land surveyor, §34-11-7.
Trade schools, §16-60-212.
Veterans.
State service commissioner, §31-5-12.
Warrants for the payment of money.
Execution with facsimile seals, §1-3-3.
Water conservation and irrigation.
Agency, §9-10-5.
Corporations, §9-10-34.
Water system assistance authority, §22-23A-6.
Weights and measures, §8-16-54.
See WEIGHTS AND MEASURES.
When undertaking without seal sufficient, §1-3-2.
Wills.
Conveyances generally.
See CONVEYANCES.

SEAMEN'S HOME OF MOBILE.

Licenses and taxation.
Exemptions, §40-9-12.

SEAPORTS.

See HARBORS AND PORTS.

SEARCHES AND SEIZURES.

Affidavits.
Seizure of property.
Procedure, ARCP, Rule 64 (b).
Alcoholic beverages, §28-1-2
Attachments.
Seizure of property.
Rules of civil procedure.
Writs of seizure or attachment, ARCP, Rule 64 (b).
Baggage.
Liens of hotel and restaurant keepers.
Seizure and sale of baggage and goods of guests, §35-11-131.
Beverage containers.
Search warrants.
Containers unlawfully use or held, §8-12-23.
Boats.
Condemnation and sale, §§9-12-4 to 9-12-8.
Brake fluid.
Seizure for violations, §8-17-7.

SEARCHES AND SEIZURES
—Cont'd
Catfish.
Marketing of catfish.
Seizure of catfish sold in
violation of provisions
of article, §2-11-39.
Constitution of Alabama,
Const. Ala., art. I, §5.
**Constitution of the United
States,** Const. U. S.,
Amendment IV.
Controlled substances,
§20-2-93.
Cotton.
Applicability of laws relative
to seizure, §2-19-26.
Crops.
Landlord and tenant.
Seizure of crops upon
abandonment of
premises, §35-9-12.
Partition of crops.
Seizure of crops to be
divided by sheriff,
§35-6-117.
Dangerous weapons.
Stop and frisk law, §15-5-31.
Definitions.
Search warrant, §15-5-1.
Detinue.
Seizure of personal property,
ARCP, Rule 64 (b).
District courts.
Seizure of person or property.
Procedure for seizure of
property.
Applicability of rules to
district courts,
ARCP, Rule 64 (b).
Drugs.
Controlled substances,
§20-2-93.
Eggs and egg products.
Seizure for violation of
chapter, §2-12-9.
Estrays, §§3-2-1 to 3-2-3.
Exclusionary rule.
Alcoholic beverages.
Admissibility of evidence
obtained by illegal
searches, §28-1-2.
**Execution of search
warrants,** §§15-5-7 to
15-5-9.
Fees.
Search warrants.
Payment of fee, §15-5-18.
Felonies.
Search warrants.
Commission of felony as
grounds for issuance,
§15-5-2.
Fertilizer.
Seizure of noncomplying
fertilizer, §2-22-21.
Fireworks.
Authority of state fire
marshal, §§8-17-221,
8-17-225.
Fish and game.
Fish farms.
Unauthorized fishing.
Seizure and disposal of
fishing equipment,
§9-11-91.1.
General provisions.
See FISH AND GAME.
Fishing boats.
Condemnation and sale,
§§9-12-4 to 9-12-8.

SEARCHES AND SEIZURES
—Cont'd
Food.
Articles sold, stored, etc., in
violation of chapter,
§20-1-4.
Forests and forestry.
Timber theft equipment.
Condemnation, §§9-13-220
to 9-13-227.
See TREES AND
TIMBER.
Forms.
Seizure of person or property,
ARCP, Forms 88 to 91.
Frisks, §§15-5-30, 15-5-31.
Gambling.
Forfeiture of devices and
proceeds, §13A-12-30.
Municipal corporations,
§11-47-111.
Grain, §2-20-6.
Adulterated grain, §2-20-4.
Grading and standards.
Applicability of laws
relative to seizure,
§2-11-102.
Grain bleached with sulphur
fumes, §2-20-5.
Hearings.
Challenging search warrants,
§15-5-15.
Seizure of person or property.
Procedure for seizure of
property, ARCP, Rule
64 (b).
**Hotels, inns and other
transient lodging places.**
Lien of hotel keepers.
Seizure and sale of
baggage and goods,
§35-11-131.
Judges.
Searching a person charged
with felony for weapon
or evidence in judge's
presence, §15-5-17.
Juvenile proceedings.
Illegally seized evidence,
§12-15-66.
Landlord and tenant.
Crops.
Seizure upon abandonment
of premises, §35-9-12.
Linseed oil.
Illegal products, §8-17-44.
Livestock running at large,
§§3-5-4 to 3-5-14.
See LIVESTOCK.
Lotteries.
Transportation of lottery
paraphernalia.
Seizures of vehicles used,
§13A-12-70.
Marine mammal protection.
Violations of article.
Custody and disposition of
equipment, etc., seized,
§9-11-396.
Marine resources.
Condemnation and sale of
boat and equipment,
§§9-12-4 to 9-12-8.
Division personnel.
Seizure of illegal items,
§9-2-85.
Military affairs.
Illegally acquired military
property, §31-2-30.
Unlawfully retained
property, §31-2-31.

SEARCHES AND SEIZURES
—Cont'd
Milk and milk products.
Applicability of laws relative
to seizure, §2-13-22.
Seizure of milk in transit,
§2-13-89.
Motor vehicles.
Municipal testing stations.
Inspections.
Uninspected vehicles,
§32-18-8.
Uniform certificate of title
and antitheft act.
Identifiable component
part, §32-8-86.
Municipal corporations.
Gambling implements,
§11-47-111.
Oaths.
Warrants.
Supported by oath or
affirmation, Const.
Ala., art. I, §5; Const.
U. S., Amendment IV.
Obscenity.
Seizure of property,
§13A-12-200.8.
Oil and gas.
Illegal oil, gas or product,
§§8-17-114, 9-17-22.
Partition.
Crops.
Seizure of crops to be
divided by sheriff,
§35-6-117.
Penalties.
Search warrants.
Procuring maliciously or
without probable
cause, §15-5-19.
Penitentiary.
Search of person and
baggage of convict,
§14-3-35.
Pesticides.
Noncomplying articles,
§2-27-15.
Petroleum products,
§§9-17-22, 9-17-114.
Presence of judge.
Searching a person charged
with felony in presence
of judge, §15-5-17.
**Public officers and
employees.**
Public property, papers, etc.
Recovery of papers,
property, etc., by
successors to office,
§§36-12-24, 36-12-25.
Public places.
Searches, etc., of persons in
public places, §§15-5-30,
15-5-31.
Restaurants.
Liens of restaurant keepers.
Seizure and sale of goods
and baggage of
customers, §35-11-131.
Rules of civil procedure,
ARCP, Rule 64.
Forms, ARCP, Forms 88 to
91.
Search warrants, §§15-5-1 to
15-5-19.
Affidavit required, §15-5-3.

SEARCHES AND SEIZURES
—Cont'd
Search warrants—Cont'd
Alcoholic beverages.
Dry counties, §§28-4-251 to
28-4-264.
See ALCOHOLIC
BEVERAGES.
Complainant.
Examination, §15-5-4.
Costs.
Payment of costs, §15-5-18.
Defined, §15-5-1.
Depositions.
Contents, §15-5-4.
Examination of complainant
and witnesses, §15-5-4.
Execution.
Authority of serving officer
to break into house,
§15-5-9.
By whom executed,
§15-5-7.
Time of execution to be
stated, §15-5-8.
When executed, §15-5-8.
Within ten days, §15-5-12.
Fees.
Payment of fees, §15-5-18.
Fish and game.
Wardens.
Execution, §9-2-65.
Forms, §15-5-6.
Grounds for issuance,
§15-5-2.
Hearings.
Challenging search
warrants, §15-5-15.
Record, §15-5-15.
Issuance, §15-5-5.
Examination of
complainant and
witnesses, §15-5-4.
Generally, §15-5-5.
Grounds, §15-5-2.
Probable cause required,
Const. Ala., art. I, §5;
Const. U. S.,
Amendment IV.
Municipal courts, §12-14-32.
Oath or affirmation, Const.
Ala., art. I, §5; Const. U.
S., Amendment IV.
Penalties.
Procuring maliciously or
without probable
cause, §15-5-19.
Probable cause.
Penalty for procuring
without probable
cause, §15-5-19.
Required, §15-5-3; Const.
Ala., art. I, §5; Const.
U. S., Amendment IV.
Return.
Contents of return,
§15-5-13.
Copies to be furnished,
§15-5-13.
Within ten days, §15-5-12.
Searching a person charged
with felony in
magistrate's presence,
§15-5-17.
Taking of property, §15-5-10.
Disposition of taken
property, §15-5-14.
Receipt for property taken,
§15-5-11.
Restoration to defendant,
§15-5-16.

SEARCHES AND SEIZURES
—Cont'd
Search warrants—Cont'd
Witnesses.
Examination, §15-5-4.
Seeds.
Elimination of fungi and
noxious weeds from seed.
Seeds in violation of rules
and regulations,
§2-26-31.
Noncomplying seeds,
§2-26-12.
**Southeast interstate low-
level radioactive waste
management compact.**
Source of ionizing radiation.
Impoundment or seizure,
§22-32-8.
Stop and frisk law.
Authority of peace officer,
§15-5-30.
Dangerous weapons,
§15-5-31.
Telegraphs.
Prohibited instruments,
§37-8-221.
Telephones.
Prohibited instruments,
§37-8-221.
Tobacco.
Use tax.
Seizure of contraband,
§40-25-41.
Trees and timber.
Condemnation of timber theft
equipment, §§9-13-220 to
9-13-227.
See TREES AND TIMBER.
Turpentine.
Illegal turpentine, §8-17-173.
Warrants.
Search warrants, §§15-5-1 to
15-5-19.
Weapons.
Pistols.
Seizure of pistols involved
in certain violations,
§13A-11-84.
Stop and frisk law, §15-5-31.
Weights and measures.
Incorrect, false or unsealed
weight, measure, device,
package or commodity.
Seizure for evidence,
§8-16-10.
Writs of seizure.
Forms, ARCP, Forms 88 to
91.

SEARCH WARRANTS,
§§15-5-1 to 15-5-19.
See SEARCHES AND
SEIZURES.

SEAT BELTS, §§32-5-217,
32-5-222.

SEAWALLS.
Bulkheads generally.
See BOOMS AND
BULKHEADS.
Constitution of Alabama.
Districts to build and
maintain seawalls,
Const. Ala., amd. 15.
Municipal corporations.
Assessments for public
improvements.
Manner of assessment,
§11-48-16.

**SECONDARY ROAD
COMMITTEE,** §40-12-270.

SECRETARY OF STATE,
§§36-14-1 to 36-14-15.
**Acts and resolutions of
legislature,** §§36-14-11 to
36-14-13.
Copies.
Library of congress,
§36-14-12.
Probate judges.
Copies to be furnished
for, §36-14-13.
Surplus copies.
Sale, §36-14-13.
Distribution, §36-14-11.
Library of congress.
Copies to be furnished,
§36-14-12.
Probate judges.
Copies to be furnished for,
§36-14-13.
Bishop of diocese.
Application for corporation,
§10-4-2.
Fees to be paid secretary of
state, §10-4-8.
Bond, §36-14-2.
Disposal of certain books,
acts, codes, etc.
Liability on bond, §36-14-9.
Filing, §36-5-1.
Recordation, §36-5-1.
Books.
Copies.
When duplicate copies to
be furnished to judicial
officers, §36-14-14.
Custody, §36-14-4.
Disposal.
Accounts.
Sales and money paid
over, §36-14-8.
Authorized, §36-14-6.
Director of finance.
Returns and payments,
§36-14-7.
Duty upon leaving office,
§36-14-9.
Governor.
Filing of list of books,
§36-14-7.
Liability on bond, §36-14-9.
List of books.
Filing with governor,
§36-14-7.
Receipt of doorkeeper.
Sufficient voucher,
§36-14-10.
Restrictions, §36-14-6.
Photographic reproduction,
§36-14-15.
Legal effect, §36-14-15.
Codes.
Disposal of certain codes,
§§36-14-6 to 36-14-10.
Commercial code.
Secured transactions.
Filing.
Central index system
program.
Promulgation of
regulations,
§7-9-410.
Place of filing, §7-9-401.
Compensation, Const. Ala.,
art. V, §118.
Constitution of Alabama.
Compensation, Const. Ala.,
art. V, §118.

SECRETARY OF STATE
—Cont'd
Constitution of Alabama
—Cont'd
Duties, Const. Ala., art. V,
§§134, 137; amd. 111.
Executive department.
Member of department,
Const. Ala., art. V,
§112.
Qualifications, Const. Ala.,
art. V, §132.
Residency requirements,
Const. Ala., art. V, §118.
Succession.
Ineligible to succeed self,
Const. Ala., art. V,
§116.
Term of office, Const. Ala.,
art. V, §116; amd. 282.
Vacancy in office, Const.
Ala., art. V, §136.
**Coosa valley development
authority.**
Application for incorporation.
Presentation to secretary,
§33-16-4.
Certificate of incorporation.
Issuance, §33-16-5.
Dissolution of authority.
Application for dissolution.
Filing with secretary,
§33-16-15.
Fees.
No fees to be paid to
secretary of state,
§33-16-5.
Corporations, §§10-2A-29,
10-2A-280, 10-2A-233,
10-2A-332.
See CORPORATIONS.
Corrections.
Institution finance authority.
Fees for incorporation or
dissolution, §14-2-35.
Duties, §36-14-1; Const. Ala.,
art. V, §§134, 137; amd.
111.
Education.
Compact for education.
Bylaws of commission and
amendments to be filed
with secretary,
§16-44-3.
Elections.
Amendments to constitution.
Returns made to secretary
of state, §17-17-2.
Canvass of election returns.
Opening in presence of
secretary, §17-14-20.
Congressional elections.
Returns.
Board of supervisors to
make returns to
secretary, §17-20-3.
Constitutional provisions,
Const. Ala., art. V,
§§114, 115.
Contests, Const. Ala., art. V,
§115.
Fair campaign practices.
Duties, §17-22A-11.
Political committees.
Filing copy of federal
report with
secretary,
§17-22A-15.
General elections.
Offices for which general
election held, §17-2-2.

SECRETARY OF STATE
—Cont'd
Elections—Cont'd
General elections—Cont'd
Time of general election,
§17-2-3.
Presidential and vice-
presidential elections.
Making returns to
secretary, §17-19-4.
Primary elections,
§§17-16-11, 17-16-40.
Results to be received by
secretary, §§17-16-35,
17-16-36.
Returns.
Opening, Const. Ala., art.
V, §115.
Publication, Const. Ala.,
art. V, §115.
Transmission to speaker of
house, Const. Ala., art.
V, §115.
State officers elected by the
people, §17-2-1.
Tie votes, Const. Ala., art. V,
§115.
Time, Const. Ala., art. V,
§114.
Electric cooperatives.
Filing of articles, §37-6-19.
**Elk river development
agency.**
Incorporation.
Application for
incorporation.
Duties as to, §33-12-3.
Executive department.
Member of department,
Const. Ala., art. V, §112.
Fees.
Alabama highway authority.
Fees not to be collected,
§23-1-153.
Institution finance authority.
Incorporation or
dissolution, §14-2-35.
Restrictions on receipt of
fees, Const. Ala., art. V,
§137; amd. 111.
Services performed, §36-14-3.
Harbors and ports.
Port authority, §§33-13-3 to
33-13-5.
**Historical preservation
authorities.**
Certificate of incorporation.
Filing with secretary,
§41-10-139.
Recordation by secretary,
§41-10-139.
Fees, taxes or costs for
incorporation, etc.
Payment to secretary,
§41-10-147.
Impeachment, Const. Ala.,
art. VII, §173.
General provisions.
See IMPEACHMENT.
**Industrial development
authority.**
Incorporation, §§41-10-23,
41-10-24.
**Industrial development
corporations.**
Approval of articles of
corporation, §10-4-131.

SECRETARY OF STATE
—Cont'd
Insurance.
Mail order insurance.
Service of process on
unauthorized insurers.
Secretary as agent for
service, §27-11-5.
Legislature.
Acts and resolutions of
legislature, §§36-14-11 to
36-14-13.
Records.
Legislation, §29-1-15.
Papers and documents of
legislature, §29-1-14.
Receipt for papers,
§29-1-17.
**Mental health finance
authority.**
Incorporation of authority.
Application for authority to
incorporate.
Presented to secretary,
§41-10-353.
Certificate of incorporation.
Issuance, §41-10-354.
Mental unsoundness, Const.
Ala., art. V, §136.
Oath of office.
General provisions, §36-4-2.
See PUBLIC OFFICERS
AND EMPLOYEES.
**Photographic reproduction
of records, etc.,**
§36-14-15.
Legal effect, §36-14-15.
Primary elections,
§§17-16-11, 17-16-40.
Public officers generally.
See PUBLIC OFFICERS
AND EMPLOYEES.
Public works.
Improvement authorities.
Incorporation, §39-7-11.
Qualifications, Const. Ala.,
art. V, §132.
Records.
Legislature, §§29-1-14 to
29-1-17.
Local government records
commission.
Member of commission,
§41-13-22.
Photographic reproduction,
§36-14-15.
Legal effect, §36-14-15.
Residency requirements,
Const. Ala., art. V, §118.
Secured transactions.
Place of filing, §7-9-401.
Securities.
Registration of securities.
Applicability of article,
§8-6-12.
Consent to service on
secretary, §8-6-12.
State records commission.
Member of commission,
§41-13-20.
Succession.
One additional term, Const.
Ala., amd. 282.
**Synfuels development
authority.**
Application for authority to
incorporate.
Review and recordation by
secretary, §9-6A-4.

SECRETARY OF STATE
—Cont'd
Synfuels development authority—Cont'd
Dissolution of authority.
Recordation of application for dissolution by secretary, §9-6A-10.
Term of office, Const. Ala., art. V, §136; amd. 282.
Tombigbee Valley development authority.
Dissolution.
Application for dissolution.
Filing with secretary, §33-17-15.
Fees.
No fees to be paid to secretary, §33-17-5.
Incorporation.
Presentation of application to secretary, §33-17-4.
Unincorporated professional associations.
Furnishing of statements to secretary, §10-10-10.
Vacancy in office, Const. Ala., art. V, §136.
Water system assistance authority.
Application to become corporation.
Filing with, §22-23A-5.

SECURED TRANSACTIONS.
Commercial code, §§7-9-101 to 7-9-507.
See COMMERCIAL CODE.
Defrauding secured creditors, §13A-9-46.
Motor vehicles.
Uniform certificate of title and antitheft act, §§32-8-60 to 32-8-67.
See MOTOR VEHICLES.
Pledge and collateral security, §§7-9-101 to 7-9-507.
See COMMERCIAL CODE.
Taxation.
Security agreements and security interests exempt, §40-9-1.
Trees and timber.
Condemnation of timber theft equipment.
Notice to secured creditor, §9-13-224.
Weapons.
Pistols.
Loans secured by pistol, §13A-11-80.

SECURITIES, §§8-6-1 to 8-6-122.
Agents.
Civil liabilities, §8-6-19.
Agriculture.
Agricultural markets and coliseum corporation, §§2-6-70 to 2-6-86.
See AGRICULTURE.
Appeals.
Action of commission, §8-6-32.
Arrest.
Director, §8-6-22.
Securities commission, §8-6-21.

SECURITIES—Cont'd
Attorneys at law.
Director.
Appointment of legal counsel, §8-6-58.
Banks and financial institutions generally.
See BANKS AND FINANCIAL INSTITUTIONS.
Blue sky law, §§8-6-1 to 8-6-60.
Bond issues.
General provisions.
See BOND ISSUES.
Investment securities, §§7-8-101 to 7-8-406.
See COMMERCIAL CODE.
Bonds, surety.
Dealers, §8-6-3.
Director, §8-6-59.
Salesmen, §8-6-3.
Securities commission.
Employees, §8-6-59.
Commercial code.
Investment securities, §§7-8-101 to 7-8-406.
See COMMERCIAL CODE.
Commission.
Securities commission, §§8-6-50 to 8-6-60. See within this heading, "Securities commission."
Constitution of Alabama.
Bonds and other securities issued by certain public corporations, Const. Ala., amd. 108.
Construction and interpretation.
Fiduciary security transfers.
Construction of article, §8-6-80.
Counties.
Bond issues.
Securities issued in anticipation of grants, §§11-11B-1 to 11-11B-8.
See COUNTIES.
Exemption from usury and interest statutes, §11-14-18.
Redemption of securities, §§11-82-1 to 11-82-7.
See COUNTIES.
Coupons.
Registered securities.
Issuance without coupons, §41-1-7.
Dealers.
Bonds, §8-6-3.
Defined, §8-6-2.
Registration, §8-6-3.
Definitions, §8-6-2.
Exemption from definition.
Burden of proving, §8-6-30.
Fiduciary security transfers, §8-6-71.
Minors.
Ownership by minors, §8-6-91.
Taxation, §40-24-1.
Dental service corporations.
Custody of securities, §22-21-370.
Hearings on posting, §22-21-370.
Modification orders, §22-21-370.

SECURITIES—Cont'd
Dental service corporations
—Cont'd
Noncompliance.
Effect, §22-21-370.
Posting, §22-21-370.
Release of securities, §22-21-370.
Detinue.
Action against purchaser based on wrongful transfer, §7-8-315.
Director.
Appointment, §8-6-55.
Arrests.
Warrants of arrest, §8-6-22.
Bond, §8-6-59.
Deputy director, §8-6-57.
Duties, §§8-6-22, 8-6-55.
Employees.
Bonds, §8-6-59.
Industrial revenue bonds.
Preissuance procedure, §§8-6-110 to 8-6-122.
See INDUSTRIAL REVENUE BONDS.
Legal counsel.
Appointment, §8-6-58.
Office.
Place of office, §8-6-60.
Personnel.
Appointment, §8-6-58.
Powers.
Exercise by commission, §8-6-53.
Qualifications, §8-6-56.
Salary, §8-6-58.
Education.
Public school corporation, §§16-14-17 to 16-14-19.
Electric cooperatives.
Bond issues.
Exemption from provisions, §37-6-29.
Evidence.
Copies of register entries or documents.
Certified copy deemed prima facie evidence, §8-6-28.
Fiduciary security transfers.
Evidence of appointment or incumbency, §8-6-76.
Executors and administrators.
Securities held by fiduciaries, §§19-4-1 to 19-4-42.
See FIDUCIARIES.
Fees.
Registration of securities, §8-6-8.
Fiduciaries.
Securities held by fiduciaries, §§19-4-1 to 19-4-42.
See FIDUCIARIES.
Fiduciary security transfers.
Adverse claims, §8-6-77.
Applicability of article, §8-6-72.
Assignment by fiduciary, §8-6-75.
Conflicts of law.
Registration and transfer governed by state of incorporation, §8-6-72.
Construction of article, §8-6-80.
Definitions, §8-6-71.
Evidence of appointment or incumbency, §8-6-76.

SECURITIES—Cont'd
Fiduciary security transfers
—Cont'd
Inquiry into fiduciary
relationship.
Not required, §8-6-74.
Liability.
Corporation or transfer
agent, §8-6-79.
Third persons.
Nonliability, §8-6-78.
Presumption that registered
owner continues to be
fiduciary, §8-6-74.
Tax obligations not affected,
§8-6-73.
Title of article.
Short title, §8-6-70.
Filing.
Document deemed filed when
received, §8-6-26.
Fees, §8-6-8.
Truth, completeness, etc., of
documents.
Filing not finding, §8-6-14.
Forgery.
First degree forgery,
§13A-9-2.
Forms.
Commission may prescribe,
§8-6-23.
Liability for acts or
omissions in good faith
under forms, §8-6-24.
Gifts to minors.
Uniform transfers to minors
act, §§35-5A-1 to
35-5A-24.
See TRANSFERS TO
MINORS.
Grants.
Issuance of securities in
anticipation of receipt of
grants, §§11-81A-1 to
11-81A-7.
Authorization, §11-81A-4.
Counties.
Power and authority,
§11-81A-3.
Definitions, §11-81A-1.
Effect of chapter,
§11-81A-7.
Exemption from taxation,
§11-81A-5.
Grantees.
Power and authority,
§11-81A-2.
Investments.
Legal investments,
§11-81A-6.
Legal investment status of
securities, §11-81A-6.
Municipalities.
Power and authority,
§11-81A-3.
Public corporations.
Power and authority,
§11-81A-3.
Taxation.
Exemption of securities,
§11-81A-5.
Health care authorities.
Additional powers.
Definition of securities,
§22-21-350.
Federal securities.
Defined, §22-21-350.
General obligations
securities, §22-21-353.
Conditions, §22-21-320.
Defined, §22-21-311.

SECURITIES—Cont'd
Health care authorities
—Cont'd
Execution and delivery,
§22-21-320.
Conditions for execution,
§22-21-322.
Indenture.
Source of payment,
§22-21-323.
Interest, §22-21-320.
Exemption from usury and
interest provisions,
§22-21-328.
Limitation of actions to
contest validity,
§22-21-329.
Negotiability, §22-21-327.
Notice of issuance,
§22-21-329.
Payment.
Remedies for default in
payment, §22-21-331.
Source of payment,
§22-21-323.
Powers of authority,
§22-21-318.
Proceeds.
Use, §22-21-324.
Refunding securities,
§22-21-321.
Remedies for default in
payment, §22-21-331.
Specific obligation securities,
§22-21-323.
State, counties or
municipalities not
indebted, §22-21-325.
Terms, §22-21-320.
Usury.
Exemption from usury
provisions, §22-21-328.
Validity.
Limitation on actions to
contest, §22-21-329.
Health care service plans.
Deposit with state treasurer,
§10-4-112.
Hearings.
Orders of commission,
§8-6-32.
Private hearings.
Request for, §8-6-25.
Public hearings, §8-6-25.
Income tax.
Deductions.
Stock bonus plans.
Contributions paid by
employer to or
under, §40-18-15.
Interest or other income
received from obligations
of United States,
§40-18-4.
Optional method for
returning as income
increases in redemption
value of securities
purchased at a discount,
§40-18-9.
Indictments.
Advertising unregistered
securities.
Form, §15-8-150.
**Industrial development
corporations.**
Applicability of laws
regulating securities,
§10-4-152.

SECURITIES—Cont'd
Injunctions.
Violations of article, §8-6-16.
Appointment of receivers
or conservators for
defendants or
defendants' assets,
§8-6-16.
Insurance.
Licensing of securities
salesmen, §27-27-11.
Interest.
Issuance of interest bearing
securities, §41-1-9.
Provisions deemed
declarative of existing
law, §41-1-10.
Investigations.
Securities commission,
§8-6-15.
Investments.
Commercial code, §§7-8-101
to 7-8-406.
See COMMERCIAL CODE.
Issuance, §§41-1-7 to 41-1-10.
Facsimile signatures,
§41-1-8.
Facsimiles of corporate seal,
§41-1-8.
Interest bearing securities,
§41-1-9.
Provisions deemed
declarative of existing
law, §41-1-10.
Registered securities.
Issuance without coupons,
§41-1-7.
Limitation of actions.
Prosecutions for violations of
article, §8-6-18.
Minors.
Gifts to minors.
Uniform transfers to
minors act, §§35-5A-1
to 35-5A-24.
See TRANSFERS TO
MINORS.
Ownership by minors,
§§8-6-90 to 8-6-95.
Bank.
Defined, §8-6-91.
Liability for treating
minor as having
capacity to exercise
rights, §8-6-92.
Broker.
Defined, §8-6-91.
Liability for treating
minor as having
capacity to exercise
rights, §8-6-92.
Definitions, §8-6-91.
Disaffirmance of security
transaction.
Minor may not disaffirm
unless prior written
notice of minority
given, §8-6-93.
Dividends.
Right of minor to
receive, §8-6-94.
Effect of article.
Certain laws not
affected, §8-6-95.
Issuer.
Defined, §8-6-91.
Liability for treating
minor as having
capacity to exercise
rights, §8-6-92.

SECURITIES—Cont'd
Minors—Cont'd
Ownership by minors
—Cont'd
Notice of minority.
Minor may not disaffirm
security transaction
unless prior written
notice given, §8-6-93.
Presumption that holder
not minor, §8-6-92.
Third parties.
Defined, §8-6-91.
Liability for treating
minor as having
capacity to exercise
rights, §8-6-92.
Title of article.
Short title, §8-6-90.
Transfer agent.
Defined, §8-6-91.
Liability for treating
minor as having
capacity to exercise
rights, §8-6-92.
Motor vehicle carriers.
Public service commission.
Members not to own
securities of carriers or
brokers, §37-3-8.
Municipal corporations.
Securities issued in
anticipation of grants,
§§11-64-1 to 11-64-7.
See MUNICIPAL
CORPORATIONS.
Notice.
Ownership by minors.
Notice of minority.
Minor may not disaffirm
security transaction
unless prior written
notice given, §8-6-93.
**Pledge and collateral
security generally.**
See PLEDGE AND
COLLATERAL
SECURITY.
Presumptions.
Fiduciary security transfers.
Presumption that
registered owner
continues to be
fiduciary, §8-6-74.
Ownership by minors.
Presumption that holder
not minor, §8-6-92.
Public school corporation,
§§16-14-17 to 16-14-19.
Public utilities, §§37-4-1 to
37-4-16.
See PUBLIC UTILITIES.
Purchase.
Prohibited acts, §8-6-17.
Remedies of purchasers,
§8-6-19.
Receivers.
Injunctions.
Appointment of receivers
or conservators for
defendants or
defendants' assets,
§8-6-16.
Register.
Commission to keep register,
§8-6-27.
Copies of entries.
Certified copy deemed
prima facie evidence,
§8-6-28.

SECURITIES—Cont'd
Register—Cont'd
Copies of entries—Cont'd
Commission to furnish,
§8-6-28.
Inspection.
Open for public inspection,
§8-6-27.
Registration of dealers,
§8-6-3.
Registration of salesmen,
§8-6-3.
Registration of securities.
Applicability of article,
§8-6-12.
Commission.
Action on application for
registration by
qualification, §8-6-8.
Discharge from supervision
by, §8-6-8.
Coordination.
Registration by, §8-6-6.
Conditions precedent,
§8-6-8.
Denial of registration, §8-6-9.
Effect.
Representations
concerning, §8-6-14.
Exemptions, §§8-6-4, 8-6-10,
8-6-11.
Fees.
Filing and registration
fees, §8-6-8.
Financial statements by
registrants, §8-6-8.
Investment securities.
Commercial code,
§§7-8-101 to 7-8-406.
See COMMERCIAL
CODE.
Notification.
Registration by, §8-6-5.
Qualification.
Registration by, §8-6-7.
Application.
Action by commission,
§8-6-8.
Conditions precedent,
§8-6-8.
Reports by registrants,
§8-6-8.
Required, §8-6-4.
Revocation, §8-6-9.
Secretary of state.
Consent to service of
process on, §8-6-12.
Service of process.
Consent to service on
secretary of state,
§8-6-12.
Statement, §8-6-8.
Suspension, §8-6-9.
Truth, completeness, etc., of
documents.
Registration not finding,
§8-6-14.
Restriction on transfer,
§§7-8-204, 10-2A-41.
Revenue.
Disposition, §8-6-33.
Rules and regulations.
Liability for acts or
omissions in good faith
under rules, §8-6-24.
Securities commission,
§8-6-23.
Sale.
Civil liabilities of sellers,
§8-6-19.
Prohibited acts, §8-6-17.

SECURITIES—Cont'd
Salesmen.
Bonds, §8-6-3.
Defined, §8-6-2.
Registration, §8-6-3.
**Savings and loan
associations,** §§5-16-24,
5-16-50.
Scienter.
Proof not required in certain
proceedings, §8-6-18.
**Seals and sealed
instruments.**
Facsimile seals.
Issuance of securities,
§41-1-8.
Securities commission,
§§8-6-50 to 8-6-60.
Appeals from, §8-6-32.
Appointment of
commissioners, §8-6-51.
Reappointment, §8-6-52.
Arrest.
Warrants of arrest,
§8-6-21.
Chairman, §8-6-53.
Civil liability of
commissioners, §8-6-51.
Compensation of members,
§8-6-54.
Confidential information.
Use or disclosure by
commissioners or
employees, §8-6-51.
Created, §8-6-50.
Director, §§8-6-55 to 8-6-60.
See within this heading,
"Director."
Duties, §8-6-50.
Forms.
Prescribing, §8-6-23.
Industrial revenue bonds.
Preissuance procedure,
§§8-6-110 to 8-6-122.
See INDUSTRIAL
REVENUE BONDS.
Investigations, §8-6-15.
Meetings, §8-6-53.
Membership, §8-6-51.
Offices.
Access to, §8-6-53.
Place of office, §8-6-60.
Opinions.
Interpretative opinions,
§8-6-29.
Orders.
Hearing on, §8-6-32.
Liability for acts or
omissions in good faith
under orders, §8-6-24.
Publication, §8-6-31.
Powers of director.
Exercise by commission,
§8-6-53.
Qualifications of
commissioners, §8-6-51.
Quorum, §8-6-53.
Records, §8-6-53.
Access to, §8-6-53.
Register.
Commission to keep,
§8-6-27.
Copies of entries.
Commission to furnish,
§8-6-28.
Registration of securities.
Action on application for
registration by
qualification, §8-6-8.
Discharge from supervision
by commission, §8-6-8.

SECURITIES—Cont'd
Securities commission
—Cont'd
Reports, §8-6-53.
Rules and regulations,
§8-6-23.
Rules of procedure, §8-6-53.
Subpoenas, §8-6-15.
Terms of office.
Appointed members,
§8-6-52.
Vacancies.
Filling, §8-6-52.
Warnings to public.
Issuance, §8-6-31.
Signatures.
Facsimile signatures.
Issuance of securities with,
§41-1-8.
Taxation.
Access to record books,
§40-24-6.
Ad valorem taxes.
Exemption of securities
included in lists,
§40-24-8.
Definitions, §40-24-1.
Issuance of securities in
anticipation of receipt of
grants.
Exemption from taxation,
§11-81A-5.
List of securities.
Access to record books,
§40-24-6.
Ad valorem taxes.
Exemption of securities
included in,
§40-24-8.
Privilege or license tax on
lists, §40-24-8.
Receipts, §40-24-5.
Recordation in bound
books, §40-24-3.
Recording of list as notice,
§40-24-7.
Transcripts, §40-24-6.
When list operates as
record, §40-24-5.
Notice.
Recording of list of
securities as notice,
§40-24-7.
Officers.
Dealing in state securities,
§40-1-25.
Owners.
Defined, §40-24-1.
Lists of securities.
Owners may file,
§40-24-2.
Privilege or license tax on
lists of securities,
§40-24-8.
Recordation of lists in bound
books, §40-24-3.
Fees, §40-24-4.
Transcripts.
Record books, §40-24-6.
Telephone companies,
§§37-2-170 to 37-2-184.
See TELEPHONES.
Title of chapter.
Short title, §8-6-1.
Transfer.
Fiduciary security transfers,
§§8-6-70 to 8-6-80. See
within this heading,
"Fiduciary security
transfers."

SECURITIES—Cont'd
Transfer—Cont'd
Restriction on transfer,
§§7-8-204, 10-2A-41.
Trusts and trustees.
Corporate fiduciaries.
Registration of securities
held by corporate
fiduciary in name of
nominee, §19-3-7.
General provisions, §19-3-10.
Proxies.
Execution by fiduciary
holding corporate
stocks, §19-3-8.
Securities held by fiduciaries,
§§19-4-1 to 19-4-42.
See FIDUCIARIES.
Uniform laws.
Commercial code.
Investments securities,
§§7-8-101 to 7-8-406.
See COMMERCIAL
CODE.
Fiduciary security transfers,
§§8-6-70 to 8-6-80. See
within this heading,
"Fiduciary security
transfers."
Universities and colleges.
Issuance of revenue
securities, Const. Ala.,
amd. 160.
Violations of article.
Civil liabilities, §8-6-19.
Injunctive relief, §8-6-16.
Limitation on prosecution,
§§8-6-18.
Penalties.
Criminal penalties,
§8-6-18.

**SECURITY TO KEEP THE
PEACE,** §§15-6-1 to 15-6-61.
See PEACE BONDS.

SEDITION.
**Anarchy and subversive
activities generally.**
See ANARCHY AND
SUBVERSIVE
ACTIVITIES.
Libel and slander, §§6-5-180
to 6-5-189.
See LIBEL AND SLANDER.
Treason generally.
See TREASON.

SEDUCTION.
Actions.
No civil claims for seduction
of any female person of
age 19 or over, §6-5-331.
Parents.
Action for seduction of
daughter, §6-5-351.
Unmarried woman under 19
years of age, §6-5-350.
Indictments.
Form, §15-8-150.
Limitation of actions, §6-2-38.

SEEDS, §§2-26-1 to 2-26-76.
Advertising.
Prohibited acts, §2-26-11.
Analyses, §2-26-8.
Attachment.
Liens of owners of plants for
drying or processing
planting seeds,
§35-11-291.

SEEDS—Cont'd
Auburn university.
Registration of symbol of
seeds or plant parts.
Cooperation of experiment
station of Auburn
university, §2-26-52.
Audits.
Records of receipts, sales and
deliveries, §2-26-10.
Bills of lading.
Maintenance by trucks, etc.,
transporting seed for
sale, §2-26-10.
**Board of agriculture and
industries.**
Rules and regulations,
§2-26-3.
Brands and marks.
Registration of symbol of
seeds or plat parts,
§§2-26-50 to 2-26-52.
Cleaning.
Elimination of fungi and
noxious weeds from seed.
Failure to clean seeds, etc.,
in accordance with
rules and regulations,
§2-26-32.
Permits, §§2-26-5, 2-26-6.
**Commissioner of agriculture
and industries.**
Powers and duties, §2-26-2.
Complaints, §§2-26-70 to
2-26-76. See within this
heading, "Investigation of
complaints."
Condemnation.
Elimination of fungi and
noxious weeds from seed.
Condemnation of seeds in
violation of rules and
regulations, §2-26-31.
Noncomplying seeds,
§2-26-12.
Cotton.
Traffic in seed cotton,
§§2-19-40 to 2-19-43.
Definitions, §2-26-1.
**Department of agriculture
and industries.**
Rules and regulations.
Sale or distribution of tree
or shrub seed, §2-26-4.
Seed investigation and
arbitration committee,
§§2-26-70 to 2-26-76.
Division.
Establishment, §2-26-4.
Powers and duties, §2-26-4.
Drying planting seeds.
Liens of owners of plants for
drying or processing
planting seeds,
§§35-11-290, 35-11-291.
**Elimination of fungi and
noxious weeds from
seed,** §§2-26-30 to 2-26-32.
Commissioner of agriculture
and industries.
Right to inspect and secure
samples, §2-26-31.
Rules and regulations,
§2-26-30.
Condemnation of seeds in
violation of rules and
regulations, §2-26-31.
Inspections.
Right of commissioner to
inspect, §2-26-31.

SEEDS—Cont'd
  **Elimination of fungi and
    noxious weeds from seed**
    —Cont'd
    Processing.
      Failure to process seeds in
        accordance with rules
        and regulations,
        §2-26-32.
      Rules and regulations.
        Failure to process, clean,
          etc., seeds, etc., in
          accordance with,
          §2-26-32.
        Promulgation, §2-26-30.
        Suspension from sale,
          seizure and
          condemnation of seeds,
          etc., in violation of
          rules and regulations,
          §2-26-31.
      Seizure of seeds, etc., in
        violation of rules and
        regulations, §2-26-31.
      Suspension from sale of
        seeds, etc., in violation of
        rules and regulations,
        §2-26-31.
  Exemptions from article,
    §2-26-14.
  Falsely named seeds.
    Sale, etc., §2-25-42.
  Fees.
    Permits for sale, §2-26-5.
  Fraud.
    Sale, etc., of falsely named
      seeds, §2-25-42.
  Fungi.
    Elimination from seed,
      §§2-26-30 to 2-26-32.
  Garnishment.
    Liens of owners of plants for
      drying or processing
      planting seeds.
      Enforcement of lien,
        §35-11-291.
  Hybrid seed corn.
    Requirements as to
      certification, etc.,
      §2-26-9.
  Injunctions.
    Permits.
      Restraining persons
        selling, processing,
        cleaning, etc., seed
        without permit,
        §2-26-6.
  Interpretations, §2-26-8.
  Investigation of complaints.
    Evidence.
      Admissibility of findings,
        §2-26-76.
      Filing procedure, §2-26-74.
      Findings.
        Admissibility as evidence,
          §2-26-76.
        Effect, §2-26-76.
      Hearings, §2-26-75.
      Hinderance or obstruction.
        Violation of article,
          §2-26-75.
      Procedure, §§2-26-74,
        2-26-75.
      Purpose of article, §2-26-70.
      Seed investigation and
        arbitration committee,
        §§2-26-70 to 2-26-76.
        Access to premises and
          records, §2-26-75.
        Creation, §2-26-71.

SEEDS—Cont'd
  Investigation of complaints
    —Cont'd
    Seed investigation and
      arbitration committee
      —Cont'd
      Findings and
        recommendations,
        §2-26-74.
      Filing, §2-26-75.
      Meetings, §2-26-71.
      Members.
        Appointment, §2-26-71.
        Compensation, §2-26-72.
        Duties, §2-26-73.
        Expenses, §2-26-72.
        Qualifications, §2-26-71.
        Terms of office, §2-26-71.
      Officers, §2-26-71.
  Labels.
    Prohibited acts, §2-26-11.
    Registration of symbol of
      seeds or plant parts,
      §§2-26-50 to 2-26-52.
    Requirements as to labeling
      of containers, §2-26-7.
  Laboratories.
    Testing laboratory.
      Establishment, §2-26-4.
  Liens.
    Owners of plants for drying
      or processing planting
      seeds.
      Attachment, §35-11-291.
      Declaration of lien,
        §35-11-290.
      Enforcement of lien,
        §35-11-291.
      Garnishment, §35-11-291.
      Liens generally.
        See LIENS.
      Priority of lien, §35-11-290.
      Sale to enforce lien,
        §35-11-291.
  Noncomplying seeds.
    Suspension from sale, seizure
      and condemnation,
      §2-26-12.
  Permits.
    Fees, §2-26-5.
    Injunctive proceedings to
      restrain persons selling,
      processing, cleaning, etc.,
      seed without permit,
      §2-26-6.
    Requirement for sale,
      cleaning, processing, etc.,
      §2-26-5.
  Planting seeds.
    Liens of owners of plants for
      drying or processing
      planting seeds,
      §§35-11-290, 35-11-291.
  Processing.
    Permits, §§2-26-5, 2-26-6.
  Prohibited acts, §2-26-11.
  Records.
    Audits, §2-26-10.
    Receipt, sale and delivery,
      §2-26-10.
    Retail sellers.
      Maintenance of sales
        records by retail
        sellers, §2-26-10.
  **Registration of symbol of
    seeds or plant parts.**
    Agricultural extension
      service.
      Cooperation, §2-26-52.

SEEDS—Cont'd
  **Registration of symbol of
    seeds or plant parts**
    —Cont'd
    Auburn university.
      Cooperation of experiment
        station, §2-26-52.
    Department of agriculture
      and industries.
      Cooperation, §2-26-52.
    Required, §2-26-50.
    Use of symbols by persons,
      associations, etc., other
      than associations
      registering symbols,
      §2-26-51.
    Violations of article deemed
      misdemeanors, §2-26-51.
  Rules and regulations.
    Promulgation by state board,
      §2-26-3.
    Violations, §2-26-11.
      Deemed misdemeanor,
        §2-26-13.
  Sales.
    Drying or processing plants.
      Liens of owners.
        Sale to enforce,
          §35-11-291.
    Permits, §§2-26-5, 2-26-6.
    Prohibited acts, §2-26-11.
    Records, §2-26-10.
    Suspension from sale.
      Elimination of fungi and
        noxious weeds from
        seed.
        Seeds, etc., in violation
          of rules and
          regulations,
          §2-26-31.
      Noncomplying seeds,
        §2-26-12.
  Sales tax.
    Exemptions.
      Sale of seeds for planting,
        §40-23-4.
  Samples.
    Elimination of fungi and
      noxious weeds from seed.
      Right of commissioner to
        secure samples,
        §2-26-31.
  Seizure.
    Elimination of fungi and
      noxious weeds from seed.
      Seeds, etc., in violation of
        rules and regulations,
        §2-26-31.
    Noncomplying seeds,
      §2-26-12.
  Shrub seeds.
    Rules and regulations.
      Enforcement of rules as to
        sale or distribution,
        §2-26-4.
  Suspension from sale.
    Elimination of fungi and
      noxious weeds from seed.
      Seeds, etc., in violation of
        rules and regulations,
        §2-26-31.
    Noncomplying seeds,
      §2-26-12.
  **Symbol of seeds or plant
    parts.**
    Adoption, §2-26-50.
    Registration, §§2-26-50 to
      2-26-52.

SEEDS—Cont'd
Symbol of seeds or plant parts—Cont'd
Use of symbols by persons, associations, etc., other than associations registering symbols, §2-26-51.
Testing laboratory.
Establishment, §2-26-4.
Tree seed.
Rules and regulations.
Sale or distribution of tree or shrub seed, §2-26-4.
Trucks.
Maintenance of bills of lading, waybills, etc., §2-26-10.
Use tax.
Exemptions, §40-23-62.
Violations of article.
Deemed misdemeanor, §2-26-13.
Suspension from sale, seizure and condemnation of articles, §2-26-12.
Weeds.
Elimination of fungi and noxious weeds from seed, §§2-26-30 to 2-26-32.
Weed seed.
Prohibited acts, §2-26-11.

SEEING EYE DOGS, §§21-7-6, 21-7-7.

SEGREGATION.
Education, Const. Ala., art. XIV, §256.

SEINES AND NETS, §§9-12-110 to 9-12-113.
See MARINE RESOURCES.

SEISIN.
Livery of seisin.
Unnecessary, §35-4-31.

SEIZURES.
See SEARCHES AND SEIZURES.

SELF-DEFENSE.
Use of force in defense of persons or property.
General provisions.
See CRIMINAL LAW AND PROCEDURE.

SELF-INCRIMINATION.
Constitution of Alabama, Const. Ala., art. I, §6.
Constitution of the United States, Const. U. S., Amendment V.
Elections.
Contests.
Witnesses, §17-15-3.
Juvenile proceedings.
Privilege, §12-15-66.
Public service commission.
Compelling testimony of employees who violate code, §37-8-3.
Hearings on rate and other regulations.
Witnesses not excused, §37-1-91.

SELF-SERVICE STORAGE FACILITIES, §§8-15-30 to 8-15-37.
Additional nature of rights, §8-15-36.
Citation of article, §8-15-30.

SELF-SERVICE STORAGE FACILITIES—Cont'd
Creditors.
Effect of laws governing rights, §8-15-37.
Definitions, §8-15-31.
Landlord and tenant.
Effect of law governing rights of landlords, §8-15-37.
Liens.
Owner's lien, §8-15-33.
Satisfaction, §8-15-34.
Posting of notice as to effect of failure to pay charges, §8-15-35.
Satisfaction of owner's lien, §8-15-34.
Notice.
Charges.
Failure to pay charges.
Posting of notice as to effect, §8-15-35.
Risk of loss.
Determination, §8-15-32.
Short title, §8-15-30.
Title of chapter, §8-15-30.
Vesting of care in occupant, §8-15-32.

SELMA, MUNICIPALITY OF.
Property tax, Const. Ala., amd. 8.
School tax.
Additional school tax, Const. Ala., amd. 6.

SEMI-TRAILERS.
General provisions.
See MOTOR VEHICLES.
Motor vehicle carriers.
See MOTOR VEHICLE CARRIERS.

SENATE.
State senate generally.
See LEGISLATURE.
United States senate generally.
See CONGRESS.

SENIOR CITIZENS.
See AGED PERSONS.

SENIOR CITIZENS HALL OF FAME, §§41-9-740 to 41-9-745.
See AGED PERSONS.

SENTENCING.
Applicability of provisions, §13A-5-1.
Attorneys at law.
Life sentence without parole.
Appointment of experienced counsel for indigent defendants, §13A-5-54.
Authorized dispositions, §13A-5-2.
Capital offenses, §§13A-5-39 to 13A-5-59.
See CAPITAL OFFENSES.
Capital punishment, §§15-18-80 to 15-18-86.
See CAPITAL PUNISHMENT.
Classification of offenses, §13A-5-3.
Commutation of sentence.
Death penalty.
Postponing execution pending commutation, §15-18-100.

SENTENCING—Cont'd
Commutation of sentence—Cont'd
Imprisonment on commuted sentence, §14-3-31.
Municipal courts.
Power of mayor, §12-14-15.
Constitution of the United States, Const. U. S., Amendment VIII.
Capital punishment, Const. U. S., Amendment V.
Contempt.
Article not to deprive court of authority, §13A-5-2.
Corporations.
Article not to deprive court of authority to dissolve corporation, §13A-5-2.
County convicts, §§14-4-9, 14-4-10.
Criminal procedure, rules of.
Judgment and sentence.
See RULES OF CRIMINAL PROCEDURE.
Death penalty, §§15-18-80 to 15-18-86.
See CAPITAL PUNISHMENT.
Drugs.
Controlled substances.
Trafficking offenses.
Habitual felony offender act.
Applicability, §13A-12-231.
Mandatory minimum terms of imprisonment, §13A-12-231.
Suspension, deferral, etc., of sentence, §13A-12-232.
Evidence.
Habitual felony offenders.
Proof of prior convictions, §13A-5-10.1.
Felonies.
Authorized dispositions, §13A-5-2.
Fines.
Authorized, §13A-5-2.
General provisions, §§13A-5-5 to 13A-5-8.
Hard labor.
Sentence of imprisonment to include, §13A-5-6.
Imprisonment.
Place, §13A-5-8.
Sentence to be for definite term, §13A-5-6.
Limitation on term of imprisonment, §13A-5-6.
Presentence investigation, §13A-5-5.
Good conduct.
Prisons and prisoners.
Deductions from sentence.
Correctional incentive time, §§14-9-40 to 14-9-43.
General provisions.
See PRISONS AND PRISONERS.
Guilty pleas.
Determination of degree of offense and fixing of punishment, §15-15-24.
Sentencing of defendant after plea, §15-15-23.

SENTENCING—Cont'd
Habitual felony act.
Additional penalties,
§13A-5-9.
Determination of whether
defendant repeat or
habitual offender,
§13A-5-10.
Proof of prior convictions,
§13A-5-10.1.
Hearings.
Habitual felony offenders.
Determining whether
defendant is repeat or
habitual offender,
§13A-5-10.
Homicide.
Authorized disposition,
§13A-5-2.
Indigent defendants.
Appointment of experienced
counsel, §13A-5-54.
Investigations.
Presentence investigation,
§13A-5-5.
Jails.
Commitment of prisoners,
§§14-6-3 to 14-6-6.
General provisions,
§§14-6-12, 14-6-22.
Licenses.
Article not to deprive court
of authority to suspend
or cancel, §13A-5-2.
Life sentence without parole.
Attorneys at law.
Appointment of
experienced counsel for
indigent defendants,
§13A-5-54.
Military affairs.
Courts-martial, §31-2-83.
Governor.
Approval prerequisite to
execution of
sentence, §31-2-103.
Persons authorized to
execute sentences,
§31-2-104.
Review of sentence by
governor, §31-2-103.
Military courts.
Actions against members
of court as to
sentences, §31-2-89.
Misdemeanors.
Authorized dispositions,
§13A-5-2.
Imprisonment.
Place, §13A-5-8.
Term, §13A-5-7.
Offenses.
Classification, §13A-5-3.
Pardons generally.
See PARDONS.
Parole.
General provisions.
See PAROLE.
Life sentence without parole.
Attorneys at law.
Appointment of
experienced counsel
for indigent
defendants,
§13A-5-54.
Penalties.
See PENALTIES.
Penitentiary.
General provisions,
§§14-3-51, 14-3-52.

SENTENCING—Cont'd
Penitentiary—Cont'd
Good conduct.
Deductions from sentence,
§§14-9-40 to 14-9-44.
Permits.
Article not to deprive court
of authority to suspend
or cancel, §13A-5-2.
Post-conviction remedies,
ARCrP, Rule 20.
Prisons and prisoners.
General provisions.
See PRISONS AND
PRISONERS.
Probation generally.
See PROBATION.
Property.
Forfeiture of property.
Article not to deprive court
of authority, §13A-5-2.
**Public officers and
employees.**
Article not to deprive court
of authority to remove
from office, §13A-5-2.
Felonies.
Conviction vacates office,
§36-9-2.
Punishment generally.
See PENALTIES.
Recorded devices.
Sales, rental, etc., in
contravention of article.
Penalties, §13A-8-86.
**Relief from conviction or
sentence.**
Post-conviction remedies,
ARCrP, Rule 20.
Rules of criminal procedure.
Post-conviction remedies,
ARCrP, Rule 20.
Split sentences.
Discretion of sentencing
judge, §15-18-8.
Stays pending appeal,
§§12-22-170 to 12-22-173.
Violations.
Imprisonment.
Place, §13A-5-8.
Term, §13A-5-7.
Youthful offenders,
§§15-19-5, 15-19-6.

SEPTIC TANKS.
Municipal corporations.
Regulation, installation, etc.,
§11-50-55.

SERVICE MARKS.
**Registration of trademarks
and service marks,**
§§8-12-6 to 8-12-19.
See TRADEMARKS.

**SERVICEMEN'S
READJUSTMENT ACT.**
Insurance.
Investments.
Life insurance companies
may invest in loans
guaranteed under act,
§27-1-9.

SERVICE OF PROCESS.
Acceptance of service,
ARCP, Rule 4 (h).
Adjoining counties.
Execution of writs,
attachments and other
process, §15-10-45.

SERVICE OF PROCESS
—Cont'd
Alternative modes of service.
Effect of availability, ARCP,
Rule 4 (g).
**Amendment of proof of
service,** ARCP, Rule 4 (d).
Appeals.
Rules of appellate procedure,
ARAP, Rule 25 (b) to (d).
Associations.
How served, ARCP, Rule 4
(c).
Attorneys at law.
Disciplinary proceedings,
ARDE, Rule 12.
Aviation.
Aeronautics commission.
Orders.
Service upon interested
persons, §4-2-50.
Avoidance of service.
Service by publication,
ARCP, Rule 4.3 (c).
Burial societies.
Validity of service of process
on trustee, §10-4-23.
Certified mail.
Additional time after service
by mail, ARCP, Rule 6
(e).
Deposit of money for postage
and registration, §6-4-22.
Foreign countries, ARCP,
Rule 4.4 (b).
Notice, etc., required to be
served by registered mail
may be served by
certified mail, §1-3-7.
Out-of-state service by
certified mail, ARCP,
Rule 4.2 (b).
Service by certified mail,
ARCP, Rule 4.1 (c).
Circuit courts.
Defendant service fees,
§12-19-73.
Fee for issuance of witness
subpoenas, §12-19-74.
Class actions, ARCP, Rule 23
(c).
Condominiums.
Association, §35-8-12.
Conservators.
Settlements of accounts of
conservators.
Compulsion of settlement
by probate court,
§§26-5-30 to 26-5-34.
Final settlement,
§§26-5-33, 26-5-34.
Partial settlement,
§26-5-30.
Costs, §26-5-32.
Issuance, §26-5-31.
Coroners.
When coroner or special
coroner may execute,
§6-4-3.
Corporations.
Churches.
Validity of service on
trustee, §10-4-23.
Dissolution.
Involuntary dissolution,
§10-2A-194.
Foreign corporations.
Doing business act,
§§10-2A-235 to
10-2A-237.

SERVICE OF PROCESS
—Cont'd
Corporations—Cont'd
Graveyard owners.
Validity of service on
trustee, §10-4-23.
How corporation served,
ARCP, Rule 4 (c).
Nonprofit corporations,
§10-3A-25.
Prosecution of corporations.
Service of notice of
indictment, §10-7-2.
Public societies.
Validity of service on
trustee, §10-4-23.
Counties.
Execution in adjoining
county, §6-4-2.
How county served, ARCP,
Rule 4 (c).
Criminal law and procedure.
Simulating legal process,
§13A-10-131.
Defendants.
Multiple defendants, ARCP,
Rule 4 (f).
Defenses.
Insufficiency of service.
Litigation on merits after
loss on defense not bar
to raising of same
defense on appeal,
§6-8-101.
Delivery by process server,
ARCP, Rule 4.1 (b).
Foreign countries, ARCP,
Rule 4.4 (b).
Out-of-state service, ARCP,
Rule 4.2 (b).
Detinue.
Action for recovery of
household furniture and
equipment, §6-6-251.
Diseases.
Notifiable diseases.
Commitment petition.
Notice of petition to be
served, §22-11A-27.
District courts.
Defendant service fees,
§12-19-73.
Witness subpoenas.
Fee for issuance, §12-19-74.
Domestic relations.
Service by publication.
Alternative to publication
in certain proceedings,
ARCP, Rule 4.3 (e).
Dual modes of service.
Effect of availability, ARCP,
Rule 4 (g).
Effect, §6-4-20.
Elections.
Contests.
Notice of contest.
Failure of officer to serve
notice, §17-15-5.
Eminent domain, §18-1A-74.
**Executors and
administrators.**
Actions by and against.
Service of summons,
§43-2-130.
Nonresident executors and
administrators,
§§43-2-198, 43-2-199.
Removal.
Service of citation,
§43-2-294.

SERVICE OF PROCESS
—Cont'd
Extradition.
Return of accused to
Alabama.
Exemption from civil
process upon return,
§15-9-63.
Extraodinary writs.
Petitions.
Rules of appellate
procedure, ARAP, Rule
21.
Fees.
Defendant service fees.
Circuit and district courts,
§12-19-73.
Witness subpoenas.
Circuit and district court
fee for issuance,
§12-19-74.
Criminal cases, §12-19-171.
Foreign countries, ARCP,
Rule 4.4.
Fraternal benefit societies,
§27-34-47.
Fraternal orders.
Declaratory actions,
§10-4-175.
Garnishment, §6-6-393.
Guardian and ward.
Curators.
Appointment, §26-7A-3.
Filing of petition,
§26-7A-2.
Uniform guardianship and
protective proceedings
act.
Conservators.
Submission personally to
jurisdiction of a
court by accepting
appointment,
§26-2A-141.
Incapacitated persons.
Guardians.
Acceptance of
appointment
constitutes consent
to jurisdiction,
§26-2A-106.
Minors.
Guardians.
Consent to service by
acceptance of
appointment,
§26-2A-77.
Habeas corpus, §15-21-16.
How served, ARCP, Rules 4
(c), 4.1 (a), 4.2 (b).
Impeachment.
Duties, liabilities and fees of
sheriffs, §36-11-17.
Proceedings where defendant
has removed, absconded
or secreted himself,
§36-11-25.
Sheriff or clerk of court
subject to, §36-11-18.
Incomplete service, ARCP,
Rule 4 (f).
Indictments.
Resisting officer in executing
process.
Form of indictment,
§15-8-150.
Instructions, ARCP, Rule 4
(a).
Insufficiency of service.
Defense of, ARCP, Rule 12
(b), (h).

SERVICE OF PROCESS
—Cont'd
Insurance.
See INSURANCE.
Jails.
How incarcerated person
served, ARCP, Rule 4 (c).
Juvenile proceedings.
Publication.
Authority of court to make
interlocutory or final
dispositional orders in
cases where parties
served by, §12-15-55.
Service of summons,
§§12-15-53, 12-15-54;
ARJP, Rule 13.
Landlord and tenant.
Demand of possession,
§35-9-7.
Notice to quit, §35-9-7.
Possession wrongfully
withheld, §35-9-82.
Limits of effective service,
ARCP, Rule 4 (b).
Long arm statute.
Foreign countries, ARCP,
Rule 4.4.
Out-of-state service, ARCP,
Rule 4.2.
Mail.
Additional time after service
by mail, ARCP, Rule 6
(e).
Deposit of money for postage
and registration, §6-4-22.
Foreign countries, ARCP,
Rule 4.4 (b).
Notice required to be served
by registered mail may
be served by certified
mail, §1-3-7.
Service by certified mail,
ARCP, Rule 4.1 (c).
Out-of-state service, ARCP,
Rule 4.2 (b).
Mandamus.
Petitions, ARAP, Rule 21.
Mentally ill.
How incompetents served,
ARCP, Rule 4 (c).
Nonresident insane
defendants.
Service in absence of other
provisions, §6-4-21.
Method, §6-4-20.
Foreign countries, ARCP,
Rule 4.4 (b).
In-state service, ARCP, Rule
4.1 (a).
Out-of-state service, ARCP,
Rule 4.2 (b).
Minors.
How infants served, ARCP,
Rule 4 (c).
Nonresident minors, §6-4-21.
Withholding orders for child
support.
New employer to be served
with order, §30-3-66.
Obligor to be served notice
and given opportunity
for hearing, §30-3-62.
When order served on
employer, §30-3-61.
Multiple defendants, ARCP,
Rule 4 (f).
Dismissal of fictitious
defendants, ARCP, Rule
4 (f).

SERVICE OF PROCESS
—Cont'd
Municipal corporations.
How city served, ARCP, Rule 4 (c).
Nonresidents.
Insane nonresident defendants.
Service in absence of other provisions, §6-4-21.
Out-of-state service, ARCP, Rule 4.2.
Out-of-state service.
Basis for out-of-state service, ARCP, Rule 4.2 (a).
Methods of out-of-state service, ARCP, Rule 4.2 (b).
Parent and child.
Termination of parental rights, §26-18-6.
Parties.
Multiple defendants, ARCP, Rule 4 (f).
Partition.
Circuit courts.
Service on certain parties defendant, §35-6-25.
Partnerships.
How partnership served, ARCP, Rule 4 (c).
Pleadings and other papers, ARCP, Rule 5.
Prisons and prisoners.
How incarcerated person served, ARCP, Rule 4 (c).
Prohibition, writ of.
Petitions.
Rules of appellate procedure, ARAP, Rule 21.
Publication.
Deposit of money for postage and registration, §6-4-22.
Service, ARCP, Rule 4.3.
Public service commission.
Rate and other regulations.
Hearings on unfair rates or inadequate service, §37-1-86.
Quieting title.
In rem proceedings, §6-6-563.
Receivers.
Foreign or domestic receivers, §6-6-627.
Refusal of service, ARCP, Rule 4 (e).
Registered mail.
Deposit of money for postage and registration, §6-4-22.
Notice, etc., required to be served by registered mail may be served by certified mail, §1-3-7.
Restitution to victims of crimes.
Employment income withholding order, §15-18-146.
Rules of appellate procedure, ARAP, Rule 25 (b) to (d).
Rules of civil procedure, ARCP, Rules 4 to 6.
Securities.
Registration of securities.
Applicability of article, §8-6-12.
Consent to service on secretary of state, §8-6-12.

SERVICE OF PROCESS
—Cont'd
Sheriffs.
When justified in executing process, §36-22-7.
Simulating legal process, §13A-10-131.
Sports.
Method where agent departs state with intent to defraud or avoid service, §8-26-37.
State.
How served, ARCP, Rule 4 (c).
State departments and agencies.
How served, ARCP, Rule 4 (c).
Subpoenas, ARCP, Rule 45 (c).
Taxation.
County boards of equalization.
Subpoenas, notices and other writings, §40-3-23.
Third-party practice, ARCP, Rule 14 (a).
Transient merchants, §34-35-6.
Waiver of service, ARCP, Rule 4 (h).

SERVICE STATIONS.
Gasoline service stations, §23-3-4.

SETOFFS.
Commercial code.
Bank deposits and collections.
When items subject to setoffs, §7-4-303.
Secured transactions.
Transactions excluded from provisions, §7-9-104.
Employer's liability for certain injuries.
Setoff of amount contributed to insurance, §25-6-4.
Executors and administrators.
Distribution or division on final settlement.
Setting off indebtedness of distributee or legatee, §43-2-627.
Insurance.
Insurers.
Reorganization, rehabilitation, liquidation or conservation.
Setoff of credits and debts, §27-32-29.
Secured transactions.
Transactions excluded from provisions, §7-9-104.

SETTLEMENTS.
Arbitration and award, §§6-6-1 to 6-6-16.
See ARBITRATION AND AWARD.
Conservators.
Settlements of accounts, §§26-5-1 to 26-5-54.
See CONSERVATORS.
Corpromise and settlement generally.
See COMPROMISE AND SETTLEMENT.

SEVERANCE TAXES.
Alligator farms.
Skins, §§9-12-204, 9-12-210, 9-12-212.
Coal, §§40-13-1 to 40-13-36.
See COAL.
Counties.
Oil and gas.
Severance tax trust funds, §40-20-50.
Forest products, §§9-13-80 to 9-13-107.
See FORESTS AND FORESTRY.
Oil and gas.
County severance tax trust funds, §40-20-50.

SEWERS.
Authorities.
Water, sewer and fire protection authorities, §§11-88-1 to 11-88-111.
See WATER, SEWER AND FIRE PROTECTION AUTHORITIES.
Barbers.
Waste disposal, §22-17-4.
Beauty shops.
Waste disposal, §22-17-4.
Boats.
Discharge of litter and sewage from watercraft, §§33-6-1 to 33-6-12.
See BOATS.
Bond issues.
Municipal corporations, §§11-81-160 to 11-81-190.
See MUNICIPAL CORPORATIONS.
Commencement of actions.
Liens for improvements on public sewers, §35-11-413.
Connections.
Municipal corporations, §§11-50-53, 11-50-54.
Requiring connections, §22-26-2.
Coosa Valley development authority.
Duties and obligations, §33-16-7.
Cosmetologists.
Waste disposal, §22-17-4.
Counties.
See COUNTIES.
Districts.
Water, sewer and fire protection districts, §§11-89-1 to 11-89-19.
See WATER, SEWER AND FIRE PROTECTION DISTRICTS.
Eminent domain.
Routes and sites.
Rights of condemning corporations in selection, §10-5-8.
Health.
Insanitary sewage facilities menancing public health, §22-26-1.
Highways.
Digging up of roads, §23-1-4.
Improvement authorities, §§39-7-1 to 39-7-34.
See PUBLIC WORKS.
Insanitary sewage facilities.
Menancing public health, §22-26-1.

SEWERS—Cont'd
Jails.
Adequate sewage
connections, §14-6-103.
Liens.
Improvements on public
streets, etc., §§35-11-410
to 35-11-417.
See HIGHWAYS.
Municipal corporations.
See MUNICIPAL
CORPORATIONS.
Penalties.
Violations of chapter,
§22-26-6.
Plans.
Approval of plans for sewage
collection treatment and
disposal facilities,
§22-26-3.
Resort areas.
Construction of sewerage
facilities in resort areas,
§§11-88-40 to 11-88-111.
See WATER, SEWER AND
FIRE PROTECTION
AUTHORITIES.
Specifications.
Approval of specifications for
collection, treatment and
disposal facilities,
§22-26-3.
State board of health.
Authority to require
installation of plumbing
facilities and connections
with sanitary sewers,
§22-26-2.
Storm sewers.
Liens.
Improvements on public
streets, etc.,
§§35-11-410 to
35-11-417.
See HIGHWAYS.
Subdivisions.
Single family residences with
no access to public
sewer.
Land not subject to
subdivision regulations
of state board of
health, §22-26-7.
**Tombigbee Valley
development authority.**
Duties and obligations which
may be undertaken,
§33-17-7.
Violations of chapter.
Penalty, §22-26-6.
**Wastewater systems and
treatment plants,**
§§22-25-1 to 22-25-15.
See WATER AND
WASTEWATER
SYSTEMS AND
TREATMENT PLANTS.
Watercraft.
Discharge of litter and
sewage from watercraft,
§§33-6-1 to 33-6-12.
See BOATS.

SEWING MACHINES.
Licenses.
Sales, §40-12-156.

SEX EDUCATION.
**Teaching not authorized by
chapter,** §16-41-8.

SEXTONS.
Duties, §22-9-76.

SEXTONS—Cont'd
Reports, §22-9-76.

SEXUAL INTERCOURSE.
Prostitution, §§13A-12-110 to
13A-12-113.
Rape.
See RAPE.
Seduction, §§6-5-350, 6-5-351.
Sexual offenses, §§13A-6-60
to 13A-6-70.
See SEXUAL OFFENSES.

**SEXUALLY TRANSMITTED
DISEASES.**
**Notifiable diseases
generally,** §§22-11A-1 to
22-11A-38.
See DISEASES.

SEXUAL OFFENSES.
Advertising, §22-20-12.
Applicability of chapter,
§15-20-1.
Arrest.
Reports.
Failure to report, §15-20-4.
Law enforcement officers to
report to department of
public safety, §15-20-2.
Carnal knowledge.
See RAPE.
Consent.
Lack of consent, §13A-6-70.
Persons deemed incapable of
consent, §13A-6-70.
Definitions, §13A-6-60.
Sexual perversion, §15-20-1.
Deviate sexual intercourse.
Defined, §13A-6-60.
Director of public safety.
Courts to forward records of
convictions, §15-20-3.
Evidence.
Prior sexual behavior of
complaining witness.
Admissibility, §12-21-203.
Rape shield law, §12-21-203.
Female.
Defined, §13A-6-60.
Forcible compulsion.
Defined, §13A-6-60.
Incest.
Incestuous marriages,
§§30-1-3, 30-1-6.
Indictment for incest.
Form, §15-8-150.
Indecent exposure,
§§13A-6-68, 13A-6-69,
13A-12-130.
Juvenile proceedings.
Hearings.
Conduct of hearings,
§12-15-65.
Limitations on prosecution,
§15-3-5.
Mentally defective.
Defined, §13A-6-60.
Persons deemed incapable of
consent, §13A-6-70.
Mentally incapacitated.
Defined, §13A-6-60.
Persons deemed incapable of
consent, §13A-6-70.
Minors.
Anatomically correct dolls or
mannequins.
Use by victim or witness
under age 10, §15-25-5.

SEXUAL OFFENSES—Cont'd
Minors—Cont'd
Child victim.
Interviewing child victim
of sexual crime.
Limitations authorized,
§15-1-2.
Prosecutions involving,
§§15-25-1 to 15-25-6.
Child witness.
Prosecutions involving,
§§15-25-1 to 15-25-6.
Enticing child to enter
vehicle, house, etc., for
immoral purposes,
§13A-6-69.
Prosecution involving child
under age 16, §§15-25-1
to 15-25-6.
Anatomically correct dolls
or mannequins.
Use during testimony or
deposition of victim
or witness under age
10, §15-25-5.
Closed circuit equipment
presentation of
testimony, §15-25-3.
Competence of victim as
witness, §15-25-3.
Costs, §15-25-3.
Leading questions,
§15-25-3.
Trier of fact to determine
weight and
credibility, §15-25-3.
Considerations and rulings
on motion for delay or
containments,
§15-25-6.
Leading questions of victim
or witness under age
10, §15-25-1.
Length of proceedings.
Actions to minimize,
§15-25-6.
Videotaped deposition of
victim or witness.
Appropriations for
equipment, §15-25-4.
Costs, §15-25-2.
Protective order,
§15-25-2.
Supreme court rules,
§15-25-2.
Motor vehicles.
Minors.
Enticing child to enter
vehicle for immoral
purposes, §13A-6-69.
Obscenity generally,
§§13A-12-130 to
13A-12-200.10.
See OBSCENITY.
Physically helpless.
Defined, §13A-6-60.
Persons deemed incapable of
consent, §13A-6-70.
Pornography.
Obscenity generally,
§§13A-12-130 to
13A-12-200.10.
See OBSCENITY.
Prostitution, §§13A-12-110 to
13A-12-113.
Rape.
See RAPE.
Rape shield law, §12-21-203.

SEXUAL OFFENSES—Cont'd
Records.
Availability to law
enforcement officers, etc.,
§15-20-5.
Courts to forward records of
convictions to director of
public safety, §15-20-3.
Report of information to be
recorded and indexed by
department of public
safety, §15-20-5.
Sexual abuse.
Confidentiality of records
of victims under
eighteen years of age,
§15-1-2.
**Registration of sex
offenders.**
Counties.
Moving from one county to
another.
Registration upon move,
§13A-11-200.
Registration with sheriff of
county of residence,
§13A-11-200.
Department of public safety.
Register, §13A-11-202.
Sheriff to maintain register
and supply information
to, §13A-11-201.
Duty to register with sheriff,
§13A-11-200.
Penalties.
Violations, §13A-11-203.
Register.
Availability for inspection,
§13A-11-202.
Maintenance,
§§13A-11-201 to
13A-11-202.
Sheriff.
Maintenance of register or
roster, §13A-11-201.
Violations of article.
Penalty for violation,
§13A-11-203.
Reports.
Failure to report arrest or
conviction, §15-20-4.
Officers to report arrests to
department of public
safety, §15-20-2.
Seduction, §§6-5-350, 6-5-351.
Sexual abuse.
Child victim.
Limitation of interviews.
Authorized, §15-1-2.
Confidentiality of records.
Victims under eighteen
years of age, §15-1-2.
First degree sexual abuse.
Class B felony, §13A-6-66.
Elements of crime,
§13A-6-66.
Interviews of victims.
Limits on interviews of
victims under twelve
years of age, §15-1-2.
Second degree sexual abuse.
Class A misdemeanor,
§13A-6-67.
Elements of crime,
§13A-6-67.
Sexual contact.
Defined, §13A-6-60.
Sexual intercourse.
Defined, §13A-6-60.

SEXUAL OFFENSES—Cont'd
Sexual misconduct.
Class A misdemeanor,
§13A-6-65.
Elements of crime,
§13A-6-65.
Sexual perversion.
Defined, §15-20-1.
Sodomy, §§13A-6-63,
13A-6-64, 13A-6-69.
Victims.
Child victim, §§15-25-1 to
15-25-6.
Anatomically correct dolls
or mannequins.
Use during testimony or
depositions,
§15-25-5.
Closed circuit equipment to
present testimony.
Competence as witness,
§15-25-3.
Leading questions
authorized, §15-25-3.
Use, §15-25-3.
Weight and credibility
assessed by trier of
fact, §15-25-3.
Competent as witness,
§15-25-3.
Interviewing child victim
of sexual crime.
Limitations by presiding
judge of circuit court
authorized, §15-1-2.
Leading questions.
Authorized, §§15-25-1,
15-25-3.
Length of proceedings
stressful to child.
Minimizing, §15-25-6.
Videotaped deposition,
§15-25-2.
Anatomically correct
dolls, §15-25-5.
Appropriation for
viewing equipment,
§15-25-4.
Videotaped recording.
Child victim.
Deposition of victim or
witness under age
sixteen, §15-25-2.
Videotaped deposition.
Anatomically correct
dolls, §15-25-5.
Appropriation for
equipment to view,
§15-25-4.
Witnesses.
Child victim or witness,
§§15-25-1 to 15-25-6.
Anatomically correct dolls
or mannequins.
Use during testimony or
deposition, §15-25-5.
Closed circuit viewing of
testimony.
Competence of victim as
witness, §15-25-3.
Leading questions,
§15-25-3.
Competence of victim as
witness, §15-25-3.
Leading questions,
§§15-25-1, 15-25-3.
Length of proceedings.
Minimizing, §15-25-6.

SEXUAL OFFENSES—Cont'd
Witnesses—Cont'd
Child victim or witness
—Cont'd
Videotaped deposition,
§15-25-2.
Anatomically correct
dolls or mannequins,
§15-25-5.
Appropriation for
viewing equipment,
§15-25-4.

**SHAKESPEARE FESTIVAL
THEATRE FINANCE
AUTHORITY,** §§41-10-200
to 41-10-215.
Article cumulative,
§41-10-214.
Bids and bidding.
Exemption from competitive
bidding laws, §41-10-212.
Board of directors.
Appointment, §41-10-203.
Composition, §41-10-203.
Copies of proceedings as
evidence, §41-10-203.
Governing of authority,
§41-10-203.
Impeachment, §41-10-203.
Meetings.
Open meetings required,
§41-10-205.
Qualifications, §41-10-203.
Quorum, §41-10-203.
Terms of office, §41-10-203.
Vacancies in office,
§41-10-203.
Bond issues, §§41-10-206 to
41-10-208.
Execution, §41-10-206.
Pledges of revenue and other
security, §41-10-206.
Proceeds, §41-10-207.
Refunding bonds, §41-10-208.
Sale.
Proceeds, §41-10-207.
Source of payment,
§41-10-206.
**Construction and
interpretation.**
Liberal construction of
article, §41-10-215.
Contracts.
Public contracts.
Competitive bidding.
Exemptions, §41-10-212.
Definitions, §41-10-201.
Dissolution, §41-10-213.
Ethics.
Inapplicability of code of
ethics, §41-10-211.
Expenses, §41-10-203.
Incorporation, §41-10-202.
Interest.
Exemption from usury and
interest laws,
§41-10-210.
Legislative findings,
§41-10-200.
**Liberal construction of
article,** §41-10-215.
Officers, §41-10-204.
Powers, §41-10-205.
Purpose, §41-10-200.
Refunding bonds, §41-10-208.
**State supervision and
control.**
Freedom from, §41-10-211.
Taxation.
Exemptions, §41-10-209.

SHAKESPEARE FESTIVAL
THEATRE FINANCE
AUTHORITY—Cont'd
Usury.
Exemption from usury and
interest laws,
§41-10-210.

SHARECROPPERS.
Landlord and tenant.
See LANDLORD AND
TENANT.
Liens of tenants in common,
§§35-11-350, 35-11-351.

SHEEP.
Estrays, §§3-2-1 to 3-2-23.
See ESTRAYS.
General provisions.
See LIVESTOCK.
Running at large, §§3-2-20 to
3-2-23.

SHEET METAL
CONTRACTORS, §§34-31-1
to 34-31-34.
See HEATING AND AIR
CONDITIONING
CONTRACTORS.

SHEFFIELD, MUNICIPALITY
OF.
Bond issues.
Debt limit, Const. Ala., art.
XII, §226.
Debt limit, Const. Ala., amd.
268.
Property tax, Const. Ala.,
amd. 8.
School tax.
Special property tax for
educational purposes,
Const. Ala., amd. 171.

SHELBY COUNTY.
Court costs and charges,
Const. Ala., amd. 249.
Economic and industrial
development promotion,
Const. Ala., amd. 429.
Officers.
Compensation, Const. Ala.,
amd. 249.
Public service districts.
Local public service districts,
Const. Ala., amd. 343.

SHELLFISH.
General provisions.
See MARINE RESOURCES.

SHELLY'S CASE.
Rule in Shelly's case.
Abolished, §35-4-230.

SHELTON STATE
TECHNICAL INSTITUTE.
Shelton State Technical
Trade School designated
as, §16-60-2.

SHELTON STATE
TECHNICAL TRADE
SCHOOL.
Designated Shelton State
Technical Institute,
§16-60-2.

SHERIFFS, §§36-22-1 to
36-22-65.
Administrators, §§43-2-84,
43-2-87, 43-2-171, 43-2-172.
See EXECUTORS AND
ADMINISTRATORS.

SHERIFFS—Cont'd
Alabama Sheriffs
Association.
Payment of membership dues
for sheriff, §36-22-19.
Alcoholic beverages.
General provisions.
See ALCOHOLIC
BEVERAGES.
Arbitration and award.
Fees and charges,
Arrest.
General provisions.
See ARREST.
Assault upon peace officer,
§§13A-6-20 to 13A-6-25.
See ASSAULT AND
BATTERY.
Attachment.
Holding of attached property,
§6-6-73.
Levy.
Indemnification by
plaintiff, §6-6-80.
Sale of perishables.
Proceedings against sheriff
for money received,
§6-6-79.
Attorneys at law.
Attorneys not deemed
sufficient sureties on
official bonds of sheriffs,
§36-5-13.
Practice of law prohibited,
§34-3-14.
Benefits.
Retirement system,
§§36-22-40 to 36-22-45.
See within this heading,
"Retirement system."
Boats.
Licenses.
Special agents to sell boat
licenses.
Sheriffs designated as
special agents,
§33-5-20.
Bonds, surety, §36-22-1.
Attorneys not deemed
sufficient sureties,
§36-5-13.
Books.
Records, §§36-22-8, 36-22-10
to 36-22-13.
Sales book, §36-22-12.
Child abuse and neglect,
§§26-14-1 to 26-14-13.
See MINORS.
Commissions.
Clerks of circuit court.
When sheriff's commissions
to be collected by
clerk, §12-17-95.
Disposition, §36-22-17.
Compensation, §36-22-16.
Conservators.
Appointment as.
Incapacitated persons,
§26-2-50.
Duty as principal
conservator, §15-6-1.
Constitution of Alabama,
Const. Ala., art. V, §138;
amd. 35.
See CONSTITUTION OF
ALABAMA.

SHERIFFS—Cont'd
Coroners.
Fees.
Payment to coroners for
services rendered in
discharging duties of
sheriff, §12-19-193.
Liability for wrongful acts
while discharging duties
of sheriff, §11-5-12.
Official acts valid through
process directed to
sheriff, etc., §11-5-8.
When coroner to discharge
duties of sheriff, §11-5-5.
Corporations.
Creditors' actions.
Subjecting unpaid
subscriptions to satisfy
payment of judgment
against corporation,
§6-6-187.
Costs.
Creditors' actions.
Discovery of assests.
Taxation of costs,
§6-6-203.
Failure to return, levy or
collect execution for.
Issuance of execution
against sheriff,
§12-19-50.
Counties generally.
See COUNTIES.
Criminal justice information
center.
Duty of sheriffs to furnish
data to center, §41-9-623.
Criminal law and procedure.
Pistols.
Who may carry pistol,
§13A-11-52.
Crops.
Partition of crops, §§35-6-110
to 35-6-126.
See PARTITION.
Dams.
Erection of dams for mills,
gins, factories or electric
generators, §§18-2-1 to
18-2-21.
See DAMS.
Death.
Jails.
Delivery of jail upon death
of sheriff, §14-6-2.
Retirement system.
Refunds of salary
deductions.
Payment upon death,
§36-22-42.
Decedent's estates.
Executors and
administrators,
§§43-2-84, 43-2-87,
43-2-171, 43-2-172.
See EXECUTORS AND
ADMINISTRATORS.
Deeds.
Evidence.
Recitals in sheriff's deed,
§12-21-99.
Deputies.
Bonds, surety.
Attorneys not deemed
sufficient sureties on
official bonds of
deputies, §36-5-13.
Claims for compensation.
Preferred claims against
counties, §36-22-4.

SHERIFFS—Cont'd
Deputies—Cont'd
Dams.
Erection of dams for mills,
gins, factories or
electric generators.
Deputy performing
duties of sheriff,
§18-2-20.
Fish and game.
Violations of fish and game
laws.
Enforcing officers to
have powers of
deputies, §9-11-8.
Overtime compensation,
§36-21-4.1.
Disability, §§36-22-40 to
36-22-45. See within this
heading, "Retirement
system."
Duties.
Generally, §36-22-3.
Impeachment.
Service of process,
§36-11-17.
Election generally.
See ELECTIONS.
Equipment.
County commission to
furnish, §36-22-18.
Evidence.
Deeds.
Recitals in sheriff's deed,
§12-21-99.
Executions, §§6-9-149,
6-9-150.
Executive department.
Members of department,
Const. Ala., art. V, §112.
**Executors and
administrators,** §§43-2-84,
43-2-87, 43-2-171, 43-2-172.
See EXECUTORS AND
ADMINISTRATORS.
Fees.
Arbitration and award,
§6-6-10.
Commissions.
When commission to be
collected by clerk of
circuit court,
§12-17-95.
Disposition, §36-22-17.
Impeachment.
Service of process,
§36-11-17.
Jails.
Feeding of prisoners,
§§14-6-40 to 14-6-50.
See JAILS.
Felonies.
Registration of felons,
§§13A-11-180 to
13A-11-186.
See FELONIES.
**Fiduciary funds in hands of
officials,** §§19-3-80 to
19-3-87.
See FIDUCIARIES.
Fish and game.
Violations of fish and game
laws.
Deputies.
Enforcing officers to
have powers of
deputies, §9-11-8.

SHERIFFS—Cont'd
**Forcible entry and unlawful
detainer.**
Process.
Neglect or refusal to
execute, §6-6-333.
Forests and forestry.
Designation as forest
wardens, §9-13-5.
Funds.
Fiduciary funds in hands of
officials, §§19-3-80 to
19-3-87.
See FIDUCIARIES.
Garnishment.
Money in hands of sheriff,
§6-6-412.
Gasoline tax.
Delinquents.
Collection of taxes and
penalties, §40-17-47.
Grand jury.
Summoning jurors,
§§12-16-70 to 12-16-90.
See GRAND JURY.
Guardian and ward.
Minors.
Appointment of sheriff as
guardian, §26-2-27.
Health.
Expenses.
Recovery of expenses by
sheriff, §22-2-13.
Impeachment, Const. Ala.,
art. V, §138; amd. 35.
Effect, Const. Ala., art. V,
§138.
Execution of process where
sheriff subject to
impeachment
proceedings, §36-11-18.
General provisions.
See IMPEACHMENT.
Service of process.
Duties, liabilities and fees
of sheriffs, §36-11-17.
Subject to impeachment,
§36-11-1; Const. Ala.,
art. VII, §174.
Imprisonment.
When coroners to discharge
duties of sheriff, §11-5-5.
Incompetence.
Coroners to discharge duties,
§11-5-5.
Information.
Furnishing on request.
Penalty for failure to
provide, §14-6-85.
Investigations.
Institution by county
solicitors, §36-22-6.
Special investigations.
Conduct, §36-22-5.
Expenses, §36-22-6.
Jails.
See JAILS.
Judgments.
Creditors' actions.
Complaint for discovery of
assets.
Order or judgment,
§6-6-185.
Evidence.
Recital in sheriff's deed,
§12-21-99.
Summoning jurors,
§§12-16-80 to 12-16-90.
See JURY.

SHERIFFS—Cont'd
Liability.
Impeachment.
Service of process,
§36-11-17.
Limitation of actions.
Nonfeasance, misfeasance or
malfeasance, §6-2-33.
Actions against surety,
§6-2-34.
Lis pendens.
Liability on bonds, §35-4-139.
Marine resources.
Posse comitatus.
Summoning into service,
§9-12-2.
Military affairs.
Courts-martial.
Compensation for
execution of process,
§31-2-106.
Delivery of certificate to
sheriff for execution of
sentence, §31-2-105.
Execution of processes and
sentences.
Persons authorized to
execute, §31-2-104.
Payment of sheriffs' fees,
§31-2-102.
Ordering out of troops.
Request to governor by
sheriff, §31-2-111.
Unlawfully retained military
property.
Seizure by sheriff,
§31-2-31.
Minors.
Guardian and ward.
Appointment of sheriff as
guardian, §26-2-27.
Money.
Conveyance of money subject
to further order or
judgment of court to
successor, §36-22-14.
Motor vehicle carriers.
Execution against property of
delinquent tax payer.
Duties of sheriff, §40-19-10.
Motor vehicles.
Tags and plates.
Amateur radio operators.
Lists to be furnished to
sheriff, §§32-6-72,
32-6-92.
Uniform certificate of title
and antitheft act,
§32-8-8.
Municipal corporations.
County deputy sheriffs.
Employment as police,
§11-43-16.
Municipal courts.
Execution of warrants and
processes, §12-14-4.
National sheriffs association.
Payment of membership dues
for sheriff, §36-22-19.
Notice.
Discovery of assets.
Notice to debtor to file
statement of assets,
§6-6-200.
Office, §36-22-2.
Overtime.
Deputies, §36-21-4.1.
Partition of crops, §§35-6-110
to 35-6-126.
See PARTITION.

SHERIFFS—Cont'd

Peace officers generally.
See PEACE OFFICERS.

Penitentiary.
Delivery of convicts,
§14-3-33.

Pensions, §§36-22-40 to
36-22-45. See within this
heading, "Retirement
system."

Personal property.
Trial of right of property.
Release of sheriff from
damages for seizure,
§6-6-168.

Prisoners.
Disposition of allowances
received for feeding,
§36-22-17.

Probate courts.
Liability for failure to take
money on or return
execution issued by
probate court, §12-13-17.

Process.
Execution of process required
of constables.
Compensation, §36-22-9.
Liability, §36-22-9.
When sheriff justified in
executing, §36-22-7.

Public officers generally.
See PUBLIC OFFICERS
AND EMPLOYEES.

Public works.
Resident workmen.
Certificates of sheriffs as to
residence.
Reliance by employers,
§39-3-3.

Quarters.
County commission to
furnish, §36-22-18.

Railroads.
Signs resembling railroad
signs.
Erection or maintenance.
Sheriff to report
violations to grand
jury, §37-8-200.

Real property.
Levy on real property.
Notice of levy.
Filing with probate
judge, §35-4-132.

Records.
Disposition of record books,
§36-22-12.
Executions or orders of sale
received.
Record book.
Entries as to amounts,
§36-22-11.
Maintenance, §36-22-10.
Inspection of record books,
§36-22-13.
Prisoners received into
county jail.
Record book, §36-22-8.

Registration.
Felons, §§13A-11-180 to
13A-11-186.
See FELONIES.
Sexual offenders,
§§13A-11-200 to
13A-11-203.

Removal from office.
Jails.
Delivery of jail upon
removal, §14-6-2.

SHERIFFS—Cont'd

Reports.
Child abuse or neglect,
§§26-14-1 to 26-14-13.
See MINORS.
Preparation of reports as to
alleged violations of law,
§36-22-5.

Resignation.
Jails.
Delivery of jail upon
resignation, §14-6-2.

Retirement system,
§§36-22-40 to 36-22-45.
Benefits.
Disability benefits,
§36-22-41.
Payment, §36-22-43.
Deductions from salary,
§36-22-42.
Refunds, §36-22-42.
Payments upon death,
§36-22-42.
Disability benefits,
§36-22-41.
Election to participate,
§36-22-44.
Eligibility, §36-22-40.
Exemptions from article,
§36-22-45.
Other retirement systems.
Effect, §36-22-42.
Payments, §36-22-43.
Salary.
Deductions, §36-22-42.
Supernumerary sheriffs,
§§36-22-60 to 36-22-65.
See within this heading,
"Supernumerary
sheriffs."

Riots.
Duty to suppress, §15-6-1.

Salary, §36-22-16.

Sales book, §36-22-12.

Sales tax.
Failure to pay tax.
Department of revenue to
issue execution
directed to sheriff,
§40-23-20.

Service of process.
When sheriff justified in
executing process,
§36-22-7.

Sexual offenses.
Registration of sex offenders,
§§13A-11-200 to
13A-11-203.
See SEXUAL OFFENSES.

Succession to office.
Sheriff not eligible to succeed
self, Const. Ala., art. V,
§138; amd. 35.

**Summary proceedings
involving officials,**
§§6-6-680 to 6-6-684.

Supernumerary sheriffs,
§§36-22-60 to 36-22-65.
Allowance for surviving
spouse, §36-22-61.
Benefits.
Amount, §36-22-62.
Effect of other retirement
plans, §36-22-61.
Election between retirement
plans, §36-22-64.
Election of program,
§36-22-60.
Minimum creditable service,
§36-22-63.
Oath of office, §36-22-65.

SHERIFFS—Cont'd

Supernumerary sheriffs
—Cont'd
Payroll deductions,
§36-22-61.
Qualifications, §36-22-60.
Service credit for prior
service.
Purchase, §36-22-63.
Time limit, §36-22-63.
Vacancies.
Filling, §36-22-60.
Subject to call, §36-22-65.

Taxation.
Sale of property under
execution.
Duty of sheriff, §40-1-24.

Term of office, Const. Ala.,
art. V, §138; amd. 35.
Jails.
Delivery of jail upon
expiration of term,
§14-6-2.

Trusts and trustees.
Fiduciary funds in hands of
officials, §§19-3-80 to
19-3-87.
See FIDUCIARIES.

Vacancies.
Coroners to discharge duties,
§11-5-5.

Weights and measures.
Powers conferred upon
commissioner and
sealers, §8-16-11.

SHIELD LAW.

News gatherers.
Exemption from disclosure of
sources, §12-21-142.

Rape shield law, §12-21-203.

SHIPS AND SHIPPING.

Abandonment.
Notice to department of
conservation and natural
resources, §33-5-16.

Advertising.
Name of country of registry
to be stated, §33-1-34.

Alabama port authority,
§§33-13-1 to 33-13-13.
See HARBORS AND PORTS.

Alcoholic beverages.
See ALCOHOLIC
BEVERAGES.

Anchorage.
State docks department.
Powers of department to
regulate, §33-3-2.

Applicability of chapter,
§33-5-2.

Arrests.
Fees of arresting officer,
§33-5-34.

**Banks and financial
institutions.**
Drafts or bills of exchange
arising from transactions
involving shipment of
goods.
Authority to accept,
§5-5A-25.
Limitations, §5-5A-26.

Bills of lading.
Commercial code, §§7-7-301
to 7-7-309.
See COMMERCIAL CODE.
Documents of title, §§7-7-101
to 7-7-603.
See COMMERCIAL CODE.

SHIPS AND SHIPPING
—Cont'd
Blind persons.
Right to use of public
conveyances and
transportation facilities,
§21-7-3.
Boarding vessels.
Harbor masters, §33-3-5.
Boats.
See BOATS.
Booms and bulkheads.
See BOOMS AND
BULKHEADS.
Certificates of registration,
§§33-5-9 to 33-5-19.
Classification of vessels.
Fees.
Schedule, §33-5-17.
Commercial code.
Secured transactions.
Transactions excluded from
article, §7-9-104.
Counties.
Local regulation, §33-5-31.
Numbering provisions.
Exemptions.
Vessels owned by
municipalities,
§33-5-19.
Country of registry.
Advertising.
Name of country of
registry to be stated in
advertising, §33-1-34.
Flags.
Mobile harbor.
Ships entering or leaving
port to fly flag of
country of registry,
§33-1-34.
Dangerous vessels.
State docks department.
Failure to remove vessels
upon order of
department, §33-1-33.
Dealers.
Certificates of registration
and numbering.
Description of vessel of
manufacturer or dealer
to be omitted from
certificate, §33-5-14.
Declaration of policy,
§33-5-1.
Definitions, §33-5-3.
**Department of conservation
and natural resources.**
Certificates of registration
and numbers.
Issuance, §33-5-10.
Change of address.
Notice to department,
§33-5-16.
Commissioner.
Rules and regulations.
Admissibility as
evidence, §33-5-30.
Supplying information to
federal agencies,
§33-5-8.
Warning citations,
§33-5-36.
Enforcement of chapter,
§33-5-6.
Records.
Keeping of records,
§33-5-7.

SHIPS AND SHIPPING
—Cont'd
Destruction.
Notice to department of
conservation and natural
resources, §33-5-16.
District courts.
Jurisdiction of offenses,
§33-5-32.
Docks.
General provisions.
See HARBORS AND
PORTS.
Drawbridges.
Railroad drawbridges.
Steamboats passing
through, §37-2-88.
Enforcement of chapter,
§33-5-6.
Evidence.
Rules and regulations of
commissioner.
Admissibility, §33-5-30.
Explosives.
Transportation of explosives,
§§37-8-180 to 37-8-184.
Fees.
Arrests.
Fees of arresting officer,
§33-5-34.
Certificates of registration
and numbers, §33-5-10.
Violations.
Fees in certain
prosecutions, §33-5-33.
Fees of arresting officer,
§33-5-34.
Fines.
Disposition, §33-5-32.
Flags.
Mobile harbor.
Ships entering or leaving
port to fly flag of
country of registry,
§33-1-34.
Foreign vessels.
Numbering, §33-5-15.
Garbage and trash.
Discharge of litter and
sewage from watercraft,
§§33-6-1 to 33-6-12.
See BOATS.
Handicapped persons.
Right to use of public
conveyances and
transportation facilities,
§21-7-3.
Harbor masters, §§33-3-1 to
33-3-6.
See HARBORS AND PORTS.
Harbors generally.
See HARBORS AND PORTS.
Inspections.
Certificates of registration
and numbering.
Availability for inspection,
§33-5-11.
Jurisdiction.
District courts.
Offenses, §33-5-32.
Licenses.
Foreign vessels.
Operation without license,
§33-5-15.
Term of license, §33-5-13.
Liens.
Declaration of lien on
watercraft, §35-11-60.

SHIPS AND SHIPPING
—Cont'd
Litter.
Discharge of litter and
sewage from watercraft,
§§33-6-1 to 33-6-12.
See BOATS.
Local regulation, §33-5-31.
Manufacturers.
Certificates of registration
and numbering.
Description of vessel of
manufacturer or dealer
to be omitted from
certificate, §33-5-14.
Operation of transportation
methods for persons or
property by
manufacturing
companies, §10-5-9.
Marine police.
General provisions, §§33-5-4
to 33-5-6.
Patrol boats, §§9-12-29,
9-12-30.
Masters.
State docks director.
Violation of orders of
director, §33-1-32.
Mines and minerals.
Operation of transportation
methods for persons or
property by mining
companies, §10-5-9.
Motor fuels.
Additional excise tax on
gasoline, motor fuel and
lubricating oil.
Ships, vessels and barges.
Exemptions, §40-17-220.
Municipal corporations.
Local regulation, §33-5-31.
Numbering.
Exemption from
numbering provisions.
Ships owned by,
§33-5-19.
Notice.
Change of address.
Notice to department of
conservation and
natural resources,
§33-5-16.
Destruction or abandonment
of vessel.
Notice to department of
conservation and
natural resources,
§33-5-16.
Transfer of interest.
Notice to department of
conservation and
natural resources,
§33-5-16.
Numbering.
Certificates of numbers.
Application, §33-5-11.
Contents, §33-5-11.
Fees, §33-5-10.
Use of funds received,
§33-5-10.
Inspection.
Availability for
inspection, §33-5-11.
Issuance, §§33-5-10,
33-5-11.
Manufacturers' and
dealers' vessels.
Description of vessel to
be omitted from
certificate, §33-5-14.

SHIPS AND SHIPPING
—Cont'd
Numbering—Cont'd
Certificates of numbers
—Cont'd
Size, §33-5-11.
Term, §33-5-13.
Display of numbers, §§33-5-9,
33-5-11.
Exemptions, §33-5-19.
Foreign vessels, §33-5-15.
Local regulation, §33-5-31.
Numbering system, §33-5-12.
Only authorized number to
be used, §33-5-18.
Required, §33-5-9.
Owners.
Change of address.
Notice to department of
conservation and
natural resources,
§33-5-16.
Defined, §33-5-3.
Passenger ships.
Advertising.
Name of country of
registry to be stated in
advertising, §33-1-34.
Penalties.
Disposition of fines, §33-5-32.
Violations of chapter
generally, §33-5-35.
Pilots and pilotage, §§33-4-1
to 33-4-57.
See PILOTS AND
PILOTAGE.
Police.
Marine police.
General provisions,
§§33-5-4 to 33-5-6.
See MARINE POLICE.
Patrol boats, §§9-12-29,
9-12-30.
See MARINE
RESOURCES.
Policy.
Declaration of policy, §33-5-1.
Port authority, §§11-94-1 to
11-94-25.
See HARBORS AND PORTS.
Ports generally.
See HARBORS AND PORTS.
Quarantine.
Free rides on public
transports for quarantine
officers, §22-12-23.
Supervision of public
conveyances affected by
quarantine, §22-12-21.
Transportation of person or
thing in violation of
quarantine, §22-12-22.
Quarries.
Operation of transportation
methods for persons or
property by quarrying
companies, §10-5-9.
Railroads.
Drawbridges.
Steamboats passing
through railroad
drawbridges, §37-2-88.
Operation of transportation
methods for persons or
property by railroad
companies, §10-5-9.
Records.
Keeping of records, §33-5-7.
Registration of vessels.
Certificates of registration.
Application, §33-5-11.

SHIPS AND SHIPPING
—Cont'd
Registration of vessels
—Cont'd
Certificates of registration
—Cont'd
Change of ownership.
Filing new application
form, §33-5-15.
Contents, §33-5-11.
Destruction or
abandonment of vessel.
Termination of
certificate, §33-5-16.
Duplicate certificates,
§33-5-16.
Fees, §33-5-10.
Use of funds received,
§33-5-10.
Inspection.
Availability for
inspection, §33-5-11.
Issuance, §§33-5-10,
33-5-11.
Manufacturers' and
dealers' vessels.
Description to be omitted
from certificate,
§33-5-14.
Size, §33-5-11.
Term, §33-5-13.
Transfer of interest.
Termination of
certificate, §33-5-16.
Destruction or abandonment
of vessel.
Termination of certificate,
§33-5-16.
Fees.
Schedule of fees, §33-5-17.
Numbering, §§33-5-9 to
33-5-19.
Required, §33-5-9.
Transfer of interest.
Termination of certificate,
§33-5-16.
Rules and regulations.
Evidence.
Admissibility, §33-5-30.
Filing, §33-5-29.
Power of commissioner to
promulgate, §33-5-28.
Publication, §33-5-29.
Safety.
Declaration of policy, §33-5-1.
Sales tax.
Exemptions, §40-23-4.
Salvage, §§35-13-1 to 35-13-10.
See SALVAGE.
Secured transactions.
Transactions excluded from
article, §7-9-104.
Sewage.
Discharge of litter and
sewage from watercraft,
§§33-6-1 to 33-6-12.
See BOATS.
State docks department.
Anchorage, berthage and
moorage.
Powers regulate, §33-3-2.
Dangerous vessels.
Failure to remove upon
order of department,
§33-1-33.
Police and supervisory duties
of department, §33-3-1.
Protection of shipping while
in harbors and ports,
§33-3-1.

SHIPS AND SHIPPING
—Cont'd
Taxation.
Motor fuels.
Additional excise tax on
gasoline, motor fuel
and lubricating oil.
Ships, vessels and
barges.
Exemptions,
§40-17-220.
Subjects of taxation,
§40-11-1.
Transfer of interest.
Notice to department of
conservation and natural
resources, §33-5-16.
Transportation companies
generally.
See TRANSPORTATION
COMPANIES.
Unemployment
compensation.
Maritime employment.
Benefits, §25-4-76.
United States.
Commissioner of
conservation and natural
resources.
Supplying information to
federal agencies,
§33-5-8.
Numbering.
Exemption from
numbering provisions.
Ships owned by United
States, §33-5-19.
Use tax.
Exemptions.
Fuels and supplies for use
aboard ships,
§40-23-62.
Violations.
District courts.
Jurisdiction of offenses,
§33-5-32.
Fees.
Arresting officer, §33-5-34.
Certain prosecutions,
§33-5-33.
Fines.
Disposition, §33-5-32.
Penalty for violations of
chapter, §33-5-35.
Warning citations, §33-5-36.
Warning citations, §33-5-36.

SHIPWRECKS.
History and archives.
Contracts for recovery or
salvage of archaeological
treasure, §41-9-249.1.

**SHOALS PRESBYTERIAN
APARTMENTS, INC.**
Taxation.
Exemption, §40-9-26.

SHOOTING GALLERIES.
Licenses, §40-12-157.
Municipal corporations,
§11-51-102.
Revocation, §11-51-103.
Municipal corporations.
Closing, §11-51-102.
Licenses, §11-51-102.
Revocation, §11-51-103.

**SHOOTING INTO OCCUPIED
VEHICLE, §32-5-11.**

SHOPPING CARTS,
§§13A-8-60 to 13A-8-64.
Abandonment on public streets, sidewalks, parking lots, etc.,
§13A-8-62.
Copy of article.
Posting in stores, §13A-8-63.
Defined, §13A-8-60.
Parking lots.
Abandonment on, §13A-8-62.
Penalties.
Violations, §13A-8-64.
Posting of article in stores,
§13A-8-63.
Premises.
Defined, §13A-8-61.
Removal from premises without consent of owner, §13A-8-61.
Sidewalks.
Abandonment on, §13A-8-62.
Streets.
Abandonment on, §13A-8-62.
Violations of article.
Penalty, §13A-8-64.

SHORE.
Coastal areas, §§9-7-10 to 9-7-20.
See COASTAL AREAS.

SHORT TITLES.
Actions.
Legal service liability actions.
Alabama Legal Services Liability Act, §6-5-571.
Medical liability actions.
Alabama Medical Liability Act, §6-5-480.
Alabama Medical Liability Act of 1987, §6-5-541.
Administrative procedure.
Alabama Administrative Procedure Act, §41-22-1.
Adoption.
Alabama Subsidized Adoption Act, §26-10-20.
Adult Protective Services Act of 1976, §38-9-1.
Advertising.
Outdoor advertising.
Highway Beautification Act, §23-1-270.
Aeronautics.
Airport Zoning Act, §4-6-1.
Alabama Aeronautics Department Act of 1945, §4-2-1.
Alabama Air Commerce Act, §37-9-1.
Africatown, U.S.A. Act of 1985, §41-10-230.
Aged persons.
Adult Protective Services Act of 1976, §38-9-1.
Long term quality health care act, §22-6-21.
Agents.
Alabama Athlete Agents Regulatory Act of 1987, §8-26-1.
Agriculture.
Feed.
Alabama Commercial Feed Law of 1978, §2-21-16.
Fertilizer.
Alabama Fertilizer Law of 1969, §2-22-1.

SHORT TITLES—Cont'd
Agriculture—Cont'd
Liming materials.
Alabama agricultural Liming Materials Act, §2-23-1.
Nonpoint Financial Assistance.
Alabama Agricultural Nonpoint Financial Assistance Act of 1988, §22-38-1.
Pollution.
Alabama Agricultural Nonpoint Financial Assistance Act of 1988, §22-38-1.
Air pollution.
Alabama Air Pollution Control Act of 1971, §22-28-1.
Airport Zoning Act, §4-6-1.
Alabama Administrative Procedure Act, §41-22-1.
Alabama Aeronautics Department Act of 1945, §4-2-1.
Alabama Agricultural Liming Materials Act, §2-23-1.
Alabama Agricultural Nonpoint Financial Assistance Act of 1988, §22-38-1.
Alabama Air Commerce Act, §37-9-1.
Alabama Air Pollution Control Act of 1971, §22-28-1.
Alabama Athlete Agents Regulatory Act of 1987, §8-26-1.
Alabama Banking Code, §5-1A-1.
Alabama Business Corporation Act, §10-2A-1.
Alabama Catfish Marketing and Consumer Act of 1975, §2-11-30.
Alabama Chemical Tests for Intoxication Act, §32-5-190.
Alabama Child Abuse Act, §26-15-1.
Alabama Coal Mine Safety Law of 1975, §25-9-1.
Alabama Cogeneration Act of 1983, §37-12-1.
Alabama Commercial Feed Law of 1978, §2-21-16.
Alabama Computer Crime Act, §13A-8-100.
Alabama Credit Card Act, §5-20-2.
Alabama Crime Victims Compensation Act, §15-23-1.
Alabama Criminal Code, §13A-1-1.
Alabama Dental Services Corporation Act, §22-21-360.
Alabama Driver License Compact Act, §32-6-30.
Alabama Educational Benefits for Dependents of Blind Parents Act, §16-33-1.

SHORT TITLES—Cont'd
Alabama Emergency Management Act of 1955, §31-9-1.
Alabama Eminent Domain Code, §18-1A-1.
Alabama Energy Management and Conservation Act of 1980, §41-6A-1.
Alabama Enterprise Zone Act, §41-23-20.
Alabama Environmental Management Act, §22-22A-1.
Alabama Exceptional Child Education Act, §16-39-1.
Alabama Fertilizer Law of 1969, §2-22-1.
Alabama G.I. and Dependents' Educational Benefit Act, §31-6-1.
Alabama Health Care Plan, §27-21-6.
Alabama Health Care Responsibility Act, §22-21-290.
Alabama Insurance Code, §27-1-1.
Alabama Insurance Guaranty Association Act, §27-42-1.
Alabama Lead Ban Act of 1988, §22-37-1.
Alabama Legal Services Liability Act, §6-5-571.
Alabama Life and Disability Insurance Guaranty Association Act, §27-44-1.
Alabama Limited Partnership Act of 1983, §10-9A-201.
Alabama Litigation Accountability Act, §12-19-270.
Alabama Livestock Dealers Financial Responsibility Act, §2-15-130.
Alabama Marine Mammal Protection Act of 1976, §9-11-390.
Alabama Medical Liability Act, §6-5-480.
Alabama Medical Liability Act of 1987, §6-5-541.
Alabama Medicare Supplement Minimum Standards Act, §27-19-50.
Alabama Motion Picture Fair Competition Act, §8-18-1.
Alabama Motor Carrier Act, §37-3-1.
Alabama Nonprofit Corporation Act, §10-3A-1.
Alabama Partnership Act, §10-8-1.
Alabama Perinatal Health Act, §22-12A-1.
Alabama Pesticide Act of 1971, §2-27-1.
Alabama Radio Utility Act, §37-4-100.
Alabama Regional Reciprocal Banking Act of 1986, §5-13A-1.
Alabama Regional Reciprocal Savings Institutions Act, §5-14A-1.

SHORT TITLES—Cont'd

Alabama Restitution Withholding Act, §15-18-140.

Alabama Rules of Appellate Procedure, ARAP, Rule 49.

Alabama Rules of Civil Procedure, ARCP, Rule 85.

Alabama Rules of Juvenile Procedure, ARJP, Rule 29.

Alabama Rules of the Road Act, §32-5A-1.

Alabama Safe Drinking Water Act of 1977, §22-23-30.

Alabama Small Estates Act, §43-2-690.

Alabama Small Loan Act, §5-18-1.

Alabama Subsidized Adoption Act, §26-10-20.

Alabama Sunset Law of 1981, §41-20-1.

Alabama Supercomputer Authority Act, §41-10-390.

Alabama Surface Mining Act of 1969, §9-16-1.

Alabama Surface Mining Control and Reclamation Act of 1981, §9-16-70.

Alabama Table Wine Act, §28-7-1.

Alabama Trade School and Junior College Authority Act, §16-60-80.

Alabama Trade Secrets Act, §8-27-1.

Alabama Underground Storage Tank and Well Head Protection Act of 1988, §22-36-1.

Alabama Underground Storage Tank Trust Fund Act, §22-35-2.

Alabama Uniform Anatomical Gift Act, §22-19-40.

Alabama Uniform Certificate of Title and Antitheft Act, §32-8-1.

Alabama Uniform Controlled Substances Act, §20-2-1.

Alabama Uniform Disclaimer of Property of Interest Act, §43-8-290.

Alabama Uniform Guardianship and Protective Proceedings Act, §26-2A-1.

Alabama Uniform Parentage Act, §26-17-1.

Alabama Uniform Transfers to Minors Act, §35-5A-1.

Alabama Water Management Act, §9-9-1.

Alabama Water Pollution Control Act, §22-22-1.

Alcoholic beverages.
Alcoholic Beverage Licensing Code, §28-3A-1.
Elections.
Special Method Referendum Act of 1971, §28-2-20.

SHORT TITLES—Cont'd

Alcoholic beverages—Cont'd
Motor vehicles.
Alabama Chemical Tests for Intoxication Act, §32-5-190.
Wine.
Alabama Table Wine Act, §28-7-1.

Anatomical gifts.
Alabama Uniform Anatomical Gift Act, §22-19-40.

Appeals.
Alabama Rules of Appellate Procedure, ARAP, Rule 49.

Aquaculture.
Catfish.
Alabama Catfish Marketing and Consumer Act of 1975, §2-11-30.

Asbestos Contractors Accreditation Act, §22-39-2.

Athletics.
Alabama Athlete Agents Regulatory Act of 1987, §8-26-1.

Attorneys at law.
Alabama Legal Services Liability Act, §6-5-571.
Legal Expense Insurance Act, §27-43-1.
Malpractice.
Alabama Legal Services Liability Act, §6-5-571.

Attorneys' fees.
Alabama Litigation Accountability Act, §12-19-270.

Banking.
Alabama Regional Reciprocal Banking Act of 1986, §5-13A-1.

Banks.
Alabama Banking Code, §5-1A-1.
Gulledge-Cates Banking Reform Act of 1980, §5-1A-1.

Black Heritage Museum of West Alabama Act, §16-62-1.

Black history.
Black Heritage Museum of West Alabama Act, §16-62-1.
State Black Archives, Research Center and Museum, §16-49-50.

Blind persons.
Education.
Alabama Educational Benefits for Dependents of Blind Parents Act, §16-33-1.
Alabama Exceptional Child Education Act, §16-39-1.

Boards and commissions.
Sunset law.
Alabama Sunset Law of 1981, §41-20-1.

Bread Flour and Cornmeal Enrichment Act, §20-1-70.

SHORT TITLES—Cont'd

Bridges.
Toll Road, Bridges and Tunnel Authority Act, §23-2-140.

Budget Management Act, §41-19-1.

Bulk transfers.
Uniform Commercial Code, §7-6-101.

Business corporations.
Alabama Business Corporation Act, §10-2A-1.

Capital improvements.
County Government Capital Improvement Act, §11-29-1.

Carriers.
Uniform Fiduciaries Act, §19-1-1.

Catfish.
Alabama Catfish Marketing and Consumer Act of 1975, §2-11-30.

Checks.
Sale of Checks Act, §8-7-1.

Child abuse.
Alabama Child Abuse Act, §26-15-1.
Child Abuse and Neglect Prevention Act, §26-16-1.
Protection from Abuse Act, §30-5-1.

Child Abuse and Neglect Prevention Act, §26-16-1.

Child Care Act of 1971, §38-7-1.

Child custody.
Uniform Child Custody Jurisdiction Act, §30-3-20.

Child Protection Act of 1984, §26-18-1.

Children.
Adoption.
Alabama Subsidized Adoption Act, §26-10-20.
Child abuse.
Alabama Child Abuse Act, §26-15-1.
Child Abuse and Neglect Prevention Act, §26-16-1.
Protection From Abuse Act, §30-5-1.
Child Care Act of 1971, §38-7-1.
Child custody.
Uniform Child Custody Jurisdiction Act, §30-3-20.
Child support.
Child Support Act of 1979, §38-10-1.
Interstate Income Withholding Act, §30-3-90.
Guardians.
Alabama Uniform Guardianship and Protective Proceedings Act, §26-2A-1.
Parentage.
Alabama Uniform Parentage Act, §26-17-1.
Perinatal health.
Alabama Perinatal Health Act, §22-12A-1.

SHORT TITLES—Cont'd
 Children—Cont'd
  Securities Ownership by
    Minors Act, §8-6-90.
  Transfers to minors.
   Alabama Uniform
     Transfers to Minors
     Act, §35-5A-1.
 Child support.
  Child Support Act of 1979,
    §38-10-1.
  Interstate Income
    Withholding Act,
    §30-3-90.
 Child Support Act of 1979,
    §38-10-1.
 Civil defense.
  Alabama Emergency
    Management Act of
    1955, §31-9-1.
 Civil procedure.
  Alabama Rules of Civil
    Procedure, ARCP, Rule
    85.
 Coal mines.
  Alabama Coal Mine Safety
    Law of 1975,
    §25-9-1.
 Coliseums.
  State Products Mart and
    Coliseum Authority Act,
    §41-10-80.
 Colleges and universities.
  Private Colleges and
    Universities Facilities
    Authority Act,
    §16-18A-1.
 Commercial Code, §7-1-101.
 Commercial Code--Bank
    Deposits and Collections,
    §7-4-101.
 Commercial Code--Bulk
    Transfers, §7-6-101.
 Commercial Code--
    Commercial Paper,
    §7-3-101.
 Commercial Code--
    Documents of Title,
    §7-7-101.
 Commercial Code--
    Investment Securities,
    §7-8-101.
 Commercial Code--Letters of
    Credit, §7-5-101.
 Commercial Code--Sales,
    §7-2-101.
 Commercial Code--Secured
    Transactions, §7-9-101.
 Commercial feeds.
  Alabama Commercial Feed
    Law of 1978, §2-21-16.
 Computers.
  Alabama Supercomputer
    Authority Act,
    §41-10-390.
  Crimes and offenses.
   Alabama Computer Crime
     Act, §13A-8-100.
 Condominium Ownership
    Act, §35-8-1.
 Confidentiality.
  Victim Counselor
    Confidentiality Act of
    1987, §15-23-40.
 Conservation.
  Alabama Energy
    Management and
    Conservation Act of
    1980, §41-6A-1.

SHORT TITLES—Cont'd
 Conservation and natural
    resources.
  Alabama Marine Mammal
    Protection Act of 1976,
    §9-11-390.
  Alabama Surface Mining Act
    of 1969, §9-16-1.
  Alabama Surface Mining
    Control and Reclamation
    Act of 1981, §9-16-70.
  Alabama Water Management
    Act, §9-9-1.
  Environmental Improvement
    Authorities Act of 1969,
    §9-6-1.
  Mines and minerals.
   Alabama Surface Mining
     Act of 1969, §9-16-1.
   Alabama Surface Mining
     Control and
     Reclamation Act of
     1981, §9-16-70.
  Timber Theft Equipment
    Condemnation Act,
    §9-13-220.
 Conservators.
  Uniform Fiduciaries Act,
    §19-1-1.
 Consumer protection.
  Catfish.
   Alabama Catfish
     Marketing and
     Consumer Act of 1975,
     §2-11-30.
 Contractors.
  Asbestos Contractors
    Accreditation Act,
    §22-39-2.
 Controlled substances.
  Alabama Uniform Controlled
    Substances Act, §20-2-1.
  Controlled Substances
    Therapeutic Research
    Act, §20-2-110.
  Drug Predator Control Act of
    1987, §13A-12-201.
  Imitation Controlled
    Substances Act,
    §20-2-140.
 Cornmeal.
  Bread, Flour and Cornmeal
    Enrichment Act,
    §20-1-70.
 Corporations.
  Alabama Business
    Corporation Act,
    §10-2A-1.
  Alabama Nonprofit
    Corporation Act,
    §10-3A-1.
  Business corporations.
   Alabama Business
     Corporation Act,
     §10-2A-1.
  Dentists.
   Alabama Dental Services
     Corporation Act,
     §22-21-360.
  Nonprofit corporations.
   Alabama Nonprofit
     Corporation Act,
     §10-3A-1.
  Professional corporations.
   Revised Alabama
     Professional
     Corporation Act,
     §10-4-380.
  Revised Alabama
    Professional Corporation
    Act, §10-4-380.

SHORT TITLES—Cont'd
 Corrections.
  Inmate Community
    Reintegration Under SIR
    Act, §15-18-110.
  Interstate Corrections
    Compact Act, §14-13-1.
  Prison-Made Goods Act of
    Alabama, §14-7-6.
 Council Manager Act of
    1982, §11-43A-1.
 County Government Capital
    Improvement Act,
    §11-29-1.
 Credit cards.
  Alabama Credit Card Act,
    §5-20-2.
 Crimes and offenses.
  Alabama Criminal Code,
    §13A-1-1.
  Computers.
   Alabama Computer Crime
     Act, §13A-8-100.
  Data processing.
   Alabama Computer Crime
     Act, §13A-8-100.
  Drugs.
   Drug Crimes
     Amendments Act of
     1987, §13A-12-210.
 Criminal procedure.
  Alabama Crime Victims
    Compensation Act,
    §15-23-1.
  Alabama Restitution
    Withholding Act,
    §15-18-140.
  Criminal Psychopath Release
    Restriction Act,
    §15-16-60.
  Detainers.
   Uniform Mandatory
     Disposition of
     Detainers Act,
     §15-9-80.
  Inmate Community
    Reintegration Under SIR
    Act, §15-18-110.
  Insanity.
   Criminal Psychopath
     Release Restriction
     Act, §15-16-60.
  Mental retardation.
   Retarded Defendant Act,
     §15-24-1.
  Psychopaths.
   Criminal Psychopath
     Release Restriction
     Act, §15-16-60.
  Restitution.
   Alabama Restitution
     Withholding Act,
     §15-18-140.
  Retarded Defendant Act,
    §15-24-1.
  Uniform Mandatory
    Disposition of Detainers
    Act, §15-9-80.
  Victims of crimes.
   Alabama Crime Victims
     Compensation Act,
     §15-23-1.
   Victim Counselor
     Confidentiality Act of
     1987, §15-23-40.

SHORT TITLES—Cont'd
Criminal procedure—Cont'd
Witnesses.
Uniform Act to Secure the
Attendance of
Witnesses from
Without a State in
Criminal Proceedings,
§12-21-280.
Data processing.
Alabama Supercomputer
Authority Act,
§41-10-390.
Crimes and offenses.
Alabama Computer Crime
Act, §13A-8-100.
Dead bodies.
Anatomical gifts.
Alabama Uniform
Anatomical Gift Act,
§22-19-40.
Death.
Anatomical gifts.
Alabama Uniform
Anatomical Gift Act,
§22-19-40.
Natural Death Act, §22-8A-1.
Simultaneous death.
Uniform Simultaneous
Death Act, §43-7-1.
Decedents' estates.
Disclaimer of property.
Alabama Uniform
Disclaimer of Property
of Interest Act, §43-8-290.
Simultaneous death.
Uniform Simultaneous
Death Act, §43-7-1.
Small estates.
Alabama Small Estates
Act, §43-2-690.
**Deceptive Trade Practices
Act,** §8-19-1.
Dentists.
Alabama Dental Services
Corporation Act,
§22-21-360.
Alabama Medical Liability
Act, §6-5-480.
Alabama Medical Liability
Act of 1987, §6-5-541.
Corporations.
Alabama Dental Service
Corporation Act,
§22-21-360.
Malpractice.
Alabama Medical Liability
Act, §6-5-480.
Alabama Medical Liability
Act of 1987, §6-5-541.
Deposits.
George Wallace, Jr., Plan for
Linked Deposits of 1988,
§5-21-1.
Detainers.
Uniform Mandatory
Disposition of Detainers
Act, §15-9-80.
Disclaimer of property.
Alabama Uniform Disclaimer
of Property of Interest
Act, §43-8-290.
Documents of title.
Uniform Commercial Code,
§7-7-101.
Drinking water.
Alabama Safe Drinking
Water Act of 1977,
§22-23-30.
**Driver Training School
License Act,** §32-14-1.

SHORT TITLES—Cont'd
Drugs.
Controlled substances.
Alabama Uniform
Controlled Substances
Act, §20-2-1.
Controlled Substances
Therapeutic Research
Act, §20-2-110.
Drug Predator Control Act
of 1987, §13A-12-201.
Imitation Controlled
Substances Act,
§20-2-140.
Crimes and offenses.
Drug Crimes
Amendments Act of
1987, §13A-12-210.
Drug Abuse Education Act of
1971, §16-41-1.
Drug Predator Control Act of
1987, §13A-12-201.
Drunk Driving.
Alabama Chemical Tests for
Intoxication Act,
§32-5-190.
Dumps.
Solid Waste Disposal Act,
§22-27-1.
**Educational Reform Act of
1984,** §16-6A-1.
Elections.
Alcoholic beverages.
Special Method
Referendum Act of
1971, §28-2-20.
1983 Election Reform Act,
§17-24-1.
Emergencies.
Alabama Emergency
Management Act of
1955, §31-9-1.
**Emergency Interim
Succession Act,** §29-3-1.
Eminent domain.
Alabama Eminent Domain
Code, §18-1A-1.
Energy conservation.
Alabama Cogeneration Act of
1983, §37-12-1.
Energy resources.
Alabama Energy
Management and
Conservation Act of
1980, §41-6A-1.
Enterprise zones.
Alabama Enterprise Zone
Act, §41-23-20.
Environment.
Air pollution.
Alabama Air Pollution
Control Act of 1971,
§22-28-1.
Hazardous Waste
Management and
Minimization Act,
§22-30-1.
**Environmental Improvement
Authorities Act of 1969,**
§9-6-1.
Environmental management.
Alabama Environmental
Management Act,
§22-22A-1.
**Excellence in Local
Education Act,** §16-13-60.
**Executors and
administrators.**
Small estates.
Alabama Small Estates
Act, §43-2-690.

SHORT TITLES—Cont'd
**Executors and
administrators**—Cont'd
Uniform Fiduciaries Act,
§19-1-1.
**Fair Campaign Practices
Act,** §17-22A-1.
Feed.
Alabama Commercial Feed
Law of 1978, §2-21-16.
Fertilizer.
Alabama Fertilizer Law of
1969, §2-22-1.
Fiduciaries.
Uniform Act for
Simplification of
Fiduciary Security
Transfers, §8-6-70.
Uniform Fiduciaries Act,
§19-1-1.
Finance.
Budget Management Act,
§41-19-1.
Financial institutions.
Alabama Banking Code,
§5-1A-1.
Alabama Credit Card Act,
§5-20-2.
Alabama Regional Reciprocal
Banking Act of 1986,
§5-13A-1.
Alabama Regional Reciprocal
Savings Institutions Act,
§5-14A-1.
Alabama Small Loan Act,
§5-18-1.
George Wallace, Jr., Plan for
Linked Deposits of 1988,
§5-21-1.
Gulledge-Cates Banking
Reform Act of 1980,
§5-1A-1.
Savings and Loan
Act, §5-16-1.
Fish and game.
Catfish.
Alabama Catfish
Marketing and
Consumer Act of 1975,
§2-11-30.
Flour.
Bread, Flour and Cornmeal
Enrichment Act,
§20-1-70.
Foreign judgments.
Enforcement.
Uniform Enforcement of
Foreign Judgments
Act, §6-9-230.
Uniform Enforcement of
Foreign Judgments Act,
§6-9-230.
Franchises.
Motor Vehicle Franchise Act,
§8-20-1.
Fuel.
Motor Fuel Marketing Act,
§8-22-1.
Funds.
Underground storage.
Alabama Underground
Storage Tank Trust
Fund Act, §22-35-2.
Garbage.
Hazardous Waste
Management and
Minimization Act,
§22-30-1.
Solid Waste Disposal Act,
§22-27-1.

SHORT TITLES—Cont'd
Garnishment.
Alabama Restitution
Withholding Act,
§15-18-140.
**George Wallace, Jr., Plan for
Linked Deposits of 1988,**
§5-21-1.
Guaranty associations.
Alabama Insurance
Guaranty Association
Act, §27-42-1.
Alabama Life and Disability
Insurance Guaranty
Association Act,
§27-44-1.
Guardians.
Alabama Uniform
Guardianship and
Protective Proceedings
Act, §26-2A-1.
Uniform Fiduciaries Act,
§19-1-1.
Uniform Veterans'
Guardianship Act,
§26-9-1.
**Gulledge-Cates Banking
Reform Act of 1980,**
§5-1A-1.
Hazardous waste.
Hazardous Waste
Management and
Minimization Act,
§22-30-1.
Solid Waste Disposal Act,
§22-27-1.
Health.
Health Care Authorities Act
of 1982, §22-21-310.
Indigent persons.
Alabama Health Care
Responsibility Act,
§22-21-290.
Long-Term Quality Health
Care Act, §22-6-21.
Long-Term Residential
Health Care Recipient
Ombudsman Act,
§22-5A-1.
Perinatal health.
Alabama Perinatal Health
Act, §22-12A-1.
Planning.
State Health Planning and
Development Act of
1975, §22-4-1.
State Health Planning and
Development Act of
1975, §22-4-1.
**Health Care Authorities Act
of 1982, §22-21-310.**
Health Care Plan, §27-21-6.
**Highway and Traffic Safety
Coordination Act of
1967, §32-4-1.**
**Highway Beautification Act--
Junkyard Control,**
§23-1-240.
**Highway Beautification Act--
Outdoor Advertising,**
§23-1-270.
**Highway Beautification Act--
Scenic Enhancement,**
§23-1-220.
Toll Road, Bridges and
Tunnel Authority Act,
§23-2-140.
Historical preservation.
Africatown, U.S.A. Act of
1985, §41-10-230.

SHORT TITLES—Cont'd
Historical preservation
—Cont'd
Authorities.
Historical Preservation
Authorities Act of
1979, §41-10-135.
Historical Preservation
Authorities Act of 1979,
§41-10-135.
Hospitals.
Alabama Medical Liability
Act, §6-5-480.
Alabama Medical Liability
Act of 1987, §6-5-541.
Health Care Authorities Act
of 1982, §22-21-310.
Malpractice.
Alabama Medical Liability
Act, §6-5-480.
Alabama Medical Liability
Act of 1987, §6-5-541.
Housing.
Housing authorities law,
§24-1-20.
Mobile homes.
Uniform Code for the
Anchoring of Mobile
Homes Act, §24-5-30.
Uniform Standards Code
for Mobile Homes Act,
§24-5-1.
Supplemental Housing
Authorities Law,
§24-1-100.
Housing Authorities Law,
§24-1-20.
**Imitation Controlled
Substances Act,**
§20-2-140.
Improvements.
County Government Capital
Improvement Act,
§11-29-1.
Municipal Government
Capital Improvement
Act, §11-66-1.
Municipal Public
Improvement Act,
§11-48-1.
Indigent persons.
Health.
Alabama Health Care
Responsibility Act,
§22-21-290.
Industrial relations.
Small Business Assistance
Act of 1975, §25-10-1.
Infants.
Adoption.
Alabama Subsidized
Adoption Act,
§26-10-20.
Child abuse.
Alabama Child Abuse Act,
§26-15-1.
Child Abuse and Neglect
Prevention Act,
§26-16-1.
Protection from Abuse Act,
§30-5-1.
Child Care Act of 1971,
§38-7-1.
Child custody.
Uniform Child Custody
Jurisdiction Act,
§30-3-20.
Child protection.
1984 Child Protection Act,
§26-18-1.

SHORT TITLES—Cont'd
Infants—Cont'd
Child support.
Child Support Act of 1979,
§38-10-1.
Interstate Income
Withholding Act,
§30-3-90.
Guardians.
Alabama Uniform
Guardianship and
Protective Proceedings
Act, §26-2A-1.
Parentage.
Alabama Uniform
Parentage Act,
§26-17-1.
Perinatal health.
Alabama Perinatal Health
Act, §22-12A-1.
Securities Ownership by
Minors Act, §8-6-90.
Transfers to minors.
Alabama Uniform
Transfers to Minors
Act, §35-5A-1.
**Inmate Community
Reintegration Under SIR
Act, §15-18-110.**
Insanity.
Criminal Psychopath Release
Restriction Act,
§15-16-60.
Insurance.
Alabama Health Care Plan,
§27-21-6.
Alabama Insurance Code,
§27-1-1.
Alabama Insurance
Guaranty Association
Act, §27-42-1.
Alabama Life and Disability
Insurance Guaranty
Association Act,
§27-44-1.
Legal Expense Insurance
Act, §27-43-1.
Medicare Supplement
Minimum Standards Act,
§27-19-50.
Rating Law, §27-13-6.
Trade Practices Law,
§27-12-1.
Unauthorized Insurers
Law, §27-11-1.
**Interstate Income
Withholding Act,**
§30-3-90.
Investment securities.
Uniform Commercial Code,
§7-8-101.
Judgments.
Foreign judgments.
Uniform Enforcement of
Foreign Judgments
Act, §6-9-230.
Uniform Enforcement of
Foreign Judgments Act,
§6-9-230.
Junkyards.
Highway Beautification Act--
Junkyard Control,
§23-1-240.
Jurisdiction.
Child custody.
Uniform Child Custody
Jurisdiction Act,
§30-3-20.

SHORT TITLES—Cont'd

Juvenile proceedings.
Alabama Rules of Juvenile Procedure, ARJP, Rule 29.

Labor.
Prison-Made Goods Act of Alabama, §14-7-6.

Landfills.
Solid Waste Disposal Act, §22-27-1.

Law enforcement officers.
Police Officer's and Firefighter's Survivors Educational Assistance Act, §36-21-100.

Lead.
Alabama Lead Ban Act of 1988, §22-37-1.

Legal Expense Insurance Act, §27-43-1.

Legal malpractice.
Alabama Legal Services Liability Act, §6-5-571.

Legislature.
Emergency Interim Succession Act, §29-3-1.

Liability.
Legal service liability actions.
Alabama Legal Services Liability Act, §6-5-571.
Medical liability actions.
Alabama Medical Liability Act, §6-5-480.
Alabama Medical Liability Act of 1987, §6-5-541.

Licenses.
Alcoholic Beverage Licensing Code, §28-3A-1.
Driver Training School License Act, §32-14-1.
Motor vehicles.
Alabama Driver License Compact Act, §32-6-30.

Liming materials.
Alabama Agricultural Liming Materials Act, §2-23-1.

Livestock.
Alabama Livestock Dealers Financial Responsibility Act, §2-15-130.
Dealers.
Alabama Livestock Dealers Financial Responsibility Act, §2-15-130.

Living will.
Natural Death Act, §22-8A-1.

Loans.
Small loans.
Alabama Small Loan Act, §5-18-1.

Long-Term Quality Health Care Act, §22-6-21.

Long-Term Residential Health Care Recipient Ombudsman Act, §22-5A-1.

Malpractice.
Alabama Legal Services Liability Act, §6-5-571.
Alabama Medical Liability Act, §6-5-480.
Alabama Medical Liability Act of 1987, §6-5-541.
Legal malpractice.
Alabama Legal Services Liability Act, §6-5-571.

SHORT TITLES—Cont'd

Malpractice—Cont'd
Medical malpractice.
Alabama Medical Liability Act, §6-5-480.
Alabama Medical Liability Act of 1987, §6-5-541.

Margarine.
Oleomargarine Fortification Act, §20-1-110.

Marine mammals.
Alabama Marine Mammal Protection Act of 1976, §9-11-390.

Marketing.
Alabama Catfish Marketing and Consumer Act of 1975, §2-11-30.
Southern Products Mart Authority Act, §41-10-50.
State Products Mart and Coliseum Authority Act, §41-10-80.

Mayor/Commission/City Manager Act of 1988, §11-44E-221.

Medical malpractice.
Alabama Medical Liability Act, §6-5-480.
Alabama Medical Liability Act of 1987, §6-5-541.

Medicare.
Alabama Medicare Supplement Minimum Standards Act, §27-19-50.

Mental health.
Criminal Psychopath Release Restriction Act, §27-19-50.

Mental retardation.
Criminal procedure.
Retarded Defendant Act, §15-24-1.

Merit System Act, §36-26-1.

Military affairs.
Education.
Alabama G.I. and Dependents' Educational Benefit Act, §31-6-1.
National Guard Educational Assistance Act, §31-10-1.

Mines and minerals.
Alabama Coal Mine Safety Law of 1975, §25-9-1.
Alabama Surface Mining Act of 1969, §9-16-1.
Alabama Surface Mining Control and Reclamation Act of 1981, §9-16-70.

Minors.
Adoption.
Alabama Subsidized Adoption Act, §26-10-20.
Child abuse.
Alabama Child Abuse Act, §26-15-1.
Child Abuse and Neglect Prevention Act, §26-16-1.
Protection from Abuse Act, §30-5-1.
Child Care Act of 1971, §38-7-1.
Child custody.
Uniform Child Custody Jurisdiction Act, §30-3-20.

SHORT TITLES—Cont'd

Minors—Cont'd
Child protection.
1984 Child Protection Act, §26-18-1.
Child support.
Child Support Act of 1979, §38-10-1.
Interstate Income Withholding Act, §30-3-90.
Guardians.
Alabama Uniform Guardianship and Protective Proceedings Act, §26-2A-1.
Parentage.
Alabama Uniform Parentage Act, §26-17-1.
Perinatal health.
Alabama Perinatal Health Act, §22-12A-1.
Securities Ownership by Minors Act, §8-6-90.
Transfers to minors.
Alabama Uniform Transfers to Minors Act, §35-5A-1.

Mobile homes.
Uniform Code for the Anchoring of Mobile Homes Act, §24-5-30.
Uniform Standards Code for Mobile Homes Act, §24-5-1.

Motion pictures.
Alabama Motion Picture Fair Competition Act, §8-18-1.

Motor Fuel Marketing Act, §8-22-1.

Motor vehicle carriers.
Alabama Motor Carrier Act, §37-3-1.

Motor Vehicle Franchise Act, §8-20-1.

Motor vehicles.
Alabama Driver License Compact Act, §32-6-30.
Alabama Rules of the Road Act, §32-5A-1.
Alabama Uniform Certificate of Title and Antitheft Act, §32-8-1.
Alcoholic beverages.
Alabama Chemical Tests for Intoxication Act, §32-5-190.
Driver Training School Licensing Act, §32-14-1.
Highway and Traffic Safety Coordination Act of 1967, §32-4-1.
Motor Vehicle Safety-Responsibility Act, §32-7-1.

Municipal corporations.
Council Manager Act of 1982, §11-43A-1.
Mayor/Commission/City Manager Act of 1988, §11-44E-221.

Municipal Government Capital Improvement Act, §11-66-1.

Municipal Public Improvement Act, §11-48-1.

SHORT TITLES—Cont'd
National guard.
  Education.
    National Guard
      Educational Assistance
      Act, §31-10-1.
Natural Death Act, §22-8A-1.
Natural resources.
  Alabama Environmental
    Management Act,
    §22-22A-1.
Negligence.
  Alabama Legal Services
    Liability Act, §6-5-571.
  Alabama Medical Liability
    Act, §6-5-480.
  Alabama Medical Liability
    Act of 1987, §6-5-541.
  Legal malpractice.
    Alabama Legal Services
      Liability Act, §6-5-571.
  Medical malpractice.
    Alabama Medical Liability
      Act, §6-5-480.
    Alabama Medical Liability
      Act of 1987, §6-5-541.
Newborns.
  Alabama Perinatal Health
    Act, §22-12A-1.
1983 Election Reform Act,
  §17-24-1.
1984 Child Protection Act,
  §26-18-1.
Nonprofit corporations.
  Alabama Nonprofit
    Corporation Act,
    §10-3A-1.
Oleomargarine Fortification
  Act, §20-1-110.
Ombudsman.
  Long-Term Residential
    Health Care Recipient
    Ombudsman Act,
    §22-5A-1.
Outdoor advertising.
  Highway Beautification Act,
    §23-1-270.
Paralegals.
  Alabama Legal Services
    Liability Act, §6-5-571.
  Malpractice.
    Alabama Legal Services
      Liability Act, §6-5-571.
Parent and child.
  Alabama Uniform Parentage
    Act, §26-17-1.
Parks and recreation.
  Africatown, U.S.A. Act of
    1985, §41-10-230.
Partnerships.
  Alabama Limited
    Partnership Act of 1983,
    §10-9A-201.
  Alabama Partnership Act,
    §10-8-1.
  Limited partnerships.
    Alabama Limited
      Partnership Act of
      1983, §10-9A-201.
Personnel.
  Merit System Act, §36-26-1.
Pesticides.
  Alabama Pesticide Act of
    1971, §2-27-1.
Physicians and surgeons.
  Alabama Medical Liability
    Act, §6-5-480.
  Alabama Medical Liability
    Act of 1987, §6-5-541.

SHORT TITLES—Cont'd
Physicians and surgeons
  —Cont'd
  Malpractice.
    Alabama Medical Liability
      Act, §6-5-480.
    Alabama Medical Liability
      Act of 1987, §6-5-541.
Planning.
  Health.
    State Health Planning and
      Development Act of
      1975, §22-4-1.
Police Officer's and
  Firefighter's Survivors
  Educational Assistance
  Act, §36-21-100.
Pollution.
  Agriculture.
    Alabama Agricultural
      Nonpoint Financial
      Assistance Act of 1988,
      §22-38-1.
  Alabama Air Pollution
    Control Act of 1971,
    §22-28-1.
  Alabama Water Pollution
    Control Act, §22-22-1.
Pregnancy.
  Alabama Perinatal Health
    Act, §22-12A-1.
Prisons and prisoners.
  Inmate Community
    Reintegration Under SIR
    Act, §15-18-110.
  Interstate Corrections
    Compact Act, §14-13-1.
  Prison-Made Goods Act of
    Alabama, §14-7-6.
Private Colleges and
  Universities Facilities
  Authority Act, §16-18A-1.
Professional corporations.
  Revised Alabama
    Professional Corporation
    Act, §10-4-380.
Proration Prevention Act of
  1988, §40-1-32.1.
Protection from Abuse Act,
  §30-5-1.
Protective proceedings.
  Alabama Uniform
    Guardianship and
    Protective Proceedings
    Act, §26-2A-1.
Psychopaths.
  Criminal Psychopath Release
    Restriction Act,
    §15-16-60.
Public officers and
  employees.
  Merit System Act, §36-26-1.
Public utilities.
  Air commerce.
    Alabama Air Commerce
      Act, §37-9-1.
  Alabama Cogeneration Act of
    1983, §37-12-1.
  Radio utilities.
    Alabama Radio Utility Act,
      §37-4-100.
Radio utilities.
  Alabama Radio Utility Act,
    §37-4-100.
Railroads.
  State Rail Preservation Act,
    §37-10-1.
Rating law.
  Insurance, §27-13-6.

SHORT TITLES—Cont'd
Real property.
  Condominium Ownership
    Act, §35-8-1.
  Eminent domain.
    Alabama Eminent Domain
      Code, §18-1A-1.
Receivers.
  Uniform Fiduciaries Act,
    §19-1-1.
Regional Vocational and
  Trade Schools Act,
  §16-60-190.
Restitution.
  Alabama Restitution
    Withholding Act,
    §15-18-140.
Retarded Defendant Act,
  §15-24-1.
Revised Alabama
  Professional
  Corporation Act,
  §10-4-380.
Rubbish.
  Solid Waste Disposal Act,
    §22-27-1.
Rules of court.
  Alabama Rules of Appellate
    Procedure, ARAP, Rule
    49.
  Alabama Rules of Juvenile
    Procedure, ARJP, Rule
    29.
Rules of the Road Act,
  §32-5A-1.
Safety.
  Alabama Coal Mine Safety
    Law of 1975, §25-9-1.
  Highway and Traffic Safety
    Coordination Act of
    1967, §32-4-1.
  Motor Vehicle Safety-
    Responsibility Act,
    §32-7-1.
Sale of Checks Act, §8-7-1.
Savings and Loan Act,
  §5-16-1.
Savings institutions.
  Alabama Regional Reciprocal
    Savings Institutions Act,
    §5-14A-1.
Schools.
  Alabama Educational
    Benefits for Dependents
    of Blind Parents Act,
    §16-33-1.
  Alabama Exceptional Child
    Education Act, §16-39-1.
  Alabama G.I. and
    Dependents' Educational
    Benefit Act, §31-6-1.
  Alabama Trade School and
    Junior College Authority
    Act, §16-60-80.
  Driver Training School
    License Act, §32-14-1.
  Drug Abuse Education Act of
    1971, §16-41-1.
  Educational Reform Act of
    1984, §16-6A-1.
  Excellence in Local
    Education Act,
    §16-13-60.
  Exceptional children.
    Alabama Exceptional Child
      Education Act,
      §16-39-1.
  National Guard Educational
    Assistance Act, §31-10-1.

SHORT TITLES—Cont'd
Schools—Cont'd
Police Officer's and
Firefighter's Survivors
Educational Assistance
Act, §36-21-100.
Private Colleges and
Universities Facilities
Authority Act,
§16-18A-1.
Regional Vocational and
Trade Schools Act,
§16-60-190.
Vocational and trade
schools.
Regional Vocational and
Trade Schools Act,
§16-60-190.
Secured transactions.
Uniform Commercial Code,
§7-9-101.
Securities.
Investment securities.
Uniform Commercial Code,
§7-8-101.
Securities Act of Alabama,
§8-6-1.
Securities Ownership by
Minors Act, §8-6-90.
Uniform Act for
Simplification of
Fiduciary Security
Transfers, §8-6-70.
Self-Service Storage Act,
§8-15-30.
Simultaneous death.
Uniform Simultaneous Death
Act, §43-7-1.
**Small Business Assistance
Act of 1975,** §25-10-1.
Small estates.
Alabama Small Estates Act,
§43-2-690.
Small loans.
Alabama Small Loan Act,
§5-18-1.
Solid Waste Disposal Act,
§22-27-1.
**Southern Products Mart
Authority Act,**
§41-10-50.
**Special Method Referendum
Act of 1971,** §28-2-20.
Sports.
Alabama Athlete Agents
Regulatory Act of 1987,
§8-26-1.
**State Black Archives,
Research Center and
Museum,** §16-49-50.
**State departments and
agencies.**
Sunset law.
Alabama Sunset Law of
1981, §41-20-1.
**State Health Planning and
Development Act of
1975,** §22-4-1.
**State Products Mart and
Coliseum Authority Act,**
§41-10-80.
State Rail Preservation Act,
§37-10-1.
Storage.
Self-Service Storage Act,
§8-15-30.
Sunset law.
Alabama Sunset Law of
1981, §41-20-1.

SHORT TITLES—Cont'd
**Supplemental Housing
Authorities Law,**
§24-1-100.
Support and maintenance.
Interstate Income
Withholding Act,
§30-3-90.
**Tax Enforcement and
Compliance Act,**
§40-29-1.
TECA, §40-29-1.
Tests.
Alabama Chemical Tests for
Intoxication Act,
§32-5-190.
**Timber Theft Equipment
Condemnation Act,**
§9-13-220.
Title.
Motor vehicles.
Alabama Uniform
Certificate of Title and
Antitheft Act, §32-8-1.
**Toll Road, Bridges and
Tunnel Authority Act,**
§23-2-140.
Trade Practices Law,
§27-12-1.
Trade secrets.
Alabama Trade Secrets Act,
§8-27-1.
Transfers to minors.
Alabama Uniform Transfers
to Minors Act, §35-5A-1.
Trusts and trustees.
Uniform Fiduciaries Act,
§19-1-1.
Tunnels.
Toll Road, Bridges and
Tunnel Authority Act,
§23-2-140.
Unauthorized Insurers Law,
§27-11-1.
Unclaimed property.
Uniform Disposition of
Unclaimed Property Act,
§35-12-20.
Underground storage.
Alabama Underground
Storage Tank and Well
Head Protection Act of
1988, §22-36-1.
Alabama Underground
Storage Tank Trust
Fund Act, §22-35-2.
**Uniform Act for
Simplification of
Fiduciary Security
Transfers,** §8-6-70.
**Uniform Act to Secure the
Attendance of Witnesses
from Without a State in
Criminal Proceedings,**
§12-21-280.
**Uniform Child Custody
Jurisdiction Act,**
§30-3-20.
**Uniform Code for the
Anchoring of Mobile
Homes Act,** §24-5-30.
Uniform Commercial Code,
§7-1-101.
**Uniform Commercial Code--
Bank Deposits and
Collections,** §7-4-101.
**Uniform Commercial Code--
Bulk Transfers,** §7-6-101.
**Uniform Commercial Code--
Commercial Paper,**
§7-3-101.

SHORT TITLES—Cont'd
**Uniform Commercial Code--
Documents of Title,**
§7-7-101.
**Uniform Commercial Code--
Investment Securities,**
§7-8-101.
**Uniform Commercial Code--
Letters of Credit,**
§7-5-101.
**Uniform Commercial Code--
Sales,** §7-2-101.
**Uniform Commercial Code--
Secured Transactions,**
§7-9-101.
**Uniform Disposition of
Unclaimed Property Act,**
§35-12-20.
**Uniform Enforcement of
Foreign Judgments Act,**
§6-9-230.
**Uniform Federal Lien
Registration Act,**
§35-11-42.
Uniform Fiduciaries Act,
§19-1-1.
**Uniform Mandatory
Disposition of Detainers
Act,** §15-9-80.
**Uniform Simultaneous Death
Act,** §43-7-1.
**Uniform Standards Code for
Mobile Homes Act,**
§24-5-1.
**Uniform Veterans'
Guardianship Act,**
§26-9-1.
Veterans.
Alabama G.I. and
Dependents' Educational
Benefit Act, §31-6-1.
Uniform Veterans'
Guardianship Act,
§26-9-1.
**Victim Counselor
Confidentiality Act of
1987,** §15-23-40.
Victims of crimes.
Alabama Crime Victims
Compensation Act,
§15-23-1.
Vocational education.
Regional Vocational and
Trade Schools Act,
§16-60-190.
Wages.
Withholding.
Alabama Restitution
Withholding Act,
§15-18-140.
**Wallace-Folsom Prepaid
College Tuition Act,**
§16-33C-2.
Waste.
Hazardous Waste
Management and
Minimization Act,
§22-30-1.
Solid Waste Disposal Act,
§22-27-1.
Water management.
Alabama Water Management
Act, §9-9-1.
Water pollution.
Alabama Water Pollution
Control Act, §22-22-1.
**Waterworks and water
supplies.**
Alabama Safe Drinking
Water Act of 1977,
§22-23-30.

SHORT TITLES—Cont'd
Wells.
Alabama Underground
Storage Tank and Well
Head Protection Act of
1988, §22-36-1.
Wills.
Disclaimer of property.
Alabama Uniform
Disclaimer of Property
of Interest Act,
§43-8-290.
Wine.
Alabama Table Wine Act,
§28-7-1.
Witnesses.
Uniform Act to Secure the
Attendance of Witnesses
from Without a State in
Criminal Proceedings,
§12-21-280.

SHOTGUNS, §§13A-11-62 to
13A-11-66.
See WEAPONS.

SHOWS.
Licenses.
Transient theatrical and
vaudeville shows,
§40-12-173.
Vaudeville and variety
shows, §40-12-166.
Livestock shows.
State aid, §§2-7-50 to 2-7-53.

SHRIMP.
See MARINE RESOURCES.

SHRINE CLUBS.
Licenses and taxation.
Exemptions.
Annual shrine circus and
other events, §40-9-13.

**SHRINE MOTORCYCLE
CLUBS,** §§32-6-190,
32-6-191.
See MOTORCYCLES.

SICKLE-CELL ANEMIA.
Insurance.
Denial of health or disability
insurance upon
diagnosis, §27-5-13.
Testing of infants, §22-20-3.

SIDEWALKS.
Blind persons.
Right to full use of
sidewalks, §21-7-2.
Definitions, §32-1-1.1.
Handicapped persons.
Right to full use of
sidewalks, §21-7-2.
Motor vehicles.
See MOTOR VEHICLES.
Municipal corporations.
Assessments for public
improvements,
§§11-48-18, 11-48-65.
Bond issues.
Public improvements
generally.
See MUNICIPAL
CORPORATIONS.
General provisions, §11-49-2.
Shopping carts.
Abandonment on sidewalks,
§13A-8-62.

**SIGHT CONSERVATION
ASSOCIATION.**
**Exemption from sales and
use taxes,** §40-23-5.

SIGHT-SEEING.
See TOURISTS.

SIGNALS.
Motor vehicles, §§32-5A-7,
32-5A-30 to 32-5A-37.
See MOTOR VEHICLES.

SIGNATURES.
Bond issues.
Execution of bonds with
facsimile signatures,
§§1-3-3, 41-1-8.
Commercial code.
See COMMERCIAL CODE.
Contracts.
Specific performance.
Contract signed by one
party only may be
enforced by other,
§8-1-44.
Conveyances, §35-4-20.
Criminal law and procedure.
Obtaining signature by
deception, §13A-9-11.
Deeds, §35-4-20.
Defined, §1-1-1.
**Environmental improvement
authorities.**
Bond issues, §9-6-9.
Certificate of incorporation,
§9-6-5.
Facsimile signatures.
Execution of bonds, notes,
etc., with, §§1-3-3,
41-1-8.
Forgery and counterfeiting.
Obtaining signature by
deception, §13A-9-11.
Fraud.
Obtaining signature by
deception, §13A-9-11.
Highways.
Authority.
Bond issues, §23-1-157.
Finance corporation.
Bond issues, §23-1-177.
Indictments.
Grand jury foreman to sign,
§12-16-204.
Obtaining signature by false
pretenses.
Form of indictment,
§15-8-150.
Investment securities.
Burden of proof, §7-8-105.
**Mental health finance
authority.**
Bond issues.
Execution of bonds,
§41-10-359.
Military affairs.
Courts-martial.
Judicial notice of signature
of commissioned
officers, §31-2-98.
Negligence.
Commercial paper.
Negligence contributing to
alteration or
unauthorized
signature, §7-3-406.
Notes.
Execution of notes with
facsimile signatures,
§§1-3-3, 41-1-8.
**Pleadings, motions and
other papers,** ARCP, Rule
11.
Probate code.
Self-proving wills, §43-8-132.

SIGNATURES—Cont'd
**Proof of execution of
documents,** §§12-21-60 to
12-21-62.
Securities.
Facsimile signatures.
Issuance of securities with,
§§1-3-3, 41-1-8.
Uniform commercial code.
See COMMERCIAL CODE.
**Warrants for the payment of
money.**
Execution of warrants with
facsimile signatures,
§1-3-3.
Wills, §43-8-131.
Conveyances generally,
§§35-4-1 to 35-4-412.
See CONVEYANCES.
General provisions.
See WILLS.
Self-proving wills, §43-8-132.
Witnesses.
Proof of execution of
documents, §§12-21-61,
12-21-62.

SIGNS.
Advertising.
General provisions,
§§23-1-270 to 23-1-288.
See ADVERTISING.
Alcoholic beverages.
Dry counties.
Exhibition of signs
containing names of
prohibited liquors or
beverages, §28-4-31.
Wet counties, §28-3-16.
Billboards.
Outdoor advertising,
§§23-1-270 to 23-1-288.
See ADVERTISING.
Billiard rooms.
Posting of law as to minors,
§34-6-11.
Bridges.
Expenditure of state funds.
Signs designating bridge in
honor or memory of
individual, §23-1-8.1.
Speed limitations.
Direction of signs on
bridges, §32-5A-176.
Erection of signs on
bridges, §32-5-92.
Chiropractors.
Place of practice, §34-24-161.
Electricity.
Operations in proximity to
high voltage overhead
conductors.
Warning signs, §37-8-53.
Highways.
Detours, §23-5-2.
See HIGHWAYS.
General provisions, §§23-1-7
to 23-1-8.1.
Outdoor advertising,
§§23-1-270 to 23-1-288.
See HIGHWAYS.
Motor vehicles, §§32-5A-7,
32-5A-30 to 32-5A-37.
See MOTOR VEHICLES.
Municipal corporations,
§§11-49-1, 11-49-5,
32-1-113.
Obscenity.
Public display, §13A-12-131.

SIGNS—Cont'd
Outdoor advertising,
§§23-1-270 to 23-1-288.
See ADVERTISING.
Public buildings.
Expenditure of state funds.
Signs designating
buildings in honor or
memory of individual,
§23-1-8.1.
Railroad, §§37-2-80, 37-2-83,
37-8-200.
Real estate brokers.
Disciplinary actions.
Unlawful placement of
signs, §34-27-36.
Tourists.
Highways.
Indications of tourist
attractions, §23-1-7.

SILVER.
Auction sales, §§8-14-20 to
8-14-24.

SILVER NITRATE.
**Prevention of infantile
blindness,** §22-20-2.

SILVERSMITHS.
Liens.
Declaration, §35-11-150.
Enforcement, §35-11-151.
Sale of articles, §35-11-151.

SIMULTANEOUS ACTIONS.
Election between actions.
Prohibition on filing action
for same cause against
same party
simultaneously, §6-5-440.

SIMULTANEOUS DEATH
ACT, §§43-7-1 to 43-7-8.
Applicability of chapter.
Chapter not applicable if
decedent provides
otherwise, §43-7-7.
**Beneficiaries of another
person's disposition of
property,** §43-7-3.
Chapter not retroactive,
§43-7-6.
**Construction and
interpretation.**
Uniformity, §43-7-8.
**Disposition of property of
decedents,** §43-7-2.
Evidence.
No sufficient evidence of
survivorship, §43-7-2.
Insurance policies, §43-7-5.
Joint tenants, §43-7-4.
Property of decedents.
Disposition, §43-7-2.
Short title, §43-7-1.
Survivorship.
No sufficient evidence of
survivorship, §43-7-2.
Tenants by the entirety,
§43-7-4.
Uniformity of interpretation,
§43-7-8.

SINGLE-TAX AND OTHER
MUTUAL ECONOMIC
ASSOCIATIONS,
§§10-4-190 to 10-4-194.
Arbitration and award.
Disputes arising under real
estate leases, §10-4-194.
Bylaws, §10-4-191.
Constitution, §10-4-191.
Incorporation, §10-4-190.

SINGLE-TAX AND OTHER
MUTUAL ECONOMIC
ASSOCIATIONS—Cont'd
Lessee associations.
Recognition, §10-4-194.
Officers, §10-4-191.
Powers, §10-4-192.
**Water supply and
waterworks.**
Exemption of certain
waterworks from ad
valorem taxes, §10-4-193.

SINKING FUNDS.
Counties, §§11-81-15, 11-81-19
to 11-81-26.
See COUNTIES.
Municipal corporations,
§§11-81-15, 11-81-19 to
11-81-26.
See MUNICIPAL
CORPORATIONS.

SKATING RINKS.
Licenses, §40-12-159.

SKIN DISEASES, §§22-17-8 to
22-17-10.
See DISEASES.

SKIPPERS ACT.
**Reciprocal state
enforcement of duty to
support act,** §§30-4-80 to
30-4-98.
See DESERTION AND
NONSUPPORT.

SLANDER.
General provisions, §§6-5-182
to 6-5-189.
See LIBEL AND
SLANDER.

SLAUGHTERHOUSES.
County boards of health.
Duties, §22-3-2.
**Days and hours when
slaughtering to be done,**
§2-17-12.
Horses, mules, etc.
Preparation in facilities
separate from those in
which cattle, sheep, etc.,
prepared, §2-17-15.
Inspection, §§2-17-11, 2-17-12.
Refusal or withdrawal of
inspection, §2-17-20.
Municipal corporations.
Establishment, §11-47-138.
Regulation, §§11-47-137,
11-47-138.
Sanitary conditions, §2-17-11.
Slaughter.
See MEAT AND MEAT
PRODUCTS.
State board of health.
Authority, §22-2-2.

SLAVERY.
Constitution of Alabama.
Prohibited, Const. Ala., art.
I, §32.
**Constitution of the United
States,** Const. U. S.,
Amendments XIII, XIV,
XV.

SLEEPING CAR
COMPANIES, §§37-2-1 to
37-2-184.
See TRANSPORTATION
COMPANIES.

SLEEPING SICKNESS.
Notifiable diseases,
§§22-11A-1 to 22-11A-38.
See DISEASES.

SLINGSHOTS.
**Possession or use
prohibited,** §13A-11-53.

SLOT MACHINES.
Gambling.
Defined, §13A-12-20.
Possession, §13A-12-27.
Possession generally,
§13A-12-27.

SMALL BUSINESS
ASSISTANCE, §§25-10-1 to
25-10-10.
Advisory council, §25-10-6.
Construction of chapter,
§25-10-10.
Declaration of public policy,
§25-10-2.
Definitions, §25-10-3.
**Department of industrial
relations.**
Administrative rules,
regulations, etc.
Adoption, §25-10-8.
Cooperation of other state
departments or agencies,
§25-10-8.
Cooperation with federal
agencies, §25-10-8.
Duties, §25-10-4.
Federal agencies.
Cooperation with, §25-10-8.
Hearings.
Conduct of public hearings,
§25-10-5.
Powers and duties, §25-10-4.
Recommendations, §25-10-7.
Reports, §25-10-7.
Witnesses.
Powers as to, §25-10-5.
Federal agencies.
Cooperation of department
with, §25-10-8.
Hearings.
Department of industrial
relations, §25-10-5.
Legislative intent.
Declaration, §25-10-2.
Public policy.
Declaration, §25-10-2.
**Purchases by state
departments or agencies.**
Meaningful percentage to be
awarded to small
businesses, §25-10-9.
Recommendations.
Department of industrial
relations, §25-10-7.
Reports.
Department of industrial
relations, §25-10-7.
Rules and regulations.
Administrative rules,
regulations, etc.,
§25-10-8.
Short title of chapter,
§25-10-1.
**State departments or
agencies.**
Cooperation with department
of industrial relations,
§25-10-8.
Purchases.
Meaningful percentage to
be awarded to small
businesses, §25-10-9.

SMALL BUSINESS ASSISTANCE—Cont'd
Witnesses.
Powers of department of industrial relations, §25-10-5.

SMALL BUSINESS OFFICE OF ADVOCACY, §§41-9-760 to 41-9-767.
Created, §41-9-760.
Definitions, §41-9-761.
Director, §41-9-762.
Duties, §41-9-763.
Employees, §41-9-762.
Functions, §41-9-763.
Information required of state agencies, §41-9-764.
New regulatory programs.
Notification of establishment, §41-9-765.
Purpose, §41-9-760.
Reports, documents and information.
Annual report, §41-9-767.
Necessary to carry on functions of office.
State agencies required to furnish, §41-9-767.
State agencies to disclose establishment of new regulatory programs, §41-9-765.
Telephones.
Toll-free telephone number.
Authorized, §41-9-766.

SMALL CLAIMS, ASCR, Rules A to N.
Answers.
Deadline, ASCR, Rule F.
Form, ASCR, Form 4.
Appeals, ASCR, Rule M.
Complaints.
Forms, ASCR, Forms 1 to 3.
Counterclaims.
Forms, ASCR, Form 4.
Default, ASCR, Rule K.
Definitions.
Rules of procedure, ASCR, Rule B.
Discovery.
Exchange of information in advance of trial, ASCR, Rule G.
District courts.
Jurisdiction, §12-12-31.
Enforcement of judgments, ASCR, Rule L.
Exchange of information in advance of trial, ASCR, Rule G.
Forms, ASCR, Forms 1 to 5.
Promulgation, ARJA, Rule 21.
Instructions.
Published instructions, ARJA, Rule 21.
Judgments.
Default judgments, ASCR, Rule K.
Enforcement, ASCR, Rule L.
Notice.
Forms.
Notice to defendant and complainant, ASCR, Forms 1 to 3, 5.
Pre-trial conference, ASCR, Rule H.
Rules of civil procedure.
Applicability to small claims cases, ASCR, Rule N.

SMALL CLAIMS—Cont'd
Rules of procedure, ASCR, Rules A to N.
Answers.
Deadlines, ASCR, Rule F.
Form, ASCR, Form 4.
Appeals, ASCR, Rule M.
Beginning the case, ASCR, Rule C.
Complaints.
Forms, ASCR, Forms 1 to 3.
Counterclaims.
Forms, ASCR, Form 4.
Default, ASCR, Rule K.
Defending the case, ASCR, Rule C.
Definitions, ASCR, Rule B.
Enforcement of judgments, ASCR, Rule L.
Exchange of information in advance of trial, ASCR, Rule G.
Forms, ASCR, Forms 1 to 5.
Judgments.
Default judgments, ASCR, Rule K.
Enforcement, ASCR, Rule L.
Notice.
Forms.
Notice to defendant and complainant, ASCR, Forms 1 to 3, 5.
Pre-trial conference, ASCR, Rule H.
Rules of civil procedure.
Applicability of ARCP, ASCR, Rule N.
Scope of rules, ASCR, Rule A.
Subpoenas.
Witnesses, ASCR, Rule I.
Summons, ASCR, Rule D.
Time, ASCR, Rule E.
Trial, ASCR, Rule J.
Witnesses.
Subpoenas, ASCR, Rule I.
Sessions of court.
Regularly held, ARJA, Rule 21.
Subpoenas.
Witnesses, ASCR, Rule I.
Summons, ASCR, Rule D.
Time.
Rules of procedure, ASCR, Rule E.
Trial.
Rules of procedure, ASCR, Rule J.
Witnesses.
Subpoenas, ASCR, Rule I.

SMALL ESTATES, §§43-2-690 to 43-2-696.
See EXECUTORS AND ADMINISTRATORS.

SMALL LOANS, §§5-18-1 to 5-18-24.
Accounts and accounting.
Generally, §5-18-11.
Actions.
Applicability of chapter to actions on debts or evidences of indebtedness, §5-18-21.
Advance payment, §5-18-16.
Advertising.
Rates, terms or conditions for loans, §5-18-13.

SMALL LOANS—Cont'd
Amendment of chapter, §5-18-22.
Appeals.
Act of bureau or supervisor, §5-2A-82.
Review of orders of supervisor, §5-18-20.
Bonds, surety.
Bureau of loans.
Supervisor, §5-2A-80.
Bureau of loans, §§5-2A-80 to 5-2A-83.
Appeals from, §5-2A-82.
Created, §5-2A-80.
Defined, §5-18-3.
Employees.
Appointment, §5-2A-80.
Expenses, §5-2A-83.
Licenses.
Revocation or suspension, §5-2A-81.
Salaries.
Payment, §5-2A-83.
Supervisor.
Appeals from, §5-2A-82.
Appointment, §5-2A-80.
Bond, surety, §5-2A-80.
Cease and desist orders, §5-18-10.
Defined, §5-18-3.
Injunctions, §5-18-10.
Investigations, §5-2A-80.
Oath, §5-2A-80.
Orders, §5-18-12.
Cease and desist orders, §5-18-10.
Review, §5-18-20.
Rules and regulations, §5-18-12.
Salary, §5-2A-83.
Witnesses, §5-18-10.
Cash advance.
Defined, §5-18-3.
Cease and desist orders, §5-18-10.
Charges for loans, §§5-18-13, 5-18-15, 5-18-18.
Circuit courts.
Appeals from acts of bureau or supervisor, §5-2A-82.
Collection of loans.
Loans made outside state, §5-18-19.
Commercial code.
Secured transactions.
Validity of security agreement, §7-9-201.
Conditions for loans, §§5-18-13, 5-18-15, 5-18-18.
Confessions of judgment, §5-18-16.
Contracts.
Copy.
Delivery to borrower, §5-18-16.
Obligation under more than one contract.
Inducing borrower to become obligated, §5-18-15.
Period.
Contract period, §5-18-15.
Preexisting contracts.
Revocation, suspension or surrender of licenses not to impair, §5-18-9.
Splitting of contracts, §5-18-15.

SMALL LOANS—Cont'd
  Contracts—Cont'd
    Void contracts, §5-18-15.
    Contract in violation of
      section void, §5-18-16.
  Copies.
    Certified copies of official
      documents, §5-18-12.
  Debts.
    Applicability of chapter to
      actions on debts or
      evidences of
      indebtedness, §5-18-21.
  Default charges, §5-18-15.
  Definitions, §5-18-3.
  Examinations.
    Annual examinations of
      licensees, §5-18-10.
    Superintendent of banks.
      Examination of small loan
        companies, §5-2A-24.
  Extension charges, §5-18-15.
  Fees.
    Examination of small loan
      companies, §5-2A-24.
    Recording fees, §5-18-13.
  Findings of fact.
    Legislative findings of fact,
      §5-18-2.
  Injunctions.
    Violations of chapter,
      §5-18-10.
    Violations of small loan act,
      §5-2A-81.
  Installment payments,
    §5-18-15.
    Form, §5-18-16.
    Interest after due date of
      final installment,
      §5-18-15.
  Insurance.
    Security for loans.
      Acceptance as additional
        security, §5-18-17.
  Intent.
    Legislative declaration of
      intent, §5-18-2.
  **Interest rates, charges and
    fees,** §§5-18-3 to 5-18-15,
    5-18-18. See within this
    heading, "Rates, terms or
    conditions for loans."
  Investigations.
    Application for licenses,
      §5-18-6.
    Generally, §5-18-10.
    Supervisor of bureau of
      loans, §5-2A-80.
  Judgments.
    Confessions of judgment,
      §5-18-16.
  Legislature.
    Findings of fact and
      declaration, §5-18-2.
  Licensee.
    Defined, §5-18-3.
  Licenses, §§5-18-3 to 5-18-12.
    Application, §5-18-5.
      Investigation of
        application, §5-18-6.
    Bureau of loans.
      Revocation and suspension
        of licenses, §5-2A-81.
    Contents, §5-18-7.
    Continuing effect, §5-18-7.
    Copies.
      Certified copies of official
        documents, §5-18-12.
    Defined, §5-18-3.
    Denial, §5-18-6.
    Evasions, §5-18-4.

SMALL LOANS—Cont'd
  Licenses—Cont'd
    Exemptions, §5-18-4.
    Fees, §5-18-5.
    Investigation of application,
      §5-18-6.
    Issuance, §5-18-6.
      New licenses, §5-18-9.
    Penalties for violation of
      section, §5-18-4.
    Place of business of licensee,
      §5-18-8.
    Posting, §5-18-7.
    Records, §§5-18-9 to 5-18-11.
    Reinstatement, §5-18-9.
    Removal of place of business,
      §5-18-8.
    Required, §5-18-4.
    Revocation, §5-18-9.
      Bureau of loans, §5-2A-81.
    Separate license for each
      place of business,
      §5-18-8.
    Surrender, §5-18-9.
      Reinstatement of license,
        §5-18-9.
    Suspension, §5-18-9.
      Bureau of loans, §5-2A-81.
    Violation of requirement.
      Penalties, §5-18-4.
  Liens.
    Acceptance of liens on real
      estate as security for
      loans, §5-18-14.
  Liquidation.
    Receiver to have power to
      liquidate upon violation
      of chapter, §5-18-10.
  **Listing of licensees doing
    business in state.**
    Maintenance, §5-18-23.
  Modification of chapter,
    §5-18-22.
  **Mortgages and deeds of
    trust.**
    Acceptance of liens on real
      estate as security for
      loans, §5-18-14.
  Oaths.
    Bureau of loans.
      Supervisor, §5-2A-80.
  Offices, §§5-18-8, 5-18-14.
  Other business.
    Conduct in office of licensee,
      §5-18-14.
  Payment.
    Advance payment, §5-18-16.
    Duties of licensees as to
      making and payment of
      loans, §5-18-16.
    Installment payments,
      §5-18-15.
    Form, §5-18-16.
    Receipts, §5-18-16.
  Penalties.
    Violation of license
      requirement, §5-18-4.
    Violations of chapter,
      §5-18-24.
  Person.
    Defined, §5-18-3.
  Place of business.
    Conduct of other business in
      office of licensee,
      §5-18-14.
    Loan business confined to
      licensed offices, §5-18-14.
    Removal, §5-18-8.
    Separate license for each
      place of business,
      §5-18-8.

SMALL LOANS—Cont'd
  **Pledge and collateral
    security.**
    Insurance.
      Acceptance as additional
        security for loans,
        §5-18-17.
    Liens on real estate,
      §5-18-14.
    Release, §5-18-16.
  Promissory notes.
    Incomplete instruments,
      §5-18-16.
  **Rates, terms or conditions
    for loans.**
    Advertising, §5-18-13.
    Charges on loans of seventy-
      five dollars or less,
      §5-18-15.
    Computation of charges,
      §5-18-15.
    Default charges, §5-18-15.
    Extension charges, §5-18-15.
    Installment payments,
      §5-18-15.
    Interest after due date of
      final installment,
      §5-18-15.
    Interest after due date of
      final installment,
      §5-18-15.
    Loans of more than $300,
      §5-18-15.
    Maximum rates of interest,
      §5-18-15.
    Method of computing
      charges, §5-18-15.
    Payments.
      Installment payments,
        §5-18-15.
    Recording fees, §5-18-13.
    Refunds, §5-18-15.
    Rules and regulations,
      §5-18-13.
    Schedule of rates to be
      displayed, §5-18-13.
  Receipts, §5-18-16.
  Receivers.
    Appointment upon violation
      of chapter, §5-18-10.
  Recordation.
    Fees, §5-18-13.
  Records.
    Access to records of licensees,
      §5-18-10.
    Generally, §5-18-11.
    Licenses.
      Suspension or revocation of
        license, §5-18-9.
  Refunds, §5-18-15.
  Release.
    Obligation and security,
      §5-18-16.
  Repeal of chapter, §5-18-22.
  Reports.
    Annual report, §5-18-11.
    Public access to reports,
      §5-18-23.
  Residence of borrower,
    §5-18-8.
  Rules and regulations.
    Copies.
      Certified copies of official
        documents, §5-18-12.
    Promulgation, §5-18-12.
    Rates, terms or conditions for
      loans, §5-18-13.
  Salaries.
    Bureau of loans.
      Payment, §5-2A-83.

SMALL LOANS—Cont'd
  Secured transactions.
    Validity of security
        agreement, §7-9-201.
  Security, §§5-18-14 to 5-18-17.
  Short title of chapter,
      §5-18-1.
  Statement.
    Delivery of written statement
        to borrower, §5-18-16.
  Terms for loans, §§5-18-13,
      5-18-15, 5-18-18.
  Violations of chapter.
    Cease and desist orders,
        §5-18-10.
    Injunctive relief, §5-2A-81.
    Penalties, §5-18-24.
    Receivers.
      Appointment upon
          violation, §5-18-10.
  Witnesses.
    Power of supervisor,
        §5-18-10.

SMALLPOX.
  Notifiable diseases,
      §§22-11A-1 to 22-11A-38.
    See DISEASES.

**SMITH'S WATER
    AUTHORITY.**
  **Exemption from gross
      receipts tax,** §40-21-82.1.

SMOKE.
  Air pollution, §§22-28-1 to
      22-28-23.
    See AIR POLLUTION.
  Motor vehicles.
    Preventing escape of
        excessive fumes or
        smoke, §32-5-216.

SMOKE DETECTORS.
  **Hotels, inns and other
      transient lodging places.**
    Duty of owners and
        operators, §34-15-4.

SNEAD JUNIOR COLLEGE.
  Advisory board.
    Generally, §16-60-152.
  Buildings.
    Governor authorized to
        accept, §16-60-150.
  Debts.
    Outstanding indebtedness,
        §16-60-151.
  Facilities.
    Governor authorized to
        accept, §16-60-150.
  Governor.
    Power, §16-60-150.
  Maintenance.
    Governor authorized to
        provide for, §16-60-150.
  Operation.
    College to be operated as
        other like institutions,
        §16-60-151.
    Governor authorized to
        provide for, §16-60-150.
  Outstanding indebtedness,
      §16-60-151.
  Property.
    Governor authorized to
        accept, §16-60-150.

SNUFF.
  Tobacco tax.
    General provisions.
      See TOBACCO.
    Sales tax, §40-25-2.

SNUFF—Cont'd
  Tobacco tax—Cont'd
    Use tax, §§40-25-40,
        40-25-41.

**SOBRIETY CHEMICAL TEST
    ACT.**
  Motor vehicles.
    Driving under the influence,
        §§32-5-190 to 32-5-194.

SOCCER.
  Agents.
    Generally, §§8-26-1 to
        8-26-41.
    See SPORTS.

**SOCIAL AND LITERARY
    CLUBS.**
  Conveyances by, §§35-4-340
      to 35-4-344.
  Tax exemption, §40-9-1.

SOCIAL SECURITY.
  Aged persons.
    Medical assistance to elderly
        persons, §§38-6-1 to
        38-6-9.
    See AGED PERSONS.
  Blind persons.
    Assistance to needy blind
        persons.
      Conflicts with social
          security act, §38-5-7.
  County employees, §§36-28-1
      to 36-28-10. See within
      this heading, "Public
      employees."
  Definitions.
    Public employees, §36-28-1.
  Municipal employees,
      §§36-28-1 to 36-28-10. See
      within this heading,
      "Public employees."
  Public employees, §§36-28-1
      to 36-28-10.
    Contributions.
      Fund, §36-28-8.
      Instrumentalities.
        Payment, §36-28-5.
      Political subdivision or
          instrumentality
          employees, §36-28-5.
      Delinquent accounts.
        Penalty, §36-28-5.
        Payment, §36-28-5.
      State employees.
        Collection of
            contributions,
            §36-28-7.
    Declaration of policy,
        §36-28-2.
    Definitions, §36-28-1.
    Federal-state agreement,
        §36-28-4.
    Funds.
      Contribution fund,
          §36-28-8.
    Instrumentalities.
      Delinquent accounts.
        Penalty, §36-28-5.
      Payment of contributions,
          §36-28-5.
      Plans for coverage of
          employees.
        Submission, approval,
            etc., §36-28-5.
      Powers of instrumentalities
          created jointly with
          other states, §36-28-4.
    Political subdivisions.
      Delinquent accounts.
        Penalties, §36-28-5.

SOCIAL SECURITY—Cont'd
  Public employees—Cont'd
    Political subdivisions—Cont'd
      Payment of contributions,
          §36-28-5.
      Plans for coverage of
          employees.
        Submission, approval,
            etc., §36-28-5.
    State comptroller.
      Rules and regulations.
        Promulgation, §36-28-10.
    State office for social
        security, §36-28-3.
    Student employees.
      Coverage, §36-28-6.
  Reports.
    Welfare, §§38-1-4, 38-2-10.
      See within this heading,
          "Welfare."
  State employees, §§36-28-1 to
      36-28-10.
  Welfare.
    Reports.
      Filing names of recipients
          of public assistance
          with probate judge.
        Conflicts with social
            security act, §38-1-4.
      State department of human
          resources.
        Reports to social security
            administration,
            §38-2-10.

SOCIAL WORKERS, §§34-30-1
      to 34-30-58.
  Appeals.
    Disciplinary proceedings,
        §34-30-5.
  Associations.
    Professional associations,
        §34-30-31.
  **Board of social work
      examiners,** §§34-30-50 to
      34-30-58.
    Appointment, §34-30-50.
    Bequests.
      Acceptance, §34-30-58.
    Compensation of members,
        §34-30-54.
    Composition, §34-30-50.
    Continuing education.
      Establishment of
          requirements and
          standards, §34-30-57.
    Contributions.
      Acceptance, §34-30-58.
    Created, §34-30-50.
    Duties, §34-30-57.
    Filling of vacancies,
        §34-30-52.
    Meetings, §34-30-56.
    Membership, §34-30-50.
    Notice of meetings,
        §34-30-56.
    Officers.
      Election, §34-30-56.
    Organization, §34-30-56.
    Qualification of members,
        §34-30-50.
      State employees, §34-30-53.
    Quorum, §34-30-56.
    Removal of members,
        §34-30-55.
    State employees.
      Eligibility for appointment,
          §34-30-53.
    Term of office, §34-30-51.
    Vacancies.
      Filling, §34-30-52.

SOCIAL WORKERS—Cont'd
Child abuse or neglect.
Mandatory reporting,
§26-14-3.
Civil service employees,
§34-30-32.
Continuing education.
Establishment of
requirements and
standards, §34-30-57.
Declaration of policy,
§34-30-2.
Definitions, §34-30-1.
Disciplinary proceedings.
Grounds, §34-30-4.
Procedure, §34-30-5.
Examinations.
Exemptions, §34-30-27.
Fees.
Licenses, §34-30-25.
Disposition, §34-30-6.
Initial fee, §34-30-23.
Funds.
Disbursement from fund,
§34-30-6.
Fees.
Disposition of fees,
§34-30-6.
Separate funds created,
§34-30-6.
Groups.
Practice of social work in
groups, §34-30-30.
Hearings.
Disciplinary proceedings,
§34-30-5.
Injunctions.
Violation of chapter,
§34-30-5.
Licenses, §§34-30-20 to
34-30-33.
Application, §34-30-23.
Disciplinary proceedings.
Grounds, §34-30-4.
Procedure, §34-30-5.
Display, §34-30-28.
Effect of license, §34-30-28.
Exemptions, §34-30-21.
Expiration date, §34-30-26.
Fees, §34-30-25.
Disposition, §34-30-6.
Initial fee, §34-30-23.
Issuance, §34-30-23.
Persons licensed in other
states, §34-30-24.
Qualifications of applicants,
§34-30-22.
Reciprocity, §34-30-24.
Renewal, §34-30-26.
Grounds for failure to
renew, §34-30-4.
Required, §34-30-20.
Exemptions, §34-30-21.
Suspension or revocation.
Grounds, §34-30-4.
Procedure, §34-30-5.
Term, §34-30-26.
Merit system, §34-30-32.
Names.
Representation to public as
social worker, §34-30-33.
Notices.
Board of social work
examiners.
Meetings, §34-30-56.
Disciplinary proceedings,
§34-30-5.
Partnerships.
Practice of social work in
partnerships, §34-30-30.

SOCIAL WORKERS—Cont'd
Policy.
Declaration, §34-30-2.
**Private independent
practice.**
Qualifications, §34-30-3.
Requirements, §34-30-3.
Professional associations,
§34-30-31.
Purposes of chapter,
§34-30-2.
Reciprocity.
Licenses, §34-30-24.
**Representation to public as
social worker,** §34-30-33.
**School of social work of
Alabama,** §§16-47-170 to
16-47-175.
See UNIVERSITY OF
ALABAMA.
Supervision.
Licensed bachelor social
worker, §34-30-29.

SOCIETIES.
**Conveyances by literary or
social societies,**
§§35-4-340 to 35-4-344.
Corporations.
Public societies, §§10-4-20 to
10-4-28.
See CORPORATIONS.
Fraternal benefit societies,
§§27-34-1 to 27-34-54.
See FRATERNAL BENEFIT
SOCIETIES.
Fraternal orders, §§10-4-170
to 10-4-179.
See FRATERNAL ORDERS.
Public societies.
Corporations, §§10-4-20 to
10-4-28.
See CORPORATIONS.
Religious societies.
Corporations, §§10-4-20 to
10-4-28.
See CORPORATIONS.
Social and literary clubs.
Conveyances by, §§35-4-340
to 35-4-344.

**SOCIETIES FOR
PREVENTION OF
CRUELTY TO ANIMALS.**
**Care and keeping of
neglected or abused
animals,** §3-1-13.
**Destruction of certain
abandoned animals by
members of societies,**
§3-1-8.

SODOMY.
First degree sodomy.
Class A felony, §13A-6-63.
Elements of crime,
§13A-6-63.
Motor vehicles.
Minors.
Enticing child to enter
vehicle for immoral
purposes, §13A-6-69.
Second degree sodomy.
Class B felony, §13A-6-64.
Elements of crime,
§13A-6-64.

SOFT DRINKS.
Adulteration, §20-1-28.
Artificial sweeteners,
§20-1-28.
Beverages generally.
See BEVERAGES.

SOFT DRINKS—Cont'd
**Names, marks, etc., on
beverage containers,**
§§8-12-20, 8-12-21.

**SOIL AND WATER
CONSERVATION,** §§9-8-1
to 9-8-67.
**Agricultural and
conservation
development
commission,** §§9-8A-3,
9-8A-15, 9-8A-16.
Bond issues.
Watershed conservancy
districts, §§9-8-61,
9-8-62.
Boundaries.
Soil and water conservation
districts.
Changes, §9-8-23.
Watershed conservancy
districts, §9-8-52.
Addition of lands to
districts, §9-8-63.
Detachment of lands from
districts, §9-8-64.
Commission, Const. Ala., amd.
451.
Contracts.
Soil and water conservation
districts.
Effect of discontinuance of
district, §9-8-31.
Powers of district, §9-8-25.
Watershed conservancy
districts.
Powers of board, §9-8-61.
Cost-share grants, §§9-8A-1
to 9-8A-16.
Accounting.
Soil and water
conservation districts,
§9-8A-12.
Agreement to maintain
conservation practices,
§9-8A-11.
Agricultural and
conservation
development commission.
Administrative procedure
act inapplicable,
§9-8A-15.
Appointment, §9-8A-3.
Compensation, §9-8A-3.
Composition, §9-8A-3.
Earnings.
Use, §9-8A-16.
Incorporation, §9-8A-15.
Independence, §9-8A-15.
Liability of officers and
members, §9-8A-3.
Meetings, §9-8A-3.
Officers, §9-8A-3.
Powers, §9-8A-4.
Exercise, §9-8A-15.
Records, §9-8A-3.
Taxation.
Exemption, §9-8A-13.
Terms of office, §9-8A-3.
Use of earnings, §9-8A-16.
Vacancies in office,
§9-8A-3.
Allocated funds.
Applications for, §9-8A-9.
Original allocation,
§9-8A-5.
Reallocation of reverted
funds, §9-8A-5.
Reversion, §9-8A-5.
Use, §9-8A-5.

SOIL AND WATER
　CONSERVATION—Cont'd
Cost-share grants—Cont'd
　Application, §9-8A-6.
　Definitions, §9-8A-1.
　Designing of proposed
　　projects, §9-8A-10.
　Eligibility, §9-8A-6.
　　Eligible soil and water
　　　conservation practices,
　　　§9-8A-7.
　　Ineligible lands, §9-8A-8.
　Funds.
　　Allocated funds, §9-8A-5.
　　Reserve funds, §9-8A-5.
　　Revolving fund, §9-8A-4.1.
　Ineligible lands, §9-8A-8.
　Legislative findings, §9-8A-2.
　Processing, §9-8A-9.
　Proposed soil and water
　　conservation practices.
　　Designing, §9-8A-10.
　Purpose of provisions,
　　§9-8A-2.
　Reports.
　　Soil and water
　　　conservation districts,
　　　§9-8A-12.
　Reserve funds, §9-8A-5.
　Revolving fund.
　　Allocation to fund,
　　　§9-8A-4.1.
　　Established, §9-8A-4.1.
　　Expenditure of funds,
　　　§9-8A-4.1.
　Sale of land.
　　Land to which agreement
　　　is in effect, §9-8A-11.
　Taxation.
　　Agricultural and
　　　conservation
　　　development
　　　commission.
　　　Exemption, §9-8A-13.
　　Exemptions, §9-8A-14.
Damages.
　Districts.
　　Land-use regulations,
　　　§9-8-27.
Definitions.
　Cost-share grants, §9-8A-1.
　Soil and water conservation
　　districts, §9-8-20.
　Watershed conservancy
　　districts, §9-8-50.
Districts, §§9-8-20 to 9-8-32.
　Applications, §9-8-23.
　Body politic and corporate,
　　§9-8-25.
　Boundaries.
　　Changes, §9-8-23.
　Certificate of dissolution,
　　§9-8-31.
　Certificates of organization.
　　Issuance, §9-8-23.
　Contracts.
　　Authority of district,
　　　§9-8-25.
　Effect of discontinuance of
　　district, §9-8-31.
　Cooperation between
　　districts, §9-8-29.
　Damages.
　　Land-use regulations.
　　　Violations, §9-8-27.
　Declaration of policy, §9-8-21.
　Definitions, §9-8-20.
　Discontinuance.
　　Effect, §9-8-31.
　　Procedure, §9-8-31.

SOIL AND WATER
　CONSERVATION—Cont'd
Districts—Cont'd
　Discontinuance—Cont'd
　　Watershed conservancy
　　　districts.
　　　Supervision of watershed
　　　　conservancy
　　　　districts, §9-8-66.
　Drainage districts, §§9-9-70
　　to 9-9-80.
　　See WATER
　　　MANAGEMENT AND
　　　DRAINAGE.
　Duties.
　　General provisions,
　　　§9-8-25.
　Elections.
　　Discontinuance of district,
　　　§9-8-31.
　　Incorporation, §9-8-23.
　　Land-use regulations,
　　　§9-8-26.
　Expenses.
　　Payment of expenses,
　　　§9-8-32.
　Gifts.
　　Acceptance, §9-8-25.
　Hearings.
　　Discontinuance of district,
　　　§9-8-31.
　　Incorporation of districts,
　　　§9-8-23.
　　Land-use regulations,
　　　§9-8-26.
　Incorporation.
　　Procedure, §9-8-23.
　Land-use regulations.
　　§§9-8-26 to 9-8-28.
　　Adoption.
　　　Procedure, §9-8-26.
　　Amendments, §9-8-26.
　　Compliance.
　　　Access to lands for
　　　　investigation,
　　　　§9-8-27.
　　Contents, §9-8-26.
　　Damages.
　　　Violations, §9-8-27.
　　Elections, §9-8-26.
　　Enforcement, §9-8-28.
　　Hearings.
　　　Procedure for adoption,
　　　　§9-8-26.
　　Ordinances, §9-8-26.
　　Publication, §9-8-26.
　　Public lands, §9-8-30.
　　Right of entry.
　　　Investigations as to
　　　　observance, §9-8-27.
　　Violations.
　　　Complaint, §9-8-28.
　　　Correction by
　　　　supervisors, §9-8-28.
　　　Damages, §9-8-27.
　　　Remedies, §9-8-28.
　Legislative findings, §9-8-21.
　Names, §9-8-23.
　Notice.
　　Discontinuance of district,
　　　§9-8-31.
　　Hearings on incorporation,
　　　§9-8-23.
　　Land-use regulations,
　　　§9-8-26.
　Performance of work on
　　private lands.
　　Conditions for
　　　performance, §9-8-25.
　Petition for incorporation,
　　§9-8-23.

SOIL AND WATER
　CONSERVATION—Cont'd
Districts—Cont'd
　Policies.
　　Declaration of policy,
　　　§9-8-21.
　Powers and duties, §9-8-25.
　Property.
　　Acquisition.
　　　Applicability of certain
　　　　provisions, §9-8-25.
　　　Powers, §9-8-25.
　　Disposal upon
　　　discontinuance,
　　　§9-8-31.
　　Private property.
　　　Conditions for
　　　　performance of work
　　　　§9-8-25.
　Reorganization, §9-8-23.
　Repeal, §9-8-26.
　Seals, §9-8-25.
　State agencies.
　　Cooperation of state
　　　agencies, §9-8-30.
　State soil and water
　　conservation committee,
　　§9-8-22.
　Subdistricts.
　　Watershed conservancy
　　　districts, §§9-8-50 to
　　　9-8-67. See within thi
　　　heading, "Watershed
　　　conservancy districts."
　Supervisors.
　　Appointment, §§9-8-23,
　　　9-8-24.
　　Chairman, §9-8-24.
　　Compensation, §9-8-24.
　　Composition, §§9-8-23,
　　　9-8-24.
　　Cooperation between
　　　districts, §9-8-29.
　　Duties, §9-8-24.
　　Expenses, §9-8-24.
　　Powers, §9-8-24.
　　Qualifications, §§9-8-23,
　　　9-8-24.
　　Quorum, §9-8-24.
　　Removal, §9-8-24.
　　Terms of office, §9-8-24.
　　Vacancies in office,
　　　§9-8-24.
　Taxation.
　　Exemptions, §9-8-25.
　United States.
　　Agent of United States,
　　　§9-8-25.
　Water management districts
　　§§9-9-1 to 9-9-58.
　　See WATER
　　　MANAGEMENT ANI
　　　DRAINAGE.
　Watershed conservancy
　　districts, §§9-8-50 to
　　9-8-67. See within this
　　heading, "Watershed
　　conservancy districts."
Elections.
　Districts.
　　Discontinuance of district,
　　　§9-8-31.
　　Incorporation of districts,
　　　§9-8-23.
　　Land-use regulations,
　　　§9-8-26.
　　Watershed conservancy
　　　districts.
　　　Board of directors, §9-8-59
　　　Referendum upon creation
　　　　§§9-8-56 to 9-8-58.

**SOIL AND WATER
CONSERVATION**—Cont'd
Eminent domain.
Watershed conservancy
districts.
Board of directors.
Powers, §9-8-61.
Funds.
Cost-share grants,
§§9-8A-4.1, 9-8A-5.
Gifts.
Districts.
Acceptance, §9-8-25.
Watershed conservancy
districts.
Acceptance, §9-8-61.
Grants.
Cost-share grants, §§9-8A-1
to 9-8A-16. See within
this heading, "Cost-share
grants."
Hearings.
Districts.
Discontinuance, §9-8-31.
Incorporation, §9-8-23.
Land-use regulations,
§9-8-26.
Watershed conservancy
districts.
Addition of lands to
districts, §9-8-63.
Bond issues.
Issuance, §9-8-62.
Detachment of lands from
districts, §9-8-64.
Discontinuance, §9-8-65.
Petition for formation,
§9-8-55.
Irrigation, §§9-10-1 to 9-10-47.
See WATER
CONSERVATION AND
IRRIGATION.
Laboratories.
Soil testing laboratories,
§§2-24-1 to 2-24-5.
Land-use regulations.
Districts, §§9-8-26 to 9-8-28.
Legislature.
Districts.
Legislative findings,
§9-8-21.
Notice.
Districts.
Discontinuance, §9-8-31.
Hearings on incorporation,
§9-8-23.
Land-use regulations,
§9-8-26.
Watershed conservancy
districts.
Addition of lands to
districts, §9-8-63.
Bond issues.
Issuance, §9-8-62.
Detachment of lands from
districts, §9-8-64.
Discontinuance, §9-8-65.
Elections.
Board of directors,
§9-8-59.
Petition for formation.
Hearings, §9-8-55.
Referendum upon creation,
§9-8-56.
Ordinances.
Districts.
Land-use regulations,
§9-8-26.
Petitions.
Districts.
Incorporation, §9-8-23.

**SOIL AND WATER
CONSERVATION**—Cont'd
Petitions—Cont'd
Watershed conservancy
districts.
Petition for formation,
§§9-8-53 to 9-8-54.
Public lands.
Districts.
Land-use regulations.
Applicability of
regulations, §9-8-30.
Recordation.
Watershed conservancy
districts.
Referendum upon creation.
Results, §9-8-58.
Records.
State soil and water
conservation committee,
§9-8-22.
Rules and regulations.
State soil and water
conservation committee.
Promulgation, §9-8-22.
**Soil and water conservation
districts,** §§9-8-20 to
9-8-32.
Soil-testing laboratories,
§§2-24-1 to 2-24-5.
State agencies.
Districts.
Cooperation, §9-8-30.
**State soil and water
conservation committee.**
Administrative officer.
General provisions,
§9-8-22.
Appointment, §9-8-22.
Composition, §9-8-22.
Districts.
General provisions. See
within this heading,
"Districts."
Duties, §9-8-22.
Establishment, §9-8-22.
Expenses.
Payment, §9-8-32.
Powers, §9-8-22.
Records, §9-8-22.
Rules and regulations.
Promulgation, §9-8-22.
Terms of office, §9-8-22.
Vacancies in office, §9-8-22.
Water management districts.
Cooperation with persons
desiring to form
districts, §9-9-3.
Establishment.
Opinion of representative
of state committee,
§9-9-10.
Subdivisions.
County regulation of
subdivisions, §11-24-1.
See COUNTIES.
Supervisors.
Districts, §§9-8-23, 9-8-24,
9-8-29.
Taxation.
Cost-share grants.
Exemption from taxation,
§9-8A-14.
Agricultural and
conservation
development
commission,
§9-8A-13.
Soil and water conservation
districts.
Exemptions, §9-8-25.

**SOIL AND WATER
CONSERVATION**—Cont'd
Taxation—Cont'd
Watershed conservancy
districts.
Exemption, §9-8-67.
United States.
Soil and water conservation
districts.
Agent of United States,
§9-8-25.
Watershed conservancy
districts.
Cooperation with or act as
agent for, §9-8-61.
**Water conservation and
irrigation,** §§9-10-1 to
9-10-47.
See WATER
CONSERVATION AND
IRRIGATION.
**Water management and
drainage,** §§9-9-1 to
9-9-80.
See WATER
MANAGEMENT AND
DRAINAGE.
**Water resources research
institute,** §§9-8-1 to 9-8-4.
Article supplementary,
§9-8-4.
Control, §9-8-3.
Declaration of policy, §9-8-1.
Duties, §9-8-3.
Establishment.
Authority to establish,
§9-8-2.
Federal funds.
Receipt of federal funds,
§9-8-2.
Management, §9-8-3.
Policies.
Declaration of policy,
§9-8-1.
Powers, §9-8-3.
Purposes of article, §9-8-1.
**Watershed conservancy
districts,** §§9-8-50 to
9-8-67.
Board of directors, §§9-8-59
to 9-8-61.
Bonds, surety.
Treasurer, §9-8-59.
Compensation, §9-8-60.
Composition, §9-8-59.
Duties, §9-8-61.
Election, §9-8-59.
Nominating petition,
§9-8-59.
Expenses.
Reimbursement, §9-8-60.
Governing body of district,
§9-8-59.
Officers, §9-8-59.
Powers, §9-8-61.
Quorum, §9-8-59.
Salaries, §9-8-60.
Terms of office, §9-8-59.
Vacancies in office,
§9-8-59.
Bond issues.
Issuance.
Powers of board, §9-8-61.
Procedure, §9-8-62.
Borrowing money.
Powers of board, §9-8-61.
Boundaries, §9-8-52.
Addition of lands to
districts, §9-8-63.
Detachment of lands from
districts, §9-8-64.

**SOIL AND WATER
        CONSERVATION**—Cont'd
**Watershed conservancy
        districts**—Cont'd
Composition, §9-8-52.
Contracts.
    Powers of board, §9-8-61.
Creation.
    Authorized, §9-8-51.
Definitions, §9-8-50.
Directors, §§9-8-59 to 9-8-61.
Discontinuance of district.
    Procedure, §9-8-65.
Elections.
    Board of directors, §9-8-59.
    Referendum upon creation,
        §§9-8-56 to 9-8-58.
Eminent domain.
    Powers of board of
        directors, §9-8-61.
Gifts.
    Acceptance, §9-8-61.
Hearings.
    Addition of lands to
        districts, §9-8-63.
    Bond issues.
        Issuance, §9-8-62.
    Detachment of lands from
        districts, §9-8-64.
    Discontinuance of district,
        §9-8-65.
Notice.
    Addition of lands to
        districts, §9-8-63.
    Bond issues.
        Issuance, §9-8-62.
    Detachment of lands from
        districts, §9-8-64.
    Discontinuance of district,
        §9-8-65.
    Elections.
        Board of directors,
            §9-8-59.
    Petition for formation.
        Hearings, §9-8-55.
    Referendum upon creation,
        §9-8-56.
Petition for formation.
    Approval, §9-8-55.
    Contents, §9-8-53.
    Denial, §9-8-55.
    District lying in more than
        one soil and water
        conservation district,
        §9-8-54.
    Filing, §9-8-53.
    Hearings, §9-8-55.
    Notice of hearing, §9-8-55.
Property.
    Acquisition of property.
        Power of board of
            directors, §9-8-61.
Purposes, §9-8-51.
Recordation.
    Referendum upon creation.
        Recordation of results,
            §9-8-58.
Referendum upon creation.
    Absentee ballots, §9-8-57.
    Ballots.
        Absentee ballots,
            §9-8-57.
        Contents, §9-8-57.
    Certification of results,
        §9-8-58.
    Conduct, §9-8-57.
    Counting of votes, §9-8-58.
    Eligibility of voters,
        §9-8-57.
    Filing of results, §9-8-58.
    Notice, §9-8-56.

**SOIL AND WATER
        CONSERVATION**—Cont'd
**Watershed conservancy
        districts**—Cont'd
Referendum upon creation
    —Cont'd
    Polling officers.
        Appointment, §9-8-56.
        Qualifications, §9-8-56.
    Purpose, §9-8-56.
    Qualifications of voters,
        §9-8-57.
    Results, §9-8-58.
Soil and water conservation
    districts.
    General provisions,
        §§9-8-20 to 9-8-32.
Supervision.
    When soil and water
        conservation district
        discontinued, §9-8-66.
Taxation.
    Exemption, §9-8-67.
United States.
    Cooperate with or act as
        agent for, §9-8-61.
Water management districts.
    Organization of district
        over lands of
        watershed conservancy
        district, §9-9-51.

SOIL CLASSIFIERS, §§34-32-1
    to 34-32-19.
Applicability of provisions,
    §34-32-5.
    Exemptions, §34-32-6.
Board.
    Advisory council, §34-32-7.
        Appointment of members,
            §34-32-7.
        Composition, §34-32-7.
        Duties, §34-32-7.
        Expenses of members,
            §34-32-7.
        Meetings, §34-32-7.
        Officers, §34-32-7.
        Qualifications of members,
            §34-32-7.
        Terms of members,
            §34-32-7.
        Vacancies, §34-32-7.
    Defined, §34-32-2.
    Duties, §34-32-7.
    Funds, §34-32-19.
    Generally, §34-32-7.
    Hearings.
        Powers generally, §34-32-8.
    Investigation of complaints,
        §34-32-13.
    Investigation of violations,
        §34-32-14.
    Powers, §34-32-8.
    Record of proceedings,
        §34-32-8.
    Rules and regulations,
        §34-32-8.
    Secretary.
        Receiving and accounting
            for moneys, §34-32-19.
Citation of act.
    Short title, §34-32-1.
**Construction and
    interpretation,** §34-32-3.
Corporations.
    Practice through corporations
        not prohibited, §34-32-4.
Definitions, §34-32-2.
Education.
    Qualifications for
        registration, §34-32-9.

SOIL CLASSIFIERS—Cont'd
Exemptions from provisions,
    §34-32-6.
Fees.
    Registration, §34-32-12.
Hearings.
    Powers of board, §34-32-8.
Injunctions.
    Power of board, §34-32-8.
Investigations.
    Board.
        Investigation of
            complaints, §34-32-13.
        Investigation of violations,
            §34-32-14.
Partnerships.
    Practice by partnerships not
        prohibited, §34-32-4.
Penalties.
    Violations of provisions,
        §34-32-18.
**Practice of soil
    classification.**
    Defined, §34-32-2.
    Partnerships or corporations,
        §34-32-4.
**Qualified professional soil
    classifiers.**
    Defined, §34-32-2.
Records.
    Board.
        Record of proceedings,
            §34-32-8.
**Registered professional soil
    classifiers.**
    Defined, §34-32-2.
    Exclusive use of title,
        §34-32-16.
Registration.
    Applications, §34-32-9.
    Denial.
        Notification, §34-32-9.
        Request for hearing,
            §34-32-9.
    Expiration of certificate,
        §34-32-10.
    Fees, §34-32-12.
    Issuance of certificates,
        §34-32-9.
    Qualifications, §34-32-9.
    Renewal of certificate,
        §34-32-10.
        Nonrenewal within five
            years.
            Effect, §34-32-11.
    Suspension or revocation.
        Unlawful to sign
            documents, §34-32-17.
Rules and regulations.
    Board, §34-32-8.
Scope of provisions, §34-32-5.
    Exemptions, §34-32-6.
Title of act.
    Short title, §34-32-1.
Violations of provisions.
    Investigation, §34-32-14.
    Penalties, §34-32-18.
    Prosecution, §34-32-15.

**SOIL TESTING
    LABORATORIES,** §§2-24-1
    to 2-24-5.
    See AGRICULTURE.

SOLAR ENERGY.
Income tax.
    Solar energy tax credits,
        §§40-18-120, 40-18-121.

SOLDIERS AND SAILORS.
Military affairs, §§31-1-1 to
    31-10-4.
    See MILITARY AFFAIRS.

SOLDIERS AND SAILORS
—Cont'd
Veterans, §§31-5-1 to 31-8-33.
See VETERANS.

SOLICITATION.
Ameraport.
Offshore harbor and terminal
commission.
Soliciting money and other
assistance, §33-10-12.
Carriers.
Soliciting claims against
carriers, §37-8-280.
Elections.
Fair campaign practices.
Force, threats, etc., to
solicit money,
§17-22A-20.
Health maintenance
organizations.
Untrue or misleading
solicitation, §27-21A-13.
Inciting to crime, §§13A-4-1,
13A-4-5.
Motor vehicle carriers.
Claims.
Soliciting claims against
carriers, §37-8-280.
Motor vehicles.
Soliciting rides, §32-5A-216.
Peace officers.
State or federal peace officer
magazines or journals.
Solicitation of
advertisements,
§13A-14-5.
Prostitution, §§13A-12-110 to
13A-12-113.
Railroads.
Soliciting claims against
carriers, §37-8-280.
Transportation companies.
Claims against
transportation
companies.
Soliciting claims forbidden,
§§37-2-43, 37-8-280.

SOLICITORS.
Circuit courts.
Abolition of office and
performance of functions
by assistant district
attorneys, §12-12-9.
Designation of circuit
solicitor as district
attorney, Const. Ala.,
amd. 226.
Constitution of Alabama,
Const. Ala., amd. 226.
Impeachment, Const. Ala.,
art. VII, §174.
District attorneys.
See DISTRICT
ATTORNEYS.
Insurance.
Casualty insurance
representatives,
§27-7-27.
Licenses, §27-7-27.
False statements, etc., in
insurance application,
§27-12-23.
Fees.
Licenses, §27-4-2.
Licenses.
Examinations.
Fees, §27-4-2.

SOLICITORS—Cont'd
Insurance—Cont'd
Licenses—Cont'd
Property, casualty and
surety insurance
representatives,
§27-7-27.
Mutual aid associations.
Authorization to act as or
for associations,
§27-30-4.
Requirements, §27-30-5.
Permits.
Solicitation permits,
§§27-27-4 to 27-27-14.
See INSURANCE.
Property insurance
representatives,
§27-7-27.
Surety insurance
representatives,
§27-7-27.

SOLID WASTE.
Authorities, §§11-89A-1 to
11-89A-25.
Definitions.
Management plan, §22-27-43.
Disposal authorities,
§§11-89A-1 to 11-89A-25.
Agreements from and with
other bodies, §11-89A-15.
Aid from and with other
bodies, §11-89A-15.
Another authority.
Incorporation by same
determining
subdivision,
§11-89A-22.
Applicability of certain
provisions, §11-89A-13.
Application for incorporation
of authority.
Filing of, §11-89A-3.
Bids.
Exemption from
competitive bid laws,
§11-89A-18.
Board of directors.
Election, §11-89A-6.
Expenses, §11-89A-6.
Impeachment, §11-89A-6.
Meetings, §11-89A-6.
Notice, §11-89A-6.
Qualifications, §11-89A-6.
Resolutions, §11-89A-6.
Dissolution of authority,
§11-89A-21.
Terms of office, §11-89A-6.
Vacancies, §11-89A-6.
Bonds.
Contest to validity,
§11-89A-23.
Contracts and agreements
to secure, §11-89A-10.
Generally, §11-89A-9.
Issuance, §11-89A-9.
Legal investments,
§11-89A-20.
Notice of bond resolution,
§11-89A-23.
Proceeds from sales,
§11-89A-11.
Refunding bonds,
§11-89A-12.
Securities for payments,
§11-89A-10.
Certificate of incorporation,
§11-89A-4.
Amendments to,
§11-89A-5.

SOLID WASTE—Cont'd
Disposal authorities—Cont'd
Construction of chapter.
Liberal construction,
§11-89A-25.
Cooperation from and with
other bodies, §11-89A-15.
Cumulative effect of chapter,
§11-89A-24.
Definitions, §11-89A-2.
Disposition of net earnings,
§11-89A-19.
Dissolution, §11-89A-21.
Eminent domain.
Power of, §11-89A-14.
Exemptions.
Competitive bid laws,
§11-89A-18.
Taxation, §11-89A-16.
Usury and interest laws,
§11-89A-17.
Facilities.
Location of, §11-89A-8.
Findings of legislature,
§11-89A-1.
Incorporation of authority.
Authorization by governing
body of county or
municipality,
§11-89A-3.
Certificate, §11-89A-4.
Amendments, §11-89A-5.
Denial, §11-89A-3.
Filing of application,
§11-89A-3.
Notice to secretary of state,
§11-89A-4.
Procedure, §11-89A-4.
Investments.
Bonds as legal
investments,
§11-89A-20.
Legislative findings,
§11-89A-1.
Liberal construction of
chapter, §11-89A-25.
Location of facilities,
§11-89A-8.
Net earnings.
Disposition of, §11-89A-19.
Officers, §11-89A-7.
Powers, §11-89A-8.
Property of authority.
Dissolution of authority.
Vesting of title,
§11-89A-21.
Refunding bonds,
§11-89A-12.
Supervision and control.
Freedom from authority of
state, §11-89A-13.
Taxation.
Exemption, §11-89A-16.
Usury and interest laws.
Exemptions, §11-89A-17.
General provisions.
See GARBAGE AND
TRASH.
Management plan, §§22-27-40
to 22-27-49.
Advisory committee.
Compensation.
Service without pay,
§22-27-44.
Composition, §22-27-44.
Created, §22-27-44.
Duties, §22-27-44.
Expenses.
Reimbursement,
§22-27-44.

SOLID WASTE—Cont'd
Management plan—Cont'd
Advisory committee—Cont'd
Number of members,
§22-27-44.
Qualifications, §22-27-44.
Commissions.
Regional planning and
development
commissions.
Duties, §22-27-46.
Definitions, §22-27-43.
Department of environmental
management.
Director.
Preparation of plan,
§22-27-45.
Findings of legislature,
§22-27-40.
Goals.
Preparation of plan,
§22-27-45.
Implementation of plans,
§22-27-48.
Intent of legislature,
§22-27-42.
Legislative findings,
§22-47-40.
Legislative purposes,
§22-27-41.
Local plans.
Required, §22-27-47.
Moratorium on issuance of
permits, §22-27-49.
Permits.
Moratorium on issuance of,
§22-27-49.
Preparation of plan,
§22-27-45.
Implementation, §22-27-48.
Local plans.
Required, §22-27-47.
Purposes.
Legislative purposes,
§22-27-41.
Regional planning and
development
commissions.
Duties, §22-27-46.
Permits.
Management plan.
Moratorium on issuance of
permits, §22-27-49.
Sewers.
See SEWERS.

SONG.
**Official state reunion theme
song, §1-2-24.**
State song, §1-2-16.

SON OF SAM LAW.
**Escrow account for benefit
of crime victims.**
Actions to defeat purpose of
provisions to as null and
void, §41-9-84.
Diversion to state of money,
§41-9-82.
Limitation of actions.
Commencement of
running, §41-9-83.
List of criminals to probate
judge, §41-9-81.
Notice to victims, §41-9-81.
Restitution to victims,
§41-9-80.

SON OF SAM LAW—Cont'd
**Restitution to victims of
crimes.**
Withholding, §§15-18-140 to
15-18-151.
See RESTITUTION TO
VICTIMS OF CRIMES.

SOUND.
Recorded devices.
Copying and sale of recorded
devices, §§13A-8-80 to
13A-8-86.
See RECORDED DEVICES.

SOUTH ALABAMA.
**University of South
Alabama, §§16-55-1 to
16-55-9.**
See UNIVERSITY OF
SOUTH ALABAMA.

**SOUTH ALABAMA STATE
FAIR ASSOCIATION.**
**Southeastern livestock
exhibition.**
Exemption from sales and
use taxes, §40-23-5.

**SOUTHEAST ASIAN WAR
PRISONERS.**
Bonus, §§31-7-1 to 31-7-5.

**SOUTHEASTERN
INTERSTATE FOREST
FIRE PROTECTION
COMPACT, §§9-13-200,
9-13-201.**
See FORESTS AND
FORESTRY.

**SOUTHEAST INTERSTATE
LOW-LEVEL
RADIOACTIVE WASTE
MANAGEMENT
COMPACT,
§§22-32-1 to 22-32-9.**
Appropriations, §22-32-5.
Auctions and auctioneers.
Seizure of source of ionizing
radiation.
Unredeemed equipment
may be auctioned,
§22-32-8.
Bonds, surety.
Contractors or leasors,
§22-32-5.
Commission.
Compact commission fund,
§22-32-5.
Composition, §22-32-2.
Cooperation of departments,
agencies, officers and
political subdivisions
with, §22-32-7.
Members, §22-32-2.
Contents of compact,
§22-32-1.
Contracts.
Bonds, surety, §22-32-5.
Operation and disposal of
waste, §22-32-4.
Counties.
Cooperation with
commission, §22-32-7.
**Delegation of authority to
stop, inspect and enforce
regulations, §22-32-6.**
Disposal sites.
Acquisition, §22-32-3.
Operation.
Authorization, §22-32-4.
Users' charges, §22-32-4.

**SOUTHEAST INTERSTATE
LOW-LEVEL
RADIOACTIVE WASTE
MANAGEMENT
COMPACT**—Cont'd
Effective date of chapter,
§22-32-9.
Eminent domain.
Acquisition of disposal sites,
§22-32-3.
Enactment, §22-32-1.
Fees.
Licensing and inspection
fees, §22-32-5.
Royalty fees, §22-32-5.
Funds.
Compact commission fund,
§22-32-5.
Operating fund, §22-32-5.
Perpetual care fund, §22-32-5.
Radiation safety fund,
§22-32-5.
**Hazardous waste or
substances.**
Fees for disposal.
Effect of chapter on,
§22-30B-18.
Inspections.
Delegation of authority to
inspect and enforce
regulations, §22-32-6.
Fees, §22-32-5.
Leases.
Bond, surety of leasor,
§22-32-5.
Operation and disposal of
waste, §22-32-4.
Licenses.
Fees, §22-32-5.
Municipal corporations.
Cooperation with
commission, §22-32-7.
Orders.
Issuance of order prohibiting
use of source of ionizing
radiation, §22-32-8.
Penalties.
Violation of chapter,
§22-32-8.
**Public officers and
employees.**
Cooperation with
commission, §22-32-7.
Royalty fees, §22-32-5.
Searches and seizures.
Source of ionizing radiation.
Impoundment or seizure,
§22-32-8.
Source of ionizing radiation.
Impoundment or seizure,
§22-32-8.
Orders prohibiting use,
§22-32-8.
**State departments and
agencies.**
Cooperation with
commission, §22-32-7.
Text of compact, §22-32-1.
Transportation.
Stopping, inspecting and
enforcing regulations.
Delegation of authority,
§22-32-6.

**SOUTHERN GROWTH
POLICIES AGREEMENT,
§§41-18-1 to 41-18-3.**
Adoption.
Effect of adoption, §41-18-3.

**SOUTHERN GROWTH
POLICIES AGREEMENT**
—Cont'd
Amendments.
Copies of amendments,
§41-18-2.
Bylaws.
Copies of bylaws, §41-18-2.
Contents, §41-18-1.
Text, §41-18-1.

**SOUTHERN INTERSTATE
NUCLEAR COMPACT,**
§§9-18-1 to 9-18-6.
See ATOMIC ENERGY.

SOUTHERN PINE.
State tree, §1-2-12.

**SOUTHERN PRODUCTS
MART AUTHORITY,**
§§41-10-50 to 41-10-69.
See PRODUCTS MARTS.

**SOUTHERN STANDARD
BUILDING CODE.**
Subdivisions.
Regulation of subdivisions by
county.
Consistency with code,
§11-24-1.

**SOUTHERN STATES
ENERGY COMPACT,**
§§9-18A-1 to 9-18A-4.
Advisory committees.
Establishment by board,
§9-18A-1.
Board, §§9-18A-1, 9-18A-2,
9-18A-4.
Advisory committees.
Establishment, §9-18A-1.
Appointment of members,
§§9-18A-1, 9-18A-2.
Budget, §9-18A-1.
Bylaws, §9-18A-1.
Chairman.
Election, §9-18A-1.
Composition, §9-18A-1.
Cooperation of state
department, officers, etc.,
§9-18A-4.
Executive director, §9-18A-1.
Members.
Appointment, §9-18A-2.
Designation of deputy or
assistant, §9-18A-2.
Personnel.
Employment policies and
employee benefits,
§9-18A-1.
Powers, §9-18A-1.
Reports.
Annual report to governors
of party states,
§9-18A-1.
Rules and regulations,
§9-18A-1.
Seal, §9-18A-1.
Terms of office, §9-18A-2.
Treasurer.
Election, §9-18A-1.
Vice-chairman.
Election, §9-18A-1.
Budget.
Distribution of costs among
party states, §9-18A-1.
Submission by board,
§9-18A-1.
Bylaws.
Adoption by board, §9-18A-1.
**Construction and
interpretation,** §9-18A-1.
Severability, §9-18A-1.

**SOUTHERN STATES
ENERGY COMPACT**
—Cont'd
Effective date.
Conditions, §9-18A-1.
Enactment, §9-18A-1.
Executive director.
Appointment, §9-18A-1.
Finances, §9-18A-1.
Membership.
Eligible parties, §9-18A-1.
Requirements, §9-18A-1.
Withdrawal, §9-18A-1.
Policy, §9-18A-1.
Purpose, §9-18A-1.
Reports.
Board.
Annual report to governors
of party states,
§9-18A-1.
Rules and regulations.
Board, §9-18A-1.
Severability, §9-18A-1.
Supplementary agreements,
§9-18A-1.
Limitation on expenditure of
funds, §9-18A-3.

**SOUTHERN UNION
COLLEGE,** §§16-60-130 to
16-60-132.
Advisory board.
Generally, §16-60-132.
Buildings.
Acceptance of facilities by
governor, §16-60-130.
Facilities.
Acceptance of facilities by
governor, §16-60-130.
Governor.
Acceptance of facilities by
governor, §16-60-130.
**Operation as other like
institutions,** §16-60-131.
**Operation as state
institution.**
Provisions for, §16-60-130.
Property.
Acceptance of facilities by
governor, §16-60-130.
State institution.
Provisions for operation as,
§16-60-130.

**SOUTHWEST STATE
TECHNICAL INSTITUTE.**
**State vocational technical
school at Mobile
designated as,** §16-60-1.

SOVEREIGN IMMUNITY.
State, Const. Ala., art. I, §14.

SOVEREIGNTY OF STATE,
§41-1-1.

SOYBEANS, §§2-8-80 to 2-8-103.
Audits.
Promotion of soybean
industry.
Annual audit of soybean
producers' associations,
§2-8-99.
Bonds, surety.
Promotion of soybean
industry.
Treasurer of soybean
producers' association,
§2-8-96.
Buyers.
Permit required, §2-8-102.

SOYBEANS—Cont'd
Constitution of Alabama.
Promotion of soybean
industry, Const. Ala.,
amd. 315.
Amendment of
amendment, Const.
Ala., amd. 401.
Permits.
Buyers, §2-8-102.
**Promotion of soybean
industry,** §§2-8-80 to
2-8-103; Const. Ala., amd.
315.
Amendment of amendment,
Const. Ala., amd. 401.
Assessments.
Collection, §2-8-91.
Remission of collections
to treasurer of
soybean producers'
association, §2-8-92.
Declared to be in public
interest, §2-8-82.
Deductions for expenses,
§2-8-91.
Expenditure of
assessments, §2-8-97.
Limitation on, §2-8-89.
Penalty for failure to
deduct and pay over
assessment, §2-8-103.
Referendum.
Application for approval
to conduct, §§2-8-83,
2-8-84.
Authority of certified
association to
conduct, §2-8-85.
Canvass of results,
§2-8-89.
Conduct, §2-8-87.
Declared to be in public
interest, §2-8-82.
Eligibility to vote,
§2-8-88.
Majority vote required
for approval of
assessment, §2-8-89.
Notice, §2-8-86.
Payment of expense,
§2-8-87.
Question to be voted on,
§2-8-88.
Subsequent referendum,
§2-8-90.
Refund of assessment to
soybean producer,
§2-8-95.
Audits.
Annual audit of soybean
producers' associations,
§2-8-99.
Authorized activities.
Not illegal or in restraint
of trade, §2-8-81.
Buyers.
Injunctions, §2-8-103.
Inspection of books and
records, §2-8-103.
Permit required, §2-8-102.
Certification of soybean
producers' association.
Application for
certification.
Action by board, §2-8-84.
Generally, §2-8-83.
Revocation of certification,
§2-8-101.

SOYBEANS—Cont'd
Promotion of soybean industry—Cont'd
Commissioner of agriculture and industries.
Enforcement duties, §2-8-101.
Examination of soybean producers' associations by department of examiners of public accounts, §2-8-99.
Exemptions from article, §2-8-94.
Joint programs with other states, §2-8-98.
Legislative purpose and intent, §2-8-80.
Penalty for failure to deduct and pay over assessment, §2-8-103.
Permit required of buyers, §2-8-102.
Rules and regulations, §2-8-100.
Statement of soybean producers' associations.
Publication, §2-8-99.
Treasurers of soybean producers' associations.
Bonds, surety, §2-8-96.
Remission of collections to treasurers, §2-8-92.
Rules and regulations.
Promotion of soybean industry, §2-8-100.

SPACE SCIENCE EXHIBIT COMMISSION, §§41-9-430 to 41-9-439.
Accounts and accounting, §41-9-437.
Advertising.
Exhibits and facilities, §41-9-436.
Appointment of members, §41-9-431.
Audits.
Records and books of account, §41-9-437.
Bond issues.
Denominations, §41-9-433.
Execution, §41-9-433.
Form, §41-9-433.
Liability upon revenue bonds issued, §41-9-435.
Payment.
Pledge of revenues and income of commission, §41-9-434.
Redemption, §41-9-433.
Sale, §41-9-433.
Security.
Pledge of revenues and income of commission, §41-9-434.
Terms, §41-9-433.
Chairman, §41-9-431.
Compensation of members, §41-9-431.
Composition, §41-9-431.
Concessions.
Operation or leasing in or on grounds and facilities, §41-9-436.
Construction of article, §41-9-439.
Creation, §41-9-430.

SPACE SCIENCE EXHIBIT COMMISSION—Cont'd
Department of army.
Commission to provide facilities for exhibits, §41-9-430.
Executive committee, §41-9-431.
Exemption from taxation, §41-9-438.
Exhibits.
Advertising, §41-9-436.
Department of army.
Commission to provide facilities for exhibits, §41-9-430.
National aeronautics and space administration.
Commission to provide facilities for exhibits, §41-9-430.
Promotion, §41-9-436.
Expenses.
Reimbursement, §41-9-431.
Leases.
Concessions, §41-9-436.
Lodging for visitors.
Commission empowered to provide, §41-9-430.
Meetings, §41-9-431.
National aeronautics and space administration.
Commission to provide facilities for exhibits, §41-9-430.
Personal property.
Purchase and acquisition of tangible personal property, §41-9-436.
Powers, §41-9-432.
Promotion.
Exhibits and facilities, §41-9-436.
Public body corporate, §41-9-430.
Qualifications of members, §41-9-431.
Quorum, §41-9-431.
Records.
Maintenance and audit, §41-9-437.
Removal of members, §41-9-431.
Taxation.
Exemption, §41-9-438.
Terms of members, §41-9-431.
Vacancies, §41-9-431.

SPACE SCIENCE EXHIBIT FINANCE AUTHORITY, §§41-10-300 to 41-10-332.
Bond issues.
Authorized, §41-10-310.
Competitive bidding, §41-10-313.
Debts of state.
Not debts of state, §41-10-321.
Deposit of government funds.
Security for, §41-10-315.
Disposition of proceeds, §41-10-316.
Investment, §41-10-317.
Execution, §41-10-309.
Investment.
Proceeds, §41-10-317.
Trust fund, §41-10-314.
Issuance.
Authorized, §41-10-310.
Refunding bonds, §41-10-311.

SPACE SCIENCE EXHIBIT FINANCE AUTHORITY—Cont'd
Bond issues—Cont'd
Negotiable instruments.
Bonds and coupons deemed, §41-10-320.
Payment.
Special funds for payment, §41-10-326.
Price, §41-10-313.
Priority of bonds, §41-10-312.
Proceeds.
Disposition, §41-10-316.
Refunding bonds.
Authority to issue, §41-10-311.
Rights of holders, §41-10-319.
Sale.
Competitive bidding, §41-10-313.
Disposition of proceeds, §41-10-316.
Investment, §41-10-317.
Expenses, §41-10-313.
Notice, §41-10-313.
Security, §41-10-318.
Specifications, §41-10-312.
Temporary loans in anticipation of issuance, §41-10-308.
Commission.
Conveyance of property by commission, §41-10-322.
Compensation, §41-10-305.
Composition, §41-10-305.
Construction of article, §41-10-301.
Construction of facilities.
Approval, §41-10-323.
Lease of vacant facilities to prevent default, §41-10-325.
Leasing to commission and other agencies, §41-10-324.
Plans, §41-10-323.
Debts.
Bond issues.
Not debt of state, §41-10-321.
Definitions, §41-10-300.
Directors, §41-10-305.
Proceedings, §41-10-306.
Resolutions, §41-10-306.
Dissolution.
Fees.
No fees, §41-10-329.
Generally, §41-10-330.
Expenses, §41-10-305.
Special funds for payment, §41-10-326.
Incorporation, §41-10-302.
Certificate of incorporation.
Application, §41-10-303.
Issuance, §41-10-304.
Recordation, §41-10-304.
Fees.
No fees for, §41-10-329.
Insurance.
Special funds for payment, §41-10-326.
Investments.
Bond issues, §41-10-314.
Lease of facilities.
Exemption from competitive bid laws, §41-10-331.
Vacant facilities to prevent default on bonds, §41-10-325.
Liability, §41-10-305.

SPACE SCIENCE EXHIBIT FINANCE AUTHORITY —Cont'd

Loans.
Temporary loans in anticipation of issuance of bonds, §41-10-308.
Members, §41-10-305.
Negotiable instruments.
Bonds and coupons deemed, §41-10-320.
Notes.
Execution, §41-10-309.
Officers, §41-10-305.
Powers, §41-10-307.
Property.
Conveyance by commission to authority, §41-10-322.
Right to possession, §41-10-322.
Purpose of article, §41-10-301.
Quorum, §41-10-305.
Sunset law.
Exemption from, §41-10-332.
Taxation.
Exemption, §41-10-327.
Vacancies in office, §41-10-305.
Venue.
Actions, §41-10-328.

SPARRING, §§41-9-90.1, 41-9-96.
See BOXING AND WRESTLING.

SPEARFISHING, §§9-11-170 to 9-11-176.
See FISH AND GAME.

SPECIAL EDUCATIONAL TRUST FUND.
Generally.
See EDUCATION.
Taxation.
Setting up treasury account, §40-1-32.
Source of fund.
Revenues, §40-1-31.

SPECIAL ELECTIONS.
Absentee voting.
See ELECTIONS.
General provisions, §§17-18-1 to 17-18-7.
See ELECTIONS.
Improvement authorities, §§39-7-8, 39-7-31.

SPECIFIC PERFORMANCE, §§8-1-40 to 8-1-47.
Arbitration.
Agreement to arbitrate cannot be specifically enforced, §8-1-41.
Commercial code.
Investment securities.
Right to obtain possession of security wrongfully transferred, §7-8-315.
Sales.
Buyer's right to specific performance, §7-2-716.
Conditions precedent.
Specific performance not enforced for party not fully performing, §8-1-42.
Consideration.
Specific performance not enforced against party who has not received adequate consideration, §8-1-40.

SPECIFIC PERFORMANCE —Cont'd
Conveyances.
Breach of agreement to transfer.
Pecuniary compensation presumed inadequate, §8-1-47.
Judgment for specific performance, §35-4-33.
Deeds.
Breach of agreement to transfer.
Pecuniary compensation deemed inadequate, §8-1-47.
Judgment for specific performance, §35-4-33.
Enforcement.
Cases in which specific performance not enforced, §8-1-40.
Conditions precedent.
Specific performance not enforced for party not fully performing, §8-1-42.
Obligations which cannot be specifically enforced, §8-1-41.
Fraud.
Cases in which specific performance not enforced, §8-1-40.
Investment securities.
Right to obtain possession of security wrongfully transferred, §7-8-315.
Judgments for specific performance.
Effect, §35-4-33.
Liquidated damages.
Imposition does not bar specific performance, §8-1-45.
Mutuality.
Generally, §8-1-43.
Penalty provisions.
Imposition does not bar specific performance, §8-1-45.
Personal property.
Breach of agreement to transfer.
Pecuniary compensation presumed adequate, §8-1-47.
Personal service.
Obligations which cannot be specifically enforced, §8-1-41.
Pleadings.
Form of complaint, ARCP, Form 4.
Presumptions.
Availability as remedy, §8-1-47.
Real property.
Breach of agreement to transfer.
Pecuniary compensation presumed inadequate, §8-1-47.
Conveyances. See within this heading, "Conveyances."
Judgment for specific performance, §35-4-33.

SPECIFIC PERFORMANCE —Cont'd
Real property—Cont'd
Obligation on real estate.
Specific enforcement against person subsequently claiming title, §8-1-46.
Rules of civil procedure.
Judgment for specific acts, ARCP, Rule 70.
Pleadings.
Form of complaint, ARCP, Form 4.
Signing by one party only.
Other party may specifically enforce, §8-1-44.

SPEECH.
Freedom of speech.
Constitution of Alabama, Const. Ala., art. I, §4.
Constitution of United States, Const. U. S., Amendment I.
Members of congress, Const. U. S., Art. I, §6.
Pathologists and audiologists, §§34-28A-1 to 34-28A-44.
See SPEECH PATHOLOGISTS AND AUDIOLOGISTS.

SPEECH PATHOLOGISTS AND AUDIOLOGISTS, §§34-28A-1 to 34-28A-44.
Appeals.
Revocation or suspension of licenses, §34-28A-26.
Attorney general.
Assistance in enforcement of chapter, §34-28A-4.
Audiology.
Defined, §34-28A-1.
Board of examiners, §§34-28A-40 to 34-28A-44.
Appointment of members, §34-28A-40.
Bylaws.
Adoption, §34-28A-43.
Compensation of members, §34-28A-41.
Composition, §34-28A-40.
Creation, §34-28A-40.
Defined, §34-28A-1.
Disposition of funds received. §34-28A-44.
Employees, §34-28A-44.
Enforcement of chapter, §34-28A-42.
Evidence.
Admissibility of copies of proceedings, records, etc., §34-28A-44.
Examinations. See within this heading, "Examinations."
Executive secretary, §34-28A-44.
Governor.
Appointment and removal of members, §34-28A-40.
Injunctions.
Authority of board, §34-28A-43.
Liability of members, §34-28A-43.
Licenses. See within this heading, "Licenses."
Meetings, §34-28A-40.

**SPEECH PATHOLOGISTS
AND AUDIOLOGISTS**
—Cont'd
Board of examiners—Cont'd
Powers and duties,
§34-28A-42.
Qualification of members,
§34-28A-40.
Quorum, §34-28A-40.
Records.
Admissibility of records as
evidence, §34-28A-44.
Removal of members,
§34-28A-40.
Reports.
Monthly reports,
§34-28A-44.
Revocation or suspension of
licenses, §§34-28A-4,
34-18A-26.
Rules and regulations,
§§34-28A-42, 34-28A-43.
Seal of board, §34-28A-43.
Terms of office, §34-28A-40.
Vacancies.
Filling, §34-28A-40.
Witnesses.
Authority to compel
attendance,
§34-28A-43.
Certificates, §§34-18A-20 to
34-18A-27.
Construction of chapter.
Rules of construction,
§34-28A-6.
Continuing education,
§34-28A-25.
**Declaration of policy and
legislative intent,**
§34-28A-2.
Definitions, §34-28A-1.
Education.
Continuing education,
§34-28A-25.
Enforcement of chapter.
Attorney general to assist,
§34-28A-4.
Duty of state officials,
§34-28A-4.
Evidence.
Board of examiners.
Admissibility of board
records, §34-28A-44.
Authority to compel
production of
documents,
§34-28A-43.
Examinations.
Applications, §34-28A-22.
Board of examiners. See
within this heading,
"Board of examiners."
Fees, §34-28A-22.
Passage prerequisite to
issuance of licenses,
§34-28A-21.
Prior practice.
Waiver of examination,
§34-28A-24.
Reexamination.
Applications, §34-28A-22.
Subjects examined,
§34-28A-23.
Time and place, §34-28A-23.
Waiver, §34-28A-24.
Exemptions from chapter.
Persons and practices exempt
from chapter, §34-28A-3.

**SPEECH PATHOLOGISTS
AND AUDIOLOGISTS**
—Cont'd
Fees.
Examinations.
Application fee,
§§34-28A-22,
34-28A-27.
Licenses, §34-28A-27.
Inactive status fee,
§34-28A-25.
Felonies.
Revocation or suspension of
licenses.
Conviction as grounds,
§34-28A-26.
Fraud.
Penalty for false information
or fraudulent practice,
§34-28A-4.
Revocation or suspension of
licenses.
Fraud as grounds,
§34-28A-26.
Free enterprise system.
Chapter not to restrict,
§34-28A-6.
Governor.
Board of examiners.
Appointment and removal
of members,
§34-28A-40.
**Hearing aid dealers and
fitters.**
Exemptions from provisions
of chapter, §34-28A-3.
Injunctions.
Board of examiners.
Authority of board,
§34-28A-43.
Liability of board
members, §34-28A-43.
Proceedings to enjoin
violations, §34-28A-5.
Legislature.
Legislative intent, §34-28A-2.
Licenses.
Continuing education,
§34-28A-25.
Duration of license term,
§34-28A-25.
Educational requirements of
applicants, §34-28A-21.
Examinations.
Generally, §§34-28A-21 to
34-28A-24.
Expiration.
Duration of license,
§34-28A-25.
Effect of failure to renew,
§34-28A-25.
Fees, §34-28A-27.
Inactive status fee,
§34-28A-25.
Fines.
Administrative fines.
Disciplining of licensees,
§34-28A-42.
Inactive status.
Placement of license on,
§34-28A-25.
Interim practice pending
action on application,
§34-28A-22.
Issuance, §34-28A-25.
Passage of examination
prerequisite,
§34-28A-21.
Qualified applicants only,
§34-28A-20.

**SPEECH PATHOLOGISTS
AND AUDIOLOGISTS**
—Cont'd
Licenses—Cont'd
Practice without license
prohibited, §34-28A-4.
Qualifications of applicants.
Generally, §34-28A-21.
Issuance only to qualified
applicants, §34-28A-20.
Renewal.
Effect of failure to renew,
§34-28A-25.
Fee, §34-28A-27.
Generally, §34-28A-25.
Required, §34-28A-20.
Penalty for unlawful
practice, §34-28A-4.
Revocation or suspension.
Appeal, §34-28A-26.
Grounds, §34-28A-26.
Hearing, §34-28A-26.
Notice of charges,
§34-28A-26.
Restoration of license,
§34-28A-26.
Using or attempting to use
revoked license,
§34-28A-4.
Term of license, §34-28A-25.
Nonresidents.
Exemption of temporary in
state practice from
provisions, §34-28A-3.
Penalties.
Administrative fines.
Disciplining of licensees,
§34-28A-42.
Disposition of collected fines,
§34-28A-4.
Violations of chapter,
§34-28A-4.
Physicians.
Exemptions from provisions
of chapter, §34-28A-3.
Policy.
Declaration of public policy,
§34-28A-2.
Prohibited acts, §34-28A-4.
Records.
Board of examiners.
Admissibility of board
records as evidence,
§34-28A-44.
Repeals.
Provisions of chapter not to
repeal other code
provisions, §34-28A-6.
Reports.
Board of examiners.
Monthly report,
§34-28A-44.
**Revocation or suspension of
licenses,** §§34-18A-4,
34-28A-26.
Rules and regulations.
Board of examiners,
§§34-28A-42, 34-28A-43.
**Seals and sealed
instruments.**
Seal of board of examiners,
§34-28A-43.
**Speech and hearing
association.**
Defined, §34-28A-1.
Speech pathology.
Defined, §34-28A-1.
Subpoenas.
Board of examiners.
Authority to issue,
§34-28A-43.

SPEECH PATHOLOGISTS AND AUDIOLOGISTS —Cont'd

Violations of chapter.
Injunctions and restraining orders, §34-28A-5.
Authority of board of examiners, §34-28A-43.
Penalties, §34-28A-4.
Witnesses.
Board of examiners.
Authority to compel attendance, §34-28A-43.

SPEED LIMITS.
See MOTOR VEHICLES.

SPEEDWAYS.
Public athletic boards, §§11-59-1 to 11-59-17.
See MUNICIPAL CORPORATIONS.

SPENDTHRIFT TRUSTS.
Authorized, §19-3-1.

SPINAL MENINGITIS.
Notifiable diseases, §§22-11A-1 to 22-11A-38.
See DISEASES.

SPIRITUOUS LIQUORS.
See ALCOHOLIC BEVERAGES.

SPLIT INTEREST TRUSTS.
Private foundations, charitable trusts and split-interest trusts.
Cemeteries, §§11-17-13 to 11-17-16.
General provisions, §§19-3-300 to 19-3-302.

SPORTS.
Actions.
Agents.
Jurisdiction determined by damages claimed, §8-26-36.
Parties to action against agent, §8-26-36.
Transfer and assignment of action, §8-26-36.
Advertising.
Agents, §8-26-33.
False information or promises, §8-26-33.
Agents, §§8-26-1 to 8-26-41.
Actions against athlete agents.
Jurisdiction.
Determined by damages claimed, §8-26-36.
Parties, §8-26-36.
Transfer and assignment, §8-26-36.
Advertising, §8-26-33.
False, fraudulent, etc., information.
Prohibited, §8-26-33.
Athlete agent regulatory commission.
Creation, §8-26-3.
Definition of "commission," §8-26-2.
Disputes.
Certification that no controversy exists, §8-26-38.
Employees, §8-26-3.

SPORTS—Cont'd
Agents—Cont'd
Athlete agent regulatory commission—Cont'd
Fees.
Setting by commission, §8-26-13.
Members, §8-26-3.
Compensation, §8-26-3.
Expenses, §8-26-3.
Reimbursement, §8-26-3.
Oath, §8-26-3.
Reappointment, §8-26-3.
Removal, §8-26-3.
Terms of office, §8-26-3.
Vacancies, §8-26-3.
Officers, §8-26-3.
Quorum, §8-26-3.
Records, §8-26-3.
Register.
Annual register, §8-26-3.
Registration.
Agents required to register with commission, §8-26-4.
Rules and regulations, §§8-26-3, 8-26-28.
Bonds, surety.
Certificate of deposit payable to commission or savings account assigned to commission in lieu of, §8-26-14.
Conditions, §8-26-15.
Damages not limited to amount of bond, §8-26-15.
Insurance.
Malpractice coverage in lieu of bond, §8-26-14.
Registration.
Renewal, §8-26-9.
Requirements, §8-26-14.
Suspension of registration.
Failure to maintain coverage, §8-26-16.
Certificate of convenience.
Duration, §8-26-21.
Eligibility, §8-26-21.
Renewal, §8-26-21.
Certificate of conveyance.
When issued, §8-26-20.
Citation of chapter, §8-26-1.
Conflicts of interest.
Disclosure of agent's interest in entity used in giving investment advice, §8-26-31.
Interest in entity directly involved in same sport.
Prohibited, §8-26-30.
Contracts.
Agent contract.
Defined, §8-26-2.
Amateur standing.
Required statement that amateur standing may be jeopardized, §8-26-23.
Contracts in violation of law.
Prohibited, §8-26-32.
Disputes.
Agreement to refer disputes to commission, §8-26-22.
Forms.
Approved form, §8-26-22.

SPORTS—Cont'd
Agents—Cont'd
Contracts—Cont'd
Player associations or organizations.
Defined, §8-26-2.
Professional sports services contracts.
Defined, §8-26-2.
Registration.
Required statement as to, §8-26-22.
Validity of certain provisions, §8-26-39.
Death.
Certificate of convenience.
Generally, §§8-26-20, 8-26-21.
Definitions, §8-26-2.
Disputes.
Appeals, §8-26-38.
Referral to commission, §8-26-38.
Effect of failure to comply with chapter, §8-26-40.
Employees of union or players association may not have interest in revenues, §8-26-34.
False information or promises concerning employment, §8-26-33.
Fees.
Limit on, §8-26-24.
Athlete fails to procure or be paid for employment, §8-26-35.
Registration, §§8-26-12, 8-26-13.
Filing of application, §§8-26-12, 8-26-13.
Schedule of fees, §8-26-24.
Incompetence of agent.
Certificates of convenience.
Generally, §§8-26-20, 8-26-21.
Inspections.
Books, records, etc., §8-26-27.
Offers of compensation to university employees for referrals.
Prohibited, §8-26-34.
Penalties.
Violations of provisions, §8-26-41.
Records, §8-26-26.
Inspection of books and records, §8-26-27.
Registration, §8-26-4.
Applicability of registration, §8-26-19.
Application, §8-26-5.
Contents, §8-26-5.
Disclosure of names and addresses of financially interested persons, §8-26-11.
Evaluation of applicants, §8-26-6.
Fee for filing, §§8-26-12, 8-26-13.
Principal place of business.
Verification, §8-26-6.
Renewal, §8-26-9.
Bond, §8-26-9.

SPORTS—Cont'd
  Agents—Cont'd
    Registration—Cont'd
      Application—Cont'd
        Renewal—Cont'd
          Disclosure of names
              and addresses of
              financially
              interested persons,
              §8-26-11.
          Fee, §8-26-9.
        Certificates of convenience,
            §§8-26-20, 8-26-21.
        Contents, §8-26-18.
        Duration, §8-26-9.
        Effect of failure to comply,
            §8-26-40.
        Fees, §§8-26-12, 8-26-13.
        Provisional registration,
            §8-26-10.
        Refusal.
          Appeals, §8-26-7.
          Determination of
              commission, §8-26-7.
          Grounds, §8-26-7.
          Hearing, §8-26-7.
          Notice, §8-26-7.
        Reinstatement, §8-26-8.
        Renewal.
          Applications, §8-26-9.
            Bond, §8-26-9.
            Fee, §8-26-9.
          Provisional registration,
              §8-26-10.
          Temporary registration,
              §8-26-10.
        Revocation, §8-26-8.
        Scope of registration,
            §8-26-19.
        Suspension, §8-26-8.
          Bonds, surety.
            Failure to maintain
                coverage, §8-26-16.
          Procedure, §8-26-8.
        Temporary registration,
            §8-26-10.
        Violations of provisions.
          Fines.
            Disposition, §8-26-17.
    Reports.
      Commission may prescribe,
          §8-26-27.
    Rules and regulations.
      Athlete agent regulatory
          commission, §8-26-28.
    Sale or transfer of agent's
        interest in profits,
        §8-26-29.
    Service of process.
      Departure from state by
          athlete agent with
          intent to defraud or
          avoid service, §8-26-37.
    Short title of chapter,
        §8-26-1.
    Title of chapter, §8-26-1.
    Trust fund.
      Deposit of money received
          on behalf of athlete,
          §8-26-25.
      Establishment required
          where agent is
          recipient of athlete's
          salary, §8-26-25.
  **Alabama high school
      athletic association.**
    Teachers' retirement system.
      Membership of certain
          employees, §16-25-7.

SPORTS—Cont'd
  Appeals.
    Agents.
      Disputes, §8-26-38.
      Registration.
        Refusal, §8-26-7.
  Baseball parks.
    Licenses, §40-12-59.
  Bonds, surety.
    Agents.
      Registration.
        Certificates of deposit
            payable to
            commission or
            savings account
            assigned to
            commission in lieu of
            bond, §8-26-14.
        Conditions of surety
            bond, §8-26-15.
        Damages.
          Not limited to amount
              of bond, §8-26-15.
        Insurance.
          Malpractice coverage
              in lieu of bond,
              §8-26-14.
        Renewal, §8-26-9.
        Surety bond required
            prior to issuance,
            §8-26-14.
          Amount, §8-26-14.
        Suspension.
          Failure to maintain
              coverage, §8-26-16.
        To whom bond payable,
            §8-26-15.
  Boxing and wrestling,
      §§41-9-90.1, 41-9-96.
  Bribery.
    Class A misdemeanor,
        §13A-11-141.
    Definitions, §13A-11-140.
    Elements of crime,
        §13A-11-141.
    Receiving a sports bribe,
        §13A-11-142.
  Conflicts of interest.
    Agents.
      Disclosure of interest in
          entity in giving
          investment advice
          required, §8-26-31.
      Interest in entity directly
          involved in same sport.
        Prohibited, §8-26-30.
  Contracts.
    Agents.
      Agent contracts.
        Defined, §8-26-2.
      Amateur standing.
        Required statement that
            amateur standing
            may be jeopardized,
            §8-26-23.
      Contracts in violation of
          law.
        Prohibited, §8-26-32.
      Disputes.
        Agreement to refer
            disputes to
            commission,
            §8-26-22.
      Forms.
        Approved form, §8-26-22.
      Professional sports services
          contracts.
        Defined, §8-26-2.
      Registration.
        Required statement as
            to, §8-26-22.

SPORTS—Cont'd
  Contracts—Cont'd
    Agents—Cont'd
      Validity of certain
          provisions, §8-26-39.
  Damages.
    Agents.
      Registration.
        Damages not limited to
            amount of bond,
            §8-26-15.
  Definitions.
    Agents, §8-26-2.
    Sports bribery, §13A-11-140.
  Fees.
    Agents.
      Changes in schedule,
          §8-26-24.
      Filing of schedule,
          §8-26-24.
      Limit on fees charged,
          §8-26-24.
        Athlete fails to procure
            or be paid for
            employment,
            §8-26-35.
      Registration, §§8-26-12,
          8-26-13.
        Application.
          Filing fees, §§8-26-12,
              8-26-13.
        Renewal, §8-26-9.
  Gambling.
    Evidence.
      Newspaper reports of
          sporting events,
          §13A-12-28.
    General provisions.
      See GAMBLING.
  Hall of fame.
    Sports hall of fame board.
      General provisions,
          §§41-9-450 to 41-9-454.
      Motor sports hall of fame
          commission,
          §§41-9-470 to 41-9-478.
        See MOTOR SPORTS
            HALL OF FAME
            COMMISSION.
  Hearings.
    Agents.
      Registration.
        Refusal, §8-26-7.
  **Influencing outcome of
      sports contest,**
      §13A-11-143.
  Insurance.
    Agents.
      Registration.
        Malpractice coverage in
            lieu of bond,
            §8-26-14.
  Judgments.
    Agents.
      Registration.
        Refusal.
          Effective date of orders
              and judgments,
              §8-26-7.
  Licenses.
    Athletic fields, §40-12-147.
    Municipal corporations.
      Licensing of athletic
          games, §11-51-104.
  **Motor sports hall of fame
      commission,** §§41-9-470 to
      41-9-478.
    See MOTOR SPORTS HALL
        OF FAME
        COMMISSION.

SPORTS—Cont'd
Municipal corporations.
Licensing of athletic games, §11-51-104.
Public athletic boards, §§11-59-1 to 11-59-17.
See MUNICIPAL CORPORATIONS.
Notice.
Agents.
Registration.
Refusal, §8-26-7.
Oaths.
Agents.
Athlete agent regulatory commission.
Members, §8-26-3.
Penalties.
Violations of chapter, §8-26-41.
Public athletic boards,
§§11-59-1 to 11-59-17.
See MUNICIPAL CORPORATIONS.
Publications.
Agents.
Publication of false, fraudulent or misleading information prohibited, §8-26-33.
Records.
Agents.
Athlete agent regulatory commission, §8-26-3.
Inspection of books and records, §8-26-27.
Records to be kept by agent, §8-26-26.
Registration.
Agents, §§8-26-4 to 8-26-21.
See within this heading, "Agents."
Rules and regulations.
Agents.
Athlete agent regulatory commission, §§8-26-3, 8-26-28.
Sales tax.
Gross proceeds from sales of admissions.
Exemptions, §40-23-4.
Tax levied on gross receipts, §40-23-2.
Service of process.
Method where agent departs state with intent to defraud or avoid service, §8-26-37.
State products mart and coliseum authority,
§§41-10-80 to 41-10-109.
See PRODUCTS MARTS.
Tampering with sports contest, §13A-11-143.
Taxation.
Stadiums.
Exemption, §40-9-1.
Unemployment compensation.
Participation in professional sports.
Disqualifications for benefits, §25-4-78.

SPORTS HALL OF FAME BOARD, §§41-9-450 to 41-9-454.
Annual function, §41-9-452.
Appointment of members, §41-9-450.

SPORTS HALL OF FAME BOARD—Cont'd
Appropriations.
Expenditure, §41-9-454.
Busts.
Display of busts in Jefferson County Civic Center, §41-9-451.
Bylaws.
Adoption, §41-9-452.
Committees.
Appointment, §41-9-452.
Compensation of members, §41-9-450.
Composition, §41-9-450.
Contributions.
Solicitation and acceptance, §41-9-453.
Creation, §41-9-450.
Donations.
Solicitation and acceptance, §41-9-453.
Executive secretary or director, §41-9-451.
Exemption from taxation, §41-9-453.
Exhibits.
Display in Jefferson county civic center, §41-9-451.
Expenditures, §41-9-454.
Expenses of members, §41-9-450.
Funds.
Expenditure, §41-9-454.
Gifts.
Solicitation and acceptance, §41-9-453.
Jefferson County Civic Center.
Display of busts, exhibits, etc., in, §41-9-451.
Meetings, §41-9-450.
Motor sports hall of fame commission, §§41-9-470 to 41-9-478.
See MOTOR SPORTS HALL OF FAME COMMISSION.
Number of members, §41-9-450.
Officers, §41-9-450.
Offices, §41-9-451.
Polls.
Conduct of polls, §41-9-452.
Purpose of board, §41-9-452.
Quarters, §41-9-451.
Quorum, §41-9-450.
Representatives.
Appointment, §41-9-452.
Rules and regulations.
Adoption, §41-9-452.
Staff, §41-9-451.
Surveys.
Conduct of surveys, §41-9-452.
Taxation.
Exemption, §41-9-453.
Terms of members, §41-9-450.

SPOTLIGHTING.
General provisions, §32-5-17.

SPRINGHILL COLLEGE.
Marine environmental sciences consortium, §§16-45-1 to 16-45-5.

SPRINKLER SYSTEMS.
Fire protection sprinkler systems, §§34-33-1 to 34-33-12.
See FIRES AND FIRE PREVENTION.

SQUARE DANCE.
State dance, §1-2-18.

STABLES.
Coal.
Mine safety.
Underground stables, §25-9-153.
Livery stables.
Liens of keepers, §§35-11-190, 35-11-191.

STADIUMS.
Bond issues.
Counties.
Public improvement bonds, §§11-81-140 to 11-81-150.
See COUNTIES.
Municipal corporations.
Public improvement bonds, §§11-81-110 to 11-81-123.
See MUNICIPAL CORPORATIONS.
Public athletic boards,
§§11-59-1 to 11-59-17.
See MUNICIPAL CORPORATIONS.

STALLIONS.
Liens.
Owners of stallions, §§35-11-330, 35-11-331.

STAMPS.
Alcoholic beverages.
See ALCOHOLIC BEVERAGES.
Counties.
Claims against counties for stamps for certain officers, §11-12-14.
Gambling.
Federal wagering occupational stamp tax, §§13A-12-90 to 13A-12-92.
Recordation.
Time stamp, §35-4-58.
Trading stamps.
Licenses, §40-12-170.

STARLINGS.
Hunting.
Unprotected birds, §9-11-233.

STATE.
Actions.
Actions by the state.
Public moneys, funds or property.
Recovery, §6-5-4.
Right to commence.
Foreign jurisdictions, §6-5-2.
Generally, §6-5-1.
Successor of public officer, §6-5-3.
Claims against state, §§41-9-60 to 41-9-74.
See CLAIMS AGAINST STATE.
Suits against state, Const. U. S., Amendment XI.
Attorney general may be required to defend, Const. Ala., amd. 111.
Aged persons.
See AGED PERSONS.
Annexation.
Foreign territory, Const. Ala., art. IV, §90.

STATE—Cont'd

Appeals.
Costs for and against state, ARAP, Rule 35 (b).
Criminal cases.
Statute under which prosecution preferred held unconstitutional, §12-22-91.

Auditor.
General provisions.
See STATE AUDITOR.

Authority.
Maintenance and defense of state authority, §41-1-2.

Aviation.
Sovereignty over airspace, §4-2-70.

Bird, §1-2-7.

Blind persons.
Employment by state, §21-7-8.

Bond issues.
When bonds of state payable, §41-1-4.

Boundaries of state, §§41-2-1 to 41-2-4; Const. Ala., art. II, §37.

Bridges.
See BRIDGES.

Camellia.
State flower, §1-2-11.

Capitol.
See CAPITOL.

Cession of land to United States, §§42-3-1 to 42-3-3.

Civil defense.
Emergency management agency, §31-9-4.
Torts.
Immunity of state from liability for, §31-9-16.

Claims against state, §§41-9-60 to 41-9-74.
See CLAIMS AGAINST STATE.

Coat of arms.
Description, §1-2-1.
Heraldic terms, §1-2-2.
Use, §1-2-3.

Compacts.
Compacts between the states or with foreign powers, Const. U. S., Art. I, §10.

Comptroller.
See COMPTROLLER.

Condemnation.
Power of eminent domain.
See EMINENT DOMAIN.

Constitution of Alabama.
Boundaries.
Defined, Const. Ala., art. II, §37.
State not to be made defendant, Const. Ala., art. I, §14.
Treason against the state, Const. Ala., art. I, §18.

Constitution of the United States.
Admission of new states, Const. U. S., Art. IV, §3.
Bill of attainder, Const. U. S., Art. I, §10.
Bills of credit, Const. U. S., Art. I, §10.
Commerce, Const. U. S., Art. I, §§8, 9.
Compacts between the states or with foreign powers, Const. U. S., Art. I, §10.

STATE—Cont'd

Constitution of the United States—Cont'd
Contracts.
Impairing obligations of contracts, Const. U. S., Art. I, §10.
Controversies between citizens of different states, Const. U. S., Art. III, §2.
Controversies between states, Const. U. S., Art. III, §2.
Duties and imposts, Const. U. S., Art. I, §10.
Equal suffrage in senate, Const. U. S., Art. V.
Exports, Const. U. S., Art. I, §§9, 10.
Ex post facto laws, Const. U. S., Art. I, §10.
Full faith and credit clause, Const. U. S., Art. IV, §1.
Gold and silver coin tender in payment of debts, Const. U. S., Art. I, §10.
Impairing obligations of contracts, Const. U. S., Art. I, §10.
Imports and exports, Const. U. S., Art. I, §10.
Invasion.
Protection against, Const. U. S., Art. IV, §4.
Legal tender, Const. U. S., Art. I, §10.
Letters of marque or reprisal, Const. U. S., Art. I, §10.
Limitations on powers of the state, Const. U. S., Art. I, §10.
Money.
Coining money, Const. U. S., Art. I, §10.
New states, Const. U. S., Art. IV, §3.
Powers, Const. U. S., Art. I, §10.
Reserved to state, Const. U. S., Amendment X.
Protection and aid of states, Const. U. S., Art. IV, §4.
Republican form of government guaranteed, Const. U. S., Art. IV, §4.
Reservation of powers to state, Const. U. S., Amendment X.
Right to coin money, Const. U. S., Art. I, §10.
Suits against, Const. U. S., Amendment XI.
Tender in payment of debts, Const. U. S., Art. I, §10.
Tonnage, Const. U. S., Art. I, §10.
Treaties, Const. U. S., Art. I, §10.
Troops or ships of war in time of peace, Const. U. S., Art. I, §10.
War, Const. U. S., Art. I, §10.

Contracts.
Impairing obligations of contracts, Const. U. S., Art. I, §10.
Public contracts, §§41-16-1 to 41-16-125.
See CONTRACTS.

STATE—Cont'd

Coosa Valley development authority.
Cooperation with state, §33-16-2.

Corporations.
Obligations and liabilities of corporations, etc., held or owned by state, Const. Ala., art. IV, §100.
State interest in corporate enterprises prohibited, Const. Ala., art. IV, §93; amd. 1.
Exceptions, Const. Ala., amds. 12, 58.

Corrections.
Institution finance authority.
Leasing of facilities to state, §14-2-29.

Counterclaim against state, ARCP, Rule 13 (d).

Counties.
Contracts with state government, §11-1-10.

Courts.
State not to be made defendant, Const. Ala., art. I, §14.

Criminal law and procedure.
Obstructing governmental operations.
Definitions, §13A-10-1.
Elements of crime, §13A-10-2.

Customs.
Exportations from any state.
Duties not to be laid on, Const. U. S., Art. I, §9.
State may not impose without consent of congress, Const. U. S., Art. I, §10.

Damages, §§41-9-60 to 41-9-74.
See CLAIMS AGAINST STATE.

Debt.
Constitution of Alabama.
Imprisonment for debts, Const. Ala., art. I, §20.

Development.
State development office, §§41-9-201 to 41-9-210.
See DEVELOPMENT.

Domestic products.
Use for public works, etc., §39-3-1.

Downtown redevelopment authorities.
Freedom from state supervision and control, §11-54A-18.

Ejectment.
Recovery of lands by or in name of state for educational or governmental institutions, §6-6-281.

Eminent domain.
See EMINENT DOMAIN.

Employees.
See PUBLIC OFFICERS AND EMPLOYEES.

Engineers.
Public works.
Supervision and preparation by professional engineers, §34-11-10.

STATE—Cont'd
Environmental improvement authorities.
Aid and cooperation of state, §9-6-13.
Escheats.
See ESCHEATS.
Fees.
Disposition of departmental and institutional fees, receipts, etc., §41-4-92.
Fires and fire prevention.
Volunteer fire departments.
Donations.
Authority of state, §9-3-18.
Fiscal year, §1-3-4.
Fish.
State fresh water fish, §1-2-9.
State saltwater fish, §1-2-8.
Flags, §§1-2-5, 1-2-6.
Flower, §1-2-11.
Forests and forestry.
Sale of timber or forest products.
Disposition of revenues, §2-30-22.
State forester, §§9-3-5, 9-3-6, 9-3-8.
State forestry commission, §§9-3-1 to 9-3-17.
See FORESTS AND FORESTRY.
State forests.
See FORESTS AND FORESTRY.
Game bird.
Designation and name, §1-2-17.
Governor.
See GOVERNOR.
Great seal of state, §1-2-4.
Handicapped persons.
Employment by state, §21-7-8.
Harbors and ports.
See HARBORS AND PORTS.
Health care authorities.
Defined, §22-21-311.
Securities not obligation of state, §22-21-325.
Hematite.
Official mineral of state, §1-2-13.
Historical research.
Contracts between counties or cities and historical corporations, etc., authorized, §16-42-3.
Counties and cities authorized to undertake research into history of state, §16-42-1.
Funds.
Use of county and municipal funds, §16-42-2.
History of state.
See HISTORY AND ARCHIVES.
Holidays, §1-3-8.
Horse, §1-2-10.
House of representatives.
See LEGISLATURE.
Immunity, Const. Ala., art. I, §14.
Industrial development corporations.
Credit of state not to be pledged, §10-4-141.

STATE—Cont'd
Jurisdiction of state, §41-1-1.
Maintenance and defense, §41-1-2.
Largemouth bass.
State fresh water fish, §1-2-9.
Legislature.
See LEGISLATURE.
Limitation of actions.
See LIMITATION OF ACTIONS.
Livestock inspectors, §§2-4-2, 2-4-3.
Marble.
Official rock of state, §1-2-14.
Military affairs.
Federal service.
Payment of expenses by state upon call into federal service, §31-2-44.
Persons exempted from military service, §31-2-6.
Proceedings by state when member of armed forces unable to account for property or money, §31-2-34.
Mineral.
Official mineral, §1-2-13.
Motor sports hall of fame commission.
Bonds not obligation of state, §41-9-475.
Motor vehicle carriers.
Vehicles owned and operated by state.
Exemptions, §37-3-4.
Motor vehicles.
State-owned motor vehicles, §§41-17-1 to 41-17-9.
See MOTOR VEHICLES.
Municipal corporations.
Streets.
Payment of costs of streets constructed, improved, etc., by county, state or federal government, §§11-49-60 to 11-49-63.
Nobility, titles of.
Titles of nobility prohibited, Const. U. S., Art. I, §§9, 10.
Obstructing governmental operations.
Class A misdemeanor, §13A-10-2.
Definitions, §13A-10-1.
Elements of crime, §13A-10-2.
Officers.
See PUBLIC OFFICERS AND EMPLOYEES.
Offices.
Director of finance.
Duty as to offices in Capitol and other locations, §41-4-34.
Official coat of arms, §§1-2-1 to 1-2-3.
Oil and gas.
Leases by state, §§9-17-60 to 9-17-69.
See OIL AND GAS.
Poet laureate, §1-2-15.
Police.
See STATE POLICE.
Prisons.
See PRISONS AND PRISONERS.

STATE—Cont'd
Private enterprise.
State interest in private enterprise prohibited, Const. Ala., art. IV, §93; amd. 1.
Exceptions, Const. Ala., amds. 12, 58.
Property.
Buildings.
Rent charged for use, §41-4-17.
Cession of land to United States, §§42-3-1 to 42-3-3.
Prisons and prisoners.
Sale and purchase of state lands for convict labor, §§14-3-2 to 14-3-4.
Property inventory control division.
General provisions, §§36-16-7 to 36-16-11.
Public buildings.
See PUBLIC BUILDINGS.
Public lands.
See PUBLIC LANDS.
Public officers and employees.
See PUBLIC OFFICERS AND EMPLOYEES.
Publicity.
Bureau of tourism and travel, §§41-7-1 to 41-7-5.
Public officers and employees.
See PUBLIC OFFICERS AND EMPLOYEES.
Public service commission.
Appeals.
State may appeal, §37-1-133.
Public utilities.
Securities.
Guarantee or obligation on part of state not to be implied, §37-4-12.
Public works.
See PUBLIC WORKS.
Quieting title.
In personam proceedings.
Maintenance of action by state, §6-6-546.
Racking horse.
State horse, §1-2-10.
Real property.
Actions for recovery of certain lands.
No limitation of time, §6-2-31.
Cession of land to United States, §§42-3-1 to 42-3-3.
Republican form of government.
Guaranteed to states, Const. U. S., Art. IV, §4.
Rock.
Official rock of state, §1-2-14.
Sales tax.
Exemptions.
Sales of tangible personal property to the state, §40-23-4.
Seal.
Great seal of state, §1-2-4.
Seat of government.
Legislation to change, Const. Ala., art. IV, §78.

STATE—Cont'd
  Secretary of state.
    See SECRETARY OF
      STATE.
  Senate.
    See LEGISLATURE.
  Service of process.
    How state served, ARCP,
      Rule 4 (c).
  Soil and water conservation.
    Districts.
      Cooperation of state
        agencies, §9-8-30.
  Southern pine.
    State tree, §1-2-12.
  Sovereign immunity, Const.
    Ala., art. I, §14.
  Sovereignty, §41-1-1.
    Airspace, §4-2-70.
  Streets.
    Municipal corporations.
      Payment of costs of streets
        constructed, improved,
        etc., by county, state
        or federal government,
        §§11-49-60 to 11-49-63.
  Tarpons.
    State saltwater fish, §1-2-8.
  Telephones.
    Securities of telephone
      companies.
      Guarantee or obligation on
        part of state not to be
        implied, §37-2-176.
  Tombigbee Valley
    development authority.
    Contracts.
      Power to enter into
        contracts with state,
        §33-17-8.
    Cooperation with state,
      §33-17-2.
  Torts.
    Claims against state,
      §§41-9-60 to 41-9-74.
    See CLAIMS AGAINST
      STATE.
  Toxicologist.
    General provisions.
      See STATE
        TOXICOLOGIST.
  Transportation companies.
    Actions.
      Rights of action by state
        not waived, §37-2-44.
    Free transportation or
      reduced rates for state of
      Alabama, §37-2-40.
  Treason against the state,
    Const. Ala., art. I, §18.
  Treasurer.
    General provisions.
      See STATE TREASURER.
  Tree, §1-2-12.
  Turkey.
    State game bird, §1-2-17.
  Use tax.
    Exemptions.
      Property stored, used or
        consumed by state,
        §40-23-62.
  Veterans.
    Bonus for Southeast Asian
      war prisoners.
      Taxation by state.
        Bonus not subject to,
          §31-7-2.

STATE—Cont'd
  Veterans—Cont'd
    Educational benefits.
      Benefits for wives or
        widows and
        dependents in addition
        to other state benefits,
        §31-6-9.
    State service commissioner.
      Representation of state
        before federal agencies,
        §31-5-6.
  Visitors.
    Protection of certain state
      officers and visitors,
      §§36-33-1 to 36-33-4.
  Warrants for the payment of
    money.
    See FINANCE.
  Water conservation and
    irrigation.
    Corporations.
      Bond issues.
        See WATER
          CONSERVATION
          AND IRRIGATION.
  Yellowhammer.
    State bird, §1-2-7.

STATE APIARISTS.
  See HONEYBEES AND
    APIARIES.

STATE AUDITOR, §§36-16-1 to
  36-16-11.
  Assistants, §36-16-3.
  Bond, §36-16-4.
  Chief clerk.
    Employment, §36-16-3.
    Official acts deemed those of
      auditor, §36-16-6.
  Claims.
    Proof of correctness.
      Authority to require,
        §36-16-2.
  Clerical help, §36-16-3.
  Compensation, Const. Ala.,
    art. V, §118.
  Constitution of Alabama.
    Compensation, Const. Ala.,
      art. V, §118.
    Duties, Const. Ala., art. V,
      §137; amd. 111.
    Executive department.
      Member of department,
        Const. Ala., art. V,
        §112.
    Fees.
      Restrictions on, Const.
        Ala., art. V, §137.
    Impeachment, Const. Ala.,
      art. VII, §173.
    Mental unsoundness, Const.
      Ala., art. V, §136.
    Qualifications, Const. Ala.,
      art. V, §132.
    Reports.
      Annual report, Const. Ala.,
        art. V, §137.
    Residency requirements,
      Const. Ala., art. V, §118.
    Succession.
      Ineligible to succeed self,
        Const. Ala., art. V,
        §116.
      One additional term,
        Const. Ala., amd. 282.
    Term of office, Const. Ala.,
      art. V, §116; amd. 282.
    Vacancy in office, Const.
      Ala., art. V, §136.

STATE AUDITOR—Cont'd
  Duties, §36-16-1; Const. Ala.,
    art. V, §137.
  Election.
    See ELECTIONS.
  Executive department.
    Member of department,
      Const. Ala., art. V, §112.
  Fees, §36-16-5.
    Restrictions on, Const. Ala.,
      art. V, §137; amd. 111.
  Impeachment, Const. Ala.,
    art. VII, §173.
    General provisions.
      See IMPEACHMENT.
  Inventories.
    Property inventory control
      division, §§36-16-7 to
      36-16-11.
  Mental unsoundness, Const.
    Ala., art. V, §136.
  Oath of office.
    General provisions.
      See PUBLIC OFFICERS
        AND EMPLOYEES.
  Printing.
    Public printing and binding.
      Approval of contract and
        bond, §41-4-136.
  Property inventory control
    division, §§36-16-7 to
    36-16-11.
    Chief.
      Authority, §36-16-10.
      Neglect of duty, §36-16-10.
    Created, §36-16-7.
    Inventories, §36-16-8.
    Officers.
      Neglect of duty, §36-16-10.
    Property exempt from
      control, §36-16-11.
    Property managers, §36-16-8.
    State personal property.
      Duty of examiners of
        public accounts,
        §36-16-9.
    Establishment of control,
      §36-16-8.
  Public officers generally.
    See PUBLIC OFFICERS
      AND EMPLOYEES.
  Qualifications, Const. Ala.,
    art. V, §132.
  Reports.
    Annual report, Const. Ala.,
      art. V, §137.
  Residency requirements,
    Const. Ala., art. V, §118.
  Succession, Const. Ala., art.
    V, §116; amd. 282.
  Term of office, Const. Ala.,
    art. V, §116; amd. 282.
  Vacancy in office, Const.
    Ala., art. V, §136.

STATE BLACK ARCHIVES,
  RESEARCH CENTER
  AND MUSEUM, §§16-49-50
  to 16-49-55.
  See HISTORY AND
    ARCHIVES.

STATE BOARD OF
  EDUCATION, §§16-3-1 to
  16-3-37.
  See EDUCATION.

STATE BOARD OF HEALTH.
  General provisions, §§22-2-1
    to 22-2-3.

STATE CAPITOL.
  Constitution of Alabama.
    Legislation to change seat of
      government of state,
      Const. Ala., art. IV, §78.
    Meeting place of legislature,
      Const. Ala., amd. 427.
  General provisions.
    See CAPITOL.
  Montgomery.
    See MONTGOMERY, CITY
      OF.

**STATE CHAMPIONSHIP
  HORSE SHOW.**
  Designation, §1-2-22.

STATE COMPTROLLER.
  See COMPTROLLER.

STATE DANCE.
  Square dance, §1-2-18.

**STATE DEPARTMENTS AND
  AGENCIES.**
  Accounts and accounting.
    Department of examiners of
      public accounts.
    General provisions,
      §§41-5-1 to 41-5-24.
      See ACCOUNTS AND
        ACCOUNTING.
  **Administrative procedure
    act,** §§41-22-1 to 41-22-27.
    See ADMINISTRATIVE
      PROCEDURE ACT.
  Agriculture.
    Department of agriculture
      and industries.
      See AGRICULTURE.
  **Alabama administrative
    monthly.**
    Cost to agencies for use of
      Alabama administrative
      monthly, §41-22-7.
  Archives and history.
    Department of archives and
      history, §§41-6-1 to
      41-6-53.
      See HISTORY AND
        ARCHIVES.
  **Banks and financial
    institutions.**
    Deposit of public funds.
      Pledge of assets of banks
        as security for
        deposits, §5-5A-28.
    State banking departments.
      See BANKS AND
        FINANCIAL
        INSTITUTIONS.
  **Bear Creek development
    authority.**
    Cooperation of state agencies,
      §33-15-17.
  Boards and commissions,
    §§41-9-20 to 41-9-873.
    See BOARDS AND
      COMMISSIONS.
  Budgets.
    Budget management act,
      §§41-19-1 to 41-19-12.
    See BUDGETS.
  **Conservation and natural
    resources department,**
    §§9-2-1 to 9-2-130.
    See CONSERVATION AND
      NATURAL
      RESOURCES.
  Continuation. See within this
    heading, "Sunset law."

**STATE DEPARTMENTS AND
  AGENCIES**—Cont'd
  Contracts.
    Public contracts.
      See CONTRACTS.
    Public improvement
      contracts.
      See PUBLIC WORKS.
  Conveyances.
    See CONVEYANCES.
  **Coosa Valley development
    authority.**
    Cooperation with, §33-16-2.
    Delegation of duties,
      §33-16-10.
  Corrections.
    Department of corrections,
      §§14-1-1.1, 14-1-1.2.
  Court management.
    Department of court
      management.
      See COURTS.
  Criminal law and procedure.
    Executive or secret sessions
      of certain boards
      prohibited, §13A-14-2.
    Obstructing governmental
      operations, §§13A-10-1,
      13A-10-2.
  **Department of agriculture
    and industries.**
    See AGRICULTURE.
  **Department of archives and
    history,** §§41-6-1 to
    41-6-53.
    See HISTORY AND
      ARCHIVES.
  **Department of conservation
    and natural resources,**
    §§9-2-1 to 9-2-130.
    See CONSERVATION AND
      NATURAL
      RESOURCES.
  Department of corrections,
    §§14-1-1.1, 14-1-1.2.
  **Department of economic and
    community affairs,**
    §§41-23-1 to 41-23-7.
    See ECONOMIC AND
      COMMUNITY
      AFFAIRS.
  Department of education,
    §§16-2-1 to 16-2-8.
    See EDUCATION.
  **Department of examiners of
    public accounts,** §§41-5-1
    to 41-5-24.
    See ACCOUNTS AND
      ACCOUNTING.
  Department of finance,
    §§41-4-1 to 41-4-263.
    See FINANCE.
  **Department of human
    resources.**
    See WELFARE.
  **Department of industrial
    relations,** §§25-2-1 to
    25-2-26.
    See LABOR.
  Department of insurance.
    See INSURANCE.
  Department of labor,
    §§25-3-1 to 25-3-5.
  **Department of mental health
    and mental retardation,**
    §§22-50-2, 22-50-3.
  Department of public safety.
    See MOTOR VEHICLES.
  Department of revenue.
    See TAXATION.

**STATE DEPARTMENTS AND
  AGENCIES**—Cont'd
  **Department of veterans'
    affairs.**
    See VETERANS.
  **Department of youth
    services,** §§44-1-20 to
    44-1-40.
    See YOUTH SERVICES.
  Development.
    State development office.
      See DEVELOPMENT.
  **District court administrative
    agency.**
    See DISTRICT COURTS.
  Docks.
    State docks department.
      See HARBORS AND
        PORTS.
  **Economic and community
    affairs.**
    Department.
      See ECONOMIC AND
        COMMUNITY
        AFFAIRS.
  Education.
    Department of education,
      §§16-2-1 to 16-2-8.
    See EDUCATION.
  **Elk River development
    agency,** §§33-12-1 to
    33-12-10.
    See ELK RIVER
      DEVELOPMENT
      AGENCY.
  Energy department.
    See ENERGY
      MANAGEMENT AND
      CONSERVATION.
  **Environmental management
    department.**
    See ENVIRONMENTAL
      MANAGEMENT.
  Evidence.
    Authentication of paper or
      documents by
      department head,
      §12-21-72.
  **Examiners of public
    accounts.**
    Department of examiners of
      public accounts, §§41-5-1
      to 41-5-24.
    See ACCOUNTS AND
      ACCOUNTING.
  Fees.
    Disposition of fees, §41-4-92.
  Finance.
    Department of finance,
      §§41-4-1 to 41-4-263.
    See FINANCE.
  Health.
    State health department.
      See HEALTH.
  Highways.
    Highway department,
      §§23-1-20 to 23-1-63.
    See HIGHWAYS.
    National highway safety act
      of 1966.
      Participation by all
        departments in
        benefits, §32-4-5.
  History.
    Department of archives and
      history, §§41-6-1 to
      41-6-53.
    See HISTORY AND
      ARCHIVES.

STATE DEPARTMENTS AND
AGENCIES—Cont'd
Holidays.
When state offices may be
open on holidays, §1-3-8.
Honorariums.
Competitive bidding laws.
Exemption of certain
departments and
agencies whose
principal business is
honorariums,
§41-16-21.2.
Human resources.
Department of human
resources.
See WELFARE.
Industrial relations.
Department of industrial
relations, §§25-2-1 to
25-2-26.
See LABOR.
Insurance.
Department of insurance.
See INSURANCE.
Interest.
Maximum rates of interest.
Exemptions, §8-8-7.
Inventories.
Nonconsumable personal
property, §41-1-6.
Labor.
Department of labor,
§§25-3-1 to 25-3-5.
Law enforcement planning
agency, §§41-8A-1 to
41-8A-13.
See LAW ENFORCEMENT
PLANNING AGENCY.
Leases.
Conveyances by governor or
state agency or
institution.
See CONVEYANCES.
Lease-sale contracts.
Authorized for
procurement of
equipment, §41-4-115.
Legislative reference service.
See LEGISLATURE.
Libraries.
Interstate library compact.
General provisions.
See LIBRARIES.
Library boards.
See LIBRARIES.
Public library service.
See LIBRARIES.
State library agency.
See LIBRARIES.
Supreme court library.
See SUPREME COURT.
Materials.
Procedure for obtaining,
§41-4-113.
Mental health.
Department of mental health
and mental retardation,
§§22-50-2, 22-50-3.
Municipal court
administrative agency.
See MUNICIPAL COURTS.
Obstructing governmental
operations, §§13A-10-1,
13A-10-2.
Personal property.
Inventory, §41-1-6.
Personnel department.
General provisions.
See PUBLIC OFFICERS
AND EMPLOYEES.

STATE DEPARTMENTS AND
AGENCIES—Cont'd
Publicity.
Bureau of tourism and
travel, §§41-7-1 to
41-7-5.
Public safety.
Department of public safety.
See MOTOR VEHICLES.
Public utilities.
Purchase by governmental
agencies.
See PUBLIC UTILITIES.
Reports.
Printing, §41-4-141.
Time for making, §41-4-141.
Revenue.
Department of revenue.
See TAXATION.
Safety.
Department of public safety.
See MOTOR VEHICLES.
Service of process.
How department or agency
served, ARCP, Rule 4 (c).
Southeast interstate low-
level radioactive waste
management compact.
Cooperation with
commission, §22-32-7.
State banking department.
See BANKS AND
FINANCIAL
INSTITUTIONS.
State development office.
See DEVELOPMENT.
State docks department.
See HARBORS AND PORTS.
State employees' retirement
system.
See PUBLIC OFFICERS
AND EMPLOYEES.
Sunset law, §§41-20-1 to
41-20-16.
Actions.
Claims or rights against
agency.
Effect of termination of
agency, §41-20-14.
Bills.
Continuing, reestablishing
or terminating
agencies.
Requirements as to bills,
§41-20-11.
Budgets.
Governor.
Zero-based review and
evaluation.
Utilization of
principles,
§41-20-15.
Citation of chapter, §41-20-1.
Construction of chapter,
§41-20-16.
Definitions, §41-20-2.
Duration of period for
cessation of affairs,
§41-20-12.
Funds.
Reversion to state of
unexpended funds,
§41-20-12.
Governor.
Review and evaluation of
agencies.
Zero-based review and
evaluation.
Use by governor in
preparation of
budget, §41-20-15.

STATE DEPARTMENTS AND
AGENCIES—Cont'd
Sunset law—Cont'd
Municipal electric authority.
Exemption, §11-50A-28.
Personnel.
Abolition of positions,
§41-20-12.
Reports.
Review and evaluation of
agencies.
Select joint committee,
§41-20-4.
Review and evaluation of
agencies.
Burden of proof.
Establishment of public
need for
continuation,
§41-20-6.
Commencement, §41-20-5.
Conclusions, §41-20-5.
Department of examiners
of public accounts.
Furnishing of
information,
§41-20-9.
Establishment of public
need for continuation.
Burden of proof,
§41-20-6.
Factors to be considered
in determining,
§41-20-7.
Hearings, §41-20-6.
Information to be provided
by agencies, §41-20-6.
Legislature.
Debate upon
recommendations,
§41-20-10.
Legislative fiscal office.
Furnishing of
information,
§41-20-9.
Legislative reference
service.
Furnishing of
information,
§41-20-9.
Voting upon
recommendations,
§41-20-10.
Select joint committee.
Chairman, §41-20-4.
Compensation of
members, §41-20-4.
Composition, §41-20-4.
Creation, §41-20-4.
Duties, §41-20-4.
Selection of members,
§41-20-4.
Voting by legislature,
§41-20-4.
Zero-based review and
evaluation, §41-20-8.
Utilization by governor
in preparation of
budget, §41-20-15.
Termination of certain
agencies.
Procedure.
Agencies not designated,
§41-20-3.
Requirements, §41-20-3.
Specifications of dates,
§41-20-3.
Title of chapter, §41-20-1.

STATE DEPARTMENTS AND
AGENCIES—Cont'd
Sunshine law.
Executive or secret sessions
of certain boards
prohibited, §13A-14-2.
Supplies.
Procedures for obtaining,
§41-4-113.
Termination. See within this
heading, "Sunset law."
Tombigbee Valley
development authority.
Contracts.
Power to enter into
contracts, §33-17-8.
Cooperation, §33-17-2.
Delegation of duties of
authority to state
departments and
agencies, §33-17-10.
Tourists.
Bureau of tourism and
travel, §§41-7-1 to
41-7-5.
Veterans' affairs.
See VETERANS.
Water conservation and
irrigation agency.
See WATER
CONSERVATION AND
IRRIGATION.
Welfare.
Department of human
resources.
See WELFARE.
Youth services.
Department of youth
services, §§44-1-20 to
44-1-40.
See YOUTH SERVICES.

STATE EMPLOYEES'
RETIREMENT SYSTEM,
§§36-27-1 to 36-27-86.
See PUBLIC OFFICERS AND
EMPLOYEES.

STATE FAIR.
Alabama state fair and
exhibit association.
Exemption from licenses and
taxes, §40-9-15.

STATE FIRE COLLEGE.
Board of trustees.
Endowment funds.
Investment, §16-13-2.
Police.
General provisions,
§§16-22-1, 16-22-2.

STATE FIRE MARSHAL,
§§36-19-1 to 36-19-29.
See FIRES AND FIRE
PREVENTION.

STATE FORESTS.
See FORESTS AND
FORESTRY.

STATE FOSSIL.
"Species basilosaurus
cetoides" designated as
state fossil, §1-2-20.

STATE FUNDS.
See FINANCE.

STATE GEOLOGIST, §§9-4-1 to
9-4-10.
See GEOLOGICAL SURVEY.

STATE GUARD.
See MILITARY AFFAIRS.

STATE HEALTH PLANNING
AND DEVELOPMENT.
Coordinating council. See
within this heading,
"Statewide health
coordinating council."
Health systems agencies.
Generally, §22-4-9.
State board of health.
Cooperation of officers,
agencies, etc., of state
with board, §22-4-10.
Statewide health
coordinating council.
Compensation of members,
§22-4-7.
Consultants.
Appointment, §22-4-7.
Meetings, §22-4-7.
State officers, agencies, etc.
Cooperation with council,
§22-4-10.
Task forces.
Appointment, §22-4-7.
Compensation of members,
§22-4-7.
Vacancies, §22-4-7.

STATE HIGHWAY PATROL,
§§32-2-20 to 32-2-26.
See MOTOR VEHICLES.

STATE HOUSE.
Constitution of Alabama,
Const. Ala., amd. 427.

STATE INSECT.
Designation, §1-2-25.

STATE LANDS.
See PUBLIC LANDS.

STATE LIQUOR STORES.
See ALCOHOLIC
BEVERAGES.

STATE MILITIA.
See MILITARY AFFAIRS.

STATE NUT.
Pecan designated as state
nut, §1-2-19.

STATE PARKS.
Acquisition of lands.
Bond issue to acquire, Const.
Ala., amd. 267.
Commissioner of
conservation and natural
resources.
Powers and duties, §9-2-9.
Counties.
Grants of lands to state
park system, §9-14-6.
Department of conservation
and natural resources.
Powers generally, §9-2-3.
Municipal corporations.
Grants of lands to state
park system, §9-14-6.
Appropriations.
Counties and municipalities.
Improvement, operation,
etc., of state park
system, §9-14-6.
Arrest.
Director of division of parks.
Powers of arrest, §9-2-9.
Police.
Deputy police officers,
§9-2-9.

STATE PARKS—Cont'd
Attorney general.
Concessions within state
park areas.
Contracts for maintenance
and operation.
Approval, §9-14-28.
Bond issues.
Acquisition, development,
etc., of parks and park
facilities, Const. Ala.,
amd. 267.
Bonds, surety.
Concessions within state
park areas.
Contracts for maintenance
and operation,
§9-14-23.
Division of parks.
Director, §9-2-102.
Bridges.
Repair and maintenance.
Bridges within state parks
system and state
owned public fishing
lake areas, §9-14-5.
Buildings and facilities.
Revenues.
Operation of certain new
facilities.
Disposition and
expenditure,
§9-2-108.
Concessions within state
park areas, §§9-14-20 to
9-14-29.
Bonds, surety.
Contracts for maintenance
and operation,
§9-14-23.
Contracts for maintenance
and operation.
Advertising.
Bids, §9-14-22.
Applicability of article,
§9-14-29.
Attorney general.
Approval, §9-14-28.
Authorized, §9-14-20.
Award, §9-14-24.
Bids.
Advertisements for
sealed bids, §9-14-22.
Financial statements,
§9-14-25.
Invitations to bid,
§9-14-21.
Opening, §9-14-22.
Public inspection,
§9-14-22.
Rejection of all bids,
§9-14-23.
Retention of original
bids, §9-14-22.
Solicitations for sealed
bids, §9-14-22.
Submission, §9-14-22.
Bonds, surety, §9-14-23.
Cancellation, §9-14-26.
Commissioner of
conservation and
natural resources.
Consummation of
contracts, §9-14-28.
Conditions.
Generally, §9-14-24.
Consummation of
contracts, §9-14-28.
Duration, §9-14-27.

STATE PARKS—Cont'd
Concessions within state park areas—Cont'd
Contracts for maintenance and operation—Cont'd
Examiner of public accounts.
Approval, §9-14-28.
Execution.
Failure of successful bidder to execute, §9-14-23.
Exemption from article, §9-14-29.
Failure of successful bidder to execute, §9-14-23.
Financial resources of persons seeking concessions, §9-14-25.
Governor.
Approval, §9-14-28.
Invitations to bid, §9-14-21.
Length of term, §9-14-27.
Negotiation of contract, §9-14-23.
Qualifications of bidders, §9-14-21.
Financial resources, §9-14-25.
Rates and charges.
Provisions of contract as to concessionaire's rates and charges, §9-14-24.
Reasonableness, §9-14-24.
Review.
Periodic review, §9-14-24.
Rejection of all bids, §9-14-23.
Responsibility for maintenance of state facilities leased, §9-14-21.
Terms and conditions.
Generally, §9-14-24.
Rates and charges.
Provisions in contracts for maintenance and operation, §9-14-24.
Confederate memorials.
Division of parks.
Director.
Powers and duties, §9-2-104.
Cooperation with citizens' committees, §9-2-105.
White house of the confederacy, §§41-12-1 to 41-12-3.
Conservation and natural resources.
Commissioner.
Powers and duties, §§9-2-9, 9-2-10.
Constitution of Alabama.
Bond issue to acquire, develop, etc., Const. Ala., amd. 267.
Contracts.
Concessions within state park areas. See within this heading, "Concessions within state park areas."
Counties.
Appropriations, §9-14-6.

STATE PARKS—Cont'd
Counties—Cont'd
Grants of lands to state park system, §9-14-6.
Definitions, §9-14-1.
Department of conservation and natural resources.
Powers and duties, §9-2-2.
Description.
Ascertainment, §9-15-6.
Designation, §9-14-2.
Director. See within this heading, "Division of parks."
Division of parks, §§9-2-100 to 9-2-107.
Creation, §9-2-100.
Director, §§9-2-100 to 9-2-105.
Appointment, §9-2-100.
Arrest.
Powers of arrest, §9-2-9.
Bond, surety, §9-2-102.
Full-time position, §9-2-101.
Head of division, §9-2-100.
Oath of office, §9-2-101.
Powers and duties.
Confederate memorials, §9-2-104.
Cooperation with citizens' committees, §9-2-105.
Exemptions, §9-2-103.
General provisions, §9-2-103.
Expenses.
Payment from state park fund, §9-2-107.
Head of division.
Director, §9-2-100.
Exchange of land.
Authority of department, §9-2-3.
Fees.
Use of parks.
Authority to charge, §9-2-9.
Fish and game.
State owned public fishing lake areas.
Roads and bridges.
Repair and maintenance, §9-14-5.
Fort Louis de la Mobile.
Monument.
Maintenance, §9-14-3.
Funds.
Composition, §9-2-107.
Creation, §§9-2-106, 9-2-107.
Expenditures, §9-2-107.
Purposes, §9-2-107.
Revolving fund.
Audit, §9-2-107.
Creation, §9-2-107.
Expenditures, §9-2-107.
Uses, §9-2-107.
Income.
Disposition of revenue, §§9-2-3, 9-2-108.
Locations.
Ascertainment, §9-15-6.
Maintenance.
Commissioner of conservation and natural resources.
Duties, §9-2-10.

STATE PARKS—Cont'd
Maintenance—Cont'd
Contracts for maintenance and operation of concessions. See within this heading, "Concessions within state park areas."
Roads, §§9-14-4, 9-14-5.
Monuments and historic sites.
Confederate memorials.
Director of division of parks.
Powers and duties, §9-2-104.
Cooperation with citizens' committees, §9-2-105.
Defined, §9-14-1.
Designation, §9-14-2.
Fort Louis de la Mobile.
Maintenance of monument, §9-14-3.
Uses, §9-14-2.
White house of the confederacy, §§41-12-1 to 41-12-3.
Municipal corporations.
Appropriations, §9-14-6.
Grants of land to state park system, §9-14-6.
Oaths.
Division of parks.
Director, §9-2-101.
Parkways.
Defined, §9-14-1.
Designation, §9-14-2.
Uses.
Generally, §9-14-2.
Penalties.
Rules and regulations.
Violations, §9-2-9.
Personnel.
Employment.
Department of conservation and natural resources, §9-2-3.
Police.
Deputy police officers.
Arrest.
Powers of arrest, §9-2-9.
Authority to designate, §9-2-9.
Public lands.
Unused public lands.
Use as state parks, §9-15-3.
Records.
Disposition, §9-15-7.
Preparation of records of ownership, §9-15-6.
Revenues.
Disposition, §§9-2-3, 9-2-108.
Revolving fund, §9-2-107.
Roads.
Construction.
Leading from state highways, §9-14-4.
Maintenance.
Leading from state highways, §9-14-4.
Within state parks system, §9-14-5.
Rules and regulations.
Penalties.
Violations, §9-2-9.

STATE PARKS—Cont'd
Rules and regulations
  —Cont'd
Promulgation.
  Commissioner of
    conservation and
    natural resources,
    §9-2-9.
  Department of
    conservation and
    natural resources,
    §9-2-3.
Violations.
  Penalties, §9-2-9.
Sales.
Public lands.
  Authority of department,
    §9-2-3.
Trees and timber.
  Disposition and
    expenditure of
    revenue, §9-2-108.
Trees and timber.
Sale.
  Disposition and
    expenditure of
    revenues, §9-2-108.
Uses.
Generally, §9-14-2.

**STATE PILOTAGE
  COMMISSION,** §§33-4-1 to
  33-4-45.
See PILOTS AND PILOTAGE.

STATE POLICE.
Aiding.
Refusing to aid, §13A-10-5.
Arrest.
Force.
  Use of force in making
    arrest, §13A-3-27.
Death.
Compensation for death from
  occupational diseases,
  §§36-30-20 to 36-30-23.
Definitions.
Occupational diseases.
  Compensation for death or
    disability, §36-30-20.
Disability.
Compensation for disability
  from occupational
  diseases, §§36-30-20 to
  36-30-23.
Diseases.
Occupational diseases,
  §§36-30-20 to 36-30-23.
Entrapment.
When defense, §13A-3-31.
Escape.
Force.
  Use of force in preventing
    escape, §13A-3-27.
Force.
Use in making arrest or
  preventing escape,
  §13A-3-27.
Good Samaritan Act.
State trooper rendering first
  aid or emergency care at
  scene of accident, etc.
  Exemption from liability,
  §6-5-332.
Highway patrol.
General provisions.
  See MOTOR VEHICLES.
Highways.
Closing highways, §32-5-16.

STATE POLICE—Cont'd
Occupational diseases.
Compensation for death or
  disability, §§36-30-20 to
  36-30-23.
  Authorized, §36-30-21.
  Definitions, §36-30-20.
  Eligibility for benefits.
    Generally, §36-30-22.
  Where physical
    examination not
    required at time of
    entry into service,
    §36-30-23.
Peace officers generally.
See PEACE OFFICERS.
Reserves, §§32-2-40 to 32-2-44.
Compensation, §32-2-40.
Composition, §32-2-40.
Department of public safety.
  Assisting, §32-2-43.
Director.
  Fitness of persons to
    serve.
    Determination,
    §32-2-42.
  Supervision of reserves,
    §32-2-41.
  Establishment of reserves,
    §32-2-40.
Duties, §32-2-43.
Establishment, §32-2-40.
Firearms.
  Authority to carry,
    §32-2-44.
Fitness to serve.
  Determination, §32-2-42.
Immunity, §32-2-41.
Supervision, §32-2-41.
Weapons.
  Authority to carry,
    §32-2-44.
Retirement.
Completion of 25 years
  service.
  State trooper may retire
    upon, §36-21-12.

STATE PRISONS.
General provisions.
See PRISONS AND
  PRISONERS.

**STATE PRODUCTS MART
  AND COLISEUM
  AUTHORITY,** §§41-10-80 to
  41-10-109.
See PRODUCTS MARTS.

**STATE RENAISSANCE
  FAIRE.**
Designation, §1-2-21.

STATE'S ATTORNEYS.
See DISTRICT ATTORNEYS.

STATE SONG.
Adoption, §1-2-16.
**Official state reunion theme
  song,** §1-2-24.

**STATE SUPERINTENDENT
  OF EDUCATION,** §§16-4-1
  to 16-4-21.
See EDUCATION.

**STATE TEACHERS
  COLLEGES.**
See UNIVERSITIES AND
  COLLEGES.

STATE TOXICOLOGIST.
**Blood and urine samples
  from certain dead
  bodies.**
Authority, §22-19-80.
Exemption from civil and
  criminal liability,
  §22-19-82.
Motor vehicles.
Safety coordinating
  committee.
  Member of committee,
    §32-3-1.
Public officers generally.
See PUBLIC OFFICERS
  AND EMPLOYEES.
**Safety coordinating
  committee.**
Member of committee,
  §32-3-1.
Samples.
Blood and urine samples
  from certain dead bodies.
  Authority, §22-19-80.
  Exemption from civil and
    criminal liability,
    §22-19-82.

STATE TREASURER,
  §§36-17-1 to 36-17-19.
Accountants.
Maintenance of funds for fees
  and charges collected,
  §34-1-22.
Additional employee,
  §36-17-4.1.
**Agricultural center
  corporation.**
Lease of corporations
  properties to board.
  Rental payments.
    Disbursement, §2-6-34.
Assistants, §36-17-4.
Bond issues, §§36-17-8,
  36-17-10 to 36-17-15.
Cancelled bonds.
  Destruction, §36-17-13.
Coupons.
  Conversion of coupon bonds
    into registered bonds
    and vice versa,
    §36-17-15.
  Custodian of paid coupons
    which must be
    cancelled, §36-17-12.
  Destruction of cancelled
    coupons, §36-17-13.
  Recordation of paid and
    cancelled coupons,
    §36-17-13.
Duplicates.
  Lost or destroyed
    registered state bonds.
    Issuance of duplicates,
    §36-17-14.
Interest payments.
  Drawing money for
    payment.
    Procedure, §36-17-8.
  Fiscal agency in New
    York.
    Duty to pay interest,
    §36-17-10.
  Liability for loss in
    providing for payment.
    When treasurer not
    liable, §36-17-11.
Paid bonds.
  Registry, §36-17-12.
Redeemed bonds.
  Custodian, §36-17-12.

STATE TREASURER—Cont'd
Bond issues—Cont'd
Registered bonds.
Conversion of coupon bonds
into registered bonds
and vice versa,
§36-17-15.
Duplicates of lost or
destroyed bonds.
Issuance, §36-17-14.
Registry of paid bonds,
§36-17-12.
Bonds, surety.
Additional bond, §§36-5-40,
36-5-41.
Amount, §36-17-1.
Deposit with treasurer,
§36-17-19.
Jurisdiction of action upon,
§36-17-2.
Payments made to treasurer,
§36-17-19.
Chief clerk, §36-17-4.
Compensation, Const. Ala.,
art. V, §118.
Constitution of Alabama.
Compensation, Const. Ala.,
art. V, §118.
Duties, Const. Ala., art. V,
§137; amd. 111.
Executive department.
Member of department,
Const. Ala., art. V,
§112.
Fees.
Restrictions on receipt,
Const. Ala., art. V,
§137.
Qualifications, Const. Ala.,
art. V, §132.
Residency requirements,
Const. Ala., art. V, §118.
Succession.
Ineligible to succeed self,
Const. Ala., art. V,
§116.
One additional term,
Const. Ala., amd. 282.
Term of office, Const. Ala.,
amd. 282.
Vacancy in office, Const.
Ala., art. V, §136.
Coosa Valley development
authority.
Bond issues.
Payment of principal and
interest, §33-16-14.
Custodian of funds, §33-16-6.
Treasurer of authority,
§33-16-6.
Corrections.
Alabama corrections
institution finance
authority.
Treasurer of authority,
§14-2-6.
Counties.
Transfer of money
erroneously paid into
county treasurer, etc.,
state treasury, §11-1-6.
Duties, §36-17-3; Const. Ala.,
art. V, §137; amd. 111.
Education.
Vocational education.
Treasurer custodian of
federal funds, §16-37-2.
Elections.
See ELECTIONS.

STATE TREASURER—Cont'd
Employees.
Additional employee.
Authority as to, §36-17-4.1.
Escheats.
Payment of receipts to state
treasurer, §43-6-7.
Executive department.
Member of department,
Const. Ala., art. V, §112.
Fees.
Restrictions on receipt of
fees, Const. Ala., art. V,
§137; amd. 111.
Funds.
Sinking funds.
Special trustee, §36-17-17.
Surplus state funds.
Investment in obligations
of United States,
§36-17-18.
Handicapped persons.
Rehabilitation and crippled
children service.
Federal funds for
rehabilitation.
Treasurer custodian,
§16-38-4.
Harbors and ports.
Port authority.
Bond issues.
State treasurer to pay
principal and
interest of bonds,
§33-13-13.
Health care service plans.
Deposit of securities with
state treasurer,
§10-4-112.
Highways.
Authority.
Bond issues.
Payments by state
treasurer, §23-1-159.
Treasurer of corporation,
§23-1-154.
Finance corporation.
Bond issues.
Payments by treasurer,
§23-1-179.
Treasurer of corporation,
§23-1-174.
Impeachment, Const. Ala.,
art. VII, §173.
General provisions.
See IMPEACHMENT.
Income tax.
Disposition of collections,
§40-18-51.
Insurance.
Custodian of insurers'
deposits, §27-6-4.
Interest payments.
Bond issues, §§36-17-8,
36-17-10 to 36-17-15.
Investments.
Surplus state funds.
Investment in obligations
of United States,
§36-17-18.
Liability.
Loss in providing for
payment of interest on
state bonds.
When treasurer not liable,
§36-17-11.

STATE TREASURER—Cont'd
Mental health finance
authority.
Bond issues.
Payment of principal and
interest, §41-10-370.
Records, §41-10-370.
Mental unsoundness, Const.
Ala., art. V, §136.
Merit system.
Officers and employees
subject to, §36-17-5.
Motor vehicles.
Surety insurance.
Sole surety.
Cosureties on bond of
state treasurer,
§27-24-4.
Oath of office.
General provisions.
See PUBLIC OFFICERS
AND EMPLOYEES.
Printing.
Public printing and binding.
Approval of contract and
bond, §41-4-136.
Public officers generally.
See PUBLIC OFFICERS
AND EMPLOYEES.
Qualifications, Const. Ala.,
art. V, §132.
Rehabilitation and crippled
children service.
Federal funds.
Treasurer custodian of
federal funds for
rehabilitation,
§16-38-4.
Removal from office.
Settlement of accounts and
delivery of books,
§36-17-6.
Reports.
Annual report by state
treasurer, Const. Ala.,
art. V, §137; amd. 111.
Residency requirements,
Const. Ala., art. V, §118.
Resignation.
Settlement of accounts and
delivery of books,
§36-17-6.
Savings and loan
associations.
Securities issued by
associations.
Deposits with state
treasurer, §5-16-50.
Voluntary liquidation.
Unclaimed dividends and
share accounts.
Certification and
transmittal to state
treasurer, §5-16-34.
Payment of creditors or
investors by state
treasurer, §5-16-35.
Sinking funds.
Special trustee, §36-17-17.
Southern products mart
authority.
Maintenance of records
pertaining to payment o
bonds, §41-10-65.
State bonds.
General provisions. See
within this heading,
"Bond issues."
Succession.
One additional term, Const.
Ala., amd. 282.

STATE TREASURER—Cont'd

Term of office, Const. Ala., art. V, §116; amd. 282.

Tombigbee Valley development authority.
Custodian of funds, §33-17-6.
Treasurer of authority, §33-17-6.

Vacancy in office, Const. Ala., art. V, §136.

Vocational education.
Custodian of federal funds, §16-37-2.

Warrants.
Destruction of cancelled state warrants, §36-17-16.

Water system assistance authority.
Investments in bond issues of authority, §22-23A-12.

STATE TROOPERS.
See STATE POLICE.

STATE VETERINARIAN.
General provisions, §§2-4-1 to 2-4-4.
Livestock.
See LIVESTOCK.

STATE VOCATIONAL TECHNICAL SCHOOL AT MOBILE.
Designated Southwest State Technical Institute, §16-60-1.

STATISTICS.
Aged persons.
Commission on the aging.
Duty to gather statistics, §38-3-2.
Agricultural statistics, §§2-2-50 to 2-2-53.
Annuity tables, §§35-16-1, 35-16-2.
Corrections.
Board of corrections.
Duty to collect, §14-1-8.
Court statistics, §12-8-7.
Data systems.
See DATA.
Highways.
Department.
Preparation, §23-1-40.
Mortality tables, §§35-16-3, 35-16-4.
Penitentiary.
Information regarding convicts, §14-3-35.
Tables.
Annuity tables, §§35-16-1, 35-16-2.
Mortality tables, §§35-16-3, 35-16-4.
Vital statistics.
See VITAL STATISTICS.

STATUTE OF FRAUDS.
Commercial code.
Investment securities, §7-8-319.
Kinds of personal property not otherwise covered, §7-1-206.
Sales contracts, §7-2-201.
Modification of sales contracts, §7-2-209.
See COMMERCIAL CODE.
Contracts.
Certain agreements void unless in writing, §8-9-2.
Commercial code.
See COMMERCIAL CODE.

STATUTE OF FRAUDS —Cont'd

Contracts—Cont'd
Sales contracts, §7-2-202.
Modification of sales contracts, §7-2-209.
Defenses.
Affirmative defense, ARCP, Rule 8 (c).
Investment securities, §7-8-319.
Sales.
Contracts, §7-2-201.
Modification of sales contracts, §7-2-209.
Trusts and trustees.
Trust concerning lands required to be in writing, §35-4-255.
Uniform commercial code.
Investment securities, §7-8-319.
Kinds of personal property not otherwise covered, §7-1-206.
Sales contracts, §7-2-201.
Modification of sales contracts, §7-2-209.
See COMMERCIAL CODE.

STATUTE OF LIMITATIONS.
Criminal law and procedure.
Limitations on prosecution.
See CRIMINAL LAW AND PROCEDURE.
General provisions.
See LIMITATION OF ACTIONS.

STATUTES.
Alabama law institute, §§29-8-1 to 29-8-5.
Amendment.
By title only, Const. Ala., art. IV, §45.
Appeals.
Briefs.
Reproduction of statutes in briefs, ARAP, Rule 28 (f).
Attorney general.
Allegations statutes unconstitutional.
Entitled to be heard, §6-6-227.
Served with copy of proceedings, §6-6-227.
Constitutional validity questioned.
Notice to attorney general, §6-6-227; ARAP, Rule 44.
Commission on uniform state laws.
General provisions, §§41-9-370 to 41-9-374.
Conservation and natural resources.
Commissioner.
Publication and distribution of laws and rules and regulations, §9-2-8.
Constitution of Alabama.
General provisions.
See CONSTITUTION OF ALABAMA.
Constitution of the United States.
Approval of laws by president, Const. U. S., Art. I, §7.

STATUTES—Cont'd

Constitution of the United States—Cont'd
Ex post facto laws, Const. U. S., Art. I, §§9, 10.
Full faith and credit clause, Const. U. S., Art. IV, §1.
Limitations on legislation, Const. U. S., Art. I, §9.
Proof, Const. U. S., Art. IV, §1.
Revenue bills, Const. U. S., Art. I, §7.
Supreme law of the land, Const. U. S., Art. VI.
Veto, Const. U. S., Art. I, §7.
Construction and interpretation.
See CONSTRUCTION AND INTERPRETATION.
Copyright.
Duty of governor, §36-13-5.
County laws, §§11-13-1 to 11-13-6.
See COUNTIES.
Declaratory judgments.
Questions of construction or validity, §6-6-223.
Distribution of acts and journals, §41-4-150.
Pamphlet form of printing.
Distribution of pamphlets, §41-4-156.
Division of laws, Const. Ala., art. IV, §45.
Evidence.
Other states and territories, §12-21-93.
Transcripts of foreign statutes, §12-21-94.
Private legislative acts.
Admissibility in evidence, §12-21-37.
Fish and game.
Commissioner.
Publication and distribution, §9-2-8.
Full faith and credit clause, Const. U. S., Art. IV, §1.
Funerals.
Board of funeral service to distribute relevant statutes upon request, §34-13-4.
Governor.
Copyright, §36-13-5.
Legislative reference service, §§29-7-1 to 29-7-7.
See LEGISLATURE.
Limitation of actions.
Foreign statutes.
Effect upon actions on contracts, §6-2-17.
Local laws.
Constitution of Alabama.
See CONSTITUTION OF ALABAMA.
Counties, §§11-13-1 to 11-13-6.
See COUNTIES.
Marine resources.
Commissioner.
Publication and distribution of statutes, §9-2-8.
Pleadings.
Special statute, ARCP, Rule 9 (d).
Population acts.
Not repealed, §1-1-10.

STATUTES—Cont'd
President.
Approval of laws by
president, Const. U. S.,
Art. I, §7.
Veto, Const. U. S., Art. I, §7.
Printing.
Public printing and binding,
§§41-4-130 to 41-4-161.
See PRINTING.
Private laws.
Special, private or local laws.
Constitution of Alabama.
See CONSTITUTION OF
ALABAMA.
Promulgation of laws.
Periodic promulgation, Const.
Ala., art. IV, §85.
Repeals.
Civil practice.
Practice and procedure in
certain courts not
affected by repeal of
prior statutes, §6-1-1.
Previous validating acts not
repealed, §1-1-13.
Repealed laws not revived,
§1-1-11.
Uncodified statutes of public,
general and permanent
nature, §1-1-10.
Restricted to one subject,
Const. Ala., art. IV, §45.
Revision of laws.
Periodic revision, Const. Ala.,
art. IV, §85.
Revival.
By title only, Const. Ala.,
art. IV, §45.
Severability of provisions of
statutes, §1-1-16.
Special, private or local
laws.
Constitution of Alabama.
See CONSTITUTION OF
ALABAMA.
Style of laws, Const. Ala., art.
IV, §45.
Suspension of laws, Const.
Ala., art. I, §21.
For benefit of individuals or
private corporations,
Const. Ala., art. IV,
§108.
Uncodified statutes of
public, general and
permanent nature.
Repeal, §1-1-10.
Uniform laws.
Commission on uniform state
laws, §§41-9-370 to
41-9-374.
United States.
Approval of laws by
president, Const. U. S.,
Art. I, §7.
Limitations on legislation,
Const. U. S., Art. I, §9.
Revenue bills, Const. U. S.,
Art. I, §7.
Validating acts.
Previous validating acts not
repealed, §1-1-13.

STAY OF PROCEEDINGS.
Appeals, ARCP, Rule 62 (d);
ARAP, Rule 8.
Automatic appeal from death
sentence.
Automatic stay of
execution, §12-22-150;
ARAP, Rule 8 (d).
Certificate of judgment,
ARAP, Rule 41 (b).
Criminal cases.
See APPEALS.
Stays pending appeal.
See APPEALS.
Writs of error.
Stay of proceedings on
judgment, §12-22-222.
Capital punishment.
Stay pending appeal,
§12-22-150; ARAP, Rule
8 (d).
Corporations.
Prosecution of corporations.
Stay of execution on
judgment, §10-7-4.
Court of civil appeals.
Powers of judges as to
issuance of stays,
§12-3-8.
Court of criminal appeals.
Powers of judges as to
issuance of stays,
§12-3-8.
Criminal appeals.
See APPEALS.
Criminal law and procedure.
Capital punishment,
§12-22-150; ARAP, Rule
8 (d).
Stays pending appeal.
See APPEALS.
Enforcement of judgment.
Stay of proceedings to
enforce a judgment,
ARCP, Rule 62.
Execution of sentence.
Capital punishment,
§12-22-150; ARAP, Rule
8 (d).
General provisions.
See SENTENCING.
Insurance.
Life and disability insurance
guaranty association,
§27-44-18.
Judgments.
Affirmation of stayed
judgment, §§12-22-72 to
12-22-74.
Applicability of
amendatory provisions,
§12-22-73.1.
Stay of proceedings to
enforce a judgment,
ARCP, Rule 62.
Quo warranto.
Appeals.
Stay of execution on
judgment, §6-6-604.
Taxation.
Insurance guaranty
association, §27-42-18.
Writs of error.
Stay of proceedings on
judgment, §12-22-222.

STEALING.
See THEFT.

STEAM FITTERS.
Licenses, §40-12-145.

STEAMSHIPS.
Alcoholic beverages.
See ALCOHOLIC
BEVERAGES.
General provisions.
See SHIPS AND SHIPPING.
Licenses.
Alcoholic beverages.
See ALCOHOLIC
BEVERAGES.
Manufacturers.
Operation of transportation
methods for persons or
property by
manufacturing
companies, §10-5-9.
Mines and minerals.
Operation of transportation
methods for persons or
property by mining
companies, §10-5-9.
Quarries.
Operation of transportation
methods for persons or
property by quarrying
companies, §10-5-9.
Railroads.
Operation of transportation
methods for persons or
property by railroad
companies, §10-5-9.
Transportation companies.
See TRANSPORTATION
COMPANIES.

STEEL.
Motor vehicles.
Size and weight of vehicles
transporting structural
steel.
Exemptions from
restrictions, §32-9-25.
Public works.
Contractors for state projects
Use of steel produced in
United States, §39-3-4

STEVENSON,
MUNICIPALITY OF.
Property tax, Const. Ala.,
amd. 8.

STILLBIRTHS.
Vital statistics.
See VITAL STATISTICS.

STILLMAN COLLEGE.
Black Heritage Museum of
West Alabama, §§16-62-1
to 16-62-6.
See BLACK HERITAGE
MUSEUM OF WEST
ALABAMA.

STILLS.
Alcoholic beverages.
See ALCOHOLIC
BEVERAGES.
Turpentine and resin stills.
Licenses, §40-12-175.

STIMULANT DRUGS.
Controlled substances.
See DRUGS.

STIPULATIONS.
Discovery.
Stipulations regarding
discovery procedure,
ARCP, Rule 29.
Dismissal of actions, ARCP,
Rule 41 (a).
Form of stipulation, ARCP,
Form 71.

**STOCK AND
    STOCKHOLDERS.**
  Agriculture.
    Marketing associations.
      Authority to acquire stock,
        §2-10-27.
      Incorporated marketing
        associations.
        Exchange of stock,
          §2-10-66.
        Stock of associations,
          §2-10-62.
    Mutual farming or trucking
      associations.
      Organization with capital
        stock, §2-10-98.
  Banks.
    See BANKS AND
      FINANCIAL
      INSTITUTIONS.
  Corporations.
    See CORPORATIONS.
  General provisions.
    See CORPORATIONS.
  **Industrial development
      corporations.**
    See INDUSTRIAL
      DEVELOPMENT
      CORPORATIONS.
  Insurance.
    Stock insurers.
      See INSURANCE.
  Licenses.
    Stock and bond brokers,
      §40-12-162.
  Minors.
    Corporations.
      See CORPORATIONS.
    Ownership of securities by
      minors, §§8-6-90 to
      8-6-95.
      See SECURITIES.
    Transfers to minors,
      §§35-5A-1 to 35-5A-24.
      See TRANSFERS TO
        MINORS.
  Public utilities.
    Taxation.
      Ad valorem taxes.
        Stockholders not
          required to list
          shares or pay ad
          valorem taxes
          thereon, §40-21-29.
  Regulations.
    Securities regulation.
      See SECURITIES.
  Securities generally.
    See SECURITIES.
  Subscription for shares.
    See CORPORATIONS.
  Taxation.
    Corporate shares of stock.
      See CORPORATIONS.
    Levy and sale of personal
      property by tax
      collectors.
      Shares of stock, §40-5-16.
    Securities tax.
      See SECURITIES.
  **Transfers to minors,
      §§35-5A-1 to 35-5A-24.**
    See TRANSFERS TO
      MINORS.

**TOCK LAWS, §§3-5-1 to
    3-5-14.**
  See LIVESTOCK.

TOLEN PROPERTY.
  **Bringing stolen property
      into this state, §13A-8-20.**

STOLEN PROPERTY—Cont'd
  False pretenses.
    Bringing into state property
      obtained by false
      pretense elsewhere,
      §13A-8-21.
  Livestock.
    Department of agriculture
      and industries to
      determine ownership of
      stolen livestock and
      furnish information to
      interested persons,
      §2-15-25.
  Municipal corporations.
    Disposition of proceeds,
      §11-47-116.
    Redemption by owner,
      §11-47-116.
    Sale, §11-47-116.
    Storage, §11-47-116.
    Taking up stolen property,
      §11-47-116.
  **Receiving stolen property,
      §§13A-8-16 to 13A-8-19.**
  Venue.
    Stolen property brought into
      state, §15-2-5.
    Stolen property carried into
      another county, §15-2-9.

STONE.
  Counties.
    Acquisition of lands for stone
      quarries, §11-14-23.
    Conduct of condemnation
      proceedings, §11-14-24.

**STONEWALL JACKSON
    MEMORIAL FUND,
    §§16-32-1 to 16-32-3.**
  See UNIVERSITIES AND
    COLLEGES.

**STOP AND FRISK LAW,
    §§15-5-30, 15-5-31.**

STOPPAGE IN TRANSIT.
  Commercial code.
    Sales.
      Seller's remedies, §7-2-705.

**STOPPING, STANDING AND
    PARKING.**
  Motor vehicles.
    See MOTOR VEHICLES.

STORAGE.
  **Self service facilities,
      §§8-15-30 to 8-15-38.**
    See SELF-SERVICE
      STORAGE FACILITIES.

STORES.
  Alcoholic beverages.
    State liquor stores.
      See ALCOHOLIC
        BEVERAGES.
  Arrest.
    Detention and arrest of
      person suspected of
      larceny of goods held for
      sale, §15-10-14.
  Definitions, §40-12-310.
  Fees, §§40-12-315, 40-12-316.
  **Licenses, §§40-12-310 to
      40-12-319.**
    Application, §40-12-312.
      Examinations, §40-12-313.
    Definitions.
      "Store," §40-12-310.
    Expiration, §40-12-314.
    Fees.
      Annual fees, §40-12-315.
      Portion of year, §40-12-316.

STORES—Cont'd
  Licenses—Cont'd
    Form.
      Furnished and prescribed
        by department of
        revenue, §40-12-318.
    Issuance, §40-12-313.
    Money collected.
      Expenses of department of
        revenue.
        Payment, §40-12-318.
      Payment into treasury,
        §40-12-318.
    Penalties.
      Failure to take out license,
        §40-12-319.
    Renewal, §40-12-314.
    Requirement.
      Who must procure license,
        §40-12-311.
    Scope of article, §40-12-317.

STRAYS.
  See ESTRAYS.

STREAMS.
  General provisions.
    See WATERS AND
      WATERCOURSES.

STREETS.
  Abandonment.
    Closing and vacating streets,
      alleys and highways,
      §§23-4-1 to 23-4-20.
      See HIGHWAYS.
  Abutting landowners.
    Vacation of street or alley,
      §§23-4-2, 23-4-20.
  Airports.
    Tax or license for use of
      public streets, etc.,
      leading to or from
      airport prohibited,
      §4-3-9.
  Bicycles generally.
    See BICYCLES.
  Blind persons.
    Right to full use of streets,
      §21-7-2.
  Capitol.
    Control of streets adjacent to
      Capitol.
      Legislature authorized to
        control, §29-1-19.1.
  **Closing and vacating streets,
      alleys and highways,
      §§23-4-1 to 23-4-20.**
    See HIGHWAYS.
  Counties.
    Public roads, bridges and
      ferries.
      See COUNTIES.
  Handicapped persons.
    Right to full use of streets,
      §21-7-2.
  Highway department.
    Construction and
      maintenance of streets,
      §23-1-42.
  Highways.
    General provisions.
      See HIGHWAYS.
  **Improvements on public
      streets, etc.**
    Liens, §§35-11-410 to
      35-11-417.
      See HIGHWAYS.
  **Interstate highway system,
      §§23-3-1 to 23-3-8.**
    See HIGHWAYS.

STREETS—Cont'd
Liens.
Improvements on public
streets, etc., §§35-11-410
to 35-11-471.
See HIGHWAYS.
Littering, §§33-5-6 to 33-5-9.
Livestock.
Markets.
Purchase of livestock on
public street within
2,500 feet of public
livestock market,
§2-15-71.
**Mechanics' and
materialmen's liens.**
Improvements on public
street, etc., §§35-11-410
to 35-11-417.
See HIGHWAYS.
Mentally ill.
State mental institutions.
Construction and
maintenance.
State highway
department,
§23-1-42.
Military affairs.
Disloyal or insulting
remarks.
Making disloyal or
insulting remarks,
gestures, etc., to or
about troops at drill on
streets, §31-2-22.
Right of troops to use streets,
§31-2-84.
Riots.
Regulation of passage and
occupancy during riot,
§31-2-122.
Motor vehicles.
See MOTOR VEHICLES.
Municipal corporations.
See MUNICIPAL
CORPORATIONS.
**Partlow state school and
hospital.**
Construction and
maintenance.
State highway department,
§23-1-42.
Prisons and prisoners.
Work on public roads,
§§14-4-6 to 14-4-8,
23-1-37.
**Public roads, bridges and
ferries.**
See COUNTIES.
Rights of way.
Vacation.
Fee, §11-49-6.
Sales tax.
Contractors, §40-23-50.
Searches and seizures.
Stop and frisk law,
§§15-5-30, 15-5-31.
Shopping carts.
Abandonment on public
streets, §13A-8-62.
Stop and frisk law, §§15-5-30,
15-5-31.
Subdivisions.
County regulation of
subdivisions, §11-24-1.
Universities and colleges.
Construction and
maintenance.
State highway department,
§23-1-42.

STREETS—Cont'd
Vacating streets, §§23-4-1 to
23-4-20.
See HIGHWAYS.

STRIKES.
See LABOR.

STRINGFELLOW.
**Stringfellow memorial
hospital nonprofit realty
company.**
Exemption from taxation,
§40-9-1.1.
**Susie Parker Stringfellow
memorial hospital.**
Exemption from taxation,
§40-9-1.1.

**STRINGFELLOW MEMORIAL
HOSPITAL NONPROFIT
REALTY COMPANY.**
Exemption from taxation,
§40-9-1.1.

STRIP MINING.
Mine safety.
Surface mining operations,
§§25-9-270 to 25-9-284.
See COAL.
**Surface mining control and
reclamation,** §§9-16-70 to
9-16-107.
See COAL.
**Surface mining reclamation
generally,** §§9-16-1 to
9-16-15.
See COAL.

**STRUCTURAL PEST
CONTROL.**
See PEST CONTROL.

STRUCTURED DAMAGES.
General provisions, §§6-11-1
to 6-11-7.
See DAMAGES.

**STUDENT GRANT
PROGRAM,** §§16-33A-1 to
16-33A-11.
Administration of program,
§16-33A-4.
**Alabama commission on
higher education
(ACHE),** §16-33A-1.
Cessation.
Responsibility for program
upon cessation of
ACHE, §16-33A-11.
Definitions, §16-33A-1.
Duties.
Basic duties, §16-33A-5.
Powers and duties.
Generally, §16-33A-5.
Alabama resident.
Defined, §16-33A-1.
Application for grants,
§16-33A-6.
Approval of grants,
§§16-33A-1, 16-33A-6.
Availability of grants,
§16-33A-6.
Award of grant, §16-33A-6.
Definitions, §16-33A-1.
Educational institutions.
Annual reports to legislature,
§16-33A-8.
Approved institution.
Defined, §16-33A-1.
Audits, §16-33A-8.
Reports.
Annual reports to
legislature, §16-33A-8.

**STUDENT GRANT
PROGRAM**—Cont'd
Eligible student.
Defined, §16-33A-1.
Full-time student.
Defined, §16-33A-1.
Funds.
Nonsectarian use required,
§16-33A-7.
Proration when funds
insufficient to provide
full grants, §16-33A-9.
Grants.
Amount for each eligible
student, §16-33A-3.
Application, §16-33A-6.
Approval, §16-33A-6.
Availability, §16-33A-6.
Awards, §16-33A-6.
Defined, §16-33A-1.
Effective date, §16-33A-3.
Payable to institutions on
behalf of students,
§16-33A-3.
Procedures, §16-33A-6.
Renewal, §16-33A-6.
Requirements, §16-33A-6.
Revocation, §16-33A-6.
**Institutional related
expenses.**
Defined, §16-33A-1.
Legislative findings,
§16-33A-2.
Misrepresentations.
Penalty, §16-33A-10.
Nonsectarian use of funds.
Required, §16-33A-7.
Part-time student.
Defined, §16-33A-1.
**Proration of funds when
insufficient to provide
full grants,** §16-33A-9.
Purpose of chapter,
§16-33A-2.
Renewal of grants,
§16-33A-6.
Revocation of grants,
§16-33A-6.
Undergraduate student.
Defined, §16-33A-1.

STUDENT LOAN PROGRAM,
§§16-33B-1 to 16-33B-8.
Administration of program,
§16-33B-3.
Commission on higher
education, §16-33B-3.
Powers and duties of
commission, §16-33B-
Officials, §16-33B-3.
Personnel, §16-33B-3.
Attorneys at law.
Legal counsel for program,
§16-33B-8.
Audits.
Institutions.
Approved and eligible
institutions, §16-33B-
**Commission on higher
education.**
Administration of program,
§16-33B-3.
Powers and duties of
commission, §16-33B-
Definitions, §16-33B-1.
Dissolution of program,
§16-33B-7.
Vesting of property,
§16-33B-7.

STUDENT LOAN PROGRAM
—Cont'd
**False statements or
misrepresentations,**
§16-33B-6.
Fraud.
False statements or
misrepresentations,
§16-33B-6.
Legal counsel for program,
§16-33B-8.
Legislative findings,
§16-33B-2.
Loans.
Application.
False statements or
misrepresentations,
§16-33B-6.
Purpose of chapter,
§16-33B-2.
STUDENTS.
Education.
See EDUCATION.
Scholarships.
See SCHOLARSHIPS.
Student grant program,
§§16-33A-1 to 16-33A-11.
See STUDENT GRANT
PROGRAM.
Student loan program,
§§16-33B-1 to 16-33B-8.
See STUDENT LOAN
PROGRAM.
Universities and colleges.
See UNIVERSITIES AND
COLLEGES.

STUMPAGE.
Liens for stumpage,
§35-11-21.
Trees and timber generally.
See TREES AND TIMBER.

SUBDIVISIONS.
Counties.
County commissions.
Powers and duties,
§11-3-11.
Flood-prone areas.
Land-use management in
flood-prone areas,
§§11-19-1 to 11-19-24.
See COUNTIES.
General provisions.
See COUNTIES.
Flood-prone areas.
Counties.
Land-use management in
flood-prone areas,
§§11-19-1 to 11-19-24.
See COUNTIES.
**Mechanics' and
materialmen's liens.**
Selection of land to be
charged, §35-11-217.
Municipal corporations.
General provisions,
§§11-52-30 to 11-52-54.
See MUNICIPAL
CORPORATIONS.
Sewers.
Single family residences with
no access to public
sewer.
Land not subject to
subdivision regulations
of state board of
health, §22-26-7.
Surveys, plats or maps.
Municipal corporations.
See MUNICIPAL
CORPORATIONS.

SUBPOENAS.
Accountants.
Board of public accountancy.
Hearings.
Accused may subpoena
witnesses, §34-1-14.
Production of documents,
evidence, etc.,
§34-1-14.
Accounts and accounting.
Department of examiner of
public accounts,
§41-5-16.
Adjoining counties.
Execution of subpoenas in
adjoining counties,
§§12-21-183, 15-10-45.
Air pollution, §22-28-22.
Appeals to circuit courts.
Criminal cases.
Issuance, execution and
return of subpoenas for
witnesses, §12-22-111.
Arbitration and award.
Subpoena of witnesses,
§§6-6-7 to 6-6-9.
Attorney general.
Power to issue, §36-15-13.
Attorneys at law.
Disciplinary proceedings,
ARDE, Rule 13.
Subpoena of witnesses and
evidence, §34-3-82.
Aviation.
Enforcement, §4-2-48.
Chiropractors.
Licenses.
Refusal, revocation or
suspension.
Compelling attendance of
witnesses and
production of
documents and
things, §34-24-173.
Coal.
Mine safety.
Expenses of executing
subpoenas, §25-9-23.
Contempt.
Failure to obey subpoena,
ARCP, Rule 45 (f).
Contents, §12-21-180.
Coroner's inquest.
Proceedings against
defaulting witnesses,
§15-4-4.
Subpoena of witnesses,
§15-4-3.
Cosmetologists.
Board of cosmetology.
Subpoena power of board,
§34-7-21.
County commissions.
Powers and duties of county
commissions, §11-3-11.
Criminal cases.
Appeals to circuit courts.
Issuance, execution and
return of subpoenas for
witnesses, §12-22-111.
Witnesses generally,
§§12-21-243 to 12-21-246.
Dental service corporations.
Examination and
investigation of
corporations.
Power to subpoena
witnesses, §22-21-386.

SUBPOENAS—Cont'd
Dentists.
Board of dental examiners.
Subpoena power of board,
§34-9-46.
**Department of examiners of
public accounts,** §41-5-16.
Depositions.
Subpoena for taking
depositions, ARCP, Rule
45 (d).
Form, ARCP, Form 75.
Disobeying.
Contempt, ARCP, Rule 45 (f).
Distance of travel,
§12-21-180.
District attorneys.
Authority to issue,
§§12-16-198, 12-21-245.
Power to issue, §12-17-184.
Documentary evidence,
ARCP, Rule 45 (b).
Production of documentary
evidence, ARCP, Form
75.
Engineers.
Board of registration.
Subpoena power of board,
§34-11-35.
Environmental management.
Commission.
Hearings and procedures
before commission,
§22-22A-7.
Execution, §12-21-180.
Criminal cases, §12-21-246.
Expert witnesses, §12-21-181.
**Failure of subpoenaed
witness to attend and
remain.**
Proceedings upon failure,
§12-21-182.
Failure to obey.
Contempt, ARCP, Rule 45 (f).
Fires and fire prevention.
Fire marshal.
Fees.
Service of subpoenas,
§36-19-22.
Fish and game.
Wardens.
Service by warden, §9-2-65.
Forests and forestry.
Board of registration for
foresters.
Subpoena power of board,
§34-12-35.
Forms, ARCP, Rule 45 (a);
ARCP, Forms 73 to 75.
Funerals.
Board of funeral service.
Power of board, §34-13-26.
Grain dealers.
Commissioner of agriculture.
Power to issue subpoenas,
§2-31-14.
Grand jury, §12-21-243.
Issuance of subpoenas for
witnesses, §12-16-197.
District attorneys,
§§12-16-198,
12-21-245.
Habeas corpus hearings.
Witnesses, §15-21-15.
**Hearing aid dealers and
fitters.**
Board of hearing aid dealers
and fitters.
Subpoena power of board,
§34-14-9.
Issuance, ARCP, Rule 45 (a).

SUBPOENAS—Cont'd
Judicial compensation commission.
Powers of members of commission as to subpoenas, §12-10-2.
Judicial inquiry commission, AJICR, Rule 7.
Limit on distance, §12-21-180.
Meat and meat products.
Failure to attend and testify or produce documentary evidence in obedience to subpoena, §2-17-33.
Issuance by commissioner, §2-17-24.
Military affairs.
Courts-martial.
Subpoena of witnesses, §31-2-100.
Motor vehicle carriers.
Examiners.
Power to issue subpoenas, §37-3-28.
Municipal corporations.
Class 5 municipalities.
Mayor/commission/city manager form of government.
Investigations as to municipal affairs, §11-44E-181.
Oil and gas.
Conservation and regulation of production.
Powers of oil and gas board, §9-17-8.
Optometrists.
Board of optometrists.
Disciplinary proceedings, §34-22-8.
Subpoena power of board, §34-22-42.
Pharmacists and pharmacies.
Board of pharmacy.
Subpoena power of board, §34-23-92.
Pilots and pilotage.
Failure of witness to answer, §33-4-42.
Issuance of subpoenas in behalf of pilot, §33-4-44.
Power of commission to subpoena witnesses, §33-4-41.
Service by sheriff, §33-4-41.
Plumbing.
Certification of plumbers and gas fitters.
Revocation of certificates.
Compelling attendance of witnesses, §34-37-12.
Polygraph examiners.
Disciplinary actions.
Board authorized to issue subpoenas, §34-25-34.
Poultry.
Failure to attend and testify or produce documentary evidence in obedience to subpoena, §2-17-33.
Issuance by commissioner, §2-17-24.
Production of documentary evidence, ARCP, Rule 45 (b).
Form, ARCP, Form 75.

SUBPOENAS—Cont'd
Psychologists.
Disciplinary actions.
Subpoena power of board, §34-26-47.
Public service commission.
Compliance with subpoenas.
Power of circuit court, §37-1-104.
Hearings on rate and other regulations.
See PUBLIC SERVICE COMMISSION.
Powers of commissioners and examiners to issue subpoenas, §37-1-63.
Real estate brokers.
Disciplinary actions.
Authority of commission, §34-27-37.
Rules of civil procedure.
See RULES OF CIVIL PROCEDURE.
Securities.
Securities commission, §8-6-15.
Service, ARCP, Rule 45 (c).
Small claims.
Witnesses, ASCR, Rule I.
Speech pathologists and audiologists.
Board of examiners.
Authority of board to issue, §34-28A-43.
Subpoena duces tecum, ARCP, Rule 45 (b).
Form, ARCP, Form 74.
Surveys and surveyors.
Board of registration.
Subpoena power of board, §34-11-35.
Taxation.
County boards of equalization.
Service, §40-3-23.
Failure to obey, §40-29-117.
Travel distance.
Permissible travel distance, §12-21-180.
Venue.
Change of venue in criminal cases.
Compelling attendants of witnesses at hearing for a change, §15-2-22.
Issuance by court to which trial removed, §15-2-27.
Welfare.
Power of state and county departments, §38-4-6.
Witnesses generally, ARCP, Rule 45 (a), (e).
Criminal cases, §§12-21-243 to 12-21-246.
Failure to attend and remain.
Proceedings upon failure, §12-21-182.
Habeas corpus hearings, §15-21-15.
Small claims, ASCR, Rule I.

SUBROGATION.
Attorneys at law.
Client security fund, ACSF, Rule 10.

SUBROGATION—Cont'd
Child support programs.
Recipients of aid.
Department subrogated to right of child or recipients to collect and receive child support payments, §38-10-4.
Commercial code.
Bank deposits and collections.
Payor bank's right to subrogation on improper payment, §7-4-407.
Crime victims compensation.
Collateral source.
Award of compensation subrogates commission to rights of claimant, §15-23-14.
Health.
Medicaid program.
Subrogation of state to rights of recipients, §22-6-6.
Liens, §§35-11-2, 35-11-3, 35-11-234.
Right to subrogation.
Suretyship generally, §§8-3-1 to 8-3-42.
See SURETYSHIP.
Suretyship generally, §§8-3-1 to 8-3-4.

SUBSCRIPTION.
Defined, §1-1-1.
Shares of stock.
See CORPORATIONS.

SUBSEQUENT OFFENSES.
Felonies.
Repeat offenders.
See FELONIES.

SUBSTITUTION OF PARTIES.
See PARTIES.

SUBVERSIVE ACTIVITIES.
See ANARCHY AND SUBVERSIVE ACTIVITIES.

SUFFRAGE.
Constitutional provisions, Const. U. S., Amendments XIV, XIX, XXVI.
Right to vote generally.
See ELECTIONS.

SUGAR.
Licenses.
Factories, §40-12-165.

SUICIDE.
Natural death act.
Life-support procedures.
Withholding or withdrawal not suicide, §22-8A-9.

SUITS.
See ACTIONS.

SULPHUR.
Grain.
Sale of grain bleached with sulphur fumes, §2-20-5.

SUMMARY JUDGMENT.
See JUDGMENTS.

SUMMONS AND PROCESS.
Amendment, ARCP, Rule 4 (d).

SUMMONS AND PROCESS
—Cont'd
Constables.
Duty to execute and return,
§36-23-6.
Execution by sheriffs.
Compensation, §36-22-9.
Liability, §36-22-9.
Coroners.
When coroner to execute
summons, §11-5-7.
Counties.
Adjoining county.
Execution, §6-4-2.
Navigable streams not
within limits of any
county.
Execution of process on
said streams, §11-1-3.
Criminal law and procedure.
Simulating legal process,
§13A-10-131.
Defenses.
Insufficiency of process.
Litigation on merits.
Appeal.
No bar to raising same
defense on appeal,
§6-8-101.
Dispossession.
Real property.
Unlawfully taking
possession of or going
back into possession of
real estate after
dispossession under
legal process,
§13A-7-60.
Education.
County boards of education.
Execution of process,
§16-8-40.
**Executors and
administrators.**
Actions by and against.
Service of summons,
§43-2-130.
**Forcible entry and unlawful
detainer,** §§6-6-332,
6-6-333.
Forms, ARCP, Rule 4 (a).
Garnishment, §6-6-393.
Insufficiency of process.
Defense of insufficiency of
process, ARCP, Rule 12
(b), (h).
Issuance, ARCP, Rule 4 (a).
Jails.
Commitment and discharge
of prisoners.
Duty to file process or
order, §14-6-16.
Juvenile proceedings.
Endorsements upon
summonses, §12-15-53.
Issuance of summonses,
§12-15-53.
Powers of courts as to
issuance, §12-15-2.
Service of summons,
§12-15-53; ARJP, Rule
13.
Manner of service,
§12-15-54.
Waiver of service,
§12-15-53.
Landlord and tenant.
Possession wrongfully
withheld.
Issuance of process,
§35-9-81.

SUMMONS AND PROCESS
—Cont'd
Landlord and tenant—Cont'd
Service of process, §§35-9-7,
35-9-82.
Legislature.
Enforcement of process,
Const. Ala., art. IV, §53.
Privilege from arrest and
process, §29-1-7; Const.
Ala., art. IV, §56.
Motor vehicles.
Uniform traffic infractions.
Complaint and summons,
ARJA, Rule 19.
Municipal corporations.
Violations of certain
ordinances.
Summons and complaint in
lieu of arrest,
§11-40-10.1.
Municipal courts, §12-14-4.
Persons not parties.
Process in behalf of and
against persons not
parties, ARCP, Rule 71.
Probate courts, §12-13-6.
Quo warranto.
Return of summons,
§6-6-593.
Return.
Time, §6-4-1.
Rules of civil procedure.
See RULES OF CIVIL
PROCEDURE.
Service of process.
See SERVICE OF PROCESS.
Sheriffs.
When sheriff justified in
executing process,
§36-22-7.
Simulating legal process,
§13A-10-131.
Small claims, ASCR, Rule D.
Style of all processes, Const.
Ala., art. VI, §170.
Sundays.
Commencement of action on
Sunday, §6-4-4.
Time for execution, §6-4-1.
Wills.
Contesting validity of wills.
Summoning witnesses,
§43-8-191.

SUMTER COUNTY.
Economic development,
Const. Ala., amd. 250.
Probate judge.
Compensation, Const. Ala.,
amd. 486.

SUNDAYS.
Alcoholic beverages.
Clubs, §28-3A-12.
Legal hours of sale,
§28-3A-25.
Attachment.
Issuance and execution,
§6-6-52.
**Banks and financial
institutions.**
Transaction of business on
Sundays, §5-5A-30.
Blue laws, §§13A-12-1,
13A-12-2.
**Certain acts prohibited on
Sunday,** §13A-12-1.

SUNDAYS—Cont'd
Circuit courts.
Clerks of court and registers.
Office hours.
Saturdays, Sundays and
other holidays,
ARJA, Rule 5.
Courts.
Clerks of court and registers.
Office hours.
Saturdays, Sundays and
other holidays,
ARJA, Rule 5.
District courts.
Clerks of court.
Office hours.
Saturdays, Sundays and
other holidays,
ARJA, Rule 5.
Gambling.
Gambling on Sundays
prohibited, §13A-12-1.
Holidays, §1-3-8.
Markets.
Holding public markets and
trading therein on
Sunday, §13A-12-2.
Merchants.
Certain acts prohibited on
Sunday, §13A-12-1.
Shooting and hunting.
Prohibited, §13A-12-1.
Summons and process.
Commencement of action on
Sunday, §6-4-4.
Weapons.
Shooting weapons on Sunday,
§13A-12-1.

SUNFISH.
See FISH AND GAME.

SUNSET LAW.
General provisions, §§41-20-1
to 41-20-16.
See STATE DEPARTMENTS
AND AGENCIES.
**Space science exhibit
finance authority.**
Exemption from law,
§41-10-332.

SUNSHINE LAW.
Boards and commissions.
Executive or secret sessions
prohibited for certain
boards, §13A-14-2.

**SUPERCOMPUTER
AUTHORITY,** §§41-10-390
to 41-10-405.
Assets.
Transfer of certain assets to
authority, §41-10-404.
Board of directors.
Proceedings.
Admissibility in evidence,
§41-10-395.
Writing, recordation and
filing, §41-10-395.
Chief executive officer.
Employment, §41-10-397.
Citation of article,
§41-10-390.
**Confidentiality of
information,** §41-10-399.
**Construction and
interpretation.**
Construction of article,
§41-10-391.
Contracts.
Liability upon contract,
§41-10-402.

**SUPERCOMPUTER
    AUTHORITY**—Cont'd
Contracts—Cont'd
  Requirements for contractual
    agreements for
    supercomputer services,
    §41-10-399.
Corporations.
  Nonprofit corporation,
    §41-10-403.
Data.
  Confidentiality, §41-10-399.
  Use by authority, §41-10-399.
Dissolution, §41-10-406.
**Duplication of services to be
    avoided,** §41-10-405.
Funds.
  Supercomputer system fund,
    §41-10-400.
Incorporation.
  Application.
    Execution, §41-10-393.
    Filing and recordation,
      §41-10-393.
  Authorization, §41-10-392.
  Certificate of incorporation.
    Issuance, §41-10-394.
    Recordation, §41-10-394.
  Contents, §41-10-393.
  Fees, §41-10-394.
  Procedure.
    Generally, §41-10-392.
Intellectual property.
  Authority to have no
    proprietary interest,
    §41-10-398.
Intent of legislature,
    §41-10-391.
Legislative findings,
    §41-10-391.
Nonprofit corporation,
    §41-10-403.
Officer, §41-10-395.
Powers.
  Generally, §41-10-396.
Records.
  Public record laws.
    Inapplicability, §41-10-399.
Staff.
  Employment, §41-10-397.
Supercomputer system fund,
    §41-10-400.
Taxation.
  Exemption from taxation,
    §41-10-401.
Title of article, §41-10-390.

SUPERMARKETS.
Shopping carts, §§13A-8-60 to
    13A-8-64.

SUPERNUMERARIES.
District attorneys,
    §§12-17-210 to 12-17-216.
  See DISTRICT
    ATTORNEYS.
License commissioners,
    §§40-6-1 to 40-6-8.
  See LICENSES.
Sheriffs, §§36-22-60 to
    36-22-65.
  See SHERIFFS.
Tax assessors, §§40-6-1 to
    40-6-8.
  See TAXATION.
Tax collectors, §§40-6-1 to
    40-6-8.
  See TAXATION.

SUPERSEDEAS.
Appeals.
  Judgments on applications
    for remedial writs,
    §12-22-6.
  Recording of order fixing
    supersedeas bond,
    §12-22-40.
Bonds, surety.
  Recording of order fixing
    supersedeas bond,
    §12-22-40.
Rules of civil procedure.
  Writ abolished, ARCP, Rule
    60 (b).

**SUPPLEMENTAL HOUSING
    AUTHORITIES LAW,**
    §§24-1-100 to 24-1-117.
  See HOUSING
    AUTHORITIES.

**SUPPORT AND
    MAINTENANCE.**
Actions.
  Enforcement of support.
    Payment of overdue
      support.
      Bond, security, or other
        guarantee to secure
        payment, §30-3-6.
Alimony, §§30-2-50 to 30-2-54.
Bonds, surety.
  Payment of overdue support.
    Bond, security, or other
      guarantee to secure,
      §30-3-6.
Child custody and support.
  See MINORS.
Child support programs,
    §§38-10-1 to 38-10-33.
  See CHILD SUPPORT
    PROGRAMS.
Conveyances.
  Voiding of conveyances based
    on consideration of
    support, §8-9-12.
Desertion and nonsupport,
    §§30-4-50 to 30-4-65.
  See DESERTION AND
    NONSUPPORT.
Divorce and alimony,
    §§30-2-1 to 30-2-54.
  See DIVORCE AND
    ALIMONY.
Duty to support.
  Reciprocal state enforcement
    of duty to support,
    §§30-4-80 to 30-4-98.
  See DESERTION AND
    NONSUPPORT.
**Enforcement of duty to
    support.**
  Reciprocal state enforcement,
    §§30-4-80 to 30-4-98.
  See DESERTION AND
    NONSUPPORT.
Hearings.
  Payment of overdue support.
    Bond, security, or other
      guarantee to secure.
      Obligor to have
        opportunity to be
        heard on matter,
        §30-3-6.
Husband and wife.
  Divorce and alimony,
    §§30-2-1 to 30-2-54.
  See DIVORCE AND
    ALIMONY.

**SUPPORT AND
    MAINTENANCE**—Cont'd
Indigent persons.
  Relief and support by
    counties.
  See INDIGENT PERSONS.
Mentally ill.
  Support of persons in state
    mental institutions,
    §§22-53-1 to 22-53-26.
  See MENTALLY ILL.
Minors.
  Custody and support.
    See MINORS.
  Divorce.
    See DIVORCE AND
      ALIMONY.
  Trusts and trustees.
    See TRUSTS AND
      TRUSTEES.
Nonsupport.
  General provisions, §§30-4-50
    to 30-4-65.
  See DESERTION AND
    NONSUPPORT.
Notice.
  Payment of overdue support.
    Bond, security, or other
      guarantee to secure.
      Petition or original
        pleading to clearly
        notify obligor,
        §30-3-6.
Overdue support.
  Bond, security, or other
    guarantee to secure
    payment, §30-3-6.
Payment of support.
  Overdue support.
    Bond, security, or other
      guarantee to secure,
      §30-3-6.
**Reciprocal state
    enforcement of duty to
    support,** §§30-4-80 to
    30-4-98.
  See DESERTION AND
    NONSUPPORT.
Trusts and trustees.
  See TRUSTS AND
    TRUSTEES.
**Unemployment
    compensation.**
  Deduction of child support
    obligations, §25-4-152.
**Uniform reciprocal
    enforcement of support
    act.**
  Reciprocal state enforcement
    of duty to support,
    §§30-4-80 to 30-4-98.
  See DESERTION AND
    NONSUPPORT.
U.R.E.S.A.
  Reciprocal state enforcement
    of duty to support,
    §§30-4-80 to 30-4-98.
  See DESERTION AND
    NONSUPPORT.

SUPREME COURT, §§12-2-1 to
    12-2-160.
Acknowledgments.
  Justices.
    Taking of
      acknowledgments,
      §12-2-3.
Adjournment, §12-2-8.
Administrative rules.
  Promulgation, §12-2-19.

SUPREME COURT—Cont'd
  Advisory committees,
    §12-2-16.
  Affidavits.
    Justices.
      Taking of affidavits,
        §12-2-3.
  Appeals.
    Criminal cases.
      Appeals to supreme court.
        See within this
          heading, "Criminal
          cases."
  Appropriations.
    Purposes for used, §12-2-20.
  Attendant.
    Employment, etc., of court
      attendant, §12-2-32.
  Attorneys at law.
    Disciplinary proceedings.
      Appeals to supreme court,
        ARDE, Rule 8.
    Roll of attorneys, ARAP,
      Rule 46.
    Special judges.
      Appointment of members
        of bar.
          Determination of certain
            cases, §12-2-14.
    Staff attorneys, §12-2-21.
  Bonds, surety.
    Clerk of court, §12-2-91.
      Additional bond, §12-2-92.
    Marshal, §12-2-153.
  Capital offenses.
    Forms.
      Supreme court to
        promulgate indictment
        and verdict forms,
        §13A-5-56.
    Jury instructions.
      Supreme court to
        promulgate jury
        instructions,
        §13A-5-56.
  **Certified questions from
    federal courts,** ARAP,
    Rule 18.
  Certiorari.
    Issuance of writs.
      Powers of justices, §12-2-2.
    Petition for certiorari.
      Review of decisions of
        courts of appeal,
        ARAP, Rule 39.
  Chief justice.
    Absence.
      Performance of duties or
        functions in absence,
        §12-2-5.
      Extended absence,
        §12-2-6.
    Administration of courts,
      Const. Ala., amd. 328.
      Powers and duties as to
        administration,
        §12-2-30.
    Administrative decisions.
      Review by justices,
        §12-5-20.
    Associations.
      Membership and
        associations devoted to
        improvement of justice,
        etc., authorized,
        §12-5-16.
    Colleges, conferences, etc.,
      pertaining to
        administration of courts,
        §12-5-17.

SUPREME COURT—Cont'd
  Chief justice—Cont'd
    Confidential secretary,
      §12-2-130.
    Consultants.
      Employment, §12-5-14.
    Court attendant.
      Employment, §12-2-32.
    Decisions.
      Review of administrative
        decisions of chief
        justice by associate
        justices, §12-5-20.
    Delegation of authority,
      §12-5-15.
    Disability.
      Performance of duties or
        functions of chief
        justice in event of
        disability, §12-2-5.
      Extended disability,
        §12-2-6.
    Elections.
      General elections.
        Offices for which general
          election held,
          §17-2-2.
        State and county officers
          elected by the people,
          §17-2-1.
        When chief justice to be
          elected, §17-2-6.
    Information.
      Provision for compilation
        and tabulation of
        information supplied to
        office, §12-2-31.
    Organizations.
      Membership in
        organizations devoted
        to improvement of
        justice, etc.,
        authorized, §12-5-16.
    Reports.
      Provision for compilation
        and tabulation,
        §12-2-31.
    Safety coordinating
      committee.
        Member of committee,
          §32-3-1.
    Secretary.
      Confidential secretary,
        §12-2-130.
    Special sessions of courts.
      Ordering attendance of
        district attorneys at
        special sessions,
        §12-2-34.
      Ordering of special sessions
        of courts, §12-2-33.
    Supervision of courts, Const.
      Ala., amd. 328.
      Powers and duties of
        supervision, §12-2-30.
    Workmen's compensation.
      Rules for circuit courts.
        Chief justice to prepare
          uniform rules,
          §25-5-12.
  Clerk.
    Additional help.
      Employment, §12-2-95.
    Appointment, §12-2-90;
      Const. Ala., art. VI,
      §164; amd. 271.
    Assistance.
      Employment of additional
        help, §12-2-95.

SUPREME COURT—Cont'd
  Clerk—Cont'd
    Assistant.
      Confidential assistant,
        §12-2-94.
    Attorneys at law.
      Roll of attorneys, ARAP,
        Rule 46.
    Blanks.
      Furnishing of blanks,
        §12-2-99.
    Bond, §12-2-91.
      Additional bond, §12-2-92.
    Clerks of court generally.
      See CLERKS OF COURT.
    Confidential assistant,
      §12-2-94.
    Costs.
      Collection and disposition,
        §12-2-100.
    Deputy clerk.
      Appointment, §12-2-110.
      Creation of office,
        §12-2-110.
      Powers, §12-2-112.
      Removal, §12-2-110.
      Salary, §12-2-111.
    Duties, §§12-2-97, 12-2-112;
      ARAP, Rule 17.
    Employment of additional
      help, §12-2-95.
    Fees, §12-19-91.
      Collection and disposition,
        §12-2-100.
      Provision to department of
        finance of quarterly
        statement of fees paid
        into treasury,
        §12-2-100.
      Schedule of fees, §12-19-91.
    Law clerks. See within this
      heading, "Justices."
    Office and office hours,
      §12-2-96.
    Powers, §12-2-97.
    Records.
      Binding.
        Payment of costs for
          binding, §12-2-98.
      Furnishing of record books,
        §12-2-99.
    Removal, §12-2-90; Const.
      Ala., art. VI, §166.
    Salary, §12-2-93.
    Stationery.
      Furnishing of stationery,
        §12-2-99.
    Term of office, Const. Ala.,
      art. VI, §164.
  Committees.
    Advisory and standing
      committees, §12-2-16.
  Composition of court,
    §12-2-1; Const. Ala., art.
    VI, §151.
  Conflicting opinions.
    Standards for decision of
      cases in which existing
      opinion and former
      ruling in case conflict,
      §12-2-13.
  Constitutional questions.
    Advisory opinions.
      Effect, §12-2-12.
      How obtained, §12-2-10.
  Constitution of Alabama.
    See CONSTITUTION OF
      ALABAMA.

SUPREME COURT—Cont'd
Constitution of the United States.
Supreme court of the United States.
See CONSTITUTION OF THE UNITED STATES.
Contempt.
Powers of court, §12-2-7.
Costs.
Clerk of court.
Collection and disposition, §12-2-100.
Court of civil appeals.
Decisions and proceedings of courts of appeals subject to general superintendence and control of supreme court, §12-3-16.
Decisions of supreme court to govern holding and decisions of courts of appeals, §12-3-16.
Review of decisions, ARAP, Rule 39.
Transfer of cases in court of civil appeals to supreme court, §12-3-15.
Court of criminal appeals.
Decisions and proceedings of courts of appeals subject to general superintendence and control of supreme court, §12-3-16.
Decisions of supreme court to govern holdings and decisions of court of criminal appeals, §12-3-16.
Review of decisions, ARAP, Rule 39.
Transfer of cases in court of criminal appeals to supreme court, §12-3-14.
Courts generally.
See COURTS.
Criminal cases.
Appeals to supreme court, §§12-22-130 to 12-22-133.
Charge to jury.
Presumption that written charges asked before jury retired, §12-22-132.
Conflict over jurisdiction, §12-22-131.
Judgment of conviction, §12-22-130.
Jurisdiction.
Decision where conflict over jurisdiction, §12-22-131.
Retention of jurisdiction by trial court, §12-22-133.
Questions of law.
Reserving questions of law, §12-22-132.
When appeal taken to wrong court, §12-22-131.
Court of criminal appeals.
See within this heading, "Court of criminal appeals."

SUPREME COURT—Cont'd
Decisions.
Reporter of decisions.
See REPORTER OF DECISIONS OF SUPREME COURT AND COURTS OF APPEALS.
Reports of decisions. See within this heading, "Reports of decisions."
Deputy clerks, §§12-2-110 to 12-2-112.
Dissent.
Court sitting in divisions, ARAP, Rule 16 (c).
District court.
Administrative agency.
Supreme court to provide rules of administration for agency, §12-17-252.
Divisions.
Court sitting in divisions, ARAP, Rule 16.
Drugs.
Controlled substances.
Manufacturers and distributors.
Registration.
Appeal from denial, refusal to renew, revocation or suspension, §20-2-53.
Elections.
Chief justice. See within this heading, "Chief justice."
Contest of elections.
See ELECTIONS.
General elections.
Officers for which general elections held, §17-2-2.
Justices elected by the people, §§12-2-1, 17-2-1.
Two or more justices to be elected at the same time.
Designation by number, §17-7-20.
When justices to be elected, §17-2-6.
Equitable process.
Applications to supreme court for equitable process, §12-22-8.
Extraordinary writs.
Review in supreme court of decisions of courts of appeals.
Rules of appellate procedure, ARAP, Rule 21.
Federal courts.
Certified questions from federal courts, ARAP, Rule 18.
Fees.
Attorney general's fee, §12-19-190.
Clerk of supreme court, §12-19-91.
Collection and disposition, §12-2-100.
Provision to department of finance of quarterly statement of fees paid into treasury, §12-2-100.
Habeas corpus.
Powers of court, §12-2-7; Const. Ala., art. VI, §140.

SUPREME COURT—Cont'd
Impeachment.
Appeals to supreme court.
See IMPEACHMENT.
Justices subject to impeachment, Const. Ala., art. VII, §173.
Proceedings in supreme court.
See IMPEACHMENT.
Improperly submitted cases.
Transfer, §12-1-4.
Injunctions.
Granting.
Powers of justices, §12-2-2.
Judges may grant, §6-6-500.
Powers of court, §12-2-7; Const. Ala., art. VI, §140.
Judges.
Duties.
Establishment of additional duties for judges, §12-2-17.
Judicial building.
Security protection, etc., §12-2-18.
Judicial inquiry commission.
Rules of procedure of judicial inquiry commission.
See JUDGES.
Jurisdiction, Const. Ala., amd. 328.
Certified questions from federal courts, ARAP, Rule 18 (b).
Generally, §12-2-7; Const. Ala., art. VI, §140.
Justices.
Acknowledgments.
Taking, §12-2-3.
Affidavits.
Taking of affidavits, §12-2-3.
Canons of judicial ethics.
See CANONS OF JUDICIAL ETHICS.
Certiorari.
Issuance of writs, §12-2-2.
Chief justice. See within this heading, "Chief justice."
Compensation, §12-2-4; Const. Ala., art. VI, §150.
Retired justices on active duty status, §12-18-10.
Composition of court, §12-2-1; Const. Ala., art. VI, §151; amd. 328.
Confidential secretaries. See within this heading, "Secretaries."
Death.
Payment of retirement benefits to spouses upon death of justices, §12-18-10.
Supernumerary justices.
Contribution for payment of retirement benefits to spouse of supernumerary justice upon death of justice, §12-18-31.
Election by surviving spouses to obtain benefits under provisions of article 1 of chapter, §12-18-33.

SUPREME COURT—Cont'd
Justices—Cont'd
  Disability benefits,
    §12-18-10.
  Disqualification.
    Appointment of members
      of bar to sit as special
      judges in
      determination of
      certain cases, §12-2-14.
    Grounds, §12-1-13.
  District attorneys.
    Retirement system.
      Time of service as full-
        time state
        prosecutor,
        §12-18-8.1.
  Dual office holding, Const.
    Ala., art. VI, §150.
  Duties.
    Retired justices, §12-18-7.
      Retired justices on active
        duty status,
        §12-18-10.
  Election of justices, §12-2-1;
    Const. Ala., art. VI,
    §152.
    Contest of elections.
      See ELECTIONS.
    General elections.
      Offices for which general
        election held,
        §17-2-2.
    State and county officers
      elected by the people,
      §§12-2-1, 17-2-1.
    Time of holding election,
      Const. Ala., art. VI,
      §156.
    Two or more justices at
      same election.
      Designating justices by
        number, §17-7-20.
    When justices to be
      elected, §17-2-6.
  Eligibility to become
    supernumerary justice,
    §12-2-50.
  Impeachment.
    See IMPEACHMENT.
  Injunctions.
    Granting, §12-2-2.
  Judges generally.
    See JUDGES.
  Law clerks, §§12-2-70 to
    12-2-72.
    Appointment, §12-2-70.
    Clerks to serve appointing
      justices, §12-2-71.
    Dismissal, §12-2-71.
    Salaries, §12-2-72.
    Sucessors.
      Appointment, §12-2-71.
  Names.
    Minutes of court and
      reports of decisions to
      state names of judges
      sitting in final decision
      of cases, §12-2-15.
  Number of justices, Const.
    Ala., amd. 328.
  Oaths.
    Administration of oaths,
      §12-2-3.
    Retired justices, §12-18-7.
  Powers.
    Retired justices, §12-18-7.
      Retired justices on active
        duty status,
        §12-18-10.

SUPREME COURT—Cont'd
Justices—Cont'd
  Retirement.
    Active duty status,
      §12-18-10.
    Applicability of provisions
      of article to justices
      elected or appointed to
      office after September
      18, 1973, §12-18-5.
    Benefits, §12-18-10.
      Age sixty, §12-18-40.
      Forfeiture of right to
        receive benefits upon
        failure to file
        declaration of
        intention to retire,
        §12-18-7.
      Payment to spouses upon
        death of justices,
        §12-18-10.
    Spouses.
      Payment of benefits to
        spouses upon
        death of justices,
        §12-18-10.
    Compensation of retired
      justices.
      Retired justices on active
        duty status,
        §12-18-10.
    Confidential secretaries.
      Retired justices
        performing active
        duty, §12-5-21.
    Construction of article,
      §12-18-13.
    Contributions made to
      employees' retirement
      system of Alabama.
      Transfer of contributions
        into judicial
        retirement fund,
        §12-18-8.
    Contributions to
      retirement fund by
      justices, §12-18-5.
    Refund of contributions
      upon termination of
      service prior to
      eligibility for
      benefits under
      article, §12-18-8.
    Creditable service as
      district or county court
      judge, §12-18-41.
    Credit for time of service
      as full-time state
      prosecutor, §12-18-8.1.
    Death.
      Payment of benefits to
        spouses upon death
        of justices,
        §12-18-10.
    Declaration as to intention
      to retire, §12-18-7.
    Duties of retired justices,
      §12-18-7.
      Retired justices on active
        duty status,
        §12-18-10.
    Election by justices holding
      office on September 18,
      1973, to come under
      provisions of article,
      §12-18-5.
    Eligibility for retirement,
      §12-18-6.
    Entitlement to retirement
      and receipt of pension,
      §12-18-4.

SUPREME COURT—Cont'd
Justices—Cont'd
  Retirement—Cont'd
    Forfeiture of right to
      receive benefits upon
      failure to file
      declaration of
      intention to retire,
      §12-18-7.
    Intention to retire.
      Declaration as to
        intention, §12-18-7.
    Judicial retirement fund,
      §§12-18-1 to 12-18-114.
      See JUDGES.
    Military service.
      Granting of credit for
        military service,
        §12-18-5.
    Powers of retired justices,
      §12-18-7.
      Justices on active duty
        status, §12-18-10.
    Prior service.
      Receipt of credit for prior
        service under
        employees'
        retirement system
        upon payment of
        contribution for prior
        years of service,
        §12-18-8.
    Prior to eligibility for
      benefits.
      Refund of contributions
        to judicial
        retirement fund,
        §12-18-8.
    Retirement order, §12-18-4.
    Spouses.
      Payment of benefits to
        spouses upon death
        of justices,
        §12-18-10.
    Vacancies in office,
      §12-18-9.
    Salary, §12-2-4; Const. Ala.,
      art. VI, §150.
    Retired justices on active
      duty status, §12-18-10.
    Secretaries.
      Confidential secretaries.
        See within this
        heading, "Secretaries."
    Special judges.
      Appointment of members
        of bar to sit as special
        judges in
        determination of
        certain cases, §12-2-14.
    Supernumerary justices.
      Continuation of laws
        concerning duties,
        benefits, etc., §12-2-50.
      Death.
        Contribution for
          payment of
          retirement benefits
          to spouse of
          supernumerary
          justice upon death of
          justice, §12-18-31.
        Election by surviving
          spouses to obtain
          retirement benefits
          under provisions of
          article 1, §12-18-33.
      Eligibility to become,
        §12-2-50.

SUPREME COURT—Cont'd
  Justices—Cont'd
    Supernumerary justices
      —Cont'd
      Retirement.
        Benefits.
          Contribution for
            payment of
            benefits to spouse
            of supernumerary
            justice upon death
            of justice,
            §12-18-31.
        Death.
          Contribution for
            payment of
            benefits to spouse
            of supernumerary
            justice upon death
            of justice,
             §12-18-31.
          Election by surviving
            spouses to obtain
            benefits under
            provisions of
            article 1,
            §12-18-33.
      Effective date of article,
        §12-18-34.
      Election by justices
        becoming
        supernumerary
        justices prior to
        September 18, 1973
        to come under
        provisions of article
        1, §12-18-30.
      Spouses.
        Contribution for
          payment of
          benefits to spouse
          of supernumerary
          justice upon death
          of justice,
          §12-18-31.
        Election by surviving
          spouses to obtain
          benefits under
          provisions of
          article 1,
          §12-18-33.
  Terms of office, §§12-2-1,
    17-2-6; Const. Ala., art.
    VI, §155.
    Incumbents.
      Terms of incumbents not
        abridged, Const.
        Ala., art. VI, §172.
    Staggered terms of office,
      Const. Ala., art. VI,
      §156.
    Vacancies, §12-18-9; Const.
      Ala., art. VI, §158.
  Law clerks. See within this
    heading, "Justices."
  Library.
    Assistant librarian.
      Appointment, §12-2-155.
      Salary, §12-2-156.
    Bond of librarian, §12-2-153.
    Clerk.
      Appointment, §12-2-155.
      Salary, §12-2-156.
    Courts of appeals, §12-3-19.
    Employees.
      Appointment, §12-2-155.
      Salaries, §12-2-156.

SUPREME COURT—Cont'd
  Library—Cont'd
    Fund, §12-2-157.
      Use for purchase of law
        books for office of
        attorney general,
        §12-2-158.
    Librarian.
      Assistant librarian.
        Appointment, §12-2-155.
        Salary, §12-2-156.
      Bond of librarian,
        §12-2-153.
      Designation of marshal as
        state law librarian,
        §12-2-151.
    Marshal.
      Designation as state law
        librarian, §12-2-151.
    Rules.
      Justices to make rules for
        preservation and
        protection library,
        §12-2-160.
    Salaries, §§12-2-154,
      12-2-156.
    Tax, §12-2-159.
  Mandamus.
    Review in supreme court of
      decisions of courts of
      appeals, ARAP, Rule 21.
  Marshal, §§12-2-150 to
    12-2-155.
    Appointment, §12-2-150.
      Entry of appointment of
        marshal on minutes of
        court, §12-2-152.
    Bond, surety, §12-2-153.
    Courts of appeals, §12-3-19.
    Deputy marshals.
      Appointment, §12-2-155.
      Salaries, §12-2-156.
    Designation as state law
      librarian, §12-2-151.
    Designation, etc., §12-2-18.
    Duties, §12-2-150.
      Discharge of duties of
        office, §12-2-151.
    Librarian.
      Designation as state law
        librarian, §12-2-151.
    Oath, §12-2-152.
    Salary, §12-2-154.
  Minutes of court.
    Marshal.
      Entry of appointment of
        marshal on minutes of
        court, §12-2-152.
    Names of justices.
      Minutes to state names of
        justices sitting in final
        decision of cases,
        §12-2-15.
  Motor vehicle carriers.
    Appeals, §37-3-29.
  Municipal courts.
    Administrative agency for
      municipal court.
      Supreme court to provide
        rules of administration
        for agency, §12-14-52.
  Notice of appeal.
    Form, ARAP, Form 1.
  Notice of orders, ARAP, Rule
    17 (a).
  Oaths.
    Justices.
      Administration of oaths,
        §12-2-3.
      Retired justices, §12-18-7.

SUPREME COURT—Cont'd
  Opinions.
    Advisory opinions on
      constitutional questions,
      §§12-2-11, 12-2-12.
    Conflict with former ruling
      in case.
      Standard for decision of
        cases in which existing
        opinion and former
        ruling conflict,
        §12-2-13.
    Copies.
      Sending copies of opinions,
        ARAP, Rule 36 (a).
    Reports of decisions. See
      within this heading,
      "Reports of decisions."
  Orders of court.
    Notice of orders, ARAP, Rule
      17 (a).
  Original writs.
    Power to issue, Const. Ala.,
      art. VI, §140.
  Overruling cases, ARAP,
    Rule 15.
  Pensions.
    Justices. See within this
      heading, "Justices."
  Place of holding, Const. Ala.,
    art. VI, §141.
  Powers of court.
    Generally, §12-2-7.
  Prohibition, writ of.
    Review in supreme court of
      decisions of courts of
      appeals, ARAP, Rule 21.
  Public service commission.
    Appeals.
      Rate cases, §§37-1-140 to
        37-1-143.
      Right of appeal to supreme
        court, §37-1-132.
  Public utilities.
    Valuation of utility property.
      Appeals to supreme court,
        §37-4-21.
  Quo warranto.
    Power of supreme court to
      issue writs, Const. Ala.,
      art. VI, §140.
  Radio.
    Radio utilities.
      Appeals to supreme court,
        §37-4-114.
  Records.
    Clerk of court.
      Binding.
        Payment of costs for
          binding, §12-2-98.
        Furnishing of record books,
          §12-2-99.
  Remedial writs.
    Power of supreme court to
      issue, §12-2-7; Const.
      Ala., art. VI, §140.
  **Reporter of decisions of
    supreme court,** §§12-4-1
    to 12-4-4.
  Reports of decisions.
    Chief justice.
      Provision for compilation
        and tabulation,
        §12-2-31.
    Furnished to law department
      of University of
      Alabama, §16-47-8.

SUPREME COURT—Cont'd
  Reports of decisions—Cont'd
    Names of judges.
      Reports to state names of
        judges sitting in final
        decision of cases,
        §12-2-15.
    University of Alabama.
      Reports furnished to law
        department, §16-47-8.
  Retirement.
    Justices. See within this
      heading, "Justices."
  Rules for mandatory
    continuing legal
    education.
    See ATTORNEYS AT LAW.
  Rules of appellate
    procedure.
    See APPEALS.
  Rules of civil procedure.
    See RULES OF CIVIL
      PROCEDURE.
  Rules of court, Const. Ala.,
    amd. 328.
    Administrative rules,
      §12-2-19.
    Code of Alabama.
      Adoption not to affect
        supreme court rules,
        §6-1-1.
    Effect, §§6-1-2, 12-1-1.
    Filing, §12-2-19.
    Powers of court, §12-2-7.
    Publication, §12-2-19.
  Rules of criminal procedure.
    See RULES OF CRIMINAL
      PROCEDURE.
  Rules of disciplinary
    enforcement.
    See ATTORNEYS AT LAW.
  Rules of judicial
    administration.
    See COURTS.
  Rules of juvenile procedure.
    See JUVENILE
      PROCEEDINGS.
  Rules of procedure of
    judicial inquiry
    commission.
    See JUDGES.
  Salaries.
    Clerks, §12-2-93.
    Justices, §12-2-4; Const. Ala.,
      art. VI, §150.
      Retired justices on active
        duty status, §12-18-10.
    Library.
      Assistant librarian,
        §12-2-156.
      State law librarian,
        §12-2-154.
    Staff attorneys, §12-2-21.
  Secretaries.
    Associate justices and
      supernumerary justices.
      Compensation, §12-2-131.
      Confidential secretaries.
        Appointment, §12-2-131.
        Duties, §12-2-132.
    Chief justice.
      Confidential secretary of
        chief justice, §12-2-130.
    Retired justices performing
      active duty.
      Confidential secretaries,
        §12-5-21.
  Small claims rules.
    See SMALL CLAIMS.
  Staff attorneys, §12-2-21.

SUPREME COURT—Cont'd
  Standing committees,
    §12-2-16.
  Supernumerary justices. See
    within this heading,
    "Justices."
  Taxation.
    Library tax, §12-2-159.
  Temporary restraining
    orders.
    Applications to supreme
      court, §12-22-8.
  Terms of court.
    Regular terms, §12-2-8.
    Special terms, §12-2-9.
    When held, §12-2-8.
  Transfer of cases.
    Improperly submitted cases,
      §12-1-4.
  University of Alabama.
    Books.
      Furnished to law
        department, §16-47-7.
    Reports.
      Furnished to law
        department, §16-47-8.
  Workmen's compensation.
    Rules for circuit courts.
      Chief justice of supreme
        court to prepare
        uniform rules,
        §25-5-12.
  Writs.
    Powers of court, §12-2-7;
      Const. Ala., art. VI,
      §140.

SURETY BONDS.
  See BONDS, SURETY.

SURETYSHIP, §§8-3-1 to
  8-3-42.
  Actions.
    Payments by surety pending
      action, §8-3-8.
    Surety may require creditor
      to bring action against
      principal, §8-3-13.
  Banks and financial
    institutions.
    Agreements between
      principal and sureties on
      bond for deposit of
      money and assets in
      bank, §5-5A-35.
  Bills.
    Relationship of joint makers,
      §8-3-1.
  Bills of lading.
    Indorser not guarantor for
      other parties, §7-7-505.
  Bonds, surety.
    See BONDS, SURETY.
  Circuit courts.
    Court in which complaints
      filed, §8-3-15.
  Collateral security.
    Replevy bonds. See within
      this heading, "Replevy
      bonds."
  Commercial code.
    Documents of title.
      Indorser not guarantor for
        other parties, §7-7-505.
    Investment securities.
      Indorser not guarantor,
        §7-8-308.
  Complaints.
    Court in which filed, §8-3-15.
  Confession of judgment.
    When surety not to confess
      judgment, §8-3-12.

SURETYSHIP—Cont'd
  Contribution by cosureties,
    §8-3-9.
  Counterclaims.
    Debt or liquidated demand
      due principal, §6-8-81.
  Discharge.
    Failure of creditor to bring
      action against principal
      when required, §8-3-13.
    Tender by surety, §8-3-4.
  Documents of title.
    Indorser not guarantor for
      other parties, §7-7-505.
  Evidence.
    Parol evidence.
      Suretyship may be proved
        by parol, §8-3-6.
  Executions.
    Levy on property of principal
      first if execution against
      sureties, §6-9-83.
    Right of surety paying
      execution, §6-9-2.
  Husband and wife.
    Insurance policy designating
      wife as beneficiary.
      Assignment as security for
        indebtedness.
        Exemption from
          prohibition against
          contracts of
          suretyship of wife,
          §30-4-10.
  Insurance.
    See INSURANCE.
  Investment securities.
    Indorser not guarantor,
      §7-8-308.
  Judgments.
    Confession of judgment.
      When surety not to confess
        judgment, §8-3-12.
    Control of judgment by
      endorser upon payment
      of debt, §8-3-10.
    Payment by surety.
      Execution.
        Collection of money from
          principal debtor or
          cosureties, §8-3-41.
        Issuance on judgment
          paid by surety,
          §8-3-41.
      Transfer of judgment to
        surety upon, §8-3-40.
    Right of surety paying
      judgment, §§6-9-2, 8-3-7.
    Summary judgment.
      Sureties entitled to
        summary judgment
        against principal and
        between each other,
        §8-3-42.
  Letters of credit, §§7-5-101 to
    7-5-117.
    See COMMERCIAL CODE.
  Limitation of actions,
    §§6-2-34, 6-2-36.
  Notes.
    Relationship of joint makers,
      §8-3-1.
  Parol evidence.
    Proof of suretyship, §8-3-6.
  Payment of debt.
    Control of judgment by
      indorser upon, §8-3-10.
    Judgments.
      Payment by surety. See
        within this heading,
        "Judgments."

SURETYSHIP—Cont'd
Payment of debt—Cont'd
Payments by surety pending action, §8-3-8.
Rights of surety who has paid debt, §§8-3-2, 8-3-5.
Surety paying debt subrogated to rights of creditor, §8-3-11.
Personal representatives.
Provisions of chapter inure to benefit of personal representatives, §8-3-14.
Reimbursement.
Rights of surety who has paid debt, §8-3-2.
Remedies of surety.
Nonexclusive, §8-3-3.
Replevy bonds.
Collateral security.
Seizure of property if collateral not given, §8-3-30.
Disposition of seized perishable property, §8-3-30.
When surety on replevy bond may demand, §8-3-30.
Rights of surety.
Judgments.
Surety paying judgment, §§6-9-2, 8-3-7.
Payment of debt.
Rights upon, §§8-3-2, 8-3-5.
Rules of civil procedure.
Proceedings against sureties, ARCP, Rule 65.1.
Subrogation.
Rights of surety paying judgment or execution, §6-9-2.
Rights of surety who has paid debt, §8-3-2.
Surety paying debt subrogated to rights of creditor, §8-3-11.
Tender.
Discharge of surety, §8-3-4.
Uniform commercial code.
See within this heading, "Commercial code."
Warehouse receipts.
Indorser not guarantor for other parties, §7-7-505.

SURFACE MINING.
General provisions.
See MINES AND MINERALS.

SURGEONS.
See PHYSICIANS.

SURPLUS PERSONAL PROPERTY, §§41-16-120 to 41-16-125.
Disposition of property owned by state.
Accounts, §41-16-122.
Authority of division, §41-16-122.
Availability of surplus property, §41-16-121.
Definitions, §41-16-120.
Director of economic and community affairs.
Responsibility, §41-16-120.
Effect of article.
Status of division employees, §41-16-124.

SURPLUS PERSONAL PROPERTY—Cont'd
Disposition of property owned by state—Cont'd
Hazardous material.
Disposition prohibited, §41-16-121.
List of property.
Publication and dissemination, §41-16-121.
Property held less than sixty days, §41-16-123.
Responsibility, §41-16-120.
Revenue.
Disposition, §41-16-122.
State agency for federal property assistance.
State plan of operation for, §41-16-125.

SURVEILLANCE.
Criminal surveillance, §13A-11-32.

SURVEYS AND SURVEYORS, §§34-11-1 to 34-11-37, 35-2-1 to 35-2-82.
Actions to determine boundaries.
Determination of boundaries in pending actions, §§35-3-20 to 35-3-25.
See BOUNDARIES.
Airports.
State airports.
Right of entry for surveys, §4-2-93.
Alabama coordinate system, §§35-2-1 to 35-2-9.
Coordinates.
Plane coordinates used in system, §35-2-3.
Recordation.
Limitation on recordation of coordinates defining position of point on land boundary, §35-2-6.
Definition of system.
United States coast and geodetic survey.
Definition of United States coast and geodetic survey adopted, §35-2-5.
Description of land.
Designation of system in land description, §35-2-2.
Purchaser or mortgagee not required to rely exclusively on description based on system, §35-2-9.
Tract of land lying in both zones, §35-2-4.
United States public land surveys.
Description by reference to subdivision, line or corner of United States public land surveys, §35-2-8.
Designation of system, §35-2-1.
Land description.
Designation of system in land description, §35-2-2.

SURVEYS AND SURVEYORS
—Cont'd
Alabama coordinate system
—Cont'd
Division of state into zones.
State divided into east and west zones, §35-2-1.
Monuments and markers.
Descriptions, §35-2-6.
Mortgagees.
Description of land.
Mortgagee not required to rely exclusively on description based on system, §35-2-9.
Name of system.
Limitation on use of name, §35-2-7.
Plane coordinates used in system, §35-2-3.
Purchasers.
Not required to rely exclusively on description based on system, §35-2-9.
United States coast and geodetic survey.
Definition of system by United States coast and geodetic survey adopted, §35-2-5.
United States public land surveys.
Description by reference to subdivision, line or corner of United States public land surveys, §35-2-8.
Zones.
State divided into east and west zones, §35-2-1.
Tract of land lying in both zones.
Description when tract in both zones, §35-2-4.
Appeals.
Board of registration.
Appeals from decisions of board, §34-11-13.
Applicability of chapter.
Persons and acts exempt from chapter, §34-11-14.
Associations.
Professional corporations, §§10-4-380 to 10-4-406.
See PROFESSIONAL CORPORATIONS.
Unincorporated professional associations, §§10-10-1 to 10-10-16.
See UNINCORPORATED PROFESSIONAL ASSOCIATIONS.
Board of registration.
Appeals from decisions of board, §34-11-13.
Appointment of members, §34-11-30.
Censure of surveyors.
Power of board, §34-11-11.
Compensation of members, §34-11-32.
Composition of board, §34-11-30.
Creation, §34-11-30.
Defined, §34-11-1.
Evidence.
Admissibility of board records, §34-11-37.

SURVEYS AND SURVEYORS
—Cont'd
Board of registration—Cont'd
Examinations.
Authority of board,
§34-11-6.
Expenses of members,
§34-11-32.
Funds.
Receipts and
disbursements by
secretary of board,
§34-11-36.
Governor.
Annual report to governor,
§34-11-37.
Filling vacancies on board,
§34-11-33.
Removal of members,
§34-11-33.
Hearings.
Disciplinary action against
surveyor, §34-11-11.
Immunity for good faith
actions, §34-11-35.
Injunctions.
Power of board, §34-11-35.
Investigation of complaints.
Powers of board, §34-11-35.
Legal office, §34-11-34.
Meetings, §34-11-34.
Notice of meetings,
§34-11-34.
Oaths.
Administration by board
members, §34-11-35.
Oath of office, §34-11-30.
Office.
Legal office of board,
§34-11-34.
Officers of board, §34-11-34.
Powers.
Generally, §34-11-35.
Qualifications of members,
§34-11-31.
Quorum, §34-11-34.
Records.
Board required to keep
certain records,
§34-11-37.
Reissuance of revoked
certificates, §34-11-12.
Removal of members,
§34-11-33.
Reports.
Annual report of board,
§34-11-37.
Rules and regulations.
Promulgation by board,
§34-11-35.
Secretary.
Receipts and
disbursements,
§34-11-36.
Roster of registrants,
§34-11-3.
Subpoena of witnesses,
§34-11-35.
Suspension or revocation of
certificates.
Power of board, §34-11-11.
Terms of office, §34-11-30.
Vacancies.
Filling vacancies,
§34-11-33.
Witnesses.
Power to compel
attendance of
witnesses, §34-11-35.

SURVEYS AND SURVEYORS
—Cont'd
Boundaries.
Determination in pending
actions.
See BOUNDARIES.
Buildings.
County surveyors.
Rights as to buildings not
lost by straightening
or location of section,
etc., lines, §11-7-10.
Certificates.
Registration. See within this
heading, "Registration."
Coal mines.
See COAL.
Contracts.
Division of land surveys,
§35-2-36.
Coordinate system.
Alabama coordinate system.
See within this heading,
"Alabama coordinate
system."
Corporations.
Certificate of authorization,
§34-11-9.
Practice of engineering.
Disciplinary action,
§34-11-11.
Practice of land surveying,
§34-11-9.
Professional corporations,
§§10-4-380 to 10-4-406.
See PROFESSIONAL
CORPORATIONS.
Registration as corporation
prohibited, §34-11-9.
Counties, §§11-7-1 to 11-7-12.
See COUNTIES.
County surveyors, §§11-7-1 to
11-7-12.
See COUNTIES.
Damages.
Division of land surveys.
Liability for damages to
private property,
§35-2-32.
Definitions, §34-11-1.
**Determination of boundaries
in pending actions.**
See BOUNDARIES.
Division of land surveys,
§§35-2-20 to 35-2-38.
Advisory board.
Chairman, §35-2-28.
Creation, §35-2-25.
Duties, §35-2-29.
Expenses.
Reimbursement of
expenses, §35-2-27.
Meetings, §35-2-28.
Membership, §35-2-25.
Oath of members, §35-2-27.
Right of entry upon private
property, §35-2-32.
Liability for damages,
§35-2-32.
Terms of members,
§35-2-26.
Trespass.
Immunity from arrest for
trespass, §35-2-32.
Vacancies.
Filling, §35-2-26.
Authorized surveys, §35-2-38.
Chief of division.
Appointment, §35-2-21.

SURVEYS AND SURVEYORS
—Cont'd
Division of land surveys
—Cont'd
Chief of division—Cont'd
Commissioner of
conservation and
natural resources.
Functions, duties and
responsibilities of
commissioner acting
through chief of
division, §35-2-24.
Duties, §35-2-23.
Functions, §35-2-23.
No other lucrative position
to be held, §35-2-22.
Oath, §35-2-22.
Qualifications, §35-2-21.
Right of entry upon private
property, §35-2-32.
Liability for damages,
§35-2-32.
Salary, §35-2-22.
Trespass.
Immunity from arrest for
trespass, §35-2-32.
Commissioner of
conservation and natural
resources.
Functions, duties and
responsibilities of
commissioner acting
through chief of
division, §35-2-24.
Compensation.
Limitation on amount of
warrants for payment
of compensation,
§35-2-37.
Contracts, §35-2-36.
Court proceedings.
Admissibility of division
records in court
proceedings, §35-2-33.
Creation, §35-2-20.
Damages to private property.
Liability, §35-2-32.
Department of conservation
and natural resources.
Division of department,
§35-2-20.
Employees.
Private surveying or
consultation not
permitted, §35-2-34.
Registration, §35-2-34.
Evidence.
Admissibility of division
records in court
proceedings, §35-2-33.
Expenses.
Warrants for payment of
expenses.
Limitation on amount of
warrants, §35-2-37.
Extent of surveys or
resurveys authorized by
article, §35-2-38.
Land.
Acquisition of land for
monuments and office,
§35-2-30.
Maps.
Production, reproduction or
sale, §35-2-35.
Monuments.
Acquisition of land for
monuments, §35-2-30.

SURVEYS AND SURVEYORS
—Cont'd
Division of land surveys
—Cont'd
Monuments—Cont'd
Commissioner of
conservation and
natural resources.
Functions, duties and
responsibilities of
commissioner acting
through chief of
division, §35-2-24.
Municipal corporations.
See MUNICIPAL
CORPORATIONS.
Office.
Acquisition of land for
office, §35-2-30.
Plats.
Production, reproduction or
sale, §35-2-35.
Private property.
Right of entry upon private
property, §35-2-32.
Private surveying or
consultation not
permitted, §35-2-34.
Purpose, §35-2-20.
Records.
Admissibility of division
records in court
proceedings, §35-2-33.
Furnishing copies of
records to division,
§35-2-33.
Production, reproduction or
sale, §35-2-35.
Registration of employees,
§35-2-34.
Reports.
Production, reproduction or
sale, §35-2-35.
Right of entry upon private
property, §35-2-32.
Liability for damages,
§35-2-32.
Sales.
Maps, plats, reports or
records, §35-2-35.
Survey corners and
accessories.
Custody and ownership of
original survey corners
and accessories,
§35-2-31.
Penalty for alteration or
destruction, §35-2-31.
Trespass.
Immunity from arrest for
trespass, §35-2-32.
Evidence.
Board of registration.
Admissibility of board
records, §34-11-37.
Division of land surveys.
Admissibility of division
records in court
proceedings, §35-2-33.
Surveyor general of United
States.
Books, maps, etc.
Admissibility of copies,
§12-21-36.
Examinations.
Board of registration.
Authority over scope and
methods of procedure,
§34-11-6.
Fees, §34-11-6.

SURVEYS AND SURVEYORS
—Cont'd
Examinations—Cont'd
Qualifications for
registration, §34-11-4.
Reexamination, §34-11-6.
Scope of examination,
§34-11-6.
Subjects examined, §34-11-6.
**Exemptions from provisions
of chapter,** §34-11-14.
Fees.
Duplicate certificates,
§34-11-12.
Examination fees, §34-11-6.
Registration fees, §34-11-5.
Fences.
County surveyors.
Rights as to fences not lost
by straightening or
location of section, etc.,
lines, §11-7-10.
Flood-prone areas.
Counties.
Land-use management in
flood-prone areas,
§§11-19-1 to 11-19-24.
See COUNTIES.
Fraud.
Grounds for disciplinary
action, §34-11-11.
Funds.
Board of registration.
Secretary to receive and
account for all funds,
§34-11-36.
Geological survey, §§9-4-1 to
9-4-19.
See GEOLOGICAL
SURVEY.
Governor.
Board of registration. See
within this heading,
"Board of registration."
Highways.
Department.
Right of entry for purposes
of making surveys,
§23-1-44.
Injunctions.
Board of registration.
Power of board, §34-11-35.
Landscape architects.
General provisions.
See LANDSCAPE
ARCHITECTS.
Surveyors exempt from
licensing provisions,
§34-17-27.
**Local government records
commission.**
Conduct of surveys
authorized, §41-13-24.
Marine resources.
Private reefs.
Surveys and markings of
reefs, §9-12-32.
Municipal corporations.
Surveys, plats or maps,
§§35-2-50 to 35-2-62.
See MUNICIPAL
CORPORATIONS.
Partnerships.
Certificate of authorization,
§34-11-9.
Practice of land surveying,
§34-11-9.
Registration as partnership
prohibited, §34-11-9.

SURVEYS AND SURVEYORS
—Cont'd
Penalties.
Survey corners and
accessories.
Penalty for alteration or
destruction, §35-2-31.
Violations of chapter,
§34-11-15.
Policy.
Public policy regarding
regulation of surveying,
§34-11-2.
Practice of surveying.
Defined, §34-11-1.
Regulation of practice,
§34-11-2.
Professional corporations,
§§10-4-380 to 10-4-406.
See PROFESSIONAL
CORPORATIONS.
Public lands.
School lands.
Surveying of lands,
§9-15-37.
Recordation.
Town surveys, plats or maps,
§§35-2-51, 35-2-57.
Records.
Division of land surveys.
General provisions. See
within this heading,
"Division of land
surveys."
Furnishing copies to division
of land surveys, §35-2-33.
Registration.
Applications, §34-11-5.
Record of applicants to be
kept by board,
§34-11-37.
Board of registration. See
within this heading,
"Board of registration."
Certificates.
Duplicate certificates,
§34-11-12.
Expiration, §34-11-8.
Issuance, §34-11-7.
Renewal, §34-11-8.
Corporations.
Registration of corporation
prohibited, §34-11-9.
Division of land surveys.
Registration of employees,
§35-2-34.
Examinations. See within
this heading,
"Examinations."
Expiration of certificates,
§34-11-8.
Fees, §34-11-5.
General requirements,
§34-11-4.
Partnerships.
Registration of partnership
prohibited, §34-11-9.
Policy regarding registration
requirements, §34-11-2.
Renewal of certificates,
§34-11-8.
Roster of registrants,
§34-11-3.
Seal, §34-11-7.
Suspension or revocation of
certificates.
Appeals from decisions of
board, §34-11-13.
Grounds, §34-11-11.
Reissuance of revoked
certificates, §34-11-12.

SURVEYS AND SURVEYORS
—Cont'd
Responsible charge.
Defined, §34-11-1.
Right of entry.
County surveyors, §§11-7-5,
11-7-11.
Division of land surveys,
§35-2-32.
Highways.
Department.
Right of entry for
purposes of making
surveys, §23-1-44.
**Rules of professional
conduct.**
Adoption, §34-11-35.
Sales.
Division of land surveys.
Maps, plats, etc., §35-2-35.
**Seal of professional land
surveyor,** §34-11-7.
State geologist, §§9-4-1 to
9-4-10.
See GEOLOGICAL
SURVEY.
State records commission.
Conduct of surveys
authorized, §41-13-24.
Subpoenas.
Board of registration.
Power of board, §34-11-35.
**Town surveys, plats or
maps,** §§35-2-50 to
35-2-62.
See MUNICIPAL
CORPORATIONS.
Trespass.
Division of land surveys.
Immunity from arrest for
trespass, §35-2-32.
**Unincorporated professional
associations,** §§10-10-1 to
10-10-16.
See UNINCORPORATED
PROFESSIONAL
ASSOCIATIONS.
United States.
Public land surveys.
Description by reference to
subdivision, line or
corner of United States
public land surveys,
§35-2-8.
Original survey corners
and accessories.
Custody and ownership,
§35-2-31.
**United States coast and
geodetic survey.**
Alabama coordinate system.
Definition of system by
United States coast
and geodetic survey
adopted, §35-2-5.
Urban renewal projects,
§24-3-4.
Waters and watercourses.
Development of docks and
other facilities along
inland waterways.
See WATERS AND
WATERCOURSES.
Witnesses.
Board of registration.
Witnesses.
Power to compel
attendance,
§34-11-35.

SURVIVAL OF ACTIONS.
See ABATEMENT, REVIVAL
AND SURVIVAL OF
ACTIONS.

SURVIVING SPOUSE.
Debts.
Exemptions from
administration and
payment of debts.
See EXEMPTIONS FROM
ADMINISTRATION
AND PAYMENT OF
DEBTS.
**District attorneys' spouses
fund,** §§12-17-201 to
12-17-207.
See DISTRICT
ATTORNEYS.
Dower.
See DOWER.
**Executors and
administrators.**
Compelling payment of
legacies.
Applicability to dissenting
widow, §43-2-580.
Exemptions.
See EXEMPTIONS FROM
ADMINISTRATION
AND PAYMENT OF
DEBTS.
Governor's pension,
§36-13-12.
Salaries.
Debt for wage owed to
intestate former
employee.
Discharge by payment to
surviving spouse,
§43-8-115.
Veterans.
Educational benefits.
See VETERANS.
Pension for widows.
Confederate veterans,
§§31-8-1 to 31-8-33.
See VETERANS.
Wages.
Debt for wage owed to
intestate former
employee.
Discharge by payment to
surviving spouse,
§43-8-115.
Wills.
Notice to surviving spouse of
probate of will,
§§43-8-164 to 43-8-166.

**SUSIE PARKER
STRINGFELLOW
MEMORIAL HOSPITAL.**
**Exemption from state,
county and municipal ad
valorem taxation,**
§40-9-1.1.

SWAMPS.
Drainage.
Assessment by municipal
corporations for costs of
swamp drainage,
§11-48-16.
Municipal corporations.
Assessments for public
improvements.
Manner of assessment of
costs for swamp
drainage, §11-48-16.
Public lands.
See PUBLIC LANDS.

SWEARING.
False swearing.
See PERJURY.
Oaths.
See OATHS.

SWEATSHOPS.
Child labor.
See LABOR.

SWIMMING POOLS.
Counties.
Bond issues.
Public improvement bonds,
§§11-81-140 to
11-81-150.
See COUNTIES.
Municipal corporations.
Bond issues.
Public improvement bonds,
§§11-81-110 to
11-81-123.
See MUNICIPAL
CORPORATIONS.
Public athletic boards,
§§11-59-1 to 11-59-17.
See MUNICIPAL
CORPORATIONS.

SWINE.
Estrays.
See ESTRAYS.
General provisions.
See LIVESTOCK.

**SYLACAUGA NURSES'
TRAINING SCHOOL.**
Board of trustees.
Endowment funds.
Investment of endowment
funds held by board,
§16-13-2.
**Commission of higher
education.**
General provisions.
See UNIVERSITIES AND
COLLEGES.
Police, §§16-22-1, 16-22-2.
Scholarships.
Amount, §16-58-3.
Conditions, §16-58-3.
Selection of recipients,
§16-58-3.
Distribution, §16-58-1.
Eligibility.
Who eligible, §16-58-2.
Established, §16-58-1.

SYMBOLS.
Brands and marks.
See BRANDS AND MARKS.
Seeds or plant parts.
Registration.
See SEEDS.
Trademarks.
See TRADEMARKS.

**SYNFUELS DEVELOPMENT
AUTHORITY,** §§9-6A-1 to
9-6A-10.
**Application for authority to
incorporate,** §9-6A-4.
Review and recordation by
secretary of state,
§9-6A-4.
Board of directors.
Compensation, §9-6A-6.
Proceedings.
Reduced to writing and
recorded, §9-6A-6.

SYNFUELS DEVELOPMENT AUTHORITY—Cont'd

Bridges.
Contracts for construction, reconstruction, etc.
Supervision or performance by highway department, §9-6A-8.
Certificate of incorporation, §9-6A-5.
Contracts.
Competitive bidding, §9-6A-8.
Highways, roads and bridges.
Supervision or performance by highway department, §9-6A-8.
Definitions, §9-6A-1.
Dissolution of authority, §9-6A-10.
Application for dissolution, §9-6A-10.
Recordation of application by secretary of state, §9-6A-10.
Duties.
Delegation of duties and obligations, §9-6A-9.
Energy department.
Director of department.
Individuals who may become public corporation, §9-6A-3.
Finance director.
Individuals who may become public corporation, §9-6A-3.
Governor.
Individuals who may become public corporation, §9-6A-3.
Highway department.
Contracts for construction, reconstruction, etc., of highways, roads and bridges, §9-6A-8.
Incorporation of authority.
Application for authority to incorporate, §9-6A-4.
Recordation by secretary of state, §9-6A-4.
Review by secretary of state, §9-6A-4.
Certificate of incorporation, §9-6A-5.
Individuals who may become public corporation, §9-6A-3.
Legislative intent, §9-6A-2.
Lieutenant governor.
Individuals who may become public corporation, §9-6A-3.
Obligations of authority.
Delegation of obligations, §9-6A-9.
Powers of authority, §9-6A-7.
Purposes of authority, §9-6A-2.
Recordation.
Application for authority to incorporate.
Secretary of state to record, §9-6A-4.
Dissolution of authority.
Application for dissolution recorded by secretary of state, §9-6A-10.

SYNFUELS DEVELOPMENT AUTHORITY—Cont'd

Records.
Board of directors.
Proceedings to be reduced to writing and recorded, §9-6A-6.
Secretary of state.
Application for authority to incorporate.
Review and recordation by secretary of state, §9-6A-4.
Dissolution of authority.
Recordation of application for dissolution by secretary of state, §9-6A-10.
Speaker of house of representatives.
Individuals who may become public corporation, §9-6A-3.

SYPHILIS.
Marriage.
Licenses.
Examination for syphilis.
Prerequisite for marriage license, §22-11A-15.
Notifiable diseases, §§22-11A-1 to 22-11A-38.
See DISEASES.

SYRUP.
Licenses.
Factories, §40-12-165.

T

TABLE WINE, §§28-7-1 to 28-7-24.
See ALCOHOLIC BEVERAGES.

TAGS.
Advertising.
Outdoor advertising.
Erection or maintenance of signs.
Exceptions, §23-1-277.
Identification tags or decals, §23-1-275.
Dogs.
Rabies tag, §§3-7-4 to 3-7-6.
Motor vehicles, §§32-6-51 to 32-6-295.
See MOTOR VEHICLES.
Rabies, §§3-7-4 to 3-7-6.

TAILGATING.
Prohibited, §32-5A-89.

TALLADEGA COUNTY.
Court costs and charges, Const. Ala., amd. 85.
Economic and industrial development promotion, Const. Ala., amd. 429.
Jail.
Construction.
Fee on civil and criminal cases for, Const. Ala., amd. 504.
Officers.
Fees, salaries, etc., Const. Ala., amd. 85.
Property tax.
Levy and collection of additional property taxes, Const. Ala., amd. 98.

TALLADEGA COUNTY —Cont'd

School taxes.
Special school district taxes, Const. Ala., amd. 310.
Special school tax, Const. Ala., amd. 181.
Special school tax in school district No. 1, Const. Ala., amd. 252.

TALLADEGA, MUNICIPALITY OF.
Property tax, Const. Ala., amd. 13.

TALLAPOOSA COUNTY.
Hospitals.
Tax and tax anticipation bonds, Const. Ala., amd. 198.
Officers.
Compensation, Const. Ala., amd. 297.
School tax.
Additional property taxes, Const. Ala., amd. 129.

TANNEHILL FURNACE AND FOUNDRY COMMISSION, §§41-9-320 to 41-9-330.
See HISTORY AND ARCHIVES.

TAPES.
Copying and sale of recorded devices, §§13A-8-80 to 13A-8-86.
See RECORDED DEVICES.

TARIFFS.
Common carriers, §§37-3-20 to 37-3-23.
Public utilities.
Rates.
See PUBLIC UTILITIES.
Transportation companies, §§37-2-10, 37-8-22.

TARPONS.
State saltwater fish, §1-2-8.

TAXATION.
Actions.
Collection of taxes, §40-5-42.
Defense of actions, §40-1-13.
Limitation. See within this heading, "Limitation of actions."
Officers.
Actions against, §§40-1-16, 40-1-17, 40-1-40.
Sale of land for taxes, §§40-10-1 to 40-10-166.
See within this heading, "Sale of land for taxes."
Supreme court library tax, §12-2-159.
Tax collectors.
Collection of taxes by action, §40-5-42.
Administration of state revenue laws.
Attempts to interfere with, §40-29-118.
Ad valorem taxes.
Classification of taxable property, Const. Ala., amd. 373.
Distribution, §40-8-3.

TAXATION—Cont'd
Ad valorem taxes—Cont'd
Exemptions from taxation.
Generally, §§40-9-1 to
40-9-49. See within
this heading,
"Exemptions from
taxation."
Hotels, inns and other
transient lodging places.
Industrial development
boards.
Hotels and motor inns
built under act not
exempt, §11-54-96.1.
Investments, §§40-1-47,
40-1-48.
Motor vehicles.
Certificate of title.
Prerequisite to
assessment,
§32-8-33.
Salaries, fees, etc., of county
officials.
Assessment and collection
of taxes, Const. Ala.,
amd. 411.
Statewide property
reappraisal, §§40-7-60 to
40-7-100. See within this
heading, "Assessments."
Aged persons.
Exemptions from taxation.
Homestead exemptions,
§40-9-19.
Verification of eligibility
by mail, §40-9-21.1.
Principal residence of
certain persons,
§§40-9-21, 40-9-21.1.
Agents.
Liability of agents, §40-1-7.
Returns.
Separate returns in
individual and
fiduciary capacity,
§40-7-20.
Agriculture.
Agricultural center
corporation.
Exemption, §2-6-37.
Agricultural development
authority.
Exemption, §2-3A-11.
Agricultural markets and
coliseum corporation.
Exemption, §2-6-85.
Exemptions from taxation,
§40-9-1.
Agricultural center
corporation, §2-6-37.
Agricultural development
authority, §2-3A-11.
Motor fuels.
Additional excise tax on
gasoline, motor fuels
and lubricating oil,
§40-17-220.
Mutual farming or trucking
associations, §2-10-105.
Air commerce.
Exemptions from taxation.
Air carriers.
Aircraft and other
equipment, §40-9-1.
Alcoholic beverage sales.
Certified licensed air
carrier with hub
operation in state,
§28-3-207.
Gasoline tax, §40-17-31.

TAXATION—Cont'd
Air commerce—Cont'd
Exemptions from taxation
—Cont'd
Air carriers—Cont'd
Sales tax, §40-23-4.
Use tax, §40-23-62.
Aircraft.
Exemptions from taxation.
Motor fuels.
Additional excise tax on
gasoline, motor fuels
and lubricating oil,
§40-17-220.
Air pollution, §§40-18-35,
40-23-62.
Airport authorities.
Exemption from taxation,
§4-3-8.
Alternate procedure for
incorporation, §4-3-59.
Alabaster, city of.
Additional ad valorem tax in
city, Const. Ala., amd.
409.
Alcoholic beverages.
See ALCOHOLIC
BEVERAGES.
Alligator farms.
Disposition of revenue,
§9-12-212.
Severance tax on skins,
§9-12-210.
Payment of severance tax
prerequisite to sale or
shipment of skin,
§9-12-204.
Aluminum.
Exemptions from taxation.
Manufacturers of
aluminum or
aluminum products,
§40-9-5.
**Ameraport offshore harbor
and terminal
commission.**
Exemption from taxation,
§33-10-25.
American Cancer Society.
Exemptions, §40-9-12.
American Legion.
Property exempt, §40-9-1.
Appeals.
Assessments, §§40-7-45 to
40-7-48, 40-7-71.
Cigarettes.
Gummed cigarette papers.
Assessment of tax,
§§40-25A-10,
40-25A-11.
County boards of
equalization, §§40-3-1 to
40-3-26.
Estate and inheritance taxes,
§40-15-20.
Hotels, inns and other
transient lodging places.
Assessments, §40-26-13.
Income tax.
See INCOME TAX.
Public utilities.
Protest of incorrect
valuation, §40-21-24.
Sale of land for taxes.
Decree of sale, §§40-10-1 to
40-10-166. See within
this heading, "Sale of
land for taxes."
Sales tax.
Assessments, §40-23-18.

TAXATION—Cont'd
Appeals—Cont'd
Use tax.
Redeterminations,
§40-23-73.
Appraisals.
Assessments, §§40-7-1 to
40-7-100. See within this
heading, "Assessments."
Appraisers.
Certified appraisers.
Payment to certain
certified appraisers,
§40-1-46.
Arbitration and award.
Multistate tax compact,
§40-27-1.
Armories.
Exemption of property used
for armory and training
purposes, §31-4-12.
Arrests.
Department of revenue.
Agents and employees.
Arrest fee, §40-2-10.
Assessments, §§40-7-1 to
40-7-100.
Appeals.
Department of revenue,
§§40-2-22, 40-2-23.
Judgment of revaluation,
§40-7-48.
Notice, §40-7-46.
Right, §40-7-45.
Statewide property
reappraisal, §40-7-71.
Time, §40-7-45.
Trial, §40-7-47.
Assessors. See within this
heading, "Tax assessors."
Assignees authorized to sell.
Property in possession,
§40-7-13.
Auctioneers, §40-7-44.
Book of assessments.
Abstracts of property,
§40-7-35.
Amount of taxes delivered
to collector.
Book showing, §40-7-36.
Certification by
department, §40-7-34.
Form, §40-7-33.
Levy of taxes from,
§40-7-42.
Lists.
Use in lieu of book,
§40-7-33.
Required, §40-7-33.
Change in condition of
property.
Fraudulent failure to
report, §40-7-12.
Class III property.
Current use value.
Appraisal of property,
§40-7-25.1.
Conversion of property to
other taxable use,
§40-7-25.3.
Defined, §40-7-25.1.
Denial of application.
Appeal from denial,
§40-7-25.2.
Qualification procedure,
§40-7-25.2.
Rules and regulations,
§40-7-25.1.

TAXATION—Cont'd
  Assessments—Cont'd
    Class III property—Cont'd
      Current use value—Cont'd
        Sale of property.
          New owner required to
            reapply upon sale,
            §40-7-25.2.
    Collection.
      Limitation of actions,
        §40-29-51.
    Commencement, §40-7-2.
    Commission merchants.
      Property in possession,
        §40-7-13.
    Completion, §40-7-2.
    Consignees authorized to sell.
      Property in possession,
        §40-7-13.
    Corporations.
      By whom property should
        be listed, §40-7-17.
      Foreign corporations.
        Allocation of tax
          obligation between
          transferor and
          foreign corporate
          transferee of certain
          property, §40-7-18.
    County boards of
      equalization, §§40-3-1 to
      40-3-26.
    Credits.
      Credit against tax liability
        for certain taxpayers
        whose property has
        been reassessed,
        §40-8-5.
    Department of revenue. See
      within this heading,
      "Department of
      revenue."
    Effective date of assessments,
      §40-7-9.1.
    Enforcement of imposed
      taxes.
      Authority, §40-7-21.
    Errors.
      Correction, §40-7-2.2.
    Escaped taxes, §40-7-23.
    Estimated values.
      Fair market value,
        §40-7-15.
      Taxpayer to give, §40-7-14.
    Executors and
      administrators.
      By whom property should
        be listed, §40-7-17.
    Exempt property.
      Allowance of statutory
        exemptions, §40-7-10.
      Entry of deductions for
        exemptions, §40-7-25.
      Listing, §40-7-6.
        Mailing or sending list,
          §40-7-7.
      Property no longer exempt,
        §40-7-10.
    Fair market value of
      property, §40-7-15.
      Estimation by assessor,
        §40-7-25.
    Guardian and ward.
      By whom property should
        be listed, §40-7-17.
    Husband and wife.
      By whom property should
        be listed, §40-7-17.

TAXATION—Cont'd
  Assessments—Cont'd
    Improvements.
      Correction of assessment
        when improvements
        nonexistent, §40-7-28.
      Failure to report, §40-7-11.
    Incompetents.
      By whom property should
        be listed, §40-7-17.
    Insurance guaranty
      association.
      Credits for assessments
        paid, §27-42-16.
    Jeopardy assessment,
      §40-29-91.
    Limitation of action.
      Suspension, §40-29-50.
    Lists.
      Failure to fill out,
        §40-7-21.
      Procedure by assessor upon
        failure to procure,
        §40-7-22.
      Use in lieu of assessment
        book, §40-7-33.
    Local taxation.
      Assessment ratios for
        purposes of, §40-8-4.
    Notice.
      Appeals, §40-7-46.
    Oaths.
      Failure to subscribe,
        §40-7-21.
      Oath to be used on bottom
        of assessment sheet,
        §40-7-8.
    "Owners unknown," §40-7-31.
    Parent and child.
      By whom property should
        be listed, §40-7-17.
    Partnerships.
      By whom property should
        be listed, §40-7-17.
    Penalties.
      Remission of penalties,
        §40-7-29.
    Plat books.
      All real estate, §40-7-38.
        Failure to comply,
          §40-7-40.
      Blocks and lots platted and
        recorded, §40-7-37.
      Revision.
        Annual revision,
          §40-7-39.
        Failure to comply,
          §40-7-40.
      Where kept, §40-7-41.
    Preceding years evaluation.
      Entry by assessor,
        §40-7-14.
    Property taxes to be assessed
      in exact proportion to
      value of property, Const.
      Ala., art. XI, §211.
    Rate, §40-8-1.
      Assessment ratios for
        purposes of local
        taxation, §40-8-4.
    Real estate.
      Description, §40-7-16.
    Reappraisals.
      Statewide property
        reappraisal, §§40-7-60
        to 40-7-100.

TAXATION—Cont'd
  Assessments—Cont'd
    Reassessment.
      Credit against tax liability
        for certain taxpayers
        whose property has
        been reassessed,
        §40-8-5.
    Receivers.
      By whom property should
        be listed, §40-7-17.
    Schedules.
      Failure to fill out,
        §40-7-21.
    Special, private or local laws
      prohibited, Const. Ala.,
      art. IV, §104.
    Statewide property
      reappraisal, §§40-7-60 to
      40-7-100.
      Administration of program
        §40-7-74.
      Ad valorem taxes.
        Basis of assessment,
          §40-7-62.
        Program for
          equalization.
          Costs to be prorated
            among county
            agencies, §40-7-68
      Appeals, §40-7-71.
      Appraisers.
        Qualifications, §40-7-67.
      Appropriations, §§40-7-70
        to 40-7-72.
      Avoidance of article,
        §40-7-73.
      Complaints.
        Hearing, §40-7-71.
      Completion.
        Schedule, §40-7-66.
        Time, §40-7-63.
      Contract work.
        Inspection and approval
        §40-7-61.
      County boards of
        equalization.
        Compensation of
          members, §40-7-71.
      County bonds for purpose
        of paying costs of
        reappraisal.
      Conflicts with other
        laws, §40-7-97.
      Definitions, §40-7-90.
      Legislative intent,
        §40-7-91.
      Pledges for payment.
        Special pledges,
          §40-7-93.
      Provisions supplemental
        §40-7-100.
      Warrants.
        Authorization to issue
          §40-7-92.
        Effect of issuance,
          §40-7-96.
        Exemption from laws
          relative to usury,
          interest, etc.,
          §40-7-99.
        Legal investments for
          trust funds,
          §40-7-95.
        Payment of pro rata
          shares of principal
          and interest,
          §40-7-98.
        Refunding warrants,
          §40-7-94.

TAXATION—Cont'd
Assessments—Cont'd
Statewide property
reappraisal—Cont'd
County employees.
Department's
requirements to be
met without
becoming employees
for state merit
system, §40-7-67.
County governing bodies.
Consultations by
department,
§40-7-66.
Equalization of
assessments.
Basis, §40-7-71.
Expenses of county
reappraisal.
County may be charged
pro rate share,
§40-7-70.
Credit against state's
portion, §40-7-70.
Fair market value.
Appraisal of property,
§40-7-62.
Certification that county
property appraised
at, §40-7-71.
Firms of appraisers.
Bona fide state resident,
§40-7-65.
Employment as
consultants,
§40-7-65.
Forms.
Department to prescribe
for counties,
§40-7-64.
Frustration of article,
§40-7-73.
Fund to maintain program
of equalization.
Establishment, §40-7-70.
Inspection of program,
§40-7-60.
Noncompliance by county.
Department may act,
§40-7-67.
Personnel, §40-7-67.
Procedures, §40-7-61.
Department to prescribe,
§40-7-64.
Records.
Department to prescribe
for counties,
§40-7-64.
Permanent uniform
record system.
Department to design,
§40-7-64.
Regulation of program,
§40-7-60.
Reports.
Department to prescribe
progress reports for
counties, §40-7-64.
Revenue bonds to finance
program.
Authority to issue,
§40-7-69.
Review.
Values subject to review,
§40-7-71.
Standards, §40-7-61.
Department to prescribe
for counties,
§40-7-64.

TAXATION—Cont'd
Assessments—Cont'd
Statewide property
reappraisal—Cont'd
Supervision of program,
§40-7-60.
System of appraisal.
Determination, §40-7-66.
Tax assessors.
Consultations by
department,
§40-7-66.
Supplemental assessment,
§40-7-2.
Tax assessors. See within
this heading, "Tax
assessors."
Tax collectors. See within
this heading, "Tax
collectors."
Taxpayers.
Duties, §40-7-1.
Time for, §40-7-9.1.
Trusts and trustees.
By whom property should
be listed, §40-7-17.
Assessors. See within this
heading, "Tax assessors."
Associations.
Exemption from taxation.
Social or literary
advancement.
Property used in
connection with
college or university,
§40-9-16.
Athletic stadiums.
Exemptions from taxation,
§40-9-1.
Atomic energy.
Exemptions from taxation.
Nuclear fuel assemblies,
§40-9-22.
Attorneys at law.
Taxing authorities acting as
attorney for taxpayer.
Unlawful, §40-1-20.
Auctions and auctioneers.
Assessment against
auctioneers, §40-7-44.
Limitations on authority of
political subdivisions,
§34-4-6.
Subjects of taxation,
§40-11-1.
Audits.
Multistate tax compact.
Interstate audits, §40-27-1.
Force and effect,
§40-27-6.
Automatic refunds,
§40-29-71.
Auxiliary state forests.
Taxation of timber on lands
designated as, §§9-13-40,
9-13-45 to 9-13-48.
Aviation.
Air commerce.
Exemptions from taxation.
Air carriers. See within
this heading, "Air
commerce."
Airport authorities.
Exemption, §4-3-8.
Alternate procedure for
incorporation,
§4-3-59.

TAXATION—Cont'd
Aviation—Cont'd
Motor fuels.
Additional excise tax on
gasoline, motor fuel
and lubricating oil.
Exemption, §40-17-220.
Bad checks.
Payment of tax with bad
check, §40-29-70.
**Banks and financial
institutions.**
Common trust funds.
Generally, §5-12A-15.
Credit unions, §5-17-24.
Equalization of taxation of
state and national bank,
§40-1-9.
Excise tax, §§40-16-1 to
40-16-8.
See BANKS AND
FINANCIAL
INSTITUTIONS.
Industrial development
corporations, §10-4-143.
Money on deposit.
Exemption, §40-9-1.
Officers.
Failure to make, swear to
and deliver required
statements, §40-1-19.
Savings and loan
associations.
Exemptions from income
tax, §10-18-32.
**Bear creek development
authority.**
Bonds and other obligations.
Exemption, §33-15-12.
Beer.
Excise tax on beer,
§§28-3-190 to 28-3-199.
See ALCOHOLIC
BEVERAGES.
**Birmingham building trades
towers.**
Exemptions, §40-9-12.
**Birmingham Football
Foundation, Inc.**
Exemptions from taxation,
§40-9-12.
Boardinghouses.
Transient occupancy tax,
§§40-26-1 to 40-26-21.
See HOTELS, INNS AND
OTHER TRANSIENT
LODGING PLACES.
Boards of equalization.
County boards, §§40-3-1 to
40-3-26. See within this
heading, "County boards
of equalization."
Bond issues.
Exemptions from taxation,
§§11-89-16, 33-16-12,
40-9-1.
Alabama state bonds,
§40-9-1.
County and municipal
bonds, §§11-81-29,
40-9-1.
Highways, §23-1-157.
Housing finance authority,
§24-1A-12.
United States bonds,
§40-9-1.
Income tax, §§40-18-4,
40-18-14.
Subjects of taxation,
§40-11-1.

TAXATION—Cont'd

Bonds, surety.
Commissioner of revenue,
§40-2-43.
Department of revenue.
Employees, §40-2-4.
Legal counsel, §40-2-62.
Lien for taxes.
Release of lien, §40-29-20.
Tax assessors, §40-4-1.
Tax collectors, §40-5-3.
Books.
Assessments, §§40-7-33 to
40-7-36, 40-7-42.
Lands on which taxes
unpaid, §§40-10-2,
40-10-3.
Plat books, §§40-7-37 to
40-7-41.
Boxing and wrestling.
Commissioner of revenue to
collect, §41-9-96.
Distribution of proceeds,
§41-9-96.
Boy Scouts of America.
Exemptions, §40-9-12.
Business trusts, §19-3-67.
Cahaba trace commission.
Exemption, §41-9-807.
Calcium cyanamide.
Exemptions from taxation.
Manufacturers of calcium
cyanamide, §40-9-5.
Canals.
Subjects of taxation,
§40-11-1.
Cancer Society.
Exemptions, §40-9-12.
Capital gain or loss.
Generally, §§40-18-6 to
40-18-9.
Capitation tax.
Constitutional provisions,
Const. U. S., Art. I, §9.
Election.
Denial or abridgement of
the right to vote for
failure to pay tax
prohibited, Const. U.
S., Amendment XXIV.
**Catholic Maritime Club of
Mobile, Inc.**
Exemptions, §40-9-12.
Cemeteries.
Exemptions, §40-9-1.
Charities.
Exemptions, §40-9-12.
Property exempt, §40-9-1.
Checks.
Bad checks.
Payment of tax with bad
check, §40-29-70.
Childhaven, Inc.
Exemptions, §40-9-12.
Church schools.
Exemptions from taxation.
Lubricating oils and
greases, §40-17-171.
Motor fuels.
Additional excise tax on
gasoline, motor fuel
and lubricating oil,
§40-17-220.
Cigarettes.
Gummed cigarette papers,
§§40-25A-1 to 40-25A-20.
See CIGARETTES.
Tobacco tax.
See TOBACCO.
Claim, §40-9-2.

TAXATION—Cont'd

Class III property.
Assessments, §§40-7-25.1 to
40-7-25.3.
Coal severance tax, §§40-13-1
to 40-13-36.
See COAL.
Collection of taxes.
Actions, §40-5-42.
Limitation, §40-1-36.
Escaped taxes, §§40-5-34,
40-5-35.
Execution sufficient warrant
for levy, §40-1-15.
Failure to collect.
Penalties, §40-29-73.
General provisions. See
within this heading,
"Tax collectors."
Insolvent taxes, §40-5-28.
Lien for taxes. See within
this heading, "Liens for
taxes."
Limitation of actions.
Collection after
assessment, §40-29-51.
Penalties.
Willful failure to collect,
§40-29-111.
Sale of land, §§40-10-1 to
40-10-166. See within
this heading, "Sale of
land for taxes."
Special, private or local laws
prohibited, Const. Ala.,
art. IV, §104.
Special taxes, §§40-5-39 to
40-5-41.
Tax collectors generally,
§§40-5-1 to 40-5-46. See
within this heading,
"Tax collectors."
Tax enforcement and
compliance act.
Generally, §§40-29-20 to
40-29-34.
Taxpayer about to jeopardize
possibility of collection,
§§40-5-31, 40-5-32.
Willful failure to collect.
Penalties, §40-29-111.
Collectors.
Tax collectors, §§40-5-1 to
40-5-46. See within this
heading, "Tax collectors."
Commissioner of revenue.
Appointment, §40-2-41.
Assistant commissioner of
revenue, §40-2-44.
Authority.
Generally, §40-2-40.
Bonds, surety, §40-2-43.
Boxing and wrestling.
Collection of taxes by
commissioner,
§41-9-96.
Chief executive officer of
department, §40-2-40.
Duties.
Generally, §40-2-40.
Gasoline tax.
Refund on gasoline used
for agricultural
purposes.
Powers of commissioner,
§40-17-106.

TAXATION—Cont'd

Commissioner of revenue
—Cont'd
Local commissioners of
revenue.
Supernumerary tax
officials, §§40-6-1 to
40-6-7. See within this
heading,
"Supernumerary."
Motor carrier fuel tax.
Rules and regulations,
§40-17-152.
Motor vehicles.
Reciprocal agreements for
registration on an
apportionment or
allocation basis.
Powers of commissioner,
§32-6-56.
Tags and plates.
Disabled veterans.
Special plates for
disabled veterans,
§32-6-131.
Rules and regulations.
Power of commissioner
to make, §32-6-53
Oath of office, §40-2-42.
Powers.
Generally, §40-2-40.
Qualifications, §40-2-41.
Reports.
Annual report, §40-29-120.
Salaries, §§40-6A-1 to
40-6A-8. See within this
heading, "Salaries."
Term of office, §40-2-41.
Unclaimed property.
Uniform disposition of
unclaimed property
act, §§35-12-20 to
35-12-48.
See LOST OR
UNCLAIMED
PROPERTY.
Compact.
Multistate tax compact,
§§40-27-1 to 40-27-6. See
within this heading,
"Multistate tax
compact."
Comptroller.
Refund of taxes paid by
mistake or error.
Duty, §40-10-162.
Sale of land for taxes.
Land sold for taxes not due
at time of sale.
Payment of refund,
§40-10-103.
Condominiums, §35-8-15.
**Confidentiality of
information.**
Returns, statements, etc.,
§40-1-33.
Congress.
Powers of congress, Const. U.
S., Art. I, §8.
Constitution of Alabama.
See CONSTITUTION OF
ALABAMA.
**Constitution of the United
States.**
Capitation tax, Const. U. S.,
Art. I, §9.

AXATION—Cont'd
Constitution of the United States—Cont'd
Elections.
Denial or abridgement of right to vote for failure to pay tax prohibited, Const. U. S., Amendment XXIV.
Excises.
Powers of congress, Const. U. S., Art. I, §8.
Exports, Const. U. S., Art. I, §§9, 10.
Income tax, Const. U. S., Amendment XVI.
Limitations on powers of states, Const. U. S., Art. I, §10.
Powers of congress, Const. U. S., Art. I, §8.
Revenue bills, Const. U. S., Art. I, §7.
Construction and interpretation.
Multistate tax compact, §40-27-1.
Controlled substances excise tax, §§40-17A-1 to 40-17A-16.
See DRUGS.
Conversion of public revenues.
Limitation on prosecution, §15-3-3.
Coosa Valley Development authority.
Bond issues.
Exemption, §33-16-12.
Corporations.
General provisions.
See CORPORATIONS.
Income tax, §§40-18-1 to 40-18-176.
See INCOME TAX.
S corporations, §§40-18-160 to 40-18-176.
See CORPORATIONS.
Corrections.
Institution finance authority.
Exemption, §14-2-32.
Corrupt or forcible interference, §40-29-118.
Costs.
Payment of court costs taxed against estate, §40-1-14.
Sale of land for taxes.
Land sold for taxes not due at time of sale.
Warrant for costs, §40-10-105.
Taxation of costs, ARCP, Rule 54 (d).
Cotton.
Exemptions from taxation, §40-9-1.
Counties.
Boards of equalization, §§40-3-1 to 40-3-26. See within this heading, "County boards of equalization."
Bond issues, §40-9-1.
See COUNTIES.
Education.
See EDUCATION.
Elimination of payments of less than five dollars to municipalities, §40-1-31.2.

TAXATION—Cont'd
Counties—Cont'd
Exemption from taxation.
Generally.
See COUNTIES.
Forest protection.
Special taxes for forest protection, §§9-13-160 to 9-13-167.
See FORESTS AND FORESTRY.
Gasoline taxes.
Issuing warrants in anticipation of, §§11-11-1 to 11-11-8.
See COUNTIES.
General provisions.
See COUNTIES.
Hospitals.
Special county tax.
See HOSPITALS.
Loans.
Making loans in anticipation of taxes, §§11-10-1 to 11-10-6.
See COUNTIES.
Public buildings, bridges or roads.
Apportionment of road and bridge taxes between counties and municipalities, §§11-83-1 to 11-83-3.
Special tax authorized, §11-14-11; Const. Ala., art. XI, §215.
Disposition of excess proceeds, §11-14-11.
Special taxes.
See COUNTIES.
Statewide property reappraisal.
County bonds for purpose of costs, §§40-7-90 to 40-7-100. See within this heading, "Assessments."
County boards of equalization, §§40-3-1 to 40-3-26.
Agents.
Powers and duties, §40-3-16.
Appeals.
Procedure, §40-3-25.
Representation of state, §40-3-26.
Right, §40-3-24.
State and county officials not to represent taxpayers, §40-3-26.
Appraisals, §§40-3-8 to 40-3-13.
Assessments.
Meetings to review, §40-3-17.
Reopening before boards, §40-7-25.
Statements of increases by boards, §40-7-25.
Chairman, §40-3-15.
Compensation of members.
Payments.
How made, §40-3-14.
Proration, §40-3-8.
Schedule of compensation, §40-3-7.
Term of service, §40-3-7.
Composition, §40-3-1.
Creation, §40-3-1.

TAXATION—Cont'd
County boards of equalization—Cont'd
Duties, §40-3-16.
Failure to perform within specified time not fatal defect, §40-3-22.
Inventory.
Appraisal of property in certain counties, §40-3-10.
Supervision of preparation, §40-3-13.
Approval, §40-3-9.
Authorized, §40-3-8.
Cost.
Authority to contribute, §40-3-8.
Payable on requisition by presiding officer, §40-3-12.
Proration, §40-3-11.
Supervision of preparations, §40-3-13.
Meetings.
Assessments.
Meetings to review, §40-3-17.
Objections to valuations.
Meetings to hear, §40-3-19.
Returns.
Meetings to inspect, §40-3-18.
Notice.
Service of notices, §40-3-23.
Valuation of property, §40-3-20.
Oath of members, §40-3-3.
Offices.
Dual office-holding, §40-3-5.
Protest procedure, §40-3-16.
Qualifications of members, §40-3-1.
Returns.
Meetings to inspect, §40-3-18.
Rules and regulations, §40-3-15.
Secretary, §40-3-6.
Selection of members, §40-3-2.
Staff.
Employment, §40-3-8.
Statewide property reappraisal.
Compensation of members, §40-7-71.
Subpoenas.
Service, §40-3-23.
Terms of office, §40-3-2.
Vacancies in office.
Filling, §40-3-4.
Valuation of property.
Corrected values.
Tax assessor to enter, §40-3-21.
Notice.
Publication, §40-3-20.
Objections.
Meetings to hear, §40-3-19.
County industrial development authorities.
Exemptions, §11-92A-18.
Bond issues, §§11-92A-16, 11-92A-18.

TAXATION—Cont'd
Courts.
  Costs.
    See COSTS.
  Creditors.
    Insurance guaranty
        association.
      Preferred creditor status,
        §27-42-19.
  Credit unions.
    General provisions, §5-17-24.
  Crime victims compensation.
    Exemption, §15-23-15.
  Criminal law and procedure.
    Financial statements.
      Issuing false statements,
        §13A-9-49.
    Limitation of actions,
        §40-29-119.
  Date taxes due, §40-11-4.
  **Daughters of the American
      Revolution.**
    Exemptions, §40-9-13.
  Deeds.
    Recordation tax, §§40-22-1 to
        40-22-12.
      See RECORDATION.
  Defeating of tax.
    Penalties, §40-29-110.
  Definitions, §40-1-1.
    Assessments.
      Statewide property
          reappraisal.
        County bonds for purpose
            of paying costs,
            §40-7-90.
    Multistate tax compact,
        §40-27-1.
  Delinquent taxes.
    Collection, §40-12-10.
  Dental service corporations.
    Exemption, §22-21-370.
    Required taxes, §22-21-374.
  Department of revenue.
    Agents.
      Peace officers, §40-2-10.
    Arrests.
      Fee of agents and
          employees, §40-2-10.
    Assessments.
      Advisory capacity,
          §40-7-26.
      Appeal from final
          assessments.
        Effect of final judgment,
            §40-2-22.
        Procedure.
          Generally, §40-2-22.
          Records and proceedings
              to be delivered by
              department,
              §40-2-23.
          Right, §40-2-22.
      Approval of valuation by
          department.
        Effect, §40-7-26.
        Nonapproved assessment
            docket, §40-7-26.
      Book of assessments.
        Certification, §40-7-34.
      Setting aside.
        Notice, §40-2-15.
    Bonds, surety.
      Employees, §40-2-4.
    Commissioner of revenue.
      See within this heading,
          "Commissioner of
          revenue."

TAXATION—Cont'd
Department of revenue
  —Cont'd
  Copies.
    Photographic reproductions
        of documents,
        §§40-2-12 to 40-2-14.
  Creation, §40-2-1.
  Divisions.
    Salaries of division chiefs,
        §40-2-24.
  Duties.
    Generally, §40-2-11.
  Employees.
    Bonds, §40-2-4.
    Employment, §40-2-2.
    Peace officers, §40-2-10.
  Equalization of valuation.
    Generally, §40-2-16.
    Revaluation by board of
        equalization to effect,
        §40-2-17.
    Procedure after,
        §40-2-18.
  Equipment, §40-2-7.
  Estate and inheritance tax.
    Computation, §40-15-3.
  Expenses.
    Legal counsel.
      Traveling expenses,
          §40-2-63.
    Payment, §40-2-2.
    How paid, §40-2-7.
    Traveling expenses,
        §§40-2-8, 40-2-9.
  Gasoline tax, §§40-17-39,
      40-17-43.
  Hazardous waste.
    Fees for disposal of
        hazardous waste or
        substances.
      General provisions,
          §§22-30B-1 to
          22-30B-18.
        See HAZARDOUS
            WASTE.
  Hearings.
    Notice, §40-2-5.
  Income tax.
    Reports to department
        providing source of
        income, §40-18-26.
    Returns.
      General provisions.
        See INCOME TAX.
  Legal counsel.
    Appointment, §40-2-61.
    Assistant counsel,
        §40-2-64.
    Bond, §40-2-62.
    Clerical help, §40-2-63.
    Creation of office, §40-2-60.
    Duties, §40-2-61.
    Expenses.
      Traveling expenses,
          §40-2-63.
    Full-time position,
        §40-2-65.
    Oath, §40-2-61.
    Office, §40-2-63.
    Powers, §40-2-61.
    Qualifications, §40-2-61.
    Special counsel.
      Employment, §40-2-66.
    Term of office, §40-2-61.
  Lubricating oils and greases.
    Tax.
      Enforcement of
          provisions,
          §40-17-179.

TAXATION—Cont'd
Department of revenue
  —Cont'd
  Motor fuels.
    Distributors of motor fuels
      Appeals from
          department's
          decisions,
          §40-12-203.
  Motor vehicles.
    Uniform certificate of title
        and antitheft act.
      General provisions,
          §§32-8-1 to 32-8-88.
        See MOTOR
            VEHICLES.
  Municipal license taxes.
    Collection by state
        department of revenue
        §§11-51-180 to
        11-51-185.
      See MUNICIPAL
          CORPORATIONS.
  Municipal sales and use
      taxes.
    Administration and
        collection by state
        department,
        §11-51-207.
  Notices.
    Hearings, §40-2-5.
    Revaluation, §40-2-15.
    Setting assessment aside,
        §40-2-15.
  Offices, §40-2-7.
  Photographic or electronic
      reproductions of
      documents.
    Authority to make,
        §40-2-12.
    Disposition of original
        documents, §40-2-12.
    Force and effect of
        originals, §40-2-13.
    Legislative intent,
        §40-2-14.
  Powers.
    Generally, §40-2-11.
  Public service commission.
    Furnishing information to
        department, §37-1-42.
  Revaluation.
    Notice, §40-2-15.
    Procedure after, §40-2-18.
  Secretary.
    Duties, §40-2-3.
    Employment, §40-2-2.
  Transient occupancy tax,
      §§40-26-1 to 40-26-19.
    See HOTELS, INNS AND
        OTHER TRANSIENT
        LODGING PLACES.
  Witnesses.
    Appearance.
      Required, §40-2-19.
    Fees, §40-2-21.
    Incriminating testimony,
        §40-2-20.
    Oaths, §40-2-6.
    Perjury, §40-2-20.
    Production of records,
        books and papers.
      Required, §40-2-19.
  Diesel fuel tax, §§40-17-1 to
      40-17-21.
    See MOTOR FUELS.
  Distraint, §§40-29-23 to
      40-29-34. See within this
      heading, "Levy and
      distraint."

AXATION—Cont'd
Distribution of payments in lieu of taxes.
Tennessee Valley authority, §§40-28-1 to 40-28-4.
Docks.
Subjects of taxation, §40-11-1.
Dog racing.
Exemptions.
Admissions and handle.
Sales tax exemption, §40-11-5.
Validity of prior exemptions, §40-11-5.
Payment of taxes.
Required, §40-11-5.
Track pari-mutuel pool tax, §§40-26A-1 to 40-26A-17.
See DOG RACING.
Tracks.
Subject of taxation, §40-11-5.
Downtown redevelopment authorities.
Exemption, §11-54A-14.
Drugs.
Controlled substances excise tax, §§40-17A-1 to 40-17A-16.
See DRUGS.
Due date, §40-11-4.
Eagles club.
Property exempt, §40-9-1.
East Alabama Services for the Elderly, Inc.
Exemption, §40-9-26.
East Presbyterian Apartments.
Exemption, §40-9-26.
Education.
Counties.
Exemptions from taxation.
See within this heading, "Exemptions from taxation."
Licenses.
County license tax for school purposes, §§40-12-4 to 40-12-7.
Exemptions from taxation.
See within this heading, "Exemptions from taxation."
General provisions.
See EDUCATION.
Educational television foundation authority.
Exemptions, §16-7A-4.
Elections.
Denial or abridgement to vote.
Failure to pay poll or other tax, Const. U. S., Amendment XXIV.
Education.
See EDUCATION.
Special taxes.
Ratification of certain municipal and county elections as to levy, §40-1-37.
Tax assessors.
Failure to elect successor vacates office, §36-9-5.
General elections.
Offices for which general election held, §17-2-2.
Time, §17-2-3.

TAXATION—Cont'd
Elections—Cont'd
Tax assessors—Cont'd
State and county officers elected by the people, §17-2-1.
Tax collectors.
Failure to elect successor vacates office, §36-9-5.
General elections.
Offices for which held, §17-2-2.
Time, §17-2-3.
State and county officers elected by the people, §17-2-1.
Electric power companies.
Public utilities generally, §§40-21-1 to 40-21-107.
See PUBLIC UTILITIES.
Elk river development agency.
Counties.
Levy by governing bodies, §33-12-6.
Exemption, §33-12-5.
Municipal corporations.
Levy by governing bodies, §33-12-6.
Elks Club.
Exemptions from taxation.
Elks memorial center, §40-9-12.
Property, §40-9-1.
Eminent domain.
Deduction of taxes from award, §18-1A-214.
Employers and employees.
Tax statements to employees.
Fraudulent statement or failure to furnish.
Penalty, §40-29-74.
Enterprise zones.
Credits, §41-23-24.
Exemptions.
Contracts with eligible businesses to provide for, §41-23-30.
Federal tax exemptions.
Complimentary to and consistent with, §41-23-32.
Incentives.
Credits, §41-23-24.
Rules to implement.
Commissioner to formulate, §41-23-24.
Rules and regulations.
Incentives.
Formulation of rules to implement, §41-23-24.
Environmental improvement authorities.
Exemptions from taxation, §9-6-15.
Episcopal Foundation of Jefferson county.
Exemptions from taxation, §40-9-13.
Equalization.
County boards of equalization, §§40-3-1 to 40-3-26. See within this heading, "County boards of equalization."
Error.
Land sold for taxes not due at time of sale, §§40-10-100 to 40-10-105.

TAXATION—Cont'd
Error—Cont'd
Refund of taxes paid by error, §§40-10-160 to 40-10-165. See within this heading, "Refunds."
Escaped taxes.
Assessments, §40-7-23.
Collection, §40-7-23.
Notice, §40-7-23.
Penalties.
Avoidance of penalty, §40-7-23.
Estate and inheritance tax, §§40-15-1 to 40-15-21.
See ESTATE AND INHERITANCE TAX.
Evasion of taxes.
Penalties, §§40-29-73, 40-29-110.
Evidence.
Actions by state against officers.
Copies of books, records, papers, etc., admitted in evidence, §40-1-16.
Sale of land for taxes.
Actions for possession.
Books and records as prima facie evidence, §40-10-81.
Recitation of fact of purchase deemed prima facie evidence, §40-10-79.
Excise taxes.
Alcoholic beverages, §§28-3-183 to 28-3-187.
Beer, §§28-3-190 to 28-3-199.
See ALCOHOLIC BEVERAGES.
Financial institutions, §§40-16-1 to 40-16-8.
See BANKS AND FINANCIAL INSTITUTIONS.
Executors and administrators.
Assessments.
By whom property should be listed, §40-7-17.
Returns.
Separate returns in individual and fiduciary capacity, §40-7-20.
Tax assessors.
Notification of appointment of fiduciaries, §40-7-30.
Exemptions from taxation, §§11-89-16, 40-9-1; Const. Ala., art. IV, §91.
Aged persons.
Homestead exemptions, §40-9-19.
Verification of eligibility by mail, §40-9-21.1.
Principal residence of certain persons, §40-9-21.
Verification of eligibility by mail, §40-9-21.1.
Agricultural center corporation, §2-6-37.
Agricultural development authority, §2-3A-11.
Agricultural products, §40-9-1.

TAXATION—Cont'd
Exemptions from taxation
—Cont'd
Agriculture.
  Motor fuels.
    Additional excise tax on
      gasoline, motor fuels
      and lubricating oil,
      §40-17-220.
Air carriers.
  Aircraft and other
    equipment, §40-9-1.
  Alcoholic beverage sales.
    Certified licensed air
      carrier with hub
      operation in state,
      §28-3-207.
  Gasoline tax, §40-17-31.
  Sales tax, §40-23-4.
  Use tax, §40-23-62.
Aircraft.
  Motor fuels.
    Additional excise tax on
      gasoline, motor fuels
      and lubricating oil,
      §40-17-220.
Airport authorities, §4-3-8.
Alternate procedure for
  incorporation, §4-3-59.
Aluminum.
  Manufacturers of
    aluminum or
    aluminum products,
    §40-9-5.
American Legion.
  Property, §40-9-1.
Association formed for social
  or literary advancement.
  Property used in
    connection with college
    or university, §40-9-16.
Athletic stadiums, §40-9-1.
Atomic energy.
  Nuclear fuel assemblies,
    §40-9-22.
Aviation hall of fame board.
  Contributions, etc.,
    §41-9-722.
Banks.
  Money on deposit, §40-9-1.
Birmingham building trades
  towers, §40-9-12.
Birmingham Football
  Foundation, Inc.,
  §40-9-12.
Boards for operation of
  water, sewer, gas and
  electric systems,
  §11-50-322.
Boards of water and sewer
  commissioners,
  §11-50-354.
Bond issues, §§11-89-16,
  33-16-12, 40-9-1.
  Alabama state bonds,
    §40-9-1.
  County and municipal
    bonds, §§11-81-29,
    40-9-1.
  Housing finance authority,
    §24-1A-12.
  United States bonds,
    §40-9-1.
Boy Scouts of America,
  §40-9-12.
Calcium cyanamide.
  Manufacturers, §40-9-5.
Cancer Society, §40-9-12.
Catholic Maritime Club of
  Mobile, Inc., §40-9-12.
Cemeteries, §40-9-1.

TAXATION—Cont'd
Exemptions from taxation
—Cont'd
Charities.
  Property, §40-9-1.
Childhaven, Inc., §40-9-12.
Church schools.
  Lubricating oils and
    greases, §40-17-171.
  Motor fuels.
    Additional excise tax on
      gasoline, motor fuel
      and lubricating oil,
      §40-17-220.
Civic organizations.
  Acquisition of projects for
    provision of buildings
    and other facilities for
    certain national
    organizations.
  Exemption from taxation
    of projects, bonds,
    etc., §11-54-61.
Colleges, §§40-9-16, 40-9-17.
Corporations.
  Mental health.
    Corporations organized
      to establish regional
      programs and
      facilities, §40-9-23.
  Nonprofit corporations,
    §§40-9-12, 40-9-13.
  Corporation formed for
    social or literary
    advancement.
    Property used in
      connection with
      college or
      university,
      §40-9-16.
  Corporation organized
    for purpose of aiding
    retired teachers,
    §40-9-18.
Corrections.
  Institution finance
    authority, §14-2-32.
Counties.
  Bond issues, §§11-81-29,
    40-9-1.
  Exemptions from county
    taxes generally.
    See COUNTIES.
  Industrial development
    boards.
    Exemptions of
      corporations,
      §11-20-47.
  Motor fuels.
    Additional excise tax on
      gasoline, motor fuel
      and lubricating oil,
      §40-17-220.
  Parks and recreation.
    Public parks and
      recreation boards,
      §11-22-13.
  Projects for promotion of
    industry and trade,
    §11-20-12.
  Property, §40-9-1.
  Public building authorities.
    Projects, income from
      leases, warrants,
      etc., §11-15-17.
County loans made in
  anticipation of payments
  under state and local
  fiscal assistance act of
  1972, §11-10-6.

TAXATION—Cont'd
Exemptions from taxation
—Cont'd
County loans made in
  anticipation of taxes,
  §11-10-5.
  When no assessment.
    See COUNTIES.
Daughters of the American
  Revolution, §40-9-13.
Dental service corporations,
  §22-21-370.
Disabled American veterans
  §40-9-1.
Disabled persons.
  Principal residence of
    totally disabled
    persons, §40-9-21.
  Verification of eligibility
    by mail, §40-9-21.1.
District electric corporations
  §11-50-531.
Dog racing.
  Validity of prior
    exemptions, §40-11-5.
East Alabama Services for
  the Elderly, Inc.,
  §40-9-26.
East Presbyterian
  Apartments, §40-9-26.
Education.
  Alabama education
    authority.
    Bond issues, §16-15-9.
  Church schools.
    Gasoline tax, §40-17-31.
    Lubricating oils and
      greases, §40-17-171.
    Motor fuels.
      Additional excise tax
        on gasoline, motor
        fuel and
        lubricating oil,
        §40-17-220.
  City and county boards of
    education.
    Gasoline tax, §40-17-31.
    Lubricating oils and
      greases, §40-17-171.
    Motor fuels.
      Additional excise tax
        on gasoline, motor
        fuel and
        lubricating oil,
        §40-17-220.
  City boards of education.
    Notes in anticipation of
      warrants,
      §16-13-216.
  Corporation organized for
    purpose of aiding
    retired teachers,
    §40-9-18.
  County boards of
    education.
    Notes in anticipation of
      warrants,
      §16-13-216.
  Private schools.
    Gasoline tax, §40-17-31.
    Lubricating oils and
      greases, §40-17-171.
    Motor fuels.
      Additional excise tax
        on gasoline, motor
        fuel and
        lubricating oil,
        §40-17-220.
  Public school and college
    authority.
    Bond issues, §16-16-9.

TAXATION—Cont'd
Exemptions from taxation
—Cont'd
Education—Cont'd
Tax anticipation warrants
in cities and counties,
§§16-13-75, 40-9-1.
Warrants for special
county and district
taxes, §16-13-106.
Educational building
authorities.
Bond issues, §16-17-14.
Educational television
foundation authority,
§16-7A-4.
Elks Club.
Elks memorial center,
§40-9-12.
Environmental control.
Environmental
improvement
authorities, §9-6-15.
Episcopal Foundation of
Jefferson county,
§40-9-13.
Factories, industries and
plants.
County taxes.
See COUNTIES.
Municipal taxes.
See MUNICIPAL
CORPORATIONS.
State ad valorem taxes.
Application, §40-9-44.
Cessation of exemption,
§40-9-45.
Generally, §40-9-43.
Inapplicability to taxes
to which factories,
plants, etc., already
subject, §40-9-46.
New or extended
factories, industries
and plants, §40-9-48.
Fairs, §40-9-1.
Family portraits, §40-9-1.
Fire departments.
Volunteer fire
departments, §40-9-13.
Foreign trade and relations
commission.
Gifts, §41-9-664.
Forests and forestry.
Standing timber, §40-11-1.
Fraternal benefit societies,
§27-34-42.
Property, §40-9-1.
Freewill Baptist children's
home, §40-9-12.
Furniture.
Claim of exemption of
household and kitchen
furniture, §40-9-2.
Gas districts, §11-50-412.
Girl Scouts of America,
§40-9-12.
Handicapped persons.
Principal residence of
totally disabled
persons, §40-9-21.
Verification of eligibility
by mail, §40-9-21.1.
Property, §40-9-1.
Health care authorities,
§22-21-333.
Heart Association, §40-9-13.
Helping Hand Club of
Anniston, §40-9-12.

TAXATION—Cont'd
Exemptions from taxation
—Cont'd
Highways.
Authority.
Bond issues, §23-1-157.
Federal aid highway
finance authority.
Bonds and notes,
§23-1-312.
Finance corporation.
Bond issues, §23-1-177.
Historical commissions.
Alabama historical
commission, §41-9-256.
Tannehill furnace and
foundry commission,
§41-9-329.
Historical preservation
authorities, §41-10-147.
Historic Blakely authority,
§41-10-179.
Holy Comforter House, Inc.,
of Gadsden, §40-9-12.
Homestead exemption,
§40-9-19.
Claim, §40-9-2.
Verification of eligibility
by mail, §40-9-21.1.
Hospitals.
County and municipal
hospital authorities,
§§22-21-182,
22-21-186.
County hospital boards,
§22-21-80.
County hospital
corporations.
Securities, §22-21-108.
Municipal hospital
building authorities,
§22-21-153.
Property, §40-9-1.
Public hospitals,
§§11-95-11, 11-95-15.
Susie Parker Stringfellow
memorial hospital,
§40-9-1.1.
Housing finance authority,
§24-1A-12.
Income tax.
See INCOME TAX.
Industrial development
authority.
Bonds of authority,
§41-10-28.
Industrial development
boards, §11-54-96.
Industrial development
corporations, §10-4-143.
Institute for deaf and blind.
Gasoline tax, §40-17-31.
Lubricating oils and
greases, §40-17-171.
Insurance guaranty
association, §27-42-15.
Insurers, §27-4-10.
Junior college for Franklin,
Marion and Winston
counties.
Property, §16-60-35.
Junior college for Jackson
and DeKalb counties.
Property, §16-60-65.
Knights of Pythias, §40-9-12.
Libraries, §40-9-1.
Public library authorities,
§11-57-25.
Literary societies.
Property, §40-9-1.

TAXATION—Cont'd
Exemptions from taxation
—Cont'd
Loyal Order of Moose,
§40-9-1.
Mail.
Verification of eligibility
by mail.
Homestead exemption,
§40-9-21.1.
Principal residence of
totally disabled
persons, §40-9-21.1.
Masonic lodges.
Alabama Masonic Home,
§40-9-12.
Mayfair Towers Corporation,
§40-9-26.
Medical clinic boards,
§11-58-14.
Mental health facilities.
Regional mental health
programs and
facilities, §22-51-13.
Corporations organized
to establish,
§40-9-23.
Methodist children's home,
§40-9-12.
Methodist home for the
aging, §40-9-12.
Military affairs.
National guard.
Property, §40-9-1.
Property owned or leased
by units of armed
forces, §31-2-80.
Mortgages, §40-9-1.
Motor sports hall of fame
commission, §41-9-474.
Municipal corporations,
§11-59-16.
Annexed territory.
See MUNICIPAL
CORPORATIONS.
Boards for operation of
water, sewer, gas and
electric systems,
§11-50-322.
Boards of water and sewer
commissioners,
§11-50-354.
Bond issues, §§11-81-29,
40-9-1.
Consolidation of contiguous
municipalities.
Industrial or
manufacturing
plants, §11-42-102.
District electric
corporations,
§11-50-531.
Exemptions from
municipal taxation
generally.
See MUNICIPAL
CORPORATIONS.
Gas districts, §11-50-412.
Medical clinic boards,
§11-58-14.
Motor fuels.
Additional excise tax on
gasoline, motor fuel
and lubricating oil,
§40-17-220.
Post-office projects,
§11-55-11.

TAXATION—Cont'd
Exemptions from taxation
 —Cont'd
Municipal corporations
 —Cont'd
Promotion of industry,
 trade and pollution
 control.
 Projects for promotion,
 §11-54-31.
Property, §§40-9-1, 40-9-14.
Public building authorities,
 §11-56-21.
Public library authorities,
 §11-57-25.
Public park and recreation
 boards, §11-60-17.
Special health care facility
 authorities, §11-62-18.
Waterworks and sewer
 boards.
 Property and income of
 corporation,
 §11-50-235.
Municipal electric authority,
 §11-50A-7.
Music hall of fame board.
 Gifts, §41-9-683.
National foundation.
 Alabama field offices,
 §40-9-12.
New hope industries of
 Dothan, §40-9-12.
Peanuts stored in licensed
 warehouses, §40-9-3.
Pecans stored in licensed
 warehouses, §40-9-3.
Personal property, §40-9-1.
 Shipment outside of state.
 Personal property stored
 for, §40-9-6.
 Warehouseman.
 Personal property held
 by for distribution,
 §40-9-7.
Pollution control devices,
 §40-9-1.
Pollution control finance
 authority, §22-29-22.
Port authority, §11-94-19.
Post-office projects,
 §11-55-11.
Poultry, §40-9-1.
Presbyterian Apartments,
 Incorporated, §40-9-13.
Presbyterian Apartments of
 Birmingham, Inc.,
 §40-9-26.
Presbyterian home for
 children, §40-9-12.
Presbyterian Homes of
 Decatur, Inc., §40-9-26.
Private schools.
 Lubricating oils and
 greases, §40-17-171.
 Motor fuels.
 Additional excise tax on
 gasoline, motor fuel
 and lubricating oil,
 §40-17-220.
Property tax relief fund,
 §40-9-24.
Public athletic boards,
 §11-59-16.
Public building authorities,
 §11-56-21.
Public library authorities,
 §11-57-25.
Public park and recreation
 boards, §11-60-17.

TAXATION—Cont'd
Exemptions from taxation
 —Cont'd
Railroad authorities,
 §37-13-16.
Railroads.
 Motor fuels.
 Additional excise tax on
 gasoline, motor fuels
 and lubricating oil,
 §40-17-220.
Religious organizations.
 Property used for religious
 worship, §40-9-1.
Rescue squad vehicles,
 §32-11-2.
Sales tax.
 See SALES TAX.
Salvation army, §40-9-12.
Schools.
 Property, §40-9-1.
Scientific institutions.
 Property, §40-9-1.
Seamen's home of Mobile,
 §40-9-12.
Security interest, §40-9-1.
Shakespeare festival theatre
 finance authority,
 §41-10-209.
Shoals Presbyterian
 Apartments, Inc.,
 §40-9-26.
Shrine clubs.
 Annual shrine circus and
 other events, §40-9-13.
Soil and water conservation.
 Districts, §9-8-25.
 Watershed conservancy
 districts, §9-8-67.
Solid waste disposal
 authorities, §11-89A-16.
Southern products mart
 authority, §41-10-61.
Space science exhibit
 commission, §41-9-438.
Special, private or local laws
 prohibited, Const. Ala.,
 art. IV, §104.
Sports hall of fame board,
 §41-9-453.
State bar building
 foundation, §34-3-105.
State fair.
 Alabama state fair and
 exhibit association,
 §40-9-15.
State products mart and
 coliseum authority,
 §41-10-107.
Stringfellow memorial
 hospital nonprofit realty
 company, §40-9-1.1.
Susie Parker Stringfellow
 memorial hospital,
 §40-9-1.1.
Tannehill furnace and
 foundry commission,
 §41-9-329.
Textiles.
 Products or materials used
 in textile manufacture,
 §40-9-4.
Tobacco, §40-9-1.
Trees and timber.
 Standing timber exempt
 from taxation,
 §40-11-1.
United States.
 Bonds, §40-9-1.
 Property, §40-9-1.

TAXATION—Cont'd
Exemptions from taxation
 —Cont'd
Universities and colleges.
 Property of corporation or
 association formed for
 social or literary
 advancement used in
 connection with colleg
 or university, §40-9-16
 Property owned and used
 or held by colleges for
 certain purposes,
 §40-9-17.
University of Alabama
 Huntsville Foundation,
 §40-9-12.
University of Montevallo.
 Property exempt from
 taxes, §16-54-12.
Use tax, §40-23-62.
 See USE TAX.
USS Alabama battleship
 commission, §41-9-358.
Utility services facilities,
 §11-97-18.
Vessels.
 Motor fuels.
 Additional excise tax on
 gasoline, motor fuels
 and lubricating oil,
 §40-17-220.
Veterans.
 Certain homes owned by
 veterans or their
 widows, §40-9-20.
 Property of incompetent
 veterans, §40-9-1.
Veterans of foreign wars.
 Property, §40-9-1.
Water conservation and
 irrigation.
 Corporations.
 Bond issues, §9-10-41.
Water system assistance
 authority.
 Bonds or other
 indebtedness of
 authority, §22-23A-13.
Waterworks and sewer
 boards.
 Property and income of
 corporation,
 §11-50-235.
Welfare, §38-4-8.
Wells.
 Artesian wells leased to
 municipalities, §40-9-8
Women's hall of fame board,
 §41-9-554.
Young Men's Christian
 Association.
 Property exempt, §40-9-9.
Young Men's Hebrew
 Association.
 Property exempt, §40-9-12.
Young Women's Christian
 Association.
 Property exempt, §40-9-10.
Young Women's Christian
 Organization.
 Property exempt, §40-9-11.
Youth services.
 Department of youth
 services school
 districts.
 Gasoline tax, §40-17-31.
 Lubricating oils and
 greases, §40-17-171.

TAXATION—Cont'd
Fairs.
Exemptions, §40-9-1.
Alabama fair and exhibit association, §40-9-15.
Fair trial tax, §§12-19-250 to 12-19-254.
Family portraits.
Exemptions from taxation, §40-9-1.
Federal tax returns.
Misuse of returns or information from by state officers, employees, etc., §40-1-43.
Fees.
Department of revenue.
Agents and employees.
Arrest fee, §40-2-10.
Witnesses, §40-2-21.
Disposition of certain fees, §40-1-31.1.
Salaried officers.
Duty as to disposition of fees collected, §40-1-10.
Sale of land for taxes, §40-10-27.
Disposition of fees, §40-1-31.1.
Land sold for taxes not due at time of sale.
Warrant for fees, §40-10-105.
Supernumerary officials.
Deductions from fees of officials charged with assessment or collection of taxes, §40-6-4.
Tax assessors. See within this heading, "Tax assessors."
Tax collectors. See within this heading, "Tax collectors."
Financial institutions.
Excise tax, §§40-16-1 to 40-16-8.
See BANKS AND FINANCIAL INSTITUTIONS.
Fire departments.
Volunteer fire departments, §40-9-13.
Fish and game.
Nonresidents.
Payment of ad valorem property taxes.
Treatment as Alabama resident, §9-11-49.2.
Forests and forestry.
See FORESTS AND FORESTRY.
Fraternal benefit societies.
Conversion into stock or mutual life insurance company.
Exemption from premium taxes, §27-35-11.
Exemption from taxation, §§27-34-42, 40-9-1.
Fraud.
Assessments.
Change in condition of property.
Fraudulent failure to report, §40-7-12.
Penalties, §40-29-115.
Returns.
Penalties, §40-29-116.

TAXATION—Cont'd
Fraud—Cont'd
Warrants.
Falsely and fraudulently procuring state warrants, §40-1-26.
Freewill Baptist children's home.
Exemptions from taxation, §40-9-12.
Furs.
Shipment of furs without tax, §9-11-253.
Gains.
Capital gains, §§40-18-6 to 40-18-9.
Gambling.
Federal wagering occupational tax stamp, §§13A-12-90 to 13A-12-92.
Garnishment.
Delinquent taxpayers, §§40-5-20 to 40-5-22.
Gas companies.
See PUBLIC UTILITIES.
Gasoline.
Additional excise tax on gasoline, motor fuel and lubricating oil, §§40-17-220 to 40-17-225.
See within this heading, "Motor fuels."
Generation-skipping tax.
General provisions, §§19-5-1 to 19-5-12.
See TRUSTS AND TRUSTEES.
Gifts.
Foreign trade and relations commission, §41-9-664.
Music hall of fame board.
Exemptions, §41-9-683.
Girl Scouts of America.
Exemptions, §40-9-12.
Grants.
Securities.
Issuance of securities in anticipation of receipt of grants.
Exemption of securities, §11-81A-5.
Grease.
Lubricating oils and greases, §§40-17-170 to 40-17-186.
See LUBRICATING OILS AND GREASES.
Gross receipts tax.
Public utilities, §§40-21-80 to 40-21-87.
See PUBLIC UTILITIES.
Guardian and ward.
Assessments.
By whom property should be listed, §40-7-17.
Returns.
Separate returns in individual and fiduciary capacity, §40-7-20.
Tax assessors.
Notification of appointment of fiduciaries, §40-7-30.
Handicapped persons.
Exemptions from taxation.
Principal residence of totally disabled persons, §40-9-21.
Verification of eligibility by mail, §40-9-21.1.
Property, §40-9-1.

TAXATION—Cont'd
Handicapped persons —Cont'd
Income tax deductions.
Removal of any architectural or transportation barriers, §40-18-15.
Harbors and ports.
Leases.
Exemption, §33-1-19.
Subjects of taxation, §40-11-1.
Hazardous waste or substances.
Fees for disposal of hazardous waste or substances, §§22-30B-1 to 22-30B-18.
See HAZARDOUS WASTE.
Health.
County health officer and health department.
Tax to establish and maintain, §22-3-10.
Health care authorities.
Exemptions, §22-21-333.
Hospital taxes.
Defined, §22-21-311.
Proceeds.
Use, §22-21-344.
Health care service plans.
License, privilege or other taxes by municipalities or counties prohibited, §10-4-107.
Health maintenance organizations, §27-21A-28.
Hearings.
Department of revenue.
Notice of hearing, §40-2-5.
Hotels, inns and other transient lodging places.
Transient occupancy tax.
Assessment, §40-26-13.
Income tax.
Assessments.
Taxpayers' protest, §40-18-40.
Setoff debt collection, §§40-18-103, 40-18-104.
Public utilities.
Incorrect valuations, §40-21-24.
Sales tax.
Assessments, §40-23-17.
Use tax.
Redeterminations, §40-23-73.
Heart Association.
Exemptions, §40-9-13.
Helping Hand Club of Anniston.
Exemption, §40-9-12.
Highways.
Authority.
Bond issues.
Exemption from taxation, §23-1-157.
Contractors.
Sales tax on street and highway contractors.
See SALES TAX.
Federal aid highway finance authority.
Bonds and notes.
Exemptions, §23-1-312.

TAXATION—Cont'd
Highways—Cont'd
Finance corporation.
Bond issues.
Exemption, §23-1-177.
Historical preservation authorities.
Exemption from taxation, §41-10-147.
Incorporation.
Payment to secretary of state or probate judge, §41-10-147.
License or excise tax.
Imposition on authority, §41-10-147.
Historic Blakeley authority.
Exemption, §41-10-179.
History and archives.
Alabama historical commission.
Exemption, §41-9-256.
Tannehill furnace and foundry commission.
Exemption, §41-9-329.
Holy Comforter House, Inc., of Gadsden.
Exemptions, §40-9-12.
Homestead exemption, §40-9-19.
Applications.
Time for acceptance, §40-7-9.1.
Effective date, §40-7-9.1.
Verification of eligibility by mail, §40-9-21.1.
Horse racing.
Exemption from certain taxes, §11-65-35.
Hospitals.
Counties.
Special county tax.
See HOSPITALS.
Exemptions from taxation.
County and municipal hospital authorities, §§22-21-182, 22-21-186.
County hospital boards, §22-21-80.
County hospital corporations, §22-21-108.
Municipal hospital building authorities, §22-21-153.
Property, §40-9-1.
Stock of hospital corporations, §40-9-1.
Stringfellow memorial hospital nonprofit realty company, §40-9-1.1.
Susie Parker Stringfellow memorial hospital, §40-9-1.1.
Public hospitals.
Exemption of corporations, §11-95-11.
Special hospital taxes.
Applicability of certain provisions, §11-95-15.
Service program for indigents.
Appropriation of proceeds of special county tax, §22-21-223.

TAXATION—Cont'd
Hotels.
Industrial development boards.
Ad valorem taxes.
Hotels and motor inns built under act not exempt from, §11-54-96.1.
Transient occupancy tax, §§40-26-1 to 40-26-21.
See HOTELS, INNS AND OTHER TRANSIENT LODGING PLACES.
Housing finance authority.
Exemption, §24-1A-12.
Husband and wife.
Assessments.
By whom property should be listed, §40-7-17.
Returns.
Separate returns in individual and fiduciary capacity, §40-7-20.
Income tax, §§40-18-1 to 40-18-121.
See INCOME TAX.
Incompetents.
Assessments.
By whom property should be listed, §40-7-17.
Indians.
Constitutional provisions, Const. U. S., Amendment XIV.
Industrial development authority.
Bond issues.
Exemption, §41-10-28.
Industrial development corporations.
Credits, §10-4-143.
Exemptions, §10-4-143.
Licenses.
Occupational license taxes, §10-4-144.
Privileges, §10-4-143.
Inheritance tax, §§40-15-1 to 40-15-21.
See ESTATE AND INHERITANCE TAX.
Inns.
Transient occupancy tax, §§40-26-1 to 40-26-21.
See HOTELS, INNS AND OTHER TRANSIENT LODGING PLACES.
Institute for deaf and blind.
Exemptions from taxation.
Gasoline tax, §40-17-31.
Lubricating oils and greases, §40-17-171.
Insurance.
Insurance guaranty association.
Exemption, §27-42-15.
Insurance companies, §§27-4-1 to 27-4-11.
See INSURANCE.
Interest.
Delinquent taxes, §40-1-44.
Overpayments, §40-1-44.
Sale of land for taxes.
Land sold for taxes not due at time of sale.
Warrant for interest, §40-10-105.

TAXATION—Cont'd
Investments.
Ad valorem taxes, §40-1-47.
Special fund.
Establishment, §40-1-47.
Use, §40-1-48.
Jails.
County jails.
Levy of tax for erection, etc., §11-14-14.
Failure to levy tax when necessary, §11-14-15.
Special tax for jail, §11-14-16.
Jeopardy assessment, §40-29-91.
Judgments.
Actions by state against officers.
Judgment on verdict in favor of state, §40-1-17.
Assessments.
Appeals.
Judgment of revaluation, §40-7-48.
Sale of land for taxes.
Rights and remedies of purchasers.
Judgment when adverse claimant to tax title has made payment or tender, §40-10-80.
Judicial building authority.
Exemption, §41-10-279.
Judicial sales.
Sale of land, §§40-10-1 to 40-10-166. See within this heading, "Sale of land for taxes."
Junior college for Franklin, Marion and Winston counties.
Exemption of property, §16-60-35.
Junior college for Jackson and DeKalb counties.
Exemption of property, §16-60-65.
Knights of Pythias.
Exemptions, §40-9-12.
Land.
Commissioners. See within this heading, "Sale of land for taxes."
Sale of land for taxes, §§40-10-1 to 40-10-166. See within this heading, "Sale of land for taxes."
Leases.
Personal property.
Leasing or renting, §§40-12-220 to 40-12-227.
See PERSONAL PROPERTY.
Legislature.
Travel expenses of legislators.
Treatment for state income tax purposes, §29-1-8.1.
Levy and distraint, §§40-29-23 to 40-29-34.
Application of proceeds, §40-29-33.
Authority, §40-29-23.
Books.
Production, §40-29-25.
Effect of honoring levy, §40-29-24.

TAXATION—Cont'd
Levy and distraint—Cont'd
Enforcement of levy,
§40-29-24.
Notice, §40-29-23.
Procedure, §40-29-23.
Proceeds.
Application, §40-29-33.
Production of books,
§40-29-25.
Release.
Authority, §40-29-34.
Seizure and sale of property,
§40-29-23.
Certificate of sale,
§40-29-29.
Legal effect, §40-29-30.
Conditions of sale,
§40-29-26.
Deed of real property,
§40-29-29.
Legal effect, §40-29-30.
Expenses, §40-29-32.
Forcible rescue of seized
property, §40-29-118.
Indivisible property.
Sale, §40-29-26.
Manner of sale, §40-29-26.
Notice.
Sale, §40-29-26.
Seizure, §40-29-26.
Perishable goods,
§40-29-27.
Proceeds.
Application, §40-29-23.
Records of sales, §40-29-31.
Redemption of property,
§40-29-28.
Return of property,
§40-29-34.
Surrender of property subject
to levy, §40-29-24.
Libraries.
Property exempt, §40-9-1.
Licenses.
Commissioners.
Supernumerary license
commissioners,
§§40-6-1 to 40-6-8.
See LICENSES.
Delinquent taxes.
Collection, §40-12-10.
Inspectors, §40-12-10.
Powers and duties,
§40-12-10.
Municipal corporations.
See MUNICIPAL
CORPORATIONS.
Lid bill.
Ad valorem taxation.
Classification of taxable
property, Const. Ala.,
amd. 373.
Lien for taxes.
Date of lien, §§40-1-3,
40-29-21.
Estate and inheritance tax.
Lien of state, §40-15-13.
Filing.
Place for filing, §40-29-22.
Generally, §§40-1-2,
40-29-20.
Lien of tax collector,
§40-5-46.
Limitation of actions.
Chapter inapplicable,
§6-2-2.
Preferred claim, §40-1-4.
Priority against certain
persons, §40-29-22.

TAXATION—Cont'd
Lien for taxes—Cont'd
Protection for certain
commercial transactions
financing agreements,
§40-29-22.
Release.
Bond, surety, §40-29-20.
Term of lien, §40-29-21.
United States taxes,
§§35-11-42 to 35-11-48.
See UNITED STATES.
Validity against certain
persons, §40-29-22.
Limitation of actions.
Actions by state or political
subdivision for recovery
taxes, §6-2-35.
Action to test validity of
municipal election for
purpose of levying taxes,
§6-2-40.
Assessments.
Suspension, §40-29-51.
Collection of taxes, §40-1-36.
Collection after
assessment, §40-29-51.
Criminal prosecution,
§40-29-119.
Lien for taxes.
Chapter inapplicable,
§6-2-2.
Sale of land for taxes.
Actions for recovery of real
estate sold, §40-10-82.
Suspension, §40-29-52.
**Liquefied petroleum gas fuel
tax,** §§40-17-160 to
40-17-166.
See LIQUEFIED
PETROLEUM GAS
FUEL TAX.
Lists.
Falsely returning as sworn
to, §40-1-18.
Literary societies.
Property exempt, §40-9-1.
Lodging houses.
Transient occupancy tax,
§§40-26-1 to 40-26-21.
See HOTELS, INNS AND
OTHER TRANSIENT
LODGING PLACES.
Loss.
Capital loss, §§40-18-6 to
40-18-9.
Loyal Order of Moose.
Exemption, §40-9-1.
Lubricating oils and greases.
Additional excise tax on
gasoline, motor fuel and
lubricating oil,
§§40-17-220 to 40-17-225.
See within this heading,
"Motor fuels."
General provisions,
§§40-17-170 to 40-17-186.
See LUBRICATING OILS
AND GREASES.
Mail.
Exemptions from taxation.
Disabled persons.
Principal residence of
totally disabled
persons.
Verification of
eligibility by mail,
§40-9-21.1.
Homestead exemption.
Verification of eligibility
by mail, §40-9-21.1.

TAXATION—Cont'd
Mail—Cont'd
Timely mailing treated as
timely filing and paying,
§40-1-45.
Mappers.
Certified mappers.
Payment to certain
certified mappers,
§40-1-46.
Maps and plats.
Assessments.
Plat book, §§40-7-37 to
40-7-41.
School tax district,
§§16-13-192, 16-13-193.
Marine resources.
See MARINE RESOURCES.
Masonic homes.
Exemption, §40-9-12.
**Mayfair Towers
Corporation.**
Exemption, §40-9-26.
Men's hall of fame.
Donations, contributions and
gifts.
Exemption, §41-9-853.
**Mental health finance
authority.**
Exemptions from taxation.
Bonds and income of
authority, §41-10-362.
Federal income tax.
Interest on bonds.
Power of authority to
pay and make
agreements for
exemption,
§41-10-371.
Mentally ill.
Exemptions from taxation.
Corporations organized to
establish regional
programs and
facilities, §40-9-23.
Methodist children's home.
Exemptions, §40-9-12.
**Methodist home for the
aging.**
Exemptions, §40-9-12.
Mileage tax, §§40-19-1 to
40-19-17.
See MOTOR VEHICLE
CARRIERS.
Military affairs.
Exemption of property owned
or leased by units of
armed forces, §31-2-80.
National guard.
Property exempt, §40-9-1.
Post exchanges and canteens.
Exemption from tobacco
and gasoline taxes,
§31-2-81.
Mineral documentary tax,
§§40-20-30 to 40-20-37.
See OIL AND GAS.
Mistake.
Land sold for taxes not due
at time of sale,
§§40-10-100 to 40-10-105.
See within this heading,
"Sale of land for taxes."
Refund of taxes paid by
mistake, §§40-10-160 to
40-10-165. See within
this heading, "Refunds."
Mobile homes.
Decals, §40-7-1.

TAXATION—Cont'd
Mobile homes—Cont'd
Gas or electric service.
Report of connection,
§40-7-1.
Real estate.
Owner to report name and
address of owner of
mobile home, §40-7-1.
**Mortgages and deeds of
trust.**
Recordation tax, §§40-22-1 to
40-22-12.
See RECORDATION.
Motels.
Transient occupancy tax,
§§40-26-1 to 40-26-21.
See HOTELS, INNS AND
OTHER TRANSIENT
LODGING PLACES.
Motor carrier fuel tax,
§§40-17-140 to 40-17-155.
See MOTOR VEHICLE
CARRIERS.
Motorcycles.
Shrine motorcycle clubs,
§32-6-191.
Motor fuels.
Additional excise tax on
gasoline, motor fuel and
lubricating oil,
§§40-17-220 to 40-17-225.
Administration of
provisions, §40-17-221.
Agriculture.
Exemptions, §40-17-220.
Aircraft.
Exemptions, §40-17-220.
Allocations of revenue
collections, §40-17-225.
Collection, §40-17-221.
Allocations of revenue
collections,
§40-17-225.
Counties.
Exemptions, §40-17-220.
Disposition of proceeds,
§§40-17-222,
40-17-223.
Education.
Church schools.
Exemptions,
§40-17-220.
City and county boards
of education.
Exemptions,
§40-17-220.
Private schools.
Exemptions,
§40-17-220.
Exemptions, §40-17-220.
Highways.
Use of net tax proceeds
for highway
purposes,
§40-17-224.
Levy, §40-17-220.
Municipal corporations.
Exemptions, §40-17-220.
Proceeds.
Disposition.
Proceeds derived from
gasoline and
lubricating oil,
§40-17-223.
Proceeds derived from
motor fuel,
§40-17-222.

TAXATION—Cont'd
Motor fuels—Cont'd
Additional excise tax on
gasoline, motor fuel and
lubricating oil—Cont'd
Proceeds—Cont'd
Use of net tax proceeds
for highway
purposes,
§40-17-224.
Railroads.
Exemptions, §40-17-220.
Rate, §40-17-220.
Remittance, §40-17-220.
United States certificates
of exemption,
§40-17-220.
Vessels.
Exemptions, §40-17-220.
General provisions.
See MOTOR FUELS.
Liquefied petroleum gas fuel
tax, §§40-17-160 to
40-17-166.
See LIQUEFIED
PETROLEUM GAS
FUEL TAX.
Motor carrier fuel tax,
§§40-17-140 to 40-17-155.
See MOTOR VEHICLE
CARRIERS.
Municipal corporations.
Exemption of class 1
municipalities,
§40-17-240.
**Motor sports hall of fame
commission.**
Exemptions, §41-9-474.
Motor vehicle carriers.
Fuel tax, §§40-17-140 to
40-17-154.
See MOTOR VEHICLE
CARRIERS.
Local authorities.
Power to tax, §32-5-1.
Mileage tax, §§40-19-1 to
40-19-17.
See MOTOR VEHICLE
CARRIERS.
Municipal privilege license
tax, §37-3-33.
Motor vehicles.
See MOTOR VEHICLES.
Multistate tax compact,
§§40-27-1 to 40-27-6.
Adopted, §40-27-1.
Arbitration, §40-27-1.
Audits.
Interstate audits, §40-27-1.
Force and effect,
§40-27-6.
Commission.
Generally, §40-27-1.
Representatives from
subdivisions affected
by compact, §40-27-5.
State representative,
§40-27-2.
Alternate state
representatives,
§40-27-3.
Counsel for, §40-27-4.
Construction, §40-27-1.
Definitions, §40-27-1.
Income taxation.
Division of income,
§40-27-1.
Elements, §40-27-1.
Multistate tax commission,
§§40-27-1 to 40-27-5.
Purposes, §40-27-1.

TAXATION—Cont'd
Multistate tax compact
—Cont'd
Sales and use taxation.
Elements, §40-27-1.
Severability, §40-27-1.
Terms, §40-27-1.
Municipal corporations.
Education.
See EDUCATION.
Elimination of payments of
less than five dollars to
municipalities,
§40-1-31.2.
Enterprise zones.
Creation with class 1
cities.
Reduction in municipal
tax and license
rates, §11-40-16.
Exemptions. See within this
heading, "Exemptions
from taxation."
General provisions, §§11-51-1
to 11-51-74.
See MUNICIPAL
CORPORATIONS.
Motor fuels.
Additional excise tax.
Exemption, §40-17-220.
Exemption of class 1
municipalities,
§40-17-240.
National foundation.
Exemptions from taxation.
Alabama field offices,
§40-9-12.
**New Hope Industries of
Dothan.**
Exemptions, §40-9-12.
Notice.
Assessments.
Appeals, §40-7-46.
County boards of
equalization.
Service of notices, §40-3-23.
Valuation of property,
§40-3-20.
Department of revenue.
Hearings, §40-2-5.
Form of notice to taxpayers,
§40-1-29.
Hotels, inns and other
transient lodging places.
Transient occupancy tax.
Assessment, §40-26-13.
Income tax.
Assessment.
Mailing of tax to be only
notice required,
§40-18-40.
Setoff debt collection,
§§40-18-103,
40-18-105.
Mailing.
Notice required to be given
by registered mail may
be given by certified
mail, §40-1-30.
Motor vehicle carriers.
Mileage tax.
See MOTOR VEHICLE
CARRIERS.
Public utilities.
Valuation notice,
§40-21-23.
Returns.
Attendance of assessor to
receive returns,
§40-7-3.

TAXATION—Cont'd
  Notice—Cont'd
    Sale of land, §§40-10-4 to
      40-10-6.
    Sales tax.
      See SALES TAX.
    Securities tax, §40-24-7.
    Tax collectors.
      Garnishment of delinquent
        taxpayers, §40-5-20.
      Levy and sale of personal
        property, §40-5-14.
    Use tax.
      Additional amounts due.
        When notice to be
          mailed, §40-23-76.
  Oaths.
    Assessments.
      Failure to subscribe,
        §40-7-21.
      Oath to be used on bottom
        of assessment sheet,
        §40-7-8.
    Commissioner of revenue.
      Oath of office, §40-2-42.
    County boards of
      equalization.
      Oath of members, §40-3-3.
    Department of revenue.
      Legal counsel.
        Oath of office, §40-2-61.
      Witnesses, §40-2-6.
    Returns.
      Administering oath before
        return made, §40-7-5.
    Supernumerary officials,
      §40-6-2.
  Officers.
    Actions against, §40-1-40.
      Evidence.
        Copies of books, records,
          papers, etc.,
          §40-1-16.
        Verdict in favor of state.
          Judgment upon,
          §40-1-17.
    Attorney for taxpayer.
      Unlawful, §40-1-20.
    Books and records.
      Access, §40-1-21.
      Copies admitted in
        evidence in actions
        against officers,
        §40-1-16.
    Conversion.
      Liability, §40-1-23.
    Fees.
      Salaried officers.
        Duty as to disposition of
          fees collected,
          §40-1-10.
    Impeachment, §40-1-28.
    Penalties.
      Neglect of duty, §40-1-22.
    Salaries, §§40-6A-1 to
      40-6A-8. See within this
      heading, "Salaries."
    Securities.
      Dealing in state securities,
        §40-1-25.
    Sheriffs.
      Sale of property under
        execution.
        Duty of sheriff, §40-1-24.
    State employees' retirement
      system.
      Exemption of benefits,
        §36-27-28.
    Tax assessors. See within
      this heading, "Tax
      assessors."

TAXATION—Cont'd
  Officers—Cont'd
    Tax collectors. See within
      this heading, "Tax
      collectors."
  Oil and gas.
    General provisions.
      See OIL AND GAS.
    Lubricating oils and greases.
      Additional tax on gasoline,
        motor fuel and
        lubricating oil,
        §§40-17-220 to
        40-17-225. See within
        this heading, "Motor
        fuels."
      General provisions,
        §§40-17-170 to
        40-17-186.
      See LUBRICATING
        OILS AND
        GREASES.
  Other states.
    Enforcement of liability for
      taxes imposed by other
      states, §40-1-35.
  **Overpayments into state
    treasury**, §40-1-42.
    Interest, §40-1-44.
  Oysters.
    Private reefs.
      Oysters harvested,
        §9-12-44.
  Parent and child.
    Assessments.
      By whom property should
        be listed, §40-7-17.
    Returns.
      Separate returns in
        individual and
        fiduciary capacity,
        §40-7-20.
  Partnerships.
    Assessments.
      By whom property should
        be listed, §40-7-17.
    Returns.
      Separate returns in
        individual and
        fiduciary capacity,
        §40-7-20.
  Payment of taxes.
    Bad checks, §40-29-70.
    Date taxes due, §40-11-4.
    Dog racetracks.
      Required, §40-11-5.
    Error.
      Refund of taxes paid by
        error. See within this
        heading, "Refunds."
    Lienors, §40-1-27.
    Mail.
      Effect of timely mailing,
        §40-1-45.
    Mistake.
      Refund of taxes paid by
        mistake. See within
        this heading,
        "Refunds."
    Payment under protest.
      Authorized, §40-1-11.
      Disposition of funds,
        §40-1-12.
      Recovery.
        Procedure, §40-1-11.
    Promptness, §40-1-39.
    Refunds. See within this
      heading, "Refunds."
    Remitting of payments,
      §40-1-5.

TAXATION—Cont'd
  Payment of taxes—Cont'd
    Sale of land for payment. See
      within this heading,
      "Sale of land for taxes."
    Time.
      Date taxes due, §40-11-4.
      Willful failure to pay.
        Penalties, §40-29-112.
  Peace officers.
    Department of revenue.
      Agents and employees
        constituted peace
        officers, §40-2-10.
    Hall of fame.
      Donations, contributions
        and gifts.
        Exemption, §41-9-872.
  Peanuts.
    Exemptions from taxation.
      Peanuts stored in licensed
        warehouses, §40-9-3.
  Pecans.
    Exemptions from taxation.
      Pecans stored in licensed
        warehouses, §40-9-3.
  Penalties, §40-1-5.
    Alcoholic beverages.
      Malt or brewed beverages.
        Excise tax, §§28-3-186,
        28-3-187.
    Assessments.
      Penalty assessed as tax,
        §40-29-72.
      Remission of penalties,
        §40-7-29.
    Cigarettes.
      Gummed cigarette papers.
        See CIGARETTES.
    Collection of taxes.
      Failure to collect,
        §40-29-73.
      Willful failure,
        §40-29-111.
    Defeating tax, §40-29-110.
    Evasion of taxes, §§40-29-73,
      40-29-110.
    Gasoline tax, §40-17-37.
    Income tax.
      See INCOME TAX.
    Insurance companies,
      §27-4-7.
    Liquefied petroleum gas fuel
      tax, §40-17-164.
    Lubricating oils and greases,
      §40-17-178.
    Motor vehicle carriers.
      Fuel tax, §§40-17-144,
        40-17-155.
      Mileage tax.
        See MOTOR VEHICLE
          CARRIERS.
    Officers who neglect duty,
      §40-1-22.
    Payment of taxes.
      Willful failure to pay,
        §40-29-112.
    Public utilities, §§40-21-17,
      40-21-31.
    Remittance.
      Authority to remit,
        §40-1-6.
    Returns.
      Failure to make,
        §40-29-112.
      Fraud, §40-29-116.
    Sale of land for taxes.
      Land sold for taxes not due
        at time of sale.
        Warrant for penalty,
          §40-10-105.

TAXATION—Cont'd
  Penalties—Cont'd
    Sales tax.
      See SALES TAX.
    Statements.
      Failure to furnish
        statement, §40-29-74.
      Failure to make,
        §40-29-113.
      False statements,
        §40-29-115.
      Fraudulent statements,
        §§40-29-74, 40-29-113,
        40-29-116.
    Tobacco.
      Sales tax.
        See TOBACCO.
    Use tax.
      Failure to pay, §40-23-69.
      Fraud, §40-23-80.
    Waiver.
      Authority to waive,
        §40-1-6.
  Penny trust fund.
    Deduction, §41-15A-3.
  Personal property.
    Exemptions, §40-9-1.
    Holding by warehousemen
      for distribution,
      §40-9-7.
    Storage for shipment
      outside of state,
      §40-9-6.
    Leasing or renting,
      §§40-12-220 to 40-12-227.
      See PERSONAL
        PROPERTY.
    Levy and sale. See within
      this heading, "Tax
      collectors."
    Subjects of taxation,
      §40-11-1.
  Pilots and pilotage.
    License tax.
      Levy, payment and
        disposition, §33-4-38.
  Pipeline companies.
    Public utilities generally,
      §§40-21-1 to 40-21-107.
      See PUBLIC UTILITIES.
  Plat books.
    Assessments, §§40-7-37 to
      40-7-41.
  Police.
    Fraternal order of police.
      Property exempt, §40-9-1.
  Poll taxes.
    Education.
      Use for support of public
        schools, Const. Ala.,
        art. XIV, §259.
    Prohibited, Const. U. S.,
      Amendment XXIV.
  Pollution control equipment.
    Exemptions, §40-9-1.
  Port authority.
    Exemption, §11-94-19.
  Poultry.
    Exemption, §40-9-1.
  Power to levy taxes.
    Delegation.
      Power not to be delegated,
        Const. Ala., art. XI,
        §212.
  Presbyterian Apartments,
    Inc.
    Exemptions, §40-9-13.
  Presbyterian Apartments of
    Birmingham, Inc.
    Exemption, §40-9-26.

TAXATION—Cont'd
  Presbyterian home for
    children.
    Exemptions, §40-9-12.
  Presbyterian Homes of
    Decatur, Inc.
    Exemption, §40-9-26.
  Printing.
    Subjects of taxation,
      §40-11-1.
  Private schools.
    Exemptions from taxation.
      Lubricating oils and
        greases, §40-17-171.
      Motor fuels.
        Additional excise tax on
          gasoline, motor fuel
          and lubricating oil,
          §40-17-220.
  Probate courts.
    Refund of taxes paid by
      mistake or error.
      Duty of judge of probate,
        §40-10-162.
  Property taxable. See within
    this heading, "Subjects of
    taxation."
  Proration prevention
    account.
    Appropriations, §40-1-32.1.
    Establishment, §40-1-32.1.
    Reversion to trust fund,
      §40-1-32.1.
    Withdrawal, §40-1-32.1.
  Protest.
    Payment under protest,
      §§40-1-11, 40-1-12.
  Public officers and
    employees. See within
    this heading, "Officers."
  Public utilities.
    General provisions, §§40-21-1
      to 40-21-107.
      See PUBLIC UTILITIES.
    Gross receipts tax,
      §§40-21-80 to 40-21-87.
      See PUBLIC UTILITIES.
    Subjects of taxation,
      §40-11-1.
  Railroad authorities.
    Exemption, §37-13-16.
  Railroads.
    Exemptions from taxation.
      Motor fuels.
        Additional excise tax on
          gasoline, motor fuels
          and lubricating oil,
          §40-17-220.
    Motor fuels.
      Additional excise tax on
        gasoline, motor fuel
        and lubricating oil.
        Exemptions, §40-17-220.
    Public utilities generally,
      §§40-21-1 to 40-21-107.
    Subjects of taxation,
      §40-11-1.
  Rate of taxation, Const. Ala.,
    amd. 325.
    Allocation, §40-8-3.
    Assessment rate, §40-8-1.
      Assessment ratios for
        purposes of local
        taxation, §40-8-4.
    Established, §40-8-2.
    Limitation on state property
      tax rate, Const. Ala., art.
      XI, §214.

TAXATION—Cont'd
  Rate of taxation—Cont'd
    Property of private
      corporations, associations
      and individuals to be
      taxed at same rate,
      Const. Ala., art. XI,
      §217.
    Exception as to religious,
      educational and
      charitable property,
      Const. Ala., art. XI,
      §217.
  Real property.
    Capital gain or loss.
      Generally, §§40-18-6 to
      40-18-9.
    Recordation tax, §§40-22-1 to
      40-22-12.
      See RECORDATION.
    Sale of land for taxes,
      §§40-10-1 to 40-10-166.
      See within this heading,
      "Sale of land for taxes."
    Subjects of taxation,
      §40-11-1.
  Reappraisals.
    Statewide property
      reappraisal, §§40-7-50 to
      40-7-100. See within this
      heading, "Assessments."
  Receivers.
    Assessments.
      By whom property should
        be listed, §40-7-17.
    Liability, §40-1-8.
    Returns.
      Separate returns in
        individual and
        fiduciary capacity,
        §40-7-20.
    Tax assessors.
      Notification of appointment
        of fiduciaries, §40-7-30.
  Recordation tax, §§40-22-1 to
    40-22-12.
    See RECORDATION.
  Records.
    Cigarettes.
      Gummed cigarette papers.
        See CIGARETTES.
    Education.
      Warrants for special
        county and district
        taxes, §16-13-106.
    Hotels, inns and other
      transient lodging places.
      Transient occupancy tax.
        See HOTELS, INNS
        AND OTHER
        TRANSIENT
        LODGING PLACES.
    Income tax, §§40-18-48,
      40-18-107.
      Custody, §40-18-48.
      Setoff debt collection.
        Confidentiality,
        §40-18-107.
    Inspection, §40-1-5.
    Lubricating oils and greases,
      §§40-17-176, 40-17-178.
    Maintenance, §40-1-5.
    Motor fuels.
      Diesel fuel tax.
        Failure to keep records,
        §40-17-9.
      Gasoline tax, §§40-17-35,
        40-17-137.
    Motor vehicle carriers.
      Fuel tax, §40-17-149.
      Mileage tax, §40-19-5.

TAXATION—Cont'd
Records—Cont'd
Public utilities.
Compelling production of
records, §40-21-19.
Tobacco sales tax,
§§40-25-13, 40-25-26.
Redemption.
Land sold for taxes,
§§40-10-120 to 40-10-143.
Redevelopment projects.
Tax status of certain land,
§24-2-7.
Refunds.
Automatic refund, §40-29-71.
Errors.
Refunds due to errors,
§40-7-2.2.
Sale of land for taxes not
due at time of sale,
§§40-10-100 to
40-10-103.
Taxes paid by mistake or
error, §§40-10-160 to
40-10-165.
Gasoline tax, §§40-17-100 to
40-17-108.
See GASOLINE.
Income tax.
See INCOME TAX.
Mistake.
Taxes paid by mistake or
error, §§40-10-160 to
40-10-165.
Overpayment made directly
to department of
revenue, §40-1-34.
Sale of land for taxes.
Land sold for taxes not due
at time of sale.
Refund to purchaser,
§§40-10-100 to
40-10-103.
Taxes paid by mistake or
error, §§40-10-160 to
40-10-165.
Comptroller.
Duty, §40-10-162.
County treasurer.
Payment by, §40-10-163.
Municipal corporations.
Application of provisions,
§40-10-166.
Payment by, §40-10-165.
Recovery from,
§40-10-164.
Petition.
Duty of probate judge
and comptroller,
§40-10-162.
Filing, §40-10-161.
Presentation to county
commission,
§40-10-163.
Probate judge.
Duty, §40-10-162.
State treasurer.
Payment by, §40-10-162.
When taxpayer entitled to
recover, §40-10-160.
Religion.
Property used for religious
worship exempt, §40-9-1.
Remedies.
Rights and remedies.
Purchasers at tax sales,
§§40-10-70 to 40-10-83.
Remittances.
Payment, §40-1-5.
Penalties, §40-1-6.

TAXATION—Cont'd
Rent.
Personal property.
Leasing or renting,
§§40-12-220 to
40-12-227.
See PERSONAL
PROPERTY.
Reports, §40-1-5.
Cigarettes.
Gummed cigarette papers.
Penalty for failure to
report, §40-25A-6.
Commissioner of revenue.
Annual report, §40-29-120.
Estate and inheritance taxes.
Failure to make.
Appraisement, §40-15-10.
Income tax.
Information from source of
income.
Definition of "report
from source,"
§40-18-1.
Report to revenue
department,
§40-18-26.
Lubricating oils and greases.
See LUBRICATING OILS
AND GREASES.
Motor fuels.
Diesel fuel tax, §§40-17-8,
40-17-9.
Gasoline tax.
See GASOLINE.
General provisions.
See MOTOR FUELS.
Motor vehicle carriers.
Fuel tax.
See MOTOR VEHICLE
CARRIERS.
Mileage tax.
See MOTOR VEHICLE
CARRIERS.
Promptness, §40-1-39.
Public utilities.
See PUBLIC UTILITIES.
Sales tax.
See SALES TAX.
Tax collectors. See within
this heading, "Tax
collectors."
Tobacco sales tax, §40-25-14.
Rescue squads.
Exemptions, §32-11-2.
Retirement.
State employees' retirement
system.
Exemption of benefits,
§36-27-28.
Supernumerary tax officials.
Election to participate in
supernumerary
retirement program,
§40-6-8.
Returns.
Agents.
Separate returns in
individual and
fiduciary capacity,
§40-7-20.
Confidentiality, §40-1-33.
County boards of
equalization.
Meetings to inspect,
§40-3-18.
Errors.
Correction, §40-7-2.2.

TAXATION—Cont'd
Returns—Cont'd
Executors and
administrators.
Separate returns in
individual and
fiduciary capacity,
§40-7-20.
Exempt property.
Listing, §40-7-6.
Failure to make.
Demand against persons
failing to make,
§40-7-19.
Penalties, §40-29-112.
Receipt on commissions
from business,
§40-7-24.
Fraud.
Penalties, §40-29-116.
Guardian and ward.
Separate returns in
individual and
fiduciary capacity,
§40-7-20.
Husband and wife.
Separate returns in
individual and
fiduciary capacity,
§40-7-20.
Income tax.
See INCOME TAX.
Interrogation as to items and
details of property,
§40-7-6.
Mail.
Effect of timely mailing,
§40-1-45.
Notice.
Attendance of assessor to
receive returns,
§40-7-3.
Oaths.
Administering oath before
return made, §40-7-5.
Parent and child.
Separate returns in
individual and
fiduciary capacity,
§40-7-20.
Partnerships.
Separate returns in
individual and
fiduciary capacity,
§40-7-20.
Promptness, §40-1-39.
Real estate.
Failure to furnish
description, §40-7-4.
Receivers.
Separate returns in
individual and
fiduciary capacity,
§40-7-20.
Tax assessors.
Copies, §40-4-7.
Duties, §40-7-27.
Taxpayers.
Duty to attend
appointment and
return list of property,
§40-7-4.
Trusts and trustees.
Separate returns in
individual and
fiduciary capacity,
§40-7-20.
Revenue bills, Const. U. S.,
Art. I, §7.
Revenues collected.
Distribution, §40-1-31.

TAXATION—Cont'd

Rooming houses.

Industrial development
boards.
Ad valorem taxes.
Hotels and motor inns
built under act not
exempt from,
§11-54-96.1.
Transient occupancy tax,
§§40-26-1 to 40-26-21.
See HOTELS, INNS AND
OTHER TRANSIENT
LODGING PLACES.

Rules and regulations.

Cigarettes.
Gummed cigarette papers,
§40-25A-16.
Hotels, inns and other
transient lodging places.
Transient occupancy tax,
§40-26-19.
Income tax, §40-18-57.
Motor fuels.
Diesel fuel tax, §40-17-18.
Motor vehicle carriers fuel
tax, §40-17-152.
Motor vehicle carriers.
Fuel tax, §40-17-152.
Mileage tax, §40-19-13.
Tobacco sales tax, §40-25-10.

Salaries.

Compensation of tax officials,
§§40-6A-1 to 40-6A-8.
Ad valorem taxes.
Officials charged with
assessing and
collecting, §40-6A-2.
Applicability of section,
§40-6A-3.
Conversion from fee basis
to salary basis.
Manner of payment of
fees due, §40-6A-7.
Salary must equal net
personal income,
§40-6A-4.
Effective date of provisions,
§40-6A-8.
Legislative intent,
§40-6A-1.
Manner of payment of fees
due prior to conversion
from fee to salary
basis, §40-6A-7.
Merit system.
Membership in merit
system, §40-6A-5.
Office personnel, §40-6A-5.
Payment of fees,
commissions, etc., into
local general fund,
§40-6A-6.
Personal income.
Salary must equal net
personal income,
§40-6A-4.
Support services provided
by local governing
bodies, §40-6A-5.
Department of revenue.
Division chiefs, §40-2-24.
Tax assessors, §40-6A-2.
Tax collectors, §40-6A-2.
Withholding tax.
See INCOME TAX.

TAXATION—Cont'd

Sale of land for taxes,
§§40-10-1 to 40-10-166.
Bidding in for state,
§40-10-18.
Certificates of purchase,
§40-10-20.
Costs when land bid in for
state, §40-10-22.
Redemption of land sold for
taxes.
Certification of sale of
lands bid in for
state, §40-10-140.
Certification when land
bid in by state sold,
§40-10-136.
Deed of state on sale of
land bid in by state,
§40-10-135.
Deposit of redemption
money when lands
bid in by state,
§40-10-129.
Duty of probate judge on
redemption of land
bid in by state,
§40-10-130.
List and sale of lands bid
in by state,
§40-10-132.
Manner of sale of land
bid in by state,
§40-10-134.
Notice to former owner
of application to
purchase land bid in
by state, §40-10-133.
Right of state or assignee
to possession when
lands are bid in for
state, §40-10-73.
Book of lands upon which
taxes have not been
paid.
Contents, §40-10-2.
Entries.
Forms, §40-10-2.
Preparation, §40-10-3.
Certificates of purchase.
Assignments, §40-10-21.
Contents, §40-10-19.
Delivery, §40-10-19.
When land bid in for state,
§40-10-20.
Cloud upon title to real
estate erroneously sold
for taxes.
Removal, §40-10-31.
Confirmation of sale,
§40-10-13.
Costs.
Paid by purchasers,
§40-10-23.
When land bid in for state,
§40-10-22.
Decree of sale, §40-10-11.
Appeal, §40-10-25.
Payment of judgment on
appeal, §40-10-26.
Issuance, §40-10-8.
Deeds.
Acknowledgment,
§40-10-30.
Delivery to purchaser,
§40-10-29.
Effect, §40-10-30.
Signature of probate judge,
§40-10-30.

TAXATION—Cont'd

Sale of land for taxes
—Cont'd
Defective sale proceedings.
Rights and remedies of
purchasers, §40-10-75.
Description of property,
§40-10-14.
Erroneous sale.
Removal of cloud upon title
to real estate
erroneously sold,
§40-10-31.
Erroneous tax payment.
Refund of taxes paid by
mistake or error,
§§40-10-160 to
40-10-165.
Excess arising from sale.
Disposition, §40-10-28.
Fees, §40-10-27.
Disposition of fees,
§40-1-31.1.
Land commissioner,
§§40-10-50 to 40-10-54.
Agents.
Appointment, §40-10-50.
Duties, §40-10-52.
Assistants.
Appointment, §40-10-50.
Certificates.
Blank certificates,
§40-10-53.
Compensation, §40-10-50.
Deeds.
Blank deeds, §40-10-53.
Designation, §40-10-50.
Duties.
Agents, §40-10-52.
Generally, §40-10-51.
Lists of lands bid in for
state.
Commissioner to furnish
assessor, §40-10-54.
Redemption of land sold for
taxes.
Duty of commissioner,
§40-10-126.
Land sold for taxes not due
at time of sale,
§§40-10-100 to 40-10-105.
Comptroller.
Payment of refund,
§40-10-103.
Costs and fees.
Warrant for, §40-10-105.
Penalties and interest.
Warrant for, §40-10-105.
Refund to purchaser,
§40-10-101.
Land purchased and sold
privately by state,
§40-10-100.
Payment by comptroller,
§40-10-103.
Procurement, §40-10-102.
Taxes.
Warrant for, §40-10-105.
Warrants, §§40-10-104,
40-10-105.
School funds, §40-10-104.
Manner of sale, §40-10-15.
Mistake.
Land sold for taxes not due
at time of sale,
§§40-10-100 to
40-10-105.
Refund of taxes paid by
mistake or error,
§§40-10-160 to
40-10-165.

TAXATION—Cont'd
Sale of land for taxes
 —Cont'd
Notice of sale, §40-10-12.
Description of property,
 §40-10-14.
Notice to taxpayer.
 Assessment to "owner
  unknown," §40-10-5.
 Publication, §40-10-6.
 Service, §40-10-4.
Officers not to be interested
 in purchase, §40-10-24.
Partial payment of taxes
 prior to sale, §40-10-7.
Payment by purchaser,
 §40-10-17.
Portion sufficient to satisfy
 decree, §40-10-16.
Probate court.
 Duties of judge, §40-10-15.
 Ordering sales, §40-10-1.
 Redemption of land sold for
  taxes.
 Duty of probate judge on
  redemption of land
  bid in by state,
  §40-10-130.
Purchase.
 Certificate, §§40-10-19 to
  40-10-21.
 Payment by purchaser,
  §40-10-17.
Purchasers at tax sales.
 Rights and remedies,
  §§40-10-70 to 40-10-83.
 Actions for possession.
  Books and records as
   prima facie
   evidence,
   §40-10-81.
  Defeat on grounds
   other than that
   taxes were not
   due, §40-10-76.
  Failure of defense on
   grounds other
   than that taxes
   were not due,
   §40-10-77.
  Recitation of fact of
   purchase deemed
   prima facie
   evidence,
   §40-10-79.
 Defective sale
  proceedings,
  §40-10-75.
 Evidence.
  Books and records,
   §40-10-81.
  Recitation of fact of
   purchase,
   §40-10-79.
 Land insufficiently
  described, §40-10-72.
 Lands sold which are not
  liable for taxes,
  §40-10-71.
 Liens.
  Purchaser to receive
   assignment,
   §40-10-70.
  Redemption when lien
   is recorded,
   §§40-10-73,
   40-10-74.
  Limitation of actions,
   §40-10-82.

TAXATION—Cont'd
Sale of land for taxes
 —Cont'd
Purchasers at tax sales
 —Cont'd
 Rights and remedies
  —Cont'd
  Payment by original
   owner or assignee.
   Effect, §40-10-83.
  Right to possession.
   Purchaser or assignee,
    §40-10-74.
   State or assignee
    where lands are
    bid in for state,
    §40-10-73.
  Tender of party claiming
   adversely to tax
   title, §40-10-78.
  Judgment in favor of
   party, §40-10-80.
Redemption of land sold for
 taxes, §§40-10-120 to
 40-10-143.
 Certificate of redemption.
  Issuance, §40-10-127.
 Deposit of redemption
  money.
  Generally, §40-10-128.
  Lands bid in by state,
   §40-10-129.
 Lands bid in by state.
  Certification upon sale,
   §§40-10-136,
   40-10-140.
  Conveyance to
   department of
   conservation and
   natural resources.
   Deed to department,
    §40-10-138.
   Notice to former
    owner, §40-10-139.
   Procedure, §40-10-137.
  Deed of state,
   §40-10-135.
  Deposit of redemption
   money, §40-10-129.
  Duty of probate judge on
   redemption,
   §40-10-130.
  List and sale,
   §40-10-132.
  Manner of sale,
   §40-10-134.
  Notice to former owner
   of application to
   purchase,
   §40-10-133.
  Lien and sale of property
   for unpaid
   installments of taxes.
   Disposition of money,
    §40-10-142.
   Persons other than
    holders of legal title.
    Expenses of
     redemption,
     §40-10-143.
   Procedure, §40-10-141.
  Manner of redemption,
   §§40-10-121,
   40-10-122.
  Probate judges.
   Duty on redemption of
    land bid in by state,
    §40-10-130.

TAXATION—Cont'd
Sale of land for taxes
 —Cont'd
Redemption of land sold for
 taxes—Cont'd
 Redeeming lots and parcels
  without redeeming
  entire property.
  Authorization,
   §§40-10-123,
   40-10-124.
  How redeemed,
   §40-10-125.
  Land commissioner.
   Duty, §40-10-126.
  Rents, issues and profits of
   redeemed land,
   §40-10-131.
  Time, §40-10-120.
  Who may redeem,
   §40-10-120.
 Refund of taxes paid by
  mistake or error,
  §§40-10-160 to 40-10-165.
 Taxes not due.
  Land sold for taxes not due
   at time of sale,
   §§40-10-100 to
   40-10-105.
 Trial of cases, §40-10-8.
  Attendance of collector,
   §40-10-9.
  When deputy may attend
   in lieu of collector,
   §40-10-10.
  Continuance, §40-10-8.
  Decree.
   Issuance, §40-10-8.
  Evidence.
   Tax book, §40-10-9.
Sales tax.
 General provisions, §§40-23-1
  to 40-23-50.
  See SALES TAX.
 Municipal corporations,
  §§11-51-200 to 11-51-207.
  See MUNICIPAL
   CORPORATIONS.
 Personal property.
  Leasing or renting,
   §§40-12-220 to
   40-12-227.
  See PERSONAL
   PROPERTY.
 Tobacco, §§40-25-1 to
  40-25-29.
  See TOBACCO.
Salvation army.
 Exemptions, §40-9-12.
Schools.
 County tax for education,
  §40-12-4.
 Property exempt, §40-9-1.
School taxes.
 General provisions.
  See EDUCATION.
Scientific institutions.
 Property exempt, §40-9-1.
S corporations, §§40-18-160 to
 40-18-176.
 See CORPORATIONS.
Seamen's home of Mobile.
 Exemptions, §40-9-12.
Securities.
 Grants.
  Issuance of securities in
   anticipation of receipt
   of grants.
   Exemption of securities,
    §11-81A-5.

TAXATION—Cont'd
  Securities—Cont'd
    Officers.
      Dealing in state securities,
        §40-1-25.
  Securities tax, §§40-24-1 to
    40-24-8.
    See SECURITIES.
  Security interests.
    Exemption, §40-9-1.
  Service of process.
    County boards of
      equalization.
      Subpoenas, notices and
        other writings,
        §40-3-23.
  Settlements.
    Correction, §40-1-41.
    Promptness, §40-1-39.
    Tax collectors. See within
      this heading, "Tax
      collectors."
  Severance taxes.
    Coal, §§40-13-1 to 40-13-36.
      See COAL.
    Forest products, §§9-13-80 to
      9-13-107.
      See FORESTS AND
        FORESTRY.
  **Shakespeare festival theatre
    finance authority.**
    Exemptions, §41-10-209.
  Sheriffs.
    Sale of property under
      execution.
      Duty of sheriff, §40-1-24.
  Ships and shipping.
    Motor fuels.
      Additional excise tax on
        gasoline, motor fuel
        and lubricating oil.
        Ships, vessels and
          barges.
          Exemptions,
            §40-17-220.
    Subjects of taxation,
      §40-11-1.
  **Shoals Presbyterian
    Apartments, Inc.**
    Exemption, §40-9-26.
  Shrine club.
    Exemptions from taxation.
      Annual shrine circus and
        other events, §40-9-13.
  Soil and water conservation.
    Cost-share grants.
      Exemption, §9-8A-14.
      Agricultural and
        conservation
        development
        commission,
        §9-8A-13.
    Districts.
      Exemption, §9-8-25.
    Watershed conservancy
      districts.
      Exemption, §9-8-67.
  **Solid waste disposal
    authorities.**
    Exemption, §11-89A-16.
  **Southern products mart
    authority.**
    Exemption, §41-10-61.
  **Space science exhibit
    commission.**
    Exemption, §41-9-438.
  **Space science exhibit
    finance authority.**
    Exemption, §41-10-327.

TAXATION—Cont'd
  **Special educational trust
    fund.**
    Setting up treasury account,
      §40-1-32.
    Source of fund.
      Revenues, §40-1-31.
  Sports hall of fame board.
    Exemption, §41-9-453.
  Stamps.
    Federal wagering
      occupational tax stamp,
      §§13A-12-90 to
      13A-12-92.
  **State bar building
    foundation.**
    Exemption, §34-3-105.
  State debt.
    Creation after ratification of
      constitution, Const. Ala.,
      art. XI, §213; amd. 26.
    Refunding bonds for existing
      indebtedness, Const.
      Ala., art. XI, §213; amd.
      26.
  Statements.
    Bank officers.
      Failing to make, swear to
        and deliver required
        statements, §40-1-19.
    Confidentiality, §40-1-33.
    Failure to furnish,
      §40-29-74.
    Failure to make.
      Penalties, §40-29-113.
    Fraudulent statements,
      §40-29-74.
    Penalties, §§40-29-113,
      40-29-115, 40-29-116.
  **State products mart and
    coliseum authority.**
    Exemption, §41-10-107.
  **Statewide property
    reappraisal,** §§40-7-60 to
    40-7-100. See within this
    heading, "Assessments."
  Stay of proceedings.
    Insurance guaranty
      association, §27-42-18.
  Stock and stockholders.
    Corporate shares, §§40-14-70
      to 40-14-74.
    Levy and sale of personal
      property by tax
      collectors.
      Shares of stock,
        §40-5-16.
    Securities tax, §§40-24-1 to
      40-24-8.
      See SECURITIES.
    Subjects of taxation,
      §40-11-1.
  **Stringfellow memorial
    hospital nonprofit realty
    company.**
    Exemption, §40-9-1.1.
  Subjects of taxation, Const.
    Ala., amd. 325.
    Auctions, §40-11-1.
    Bond issues, §40-11-1.
    Canals, §40-11-1.
    Construction equipment,
      §40-11-1.
    Definitions, §40-11-1.
    Docks, §40-11-1.
    Dog race tracks, §40-11-5.
    Enumeration, §40-11-1.
    Harbors and ports, §40-11-1.
    Personal property, §40-11-1.
    Printing, §40-11-1.
    Public utilities, §40-11-1.

TAXATION—Cont'd
  Subjects of taxation—Cont'd
    Railroads, §40-11-1.
    Real property, §40-11-1.
    Ships and shipping, §40-11-1.
    Stock and stockholders,
      §40-11-1.
    Stocks of goods, §40-11-1.
    United States.
      Property and activities,
        §§40-11-2, 40-11-3.
    Warehouses, §40-11-1.
  Subpoenas.
    County boards of
      equalization.
      Service, §40-3-23.
    Failure to obey, §40-29-117.
  Supercomputer authority.
    Exemption, §41-10-401.
  Supernumerary tax officials.
    Commission as
      supernumeraries,
      §§40-6-1 to 40-6-7.
    Applicability of retirement
      system established for
      elected officials,
      §40-6-6.
    Assumption of duties in
      case of vacancy,
      §40-6-2.
    Compensation, §40-6-3.
    Deduction from salaries of
      officials charged with
      assessment of
      collection of taxes,
      §40-6-4.
    Election by officials
      eligible for retirement
      under another plan,
      §40-6-5.
    Exceptions to provisions,
      §40-6-7.
    Life tenure, §40-6-3.
    Oath, §40-6-2.
    Vacancies.
      Assumption of duties,
        §40-6-2.
    When officials
      commissioned, §40-6-1.
    Retirement.
      Election to participate in
        supernumerary
        retirement program,
        §40-6-8.
  Supreme court.
    Library tax, §12-2-159.
  **Susie Parker Stringfellow
    memorial hospital.**
    Exemption from taxation,
      §40-9-1.1.
  Taxable property. See within
    this heading, "Subjects of
    taxation."
  Tax administrators.
    Certified tax administrators.
      Payment to certain
        certified tax
        administrators,
        §40-1-46.
  Tax assessors.
    Authority as to assessments,
      §40-7-1.
    Bonds, §40-4-1.
    Commissions.
      Amount, §40-4-2.
      Erroneous assessments.
        No commissions, §40-4-4.
      Payment, §40-4-2.
    Counties.
      See COUNTIES.
    Deputies, §40-4-6.

TAXATION—Cont'd
Tax assessors—Cont'd
Duties.
Removal of property.
Duties of assessor when
reason to believe
property may be
removed, §40-7-43.
Visiting voting places for
purpose of listing,
§40-7-3.
Elections.
Failure to elect successor
vacates office, §36-9-5.
General elections.
Offices for which general
election held,
§17-2-2.
Time, §17-2-3.
State and county officers
elected by the people,
§17-2-1.
Error in computing taxes
due.
Correction, §40-7-9.
Executors and
administrators.
Notification of appointment
of fiduciaries, §40-7-30.
Fees.
Demand against persons
failing to make,
§40-7-19.
Disposition, §40-1-31.1.
Fees of assessor paid on
salary basis, §40-4-3.
Returns on escaped
property, §40-7-32.
Disposition of fees,
§40-1-31.1.
Schedule, §40-4-5.
Forms.
Printing and furnishing
blank forms, §40-4-7.
Guardian and ward.
Notification of appointment
of fiduciaries, §40-7-30.
Impeachment.
General provisions.
See IMPEACHMENT.
Subject to impeachment,
§36-11-1; Const. Ala.,
art. VII, §175.
Officers generally. See within
this heading, "Officers."
Public utilities.
Local taxes.
Entry and collection,
§40-21-28.
Report to tax assessor,
§40-21-17.
What considered in
arriving at taxable
value of property,
§40-21-20.
Receivers.
Notification of appointment
of fiduciaries, §40-7-30.
Returns.
Copies, §40-4-7.
Demand against persons
failing to make
returns, §40-7-19.
Duties of assessors,
§40-7-27.
Escaped property.
Fees of assessor for
returns on escaped
property, §40-7-32.
Salaries, §40-6A-2.

TAXATION—Cont'd
Tax assessors—Cont'd
Summary proceedings
involving officials.
See PUBLIC OFFICERS
AND EMPLOYEES.
Supernumerary tax
assessors.
Applicability of retirement
system established for
elected officials,
§40-6-6.
Commission as
supernumeraries,
§40-6-1.
Compensation, §40-6-3.
Deductions from salaries of
officials charged with
assessment or
collection of taxes,
§40-6-4.
Election by officials
eligible for retirement
under another plan,
§40-6-5.
Exceptions to provisions,
§40-6-7.
Fees.
Deductions from fees of
officials charged
with assessment or
collection of taxes,
§40-6-4.
Life tenure, §40-6-3.
Oath, §40-6-2.
Retirement.
Election to participate in
supernumerary
retirement program,
§40-6-8.
Vacancies.
Assumption of duties,
§40-6-2.
Supplies.
Duty of county officials to
furnish, §40-4-8.
Terms of office, §36-3-5.
Trusts and trustees.
Notification of appointment
of fiduciaries, §40-7-30.
Vacancies in office.
Failure to elect successor,
§36-9-5.
Voting places.
Duty to visit for purpose of
listing, §40-7-3.
Tax collectors.
Actions.
Collection of taxes by
action, §40-5-42.
Assessments.
List of errors in
assessments.
Advertisement costs,
§40-5-23.
Certification of corrected
list to department of
revenue, §40-5-25.
Correction, §40-5-24.
Examination, §40-5-24.
Publication, §40-5-23.
Reports, §40-5-23.
Bond, §40-5-3.
Commissions, §40-5-4.
County tax collectors.
See COUNTIES.
Countywide taxes.
Collection and report,
§40-5-33.
Death, §40-5-38.

TAXATION—Cont'd
Tax collectors—Cont'd
Delinquent taxes.
Costs on payment, §40-5-8.
Demand on delinquent
taxpayers, §40-5-7.
Fee, §40-5-6.
Garnishment of delinquent
taxpayers, §§40-5-20 to
40-5-22.
Interest, §40-5-9.
Receipts on payment,
§40-5-10.
Deputies, §40-5-2.
Elections.
Failure to elect successor
vacates office, §36-9-5.
General elections.
Offices for which general
election held,
§17-2-2.
Time, §17-2-3.
State and county officers
elected by the people,
§17-2-1.
Escaped taxes.
Assessment and collection.
Procedure, §40-5-34.
Report to assessor,
§40-5-35.
Expenses.
Mileage to and from seat of
government, §40-5-45.
Fees.
Demand on delinquent
taxpayers, §40-5-6.
Disposition of fees paid to
collector on salary
basis, §40-5-5.
Garnishment of delinquent
taxpayers, §40-5-22.
Levy and sale of property,
§40-5-6.
When delinquent
taxpayer has left
county, §40-5-17.
Garnishment of delinquent
taxpayers.
Fees, §40-5-22.
Notice, §40-5-20.
Procedure, §40-5-21.
Impeachment.
General provisions.
See IMPEACHMENT.
Subject to impeachment,
§36-11-1; Const. Ala.,
art. VII, §175.
Insolvent taxes, §§40-5-23 to
40-5-30.
Collection, §40-5-28.
Final report of uncollected
balances, §40-5-29.
List.
Advertisement costs,
§40-5-23.
Certification of corrected
list to department of
revenue, §40-5-25.
Correction, §40-5-24.
Court to deliver to
collector, §40-5-27.
Examination, §40-5-24.
Publication, §40-5-23.
Reports, §40-5-23.
New accounts stated with
collector, §40-5-26.
Retirement.
Report when collector
retires from office,
§40-5-30.

TAXATION—Cont'd
  Tax collectors—Cont'd
    Insolvent taxes—Cont'd
      Uncollected balances.
        Final report, §40-5-29.
    Levy and sale of personal
      property.
      Exemptions.
        No property exempt,
          §40-5-18.
      Fees, §40-5-6.
        Disposition, §40-1-31.1.
        When delinquent
          taxpayer has left
          county, §40-5-17.
      Location, §40-5-14.
      Notice, §40-5-14.
      Proceeds.
        Application and
          disposition, §40-5-15.
      Real property.
        Sale if personalty
          insufficient,
          §40-5-19.
      Shares of stock, §40-5-16.
      Time, §40-5-14.
      When delinquent taxpayer
        has left county,
        §40-5-17.
    Lienholders of real estate.
      Payments by, §40-5-12.
    Lien of tax collector,
      §40-5-46.
    Mortgagees of real estate.
      Payments by, §40-5-12.
    Notice.
      Garnishment of delinquent
        taxpayers, §40-5-20.
      Levy and sale of personal
        property, §40-5-14.
    Officers generally. See within
      this heading, "Officers."
    Offices.
      Keeping open, §40-5-1.
    Parcels of real estate.
      Payment when listed
        separately, §40-5-13.
    Purchasers of real estate.
      Payments by, §40-5-12.
    Receipts.
      Book of receipts with
        duplicate sheets,
        §40-5-11.
      Delinquent taxes.
        Receipts on payment,
          §40-5-10.
    Reports.
      Assessment and collection
        of escaped taxes.
        Report to assessor,
          §40-5-35.
      Errors in assessments.
        List, §40-5-23.
      Insolvent taxes.
        List, §40-5-23.
      Payments into particular
        treasuries, §40-5-36.
      Failure to make reported
        to comptroller,
        §40-5-37.
      Procedure, §40-5-36.
    Retirement.
      Report when collector
        retires, §40-5-30.
    Salaries, §40-6A-2.
    School district taxes.
      Collection and report,
        §40-5-33.
    Settlements.
      Final settlements and
        payments, §40-5-44.

TAXATION—Cont'd
  Tax collectors—Cont'd
    Settlements—Cont'd
      Settlements with
        particular treasurers,
        §40-5-43.
      Special taxes.
        Closing accounts on
          accomplishing purpose
          for which collected,
          §40-5-41.
        Payments on collection,
          §40-5-40.
        Receipts on collection,
          §40-5-39.
    Summary proceedings
      involving officials.
      See PUBLIC OFFICERS
        AND EMPLOYEES.
    Supernumerary tax
      collectors, §§40-6-1 to
      40-6-8.
      Applicability of retirement
        system established for
        elected officials,
        §40-6-6.
      Commission as
        supernumeraries,
        §40-6-1.
      Compensation, §40-6-3.
      Deductions from salaries
        of officials charged
        with assessment or
        collection of taxes,
        §40-6-4.
      Election by officials
        eligible for retirement
        under another plan,
        §40-6-5.
      Exceptions to provisions,
        §40-6-7.
      Fees.
        Deductions from fees of
          officials charged
          with assessment or
          collection of taxes,
          §40-6-4.
      Life tenure, §40-6-3.
      Oath, §40-6-2.
      Retirement.
        Election to participate in
          supernumerary
          retirement program,
          §40-6-8.
      Vacancies.
        Assumption of duties in
          case of vacancy,
          §40-6-2.
    Supplies.
      Duty of county officials to
        furnish, §40-4-8.
    Taxpayer about to jeopardize
      possibility of collection.
      Duty of collector, §40-5-31.
    Liability of collector for
      failure to act, §40-5-32.
    Terms of office, §36-3-6.
    Vacancies in office.
      Failure to elect successor,
        §36-9-5.
    Visits to precincts, §40-5-1.
  **Tax enforcement and
    compliance act,** §§40-19-1
    to 40-29-120.
    Applicability of chapter,
      §40-29-2.
    Citation of chapter, §40-29-1.
    Legislative intent, §40-29-2.
    Purpose of chapter, §40-29-2.
    Short title of act, §40-29-1.

TAXATION—Cont'd
  Tax increment districts,
    §§11-99-1 to 11-99-10;
    Const. Ala., amd. 475.
    See TAX INCREMENT
      DISTRICTS.
  Telegraph companies.
    Public utilities generally,
      §§40-21-1 to 40-21-107.
    See PUBLIC UTILITIES.
  Telephone companies.
    Public utilities generally,
      §§40-21-1 to 40-21-107.
    See PUBLIC UTILITIES.
  Television.
    Community antenna
      television facilities.
      License tax, §11-27-3.
  Tennessee valley authority.
    Distribution of payments in
      lieu of taxes.
      Counties served by
        Tennessee valley
        authority, §40-28-2.
      Basis for allocation of
        payments, §40-28-3.
      Manner of making
        payments, §40-28-4.
      Sharing payments with
        municipalities,
        §40-28-3.
      When payments to be
        made by state,
        §40-28-4.
    Definitions, §40-28-1.
    Dry counties not served by
      Tennessee valley
      authority, §40-28-2.
    Exhibit commission.
      Bonds, etc., exempt from
        taxation, §41-9-786.
  Terrapins.
    Tax on terrapins caught for
      commercial purposes,
      §9-12-45.
  Textiles.
    Exemptions from taxation.
      Product for materials used
        in textile manufacture,
        §40-9-4.
  Time.
    Date taxes due, §40-11-4.
  Tobacco.
    Exemptions from taxation,
      §40-9-1.
    Sales tax, §§40-25-1 to
      40-25-29.
    See TOBACCO.
    Use tax, §§40-25-40 to
      40-25-47.
    See TOBACCO.
  Tourist camps.
    Transient occupancy tax,
      §§40-26-1 to 40-26-21.
    See HOTELS, INNS AND
      OTHER TRANSIENT
      LODGING PLACES.
  Transient occupancy tax,
    §§40-26-1 to 40-26-21.
    See HOTELS, INNS AND
      OTHER TRANSIENT
      LODGING PLACES.
  Trees and timber.
    Forests products privilege
      and severance tax,
      §§9-13-80 to 9-13-107.
    See FORESTS AND
      FORESTRY.
    Standing timber.
      Exempted, §40-11-1.

TAXATION—Cont'd
Trees and timber—Cont'd
State forests.
Taxation of timber on
lands designated as
auxiliary state forests.
See FORESTS AND
FORESTRY.
Trial.
Assessments.
Appeals, §40-7-47.
Trial tax, §40-1-38.
Trusts and trustees.
Assessments.
By whom property should
be listed, §40-7-17.
Business trusts, §19-3-67.
Generation-skipping tax.
General provisions,
§§19-5-1 to 19-5-12.
See TRUSTS AND
TRUSTEES.
Levy, §§40-15A-1 to
40-15A-14.
See TRUSTS AND
TRUSTEES.
Preclusion and
minimization, §§19-5-1
to 19-5-12.
See TRUSTS AND
TRUSTEES.
Liability of trustees, §40-1-8.
Private foundations,
charitable trusts and
split-interest trusts.
Trustee not to engage in
certain acts subjecting
trust to federal
taxation, §19-3-300.
Returns.
Separate returns in
individual and
fiduciary capacity,
§40-7-20.
Tax assessors.
Notification of appointment
of fiduciaries, §40-7-30.
Turkey hunters hall of fame.
Exemption, §41-9-833.
Uniform transfers to minors act.
General provisions,
§§35-5A-1 to 35-5A-24.
See TRANSFERS TO
MINORS.
United States.
Exemptions from taxation.
United States bonds,
§40-9-1.
Gambling.
Federal wagering
occupational tax
stamp, §§13A-12-90 to
13A-12-92.
See GAMBLING.
Lien for United States taxes,
§§35-11-42 to 35-11-48.
See UNITED STATES.
Universities and colleges.
Exemptions, §§40-9-16,
40-9-17.
University of Alabama Huntsville Foundation.
Exemptions, §40-9-12.
University of Montevallo.
Exemptions, §16-54-12.
Property exempt from taxes,
§16-54-12.

TAXATION—Cont'd
Use tax.
General provisions,
§§40-23-60 to 40-23-88.
See USE TAX.
Municipal corporations,
§§11-51-200 to 11-51-207.
See MUNICIPAL
CORPORATIONS.
Tobacco, §§40-25-40 to
40-25-46.
See TOBACCO.
Utility service use tax,
§§40-21-100 to 40-21-107.
See PUBLIC UTILITIES.
USS Alabama battleship commission.
Exemption, §41-9-358.
Utility services facilities.
Exemption, §11-97-18.
Vacation time-sharing plans.
Proceeds from sale or resale
of lease plans.
Exempt from transient
occupancy tax,
§34-27-65.
Vessels.
Motor fuels.
Additional excise tax on
gasoline, motor fuels
and lubricating oil.
Exemption, §40-17-220.
Veterans.
Exemptions from taxation.
Bonus for Southeast Asian
war prisoners, §31-7-2.
Certain homes owned by
veterans or their
widows, §40-9-20.
Disabled American
veterans, §40-9-1.
Property of incompetent
veterans, §40-9-1.
Veterans of foreign wars.
Property exempt, §40-9-1.
Wagering.
Federal wagering
occupational stamp tax,
§§13A-12-90 to
13A-12-92.
Wage winnings withholding tax, §§40-18-90, 40-18-91.
Waiver.
Authority to waive, §40-1-6.
Warehouses.
Subjects of taxation,
§40-11-1.
Warrants.
Assessments.
Statewide property
reappraisal.
Falsely and fraudulently
procuring, §40-1-26.
Special county and district
taxes.
Costs.
Payment of incidental
costs, §16-13-100.
Incidental costs.
Payment, §16-13-100.
Method of payment,
§16-13-99.
Place of payment,
§16-13-99.
Redemption of warrants
prior to maturity,
§16-13-101.
Water companies.
See PUBLIC UTILITIES.

TAXATION—Cont'd
Water conservation and irrigation.
Agency, §§9-10-5, 9-10-9.
Corporations.
Bond issues.
Exemptions, §9-10-41.
Water management and drainage.
Districts.
General provisions.
See WATER
MANAGEMENT
AND DRAINAGE.
Water pollution control authority.
Bonds exempt, §22-34-13.
Waters and watercourses.
Development of docks
along inland
waterways.
Bonds and interest exempt
from taxation,
§§33-2-17, 33-2-44,
33-2-77, 33-2-107,
33-2-136, 33-2-163.
Water system assistance authority.
Bonds or other indebtedness
of authority.
Exemption, §22-23A-13.
Welfare.
Exemption of payments,
§38-4-8.
Wells.
Exemptions from taxation.
Artesian wells leased to
municipalities, §40-9-8.
Witnesses.
Department of revenue.
Appearance.
Required, §40-2-19.
Fees, §40-2-21.
Incriminating testimony,
§40-2-20.
Oaths, §40-2-6.
Perjury, §40-2-20.
Production of records,
books and papers.
Required, §40-2-19.
Young Men's Christian Association.
Exemptions, §40-9-9.
Young Men's Hebrew Association.
Exemptions, §40-9-12.
Young Women's Christian Association.
Exemptions, §40-9-10.
Young Women's Christian Organization.
Exemptions, §40-9-11.
Youth services.
Exemptions from taxation.
Department of youth
services school
districts.
Gasoline tax, §40-17-31.
Lubricating oils and
greases, §40-17-171.

TAX ENFORCEMENT AND COMPLIANCE ACT,
§§40-29-1 to 40-29-120.
See TAXATION.

TAXICABS.
Motor vehicles generally.
See MOTOR VEHICLES.
Radio utilities.
See RADIO.

TAX INCREMENT BASE.
Payments to local finance officer, §11-99-6.
Positive tax increments.
Allocation, §11-99-6.
Tax increment fund, §11-99-6.

TAX INCREMENT DISTRICTS, §§11-99-1 to 11-99-10.
Apportionment of property taxes.
Equalized valuation for, §11-99-10.
Boundaries.
Powers of municipalities and counties, §11-99-3.
Constitution of Alabama.
Authority for legislation, Const. Ala., amd. 475.
Costs.
Financing, §11-99-8.
Creation.
Powers of municipalities and counties, §11-99-3.
Procedure, §11-99-4.
Definitions, §11-99-2.
Equalized valuation for apportionment of property taxes, §11-99-10.
Financing of project costs, §11-99-8.
Findings and declarations of legislature, §11-99-1.
Identification of property within each district, §11-99-5.
Legislative findings and declarations, §11-99-1.
Notice.
Assessed and equalized value of property and tax increment base, §11-99-5.
Overlapping districts, §11-99-9.
Powers of municipalities and counties, §11-99-3.
Project costs.
Financing, §11-99-8.
Project plans.
Amendment.
Redetermination of tax increment base, §11-99-5.
Approval, §11-99-4.
Tax increment base.
Determination, §11-99-5.
Termination, §11-99-7.
Valuation of taxable property.
Aggregate valuation, §11-99-5.

TEACHERS.
General provisions.
See EDUCATION.

TECHNICAL COLLEGES.
Alabama Mining Academy.
Walker state technical college, §§16-60-260 to 16-60-264.
Alabama Technical College.
Merger of institutions, §16-60-270.
New college designated and named, §16-60-270.
Gadsden State Technical Institute.
Merger of institutions, §16-60-270.

TECHNICAL COLLEGES —Cont'd
National guard.
Educational assistance, §§31-10-1 to 31-10-4.
School buses.
Transportation of students on public school buses, §16-27-2.
Walker State Technical College.
Alabama Mining Academy, §§16-60-260 to 16-60-264.

TELEGRAPHS.
Billing.
Avoiding or attempting to avoid lawful charge, price or toll.
Prohibited instruments.
See within this heading, "Prohibited instruments."
Charges.
Avoiding or attempting to avoid lawful charge.
Prohibited instruments.
See within this heading, "Prohibited instruments."
Companies, Const. Ala., art. XII, §239.
Counties.
Public roads, bridges and ferries.
Rights of way.
Construction of facilities, §23-1-85.
Easements.
Eminent domain.
Foreign telegraph companies.
Acquisition of easements, §18-1A-272.
Highways.
Rights of way.
Contracts with department, §23-1-59.
Licenses.
Municipal license schedule, §11-51-127.
Municipal corporations.
License schedule, §11-51-127.
Rights of way.
Rules and regulations.
Highway department, §23-1-59.
Definitions.
Prohibited instruments, §37-8-217.
Disclosure of messages.
Unlawful disclosure by employees of companies, §37-8-212.
Easements.
Foreign companies.
Eminent domain.
Acquisition of easements, §18-1A-272.
Eminent domain.
Easements.
Foreign telegraph companies.
Acquisition of easements, §18-1A-272.
Employees.
Unlawful disclosure of messages, §37-8-212.

TELEGRAPHS—Cont'd
Harassing communications, §13A-11-8.
License tax, §40-21-59.
Municipal corporations.
Streets.
Regulation of use of streets for telegraph lines, §11-43-62.
Penalties.
Prohibited instruments.
Violations, §37-8-220.
Prohibited instruments.
Defined, §37-8-217.
Manufacture or sale, §37-8-218.
Penalties, §37-8-220.
Search and seizure, §37-8-221.
Radio.
Radio utility systems.
Construction and maintenance of antennas and towers.
Right of eminent domain, §37-4-113.
Interconnecting radio utility systems with existing telephone or telegraph companies, §37-4-112.
Certificate of public convenience and necessity required, §37-4-103.
Rights of way.
Rules and regulations of company promulgated by highway department, §23-1-59.
Searches and seizures.
Prohibited instruments, §37-8-221.
Taxation.
General provisions.
See PUBLIC UTILITIES.
Transportation companies generally.
See TRANSPORTATION COMPANIES.

TELEPHONES.
Actions.
Securities of telephone companies.
Penalties.
Actions to recover, §37-2-182.
Bait advertising.
Limitation on criminal liability of telephone companies, §13A-9-44.
Billing.
Avoiding or attempting to avoid lawful charge, price or toll.
Prohibited instruments.
See within this heading, "Prohibited instruments."
Bond issues.
Securities of telephone companies, §§37-2-170 to 37-2-184. See within this heading, "Securities of telephone companies."

TELEPHONES—Cont'd
Charges.
Avoiding or attempting to
avoid lawful charge.
Prohibited instruments.
See within this
heading, "Prohibited
instruments."
Coal.
Mine safety, §25-9-174.
Telephone wires,
§25-9-171.
Commercial code.
Secured transactions.
Applicability of filing
provisions, §7-9-302.
Companies, Const. Ala., art.
XII, §239.
Connecting companies.
Review and adjustment of
rates when South
Central Bell receives
increase, §37-1-80.1.
Counties.
Public roads, bridges and
ferries.
Rights of way.
Construction of
facilities, §23-1-85.
Eminent domain generally.
See within this heading,
"Eminent domain."
General provisions.
See TRANSPORTATION
COMPANIES.
Highways.
Rights of way.
Contracts with highway
department,
§23-1-59.
Rules and regulations.
Highway department,
§23-1-59.
Licenses.
Municipal license schedule,
§11-51-128.
Rates.
Deaf and hearing-impaired
customers.
Telephone surcharge for
service, §37-1-80.2.
General provisions,
§§37-1-80 to 37-1-105.
See PUBLIC SERVICE
COMMISSION.
Review and adjustment of
rates of connecting
companies when South
Central Bell receives
increase, §37-1-80.1.
Securities of telephone
companies, §§37-2-170 to
37-2-184. See within this
heading, "Securities of
telephone companies."
South Central Bell.
Review and adjustment of
rates of connecting
companies when South
Central Bell receives
increase, §37-1-80.1.
Condemnation.
Companies constructing,
operating or maintaining
public utility, §10-5-4.
**Construction of public
utility.**
Condemnation of ways and
rights of way, §10-5-4.

TELEPHONES—Cont'd
**Construction of telephone
lines.**
Through curtilage of house
without consent, §10-5-5.
Corporations.
Foreign corporations.
Extension of lines into
state, §10-2A-225.
Counties.
Claims and demands against
counties.
Telephones for certain
officers, §11-12-14.
Courthouses.
Designation of courthouse
offices for installation
of telephones, §11-3-12.
Powers and duties of
county commissions,
§11-3-11.
Procuring and providing for
offices, §11-3-11.
Criminal law and procedure.
Harassment, §13A-11-8.
Party lines.
Falsely requesting use for
emergency,
§13A-11-223.
Unlawfully refusing to
yield, §13A-11-222.
Deaf persons.
Surcharge for service to deaf
and hearing-impaired
customers, §37-1-80.2.
Definitions.
Emergency telephone service,
§11-98-1.
Prohibited instruments,
§37-8-217.
Rural telephone service,
§37-6-40.
Securities of telephone
companies, §37-2-170.
Directories.
Party lines.
Failure to relinquish party
line for emergency call
or falsely requesting
party line for
emergency.
Notice in directories,
§37-8-213.
Disclosure of messages.
Unlawful disclosure by
employees of telephone
or telegraph companies,
§37-8-212.
Dwellings.
Construction through
curtilage of house
without consent, §10-5-5.
Electric cooperatives.
Rural telephone service,
§§37-6-40 to 37-6-49. See
within this heading,
"Rural telephone
service."
Emergencies.
Party lines.
Failure to relinquish party
line for emergency
call, §37-8-213.
Falsely requesting use of
party line for
emergency,
§§13A-11-223,
37-8-213.

TELEPHONES—Cont'd
**Emergency telephone
service.**
Board of commissioners.
Composition, §11-98-4.
Creation, §11-98-4.
Officers, §11-98-4.
Powers and duties.
Generally, §11-98-4.
Qualifications of members,
§11-98-4.
Quorum, §11-98-4.
Terms of office, §11-98-4.
Charges, §11-98-5.
Communications districts.
Board of commissioners,
§11-98-4.
Powers and duties.
Generally, §11-98-2.
Definitions, §11-98-1.
Methods of response to calls,
§11-98-7.
Number.
Digits 911 established,
§11-98-3.
Secondary backup
emergency number,
§11-98-6.
Response to calls.
Methods, §11-98-7.
Eminent domain.
Condemnation of ways and
rights of way by
companies constructing,
operating or maintaining
public utility, §10-5-4.
Foreign telephone companies.
Acquisition of easements
for connecting lines,
§18-1A-272.
Grant of easements to
telephone and telegraph
companies, Const. Ala.,
art. IV, §99.
Power of public utility
corporations, §10-5-1.
Routes and sites.
Rights of condemning
corporations in
selection of routes and
sites, §10-5-8.
Employees.
Unlawful disclosure of
messages, §37-8-212.
False advertising.
Limitation on criminal
liability of telephone
companies, §13A-9-44.
**Foreign telephone
companies.**
Easements.
Acquisition for connecting
lines, §18-1A-272.
Harassing communications,
§13A-11-8.
Housing.
Construction of line through
curtilage of house
without consent, §10-5-5.
Improvement authorities.
General provisions, §§39-7-1
to 39-7-34.
See PUBLIC WORKS.
Larceny.
See LARCENY.
Licenses.
Municipal license schedule
for telephone companies,
§11-51-128.
Tax, §40-21-58.

TELEPHONES—Cont'd
Mobile radio telephone service.
Radio utilities.
Exceptions to provisions, §37-4-111.
Municipal corporations.
Annexation.
Territory exempt from taxation.
Assessment and collection of privilege or license tax from operators, §11-42-84.
Commission form of government.
Municipal officers or employees.
Conflicts of interest, §§11-44-46 to 11-44-48.
License tax on coin telephones, §11-51-98.
Licensing of telephone companies.
Schedule, §11-51-128.
Streets.
Regulation of use of streets for telephone or telegraph lines, §11-43-62.
Trees.
Attaching wires to trees in municipalities, §9-13-15.
Oaths.
Securities of telephone companies.
Applications to issue, §37-2-172.
Operation of public utility.
Condemnation of ways and rights of way, §10-5-4.
Party lines.
Failure to relinquish for emergency call, §37-8-213.
Falsely requesting use for emergency, §§13A-11-223, 37-8-213.
Unlawfully refusing to yield, §13A-11-222.
Penalties.
Prohibited instruments.
Violations, §37-8-220.
Prices.
Avoiding or attempting to avoid lawful price.
Prohibited instruments.
See within this heading, "Prohibited instruments."
Prohibited instruments.
Court order.
Seizure by court order, §37-8-221.
Defined, §37-8-217.
Manufacture or sale, §37-8-218.
Penalties, §37-8-220.
Search and seizure, §37-8-221.
Seizure incident to lawful arrest, §37-8-221.
Violations.
Penalties, §37-8-220.
Public service commission.
General provisions.
See PUBLIC SERVICE COMMISSION.

TELEPHONES—Cont'd
Public service commission —Cont'd
Rural telephone service, §§37-6-40 to 37-6-49. See within this heading, "Rural telephone service."
Securities of telephone companies, §§37-2-170 to 37-2-184. See within this heading, "Securities of telephone companies."
Radio.
Radio utility systems.
Construction and maintenance of antennas and towers.
Right of eminent domain, §37-4-113.
Interconnecting systems with existing telephone or telegraph companies, §37-4-112.
Certificate of public convenience and necessity required, §37-4-103.
Mobile radio telephone service.
Article not applicable to, §37-4-111.
Rates.
Connecting telephone companies.
Review and adjustment of rates when South Central Bell receives increase, §37-1-80.1.
Deaf and hearing-impaired customers.
Telephone surcharge for service, §37-1-80.2.
General provisions, §§37-1-80 to 37-1-105.
See PUBLIC SERVICE COMMISSION.
Reports.
Securities of telephone companies.
Company reports, §37-2-179.
Respondeat superior.
Securities of telephone companies.
Acts of employees or officers deemed acts of company, §37-2-181.
Rights of way.
Eminent domain generally.
See within this heading, "Eminent domain."
Rural telephone service, §§37-6-40 to 37-6-49.
Definitions, §37-6-40.
Electric cooperatives.
Furnishing telephone service exclusively, §37-6-46.
Name of cooperative furnishing service, §37-6-43.
Organization.
Validation of acts relating to organization, §37-6-49.

TELEPHONES—Cont'd
Rural telephone service —Cont'd
Electric cooperatives—Cont'd
Powers, §§37-6-41, 37-6-42, 37-6-44.
Authority to supply electrical energy or telephone service or both, §37-6-45.
Furnishing telephone service exclusively, §37-6-46.
Vesting of certain powers, §37-6-49.
Improvement and expansion of facilities.
Duty of public service commission to encourage, §37-6-47.
Public service commission.
Additional compensation for members, §37-6-48.
Duty to encourage improvement and expansion of facilities, §37-6-47.
Searches and seizures.
Prohibited instruments, §37-8-221.
Secured transactions.
Applicability of filing provisions, §7-9-302.
Securities of telephone companies, §§37-2-170 to 37-2-184.
Actions.
Recovery of penalties, §37-2-182.
Applicability of article.
Exceptions, §§37-2-177, 37-2-184.
Application to issue securities or assume obligations, §§37-2-171 to 37-2-174.
Contents, §37-2-172.
Continuing applications.
Order making such continuance, §37-2-173.
Disposition by public service commission.
Time for disposition, §37-2-173.
Docket.
Placing application at head of commission docket, §37-2-173.
Filing.
By whom filed, §37-2-172.
Form, §37-2-172.
Grant or denial, §37-2-174.
Modifications, §37-2-174.
Oath.
Application to be made under oath, §37-2-172.
Order of public service commission, §37-2-171.
Signatures, §37-2-172.
Supplemental orders of commission, §37-2-174.
Time for disposition by commission, §37-2-173.
When required, §37-2-171.
Certificate of notification.
Notes not covered by provisions of article, §37-2-177.

TELEPHONES—Cont'd
**Securities of telephone
companies**—Cont'd
Certificate of notification
—Cont'd
Sale, pledge or other
disposition of
securities, §37-2-175.
Debentures.
Receiver's certificate or
debentures, §37-2-178.
Definitions, §37-2-170.
Employees.
Acts of employees deemed
acts of company,
§37-2-181.
Exemptions.
Certain companies
exempted from
provisions, §37-2-184.
Guarantee or obligation on
part of state not to be
implied, §37-2-176.
Issuance.
Application to issue
securities, §§37-2-171
to 37-2-174.
Validity of securities
issued without
authorization,
§37-2-180.
Notice.
Sale, pledge or other
disposition of
securities, §37-2-175.
Obligations.
Assuming obligations,
§§37-2-171 to 37-2-174.
Officers.
Acts of officers deemed acts
of company, §37-2-181.
Securities issued without
authorization.
Penalty for willful
violation, §37-2-180.
Penalties.
Actions to recover
penalties, §37-2-182.
Payment into treasury,
§37-2-183.
Willful violations,
§37-2-180.
Pledges.
Subsequent to filing
application, §37-2-175.
Public service commission.
Application to issue
securities or assume
obligations.
Form and contents.
Commission to
prescribe,
§37-2-172.
Grant or denial by
commission,
§37-2-174.
Time, §37-2-173.
Order of commission,
§37-2-171.
Supplemental orders,
§37-2-174.
Receiver's certificate or
debentures, §37-2-178.
Reports.
Company reports,
§37-2-179.
Sales.
Subsequent to filing of
application, §37-2-175.

TELEPHONES—Cont'd
**Securities of telephone
companies**—Cont'd
State.
Guarantee or obligation on
part of state not to be
implied, §37-2-176.
Validity of securities issued
without authorization,
§37-2-180.
Violations.
Penalty for willful
violation, §37-2-180.
**Small business office of
advocacy.**
Toll-free telephone number
authorized, §41-9-766.
**South Central Bell telephone
company.**
Review and adjustment of
rates of connecting
companies when South
Central Bell receives
increase, §37-1-80.1.
State.
Securities of telephone
companies.
Guarantee or obligation on
part of state not to be
implied, §37-2-176.
Taxation.
General provisions.
See PUBLIC UTILITIES.
Tolls.
Avoiding or attempting to
avoid lawful tolls.
Prohibited instruments.
See within this
heading, "Prohibited
instruments."
**Transportation companies
generally.**
See TRANSPORTATION
COMPANIES.

TELEVISION.
Bait advertising.
Limitation on criminal
liability for, §13A-9-44.
Cable TV, §§11-27-1 to
11-27-3, 23-1-59.
Canons of judicial ethics.
When broadcasting in
courtroom permitted,
ACJE, Canon 3A.
**Community antenna
television facilities,**
§§11-27-1 to 11-27-3.
Cable television facilities.
Included within term,
§11-27-1.
County commissions.
Levy and collection of
license tax, §11-27-3.
Powers generally, §11-27-1.
Definitions, §11-27-1.
Franchises.
Applicability of provisions,
§11-27-1.
Authority of county
commissions, §11-27-1.
Conditions, §11-27-2.
Governing provisions,
§11-27-2.
Granting by county
commissions,
§§11-27-1, 11-27-2.
License tax on gross
revenue, §11-27-3.
Powers of county
commissions, §11-27-1.

TELEVISION—Cont'd
**Community antenna
television facilities**
—Cont'd
Franchises—Cont'd
Revocation for continued
violations, §11-27-2.
Rights of way, §11-27-2.
Licenses.
Taxation, §11-27-3.
Powers of county
commissions, §11-27-1.
Rights of way.
Contracts.
Highway department,
§23-1-59.
Rules and regulations.
Highway department,
§23-1-59.
Taxation.
License taxes, §11-27-3.
Theft of cable television
services.
Acts prohibited,
§13A-8-121.
"Cable television company"
defined, §13A-8-120.
Damages, §13A-8-124.
Evidence.
Possession of certain
devices.
Prima facie evidence of
intent to violate
article,
§13A-8-122.
Possession of certain
devices.
Prima facie evidence of
intent to violate
article, §13A-8-122.
Satellite reception dishes.
Article not applicable to,
§13A-8-126.
Violation of provisions.
Damages, §13A-8-124.
Equipment used deemed
contraband,
§13A-8-125.
Injunctive relief,
§13A-8-124.
Seizure and forfeiture of
equipment used,
§13A-8-125.
Violation of provisions.
Civil liability, §13A-8-123.
Courts.
When broadcasting in
courtroom permitted,
ACJE, Canon 3A.
Definitions.
Community antenna
television facilities,
§11-27-1.
**Educational television
commission,** §§16-7-1 to
16-7-6.
See EDUCATION.
**Educational television
foundation authority,**
§§16-7A-1 to 16-7A-8.
See EDUCATIONAL
TELEVISION
FOUNDATION
AUTHORITY.
False advertising.
Limitation on criminal
liability for, §13A-9-44.

TELEVISION—Cont'd
Franchises.
  Community antenna
    television facilities,
    §§11-27-1 to 11-27-3,
    23-1-59.
Horse racing.
  Transmission of racing
    events, §11-65-32.
Judges.
  When broadcasting in
    courtroom permitted,
    ACJE, Canon 3A.
Lost or unclaimed property.
  Disposition of unclaimed
    articles left for service,
    §35-12-6.
Motor vehicles.
  Location of television viewers
    in vehicle, §32-5-219.
Taxation.
  Community antenna
    television facilities.
    License tax, §11-27-3.
Theft.
  Cable television services,
    §§13A-8-120 to
    13A-8-126. See within
    this heading,
    "Community antenna
    television facilities."
Unclaimed property.
  Disposition of unclaimed
    televisions left for
    service, §35-12-6.

TEMPERANCE.
Judges.
  Maintenance of temperance
    at all times, ACJE,
    Canon 2B.
Municipal corporations.
  Promotion of temperance,
    §11-47-112.

**TEMPORARY RESTRAINING
  ORDERS.**
See INJUNCTIONS.

TENANTS.
**Joint tenants and tenants in
  common.**
  See JOINT TENANTS AND
    TENANTS IN
    COMMON.
Landlord and tenant.
  See LANDLORD AND
    TENANT.

**TENANTS BY THE
  ENTIRETIES.**
Simultaneous death act,
  §43-7-4.

TENANTS IN COMMON.
See JOINT TENANTS AND
  TENANTS IN COMMON.

TENDER.
Commercial code.
  Sales.
    See COMMERCIAL CODE.
Legal tender, Const. U. S.,
  Art. I, §10.
Libel and slander.
  Tender of money, §§6-5-188,
    6-5-189.
Trial.
  Answer of tender, §6-8-100.
  Judgment on, §6-8-100.

TENNESSEE RIVER.
**Tombigbee-Tennessee
  waterway development
  compact,** §§33-8-1 to
  33-8-4.

**TENNESSEE VALLEY
  AUTHORITY.**
Appropriations.
  Exhibit commission.
    Bond issues.
      Payment of principal and
        interest.
        Appropriation from
          revenues retained
          by state,
          §41-9-783.
Audits.
  Exhibit commission,
    §41-9-785.
Bond issues.
  Exhibit commission.
    Exclusive obligation of
      commission, §41-9-783.
    Exemption from taxation,
      §41-9-786.
    Payment of principal and
      interest.
      Appropriation and pledge
        from revenues
        retained by state,
        §41-9-783.
Contracts.
  Exhibit commission.
    Powers, §41-9-782.
Exhibit commission,
  §§41-9-780 to 41-9-787.
  Appointment, §41-9-781.
  Audit, §41-9-785.
  Authority.
    Additional authority,
      §41-9-784.
    Generally, §41-9-782.
  Bond issues.
    Appropriations.
      Payment of principal and
        interest.
        Appropriation from
          revenues retained
          by state,
          §41-9-783.
    Exclusive obligation of
      commission, §41-9-783.
    Exempt from taxation,
      §41-9-786.
    Payment of principal and
      interest.
      Appropriations and
        pledges, §41-9-783.
    Pledge.
      Payment of principal and
        interest, §41-9-783.
  Chairman, §41-9-781.
  Compensation, §41-9-781.
  Composition, §41-9-781.
  Construction and
    interpretation.
    Article liberally construed,
      §41-9-787.
  Contracts.
    Powers, §41-9-782.
  Creation, §41-9-780.
  Donations.
    Power to accept, §41-9-782.
  Executive committee,
    §41-9-781.
  Executive director.
    Power to employ,
      §41-9-782.
  Gifts.
    Power to accept, §41-9-782.

**TENNESSEE VALLEY
  AUTHORITY**—Cont'd
Exhibit commission—Cont'd
  Grants.
    Power to accept, §41-9-782.
  Liberal construction of
    article, §41-9-787.
  Meetings, §41-9-781.
  Obligations.
    Exemption from taxation,
      §41-9-786.
  Personnel.
    Power to employ additional
      personnel, §41-9-782.
  Powers, §41-9-780.
    Additional powers,
      §41-9-784.
  Privileges, §41-9-780.
  Property.
    Powers as to, §41-9-782.
  Purpose, §41-9-780.
  Qualifications of members,
    §41-9-781.
  Quorum, §41-9-781.
  Records.
    Maintenance of accurate
      record, §41-9-785.
  Rules and regulations.
    Power to adopt, §41-9-782.
  Taxation.
    Bonds, etc., exempt from
      taxation, §41-9-786.
  Terms of office, §41-9-781.
  Vacancies in office,
    §41-9-781.
Gifts.
  Exhibit commission.
    Power to accept, §41-9-782.
Grants.
  Exhibit commission.
    Power to accept, §41-9-782.
**Pledge and collateral
  security.**
  Exhibit commission.
    Bond issues.
      Payment of principal or
        interest, §41-9-783.
Property.
  Exhibit commission.
    Powers as to, §41-9-782.
Records.
  Exhibit commission.
    Maintenance, §41-9-785.
Rules and regulations.
  Exhibit commission.
    Power to adopt, §41-9-782.
Taxation.
  Distribution of payments in
    lieu of taxes, §§40-28-1
    to 40-28-4.
  Exhibit commission.
    Exemptions, §41-9-786.
Trusts and trustees.
  Bond issues.
    Investment of trust estates
      in bonds of authority,
      §19-3-127.

TENNIS COURTS.
Bond issues.
  Public improvement bonds
    generally.
    Counties, §§11-81-140 to
      11-81-150.
    See COUNTIES.
    Municipal corporations,
      §§11-81-110 to
      11-81-150.
    See COUNTIES.

TENNIS COURTS—Cont'd
  Public athletic boards.
    General provisions, §§11-59-1
      to 11-59-17.
      See MUNICIPAL
        CORPORATIONS.

TENSES.
  **Past or present includes
    future,** §1-1-2.

TENURE.
  Teachers, §§16-24-1 to
    16-24-38.
    See EDUCATION.

**TERMINAL ILLNESS OR
  CONDITION.**
  Natural death act, §§22-8A-1
    to 22-8A-10.
    See NATURAL DEATH
      ACT.

**TERMINATION OF LIFE-
  SUPPORT
  PROCEDURES,** §§22-8A-1
    to 22-8A-10.
  See NATURAL DEATH ACT.

**TERMINATION OF
  PARENTAL RIGHTS,**
    §§26-18-1 to 26-18-10.
  See PARENT AND CHILD.

TERMITES.
  Pest control generally.
    See PEST CONTROL.

TERRAPINS, §9-12-45.
  Flattened musk turtle.
    Protection, §9-11-269.

TERRITORIES.
  **Constitution of the United
    States,** Const. U. S., Art.
    IV, §3.

TETANUS.
  **Notifiable diseases
    generally,** §§22-11A-1 to
    22-11A-38.
    See DISEASES.

TEXTBOOKS.
  General provisions, §§16-36-1
    to 16-36-39.
    See EDUCATION.
  University of Alabama.
    Law department.
      Books may be furnished to,
        §16-47-7.

TEXTILES.
  Taxation.
    Exemptions.
      Products and materials
        used in textile
        manufacture, §40-9-4.

THEATERS.
  Building code.
    Minimum building standards
      code, §§41-9-160 to
      41-9-166.
      See BUILDINGS.
  County boards of health.
    Duties, §22-3-2.
  Health.
    Authority of state board of
      health, §22-2-2.
    Duties of county boards of
      health, §22-3-2.
  Licenses.
    Municipal corporations,
      §11-51-102.
    Revocation, §11-51-103.
  Municipal corporations.
    Closing, §11-51-102.

THEATERS—Cont'd
  Municipal corporations
    —Cont'd
    Licenses, §11-51-103.
  **Shakespeare festival theatre
    finance authority,**
    §§41-10-200 to 41-10-215.
    See SHAKESPEARE
      FESTIVAL THEATRE
      FINANCE
      AUTHORITY.
  State board of health.
    Authority, §22-2-2.

THEFT.
  Authorized use of vehicle.
    Defenses for prosecutions,
      §13A-8-12.
  Cable television services,
    §§13A-8-120 to 13A-8-126.
    See TELEVISION.
  Commercial code.
    Commercial paper.
      Defenses, §7-3-306.
      Stolen instruments,
        §7-3-804.
  Computer services,
    §13A-8-10.
  Controlled substances.
    Second degree theft of
      property, §13A-8-4.
  Credit cards.
    Second degree theft of
      property, §13A-8-4.
  Debit cards.
    Second degree theft of
      property, §13A-8-4.
  Deception.
    Defined, §13A-8-1.
  **Defenses to prosecutions for
    theft,** §13A-8-12.
  Definitions, §§13A-8-1,
    13A-8-2.
    Lost property, §13A-8-6.
    Theft of trademark or trade
      secrets, §13A-8-10.4.
    Trademarks or trade secrets,
      §13A-8-10.4.
  Deprive.
    Defined, §13A-8-1.
  Electricity.
    Acts which make electricity
      unlawfully available,
      §13A-8-23.
  Elements of crime, §13A-8-2.
  Embezzlement.
    See EMBEZZLEMENT.
  Exhibitions.
    Admission to exhibitions,
      §13A-8-10.
  Financial institution.
    Defined, §13A-8-1.
  Firearms.
    Defined, §13A-8-1.
    Second degree theft of
      property, §13A-8-4.
  **First degree theft of
    property.**
    Class B felony, §13A-8-3.
    Elements of crime, §13A-8-3.
  Forests and forestry.
    Timber theft equipment.
      Condemnation, §§9-13-220
        to 9-13-227.
        See TREES AND
          TIMBER.
  Fraud.
    Charitable fraud.
      Theft of property by
        charitable fraud,
        §13A-9-72.

THEFT—Cont'd
  **Fraudulent leasing or rental
    of property.**
    Elements of offense,
      §13A-8-140.
    Evidence.
      Prima facie evidence,
        §13A-8-141.
    Penalties, §13A-8-144.
    Written demand for return,
      §13A-8-142.
    Notice, §§13A-8-142,
      13A-8-143.
      Immunity from liability
        for giving of notice,
        §13A-8-143.
  Gas.
    Acts which make gas
      unlawfully available,
      §13A-8-23.
  **Hotels, inns and other
    transient lodging places.**
    Theft of services, §13A-8-10.
  Insurance.
    Casualty insurance
      generally.
      See INSURANCE.
  Livestock, §2-2-14.
    Arrest.
      Appearance upon arrest,
        §2-2-14.1.
    Forfeiture of vehicles, etc.,
      used in theft, §2-2-14.2.
    Investigator, §2-2-14.
    Second degree theft of
      property, §13A-8-4.
  Lost property.
    Defenses to prosecutions,
      §13A-8-12.
    Definitions, §13A-8-6.
    First degree theft of lost
      property, §13A-8-7.
    Second degree theft of lost
      property, §13A-8-8.
    Third degree theft of lost
      property, §13A-8-9.
  Misapplication of property.
    See EMBEZZLEMENT.
  Motor vehicles.
    First degree theft of
      property, §13A-8-3.
    Unauthorized use of vehicle,
      §13A-8-11.
    Uniform certificate of title
      and antitheft act,
      §§32-8-1 to 32-8-87.
      See MOTOR VEHICLES.
    Unlawful breaking and
      entering, §13A-8-11.
  Personal property.
    Fraudulent leasing or rental
      of property.
      Elements of offense,
        §13A-8-140.
      Evidence.
        Prima facie evidence,
          §13A-8-141.
      Penalties, §13A-8-144.
      Written demand for return,
        §13A-8-142.
      Notice, §§13A-8-142,
        13A-8-143.
  Professional services,
    §13A-8-10.
  Receiving stolen property.
    See RECEIVING STOLEN
      PROPERTY.
  Restaurants.
    Theft of services, §13A-8-10.
  Robbery.
    See ROBBERY.

THEFT—Cont'd
  Second degree theft of property.
    Class C felony, §13A-8-4.
    Elements of crime, §13A-8-4.
  Services.
    Cable television services, §§13A-8-120 to 13A-8-126.
      See TELEVISION.
    Defenses to theft of services, §13A-8-12.
    Defined, §13A-8-10.
    Elements of crime, §13A-8-10.
    First degree theft, §13A-8-10.1.
    Second degree theft, §13A-8-10.2.
    Third degree theft, §13A-8-10.3.
  Shopping carts, §13A-8-61.
  Stolen property.
    General provisions.
      See STOLEN PROPERTY.
    Receiving stolen property.
      See RECEIVING STOLEN PROPERTY.
  Telephone or other public services, §13A-8-10.
  Television.
    Cable television services, §§13A-8-120 to 13A-8-126.
      See TELEVISION.
  Third degree theft of property.
    Class A misdemeanor, §13A-8-5.
    Elements of crime, §13A-8-5.
  Threats.
    Defined, §13A-8-1.
  Trademarks or trade secrets, §13A-8-10.4.
    Class C felony, §13A-8-10.4.
    Definitions, §13A-8-10.4.
    Elements of offense, §13A-8-10.4.
  Transportation services, §13A-8-10.
  Trees and timber.
    Condemnation of timber theft equipment, §§9-13-220 to 9-13-227.
      See TREES AND TIMBER.
  Unauthorized use of vehicle, §13A-8-11.
  Uniform certificate of title and antitheft act, §§32-8-1 to 32-8-87.
      See MOTOR VEHICLES.
  Value.
    Defined, §13A-8-1.
    First degree theft of property, §13A-8-3.
    Second degree theft of property, §13A-8-4.
    Third degree theft of property, §13A-8-5.
  Water.
    Acts which water make unlawfully available, §13A-8-23.
  Weapons.
    Second degree theft of property, §13A-8-4.

THERAPEUTIC RESEARCH.
  Drugs, §§20-2-110 to 20-2-120.
    See DRUGS.

THERAPY.
  Physical therapists, §§34-24-190 to 34-24-196.
    See PHYSICAL THERAPISTS.

THIRD-PARTY PRACTICE.
  Defendant.
    When defendant may bring in third-party, ARCP, Rule 14 (a).
  Dismissal of third-party claim, ARCP, Rule 41 (c).
  Forms, ARCP, Forms 28, 29.
  Plaintiff.
    When plaintiff may bring in third-party, ARCP, Rule 14 (b).
  Pleadings, ARCP, Rule 14.
    Forms, ARCP, Form 29.
  Service of process, ARCP, Rule 14 (a).
  When third-party may be brought in, ARCP, Rule 14.

THORSBY, MUNICIPALITY OF.
  Property tax, Const. Ala., amd. 17.

THREATS.
  Assault and battery.
    See ASSAULT AND BATTERY.
  Criminal coercion.
    Class A misdemeanor, §13A-6-25.
    Elements of crime, §13A-6-25.
  Defined, §13A-8-1.
  Disorderly conduct, §13A-11-7.
  Elections.
    Fair campaign practices.
      Solicitation of money by threats, §17-22A-20.
  Extortion.
    Generally, §§13A-8-13 to 13A-8-15.
  Felonies.
    Compelling persons to engage in prostitution, §13A-12-111.
  Insurance.
    Intimidation, §27-12-8.
  Jury.
    Intimidating jurors, §13A-10-127.
  Labor unions and labor relations.
    General provisions, §§25-7-1 to 25-7-16.
      See LABOR.
  Peace bonds.
    General provisions, §§15-6-1 to 15-6-61.
      See PEACE BONDS.
  Protection of certain state officers and visitors, §§36-3-1 to 36-3-4.
  Robberies.
    See ROBBERY.
  Security to keep the peace.
    Generally, §§15-6-1 to 15-6-61.
      See PEACE BONDS.
  Witnesses.
    Intimidating witnesses, §13A-10-123.

TICKETS.
  Carriers.
    Free tickets.
      Persons passing free of charge on all common carriers, §37-1-15.
    Transportation companies.
      List of tickets to be filed, §37-2-8.
  Police.
    Unauthorized disposition of traffic ticket, §12-12-56.
  Records.
    Traffic tickets, §12-12-54.
  Reports.
    Traffic tickets, §12-12-54.
  Requirement of use of uniform traffic ticket and complaint, §12-12-53.
  Responsibility for accounting for uniform traffic tickets and complaints, §12-12-54.
  Unauthorized disposition of traffic ticket, §12-12-56.

TICKET SCALPERS.
  Licenses, §40-12-167.

TICK FEVER.
  Notifiable diseases generally, §§22-11A-1 to 22-11A-38.
    See DISEASES.

TICKS.
  Eradication, §§2-15-290 to 2-15-299.
    See LIVESTOCK.

TIMBER.
  See TREES AND TIMBER.

TIME-SHARING.
  Vacation time-sharing plans, §§34-27-50 to 34-27-69.
    See VACATION TIME-SHARING PLANS.

TIRES.
  Motor vehicle carriers, §32-5-210.
  Motor vehicles.
    See MOTOR VEHICLES.

TISSUE.
  Commercial code.
    Human blood and tissues.
      Implied warranty, §7-2-314.

TITLE.
  Abstracts of title.
    Ejectment, §6-6-283.
    Forests and forestry.
      State forests.
        When abstract of title required, §9-13-42.
    Judicial sales, §6-8-30.
  Bare title.
    Action for trespass by person having, §6-5-214.
  Bonds for title.
    Recordation, §35-4-53.
  Code of Alabama.
    Sets of code.
      Vesting of title, §41-21-5.
  Color of title.
    Ejectment.
      Liability of person holding possession under color of title, §6-6-289.
  Commercial code.
    General provisions.
      See COMMERCIAL CODE.

TITLE—Cont'd

Disputed possession.
Party with legal title deemed in possession, §6-5-215.
Documents of title, §§7-7-101 to 7-7-603.
See COMMERCIAL CODE.
Eminent domain.
Adverse claim or title.
Distribution of award among property owners, §18-1A-292.
Transfer of title.
Expenses incidental to, §18-1A-30.
Evidence.
Admissibility of evidence of title to lands, §12-21-41.
Certificate and transcripts as evidence of land title and facts, §12-21-98.
Executions.
Conveyance by sale under judicial process, §6-9-140.
Caveat emptor, §6-9-142.
Exemptions from administration and payment of debts.
Vesting for life of title to property in deserted spouse or minors, §§6-10-101, 6-10-107.
Fish and game.
Freshwater fish.
Vesting in state, §9-11-81.
State game lands, §9-11-3.
Wild birds and animals.
Vested in state, §9-11-230.
Forcible entry and unlawful detainer.
Limitations on inquiry into title, §6-6-336.
Forests and forestry.
Forest products.
Unauthorized cutting.
Proof of title, §9-13-61.
State forests.
Auxiliary state forests.
Designation of land.
When abstract of title required, §9-13-42.
Guardian and ward.
Uniform guardianship and protective proceedings act.
Conservators.
Title by appointment, §26-2A-148.
Insurance, §27-25-1.
Investment securities.
Title acquired by bona fide purchaser, §7-8-301.
Landlord and tenant.
Tenant estopped to deny landlord's title, §35-9-1.
Livestock.
Brands.
Admissibility of certificate of registration of brand in proceedings as to title, §2-15-22.
Mortgages and deeds of trust.
Foreclosure deed conveys legal title, §35-10-5.
Revested upon payment of debt, §35-10-26.

TITLE—Cont'd

Motor vehicles.
Uniform certificate of title and antitheft act, §§32-8-1 to 32-8-88.
See MOTOR VEHICLES.
Ownership of title instruments, §35-4-9.
Partition.
See PARTITION.
Public lands.
General provisions.
See PUBLIC LANDS.
Quieting title.
General provisions, §§6-6-540 to 6-6-573.
See QUIETING TITLE.
Recordation.
Bonds for title, §35-4-53.
Redemption of real estate.
Failure or refusal of purchaser to reconvey title, §6-5-255.
Rules of civil procedure.
Vesting title, ARCP, Rule 70.
Secured transactions, §§7-9-101 to 7-9-507.
See COMMERCIAL CODE.
Slander of title.
Right of action, §6-5-211.
Trusts and trustees.
Necessity for legal title to vest in trustees, §35-4-251.
Uniform commercial code.
See COMMERCIAL CODE.

TOBACCO.

Cigarettes.
See CIGARETTES.
Counties.
Sales tax.
Basis of tax levy, §40-25-29.
Definitions.
Sales tax, §40-25-1.
Use tax, §40-25-40.
Executions.
Sales tax.
Unpaid taxes or penalties, §40-25-21.
Use tax, §40-25-44.
Forgery and counterfeiting.
Sales tax.
Counterfeit stamps, §40-25-6.
Fraud.
Sales tax.
Use or reuse of stamps, §40-25-6.
Garnishment.
Use tax, §40-25-44.
Inspections.
Sales tax.
Enforcement by inspection, §40-25-12.
Interference.
Penalties, §40-25-12.
Licenses.
Cigars, cigarettes, cheroots, etc.
Retailers, §40-12-72.
Wholesalers, §40-12-73.
Liens.
Sales tax.
Tax lien, §40-25-21.
Use tax, §40-25-45.

TOBACCO—Cont'd

Military affairs.
Taxation.
Exemption of certain post exchanges and canteens from tobacco taxes, §31-2-81.
Municipal corporations.
Sales tax.
Basis of tax levy, §40-25-29.
Permits.
Sales tax.
Permit for wholesalers or jobbers, §40-25-16.
Presumptions.
Sales tax.
Possession of unstamped tobacco products, §40-25-25.
Prisons and prisoners.
County convicts.
Work on public roads.
Tobacco allowance, §14-4-8.
Records.
Sales tax, §§40-25-13, 40-25-26.
Use tax, §40-25-46.
Reports.
Administration of article, §40-25-26.
Assessments, §40-25-18.
Boxes.
Reusing or refilling, §40-25-20.
Buses.
Statements, §40-25-11.
Chewing tobacco.
Liability for tax, §40-25-2.
Cigarettes.
Liability for tax, §40-25-2.
Cigars.
Liability for tax, §40-25-2.
Common carriers.
Interstate common carriers.
Rules and regulations, §40-25-10.
Statements, §40-25-11.
Confiscation.
Commodities subject to, §40-25-8.
Department may compromise, §40-25-10.
Procedure when goods confiscated, §40-25-9.
Containers.
Reusing or refilling, §40-25-20.
Contract carriers.
Statements, §40-25-11.
Counties.
Basis of tax levy, §40-25-29.
Debt due state, §40-25-21.
Definitions, §40-25-1.
Department of revenue.
Expenses deducted from collected taxes, §40-25-27.
Supplies provided, §40-25-27.
Distribution of tobacco products, §40-25-19.
Drop shipments, §40-25-7.
Effect of article, §40-25-28.
Enforcement, §40-25-26.
Inspections, §40-25-11.

TOBACCO—Cont'd
Reports—Cont'd
Executions.
Unpaid taxes or penalties,
§40-25-21.
Inspection.
Enforcement by inspection,
§40-25-12.
Interference.
Penalties, §40-25-12.
Interstate commerce.
Nontaxable sales,
§40-25-15.
Liability for tax, §40-25-2.
Liens.
Tax lien, §40-25-21.
Municipal corporations.
Basis of tax levy,
§40-25-29.
Nontaxable sales, §40-25-15.
Packages.
Reusing or refilling,
§40-25-20.
Payment.
Unpaid taxes.
Execution, §40-25-21.
Penalties.
Execution for unpaid
penalties, §40-25-21.
Inspections.
Interference, §40-25-12.
Unstamped goods.
Sale, purchase, receipt,
etc., §40-25-24.
Permits.
Wholesale dealers and
jobbers, §40-25-16.
Presumptions.
Possession of unstamped
tobacco products,
§40-25-25.
Records, §40-25-13.
Examination of books,
records, etc., §40-25-26.
Reports.
Wholesalers, §40-25-14.
Revenues collected.
Disposition, §40-25-23.
Expenses of department
deducted from collected
taxes, §40-25-27.
Payment, §40-25-23.
Rules and regulations.
Interstate common
carriers, §40-25-10.
Sales tax.
Wholesalers, §§40-25-1 to
40-25-29.
Snuff.
Liability for tax, §40-25-2.
Stamps.
Affixing.
Method and time,
§40-25-4.
Consignment, §40-25-5.
Counterfeit stamps,
§40-25-6.
Defined, §40-25-1.
Design, etc., §40-25-3.
Discounts for handling,
§40-25-5.
Evasion of stamp tax,
§40-25-18.
Fraud.
Use or reuse of stamps,
§40-25-6.
Goods not stamped.
Presumption arising
from possession,
§40-25-25.

TOBACCO—Cont'd
Reports—Cont'd
Stamps—Cont'd
Goods not stamped—Cont'd
Sale, purchase, receipt,
etc.
Penalty, §40-25-24.
Supplying to department,
§40-25-27.
Transportation of tobacco
products, §40-25-19.
United States.
Effect of federal
legislations, §40-25-22.
Wholesale dealers and
jobbers.
Defined, §40-25-1.
Nontaxable sales,
§40-25-15.
Permit, §40-25-16.
Qualifications.
Persons not qualified,
§40-25-16.
Reports, §40-25-14.
Requirements for sales,
§40-25-17.
Searches and seizures.
Use tax.
Seizure of contraband,
§40-25-41.
Taxation.
Exemptions from taxation,
§40-9-1.
Sales tax, §§40-25-1 to
40-25-29.
Use tax, §§40-25-40 to
40-25-47. See within this
heading, "Use tax."
United States.
Sales tax.
Effect of federal legislation,
§40-25-22.
Use tax, §§40-25-40 to
40-25-47.
Amount, §40-25-41.
Assessment, §40-25-43.
Contraband.
Seizure, §40-25-41.
Definitions, §40-25-40.
Execution, §40-25-44.
Garnishment, §40-25-44.
Levy, §40-25-41.
Lien, §40-25-45.
Payment.
Liability for payment,
§40-25-41.
Records, §40-25-46.
Registration as responsible
taxpayer, §40-25-41.
Returns, §40-25-42.
Revenues collected.
Disposition, §40-25-47.
Scope of article, §40-25-41.
Seizure of contraband,
§40-25-41.

**TOLL ROAD, BRIDGE AND
TUNNEL AUTHORITY,**
§§23-2-140 to 23-2-161.
Advertising.
Bids for construction,
§23-2-145.
Annual report to legislature.
Contents, §23-2-158.
Audits.
Annual audit, §23-2-158.
Costs, §23-2-158.
**Authority to enter private
lands to drill, survey,
etc.,** §23-2-146.

**TOLL ROAD, BRIDGE AND
TUNNEL AUTHORITY**
—Cont'd
Bonds.
Defined, §23-2-142.
Refunding bonds, §23-2-148.
Purposes, §23-2-148.
Revenue bonds. See within
this heading, "Revenue
bonds."
Toll road revenue bonds.
Defined, §23-2-142.
Tunnel revenue bonds.
Defined, §23-2-142.
Bonds, surety, §23-2-143.
Bridge.
Revenue bonds.
Defined, §23-2-142.
Chairman.
Governor, §23-2-143.
Citation, §23-2-140.
Collection.
Authority to collect tolls,
revenues, etc., §23-2-150.
Compensation, §23-2-143.
Conflicts of interest,
§23-2-159.
Penalty, §23-2-159.
Costs.
Defined, §23-2-142.
Definitions, §23-2-142.
Enforcement.
Rights of bondholders and
trustees, §23-2-152.
Scope of rights, §23-2-152.
Established, §23-2-143.
Governor.
Chairman, §23-2-143.
Ex officio member, §23-2-143.
**Grade separations at
intersections,** §23-2-146.
Incorporated, §23-2-143.
Indebtedness.
Limitations, §23-2-161.
Intent, §23-2-141.
Interstate highway system.
Toll bridges designated as
part of system,
§§23-2-121, 23-2-122.
Leases.
Authority, §23-2-150.
Legislative intent, §23-2-141.
Lieutenant governor.
Ex officio member, §23-2-143.
Maintenance.
Responsibility of authority,
§23-2-155.
Members, §23-2-143.
Officers, §23-2-143.
Secretary.
Election, §23-2-143.
Owners.
Defined, §23-2-142.
Powers.
Generally, §23-2-144.
Projects.
Bridge projects.
Defined, §23-2-142.
Defined, §23-2-142.
Toll road projects.
Defined, §23-2-142.
Tunnel projects.
Defined, §23-2-142.
Property.
Acquisition from counties,
cities, etc., §23-2-157.
Taxation.
Exemption of authority's
property, §23-2-153.

TOLL ROAD, BRIDGE AND TUNNEL AUTHORITY —Cont'd

Proposed projects.
Studies by state highway department, §23-2-161.
Reimbursement by authority, §23-2-161.
Public highways.
Defined, §23-2-142.
Public utility facilities.
Relocation, etc., §23-2-146.
Purpose of article, §23-2-141.
Quorum, §23-2-143.
Relocation of public highways, §23-2-146.
Reports.
Annual report to legislature, §23-2-158.
Revenue bonds.
Authorized provisions protecting holders, §23-2-149.
Bond anticipation notes, §23-2-147.
Bondholders.
Rights of enforcement, §23-2-152.
Definitions, §23-2-142.
Deposit with state officers or agencies, §23-2-154.
Forms, §23-2-147.
Issuance, §23-2-147.
Legal investments for all purposes, §23-2-154.
Payment of principal and interest.
Sources, §23-2-147.
Pledge of revenues, §23-2-149.
Procedures, §23-2-147.
Proceeds.
Use, §23-2-147.
Terms of bonds, §23-2-147.
Trust agreements securing bond issues, §23-2-149.
Revenues.
Authority to collect, §23-2-150.
Deemed trust funds, §23-2-151.
Tax exempt status, §23-2-153.
Rights of way.
Authority to lease, §23-2-150.
Rules and regulations.
Enforcement.
Police force, §23-2-156.
Jurisdiction, §23-2-156.
Use of toll roads, bridges and tunnels, §23-2-156.
Violations, §23-2-156.
Penalties, §23-2-156.
Taxation.
Exemption of authority's property and revenues, §23-2-153.
Title.
Short title, §23-2-140.
Tolls.
Authority to collect, §23-2-150.
Rates adjusted to conform to trust agreement, §23-2-150.
Transfer of toll roads, bridges and tunnels to state, §23-2-160.
Trustees.
Depositary deemed trustee, §23-2-151.

TOLL ROAD, BRIDGE AND TUNNEL AUTHORITY —Cont'd

Trustees—Cont'd
Rights of enforcement, §23-2-152.
Vacancies.
Filling, §23-2-143.
Violations.
Rules and regulations, §23-2-156.
Penalty, §23-2-156.
Work done by force account, §23-2-145.

TOLLS.
Bridges.
Interstate highway system.
Toll bridges designated as part of, §§23-2-121, 23-2-122.
Toll road, bridge and tunnel authority, §§23-2-140 to 23-2-161.
See TOLL ROAD, BRIDGE AND TUNNEL AUTHORITY.
Interstate highway system.
Bridges, §§23-2-121, 23-2-122.
Tunnels, §§23-2-120 to 23-2-122.
Toll road, bridge and tunnel authority, §§23-2-140 to 23-2-161.
See TOLL ROAD, BRIDGE AND TUNNEL AUTHORITY.
Tunnels.
General provisions.
See TUNNELS.
Toll road, bridge and tunnel authority, §§23-2-140 to 23-2-161.
See TOLL ROAD, BRIDGE AND TUNNEL AUTHORITY.
Waters and watercourses.
Riparian owners.
Right to charge tolls, §§33-7-50 to 33-7-52.

TOMATOES.
Sales tax.
Exemptions.
Certain items in production of tomatoes, §40-23-4.
Vegetables generally.
See FRUITS AND VEGETABLES.

TOMBIGBEE-TENNESSEE WATERWAY DEVELOPMENT COMPACT, §§33-8-1 to 33-8-4.
Appropriations, §33-8-2.
Authorization, §33-8-1.
Compact administrator.
Powers, §33-8-3.
Governor.
Authority to execute, §33-8-1.
Powers of governor, §33-8-3.
When chapter to become effective, §33-8-4.
Legislature.
Ratification, §33-8-1.
Members of authority.
Powers, §33-8-3.
Provisions.
Generally, §33-8-1.

TOMBIGBEE-TENNESSEE WATERWAY DEVELOPMENT COMPACT—Cont'd

State officers.
Powers, §33-8-3.
Time.
When chapter to become effective, §33-8-4.

TOMBIGBEE VALLEY DEVELOPMENT AUTHORITY, §§33-17-1 to 33-17-15.
Actions.
Power to sue and be sued, §33-17-8.
Bond issues, §§33-17-12 to 33-17-14.
Delivery, §33-17-12.
Directors.
Authority for sale, §33-17-12.
Execution, §33-17-12.
Form, §33-17-12.
Full faith and credit of state.
Pledged for payment, §33-17-12.
General obligations of state, §33-17-12.
Governor.
Approval of terms and conditions, §33-17-12.
Interest.
Rates, §33-17-12.
State treasurer to pay interest, §33-17-14.
Investments.
Proceeds of sales, §33-17-13.
Issuance.
Authority to issue, §33-17-12.
Legislative intent, §33-17-2.
Maximum amount, §33-17-12.
Payment.
Full faith and credit of state pledged for, §33-17-12.
Principal.
Maturity and annual installments, §33-17-12.
State treasurer to pay principal, §33-17-14.
Proceeds.
Disposition, §33-17-13.
Investments, §33-17-13.
Records.
Payment of principal and interest by state treasurer, §33-17-14.
Sale.
Directors, §33-17-12.
Proceeds.
Disposition, §33-17-13.
Public sale, §33-17-12.
Sale for less than face value, §33-17-12.
State treasurer.
Payment of principal and interest, §33-17-14.
Taxation.
Exemption, §33-17-12.
Bridges.
Duties to highway bridges, §33-17-7.
Construction of chapter, §33-17-2.

**TOMBIGBEE VALLEY
    DEVELOPMENT
    AUTHORITY**—Cont'd
Contracts.
    Approval by directors,
        §33-17-9.
    Counties.
        Power to contract with,
            §33-17-8.
    Maximum monetary
        obligations, §33-17-9.
    Municipal corporations.
        Power to contract with,
            §33-17-8.
    State departments and
        agencies.
        Power to contract with,
            §33-17-8.
    United States.
        Power to contract with,
            §33-17-8.
Counties.
    Contracts.
        Power to contract with,
            §33-17-8.
Definitions, §33-17-1.
Directors, §33-17-6.
    Bond issues.
        Authority for sale,
            §33-17-12.
    Compensation, §33-17-6.
    Contracts.
        Approval by directors,
            §33-17-9.
Dissolution, §33-17-15.
    Application of dissolution.
        Filing with secretary of
            state, §33-17-15.
Duties.
    Delegation, §33-17-10.
    Generally, §33-17-7.
Eminent domain.
    Exercise of power, §33-17-8.
Fees.
    Secretary of state.
        No fees to be paid to
            secretary, §33-17-5.
Flood control project.
    Defined, §33-17-1.
Governor.
    Bond issues.
        Approval of terms and
            conditions, §33-17-12.
    President of authority,
        §33-17-6.
    Public corporation, §33-17-3.
Highways.
    Duties as to highway
        relocation, §33-17-7.
Incorporation.
    Application.
        Presentation to secretary of
            state, §33-17-4.
        Signatures required,
            §33-17-4.
    Certificate of incorporation,
        §33-17-5.
    Records, §33-17-5.
    Procedure, §33-17-4.
    Public corporation.
        Authorization to form,
            §33-17-3.
    Seal, §33-17-5.
    Succession by corporate
        name, §33-17-8.
Interest.
    Bond issues, §§33-17-12,
        33-17-14.
Legislative intent, §33-17-2.
Members, §33-17-6.
    Compensation, §33-17-6.

**TOMBIGBEE VALLEY
    DEVELOPMENT
    AUTHORITY**—Cont'd
Municipal corporations.
    Contracts.
        Power to contract with,
            §33-17-8.
Obligations.
    Generally, §33-17-7.
Officers, §33-17-6.
    Compensation, §33-17-6.
Powers.
    Enumerated, §33-17-8.
Public corporations.
    Authorization to form,
        §33-17-3.
    Delegation of duties to other
        public corporations,
        §33-17-10.
Quorum, §33-17-6.
Real property.
    Dissolution.
        Disposition upon,
            §33-17-15.
    Power to receive, take and
        hold, §33-17-8.
Records.
    Bond issues.
        Payment of principal and
            interest by state
            treasurer, §33-17-14.
    Certificate of incorporation,
        §33-17-5.
    Proceedings, §33-17-6.
Sales.
    Bond issues, §§33-17-12,
        33-17-13.
Seal, §33-17-5.
Secretary of state.
    Dissolution.
        Application for dissolution.
            Filing with secretary,
                §33-17-15.
    Fees.
        No fees to be paid to
            secretary, §33-17-5.
    Incorporation.
        Presentation of application
            to secretary, §33-17-4.
Sewers.
    Duties and obligations which
        may be undertaken,
        §33-17-7.
**State departments and
    agencies.**
    Contracts.
        Power to contract with,
            §33-17-8.
    Cooperation, §33-17-2.
    Delegation of duties to state
        departments and
        agencies, §33-17-10.
State docks department.
    River and canal terminals.
        Authority to provide and
            maintain, §33-17-11.
State treasurer.
    Bond issues.
        Payment of principal and
            interest, §33-17-14.
    Custodian of funds, §33-17-6.
    Treasurer of authority,
        §33-17-6.
United States.
    Contracts.
        Power to contract with,
            §33-17-8.
    Cooperation with United
        States, §33-17-2.

**TOMBIGBEE VALLEY
    DEVELOPMENT
    AUTHORITY**—Cont'd
**Water supply and
    waterworks.**
    Duties as to, §33-17-7.

TOMBS AND TOMBSTONES.
**Aboriginal mounds,
    earthworks and other
    antiquities,** §§41-3-1 to
    41-3-6.
    See HISTORY AND
        ARCHIVES.
Cemeteries.
    Defacing, §13A-7-23.1.
    Licenses.
        Selling or erecting
            tombstones,
            §40-12-131.

TORTS.
Actions.
    Foreign causes of action.
        Enforcement when
            jurisdiction of
            defendant can be
            obtained in this state,
            §6-5-430.
Agents.
    Employer's liability for
        certain injuries,
        §§25-5-31, 25-5-32,
        25-6-1 to 25-6-4.
    See EMPLOYERS AND
        EMPLOYEES.
Associations.
    Officers.
        Liability of officers of
            nonprofit associations,
            §§10-11-1 to 10-11-5.
Authorities.
    Officers.
        Liability, §§10-11-1 to
            10-11-5.
Aviation.
    Jurisdiction, §4-2-4.
    State, municipal, etc.,
        immunity from tort
        liability, §4-2-4.
Boards and commissions.
    Officers.
        Liability, §§10-11-1 to
            10-11-5.
Civil defense.
    Immunity of state from
        liability for torts,
        §31-9-16.
    Shelters.
        Exemption from tort
            liability.
            Persons granting license
                or privilege for use
                of real estate, etc.,
                §31-9-17.
**Claims against state
    generally.**
    See CLAIMS AGAINST
        STATE.
Commercial code.
    Secured transactions.
        Transfer of claims exclude
            from provisions of
            article, §7-9-104.
Corporations.
    Nonprofit corporations.
        Officers.
            Liability, §§10-11-1 to
                10-11-5.

TORTS—Cont'd

Counties.
Claims and demands against counties, §§11-93-1 to 11-93-3.

Education.
Insurance.
Risk management cooperatives.
Boards of education.
Liability for tort claims, §16-8-42.1.

Employers and employees.
Employer's liability for certain injuries, §§25-5-31, 25-5-32, 25-6-1 to 25-6-4.
See EMPLOYERS AND EMPLOYEES.

Environmental improvement authorities.
Immunity from tort liability, §9-6-14.

Guardian and ward.
Uniform guardianship and protective proceedings act.
Conservators.
Personal liability, §26-2A-157.

Guests.
Duty of care owed persons on premises for sporting or recreational purposes, §§35-15-1 to 35-15-5.

Husband and wife.
See HUSBAND AND WIFE.

Invitees.
Duty of care owed persons on premises for sporting or recreational purposes, §§35-15-1 to 35-15-5.

Libel and slander.
See LIBEL AND SLANDER.

Licensees.
Duty of care owed persons on premises for sporting or recreational purposes, §§35-15-1 to 35-15-5.

Malpractice.
Medical malpractice, §§6-5-540 to 6-5-552.
See MALPRACTICE.

Mentally ill.
Regional mental health programs and facilities.
Officers.
Liability, §§10-11-1 to 10-11-5.

Minors.
Torts to property.
Liability for, §6-5-380.

Municipal corporations.
Claims and demands against municipal corporations, §§11-93-1 to 11-93-3.
Liability for negligence of agents, etc.
See MUNICIPAL CORPORATIONS.

Parent and child.
Liability.
Destruction of property by minor, §6-5-380.

Products liability, §§6-5-500 to 6-5-525.
See PRODUCTS LIABILITY.

TORTS—Cont'd

Railroads.
Railway policemen.
Liability of corporation for acts of policemen, §37-2-155.

Recreation.
Duty of care owed persons on premises for recreational purposes, §§35-15-1 to 35-15-5.

Respondeat superior.
Employer's liability for certain injuries.
See EMPLOYERS AND EMPLOYEES.

Secured transactions.
Transfer of claims excluded from provisions of article, §7-9-104.

State.
Claims against state generally.
See CLAIMS AGAINST STATE.

Transfers to minors.
Liability of minor, §35-5A-18.

Water, sewer and fire protection authorities.
Immunity from tort liability, §11-88-15.

Water, sewer and fire protection districts.
Immunity from tort liability, §11-89-15.

Workmen's compensation, §§25-5-1 to 25-5-231.
See WORKMEN'S COMPENSATION.

TOURISTS.

Bureau of tourism and travel, §§41-7-1 to 41-7-5.

Camps.
Licenses, §40-12-168.

Duty of care owed persons on premises for certain purposes, §§35-15-1 to 35-15-5.

Highways.
Signs and markers.
Indications of tourist attractions, §23-1-7.

Hotels, inns and other transient lodging places.
General provisions.
See HOTELS, INNS AND OTHER TRANSIENT LODGING PLACES.

Licenses.
Tourist camps, §40-12-168.

Transient occupancy tax, §§40-26-1 to 40-26-21.
See HOTELS, INNS AND OTHER TRANSIENT LODGING PLACES.

TOWELS.

Common towels.
Use in public places prohibited, §22-20-1.

TOWING.

Motor vehicles.
See MOTOR VEHICLES.

TOWNS.

Municipal corporations.
See MUNICIPAL CORPORATIONS.

TOXICOLOGY.

Caustic or corrosive substances.
See CAUSTIC OR CORROSIVE SUBSTANCES.

General provisions.
See POISONS AND POISONING.

State toxicologist.
General provisions, §§22-19-80 to 22-19-82.

TOXIC SUBSTANCES IN THE WORKPLACE, §§22-33-1 to 22-33-15.

Alabama substance list.
Contents, §22-33-4.
Defined, §22-33-2.
Promulgation, §22-33-4.
Revisions, §22-33-4.

Concentration levels.
Promulgation of standards, §22-33-4.

Contractors.
Liability and responsibility, §22-33-3.

Definitions, §22-33-2.

Education.
Employee education and training, §22-33-7.

Emergency medical service providers.
Notice, §22-33-10.

Employee education and training, §22-33-7.

Exemptions, §22-33-4.

Federal provisions.
When to prevail, §22-33-15.

Fire departments.
Notice to, §22-33-10.

General contractors.
Liability and responsibility, §22-33-3.

Independent contractors.
Liability and responsibility, §22-33-3.

Injunctions.
Violation of provisions, §22-33-13.

Intent of legislature, §22-33-1.

Law enforcement agencies.
Notice, §22-33-10.

Legislative intent, §22-33-1.

Local standards prohibited, §22-33-14.

Material safety data sheet.
Availability at workplace, §22-33-6.
Defined, §22-33-2.
Failure to provide, §22-33-6.
Provisions, §22-33-6.
Rights of employees, §22-33-6.
When to be provided, §22-33-6.

Notice.
Fire departments, emergency medical service providers and law enforcement agencies, §22-33-10.

Records.
Employers, §22-33-11.

Reports.
Annual report of director, §22-33-12.

Retaliatory acts by employer.
Cause of action, §22-33-8.
Prohibited, §22-33-8.

TOXIC SUBSTANCES IN THE WORKPLACE—Cont'd

Subcontractors.
  Liability and responsibility, §22-33-3.

Toxic substances advisory council.
  Advice and recommendations, §22-33-5.
  Appointment, §22-33-5.
  Compensation, §22-33-5.
  Composition, §22-33-5.
  Creation, §22-33-5.
  Expenses, §22-33-5.
  Meetings, §22-33-5.

Trade secrets.
  Protection, §22-33-9.
  When disclosure authorized or required, §22-33-9.

Violations of chapter.
  Remedies, §22-33-13.

TRACHOMA.

Notifiable diseases, §§22-11A-1 to 22-11A-38.
  See DISEASES.

TRACTORS.

See MOTOR VEHICLES.

TRADE AND COMMERCE.

Antiblacklist act, §13A-11-123.

Commerce and business in the state.
  Constitutional provisions, Const. U. S., Art. I, §§8, 9.

Commercial code, §§7-1-101 to 7-10-104.

Commercial lists.
  Evidence, §12-21-113.

Constitution of the United States, Const. U. S., Art. I, §§8, 9.

Consumer finance.
  General provisions, §§5-19-1 to 5-19-31.
  See CONSUMER FINANCE.

Counties.
  Projects for promotion of industry and trade.
  See COUNTIES.

Deceptive trade practices, §§8-19-1 to 8-19-15.
  See DECEPTIVE TRADE PRACTICES.

Fair trade.
  Insurance.
    Trade practices law, §§27-12-1 to 27-12-24.
    See INSURANCE.
  Monopolies.
    See MONOPOLIES.
  Motion picture fair competition, §§8-18-1 to 8-18-6.
    See MOTION PICTURES.
  Restraint of trade or production. See within this heading, "Restraint of trade or production."

Foreign trade zones.
  Harbors and ports.
    Establishment, §33-1-30.

Insurance.
  Trade practices law, §§27-12-1 to 27-12-24.
  See INSURANCE.

Monopolies.
  See MONOPOLIES.

TRADE AND COMMERCE —Cont'd

Motion picture fair competition, §§8-18-1 to 8-18-6.
  See MOTION PICTURES.

Municipal corporations.
  Promotion of industry, trade and pollution control, §§11-54-20 to 11-54-32.
  See MUNICIPAL CORPORATIONS.

Price current.
  Evidence of price current, §12-21-113.

Promotion by counties or municipalities.
  Counties.
    Industrial development boards, §§11-20-30 to 11-20-50.
    See COUNTIES.
    Projects for promotion of industry and trade, §§11-20-1 to 11-20-50.
    See COUNTIES.
  Municipal corporations.
    Promotion of industry, trade and pollution control, §§11-54-20 to 11-54-32.
    See MUNICIPAL CORPORATIONS.

Railroads.
  Restraint of trade.
    Unlawful pooling of freights, §37-8-30.

Restraint of trade or production.
  Blacklisting.
    Unlawful, §13A-11-123.
  Combinations.
    Prohibited purposes, §§8-10-1, 8-10-2.
  Competition.
    Destruction, §8-10-3.
  Contracts.
    Contracts restraining business void, §8-1-1.
    Exceptions, §8-1-1.
  Generally, §8-10-3.
  Monopolies.
    See MONOPOLIES.
  Motion picture fair competition, §§8-18-1 to 8-18-6.
    See MOTION PICTURES.
  Pools.
    Entering pool to fix price or limit quantity of commodity, §8-10-1.
  Railroads.
    Unlawful pooling of freights, §37-8-30.

Securities.
  See SECURITIES.

Unfair trade.
  Deceptive trade practices, §§8-19-1 to 8-19-15.
    See DECEPTIVE TRADE PRACTICES.
  Insurance.
    Trade practices law, §§27-12-1 to 27-12-24.
    See INSURANCE.
  Monopolies.
    See MONOPOLIES.
  Motion picture fair competition, §§8-18-1 to 8-18-6.
    See MOTION PICTURES.

TRADE AND COMMERCE —Cont'd

Unfair trade—Cont'd
  Restraint of trade or production. See within this heading, "Restraint of trade or production."

TRADEMARKS.

Agriculture.
  Grading and standards of farm products and fish, §§2-11-53 to 2-11-55.

Appropriation to designate origin or ownership, §8-12-1.

Brands and marks generally.
  See BRANDS AND MARKS.

Definitions.
  Registration of trademarks and service marks, §8-12-6.
  Theft of trademarks, §13A-8-10.4.

Labels generally.
  See LABELS.

Milk and milk products.
  Marked containers.
    See MILK AND MILK PRODUCTS.

Plant parts.
  Registration of symbol of seeds or plant parts.
    See SEEDS.

Registration of trademarks and service marks, §§8-12-8 to 8-12-18.
  Application, §8-12-8.
  Assignment of mark and registration, §8-12-11.
    Fee, §8-12-11.
  Business reputation.
    Injunctive relief.
      Injury to business reputation grounds for, §8-12-17.
  Cancellation of registration, §8-12-13.
  Certificate of registration, §8-12-9.
    Duration, §8-12-10.
    Evidence.
      Use as, §8-12-9.
    Issuance, §8-12-9.
      New certificate, §8-12-11.
    Recordation of new certificate, §8-12-11.
      Effect of failure to record, §8-12-11.
    Renewal, §8-12-10.
      Fee, §8-12-10.
  Common law rights, §8-12-19.
  Damages.
    Fraudulent filing or registration.
      Liability, §8-12-15.
  Definitions, §8-12-6.
  Fee.
    Application filing fee, §8-12-8.
    Assignment of mark and registration, §8-12-11.
    Renewal fee, §8-12-10.
  Fraudulent filing or registration.
    Liability for damages, §8-12-15.
  Goods and services.
    Classification of, §8-12-14.

TRADEMARKS—Cont'd
Registration of trademarks and service marks —Cont'd
Infringement.
Liability to civil action for, §8-12-16.
Injunctive relief.
Grounds for.
Injury to business reputation or dilution of quality of mark, §8-12-17.
Quality of mark.
Dilution of.
Injunctive relief.
Grounds, §8-12-17.
Records.
Maintenance of, §8-12-12.
Registrability, §8-12-7.
Remedies, §8-12-18.
Services.
Classification, §8-12-14.
Seeds.
Registration of symbol of seeds or plant parts.
See SEEDS.
Theft.
Class C felony, §13A-8-10.4.
Definitions, §13A-8-10.4.
Elements of offense, §13A-8-10.4.

TRADE SCHOOLS.
Alabama Institute of Aviation Technology at Ozark.
Operation as additional vocational trade school, §16-60-198.
Alabama school of trades, §§16-60-210 to 16-60-221.
Board of control.
Acceptance of donations, §16-60-217.
Records to be preserved, §16-60-220.
Rules and regulations, §16-60-219.
State board of education to constitute, §16-60-216.
Board of trustees.
Appointment of members, §16-60-213.
Compensation of members, §16-60-214.
Composition, §16-60-213.
Duties, §16-60-215.
Established, §16-60-213.
Expenses of members, §16-60-214.
Meetings, §16-60-214.
Powers, §16-60-215.
State superintendent of education ex officio member, §16-60-213.
Terms of members, §16-60-213.
Control of school.
Rules and regulations for control, §16-60-219.
Courses of study, §16-60-221.
Powers of board of trustees, §16-60-215.
Donations.
Acceptance by board of control, §16-60-217.
Acceptance by board of trustees, §16-60-215.

TRADE SCHOOLS—Cont'd
Alabama school of trades —Cont'd
Gifts.
Acceptance by board of control, §16-60-217.
Acceptance by board of trustees, §16-60-215.
Location, §16-60-210.
Management of school.
Board of control, §16-60-216.
Operation.
Powers of board of trustees, §16-60-215.
Placement of graduates.
Powers of board of trustees, §16-60-215.
Records.
Preservation of records, §16-60-220.
Rules and regulations, §16-60-219.
Seals and sealed instruments.
Corporate seal, §16-60-212.
State board of education.
Board of control, §16-60-216.
State superintendent of education.
Courses of study, §16-60-221.
Ex officio member of board of trustees, §16-60-213.
Training of students, §16-60-218.
Training standards.
Powers of board of trustees, §16-60-215.
Alabama trade school and junior college authority act, §§16-60-80 to 16-60-96.
See JUNIOR COLLEGES.
Appropriation, §16-60-193.
Aviation.
Alabama Institute of Aviation Technology at Ozark.
Operation as additional vocational trade school, §16-60-198.
Bond issues.
Trade school and junior college authority, §§16-60-90 to 16-60-93.
Buildings.
Approval of plans, §16-60-89.
Expenditures for building, §16-60-89.
Frank Lee youth center, §16-60-172.
Chancellor.
Appointment, §16-60-111.1.
Chief executive officer of postsecondary education department, §16-60-111.5.
Delegation of decision-making authority to chancellor, §16-60-111.6.
Powers and duties, §§16-60-111.1, 16-60-111.2, 16-60-111.5.
Transfer from state superintendent of education, §16-60-114.
Qualifications, §16-60-111.1.

TRADE SCHOOLS—Cont'd
Chancellor—Cont'd
Responsibility for operation of junior colleges and trade schools, §16-60-111.2.
Salary, §16-60-111.3.
Term of office, §16-60-111.1.
Construction.
Under supervision of state building commission, §16-60-192.
Contracts.
Competitive bidding, §16-60-89.
Control. See within this heading, "Management and control."
Corporate powers, §16-60-211.
Corporate seal, §16-60-212.
Definitions.
Management and control, §16-60-110.
Trade school and junior college authority, §16-60-81.
Equipment.
Expenditures for equipping, §16-60-89.
Establishment.
Order of establishment, §16-60-193.
State board of education authorized to establish, §16-60-191.
When schools to be established, §16-60-192.
Expenditure of appropriation, §16-60-193.
Faculty.
Appointment, §16-60-111.7.
Qualifications, §16-60-111.7.
Frank Lee youth center, §§16-60-170 to 16-60-173.
Authorization to maintain, §16-60-170.
Construction, §16-60-171.
Funds, §16-60-172.
Supervision, §16-60-172.
Enrollment.
Selection, §16-60-171.
Equipment, §16-60-171.
Funds.
Construction, §16-60-172.
Maintenance, §16-60-171.
Authority to maintain, §16-60-170.
Reversion of property and buildings to board of corrections, §16-60-173.
Teachers, §16-60-171.
Transfer of property and buildings to board of education, §16-60-173.
Franklin county.
Conversion of junior college for Franklin, Marion and Winston counties to trade school and junior college, §§16-60-38 to 16-60-40.
Junior college for Franklin, Marion and Winston counties.
Conversion to trade school and junior college, §§16-60-38 to 16-60-40.
Limestone county.
Trade school in, §16-60-193.

TRADE SCHOOLS—Cont'd
Location of schools,
§16-60-193.
Determination by trade
school and junior college
authority, §16-60-88.
Maintenance.
State board of education
authorized to maintain,
§16-60-191.
Management and control.
Borrowing money.
Authority to borrow in
anticipation of current
revenues, §16-60-113.
Definitions, §16-60-110.
Interpretation of sections
16-60-110 and 16-60-111,
§16-60-112.
Regional vocational and
trade schools,
§16-60-194.
Teachers' salaries.
Authority to borrow in
anticipation of current
revenues if funds not
sufficient to pay,
§16-60-113.
Marion county.
Conversion of junior college
for Franklin, Marion and
Winston counties to
trade school and junior
college, §§16-60-38 to
16-60-40.
Mining.
Alabama mining academy,
§§16-60-260 to 16-60-264.
Order of establishment,
§16-60-193.
Powers.
Corporate powers,
§16-60-211.
**Regional vocational and
trade schools,**
§§16-60-190 to 16-60-198.
Additional vocational trade
schools authorized,
§16-60-197.
Advisory council, §16-60-195.
Alabama Institute of
Aviation Technology at
Ozark.
Operation as additional
vocational trade
school, §16-60-198.
Appropriations.
Council of appropriations
for support of
vocational trade
schools, §16-60-196.
Management and control,
§16-60-194.
Short title of article,
§16-60-190.
State board of control.
Management and control,
§16-60-194.
Teachers.
Leaves of absence,
§16-60-194.
Veteran training programs.
Schools to be suitable for,
§16-60-194.
Rules and regulations.
Alabama school of trades,
§16-60-219.

TRADE SCHOOLS—Cont'd
Salaries.
Teachers' salaries.
Authority to borrow in
anticipation of current
revenues if funds not
sufficient to pay,
§16-60-113.
**Seals and sealed
instruments.**
Corporate seal, §16-60-212.
**Shelton State Technical
Institute.**
Shelton State Technical
Trade School designated
as, §16-60-2.
**Shelton State Technical
Trade School.**
Designated Shelton State
Technical Institute,
§16-60-2.
Sites.
When sites must be donated,
§16-60-88.
**Southwest State Technical
Institute.**
State Vocational Technical
School at Mobile
designated as, §16-60-1.
State board of control.
Alabama school of trades.
See within this heading,
"Alabama school of
trades."
Authorized to establish and
maintain, §16-60-191.
Management and control. See
within this heading,
"Management and
control."
Regional vocational and
trade schools,
§16-60-194.
**State superintendent of
education.**
Powers and duties.
Transfer to chancellor,
§16-60-114.
**State Vocational Technical
School at Mobile
designated Southwest
State Technical Institute,**
§16-60-1.
Teachers.
Frank Lee youth center,
§16-60-171.
Regional vocational and
trade schools.
Leaves of absence,
§16-60-194.
Salaries.
Authority to borrow in
anticipation of current
revenues if funds not
sufficient to pay,
§16-60-113.
**Trade school and junior
college authority,**
§§16-60-80 to 16-60-96.
See JUNIOR COLLEGES.
Unaccredited schools,
§§16-46-1 to 16-46-10.
Veterans.
Regional vocational and
trade schools.
Schools to be suitable for
veteran training
programs, §16-60-194.

TRADE SCHOOLS—Cont'd
**Wenonah State Technical
School.**
Wenonah State Technical
Trade School designated
as, §16-60-3.
**Wenonah State Technical
Trade School.**
Designated Wenonah State
Technical School,
§16-60-3.
**When schools to be
established,** §16-60-192.
Winston county.
Conversion of junior college
for Franklin, Marion and
Winston counties to
trade school and junior
college, §§16-60-38 to
16-60-40.

TRADE SECRETS.
Damages.
Misappropriation.
Violations of trade secret,
§8-27-3.
Definitions, §8-27-2.
Effect on other law, §8-27-6.
Limitation of actions.
Misappropriation, §8-27-4.
Remedies.
Misappropriation.
Actual or threatened
misappropriation of
trade secrets, §8-27-4.
Short title, §8-27-6.
Theft.
Class C felony, §13A-8-10.4.
Definitions, §13A-8-10.4.
Elements of offense,
§13A-8-10.4.
Title of chapter, §8-27-1.

TRADING STAMPS.
Licenses, §40-12-170.

TRAFFIC REGULATIONS.
District courts.
Traffic offenses, §§12-12-50 to
12-12-56.
See DISTRICT COURTS.
General provisions.
See MOTOR VEHICLES.

TRAILERS.
Mobile homes.
General provisions, §§24-5-1
to 24-5-34.
See MOBILE HOMES.
**Trucks, trailers and semi-
trailers.**
See MOTOR VEHICLES.

TRAINERS.
Animals.
Lien on animals for feeding,
boarding or training,
§35-11-71.
Birds.
Lien on birds for feeding,
boarding or training,
§35-11-71.
Dogs, §9-11-52.
Liens.
Birds or animals.
Feeding, boarding or
training, §35-11-71.
Livestock.
Lien on stock for training,
§35-11-70.
Livestock.
Lien on stock for pasturage
or training, §35-11-70.

TRAINS.
See RAILROADS.

TRANSCRIPTS.
  Admissibility in evidence,
    ARCP, Rule 80.
  Court reporters.
    Fees.
      Preparation of original and
        providing copies,
        ARJA, Rule 29.
  District courts.
    Provision for transcripts of
      proceedings by courts,
      §12-12-2.
  Fees, ARJA, Rule 29.
    Court reporters.
      Preparation of original and
        providing copies,
        ARJA, Rule 29.
  Preparation.
    Requirements, ARJA, Rule
      29.
  Record on appeal.
    See APPEALS.

TRANSFERS.
  Bulk transfers, §§7-6-101 to
    7-6-111.
    See COMMERCIAL CODE.
  Conveyances.
    See CONVEYANCES.
  Fraudulent transfers,
    §§8-9A-1 to 8-9A-12.
    See FRAUDULENT
      TRANSFERS.

TRANSFERS TO MINORS,
  §§35-5A-1 to 35-5A-24.
  Accounts and accounting.
    Custodians, §35-5A-20.
      Permission of court to
        account, §35-5A-20.
      Petitions for accounting,
        §35-5A-20.
  Applicability of chapter,
    §§35-5A-3, 35-5A-22,
    35-5A-23.
    Uniformity of application and
      construction, §35-5A-24.
  Bonds, surety.
    Custodians, §35-5A-16.
  Citation of chapter, §35-5A-1.
  Conservators.
    Irrevocable transfers to other
      adults or trust
      companies, §35-5A-7.
  Construction and
    interpretation.
    Uniformity of application and
      construction, §35-5A-24.
  Corporate stock.
    Infant stockholders.
      Effect of chapter on
        transfers to minors act,
        §10-6-4.
  Custodial property.
    Acknowledgment of delivery,
      §35-5A-9.
    Care of custodial property,
      §35-5A-13.
    Claims against property,
      §35-5A-18.
    Creation, §35-5A-10.
    Delivery or payment to
      minor, §35-5A-15.
    Duty of custodian to keep
      property separate and
      distinct, §35-5A-13.
    How transfers effected,
      §35-5A-10.
    Manner of creating,
      §35-5A-10.

TRANSFERS TO MINORS
  —Cont'd
  Custodial property—Cont'd
    Order by court to pay minor,
      §35-5A-15.
    Standard of care of
      custodian, §35-5A-13.
    Use by minor, §35-5A-15.
  Custodians.
    Accounts and accounting,
      §35-5A-20.
      Permission by court to
        make account,
        §35-5A-20.
      Petition to court for
        accounting by
        custodian, §35-5A-20.
    Acknowledgment of delivery
      of custodial property,
      §35-5A-9.
    Bonds, surety, §35-5A-16.
    Care.
      Standards, §35-5A-13.
    Compensation, §35-5A-16.
    Death, §35-5A-19.
      Validity of transfers,
        §35-5A-12.
    Declining to serve,
      §35-5A-19.
    Duty to keep custodial
      property separate and
      distinct, §35-5A-13.
    Expenses, §35-5A-16.
    Future events.
      Nomination of custodian to
        serve upon, §35-5A-4.
    Investments, §35-5A-13.
    Liability, §35-5A-19.
    Life insurance policies.
      Use of funds to purchase,
        §35-5A-13.
    Nomination.
      Custodian to serve upon
        future events,
        §35-5A-4.
    Personal jurisdiction over,
      §35-5A-3.
    Powers, §§35-5A-13,
      35-5A-14.
    Records, §35-5A-13.
    Removal, §35-5A-19.
    Resignation, §35-5A-19.
    Single custodianship,
      §35-5A-11.
    Special skills or expertise,
      §35-5A-13.
    Standards of care, §35-5A-13.
    Successor custodians.
      Designation, §35-5A-19.
    Termination, §35-5A-21.
  Death.
    Termination of custodianship
      upon minor's death,
      §35-5A-21.
    Validity and effect of
      transfer not affected,
      §35-5A-12.
  Debts.
    Person owing liquidated debt
      to minor, §35-5A-8.
  Definitions, §35-5A-2.
  Gifts.
    Transfer by irrevocable gift,
      §35-5A-5.
  Insurance.
    Life insurance.
      Purchase of policies by
        custodian, §35-5A-13.
  Investments.
    Custodians, §35-5A-13.

TRANSFERS TO MINORS
  —Cont'd
  Irrevocability of transfer,
    §35-5A-12.
  Liability.
    Custodians, §35-5A-18.
    Exemption of third persons,
      §35-5A-17.
    Minors.
      Personal liability,
        §35-5A-18.
  Life insurance.
    Purchase of policies by
      custodian, §35-5A-13.
  Manner of making transfers.
    Transfer to only one minor,
      §35-5A-11.
  Obligation to support minor.
    Delivery, payment or
      expenditure of custodial
      property in addition to
      and not substitution for
      obligation, §35-5A-15.
  Personal representatives.
    Transfer not authorized in
      will or trust, §35-5A-7.
  Petitions.
    Accounting by custodian,
      §35-5A-20.
  Powers of appointment.
    Transfer by exercise of
      power, §35-5A-5.
  Records.
    Custodians, §35-5A-13.
  Short title of chapter,
    §35-5A-1.
  Standard of care of
    custodian, §35-5A-13.
  Third parties.
    Exemption from liability,
      §35-5A-17.
  Torts.
    Liability of minor, §35-5A-18.
  Transfer incorporates in
    disposition all provisions
    of chapter, §35-5A-12.
  Transfers made under law
    of another state,
    §35-5A-3.
  Trust companies.
    Fiduciaries.
      Irrevocable transfer to
        trust company and
        custodian, §35-5A-7.
  Trusts and trustees.
    Transfer authorized by trust,
      §35-5A-6.
  Validity of transfer,
    §35-5A-12.
  Wills.
    Transfer authorized by will
      or trust, §35-5A-6.

TRANSIENT LODGING
  PLACES.
  See HOTELS, INNS AND
    OTHER TRANSIENT
    LODGING PLACES.

TRANSIENT MERCHANTS,
  §§34-35-1 to 34-35-9.
  Agents.
    Registered agents, §34-35-6.
  Bonds, surety, §34-35-7.
  Definitions, §34-35-1.
  Exemptions from chapter,
    §34-35-2.
  Fees.
    Licenses, §34-35-7.
  Licenses.
    Applications, §34-35-4.
      Form, §34-35-5.

TRANSIENT MERCHANTS
—Cont'd
Licenses—Cont'd
Expiration, §34-35-8.
Fees, §34-35-7.
Forms, §34-35-5.
Issuance, §34-35-8.
Nontransferrable, §34-35-8.
Renewal, §34-35-8.
Required, §§34-35-3, 34-35-4.
Territorial validity, §34-35-8.
Lists, §34-35-6.
Penalties.
Violations of chapter,
§34-35-9.
Registered agents, §34-35-6.
Lists, §34-35-6.
Requirements for
transacting business,
§34-35-3.
Service of process, §34-35-6.
Violations of chapter,
§34-35-9.

TRANSIENT OCCUPANCY
TAX, §§40-26-1 to 40-26-21.
See HOTELS, INNS AND
OTHER TRANSIENT
LODGING PLACES.

TRANSPORTATION.
Alligator farms.
Carcasses, parts, etc.
Tags required, §9-12-204.
Definition of transport,
§9-12-200.
Blind persons.
Right to use of public
transportation facilities,
§21-7-3.
Companies.
General provisions, §§37-2-1
to 37-2-184.
See TRANSPORTATION
COMPANIES.
Dead bodies, §22-19-1.
Explosives.
See EXPLOSIVES AND
EXPLOSIONS.
Fish and game.
See FISH AND GAME.
Handicapped persons.
Right to use of public
transportation facilities,
§21-7-3.
Hazardous waste.
Exemptions.
Certain transporters
exempt, §22-30-21.
Facility or site which does
not have permit.
Transporting to.
Prohibited, §22-30-19.
Highways generally.
See HIGHWAYS.
Motor vehicle carriers.
See MOTOR VEHICLE
CARRIERS.
Motor vehicles generally.
See MOTOR VEHICLES.
Municipal corporations.
Public transportation service
in Class 3 municipalities,
§§11-49A-1 to 11-49A-20.
See MUNICIPAL
CORPORATIONS.
Prisons and prisoners.
Discharging convicts.
Furnishing to discharged
convicts, §14-10-1.
Quarantine, §§22-12-21,
22-12-22.

TRANSPORTATION—Cont'd
Railroads generally.
See RAILROADS.

TRANSPORTATION
COMPANIES, §§37-2-1 to
37-2-184.
Abandonment of service.
Permit, §§37-2-5 to 37-2-7.
Actions.
Connecting carriers.
Joint actions against,
§37-2-34.
Damages for loss, injury or
delay in delivery.
Action for, §37-2-62.
Joint actions against
connecting carriers,
§37-2-34.
Overcharges.
Actions for recovery of
overcharge, §37-2-33.
Penalties.
Recovery of penalties,
§§37-2-17, 37-2-45.
Rights of action not waived,
§37-2-44.
Agriculture.
Special rates for agricultural
enterprises, §37-2-15.
Air commerce.
See AIR COMMERCE.
Applicability of chapter.
Governmentally owned
companies, §37-2-2.
Baggage.
Personal baggage of
passengers. See within
this heading,
"Passengers."
Bills of lading or receipts,
§§37-2-21 to 37-2-26.
Charges.
Settling charges according
to stipulated rate,
§37-2-26.
Common-law liability of
common carrier.
Not affected, §37-2-21.
Contents, §37-2-21.
Cotton.
Delivery to cotton
compress, §37-2-24.
Receipt for cotton in bales,
§37-2-21.
Delivery to carrier.
Bill of lading not given
until property
delivered, §37-2-22.
Liability for failure to
indorse partial
delivery, §37-2-23.
Duplicates, §37-2-22.
Liability for false or second
bill of lading or
receipt, §37-2-23.
False or second bill of lading
or receipt.
Liability, §37-2-23.
Penalty, §37-2-16.
Freight generally. See within
this heading, "Freight."
Indorsements.
Partial delivery.
Liability for failure to
indorse, §37-2-23.
Issuance.
When issued, §37-2-21.
Liability, §§37-2-21, 37-2-23.

TRANSPORTATION
COMPANIES—Cont'd
Bills of lading or receipts
—Cont'd
Rates.
Charges to be settled
according to stipulated
rate in bill of lading,
§37-2-26.
Sales.
Unauthorized sale of
property prohibited,
§37-2-25.
Unauthorized sale or transfer
of property.
Prohibited, §37-2-25.
Certificates of convenience
and necessity.
Notice of filing of application
for certificate.
Owners of land proposed to
be acquired by utility
or telephone company
to be given notice,
§37-2-4.1.
When required, §37-2-4.
Charges.
Freight charges. See within
this heading, "Freight."
Charities.
Discounts.
Exemptions for charities,
§37-8-28.
Free passes.
Exemptions for charities,
§37-8-28.
Free transportation or
reduced rates for
charitable purposes,
§37-2-40.
Rebates.
Exemptions, §37-8-28.
Claims.
Prohibited acts, §§37-2-43,
37-8-280.
Soliciting claims from
shippers or consignees
against carriers,
§37-8-280.
Common carriers.
Bills of lading or receipts.
See within this heading,
"Bills of lading or
receipts."
Common-law liability for
injuries, §37-2-21.
Complaints.
Reparation.
Complaints for recovery of
reparation, §37-2-19.
Concentration and transit
privileges and rates.
When permitted,
§37-2-20.
Connecting carriers.
Joint actions against,
§37-2-34.
Cotton.
Bills of lading or receipts.
See within this heading,
"Bills of lading or
receipts."
Delivery of cotton to
compress.
Issuance of bill of lading,
§37-2-24.

TRANSPORTATION
    COMPANIES—Cont'd
Damages.
  Loss, injury or delay in
    delivery.
    Action for damages,
      §37-2-62.
    Limitation of actions,
      §37-2-62.
    Claim for damages,
      §37-2-61.
    Failure to present
      verified claim,
      §37-2-61.
    Itemized statement of
      goods, §37-2-61.
    Measure of damages,
      §37-2-60.
  Treble damages, §37-2-18.
Definitions, §37-2-1.
Delay in delivery.
  Damages, §§37-2-60 to
    37-2-62.
  Unreasonable delay.
    Joint actions against
      connecting carriers,
      §37-2-34.
Delivery.
  Connecting carriers.
    Joint actions against
      connecting carriers for
      unreasonable delay,
      §37-2-34.
  Partial delivery of
    consignment, §37-2-32.
Depots.
  Storage of freight in depot or
    warehouse.
    Liability of company,
      §37-2-27.
Devices.
  Repairs, improvements or
    changes in property or
    devices.
    Order by public service
      commission, §37-2-9.
Discounts.
  Exemptions, §37-8-28.
  Penalties for violations,
    §37-8-27.
Discrimination.
  Charging or collecting higher
    than lawful rate,
    §37-8-23.
  Penalty, §37-2-16.
  Public utilities generally.
    See PUBLIC UTILITIES.
  Reparation, §37-2-19.
  Violation of statutes relating
    to, §37-8-20.
Drawbacks.
  Discrimination by drawback.
    Penalty, §37-2-16.
Employees.
  Act of employee.
    Act of company, §37-2-46.
  Discounts.
    Exemptions, §37-8-28.
  Free transportation or
    reduced rates, §37-2-40.
    Exemptions, §37-8-28.
  Rebates.
    Exemptions, §37-8-28.
  Respondeat superior,
    §37-2-46.
  Wages.
    Biweekly payment,
      §37-8-270.

TRANSPORTATION
    COMPANIES—Cont'd
Fairs.
  Free transportation or
    reduced rates to or from
    fairs and expositions,
    §37-2-40.
Fees.
  Inspection and supervision
    fees.
    Liens, §37-2-41.
    Payment to public service
      commission, §37-2-41.
    Supervision fees, §37-2-41.
Free transportation, §37-2-40.
  Exemptions, §37-8-28.
  Penalties for violations,
    §37-8-27.
Freight.
  Charges.
    Baggage.
      Personal baggage of
        passengers. See
        within this heading,
        "Passengers."
    Charges to be settled
      according to rates
      stipulated in bill of
      lading, §37-2-26.
    Overcharges, §37-2-33.
    Partial delivery of
      consignment, §37-2-32.
    Refund of excessive
      charges upon
      submission of expense
      bill or receipt,
      §37-2-42.
  Charging or collecting higher
    than lawful rate for
    transportation of freight,
    §37-8-23.
  Claims.
    Soliciting claims from
      shippers or consignees
      against carriers,
      §37-8-280.
  Classes of freight.
    Bills of lading or receipts.
      Classes to be stated in
      bill, §37-2-21.
  Damages for loss, injury or
    delay in delivery,
    §§37-2-60 to 37-2-62.
  Duty to receive or transport
    freight, §37-2-31.
  Liability for failure or
    delay, §37-2-31.
  Freight bureaus.
    Soliciting claims against
      transportation
      companies forbidden,
      §37-2-43.
  Live freight.
    Sale of unclaimed freight,
      §§37-2-28 to 37-2-30.
  Partial delivery of
    consignment, §37-2-32.
  Sale of unclaimed freight,
    §§37-2-28 to 37-2-30.
  Storage of freight in depot or
    warehouse.
    Liability of transportation
      company, §37-2-27.
  Unclaimed freight.
    Sale of unclaimed freight,
      §§37-2-28 to 37-2-30.

TRANSPORTATION
    COMPANIES—Cont'd
**Governmentally owned
    transportation
    companies,** §37-2-2.
  Inspection and supervision
    fees.
    Fees to be measured by
      amount of gross
      receipts, §37-2-41.
Hearings.
  Abandonment of service.
    Application for permit to
      abandon, §37-2-6.
Injury in delivery.
  Damages, §§37-2-60 to
    37-2-62.
Inspections.
  Public service commission.
    Inspection fee, §37-2-41.
Insurance.
  Unclaimed freight.
    Sale.
      Application of proceeds
        for insurance,
        §37-2-30.
Interstate commerce.
  Concentration and transit
    privileges and rates,
    §37-2-20.
Joint rates, §§37-2-10, 37-2-11.
Liability.
  Bills of lading or receipts.
    Common-law liability of
      common carriers not
      affected, §37-2-21.
    Failure to indorse partial
      delivery, §37-2-23.
    False or second bill of
      lading, §37-2-23.
  Employees.
    Act of employee as act of
      company, §37-2-46.
  Failure or delay in
    transporting or receiving
    freight, §37-2-31.
  Joint actions against
    connecting carriers,
    §37-2-34.
  Storage of freight in depot or
    warehouse, §37-2-27.
Liens.
  Inspection and supervision
    fees, §37-2-41.
Limitation of actions.
  Damages for loss, injury or
    delay in delivery.
    Action for damages,
      §37-2-62.
Littering.
  Vehicles loaded with gravel,
    rock, sawdust, wood, etc.
    Spilling loads, §32-5-76.
Loss.
  Connecting carriers.
    Joint actions against,
      §37-2-34.
  Damages for loss of
    deliveries, §§37-2-60 to
    37-2-62.
  Liability for losses, §37-2-21.
Mileage books.
  List of books to be filed with
    public service
    commission, §37-2-8.
Municipal corporations.
  Abandonment of service.
    Permit for abandonment.
      Notice of application to
        municipalities
        affected, §37-2-6.

TRANSPORTATION COMPANIES—Cont'd
Municipal corporations—Cont'd
Free transportation or reduced rates, §37-2-40.
Governmentally owned companies.
Applicability of chapter, §37-2-2.
Notice.
Abandonment of service.
Application for permit to abandon, §37-2-6.
Arrival of freight.
Notice to consignee, §37-2-27.
Change in rates, §37-2-12.
Storage of freight in depot or warehouse.
Notice to consignee, §37-2-27.
Officers.
Free transportation or reduced rates, §37-2-40.
Passengers.
Personal baggage, §§37-2-35 to 37-2-39.
Abandoned baggage.
Storage charges, §37-2-39.
Charges.
Excess baggage, §37-2-36.
Free transportation within certain weight limits, §37-2-35.
Storage charges for baggage left in baggage rooms or station houses, §37-2-39.
Commercial travelers, §37-2-37.
Excess baggage.
Charge, §37-2-36.
Free transportation within certain weight limits, §37-2-35.
Size.
Maximum size and weight limits, §37-2-38.
Storage charges.
Baggage left in baggage rooms or station houses, §37-2-39.
Weight.
Free transportation within certain weight limits, §37-2-35.
Maximum size and weight limits, §37-2-38.
Railroads.
General provisions.
See RAILROADS.
Passes, §§37-2-8, 37-8-27.
Penalties.
Action for, §37-2-17.
Cumulative, §37-2-44.
Discrimination, §37-2-16.
Excessive rates, §37-2-17.
Free passes, rebates or discounts.
Violations, §37-8-27.
Rates.
Excessive rates, §37-2-17.

TRANSPORTATION COMPANIES—Cont'd
Penalties—Cont'd
Recovery of penalties or forfeitures, §37-2-45.
Treble damages, §37-2-18.
Permits.
Abandonment of service.
Application for permit, §37-2-6.
Conditions, §37-2-7.
Exceptions, §37-2-7.
Grant or refusal, §37-2-7.
Hearing, §37-2-6.
Notice to municipalities affected, §37-2-6.
Revocation, §37-2-7.
When permit required, §37-2-5.
Certificates of convenience and necessity, §§37-2-4, 37-2-4.1.
Plants.
Abandonment of service.
When permit required, §37-2-5.
Construction of new plants.
Certificate of convenience and necessity, §37-2-4.
Police.
Railway policemen, §§37-2-150 to 37-2-157.
See RAILROADS.
Property.
Abandoning operation of property.
When permit to abandon required, §37-2-5.
Acquiring property of other companies.
Certificate of convenience and necessity, §37-2-4.
Notice of filing of application for certificate of convenience and necessity.
Owners of land proposed to be acquired by company to be given notice, §37-2-4.1.
Unauthorized sale or transfer of property prohibited, §37-2-25.
Public service commission.
General provisions, §§37-1-1 to 37-1-157.
See PUBLIC SERVICE COMMISSION.
Public utilities generally.
See PUBLIC UTILITIES.
Railroads generally.
See RAILROADS.
Railway policemen, §§37-2-150 to 37-2-157.
See RAILROADS.
Rates.
Bills of lading.
Charges to be settled according to rates stipulated in bill of lading, §37-2-26.
Changes in rates.
Notice of proposed change, §37-2-12.
Charges to be settled according to rates stipulated in bill of lading, §37-2-26.
Charging or accepting rate lower than published tariff, §37-8-22.

TRANSPORTATION COMPANIES—Cont'd
Rates—Cont'd
Charging or collecting higher than lawful rate, §37-8-23.
Concentration and transit rates.
When permitted, §37-2-20.
Emergency rates, §37-2-14.
Excessive rates.
Penalty, §37-2-17.
Free transportation or reduced rates for certain purposes, §37-2-40.
Joint rates.
Apportionment, §37-2-11.
Publication, §37-2-10.
Public service commission.
Establishment of rates, §37-2-11.
Refusal by companies to establish, §37-2-11.
Legally applicable rates.
Posted rates to be legally applicable, §37-2-13.
Overcharges, §37-2-33.
Posted rates to be legally applicable rates, §37-2-13.
Reparation for excessive or unjust rates, §37-2-19.
Schedules of rates.
Public inspection, §37-2-10.
Special rates.
Agricultural enterprises, §37-2-15.
Authority of public service commission, §37-2-15.
Discrimination by special rate.
Penalty, §37-2-16.
Publication, §37-2-15.
Revocation by commission, §37-2-15.
Temporary rates.
Power of public service commission, §37-2-14.
Violation of statutes relating to reasonable rates, §37-8-20.
Rebates.
Discrimination by rebate.
Penalty, §37-2-16.
Employees.
Exemptions, §37-8-28.
Exemptions, §37-8-28.
Penalties for violations, §37-8-27.
Public utilities generally.
See PUBLIC UTILITIES.
Receipts. See within this heading, "Bills of lading or receipts."
Records.
Sale of unclaimed freight, §37-2-30.
Refunds.
Excessive charges.
Refund upon submission of expense bill or receipt, §37-2-42.
Overcharges, §37-2-33.
Repairs and improvements.
Public service commission.
Order directing, §37-2-9.
Reparation, §37-2-19.
Reports.
False report of weight.
Penalty, §37-2-16.

TRANSPORTATION COMPANIES—Cont'd
Sale of unclaimed freight,
§§37-2-28 to 37-2-30.
Insurance.
Transportation company may insure freight at expense of owner, §37-2-30.
Nonperishable freight.
Generally, §37-2-28.
Notice of sale, §37-2-28.
Proceeds, §37-2-28.
Notice of sale.
Nonperishable freight, §37-2-28.
Perishable or live freight, §37-2-29.
Perishable or live freight.
Notice of sale, §37-2-29.
When sale may be made, §37-2-29.
Proceeds.
Application of proceeds, §37-2-30.
Insurance.
Application of proceeds, §37-2-30.
Nonperishable freight, §37-2-28.
Records.
Article sold and price obtained, §37-2-30.
Surplus.
Disposition, §37-2-30.
Sales.
Unauthorized sale or transfer of property prohibited, §37-2-25.
Unclaimed freight, §§37-2-28 to 37-2-30.
Schedules.
Rates.
Public inspection, §37-2-10.
Service.
Abandonment of service.
Permit, §§37-2-5 to 37-2-7.
Violation of statutes relating to, §37-8-20.
Solicitation.
Claims.
Prohibited acts, §§37-2-43, 37-8-280.
Special rates, §§37-2-15, 37-2-16.
State.
Actions.
Rights of actions by state not waived, §37-2-44.
Free transportation or reduced rates for state of Alabama, §37-2-40.
Tariffs.
Charging or accepting rate lower than published tariff, §37-8-22.
Filing with public service commission, §37-2-10.
Posting, §37-2-10.
Public inspection, §37-2-10.
Tickets and passes.
Free passes, §37-8-27.
List of tickets, passes and mileage books to be filed with public service commission, §37-2-8.
Traffic associations.
Soliciting claims against transportation companies forbidden, §37-2-43.

TRANSPORTATION COMPANIES—Cont'd
Unclaimed freight.
Sale of unclaimed freight, §§37-2-28 to 37-2-30.
United States.
Free transportation or reduced rates, §37-2-40.
Governmentally owned companies.
Applicability of chapter, §37-2-2.
Violations.
Each violation constitutes separate offense, §37-2-46.
Free passes, rebates or discounts.
Penalties for violations, §37-8-27.
Wages.
Bi-weekly payment, §37-8-270.
Waiver.
Rights of action not waived, §37-2-44.
Warehouses.
Storage of freight in depot or warehouse.
Liability of company, §37-2-27.
Weight.
Baggage.
Personal baggage of passengers, §§37-2-35, 37-2-38.
False weighing.
Penalty, §37-2-16.
Reports.
False report of weight.
Penalty, §37-2-16.

TRAPPING.
Duty of care owed persons on premises for certain purposes, §§35-15-1 to 35-15-5.
General provisions.
See FISH AND GAME.

TRASH.
See GARBAGE AND TRASH.

TRAVEL.
Bureau of tourism and travel, §§41-7-1 to 41-7-5.

TRAVELERS' CHECKS.
Sale of checks, §§8-7-1 to 8-7-15.
See CHECKS.

TREASON.
Anarchy and subversive activities, §31-9-20.
Bills of attainder.
Bills of attainder of treason by legislature prohibited, Const. Ala., art. I, §19.
Class A felony, §13A-11-2.
Constitution of Alabama.
Against the state, Const. Ala., art. I, §18.
Bills of attainder of treason by legislature prohibited, Const. Ala., art. I, §19.
Conviction not to work corruption of blood or forfeiture of estate, Const. Ala., art. I, §19.
Constitution of the United States, Const. U. S., Arts. I, §6; II, §4; III, §3; VI.
Elements of crime, §13A-11-2.

TREASON—Cont'd
Subversive activities, §31-9-20.
Witnesses.
Two witnesses required, §13A-11-2.

TREASURER OF STATE.
See STATE TREASURER.

TREATIES.
Supreme law of the land, Const. U. S., Art. VI.

TREES AND TIMBER.
Actions.
Damages for destruction, injury or removal of trees, §§35-14-1 to 35-14-3.
Arrests.
Fees, §9-13-24.
Attachment.
Employees' or laborers' liens, §§35-11-270 to 35-11-273.
Liens for stumpage, §35-11-21.
Auxiliary state forests, §§9-13-40 to 9-13-50.
See FORESTS AND FORESTRY.
Booms and bulkheads.
Opening or cutting loose without authority, §33-7-8.
Turning logs, timber or lumber out of boom without notice to owner, §33-7-7.
Chattels.
Conveyances of standing timber.
When standing timber and trees, etc., deemed chattels, §35-4-363.
Commercial code.
Sales.
Goods to be severed from realty, §7-2-107.
Secured transactions.
Description of land, §7-9-203.
Financing statement, §7-9-402.
Place of filing, §7-9-401.
Condemnation of timber theft equipment, §§9-13-220 to 9-13-227.
Citation of act.
Short title, §9-13-220.
Construction and interpretation.
Cumulative nature of provisions, §9-13-227.
Conviction for theft of timber or lumber.
Report to district attorney, §9-13-223.
Costs of proceedings.
Payment, §9-13-225.
From proceeds of sale, §§9-13-225, 9-13-226.
Cumulative nature of provisions, §9-13-227.
District attorneys.
Institution of proceedings, §9-13-224.
Reports to district attorney.
Conviction of person for theft of timber or lumber, §9-13-223.
Seizure, §9-13-222.

TREES AND TIMBER—Cont'd
Condemnation of timber theft equipment—Cont'd
District forester.
Delivery of equipment to, §9-13-221.
Duty of law enforcement officers, §9-13-221.
Institution of proceedings, §9-13-224.
Judgments, §9-13-225.
Presumptions.
Legal title to equipment, §9-13-224.
Records.
State forester, §9-13-225.
Sale.
Order of court, §9-13-225.
Use of proceeds, §9-13-226.
Secured transactions.
Notice to creditor, §9-13-224.
Seizure of vehicle or equipment.
Duties of law enforcement officers, §9-13-221.
Report to district attorney, §9-13-222.
Short title of act, §9-13-220.
Title of act.
Short title, §9-13-220.
Title to equipment.
Presumption as to vesting of legal title, §9-13-224.
Vehicles.
Seizure, §§9-13-221, 9-13-222.
Construction and interpretation.
Condemnation of timber theft equipment.
Cumulative nature of provisions, §9-13-227.
Conveyances of standing timber.
Chattels.
When standing timber deemed chattels, §35-4-363.
Cutting timber.
Reversion of title to uncut timber, §35-4-362.
Time for cutting, §35-4-360.
Removal of timber.
Time for removal, §35-4-360.
Reversion of title to uncut timber, §35-4-362.
Right of way over timberlands, §35-4-361.
Time for cutting and removal of timber, §35-4-360.
Transfers of standing timber, trees and cutting rights.
Void and inoperative as against certain persons, §35-4-92.
Uncut timber.
Reversion of title to uncut timber, §35-4-362.
Counties.
Developing, advertising and promoting timber resources, §11-3-11.

TREES AND TIMBER—Cont'd
Damages for destruction, injury or removal of trees, §§35-14-1 to 35-14-3.
Actions.
Court in which action may be brought, §35-14-3.
Further proceedings not barred, §35-14-3.
Joinder, §35-14-1.
Criminal proceedings.
Not barred, §35-14-3.
Fruit trees, §35-14-2.
Further proceedings.
Not barred, §35-14-3.
Generally, §35-14-1.
Joinder of actions, §35-14-1.
Limitation of actions, §35-14-3.
Ornamental trees, §35-14-2.
Owner of trees.
When owner of trees deemed owner of land, §35-14-1.
Deeds.
Conveyance of standing timber.
Generally, §§35-4-360 to 35-4-363.
Definitions.
Tree surgery, §2-28-1.
Destruction.
Damages for destruction, §§35-14-1 to 35-14-3.
Diseases.
Control of disease, §§2-25-1 to 2-25-22.
See NURSERIES.
Insect infestation or tree disease infection, §§9-13-120 to 9-13-126.
See FORESTS AND FORESTRY.
Pathologists.
See PLANTS.
Tree surgery, §§2-28-1 to 2-28-12.
Electricity.
Condemnation by electric utilities.
Right to remove timber, §37-4-130.
Employees' or laborers' liens, §§35-11-270 to 35-11-273.
Attachment, §35-11-273.
Declaration of lien, §35-11-270.
Enforcement of lien, §35-11-273.
Liens generally.
See LIENS.
Limitations, §35-11-272.
Priority of lien, §35-11-271.
Fees.
Arrests.
Arresting officers, §9-13-24.
Informers' fees, §9-13-24.
Tree surgery.
Permit fee, §2-28-4.
Forests and forestry.
General provisions.
See FORESTS AND FORESTRY.

TREES AND TIMBER—Cont'd
Fraud.
Fruit trees.
Delivery of fruit trees of different kind, variety etc., than sold, §2-25-40.
Limitation of prosecutions, §2-25-41.
Sale, etc., of falsely named trees, §2-25-42.
Fruit trees.
Damages for destruction, injury or removal, §35-14-2.
Delivery of fruit trees of different kind, variety, etc., than sold, §2-25-40.
Limitation period for prosecutions, §2-25-41.
Income tax.
Deductions.
Depletion allowance, §40-18-15.
Corporations, §40-18-35.
Informers.
Violation of chapter.
Fees, §9-13-24.
Injury.
Damages for injury, §§35-14-1 to 35-14-3.
Insects.
Control of insects, §§2-25-1 to 2-25-22.
See NURSERIES.
Insect infestation or tree disease infection, §§9-13-120 to 9-13-126.
See FORESTS AND FORESTRY.
Tree surgery. See within this heading, "Tree surgery."
Joinder.
Damages for destruction, injury or removal of trees.
Joinder of actions, §35-14-1.
Judgments.
Condemnation of timber theft equipment, §9-13-225.
Laborers' liens, §§35-11-270 to 35-11-273.
Landscape architects.
See LANDSCAPE ARCHITECTS.
Landscaping.
See LANDSCAPING.
Licenses.
Dealers, §40-12-121.
Funds from licenses pertaining to.
Disposition of proceeds, §40-12-28.
Lumberyards, §40-12-122.
Mills.
Veneer mills, planing mills, box factories, etc., §40-12-177.
Liens.
Employees' or laborers' liens, §§35-11-270 to 35-11-273.
Sawmills.
See SAWMILLS.
Stumpage, §§35-11-20, 35-11-21.
Limitation of actions.
Damages for destruction, injury or removal of trees, §35-14-3.

TREES AND TIMBER—Cont'd
Limitation of actions—Cont'd
Timber employees' or
laborers' liens,
§35-11-272.
Mobile harbor.
Fastening collection of logs,
lumber or timber to
beacon lights or pilings,
§33-7-10.
**Mortgages and deeds of
trust.**
Transfers of standing timber,
trees and cutting rights.
Void and inoperative as
aginst mortgagees
without notice or prior
recordation, §35-4-92.
Motor vehicle carriers.
Vehicles hauling trees or
timber.
Exemptions from chapter,
§37-3-4.
Motor vehicles.
Loads which must be
fastened, §32-5-75.
Size and weight of vehicles
transporting.
Exemption from article,
§32-9-25.
Unloading logs, lumber, etc.,
on or near highways,
§32-5-4.
Municipal corporations.
Public utilities.
Attachment of wires to
trees, §9-13-15.
Navigation.
Floating logs, timber or
lumber upon watercourse
without sufficient force
to prevent obstruction,
§33-7-6.
Obstructing streams used for
floating timber to
market, §33-7-5.
Opening or cutting loose of
boom without authority,
§33-7-8.
Turning logs, timber or
lumber out of boom
without notice to owner,
§33-7-7.
Notice.
Transfers of standing timber,
trees and cutting rights.
Void and inoperative as
against certain persons
without notice or prior
recordation, §35-4-92.
Nurseries.
See NURSERIES.
Ornamental trees.
Damages for destruction,
injury or removal,
§35-14-2.
Pathologists.
See PLANTS.
Penalties.
Tree surgery.
Violations of chapter or
rules or regulations,
§2-28-11.
Permits.
Tree surgery. See within this
heading, "Tree surgery."
Public lands.
Sale of timber from lands,
§9-15-18.

TREES AND TIMBER—Cont'd
Public lands—Cont'd
School lands.
Cruising of timber,
§9-15-37.
Sale of timber.
See PUBLIC LANDS.
Swamp and overflowed lands.
Sale of timber.
See PUBLIC LANDS.
Recordation.
Transfers of standing timber,
trees and cutting rights.
Void and inoperative as
against certain persons
without notice or prior
recordation, §35-4-92.
Records.
Condemnation of timber theft
equipment.
State forester, §9-13-225.
**Remainders, reversions and
executory interests.**
Conveyances of standing
timber.
Reversion of title to uncut
timber, §35-4-362.
Removal.
Timber.
Conveyances of standing
timber.
Time for removal,
§35-4-360.
Trees.
Damages, §§35-14-1 to
35-14-3.
Rights of way.
Conveyances of standing
timber.
Right of way over
timberlands,
§35-4-361.
Sales.
Condemnation of timber theft
equipment.
Sale of equipment seized,
§§9-13-225, 9-13-226.
Public lands.
Sale of timber from lands,
§9-15-18.
State parks.
Disposition and
expenditure of
revenues, §9-2-108.
Transfers of standing timber,
trees and cutting rights
inoperative and void as
against without notice or
prior recordation,
§35-4-92.
Sawmills.
See SAWMILLS.
Searches and seizures.
Condemnation of timber theft
equipment, §§9-13-220 to
9-13-227. See within this
heading, "Condemnation
of timber theft
equipment."
Secured transactions.
Condemnation of timber theft
equipment.
Notice to secured creditor,
§9-13-224.
Description of land, §7-9-203.
Place of filing, §7-9-401.
Seeds.
See SEEDS.

TREES AND TIMBER—Cont'd
Severance tax.
Forest products privilege and
severance taxes,
§§9-13-80 to 9-13-107.
See FORESTS AND
FORESTRY.
Southern pine.
State tree, §1-2-12.
Standing timber.
Conveyances of standing
timber. See within this
heading, "Conveyances of
standing timber."
Tax exemption, §40-11-1.
State forests.
See FORESTS AND
FORESTRY.
State parks.
Sale.
Disposition and
expenditure of
revenues, §9-2-108.
State tree, §1-2-12.
Stumpage.
Liens for stumpage.
Attachment, §35-11-21.
Declaration of lien,
§35-11-20.
Enforcement, §35-11-21.
Liens generally.
See LIENS.
Taxation.
Forest products privilege and
severance taxes,
§§9-13-80 to 9-13-107.
See FORESTS AND
FORESTRY.
Standing timber.
Exempted from taxation,
§40-11-1.
State forests.
Auxiliary state forests.
Taxation of timber on
lands designated as
auxiliary state
forests.
See FORESTS AND
FORESTRY.
Theft.
Condemnation of timber theft
equipment, §§9-13-220 to
9-13-227. See within this
heading, "Condemnation
of timber theft
equipment."
Tree surgery, §§2-28-1 to
2-28-12.
Appeals from denial or
revocation of permits,
§2-28-7.
Applicability of chapter,
§2-28-12.
Definitions, §2-28-1.
Examinations.
Applicants for permits,
§§2-28-4, 2-28-6.
Persons engaged in work
or services, §2-28-2.
Examining board, §2-28-2.
Fees.
Permit fees, §2-28-4.
Injunctions.
Restraining performance of
professional work or
services without
permit, §2-28-11.
Penalties, §2-28-11.
Commissioner of
agriculture may
impose, §2-2-18.

TREES AND TIMBER—Cont'd
Tree surgery—Cont'd
Penalties—Cont'd
Commissioner of
agriculture may
impose penalty,
§2-2-18.
Permits.
Appeal from denial or
revocation, §2-28-7.
Denial, §2-28-7.
Duration, §2-28-4.
Examination of applicants,
§§2-28-4, 2-28-6.
Experience of applicants.
Submission of statements
as to experience,
§2-28-4.
Fees, §2-28-4.
Injunctions to restrain
performance of
professional work or
services without
permit, §2-28-11.
Issuance, §2-28-4.
Qualifications of
applicants.
Submission of statements
as to, §2-28-4.
Required for performance
of work or services
governed by chapter,
§2-28-4.
Revocation, §2-28-7.
Testing of applicants,
§2-28-4.
Training of applicants.
Submission of statements
as to, §2-28-4.
Rules and regulations.
Penalties for violations,
§2-28-11.
Qualifications and practice
of persons engaged in
work or services
governed by chapter,
§2-28-3.
Violations of chapter.
Penalties for violations,
§2-28-11.
Violations of chapter.
Informers.
Fees, §9-13-24.
Tree surgery.
Penalties for violation,
§2-28-11.
Waters and watercourses.
Floating logs, timber or
lumber upon watercourse
without sufficient force
to prevent obstruction,
§33-7-6.
Obstructing streams used for
floating timber to
market, §33-7-5.
Opening or cutting loose of
boom without authority,
§33-7-8.
Turning logs, timber or
lumber out of boom
without notice to owner,
§33-7-7.

TRESPASS.
Actions.
Personal property.
Bailments, §6-5-263.
Generally, §6-5-262.

TRESPASS—Cont'd
Actions—Cont'd
Person having bare title to
real property.
Action for trespass by,
§6-5-214.
Right of action against
executor or
administrator, §6-5-90.
Airports.
Vehicles.
Trespass and operation on
airports, landing fields,
etc., §4-2-7.
Animals.
Wanton, malicious, etc.,
destruction, injury, etc.,
of animal of another.
Proof of trespassing by
animal in mitigation
or justification,
§3-1-11.
Boats.
Warnings.
Trespass after warning on
booms, bulkheads or
piles erected by
riparian proprietors,
§33-7-9.
Booms and bulkheads.
Warnings.
Trespass after warning on
booms, bulkheads or
piles erected by
riparian proprietors,
§33-7-9.
Bridges.
Rules and regulations.
Highway department,
§23-1-59.
Buildings.
Defined, §13A-7-1.
Continuous trespass.
Damages, §6-5-217.
Contracts.
Actions on premises in
writing not under seal.
Six year limitation,
§6-2-34.
Decedents' estates.
Right of action against
executor or
administrator, §6-5-90.
Definitions, §13A-7-1.
**Duty of care owed persons
on premises for sporting
or recreational purposes,**
§§35-15-1 to 35-15-5.
Dwellings.
Defined, §13A-7-1.
Education.
Reports of property damage
and physical assaults on
students and school
personnel, §16-1-24.
Enter or remain unlawfully.
Defined, §13A-7-1.
**Executors and
administrators.**
Right of action against,
§6-5-90.
**First degree criminal
trespass.**
Class A misdemeanor,
§13A-7-2.
Elements of crime, §13A-7-2.
Force.
Use of force to prevent
commission of trespass,
§13A-3-25.

TRESPASS—Cont'd
**Forcible entry and unlawful
detainer.**
Action of trespass not
precluded, §6-6-316.
Highways.
Rules and regulations.
Highway department,
§23-1-59.
Indictments.
Unlawful entry after
warning.
Form of indictment,
§15-8-150.
Limitation of actions, §6-2-34.
Livestock.
Destruction or injury of
animal of another.
Proof of trespassing by
animal in mitigation
or justification,
§3-1-11.
Fences.
Liability of owner of
animal breaking into
lands not enclosed by
lawful fence for
trespass or damages,
§3-4-6.
Running at large.
See LIVESTOCK.
Personal property.
Actions.
Bailments, §6-5-263.
Generally, §6-5-262.
Detention or conversion.
Six year limitation,
§6-2-34.
Six year limitation, §6-2-34.
Premises.
Defined, §13A-7-1.
Prisons and prisoners.
Trespassing about prisons.
Penalties, §14-11-9.
Public lands.
School lands.
Enforcement of state
trespass laws,
§9-15-34.
Swamp and overflowed lands.
Enforcement of state
trespass laws,
§9-15-35.
Real property.
Six year limitation, §6-2-34.
Right of way.
Unlawful interference,
§6-5-216.
Rules and regulations.
Bridges.
Highway department,
§23-1-59.
Highways.
Highway department,
§23-1-59.
**Second degree criminal
trespass.**
Class C misdemeanor,
§13A-7-3.
Elements of crime, §13A-7-3.
Surveillance.
Criminal surveillance while
trespassing in private
place, §13A-11-32.
Surveys and surveyors.
Division of land surveys.
Immunity from arrest for
trespass, §35-2-32.
**Third degree criminal
trespass.**
Elements of crime, §13A-7-4.

TRESPASS—Cont'd
Third degree criminal trespass—Cont'd
Violation, §13A-7-4.
Trees and timber.
Cutting timber on lands of another.
See TREES AND TIMBER.
Venue.
Actions against individuals for trespass to lands, §6-3-2.

TRIAL.
Appeals to circuit courts.
De novo trial in circuit court, §12-22-113.
Assignment of cases for trial, ARCP, Rule 40.
Calendar.
Setting of cases, ARCP, Rule 40 (a).
Capital offenses.
See CAPITAL OFFENSES.
Circuit courts.
Conduct in open court, ARCP, Rule 77 (b).
Consolidation, ARCP, Rule 42 (a).
Form of motion, ARCP, Form 72.
Constitution of Alabama.
Right to speedy, public trial, Const. Ala., art. I, §6.
Constitution of the United States.
Public trial, Const. U. S., Amendment VI.
Speedy trial, Const. U. S., Amendment VI.
Construction and interpretation.
Crime victims' court attendance, §15-14-51.
Corporations.
Prosecution of corporations.
When case stands for trial, §10-7-2.
Costs.
See COSTS.
Counterclaims and cross-claims.
Separate trials, ARCP, Rule 13 (i).
Court.
Trial by court, ARCP, Rule 39.
Crime victims' court attendance, §§15-14-50 to 15-14-57.
Citation of article, §15-14-50.
Construction of article, §15-14-51.
Criminal offense.
Defined, §15-14-52.
Definitions, §15-14-52.
Designation of representative.
When victim unable to attend, §15-14-56.
Effect of nonattendance of representative, §15-14-57.
Exclusion from courtroom.
Exemption from rule requiring exclusion of witnesses from court, §15-14-55.
Removal generally, §15-14-54.

TRIAL—Cont'd
Crime victims' court attendance—Cont'd
Exclusion from courtroom —Cont'd
Victim may not be excluded, §15-14-54.
Legislative findings, §15-14-51.
Nonattendance of representative.
Effect, §15-14-57.
Person.
Defined, §15-14-52.
Presence in courtroom.
Right of victim to be present, §15-14-53.
Purpose of article, §15-14-51.
Removal generally, §15-14-54.
Representatives.
Designation when victim unable to attend, §15-14-56.
Effect of nonattendance of representative, §15-14-57.
Right of victim to be present in courtroom, §15-14-53.
Seating at counsel table of prosecutor, §15-14-53.
Short title of act, §15-14-50.
Victim.
Defined, §15-14-52.
Exclusion from courtroom not allowed, §15-14-54.
Witnesses.
Exemption from rule requiring exclusion from court, §15-14-55.
Criminal law and procedure.
Crime victims' court attendance, §§15-14-50 to 15-14-57. See within this heading, "Crime victims' court attendance."
Preliminary hearings, §§15-11-1 to 15-11-15.
See PRELIMINARY HEARINGS.
Verdict, §§15-17-2 to 15-17-5.
Defenses.
See DEFENSES.
Definitions.
Crime victims' court attendance, §15-14-52.
Depositions.
Use at trial, §12-21-262; ARCP, Rule 32.
District courts.
Generally, §12-12-3.
Eminent domain.
See EMINENT DOMAIN.
Executors and administrators.
Insolvent estates.
Trial of issue of insolvency to be by jury, §43-2-705.
Removal, §43-2-296.
Exemptions from levy and sale under process.
Contest of exemption claims, §§6-10-30, 6-10-31.
Fair trial tax, §§12-19-250 to 12-19-254.

TRIAL—Cont'd
Findings by court, ARCP, Rule 52.
Stay on motion for amendment to findings or for additional findings, ARCP, Rule 62 (b).
Guardian and ward.
Uniform guardianship and protective proceedings act.
Jury trial, §26-2A-35.
Hearings generally.
See HEARINGS.
Highways.
Closing and vacating streets, alleys and highways.
Appeals, §23-4-5.
Interrogatories.
Use at trial, ARCP, Rule 33 (b).
Joint or several trials.
Election by jointly indicted defendants, §15-14-20.
Jury.
Advisory jury, ARCP, Rule 39 (c).
General provisions.
See JURY.
Selection.
Procedure, §18-1A-151.
Trial by consent, ARCP, Rule 39 (c).
Trial by jury, ARCP, Rule 39 (a).
Guardian and ward.
Uniform guardianship and protective proceedings act, §26-2A-35.
Right to trial by jury, Const. Ala., art. I, §11; Const. U. S., Amendments VI, VII.
Waiver, §18-1A-151; ARCP, Rule 38 (d).
Juveniles.
Youthful offenders, §§15-19-1, 15-19-3 to 15-19-5.
See YOUTHFUL OFFENDERS.
Landlord and tenant.
Liens for advances and rent of lands.
Attachment, §35-9-36.
Liens.
Attachment, §35-11-6.
Minors.
Youthful offenders, §§15-19-1, 15-19-3 to 15-19-5.
Motor vehicles.
Uniform traffic infractions.
Defendant's appearance.
Plea and waiver of trial, ARJA, Rule 19.
Municipal courts.
Cases to be tried by judge without jury, §12-14-6.
Powers of courts as to trial, §12-14-10.
New trial.
See NEW TRIAL.
Notice.
Notice that case has been placed on trial docket, ARCP, Rule 40 (b).

TRIAL—Cont'd
Omission in testimony.
Court may allow introduction
before argument
concluded, §15-14-4.
Partition.
Crops.
Trial by jury, §35-6-122.
Preliminary hearings.
General provisions, §§15-11-1
to 15-11-15.
See PRELIMINARY
HEARINGS.
Preparation for trial.
Discovery of trial
preparation, ARCP, Rule
26 (b).
Public trial, Const. Ala., art.
I, §6; Const. U. S.,
Amendment VI.
Quo warranto, §6-6-593.
Rules of criminal procedure,
ARCrP, Rules 15.3 (c), 15.4
(c).
Separate trials, ARCP, Rules
20 (b), 42 (b).
Counterclaims and cross-
claims, ARCP, Rule 13
(i).
Setting cases for trial, ARCP,
Rule 40 (a).
Capital cases, §15-14-3.
Defendant not to be tried
until case on docket one
day, §15-14-2.
Duty of circuit clerks,
§15-14-1.
Small claims.
Rules of procedure, ASCR,
Rule J.
Speedy trial, Const. Ala., art.
I, §6; Const. U. S.,
Amendment VI.
Subpoena for trial, ARCP,
Rule 45 (e).
Taxation.
Assessments.
Appeals, §40-7-47.
Costs.
See COSTS.
Fair trial tax, §§12-19-250 to
12-19-254.
Sale of land for taxes,
§§4-10-8 to 4-10-10.
Trial tax, §40-1-38.
Tender.
Answer of tender, §6-8-100.
Judgment on, §6-8-100.
Transcripts.
Record on appeal.
See APPEALS.
Venue.
See VENUE.
Verdict.
General provisions.
See VERDICT.
Wills.
Contesting validity of wills
generally.
See WILLS.
Youthful offenders,
§§15-19-1, 15-19-3 to
15-19-5.

TRICHINOSIS.
Notifiable diseases,
§§22-11A-1 to 22-11A-38.
See DISEASES.

TROOPERS.
See STATE POLICE.

TROY STATE UNIVERSITY.
Administration of university.
Board of trustees.
Powers, §16-56-6.
Agents.
Default, etc., not to work
forfeiture, §16-56-11.
**American legion
scholarships.**
See UNIVERSITIES AND
COLLEGES.
Board of trustees.
Administration of university.
Powers, §16-56-6.
Appointment of members,
§16-56-3.
Body corporate, §16-56-1.
Compensation of members,
§16-56-3.
Composition, §16-56-3.
Courses of instruction.
Powers of board, §16-56-6.
Created, §16-56-3.
Default, etc., not to work
forfeiture, §16-56-11.
Degrees.
Powers of board, §16-56-6.
Endowment funds.
Investment, §16-13-2.
Expenses of members,
§16-56-3.
Payment, §16-56-9.
Governor.
Ex officio president of
board, §16-56-3.
Jurisdiction.
Transfer of jurisdiction,
etc., to board, §16-56-7.
Legislature.
Reports to legislature,
§16-56-10.
Meetings, §16-56-4.
Membership, §16-56-3.
Organization of university.
Powers, §16-56-6.
Quorum, §16-56-5.
Reports to legislature,
§16-56-10.
State superintendent of
education.
Member of board, §16-56-3.
Terms of members, §16-56-3.
Transfer of jurisdiction, etc.,
to board, §16-56-7.
Tuition.
Powers of board, §16-56-6.
Vacancies, §16-56-8.
Body corporate, §16-56-1.
**Commission of higher
education.**
General provisions.
See UNIVERSITIES AND
COLLEGES.
Corporation.
Body corporate, §16-56-1.
Rights, privileges,
responsibilities, etc.,
§16-56-2.
Courses of instruction.
Board of trustees.
Powers of board, §16-56-6.
Degrees.
Board of trustees.
Powers of board, §16-56-6.
Faculty.
Appointment, §16-56-6.
Eminent scholars trust fund,
§§16-61-1 to 16-61-10.
See UNIVERSITIES AND
COLLEGES.
Removal, §16-56-6.

TROY STATE UNIVERSITY
—Cont'd
Faculty—Cont'd
Salary, §16-56-6.
Funds.
Eminent scholars trust fund,
§§16-61-1 to 16-61-10.
See UNIVERSITIES AND
COLLEGES.
Gifts.
Not to fail for informality,
§16-56-11.
Governor.
Board of trustees.
Ex officio president of
board, §16-56-3.
Grants.
Not to fail for informality,
§16-56-11.
Jurisdiction.
Board of trustees.
Transfer of jurisdiction,
etc., to board, §16-56-7
Legislature.
Board of trustees.
Reports to legislature,
§16-56-10.
**Marine environmental
sciences consortium,**
§§16-45-1 to 16-45-5.
Names.
Grant or gift not to fail for
misnomer, §16-56-11.
Nursing.
School of nursing, §§16-56-13
to 16-56-15.
Officers.
Appointment, §16-56-6.
Default, etc., not to work
forfeiture, §16-56-11.
Police officers, §16-56-12.
Removal, §16-56-6.
Salaries, §16-56-6.
Organization of university.
Board of trustees.
Powers, §16-56-6.
Police.
Generally, §§16-22-1,
16-22-2.
Property.
Rights, privileges,
responsibilities, etc., of
corporation, §16-56-2.
Reports.
Board of trustees.
Reports to legislature,
§16-56-10.
Salaries.
Faculty, §16-56-6.
Officers, §16-56-6.
Powers of board of trustees,
§16-56-6.
Scholarships.
American Legion
scholarships, §§16-31-1
to 16-31-4.
School of nursing, §§16-56-13
to 16-56-15.
School of nursing.
Scholarships.
Amount, §16-56-15.
Conditions, §16-56-15.
Distribution, §16-56-13.
Eligibility.
Selection of recipients,
§16-56-15.
Who eligible, §16-56-14.
**State superintendent of
education.**
Ex officio member of board of
trustees, §16-56-3.

TROY STATE UNIVERSITY
—Cont'd
Trustees.
Board of trustees. See within
this heading, "Board of
trustees."
Tuition.
Board of trustees.
Powers of board, §16-56-6.
TRUANCY.
Juvenile proceedings,
§§16-28-21 to 16-28-23.
School attendance.
See EDUCATION.
TRUCKS.
General provisions.
See MOTOR VEHICLES.
Motor vehicle carriers.
See MOTOR VEHICLE
CARRIERS.
TRUST AND TRUSTEES.
Cemeteries.
Charitable trusts.
Conveyances, devises, etc.,
for preservation,
repair, etc., of burial
places deemed to
create charitable
trusts, §11-17-13.
Counties.
Cemeteries.
Conveyances, devises, etc.,
for preservation,
repair, etc., of burial
places deemed to
create charitable
trusts, §11-17-13.
TRUST COMPANIES.
See BANKS AND FINANCIAL
INSTITUTIONS.
TRUSTS AND TRUSTEES.
Accounts and accounting.
Evidence.
Books of account kept by
deceased trustee.
Admissibility in
evidence, §12-21-32.
Accumulation trust.
Minors.
Application of income for
accumulation to
support of minor,
§35-4-253.
Term, §35-4-252.
**Alabama Agricultural and
Mechanical University.**
Board of trustees, §§16-49-1
to 16-49-30.
See ALABAMA
AGRICULTURAL
AND MECHANICAL
UNIVERSITY.
Alabama school of trades.
Board of trustees,
§§16-60-210 to 16-60-221.
See TRADE SCHOOLS.
Alabama State University.
Board of trustees, §§16-50-20
to 16-50-30.
See ALABAMA STATE
UNIVERSITY.
Alabama trust fund, Const.
Ala., amd. 450.
Animals.
Principal and income.
Principal comprising
animals, §19-3-277.

TRUSTS AND TRUSTEES
—Cont'd
Appointment of trustees.
New trustees.
Power of circuit court to
fill vacancy, §19-3-250.
When circuit court must
appoint, §19-3-251.
Removal of trust estate from
another state, §§19-3-230
to 19-3-232.
Successor trustees, §19-3-212.
Attorneys at law.
Fees.
Costs in trust proceedings,
§34-3-60.
Auburn University, §§16-48-1
to 16-48-12.
See AUBURN
UNIVERSITY.
Bankruptcy.
Secured transactions.
Priority over unperfected
security interests,
§7-9-301.
**Banks and financial
institutions.**
Administration of common
trust funds, §§15-12A-1
to 15-12A-15.
See BANKS AND
FINANCIAL
INSTITUTIONS.
Regulation of trust business,
§§5-11A-1 to 5-11A-12.
See BANKS AND
FINANCIAL
INSTITUTIONS.
**Bequests to trustee of
existing trust,** §43-8-140.
Bonds, surety.
Express trusts for payment
or security of debts,
§§19-3-20 to 19-3-23.
Removal of trust estate from
another state.
Bond of new trustee,
§19-3-233.
Tennessee Valley Authority.
Investment of trust estate
in bonds of authority,
§19-3-127.
Business trusts, §§19-3-60 to
19-3-67.
Actions.
Suits against trust,
§19-3-66.
Attachments.
Property subject to
attachment, §19-3-66.
Beneficial owners.
Liability, §19-3-63.
Certificates of ownership,
§19-3-63.
Declaration of trust.
Contents and recordation,
§19-3-64.
Defined, §19-3-60.
Duration, §19-3-65.
Establishment, §19-3-61.
Execution.
Property subject to
execution, §19-3-66.
Lawful purposes, §19-3-61.
Liability of beneficial owners,
§19-3-63.
Liability of trustees,
§19-3-62.
Powers of trustees, §19-3-62.

TRUSTS AND TRUSTEES
—Cont'd
Business trusts—Cont'd
Recordation.
Declaration of trust,
§19-3-64.
Restraint of alienation not
violated, §19-3-65.
Rules against perpetuities.
Not violated, §19-3-65.
Suits against trust, §19-3-65.
Taxation, §19-3-67.
Cemeteries.
Charitable trusts, §§11-17-13
to 11-17-16.
Burial societies,
cemeteries, etc.,
empowered to accept
conveyances, devises,
etc., and to act as
trustees, §11-17-14.
Empowered to accept
conveyances, devises,
etc., and to act as
trustees, §11-17-14.
Perpetual trusts.
Terms and conditions,
§11-17-15.
Trust created by
conveyances, devises,
etc., may be
perpetual, §11-17-15.
Validation, etc., of prior
conveyances, bequests,
etc., §11-17-16.
Generally, §§19-3-300 to
19-3-303.
Charitable trusts.
Cemeteries, §§11-17-13 to
11-17-16.
Circuit courts.
Removal of trust estate to
another state.
Power of circuit court to
authorize, §19-3-190.
Common trust funds.
Banks and financial
institutions.
Administration, etc.,
§§5-12A-1 to 5-12A-15.
See BANKS AND
FINANCIAL
INSTITUTIONS.
Conflict of laws.
Investment of trust estate.
Repeal of conflicting
statutes, §19-3-120.
Constitution of Alabama.
Regulation of trusts, Const.
Ala., art. IV, §103.
Conveyances.
Powers of disposition,
§§35-4-290 to 35-4-306.
See CONVEYANCES.
Corporations.
Application of corporations
provisions, §10-2A-336.
Foreign corporations.
Acting in fiduciary
capacity, §§10-2A-21 to
10-2A-224.1.
See CORPORATIONS.
Voting of shares by trustee,
§10-2A-53.
Voting trusts.
Creation by stockholders,
§10-2A-55.

TRUSTS AND TRUSTEES
—Cont'd

Corrections.
Institution finance authority.
Bond issues.
Investment of trust
funds, §14-2-17.

Cotrustees.
Survivorship, §19-3-252.

Counties.
Acquisition of lands for
public purposes.
Trust fund, §11-18-3.
Claims and demands against
counties.
Verification, §11-12-6.
Sinking funds.
Trustee of sinking fund,
§§11-81-24, 11-81-25.
Warrants for construction of
public buildings, bridges
and roads.
Deemed legal investments
for trust funds,
§11-28-5.
Warrants or certificates of
indebtedness for sanitary
sewer systems.
Investment of trust funds,
§11-9-4.
Waterworks systems
warrants.
Investment of trust funds
in warrants, §11-9-25.

Creation.
Lawful purpose.
Trust may be created for
lawful purpose,
§35-4-251.

Creditors.
Trust void as to creditors
without notice,
§35-4-256.

Credit unions.
Deposits for trust
beneficiaries, §5-17-15.

Crime victims compensation.
Collateral source.
Funds recovered from
collateral source held
in trust for
commission, §15-23-14.
Disposition of trust funds,
§15-23-14.

Cy pres act, §35-4-251.

Death.
Books of account kept by
deceased trustee.
Admissibility in evidence,
§12-21-32.
Powers of disposition.
Execution of power upon
death of trustee with
right of selection,
§35-4-298.
Representative of deceased
sole trustee to settle
with succeeding trustee,
§19-3-253.
Survivorship between
cotrustees, §19-3-252.
Trust estate not descendible
upon death of trustee,
§35-4-258.
Trusts for employees or self-
employed persons.
Death benefit plans,
§35-4-259.

TRUSTS AND TRUSTEES
—Cont'd

Debts.
Express trusts for payment
or security of debts,
§§19-3-20 to 19-3-41.
Accounts.
Auditing of account,
§19-3-37.
Duty of trustee to
render, §19-3-35.
Examination of account,
§19-3-37.
Allowance of claims.
Claims presented and
not objected to stand
allowed, §19-3-31.
Order allowing or
disallowing claim,
§19-3-34.
Appeals, §19-3-38.
Appraisers.
Appointment, §19-3-25.
Duties, §19-3-25.
Bad debts.
Compromise or sale,
§19-3-39.
Bonds, surety.
Application for order
requiring trustee to
give bond.
Contents, §19-3-21.
Hearing, §19-3-22.
Notice of hearing,
§19-3-21.
Right of creditors to
apply for order,
§19-3-20.
Failure of trustee to give
bond, §19-3-23.
Order requiring trustee
to give bond,
§19-3-22.
Application for,
§§19-3-20, 19-3-21.
Claims docket, §19-3-30.
Compromise of bad debts,
§19-3-39.
Creditors.
Notice to creditors,
§§19-3-28, 19-3-36,
19-3-40.
Disallowing claims.
Order allowing or
disallowing claim,
§19-3-34.
Docket.
Claims docket, §19-3-30.
Evidence.
Admissibility at
hearings, §19-3-38.
Hearings.
Application for order
requiring trustee to
give bond, §19-3-22.
Evidence.
Admissibility at
hearings, §19-3-38.
Objections to claims,
§19-3-34.
Inventories.
Duty of trustee to make
inventory, §19-3-24.
Filing of copies, §19-3-24.
Supplemental
inventories,
§19-3-24.
Notice to creditors,
§§19-3-28, 19-3-36,
19-3-40.

TRUSTS AND TRUSTEES
—Cont'd

Debts—Cont'd
Express trusts for payment
or security of debts
—Cont'd
Objections to claims.
Conduct of hearing,
§19-3-34.
Filing, §19-3-32.
Hearing.
Conduct, §19-3-34.
Time, §19-3-33.
Notice, §19-3-33.
Order allowing or
disallowing claim,
§19-3-34.
Time for hearing,
§19-3-33.
Petition for administration.
Contents, §19-3-26.
Submission to circuit
judge, §19-3-27.
When filed, §19-3-26.
Presentation of claims,
§19-3-29.
Claims presented and
not objected to stand
allowed, §19-3-31.
Notice to creditors,
§19-3-28.
Order designating time
for, §19-3-27.
Receipt, §19-3-29.
Time for presenting,
§19-3-27.
Real estate.
Sale, §19-3-40.
Removal of trustee,
§19-3-41.
Sale of bad debts, §19-3-39.
Sale of real estate,
§19-3-40.
Settlement.
Notice to creditors,
§19-3-36.
Time for settlement,
§19-3-36.
When settlements
compelled, §19-3-41.
Successor trustees.
Appointment, §19-3-23.
Verification of claims,
§19-3-29.

Decedents' estates.
Trust estate not descendible
upon death of trustee,
§35-4-258.

Declaratory judgments.
Questions on administration
of trust, §6-6-225.

Deeds of trust.
See MORTGAGES AND
DEEDS OF TRUST.

Definitions.
Generation-skipping tax,
§19-5-1.
Generation-skipping
transfer, §40-15A-1.
Principal and income,
§19-3-270.

Descent and distribution.
Trust estate not descendible
upon death of trustee,
§35-4-258.

**Devise to trustee of existing
trust,** §43-8-140.

Discharge of trustee.
Survivorship between
cotrustees, §19-3-252.

TRUSTS AND TRUSTEES
—Cont'd
Education.
Board of school trustees.
General provisions,
§§16-10-1 to 16-10-11.
See EDUCATION.
Support and maintenance of
relatives.
Express trust for support
and maintenance,
§19-3-1.
Employers and employees.
Income tax.
Contributions to trust
made by employer,
§40-18-25.
Trusts for employees or self-
employed persons,
§35-4-259.
Estate of trustee, §19-3-3.
Evidence.
Books of accounts kept by
deceased trustee.
Admissibility in evidence,
§12-21-32.
Express trusts.
Payment or security of debts.
See within this heading,
"Debts."
Spendthrift trusts.
Authorized, §19-3-1.
Support and maintenance of
relatives, §19-3-1.
Extinguishment of trust,
§19-3-2.
Fees.
Allowance of fees, §19-3-6.
Attorney's fees paid as part
of costs, §34-3-60.
Removal of trust estate from
another state.
Register or clerk,
§19-3-234.
Fiduciaries generally.
See FIDUCIARIES.
Foundation.
Private foundations,
§§19-3-300 to 19-3-303.
Garnishment.
Money or effects in hands of
trustee, §6-6-413.
Generation-skipping tax,
§§19-5-1 to 19-5-12.
Administration of chapter,
§40-15A-13.
Allocation of exemptions,
§19-5-2.
Division of trust, §§19-5-3
to 19-5-6.
Amount, §40-15A-2.
Applicability of chapter,
§§19-5-11, 19-5-12.
Assessment.
Final assessment,
§40-15A-6.
Computation, §40-15A-5.
Construction and
interpretation.
Applicability of chapter,
§§19-5-11, 19-5-12.
Purpose of chapter,
§19-5-8.
Definitions, §19-5-1.
Generation-skipping
transfer, §40-15A-1.
Delinquent tax.
Interest, §40-15A-11.
Time limit for collection of,
§40-15A-10.

TRUSTS AND TRUSTEES
—Cont'd
Generation-skipping tax
—Cont'd
Division of trust.
Allocation of distributions
from separate trusts,
§19-5-7.
More than one beneficiary
or class, §19-5-5.
Qualified terminable
interest property trust,
§19-5-6.
Separate trust for exempt
and nonexempt
property, §19-5-3.
Separate trust for property
transferred from
another trust in order
to preclude or
minimize GST,
§19-5-4.
Evidence.
Required production of
evidence, §40-15A-6.
Exemptions.
Allocation, §19-5-2.
Exercise of authority by
fiduciary, §19-5-9.
Failure to timely file,
§40-15A-6.
Federal returns.
Duplicates, §40-15A-5.
Fiduciaries.
Exercise of authority by
fiduciary, §19-5-9.
Not liable for acts in good
faith, §19-5-10.
Force and effect of judgment,
§40-15A-8.
Levy, §40-15A-2.
Liability.
Fiduciary not liable for
acts in good faith,
§19-5-10.
Lien, §40-15A-9.
Payment, §40-15A-4.
Delinquent payments.
Collection.
Time limit,
§40-15A-10.
Interest, §40-15A-11.
Demand not to exceed total
tax, §40-15A-7.
Extension of time,
§40-15A-7.
Refund of excessive
payments, §40-15A-12.
Proceeds.
Disposition, §40-15A-5.
Property outside of state.
Allocation of tax,
§40-15A-14.
Protest.
Notice, §40-15A-8.
Purpose of chapter, §19-5-8.
Refunds.
Application for refund of
excessive payments,
§40-15A-12.
Taxable property, §40-15A-3.
Property charge,
§40-15A-4.
Gifts.
Satisfaction of pecuniary
gifts by distribution of
property in kind, §19-3-9.
Group trusts.
Trusts for employees or self-
employed persons,
§35-4-259.

TRUSTS AND TRUSTEES
—Cont'd
Hospitals.
Trusts for payment of
liability claims against
hospitals, §§22-21-240 to
22-21-243.
Housing.
National housing act.
Investment of trust estate
in debts incurred
under, §19-3-128.
Income.
Accumulation trust.
Application to support of
minor, §35-4-253.
Principal and income,
§§19-3-270 to 19-3-282.
See within this heading,
"Principal and income."
Income tax.
Application of tax, §40-18-25.
Computation of net income of
trust, §40-18-25.
Employers and employees.
Contributions to trust
made by employer,
§40-18-25.
Exemptions.
Trust income, §40-18-25.
Gain or loss.
Basis of property.
Gift or transfer in trust,
§40-18-6.
Payment of tax by fiduciary,
§40-18-25.
Returns.
Responsibility of fiduciary
for making, §40-18-25.
Indemnification of trustee,
§19-3-4.
Insurance.
Investment of trust estate.
Life, endowment or
annuity contracts,
§19-3-125.
Mutual aid associations.
Trustees, §27-30-30.
Policies or proceeds.
Trusts consisting of,
§35-4-260.
Trusteed assets of alien
insurers.
See INSURANCE.
Intemperates and inebriates.
Waste of estate, §§6-6-522 to
6-6-526.
Investment of trust estate,
§§19-3-120 to 19-3-132.
Annuity contracts, §19-3-125.
Authority.
Judgment on hearing,
§19-3-132.
Notice of petition to obtain,
§19-3-131.
Petition to obtain
authority, §19-3-131.
Authorization of investment
of trust funds in bonds or
stock of private
corporations prohibited,
Const. Ala., art. IV, §74.
Authorized investments,
§§19-3-120, 19-3-120.1.
Classes of authorized
investments, §19-3-120.
Collective investment funds,
§19-3-120.1.
Common trusts, §19-3-120.1.
Conflicting statutes.
Repeal, §19-3-120.

TRUSTS AND TRUSTEES
—Cont'd
Investment of trust estate
—Cont'd
Counties.
Tax anticipation bonds,
etc., of certain
counties, §19-3-126.
Endowment contracts,
§19-3-125.
Housing and urban
development.
Mortgages insured by
secretary, §§19-3-123,
19-3-124.
Securities issued or insured
by secretary,
§19-3-122.
Insurance.
Life, endowment or
annuity contracts,
§19-3-125.
Interest of investment
companies and trusts,
§19-3-120.1.
Liability of trustees.
General rules of law
govern, §19-3-129.
Life insurance contracts,
§19-3-125.
National housing act.
Debts incurred under act,
§19-3-128.
Outside state, §19-3-130.
Petition to obtain authority,
§19-3-131.
Restrictions on investment of
trust funds by trustees
in private corporations,
Const. Ala., amd. 40.
Standards for fiduciary
investment and
management,
§19-3-120.2.
Tennessee Valley Authority.
Bonds of authority,
§19-3-127.
Veterans.
Debts incurred under acts
of congress relating to
benefits, §19-3-128.
Warrants.
Interest-bearing warrants,
§19-3-121.
**Jacksonville State
University.**
Board of trustees, §§16-52-1
to 16-52-15.
See JACKSONVILLE
STATE UNIVERSITY.
**Junior college for Franklin,
Marion and Winston
counties.**
Board of trustees.
See JUNIOR COLLEGES.
**Junior college for Jackson
and DeKalb counties.**
Board of trustees, §§16-60-50
to 16-60-67.
See JUNIOR COLLEGES.
Labor.
Trusts for employees or self-
employed persons,
§35-4-259.
Liability of trust estate,
§§19-3-100 to 19-3-107. See
within this heading, "Trust
estate."

TRUSTS AND TRUSTEES
—Cont'd
Livingston University.
Board of trustees, §§16-53-1
to 16-53-12.
See LIVINGSTON
UNIVERSITY.
Management.
Standards for fiduciary
investment and
management,
§19-3-120.2.
Minors.
Accumulation trust.
Application of income for
accumulation to
support of minor,
§35-4-253.
Transfers to minors
generally, §§35-5A-1 to
35-5A-24.
See TRANSFERS TO
MINORS.
Misapplication of assets,
§19-3-105.
Tracing misapplied assets,
§19-3-106.
Municipal corporations.
Sinking fund, §§11-81-24,
11-81-25.
Natural resources.
Principal and income.
Disposition of natural
resources, §19-3-278.
Notice.
Creditors or purchasers
without notice.
Trust void as to, §35-4-256.
Recording as notice of trust,
§35-4-257.
Settlement, §19-3-5.
Oral testimony.
Trust concerning lands
required to be in writing,
§35-4-255.
Parol testimony.
Trust concerning lands
required to be in writing,
§35-4-255.
Payment to trustee.
Responsibility of payor for,
§35-4-254.
Penny trust fund, §§41-15A-1
to 41-15A-5.
See PENNY TRUST FUND.
Pensions.
Trusts for employees or self-
employed persons,
§35-4-259.
Pour-over trusts, §43-8-140.
Powers of disposition.
Conveyances, §§35-4-290 to
35-4-306.
See CONVEYANCES.
Principal and income,
§§19-3-270 to 19-3-282.
Animals.
Principal comprising
animals, §19-3-277.
Applicability of article,
§19-3-271.
Apportionment of income,
§19-3-273.
Business.
Principal used in business,
§19-3-276.
Definitions, §19-3-270.
Depletion.
Principal subject to
depletion, §19-3-279.

TRUSTS AND TRUSTEES
—Cont'd
Principal and income
—Cont'd
Discount obligations,
§19-3-275.
Disposition, §19-3-272.
Dividends.
Corporate dividends,
§19-3-274.
Division, §19-3-272.
Expenses.
Nontrust estates,
§19-3-282.
Trust estates, §19-3-281.
Natural resources.
Disposition, §19-3-278.
Powers of settlor, §19-3-271.
Premium and discount
obligations, §19-3-275.
Principal comprising
animals, §19-3-277.
Principal subject to depletion,
§19-3-279.
Principal used in business,
§19-3-276.
Settlor.
Powers, §19-3-271.
Share rights, §19-3-274.
Unproductive estate,
§19-3-280.
**Private foundations,
charitable trusts and
split-interest trusts,**
§§19-3-300 to 19-3-303.
Amendment of trust
instrument.
Power to amend, §19-3-301.
Attorney general.
Rights and powers not
impaired, §19-3-302.
Cemeteries, §§11-17-13 to
11-17-16.
Courts.
Rights and powers not
impaired, §19-3-302.
Future provisions of federal
internal revenue laws
included, §19-3-303.
Taxation.
Future provisions of
federal internal
revenue laws included,
§19-3-303.
Trustee not to engage in
certain acts subjecting
trust to federal
taxation, §19-3-300.
Professional corporations.
Voting trusts.
All trustees and
beneficiaries to be
qualified persons,
§10-4-392.
Public lands.
Unused public lands.
Rights of trust
beneficiaries.
Duties of department to
be performed
without prejudice,
§9-15-5.
Public officers.
Fiduciary funds in hand of
officials, §§19-3-80 to
19-3-87.
See FIDUCIARIES.
Purchasers.
Trust void as to purchasers
without notice,
§35-4-256.

TRUSTS AND TRUSTEES
—Cont'd

Purposes.
Trust may be created for lawful purpose, §35-4-251.

Railroad authorities.
Bonds of authorities.
Eligibility as investments for trust funds, §37-13-18.

Real property.
Sale of land devised and held in trust, §19-3-172.
Investment of proceeds of sale, §19-3-173.

Recordation.
Business trusts.
Declaration of trust, §19-3-64.
Notice of trust, §35-4-257.

Relatives.
Support and maintenance of relatives.
Express trust for support and maintenance, §19-3-1.

Removal of trustees.
Appointment of successor, §19-3-212.
Grounds, §19-3-211.
Survivorship between cotrustees, §19-3-252.

Removal of trust estate from another state, §§19-3-230 to 19-3-234.
Appointment of trustee, §19-3-232.
Application to appoint, §19-3-230.
Notice of hearing on application, §19-3-231.
Bond of new trustee, §19-3-233.
Fees.
Register or clerk, §19-3-234.

Removal of trust estate to another state, §§19-3-190 to 19-3-192.
Authorization.
Power of circuit court to authorize removal, §19-3-190.
Circuit courts.
Power to authorize removal, §19-3-190.
Hearings.
Judgment on hearing, §19-3-192.
Judgment on hearing, §19-3-192.
Notice of petition to obtain removal, §19-3-191.
Petition to obtain removal, §19-3-191.

Renunciation by trustee.
Survivorship between cotrustees, §19-3-252.

Resignation of trustees, §19-3-210.

Retirement.
Trusts for employees or self-employed persons, §35-4-259.

Rules against perpetuities.
Business trusts.
Rule not violated, §19-3-65.

TRUSTS AND TRUSTEES
—Cont'd

Sales.
Land devised and held in trust, §§19-3-172, 19-3-173.

Savings and loan associations.
Accounts, §5-16-43.
Death.
Disposition of deposit in trust for another upon death, §5-16-47.

School trustees.
Boards of school trustees.
General provisions, §§16-10-1 to 16-10-11.
See EDUCATION.

Securities.
Conversion or exchange, etc., upon merger, consolidation, §19-3-10.
Corporate fiduciaries.
Registration of securities held by corporate fiduciary in name of nominee, §19-3-7.
Fiduciary security transfers.
See SECURITIES.
Liquidation.
Conversion or exchange of securities upon liquidation, §19-3-10.
Merger or consolidation.
Conversion or exchange, etc., of securities upon, §19-3-10.
Proxies.
Execution by fiduciary holding corporate stocks, §19-3-8.
Securities held by fiduciaries, §§19-4-1 to 19-4-42.
See FIDUCIARIES.

Self-employed persons.
Trusts for, §35-4-259.

Settlement.
Notice of settlement, §19-3-5.

Spendthrift trusts.
Authorized, §19-3-1.

Split-interest trusts, §§19-3-300 to 19-3-303.

Standards for fiduciary investment and management, §19-3-120.2.

Statute of frauds.
Trust concerning lands required to be in writing, §35-4-255.

Successor trustees.
Appointment, §19-3-212.
Number of new trustees, §19-3-251.
Power of circuit court to fill vacancy, §19-3-250.
Representative of deceased sole trustee to settle with succeeding trustee, §19-3-253.
When circuit court must appoint, §19-3-251.

Support and maintenance.
Express trust for support and maintenance of relative, §19-3-1.
Minors.
Generally, §35-4-253.

TRUSTS AND TRUSTEES
—Cont'd

Support and maintenance —Cont'd
Minors—Cont'd
Transfers to minors generally, §§35-5A-1 to 35-5A-24.
See TRANSFERS TO MINORS.

Survivorship between cotrustees, §19-3-252.

Taxation.
Assessments.
By whom property should be listed, §40-7-17.
Business trusts, §19-3-67.
Generation-skipping tax.
Levy, §§40-15A-1 to 40-15A-14. See within this heading, "Generation-skipping tax."
Preclusion and minimization, §§19-5-1 to 19-5-12. See within this heading, "Generation-skipping tax."
Liability of trustees, §40-1-8.
Private foundations, charitable trusts and split-interest trusts.
Trustee not to engage in certain acts subjecting trust to federal taxation, §19-3-300.
Returns.
Separate returns in individual and fiduciary capacity, §40-7-20.
Tax assessors.
Notification of appointment of fiduciaries, §40-7-30.

Tennessee Valley Authority.
Bonds, surety.
Investment of trust estate in bonds of authority, §19-3-127.

Termination of trust estate, §19-3-3.

Term of trusts.
Accumulative trust, §35-4-252.

Third persons.
Effect of use, trust or confidence for mere benefit of third person, §35-4-250.

Title.
Necessity for legal title to vest in trustees, §35-4-251.

Transfers to minors generally, §§35-5A-1 to 35-5A-24.
See TRANSFERS TO MINORS.

Troy State University.
Board of trustees, §§16-56-1 to 16-56-15.
See TROY STATE UNIVERSITY.

Trust companies.
Financial institutions generally.
See BANKS AND FINANCIAL INSTITUTIONS.

TRUSTS AND TRUSTEES
—Cont'd

Trust estate.

Investment of trust estate, §§19-3-120 to 19-3-132.
See within this heading, "Investment of trust estate."

Liability of trust estate, §§19-3-100 to 19-3-107.

Administration.
Pending action for, §19-3-103.

Enforcement.
Charging real property, §19-3-104.
Judgment charging estate, §19-3-102.
Petition to enforce liability, §19-3-101.
Substitution of parties, §19-3-101.

Framing relief so as to render trust effectual, §19-3-107.

Investment of trust estate.
General rules of law govern trustee's liability, §19-3-129.

Misapplication of assets, §19-3-105.

Tracing misapplied assets, §19-3-106.

When trust estate may become liable, §19-3-100.

Removal of trust estate from another state, §§19-3-230 to 19-3-234.

Termination, §19-3-3.

Unemployment compensation trust fund, §§25-4-1 to 25-4-152.
See UNEMPLOYMENT COMPENSATION.

Uniform fiduciaries act, §§19-1-1 to 19-1-13.
See FIDUCIARIES.

University of Alabama.
Board of trustees.
General provisions, §§16-47-30 to 16-47-37.
See UNIVERSITY OF ALABAMA.

University of Montevallo.
Board of trustees, §§16-54-1 to 16-54-18.
See UNIVERSITY OF MONTEVALLO.

University of North Alabama.
Board of trustees, §§16-51-1 to 16-51-15.
See UNIVERSITY OF NORTH ALABAMA.

University of South Alabama.
Board of trustees, §§16-55-1 to 16-55-9.
See UNIVERSITY OF SOUTH ALABAMA.

Vacancies.
Power of circuit court to fill, §19-3-250.

Veterans.
Investment of trust estate in debts incurred under acts of congress relating to veterans' benefits, §19-3-128.

TRUSTS AND TRUSTEES
—Cont'd

Void trusts.
Creditors or purchasers without notice.
Trust void as to, §35-4-256.

Water system assistance authority.
Investments in bonds of authority, §22-23A-12.

Welfare.
State public welfare trust fund, §38-4-13.

Wills, §43-8-140.

Workmen's compensation.
Payment of compensation to court appointed trustee, §25-5-85.
Second injury trust fund, §§25-5-70 to 25-5-75.
See WORKMEN'S COMPENSATION.

Writing.
Trust concerning lands required to be in writing, §35-4-255.

TUBERCULOSIS.

Constitution of Alabama.
District tuberculosis sanitoria.
Bonds, Const. Ala., amd. 74.

Education.
Employment of teachers, janitors, food handlers or bus drivers with tuberculosis, §16-22-3.

Faith healing.
Treatment by prayer or spiritual means.
Preservation of religious freedom, §22-11A-10.

Jails.
Tubercular prisoners.
See JAILS.

Jefferson tuberculosis sanatorium.
Sales tax.
Exemptions, §40-23-4.
Use tax.
Exemptions, §40-23-62.

Notifiable diseases, §§22-11A-1 to 22-11A-38.
See DISEASES.

Penitentiary.
Separation of convicts, §14-3-41.

Prisons and prisoners.
General provisions.
See PRISONS AND PRISONERS.
Jails.
Tubercular prisoners.
See JAILS.
Penitentiary.
Separation of convicts, §14-3-41.

Quarantine.
Probate court may order, §22-11A-10.

Sales tax.
Exemptions.
Jefferson tuberculosis sanatorium, §40-23-4.

Sanatoria.
District tuberculosis sanitoria.
Bonds, Const. Ala., amd. 74.

TUBERCULOSIS—Cont'd

Schools.
Employment of teachers, janitors, food handlers or bus drivers with tuberculosis, §16-22-3.

Teachers.
Employment of teachers with tuberculosis, §16-22-3.

Use tax.
Jefferson tuberculosis sanatorium.
Exemptions, §40-23-62.

TULAREMIA.

Notifiable diseases, §§22-11A-1 to 22-11A-38.
See DISEASES.

TUNNELS.

Beautification.
Contracts.
Federal assistance, §23-1-1.
Rules and regulations.
Federal assistance, §23-1-1.

Bond issues.
Interstate highway system, §§23-2-120, 23-2-122.

Public improvement bonds.
Counties.
General provisions, §§11-81-140 to 11-81-150.
See COUNTIES.

Municipal corporations.
Certain revenue-producing undertakings, §§11-81-140 to 11-81-150.
See COUNTIES.

Toll road, bridge and tunnel authority.
See TOLL ROAD, BRIDGE AND TUNNEL AUTHORITY.

Construction.
Contracts.
Federal assistance, §23-1-1.
Rules and regulations.
Federal assistance, §23-1-1.
Through curtilage of house without consent, §10-5-5.

Contracts.
Beautification, construction or maintenance.
Federal assistance, §23-1-1.

Dwellings.
Construction through curtilage of house without consent, §10-5-5.

Housing.
Construction through curtilage of house without consent, §10-5-5.

Interstate highway system.
Toll tunnels designated as parts of interstate highway system.
Bond issues.
Payment.
Toll facilities to be operated as free facilities after payment, §23-2-122.
Prohibition against further bonded indebtedness, §23-2-120.

TUNNELS—Cont'd
  Interstate highway system
    —Cont'd
    Toll tunnels designated as
      parts of interstate
      highway system—Cont'd
      Construction.
        When newly constructed
          tunnel deemed part
          of existing facility,
          §23-2-121.
      Tolls.
        Free facilities after
          payment of
          outstanding
          indebtedness,
          §23-2-122.
        Maintenance of tolls,
          §23-2-120.
        When newly constructed
          tunnel deemed part
          of existing facility,
          §23-2-121.
  Maintenance.
    Contracts.
      Federal assistance, §23-1-1.
    Rules and regulations.
      Federal assistance, §23-1-1.
  Manufacturers.
    Connections to public ways.
      Construction and operation
        by manufacturing
        corporations, §10-5-13.
  Mines and minerals.
    Connections to public ways.
      Construction and operation
        by mining
        corporations, §10-5-13.
    Railroads.
      Requirement of
        construction and
        maintenance by
        railroads of bridges,
        tunnels, etc., within
        limits of certain cities,
        §§11-49-40 to 11-49-45.
      See MUNICIPAL
        CORPORATIONS.
  Quarries.
    Connections to public ways.
      Construction and operation
        by quarrying
        corporations, §10-5-13.
  Railroads.
    Grade crossings generally.
      See RAILROADS.
    Municipal corporations.
      Requirement of
        construction and
        maintenance by
        railroads of bridges,
        tunnels, etc., within
        limits of certain cities,
        §§11-49-40 to 11-49-45.
      See MUNICIPAL
        CORPORATIONS.
  Rules and regulations.
    Federal assistance, §23-1-1.
  Sales tax.
    Exemptions.
      Fabricated steel tube
        sections, §40-23-4.
  Tolls.
    Toll road, bridge and tunnel
      authority, §§23-2-140 to
      23-2-161.
    See TOLL ROAD, BRIDGE
      AND TUNNEL
      AUTHORITY.

TUNNELS—Cont'd
  Tolls—Cont'd
    Toll tunnels designated as
      parts of interstate
      highway system. See
      within this heading,
      "Interstate highway
      system."
  Use tax.
    Fabricated steel tube
      sections.
      Exemptions, §40-23-62.

**TURKEY HUNTERS HALL
  OF FAME,** §§41-9-830 to
  41-9-833.
  Board.
    Appointment, §41-9-830.
    Composition, §41-9-830.
    Creation, §41-9-830.
    Functions, §41-9-832.
    Location, §41-9-831.
    Meetings, §41-9-830.
    Purposes, §41-9-832.
    Quorum, §41-9-830.
    Responsibility for museum,
      §41-9-833.
    Terms of office, §41-9-830.
    Vacancies in office,
      §41-9-830.
  Creation, §41-9-830.
  Donations, §41-9-833.
  Election to hall of fame,
    §41-9-832.
  Location, §41-9-831.
  Taxation.
    Exemption, §41-9-833.

TURKEYS.
  Hunting generally.
    See FISH AND GAME.
  Poultry generally.
    See POULTRY.

TURNPIKES.
  Highways.
    General provisions.
      See HIGHWAYS.
  **Toll road, bridge and tunnel
    authority,** §§23-2-140 to
    23-2-161.
    See TOLL ROAD, BRIDGE
      AND TUNNEL
      AUTHORITY.

TURPENTINE, §§8-17-170 to
  8-17-175.
  Enforcement of article,
    §8-17-173.
  Labels.
    Requirements, §8-17-171.
    Tanks, etc., containing
      substitutes, §8-17-172.
  Licenses.
    Turpentine stills, §40-12-175.
  Penalties.
    Violations, §8-17-174.
  Sales.
    Illegal turpentine.
      Suspension from sale,
        §8-17-173.
    Substitutes, §8-17-172.
  Searches and seizures.
    Illegal turpentine, §8-17-173.
  Standards, §8-17-170.
  Substitutes.
    Sales, §8-17-172.
    Tanks containing.
      Labeling, §8-17-172.
  Violations of article.
    Penalty, §8-17-174.

TURTLES.
  Flattened musk turtle.
    Protection, §9-11-269.
  Marine resources, §19-12-145.

TUSCALOOSA COUNTY.
  Bond issues.
    Extension of debt limit,
      Const. Ala., amd. 115.
  Debt limit.
    Extension of debt limit,
      Const. Ala., amd. 115.
  **Economic and industrial
    development promotion,**
    Const. Ala., amd. 429.
  Fire protection districts,
    Const. Ala., amd. 358.
  **Garbage and trash disposal
    districts,** Const. Ala., amd.
    358.
  Officers.
    Regulation of salaries, etc.,
      Const. Ala., amd. 33.
  Recreation.
    Special property tax for
      recreational purposes,
      Const. Ala., amd. 333.
  School tax.
    Special property tax, Const.
      Ala., amd. 164.
    Special school tax, Const.
      Ala., amd. 71.

**TUSCALOOSA,
  MUNICIPALITY OF.**
  Property tax, Const. Ala.,
    amd. 13.

**TUSCUMBIA,
  MUNICIPALITY OF.**
  Debt limit, Const. Ala., art.
    XII, §226; amd. 268.
  Property tax, Const. Ala.,
    amd. 8.
  School tax.
    Special property tax, Const.
      Ala., amd. 170.

TUSKEGEE INSTITUTE.
  Appropriations.
    Purpose, §16-57-1.
  Board of commissioners.
    Generally, §16-57-1.
  Board of trustees.
    Endowment funds.
      Investment, §16-13-2.
  Bonds, surety.
    Treasurer, §16-57-1.
  **Commission of higher
    education.**
    General provisions, §§16-5-1
      to 16-5-14.
    See UNIVERSITIES AND
      COLLEGES.
  **Contracts for education of
    Alabama students,**
    §16-3-35.
  Governor.
    Appointment of
      commissioner, §16-57-1.
  **Marine environmental
    sciences consortium,**
    §§16-45-1 to 16-45-5.
  Nursing school, §§16-57-2 to
    16-57-4.
  Police.
    Generally, §§16-22-1,
      16-22-2.
  School of nursing.
    Scholarships, §§16-57-2 to
      16-57-4.
      Amount, §16-57-4.
      Conditions, §16-57-4.

TUSKEGEE INSTITUTE
—Cont'd
School of nursing—Cont'd
Scholarships—Cont'd
Distribution.
How distributed,
§16-57-2.
Eligibility.
Who eligible, §16-57-3.
Established, §16-57-2.
How distributed, §16-57-2.
Selection of recipients,
§16-57-4.
State board of education.
Contracts with Tuskegee
Institute for education of
Alabama students,
§16-3-35.
Treasurer.
Bond of treasurer, §16-57-1.

**TUSKEGEE, MUNICIPALITY
OF.**
**Daniel "Chappie" James
Aerospace Memorial.**
Indebtedness for, Const. Ala.,
amd. 438.
Property tax, Const. Ala.,
amd. 8.

TYPEWRITERS.
Licenses for sale, §40-12-44.

TYPHOID FEVER.
Notifiable diseases,
§§22-11A-1 to 22-11A-38.
See DISEASES.

TYPHUS.
Notifiable diseases,
§§22-11A-1 to 22-11A-38.
See DISEASES.

                  U

U-HAUL-IT VEHICLES.
Renting and hiring vehicles.
See MOTOR VEHICLES.

UNCLAIMED BODIES.
Distribution, §§22-19-20 to
22-19-30.
See DEAD BODIES.

UNCLAIMED PROPERTY.
Lost or unclaimed property.
See LOST OR UNCLAIMED
PROPERTY.

**UNDERGROUND STORAGE
TANKS,** §§22-35-1 to
23-35-13.
Administration of chapter.
Budgets, §22-35-9.
Costs, §22-35-9.
Advisory board.
Chairman, §22-35-6.
Composition, §22-35-6.
Creation, §22-35-6.
Duties, §22-35-6.
Meetings, §22-35-6.
Citation of chapter, §22-35-2.
Contamination. See within
this heading, "Water
contamination."
Definitions, §22-35-3.
Tank and wellhead
protection, §22-36-2.
Financial responsibility.
Response action, §22-35-7.
Intent of legislature,
§22-35-1.
Legislative findings, §22-35-1.

**UNDERGROUND STORAGE
TANKS**—Cont'd
Liability of owners,
§22-35-12.
Notice of provisions.
Underground storage tank
owners, §22-35-11.
**Rehabilitation of
contamination sites,**
§22-35-8.
Response action.
Financial responsibility
requirements, §22-35-7.
Rules and regulations.
Adoption, §22-35-10.
Tank and wellhead
protection, §22-36-3.
Adoption, §22-36-10.
Establish and protect
wellhead areas,
§22-36-7.
Trust fund.
No disbursements until
adoption of rules and
regulations, §22-35-13.
Short title of chapter,
§22-35-2.
**Tank and wellhead
protection,** §§22-36-1 to
22-36-10.
Citation of chapter, §22-36-1.
Definitions, §22-36-2.
Fees.
Tank regulation fee,
§22-36-5.
Leaking underground storage
tank trust fund.
Administration, §22-36-6.
Expenditures, §22-36-6.
Owners.
Information to be furnished
by owners, §22-36-4.
Liability for costs,
§22-36-6.
Permitting access to
records and entry and
inspection of facilities,
§22-36-4.
Penalties.
Violation of chapter,
§22-36-9.
Records.
Availability to public,
§22-36-8.
Reports.
Availability to public,
§22-36-8.
Rules and regulations,
§22-36-3.
Adoption, §22-36-10.
Establish and protect
wellhead areas,
§22-36-7.
Short title of chapter,
§22-36-1.
Violation of chapter.
Penalties, §22-36-9.
Trust fund.
Assessments.
Special assessments when
fund depleted,
§22-35-5.
Audits, §22-35-5.
Charges against fund,
§22-35-4.
Creation, §22-35-4.
Credits to fund, §22-35-4.
Disbursements.
No disbursements until
adoption of rules and
regulations, §22-35-13.

**UNDERGROUND STORAGE
TANKS**—Cont'd
Trust fund—Cont'd
Fees.
Deposited in fund,
§22-35-5.
Failure to pay, §22-35-5.
Owners to pay, §22-35-5.
Indemnification.
Limitation as to third
party claim, §22-35-4.
Investments, §22-35-5.
Payments from fund.
Procedure for obtaining,
§22-35-5.
Use of fund, §22-35-5.
Water contamination.
Clean-up costs.
Limit on liability, §22-35-5.
Investigation, §22-35-4.
Liability of owner for costs,
§22-35-4.
Rehabilitation of
contamination sites,
§22-35-8.

UNDERTAKERS.
General provisions.
See FUNERALS.

UNDERTAKINGS.
Bail and recognizance.
See BAIL AND
RECOGNIZANCE.
Bonds, surety.
See BONDS, SURETY.
Peace bonds.
See PEACE BONDS.

UNDULANT FEVER.
Notifiable diseases,
§§22-11A-1 to 22-11A-38.
See DISEASES.

**UNEMPLOYMENT
COMPENSATION,** §§25-4-1
to 25-4-152.
Actions.
Limitation of actions,
§25-4-145.
Procedures for collection of
delinquent payments,
§25-4-134.
Administration fund,
§25-4-142.
Defined, §25-4-15.
Replacement of certain funds
§25-4-142.
Special employment security
administration fund,
§25-4-142.
Advisory council, §25-4-114.
Agencies.
Cooperation with, §25-4-118.
Reciprocal arrangements
with, §25-4-120.
Aliens.
Disqualifications for benefits,
§25-4-78.
Amendment of chapter.
Reservation of right,
§25-4-144.
Appeals.
Benefits.
Appeals tribunals.
Appeals from, §25-4-95.
Appointment, §25-4-92.
Decisions.
Appeals from,
§25-4-95.
Notification of parties,
§25-4-93.

**UNEMPLOYMENT
COMPENSATION**—Cont'd
Appeals—Cont'd
Benefits—Cont'd
Appeals tribunals—Cont'd
Decisions—Cont'd
Power to affirm,
modify or set
aside, §25-4-93.
When final, §25-4-92.
Notice of decision,
§25-4-93.
Procedure, §25-4-92.
Witnesses.
Powers as to, §25-4-97.
Industrial relations board
of appeals.
Appeals from, §25-4-95.
Powers and duties,
§25-4-94.
Witnesses.
Powers as to, §25-4-97.
Appropriations, §25-4-143.
Arrest.
Fee, §25-4-147.
Assignments.
Benefits.
Assignment of right to
benefits void,
§25-4-140.
Attachments.
Benefits.
Exemption from
attachment, §25-4-140.
Contributions.
Procedures for collection of
delinquent
contributions,
§25-4-134.
Attorneys at law.
Fees for attorneys or agents.
Limitation of fees and
proceedings under
chapter, §25-4-139.
Available suitable work.
Failure to accept.
Disqualifications for
benefits, §25-4-78.
Bankruptcy and insolvency.
Employers.
Effect of bankruptcy of
employer, §25-4-135.
Base period.
Defined, §25-4-1.
Benefits.
Accrual, §25-4-70.
Agreement to waive right to
benefits, §25-4-138.
Amount.
Maximum individual
benefit entitlement
during benefit year,
§25-4-74.
Weekly benefit amount.
Individual weekly
benefit amount,
§25-4-72.
Assignments of right to
benefits void, §25-4-140.
Attachment.
Exemption, §25-4-140.
Base period.
Defined, §25-4-1.
Benefit year.
Defined, §25-4-3.
Claims for benefits.
Appeals tribunals.
Appeals from, §25-4-95.
Appointment, §25-4-92.

**UNEMPLOYMENT
COMPENSATION**—Cont'd
Benefits—Cont'd
Claims for benefits—Cont'd
Appeals tribunals—Cont'd
Decisions.
Appeals from,
§25-4-95.
Notification of parties,
§25-4-93.
Power to affirm,
modify or set
aside, §25-4-93.
When final, §25-4-92.
Notice of decision,
§25-4-93.
Procedure, §25-4-92.
When decisions final,
§25-4-92.
Witnesses.
Powers as to witnesses,
§25-4-97.
Attorneys' fees, §25-4-139.
Determinations upon
claims, §25-4-91.
Exclusiveness of procedure,
§25-4-96.
Fees, §25-4-139.
Witness fees, §25-4-97.
Filing, §25-4-90.
Industrial relations board
of appeals.
Appeals from, §25-4-95.
Powers and duties,
§25-4-94.
Witnesses.
Powers as to witnesses,
§25-4-97.
Procedure exclusive,
§25-4-96.
Redeterminations upon
claims, §25-4-91.
Witnesses, §25-4-97.
Collection of overpayment,
§25-4-145.
Defined, §25-4-2.
Determination of benefit
charges, §25-4-54.
Disqualifications for benefits,
§25-4-78.
Eligibility conditions,
§25-4-77.
Encumbrance of right to
benefits void, §25-4-140.
Executions.
Exemption, §25-4-140.
Extension of benefit period,
§25-4-75.
Garnishment.
Exemption, §25-4-140.
Interstate benefit payments,
§25-4-120.
Invalidity of provisions
pertaining to payment.
Disposition of trust funds
in event of, §25-4-148.
Manner of payment,
§25-4-70.
Maritime employment,
§25-4-76.
Maximum individual benefit
entitlement during
benefit year, §25-4-74.
Overpayment.
Collection, §25-4-145.
Payment.
Interstate benefit
payments, §25-4-120.

**UNEMPLOYMENT
COMPENSATION**—Cont'd
Benefits—Cont'd
Payment—Cont'd
Invalidity of provisions
pertaining to payment.
Disposition of trust funds
in event of
invalidity, §25-4-148.
Manner of payment,
§25-4-70.
Notice of payment,
§25-4-91.
Overpayment, §25-4-145.
Time of payment, §25-4-70.
Weekly benefit payment.
Individual weekly
benefit payment,
§25-4-73.
Period.
Extension of benefit period,
§25-4-75.
Pledge of right to benefits
void, §25-4-140.
Requisition of moneys from
trust fund, §25-4-32.
School systems.
Appropriation of funds for
payment of benefits for
employees of,
§25-4-150.
State employees.
Appropriation of funds for
payment of, §25-4-149.
Time of payment, §25-4-70.
Trust fund.
Requisition of moneys from
trust fund, §25-4-32.
Waiver of right to benefits.
Agreement to waive right,
§25-4-138.
When individuals deemed
unemployed, §25-4-71.
Calendar quarter.
Defined, §25-4-4.
Child support obligations.
Deduction, §25-4-152.
Contributions.
Accrual, §25-4-50.
Adjustments, §25-4-137.
Agreement to pay employer's
contributions, §25-4-138.
Benefit charges.
Contribution rates for
employers subject to,
§25-4-54.
Defined, §25-4-5.
Delinquent payments.
Assessment of interest,
§25-4-132.
Collection.
Procedures for collection,
§25-4-134.
Interest.
Assessment of interest
on delinquent
payments, §25-4-132.
Penalties for delinquent
payments, §25-4-133.
Procedures for collection,
§25-4-134.
Employees' contributions,
§25-4-52.
Withholding of employee
contributions,
§25-4-53.
Extension of time for
payment.
Director may extend time,
§25-4-136.

**UNEMPLOYMENT
COMPENSATION**—Cont'd
Contributions—Cont'd
Interest.
Payment of interest on
moneys advanced by
federal government,
§25-4-55.
Assessment to
discontinue when all
interest paid,
§25-4-57.
Creation of special
payment fund,
§25-4-56.
Disposition of moneys in
fund when
assessment
discontinued,
§25-4-58.
Money advanced after
previously borrowed
funds repaid,
§25-4-57.
Invalidity of provisions
pertaining to payment.
Disposition of trust funds
in event of invalidity,
§25-4-148.
Manner of payment,
§25-4-50.
Payments in lieu of
contributions.
Accrual, §25-4-50.
Defined, §25-4-5.
Manner of payment,
§25-4-50.
Rates, §25-4-51.
Time of payment, §25-4-50.
Penalties.
Delinquent payments,
§25-4-133.
Rates of contributions, etc.,
by employers, §25-4-51.
Adjustments, §25-4-137.
Decrease, §25-4-54.
Determination of
contribution rates,
§25-4-54.
Employers chargeable with
benefit charges,
§25-4-54.
Increase.
Employment security
administration
enhancement fund,
§25-4-40.
Increase of contribution
rate, §25-4-54.
Interest on moneys
advanced by federal
government, §25-4-55.
Maximum rate, §25-4-54.
Notice of contribution rate,
§25-4-54.
Review of contribution
rate, §25-4-54.
Successor employers,
§25-4-54.
Reduction of wages to
finance employer's
contributions, §25-4-138.
Refunds, §25-4-137.
Time for payment, §25-4-50.
Director may extend,
§25-4-136.
Trust fund.
Composition, §25-4-30.
Withholding of employee
contributions, §25-4-53.

**UNEMPLOYMENT
COMPENSATION**—Cont'd
Counties.
Coverage.
Election, §25-4-131.
Coverage.
Employer's coverage,
§§25-4-130, 25-4-131.
Criminal acts.
Discharge for criminal act.
Disqualifications for
benefits, §25-4-78.
Definitions, §§25-4-1 to
25-4-17.
**Department of industrial
relations.**
Board of appeals.
Claims for benefits.
Appeals from board,
§25-4-95.
Powers and duties of
board, §25-4-94.
Witnesses.
Powers of board as to
witnesses,
§25-4-97.
Employees, §25-4-113.
Certain employees
constituted peace
officers to enforce
certain provisions,
§25-4-146.
Immunity from civil suit,
§25-4-113.
Exceptions, §25-4-113.
Representation in court
actions, §25-4-117.
Desertion and nonsupport.
Deduction of child support
obligations, §25-4-152.
**Director of industrial
relations.**
Administration of chapter.
Powers and duties,
§25-4-110.
Benefits.
Claims for benefits.
Redeterminations upon
claims, §25-4-91.
Compromise or waiver of
civil penalties or interest
charges, §25-4-119.
Contributions.
Director may extend time
for, §25-4-136.
Cooperation with state and
federal agencies,
§25-4-118.
Defined, §25-4-6.
Immunity from civil suit,
§25-4-113.
Exceptions, §25-4-113.
Information.
Release, §25-4-118.
Reciprocal arrangements
with state and federal
agencies, §25-4-120.
Reduction of unemployment.
Duties of director with
respect to reduction,
§25-4-115.
Representation in court
actions, §25-4-117.
Universities and colleges.
Release of information to
institutions of higher
education, §25-4-118.
**Discharge for dishonest or
criminal act.**
Disqualifications for benefits,
§25-4-78.

**UNEMPLOYMENT
COMPENSATION**—Cont'd
Dishonest acts.
Discharge for dishonest act.
Disqualifications for
benefits, §25-4-78.
**Division of unemployment
compensation.**
Director of industrial
relations designated
chief of division,
§25-2-10.
Eligibility for benefits.
Conditions, §25-4-77.
Employees.
Contributions, §§25-4-52,
25-4-53.
Defined, §25-4-7.
Department of industrial
relations. See within this
heading, "Department of
industrial relations."
Employers.
Bankruptcy.
Effect of bankruptcy,
§25-4-135.
Contributions.
Rates of contributions,
etc., by employers. See
within this heading,
"Contributions."
Coverage.
Duration, §25-4-130.
Election of coverage by
employing units and
political subdivisions,
§25-4-131.
Termination, §25-4-130.
Defined, §25-4-8.
Liquidation.
Effect of liquidation,
§25-4-135.
Payments in lieu of
contributions, §§25-4-5,
25-4-50, 25-4-51.
Rates of contributions by
employers. See within
this heading,
"Contributions."
Employing units.
Coverage.
Election of coverage under
chapter, §25-4-131.
Defined, §25-4-9.
Records, §25-4-116.
Reports, §25-4-116.
Employment.
Defined, §25-4-10.
Employment office.
Defined, §25-4-11.
**Employment security
administration fund,**
§§25-4-15, 25-4-142.
Executions.
Benefits.
Exemption, §25-4-140.
**Failure to accept available
suitable work.**
Disqualifications for benefits,
§25-4-78.
Federal agencies.
Cooperation with, §25-4-118.
Reciprocal arrangements
with, §25-4-120.
**Federal unemployment
compensation
amendments of 1976.**
Effect of challenges or
invalidation, §25-4-151.
Fees.
Arrest fee, §25-4-147.

UNEMPLOYMENT COMPENSATION—Cont'd

Fees—Cont'd
Attorneys' fees, §25-4-139.
Generally, §25-4-139.
Fiscal year.
Defined, §25-4-4.
Fraud.
Arrest fee, §25-4-147.
Enforcement of fraud provisions of chapter.
Certain employees of department of industrial relations constituted peace officers, §25-4-146.
Funds.
Administration fund, §§25-4-15, 25-4-142.
Definitions, §§25-4-12, 25-4-15.
Employment security administration enhancement fund, §25-4-40.
Trust fund. See within this heading, "Trust fund."
Garnishment.
Benefits.
Exemption, §25-4-140.
Insured work.
Defined, §25-4-13.
Interest.
Compromise or waiver of interest charges, §25-4-119.
Payment of interest on moneys advanced by federal government, §25-4-55.
Assessment to discontinue when all interest paid, §25-4-57.
Creation of special payment fund, §25-4-56.
Disposition of moneys in fund when assessment discontinued, §25-4-58.
Money advanced after previously borrowed funds repaid, §25-4-57.
Labor dispute in place of employment.
Disqualifications for benefits, §25-4-78.
Legislature.
Reservation of right to repeal or amend chapter, §25-4-144.
Licenses.
Revocation or suspension of required license.
Disqualifications for benefits, §25-4-78.
Limitation of actions, §25-4-145.
Maritime employment.
Benefits, §25-4-76.
Municipal corporations.
Coverage.
Election, §25-4-131.
Office.
Employment office.
Defined, §25-4-11.
Payments in lieu of contributions, §§25-4-5, 25-4-50, 25-4-51.
Penalties.
Compromise or waiver of civil penalties, §25-4-119.

UNEMPLOYMENT COMPENSATION—Cont'd

Penalties—Cont'd
Delinquent contribution payments and reports, §25-4-133.
Generally, §25-4-145.
Trust fund.
Disposition of penalties, §25-4-31.
Police.
Certain employees of department of industrial relations constituted peace officers to enforce certain provisions, §25-4-146.
Political subdivisions.
Coverage.
Election, §25-4-131.
Reciprocity.
Reciprocal arrangements with state and federal agencies, §25-4-120.
Records.
Employing units, §25-4-116.
Reduction of unemployment.
Duties of director with respect to, §25-4-115.
Repeal of chapter.
Reservation of right, §25-4-144.
Reports.
Employing units, §25-4-116.
Penalties for delinquent reports, §25-4-133.
Rules and regulations.
Adoption, §25-4-111.
Distribution, §25-4-112.
Publication, §25-4-112.
School systems.
Benefits for employees of local school systems.
Appropriation of funds for payment of, §25-4-150.
Self-employment.
Disqualifications for benefits, §25-4-78.
Ships and shipping.
Maritime employment.
Benefits, §25-4-76.
Sports.
Participation in professional sports.
Disqualifications for benefits, §25-4-78.
State.
Defined, §25-4-14.
State agencies.
Cooperation with, §25-4-118.
Reciprocal arrangements with, §25-4-120.
State employees.
Appropriation of funds for payment of benefits for, §25-4-149.
Support and maintenance.
Deduction of child support obligations, §25-4-152.
Trust fund.
Administration, §25-4-30.
Composition, §25-4-30.
Defined, §25-4-12.
Disposition in event of certain provisions, §25-4-148.
Interest.
Disposition, §25-4-31.
Penalties.
Disposition, §25-4-31.

UNEMPLOYMENT COMPENSATION—Cont'd

Trust fund—Cont'd
Requisition of moneys from fund, §25-4-32.
Separate accounts, §25-4-31.
Treasurer, §25-4-31.
Universities and colleges.
Director of industrial relations.
Release of information to institutions of higher education, §25-4-118.
Voluntary departure from work.
Disqualifications for benefits, §25-4-78.
Wages.
Defined, §25-4-16.
Determination of invididual benefit charges, §25-4-54.
Employers chargeable with benefit charges.
Contribution rates for employers, §25-4-54.
Reciprocal arrangements with state and federal agencies.
Combination of wage credits, §25-4-120.
Reduction of wages to finance employers' contributions, §25-4-138.
Week.
Defined, §25-4-17.
Witnesses.
Benefits.
Claims for benefits, §25-4-97.

UNFAIR TRADE.
General provisions.
See TRADE AND COMMERCE.

UNIFIED JUDICIAL SYSTEM.
Records.
Disposal of records according to supreme court rule, §41-13-21.

UNIFORM LAWS.
Anatomical gift act, §§22-19-40 to 22-19-47.
See ANATOMICAL GIFTS.
Child custody jurisdiction act, §§30-3-20 to 30-3-44.
See MINORS.
Commercial code.
See COMMERCIAL CODE.
Commission on uniform state laws.
Appointment of members, §41-9-370.
Appropriation, §41-9-374.
Composition, §41-9-370.
Contributions.
Payment, §41-9-374.
Creation, §41-9-370.
Duties, §41-9-373.
Expenses.
Payment, §41-9-374.
Meetings, §41-9-372.
Organization, §41-9-372.
Reports to legislature, §41-9-373.
Terms of members, §41-9-370.
Vacancies, §41-9-371.

UNIFORM LAWS—Cont'd
Conservators.
Uniform guardianship and
protective proceedings
act, §§26-2A-1 to
26-2A-160.
See GUARDIAN AND
WARD.
Custody.
Uniform child custody
jurisdiction act,
§§30-3-20 to 30-3-44.
See MINORS.
Desertion and nonsupport.
Reciprocal state enforcement
of duty to support,
§§30-4-80 to 30-4-98.
See DESERTION AND
NONSUPPORT.
Detainers.
Mandatory disposition of
detainers, §§15-9-80 to
15-9-88.
See DETAINERS.
Federal lien registration act,
§§35-11-42 to 35-11-48.
See UNITED STATES.
Fiduciaries.
Fiduciary security transfers,
§§8-6-70 to 8-6-80.
See SECURITIES.
Uniform fiduciaries act,
§§19-1-1 to 19-1-13.
See FIDUCIARIES.
Foreign judgments.
Uniform enforcement of
foreign judgments act,
§§6-9-230 to 6-9-238.
See JUDGMENTS.
Guardian and ward.
Uniform guardianship and
protective proceedings
act, §§26-2A-1 to
26-2A-160.
See GUARDIAN AND
WARD.
Insurers' liquidation act.
Liquidation, §§27-32-1 to
27-32-41.
See INSURANCE.
Judgments.
Foreign judgments.
Uniform enforcement of
foreign judgment act,
§§6-9-230 to 6-9-238.
See JUDGMENTS.
Legislature.
Commission on uniform state
laws.
Reports to legislature,
§41-9-373.
**Mandatory disposition of
detainers,** §§15-9-80 to
15-9-88.
See DETAINERS.
Minors.
Child custody jurisdiction
act, §§30-3-20 to 30-3-44.
See MINORS.
Reciprocal state enforcement
of duty to support,
§§30-4-80 to 30-4-98.
See DESERTION AND
NONSUPPORT.
Uniform transfers to minors
act, §§35-5A-1 to
35-5A-24.
See TRANSFERS TO
MINORS.

UNIFORM LAWS—Cont'd
Motor vehicles.
Uniform certificate of title
and antitheft act,
§§32-8-1 to 32-8-88.
See MOTOR VEHICLES.
Uniform vehicle code.
Use in interpretation and
construction of rules of
the road act,
§32-5A-11.
Parent and child.
Uniform parentage act,
§§26-17-1 to 26-17-21.
See PARENT AND
CHILD.
Probate code, §§43-8-1 to
43-8-298.
See WILLS.
Reports.
Commission on uniform state
laws, §41-9-373.
Securities.
Fiduciary security transfers,
§§8-6-70 to 8-6-80.
See SECURITIES.
Simultaneous death act,
§§43-7-1 to 43-7-8.
See SIMULTANEOUS
DEATH ACT.
Support.
Reciprocal state enforcement
of duty to support,
§§30-4-80 to 30-4-98.
See DESERTION AND
NONSUPPORT.
Transfers to minors,
§§35-5A-1 to 35-5A-24.
See TRANSFERS TO
MINORS.
Unclaimed property.
Uniform disposition of
unclaimed property act,
§§35-12-20 to 35-12-48.
See LOST OR
UNCLAIMED
PROPERTY.
U.R.E.S.A.
Reciprocal state enforcement
of duty to support,
§§30-4-80 to 30-4-98.
See DESERTION AND
NONSUPPORT.

**UNINCORPORATED
ASSOCIATIONS.**
Actions, ARCP, Rule 23.2.
Venue.
See VENUE.

**UNINCORPORATED
PROFESSIONAL
ASSOCIATIONS,** §§10-10-1
to 10-10-16.
Accountants.
See ACCOUNTANTS.
Actions.
Laws governing actions,
§10-10-3.
Agents.
Disqualification to practice.
Withdrawal of agents
becoming disqualified
to practice, §10-10-13.
Professional services to be
rendered only through
licensed officers or
employees, §10-10-12.
Applicability of chapter,
§10-10-2.
Articles of association,
§10-10-5.

**UNINCORPORATED
PROFESSIONAL
ASSOCIATIONS**—Cont'd
Assets.
Distribution on dissolution,
§10-10-16.
Board of governors, §10-10-8.
Bylaws, §10-10-8.
Charter.
Alteration, §10-1-1.
Amendment, §10-1-1.
Extension, §10-1-1.
Continuity of associations.
Independent of members or
shareholders, §10-10-15.
Purchase of membership or
shares of former
member, §10-10-14.
Conveyances, §10-10-9.
Definitions, §10-10-1.
Disqualification to practice.
Withdrawal of members and
employees becoming
disqualified, §10-10-13.
Dissolution, §10-10-5.
Distribution of assets on
dissolution, §10-10-16.
Members and employees
becoming disqualified to
practice.
Proceedings to dissolve
noncomplying
association, §10-10-13.
Employees.
Disqualification to practice.
Withdrawal of employees
becoming disqualified,
§10-10-13.
Professional services to be
rendered only through
licensed officers or
employees, §10-10-12.
Exemption from liability,
§10-10-9.
Formation, §10-10-4.
Governors.
Board of governors, §10-10-8.
Laws governing, §10-10-2.
Action, §10-10-3.
Liability.
Exemption, §10-10-9.
Members or shareholders,
§10-10-11.
Membership.
Purchase of membership of
former member,
§10-10-14.
Member's interest.
Nature and transferability,
§10-10-7.
Names, §10-10-5.
Nonstock associations.
Continuity independent of
members, §10-10-15.
Disqualification to practice.
Withdrawal of members
becoming disqualified,
§10-10-13.
Liability of members,
§10-10-11.
Nature of member's interest,
§10-10-7.
Purchase of membership of
former member,
§10-10-7.
Transferability of member's
interest, §10-10-7.
Voting by members,
§10-10-8.

UNINCORPORATED
PROFESSIONAL
ASSOCIATIONS—Cont'd
Officers, §10-10-8.
Disqualification to practice.
Withdrawal of officers
becoming disqualified,
§10-10-13.
Professional services to be
rendered only through
licensed officers or
employees, §10-10-12.
Partnerships.
Certain statutes not affected
by chapter, §10-8-7.
Personal property.
Conveyances, §10-10-9.
Powers, §10-10-9.
Professional relationships.
Effect of chapter on,
§10-10-11.
Property.
Conveyances, §10-10-9.
Purposes, §10-10-6.
Real property.
Conveyances, §10-10-9.
Reports.
Furnishing of statements to
secretary of state,
§10-10-10.
Restriction on service
rendered, §10-10-4.
Secretary of state.
Furnishing of statements to
secretary of state,
§10-10-10.
Services rendered.
Professional services to be
rendered only licensed
officers or employees,
§10-10-12.
Restriction on service
rendered, §10-10-4.
Statements to secretary of
state.
Furnishing of statements,
§10-10-10.
Stock associations.
Continuity independent of
shareholders, §10-10-15.
Disqualification to practice.
Withdrawal of
shareholders becoming
disqualified, §10-10-13.
Liability of shareholders,
§10-10-11.
Nature of member's interest,
§10-10-7.
Purchase of shares of former
shareholder, §10-10-14.
Transferability of member's
interest, §10-10-14.
Voting by shareholders,
§10-10-8.
Voting by members or
shareholders, §10-10-8.

UNINSURED MOTORISTS.
Safety-responsibility act,
§§32-7-1 to 32-7-42.
See MOTOR VEHICLES.

UNIONS.
Labor unions, §§25-7-1 to
25-7-54.
See LABOR.

UNIONTOWN,
MUNICIPALITY OF.
Economic development,
Const. Ala., amd. 155.

UNITED STATES.
Acquisition of land.
Authorized, §42-1-1.
Consent to acquisition of
lands needed for
consolidation and
administration of
national forests, §42-1-2.
Actions.
Parties.
Persons in federal service
and spouses living in
state deemed residents
for purpose of
commencing actions,
§6-7-20.
Advertising.
Outdoor advertising.
Federal funds.
Director authorized to
accept, §23-1-285.
Secretary of transportation.
Agreements with,
§23-1-284.
Agriculture.
Offense under federal
jurisdiction, §2-1-10.
Air commerce.
Cooperation with federal
authorities, §37-9-12.
United States mail exempt
from regulation, §37-9-3.
Airports.
Federal funding.
See AVIATION.
Appeals.
Condemnation of land or
rights of way.
Assessment of damages,
§42-2-9.
Grant or refusal of
application, §42-2-6.
Appropriations, Const. U. S.,
Art. I, §9.
Atomic energy.
Disposal of nuclear waste.
Nonconsent of state to
acquisition of land by
federal government,
§22-14-16.
Radiation.
Agreements with federal
goverment, §22-14-9.
Attorneys at law.
Condemnation of land or
rights of way.
Appointment of counsel for
infants and persons of
unsound mind, §42-2-4.
Boats.
Commissioner of
conservation and natural
resources.
Supplying information to
federal agencies,
§33-5-8.
Discharge of litter and
sewage from watercraft.
Marine toilets.
Standards for marine
toilets.
Conformity with
federal standards,
§33-6-5.
Numbering.
Exemption from
numbering provisions.
Boats owned by United
States, §33-5-19.

UNITED STATES—Cont'd
Bond issues.
Bridges.
Acquiring in conjunction
with United States,
Const. Ala., amd. 87.
Income tax.
Interest or other income
received from
obligations of United
States, §40-18-4.
Taxation.
Exemption, §40-9-1.
Bridges.
Bond issues for acquiring
bridges in conjunction
with United States,
Const. Ala., amd. 87.
Contracts.
Rivers forming boundaries
between states,
§23-1-57.
Cession of land by state.
Governor.
Authority to cede
jurisdiction, §42-3-1.
Navigable waters.
Cession of sites covered by
navigable waters,
§42-3-2.
Reservation of rights by
state, §42-3-3.
Civil defense.
Acceptance of services from
federal government by
governor, §31-9-18.
Condemnation of land or
rights of way, §§42-2-1 to
42-2-12.
Appeal from assessment of
damages, §42-2-9.
Appeal from grant or refusal
of application, §42-2-6.
Application, §42-2-2.
Appeal from grant or
refusal, §42-2-6.
Order granting or refusing
application, §42-2-6.
Assessment of damages.
Appeal from, §42-2-9.
Commissioners for
assessment of damages
and compensation,
§§42-2-7, 42-2-8.
Attorneys at law.
Appointment of counsel for
infants and persons of
unsound mind, §42-2-4.
Commissioners for
assessment of damages
and compensation,
§§42-2-7, 42-2-8.
Appointment, §42-2-7.
Duties, §42-2-7.
Notice to commissioner,
§42-2-7.
Report, §42-2-8.
Compensation.
Commissioners for
assessment of damages
and compensation,
§§42-2-7, 42-2-8.
Conveyance.
Appointment of
commissioner to
execute conveyance,
§42-2-12.
Damages.
Assessment of damages,
§42-2-8.
Appeal from, §42-2-9.

UNITED STATES—Cont'd

Condemnation of land or rights of way—Cont'd

Damages—Cont'd

Assessment of damages —Cont'd

Commissioners for assessment of damages and compensation, §§42-2-7, 42-2-8.

Failure to pay damages, §42-2-11.

Payment, §42-2-11.

Guardian ad litem.

Appointment for infants and persons of unsound mind, §42-2-4.

Hearings.

Conduct, §42-2-6.

Failure of owner to appear at hearing, §42-2-5.

Notice, §42-2-3.

Order appointing day of hearing, §42-2-3.

Jurisdiction of probate court, §42-2-1.

Mentally ill.

Appointment of guardian ad litem and counsel for persons of unsound mind, §42-2-4.

Minors.

Appointment of guardian ad litem and counsel for infants, §42-2-4.

Order of condemnation.

Vests title, §42-2-10.

Probate courts.

Jurisdiction, §42-2-1.

Reports.

Commissioners for assessment of damages and compensation, §42-2-7.

Right of entry on land pending appeal, §42-2-10.

Vesting of title.

Order of condemnation vests title, §42-2-10.

When authorized, §42-2-1.

Congress.

See CONGRESS.

Conservation and natural resources.

Department.

Cooperation with federal agencies, §9-2-26.

Uniform relocation assistance and land acquisition policies act.

Department to comply with, §9-2-27.

Constitution.

See CONSTITUTION OF THE UNITED STATES.

Contracts.

Bridges.

Rivers forming boundaries between states, §23-1-57.

Coosa valley development authority.

Cooperation with United States, §33-16-2.

UNITED STATES—Cont'd

Corrections.

Institution finance authority.

Kilby property.

Lease.

Environmental protection agency, §14-2-27.

Leasing of facilities, §14-2-30.

Cotton.

Standards.

United States standards adopted, §2-19-80.

Counties.

Contracts with federal government, §11-1-10.

Surplus funds.

Investment in United States securities, §11-8-11.

Courts.

Certified questions from federal courts, ARAP, Rule 18.

Constitution of the United States.

See CONSTITUTION OF THE UNITED STATES.

Criminal law and procedure.

Gambling.

Federal wagering occupational tax stamp, §§13A-12-90 to 13A-12-92.

Marshals.

Pistols.

Carrying, §13A-11-52.

Customs.

Congress.

Power to lay and collect, Const. U. S., Art. I, §8.

Duty of tonnage, Const. U. S., Art. I, §10.

Importation of persons, Const. U. S., Art. I, §9.

Tonnage, Const. U. S., Art. I, §10.

Dams.

Dams on navigable rivers.

Consent of federal government, §33-7-31.

Decedents' estates.

Persons in federal service.

Jurisdiction of probate courts, §12-13-2.

Education.

Federal grants.

See EDUCATION.

Illiteracy.

Authority of state and local boards to cooperate with federal government, §16-34-3.

Eminent domain.

Atomic energy.

Disposal of nuclear waste.

Nonconsent of state to acquisition of land by federal government, §22-14-16.

Condemnation of land or rights of way, §§42-2-1 to 42-2-12. See within this heading, "Condemnation of lands or rights of way."

UNITED STATES—Cont'd

Environmental improvement authorities.

Cooperation with United States and agencies, §9-6-8.

Evidence.

Authentication of certain official documents, §12-21-73.

Land office deeds or written instruments for conveyance or sale of land.

Proof of deeds, §12-21-66.

Fish and game.

Fish restoration and management projects.

Assent to federal act, §9-11-19.

Migratory birds.

Reservations.

Acquisition of lands, §9-11-263.

Shooting preserves.

Federal lands, §9-11-4.

Flag.

Display at schools, §§16-43-1 to 16-43-3.

Forests and forestry.

Insect infestation or tree disease infection.

Protection of forest trees.

Cooperative agreements, §9-13-125.

National forests.

See FORESTS AND FORESTRY.

State forestry commission.

Cooperative agreements and stipulations.

Authority of commission to enter, §9-3-4.

Gambling.

Federal wagering occupational stamp tax, §§13A-12-90 to 13A-12-92.

Geological survey.

Cooperation with United States geological survey, §9-4-11.

Topographic survey.

Agreements as to payment of expenses, §9-4-12.

Gifts.

Foreign presents to United States officials, Const. U. S., Art. I, §9.

Governor.

Cession of land by state to United States.

Authority of governor, §42-3-1.

Guardian ad litem.

Condemnation of land or rights of way.

Appointment for infants and persons of unsound mind, §42-2-4.

Harbors and ports.

Foreign trade zones.

Establishment, §33-1-30.

State docks department.

Authority to contract with federal government for certain purposes, §33-1-36.

UNITED STATES—Cont'd
Highways.
Bond issue for acquiring highways in conjunction with United States, Const. Ala., amd. 87.
Federal aid, §§23-1-300 to 23-1-318.
See HIGHWAYS.
Interstate highway system.
See HIGHWAYS.
National highway safety act of 1966.
Participation in benefits, §32-4-5.
Rivers forming boundaries between states.
Agreements and contracts with federal government relative to bridges, §23-1-57.
House of representatives.
See CONGRESS.
Housing authorities.
Contracts with federal government for construction of projects, §§24-1-34, 24-1-73.
Federal contributions.
Agreements of authorities to secure federal contributions, §24-1-4.
Illiteracy.
Authority of state and local boards of education to cooperate with federal government, §16-34-3.
Income tax.
Armed forces.
Persons and subjects taxable, §40-18-3.
Bond issues.
Interest or other income received from obligations of United States, §40-18-4.
Corporations.
Deductions allowed corporations.
Taxes imposed by authority of United States, §40-18-35.
Deductions, §40-18-15.
Corporations.
Taxes imposed by authority of United States, §40-18-35.
Exemptions.
Interest upon obligations of the United States, §40-18-14.
Income of officers or agents, §40-18-3.
Interest.
Interest received from obligations of United States, §40-18-4.
Persons and subjects taxable, §40-18-3.
Returns.
Inspection by federal agents, §40-18-53.
Securities.
Interest or other income received from obligations of United States, §40-18-4.

UNITED STATES—Cont'd
Investments.
State funds.
Notes and bonds of United States or federal agencies, §41-14-30.
Jails.
Federal prisoners, §§14-6-3, 14-6-4.
Judges.
United States courts, Const. U. S., Art. III, §1.
Junkyard control.
Agreements with department of transportation.
Authority of highway director, §23-1-249.
Land.
Condemnation, §§42-2-1 to 42-2-12. See within this heading, "Condemnation of land or rights of way."
Letters of marque and reprisal, Const. U. S., Art. I, §§8, 10.
Liens.
Uniform federal lien registration.
Applicability of article, §35-11-43.
Certificates.
Execution, §35-11-45.
Citation of article, §35-11-42.
Construction and interpretation.
Uniformity, §35-11-48.
Duties of filing officer, §35-11-46.
Fees, §35-11-47.
Filing.
Fees, §35-11-47.
Place, §35-11-44.
Notice.
Duties of filing officer, §35-11-46.
Execution, §35-11-45.
Place of filing, §35-11-44.
Scope of article, §35-11-451.
Short title of article, §35-11-42.
Uniformity of application and construction of article, §35-11-48.
Meat and meat products.
Department of agriculture.
Exemption of meat inspected and passed by United States department of agriculture, §2-17-28.
Mentally ill.
Condemnation of land or rights of way.
Appointment of guardian ad litem and counsel for infants and persons of unsound mind, §42-2-4.
Military affairs.
Active federal service.
Credit for federal service, §31-2-13.
Commission and United States reserve.
Acceptance not incompatible with holding of civil office, §31-2-36.

UNITED STATES—Cont'd
Military affairs—Cont'd
Compensation for death of national guardsmen.
Dependents must be residents of United States, §31-3-4.
Customs and usage of United States armed forces.
Matters governed by, §31-2-35.
Federally recognized national guard.
Qualifications, §31-2-69.
Officers to have same powers and duties as officers in armed forces of United States, §31-2-70.
Persons exempted from military service.
Officers of United States, §31-2-6.
Release from active federal service.
Status members of national guard and naval militia upon release, §31-2-43.
Uniforms.
Unauthorized wearing of uniform of United States armed forces, §31-2-17.
Minors.
Condemnation of land or rights of way.
Appointment of guardian ad litem and counsel for infants, §42-2-4.
Motor vehicle carriers.
Vehicles owned and operated by the United States.
Exemptions from chapter, §37-3-4.
Motor vehicles.
Certificate of title.
Exemption, §32-8-31.
Drivers' licenses.
Persons in service of federal government driving official motor vehicles.
Exemptions, §32-6-2.
Reciprocal agreements.
Authorities in charge of federal military installations, §32-6-11.
Safety-responsibility act.
Exceptions to act, §32-7-36.
Trucks, trailers and semi-trailers.
Size and weight of vehicles.
Exemption, §32-9-22.
Municipal corporations.
Donation of property to for defense purposes.
Authority, §11-54-211.
Legislative findings and declarations, §11-54-210.
Post office projects, §§11-55-1 to 11-55-13.
See MUNICIPAL CORPORATIONS.

UNITED STATES—Cont'd
Municipal corporations
—Cont'd
Streets.
Payment of costs of streets
constructed, improved,
etc., by federal
government,
§§11-49-60 to 11-49-63.
National forests.
See FORESTS AND
FORESTRY.
Obligations.
Investment of surplus state
funds.
Treasurer authorized to
invest, §36-17-18.
Parties.
Actions to which United
States a party, Const. U.
S., Art. III.
Persons in federal service
and spouses living in
state deemed residents
for purpose of
commencing actions,
§6-7-20.
Pipelines.
Gas pipeline systems.
Federal minimum safety
standards.
Compliance with,
§37-4-81.
Planning.
Office of state planning and
federal programs.
See DEVELOPMENT.
Post office.
Constitutional provisions,
Const. U. S., Art. I, §8.
Municipal corporations.
Post office projects,
§§11-55-1 to 11-55-13.
See MUNICIPAL
CORPORATIONS.
Poultry.
Department of agriculture.
Exemption of poultry
inspected and passed
by United States
department of
agriculture, §2-17-28.
**President of the United
States.**
See PRESIDENT OF THE
UNITED STATES.
Prisons and prisoners.
Federal prisoners, §§14-6-3,
14-6-4.
Penitentiary.
Board of corrections to
receive federal
prisoners, §14-3-32.
Public service commission,
§§37-1-46, 37-1-47.
Public utilities.
Sale or lease of utility
property.
Sale of property in
interstate commerce
contrary to federal law
not authorized,
§37-4-44.
Purchases and stores.
Purchase of property from
United States or its
agencies, §41-4-114.
Real property.
Acquisition of land, §42-1-1.
Redevelopment projects.
Federal aid, §24-2-8.

UNITED STATES—Cont'd
Reports.
Condemnation of land or
rights of way.
Commissioners for
assessment of damages
and compensation,
§42-2-8.
Rights of way.
Condemnation of land or
rights of way, §§42-2-1 to
42-2-12. See within this
heading, "Condemnation
of land or rights of way."
Roads.
Bond issue for acquiring
roads in conjunction with
United States, Const.
Ala., amd. 87.
**Savings and loan
associations.**
Federal savings and loan
associations.
See SAVINGS AND LOAN
ASSOCIATIONS.
Senate.
See CONGRESS.
Ships and shipping.
Commissioner of
conservation and natural
resources.
Supplying information to
federal agencies,
§33-5-8.
Numbering.
Exemptions.
Ships owned by United
States, §33-5-19.
Soil and water conservation.
Districts.
Agents of United States,
§9-8-25.
Watershed conservancy
districts.
Cooperate with or act as
agent for, §9-8-61.
Statutes.
Approval of laws by
president, Const. U. S.,
Art. I, §7.
Limitations on legislation,
Const. U. S., Art. I, §9.
Revenue bills, Const. U. S.,
Art. I, §7.
Streets.
Municipal corporations.
Payment of costs of streets
constructed, improved,
etc., by federal
government,
§§11-49-60 to 11-49-63.
Suits against, Const. U. S.,
Art. III, §2.
Surveys and surveyors.
Public land surveys.
Description by reference to
United States public
land surveys, §35-2-8.
Original survey corners
and accessories.
Custody and ownership,
§35-2-31.
United States coast and
geodetic survey.
Alabama coordinate
system.
Definition of system by
United States coast
and geodetic survey
adopted, §35-2-5.

UNITED STATES—Cont'd
Taxation.
Estate and inheritance tax.
Federal tax.
See ESTATE AND
INHERITANCE
TAX.
Subjects of state taxation.
Property and activities of
United States and its
agencies, §40-11-2.
Taxation where
immunity waived,
§40-11-3.
Titles of nobility.
Prohibited, Const. U. S., Art.
I, §§9, 10.
Tobacco.
Sales tax.
Effect of federal legislation,
§40-25-22.
**Tombigbee valley
development authority.**
Cooperation with United
States, §33-17-2.
Transportation companies.
Free transportation or
reduced rates, §37-2-40.
Governmentally owned
companies.
Applicability of chapter,
§37-2-2.
Unclaimed property.
Property held by federal
courts, officers,
authorities or agencies.
Presumption of
abandonment,
§35-12-28.
Veterans.
Educational benefits for
veterans, §31-6-8.
State service commissioner.
Representation of state
before federal agencies,
§31-5-6.
**Vice-president of the United
States.**
See VICE-PRESIDENT OF
THE UNITED STATES.
**Water conservation and
irrigation.**
Agency.
Power to enter into
agreements with,
§9-10-5.
Corporations.
Powers to enter into
agreements and
contracts with,
§9-10-34.
Waters and watercourses.
Navigable waters.
Cession of sites by state.
Lands covered by
navigable waters,
§42-3-2.
Weights and measures.
Constitutional provisions,
Const. U. S., Art. I, §8.
Youth services.
Department of youth
services.
Agreements with federal
government, §44-1-40.

UNITED STATES COAST AND GEODETIC SURVEY.

Alabama coordinate system.
Definition of system by United States coast and geodetic survey adopted, §35-2-5.

UNIVERSITIES AND COLLEGES.

Age.
Majority.
Age of majority.
Contracting for educational loans, §26-1-5.

Alabama Agricultural and Mechanical University, §§16-49-1 to 16-49-30.
See ALABAMA AGRICULTURAL AND MECHANICAL UNIVERSITY.

Alabama commission on higher education, §§16-5-1 to 16-5-14. See within this heading, "Commission on higher education."

Alabama state university, §§16-50-1 to 16-50-30.
See ALABAMA STATE UNIVERSITY.

American Legion scholarships, §§16-31-1 to 16-31-4.
Amount, §16-31-1.
Appropriation from Alabama special educational trust fund, §16-31-4.
Credit to account of beneficiary, §16-31-3.
Designation of institution.
Fund paid to institution designated, §16-31-2.
What institutions may be designated, §16-31-1.
Enumeration of eligible universities, §16-31-1.
Established, §16-31-1.
Fund paid to university designated, §16-31-2.
Special educational trust fund.
Appropriation from, §16-31-4.
Use, §16-31-1.

Armory commission.
Bonds, surety.
Care of arms, equipment, etc., of reserve units of state colleges, etc., §31-4-4.

Athens State College.
Teachers retirement system.
Purchase of credit for total years of service rendered by employees participating in system, §16-25-13.1.

Auburn University, §§16-48-1 to 16-48-12.
See AUBURN UNIVERSITY.

Authorities.
Educational building authorities, §§16-17-1 to 16-17-19.
See EDUCATION.

UNIVERSITIES AND COLLEGES—Cont'd

Authorities—Cont'd
Public school and college authority, §§16-16-1 to 16-16-13.
See EDUCATION.

Barber colleges.
See BARBERS.

Blind persons.
Educational benefits for dependents of blind parents, §§16-33-1 to 16-33-12. See within this heading, "Educational benefits for dependents of blind parents."

Boards and commissions.
Commission on higher education, §§16-5-1 to 16-5-14.

Bond issues.
Issuance of revenue securities by institutions of learning, Const. Ala., amd. 160.
Private colleges and universities. See within this heading, "Private colleges and universities facilities authority."

Budgets.
Proprosal and recommendations, §16-5-9.

Buildings.
Educational building authorities, §§16-17-1 to 16-17-19.
See EDUCATION.

Chiropractic students enrolled in board approved chiropractic colleges.
Preceptorship and extern programs, §34-24-145.

Churches.
Conventions or associations of churches.
Establishment by state, sectional or national conventions or associations, §10-4-61.

Commission on higher education, §§16-5-1 to 16-5-14.
Additional powers and duties, §16-5-10.
Advisory committee, §16-5-7.
Appointment of members, §16-5-2.
Budget.
Proposals and recommendations, §16-5-9.
Composition, §16-5-2.
Consultants.
Appointment to evaluate commission, §16-5-12.
Assistants to commission, §16-5-5.
Council of presidents, §16-5-5.
Definitions, §16-5-1.
Duties, §16-5-10.
Employees, §16-5-4.
Evaluating commission, §16-5-12.
Executive officer, §16-5-4.
Expenses, §16-5-4.
Functions, §16-5-2.

UNIVERSITIES AND COLLEGES—Cont'd

Commission on higher education—Cont'd
Gift to commission, §16-5-14.
Governing boards and commissions.
Powers and duties of governing boards.
Cooperation from commission, §16-5-13.
Grants to commission, §16-5-14.
Instructional programs.
Coordination of programs, §§16-5-7, 16-5-8.
Defined, §16-5-1.
Meetings, §16-5-4.
Military reservation.
Exemption from powers, §16-5-8.
New members, §16-5-3.
Off-campus offerings.
Defined, §16-5-1.
Organization, §16-5-4.
Planning.
Long-range planning, §16-5-6.
Powers.
Additional powers, §16-5-10.
Military reservation exemption, §16-5-8.
Public institutions for higher education.
Defined, §16-5-1.
Powers and duties of governing boards, §16-5-10.
Public service.
Coordination of program, §§16-5-7, 16-5-8.
Qualifications of members, §16-5-2.
Quorum, §16-5-4.
Reappointments, §16-5-3.
Reconfirmation of current members, §16-5-3.
Research.
Coordination of program, §§16-5-7, 16-5-8.
Retirement system, §16-5-4.
Revising commission, §16-5-12.
Scholarships.
Emergency secondary education scholarship fund.
Administrative authority of commission, §16-23-23.
Southern regional compact for education.
Commission designated agency responsible for functions, §16-5-11.
State board.
Commission relationship, §16-5-13.
State university and college information system.
Designing and establishing, §16-5-7.
Student loan program, §§16-33B-1 to 16-33B-8.
See STUDENT LOAN PROGRAM.
Terms of members, §16-5-3.
Units.
Defined, §16-5-1.

UNIVERSITIES AND COLLEGES—Cont'd
Commission on higher education—Cont'd
Vacancies, §16-5-3.
Compact.
Authority of institutions of higher learning to make interstate educational agreements, §16-3-34.
Constitution of Alabama.
Revenue securities.
Issuance by institutions of learning, Const. Ala., amd. 160.
Contest.
Stonewall Jackson memorial fund generally, §§16-32-1 to 16-32-3.
Contingent interests.
Sale by state institutions, §35-4-384.
Contracts.
Age of majority.
Contracting for educational loans, §26-1-5.
Prepaid tuition contracts, §§16-33C-7, 16-33C-8.
Corporations.
Nonprofit corporations.
See CORPORATIONS.
Counties.
Local aid to state educational institutions, §§16-19-1 to 16-19-8.
Dead bodies.
Distribution of unclaimed bodies for scientific study, §§22-19-20 to 22-19-30.
See DEAD BODIES.
Definitions.
Commission of higher education, §16-5-1.
Local aid to state educational institutions, §16-19-1.
Prepaid tuition, §16-33C-3.
Dental college of Alabama.
See UNIVERSITY OF ALABAMA.
Designating, §16-3-37.
Educational benefits for dependents of blind parents, §§16-33-1 to 16-33-12.
Application for benefits.
Determination of eligibility, §16-33-6.
Duties of state department and state superintendent of education, §16-33-7.
Made to state department of education, §16-33-6.
Proof of residence, eligibility and qualifications.
Applicant to present proof, §16-33-5.
Scholastic and other entrance requirements.
Applicants to meet, §16-33-9.
City superintendent of schools.
Duties, §16-33-8.
Construction of chapter.
Liberal construction, §16-33-3.

UNIVERSITIES AND COLLEGES—Cont'd
Educational benefits for dependents of blind parents—Cont'd
County superintendent of education.
Duties, §16-33-8.
Eligibility.
Applicant to present proof of eligibility, §16-33-5.
Benefits not extended beyond lives of immediate children of blind person, §16-33-10.
Benefits not payable if equal benefits available from federal or state government, §16-33-11.
Determination of eligibility, §16-33-6.
Equal benefits from federal or state government.
Benefits not payable if available, §16-33-11.
Extension of benefits.
Benefits not extended beyond lives of immediate children of blind person, §16-33-10.
Federal benefits.
Benefits not payable if equal benefits available from federal government, §16-33-11.
Liberal construction of chapter, §16-33-3.
Low income families.
Attendance at state institutions or trade schools without payment of fees or tuition, §16-33-4.
Purpose of chapter, §16-33-3.
Qualifications.
Applicant to present proof, §16-33-5.
Residence.
Applicant to present proof of residence, §16-33-5.
Short title of chapter, §16-33-1.
Standards of institutions.
Applicants to meet, §16-33-9.
Not lowered by chapter, §16-33-9.
State benefits.
Benefits not payable if equal benefits available from state government, §16-33-11.
State department of education.
Application to be made to state department, §16-33-6.
Duties, §16-33-7.
State superintendent of education.
Duties, §16-33-7.
Teachers.
Duties, §16-33-8.
Textbooks.
Free textbooks, §16-33-4.
Title of benefits, §16-33-12.

UNIVERSITIES AND COLLEGES—Cont'd
Educational benefits for dependents of blind parents—Cont'd
Tuition and fees.
Attendance at state institutions or trade schools without payment of fees or tuition, §16-33-4.
Defined, §16-33-2.
Educational building authorities, §§16-17-1 to 16-17-19.
See EDUCATION.
Elections.
Registrars.
Duty to visit for purpose of registering voters, §17-4-160.
Registration by mail when absent at institution of higher learning, §17-4-134.
Eminent domain, §18-1A-295.
Eminent scholars trust fund, §§16-61-1 to 16-61-10.
Administration, §16-61-2.
Applicability of provisions.
Future appropriations to eminent scholars programs, §16-61-10.
Appropriations.
Funds.
Allocation per university, §16-61-3.
Applicability of provisions to future appropriations, §16-61-10.
Generally, §16-61-2.
Matching funds, §§16-61-4, 16-61-5.
Commission of higher education.
Annual report, §16-61-6.
Endowed chairs.
Establishment, §16-61-7.
Selection process for holder of chair, §16-61-8.
Established, §16-61-2.
Funding.
Accounting, §16-61-4.
Appropriated funds.
Allocation per university, §16-61-3.
Applicability of provisions to future appropriations, §16-61-10.
Generally, §16-61-2.
Matching funds, §§16-61-4, 16-61-5.
Challenge grants, §16-61-4.
Written agreement between university and respective foundation, §16-61-9.
Endowment funds.
Amount required for endowed chair, §16-61-7.
Use of endowment funds, §16-61-8.
Agreement between university and respective foundation, §16-61-9.

**UNIVERSITIES AND
COLLEGES**—Cont'd
Eminent scholars trust fund
—Cont'd
Funding—Cont'd
Investment of funds,
§16-61-6.
Limitations on total funds
received, §16-61-6.
Maintenance and
investment of funds,
§16-61-6.
Matching funds, §§16-61-4,
16-61-5.
Raising funds, §16-61-3.
Investments, §16-61-6.
Legislative intent, §16-61-1.
Purpose, §16-61-1.
Reports.
Annual report, §16-61-6.
**Extension or
correspondence courses.**
Veterans.
Educational benefits for
veterans, §§31-6-1 to
31-6-17.
See VETERANS.
Fires and fire prevention.
Survivor's education
assistance act.
General provisions,
§§36-21-100 to
36-21-105.
See FIRES AND FIRE
PREVENTION.
Fraternal orders.
General provisions,
§§10-4-170 to 10-4-179.
See FRATERNAL
ORDERS.
Funds.
Eminent scholars trust fund,
§§16-61-1 to 16-61-10.
See within this heading,
"Eminent scholars trust
fund."
Funeral services.
School or college of mortuary
science, §§34-13-1,
34-13-50.
Geological survey.
General provisions.
See GEOLOGICAL
SURVEY.
Handicapped persons.
Rehabilitation and crippled
children service.
Cooperation in
rehabilitation work,
§16-38-7.
Hazing.
Prohibited, §16-1-23.
Highways.
See HIGHWAYS.
Huntington College.
Marine environmental
sciences consortium,
§§16-45-1 to 16-45-5.
Information system.
State university and college
information system.
Commission on higher
education.
Designing and
establishing, §16-5-7.
Insurance.
Appropriations.
Consideration in
determining patient
care reimbursement,
§27-1-11.1.

**UNIVERSITIES AND
COLLEGES**—Cont'd
Insurance—Cont'd
Life insurers organized to aid
nonprofit educational
and scientific
institutions.
Annual license fee, §27-4-8.
**Interstate educational
agreements.**
Authority of institutions of
higher learning to make,
§16-3-34.
**Jacksonville State
University,** §§16-52-1 to
16-52-15.
See JACKSONVILLE
STATE UNIVERSITY.
Judges.
Expenses, §12-5-11.
Junior colleges.
See JUNIOR COLLEGES.
Livingston university,
§§16-53-1 to 16-53-12.
See LIVINGSTON
UNIVERSITY.
Loans.
Age of majority.
Contracting for educational
loans, §26-1-5.
**Local aid to state
educational institutions,**
§§16-19-1 to 16-19-8.
Appropriations.
Authorized, §16-19-2.
Definitions, §16-19-1.
Donations.
Authorized, §16-19-2.
Inconsistent legislation.
Provisions of chapter
control, §16-19-6.
Powers cumulative, §16-19-8.
Schoolhouses.
Warrants deemed issued
for purpose of
constructing, §16-19-7.
Warrants.
Issuance.
Authorization, §16-19-3.
Deemed audit and
allowance of claim,
§16-19-5.
Purposes, §16-19-7.
Payment.
Pledge of revenues for
payment, §16-19-4.
Pledge of revenues for
payment, §16-19-4.
Preferred claims.
County general
obligation warrants
to constitute,
§16-19-5.
Loitering.
Loitering without legitimate
reason or permission,
§13A-11-9.
Majority.
Age of majority.
Contracting for educational
loans, §26-1-5.
**Marine environmental
sciences consortium,**
§§9-7-13, 16-45-1 to
16-45-5.
See MARINE
ENVIRONMENTAL
SCIENCES
CONSORTIUM.

**UNIVERSITIES AND
COLLEGES**—Cont'd
Medical schools.
Meharry Medical College,
§16-3-35.
University of Alabama
School of Medicine.
Generally, §§16-47-90 to
16-47-129.
See UNIVERSITY OF
ALABAMA.
Meharry Medical College,
§16-3-35.
Military affairs.
Armory commission.
Bonds, surety.
Arms and equipment.
Care of arms,
equipment, etc., of
United States
reserve units of
state colleges,
§31-4-4.
National guard.
Educational assistance,
§§31-10-1 to 31-10-4.
Minors.
Age of majority.
Contracting for educational
loans, §26-1-5.
Montevallo.
University of Montevallo,
§§16-54-1 to 16-54-18.
See UNIVERSITY OF
MONTEVALLO.
Municipal corporations.
Local aid to state educational
institutions, §§16-19-1 to
16-19-8.
Naming, §16-3-37.
National guard.
Educational assistance,
§§31-10-1 to 31-10-4.
Nonprofit corporations.
General provisions.
See CORPORATIONS.
North Alabama.
University of North
Alabama, §§16-51-1 to
16-51-15.
See UNIVERSITY OF
NORTH ALABAMA.
Nursing.
Sylacauga Nurses' Training
School, §§16-58-1 to
16-58-3.
Tuskegee Institute, §§16-57-1
to 16-57-4.
University of Alabama
School of Nursing.
General provisions,
§§16-47-130 to
16-47-137.
See UNIVERSITY OF
ALABAMA.
Huntsville.
Scholarships to division
of nursing,
§§16-47-150 to
16-47-152.
University of South
Alabama, §§16-55-7 to
16-55-9.
Obscenity.
Libraries.
Anti-obscenity enforcement
act.
Inapplicability of
criminal provisions
to, §13A-12-200.10.

UNIVERSITIES AND COLLEGES—Cont'd

Parent and child.

Educational benefits for dependents of blind parents, §§16-33-1 to 16-33-12. See within this heading, "Educational benefits for dependents of blind parents."

Peace officers.

Survivor's education assistance act, §§36-21-100 to 36-21-105. See PEACE OFFICERS.

Pharmacists and pharmacies.

Schools and colleges of pharmacy, §§34-23-4, 34-23-50.

Police.

Duties, §16-22-1.

Employment, §16-22-1.

Jurisdiction.

Extension of jurisdiction, §16-22-2.

Powers, §16-22-1.

Prepaid tuition.

Beneficiary.

Qualified beneficiary.

Defined, §16-33C-3.

Contracts.

Conditions, §16-33C-7.

Contents, §16-33C-7.

Definition, §16-33C-3.

Terms, §16-33C-7.

Definitions, §16-33C-3.

Fees.

Outside tuition fees.

Defined, §16-33C-3.

Legislative intent, §16-33C-1.

Purchasers.

Defined, §16-33C-3.

Information to be provided to purchasers, §16-33C-8.

Short title, §16-33C-2.

State colleges.

Defined, §16-33C-3.

Title of act.

Short title, §16-33C-2.

Trust fund.

Board of trustees.

Administrative procedure.

Exemption from provisions, §16-33C-5.

Compensation, §16-33C-4.

Composition, §16-33C-4.

Defined, §16-33C-3.

Officers, §16-33C-4.

Powers, §16-33C-5.

Qualifications, §16-33C-4.

Quorum, §16-33C-4.

Created, §16-33C-6.

Defined, §16-33C-3.

Information provided to purchasers, §16-33C-8.

Investment of funds, §16-33C-6.

Source of funds, §16-33C-6.

Tuition.

Defined, §16-33C-3.

Universities.

Defined, §16-33C-3.

UNIVERSITIES AND COLLEGES—Cont'd

Private colleges and universities facilities authority, §§16-18A-1 to 16-18A-13.

Actions.

Venue and jurisdiction, §16-18A-10.

Bond issues.

Costs, §16-18A-9.

Defined, §16-18A-2.

Disposition of proceeds, §16-18A-8.

Enforceability, §16-18A-11.

Fees, §16-18A-9.

Form, §16-18A-5.

Issuance, §16-18A-5.

Liens.

Creation of statutory mortgage lien, §16-18A-7.

Negotiability, §16-18A-5.

Proceeds.

Deemed trust funds, §16-18A-12.

Disposition, §16-18A-8.

Records, §16-18A-7.

Refunding bonds, §16-18A-5.

Security, §16-18A-5.

Contracts to secure payment, §16-18A-6.

Taxation.

Exemptions, §16-18A-9.

Terms, §16-18A-5.

Citation, §16-18A-1.

Costs.

Bond issues, §16-18A-9.

Defined, §16-18A-2.

Creation, §16-18A-3.

Definitions, §16-18A-2.

Duties, §16-18A-4.

Fees.

Bond issues, §16-18A-9.

Institutions for higher education.

Defined, §16-18A-2.

Litigation.

Venue and jurisdiction, §16-18A-10.

Meetings, §16-18A-3.

Members, §16-18A-3.

Powers and duties, §16-18A-4.

Projects.

Defined, §16-18A-2.

Title to, §16-18A-13.

Property.

Defined, §16-18A-2.

Revenues.

Defined, §16-18A-2.

Rules and regulations.

Promulgation, §16-18A-3.

Short title, §16-18A-1.

Professors.

Retirement system.

Teachers' retirement system, §§16-25-1 to 16-25-28.

See EDUCATION.

Providing instruction not available at state-supported institutions, §16-3-33.

Public school and college authority, §§16-16-1 to 16-16-13.

See EDUCATION.

UNIVERSITIES AND COLLEGES—Cont'd

Rehabilitation and crippled children's service.

Cooperation in rehabilitation work, §16-38-7.

Residency requirements.

Parent or guardian.

Employed by congressman or in executive branch of federal government, §16-1-19.

Scholarships.

American Legion scholarships, §§16-31-1 to 16-31-4.

Blind persons.

Educational benefits for dependents of blind parents, §§16-33-1 to 16-33-12. See within this heading, "Educational benefits for dependents of blind parents."

Dental college of Alabama, §§16-47-76 to 16-47-81. See UNIVERSITY OF ALABAMA.

Jacksonville State University, §§16-52-13 to 16-52-15.

Library science and library education, §41-8-6.

Stonewall Jackson memorial fund, §§16-32-1 to 16-32-3.

Sylacauga Nurses' Training School, §§16-58-1 to 16-58-3.

Troy State University.

School of nursing, §§16-56-13 to 16-56-15.

Tuskegee Institute.

School of nursing, §§16-57-2 to 16-57-4.

University of Alabama.

See UNIVERSITY OF ALABAMA.

University of Alabama, Huntsville.

Scholarships to division of nursing, §§16-47-150 to 16-47-152.

University of Alabama School of Medicine, §§16-47-121 to 16-47-129. See UNIVERSITY OF ALABAMA.

University of Alabama School of Nursing.

General provisions, §§16-47-135 to 16-47-137.

University of North Alabama.

School of nursing, §§16-51-13 to 16-51-15.

University of South Alabama.

School of nursing, §§16-55-7 to 16-55-9.

School buses.

Transportation of students on public school buses, §16-27-2.

School of medicine, §§16-47-90 to 16-47-129. See UNIVERSITY OF ALABAMA.

UNIVERSITIES AND
COLLEGES—Cont'd
Securities.
Issuance of revenue
securities, Const. Ala.,
amd. 160.
Snead Junior College,
§§16-60-150 to 16-60-152.
Social workers.
School of Social Work of
Alabama, §§16-47-170 to
16-47-175.
See UNIVERSITY OF
ALABAMA.
South Alabama University,
§§16-55-1 to 16-55-9.
See UNIVERSITY OF
SOUTH ALABAMA.
Southern regional compact
for education.
Commission on higher
education.
Commission designated
agency responsible for
functions, §16-5-11.
Southern Union College,
§§16-60-130 to 16-60-132.
State board.
Commission on higher
education.
Commission relationship,
§16-5-13.
State board of education.
Naming or designating
institutions of higher
learning, §16-3-37.
Providing instruction not
available at state-
supported institutions,
§16-3-33.
State university and college
information system.
Commission on higher
education.
Designing and
establishing, §16-5-7.
Stonewall Jackson memorial
fund.
Administration, §16-32-2.
Appropriation, §16-32-3.
Award in scholarships,
§16-32-2.
Board of trustees.
Administration of fund,
§16-32-2.
Compensation, §16-32-2.
Composition, §16-32-2.
Created, §16-32-2.
Creation, §16-32-1.
Depository for fund, §16-32-2.
Disbursements, §16-32-2.
Essay contests, §16-32-2.
Establishment, §16-32-1.
Investment of fund, §16-32-2.
Purpose, §16-32-1.
Student loan program.
General provisions,
§§16-33B-1 to 16-33B-8.
See STUDENT LOAN
PROGRAM.
Sylacauga Nurses' Training
School, §§16-58-1 to
16-58-3.
Taxation.
Exemptions from taxation,
§§40-9-16, 40-9-17.
Textbooks.
Education benefits for
dependents of blind
parents.
Free textbooks, §16-33-4.

UNIVERSITIES AND
COLLEGES—Cont'd
Troy State University,
§§16-56-1 to 16-56-15.
See TROY STATE
UNIVERSITY.
Trust fund for eminent
scholars, §§16-61-1 to
16-61-10. See within this
heading, "Eminent scholars
trust fund."
Tuition.
Prepaid tuition.
Wallace-Folsom prepaid
college tuition trust
fund, §§16-33C-1 to
16-33C-8.
Residency requirements.
Parent or guardian.
Employment by
congressman or in
executive branch of
federal government,
§16-1-19.
Tuskegee Institute, §§16-57-1
to 16-57-4.
Unemployment
compensation.
Director of industrial
relations.
Release of information to
institutions of higher
education, §25-4-118.
University of Alabama,
§§16-47-1 to 16-47-204.
See UNIVERSITY OF
ALABAMA.
University of Montevallo,
§§16-54-1 to 16-54-18.
See UNIVERSITY OF
MONTEVALLO.
University of North
Alabama, §§16-51-1 to
16-51-15.
See UNIVERSITY OF
NORTH ALABAMA.
University of South
Alabama, §§16-55-1 to
16-55-9.
See UNIVERSITY OF
SOUTH ALABAMA.
Veterans.
Educational benefits,
§§31-6-1 to 31-6-17.
See VETERANS.
Walker state technical
college.
Alabama mining academy,
§§16-60-260, 16-60-261.
Wallace-Folsom prepaid
college tuition trust
fund, §§16-33C-1 to
16-33C-8. See within this
heading, "Prepaid tuition."

UNIVERSITY OF ALABAMA.
American Legion
scholarships, §§16-31-1 to
16-31-4.
Appropriations.
Dentists advisory board.
Appropriations to
university not affected,
§16-47-52.
School of medicine.
Appropriations to
university not affected,
§16-47-92.

UNIVERSITY OF ALABAMA
—Cont'd
Appropriations—Cont'd
School of nursing.
Appropriations to
university not affected,
§16-47-133.
School of social work.
Appropriations to
university not affected,
§16-47-174.
Asbestos.
Contractors accreditation.
Safe-state program.
Division of university.
Designated
accreditation
agency, §22-39-4.
Board of trustees, Const.
Ala., art. XIV, §264.
Amendment, Const. Ala.,
amd. 399.
Body corporate, §16-47-1.
Compensation of trustees,
§16-47-30.
Composition, §16-47-1.
Dentists advisory board.
Authority, §16-47-54.
Report to legislature,
§16-47-53.
Election of trustees,
§16-47-30.
Endowment funds.
Investment, §16-13-2.
Executive committee,
§16-47-37.
Expenses.
Payment, §16-47-33.
Governor.
Ex officio president of
board, §16-47-30.
Legislature.
Report to legislature,
§16-47-36.
Dentists advisory board,
§16-47-53.
School of medicine,
§16-47-93.
School of nursing,
§16-47-134.
School of social work,
§16-47-175.
Majority vote, §16-47-31.
Meetings, §16-47-32.
Powers.
Corporate powers,
§16-47-2.
Generally, §16-47-34.
President pro tempore,
§16-47-31.
Property.
Authority to dispose of
property, §16-47-35.
Quorum, §16-47-31.
Records.
Preservation of records of
proceedings, §16-47-33.
Reports to legislature,
§16-47-36.
Dental college of Alabama,
§16-47-53.
School of medicine,
§16-47-93.
School of nursing,
§16-47-134.
School of social work,
§16-47-175.
School of medicine.
Annual report to
legislature, §16-47-93.
Authority, §16-47-94.

UNIVERSITY OF ALABAMA
—Cont'd
Board of trustees—Cont'd
School of medicine—Cont'd
Power, §16-47-94.
School of nursing.
Report to legislature,
§16-47-134.
School of social work.
Powers and duties,
§16-47-171.
Reports, §16-47-175.
State superintendent of
education.
Member of board,
§16-47-30.
Terms of members,
§16-47-30.
Vacancies, §16-47-30.
Voting.
Majority vote, §16-47-31.
Body corporate, §16-47-1.
Bond issues.
Construction and
improvement purposes,
Const. Ala., amd. 157.
Medical center, Const.
Ala., amd. 119.
Mental hospital, Const.
Ala., amd. 141.
School of medicine.
Issuance of bonds,
§16-47-95.
Bureau of mines.
Cooperation of university
with, §16-47-13.
Cement.
Testing laboratories,
§16-47-14.
Code of Alabama.
Furnished to law
department, §16-47-8.
**Commission of higher
education.**
General provisions, §§16-5-1
to 16-5-14.
See UNIVERSITIES AND
COLLEGES.
Constitution of Alabama.
Board of trustees, Const.
Ala., art. XIV, §264.
Amendment, Const. Ala.,
amd. 399.
Bond issues.
Bonds for construction and
improvement purposes,
Const. Ala., amd. 157.
Medical center, Const. Ala.
amds. 119, 141.
Funds.
Interest.
Annual payment, Const.
Ala., art. XIV, §265.
Corporation.
Body corporate, §16-47-1.
Definitions.
Museum, §16-47-190.
Degrees.
Powers of board of trustees,
§16-47-34.
Dental college of Alabama,
§§16-47-50 to 16-47-81.
Establishment, §16-47-50.
Scholarships.
Board of dental scholarship
awards.
Authorization to
establish
scholarships,
§16-47-76.
Composition, §16-47-76.

UNIVERSITY OF ALABAMA
—Cont'd
Dental college of Alabama
—Cont'd
Scholarships—Cont'd
Board of dental scholarship
awards—Cont'd
Created, §16-47-76.
Duties, §16-47-77.
Powers, §16-47-77.
Terms of members,
§16-47-76.
Contractual agreement of
recipients, §16-47-80.
Established.
Board of dental
scholarship awards.
Authorized to
establish,
§16-47-76.
Loans.
Contractual agreement
of recipients,
§16-47-80.
Penalties for breach of
contract, §16-47-80.
Repayment of loans,
§16-47-79.
Localities in need of
dentists, §16-47-81.
Merit scholarships,
§16-47-78.
Penalties for breach of
contractual agreement,
§16-47-80.
Repayment of loans,
§16-47-79.
Types of scholarships,
§16-47-78.
Teaching permits.
Issuance, §34-9-8.
Dentists advisory board.
Appropriations not to affect
other appropriations to
university, §16-47-52.
Board of trustees.
Authority, §16-47-54.
Report to legislature,
§16-47-53.
General provisions,
§16-47-51.
Reports.
Board of trustees to report
to legislature,
§16-47-53.
Ejectment.
Recovery of lands by or in
name of state for
university, §6-6-281.
Elections.
Board of trustees, §16-47-30.
Eminent domain.
General provisions.
See EMINENT DOMAIN.
Faculty.
Appointment by board of
trustees, §16-47-34.
Eminent scholars trust fund,
§§16-61-1 to 16-61-10.
See UNIVERSITIES AND
COLLEGES.
Franchises.
Previous franchises retained,
§16-47-6.
Funds.
Eminent scholars trust fund,
§§16-61-1 to 16-61-10.
See UNIVERSITIES AND
COLLEGES.

UNIVERSITY OF ALABAMA
—Cont'd
Funds—Cont'd
Interest.
Annual payment, Const.
Ala., art. XIV, §265.
Museum.
Contributions, §16-47-202.
University of Alabama
museum fund,
§16-47-203.
University fund, §16-47-4.
Genetic service.
Diagnostic facilities, genetic
counseling and prenatal
testing, §22-10A-2.
Geological survey.
State geologist.
See GEOLOGICAL
SURVEY.
Gifts.
Preserved, §16-47-5.
Governor.
Museum.
Governor may convey
interest of state in
museum lands to
university, §16-47-204
Grants.
Preserved, §16-47-5.
Huntsville, §§16-47-150 to
16-47-152.
Bonds for construction and
improvement purposes a
University of Alabama
research institute, Const
Ala., amd. 157.
Scholarships to division of
nursing, §§16-47-150 to
16-47-152.
Amount, §16-47-152.
Conditions, §16-47-152.
Distribution, §16-47-150.
Eligibility.
Who eligible, §16-47-151
Established, §16-47-150.
Selection of recipients,
§16-47-152.
Insurance.
Appropriations to university
Consideration in patient
care reimbursements,
§27-1-11.1.
Laboratories.
Testing laboratories,
§16-47-14.
Law department.
Books may be furnished.
Law department, §16-47-7
Code of Alabama.
Furnished law department
§16-47-8.
State publications.
Additional copies furnishe
to law department for
exchange, §16-47-9.
Supreme court reports.
Furnished law department
§16-47-8.
Legislature.
Board of trustees.
Report to legislature,
§§16-47-36, 16-47-53,
16-47-93, 16-47-134,
16-47-175.
Dental college of Alabama.
Report to legislature,
§16-47-53.
School of medicine.
Annual report to
legislature, §16-47-93.

UNIVERSITY OF ALABAMA
—Cont'd
Legislature—Cont'd
  School of nursing.
    Report to legislature,
      §16-47-134.
  School of social work.
    Report to legislature,
      §16-47-175.
Marine environmental
  sciences consortium,
  §§16-45-1 to 16-45-5.
Medical school, §§16-47-90 to
  16-47-129. See within this
  heading, "School of
  medicine."
Military system.
  Authority to abolish, Const.
    Ala., art. XIV, §265.
Mines and minerals.
  Bureau of mines.
    Cooperation of university
      with, §16-47-13.
  Department of mining
    engineering.
    Declared to be school of
      mines, §16-47-12.
  School of mines of Alabama,
    §16-47-12.
Museum, §§16-47-190 to
  16-47-204.
  Acquisition of land for
    museum, §§16-47-191,
    16-47-192.
  Acquisition of personal
    property for museum,
    §16-47-194.
  Geological survey
    authorized to transfer
    property and make
    collection, §16-47-196.
  Powers of university over
    personal property
    acquired for use or
    display, §16-47-197.
  Buildings.
    Erection, maintenance and
      improvements,
      §16-47-193.
  Collections.
    Geological survey
      authorized to,
      §16-47-196.
  Contributions.
    Generally, §16-47-202.
  Counties.
    Contributions, §16-47-202.
  Definitions, §16-47-190.
  Display.
    Place of display,
      §16-47-194.
    Powers of university over
      personal property
      acquired for display,
      §16-47-197.
  Employees for museum,
    §16-47-198.
  Erection of buildings,
    §16-47-193.
  Funds.
    Contributions, §16-47-202.
    University of Alabama
      museum fund,
      §16-47-203.
  Governor.
    Conveying interest of state
      in museum lands to
      university, §16-47-204.
  Improvement of buildings,
    §16-47-193.

UNIVERSITY OF ALABAMA
—Cont'd
Museum—Cont'd
  Maintenance of buildings,
    §16-47-193.
  Municipal corporations.
    Contribution to museum,
      §16-47-202.
  Police.
    Powers of police officers
      appointed by
      university president,
      §16-47-199.
  Property.
    Acquisition of land for
      museum.
      Authorization,
        §16-47-191.
      Cooperation with others,
        §16-47-191.
      From Alabama museum
        of natural history,
        §16-47-192.
    Acquisition of personal
      property for museum,
      §16-47-194.
    Powers of university over
      personal property
      acquired, §16-47-197.
    Contributions, §16-47-202.
    Governor may convey
      interest of state in
      museum lands to
      university, §16-47-204.
  Recreational facilities.
    Construction and
      operation, §16-47-195.
  Roads to and within museum
    grounds.
    Construction and
      maintenance,
      §16-47-201.
  Rules and regulations,
    §16-47-199.
    Violations, §16-47-199.
    Disposition of fines,
      §16-47-200.
  Teaching at museum,
    §16-47-198.
Nursing school, §§16-47-130
  to 16-47-137. See within
  this heading, "School of
  nursing."
Police.
  Appointed by president,
    §16-47-10.
  Duties, §16-47-10.
  Extended jurisdiction,
    §16-47-11.
  Jurisdiction.
    Extended jurisdiction,
      §16-47-11.
  Museum.
    Powers of police officers
      appointed by
      university president,
      §16-47-199.
  Powers, §§16-47-10,
    16-47-199.
  Universities generally,
    §§16-22-1, 16-22-2.
Powers.
  Corporate powers, §16-47-2.
  Property.
    Power to hold and dispose
      of property, §16-47-3.
President.
  Agricultural and industrial
    exhibit commission.
    Member of commission,
      §2-7-1.

UNIVERSITY OF ALABAMA
—Cont'd
Privileges.
  Previous privileges retained,
    §16-47-6.
Professors.
  State geologist.
    See GEOLOGICAL
      SURVEY.
Property.
  Board of trustees.
    Authority to dispose of
      property, §16-47-35.
  Museum.
    Acquisition of land for
      museum.
      Authorization,
        §16-47-191.
      Cooperation with others,
        §16-47-191.
      From Alabama museum
        of natural history,
        §16-47-192.
    Acquisition of personal
      property for museum,
      §16-47-194.
    Powers of university over
      personal property
      acquired, §16-47-197.
    Contributions, §16-47-202.
    Geological survey
      authorized to transfer
      property and make
      collections, §16-47-196.
    Governor may convey
      interest of state in
      museum lands to
      university, §16-47-204.
  Power to hold and dispose of
    property, §16-47-3.
  Previous property retained,
    §16-47-6.
  School of medicine.
    Acquisition of property for,
      §16-47-95.
Records.
  Board of trustees.
    Preservation of records of
      proceedings, §16-47-33.
Recreational facilities.
  Construction and operation,
    §16-47-195.
Reports.
  Board of trustees.
    Report to legislature,
      §§16-47-36, 16-47-53,
      16-47-93, 16-47-134,
      16-47-175.
  Dentists advisory board.
    Board of trustees to report
      to legislature,
      §16-47-53.
  School of medicine.
    Annual report to
      legislature, §16-47-93.
  School of nursing.
    Report to legislature,
      §16-47-134.
  Supreme court reports.
    Furnished to law
      department, §16-47-8.
Research institute.
  Bonds for construction and
    improvement purposes,
    Const. Ala., amd. 157.
Rights.
  Retained, §16-47-6.

UNIVERSITY OF ALABAMA
—Cont'd
Rules and regulations.
Museum, §16-47-199.
Violations, §16-47-199.
Disposition of fines for
violations,
§16-47-200.
Salaries.
Powers of board of trustees,
§16-47-34.
State geologist.
Compensation for teaching,
§9-4-6.
Sales tax.
Tax levied on gross receipts,
§40-23-2.
Scholarships.
American Legion
scholarships, §§16-31-1
to 16-31-4.
Dental college of Alabama,
§§16-47-76 to 16-47-81.
See within this heading,
"Dental college of
Alabama."
School of medicine,
§§16-47-121 to 16-47-129.
See within this heading,
"School of medicine."
School of nursing.
Generally, §§16-47-135 to
16-47-137.
Huntsville.
Scholarships to division
of nursing,
§§16-47-150 to
16-47-152.
School of social work,
§16-47-172.
School of medicine,
§§16-47-90 to 16-47-129.
Anatomical gifts.
See ANATOMICAL
GIFTS.
Appropriations.
Appropriations to
university not affected,
§16-47-92.
Board of trustees.
Annual report to
legislature, §16-47-93.
Authority, §16-47-94.
Power, §16-47-94.
Bond issues.
Authorized, Const. Ala.,
amds. 119, 141.
Issuance, §16-47-95.
Creation, §16-47-90.
Dead bodies.
Distribution of unclaimed
bodies for scientific
study, §§22-19-20 to
22-19-30.
See DEAD BODIES.
Establishment, §16-47-90.
Legislature.
Annual report to
legislature, §16-47-93.
Medical center.
Bond issues, Const. Ala.,
amds. 119, 141.
Mental hospital at
University of Alabama
medical center.
Bond issue, Const. Ala.,
amd. 141.
Name, §16-47-90.
Physicians advisory board.
General provisions,
§16-47-91.

UNIVERSITY OF ALABAMA
—Cont'd
School of medicine—Cont'd
Property.
Acquisition for school of
medicine, §16-47-95.
Reports.
Annual report to
legislature, §16-47-93.
Scholarships, §§16-47-121 to
16-47-129.
Board of medical
scholarship awards,
§§16-47-121 to
16-47-123.
Authorization to
establish,
§16-47-121.
Chairman, §16-47-122.
Composition, §16-47-122.
Created, §16-47-121.
Powers and duties,
§16-47-123.
Terms of members,
§16-47-122.
Establishment.
Board of medical
scholarship awards.
Authorization to
establish,
§16-47-121.
Loans, §16-47-124.
Localities in need of
physicians, §16-47-129.
Agreement of recipient
to practice in certain
area, §16-47-127.
Penalty for failure of
recipient to
perform loan
agreement,
§16-47-128.
Merit scholarships,
§16-47-124.
Penalty for failure of
recipient to perform
loan agreement,
§16-47-128.
Recipients.
Agreement to practice in
certain area,
§16-47-127.
Penalty for failure to
perform loan
agreement,
§16-47-128.
Repayment of loans.
Generally, §16-47-125.
Performance of certain
services, §16-47-126.
Types of scholarships,
§16-47-124.
School of nursing,
§§16-47-130 to 16-47-137.
Appropriations.
Appropriations to
university not affected,
§16-47-133.
Board of trustees.
Report to legislature,
§16-47-134.
Clinical facilities, §16-47-131.
Creation, §16-47-130.
Dean.
Director of school,
§16-47-130.
Director of school,
§16-47-130.
Educational facilities,
§16-47-131.
Establishment, §16-47-130.

UNIVERSITY OF ALABAMA
—Cont'd
School of nursing—Cont'd
Expenses.
Payment, §16-47-132.
Facilities, §16-47-131.
Legislature.
Report to legislature,
§16-47-134.
Name, §16-47-130.
Purpose, §16-47-130.
Reports.
Report to legislature,
§16-47-134.
Scholarships.
Amount, §16-47-137.
Conditions, §16-47-137.
Eligibility, §16-47-136.
How distributed,
§16-47-135.
Selection of recipients,
§16-47-137.
University of Alabama,
Huntsville,
§§16-47-150 to
16-47-152.
School of social work,
§§16-47-170 to 16-47-175.
Admission.
Preferential consideration
for residents,
§16-47-173.
Requirements, §16-47-172.
Residents to have
preferential
consideration,
§16-47-173.
Standards, §16-47-172.
Appropriations.
Appropriations to
university not affected,
§16-47-174.
Board of trustees.
Powers and duties,
§16-47-171.
Reports, §16-47-175.
Course of instruction.
Minimum course,
§16-47-170.
Created, §16-47-170.
Dean.
Qualifications, §16-47-171.
Established, §16-47-170.
Legislature.
Report of board of trustees,
§16-47-175.
Minimum course of
instruction, §16-47-170.
Name, §16-47-170.
Requirements for admission,
§16-47-172.
Residents.
Preferential consideration
for admission,
§16-47-173.
Scholarships, §16-47-172.
Separate graduate school.
School to be separate
graduate school,
§16-47-171.
Standards for admission,
§16-47-172.
Soil and water conservation
Water resources research
institute.
General provisions.
See SOIL AND WATER
CONSERVATION.
State geologist.
See GEOLOGICAL
SURVEY.

UNIVERSITY OF ALABAMA
—Cont'd
State superintendent of education.
Member of board of trustees, §16-47-30.
Supreme court.
Books may be furnished law department, §16-47-7.
Reports.
Furnished to law department, §16-47-8.
Teachers.
Summer school for teachers.
Establishment, §16-47-15.
Maintenance, §16-47-16.
Testing laboratories, §16-47-14.
Textbooks.
Law department.
Books may be furnished law department, §16-47-7.
Trustees.
Board of trustees. See within this heading, "Board of trustees."
Tuition.
Powers of board of trustees, §16-47-34.
University fund.
Eminent scholars trust fund, §§16-61-1 to 16-61-10.
See UNIVERSITIES AND COLLEGES.
Generally. See within this heading, "Funds."
University of Alabama, Huntsville, §§16-47-150 to 16-47-152.
Water resources research institute.
Article supplementary, §9-8-4.

UNIVERSITY OF ALABAMA HUNTSVILLE FOUNDATION.
Licenses.
Exemptions, §40-9-12.
Taxation.
Exemptions, §40-9-12.

UNIVERSITY OF MONTEVALLO, §§16-54-1 to 16-54-18.
Actions.
Corporate powers, §16-54-1.
Admission to university.
Eligibility, §16-54-11.
Qualifications, §16-54-11.
Agents.
Records of transactions.
Required, §16-54-10.
American Legion scholarships, §§16-31-1 to 16-31-4.
Board of trustees.
Appointment of members, §16-54-2.
Composition, §16-54-2.
Election of president, §16-54-5.
Endowment funds.
Investment of endowment funds held by board, §16-13-2.
Expenses of members, §16-54-2.
Governor.
President ex officio, §16-54-2.

UNIVERSITY OF MONTEVALLO—Cont'd
Board of trustees—Cont'd
Secretary.
Election, §16-54-7.
Superintendent of education.
Ex officio member, §16-54-2.
Terms of members, §16-54-2.
Treasurer of university.
Election, §16-54-8.
Vacancies, §16-54-2.
Body corporate, §16-54-1.
Bonds, surety.
Treasurer of university, §16-54-8.
Commission of higher education.
General provisions, §§16-5-1 to 16-5-14.
See UNIVERSITIES AND COLLEGES.
Corporation.
Body corporate, §16-54-1.
Powers, §16-54-1.
Degrees, §16-54-4.
Diplomas, §16-54-4.
Eligibility for admission, §16-54-11.
Eminent domain.
Lands may be condemned, §16-54-15.
Faculty.
Appointment, §16-54-6.
Compensation, §16-54-6.
Composition, §16-54-6.
Eminent scholars trust fund, §§16-61-1 to 16-61-10.
See UNIVERSITIES AND COLLEGES.
Federal grants.
Lease or disposal of lands received, §16-54-16.
Funds.
Eminent scholars trust fund, §§16-61-1 to 16-61-10.
See UNIVERSITIES AND COLLEGES.
Governor.
Board of trustees.
Ex officio president, §16-54-2.
Grants.
Federal grants.
Lease or disposal of lands received, §16-54-16.
Preserved, §16-54-14.
Licenses.
Employees exempt from license taxes, §16-54-12.
Marine environmental sciences consortium, §§16-45-1 to 16-45-5.
Name, §16-54-1.
Officers.
Records of transactions.
Required, §16-54-10.
Police.
University police generally, §§16-22-1, 16-22-2.
Powers.
Generally, §16-54-1.
President of university.
Election, §16-54-5.
Faculty.
Powers as to, §16-54-6.
Qualifications, §16-54-5.
Removal, §16-54-5.
Salary, §16-54-5.
Property.
Corporate powers, §16-54-1.

UNIVERSITY OF MONTEVALLO—Cont'd
Property—Cont'd
Disposition of proceeds from lands, §16-54-17.
Exemption from taxes, §16-54-12.
Federal grants.
Lease or disposal of lands received, §16-54-16.
Funds.
Previously generated by proceeds from lands dedicated to university.
Deposit in restricted endowment fund, §16-54-18.
Lands may be purchased or condemned, §16-54-15.
Purpose, §16-54-3.
Records.
Transactions, §16-54-10.
Rights.
Preservation, §16-54-14.
Salaries.
Faculty, §16-54-6.
President of university, §16-54-5.
Secretary of university, §16-54-7.
Treasurer of university, §16-54-8.
Scholarships.
American Legion scholarships, §§16-31-1 to 16-31-4.
See UNIVERSITIES AND COLLEGES.
Secretary of university.
Compensation, §16-54-7.
Duties, §16-54-7.
Election, §16-54-7.
Records of transactions.
Required, §16-54-10.
State superintendent of education.
Members of board of trustees, §16-54-2.
Students.
Employment of student assistants, §16-54-13.
Taxation.
Employees exempt from license taxes, §16-54-12.
Property exempt from taxes, §16-54-12.
Treasurer of university.
Bonds, surety, §16-54-8.
Compensation, §16-54-8.
Duties, §16-54-8.
Election, §16-54-8.
Records of transactions.
Required, §16-54-10.
Removal from office, §16-54-9.
Term of office, §16-54-8.
Trustees.
Board of trustees. See within this heading, "'Board of trustees."

UNIVERSITY OF NORTH ALABAMA, §§16-51-1 to 16-51-15.
Administration.
Board of trustees.
Powers, §16-51-6.
Agents.
Default, etc., not to work forfeiture, §16-51-11.

UNIVERSITY OF NORTH ALABAMA—Cont'd
Board of trustees.
Administration.
Powers, §16-51-6.
Appointment of members, §16-51-3.
Body corporate, §16-51-1.
Compensation of members, §16-51-3.
Composition, §16-51-3.
Courses of instruction.
Powers of board, §16-51-6.
Created, §16-51-3.
Default, etc., not to work forfeiture, §16-51-11.
Degrees.
Powers of board, §16-51-6.
Endowment funds.
Investment, §16-13-2.
Expenses of members, §16-51-3.
Payment, §16-51-9.
Faculty.
Powers as to, §16-51-6.
Jurisdiction.
Transfer of jurisdiction, §16-51-7.
Legislature.
Reports to legislature, §16-51-10.
Meetings, §16-51-4.
Membership, §16-51-3.
Organization.
Powers, §16-51-6.
Powers, §16-51-6.
President of university.
Powers of board, §16-51-6.
Quorum, §16-51-5.
Reports to legislature, §16-51-10.
Terms of members, §16-51-3.
Transfer of jurisdiction, §16-51-7.
Tuition.
Powers of board, §16-51-6.
Vacancies in office, §16-51-8.
Body corporate, §16-51-1.
Commission of higher education.
General provisions, §§16-5-1 to 16-5-14.
See UNIVERSITIES AND COLLEGES.
Corporation.
Body corporate, §16-51-1.
Rights, privileges, responsibilities, etc., §16-51-2.
Courses of instruction.
Board of trustees.
Powers of board, §16-51-6.
Degrees.
Board of trustees.
Powers of board, §16-51-6.
Faculty.
Board of trustees.
Powers as to faculty, §16-51-6.
Eminent scholars trust fund, §§16-61-1 to 16-61-10.
See UNIVERSITIES AND COLLEGES.
Employment, §16-51-6.
Salaries, §16-51-6.
Funds.
Eminent scholars trust fund, §§16-61-1 to 16-61-10.
See UNIVERSITIES AND COLLEGES.

UNIVERSITY OF NORTH ALABAMA—Cont'd
Gifts and grants.
Not to fail for informality, §16-51-11.
Jurisdiction.
Board of trustees.
Transfer of jurisdiction, §16-51-7.
Legislature.
Board of trustees.
Reports to legislature, §16-51-10.
Marine environmental sciences consortium, §§16-45-1 to 16-45-5.
Nursing school.
Scholarships, §§16-51-13 to 16-51-15.
Officers and employees.
Default, etc., not to work forfeiture, §16-51-11.
Police officers, §16-51-12.
Organization.
Board of trustees.
Powers, §16-51-6.
Police.
University police generally, §§16-22-1, 16-22-2.
President of university.
Appointment, §16-51-6.
Board of trustees.
Powers of board, §16-51-6.
Salaries, §16-51-6.
Property.
Rights, privileges, responsibilities, etc., of corporation, §16-51-2.
Reports.
Board of trustees.
Reports to legislature, §16-51-10.
Salaries.
Board of trustees.
Powers of board, §16-51-6.
Faculty, §16-51-6.
President of university, §16-51-6.
School of nursing.
Scholarships.
Amount, §16-51-15.
Conditions, §16-51-15.
Distribution, §16-51-13.
Eligibility, §16-51-14.
Selection of recipients, §16-51-15.
Trustees.
Board of trustees. See within this heading, "Board of trustees."
Tuition.
Board of trustees.
Powers of board, §16-51-6.

UNIVERSITY OF SOUTH ALABAMA, §§16-55-1 to 16-55-9.
Administration of university.
Powers of board of trustees, §16-55-4.
Board of trustees, §§16-55-1 to 16-55-6.
Appointment of members, §16-55-2.
Authority, §16-55-3.
Body corporate, §16-55-1.
Classifications.
Trustees divided into classes, §16-55-5.
Compensation of members, §16-55-2.

UNIVERSITY OF SOUTH ALABAMA—Cont'd
Board of trustees—Cont'd
Courses of instruction.
Powers of board, §16-55-4.
Degrees.
Powers of board, §16-55-4.
Divided into classes, §16-55-5.
Endowment funds.
Investment, §16-13-2.
Expenses of members, §16-55-2.
Faculty.
Powers of board, §16-55-4.
Governor.
Ex officio president of board, §16-55-2.
Meetings, §16-55-6.
Officers and employees.
Powers of board, §16-55-4.
Powers, §§16-55-3, 16-55-4.
Privileges, §16-55-3.
Quorum, §16-55-6.
Rights, §16-55-3.
State superintendent of education.
Member of board of trustees, §16-55-2.
Terms of members, §16-55-2.
Initial terms, §16-55-5.
Tuition.
Powers of board, §16-55-4.
Vacancies, §16-55-2.
Body corporate, §16-55-1.
Commission of higher education.
General provisions, §§16-5-1 to 16-5-14.
See UNIVERSITIES AND COLLEGES.
Courses of instruction.
Board of trustees.
Powers of board, §16-55-4.
Degrees.
Board of trustees.
Powers of board, §16-55-4.
Faculty.
Appointment, §16-55-4.
Board of trustees.
Powers of board, §16-55-4.
Eminent scholars trust fund, §§16-61-1 to 16-61-10.
See UNIVERSITIES AND COLLEGES.
Removal by board, §16-55-4.
Salaries, §16-55-4.
Funds.
Eminent scholars trust fund, §§16-61-1 to 16-61-10.
See UNIVERSITIES AND COLLEGES.
Genetic service.
Diagnostic facilities, genetic counseling and prenatal testing, §22-10A-2.
Governor.
Board of trustees.
Ex officio president of board, §16-55-2.
Marine environmental sciences consortium, §§16-45-1 to 16-45-5.
Nursing school.
Scholarships, §§16-55-7 to 16-55-9.
Officers and employees.
Appointment, §16-55-4.
Board of trustees.
Powers of board, §16-55-4.
Removal, §16-55-4.

UNIVERSITY OF SOUTH ALABAMA—Cont'd
Organization.
Powers of board of trustees, §16-55-4.
Police.
University police generally, §§16-22-1, 16-22-2.
Public lands.
Settlement of dispute as to certain property.
Conveyance to University of South Alabama Foundation, §35-4-393.
Salaries.
Faculty, §16-55-4.
Officers and employees, §16-55-4.
Powers of board of trustees, §16-55-4.
School of nursing.
Scholarships.
Amount, §16-55-9.
Conditions, §16-55-9.
Distribution, §16-55-7.
Eligibility.
Who eligible, §16-55-8.
Selection of recipients, §16-55-9.
State superintendent of education.
Member of board of trustees, §16-55-2.
Trustees.
Board of trustees. See within this heading, "Board of trustees."
Tuition.
Board of trustees.
Powers of board, §16-55-4.

UNLAWFUL DETAINER,
§§6-6-310 to 6-6-353.
See FORCIBLE ENTRY AND UNLAWFUL DETAINER.

UNSOLICITED MERCHANDISE.
Delivery by mail or common carrier.
Disposition, §35-1-3.

UNUSED PUBLIC LANDS,
§§9-15-1 to 9-15-19.
See PUBLIC LANDS.

UPHOLSTERERS.
Licenses, §40-12-125.

URBAN ENTERPRISE ZONES.
Creation within Class 1 cities, §11-40-16.

URBAN RENEWAL PROJECTS, §§24-3-1 to 24-3-19.
Acquisition, §24-3-7.
Conflict of laws, §24-3-9.
Definitions.
Urban renewal plans, §24-3-3.
Development of undeveloped vacant land.
Preparation for development, §24-3-7.
Disposal of undeveloped vacant land.
Preparation for disposal, §24-3-7.
Housing authorities.
Authorized to plan and undertake projects, §24-3-2.

URBAN RENEWAL PROJECTS—Cont'd
Housing authorities—Cont'd
Delegation of powers to municipalities, §24-3-5.
Powers conferred by chapter supplemental, §24-3-8.
Powers with respect to projects, §24-3-4.
Legislative findings and declaration of necessity, §24-3-1.
Municipal corporations.
Assistance of urban renewal projects by municipalities, §24-3-5.
Authorized to plan and undertake projects, §24-3-2.
Delegation of powers of authority to municipalities, §24-3-5.
Powers conferred by chapter supplemental, §24-3-8.
Private enterprise.
Municipalities to afford opportunities for redevelopment, etc., §24-3-1.
Plans, §24-3-4.
Defined, §24-3-3.
Housing authorities and municipalities authorized to plan projects, §24-3-2.
Preparation and approval, §24-3-3.
What constitutes urban renewal projects and plans, §§24-3-2, 24-3-3.
Powers conferred by chapter supplemental, §24-3-8.
Private enterprise.
Municipalities to afford opportunities for redevelopment, etc., §24-3-1.
Program.
Workable program, §24-3-6.
Provisions of chapter cumulative, §24-3-9.
Redevelopment projects.
See REDEVELOPMENT PROJECTS.
Surveys, §24-3-4.
Vacant land.
Preparation for development or disposal, §24-3-7.
Workable program, §24-3-6.

U.R.E.S.A.
Reciprocal state enforcement of duty to support, §§30-4-80 to 30-4-98.
See DESERTION AND NONSUPPORT.

USED CAR SALES, §§32-16-1 to 32-16-4.
See MOTOR VEHICLES.

USE TAX, §§40-23-60 to 40-23-88.
Actions.
Actions to prevent or enjoin collection of tax, §40-23-87.
Delinquent taxes.
Actions to collect, §40-23-86.

USE TAX—Cont'd
Actions—Cont'd
Penalties.
Returns.
Failing or refusing to furnish returns, §40-23-88.
Additional amounts.
When notice of additional amount due to be mailed, §40-23-76.
Advertising.
Assumption or absorption of tax by sellers.
Advertising prohibited, §40-23-67.
Aged persons.
Medicines prescribed by physicians,
Exemptions, §40-23-62.
Agriculture, §§40-23-63, 40-23-64.
Air commerce.
Air carriers.
Exemptions, §40-23-62.
Air pollution.
Exemptions.
Devices or facilities for control, reduction or elimination, §40-23-62.
American Legion.
Exemption from tax, §40-23-5.
Appeals.
Redeterminations, §40-23-73.
Attorney general.
Delinquent taxes.
Actions to collect, §40-23-86.
Bonds, surety.
Deposit of security.
Department may require, §40-23-75.
Chilton county rescue squad.
Exemptions, §40-23-5.
Coal.
Exemptions, §40-23-62.
Collection.
Collection of tax on same sale.
Only one municipal or county use tax collectible, §40-23-2.1.
Retail sellers to collect, §40-23-67.
Confidential information.
Divulging, §40-23-84.
Constitution of Alabama.
Exemptions.
Property exempt under constitution, §40-23-62.
Constitution of the United States.
Exemptions.
Property prohibited from being taxed under constitution, §40-23-62.
Cottonseed meal.
Exemptions, §40-23-62.
Council of state governments.
Exemptions, §40-23-5.
Counties.
Collection of tax on same sale.
Only one county use tax collectible, §40-23-2.1.
Exemptions, §40-23-62.

USE TAX—Cont'd
  Credits.
    Taxes paid to another state, §40-23-65.
  Cystic fibrosis research foundation.
    Exemptions, §40-23-62.
  Declaratory judgments.
    Fixing tax liability, §40-23-87.
  Definitions, §40-23-60.
  Delinquent taxes.
    Collection, §40-23-86.
  Department of revenue.
    Determination of true amount of tax due, §40-23-70.
    Disposition of funds derived from tax, §40-23-85.
    Divulging confidential information, §40-23-84.
    Enforcement of article, §40-23-83.
    Examination of records, §40-23-83.
    Rules and regulations, §40-23-83.
  Determination of true amount of tax due.
    Authority of department of revenue, §40-23-70.
  Diabetes Trust Fund, Inc.
    Exemption, §40-23-5.
  Disabled American veterans.
    Exemption, §40-23-5.
  Discounts, §40-23-77.
  Disposition of funds derived from tax, §40-23-85.
  Drugs.
    Exemptions, §40-23-62.
  Education.
    Exemptions.
      Certain tangible personal property, §40-23-62.
    Use of county sales and use tax funds for general educational purposes, §16-13-37.
  Enforcement of article.
    Department of revenue to enforce, §40-23-83.
  Estimates of tax due when no return made, §40-23-71.
  Exemptions, §40-23-62.
    Aged persons.
      Medicines prescribed by physicians, §40-23-62.
    Air carriers, §40-23-62.
    Air pollution.
      Devices or facilities for control, reduction or elimination, §40-23-62.
    Alabama Special Olympics, Inc., §40-9-25.
    American Legion, §40-23-5.
    Chilton county rescue squad, §40-23-5.
    Coal, §40-23-62.
    Constitution of Alabama.
      Property exempt from taxation under, §40-23-62.
    Constitution of the United States.
      Property exempt from taxation under, §40-23-62.
    Cottonseed meal, §40-23-62.
    Council of state governments, §40-23-5.

USE TAX—Cont'd
  Exemptions—Cont'd
    Counties.
      Property stored, used or consumed by counties, §40-23-62.
    Cystic fibrosis research foundation, §40-23-62.
    Diabetes Trust Fund, Inc., §40-23-5.
    Diesel fuel used for off-highway agricultural purposes, §40-23-62.
    Disabled American veterans, §40-23-5.
    Drugs, §40-23-62.
    Education.
      Certain tangible personal property, §40-23-62.
    Fertilizer, §40-23-62.
    George Lindsey Celebrity Benefit, Inc., §40-9-25.
    Goodwill industries, §40-23-5.
    Insecticides, §40-23-62.
    Livestock, §40-23-62.
    Lubricating oil and gasoline, §40-23-62.
    Mines and minerals.
      Exploration in offshore federal waters.
        Equipment, machinery, fuel, etc., used in, §40-23-62.
    Motor fuels.
      Diesel fuel used for off-highway agricultural purposes, §40-23-62.
    Municipal corporations.
      Property stored, used or consumed by municipalities, §40-23-62.
    National conference of state legislatures, §40-23-5.
    Nonresidents.
      Tangible personal property brought into state by nonresident, §40-23-62.
    Oil and gas, §40-23-62.
      Exploration in offshore federal waters.
        Equipment, fuel, machinery, etc., used in, §40-23-62.
    Poultry, §40-23-62.
    Public utilities, §40-23-62.
    Railroads.
      Railroad cars, vessels and barges, §40-23-62.
    Religion.
      Religious magazines and publications, §40-23-62.
    Ships and shipping.
      Fuels and supplies for use aboard ships, §40-23-62.
    Sight conservation association, §40-23-5.
    State.
      Property stored, used or consumed by state, §40-23-62.
    Tuberculosis.
      Jefferson tuberculosis sanatorium, §40-23-62.
    Tunnels.
      Fabricated steel tube sections, §40-23-62.
    Veterans, §40-23-5.

USE TAX—Cont'd
  Exemptions—Cont'd
    Warranty agreements, §40-23-62.
    Water pollution.
      Devices or facilities for control, reduction or elimination, §40-23-62.
    Women's clubs, §40-23-5.
  Fertilizer.
    Exemptions, §40-23-62.
  Fraud.
    Penalty for fraud, §40-23-80.
  Goodwill industries.
    Exemptions, §40-23-5.
  Hearings.
    Redeterminations, §40-23-73.
  Imposition, §40-23-61.
  Injunctions.
    Injunctions against collection of tax prohibited, §40-23-87.
  Insecticides.
    Exemptions, §40-23-62.
  Interest.
    Estimate of tax due when no return made, §40-23-71.
    Excess payments, §40-23-79.
    Fraud, §40-23-80.
    Taxes not paid when due, §40-23-77.
  Jeopardy determinations, §40-23-72.
  Liens.
    Tax a lien, §40-23-81.
  Limitation of actions.
    Collection of tax, §40-23-87.
  Livestock.
    Exemptions, §40-23-62.
  Mandamus.
    Writ of mandamus against collection of tax, §40-23-87.
  Mines and minerals.
    Exemptions.
      Exploration in offshore federal waters.
        Equipment, machinery, fuel, etc., used in, §40-23-62.
    Tax on machines used in mining, §40-23-61.
  Motor fuel.
    Diesel fuel used for off-highway agricultural purposes.
      Exemption, §40-23-62.
  Motor vehicles, §40-23-61.
  Municipal corporations.
    Collection of tax on same sale.
    Only one municipal sales or use tax collectible, §40-23-2.1.
    Exemptions, §40-23-62.
    Municipal sales and use tax.
    See MUNICIPAL CORPORATIONS.
  National conference of state legislatures.
    Exemptions, §40-23-5.
  Nonresidents.
    Exemptions.
      Tangible personal property brought into state by nonresident, §40-23-62.
  Notice.
    Additional amounts due.
      When notice to be mailed, §40-23-76.

USE TAX—Cont'd
Oil and gas.
Exemptions, §40-23-62.
Exploration in offshore
federal waters.
Equipment, machinery,
fuel, etc., used in,
§40-23-62.
Other states.
Credit for sales or use tax
paid to, §40-23-65.
Payment.
Delay.
Jeopardy determinations,
§40-23-72.
Excess payments, §40-23-78.
Interest, §40-23-79.
Failure to pay.
Penalty, §40-23-69.
Jeopardy determinations,
§40-23-72.
When due, §40-23-68.
Penalties.
Failure to pay tax, §40-23-69.
Fraud, §40-23-80.
Poultry.
Exemptions, §40-23-62.
Property tax, §40-23-61.
Public utilities.
Exemptions, §40-23-62.
Service use tax, §§40-21-100
to 40-21-107.
See PUBLIC UTILITIES.
Purchase money.
Retailers selling out.
Purchaser to retain part of
purchase money,
§40-23-82.
Railroads.
Exemptions.
Railroad cars, vessels and
barges, §40-23-62.
Records.
Examination by department,
§40-23-83.
Required, §40-23-83.
Redeterminations.
Appeals, §40-23-73.
Hearings, §40-23-73.
Petition, §40-23-72.
Procedure, §40-23-73.
Religion.
Exemptions.
Religious magazines and
publications,
§40-23-62.
Retail sales.
Defined, §40-23-60.
Retail sellers.
Collection of tax, §40-23-67.
Information, §40-23-66.
Not to assume or absorb tax,
§40-23-67.
Registration.
Required, §40-23-66.
Returns.
Final return of retailers
selling out, §40-23-82.
Seller to file, §40-23-68.
Returns.
Determining true amount of
tax due, §40-23-70.
Estimate of tax due when no
return made, §40-23-71.
Extension of time for
making, §40-23-74.
Failing to furnish return,
§40-23-88.
Final return of retailers
selling out, §40-23-82.

USE TAX—Cont'd
Returns—Cont'd
Sellers to file returns,
§40-23-68.
Signature of seller required,
§40-23-68.
Rules and regulations.
Department of revenue,
§40-23-83.
Sales price.
Defined, §40-23-60.
Sales tax.
General provisions, §§40-23-1
to 40-23-50.
See SALES TAX.
Security.
Department may require,
§40-23-75.
Sale at public auction,
§40-23-75.
Seeds.
Exemptions, §40-23-62.
**Selling out or quitting
business.**
Final return of retailers
selling out, §40-23-82.
Ships and shipping.
Exemptions.
Fuels and supplies for use
aboard ships,
§40-23-62.
**Sight conservation
association.**
Exemption, §40-23-5.
State.
Exemptions.
Property stored, used or
consumed by state,
§40-23-62.
**Tax enforcement and
compliance act, §§40-29-1
to 40-29-120.**
See TAXATION.
**Tobacco, §§40-25-40 to
40-25-47.**
See TOBACCO.
Tuberculosis.
Jefferson tuberculosis
sanatorium.
Exemptions, §40-23-62.
Tunnels.
Fabricated steel tube
sections.
Exemptions, §40-23-62.
**Utility service use tax,
§§40-21-100 to 40-21-107.**
See PUBLIC UTILITIES.
Veterans.
Exemptions, §40-23-5.
Violations.
Penalty, §40-23-88.
Warranty.
Exemptions.
Repairs done pursuant to
warranty agreements,
§40-23-62.
Water pollution.
Exemptions.
Devices or facilities for
control, reduction or
elimination, §40-23-62.
When due, §40-23-68.
Wholesale sales.
Defined, §40-23-60.

**USS ALABAMA
BATTLESHIP
COMMISSION, §§41-9-340
to 41-9-358.**
Accounts and accounting,
§41-9-350.

USS ALABAMA
BATTLESHIP
COMMISSION—Cont'd
Acquisition of battleship,
§41-9-347.
Appointment of members,
§41-9-340.
Appropriations.
Counties and municipalities,
§41-9-356.
Audits.
Records and books of
account, §41-9-350.
**Banks and financial
institutions.**
Bond issues.
Legal investments for
banks, §41-9-353.
Borrowing from bank.
Authorized pending loan
from state docks
department, §41-9-355.
Battleship fund, §41-9-357.
**Bond issues, §§11-97-9 to
11-97-12.**
Authority for issuance and
sale, §41-9-352.
Banks.
Legal investments for
banks, §41-9-353.
Denominations, §41-9-352.
Exclusively obligations of
commission, §41-9-353.
Fiduciaries.
Legal investments for
fiduciaries, §41-9-353.
Form, §41-9-352.
Insurance companies.
Legal investments,
§41-9-353.
Investments.
Legal investments,
§41-9-353.
Negotiable instruments,
§41-9-353.
Payment, §41-9-352.
Security for payment,
§41-9-352.
Redemption, §41-9-352.
Resolution authorizing bonds.
Effect of recital as to
issuance in resolution,
§41-9-353.
Sale, §41-9-352.
Security for payment,
§41-9-352.
Terms of bonds, §41-9-352.
Bonds, surety.
Requirement of bond from
treasurer, §41-9-342.
Borrowing money.
Authorized, §41-9-354.
Banks.
Commission may borrow
from banks.
Pending loan from state
docks department,
§41-9-355.
Bond issues, §§11-97-9 to
11-97-12. See within this
heading, "Bond issues."
Pledge of future revenues as
security for repayment of
loans, §41-9-354.
State docks department.
Loan from state docks
department, §41-9-355.
Forgiveness of
outstanding
indebtedness,
§41-9-355.

USS ALABAMA
BATTLESHIP
COMMISSION—Cont'd
Compensation of members,
§41-9-341.
Composition, §41-9-340.
Conflicts of interest.
Members or employees,
§41-9-341.
Corporation.
Commission as public body
corporate, §41-9-346.
Counties.
Appropriations, §41-9-356.
Creation, §41-9-340.
Director.
Executive director, §41-9-344.
Duties, §41-9-349.
Emergencies.
Reserve fund for
emergencies, §41-9-350.
Employees, §41-9-345.
Conflicts of interest,
§41-9-341.
Insurance, §41-9-351.
Executive committee,
§41-9-343.
Executive director, §41-9-344.
Exemption from taxation,
§41-9-358.
Exhibition of battleship,
§41-9-347.
Expenses of members,
§41-9-341.
Fiduciaries.
Bond issues.
Legal investments for
fiduciaries, §41-9-353.
Funds.
Battleship fund, §41-9-357.
Reserve fund for special
contingencies and
emergencies, §41-9-350.
Insurance.
Bond issues.
Legal investments for
insurance companies,
§41-9-353.
Employees and property,
§41-9-351.
Jurisdiction.
Exclusive control over
battleship, park, etc.,
§41-9-348.
Loans, §§41-9-354, 41-9-355.
Meetings, §41-9-342.
Memorial park.
Commission to establish,
operate, etc., §41-9-347.
Motor vehicles.
Tags and plates.
Special tag number for
chairman, §32-6-55.
Municipal corporations.
Appropriations, §41-9-356.
Obligations.
Bond issues. See within this
heading, "Bond issues."
To be exclusively obligations
of commission, §41-9-353.
Officers, §41-9-342.
Organization, §41-9-342.
Powers, §41-9-349.
Procedure, §41-9-342.
Property.
Insurance, §41-9-351.
Public body corporate,
§41-9-346.
Qualifications of members,
§41-9-340.
Quorum, §41-9-342.

USS ALABAMA
BATTLESHIP
COMMISSION—Cont'd
Records, §41-9-350.
Removal of members,
§41-9-340.
Reserve fund, §41-9-350.
Seal, §41-9-342.
State agency.
Commission as, §41-9-348.
Taxation.
Exemption, §41-9-358.
Terms of members, §41-9-340.
Vacancies, §41-9-340.

USURY.
See INTEREST.

UTILITIES.
Actions.
Utility services actions,
§§6-5-600 to 6-5-605.
See UTILITY SERVICES
ACTIONS.
Bonds, surety.
Highways.
Digging up of roads,
§23-1-4.
General provisions.
See PUBLIC UTILITIES.
Highways.
Digging up of roads, §23-1-4.
Permits.
Digging up of roads, §23-1-4.
Public service commission.
General provisions, §§37-1-1
to 37-1-157.
See PUBLIC SERVICE
COMMISSION.
Redevelopment projects,
§§24-2-1 to 24-2-10.
See REDEVELOPMENT
PROJECTS.
Subdivisions.
County regulation of
subdivisions generally,
§§11-24-1 to 11-24-11.
See COUNTIES.
Utility services facilities,
§§11-97-1 to 11-97-27.
See UTILITY SERVICES
FACILITIES.

UTILITY GROSS RECEIPTS
TAX.
Public utilities.
Gross receipts tax,
§§40-21-80 to 40-21-87.
See PUBLIC UTILITIES.

UTILITY SERVICES
ACTIONS, §§6-5-600 to
6-5-605.
Convictions.
Effect of criminal conviction,
§6-5-603.
Damages.
Effect of criminal conviction,
§6-5-603.
Estimated lost revenue.
Determination, §6-5-604.
Treble damages, §6-5-602.
Definitions, §6-5-600.
Diversion or unauthorized
use of utility services.
Right of action, §6-5-601.
Estimated lost revenue.
Determination, §6-5-604.
Public utility.
Application of term, §6-5-605.

UTILITY SERVICES
ACTIONS—Cont'd
Right of action.
Diversion or unauthorized
use of utility services,
§6-5-601.
Utilities.
Application of term, §6-5-605

UTILITY SERVICES
FACILITIES, §§11-97-1 to
11-97-27.
Aid and cooperation from
other bodies, §11-97-15.
Bids and bidding.
Exemption from competitive
bid laws, §11-97-20.
Bond issues.
Cancellation, §11-97-10.
Contracts.
Security for payment of
bonds, §11-97-10.
Generally, §11-97-9.
Issuance, §11-97-9.
Negotiable instruments,
§11-97-10.
Notice of resolution,
§11-97-25.
Proceeds from sale,
§11-97-11.
Refunding bonds, §11-97-12.
Sales.
Proceeds, §11-97-11.
Security for payment of
bonds, §11-97-10.
Validity.
Contest to validity,
§11-97-25.
Bonds.
Investments.
Legal investments,
§11-97-22.
Chapter cumulative,
§11-97-26.
Competitive bidding.
Exemption from laws,
§11-97-20.
Construction and
interpretation.
Liberal construction of
chapter, §11-97-27.
Contracts.
Public contracts.
Competitive bidding.
Exemption from article,
§11-97-20.
Corporations.
Aid and cooperation from
other bodies, §11-97-15.
Board of directors.
Composition, §11-97-6.
Election, §11-97-6.
Expenses, §11-97-6.
Qualifications of members,
§11-97-6.
Quorum, §11-97-6.
Removal from office,
§11-97-6.
Term of office, §11-97-6.
Vacancies in office,
§11-97-6.
Bond issues. See within this
heading, "Bond issues."
Certificate of incorporation,
§11-97-4.
Amendments, §11-97-5.
Dissolution, §11-97-23.
Earnings.
Disposition, §11-97-21.
Eminent domain.
Powers, §11-97-14.

UTILITY SERVICES
FACILITIES—Cont'd
Corporations—Cont'd
Freedom from supervision
and control of state,
§11-97-13.
Incorporation.
Another corporation by
same determining
subdivision, §11-97-24.
Application.
Contents, §11-97-3.
Authorization, §11-97-3.
Filing of application,
§11-97-3.
Procedure, §11-97-4.
Laws respecting operation of
facilities.
Applicability, §11-97-13.
Nonprofit public corporation,
§11-97-21.
Officers, §11-97-7.
Powers, §11-97-8.
Eminent domain,
§11-97-14.
Taxation.
Exemption, §11-97-18.
Vesting of title to property in
determining subdivision,
§11-97-23.
Declaration of legislature,
§11-97-1.
Definitions, §11-97-2.
Eminent domain.
Powers of corporation,
§11-97-14.
Findings of legislature,
§11-97-1.
Interest.
Exemption from usury and
interest laws, §11-97-19.
Investments.
Bond issues.
Legal investments,
§11-97-22.
Legislative declaration and
findings, §11-97-1.
Location of facilities,
§11-97-8.
Notice.
Bond issues.
Notice of bond resolution,
§11-97-25.
Provisions of chapter
cumulative, §11-97-26.
Refunding bonds, §11-97-12.
Taxation.
Exemption from taxation,
§11-97-18.
Usury.
Exemption from usury and
interest laws, §11-97-19.
Utility services agreements.
Approval.
Prior approval of
agreements with
governmental users,
§11-97-17.
Authority to enter into,
§11-97-16.
Contents, §11-97-16.
Enforceability, §11-97-16.
Prior approval, §11-97-17.

V

VACATION TIME-SHARING
PLANS, §§34-27-50 to
34-27-69.
Accommodations.
Defined, §34-27-50.
Accounts and accounting.
Escrow accounts.
Deficiency, §34-27-61.
Defined, §34-27-50.
Failure to place all funds
in escrow accounts,
§34-27-55.
Failure to place 50 percent
of cash, etc., received
in escrow, §34-27-58.
Actions.
Commission notified of legal
action against licensee,
§34-27-69.
Advertising.
Failure to follow rules of
advertising, §34-27-51.
Bad checks, §34-27-60.
Bonds, surety, §34-27-51.
Applicants for licenses,
§34-27-69.
Business entities.
Defined, §34-27-50.
Construction and
interpretation, §34-27-62.
Contracts.
Cancellation, §§34-27-53,
34-27-54.
Defined, §34-27-50.
Failure, etc., to honor buyer's
request to cancel
contract, §34-27-54.
Failure to disclose financial
obligations and interests,
§34-27-59.
Failure to include certain
provisions, §34-27-53.
Failure to keep copies of
contracts, §34-27-53.
Failure to utilize and furnish
buyer fully completed
copy of contract,
§34-27-53.
Definitions, §34-27-50.
Willful violation, §34-27-61.
Documents.
Failure to provide certain
documents at
registration, §34-27-51.
Enforcement of article,
§34-27-62.
Real estate commission,
§34-27-62.
Escrow accounts.
Deficiency, §34-27-61.
Defined, §34-27-50.
Failure to place all funds in
escrow accounts,
§34-27-55.
Failure to place 50 percent of
cash, etc., received in
escrow, §34-27-58.
Escrow agents.
Defined, §34-27-50.
Examinations.
Persons desiring to act as
sellers, §34-27-66.
Exchange companies.
Defined, §34-27-50.
Exchange programs.
Defined, §34-27-50.
Facilities.
Defined, §34-27-50.

VACATION TIME-SHARING
PLANS—Cont'd
Fees.
Examination fees, §34-27-66.
License fees, §34-27-66.
Registration fees, §34-27-64.
Violations of article.
Investigation costs,
§34-27-64.
Fraud, §§34-27-56, 34-27-60.
Hearings.
Violation of article,
§34-27-61.
Implementation of article,
§34-27-62.
Real estate commission,
§34-27-62.
Injunctions against
violations of article,
§34-27-68.
Insurance.
Failure to provide liability
insurance, §34-27-58.
Inventories.
Failure to furnish buyer with
inventory, §34-27-53.
Investigations.
Violations of article,
§34-27-68.
Assessment of
investigation costs,
§34-27-64.
Licensees.
Defined, §34-27-50.
Licenses.
Actions.
Commission notified of
actions against
licensees, §34-27-69.
Bonds, surety.
Applicants for licenses,
§34-27-69.
Change of address of
licensee, §34-27-66.
Examinations, §34-27-66.
Fees, §34-27-66.
Issuance, §34-27-66.
Refusal, suspension or
revocation, §§34-27-61,
34-27-69.
Reinstatement, §34-27-69.
Relicensure, §34-27-69.
Renewal, §34-27-66.
Selling, etc., without license,
§34-27-51.
When required, §34-27-51.
Liens.
Statement of liens.
When required, §34-27-51.
Managing agents.
Defined, §34-27-50.
Misrepresentation,
§§34-27-56, 34-27-60.
Penalties, §34-27-61.
Promotional devices.
Violations of article,
§34-27-60.
Qualifying brokers.
Defined, §34-27-50.
Real estate commission.
Commissioner.
Defined, §34-27-50.
Defined, §34-27-50.
Enforcement of article,
§34-27-62.
Implementation of article,
§34-27-62.
Receivable.
Defined, §34-27-50.

VACATION TIME-SHARING PLANS—Cont'd

Records.
Failure to keep certain items among business records, §34-27-52.
Failure to provide certain documents at registration, §34-27-51.
Minutes not substantially completed.
Additional documents required upon filing of plan, §34-27-63.

Refunding of payments.
Failure to refund all payments, §34-27-55.

Registration.
Fees, §34-27-64.
Prerequisites, §34-27-51.
Procedure, §34-27-67.
Required, §§34-27-51, 34-27-67.
Revocation, §34-27-68.
Voidable sales.
Nonregistered plan, §34-27-62.

Rights of other owners.
Sale, lease or transfer of seller's interest substantially affecting rights, §34-27-57.

Rules and regulations.
Promulgation, §34-27-62.

Sales.
Licenses.
General provisions, §§34-27-66, 34-27-69.
Violations of article.
Refusal, suspension or revocation, §34-27-61.
Selling, etc., without license, §§34-27-51, 34-27-60.
Suspension or revocation for violations of article, §34-27-69.
Voidable sales, §34-27-62.

Substantially complete.
Defined, §34-27-50.

Taxation.
Proceeds from sale or resale of lease plans.
Exempt from transient occupancy tax, §34-27-65.

Third persons.
Violations of article.
Certain sales, leases or transfers to third persons, §34-27-57.

Time-sharing project.
Defined, §34-27-50.

Time-sharing units.
Defined, §34-27-50.

Transient occupancy tax.
Proceeds from sale or resale of lease plans exempt, §34-27-65.

Units not substantially completed.
Additional documents required upon filing of plan, §34-27-63.

Unit week.
Defined, §34-27-50.

Vacation time-sharing lease plans.
Cancellation of contracts, §§34-27-53, 34-27-54.

VACATION TIME-SHARING PLANS—Cont'd

Vacation time-sharing lease plans—Cont'd
Defined, §34-27-50.
Failure to place 50 percent of cash, etc., received in escrow, §34-27-58.
Proceeds exempt from transient occupancy tax, §34-27-65.

Vacation time-sharing ownership plans.
Cancellation of contracts, §§34-27-53, 34-27-54.

Vacation time-sharing sales licenses.
Defined, §34-27-50.

Violations of article, §§34-27-51 to 34-27-60.

Waiver.
Rights of purchasers.
Violations of article, §34-27-60.

VACCINATION.
Compulsory vaccination.
Provision for system, §11-47-132.

Hog cholera vaccine, §§2-15-250 to 2-15-274.
See LIVESTOCK.

Rabies, §§3-7-1 to 3-7-13.
See RABIES.

School children.
Immunization, §§16-30-1 to 16-30-5.

VALIDATION.
Bond issues.
Counties, §§11-81-220 to 11-81-227.
See COUNTIES.
Municipal corporations, §§11-81-220 to 11-81-227.
See MUNICIPAL CORPORATIONS.

County obligations, §§6-6-750 to 6-6-757.
See COUNTIES.

Housing authorities, §§24-1-7 to 24-1-9.

Municipal corporations.
City obligations, §§6-6-750 to 6-6-757.
See MUNICIPAL CORPORATIONS.

Previous validating acts not repealed, §1-1-13.

Public officers and employees.
De facto officials.
Official act, §36-1-2.

VANDALISM.
Caves, §9-19-3.
Minors.
Liability of parents, §6-5-380.
Schools, §16-1-24.

VEGETABLES.
See FRUITS AND VEGETABLES.

VEHICLES.
Bicycles.
General provisions, §§32-5A-260 to 32-5A-266.
See BICYCLES.

Brake fluid.
Regulation of brake fluid, §§8-17-1 to 8-17-9.
See BRAKE FLUID.

VEHICLES—Cont'd
Motorcycles, §§32-12-1 to 32-12-44.
See MOTORCYCLES.

Motor vehicle carriers.
General provisions, §§37-3-1 to 37-3-34.
See MOTOR VEHICLE CARRIERS.

Motor vehicles, §§32-1-1 to 32-18-8.
See MOTOR VEHICLES.

VENDING MACHINES.
Banks and financial institutions.
Use of automatic tellers, §5-5A-30.

Cigarettes.
Municipal license tax, §11-51-98.

Insurance.
See INSURANCE.

Larceny.
See LARCENY.

Licenses, §40-12-176.
Municipal corporations, §§11-51-98, 11-51-100.

Municipal corporations.
License tax.
Authorized, §11-51-98.
Vending machines on which music is played, §11-51-100.
Music machines.
Regulation and control, §11-51-100.

Slugs.
Unlawful use.
Class B misdemeanor, §13A-9-17.
Definitions, §13A-9-16.
Prohibited, §13A-9-17.

VENDING STANDS.
Blind persons.
Operation by, §§21-1-40, 21-1-41.

Licenses.
Blind persons.
Preference in issuance, §21-1-41.

VENDITIONI EXPONAS.
Executions, §§6-9-120, 6-9-121.
See EXECUTIONS.

VENDORS' LIENS.
Literary or social societies.
Conveyances by, §35-4-343.

Payment.
When indebtedness presumed paid, §35-10-20.

Recordation.
Purchasers protected, §35-4-64.

Satisfaction.
Recordation, §35-10-29.
When indebtedness presumed paid, §35-10-20.

VENEREAL DISEASES.
Barbers and cosmetologists.
Service by persons having venereal disease, §22-17-8.

Marriage.
Syphilis examination for marriage license, §22-11A-15.

Notifiable diseases, §§22-11A-1 to 22-11A-38.
See DISEASES.

VENIRE.
  Grand juries.
    See GRAND JURY.
  Jury.
    See JURY.

VENTILATION.
  Coal mine safety, §§25-9-80 to
    25-9-91.
    See COAL.

VENUE.
  Abortion.
    Parental consent.
      Waiver of written consent
        requirement, §26-21-4.
  Agreements contrary to
    article void, §6-3-1.
  Agricultural center
    corporation.
    Actions under article,
      §2-6-35.
  Attachment.
    Actions by defendant,
      §6-6-149.
  Bonds, surety.
    Breach of official bond,
      §6-3-8.
  Buses.
    Violations committed on
      buses, §37-8-94.
  Change of venue.
    Civil actions.
      Convenience of parties and
        witnesses or in interest
        of justice, §6-3-21.1.
      Docket sheet and other
        papers.
        Certification and
          delivery, §6-3-22.
        Notice, §6-3-22.
        Time for answer, §6-3-22.
      One change for cause
        permitted on motion of
        party, §6-3-20.
    Constitution of Alabama,
      Const. Ala., art. I, §6;
      art. IV, §75.
    Criminal law and procedure,
      §§15-2-1 to 15-2-27.
    Probate courts, §12-13-10.
    Special, private or local laws
      prohibited, Const. Ala.,
      art. IV, §104.
    Wills.
      Contesting validity,
        §43-8-197.
  Child custody.
    Modification, §30-3-5.
  Child support.
    Modification, §30-3-5.
  Conservators.
    Proceedings under division,
      §26-2A-132.
  Constitution of Alabama.
    Change of venue, Const.
      Ala., art. I, §6; art. IV,
      §75.
    Special, private or local
      laws prohibited, Const.
      Ala., art. IV, §104.
  Constitution of the United
    States, Const. U. S., Art.
    III, §2.
  Contracts.
    Actions against individuals,
      §6-3-2.
    Easement or right-of-way
      contracts, §6-3-3.

VENUE—Cont'd
  Corporations.
    Actions against foreign and
      domestic corporations,
      §6-3-7.
    Foreign corporations, Const.
      Ala., art. XII, §232.
    Insurance.
      Actions against
        corporations issuing,
        §6-3-5.
    Involuntary dissolution
      actions, §§10-2A-194,
      10-3A-148.
    Nonprofit corporations.
      Involuntary dissolution,
        §10-3A-148.
    Liquidation, §10-3A-149.
  Corrections.
    Institution finance authority.
      Actions, §14-2-33.
  Counties.
    Damages for personal injury,
      death or property
      damage, §6-3-11.
    Local laws in counties
      having two courthouses
      unaffected, §6-3-10.
  Criminal law and procedure.
    Change of venue.
      Appeal from denial,
        §15-2-20.
      Application, §15-2-20.
      Forwarding case materials.
        Duty of clerk of court,
        §15-2-25.
      Hearings.
        Presence of defendant in
          confinement
          unnecessary,
          §15-2-20.
        Subpoena of witnesses,
          §15-2-22.
      Indictment.
        Trial on certified copy
          after change
          granted, §15-2-26.
      Judge.
        Change on motion of
          trial judge, §15-2-21.
      One removal only allowed,
        §15-2-24.
      Removal to nearest county,
        §15-2-24.
      Transcript.
        Certification of admitted
          portions of record,
          §15-2-26.
        Correction of transcript
          mistakes, §15-2-26.
      Witnesses.
        Compelling attendance
          at hearing, §15-2-22.
        Examination of
          prosecution
          witnesses on
          interrogatories,
          §15-2-23.
        Issuance of subpoenas for
          trial witnesses,
          §15-2-27.
    Commencement of offense in
      state and consummation
      elsewhere, §15-2-3.
    Commencement outside state
      and consummation
      within state, §15-2-4.
    County where offense
      committed, §15-2-2.
    Commission in more than
      one county, §15-2-6.

VENUE—Cont'd
  Criminal law and procedure
    —Cont'd
    County where offense
      committed—Cont'd
      Commission on or near
        county border, §15-2-7.
      Forcible marriage, §15-2-8.
      Kidnapping, §15-2-8.
      Property brought into state,
        §15-2-5.
      Prostitution, §15-2-8.
      Stolen property.
        Carrying into another
          county, §15-2-9.
  Defenses.
    Improper venue, ARCP, Rule
      12 (b), (h).
    Raising again on appeal,
      §6-8-101.
  District courts, §12-12-36.
  Divorce.
    A vinculo, §30-2-4.
  Easements.
    Actions for breach of
      easement contracts,
      §6-3-3.
  Eminent domain.
    Actions, §18-1A-71.
  Executors and
    administrators.
    Actions by and against,
      §43-2-130.
    Nonresident executors and
      administrators,
      §43-2-197.
  Forcible entry and unlawful
    detainer, §6-6-331.
  Forcible marriage, §15-2-8.
  Guardian and ward.
    Curators.
      Appointment, §26-7A-2.
    Uniform guardianship and
      protective proceedings
      act.
      Incapacitated persons.
        Guardianship
          proceedings,
          §26-2A-101.
        Proceedings
          subsequent to
          appointment,
          §26-2A-111.
      Minors.
        Guardians.
          Appointment,
            §26-2A-74.
          Proceedings
            subsequent to
            appointment,
            §26-2A-80.
        Multiple proceedings,
          §26-2A-32.
        Protective proceedings,
          §26-2A-132.
  Improper venue, §6-8-101;
    ARCP, Rule 82 (d).
  Indictments.
    Allegation of venue
      unnecessary, §15-8-31.
  Injunctions.
    Action to enjoin proceedings
      or judgments in other
      courts, §6-3-2.
  Insurance.
    Insurers.
      Delinquency proceedings,
        §27-32-3.

VENUE—Cont'd
Insurance—Cont'd
Issuance of policies.
Actions against persons, firms or corporations issuing, §6-3-5.
Actions against unincorporated groups issuing, §6-3-4.
Joinder, ARCP, Rule 82 (c).
Judgments.
Action to enjoin judgments, §6-3-2.
Jurisdiction.
General provisions.
See JURISDICTION.
Juvenile proceedings, §12-15-35.
Malpractice, §6-5-546.
Military affairs.
Change of venue.
National guard members under indictment, §31-2-118.
Minors.
Child custody, visitation rights or child support.
Modification, §30-3-5.
Juvenile proceedings, §12-15-35.
Unlawfully detaining, §15-2-8.
Monopolies.
Actions by and against, §6-5-60.
Motor vehicle carriers.
Violations committed on trains or buses, §37-8-94.
Municipal corporations.
Damages for personal injury, death or property damage, §6-3-11.
Nonresidents, §6-3-2.
Notice.
Change or transfer, §6-3-22.
Nuisances.
Lewdness, assignation or prostitution.
Action to abate and perpetually enjoin, §6-5-143.
Personal actions generally, §6-3-2.
Physicians.
Judicial review of administrative decisions of medical licensure commission, §34-24-367.
Post-conviction remedies, ARCrP, Rule 20.5.
Prisons and prisoners.
Actions where prison system involved, §6-3-9.
Violations of law.
Where tried, §14-3-9.
Probate courts.
Change of venue, §12-13-10.
Prostitution, §15-2-8.
Public officers and employees.
Bonds, surety.
Breach of official bond, §6-3-8.
Code of ethics.
Actions for violations of chapter, §36-25-27.
Summary proceedings involving officials, §6-6-661.

VENUE—Cont'd
Public printing and binding.
Venue of actions on contracts, §41-4-138.
Public service commission.
Violations of rules, orders or statutes, §37-8-2.
Quo warranto, §§6-6-590, 6-6-591.
Railroads.
Violations committed on trains, §37-8-94.
Real property.
Actions against individuals for recovery or possession, §6-3-2.
Equitable proceedings where real estate is subject matter, §6-3-2.
Rights of way.
Actions for breach of right-of-way contracts, §6-3-3.
Rules of civil procedure, ARCP, Rule 82.
See RULES OF CIVIL PROCEDURE.
Rules of criminal procedure.
Post-conviction remedies, ARCrP, Rule 20.5.
Space science exhibit finance authority.
Actions, §41-10-328.
Stolen property.
Bringing into state, §15-2-5.
Carrying into another county, §15-2-9.
Transfer of venue, §6-3-21.
Civil actions, §6-3-21.1.
Docket sheet and other papers.
Certification and delivery, §6-3-22.
Notice, §6-3-22.
Time for answer, §6-3-22.
Trespass to lands.
Actions against individuals, §6-3-2.
Unincorporated associations.
Actions against, §6-3-6.
Unincorporated groups issuing insurance policies, §6-3-4.
Visitation rights.
Modification, §30-3-5.
Wills.
Contesting validity.
Change of venue, §43-8-197.
Probate code, §§43-8-21, 43-8-162.
Work or labor done.
Actions for, §6-3-3.

VERDICT.
Attorneys at law.
Court to provide attorneys with questions or interrogatories, ARCP, Rule 49 (d).
Criminal law and procedure.
Conviction if any result charged produced by act, §15-17-4.
Conviction where act may be committed by different intents, modes or means, §15-17-3.

VERDICT—Cont'd
Criminal law and procedure —Cont'd
Jointly tried defendants.
When jury cannot agree upon verdict as to all, §15-17-2.
Mentally ill.
Special verdict of not guilty due to insanity, §15-16-24.
Directed verdict.
Motion for directed verdict.
Effect, ARCP, Rule 50 (a).
Form, ARCP, Form 77.
Stay on motion, ARCP, Rule 62 (b).
When court may grant, ARCP, Rule 50 (e).
When made, ARCP, Rule 50 (a).
Ejectment.
Verdict for plaintiff, §6-6-291.
Forms.
Majority verdict.
Stipulation, ARCP, Form 76.
Motion for directed verdict, ARCP, Form 77.
Motion for judgment notwithstanding verdict, ARCP, Form 78.
General provisions.
See JURY.
General verdicts, ARCP, Rule 49 (a).
Accompanied by answer to interrogatories, ARCP, Rule 49 (c).
Interrogatories to jury, ARCP, Rule 49 (d).
Court to provide attorneys with questions or interrogatories, ARCP, Rule 49 (d).
General verdict accompanied by answer to interrogatories, ARCP, Rule 49 (c).
Judgment notwithstanding verdict.
Motion, ARCP, Rule 50 (b).
Conditional rulings on grant of motion, ARCP, Rule 50 (c).
Denial of motion, ARCP, Rule 50 (d).
Form, ARCP, Form 78.
When court may grant, ARCP, Rule 50 (e).
Jury.
General provisions.
See JURY.
Majority verdict, ARCP, Rule 48.
Form of stipulation for majority verdict, ARCP, Form 76.
Mechanics' and materialmen's liens.
Enforcement, §35-11-224.
Mentally ill.
Criminal law and procedure.
General verdict of not guilty or verdict of conviction, §15-16-24.
Special verdict of not guilty due to insanity, §15-16-24.

VERDICT—Cont'd
  Motions.
    Directed verdict. See within
      this heading, "Directed
      verdict."
    Judgment notwithstanding
      verdict. See within this
      heading, "Judgment
      notwithstanding verdict."
      §15-17-2.
  New trial.
    Grounds, §15-17-5.
  Polling of jurors, §12-16-15.
  Questions to jury, ARCP,
    Rule 49.
  Rules of civil procedure.
    See RULES OF CIVIL
      PROCEDURE.
  Special verdicts, ARCP, Rule
    49 (b).

VESSELS.
  Boats.
    Discharge of litter and
      sewage from watercraft,
      §§33-6-1 to 33-6-12.
    See BOATS.
    General provisions, §§33-5-1
      to 33-5-36.
    See BOATS.
  **Constitution of the United
    States.**
    Bound to and from one state
      not to be obliged to clear,
      etc., in another, Const.
      U. S., Art. I, §9.
  Ships and shipping.
    General provisions, §§33-5-1
      to 33-5-36.
    See SHIPS AND
      SHIPPING.

**VESTAVIA HILLS,
  MUNICIPALITY OF.**
  Property tax, Const. Ala.,
    amd. 352.

VETERANS,
  Aged veterans.
    Incompetent veterans,
      §§26-9-1 to 26-9-19. See
      within this heading,
      "Incompetent veterans
      and dependents."
  Appropriations.
    Pensions.
      Widows of Confederate
        veterans, §§31-8-1 to
        31-8-33.
  Assignments.
    Bonus for Southeast Asian
      war prisoners, §31-7-2.
  Attachments.
    Bonus for Southeast Asian
      war prisoners, §31-7-2.
  **Banks and financial
    institutions.**
    Regulation of trust business.
      Exemption of trust
        companies acting as
        administrator from
        bond requirement,
        §5-11A-9.
  Benefits.
    Educational benefits,
      §§31-6-1 to 31-6-17.
    Federal benefits, §§31-6-1 to
      31-6-17.
  Board of veterans' affairs.
    Generally, §31-5-3.
    State veterans' homes.
      Powers, §31-5A-6.

VETERANS—Cont'd
  Board of veterans' affairs
    —Cont'd
    State veterans' homes
      —Cont'd
      Rules and regulations.
        Admissions and
          discharges, §31-5A-8.
  Bonds, surety.
    Assistant service
      commissioner, §31-5-11.
    County service
      commissioners, §31-5-11.
    District service
      commissioners, §31-5-11.
    State service commissioner,
      §31-5-11.
  **Bonus for Southeast Asian
    war prisoners,** §§31-7-1 to
    31-7-5.
    Amount, §31-7-1.
    Applications, §§31-7-3 to
      31-7-5.
    Assignments.
      Prohibited, §31-7-2.
    Attachments.
      Prohibited, §31-7-2.
    Department of veterans'
      affairs.
      Rules and procedures.
        Establishment, §31-7-3.
    Determination of eligibility.
      Rules and procedures.
        Adoption by department,
          §31-7-3.
    Next of kin.
      Defined, §31-7-1.
      Payments to next of kin of
        persons who died while
        imprisoned, §31-7-1.
    Payments.
      Next of kin of persons who
        died while imprisoned,
        §31-7-1.
      Rules and procedures.
        Adoption by department,
          §31-7-3.
      To whom payable, §31-7-1.
    Persons who died while
      imprisoned.
      Payments to next of kin,
        §31-7-1.
    Tax exempt, §31-7-2.
    Warrants.
      Issuance and payment,
        §31-7-5.
  Budgets.
    State veterans' homes.
      Budget request, §31-5A-9.
  Claims.
    Assistance in processing,
      §§31-5-4, 31-5-5.
  Commitment.
    Incompetent veterans,
      §26-9-13.
  Confederate veterans.
    Widows.
      Old age assistance,
        §§38-4-11, 38-4-12.
      Pensions, §§31-8-1 to
        31-8-33.
  Constitution of Alabama.
    Exemptions from poll tax,
      Const. Ala., amds. 7, 10,
      14, 49, 90.
  Contracts.
    Minor veterans empowered to
      contract liability for
      repayment of certain
      loans, §31-1-2.

VETERANS—Cont'd
  Contracts—Cont'd
    State veterans' homes.
      Operation of homes,
        §31-5A-4.
    Veterans' organizations.
      Contracts for assistance in
        processing claims,
        §31-5-5.
  Counties.
    County service
      commissioners, §§31-5-9
      to 31-5-11, 31-5-14.
    District service
      commissioners, §§31-5-9
      to 31-5-11, 31-5-14.
  Definitions, §31-5-1.
    Educational benefits, §31-6-2.
    Incompetent veterans and
      dependents, §26-9-2.
    State veterans' homes,
      §31-5A-2.
  **Department of veterans'
    affairs,** §§31-5-1 to
    31-5-14.
    Assistance to veterans in
      presenting claims,
      §31-5-4.
    Board of veterans' affairs.
      Department to operate
        under board, §31-5-2.
    Bonus for Southeast Asian
      war prisoners, §§31-7-1
      to 31-7-5.
    Bureaus and divisions.
      Subordinate bureaus and
        divisions, §31-5-2.
    Composition, §31-5-2.
    Contracts with veterans'
      organizations for
      assistance in processing
      claims, §31-5-5.
    Definitions, §31-5-1.
    Educational benefits,
      §§31-6-1 to 31-6-17. See
      within this heading,
      "Educational benefits."
    Employees.
      Salaries, §31-5-14.
    Establishment of rights,
      §§31-5-2, 31-5-4.
    Expenses.
      Payment, §31-5-14.
    Head of department.
      State service commissioner,
        §31-5-6.
    Offices, §31-5-13.
    Power of attorney.
      Execution, §31-5-4.
    State service commissioner.
      Head of department,
        §31-5-6.
    State veterans' homes.
      Administration of homes,
        §31-5A-5.
      Contracts.
        Operation of homes,
          §31-5A-4.
      Expenditure of funds,
        §31-5A-3.
      Federal aid and gifts.
        Authorization to receive,
          §31-5A-3.
  Dependents.
    Educational benefits,
      §§31-6-1 to 31-6-17.
    Incompetent veterans and
      dependents, §§26-9-1 to
      26-9-19.

VETERANS—Cont'd
  Disabled veterans.
    Educational benefits,
      §§31-6-1 to 31-6-17. See
      within this heading,
      "Educational benefits."
    Exemption from licenses.
      See LICENSES.
    Incompetent veterans,
      §§26-9-1 to 26-9-19. See
      within this heading,
      "Incompetent veterans
      and dependents."
    Licenses.
      Exemption from licenses,
        §§40-12-340 to
        40-12-352.
      See LICENSES.
    Motor vehicle tags and
      plates, §§32-6-130 to
      32-6-133.
  District service
    commissioners, §§31-5-9
    to 31-5-11, 31-5-14.
  Educational benefits,
    §§31-6-1 to 31-6-17.
    Application for benefits,
      §31-6-10.
    Proof to be submitted,
      §31-6-11.
    Armed forces.
      Defined, §31-6-2.
    Certificate of eligibility,
      §31-6-10.
    State service commission to
      forward, §31-6-12.
    Children.
      County and city teachers
        to be informed and to
        inform dependents of
        benefits provided,
        §31-6-14.
      Deceased or totally
        disabled veterans or
        prisoners of war,
        §31-6-4.
      Limited to lives of
        veterans' immediate
        children, §31-6-7.
      Partially disabled veterans.
        §31-6-6.
    City superintendent of
      schools.
      Informing dependents of
        benefits provided,
        §31-6-14.
    Deceased or totally disabled
      veterans or prisoners of
      war.
      Benefits for children,
        §31-6-4.
      Wives or widows, §31-6-5.
    Definitions, §31-6-2.
    Department of veterans'
      affairs.
      Forms.
        Furnishing forms and
          assistance in
          preparing, §31-6-12.
      Informing veterans of
        benefits under chapter,
        §31-6-12.
    Designation of benefits,
      §31-6-3.
    Eligibility.
      Certificate of eligibility,
        §§31-6-10, 31-6-12.
      Determination of
        eligibility, §31-6-10.

VETERANS—Cont'd
  Educational benefits—Cont'd
    Eligibility—Cont'd
      Entrance requirements of
        educational
        institutions.
        Chapter not to affect,
          §31-6-16.
    Extension or correspondence
      courses, §31-6-8.
    Federal benefits.
      Benefits provided not to be
        in addition to, §31-6-8.
      Wives or widows.
        Benefits for wives or
          widows in addition
          to other benefits,
          §31-6-9.
    Fees.
      Defined, §31-6-2.
      Waiver by institutions,
        §31-6-15.
    Funds.
      Special educational trust
        fund.
        Reimbursement of
          institutions
          providing benefits,
          §31-6-15.
    Honorable discharge.
      Proof required by
        applicants, §31-6-11.
    Interruption of benefits,
      §31-6-9.
    Partially disabled veterans.
      Children.
        Benefits for, §31-6-6.
      Wives or widows.
        Benefits for, §31-6-6.
    Prior statutes.
      Rights under prior
        statutes, §31-6-17.
    Prisoners of war.
      Benefits for children,
        §31-6-4.
      Wives or widows, §31-6-5.
    Reimbursement of
      educational institutions
      providing benefits,
      §31-6-15.
    Reinstatement of
      entitlement, §31-6-6.
    Residents.
      Proof to be submitted by
        applicants for benefits,
        §31-6-11.
    Short title, §31-6-1.
    Teachers.
      County and city teachers
        to be informed and to
        inform veterans'
        dependents of benefits
        provided, §31-6-14.
    Title.
      Short title, §31-6-1.
    Totally disabled veterans or
      prisoners of war.
      Benefits for children,
        §31-6-4.
      Wives or widows, §31-6-5.
    Trade schools.
      Faculties to be informed of
        benefits provided,
        §31-6-13.
    Tuition.
      Defined, §31-6-2.
    Universities and colleges.
      Faculties to be informed of
        benefits provided,
        §31-6-13.

VETERANS—Cont'd
  Educational benefits—Cont'd
    Universities and colleges
      —Cont'd
      Reimbursement of
        institutions providing
        benefits, §31-6-15.
    Wartime or extrahazardous
      conditions.
      Proof to be submitted by
        applicants for benefits,
        §31-6-11.
    Wives or widows.
      Deceased or totally
        disabled veterans or
        prisoners of war,
        §31-6-5.
      Other state or federal
        benefits.
        Benefits for wives or
          widows in addition
          to other state or
          federal benefits,
          §31-6-9.
      Partially disabled veterans,
        §31-6-6.
  Exemption from licenses.
    Disabled veterans,
      §§40-12-340 to 40-12-352.
    See LICENSES.
    World War II veterans,
      §§40-12-370 to 40-12-377.
    See LICENSES.
  Fraud.
    Pensions for widows of
      Confederate veterans,
      §31-8-18.
  Funds.
    Educational benefits.
      Special educational trust
        fund.
        Reimbursement of
          institutions
          providing benefits,
          §31-6-15.
    State veterans' home trust
      fund, §31-5A-7.
  Governor.
    Board of veterans' affairs.
      Member, §31-5-3.
  Grand jury.
    Pensions for widows of
      Confederate veterans.
      Investigations of county
        pension list, §31-8-29.
  Guardian and ward.
    Incompetent veterans,
      §§26-9-1 to 26-9-19. See
      within this heading,
      "Incompetent veterans
      and dependents."
  Hospitals.
    Commitment of incompetent
      veteran to veterans'
      hospital, §26-9-13.
  Husband and wife.
    Educational benefits,
      §§31-6-1 to 31-6-17.
  Incompetent veterans and
    dependents, §§26-9-1 to
    26-9-19.
    Administration.
      Defined, §26-9-2.
    Administrator.
      Defined, §26-9-2.
    Applicability of chapter,
      §26-9-19.
    Appointment of guardian.
      Bonds, surety, §26-9-9.
      Fitness of guardian,
      §26-9-9.

VETERANS—Cont'd
Incompetent veterans and dependents—Cont'd
Appointment of guardian—Cont'd
Limitations, §26-9-4.
Petitions.
Certification as to age of minor ward, §26-9-6.
Certification as to incompetence, §26-9-7.
Contents, §26-9-5.
Filing, §26-9-5.
Notice of filing of petition, §26-9-8.
When guardian to be appointed, §26-9-3.
Benefits.
Defined, §26-9-2.
Commitment to veterans' hospital, §26-9-13.
Compensation.
Guardian, §26-9-17.
Construction of chapter, §26-9-19.
Definitions, §26-9-2.
Discharge of guardians, §26-9-16.
Estate and income.
Defined, §26-9-2.
Fees.
Settlements of accounts of guardians, §26-9-18.
Funds of ward.
Investment, §26-9-10.
Loans, §26-9-10.
Guardians.
Defined, §26-9-2.
Income.
Defined, §26-9-2.
Investments.
Maintenance and support.
Persons other than ward, §26-9-11.
Loans.
Limitations, §26-9-10.
Maintenance and support.
Persons other than ward, §26-9-11.
Notices.
Petition for appointment of guardian, §26-9-8.
Person.
Defined, §26-9-2.
Records.
Public record used to determine eligibility for benefits.
Furnishing copy, §26-9-12.
Removal of guardian, §26-9-16.
Failure to file account of money received for ward, §26-9-15.
Settlements of accounts of guardians.
Compensation.
Guardian, §26-9-17.
Costs, §26-9-18.
Fees, §26-9-18.
Filing of account.
Annually, §26-9-14.
Failure to file, §26-9-15.
Receipts and disbursements, §26-9-14.
Notice of hearing, §26-9-14.

VETERANS—Cont'd
Incompetent veterans and dependents—Cont'd
Settlements of accounts of guardians—Cont'd
Removal of guardians.
Failure to file account, §26-9-15.
Veterans' administration.
Certified copy of account sent to veterans' administration, §26-9-14.
Short title, §26-9-1.
Support and maintenance.
Persons other than ward, §26-9-11.
Uniform veterans' guardianship act.
Short title, §26-9-1.
Veterans' hospital.
Commitment of incompetent veteran, §26-9-13.
Ward.
Defined, §26-9-2.
Interest.
Maximum rates of interest.
Exemption of debts incurred pursuant to veterans' benefits, §8-8-6.
Licenses.
Exemption from licenses.
Disabled veterans, §§40-12-340 to 40-12-352.
See LICENSES.
World War II veterans, §§40-12-370 to 40-12-377.
See LICENSES.
Loans.
Minor veterans empowered to contract liability for repayment of certain loans, §31-1-2.
Mentally ill.
Commitment.
Veterans' administration, §22-52-13.
Incompetent veterans, §§26-9-1 to 26-9-19. See within this heading, "Incompetent veterans and dependents."
Military affairs.
See MILITARY AFFAIRS.
Militia.
Unorganized militia.
See MILITARY AFFAIRS.
Minors.
Educational benefits, §§31-6-1 to 31-6-17. See within this heading, "Educational benefits."
Loans.
Minor veterans empowered to contract liability for repayment of certain loans, §31-1-2.
Misrepresentation.
Pensions for widows of Confederate veterans, §31-8-17.
Motor vehicles.
Disabled veterans.
Ad valorem taxes.
Exemption for vehicles issued to disabled veterans, §40-12-254.

VETERANS—Cont'd
Motor vehicles—Cont'd
Disabled veterans—Cont'd
License taxes and registration fees.
Exemption, §40-12-244.
Motor vehicles issued to disabled veterans, §40-12-254.
Tags and plates.
See MOTOR VEHICLES.
Municipal corporations.
Exemptions from licenses, §§40-12-343, 40-12-373.
Nonresidents.
Pensions for widows of Confederate veterans.
Persons becoming resident citizens of other states to be dropped from pension roll, §31-8-13.
Notaries public.
State service commissioner, §31-5-12.
Oaths.
County service commissioners, §31-5-11.
State service commissioner, §31-5-11.
Penalties.
Pensions for widows of Confederate veterans.
Violation of laws, §31-8-33.
Pensions for widows of Confederate veterans, §§31-8-1 to 31-8-33.
Absence from state.
Temporary absence, §31-8-13.
Affidavits.
Certificates to accompany application, §31-8-8.
Amount of pension, §31-8-19.
Applications.
Certificates to accompany, §31-8-8.
Contents, §31-8-7.
Filing, §31-8-6.
Forms.
State department of human resources to provide, §31-8-5.
Forwarding of applications by county department of human resources, §31-8-6.
Oath, §31-8-7.
Placement on pension roll, §31-8-7.
Reapplication.
When allowed, §31-8-12.
Reinstatement to pension roll, §31-8-14.
Rejected applications.
Disposition, §31-8-11.
Verification of applications, §31-8-31.
Appropriations, §31-8-19.
Confederate pension funds for old age pension purposes, §38-4-12.
Back pay, §31-8-16.
Claims.
Transfer or discount of claims, §31-8-25.
Unauthorized purchase or receipt of transfer, §31-8-26.

VETERANS—Cont'd
**Pensions for widows of
  Confederate veterans**
  —Cont'd
Confederate archives.
  Certificates to accompany
    application, §31-8-8.
County department of human
  resources.
  Applications.
    Filing and forwarding by
      county department,
      §31-8-6.
  Payment of pensions,
    §31-8-21.
Death of pensioner.
  Disposition of pension after
    death, §31-8-24.
Discounts.
  Pension claims or
    warrants, §31-8-25.
Dropping persons from
  pension roll.
  Back pay, §31-8-16.
  Errors.
    Restoration of pensioner
      dropped from roll
      through error,
      §31-8-15.
  Misrepresentation,
    §31-8-17.
  Persons becoming resident
    citizens of other states,
    §31-8-13.
  Reinstatement.
    Application, §31-8-14.
    Right of reinstatement,
      §31-8-13.
Eligibility.
  Certain persons not to be
    placed on pension roll,
    §31-8-4.
  Remarried widows, §31-8-3.
Federal benefits.
  Wives or widows, §31-6-9.
Forms.
  State department of
    pensions and security
    to furnish forms,
    §31-8-5.
Fraud, §31-8-18.
Grand jury.
  Investigations of lists,
    §31-8-29.
Lists.
  Annual publication of
    county pension list,
    §31-8-28.
  Grand jury investigations
    of county pension list,
    §31-8-29.
Misrepresentation, §31-8-17.
Nonresidents.
  Persons becoming resident
    citizens of other states
    to be dropped from
    pension roll, §31-8-13.
Oaths.
  Application, §31-8-7.
Other states.
  Persons becoming resident
    citizens of other states
    to be dropped from
    pension roll, §31-8-13.
Payment.
  Amount of pension,
    §31-8-19.
  Monthly payment,
    §31-8-19.
  Proof of identity of payee.
    When required, §31-8-23.

VETERANS—Cont'd
**Pensions for widows of
  Confederate veterans**
  —Cont'd
Payment—Cont'd
  State department of human
    resources.
    Authority to make
      payment of pensions
      under chapter,
      §31-8-1.
  Warrants, §31-8-20.
    Delivery of warrants to
      payees, §31-8-22.
    Undelivered warrants.
      Disposition, §31-8-22.
    Warrants to reach
      county departments
      of human resources
      by last day of
      month, §31-8-21.
Penalties.
  Violations, §31-8-33.
Permanent state pension roll.
  Maintenance, §31-8-31.
Persons entitled to pension,
  §31-8-2.
Placement on pension roll.
  Application for placement,
    §31-8-7.
  Certain persons ineligible,
    §31-8-4.
  Certificates to accompany
    application, §31-8-8.
Proof of service of husband,
  §§31-8-8, 31-8-9.
Publication.
  Annual publication of
    county pension list,
    §31-8-28.
Reapplication.
  When allowed, §31-8-12.
Records.
  Permanent state record of
    pensioners, §31-8-30.
  Rejected applications,
    §31-8-11.
Remarried widows, §31-8-3.
Reports.
  Grand jury investigations
    of county pension list,
    §31-8-29.
  Operation of state pension
    law, §31-8-32.
State department of human
  resources.
  Certain persons not to be
    placed on pension roll,
    §31-8-4.
  Forms.
    State department to
      furnish, §31-8-5.
  Payment of pensions under
    chapter, §31-8-1.
  Rejected applications.
    Disposition, §31-8-11.
  Warrants.
    Delivery to county
      departments,
      §31-8-22.
State pension law.
  Report on operation,
    §31-8-32.
Transfer or discount of
  pension claims or
  warrants, §31-8-25.
Unauthorized purchase or
  receipt of transfer,
  §31-8-26.
Warrants.
  Payment, §31-8-20.

VETERANS—Cont'd
**Pensions for widows of
  Confederate veterans**
  —Cont'd
Warrants—Cont'd
  Pension warrants to reach
    county departments of
    human resources by
    last day of month,
    §31-8-21.
  Transfer or discount of
    pension warrants,
    §31-8-25.
  Unauthorized purchase or
    receipt of transfer,
    §31-8-26.
  Undelivered warrants.
    Disposition, §31-8-22.
Witnesses.
  Certification to accompany
    application, §31-8-8.
Poll tax.
  Exemptions, Const. Ala.,
    amds. 7, 10, 14, 49, 90.
Power of attorney.
  Department of veterans'
    affairs.
    Execution of power,
      §31-5-4.
Prisoners of war.
  Bonus for Southeast Asian
    war prisoners, §§31-7-1
    to 31-7-5.
  Educational benefits,
    §§31-6-1 to 31-6-17.
**Reciprocal agreements with
  other states, §31-5-6.**
Reports.
  Pensions.
    Widows of Confederate
      veterans, §§31-8-1 to
      31-8-33.
  State veterans' homes,
    §31-5A-9.
    Administration of homes,
      §31-5A-5.
Rules and regulations.
  State veterans' homes.
    Admissions and discharges,
      §31-5A-8.
    Applicable regulations,
      §31-5A-11.
**Seals and sealed
  instruments.**
  State service commissioner.
    Seal of office, §31-5-12.
**Southeaste Asian war
  prisoners.**
  Bonus, §§31-7-1 to 31-7-5.
State service commissioner.
  Appointment, §31-5-6.
  Assistant state service
    commissioners, §§31-5-8,
    31-5-11.
  Bond, §31-5-11.
  Compensation, §31-5-7.
  Department of veterans'
    affairs.
    Head of department,
      §31-5-6.
  Duties.
    Generally, §31-5-7.
  Federal agencies.
    Representation of state
      before, §31-5-6.
  Notary public.
    Appointment and powers
      as, §31-5-12.
  Oath of office, §31-5-11.
  Offices, §31-5-13.
  Qualifications, §31-5-6.

VETERANS—Cont'd
State service commissioner
—Cont'd
Reciprocal agreements with
other states, §31-5-6.
Removal, §31-5-6.
Seal of office, §31-5-12.
Term of office, §31-5-6.
State veterans' homes.
Administration of homes,
§31-5A-5.
Admissions, §31-5A-8.
Board of veterans' affairs.
Powers, §31-5A-6.
Rules and regulations.
Admissions and
discharges, §31-5A-8.
Budget request, §31-5A-9.
Certification, §31-5A-11.
Contracts.
Operation of homes,
§31-5A-4.
Cost of care.
Reimbursement by
residents, §31-5A-10.
Definition of "veteran,"
§31-5A-2.
Department of veterans'
affairs.
Administration of homes,
§31-5A-5.
Contracts.
Operation of homes,
§31-5A-4.
Expenditure of funds,
§31-5A-3.
Federal aid and gifts.
Authority to receive,
§31-5A-3.
Discharges, §31-5A-8.
Federal aid.
Board of veterans' affairs.
Power to accept and use,
§31-5A-6.
Department of veterans'
affairs.
Authorization to receive,
§31-5A-3.
Findings of legislature,
§31-5A-1.
Funds.
Trust fund, §31-5A-7.
Gifts.
Board of veterans' affairs.
Power to accept and use,
§31-5A-6.
Department of veterans'
affairs.
Authorization to receive
private gifts,
§31-5A-3.
Legislative intent, §31-5A-1.
Reimbursement of cost by
residents, §31-5A-10.
Reports, §31-5A-9.
Administration of homes,
§31-5A-5.
Rules and regulations.
Admissions and discharges,
§31-5A-8.
Applicable regulations,
§31-5A-11.
Trust fund, §31-5A-7.
Taxation.
Exemptions.
Disabled American
veterans, §40-9-1.
Property of incompetent
veterans, §40-9-1.
Sales and use taxes,
§40-23-5.

VETERANS—Cont'd
Taxation—Cont'd
Motor vehicles.
Disabled veterans,
§§40-12-244,
40-12-254.
Property exempt, §40-9-1.
Trade schools.
Regional vocational and
trade schools.
Schools to be suitable for
veteran training
programs, §16-60-194.
Trusts and trustees.
Investment of trust estate in
debts incurred under acts
of congress relating to
veterans' benefits,
§19-3-128.
United States.
Educational benefits for
veterans.
Federal benefits, §§31-6-1
to 31-6-17.
State service commissioner.
Representation of state
before federal agencies,
§31-5-6.
Universities and colleges.
Educational benefits,
§§31-6-1 to 31-6-17.
Vietnam war.
Bonus for Southeast Asian
war prisoners, §§31-7-1
to 31-7-5.
Warrants for the payment of
money.
Bonus for Southeast Asian
war prisoners.
Issuance of warrant upon
approval of
application, §31-7-5.
Payment of warrant out of
general fund, §31-7-5.
Pensions.
Widows of Confederate
veterans, §§31-8-1 to
31-8-33.
Welfare.
Pensions.
Widows of Confederate
veterans, §§31-8-1 to
31-8-33.
Widows.
Confederate veterans.
Old age assistance.
Eligibility, §38-4-11.
Pensions for widows,
§§31-8-1 to 31-8-33.
Educational benefits,
§§31-6-1 to 31-6-17.
Wives.
Educational benefits,
§§31-6-1 to 31-6-17.
World War II veterans.
Licenses.
Exemption from licenses,
§§40-12-370 to
40-12-377.
See LICENSES.

VETERANS' DAY.
Observance by closing of
schools, banks and
government offices,
§1-3-8.

VETERINARIANS, §§34-29-1 to
34-29-94.
Abandoned animals.
Disposition, §34-29-86.

VETERINARIANS—Cont'd
Acts prohibited.
Certain acts not prohibited,
§34-29-77.
Appeals.
Disciplinary action,
§34-29-83.
Board of veterinary medical
examiners, §§34-29-63 to
34-29-69.
Appointment, §34-29-63.
Body corporate, §34-29-69.
Bylaws, §34-29-66.
Compensation, §34-29-67.
Composition, §34-29-63.
Confidentiality of
information, §34-29-68.
Established, §34-29-63.
Executive secretary,
§34-29-65.
Salary, §34-29-65.
Expenditures, §34-29-70.
Expenses, §34-29-67.
Funds, §34-29-70.
Expenditure, §34-29-67.
Transfer of excess,
§34-29-70.
Meetings, §34-29-66.
Powers.
Generally, §34-29-69.
President, §34-29-66.
Qualifications of members,
§34-29-64.
Quorum, §34-29-66.
Records, §§34-29-66,
34-29-68.
Removal of members,
§34-29-64.
Reports.
Semiannual report,
§34-29-66.
Term of office, §34-29-63.
Vacancies, §34-29-63.
Vice-president, §34-29-66.
Certificate of registration.
Issuance, §34-29-73.
Citation of article, §34-29-60.
Complaints.
Privileged communications,
§34-29-80.
Continuing education
requirements, §34-29-75.
Veterinary technicians,
§34-29-94.
Definitions, §34-29-61.
Drugs.
Controlled substances.
Prescription,
administration, etc.,
for use by human
beings, §20-2-74.
Emergency care of animals
or human victims.
Immunity, §34-29-90.
Employment by other
licensed veterinarian,
§34-29-87.
Examinations.
Conduct, §34-29-73.
Graduate of nonaccredited
school, §34-29-91.
Issuance of license without
written examination,
§34-29-74.
Notice, §34-29-73.
Passing score, §34-29-73.
Retaking, §34-29-73.
Veterinary technicians,
§34-29-94.

VETERINARIANS—Cont'd
Federal veterinarians.
Appointment as assistant
state veterinarians,
§2-4-3.
Hearings.
Administrative hearings,
§34-29-79.
Immunities.
Emergency care of animals
or human victims,
§34-29-90.
Veterinary technicians,
§34-29-94.
Persons investigating
complaint, §34-29-80.
Injunctions.
Unauthorized practice of
veterinary medicine,
§34-29-78.
Internship, §34-29-91.
Six month requirement,
§34-29-93.
Legislative intent, §34-29-62.
Licenses.
Application, §34-29-72.
Continuing education
requirement, §34-29-75.
Display, §34-29-89.
Expiration, §34-29-75.
Fees, §34-29-75.
Filing with probate office,
§34-29-84.
Issuance, §34-29-73.
Without written
examination,
§34-29-74.
Persons holding license on
April 30, 1986.
Status, §34-29-85.
Prohibited acts, §34-29-76.
Qualifications of applicant,
§34-29-72.
Recording, §34-29-66.
Renewal, §34-29-75.
Required, §§34-29-76,
34-29-77.
Suspension or revocation.
Appeals, §34-29-83.
Hearing, §34-29-79.
Reinstatement, §34-29-81.
Relicensing, §34-29-81.
Stay of revocation,
§34-29-83.
Temporary licenses,
§34-29-71.
Veterinary surgery,
§40-12-178.
Veterinary technician
license, §34-29-94.
Liens.
Declaration, §35-11-390.
Enforcement, §35-11-391.
Mobile clinics.
Premise permits.
Requirements, §34-29-88.
Partnerships.
All partners to be licensed,
§34-29-87.
Penalties.
Unauthorized practice of
veterinary medicine,
§34-29-82.
Permits.
Premise permits, §§34-29-88,
34-29-89.
Veterinary technician
permit, §34-29-94.
Premise permits, §§34-29-88,
34-29-89.
Prohibited acts, §34-29-76.

VETERINARIANS—Cont'd
Rabies.
Sale, etc., of antirabies
vaccine to persons other
than rabies inspectors or
licensed veterinarians,
§3-7-2.
Reports.
State veterinarian.
Annual report, §2-4-4.
Satellite clinics.
Premise permits.
Requirements, §34-29-88.
Short title of article,
§34-29-60.
State veterinarian.
Appointment, §2-4-1.
Assistant state veterinarians.
Appointment, §2-4-2.
Federal veterinarians,
§2-4-3.
Brucellosis or Bang's disease.
General provisions,
§§2-15-193, 2-15-194.
Compensation, §2-4-1.
Duties, §2-4-1.
Livestock.
Brucellosis or Bang's
disease, §§2-15-193,
2-15-194.
Diseases, §§2-15-155,
2-15-158.
Livestock markets.
Interference with
performance of duties
by state veterinarian,
§2-15-69.
Right of entry and
inspection, §2-15-69.
Powers, §2-4-1.
Qualifications, §2-4-1.
Reports.
Annual report, §2-4-4.
State livestock inspectors.
Appointment, §2-4-2.
Federal livestock
inspectors, §2-4-3.
Student preceptees.
Service for minimum period,
§34-29-92.
**Unauthorized practice of
veterinary medicine.**
Injunctions, §34-29-78.
Penalties, §34-29-82.
Veterinary technicians.
Licenses and permits,
§34-29-94.

VETO.
Governor's veto power,
Const. Ala., art. V, §§125,
126.

VIADUCTS.
Eminent domain.
Internal improvement
corporations, §10-5-1.
Fishing from, §32-5A-216.

**VICE-PRESIDENT OF THE
UNITED STATES.**
Age, Const. U. S., Amendment
XII.
Bribery, Const. U. S., Art. II,
§4.
Elections.
Electors.
Majority vote is necessary
to elect president or
vice-president, Const.
U. S., Amendment XII.

**VICE-PRESIDENT OF THE
UNITED STATES**—Cont'd
Elections—Cont'd
General provisions, §§17-19-1
to 17-19-8.
See ELECTIONS.
Failure to qualify, Const. U.
S., Amendment XX.
Impeachment, Const. U. S.,
Art. II, §4.
Oaths, Const. U. S., Art. VI;
Amendment XIV.
President of the senate,
Const. U. S., Art. I, §3.
Qualifications, Const. U. S.,
Amendment XII.
Removal, Const. U. S., Art. II,
§4.
**Succession to office of
president,** Const. U. S.,
Art. II, §1; Amendment
XX.
Upon death, resignation or
removal of president,
Const. U. S., Amendment
XXV, §1.
Treason, Const. U. S., Art. II,
§4.
Vacancy in office, Const. U.
S., Art. II, §1; Amendment
XX.
Nomination by president,
Const. U. S., Amendment
XXV, §2.
Confirmation by majority
vote of both houses of
congress, Const. U. S.,
Amendment XXV, §2.

VICTIM COUNSELORS.
Confidentiality.
Child abuse or neglect.
Duty to report, §15-23-45.
Citation of act.
Short title, §15-23-40.
Communications with victim
counselor, §15-23-42.
Construction and
interpretation.
Other testimonial
privileges not limited,
§15-23-44.
Practice of medicine.
Provisions not to be
construed as
authorizing,
§15-23-46.
Prescribing drugs.
Provisions not to be
construed as
authorizing,
§15-23-46.
Reporting crimes.
Duty to report certain
crimes, §15-23-45.
Definitions, §15-23-41.
Drugs.
Victim counselor not to
prescribe, §15-23-46.
Exceptions.
Duty of victim counselor to
report certain crimes,
§15-23-45.
Suit against victim
counselor by victim,
§15-23-43.
Generally, §15-23-42.
Other testimonial privileges.
Not limited by provisions,
§15-23-44.

VICTIM COUNSELORS
—Cont'd
Confidentiality—Cont'd
Practice of medicine by
victim counselor.
Not authorized, §15-23-46.
Short title of act, §15-23-40.
Suit against counselor by
victim.
Exception as to, §15-23-43.
Title of act.
Short title, §15-23-40.
Waiver of protection,
§15-23-43.
Definitions, §15-23-41.
Prescriptions.
Confidentiality provisions not
to authorize prescribing
of drugs, §15-23-46.
Reports.
Confidentiality.
Duty to report certain
crimes, §15-23-45.

VICTIMS.
Crime victims compensation,
§§15-23-1 to 15-23-23.
See CRIME VICTIMS
COMPENSATION.
**Crime victims' court
attendance,** §§15-14-50 to
15-14-57.
See TRIAL.
**Restitution to victims of
crimes,** §§15-18-65 to
15-18-78.
See RESTITUTION TO
VICTIMS OF CRIMES.
Sexual offenses.
Child victim.
Anatomically correct dolls
or mannequins.
Use during testimony or
depositions,
§15-25-5.
Child sexual abuse victim
protection act,
§§15-25-30 to 15-25-40.
See MINORS.
Closed circuit equipment to
present testimony.
Competence of child
victim as witness,
§15-25-3.
Leading questions
authorized, §15-25-3.
Use, §15-25-3.
Weight and credibility
assessed by trier of
fact, §15-25-3.
Competent as witness,
§15-25-3.
Weight and credibility
determined by trier
of fact, §15-25-3.
Interviewing child victim
of sexual crime.
Limitations by presiding
judge of circuit court
authorized, §15-1-2.
Leading questions.
Authorized, §§15-25-1,
15-25-3.
Length of proceedings
stressful to child.
Minimizing, §15-25-6.
Videotaped deposition,
§15-25-2.
Anatomically correct
dolls, §15-25-5.

VICTIMS—Cont'd
Sexual offenses—Cont'd
Child victim—Cont'd
Videotaped deposition
—Cont'd
Appropriation for
viewing equipment,
§15-25-4.

VIDEO CASSETTES AND VIDEOTAPING.
Appeals.
Record on appeal, ARAP,
Rule 14.
**Copying and sale of
recorded devices
generally,** §§13A-8-80 to
13A-8-86.
See RECORDED DEVICES.
Sexual offenses.
Child victim.
See VICTIMS.

VIETNAM WAR.
**Bonus for Southeast Asian
war prisoners,** §§31-7-1 to
31-7-5.

VISITATION.
Adoption.
Visitation rights.
Natural grandparents,
§26-10-5.
Bonds, surety.
Compliance with visitation
order, §30-3-6.
**Compliance with visitation
order.**
Bond, security, or other
guarantee to secure,
§30-3-6.
Grandparents.
Rights, §30-3-4.
Hearings.
Compliance with visitation
order.
Bond, security, or other
guarantee to secure.
Obligor to have
opportunity to be
heard on matter,
§30-3-6.
**Modification of child
custody, visitation rights
or child support.**
Venue of proceedings,
§30-3-5.
Notice.
Compliance with visitation
order.
Bond, security, or other
guarantee to secure.
Petition or other original
pleading to clearly
notify obligor,
§30-3-6.
Rights of grandparents,
§30-3-4.

VISITORS.
**Protection of certain state
officers and visitors,**
§§36-33-2 to 36-33-4.

VISUALLY HANDICAPPED.
See BLIND PERSONS.

VITAL STATISTICS, §§22-9-1
to 22-9-79.
Abortion.
Reports by persons
performing abortions or
agents, §26-21-8.

VITAL STATISTICS—Cont'd
Adoption.
Birth certificates, §26-10-4.
Registrars.
Order of adoption,
§26-10-4.
**Annuity and mortality
tables,** §§35-16-1 to
35-16-4.
Births.
Certificates.
Additional information,
§22-9-6.
Adoption.
Inspections, §26-10-4.
Issuance of new birth
certificate, §26-10-4.
Original certificate to be
sealed and filed,
§26-10-4.
Compensation of local and
deputy registrars for
certificates, §22-9-9.
Correction, §22-9-6.
Crimes and offenses,
§22-19-3.
Delayed certificates,
§22-9-34.
Certificate based on
court order or
decree, §22-9-35.
Examination, §22-9-7.
Forms, §§22-9-6, 22-9-31.
Foundlings, §22-9-33.
Furnishing certificates,
§22-9-7.
Manner of preparation,
§22-9-31.
Processing of certificates,
§22-9-7.
Required, §22-9-30.
Supplemental report of
child's name or other
information, §22-9-32.
Delayed certificates,
§§22-9-34, 22-9-35.
Hospitals and institutions.
Records and reports of
births, §22-9-11.
Records.
Births in institutions,
§22-9-11.
Registration of births.
Certificates, §§22-9-6,
22-9-7.
Registration districts,
§22-9-4.
State board of health,
§22-9-2.
Stillbirths, §§22-9-6, 22-9-7.
Certificates.
Compensation of local
and deputy
registrars, §22-9-9.
Examination, §22-9-7.
Execution, §22-9-72.
Filing, §22-9-72.
Forms, §22-9-6.
Processing, §22-9-7.
Registration of stillbirths,
§22-9-2.
Bureau of vital statistics,
§22-9-3.
Burial generally.
See BURIAL.
Certificates.
Additional information,
§22-9-6.
Births. See within this
heading, "Births."
Corrections, §22-9-6.

VITAL STATISTICS—Cont'd
Certificates—Cont'd
  Death. See within this
    heading, "Death."
  Deputy registrars of vital
    statistics.
    Compensation for birth,
      death and stillbirth
      certificates, §22-9-9.
  Divorces. See within this
    heading, "Divorces."
  Examination, §22-9-7.
  Forms, §§22-9-6, 22-9-31.
  Furnishing, §22-9-7.
  Local registrars of vital
    statistics.
    Compensation for birth,
      death and stillbirth
      certificates, §22-9-9.
  Marriages. See within this
    heading, "Marriages."
  Stillbirths. See within this
    heading, "Births."
County boards of health.
  Duties, §22-3-2.
County health officers.
  Duties, §22-3-5.
Death.
  Burial generally.
    See BURIAL.
  Certificates.
    Additional information,
      §§22-9-6, 22-9-70.
    Authentication, §22-9-70.
    Caskets.
      Certificates to be
        enclosed in sold
        casket, §22-9-77.
    Certification of medical
      data, §22-9-71.
    Compensation of local and
      deputy registrars for
      death certificates,
      §22-9-9.
    Corrections, §22-9-6.
    Crimes and offenses,
      §22-19-3.
    Diseases.
      When death due to
        infectious, etc.,
        disease, §22-9-7.
    Examination, §22-9-7.
    Filing, §22-9-70.
    Forms, §22-9-6.
    Furnishing of certificates,
      §22-9-7.
    Medical data.
      Certification, §22-9-71.
    Processing, §22-9-7.
    Stillbirths, §§22-9-6,
      22-9-7.
  Diseases.
    Proceedings when death
      due to infectious, etc.,
      disease, §22-9-7.
  Hospitals and institutions.
    Records and reports of
      deaths, §22-9-11.
  Midwives.
    Failure to report death,
      §22-9-78.
  Penalty for violations,
    §22-9-79.
  Registration of deaths,
    §22-9-2.
  Reports.
    Deaths in institutions,
      §22-9-11.
  Rules and regulations.
    Penalty for violation,
      §22-9-79.

VITAL STATISTICS—Cont'd
Death—Cont'd
  Sextons.
    Duties, §22-9-76.
  Violations of article.
    Penalty, §22-9-79.
Definitions, §22-9-1.
Deputy registrars, §22-9-5.
  Certificates.
    Compensation for birth,
      death and stillbirth
      certificates, §22-9-9.
Districts.
  Registration districts,
    §22-9-4.
Divorces.
  Certificates, §22-9-51.
    Additional information,
      §22-9-6.
    Corrections, §22-9-6.
    Examination of certificates,
      §22-9-7.
    Forms, §22-9-6.
    Furnishing of certificates,
      §22-9-7.
  Record of divorces, §22-9-51.
Elections.
  Statewide registration.
    Information provided to
      director of voter
      registration, §17-4-212.
Enforcement of chapter,
  §22-9-12.
Evidence.
  Certified registers of
    marriages, births and
    deaths, §12-21-101.
Fees.
  Local registrars of vital
    statistics.
    Priority of fees, §22-9-10.
  Registration.
    Certified copies or
      authentication of
      registered records,
      §22-9-8.
  State registrar of vital
    statistics, §22-9-8.
Forms.
  Certificates, §§22-9-6,
    22-9-31.
Foundlings.
  Registration, §22-9-33.
Funerals.
  Record and report of casket
    sales or funerals,
    §22-9-77.
Hospitals and institutions.
  Births and deaths.
    Records and reports,
      §22-9-11.
Inmates.
  Records and reports of
    inmates in institutions,
    §22-9-11.
Juvenile proceedings.
  Release of information,
    ARJP, Rule 18.
**Local registrars of vital
  statistics,** §22-9-5.
  Certificates.
    Compensation for birth,
      death and stillbirth
      certificates, §22-9-9.
  Claims.
    Priority, §22-9-10.
  Enforcement of chapter,
    §22-9-12.
  Fees.
    Priority, §22-9-10.

VITAL STATISTICS—Cont'd
Marriages.
  Certificates.
    Additional information,
      §22-9-6.
    Corrections, §22-9-6.
    Examination of certificates,
      §22-9-7.
    Forms, §22-9-6.
    Furnishing of certificates,
      §22-9-7.
    Record of certificates,
      §22-9-50.
  Divorces, §§22-9-6, 22-9-7,
    22-9-51.
  Licenses.
    Record, §22-9-50.
Midwives.
  Failure to report death,
    §22-9-78.
Mortality tables, §§35-16-1 to
  35-16-4.
Penalties.
  Death.
    Violation of article or state
      board of health
      regulations, §22-9-79.
Permits.
  Burial generally.
    See BURIAL.
**Receipts for burial, removal
  or other disposition of
  dead human bodies,**
  §§22-9-73, 22-9-74.
Records.
  Births in institutions,
    §22-9-11.
Registrars.
  Local registrars, §22-9-5.
    General provisions. See
      within this heading,
      "Local registrars of
      vital statistics."
  State board of health,
    §22-9-3.
    General provisions. See
      within this heading,
      "State registrar of
      vital statistics."
Registration.
  Authentication of registered
    records, §22-9-8.
  Births, §§22-9-30 to 22-9-32.
  Certificates, §§22-9-6, 22-9-7.
  Certified copies of registered
    records, §22-9-8.
  Deaths, §22-9-2.
  Deputy registrars, §22-9-5.
  Districts, §22-9-4.
  Fees.
    Certified copies or
      authentication of
      registered records,
      §22-9-8.
  Foundlings, §22-9-33.
  Local registrars, §22-9-5.
  State board of health.
    Registration of births,
      deaths and stillbirths,
      §22-9-2.
  State registrar, §22-9-3.
  Stillbirths, §22-9-2.
Reports.
  Deaths in institutions,
    §22-9-11.
Rules and regulations.
  State board of health.
    Penalty for violation,
      §22-9-79.

VITAL STATISTICS—Cont'd
State board of health.
Registration of births, deaths
and stillbirths, §22-9-2.
Rules and regulations.
Penalty for violation,
§22-9-79.
State registrar of vital
statistics, §22-9-3.
Enforcement of chapter,
§22-9-12.
Fees, §22-9-8.
Statewide system of vital
statistics, §22-9-2.
Stillbirths, §§22-9-6, 22-9-7.
Tables.
Annuity and mortality
tables, §§35-16-1 to
35-16-4.

VITAMINS.
Oleomargarine.
Minimum requirements as to
units of vitamin A,
§20-1-111.
Sales tax exemption.
Prescriptions for vitamins
and supplements,
§40-9-27.

VOCATIONAL EDUCATION.
Alabama mining academy,
§§16-60-260 to 16-60-264.
General provisions, §§16-37-1
to 16-37-8.
See EDUCATION.
Regional vocational and
trade schools act,
§§16-60-190 to 16-60-198.
See TRADE SCHOOLS.
Retirement.
Participation in teachers'
retirement system,
§16-25-10.3.
Trade schools, §§16-60-1 to
16-60-270.
See TRADE SCHOOLS.

VOLUNTARY
CONVEYANCES.
Bulk transfers, §§7-6-101 to
7-6-111.
See COMMERCIAL CODE.
Commercial code.
Bulk transfers, §§7-6-101 to
7-6-111.
See COMMERCIAL CODE.

VOTING, §§17-1-1 to 17-24-11.
See ELECTIONS.

VOTING MACHINES, §§17-9-1
to 17-9-41.
See ELECTIONS.

W

WAGERING.
Federal wagering
occupational tax stamp,
§§13A-12-90 to 13A-12-92.
General provisions,
§§13A-12-20 to 13A-12-92.
See GAMBLING.
Horse racing, §§11-65-1 to
11-65-47.
See HORSE RACING.
Lotteries, §§13A-12-22,
13A-12-29, 13A-12-70 to
13A-12-75.
See LOTTERIES.

WAGES.
Agricultural laborers.
Liens for wages, §§35-11-91
to 35-11-97.
See AGRICULTURE.
Assignments.
Future wages, §8-5-21.
Buses.
Bi-weekly payment of wages,
§37-8-270.
Commercial code.
Secured transactions.
Transactions excluded,
§7-9-104.
Counterclaims.
Exemption of wages of head
of family, §6-8-82.
Debts.
Intestate former employee
owed wages.
Discharge of debtor,
§43-8-115.
Enterprise zones.
Subsidies.
Agreements with
employers to receive,
§41-23-30.
Exemptions from levy and
sale under process.
Personal services, §6-10-7.
Garnishment, §§5-19-15,
6-6-480 to 6-6-484, 6-10-7.
See GARNISHMENT.
Income tax.
Withholding tax, §§40-18-70
to 40-18-85.
See INCOME TAX.
Intestate succession.
Debt for wages owed to
intestate former
employee.
Discharge of debtor,
§43-8-115.
Liens.
Agricultural superintendents
and laborers, §§35-11-91
to 35-11-97.
See AGRICULTURE.
Lumber employees or
laborers, §§35-11-270 to
35-11-273.
See LUMBER.
Railroad employees,
§§35-11-90 to 35-11-97.
See RAILROADS.
Sawmill employees or
laborers, §§35-11-270 to
35-11-273.
Timber employees or
laborers, §§35-11-270 to
35-11-273.
Limitation of actions.
Recovery of wages, §6-2-38.
Lumber employees or
laborers.
Liens for wages, §§35-11-270
to 35-11-273.
Motor vehicle carriers.
Biweekly payment of wages,
§37-8-270.
Pilots and pilotage, §§33-4-48
to 33-4-52.
Railroads.
Bi-weekly payment of wages,
§37-8-270.
Liens for wages, §§35-11-90
to 35-11-97.
See RAILROADS.
Salaries.
See SALARIES.

WAGES—Cont'd
Sawmill employees or
laborers.
Liens for wages, §§35-11-270
to 35-11-273.
Secured transactions.
Transactions excluded from
article, §7-9-104.
Surviving spouse.
Debt for wage owed to
intestate former
employee.
Discharge by payment to
surviving spouse,
§43-8-115.
Timber employers or
laborers.
Liens for wages, §§35-11-270
to 35-11-273.
Transportation companies.
Bi-weekly payment,
§37-8-270.
Unemployment
compensation.
General provisions, §§25-4-1
to 25-4-152.
See UNEMPLOYMENT
COMPENSATION.
Widows.
Debt for wages owed to
intestate former
employee.
Discharge by payment to
surviving spouse,
§43-8-115.
Withholding tax, §§40-18-70
to 40-18-85.
See INCOME TAX.

WAGONS.
Municipal corporations.
Licensing, §11-51-101.

WALKER COUNTY.
Court costs and fees, Const.
Ala., amd. 127.
Hospitals.
Tax in district two, Const.
Ala., amd. 276.
Officers.
Allowances, etc., of officers,
Const. Ala., amd. 127.
Fees, salaries, etc., of certain
public officers, Const.
Ala., amd. 50.
Roads.
Special road tax, Const. Ala.,
amd. 19.
Salaries and wages.
License, excise, etc., taxes on
salaries and wages by
municipal corporations,
Const. Ala., amd. 133.
School tax.
Special school taxes, Const.
Ala., amd. 204.

WALKER STATE
TECHNICAL COLLEGE.
Alabama mining academy,
§§16-60-260 to 16-60-264.

WALLACE-CATER ACT.
Municipal corporations.
Industrial development
board, §§11-54-80 to
11-54-101.
See MUNICIPAL
CORPORATIONS.

WALLACE-CATER ACT
—Cont'd
Municipal corporations
—Cont'd
Promotion of industry, trade
and pollution control,
§§11-54-20 to 11-54-32.
See MUNICIPAL
CORPORATIONS.

**WALLACE-FOLSOM
PREPAID COLLEGE
TUITION TRUST FUND,**
§§16-33C-1 to 16-33C-8.
See UNIVERSITIES AND
COLLEGES.

WALNUTS.
See NUTS.

WAR.
Articles of war, Const. U. S.,
Art. I, §8.
**Bonus for Southeast Asian
war prisoners,** §§31-7-1 to
31-7-5.
Civil defense, §§31-9-1 to
31-9-24.
See CIVIL DEFENSE.
Congress.
Articles of war, Const. U. S.,
Art. I, §8.
Declaration of war, Const. U.
S., Art. I, §8.
Constitution of Alabama.
Continuity of legislature in
event of enemy attack,
Const. Ala., amd. 159.
**Constitution of the United
States.**
Articles of war, Const. U. S.,
Art. I, §8.
Declaration by congress,
Const. U. S., Art. I, §8.
State engaging in, Const. U.
S., Art. I, §10.
Counties.
Financial provisions,
§11-8-15.
Officers.
Military service of officers
in time of national
emergency, §§36-8-1 to
36-8-6.
See PUBLIC OFFICERS
AND EMPLOYEES.
Fiduciaries in war service,
§§19-2-1 to 19-2-5.
Grand jury.
Dispensability of
presentment, Const. U.
S., Amendment V.
Insurance.
Foreign insurers.
Effect of war on contracts
of, §27-14-23.
Legislature.
Continuity in event of enemy
attack, Const. Ala., amd.
159.
Emergency interim
succession, §§29-3-1 to
29-3-16.
See LEGISLATURE.
Limitation of actions.
Contracts during war.
Computation of time,
§6-2-13.
Military affairs, §§31-1-1 to
31-6-17.
See MILITARY AFFAIRS.

WAR—Cont'd
**Public officers and
employees.**
Military service.
General provisions,
§§36-8-1 to 36-8-6.
See PUBLIC OFFICERS
AND EMPLOYEES.
**Quartering soldiers in
homes,** Const. U. S.,
Amendment III.
Southeast Asian war.
Bonus for Southeast Asian
war prisoners, §§31-7-1
to 31-7-5.
State.
May not make without
consent of congress,
Const. U. S., Art. I, §10.
Treason.
In levying against the
United States, Const. U.
S., Art. III, §3.
Vietnam war.
Bonus for Southeast Asian
war prisoners, §§31-7-1
to 31-7-5.

WARDENS.
Forest fire wardens, §§9-13-6
to 9-13-9.
Forest wardens, §9-13-5.
Game and fish wardens,
§§9-2-64, 9-2-65.

WARDS.
Conservators.
Generally.
See CONSERVATORS.
Removal of person or
property of minors and
wards, §§26-8-1 to
26-8-52.
See GUARDIAN AND
WARD.
Guardian and ward.
See GUARDIAN AND
WARD.
Municipal corporations.
See MUNICIPAL
CORPORATIONS.

WAREHOUSE RECEIPTS.
Documents of title, §§7-7-101
to 7-7-603.
Commercial code.
See COMMERCIAL CODE.
Endorsement.
When endorsed "stored in the
open," §8-15-16.
Issuance by warehouseman,
§8-15-15.

WAREHOUSES, §§8-15-1 to
8-15-38.
Appeals.
Denial of permit, §8-15-6.
**Board of agriculture and
industries.**
Promulgation of standards,
character of records,
rules and regulations,
§8-15-2.
Bond issues.
Counties.
Public improvement bonds,
§§11-81-140 to
11-81-150.
See COUNTIES.

WAREHOUSES—Cont'd
Bond issues—Cont'd
Municipal corporations.
Public improvement bonds,
§§11-81-110 to
11-81-150.
See MUNICIPAL
CORPORATIONS.
Bonds, surety.
Permits, §8-15-7.
Recordation, §8-15-8.
State bond not required for
federally bonded
warehouses, §8-15-3.
Commercial code.
Warehouse receipts,
§§7-7-101 to 7-7-603.
See COMMERCIAL CODE.
**Commissioner of agriculture
and industries.**
Inspection by commissioner
and agents, §8-15-11.
Supervision, §8-15-1.
Complaints.
Investigation of complaints
against warehouses,
§8-15-12.
Cotton, §§2-19-3, 2-19-19,
2-19-82.
Definitions, §8-15-1.
Self-service storage facilities,
§8-15-31.
Fees.
Permits.
Filing fee, §8-15-3.
Witness fees, §8-15-13.
Harbors and ports.
Acquisition and operation,
§§33-1-12, 33-1-22.
Hearings.
Public hearing on operations,
§8-15-13.
Inland waterways.
Development of docks and
other facilities along
inland waterways ,
§§33-2-1 to 33-2-213.
See WATERS AND
WATERCOURSES.
Inspections.
Commissioner and agents,
§8-15-11.
Insurance.
Permits.
Bond requirement.
Proof of insurance,
§8-15-7.
Raw agricultural
commodities, §8-15-18.
Requirement for articles not
stored in warehouse,
§8-15-17.
Stored cotton, §8-15-18.
Investigations.
Complaints against
warehouses, §8-15-12.
Liability of warehouseman.
Articles not stored in
warehouse, §8-15-17.
Licenses, §40-12-179.
Cotton warehouses,
§40-12-88.
Refrigerated warehouses,
§40-12-137.
Liens.
Warehouseman's lien,
§7-7-209.
Enforcement, §7-7-210.
Liquidation of operation,
§8-15-14.

WAREHOUSES—Cont'd
Motor fuel taxes.
Reports.
Information not public,
§40-17-202.
Penalty for failure to
comply, §40-17-203.
When reports to be made
by warehousemen and
transfer companies,
§40-17-201.
Notice.
Grant or denial of permit,
§8-15-6.
Penalties.
Operating without permit,
§8-15-10.
Permits, §§8-15-3 to 8-15-10,
8-15-14.
Application, §8-15-3.
False statements, §8-15-4.
Bonds, surety, §8-15-7.
Recordation, §8-15-8.
State bond not required for
federally bonded
warehouses, §8-15-3.
Denial.
Appeals, §8-15-6.
Notification, §8-15-6.
Expiration date, §8-15-9.
Filing fee, §8-15-3.
Grant.
Notification, §8-15-6.
Investigation of building and
applicant, §8-15-5.
Issuance, §8-15-9.
Bond prerequisite, §8-15-7.
License.
Prerequisite to issuance,
§8-15-3.
Penalties.
Operating without permit,
§8-15-10.
Disposition of proceeds,
§8-15-10.
Required, §8-15-3.
Revocation, §8-15-14.
Term, §8-15-9.
Receipts.
Documents of title, §§7-7-101
to 7-7-603.
Commercial code,
§§7-7-101 to 7-7-603.
See COMMERCIAL
CODE.
Endorsement.
When endorsed "stored in
the open," §8-15-16.
Issuance by warehouseman,
§8-15-15.
Records.
Character of records.
Promulgation by state
board of agriculture
and industries,
§8-15-2.
Reports.
Motor fuel taxes, §§40-17-201
to 40-17-203.
Rules and regulations.
Promulgation by board of
agriculture and
industries, §8-15-2.
Self-service storage facilities,
§§8-15-30 to 8-15-38.
Applicability of article,
§8-15-38.
Citation of article, §8-15-30.

WAREHOUSES—Cont'd
Self-service storage facilities
—Cont'd
Creditors.
Effect of laws governing
rights of creditors,
§8-15-37.
Definitions, §8-15-31.
Failure to pay charges.
Posting of notice as to
effect, §8-15-35.
Landlords.
Effect of laws governing
rights of landlord
against tenants,
§8-15-37.
Liens.
Owner's liens, §8-15-33.
Satisfaction, §8-15-34.
Posting of notice as to
effect of failure to pay
charges, §8-15-35.
Satisfaction of owner's lien,
§8-15-34.
Notice.
Posting of notice as to
effect of failure to pay
charges, §8-15-35.
Rights provided by article as
additional to other rights
allowed by law, §8-15-36.
Risk of loss.
Determination, §8-15-32.
Short title, §8-15-30.
Vesting of care in occupant,
§8-15-32.
Standards.
Promulgation by board of
agriculture and
industries, §8-15-2.
Taxation.
Subjects of taxation,
§40-11-1.
Transportation companies.
Storage of freight in
warehouse.
Liability, §37-2-27.
Waters and watercourses.
Development of docks and
other facilities along
inland waterways,
§§33-2-1 to 33-2-213.
See WATERS AND
WATERCOURSES.
Witnesses.
Public hearing on operations,
§8-15-13.

WARRANTS.
Arrest warrants, §§15-7-3,
15-7-4.
General provisions.
See ARREST.
Bench warrants, §15-10-60.
Boats.
Discharge of litter and
sewage from watercraft,
§33-6-10.
Capital punishment.
Warrant for execution of
death penalty.
Issuance and delivery for
execution, §§15-18-80,
15-18-85.
Civil defense.
Orders, rules and regulations
of governor.
Arrest without warrant for
violating or attempting
to violate, §31-9-15.

WARRANTS—Cont'd
Claims against state,
§§41-9-71, 41-9-72.
Complaints.
Arrest warrant on complaint,
§§15-7-1 to 15-7-4.
Constitution of Alabama.
Searches and seizures.
Conditions for issuance,
Const. Ala., art. I, §5.
**Constitution of the United
States.**
Searches and seizures.
Conditions for issuance,
Const. U. S.,
Amendment IV.
Death penalty.
Warrant for execution,
§§15-18-80, 15-18-85.
Extradition.
Arrest warrants, §§15-9-30 to
15-9-65.
See EXTRADITION.
Finance, §§41-4-57 to 41-4-60.
Fish and game.
Violations of fish and game
laws.
Arrest without warrant,
§9-11-8.
Corporations.
Service and return of
warrant, §9-11-9.
Wardens.
Execution of search
warrants, §9-2-65.
Industrial parks, §§11-92-6 to
11-92-10.
Libel and slander.
Publication of certain
documents considered
privileged, §13A-11-161.
Military affairs.
Courts-martial.
Disruption of proceedings,
§31-2-101.
Military courts.
Actions against members
of courts as to
warrants, §31-2-89.
Money, §§1-3-3, 35-2-37.
Motor vehicles.
Uniform traffic infractions.
Failure of defendant to
appear.
Issuance of supplemental
warrant, ARJA,
Rule 19.
Municipal courts.
See MUNICIPAL COURTS.
Parole.
Retaking of parolee,
§15-22-31.
Peace bonds, §§15-6-21,
15-6-25.
Quarantine.
Arrests without warrants,
§22-12-26.
Search warrants, §§15-5-1 to
15-5-19.
See SEARCHES AND
SEIZURES.
Witnesses.
Execution of warrants for
arrest of witnesses in
adjoining counties,
§12-21-183.
Youth services.
Detention without order or
warrant of escaped
youths, §44-1-9.

WARRANTS FOR THE PAYMENT OF MONEY.
Division of land surveys.
Expenses and compensation.
Limitation on amount,
§35-2-37.
Facsimile signatures or seals.
Execution of warrants with,
§1-3-3.
Municipal corporations,
§§11-44E-44, 11-44E-76.
State warrants.
General provisions, §§41-4-57
to 41-4-60.

WARRANTY.
Agents.
Warranty of authority
assumed, §8-2-5.
Auctions and auctioneers.
Gold, silver, watches,
jewelry, china, etc.
Descriptions of goods
considered warranties,
§8-14-23.
Commercial code.
See COMMERCIAL CODE.
Conveyances.
When covenants of warranty
implied, §35-4-271.
Words "grant," "bargain," or
"sell," §35-4-271.
Cotton.
Implied warranty as to
packing, §2-19-22.
Deeds.
When covenants of warranty
implied, §35-4-271.
Documents of title.
Collecting bank.
Warranties of collecting
bank, §7-7-508.
Warranties on negotiation or
transfer, §7-7-507.
Investment securities.
Effect of signature of
authenticating trustee,
registrar or transfer
agent, §7-8-208.
Warranties on presentment
and transfer, §7-8-306.
Life tenants, §35-4-270.
Livestock.
No implied warranty that
livestock disease free,
§2-15-4.
Motor vehicles.
Warranty work on motor
vehicles, §§32-17-1,
32-17-2.
Pleadings.
Form of complaint on a
warranty, ARCP, Form
21.
Secured transactions.
Modification of sales
warranties where
security agreement
exists, §7-9-206.
Uniform commercial code.
See COMMERCIAL CODE.
Use tax.
Exemptions.
Repairs done pursuant to
warranty agreements,
§40-23-62.

WASHINGTON COUNTY.
Court costs and charges,
Const. Ala., amd. 349.

WASHINGTON COUNTY
—Cont'd
Officers.
Compensation of certain
officers, Const. Ala.,
amd. 349.
Port authority, Const. Ala.,
amd. 470.
Public buildings.
Special tax and bond issues
for public buildings,
Const. Ala., amd. 199.
Roads and bridges.
Indebtedness to improve,
Const. Ala., amd. 410.
School tax.
Additional tax, Const. Ala.,
amd. 182.

WASTE.
Actions.
Against executor or
administrator, §6-5-90.
Executors and administrators.
Grounds for removal,
§43-2-290.
Right of action against
executor or
administrator, §6-5-90.
Intemperates and inebriates.
Complaint to preserve estate
from waste, §6-6-520.
Restoration of estate,
§6-6-527.
Securing estate against
further waste pending
action, §6-6-521.
Trustee.
Appointment, §6-6-522.
Compensation, §6-6-526.
Control by appointing
court, §6-6-524.
Duties, §6-6-523.
Settlement of account,
§6-6-525.
Solid waste, §§11-89A-1 to
11-89A-25.
See SOLID WASTE.
Trustees.
Preservation of estate of
intemperates and
inebriates, §§6-6-520 to
6-6-527. See within this
heading, "Intemperates
and inebriates."

WASTEWATER SYSTEMS AND TREATMENT PLANTS, §§22-25-1 to 22-25-15.
See WATER AND
WASTEWATER SYSTEMS
AND TREATMENT
PLANTS.

WATCHES.
Auction sales, §§8-14-20 to
8-14-24.

WATCHMAKERS' LIENS,
§§35-11-150, 35-11-151.

WATER AND WASTEWATER SYSTEMS AND TREATMENT PLANTS.
Certification of operators.
Examinations, §22-25-8.
Failure of operator to be
certified, §22-25-14.
Issuance, §22-25-9.
Renewal, §22-25-11.
Revocation, §22-25-12.

WATER AND WASTEWATER SYSTEMS AND TREATMENT PLANTS
—Cont'd
Certification of operators
—Cont'd
State health officer's duty,
§22-25-7.
Term, §22-25-11.
**Classification of plants and
systems,** §22-25-2.
Definitions, §22-25-1.
**Environmental management
department.**
Rules and regulations,
§22-25-13.
Examination of operators,
§22-25-8.
Penalties, §22-25-15.
Rules and regulations,
§22-25-13.
State health officer.
Certification of operators,
§22-25-7.
Violations of chapter.
Penalty, §22-25-15.

WATER CLOSETS.
Municipal corporations.
Regulation, installation, etc.,
§11-50-55.

WATER CONSERVATION AND IRRIGATION,
§§9-10-1 to 9-10-47.
Agency, §§9-10-1 to 9-10-14.
Actions.
Power to sue and be sued,
§9-10-5.
Article supplementary,
§9-10-14.
Assistance of other state
agencies, §9-10-11.
Board of directors.
Application for
incorporation, §9-10-3.
Compensation, §9-10-4.
Composition, §9-10-2.
Election, §9-10-2.
Exercise of corporation
powers, §9-10-4.
Expenses, §9-10-4.
Meetings, §9-10-4.
Officers, §9-10-4.
Qualification of members,
§9-10-2.
Quorum, §9-10-4.
Records of proceedings,
§9-10-4.
Reports.
Annual report, §9-10-10.
Terms of office, §9-10-2.
Vacancies, §9-10-2.
Bond issues, §§9-10-5, 9-10-8.
Bylaws, §9-10-5.
Certificate of incorporation,
§9-10-3.
Commissioner of
conservation and natural
resources.
Construction of term,
§9-10-13.
Composition, §9-10-2.
Conflicts of interest.
Officers of corporation,
§9-10-12.
Construction and building.
Contracts, §9-10-7.
Permits, §9-10-6.
Study of water needs,
§9-10-6.

**WATER CONSERVATION
AND IRRIGATION**—Cont'd
Agency—Cont'd
Construction of article,
§9-10-14.
Contracts.
Construction work, §9-10-7.
Officers not to be
interested in contracts,
§9-10-12.
Powers of corporation,
§9-10-5.
Purchases of materials,
§9-10-7.
Cooperation of other state
agencies, §9-10-11.
Counties.
Collection of taxes for work
of agency, §9-10-9.
Contribution of money for
work of agency,
§9-10-9.
Duties generally, §9-10-5.
Eminent domain.
Powers of corporation,
§9-10-5.
Establishment, §§9-10-1 to
9-10-3.
Gifts.
Power to accept, §9-10-5.
Incorporation, §9-10-3.
Membership, §9-10-2.
Municipal corporations.
Collection of taxes for work
of agency, §9-10-9.
Contributing money for
work of agency,
§9-10-9.
Officers.
Conflicts of interest,
§9-10-12.
Offices, §9-10-5.
Penalties.
Conflicts of interest,
§9-10-12.
Powers, §§9-10-4, 9-10-5.
Property.
Powers of corporation,
§9-10-5.
Reports.
Annual reports, §9-10-10.
Seal, §9-10-5.
State agencies and
institutions.
Cooperation and
assistance, §9-10-11.
Supplementary provisions,
§9-10-14.
Taxation.
Counties and
municipalities.
Collection of taxes for
work of agency,
§9-10-9.
Powers of corporation,
§9-10-5.
United States.
Power to enter into
agreements with,
§9-10-5.
**Banks and financial
institutions.**
Corporations.
Bond issues.
Investments, §9-10-39.
Bond issues.
Agency, §§9-10-5, 9-10-8.
Corporations, §§9-10-36 to
9-10-41. See within this
heading, "Corporations."

**WATER CONSERVATION
AND IRRIGATION**—Cont'd
Bylaws.
Agency, §9-10-5.
Corporations, §9-10-34.
Coal.
Replacement and water
rights, §9-16-97.
Conflicts of interest.
Agency.
Officers of corporation,
§9-10-12.
Corporations.
Officers, §9-10-45.
Constitution of Alabama.
Development of irrigation
districts, Const. Ala.,
amd. 227.
Contracts.
Agency. See within this
heading, "Agency."
Corporations. See within this
heading, "Corporations."
Corporations, §§9-10-30 to
9-10-47.
Actions.
Power to sue and be sued,
§9-10-34.
Board of directors.
Appointment, §9-10-33.
Compensation, §9-10-33.
Composition, §9-10-30.
Exercise of powers of
corporation, §9-10-33.
Expenses, §9-10-33.
Officers, §9-10-33.
Qualifications of members,
§9-10-30.
Quorum, §9-10-33.
Records of proceedings,
§9-10-33.
Terms of office, §9-10-33.
Vacancies, §9-10-33.
Bond issues, §§9-10-36 to
9-10-41.
Counties.
Not obligations of
counties, §9-10-40.
Deposit with state or
municipal officers or
agencies, §9-10-39.
Execution, §9-10-36.
Interest, §9-10-36.
Investments.
Banks, insurance
companies, etc.,
§9-10-39.
Issuance.
Procedure, §9-10-36.
Refunding bonds,
§9-10-37.
Maturity, §9-10-36.
Negotiable instruments,
§9-10-36.
Pledge of revenues,
§9-10-38.
Powers of corporation,
§9-10-34.
Proceeds.
Use, §9-10-36.
Purposes, §9-10-36.
Refunding bonds.
Issuance, §9-10-37.
Purposes, §9-10-37.
Sale, §9-10-36.
Security for bonds,
§9-10-38.
State.
Not obligations of state,
§9-10-40.
Tax exemptions, §9-10-41.

**WATER CONSERVATION
AND IRRIGATION**—Cont'd
Corporations—Cont'd
Bylaws.
Adoption, §9-10-34.
Certificate of incorporation,
§§9-10-31, 9-10-32.
Construction and building.
Contracts, §§9-10-34,
9-10-43, 9-10-45.
Permits, §9-10-35.
Projects to be maintained
in good condition,
§9-10-44.
Construction of terms.
Change in responsible
state agency, §9-10-47.
Contracts.
Advertising for bids,
§9-10-43.
Awarding, §9-10-43.
Conflicts of interest,
§9-10-45.
Notice, §9-10-43.
Powers of corporation,
§9-10-34.
Counties.
Bond issues.
Not obligations of
counties, §9-10-40.
Lease, conveyance, etc., of
real property, §9-10-42.
Damages.
Entry on property.
Reimbursement for
actual damages,
§9-10-46.
Definitions.
Construction of terms.
Change in responsible
state agency,
§9-10-47.
Duties generally, §9-10-34.
Eminent domain power,
§9-10-34.
Gifts.
Acceptance, §9-10-34.
Incorporation, §§9-10-30 to
9-10-32.
Interest.
Bond issues, §9-10-36.
Investments.
Bond issues, §9-10-39.
Leases.
Counties, cities, public
departments, etc.,
§9-10-42.
Maintenance of projects,
§9-10-44.
Municipal corporations.
Lease or conveyance of real
property, §9-10-42.
Notes.
Issuance, §9-10-36.
Officers.
Conflicts of interest,
§9-10-45.
Offices, §9-10-34.
Penalties.
Conflicts of interest,
§9-10-45.
Permits.
Construction permits,
§9-10-35.
Powers generally, §§9-10-33,
9-10-34.
Property.
Lease or conveyance by
counties, cities, etc.,
§9-10-42.

**WATER CONSERVATION
AND IRRIGATION**—Cont'd
Corporations—Cont'd
  Property—Cont'd
    Powers of corporation,
      §9-10-34.
    Right of entry.
      Agents and employees,
        §9-10-46.
      Damages.
        Reimbursement for
          actual damages,
          §9-10-46.
  Rules and regulations.
    Promulgation, §9-10-34.
  Seals.
    Adoption, §9-10-34.
  State.
    Bonds not obligations of
      state, §9-10-40.
    Investment in bonds,
      §9-10-39.
  Tax exemption.
    Bond issues, §9-10-41.
  United States.
    Power to enter into
      agreements and
      contracts with,
      §9-10-34.
Counties.
  Agency.
    Collection of taxes for work
      of agency, §9-10-9.
    Contributing money for
      work of agency,
      §9-10-9.
  Corporations.
    Bond issues.
      Not obligations of
        counties, §9-10-40.
    Property.
      Lease or conveyance of
        real property,
        §9-10-42.
Damages.
  Corporations.
    Entry on property.
      Reimbursement for
        actual damages,
        §9-10-46.
Definitions.
  Corporations.
    Construction of terms.
      Change in responsible
        state agency,
        §9-10-47.
Director of irrigation,
  §9-2-16.
Districts.
  Development of irrigation
    districts, Const. Ala.,
    amd. 227.
  Drainage subdistricts,
    §§9-9-70 to 9-9-80.
    See WATER
      MANAGEMENT AND
      DRAINAGE.
  Soil and water conservation
    districts, §§9-8-20 to
    9-8-32.
    See SOIL AND WATER
      CONSERVATION.
  Water management districts,
    §§9-9-1 to 9-9-58.
    See WATER
      MANAGEMENT AND
      DRAINAGE.

**WATER CONSERVATION
AND IRRIGATION**—Cont'd
Districts—Cont'd
  Watershed conservancy
    districts, §§9-8-50 to
    9-8-67.
    See SOIL AND WATER
      CONSERVATION.
Eminent domain.
  Agency.
    Powers of corporation,
      §9-10-5.
  Corporations.
    Right of eminent domain,
      §9-10-34.
Geological survey.
  General provisions, §§9-4-1 to
    9-4-19.
  See GEOLOGICAL
    SURVEY.
Gifts.
  Agency.
    Power to accept, §9-10-5.
  Corporations.
    Acceptance, §9-10-34.
Insurance.
  Corporations.
    Bond issues.
      Investments, §9-10-39.
Interest.
  Corporations.
    Bond issues, §9-10-36.
Investments.
  Corporations.
    Bond issues, §9-10-39.
Leases.
  Corporations.
    Counties, cities, public
      departments, etc.,
      §9-10-42.
Municipal corporations.
  Agency.
    Collection of taxes for work
      of agency, §9-10-9.
    Contributing money for
      work of agency,
      §9-10-9.
  Corporations.
    Lease or conveyance of real
      property, §9-10-42.
Penalties.
  Agency.
    Conflicts of interest,
      §9-10-12.
  Corporations.
    Conflicts of interest,
      §9-10-45.
Permits.
  Agency.
    Construction work,
      §§9-10-6, 9-10-7.
Property.
  Agency.
    Powers, §9-10-5.
  Corporations, §§9-10-34,
    9-10-42.
Quorum.
  Agency.
    Board of directors, §9-10-4.
  Corporations.
    Board of directors,
      §9-10-33.
Records.
  Agency.
    Proceedings of board,
      §9-10-4.
  Corporations.
    Proceedings of board,
      §9-10-33.

**WATER CONSERVATION
AND IRRIGATION**—Cont'd
Reports.
  Agency.
    Annual reports, §9-10-10.
Rules and regulations.
  Corporations.
    Promulgation, §9-10-34.
Salaries.
  Director of irrigation,
    §9-2-16.
Sales.
  Corporations.
    Bond issues, §9-10-36.
**Seals and sealed
  instruments.**
  Agency.
    Adoption and use of seal,
      §9-10-5.
  Corporations.
    Adoption of seal, §9-10-34.
State.
  Corporations.
    Bond issues.
      Deposit of bonds with
        state officers or
        agencies, §9-10-39.
      Investment in bonds,
        §9-10-39.
      Not obligations of state,
        §9-10-40.
Taxation.
  Agency, §§9-10-5, 9-10-9.
  Corporations.
    Bond issues, §9-10-41.
United States.
  Agency.
    Power to enter into
      agreements with,
      §9-10-5.
  Corporations.
    Power to enter into
      agreements with,
      §9-10-34.
**Water management and
  drainage, §§9-9-1 to
  9-9-80.**
  See WATER
    MANAGEMENT AND
    DRAINAGE.
**Water resources research
  institute, §§9-8-1 to 9-8-4.**
**Watershed conservancy
  districts, §§9-8-50 to
  9-8-67.**
  See SOIL AND WATER
    CONSERVATION.

WATERCRAFT.
Boats, §§33-5-1 to 33-6-12.
  See BOATS.
Harbors and ports.
  Generally, §§33-1-1 to
    33-1-36.
  See HARBORS AND
    PORTS.
Navigation.
  Generally, §§33-7-1 to
    33-7-54.
  See NAVIGATION.
Ships and shipping.
  Generally, §§33-5-1 to
    33-6-12.
  See SHIPS AND
    SHIPPING.

**WATER IMPROVEMENT
COMMISSION.**
**Functions transferred to
department of
environmental
management, §22-22A-4.**

WATER MANAGEMENT AND DRAINAGE, §§9-9-1 to 9-9-80.

Accounts and accounting.
Auditing of accounts.
Board of water management commissioners, §9-9-18.
Districts, §9-9-18.
Actions.
Districts.
Bond issues.
Proceedings upon default, §9-9-40.
Annexation.
Districts.
Annexation of land to district, §9-9-50.
Appeals.
Districts.
Board of viewers.
Confirmation of report, §9-9-30.
Inclusion or exclusion of property from district, §9-9-12.
Drainage subdistricts.
Orders of commission, §9-9-77.
Effect of failure to appeal, §9-9-80.
Assessments.
Drainage subdistricts.
Improvements, §§9-9-76, 9-9-77, 9-9-80.
Audits of accounts.
Board of water management commissioners, §9-9-18.
Districts, §9-9-18.
Board of viewers, §§9-9-26 to 9-9-30.
Board of water management commissioners.
Accounts.
Auditing, §9-9-18.
Appointment, §9-9-14.
Bond issues.
Authority to issue, §9-9-15.
Bonds, surety, §9-9-41.
Borrowing money, §9-9-15.
Composition, §9-9-14.
Contracting power, §9-9-15.
Damages.
Entering lands to make surveys, §9-9-22.
District.
General provisions, §§9-9-1 to 9-9-58. See within this heading, "Districts."
Duties generally, §9-9-15.
Employees, §9-9-14.
Compensation, §9-9-19.
Fiscal agent, §9-9-17.
Meetings, §9-9-14.
Notice of annual meeting, §9-9-18.
Oath of office, §9-9-14.
Officers.
Compensation, §9-9-19.
Election, §9-9-14.
Powers and duties, §9-9-15.
Qualifications of members, §9-9-14.
Quorum, §9-9-14.
Removal of commissioners, §9-9-20.
Reports, §9-9-18.

WATER MANAGEMENT AND DRAINAGE—Cont'd
Board of water management commissioners—Cont'd
Right of entry, §9-9-22.
Obstruction of entrance, §9-9-22.
Rulemaking power, §9-9-14.
Secretary.
Compensation, §9-9-19.
Surveys, §9-9-22.
Terms of office, §9-9-14.
Treasurer, §9-9-16.
Vacancies, §9-9-14.
Bond issues.
Board of water management commissioners.
Authority to issue, §9-9-15.
Districts, §§9-9-36 to 9-9-40.
Bonds, surety.
Board of water management commissioners, §9-9-41.
Districts.
Contractors, §§9-9-42, 9-9-44.
Employees, §9-9-41.
Engineers, §9-9-41.
Treasurer, §9-9-16.
Constitution of Alabama.
Districts, Const. Ala., amd. 257.
Construction of article, §9-9-58.
Contractors.
Districts.
Construction of improvements, §§9-9-42 to 9-9-45.
Contracts.
Board of water management commissioners.
Power to contract, §9-9-15.
Districts.
Construction of improvements, §9-9-42.
Costs.
Drainage subdistricts.
Establishment, operation, etc., §9-9-79.
Counties.
Drainage subdistricts, §§9-9-72, 9-9-73, 9-9-77.
Damages.
Board of water management commissioners.
Entry on lands to make surveys, §9-9-22.
Districts.
Damages to improvements, §9-9-48.
Drainage subdistricts.
Eminent domain, §9-9-78.
Definitions.
Districts, §9-9-2.
Drainage subdistricts, §9-9-70.
Costs and expenses, §9-9-79.
Districts, §§9-9-1 to 9-9-58; Const. Ala., amd. 257.
Actions.
Bond issues.
Proceedings upon default, §9-9-40.
Annexation of land, §9-9-50.
Appeals.
Board of viewers.
Confirmation of report, §9-9-30.

WATER MANAGEMENT AND DRAINAGE—Cont'd
Districts—Cont'd
Appeals—Cont'd
Inclusion or exclusion of property from district, §9-9-12.
Audits.
District accounts, §9-9-18.
Reports, §9-9-18.
Board of viewers.
Appointment, §9-9-26.
Assessment of lands, §9-9-27.
Compensation, §9-9-19.
Composition, §9-9-26.
Petition for appointment, §9-9-26.
Qualifications of members, §9-9-26.
Quorum, §9-9-26.
Removal of viewers, §9-9-20.
Report of findings, §9-9-27.
Approval, §9-9-29.
Assessment of lands, §9-9-27.
Confirmation, §9-9-29.
Appeal from confirmation, §9-9-30.
Exceptions, §9-9-29.
Hearings, §9-9-29.
Notice of hearing, §9-9-28.
Viewing of property, §9-9-27.
Board of water management commissioners, §§9-9-14 to 9-9-22. See within this heading, "Board of water management commissioners."
Bond issues, §§9-9-36 to 9-9-40.
Actions.
Proceedings upon default, §9-9-40.
Amount, §9-9-37.
Default, §9-9-40.
Execution, §9-9-37.
Interest, §§9-9-39, 9-9-40.
Issuance.
Failure to pay tax deemed consent to issue, §9-9-36.
Order of issuance, §9-9-37.
Powers of board of water management commissioners, §§9-9-15, 9-9-37.
Waiver of defenses.
Failure to pay tax, §9-9-36.
Mandamus.
Default, §9-9-40.
Maturity, §9-9-37.
Negotiable instruments, §9-9-37.
Payment.
Principal and interest, §9-9-39.
Receiver.
Remedies upon default, §9-9-40.
Sales.
Disposition of proceeds, §9-9-38.

WATER MANAGEMENT AND DRAINAGE—Cont'd
Districts—Cont'd
Bonds, surety.
  Contractors, §§9-9-42 to
    9-9-45.
  Employees, §9-9-41.
  Treasurer, §9-9-16.
Citation of article, §9-9-1.
Construction of article,
  §9-9-58.
Construction of
  improvements.
  Bridges and culverts.
    Cost of construction
      when ditch, drain or
      watercourse crosses
      public highway,
      §9-9-46.
  Contractors, §§9-9-42 to
    9-9-45.
  Contracts.
    Authority for letting
      contracts, §9-9-42.
    Forfeiture upon default
      of contractor,
      §9-9-42.
    Procedures, §9-9-42.
  Engineer.
    Duties of water
      management
      engineer, §9-9-43.
  Highways.
    Ditches, drains or
      watercourses
      crossing public
      highway.
      Cost of construction of
        bridges and
        culverts, §9-9-46.
  Notice.
    Awarding of contracts,
      §9-9-42.
  Railroads.
    Improvements crossing
      railroad right of
      way, §9-9-47.
Contractors, §§9-9-42 to
  9-9-45.
Contracts.
  Construction of
    improvements, §9-9-42.
Damages.
  Improvements, §9-9-48.
Declaration of benefits of
  drainage, etc., §9-9-3.
Definitions, §9-9-2.
Dissolution.
  Damages assessed exceed
    90 percent of benefits
    assessed, §9-9-29.
  Decree of probate court,
    §9-9-29.
  Procedure, §9-9-57.
  Drainage districts, §9-9-56.
  Drainage subdistricts,
    §§9-9-70 to 9-9-80. See
    within this heading,
    "Drainage subdistricts."
Eminent domain.
  Right of condemnation,
    §9-9-21.
Employees.
  Bonds, surety, §9-9-41.
  Compensation, §9-9-19.
Engineers.
  Appointment, §9-9-23.
  Board of viewers.
    Engineer to accompany
      when assessing land,
      §9-9-27.

WATER MANAGEMENT AND DRAINAGE—Cont'd
Districts—Cont'd
Engineers—Cont'd
  Bonds, surety, §9-9-41.
  Construction of
    improvements.
    Duties, §9-9-43.
  Improvements.
    Reports, §9-9-23.
  Qualifications, §9-9-23.
Establishment, §§9-9-5 to
  9-9-13.
Inclusion of lands in
  another water
  management district,
  §9-9-52.
Over lands of watershed
  conservancy district,
  §9-9-51.
Fiscal agent, §9-9-17.
Forms.
  Taxation.
    Certificate and order
      directing collection,
      §9-9-32.
    Tax records, §9-9-31.
Hearings.
  Annexation of land to
    district, §9-9-50.
  Board of viewers.
    Reports, §9-9-29.
    Notice of hearing on
      report, §9-9-28.
  Establishment of districts.
    Notice of hearing, §9-9-9.
    Opinion of representative
      of state committee,
      §9-9-10.
    Procedure, §9-9-11.
Improvements.
  Adjoining states.
    Joint works of
      improvement,
      §9-9-53.
  Construction, §§9-9-42 to
    9-9-47.
  Control of completed
    improvements, §9-9-48.
  Crossing railroad right of
    way.
    Procedure as to proposed
      improvement,
      §9-9-24.
  Damages.
    Liabilities, §9-9-48.
  Injuries.
    Liabilities, §9-9-48.
  Joint works with adjoining
    states, §9-9-53.
  Lateral drains from lands.
    Rights of landowners to
      use as, §9-9-49.
  Maintenance, §9-9-48.
  Obstruction of
    improvements, §9-9-48.
  Reports, §9-9-23.
    Adoption, §9-9-23.
  Supervision of completed
    improvements, §9-9-48.
  Taxation, §§9-9-31 to
    9-9-36.
Inclusion of lands in another
  district, §9-9-52.
Interest.
  Bond issues, §§9-9-36 to
    9-9-40.
  Warrants.
    Interest on warrants not
      paid because of lack
      of funds, §9-9-54.

WATER MANAGEMENT AND DRAINAGE—Cont'd
Districts—Cont'd
Liens.
  Tax liens, §9-9-32.
Notice.
  Board of viewers.
    Hearing on report,
      §9-9-28.
  Construction of
    improvements.
    Awarding of contracts,
      §9-9-42.
  Establishment.
    Notice of filing of
      petition and of
      hearing, §9-9-9.
  Request of additional
    powers by drainage
    districts, §9-9-56.
Officers.
  Compensation, §9-9-19.
  Removal, §9-9-20.
Penalties.
  Taxation.
    Delinquent taxes,
      §9-9-32.
    Tax collector failing to
      make prompt
      payment to
      treasurer, §9-9-34.
Petitions.
  Annexation of land to
    district, §9-9-50.
  Dissolution of districts,
    §9-9-57.
  Eligibility to sign, §9-9-4.
  Establishment of districts.
    General provisions,
      §§9-9-5 to 9-9-13.
  Signatures, §9-9-4.
  Who may sign petitions,
    §9-9-4.
Probate courts.
  Annexation of land to
    district, §9-9-50.
  Dissolution of districts,
    §9-9-57.
  Errors.
    Correction in
      proceedings, §9-9-55.
  Hearings.
    Establishment of
      districts, §9-9-11.
  Jurisdiction to establish,
    §9-9-5.
    Original and exclusive
      jurisdiction, §9-9-8.
  Records of proceedings,
    §9-9-6.
  Water management plan.
    Transmittal of certified
      copy to court,
      §9-9-26.
Property.
  Annexation of land to
    district, §9-9-50.
Purposes, §9-9-5.
Railroads.
  Construction of
    improvements.
    Crossing railroad right of
      way, §9-9-47.
  Proposed improvements
    crossing railroads.
    Procedure, §9-9-24.
Receivers.
  Bond issues.
    Default in payment,
      §9-9-40.

WATER MANAGEMENT AND DRAINAGE—Cont'd

Districts—Cont'd

Records.
  District record book, §9-9-6.
  Tax records, §9-9-31.
    Preparation, §9-9-32.
    Treasurer, §9-9-35.
Remedies.
  Exclusive remedies, §9-9-58.
Reports.
  Annual report, §9-9-18.
  Board of viewers.
    General provisions, §§9-9-26 to 9-9-30.
  Engineer's report, §9-9-7.
  Improvements in districts, §9-9-23.
Sales.
  Bond issues, §9-9-38.
  Delinquent tax lands, §9-9-40.
State soil and water conservation committee.
  Cooperation with persons desiring to form districts, §9-9-3.
Subdistricts, §§9-9-70 to 9-9-80. See within this heading, "Drainage subdistricts."
Taxation.
  Additional taxes, §9-9-31.
  Annexation of land to district, §9-9-50.
  Bond issues.
    Additional taxes, §9-9-39.
    Payment of principal and interest, §9-9-39.
  Collection.
    Certificates.
      Form, §9-9-32.
    Effect of defect in proceedings, §9-9-58.
    Order directing collection.
      Form, §9-9-32.
    Property divided, sold or transferred, §9-9-33.
    Tax collector.
      Compensation, §9-9-34.
      Failure to make prompt payment to treasurer, §9-9-34.
  Cost of establishing district.
    Levy of tax, §9-9-13.
  Delinquent taxes.
    Proceedings as to, §9-9-32.
    Sale of land, §9-9-32.
  District treasurer.
    Records, §9-9-35.
  Divided property, §9-9-33.
  Levy.
    Additional taxes, §9-9-31.
    Annual installment of tax, §9-9-32.
    Cost of establishing district, §9-9-13.
    Expenses of proposed works and improvements, §9-9-31.
  Lien for taxes, §9-9-32.
  Maintenance of improvements, §9-9-48.

WATER MANAGEMENT AND DRAINAGE—Cont'd

Districts—Cont'd

Taxation—Cont'd
  Payment.
    District treasurer.
      Effect of failure to pay, §9-9-36.
      Privilege of paying to, §9-9-35.
      When due and payable, §9-9-32.
  Penalties.
    Delinquent taxes, §9-9-32.
    Tax collector failing to make payment to treasurer, §9-9-34.
  Records, §9-9-31.
    District treasurer, §9-9-35.
    Preparation, §9-9-32.
  Tax collector.
    Compensation, §9-9-34.
    Failure to make prompt payment to treasurer, §9-9-34.
  Transferred property, §9-9-33.
Title of article, §9-9-1.
Treasurer, §9-9-16.
Warrants.
  Failure to pay for lack of funds.
    Procedure as to warrants, §9-9-54.
Water management plan.
  Adoption, §9-9-23.
  Amendments, §9-9-25.
  Board of viewers, §§9-9-26 to 9-9-30.
  Construction of improvements under plan, §§9-9-42 to 9-9-47.
  Errors.
    Correction, §9-9-25.
  Probate court.
    Transmittal of certified copy to court, §9-9-26.
  Report of engineer, §9-9-23.
Watershed conservancy district.
  Organization of district over lands of, §9-9-51.

Drainage districts.

General provisions, §§9-9-1 to 9-9-58. See within this heading, "Districts."

Drainage subdistricts, §§9-9-70 to 9-9-80.

Appeals.
  Orders of commission, §9-9-77.
  Effect of failure to appeal, §9-9-80.
Assessments for improvements, §9-9-76.
Collection.
  Effect of defect in proceedings, §9-9-80.
Construction of article, §9-9-80.
Costs.
  Defined, §9-9-79.
  Establishment, operation, etc., §9-9-79.

WATER MANAGEMENT AND DRAINAGE—Cont'd

Drainage subdistricts —Cont'd

County commissions, §§9-9-72, 9-9-73.
  Appeals from orders of commission, §9-9-77.
Damages.
  Eminent domain, §9-9-78.
Declaration of benefits and public policy, §9-9-71.
Definitions, §9-9-70.
  Costs and expenses, §9-9-79.
Effect of defect in proceedings, §9-9-80.
Eminent domain.
  Damages, §9-9-78.
  Right of condemnation, §9-9-78.
Establishment, §§9-9-74, 9-9-75, 9-9-79.
Exclusive remedies provided in article, §9-9-80.
Expenses, §9-9-79.
Jurisdiction, §9-9-74.
Policy of state, §9-9-71.
Purposes, §9-9-74.
Remedies of article exclusive, §9-9-80.

Eminent domain.

Districts.
  Power of eminent domain, §9-9-21.
Drainage subdistricts.
  Right of condemnation, §9-9-78.

Engineers.

Districts, §9-9-23.

Forms.

Districts.
  Taxation.
    Certificate and order directing collection, §9-9-32.
    Tax records, §9-9-31.

Hearings.

Districts. See within this heading, "Districts."
Drainage subdistricts.
  Establishment, §9-9-75.

Injuries.

Districts.
  Injuries to improvements, §9-9-48.

Interest.

Districts.
  Bond issues, §§9-9-36 to 9-9-40.
  Warrants.
    Interest on warrants not paid because of lack of funds, §9-9-54.

Liens.

Districts.
  Tax liens, §9-9-32.

Mandamus.

Districts.
  Bond issues.
    Default, §9-9-40.

Notice.

Board of water management commissioners.
  Annual reports and annual meetings, §9-9-18.
Districts. See within this heading, "Districts."
Drainage subdistricts.
  Hearings on establishment, §9-9-75.

**WATER MANAGEMENT AND
    DRAINAGE**—Cont'd
Oaths.
  Board of water management
      commissioners.
    Oath of office, §9-9-14.
Penalties.
  Districts.
    Taxation.
      Delinquent taxes,
          §9-9-32.
      Tax collector failing to
          make prompt
          payment to
          treasurer, §9-9-34.
Petitions.
  Water management districts,
      §§9-9-4, 9-9-50, 9-9-57.
Probate courts.
  Districts. See within this
      heading, "Districts."
Property.
  Districts.
    Annexation of land to
        district, §9-9-50.
Railroads.
  Districts.
    Improvements.
      Construction of
          improvements
          crossing railroad
          right of way,
          §9-9-47.
      Procedure as to proposed
          improvements
          crossing right of
          way, §9-9-24.
Receivers.
  Districts.
    Bond issues.
      Remedies upon default,
          §9-9-40.
Records.
  Districts.
    Record book, §9-9-6.
    Tax records, §9-9-31.
    District treasurer,
        §9-9-35.
    Preparation of tax
        records, §9-9-32.
Remedies.
  Exclusive remedies, §9-9-58.
Reports.
  Board of water management
      commissioners.
    Annual reports, §9-9-18.
  Districts, §§9-9-7, 9-9-18,
      9-9-23.
Rules and regulations.
  Board of water management
      commissioners.
    Promulgation, §9-9-14.
Sales.
  Districts.
    Bond issues, §9-9-38.
      Delinquent tax lands,
          §9-9-40.
Soil and water conservation,
    §§9-8-1 to 9-8-67.
  See SOIL AND WATER
      CONSERVATION.
Taxation.
  Districts, §§9-9-31 to 9-9-36.
    See within this heading,
        "Districts."
Warrants.
  Districts, §9-9-54.

**WATER MANAGEMENT AND
    DRAINAGE**—Cont'd
**Water conservation and
    irrigation,** §§9-10-1 to
    9-10-47.
  See WATER
      CONSERVATION AND
      IRRIGATION.

WATER POLLUTION.
**Agricultural nonpoint
    source pollution.**
  Citation of chapter, §22-38-1.
  Committee.
    Personnel, §22-38-8.
  Definitions, §22-38-2.
  Department.
    Contracting power,
        §22-38-7.
    Lead agency in developing
        state plan, §22-38-7.
  Federal funds, §§22-38-4 to
      22-38-6.
  Legislative intent, §22-38-3.
  Priorities for pollution
      control, §22-38-6.
  Progress in water quality.
    Providing information to
        department, §22-38-6.
  Rules and regulations,
      §22-38-8.
  Short title of chapter,
      §22-38-1.
Authorities.
  Environmental improvement
      authorities, §§9-6-1 to
      9-6-17.
    See ENVIRONMENTAL
        IMPROVEMENT
        AUTHORITIES.
  Pollution control finance
      authority, §§22-29-1 to
      22-29-23.
  Water pollution control
      authority, §§22-34-1 to
      22-34-17.
    See WATER POLLUTION
        CONTROL
        AUTHORITY.
Boats.
  Discharge of litter and
      sewage from watercraft,
      §§33-6-1 to 33-6-12.
    See BOATS.
Bond issues.
  Pollution control finance
      authority, §§22-29-1 to
      22-29-23.
Definitions.
  Agricultural nonpoint source
      pollution, §22-38-2.
  Pollution control finance
      authority, §22-29-1.
**Discharge of litter and
    sewage from watercraft,**
    §§33-6-1 to 33-6-12.
  See BOATS.
Drinking water.
  Safe drinking water act.
    Polluting public water
        supply prohibited,
        §22-23-47.
**Environmental improvement
    authorities.**
  General provisions, §§9-6-1 to
      9-6-17.
    See ENVIRONMENTAL
        IMPROVEMENT
        AUTHORITIES.

WATER POLLUTION—Cont'd
Finance authority.
  Pollution control finance
      authority, §§22-29-1 to
      22-29-23.
Funds.
  Pollution control finance
      authority.
    Custody and disposition,
        §22-29-16.
Income tax.
  Corporate deductions.
    Amounts invested in water
        pollution control,
        §40-18-35.
Litter.
  Discharge of litter and
      sewage from watercraft,
      §§33-6-1 to 33-6-12.
    See BOATS.
**Pollution control finance
    authority,** §§22-29-1 to
    22-29-23.
  Anticipatory borrowing,
      §22-29-11.
  Bond issues, §§22-29-8 to
      22-29-15.
    Anticipatory borrowing,
        §22-29-11.
    Authorization to issue and
        sell, §22-29-8.
    Contest of validity,
        §22-29-10.
    Execution, §22-29-13.
    Issuance.
      Authorized, §22-29-8.
    Negotiable instruments,
        §22-29-14.
    Not debt of state,
        §22-29-15.
    Payments.
      Security, §22-29-8.
    Presumption of validity,
        §22-29-10.
    Refunding bonds,
        §22-29-12.
    Sale.
      Authorization to sell,
          §22-29-8.
      Procedure for sale,
          §22-29-9.
    Security for payment,
        §22-29-8.
    Tax exemption, §22-29-22.
    Validity.
      Contesting, §22-29-10.
      Presumed, §22-29-10.
  Certificate of incorporation,
      §22-29-5.
  Certificates.
    Execution, §22-29-13.
    Not debt of state,
        §22-29-15.
    Temporary financing,
        §22-29-11.
  Definitions, §22-29-1.
  Directors, §22-29-6.
  Dissolution, §22-29-23.
  Funds.
    Custody and disposition,
        §22-29-16.
  Grants to local public bodies.
    Applications, §22-29-19.
    Appropriations, §22-29-18.
    Authorized, §22-29-17.
    Plan or program,
        §22-29-20.
    Powers of local public
        bodies, §22-29-21.
  Incorporation.
    Application, §22-29-4.

WATER POLLUTION—Cont'd
Pollution control finance authority—Cont'd
Incorporation—Cont'd
Authorized, §22-29-3.
Certificate of incorporation, §22-29-5.
Members, §22-29-6.
Money.
Custody and disposition, §22-29-16.
Officers, §22-29-6.
Orders, §22-29-6.
Powers, §22-29-7.
Promissory notes.
Execution, §22-29-13.
Not debt of state, §22-29-15.
Temporary financing, §22-29-11.
Purpose of chapter, §22-29-2.
Quorum, §22-29-6.
Refunding bonds, §22-29-12.
Resolutions, §22-29-6.
Tax exemptions, §22-29-22.
Temporary financing, §22-29-11.
Safe drinking water act.
Polluting public water supply prohibited, §22-23-47.
Sales tax.
Exemptions for water pollution control equipment, §40-23-4.
Sewage.
Discharge of litter and sewage from watercraft, §§33-6-1 to 33-6-12.
See BOATS.
Taxation.
Pollution control finance authority.
Tax exemptions, §22-29-22.
Use tax exemption.
Devices or facilities for control reduction or elimination, §40-23-62.
Water improvement commission.
Functions transferred, §22-22A-4.
Water pollution control authority, §§22-34-1 to 22-34-17.
See WATER POLLUTION CONTROL AUTHORITY.

WATER POLLUTION CONTROL ACT, §§22-22-1 to 22-22-14.
Chapter supplementary to other laws, §22-22-13.
Citation of chapter, §22-22-1.
Declaration of policy, §22-22-2.
Definitions, §22-22-1.
Department of environmental management.
Chapter supplementary to other laws, §22-22-13.
Citation of chapter, §22-22-1.
Duties, §22-22-9.
Enforcement of orders, §22-22-9.
Disbursement of funds, §22-22-11.
Notice of hearing.
Establishment of standards, §22-22-9.

WATER POLLUTION CONTROL ACT—Cont'd
Department of environmental management—Cont'd
Penalties.
Civil penalties, §22-22-9.
Criminal penalty, §22-22-14.
Permits, §22-22-9.
Powers, §22-22-9.
Technical committees, §22-22-7.
Director.
Defined, §22-22A-3.
Rules and regulations.
Review by director, §22-22A-8.
Division.
Defined, §22-22A-3.
Ethics commission, §22-22A-6.
Evidence.
Hearings and procedures before commission, §22-22A-7.
Funds.
Alabama department of environmental management fund, §22-22A-11.
Garbage and trash.
Department.
Supervision of regulatory control, §22-27-7.
Hazardous waste, §§22-30-1 to 22-30-20.
See HAZARDOUS WASTE.
Health department.
Routine bacteriological analyses.
Contracts with environmental management department, §22-22A-4.
Hearing officers, §§22-22A-3, 22-22A-7.
Hearings.
Commission hearings, §22-22A-7.
Rules and regulations.
Adoption of rules, regulations and standards, §22-22A-8.
Subpoenas.
Judicial enforcement, §22-22A-7.
Legislative intent, §22-22A-2.
Notice.
Commission.
Hearings and procedures before commission, §22-22A-7.
Department of environmental management.
Hearings.
Establishment of standards, §22-22-9.
Rules and regulations.
Adoption of rules, regulations and standards, §22-22A-8.
Office of state planning and federal programs.
Coastal area boards.
Transfer of functions of board to office, §22-22A-10.

WATER POLLUTION CONTROL ACT—Cont'd
Office of state planning and federal programs—Cont'd
Coastal resources advisory committee.
Advice to office, §22-22A-12.
Penalties.
Civil penalty, §22-22-9.
Criminal penalty, §22-22-14.
Purpose of chapter, §22-22-2.
Records.
Commission, §§22-22A-6, 22-22A-7.
Rules and regulations.
Procedure for adoption, §22-22A-8.
Safe drinking water act, §§22-23-30 to 22-23-53.
See WATER SUPPLY AND WATERWORKS.
Short title, §22-22-1.
Subpoenas.
Commission hearings and procedures, §22-22A-7.
Title of act.
Short title, §22-22A-1.
Water well standards, §§22-24-1 to 22-24-12.
See WATER SUPPLY AND WATERWORKS.

WATER POLLUTION CONTROL AUTHORITY, §§22-34-1 to 22-34-17.
Accounts and accounting, §22-34-11.
Authority.
Defined, §22-34-1.
Board of directors.
Defined, §22-34-1.
Provisions applicable to board, §22-34-5.
Bond issues.
Authorization to issue, §22-34-7.
Certificates of notes in anticipation of bonds, §22-34-9.
Dedicated source of revenue to repay money, §22-34-11.
Default, §22-34-11.
Definitions, §22-34-1.
Interest.
Exemption from usury laws, §22-34-14.
Investments legal, §22-34-12.
Negotiability, §22-34-16.
Obligations only of authority, §22-34-17.
Refunding bonds, §22-34-10.
Sale, §22-34-8.
Special obligation bonds, §22-34-17.
State not indebted, §22-34-17.
Tax exemption, §22-34-13.
Usury laws.
Exempt, §22-34-14.
Composition, §22-34-4.
Definitions, §22-34-1.
Department.
Defined, §22-34-1.
Directors.
Generally, §§22-34-1, 22-34-5.

**WATER POLLUTION
 CONTROL AUTHORITY**
 —Cont'd
**Environmental management
 department.**
 Definition of department,
 §22-34-1.
Establishment, §22-34-4.
Federal clean water act.
 Defined, §22-34-1.
Funds.
 Water pollution control
 revolving loan fund,
 §22-34-3.
General powers, §22-34-6.
Incorporation, §§22-34-5,
 22-34-15.
Interest.
 Bond issues.
 Exemption from usury
 laws, §22-34-14.
Legislative intent, §22-34-2.
Loans.
 Accounting, §22-34-11.
 Default, §22-34-11.
Notice.
 Incorporation of authority,
 §22-34-15.
Officers, §22-34-5.
Powers generally, §22-34-6.
Projects.
 Defined, §22-34-1.
Public bodies.
 Defined, §22-34-1.
Refunding bonds, §22-34-10.
Reports.
 Water pollution control
 revolving loan fund,
 §22-34-3.
Resolutions.
 Authorizing resolution.
 Defined, §22-34-1.
Sales.
 Bond issues, §22-34-8.
Taxation.
 Bonds exempt, §22-34-13.
Usury.
 Bond issues.
 Authority exempt from
 usury laws, §22-34-14.
**Water pollution control
 revolving loan fund,**
 §22-34-3.

**WATER POWER
 COMPANIES,** §§10-4-320 to
 10-4-323.
 See DAMS.

**WATER RESOURCES
 RESEARCH INSTITUTE,**
 §§9-8-1 to 9-8-4.
 See SOIL AND WATER
 CONSERVATION.

**WATERS AND
 WATERCOURSES,**
 §§33-1-1 to 33-17-15.
Alabama port authority,
 §§33-13-1 to 33-13-13.
 See HARBORS AND PORTS.
Ameraport.
 General provisions, §§33-9-1,
 33-9-2, 33-10-1 to
 33-10-26.
 See AMERAPORT.
Animals.
 Depositing dead animals or
 fowl in running streams,
 §22-20-9.

**WATERS AND
 WATERCOURSES**—Cont'd
Appropriations.
 Development of docks along
 inland waterways.
 Bonds.
 Payment of principal and
 interest, §§33-2-70,
 33-2-100, 33-2-129,
 33-2-159.
**Bear creek development
 authority,** §§33-15-1 to
 33-15-19.
 See BEAR CREEK
 DEVELOPMENT
 AUTHORITY.
Beavers.
 Hunting, §9-11-262.
Bond issues.
 Development of docks along
 inland waterways,
 §§33-2-8, 33-2-37,
 33-2-67, 33-2-97,
 33-2-126, 33-2-156.
 Navigable waterway between
 Demopolis and
 Tennessee river and
 Tombigbee valley
 projects, Const. Ala.,
 amd. 355.
Booms and bulkheads.
 Generally, §§33-7-7 to 33-7-9.
 Liens of owners.
 Attachment, §35-11-311.
 Declaration, §35-11-310.
 Enforcement, §35-11-311.
 Liens generally.
 See LIENS.
Bridges.
 General provisions.
 See BRIDGES.
Coastal areas, §§9-7-10 to
 9-7-20.
 See COASTAL AREAS.
Commercial fishing,
 §§9-11-140 to 9-11-156.
 See FISH AND GAME.
Constitution of Alabama.
 Development of docks along
 inland waterways, Const.
 Ala., amds. 116, 274,
 288.
 Navigable waters declared
 free public highways,
 Const. Ala., art. I, §24.
 Navigable waterway between
 Demopolis and
 Tennessee river, Const.
 Ala., amd. 270.
 Navigable waterway between
 Demopolis and
 Tennessee river and
 Tombigbee valley
 projects, Const. Ala.,
 amd. 355.
 Navigable waterway between
 Montgomery and
 Gadsden and to the
 Alabama-Georgia
 boundary, Const. Ala.,
 amd. 287.
Construction works.
 Development of docks along
 inland waterways.
 Authority to construct new
 facilities, §§33-2-33,
 33-2-63, 33-2-93,
 33-2-122, 33-2-152.
 New facilities.

**WATERS AND
 WATERCOURSES**—Cont'd
Construction works—Cont'd
 Duty to drain areas in
 construction works,
 §22-20-10.
Contracts.
 Department may constract
 current indebtedness,
 §§33-2-7, 33-2-36,
 33-2-66, 33-2-96,
 33-2-125, 33-2-155.
 Development of docks
 along inland
 waterways.
 Opening and cleaning
 navigable streams.
 County commission
 authorized to make
 contracts, §33-7-2.
**Coosa valley development
 authority,** §§33-16-1 to
 33-16-15.
 See COOSA VALLEY
 DEVELOPMENT
 AUTHORITY.
Costs.
 Development of docks and
 other facilities along
 inland waterways,
 §§33-2-32, 33-2-62,
 33-2-92.
Counties.
 Acquisition of lands for
 public purposes,
 §11-18-2.
 County commission.
 Opening and cleaning
 navigable streams.
 Contracting power,
 §33-7-2.
 Developing, advertising and
 promoting water
 resources, §11-3-11.
 Navigable streams.
 Execution of process on
 streams, §11-1-3.
 Not within limits of any
 county.
 Jurisdiction over,
 §11-1-3.
 Operation, etc., of bridges
 over navigable, etc.,
 streams, §§11-3-15 to
 11-3-17.
Damages.
 Diverting streams, §33-7-4.
Dams.
 General provisions.
 See DAMS.
Definitions.
 Development of docks along
 inland waterways,
 §§33-2-30, 33-2-60,
 33-2-90, 33-2-150. See
 within this heading,
 "Development of docks
 along inland waterways."
**Development of docks along
 inland waterways,**
 §§33-2-1 to 33-2-196.
 Appropriations.
 Bonds.
 Payment of principal and
 interest, §§33-2-70,
 33-2-100, 33-2-129,
 33-2-159.
 Article cumulative, §33-2-18.
 Authorized, Const. Ala.,
 amds. 116, 274, 288.

WATERS AND WATERCOURSES—Cont'd
Development of docks along inland waterways—Cont'd

Bonds, Const. Ala., amds. 116, 274, 288.
Defined, §§33-2-30, 33-2-60, 33-2-90, 33-2-120, 33-2-150.
Completion of facilities acquired under earlier acts, §§33-2-33, 33-2-63, 33-2-93, 33-2-122, 33-2-152.
Construction.
New facilities.
Authority to construct, §§33-2-33, 33-2-63, 33-2-93, 33-2-122, 33-2-152.
Construction and interpretation of article.
Article cumulative, §33-2-18.
Contracts.
Department may contract current indebtedness, §§33-2-7, 33-2-36, 33-2-66, 33-2-96, 33-2-125, 33-2-155.
Costs.
Additional cost authorized, §§33-2-32, 33-2-62, 33-2-92.
1957 provisions.
Maximum cost of development, §33-2-2.
1967 provisions.
Facilities at additional cost of $2,000,000 authorized, §33-2-121.
Total cost to state, §§33-2-32, 33-2-62, 33-2-92.
Current indebtedness.
Department may contract.
1957 provisions, §33-2-7.
1959 provisions, §33-2-36.
1961 provisions, §33-2-66.
1963 provisions, §33-2-96.
1967 provisions, §33-2-125.
1969 provisions, §33-2-155.
Definitions.
1957 provisions, §33-2-90.
1959 provisions, §33-2-30.
1961 provisions, §33-2-60.
1963 provisions, §33-2-90.
1967 provisions, §33-2-120.
1969 provisions, §33-2-150.
Docks department.
Authority under article cumulative, §§33-2-94, 33-2-123.
Eminent domain, §33-2-124.
Earlier acts.
Completion of facilities acquired under earlier acts, §§33-2-33, 33-2-63, 33-2-93, 33-2-122, 33-2-152.

WATERS AND WATERCOURSES—Cont'd
Development of docks along inland waterways—Cont'd

Eminent domain.
1957 provisions, §§33-2-3, 33-2-5, 33-2-6.
1959 provisions.
Proceedings, §33-2-35.
1961 provisions.
Proceedings, §33-2-65.
1963 provisions, §33-2-95.
1967 provisions, §33-2-124.
1969 provisions, §33-2-154.
Federal authorities.
Permit or consent, §§33-2-33, 33-2-63, 33-2-93, 33-2-122, 33-2-152.
Governor.
1957 provisions.
Exercise of authority, §33-2-14.
1959 provisions.
Approval, §33-2-33.
1961 provisions.
Approval, §33-2-63.
1963 provisions.
Approval, §33-2-93.
1969 provisions.
Approval, §33-2-152.
Inland facilities.
Application of revenues, §§33-2-9, 33-2-40, 33-2-71, 33-2-101, 33-2-130, 33-2-160.
Inland waterways improvement bonds, §§33-2-8, 33-2-37, 33-2-67, 33-2-97, 33-2-126, 33-2-156.
Interest.
Exemption from taxation, §§33-2-17, 33-2-44, 33-2-77, 33-2-107, 33-2-136, 33-2-166.
Investments.
Proceeds of bonds, §§33-2-102, 33-2-131.
Legislative intent, §33-2-18.
Licenses.
Occupying state property.
Revocation and suspension of licenses to occupy, §§33-2-16, 33-2-43, 33-2-76, 33-2-100, 33-2-135, 33-2-165.
New facilities.
Authority to acquire, construct and maintain, §§33-2-3, 33-2-33, 33-2-63, 33-2-93, 33-2-122, 33-2-152.
1957 provisions, §§33-2-1 to 33-2-18.
Acquisition of facilities.
Power of state to acquire, §33-2-3.
Ascertainment of cost of each unit, §33-2-10.
Authority of state and state docks department generally, §33-2-1.
Bonds.
Faith and credit of state pledged to payment of bonds, §33-2-11.

WATERS AND WATERCOURSES—Cont'd
Development of docks along inland waterways—Cont'd

1957 provisions—Cont'd
Bonds—Cont'd
Inland waterways improvement bonds, §33-2-8.
Construction of facilities.
Authority of state, §33-2-3.
Contracts.
State docks department.
Department may contract current indebtedness, §33-2-7.
Costs.
Maximum cost of development, §33-2-2.
Definitions, §33-2-90.
Dredging.
Authority, §33-2-3.
Eminent domain.
Limitation upon right, §33-2-3.
Powers generally, §33-2-5.
Proceedings, §33-2-6.
Expenses.
Payment of deficiency where proceeds are insufficient to cover expenses, §33-2-9.
Faith and credit of state pledged to payment of bonds, §33-2-11.
Governor.
Exercise of authority, §33-2-14.
Legislature.
Reports.
Department to make reports to legislature, §33-2-13.
Loans.
Temporary loans, §33-2-8.
Maintenance of facilities, §33-2-3.
Operation of facilities, §33-2-3.
Plans, §33-2-3.
Privately-owned facilities.
Eminent domain.
Limitation upon right, §33-2-3.
Proceeds.
Application of proceeds of facilities, §33-2-9.
Payment of deficiency where proceeds are insufficient to cover expenses, §33-2-9.
Rates and charges.
Use of facilities, §33-2-11.
Real property.
Acquisition, §33-2-6.
Reports, §33-2-13.
Rights of way.
Acquisition, §33-2-6.
Sinking fund, §33-2-10.
State.
Authority of state generally, §33-2-1.

WATERS AND WATERCOURSES—Cont'd
Development of docks along inland waterways —Cont'd
1957 provisions—Cont'd
State—Cont'd
Payment of bonds.
Faith and credit of state pledged to payment, §33-2-11.
State docks department.
Authority.
Generally, §33-2-1.
Contracts.
Department may contract current indebtedness, §33-2-7.
Eminent domain power, §33-2-5.
Powers and duties under article cumulative, §33-2-4.
Rates and charges.
Department to have right and power to fix, §33-2-12.
Reports to legislature, §33-2-13.
Surveys, §33-2-3.
1959 provisions, §§33-2-30 to 33-2-44.
Authority to acquire, construct, maintain, etc., new facilities, §33-2-33.
Bonds.
Additional inland waterways improvement bonds, §33-2-37.
Defined, §33-2-30.
Interest.
Exemption from taxation, §33-2-44.
Sale.
Disposition of proceeds, §33-2-39.
Requirements, §33-2-38.
Completion of facilities acquired under 1957 act, §33-2-33.
Contracts.
Department may contract current indebtedness, §33-2-36.
Costs.
Authorized cost additional, §33-2-32.
Dock facilities.
Authorization at additional cost of $3,500,000, §33-2-31.
Total cost to state, §33-2-32.
Current indebtedness.
Department may contract, §33-2-36.
Definitions, §33-2-30.
Dock facilities.
Authorization at additional cost of $3,500,000, §33-2-31.
Defined, §33-2-30.
Eminent domain proceedings, §33-2-35.

WATERS AND WATERCOURSES—Cont'd
Development of docks along inland waterways —Cont'd
1959 provisions—Cont'd
Federal authorities.
Permit or consent from, §33-2-33.
Governor.
Approval, §33-2-33.
Interest.
Exemption from taxation, §33-2-44.
Licenses.
Occupation of state property.
Revocation or cancellation of licenses, §33-2-43.
New facilities.
Authority to acquire, construct, maintain, etc., new facilities, §33-2-33.
1957 provisions.
Completion of facilities acquired, §33-2-33.
Permits.
Federal authorities, §33-2-33.
Plans, §33-2-33.
Property.
Acquisition, §33-2-35.
Rates and charges.
Use of facilities, §33-2-42.
Records.
Unit of development.
Separate records as to each unit, §33-2-41.
Revenues from dock facilities, §33-2-40.
Rights of way.
Acquisition, §33-2-35.
State docks department.
Authority under article cumulative, §33-2-34.
Current indebtedness.
Department may contract, §33-2-36.
Eminent domain.
Powers, §33-2-35.
Sale of bonds.
Fixing terms and conditions, §33-2-38.
State property.
License to occupy.
Revocation or cancellation, §33-2-43.
Survey, §33-2-33.
Taxation.
Bonds exempt, §33-2-44.
Interest exemption, §33-2-44.
Unit of development.
Defined, §33-2-30.
Proceeds derived from operation.
Application of proceeds, §33-2-40.
Records.
Separate records, §33-2-41.
Use of facilities.
Rates and charges, §33-2-42.

WATERS AND WATERCOURSES—Cont'd
Development of docks along inland waterways —Cont'd
1961 provisions, §§33-2-60 to 33-2-77.
Appropriations.
Principal and interest on bonds.
Appropriation for payment, §33-2-70.
Bonds.
Exemption from taxation, §33-2-77.
Interest.
Appropriation for payment, §33-2-70.
Tax exempt, §33-2-77.
Principal.
Appropriation for payment, §33-2-70.
Refunding bonds, §33-2-72.
Sale.
Disposition of proceeds, §33-2-69.
Requirements, §33-2-68.
Contracts.
Current indebtedness.
Department may contract, §33-2-66.
Costs.
Authorized cost additional, §33-2-62.
Dock facilities at additional cost of $1,500,000 authorized, §33-2-61.
Total cost to state, §33-2-62.
Current indebtedness.
State docks department may contract, §33-2-66.
Definitions, §33-2-60.
Dock facilities.
Additional cost of $1,500,000 authorized, §33-2-61.
Defined, §33-2-60.
Eminent domain proceedings, §33-2-65.
Governor.
Approval of plans, §33-2-63.
Inland waterways facilities.
Application of revenues, §33-2-71.
Defined, §33-2-60.
Inland waterways improvement bonds.
Additional bonds generally, §33-2-67.
Licenses.
Occupying state property.
Revocation or cancellation, §33-2-76.
New facilities.
Authority to acquire, construct, maintain, etc., new facilities, §33-2-63.
1957 provisions.
Completion of facilities acquired, §33-2-63.

WATERS AND WATERCOURSES—Cont'd

Development of docks along inland waterways —Cont'd

1961 provisions—Cont'd

1959 provisions.

Completion of facilities acquired, §33-2-63.

Plans, §33-2-63.

Approval of governor, §33-2-63.

Port of Mobile facilities.

Defined, §33-2-60.

Use of surplus revenues to pay operating deficit, §33-2-74.

Property.

Acquisition, §33-2-65.

Rates and charges.

Use of facilities, §33-2-75.

Records.

Separate records as to each unit of development, §33-2-73.

Refunding bonds, §33-2-72.

Rights of way.

Acquisition, §33-2-65.

State docks department.

Authority under article cumulative, §33-2-64.

Current indebtedness.

Department may contract, §33-2-66.

Rates and charges.

Fixing, §33-2-75.

State property.

Licenses to occupy.

Revocation or cancellation, §33-2-76.

Surveys, §33-2-63.

Taxation.

Bonds and interest exempt, §33-2-77.

United States.

Permit or consent from federal authorities, §33-2-63.

Unit of development.

Defined, §33-2-60.

Records.

Separate records, §33-2-73.

1963 provisions, §§33-2-90 to 33-2-107.

Acquisition.

Authority to acquire new facilities, §33-2-93.

Completion of facilities acquired under earlier acts, §33-2-93.

How property acquired, §33-2-95.

Rights of way, §33-2-95.

Construction.

New facilities.

Authority to construct, §33-2-93.

Contracts.

Current indebtedness.

State docks department may contract, §33-2-96.

Costs.

Additional costs.

Authorized, §33-2-92.

WATERS AND WATERCOURSES—Cont'd

Development of docks along inland waterways —Cont'd

1963 provisions—Cont'd

Costs—Cont'd

Additional costs—Cont'd

Facilities at additional costs of $2,000,000 authorized, §33-2-91.

Total cost to state, §33-2-92.

Total cost to state, §33-2-92.

Current indebtedness.

State docks department may contract, §33-2-96.

Definitions, §33-2-90.

Docks department.

Authority under article cumulative, §33-2-94.

Earlier acts.

Completion of facilities acquired under earlier acts, §33-2-93.

Eminent domain, §33-2-95.

Federal authorities.

Permit or consent, §33-2-93.

Governor.

Approval of plans, §33-2-93.

Inland facilities.

Application of revenues, §33-2-101.

Bonds generally, §33-2-97.

Interest.

Appropriation for payment, §33-2-100.

Investments.

Proceeds, §33-2-102.

Licenses.

Occupying state property.

Revocation of licenses, §33-2-106.

Mobile.

Surplus revenues.

Use to pay operating deficits, §33-2-104.

New facilities.

Authority to acquire, construct and maintain, §33-2-93.

Permits.

Federal authorities, §33-2-93.

Plans, §33-2-93.

Approval by governor, §33-2-93.

Proceeds.

Disposition of proceeds from sale of bonds, §33-2-99.

Inland facilities.

Application of revenues, §33-2-101.

Investment of proceeds, §33-2-102.

Refunding bonds, §33-2-102.

Property.

Acquisition, §33-2-95.

WATERS AND WATERCOURSES—Cont'd

Development of docks along inland waterways —Cont'd

1963 provisions—Cont'd

Rates and charges.

Use of facilities, §33-2-105.

Records.

Unit of development.

Separate records as to each unit, §33-2-102.

Refunding bonds.

Provisions of article applicable to, §33-2-102.

Rights of way.

Acquisition, §33-2-95.

Sale of bonds.

Disposition of proceeds, §33-2-99.

State docks department.

Authority, etc., under article cumulative, §33-2-94.

Defined, §33-2-90.

Eminent domain, §33-2-95.

Licenses.

Revocation or cancellation, §33-2-106.

Rates and charges.

Fixing, §33-2-105.

Surplus revenues.

Port of Mobile.

Use to pay operating deficits, §33-2-104.

Surveys, §33-2-93.

Taxation.

Bonds exempt, §33-2-107.

United States.

Permit or consent from federal authorities, §33-2-93.

Unit of development.

Defined, §33-2-90.

Records.

Separate records as to each unit, §33-2-103.

1967 provisions.

Costs.

Facilities at additional cost of $2,000,000 authorized, §33-2-121.

Definitions, §33-2-120.

Dock facilities.

Defined, §33-2-120.

Eminent domain.

Proceedings, §33-2-124.

Exemption from taxation, §§33-2-17, 33-2-44, 33-2-77, 33-2-107, 33-2-136, 33-2-166.

Inland waterways facilities.

Defined, §33-2-120.

Inland waterways improvement bonds.

General provisions relative to additional bonds, §§33-2-8, 33-2-37, 33-2-67, 33-2-97, 33-2-126, 33-2-156.

**WATERS AND
WATERCOURSES**—Cont'd
**Development of docks along
inland waterways**
—Cont'd
1967 provisions—Cont'd
Interest.
Appropriation for
payment, §§33-2-70,
33-2-100, 33-2-129,
33-2-159.
Exemption from
taxation, §§33-2-17,
33-2-44, 33-2-77,
33-2-107, 33-2-136,
33-2-166.
Investment of proceeds,
§§33-2-102, 33-2-131.
Port of mobile facilities.
Defined, §33-2-120.
Property.
Acquisition, §33-2-124.
Refunding bonds,
§§33-2-72, 33-2-102,
33-2-131, 33-2-162.
Rights of way.
Acquisition, §33-2-124.
Sale of bonds.
Disposition of proceeds,
§§33-2-9, 33-2-39,
33-2-69, 33-2-99,
33-2-128, 33-2-158.
Requirements, §§33-2-38,
33-2-68, 33-2-98,
33-2-127, 33-2-157.
State docks department.
Authority under
department
cumulative,
§33-2-123.
Eminent domain
proceedings,
§33-2-124.
Taxation.
Exemption from
taxation, §§33-2-17,
33-2-44, 33-2-77,
33-2-107, 33-2-136,
33-2-166.
Unit of development.
Defined, §33-2-120.
1969 provisions, §§33-2-150
to 33-2-166.
Acquisition.
Authority to acquire new
facilities, §33-2-152.
Completion of facilities
acquired under
earlier acts,
§33-2-152.
How property acquired,
§33-2-154.
Rights of way.
How acquired,
§33-2-154.
Appropriations.
Bonds.
Payment of principal
and interest,
§33-2-159.
Bonds.
Appropriations.
Payment of principal
and interest,
§33-2-159.
Inland facilities bonds.
General provisions
relative to,
§33-2-156.

**WATERS AND
WATERCOURSES**—Cont'd
**Development of docks along
inland waterways**
—Cont'd
1969 provisions—Cont'd
Bonds—Cont'd
Interest.
Appropriation for
payment,
§33-2-159.
Tax exempt, §33-2-166.
Principal.
Appropriation for
payment,
§33-2-159.
Refunding bonds.
Issuance, §33-2-161.
Sale of bonds.
Disposition of proceeds,
§33-2-158.
Requirements,
§33-2-157.
Taxation.
Exemption, §33-2-166.
Construction.
New facilities.
Authority to construct,
§33-2-152.
Contracts.
Current indebtedness.
State docks
department may
contract,
§33-2-155.
Costs.
Additional cost.
Facilities at additional
cost of $10,000,000
authorized,
§33-2-151.
Facilities at additional
cost of $10,000,000
authorized,
§33-2-151.
Current indebtedness.
State docks department
may contract,
§33-2-155.
Definitions, §33-2-150.
Earlier acts.
Completion of facilities
acquired under
earlier acts,
§33-2-152.
Eminent domain,
§33-2-154.
Federal authorities.
Permit or consent,
§33-2-152.
Governor.
Approval of plans,
§33-2-152.
Inland facilities.
Application of revenues,
§33-2-160.
Bonds.
General provisions
relative to,
§33-2-156.
Defined, §33-2-150.
Interest.
Appropriation for
payment, §33-2-159.
Exempt from taxation,
§33-2-166.
Investments.
Proceeds, §33-2-161.

**WATERS AND
WATERCOURSES**—Cont'd
**Development of docks along
inland waterways**
—Cont'd
1969 provisions—Cont'd
Licenses.
Occupying state
property.
Revocation of licenses,
§33-2-165.
New facilities.
Authority to acquire,
construct, and
maintain, §33-2-152.
Occupying state property.
Licenses.
Revocation, §33-2-165.
Plans, §33-2-152.
Approval of governor,
§33-2-152.
Port of Mobile facilities.
Defined, §33-2-150.
Use of surplus revenues
to pay operating
deficit, §33-2-163.
Proceeds.
Disposition of proceeds
from sale of bonds,
§33-2-158.
Inland facilities.
Application of
revenues,
§33-2-160.
Investment of proceeds,
§33-2-161.
Refunding bonds,
§33-2-161.
Property.
How acquired, §33-2-154.
Rates and charges.
State docks department.
Power to fix,
§33-2-164.
Use of facilities,
§33-2-164.
Records.
Unit of development.
Separate records as to
each unit,
§33-2-162.
Refunding bonds.
Issuance, §33-2-161.
Proceeds.
Disposition, §33-2-161.
Rights of way.
How acquired, §33-2-154.
State docks department.
Authority of department
under article
cumulative,
§33-2-153.
Current indebtedness.
Department may
contract,
§33-2-155.
Eminent domain power,
§33-2-154.
Rates and charges.
Power to fix,
§33-2-164.
Records.
Separate records as to
each unit of
development,
§33-2-162.
Surveys, §33-2-152.
Taxation.
Bond exemption,
§33-2-166.

WATERS AND WATERCOURSES—Cont'd
Development of docks along inland waterways —Cont'd
1969 provisions—Cont'd
Taxation—Cont'd
Interest exemption, §33-2-166.
United States.
Permit or consent from federal authorities, §33-2-152.
Unit of development.
Defined, §33-2-150.
Separate records as to each unit, §33-2-162.
Occupying state property.
Licenses.
Revocation and suspension, §§33-2-16, 33-2-43, 33-2-76, 33-2-106, 33-2-135, 33-2-165.
Plans.
1957 provisions, §33-2-3.
1959 provisions, §33-2-33.
1961 provisions, §33-2-63.
1963 provisions, §33-2-93.
1969 provisions, §33-2-152.
Port of Mobile facilities.
Surplus revenues.
Use to pay operating deficit, §§33-2-74, 33-2-104, 33-2-133, 33-2-163.
Prior indebtedness.
No prior indebtedness to be paid from funds received, §33-2-15.
Property.
Acquisition.
1957 provisions, §33-2-6.
1959 provisions, §33-2-35.
1961 provisions, §33-2-65.
1963 provisions, §33-2-95.
1967 provisions, §33-2-124.
1969 provisions, §33-2-154.
Rates and charges for use of facilities.
State docks department.
1957 provisions, §33-2-12.
1959 provisions, §33-2-42.
1961 provisions, §33-2-75.
1963 provisions, §33-2-105.
1967 provisions, §33-2-134.
1969 provisions, §33-2-164.
Records.
Units of development.
Separate records as to each unit, §§33-2-41, 33-2-73, 33-2-103, 33-2-132, 33-2-162.
Refunding bonds, §§33-2-72, 33-2-102, 33-2-131, 33-2-162.
Rights of way.
1957 provisions, §33-2-6.
1959 provisions, §33-2-35.
1961 provisions, §33-2-65.

WATERS AND WATERCOURSES—Cont'd
Development of docks along inland waterways —Cont'd
Rights of way—Cont'd
1963 provisions, §33-2-95.
1967 provisions, §33-2-124.
1969 provisions, §33-2-154.
Surveys.
1957 provisions, §33-2-3.
1959 provisions, §33-2-33.
1961 provisions, §33-2-63.
1963 provisions, §33-2-93.
1969 provisions, §33-2-152.
Taxation.
Bonds and interest exempt from taxation, §§33-2-17, 33-2-44, 33-2-77, 33-2-107, 33-2-136, 33-2-163.
United States.
Permit or consent from federal authorities, §§33-2-33, 33-2-63, 33-2-93, 33-2-122, 33-2-152.
Diverting streams.
Damages for diverting stream, §33-7-4.
Docks.
Development of docks along inland waterways, §§33-2-94, 33-2-123, 33-2-124.
General provisions, §§33-1-1 to 33-1-36.
See HARBORS AND PORTS.
Riparian owners.
Installing docks, §33-7-50.
Obstructing navigation, §33-7-51.
State docks department. See within this heading, "Development of docks along inland waterways."
Duty of care owed persons on premises for sporting or recreational purposes, §§35-15-1 to 35-15-5.
Elk river development agency, §§33-12-1 to 33-12-10.
See ELK RIVER DEVELOPMENT AGENCY.
Eminent domain.
Development of docks along inland waterways. See within this heading, "Development of docks along inland waterways."
Environmental protection.
Ameraport offshore harbor and terminal commission, §33-10-20.
Fish and game.
General provisions, §§9-11-140 to 9-11-156.
See FISH AND GAME.
Fishing, §§9-11-140 to 9-11-156.
See FISH AND GAME.
Fowl.
Depositing dead fowl in running streams, §22-20-9.

WATERS AND WATERCOURSES—Cont'd
Geological survey.
General provisions, §§9-4-1 to 9-4-19.
See GEOLOGICAL SURVEY.
Governor.
Development of docks along inland waterways. See within this heading, "Development of docks along inland waterways."
Gravel.
Sale or leasing.
Public water bottoms, §§9-15-52, 9-15-53.
Harbors, §§33-1-1 to 33-1-36.
See HARBORS AND PORTS.
Health.
Nuisances menacing public health, §§22-10-1 to 22-10-3.
Highways.
Navigable waters declared free public highways, Const. Ala., art. I, §24.
Hunting.
General provisions, §§9-11-250, 9-11-252.
Impounded waters.
Commercial fishing, §§9-11-140 to 9-11-156.
See FISH AND GAME.
Inland waterways.
Development of docks along inland waterways. See within this heading, "Development of docks along inland waterways."
Legislature.
Riparian owners.
Repossession of structures by legislature, §33-7-51.
Toll regulation, §33-7-52.
Licenses.
Development of docks along inland waterways.
Occupying state property.
Revocation and suspension of license to occupy, §§33-2-3, 33-2-33, 33-2-63, 33-2-93, 33-2-122, 33-2-152.
Upland owners.
Revocation or suspension, §33-1-29.
Litter.
Discharge of litter and sewage from watercraft, §§33-6-1 to 33-6-12.
See BOATS.
Manufacturers.
Construction and operation of connections to navigable watercourses by manufacturing corporations, §10-5-13.
Marine environmental sciences consortium, §§16-45-1 to 16-45-5.
Marine police, §§33-5-4 to 33-5-6.
Marine resources, §§9-12-1 to 9-12-184.
See MARINE RESOURCES.

WATERS AND
WATERCOURSES—Cont'd
Mines and minerals.
Construction and operation of
connections to navigable
watercourses by mining
corporations, §10-5-13.
Mobile harbor.
Development of docks along
inland waterways,
§§33-2-74, 33-2-104,
33-2-133, 33-2-163. See
within this heading,
"Development of docks
along inland waterways."
Municipal corporations.
Alteration of channel of
watercourses, §11-47-15.
Navigation.
General provisions, §§33-1-1
to 33-17-15.
See NAVIGATION.
Harbors and ports, §§33-1-1
to 33-17-15.
See HARBORS AND
PORTS.
Obstructing navigation.
General provisions,
§§33-7-1 to 33-7-54.
See NAVIGATION.
Pilots and pilotage, §§33-4-1
to 33-4-57.
See PILOTS AND
PILOTAGE.
Nuisances menacing public
health, §§22-10-1 to
22-10-3.
Obstructions.
Dams, §§33-7-1 to 33-7-54.
See DAMS.
General provisions, §§33-7-1
to 33-7-54.
See NAVIGATION.
Opening and cleaning
navigable streams,
§33-7-2.
Penalties.
Fish and game.
Preventing passage of fish
up creeks or rivers,
§9-11-92.
Obstructing navigable
watercourse, §33-7-3.
Pilots and pilotage, §§33-4-1
to 33-4-57.
See PILOTS AND
PILOTAGE.
Plans.
Development of docks along
inland waterways. See
within this heading,
"Development of docks
along inland waterways."
Police.
Marine police. §§33-5-4 to
33-5-6.
Pollution.
Water pollution.
See WATER POLLUTION.
Port authority.
Alabama port authority,
§§33-13-1 to 33-13-13.
See HARBORS AND
PORTS.
Generally, §§11-94-1 to
11-94-24.
See HARBORS AND
PORTS.
Ports, §§33-1-1 to 33-1-36.
See HARBORS AND PORTS.

WATERS AND
WATERCOURSES—Cont'd
Power companies, §§10-4-320
to 10-4-323.
Public thoroughfares.
Navigable waters as, §33-7-1.
Quarries.
Construction and operation of
connections to navigable
watercourses by
quarrying corporations,
§10-5-13.
Records.
Development of docks along
inland waterways.
Units of development.
Separate records as to
each unit, §§33-2-41,
33-2-73, 33-2-103,
33-2-132, 33-2-162.
Recreational purposes.
Duty of care owed persons on
premises, §§35-15-1 to
35-15-5.
Refunding bonds.
Development of docks along
inland waterways,
§§33-2-72, 33-2-102,
33-2-131, 33-2-162. See
within this heading,
"Development of docks
along inland waterways."
Rights of riparian owners,
§§33-7-50 to 33-7-54.
Rights of way.
Development of docks along
inland waterways. See
within this heading,
"Development of docks
along inland waterways."
Navigable waters as public
thoroughfares, §33-7-1.
Riparian owners.
Coastal areas.
Permissible areas, §9-7-13.
Development and relief work.
Tidelands, §33-7-53.
Diverting streams.
Damages for diversion,
§33-7-4.
Docks.
Installing docks, §33-7-50.
Obstructing navigation,
§33-7-51.
Dredging or cleaning creeks,
etc., running through
property, §33-7-54.
Limitations on right,
§33-7-54.
Legislature.
Repossession of structures
by legislature,
§33-7-51.
Toll regulation, §33-7-52.
Obstructing navigation.
Structures not to obstruct,
§33-7-51.
Repossession by legislature,
§33-7-51.
Tidelands.
Development and relief
work upon and
abutting on tidelands,
§33-7-53.
Tolls.
Charging tolls, §33-7-50.
Regulation by legislature,
§33-7-52.
Restriction on tolls,
§33-7-51.

WATERS AND
WATERCOURSES—Cont'd
Riparian owners—Cont'd
Trespass after warning on
booms, bulkheads or
piles erected by riparian
proprietors, §33-7-9.
Wharves.
Installing wharves,
§33-7-50.
Obstructions to navigation.
Structures not to
obstruct, §33-7-51.
Riparian rights.
Condemnation by
waterworks corporation,
§10-5-6.
Rivers.
Dams on navigable rivers,
§§33-7-30 to 33-7-32.
Development of docks along
inland waterways. See
within this heading,
"Development of docks
along inland waterways."
Salvage, §§35-13-1 to 35-13-10.
See SALVAGE.
Sand or gravel.
Sale or leasing.
Public water bottoms,
§§9-15-52, 9-15-53.
Sewage.
Discharge of litter and
sewage from watercraft,
§§33-6-1 to 33-6-12.
See BOATS.
State.
Development of docks along
inland waterways. See
within this heading,
"Development of docks
along inland waterways."
State docks department.
Development of docks along
inland waterways. See
within this heading,
"Development of docks
along inland waterways."
Jurisdiction of department,
§33-1-11.
Submerged lands.
Sales, §33-1-18.
Surveys and surveyors.
Development of docks along
inland waterways. See
within this heading,
"Development of docks
along inland waterways."
Taxation.
Development of docks along
inland waterways.
Bonds and interest exempt
from taxation,
§§33-2-17, 33-2-44,
33-2-77, 33-2-107,
33-2-136, 33-2-163.
Tidal waters.
Lands lying under or
abutting tidal waters.
Sales, §33-1-18.
Tolls.
Riparian owners, §§33-7-50
to 33-7-52.
Tombigbee-Tennessee
waterway development
compact, §§33-8-1 to
33-8-4.

WATERS AND WATERCOURSES—Cont'd

Tombigbee Valley development authority, §§33-17-1 to 33-17-15.
See TOMBIGBEE VALLEY DEVELOPMENT AUTHORITY.

Torts.
Duty of care owed persons on premises for sporting or recreational purposes, §§33-15-1 to 33-15-5.

Trees and timber.
Floating logs, timber or lumber upon watercourse without sufficient force to prevent obstruction, §33-7-6.
Obstructing streams used for floating timber to market, §33-7-5.
Opening or cutting loose of boom without authority, §33-7-8.
Turning logs, timber or lumber out of boom without notice to owner, §33-7-7.

United States.
Development of docks along inland waterways.
Permit or consent from federal authorities, §§33-2-33, 33-2-63, 33-2-93, 33-2-122, 33-2-152.
Navigable waters.
Cession of sites by state of lands covered by navigable waters to United States, §42-3-2.

Upland owners.
Revocation or suspension of licenses, §33-1-29.

Waterbottoms.
Ameraport offshore harbor and terminal commission, §§33-10-1 to 33-10-26.
See AMERAPORT.

Water pollution control act, §§22-22-1 to 22-22-14.
See WATER POLLUTION CONTROL ACT.

Water resources research institute, §§9-8-1 to 9-8-4.

Watershed conservancy districts, §§9-8-50 to 9-8-67.
See SOIL AND WATER CONSERVATION.

WATER, SEWER AND FIRE PROTECTION AUTHORITIES.

Acquisition, operation, etc., of systems.
Outside service area.
Power of authority outside service area, §11-88-7.
Sewer systems, §11-88-7.
Applicability of rates and charges provisions, §11-88-12.

Assessments for cost of improvement.
Abatement of assessments, §11-88-62.
Final assessment, §11-88-60.

WATER, SEWER AND FIRE PROTECTION AUTHORITIES—Cont'd

Assessments for cost of improvement—Cont'd
Amount of assessment.
Fixing by board, §11-88-60.
Appeal from assessments to circuit court.
Appeal bond, §11-88-68.
Appeal from circuit court to supreme court, §§11-88-74 to 11-88-77.
Authorization, §11-88-67.
Bonds, surety, §11-88-68.
Costs of appeal and trial, §§11-88-72, 11-88-73.
Entry of appeal on trial docket, §11-88-69.
Judgments, §11-88-73.
Procedure, §11-88-67.
Transcript of proceedings, §§11-88-70, 11-88-71.
Trial, §11-88-72.
Appeal from judgment of circuit court to supreme court, §§11-88-74, 11-88-77.
Assessment book.
Contents, §11-88-54.
Entry of list of property owners to be assessed in book, §11-88-54.
Publication of notice as to book, §11-88-55.
Status, §11-88-54.
Defective assessments.
Judgment, §11-88-73.
Defects in notice or proceedings.
Effect of defects, §11-88-61.
Supplementary proceedings for correction, §11-88-61.
Enforcement of liens.
Amounts recovered in actions to enforce, §11-88-64.
Circuit courts, §11-88-64.
Effect, §§11-88-65, 11-88-66.
Liens.
Assessment as lien on property, §11-88-60.
Assignment of liens, §11-88-63.
Duration of liens, §11-88-65.
Enforcement of liens, §§11-88-64 to 11-88-66.
Transfer of liens, §11-88-63.
List of property owners to be assessed.
Entry of list in assessment book, §11-88-54.
Preparation, §11-88-53.
Notice.
Defects in notice, §11-88-61.
Objections or defenses to proposed assessments.
Failure to file, §11-88-56.
Filing of written objecitons or defenses, §11-88-56.
Hearing of objections and defenses, §11-88-59.
Subpoena of witnesses by board, §11-88-58.
Reduction of assessments, §11-88-62.

WATER, SEWER AND FIRE PROTECTION AUTHORITIES—Cont'd

Assessments for costs of improvements.
Construction of sewerage facilities in resort areas, §§11-88-40 to 11-88-111.

Board of directors, §11-88-6.

Bond issues.
Construction of sewerage facilities in resort areas, §§11-88-91 to 11-88-108.
Contracts to secure payment, §11-88-9.
Delivery, §11-88-8.
Denominations, §11-88-8.
Disposition of proceeds from sale, §11-88-11.
Execution, §11-88-8.
Exemption from taxation, §11-88-16.
Form, §11-88-8.
Liability on bonds, §11-88-8.
Mortgages and deeds of trust.
Security for payment, §11-88-8.
Statutory mortgage lien to secure, §11-88-9.
Notice.
When required for issuance, §11-88-21.
Payment.
Security for payment, §11-88-8.
Contracts to secure, §11-88-9.
Statutory mortgage lien, §11-88-10.
Proceeds from sale.
Disposition, §§11-88-8, 11-88-11.
Refunding bonds, §11-88-8.
Sale, §11-88-8.
Proceeds.
Disposition, §11-88-11.
Security for payment, §11-88-8.
Contracts to secure payment, §11-88-9.
Statutory mortgage lien, §11-88-10.
Taxation.
Exemption from taxation, §11-88-16.
Terms, §11-88-8.
Trust indentures.
Security for payment, §11-88-8.
When proceedings, notice, etc., for issuance of bonds required, §11-88-21.

Certificate of incorporation, §§11-88-4, 11-88-5.

City takeover of authority's water system, §§11-88-130 to 11-88-135.
Board of water and sewer commissioners.
Inclusion of governing board of authority in, §11-88-131.
Consent to acquisition.
Vote, §11-88-135.
County customers.
Excessive rates.
Prohibited, §11-88-130.
Treatment, §11-88-130.

WATER, SEWER AND FIRE PROTECTION AUTHORITIES—Cont'd

City takeover of authority's water system—Cont'd

Escrow account for construction of water service improvements, §11-88-133.

Fire protection system.
Conveyance of funds in trust for authority's system, §11-88-132.

Governing board of authority.
Inclusion in governing board of commissioners, §11-88-131.
Trustees for funds for authority's fire protection system, §11-88-132.

Improvements.
Escrow account for construction, §11-88-133.

Notice.
Vote on consent to acquisition, §11-88-135.

Sanitary sewer service system plan, §11-88-134.

Sewers.
Sanitary sewer service system plan, §11-88-134.

Construction of sewerage facilities in resort areas, §§11-88-40 to 11-88-111.

Acceptance of work, §11-88-49.

Acquisition of lands, §11-88-110.

Amount of assessment.
Annexation.
Effect upon assessments, §11-88-111.
Appeal bond, §11-88-68.
Issuance of execution on appeal bond, §11-88-78.
Appeal from judgment of circuit court to supreme court.
By authority, §11-88-77.
Interest to judgment upon affirmance, §11-88-76.
Procedure for appeal by property owner, §11-88-74.
Record of appeal by property owner, §11-88-75.
Authorization of levy, §11-88-51.
Bond issues.
Disposition of assessments collected for improvements financed by outstanding issues, §11-88-104.
Default in payment, §11-88-80.

WATER, SEWER AND FIRE PROTECTION AUTHORITIES—Cont'd

Construction of sewerage facilities in resort areas —Cont'd

Amount of assessment —Cont'd
Incorporation of area in which assessments made.
Effect upon assessments, §11-88-111.
Levy authorized, §11-88-51.
Liens.
Effect of annexation or incorporation upon liens, §11-88-111.
Limitation as to amount of assessment, §11-88-52.
Mailing of copies of resolution, §11-88-45.
Manner of assessment, §11-88-52.
Manner of payment, §11-88-79.
Official charged with duty of collecting.
Bond, §11-88-107.
Duties, §11-88-107.
Payment.
Default in payment, §§11-88-80, 11-88-81.
Manner of payment, §11-88-79.
Redemption of property after sale.
Authorization, §11-88-85.
Certificate of warning to redeem, §§11-88-87, 11-88-88.
Deeds of certificate of warning to redeem, §§11-88-87, 11-88-88.
During extended redemption period, §11-88-90.
Errors by probate judge, §11-88-89.
Extension of redemption period, §11-88-86.
Liability of probate judge for errors or mistakes, §11-88-89.
Procedure, §11-88-85.
Termination of redemption rights, §11-88-89.
Sale of property assessed, §11-88-80.
Annexation of area in which assessments made.
Effect upon assessments, liens, bonds, etc., §11-88-111.
Assessments for cost of improvement.
Abatement, §11-88-62.
Final assessment, §11-88-60.
Advertisement of property to be sold for assessments, §11-88-80.
Cost of advertisement as charge against property to be sold, §11-88-82.

WATER, SEWER AND FIRE PROTECTION AUTHORITIES—Cont'd

Construction of sewerage facilities in resort areas —Cont'd

Assessments for cost of improvement—Cont'd
Advertisement of property to be sold for assessments—Cont'd
Effect of mistakes in advertisement, §11-88-84.
Amount of assessment.
Fixing by board, §11-88-60.
Limitation, §11-88-52.
Appeal from assessments to circuit court, §§11-88-67 to 11-88-73.
Appeal bond, §11-88-68.
Authorization, §11-88-67.
Bonds, surety, §11-88-68.
Conduct of trial, §11-88-72.
Costs, §§11-88-72, 11-88-73.
Docket, §11-88-69.
Entry of appeal on trial docket, §11-88-69.
Judgment, §11-88-73.
Procedure, §11-88-67.
Sale upon judgment in favor of authority, §11-88-78.
Transcript of proceedings, §§11-88-70, 11-88-7
Trial, §11-88-72.
Assessment book.
Contents, §11-88-54.
Entry of list of property owners to be assessed, §11-88-54.
Publication of notice as to assessment book, §11-88-55.
Status, §11-88-54.
Collection of assessments.
Bond of official charged with duty of collecting, §11-88-107.
Excess amounts collected, §11-88-10
Correctness of assessment
Transcript as evidence correctness, §11-88-71.
Deed to property to be soled for assessments
Execution to purchaser, §11-88-83.
Redemption of property after sale for assessment, §11-88-88.
Rights, titles, etc., conveyed to purchaser by deed, §11-88-83.
Defective assessments.
Judgment, §11-88-73.
Defects in notice or proceedings, §11-88-6
Enforcement of liens.
Amounts recovered in civil actions to enforce liens, §11-88-64.

WATER, SEWER AND FIRE PROTECTION AUTHORITIES—Cont'd
Construction of sewerage facilities in resort areas —Cont'd
Assessments for cost of improvement—Cont'd
Enforcement of liens —Cont'd
Circuit courts, §11-88-64.
Duration of liens, §11-88-65.
Effect of enforcement, §§11-88-65, 11-88-66.
Excess amounts collected, §11-88-109.
Hearing of objections and defenses to proposed assessments, §§11-88-57, 11-88-59.
Subpoena of witnesses by board, §11-88-58.
Liens.
Assessment as lien on property, §11-88-60.
Assignment by authorities, §11-88-63.
Duration, §11-88-65.
Enforcement of liens, §§11-88-64 to 11-88-66.
Transfer of liens by authorities, §11-88-63.
Limitation period for claims for refunds, §11-88-109.
List of property owners to be assessed.
Entry of list in assessment book, §11-88-54.
Preparation of lists, §11-88-53.
Notice.
Defects in notice, §11-88-61.
Objections and defenses to proposed assessments, §§11-88-56 to 11-88-59.
Failure to file, §11-88-56.
Filing of written objections or defenses, §11-88-56.
Hearing of objections and defenses, §§11-88-57, 11-88-59.
Subpoena of witnesses by board, §11-88-58.
Payment.
When due and payable, §11-88-80.
Purchase of property by board, §11-88-83.
Reduction, §11-88-62.
Final assessment, §11-88-60.
Refunding excess amounts collected upon demand, §11-88-109.
Sale of property assessed, §11-88-80.
Advertisement, §§11-88-80, 11-88-82, 11-88-84.
Correction of errors, §11-88-84.

WATER, SEWER AND FIRE PROTECTION AUTHORITIES—Cont'd
Construction of sewerage facilities in resort areas —Cont'd
Assessments for cost of improvement—Cont'd
Sale of property assessed —Cont'd
Cost of advertisement and sale as charge against property, §11-88-82.
Deed, §§11-88-83, 11-88-88.
Defaulting property owner may pay assessment prior to sale, §11-88-81.
Enforcement of lien, §11-88-84.
Mistakes in advertisement or sale, §11-88-84.
Purchase of property by board, §11-88-83.
Redemption of property after sale, §§11-88-85 to 11-88-90.
Supplementary proceedings for correction of errors, §11-88-84.
Surplus proceeds, §11-88-83.
Title conveyed to purchaser by deed, §11-88-83.
When final judgment entered in favor of authority, §11-88-78.
Supreme court.
Appeal from judgment of circuit court, §§11-88-74 to 11-88-77.
Tax liens.
Effect on assessment lien, §11-88-65.
Transcript of proceedings of authority as to assessment.
Contents, §11-88-70.
Evidentiary effect, §11-88-71.
Transmittal to circuit court, §11-88-70.
Trial by circuit court, §11-88-72.
Unclaimed excess collections.
Disposition, §11-88-109.
When due and payable, §11-88-80.
Witnesses.
Subpoena, §11-88-58.
Bonds or notes, §§11-88-91 to 11-88-108.
Adjustment of bonds.
Authorization and procedure, §11-88-102.
Annexation.
Effect, §11-88-111.
Applicability of certain other provisions of law, §11-88-94.

WATER, SEWER AND FIRE PROTECTION AUTHORITIES—Cont'd
Construction of sewerage facilities in resort areas —Cont'd
Bonds or notes—Cont'd
Bids, §11-88-95.
Determination of highest bidder, §11-88-96.
Commercial paper.
Bonds to resemble commercial paper, §11-88-99.
Consolidation of improvements, §11-88-93.
Consolidation of outstanding bond issues for refunding, §11-88-104.
Denominations, §11-88-94.
Destroyed bonds.
Replacement, §11-88-101.
Disposition of proceeds, §11-88-97.
Diversion of funds for payment of bonds and coupons, §11-88-107.
Duplicate bonds.
Replacement of lsot, mutilated or destroyed bonds, §11-88-101.
Exchange, §§11-88-94, 11-88-95.
Execution of short term notes before or during improvement, §11-88-91.
Exemption from taxation, §11-88-100.
Form, §11-88-94.
Incorporation.
Effect on bonds or notes, §11-88-111.
Issuance of bonds.
After completion of work on improvement, §11-88-92.
Consolidation of improvements, §11-88-93.
Duplicates, §11-88-101.
Irregularities in proceedings not to affect validity, §11-88-99.
Limitation of actions as to, §11-88-98.
Prior to letting of contract or during progress of work on improvement, §11-88-91.
Recitals, §11-88-98.
Validity, §§11-88-98, 11-88-99.
Liability.
Misappropration of funds, §11-88-107.
Limitation of actions or proceedings as to issuance, §11-88-98.
Lost bonds.
Replacement, §11-88-101.
Mandamus proceedings.
Institution against officer failing to pay bonds or interest, §11-88-106.

**WATER, SEWER AND FIRE
 PROTECTION
 AUTHORITIES**—Cont'd
**Construction of sewerage
 facilities in resort areas**
 —Cont'd
Bonds or notes—Cont'd
 Misappropriation of funds
  for payment,
  §11-88-107.
 Mutilated bonds.
  Replacement, §11-88-101.
 Neglect of duties by
  officers not to affect
  validity, §11-88-99.
 Notice of sale or exchange,
  §11-88-95.
 Payment.
  Diversion of funds for
   payment,
   §11-88-107.
  Liability for
   misappropriation of
   funds, §11-88-107.
  Mandamus against
   officer failing to pay
   bonds or interest,
   §11-88-106.
  Misappropriation of
   funds for payment,
   §11-88-107.
 Price.
  Sale price, §11-88-94.
 Proceeds from sale.
  Disposition, §11-88-97.
 Redemption of bonds,
  §11-88-108.
 Refunding bonds.
  Authorization for
   refunding,
   §11-88-102.
  Consolidation of
   outstanding bond
   issues for refunding,
   §11-88-104.
  Exchange, §11-88-95.
  Procedure for refunding
   of bonds, §11-88-102.
  Special fund used in
   taking up bonds or
   coupons
   representing
   principal and
   maturity,
   §11-88-103.
  Sale, §11-88-95.
  Sinking fund accounts,
   §§11-88-105,
   11-88-106.
 Replacement of lost,
  mutilated or destroyed
  bonds, §11-88-101.
 Sale, §§11-88-94, 11-88-95.
  Determination of highest
   bidder, §11-88-96.
  Disposition of proceeds,
   §11-88-97.
  Notice, §11-88-95.
  Price, §11-88-94.
  Proceeds, §11-88-97.
  Recitals, §11-88-98.
  Refunding bonds,
   §11-88-95.
  Validity, §11-88-98.
 Settlement of bonds.
  Authorization and
   procedure,
   §11-88-102.
  Sinking fund accounts,
   §§11-88-105,
   11-88-106.

**WATER, SEWER AND FIRE
 PROTECTION
 AUTHORITIES**—Cont'd
**Construction of sewerage
 facilities in resort areas**
 —Cont'd
Bonds or notes—Cont'd
 Taxation.
  Exemption from
   taxation, §11-88-100.
  Terms, §11-88-94.
 Validity of bonds,
  §§11-88-98,
  11-88-99.
Completion of work.
 Issuance of bonds after,
  §11-88-92.
Consent of county governing
 bond, §11-88-41.
Consolidation of
 improvements after
 issuance,
 §11-88-93.
Construction of improvement.
 Acceptance of work,
  §11-88-49.
 Bonds or notes.
  Issuance before
   contract or
   during work,
   §11-88-91.
  Issuance of bonds
   after completion
   of work,
   §11-88-92.
 By authority,
  §11-88-47.
 Rejection of work,
  §11-88-49.
 Supervision of work,
  §11-88-48.
Contracts.
 Bids.
  Publication of notice
   for bids,
   §11-88-47.
  Requirement of bonds,
   etc., from bidders,
   §11-88-47.
 Bonds, surety.
  Requirement of bonds
   from bidders,
   §11-88-47.
 Letting of contract,
  §11-88-47.
Costs of improvement.
 Assessments for costs,
  §§11-88-51 to
  11-88-90.
 Bonds or notes to pay
  costs, §§11-88-91 to
  11-88-108.
 Payment by board,
  §11-88-50.
 Specification,
  §11-88-50.
Definitions, §11-88-40.
Details, drawings, plans, etc.
 Adoption of resolution
  directing drawing,
  §11-88-43.
 Filing for examination by
  property owners,
  §11-88-44.
Eminent domain.
 Acquisition of lands by
  authority, §11-88-110.

**WATER, SEWER AND FIRE
 PROTECTION
 AUTHORITIES**—Cont'd
**Construction of sewerage
 facilities in resort areas**
 —Cont'd
Hearing on objections as to
 improvement, §11-88-46.
 Appointment of date for
  hearing, §11-88-44.
Incorporation of area in
 which assessments made
 Effect upon assessments,
  liens, bonds, etc.,
  §11-88-111.
Labor.
 Furnishing of labor for
  improvement by
  authority, §11-88-47.
Legislative findings and
 declarations, §11-88-41.
Liens.
 Effect of annexation or
  incorporation upon
  liens, §11-88-111.
Objections to improvement.
 Hearing of objections,
  §11-88-46.
 Appointment of date for
  hearing, §11-88-44.
Powers of authorities,
 §11-88-42.
 To be exercised only in
  resort areas, §11-88-41
Property.
 Acquisition of lands by
  authority, §11-88-110.
Rejection of work, §11-88-49.
Resolution by board
 describing improvement,
 property benefited, etc.
 Adoption, §11-88-43.
 Amendment of resolution,
  §11-88-46.
 Mailing of copies,
  §11-88-45.
 Publication, §11-88-45.
 Rescission of resolution,
  §11-88-46.
 When unanimous vote
  required to approve
  resolution, §11-88-46.
Sinking fund accounts.
 Disposition, §11-88-105.
 Maintenance, §11-88-106.
 Mandamus for failing to
  maintain separate
  accounts, §11-88-106.
 Separate accounts to be
  maintained for
  refunding bond issues
  §11-88-105.
Supervision of work,
 §11-88-48.
Tax leins.
 Assessments for cost of
  improvement.
  Effect on assessmentl
   ien, §11-88-65.
 Bonds or notes.
  Exemption from
   taxation, §11-88-10
Contracts.
 Bond issues.
  Contracts to secure
   payment, §11-88-9.
Definitions, §11-88-1.
 Construction of sewage
  treatment or disposal
  plants in resort areas,
  §11-88-40.

WATER, SEWER AND FIRE PROTECTION AUTHORITIES—Cont'd

Directors.
Board of directors, §11-88-6.
Dissolution of authority.
Authorization and procedure for dissolution, §11-88-18.
Excise tax.
Imposition upon authority, §11-88-16.
Exemption from taxation, §11-88-16.
Fire protection service.
Furnishing declared governmental function, §11-88-15.
Governmental function.
Fire protection service as governmental function, §11-88-15.
Grants to authority by public body, §11-88-13.
Importation of authority.
Existence not to prevent subsequent incorporation of another authority, §11-88-19.
When required, §11-88-21.
Incorporation of authority.
Application for incorporation.
Filing, §11-88-3.
Resolution approving or denying, §11-88-3.
Filing copy with probate judge, §11-88-4.
Certificate of incorporation.
Amendment.
Procedure for amendment, §11-88-5.
Contents, §11-88-4.
Execution, §11-88-4.
Filing, §11-88-4.
Recordation.
Entry of order, §11-88-4.
Notification of secretary of state, §11-88-4.
Costs.
Payment to probate judge, §11-88-16.
Defective incorporations.
Validation of prior defective incorporations, §11-88-20.
Fees.
Payment to probate judge, §11-88-16.
Notice.
When required, §11-88-21.
Resolution approving or denying application for incorporation, §§11-88-3, 11-88-4.
Subsequent incorporation of another authority.
Existence of authority not to prevent, §11-88-19.
Taxes.
Payment to probate judge, §11-88-16.
Validation of prior defective incorporations, §11-88-20.
When proceedings, notice, etc., required, §11-88-21.
Leases.
Exemption from taxation, §11-88-16.

WATER, SEWER AND FIRE PROTECTION AUTHORITIES—Cont'd

Liability on bonds, §11-88-8.
Tort liability.
Immunity from tort liability of authority, §11-88-15.
Licenses.
Imposition of license tax upon authority, §11-88-16.
Loans to authority by public body, §11-88-13.
Mortgages and deeds of trust.
Security for payment of bonds, §11-88-8
Statutory mortgage lien to secure payment of bonds, §11-88-10.
Powers of authorities, §11-88-7.
Additional powers, §11-88-7.1.
Construction of sewerage facilities in resort areas, §§11-88-41, 11-88-42.
Property.
Dissolution of authority.
Vesting upon dissolution, §11-88-18.
Exemption from taxation, §11-88-16.
Loans, sales, grants, etc., to authority by public body, §11-88-13.
When proceedings, notice, etc., for acquisition of property required, §11-88-21.
Public roads, bridges and ferries.
Use of rights-of-way of public roads by authorities, §11-88-14.
Public service commission.
Exemption of authority from jurisdiction, §11-88-21.
Purpose of article, §11-88-2.
Rates and charges.
Establishment, §11-88-12.
Revision, §11-88-12.
Schedules, §11-88-7.
Sewer charges, §11-88-12.
Resolutions.
Construction of sewerage facilities in resort areas, §§11-88-43, 11-88-45.
Incorporation of authority.
Approving or denying application, §§11-88-3, 11-88-4.
Resort areas.
Construction of sewerage facilities, §§11-88-40 to 11-88-111.
Rights-of-way.
Use of rights-of-way of public roads by authorities, §11-88-14.
Roads.
Use of rights-of-way of public roads by authority, §11-88-14.
Sales to authority by public body, §11-88-13.
Taxation.
Exemption from taxation, §11-88-16.

WATER, SEWER AND FIRE PROTECTION AUTHORITIES—Cont'd

Torts.
Immunity from tort liability of authority, §11-88-15.
Usury laws.
Exemption of authority from usury laws, §11-88-17.

WATER, SEWER AND FIRE PROTECTION DISTRICTS.

Acquisition, operation, etc., of systems.
Exclusiveness of provisions, §11-89-19.
Outside service area, §11-89-7.
Board of directors, §11-89-6.
Bond issues.
Contracts to secure payment, §11-89-9.
Delivery, §11-89-8.
Denominations, §11-89-8.
Disposition of proceeds, §11-89-11.
Execution, §11-89-8.
Form, §11-89-8.
Liability on bonds, §11-89-8.
Mortgages and deeds of trust.
Securing payment, §11-89-8.
Statutory mortgage lien to secure payment of bonds, §11-89-10.
Payment, §11-89-8.
Contracts to secure, §11-89-9.
Security, §11-89-8.
Contracts to secure, §11-89-9.
Statutory mortgage lien to secure, §11-89-10.
Proceeds from sale.
Disposition, §11-89-11.
Provisions of chapter as to issuance of bonds exclusive, §11-89-19.
Refunding bonds, §11-89-8.
Sale, §11-89-8.
Disposition of proceeds, §11-89-11.
Security for payment, §11-89-8.
Contracts, §11-89-9.
Statutory mortgage lien, §11-89-10.
Tax exemption, §11-89-16.
Terms, §11-89-8.
Trust indentures.
Security for payment, §11-89-8.
Definitions, §11-89-1.
Directors.
Board of directors, §11-89-6.
Dissolution of districts.
Authorization and procedure for dissolution, §11-89-17.
Fire protection service.
Furnishing as governmental function, §11-89-15.
Governmental function.
Fire protection service as governmental function, §11-89-15.
Grants to district by public bodies, §11-89-13.

WATER, SEWER AND FIRE PROTECTION DISTRICTS—Cont'd

Incorporation of district.
Application for incorporation.
Filing, §11-89-3.
Resolutions approving or denying.
Adoption, §11-89-3.
Filing copies with probate judge, §11-89-4.
Certificate of incorporation.
Amendment, §11-89-5.
Payment of fees, taxes or costs to probate judge, §11-89-16.
Contents, §11-89-4.
Execution, §11-89-4.
Filing, §11-89-4.
Recordation.
Notification to secretary of state of recordation, §11-89-4.
Costs.
Payment to probate judge, §11-89-16.
Existence of district not to prevent subsequent incorporation of another district, §11-89-18.
Fees, §11-89-16.
Provisions of chapter as to incorporation exclusive, §11-89-19.
Resolutions approving or denying application for.
Adoption, §11-89-3.
Filing copies of resolutions with probate judge, §11-89-4.
Subsequent incorporation.
Existence of district not to prevent, §11-89-18.
Taxes.
Payment to probate judge, §11-89-16.
Leases.
Tax exemption, §11-89-10.
Liability on bonds, §11-89-8.
Immunity from tort liability of district, §11-89-15.
Loans to district by public bodies, §11-89-13.
Mortgages and deeds of trust.
Bond issues.
Security for payment of bonds, §11-89-8.
Statutory mortgage lien to secure payment of bonds, §11-89-10.
Outside service area.
Power as to such systems, §11-89-7.
Powers of distirct, §11-89-7.
Property.
Acquisition of property.
Provisions of chapter as to acquisition exclusive, §11-89-19.
Apportionment of property of district upon dissolution, §11-89-17.
Loans, sales, grants, etc., of property to district by public bodies, §11-89-13.
Tax exemption, §11-89-16.

WATER, SEWER AND FIRE PROTECTION DISTRICTS—Cont'd

Property—Cont'd
Vesting of title to property of district upon dissolution, §11-89-17.
Public roads, bridges and ferries.
Use of rights-of-way of public roads by district, §11-89-14.
Public service commission.
Jurisdiction of commission, §11-89-19.
Purpose of chapter, §11-89-2.
Rates and charges.
Establishment, §11-89-12.
Revision, §11-89-12.
Schedules.
Provisions in schedules of rates and charges, §11-89-7.
Resolutions.
Incorporation of district.
Approving or denying application, §11-89-3.
Filing copies with probate judge, §11-89-4.
Rights-of-way.
Use of rights-of-way of public roads by district, §11-89-14.
Sales to district by public bodies, §11-89-13.
State board of health.
Jurisdiction over and regulation of district, §11-89-19.
Tax exemption, §11-89-16.
Tort liability.
Immunity of district, §11-89-15.

WATERSHED CONSERVANCY DISTRICTS, §§9-8-50 to 9-8-67.

See SOIL AND WATER CONSERVATION.

WATER SUPPLY AND WATERWORKS.

Alabama water system assistance authority, §§22-23A-1 to 22-23A-17.
See WATER SYSTEM ASSISTANCE AUTHORITY.
Animals.
Dead animals.
Depositing in water supplies, §22-20-8.
Authorities.
Improvement authorities, §§39-7-1 to 39-7-34.
See PUBLIC WORKS.
Water system assistance authority, §§22-23A-1 to 22-23A-17.
See WATER SYSTEM ASSISTANCE AUTHORITY.
Barbers and beauty shops.
Water connections, §22-17-4.

WATER SUPPLY AND WATERWORKS—Cont'd

Certification.
General provisions, §§22-25-7 to 22-25-12, 22-25-14.
See WATER AND WASTEWATER SYSTEMS AND TREATMENT PLANTS.
Commercial code.
Secured transactions.
Applicability of filing provisions, §7-9-302.
Contaminated water.
Nuisances menacing public health, §§22-10-1 to 22-10-3.
Conveyances.
Water distribution facilities.
Conveyance without approval of public service commission, §37-4-45.
Coosa Valley development authority.
Duties and obligations with respect to, §33-16-7.
Counties, §§11-21-1 to 11-21-4.
County boards of health.
Duties, §22-3-2.
County health officers.
Duties, §22-3-5.
Definitions.
Safe drinking water act, §22-23-31.
Wells, §22-24-1.
Department of environmental management.
Wells.
Definition of board, §22-24-1.
Promulgation and enforcement of rules and regulations, §22-24-3.
Drinking water, §§22-23-30 to 22-23-53. See within this heading, "Safe drinking water act."
Eminent domain.
Companies constructing, operating or maintaining public utility, §10-5-4.
Public utility corporations, §10-5-1.
Routes and sites.
Rights of condemning corporations in selecting, §10-5-8.
Water sources, riparian rights and necessary lands.
Condemnation by waterworks corporation, §10-5-6.
Health.
Authority and jurisdiction of state board of health, §22-2-2.
Duties of county boards of health, §22-3-2.
Duties of county health officers, §22-3-5.
Nuisances menacing public health, §§22-10-1 to 22-10-3.

WATER SUPPLY AND WATERWORKS—Cont'd

Highways.
Contracting with local authorities as to use by public utility corporations, §10-5-14.

Improvement authorities, §§39-7-1 to 39-7-34.
See PUBLIC WORKS.

Insanitary water.
Nuisances menacing public health, §§22-10-1 to 22-10-3.

Lead contamination.
Notice to customers, §22-37-5.
Use or sale of materials not lead-free, §22-37-6.

Leases.
Water distribution facilities, §37-4-45.

Licenses.
Well driller's license, §§22-24-5, 22-24-7.

Marion county.
Public water authority.
Creation authorized, Const. Ala., amd. 490.

Municipal corporations.
General provisions.
See MUNICIPAL CORPORATIONS.
Waterworks utility boards, §§11-50-430 to 11-50-445.
See MUNICIPAL CORPORATIONS.

Noxious substances.
Depositing in water supplies, §22-20-8.

Nuisances.
Nuisances menacing public health, §§22-10-1 to 22-10-3.
Safe drinking water act.
Violations deemed public nuisances, §22-23-53.

Operators.
Certification, §§22-25-7 to 22-25-12, 22-25-14.
See WATER AND WASTEWATER SYSTEMS AND TREATMENT PLANTS.

Penalties.
Wells, §22-24-11.

Permits.
Safe drinking water act.
Permit to construct or modify water system, §§22-23-40 to 22-23-44.

Pollution.
Safe drinking water act.
Polluting public water supply prohibited, §22-23-47.

Reports.
Safe drinking water act.
Applicants or suppliers, §22-23-46.

Right of entry.
Safe drinking water act, §22-23-45.

Riparian rights.
Condemnation of riparian rights by waterworks corporation, §10-5-6.

WATER SUPPLY AND WATERWORKS—Cont'd

Rules and regulations.
Safe drinking water act, §§22-23-32 to 22-23-35, 22-23-48.
Wells, §22-24-3.

Safe drinking water act, §§22-23-30 to 22-23-53.
Board of health.
Administration of article, §22-23-49.
Duties, §22-23-49.
Emergencies, §22-23-36.
Permits to construct or modify water system, §§22-23-40 to 22-23-44.
Powers, §22-23-49.
Regulatory authority, §22-23-32.
State primary drinking water regulations, §22-23-33.
State secondary drinking water regulations, §22-23-34.
Variances and exceptions from regulations, §22-23-35.
Right of entry for investigations and inspections, §22-23-45.
Citation.
Short title, §22-23-30.
Construction of water systems.
Permit, §§22-23-40 to 22-23-44.
Definitions, §22-23-31.
Emergencies.
Action by board, §22-23-36.
Environmental management department.
"Board" defined, §22-23-31.
Modification of water systems.
Permit, §§22-23-40 to 22-23-44.
Notices.
Violations, §22-23-37.
Nuisances.
Violations deemed public nuisances, §22-23-53.
Penalties, §22-23-52.
Permit to construct or modify water system, §§22-23-40 to 22-23-44.
Polluting public water supply prohibited, §22-23-47.
Prohibited acts, §§22-23-47, 22-23-48.
Reports.
Condition of water supply, plant, etc., §22-23-46.
Rules and regulations.
Failure to comply prohibited, §22-23-48.
Regulatory authority of board, §§22-23-32 to 22-23-35.
Samples.
Analysis, §22-23-39.
Failure to supply prohibited, §22-23-48.
Required, §22-23-38.
Title, §22-23-30.

Secured transactions.
Applicability of filing provisions, §7-9-302.

WATER SUPPLY AND WATERWORKS—Cont'd

Single-tax and other mutual economic associations.
Exemption from ad valorem taxes, §10-4-193.

Smith's water authority in Lee county.
Exemption from gross receipt tax, §40-21-82.1.

State board of health.
Authority and jurisdiction, §22-2-2.

Taxation.
General provisions, §§40-21-1 to 40-21-34.
See PUBLIC UTILITIES.

Theft.
Acts which make water unlawfully available, §13A-8-23.

Tombigbee Valley development authority.
Duties and obligations as to construction and maintenance, §33-17-7.

Water distribution facilities.
Conveyance without approval of public service commission, §37-4-45.

Water pollution control act, §§22-22-1 to 22-22-14.
See WATER POLLUTION CONTROL ACT.

Water resources research institute, §§9-8-1 to 9-8-4.

Water, sewer and fire protection authorities, §§11-88-1 to 11-88-111.
See WATER, SEWER AND FIRE PROTECTION AUTHORITIES.

Water, sewer and fire protection districts, §§11-89-1 to 11-89-19.
See WATER, SEWER AND FIRE PROTECTION DISTRICTS.

Water system assistance authority.
General provisions, §§22-23A-1 to 22-23A-17.
See WATER SYSTEM ASSISTANCE AUTHORITY.

Wells, §§22-24-1 to 22-24-12.
Applicability of chapter, §22-24-2.
Definitions, §22-24-1.
Department of environmental management.
Definition of board, §22-24-1.
Promulgation and enforcement of rules and regulations, §22-24-3.
Drilling.
Supervision of drilling by licensed driller, §22-24-4.
Well driller's license, §§22-24-5, 22-24-7.
Exemption from chapter.
Baldwin county, §22-24-12.
Fines.
Disposition of fines, §22-24-11.
Licenses.
Well driller's license, §§22-24-5, 22-24-7.

WATER SUPPLY AND WATERWORKS—Cont'd
Wells—Cont'd
Penalty for violation of chapter, §22-24-11.
Repair.
Supervision of repair by licensed driller, §22-24-4.
Rules and regulations.
Promulgation, §22-24-3.

WATER SYSTEM ASSISTANCE AUTHORITY, §§22-23A-1 to 22-23A-17.
Actions.
Power to sue and be sued, §22-23A-6.
Application to become corporation, §22-23A-5.
Attorneys at law.
Power to appoint and employ, §22-23A-6.
Board of directors, §22-23A-5.
Quorum, §22-23A-5.
Record of proceedings, §22-23A-5.
Vacancies, §22-23A-5.
Bond issues.
Approval not required, §22-23A-15.
Authority to issue, §22-23A-7.
Refunding bonds, §22-23A-10.
Defined, §22-23A-1.
Exclusively obligations of authority, §22-23A-17.
Interest, §22-23A-7.
Exempt from usury, §22-23A-14.
Investments in, §22-23A-12.
Loans in anticipation of issuance, §22-23A-9.
Negotiable instruments.
Bonds and coupons deemed, §22-23A-16.
Notice of public sale, §22-23A-8.
Power to issue, §22-23A-6.
Proceeds.
Defined, §22-23A-1.
Refunding bonds.
Authority to issue, §22-23A-10.
Sales.
Authority, §22-23A-7.
Procedure, §22-23A-8.
Security for payment of principal and interest, §22-23A-7.
Tax exemptions, §22-23A-13.
Terms, §22-23A-7.
Community water systems.
Dedicated sources of revenue.
Establishment, §22-23A-11.
Defined, §22-23A-1.
Powers, §22-23A-6.
Corporations.
Application to become corporation, §22-23A-5.
Incorporation of authority.
Proceedings, notice or approval not required, §22-23A-15.
Counties.
Investments in bonds of authority, §22-23A-12.

WATER SYSTEM ASSISTANCE AUTHORITY—Cont'd
Creation.
How created, §22-23A-3.
Dedicated sources of revenue.
Community water systems.
Authority to establish, §22-23A-11.
Definitions, §22-23A-1.
Department of economic and community affairs.
Department defined, §22-23A-1.
Director.
Vice-president of authority, §22-23A-5.
Deposits.
Water supply assistance fund, §22-23A-4.
Employees.
Power to appoint, §22-23A-6.
Executors and administrators.
Investments in bonds of authority, §22-23A-12.
Fiduciaries.
Investments in bonds of authority, §22-23A-12.
Fiscal year.
Power to establish, §22-23A-6.
Funds.
Water supply assistance fund.
Established, §22-23A-4.
Governor.
Annual report, §22-23A-6.
President of authority, §22-23A-5.
Insurance companies.
Investments in bonds of authority, §22-23A-12.
Interest.
Bond issues, §22-23A-7.
Exemption from usury, §22-23A-14.
Loans in anticipation of bond issues, §22-23A-9.
Investments.
Bond issues, §22-23A-12.
Water supply assistance fund, §22-23A-4.
Legislative intent, §22-23A-2.
Legislature.
Speaker of house.
Appointments to authority or committee, §22-23A-3.
Water assistance legislative oversight committee, §22-23A-3.
Lieutenant governor.
Appointments to authority or committee, §22-23A-3.
Loans.
Approval not required, §22-23A-15.
In anticipation of bond issues, §22-23A-9.
Municipal corporations.
Investments in bonds of authority, §22-23A-12.
Negotiable instruments.
Bonds and coupons deemed, §22-23A-16.
Notice of public sale.
Bond issues, §22-23A-8.

WATER SYSTEM ASSISTANCE AUTHORITY—Cont'd
Obligations of authority.
Bonds, notes and certificates exclusively obligations of authority, §22-23A-17.
Powers of authority, §22-23A-6.
President of authority.
Governor, §22-23A-5.
Projects.
Defined, §22-23A-1.
Promissory notes.
Loans in anticipation of bond issues, §22-23A-9.
Purposes of chapter, §22-23A-15.
Recordation.
Application to become corporation, §22-23A-5.
Records.
Proceedings of board of directors, §22-23A-5.
Reports.
Governor to deliver annual report, §22-23A-6.
Resolutions.
Authorizing resolutions.
Defined, §22-23A-1.
Sales.
Bond issues.
Authority, §22-23A-7.
Procedure, §22-23A-8.
Seals and sealed instruments.
Power to have, use or alter corporate seal, §22-23A-6.
Secretary of state.
Application to become corporation.
Filing with, §22-23A-5.
State treasurer.
Investments in bond issues of authority, §22-23A-12.
Tax exemption.
Bonds or other indebtedness of authority, §22-23A-13.
Trusts and trustees.
Investments in bonds of authority, §22-23A-12.
Vice-president of authority.
Director of department, §22-23A-5.
Water assistance legislative oversight committee, §22-23A-3.
Water supply assistance fund.
Established, §22-23A-4.

WEAPONS, §§13A-11-50 to 13A-11-84.
Ammunition.
Brass or steel teflon-coated handgun ammunition, §13A-11-60.
Licenses.
Dealers, §40-12-158.
Nonresidents.
Sale of ammunition to, §13A-11-58.
Purchase in adjoining states, §13A-11-58.
Antique pistols, §13A-11-83.
Apprehension of attack.
Carrying concealed weapons.
Mitigation of punishment, §13A-11-51.

WEAPONS—Cont'd

Armory commission, §§31-4-1
to 31-4-19.
See MILITARY AFFAIRS.
Assault and battery,
§§13A-6-20 to 13A-6-25.
See ASSAULT AND
BATTERY.
Aviation.
Discharging firearm into
aircraft, §13A-11-61.
Bowie knives.
Selling to minor prohibited,
§13A-11-57.
Brass knuckles.
Prohibited, §13A-11-53.
**Brass or steel teflon-coated
handgun ammunition.**
Possession or sale,
§13A-11-60.
Buildings.
Discharging firearm into,
§13A-11-61.
Bullets.
Brass or steel teflon-coated
handgun ammunition.
Possession or sale,
§13A-11-60.
Motor vehicle accidents.
Garages to report bullet
damage, §32-10-10.
Canes.
Carrying rifle or shotgun
walking cane,
§13A-11-54.
**Carrying concealed
weapons.**
Apprehension of attack may
mitigate punishment,
§13A-11-51.
Indictment, §13A-11-55.
Prohibited, §13A-11-50.
**Committing crime when
armed,** §13A-11-71.
Constitution of Alabama.
Right to bear arms, Const.
Ala., art. I, §26.
**Constitution of the United
States.**
Right to bear arms, Const. U.
S., Amendment II.
Stop and frisk law,
§§15-5-30, 15-5-31.
Dealers.
Pistols, §§13A-11-78,
13A-11-79, 40-12-143.
Defense of persons.
Use of deadly physical force
in defense of persons.
When justified, §13A-3-23.
Definitions.
Pistols, §13A-11-70.
**Demonstration in public
places.**
Possession of firearms by
persons at, §13A-11-59.
Drug addicts.
Pistols.
Delivery to addicts,
§13A-11-76.
Possession by addicts,
§13A-11-72.
Drunkards.
Pistols.
Delivery of pistols to
drunkards,
§13A-11-76.
Habitual drunkards
forbidden to possess,
§13A-11-72.

WEAPONS—Cont'd

Evidence.
Committing crime when
armed.
Evidence of intent,
§13A-11-71.
Felonies.
Delivery of pistols to
convicted felons,
§13A-11-76.
Fighting in public places.
Using firearms while
fighting, §13A-11-56.
Firearms.
Aircraft.
Discharging firearm into
aircraft, §13A-11-61.
Buildings.
Discharging firearm into
building, §13A-11-61.
Demonstrations at public
places.
Possession of firearms by
persons at, §13A-11-59.
Fish and game.
Wardens.
Carrying of firearms,
§9-2-65.
Wildlife management
areas.
Carrying or possession of
firearms, §9-11-304.
Licenses.
Pistols, §§13A-11-73 to
13A-11-75, 13A-11-81.
Shotguns, rifles,
ammunition, etc.
Dealers, §40-12-158.
Motor vehicles.
Discharging firearm into
automobile or truck,
§13A-11-61.
Garages to report bullet
damage, §32-10-10.
Peace officers.
Eligibility of honorably
retired law
enforcement officers to
carry handguns,
§36-21-9.
Pistols, §§13A-11-70 to
13A-11-84. See within
this heading, "Pistols."
Purchase in adjoining states,
§13A-11-58.
Railroads.
Discharging firearm into
locomotive or car,
§13A-11-61.
Residents of adjoining states.
Sales to prohibited,
§13A-11-58.
State trooper reserves.
Authority to carry,
§32-2-44.
Theft.
Second degree theft of
property, §13A-8-4.
Use while fighting in public
place, §13A-11-56.
Watercraft.
Discharging firearm into,
§13A-11-61.
Fish and game.
Firearms.
Wardens.
Carrying of firearms,
§9-2-65.

WEAPONS—Cont'd

Fish and game—Cont'd
Firearms—Cont'd
Wildlife management
areas.
Carrying or possession of
firearms, §9-11-304.
Hunting, §§9-11-230 to
9-11-283.
See FISH AND GAME.
Forfeitures.
Seizure of pistols involved in
violations of certain
sections, §13A-11-84.
Frisks.
Stop and frisk law,
§§15-5-30, 15-5-31.
Handguns.
Ammunition.
Brass or steel teflon-coated
handgun ammunition.
Possession or sale,
§13A-11-60.
Peace officers.
Eligibility of honorably
retired law
enforcement officers to
carry handguns,
§36-21-9.
Pistols, §§13A-11-70 to
13A-11-84. See within
this heading, "Pistols."
Highway patrol.
Officers to receive pistol as
part of retirement
benefits, §32-2-26.
Hunting, §§9-11-230 to
9-11-283.
See FISH AND GAME.
Indictments.
Unlawful carrying of
weapons, §13A-11-55.
Unlawful sale of weapons,
§15-8-150.
Unlawful use of weapons,
§15-8-150.
Knives.
Dealer licenses.
Bowie and dirk knives,
§40-12-143.
Licenses.
Bowie and dirk knife dealers,
§40-12-143.
False information in
applications, §13A-11-81.
Pistols, §§13A-11-73 to
13A-11-75, 13A-11-81.
Shotguns, rifles, ammunition,
etc.
Dealers, §40-12-158.
Loans.
Loans secured by pistol,
§13A-11-80.
Marine resources.
Authority to carry firearms,
§9-2-86.
Mentally ill.
Delivery of pistols to persons
of unsound mind,
§13A-11-76.
Military affairs.
Arms and equipment,
§§31-2-23 to 31-2-34.
See MILITARY AFFAIRS.
National guard commanders.
Forbidding sale of
weapons, §31-2-124.
Minors.
Bowie knives.
Selling to minor,
§13A-11-57.

WEAPONS—Cont'd
Minors—Cont'd
Pistols.
Delivery to minors,
§13A-11-76.
Selling to minor,
§13A-11-57.
Motor vehicles.
Discharging firearm into
automobile or truck,
§13A-11-61.
Garages to report bullet
damage, §32-10-10.
Throwing or shooting deadly
or dangerous missile into
occupied vehicle,
§32-5-11.
Municipal corporations.
Closing places for sale of
firearms, §11-51-102.
Ordinances and resolutions.
Subject matter of handguns
reserved to state
legislature, §11-45-1.1.
Revocation of licenses of
places where firearms
kept for sale, §11-51-103.
Riots.
Issuance of proclamation
for forbidding sale of
arms, ammunition,
etc., during riots, etc.,
§11-43-82.
National guard.
Commanders may forbid sale
of weapons, §31-2-124.
Nonresidents.
Sale of firearms or
ammunition to
nonresidents,
§13A-11-58.
Parole officers.
Pistol of officer included in
retirement benefits,
§15-22-24.
Peace officers.
Handguns.
Eligibility to carry upon
retirement, §36-21-9.
Pistols, §§13A-11-70 to
13A-11-84.
Antique pistols, §13A-11-83.
Application for purchase,
§13A-11-77.
Carrying pistols on premises
not one's own,
§13A-11-52.
Committing crime when
armed, §13A-11-71.
Evidence of intent,
§13A-11-71.
Dealers.
Licenses, §§13A-11-78,
13A-11-79, 40-12-143.
Definitions, §13A-11-70.
Drug addicts.
Delivery to, §13A-11-76.
Possession, §13A-11-72.
Drunkards.
Delivery to, §13A-11-76.
Possession by habitual
drunkards,
§13A-11-72.
Firearms generally. See
within this heading,
"Firearms."
Highway patrol.
Officers to receive pistol as
part of retirement
benefits, §32-2-26.

WEAPONS—Cont'd
Pistols—Cont'd
Intent.
Committing crime when
armed, §13A-11-71.
Law enforcement officers.
Eligibility to carry upon
retirement, §36-21-9.
Licenses.
Dealers' licenses,
§§13A-11-78,
13A-11-79, 40-12-143.
Exceptions, §13A-11-74.
False information in
applications,
§13A-11-81.
Generally, §13A-11-75.
Required, §13A-11-73.
Loans secured by pistol
prohibited, §13A-11-80.
Mentally ill.
Delivery to, §13A-11-76.
Minors.
Delivery to, §13A-11-76.
Selling to, §13A-11-57.
Penalties, §13A-11-84.
Possession.
Certain persons forbidden,
§13A-11-72.
Sales, §13A-11-77.
Dealers, §§13A-11-78,
13A-11-79, 40-12-143.
Security.
Loans secured by pistol,
§13A-11-80.
Seizure of pistols involved in
violations, §13A-11-84.
Violent convicts.
Delivery to, §13A-11-76.
Who may carry, §13A-11-52.
Prison contraband.
Promoting, §§13A-10-36 to
13A-10-38.
Railroads.
Discharging firearm into
railroad locomotive or
car, §13A-11-61.
Rifles and shotguns,
§§13A-11-62 to 13A-11-66.
Alteration, etc., of
manufacturer's number
of firearm, §13A-11-64.
Applicability of section,
§13A-11-63.
Carrying rifle or shotgun
walking cane,
§13A-11-54.
Definitions, §13A-11-62.
Division supplemental to
other laws and penalties,
§13A-11-66.
Licenses.
Dealers, §40-12-158.
Penalties, §§13A-11-65,
13A-11-66.
Possession after
indentification altered,
§13A-11-64.
Purchase in adjoining states,
§13A-11-58.
Short-barreled rifles.
Defined, §13A-11-62.
Possession, sale, etc.,
§13A-11-63.
Right to keep and bear
arms, Const. Ala., art. I,
§26.
Robbery, §§13A-8-40 to
13A-8-44.

WEAPONS—Cont'd
Sales.
Dealers, §§13A-11-78,
13A-11-79, 40-12-143.
Pistols, §13A-11-77.
Searches and seizures.
Pistols.
Seizure when involved in
certain violations,
§13A-11-84.
Stop and frisk law,
§§15-5-30, 15-5-31.
Secured transactions.
Loans secured by pistol,
§13A-11-80.
Shotguns. See within this
heading, "Rifles and
shotguns."
Slingshots.
Prohibited, §13A-11-53.
Steel teflon-coated or brass
handgun ammunition.
Possession or sale,
§13A-11-60.
Stop and frisk law, §§15-5-30,
15-5-31.
Sunday.
Shooting weapons on,
§13A-12-1.
Teflon-coated handgun
ammunition.
Possession or sale,
§13A-11-60.
Theft.
Second degree theft of
property, §13A-8-4.

WEEDS.
Jefferson county.
Prohibition of overgrowth,
Const. Ala., amd. 497.
Municipal corporations.
Abatement of weeds.
Class 2 municipalities,
§§11-67-1 to 11-67-9.
See MUNICIPAL
CORPORATIONS.
Class 5 municipalities,
§§11-67-20 to 11-67-28.
See MUNICIPAL
CORPORATIONS.
Requirement of cutting,
§11-47-140.
Seeds.
Elimination of fungi and
noxious weeds from seed,
§§2-26-30 to 2-26-32.

WEIGHTS AND MEASURES,
§§8-16-1 to 8-16-123.
Arrests.
Power of commissioner and
sealers, §8-16-11.
Barrel.
Certain commodities,
§8-16-94.
Board of agriculture and
industries.
Rulemaking power, §8-16-15.
Specifications and tolerances,
§8-16-15.
Standards for containers of
farm products, §§8-16-16
8-16-17.
Bonds, surety.
Local sealers, §8-16-31.
Milk and cream bottles and
containers.
Manufacturers, §8-16-95.
Weighmasters, §8-16-52.
Bridges.
Weight on, §32-9-20.

WEIGHTS AND MEASURES
—Cont'd

Certificate.
Weighmasters.
Weight certificate,
§§8-16-50 to 8-16-59,
8-16-106. See within
this heading,
"Weighmasters."

Charcoal, coal and coke.
General provisions, §§8-16-98
to 8-16-100.
Scales and weighing,
§§25-9-340 to 25-9-345.
See COAL.

Commercial code.
Official certificate as prima
facie evidence, §7-1-202.

**Commercial weighing and
measuring technicians.**
Registration, §§8-16-120 to
8-16-123.

**Commissioner of agriculture
and industries.**
Arrest.
Power of, §8-16-11.
Badge.
Exhibition, §8-16-11.
Duties generally, §8-16-6.
Powers, §8-16-7.
Powers of sheriff, §8-16-11.
Standards.
Duties as to, §8-16-5.

Condemnation.
Nonstandard weights and
measures, §8-16-9.

Congress, Const. U. S., Art. I,
§8.

Constitution of Alabama.
State office for inspection or
measuring of
merchandise,
commodities, etc.,
prohibited, Const. Ala.,
art. IV, §77.

**Constitution of the United
States,** Const. U. S., Art. I,
§8.

Contracts.
Construction according to
standards ascertained by
congress, §8-16-4.

Cornmeal.
Sale in 5 to 200 pound
packages, §8-16-102.
Exceptions, §8-16-102.

Cotton, §§2-19-1, 2-19-19,
2-19-21.

Counties.
Local sealers, §§8-16-30 to
8-16-32.

Definitions, §8-16-1.
Coal, coke or charcoal.
"Ton" defined, §8-16-98.

Eggs and egg products.
Weight classes, §2-12-3.

Evidence.
Altered weight, measure or
device.
Possession prima facie
evidence of guilt,
§8-16-12.
Incorrect, false or unsealed
weight, measure, device,
package or commodity.
Seizure for evidence,
§8-16-10.
Weight certificate.
Prima facie evidence of
weight, §8-16-56.

WEIGHTS AND MEASURES
—Cont'd

False weights and measures.
Deceptive business practices,
§13A-9-41.

Farm products.
Standards for containers,
§§8-16-16, 8-16-17.

Fees.
Commercial weighing and
measuring technicians.
Registration, §8-16-122.
Probate judges' fees,
§12-19-90.
State and federal employees.
Weighing agricultural
commodities, §8-16-71.
Weighmasters.
Appointment fee, §8-16-51.

Fertilizer.
Penalty for manufacture of
commercial fertilizer
short in weight,
§2-22-18.

Flour.
Sale in 5 to 200 pound
packages, §8-16-103.
Exceptions, §8-16-103.

Fraud.
Using false weights or
measures, §13A-9-41.

**Fruits, nuts, vegetables and
grain.**
Sale by avoirdupois weight
or numerical count,
§8-16-101.

Grits.
Sale in 5 to 200 pound
packages, §8-16-102.

Ice.
Sale regulated, §8-16-104.

Liquefied petroleum gas.
Weighing or metering upon
purchase, §8-17-190.

Livestock.
Markets.
Weighing livestock at
markets, §§2-15-90 to
2-15-96.
See LIVESTOCK.

Local sealers.
Appointment, §8-16-30.
Arrest.
Power of, §8-16-11.
Badges.
Exhibition, §8-16-11.
Bond, §8-16-31.
Powers, §8-16-7.
Powers of sheriff, §8-16-11.
Qualifications, §8-16-30.
Records, §8-16-32.
Removal, §8-16-31.
Reports, §8-16-32.
Salary, §8-16-31.
Standards and apparatus.
Keeping by cities and
counties, §8-16-30.
Term of office, §8-16-31.

Marine resources.
Oysters, §§9-12-27, 9-12-61.
Shrimp, §§9-12-27, 9-12-46,
9-12-49.

Meters.
Electric meters, §37-8-6.
Gas meters, §37-8-6.

**Milk and cream bottles and
containers.**
Bond required of
manufacturers, §8-16-95.
Capacities, §8-16-95.

WEIGHTS AND MEASURES
—Cont'd

**Milk and cream bottles and
containers**—Cont'd
Local sealers.
Duties, §8-16-97.
Markings, §8-16-95.
Penalty for selling or using
noncomplying containers,
§8-16-96.

Motor vehicles.
Size and weight of vehicles,
§§32-9-20 to 32-9-32.
See MOTOR VEHICLES.

Municipal corporations.
Inspections, §11-47-17.
Charges for, §11-43-59.
Local sealers, §§8-16-30 to
8-16-32.
Provision of public scales,
§11-47-17.
Weighing machines.
License tax, §11-51-98.

Net weight.
Basis for sales by weight,
§8-16-91.

Oaths.
Weighmasters, §8-16-50.

Oil.
Sale at retail regulated,
§8-16-105.

Oysters, §§9-12-27, 9-12-61.

Packages.
Net quantities of contents to
be marked on outside,
§8-16-93.

Penalties.
Milk and cream bottles and
containers.
Selling or using
noncomplying
containers, §8-16-96.
Violations of chapter,
§8-16-18.

Presumptions.
Existence of weights,
measures or devices in
place of sale, §8-16-13.

Prohibited acts, §8-16-90.
Operating weighing or
measuring device other
than as intended,
§8-16-107.
Requesting false or incorrect
weighing or certificate,
§8-16-106.

Records.
Local sealers, §8-16-32.

Registration.
Commercial weighing and
measuring technicians,
§§8-16-120 to 8-16-123.

Repair.
Nonstandard weights and
measures, §8-16-9.

Reports.
Local sealers, §8-16-32.

Rules and regulations.
Adoption, §8-16-15.
Commercial weighing and
measuring technicians.
Registration, §8-16-121.
State and federal employees.
Weighing agricultural
commodities, §8-16-72.

Salaries.
Local sealers, §8-16-31.

Sealers.
Local sealers, §§8-16-30 to
8-16-32.

WEIGHTS AND MEASURES
—Cont'd
**Seals and sealed
instruments.**
Weighmasters, §8-16-54.
Searches and seizures.
Incorrect, false or unsealed
weight, measure, device,
package or commodity.
Seizure for evidence,
§8-16-10.
Sheriffs.
Powers conferred upon
commissioner and
sealers, §8-16-11.
Shrimp, §§9-12-27, 9-12-46,
9-12-49.
Specifications.
Prescription, §8-16-15.
Standards.
Containers of farm products.
Establishment, §8-16-16.
Federal standards.
Adoption, §8-16-17.
Requirements, §8-16-2.
Sealing or marking of
weights or measures
corresponding with
standards, §8-16-8.
State standards.
Custody, §8-16-5.
Standards approved by
congress, §8-16-3.
State and federal employees.
Appointment, §8-16-70.
Fees and charges.
Weighing agricultural
commodities, §8-16-71.
Disposition of collected
amounts, §8-16-71.
Rules and regulations.
Weighing agricultural
commodities, §8-16-72.
**State office for inspection or
measuring of
merchandise,
commodities, etc.,
prohibited,** Const. Ala.,
art. IV, §77.
Tolerances.
Prescription, §8-16-15.
Transportation companies.
False weighing.
Penalty, §37-2-16.
Passengers.
Personal baggage of
passengers, §§37-2-35,
37-2-38.
Weighmasters, §§8-16-50 to
8-16-59.
Appointment, §§8-16-50,
8-16-51.
Bond, §8-16-52.
Certificate of appointment,
§8-16-50.
Sheriffs.
Compensation.
Not to be paid by state,
§8-16-53.
Duties, §8-16-53.
Oath, §8-16-50.
Records, §8-16-55.
Reweighing of certified
commodity, produce or
article, §8-16-58.
Rights, §8-16-53.
Seal, §8-16-54.
Weight certificate.
Accurate weight, §8-16-57.
False certificates, §8-16-59.
Form, §8-16-56.

WEIGHTS AND MEASURES
—Cont'd
Weighmasters—Cont'd
Weight certificate—Cont'd
Prima facie evidence of
weight, §8-16-56.
Requesting false or
incorrect certificate,
§8-16-106.
Unauthorized issuance,
§8-16-106.

WELDING.
Education.
Eye protective devices for
pupils and teachers
participating in certain
courses, §16-1-7.

WELFARE, §§38-1-1 to
38-11-12.
Actions.
Civil actions against certain
persons, §38-1-5.
Adoption.
Child-placing agencies,
§§38-7-1 to 38-7-17. See
within this heading,
"Child care facilities."
Nonresident child.
Conditions precedent to
bringing child into
state, §38-7-15.
Subsidized adoption,
§§26-10-20 to 26-10-30.
See ADOPTION.
Adult protective services,
§§38-9-1 to 38-9-11.
See ADULT PROTECTIVE
SERVICES.
Advertisements.
Child care facilities,
§38-7-12.
Penalties, §38-7-16.
Aged persons.
Commission on the aging,
§§38-3-1 to 38-3-6.
See AGED PERSONS.
Medical assistance, §§38-6-1
to 38-6-9.
See AGED PERSONS.
Programs of assistance.
State and local government
participation, §38-1-6.
Aid to dependent children,
§38-4-1.
Appeals.
Actions of state department.
Final and binding, §38-4-5.
Child care facilities.
Revocation or refusal to
renew license, §38-7-9.
§38-4-5.
Fair hearing, §38-4-5.
Hearings.
Notice, §38-4-5.
Party at interest.
Right to appear, §38-4-5.
Reduction or cancellation of
assistance grants,
§38-4-4.
Right of appeal, §38-4-5.
Witnesses, §38-4-6.
Applications for assistance.
Contents, §38-4-2.
Denial.
Appeals, §§38-4-5, 38-4-6.
Incapacitated applicants.
Hospitalization, §38-4-9.
Investigations, §38-4-2.
Made to county department,
§38-4-2.

WELFARE—Cont'd
Applications for assistance
—Cont'd
Notice of action taken,
§38-4-2.
Records, §38-4-2.
Review, §38-2-10.
Appropriations.
Child care facilities,
§38-7-18.
Confederate veterans.
Old age pension purposes,
§38-4-12.
Counties, §38-2-9.
Municipalities, §38-2-9.
Attorney general.
Child care facilities.
Operating without license.
Report for prosecution,
§38-7-10.
Attorneys at law.
Department of human
resources.
Legal counsel for
department, §38-2-4.
Award of assistance.
Review.
Amounts of awards or
modifications of
awards, §38-2-10.
Awards and findings of
county department.
Review by county board,
§38-4-10.
Disallowances, §38-2-10.
Blind persons.
Assistance to needy blind
persons, §§38-5-1 to
38-5-7.
See BLIND PERSONS.
Board of human resources,
§38-2-2.
County boards, §38-2-7.
Department of human
resources. See within
this heading,
"Department of human
resources."
Bonds, surety.
Commodity distributor,
§38-2-13.
Department of human
resources.
Officers, §38-2-13.
Budgets.
Department of human
resources, §38-2-3.
Burden of proof.
Child care facilities.
Relationship to child,
§38-7-16.
Child abuse or neglect.
See MINORS.
Child care facilities, §§38-7-1
to 38-7-17.
Adoption.
Nonresident child.
Conditions precedent to
bringing child into
state, §38-7-15.
Advertisements.
Penalties, §38-7-16.
Right to advertise,
§38-7-12.
Aid to dependent children.
Eligibility, §38-4-1.
Appropriations, §38-7-18.
Boarding homes.
Defined, §38-7-2.
Licenses.
Renewal, §38-7-6.

WELFARE—Cont'd
Child care facilities—Cont'd
Burden of proof.
Relationship to child,
§38-7-16.
Child.
Defined, §38-7-2.
Child abuse or neglect.
Mandatory reporting,
§26-14-3.
Child care institutions.
Defined, §38-7-2.
Child placing agencies.
Defined, §38-7-2.
Church schools, §38-7-3.
Citation of chapter, §38-7-1.
Day care centers.
Defined, §38-7-2.
Day care homes.
Defined, §38-7-2.
Group day care homes.
Defined, §38-7-2.
Definitions, §38-7-2.
Department of human
resources.
Defined, §38-7-2.
Inspection of facilities,
§38-7-11.
Minimum standards for
licensing.
Establishment, §38-7-7.
Diseases.
Notifiable diseases.
General provisions,
§§22-11A-1 to
22-11A-38.
See DISEASES.
Persons responsible for
reporting, §22-11A-2.
District attorney.
Duty to enforce chapter or
prosecute violations,
§38-7-17.
Education.
State board of education.
Supervision of
educational work of
special institutions,
§16-3-20.
Enforcement of chapter,
§38-7-17.
Facility for child care.
Defined, §38-7-2.
Forms.
Affidavit for church school,
§38-7-3.
Foster family homes.
Defined, §38-7-2.
Interstate compact on child
placement, §§44-2-20
to 44-2-26.
See MINORS.
Licenses.
Applications, §38-7-4.
Free homes.
Defined, §38-7-2.
Group day care homes.
Defined, §38-7-2.
Group homes.
Defined, §38-7-2.
Group day care homes.
Defined, §38-7-2.
Inspections.
Defects.
Reports, §38-7-11.
Department of human
resources, §38-2-6.
Right to inspect, §38-7-11.
Scope of, §38-7-11.
Institution for child care.
Defined, §38-7-2.

WELFARE—Cont'd
Child care facilities—Cont'd
Investigations.
Licenses.
Issuance, §38-7-4.
Operating without
license, §38-7-10.
Renewal, §38-7-6.
Licenses, §§38-7-3 to 38-7-10.
Appeals.
Revocation or refusal to
renew, §38-7-9.
Applications, §38-7-4.
Foster family homes,
§38-7-4.
Renewal, §38-7-6.
Children in need of special
treatment, §38-7-7.
Department of human
resources.
Authority, §38-2-6.
Form, §38-7-5.
Investigations generally,
§38-7-4.
Issuance, §§38-7-4, 38-7-5.
Minimum standards for
licensing.
Establishment, §38-7-7.
Operating without license.
Investigations, §38-7-10.
Penalties, §38-7-16.
Report to attorney
general, §38-7-10.
Renewal, §38-7-6.
Boarding homes, §38-7-6.
Refusal to renew.
Grounds, §38-7-8.
Hearing, §38-7-9.
Review of final
decision, §38-7-9.
Required, §38-7-3.
Exception as to religious
organizations,
§38-7-3.
Revocation.
Grounds, §38-7-8.
Defects discovered
during inspection,
§38-7-11.
Hearings, §38-7-9.
Review of final decision,
§38-7-9.
Section not applicable to
boarding homes and
free homes, §38-7-9.
Standards.
Establishment of
minimum standards,
§38-7-7.
Temporary permits,
§38-7-5.
Term, §38-7-5.
Mandatory state subsidized
child day-care services
program, §38-7-18.
Maternity centers.
Defined, §38-7-2.
Minimum standards for
licensing, §38-7-7.
Night care facilities.
Defined, §38-7-2.
Nonresident child.
Conditions precedent to
bringing into state for
placement, §38-7-15.
Penalties, §38-7-16.
Permits.
Temporary permits,
§38-7-5.

WELFARE—Cont'd
Child care facilities—Cont'd
Placement of children.
Interstate compact on child
placement, §§44-2-20
to 44-2-26.
See MINORS.
Records.
Disclosure of information,
§38-7-13.
Failure to maintain.
Penalties, §38-7-16.
Maintenance, §38-7-13.
Use, §38-7-13.
Related.
Defined, §38-7-2.
Reports.
Child abuse and neglect,
§26-14-3.
Failure to make.
Penalty, §38-7-16.
When acquired, §38-7-14.
Short title of chapter,
§38-7-1.
Subsidized child day-care
services.
Mandatory state program,
§38-7-18.
Child support, §§38-10-1 to
38-10-33.
See CHILD SUPPORT
PROGRAMS.
Commissioner. See within
this heading, "Department
of human resources."
Commission on the aging,
See AGED PERSONS.
Confederate veterans.
Appropriations.
Old age pension purposes,
§38-4-12.
Widows.
Old age assistance,
§38-4-11.
Congress.
Power to provide for general
welfare, Const. U. S.,
Art. I, §8.
**Constitution of the United
States.**
General welfare.
Powers of congress, Const.
U. S., Art. I, §8.
Counties.
Aged persons.
Programs of assistance.
Participation, §38-1-6.
Allocation of funds.
Department of pensions
and security, §38-2-5.
Appropriations, §38-2-9.
Boards of human resources,
§38-2-7.
County commissions.
Powers and duties,
§11-3-11.
Departments of human
resources. See within
this heading, "County
departments of human
resources."
Relief and support of poor
persons by counties,
§§38-8-1 to 38-8-3.
**County boards of human
resources,** §38-2-7.
Reports.
Filing names of recipients
of public assistance
with probate judge,
§38-1-4.

WELFARE—Cont'd
County boards of human resources—Cont'd
Review of awards, §38-4-10.
County departments of human resources.
Agents.
State department of human resources, §38-2-6.
Awards.
Review by county board, §38-4-10.
Composition, §38-2-8.
Creation, §38-2-8.
Directors, §§38-2-7, 38-2-8.
Expenditures.
Approval by state department, §38-2-9.
Findings.
Review by county board, §38-4-10.
Hospitalization.
Incapacitated applicants and recipients of old age pensions, §38-4-9.
Merit system.
Personnel, §38-2-9.
Oaths.
Witnesses, §38-4-6.
Pensions for widows of Confederate veterans, §§31-8-1 to 31-8-33.
See VETERANS.
Personnel.
Appointment, §38-2-8.
Reports.
Duty to furnish state department, §38-2-9.
Subpoenas.
Witnesses, §38-4-6.
Day care centers, §§38-7-3 to 38-7-10.
Death.
Payments of assistance.
After death, §38-4-3.
Definitions, §38-1-1.
Child care facilities, §38-7-2.
Department of human resources.
Adoption, §§26-10-20 to 26-10-30.
See ADOPTION.
Aged persons.
Medical assistance to elderly persons, §§38-6-1 to 38-6-9.
See AGED PERSONS.
Attorneys at law.
Legal counsel for department, §38-2-4.
Awards of public assistance.
Authority of department, §38-2-10.
Board of human resources.
County boards, §38-2-7.
Generally, §38-2-2.
Bonds, surety.
Officers, §38-2-13.
Budget, §38-2-3.
Bureaus, §38-2-3.
Commissioner.
Appointment, §38-2-3.
Bonds, surety, §38-2-13.
Chief executive officer of department, §38-2-3.
Defined, §38-1-1.
Interstate compact on child placement, §§44-2-20 to 44-2-26.
See MINORS.
Powers and duties, §38-2-3.

WELFARE—Cont'd
Department of human resources—Cont'd
Commissioner—Cont'd
Qualifications, §38-2-3.
Records.
Destruction, §38-2-12.
Commodity distributor.
Bonds, surety, §38-2-13.
Composition, §38-2-1.
Corrections.
Board of corrections.
Cooperation with state board of corrections, §38-2-6.
Duty to cooperate with state department, §14-1-8.
County departments of human resources, §38-2-7.
Creation, §38-2-1.
Duties generally, §38-2-6.
Executive officer.
Commissioner, §38-2-3.
Expenditures by county departments.
Approval, §38-2-9.
Food stamp program, §38-2-6.
Funds.
Allocation, §38-2-5.
Gifts.
Authority to receive, §38-2-6.
Inspections, §38-2-6.
Interstate compact on child placement, §§44-2-20 to 44-2-26.
See MINORS.
Juvenile courts.
Advising judges and officers, §38-2-6.
Oaths.
Witnesses, §38-4-6.
Office of state parent locator, §38-2-6.1.
Pensions for widows of Confederate veterans, §§31-8-1 to 31-8-33.
See VETERANS.
Personnel.
Appointment, §38-2-3.
Bonds, surety, §38-2-13.
Powers generally, §38-2-6.
Records.
Destruction, §38-2-12.
Photographic reproductions, §38-2-11.
Reports.
Annual report, §38-2-3.
Responsibilities generally, §38-2-6.
Rules and regulations, §38-2-6.
Adoption, §38-2-3.
Standards of assistance.
Development, §38-2-10.
State parent locator, §38-2-6.1.
Subpoenas, §38-4-6.
District attorneys.
Child care facilities.
Duty to enforce chapter or prosecute violations, §38-7-17.
Eligibility for public assistance, §38-4-1.
Confederate veterans.
Widows, §38-4-11.
Determination, §38-4-2.

WELFARE—Cont'd
Eligibility for public assistance—Cont'd
Reduction, cancellation or continuance of assistance, §38-4-4.
Employment program.
Administration, §38-11A-2.
Application for public assistance, §38-11A-4.
Establishment, §38-11A-2.
Exemption options, §38-11A-4.
Funding, §38-11A-3.
Legislative intent, §38-11A-1.
Evidence.
Photographic reproductions, §38-2-11.
Expenditures.
Approval by state department of human resources, §38-2-9.
Federal government.
Agent.
Department of human resources, §38-2-6.
Allocation of funds.
Department of human resources, §38-2-5.
Food stamp program.
Department of human resources responsibility, §38-2-6.
Funds.
Allocation, §38-2-5.
Appropriations.
County municipalities, §38-2-9.
Expenditures.
Approval by state department of human resources, §38-2-9.
State public welfare trust fund, §38-4-13.
Garnishment.
Exemption of assistance grants, §38-4-8.
Gifts.
Department of human resources.
Authority to receive, §38-2-6.
Grand jury investigations.
Recipients of public assistance, §38-2-6.
Grants.
Payments of assistance grants, §§38-4-2 to 38-4-4, 38-4-8.
Group homes, §§38-7-1 to 38-7-17. See within this heading, "Child care facilities."
Guardian and ward.
Handling public assistance payments of incompetents, §38-1-3.
Hearings.
Child care facilities.
Revocation or refusal to renew license, §38-7-9.
Hospitals.
Hospitalization of incapacitated applicants and recipients, §38-4-9.
Human relations resources board, §§38-11-1 to 38-11-12.
Inspections.
Child care facilities, §38-7-11.

WELFARE—Cont'd
Inspections—Cont'd
Department of human
resources.
Powers and duties, §38-2-6.
Reports.
Names of recipients of
public assistance,
§38-1-4.
Investigations.
Application for assistance,
§38-4-2.
Child care facilities.
Licenses.
Issuance, §38-7-4.
Operating without
license, §38-7-10.
Renewal, §38-7-6.
Grand jury.
Recipients of public
assistance, §38-2-6.
Reduction or cancellation of
assistance grants,
§38-4-4.
Juvenile courts.
Department of human
resources.
Advising judges and
officers, §38-2-6.
Licenses.
Child care facilities, §§38-7-3
to 38-7-10. See within
this heading, "Child care
facilities."
Limitation of actions.
Persons owning property and
supported at public
charge.
Civil actions against,
§38-1-5.
**Medical assistance to elderly
persons,** §§38-6-1 to
38-6-9.
See AGED PERSONS.
Minors.
Aid to dependent children.
Eligibility, §38-4-1.
Child care facilities, §§38-7-1
to 38-7-17.
Municipal corporations.
Appropriations, §38-2-9.
Assistance to aged persons.
Authority to participate in
programs, §38-1-6.
Names.
Recipients of public
assistance.
Filing names with probate
judge, §38-1-4.
Nonresidents.
Child care facilities.
Conditions precedent to
bringing child into
state for purposes of
placement, §38-7-15.
Notice.
Appeals, §38-4-5.
Application for assistance.
Action taken, §38-4-2.
Oaths.
Witnesses, §38-4-6.
**Office of state parent
locator,** §38-2-6.1.
Old age.
Commission on the aging,
§§38-3-1 to 38-3-6.
See AGED PERSONS.
Medical assistance, §§38-6-1
to 38-6-9.
See AGED PERSONS.

WELFARE—Cont'd
Old age—Cont'd
Programs of assistance.
State and local government
participation. §38-1-6.
Payments of assistance.
Amount of assistance.
Appeals, §§38-4-4 to 38-4-6.
Determination, §38-4-2.
Bankruptcy.
Not to pass to trustee,
§38-4-8.
Cancellation, §38-4-4.
Death.
Payments after death.
Endorsement of checks,
§38-4-3.
Eligibility, §38-4-1.
Exemptions.
Taxes, levy, etc., §38-4-8.
Garnishments.
Exemptions, §38-4-8.
Guardian of incompetent,
§38-1-3.
Legal representatives of
incompetents, §38-1-3.
Levy.
Exemptions, §38-4-8.
Persons owning property and
supported at public
charge.
Civil actions against,
§38-1-5.
Process.
Exemptions, §38-4-8.
Reduction.
Recipients becoming
possessed of income or
resources, §38-4-4.
Reports.
Recipients of public
assistance, §38-1-4.
Review of awards.
County boards of human
resources, §38-4-10.
Taxation.
Exemptions, §38-4-8.
Penalties.
Child care facilities,
§38-7-16.
Recipients of public
assistance.
Disclosure of names,
§38-1-4.
Permits.
Child care facilities.
Temporary permits,
§38-7-5.
Prisons and prisoners.
Department of human
resources.
Board of corrections.
Cooperation with state
board of corrections,
§38-2-6.
Probate courts.
County boards of human
resources.
Filing names of recipients
of public assistance
with probate judge,
§38-1-4.
Guardian and ward.
Handling payments to
incompetents, §38-1-3.
Property.
Persons owning property and
supported at public
charge.
Civil actions against,
§38-1-5.

WELFARE—Cont'd
Property—Cont'd
Reduction, cancellation or
continuance of assistance
grants.
Recipients becoming
possessed of income or
resources, §38-4-4.
**Recipients of public
assistance.**
Eligibility, §38-4-1.
Grand jury investigations.
Submission of lists of
recipients, §38-2-6.
Hospitalization.
Old age pensions, §38-4-9.
Names.
Filing with probate judge,
§38-1-4.
Unlawful disclosure or use
of names, §38-1-4.
Payments of assistance,
§§38-4-2 to 38-4-4,
38-4-8.
Persons owning property and
supported at public
charge.
Civil actions against
certain persons,
§38-1-5.
Records.
Application for assistance,
§38-4-2.
Case record material.
Confidentiality, §38-2-6.
Defined, §38-1-1.
Child care facilities,
§38-7-13.
Destruction, §38-2-12.
Photographic
reproductions.
Destruction of originals,
§38-2-11.
Evidence.
Persons owning property
and supported at
public charge.
Prima facie evidence of
indebtedness,
§38-1-5.
Photographic reproductions,
§38-2-11.
Reports.
Child care facilities,
§§38-7-14, 38-7-16 to
38-7-18.
County boards of human
resources.
Authority to require from
county departments,
§38-4-10.
County departments of
human resources.
Duty to furnish state
department, §38-2-8.
Department of human
resources.
Annual report, §38-2-3.
Reports to social security
administration,
§38-2-10.
Recipients of public
assistance.
Conflicts with social
security act, §38-1-4.
Filing names with probate
judge, §38-1-4.
Inspection of reports,
§38-1-4.
Unlawful disclosure or use
of names, §38-1-4.

WELFARE—Cont'd
Rules and regulations.
Department of human
resources, §§38-2-3,
38-2-6.
Salaries.
Board of human resources,
§38-2-2.
County boards of human
resources, §38-2-7.
Social security act.
Filing names of recipients of
public assistance with
probate judge.
Conflict with social
security act, §38-1-4.
**Social security
administration.**
Department of human
resources.
Reports to security
administration,
§38-2-10.
Standards of assistance.
Development by department
of human resources,
§38-2-10.
**State board of human
resources,** §38-2-2.
**State department of human
resources.** See within this
heading, "Department of
human resources."
State parent locator,
§38-2-6.1.
**State public welfare trust
fund,** §38-4-13.
Subpoenas, §38-4-6.
Subsidized adoption,
§§26-10-20 to 26-10-30.
See ADOPTION.
Taxation.
Exemption of payments,
§38-4-8.
Trusts and trustees.
State public welfare trust
fund, §38-4-13.
Veterans.
Confederate veterans.
Old age assistance to
widows, §§38-4-11,
38-4-12.
**Warrants for the payment of
money.**
State public welfare trust
fund.
Disbursements, §38-4-13.
Witnesses, §38-4-6.

WELLS.
Abandoned wells.
Creating hazards,
§13A-11-220.
Drillers.
Water wells, §§22-24-1 to
22-24-12.
See WATER SUPPLY
AND WATERWORKS.
Municipal corporations.
Construction, regulation, etc.,
of water wells,
§11-47-140.
Oil and gas.
Conservation and regulation
of production, §§9-17-1 to
9-17-33.
See OIL AND GAS.
Privilege tax on production,
§§40-20-1 to 40-20-13.
See OIL AND GAS.

WELLS—Cont'd
Taxation.
Exemption of artesian wells
leased to municipalities,
§40-9-8.
Water wells, §§22-24-1 to
22-24-12.
See WATER SUPPLY AND
WATERWORKS.

**WENONAH STATE JUNIOR
COLLEGE.**
**Wenonah state technical
junior college designated
as,** §16-60-3.

**WENONAH STATE
TECHNICAL SCHOOL.**
**Wenonah state technical
trade school designated
as,** §16-60-3.

WET COUNTIES, §§28-3-1 to
28-3-286.
See ALCOHOLIC
BEVERAGES.

WHALES.
Marine mammal protection.
General provisions,
§§9-11-390 to 9-11-398.
See MARINE MAMMAL
PROTECTION.

WHARVES.
Bond issues.
Public improvement bonds,
§§11-81-140 to 11-81-150.
See COUNTIES.
Booms and bulkheads.
See BOOMS AND
BULKHEADS.
General provisions.
See HARBORS AND PORTS.
Inland waterways.
Development of docks and
other facilities along
inland waterways,
§§33-2-1 to 33-2-213.
See WATERS AND
WATERCOURSES.
Municipal corporations.
Operation of wharves,
§11-47-15.
Riparian owners, §§33-7-50 to
33-7-54.
**Transportation companies
generally.**
See TRANSPORTATION
COMPANIES.

WHEAT, §§2-20-1 to 2-20-6.
See GRAIN.

WHITE CANES.
**Annual proclamation of
white cane safety day,**
§21-7-10.
**Crossing streets with white
canes,** §32-5A-220.

**WHITE HOUSE OF THE
CONFEDERACY.**
Designation as memorial,
§41-12-1.
Maintenance of building.
Department of finance to
maintain, §41-12-2.
Expenses, §41-12-2.
Management of building.
Association to manage
building, §41-12-3.
**Purposes for which
memorial may be used,**
§41-12-1.

**WHOLESALE MERCHANTS
ASSOCIATIONS.**
Incorporation, §10-4-280.

WHOOPING COUGH.
Notifiable diseases,
§§22-11A-1 to 22-11A-38.
See DISEASES.

WIDOWS.
Debts.
Exemptions from
administration and
payment of debts,
§§6-10-60 to 6-10-107.
See EXEMPTIONS FROM
ADMINISTRATION
AND PAYMENT OF
DEBTS.
Dower, §§35-4-190 to 35-4-192.
**Executors and
administrators.**
Compelling payment of
legacies.
Applicability to dissenting
widow, §43-2-586.
**Exemptions from
administration and
payment of debts,**
§§6-10-60 to 6-10-107.
See EXEMPTIONS FROM
ADMINISTRATION
AND PAYMENT OF
DEBTS.
Governors' widows.
Pension, §36-13-12.
Veterans.
Educational benefits,
§§31-6-5, 31-6-6, 31-6-9.
Pensions for widows of
Confederate veterans,
§§31-8-1 to 31-8-33.
See VETERANS.
Wages.
Debt for wages owed to
intestate former
employee.
Discharge by payment to
surviving spouse,
§43-8-115.
Wills.
Notice to surviving spouse of
probate of will,
§§43-8-164 to 43-8-166.

WILCOX COUNTY.
Court costs and charges,
Const. Ala., amd. 434.
Probate judge.
Compensation, Const. Ala.,
amd. 487.
Taxation.
Additional ad valorem tax,
Const. Ala., amd. 461.

WILDLIFE.
Counties.
Acquisition of lands for
public purposes.
Use of land for betterment
of wildlife, §11-18-2.
General provisions, §§9-11-1
to 9-11-457.
See FISH AND GAME.

**WILDLIFE MANAGEMENT
AREAS.**
General provisions,
§§9-11-300 to 9-11-307.
See FISH AND GAME.

WILDLIFE PARKS.
  Possession of wildlife for
    public exhibition
    purposes, §§9-11-320 to
    9-11-328.
    See FISH AND GAME.

WILLS, §§43-2-1 to 43-8-298.
  Accounts and accounting.
    Exemption of executor from
      filing inventory or
      making report or final
      settlement, §43-2-311.
  Acknowledgments.
    Conveyances generally,
      §§35-4-23 to 35-4-29.
    See CONVEYANCES.
  Actions.
    Legatees.
      Recovery of legacy,
        §43-2-138.
  Ademption.
    Satisfaction, §43-8-231.
  Administrators generally.
    See EXECUTORS AND
      ADMINISTRATORS.
  After-acquired property.
    Construction of wills to pass,
      §43-8-223.
  Age.
    Who may make will,
      §43-8-130.
  Aliens.
    Intestate succession,
      §43-8-56.
    Probate of foreign will,
      §43-8-175.
  Annulment.
    Revocation by annulment,
      §43-8-137.
  Anti-lapse provisions,
    §43-8-224.
  Bequests.
    Anti-lapse statute, §43-8-224.
    Bequest to trustee of existing
      trust, §43-8-140.
    Death of devisee before
      testator, §43-8-224.
  Bona fide purchase.
    Effect on will, §43-8-253.
  Burning, §43-8-136.
  Cancelling, §43-8-136.
  Capacity to convey lands by
    will, §35-4-1.
  Cemeteries.
    Charitable trusts, §§11-17-13
      to 11-17-16.
  Children.
    Generally. See within this
      heading, "Minors."
  Circuit courts.
    Contesting validity after
      admission to probate,
      §§43-8-190 to 43-8-202.
  Codicils.
    Inclusion of term "codicil"
      within term "will,"
      §43-8-1.
    Revocation by writing or by
      act, §43-8-136.
  Condominiums.
    Devise includes undivided
      interest in common and
      limited common
      elements, §35-8-6.
  Constitution of Alabama.
    Giving effect to invalid will.
      Special, private or local
        laws prohibited, Const.
        Ala., art. IV, §104.

WILLS—Cont'd
  Constitution of Alabama
    —Cont'd
    Probate courts.
      Power to grant letters
        testamentary, Const.
        Ala., amd. 364.
  Construction.
    Anti-lapse provision,
      §43-8-224.
    Choice of law as to meaning
      and effect of wills,
      §43-8-221.
    Devise construed to convey
      all of estate, §43-8-223.
    Devisee required to survive
      testator by five days,
      §43-8-220.
    Failure of testimentary
      provisions, §43-8-225.
    Generic terms, §43-8-230.
    Intention of testator.
      Controlling effect,
        §43-8-222.
    Passing of all property,
      including after-acquired
      property, §43-8-223.
  Contesting validity,
    §§43-8-190 to 43-8-202.
    After admission to probate.
      Generally, §43-8-199.
      Judgment.
        Conclusiveness,
          §43-8-200.
      Jury trial, §43-8-202.
      Parties, §43-8-200.
      Time for contest,
        §43-8-199.
        Additional time for
          infants and persons
          of unsound mind,
          §43-8-201.
      Witnesses.
        Consideration of
          witnesses' testimony,
          §43-8-202.
    Appeals from probate court,
      §§12-22-20 to 12-22-27.
      See PROBATE COURTS.
    Before probate.
      Admission of will to
        probate, §43-8-195.
      Appeal from judgment of
        circuit court,
        §43-8-198.
      Certification of judgment
        to probate court,
        §43-8-198.
      Circuit courts.
        Appeal from judgment of
          circuit court,
          §43-8-198.
        Certification of judgment
          to probate court,
          §43-8-198.
        Transfer of contest to
          circuit court,
          §43-8-198.
      Continuance, §43-8-191.
      Costs, §43-8-196.
        Change of venue,
          §43-8-197.
      Depositions, §43-8-194.
      Filing objections,
        §43-8-190.
      Jury trial,
        Drawing of jurors,
          §43-8-192.
        Penalty for default by
          jurors, §43-8-192.

WILLS—Cont'd
  Contesting validity—Cont'd
    Before probate—Cont'd
      Jury trial—Cont'd
        Summoning of jurors,
          §§43-8-190, 43-8-192.
        Procedural rules,
          §43-8-194.
        Rejection of will, §43-8-195.
        Summoning witnesses,
          §43-8-191.
        Time for trial, §43-8-191.
        Transfer of contest to
          circuit court,
          §43-8-198.
        Venue.
          Change of venue,
            §43-8-197.
        Who may contest will,
          §43-8-190.
        Witnesses.
          Depositions of witnesses,
           §43-8-194.
          Proceedings against
           defaulting witness,
           §43-8-193.
          Summoning witnesses,
           §43-8-191.
      Making up issue, §43-8-190.
  Contracts, §43-8-250.
  Conveyances generally,
    §§35-4-1 to 35-4-412.
    See CONVEYANCES.
  Costs.
    Contesting validity of wills,
      §43-8-196.
    Change of venue,
      §43-8-197.
  Curtesy.
    Abolished, §43-8-57.
  Custody.
    Duty of custodian after death
      of testator, §43-8-250.
    Production of will, §43-8-270.
  Cy pres act, §35-4-251.
  Debtors.
    Appointment as executor,
      §43-8-254.
    Intestate succession.
      Debts owed decedent.
        Against whom charged,
          §43-8-55.
  Declaratory judgments.
    Questions of construction or
      validity, §6-6-223.
  Definitions.
    Codicils.
      Inclusion of term "codicil"
        within term "will,"
        §43-8-1.
    Probate code, §43-8-1.
  Delivery, §43-8-270.
  Depositions.
    Witnesses, §43-8-168.
    Contesting validity of
      wills, §43-8-194.
  Destruction, §43-8-136.
  Devises and devisees.
    Anti-lapse statute, §43-8-224.
    Death of devisee before
      testator.
      Effect, §43-8-224.
    Failure of devise.
      Effect, §43-8-225.
    Securities.
      Specific devise, §43-8-226.
    Specific devises.
      Exoneration, §43-8-228.
      Nonademption, §43-8-227.
      Securities, §43-8-226.
      Nonexoneration, §43-8-228.

WILLS—Cont'd
  Devises and devisees—Cont'd
    Specific devises—Cont'd
      Sale by guardian or
        curator, §43-8-227.
      Trustee of existing trust.
        Devise to, §43-8-140.
  **Disclaimer of property
    interests.**
    General provisions,
      §§43-8-290 to 43-8-298.
    See DISCLAIMER OF
      INTERESTS IN
      PROPERTY.
    Renunciation of succession,
      §43-8-251.
  Divorce.
    Effect, §43-8-252.
    Revocation of will, §43-8-137.
  Dower.
    Abolished, §43-8-57.
  **Elective share of surviving
    spouse.**
    Abatement of shares of
      distributees, §43-8-76.
    Amount, §43-8-70.
      Order of court, §43-8-73.
    Apportionment of others'
      liability for balance of
      elective share, §43-8-75.
    Benefits regardless of
      election, §43-8-74.
    Election by guardian,
      §43-8-71.
    Homestead exemption.
      Entitlement regardless of
        election, §43-8-74.
    Nonresident decedent,
      §43-8-70.
    Notice, §43-8-73.
    Petition, §43-8-73.
    Procedure, §43-8-73.
    Right to elective share,
      §43-8-70.
    Satisfaction, §43-8-75.
    Time limitation, §43-8-73.
    Waiver, §43-8-72.
    What property applied first,
      §43-8-75.
    Withdrawal of demand,
      §43-8-73.
  Evidence.
    Admission of will, §43-8-171.
    Probate code.
      Death or status, §43-8-6.
      Rules of evidence, §43-8-6.
    Wills executed by persons
      without the state.
      Appointment of
        commissioners in other
        states and territories
        to take, §36-1-1.
  Execution.
    Choice of law as to validity,
      §43-8-135.
    Incorporation of writings by
      reference, §43-8-139.
    Minors.
      Who may make a will,
        §43-8-130.
    Reference to events of
      independent significance,
      §43-8-141.
    Self-proving wills, §43-8-132.
      Making attested will self-
        proved, §43-8-133.
    Signature, §43-8-131.
    Who may make a will,
      §43-8-130.

WILLS—Cont'd
  Execution—Cont'd
    Witnesses.
      Contesting validity of
        wills, §§43-8-190 to
        43-8-202. See within
        this heading,
        "Contesting validity."
      Conveyances generally,
        §§35-4-1 to 35-4-412.
      See CONVEYANCES.
      Generally, §§43-8-167 to
        43-8-169.
  **Executors and
    administrators generally.**
    See EXECUTORS AND
      ADMINISTRATORS.
  **Exempt property and
    allowances.**
    Family allowance, §43-8-112.
    Homestead exemptions,
      §§43-8-110, 43-8-114.
    Personal property, §43-8-111.
    Petition for relief of personal
      representative or
      interested persons,
      §43-8-113.
    Source, determination and
      documentation of,
      §43-8-113.
  **Failure of testamentary
    provisions.**
    Effect, §43-8-225.
  Fees.
    Probate judges' fees,
      §12-19-90.
  Foreign wills.
    Probate, §43-8-175.
  Forgery.
    Second degree forgery,
      §13A-9-3.
  **Former will not revived by
    revocation,** §43-8-138.
  Forms.
    Self-proving wills,
      §43-8-132.
  Fraud.
    Probate code.
      Relief against fraud,
        §43-8-5.
  Guardian and ward.
    Parental appointment of
      guardians, §§26-2A-71,
      26-2A-100.
    Uniform guardianship and
      protective proceedings
      act.
      Conservators.
        Examination of will of
          protected persons,
          §26-2A-155.
  Homestead exemptions.
    Amount of allowance,
      §43-8-110.
    Elective share of surviving
      spouse.
      Entitlement to exemption
        regardless of election,
        §43-8-74.
    Surviving spouse entitled to
      allowance, §43-8-110.
    Surviving spouse may retain
      dwelling, etc., until
      assignment, §43-8-114.
    Waiver, §43-8-72.
  Homicide.
    Effect on intestate
      succession, wills, joint
      assets, etc., §43-8-253.
    Slayer act, §43-8-253.

WILLS—Cont'd
  Incorporations by reference,
    §43-8-139.
  Intention of testator.
    Controlling effect, §43-8-222.
  Invalidity.
    Special, private or local laws
      giving effect to invalid
      will prohibited, Const.
      Ala., art. IV, §104.
  Jefferson county.
    Probate code.
      Savings provisions for,
        §43-8-9.
  Joint wills.
    No presumption of
      nonrevocation, §43-8-250.
  Judgments.
    Contesting validity of will,
      §§43-8-190 to 43-8-202.
      See within this heading,
      "Contesting validity."
  Jury.
    Contesting validity of will,
      §§43-8-190 to 43-8-192,
      43-8-202.
  Life estates.
    General provisions.
      See LIFE ESTATES.
  Limitation of actions.
    Probate code.
      Fraud, §43-8-5.
  Living will, §§22-8A-1 to
    22-8A-10.
    See NATURAL DEATH
      ACT.
  Marriage.
    Annulment.
      Revocation of will by
        annulment, §43-8-137.
    Remarriage.
      Revival of will, §43-8-137.
  Mentally ill.
    Contesting validity of will.
      Additional time allowed,
        §43-8-201.
  Minors.
    Contesting validity of will.
      Additional time allowed,
        §43-8-201.
    Notice of probate, §43-8-165.
    Pretermitted children,
      §43-8-91.
    Who may make will,
      §43-8-130.
  Mobile county.
    Probate code.
      Savings provisions for,
        §43-8-9.
  Mutual wills.
    No presumption of
      nonrevocation, §43-8-250.
  Natural death act, §§22-8A-1
    to 22-8A-10.
  Next of kin.
    Notice of probate.
      Generally, §43-8-164.
      Minors, §43-8-165.
      Persons outside state,
        §43-8-166.
  Nonresidents.
    Notice of probate, §43-8-166.
    Probate of foreign will,
      §43-8-175.
  Notice.
    Probate.
      Notice to surviving spouse
        and next of kin,
        §§43-8-164 to 43-8-166.

WILLS—Cont'd
  Objections.
    Contesting validity of will,
      §§43-8-190 to 43-8-202.
      See within this heading,
      "Contesting validity."
  Obliteration, §43-8-136.
  Omitted spouse, §43-8-90.
  Parties.
    Contesting validity of will,
      §43-8-200.
  Pour-over trusts, §43-8-140.
  Power of appointment.
    Effect of acts by holder of
      general power on
      beneficiaries, §43-8-7.
    Exercise of, §43-8-229.
  Powers of disposition.
    Conveyances generally,
      §§35-4-290 to 35-4-306.
      See CONVEYANCES.
    Requirements for disposition
      by devise or will,
      §35-4-295.
  Presumptions.
    Probate code.
      Presumption of death,
      §43-8-6.
  Pretermitted child act,
    §43-8-91.
  Probate code, §§43-8-1 to
    43-8-298.
    Admission to probate after
      contest of validity,
      §43-8-195.
    Advancements, §§43-8-50 to
      43-8-53.
    Applicability of chapter,
      §43-8-20.
    Bona fide purchasers.
      Protection, §43-8-172.
    Certificate endorsed on will,
      §43-8-170.
    Construction of chapter,
      §43-8-2.
      Construction against
        implied repeal,
        §43-8-4.
    Construction of wills,
      §§43-8-220 to 43-8-231.
    Contesting validity,
      §§43-8-190 to 43-8-202.
      See within this heading,
      "Contesting validity."
    Death.
      Evidence, §43-8-6.
    Definitions, §43-8-1.
    Depositions of witnesses,
      §43-8-168.
    Effective date, §43-8-8.
    Elective share of surviving
      spouse, §§43-8-70 to
      43-8-76. See within this
      heading, "Elective share
      of surviving spouse."
    Endorsement on will.
      Certificate endorsed on
        will, §43-8-170.
    Evidence.
      Admission of will,
        §43-8-171.
      Death or status, §43-8-6.
      Rules of evidence, §43-8-6.
    Execution of wills,
      §§43-8-130 to 43-8-141.
      See within this heading,
      "Execution."
    Exempt property and
      allowances, §§43-8-111 to
      43-8-113.

WILLS—Cont'd
  Probate code—Cont'd
    Fees.
      Probate judges' fees,
        §12-19-90.
    Filed documents.
      Deemed to include oath or
        affirmation, §43-8-22.
    Foreign wills, §43-8-175.
    Fraud.
      Relief against, §43-8-5.
    Homestead exemptions.
      Waiver, §43-8-72.
    Incompetency of witnesses.
      Probate not prevented by
        subsequent
        incompetency,
        §43-8-163.
    Jefferson county.
      Savings provision for,
        §43-8-9.
    Jurisdiction of probate
      courts, §12-13-1.
    Limitation of actions.
      Fraud, §43-8-5.
    Minors.
      Notice to, §43-8-165.
    Mobile county.
      Savings provisions for,
        §43-8-9.
    Mode of proving will,
      §43-8-167.
    Multiple proceedings,
      §43-8-21.
    Next of kin.
      Notice to, §§43-8-164 to
        43-8-166.
    Nonresidents.
      Notice to, §43-8-166.
    Notice to surviving spouse
      and next of kin,
      §§43-8-164 to 43-8-166.
    Omitted spouse, §43-8-90.
    Order of abatement of shares
      of distributees, §43-8-76.
    Policies, §43-8-2.
    Power of appointment.
      Effect of acts by holder of
        general power on
        beneficiaries, §43-8-7.
    Presumption of death,
      §43-8-6.
    Pretermitted children,
      §43-8-91.
    Principles of law and equity
      supplement code,
      §43-8-3.
    Production of will, §43-8-270.
    Purposes, §43-8-2.
    Recordation of witnesses'
      testimony, §43-8-169.
    Rejection of will after contest
      of validity, §43-8-195.
    Repeal.
      Construction against
        implied repeal,
        §43-8-4.
    Surviving spouse.
      Elective share, §§43-8-70 to
        43-8-76. See within
        this heading, "Elective
        share of surviving
        spouse."
      Notice to, §§43-8-164 to
        43-8-166.
    Time limit for probate,
      §43-8-161.
      Protection of bona fide
        purchasers, etc.,
        §43-8-172.

WILLS—Cont'd
  Probate code—Cont'd
    Transfer of proceedings,
      §43-8-21.
    Transition provisions,
      §43-8-8.
    Venue, §§43-8-21, 43-8-162.
    Where will probated,
      §43-8-162.
    Who may have will probated,
      §43-8-160.
    Withdrawal of will.
      Before probate, §43-8-173.
      For proof out of state,
        §43-8-174.
    Witnesses.
      Contesting validity of
        wills, §§43-8-190 to
        43-8-202. See within
        this heading,
        "Contesting validity."
      Conveyances generally,
        §§35-4-1 to 35-4-412.
        See CONVEYANCES.
      Generally, §§43-8-167 to
        43-8-169.
  Production of will, §43-8-270.
  Property not disposed of.
    Distributed as prescribed by
      provisions of chapter,
      §43-8-40.
  Real property.
    Who may convey lands by
      will, §35-4-1.
  Recordation.
    Witnesses' testimony,
      §43-8-169.
  Reference to events of
    independent
    significance, §43-8-141.
  Renunciation of succession,
    §43-8-251.
  Revocation.
    By writing or by act,
      §43-8-136.
    Contracts not to revoke.
      Establishment, §43-8-250.
    Divorce.
      Revocation by, §43-8-137.
    Former will not revived by
      revocation, §43-8-138.
    No presumption of
      nonrevocation from joint
      or mutual will,
      §43-8-250.
    Witnesses.
      When required, §43-8-136.
  Satisfaction.
    Ademption by satisfaction,
      §43-8-231.
  Seals and sealed
    instruments.
    Conveyances generally,
      §§35-4-1 to 35-4-412.
      See CONVEYANCES.
  Securities.
    Specific devise, §43-8-226.
  Self-proving wills, §43-8-132.
    Making attested will self-
      proved, §43-8-133.
  Separation.
    Effect of decree, §43-8-252.
  Signatures, §43-8-131.
    Self-proved wills, §43-8-132.
  Simultaneous death act,
    §§43-7-1 to 43-7-8.
    See SIMULTANEOUS
      DEATH ACT.

WILLS—Cont'd
Summons and process.
Contesting validity of wills.
Summoning witnesses,
§43-8-191.
Surviving spouse.
Elective share, §§43-8-70 to
43-8-76. See within this
heading, "Elective share
of surviving spouse."
Exempt property and
allowances, §§43-8-111 to
43-8-113.
Notice of probate.
Generally, §43-8-164.
Minors, §43-8-165.
Persons outside state,
§43-8-166.
Survivorship.
Construction of wills.
Devisee required to survive
testator by five days,
§43-8-220.
Heir required to survive
decedent by five days,
§43-8-43.
Tearing, §43-8-136.
Time.
Contesting validity of wills,
§§43-8-199, 43-8-201.
Time for trial, §43-8-191.
Probate, §43-8-161.
Protection of bona fide
purchasers, etc.,
§43-8-172.
Transfers to minors.
Transfer authorized by will
or trust, §35-5A-6.
Trial.
Contesting validity of wills,
§§43-8-190 to 43-8-202.
See within this heading,
"Contesting validity."
Trusts and trustees.
Devise or bequest to trustee
of existing trust,
§43-8-140.
Pour-over trusts, §43-8-140.
**Uniform simultaneous death
act,** §§43-7-1 to 43-7-8.
See SIMULTANEOUS
DEATH ACT.
Validity.
Contesting validity,
§§43-8-190 to 43-8-202.
See within this heading,
"Contesting validity."
Special, private or local laws
giving effect to invalid
will prohibited, Const.
Ala., art. IV, §104.
Venue.
Contesting validity of wills.
Change of venue,
§43-8-197.
Probate code, §§43-8-21,
43-8-162.
**Who may convey lands by
will,** §35-4-1.
Widows and widowers.
Elective share, §§43-8-70 to
43-8-76. See within this
heading, "Elective share
of surviving spouse."
Exempt property and
allowances, §§43-8-111
to 43-8-113.
General provisions,
§§43-8-164 to 43-8-166.
Withdrawal from probate.
Before probate, §43-8-173.

WILLS—Cont'd
Withdrawal from probate
—Cont'd
Withdrawal for proof out of
state, §43-8-174.
Witnesses.
Contesting validity of wills,
§§43-8-190 to 43-8-202.
Conveyances generally,
§§35-4-1 to 35-4-412.
See CONVEYANCES.
Depositions, §43-8-168.
Contesting validity of
wills, §43-8-194.
Incompetency of witnesses.
Probate not prevented by
subsequent
incompetency of
witnesses, §43-8-163.
Mode of proving will,
§43-8-167.
Presence, §43-8-131.
Recordation of testimony,
§43-8-169.
Revocation by writing or by
act, §43-8-136.
Signatures, §43-8-131.
Testimony.
Recordation, §43-8-169.
Who may witness will,
§43-8-134.
**Wives may dispose of
separate estates by will,**
§30-4-14.

WINE.
See ALCOHOLIC
BEVERAGES.

WINSTON COUNTY.
**County revenue
commissioner.**
Consolidation of offices of tax
assessor and tax
collector, Const. Ala.,
amd. 423.
Court costs and charges,
Const. Ala., amd. 424.
Hospitals.
Additional taxes for hospital
purposes, Const. Ala.,
amd. 254.
**Junior college for Winston
county,** §§16-60-20 to
16-60-40.
See JUNIOR COLLEGES.
**Legislation as to Winston
county,** Const. Ala., amd.
255.
School tax.
Special tax for school
purposes, Const. Ala.,
amd. 153.
Trade schools.
Conversion of junior college
for Franklin, Marion and
Winston counties to
trade school and junior
college, §§16-60-38 to
16-60-40.

WITNESSES, §§12-21-1 to
12-21-285.
Accomplices.
Testimony for felony
conviction, §12-21-222.
Accountants.
Hearings before board of
public accountancy.
Compelling attendance of
witnesses, §34-1-14.

WITNESSES—Cont'd
Accountants—Cont'd
Hearings before board of
public accountancy
—Cont'd
Right of confrontation and
cross-examination,
§34-1-14.
Accounts and accounting.
Verified itemized statement
as evidence of account's
correctness, §12-21-111.
Adjoining counties.
Execution of warrants for
witnesses and other
process in adjoining
counties, §12-21-183.
Affirmation.
All testimony, §12-21-136.
In lieu of oath, ARCP, Rule
43 (d).
Required, §12-21-135.
Agriculture.
Commissioner of agriculture
and industries.
Examination of witnesses,
§2-2-6.
**Applicability of provisions
regulating admissibility,**
§12-21-145.
Arbitration and award.
Delivery of list with
submissions, §6-6-3.
Subpoena, §§6-6-7 to 6-6-9.
Arrest.
Attendance of out-of-state
witnesses.
Exemption from arrest,
§12-21-284.
Arrest warrants.
Complaints.
Examination of witnesses,
§15-7-2.
Attachment.
Execution of attachments for
witnesses in adjoining
counties, §12-21-183.
Attendance.
Adjoining counties,
§12-21-183.
Criminal cases, §§12-21-240
to 12-21-242.
Out-of-state witnesses,
§§12-21-280 to
12-21-285.
Expert witnesses, §12-21-181.
Failure to attend and
remain.
Proceedings upon failure of
subpoenaed witness,
§12-21-182.
Securing attendance of
witnesses until case
disposed of, §12-21-184.
Subpoenas, §§12-21-243 to
12-21-246.
Attorneys at law.
Disciplinary proceedings,
§§34-3-82 to 34-3-84.
Testimony for or against
client, §12-21-161.
**Banks and financial
institutions.**
Powers of superintendents
and bank examiners,
§5-3A-6.
Barbers.
Proceedings before board of
barber examiners.
Compelling attendance of
witnesses, §34-5-8.

WITNESSES—Cont'd
Bribery, §13A-10-121.
  Receiving a bribe by a
    witness, §13A-10-122.
Child custody.
  Uniform child custody
    jurisdiction act.
    Taking testimony in
      another state,
      §30-3-38.
Chiropractors.
  Refusal, revocation or
    suspension of licenses,
    §34-24-173.
Circuit courts.
  Criminal cases, §12-22-111.
  Fees, §§12-19-130 to
    12-19-138. See within
    this heading, "Fees."
  Special sessions, §12-11-7.
Coal.
  Mine safety, §§25-9-22,
    25-9-23.
  Surface mining control and
    reclamation.
    Fees for witnesses and
      proceedings, §9-16-78.
Competency.
  Attorneys at law.
    Testimony for or against
      client, §12-21-161.
  Convicts, §12-21-162.
  Criminal cases, §§12-21-220
    to 12-21-227. See within
    this heading, "Criminal
    cases."
  Dead man's statute,
    §12-21-163.
  Deceased borrower's
    representative as usury
    witness, §12-21-164.
  Expert witnesses, §12-21-160.
  Incompetent witnesses,
    §12-21-165.
  Interested witnesses,
    §12-21-163.
Complaints.
  Examination of witnesses,
    §15-7-2.
Constitution of Alabama.
  Right to be confronted by
    witnesses, Const. Ala.,
    art. I, §6.
**Constitution of the United
  States.**
  Confrontation with
    witnesses, Const. U. S.,
    Amendment VI.
  Process to obtain, Const. U.
    S., Amendment VI.
  Self-incrimination, Const. U.
    S., Amendment V.
  Treason.
    Number in treason cases,
      Const. U. S., Art. III,
      §3.
Contracts.
  Future delivery.
    Person involved in futures
      contracts, §8-1-130.
Conveyances.
  Acknowledgments, §35-4-23.
  Attestation by witnesses,
    §35-4-20.
  Form of proof, §35-4-68.
Convicts.
  Competency, §12-21-162.
  Criminal cases.
    Testimony for state or
      defendant, §12-21-225.

WITNESSES—Cont'd
Coroner's inquest, §§15-4-3,
  15-4-4, 15-4-8.
Corporations.
  Franchise tax.
    Summoning witnesses,
      §40-14-51.
Corroboration.
  Required for perjury
    conviction, §13A-10-105.
Cosmetologists.
  Board of cosmetology.
    Proceedings before board,
      §34-7-21.
County commissions.
  Powers, §11-3-11.
Criminal cases, §§12-21-200 to
  12-21-285.
  Abandonment cases.
    Wife against husband in
      abandonment case,
      §12-21-226.
  Accomplices.
    Testimony for felony
      conviction, §12-21-222.
  Appeals to circuit courts.
    Issuance, execution and
      return of subpoenas for
      witnesses, §12-22-111.
  Attendance of out-of-state
    witnesses.
    Citation of subdivision,
      §12-21-280.
    Construction of
      subdivision,
      §12-21-285.
    Definitions, §12-21-281.
    Exemption from arrest or
      service of process,
      §12-21-284.
    Securing attendance of
      witnesses within state.
      Failure to attend and
        testify, §12-21-282.
      Fees and allowances,
        §12-21-282.
      Procedure, §12-21-282.
    Securing attendance of
      witness in another
      state.
      Failure to attend and
        testify, §12-21-283.
      Fees and allowances,
        §12-21-283.
      Procedure, §12-21-283.
  Attendance of witnesses.
    Continuation of case,
      §12-21-241.
    Failure to appear,
      §§12-21-247 to
      12-21-249.
    Generally, §12-21-240.
    Out-of-state witnesses,
      §§12-21-280 to
      12-21-285.
    Remand for new trial,
      §12-21-242.
    Subpoenas, §§12-21-243 to
      12-21-246.
  Change of venue.
    Compelling attendance at
      hearing for, §15-2-22.
    Examination of prosecution
      witnesses on
      interrogatories,
      §15-2-23.
    Subpoena of trial witnesses
      after removal,
      §15-2-27.

WITNESSES—Cont'd
Criminal cases—Cont'd
  Codefendants.
    Acquitted codefendant as
      witness, §12-21-224.
    Discharged codefendant as
      prosecution witness,
      §12-21-223.
  Competency.
    Abandonment cases.
      Wife against husband in
        abandonment cases,
        §12-21-226.
    Accomplice's testimony for
      felony conviction,
      §12-21-222.
    Codefendnats, §§12-21-223,
      12-21-224.
    Convicts, §12-21-225.
    Husband and wife,
      §§12-21-226,
      12-21-227.
    Interested witnesses,
      §12-21-221.
    Right of defendant to be
      witness, §12-21-220.
  Convicts, §12-21-225.
  Defaulting witnesses.
    Conditional judgment
      against, §§12-21-247 to
      12-21-249.
  Defendant's failure to testify.
    Effect of prosecution's
      comment, §12-21-220.
  Depositions, §§12-21-260 to
    12-21-263.
  Fees, §§12-19-171, 12-21-282,
    12-21-283.
  Husband and wife.
    Abandonment cases,
      §12-21-226.
    For or against one another,
      §12-21-227.
  Interested witnesses,
    §12-21-221.
  Right of defendant to be
    witness, §12-21-220.
  Right to be confronted by
    witnesses, Const. Ala.,
    art. I, §6; Const. U. S.,
    Amendment VI.
  Subpoenas.
    Authority of district
      attorney, §12-21-245.
    Execution, §12-21-246.
    Failure to appear,
      §§12-21-247 to
      12-21-249.
    Fee for issuance,
      §12-19-171.
    Grand jury appearance,
      §12-21-243.
    Trial appearance,
      §12-21-244.
Cross-examination.
  Leading questions,
    §12-21-138; ARCP, Rule
    43 (b).
  Right of cross-examination,
    §12-21-137.
  Scope of cross-examination,
    ARCP, Rule 43 (b).
Dead man's statute,
  §12-21-163.
Deaf persons.
  Interpreters, §§12-21-130 to
    12-21-134.

WITNESSES—Cont'd
Death.
Proof of execution of documents when subscribing witnesses dead, §12-21-62.
Debts.
Deceased borrower's representative as usury witness, §12-21-164.
Deeds.
Attestation by witnesses, §35-4-20.
Form of proof of conveyances, §35-4-68.
Definitions.
Offenses against public administration.
Testimony defined, §13A-10-120.
Securing attendance of out-of-state witnesses, §12-21-281.
Dental service corporations.
Examination and investigation.
Power to summon and examine witnesses, §22-21-386.
Dentists.
Board of dental examiners.
Authority to compel attendance, §34-9-46.
Department of examiners of public accounts, §41-5-16.
Department of industrial relations.
Powers, §25-2-23.
Depositions, §§12-21-260 to 12-21-263.
Desertion and nonsupport.
Competency of wife against husband in abandonment cases, §12-21-226.
Dower interests.
Ascertainment and payment, §35-4-191.
Drunkenness.
Incompetent witnesses, §12-21-165.
Education.
State board of education.
Examination of witnesses, §16-3-24.
Elections.
Contests.
Generally, §§17-15-28, 17-15-29.
Primary elections, §§17-16-74 to 17-16-76.
Engineers.
Board of registration.
Authority to compel attendance, §34-11-35.
Exclusion of answers.
Motion to exclude answer unnecessary, §12-21-140.
Executors and administrators.
Letters of administration.
Examination of witnesses, §43-2-45.
Expert witnesses.
Compelling appearance and testimony, §12-21-181.
Competency, §12-21-160.
Discovery of trial preparation, ARCP, Rule 26 (b).
Handwriting analysis, §12-21-40.

WITNESSES—Cont'd
Failure to testify, §12-21-143.
Fees, §§12-19-130 to 12-19-138.
Civil cases.
Attendance fees, §12-19-131.
Certificate of attendance.
Effect, §12-19-133.
Issuance, §12-19-132.
Circuit court fees generally, §12-19-130.
Claims for payment.
Presentment, §12-19-137.
Collection of amount proved, §12-19-134.
Claims for payment.
Presentment, §12-19-137.
District court fees generally, §12-19-130.
Limitation on number of witnesses to prove any one matter, §12-19-134.
Mileage fees, §12-19-131.
Nondisbursed fees.
Payment to successors, §12-19-138.
Payment of claims, §12-19-137.
Probate court, §§12-19-135, 12-19-136.
Proof of attendance, §12-19-132.
Statement as to fees.
Furnishing, §12-19-138.
Taxation of amount proved, §12-19-134.
Unpaid fees.
Witnesses not obligated to appear in same case, §12-19-133.
Criminal cases.
Attendance of out-of-state witnesses.
Securing attendance of witness in another state, §12-21-283.
Securing attendance of witness within state, §12-21-282.
Subpoenas, §12-19-171.
Impeachment trials, §36-11-21.
Payment.
Establishment and filing of special procedures, §12-19-7.
Probate judges' fees, §12-19-90.
Service of witness subpoenas, §12-19-74.
Finance.
Examination of witnesses by director of finance, §41-4-36.
Fires and fire prevention.
Fire marshal, §§36-19-19 to 36-19-22.
Forcible entry and unlawful detainer.
Failure to attend or refusal to testify, §6-6-334.
Forests and forestry.
Board of registration for foresters.
Authority to compel attendance, §34-12-35.

WITNESSES—Cont'd
Forests and forestry—Cont'd
Forest products.
Privilege and severance taxes.
Power of department as to witnesses, §9-13-102.
Funerals.
Board of funeral service.
Power to compel attendance, §34-13-26.
Gambling.
Grand jury.
Examinations, §12-16-212.
Refusal to testify, §12-16-213.
Grain dealers.
Powers of commissioner of agriculture as to, §2-31-14.
Grand jury, §§12-16-190 to 12-16-213.
See GRAND JURY.
Habeas corpus.
Proceedings against defaulting witnesses, §15-21-32.
Subpoenas for witnesses, §15-21-15.
Taxation and collection of costs, §15-21-33.
Handicapped persons.
Interpreters, §§12-21-130 to 12-21-134.
Harsh demeanor.
Right of witness to be protected, §12-21-141.
Hearing aid dealers and fitters.
Board of hearing aid dealers and fitters.
Authority to compel attendance, §34-14-9.
How testimony given, §12-21-135.
Husband and wife.
Criminal cases.
Competency, §§12-21-226, 12-21-227.
Impeachment of witnesses, ARCP, Rule 43 (b).
Impeachment trials.
Compensation and fees, §36-11-21.
Improper questions.
Right of witness to be protected, §12-21-141.
Income tax.
Failure to appear before the department of revenue, §40-18-56.
Incompetent witnesses, §12-21-165.
Insulting demeanor.
Right of witness to be protected, §12-21-141.
Insurance.
Commissioner of insurance.
Examinations, investigations or hearings, §27-2-26.
Compelling testimony or production of documents, §27-2-27.
Immunity from prosecution, §27-2-27.
Interested parties.
Competency of witness having interest, §12-21-163.

WITNESSES—Cont'd
Interested parties—Cont'd
Criminal cases, §12-21-221.
Interpreters.
Appointment, ARCP, Rule 43 (f).
Compensation, §12-21-130; ARCP, Rule 43 (f).
Generally, §12-21-130; ARCP, Rule 43 (f).
Handicapped persons, §§12-21-131 to 12-21-134.
Compensation and expenses, §12-21-134.
Confidentiality, §12-21-131.
Duty of handicapped person, §12-21-133.
Fee for services, §12-21-131.
How interpreters furnished, §12-21-132.
Notice of need, §12-21-131.
Proof of deafness, §12-21-131.
Qualifications of interpreters, §12-21-131.
Request to be channeled through certain organizations listing of qualified interpreters, §12-21-131.
When interpreters furnished, §12-21-131.
Oath of interpreters, §12-21-131.
Oath required, §12-21-130.
Intimidating witnesses, §13A-10-123.
Jails.
Commitment of prisoners.
Witnesses failing to give security for their appearance, §14-6-3.
Judges.
Canons of judicial ethics.
Character witness.
Judge not to testify voluntarily as character witness, ACJE, Canon 2C.
Disqualification of judge where judge has been a material witness, ACJE, Canon 3C.
Judicial compensation commission.
Powers, §12-10-2.
Jury.
Personal knowledge of juror as to fact in controversy during trial, §12-16-7.
Labor.
Department of industrial relations.
False statements under oath, §25-2-25.
Powers, §25-2-23.
Unions and labor relations.
Local boards of arbitration.
Powers, §25-7-51.
Leading questions, §12-21-138; ARCP, Rule 43 (b).
Life interests.
Ascertainment and payment, §35-4-191.
Lotteries.
Grand jury.
Examinations, §12-16-212.

WITNESSES—Cont'd
Lotteries—Cont'd
Grand jury—Cont'd
Refusal to testify, §12-16-213.
Marine resources.
Violation of chapter.
Summoning of witnesses, §9-12-4.
Masters, ARCP, Rule 53 (d).
Meat and meat products.
Commissioner of agriculture and industries.
Powers, §2-17-24.
Failure to attend and testify, §2-17-33.
Generally, §2-17-24.
Mentally ill.
Fees in probate court.
Inquisition proceedings, §12-19-135.
Incompetent witnesses, §12-21-165.
Superintendent and physician of state mental health facilities.
Exemption from attending as witnesses, §22-50-22.
Military affairs.
Courts-martial.
Payment of witness fees, §31-2-102.
Subpoena of witnesses, §31-2-100.
Minors.
Incompetent witnesses, §12-21-165.
Mortgages and deeds of trust.
Form of proof of conveyances, §35-4-68.
Motor vehicle accidents.
Police to interview witnesses, §32-10-7.
Motor vehicle carriers.
Examiners.
Power to compel attendance, §37-3-28.
Mute persons.
Interpreters for handicapped persons, §§12-21-131 to 12-21-134.
News-gathering persons.
Exemption from disclosing sources, §12-21-142.
Notaries public, §§36-20-1 to 36-20-32.
See NOTARIES PUBLIC.
Number of witnesses.
Limitation, §12-19-134.
Oaths.
Affirmation in lieu of oath, ARCP, Rule 43 (d).
All testimony, §12-21-136.
Incompetent witnesses, §12-21-165.
Required, §12-21-135.
Objections.
Disclosure of evidence sought by objected to question, §12-21-139.
Motion to exclude answer unnecessary, §12-21-140.
Oil and gas board.
Conservation and regulation of production.
Powers, §9-17-8.

WITNESSES—Cont'd
Optometrists.
Board of optometrists.
Authority to compel attendance and administer oaths, §34-22-42.
Disciplinary proceedings before board, §34-22-8.
Out-of-state witnesses.
Securing attendance.
Criminal cases, §§12-21-280 to 12-21-285. See within this heading, "Criminal cases."
Peace bonds.
Examination of witnesses, §15-6-20.
Penalties.
Failure of subpoenaed witness to attend and remain, §12-21-182.
Failure or refusal to testify, §12-21-143.
Perjury.
Corroboration required, §13A-10-105.
General provisions.
See PERJURY.
Pharmacists and pharmacies.
Board of pharmacy.
Compelling attendance at board proceedings, §34-23-92.
Physicians.
Revocation or suspension of licenses, §§34-24-363 to 34-24-365.
Pilots and pilotage.
Failure to answer subpoena, §33-4-42.
Fees, §33-4-43.
Issuance of subpoenas in behalf of pilot, §33-4-44.
State pilotage commission.
Power to subpoena witnesses, §33-4-41.
Plumbing.
Certification of plumbers and gas fitters.
Revocation, §34-37-12.
Poultry.
Commissioner of agriculture and industries.
Powers, §2-17-24.
Failure to attend and testify, §2-17-33.
Generally, §2-17-24.
Preliminary hearings.
Examination of witnesses, §15-11-6.
Court's duty, §15-11-8.
Separation of witnesses, §15-11-7.
Undertaking.
Discharge of witness upon entering, §15-11-14.
Form, §15-11-12.
Married women and minors, §15-11-13.
Refusal or failure of witness to enter, §15-11-14.
Requiring witness to enter, §15-11-12.

WITNESSES—Cont'd

Prisons and prisoners.
Management and treatment of convicts.
Failure to appear or testify, §14-11-3.

Privileges.
See PRIVILEGES.

Proof of facts.
Applicability of provisions regulating, §12-21-145.

Protection.
Right of witness, §12-21-141.

Public officers and employees.
Merit system.
Investigations and hearings, §36-26-41.

Public service commission,
§§37-1-63, 37-1-93, 37-8-3, 37-8-4.

Real estate brokers.
Disciplinary actions.
Authority of commission to compel attendance, §34-27-37.

Recordation.
Form of proof of conveyances, §35-4-68.

Refusal to testify, §12-21-143.

Reporters of news.
Exemption from disclosing sources, §12-21-142.

Rules of civil procedure,
ARCP, Rule 43 (b), (d), (f).
Applicability of provisions regulating admissibility or proof of facts, §12-21-145.

Sales tax.
Department of revenue.
Failure to appear before department, §40-23-22.

Scope of examination, ARCP, Rule 43 (b).

Securing attendance until case disposed of,
§12-21-184.

Self-incrimination.
Constitutional provisions, Const. U. S., Amendment V.

Service of process.
Out-of-state witnesses.
Exemption from service, §12-21-284.

Service of subpoenas.
Circuit and district court fee for issuance of witness subpoenas, §12-19-74.

Sexual offenses.
Child victim or witness.
See SEXUAL OFFENSES.

Signatures.
Proof of execution of documents, §§12-21-61, 12-21-62.

Small business assistance.
Powers of department of industrial relations, §25-10-5.

Small claims.
Subpoenas, ASCR, Rule I.

Small loans.
Power of supervisor, §5-18-10.

WITNESSES—Cont'd

Speech pathologists and audiologists.
Board of examiners.
Authority to compel attendance, §34-28A-43.

Stenographic reports of testimony.
Admissibility, ARCP, Rule 80.

Subpoenas, ARCP, Rule 45 (a).
Circuit and district court fee for issuance of witness subpoenas, §12-19-74.
Criminal cases.
Fee for issuance, §12-19-171.
Criminal cases, §§12-21-243 to 12-21-246.

Subscribing witnesses.
Proof of execution of documents, §§12-21-61, 12-21-62.

Surveys and surveyors.
Board of registration.
Authority to compel attendance, §34-11-35.

Tampering with witnesses,
§13A-10-124.

Taxation.
Department of revenue.
Appearance.
Required, §40-2-19.
Fees, §40-2-21.
Incriminating testimony, §40-2-20.
Oaths, §40-2-6.
Perjury, §40-2-20.
Production of records, books and papers.
Required, §40-2-19.

Threats.
Intimidating witnesses, §13A-10-123.

Transcripts of testimony.
Admissibility, ARCP, Rule 80.

Treason.
Two witnesses required, §13A-11-2.

Unemployment compensation.
Claims for benefits, §25-4-97.

Usury.
Deceased borrower's representative as usury witness, §12-21-164.

Warehouses.
Public hearing on operations, §8-15-13.

Warrants.
Execution of warrants for arrest of witnesses in adjoining counties, §12-21-183.

Welfare, §38-4-6.

Wills.
Contesting validity of wills, §§43-8-190 to 43-8-202.
See WILLS.
Conveyances generally, §§35-4-20, 35-4-23, 35-4-68.
General provisions, §§43-8-131, 43-8-167 to 43-8-169.
See WILLS.

WIVES.

Husband and wife.
See HUSBAND AND WIFE.

WOMEN.

Abortion, §§26-21-1 to 26-21-8.
See ABORTION.

Constitution of Alabama.
Property rights of females, Const. Ala., art. X, §209.

Constitution of the United States.
Woman suffrage, Const. U. S., Amendment XIX.

Continuing women's commission, §§41-9-410 to 41-9-414.
Appointment of members, §41-9-410.
Chairman.
Selection, §41-9-411.
Committees.
Appointment, §41-9-411.
Compensation of members, §41-9-410.
Composition, §41-9-410.
Consultants, §41-9-411.
Creation, §41-9-410.
Employees, §41-9-411.
Expenses of members, §41-9-410.
Functions, §41-9-413.
Meetings, §41-9-412.
Officers.
Selection, §41-9-411.
Office space and equipment, §41-9-411.
Procedures.
Adoption, §41-9-411.
Public hearings, §41-9-411.
Qualifications of members, §41-9-410.
Reports.
Annual report to governor and legislature, §41-9-414.
Rules.
Adoption, §41-9-411.
Task forces.
Appointment, §41-9-411.
Terms of members, §41-9-410.
Vacancies, §41-9-410.

Debts.
Property of wife not liable for debts, etc., of husband, Const. Ala., art. X, §209.

Dower, §§35-4-190 to 35-4-192.

Elections.
Woman suffrage, Const. U. S., Amendment XIX.

Executors and administrators.
Letters testamentary.
Issuance to married women, §43-2-23.
Supplemental letters for married women upon removal of disability, §43-2-24.

Hall of fame board,
§§41-9-550 to 41-9-554.
Appointment of members, §41-9-550.
Appropriations to board, §41-9-553.
Chairman, §41-9-550.
Compensation of members, §41-9-550.
Composition, §41-9-550.
Contributions, §41-9-554.

WOMEN—Cont'd
Hall of fame board—Cont'd
Creation, §41-9-550.
Donations, §41-9-554.
Election of members,
§41-9-552.
Executive secretary,
§41-9-550.
Expenses of members,
§41-9-550.
Functions, §41-9-552.
Gifts, §41-9-554.
Installation of members,
§41-9-552.
Location of board and hall of
fame, §41-9-551.
Meetings, §41-9-550.
Offices of board, §41-9-551.
Purposes, §41-9-552.
Qualifications of members,
§41-9-550.
Quorum, §41-9-550.
Taxation.
Exemption, §41-9-554.
Terms of members,
§41-9-550.
Vacancies, §41-9-550.
Jails.
Separation from men,
§14-6-13.
Labor.
Sitting accommodations.
Duty of employer to
provide, §25-1-2.
Water closets.
Duty of employer to
provide separate water
closets, §25-1-2.
Penitentiary.
Officers and guards,
§14-3-39.
Separation from men,
§14-3-40.
Pregnant women.
Inducing or attempting to
induce abortion,
miscarriage or
premature delivery,
§13A-13-7.
Prisons and prisoners.
Penitentiary, §§14-3-39,
14-3-40.
Working female convicts on
public roads, §14-4-7.
Property rights, Const. Ala.,
art. X, §209.
Prostitution, §§13A-12-110 to
13A-12-113.
**Savings and loan
associations.**
Married women.
Accounts, §5-16-43.
Seduction, §§6-5-350, 6-5-351.
Suffrage, Const. U. S.,
Amendment XIX.
Wills.
Disposal of separate estate,
§30-4-14.

WOODWORKMEN.
Liens.
Attachment, §§35-11-111,
35-11-112.
Declaration of lien,
§35-11-110.
Enforcement, §§35-11-111,
35-11-112.
Joinder of persons having
liens on same property,
§35-11-112.

WORDS AND PHRASES.
**Construction and
interpretation.**
See CONSTRUCTION AND
INTERPRETATION.
Definitions.
See DEFINITIONS.

**WORKMEN'S
COMPENSATION,** §§25-5-1
to 25-5-231.
Acceptance of article,
§25-5-54.
Accidents.
Defined, §25-5-1.
Injuries by an accident
arising out of and in the
course of his
employment.
Defined, §25-5-1.
Notice to employer,
§§25-5-78, 25-5-79.
Outside state, §25-5-35.
Actions.
Co-employee law suits. See
within this heading, "Co-
employee law suits."
Commencement.
Disputed claims for
compensation,
§§25-5-81, 25-5-88.
Compensation by civil action.
Applicability of article,
§25-5-30.
Applicability of sections
25-5-31 and 25-5-32 to
other claims for
personal injury or
death, §25-5-33.
Common law.
Article deemed extension
or modification of,
§25-5-30.
Damages.
Right of action, §25-5-31.
Defenses.
Excluded defenses,
§25-5-32.
Minors.
Applicability of certain
articles to minors,
§25-5-34.
Double compensation
when minor illegally
employed, §25-5-34.
Misconduct of employee.
Burden of proof,
§25-5-36.
Other states.
Effect of compensation
under laws in other
state, §25-5-35.
Outside state.
Employment principally
located outside state,
§25-5-35.
Recovery where accident
occurs outside state,
§25-5-35.
Right of action for
damages for injuries or
death of employee,
§25-5-31.
Disputed claims.
Determination, §25-5-81.
Proceedings, §§25-5-88 to
25-5-90.
Judgments, §§25-5-91 to
25-9-93.
Limitation of actions,
§25-5-80.

**WORKMEN'S
COMPENSATION**—Cont'd
Actions—Cont'd
Pneumoconiosis. See within
this heading,
"Pneumoconiosis."
Radiation.
Occupational exposure.
Limitation of actions,
§25-5-197.
Reports.
Disposition of cases,
§25-5-6.
Settlements, §25-5-5.
Settlements.
Reports, §25-5-5.
Third parties.
Attorney's fees, §25-5-11.
Third parties.
Actions against where
jointly liable with
employers, §25-5-11.
Appeals.
Determination of disputed
compensation claims
generally, §25-5-81.
Assignments.
Acceptance of assignment of
claim, §25-5-231.
Claims not to be assignable,
§25-5-86.
Pneumoconiosis.
Coal miners.
Assignment of benefits
void, §25-5-179.
Atomic energy.
Compensation for
occupational exposure to
radiation, §§25-5-190 to
25-5-203. See within this
heading, "Radiation."
Attachment.
Exemption of claims,
§25-5-86.
Pneumoconiosis.
Coal miners' benefits.
Exempt from
attachment,
§25-5-179.
Attorneys at law.
Fees.
Disputed claims for
compensation,
§25-5-90.
Settlements with third
parties, §25-5-11.
Persons not authorized to
practice law.
Solicitation of claims or
representation of
claimants, §25-5-227.
Solicitation of employment or
acceptance of solicited
employment, §25-5-226.
Average weekly wage.
Determination, §25-5-57.
**Avoiding liability to
workmen.**
Liabilities of persons engaged
in schemes, §25-5-10.
Awards.
Disability benefits, §25-5-57.
Minors.
Effect of payment,
§25-5-55.
Benefits.
Alteration.
Disability compensation,
§25-5-57.

WORKMEN'S
COMPENSATION—Cont'd
Benefits—Cont'd
Amendment.
Disability compensation,
§25-5-57.
Amount.
Death benefits, §25-5-60.
Disability benefits,
§25-5-57.
Assignment.
Acceptance of assignment
of claim, §25-5-231.
Blindness, §25-5-57.
Burial expenses, §25-5-67.
Commutation of
compensation to lump-
sum payments, §25-5-83.
Computation.
Disability benefits,
§25-5-57.
Death benefits, §25-5-60.
Burial expenses, §25-5-67.
Death following disability,
§25-5-57.
Maximum and minimum
weekly compensation,
§25-5-68.
To be paid only to United
States residents,
§25-5-82.
Default upon periodic
compensation payments.
Remedy for default,
§25-5-86.
Dependents.
Children, §25-5-65.
Death benefits, §25-5-60.
Cessation upon death of
dependent, §25-5-69.
Marriage.
Cessation of benefits
upon remarriage,
§25-5-69.
Disposition of
compensation upon
remarriage of widow
with dependent
children, §25-5-66.
Maximum compensation
for total dependents,
§25-5-63.
Order of compensation,
§25-5-62.
Orphans, §25-5-65.
Partial dependents,
§25-5-64.
Persons presumed wholly
dependent, §25-5-61.
Proportional benefits,
§25-5-69.
Total dependents.
Designated, §25-5-62.
Maximum compensation,
§25-5-63.
Disability benefits, §25-5-57.
Maximum and minimum
weekly compensation,
§25-5-68.
Preexisting injuries or
infirmities.
Effect, §25-5-58.
Waiting period for
temporary disabilities,
§25-5-59.
Disputed claims for
compensation.
Determination, §25-5-81.
Proceedings, §§25-5-88 to
25-5-90.

WORKMEN'S
COMPENSATION—Cont'd
Benefits—Cont'd
Disputed claims for
compensation—Cont'd
Judgments. See within this
heading, "Judgments."
Eligibility for benefits.
Death benefits, §25-5-60.
Disability benefits,
§25-5-57.
Future benefits.
Commutation to lump sum
payment, §25-5-83.
Limitation period for claims,
§25-5-80.
Lump-sum payments.
Commutation of
compensation,
§25-5-83.
Medical treatment, §25-5-77.
Medicine, §25-5-77.
Modification of payments,
§25-5-84.
Occupational diseases.
General provisions,
§§25-5-110 to 25-5-123.
Pneumoconiosis,
§§25-5-140 to 25-5-180.
See within this
heading,
"Pneumoconiosis."
Orphans, §25-5-65.
Overdue compensation
payments.
Penalty, §25-5-59.
Penalty for overdue
compensation payments,
§25-5-59.
Periodic payments.
Remedy for default,
§25-5-86.
Pneumoconiosis, §§25-5-140
to 25-5-180. See within
this heading,
"Pneumoconiosis."
Preexisting injuries or
infirmities.
Effect, §25-5-58.
Radiation.
Occupational exposure to
radiation, §§25-5-190
to 25-5-203. See within
this heading,
"Radiation."
Rehabilitation or recovery.
Effect on permanent total
disability benefits,
§25-5-57.
Revision.
Disability compensation,
§25-5-57.
Second injury trust fund,
§§25-5-70 to 25-5-75. See
within this heading,
"Second injury trust
fund."
Surgical treatment, §25-5-77.
Trustees.
Procedure for and effect of
payment to court
appointed trustee,
§25-5-85.
Vocational rehabilitation,
§25-5-77.
Waiting period for temporary
disabilities, §25-5-59.
Blind persons.
Disability compensation,
§25-5-57.

WORKMEN'S
COMPENSATION—Cont'd
Burden of proof.
Misconduct of employees,
§25-5-36.
Occupational diseases.
Right to compensation,
§25-5-120.
Radiation exposure,
§25-5-200.
Burial.
Expenses, §25-5-67.
Children.
Defined, §25-5-1.
Dependent child or orphan.
Defined, §25-5-1.
Disposition of compensation
upon remarriage of
widow with dependent
children, §25-5-66.
Circuit courts.
Chief justice of supreme
court to prepare uniform
rules for circuit courts,
§25-5-12.
Determination of disputed
compensation claims,
§25-5-81.
Report of disposition of cases.
Circuit court clerks,
§25-5-6.
Claims.
Assignment.
Acceptance, §25-5-231.
Disputed claims.
Determination, §25-5-81.
Proceedings, §§25-5-88 to
25-5-90.
Limitation period, §25-5-80.
Solicitation of claims or
representation of
claimants by persons not
authorized to practice
law, §25-5-227.
Coal.
Abandoned mine
reclamation, §9-16-134.
Coal miners.
Occupational diseases.
Settlements between
parties, §25-5-121.
Penumoconiosis, §§25-5-170
to 25-5-180. See within
this heading,
"Pneumoconiosis."
Radiation exposure.
Settlements, §25-5-201.
Reports of settlements,
§25-5-5.
Third parties.
Attorney's fees in
settlements with,
§25-5-11.
Co-employee law suits.
Compensation.
Disability generally,
§25-5-57.
Injuries or death, §25-5-51.
Maximum and minimum
weekly compensation,
§25-5-68.
Limitation of actions,
§25-5-80.
Medical expenses, §25-5-77.
Rights and remedies of
employees, §25-5-53.
Right to compensation,
§25-5-51.
Third parties.
Actions against, §25-5-11.

WORKMEN'S
 COMPENSATION—Cont'd
Co-employee law suits
 —Cont'd
Willful conduct.
 Injury or death resulting
  from, §25-5-11.
Commutation of
 compensation to lump
 sum payment, §25-5-83.
Construction and
 interpretation.
Workmen's compensation
 self-insurance groups.
 Construction of provisions,
  §11-26-6.
Costs.
Proceedings for
 determination of
 disputed claims for
 compensation, §25-5-89.
Counties.
Applicability of chapter to
 counties, §25-5-13.
Workmen's compensation
 self-insurance group.
 Attorneys and employees,
  §11-26-3.
 Bylaws.
  Establishment, §11-26-3.
 Construction of provisions,
  §11-26-6.
 Contract with solvent
  insurance companies,
  §11-26-3.
 Establishment, §11-26-1.
 Governing body of trustees.
  Establishment, §11-26-3.
 Management and
  consultant contracts,
  §11-26-3.
 Officers.
  Liability of officers of
   nonprofit
   associations,
   §§10-11-1 to 10-11-5.
 Powers generally, §11-26-3.
 Schedule of benefits.
  Establishment, §11-26-3.
 Schedule of charges.
  Establishment, §11-26-3.
Coverage.
Corporate officers.
 Exemption, §25-5-50.
Exempt employers.
 Election of coverage by,
  §25-5-50.
Withdrawal of acceptance of
 coverage, §25-5-50.
Death.
Burial expenses, §25-5-67.
Compensation for death,
 §25-5-60.
 Burial expenses, §25-5-67.
Maximum and minimum
 weekly compensation,
 §25-5-68.
U. S. residency
 requirement, §25-5-82.
Disability.
 Death following disability,
  §25-5-57.
Joint liability.
 Actions against third
  parties jointly liable
  with employers,
  §25-5-11.

WORKMEN'S
 COMPENSATION—Cont'd
Death—Cont'd
Occupational diseases.
 General provisions,
  §§25-5-110 to 25-5-123.
  See within this
  heading, "Occupational
  diseases."
 Pneumoconiosis,
  §§25-5-140 to 25-5-180.
  See within this
  heading,
  "Pneumoconiosis."
Radiation.
 Occupational exposure to
  radiation, §§25-5-190
  to 25-5-203. See within
  this heading,
  "Radiation."
Second injury trust fund,
 §§25-5-70 to 25-5-75. See
 within this heading,
 "Second injury trust
 fund."
Willful conduct.
 Actions for death resulting
  from willful conduct,
  §25-5-11.
Definitions, §25-5-1.
Average weekly wage,
 §25-5-57.
Occupational diseases,
 §25-5-110.
Pneumoconiosis, §25-5-140.
 Coal miners, §25-5-170.
Radiation.
 Occupational exposure to
  radiation, §25-5-190.
Denial of compensation.
Grounds for denial, §25-5-51.
Dependents.
Death benefits, §25-5-60.
 Cessation upon death of
  dependent, §25-5-69.
Marriage.
 Cessation upon marriage of
  dependent, §25-5-69.
Partial dependents, §25-5-64.
Persons presumed wholly
 dependent, §25-5-61.
Proportional benefits,
 §25-5-69.
Total dependents.
 Designated, §25-5-62.
 Maximum compensation,
  §25-5-63.
 Order of compensation,
  §25-5-62.
Director of industrial
 relations.
Administration of chapter,
 §25-5-2.
Defined, §25-5-2.
Forms.
 Preparation and
  distribution, §25-5-3.
Disability.
Compensation for disability,
 §25-5-57.
Maximum and minimum
 weekly compensation,
 §25-5-68.
Penalty for overdue
 payments, §25-5-59.
Death following disability.
 Compensation, §25-5-57.
Occupational diseases.
 General provisions,
  §§25-5-110 to 25-5-123.

WORKMEN'S
 COMPENSATION—Cont'd
Disability—Cont'd
Occupational diseases
 —Cont'd
 Pneumoconiosis,
  §§25-5-140 to 25-5-180.
  See within this
  heading,
  "Pneumoconiosis."
Penalty for overdue
 compensation payments,
 §25-5-59.
Pneumoconiosis, §§25-5-140
 to 25-5-180. See within
 this heading,
 "Pneumoconiosis."
Preexisting injuries or
 infirmities.
 Effect, §25-5-58.
Rehabilitation or recovery.
 Effect on permanent total
  disability benefits,
  §25-5-57.
Waiting period for temporary
 disabilities, §25-5-59.
Diseases.
Occupational diseases
 generally, §§25-5-110 to
 25-5-123. See within this
 heading, "Occupational
 diseases."
Pneumoconiosis, §§25-5-140
 to 25-5-180. See within
 this heading,
 "Pneumoconiosis."
Drunkenness.
Grounds for denial of
 compensation, §25-5-51.
Elective compensation under
 contract of employment.
Minors.
 Applicability of certain
  articles to minors,
  §25-5-34.
Outside state.
 Recovery where accident or
  employment outside
  state, §25-5-35.
Employees.
Defined, §25-5-1.
Misconduct by employees.
 Burden of proof, §25-5-36.
 Grounds for denial of
  compensation,
  §25-5-51.
Occupational diseases.
 General provisions,
  §§25-5-110 to 25-5-123.
  See within this
  heading, "Occupational
  diseases."
 Pneumoconiosis,
  §§25-5-140 to 25-5-180.
  See within this
  heading,
  "Pneumoconiosis."
Radiation.
 Occupational exposure to
  radiation, §§25-5-190
  to 25-5-203. See within
  this heading,
  "Radiation."
Rights and remedies
 exclusive, §25-5-53.
Legislative findings and
 intent, §25-5-14.

**WORKMEN'S
 COMPENSATION**—Cont'd
Employers.
 Civil and criminal liability,
   §25-5-53.
 Legislative findings and
   intent, §25-5-14.
 Corporate officers.
   Exemptions, §25-5-50.
 Defined, §25-5-1.
 Exempt employers, §25-5-50.
   Election of coverage,
     §25-5-50.
 Filing of actions against
   officers, directors, etc.,
   §25-5-14.
 Insurance.
   Options to secure payment
     of compensation,
     §25-5-8.
   Self-insurers, §25-5-8.
     Pooling of employers'
       liabilities for
       qualification as self-
       insurers, §25-5-9.
 Joint employers.
   Liability, §25-5-76.
 Notice of accident, §§25-5-78,
   25-5-79.
 Occupational diseases.
   General provisions,
     §§25-5-110 to 25-5-123.
     See within this
     heading, "Occupational
     diseases."
   Pneumoconiosis,
     §§25-5-140 to 25-5-180.
     See within this
     heading,
     "Pneumoconiosis."
 Options.
   Employers' options to
     secure payment of
     compensation, §25-5-8.
   Pneumoconiosis, §§25-5-140
     to 25-5-180. See within
     this heading,
     "Pneumoconiosis."
 Radiation.
   Occupational exposure to
     radiation, §§25-5-190
     to 25-5-203. See within
     this heading,
     "Radiation."
Evidence.
 Pneumoconiosis, §25-5-174.
Examinations.
 Medical examinations,
   §25-5-77.
**Exclusive manner of
 compensation,** §25-5-52.
Executions.
 Pneumoconiosis.
   Coal miners.
     Exemption of benefits,
       §25-5-179.
Fees.
 Proceedings for
   determination of
   disputed claims for
   compensation, §25-5-89.
Funds.
 Second injury trust fund,
   §§25-5-70 to 25-5-75. See
   within this heading,
   "Second injury trust
   fund."
Future benefits.
 Commutation to lump sum
   payment, §25-5-83.

**WORKMEN'S
 COMPENSATION**—Cont'd
Garnishment.
 Exemption of claims,
   §25-5-86.
 Pneumoconiosis.
   Coal miners.
     Benefits exempt,
       §25-5-179.
Hospitals' liens.
 Division not applicable to
   moneys due under
   workmen's compensation
   act, §35-11-374.
Immunity.
 Officers, directors, etc.,
   §25-5-53.
Income tax.
 Exemptions, §40-18-14.
Injuries.
 Compensation for disability,
   §25-5-57.
 Joint liability.
   Actions against third
     parties jointly liable
     with employers for
     injuries, §25-5-11.
 Occupational diseases.
   General provisions,
     §§25-5-190 to 25-5-203.
     See within this
     heading, "Occupational
     diseases."
   Pneumoconiosis,
     §§25-5-140 to 25-5-180.
     See within this
     heading,
     "Pneumoconiosis."
 Preexisting injuries or
   infirmities.
   Effect, §25-5-58.
 Radiation.
   Occupational exposure to
     radiation, §§25-5-190
     to 25-5-203. See within
     this heading,
     "Radiation."
 Records, §25-5-4.
 Reports, §25-5-4.
 Second injury trust fund,
   §§25-5-70 to 25-5-75. See
   within this heading,
   "Second injury trust
   fund."
 Willful conduct.
   Actions for injury resulting
     from willful conduct,
     §25-5-11.
Insurance.
 Actions.
   Actions against third
     parties jointly liable
     with employers for
     injuries or death,
     §25-5-11.
   Direct actions against
     insurers, §25-5-8.
 Employees.
   Payment of insurance costs
     by employees, §25-5-8.
 Employers' options to secure
   payment, §25-5-8.
 Self-insurers, §25-5-8.
   Guaranty association.
     Assessments.
       Annual assessment for
         administration,
         §25-5-254.
       Deductible as business
         expenses,
         §25-5-257.

**WORKMEN'S
 COMPENSATION**—Cont'd
Insurance—Cont'd
 Self-insurers—Cont'd
   Guaranty association
     —Cont'd
     Board of directors,
       §25-5-252.
     By-laws, §25-5-253.
     Creation, §25-5-250.
     Examination and
       regulation by
       department,
       §25-5-256.
     Insolvency fund,
       §25-5-255.
     Membership
       requirements,
       §25-5-251.
     Powers, §25-5-250.
     Purposes, §25-5-250.
     Termination of
       membership,
       §25-5-251.
   Pooling of employers'
     liabilities for
     qualification as self-
     insurers, §25-5-9.
 Solicitation or writing of
   workmen's compensation
   insurance by insurance
   companies not in
   compliance with code,
   §25-5-229.
Intentional injury.
 Grounds for denial of
   compensation, §25-5-51.
Investments.
 Second injury trust fund.
   Investment of moneys in
     fund, §25-5-72.
Joint employers.
 Liability, §25-5-76.
Judgments.
 Discharged and marked
   satisfied upon proof of
   release or satisfaction of
   judgment, §25-5-93.
 Forwarding copy to probate
   court, §25-5-91.
 Liens.
   Creation, §25-5-91.
   Discharge, §25-5-92.
Liability.
 Joint liability.
   Actions against third
     parties jointly liable
     with employers for
     injuries or death,
     §25-5-11.
 Persons engaged in schemes
   to avoid liability to
   workmen, §25-5-10.
Liens.
 Judgment liens.
   Creation, §25-5-91.
   Discharge, §25-5-92.
Limitation of actions,
   §25-5-80.
 Occupational diseases,
   §25-5-117.
 Pneumoconiosis, §25-5-147.
   Coal miners, §25-5-178.
 Radiation exposure,
   §25-5-197.
Lump sum settlements.
 Commutation of
   compensation, §25-5-83.

**WORKMEN'S
COMPENSATION**—Cont'd
Marriage.
Dependents.
Cessation of benefits upon
death or marriage of
dependent, §25-5-69.
Medical examinations,
§25-5-77.
Medical treatment, §25-5-77.
Minors.
Applicability of certain
articles to minors,
§25-5-34.
Double compensation when
minor illegally employed,
§25-5-34.
Payment of awards to
minors.
Effect, §25-5-55.
Rights and powers, §25-5-55.
Misconduct of employees.
Burden of proof, §25-5-36.
Grounds for denial of
compensation, §25-5-51.
Municipal corporations.
Applicability of chapter to
municipalities, §25-5-13.
Notice to employer.
Accidents, §§25-5-78, 25-5-79.
Occupational diseases.
Actions.
Limitation period,
§25-5-117.
Applicability of article,
§§25-5-16, 25-5-122.
Presumptions as to
applicability,
§25-5-112.
Applicability of other
provisions of chapter to
article, §25-5-123.
Benefits.
Computation, §25-5-119.
Exposures prior to
September 1, 1971,
§25-5-118.
Presumptions and burden
of proof as to right to
compensation,
§25-5-120.
Right to compensation for
death or disablement,
§25-5-111.
Burden of proof as to right to
compensation, §25-5-120.
Civil and criminal liability of
employers, §25-5-114.
Coal miners.
Pneumoconiosis,
§§25-5-170 to 25-5-180.
See within this
heading,
"Pneumoconiosis."
Computation of compensation
and benefits payable
under article, §25-5-119.
Contribution not required
from nonliable employer,
§25-5-116.
Definitions, §25-5-110.
Disputed compensation
claims.
Determination, §25-5-121.
Employers.
Civil and criminal liability,
§25-5-114.
Exposures to hazards prior to
September 1, 1971.
Rights and remedies,
§25-5-118.

**WORKMEN'S
COMPENSATION**—Cont'd
Occupational diseases
—Cont'd
Exposure to radiation,
§§25-5-190 to 25-5-203.
See within this heading,
"Radiation."
False written representation
to employer as to
previous compensation,
§25-5-115.
Limitation period for claims
or actions for
compensation, §25-5-117.
Manner of compensation,
etc., provided by article
exclusive, §25-5-113.
Pneumoconiosis, §§25-5-140
to 25-5-180. See within
this heading,
"Pneumoconiosis."
Presumptions as to
applicability and
acceptance of provisions
of article, §25-5-112.
Presumptions as to right to
compensation, §25-5-120.
Previous compensation.
False written
representation to
employer as to,
§25-5-115.
Rights and remedies of
employees under article
exclusive, §25-5-114.
Right to compensation for
death or disablement,
§25-5-111.
Presumptions and burden
of proof, §25-5-120.
Settlements between parties,
§25-5-121.
Which employer liable for
compensation, §25-5-116.
**Occupational exposure to
radiation,** §§25-5-190 to
25-5-203. See within this
heading, "Radiation."
Payments.
Reports.
Supplementary reports as
to initiation, cessation,
etc., of compensation
payments, §25-5-7.
Security for payment.
Employers' options to
secure payment,
§25-5-8.
Penalties.
Overdue compensation
payments, §25-5-59.
Physicians.
Defined, §25-5-1.
Pneumoconiosis, §§25-5-140
to 25-5-180.
Actions.
Limitation period,
§25-5-147.
Coal miners, §25-5-178.
Settlements, §25-5-150.
Amount of compensation and
benefits payable under
article, §§25-5-149,
25-5-172.
Coal miners, §25-5-172.
Evidence of
pneumoconiosis,
§25-5-174.

**WORKMEN'S
COMPENSATION**—Cont'd
Pneumoconiosis—Cont'd
Amount of compensation and
benefits payable under
article—Cont'd
When miner deemed
totally disabled,
§25-5-173.
Applicability of article,
§§25-5-16, 25-5-151.
Presumptions as to
applicability,
§25-5-142.
Applicability of other
provisions of chapter to
article, §25-5-152.
Benefits.
Amount, §25-5-149.
Computation, §25-5-149.
Right to compensation for
injury or death,
§25-5-141.
Civil and criminal liability of
employers, §25-5-144.
Coal miners.
Amount of compensation
payable, §25-5-172.
Applicability of other
provisions of chapter to
article, §25-5-180.
Assignment of benefits
void, §25-5-179.
Attachments.
Exemption of benefits,
etc., §25-5-179.
Death.
When presumed due to
penumoconiosis,
§25-5-176.
Definitions, §25-5-170.
Executions.
Exemption of benefits,
§25-5-179.
Garnishment.
Exemption of benefits,
§25-5-179.
Origin of pneumoconiosis.
Presumptions, §25-5-175.
Rights and remedies of
miners under article
exclusive, §25-5-177.
Right to compensation for
total disability or
death, §25-5-171.
Computation of compensation
and benefits payable,
§25-5-149.
Contribution not required
from nonliable employer,
§25-5-146.
Definitions, §25-5-140.
Coal miners, §25-5-170.
Disputed claims.
Determination, §25-5-150.
Evidence of pneumoconiosis,
§25-5-174.
Exposures to hazards
occurring prior to June
29, 1951.
Rights and remedies,
§25-5-148.
False written representation
to employer as to
previous compensation,
§25-5-145.
Liability of employers.
Civil and criminal liability,
§25-5-144.

**WORKMEN'S
COMPENSATION**—Cont'd
Pneumoconiosis—Cont'd
Liability of employers
—Cont'd
Which employer liable for
compensation,
§25-5-146.
Limitation period for claims
or actions, §25-5-147.
Coal miners, §25-5-178.
Manner of compensation,
etc., provided by article
exclusive, §25-5-143.
Presumptions.
Applicability and
acceptance of
provisions of article,
§25-5-142.
Coal miners.
Presumptions as to
origin of
pneumoconiosis,
§25-5-175.
When death presumed
due to
pneumoconiosis,
§25-5-176.
Previous compensation for
disease.
False written
representation to
employer, §25-5-145.
Rights and remedies of
employees, etc., under
article exclusive,
§25-5-144.
Coal miners, §25-5-177.
Right to compensation for
injury or death,
§25-5-171.
Exposures to hazards
occurring prior to June
29, 1951, §25-5-148.
Settlements, §25-5-150.
Which employer liable for
compensation, §25-5-146.
Presumptions, §25-5-54.
Dependency, §25-5-61.
Occupational diseases.
Applicability of article,
§25-5-112.
Right to compensation,
§25-5-120.
Pneumoconiosis.
Applicability and
acceptance of
provisions of article,
§25-5-142.
Coal miners.
Origin of
pneumoconiosis,
§25-5-175.
When death presumed
due to
pneumoconiosis,
§25-5-176.
Radiation exposure.
Occupational exposure to
radiation.
Applicability and
acceptance of
provisions of article,
§25-5-192.
Right to compensation,
§25-5-200.

**WORKMEN'S
COMPENSATION**—Cont'd
Radiation, §§25-5-190 to
25-5-203.
Occupational exposure to
radiation.
Acceptance and
applicability of article.
Applicability of article,
§§25-5-16, 25-5-202.
Presumptions, §25-5-192.
Applicability of other
provisions of chapter to
article, §25-5-203.
Burden of proof as to right
to compensation,
§25-5-200.
Civil and criminal liability
of employers,
§25-5-194.
Computation of
compensation and
benefits, §25-5-199.
Contribution not required
from nonliable
employer, §25-5-196.
Definitions, §25-5-190.
Disputed compensation
claims.
Determination,
§25-5-201.
Exposures prior to
September 7, 1967.
Rights and remedies,
§25-5-198.
False written
representation to
employer as to
previous compensation
for exposure,
§25-5-195.
Liability of employers.
Civil and criminal
liability, §25-5-194.
Which employer liable
for compensation,
§25-5-196.
Limitation period for
claims or actions,
§25-5-197.
Manner of compensation
provided by article
exclusive, §25-5-193.
Presumptions.
Applicability and
acceptance of
provisions of article,
§25-5-192.
Right to compensation,
§25-5-200.
Previous compensation for
exposure.
False written
representation to
employer, §25-5-195.
Rights and remedies as to
exposures to hazards
occurring prior to
September 7, 1967,
§25-5-198.
Rights and remedies of
employees under
article exclusive,
§25-5-194.
Right to compensation for
injury or death,
§25-5-191.
Presumptions and
burden of proof,
§25-5-200.
Settlements, §25-5-201.

**WORKMEN'S
COMPENSATION**—Cont'd
Radiation—Cont'd
Occupational exposure to
radiation—Cont'd
Which employer liable for
compensation,
§25-5-196.
Records.
Injuries for which
compensation claimed,
§25-5-4.
Rehabilitation or recovery.
Effect on permanent total
disability benefits,
§25-5-57.
Reports.
Injuries for which
compensation claimed,
§25-5-4.
Settlement of cases, §25-5-5.
Right to compensation,
§25-5-51.
Preference, §25-5-87.
Rules and regulations.
Violations.
Denial of compensation,
§25-5-51.
Safety appliances.
Wilful failure to use.
Denial of compensation,
§25-5-51.
Safety committee, §25-5-15.
**Schemes to avoid liability to
workmen.**
Liabilities of persons engaged
in schemes, §25-5-10.
Second injury trust fund.
Administration of fund.
Rules and regulations,
§25-5-75.
Claims.
Priority, §25-5-73.
Contributions.
Employer contributions,
§25-5-71.
Created, §25-5-70.
Custodian of fund, §25-5-70.
Employers.
Contributions, §25-5-71.
Escheat of judgments
under employer's
liability act, §25-5-71.
Refunds to employers,
§25-5-71.
Escheat of judgments under
employer's liability act,
§25-5-71.
Investment of moneys in
fund, §25-5-72.
Liability of fund.
Determination, §25-5-74.
Payments from fund,
§25-5-73.
Priority of claims, §25-5-73.
Refunds to employers,
§25-5-71.
Rules and regulations.
Administration of fund,
§25-5-75.
Trustee of fund, §25-5-70.
Settlement of cases, §25-5-56.
Lump sum settlements,
§25-5-83.
Occupational diseases,
§25-5-121.
Pneumoconiosis, §25-5-150.
Radiation exposure,
§25-5-201.
Reports, §25-5-5.

WORKMEN'S
COMPENSATION—Cont'd
Settlement of cases—Cont'd
Third parties.
Attorney's fees, §25-5-11.
Severability of act, §25-5-17.
Supreme court.
Rules for circuit courts.
Chief justice of supreme
court to prepare
uniform rules,
§25-5-12.
Surgical treatment, §25-5-77.
Third parties.
Actions against third parties
jointly liable with
employers for injuries or
death, §25-5-11.
Trusts and trustees.
Payment of compensation to
court appointed trustee,
§25-5-85.
Second injury trust fund,
§§25-5-70 to 25-5-75. See
within this heading,
"Second injury trust
fund."
Vocational rehabilitation,
§25-5-77.
Wages.
Defined, §25-5-1.
Whistleblower protection,
§25-5-11.1.
Willful conduct.
Action for injury or death
resulting from, §25-5-11.

WORK RELEASE.
General provisions, §§14-8-1
to 14-8-44.
See PRISONS AND
PRISONERS.

WORTHLESS CHECKS.
Actions.
Holder's right of action,
§6-5-285.
Criminal law and procedure.
Negotiating worthless
instrument, §§13A-9-13.1
to 13A-9-13.3.
District attorneys.
Special services division.
Worthless check unit,
§12-17-224.
Penalty and service charge,
§8-8-15.
Taxes.
Payment with bad check,
§40-29-70.

WRECKS.
Motor vehicles, §§32-10-1 to
32-10-12.
See MOTOR VEHICLES.

WRESTLING.
See BOXING AND
WRESTLING.

WRITING.
Authors.
Protection of rights, Const.
U. S., Art. I, §8.
Deeds.
Writing required, §35-4-20.
Defined, §1-1-1.
Depositions upon written
questions, ARCP, Rule 31
(a) to (c).
Evidence.
See EVIDENCE.

WRITING—Cont'd
Forgery, §§13A-9-1 to
13A-9-11.
See FORGERY AND
COUNTERFEITING.
Wills, §§43-8-220 to 43-8-321.
See WILLS.

WRITS.
Appeals.
Remedial writs, §6-6-641.
Writs of error.
Criminal cases, §12-22-222.
Arrest, §§15-10-40 to 15-10-47.
See ARREST.
Attachment, §§6-6-70, 6-6-74,
6-6-75.
Certiorari, §§12-2-2, 12-3-8.
Coroners.
Execution of writs, §11-5-7.
Court of civil appeals.
Issuance of remedial and
original writs, §12-3-11.
Court of criminal appeals.
Issuance of remedial and
original writs, §12-3-11.
Dams.
Erection of dams for mills,
gins, etc., §§18-2-1 to
18-2-21.
See DAMS.
Detinue, §§6-6-263, 6-6-264.
District courts.
Issuance, §12-12-7.
Ejectment.
Issuance before judgment
satisfied, §6-6-297.
Error.
Writs of error.
Criminal cases, §12-22-222.
Executions.
Endorsements, §§6-9-98 to
6-9-101.
Extraordinary writs, ARAP,
Rule 21.
Certiorari, §§12-2-2, 12-3-8.
Habeas corpus, §§15-21-1 to
15-21-34.
See HABEAS CORPUS.
Mandamus generally.
See MANDAMUS.
Prohibition, writ of, §6-6-640.
Quo warranto, §§6-6-590 to
6-6-604.
See QUO WARRANTO.
Forcible entry and unlawful
detainer.
Writ of restitution or
possession, §§6-6-350 to
6-6-353.
Habeas corpus, §§15-21-1 to
15-21-34.
See HABEAS CORPUS.
Injunctions generally.
See INJUNCTIONS.
Juvenile proceedings.
Issuance of writs, §12-15-2.
Landlord and tenant.
Possession wrongfully
withheld.
Issuance of writ, §35-9-81.
Service of writ, §35-9-82.
Mandamus generally.
See MANDAMUS.
Ne exeat.
Removal of personality by life
tenant.
Remainderman or
reversioner entitled to
writ of ne exeat,
§35-4-171.

WRITS—Cont'd
Prohibition, writ of, §6-6-640.
Public officers and
employees.
Summary proceedings
involving officials.
Judgment against sheriff,
etc., receiving or
executing writ,
§6-6-680.
Quo warranto, §§6-6-590 to
6-6-604.
See QUO WARRANTO.
Remedial writs.
Appeals, §6-6-641.
Application, §6-6-640.
Effect of article, §6-6-642.
Generally, §6-9-1.
Relief upon issues presented,
§6-6-640.
Restitution or possession,
writ of, §§6-6-350 to
6-6-353.
Rules of appellate
procedure.
Extraordinary writs directed
to judges, ARAP, Rule
21.
Rules of civil procedure.
Seizure of property.
Writs of seizure or
attachment, ARCP,
Rule 64 (b).
Supreme court.
Powers, §12-2-7; Const. Ala.,
art. VI, §140.
Venditioni exponas,
§§6-9-120, 6-9-121.

WRONGFUL DEATH.
Abatement, revival and
survival, §6-5-410.
Actions, §6-5-410.
Injuries to decedent's
property, §6-5-411.
Wrongful death of minor,
§6-5-391.
Claims by and against state.
Claims to be made by
personal representative,
§41-9-64.
Limitation on amount of
award, §41-9-70.
Executors and
administrators.
Right of action, §6-5-410.
Limitation of actions,
§§6-2-38, 6-5-410.
Minors, §6-5-391.
Pleadings.
Form of complaint, ARCP,
Form 31.

X

X-RAYS.
Regulation of sources of
ionizing radiation,
§§22-14-1 to 22-14-16.
See ATOMIC ENERGY.
Tuberculosis, §§22-11A-9 to
22-11A-12.

Y

YEAR.
Defined, §1-1-1.
Education.
Fiscal year.
Defined, §16-1-1.

YEAR—Cont'd
Education—Cont'd
Scholastic year.
Defined, §16-1-1.
Fiscal year of state, §1-3-4.

YELLOW FEVER.
Notifiable diseases,
§§22-11A-1 to 22-11A-38.
See DISEASES.

YELLOW-HAMMER.
State bird, §1-2-7.

YORK, MUNICIPALITY OF.
Economic development,
Const. Ala., amd. 221.

**YOUNG MEN'S CHRISTIAN
ASSOCIATION.**
Conveyances by literary or
social societies,
§§35-4-340 to 35-4-344.
Licenses.
Exemptions, §40-9-9.
Taxation.
Exemptions, §40-9-9.

**YOUNG MEN'S HEBREW
ASSOCIATION.**
Licenses.
Exemptions, §40-9-12.
Taxation.
Exemptions, §40-9-12.

**YOUNG WOMEN'S
CHRISTIAN
ASSOCIATION.**
Conveyances by literary or
social societies,
§§35-4-340 to 35-4-344.
Licenses.
Exemptions, §40-9-10.
Taxation.
Exemptions, §40-9-10.

**YOUNG WOMEN'S
CHRISTIAN
ORGANIZATION.**
Licenses.
Exemptions, §40-9-11.
Taxation.
Exemptions, §40-9-11.

YOUTHFUL OFFENDERS,
§§15-19-1 to 15-19-7.
Arraignment, §15-19-1.
**Effect of determination of
youthful offender,**
§15-19-7.
Examination.
Court to determine how
youth to be tried,
§15-19-1.
Inadmissibility of statements,
admissions and
confessions, §15-19-5.
Felonies.
Disposition of case upon
adjudication, §15-19-6.
Fingerprints.
Confidentiality of records,
§15-19-7.
Investigation.
Inadmissibility of statements,
admissions and
confessions, §15-19-5.
Probation officers to assist
court, §15-19-2.
Misdemeanors.
Disposition of case upon
adjudication, §15-19-6.
Probation.
Court authorized to post
probation, §15-19-6.

YOUTHFUL OFFENDERS
—Cont'd
Probation—Cont'd
Juvenile probation generally,
§§12-15-74, 12-15-75.
Record.
Confidentiality, §15-19-7.
Inspection, §15-19-7.
Sentencing.
Consideration of statements,
etc., §15-19-5.
Disposition upon
adjudication, §15-19-6.
Trial.
Inadmissibility of
examination and
investigation statements,
etc., §15-19-5.
Investigation.
Court to determine how
youth to be tried,
§15-19-1.
Sessions to be separate from
adult trial, §15-19-3.
Without jury, §15-19-4.
Consent of minor, §15-19-1.

YOUTH SERVICES, §§44-1-1 to
44-1-77.
Administrator.
Compact administrator,
§44-2-2.
Aftercare.
Release of youth into
aftercare, §44-1-36.
**Alabama boys industrial
school, Alabama training
school for girls and
Alabama industrial
school.**
Advisory boards.
Separate advisory boards,
§44-1-4.
Appropriations.
Restrictions, §44-1-6.
Control, §44-1-3.
Custody of inhabitants.
Legal custody, §44-1-3.
Donations, §44-1-7.
Employees.
Continuation of rights, etc.,
§44-1-5.
Funds of department.
Endowment funds, §44-1-7.
Priority as to use, §44-1-3.
Regulations, §44-1-4.
Teachers.
Continuation of rights, etc.,
§44-1-5.
Personal leave for teachers,
§44-1-5.
Textbooks.
Purchase and furnishing of
state-owned textbooks,
§16-36-25.
**Alabama girls' industrial
school,** §§16-54-1 to
16-54-18.
See UNIVERSITY OF
MONTEVALLO.
Attorneys at law.
Department of youth
services.
Legal counsel, §44-1-23.
Board.
Youth services board,
§§44-1-50 to 44-1-56. See
within this heading,
"Youth services board."

YOUTH SERVICES—Cont'd
Budgets.
Youth services board,
§44-1-56.
Children.
Interstate compact on child
placement, §§44-2-1 to
44-2-26.
See MINORS.
Commitment.
Dental treatment.
Authorization, §44-1-33.
Determination of social
service plan, §44-1-32.
Discharge.
Clothing, money and
transportation to be
furnished upon release,
§44-1-37.
Rehabilitated youth,
§44-1-36.
Evaluation of youth,
§44-1-30.
Petition for examination,
§44-1-35.
Extension of orders of
commitment, §44-1-36.
Guardianship, §44-1-31.
Medical treatment.
Authorization, §44-1-33.
Mentally ill youth, §44-1-36.
Psychiatric treatment.
Authorization, §44-1-33.
Release of youth into
aftercare, §44-1-36.
Clothing, money and
transportation to be
furnished upon release,
§44-1-37.
Retarded youth, §44-1-36.
Review of committed youth,
§44-1-34.
Petition for review,
§44-1-35.
Study of youth, §44-1-30.
Petition for examination,
§44-1-35.
Surgical treatment.
Authorization, §44-1-33.
Termination of orders of
commitment, §44-1-36.
Compacts.
Interstate compact on child
placement, §§44-2-1 to
44-2-26.
See MINORS.
Interstate compact on
juveniles, §§44-2-1 to
44-2-7. See within this
heading, "Interstate
compact on juveniles."
Conflicts of interest, §44-1-29.
**Construction and
interpretation.**
Youth services department
district, §44-1-77.
Contracts.
Competitive bids, §44-1-29.
Conflicts of interest,
§44-1-29.
Definitions, §44-1-2.
Dental treatment.
Authorization, §44-1-33.
**Department of youth
services.**
Agreements with federal
government, §44-1-40.
Attorneys at law.
Legal counsel, §44-1-23.

YOUTH SERVICES—Cont'd
Department of youth
services—Cont'd
Commitment, §§44-1-30 to
44-1-37. See within this
heading, "Commitment."
Composition, §44-1-20.
Confinement of youth in
adult penal institutions,
§44-1-8.
Conflicts of interest,
§44-1-29.
Created, §44-1-20.
Custody, §§44-1-30 to
44-1-32.
Evaluation and study of
youth, §44-1-30.
Development of department
program, §44-1-25.
Director of youth services,
§44-1-21.
Districts, §§44-1-70 to
44-1-77. See within this
heading, "Department of
youth services districts."
Duties, §44-1-24.
Employees, §44-1-22.
Evaluation of youth in
custody of department,
§44-1-30.
Petition for examination,
§44-1-35.
Federal government.
Agreements with, §44-1-40.
Guardianship of youth in
custody of department,
§44-1-31.
Legal counsel, §44-1-23.
Offices.
Principal offices, §44-1-20.
Penal institutions.
Confinement of youth in
adult penal
institutions, §44-1-8.
Powers, §44-1-24.
Program.
Development of
department program,
§44-1-25.
Standards for programs,
§44-1-27.
Records of examinations, etc.,
§44-1-38.
Restrictions on release or
use, §44-1-39.
State youth sevices director,
§44-1-21.
Study of youth in custody of
department, §44-1-30.
Petition for examination,
§44-1-35.
Department of youth
services districts,
§§44-1-70 to 44-1-77.
Benefits, §44-1-75.
Budgets.
Submission, §44-1-72.
Construction of article,
§44-1-77.
Department designated
district, §44-1-70.
Expenses of members and
employees for
participation in
conferences, etc.
Advancements and
accounting, §16-13-14.
Functioning of district,
§44-1-76.
Funding, §44-1-73.

YOUTH SERVICES—Cont'd
Department of youth
services districts—Cont'd
Gasoline tax.
Exemptions, §40-17-31.
Insurance, §44-1-75.
Leaves, §44-1-75.
Lubricating oils and greases.
Tax exemption, §40-17-171.
Personnel.
Employment of new
teaching personnel,
§44-1-74.
Employment of
nonteaching personnel,
§44-1-74.
Retention, §44-1-74.
Records, §44-1-38.
Restrictions on release or
use, §44-1-39.
Salary schedule for teachers,
§44-1-75.
Special school district,
§44-1-70.
State board of education.
Relationship between
district and board,
§44-1-70.
Relationship of board of
youth services and
superintendent to state
board, §44-1-76.
Superintendent of education,
§§44-1-71, 44-1-72.
Detention facilities,
§§44-1-27, 44-1-28.
Director of youth services,
§44-1-21.
Discharge, §44-1-36.
Clothing, money and
transportation to be
furnished upon release,
§44-1-37.
Districts.
Department of youth services
districts, §§44-1-70 to
44-1-77. See within this
heading, "Department of
youth service districts."
Enforcement of chapter,
§44-1-10.
Escape.
Detention without order or
warrant of escaped
youths, §44-1-9.
Federal government.
Agreements with
department, §44-1-40.
Foster care facilities,
§44-1-27.
Guardianship of youth in
custody of department,
§44-1-31.
Inspections.
Detention facilities, §44-1-27.
Foster care facilities,
§44-1-27.
Interstate compact on child
placement, §§44-2-1 to
44-2-26.
See MINORS.
Interstate compact on
juveniles.
Agreements.
Supplementary
agreements, §44-2-3.
Amendment.
Rendition amendment,
§44-2-8.

YOUTH SERVICES—Cont'd
Interstate compact on
juveniles—Cont'd
Cooperation with state
departments, agencies,
etc., §44-2-2.
Declaration of legislative
policy, §44-2-1.
Director of youth services.
Administrator of compact,
§44-2-2.
Enforcement, §44-2-5.
Financial arrangements,
§44-2-4.
Legislative findings and
declaration of policy,
§44-2-1.
Procedures.
Additional procedures not
precluded, §44-2-6.
Rules and regulations.
Promulgation, §44-2-2.
State departments, agencies,
etc.
Responsibilities, §44-2-5.
Licenses.
Detention facilities, §44-1-27.
Foster care facilities,
§44-1-27.
Medical treatment.
Authorization, §44-1-33.
Mentally ill.
Commitment to state
hospitals, §44-1-36.
Mentally retarded persons.
Commitment to state
hospitals, §44-1-36.
Penalties.
Violations of chapter,
§44-1-10.
Probation.
Juvenile probation officers,
§44-1-26.
Powers and duties of
department, §44-1-24.
Responsibilities of
department of pensions
and security, §44-1-26.
Salary subsidies for
probation services,
§44-1-26.
Programs.
Development, §44-1-25.
Standards, §44-1-27.
Psychiatric treatment.
Authorization, §44-1-33.
Purpose of chapter, §44-1-1.
Records.
Department of youth
services.
Examinations, etc.,
§44-1-38.
Restrictions on release or
use, §44-1-39.
Youth services board
proceedings, §44-1-51.
Rehabilitation.
Discharge of rehabilitated
youth, §44-1-36.
Reports.
Youth services board.
Annual report to governor,
§44-1-55.
Salaries.
Responsibilities of
department of pensions
and security, §44-1-26.
Subsidies for probation
services, §44-1-26.
Social service plan.
Determination, §44-1-32.

YOUTH SERVICES—Cont'd
  **State youth services
      director,** §44-1-21.
  Surgical treatment.
    Authorization, §44-1-33.
  **Trade school at Frank Lee
      youth center,** §§16-60-170
      to 16-60-173.
  United States.
    Department of youth
        services.
      Agreements with federal
          government, §44-1-40.
  Warrants.
    Detention without order or
        warrant of escaped
        youths, §44-1-9.
  Youth services board,
      §§44-1-50 to 44-1-56.
    Appointment of members,
        §44-1-51.
    Budget requests, §44-1-56.
    Compensation of members,
        §44-1-51.
    Conflicts of interest,
        §44-1-29.
    Created, §44-1-50.
    Decisions.
      Judicial review, §44-1-54.
    Governor.
      Annual report to governor,
          §44-1-55.
      Ex officio chairman,
          §44-1-51.
    Judicial review, §44-1-54.
    Meetings, §44-1-53.
    Membership, §44-1-51.
    Officers, §44-1-51.
    Offices.
      Principal offices, §44-1-50.
    Orders.
      Judicial review, §44-1-54.

YOUTH SERVICES—Cont'd
  Youth services board—Cont'd
    Powers generally, §44-1-52.
    Quorum, §44-1-53.
    Records of proceedings,
        §44-1-51.
    Reports.
      Annual report to governor,
          §44-1-55.
    Terms of members, §44-1-51.
    Vacancies, §44-1-51.

                    Z

ZONING.
  Airport authorities.
    Exemption from state zoning
        restrictions, §4-3-10.
    Alternate procedure for
        incorporation, §4-3-60.
    Powers, §4-3-10.
      Alternate procedure for
          incorporation, §4-3-60.
  Airports.
    General provisions, §§4-6-1 to
        4-6-15.
      See AVIATION.
  Appeals.
    Airports, §4-6-11.
    Municipal corporations,
        §§11-52-80, 11-52-81.
  Condominiums.
    Construction and application
        of zoning laws, §35-8-21.
  Conflict of laws, §11-52-82.
  Counties, §§11-19-1 to
      11-19-24.
    See COUNTIES.

ZONING—Cont'd
  Districts.
    Municipal corporations,
        §§11-52-70 to 11-52-84.
    See MUNICIPAL
        CORPORATIONS.
  Flood-prone areas.
    Land-use management in
        flood-prone areas,
        §§11-19-1 to 11-19-24.
    See COUNTIES.
  Housing authorities.
    County housing authorities.
      Authority projects subject
          to local zoning laws,
          §24-1-69.
    Municipal housing
        authorities.
      Authority projects subject
          to local zoning laws,
          §24-1-30.
  Municipal corporations.
    Classified municipalities.
      Mayor-council form of
          government,
          §11-43C-30.
    General provisions,
        §§11-52-70 to 11-52-84.
    See MUNICIPAL
        CORPORATIONS.
  Ordinances.
    Municipal corporations,
        §§11-52-76 to 11-52-78,
        11-52-82 to 11-52-84.
    See MUNICIPAL
        CORPORATIONS.

ZOOS.
  Wildlife.
    Possession for public
        exhibition purposes,
        §§9-11-320 to 9-11-328.
    See FISH AND GAME.